THE AUTHORITY SINCE 1868

THE WORLD ALMANAC & BOOK OF FACTS 1982

Published Annually by
NEWSPAPER ENTERPRISE ASSOCIATION, INC.
New York

THE
WORLD
ALMANAC
& BOOK OF FACTS
1982

Publisher: Jane D. Flatt
Editor: Hana Umlauf Lane
Managing Editor: Vincent P. Bannan
Assistant Managing Editor: Aaron Kinne

Assistant Editors: Patricia Fisher, June Foley, Thomas J. McGuire
Assistant to the Publisher: Reva S. Moore

Canadian Editor: John Filion

Paperback cover design: Barbara Wilhelm, Elke Raedisch

The editors acknowledge with thanks the many letters of helpful comment and criticism from users of THE WORLD ALMANAC, and invite further suggestions and observations. Because of the volume of mail directed to the editorial offices, it is not possible personally to reply to each letter writer. However, every communication is read by the editors and all comments and suggestions receive careful attention. Inquiries regarding contents should be sent to: The World Almanac, 200 Park Avenue, New York, NY 10166.

THE WORLD ALMANAC is published annually in November. Purchase orders should be sent to: World Almanac Education Division, 1278 W. 9th St., Cleveland, OH 44113.

THE WORLD ALMANAC does not decide wagers.

The first edition of THE WORLD ALMANAC, a 120-page volume with 12 pages of advertising, was published by the New York World in 1868, 114 years ago. Annual publication was suspended in 1876. Joseph Pulitzer, publisher of the New York World, revived THE WORLD ALMANAC in 1886 with the goal of making it a "compendium of universal knowledge." It has been published annually since then. In 1931, it was acquired by the Scripps-Howard Newspapers; until 1951, it bore the imprint of the New York World-Telegram and thereafter, until 1967, that of the New York World-Telegram and Sun. It is now published in paper and clothbound editions by Newspaper Enterprise Association, Inc., a Scripps-Howard company.

THE WORLD ALMANAC & BOOK OF FACTS 1982
Copyright© Newspaper Enterprise Association, Inc. 1981
Library of Congress Catalog Card Number 4-3781
International Standard Serial Number (ISSN) 0084-1382
Newspaper Enterprise Association, Inc. (softcover) ISBN 0-911818-22-7
Newspaper Enterprise Association Inc. (hardcover) ISBN 0-911818-23-5
Doubleday and Co., Inc. ISBN 0-385-17886-7
Ballantine Books ISBN 0-345-29862-4
Windward/W.H. Smith & Son Ltd. ISBN 0-7112-0224-9
Microfilm Edition since 1868: Bell and Howell Co.
Printed in the United States of America
The Ballantine paperback edition distributed in the United States by Ballantine Books, a division of Random House, Inc. and in Canada by Random House of Canada, Ltd.

NEWSPAPER ENTERPRISE ASSOCIATION, INC.
200 Park Avenue, New York, NY 10166

1982 HIGHLIGHTS

GENERAL INDEX

3

Addenda, Late News, Changes

Awards (p. 408-419)

Nobel Prize in Physics: Nicolaas Boembergen and Arthur Schlawlow, both U.S., to split $180,000 prize with Kai M. Siegbahn, Sweden, for their work in developing technologies with lasers and other devices that can seek out the innermost secrets of complex forms of matter (p. 408).

Nobel Prize in Chemistry: Kenichi Fukui, Japan, and Roald Hoffmann, U.S., to share $180,000 prize for work in explaining chemical reactions (p. 408).

Nobel Prize in Medicine or Physiology: Roger W. Sperry, U.S., split the $180,000 prize with Dr. David H. Hubel, and Dr. Tosten N. Wiesel, both U.S., for research that has proved vital to understanding the organization and functioning of the brain (p. 408-409).

Nobel Prize in Literature: Elias Cenetti, who was born in Bulgaria, writes in German, and is living in London, was cited by the Swedish Academy for his "writings marked by a broad outlook, a wealth of ideas and artistic power"(p. 409).

Nobel Peace Prize: The Office of the United Nations High Commissioner for Refugees was awarded the prize for aiding the growing numbers of homeless and displaced people around the world (p. 409-410).

Nobel Memorial Prize in Economics: James Tobin, U.S., won the award for his analyses of financial markets and their effect on how businesses and families spend and save money (p. 410).

Broadcasting and Theater (pp. 417)

Emmy Awards, by Academy of Television Arts and Sciences, for nighttime programs, 1980-81: Dramatic series: *Hill Street Blues;* actor: Daniel J. Travanti, *Hill Street Blues;* supporting actor: Michael Conrad, *Hill Street Blues;* actress: Nancy Marchand, *Lou Grant;* director: Robert Butler, *Hill Street Blues;* writer: Michael Kozoll and Steven Bochco, *Hill Street Blues.* Comedy series: *Taxi;* actor: Judd Hirsch, *Taxi;* actress: Isabel Sanford, *The Jeffersons;* supporting actor: Danny DeVito, *Taxi;* supporting actress: Eileen Brennan, *Private Benjamin;* director: James Burrows, *Taxi;* writer: Michael Leeson, *Taxi.* Limited series or specials: *Shogun;* actor: Anthony Hopkins, *The Bunker;* actress: Vanessa Redgrave, *Playing for Time;* supporting actor: David Warner Falco, *Masada;* supporting actress: Jane Alexander, *Playing for Time;* writer: Arthur Miller, *Playing for Time;* director: James Goldstone, Kent State. Information: *The Body Human: The Bionic Breakthrough.* Variety or Music: *Lily: Sold Out.* Classical performing arts: *Kennedy Center Honors: A Celebration of the Performing Arts.* Animated: *Life is a Circus, Charlie Brown.*

Miscellaneous Awards

International American Music Competition, by Rockefeller Foundation and Carnegie Hall, $10,000, and additional $5,000 for second year, $25,000 recording contract, $35,000 for "career development": Randall Hodgkinson.

Books, Allied Arts (pp. 415-416)

Nebula Awards, by Science Fiction Writers of America: novel: *Timescape,* Gregory Benford; *The Unicorn Tapestry,* Suzy McKee; novelette: *The Ugly Chicken,* Howard Waldrup; short story: "Grotto of the Dancing Deer," Clifford D. Simak; Grand Master Award: Fritz Leiber.

Hemingway Foundation Award, by PEN American Center, -$6,000: *Household Words,* Joan Silber; special award, $1,500: *Childhood and Other Neighborhoods,* Stuart Dybek.

Crime in the U.S. (pp. 965-969)

The **F.B.I.** index of reported serious crimes rose by 9 percent in 1980 over 1979. Murder, rape, robbery, and aggravated assault increased 11 percent in 1980. Every crime in the bureau's crime index increased. Murder was up to 7 percent, rape 8 percent, robbery 18 percent, aggravated assault 7 percent, burglary 14 percent, larceny 8 percent and motor vehicle theft 2 percent. Men from the ages of 20 to 29 were the largest group of murder victims; 45 percent of the murders resulted from quarrels and 18 percent occurred as the result of felony activities.

Arts and Media (pp. 420-432)

Elizabeth Ward, of Russelville, Ark., was chosen **Miss America 1982** (p. 419).

Death Roll (pp. 951-953)

Chase, Mary, 74; playwright who is best known as the creator of the invisible 6 ft. 1 in. tall rabbit "Harvey"; Denver, Oct. 20.

Sports (pp. 822-917)

WBC welterweight champion Sugar Ray Leonard knocked out the WBA welterweight champion Thomas Hearns in the 14th round of their bout in Las Vegas, Nev. on Sept. 16.

Ambassadors and Envoys (pp. 601-602)

The new acting U.S. ambassador to **Pakistan** is Barrington King.

The new U.S. ambassador to **Saudi Arabia** is Richard Murphy.

The new U.S. ambassador to the **USSR** is Arthur A. Hartman.

Nations of the World (pp. 514-599)

Belize: The British colony British Honduras became the independent nation Belize, Sept. 21. The Prime Minister of the new nation is George Price (p. 591).

Boliva: President Luis Garcia Meza was forced to resign, Aug. 4 in a coup that began Aug. 3. He was replaced by a juanta composed of commanders of the army, air force and navy. (pp. 520-521).

Brazil: A heart attack, Sept. 20, temporarily idled President Jaoa Baptista Figueiredo. Vice President Aureliano, a civilian, filled the vacancy (pp. 521-522).

Central African Empire: The new ruler is Gen. Andre Kolingba who overthrew the civilian government of President David Dacko in an army coup, Sept. 1 (p. 525).

Egypt: Hosni Mubarak, a 53-year-old former commander of the Egyptian Air Force, was sworn in as President, Oct. 14, to succeed Anwar el-Sadat, who was assassinated Oct. 6 (pp. 534-535).

Greece: The Panhellenic Socialist Movement of Andreas Papandreou won the Greek parliamentary elections, Oct. 18, defeating Prime Minister George Rallis (p. 541).

Iran: Hojatolislam Ali Khamenei, age 42, was sworn in Oct. 13, as the new president, succeeding Mohammed Ali Rajai, who was assassinated Aug. 30, only 37 days after being elected. Rajai's predecessor, Abolhassan Bani-Sadr, who was elected in January 1980, was dismissed by Ayatollah Ruhollah Khomeini on June 22, 1981. On Oct. 22, the Iranian Parliament rejected the nomination of Ali Akbar Vellayati as premier (pp. 547-548).

Norway: The Labor Party of Prime Minister Gro Harlem Bruntland, Scandinavia's first female prime minister, was defeated in parlimentary elections by the conservative party of Kare Willoch, Sept. 14. He was sworn in Oct. 14 (pp. 566-567).

Panama: General Omar Torrijos Herrera was killed in a plane crash, July 31. Aristides Royo was confirmed in the role of president (p. 568).

Poland: Prime Minister Wojciech Jaruzelski replaced Stanislaw Kania as the Communist leader of Poland, Oct. 18 (p. 571).

Portugal: Francisco Pinto Balsemao resigned as prime minister, Aug. 10, but returned to office when no alternative leader emerged in the Social Democratic Party. (pp. 571-572).

North American Cities (p. 670)

Harold R. Lifvendahl is the president and publisher, Joseph D. Cantrell is the general manager, and Stephen R. Vaughn is the executive editor of the **Orlando,** Florida **Sentinel Star.**

The World Almanac

and Book of Facts for 1982

The Top 10 News Stories of 1981 .

Terrorism, both political and personal, made top headlines, as Egypt's Pres. Anwar el-Sadat was gunned down by Moslem extremists, U.S. Pres. Ronald Reagan and Pope John Paul II fell victim to assassination attempts and, late in 1980, former Beatle John Lennon was killed by a lone assassin.

Only minutes after Pres. Reagan's inauguration, the 52 Americans who had been held hostage in Iran, were flown to freedom, ending their 444-day ordeal.

Marriage, a royal marriage specifically, captivated hearts worldwide when England's Prince Charles wed Lady Diana Spencer.

Jousting successfully with Congress, Pres. Reagan succeeded in cutting $35.1 billion in spending from the 1982 budget and enacting his tax-cut proposals calling for about a 23 percent reduction through 1983.

Elections by secret ballot for Polish communist party leaders highlighted a turbulent year also marked by continued labor unrest, severe economic decline, the threat of Soviet intervention, and governmental shuffling.

Space Shuttle Columbia shot successfully into orbit, despite some non-critical defects in heat-shielding tiles, and landed safely back on Earth 2 days later.

Sandra Day O'Connor, a judge on the Arizona Court of Appeals, became the first woman to serve on the Supreme Court.

Inflicting delays and flight cancellations on the nation's travelers, air traffic controllers went on strike, rejecting the government's final offer for a new contract.

Claiming defensive objectives, Israel destroyed an Iraqi atomic reactor near Baghdad; Israel stated that the reactor would have enabled Iraq to produce nuclear weapons that could be used against Israel.

An Atlanta, Ga., grand jury indicted Wayne B. Williams on charges of murdering 2 of the 28 young black people killed over the last 2 years in the Atlanta area.

President Reagan's First Year: An Overview

By Donald Lambro
Syndicated Columnist, United Feature Syndicate

Ronald Wilson Reagan, the 40th president of the United States, began his first day in office by telling Americans that "government is not the solution" to our problems. "Government is the problem," Reagan stated in his inaugural address. For Reagan, our oldest chief executive to take office, this was the bedrock conservative gospel he had preached for more than 20 years. Yet, more than any other statement he has made or will make as president, these words have been the overriding theme of his administration.

In a whirlwind of executive decrees, legislative initiatives, and supersalesmanship, the former Hollywood actor and California governor has left political observers and Washington journalists reaching for historical comparisons. His goal: a radical reshaping of American government aimed at slowing the inexorable growth in federal spending and taxation that has continued uninterrupted for the last 50 years.

"Hit the Ground Running"

As he promised in his campaign for the presidency, Reagan "hit the ground running" as soon as he took the oath of office. Minutes after his inauguration he ordered a federal hiring freeze to trim back the government's sizeable workforce of nearly 5 million people.

In a tenacious blitz on the bureaucracy, Reagan ordered reductions in government travel, film-making, publications, and consulting contracts. Decreeing a 3-month delay in the adoption of new regulations, he created a Cabinet-level Task Force on Regulatory Relief headed by Vice President George Bush to review and reduce future federal regulatory activities. He abolished the Council of Wage and Price Stability, and created the Council on Integrity and Efficiency to conduct a coordinated attack against waste and fraud in government.

Then, one month after taking office, Reagan sent Congress an ambitious budget and tax-cutting program aimed at reviving a stagnant economy. His plan called for nearly $49 billion in budget savings and an unprecedented 3-year, 30 percent income tax reduction modeled after the Kemp-Roth plan he supported during the campaign. The conventional wisdom at the time predicted Reagan would be lucky to get half of what he sought, if that.

Assassination Attempt Recovery Wins Admiration

Indeed, by late March Reagan's popularity had declined in the polls amid widening predictions that his economic package would not survive the Democratic-controlled House. Then an assassination attempt, March 30, that came perilously close to taking Reagan's life altered the political equation and in the process temporarily raised Reagan's presidency to almost heroic proportions.

Reagan's remarkable physical stamina and wit during his convalescence won him the nation's admiration and respect and served to extend the presidential honeymoon. His approval rating in the polls shot up from 66 to 80 percent.

Yet Reagan's long recuperation also prevented him from aggressively lobbying Congress personally in behalf of his economic package, which was becoming bogged down. Nonetheless, Reagan slowly returned to his duties; signing legislation just days after removal of a bullet from his chest; talking by phone to congressmen during the Easter recess in his robe and pajamas.

His triumphant return to the presidential arena came in a dramatic, televised address before a joint session of Congress on the eve of his 100th day in office to push his stalled economic recovery package off dead center. A moving plea to lawmakers to help him "clean up our economic mess" was followed by a sophisticated White House lobbying campaign that led to final enactment of the lion's share of his proposals on July 29.

Forges Bi-Partisan Coalition

After a 6-month assault on Congress, Reagan had managed to forge a bipartisan coalition to pass the biggest tax and budget cuts in American history in a little over 5 months time.

With the support of the Republican majority in the Senate and the conservative Democratic "Boll Weevils" in the House, Reagan succeeded in cutting $35.1 billion in spending from the fiscal 1982 budget. At the same time, Congress enacted his tax proposals to cut marginal income tax rates by 5 percent as of October 1981, 10 percent in 1982, and another 10 percent in 1983. He signed both bills into law at his Santa Barbara ranch, **August 13.**

The New York Times called Reagan's first few months in office "the most dramatic first 100 days since F.D.R." His lightning blitz on Congress represented an extraordinary legislative achievement that brought about hundreds of legislative changes and spending cuts in federal programs. Through it all, Reasan deftly avoided serious controversy as he massaged lawmakers with legislative tradeoffs and special favors in a display of professional political adroitness that surprised both friends and foes alike.

Honeymoon Dissipates

But sunny July quickly gave way to the dog days of August and the Reagan honeymoon began to dissipate. Interest rates rose to double digit levels and Reagan began making a series of controversial decisions:

— **August 3:** Fired striking Air Traffic Controllers.
— **August 5:** Proposed the sale of advance radar AWACS aircraft to Saudi Arabia.
— **August 13:** Moved ahead with development of the neutron warhead.

Meanwhile, as Reagan's budget advisers began recalculating the tax cut's effect on future revenues versus the $35 billion spending cut, larger than expected budget deficits loomed on the horizon — as high as $80 billion in fiscal 1982.

And Democratic critics unleashed a barrage of attacks on Reagan's economic policies, charging that Wall Street's reluctance to respond to tax and budget cuts proved they had failed. Those charges mounted during September, despite the fact that the cuts would not take effect until October 1. Even Republican leaders, freshly returned from their states over the August recess, began expressing fears that perhaps the tax cuts were too deep and should be partially delayed. Many said that the government would be saddled with an enormous debt that would reignite inflation which had fallen from 12.4 percent in 1980 to around 9.6 percent in 1981.

Alarmed at the prospect of racking up the single biggest deficit in history, Reagan sent Budget Director David Stockman back to the budget books for further cuts. Girding for another battle with Congress, Reagan told the nation on **September 24** that still deeper cuts were called for. He proposed an additional $13 billion in spending reductions, including the dismantling of the Education and Energy Departments, and a $2 billion cut in defense spending.

In foreign affairs, Reagan's hardnosed approach toward the Soviets became immediately evident when Soviet Ambassador Anatoly Dobrynin made the customary first visit to Secretary of State Alexander Haig in January. Haig saw

Hard-Nosed Stance on Soviets

to it that the Russian ambassador used the front entrance at State instead of the private VIP underground entrance to which he had become accustomed.

Significantly, however, it is the "linkage" of Soviet military and foreign policy actions to any future improvement in relations with the United States that has been Reagan's most significant change in U.S. foreign policy. If the front door rebuff to Dobrynin was not strong enough for the Soviets to understand, Reagan bluntly laid out his attitude toward the Soviets **January 29,** when he said the U.S.S.R.

was "prepared to commit any crime, to lie, to cheat" to further its "world revolution" aims.

In February, Reagan drew the line on further "Soviet expansion" into Third World countries and backed up his words by sending military advisers into El Salvador.

Critics charged Reagan's foreign policy statements marked a dangerous return to the Cold War days, but supporters hailed the president's tough talk as realistic and necessary in the face of a massive Russian military buildup and international adventurism.

By September, Reagan said that any serious arms limitation treaty with the Soviet Union must be legitimate and verifiable or, he warned, "they will be in an arms race which they can't win." Amassing the bargaining chips he believes are pivotal to future arms limitation talks, Reagan announced his long-awaited strategic arms program in early October. It called for deployment of 100 MX land-based missiles, production of 100 B1 bombers, and development of the "Stealth" radar-evading bomber.

Despite Reagan's intention to substantially beef up the U.S. defense posture by spending $1.5 trillion over the next 5 years, the administration has also held out the olive branch to the Soviet Union. In April, Reagan ended the ban on grain exports to Russia, and, in September, Haig held his first meeting with Soviet foreign minister Andrei Gromyko to begin discussion of a broad range of U.S.-Soviet differences.

Will the "Reagan Revolution" Work?

Whether Reagan's attempts to substantially reshape American government will succeed, no one can say for sure. The so-called "Reagan Revolution" is occurring at a time when Americans clearly believe that government has grown excessively; and that government's appetite for the nation's income — now nearly 23 percent of GNP — has to a large degree been the source of America's economic anemia.

More than anything else, it has been these factors within the nation's consciousness that have laid the groundwork for Reagan's impressive and unprecedented legislative achievements. Equally important has been Reagan's obviously persuasive talent as a communicator, which in the end sold his tax and budget cuts to a nation waiting for a plan to lift the country out of its economic malaise.

Not only has Reagan changed the direction of government, but he has also significantly altered the presidential style. Foregoing the punishing 12-hour days of his predecessor, Reagan's 9-to-5 routine — with Wednesday afternoons off for horseback riding — has made the presidency less frenetic and, perhaps, in some ways more reassuring. His decision to take off the month of August to vacation at his ranch is unprecedented among modern presidents.

Reagan's style of governing is built upon a Cabinet government to which he has delegated substantial authority among his closest aides and department heads. His own role, in his words, is "the chairman of the board," charting the overall policies they will implement. One must go back to the days of Dwight Eisenhower, whom Reagan greatly admires, for a comparison to Reagan's brand of governing.

In spite of his early successes, Reagan's record thus far is a mixed one and the future of his administration is uncertain. Deeper budget cuts will be made over the next 3 years in order to balance the budget by 1984. This will no doubt spark bitter opposition among special interest groups. Indeed, the full impact of spending cuts made, and to be made, have not yet filtered through our national consciousness. When it does, the pressure on Congress to resume spending levels of old is likely to intensify.

Still, the most fundamental economic question facing the nation is whether Reagan's combined spending and tax cuts will work? There are as many answers to that question as there are economists.

Whether this 70-year-old president succeeds where others have failed on the economy is impossible to say. But one thing is certain. His efforts to reduce the size and growth of the federal bureaucracy, however tentative, have changed the way government will be run for many years to come.

Heroes of Young America: The Second Annual Poll

Who is the top hero of America's youth? This year, it's no surprise. For the second year in a row, The World Almanac's nationwide poll of 8th graders has chosen Burt Reynolds. The handsome actor, who far outdistanced the rest of the field, won, based on an analysis of the ballots, because his admirers are equally male and female and come from every corner of the United States.

The remainder of the top 30 also showed no great surprises. The top heroes are almost exclusively entertainers, many of them comedians who often play inconoclastic figures. Today's youth admires those who fill TV or screen roles that make fun and often get the better of authority. The actual figures of authority in the U.S., i.e. political leaders, government officials, businessmen, are totally absent from the list.

An interesting aside of the entertainers' predominance is that they are, in fact, almost exclusively actors. Only 3, Kenny Rogers, Olivia Newton-John, and Billy Joel, are singers and musicians. This comes as somewhat of a surprise in light of young America's involvement with pop music. This phenomenon may result from the fact that actors have a strong visual presence, whereas musicians are associated more with the sound of their music.

Also notably down in numbers are sports stars. This year's list of top 30 heroes holds only 3 sports figures, "Sugar" Ray Leonard, Earl Campbell, and "Magic" Johnson, whereas last year 10 of the top 30 heroes came from the sports world, possibly the influence of the Olympic year. Also conspicuously absent are baseball players. This may well reflect the fact that the balloting was conducted in the first weeks of September, not long after the conclusion of the baseball strike.

The second annual World Almanac survey was, again, based on a geographic cross-section of junior high school students, most of them 13 and 14 years old and from both intercity and suburban schools. The young students were asked to consider the persons they admired most and wanted to be like when they grew up. The students were chosen to participate in the poll through representatives of World Almanac co-sponsoring newspapers.

An examination of the results shows one heartening surprise. George Burns, the 85-year-old comedian and actor, who made a strong showing last year but did not place in the top 30, made it into the top 10, ending up in 8th place. In fact, the top 3 are over 40, although two of them, Burt Reynolds and Alan Alda, along with Bill Cosby, are, at 45, the oldest on the list, aside from George Burns, of course. Brooke Shields, at 16, is the youngest, and at least 10 of the others are under 30. In general, there's no question that, not unlike last year's results showed, young America associates its heroes with youthfulness.

Again, reflecting the results seen in the previous year's poll, very few women reach the top 30, only 5 in fact, down one from last year. An examination of the voting shows that while many girls voted for male heroes, very few boys voted for female heroes. The only exceptions in this pattern were Brooke Shields and Bo Derek, the top female vote-getters, who reached spots 4 and 7 respectively on the strength of male support.

Here they are, the heroes of young America:

1. **Burt Reynolds**, actor, popular TV "talk show" personality, has starred in many movies, including *Smokey and the Bandit, Starting Over.*
2. **Richard Pryor**, comedian, actor, starred in *Stir Crazy* and *Bustin' Loose.*
3. **Alan Alda**, TV and movie actor, is best known for his role as "Hawkeye" Pierce on the TV series "M*A*S*H," and recently starred in *The Four Seasons.*
4. **Brooke Shields**, movie actress, model, has starred in *The Blue Lagoon* and *Endless Love.*
5. **John Ritter**, actor, stars in the popular TV series "Three's Company" and recently appeared in *Hero at Large.*
6. **Scott Baio**, TV actor, created the role of "Chachi Arcola" on "Happy Days" and stars in many made-for-television movies.
7. **Bo Derek**, actress, starred in *10* and *Tarzan The Ape Man.*
8. **George Burns**, TV and movie star, recently starred in *Oh God! Book II.*
9. **"Sugar" Ray Leonard**, boxer, current holder of both the WBC and WBA welter-weight boxing titles and won a gold medal in the 1976 Summer Olympics.
10. **Steve Martin**, TV and movie comedian, author of *Cruel Shoes*, starred in *The Jerk.*
11. **Bill Murray**, TV and movie actor, gained fame on "Saturday Night Live" and has starred in *Stripes, Meatballs,* and *Where the Buffalo Roam.*
12. **John Schneider**, TV actor, stars as Bo Duke on the "Dukes of Hazard."
13. **Erik Estrada**, TV actor, stars in the popular TV show "CHiPs."
14. **Robin Williams**, TV and movie actor, star of "Mork and Mindy," will play Garp in the movie version of *The World According to Garp.*
15. **Henry Winkler**, actor, created the role of Fonzie on "Happy Days."
16. **Bill Cosby**, actor, comedian, was the first black to star in a TV series, "I Spy," and has appeared in numerous movies.
17. **John Belushi**, actor, comedian, gained fame on "Saturday Night Live" and in the movie *Animal House* and has recently starred in *Continental Divide.*
18. **Kristy McNichol**, TV and movie actress, has recently appeared in *Only When I Laugh* and *The Night The Lights Went Out in Georgia.*
19. **Tom Selleck**, TV actor, plays the title role on "Magnum, P.I."
20. **Lou Ferrigno**, TV actor, is "The Hulk" on "The Incredible Hulk."
21. **Kenny Rogers**, country and pop singer, composer, whose most popular songs include "The Gambler," "Lucille," and "Coward of the County."
22. **"Magic" Johnson**, basketball player, star guard for the Los Angeles Lakers.
23. **Tom Wopat**, TV actor, plays Luke Duke on "The Dukes of Hazard."
24. **Earl Campbell**, running back for the Houston Oilers, won the Heisman Trophy in 1977, the NFL Rookie of the Year and MVP in 1978, and MVP again in 1979 and 1980.
25. **Goldie Hawn**, actress, both starred in and produced the movie *Private Benjamin.*
26. **Olivia Newton-John**, singer, starred in the movies *Grease* and *Xanadu.*
27. **Christopher Reeve**, actor, played Superman in the recent revival and in the sequal Superman II and starred on Broadway in *The Fifth of July.*
28. **Robert Redford**, actor, director, won an Academy Award for best direction for *Ordinary People.*
29. **Sylvester Stallone**, actor, author, shot to stardom in the title role of the film *Rocky* and recently starred in *Victory.*
30. **Billy Joel**, rock singer, is best known for his hit song "Just the Way You Are."

Mayors and City Managers of Larger North American Cities

As of Oct., 1981

*Asterisk before name denotes city manager. All others are mayors. For mayors, dates are those of next election; for city managers, they are dates of appointment.

D, Democrat; R, Republican; N-P, Non-Partisan

City	Name	Term
Abilene, Tex.	Elbert E. Hall, N-P	1984, Apr.
Abington, Pa.	*Albert Herrmann	1978, May
Akron, Oh.	Roy L. Ray, R	1983, Nov.
Alameda, Cal.	*J. Bruce Rupp	1980, Jan.
Albany, Ga.	*Carl Leay	1980, Jan.
Albany, N.Y.	Erastus Corning 2d, D	1983, Nov.
Albuquerque, N.M.	David Rusk, D	1981, Oct.
Alexandria, La.	Carroll E. Lanier, D	1982, Sept.
Alexandria, Va.	*Douglas Harman	1976, Jan.
Alhambra, Cal.	*Andrew Lazzaretto Jr.	1980, Jan.
Allen Park, Mich.	Frank J. Lada, D	1981, Nov.
Allentown, Pa.	Frank Fischl Jr., R	1981, Nov.
Alton, Ill.	Paul A. Lenz, N-P	1981, Apr.
Altoona, Pa.	Alan Hancock, R	1983, Nov.
Amarillo, Tex.	*John S. Stiff.	1963, Sept.
Ames, La.	*John Elwell	1980, Mar.
Anaheim, Cal.	*William O. Talley	1976, July
Anchorage, Alas.	George M. Sullivan, R.	1981, Nov.
Anderson, Ind.	Thomas McMahan, R	1983, Nov.
Anderson, S.C.	*Richard Burnette	1976, Sept.
Ann Arbor, Mich.	*Terry V. Sprenkel	1980, Jan.
Appleton, Wis.	Dorothy Johnson, N-P	1984, Apr.
Arcadia, Cal.	*George J. Watts	1981, July
Arlington, Mass.	*Donald R. Marquis	1966, Nov.
Arlington, Tex.	*Ross Calhoun	1973, Mar.
Arlington, Va.	*W.V. Ford	1976, Mar.
Arlington Hts., Ill.	*L.A. Hanson	1958, Oct.
Arvada, Col.	*Craig Kocian	1977, Mar.
Asheville, N.C.	Roy Trantham, D	1981, Nov.
Atlanta, Ga.	Maynard Jackson, D	1981, Nov.
Atlantic City, N.J.	Joseph Lazarow, R	1984, May
Auburn, N.Y.	*Bruce Clifford.	1966, Aug.
Augusta, Ga.	Lewis A. Newman, N-P	1981, Nov.
Aurora, Col.	*Robert E. Brown	1978, June
Austin, Tex.	*Dan H. Davidson	1972, Aug.
Bakersfield, Cal.	*Harold E. Bergen.	1966, July
Baldwin Park, Cal.	*Philip R. Sexton	1977, Dec.
Baltimore, Md.	William Schaefer, D	1983, Nov.
Bangor, Me.	*John W. Flynn	1977, Feb.
Baton Rouge, La.	Pat Screen, D	1984, Nov.
Battle Creek, Mich.	*Gordon Jaeger	1976, Mar.
Bay City, Mich.	*David D. Barnes	1979, May
Bayonne, N.J.	Dennis Collins, D	1982, May
Baytown, Tex.	*Fritz Lanham	1972, May
Beaumont, Tex.	*Ray A. Riley	1978, Apr.
Belleville, Ill.	Richard Brauer, N-P	1985, Apr.
Bellevue, Wash.	*Andrea Beatty	1980, June
Bellflower, Cal.	*Jack Simpson	1980, July
Beloit, Wis.	*H. Herbert Holt	1971, Mar.
Berkeley, Cal.	*vacant	
Berwyn, Ill.	Joseph Lanzilotti, D	1985, Apr.
Bessemer, Ala.	Ed Porter, D	1982, Sept.
Bethlehem, Pa.	Paul M. Marcincin, D	1981, Nov.
Beverly Hills, Cal.	*Edward Kreins	1979, Oct.
Billings, Mont.	*Al Thelen	1979, Nov.
Biloxi, Miss.	Gerald Blessey, D	1985, June
Binghamton, N.Y.	Alfred J. Libous, R	1981, Nov.
Birmingham, Ala.	Richard Arrington Jr., D	1983, Oct.
Bismarck, N.D.	Bus Leary, N-P	1982, Apr.
Bloomfield, Minn.	*John Pidgeon	1967, Dec.
Bloomington, Ill.	Richard Buchanan, R	1985, Apr.
Bloomington, Ind.	Francis X. McCloskey, D	1983, Oct.
Bloomington, Minn.	*John Pidgeon	1967, Dec.
Boise, Ida.	Dick Eardley, N-P	1981, Nov.
Bossier City, La.	Marvin E. Anding, D	1985, Mar.
Boston, Mass.	Kevin White, D	1983 Nov.
Boulder, Col.	*Robert Westdyke	1976, Aug.
Bowie, Md.	*G. Charles Moore	1975, Aug.
Bowling Green, Ky.	*Charles W. Coates.	1977, Feb.
Bridgeport, Conn.	John Mandanici, D	1981, Nov.
Bristol, Conn.	Michael Werner, R	1981, Nov.
Brockton, Mass.	David E. Crosby, D	1981, Nov.
Brookline, Mass.	Board of Selectmen	
Brooklyn Center, Minn.	*Gerald G. Splinter	1977, Oct.
Bryan, Tex.	*Ernest R. Clark.	1979, Feb.
Buffalo, N.Y.	James D. Griffen, D	1981, Nov.

City	Name	Term
Burlington, Vt.	Bernard Sanders, N-P	1983, Mar.
Calumet City, Ill.	Robert C. Stefaniak, D	1985, Apr.
Cambridge, Mass.	*Robert Healy, Act.	1981, July
Camden, N.J.	Melvin Primas Jr., D.	1985, May
Canton, Oh.	Stanley A. Cmich, R.	1983, Nov.
Carson, Cal.	*vacant	
Casper, Wyo.	*Kenneth Erickson	1969, Oct.
Cedar Rapids, Ia.	Donald J. Canney, N-P	1981, Nov.
Champaign, Ill.	*V. Eugene Miller	1974, Sept.
Charleston, S.C.	Joseph P. Riley Jr., D.	1983, Nov.
Charleston, W. Va.	Joe F. Smith, D	1983, Mar.
Charlotte, N.C.	*O. Wendell White	1981, Mar.
Charlottesville, Va.	*Cole Hendrix	1971, Jan.
Chattanooga, Tenn.	Charles A. Rose, N-P	1983, Mar.
Chesapeake, Va.	*John T. Maxwell	1978, Sept.
Chester, Pa.	Joseph Battle, R.	1983, Nov.
Cheyenne, Wyo.	Donald Erickson, R	1984, Nov.
Chicago, Ill.	Jane M. Byrne, D	1983, Apr.
Chicago Hts., Ill.	Charles Panici, R	1983, Apr.
Chicopee, Mass.	Robert Kumor Jr., D.	1981, Nov.
Chula Vista, Cal.	*Lane F. Cole	1975, Feb.
Cicero, Ill.	Henry J. Klosak, R	1985, Apr.
Cincinnati, Oh.	*Sylvester Murray	1979, Sept.
Clarksville, Tenn.	Ted Crozier, N-P	1982, Nov.
Clearwater, Fla.	*Anthony Shoemaker .	1977, June
Cleveland, Oh.	George Voinovich, R	1981, Nov.
Cleveland Hgts., Oh.	*Richard Robinson	1978, July
Clifton, N.J.	*William Holster	1957, Mar.
Col. Spgs., Col.	*George H. Fellows	1966, July
Columbia, Mo.	*Richard Gray	1980, Nov.
Columbia, S.C.	*Graydon V. Olive Jr.	1970, Mar.
Columbus, Ga.	Harry Jackson, D	1982, Nov.
Columbus, Oh.	Tom Moody, R.	1983, Nov.
Commerce, Cal.	*Robert Hinderliter	1973, Aug.
Compton, Cal.	*Ronald D. Nelson	1981, July
Concord, Cal.	*Farrel A. Stewart.	1960, Apr.
Coon Rapids., Minn.	*Richard Thistle	1979, July
Coral Gables, Fla.	*J. Martin Gainer	1975, Jan.
Corpus Christi, Tex.	*R. Marvin Townsend .	1968, Jan.
Corvallis, Ore.	*Gary F. Pokorny	1978, Nov.
Costa Mesa, Cal.	*Fred Sorsabel	1970
Council Bluffs, Ia.	*Michael G. Miller	1978, Aug.
Covington, Ky.	Bernard Moorman, N-P	1983, Nov.
Cranston, R.I.	Edward DiPrefe, R	1982, Nov.
Crystal, Minn.	*John Irving	1963, Jan.
Culver City, Cal.	*Dale Jones	1969, Aug.
Cuyahoga Falls, Oh.	Robert Quirk, D	1981, Nov.
Dallas, Tex.	*Charles S. Anderson.	1981, Oct.
Daly City, Cal.	*David R. Rowe	1969, July
Danbury, Conn.	James Dyer, D.	1981, Nov.
Danville, Ill.	David S. Palmer, N-P	1983, Apr.
Danville, Va.	*Charles Church	1981, June
Dayton, Oh.	*Earl Sterzer.	1979, Feb.
Daytona Bch., Fla.	*Howard D. Tipton	1978, Oct.
Dearborn, Mich.	John O'Reilly, N-P	1981, Nov.
Dearborn Hgts., Mich.	Donald Bishop, D	1981, Nov.
Decatur, Ala.	Bill Dukes, N-P.	1984, Aug.
Decatur, Ill.	*Leslie T. Allen	1972, Sept.
Denton, Tex.	*G. Charles Hartung	1977, Sept.
Denver, Col.	William H. McNichols, D	1983, May
Des Moines, Ia.	*Richard Wilkey	1974, Mar.
Des Plaines, Ill.	John Seitz, R.	1985, Apr.
Detroit, Mich.	Coleman A. Young, N-P	1981, Nov.
Dover, Del.	*John P. Mogan	1979, Mar.
Downers Grove, Ill.	*James R. Griesemer.	1972, Sept.
Downey, Cal.	*John W. Donlevy	1981, Aug.
Dubuque, Ia.	*W. Kenneth Gearhart	1979, Aug.
Duluth, Minn.	John Fedo, D	1983, Nov.
Durham, N.C.	*Barry Del Castilho	1980, Oct.
E. Chicago, Ind.	Robert A. Pastrick, D	1983, Nov.
E. Cleveland, Oh.	*Frank Wise	1979, Jan.
E. Detroit, Mich.	*J. Scott Miller.	1979, Oct.
E. Hartford, Conn.	George Dagon, D	1981, Nov.
E. Lansing, Mich.	*Jerry Coffman	1977, Jan.
E. Orange, N.J.	Thomas H. Cooke Jr., D	1981, Nov.

City	Name	Term
E. Providence, R.I.	Mark Hayward, R	1982, Nov.
E. St. Louis, Ill.	Carl E. Officer, D	1983, Apr.
Eau Claire, Wis.	*Stephen Atkins	1978, Sept.
Edina, Minn.	*Kenneth Rosland	1977, Nov.
Edison, N.J.	Anthony Yelencsics, D	1981, Nov.
El Cajon, Cal.	*Robert Applegate	1958, Sept.
El Monte, Cal.	*Douglas Dunlap	1981, Jan.
El Paso, Tex.	Johnathan W. Rogers, N-P	1983, Apr.
Elgin, Ill.	*Leo Wilson	1972, Dec.
Elizabeth, N.J.	Thomas G. Dunn, D	1984, Nov.
Elkhart, Ind.	Eleanor Kesim, D	1983, Nov.
Elmhurst, Ill.	*Robert T. Palmer	1953, Aug.
Elmira, N.Y.	*Joseph E. Sartori	1972, June
Elyria, Oh.	Michael Keys, D	1983, Nov.
Enfield, Conn.	*Robert F. Ledger Jr.	1977, Mar.
Enid, Okla.	*Lyle Smith	1979, Feb.
Erie, Pa.	Louis J. Tullio, D	1981, Nov.
Escondido, Cal.	*Ray Windsor	1980, Jan.
Euclid, Oh.	Anthony Giunta, D	1983, Nov.
Eugene, Ore.	*Michael Gleason	1981, Jan.
Evanston, Ill.	*Edward A. Martin	1971, Apr.
Evansville, Ind.	Michael Vandiver, D	1983, Nov.
Everett, Mass.	Edward Connolly, D	1981, Nov.
Everett, Wash.	Bill Moore, N-P	1981, Nov.
Fairborn, Oh.	*William Burns	1977, Feb.
Fairfield, Cal.	*B. Gale Wilson	1956, Mar.
Fairfield, Conn.	John J. Sullivan, D	1981, Nov.
Fair Lawn, N.J.	*Frank Peruggi	1977, July
Fall River, Mass.	Carlton Viveiros, N-P	1981, Nov.
Fargo, N.D.	Jon Lindgren, D	1982, Apr.
Farmington Hills, Mich.	*Lawrence Savage	1979, Feb.
Fayetteville, Ark.	*Donald Grimes	1972, Apr.
Fayetteville, N.C.	*William G. Thomas 3d	1976, Sept.
Fitchburg, Mass.	David Gilmartin, D	1983, Oct.
Flagstaff, Ariz.	Paul Babbitt Jr., N-P	1982, Apr.
Flint, Mich.	James Rutherford, N-P	1983, Nov.
Florissant, Mo.	James J. Eagan, N-P	1983, Apr.
Fond du Lac, Wis.	David Metzger, N-P	1982, Apr.
Ft. Collins, Col.	*John Arnold	1977, Oct.
Ft. Lauderdale, Fla.	*Constance Hoffmann	1980, Oct.
Ft. Lee, N.J.	Nicholas Corbiscello, R.	1984, Nov.
Ft. Smith, Ark.	*William Faught	1981, July
Ft. Wayne, Ind.	Wilfred Moses, D	1983, Nov.
Ft. Worth, Tex.	*Robert Herchert	1978, Aug.
Fremont, Cal.	*Charles Kent McClain	1981, May
Fresno, Cal.	*Gerald E. Newfarmer	1978, Sept.
Fullerton, Cal.	*William C. Winter	1979, Oct.
Gadsden, Ala.	Steve Means, D.	1982, July
Gainesville, Fla.	*Orville Powell	1980, Jan.
Galesburg, Ill.	*Lawrence Asaro	1979, Sept.
Galveston, Tex.	*Stephen Huffman	1980, Apr.
Gardena, Cal.	*John Sheehan	1979, Oct.
Garden Grove, Cal.	*Delbert L. Powers	1980, July
Garfield Hts., Oh.	Theodore Holtz, D	1981, Nov.
Garland, Tex.	*Fred Greene	1979, Sept.
Gary, Ind.	Richard G. Hatcher, D	1983, Nov.
Gastonia, N.C.	*Gary Hicks	1973, Dec.
Glendale, Ariz.	*S.F. Van de Putte	1960, Aug.
Grand Forks, N.D.	H.C. Wessman, R	1982, Apr.
Gr. Island, Neb.	Robert L. Kriz, N-P	1982, Nov.
Gr. Prairie, Tex.	*Ted C. Willis	1981, Aug.
Gr. Rapids, Mich.	*Joseph G. Zainea	1976, Oct.
Great Falls, Mont.	*Richard D. Thomas	1973, May
Greeley, Col.	*Peter Morrell	1973, Dec.
Green Bay, Wis.	Samuel Halloin, N-P.	1983, Apr.
Greensboro, N.C.	*T.Z. Osborne	1973, Feb.
Greenville, Miss.	William Burnley Jr., D	1983, Dec.
Greenville, S.C.	Jesse L. Helms, R.	1983, May
Greenwich, Conn.	Ruth L. Sims, D	1981, Nov.
Groton, Conn.	Catherine Kolnaski, D	1983, May
Hackensack, N.J.	*Joseph J. Squillace	1964, Oct.
Hagerstown, Md.	Donald Frush, R	1985, Mar.
Hamden, Conn.	Richard Harris, D	1981, Nov.
Hamilton, Oh.	*Jack Kirsch	1975, Dec.
Hammond, Ind.	Edward J. Raskosky, D.	1983, May
Hampton, Va.	*Thomas Miller	1981, Mar.
Harlingen, Tex.	Randy Whittington, N-P	1982, Nov.
Harrisburg, Pa.	Paul Doutrich, R	1981, Nov.
Hartford, Conn.	*W. Wilson Gaitor	1980, July
Harvey, Ill.	James A. Haines, R.	1983, Feb.
Hattiesburg, Miss.	Bobby L. Chain, R	1985, Apr.
Haverhill, Mass.	Thomas Vathally, D	1981, Nov.

City	Name	Term
Hawthorne, Cal.	*R. Kenneth Jue	1977, Jan.
Hayward, Cal.	*Donald Blubaugh	1979, Nov.
Hialeah, Fla.	Dale Bennett, D	1981, Nov.
High Point, N.C.	*Cyrus L. Books	1976, Aug.
Highland Pk., Ill.	Robert Buhai, N-P.	1983, Apr.
Hoboken, N.J.	Steve Cappiello, D	1985, May
Hollywood, Fla.	*James Chandler	1976, Nov.
Holyoke, Mass.	Ernest Proulx, D.	1983, Nov.
Honolulu, Ha.	Eileen Anderson, D	1984, Nov.
Hot Springs, Ark.	Tom Ellsworth, N-P	1982, Nov.
Houston, Tex.	James McConn, N-P	1981, Nov.
Huntington, W. Va.	*Richard Barton	1978, Feb.
Huntington Beach, Cal.	*Floyd Belsito	1976, June
Huntsville, Ala.	Joe W. Davis, N-P.	1984, July
Hutchinson, Kan.	*George Pyle	1967, Sept.
Idaho Falls, Ida.	Thomas Campbell, N-P	1981, Nov.
Independence, Mo.	*Keith Wilson Jr.	1980, July
Indianapolis, Ind.	William Hudnut, R	1983, Nov.
Inglewood, Cal.	*Paul Eckles	1975, Nov.
Inkster, Mich.	William Daniels, D	1983, Nov.
Iowa City, Ia.	*Neal Berlin	1975, Feb.
Irving, Tex.	*Jack Huffman	1974, Jan.
Irvington, N.J.	Robert Miller, D	1982, Apr.
Jackson, Mich.	*S.W. McAllister Jr.	1974, Mar.
Jackson, Miss.	Dale Danks, D	1985, May
Jackson, Tenn.	Bob Conger, D.	1983, June
Jacksonville, Fla.	Jake Godbold, D.	1983, May
Jamestown, N.Y.	Steve Carlson, D	1981, Nov.
Janesville, Wis.	*Philip L. Deaton.	1976, Mar.
Jefferson City, Mo.	George Hartsfield, D	1983, Apr.
Jersey City, N.J.	Gerald McCann, N-P	1985, May
Johnson City, Tenn.	*Charles Tyson	1979, Jan.
Johnstown, Pa.	Charles Tomljanovic, D.	1981, Nov.
Joliet, Ill.	*vacant	
Joplin, Mo.	*James P. Berzina	1977, Mar.
Kalamazoo, Mich.	*Robert C. Bobb.	1976, Nov.
Kansas City, Kan.	John Reardon, D	1983, Apr.
Kansas City, Mo.	Richard Berkley, N-P	1983, May
Kenosha, Wis.	John Bilotti, N-P	1984, Apr.
Kettering, Oh.	Charles Horn, R	1981, Nov.
Key West, Fla.	*Robert Bensko	1981, Mar.
Killeen, Tex.	*Mike Eastland	1974, Apr.
Knoxville, Tenn.	Randell L. Tyree, D	1983, Oct.
Kokomo, Ind.	Stephen Daily, D	1983, Nov.
LaCrosse, Wis.	Patrick Zielke, N-P	1983, Apr.
La Habra, Cal.	*Lee Risner	1970, Nov.
La Mesa, Cal.	*Ronald Bradley	1980, May
La Mirada, Cal.	*Gary K. Sloan	1981, Apr.
Lafayette, Ind.	James Riehle, D.	1983, Nov.
Lafayette, La.	Dud Lastrapes, R	1984, Apr.
Lake Charles, La.	Paul Savoie, D.	1985, Apr.
Lakeland, Fla.	*Robert V. Youkey	1960, Jan.
Lakewood, Cal.	*Howard L. Chambers	1976, May
Lakewood, Col.	*Bill Kirchhoff	1980, Oct.
Lakewood, Oh.	Anthony Sinagra, R	1983, Nov.
Lancaster, Pa.	Arthur E. Morris, R	1981, Nov.
Lansing, Mich.	Gerald Graves, N-P.	1981, Nov.
Laredo, Tex.	Aldo Tatangelo, D	1982, Apr.
Las Cruces, N.M.	*J.W. Harrison	1980, Aug.
Las Vegas, Nev.	William Briare, N-P	1983, June
Lawrence, Kan.	*Buford M. Watson Jr.	1970, Jan.
Lawton, Okla.	*Robert Metzinger	1977, Jan.
Lewiston, Me.	*Lucien Gosselin	1980, Jan.
Lexington, Ky.	James Amato, N-P	1981, Nov.
Lima, Oh.	Harry Moyer, N-P	1981, Nov.
Lincoln, Neb.	Helen Boosalis, N-P.	1983, May
Linden, N.J.	John Gregorio, D	1982, Nov.
Little Rock, Ark.	*Mahlon Martin	1980, July
Livermore, Cal.	*Leland Horner	1978, Oct.
Long Beach, Cal.	*John Dever	1977, Jan.
Long Beach, N.Y.	*William McKenney	1978, Jan.
Longview, Tex.	*C. Ray Jackson	1980, Apr.
Lorain, Oh.	William Parker, D	1983, Nov.
Los Angeles, Cal.	Thomas Bradley, N-P	1985, June
Louisville, Ky.	William Stansbury, D	1981, Nov.
Lowell, Mass.	*B. Joseph Tully	1979, June
L. Merion, Pa.	*Thomas B. Fulweiler	1968, Jan.
Lubbock, Tex.	*Larry Cunningham	1976, Sept.
Lynchburg, Va.	*E. Allen Culverhouse	1979, June
Lynn, Mass.	Antonio J. Marino, D.	1981, Nov.
Lynwood, Cal.	*James Weaver	1980, Nov.

City	Name	Term
Macon, Ga.	George Israel, R	1983, Nov.
Madison, Wis.	Joel Skornicka, N-P	1983, Apr.
Malden, Mass.	James Conway, D	1981, Nov.
Manchester, Conn.	Stephen Penny, D	1981, Nov.
Manchester, N.H.	Charles Stanton, D	1981, Nov.
Manitowoc, Wis.	Anthony V. Dufek, D	1983, Apr.
Mansfield, Oh.	Edward Meehan, R	1983, Nov.
Marion, Ind.	Fred Weagley, R	1983, Nov.
Marion, Oh.	Ronald Malone, R	1983, Nov.
McAllen, Tex.	Othal Brand, N-P	1983, Apr.
McKeesport, Pa.	Lou Washowich, D	1983, May
Medford, Mass.	*Carroll P. Sheehan.	1980, Aug.
Melbourne, Fla.	*Samuel Halter	1978, July
Memphis, Tenn.	Wyeth Chandler, N-P	1983, Nov.
Mentor, Oh.	*Edward Podojil.	1977, Nov.
Meridian, Miss.	*Joel W. Forrester	1959, July
Mesa, Ariz.	*C.K. Luster	1979, June
Mesquite, Tex.	*C.K. Duggins	1976, Feb.
Miami, Fla.	*Howard V. Gary	1981, Apr.
Miami Beach, Fla.	Murray Meyerson, N-P	1981, Nov.
Middletown, Oh.	*Dale F. Helsel	1970, Oct.
Midland, Tex.	G. Thane Akins, N-P	1982, Apr.
Midwest City, Okla.	*Irving P. Frank	1978, Apr.
Milford, Conn.	Henry Povinelli, R	1981, Nov.
Milwaukee, Wis.	Henry W. Maier, D	1984, Apr.
Minneapolis, Minn.	Donald Fraser, D	1981, Nov.
Minnetonka, Minn.	*James F. Miller	1979, Jan.
Minot, N.D.	*R.A. Schempp	1977, Nov.
Mobile, Ala.	Gary Greenough, N-P	1985, July
Modesto, Cal.	*Garth Lipsky	1974, Jan.
Monroe, La.	Robert Powell, D	1984, May
Montclair, N.J.	*Bertrand Kendall	1980, Sept.
Montebello, Cal.	*Joseph Goeden	1980, May
Monterey Park, Cal.	*Lloyd de Llamas	1976, Sept.
Montgomery, Ala.	Emory Folmar, R	1983, Nov.
Mt. Prospect, Ill.	*Terrance Burghard.	1978, Oct.
Mt. Vernon, N.Y.	Thomas E. Sharpe, D	1983, Nov.
Mountain View, Cal.	*Bruce Liedstrand	1976, Aug.
Muncie, Ind.	Alan K. Wilson, R	1983, Nov.
Muskegon, Mich.	*William Gleason	1979, June
Muskogee, Okla.	*C. Clay Harrell	1979, June
Napa, Cal.	Phyllis Moore, R	1984, Apr.
Nashua, N.H.	Maurice Arel, D	1983, Nov.
Nashville, Tenn.	Richard Fulton, D	1984, Sept.
National City, Cal.	*Tom McCabe	1979, Feb.
New Bedford, Mass.	John Markey, N-P	1981, Nov.
New Britain, Conn.	William J. McNamara, D	1981, Nov.
New Brunswick, N.J.	John Lynch, D	1982, Nov.
New Castle, Pa.	Angelo Sands, D	1983, Nov.
New Haven, Conn.	Biagio DiLieto, D	1981, Nov.
New Kensington, Pa.	Verle N. Bevan, D	1981, Nov.
New London, Conn.	*C.F. Driscoll.	1969, May
New Orleans, La.	Ernest Morial, D	1982, Feb.
New Rochelle, N.Y.	*C. Samuel Kissinger	1975, Apr.
New York, N.Y.	Edward Koch, D	1981, Nov.
Newark, N.J.	Kenneth Gibson, D	1982, July
Newark, Oh.	Mary M. Lusk, D	1983, Nov.
Newport, R.I.	*John Connors Jr.	1981, Mar.
Newport Beach, Cal.	*Robert L. Wynn.	1971, Aug.
Newport News, Va.	*Robert T. Williams	1981, Feb.
Newton, Mass.	Theodore Mann, N-P	1981, Nov.
Niagara Falls, N.Y.	*William Sdao	1980, Mar.
Norfolk, Va.	*Julian Hirst	1975, July
Norman, Okla.	*James D. Crosby.	1976, Feb.
Norristown, Pa.	*John Plonski	1979, Apr.
No. Charleston, S.C.	John Bourne, R	1982, May
North Chicago, Ill.	Leo F. Kukla, D	1985, Apr.
No. Little Rock, Ark.	Reed Thompson, N-P	1984, Nov.
Norwalk, Cal.	Cecil Green, D	1982, Apr.
Norwalk, Conn.	William A. Collins, D	1981, Nov.
Norwich, Conn.	*Charles Whitty	1973, June
Novato, Cal.	*Phillip J. Brown	1974, May
Oak Lawn, Ill.	*Richard E. O'Neill	1976, May
Oak Park, Ill.	*Jack Grundy	1976, Oct.
Oak Ridge, Tenn.	*M. Lyle Lacy 3d	1978, July
Oakland, Cal.	*Henry L. Gardner	1981, June
Oceanside, Cal.	*Robert Bourcier	1978, June
Odessa, Tex.	*Kerry R. Sweatt	1978, Jan.
Ogden, Ut.	*Cowles Mallory.	1981, Mar.
Oklahoma City, Okla.	*James Cook	1976, Apr.
Omaha, Neb.	Michael Boyle, D	1985 May
Ontario, Cal.	R.E. Ellingwood, N-P	1982, Apr.
Orange, Cal.	*Joseph Baker.	1978, Dec.
Orange, N.J.	Joel Shain, D.	1984, May

City	Name	Term
Orlando, Fla.	Bill Frederick, N-P	1984, Sept.
Oshkosh, Wis.	*W. O. Frueh.	1976, Aug.
Overland Park, Kan.	*Donald Pipes	1977, June
Owensboro, Ky.	*William Sequino	1981, Apr.
Oxnard, Cal.	*Stephen Cook	1979, Apr.
Pacifica, Cal.	*David Finigan	1981, May
Palm Springs, Cal.	*Norman R. King	1979, Dec.
Palo Alto, Cal.	*William Zaner	1979, Sept.
Parkersburg, W. Va.	Alvin K. Smith, D	1981, Nov.
Parma, Oh.	John Petruska, D	1983, Nov.
Pasadena, Cal.	*Donald F. McIntyre.	1973, June
Pasadena, Tex.	Johnny Isbell, N-P	1983, Apr.
Passaic, N.J.	Robert Hare, N-P	1985, May
Paterson, N.J.	Lawrence Kramer, R	1982, May
Pawtucket, R.I.	William Harty Jr., D	1981, Nov.
Peabody, Mass.	Peter Torigian, D	1981, Nov.
Pekin, Ill.	Willard Birkmeier, D	1983, Apr.
Pensacola, Fla.	*Steve Garman	1978, June
Peoria, Ill.	*James B. Daken	1979, Jan.
Petersburg, Va.	*John P. Bond 3d	1979, Oct.
Perth Amboy, N.J.	George J. Otlowski, D	1984, May
Philadelphia, Pa.	William Green, D	1983, Nov.
Phoenix, Ariz.	*Marvin Andrews	1976, Oct.
Pico Rivera, Cal.	*vacant	
Pine Bluff, Ark.	D.W. Wallis, D	1984, Nov.
Pittsburgh, Pa.	Richard S. Caliguiri, D.	1981, Nov.
Pittsfield, Mass.	Charles Smith, D	1981, Nov.
Plainfield, N.J.	Paul O'Keeffe, R	1981, Nov.
Pocatello, Ida.	*Charles W. Moss.	1970, Jan.
Pomona, Cal.	*Ora E. Lampman.	1978, July
Pompano Bch., Fla.	*John Schoeberlein.	1975, May
Pontiac, Mich.	*Joseph Neipling	1979, May
Port Arthur, Tex.	*George Dibrell	1962, Oct.
Port Huron, Mich.	*Gerald R. Bouchard	1965, June
Portage, Mich.	*Donald Ziemke	1974, Aug.
Portland, Me.	*Stephen Honey.	1980, Oct.
Portland, Ore.	Frank Ivancie, N-P	1984, Nov.
Portsmouth, Oh.	*Barry Feldman	1977, Jan.
Portsmouth, Va.	*G. Robert House Jr.	1981, Mar.
Poughkeepsie, N.Y.	*John St. Leger, Act.	1981, Sept.
Prichard, Ala.	John H. Smith, D	1984, June
Providence, R.I.	Vincent Cianci Jr., R	1982, Nov.
Provo, Ut.	Jim Ferguson, N-P	1981, Nov.
Pueblo, Col.	*Fred E. Weisbroad	1967, Feb.
Quincy, Ill.	C. David Neussen, R	1985, Apr.
Quincy, Mass.	Arthur H. Tobin, D	1981, Nov.
Racine, Wis.	Stephen Olson, N-P	1983, Apr.
Raleigh, N.C.	G. Smedes York, N-P	1983, Oct.
Rapid City, S.D.	Arthur La Croix, R	1983, Apr.
Reading, Pa.	Karen Miller, D	1983, Nov.
Redlands, Cal.	*Chris Christiansen	1978, Nov.
Redondo Beach, Cal.	*Timothy Casey	1981, May
Redwood City, Cal.	*James M. Fales Jr.	1971, Aug.
Reno, Nev.	*Chris Cherches	1980, Nov.
Revere, Mass.	George V. Colella, D	1981, Nov.
Richardson, Tex.	Raymond Noah, R.	1983, Apr.
Richfield, Minn.	*Karl Nollenberger	1979, July
Richmond, Cal.	*Joseph Salvato.	1980, July
Richmond, Ind.	Clifford Dickman, R	1983, Nov.
Richmond, Va.	*Manuel Deese	1979, Jan.
Riverside, Cal.	*Douglas Weiford	1980, Mar.
Roanoke, Va.	*H. Bern Ewert	1978, Jan.
Rochester, Minn.	*Steven Kvenvold	1979, June
Rochester, N.Y.	*Peter Korn	1980, Mar.
Rock Hill, S.C.	*Joe Lanford	1979, July
Rock Island, Ill.	James R. Davis, N-P	1981, Apr.
Rockford, Ill.	John McNamara, D	1985, Mar.
Rockville, Md.	*Larry N. Blick	1972, Nov.
Rome, N.Y.	Carl Eilenberg, R	1983, Nov.
Rosemead, Cal.	*Frank Tripepi	1975, Jan.
Roseville, Mich.	*B. J. Nardelli	1976, Mar.
Roseville, Minn.	*James Andre	1974, May
Rosewell, N.M.	*Robert Owen	1973, Oct.
Royal Oak, Mich.	*William Baldridge	1975, Sept.
Sacramento, Cal.	*Walter Slipe.	1976, Mar.
Saginaw, Mich.	*Thomas Dalton	1978, Nov.
St. Clair Shores, Mich.	*Robert James	1979, Feb.
St. Cloud, Minn.	Robert Huston, N-P	1982, Apr.
St. Joseph, Mo.	Gordon Weaver, R	1982, Apr.
St. Louis, Mo.	Vincent Schoemehl, D	1985, Apr.
St. Louis Pk., Minn.	*James Brimeyer	1980, Aug.
St. Paul, Minn.	George Latimer, D	1982, Apr.

City	Name	Term
St. Petersburg, Fla.	*Alan Harvey	1980, Mar.
Salem, Mass.	Jean Levesque, D	1981, Nov.
Salem, Ore.	*Ralph Hanley	1978, June
Salina, Kan.	*Rufus L. Nye	1979, May
Salinas, Cal.	*Robert Christofferson	1972, Dec.
Salt Lake City, Ut.	Ted Wilson, D	1983, Nov.
San Angelo, Tex.	*H. D. Howard	1958
San Antonio, Tex.	*Thomas Huebner.	1977, Jan.
San Bernardino, Cal.	W. R. Holcomb, R.	1985, Mar.
San Bruno, Cal.	*Gerald Minford	1971, Dec.
San Diego, Cal.	*Ray Blair Jr.	1978, May
San Francisco, Cal.	Dianne Feinstein, D	1983, Nov.
San Jose, Cal.	*Francis T. Fox	1980, May
San Leandro, Cal.	*Lee Riordan.	1976, Apr.
San Mateo, Cal.	*Richard Delong.	1976, Sept.
Sandusky, Oh.	*Frank Link.	1972, Jan.
Santa Ana, Cal.	*A. J. Wilson	1980, July
Santa Barbara, Cal.	*Richard Thomas	1977, Jan.
Santa Cruz, Cal.	*Richard Wilson	1981, June
Santa Fe, N.M.	*W.C. Sisneros	1979, Oct.
Santa Maria, Cal.	*Robert Grogan	1963, Jan.
Santa Monica, Cal.	*vacant	
Santa Rosa, Cal.	*Kenneth Blackman.	1969, July
Sarasota, Fla.	*Kenneth Thompson	1950, Feb.
Savannah, Ga.	*Arthur A. Mendonsa	1971, Sept.
Schenectady, N.Y.	Frank J. Duci, R	1983, Nov.
Scottsdale, Ariz.	*Roy Pederson	1980, Mar.
Scranton, Pa.	Eugene Hickey, D	1981, Nov.
Seattle, Wash.	Charles Royer, N-P	1981, Nov.
Shaker Heights, Oh.	Walter C. Kelley, N-P	1983, Nov.
Sheboygan, Wis.	Richard Suscha, N-P	1985, Apr.
Shreveport, La.	W. T. (Billy) Hanna Jr., D	1982, Nov.
Simi Valley, Cal.	*Lin Koester	1979, June
Sioux City, Ia.	*Paul Flynn.	1979, May
Sioux Falls, S.D.	Rick Knobe, R	1984, Apr.
Skokie, Ill.	*Robert Eppley	1979, Jan.
Somerville, Mass.	Eugene Brune, D	1981, Nov.
South Bend, Ind.	Roger Parent, D	1983, Nov.
So. Gate, Cal.	*John Gottes, Act.	1981, Aug.
So. S.F., Cal.	*C. W. Birkelo	1978
Southfield, Mich.	*Del Borgsdorf.	1980, June
Spartanburg, S.C.	*W. H. Carstarphen.	1975, Apr.
Spokane, Wash.	*Terry Novak	1978, July
Springfield, Ill.	J. Michael Houston, R.	1983, Apr.
Springfield, Mass	Theodore Dimauro, D.	1981, Nov.
Springfield, Mo.	*Don G. Busch.	1971, Oct.
Springfield, Oh.	*Thomas M. Bay	1978, Nov.
Stamford, Conn.	Louis A. Clapes, R	1981, Nov.
Sterling Hts., Mich.	*Leonard Hendricks.	1968, Aug.
Stillwater, Okla.	*Lawrence Gish	1966, Aug.
Stockton, Cal.	*Ray Cezar	1980, Dec.
Stratford, Conn.	*Michael Brown	1978, May
Suffolk, Va.	*John Rowe Jr.	1981, Mar.
Sunnyvale, Cal.	*Thomas Lewcock	1980, Apr.
Syracuse, N.Y.	Lee Alexander, D	1981, Nov.
Tacoma, Wash.	*Erling O. Mork	1975, June
Tallahassee, Fla.	*Daniel A. Kleman.	1974, Aug.
Tampa, Fla.	Bob Martinez, N-P	1983, Mar.
Taunton, Mass.	Joseph Amaral, D	1981, Nov.
Taylor, Mich.	Donald L. Zub, D	1981, Nov.
Teaneck, N.J.	*Werner H. Schmid	1959, Mar.
Tempe, Ariz.	Harry E. Mitchell, D	1982, Apr.
Temple, Tex.	*Barney Knight	1978, Dec.
Terre Haute, Ind.	P. Pete Chalos, D	1983, Nov.
Thousand Oaks, Cal.	*Grant Brimhall	1978, Jan.
Titusville, Fla.	*Norman Hickey	1974, June
Toledo, Oh.	*J. Michael Porter	1979, Feb.
Topeka, Kan.	William McCormick, N-P	1983, Apr.
Torrance, Cal.	*Edward J. Ferraro	1964, Mar.
Trenton, N.J.	Arthur Holland, N-P	1982, May
Troy, Mich.	*Frank Gerstenecker	1970, Feb.
Troy, N.Y.	*John P. Buckley	1972, June
Tucson, Ariz.	*Joel Valdez	1974, May
Tulsa, Okla.	James M. Inhofe, R	1982, Apr.
Tuscaloosa, Ala.	Ernest Collins, N-P	1981, Oct.
Tyler, Tex.	*Ed Wagoner	1977, June
Union City, N.J.	William Musto, D	1982, May
Univ. City, Mo.	*Frank Ollendorff	1980, Mar.
Upland, Cal.	*S. Lee Travers	1974, June
Upper Arlington, Oh.	*H. W. Hyrne	1968, May
Urbana, Ill.	Jeffrey Markland, R	1985, Apr.
Utica, N.Y.	Stephen Pawlinga, D	1981, Nov.
Vallejo, Cal.	*Ted McDonell.	1979, Jan.
Vancouver, Wash.	*Paul Grattet.	1980, June
Victoria, Tex.	*James J. Miller	1980, June
Vineland, N.J.	Patrick R. Fiorilli, N-P	1984, May
Virginia Beach, Va.	*George L. Hanbury	1974, Nov.
Waco, Tex.	*David F. Smith Jr.	1971, Aug.
Walnut Creek, Cal.	*Thomas Dunne	1972, May
Waltham, Mass.	Arthur J. Clark, N-P	1981, Nov.
Warren, Mich.	Ted Bates, N-P	1981, Nov.
Warwick, R.I.	Joseph Walsh, D	1982, Nov.
Wash, D.C.	Marion Barry, D	1982, Nov.
Waterbury, Conn.	Edward Bergin, D	1981, Nov.
Waterloo, Ia.	Leo Rooff, N-P	1981, Nov.
Waukegan, Ill.	Bill Morris, D	1981, Apr.
Waukesha, Wis.	Joseph LaPorte, N-P	1982, Apr.
Wausau, Wis.	John Kannenberg, N-P	1984, Apr.
Wauwatosa, Wis.	James A. Benz, N-P	1984, Apr.
W. Allis, Wis.	Jack Barlich, N-P	1984, Feb.
W. Covina, Cal.	*Herman Fast	1976, Aug.
W. Hartford, Conn.	*William Brady	1977, Sept.
W. Haven, Conn.	Robert A. Johnson, D	1981, Nov.
W. New York, N.J.	Anthony DeFino, D	1983, May
W. Palm Beach, Fla.	*Richard Simmons	1969, Nov.
Westland, Mich.	Thomas F. Taylor, N-P	1981, Nov.
Westminster, Cal.	*vacant	
Weymouth, Mass.	Board of Selectmen	
Wheaton, Ill.	Ralph Barger, R	1983, Apr.
Wheeling, W. Va.	*F. Wayne Barte.	1979, Nov.
White Plains, N.Y.	Alfred Del Vecchio, R	1981, Nov.
Whittier, Cal.	*Tom Mauk	1980, Sept.
Wichita, Kan.	*E. H. Denton	1976, July
Wichita Falls, Tex.	*Stuart A. Bach	1980, Oct.
Wilkes-Barre, Pa.	Thomas McLaughlin, D	1983, Nov.
Williamsport, Pa.	Stephen Lucasi, R.	1983, Nov.
Wilmington, Del.	William T. McLaughlin, D	1984, Nov.
Wilmington, N.C.	*Robert Cobb	1977, Dec.
Winston-Salem, N.C.	*Bryce A. Stuart.	1980, Jan.
Woonsocket, R.I.	Gaston Ayotte Jr., D	1981, Nov.
Worcester, Mass.	*Francis J. McGrath.	1951, Apr.
Wyoming, Mich.	*James Sheeran	1976, Nov.
Yakima, Wash.	*Richard Zais Jr.	1979, Jan.
Yonkers, N.Y.	*Eugene J. Fox	1980, Nov.
York, Pa.	Elizabeth Marshall, D	1981, Nov.
Youngstown, Oh.	George Vukovich, D	1981, Nov.
Zanesville, Oh.	Cameron R. Agin, N-P	1983, Nov.

Canadian Cities

(as of Oct. 23, 1981)

City	Name	Term
Calgary, Alta.	Ralph Klein.	1983, Oct.
Charlottetown, P.E.I.	Frank Moran	1982, Nov.
Edmonton, Alta.	Cec Purves.	1983, Oct.
Fredericton, N.B.	Elbridge Wilkins	1983, May
Guelph, Ont.	Norman Jary	1982, Nov.
Halifax, N.S.	Robert Wallace	1982, Oct.
Hamilton, Ont.	Bill Powell	1982, Nov.
Hull, Que.	Michel Legere	1982, Nov.
Kingston, Ont.	John Gerretsen	1982, Nov.
Kitchener, Ont.	Morley Rosenberg	1982, Nov.
London, Ont.	Al Gleeson	1982, Nov.
Moncton, N.B.	Dennis Cochrane	1983, May
Montreal, Que.	Jean Drapeau	1982, Nov.
North York, Ont.	Mel Lastman	1982, Nov.
Oshawa, Ont.	Allan Pilkey.	1982, Nov.
Ottawa, Ont.	Mrs. Marion Dewar	1982, Nov.
Peterborough, Ont.	Bob Barker	1982, Nov.
Quebec, Que.	Jean Pelletier	1981, Nov.
Regina, Sask.	Larry Schneider	1982, Oct.
Saint John, N.B.	Bob Lockhart	1983, May
St. John's, Nfld.	Mrs. Dorothy Wyatt	1981, Nov.
Saskatoon, Sask.	Clifford Wright	1982, Oct.
Sault Ste. Marie	Don MacGregor	1982, Nov.
Sherbrooke, Que.	Jacques O'Bready	1982, Nov.
Sudbury, Ont.	Jim Gordon.	1982, Nov.
Toronto, Ont.	Art Eggleton	1982, Nov.
Vancouver, B.C.	Mike Harcourt	1982, Nov.
Victoria, B.C.	Bill Tindall	1981, Nov.
Waterloo, Ont.	Mrs. Marjorie Carroll	1982, Nov.
Windsor, Ont.	Bert Weeks	1982, Nov.
Winnipeg, Man.	Bill Norrie.	1983, Oct.

CONSUMER SURVIVAL KIT

Your Federal Income Tax: Facts on Filing

Source: Internal Revenue Service, U.S. Treasury Department.

Who Must File

Every individual under 65 years of age who resided in the United States and had a gross income of $3,300 or more during the year must file a federal income tax return. Anyone 65 or older on the last day of the tax year is not required to file a return unless he had gross income of $4,300 or more during the year. A married couple, both 65 or older, need not file unless their gross income is $7,400 or more.

A taxpayer with gross income of less than $3,300 (or less than $4,300 if 65 or older) should file a return to claim the refund of any taxes withheld, even if he is listed as a dependent by another taxpayer.

If you are married, you must file a tax return if your combined gross income was $5,400 or more, provided you are eligible to file a joint return and are living together at the close of the tax year. The requirement is $6,400 if one spouse is 65 or older, and $7,400 if both of you are 65 or older. If you are married and your spouse files a separate return, or you did not share the same household at the end of the year, you must file a tax return if your gross income was $1,000 or more.

Forms to Use

A taxpayer may, at his election, use form 1040 or Form

New Tax Cuts Can Mean Savings On 1981 Tax

The new tax law could mean big savings for the individual. Many of the provisions will not take affect until next year or the year after. However, some of the changes could affect individual 1981 taxes, including:

• **Tax Rate Cut.** All taxpayers will find their 1981 tax rate cut by 1¼ percent (not the 5 percent you may have heard about—that applies only to the last 3 months, the last quarter of the year).

• **Sale of a Home.** Two new provisions, both of which apply to the sale of a principal residence only, may shield some of the gains made on the sale from taxes.

1. For those 55 or older, the tax exclusion on profit on selling a home rises from $100,000 to $125,000 on all sales made after July 20, 1981.

2. The period during which payment of income tax on the profit from selling a home can be delayed if the profit is reinvested in another principal residence increases from 18 months to 2 years.

• **Tax Incentives for Savings.** The taxpayer has the option of investing in the new All Savers Certificates from which interest will be tax-exempt.

• **Capital Gains Tax Reduced.** The tax rate on long-term capital gains (profits from the sale of an asset such as stocks or real estate held for more than a year) decreases from a maximum of 28 percent to no more than 20 percent on sales and exchanges that took place after June 9, 1981.

• **Windfall Profit Tax Credit.** For those who own a royalty in oil production, the credit against the Crude Oil Windfall Profit Tax in 1981 rises from $1,000 to $2,500.

• **Tougher Penalties for Late Taxes.** If you face the possibility of filing late, closely examine the new penalties—the IRA can, as of Jan. 1, 1982 charge the full prime lending rate (the rate banks often charge their best customers) on taxes paid late.

1040A. However, those taxpayers who choose to itemize deductions must use the longer form 1040.

Deductions

A taxpayer may either itemize deductions or choose the zero bracket amount. For single taxpayers the zero bracket amount is $2,300. For married taxpayers filing a joint return it is $3,400. For married taxpayers filing separate returns the deduction is $1,700 each.

Dates for Filing Returns

For individuals using the calendar year, Apr. 15 is final date (unless it falls on a Saturday, Sunday, or a legal holiday) for filing income tax returns and for payment of any tax due, and the first quarterly installment of the estimated tax. Other installments of estimated tax to be paid June 15, Sept. 15, and Jan. 15.

Apr. 15 is final date for filing declaration of estimated tax. Amended declarations may be filed June 15, Sept. 15, and Jan. 15.

Instead of paying the 4th installment a final income return may be filed by Jan. 31. Farmers may file a final return by Mar. 1 to satisfy estimated tax requirements.

Joint Return

A husband and wife may make a return jointly, even if one has no income personally.

One provision stipulates that if one spouse dies, the survivor may compute his tax using joint return rates for the first two taxable years following, provided he or she was also entitled to file a joint return the year of the death, and furnishes over half the cost of maintaining in his household a home for a dependent child or stepchild. If the taxpayer remarries before the end of the taxable year these privileges are lost but he is permitted to file a joint return with his new spouse.

Estimated Tax

If total tax exceeds withheld tax by at least $100, declarations of estimated tax are required from (1) single individuals, heads of a household or surviving spouses, or a married person entitled to file a joint return whose spouse does not receive wages, who expects a gross income over $20,000; (2) married individuals with over $10,000 where both spouses receive wages; (3) married individuals with over $5,000 not entitled to file a joint return; and (4) individuals whose gross income can reasonably be expected to include more than $500 from sources other than wages subject to withholdings.

Exemptions

Personal exemption is $1,000.

Every individual has an exemption of $1,000, to be deducted from gross income. A husband and a wife are each entitled to a $1,000 exemption. A taxpayer 65 or over on the last day of the year gets another exemption of $1,000. A person blind on the last day of the year gets another exemption of $1,000.

Exemption for dependents, over one-half of whose total support comes from the taxpayer and for whom the other dependency tests have been met, is $1,000. This applies to a child, stepchild, or adopted child as well as certain other relatives with less than $1,000 gross income; also to a child, stepchild, or adopted child of the taxpayer who is under 19 at the end of the year or was a full-time student during 5 months of the year even if he makes $1,000 or more. A dependent can be a non-relative if a member of the taxpayer's household and living there all year.

Taxpayer gets the exemption for his child who is a student regardless of the student's age or earnings, provided the taxpayer provides over half of the student's total support. If the student gets a scholarship, this is not counted as support.

Child and Disabled Dependent Care

To qualify, a taxpayer must be employed and provide over one-half the cost of maintaining a household for a dependent child under 15, a disabled dependent of any age, or a disabled spouse.

Taxpayers may be allowed a credit based on a percentage of employment related expenses.

For further information consult your local IRS office or the instructional material attached to your return form.

Life Insurance

Life insurance paid to survivors is not taxed as income. Interest on life insurance left with the insurance company and paid to survivors at intervals is taxable when available. Surviving spouse has an exclusion of the prorata amount of principal payable at death plus up to $1,000 per year of interest earned when life insurance proceeds are payable in installments.

Regular payments under the Railroad Retirement Act, and those received as social security, are exempt.

Dividends

The first $100 in dividends can be excluded from income. If husband and wife both receive $100 on their joint return they can exclude $200. An individual is also entitled to exclude up to $750 ($1,500 on a joint return) for certain dividends received from qualifying public utilities.

The exclusion does not apply to dividends from tax-exempt corporations, mutual savings banks, building and loan associations, and several others.

Dividends paid in stock or in stock rights are generally exempt from tax, except when paid in place of preferred stock dividends of the current or preceding year, or when the stockholder has an option to take stock or property or when the stock distribution is disproportionate.

Deductible Medical Expenses

Expenses for medical care, not compensated for by insurance or other payment for taxpayer, spouse, and dependents, in excess of 3% of adjusted gross income are deductible. There is no limit to the maximum amount of medical expenses that can be deducted.

Medical care includes diagnosis, treatment and prevention of disease or for the purpose of affecting any structure or function of the body, and amounts paid for insurance to reimburse for hospitalization, surgical fees and other medical expenses.

Only medicine and drugs in excess of 1% of adjusted gross income may be deducted.

One-half the cost of medical care insurance premiums up to $150 can be deducted without regard to the 3% limitation. The other half plus any excess over $150 is included with other medical expenses subject to the 3% limit.

Medical expenses for a decedent paid by his estate within one year after his death may be treated as expenses of the decedent taxpayer.

Medical and hospital benefits provided by the employer may be exempt from individual income tax.

Disability income payments are excludable only if the payee is totally and permanently disabled and under age 65 at the end of the tax year. Up to $5,200 can be excluded but must be reduced by income above certain limits.

Deductions for Contributions

Deductions up to 50% of taxpayers' adjusted gross income may be taken for contribution to most publicly supported charitable organizations, including churches or associations of churches, tax-exempt educational institutions, tax-exempt hospitals, and medical research organizations associated with a hospital. The deduction is generally limited to 20% for such organizations as private nonoperating foundations, and certain organizations that do not qualify for the 50% limitation.

Taxpayers also are permitted to carry over for five years certain contributions, generally to publicly supported organizations, which exceed the 50% allowable deduction the year the contribution was made.

Also permissible is the deduction as a charitable contribution of unreimbursed amounts up to $50 a school month spent to maintain an elementary or high school student, other than a dependent or relative, in taxpayer's home. There must be a written agreement between you and a quali-

---

New Tax Changes for 1982 and After

The changes most likely to affect millions of tax payers include:

- **Tax Rate Cuts Will Continue.** Tax rates will fall by about another 10 percent on July 1, 1982, and another 10 percent on July 1, 1983, adding to a total of approximately 23 percent.
- **Top Tax Rate to Drop.** The maximum rate for high-bracket individuals (currently as much as 70 percent on unearned income such as interest, dividends, rent, and royalties) will fall to 50 percent.
- **"Marriage Penalty" to Decrease.** If both spouses work outside the home, they will be allowed a deduction from their gross income of 5 percent of whichever salary is lower, with the maximum deduction being $1,500. The next year, the percentage will rise to 10 and the maximum to $3,000.
- **Higher Tax Credits for Child Care.**
- **Individual Retirement Accounts (IRAs) Will Broaden.** Even those persons covered by company pension plans will be able to open IRAs. The tax-free investment in an IRA will increase from $1,500 to $2,000. Self-employed people will be allowed to shelter as much as $15,000 (up from $7,500) of their income in a Keogh Retirement Plan.
- **Interest Exclusion to Drop.** The $200 exclusion for the single tax payer ($400 for married couples) for tax-free interest and dividends will be cut in half and apply only to dividends.
- **Charitable Contributions Deductible on All Forms.** Even the taxpayer who does not itemize will be able to write off 25 percent of the first $100 donated to charitable organizations. By 1986, non-itemizers will be able to deduct all charitable contributions.

---

fied organization.

For changes applying to 1982 income tax and thereafter see box this page.

Deductions for Interest Paid

Interest paid by the taxpayer is deductible.

To deduct interest on a debt, you must be legally liable for that debt. No deduction will be allowed for payments you make for another person if you were not legally liable to make them.

Prizes and Awards

All prizes and awards must be reported in gross income, except when received without action by the recipient. To be exempt, awards must be received primarily in recognition of religious, charitable, scientific, educational, artistic, literary, or civic achievement. (Nobel and Pulitzer prizes exempt.)

Deductions for Employees

An employee may use the zero bracket amount and deduct as well the following if in connection with his employment: transportation, except commuting; automobile expense, including gas, oil, and depreciation; however, meals and lodging are deductible as traveling expense only if the employee is away from home overnight.

An outside salesman—a salesman who works fulltime outside the office, using the latter only for incidentals—may use the zero bracket amount and deduct all his business expenses.

An employee who is reimbursed and is required to account to his employer for his business expenses will not be required to report either the reimbursement or the expenses on his tax return. Any allowance to the employee in excess of his expenses must be included in gross income. If he claims a deduction for an excess of expenses over reimbursement he will have to report the reimbursement and claim actual expenses.

An employee who is not required to account to his employer must report on his return the total amounts of reimbursements and expenses for travel, transportation, entertainment, etc., that he incurs under a reimbursement arrangement with his employer.

The expense of moving to a new place of employment may be deducted under certain circumstances regardless of whether the taxpayer is a new or continuing employee, or whether he pays his own expenses or is reimbursed by his employer. Reimbursement must be reported as income.

Tax Credit for the Elderly

Subject to certain rules or exclusions, taxpayers 65 or older may claim a credit which varies according to filing status. Taxpayers should read IRS instructions carefully for full details. You may also be eligible for a credit if you are under age 65 and receive a taxable pension from a public retirement system.

The credit is limited to 15% of $2,500 for single taxpayers; 15% of $2,500 for married taxpayers filing a joint return when only one taxpayer is 65 or older; 15% of $3,750 for married taxpayers both 65 or older filing a joint return; and 15% of $1,875 for a married taxpayer filing a separate return.

Net Capital Losses

An individual taxpayer may deduct capital losses up to $3,000 against his ordinary income. However, it takes $2 of net long-term capital loss to get $1 of offset against other income. He may carry the rest over to subsequent years at the same rate, no legal limit on the number of years.

Income Averaging

Individuals with large fluctuations in their annual income may be able to take advantage of averaging provisions available to taxpayers whose income for a particular year exceeds 120% of their average income for the prior 4 years, if the excess is more than $3,000.

Individual Income Tax Returns for 1979

	All returns				Taxable returns		
	Returns		Adjusted gross income less deficit		Returns		Adjusted gross income less deficit
	Number	Percent of total	Amount ($000)	Average (dollars)	Number	Percent of total	Amount ($000)
Size of adjusted gross income							
Total.	92,616,213	100.0	1,463,666,582	15,804	71,577,417	100.0	1,399,393,725
No adjusted gross income . . .	525,926	0.6	−7,936,655	−15,091	5,927	(1)	−375,529
$1 under $1,000.	3,253,653	3.5	1,878,880	577	*1,973	(1)	*1,779
$1,000 under $2,000	4,553,347	4.9	6,838,317	1,502	99,404	0.1	150,633
$2,000 under $3,000	4,508,574	4.9	11,181,659	2,480	126,944	0.2	320,095
$3,000 under $4,000	4,132,656	4.5	14,467,929	3,501	1,953,373	2.7	7,071,419
$4,000 under $5,000	3,878,952	4.2	17,407,687	4,488	2,494,539	3.5	11,217,897
$5,000 under $6,000	4,061,083	4.4	22,368,548	5,508	2,714,334	3.8	14,983,496
$6,000 under $7,000	4,267,397	4.6	27,707,117	6,493	2,982,051	4.2	19,393,918
$7,000 under $8,000	4,043,370	4.4	30,285,021	7,490	3,106,087	4.3	23,302,531
$8,000 under $9,000	3,718,707	4.0	31,596,663	8,497	3,251,848	4.5	27,660,219
$9,000 under $10,000	3,544,269	3.8	33,633,335	9,489	3,334,728	4.7	31,665,218
$10,000 under $11,000.	3,204,766	3.5	33,638,824	10,496	3,076,058	4.3	32,293,313
$11,000 under $12,000.	3,011,101	3.3	34,601,755	11,491	2,924,005	4.1	33,606,995
$12,000 under $13,000.	2,911,977	3.1	36,362,047	12,487	2,853,348	4.0	35,632,080
$13,000 under $14,000.	2,736,544	3.0	36,946,496	13,501	2,686,043	3.8	36,265,691
$14,000 under $15,000.	2,566,552	2.8	37,217,775	14,501	2,527,621	3.5	36,651,882
$15,000 under $20,000.	11,387,764	12.3	198,625,566	17,442	11,251,622	15.7	196,285,827
$20,000 under $25,000.	9,009,214	9.7	201,424,044	22,358	8,953,081	12.5	200,189,331
$25,000 under $30,000.	6,314,186	6.8	172,472,245	27,315	6,283,409	8.8	171,637,415
$30,000 under $40,000.	6,454,074	7.0	220,130,631	34,107	6,430,778	9.0	219,345,869
$40,000 under $50,000.	2,205,166	2.4	97,230,478	44,092	2,200,923	3.1	97,043,573
$50,000 under $75,000.	1,463,365	1.6	86,605,139	59,182	1,457,283	2.0	86,245,146
$75,000 under $100,000 . . .	417,117	0.5	35,802,515	85,833	416,254	0.6	35,731,180
$100,000 under $200,000 . . .	353,945	0.4	46,503,656	131,387	353,348	0.5	46,430,577
$200,000 under $500,000 . . .	78,912	0.1	22,242,466	281,864	78,866	0.1	22,229,090
$500,000 under $1,000,000 . .	10,054	(1)	6,661,556	662,578	10,036	(1)	6,650,528
$1,000,000 or more.	3,542	(1)	7,772,888	2,194,491	3,534	(1)	7,763,552

	Taxable returns—continued					
	Taxable income	Income tax after credits		Total income tax		
	Amount ($000)	Number of returns	Amount ($000)	Amount ($000)	Percent of adjusted gross income	Average (dollars)
Size of adjusted gross income						
Total.	1,125,105,348	71,513,473	212,749,638	213,754,094	15.3	2,986
No adjusted gross income.	—	*208	*197	49,978	(1)	8,432
$1 under $1,000	—	*1,718	*5,498	*6,305	(1)	*3,196
$1,000 under $2,000	267,804	98,555	5,833	7,281	4.8	73
$2,000 under $3,000	374,001	126,172	15,573	15,855	5.0	125
$3,000 under $4,000	5,163,975	1,953,225	100,613	101,012	1.4	52
$4,000 under $5,000	8,431,126	2,493,716	390,739	392,529	3.5	157

	Taxable income —	Income tax after credits		Total income tax		
Size of adjusted gross income	Amount ($000)	Number of returns	Amount ($000)	Amount ($000)	Percent of adjusted gross income	Average (dollars)
$5,000 under $6,000	11,633,567	2,714,098	795,894	796,773	5.3	294
$6,000 under $7,000	15,422,934	2,981,988	1,283,038	1,283,371	6.6	430
$7,000 under $8,000	18,417,003	3,105,830	1,638,686	1,640,848	7.0	528
$8,000 under $9,000	21,625,427	3,251,409	2,026,255	2,028,058	7.3	624
$9,000 under $10,000	24,732,665	3,333,297	2,544,568	2,545,442	8.0	763
$10,000 under $11,000 . . . ./	25,257,530	3,075,071	2,824,409	2,827,539	8.8	919
$11,000 under $12,000	26,371,919	2,922,665	3,098,237	3,099,689	9.2	1,060
$12,000 under $13,000	28,015,079	2,852,661	3,433,366	3,434,276	9.6	1,204
$13,000 under $14,000	28,744,209	2,685,823	3,672,112	3,673,229	10.1	1,368
$14,000 under $15,000	29,139,861	2,526,710	3,852,080	3,853,745	10.5	1,525
$15,000 under $20,000	157,210,165	11,247,352	22,623,165	22,631,388	11.5	2,011
$20,000 under $25,000	161,245,203	8,947,879	25,665,824	25,680,080	12.8	2,868
$25,000 under $30,000	139,106,426	6,274,329	24,385,427	24,412,408	14.2	3,885
$30,000 under $40,000	178,221,655	6,418,311	35,471,755	35,525,795	16.2	5,524
$40,000 under $50,000	79,019,715	2,193,936	18,366,690	18,423,057	19.0	8,371
$50,000 under $75,000	70,176,041	1,450,656	19,621,494	19,744,918	22.9	13,549
$75,000 under $100,000	29,006,476	414,166	9,829,678	9,929,498	27.8	23,854
$100,000 under $200,000	38,017,421	351,724	15,328,310	15,554,030	33.5	44,019
$200,000 under $500,000	18,103,642	78,461	8,919,989	9,098,091	40.9	115,361
$500,000 under $1,000,000	5,269,023	9,991	2,957,195	3,029,782	45.6	301,891
$1,000,000 or more	6,132,483	3,522	3,893,015	3,969,117	51.1	1,123,123

(1) Less than 0.05 per cent. *Estimate based on very small sample. **Sample too small for usage data.

State Individual Income Taxes: Rates, Exemptions

Source: Tax Foundation, Inc. Data as of Sept. 1, 1981
Footnotes at end of table.

State	Taxable income	Percentage rates	Taxable income	Percentage rates	Personal exemp. Single	Personal exemp. Married family head	Credit per depend.
Alabama[1] . . . . . First	$1,000	1.5	$3,001-$5,000	4.5	$1,500	$3,000	$300
	1,001-3,000	3	Over 5,000	5			
Arizona[1 2 4] . . . . First	1,000	2	3,001-4,000	5	1,422	2,844	854
	1,001-2,000	3	4,001-5,000	6			
	2,001-3,000	4	5,001-6,000	7	Over 6,000 8		—
Arkansas[3] . . . . . First	2,999	1	9,000-14,999	4.5	17.50	35	6
	3,000-5,999	2.5	15,000-24,999	6	(tax credit)		
	6,000-8,999	3.5	25,000 and over	7			
California[1 2 4 6] . . First	2,630	1	10,561-12,540	6	(tax credit)		
	2,631-4,610	2	12,541-14,510	7	25	50	8
	4,611-6,590	3	14,511-16,500	8	Heads of households have slightly lower		
	6,591-8,580	4	16,501-18,470	9	tax rates.		
	8,581-10,560	5	18,471-20,450	10	Over 20,450 11		
Colorado[1 4 6] . . . First	1,236	2.5	7,419-8,654	5.5	1,051	2,102	1,051
	1,237-2,473	3	8,655-9,890	6			
	2,474-3,709	3.5	9,891-11,127	6.5	Surtax on intangible income over $15,000,		
	3,710-4,945	4	11,128-12,363	7.5	2%. A credit equal to ½ of 1% of net		
	4,946-6,181	4.5	12,364 and over	8	taxable income is allowed for income under		
	6,182-7,418	5			$9,000.		
Connecticut.	7% capital gains tax; tax on dividends earned if federal adjusted gross income is greater than or equal to $20,000; tax ranges from 1% on $20,000 through 9% on $100,000 and over.						
					100	200	
Delaware[3] . . . . . First	1,000	1.4	8,000-10,000	8.0	Exemptions apply only to adjusted gross		
	1,001-2,000	2.0	10,001-15,000	8.2	incomes of more than $20,000 and net		
	2,001-3,000	3.0	15,001-20,000	8.4	capital gains more than $100 (or $200 on		
	3,001-4,000	4.2	20,001-25,000	8.8	joint returns).		
	4,001-5,000	5.2	25,001-30,000	9.4	600	1,200	600
	5,001-6,000	6.2	30,001-40,000	11.0			
	6,001-8,000	7.2	40,001-50,000	12.2	Over 50,000 13.5		
Dist. of Col.[1 4] . . . First	1,000	2	5,001-10,000	7	750	1,500	750
	1,001-2,000	3	10,001-13,000	8			
	2,001-3,000	4	13,001-17,000	9			

State	Taxable income	Percentage rates	Taxable income	Per- centage rates	Personal exemp. Single	Personal exemp. Married family head	Personal exemp. Credit per depend.
	3,001-4,000	5	17,001-25,000	10			
	4,001-5,000	6	Over 25,000	11			
Georgia[3][5] . . . . . First	1,000	1	5,000-6,999	4	1,500	3,000	700
	1,001-2,999	2	7,000-10,000	5			
	3,000-4,999	3	Over 10,000	6	For married persons filing separately, rates range from 1% on the first $500		
	to 6% on $5,000 or more. For single persons rates range from 1% on first $750 to 6% on $7,000 or more.						
Hawaii[1] . . . . . . First	500	2.25	3,001-5,000	7.5	1,000	2,000	1,000
	501-1,000	3.25	5,001-10,000	8.5	Special tax rates for heads of households.		
	1,001-1,500	4.5	10,001-14,000	9.5			
	1,501-2,000	5	14,001-20,000	10			
	2,001-3,000	6.5	20,001-30,000	10.5	Over 30,000	11	
Idaho[2][3][4] . . . . . First	1,000	2	3,001-4,000	5.5			Federal exemptions
	1,001-2,000	4	4,001-5,000	6.5	Each person (husband and wife filing jointly are deemed one person) filing return pays additional $10.		
	2,001-3,000	4.5	Over 5,000	7.5			
Illinois	Total net income			2.5	1,000	2,000	1,000
Indiana[4]	Adjusted gross	1.9			1,000	*2,000	500
*Lesser of $1,000 or adjusted gross income of each spouse, but not less than $500.							
Iowa[3][6] . . . . . . First	1,023	0.5	3,070-4,092	3.5	(tax credit) 15	30	10
	1,024-2,046	1.25	4,093-7,161	5	Net incomes $5,000 or less are not taxable.		
	2,047-3,069	2.75	7,162-9,207	6	On up to 13% over $76,725		
Kansas[2][4] . . . . . First	2,000	2	5,001-7,000	5	1,000	2,000	1,000
	2,001-3,000	3.5	7,001-10,000	6.5	20,001-25,000 8.5		
	3,001-5,000	4	10,001-20,000	7.5	Over 25,000 9.0		
Kentucky[3] . . . . . First	3,000	2	4,001-5,000	4	(tax credit)		
	3,001-4,000	3	5,001-8,000	5	20	40	20
			Over 8,000	6			
Louisiana[1][2]	First 10,000	2	Over 50,000	6	6,000	12,000	1,000
	10,001-50,000	4					
Credits are allowed new income which is taxed at 2%; additional $1,000 exemp. for blindness allowed for dependents.							
Maine[1][3] . . . . . . First	2,000	1	8,001-10,000	7	1,000	2,000	1,000
	2,001-4,000	2	10,001-15,000	8			
	4,001-6,000	3	15,001-25,000	9.2			
	6,001-8,000	6	Over 25,000	10			
Maryland[1][3][4] . . . First	1,000	2	2,001-3,000	4	800	1,600	800
	1,001-2,000	3	Over 3,000	5			
	An additional exemption of $800 is allowed for each dependent 65 or over.						
Massachusetts	Earned and business income:	5*			2,000	4,000	700
	Interest, divs., capital gains on intangibles:	10*	The exemptions shown are those allowed against business income, including salaries and wages. A specific exemption of $2,000 is allowed for each taxpayer. In addition, a dependency exemption of $600 is allowed for a dependent spouse who has income from all sources of less than $2,000. In the case of a joint return, the exemption is the smaller of (1) $4,600 or (2) $2,600 plus the income of the spouse having the smaller income.			
	*Plus 7.5% surtax.						
Michigan[4]	All taxable income	4.6			1,500	3,000	1,500
Minnesota[1][3][4][6] . First	599	1.6	5,983-8,374	10.2	60	120	60
	600-1,198	2.2	8,375-10,766	11.5			
	1,199-2,394	3.5	10,767-14,952	12.8			
	2,395-3,590	5.8	14,953-23,921	14	An additional tax credit of $60 is allowed for each unmarried taxpayer aged 65 or older.		
	3,591-4,786	7.3	23,922-32,890	15			
	4,787-5,982	8.8	Over 32,890	16			
Mississippi[3] . . . . First	5,000	3	Over 5,000	4	6,000	9,500	1,500
Missouri[4] . . . . . First	1,000	1.5	5,001- 6,000	4	1,200	2,400	400
	1,001-2,000	2	6,001- 7,000	4.5			
	2,001-3,000	2.5	7,001- 8,000	5	An additional $800 exemption is allowed unmarried head of household.		
	3,001-4,000	3	8,001-9,000	5.5			
	4,001-5,000	3.5	Over 9,000	6			
Montana[3] . . . . . First	1,000	2	8,001-10,000	7	800	1,600	800
	1,001-2,000	3	10,001-14,000	8			
	2,001-4,000	4	14,001-20,000	9	Additional surtax of 10% on tax liability.		
	4,001-6,000	5	20,001-35,000	10			
	6,001-8,000	6	Over 35,000	11			

State	Taxable income	Percentage rates	Taxable income	Percentage rates	Personal exemp. Single	Married family head	Credit per depend.
Nebraska[3, 4]				Federal exemptions			

The tax is imposed as a % of the taxpayer's Fed. income tax liability (not including surtax) before credits, with limited adjustments. For the year 1981 the rate was set at 15% by State Board of Equalization and Assessment.

New Hampshire	Interest and dividends (except interest on savings accounts).	5	4% commuter tax		$600 of each income is exempt; additional $600 exemptions are allowed to persons who are 65 or older, blind or handicapped and unable to work.		

New Jersey[2]	First 20,000	2				1,000	2,000	1,000
	Over 20,000	2.5			Additional credit of $1,000 allowed for the elderly, and disabled.		

Commuter tax from 2% on net income under $1,000 to 14% on income over $23,000. (Will cease after 12/31/90)

New Mexico[2, 3, 4]	First 2,000	.6	12,001-14,000	3.1			
	2,001-3,000	.7	14,001-16,000	3.6	Federal exemptions		
	3,001-4,000	.8	16,001-18,000	4.2			
	4,001-5,000	.9	18,001-20,000	4.7	The income classes reported are for		
	5,001-6,000	1.1	20,001-25,000	5.2	individuals. For joint returns and heads		
	6,001-7,000	1.3	25,001-35,000	5.6	of households, a separate rate schedule is		
	7,001-8,000	1.7	35,001-50,000	6.0	provided. A credit is allowed for state and		
	8,001-10,000	2.1	50,001-100,000	6.3	local taxes for gross income of less than		
	10,000-12,000	2.6	Over 100,000	6.7	$9,000		

New York[1, 4]	First 1,000	2	13,001-15,000	9	750	1,500	750
	1,001-3,000	3	15,001-17,000	10	Income from unincorporated business is		
	3,001-5,000	4	17,001-19,000	11	taxed at 4%. The following credit is al-		
	5,001-7,000	5	19,001-21,000	12	lowed: $100 tax or less, full amount; $100		
	7,001-9,000	6	21,001-23,000	13	to $200 difference between $200.00 and		
	9,001-11,000	7	Over 23,000	14	amount of tax; $200 or more, no credit.		
	11,001-13,000	8		The maximum tax	rate on personal service income is 10%.		

North Carolina[3,4]	First 2,000	3	6,001-10,000	6	1,100	2,200*	700
	2,001-4,000	4	Over 10,000	7	*An additional exemption of $1,000		
	4,001-6,000	5					

is allowed the spouse having the lower income; joint returns are not permitted.

North Dakota[3]	First 3,000	1	8,001-12,000	4	750	1,500	750
	3,001-5,000	2	12,001-30,000	5	A credit of 25% of income tax liability		
	5,001-8,000	3	Over 30,000	7.5	is allowed up to a maximum of $100.		

Ohio[4]	First 5,000	0.5	15,001-20,000	2.5	650	1,300	650
	5,001-10,000	1	20,001-40,000	3			
	10,001-15,000	2	over 40,000	3.5			

Taxpayers age 65 or older are allowed a $25 credit, or if they have received a lump sum distribution from a pension, retirement or profit sharing plan during the tax year, they are allowed a credit equal to $25 times the taxpayer's expected remaining life. Credit may not exceed tax otherwise due. Credit is also allowed for an amount paid during the school year for elementary and secondary education or instruction or training of dependents who do not have a high school diploma.

Oklahoma[1,4]	First 2,000	0.5	10,001-12,500	4	750	1,500	750
	2,001-5,000	1	12,501-15,000	5	Rates for single persons, married couples		
	5,001-7,500	2	Over 15,000	6	filing separately, and estates and trusts		
	7,501-10,000	3			range from .5% on the first $1,000 to		

Non-resident aliens are taxed at a flat rate of 6% of Oklahoma taxable income.   6% over $7,500.

Oregon[3,4]	First 500	4	3,001-4,000	8	1,000	2,000	1,000
	501-1,000	5	4,001-5,000	9	A credit is provided in an amount and equal		
	1,001-2,000	6	Over 5,000	10	to 25% of the federal retirement income		
	2,001-3,000	7			tax credit to the extent that such a credit is based on Oregon taxable income.		

Pennsylvania	2.2% of specified classes of taxable income						

Rhode Island	19% of modified federal income tax liability				Federal Exemptions		

South Carolina[1]	First 2,000	2	6,001-8,000	5	800	1,600	800
	2,001-4,000	3	8,001-10,000	6			
	4,001-6,000	4	Over 10,000	7			

Tennessee	Interest and dividends	6			Dividends from corporations, 75% of whose property is taxable in Tenn., are taxed at 4%.		

Utah[1]	First 1,500	2.25	4,501-6,000	5.75	750	1,000	750
	1,501-3,000	3.75	6,001-7,500	6.75	Married taxpayers filing separately, single		
	3,001-4,500	4.75	Over 7,500	7.75	taxpayers, estates and trusts, pay rates		

ranging from 2.75% on first $750 of taxable income to 7.75% on taxable income over $3,750.

Vermont[4]	Federal exemptions.						

The tax is imposed at a rate of 23% of the fed. income tax liability of the taxpayer for the taxable year after certain credits (retirement income, investment, foreign tax, child and dependent care, and tax-free covenant bonds) but before any surtax on fed. liability, reduced by a % equal to the % of the taxpayer's adjusted gross income for the taxable year which is not Vermont income.

Virginia[3]	First 3,000	2	5,001-12,000	5	600	1,200	600
	3,001-5,000	3	Over 12,000	5.75			

State	Taxable Income	Percentage rates	Taxable income	Percentage rates	Personal exemp. Single	Married family head	Credit depend.
West Virginia[1,3]. First	2,000	2.1	20,001-22,000	6	600	1,200	600
	2,001-4,000	2.3	22,001-26,000	6.1	For joint returns and a return of a surviving spouse, a separate rate schedule is provided.		
	4,001-6,000	2.8	26,001-32,000	6.5			
	6,001-8,000	3.2	32,001-38,000	6.8			
	8,001-10,000	3.5	38,001-44,000	7.2			
	10,001-12,000	4	44,001-50,000	7.5			
	12,001-14,000	4.6	50,001-60,000	7.9	90,001-100,000		9.1
	14,001-16,000	4.9	60,001-70,000	8.2	100,001-150,000		9.3
	16,001-18,000	5.3	70,001-80,000	8.6	150,001-200,000		9.5
	18,001-20,000	5.4	80,001-90,000	8.8	Over 200,000		9.6
Wisconsin[1,4] . . First	3,300	3.4	13,201-16,500	8.7	(Tax Credit)		
	3,301-6,600	5.2	16,501-22,000	9.1	20	40	20
	6,601-9,900	7.0	22,001-44,000	9.5			
	9,901-13,200	8.2	Over $44,000	10.0			

(1) A standard deduction and optional tax table are provided. In Louisiana, standard deduction is incorporated in tax tables.

(2) Community property state in which, in general, one-half of the community income is taxable to each spouse.

(3) A standard deduction is allowed.

(4) A limited general tax credit for taxpayers filing joint returns and a credit for home improvements is allowed in Ohio; a limited tax credit is allowed for sales taxes in Colorado, Massachusetts, Nebraska, and Vermont; for property taxes and city income taxes in Michigan; for personal property taxes in Maryland and Wisconsin; for property taxes in D.C. if household income is less than $10,000, and in N.Y. if household income is less than $12,000; for installation of solar energy devices in Arizona, California, Kansas, New Mexico, North Carolina, and Oregon; for property taxes paid on pollution control property in Colorado; for installation of insulation in residences in Idaho; and for making an existing building accessible to the handicapped in Kansas.

(5) Tax credits are allowed: $15 for single person or married person filing separately if AGI is $3,000 or less. (For each dollar by which the federal AGI exceeds $3,000 the credit is reduced by $1 until no credit is allowed if federal AGI is $3,015 or more.) $30 for heads of households or married persons filing jointly with $6,000 or less AGI. (For each dollar by which federal AGI exceeds $6,000, credit is reduced by $1 until no credit is allowed if federal AGI is $6,030 or more.)

(6) Tax bracket adjusted for inflation.

State Estate Tax Rates and Exemptions

Source: Compiled by Tax Foundation from Commerce Clearing House data

As of Sept. 1, 1980. See index for state inheritance tax rates and exemptions.

State (a)	Rates (on net estate after exemptions) (b)	Maximum rate applies above	Exemption
Alabama.	Maximum federal credit (c, d)	$10,040,000	$60,000
Alaska	Maximum federal credit (c, d)	10,040,000	60,000
Arizona	Maximum federal credit (c, d)	10,000,000	60,000 (f, g)
Arkansas	Maximum federal credit (c, d)	10,040,000	60,000 (g)
Colorado	Maximum federal credit (c, d)	10,040,000	60,000
Florida	Maximum federal credit (c, d)	10,040,000	60,000
Georgia	Maximum federal credit (c, d)	10,040,000	60,000
Massachusetts	5% on first $50,000 to 16%	4,000,000	30,000 (h)
Minnesota	7% on first $100,000 to 12% (e)	1,000,000	200,000 (g)
Mississippi	1% on first $60,000 to 16%	10,000,000	161,563 (f, g)
Missouri	Maximum federal credit (c, d)	10,040,000	60,000
New Mexico	Maximum federal credit (c, d)	10,040,000	60,000
New York	2% on first $50,000 to 21% (e,i)	10,100,000	(f,g,i)
North Dakota	Maximum federal credit (c, d)	10,040,000	60,000 (g)
Ohio	2% on first $40,000 to 7% (e)	500,000	5,000 (g, k)
Oklahoma	1% on first $10,000 to 10% (e)	10,000,000	60,000 (g,l,m)
Rhode Island	2% on first $25,000 to 9% (c)	1,000,000	25,000
South Carolina	5% on first $40,000 to 7%.	100,000	120,000 (g)
Utah	Maximum federal credit (c, d)	10,040,000	60,000 (g)
Vermont	Maximum federal credit (e, n)	10,040,000	60,000 (g)
Virginia	Maximum federal credit (c, d)	10,040,000	60,000

(a) Excludes states shown in table on page 53 which levy an estate tax, in addition to their inheritance taxes, to assure full absorption of the federal credit.

(b) The rates generally are in addition to graduated absolute amounts.

(c) Maximum federal credit allowed under the 1954 code for state estate taxes paid is expressed as a percentage of the taxable estate (after $60,000 exemption) in excess of $40,000, plus a graduated absolute amount.

(d) A tax on nonresident estates is imposed on the proportionate share of the net estate which the property located in the state bears to the entire estate wherever situated.

(e) An additional estate tax is imposed to assure full absorption of the federal credit.

(f) Insurance receives special treatment.

(g) Transfers to religious, charitable, educational, and municipal corporations are fully exempt. Limited in Mississippi to those located in U.S. or its possessions.

(h) Applies to net estates above $60,000.

(i) On net estate before exemption.

(j) The specific exemptions ($20,000 of the net estate transferred to spouse and $5,000 to lineal ancestors and descendants and certain other named relatives) are allowed in an amount equal to 2% of the first $50,000 and 3% of the next $100,000.

(k) Property is exempt to the extent transferred to surviving spouse not exceeding $30,000; for a child under 18, $7,000, and for each child 18 or over, $3,000.

(l) An estate valued at $100 or less is exempt.

(m) Exemption is a total aggregate of $60,000 for father, mother, child, and other named relatives.

(n) The tax is 30% of the federal estate tax liability. Taxes on estates of decedents dying after 12/31/76, but before 1/1/79, are reduced by the percentage that $120,000 is of the amount of the federal taxable estate; after 12/31/78, $240,000. The reduction shall not be more than 100%.

State Retail Sales Taxes: Types and Rates

April 1, 1981

State	Tangible personal property	Admissions	Selected service — Rest. meals	Transient lodging	Public utilities	Rates on other services and nonretail business
Alabama[2]	4%[3]	4%	4%	4%	...	Gross rcpts of amus't operators, 4%, agric., mining and mfg. mach., 1.5%
Arizona[2]	4	4	4	3	4	Timbering, 1.5%; storage, apt., office rental, 3%.
Arkansas[2]	3	3	3	3	3	Printing, photographic services; rcpts. from coin-operated dev.; repair services incl. auto and elect., 3%.
California[2]	4.75[5]	...	4.75	...	[14]	Renting, leasing, producing, fabricating, processing, pringting, 4.75%
Colorado[2]	3	...	3	3[10]	3	
Connecticut	7.5	...	7[7]	7[10]	7[13]	Storing for use or consumption of personal property items, 7%.
D. of C.	6	5	6	6	5	Duplicating, mailing, addressing and public stenographic services, 5%; sales of food for off-premise consumption, nonprescription medicines, 2%.
Florida	4	4	4	4	...	Rental income of amus't mach., 4%.
Georgia	3	3	3	3 / 3		Levies on amus's dev., 3%.
Hawaii[1]	4	4	4	4	...	Sugar processors, pineapple farmers and selected businesses, 0.5%; insur. solicitors, 2% contractors, sales rep., professions, radio stations, 4%.
Idaho[6]	3	3	3	3	...	Closed circuit TV boxing, wrestling, 5%.
Illinois[2]	4	...	4	...	...	Property sold in connection with a sale of service, 4%, remodeling repairing and reconditioning of tangible personal property, 4%.
Indiana	4	...	4	4	4	
Iowa	3	3	3	3	3	Laundry, dry cleaning, automobile and cold storage, photography, printing, repairs, barber and beauty parlor services, advt., dry cleaning equip. rentals and gross rcpts. from amus't dev., 3%.
Kansas[2]	3	3	3	3	3	Gross rcpts. from operation of coin-operated devices; commer. amus't, 3%.
Kentucky[2]	5	5	5	5	5	Storage, sewer services, photog. and photo fin., 5%; ticket sales to boxing or wrestling on closed circuit TV, 5% of gross rcpts; tax also applies to pay'ts for right to broadcast matches.
Louisana[2]	3	3	3	3	...	Food and prescpt'n. drugs, exempt.
Maine	5	...	5	5	5	Proceeds from closed circuit TV, 5%.
Maryland[2]	5[3]	[11]	5[7]	5	5	Farm equip., 2%; mfg. equip., including that used in generation of electricity or in R.&S. sold to mfrs., 2%; watercraft, 3%
Mass.	5	...	[7]	5.7[9]	...	
Michigan	4	...	4	4	4	
Minnesota[2]	4[3]	4	4	4	4	Food, medicines and clothing are exempt; coin-operated vending mach., 3% of gross sales.
Mississippi[1]	5[3]	...	5	5	5	Wholesaling, 0.125% (0.5% on sales of meat for human consumption; 5% on beer, alc. bevs., soft drinks and motor fuel); extracting or mining of minerals, specified miscellaneous bus. incl. bowling, pool halls, warehouses, laundry and dry cleaning, pest control services, specified repair services, 5%; cotton ginning, 15c per bale; sales of materials to railroads for use in track structures, 3%; tractors, indust. fuel and mfg. mach. sales over $500, 1%.
Missouri[2]	3.125	3.125	3.125	3.125	3.125	
Nebraska[2]	3	3	3	3	3	
Nevada[2]	3[10]	...	3	...	...	
New Jersey[1] [2]	5	5[11]	5	5[9]	...	
New Mexico[1] [2]	3.75[3]	3.75	3.75	3.75	3.75	
New York[2]	4	4[11]	4[7]	4[9]	4	Safe deposit rentals, 4%.
North Carolina[2]	3[3]	...	3	3	...	Farm and industrial machinery, 1% ($80 max.); airplanes, boats and locomotives, 2% ($120 max); sales of horses and mules, 1%.

State	Tangible personal property	Admissions	Selected service			Rates on other services and nonretail business
			Rest. meals	Trans-ient lodging	Public utilities	
North Dakota	3[3]	3	3	,3	3	Severance of sand or gravel from the soil, 3%.
Ohio[2]	4	...	4	4	...	
Oklahoma[2]	2[3]	2	2	2	2	Advert. (exclusive of newspapers, periodicals, billboards), printing, auto storage, gross proceeds from amusement dev., 2%.
Pennsylvania[2]	6	...	6[7]	6	6	Cleaning, polishing, lubr. and insp. motor vehicles, rental income of coin-operated amuse. dev., 6%.
Rhode Island	6	...	6	6	6	
South Carolina	4	...	4	4	4	
South Dakota[1][2]	5	4	4	3	3	Farm mach. and agric. irrigation equip., 2%; gross rcpts. from professions (other than medical), 4%.
Tennessee[2]	4.5	...	4.5	4.5	4.5	Vending machines, 1.5% (except tobacco products, 2.5%); industrial, farm equipment and machinery, 1%.
Texas[2]	4[3]	...	4	...	4	
Utah[2]	4	4	4	4	4	
Vermont	3	3	12	12	3	
Virginia[2]	3[3]	...	3	3	...	
Washington[1][2]	4.5	4.5	4.5	4.5		Rentals, auto, parking, other specified services, amusements, recreations, 4.5% (unless subject to county or city adm. taxes, when they remain taxable under the state business, occupation levy, 1%).
West Virginia[1]	3[3]	3	3	3	...	All services except public util. and personal and professional services, 3%.
Wisconsin[2]	4	4[11]	4	4	4	
Wyoming[2]	3	3	3	3	3	

(1) All but a few states levy sales taxes of the single-stage retail type. Ha. and Miss. levy multiple-stage sales taxes. The N.M. and S.D. taxes have broad bases with respect to taxable services but they are not multiple-stage taxes. Wash. and W.Va. levy gross receipts taxes on all business, distinct from their sales taxes. Alaska also levies a gross receipts tax on businesses. The rates applicable to retailers, with exceptions, under these gross receipts taxes are as follows: Alaska 0.5% on gross receipts of $20,000-$100,000 and 0.25% on gross receipts in excess of $100,000; Wash., 0.44%, plus a 6% surtax; and W.Va., 0.55%. N.J. imposes a tax of 0.05% on retail stores with income in excess of $150,000, and an unincorporated business tax at the rate of 0.25% of 1% if gross receipts exceed $5,000.

(2) In addition to the State tax, sales taxes are also levied by certain cities and/or counties.

(3) Motor vehicles are taxed at the general sales tax rates with the following exceptions: Ala., 1.5%; Miss., 3%; and N.C., 2% ($120 maximum). Motor vehicles are exempt from the general sales and use taxes but are taxed under motor vehicle tax laws in Md., 4%; Minn., 4%; N.M., 2%; N.D. 4%; Okla., 2%; S.D. and W.Va., 3%; Tex., 4%; Va., 2%; and the D.C., 4%.

(4) Ariz. and Miss. also tax the transportation of oil and gas by pipeline. Ga., Mo., Okla., and Utah do not tax transportation of property. Miss. taxes taxicab transportation at the rate of 2%. Okla. does not tax fares of 15¢ or less on local transportation. Utah does not tax street railway fares.

(5) "Lease" excludes the use of tangible personal property for a period of less than one day for a charge of less than $10 when the privilege of using the property is restricted to use on the premises or at a business location of the grantor.

(6) A limited credit (or refund) in the form of a flat dollar amount per personal exemption is allowed against the personal income tax to compensate for (1) sales taxes paid on food in Col., D.C., and Neb.; and (2) all sales taxes paid in Ida., Mass., and Vt. Low-income taxpayers (adjusted gross income not over $6,000) are allowed a credit against D.C. tax liability ranging from $2 to $6 per personal exemption, depending on taxpayer's income bracket. A refund is allowed if credit exceeds tax liability.

(7) Restaurant meals below a specified price are exempt: Conn. and Md. less than $1; N.Y. less than $1 (when alcoholic beverages are sold, meals are taxable regardless of price); and Pa., 50¢ or less. In Mass., restaurant meals ($1 or more) which are taxed at 8% under the meals excise tax are exempt.

(8) Conn., exempts clothing for children under 10 years of age. Pa. and Wisc. exempt clothing with certain exceptions.

(9) In Col. and Conn., the first 30 consecutive days of rental or occupancy of rooms is taxable. Over 30 days is exempt. In Mass., transient lodging (in excess of $2 a day) is subject to a 5.7% (5% plus 14% surtax) room occupancy excise tax. In N.J. and N.Y., rooms which rent for $2 a day or less are exempt.

(10) Includes a statewide mandatory 1% county sales tax collected by the state and paid to the counties for support of local school districts.

(11) Md. taxes at 0.5% gross receipts derived from charges for rentals of sporting or recreational equipment, and admissions, cover charges for tables, services or merchandise at any roof garden or cabaret. In N.J., admissions to a place of amusement are taxable if the charge is in excess of 75¢. N.Y. taxes admissions when the charge is over 10¢; exempt are participating sports (such as bowling and swimming), motion picture theaters, race tracks, boxing, wrestling, and live dramatic or musical performances. In Wis., sales of admissions to motion picture theaters costing 75¢ or less are exempt.

(12) Meals and rooms are exempt from sales tax, but are subject to a special excise tax of 5%.

(13) Gas, water, electricity, telephone and telegraph services provided to consumers through mains, lines or pipes are exempt. Gas and electric energy used for domestic heating are exempt. Interstate telephone calls are exempt, as are calls from coin-operated telephones.

(14) Beginning Jan. 1, 1975, a surcharge for efficiency is imposed at the rate of 1/10th mill ($0.0001) per kwh.

State Inheritance Tax Rates and Exemptions

Source: Compiled by Tax Foundation from Commerce Clearing House data.
As of Apr. 1, 1981

State (a)	Rates (b) (percent) Spouse, child, or parent	Brother or sister	Other than relative	Max. rate applies above ($1,000)	Exemptions (c) ($1,000) Spouse	Child or parent	Brother or sister	Other than relative
California	3-14(v)	6-20	10-24	$400	All	$20(e)	$10	$3
Connecticut (f)	2-8	4-10	8-14	1,000	100	20	6	1
Delaware	1-6	5-10	10-16	200	70	3	1	None
District of Columbia	1-8	5-23	5-23	1,000	5	5	1	1
Hawaii	2-7	3-10	3-10	200	100	50	5	5
Idaho	2-15	4-20	8-30	500	50(d)	30(e)	10	10
Illinois	2-14	2-14	10-30	500	20	20	10	0.1
Indiana	1-10	7-15	10-20	1,500(g)	All	5(e)	0.5	0.1
Iowa	1-8	5-10	10-15	150	80	10(e)	None	None
Kansas	0.5-5	3-12.5	10-15	500	250	30	5	None
Kentucky	2-10	4-16	6-16	500(u)	50	5(e)	1	0.5
Louisiana	2-3	5-7	5-10	25	5(d)	5	1	0.5
Maine	5-10	8-14	14-18	250(g)	50	25	1	1
Maryland (j)	1	10	10	(k)	.15 (h)	.15 (h)	0.15 (h)	0.15 (h)
Michigan	2-10 (l)	2-10 (l)	12-17 (l)	750	65(e)	10	10	None
Montana	2-8	4-16	8-32	100	All	7(e)	1.0	None
Nebraska	1	1	6-18	60	10	10	10	0.5
New Hampshire	(n)	15	15	(k)	(n)	(n)	None	None
New Jersey	2-16	11-16	15-16	3,200	15	15	0.5 (h)	0.5 (h)
North Carolina	1-12	4-16	8-17	3,000	3-15	2(e)	None	None
Oregon	12	12	12	(k)	(p)	(r)	2	None
Pennsylvania	6	15	15	(k)	None(q)	None(q)	None	None
South Dakota (a)	(s)	4-16	6-24	100	All	30(e)	0.5	0.1
Tennessee	5.5-9.5	5.5-9.5	6.5-16	440	120	120	120	10
Texas	1-6	3-10	5-20	1,000	200(t)	200(t)	10	0.5
Washington	1-10	3-20	10-25	500	(d)	(v)	10	None
West Virginia	3-13	4-18	10-30	1,000	30	10	None	None
Wisconsin	1.25-12.5	5-25	10-30(u)	500	250	10	1	0.5
Wyoming	2	2	2	(k)	200	33	33	None

(a) In addition to an inheritance tax, all states listed also levy an estate tax, generally to assure full absorption of the federal credit. Exception is S.D.

(b) Rates generally apply to excess above graduated absolute amounts.

(c) Generally, transfers to governments or to solely charitable, educational, scientific, religious, literary, public, and other similar organizations in the U.S. are wholly exempt. Some states grant additional exemptions either for insurance, homestead, joint deposits, support allowance, disinherited minor children, orphaned, incompetent or blind children, and for previously or later taxed transfers. In many states, exemptions are deducted from the first bracket only.

(d) Community property state in which, in general, either all community property to the surviving spouse is exempt, or only one-half of the community property is taxable on the death of either spouse.

(e) Exemption for child (in thousands): $30 in Iowa; and $30 in S.D. Exemption for minor child is (in thousands): $40 in Cal.; $50 in Idaho; $5 in Ind.; $20 in Ky.; $15 in Mon. In Mo. the exemption for an insane, blind or otherwise incapacitated lineal descendant is (thousands) $15. In Mich. a widow receives $5,000 for every minor child to whom no property is transferred in addition to the normal exemption for a spouse.

(f) On estates an additional inheritance tax equal to 30% of the basic tax is imposed.

(g) Maximum rate for brother or sister and any other than relative in Indiana is $1 million. In Maine the maximum rate for any other than relative is $150 thousand.

(h) No exemption if share exceeds amount stated.

(i) Estates over $3 million are not subject to the inheritance tax but are subject to an estate tax equal to the amount of the federal credit.

(j) Where property of a decedent subject to administration in Md. is $5,000 or less, no inheritance taxes are due.

(k) Rate applies to entire share.

(l) There is no tax on the share of any beneficiary if the value of the share is less than $100. In addition each county collects an additional 0.5% of the tax collected.

(m) In addition, an exemption of $1/2$ of the decedent's estate, or $1/3$ if decedent is survived by lineal descendents.

(n) Spouses, children, parents, and adopted children in the decedent's line of succession are exempt.

(o) Net taxable estates are allowed an exemption of $50,000 if the decedent died in 1978, $70,000 if death occurs in 1979 or 1980, $100,000 if death occurs in 1981 or 1982, $200,000 if death occurs in 1983 or 1984 and $500,000 if death occurs in 1985 or 1986.

(p) Credit is allowed to surviving spouse, child or stepchild under 18 years or child who is incapable of self support. The credit is $54,000 in 1978, $51,000 in 1979 and 1980, $48,000 in 1981 and 1982, $36,000 in 1983 and 1984 and zero thereafter. Estates of descendants dying on or after 1/1/87 are not subject to inheritance tax.

(q) However, the $2,000 family exemption is specifically allowed as a deduction.

(r) Beneficiaries of estates worth more than $250,000 are liable for their share of the additional estate tax.

(s) The rates range from 3-6% for a spouse and child and from 3-12% for parents. Effective 7/1/79, exemption for spouse is $100,000. Parent exemption $3,000.

(t) Increased to $250,000 from 1/1/82 through 8/31/85 and to $300,000 beginning 9/1/85. When more than one beneficiary (spouse, child or parent) receives property, and when the total exceeds the amount of the exemption, the exemption is divided proportionally.

(u) Maximum rate applies above $50,000.

(v) Rates for surviving spouse 6-14%.

Federal Estate and Gift Tax

Source: Tax Foundation, Inc.

Estate Tax

As a result of the Economic Recovery Tax Act of 1981, the lifetime unified credit against combined estate and gift taxes is increased in steps from $47,000 in 1981 to $62,800 in 1982, $79,300 in 1983, $96,300 in 1984, $121,800 in 1985, $155,800 in 1986, and $192,800 in 1987. Thus, cumulative transfers exempt from estate and gift taxes are increased from $175,625 in 1981, to $225,000 in 1982, $275,000 in 1983, $325,000 in 1984, $400,000 in 1985, $500,000 in 1986, and $600,000 in 1987 and thereafter. The act also reduced the maximum estate and gift tax rate over a four-year period from 70 percent in 1981, decreasing to 50 percent in 1985 and thereafter. The schedules for 1982 through 1985 are shown below.

Estate taxes are computed by applying the unified rate schedule, shown below, to the total estate minus allowable deductions, such as funeral expenses, administrative expenses, debts and charitable contributions, plus taxable gifts made after 1976. Gift taxes paid are subtracted from tax due, and credit also may be taken for state death taxes. The amount of the state tax credit is determined by the schedule shown in the table below or the actual state taxes paid, whichever is less. No state tax credit is available to an adjustable taxable estate (i.e., taxable estate minus $60,000) smaller than $40,000. Transfers to a surviving spouse are generally tax exempt.

The law provides for real property passed on to family members for use in a closely held business, such as farming, to be valued in basis of such use, rather than fair market value on basis of highest and best use. In no case may this special valuation reduce the gross estate by more than $600,000 in 1981, $700,000 in 1982, and $750,000 in 1983 and thereafter.

Generation-skipping transfers that occur after April 30, 1976, in general are now subject to taxes substantially equivalent to those that would have been imposed had the property been transferred outright to each successive generation. However, an exclusion is provided for transfers to grandchildren up to $250,000 for each child of the decedent who serves as a conduit for the transfer (not for each grandchild).

A return must be filed for the estate of every U.S. citizen or resident whose gross estate exceeds $175,600 in 1981 ($36,000 for the estate of a nonresident not a citizen). The return is due nine months after death unless an extension is granted.

Gift Tax

Any citizen or resident alien whose gifts to any one person exceed $3,000 ($10,000 after 1981) within a calender year will be liable for payment of a gift tax, at rates determined under the unified estate and gift tax schedule. Gift tax returns are filed on an annual basis and ordinarily are due by April 15 of the following year.

Gifts made by a husband and wife to a third party may be considered as having been made one-half by each, provided both spouses consent to such division.

Unified Rate Schedule for Estate and Gift Tax for 1981

If the amount with respect to which the tentative tax to be computed is:			The tentative tax is:		
Not over $10,000			18 percent of such amount.		
Over	$10,000 but not over	$20,000.	$1,800, plus 20%	of the excess over	$10,000.
Over	$20,000 but not over	$40,000.	$3,800, plus 22%	of the excess over	$20,000.
Over	$40,000 but not over	$60,000.	$8,200, plus 24%	of the excess over	$40,000.
Over	$60,000 but not over	$80,000.	$13,000, plus 26%	of the excess over	$60,000.
Over	$80,000 but not over	$100,000.	$18,200, plus 28%	of the excess over	$80,000.
Over	$100,000 but not over	$150,000.	$23,800, plus 30%	of the excess over	$100,000.
Over	$150,000 but not over	$250,000.	$38,800, plus 32%	of the excess over	$150,000.
Over	$250,000 but not over	$500,000.	$70,800, plus 34%	of the excess over	$250,000.
Over	$500,000 but not over	$750,000.	$155,800, plus 37%	of the excess over	$500,000.
Over	$750,000 but not over	$1,000,000.	$248,300, plus 39%	of the excess over	$750,000.
Over	$1,000,000 but not over	$1,250,000.	$345,800, plus 41%	of the excess over	$1,000,000.
Over	$1,250,000 but not over	$1,500,000.	$448,300, plus 43%	of the excess over	$1,250,000.
Over	$1,500,000 but not over	$2,000,000.	$555,800, plus 45%	of the excess over	$1,500,000.
Over	$2,000,000 but not over	$2,500,000.	$780,800, plus 49%	of the excess over	$2,000,000.
Over	$2,500,000 but not over	$3,000,000.	$1,025,800, plus 53%	of the excess over	$2,500,000.
Over	$3,000,000 but not over	$3,500,000.	$1,290,800, plus 57%	of the excess over	$3,000,000.
Over	$3,500,000 but not over	$4,000,000.	$1,575,800, plus 61%	of the excess over	$3,500,000.
Over	$4,000,000 but not over	$4,500,000.	$1,880,800, plus 65%	of the excess over	$4,000,000.
Over	$4,500,000 but not over	$5,000,000.	$2,205,800, plus 69%	of the excess over	$4,500,000.
Over $5,000,000			$2,550,800, plus 70%	of the excess over	$5,000,000.
Rates remain the same for subsequent years except for the maximums:					
1982:		Over $4,000,000.	$1,880,800, plus 65%	of the excess over	$4,000,000
1983:		Over $3,500,000.	$1,575,800, plus 60%	of the excess over	$3,500,000
1984:		Over $2,500,000.	$1,025,800, plus 55%	of the excess over	$2,500,000
1985:		Over $2,500,000.	$1,025,800, plus 50%	of the excess over	$2,500,000

State Death Tax Credit for Estate Tax

Adjusted taxable estate from	to	Credit = +	%	Of excess over	Adjusted taxable estate from	to	Credit = +	%	Of excess over
$ 0	$ 40,000	- 0	0	$ 0	2,540,000	3,040,000	146,800	8.8	2,540,000
40,000	90,000	0	.8	40,000	3,040,000	3,540,000	190,800	9.6	3,040,000
90,000	140,000	400	1.6	90,000	3,540,000	4,040,000	238,800	10.4	3,540,000
140,000	240,000	1,200	2.4	140,000	4,040,000	5,040,000	290,800	11.2	4,040,000
240,000	440,000	3,600	3.2	240,000	5,040,000	6,040,000	402,800	12	5,040,000
440,000	640,000	10,000	4.0	440,000	6,040,000	7,040,000	522,800	12.8	6,040,000
640,000	840,000	18,000	4.8	640,000	7,040,000	8,040,000	650,800	13.6	7,040,000
840,000	1,040,000	27,600	5.6	840,000	8,040,000	9,040,000	786,800	14.4	8,040,000
1,040,000	1,540,000	38,800	6.4	1,040,000	9,040,000	10,040,000	930,800	15.2	9,040,000
1,540,000	2,040,000	70,800	7.2	1,540,000	10,040,000		1,082,800	16	10,040,000
2,040,000	2,540,000	106,800	8.0	2,040,000					

(1) The adjusted taxable estate equals the taxable estate minus $60,000.

City Income Tax in U.S. Cities over 50,000

Compiled by Tax Foundation from Commerce Clearing House data and other sources.

City	Rates % 1981	Orig.	Year began	City	Rates % 1981	Orig.	Year began
Cities with 500,000 or more inhabitants				Scranton, Pa.	2.6	1.0	1948
Baltimore, Md.	(50% of state tax)	1.0	1966	Toledo, Oh.	1.5	1.0	1946
Cleveland, Oh.	2.0	0.5	1967	Youngstown, Oh.	1.5	0.3	1948
Columbus, Oh.	1.5	0.5	1947	**Cities with 50,000 to 99,999 Inhabitants**			
Detroit, Mich.	2.0	1.0	1965	Altoona, Pa.	1.0	1.0	1948
Kansas City, Mo.	1.0	0.5	1964	Bethlehem, Pa.	1.0	1.0	1957
New York, N.Y.	.9-4.3	0.4-2.0	1966	Chester, Pa.	1.0	1.0	1956
Philadelphia, Pa.	4.3125	1.5	1939	Covington, Ky.	2.5	1.0	1956
Pittsburgh, Pa.	2.25	1.0	1954	Euclid, Oh.	1.5	0.5	1967
St. Louis, Mo.	1.0	.25	1948	Gadsden, Ala.	2.0	1.0	1956
Cities with 100,000 to 499,999 inhabitants				Hamilton, Oh.	1.5	0.8	1960
Akron, Oh.	1.8	1.0	1962	Harrisburg, Pa.	1.0	1.0	1966
Allentown, Pa.	1.0	1.0	1958	Lakewood, Oh.	1.0	1.0	1968
Birmingham, Ala.	1.0	1.0	1970	Lancaster, Pa.	0.5	0.5	1959
Canton, Oh.	1.5	0.6	1954	Lima, Oh.	1.0	.75	1959
Cincinnati, Oh.	2.0	1.0	1954	Lorain, Oh.	1.0	0.5	1967
Dayton, Oh.	1.75	0.5	1949	Pontiac, Mich.	1.0	1.0	1968
Erie, Pa.	1.0	1.0	1948	Reading, Pa.	1.0	1.0	1969
Flint, Mich.	1.0	1.0	1965	Saginaw, Mich.	1.0	1.0	1965
Grand Rapids, Mich.	1.0	1.0	1967	Springfield, Oh.	2.0	1.0	1948
Lansing, Mich.	1.0	1.0	1968	Warren, Oh.	1.0	0.5	1952
Lexington, Ky.	2.0	1.0	1952	Wilkes-Barre, Pa.	3.0	1.0	1966
Louisville, Ky.[1]	2.2	0.75	1948	Wilmington, Del.	1.0	0.5	1970
Parma, Oh.	1.5	0.5	1967	York, Pa.	1.0	1.0	1965

(1) Includes rates for Jefferson City and school board.

Canadian Income Tax Rates

Source: Revenue Canada

1981 Rates of Federal Income Tax

Taxable income $		Tax	
1,874- or less		—	
1,875	—	23.12% on next	$ 108
1,983	$ 47	+ 25% on next	75
2,058	141	+ 25.16% on next	1,908
3,966	621	+ 26.64% on next	1,983
5,949	1,150	+ 28.12% on next	3,966
9,915	2,265	+ 31.08% on next	2,648
12,563	3,088	+ 29.19% on next	1,318
13,881	3,473	+ 31.97% on next	3,966
17,847	4,740	+ 34.75% on next	3,966
21,813	6,118	+ 38.92% on next	4,121

Taxable income		Tax	
25,934	7,722	+ 41.44% on next	1,828
27,762	8,480	+ 47.36% on next	19,830
47,592	17,872	+ 53.28% on next	29,745
77,337	33,721	+ 57.72% on next	41,643
118,980	57,757	+ 63.64% on remainder	

(1) Rates are applied to basic federal tax payable. (2) Plus provincial surtax.

1981 Rates of Provincial Income Tax[1]

Newfoundland	58%	Manitoba	54%
Prince Edward Island	52.5%	Saskatchewan	53%[2]
Nova Scotia	52.5%	Alberta	38.5%
New Brunswick	55.5%	British Columbia	44%
Ontario	46%	N.W.T. and Yukon	43%

Canada: Taxable Returns by Income, 1978

Source: Revenue Canada Taxation Statistics

Total income in dollars	Number	Per-cent	Total income (millions)	Per-cent	Taxed income (millions)	Federal tax (millions)	Per-cent	Fed. Tax rate on total income
$1-1,500	873,116	13.95	652.8	.42	1.3	—	—	—
1,500-3,000	1,167,494	8.18	2,613.5	1.66	30.0	—	—	—
3,000-4,000	740,108	5.16	2,589.0	1.64	319.8	—	—	—
4,000-5,000	722,229	5.05	3,245.9	2.07	786.2	.1	—	.02%
5,000-10,000	3,268,060	22.82	24,384.7	15.51	11,227.9	.5	—	.03%
10,000-15,000	2,573,068	17.97	31,795.2	20.22	19,345.5	689.9	4.86	2.83%
15,000-20,000	1,841,415	12.86	31,874.3	20.27	21,371.7	2,240.2	15.77	7.1%
20,000-25,000	992,565	6.93	22,044.4	14.03	15,451.5	3,090.4	21.76	8.7%
25,000-30,000	460,821	3.22	12,537.8	7.97	9,049.1	2,523.9	17.77	11.5%
30,000-50,000	437,343	3.05	15,895.5	10.11	11,835.9	1,587.8	11.18	12.7%
50,000-100,000	100,826	.70	6,562.4	4.17	5,208.7	2,262.1	15.93	14.2%
100,000-200,000	14,967	.11	1,937.2	1.24	1,586.4	1,146.7	8.07	17.5%
200,000 and over	3,189	.02	1,091.6	.69	856.6	409.1	2.88	21.1%
						252.7	1.78	23.15%

Understanding the Economy: A Glossary of Terms

Balance of payments: The difference between all payments made to foreign countries and all payments coming in from abroad over a set period of time. A *favorable* balance exists when more payments are coming in than going out and an *unfavorable* balance exists when the reverse is true. Payments include gold, the cost of merchandise and services, interest and dividend payments, money spent by travelers, and repayment of principal on loans.

Balance of trade (trade gap): The difference between exports and imports, both in actual funds and credit. A nation's balance of trade is *favorable* when exports exceed imports and *unfavorable* when the reverse is true.

Cost of living: The cost of maintaining a particular standard of living measured in terms of purchased goods and services. The rise in the cost of living is the same as the rate of inflation.

Cost-of-living benefits: Benefits that go to those persons whose money receipts increase automatically as prices rise.

Credit crunch (liquidity crisis): The period when cash for lending to business and consumers is in short supply.

Deficit spending: The practice whereby a government goes into debt to finance some of its expenditures.

Depression: A long period of little business activity when prices are low, unemployment is high, and purchasing power decreases sharply.

Devaluation: The official lowering of a nation's currency, decreasing its value in relations to foreign currencies.

Disposable income: Income after taxes which is available to persons for spending and saving.

Federal Reserve System: The entire banking system of the U.S., incorporating 12 Federal Reserve banks (one in each of 12 Federal Reserve districts), and 24 Federal Reserve branch banks, all national banks and state-chartered commercial banks and trust companies that have been admitted to its membership. The system wields a great deal of influence on the nation's monetary and credit policies.

Gross National Product (GNP): The total dollar value of all goods that have been bought for final use and services during a year. The GNP is generally considered to be the most comprehensive measure of a nation's economic activity. The *Real* GNP is the GNP adjusted for inflation.

GNP price deflator: A statistical measure that shows changes, both up and down, in the price level of the GNP over a span of years. It covers a larger segment of the economy than is usually covered by other price indexes.

Inflation: An increase in the average level of prices; double-digit inflation occurs when the percent increase rises above 10.

Key leading indicators: A series of a dozen indicators from different segments of the economy used by the Commerce Department to try to foretell what will happen in the economy in the near future.

Money supply: The currency held by the public plus checking accounts in commercial banks and savings institutions.

National debt: The debt of the central government as distinguished from the debts of the political subdivisions of the nation and private business and individuals.

National debt ceiling:—Limit set by Congress beyond which the national debt cannot rise. This limit is periodically raised by Congressional vote.

Per capita income: The nation's total income divided by the number of people in the nation.

Prime interest rate: The rate charged by banks on short-term loans to their large commercial customers with the highest credit rating.

Producer price index (formerly the wholesale price index): A statistical measure of the change in the price of wholesale goods. It is reported for 3 different stages of the production chain: crude, intermediate, and finished goods.

Public debt: The total of the nation's debts owed by state, local, and national government. This is considered a good measure of how much of the nation's spending is financed by borrowing rather than taxation.

Recession: A mild decrease in economic activity marked by a decline in real GNP, employment, and trade, usually lasting 6 months to a year, and marked by widespread decline in many sectors of the economy. Not as severe as a depression.

Seasonal adjustment: Statistical changes made to compensate for regular fluctuations in data that are so great they tend to distort the statistics and make comparisons meaningless. For instance, seasonal adjustments are made in mid winter for a slowdown in housing construction and for the rise in farm income in the fall after the summer crops are harvested.

Stagflation (slumpflation): The combination in the economy in which a high rate of inflation coincides with a high rate of unemployment.

Supply-side economics: The school of economic thinking which stresses the importance of the costs of production as a means of revitalizing the economy. Advocates policies that raise capital and labor output by increasing the incentives to produce.

Wage-price controls: A policy under which the level of wages, salaries and prices are set by law or the administration.

Wage-price spiral: The phenomenon that takes place when workers succeed in obtaining pay raises greater than their increase in productivity. Since the higher wages mean increased cost to the employers, prices tend to increase; the resulting higher prices give workers an incentive to bargain for even higher wages.

Windfall profits tax: A tax on the profits received by oil producers as a result of the decontrol of oil prices and their resulting rise.

Annual Average Purchasing Power of the Dollar

Source: Bureau of Labor Statistics, U.S. Labor Department

Obtained by dividing the index for 1967 (100.00) by the index for the given period and expressing the result in dollars and cents. Beginning 1961, wholesale prices include data for Alaska and Hawaii; beginning 1964, consumer prices include them.

Year	As measured by—		Year	Wholesale prices	Consumer prices	Year	Wholesale prices	Consumer prices
	Wholesale prices	Consumer prices						
1940	$2.469	$2.381	1969	$ .939	$ .960	1976	$ .546	$ .587
1950	1.222	1.387	1970	.906	.860	1977	.515	.551
1955	1.139	1.247	1971	.878	.824	1978	.478	.493
1960	1.054	1.127	1972	.840	.799	1979	.463	.461
1965	1.035	1.058	1973	.744	.752	1980	.405	.406
1967	1.000	1.000	1974	.625	.677	1981, June	.371	.368
1968	.976	.960	1975	.572	.620			

How Much Do You Really Make?
Is Your Salary Keeping Up With Inflation?

Beginning in January 1978, the Bureau of Labor Statistics introduced a revised consumer price index for urban wage earners and clerical workers — about 40% of the population. The revised index (CPI-W) is based on a new, larger market basket of goods priced in 85 areas (29 more areas than for the old CPI). The new market basket includes TV and sound equipment and repairs, additional children's clothes, luggage, automotive body work, medical supplies such as crutches, and a variety of other goods and services which were not included in the old CPI.

In addition to the revised CPI, the Bureau also began to publish a completely new index for all urban dwellers, including the unemployed, the retired, and professional and managerial workers — about 80% of the U.S. population. This new urban index (CPI-U) takes into account the different ways price changes affect the purchasing habits of the poor and the moderately rich.

Both the CPI-W and the CPI-U use the same base year as the old CPI (1967=100) and were dovetailed into the old CPI. However, because of the many changes in sampling procedures, neither of the new indexes are strictly comparable with the old index.

Which Index For You?

Which index should you use to calculate the impact of inflation on your life? If your income is near the poverty level, or if you are retired on a moderate income, you should probably use the new CPI-U. Otherwise, even if you are moderately rich, the CPI-W will probably be the best indicator for you.

The CPI (W and U) emerges each month as single numbers. At the end of the year an average is computed from the monthly figures. (Averaging does away with fluctuations caused by special situations that have nothing to do with inflation.)

For example, the average CPI for 1980 was 247.0. This means that the value of goods and services, which was set at 100% in 1967, cost 147.0% more in 1980.

Changes in prices and how they affect you can be calculated by comparing the CPI of one period against another. The 1980 CPI reading of 247.0 can be compared to the 1979 reading of 217.7. Dividing by 217.7, the excess over 1 is the

Consumer Price Indexes, 1981

Source: Bureau of Labor Statistics, U.S. Labor Department

(1967=100)	December 1980 CPI-U	December 1980 CPI-W	January CPI-U	January CPI-W	March CPI-U	March CPI-W	May CPI-U	May CPI-W
All Items	258.4	258.7	260.5	260.7	265.1	265.2	269.0	269.1
Food, beverages	259.3	260.5	261.4	262.1	265.0	265.5	265.4	265.9
Housing	276.9	277.1	279.1	279.1	282.6	282.2	288.5	288.1
Apparel, upkeep	183.9	182.9	181.1	180.8	185.1	184.3	186.4	186.2
Transportation	261.1	261.9	264.7	265.7	273.5	274.4	277.8	278.9
Medical care	275.8	277.6	279.5	281.4	284.7	287.0	289.0	290.8
Entertainment	212.0	210.1	214.4	212.2	218.2	216.1	220.3	217.7
Other goods, services	224.6	223.0	226.2	224.4	228.7	226.8	232.2	230.4
Services	284.7	285.5	287.7	288.4	292.5	293.1	299.6	300.0
Rent, for home	199.6	199.4	200.9	200.6	203.0	202.7	205.9	205.5
Household, less rent	338.4	341.9	342.3	345.5	348.8	351.8	360.4	363.5
Transportation	255.8	254.7	258.7	257.7	262.5	261.3	266.6	265.5
Medical care	297.9	300.0	302.1	304.3	307.5	310.2	311.7	313.6
Other services	228.1	228.4	230.4	230.2	233.2	233.0	235.3	234.5
All items less food	255.5	255.7	257.6	257.9	262.3	262.6	267.0	267.2
Commodities	243.8	244.3	245.4	245.8	249.8	250.2	251.9	252.4
Commodities less food	231.0	231.2	232.4	232.7	237.0	237.4	239.6	240.3
Nondurables	254.1	255.6	256.9	258.3	265.2	266.6	265.8	267.2
Energy	370.4	373.7	381.7	385.2	409.3	413.7	411.3	414.9
All items less energy	249.7	249.3	251.2	250.6	253.8	252.9	257.9	257.0

Average Consumer Price Indexes

Source: Bureau of Labor Statistics, U.S. Labor Department

The Consumer Price Index (CPI-W) measures the average change in prices of goods and services purchased by urban wage earners and clerical workers. (1967 = 100)

	1974 Index	1974 %+	1975 Index	1975 %+	1976 Index	1976 %+	1977 Index	1977 %+	1978 Index	1978 %+	1979 Index	1979 %+	1980 Index	1980 %+
All items	147.7	11.0	161.2	9.1	170.5	5.8	181.5	6.5	195.3	7.6	217.7	11.5	247.0	13.5
Food, drink	158.7	13.8	172.1	8.4	177.4	3.1	188.0	6.0	206.2	9.7	228.7	10.9	248.7	8.7
Housing	148.8	11.3	164.5	10.6	174.6	6.1	186.5	6.8	202.6	8.6	227.5	12.3	263.2	12.3
Apparel, upkeep	136.2	7.4	142.3	4.5	147.6	3.7	154.2	4.5	159.5	3.4	166.4	4.3	177.4	6.6
Transportation	137.7	11.2	150.6	9.4	165.5	9.9	177.2	7.1	185.8	4.9	212.8	14.5	250.5	17.7
Medical care	150.5	9.3	168.6	12.0	184.7	9.5	202.4	9.6	219.4	8.4	240.1	9.4	267.2	11.3
Entertainment	139.8	7.5	152.2	8.9	159.8	5.0	167.7	4.9	176.2	5.1	187.7	6.5	203.7	8.5
Other	142.0	7.2	153.9	8.4	162.7	5.7	172.2	5.8	183.2	6.4	196.3	7.2	213.6	8.8

percentage increase for the year 1980; in this case, 13.5%.

Did your income increase by enough to keep up with this inflation? To make the comparison, dig out your old W-2 or income tax return forms, or find your old paycheck stubs. Both gross and takehome pay comparisons will be of interest to you, but take care to compare equals. Overtime pay should not be counted. Also, watch out for changes in deductions such as those for tax exemptions, credit union payments, payroll bonds, and the like. These have nothing to do with inflation and should be added back to your take home pay.

Measuring Your Paycheck

A. To compare year-to-year earnings in percent form, divide your 1980 earnings by those of 1979 and express the result as a percentage. For example, if you earned the gross wages of the average U.S. worker, your paychecks in 1979 showed about $219.30 per week as compared with $235.10 per week in 1980, an increase of 7.20%. Since prices rose by 13.5% during 1980, the average worker had a loss of 6.3% in real gross income that year. You can do the same kind of

calculation on your total 1979 and 1980 earnings by using your total annual income figures in place of weekly earnings figures.

B. Another way to handle the same figures takes a dollar form. For this calculation, assume your wage was $219.30 at the end of 1979. During 1980, prices increased by 13.5%. To match that price increase, your wages should have gone up to $248.91 (219.30 times 1.135) by the end of 1980.

While readings on a monthly basis may be misleading, you may want a rough idea of how much you are being affected by inflation right now. For example, if you had weekly earnings of $252.38 in May of 1981, compared to earnings of $235.10 in December, 1980, your income went up 7.35% (The difference, $17.28, divided by 235.10). The CPI-W went from 258.7 to 269.1 during the same period, a gain of 4.02%. This means you had a gain on inflation in the first 5 months of 1981. You can make the same calculation for any month by using the latest CPI figures as they are issued by the Department of Labor and published in your local newspaper.

Consumer Price Index by Cities

(1967-100, except Anchorage and Miami)

City[1]	1978 avg.	1979 avg.	1980 avg.	March, 1981 CPI-U	March, 1981 CPI-W	June, 1981 CPI-U	June, 1981 CPI-W
Anchorage, Alas. (10/67=100)	187.5	207.0	228.2	241.1	236.2	272.8	—
Atlanta, Ga.	192.6	212.7	242.3	—	—	269.2	272.8
Baltimore, Md.	199.6	218.8	250.3	270.3	269.3	—	—
Boston, Mass.	193.1	212.9	240.0	262.2	261.8	—	—
Buffalo, N.Y.	193.0	211.3	235.6	—	—	257.2	256.1
Chicago, Ill.-Northwest Ind.	190.7	214.6	245.5	—	258.9	269.1	267.9
Cincinnati, Ohio-Ky.-Ind.	199.1	223.8	254	256.1	267.7	—	—
Cleveland, Ohio	193.9	219.5	25	—	—	285.3	283.8
Dallas-Ft. Worth, Tex.	194.0	218.6	25	—	—	286.0	284.0
Denver-Boulder, Col.	202.1	233.5	261.5	281.4	285.8	—	—
Detroit, Mich.	194.1	218.8	252.1	268.2	263.6	280.5	275.9
Honolulu, Ha.	184.1	204.6	228.5	—	—	252.8	253.8
Houston, Tex.	208.2	235.7	265.4	—	—	292.9	289.4
Kansas City, Mo.-Kan.	191.8	219.2	248.1	—	—	270.5	269.1
Los Angeles-Long Beach, Anaheim, Cal.	192.8	213.7	247.3	263.3	266.5	267.9	271.7
Miami, Fla. (11/77=100)	104.8	114.8	130.8	140.0	141.7	—	—
Milwaukee, Wis.	192.3	218.8	251.5	269.9	274.6	—	—
Minneapolis-St. Paul, Minn-Wis.	199.7	222.6	247.8	—	—	276.1	276.6
New York, N.Y.-Northeast N.J.	196.1	213.1	237.2	253.9	253.7	258.6	257.9
Northeast Pa. (Scranton)	191.9	210.7	237.1	257.6	260.6	—	—
Philadelphia, Pa.-N.J.	194.3	213.6	241.4	258.3	259.5	265.4	265.6
Pittsburgh, Pa.	195.5	217.3	247.2	—	—	271.3	273.0
Portland, Ore.-Wash.	198.4	225.4	255.4	268.1	267.0	—	—
St. Louis, Mo.-Ill.	191.5	215.8	244.9	259.3	259.4	—	—
San Diego, Cal.	200.1	233.1	268.5	293.1	288.0	—	—
San Francisco-Oakland, Cal.	197.8	214.6	247.3	—	—	274.0	274.3
Seattle-Everett, Wash.	194.8	216.3	252.1	271.1	267.9	—	—
Washington, D.C.-Md.-Va.	197.0	218.6	244.7	262.3	264.2	—	—

(1) The area listed includes the entire Standard Metropolitan Statistical Area, except New York and Chicago, which include the Standard Consolidated Area.

Annual Percent Change in Productivity and Related Data, 1970-80

Source: Bureau of Labor Statistics, U.S. Labor Department

Item	1970	1971	1972	1973	1974	1975	1976	1977	1978	1979	1980
Private business sector:											
Output per hour of all persons	0.7	3.4	3.5	1.9	-3.0	2.1	3.5	1.6	0.3	-0.8	-0.3
Real compensation per hour	1.1	2.4	2.9	1.9	-1.7	0.7	2.8	1.6	1.5	-1.7	-3.1
Unit labor cost	6.4	3.2	2.8	6.2	12.5	7.7	5.0	6.4	9.0	10.3	10.3
Unit nonlabor payments	1.2	6.8	5.2	5.0	4.4	15.3	5.2	4.2	4.3	5.8	6.8
Implicit price deflator	4.7	4.4	3.6	5.8	9.8	10.1	5.1	5.7	7.5	8.9	9.2
Nonfarm business sector:											
Output per hour of all persons	0.2	3.1	3.7	1.7	-3.1	1.9	3.5	1.3	0.5	-1.1	-0.4
Real compensation per hour	0.7	2.3	3.1	1.5	-1.7	0.7	2.5	1.5	1.5	-2.1	-3.3
Unit labor cost	6.5	3.5	2.8	6.0	12.6	7.8	4.7	6.7	8.8	10.2	10.3
Unit nonlabor payments	1.6	6.7	3.8	0.3	5.9	17.1	6.9	4.3	3.3	5.1	8.3
Implicit price deflator	4.9	4.5	3.1	4.1	10.5	10.6	5.4	5.9	7.0	8.6	9.7
Manufacturing:											
Output per hour of all persons	-0.3	5.3	5.1	2.7	-5.2	4.9	4.3	2.4	2.5	0.8	-0.5
Real compensation per hour	0.9	1.9	2.1	0.9	-0.8	2.4	2.4	2.2	1.8	-2.0	-0.2
Unit labor cost	7.2	0.9	0.4	4.3	16.1	6.6	3.9	6.3	6.9	8.2	11.0
Unit nonlabor payments	-3.2	9.2	2.3	-1.0	-0.7	21.6	8.5	3.3	NA	NA	273.7
Implicit price deflator	4.2	3.1	1.0	2.8	11.5	10.2	5.1	5.5	NA	NA	82.2

Consumer Price Index (CPI-U) by Region and City Size

Source: Bureau of Labor Statistics, U.S. Labor Department

(City sizes: A=1.25 million or more; B=385,000 to 1.25 million; C=75,000 to 385,000; D=75,000 or less.)

June, 1981 (Dec. 1977 = 100)	All items	Food and beverages	Housing	Apparel, upkeep	Transpor- tation	Medical care	Enter- tainment	Other goods and services
Northeast								
Size A	139.1	137.5	142.1	116.2	151.5	134.8	127.9	125.9
Size B	146.8	139.2	153.2	118.9	159.1	134.0	129.6	132.1
Size C	152.5	141.1	166.0	123.1	158.4	137.8	125.9	134.1
Size D	146.3	136.1	154.0	122.9	156.6	137.2	130.2	128.8
North Central								
Size A	150.0	138.1	162.9	110.8	156.4	139.1	130.6	130.1
Size B	146.6	137.5	152.6	118.9	157.3	139.9	124.4	136.0
Size C	142.3	139.6	143.5	115.3	157.0	140.4	129.8	129.3
Size D	143.1	140.7	144.0	118.6	155.9	144.0	126.9	134.3
South								
Size A	146.2	138.2	152.3	121.1	158.1	135.0	124.9	133.1
Size B	148.7	139.4	156.4	119.9	158.3	138.8	130.7	134.1
Size C	145.9	138.7	151.9	115.3	156.6	142.1	132.1	131.5
Size D	144.8	141.9	147.5	109.5	157.7	148.1	133.5	134.1
West								
Size A	147.5	138.3	153.2	120.7	157.4	141.0	127.7	134.8
Size B	149.1	142.6	155.1	123.1	157.5	141.2	128.9	134.7
Size C	143.9	137.5	146.7	113.4	158.7	141.5	130.8	130.2
Size D	146.9	143.2	146.1	133.5	159.3	146.2	143.7	137.8

The Northeast region includes cities from Boston to Pittsburgh; the North Central, cities from Cleveland to Grand Island, Neb. and from Minneapolis to St. Louis and Cincinnati; the South, cities from Baltimore to Dallas; the West, cities from Alamogordo, N. Mex., to Butte, Mont. Anchorage, and Honolulu.

Average Weekly Earnings of Production Workers[1]

Source: Bureau of Labor Statistics, U.S. Labor Department

	Manufacturing workers						Private nonagricultural workers					
			Spendable average weekly earnings[2]						Spendable average weekly earnings[2]			
	Gross average weekly earnings		Worker with no dependents		Worker with 3 dependents		Gross average weekly earnings		Worker with no dependents		Worker with 3 dependents	
Year and month	Current dollars	1977 dollars	Current dollars	1977 dollars	Current dollars	1977 dollars	Current dollars	1977 dollars	Current dollars	1977 dollars	Current dollars	1977 dollars
1973	166.46	227.09	132.57	180.86	143.50	195.77	145.39	198.35	117.71	160.31	143.50	173.78
1974	176.80	217.20	140.19	172.22	151.56	186.19	154.76	190.12	124.37	152.79	151.56	165.37
1975	190.79	214.85	151.61	170.73	166.29	187.26	163.53	184.16	132.49	149.20	166.29	164.02
1976	209.32	222.92	167.83	178.73	181.32	193.10	175.45	186.85	143.30	152.61	181.32	166.00
1977	228.90	228.90	183.80	183.80	200.06	200.06	189.00	189.00	155.19	155.19	200.06	169.93
1978	249.27	231.66	197.40	183.46	214.87	199.69	203.70	189.31	165.39	153.71	214.87	167.95
1979	268.94	224.64	212.70	177.40	232.38	193.81	219.91	183.41	178.00	148.46	194.82	162.49
1980	288.62	212.64	225.79	165.90	247.01	181.49	235.10	172.74	188.82	138.74	206.40	151.65
1981 Jan. . .	308.43	214.78	237.60	165.46	260.36	181.31	246.75	171.83	195.68	136.27	213.96	149.00
Feb. . .	306.13	210.83	236.08	162.59	258.70	178.17	247.10	170.18	195.92	134.93	214.22	147.53
Mar. . .	311.22	213.02	239.37	163.84	262.38	179.59	249.92	171.06	197.88	135.44	216.34	148.08
Apr. . .	312.84	212.82	240.39	163.53	263.55	179.29	250.98	170.73	198.61	135.11	217.14	147.71
May[p] . .	317.59	214.15	243.40	164.13	266.99	180.03	252.38	170.14	199.59	134.59	218.20	147.13
June[p] .	319.20	213.51	244.42	163.49	268.15	179.36	254.88	170.49	201.32	134.66	220.08	147.21

(1) Data relate to production workers in mining and manufacturing; to construction workers in contract construction; and to nonsupervisory workers in transportation and public utilities; wholesale and retail trade; finance, insurance, and real estate; and services. (2) Spendable average weekly earnings are based on gross average weekly earnings less the estimated amount of the worker's Federal, social security, and income taxes. (p) preliminary.

Shopping for Credit: Ask the Right Questions

Source: New York State Banking Department

Under federal law, all institutions that extend or arrange for the extension of consumer credit must give the borrower meaningful information about the cost of each loan. The cost must be expressed as the dollar amount of the interest or finance charge, and as the annual percentage rate computed on the amount financed.

To be sure the loan or credit agreement you are considering suits both your budget and your individual needs, shop around. And ask questions to compare and evaluate a lender's rate and services. For instance:

1. What is the annual percentage rate?
2. What is the total cost of the loan in dollars?

3. How long do you have to pay off the loan?
4. What are the number, amounts, and due dates of payments?
5. What is the cost of deferring or extending the time period of the loan?
6. What is the cost of late charges for overdue payments?
7. If you pay the loan off early, are there any prepayment penalties?
8. Does the loan have to be secured? If so, what collateral is required?
9. What is the cost of credit life or other insurance that is being offered or may be required?
10. Are there any other charges you may have to pay?

Interest Laws and Consumer Finance Loan Rates

Source: Revised by Christian T. Jones. Editor Consumer Finance Law Bulletin, Prospect Heights, Ill.

Most states have laws regulating interest rates. These laws fix a legal or conventional rate which applies when there is no contract for interest. They also fix a general maximum contract rate, but in many states there are so many exceptions that the general contract maximum actually applies only to exceptional cases. Also, federal law has preempted state limits on first home mortgages and, over $1,000, business and agricultural credit, subject to each state's right to reinstate its own law.

Legal rate of interest. The legal or conventional rate of interest applies to money obligations when no interest rate is contracted for and also to judgments. The rate is usually somewhat below the general interest rate.

General maximum contract rates. General interest laws in most states set the maximum rate between 8% and 16% per year. The general maximum is fixed by the state constitution at 10% per year in Arkansas. Loans to corporations are frequently exempted or subject to a higher maximum. In recent years, it has also been common to provide special rates for home mortgage loans and variable rates that are indexed to federal rates. In 1981, a number of states allowed regulated lenders to charge any rate agreed to with the customer.

Specific enabling acts. In many states special statutes permit industrial loan companies, second mortgage lenders, and banks to charge 1.5% a month or more. Laws regulating revolving loans, charge accounts and credit cards generally limit charges to 1.5% per month plus annual fees for credit cards. Rates for installment sales contracts in most states are somewhat higher. Credit unions may generally charge 1% to 1½% a month. Pawnbrokers' rates vary widely. Savings and loan associations, and loans insured by federal agencies, are also specially regulated.

Consumer finance loan statutes. Most consumer finance loan statutes are based on early models drafted by the Russell Sage Foundation (1916-42) to provide small loans to wage earners under license and other protective regulations. Since 1969 the model has frequently been the Uniform Consumer Credit Code which applies to credit sales and loans for consumer purposes. In general, licensed lenders may charge 3% a month for amounts to $500 and reduced rates for additional amounts. A number of states permit add-on rates of 17% to 20% ($17 to $20 per $100) a year of the original principal for $300 and lower rates for additional amounts. An add-on of 17% ($17 per $100) per year yields about 2.5% per month if paid in equal monthly installments. In the table below unless otherwise stated, monthly and annual rates are based on reducing principal balances, annual add-on rates are based on the original principal for the full term, and two or more rates apply to different portions of balance or original principal.

States with consumer finance loan laws and the rates of charge as of Oct. 1, 1981:

Maximum monthly rates computed on unpaid balances, unless otherwise stated.

Ala.. . . Annual add-on: 15% to $750, 10% to $2,000, 8% over $2,000 (min. 1.5% on unpaid balances). Higher rates for loans up to $749. To 7/1/87, no limit over $5,000.

Alas.. . 3% to $500, 2% to $1,000, and 1% over; or equivalent flat rate to $25,000. Over $5,000 1.5% or 8% over FRB discount rate to $25,000.

Ariz.. . Up to $1,000: 3% to $300, 2% to $600, 1.5% over $600. Over $1,000: 2.5% to $300, 2% to $1,000, 1.5% to $1,500, 1% to $10,000; (1.625% min.): 1% fee to $1,500.

Cal.. . . 2.5% to $225, 2% to $900, 1.5% to $1,650, 1% to $10,000 (1.5% min.). No max. over $10,000.

Colo.. . 36% per year to $630, 21% to $2,100, 15% to $25,000 (21% min.).

Conn. . Annual Add-on: 17% to $600, 11% to $5,000; 11% over $1,800 to $5,000 for certain secured loans.

Del.. . . Any agreed rate.

Fla.. . . 30% per year to $500, 24% to $1,000, 18% to $2,500; 18% per year on any amount over $2,500 to $25,000.

Ga.. . . 10% per year discount to 18 months, add-on to 36½ months; 8% fee to $600, 4% on excess plus $2 per month; max. $3,000.

Ha.. . . 3.5% to $100, 2.5% to $300; 2% on entire balance over $300 (temporary rate to 7/1/85).

Ida.. . . 36% per year to $660, 24% to $2,200, 18% to $55,000 (21% min.).

Ill.. . . . Any agreed rate.

Ind.. . . 36% per year to $540, 21% to $1,800, 15% to $45,000 (21% min.).

Ia.. . . 3% to $500, 2% to $1,200, 1.5% to $2,000; or equivalent flat rate.

Kan. . . 36% per year to $420, 21% to $1,400, 14.45% to $25,000 (18% min.).

Ky.. . . 3% to $600, 2% to $1,500, 1.5% to $2,000.

La.. . . 36% per year to $1,400, 27% to $4,000, 24% to $7,000, 21% over $7,000.

Me.. . . 30% per year to $540, 21% to $1,800, 15% to $45,000 (18% min.).

Md.. . . 2.75% to $500, 2% to $700, 1.25% to $1,200; 1.75% to $3,500; 1.5% to $5,000; 1.35% to $6,000.

Mass. . 23% per year plus $20 fee to $6,000.

Mich.. . 31% per year to $500, 13% to $3,000 (18% min.).

Minn.. . 33% per year to $350, 19% to $35,000 (21.75% min.).

Miss.. . 36% per year to $800, 33% to $1,800, 24% to $4,500,

12% over $4,500.

Mo.. . . 2.218% to $800, 1.25% to $2,500, 10% per year over $2,500, plus 5% fee (max. $15).

Mont.. . Annual add-on: 20% to $500, 16% to $1,000, 12% to $7,500. 2% per mo. over $7,500 to $25,000.

Neb.. . 24% to $1,000, 18% to $5,000, 16% to $7,000.

Nev.. . Any agreed rate.

N.H.. . 2% to $600, 1.5% to $1,500; Any agreed rate to $10,000.

N.J.. . . 30% per year to $5,000.

N.M.. . Any agreed rate.

N.Y.. . Any agreed rate.

N.C.. . 3% to $600, 1.25% to $3,000.

N.D.. . 2.5% to $250, 2% to $500, 1.75% to $750, 1.5% to $1,000; any agreed rate on entire amount over $1,000 to $15,000.

Ohio . . 28% per year to $1,000, 22% to $3,000; 21% on entire amount over $3,000.

Okla.. . 30% per annum to $540, 21% to $1,800, 15% to $45,000. (21% min.). Special rates to $100.

Ore. . . Any agreed rate.

Pa.. . . 9.5% per year discount to 36 months, 6% for remaining time plus 2% fee (min. 2%) to $5,000.

P.R.. . Annual Add-on: 20% to $300, 7% to $600.

R.I.. . . 3% to $300, 2.5% for loans between $300 and $800; 2% for larger loans to $2,500.

S.C. . . 36% per year to $390, 21% to $1,300, 15% to $32,500 (18% min.). Special rate to $150.

S.D. . . 2.5% to $500, 2% to $1,200, 1.5% to $2,000, 1% to $2,500. Over $2,500, 19.5% per year to $30,000.

Tenn.. . 7.5% per year discount plus fees; no size limit (max. 18% per year on unpaid balances).

Texas . Annual add-on: 18% to $750, 8% to $6,250 or formula rate (max. 24% per year on unpaid balances.)

Utah . . 36% per year to $660, 21% to $2,200, 15% to $55,000 (21% min.) or, by rule, 24%.

Vt. . . . 2% to $1,000, 1% to $3,000 (min. 1.5%).

Va.. . . 3% to $500, 2.25% to $1,500, 1.5% to $2,500; or annual add-on of 21% to $500, 17% to $1,500, 13% to $2,500; 2% fee.

Wash. . 2.5% to $500, 1.5% to $1,000, 1% to $2,500.

W.Va.. . 36% per year to $500, 24% to $1,501, 18% to $1,600.

Wis. . . Annual discount: 9.5% on first $2,000, 8% to $3,000 up to 36 months; 19% per year for larger loans. (temporary rate to 10/31/81).

Wyo.. . 36% per year to $300, 21% to $1,000, 15% to $25,000 (21% min.).

Fair Credit: What You Should Know

Source: Federal Trade Commission

Federal legislation has made it easier for you to be treated fairly in credit-related areas:

Billing. Don't let the anonymous computer get you down. The Fair Credit Billing Act states that, if you find an error in the amount of $50 or more in your credit card statement or department store revolving charge statement and you write to the company about it (on a separate sheet of paper, not the bill), the company must acknowledge your letter within 30 days and must resolve the dispute within 90 days.

Equal Credit. The Equal Credit Opportunity Act (ECOA) bans any discrimination according to sex or marital status in the granting of credit. Discrimination is also prohibited on the basis of age, race, color, religion, national origin, or receipt of public assistance payments.

However, the creditor may ask questions relating to these areas if they have bearing on your credit worthiness. The creditor does have the right to determine whether you are willing and able to repay your debts. For instance, the creditor can ask you if you are "married," "unmarried," or "separated" if, and only if, (1) you are applying jointly with your spouse; (2) your spouse will be an authorized user of the account; (3) you live in a community property state or you list assets located in a community property state. Similarly, a creditor may ask about alimony, child support, and separate maintenance if, and only if, you are depending on these as sources to establish your ability to repay your debts. In this case, the creditor may ask whether there is a court order that requires the payments or may inquire about the length of time and regularity of the payments, as well as your ex-spouse's credit history.

The ECOA also requires that if you are turned down for credit, the creditor must tell you the reason you were turned down.

Mail-Order Merchandise. By law, you have the right to receive merchandise ordered through the mail within 30 days, unless another deadline has been specified. Promises such as "one week" or "4 to 6 weeks" must be met. If either the seller's or the FTC's deadline is missed, you have the right to cancel and have all your money returned. If you run into a problem with late or non-delivery, contact the Federal Trade Commission for help.

Consumer Installment Credit

Source: Federal Reserve System (amounts outstanding, millions of dollars)

| End of year or month | Total | By holder | | | | | | By type | | | |
		Commercial banks	Finance companies	Credit unions	Retailers	Savings and loans and other	Automobile	Mobile homes	Revolving	All others
1974	164,594	80,054	36,087	21,895	18,114	8,444	54,266	14,642	13,681	82,005
1975	171,996	82,936	35,995	25,666	18,201	9,198	57,242	14,434	15,019	85,301
1976	193,525	93,728	38,918	31,169	19,260	10,450	67,707	14,573	17,189	94,056
1977	230,564	112,373	44,868	37,605	23,490	12,228	82,911	14,945	39,274	93,434
1978	273,645	136,016	54,298	44,334	25,987	13,010	101,647	15,235	48,309	108,454
1979	312,024	154,177	68,318	46,517	28,119	14,893	116,362	16,838	56,937	121,887
1980	313,435	145,765	76,756	44,041	29,410	17,463	116,327	17,327	59,862	119,919
1981, June(e) e-estimated	318,459	143,310	82,723	45,686	27,412	19,328	119,685	17,724	58,470	122,580

Managing Credit: How Much Debt is Safe?

Source: Citibank

With the current rate of inflation, it is extremely important for consumers to keep close track of their individual use of credit and debt.

Before you make any new purchases, which involve moving income from the optional spending part of your budget to your fixed budget as a loan to be repaid, you must be sure you have those extra dollars and that you can do without them each month.

How Much Average Debt is Safe?

Once you've decided to apply for credit, you face the most-asked question about consumer debt: how much is safe?

There is no simple answer that applies to each consumer's situation. Most experts, today, avoid general rules of thumb.

Don't be misled by the percents of gross income that lenders may use to decide how much institutional risk they run in any specific application for a loan. The lending institution can use only gross income and loan-commitment averages to estimate its own average risk, and cannot know how any individual consumer will actually repay. Only you can gauge that, based on your own habits, values, and needs.

How do you determine what you can handle? To help decide, you must know at a given time how many dollars you have for optional spending, and then how many of those dollars you can move into fixed repayments.

Here's one technique for determining how many optional dollars you have:
1. Write down your annual take-home income after deductions (for taxes, etc.) and divide by 12 to get your monthly take-home income.
2. From the monthly figure, subtract all your current monthly fixed expenses—those to which you are currently committed or must cover over the next year. Include your gasoline and car costs, other transportation, heating, utilities, food, rent, or mortgage (but no other loan repayments), real estate taxes, insurance, etc.
3. Next, total your monthly nonmortgage loan repayments

and subtract them from the previous amount.

The total figure you're left with is your monthly optional spending amount. Now you must consider how comfortably you're managing with this amount. Consider that amount less the new monthly repayment. Can you still manage on the remaining amount, or should you wait until your take-home income goes up or your present debt loan goes down?

Are You Headed for Financial Trouble?

Although there is no dependable formula for determining your individual debt ratio, there are certain clear warning signals that you may have reached or have already passed it. Consider the following signals and, if several of them describe your financial situation, it may be time to look for help.

1. Your checkbook balance is getting lower and lower each month.
2. You don't seem to be able to make it from month to month without writing overdrafts on your checking account.
3. You pay only the minimum due or even less on your charge accounts each month.
4. You have borrowed on your life insurance and see little possibility of paying it back soon.
5. Your savings account is slowly disappearing or has completely disappeared, and you're not able to put any of your regular income into savings.
6. You manage to get through each month by depending on undependable extra income like overtime or odd jobs.
7. You find yourself depending on credit cards for day-to-day living expenses and using cash advances to pay off other debts.
8. You are behind on one or more of your installment payments.
9. You don't really know how much money you owe.
10. You are receiving overdue notices or phone calls from creditors.
11. Family disputes over money are growing.
12. You occasionally juggle paying bills, paying one creditor while giving excuses to another.
13. You've had to ask creditors for extensions on due dates.
14. You've taken out loans to pay debts, or taken out a debt consolidation loan.
15. You are at or near the limit on the credit lines allowed on your credit cards.
16. When you use credit, you try to get it for the longest time period and the lowest payments without considering how much more this will cost you in interest.
17. You must borrow money to pay bills you can anticipate, like quarterly property taxes.
18. Although you regularly pay all of your debts, you are forced to continue living on credit and, as a result, your debt loan never really shrinks or is even increasing.

What can you do if you find yourself in financial trouble? The first step is to drastically cut your optional spending. Put yourself and your family on a crash tight-cash program until you can stabilize your financial situation. Also, you may need to turn some assets into cash and apply it to your debts.

If these attempts fail, get in touch with your creditors. Candidly, explain your situation. Some of them may agree to a longer repayment schedule which will insure that they get their money back and that they will keep you as a customer. You may pay more in interest, but you'll have a better credit record.

If you're still in trouble, you probably need good financial counseling.

How to Find Credit Counseling

In the U.S., there are hundreds of free volunteer-staffed credit counseling sources. Others, staffed by professionals, charge a fee.

Look up Consumer Credit Counseling in your local phone book. Call the Consumer Affairs Department of your city for referrals. Contact community-centered organizations, church, local banks, consumer finance company, credit union, labor union, or your employer's personnel department.

If you can't find a local agency, write to the Family Service Association of America (44 E. 23rd St., New York, NY 10010) or the National Foundation for Consumer Credit (1819 H Street N.W., Washington, DC 20006).

Mortgages: New Alternatives to the Long-term Fixed-rate Loan

Source: Federal Home Loan Bank Board

Until quite recently the only type mortgage generally available in most parts of the country was the long-term fixed-rate mortgage. This mortgage had identical monthly payments and a term of 25 to 30 years. In the past several years, new mortgage forms have been developed, which have more flexible payment schedules and/or adjustable interest rates. These mortgages include:

Graduated-Payment Mortgage: The graduated-payment mortgage (GPM) has a fixed interest rate, but the payments start out at a lower level than on a fixed-rate mortgage. The payments on a GPM increase at a known rate during the early years of the loan. On the most popular GPM plan, the payments increase at $7\frac{1}{2}$ percent each year for the first 5 years of the loan. Payments on a GPM ultimately rise to a level higher than on a comparable fixed-payment mortgage.

Because the payments on a GPM start out at a low level, they may be insufficient to pay all the interest owed. That portion of the monthly interest in excess of the monthly payment is added to the loan balance. The outstanding balance on most GPM's actually increases for the first several years. This addition to the loan balance is called negative amortization.

A GPM is advantageous for a first-time homeowner who cannot, at the outset, handle the payments of a conventional loan, but hopes to be able to when his income rises.

Pledged-Account Mortgage: The pledged-account mortgage (PAM) is a special type of GPM. On most GPM plans the low initial payments are insufficient to pay all the interest owed. On a PAM, that portion of the interest due that is not covered by the monthly payment is deducted from a savings account pledged by the borrower. A part of the borrower's down payment is used to establish the savings account which is then pledged over to the lender. Some, but not all graduated payment mortgages have the pledged account feature.

Adjustable Mortgages: Adjustable mortgages are the newest and most complex of the new mortgage forms. The common feature of adjustable mortgages is that the interest rate is not fixed and will vary according to some interest rate index that is selected at the time the loan is originated. Lenders are not required to increase the interest rate on the mortgage as the index increases, but they are required to lower the interest rate if the index decreases. Adjustable mortgage contracts may contain limitations on the minimum and maximum size of an interest rate change.

Savings by Individuals in the U.S.

Source: Federal Reserve System

(annual flow in billions of dollars)

	1970	1975	1976	1977	1978	1979	1980
Increase in financial assets.	81.5	171.7	211.2	234.3	270.5	286.0	303.8
Currency and demand deposits	8.9	6.9	15.7	21.3	22.3	23.4	11.0
Savings accounts	43.6	83.4	107.5	107.5	100.1	79.2	131.2
Money market fund shares	—	1.3	—	.2	6.9	34.4	29.2
Securities	.2	25.5	16.3	17.0	40.1	55.2	17.5
U.S. Savings Bonds	.3	4.0	4.7	4.7	3.9	−.8	−7.3
Other U.S. Treasury securities	−11.3	15.7	1.8	6.4	19.2	32.5	18.1
U.S. Govt. agency securities	6.4	−1.0	3.8	5.7	7.6	20.1	9.7
State & local obligations	−.9	6.2	2.0	−1.5	1.8	2.4	3.0
Corporation & foreign bonds	10.7	8.9	11.8	−3.8	−2.9	10.3	3.6
Open market paper	−3.8	−4.4	−3.1	9.8	16.3	7.5	−7.6
Mutual fund shares	2.6	−.3	−2.4	.4	−.5	−.6	4.4
Other corporate equities	−4.3	−3.5	−2.2	−4.8	−5.2	−16.2	−6.3
Private life insurance reserves	5.4	8.5	8.2	11.3	11.7	12.3	11.4
Private insured pension reserves	2.8	8.1	15.3	14.9	18.3	16.2	20.0
Private noninsured pension reserves	6.9	11.8	11.2	17.4	15.9	14.0	22.3
Government ins. & pension reserves	8.9	15.1	17.7	22.5	27.9	24.4	35.3
Miscellaneous financial assets	5.4	11.1	19.3	22.0	27.3	26.9	25.7
Gross investment in tangible assets	144.7	222.3	262.6	320.7	366.4	398.7	381.6
Owner-occupied homes	25.7	45.6	60.6	80.7	97.1	106.6	93.8
Other fixed assets	33.2	42.1	46.2	58.6	67.7	75.9	79.5
Consumer durables	85.2	133.2	156.8	178.8	199.3	212.3	211.9
Inventories	.5	2.4	−1.0	2.5	2.3	3.9	−3.5
Capital consumption allowances	99.6	166.6	183.2	203.7	229.5	260.0	292.1
Owner-occupied homes	12.1	22.2	24.5	28.6	33.6	39.1	45.6
Other fixed assets	22.3	38.7	41.8	46.5	52.9	61.0	68.4
Consumer durables	65.2	105.7	116.9	128.6	143.1	159.9	178.1
Net investment in tangible assets	45.1	55.7	79.4	117.0	137.0	138.7	89.5
Owner-occupied homes	13.6	23.5	36.1	52.1	63.6	67.5	48.2
Other fixed assets	10.9	3.4	4.4	12.2	14.9	14.8	11.0
Consumer durables	20.0	26.5	40.0	50.2	56.3	52.4	33.8
Inventories	.5	2.4	−1.0	2.5	2.3	3.9	−3.5
Net increase in debt	34.4	63.5	115.1	169.2	203.2	210.8	142.1
Mortgage debt on nonfarm homes	14.1	38.0	61.5	93.0	107.6	114.6	83.4
Other mortgage debt	8.4	7.0	11.6	16.7	17.8	20.0	18.1
Consumer credit	5.4	9.6	25.4	40.2	47.6	46.3	2.3
Security credit	−1.8	.7	4.8	1.3	1.3	−1.2	5.0
Policy loans	2.3	1.6	1.4	1.7	2.6	4.7	6.7
Other debt	5.9	6.5	10.4	16.3	26.3	26.3	26.6
Individuals' saving	92.2	164.0	175.5	182.1	204.2	213.9	251.2
Less Govt. ins. & pen. reserves	8.9	15.1	17.7	22.5	27.9	24.4	35.3
Net inv. in consumer durables	20.0	26.5	40.0	50.2	56.3	52.4	33.8
Capital gains dividends from mutual funds	.9	.2	.5	.6	.7	.9	1.7
Net savings by farm corps.	−.1	.1	.1	−.2	−.2	−?	−.5
Equals pers. saving, F/F basis	62.5	122.1	117.5	109.0	119.6	136.4	180.9
Personal saving, NIPA basis	55.8	94.3	82.5	74.1	76.3	86.2	101.3
Difference	6.8	27.8	35.0	34.9	43.3	50.3	79.6

Depending upon a particular lender's adjustable mortgage plan, a change in the interest rate may result in a change in the monthly payment, the term of the loan, the outstanding balance of the loan, or some combination of these. A number of lenders offer plans in which the interest rate can change every 3 or 6 months, but the payment changes every 3 years. Under such a plan an increase in the interest rate may mean that the monthly payment is insufficient to pay all the interest due that month. When this happens the unpaid interest will be added to the loan balance. Negative amortization can occur on adjustable mortgages if payments are adjusted less frequently than the interest rate.

Some lenders have adjustable mortgage plans with interest rate caps, that is, limitations on the amount by which payments may change. The adjustable mortgages made by federal savings and loan associations are known as AML's (adjustable mortgage loans) and the adjustable mortgages made by national banks are known as ARM's (adjustable rate mortgages). Variable-rate mortgages (VRM) and renegotiable-rate mortgages (RRM) are specific types of adjustable mortgages.

Graduated-Payment Adjustable Mortgage: The graduated-payment adjustable mortgage (GPAM) combines the scheduled payment increase feature of the GPM with an adjustable interest rate. All of the variations involve a deferral of some of the interest owed during the early years of the loan.

Some plans have payments rising by a set amount each year for the first several years; other plans fix the low payments for the first 3 or 5 years. There are a limitless number of possible GPAM variations. Very few lenders are now offering this form of loan.

Wraparound Mortgages: The wraparound mortgage is a technique by which a homebuyer can assume a low interest rate mortgage from the seller. Suppose a buyer needs a $50,000 mortgage and the previous owner has an assumable mortgage with a relatively low interest rate and a remaining balance of $30,000. The buyer might obtain a wraparound mortage for $50,000. The payments to the wraparound lender must be large enough to continue to make payments on the assumed mortgage and to amortize the additional $20,000 loan. The advantage to the buyer is that the "blended" interest rate is lower than the new mortgage rates and the payments to the wraparound lender are lower than the payments on a new $50,000 mortgage at current interest rates.

Shared-Appreciation Mortgage: A shared-appreciation mortgage (SAM) is a mortgage loan in which the borrower agrees to share the appreciation, or increase in value, of the property with the lender in return for an interest rate lower than that on a standard mortgage. SAMs have a contingent interest feature; a portion of the total interest due is contingent upon the appreciation of the property. At either the sale or transfer of the property, or the refinancing or maturity of the loan, the borrower must pay the lender a share of the appreciation of the property securing the loan. Payments on SAMs are based on a long amortization schedule, but the loan may become due at the end of 5 to 10 years.

The borrower and the lender jointly determine the size of the interest rate discount, the term of the loan, and the share of the appreciation due to the lender. The amount of appreciation is unknown at the time of origination, hence the total interest due and the effective interest rate are also uncertain. Although SAMs have a relatively low initial payment, the household's mortgage payment could increase very significantly if the lender's share of the appreciation and remaining principal balance had to be refinanced at market rate. At the current time, SAMs are offered by relatively few lenders.

Investment: A Basic Glossary

Source: Merrill, Lynch, Pierce, Fenner & Smith, Inc.

The investment possibilities in securities for you as an individual are extremely varied. If you are beginning to consider what is best for your personal needs and find the world of securities somewhat bewildering, we hope the following glossary may offer some help.

Bear Market: A market in which prices are on the rise.

Bond: A written promise or IOU by the issuer to repay a fixed amount of borrowed money on a specified date and to pay a set annual rate of interest in the meantime, generally at semi-annual intervals. Bonds are generally considered safe because the lender (whether a company or the government) must make interest payments before their money is spent on anything else. Some of the most common bonds include:

Commercial Paper; An extremely short-term corporate IOU, generally due in 270 days or less. Available in face amounts of $100,000, $250,000, $500,000, $1,000,000 and combinations thereof. Yield in recent years has averaged from 12 to 17 percent.

Convertible Bond: A corporate bond (see below) which may be converted into a stated number of shares of the corporations common stock. Its price tends to fluctuate along with fluctuations in the price of the stock as well as with changes in interest rates. Average yield in recent years has ranged from 8 to 12 percent.

Corporate Bond; Evidence of debt by a corporation. Differs from a municipal bond in various ways, but particularly in taxability of interest. Considered safer than the common or preferred stock of the same company. Yield has averaged in recent years from 12 to 17 percent.

Government Bond: An IOU of the U.S. Treasury, considered the safest security in the investment world. They are divided into two categories, those that are not marketable and those that are. *Savings Bonds* cannot be bought and sold once the original purchase is made. These include the familiar Series E bonds. You buy them at 75 percent of their face value and when they mature, 5 years later, they will pay you back 100 percent of face value if you cash them in. Recently they have been paying about 6 percent interest compounded semiannually to maturity. Another type, Series H, are not discounted, but issued in amounts of $500, $1,000, $5,000, and $10,000 and pay their interest in semiannual checks. They pay 8 percent the first year of their 10-year life, 5.8 percent for the next 4 years, and 6 percent for the last 5 years. Marketable bonds fall into 3 categories. *Treasury Bills* are short-term U.S. obligations, maturing in 3, 6, or 12 months. They are sold at a discount of the face value, and the minimum denomination is $10,000. Yield in recent years has ranged from 7½ percent to 16½ percent. *Treasury Notes* mature in up to 10 years. Denominations range from $500, $1,000 to $5,000, $10,000 and up. In recent years the yield has ranged from 8¼ percent to 15 percent. *Treasury Bonds* mature in 10 to 30 years. The minimum investment is $1,000 and yield has ranged from 8⅜ to 12⅝ percent in recent years.

Municipal Bond: Issued by governmental units such as states, cities, local taxing authorities and other agencies. Interest is exempt from U.S. — and sometimes state and local — income tax. Yield in recent years has averaged from 8 to 15 percent.

Bull Market: A market in which prices are falling.

Stock: *Common Stocks* are shares of ownership in a corporation; they are the most direct way to participate in the fortunes of a company. The sometimes wide swings in the prices of this kind of stock may mean a chance for big profits (or equally big losses). *Preferred Stock* is a type of stock on which a fixed dividend must be paid before holders of common stock are issued their share of the issuing corporation's earnings. Prices are higher and yields lower than comparable bonds and are, consequently, not the best investment for individuals. Payments are usually made quarterly. They are especially attractive to corporate investors because 85 percent of preferred dividends are tax exempt to corporations. Many high-grade preferreds currently pay about 10¼ percent to 11¼ percent interest. *Convertible Preferred Stock* can be converted into the common stock of the company that issued the preferred. This stock has the advantage of producing a higher yield than common stock and it also has appreciation potential. *Over-the-Counter Stock* is not traded on the major or regional exchanges, but rather through dealers from whom you buy directly. These stocks tend to belong to smaller companies. Prices of OTC stocks are based on the dealer's supply, what he paid for them, the demand for them, and the prices of competitive dealers. *Blue Chip* stocks are so called because they have been leading stocks for a long time. They do not show dramatic growth, but yield good dividends over time. *Growth* stocks are stocks which grow yearly by a growing percentage; they do well even in bad times.

Dow-Jones Industrial Average: A measure of stock market prices, based on the 30 leading manufacturing companies on the New York Stock Exchange.

Mutual Fund: A portfolio, or selection, of professionally bought and managed stocks in which you pool your money along with thousands of other people. A share price is based on net asset value, or the value of all the investments owned by the funds, less any debt, and divided by the total number of shares. The major advantage is less risk — it is spread out over many stocks and, if one or two do badly, the remainder may shield you from the losses. *Bond Funds* are mutual funds that deal in the bond market exclusively. *Money Market Mutual Funds* buy in the so-called "Money Market" — institutions that need to borrow large sums of money for short terms. Usually the individual investor cannot afford the denominations required in the "Money Market" (i.e. treasury bills, commercial paper, certificates of deposit), but through a money market mutual fund he can take advantage of these money makers when interest rates are high. These funds offer special checking account advantages, as you can generally write a check against your investment at any time in amounts of $500 or more. The minimum investment is generally $1,000. Average yield over recent years has been from 12 to 17 percent.

Directory of Consumer and Information Offices

Source: Office of Consumer Affairs, U.S. Department of Health and Human Services

Advertising:
National Advertising Division, Council of Better Business Bureaus, 845 Third Avenue, New York, New York 10022; (212) 754-1320.
Political advertising on TV and radio
Consumer Assistance Office, Federal Communications Commission, Washington, DC 20260; (202) 245-5445.

Aging:
Director, National Clearinghouse on Aging, Department of Health and Human Services, Washington, DC 20201; (202) 245-0188.

Air Travel:
Fares and routes
Consumer Assistance Division, Civil Aeronautics Board, Washington, DC 20428; (202) 673-6047.
Safety
Chief, Community and Consumer Liaison Division, Federal Aviation Administration, APA-400, Department of Transportation; (202) 426-1960.

Alcohol and Alcoholism:
Director, National Clearinghouse for Alcohol Information, P.O. Box 2345, Rockville, MD 20852; (301) 468-2600.

Appliances:
Major Appliance Consumer Action Panel (MACAP), 20 No. Wacker Dr., Chicago, IL 60606; (312) 984-5858.
Product Safety
Public Inquiries Office, Consumer Product Safety Commission, Washington, DC 20207; (800) 638-8326; (800) 492-8363 in Maryland; (800) 638-8333 in Puerto Rico, Virgin Islands, Alaska, Hawaii.
Radiation
Director, Technical Information Staff (HFX-25), Bureau of Radiological Health, Food and Drug Administration, Department of Human Services, 5600 Fishers Lane, Rockville, MD 20857; (301) 443-3434.

Automobiles:
Safety and recalls
Administrator, National Highway Traffic Safety Administration, Department of Transportation, Washington, DC 20590; (800) 424-9393; (202) 426-1023 in Washington, DC.
Fuel-saving devices and additives
Fuel-Saving Device Evaluation Coordinator, Vehicle Emission Laboratory, Environmental Protection Agency, 2565 Plymouth Rd., Ann Arbor, MI 48105; (313) 668-4299.
Office of Consumer Affairs, Department of Energy, Washington, DC 20585; (202) 252-5373.

Banking:
American Bankers Association, 1120 Connecticut Ave., NW, Washington, DC 20036; (202) 467-4000.

Child Abuse:
National Center on Child Abuse and Neglect, P.O. Box 1182, Washington, DC 20013; (202) 245-2840.
Parents Anonymous, Suite 208, 22330 Hawthorne Blvd., Torrance, CA 90505; (800) 421-0353; (800) 352-0386 in California.

Child Support:
Director, Office of Child Support Enforcement, Department of Health and Human Services, 61110 Executive Blvd., Rockville, MD 20850; (301) 443-4442.

Civil Rights:
Civil Rights Division, Department of Justice, Main Justice Bldg., Washington, DC 20530; (202) 633-3828.

Employment
Office of Executive Director, Equal Employment Opportunity Commission, Washington, DC 20506; (202) 634-6814.
Housing
Office of Fair Housing and Equal Opportunity, Department of Housing and Urban Development, Washington, DC 20410; (800) 424-8590; (202) 426-3500 in Washington, DC.
Unfair Labor Practices
Offices of Executive Secretary, National Labor Relations Board, Washington, DC 20570; (202) 254-9430.

Consumer Information:
For a copy of the free Consumer Information Catalog, a listing of more than 200 Federal consumer publications, write to: Consumer Information Center, Pueblo, CO 81009. An annual listing of Federal consumer publications in Spanish can also be obtained from the same address.

Copyrights:
Information and Publication Section, Copyright Office, Library of Congress, Washington, DC 20559; (202) 287-8700.

Cosmetics:
Director, Consumer Communications, HFE-88, Food and Drug Administration, Department of Health and Human Services, 5600 Fishers Lane, Rockville, MD 20857; (301) 443-3170.

Credit Counseling:
Executive Director, National Foundation for Consumer Credit, 1819 H St. NW, Washington, DC 20006; (202) 223-2040.

Credit Unions:
Credit Union National Association, 1730 Rhode Island Ave. NW, Washington, DC 20036; (202) 828-4500.

Drugs, Drug Abuse:
Abuse
Director, Office of Communications and Public Affairs, Alcohol, Drug Abuse, and Mental Health Administration, Department of Health and Human Services, 5600 Fishers Lane, Rockville, MD 20857; (301) 443-3783, (301) 443-6500.
Effectiveness and Safety
Director, Consumer Communications, HFE-88, Food and Drug Administration, Department of Health and Human Services, 5600 Fishers Lane, Rockville, MD 20857, (301) 443-3170.

Education:
Office of Public Participation and Special Concerns, Department of Education, Washington, DC 20202; (202) 472-9020.
National Education Association of the United States, 1201 16th St. NW, Washington, DC 20036; (202) 833-4000.

Employment:
Coordinator of Consumer Affairs, Department of Labor, Washington, DC 20210; (202) 523-6060.
Discrimination
Director, Equal Opportunity Employment Commission, Washington, DC 20506; (202) 634-6930.
Safety and Health
Hazards Evaluation and Technical Assistance Branch, National Institute of Occupational Safety and Health, 4676 Columbia Parkway, Cincinnati, OH 45226; (513) 684-2176.
Training

For information on employment and training programs, such as the Comprehensive Employment and Training Act (CETA) programs, most of which are handled by state and local governments, check with state or local employment offices listed in the white pages of the phone book, or your mayor's office. General information can be obtained from the Director, Employment and Training Administration, Department of Labor, Washington, DC 20213; (202) 376-6905.

Energy:
Conservation and Renewable Energy Referral Service; (800) 523-2929; (800) 426-4983 in Pennsylvania.
Nuclear regulation
Office of Public Affairs, Nuclear Regulatory Commission, Washington, DC 20555; (808) 638-8282; (800) 426-2943 in Washington, DC.

Environment:
Public Inquiries Center (A-107), Environmental Protection Agency, Washington, DC 20460; (202) 755-0707.

Federal Regulations:
Federal Register
For information on federal regulations and proposals, the Office of the Federal Register is offering, among other services, recorded "Dial-a-Reg" phone messages, which give advance information on significant documents to be published in the Federal Register the following work day. The service is currently available in Washington, DC at (202) ⁓-5022; Chicago at (312) 663-0884; and Los Angeles at (213) 688-3800. The *Federal Register*, published five days a week, informs the public about proposed and new government regulations. It includes Presidential proclamations, Executive Orders, and other Presidential documents. It may be ordered from the Superintendent of Documents, U.S. Government Printing Office, Washington, DC 20402 for $1.00 per copy, $45.00 for six months, or $75.00 per year. Contact the Library, Office of the Federal Register, National Archives, Washington, DC 20408; (202) 633-6930.

Food:
Consumer information
Office of the Consumer Advisor, Department of Agriculture, Washington, DC 20250; (202) 447-3975.
Labeling, quality, and safety (all foods except meat and poultry products)
Director, Consumer Communications, Food and Drug Administration, Department of Health and Human Services, 5600 Fishers Lane, Rockville, MD 20857; (301) 443-3170.
Labeling, quality, and safety (meat and poultry products)
Food and Safety Inspection Service, Department of Agriculture, Washington, DC 20250; (202) 472-4485.
Food Stamps and Food Assistance Programs
Contact local or state Welfare Office, or local health department.

Freight Shipments:
Office of Consumer Protection, Interstate Commerce Commission, Washington, DC 20423; (800) 424-9312; (202) 275-0860 in Washington, DC.
Office of Consumer Affairs, Federal Maritime Commission, Washington, DC 20573; (202) 523-5807.
Community and Consumer Liaison Division (APA-400), Federal Aviation Administration, Department of Transportation, Washington, DC 20591; (202) 426-1960.
Office of Public Affairs (ROA-30), Federal Railroad Administration, Department of Transportation, Washington, DC 20590; (202) 426-0881.

Handicapped:
Chief, Clearinghouse on the Handicapped, Office for Handicapped Individuals, Department of Health and Human Services, Washington, DC 20201; (202) 245-0080.
Architectural barriers
National Center for a Barrier-Free Environment, 1140 Connecticut Ave. NW, Washington, DC 20036; (800)

424-2809; (202) 466-6896 in Washington, DC.
Employment
President's Committee on Employment of the Handicapped, 1111 20th St. NW, Washington, DC 20036; (202) 653-5044.
Reading material for the blind and physically handicapped
Director, National Library Service for the Blind and Physically Handicapped, 1291 Taylor St. NW, Washington, DC 20542; (800) 424-8567; (202) 287-5100, in Washington, DC.

Health:
National Health Information Clearinghouse, Department of Health and Human Services, P.O. Box 1133, Washington, DC 20013; (800) 336-4797; (703) 522-2590 in Washington, DC, Virginia, Alaska, and Hawaii.
Second Surgical Opinion Program, Department of Health and Human Services, Humphrey Bldg., Room 313 H, Washington, DC 20201; (800) 683-6833; (800) 492-6603 in Maryland.

Housing:
Information Center, Department of Housing and Urban Development, Washington, DC 20410; (202) 755-6420.
FHA Loans
Federal Housing Administration, Department of Housing and Urban Development, Washington, DC 20410; (202) 755-6600.
FmHA Insured Loans
Farmer's Home Administration, Department of Agriculture, Washington, DC 20250; (202) 447-4323.
Mobile Homes
Office of Mobile Home Standards, Department of Housing and Urban Development, Washington, DC 20410; (202) 755-6920.
Real Estate Settlement Procedures
Office of Real Estate Practices, Department of Housing and Urban Development, Washington, DC 20410; (202) 755-6524.

Insurance:
Flood insurance
Federal Insurance Administrator, Federal Emergency Management Agency, Washington, DC 20472; (800) 424-8872, 8873; (202) 287-0750.

Mail:
Fraud
Check with your local postal inspector, or the Chief Postal Inspector, U.S. Postal Service, Washington, DC 20260; (202) 245-5445.
Mail orders
Mail Order Action Line, 6 E. 43rd St., New York, New York 10018; (212) 689-4977.
Unordered merchandise
Check with your local postmaster, or the Chief Postal Inspector, above.
Unsolicited mail
To remove your name from a mailing list, contact the Mail Preference Service, Name-Removal Program, 6 E. 43rd St., New York, New York 10017; (212) 689-4977.

Medicare:
Contact your local Social Security Office, or your area Medicare carrier, by looking under Medicare in the local telephone directory. Or contact Medicare Inquiries, Health Care Financing Administration, Department of Health and Human Services, 6325 Security Blvd., Baltimore, MD 21207; (301) 594-9086.

Medicaid:
Contact your local Welfare or social services offices.

Moving and Movers:
Office of Consumer Protection, Interstate Commerce Commission, Washington, DC 20423; (800) 424-9312; (202) 275-0860 in Washington, DC.

Nursing Homes:
Division of Long-Term Care, Health Care Financing Administration, Department of Health and Human Services, 1849 Gwyn Oak Ave., Dogwood East Bldg., Baltimore, MD 21207; (301) 594-3642.
Consumer Services, American Health Care Association, 1200 15th St. NW, Washington, DC 20005; (202) 833-2050.

Passports:
Citizens Counselor Services, Department of State, Room 4811, Washington, DC 20520; emergencies (202) 632-5225; non-emergencies (202) 632-3444.

Patents and Trademarks:
Commissioner of Patents and Trademarks, Washington, DC 20231; (703) 557-3268.

Pensions:
Pension Benefit Guaranty Corp., 2020 K Street NW, Washington, DC 20006; (202) 254-4817.
PBGC Field Office, Federal Office Building, 300 No. Los Angeles St., Los Angeles, CA 90012; (213) 688-6428.

Product Quality:
Office of Consumer Affairs, Department of Commerce, Washington, DC 20230; (202) 377-5001.

Product Safety:
Public Inquiries, Consumer Product Safety Commission, Washington, DC 20207; (800) 638-8326; (800) 492-8363 in Maryland; (800) 638-8333 in Alaska, Hawaii, Puerto Rico, Virgin Islands.

Social Security:
Local Social Security Office.

Stocks and Bonds:
Director, Office of Consumer Affairs, Securities and Exchange Commission, Washington, DC 20549; (202) 523-3952.

Taxes:
The Internal Revenue Service (IRS) has 58 district offices that provide tax assistance by toll-free telephone. Toll-free numbers are listed in IRS tax packages and in local telephone directories. Taxpayers may also use the toll-free network to clarify bills and notices, and to contact the Problem Resolution Officer for complaints unresolved through normal channels.

Train Travel:
Amtrak, Office of Customer Relations, P.O. Box 2709, Washington, DC 20013; (202) 383-2121.
Director, Public Information Office, Interstate Commerce Commission, Washington, DC 20423; (800) 424-9312; (202) 275-0860 in Washington, DC.
Consumer Affairs Officer, Federal Railroad Administration, Department of Transportation, Washington, DC 20590; (202) 426-0881.

Veterans:
Veterans Administration, Washington, DC 20420; (202) 393-4120.

Warranties:
Federal Trade Commission, Washington, DC 20420; (202) 389-2567.

Canadian Consumer Associations

Automobile Protection Association

The Automobile Protection Association (APA) is a non-profit, independently-financed consumer group founded in 1969 to advise motorists on the quality of automotive products and services, to publicize and encourage legal action against what it considers dishonest or dangerous practices in the automobile industry, and to press federal and provincial governments for protective legislation. For a $20 annual fee members receive periodic APA bulletins as well as free legal consultation when needed. Accredited garage service is provided in Montreal and Ottawa. Headquarters are at 292 St-Joseph West, Montreal, Quebec H2V 2N7. Branch office at 255 Argyle, Ottawa, Ont. K2P 1B8.

Consumers' Association of Canada

The Consumers' Association of Canada (CAC) is a voluntary, non-profit organization founded in 1947 to represent consumer interests. It also provides members with information on consumer legislation and the results of its research and tests on consumer goods and services. The national office is at 2660 Southvale Cres., Level 3, Ottawa, Ont. K1B 5C4; branch offices are in each province and territory. CAC publishes monthly, bilingual magazines, *Canadian Consumer* and *Le Consommateur Canadien* (circulation 180,000). Annual membership fee is $16.

Average Canadian Income and Taxes by Occupation, 1978

Source: Revenue Canada Taxation Statistics

Occupation	Number[1]	Average income[2]	Average federal tax	Occupation	Number[1]	Average income[2]	Average federal tax
Self-employed doctors and surgeons	27,541	$53,422	$10,658	Municipal government employees	518,255	13,374	1,220
Self-employed dentists	7,223	45,985	8,827	Investors	736,191	12,849	920
Self-employed lawyers and notaries	15,187	40,587	7,564	Business employees	6,685,744	12,614	1,205
Self-employed accountants	9,374	33,440	5,468	Self-employed salesmen	30,038	12,263	1,163
Self-employed engineers and architects	3,503	30,825	5,051	Fishermen	30,869	12,231	1,202
Teachers and professors	364,073	19,451	2,193	Property owners	107,279	11,784	1,137
Armed Forces employees	84,615	16,397	1,649	Business proprietors	485,205	10,755	892
Federal government employees	374,929	16,186	1,665	Farmers	268,791	10,741	592
Provincial government employees	518,822	15,414	1,581	Self-employed entertainers and artists	14,882	7,987	583
Other self-employed professionals	34,346	14,584	1,694	Unclassified employees	279,760	7,258	427
				Pensioners	1,090,573	5,590	150
				Unclassified	1,883,011	1,911	56
				Total	14,320,313	10,964	992

(1) Based on number of tax returns (2) Average total income after business expense deductions but before personal deductions.

Average Income in Selected Canadian Cities, 1978

Source: Revenue Canada Taxation Statistics

City	Average income[1]	Rank	No. of tax returns	City	Average income[1]	Rank	No. of tax returns
Oakville, Ont.	$14,287	1	43,896	Brampton, Ont.	11,861	20	48,892
Burlington, Ont.	13,506	2	67,136	Repentigny, Que.	11,831	21	19,432
Calgary, Alta.	13,072	3	334,005	New Westminster, B.C.	11,805	22	26,931
Port Alberni, B.C.	12,887	4	15,876	Lethbridge, Alta.	11,700	23	32,351
Mississauga, Ont.	12,858	5	163,917	Langley, B.C.	11,682	24	31,563
Edmonton, Alta.	12,771	6	378,402	Ottawa, Ont.	11,644	25	325,190
Vancouver, B.C.	12,633	7	694,641	Windsor, Ont.	11,641	27	164,498
Prince George, B.C.	12,487	8	43,259	Toronto, Ont.	11,618	28	1,581,044
Pickering, Ont.	12,470	9	20,496	Montreal, Que.	11,394	33	1,206,670
Brossard, Que.	12,468	10	25,297	Quebec, Que.	11,310	35	244,861
Dundas, Ont.	12,341	11	15,658	Halifax, N.S.	11,134	38	88,575
Sarnia, Ont.	12,289	12	50,925	London, Ont.	11,053	39	176,056
Red Deer, Alta.	12,288	13	25,313	Kitchener, Ont.	10,988	41	127,868
Bramalea, Ont.	12,096	14	29,454	Fredericton, N.B.	10,461	58	34,959
Nanaimo, B.C.	12,051	15	25,898	Hamilton, Ont.	10,399	59	229,259
Kamloops, B.C.	11,962	16	36,856	Winnipeg, Man.	10,153	65	395,498
Regina, Sask.	11,958	17	98,048	St. John's, Nfld.	10,062	71	67,167
Victoria, B.C.	11,946	18	153,086	Charlottetown, P.E.I.	9,754	85	16,523
Whitby, Ont.	11,940	19	20,283	Sydney, N.S.	8,043	100	64,242

(1) Average total income after business deductions but before personal deductions.

Employment and Training Services and Unemployment Insurance

Source: Employment and Training Administration, U.S. Labor Department

Employment Service

The Federal-State Employment Service consists of the U.S. Employment Service and affiliated state employment services with their network of about 3,500 local offices. During fiscal year 1980, these offices made 6.1 million placements, 5.7 million in nonagricultural and 381,000 in agricultural industries. Overall, 4.1 million different individuals were placed in employment.

The employment service works to refer employable applicants to job openings that use their highest skills and helps the unemployed obtain services or training to make them employable. It also provides special attention to help older workers, youth, minorities, the poor, handicapped workers, migrants, seasonal farmworkers, and workers who lose their jobs because of foreign trade competition.

Veterans receive priority services including referral to jobs and training at all employment service offices. During fiscal year 1980, these offices placed over 586,000 veterans in jobs.

Comprehensive Employment and Training Services

The Comprehensive Employment and Training Act (CETA) of 1973 sets up a community system to give people training and job-related services and place them in jobs. Under this system all states and cities, counties, and combinations of local units with populations of 100,000 or more receive federal grants to plan and run comprehensive employment and training programs in their localities. Under the Private Sector Initiative Program, every program sponsor sets up a Private Industry Council to help involve businesses in hiring and training economically disadvantaged workers. A major inducement for employers to hire certain disadvantaged workers is the Targeted Jobs Tax Credit, amounting to $3,000 for each eligible worker paid $6,000 or more for the first year of employment.

National Activities

The federal role under CETA is to provide support and technical assistance to local programs, insure proper use of federal money, and serve groups with special job disadvantages.

In addition to continuing programs for Indians and migrant and seasonal farmworkers, there are continuing efforts for youth. These efforts include the Young Adult Conservation Corps, which hires unemployed young people to work on public lands; Youth Incentive Entitlement Pilot Projects, providing part-time jobs and training to youth attending school; Youth Community Conservation and Improvement Projects, which give unemployed youth paid work in community betterment; and Youth Employment and Training Programs to improve young people's job prospects. In addition, Job Corps, which was training disadvantaged youth at 97 residential centers at the end of fiscal year 1980, plans continued expansion so that it can serve 44,000 youth at any one time. The Summer Youth Employment Programs supported over 900,000 part-time jobs in 1980. The Employment and Training Administration also has programs to promote apprenticeship and to help employable people on Aid to Families with Dependent Children find jobs.

Unemployment Insurance

Unlike old-age and survivors insurance, entirely a federal program, the unemployment insurance program is a Federal-State system that provides insured wage earners with partial replacement of wages lost during involuntary unemployment. The program protects most workers in industry. During calendar year 1978, an estimated 86.2 million jobs in commerce, industry, agriculture, and government, including the armed forces, were covered under the Federal-State system. In addition, an estimated 531,000 railroad workers were insured against unemployment by the Railroad Retirement Board.

Each state, as well as the District of Columbia, Puerto Rico, and the Virgin Islands, has its own law and operates its own program. The amount and duration of the weekly benefits are determined by state laws, based on prior wages and length of employment. States are required to extend the duration of benefits when unemployment rises to and remains above specified state or national levels; costs of extended benefits are shared by the state and federal governments.

Under the Federal Unemployment Tax Act, as amended in 1976, the tax rate is 3.4% on the first $6,000 paid to each employee of employers with one or more employees in 20 weeks of the year or a quarterly payroll of $1,500. A credit of up to 2.7% is allowed for taxes paid under state unemployment insurance laws that meet certain criteria, leaving the federal share at 0.7% of taxable wages.

Social Security Requirement

The Social Security Act requires, as a condition of such grants, prompt payment of due benefits. The Federal Unemployment Tax Act provides safeguards for workers' right to benefits if they refuse jobs that fail to meet certain labor standards. Through the Unemployment Insurance Service of the Employment and Training Administration, the Secretary of Labor determines whether states qualify for grants and for tax offset credit for employers.

Benefits are financed solely by employer contributions, except in Alaska, Alabama, and New Jersey, where employees also contribute. Benefits are paid through the public employment offices, at which unemployed workers must register for work and to which they must report regularly for referral to a possible job during the time when they are drawing weekly benefit payments. During the 1980 calendar year, $13.8 billion in benefits was paid under state unemployment insurance programs to 9,991,500 beneficiaries, representing compensation for 174,216,900 weeks of unemployment. They received an average weekly payment of $98.92 for total unemployment for an average of 14.9 weeks.

Federal Worker Benefits

Title 5, chapter 85 of the U.S. Code provided unemployment insurance protection during calendar year 1980 to about 3,015,500 federal civilian employees and about 2,102,300 members of the armed forces. Benefits for unemployed federal workers and ex-servicemen are financed through direct federal appropriations but are paid by the state agencies as agents of the federal government.

During calendar year 1980, a total of $129,578,000 was paid to 81,500 unemployed federal civilian workers for a total of 1,545,800 weeks of unemployment. The average weekly payment was $94.33 and was paid for an average of 16.8 weeks. A total of $294,923,100 was paid to 187,700 unemployed ex-servicemen for 2,899,100 weeks of unemployment. The average weekly benefit was $100.00 and was paid for an average of 15.7 weeks.

Employment Security

Selected unemployment insurance data by state. Calendar year 1980, state programs only.

	Insured claimants[1] (1,000)	Bene- fici- aries[2] (1,000)	Exhaus- tions[3] (1,000)	Initial claims[4] (1,000)	Benefits paid[5] (1,000)	Avg. weekly benefit for total unemployment[p]	Funds avail- able for benefits Dec. 31, 1980[6] (millions)	Employers subject to state law Dec. 31, 1980 (1,000)
Alabama	240	210	54	507	$176,024	$76.76	$83	67
Alaska	35	32	9	62	44,134	85.13	90	11
Arizona	99	72	17	184	71,151	83.44	269	53
Arkansas	157	118	31	316	113,321	88.95	3	44
California	1,479	1,068	337	2,892	1,357,892	86.41	3,038	584
Colorado	103	77	22	181	86,363	110.99	125	72
Connecticut	169	137	20	312	163,744	102.73	109	81
Delaware	37	31	6	79	42,442	108.47	7	14
District of Columbia	37	26	11	40	55,146	122.22	23	17
Florida	235	185	66	393	153,013	74.49	797	210
Georgia	316	248	70	614	176,268	78.68	471	100
Hawaii	45	33	7	75	40,991	106.11	102	22
Idaho	54	50	15	127	54,101	97.46	87	23
Illinois	650	555	232	1,116	1,205,902	114.60	77	249
Indiana	383	297	111	748	319,084	84.96	244	93
Iowa	161	142	32	265	188,528	117.02	114	66
Kansas	98	88	22	166	113,832	105.84	224	54
Kentucky	239	185	63	467	255,589	101.33	42	62
Louisiana	177	135	42	284	207,890	108.52	221	77
Maine	77	72	19	191	56,774	85.55	34	30
Maryland	172	149	38	338	178,487	91.72	385	78
Massachusetts	314	246	62	580	315,789	97.38	238	117
Michigan	649	650	308	1,996	1,141,476	101.87	276	160
Minnesota	185	159	54	316	284,145	117.72	12	86
Mississippi	118	100	22	250	85,066	69.26	237	43
Missouri	312	244	83	704	278,426	88.41	125	112
Montana	42	36	12	80	41,194	98.11	18	23
Nebraska	63	44	13	83	43,823	93.78	79	37
Nevada	52	45	10	103	53,230	100.09	130	20
New Hampshire	54	45	3	81	30,199	84.82	82	23
New Jersey	485	424	157	861	675,735	100.69	134	165
New Mexico	41	30	9	80	33,465	82.74	91	29
New York	794	611	213	1,756	1,007,601	93.07	514	393
North Carolina	432	304	48	973	230,529	87.09	600	103
North Dakota	27	24	8	47	32,424	105.94	16	20
Ohio	655	556	182	1,461	1,075,705	124.95	57	196
Oklahoma	84	59	18	150	63,171	99.75	193	63
Oregon	181	163	35	431	202,748	98.86	345	67
Pennsylvania	783	678	156	1,890	1,164,447	115.56	151	207
Puerto Rico	144	69	42	294	83,677	53.29	67	46
Rhode Island	85	68	25	178	76,174	89.04	27	24
South Carolina	199	171	31	502	124,314	82.19	198	53
South Dakota	17	16	3	34	16,584	96.87	11	18
Tennessee	287	228	65	661	233,519	78.04	200	79
Texas	370	256	90	553	251,261	86.22	277	263
Utah	60	48	13	94	61,728	105.70	61	30
Vermont	32	27	5	58	28,077	90.13	18	14
Virginia	227	145	39	404	154,388	95.54	67	92
Virgin Islands	3	4	1	6	3,194	69.44	3	2
Washington	248	205	44	530	299,588	110.43	357	96
West Virginia	124	120	26	189	158,148	105.92	1	36
Wisconsin	386	293	69	655	451,009	117.47	257	93
Wyoming	29	12	2	24	16,014	107.51	73	15
TOTAL	**12,448**	**9,992**	**3,072**	**25,411**	**$13,777,521**	**$98.85**	**$11,464**	**4,730**

(p.) Preliminary. (1) Claimants whose base-period earnings or whose employment — covered by the unemployment insurance program — was sufficient to make them eligible for unemployment insurance benefits as provided by state law. (2) Based on number of first payments. (3) Based on final payments. Some claimants shown, therefore, actually experienced their final week of compensable unemployment toward the end of the previous calendar year but received their final payments in the current calendar year. Similarly, some claimants who served their last week of compensable unemployment toward the end of the current calendar year did not receive their final payment in this calendar year and hence are not shown. A final week of compensable unemployment in a benefit year results in the exhaustion of benefit rights for the benefit year. Claimants who exhaust their benefit rights in one benefit year may be entitled to further benefits in the following benefit year. (4) Excludes intrastate transitional claims to reflect more nearly instances of new unemployment. Includes claims filed by interstate claimants in the Virgin Islands. (5) Adjusted for voided benefit checks and transfers under interstate combined wage plan. (6) Sum of balance in state clearing accounts, benefit payment accounts, and unemployment trust fund accounts in the U.S. Treasury.

Jobs: Job Openings to 1990 and Current Earnings

Source: Bureau of Labor Statistics, U.S. Labor Department. For more detailed information on job categories, see the Occupational Outlook Handbook, 1980-81 Edition.

Occupation	Est. No. of Jobs, 1978	% Change 1978-90 (est.)	Average Earnings[1] (dollars)
Industrial			
Assemblers	1,164,000	43.0	3-8/hr.
Blue-collar worker supv.	1,671,000	16.0	18,000/yr.
Compositors	181,000	-12.8	9/hr.
Machine tool oper.	542,000	12.4	8/hr.
Power truck oper.	363,000	24.0	6.50/hr.
Printing press oper.	167,000	8.9	8.70-9.32/hr.
Tool-and-die makers	170,000	23.5	8.53/hr.
Welders	679,000	33.6	6-7/hr.
Office			
Accountants	985,000	29.4	15,700-27,300/yr.
Bank officers, mgrs.	330,000	54.5	900-1,600/mo.[2]
Bank tellers	410,000	11.0	135-180/wk.
Bookkeepers	1,830,000	11.8	916/wk.
Cashiers	1,400,000	49.7	3.72-7.64/wk.
Computer operating pers.	660,000	62.2	160-300/wk.
Computer programmers	247,000	102.4	360-465/wk.
Computer systems analysts	182,000	119.8	370-460/wk.
Insurance claim reps.	169,000	40.5	11,215-14,760/yr.
Lawyers	487,000	25.0	50,000/yr.
Office machine oper.	160,000	26.2	167/wk.
Personnel & labor relations	405,000	16.8	22,600/yr.
Postal clerks	260,000	-19.0	17,058 /yr.
Purchasing agents	185,000	44.3	16,200/yr.
Receptionists	588,000	27.9	155/wk.
Secretaries, stenographers	3,684,000	45.4	817-1,085/mo.
Shipping, receiving clerks	462,000	23.0	232/wk.
Typists	1,044,000	19.4	193/wk.
Service Occupations			
Barbers	121,000	15.7	230-290/wk.
Bartenders	282,000	30.9	3.34-6.53/hr.
Building custodians	2,251,000	20.1	4.21/hr.
Correction officers	110,000	38.9	14,900/yr.[3]
Cooks and chefs	1,186,000	31.9	(4)
Firefighters	220,000	21.0	12,700-15,800[5]
Guards	550,000	50.0	3.63/hr.
Meatcutters	204,000	-8.3	8.32/hr.
Police officers	450,000	22.7	9-18,000/yr.[5]
Private household workers	1,162,000	-23.2	(6)
Waiters and waitresses	1,383,000	18.2	1.31-3.45/hr.[7]
Educational and related occupations			
K-6 teachers	1,322,000	24.9	14,669/yr.
Second. school teach.	1,087,000	-20.8	15,474/yr.
Coll., univ. faculty	673,000	-9.2	18,700/yr.[8]
Sales occupations			
Auto. sales workers	158,000	26.5	335/wk.
Gas station workers	340,000	-5.6	2.50-5.00/hr.
Retail trade sales workers	2,851,000	32.8	3.13-7.12/hr.
Construction occupations			
Carpenters	1,253,000	10.9	10.05/hr.
Constr. laborers	860,000	12.8	8.45/hr.
Electricians (constrs.)	290,000	20.7	11.25/hr.
Painters	484,000	13.6	9.38/hr.
Plumbers, pipefitters	428,000	19.9	10.10/hr.
Roofers	114,000	22.8	9.60/hr.

Occupation	Est. No. of Jobs, 1978	% Change 1978-90 (est.)	Average Earnings[1] (dollars)
Transportation occupations			
Airplane mechanics	132,000	10.1	26,600/yr.
Airplane pilots	76,000	43.9	57,000/yr.
Airline reser. agts.	56,000	15.0	3.17/wk.
Conductors (RR)	37,000	6.2	1,064-1,637/mo.
Flight attendants	48,000	56.2	1,200/mo.
Busdrivers (local)	77,000	18.9	7.35/hr.
Taxicab drivers	94,000	0.0	3.90/hr.
Truckdrivers (local)	1,720,000	18.4	9.10/hr.
Truckdrivers (long-dist.)	584,000	18.0	29,000/yr.
Scientific and technical occupations			
Aerospace engineers	60,000	20.7	NA
Chemical engineers	53,000	20.0	NA
Chemists	143,000	24.0	23,900-29,200/yr.
Civil engineers	155,000	22.8	NA
Drafters	296,000	24.0	9,800-16,900/yr.
Electrical engineers	300,000	21.5	NA
Industrial enginners	185,000	26.0	NA
Mathematicians	33,500	9.9	14,800-22,500[2]
Mechanical engineers	195,000	19.1	NA
Mechanics and repairers			
Appliance repairers	145,000	24.1	5-10/hr.
Automobile mechanics	860,000	22.7	9.32/hr.
Bus. machine operators	63,000	56.0	200-300/wk.
Computer serv. technicians	63,000	92.5	240-400/wk.
Indust. machinery repairers	655,000	66.0	7.74/hr.
Shoe repairers	22,000	-4.5	3-5/hr.
Telephone, PBX installers and repairers	115,000	17.5	8.58-8.90/hr.
TV, radio serv. technicians	131,000	26.7	4.00-8.75/hr.
Health and medical occupations			
Dentists	120,000	29.2	50,000/yr.
Dental assistants	150,000	50.0	7,800-8,400/yr.
Dental hygienists	35,000	85.7	12-13,000
Dietitians	35,000	42.9	15,800[9]
Health serv. administrators	180,000	57.1	36,000/yr.[10]
Medical laboratory workers	210,000	26.2	15,700/yr.[11]
Nurses, registered	1,060,000	49.6	275/wk.
Nurses, licensed practical	518,000	62.2	9,000/yr.[2]
Nursing aides, orderlies, attendants	1,037,000	52.0	160/wk.[2]
Operating room technicians	35,000	49.9	10,700/yr.
Pharmacists	135,000	37.0	21,000/yr.[11]
Physical therapists	30,000	50.0	16,000/yr.
Physicians, osteopaths	405,000	38.1	(12)
Radiologic technologists	100,000	40.0	13,300/yr.
Veterinarians	33,500	35.6	33,000/yr.
Social scientists			
Economists	130,000	39.2	33,000/yr.[13]
Political scientists	14,000	13.8	13-26,000
Psychologists	130,000	32.1	22,300-33,800/yr.[9]
Sociologists	19,000	8.1	23,800/yr.
Social service occupations			
School counselors	45,000	11.1	17,700/yr.
Homemaker-home hlth. aides	110,000	70.0	2.65-4.15/hr.[2]
Social workers	385,000	24.2	10,300-13,300/yr.[2]
Design occupations			
Architects	54,000	42.6	25,000+/yr.
Interior designers	79,000	20.9	12-50,000/yr.
Communications occupations			
Newspaper reporters	45,000	19.6	370/wk.
Public relations workers	131,000	24.4	22,700-36,000/yr.

(1) Figures are 1978 estimates based on average salary of experienced worker in non-government job. For federal civilian job earnings see p. 115. Ranges of earnings reflect regional and job level differences. (2) Starting salaries. (3) Federal correction officers. (4) Chefs, $3.68-7.15/hr.; cooks, $2.90-6.36/hr. (5) Starting to maximum range. (6) By law, must earn minimum wage, currently 3.35/hr. (7) Excluding tips. (8) Full-time faculty member on 9-mo. contract. (9) Median salary. (10) Administrator of 100-150 bed-hospital. (11) Working in hospitals. (12) Median annual salary of private office-based MD's was $65,400 in 1977; osteopathic physicians earned average starting salaries at VA hospitals of $32,500 in 1979. (13) Median salary in private business; $13,300-29,500 in universities.

Quality of Life in U.S. Metropolitan Areas: A Comparative Table

Source: For personal per capita income, *Survey of Current Business,* April 1981; for unemployment rate, Bureau of Labor Statistics; for projected growth in employment and in personal income, Chase Econometrics Regional Forecasting Service; for average purchase price of a home, Federal Home Loan Bank Board; for crime rate, *Uniform Crime Reports 1980,* Federal Bureau of Investigation; for weather data, *Comparative Climatic Data for the United States Through 1980,* National Oceanic and Atmospheric Administration. Data given is for Standard Metropolitan Statistical Area (SMSAs) whenever possible; in all other cases, data given is for segment of SMSA for which data is available.

	Per capita personal income 1979	% Jobless June 1981	Projected annual % growth in jobs 1979-1990	Projected annual % growth in income 1979-1990	Average price of a home August 1981 $000	Crime rate per 100,000 1980[7]	Mean no. of days[8] clr.— pt. cldy.— cldy.	Mean no. of days below 32°F	Normal daily max. temp. August °F
Anaheim-Santa Ana Garden Gr., Cal.	10,547	4.5	3.4	3.2	118.8	6,847.0	NA	NA	NA
Atlanta, Ga.	9,294	5.4	2.1	2.8	111.3	7,575.2	107—110—148	60	86.4
Baltimore, Md.	8,967	8.1	1.0	2.0	113.9	7,473.0	109—108—148	99	85.1
Birmingham, Ala.	8,429	9.8	2.1	2.8	NA	7,079.0	99—111—155	61	89.7
Boston-Lowell-Brock-ton-Lawrence-Haverhill, Mass.-N.H.	9,351	5.8[1]	1.1	2.1	77.2	6,493.3	100—105—160	99	79.3
Bridgeport-Stam-ford-Norwalk-Danbury, Ct.	12,266	5.9[2]	1.3	1.6	NA	6,183.0	100—107—158	100	80.4
Buffalo, N.Y.	8,401	9.5	0.2	1.3	NA	5,305.8	55—102—208	135	77.6
Chicago, Ill.	10,455	8.0	0.6	1.4	78.4	5,721.8	86—107—172	132	82.3
Cincinnati, Oh., Ky., Ind.	8,995	7.8	1.4	1.9	62.6	5,774.2	NA	110	85.8
Cleveland, Oh.	10,167	7.6	0.3	1.2	82.9	5,634.4	69— 98—198	125	80.4
Columbus, Oh.	8,639	7.1	1.3	2.0	62.6	7,541.4	74—106—185	121	83.7
Dallas-Ft. Worth, Tex.	9,931	6.6	3.2	3.6	114.9	8,270.7	141— 93—131	41	96.1
Dayton, Oh.	8,740	7.5	0.8	1.6	NA	7,430.2	80—102—183	118	83.4
Denver-Boulder, Col.	10,133	5.6	3.0	3.6	71.8	8,356.9	118—128—119	159	85.8
Detroit, Mich.	10,433	11.4	0.4	1.8	80.3	7,582.3	77—105—183	124-139	81.6-82.0
Ft. Lauderdale-Hollywood, Fla.	10,002	5.0	NA	4.3	93.9	9,345.4	NA	NA	NA
Hartford-New Bri-tain-Bristol, Ct.	9,862	5.5[3]	1.4	2.0	NA	6,606.9	80—110—175	137	81.9
Honolulu, Ha.	9,573	5.8	2.0	2.6	104.9	7,574.3	88—176—101	0	87.4
Houston, Tex.	10,638	6.2	4.1	4.5	97.4	6,900.1	97—110—158	26	94.3
Indianapolis, Ind.	9,361	7.8	0.9	1.7	62.7	6,009.2	91— 99—175	121	84.0
Kansas City, Mo.-Kan.	9,632	6.1	1.3	2.2	75.2	7,720.3	119—102—144	104	88.7
Los Angeles-Long Beach, Cal.	10,606	6.6	1.5	2.2	118.8	8,418.7	165—114— 91	0-1	75.8-84.0
Louisville, Ky.-Ind.	8,810	7.6	1.1	2.2	61.0	5,570.3	94—103—168	92	86.8
Memphis, Tenn.-Ark.-Miss.	8,041	8.2	1.4	2.3	NA	6,492.3	120— 96—149	59	90.6
Miami, Fla.	9,714	6.0	2.6	3.1	93.9	11,581.8	73—173—119	0	89.9
Milwaukee, Wis.	9,715	7.3	1.5	2.2	85.2	5,364.2	94—100—171	145	79.7
Minneapolis-St. Paul, Minn.-Wis.	10,025	4.7	2.0	2.6	92.7[6]	6,137.1	99—102—164	157	80.8
Nashville-Davidson, Tenn.	8,510	6.7	2.8	3.3	NA	5,761.7	102—108—155	77	89.2
Newark, N.J.	10,500	7.4	0.6	0.9	92.5	6,990.4	95—112—158	87	83.7
New Orleans, La.	8,605	7.6	2.1	3.0	NA	7,890.2	108—119—138	13	90.6
New York, N.Y.-N.J.	9,839	8.1	0.1	1.3	92.5	8,592.8	100—122—143	80	82.5
Philadelphia, Pa.-N.J.	8,958	8.5	0.5	1.2	72.0	5,357.8	93—110—162	100	84.8
Phoenix, Ariz.	9,322	5.1	3.7	4.2	97.9	9,308.4	213— 82— 70	11	102.2
Pittsburgh, Pa.	9,218	7.9	0.8	1.6	58.2	3,485.3	58—103—204	124	80.9
Portland, Ore.-Wash.	10,067	7.8	2.8	3.2	97.4	7,324.9	69— 69—227	44	78.1
Providence-War-wick-Pawtucket, R.I.	8,551	7.2	0.7	1.5	NA	5,859.4	103—103—159	123	79.8
Riverside-San Bernadino- Ontario, Cal.	8,403	7.8	2.6	3.1	NA	8,231.9	NA	NA	NA
Rochester, N.Y.	9,218	6.4	1.1	2.0	73.0	6,111.2	61—108—196	135	80.1
Sacramento, Cal.	9,188	7.8	1.9	2.8	NA	9,373.1	190— 75—100	17	91.3
St. Louis, Mo.-Ill.	9,171	8.7	0.4	1.7	57.3	6,488.0	104—101—160	106	87.2
Salt Lake City-Ogden, Ut.	7,924	6.1	3.33.9		91.2[5]	7,247.1	127—104—134	130	90.2
San Antonio, Tex.	7,518	9.2	2.8	3.5	NA	6,411.1	107—120—138	23	95.9
San Diego, Cal.	8,908	6.5	3.4	3.7	130.5	7,038.4	148—118— 99	0	77.3
San Francisco-Oakland, Cal.	11,741	5.5	1.0	2.0	113.3	8,540.6	161—102—102	1.5	68.2
San Jose, Cal.	11,064	5.9	3.2	3.4	113.3	7,612.2	NA	NA	NA
Seattle-Everett, Wash.	10,788	8.3	2.4	3.1	92.9	7,862.0	65— 86—215	24	74
Tampa-St. Petersburg, Fla.	8,173	5.7	3.2	3.7	73.9	8,071.1	95—143—127	4	90.4
Washington D.C.-Md.-Va.	11,313	5.4	1.5	2.3	101.2	6,938.8	101—103—162	95	86

(1) Boston only; Lowell, 7.1; Brockton, 8.5; Lawrence-Haverhill, 6.2. (2) Bridgeport only; Stamford, 3.8. (3) Hartford only. (4) Worcester only. (5) June 1981. (6) July 1981. (7) Includes all crime. (8) Categories are determined for daylight hours only; clear denotes zero to 0.3 sky cover; partly cloudy denotes 0.4 to 0.7 average sky cover; cloudy denotes 0.8 to complete sky cover. Figures may not add to 365 days in all cases; discrepancy is due to averaging based on several reporting sites in the area.

Heating Your Home: Which Fuel is Most Economical?

Source: John W. Bartok, Jr., Assoc. Res. Professor in Agricultural Engineering, University of Connecticut, Storrs.

Average Annual Home Heating Costs with Alternate Fuels*

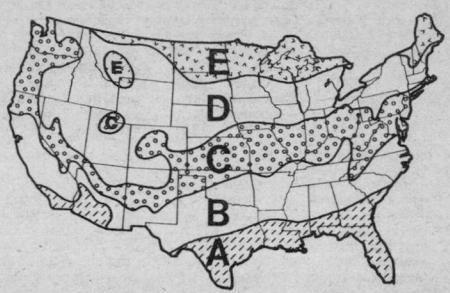

Fuel	A	B	C	D	E
Oil	$250	$625	$875	$1,050	$1,250
Gas	175	440	500	685	910
Electricity	400	990	1,390	1,680	1,975
Coal	175	315	445	540	640
Wood	150	345	520	620	730

*Based on a 1,000-square foot home with average insulation and weatherization, 1981 fuel prices. Local climate and fuel price difference will cause heating costs to vary.

Tips on Cutting Energy Costs in Your Home

Source: Con Edison Conservation Services

Heating

In many homes, in areas where temperatures drop during the winter, more energy is used for heating than anything else. Conservation measures pay off in a home which is losing heat excessively. Installing the right amount of insulation, storm windows and doors, caulking and weatherstripping are important. Also consider the following advice:

- Make sure the thermostat and heating system are in good working order. An annual checkup is recommended.
- Set the thermostat no higher than 68 degrees. When no one is home, or when everyone is sleeping, the setting should be turned down to 60 degrees or lower. An automatic setback thermostat can raise and lower your home's temperature at times you specify.
- Close off and do not heat unused areas.
- If you do not have conventional storm windows or doors use kits to make plastic storm windows.
- Keep the outside doors closed as much as possible.
- Special glass fireplace doors help keep a room's heat from being drawn up the chimney when the fire is burning low. In any case, close the damper when a fireplace is not in use.
- Use the sun's heat by opening blinds and draperies closed at night or on cold cloudy days to reduce heat loss.
- Keep radiators and warm air outlets clean. Do not block them with furniture or draperies.

Water Heater

In many homes, the water heater ranks second only to the heating system in total energy consumption. It pays to keep the water heater operating efficiently, and not to waste hot water.

- Put an insulation blanket on your water heater when you go on vacation, or turn it to a minimum setting if there is danger of freezing pipes.
- If you have a dishwasher, set the water heater thermostat no higher than 140 degrees. If not, or if you have a separate water heater for baths, a setting as low as 110 degrees may be sufficient.
- Run the dishwasher and clothes washer only when you have a full load. Use warm or cold water cycles for laundry when you can.
- Take showers instead of tub baths. About half as much hot water is used for a shower.

- Install a water-saver shower head.
- Do not leave the hot water running when rinsing dishes or shaving. Plug and partially fill the basin, or fill a pan with water.
- Use the right size water heater for your needs. An oversized unit wastes energy heating unneeded water. An undersized unit will not deliver all the hot water you want when you need it.
- When shopping for a water heater, look for the yellow-and-black federal EnergyGuide label to learn the estimated yearly energy cost of a unit.

Air Conditioning

- Clean or replace the filter in an air conditioner at the beginning of the cooling season. Then check it once a month and clean or change the filter if necessary. A dirty filter blocks the flow of air and keeps the air conditioner from doing its best job of cooling.
- Adjust the temperature control setting to provide a room temperature no lower than 78 degrees. Since most air conditioner thermostats are not marked in degrees but by words such as "cold" and "colder," use a good wall thermometer to tell which setting will provide the desired temperature.
- Close windows and doors when the air conditioner is running.
- When the outside temperature is 78 degrees or cooler, turn off the air conditioner and open windows to cool your home.
- Always keep your air conditioner turned off when you are away from home or not using the areas that it cools. An air conditioner timer can be set to turn it off when family members go to work, and to turn it on just before the first one arrives home. These timers are available at hardware stores.
- Close draperies and shades to block out the sun's heat.
- When shopping for a new room air conditioner, look for the yellow-and-black federal EnergyGuide label to learn the Energy Efficiency Rating (EER) and the estimated yearly operating cost. The higher the EER, the less electricity will be used for a cooling job.
- Read the manufacturer's instructions and follow them closely.
- If you have a central air conditioning system, run your hands along the ducts while it is operating to check for

air leaks. Repair leaks with duct tape. Make sure the duct system is properly insulated.

Refrigerators and Freezers

The refrigerator operates 24 hours a day, every day, so it is important to make sure your refrigerator is working efficiently. It is one of the biggest users of energy in the home all year round.

- Keep the condenser coils clean. The coils are on the back or at the bottom of the refrigerator. Carefully wipe, vacuum or brush the coils to remove dust and dirt at least once a year.
- Examine door gaskets and hinges regularly for air leaks. The doors should fit tightly. To check, place a piece of paper between the door and the cabinet. Close the door with normal force, then try to pull the paper straight out. There will be a slight resistance. Test all around the door, including the hinge side. If there are any places where the paper slides out easily, you need to adjust the hinges or replace the gasket, or both.
- Pause before opening your refrigerator door. Think of everything you will need before you open the door so you do not have to go back several times. When you open the door, close it quickly to keep the cool air in.
- Adjust the temperature-setting dial of the refrigerator as the manufacturer recommends. Use a thermometer to check the temperature (38 to 40 degrees is usually recommended for the refrigerator; zero degrees for the freezer). Settings that are too cold waste electricity and can ruin foods.
- If you have a manual-defrost refrigerator, do not allow the ice to build up more than $1/4$ inch thick.
- For greatest efficiency, keep your refrigerator well-stocked but allow room for air to circulate around the food.
- The freezer, on the other hand, should be packed full. If necessary, fill empty spaces with bags of ice cubes or fill milk cartons with water and freeze.
- When you are going to be away from home for a week or more, turn off and unplug the refrigerator, empty and clean it, and prop the door open.
- If you are buying a new refrigerator, look for one with a humid-dry ("power-saver") switch. This switch is used to turn off "anti-sweat" heaters in the doors to save electricity when the heaters are not needed.
- When shopping for a new refrigerator or freezer, look for the federal EnergyGuide label to help you select an efficient unit.

Cooking

There are many ways to save electricity or gas by careful use of the range or oven.

- Cook as many dishes in the oven at one time as you can instead of cooking each separately. If recipes call for slightly different temperatures, ay 325, 350, and 375 degrees, pick the middle temperature of 350 to cook all 3 dishes and remove each dish as it's done.
- Don't preheat the oven unnecessarily. Usually, any food that takes more than an hour of cooking can be started in a cold oven.
- Turn off your oven or range just before the cooking is finished. The heat that is left will usually finish the cooking.
- Whenever you peek into an oven by opening a door, the temperature drops about 25 degrees. So open the oven door as little as possible.
- Use the lowest possible heat setting to cook foods on top of the range.
- Match the pot to the size of the surface unit. Putting a small pot on a large surface unit wastes energy without cooking the food any faster.
- On gas ranges, the flame should burn in a firm, blue cone. If the flame is not blue, the range is probably not working efficiently. Get a service representative to check it.

Lighting

The first rule is to turn off lights no one is using. There also are ways to improve your home's lighting level and save energy at the same time.

- Get all family members in the habit of turning off lights when they leave a room, even if they will be gone only for a short time.
- During the day, try to get along with as few lights as possible. Let the daylight do the work. White or light-colored walls make a room seem brighter.
- Use bulbs of lower wattage where you don't need strong light.
- When you need strong light, use one large bulb instead of several smaller ones. One 100-watt incandescent bulb produces more light than 2 60-watt bulbs, with 20 percent less energy consumption. But never use bulbs of a higher wattage than a fixture was designed to take.
- Use 3-way bulbs where possible, so you can choose the amount of light you need.
- Modern solid-state dimmer controls let you save energy by reducing your lighting level and wattage. Many are easy to install.
- Consider changing to fluorescent lighting, especially in kitchens, bathrooms, and work areas. Fluorescent tubes give more light at lower energy cost than incandescent bulbs with the same wattage. Plug-in fluorescent fixtures are available at hardware stores, or an electrician can install permanent fixtures.

Measuring Energy

Source: Energy Information Administration, U.S. Energy Dept.

The following tables of equivalents contain those figures commonly used to compare different types of energy sources and their various measurements.

Btu — a British thermal unit — the amount of heat required to raise one pound of water one degree Fahrenheit. Equivalent to 1,055 joules or about 252 gram calories. A therm is usually 100,000 Btu but is sometimes used to refer to other units.

Calorie — The amount of heat required to raise one gram of water one degree Centigrade; abbreviated cal.; equivalent to about .003968 Btu. More common is the kilogram calorie, also called a kilocalorie and abbreviated Cal. or Kcal; equivalent to about 3.97 Btu. (One Kcal is equivalent to one food calorie.)

Btu Values of Energy Sources
(These are conventional or average values, not precise equivalents.)

Coal (per 2,000 lb. ton of U.S. production):
Anthracite = 22.9×10^6 Btu
Bituminous coal and lignite = 22.6×10^6

Average heating value of coal used to generate electricity in 1979 was 21.4 x 10^6 Btu per metric ton.

Natural Gas:

Dry (per cubic foot)	=	1,021 Btu
Liquefied Natural Gas (Methane) (per barrel)	=	3.0×10^6

Electricity — 1 kwh   = 3,412 Btu

Petroleum (per barrel):

Crude oil	=	5.80×10^6 Btu
Residual fuel oil	=	6.29×10^6
Distillate fuel oil	=	5.83×10^6
Gasoline (including aviation gas)	=	5.25×10^6
Jet fuel (kerosene)	=	5.67×10^6
Jet fuel (naphtha)	=	5.36×10^6
Kerosene	=	5.67×10^6

Nuclear — (per kilowatt hour)   = 10,769

The Btu and calorie, being small amounts of energy, are usually expressed as follows when large numbers are involved.

1×10^3 Btu	= 1,000
1×10^6	= 1,000,000
1×10^9	= 1,000,000,000
1×10^{12}	= 1 trillion
1×10^{15}	= 1 quadrillion
1×10^{18}	= 1 quintillion or 1 Q unit
One Q unit	= 44.3 billion short tons of coal
	= 172.4 billion tons of oil
	= 980 trillion cubic feet of natural gas

Other Conversion Factors

Electricity — 1 kwh

=	0.3 pounds of coal
=	0.25 gallon of crude oil
=	3.3 cubic feet of natural gas

Natural gas — 1 tcf (trillion cubic feet)

	=	45×10^6 short tons of bituminous and lignite coal produced
	=	176×10^6 barrels of crude oil

Coal — 1 mstce (million short tons of coal equivalent)

	=	3.9×10^6 barrels of crude oil
	=	1.7×10^6 short tons of crude oil
	=	22.1×10^9 cubic feet of natural gas

Oil — 1 million short tons (6.65×10^6 barrels)

	=	4×10^9 kwh of electricity (when used to generate power)
	=	12×10^9 kwh uncoverted
	=	1.7×10^6 short tons of coal
	=	37×10^9 cubic feet of natural gas

Approximate Conversion Factors for Oils

To convert	Barrels to metric tons	Metric tons to barrels	Barrels/ day to tons/ year	Tons/year to barrels/ day
		Multiply by:		
Crude oil[1]	.136	7.33	49.8	.0201
Gasoline	.118	8.45	43.2	.0232
Kerosene	.128	7.80	46.8	.0214
Diesel fuel	.133	7.50	48.7	.0205
Fuel oil	.149	6.70	54.5	.0184

(1) Based on world average gravity (excluding natural gas liquids).

Fuel Economy in 1982 Autos; Comparative Miles per Gallon

Source: U.S. Environmental Protection Agency

The mileage numbers and rankings below refer to testing completed through September 11, 1981. The testing of several major model types has not been completed when these data were released.

Make, model	Cu. In. displcmt.	Cylinders	Trans.[1]	Mileage
Alfa Romeo Spider	120	4	m	22
AMC Concord	258	6	a	20
AMC Spirit	258	6	a	21
Audi 4000	97	4	m	38
Audi 5000	131	5	a	19
BMW 320	108	4	m	25
BMW 633 CSI	196	6	m	19
BMW 733 I	196	6	a	18
Buick Century	231	6	a	21
Buick Electra	252	6	a	18
Buick LeSabre	252	6	a	18
Buick Regal	231	6	a	21
Buick Riviera	350	8	a	20
Buick Skyhawk	231	6	a	19
Buick Skylark	173	6	a	22
Cadillac Deville/ Brougham	350	8	a	22
Cadillac Eldorado, Seville	350	8	a	20
Chevrolet Camaro	151	4	a	23
Chevrolet Cavalier	112	4	m	30
Chevrolet Chevette	111	4	a	36
Chev. Chevette Diesl	111	4	m	40
Chevrolet Citation	173	6	a	22
Chevrolet Impala/ Caprice	267	8	a	17
Chevrolet Corvette	350	8	a	15
Chevrolet Malibu	229	6	a	21
Chevrolet Monte Carlo	229	6	a	21
Chrysler Cordoba/300	225	6	a	18
Chrysler LeBaron	156	4	a	23
Chrysler New Yorker	225	6	a	17
Datsun 2-Seater 280zx	168	6	a	31
Datsun 210	85	4	m	36
Datsun 200SX	133	4	a	25
Datsun 310	91	4	m	34
Datsun 510	119	4	a	27
Datsun 810	146	6	m	22
Dodge Aries	135	4	m	26
Dodge Challenger	156	4	a	21
Dodge Colt	98	4	a	28
Dodge DeTomaso	105	4	m	27
Dodge Diplomat	225	6	a	18
Dodge Miranda	225	6	a	18
Dodge Omni	105	4	m	30
Dodge 024	105	4	m	30
Fiat Brava	122	4	a	24
Fiat Spider 2000	122	4	a	22
Fiat Strada	91	4	a	26
Ford Escort	98	4	m	31
Ford Fairmont	200	6	a	20
Ford Granada	200	6	a	20
Ford LTD	302	8	a	17
Ford Mustang	200	6	a	20
Ford Thunderbird	231	6	a	19
Honda Accord	107	4	m	30
Honda Civic	91	4	m	35
Jaguar XJ	258	6	a	17
Mazda GLC	91	4	a	30
Mazda Rx7	70	2	a	19
Mercury Capri	200	6	a	20
Merc. Cougar	302	8	a	16
Mercury Lynx	98	4	m	31
Mercury Marquis	302	8	a	17
Mercury Zephyr	200	6	a	20
Olds. Cutlass Sup.	260	8	a	19
Oldsmobile Delta 88	231	6	a	19
Oldsmobile 98	307	8	a	17
Oldsmobile Omega	151	4	a	25
Oldsmobile Toronado	307	8	a	16
Plymouth Champ	86	4	m	39
Plymouth Gran Fury	318	8	a	17
Plymouth Horizon	105	4	m	30
Plymouth Reliant	135	4	m	26
Plym. Sapporo	156	4	a	23
Plymouth TC3/Turismo	105	4	m	30
Pontiac Bonneville	231	6	a	21
Pontiac Grand Prix	231	6	a	21
Pontiac J2000	112	4	m	30
Pontiac Phoenix	173	6	a	22
Porsche 924	121	4	m	20
Porsche 928	273	8	m	16
Subaru	109	4	m	31
Toyota Celica	144	4	m	24
Toy. Cel. Supra	168	6	m	21
Toyota Corolla	108	4	a	27
Toyota Corona	144	4	a	24
Toyota Cressida	168	6	a	22
Toyota Starlet	79	4	m	38
Toyota Tercel	89	4	a	29
Volkswgn Diesl Rabt.	97	4	m	45
Volkswgn Jetta	105	4	m	28
Volkswgn Rabbit	105	4	a	24
Volkswgn Scirocco	105	4	a	24

(1) Type of transmission: a=automatic; m=manual.

Social Security Programs: After the Paychecks Stop
Old-Age, Survivors, and Disability Insurance; Medicare; Supplemental Security Income

New Legislation

On August 13, 1981, President Reagan signed into law the Omnibus Budget Reconciliation Act of 1981 (Public law 97-35). Following are some of the provisions under the new law that affect Social Security and other related programs:

(1) Elimination of the minimum Social Security benefit for both current and future beneficiaries and payment instead of a wage-related benefit based on the worker's average earnings.

(2) Phasing out of student benefits for persons aged 19 or over or in postsecondary schools.

(3) Payment of the lump-sum death benefit only when there is a spouse who was living with the worker or a spouse or child eligible for immediate monthly survivor benefits.

(4) Offset of Social Security disability benefits when total public plan benefits based on disability exceed predisability earnings—a "Megacap" provision.

Department Renamed

The Department of Health, Education, and Welfare officially became the Department of Health and Human Services on May 4, 1980. The new Department name was necessitated by the Department of Education Organization Act, signed on October 17, 1979, which provided for establishment of a separate Department of Education. The Department of Health and Human Services has four principal components; Public Health Service, the Health Care Financing Administration, the Office of Human Development Services, and the Social Security Administration.

New Commissioner of Social Security

On May 4, 1981, John A. Svahn was confirmed as Commissioner of Social Security. He succeeded William J. Driver, who left the post in January. In the interim, Herbert R. Doggette, Jr., Deputy Commissioner for Operations, served as Acting Commissioner.

Old-Age, Survivors, and Disability Insurance

Old-Age, Survivors, and Disability Insurance covers almost all jobs in which people work for wages or salaries, as well as most work of self-employed persons, whether in a city job, or in business, or on a farm.

Old-Age, Survivors, and Disability Insurance is paid for by a tax on earnings (for 1981, up to $29,700; the taxable earnings base is now subject to adjustment based on increases in average wages in the economy). The employed worker and his or her employer share the tax equally (cash tips count as covered wages if they amount to $20 or more from one place of employment. The worker reports them to the employer, who includes them in the social security tax reports, but only the worker pays contributions on the amount of the tips).

The employer deducts the tax each payday and sends it, with an equal amount (the employer's share), to the District Director of Internal Revenue. The collected taxes are deposited in the Federal Old-Age and Survivors Insurance Trust Fund and the Federal Disability Insurance Trust Fund; they can be used only to pay benefits, the cost of rehabilitation services, and administrative expenses.

Benefit Increase, June 1981

Social Security checks delivered to beneficiaries in the first week of July 1981 reflected the seventh automatic cost-of-living increase in cash benefits under legislation enacted in 1972 and 1973. The 11.2-percent increase, which became effective in June, applied to benefits for all persons on the Social Security benefit rolls at the end of May.

Automatic increases are initiated whenever the Consumer Price Index (CPI) of the Bureau of Labor Statistics for the first calendar quarter of a year exceeds by at least 3 percent the CPI for the base quarter, which is either the first calendar quarter of the preceding year or the quarter in which an increase was legislated by Congress. In this case, the base quarter was the first quarter of 1980. The size of the benefit increase is determined by the actual percentage rise of the CPI during the quarters measured.

As a result of the benefit increase, average monthly benefits payable to retired workers rose to $427.22 for men and $331.92 for women. Average amounts for disabled workers were $454.21 for men and $329.48 for women.

Social Security benefits are based on a worker's primary insurance amount (PIA), which is related by law to the average indexed monthly earnings (AIME) on which social security contributions have been paid. The full PIA is payable to a retired worker who becomes entitled to benefits at age 65 and to an entitled disabled worker at any age. Spouses and children of retired or disabled workers and survivors of deceased workers receive set proportions of the PIA subject to a family maximum amount. The PIA is calculated by applying varying percentages to succeeding parts of the AIME. Whenever a cost-of-living benefit increase is implemented, these percentages are changed to reflect the percentage increase in benefits.

Amount of Work Required

To qualify for benefits, the worker must have been in covered employment long enough to become insured. Just how long depends on the date of birth (or if the worker dies or becomes disabled, the date of death or disability).

A person is fully covered if he or she has one quarter of coverage for every year after 1950 (or year age 21 is reached) up to but not including the year in which the worker reaches age 62 or dies.

Certain provisions in the law permit special monthly payments under the Social Security program to persons aged 72 and over who are not eligible for regular social security benefits since they had little or no opportunity to earn social security work credits during their working lifetime.

To get disability benefits, the worker must also have credit for 5 out of 10 years before he or she becomes disabled. Persons disabled before age 31 can qualify with a briefer period of coverage.

Work Years Required

The following table shows the number of work years required to be fully insured for Old-Age or Survivors benefits, according to the year worker reaches retirement age or dies.

Work credit for retirement benefits

If you reach 62 in	Years you need	If you reach 62 in	Years you need
1974	6*	1979	7
1975	6	1981	7½
1976	6¼	1983	8
1977	6½	1987	9
1978	6¾	1991 or later.	10

*For 1974 a woman needs only 5¾ years.

Work credit for survivors and disability benefits

Born after 1929, die or become disabled at	Born before 1930, die or become disabled before age 62 in	Years needed
32		2½
34		3
36		3½
38		4
40		4½
42		5
44		5½
45		5¾
46		6
48		6½
50	1979	7
52	1981	7½
54	1983	8
56	1985	8½
58	1987	9
60	1989	9½
62 or older	1991 or later.	10

Tax-rate schedule
[Percent of covered earnings]

Year	Total Employees and employers, each	OASDI	HI
1977	5.85	4.95	0.90
1978	6.05	5.05	1.00
1979-80	6.13	5.08	1.05
1981	6.65	5.35	1.30
1982-84	6.70	5.40	1.30
1985	7.05	5.70	1.35
1986-89	7.15	5.70	1.45
1990-2010	7.65	6.20	1.45
2011 and after.	7.65	6.20	1.45

	Self-employed		
1977	7.90	7.00	0.90
1978	8.10	7.10	1.00
1979-80	8.10	7.05	1.05
1981	9.30	8.00	1.30
1982-84	9.35	8.05	1.30
1985	9.90	8.55	1.35
1986-89	10.00	8.55	1.45
1990-2010	10.75	9.30	1.45
2011 and after.	10.75	9.30	1.45

What Aged Workers Get

When a person has enough work in covered employment and reaches retirement age (65 for full benefit, 62 for reduced benefit), he or she may retire and get monthly old-age benefits. If a person aged 65 or older continues to work and has earnings of more than $5,500 in 1981, $1 in benefits will be withheld for every $2 above $5,500. The annual exempt amount and the monthly test are raised automatically or according to the rise in general earnings levels. (The annual exempt amount for retirees 65 or older increases to $6,000 in 1982.) The eligible worker who is 72 receives the full amount of benefit regardless of earnings.

A worker's benefit will be raised by 1% for each year after 1970 for which the worker between 65 and 72 did not receive benefits because of earnings from work. The delayed retirement credit is increased to 3 percent a year for workers reaching age 62 after 1978. No increases are to be paid to the worker's dependents or survivors under this provision.

In 1980, the special benefit for persons aged 72 or over who do not meet the regular coverage requirements is $105.20 a month ($157.80 for a couple if both members are eligible). Like the monthly benefits, these payments are now subject to cost-of-living increases. The special payment is not made to persons on the public assistance or supplemental security income rolls.

Social Security benefits are not subject to income taxes.

A woman worker is eligible for a full old-age benefit at age 65, but she may retire at 62 and get 80% of her full benefit for the rest of her life; the nearer she is to 65 when she begins collecting her benefit, the larger it will be. (Benefits for men retiring before 65 are reduced at the same rate as benefits for women retiring before 65.)

A child can get benefits based on his mother's earnings on the same conditions as those entitling a child to benefits based on his father's earnings record.

Benefits for Worker's Spouse

The wife of a man who is getting social security retirement or disability payments may become entitled to wife's insurance benefits in a reduced amount when she reaches 62, or she may wait until she reaches 65 and get the entire amount of the wife's benefit, which is one-half of the husband's benefit. Benefits are also payable to the divorced wife of an insured worker if she was married to him for at least 20 years (10 years eff. Jan. 1979) and he was contributing to or was ordered by a court to contribute to her support.

If a woman worker entitled to an old-age benefit has a dependent husband aged 65 or over, he may draw a benefit similar to a wife's benefit at 65 (or a reduced benefit at age 62).

Benefits for Children of Retired or Disabled Workers

If a worker has children under 18 when he retires for age or disability they will get a benefit that is half his benefit, and so will his wife, even if she is under 62. Total benefits paid on a worker's earnings record are subject to a maxi-

mum and if the total paid to a family exceed that maximum, the individual dependents' benefits are adjusted downward. (Total benefits paid to the family of a worker who retired in June 1980 at age 65 with average monthly earnings of $750 can be no higher than $1,121.40.)

When entitled children reach 18, their benefits will stop, except that a child permanently and totally disabled before 22 may get a benefit as long as his disability meets the definition in the law. Benefits may now be paid to a grandchild or step-grandchild of a worker or of his spouse, in special circumstances.

OASDI	July 1981	July 1980	July 1979
Monthly beneficiaries, total (in thousands)	35,698	35,146	34,737
Aged 65 and over, total	24,036	23,437	22,858
Retired workers	17,734	17,213	16,729
Survivors and dependents . . .	6,220	6,124	6,010
Special age-72 beneficiaries. .	82	100	120
Under age 65, total	11,662	11,709	11,815
Retired workers	2,121	2,008	1,924
Disabled workers	2,827	2,861	2,881
Survivors and dependents . . .	6,714	6,840	7,010
Total monthly benefits (in millions)	$12,054	$10,466	$8,871

What Disabled Workers Get

If a worker becomes so severely disabled that he is unable to work, he may be eligible to receive a monthly disability benefit that is the same amount he would receive as a retired-worker benefit if he were 65 at the start of his disability. When he reaches 65, his disability benefit becomes a retired-worker benefit.

Benefits like those provided for dependents of retired-worker beneficiaries may be paid to dependents of disabled beneficiaries.

Survivor Benefits

If a worker should die while insured, one or more types of benefits would be payable to survivors.

1. A cash payment to cover burial expenses that amounts to 3 times the basic benefit but not more than $255, paid at the death of every insured worker.

2. A benefit for each child until the child reaches 18. The monthly benefit of each child of a worker who has died is three-quarters of the amount the worker would have received if he had lived and drawn retirement benefits. A child with a permanent disability that began before age 22 may receive his benefit after that age.

3. A mother's benefit for the widow, if children under 16 are left in her care. Her benefit is 75% of the basic benefit and she draws it until the youngest child reaches 16. Payments stop then even if the child's benefit continues because he is attending school. They will start again when she is 62 (or 60), unless she marries. If she marries and the marriage is ended, she regains benefit rights. If she has a disabled child beneficiary aged 18 or over in her care, her benefits also continue. (Beginning March 1975, widowed father's benefits are payable on same basis as widowed mother's benefits).

Disabled widows and widowers qualify for benefits at age 50 at reduced rates that depend on age at entitlement. The widow or widower must have become totally disabled before or within 7 years after the spouse's death.

4. If there are no children entitled to receive benefits, the surviving spouse will receive a benefit that is 100% of the deceased worker's basic amount, if it is first payable when the spouse is 65. The surviving spouse may choose to get the benefit at age 60; the benefit is then reduced by 19/40 of 1% for each month it is paid before age 65. However, for those aged 62 and over whose spouses claimed their benefits before 65, the benefit is the reduced amount the worker would be getting if alive but not less than 82 1/2% of the basic benefit.

5. Dependent parents may be eligible for benefits, if they have been receiving at least half their support from the worker before his or her death, have reached age 62, and (except in certain circumstances) have not remarried since the worker's death. Each parent gets 75% of the basic benefit except that if only one parent survives the benefit is 82 1/2%.

Maximum Benefits Payable

The illustrative table on page 78 shows a column heading for average monthly earnings of $2,158, but the benefit amounts shown in the column are not in general payable yet, since it will be some time before workers can have an average that high (years when the maximum creditable amount of earnings was lower than $25,900 — the 1980 maximum — must currently be included when the average is figured).

Contribution and benefit base

Calendar year Current base[1]		
	1979	22,900
	1980	25,900
1977	$16,500	1981	29,700
1978	17,700	1982	32,400

(1) Stated in law for 1979-81. Estimated under automatic adjustment-provisions for 1982.

Self-Employed

A self-employed person who has earnings of $400 or more in a year must report his earnings for income tax and social security tax purposes. If the person is not a farmer he or she reports only net returns from the business. Income from real estate, savings, dividends, loans, pensions or insurance policies need not be added if these are not part of the business.

A self-employed person who has net earnings of $400 or more in a year gets 4 quarters of coverage for that year. If earnings are less than $400 in a year they do not count toward social security credits. The nonfarm self-employed person must make estimated payments of his or her social security taxes, on a quarterly basis, for taxable years after 1966, if combined estimated income tax and social security tax amount to at least $40.

The self-employed have the option, comparable to that for farm workers, of reporting their earnings as 2/3 of their gross income from self-employment but not more than $1,600 a year. This option can be used only if actual net earnings from self-employment income is less than $1,600 and less than 2/3 of gross income and may be used only 5 times.

When a person has both taxable wages and earnings from self-employment, only as much of the self-employment income as will bring total earnings up to the current taxable maximum is subject to tax for social security purposes. A self-employed person pays the tax at a lower rate than the combined rate for an employee and his employer — about 1 1/2 times what the employee alone pays.

Farm Owners and Workers

Self-employed farmers whose gross annual earnings from farming are under $2,400 may report 2/3 of their gross earnings instead of net earnings for social security purposes. Cash or crop shares received from a tenant or share farmer count if the owner participated materially in production or management. The self-employed farmer pays contributions at the same rate as other self-employed, but may make his or her tax returns annually.

Farm workers. Earnings from farm work count toward benefits (1) if the employer pays $150 or more in cash during the year; (2) if the employee works on 20 or more days for cash pay figured on a time basis. Under these rules a person gets credit for one calendar quarter for each $250 in cash pay in a year but no more than four quarters in any one year.

Foreign farm workers admitted to the United States on a temporary basis are not covered.

Household Workers

Anyone working as maid, cook, laundress, nursemaid, baby-sitter, chauffeur, gardener and at other household tasks in the house of another, is covered by social security if he or she earns $50 or more in cash in three months from any one employer. Room and board do not count, but carfare counts if paid in cash. The job does not have to be regular or fulltime. The employee should get a card at the social security office and show it to the employer.

The employer deducts the amount of the social security tax from the worker's pay, adds an identical amount as the employer's own tax and sends the total amount to the federal government, with the number of the employee's social security card.

Medicare

Under Medicare, protection against the costs of hospital care is provided for social security and railroad retirement beneficiaries aged 65 and over and, for persons entitled for 24 months to receive a social security disability benefit, certain persons (and their dependents) with end-stage renal disease, and, on a voluntary basis with payment of a special premium, persons aged 65 and over not otherwise eligible for hospital benefits; all those eligible for hospital benefits may enroll for medical benefits and pay a monthly premium and so may persons aged 65 and over who are not eligible for hospital benefits.

Persons eligible for both hospital and medical insurance may choose to have their covered services provided through a Health Maintenance Organization.

Hospital insurance.—From October 1980 to September 1981, about $23.8 billion was withdrawn from the hospital insurance trust fund for hospital and related benefits.

As of January 1981, the hospital insurance program paid the cost of covered services for hospital and posthospital care as follows:

- Up to 90 days of hospital care during a benefit period (spell of illness) starting the first day that care as a bed-patient is received in a hospital or skilled-nursing facility and ending when the individual has not been a bed-patient for 60 consecutive days. For the first 60 days, the hospital insurance pays for all but the first $204 of expenses; for the 61st day to 90th day, the program pays all but $51 a day for covered services. In addition, each person has a 60-day lifetime reserve that can be used after the 90 days of hospital care in a benefit period are exhausted, and all but $102 a day of expenses during the reserve days are paid. Once used, the reserve days are not replaced. (Payment for care in a mental hospital is limited to 190 days.)
- Up to 100 days' care in a skilled-nursing facility (skilled-nursing home) in each benefit period. Hospital insurance pays for all covered services for the first 20 days and all but $25.50 daily for the next 80 days. At least 3 days' hospital stay must precede these services, and the skilled-nursing facility must be entered within 14 days after leaving the hospital. (The 1972 law permits more than 14 days in certain circumstances.)
- Up to 100 visits by nurses or other health workers (not doctors) from a home health agency in the 365 days after release from a hospital or extended-care facility.

Medical insurance. Aged persons can receive benefits under this supplementary program only if they sign up for them and agree to a monthly premium ($11.00 beginning July 1981). The Federal Government pays the rest of the cost. In December of each year the Secretary of Health and Human Services announces the premium payable starting in July of the following year. The premiums are to be increased only when there is a general benefit increase in the year and it will rise no more than the percent by which the cash benefits have been increased since the last premium increase.

About 142 million bills were reimbursed under the medical insurance program from July 1979 to June 1980 for a total of $9.2 billion. As of July 1979, about 26,757,300 persons were enrolled — 2,658,800 of them disabled persons under age 65.

The medical insurance program pays 80% of the reasonable charges (after the first $60 in each calendar year) for the following services:

- Physicians' and surgeons' services, whether in the doctor's office, a clinic, or hospital or at home (but physician's charges for X-ray or clinical laboratory services for hospital bed-patients are paid in full and without meeting the deductible).
- Other medical and health services, such as diagnostic tests, surgical dressings and splints, and rental or purchase of medical equipment. Services of a physical therapist in independent practice, furnished in his office or the patient's home. A hospital or extended-care facility may provide covered outpatient physical therapy services under the medical insurance program to its patients who have exhausted their hospital insurance coverage.
- Physical therapy services furnished under the supervision

of a practicing hospital, clinic, skilled nursing facility, or agency.

- Certain services by podiatrists.
- All outpatient services of a participating hospital (including diagnostic tests).
- Outpatient speech pathology services, under the same requirements as physical therapy.
- Services of licensed chiropractors who meet uniform standards, but only for treatment by means of manual manipulation of the spine and treatment of subluxation of the spine demonstrated by X-ray.
- Supplies related to colostomies are considered prosthetic devices and payable under the program.
- Home health services even without a hospital stay (up to 100 visits a year) are paid up to 100%.

To get medical insurance protection, persons approaching age 65 may enroll in the 7-month period that includes 3 months before the 65th birthday, the month of the birthday, and 3 months after the birthday, but if they wish coverage to begin in the month they reach 65 they must enroll in the 3 months **before** their birthday. Persons not enrolling within their first enrollment period may enroll later, during the first 3 months of each year but their premium is 10% higher for each 12-month period elapsed since they first could have enrolled.

The monthly premium is deducted from the cash benefit for persons receiving social security, railroad retirement, or civil service retirement benefits. Income from the medical premiums and the federal matching payments are put in a Supplementary Medical Insurance Trust Fund, from which benefits and administrative expenses are paid.

Medicare card. Persons qualifying for hospital insurance under social security receive a health insurance card similar to cards now used by Blue Cross and other health agencies. The card indicates whether the individual has taken out medical insurance protection. It is to be shown to the hospital, skilled-nursing facility, home health agency, doctor, or whoever provides the covered services.

Payments are made only in the 50 states, Puerto Rico, the Virgin Islands, Guam, and American Samoa, except that hospital services may be provided in border areas immediately outside the U.S. if comparable services are not accessible in the U.S. for a beneficiary who becomes ill or is injured in the U.S.

Supplemental Security Income

On Jan. 1, 1974, the Supplemental Security Income (SSI) program established by the 1972 Social Security Act amendments replaced the former federal grants to states for aid to the needy aged, blind, and disabled in the 50 states and the District of Columbia. The program provides both for federal payments based on uniform national standards and eligibility requirements and for state supplementary payments varying from state to state. The Social Security Administration administers the federal payments financed from general funds of the Treasury—and the state supplements as well, if the state elects to have its supplementary program federally administered. The states may supplement the federal payment for all recipients and must supplement it for persons otherwise adversely affected by the transition from the former public assistance programs. In July 1981, the number of persons receiving federal payments and federally administered state payments was 4,069,700, and the amount of these payments was $741.7 million.

As a result of the 11.2-percent benefit increase the maximum federal SSI payment for an individual with no other countable income, living in his own household, rises from $238.00 to $264.70, and that for a couple, similarly situated, goes from $357.00 to $397.00.

Minimum and maximum monthly retired-worker benefits payable to individuals who retired at age 65, 1960—81

Year of attainment of age 65[1]	Minimum benefit		Maximum benefit			
	Payable at the time of retirement	Payable effective June 1981	Payable at the time of retirement		Payable effective June 1981	
			Men[2]	Women	Men[2]	Women
1960 . . .	$30.00	$170.30	$119.00-			
					. . . $440.00	. . .
1961 . . .	33.00	170.30	120.00	. . .	443.40	. . .
1962 . . .	40.00	170.30	121.00	$123.00	447.40	$455.00-
1963 . . .	40.00	170.30	122.00	125.00	451.20	461.90
1964 . . .	40.00	170.30	123.00	127.00	455.00	469.50
1965 . . .	44.00	170.30	131.70	135.90	455.00	469.50
1966 . . .	44.00	170.30	132.70	135.90	458.30	469.50
1967 . . .	44.00	170.30	135.90	140.00	469.50	493.60
1968 . . .	[3]55.00	170.30	[3]156.00	[3]161.60	476.70	493.60
1969 . . .	55.00	170.30	160.50	167.30	490.60	511.30
1970 . . .	64.00	170.30	189.80	196.40	504.20	521.90
1971 . . .	70.40	170.30	213.10	220.40	514.60	531.90
1972 . . .	70.40	170.30	216.10	224.70	521.90	542.50
1973 . . .	84.50	170.30	266.10	270.70	535.40	556.20
1974 . . .	84.50	170.30	274.60	284.90	552.40	573.20
1975 . . .	93.80	170.30	316.30	333.70	573.20	604.60
1976 . . .	101.40	170.30	364.00	378.80	610.40	635.30
1977 . . .	107.90	170.30	412.70	422.40	650.50	665.70
1978 . . .	114.30	170.30	459.80	. . .	684.20	. . .
1979 . . .	121.80	170.30	503.40	. . .	703.40	. . .
1980 . . .	133.90	170.30	572.00	. . .	727.10	. . .
1981 . . .	153.10	170.30	677.00	. . .	752.90	. . .

(1) Assumes retirement at beginning of year. (2) Benefit for both men and women, except where women's benefit shown separately. (3) Effective for February 1968.

Examples of OASDI monthly cash benefit awards for selected beneficiary families, effective June 1980

Beneficiary family	Average monthly earnings of insured worker								
	$76 or less	$100	$300	$550	$750	$900	$1,100	$1,475	$2,158
Retired worker claiming benefits at age 65, or disabled worker:									
Worker alone.	$153.10	$197.00	$349.50	$521.80	$640.80	$695.20	$764.10	$873.60	$1,040.10
Worker with spouse claiming benefits at—									
Age 65 or over	229.70	295.50	524.30	782.70	961.20	1,042.80	1,146.20	1,310.40	1,560.20
Age 62	210.60	270.90	480.60	717.50	881.10	955.90	1,050.70	1,201.20	1,456.20
Worker, spouse, and 1 child	229.70	295.50	573.00	944.30	1,121.40	1,216.40	1,336.70	1,528.70	1,820.20
Retired worker claiming benefits at age 62:									
Worker alone.	122.50	157.60	279.60	417.50	512.70	556.20	611.30	698.90	832.10
Worker with spouse claiming benefits at—									
Age 65 or over	199.10	256.10	454.40	678.40	833.10	903.80	993.40	1,135.70	1,352.20
Age 62	180.00	231.50	410.70	613.20	753.00	816.90	897.90	1,025.50	1,248.20
Widow or widower claiming benefits at—									
Age 65 or over[1]	153.10	197.00	349.50	521.80	640.80	695.20	764.10	873.60	1,040.10
Age 60	109.50	140.90	249.90	373.10	458.20	497.10	546.40	624.70	743.70
Disabled widow or widower claiming benefits at age 50	76.70	98.50	174.80	260.90	320.40	347.60	382.10	436.80	520.10
1 surviving child.	[2]153.10	[2]153.10	262.20	391.40	480.60	521.40	573.10	655.20	780.10
Widow or widower aged 65 and over and 1 child[1] . .	229.70	295.50	573.00	913.20	1,121.40	1,216.40	1,336.70	1,528.70	1,820.20
Widowed mother or father and 1 child	229.70	295.50	524.40	782.80	961.20	1,042.80	1,146.20	1,310.40	1,560.20
Widowed mother or father and 2 children	229.70	295.50	573.00	944.30	1,121.40	1,216.40	1,336.70	1,528.70	1,820.20
Maximum family benefits	229.70	295.50	573.00	944.30	1,121.40	1,216.40	1,336.70	1,528.70	1,820.20

(1) Widow's or widower's benefit limited to amount spouse would have been receiving if still living but not less than 82½ percent of the PIA. (2) Sole survivor. NOTE: The higher monthly earnings shown in column headings on the right are not, in general, possible now, since earnings in some of the earlier years—when the maximum amount creditable was lower—must be included in the average. Therefore, the benefit amounts shown in these columns are not generally currently payable. (Effective June 1980, the highest average monthly creditable earnings possible for a worker retiring at age 65 is $784).

Social Security Trust Funds
Old-Age, Survivors, and Disability Insurance Trust Funds, 1937-1980
(thousands)

| | Receipts | | | Expenditures | | |
| | Net contrib. inc., reimb. from gen'l rev. | Net interest received | Cash benefit payments and rehab. services | Transfers to R.R. ret. acct. | Administrative expenses | Total assets at end of period |
Fiscal year:						
1937	$ 265,000	$ 2,262	$ 27	$...	$ 26,840	$ 267,235
1940	550,000	42,489	15,805	...	12,288	1,744,698
1950	2,109,912	256,778	727,266	...	56,841	12,892,612
1960	10,829,664	564,040	10,798,013	573,606	234,291	22,995,939
1970	34,554,182	1,572,375	29,062,772	589,257	623,055	37,719,951
1976	67,867,099	2,815,197	71,462,416	1,238,669	1,200,326	44,919,209
1976 (July-Sept.)[1] ...	18,264,899	93,726	19,459,572		304,448	43,513,811
1977	78,511,213	2,658,629	82,490,402	1,207,523	1,370,386	39,615,344
1978	87,192,105	2,403,128	90,828,787	1,618,461	1,413,414	35,349,916
1979	99,864,545	2,224,797	101,116,288	1,477,438	1,478,975	33,366,557
1980	115,087,980	2,340,600	115,624,227	1,441,988	1,493,990	32,245,930
Cum. (1937-80)	994,752,258	38,542,386	966,946,536	16,364,631	17,747,163	32,245,930

(1) Transitional quarter. Beginning Oct. 1976, federal fiscal year begins Oct. 1.

Hospital Insurance Trust Fund, 1966-80
(thousands)

| | Receipts | | | | Expenditures | | |
| | Net contribution income[1] | Transfers from railroad retirement account[2] | Reimbursements from general revenues[3] | Net interest[4] | Net hospital and related service benefits[5] | Administrative expenses[6] | Total assets |
Fiscal year:							
1966	$908,797	...	...	$5,970	...	$63,564	$851,204
1967	2,688,684	$16,200	$337,850	45,903	$2,507,773	88,848	1,343,221
1970	4,784,789	61,307	628,262	139,423	4,804,242	148,660	2,677,401
1975	11,296,773	126,749	520,353	614,909	10,355,390	256,134	9,870,039
1976	12,039,194	130,904	658,430	715,744	12,270,382	308,215	10,835,314
1976 (July-Sept)[7] ...	3,367,940	135,863	...	11,951	3,315,251	88,408	10,947,810
1979	19,943,084	175,600	874,849	883,158	19,898,459	411,565	13,362,750
1980	23,260,335	221,800	837,906	1,061,433	23,793,420	460,841	14,489,913
Cum. (1966-80)	144,975,825	1,446,740	9,049,582	6,183,149	143,727,333	3,488,054	14,489,913

(1) Represents amounts appropriated (estimated tax collections with suitable subsequent adjustments) after deductions for refund of estimated amount of employee-tax overpayment; and, beginning July 1973, premiums for coverage of uninsured individuals aged 65 and over. (2) Transfers (principal only) from the railroad retirement account with respect to contributions for hospital insurance coverage of railroad workers. (3) Represents Federal Government transfers from general funds appropriations to meet costs of benefits for persons not insured for cash benefits under OASHDI or railroad retirement and for costs of benefits arising from military wage credits. (4) Interest and profit on investments after transfers of interest or reimbursed administrative expenses (see footnote 6) and interest on amounts transferred from railroad retirement account (see footnote 3). (5) Represents (1) payment vouchers on letters of credit issued to fiscal intermediaries under sec. 1816 and (2) direct payments to providers of services under sec. 1815 of the Social Security Act. (6) Subject to subsequent adjustment among all four social security trust funds for allocated cost of each operation. Fiscal year 1966 includes "tool-up" period from date of enactment of Social Security Amendments of 1965 (July 20). (7) Between end of fiscal year 1976 (June 30) and start of fiscal year 1977 (Oct. 1, 1976).

Supplementary Medical Insurance Trust Fund: Status, 1967-80
(thousands)

| | Receipts | | | Expenditures | | |
| | Premium income[1] | Transfers from general revenues[2] | Net interest[3] | Net medical service benefits[4] | Administrative expenses[5] | Total assets |
Fiscal year:						
1967	$646,682	$623,000	$14,052	$664,261	$133,682	$485,791
1970	936,000	928,151	11,536	1,979,287	216,993	57,181
1975	1,886,962	2,329,590	105,539	3,765,397	404,458	1,424,413
1976	1,951,221	2,939,338	103,645	4,671,847	528,214	1,218,555
1976 (July-Sept)[6] ...	538,648	878,000	4,420	1,269,038	132,077	1,238,508
1978	2,431,133	6,385,503	228,848	6,852,252	504,234	3,968,425
1979	2,635,492	6,840,785	362,787	8,259,077	554,496	4,993,913
1980	2,927,711	6,931,713	415,510	10,143,930	593,327	4,531,591
Cum. (1967-80)	23,472,004	40,606,265	1,594,424	56,061,424	5,070,675	4,531,591

(1) Represents voluntary premium payments from and in behalf of the insured aged and (beginning July 1973) disabled. (2) Represents Federal Government transfers from general funds appropriations to match aggregate premiums paid. (3) Represents interest and profit on investments, after transfers of interest on reimbursed administrative expenses (see footnote 5). (4) Represents payment vouchers on letters of credit issued to carriers under section 1842 of the Social Security Act. (5) Subject to subsequent adjustment among all 4 social security trust funds for allocated cost of each operation. Fiscal year 1966 includes "tool-up" period from date of enactment of Social Security Amendments of 1965 (July 30). (6) Between end of fiscal year 1976 (June 30) and start of fiscal year 1977 (Oct. 1, 1976).

How Is Your Life Insurance Dollar Used?
Source: American Council of Life Insurance, 1980 figures.

Of each dollar of income received by U.S. insurance companies, $ .73 comes from premiums and $ .27 from net investment earning and other income.

The following breakdown shows how each premium dollar received from insurance purchasers is spent:

Benefit payments to policy holders	$ .494	Home and field office expenses	$ .095
Additions to policy reserve funds	$ .280	Taxes..................	$ .034
Additions to special reserves & surplus funds	$ .029	Dividends to shareholders	$ .011
Commissions to agents	$ .057	**Total**	$ 1.000

Life Insurance: Facts You Need to Know

Source: American Council of Insurance

One of the most important purchases you can make—and one you need to be well-informed about—is life insurance.

Most insurance companies are currently simplifying their life insurance plans in order that consumers might have a better idea of what they're really buying. In addition to making policies easier to read and understand, the companies are developing new premium payment methods to lower the financial burden of insurance purchase. Since almost one-third of all life insurance is bought by people aged 25-43, with over 60% paying more than $260 annually for insurance, such innovations as monthly payment plans (instead of annual or semi-annual, lump sum payments) are becoming common.

There are 3 basic types of insurance policies: (1) whole life—a policy that continues in effect as long as you pay the fixed premium; (2) endowment—a policy that will pay you or your beneficiary its face amount after a designated time; and (3) term—the policy pays your beneficiary the face amount if you die while the policy is in force.

Life Insurance as an Investment?

There's a good deal of controversy about the value of insurance as an investment, especially in times of double-digit inflation. Whole life policies, with their fixed premiums and cash value that grows over the course of the years (that can be collected when you decide to terminate the policy or borrowed against up to the current value of the policy) are considered by many to be an effective way to protect a family financially, while also having money wisely invested. Term insurance, on the other hand, is a much less expensive type of insurance, and achieves much the same purpose as whole

life (of course, only during the "term" of its existence). But there is no cash surrender value or borrowing privilege.

Since both current protection and a good future investment are necessary, the consumer must carefully weigh the advantages of life insurance before making a purchase.

How to Read a Life Insurance Policy

All life insurance policies, regardless of type, can be divided into 3 parts:

1. **Summary**—This is the basic agreement of the policy. It includes the name of the insured, the face amount of the policy, the beneficiary's name, and premium amount, as well as the type of policy, any riders (additions to the policy you might have bought), and whether or not the cost of the insurance has been figured on a guaranteed basis or a participating basis.

2. **Details**—Approximately 10 clauses giving the specifics of the policy's operation, such as due date of premium, value of the policy when you surrender it for either cash or a loan, the amount paid on your death, options for how your beneficiary can receive that money.

3. **Application**—A two-fold section that gives personal information about you and it lets you make some decisions about how the policy will work. Among typical items covered are what happens in the event of your suicide, whether you engage in dangerous sports or occupations, what your rights are under the policy, etc.

As with any legal document, it is important to read and understand what you are purchasing. If you need further information, a good source is the American Council of Insurance, 1850 K St. N.W., Washington, DC 20006.

Basic First Aid

First aid experts stress that knowing what to do for an injured person until a doctor or trained person gets to an accident scene can save a life, especially in cases of stoppage of breath, severe bleeding, and shock.

People with special medical problems, such as diabetes, cardiovascular disease, epilepsy, or allergy, are also urged to wear some sort of emblem identifying it, as a safeguard against use of medication that might be injurious or fatal in an emergency. For instance, there are many epileptics, as well as diabetics, who can mistakenly be taken for drunk or ill, according to Medic Alert, a nonprofit organization which pioneered the wearing of an informative emblem. Emblems may be obtained from Medic Alert Foundation, Turlock, CA 95380.

Most accidents occur in homes. National Safety Council figures show that home accidents annually far outstrip those in other locations, such as in autos, at work, or in public places.

Measures for some of the most frequent emergencies follow:

Animal bites — Wounds should be washed with soap under running water and animal should be caught alive for rabies test. Call doctor or take patient to him.

Asphyxiation — Start mouth-to-mouth resuscitation immediately after getting patient to fresh air. Call physician.

Bleeding — Elevate the wound above the heart if possible. Press hard on wound with sterile compress until bleeding stops. Send for doctor if it is severe.

Burns — If mild, with skin unbroken and no blisters, plunge into ice water until pain subsides. Apply mild burn ointment or petroleum jelly if pain persists. Send for physician if burn is severe. Apply sterile compresses and keep patient quiet and comfortably warm until doctor's arrival. Do not try to clean burn, or to break blisters.

Chemicals in eye — With patient lying down, pour cupfuls of water immediately into corner of eye, letting it run to

other side to remove chemicals thoroughly. Cover with sterile compress and call doctor.

Choking — Get behind the victim, wrap your arms about him above his waist. Make a fist with one hand and place it, with large thumb knuckle pressing inward, just below the point of the "V" of the rib cage. Grasp the fist with the other hand and give several hard upward thrusts or hugs. As last resort, lean victim forward and slap back between shoulder blades. Start mouth-to-mouth resuscitation if breathing stops. Send for physician or rush victim to hospital.

Convulsions — Place person on back on bed or rug so he can't hurt himself. Loosen clothing. Turn head to side. Put thick wad of cloth between jaws so patient can't bite tongue. Raise and pull lower jaw forward. Sponge head and neck with cool water if convulsions do not stop. Send for doctor.

Cuts (minor) — Apply mild antiseptic and sterile compress after washing with soap under warm running water.

Electric shock — If possible, turn off power. Don't touch victim until contact is broken; pull him from contact with rope, wooden pole, or loop of dry cloth. Start artificial respiration if breathing has stopped. Send for doctor.

Foreign body in eye — Touch object with moistened corner of handkerchief if it can be seen. If it cannot be seen or does not come out after a few attempts, take patient to doctor. Do not rub eye, since this may force item in deeper.

Fainting — Seat patient and fan his face if he feels faint. Lower head to knees. Lay him down with head turned to side if he becomes unconscious. Loosen clothing and open windows. Wave aromatic spirits of ammonia or smelling salts under nose. Keep patient lying quietly for at least 15 minutes after he regains consciousness. Call doctor if faint lasts for more than a few minutes.

Falls — Send for physician if patient has continued pain.

Cover wound with sterile dressing and stop any severe bleeding. Do not move patient unless absolutely necessary — as in case of fire — if broken bone is suspected. Keep patient warm and comfortable.

Poisoning — Call doctor. Use antidote listed on label if container is found. Call local Poison Control Center if possible. Except for lye, other caustics, and pertroleum products, induce vomiting unless victim is unconscious. Give milk if poision or antidote is unknown.

Shock (injury-related) — Keep the victim lying down; if uncertain as to his injuries, keep the victim flat on his back. Maintain the victim's normal body temperature; if the weather is cold or damp, place blankets or extra clothing over and under the victim; if weather is hot, provide shade. Get medical care as soon as possible.

Snakebites — Immediately get victim to a hospital. If there is mild swelling or pain, apply a consticting band 2 to 4 inches above the bite. Keep the victim calm and immobilize the bitten extremity, keeping it at or below heart level. Cold therapy is not recommended. If the snake can be killed without risk or delay, it should be brought, with care, to the hospital for identification. If symptoms such as rapid swelling and severe pain develop, a $1/2$-inch incision over the fang marks and suction should be performed immediately. The cut should be made with a sharp sterilized blade just through the skin and suction done for 30 minutes with a suction cup or mouth.

Stings from insects — If possible, remove stinger and apply solution of ammonia and water, or paste of baking soda. Call physician immediately if body swells or patient collapses. Prevent recurrence of severe allergic reaction via desensitization treatment from doctor.

Unconsciousness — Send for doctor and place person on stomach with his head turned to side. Start resuscitation if he stops breathing. Never give food or liquids to an unconscious person.

Mouth-to-Mouth Resuscitation

Stressing that your breath can save a life, the American Red Cross gives the following directions for mouth-to-mouth resuscitation if the victim is not breathing:

- Turn victim on his back and begin artificial respiration at once.
- Wipe out quickly any foreign matter visible in the mouth, using your fingers or a cloth wrapped around your fingers.
- Tilt victim's head back.
- Pull or push jaw into jutting-out position.
- If victim is a small child, place your mouth tightly over his mouth and nose and blow gently into his lungs about 20 times a minute. If victim is adult, cover the mouth with the mouth, pinch his nostrils shut, and blow vigorously about 12 times a minute.
- If unable to get air into lungs of victim, and if head and jaw positions are correct, suspect foreign matter in the throat. To remove it, suspend a small child momentarily by the ankles or hold child with head down for a moment and slap sharply between shoulder blades.
- If victim is an adult, turn him on his side and use same procedure.
- Again, wipe mouth to remove foreign matter.
- Repeat breathing, removing mouth each time to allow for escape of air. Continue until victim breathes for himself.

A Patient's Bill of Rights
Source: American Hospital Association. © copyright 1972.

Often, as a hospital patient, you feel you have little control over your circumstances. You do, however, have some important rights. They have been enumerated by the American Hospital Association.

1. The patient has the right to considerate and respectful care.

2. The patient has the right to obtain from his physician complete current information concerning his diagnosis, treatment, and prognosis in terms the patient can be reasonably expected to understand. When it is not medically advisable to give such information to the patient, the information should be made available to an appropriate person in his behalf. He has the right to know, by name, the physician responsible for coordinating his care.

3. The patient has the right to receive from his physician information necessary to give informed consent prior to the start of any procedure and/or treatment. Except in emergencies, such information for informed consent should include but not necessarily be limited to the specific procedure and/or treatment, the medically significant risks involved, and the probable duration of incapacitation. Where medically significant alternatives for care or treatment exist, or when the patient requests information concerning medical alternatives, the patient has the right to such information. The patient also has the right to know the name of the person responsible for the procedures and/or treatment.

4. The patient has the right to refuse treatment to the extent permitted by law and to be informed of the medical consequences of his action.

5. The patient has the right to every consideration of his privacy concerning his own medical care program. Case discussion, consultation, examination, and treatment are confidential and should be conducted discreetly. Those not directly involved in his care must have the permission of the patient to be present.

6. The patient has the right to expect that all communications and records pertaining to his care should be treated as confidential.

7. The patient has the right to expect that within its capacity a hospital must make reasonable response to the request of a patient for services. The hospital must provide evaluation, service, and/or referral as indicated by the urgency of the case. When medically permissable, a patient may be transferred to another facility only after he has received complete information and explanation concerning the need for and alternatives to such a transfer. The institution to which the patient is to be transferred must first have accepted the patient for transfer.

8. The patient has the right to obtain information as to any relationship of his hospital to other health care and education institutions insofar as this care is concerned. The patient has the right to obtain information as to the existence of any professional relationships among individuals, by name, who are treating him.

9. The patient has the right to be advised if the hospital proposes to engage in or perform human experimentation affecting his care or treatment. The patient has the right to refuse to participate in such research projects.

10. The patient has the right to expect reasonable continuity of care. He has the right to know in advance what appointment times and physicians are available and where. The patient has the right to expect that the hospital will provide a mechanism whereby he is informed by his physician of the patient's continuing health care requirements following discharge.

11. The patient has the right to examine and receive an explanation of his bill, regardless of the source of payment.

12. The patient has the right to know what hospital rules and regulations apply to his conduct as a patient

Heart Disease

Warning Signs

Source: American Heart Association

Of Heart Attack
• Prolonged, oppressive pain or unusual discomfort in the center of the chest
• Pain may radiate to the shoulder, arm, neck or jaw
• Sweating may accompany pain or discomfort
• Nausea and vomiting may also occur
• Shortness of breath may accompany other signs
The American Heart Association advises immediate action at the onset of these symptoms. The Association points out that over half of heart attack victims die before they reach the hospital and that the average victim waits 3 hours before seeking help.

Of Stroke
• Sudden temporary weakness or numbness of face or limbs on one side of the body
• Temporary loss of speech, or trouble speaking or understanding speech
• Temporary dimness or loss of vision, particularly in one eye
• An episode of double vision
• Unexplained dizziness or unsteadiness
• Change in personality, mental ability
• New or unusual pattern of headaches

Major Risk Factors

Blood pressure— systolic pressure under 120 is normal; systolic pressure over 150
= 2 times the risk of heart attack
= 4 times the risk of stroke

Cholesterol— level under 194 is normal;
level of 250 or over
= 3 times the risk of heart attack or stroke

Cigarettes— with non-smoking considered normal;
smoking one pack a day
= 2 times the risk of heart attack
= 4 times the risk of stroke

U.S. DEATHS DUE TO CARDIOVASCULAR DISEASES BY MAJOR TYPE OF DISORDER, 1979

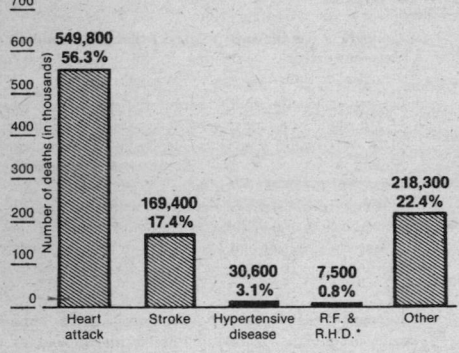

*Rheumatic Fever and Rheumatic Heart Disease
Source: National Center for Health Statistics
U.S. Department of Health and Human Services

ESTIMATED ECONOMIC COSTS IN BILLIONS OF DOLLARS OF CARDIOVASCULAR DISEASES BY TYPE OF EXPENDITURE, 1982

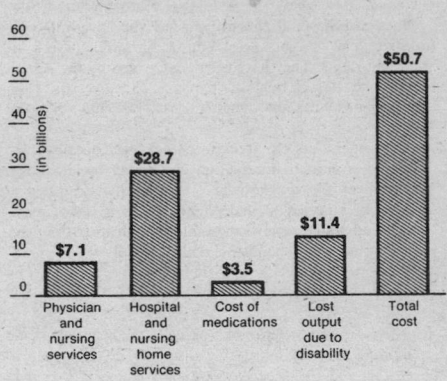

Source: American Heart Association

Cardiovascular Disease Statistical Summary

Cost — 50.7 billion (AHA est.) in 1982.

Prevalence — 41,290,000 Americans have some form of heart and blood vessel disease.
• hypertension — 35,520,000 (nearly one in 4 adults).
• coronary heart disease — 4,400,000.
• rheumatic heart disease — 1,920,000.
• stroke — 1,780,000.

Mortality — 997,766 in 1976 (52% of all deaths). 1979 (AHA est.): 975,550 (51%).
• one-fourth of all persons killed by CVD are under age 65.

Congenital or inborn heart defects — 35 recognizable types of defects.
• about 25,000 babies are born every year with heart defects.
• post-natal mortality from heart defects had been reduced to 6,500 in 1979.

Heart attack — caused 549,800 deaths in 1979.
• 4,400,000 alive today have history of heart attack and/or angina pectoris.
• 350,000 a year die of heart attack before they reach hospital.
• As many as 1,500,000 Americans will have a heart attack this year and about 550,000 of them will die.
Stroke — killed 169,400 in 1979; afflicts 1,780,000.
CCU — most of the 7,000 general hospitals in U.S. have coronary care capability.
Hypertension (high blood pressure) — 35,520,000 adults.
• easily detected and usually controllable, but only a minority have it under adequate control.
Rheumatic heart disease — 100,000 children; 1,820,000 adults.
• killed 13,110 in 1976, 7,500 in 1979.
Note: All mortality data are estimates based on 1979 provisional data.

Stress: How Much Can Affect Your Health?

Source: Reprinted with permission from the *Journal of Psychosomatic Research*, Vol. 11, pp. 213-218, T.H. Holmes, M.D.; The Social Readjustment Rating Scale © 1967, Pergamon Press, Ltd.

Change, both good and bad, can create stress and stress, if sufficiently severe, can lead to illness. Drs. Thomas Holmes and Minoru Masudu, psychiatrists at the University of Washington in Seattle, have developed the Social Readjustment Rating Scale. In their study, they gave a point value to stressful events. The psychiatrists discovered that in 79 percent of the persons studied major illness followed the accumulation of stress-related changes totaling over 300 points in one year. The scale follows:

The Social Readjustment Rating Scale

Life Event	Value
Death of Spouse	100
Divorce	73
Marital separation from mate	65
Detention in jail or other institution	63
Death of a close family member	63
Major personal injury or illness	53
Marriage	50
Being fired at work	47
Marital reconciliation with mate	45
Retirement from work	45
Major change in the health or behavior of a family member	44
Pregnancy	40
Sexual difficulties	39
Gaining a new family member (e.g., through birth, adoption, oldster moving in, etc.)	39
Major business readjustment (e.g., merger, reorganization, bankruptcy, etc.)	39
Major change in financial state (e.g., a lot worse off or a lot better off than usual)	38
Death of a close friend	37
Changing to a different line of work	36
Major change in the number of arguments with spouse (e.g., either a lot more or a lot less than usual regarding child-rearing, personal habits, etc.)	35
Taking out a mortgage or loan for a major purchase (e.g. for a home, business, etc.)	31
Foreclosure on a mortgage or loan	30
Major change in responsibilities at work (e.g., promotion, demotion, lateral transfer)	29
Son or daughter leaving home (e.g., marriage, attending college, etc.)	29
In-law troubles	29
Outstanding personal achievement	28
Wife beginning or ceasing work outside the home	26
Beginning or ceasing formal schooling	26
Major change in living conditions (e.g., building a new home, remodeling, deterioration of home or neighborhood)	25
Revision of personal habits (dress, manners, association, etc.)	24
Troubles with the boss	23
Major change in working hours or conditions	20
Change in residence	20
Changing to a new school	20
Major change in usual type and/or amount of recreation	19
Major change in church activities (e.g., a lot more or a lot less than usual)	19
Major change in social activities (e.g., clubs, dancing, movies, visiting, etc.)	18
Taking out a mortgage or loan for a lesser purchase (e.g., for a car, TV, freezer, etc.)	17
Major change in sleeping habits (a lot more or a lot less sleep, or change in part of day when asleep)	16
Major change in number of family get-togethers (e.g., a lot more or a lot less than usual)	15
Major change in eating habits (a lot more or a lot less food intake, or very different meal hours or surroundings)	15
Vacation	13
Christmas	12
Minor violations of the law (e.g., traffic tickets, jaywalking, disturbing the peace, etc.)	11

Cancer Warnings

Source: American Cancer Society

Site	Warning signal— see your doctor	Comment
Breast	Lump or thickening in the breast, or unusual discharge from nipple.	The leading cause of cancer death in women.
Colon and rectum	Change in bowel habits; bleeding.	Considered a highly curable disease when digital and proctoscopic examinations are included in routine checkups.
Lung	Persistent cough, or lingering respiratory ailment.	The leading cause of cancer death among men and rising mortality among women.
Oral (including pharynx)	Sore that does not heal; difficulty in swallowing.	Many more lives should be saved because the mouth is easily accessible to visual examination by physicians and dentists.
Skin	Sore that does not heal, or change in wart or mole.	Skin cancer is readily detected by observation, and diagnosed by simple biopsy.
Uterus	Unusual bleeding or discharge.	Uterine cancer mortality has declined 70% during the last 40 years with wider application of the Pap test. Postmenopausal women with abnormal bleeding should be checked.
Kidney and bladder	Urinary difficulty, bleeding.	Protective measures for workers in high-risk industries are helping to eliminate one of the important causes of these cancers.
Larynx	Hoarseness, difficulty in swallowing.	Readily curable if caught early.

Prostate	Urinary diffculty.	Occurs mainly in men over 60, the disease can be detected by palpation at regular checkup.
Stomach	Indigestion.	An 80% decline in mortality in 50 years, for reasons yet unknown.
Leukemia	Leukemia is a cancer of blood-forming tissues and is characterized by the abnormal production of immature white blood cells. Acute lymphocytic leukemia strikes mainly children and is treated by drugs which have extended life from a few months to as much as 10 years. Chronic leukemia strikes usually after age 25 and progresses less rapidly.	
Lymphomas (including multiple myeloma)	These cancers arise in the lymph system and include Hodgkin's disease and lymphosarcoma. Some patients with lymphatic cancers can lead normal lives for many years. Five-year survival rate for Hodgkin's disease increased from 25% to 54% in 20 years.	

Common Food Additives: How Safe Are They?

Source: Reprinted from "Chemical Cuisine" which is available from Center for Science in the Public Interest, 1755 S St., N.W., Washington, D.C. 20009, for $2.50, copyright 1978.

Avoid

Artificial Colorings: Most are synthetic chemicals not found in nature. Some are safer than others, but names of colorings are not listed on label. Used mostly in foods of low nutritional value, usually indicating that fruit or natural ingredient omitted.

Additive	Use	Comment
Blue No. 1	In beverages, candy, baked goods.	Very poorly tested.
Blue No. 2	Pet food, beverages, candy.	Very poorly tested.
Citrus Red No. 2	Skin of some Florida oranges.	May cause cancer. Does not seep through into pulp.
Green No. 3	Candy, beverages.	Needs better testing.
Orange B	Hot dogs.	Causes cancer in animals.
Red No. 3	Cherries in fruit cocktail, candy, baked goods.	May cause cancer.
Red. No. 40	Soda, candy, gelatin, desserts, pastry, pet food, sausage.	Causes cancer in mice. Widely used.
Yellow No. 5	Gelatin dessert, candy, pet food, baked goods.	Poorly tested; might cause cancer. Some people allergic to it. Widely used.
Brominated Vegetable Oil (BVO)	Emulsifier, clouding agent. Citrus-flavored soft drinks.	Residue found in body fat; safer substitutes available.
Butylated Hydroxytoluene (BHT)	Antioxidant. Cereals, chewing gum, potato chips, oils, etc.	May cause cancer; stored in body fat; can cause allergic reaction. Safer alternatives.
Caffeine	Stimulant. Naturally in coffee, tea cocoa; added to soft drinks.	Causes sleeplessness; may cause miscarriages or birth defects.
Quinine	Flavoring. Tonic water, quinine water, bitter lemon.	Poorly tested; some possibility that may cause birth defects.
Saccharin	Noncaloric sweetener. "Diet" products.	Causes cancer in animals.
Sodium Nitrite, Sodium Nitrate	Preservative, coloring, flavoring. Bacon, ham, frankfurters, luncheon meats, smoked fish, corned beef.	Prevents growth of botulism bacteria but can lead to formation of small amounts of cancer-causing nitrosamines, particularly in fried bacon.

Caution

Artificial Coloring: Yellow No. 6	Beverages, sausage, baked goods, candy, gelatin.	Appears safe, but can cause allergic reactions.
Artificial Flavoring	Soda, candy, breakfast cereals, gelatin deserts.	Hundreds of chemicals used to mimic natural flavors, almost exclusively in "junk" foods; indicates "real thing" is left out. May cause hyperactivity in some children.
Butylated Hydroxyanisole (BHA)	Antioxidant. Cereals, chewing gum, potato chips, oils.	Appears safer than BHT but needs better testing. Safer substitutes available.
Heptyl Paraben	Preservative. Beer.	Probably safe, has not been tested in presence of alcohol.
Monosodium Glutamate (MSG)	Flavor enhancer. Soup, seafood, poultry, cheese, sauces, stews, etc.	Damages brain cells in infant mice, causes "Chinese restaurant syndrome" (headache and burning or tightness in head, neck, arms) in some sensitive adults.
Phosphoric Acid; Phosphates	Acidifier, chelating agent, buffer, emulsifier, nutrient, discoloration inhibitor. Baked goods, cheese, powdered foods, cured meat, soda, breakfast cereals, dried potatoes.	Useful chemicals that are not toxic, but their widespread use creates dietary imbalance that may be causing osteoporosis.
Propyl Gallate	Antioxidant. Oil, meat products, potato stocks, chicken soup base, chewing gum.	Not adequately tested, use in frequently unnecessary.
Sulfur Dioxide; Sodium Bisulfite	Preservative, bleach. Sliced fruit, wine, grape juice, dried potatoes, dried fruit.	Can destroy vitamin B-1, but otherwise safe.

Safe

The following common food additives are rated as safe by the Center for Science in the Public Interest. Space restrictions prohibit a detailed description of each additive. The additives are: Alginate, Propylene & Glycol Alginate, Alpha Tocopherol, Ascorbic Acid, Erythorbic Acid, Beta Carotene, Calcium (Sodium) Propionate, Calcium (or Sodium) Stearoyl Lactylate, Carrageenan, Casein, Sodium Caseinate, Citric Acid, Sodium Citrate, EDTA, Ferrous Gluconate, Fumaric Acid, Gelatin, Glycerin (Glycerol), gums (Locust Bean, Guar, Furcelleran, Arabic, Karaya, Tragacanth, Ghatti), Hydrolyzed Vegetable Protein (HVP), Lactic Acid, Lactose, Lecithin, Mannitol, Mon-and-Diglycerides, Polysorbate 60, 65 and 80, Sodium Benzoate, Sodium Carboxymethylcellulose (CMC), Sorbic Acid, Potassium Sorbate, Sorbitan Monostearate, Sorbitol, Starch and Modified Starch, Vanillan, Ethyl Vanillan.

Special Considerations

Salt (Sodium chloride)	Flavoring. Most processed foods: soup, potato chips, crackers, cured meat, etc.	Large amounts of sodium may cause high blood pressure in susceptible persons and increase risk of heart attack and stroke.
Sugars: Corn Syrup, Dextrose, Glucose, Invert Sugar, Sugar	Sweeteners. Candy, soft drinks, cookies, syrups, toppings, sweetened cereals and many other foods.	Mostly in foods with low, if any, nutritional value. Excess sugars may promote tooth decay and precipitate diabetes in susceptible persons; condensed sources of calories.

Food and Nutrition

Food contains proteins, carbohydrates, fats, water, vitamins and minerals. Nutrition is the way your body takes in and uses these ingredients to maintain proper functioning. If you aren't eating foods that your body needs, you suffer from poor nutrition and, sooner or later, your health will deteriorate.

Protein

Proteins are composed of amino acids and are indispensable in the diet. They build, maintain, and repair the body. Best sources: eggs, milk, soybeans, nuts, fish, meat, poultry. No one of these foods will supply all the necessary proteins.

Fats

Fats provide energy by furnishing calories to the body, and by carrying vitamins A, D, E, and K. They are the most concentrated source of energy in the diet. Best sources: butter, margarine, salad oils, nuts, cream, eggs, most cheeses, lard, meat.

Carbohydrates

Carbohydrates provide energy for body function and activity by supplying immediate calories. The 3 forms of carbohydrates are sugars, starches, and cellulose. Best sources: wheats and cereals, legumes, nuts, potatoes (with skin), fruits, honey.

Water

Water dissolves and transports other nutrients throughout the body aiding the process of digestion, absorption, circulation, and excretion. It also helps regulate body temperature. We get water from all foods.

Vitamins

Vitamin A—promotes good eyesight and helps keep the skin and mucous membranes resistant to infection. Best sources: liver, carrots, sweet potatoes, kale, collard greens, turnips, whole milk.

Vitamin B1 (thiamine)—essential to the nervous system, heart, liver. Best sources: meat, fish, poultry, wheat germ, brewers' yeast, brown rice, whole grain cereals.

Vitamin B2 (riboflavin)—an aid to healthy eyes. Best sources: liver, almonds, wheat germ, mushrooms, turnip greens, whole milk, milk products.

Vitamin B6 (pyridoxine)—important in the regulation of the central nervous system. Best sources: whole grains, meats, nuts, brewers' yeast.

Vitamin B12 (cobalamin)—necessary for the formation of red blood cells. Best sources: meat, fish, eggs, soybeans.

Niacin—maintains the health of skin, tongue, and digestive system. Best sources: poultry, peanuts, fish, organ meats, milk and milk products, eggs.

Other B vitamins are—biotin, choline, folic acid (folacin), inositol, PABA (para-aminobenzoic acid), and pantothenic acid.

Vitamin C (ascorbic acid)—maintains collagen, a protein necessary for the formation of skin, ligaments, and bones. It helps heal wounds and mend fractures, and aids in resisting some types of virus and bacterial infections. Best sources: citrus fruits and juices, turnips, broccoli, Brussels sprouts, potatoes and sweet potatoes, tomatoes, cabbage.

Vitamin D—important for bone development. Best sources: sunlight, fortified milk and milk products, fish, egg yolks, organ meats.

Vitamin E (tocopherol)—helps protect red blood cells. May aid the circulatory system and counteract the aging process. Best sources: wheat germ, whole grains, eggs, peanuts, organ meats, margarine, vegetable oils, green leafy vegetables.

Vitamin K—necessary for formation of prothrombin, which helps blood to clot. Best sources: green leafy vegetables, tomatoes, egg yolks, oats, wheat, rye.

Minerals

Calcium—the most abundant mineral in the body, works with phosphorus in building and maintaining bones and teeth. Best sources: whole sesame seeds, cheese, milk and milk products, and blackstrap molasses.

Phosphorus—the 2d most abundant mineral, performs more functions than any other mineral, and plays a part in nearly every chemical reaction in the body. Best source: wheat germ, brewers' yeast, powdered skim milk.

Iron—the 2d most essential trace element in the body, it is necessary for the formation of myoglobin, which transports oxygen to muscle tissue, and hemoglobin, which transports oxygen in the blood. Best sources: organ meats, molasses, beans, green leafy vegetables, and shellfish.

Other minerals—chromium, cobalt, copper, fluorine, iodine, magnesium, manganese, molybdenum, potassium, selenium, sodium, sulfur, and zinc.

Recommended Daily Dietary Allowances

Source: Food and Nutrition Board, National Academy of Sciences—National Research Council (Revised 1980)

The allowances are amounts of nutrients recommended as adequate for maintenance of good nutrition in almost all healthy persons in the U.S. Diets should be based on a variety of common foods in order to provide other nutrients for which human requirements have been less well defined.

	Age (years)	Weight (lbs.)	Protein (grams)	Fat soluble Vitamins			Water soluble Vitamins							Minerals					
				Vitamin A[1]	Vitamin D[2]	Vitamin E[3]	Vitamin C (mg.)	Thiamin (mg.)	Riboflavin (mg.)	Niacin (mg.)[4]	Folacin (micrograms)	Vitamin B6 (mg.)	Vitamin B12 (micrograms)	Calcium (mg.)	Phosphorus (mg.)	Magnesium (mg.)	Iron (mg.)	Zinc (mg.)	Iodine (micrograms)
Infants	to 6 mos.	13 kg	2.2	420	10	3	35	0.3	0.4	6	30	0.3	0.5	360	240	50	10	3	40
	to 1 yr.	20 kg	2.0	400	10	4	35	0.5	0.6	8	45	0.6	1.5	540	360	70	15	5	50
Children	1-3	29	23	400	10	5	45	0.7	0.8	9	100	0.9	2.0	800	800	150	15	10	70
	4-6	44	30	500	10	6	45	0.9	1.0	11	200	1.3	2.5	800	800	200	10	10	90
	7-10	62	34	700	10	7	45	1.2	1.4	16	300	1.6	3.0	800	800	250	10	10	120
Males	11-14	99	45	1000	10	8	50	1.4	1.6	18	400	1.8	3.0	1200	1200	350	18	15	150
	15-18	145	56	1000	10	10	60	1.4	1.7	18	400	2.0	3.0	1200	1200	400	18	15	150
	19-22	154	56	1000	7.5	10	60	1.5	1.7	19	400	2.2	3.0	800	800	350	10	15	150
	23-50	154	56	1000	5	10	60	1.4	1.6	18	400	2.2	3.0	800	800	350	10	15	150
	51+	154	56	1000	5	10	60	1.2	1.4	16	400	2.2	3.0	800	800	350	10	15	150
Females	11-14	101	46	800	10	8	50	1.1	1.3	15	400	1.8	3.0	1200	1200	300	18	15	150
	15-18	120	46	800	10	8	60	1.1	1.3	14	400	2.0	3.0	1200	1200	300	18	15	150
	19-22	120	44	800	7.5	8	60	1.1	1.3	14	400	2.0	3.0	800	800	300	18	15	150
	23-50	120	44	800	5	8	60	1.0	1.2	13	400	2.0	3.0	800	800	300	18	15	150
	51+	120	44	800	5	8	60	1.0	1.2	13	400	2.0	3.0	800	800	300	10	15	150
Pregnant		+30		+200	+5	+2	+20	+0.4	+0.3	+2	+400	+0.6	+1.0	+400	+400	+150	[5]	+5	+25
Lactating		+20		+400	+5	+3	+40	+0.5	+0.5	+5	+100	+0.5	+1.0	+400	+400	+150	[5]	+10	+50

(1) Retinol equivalents. (2) Micrograms of cholecalciferol. (3) Milligrams alpha-tocopherol equivalents. (4) Niacin equivalents. (5) The use of 30-60 milligrams of supplemental iron is recommended.

Nutritive Value of Food (Calories, Proteins, etc.)

Source: Home and Garden Bulletin No. 72 (revised Sept. 1978). U.S. Agriculture Department

Available from Supt. of Documents. U. S. Government Printing Office. Washington, DC 20402

Food	Measure	Food Energy (calories)	Protein (grams)	Fat (grams)	Saturated fats (grams)	Carbohydrate (grams)	Calcium (milligrams)	Iron (milligrams)	Vitamin A (I.U.)	Thiamin (milligrams)	Riboflavin (milligrams)	Niacin (milligrams)	Ascorbic acid (milligrams)
Dairy products													
Cheese, cheddar	1 oz.	115	7	9	6.1	T	204	.2	300	.01	.11	T	0
Cheese, cottage, small curd	1 cup	220	26	9	6.0	6	126	.3	340	.04	.34	.3	T
Cheese, cream	1 oz.	100	2	10	6.2	1	23	.3	400	T	.06	T	0
Cheese, Swiss	1 oz.	105	8	8	5.0	1	272	T	240	.01	.10	T	0
Cheese, pasteurized-process spread, American	1 oz.	82	5	6	3.8	2	159	.1	220	.01	.12	T	0
Half-and-Half	1 tbsp	20	T	2	1.1	1	16	T	20	.01	.02	T	T
Cream, sour	1 tbsp.	25	T	3	1.6	1	14	T	90	T	.02	T	T
Milk, whole	1 cup	150	8	8	5.1	11	291	.1	310	.09	.40	.2	2
Milk, nonfat (skim)	1 cup	85	8	T	.3	12	302	.1	500	.09	.37	.2	2
Buttermilk	1 cup	100	8	2	1.3	12	285	.1	80	.08	.38	.1	2
Milkshake, chocolate	10.6 oz	355	9	8	5.0	63	396	.9	260	.14	.67	.4	0
Ice Cream, hardened	1 cup	270	5	14	8.9	32	176	.1	540	.05	.33	.1	1
Sherbet	1 cup	270	2	4	2.4	59	103	.3	190	.03	.09	.1	4
Yogurt, fruit-flavored	8 oz	230	10	3	1.8	42	343	.2	120	.08	.40	.2	1
Eggs													
Fried in butter	1	85	5	6	2.4	1	26	.9	290	.03	.13	T	0
Hard-cooked	1	80	6	6	1.7	1	28	1.0	260	.04	.14	T	0
Scrambled in butter (milk added)	1	95	6	7	2.8	1	47	.9	310	.04	.16	T	0
Fats & oils													
Butter	1 tbsp.	100	T	12	7.2	T	3	T	430	T	T	T	0
Margarine	1 tbsp.	100	T	12	2.1	T	3	T	470	T	T	T	0
Salad dressing, blue cheese	1 tbsp	75	1	8	1.6	1	12	T	30	T	.02	T	T
Salad dressing, French	1 tbsp	65	T	6	1.1	3	2	.1	-	-	-	-	-
Salad dressing, Italian	1 tbsp.	85	T	9	1.6	1	2	T	T	T	T	T	-
Mayonnaise	1 tbsp.	100	T	11	2.0	T	3	.1	40	T	.01	T	-
Meat, poultry, fish													
Bluefish, baked with butter or margarine	3 oz	135	22	4	-	0	25	0.6	40	.09	.08	1.6	-
Clams, raw, meat only	3 oz.	65	11	1	-	2	59	5.2	90	.08	.15	1.1	8
Crabmeat, white or king, canned	1 cup	135	24	3	.6	1	61	1.1	-	.11	.11	2.6	-
Fish sticks, breaded, cooked, frozen	1 oz.	50	5	3	-	2	3	.1	0	.01	.02	.5	-
Salmon, pink, canned	3 oz.	120	17	5	.9	0	167	.7	60	.03	.16	6.8	-
Sardines, Atlantic, canned in oil	3 oz.	175	20	9	3.0	0	372	2.5	190	.02	.17	4.6	-
Shrimp, French fried	3 oz.	190	17	9	2.3	9	61	1.7	-	.03	.07	2.3	-
Tuna, canned in oil	3 oz.	170	24	7	1.7	0	7	1.6	70	.04	.10	10.1	-
Bacon, broiled or fried crisp	2 slices	85	4	8	2.5	T	2	.5	0	.08	.05	.8	-
Ground beef, broiled, 10% fat	3 oz.	185	23	10	4.0	0	10	3.0	20	.08	.20	5.1	-
Roast beef, relatively lean	3 oz.	165	25	7	2.8	0	11	3.2	10	.06	.19	4.5	-
Beef steak, lean and fat	3 oz.	330	20	27	11.3	0	9	2.5	50	.05	.15	4.0	-
Beef & vegetable stew	1 cup	220	16	11	4.9	15	29	2.9	2,400	.15	.17	4.7	17
Lamb, chop, lean and fat	3.1 oz.	360	18	32	14.8	0	8	1.0	-	.11	.19	4.1	-
Ham, light cure, lean and fat	3 oz.	245	18	19	6.8	0	8	2.2	0	.40	.15	3.1	-
Pork, chop, lean and fat	2.7 oz	305	19	25	8.9	0	9	2.7	0	.75	.22	4.5	-
Bologna	1 slice	85	3	8	3.0	T	2	.5	-	.05	.06	.7	-
Frankfurter, cooked	1	170	7	15	5.6	1	3	.8	-	.08	.11	1.4	-
Sausage, pork link, cooked	1 link	60	2	6	2.1	T	1	.3	0	.10	.04	.5	-
Veal, cutlet, braised or boiled	3 oz.	185	23	9	4.0	0	9	2.7	-	.06	.21	4.6	-
Chicken, drumstick, fried, bones removed	1.3 oz	90	12	4	1.1	T	6	.9	50	.03	.15	2.7	-
Chicken, half broiler, broiled, bones removed	6.2 oz.	240	42	7	2.2	0	16	3.0	160	.09	.34	15.5	-
Chicken a la king	1 cup	470	27	34	12.7	12	127	2.5	1,130	.10	.42	5.4	12
Chicken potpie, baked, 1/3 of 9 in. diam. pie	1 piece	545	23	31	11.3	42	70	3.0	3,090	.34	.31	5.5	5
Fruits & products													
Apple, raw, 2-3/4 in. diam.	1	80	T	1	-	20	10	.4	120	.04	.03	.1	6
Applejuice	1 cup	120	T	T	-	30	15	1.5	-	.02	.05	.2	2
Applesauce, canned, sweetened	1 cup	230	1	T	-	61	10	1.3	100	.05	.03	.1	3
Banana, raw	1	100	1	T	-	26	10	.8	230	.06	.07	.8	12
Cherries, sweet, raw	10	45	1	T	-	12	15	.3	70	.03	.04	.3	7
Fruit cocktail, canned, in heavy syrup	1 cup	195	1	T	-	50	23	1.0	360	.05	.03	1.0	5
Grapefruit, raw, medium, white	1/2	45	1	T	-	12	19	.5	10	.05	.02	.2	44
Grapes, Thompson seedless	10	35	T	T	-	9	6	.2	50	.03	.02	.2	2
Lemonade, frozen, diluted	1 cup	105	T	T	-	28	2	.1	10	.01	.02	.2	17
Cantaloupe, 5-in. diam.	1/2	80	2	T	-	20	38	1.1	9,240	.11	.08	1.6	90
Orange, 2-5/8 in. diam.	1	65	1	T	-	16	54	.5	260	.13	.05	.5	66
Orange juice, frozen, diluted	1 cup	120	2	T	-	29	25	.2	540	.23	.03	.9	120
Peach, raw, 2-1/2 in. diam.	1	40	1	T	-	10	9	.5	1,330	.02	.05	1.0	7
Peaches, canned in syrup	1 cup	200	1	T	-	51	10	.8	1,100	.03	.05	1.5	8
Pear, raw, Bartlett, 2-1/2 in. diam.	1	100	1	1	-	25	13	.5	30	.03	.07	.2	7
Pineapple, heavy syrup pack, crushed, chunks	1 cup	190	1	T	-	49	28	.8	130	.20	.05	.5	18
Raisins, seedless	1 cup	420	4	T	-	112	90	5.1	30	.16	.12	.7	1
Strawberries, whole	1 cup	55	1	1	-	13	31	1.5	90	.04	.10	.9	88
Watermelon, 4 by 8 in. wedge	1 wedge	110	2	1	-	27	30	2.1	2,510	.13	.13	.9	30
Grain products													
Bagel, egg	1	165	6	2	.5	28	9	1.2	30	.14	.10	1.2	0
Biscuit, 2 in. diam., from home recipe	1	105	2	5	1.2	13	34	.4	T	.08	.08	.7	T
Bread, raisin	1 slice	65	2	1	.2	13	18	.6	T	.09	.06	.6	T
Bread, white, enriched, soft-crumb	1 slice	70	2	1	.2	13	21	.6	T	.10	.06	.8	T
Bread, whole wheat, soft-crumb	1 slice	65	3	1	.1	14	24	.8	T	.09	.03	.8	T
Oatmeal or rolled oats	1 cup	130	5	2	.4	23	22	1.4	0	.19	.05	.2	0
Bran flakes (40% bran), added sugar, salt, iron, vitamins	1 cup	105	4	1	-	28	19	12.4	1,650	.41	.49	4.1	12
Corn flakes, added sugar, salt, iron, vitamins	1 cup	95	2	T	-	21	*	0.6	1,180	.29	.35	2.9	9
Rice, puffed, added iron, thiamin, niacin	1 cup	60	1	T	-	13	3	.3	0	.07	.01	.7	0

(continued)

(continued)

Food	Measure	Food Energy (calories)	Protein (grams)	Fat (grams)	Saturated fats (grams)	Carbohydrate (grams)	Calcium (milligrams)	Iron (milligrams)	Vitamin A (I.U.)	Thiamin (milligrams)	Riboflavin (milligrams)	Niacin (milligrams)	Ascorbic acid (milligrams)
Wheat, shredded, plain, 1 biscuit or 1/2 cup	1 serving	90	2	1	-	20	11	.9	0	.06	.03	1.1	0
Cake, angel food, 1/12 of cake	1	135	3	T	-	32	50	.2	0	.03	.08	.3	0
Coffeecake, 1/6 cake	1	230	5	7	2.0	38	44	1.2	120	.14	.15	1.8	T
Cupcake, 2-1/2 in. diam., with chocolate icing	1	130	2	5	2.0	21	47	.4	60	.05	.06	.4	T
Boston cream pie with custard filling, 1/12 of cake	1	210	3	6	1.9	34	46	.7	140	.09	.11	.8	T
Fruitcake, dark, 1/30 of loaf	1	55	1	2	.5	9	11	.4	20	.02	.02	.2	T
Cake, pound, 1/17 of loaf	1	160	2	10	2.5	16	6	.5	80	.05	.06	.4	0
Brownies, with nuts, from commercial recipe	1	85	1	4	.9	13	9	.4	20	.03	.02	.2	T
Cookies, chocolate chip, from home recipe	4	205	2	12	3.5	24	14	.8	40	.06	.06	.5	T
Vanilla wafers	10	185	2	6		30	16	.6	50	.10	.09	.8	0
Crackers, graham	2	55	1	1	.3	10	6	.5	0	.02	.08	.5	0
Crackers, saltines	4	50	1	1	.3	8	2	.5	0	.05	.05	.4	0
Danish pastry, round piece	1	275	5	15	4.7	30	33	1.2	200	.18	.19	1.7	T
Doughnut, cake type	1	100	1	5	1.2	13	10	.4	20	.05	.05	.4	T
Macaroni and cheese, from home recipe	1 cup	430	17	22	8.9	40	362	1.8	860	.20	.40	1.8	T
Muffin, corn	1	125	3	4	1.2	19	42	.7	120	.10	.10	.7	T
Noodles, enriched, cooked	1 cup	200	7	2		37	16	1.4	110	.22	.13	1.9	0
Pancake, plain, from home recipe	1	60	2	2	.5	9	27	.4	30	.06	.07	.5	T
Pie, apple, 1/7 of pie	1	345	3	15	3.9	51	11	.9	40	.15	.11	1.3	2
Pie, banana cream, 1/7 of pie	1	285	6	12	3.8	40	86	1.0	330	.11	.22	1.0	1
Pie, cherry	1	350	4	15	4.0	52	19	.9	590	.16	.12	1.4	T
Pie, lemon, 1/7 of pie	1	305	4	12	3.7	45	17	1.0	200	.09	.12	.7	4
Pie, pecan, 1/7 of pie	1	495	6	27	4.0	61	55	3.7	190	.26	.14	1.0	T
Pie, pumpkin, 1/7 of pie	1	275	5	15	5.4	32	66	1.0	3,210	.11	.18	1.0	T
Pizza, cheese, 1/8 of 12 in. diam. pie	1	145	6	4	1.7	22	86	1.1	230	.16	.18	1.6	4
Popcorn, popped, plain	1 cup	25	1	T	T	5	1	.2	-	-	.01	.1	0
Pretzels, stick	10	10	T	T	-	2	1	T	0	.01	.01	.1	0
Rice, white, enriched, instant, cooked	1 cup	180	4	T	T	40	5	1.3	0	.21	**	1.7	0
Rolls, enriched, brown & serve	1	85	2	2	.4	14	20	.5	T	.10	.06	.9	T
Rolls, frankfurter & hamburger	1	120	3	2	.5	21	30	.8	T	.16	.10	1.3	T
Spaghetti with meat balls & tomato sauce, from home recipe	1 cup	330	19	12	3.3	39	124	3.7	1,590	.25	.30	4.0	22
Legumes, nuts, seeds													
Beans, Great Northern, cooked	1 cup	210	14	1		38	90	4.9	0	.25	.13	1.3	0
Peanuts, roasted in oil, salted	1 cup	840	37	72	13.7	27	107	3.0	-	.46	.19	24.8	0
Peanut butter	1 tbsp.	95	4	8	1.5	3	9	.3	-	.02	.02	2.4	0
Sunflower seeds	1 cup	810	35	69	8.2	29	174	10.3	70	2.84	.33	7.8	-
Sugars & sweets													
Candy, caramels	1 oz.	115	1	3	1.6	22	42	.4	T	.01	.05	.1	T
Candy, milk chocolate	1 oz.	145	2	9	5.5	16	65	.3	80	.02	.10	.1	T
Fudge, chocolate	1 oz.	115	1	3	1.3	21	22	.3	T	.01	.03	.1	T
Candy, hard	1 oz.	110	0	T	-	28	6	.5	0	0	0	0	0
Honey	1 tbsp.	65	T	0	0	17	1	.1	0	T	.01	.1	T
Jams & Preserves	1 tbsp.	55	T	T	-	14	4	.2	T	T	.01	T	T
Sugar, white, granulated	1 tbsp.	45	0	0	0	12	0	T	0	0	0	0	0
Vegetables													
Asparagus, canned, spears	4 spears	15	2	T	-	3	15	1.5	640	.05	.08	.6	12
Beans, lima, thick-seeded	1 cup	170	10	T	-	32	34	2.9	390	.12	.09	1.7	29
Beans, green, from frozen, cuts	1 cup	35	2	T	-	8	54	.9	780	.09	.12	.5	7
Beets, canned, diced or sliced	1 cup	65	2	T	-	15	32	1.2	30	.02	.05	.2	5
Broccoli, cooked	1 stalk	45	6	1	-	8	158	1.4	4,500	.16	.36	1.4	162
Cabbage, raw, coarsely shredded or sliced	1 cup	15	1	T	-	4	34	.3	90	.04	.04	.02	33
Carrots, raw, 7-1/2 by 1-1/8 in.	1	30	1	T	-	7	27	.5	7,930	.04	.04	.4	6
Cauliflower, raw	1 cup	31	3	T	-	6	29	1.3	70	.13	.12	.8	90
Celery, raw	1 stalk	5	T	T	-	2	16	.1	110	.01	.01	.1	4
Collards, cooked	1 cup	65	7	1	-	10	357	1.5	14,820	.21	.38	2.3	144
Corn, sweet, cooked	1 ear	70	2	1	-	16	2	.5	310	.09	.08	1.1	7
Corn, cream style	1 cup	210	5	2	-	51	8	1.5	840	.08	.13	2.6	13
Cucumber, with peel	6-8 slices	5	T	T	-	1	7	.3	70	.01	.01	.1	3
Lettuce, iceberg, chopped	1 cup	5	T	T	-	2	11	.3	180	.03	.03	.2	3
Mushrooms, raw	1 cup	20	2	T	-	3	4	.6	T	.07	.32	2.9	2
Onions, raw, chopped	1 cup	65	3	T	-	15	46	.9	T	.05	.07	.3	17
Peas, frozen, cooked	1 cup	110	8	T	-	19	30	3.0	960	.43	.14	2.7	21
Potatoes, baked, peeled	1	145	4	T	-	33	14	1.1	T	.15	.07	2.7	31
Potatoes, mashed, milk added	1 cup	135	4	2	.7	27	50	.8	40	.17	.11	2.1	21
Potato chips	10	115	1	8	2.1	10	8	.4	T	.04	.01	1.0	3
Potato salad	1 cup	250	7	7	2.0	41	80	1.5	350	.20	.18	2.8	28
Sauerkraut, canned	1 cup	40	2	T	-	9	85	1.2	120	.07	.09	.5	33
Spinach, chopped, from frozen	1 cup	45	6	1	-	8	232	4.3	16,200	.14	.31	.8	39
Squash, summer, cooked	1 cup	30	2	T	-	7	53	.8	820	.11	.17	1.7	21
Sweet potatoes, baked in skin, peeled	1	160	2	1	-	37	46	1.0	9,230	.10	.08	.8	25
Tomatoes, raw	1	25	1	T	-	6	16	.6	1,110	.07	.05	.9	28
Tomato catsup	1 tbsp.	15	T	T	-	4	3	.1	210	.01	.01	.2	2
Tomato juice	1 cup	45	2	T	-	10	17	2.2	1,940	.12	.07	1.9	39
Miscellaneous													
Beer	12 fl. oz.	150	1	0	0	14	18	T		.01	.11	2.2	-
Gin, rum, vodka, whisky, 86 proof	1-1/2 fl. oz.	105	-	0	T	-	-	-	-	-	-	-	-
Wine, table	3-1/2 fl. oz.	85	T	0	0	4	9	.4	-	T	.01	.1	-
Cola-type beverage	12 fl. oz.	145	0	0	0	37	-	-	0	0	0	0	0
Ginger ale	12 fl. oz.	115	0	0	0	29	-	-	0	0	0	0	0
Gelatin dessert	1 cup	140	4	0	0	34	-	-	-	-	-	-	-
Mustard, prepared	1 tsp.	5	T	T	-	T	4	.1	-	-	-	-	-
Olives, pickled, green	4 medium	15	T	2	.2	T	8	.2	40	-	-	-	-
Pickles, dill, whole	1	5	T	T	-	1	17	.7	70	T	.01	T	4
Popsicle, 3 fl. oz.	1	70	0	0	0	18	0	T	0	0	0	0	0
Soup, cream of chicken, prepared with milk	1 cup	180	7	10	4.2	15	172	.5	610	.05	.27	.7	2
Soup, cream of mushroom, prepared with milk	1 cup	215	7	14	5.4	16	191	.5	250	.05	.34	.7	1
Soup, tomato, prepared with water	1 cup	90	2	3	.5	16	15	.7	1,000	.05	.05	1.2	12

T — Indicates trace * — Varies by brand

Birthstones

Source: Jewelry Industry Council

Month	Ancient	Modern	Month	Ancient	Modern
January	Garnet	Garnet	July	Onyx	Ruby
February	Amethyst	Amethyst	August	Carnelian	Sardonyx or Peridot
March	Jasper	Bloodstone or Aquamarine	September	Chrysolite	Sapphire
April	Sapphire	Diamond	October	Aquamarine	Opal or Tourmaline
May	Agate	Emerald	November	Topaz	Topaz
June	Emerald	Pearl, Moonstone, or Alexandrite	December	Ruby	Turquoise or Zircon

Wedding Anniversaries

The traditional names for wedding anniversaries go back many years in social usage. As such names as wooden, crystal, silver, and golden were applied it was considered proper to present the married pair with gifts made of these products or of something related. The list of traditional gifts, with a few allowable revisions in parentheses, is presented below, followed by modern gifts in **bold face**.

1st-Paper, **clocks**
2d-Cotton, **china**
3d-Leather, **crystal & glass**
4th-Linen (silk), **electrical appliances**
5th-Wood, **silverware**
6th-Iron, **wood**
7th-Wool (copper), **desk sets**
8th-Bronze, **linens & lace**
9th-Pottery (china), **leather**

10th-Tin (aluminum), **diamond jewelry**
11th-Steel, **fashion jewelry, accessories**
12th-Silk, **pearls or colored gems**
13th-Lace, **textiles & furs**
14th-Ivory, **gold jewelry**
15th-Crystal, **watches**
20th-China, **platinum**
25th-Silver, **sterling silver**

30th-Pearl, **diamond**
35th-Coral (jade), **jade**
40th-Ruby, **ruby**
45th-Sapphire, **sapphire**
50th-Gold, **gold**
55th-Emerald, **emerald**
60th-Diamond, **diamond**

Canadian Marriage Information

Source: Compiled from information provided by the various provincial government departments and agencies concerned.

Marriageable age, by provinces, for both males and females with and without consent of parents or guardians. In some provinces, the court has authority, given special circumstances, to marry young couples below the minimum age. Most provinces waive the blood test requirement and the waiting period varies across the provinces.

Province	With consent		Without consent		Blood test other province		Wait for license	Wait after license
	Men	Women	Men	Women	Required	Accepted		
Newfoundland	16	16	19	19	None	None	4 days	4 days
Prince Edward Island	16	16	18	18	Yes	Yes	5 days	None
Nova Scotia	(1)	(1)	19	19	None	None	5 days	None
New Brunswick	16	14	18	18	None	None	5 days	None
Quebec	14	12	18	18	None	—	—	None
Ontario	16	16	18	18	None	—	None[2]	3 days
Manitoba	16	16	18	18	Yes	Yes	None	24 hours
Saskatchewan	15	15	18	18	Yes	Yes	5 days	24 hours
Alberta	16[8]	16[8]	18	18	Yes[3]	Yes[4]	None[5]	None
British Columbia	16[6]	16[6]	19	19	None	None	2 days[7]	None
Yukon Territory	15	15	19	19	None	None	None	24 hours
Northwest Territories	15	15	19	19	None	Yes	None	None

(1) There is no statutory minimum age in the province. Anyone under the age of 19 years must have consent for marriage and no person under the age of 16 may be married without authorization of a Family Court judge and in addition must have the necessary consent of the parent or guardian. (2) Special requirements applicable to nonresidents. (3) Applies only to applicants under 60 years of age. (4) This is upon filing of negative lab report indicating blood test was taken within 14 days preceding date of application for license. (5) Exception where consent is required by mail; depending receipt of divorce documents, etc. (6) Persons under 16 years of age (no minimum age specified) may also be married if they have obtained, in addition to the usual consent from parents or guardian, an order from a judge of the Supreme or County Court in this province. (7) Including day of application, e.g., a license applied for on a Monday cannot be issued until Wednesday. (8) Under 16 allowed if pregnant or the mother of a living child.

Grounds for Divorce in Canada

Source: Government of Canada Divorce Act

The grounds for divorce in Canada are the same for all the provinces and its territories. There are two categories of offense:

A. Marital Offense:
Adultery
Sodomy
Bestiality
Rape
Homosexual act
Subsequent marriage
Physical cruelty
Mental cruelty

B. Marriage breakdown by reason of:
Imprisonment for aggregate period of not less than 3 years
Imprisonment for not less than 2 years on sentence of death or sentence of 10 years or more
Addiction to alcohol
Addiction to narcotics
Whereabouts of spouse unknown
Non-consummation
Separation for not less than 3 years
Desertion by petitioner for not less than 5 years

Residence time: Domicile in Canada. Time between interlocutory and final decree: normally 3 months before final can be applied for.

Marriage Information

Source: Compiled by William E. Mariano, Council on Marriage Relations, Inc.,
110 E. 42d St., New York, NY 10017 (as of Mar. 15, 1981)

Marriageable age, by states, for both males and females with and without consent of parents or guardians. But in most states, the court has authority to marry young couples below the ordinary age of consent, where due regard for their morals and welfare so requires. In many states, under special circumstances, blood test and waiting period may be waived.

State	With consent		Without consent		Blood test		Wait for license	Wait after license
	Men	Women	Men	Women	Required	Other state accepted*		
Alabama(b)	14	14	18	18	Yes	Yes	none	none
Alaska	16	16	18	18	Yes	No	3 days	none
Arizona	16(i)	16	18	18	Yes	Yes	none	none
Arkansas	17	16(j)	18	18	Yes	No	3 days	none
California	18(i)	18	18	18	Yes (n)	Yes	none	none
Colorado	16	16	18	18	Yes (n)	...	none	none
Connecticut	16	16(l)	18	18	Yes	Yes	4 days	none
Delaware	18	16(o)	18	18	Yes	Yes	none	24 hrs. (c)
District of Columbia	16	16	18	18	Yes	Yes	3 days	none
Florida	18	18	18	18	Yes	Yes	3 days	none
Georgia	16	16	18	18	Yes	Yes	none (k)	none
Hawaii	16	16	18	18	Yes	Yes	none	none
Idaho	16	16	18	18	Yes (n)	Yes	none (k)	none
Illinois (a)	16	16	18	18	Yes (p)	Yes	none	1 day
Indiana	17(o)	17(o)	18	18	Yes (p)	No	72 hours	none
Iowa	16(o)	16(o)	18	18	Yes	Yes	3 days	none
Kansas	14	12	18	18	Yes	Yes	3 days	none
Kentucky	—(o)	—(o)	18	18	Yes	No	3 days	none
Louisiana (a)	18(o)	16(j)	18	16	Yes	No	none	72 hours
Maine	16(j)	16(j)	18	18	No	No	5 days	none
Maryland	16	16	18	18	none	none	48 hours	none
Massachusetts	—(o)	—(o)	18	18	Yes	Yes	3 days	none
Michigan (a)	18	16	18	18	Yes	No	3 days	none
Minnesota	—	16(e)	18	18	none	...	5 days	none
Mississippi (b)	—	—	17	15	Yes	...	3 days	none
Missouri	15	15	18	18	none	Yes	3 days	none
Montana	15	15	18	18	Yes (n)	Yes	none	3 days
Nebraska	17	17	18	18	Yes (n)	Yes	2 days	none
Nevada	16	16	18	18	none	none	none	none
New Hampshire (a)	14(e)	13(e)	18	18	Yes	Yes	5 days	none
New Jersey (a)	—	12	18	18	Yes	Yes	72 hours	none
New Mexico	16	16	18	18	Yes	Yes	none	none
New York	16	14	18	18	Yes (p)	No	none	24 hrs.(g)
North Carolina (a)	16	16	18	18	Yes (p)	Yes	none	none
North Dakota (a)	16	16	18	18	Yes	...	none	none
Ohio (a)	18	16	18	18	Yes	Yes	5 days	none
Oklahoma	16	16	18	18	Yes	No	none (f)(h)	none
Oregon	17	17	18	18	Yes	No	3 days	none
Pennsylvania	16	16	18	18	Yes	Yes	3 days	none
Rhode Island (a) (b)	18	16	18	18	Yes (n)	No	none	none
South Carolina	16	14	18	18	none	none	24 hrs.	none
South Dakota	16	16	18	18	Yes	Yes	none	none
Tennessee (b)	16	16	18	18	Yes	Yes	3 days	none
Texas	14	14	18	18	Yes	Yes	none	none
Utah (a)	14	14	18	18	none	Yes	none	none
Vermont (a)	18	16	18	18	Yes	...	none	5 days
Virginia (a)	16	16	18	18	Yes	Yes (m)	none	none
Washington	17	17	18	18	(d)	...	3 days	none
West Virginia	18	16	18	18	Yes	No	3 days	none
Wisconsin	16	16	18	18	Yes	Yes	5 days	none
Wyoming	16	16	19	19	Yes	Yes	none	none
Puerto Rico	18	16	21	21	(f)	none	none	none
Virgin Islands	16	14	18	18	none	none	8 days	none

*Many states have additional special requirements; contact individual state. (a) Special laws applicable to non-residents. (b) Special laws applicable to those under 21 years; Ala.; bond required if male is under 18, female under 18. (c) 24 hours if one or both parties resident of state; 96 hours if both parties are non-residents. (d) None, but both must file affidavit. (e) Parental consent plus court's consent required. (f) None, but a medical certificate is required. (g) Marriage may not be solemnized within 10 days from date of blood test. (h) If either under 18, 72 hrs. (i) Statute provides for obtaining license with parental or court consent with no state minimum age. (j) Under 16, with parental and court consent. (k) If either under 18, wait 3 full days. (l) If under stated age, court consent required. (m) Va. blood test form must be used. (n) Applicant must also supply a certificate of immunity against German measles (rubella). (o) If under 18, parental and/or court consent required. (p) Statement whether person is carrier of sickle-cell anemia may be required.

How to Obtain Birth, Marriage, Death Records

The United States government has published a series of inexpensive booklets entitled: Where to Write for Birth & Death Records; Where to Write for Marriage Records; Where to Write for Divorce Records; Where to Write for Birth and Death Records of U. S. Citizens Who were Born or Died Outside of the U. S.; Birth Certifications for Alien Children Adopted by

U. S. Citizens; You May Save Time Proving Your Age and Other Birth Facts. They tell where to write to get a certified copy of an original vital record. Supt. of Documents, Government Printing Office, Washington, DC 20402.

Grounds for Divorce

Source: Compiled by William E. Mariano, Council on Marriage Relations, Inc.,
110 E. 42d St., New York, NY 10017 (as of Mar. 15, 1981)

Persons contemplating divorce should study latest decisions or secure legal advice before initiating proceedings since different interpretations or exceptions in each case can change the conclusion reached.

State	Breakdown of marriage/ incompatibility	Cruelty	Desertion	Non-support	Alcohol &/or drug addiction	Felony	Impotency	Insanity	Living separate and apart	Other grounds	Residence time	Time between interlocut'y and final decrees
Alabama	X	X	X	...	X	X	X	X	2 yrs.	A-B-E	6 mos.	none-M
Alaska	X	X	X	...	X	X	X	X		B-C-F	1 yr.	none
Arizona	X	...	...	...	...	...	...	...			90 days	none
Arkansas	...	X	X	X	X	X	X	X	3 yrs.	C-I	3 mos.	none
California[2]	X	...	...	...	...	...	...	X			6 mos.	6 mos.
Colorado	X	...	...	...	...	...	...	...			90 days	none
Connecticut	X	X	X	X	X	X	...	X	18 mos.	B	1 yr.	none
Delaware	X[4]	...	...	...	...	...	...	...	6 mos.		6 mos.	none
Dist. of Columbia	...	...	...	...	...	...	...	...	6 mos.-1 yr.		6 mos.	none
Florida	X	...	...	...	...	...	...	X			6 mos.	none
Georgia	X	X	X	X	X	X	X	X		A-B-F	6 mos.	L
Hawaii	X	...	...	...	...	...	...		2 yrs.	K	6 mos.	none
Idaho	X	X	X	X	X	X	...		5 yrs.	H	6 wks.	none
Illinois	...	X	X	X	X	X	X	...		I-J	90 days	none
Indiana	X	...	...	...	...	X	X	X			6 mos.	none
Iowa	X	...	...	...	...	...	...				1 yr.	none-N
Kansas	X	X	X	X	X	X	X	X		H	60 days	none-M
Kentucky	X	...	...	...	...	...	...		1 yr.		180 days	none
Louisiana	...	X	X	X	X	X	...	X	2 yrs.	C-J-K	none	none-N
Maine	...	X	X	X	X	X	X	X		H	6 mos.	none
Maryland	...	X	X	...	...	X	X	X	1-3 yrs.	D-I	1 yr.	none
Massachusetts	X[4]	X	X	X	X	X	X	X	6 mos.-1 yr.		1 yr.	6 mos.
Michigan	X[4]	...	...	...	...	...	...	...			180 days	none
Minnesota	X[4]	...	...	...	...	...	...	...		K	180 days	none-O
Mississippi	X[4]	X	X	X	X	X	X	X		A	6 mos.	none-P
Missouri	X[4]	...	...	...	...	...	...	...			90 days	none
Montana	X	...	...	...	...	...	...	...			90 days	none
Nebraska	X	...	...	...	...	...	...	...			1 yr.	6 mos.
Nevada	X	...	...	...	...	...	...	X	1 yr.		6 wks.	none
New Hampshire[3]	X	X	X	X	X	X	X	...	2 yrs.	K	1 yr.	none
New Jersey	...	X	X	...	X	X	...	X	18 mos.	E-K	1 yr.	none
New Mexico	X	X	X	...	...	...	...	...			6 mos.	none
New York	...	X	X	...	...	...	...		1 yr.	K	1 yr.	none
North Carolina	...	...	...	...	...	...	...	X	1 yr.	A-E	6 mos.	none
North Dakota	X	X	X	X	X	X	X	X		H-K	12 mos.	none
Ohio	X	X	X	X	X	X	X	X	2 yrs.	B-G-H-I	6 mos.	none
Oklahoma	X	X	X	X	X	X	X	X		A-B-G-H	6 mos.	none
Oregon	X	...	...	...	...	...	...			B	6 mos.	90 days
Pennsylvania	...	X	X	...	...	X	X	X		C-D-I	1 yr.	none
Rhode Island	X	X	X	X	X	X	X	...	3 yrs.		1 yr.	3 mos.
South Carolina	...	X	X	X	X	X	...		1 yr.		1 yr.	none
South Dakota	...	X	X	X	X	X	...				none	none
Tennessee	X	X	X	X	X	X	...	X		A-H-I-J-K	6 mos.	none
Texas	X	X	X	X	X	X	...	X	3 yrs.		6 mos.	none-O
Utah	...	X	X	X	X	X	X	X		K	3 mos.	none
Vermont	...	X	X	X	...	...	...	X	6 mos.		6 mos.	3 mos.
Virginia	...	X	X	...	...	X	...	X	1 yr.	E	6 mos.	none-P
Washington	X	...	...	...	...	...	...	...			none	none-R
West Virginia	X	X	X	X	...	X	X	...	1 yr.		1 yr.	none
Wisconsin	X[4]	...	...	...	...	...	...	...	1 yr.	K	6 mos.	none-O
Wyoming	X	...	...	...	...	...	...	X	2 yrs.		60 days	none

Adultery is either grounds for divorce or evidence of irreconcilable differences and a breakdown of the marriage in all states. The plaintiff can invariably remarry in the same state where he or she procured a decree of divorce or annulment. Not so the defendant, who is barred in certain states for some offenses. After a period of time has elapsed even the offender can apply for permission.

(1) Generally 5 yrs. insanity but: permanent insanity in Ut.; incurable insanity in Col.; 1 yr. Wis.; 18 mos. Alas.; 2 yrs. Ga., Ha., Ind., Nev., N.J., Ore., Wash., Wy.; 3 yrs. Ark., Cal., Fla., Kan., Md., Minn., Miss., N.C., Tex., W. Va.; 6 yrs. Ida. (2) Cal. has a procedure whereby if the couple has been married less than 2 years, have no children, no real estate, little personal property, and few debts they can get a divorce without an attorney and without appearing in court. (3) Other grounds existing only in N.H. are: Joining a religious order disbelieving in marriage, treatment which injures health or endangers reason, wife without the state for 10 years, and wife in state 2 yrs. husband never in state and intends to become a citizen of a foreign country. (4) Provable only by fault grounds, separation for some period, generally a year, proof of marital discord or commitment for mental illness. (A) Pregnancy at marriage. (B) Fraudulent contract. (C) Indignities. (D) Consanguinity. (E) Crime against nature. (F) Mental incapacity at time of marriage. (G) Procurement of out-of-state divorce. (H) Gross neglect of duty. (I) Bigamy. (J) Attempted homicide. (K) Separation by decree in Conn.; after decree: one yr. in La., N.Y., Wis.; 18 mos. in N.H.; 2 yrs. in Ala., Ha., Minn., N.C. Tenn.; 3 yrs. in Ut.; 4 yrs. in N.J., N.D.; 5 yrs. in Md. (L) Determined by court order. (M) 60 days to remarry. (N) One yr. to remarry except Ha. one yr. with minor child; La. 90 days. (O) 6 mos. to remarry. (P) Adultery cases, remarriage in court's discretion. (Q) Plaintiff, 6 mos.; defendant 2 yrs. to remarry. (R) No remarriage if an appeal is pending. (S) Actual domicile in adultery cases. **Enoch Arden Laws:** disappearance and unknown to be alive - Conn., S.C., Va., Vt., 7 yrs. absence; Ala., Ark., N.Y. 5 yrs. (called dissolution); N.H. 2 yrs.

N.B. Grounds not recognized for divorce may be recognized for separation or annulment. Local laws should be consulted.

Who Owns What: Familiar Consumer Products

The following is a list of familiar consumer products and their parent companies. If you wish to register a complaint beyond the local level, the address of the parent company can be found on pages 92–98.

Admiral appliances: Magic Chef
Ajax cleanser: Colgate-Palmolive
Allstate Insurance Co.: Sears, Roebuck
Anacin: American Home Products
Aqua Velva: Nabisco
Arby's restaurants: Royal Crown
Armour meats: Greyhound
Arrid anti-perspirant: Carter-Wallace
Arrow shirts: Cluett, Peabody
Avis car rental: Norton Simon
Ban anti-perspirant: Bristol-Myers
Bayer aspirin: Sterling Drug
Beech Aircraft: Raytheon
Benson & Hedges cigarettes; Philip Morris
Betty Crocker products: General Mills
Birds Eye frozen foods: General Foods
Black & White scotch: Heublein
Bounty towels: Campbell Soup
Brillo pads: Purex
Brut toiletries: Faberge
Budget Rent A Car: Transamerica
Budweiser beer: Anheuser-Busch
Bufferin: Bristol-Myers
Bumble Bee canned fish: Castle & Cooke
Burger King restaurants: Pillsbury
Business Week magazine: McGraw-Hill
Buster Brown shoes: Brown Group
Cadillac pet foods: U.S. Tobacco
Cap'n Crunch cereal: Quaker Oats
Carrier air conditioners: United Technologies
Chap Stick: A.H. Robins
Chef Boy-ar-dee products: American Home Products
Cheerios cereal: General Mills
Chicken Of the Sea tuna: Ralston Purina
Clairol hair products: Bristol-Myers
Cold Power detergent: Colgate-Palmolive
Colt 45 malt liquor: Heileman Brewing
Copenhagen snuff: U.S. Tobacco
Cracker Jack: Borden
Crest toothpaste: Procter & Gamble
Crisco shortening: Procter & Gamble
Curtiss candy: Standard Brands
Cycle dog food: General Foods
Dash detergent: Procter & Gamble
Del Monte foods: R.J. Reynolds
Dixie Cups: American Can
Doan's Pills: Purex
Dole pineapple products: Castle & Cooke
Dristan: American Home Products
Duracell batteries: Dart & Kraft
Easy-Off oven cleaner: American Home Products
Elizabeth Arden cosmetics: Eli Lilly
Ethan Allen furniture: Interco
Excedrin: Bristol-Myers
Fab detergent: Colgate-Palmolive
Fisher Price toys: Quaker Oats
Flagg Bros. shoe stores: Genesco
Foamy shaving cream: Gillette
Folger coffee: Procter & Gamble
Formula 409 spray cleaner: Clorox
Franco-American foods: Campbell Soup
Friendly Ice Cream restaurants: Hershey Foods
Friskies pet foods: Carnation
Frito-Lay snacks: PepsiCo
Gatorade: Stokely-Van Camp
Geritol: Nabisco
Gleem toothpaste: Procter & Gamble
Good Seasons salad dressing: General Foods
Green Giant vegetables: Pillsbury
Halston fashions: Norton Simon
Hamilton Beach appliances: Scovill
Handy Wipes: Colgate-Palmolive
Head and Shoulders shampoo: Procter & Gamble
Hellman's mayonnaise: CPC International
Hertz car rental: RCA
Hi-C fruit drinks: Coca Cola
Hunt-Wesson foods: Norton Simon
Inside Sports magazine: Washington Post
Ivory soap products: Procter & Gamble
Jack in the Box restaurants: Ralston Purina
Jell-o: General Foods
Jim Beam whiskey: American Brands
Johnnie Walker scotch: Norton Simon

Karastan rugs: Fieldcrest Mills
Ken-L-Ration pet foods: Quaker Oats
Kentucky Fried Chicken: Heublein
Kinney shoe stores: F.W. Woolworth
Knorr soups: CPC International
Kool Aid soft drinks: General Foods
Ladies' Home Journal magazine: Charter
Lestoil: Noxell
Log Cabin syrup: General Foods
Lowenbrau beer: Philip Morris
Lysol cleanser: Sterling Drug
Magnavox products: North American Philips
Marlboro cigarettes: Philip Morris
Max Factor cosmetics: Norton Simon
Maxwell House coffee: General Foods
Mazola oil: CPC International
Michelob beer: Anheuser-Busch
Miller beer: Philip Morris
Minute Maid frozen juices: Coca-Cola
Minute Rice: General Foods
Mountain Dew soda: PepsiCo
NBC broadcasting: RCA
National Car Rental: Household International
Newsweek magazine: Washington Post
9-Lives cat food: H.J. Heinz
North American Van Lines: PepsiCo
Noxzema skin products: Noxell
Old Milwaukee beer: Schlitz
Ore-Ida frozen foods: H.J. Heinz
Oreo cookies: Nabisco
Oscar Mayer meats: General Foods
Pall Mall cigarettes: American Brands
Paper Mate pens: Gillette
Paul Masson wines: Seagram
People magazine: Time
Pepto-Bismol: Norton-Norwich
Pizza Hut restaurants: PepsiCo
Planter's nuts: Standard Brands
Playschool toys: Milton Bradley
Playtex products: Esmark
Prell shampoo: Procter & Gamble
Prince Matchabelli fragrances: Chesebrough-Pond's
Q-Tips: Chesebrough-Pond's
Radio Shack retail outlets: Tandy
Ragu foods: Chesebrough-Pond's
Rawlings sporting goods: Figgie International
Red Devil paints: Insilco
Red Lobster Inns: General Mills
Redbook magazine: Charter
Right Guard deodorant: Gillette
Ritz crackers: Nabisco
Samsonite luggage: Beatrice Foods
Sanka coffee: General Foods
Sergeant's pet care products: A.H. Robins
7-Eleven stores: Southland
Seven-Up: Philip Morris
Smirnoff vodka: Heublein
Smith & Wesson handguns: Bangor Punta
Sports Illustrated magazine: Time
Steak and Ale restaurants: Pillsbury
Sunkist orange soda: General Cinema
Taco Bell restaurants: PepsiCo
Tang soft drink: General Foods
Thom McAn shoe stores: Melville
Tide detergent: Procter & Gamble
Tiffany jewelry: Avon
Tiparillo's: Culbro
Tropicana foods: Beatrice Foods
Tupperware products: Dart & Kraft
Ultra Brite toothpaste: Colgate-Palmolive
V-8 vegetable juice: Campbell Soup
Virginia Slims cigarettes: Philip Morris
Vitalis hair tonic: Bristol-Myers
Wall Street Journal: Dow Jones
Weight Watchers: H.J. Heinz
Western Electric Co.: American Telephone & Telegraph
Wheaties cereal: General Mills
White Owl cigars: Culbro
White Rain shampoo: Gillette
Wilson Sporting Goods: PepsiCo
Wyler's drink mixes: Borden
Yuban coffee: General Foods

Business Directory

Listed below are major U.S. corporations, and major foreign corporations with their U.S. headquarters, whose operations—products and services—directly concern the American consumer. At the end of each listing is a representative sample of some of the company's products.

Should you, as a dissatisfied consumer, wish to register a complaint beyond the local level, address your correspondence to the attention of the Consumer Complaint Office of the individual company. Be as specific as possible about the dealer's name and address, purchase date or date of service, price, name and serial number (if any) of the product, and places you may have sought relief, with dates. Include copies of receipts and guarantees and/or warranties. Don't forget your name and complete address and telephone number with area code.

Company...Address...Chief executive officer...Business.

AMF Inc....777 Westchester Ave., White Plains, NY 10604...W.T. York...producer bowling equip., industrial prods.

AM International, Inc....1900 Ave. of the Stars, Los Angeles, CA 90067...Roy L. Ash...communications information management.

Abbott Laboratories.. Abbott Park, No. Chicago, IL 60064...R.A. Schoellhorn...health care prods.

Alberto-Culver Co....2525 Armitage Ave., Melrose Park, IL 60160...Leonard H. Lavin...hair care preparations, feminine hygiene products, household and grocery items.

Albertson's Inc....250 Parkchester Blvd., Boise, ID 83726...W.E. McCain...supermarkets.

Alcan Aluminium Ltd....1 Place Ville Marie, Montreal, Que., Canada H3C 3H2...aluminum producer.

Allegheny International, Inc....2 Oliver Plaza, Pittsburgh, PA 15222...Robert J. Buckley...steel specialty metals & materials, consumer products.

Allied Corp....Box 2245R, Morristown, NJ 07960...Edward L. Hennessy Jr...oil, gas, chemicals, fibers & plastics, electrical products, auto safety restraints.

Allied Stores Corp....1114 Ave. of the Americas, N.Y., NY 10036...Thomas M. Macioce...dept. stores incl. Bonwit Teller; Plymouth Shops; Bon Marche.

Allis Chalmers Corp....1205 S. 70th St., West Allis, WI 53214...David C. Scott...manuf. of processing equip., electrical power equip., industrial trucks, farm machinery.

Aluminum Co. of America...1501 Alcoa Bldg., Pittsburgh, PA 15219...W.H. Krome George...mining, refining, & processing of aluminum.

AMAX Inc....AMAX Center, Greenwich, CT 06830...J. Towers...natural resources and mineral development.

Amerada Hess Corp....1185 Ave. of the Americas, N.Y., NY 10036...Leon Hess...integrated petroleum co.

American Airlines...P.O. Box 61616, Dallas/Ft.Worth Airport, TX 75261...Albert V. Casey...air transportation.

American Bakeries Co....10 Riverside Plaza, Chicago, IL 60606...G.P. Turci...wholesale bakery goods.

American Brands, Inc....245 Park Ave., N.Y., NY 10017...R. K. Heimann...tobacco (Pall Mall, Carlton, Lucky Strike cigarettes; Half and Half, Paleden pipe tobacco); whiskey (Jim Beam); snack foods, golf equipment, office supplies, toiletries, insurance.

American Broadcasting Companies Inc....1330 Ave. of the Americas, N.Y., NY 10019...L.H. Goldenson...broadcasting, recordings, publishing.

American Can Co....American Lane, Greenwich, CT 06830...William S. Woodside...manuf. containers and packaging prods.

American Cyanamid Co....859 Berdan Ave., Wayne, NJ 07470...J.G. Affleck...medical, agricultural prods., specialty chemicals.

American Greetings Corp....10500 American Rd., Cleveland, OH 44144...Irving I. Stone...greeting cards.

American Hoist & Derrick Co....63 S. Robert, St. Paul, MN 55107...Robert P. Fox...heavy equip.

American Home Products Corp....685 3d Ave., N.Y., NY 10017...J. W. Culligan...household prods. (Woolite, Easy-Off oven cleaner); food (Chef Boy-ar-dee); drugs (Anacin, Dristan).

American Motors Corp....2777 Franklin Rd., Southfield, MI 48034...G.C. Meyers...passenger vehicles, service parts; Jeep Corp.

American Standard Inc....40 W. 40th St., N.Y., NY 10018...William M. Marquard...building, transportation, industrial, security, and graphic prods., construction and mining equip.

American Sterilizer Co....2222 W. Grandview Blvd., Erie, PA 16512...H.E. Fish...health care equip.

American Stores Co....709 East South Temple, Salt Lake City, UT 84127...L.S. Skaggs...retail food markets, dept. & drug stores, restaurants.

American Telephone & Telegraph Co....195 Broadway, N.Y., NY 10007...Charles L. Brown...communications...Western Electric.

Amstar Corp....1251 Ave. of Americas, N.Y., NY 10020...Robert T. Quittmeyer...sweeteners, industrial tools and equip.

Anchor Hocking Corp....109 N. Broad, Lancaster, OH 43130...G.C. Barber...glass containers, metal and plastic closures.

Anheuser-Busch, Inc....721 Pestalozzi St., St. Louis, MO 63118...A.A. Busch 3d...brewing (Budweiser, Michelob, Natural Light).

Armstrong Rubber Co....500 Sargent Dr., New Haven, CT 06507...James A. Walsh...tires.

Armstrong World Industries...P.O. Box 3001, Lancaster, PA 17604...Harry A. Jensen...interior furnishings.

Arvin Industries, Inc....1531 13th St., Columbus, IN 47201...Eugene I. Anderson...auto exhaust systems, record players.

Ashland Oil, Inc....P.O. Box 391, Ashland, KY 41101...Orin E. Atkins...petroleum refiner; chemicals, coal, insurance.

Atlantic Richfield Co....515 S. Flower St., Los Angeles, CA 90071...Robert O. Anderson...petroleum.

Automatic Data Processing, Inc....405 Route 3, Clifton, NJ 07015...F.R. Lautenberg...computer services.

Avco Corp....1275 King St., Greenwich, CT 06830...J.R. Kerr...consumer finance, insurance and management services.

Avery International Corp....415 Huntington Dr., San Marino, CA 91108...Charles D. Miller...self-adhesive labels.

Avon Products, Inc....9 West 57th St., N.Y., NY 10019...David W. Mitchell...cosmetics, fragrances, toiletries; Tiffany & Co.

Ball Corp....345 S. High St., Muncie, IN 47302...R.M. Ringoen...packaging and industrial prods.

Bally Manufacturing Corp....2640 W. Belmont Ave., Chicago, IL...R.E. Mullane...coin-operated amusement and gaming equip.; hotel-casino operator.

Bangor Punta Corp....1 Greenwich Plaza, Greenwich, CT 06830...D.W. Wallace...general aviation (Piper) handguns (Smith & Wesson), sailboats (O'day Cal; Ranger), recreational prods.

Bausch & Lomb... One Lincoln First Square, Rochester, NY 14601...Daniel G. Schuman...manuf. of vision care products, accessories.

Baxter Travenol Labs Inc....One Baxter Pky., Deerfield, IL 60015...Vernon R. Loucks Jr...medical care prods.

Beatrice Foods Co....2 La Salle St., Chicago, IL 60602...James L. Dutt...foods (Tropicana); recreational, travel, home prods.

Bell & Howell Co....7100 McCormick Rd., Chicago, IL 60645...Donald N. Frey...audio-visual instruments, business equip. and supplies.

Bendix Corp....Bendix Center, Southfield, MI 48076...M. Agee automotive, aerospace, industrial prods.

Best Products Co....Box 26303, Richmond, VA 23260...Sydney Lewis...catalog/showroom merchandiser.

Bethlehem Steel Corp....8th & Eaton Ave., Bethlehem, PA 18016...D.H. Trautlein...steel & steel prods.

Binney & Smith Inc....1100 Church La., Easton, PA 18042...Russell J. McChesney...art material and supplies...Crayola crayons, Liquitex artists colors.

Black & Decker Mfg. Co....701 E. Joppa Rd., Towson, MD 21204...Francis P. Lucier...power tools.

H & R Block, Inc....4410 Main St., Kansas City, MO 64111...Henry W. Block...tax preparation.

Blue Bell, Inc....335 Church Ct., Greensboro, NC 27420...L.K. Mann...manuf. western wear, sportswear.

Boeing Company...7755 E. Marginal Way So., Seattle, WA 98108...T.A. Wilson...aerospace.

Boise Cascade Corp....P.O. Box 50, Boise, ID 83728...J.B. Fery...timber, paper, wood prod.

Borden, Inc....277 Park Ave., N.Y., NY 10172...E.J. Sullivan...food, cheese and cheese products, snacks (Cracker Jack), beverages.

Borg-Warner Corp....200 S. Michigan Ave., Chicago, IL 60604...J.F. Bere...air conditioning, plastics, chemicals, industrial prods., financial & protection services.

Braniff International Corp....Braniff Blvd., Dallas-Ft. Worth Airport, TX 75261...J.J. Casey...air transportation.

Bristol-Myers Co....345 Park Ave., N.Y., NY 10022...Richard L. Gelb...toiletries (Ban anti-perspirant), hair items (Clairol, Vitalis), drugs (Bufferin, Excedrin), household prods., infant formula.

Brown Group, Inc....8400 Maryland Ave., St. Louis, MO 63105...W.L.H. Griffin...manuf. and wholesaler of women's and children's shoes (Buster Brown).

Brunswick Corp....One Brunswick Plaza, Skokie, IL 60077...K.B. Abernathy...marine, medical, recreation prods.

Bucyrus-Erie Co....P.O. Box 56, S. Milwaukee, WI 53172...N.K. Elstrom...mining, construction equip.

Burlington Industries, Inc....3330 W. Friendly Ave., Greensboro, NC...W. A. Klopman...textile mfg.

Burlington Northern Inc....176 E. 5th St., St. Paul, MN 55101...N.M. Lorentzsen...rail transportation, natural resources.

Burroughs Corp....Burroughs Place, Detroit, MI...W.M. Blumenthal...business equipment.

CBS Inc....51 W. 52d St., N.Y., NY 10019...W. S. Paley...broadcasting, publishing, recorded music, leisure prods.

CPC International, Inc....International Plaza, Englewood Cliffs, NJ 07632...J.W. McKee Jr....branded food items (Hellman's; Best Foods; Mazola; Skippy; Knorr Soups), corn wet milling prods.

Campbell Soup Co....Campbell Pl., Camden, NJ 08101...R. G. McGovern...canned soups, spaghetti (Franco-American), vegetable juice (V-8), pork and beans; pet foods, restaurants, confections.

Campbell Taggart, Inc....6211 Lemmon Ave., Dallas, TX 75209...C.B. Lane...bakeries, food prods., Mexican restaurants, canned and frozen Mexican foods.

Cannon Mills Co....P.O. Box 107, Kannapolis, NC 28081...O. G. Stolz...textile mfg. and marketing.

Capital Cities Communications, Inc....485 Madison Ave., New York, NY 10022...T.S. Murphy...operates television and radio stations, newspapers.

Carnation Co....5045 Wilshire Blvd., Los Angeles, CA 90036...H.E. Olson...canned evaporated milk, tomato prods., pet foods (Friskies).

Carter-Wallace, Inc....767 5th Ave., New York, NY 10022...H.H. Hoyt Jr....personal care items, anti-perspirant (Arrid), shave lathers (Rise), laxative (Carter's Pills), pet products.

Castle & Cooke, Inc....Financial Plaza of the Pacific, P.O. Box 2990, Honolulu, HI 96802...D.J. Kirchhoff...food processing...Dole, Bumble Bee.

Caterpillar Tractor Co....100 N.E. Adams St., Peoria, IL 61629...Robert E. Gilmore...heavy duty earth-moving equip., diesel engines.

Celanese Corp....1211 Ave. of the Americas, N.Y., NY 10036...John D. Macomber...chemicals, fibers, plastics, and specialties.

Cessna Aircraft Co....5800 East Pawnee Rd., Wichita, KS 67201...Russell W. Meyer Jr....general aviation aircraft, propellers, fluid power systems.

Champion International Corp....1 Champion Plaza, Stamford, CT 06921...A.C. Sigler...forest prods.

Champion Spark Plug Co....900 Upton Ave., Toledo, OH 43661...R.A. Stranahan Jr....spark plugs.

Charter Co....208 Laura St., Jacksonville FL 32202...R.K. Mason...oil refining & marketing, magazine publishing (Redbook; Ladies' Home Journal).

Chesebrough-Pond's Inc....33 Benedict Pl., Greenwich, CT 06830...Ralph E. Ward...cosmetics, toiletries, clothing, food prods., footwear...Adolph's; Health-Tex; Vaseline; Q-Tips; Pertussin; Prince Matchabelli; Ragu.

Chicago Pneumatic Tool Co....6 E. 44th St., N.Y., NY 10017...T.P. Latimer...compressors, pneumatic tools, automotive service tools, rotary water wells, blast hole drills.

Chromalloy American Corp....120 S. Central Ave., St. Louis, MO 63105...F.P. Nykiel...agricultural equip., metal fabrication, petroleum services, transportation, apparel, industrial/-commercial equip.

Chrysler Corp....1200 Lynn Townsend Dr., Detroit, MI 48231...Lee Iacocca...cars, trucks.

Church's Fried Chicken, Inc....355A Spencer Lane, San Antonio, TX 78284...R.A. Harvin...fried chicken restaurants.

Cities Service Co....P.O. Box 300, Tulsa, OK 74102...Charles J. Waidelich...industrial chemicals, petroleum, natural gas.

Clorox Co....1221 Broadway, Oakland, CA 94612...Edwin H. Shutt Jr....retail consumer prods.

Cluett, Peabody & Co....510 5th Ave., New York, NY 10036...H.H. Henley Jr....apparel (Arrow; RPM Fashions; Dobie Originals).

Coastal Corp....9 Greenway Plaza East, Houston, TX 77046...O. S. Wyatt Jr....petroleum products, and natural gas.

Coca-Cola Co....310 North Ave., Atlanta, GA 30313...R.C. Goizueta...soft drink syrups, citrus and fruit juices (Minute Maid, Hi-C), wines (Taylor).

Coleman Co., Inc....250 N. St. Francis Ave., Wichita, KS 67202...S. Coleman...outdoor recreation prods., heating & air conditioning equip.

Colgate-Palmolive Co....300 Park Ave., N.Y., NY 10022...Keith Crane...soaps and detergents (Fab; Ajax; Cold Power), tooth paste (Colgate; Ultra Brite), household prods. (Baggies; Handy Wipes; Curad bandages), restaurants (Ranch House; Lum's).

Collins & Aikman Corp....210 Madison Ave., N.Y., NY 10016...Donald F. McCullough...textiles.

Columbia Pictures Industries, Inc....711 5th Ave., N.Y., NY 10022...Francis T. Vincent Jr....film making, amusement games.

Conagra, Inc....Kiewit Plaza, Omaha, NE 68131...Charles M. Harper...grain processing & merchandising, poultry products.

Consolidated Foods Corp....135 S. La Salle, Chicago, IL 60603...John H. Bryan Jr....foods, indentification prods., housewares, appliances, clothing...Electrolux; Fuller Brush; Hanes; Gant; Popsicle; Sara Lee; Shasta; Tyco.

Continental Air Lines, Inc....7300 World Way West, Los Angeles, CA 90009...R. F. Six...commercial air carrier.

Continental Group, Inc....One Harbor Plaza, Stamford, CT 06902...S. B. Smart Jr....natural resources, financial services, packaging, insurance.

Control Data Corp....8100-34th Ave. South, Minneapolis, MN 55420...Wm. C. Norris...computer services and systems, financial and insurance services.

Adolph Coors Co....East of Town, Golden, CO 80401...W. K. Coors...brewery.

Corning Glass Works...Houghton Park, Corning, NY 14831...Amory Houghton Jr....glass mfg.

Crane Co....300 Park Ave., N.Y., NY 10022...Thomas M. Evans...fluid & pollution controls, steel, aircraft and aerospace, building prods.

Crouse-Hinds Co....P.O. Box 4999, Syracuse, NY 13221...C. J. Witting...electrical equip.

Crown Cork & Seal Co....9300 Ashton Rd., Phila., PA 19136...J.F. Connelly...cans, packaging machinery & equip.

Crown Zellerbach Corp....One Bush St., San Francisco, CA 94104...C.R. Dahl...pulp and paper products; forest products.

Culbro Corp....605 3rd Ave., New York, NY 10016...E. M. Cullman...cigars (Corina; Robert Burns; White Owl; Tiparillo's), snack foods.

Dan River, Inc....107 Frederick St., Greenville, SC 29606...D. W. Johnson Jr....textiles.

Dana Corp....4500 Dorr St., Toledo, OH 43697...Gerald B. Mitchell...truck and auto parts supplies.

Dart & Kraft, Inc....Kraft Court, Glenview, IL 60025...J. R. Richmond...food prods. (cheese, mayonnaise), direct selling (Tupperware), consumer products (Duracell batteries).

Data General Corp....Southboro, MA 01772...E. D. deCastro...digital computers.

Dayton-Hudson Corp....777 Nicollet Mall, Minneapolis, MN 55402...W. A. Andres...department, specialty, book stores; B. Dalton; Mervyns.

Deere & Company...John Deere Rd., Moline, IL 61265...William A. Hewitt...farm, industrial, and outdoor power equip.

Delta Air Lines, Inc....Hartsfield Atlanta Intl. Airport, Atlanta, GA 30320...David C. Garrett Jr....air transportation.

Diamond International Corp....733 3d Ave., N.Y., NY

10017...William J. Koslo...mfg. lumber, matches, pulp & paper, packaging, specialty printing.

Diamond Shamrock Corp....717 North Harwood St., Dallas, TX 75201...W.H. Bricker...energy, technology, and chemicals.

DiGiorgio Corp... One Maritime Plaza, San Francisco, CA 94111...R. DiGiorgio...food processing and distribution.

Digital Equipment Corp...146 Main St., Maynard, MA 01754...Kenneth H. Olsen...small computers.

Walt Disney Productions...500 S. Buena Vista St., Burbank, CA 91505...E. Cardon Walker...motion pictures, amusement parks...Disneyland, Walt Disney World.

Dr Pepper Co....5523 E. Mockingbird Lane, Dallas, TX 75265...W.W. Clements...soft drinks.

Dow Chemical Co....2020 Dow Center, Midland, MI 48640...P.F. Oreffice...chemicals, plastics, metals, consumer prods.

Dow Jones & Co....22 Courtlandt St., New York, NY 10007...W. H. Phillips...financial news service, publishing (Wall Street Journal; Barron's; Ottaway Newspapers).

Dresser Industries, Inc... The Dresser Bldg., Dallas, TX 75201...J. V. James...supplier of technology and services to energy related industries.

E.I. du Pont de Nemours & Co....1007 Market St., Wilmington, DE 19898...E. G. Jefferson...chemical mfg.

Dun & Bradstreet Corp....299 Park Ave., New York, NY 10171...H. Drake...business information and computer services, publishing, broadcasting.

Eastern Air Lines Inc....Miami International Airport, Miami, FL 33148...Frank Borman...air transportation.

Eastman Kodak Co....343 State St., Rochester, NY 14650...Walter A. Fallon...photographic materials & equip.

Jack Eckerd Corp....8333 Dryan Dairy Rd., Clearwater, FL 33518...S. Turley...drug store chain.

Emerson Electric Co....8100 W. Florissant Ave., St. Louis, MO 63136...C.F. Knight...electrical/electronics products.

Emery Air Freight Corp... Old Danbury Rd., Wilton, CT 06897...John C. Emery Jr...air freight forwarder.

Envirotech Corp....3000 Sand Hill Rd., Menlo Park, CA 94025...Robert L. Chambers...supplier of equipment and technology for air and water pollution control.

Esmark, Inc....55 E. Monroe St., Chicago, IL 60603...Donald P. Kelly...food (Swift processed meats), personal products (Playtex), auto products (STP), hosiery, knitwear.

Ethyl Corp....330 S. 4th St., Richmond, VA 23217...Floyd D. Gottwald Jr...petroleum and industrial chemicals, plastics, aluminum, energy-related prods.

Ex-Cell-O Corp....2855 Coolidge Rd., Troy, MI 48084...E. Paul Casey...precision parts and tools for aircraft, auto markets.

Exxon Corp....1251 Ave. of the Americas, N.Y., NY 10020...C.C. Garvin Jr...world's largest oil co.

FMC Corp....200 E. Randolph Dr., Chicago, IL 60601...R.H. Malotti...machinery, chemicals.

Fabergé, Inc....1345 Ave. of the Americas, N.Y., NY 10019...George Barrie...cosmetics, toiletries (Brut; Babe).

Fairchild Industries, Inc....20301 Century Blvd., Germantown, MD 20767...E.G. Uhl...aircraft manuf.

Federated Department Stores, Inc....7 W. 7th St., Cincinnati, OH 45202...H. Goldfeder...dept. stores...Abraham & Straus; Bloomingdale's; Boston Store; Bullock's; Burdines; Foley's; Goldsmith's; Lazarus; I. Magnin; Rich's; Rike's; Sanger-Harris.

Fiat Motors of North America, Inc....155 Chestnut Ridge Rd., Montvale, NJ 07645...Claudio Ferrari...automobiles.

Fieldcrest Mills, Inc....326 East Stadium Dr., Eden, NC 27288...William C. Battle...household textile prods., rugs (Karastan, Laurelcrest).

Figgie International Inc....4420 Sherwin Dr., Willoughby, OH 44094...H. E. Figgie Jr...serves consumer, industrial, technical, service markets; Rawlings Sporting Goods.

Firestone Tire & Rubber Co....1200 Firestone Pkwy., Akron, OH 44317...Richard A. Riley...tires, rubber and metal prods.

Fleetwood Enterprises, Inc....3125 Myers St., Riverside, CA 92523...John C. Crean...mobile homes, travel trailers.

Fluor Corp....3333 Michelson Dr., Irvine, CA 92730...J. R. Fluor...engineering and construction.

Ford Motor Co... The American Rd., Dearborn, MI 48121...Philip Caldwell...motor vehicles, Ford Tractor; Lincoln-Mercury.

Fort Howard Paper Co....1919 S. Broadway, Green Bay, WI

54305...disposable paper prods.

Fruehauf Corp....10900 Harper Ave., Detroit, MI 48213...R. D. Rowen...transportation equip.

GAF Corp....140 W. 51st St., New York, NY 10020...Dr. Jesse Werner...chemicals, bldg. materials.

General Cinema Corp....27 Boylston St., Chestnut Hill, MA...R. A. Smith...movie exhibitor, soft drinks (Sunkist).

General Dynamics Corp....Pierre Laclede Ctr., St. Louis, MO 63105...D. S. Lewis...military and commercial aircraft, tactical missiles.

General Electric Co....3135 Easton Ave., Fairfield, CT 06431...J. F. Welch Jr...electrical, electronic equip.

General Foods Corp....250 North, White Plains, NY 10625...J.L. Ferguson...packaged foods (Maxwell House; Yuban; Sanka; Jell-O; Post cereals; Birds Eye frozen foods; Gaines, Cycle dog foods; Tang, Kool Aid soft drinks; Minute Rice; Oscar Mayer meats.

General Instruments Corp....1775 Broadway, New York, NY 10019...F. G. Hickey...race track betting systems, CATV, semiconductors, electronic equip.

General Mills Inc....9200 Wayzatta Blvd., Minneapolis, MN 55440...E. Robert Kinney...foods, toys, restaurants, fashion and specialty retailing...Wheaties; Cheerios; Betty Crocker; Red Lobster Inns).

General Motors Corp....Gen. Motors Bldg., Detroit, MI 48202...R. B. Smith...world's largest auto manuf.

General Telephone & Electronics Corp....One Stamford Forum, Stamford, CT 06904...Theodore F. Brophy...operates largest U.S. independent telephone system.

General Tire & Rubber Co....One General St., Akron, OH 44329...M.G. O'Neil...tires, rubber prods.

Genesco Inc....Genesco Park, Nashville, TN 37202...John Hanigan...footwear and men's clothing...Hardy; Cover Girl; Jarman; Flagg Bros.; Bell Bros.; Johnston & Murphy.

Georgia-Pacific Corp....900 S.W. 5th Ave., Portland, OR 97204...Robert F. Flowerree...wood and gypsum building prods., pulp, paper, chemicals.

Gerber Products Co....445 State St., Fremont, MI 49412...Arthur J. Frens...baby foods, clothing, nursery accessories; life insurance.

Getty Oil Co....3810 Wilshire Blvd., Los Angeles, CA 90010...Sidney R. Petersen...petroleum exploration & production.

Gillette Co....Prudential Tower Bldg., Boston, MA 02199...Colman M. Mockler Jr...razors, pens (Paper Mate; Flair), toiletries (Right Guard, Dri, Soft deodorants; Foamy shaving cream; Earth Born shampoo), hair products (Toni; Adorn; White Rain).

Global Marine, Inc....811 W. 7th St., Los Angeles, CA 90017...C. R. Luigs...offshore oil and gas drilling.

B.F. Goodrich Company...500 S. Main St., Akron, OH 44318...John D. Ong...rubber, chemical, plastic prods.

Goodyear Tire & Rubber Co....1144 E. Market St., Akron, OH 44316...Charles J. Pilliod Jr...tires, rubber prods.

Gould Inc....10 Gould Center, Rolling Meadows, IL 60008...W.T. Ylvisaker...electrical and industrial prods.

W.R. Grace & Co....Grace Plaza, 1114 Ave. of the Americas, N.Y., NY 10036...J. Peter Grace...chemicals, natural resources, consumer prods. and services, restaurants...Channel Home Centers; Herman's World of Sporting Goods.

Great Atlantic & Pacific Tea Co....2 Paragon Dr., Montvale, NJ 07645...James Wood...retail food stores.

Greyhound Corp... Greyhound Tower, Phoenix, AZ 85077...John W. Teets...meat and poultry packer (Armour), bus transportation, soap prods., food, financial services.

Grumman Corp....111 Stewart, Bethpage, NY 11714...John C. Bierwirth...aerospace, buses, truck bodies, data computing services.

Gulf Oil Corp....Gulf Blvd., Pittsburgh, PA 15230...Jerry McAfee...production and marketing of petroleum and related products.

Gulf + Western Industries, Inc....One Gulf & Western Plaza, N.Y., NY 10023...David N. Judelson...diversified manufacturing, financial services, consumer and food products, natural resources, home furnishings, entertainment (Paramount Pictures; Madison Square Garden).

Halliburton Co....2600 Southland Center, Dallas, TX 75201...J. P. Harbin...oil field services, engineering, construction.

Hart Schaffner & Marx....36 S. Franklin St., Chicago, IL

60606.. Jerome S. Gore.. .apparel manufacturer and retailer (Hickey-Freeman).

Heileman (G.) Brewing Co.. .100 Harborview Plaza, La Crosse, WI 54601.. .R. G. Cleary.. .brewery (Tuborg Gold; Carling Black Label; Colt 45 Malt Liquor).

H.J. Heinz Co.. .P.O. Box 57, Pittsburgh, PA 15230.. .Anthony J.F. O'Reilly.. .foods (Star-Kist; Ore-Ida; '57 Varieties), 9-Lives cat food, Weight Watchers.

Hershey Food Corp.. .100 Manson Rd., Hershey, PA 17033.. .William Dearden.. .chocolate & confectionery prods., pasta (San Giorgio); restaurants (Friendly Ice Cream).

Heublein, Inc.. . Farmington, CT 06032.. .Hicks B. Waldron.. . alcoholic beverages (Smirnoff Vodka; Black & White Scotch; Lancers Portuguese wines); food (Kentucky Fried Chicken).

Hewlett-Packard Co.. .1501 Page Mill Rd., Palo Alto, CA 94304.. .John A. Young.. .electronic instruments.

Hilton Hotels Corp.. .9880 Wilshire Blvd., Beverly Hills, CA 90210.. .Barron Hilton.. .hotels, casinos.

Holiday Inns, Inc.. .3742 Lamar Ave., Memphis, TN 38195.. .Roy E. Winegardner.. .hotels, motels, casinos; Delta Steamship Lines.

Honeywell, Inc.. . Honeywell Plaza, Minneapolis, MN 55408.. .E.W. Spencer.. .information and control systems, aerospace, defense.

Hoover Universal Inc.. .P.O. Box 1003, Ann Arbor, MI 41806.. .D. T. Carroll.. .aluminum, steel, plastic prods.

Hoover Co.. .101 E. Maple St., No. Canton, OH 44720.. .M. R. Rawson.. .manuf. vacuum cleaners, washing machines, dryers.

Geo. A. Hormel & Co.. .501 16th Ave. N.E., Austin, MN 55912.. .I.J. Holton.. .meat packaging, pork and beef prods.

Household International Inc.. .2700 Sanders Rd., Prospect Heights, IL 60070.. .G.R. Ellis.. .financial and insurance services, merchandising, manufacturing, transportation.. .King-Seeley Thermos; National Car Rental; Household Finance.

Hughes Tool Co.. .5425 Polk Ave., Houston, TX 77023.. .supplier of products and services to the oil, gas, & mining industries; mfg. of rock drilling bits & tool joints.

Humana, Inc.. .P.O. Box 1438, Louisville, KY 40201.. .D. A. Jones.. .operates hospitals.

IC Industries, Inc.. . One Illinois Ctr., 111 E. Wacker Dr., Chicago, IL 60601.. .William B. Johnson.. .diversified prods. and services.. .railroads, consumer products, food, auto products.

Imperial Oil Ltd.. .111 St. Clair Ave. W., Toronto, Ont., Canada.. .Canada's largest oil co.

Insilco Corp.. .1000 Research Pkwy., Meriden, Ct 06450.. .Durand B. Blatz.. .diversified manufacturer.. .International Silver; Red Devil Paints and Chemicals; Rolodex; Taylor Publishing.

Intel Corp.. .3065 Bowers Ave., Santa Clara, CA 95051.. .G. E. Moore.. .semiconductor memory components.

Interco Incorporated.. .P.O. Box 8777, St. Louis, MO 63102.. .W. L. Edwards Jr.. .apparel, footwear mfg.; specialty apparel shops, home furnishings (Ethan Allen).

International Business Machines Corp.. . Old Orchard Rd., Armonk, NY 10504.. .Frank T. Cary.. .world's largest manuf. of data processing equip.

International Harvester Co.. .401 N. Michigan Ave., Chicago, IL 60611.. .A. R. McCardell.. .manuf. farm tractors and machinery, truck and construction equip.

International Paper Co.. .77 W. 45th St., New York, NY 10036.. .E. A. Gee.. .paper, wood prods.

International Telephone and Telegraph Corp.. .320 Park Ave., N.Y., NY 10022.. .R.V. Araskog.. .world's largest manuf. of telecommunications equip.

Johns-Manville Corp.. .P.O. Box 5108, Denver, CO 80217.. .J. A. McKinney.. .mining and manuf. of materials used for the production of buildings and residences.

Johnson & Johnson.. .501 George St., New Brunswick, NJ 08903.. .James E. Burke.. .surgical dressings, pharmaceuticals, health and baby prods.

Jonathan Logan, Inc.. .50 Terminal Rd., Secaucus, NJ 07094.. .Richard J. Schwartz.. .apparel.

Jostens, Inc.. .5501 Norman Center Dr., Minneapolis, MN 55437.. .H. W. Lurton.. .school rings, yearbooks.

Kaiser Aluminum & Chemical Corp.. .300 Lakeside Dr., Oak-

land, CA 94643.. .Cornell C. Maier.. .aluminum, agricultural chemicals.

Kaiser Steel Corp.. .P.O. Box 58, Oakland, CA 94604.. .R. A. Kjelland.. .steelmaker.

Kane-Miller Corp.. .555 White Plains Rd., Tarrytown, NY 10591.. .Stanley B. Kane.. .food processing.

Kaufman and Broad, Inc.. .10801 National Blvd., Los Angeles, CA 90064.. .Eli Broad.. .home builder.

Kellogg Co.. .235 Porter, Battle Creek, MI 49016.. .William E. LaMothe.. .ready to eat cereals & other food prods.. .Mrs. Smith's Pie Co.; Salada Foods.

Kerr-McGee Corp.. .P.O. Box 25861, Ave., Oklahoma City, OK 73125.. .Dean A. McGee.. .oil, natural gas, uranium, coal.

Kidde, Inc.. .9 Brighton Rd., Clifton, NJ 07015.. .Fred R. Sullivan.. .mfgr. safety, security, protection, industrial, commercial, consumer and recreation prods. and services.

Kimberly-Clark Corp.. .N. Lake St., Neenah, WI 54956.. .Darwin E. Smith.. .paper and lumber prods.

K mart Corp.. .3100 W. Big Beaver Rd., Troy, MI 48084.. .B. M. Fauber.. .chain of discount stores.

Koppers Co., Inc.. . Koppers Bldg., Pittsburgh, PA 15219.. .F. L. Byrom.. .diversified manuf.

Kroger Co.. .1014 Vine St., Cincinnati, OH 45201.. .Lyle Everingham.. .grocery chain, drugstores (SuperRx), amusement parks.

LTV Corporation.. .P.O. Box 225003, Dallas, TX 75265.. .Paul Thayer.. .steel, aerospace, meat & food prods. (Wilson Foods), shipping, energy-oriented prods.

Lane Bryant, Inc.. .11 W. 42d St., New York, NY 10036.. .A. Malsin.. .women's apparel stores, shoe stores (Coward; Farr's).

Lenox, Inc.. . Old Princeton Pike, Lawrenceville, NJ 08648.. . S. Chamberlin.. .fine china dinnerwear, glasswear, jewelry.

Levi Strauss & Co.. .2 Embarcadero Center, San Francisco, CA 94106.. .P. E. Haas.. .blue denim jeans, other apparel.

Levitz Furniture Corp.. .1317 NW 167th St., Miami, FL 33169.. .Robert M. Elliott.. .furniture stores.

Libbey-Owens-Ford Co.. .811 Madison Ave., Toledo, OH 43695.. .Don T. Mc Kone.. .glass and fabricated prods.

Eli Lilly & Company.. .307 E. McCarty St., Indianapolis, IN 46285.. .Richard D. Wood.. .mfg. human health and agricultural products, cosmetics (Elizabeth Arden).

Litton Industries, Inc.. .360 N. Crescent, Beverly Hills, CA 90210.. .Charles B. Thornton.. .industrial systems & services, advanced electronic systems, electronic & electrical prods., marine engineering, printing & publishing.

Lockheed Corp.. .2555 N. Hollywood Way, Burbank, CA 91520.. .Lawrence O. Kitchen.. .commercial and military aircraft, missiles.

Loews Corp.. .666 5th Ave., N.Y., NY 10019.. .Laurence A. Tisch.. .tobacco prods., motion picture theaters, hotels, real estate, insurance.

M. Lowenstein Corp.. .1430 Broadway, N.Y., NY 10018.. .R. Bendheim.. .textiles.

Lucky Stores, Inc.. .6300 Clark Ave., Dublin, CA 94566.. .S. D. Ritchie.. .supermarkets, restaurants, dept., fabric, and automotive stores.

MCA Inc.. .100 Universal City Plaza, Universal City, CA 91608.. .Lew R. Wasserman.. .motion pictures, television; music publishing, mail order, novelty, and gift merchandise, book publishing, records, savings and loan assn.

MEI Corp.. .733 Marquette Ave., Minneapolis, MN 55402.. .Donald E. Benson.. .soft drink bottler, distributor.

MacMillian, Inc.. .866 3d Ave., New York, NY 10022.. .E. P. Evans.. .book printing and publishing, instruction, distribution.

R. H. Macy & Co. Inc.. .151 W. 74th St., New York, NY 10001.. .E. S. Finkelstein.. .department stores.

Magic Chef, Inc.. .740 King Edward Ave., Cleveland, TN 37311.. .S.B. Rymer Jr.. .major household appliances, heating and air conditioning equip., soft drink vending equip.. .Admiral; Norge; Gaffers & Sattler; Johnson; Dixie-Narco.

MAPCO, Inc.. .1800 South Baltimore Ave., Tulsa, OK 74119.. .W. H. Thompson Jr.. .coal, gas, natural gas liquids.

Marriott Corp.. . Marriott Dr., Wash., DC 20058.. .J. Willard Marriott Jr.. .restaurants (Roy Rogers; Big Boy), hotels, food services.

Martin Marietta Corp.. .6801 Rockledge Dr., Bethesda, MD 20034.. .J. D. Rauth.. .aluminum, aerospace, cement, chemi-

cals.
Mary Kay Cosmetics, Inc....8787 Stemmon Freeway, Dallas, TX 75247...Mary Kay Ash...cosmetics, toiletries.
Masonite Corp....29 N. Wacker Dr., Chicago, IL 60606...Samuel S. Greely...building materials.
Mattel, Inc....5150 Rosecrans Ave., Hawthorne, CA 90250...A. S. Spear...toy & hobby prods., publishing, entertainment...Ringling Bros.-Barnum & Bailey; Western Publishing.
Maytag Co....403 W. 4th St. N., Newton, IA 50208...Daniel J. Krumm...manuf. home laundry equip.
McCormick & Co., Inc....11350 McCormick Rd., Hunt Valley, MD 21031...H. K. Wells...world's leading manuf. of seasoning & flavoring prods.
McDonald's Corp....McDonald's Plaza, Oak Brook, IL 60521...F. L. Turner...fast service restaurants.
McDonnell Douglas Corp....P.O. Box 516, St. Louis, MO 63131...Sanford N. McDonnell...commercial & military aircraft, space systems & missiles.
McGraw-Edison Co....333 W. River Rd., Elgin, IL 60120...E.J. Williams...electrical and mechanical prods.
McGraw-Hill, Inc....1221 Ave. of the Americas, New York, NY 10020...H. W. McGraw Jr...book, magazine publishing (Business Week), information & financial services (Standard and Poor's), TV stations.
Mead Corp....Courthouse Plaza N.E., Dayton, OH 45463 ...C. G. Garner...pulp, paper, school and office prods., furniture.
Melville Corp....3000 Westchester Ave., Harrison, NY 10528...Francis C. Rooney Jr...shoe stores (Thom McAn), apparel, drug stores.
Memorex Corp....San Tomas at Central Exp., Santa Clara, CA 95052...C.W. Spangle...computer peripheral equip.
Merck & Co., Inc....P.O. Box 2000, Rahway, NJ 07065...John L. Huck...human & animal health care prods.
Metromedia, Inc....One Harmon Plaza, Secaucus, NJ 07094...J. W. Kluge...television & radio broadcasting, publishing, entertainment (Ice Capades; Harlem Globetrotters).
Milton Bradley Co....1500 Main St., Springfield, MA 01115...James J. Shea Jr...board and card games, electronic games, toys (Playskool), school supplies.
Mobil Corp....150 E. 42d St., N.Y., NY 10017...Rawleigh Warner Jr...international oil co.; chemicals, dept. stores (Montgomery Ward).
Mohasco Corp....57 Lyon St., Amsterdam, NY 12010...S. I. Landgraf...home furnishings.
Monsanto Company....800 N. Lindbergh Blvd., St. Louis, MO 63166...John W. Hanley...chemicals, plastics, agricultural prods., textiles.
Morton Norwich...110 N. Wacker Dr., Chicago, IL 60606...Charles S. Locke...pharmaceuticals, (Pepto-Bismol), salt (Morton), household cleaning prods. (Fantastik; Spray 'n Wash), specialty chemicals.
Motorola, Inc....1303 E. Algonquin Rd., Schaumburg, IL 60196...R. W. Galvin...electronic equipment and components.
Murray Ohio Manuf. Co....Franklin Rd., Brentwood, TN 37027...bicycles, power mowers.

NCR Corp....1700 S. Patterson Blvd., Dayton, OH 45479...Charles E. Exley Jr...business information processing systems.
NL Industries...1230 Ave. of the Americas, New York, NY 10020...Ray C. Adam...petroleum services & equipment, specialty chemicals, fabricated metal products.
Nabisco, Inc....DeForest Ave., E. Hanover, NJ 07936...Robert M. Schaeberle...crackers (Ritz; Premium), cookies (Oreo; Fig Newton), toiletries (Aqua Velva; 'Lectric Shave), pharmaceutical prods. (Geritol). *Merged with Standard Brands Inc., 1981.*
National Distillers & Chemical Corp....99 Park Ave., N.Y., NY 10016...Drummond C. Bell...wines and liquors, chemicals, textiles, metals...Almaden Vineyards.
National Medical Care, Inc....Hancock Tower, Boston, MA 02116...C. L. Hampers...medical services and prods.
National Semiconductor Corp....2900 Semiconductor Dr., Santa Clara, CA 95051...Charles E. Sporck...semiconductors.
A.C. Nielson Co....Nielson Plaza, Northbrook, IL 60062...Arthur C. Nielson Jr...market research.
North American Philips Corp....100 E. 42d St., N.Y., NY 10017...P. C. Vink...consumer prods., electrical, electronic prods., professional equip., chemicals and pharmaceutical prods...Magnavox; Norelco; Sylvania; Philco.

Northrop Corp....1800 Century Park E., Los Angeles, CA 90067...Thomas V. Jones...aircraft, electronics, communications.
Northwest Airlines, Inc....Minneapolis-St. Paul Intl. Airport, St. Paul, MN 55111...M. J. Lapensky...air transportation.
Northwest Industries, Inc....6300 Sears Tower, Chicago, IL 60606...Ben W. Heineman...industrial & chemical prods., consumer prods., oil and gas drilling supplies.
Norton Simon Inc....277 Park Ave., N.Y., NY 10017...David J. Mahoney...foods (Hunt-Wesson), beverages (Johnnie Walker Scotch; Tanqueray Gin), cosmetics & fashions (Max Factor; Halston), car rental (Avis).
Noxell Corp....11050 York Rd., Cockeysville, MD...G. L. Bunting Jr...toiletry, household, consumer prods. (Noxzema; Rain Tree; Lestoil; Cover Girl).

Occidental Petroleum Corp....10889 Wilshire Blvd., Los Angeles, CA 90024...Dr. Armand Hammer...oil, gas, chemicals, coal.
Ogden Corp....277 Park Ave., New York NY 10017...R. E. Ablon...transportation, foods, metals.
Olin Corp....120 Long Ridge Rd., Stamford, CT 06904...John M. Henske...chemicals, metals, paper, sporting and defense ammunition.
Outboard Marine Corp....100 Sea Horse Dr., Waukegan, IL 60085...C.D. Strang...outboard motors, mowers (Lawn Boy).
Owens-Corning Fiberglas Corp....Fiberglas Tower, Toledo, OH 43659...W.W. Boeschenstein...glass fiber and related prods.
Owens-Illinois, Inc....P.O. Box 1035, Toledo, OH 43666...Edwin D. Dodd...glass, corrugated, and plastic containers.

Pabst Brewing Co....917 W. Juneau Ave., Milwaukee, WI 53201...Frank C. DeGuire...brewery.
Pan American World Airways...Pan Am Bldg., 200 Park Ave., N.Y., NY 10017...C. Edward Acker...air transportation.
Pargas, Inc....P.O. Box 67, Waldorf, MD 20601...N. L. Langley...distributes liquified petroleum gas.
Parker Drilling Co....Parker Bldg., Tulsa, OK 74103...R. L. Parker Jr...oil and gas drilling services.
Parker Pen Co....219 E. Court St., Janesville, WI 53545...E. William Swanson...writing instruments, recreational equip., temp. help service (Manpower, Inc.).
J.C. Penney Co., Inc....1301 Ave. of the Americas, N.Y., NY 10019...Donald V. Seibert...dept. stores, catalog sales, food, drugs, insurance.
Pennwalt Corp....Pennwalt Bldg., 3 Pkwy., Phila., PA 19102...Edwin E. Tuttle...chemicals, health prods., precision equip.
Pennzoil Co....Pennzoil Pl., Houston, TX 77001...B. P. Kerr...Integrated oil and gas co.
PepsiCo, Inc....Anderson Hill Rd., Purchase, NY 10577...D. M. Kendall...soft drinks, (Pepsi-Cola; Mountain Dew), snack foods (Frito-Lay; Doritos) restaurants (Pizza Hut; Taco Bell), sporting goods (Wilson), transportation (North American Van Lines).
Pfizer Inc....235 E. 42d St., N.Y., NY 10017...E.T. Pratt Jr...pharmaceutical, hospital, agricultural, chemical prods.
Philip Morris Inc....100 Park Ave., N.Y., NY 10017...George Weissman...cigarettes (Marlboro, Benson & Hedges 100's, Merit, Virginia Slims, Parliament Lights); beer (Miller High Life, Lite; Lowenbrau brands); soft drinks (Seven-up); specialty chemicals, paper, packaging materials, land development.
Phillips-Van Heusen Corp....1290 Ave. of the Americas, New York, NY 10019...L. S. Phillips...men, boys apparel.
Pillsbury Co. 608 2d Ave. So., Minneapolis, MN 55402...W. H. Spoor...canned & frozen vegetables (Green Giant), bakery, flower mixes, restaurants (Burger King; Steak and Ale)
Pinkerton's, Inc....100 Church St., New York, NY 10007...E. C. Fey...security and investigative services.
Pitney Bowes, Inc....Walter H. Wheeler Dr., Stamford, CT 06904...Fred T. Allen...postage meters, mail handling equip., office equipment, retail systems.
Polaroid Corp....549 Technology Sq., Cambridge, MA 02139...William J. McCune Jr...photographic equip., supplies and optical goods.
Ponderosa System, Inc....P.O. Box 578, Dayton, OH 45401...G. S. Office Jr...Steakhouse Restaurants.
Potlatch Corp....Golden Gateway Center, San Francisco, CA

94119...R. B. Madden...lumber, paper prods.

Procter & Gamble Co...301 E. 6th St., Cincinnati, OH 45202...E.G. Harness...soap & detergent (Ivory; Dash; Tide; Spic and Span), shortenings (Crisco; Fluffo), toiletries (Crest and Gleem toothpastes; Prell and Head and Shoulders Shampoos), Folger coffee.

Purex Corp...5101 Clark Ave., Lakewood, CA 90712...William R. Tincher...household cleaning prods. (Brillo; Old Dutch Cleanser; Purex), drugs & toiletries (Ayds; Doan's Pills; Cuticura).

Purolator, Inc...255 Old New Brunswick Rd., Piscataway, NJ 08854...P. A. Cameron...auto equip., courier and guard services.

Quaker Oats Co... Merchandise Mart Plaza, Chicago, IL 60654...Robert D. Stuart Jr...foods, cereal (Life; Cap'n Crunch; Puffed Wheat; Puffed Rice), foods (Aunt Jemima; Celeste), pet foods (Ken-L-Ration; Puss 'n Boots), Fisher Price toys, Magic Pan restaurants.

Quaker State Oil Refining Corp...255 Elm St., Oil City, PA 16301...Q.E. Wood...refining, marketing petroleum prods., filters, mining & marketing coal.

RCA Corp... Rockefeller Plaza, N.Y., NY 10020...Edgar H. Griffiths...radio, television (NBC), electronics, communications, financial services, vehicle renting (Hertz).

Ralston Purina Co... Checkerboard Sq., St. Louis, MO 63188...W. R. Stritz...pet and livestock food, Jack In the Box restaurants.

Ramada Inns, Inc...3838 E. Van Buren, Phoenix, AZ 85008...Richard Snell...hotel operation, casinos.

Raytheon Company...141 Spring St., Lexington, MA 02173...Thomas L. Phillips...electronics, aviation, appliances...Amana Refrigeration; Beech Aircraft.

Revere Copper & Brass Inc...605 3d Ave., N.Y., NY 10016...William F. Collins...fabricator of nonferrous metals.

Revlon, Inc...767 5th Ave., N.Y., NY 10153...Michael C. Bergerac...cosmetics, pharmaceuticals.

Reynolds Metals Co...6601 W. Broad St., Richmond, VA 23261...D. P. Reynolds...aluminum prods.

R.J. Reynolds Industries, Inc... Reynolds Blvd., Winston-Salem, NC 27102...J. P. Sticht...crude oil, petroleum, transportation, tobacco, food, and beverage prods.

Richardson-Vicks Inc...10 Westport Rd., Wilton, CT 06897...J.S. Scott...health and personal care prods., drugs, specialty chemicals.

Rite Aid Corp... Shiremanstown, PA 17011...A. Glass...discount drug stores.

Robertshaw Controls Co...P.O. Box 26544, Richmond, VA 23261...Ralph S. Thomas...controls, control systems.

A.H. Robins Co., Inc...1407 Cummings Dr., Richmond, VA 23220...E.C. Robins Jr...health care, consumer prods. (Chap Stick).

Rockwell Intl. Corp...600 Grant St., Pittsburgh, PA 15219...Robert Anderson...aerospace, electronics, automotive.

Roper Corp...1905 W. Court St., Kankakee, IL 60901...C.M. Hoover...appliances, home and lawn prods.

Royal Crown Cos., Inc...41 Perimeter Center East, Atlanta, GA 30346...D.A. McMahon...soft drinks (Nehi; RC Cola) restaurants (Arby's), citrus prods., home furnishings.

Rubbermaid Inc...1147 Akron Rd., Wooster, OH 44691...S. C. Gault...rubber and plastic prods.

SCM Corp...299 Park Ave., N.Y., NY 10171...Paul H. Elicker...diversified manufacturer...Smith Corona.

Safeway Stores, Inc... Oakland, CA 94660...P. A. Magowan...retail food stores.

St. Regis Paper Co...150 E. 42d St., N.Y., NY 10017...William R. Haselton...pulp and paper, building prods.

Santa Fe Industries, Inc...224 S. Michigan Ave., Chicago, IL 60604...J. S. Reed...transport, real estate, construction, natural resources...Atchison, Topeka and Santa Fe Railway.

Savin Corp... Columbus Ave., Valhalla, NY 10595...R. K. Low...office copiers.

Schering-Plough Corp...1000 Galloping Hill Rd., Kenilworth, NJ 07033...Richard J. Bennett...pharmaceuticals, consumer prods.

Jos. Schlitz Brewing Co...235 W. Galena St., Milwaukee, WI 53212...Frank Sellinger...brewery (Schlitz; Old Milwaukee; Erlanger).

Schlumberger Ltd...277 Park Ave., New York, NY 10172...Jean Riboud...oilfield services, electronics, measurement and control devices.

Scientific-Atlanta, Inc...3845 Pleasantdale Rd., Atlanta, GA 30340...S. Topol...communications & instrumentation prods.

Scott Paper Co... Scott Plaza, Phila., PA 19113...Charles D. Dickey Jr...paper prods. 06720.

Scovill Inc...99 Mill St., Waterbury, CT 06720...W. F. Andrews...automotive, security, housing prods., small appliances.

Seagram Co. Ltd...1430 Peel St., Montreal, Que., Canada H3A 1S9...E. M. Bronfman...distilled spirits & wine (Seven Crown; Chivas Regal; Calvert; Wolfschmidt Vodka; Paul Masson; Christian Brothers; Gold Seal).

G.D. Searle & Co...P.O. Box 1045, Skokie, IL 60076...Donald Rumsfeld...pharmaceutical/consumer, medical, optical prods., vision centers.

Sears Roebuck & Co:... Sears Tower, Chicago, IL 60684...Edward R. Telling...merchandising, insurance (Allstate), financial services.

Shell Oil Co...P.O. Box 2463, Houston, TX 77001...John F. Bookout...oil, gas, chemicals.

Sherwin-Williams Co...101 Prospect Ave. N.W., Cleveland, OH 44115...John G. Breen...world's largest paint producer.

Simplicity Pattern Co., Inc...200 Madison Ave., New York, NY 10016...H. Cooper...paper patterns for home sewing.

Singer Co...30 Rockefeller Plaza, N.Y., NY 10020...Joseph B. Flavin...sewing prods., furniture, power tools.

Skyline Corp...2520 By-Pass Rd., Elkhart, IN 46515...Arthur J. Decio...mfg. housing and recreational vehicles.

A.O. Smith...3533 N. 27th St., Milwaukee, WI 53201...L.B. Smith...auto and truck-frames, agricultural prods.

Smithkline Corp... One Franklin Plaza, Phila., PA 19101...R. F. Dee...pharmaceuticals, animal health prods., diagnostic instruments, cosmetics.

Sony Corp. of America... Tokyo, Japan...Kazuo Iwama...manuf. televisions, radios, tape recorders, audio equip., video tape recorders.

Southland Corp...2828 N. Haskell Ave., Dallas, TX 75204...J. P. Thompson...convenience stores (7-Eleven; Gristede's).

Southern Pacific Co... One Market Plaza, San Francisco, CA 94105...B.F. Biaggini...transportation, leasing, communications, real estate, natural resources.

Sperry Corp...1290 Ave. of the Americas, N.Y., NY 10019...J. Paul Lyet...computers and data processing, farm, guidance & control equip.

Sperry and Hutchinson Co...S & H Bldg., 330 Madison Ave., N.Y., NY 10017...F. Collins...S & H stamps, carpeting, furniture, insurance.

Spring Mills, Inc...205 N. White St., Ft. Mill, SC 29715...W. Y. Elisha...textiles.

Squibb Corp...40 W. 57th St., N.Y., NY 10019...Richard M. Furlaud...drugs, confectionery, household prods...Charles of the Ritz; Life Savers.

A.E. Staley Manufacturing Co...2200 E. Eldorado, Decatur, IL 62525...Donald E. Nordlund...corn and soybean processing, consumer prods.

Standard Brands Incorporated. 625 Madison Ave., N.Y., NY 10022...F. Ross Johnson...foods, related prods...(Chase and Sanborn coffee; Planter's nuts; Curtiss candy). *merged with Nabisco Brands, Inc., 1981.*

Standard Oil Co. of California...225 Bush, San Francisco, CA 94104...H.J. Haynes...integrated oil co.

Standard Oil Co. (Indiana)...200 E. Randolph Dr., Chicago, IL 60601...John E. Swearinger...oil and gas exploitation & prod., chemicals, fertilizers.

Standard Oil Co. (Ohio)... Midland Bldg., Cleveland, OH 44115...Alton W. Whitehouse Jr...oil & natural gas.

Stanley Works...195 Lake St., New Britain, CT 06050...D.W. Davis...hand tools, hardware, door opening equipment.

Sterling Drug Inc...90 Park Ave., N.Y., NY 10016...W. Clarke Wescoe...pharmaceuticals, cosmetics & toiletries, household, proprietary prods., chemicals, environmental control (Bayer Aspirin, Lysol Dorothy Gray; Parfums Givenchy).

J.P. Stevens & Co., Inc...1185 Ave. of the Americas, N.Y., NY 10036...W. Stevens...fabrics, carpets, other textile home furnishings.

Stokely-Van Camp, Inc...941 N. Meridian, Indianapolis, IN 46206...A.J. Stokley...canned fruits, vegetables, and frozen foods, soft drinks (Gatorade).

Storer Broadcasting Co...1177 Kane Concourse, Miami Beach, FL 33154...P. Storer...television & radio broadcast-

ing, CATV.
Subaru of America, Inc... .7040 Central Hwy., Pennsauken, NJ 08109...Harvey Lamm...auto importer.
Sunbeam Corp... .5400 W. Roosevelt Rd., Chicago, IL 60650...R. P. Gwinn...manuf. of small appliances (Oster; Rowenta; Victa).
Sun Company, Inc... 100 Matsonford Rd., Radnor, PA 19087...T. A. Burtis...petroleum.

Taft Broadcasting Co... .1718 Young St., Cincinnati, OH 45210...D. S. Taft...radio, TV broadcasting, TV cartoons (Hanna-Barbera), amusement parks.
Tandy Corp... .1900 One Tandy Center, Fort Worth, TX 76102...Phil R. North...consumer electronics retailing & mfg....Radio Shack.
Teledyne, Inc... .1901 Ave. of the Stars, Los Angeles, CA 90067...H. E. Singleton...electronics, aerospace prods., industrial prods., insurance, finance.
Tenneco, Inc... .P.O. Box 2511, Houston, TX 77001...J. L. Ketelsen...oil, natural gas pipelines, construction and farm equip.
Texaco Inc... .2000 Westchester Ave., White Plains, NY 10650...Maurice F. Granville...petroleum and petroleum prods.
Texas Instruments Inc... .13500 North Central, Dallas, TX 75265...Mark Shepherd Jr...electrical & electronics mfg.
Textron Inc... .40 Westminster St., Providence, RI 02903...Robert P. Straetz...aerospace, consumer, industrial, metal prods.
3M... 3M Center, St. Paul, MN 55101...Lewis W. Lehr...abrasives, adhesives, building services & chemicals, electrical, health care, photographic, printing, recording materials.
Tidewater Inc... .1440 Canal St., New Orleans, LA 70112...J. P. Laborde...marine equip. for oil industry.
Time Inc... Time & Life Bldg., New York, NY 10020...R. P. Davidson...magazine publisher (Time; Sports Illustrated; Fortune; Money; People), CATV (Home Box Office).
Toro Co... .8009-34th Ave. South, Minneapolis, MN 55420...K. B. Melrose...lawn, snow removal equip.
Trane Co., The... .3600 Pammel Creek Rd., La Crosse, WI 54601...W. G. Roth...air conditioning and heat transfer equip.
Transamerica Corp... .600 Montgomery St., San Francisco, CA 94111...John R. Beckett...insurance, financial, leisure, business services (Occidental Life Ins.; Budget Rent A Car).
Trans World Corp... .605 3d Ave., N.Y., NY 10158...L. Edwin Smart...holding co...Trans World Airlines; Hilton International; Spartan Food Systems.
Travelers Corp... One Tower Sq., Hartford, CT 06115...E. H. Budd...insurance.
Twentieth Century-Fox Film Corp... .10201 West Pico Blvd., Los Angeles, CA 90035...Dennis C. Stanfill...motion pictures and TV program production and distribution, soft drink bottling, music publishing, ski resort.

UAL, Inc... .1200 Algonquin Rd., Elk Grove Township, IL...R. J. Ferris...United Airlines, Western Hotels.
Union Carbide Corp... .270 Park Ave., N.Y. NY 10017...William S. Sneath...chemicals.
Union Oil Co. of California... Union Oil Center, Los Angeles, CA 90017...F. L. Hartley...integrated oil co., mining, chemicals.
Union Pacific Corp... .345 Park Ave., N.Y., NY 10022...J.H. Evans...railroad, petroleum, mining.
Uniroyal, Inc... World Headquarters, Middlebury, CT 06749...Joseph P. Flannery...tires, chemical, plastic prods.
United States Gypsum Co... .101 S. Wacker Dr., Chicago, IL 60606...G. J. Morgan...largest U.S. producer of gypsum & related prods.
United States Steel Corp... .600 Grant St., Pittsburgh, PA 15230...David M. Roderick...largest U.S. steel co., chemicals, transportation.
United States Tobacco Co... .100 W. Putnam Ave., Greenwich, CT 06830...L.F. Bantle...smokeless tobacco (Copenhagen; Skoal; Happy Days), pipes & pipe tobacco, pet foods.
United Technologies... United Technologies Bldg., Hartford, CT 06101...Harry J. Gray...high-technology prods...Carrier Corp.; Otis Elevator; Pratt & Whitney, Sikorsky Aircraft.
Upjohn Co... .7000 Portage Rd., Kalamazoo, MI 49001...R.T. Parfet Jr...pharmaceuticals, chemicals, agricultural and health care prods.
USAir, Inc... .Washington National Airport, Wash., DC

20001...Edwin I. Colodny...air transportation.
U.S. Home Corp... .1177 West Loop South, Dallas, TX 77001...G. R. Odom...manuf. single family homes.

VF Corp... .1047 No. Park Rd., Wyomissing, PA 19610...M.O. Lee...apparel...Vanity Fair; Kay Windsor; Lee.
Vulcan Materials Co... One Metroplex Dr., Birmingham, AL 35209...B. A. Monagham...construction materials, chemicals, metals.

Walgreen Co... .200 Wilmot Rd., Deerfield, IL 60015...Charles R. Walgreen 3d...retail drug chain, restaurants.
Wang Laboratories, Inc... One Industrial Ave., Lowell, MA 01851...A. Wang...word processors.
Warnaco Inc... .350 Lafayette St., Bridgeport, CT 06602...James C. Walker...apparel...Hathaway, Puritan, High Tide, White Stag.
Warner Communications Inc... .75 Rockefeller Plaza, N.Y., NY 10019...Steven J. Ross...filmed entertainment, records & music publishing, book publishing, CATV system, consumer prods., Atari, Franklin Mint.
Warner-Lambert Co... .201 Tabor Rd., Morris Plains, NJ 07950...Ward S. Hagan...health care, optical prods., candy.
Washington Post Co... .1150 15th St., N.W., Washington, DC 20071...Katharine Graham...newspapers, magazines (Newsweek; Inside Sports), TV stations.
Western Airlines, Inc... .6060 Avion Dr., Los Angeles, CA 90045...A. F. Kelly...air transportation.
Western Union Corp... One Lake St., Upper Saddle River, NJ 07458...Robert M. Flanagan...telecommunications.
Westinghouse Electric Corp... Westinghouse Bldg., Gateway Center, Pittsburgh, PA 15222...R.E. Kirby...manuf. products that generate, transmit, distribute, and use electricity, radio and television stations.
West Point-Pepperell Inc... .400 W. 10th St., West Point, GA 31833...J. L. Lanier Jr...apparel, industrial & household fabrics.
Weyerhaeuser Co... Tacoma, WA 98477...George H. Weyerhaeuser...manuf., distribution forest prods., including bldg. materials, pulp, paper, newsprint.
Wheelabrator-Frye Inc... Liberty Lane, Hampton, NH 03842...M. D. Dingman...environmental, energy, engineered prods., chemicals and specialty prods., railroad freight cars and equip.
Whirlpool Corp... Administrative Center, Benton Harbor, MI 49022...John H. Platts...major home appliances.
White Consolidated Industries, Inc... .11770 Berea Rd., Cleveland, OH 44111...R.H. Holdt...major home appliances, industrial equip. and machinery.
Willamette Industries, Inc... First Natl. Bank Tower, Portland, OR 97201...Gene D. Knudson...building materials and paper prods.
Williams Cos... One Williams Center, Tulsa, OK 74172...J. H. Williams...fertilizer, energy, metals.
Winn-Dixie Stores, Inc... .5050 Edgewood Ct., Jacksonville, FL 32203...B.L. Thomas...retail grocery chain.
Wometco Enterprises, Inc... .306 N. Miami Ave., Miami, FL 33128...M. Wolfson...television broadcasting, CATV, soft drink bottler.
F.W. Woolworth Co... .233 Broadway, N.Y., NY 10007...Edward F. Gibbons...variety stores, dept. stores, shoestores... Woolco, Kinney.
Wm. Wrigley Jr. Co... .410 N. Michigan Ave., Chicago, IL 60611...William Wrigley...chewing gum.

Xerox Corporation... Stamford, CT 06904...C. Peter McColough...equip. for reproduction, reduction, and transmission of printed information.

Zale Corp... .3000 Diamond Park, Dallas TX 75247... D. Zale...jewelry retailer.
Zayre Corp... Framingham, MA 01701...S. L. Feldberg...self-service discount dept. stores, specialty shops.
Zenith Radio Corp... .100 Milwaukee Ave., Glenview, IL 60025...R. W. Kluckman...electronic home entertainment prods.
Zurn Industries, Inc... One Zurn Place, Erie, PA 16512...D. M. Zurn...pollution control, energy, mechanical systems.

ECONOMICS

U.S. Budget Receipts and Outlays—1977-1980

Source: Treasury Department; Office of Management and Budget.
(Fiscal years end Sept. 30)
(thousands of dollars)

Classification	Fiscal 1977	Fiscal 1978	Fiscal 1979	Fiscal 1980[1]
Net Receipts				
Individual income taxes	156,725,183	180,987,773	217,840,966	244,068,898
Corporation income taxes	54,892,364	59,951,865	65,676,588	64,599,673
Social insurance taxes and contributions:				
Federal old-age and survivors insurance	68,031,809	73,140,779	83,409,910	95,580,645
Federal disability insurance	8,785,502	12,250,395	14,583,743	16,639,155
Federal hospital insurance	13,484,042	16,679,867	19,890,684	23,233,135
Railroad retirement taxes	1,908,494	1,822,006	2,189,887	2,311,977
Total employment taxes and contributions	92,209,847	103,893,048	120,074,224	138,764,911
Other insurance and retirement:				
Unemployment	11,311,506	13,849,597	15,386,733	15,335,788
Federal supplementary medical insurance	2,192,903	2,431,133	2,636,005	2,927,711
Federal employees retirement	2,909,697	3,174,262	3,428,322	3,659,505
Civil service retirement and disability	58,923	62,323	66,042	59,228
Total social insurance taxes and contributions	108,682,876	123,410,366	141,591,326	160,747,143
Excise taxes	17,547,715	18,376,183	18,744,953	24,329,156
Estate and gift taxes	7,326,877	5,285,401	5,410,556	6,389,480
Customs duties	5,150,151	6,572,717	7,438,533	7,173,836
Deposits of earnings-Federal Reserve Banks	5,908,214	6,641,091	8,326,930	11,767,143
All other miscellaneous receipts	640,568	771,976	910,317	974,589
Net Budget Receipts	356,861,331	401,997,000	465,940,168	520,049,919
Net Outlays				
Legislative Branch	976,492	1,048,776	1,077,101	1,217,983
The Judiciary	391,039	435,124	479,665	564,144
Executive Office of the President:				
The White House Office	17,236	16,571	16,159	18,967
Office of Management and Budget	26,536	29,299	29,788	34,971
Total Executive Office	73,386	74,566	79,589	95,385
Funds appropriated to the President:				
Appalachian regional development	248,868	261,674	304,337	340,531
Disaster relief	294,016	470,290	284,220	573,760
Foreign assistance-security	347,287	2,019,665	1,786,014	3,903,034
Foreign assistance-development-bilateral	507,098	434,972	593,058	750,062
Int. narcotics control assistance	NA	34,987	46,702	26,875
Total funds appropriated to the President	2,497,204	4,475,091	2,536,618	7,537,858
Agriculture Department:				
Food stamp program	5,398,795	5,498,774	6,821,746	9,117,136
Child Nutrition Program	2,635,039	2,526,732	2,879,668	3,377,056
Total Agriculture Department	16,737,730	20,368,401	20,633,725	24,554,916
Commerce Department	2,606,804	5,252,159	4,071,765	3,755,513
Defense Department:				
Military personnel	25,714,935	27,075,347	28,407,171	30,841,732
Retired military personnel	8,216,429	9,171,474	10,279,058	11,919,776
Operation and maintenance	30,688,742	33,577,970	36,424,304	44,770,126
Procurement	18,178,230	19,975,553	25,404,254	29,020,667
Research and development	9,795,166	10,507,963	11,152,177	13,126,878
Military construction	1,913,804	1,931,504	2,079,987	2,449,521
Family housing	1,357,866	1,404,772	1,467,517	1,680,174
Corps of Engineers and civil functions	2,279,998	2,611,625	2,886,226	3,204,436
Total Defense Department	98,031,451	105,677,084	117,921,453	136,137,929
Energy Department	5,020,477	6,429,745	7,888,792	6,456,865
Health, Education and Welfare Department:				
Food and Drug Administration	NA	275,971	299,834	325,736
National Institutes of Health	2,253,040	2,675,703	2,869,565	3,222,304
Public Health Service	NA	6,757,527	6,928,528	7,817,750
Old-age and survivors benefits	73,478,596	81,205,460	87,591,968	100,614,178
Social Security Administration	NA	108,221,236	118,041,422	134,353,608
Education Division	7,783,479	8,763,618	10,713,037	13,124,229
Human Development Services	NA	5,252,264	5,718,598	5,343,312
Total HEW	147,455,436	162,809,429	181,185,638	207,815,006
Housing and Urban Development Department	5,832,430	7,760,944	9,218,091	12,576,186
Interior Department	3,085,260	3,677,605	4,087,007	4,376,994
Justice Department:				
Federal Bureau of Investigation	520,218	552,001	585,991	-609,181
Total Justice Department	2,349,726	2,397,372	2,521,715	2,631,677
Labor Department:				
Unemployment Trust Fund	14,102,958	11,169,127	11,172,982	16,440,284
Total Labor Department	22,374,056	22,902,043	22,650,336	29,750,870
State Department	1,131,820	1,251,536	1,548,046	1,911,530
Transportation Department	12,513,984	13,451,791	15,485,569	18,962,803
Treasury Department:				
Internal Revenue Service	2,265,183	3,325,766	3,422,178	4,331,945
Interest on the public debt	41,899,720	48,694,855	59,837,203	74,860,226
General revenue sharing	6,760,092	6,854,924	6,847,709	6,828,835
Total Treasury Department	49,560,182	56,309,144	64,595,923	76,642,057
Environmental Protection Agency	4,364,808	4,071,472	4,799,768	5,601,883

Classification Net Outlays (cont'd)	Fiscal 1977	Fiscal 1978	Fiscal 1979	Fiscal 1980[1]
General Services Administration.	−31,100	117,042	172,761	169,331
National Aeronautics and Space Administration . . .	3,943,817	3,980,022	4,187,232	4,849,924
Veterans Administration	18,019,353	18,962,152	19,887,171	21,134,538
Independent agencies:				
ACTION.	186,296	203,163	211,325	133,193
Arms Control and Disarmament Agency	11,863	13,990	14,653	17,256
Board for International Broadcasting.	57,837	65,451	82,692	98,372
Civil Aeronautics Board	102,707	101,359	99,336	116,657
Commission on Civil Rights	9,476	10,464	10,257	12,035
Community Services Administration	639,363	767,918	778,894	2,166,279
Consumer Product Safety Commission	39,867	40,058	39,270	44,177
Corporation for Public Broadcasting	103,000	119,200	120,200	152,000
District of Columbia	315,717	370,968	393,151	424,694
Equal Employment Opportunity Commission . .	71,729	74,160	92,453	130,782
Export-Import Bank of the United States	NA	−105,904	200,052	1,836,003
Federal Communications Commission.	55,776	64,065	69,542	75,804
Federal Deposit Insurance Corporation	−851,645	−566,610	−1,218,370	−922,130
Federal Emergency Management Agency	NA	259,290	417,422	660,106
Federal Home Loan Bank Board.	1,913,355	−403,045	−488,357	552,046
Federal Trade Commission	51,703	58,815	62,605	68,474
Intragovernmental Agencies	292,403	153,247	88,911	104,927
International Communications Agency.	NA	352,116	373,463	432,752
Interstate Commerce Commission	60,602	64,899	54,797	155,682
Legal Services Corporation	125,004	157,429	254,307	320,308
Merit Systems Protection Board	NA	NA	6,476	13,086
National Foundation on the Arts and Humanities	192,753	247,261	283,630	320,702
National Labor Relations Board	80,546	90,414	97,190	108,867
National Science Foundation	752,035	802,783	869,647	911,907
National Transportation Safety Board	NA	15,513	15,515	17,754
Nuclear Regulatory Commission	230,547	270,862	309,475	377,872
Office of Personnel Management	NA	10,962,658	12,654,562	15,052,426
Postal Service	2,267,449	1,778,240	1,786,509	1,676,878
Railroad Retirement Board	3,858,848	4,074,556	4,365,399	4,788,046
Securities and Exchange Commission.	53,635	61,302	65,978	74,140
Small Business Administration	699,974	2,766,028	1,631,142	1,898,932
Smithsonian Institution.	114,988	125,239	132,182	138,758
Tennessee Valley Authority.	1,099,559	1,412,228	1,884,141	1,869,233
U.S. Railway Association	735,500	753,725	737,150	672,055
Other Independent agencies	85,569	177,152	186,299	287,139
Total independent agencies	**20,014,438**	**25,078,715**	**26,681,897**	**34,931,040**
Undistributed offsetting receipts	−15,053,215	−15,772,226	−18,488,845	−22,493,807
Net Budget Outlays	**401,896,376**	**450,758,000**	**493,221,018**	**579,011,294**
Less net receipts.	356,861,331	401,997,000	465,940,168	520,049,919
Deficit	**−45,035,045**	**−48,761,000**	**−27,280,850**	**−58,961,375**

(1) Estimate. (NA) Not available.

U.S. Net Receipts and Outlays

Source: Treasury Department; annual statements for year ending June 30[1] (thousands of dollars)

Yearly average	Receipts	Expenditures	Yearly average	Receipts	Expenditures	Yearly average	Receipts	Expenditures
1789-1800[1]	5,717	5,776	1871-1875	336,830	287,460	1916-1920[6]	3,483,652	8,065,333
1801-1810[2].	13,056	9,086	1876-1880	288,124	255,598	1921-1925	4,306,673	3,578,989
1811-1820[2].	21,032	23,943	1881-1885	366,961	257,691	1926-1930	4,069,138	3,182,807
1821-1830[2].	21,928	16,162	1886-1890	375,448	279,134	1931-1935[4]	2,770,973	5,214,874
1831-1840[2].	30,461	24,495	1891-1895	352,891	363,599	1936-1940[4]	4,960,614	10,192,367
1841-1850[2]	28,545	34,097	1896-1900	434,877	457,451	1941-1945[4]	25,951,137	66,037,928
1851-1860	60,237	60,163	1901-1905	559,481	535,559	1946-1950[5][7]	39,047,243	42,334,534
1861-1865	160,907	683,735	1906-1910	628,507	639,178			
1866-1870	447,301	377,642	1911-1915	710,227	720,252			

Fiscal year	Receipts	Expenditures	Fiscal year	Receipts	Expenditures	Fiscal year	Receipts	Expenditures
1955.	60,389,744	64,569,973	1971	188,332,129	210,652,667	1976 Trans[3]. .	81,772,766	94,472,996
1960.	77,763,460	76,539,413	1972[8].	215,262,639	238,285,907	1977[3].	356,861,331	401,896,376
1964.	89,458,664	97,684,375	1973	232,191,842	246,603,359	1978	401,997,000	450,758,000
1965.	93,071,797	96,506,904	1974	264,847,484	268,342,952	1979	465,954,656	493,607,095
1968[9].	153,675,705	172,803,186	1975	281,037,466	324,641,586	1980	520,049,919	579,011,294
1970	193,843,791	194,968,258	1976	300,005,077	365,610,129	1981[10]	605,640,000	661,237,000

(1) Average for period March 4, 1789, to Dec. 31, 1800. (2) Years ended Dec. 31, 1801 to 1842; average for 1841-1850 is for the period Jan. 1, 1841, to June 30, 1850. (3) Effective fiscal year 1977, fiscal year is reckoned Oct. 1-Sept. 30; transition quarter covers July 1, 1976-Sept. 30, 1976. (4) Expenditures for years 1932 through 1946 have been revised to include Government corps. (wholly owned) etc. (net). (5) Effective January 3, 1949, amounts refunded by the Government, principally for the overpayment of taxes, are being reported as deductions from total receipts rather than as expenditures. Also, effective July 1, 1948, payments to the Treasury, principally by wholly owned Government corporations for retirement of capital stock and for disposition of earnings, are excluded in reporting both budget receipts and expenditures. Neither of these changes affects the size of the budget surplus or deficit. Beginning 1931 figures in each case have been adjusted accordingly for comparative purposes. (6) Figures for 1918 through 1946 are revised to exclude statutory debt retirement (sinking fund, etc.). (7) Excludes $3 billion transferred to Foreign Economics Corporation Trust Fund, and includes $3 billion representing expenditures made from the FEC Trust Fund. (8) Effective fiscal year 1972 loan repayments will be netted against expenditures and known as outlays. (9) From 1968, figures include trust funds (e.g. Social Security). (10) Estimate.

Summary of U.S. Receipts by Source and Outlays by Function

Source: U.S. Treasury Department, and the Office of Management and Budget

(in millions)

Net Receipts	Fiscal 1977	Fiscal 1978	Fiscal 1979	Fiscal 1980[1]
Individual income taxes	$156,725	$180,988	$217,800	$244,069
Corporation income taxes	54,892	59,952	65,700	64,600
Social insurance taxes and contributions	108,689	117,743	141,600	160,747
Excise taxes	17,548	18,376	18,700	24,329
Estate and gift taxes	7,327	5,285	5,400	6,389
Customs duties	5,150	6,572	7,400	7,174
Miscellaneous receipts	6,531	7,400	9,200	12,742
Total	**356,861**	**401,997**	**465,900**	**520,050**
Net outlays				
National defense	97,501	105,200	117,700	135,880
International affairs	4,831	5,900	6,100	10,476
General science, space, and technology	4,677	4,700	5,000	5,999
Energy	4,172	5,900	6,900	6,339
Natural resources and environment	10,000	10,900	12,100	14,142
Agriculture	5,526	7,700	6,200	4,951
Commerce and housing credit	-31	3,300	2,600	7,537
Transportation	14,636	15,400	17,500	20,840
Community and regional development	6,283	11,000	9,500	10,182
Education, training, employment and social services	20,985	26,500	29,700	31,397
Health	38,785	43,700	49,600	58,165
Income security	137,004	146,200	160,200	192,160
Veterans benefits and services	18,038	19,000	19,900	21,167
Administration of justice	3,600	3,800	4,200	4,553
General government	3,357	3,800	4,200	4,878
General purpose fiscal assistance	9,499	9,600	8,400	8,268
Interest	38,092	44,000	52,600	64,571
Undistributed offsetting receipts	-15,053	-15,800	-18,500	-22,494
Total	**401,902**	**450,800**	**493,700**	**579,011**

(1) Estimate

U.S. Direct Investment Abroad, Countries and Industries

Source: Bureau of Economic Analysis, U.S. Commerce Department

(millions of dollars)

	Direct investment position		Equity and intercompany account outflows (inflows (−))		Reinvested earnings		Fees and royalties		Income	
	1979	1980	1979	1980	1979	1980	1979	1980	1979	1980
All areas	186,760	213,468	4,984	1,548	18,964	16,998	4,980	5,695	38,330	36,482
Petroleum	38,744	46,920	3,120	-2,757	5,414	4,553	325	237	13,413	13,022
Manufacturing	78,640	89,063	1,175	3,543	7,616	6,364	3,429	3,975	13,054	11,263
Other	69,376	77,485	688	763	5,934	6,080	1,226	1,483	11,863	12,558
Developed countries	138,668	157,084	2,723	5,055	14,679	12,481	4,181	4,748	24,942	24,582
Petroleum	30,220	34,173	918	-	4,204	3,917	225	253	6,962	8,566
Manufacturing	63,518	71,399	537	3,145	6,568	4,491	3,100	3,562	11,018	8,557
Other	44,931	51,512	1,268	1,911	3,906	4,074	857	933	6,962	7,459
Canada	40,243	44,640	1,035	370	3,003	3,490	886	931	5,517	5,733
Petroleum	8,648	10,573	156	518	1,052	1,389	50	67	1,890	2,003
Manufacturing	17,392	18,802	455	365	1,156	1,040	658	713	2,031	1,838
Other	14,203	15,266	424	-513	795	1,061	178	151	1,596	1,892
Europe	82,622	95,686	1,225	4,962	10,627	7,821	2,646	3,083	17,116	16,078
Petroleum	17,755	19,924	523	-101	2,884	2,251	149	156	4,483	5,856
Manufacturing	39,403	45,425	-183	2,754	4,873	3,057	1,997	2,366	7,965	5,804
Other	25,463	30,337	885	2,309	2,870	2,513	500	561	4,668	4,419
Other	15,803	16,758	462	-277	1,043	1,170	650	734	2,309	2,771
Petroleum	3,816	3,676	239	-417	269	277	26	30	588	707
Manufacturing	6,723	7,172	264	25	539	394	445	483	1,023	916
Other	5,265	5,910	-41	114	242	499	178	221	698	1,149
Developing countries	44,525	52,684	2,745	-3,454	4,149	4,387	1,008	1,235	13,127	11,712
Petroleum	6,093	10,271	2,335	-2,812	1,189	-	315	276	6,333	4,112
Manufacturing	15,122	17,664	639	398	1,048	1,874	329	413	2,036	2,706
Other	23,309	24,749	-228	-1,041	1,913	-	364	545	4,758	4,894
Latin America	35,056	38,275	270	-691	2,924	3,347	422	591	6,546	6,580
Petroleum	3,948	4,336	58	96	788	288	49	48	1,392	963
Manufacturing	12,410	14,489	555	462	687	1,509	200	265	1,501	2,161
Other	18,697	19,450	-342	-1,250	1,449	1,550	173	278	3,652	3,726
Other	9,469	14,409	2,475	-2,763	1,226	1,040	587	644	6,581	4,862
Petroleum	2,145	5,935	2,277	-2,908	400	-	266	228	4,940	3,149
Manufacturing	2,712	3,175	84	-64	361	365	129	149	535	545
Other	4,612	5,299	114	209	464	-	191	267	1,106	1,168
International	3,567	3,701	-484	-52	137	130	-210	-288	262	548

State Finances
Revenues, Expenditures, Debts, Taxes, U.S. Aid, Military Contracts

For fiscal 1980 (year ending June 30, 1980, except: Alabama and Michigan, Sept. 30; New York, Mar. 31; Texas, Aug. 31.
*Military prime contracts. Taxes are State income and sales (or gross receipts) taxes, and vehicle, etc., fees.

Sources: Census Bureau, U.S. Treasury and Defense Depts.

State	Receipts (thousands)	Outlays (thousands)	Total debt (thousands)	Per cap. debt	Per cap. taxes	Per cap. U.S. aid	Military contracts (thousands)
Alabama	$4,153,588	$4,001,856	$1,032,338	$265.38	$477.32	$407	$746,415
Alaska	3,229,513	2,032,718	1,544,554	3,861.38	3,594.02	1,462	257,355
Arizona.	3,187,080	2,637,287	94,007	34.59	619.72	308	729,656
Arkansas. . . .	2,295,172	2,147,542	362,579	158.68	507.99	411	172,384
California. . . .	36,087,253	32,812,199	8,361,705	353.28	818.23	371	13,914,411
Colorado. . . .	3,365,513	2,804,770	460,497	159.40	516.06	344	518,300
Connecticut . .	3,472,328	3,341,266	3,879,197	1,248.13	591.92	372	3,879,061
Delaware. . . .	970,333	886,151	1,044,499	1,755.46	866.75	426	243,828
Florida	8,222,693	7,386,754	2,626,926	269.70	493.25	293	2,053,198
Georgia	5,194,061	4,900,734	1,404,635	257.07	499.44	434	960,992
Hawaii	1,895,329	1,660,028	1,864,213	1,931.83	1,034.59	480	315,410
Idaho	1,107,804	1,041,287	327,334	346.75	519.43	416	28,115
Illinois.	12,729,900	12,428,758	6,277,201	549.76	619.47	392	1,006,783
Indiana	4,794,271	4,866,803	607,581	110.67	491.03	292	1,297,786
Iowa	3,479,012	3,411,812	380,999	130.79	599.67	341	303,102
Kansas	2,418,808	2,254,031	438,137	185.42	537.31	346	806,245
Kentucky. . . .	4,168,415	4,569,135	3,035,267	829.08	585.89	401	277,519
Louisiana. . . .	5,412,417	4,886,708	2,977,031	708.14	570.22	372	694,643
Maine.	1,369,397	1,325,879	730,266	649.13	550.36	464	459,418
Maryland. . . .	5,564,324	5,434,815	3,502,248	830.70	654.84	437	1,795,400
Massachusetts	7,457,128	7,336,101	5,784,878	1,008.35	684.56	503	3,743,171
Michigan	12,356,577	12,633,601	2,916,082	314.98	642.43	424	1,701,749
Minnesota . . .	5,700,144	5,417,876	2,069,902	507.70	785.52	408	1,070,273
Mississippi . . .	2,884,870	2,690,817	815,045	323.30	498.98	472	808,291
Missouri	4,257,652	3,996,072	1,017,862	207.01	425.98	391	3,264,063
Montana	1,153,208	1,004,971	309,533	393.31	553.69	618	35,241
Nebraska . . .	1,505,994	1,392,220	199,341	126.97	520.23	348	103,631
Nevada.	1,220,521	1,097,558	527,969	660.79	596.50	419	50,390
New Hampshire	893,832	889,448	899,050	976.17	290.44	375	306,481
New Jersey . .	8,822,117	8,536,848	6,526,797	886.31	579.28	384	1,532,102
New Mexico . .	2,183,291	1,744,172	707,783	544.45	712.34	514	294,877
New York . . .	27,199,172	24,977,939	23,640,088	1,346.48	724.31	545	5,678,789
North Carolina.	6,201,827	5,732,542	1,265,720	215.48	547.39	328	676,759
North Dakota .	1,013,327	909,915	219,276	335.80	569.47	531	73,150
Ohio	12,180,344	11,397,371	4,014,977	371.86	441.48	318	1,633,335
Oklahoma . . .	3,433,126	3,248,996	1,525,740	504.38	587.12	350	466,880
Oregon.	4,040,741	3,455,956	4,886,286	1,855.79	552.74	469	196,182
Pennsylvania .	14,004,267	12,644,004	6,347,873	534.92	610.16	380	2,215,927
Rhode Island .	1,392,699	1,361,003	1,463,092	1,544.98	581.61	504	261,792
South Carolina	3,484,289	3,325,311	1,937,234	621.11	538.01	342	331,444
South Dakota .	762,190	739,503	714,274	1,035.18	392.06	642	20,971
Tennessee. . .	4,028,047	3,873,736	1,405,948	306.24	411.02	442	533,406
Texas.	12,924,347	11,486,851	2,468,627	173.50	475.03	278	5,413,352
Utah	1,888,807	1,754,804	537,074	367.61	537.82	391	251,355
Vermont	711,123	675,867	654,159	1,280.15	521.17	635	125,138
Virginia	5,655,917	5,393,220	1,926,291	360.32	513.15	332	3,366,493
Washington . .	6,323,963	5,714,612	1,600,407	387.51	706.40	405	2,316,807
West Virginia .	2,640,308	2,678,563	1,816,478	931.53	625.38	487	123,897
Wisconsin . . .	6,587,518	6,074,117	2,445,967	519.87	715.48	430	377,565
Wyoming. . . .	937,196	797,449	362,895	770.48	824.04	625	33,295
Total or average	**$276,961,733**	**$257,811,981**	**$121,957,862**	**$539.95**	**$606.88**	**$441**	**$68,069,561**

U.S. Customs and Internal Revenue Receipts

Source: Treasury Department

Gross. Not reduced by appropriations to Federal old-age and survivors insurance trust fund or refunds or receipts.

Fiscal year	Customs	Internal Revenue	Fiscal year	Customs	Internal Revenue	Fiscal year	Customs	Internal Revenue
1930	$587,000,903	$3,039,295,014	1955	$606,396,634	$66,288,691,586	1976	$4,074,176,000	$302,520,000,000
1935	343,353,034	3,277,690,028	1960	1,123,037,579	91,774,802,823	1977	5,150,151,000	358,139,000,000
1940	348,590,635	5,303,133,988	1965	1,477,548,820	114,428,991,753	1978	6,728,612,000	399,776,000,000
1945	354,775,542	43,902,001,929	1970 [1]	2,429,799,000	195,700,000,000	1979	7,639,620,000	460,412,185,000
1950	422,650,329	39,448,607,109	1975	3,675,532,000	293,800,000,000	1980	7,481,593,000	565,159,678,000

(1) Transitional quarter; July 1, 1976 through Sept. 30, 1976. Through 1976 the fiscal year ended June 30. From 1977 on, fiscal year ends Sept. 30.

U.S. Business Indexes

Source: Federal Reserve System; F.W. Dodge Div., McGraw-Hill; U.S. Labor Department; U.S. Commerce Department

(1967 = 100, except as noted)

Period	Total	Industrial production Market					Industry Manufacturing	Capacity utilization in mfg.[1]	Construction contracts	Nonagricultural employment Total[2]	Manufacturing		Total retail sales[4]	Prices[4]	
		Total	Products			Materials					Employment[3]	Payrolls		Consumer	Producer finished goods
			Final Total		Equipment	Intermediate									
				Consumer goods											
1963 .	76.5	76.4	75.5	81.3	67.5	79.9	76.7	75.8	83.5	86.1	86.1	87.7	76.0	79	91.8	93.8
1965 .	89.8	88.2	87.6	92.6	80.7	90.6	92.4	89.7	89.5	93.2	92.3	93.9	88.1	90	94.5	95.7
1970 .	107.8	106.9	105.3	109.0	100.1	112.9	109.2	106.4	79.3	123.1	107.7	98.0	114.1	119	116.3	110.3
1975 .	117.8	119.3	118.2	124.0	110.2	123.1	115.5	116.3	72.9	162.3	116.9	91.3	157.3	185	161.2	163.4
1976 .	130.5	129.7	127.6	137.1	114.6	137.2	131.7	130.3	79.5	190.2	120.7	95.3	177.0	204	170.5	170.3
1977 .	138.2	137.9	135.9	145.3	123.0	145.1	138.6	138.4	81.9	160.5	125.0	98.6	198.3	224	181.5	180.6
1978 .	146.1	144.8	142.2	149.1	132.8	154.1	148.3	146.8	84.4	174.3	130.3	102.1	222.4	248	195.4	194.6
1979 .	152.5	150.0	147.2	150.8	142.2	160.5	154.6	153.6	85.7	183.0	136.0	104.9	246.8	282	217.4	216.1
1980[5] .	140.5	142.3	141.7	141.7	141.6	144.4	137.8	138.9	74.5	148.0	136.9	96.8	251.5	304	247.8	249.0

(1) Percent of capacity; based on output and capacity indexes, 1967 = 100. (2) Employees only; excludes personnel in the Armed Forces. (3) Production workers only. (4) FR index based on Census Bureau figures. (5) Seasonally adjusted indexes except for prices. Figures shown are for Aug. 1980 except for construction contracts and consumer prices which are for July 1980.

Producer Price Indexes

Source: Bureau of Labor Statistics, U.S. Labor Department

Producer Price Indexes measure average changes in prices received in primary markets of the U.S. by producers of commodities in all stages of processing.

Commodity group (1967 = 100)	Annual Avg. 1978	1979 June	1979 Dec.	1980 Jan.	1980 June
All commodities	209.3	233.5	249.7	254.9	265.2
Farm products, processed foods, and feeds	206.6	229.0	234.6	231.9	234.2
Farm products	212.5	242.8	242.5	236.4	233.4
Processed foods and feeds	202.6	220.6	229.3	228.5	233.8
Industrial commodities	209.4	234.0	253.1	260.6	273.0
Textile products and apparel	159.8	168.4	173.1	175.2	182.4
Hides, skins, leathers, and related products	200.0	268.0	249.2	255.7	241.0
Fuels and related products and power	322.5	393.7	487.9	508.0	574.8
Chemicals and allied products	198.8	219.2	238.2	246.0	261.7
Rubber and plastic products	174.8	193.1	205.9	207.8	217.1
Lumber and wood products	276.0	299.8	290.1	290.0	279.8
Pulp, paper, and allied products	195.6	216.6	231.7	237.4	251.3
Metals and metal products	227.1	258.2	273.6	284.6	282.4
Machinery and equipment	196.1	212.4	223.4	227.6	238.8
Furniture and household durables	160.4	170.2	177.9	183.4	185.3
Nonmetallic mineral products	222.8	246.9	259.6	268.4	283.2
Transportation equipment (Dec. 1968 = 100)	173.5	187.5	195.6	198.7	202.2
Miscellaneous products	184.3	205.2	227.4	242.9	257.4

Indexes of Manufacturing, Industrial Countries

Source: Bureau of Labor Statistics, U.S. Labor Department (1967 = 100)

Output per hour

Country	1960	1965	1970	1973	1974	1975	1976	1977	1978
United States	78.9	98.3	104.5	118.8	112.6	118.2	123.2	126.1	129.2
10 Foreign countries	67.5	89.6	124.7	150.0	154.6	154.2	164.5	170.5	178.6
Canada	75.1	93.7	114.7	134.3	136.6	133.3	139.4	146.1	152.2
Japan	52.6	79.1	146.5	181.2	181.7	174.6	188.7	199.2	215.7
Belgium	69.9	87.5	129.5	168.8	178.8	186.9	205.0	217.7	N.A.
Denmark	66.6	86.7	129.3	159.8	165.1	178.0	191.4	195.4	200.8
France	68.7	88.5	121.2	142.5	146.5	150.3	164.0	172.6	181.2
W. Germany	67.8	90.7	116.1	136.6	145.0	151.3	160.3	169.0	175.3
Italy	61.2	88.5	121.7	151.7	159.7	152.9	165.9	167.8	172.7
Netherlands	67.5	87.8	134.0	170.2	184.3	181.1	199.1	206.0	N.A.
Sweden	64.1	88.8	123.5	148.9	153.9	151.9	152.9	151.9	160.2
United Kingdom	77.0	92.5	108.8	127.6	127.7	124.2	127.9	126.5	128.6
8 European countries	68.8	90.9	119.7	143.3	149.0	150.5	160.5	165.1	170.7
Original EEC	68.2	91.1	120.7	144.5	151.2	154.4	165.3	172.5	179.1

Unit labor costs in U.S. dollars

Country	1960	1965	1970	1973	1974	1975	1976	1977	1978
United States	97.7	92.6	116.5	123.2	143.1	152.4	158.4	168.3	179.9
10 Foreign countries	82.4	97.4	112.4	174.1	198.8	238.7	234.4	259.9	311.4
Canada	106.9	92.0	111.7	127.0	147.7	166.6	187.4	183.7	175.8
Japan	82.5	102.5	113.2	195.2	237.3	284.8	285.3	326.5	412.0
Belgium	74.9	94.3	101.4	152.0	173.8	212.3	204.5	230.6	N.A.
Denmark	74.7	91.8	104.4	147.6	170.3	199.2	195.8	212.7	248.1
France	81.5	98.2	96.7	146.4	157.8	206.7	194.5	206.4	244.4
W. Germany	76.5	94.4	125.7	211.7	236.2	268.5	265.4	299.4	358.3
Italy	76.5	97.1	119.2	172.5	182.6	245.1	212.5	234.9	270.4
Netherlands	65.4	91.8	108.7	174.0	198.3	245.4	238.8	268.7	N.A.
Sweden	79.2	93.0	105.0	145.8	161.4	212.2	239.4	262.5	278.2
United Kingdom	85.5	98.6	104.8	130.2	154.7	196.2	182.9	196.9	249.0
8 European countries	78.7	95.9	113.6	175.5	195.2	236.1	228.3	252.7	301.5
Original EEC	77.1	95.7	116.0	185.5	204.5	245.0	235.7	262.0	312.4

Gross National Product, National Income, and Personal Income

Source: Bureau of Economic Analysis, U.S. Commerce Department
includes Alaska and Hawaii beginning in 1960 (millions of dollars)

	1950	1960	1970	1975	1979	1980
Gross national product	286,172	505,978	982,419	1,528,833	2,368,818	2,626,100
Less: Capital consumption allowances.	23,853	47,712	90,827	161,954	242,953	287,300
Equals: Net national product	262,319	458,266	894,592	1,366,879	2,125,865	2,338,900
Less: Indirect business tax and nontax liability .	23,422	45,389	94,027	139,246	189,490	212,300
Business transfer payments	778	1,974	3,983	7,599	10,175	10,500
Statistical discrepancy	2,030	−683	−2,076	7,371	3,720	−700
Plus: Subsidies minus current surplus of government enterprises	114	422	2,716	2,339	2,334	4,600
Equals: National income	236,203	412,008	798,374	1,215,002	1,924,814	2,121,400
Less: Corporate profits and inventory valuation adjustment	2,272	9,760	37,549	95,902	178,158	182,700
Net interest	...	...	...	78,615	129,741	179,800
Contributions for social insurance	7,058	21,058	58,712	110,579	189,816	203,700
Wage accruals less disbursement	24	0	0	0	−181	0
Plus: Government transfer payment to persons.	14,404	26,966	75,898	170,567	241,866	283,800
Personal interest income.	8,929	23,284	64,284	115,529	192,117	256,300
Dividends.	8,803	12,890	22,884	31,885	52,735	54,400
Business transfer payments	778	1,974	3,983	7,599	10,175	10,500
Equals: Personal income	226,102	399,724	801,271	1,255,486	1,924,173	2,160,200

National Income by Type of Income

(millions of dollars)

	1960	1965	1970	1975	1979	1980
Compensation of employees.	294,932	396,543	609,150	931,079	1,459,234	1,596,500
Wages and salaries.	271,932	362,005	546,453	805,872	1,227,397	1,343,600
Private	222,782	292,145	430,481	630,431	993,910	1,090,000
Government	49,150	69,860	115,972	175,441	233,487	253,600
Supplements to wages, salary.	23,000	34,538	62,697	125,207	231,837	252,900
Employer contrib. for social insurance . .	11,780	16,698	30,680	60,079	109,147	115,800
Other labor income	11,220	17,840	32,017	65,128	122,690	137,100
Proprietors' income	46,978	56,674	65,140	86,980	130,775	130,600
Business and professional	35,558	44,106	51,208	63,509	97,965	107,200
Inventory valuation adj.	91	−198	−506	−1,164	−2,974	−3,700
Farm	11,420	12,568	13,932	23,471	32,810	23,400
Rental income of persons.	13,758	17,117	18,644	22,426	26,908	31,800
Corp. prof., with inv. adjust..	46,580	77,096	67,891	95,902	178,158	182,700
Corp. profits before tax.	48,540	75,209	71,485	120,378	236,638	245,500
Corp. profits tax liability.	22,696	30,876	34,477	49,811	92,531	82,300
Corp. profits after tax	25,844	44,333	37,008	70,567	144,107	163,200
Dividends	12,890	19,120	22,884	31,885	52,735	56,000
Undistributed profits	12,954	25,213	14,124	38,682	91,372	107,200
Inventory valuation adj..	327	−1,865	−5,067	−12,432	−41,769	−45,700
Net interest	9,760	18,529	37,549	78,615	129,741	179,800
National income.	412,008	565,959	798,374	1,215,002	1,924,814	2,121,400

Appropriations by the Federal Government

Source: U.S. Treasury Department (fiscal year)

Year	Appropriations	Year	Appropriations	Year	Appropriations	Year	Appropriations
1890	$395,430,284.26	1940	$13,349,202,681.73	1959	$82,055,863,758.58	1972	$247,638,104,722.57
1895	492,477,759.97	1944	118,411,173,965.24	1960	80,169,728,902.87	1973	275,554,945,383.88
1900	698,912,982.83	1945	73,067,712,071.39	1961	89,229,575,129.94	1974	311,728,034,120.95
1905	781,288,215.95	1950	52,867,672,466.21	1962	91,447,827,731.00	1975	374,124,469,875.62
1910	1,044,433,622.64	1952	127,788,153,262.97	1963	102,149,886,566.52	1976	403,740,395,600.61
1915	1,122,471,919.12	1953	94,916,821,231.67	1965	107,555,087,622.62	T.Q.[1]	111,767,892,878.83
1920	6,454,596,649.56	1954	74,744,844,304.88	1967	140,861,235,376.56	1977	466,559,809,964.06
1925	3,748,651,750.35	1955	54,761,172,461.58	1969	203,049,351,090.91	1978	507,782,291,489.99
1930	4,665,236,678.04	1956	63,857,731,203.86	1970	222,200,021,901.52	1979	563,960,833,788.25
1935	7,527,559,327.66	1958	77,145,934,082.25	1971	247,623,820,964.75	1980	690,391,124,920.77

(1) Transitional Quarter; July 1, 1976 through Sept. 30, 1976. Through 1976 the fiscal year ended June 30. From 1977 on, fiscal year ends Sept. 30.

Public Debt of the U.S.

Source: U.S. Treasury Department

Fiscal year	Gross debt	Per cap.	Fiscal year	Gross debt	Per cap.	Fiscal year	Gross debt	Per cap.
1870	$2,436,453,269	$61.06	1930	$16,185,309,831	$131.51	1975	$533,188,976,772	$2,496.90
1880	2,090,908,872	41.60	1940	42,967,531,038	325.23	T.Q.[1]	634,701,954,322	2,950.15
1890	1,132,396,584	17.80	1950	256,087,352,351	1,688.30	1977	698,839,928,356	3,215.59
1900	1,263,416,913	16.60	1960	284,092,760,848	1,572.31	1978	771,544,478,952	3,521.78
1910	1,146,939,969	12.41	1965	313,818,898,984	1,612.70	1979	826,519,096,841	3,736.86
1920	24,299,321,467	228.23	1970	370,093,706,950	1,807.09	1980	907,701,290,900	p4,063.08

(p) Preliminary. (1) Transitional Quarter; July 1, 1976 through Sept. 30, 1976. Through 1976 the fiscal year ended June 30. From 1977 on, fiscal year ends Sept. 30.

National Income by Industry

Source: Bureau of Economic Analysis, U.S. Commerce Department
(millions of dollars)

	1960	1965	1970	1975	1977	1978	1979
Agricul., forestry, fisheries	**17,468**	**20,366**	**24,455**	**42,827**	**43,345**	**54,723**	**64,682**
Farms	16,452	18,805	22,191	39,379	38,488	48,823	57,882
Agri. services, forestry, fisheries	1,016	1,561	2,264	3,448	4,857	5,900	6,800
Mining	**5,613**	**6,013**	**7,810**	**18,149**	**22,445**	**26,470**	**30,131**
Metal mining	807	856	1,179	1,635	1,963	2,287	2,294
Coal mining	1,286	1,372	2,231	6,228	6,550	6,930	8,444
Crude petroleum, natural gas	2,606	2,670	3,099	8,075	11,428	14,298	16,096
Nonmetallic min. & quar.	914	1,115	1,301	2,211	2,504	2,955	3,297
Contract construction	**20,972**	**29,840**	**43,821**	**61,795**	**76,276**	**87,593**	**102,641**
Manufacturing	**125,448**	**170,361**	**215,388**	**312,467**	**409,404**	**459,502**	**514,510**
Nondurable goods	**51,818**	**65,416**	**88,088**	**127,942**	**161,629**	**175,998**	**199,061**
Food, kindred products	12,150	14,232	19,579	30,020	32,611	34,513	38,518
Tobacco manufactures	1,020	1,096	1,696	2,155	2,849	3,208	3,513
Textile mill products	4,484	5,872	7,525	8,754	11,852	12,906	14,702
Apparel, other fabric prod.	4,933	6,494	8,722	10,773	13,603	14,896	15,770
Paper, allied products	4,706	6,005	7,968	11,833	15,677	17,094	19,348
Printing, pub., allied industry	6,666	8,725	11,883	16,672	20,987	23,715	26,341
Chemicals, allied products	9,106	12,398	16,042	23,820	30,100	30,694	36,131
Petroleum and coal products	4,396	4,811	6,632	12,893	18,739	20,303	27,117
Rubber, misc. plastic products	2,751	3,939	5,804	8,661	12,441	13,745	14,524
Leather, leather products	1,606	1,844	2,237	2,361	2,770	2,924	3,097
Durable goods	**73,630**	**104,945**	**127,300**	**184,525**	**247,775**	**283,504**	**315,449**
Lumber, wood, except furn.	3,362	4,534	5,537	8,936	13,645	16,230	17,586
Furniture and fixtures	2,098	2,904	3,715	4,588	6,053	6,924	7,804
Stone, clay, glass products	4,620	5,654	6,891	9,858	13,071	15,445	16,905
Primary metal industries	11,066	14,491	15,757	24,231	28,673	33,396	39,519
Fabricated metal products	8,124	11,475	14,812	24,300	31,365	35,252	39,243
Machinery, except electrical	11,919	18,239	24,353	36,801	47,554	55,100	63,213
Electric and electronic equipment	10,496	14,855	20,132	26,646	35,258	41,037	47,220
Transport equip. exc. autos.	8,266	11,330	14,480	15,715	18,492	21,317	26,333
Motor vehicles and equipment.	8,399	14,455	12,086	19,045	34,622	37,236	33,697
Instruments	2,948	4,128	5,797	9,006	12,036	13,668	15,110
Misc. manufacturing	2,332	2,880	3,740	5,399	7,006	7,898	8,819
Transportation	**18,141**	**23,069**	**30,308**	**44,455**	**58,779**	**68,175**	**76,341**
Railroad	6,710	7,016	7,612	9,987	12,882	14,217	16,984
Local; interurban passenger transit	1,619	1,897	2,308	2,933	3,520	3,771	3,957
Motor freight trans., warehousing	5,886	8,396	11,830	18,935	24,387	28,508	31,413
Water transportation	1,635	1,982	2,503	3,323	3,914	4,673	5,220
Air transportation	1,370	2,636	4,358	7,062	10,031	12,054	13,025
Pipeline transportation	350	390	528	820	1,054	1,336	1,439
Transportation service	571	752	1,169	1,935	2,991	3,616	4,303
Communication	**8,228**	**11,497**	**17,600**	**27,066**	**35,192**	**40,533**	**43,508**
Telephone and telegraph	7,293	10,255	15,887	24,358	31,113	35,792	38,532
Radio broadcasting, television.	935	1,242	1,713	2,708	4,079	4,741	4,976
Electric, gas, sanitary services	**8,923**	**11,442**	**14,864**	**24,302**	**31,127**	**34,912**	**38,416**
Wholesale and retail trade	**64,737**	**84,662**	**122,213**	**194,227**	**234,471**	**261,780**	**290,825**
Wholesale trade.	23,420	30,469	44,860	80,564	96,041	106,950	121,924
Retail trade	41,317	54,193	77,353	113,663	138,430	154,830	168,901
Finance, ins. and real estate	**48,608**	**63,987**	**92,625**	**140,375**	**184,437**	**210,735**	**256,316**
Banking	7,255	8,943	16,448	20,109	23,368	24,649	34,025
Credit agencies, other than banks	−1,076	−1,617	−1,981	−4,729	−4,261	−4,164	2,401
Security, commodity brokers	1,219	1,942	2,733	4,144	4,576	5,428	6,328
Insurance carriers	4,816	5,880	9,269	12,751	18,903	22,616	24,104
Insurance agents, brokers, service	2,070	2,957	4,223	6,704	9,605	11,182	12,162
Real estate	33,940	45,741	61,812	100,078	130,258	148,858	176,660
Holding and other investment cos.	384	141	121	1,318	1,988	2,166	636
Services	**44,648**	**64,142**	**103,304**	**168,516**	**213,379**	**245,246**	**275,334**
Hotels, other lodging places	2,114	2,964	4,659	6,952	8,722	10,372	12,342
Personal services	4,608	5,965	7,436	8,329	10,058	11,284	12,727
Misc. business services	5,091	8,399	14,051	23,928	31,989	38,311	45,882
Automobile repair, serv., garages	1,746	2,402	3,616	5,944	7,863	9,451	10,985
Misc. repair services	1,094	1,494	2,149	3,478	4,414	5,188	6,129
Motion pictures	891	1,201	1,581	1,842	2,761	3,347	3,901
Amusement, recreation services	1,662	2,201	3,321	5,268	6,846	7,973	8,143
Medical, other health services	10,636	15,790	29,472	54,075	68,762	77,784	86,898
Legal services	2,695	4,197	6,691	11,828	14,379	16,232	18,083
Education services	2,419	4,145	6,688	10,014	12,402	13,808	14,091
Social Services	—	—	—	5,003	6,449	7,420	8,376
Nonprofit membership org.	4,176	5,787	8,912	11,016	12,638	13,858	14,373
Misc. professional services	3,719	5,629	9,673	15,030	19,254	22,688	27,045
Private households	3,797	3,968	5,055	5,809	6,842	7,530	6,359
Government, government enterprises	**52,707**	**75,374**	**127,421**	**199,875**	**235,048**	**256,570**	**277,794**
Federal	25,303	33,303	53,093	72,007	81,295	87,858	93,422
General Government	21,676	28,298	44,723	58,976	66,409	71,814	75,801
Government enterprises.	3,627	5,005	8,370	13,031	14,886	16,044	17,621
State & local.	27,404	42,071	74,328	127,868	153,753	168,712	184,372
General Government	25,470	39,294	69,964	119,641	143,730	157,763	172,329
Government enterprises.	1,934	2,777	4,364	8,227	10,023	10,949	12,043
Domestic income	**415,493**	**560,753**	**799,809**	**1,234,054**	**1,543,903**	**1,746,239**	**1,970,498**
Rest of the world	**2,477**	**4,681**	**4,616**	**10,534**	**17,813**	**20,547**	**43,794**
All industries, total	**417,970**	**565,434**	**804,425**	**1,244,588**	**1,561,716**	**1,766,786**	**2,014,292**

U.S. Currency and Coin — June 30, 1981,

Source: U.S. Treasury Department

Amounts in Circulation and Outstanding

Currency	Amounts in circulation	Add amounts held by: United States Treasury	Federal Reserve Banks	Amounts outstanding
Federal Reserve Notes[1]	$124,778,082,541	$3,553,734	$20,279,923,104	$145,061,559,379
United States Notes	307,559,175	14,979,839	2	322,539,016
Currency No Longer Issued	276,428,189	230,764	42,705	276,701,658
Total	125,362,069,905	18,764,337	20,279,965,811	145,660,800,053
Coin[2]				
Dollars[3]	$1,485,899,047	$368,623,411	$166,007,440	[3]$2,020,529,898
Fractional Coin	11,232,264,551	90,598,560	215,309,889	11,538,173,000
Total	12,718,163,598	459,221,971	381,317,329	13,558,702,898
Total currency and coin.	138,080,233,503	477,986,308	20,661,283,140	159,219,502,951

Currency in Circulation by Denominations

Denomination	Total currency in circulation	Federal Reserve Notes[1]	United States Notes	Currency no longer issued
1 Dollar	$3,393,756,324	$3,239,171,657	$143,479	$154,441,188
2 Dollars	673,649,834	539,237,804	134,398,866	13,164
5 Dollars	4,473,926,025	4,319,437,010	114,184,110	40,304,905
10 Dollars	11,223,808,800	11,197,934,470	5,950	25,868,380
20 Dollars	40,153,522,520	40,133,159,400	3,380	20,359,740
50 Dollars	13,924,536,100	13,912,651,000	.....	11,885,100
100 Dollars	51,163,617,200	51,081,792,700	58,823,300	23,001,200
500 Dollars	161,867,500	161,674,500	.....	193,000
1,000 Dollars	188,050,000	187,839,000	.....	211,000
5,000 Dollars	1,835,000	1,785,000	.....	50,000
10,000 Dollars	3,500,000	3,400,000	.....	100,000
Fractional parts	487	. . .	.....	487
Partial notes[4]	115		90	25
Total currency	**125,362,069,905**	**124,778,082,541**	**307,559,175**	**276,428,189**

Comparative Totals of Money in Circulation — Selected Dates

Date	Amounts (in millions)	Per capita[5]	Date	Amounts (in millions)	Per capita[5]	Date	Amounts (in millions)	Per capita[5]
June 30, 1981	[6]$138,080.2	$600.89	June 30, 1950	27,156.3	179.03	June 30, 1920	5,467.6	51.36
June 30, 1975	81,196.4	380.08	June 30, 1945	26,746.4	191.14	June 30, 1915	3,319.6	33.01
June 30, 1970	54,351.0	265.39	June 30, 1940	7,847.5	59.40	June 30, 1910	3,148.7	34.07
June 30, 1965	39,719.8	204.14	June 30, 1935	5,567.1	43.75			
June 30, 1960	32,064.6	177.47	June 30, 1930	$4,522.0	$36.74			
June 30, 1955	$30,229.3	$182.90	June 30, 1925	4,815.2	41.56			

(1) Issued on and after July 1, 1929. (2) Excludes coin sold to collectors at premium prices. (3) Includes $481,781,898 in standard silver dollars. (4) Represents value of certain partial denominations not presented for redemption. (5) Based on Bureau of the Census estimates of population. (6) Highest amount to date.

The requirement for a gold reserve against U.S. notes was repealed by Public Law 90-269 approved Mar. 18, 1968. Silver certificates issued on and after July 1, 1929 became redeemable from the general fund on June 24, 1968. The amount of security after those dates has been reduced accordingly.

U.S. Money in Circulation, by Denominations

Source: Fiscal Service, Bureau of Government Financial Operations, U.S. Treasury Department

Outside Treasury and Federal Reserve Banks. (millions of dollars)

End of year	Total in circulation	Coin and small denomination Total	Coin	$1	$2	$5	$10	$20	Large denomination currency Total	$50	$100	$500	$1,000	$5,000	$10,000
1950	27,741	19,305	1,554	1,113	64	2,049	5,998	8,529	8,438	2,422	5,043	368	588	4	12
1960	32,869	23,521	2,427	1,533	88	2,246	6,691	10,536	9,348	2,815	5,954	249	316	3	10
1970	57,093	39,639	6,281	2,310	136	3,161	9,170	18,581	17,454	4,896	12,084	215	252	3	4
1975	86,547	54,866	8,959	2,809	135	3,841	10,777	28,344	31,681	8,157	23,139	175	204	2	4
1978	114,645	66,693	10,739	3,194	661	4,393	11,661	36,045	47,952	11,279	36,306	167	194	2	4
1979	125,600	70,693	11,658	3,308	671	4,549	11,894	38,613	54,907	12,585	41,960	164	192	2	4
1980	137,244	73,893	12,419	3,499	677	4,635	11,924	40,739	63,352	13,731	49,264	163	189	2	3

Seigniorage on Coin and Silver Bullion

Source: Fiscal Service, U.S. Treasury Department

Seigniorage is the profit from coining money; it is the difference between the monetary value of coins and their cost, including the manufacturing expense.

Fiscal year	Total		Total
Jan. 1, 1935–June 30, 1965, cumulative	$2,525,927,763.84	1975	$660,898,070.69
1968	383,141,339.00[1]	1976	769,722,066.00
1970	274,217,884.01	1977	407,022,950.00
1972	580,586,683.00	1978	367,156,260.25
1973	399,799,682.00	1979	991,909,496.55
1974	320,706,638.49	1980	662,814,791.48
(1) Revised to include seigniorage on clad coins.		Cumulative Jan. 1, 1935–Sept. 30, 1980	10,479,265,076.97

Bureau of the Mint

Source: Bureau of the Mint, U.S. Treasury Department

The first United States Mint was established in Philadelphia, Pa., then the nation's capital, by the Act of April 2, 1792, which provided for gold, silver, and copper coinage. Originally, supervision of the Mint was a function of the secretary of state, but it became (1799) an independent agency reporting directly to the president. When the Coinage Act of 1873 was passed, all mint and assay office activities were placed under a newly organized Bureau of the Mint in the Department of the Treasury.

The Bureau of the Mint manufactures all U.S. coins and distributes them through the Federal Reserve banks and branches. The Mint also maintains physical custody of the Treasury's monetary stocks of gold and silver, and refines and processes gold and silver bullion. Functions performed by the Mint on a reimbursable basis include: the manufacture and sale of medals of a national character, the production and sale of numismatic coins and coin sets, and, as scheduling permits, the manufacture of foreign coins.

Amendments to the Coinage Act of 1965 (Public Law 19-607, Dec. 31, 1970) authorized the production of dollar coins and provided that the dollar and half dollar coins for general circulation be of the same nonsilver clad composition as the quarter dollars and dimes. The cladding is an alloy of 75 percent copper and 25 percent nickel, bonded to a core of pure copper. The coins were first minted in calendar year 1971. The legislation authorized the secretary of the treasury to mint and issue not more than 150 million one dollar pieces containing 40-percent silver for sale to the public at premium prices. The dollar coins which bore the likeness of President Eisenhower and a reverse design emblematic of the Apollo 11 moon landing were minted and issued from 1971 until early in 1975.

Public Law 93-127, Oct. 18, 1973, authorized the minting for issue after July 4, 1975, of dollar, half dollar, and quarter dollar coins with reverse designs emblematic of the Bicentennial and the obverse dates 1776-1976, for general issue; and the production of 45 million numismatic 40-percent silver coins of the same designs and denominations to be sold to the public at premium prices. Although the production of Bicentennial-design coins was terminated on Dec. 31, 1976, 40-percent silver coin sets continued to be packaged and sold after that date.

Public Law 95-447, Oct. 10, 1978, amended the Coinage Act of 1965 to provide for changes in the design, weight, and size of the $1 coin. From Jan. 1979, the $1 coins bore the likeness of Susan B. Anthony on the obverse and the Apollo 11 Moon landing on the reverse; these cupronickel clad coins weigh 8.1 grams and have a diameter of 26.5 mms.

The composition of the five cent coin continues to be 75 percent copper, 25 percent nickel, while the one cent coins are 95 percent copper and 5 percent zinc.

Calendar year 1979 coinage production follows:

Domestic Coinage Executed During Calendar Year 1980

Denomination	Philadelphia	Denver	San Francisco	Total value	Total pieces
Dollars — non-silver					
1980	$27,610,000.00	$41,628,708.00	$20,422,000.00	$89,660,708.00	89,660,708
Total dollars	$27,610,000.00	$41,628,708.00	$20,422,000.00	$89,660,708.00	89,660,708
Subsidiary					
Half dollars - 1980	$22,067,000.00	$16,728,224.50	-0-	$38,795,224.50	77,590,449
Quarters - 1980	158,958,000.00	129,581,871.75	-0-	288,539,871.75	1,154,159,487
Dimes	73,517,000.00	71,935,432.10	-0-	145,452,432.10	1,454,524,321
Total Subsidiary	$254,542,000.00	$218,245,528.35	-0-	$472,787,528.35	2,686,274,257
Minor					
Five-cent pieces	$29,650,200.00	$25,116,172.40	-0-	$54,766,372.40	1,095,327,448
One-cent pieces[1]	62,301,150.00	51,400,986.60	$11,845,900.00	125,548,036.60	12,554,803,660
Total minor	$91,951,350.00	$76,517,159.00	$11,845,900.00	$180,314,409.00	13,650,131,108
Total domestic coinage	$374,103,350.00	$335,391,395.35	$32,267,900.00	$742,762,645.35	16,426,066,073

Delivered at San Francisco Assay Office	
1980 Proof sets	2,144,231
Bicentennial 40% silver proof sets	93,219
Bicentennial 40% silver uncirc. sets	40,582

Coinage executed for foreign governments	
Country	No. of Pieces
Dominican Republic	1,658,000
Panama	18,000,000
Total	**19,658,000**

(1) Manufactured at West Point Depository - $15,762,000 (1,576,200,000 pieces)

Portraits on U.S. Treasury Bills, Bonds, Notes and Savings Bonds

Denomination	Savings bonds	Treas. bills	Treas. bonds	Treas. notes
25	Washington			
50	F.D. Roosevelt		Jefferson	
75	Truman			
100	Eisenhower		Jackson	
200	Kennedy			
500	Wilson		Washington	
1,000	T. Roosevelt	H. McCulloch	Lincoln	Lincoln
5,000	McKinley	J.G. Carlisle	Monroe	Monroe
10,000	Cleveland	J. Sherman	Cleveland	Cleveland
50,000		C. Glass		
100,000		A Gallatin	Grant	Grant
1,000,000		O. Wolcott	T. Roosevelt	T. Roosevelt
100,000,000				Madison
500,000,000				McKinley

Large Denominations of U.S. Currency Discontinued

The largest denomination of United States currency now being issued is the $100 bill. Issuance of currency in denominations of $500, $1000, $5,000 and $10,000 has been discontinued because their use has declined sharply over the past two decades.

As large denomination bills reach the Federal Reserve Bank they are removed from circulation.

Because some of the discontinued currency is expected to be in the hands of holders for many years, the description of the various denominations below is continued:

Amt.	Portrait	Embellishment on back	Amt.	Portrait	Embellishment on back
$ 1	Washington	Great Seal of U.S.	$ 100	Franklin	Independence Hall
2	Jefferson	Signers of Declaration	500*	McKinley	Ornate denominational marking
5	Lincoln	Lincoln Memorial	1,000*	Cleveland	Ornate denominational marking
10	Hamilton	U.S. Treasury	5,000*	Madison	Ornate denominational marking
20	Jackson	White House	10,000*	Chase	Ornate denominational marking
50	Grant	U.S. Capitol	100,000*	Wilson	Ornate denominational marking

*For use only in transactions between Federal Reserve System and Treasury Department.

Gold Reserves of Central Banks and Governments

Source: IMF, *International Financial Statistics*
(Million fine troy ounces)

Year end	All countries[1]	Int'l Monetary Fund	United States	Canada	Japan	Belgium	France	Fed. Rep. of Germany	Italy	Netherlands	Switzerland	United Kingdom
1964	1,156.84	62.26	442.03	29.31	8.69	41.46	106.54	121.37	60.19	48.23	77.86	61.04
1965	1,186.52	53.40	401.86	32.88	9.37	44.52	134.46	126.00	68.68	50.19	86.91	64.72
1966	1,165.02	75.77	378.14	29.87	9.40	43.56	149.66	122.62	68.97	49.45	81.17	55.44
1967	1,125.52	76.63	344.71	29.00	9.66	42.26	149.54	120.79	68.57	48.91	88.26	36.89
1968	1,106.56	65.37	311.20	24.66	10.17	43.53	110.77	129.69	83.52	48.51	74.97	42.10
1969	1,112.05	66.00	338.83	24.92	11.80	43.40	101.34	116.56	84.46	49.16	75.49	42.03
1970	1,056.83	123.97	316.34	22.59	15.20	42.01	100.91	113.70	82.48	51.06	78.03	38.54
1971	1,026.12	135.20	291.60	22.69	19.43	44.12	100.66	116.47	82.40	54.53	83.11	22.15
1972	1,017.41	153.43	275.97	21.95	21.11	43.08	100.69	117.36	82.37	54.17	83.11	21.05
1973	1,017.45	153.43	275.97	21.95	21.11	42.17	100.91	117.61	82.48	54.33	83.20	21.03
1974	1,015.96	153.40	275.97	21.95	21.11	42.17	100.93	117.61	82.48	54.33	83.20	21.03
1975	1,014.82	153.43	274.71	21.95	21.11	42.17	100.93	117.61	82.48	54.33	83.20	21.03
1976	1,009.90	149.51	274.68	21.62	21.11	42.17	101.02	117.61	82.48	54.33	83.28	21.03
1977	1,011.74	131.57	277.55	22.01	21.62	42.45	101.67	118.30	82.91	54.63	83.28	22.22
1978	1,018.53	118.20	276.41	22.13	23.97	42.59	101.99	118.64	83.12	54.78	83.28	22.82
1979	929.96	106.83	264.60	22.18	24.23	34.21	81.92	95.25	66.71	43.97	83.28	18.25

(1) Covers IMF members with reported gold holdings, Switzerland and Netherlands Antilles. For countries not listed above, see *International Financial Statistics*, a monthly publication of the International Monetary Fund.

World Gold Production

Source: Bureau of Mines, U.S. Interior Department (in troy ounces)

Year	Estimated world prod.	South Africa	Ghana	Zaire	United States	Canada	Mexico	Nicaragua	Colombia	Australia	India	Japan	Philippines	All other
1970	47,522,342	32,164,107	707,900	180,590	1,743,322	2,408,574	198,241	115,173	201,519	619,922	104,200	225,189	602,715	8,220,890
1971	46,494,837	31,388,631	697,517	171,685	1,495,108	2,243,000	150,915	121,134	188,847	672,106	118,569	255,255	637,048	8,355,022
1972	44,843,374	29,245,273	724,051	140,724	1,449,943	2,078,567	146,061	112,340	188,137	754,866	105,776	243,027	606,730	9,047,879
1973	43,296,755	27,494,603	722,531	133,642	1,175,750	1,954,340	132,557	85,051	215,876	554,278	105,390	274,850	572,250	9,962,213
1974	39,941,080	24,388,203	566,617	130,603	1,126,886	1,698,392	134,454	82,639	265,195	522,127	101,114	139,727	536,338	10,248,785
1975	38,574,162	22,937,820	523,889	103,217	1,052,252	1,674,000	132,236	70,281	299,366	514,186	91,437	143,489	501,776	10,530,213
1976	39,233,798	22,935,988	532,473	91,093	1,048,031	1,691,806	126,811	75,841	300,307	502,741	100,696	137,669	501,210	11,152,852
1977	39,121,056	22,501,886	480,884	80,418	1,100,347	1,733,609	212,709	65,764	263,437	630,155	96,902	149,018	558,235	11,247,692
1978	38,985,286	22,648,558	402,034	76,077	998,832	1,735,077	202,003	65,800	257,632	647,579	89,186	145,240	586,531	11,332,740
1979	38,801,703	22,617,178	362,000	69,992	969,920	1,644,265	188,000	61,086	269,369	596,910	84,749	127,626	561,040	11,437,567
1980[p]	38,882,318	21,669,468	410,000	39,963	951,348	1,552,366	—	66,000	280,000	556,850	78,834	130,000	701,000	12,446,489

(p) preliminary.

U.S. and World Silver Production

Source: Bureau of Mines, U.S. Interior Department

Largest production of silver in the United States in 1915—74,961,075 fine ounces.

Year (Cal.)	United States Fine ozs.	United States Value	World Fine ozs.	Year (Cal.)	United States Fine ozs.	United States Value	World Fine ozs.
1930	50,748,127	$19,538,000	248,708,426	1965. . . .	39,806,033	51,469,201	257,415,000
1935	45,924,454	33,008,000	220,704,231	1970. . . .	45,006,000	79,697,000	310,891,000
1940	69,585,734	49,483,000	275,387,000	1975. . . .	34,938,000	154,424,000	303,112,000
1945	29,063,255	20,667,200	162,000,000	1978. . . .	39,385,000	212,681,000	344,657,000
1950	43,308,739	38,291,545	203,300,000	1979. . . .	38,055,000	422,032,000	345,958,000
1955	36,469,610	33,006,839	224,000,000	1980. . . .	31,327,000	64,628,000	341,370,000
1960	36,000,000	$33,305,858	241,300,000				

---

50 Stocks Most Widely Held by Investment Companies

Source: Vickers Associates, Inc.

Publicly-held issues throughout the U.S. in order of number of institutions, etc., which held shares, as of Mar. 31, 1981.

Intl. Bus. Machines
Schlumberger, Ltd.
Exxon Corp.
Amer. Tel. & Tel.
Atlantic Richfield
Philip Morris
Halliburton Co.
Digital Equipment
General Electric Co.
Union Oil of Cal.

Eastman Kodak
Standard Oil Ind.
Smithkline Corp.
Xerox Corp.
Union Carbide
Warner Comm.
Alcan Aluminum
Mobil Corp.
Conaco, Inc.
General Motors

Phillips Petroleum
Dome Petroleum
E. I. Du Pont
Minnesota Mining
McDonald's Corp.
Hewlett Packard
Texaco
Superior Oil Co.
Honeywell, Inc.
Pizer, Inc.

Hospital Corp. of Amer.
Raytheon
Standard Oil of Cal.
Gulf Oil Corp.
Union Pacific Corp.
Johnson & Johnson
Dresser Ind., Inc.
Monsanto Co.
Standard Oil of Ohio
Armco, Inc.

Texas Oil & Gas
Northwest Airlines
Tandy Corp.
Royal Dutch Petrol.
Merck & Co.
R. J. Reynolds
Matsushita Elec.
Tenneco, Inc.
NCR Corp.
Pepsi Co., Inc.

Corporations and Stocks

Stock Exchanges Trade 15.5 Billion Shares in U.S. Firms in 1980

The Securities and Exchange Commission reported in 1981 that 15.5 billion shares of stock were traded on the New York, American, and other U.S. stock exchanges in 1980, valued at $476 billion.

The N.Y. Stock Exchange listed 2,213 issues of 1,565 companies for a total of 37.4 billion shares, valued on July 31, 1981, at $1.2 trillion. Average daily trading was 47.8 million through July 31, 1981, compared to 42.4 million in 1980.

The American Stock Exchange listed 957 issues of 857 companies. Average daily volume through July 31, 1981, was 5.54 million shares.

A 1980 count indicated that 29.8 million persons owned shares in American corporations.

N.Y. Stock Exchange Transactions and Seat Prices

Source: New York Stock Exchange

Year	Yearly volumes Stock shares	Bonds par values	Seat price High	Low	Year	Yearly volumes Stock shares	Bonds par values	Seat price High	Low
1900	138,981,000	$579,293,000	$47,500	$37,500	1940	207,599,749	$1,669,438,000	$60,000	$33,000
1905	260,569,000	1,026,254,000	85,000	72,000	1950	524,799,621	1,112,425,170	54,000	46,000
1910	163,705,000	634,863,000	94,000	65,000	1960	766,693,818	1,346,419,750	162,000	135,000
1915	172,497,000	961,700,000	74,000	38,000	1970	2,937,359,448	4,494,864,600	320,000	130,000
1920	227,636,000	3,868,422,000	115,000	85,000	1975	4,693,427,000	5,178,300,000	138,000	55,000
1925	459,717,623	3,427,042,210	150,000	99,000	1978	7,205,059,000	4,554,013,000	105,000	46,000
1929	1,124,800,410	2,996,398,000	625,000	550,000	1979	8,155,914,000	4,087,890,000	210,000	82,000
1930	810,632,546	2,720,301,800	480,000	205,000	1980	*11,352,294,000	5,190,304,000	275,000	175,000
1935	381,635,752	3,339,458,000	140,000	65,000	*Record high for trading in stocks.				

American Stock Exchange Transactions and Seat Prices

Source: American Stock Exchange

Year	Yearly volumes Stock shares	Bonds[1] princ. amts.	Seat price High	Low	Year	Yearly volumes Stock shares	Bonds[1] princ. amts.	Seat price High	Low
1929	476,140,375	$513,551,000	$254,000	$150,000	1960	286,039,982	$32,670,000	$60,000	$51,000
1930	222,270,065	863,541,000	225,000	70,000	1970	843,116,260	641,270,000	180,000	70,000
1940	42,928,337	303,902,000	7,250	6,900	1975	457,610,360	259,128,000	72,000	34,000
1945	143,309,392	167,333,000	32,000	12,000	1979	1,100,263,500	225,892,000	90,000	40,000
1950	107,792,340	47,549,000	11,000	6,500	1980	1,626,072,625	355,723,000	252,000	95,000
(1) corporate									

50 U.S. Industrials with Largest Annual Sales and Income

Source: Reprinted by permission from The FORTUNE Directory; © 1981 Time Inc.

Company	Sales (thousands)	Income (or loss) (thousands)	Company	Sales (thousands)	Income (or loss) (thousands)
Exxon	$103,142,834	$5,650,090	Dow Chemical	$10,626,000	$805,000
Mobil	59,510,000	3,272,000	Getty Oil	10,150,411	871,866
General Motors	57,728,500	(762,500)	Union Carbide	9,994,000	890,000
Texaco	51,195,830	2,642,542	Union Oil of California	9,984,100	647,000
Standard Oil of California	40,479,000	2,401,000	Eastman Kodak	9,734,303	1,153,579
Ford Motor	37,085,500	(1,543,300)	Boeing	9,426,200	600,500
Gulf Oil	26,483,000	1,407,000	Dart & Kraft	9,411,500	383,100
International Business Machines	26,213,000	3,562,000	Chrysler	9,225,300	(1,709,700)
Standard Oil (Ind.)	26,133,080	1,915,314	Caterpillar Tractor	8,597,800	564,800
General Electric	24,959,000	1,514,000	Westinghouse Electric	8,514,300	402,900
Atlantic Richfield	23,744,302	1,651,423	R.J. Reynolds Industries	8,449,000	670,400
Shell Oil	19,830,000	1,542,000	Goodyear Tire & Rubber	8,444,015	230,689
International Telephone & Telegraph	18,529,655	894,326	Beatrice Foods	8,290,509	290,140
			Xerox	8,196,500	619,200
Conoco	18,325,400	1,026,195	Marathon Oil	8,179,751	379,016
E.I. du Pont de Nemours	13,652,000	716,000	Ashland Oil	8,118,369	205,129
Phillips Petroleum	13,376,563	1,069,614	RCA	8,011,300	315,300
Tenneco	13,226,000	726,000	LTV	8,009,958	127,893
Sun	12,945,000	723,000	Amerada Hess	7,868,963	540,242
U.S. Steel	12,492,100	504,500	Cities Service	7,786,300	477,500
Occidental Petroleum	12,476,125	710,785	Philip Morris	7,328,300	576,800
United Technologies	12,323,944	393,383	Rockwell International	6,906,500	280,200
Western Electric	12,032,100	693,200	Bethlehem Steel	6,743,000	121,000
Standard Oil (Ohio)	11,023,196	1,811,224	Monsanto	6,573,600	148,800
Procter & Gamble	10,772,186	642,838	International Harvester	6,311,804	(397,328)
			Esmark	6,108,355	471,808

30 Largest Industrials Outside the U.S.

Source: Reprinted by permission from The FORTUNE World Business Directory; © 1981 Time Inc.

Company	Sales (thousands)	Income (or loss) (thousands)	Company	Sales (thousands)	Income (or loss) (thousands)
Royal Dutch/Shell Group, N-B	$77,114,243	$5,174,282	Bayer, G.	15,880,596	356,342
British Petroleum, B	48,035,941	3,337,121	BASF, G.	15,277,348	197,641
ENI, It	27,186,939	98,046	Thyssen, G	15,235,998	61,611
Fiat, It	25,155,000	NA	Petrobrás, Br.	14,836,326	767,419
Française des Pétroles, F	23,940,355	946,772	Pemex, M	14,813,514	17,316
Unilever, B-N	23,607,516	658,820	Nestlé, S.	14,615,187	407,785
Renault, F	18,979,278	160,165	Toyota Motor, J.	14,233,779	616,051
Petróleos de Venezuela, V	18,818,931	3,450,921	Nissan Motor, J.	13,853,503	461,647
Elf Aquitaine, E	18,430,074	1,378,222	Imperial Chemical Industries, B	13,290,347	(46,510)
Philips' Gloeilampenfabrieken, N.	18,402,818	165,210	Nippon Steel, J.	13,104,996	496,205
Volkswagenwerk, G	18,339,046	170,964	Hitachi, J.	12,871,328	503,385
Siemens, G	17,950,253	332,434	Matsushita Electric Industrial, J	12,684,404	541,923
Daimler-Benz, G	17,108,100	605,149	Mitsubishi Heavy Industries, J.	10,997,586	100,659
Peugeot, F.	16,846,434	(348,998)	BAT Industries, B	10,987,175	323,247
Hoechst, G	16,480,551	251,605	Générale d'Electricite,	10,847,129	96,407

National headquarters: B, Britain; Br. Brazil; F, France; G, West Germany; Ir, Iran; It, Italy; J, Japan; M, Mexico; N, Netherlands; S, Switzerland; V, Venezuela. NA—not available.

All Banks in U.S.—Number, Deposits

Source: Federal Reserve System

Comprises all national banks in the United States and all state commercial banks, trust companies, mutual stock savings banks, private and industrial banks, and special types of institutions that are treated as banks by the federal bank supervisory agencies.

Year (As of June 30)	Total all banks	Number of banks F.R.S. members			Nonmembers		Total all banks	Total deposits (millions of dollars) F.R.S. members			Nonmembers	
		Total	Nat'l	State	Mutual savings	Other		Total	Nat'l	State	Mutual savings	Other
1925	26,479	9,538	8,066	1,472	621	18,320	51,641	32,457	19,912	12,546	7,089	12,095
1930	23,855	8,315	7,247	1,068	604	14,936	59,828	38,069	23,235	14,834	9,117	12,642
1935	16,047	6,410	5,425	985	569	9,068	51,149	34,938	22,477	12,461	9,830	6,381
1940	14,955	6,398	5,164	1,234	551	8,008	70,770	51,729	33,014	18,715	10,631	8,410
1945	14,542	6,840	5,015	1,825	539	7,163	151,033	118,378	76,534	41,844	14,413	18,242
1950	14,674	6,885	4,971	1,914	527	7,262	163,770	122,707	82,430	40,277	19,927	21,137
1955	14,309	6,611	4,744	1,867	525	7,173	208,850	154,670	98,636	56,034	27,310	26,870
1960	14,006	6,217	4,542	1,675	513	7,276	249,163	179,519	116,178	63,341	35,316	34,328
1965	14,295	6,235	4,803	1,432	504	7,556	362,611	259,743	171,528	88,215	50,980	51,889
1970	14,167	5,803	4,637	1,166	496	7,868	502,658	346,229	254,261	91,967	69,285	87,145
1975, Dec. 31	15,108	5,787	4,741	1,046	475	8,846	897,101	590,999	447,590	143,409	110,569	195,533
1977, Dec. 31	15,174	5,668	4,654	1,014	467	9,039	1,074,426	683,611	520,167	163,443	134,916	255,898
1978, Dec. 31	14,712	5,564	4,564	1,000	465	8,848	1,176,247	737,127	559,284	177,843	143,684	295,436

Bank Rates on Short-term Business Loans

Source: Federal Reserve System

Percent per annum. Short-term loans mature within one year.

		All size loans							Size of loan in $1,000				
		Ave. 35 cities	N.Y. C.	7 Other N.E.	8 No. Cent.	7 S.E.	8 S.W.	4 West	1-9	10-99	100 to 499	500 to 999	1,000 and over
1967	Aug. 1-15	5.95	5.66	6.29	5.92	5.92	6.01	6.02	6.58	6.46	6.16	5.89	5.72
1970	Aug. 1-15	8.50	8.24	8.89	8.47	8.49	8.53	8.54	9.15	9.07	8.75	8.46	8.25
1974	May	11.15	11.08	11.65	11.09	10.88	10.82	11.19	10.50	11.06	11.41	11.32	11.06
1975	May	8.16	7.88	8.37	8.00	8.70	8.34	8.33	9.57	9.10	8.52	8.18	7.90
1976	Aug.	7.80	7.48	8.18	7.70	7.95	7.75	8.15	8.85	9.41	8.65	9.33	9.26
	Nov.	7.28	6.88	7.62	7.28	7.51	7.33	7.52	8.56	9.22	8.45	9.13	8.69

		All sizes	Size of Loan in $1,000[1]					
			1-24	25-49	50-99	100-499	500-999	1,000 and over
1977	Feb.	7.50	9.03	8.46	8.47	7.67	7.17	6.58
	May	7.40	9.09	8.43	8.07	7.60	7.13	6.67
1978	Feb.	8.90	9.65	9.45	9.29	9.05	8.79	8.34
	May	8.96	9.81	9.63	9.40	9.08	8.90	8.53
1979	Feb.	12.27	12.14	12.01	12.83	12.55	12.63	11.99
	May	12.34	12.30	12.69	13.02	12.61	12.68	12.07
1980	Feb.	15.67	15.06	15.54	15.91	16.23	16.34	15.50
	May	17.75	17.90	18.74	18.95	18.49	19.13	17.10

(1) In Feb. 1977, The Quarterly Interest Rate Survey was replaced by the Survey of Terms of Bank Lending (STBL). The STBL is conducted in the middle month of each quarter at about 340 member and nonmember banks. The regional breakdown was discontinued at that time. The last previous revision began with the survey period of Feb. 1971. It incorporated a number of technical changes in coverage, sampling, and interest rate calculations.

Federal Reserve System

The Federal Reserve System, central banking system of the U.S., was established Dec. 23, 1913, by an Act of Congress to give the country an elastic currency, to provide facilities for discounting commercial paper, and to improve supervision of banking. Today it is generally recognized that the primary function of the system is to foster a flow of credit and money that will facilitate orderly economic growth, a stable dollar, and a long-run balance in international payments.

The Federal Reserve System consists of the (1) Board of Governors of the Federal Reserve System; (2) Federal Open Market Committee; (3) 12 Fed. Reserve Banks and 25 branches; (4) member banks; (5) Fed. Advisory Council, and (6) the Consumer Advisory Council.

The 7 members of the Board of Governors in Washington are appointed by the President with the advice and consent of the Senate; Paul A. Volcker is chairman. The Board's principal function is in the area of monetary policy. Under the Monetary Control Act of 1980, uniform reserve requirements, set by the Federal Reserve Board, are applied to the transaction accounts and non-personal time deposits of all depository institutions; extends access to Federal Reserve discount and borrowing privileges and other services to nonmember depository institutions; and requires the Federal Reserve to set a schedule of fees for Federal Reserve services. The Depository Institutions Deregulation Committee (DIDC) was established by this act to provide for the orderly phase-out and the ultimate elimination of the limitations on the maximum rates of interest and dividends which may be paid on deposits and accounts by commercial banks, mutual savings banks, and savings and loan associations. Credit unions are not subject to the Act. Congress intended that the phase-out be completed by March 31, 1986. The DIDC consists of the Secretary of the Treasury, the Chairman of the Board of Governors of the Federal Reserve System, the Chairman of the Board of Directors of the Federal Deposit Insurance Corporation, the Chairman of the Federal Home Loan Bank Board, and the Chairman of the National Credit Union Administration Board, each of whom has one vote, and the Comptroller of the Currency who is a nonvoting member. The Board has authority to approve changes in discount rates, and to set margin requirements for certain kinds of stock transactions. Another important duty of the Board relates to supervision of state chartered member banks, and bank holding companies. The Federal Reserve has also been given responsibility by the Congress for rule writing and enforcement of a number of consumer credit protection laws.

Expenses of the Board of Governors are paid out of assessments upon the Reserve Banks.

The Federal Open Market Committee is composed of the 7 members of the Board of Governors, the president of the Federal Reserve Bank of New York, and 4 other Federal Reserve Bank presidents elected annually. The Committee establishes System open market policy for the purchases and sales of securities and for operations in foreign currencies.

Under policy adopted by the Board in 1964 all net earnings of the System (about $9 billion in 1979) are paid to the U.S. Treasury.

The Federal Advisory Council is composed of representatives of the banking industry from the 12 Federal Reserve Districts. The Council is required by law to meet with the Board at least 4 times yearly, to consult with and advise the Board on all matters within the Board's jurisdiction.

Congress established the Consumer Advisory Council in 1976. It consults with the Board at least 4 times a year on consumer-related matters. The Council has an authorized membership of 30, appointed by the Board for terms of 3 years. Members have a wide range of experience in the area of consumer credit.

Rather than having one central bank in the political capital, as in central banking systems of most countries, the Federal Reserve System is divided into 12 districts, each with a Federal Reserve Bank—in Boston, New York, Philadelphia, Cleveland, Richmond, Atlanta, Chicago, St. Louis, Minneapolis, Kansas City, Dallas, and San Francisco. The Federal Reserve Board is the policy-making organ of the System. The Board supervises the budgets and operations of the Reserve Banks, approves appointment of their presidents and first vice presidents and appoints 3 of each district bank's directors, including the chairman and vice chairman of each Reserve Bank's board. Reserve Banks are operated for public service. By statute, their stock is held entirely by member banks, which include all national banks and such state banks and trust companies as have elected to be members. Ownership of Reserve Bank stock is in the nature of an obligation incident to membership in the System and does not carry with it the attributes of control and financial interest ordinarily attached to stock ownership in corporations that are operated for profit. The amount of stock that member banks own is specified by law and dividends are limited to 6% per annum. In case of the liquidation of any Reserve Bank, its surplus would be paid entirely to the U.S. Each Reserve Bank has 9 directors, 6 of whom are chosen by member banks and 3 by the Board of Governors, including the chairman of the Reserve Bank board.

Largest Bank in Each of 48 Foreign Countries

Source: 500 Largest Banks in the Free World, compiled by the American Banker, New York. (Copyright 1981) Based on deposits Dec. 31, 1980, or nearest fiscal year-end. For Canada, see Index.

(thousands)

Country, bank	Deposits in U.S. $	Country, bank	Deposits in U.S. $
Argentina, Banco de la Nacion	10,228,834	Luxembourg, Cie, Luxembourgeoise	9,823,402
Australia, Commonwealth Bkng. Corp.	16,850,067	Malaysia, Bank Bumiputra Malaysia Berhad	3,867,568
Austria, Creditanstalt-Bankverein.	17,008,487	Mexico, Bancomer	13,476,336
Belgium, Societe Generale de Banque.	31,620,645	Netherlands, Algemene Bank Nederland	45,307,030
Brazil, Banco do Brasil.	27,137,230	New Zealand, Bank of	2,933,035
Denmark, Copenhagen Handelsbank	5,966,732	Nigeria, United Bank for Africa, Ltd.	4,347,436
Egypt, National Bank of Egypt	2,595,220	Norway, Norske Creditbank.	3,826,665
Finland, Kansallis-Osake Pankki	6,324,419	Pakistan, Habib Bank	2,818,174
France, Banque Nationale de Paris	93,643,943	Peru, Arab Latin American Bank	1,373,100
Germany, Deutsche Bank.	81,821,426	Philippines, Philippine National Bank	2,606,518
Ghana, Ghana Commercial Bank.	1,413,153	Portugal, Banco Portugues Do Atlantico.	3,370,578
Greece, National Bank of Greece	11,704,802	Saudi Arabia, National Commercial Bank	8,089,967
Hong Kong, Hongkong & Shanghai	42,207,647	Singapore, United Overseas Bank Ltd.	2,107,944
India, State Bank of India	15,349,824	South Africa, Barclays Nat'l Bank Ltd.	7,932,646
Indonesia, Bank Negara	2,194,056	Spain, Banco Espanol de Credito.	19,064,606
Iran, Bank Melli Iran	18,467,328	Sweden, Skandinaviska Enskilda Banken	16,877,238
Iraq, Rafidain Bank	10,479,832	Switzerland, Swiss Bank Corp.	36,669,944
Ireland, Allied Irish Banks, Ltd.	7,146,630	Taiwan, Bank of	5,861,917
Israel, Bank Leumi le-Israel	14,228,102	Thailand, Bangkok Bank Ltd.	3,883,762
Italy, Banca Nazionale del Lavoro	42,609,624	Turkey, Turkiye Cumhuriyeti Ziraat.	1,684,831
Japan, Dai-Ichi Kangyo Bank Ltd.	61,969,515	United Arab Emirates, Nat'l Bank of Abu Dhabi.	4,251,762
Jordan, Arab Bank, Ltd.	4,776,881	United Kingdom, Barclays Bank Ltd.	76,496,160
Korea, Bank of Seoul & Trust Co.	4,644,871	Venezuela, Banco Industrial.	2,128,513
Kuwait, National Bank of.	4,729,790	Yugoslavia, Udruzena Beogradska Banka.	7,388,796

100 Largest U.S. Commercial Banks

Source: 300 Largest Commercial Banks in U.S., compiled by the American Banker, New York. (Copyright 1980) Based on deposits June 30, 1980.

Rank		Deposits	Rank		Deposits
1	Bank of America NT&SA, San Francisco	$85,069,944,000	53	Lincoln First Bank NA, Rochester, N.Y.	2,362,018,475
2	Citibank NA, New York	72,429,528,000	54	Riggs National Bank, Washington, D.C.	2,328,020,000
3	Chase Manhattan Bank NA, New York	56,173,381,000	55	Connecticut Bank & Trust Co., Hartford	2,269,488,392
4	Manufacturers Hanover Trust Co. New York	39,000,618,000	56	Lloyds Bank California, Los Angeles	2,265,630,016
5	Morgan Guaranty Trust Co., New York	35,485,994,000	57	Bank of California NA, San Francisco.	2,263,756,000
6	Chemical Bank, New York	30,521,757,000	58	Industrial National Bank of Rhode Island, Providence	2,248,013,000
7	Continental Illinois National Bank & Trust Co., Chicago	25,566,850,000	59	First Union National Bank of North Carolina, Charlotte	2,241,638,000
8	Bankers Trust Co., New York	22,121,919,000	60	Southeast First National Bank, Miami.	2,195,645,000
9	First National Bank, Chicago	20,784,969,000	61	Citibank (New York State) NA, Buffalo	2,175,663,000
10	Security Pacific National Bank, Los Angeles	19,590,575,898	62	First National Bank, Minneapolis.	2,130,276,000
11	Wells Fargo Bank NA, San Francisco.	16,153,222,000	63	Fidelity Bank, Philadelphia	2,115,233,000
12	Marine Midland Bank NA, Buffalo, NY	13,418,696,000	64	Equibank, Pittsburgh	2,074,084,000
13	Crocker National Bank, San Francisco	12,989,763,000	65	Virginia National Bank, Norfolk.	2,073,759,000
14	United California Bank, Los Angeles	11,351,080,000	66	First Wisconsin National Bank, Milwaukee.	2,058,886,000
15	Mellon Bank NA, Pittsburgh	11,341,341,000	67	Huntington National Bank, Columbus, Ohio.	2,029,701,155
16	Irving Trust Co., New York	11,117,347,000	68	Banco Popular de Puerto Rico, San Juan	1,983,564,256
17	First National Bank, Boston	9,189,275,000	69	American Security Bank NA, Washington, D.C.	1,925,046,000
18	Bank of New York	7,990,304,303	70	First National Bank, Atlanta	1,916,421,000
19	National Bank of Detroit	6,866,871,000	71	Mercantile National Bank, Dallas	1,911,307,000
20	Seattle First National Bank	6,674,777,000	72	Bank of Hawaii, Honolulu.	1,858,401,000
21	Republic National Bank, Dallas	5,968,133,183	73	Central National Bank, Cleveland.	1,822,703,000
22	First National Bank, Dallas	5,703,883,000	74	American National Bank & Trust Co., Chicago	1,767,301,401
23	First City National Bank, Houston	4,799,288,809	75	New England Merchants National Bank, Boston	1,765,956,030
24	North Carolina National Bank, Charlotte	4,654,681,000	76	Provident National Bank, Philadelphia.	1,741,963,000
25	Union Bank, Los Angeles	4,578,524,000	77	Hartford National Bank & Trust Co., Conn.	1,724,139,000
26	Harris Trust & Savings Bank, Chicago	4,536,100,334	78	First National Bank, Baltimore	1,714,993,000
27	Valley National Bank, Phoenix	4,490,585,000	79	First & Merchants National Bank, Richmond, Va.	1,693,517,000
28	National Bank of North America, New York	4,265,985,000	80	American Fletcher National Bank & Trust Co., Indianapolis.	1,678,955,000
29	Republic National Bank, New York	4,190,031,824	81	Mercantile Trust Co. NA, St. Louis	1,650,015,000
30	Texas Commerce Bank NA, Houston.	4,045,414,000	82	Bank of Virginia, Richmond.	1,640,089,255
31	Pittsburgh National Bank	3,943,321,026	83	Sumitomo Bank of California, San Francisco	1,628,460,900
32	Northern Trust Co., Chicago	3,912,677,000	84	First National Bank, St. Louis	1,626,534,000
33	Philadelphia National Bank	3,875,088,000	85	American Bank & Trust Co., Reading, Pa.	1,609,246,000
34	Wachovia Bank & Trust Co. NA, Winston-Salem, N.C.	3,755,788,141	86	Indiana National Bank, Indianapolis	1,606,206,779
35	First Pennsylvania Bank NA, Philadelphia	3,686,497,000	87	Arizona Bank, Phoenix	1,604,820,169
36	BancOhio National Bank, Columbus	3,623,171,886	88	Equitable Trust Co., Baltimore	1,558,679,775
37	Rainier National Bank, Seattle	3,596,677,000	89	Shawmut Bank of Boston NA	1,538,088,000
38	First National Bank of Oregon, Portland	3,583,299,000	90	First National Bank of Nevada, Reno	1,533,096,000
39	United States National Bank of Oregon, Portland	3,443,582,000	91	J. Henry Schroder Bank & Trust Co., New York	1,518,304,000
40	AmeriTrust Co., Cleveland	3,434,256,000	92	Hamilton Bank, Lancaster, Pa.	1,491,852,000
41	Citizens & Southern National Bank, Atlanta	3,320,758,000	93	State Street Bank & Trust Co., Boston	1,481,139,000
42	European American Bank & Trust Co. New York	3,264,552,000	94	First National State Bank of New Jersey, Newark	1,462,086,000
43	Manufacturers National Bank, Detroit.	3,177,467,000	95	Northwestern Bank, North Wilkesboro, N.C.	1,445,378,578
44	Detroit Bank & Trust Co.	3,142,553,000	96	First National Bank, St. Paul, Minn.	1,442,767,000
45	Bank of Tokyo Trust Co., New York.	3,127,449,766	97	Idaho First National Bank, Boise.	1,432,075,569
46	California First Bank of San Francisco	2,967,404,000	98	Bank Leumi Trust Co. of New York	1,431,957,779
47	First National Bank of Arizona, Phoenix	2,945,239,000	99	First Hawaiian Bank, Honolulu.	1,403,338,000
48	Maryland National Bank, Baltimore	2,882,531,000	100	United States Trust Co., New York	1,390,112,672
49	Girard Bank, Philadelphia.	2,807,592,000			
50	United Virginia Bank, Richmond	2,666,910,000			
51	Northwestern National Bank, Minneapolis	2,660,919,000			
52	National City Bank, Cleveland	2,402,379,000			

Bank Suspensions

Source: Federal Deposit Insurance Corp. Deposits in thousands of dollars. The figures represent banks which, during the periods shown, closed temporarily or permanently on account of financial difficulties; does not include banks whose deposit liabilities were assumed by other banks.

Year	Susp.	Deposits	Year	Susp.	Deposits	Year	Susp.	Deposits	Year	Susp.	Deposits
1929	659	230,643	1937	50	14,960	1961	5	8,936	1971	5	74,605
1930	1,352	853,363	1938	50	10,296	1963	2	23,444	1972	1	20,482
1931	2,294	1,690,669	1939	32	32,738	1964	7	23,438	1973	3	25,811
1932	1,456	715,626	1940	19	5,657	1965	3	42,889	1975	1	18,248
1933*	4,004	3,598,975	1955(a)	4	6,503	1966	1	774	1976	3	18,859
1934	9	1,968	1958	3	4,156	1967	4	10,878	1978	1	1,284
1935	24	9,091	1959	3	2,593	1969	4	9,011	1979	3	12,795
1936	42	11,241	1960	1	6,930	1970	4	34,040	1980	3	15,500

*Figures for 1933 comprise 628 banks with deposits of $360,413,000 suspended before or after the banking holiday (the holiday began March 6 and closed March 15) or placed in receivership during the holiday; 2,124 banks with deposits of $2,520,391,000 which were not licensed following the banking holiday and were placed in liquidation or receivership; and 1,252 banks with deposits of $718,171,000 which had not been licensed by June 20, 1933. (a) No suspensions in years 1945-1954, 1962, 1968, 1974, 1977.

Civilian Employment of the Federal Government

Source: Workforce Analysis and Statistics Division, U.S. Office of Personnel Management as of June 30, 1979

Agency	All areas	United States			Outside United States		
		Total	Full-time	Part-time & intermittent	Total	Territories	Foreign countries
Total, all agencies[1]	2,956,426	2,824,320	2,562,665	261,655	132,106	35,485	96,621
Percent distribution	100	96	87	9	4	1	3
Legislative branch	41,114	41,041	39,690	1,351	73	13	60
Congress	19,970	19,970	19,969	1	...	...	...
Senate	7,527	7,527	7,527		...	...	...
House of Representatives	12,431	12,431	12,431	...	...	...	...
Comm. on Security and Coop. in Europe	12	12	11	1	...	...	...
Architect of the Capitol	2,368	2,368	1,730	638	...	...	...
General Accounting Office	5,437	5,374	5,208	166	63	13	50
Government Printing Office	7,342	7,342	7,175	167	...	...	...
Library of Congress	5,318	5,308	4,961	347	10	...	10
Tax Court	216	216	213	3	...	...	...
Other	463	463	434	29	...	...	...
Judicial branch	13,276	13,107	12,541	566	169	169	...
United States Courts	12,956	12,787	12,248	539	169	169	
Supreme Court	320	320	293	27	...	...	...
Executive branch	2,902,036	2,770,172	2,510,434	259,738	131,864	35,303	96,561
Executive Office of the President	1,731	1,731	1,583	148	...	...	...
White House Office	404	404	372	32	...	...	...
Office of the Vice President	25	25	24	1	...	...	...
Office of Management and Budget	643	643	613	30	...	...	...
Council of Economic Advisors	34	34	32	2	...	...	...
Council on Environmental Quality	69	69	56	13	...	...	...
Council on Wage and Price Stability	46	46	42	4	...	...	...
Domestic Council	60	60	56	4	...	...	...
Executive Mansions and Grounds	85	85	85	...	...	...	...
Office of Administration	185	185	158	27	...	...	...
Office of Special Representatives Trade Negotiations	67	67	54	13	...	...	...
Office of Science and Technology Policy	43	43	30	13	...	...	...
National Security Council	70	70	61	9	...	...	...
Executive departments	1,790,579	1,685,863	1,592,982	92,881	104,716	14,317	90,399
State[2]	30,351	10,849	10,178	671	19,502		19,502
Treasury	130,990	129,968	124,638	5,330	1,022	624	398
Defense	985,727	906,569	891,434	15,135	79,158	10,374	68,784
Department of the Army	357,050	321,645	315,128	6,517	35,405	3,698	31,707
Department of the Navy	313,164	291,581	286,658	4,923	21,583	4,909	16,674
Department of the Air Force	237,785	225,361	222,406	2,955	12,424	1,573	10,851
Defense Logistics Agency	47,541	47,116	46,754	362	425	62	363
Other Defense Activities	30,187	20,866	20,488	378	9,321	132	9,189
Justice	55,305	54,411	52,898	1,513	894	407	487
Interior	89,418	89,060	78,872	10,188	358	289	69
Agriculture	137,669	136,153	107,597	28,556	1,516	755	761
Commerce	52,865	52,621	38,073	14,548	244	89	155
Labor	24,122	24,017	22,993	1,024	105	64	41
Health, Education, and Welfare	169,553	168,658	155,627	13,031	895	847	48
Housing and Urban Development	19,263	19,074	18,165	909	189	189	...
Transportation	74,908	74,087	72,896	1,191	821	678	143
Department of Energy	20,408	20,396	19,611	785	12	1	11
Independent agencies	1,109,726	1,082,578	915,869	166,709	27,148	20,986	6,162
Action	1,969	1,436	1,371	65	533	24	509
Board of Governors, Fed. Res. System	1,494	1,494	1,455	39	...	...	...
Canal Zone Government	3,210	...	...	...	3,210	3,210	...
Community Service Admin.	1,118	1,118	1,094	24	...	...	...
Environmental Protection Agency	13,962	13,951	12,226	1,725	11	11	...
Federal Communications Comm.	2,241	2,233	2,191	42	8	8	...
Federal Trade Commission	1,953	1,953	1,767	186	...	...	...
General Services Admin.	38,949	38,828	36,496	2,332	121	106	15
International Communications Agency	8,405	3,417	3,329	88	4,988	...	4,988
Interstate Commerce Commission	2,130	2,130	2,073	57	...	...	...
National Aeronautics and Space Admin.	24,449	24,426	24,272	154	23	1	22
National Labor Relations Board	3,054	3,030	2,987	43	24	24	...
Nuclear Regulatory Comm.	3,160	3,160	3,025	135	...	...	...
Office of Personnel Mgmt.	8,405	8,384	6,425	1,959	21	21	...
Panama Canal Company	12,368	76	75	1	12,292	12,292	...
Securities and Exchange Comm.	2,007	2,007	1,969	38	...	...	...
Selective Service System	70	70	70	...	...	...	...
Small Business Admin.	5,993	5,890	5,779	111	103	103	...
Tennessee Valley Authority	48,353	48,349	48,074	275	4	...	4
U. S. Postal Service	665,980	663,156	533,026	130,130	2,824	2,824	...
Veterans Administration	233,153	230,696	203,025	27,671	2,457	2,213	244
All other agencies	27,303	26,774	25,140	1,634	529	149	380

(1) Excludes employees of Central Intelligence Agency, National Security Agency (not reported to the Office of Personnel Management) and uncompensated employees. June 1979 total includes 41,792 employees exempted from personnel ceilings in the Youth Programs and Worker Trainee Opportunities Program. (2) Includes 6,263 employees in Agency for International Development (2,712 in the Washington, D.C. metropolitan area); employees in foreign countries include 381 paid from local currency trust funds established by foreign governments.

U.S. Labor Force, Employment and Unemployment

Source: Bureau of Labor Statistics, U.S. Labor Department

(numbers in thousands; seasonally adjusted)

Labor force	Annual average			1980				
	1977	1978[1]	1979	Jan.	Feb.	Mar.	Apr.	May
Civilian labor force	97,401	100,420	102,908	104,229	104,260	104,094	104,419	104,542
Employed	90,546	94,373	96,945	97,804	97,953	97,656	97,154	96,537
Agriculture	3,244	3,342	3,297	3,270	3,326	3,358	3,242	3,191
Nonagricultural industries	87,302	91,031	93,648	94,534	94,626	94,298	93,912	93,346
Unemployed	6,855	6,047	5,963	6,425	6,307	6,438	7,265	8,006
Long term, 15 weeks and over	1,911	1,379	1,202	1,334	1,286	1,363	1,629	1,766
Unemployment rates (unemployment in each group as a percent of the groups' civilian labor force)								
Total, 16 years and over	7.0	6.0	5.8	6.2	6.0	6.2	7.0	7.7
Men, 20 years and over	5.2	4.2	4.1	4.7	4.6	4.9	5.9	6.7
Women, 20 years and over	7.0	6.0	5.7	5.8	5.7	5.7	6.3	6.5
Both sexes, 16 to 19 years	17.7	16.3	16.1	16.3	16.5	15.9	16.2	18.5
White, total	6.2	5.2	5.1	5.4	5.3	5.4	6.2	6.8
Men, 20 years and over	4.6	3.7	3.6	4.1	4.0	4.4	5.3	6.0
Women, 20 years and over	6.2	5.2	5.0	5.1	5.2	4.9	5.5	5.8
Both sexes, 16 to 19 years	15.4	13.9	13.9	14.0	13.8	13.8	14.6	14.6
Black and other, total	13.1	11.9	11.3	11.8	11.5	11.8	12.6	13.6
Men, 20 years and over	10.0	8.6	8.4	9.6	9.2	9.3	10.9	12.6
Women, 20 years and over	11.7	10.6	10.1	10.0	9.0	10.5	11.4	10.9
Both sexes, 16 to 19 years	38.3	36.3	33.5	34.6	37.9	33.0	29.8	36.3
Married men, spouse present	3.6	2.8	2.7	3.4	3.1	3.4	4.1	4.9
Married women, spouse present	6.5	5.5	5.1	5.2	5.4	5.3	5.7	6.1
Women who head families	9.3	8.5	8.3	9.2	8.5	8.7	9.3	8.4
Full-time workers	6.5	5.5	5.3	5.7	5.6	5.8	6.6	7.4
Part-time workers	9.8	9.0	8.7	8.7	8.9	8.3	8.9	8.8
White-collar workers	4.3	3.5	3.3	3.4	3.4	3.3	3.7	3.7
Blue-collar workers	8.1	6.9	6.9	8.0	7.7	8.0	9.7	11.5
Service workers	8.2	7.4	7.1	6.9	6.9	7.1	8.0	8.1
Farm workers	4.6	3.8	3.8	4.4	3.9	4.0	5.0	4.2
Nonagricultural private wage and salary workers[2]	7.0	5.9	5.7	6.2	6.0	6.2	7.1	8.3
Construction	12.7	10.6	10.2	10.8	10.5	13.0	15.1	16.5
Manufacturing	6.7	5.5	5.5	6.7	6.4	6.5	7.9	9.9
Durable goods	6.2	4.9	5.0	6.7	6.3	6.4	8.3	11.2
Nondurable goods	7.4	6.3	6.4	6.8	6.7	6.7	7.4	8.0
Wholesale and retail trade	8.0	6.9	6.5	6.6	6.4	6.3	7.0	8.0
Finance and service industries	6.0	5.1	4.9	4.6	4.6	4.9	5.1	5.7
Government workers	4.2	3.9	3.7	3.8	4.0	4.2	4.4	3.5

(1) Data for periods prior to 1978 are not strictly comparable with current data because of an expansion/in the sample and revisions in the estimation procedures. (2) Includes mining, not shown separately.

Employed Persons by Major Occupational Groups and Sex

Annual averages 1978	Thousands of persons			Percent distribution		
Occupational group	Both sexes	Males	Females	Both sexes	Males	Females
Total employed	94,773	55,491	38,882	100.0	100.0	100.0
White-collar workers	47,205	22,633	24,572	50.0	40.8	63.2
Professional and technical	14,245	8,163	6,082	15.1	14.7	15.6
Managers and administrators, except farm	10,105	7,744	2,361	10.7	14.0	6.1
Sales workers	5,951	3,285	2,666	6.3	5.9	6.9
Clerical workers	16,904	3,442	13,463	17.9	6.2	34.6
Blue-collar workers	31,531	25,765	5,766	33.4	46.4	14.8
Craft and kindred workers	12,386	11,689	697	13.1	21.1	1.8
Operatives, except transport	10,875	6,554	4,321	11.5	11.8	11.1
Transport equipment operatives	3,541	3,284	257	3.8	5.9	.7
Nonfarm laborers	4,729	4,238	491	5.0	7.6	1.3
Service workers	12,839	4,804	8,035	13.6	8.7	20.7
Private household workers	1,162	27	1,135	1.2	(1)	2.9
Other service workers	11,677	4,277	6,900	12.4	8.6	17.7
Farm workers	2,798	2,289	509	3.0	4.1	1.3
Farmers and farm managers	1,480	1,349	131	1.6	2.4	.3
Farm laborers and supervisors	1,318	940	377	1.4	1.7	1.0

(1) Less than 0.05 percent.

Employment and Unemployment in the U.S.

Civilian labor force, persons 16 years of age and over (in thousands)

Year	Civilian labor force	Employed	Unemployed	Year	Civilian labor force	Employed	Unemployed
1940	52,705	45,070	7,635	1974	91,011	85,936	5,076
1950	62,208	58,918	3,288	1975	92,613	84,783	7,830
1960	69,628	65,778	3,852	1976	94,773	87,485	7,288
1965	74,455	71,088	3,366	1977	97,401	90,546	6,855
1970	82,715	78,627	4,088	1978	100,420	94,373	6,047
1973	88,714	84,409	4,304	1979	102,908	96,945	5,963

Average Salaries of Full-time Federal Civilian Employees

Source: Office of Personnel Management, Oct. 31, 1980

Occupation Blue Collar	Men No. of employ	Men Average salary	Women No. of employ	Women Average salary	Occupation White-Collar	Men No. of employ	Men Average salary	Women No. of employ	Women Average salary
Baker	210	$17,604	17	$16,582	Accountant	18,449	$30,258	3,220	$23,215
Barber	30	17,248	1	18,283	Architect	1,544	26,386	79	22,810
Beautician	—	—	9	17,932	Attorney	13,460	38,493	3,808	32,358
Boiler operator	6,705	19,101	19	16,101	Chaplain	511	31,185	4	21,118
Carpenter	9,166	19,105	89	16,275	Chemist	6,605	32,765	1,478	25,912
Cook	4,023	18,769	1,211	16,805	Clerk/Typist	3,754	11,258	62,643	11,106
Electrician	12,864	19,963	222	16,248	Dental assistant	218	12,915	2,716	12,885
Elevator operator	383	15,723	199	13,383	Dietitian	35	26,543	1,153	23,796
Forklift operator	3,344	16,795	119	16,446	Editor/Writer	949	28,876	1,323	22,796
Janitor	17,578	13,764	5,893	13,494	Editor, technical	1,121	27,254	601	23,347
Laborer	23,821	14,278	2,168	14,037	Engineer, civil	15,431	32,644	329	23,739
Locksmith	177	18,588	4	17,321	Engineer, electrical	4,417	31,819	82	24,902
Machinist	13,343	20,613	260	16,442	Engineer, mechanical	10,067	32,259	133	24,000
Mechanic, A/C	5,343	19,722	34	15,435	Law clerk	448	21,660	401	21,482
Mechanic, aircraft	4,991	20,019	183	17,363	Librarian	1,128	29,451	2,194	26,322
Mechanic, general	6,493	19,983	59	16,459	Messenger	565	10,097	89	10,721
Painter	9,487	18,814	303	16,537	Nurse	2,541	19,918	33,469	21,326
Pipefitter	15,418	21,081	120	17,132	Paralegal	865	28,023	1,173	22,013
Plumber	2,488	18,742	13	16,974	Personnel mgmt.	19,361	28,544	29,103	18,278
Pressman	2,411	19,452	264	17,989	Pharmacist	1,986	25,808	434	23,452
Sheet metal	11,892	20,001	520	17,851	Public relations	1,947	33,745	1,086	25,954
Store clerk	1,297	15,908	401	14,608	Purchasing	1,157	16,227	3,613	15,116
Toolmaker	989	23,306	8	19,463	Secretary	734	14,439	78,736	15,293
Trainman	103	17,752	—	—	Social work	2,008	27,431	1,554	25,897
Tractor operator	2,208	16,058	29	14,853	Statistician	2,042	32,462	831	26,338
Vehicle operator	17,301	17,212	390	15,651	Technician, medical	1,170	16,339	1,481	15,225
Warehouseman	20,903	16,452	1,877	15,413	Therapist, occupational	88	21,727	580	20,726
Welder	6,463	19,698	107	17,015	Therapist, physical	263	22,554	453	20,611

Per Capita Personal Income, by States and Regions

Source: Bureau of Economic Analysis, U.S. Commerce Department (dollars)

State and Region	1970	1975	1978	1979	1980
United States	3,893	5,861	7,854	8,773	9,521
New England	4,245	6,030	7,956	8,910	10,105
Connecticut	4,871	6,779	8,973	10,129	11,720
Maine	3,250	4,766	6,334	7,039	7,925
Massachusetts	4,276	6,077	7,952	8,893	10,125
New Hampshire . . .	3,720	5,417	7,483	8,351	9,131
Rhode Island	3,878	5,709	7,628	8,510	9,444
Vermont	3,447	4,924	6,609	7,329	7,827
Mideast	4,384	6,380	8,206	9,112	10,192
Delaware	4,468	6,547	8,427	9,327	10,339
District of Columbia .	4,644	7,262	9,513	10,570	12,039
Maryland	4,267	6,403	8,514	9,331	10,460
New Jersey	4,684	6,794	8,792	9,747	10,924
New York	4,605	6,519	8,192	9,104	10,260
Pennsylvania	3,879	5,841	7,669	8,558	9,434
Great Lakes	4,050	6,047	8,224	9,118	9,779
Illinois	4,446	6,735	8,887	9,799	10,521
Indiana	3,709	5,609	7,701	8,570	8,936
Michigan	4,041	5,991	8,514	9,403	9,950
Ohio	3,949	5,778	7,836	8,715	9,462
Wisconsin	3,712	5,616	7,555	8,484	9,348
Plains.	3,657	5,719	7,637	8,628	9,338
Iowa	3,643	5,894	7,905	8,772	9,358
Kansas.	3,725	5,958	7,975	9,233	9,983
Minnesota	3,819	5,779	7,858	8,865	9,724
Missouri	3,654	5,476	7,341	8,251	8,982
Nebraska	3,657	5,882	7,491	8,684	9,365
North Dakota	3,077	5,888	7,642	8,231	8,747
South Dakota	3,108	5,009	6,580	7,455	7,806

State and Region	1970	1975	1978	1979	1980
Southeast	3,208	5,028	6,836	7,624	8,111
Alabama	2,892	4,635	6,347	6,962	7,488
Arkansas	2,791	4,510	6,236	6,933	7,268
Florida	3,698	5,631	7,605	8,546	8,996
Georgia	3,300	5,029	6,830	7,630	8,073
Kentucky	3,076	4,887	6,618	7,390	7,613
Louisiana	3,023	4,803	6,748	7,583	8,458
Mississippi	2,547	4,047	5,582	6,178	6,580
North Carolina	3,200	4,940	6,693	7,385	7,819
South Carolina	2,951	4,665	6,344	7,057	7,266
Tennessee	3,079	4,804	6,602	7,343	7,720
Virginia.	3,677	5,772	7,670	8,587	9,392
West Virginia.	3,038	4,962	6,593	7,372	7,800
Southwest	3,465	5,469	7,608	8,627	9,284
Arizona	3,614	5,391	7,411	8,423	8,791
New Mexico	3,045	4,843	6,733	7,560	7,841
Oklahoma	3,341	5,280	7,376	8,509	9,116
Texas	3,507	5,584	7,776	8,788	9,545
Rocky Mountain	3,540	5,571	7,512	8,357	9,095
Colorado	3,838	5,987	8,070	9,122	10,025
Idaho.	3,243	5,179	6,995	7,571	8,056
Montana	3,395	5,388	7,067	7,684	8,536
Utah	3,169	4,900	6,600	7,197	7,649
Wyoming	3,672	6,123	8,668	9,922	10,898
Far West.	4,310	6,474	8,807	9,901	10,713
California	4,423	6,575	8,900	10,047	10,938
Nevada	4,583	6,625	9,529	10,521	10,727
Oregon	3,677	5,769	8,112	8,938	9,317
Washington	3,997	6,298	8,581	9,565	10,309
Alaska	4,638	9,636	10,485	11,219	12,790
Hawaii	4,599	6,708	8,438	9,223	10,101

U.S. Balance of International Payments

Source: Bureau of Economic Analysis, U.S. Commerce Department
(millions of dollars)

	1955	1960	1965	1970	1975	1978	1979	1980
Exports of goods and services.	19,948	28,861	41,086	65,673	155,729	221,036	286,508	344,667
Merchandise, adjusted	14,424	19,650	26,461	42,469	107,088	142,054	182,055	223,966
Transfers under U.S. military agency sales contracts.	200	335	830	1,501	4,049	8,240	7,194	8,231
Receipts of income on U.S. investments abroad	2,817	4,616	7,436	11,746	25,351	42,972	65,970	75,936
Other services	2,507	4,261	6,359	9,957	19,242	27,772	31,289	36,534
Imports of goods and services.	−17,795	−23,729	−32,801	−60,050	−132,836	−230,240	−281,630	−333,888
Merchandise, adjusted	−11,527	−14,758	−21,510	−39,866	−98,041	−175,813	−211,524	−249,308
Direct defense expenditures	−2,901	−3,087	−2,952	−4,855	−4,795	−7,354	−8,469	−10,746
Payments of income on foreign investments in the U.S..	−520	−1,237	−2,088	−5,516	−12,564	−22,073	−33,460	−43,174
Other services	−2,847	−4,646	−6,251	−9,815	−17,436	−25,001	−28,178	−30,660
Unilateral transfers, net.	−2,498	−2,308	−2,854	−3,294	−4,613	−5,055	−5,666	−7,056
U.S. official reserve assets, net	182	2,145	1,225	2,481	−849	−732	−1,107	−8,155
U.S. Government assets, other than official reserve assets, net.	−310	−1,100	−1,605	−1,589	−3,474	−4,644	−3,783	−5,165
U.S. private assets, net.	−1,255	−5,144	−5,335	−10,228	−35,380	−57,279	−56,858	−71,456
Foreign official assets in the U.S., net.		1,473	134	6,908	7,027	33,293	−14,271	15,492
Other foreign assets in the U.S., net		821	607	−550	8,643	30,804	51,845	34,769
Allocations of special drawing rights	—	—	—	867	—	—	1,139	1,152
Statistical discrepancy	371	−1,019	−458	−219	5,753	11,354	23,822	29,640
Memoranda:								
Balance on merchandise trade	2,897	4,892	4,951	2,603	9,047	−33,759	−29,469	−25,342
Balance on goods and services	2,153	5,132	8,284	5,624	22,893	−9,204	4,878	10,779
Balance on goods, services, and remittances	1,556	4,496	7,238	4,066	21,175	−11,088	2,736	8,382
Balance on current account.	−345	2,824	5,431	2,330	18,280	−14,259	1,414	3,723

Note.—Details may not add to totals because of rounding.

Average Weekly Canadian Wages and Salaries, by Province

Source: Canadian Statistical Review, July 1981 (Canadian dollars)

Year & month	Canada[1]	Nfld.	P.E.I.	N.S.	N.B.	Que.	Ont.	Man.	Sask.	Alta.	B.C.
1970	126.82	117.70	83.82	104.21	104.01	122.38	131.52	115.88	114.87	128.15	137.97
1975	203.34	196.50	149.84	172.40	182.40	199.22	204.86	186.01	188.31	207.39	229.97
1977	249.95	242.43	187.73	212.09	223.34	244.77	249.46	226.28	235.61	261.96	284.13
1978	265.37	248.36	196.72	223.72	232.89	262.82	264.04	239.71	250.44	276.32	301.26
1979	288.25	271.64	209.77	245.23	256.49	284.35	285.57	259.00	275.79	306.79	327.14
1980	320.32	288.90	230.03	265.95	283.84	315.35	311.45	283.20	303.71	341.93	363.50
1981 (Jan.). . .	336.95	316.01	246.70	286.99	297.26	333.71	329.54	298.35	322.27	373.25	381.48

Includes Yukon and Northwest Territories.

Canadian Labor Force

Source: Statistics Canada; April, 1981, seasonally adjusted (thousands of persons)

	Can.	Nfld.	P.E.I.	N.S.	N.B.	Que.	Ont.	Man.	Sask.	Alta.	B.C.
Labor force	11,785	217	53	368	296	2,993	4,447	492	450	1,137	1,325
Employed	10,959	190	47	336	263	2,713	4,171	463	432	1,096	1,245
Unemployed	826	27	6	32	33	280	276	29	18	41	80
Percent unemployed. . .	7.0	12.4	11.1	8.7	11.1	9.4	6.2	5.9	4.0	3.6	6.0

Canadian Labor Force Characteristics

Source: Statistics Canada (thousands of workers)

Year	Labor force	Employed — All workers[1] Total	Agri-culture	Non-agri-culture	Employed — Paid workers Total	Non-agri-culture	Unem-ployed	Unem-ployed %
1950	5,163	4,976	1,018	3,958	3,522	3,411	186	3.6
1955	5,610	5,364	819	4,546	4,133	4,027	245	4.4
1960	6,411	5,965	683	5,282	4,843	4,732	446	7.0
1965	7,141	6,862	594	6,268	5,760	5,655	280	3.9
1970	8,374	7,879	511	7,368	6,839	6,740	495	5.9
1975	9,974	9,284	497	8,787	8,951	8,814	690	6.9
1978	10,882	9,972	494	9,478	9,740	9,608	911	8.4
1979	11,207	10,369	504	9,865	10,032	9,871	838	7.5
1980	11,522	10,655	477	10,178	9,604	9,449	867	7.5

(1) Including self-employed.

Federal Deposit Insurance Corporation (FDIC)

The primary purpose of the Federal Deposit Insurance Corporation (FDIC) is to insure deposits in all banks approved for insurance coverage benefits under the Federal Deposit Insurance Act. The major functions of the FDIC are to pay off depositors of insured banks closed without adequate provision having been made to pay depositors' claims, to act as receiver for all national banks placed in receivership and for state banks placed in receivership when appointed receiver by state authorities, and to prevent the continuance or development of unsafe and unsound banking practices. The FDIC's entire income consists of assessments on insured banks and income from investments; it receives no appropriations from Congress. It may borrow from the U.S. Treasury not to exceed $3 billion outstanding, but has made no such borrowings since it was organized in 1933. The FDIC surplus (Deposit Insurance Fund) as of Dec. 31, 1980 was $11 billion.

Foreign Direct Investment in the U.S.

Source: Bureau of Economic Analysis, U.S. Commerce Department

(millions of dollars)

Country	Position at yearend		Equity and inter-company ac-count inflows (outflows (-))[1]		Reinvested earnings of incorporated affiliates[2]		Income[3]		Interest, divi-dends, and earn-ings of unincor-porated affiliates[4]	
	1978	1979	1978	1979	1978	1979	1978	1979	1978	1979
Total.	42,471	52,260	5,313	5,984	2,583	3,729	4,211	6,033	1,628	2,303
By country:										
Canada	6,180	6,974	449	356	231	402	354	590	123	188
Europe.	29,180	35,999	3,350	4,201	1,866	2,600	3,038	4,246	1,172	1,646
Belgium and Luxembourg .	1,303	1,658	8	95	168	260	174	267	6	7
France	1,978	2,214	101	117	79	106	163	222	84	115
Germany	3,654	5,004	1,010	1,246	96	162	194	256	98	94
Italy	243	212	−41	−38	4	6	16	28	12	22
Netherlands	10,078	12,462	979	699	967	1,622	1,392	2,240	425	618
Denmark and Ireland	125	142	6	18	6	−1	8	1	2	1
United Kingdom	7,638	9,391	799	1,424	521	314	813	783	292	469
Sweden.	893	1,150	165	155	33	106	73	165	40	59
Switzerland.	2,879	3,290	237	430	−34	−9	177	242	210	251
Other	388	476	87	55	26	33	29	41	3	8
Japan	2,749	3,441	770	287	217	405	301	510	84	105
Australia, New Zealand, and South Africa	128	199	76	60	2	(*)	22	35	20	35
Latin America	3,603	4,878	459	967	254	304	407	525	153	221
Panama.	495	573	14	25	42	53	45	56	3	2
Other Latin America.	65	185	−52	138	−9	−17	6	44	25	60
Other Western Hemisphere	3,043	4,119	497	804	222	267	346	426	125	158
Middle East	415	474	142	45	7	14	37	59	30	45
Israel	105	139	44	31	3	4	10	14	7	10
Other	311	335	98	14	4	10	27	45	23	35
Other Africa, Asia, and Pacific	217	295	67	68	6	5	52	68	46	63
Memorandum: OPEC[5]	366	401	107	24	4	11	27	52	23	41
By industry:										
Petroleum	7,762	9,903	303	526	940	1,615	1,239	2,003	299	388
Manufacturing.	17,202	20,029	2,537	1,914	660	910	1,146	1,512	490	603
Trade	9,161	11,167	1,430	1,386	488	620	805	1,082	317	462
Finance	2,458	3,701	52	1,012	171	231	445	638	274	407
Insurance	2,773	3,454	268	482	270	188	445	528	175	341
Real Estate	1,161	1,566	262	350	−20	−8	41	73	61	81
Other.	1,954	2,439	461	313	74	173	86	195	12	21

* Less than $500,000 (+). (1) Foreign parents' shares in net changes in capital stock and intercompany accounts with incor-porated U.S. affiliates, and in equity in unincorporated U.S. affiliates. (2) Foreign parents' shares in the earnings of incorpo-rated U.S. affiliates (net of U.S. income taxes), less their shares in the gross dividends of these affiliates. (3) Foreign parents' shares in the earnings of U.S. affiliates (net of U.S. income taxes), plus net interest paid on intercompany debt, less withhold-ing taxes on dividends and interest. Also equals interest, dividends, and earnings of unincorporated affiliates plus reinvested earnings of incorporated affiliates. (4) Dividends and interest on intercompany debt credited to foreign parents by affiliates, less interest credited by foreign parents to affiliates, exclusive of withholding taxes; plus foreign parents' shares in the earnings of unincorporated U.S. affiliates. (5) Countries in the Organization of Petroleum Exporting Countries (OPEC) are: Algeria, Ecuador, Gabon, Indonesia, Iran, Iraq, Kuwait, Libya, Nigeria, Qatar, Saudi Arabia, Venezuela, and United Arab Emirates.

Canadian Unemployment Insurance Commission

Source: Canadian Statistical Review, May 1981
(Canadian dollars)

	Claims data				Benefits paid				
Year	Benefi-ciaries[1][2] (000)	Claims received (000)	Weeks paid	Total paid (thousands of dollars)	Regular	Sickness	Maternity	Retirement	Fishing
1977 . .	750	2,807	38,701	3,909,045	3,485,080	155,828	172,228	13,543	48,400
1978 . .	803	2,809	41,355	4,536,910	4,006,868	157,405	195,297	14,831	63,434
1979 . .	713	2,602	36,896	4,008,002	3,431,216	145,183	207,649	15,055	70,897
1980 . .	701	2,762	36,333	4,393,307	3,748,551	154,671	234,746	15,950	85,570

(1) Refer to the number of persons receiving $1.00 or more in unemployment insurance benefits during a specific week each month. (2) Annual figures are average of 12 months.

Canadian Provincial Unemployment Rates

Source: Statistics Canada

Year	Can.	Nfld.	P.E.I.	N.S.	N.B.	Que.	Ont.	Man.	Sask.	Alta.	B.C.
1976 . .	7.1	13.6	9.8	9.6	11.1	8.7	6.2	4.7	4.0	3.9	8.6
1977 . .	8.1	15.9	10.0	10.7	13.4	10.3	7.0	5.9	4.5	4.4	8.5
1978 . .	8.4	16.4	9.9	10.6	12.6	10.9	7.2	6.5	4.9	4.7	8.3
1979 . .	7.5	15.4	11.3	10.2	11.1	9.6	6.5	5.4	4.2	3.9	7.7
1980 . .	7.5	13.5	10.8	9.8	11.1	9.9	6.9	5.5	4.4	3.7	6.8

Total Value of Canadian Construction Work

Source: Statistics Canada (thousands of Canadian dollars)

Province	1980 New	1980 Repair	1980 Total	1981 New	1981 Repair	1981 Total
Newfoundland.	709,448	125,032	834,480	945,836	145,207	1,091,043
Prince Edward Island. .	129,180	34,660	163,840	123,683	38,102	161,785
Nova Scotia	957,567	244,415	1,201,982	1,314,429	268,029	1,582,458
New Brunswick	798,302	166,662	964,964	864,271	180,975	1,045,246
Quebec	7,524,629	1,768,598	9,293,227	8,452,179	1,923,327	10,375,506
Ontario.	9,470,309	2,537,332	12,007,641	10,645,740	2,743,807	13,389,547
Manitoba.	1,063,409	298,677	1,362,086	1,126,179	318,650	1,444,829
Saskatchewan	1,838,325	375,054	2,213,379	2,438,306	415,513	2,853,819
Alberta	10,127,849	1,090,576	11,218,425	12,406,366	1,197,761	13,604,127
British Columbia . . .	6,843,669	965,463	7,809,132	7,807,835	1,062,507	8,870,342
Total	39,462,687	7,606,469	47,069,156	46,124,824	8,293,878	54,418,702

Canadian Pulpwood, Wood Pulp, and Newsprint

Source: Canadian Statistical Review, June 1981 (thousands of metric tons)

Year	Pulpwood production[1] (thousands of cubic meters)	Wood pulp production[2] Total	Wood pulp production[2] Mechanical	Wood pulp production[2] Chemical	Wood pulp exports[3]	News-print production	Newsprint shipments Total	Newsprint shipments Domestic	Newsprint shipments Exports[4]
1977 . . .		17,772.2	6,830.1	10,916.8	6,715	8,988	9,005	909	8,096
1978 . . .	45,308	19,185.6	7,480.2	11,671.0	7,320	8,811	8,883	908	7,975
1979 . . .	48,729	19,571.6	7,441.1	12,104.6	7,828	8,710	8,730	948	7,781
1980 . . .	50,386	19,838.9	7,361.4	12,452.0	7,990	8,625	8,621	982	7,639

(1) Pulpwood produced for domestic use, excluding exports, but including receipts of purchased roundwood. (2) Total pulp production covers "screenings" which are already included in exports. "Screenings" are excluded throughout from mechanical and chemical pulp. (3) Customs exports. (4) Mill shipments destined for export.

Telephones in North American Cities

Source: American Telephone and Telegraph Co., and Trans-Canada Telephone Systems (Jan. 1, 1980)

City	Number
Akron, Oh.	351,179
Albany, N.Y.	169,663
Albuquerque, N.M. . . .	321,785
Alexandria, Va.	449,131
Allentown, Pa.	156,671
Amarillo, Tex.	145,677
Anaheim, Cal.	232,628
Anchorage, Alas.	137,123
Ann Arbor, Mich.	131,904
Atlanta, Ga.	929,663
Augusta, Ga.	162,381
Austin, Tex.	338,482
Bakersfield, Cal.	194,058
Baltimore, Md.	1,456,284
Baton Rouge, La.	306,376
Birmingham, Ala.	482,105
Boise, Ida.	138,214
Boston, Mass.	540,262
Bridgeport, Conn.	187,577
Buffalo, N.Y.	401,467
Calgary, Alta.	447,649
Cambridge, Mass.	114,076
Canton, Oh.	129,822
Cedar Rapids, Ia.	134,100
Champaign, Ill.	116,250
Charleston, S.C.	220,370
Charleston, W. Va. . . .	209,147
Charlotte, N.C.	384,927
Chattanooga, Tenn. . . .	257,752
Chicago, Ill.	2,734,837
Cincinnati, Oh.	775,864
Clearwater, Fla.	230,259
Cleveland, Oh.	934,687
Colorado Springs, Col. .	236,828
Columbia, S.C.	294,830
Columbus, Ga.	144,752
Columbus, Oh.	491,608
Corpus Christi, Tex. . . .	161,882
Covington, Ky.	126,114
Dallas, Tex.	848,964
Davenport, Ia.	123,900
Dayton, Oh.	380,426
Denver, Col.	1,349,977
Des Moines, Ia.	286,800
Detroit, Mich.	1,551,048
Durham, N.C.	125,988
East Orange, N.J.	138,089
Edmonton, Alta.	405,139
El Paso, Tex.	273,185

City	Number
Erie, Pa.	147,419
Eugene-Spring-field, Ore.	164,512
Evansville, Ind.	131,173
Fayetteville, N.C.	151,209
Flint, Mich.	234,897
Ft. Lauderdale, Fla. . . .	440,098
Fort Wayne, Ind.	186,258
Fort Worth, Tex.	364,455
Fremont City, Cal. . . .	142,651
Fresno, Cal.	284,714
Gary, Ind.	98,326
Grand Rapids, Mich. . .	321,615
Greensboro, N.C.	213,410
Greenville, S.C.	186,581
Guadalajara, Mex. . . .	286,123
Halifax, N.S.	151,836
Hamilton, Ont.	219,215
Harrisburg, Pa.	217,767
Hartford, Conn.	333,463
Hayward, Cal.	155,388
Hollywood, Fla.	239,526
Honolulu, Ha.	385,989
Houston, Tex.	1,496,626
Huntington Beach, Cal. .	154,585
Huntsville, Ala.	150,152
Indianapolis, Ind.	690,187
Jackson, Miss.	221,066
Jacksonville, Fla.	440,664
Jersey City, N.J.	187,486
Kalamazoo, Mich.	160,997
Kansas City, Kan.	174,869
Kansas City, Mo.	348,419
Kitchener, Ont.	131,878
Knoxville, Tenn.	230,260
Lancaster, Pa.	114,723
Lansing, Mich.	236,369
Las Vegas, Nev.	429,715
Lexington, Ky.	177,338
Lincoln, Neb.	165,300
Little Rock, Ark.	276,881
Livonia, Mich.	196,265
London, Ont.	142,495
Los Angeles, Cal. (Area)	6,322,018
Louisville, Ky.	592,568
Lubbock, Tex.	171,609
Macon, Ga.	122,977
Madison, Wis.	201,599

City	Number
Memphis, Tenn.	639,852
Mexico City (area) . . .	1,904,742
Miami, Fla.	1,129,870
Milwaukee, Wis. . . .	914,183
Minn.-St. Paul, Minn. . .	1,666,300
Mobile, Ala.	251,325
Modesto, Cal.	133,375
Monterrey, Mex.	255,535
Montgomery, Ala.	164,637
Montreal, Que.	1,244,494
Mt. Vernon, N.Y.	119,607
Nashville, Tenn.	434,240
New Haven, Conn. . . .	282,553
New Orleans, La.	780,660
New York, N.Y.	5,785,384
Newark, N.J.	334,773
Newport Beach, Cal. . .	132,143
Newport News, Va. . . .	218,863
Norfolk (Area), Va. . . .	494,076
Oak Lawn, Ill.	130,065
Oklahoma City, Okla. . .	670,681
Omaha, Neb.	485,500
Orange, Cal.	134,308
Orlando, Fla.	278,794
Ottawa, Ont.	463,327
Overland Pk., Kan. . . .	144,356
Palo Alto, Cal.	166,270
Passaic, N.J.	146,722
Paterson, N.J.	130,239
Pensacola, Fla.	159,710
Peoria, Ill.	206,993
Philadelphia, Pa.	1,717,363
Phoenix, Ariz.	1,131,519
Pittsburgh, Pa.	826,417
Pomona, Cal.	227,810
Pompano Beach, Fla. . .	182,694
Pontiac, Mich.	131,305
Portland, Ore.	528,099
Providence, R.I.	285,557
Quebec City	285,622
Raleigh, N.C.	222,321
Reading, Pa.	197,309
Regina, Sask.	124,322
Reno, Nev.	168,979
Richmond, Va.	412,709
Riverside, Cal.	190,624
Roanoke, Va.	139,431
Rochester, N.Y.	348,143
Rockford, Ill.	203,315

City	Number
Royal Oak, Mich.	215,090
Sacramento, Cal.	567,782
Saginaw, Mich.	140,464
St. Louis, Mo.	590,882
St. Petersburg, Fla. . . .	315,881
Salt Lake City, Ut. . . .	537,040
San Antonio, Tex.	441,689
San Diego, Cal. (area) . .	1,161,954
San Francisco, Cal. . . .	868,040
San Jose, Cal.	694,566
San Mateo, Cal.	140,179
Santa Ana, Cal.	534,726
Santa Barbara, Cal. . . .	150,581
Savannah, Ga.	155,462
Schenectady, N.Y.	132,264
Seattle, Wash.	688,041
Shreveport, La.	226,498
Skokie, Ill.	157,604
South Bend, Ind.	146,276
Southfield, Mich.	127,443
Spokane, Wash.	245,090
Springfield, Ill.	160,174
Springfield, Mass.	160,905
Springfield, Mo.	136,903
Stamford, Conn.	119,367
Stockton, Cal.	160,658
Sunnyvale, Cal.	125,146
Syracuse, N.Y.	246,950
Tacoma, Wash.	266,363
Tampa, Fla.	435,598
Toledo, Oh.	322,523
Topeka, Kan.	149,275
Toronto, Ont.	1,741,760
Tucson, Ariz.	364,746
Tulsa, Okla.	429,471
Union City, N.J.	136,277
Vancouver, B.C.	445,671
Victoria, B.C.	146,193
Warren, Mich.	338,706
Washington, D.C.	1,087,781
West Palm Beach, Fla. . .	325,977
Wichita, Kan.	252,069
Wilmington, Del.	208,408
Windsor, Ont.	135,076
Winnipeg, Man.	421,158
Winston-Salem, N.C. . .	186,683
Winter Park, Fla.	158,543
Worcester, Mass.	146,194
Youngstown, Oh.	191,703

MANUFACTURES AND MINERALS

General Statistics for Major Industry Groups

Source: Bureau of the Census

The estimates for 1978 in the following table are based upon reports from a representative sample of about 70,000 manufacturing establishments.

Industry	All employees		Production workers			Value added by mfr. (millions)
	Number (1,000)	Payroll (millions)	Number (1,000)	Manhours (millions)	Wages (millions)	
Food & kindred products	1,546.8	$ 20,310.8	1,097.7	2,158.8	$ 12,865.3	$ 62,919.5
Tobacco mfg.	59.1	812.5	49.1	92.2	611.8	4,606.7
Textile mill prods.	861.8	8,367.9	752.5	1,495.8	6,591.5	17,130.9
Apparel and other textile prods.	1,321.8	10,190.8	1,151.9	2,020.5	7,671.2	21,287.0
Lumber & wood prods.	723.2	8,411.1	618.6	1,188.0	6,495.6	18,971.5
Furniture & fixtures	481.0	5,029.2	396.5	769.0	3,610.9	10,136.2
Paper & allied prods.	638.6	9,852.3	491.8	995.6	6,939.6	24,396.0
Printing & publishing	1,144.8	15,535.8	651.9	1,201.5	8,021.3	35,828.9
Chemicals & allied prods.	903.4	15,459.3	549.6	1,103.4	8,184.3	61,505.8
Petroleum & coal prods.	148.2	3,001.0	103.1	217.4	1,983.0	16,301.0
Rubber & plastic prods.	748.0	9,422.2	587.1	1,142.6	6,448.5	21,157.2
Leather & leather prods.	244.4	1,996.0	213.9	382.8	1,513.5	4,010.1
Stone, clay & glass prods.	639.3	9,076.7	509.4	1,019.3	6,622.3	22,534.9
Primary metal industries	1,149.4	21,331.0	920.5	1,837.4	16,179.5	44,246.4
Fabricated metal prods.	1,625.1	23,382.5	1,251.2	2,475.5	16,106.8	50,385.0
Machinery, except electric	2,235.4	35,385.7	1,519.2	2,496.1	21,222.1	78,938.5
Electric, electronic equip.	1,863.0	25,853.9	1,284.6	2,464.5	14,684.1	57,187.9
Transportation equip.	1,865.7	34,961.6	1,364.5	2,750.7	23,260.8	72,956.5
Instruments & related prods.	600.1	8,570.3	374.8	730.9	4,281.7	21,883.0
Misc. mfg. industries	447.3	4,765.4	343.1	639.8	2,972.8	10,862.8
Administrative & auxiliary[1]	1,262.5	27,426.5				
All industries total	**20,508.9**	**299,142.6**	**14,231.0**	**27,681.8**	**176,446.6**	**657,245.8**

(1) In addition to the employment and payroll for operating manufacturing establishments, manufacturing concerns reported separately for central administrative offices or auxiliary units (e.g., research laboratories, storage warehouses, power plants, garages, repair shops, etc.) which serve the manufacturing establishments of a company rather than the public.

Manufacturing Production Worker Statistics

Source: Bureau of Labor Statistics, U.S. Labor Department (p -- preliminary)

Year	All employees	Production workers	Payroll index 1967 = 100	Avg. weekly earnings	Avg. hourly earnings	Avg. hrs. per wk.
1955	16,882,000	13,288,000	61.1	$75.30	$1.85	40.7
1960	16,796,000	12,586,000	68.9	89.72	2.26	39.7
1965	18,062,000	13,434,000	88.1	107.53	2.61	41.2
1970	19,367,000	14,044,000	114.3	133.33	3.35	39.8
1973	20,154,000	14,834,000	150.5	166.46	4.09	40.7
1974	20,077,000	14,638,000	158.1	176.80	4.42	40.0
1975	18,323,000	13,043,000	151.6	190.79	4.83	39.5
1976	18,997,000	13,638,000	174.1	209.32	5.22	40.1
1977	19,647,000	14,110,000	197.1	228.90	5.68	40.3
1978	20,476,000	14,714,000	222.1	249.27	6.17	40.4
1979	20,972,000	15,010,000	234.7	268.94	6.69	40.2
1980, Jan.	20,699,000	14,674,000	245.3	277.01	6.96	39.8
Feb.	20,648,000	14,615,000	248.1	278.20	6.99	39.8
Mar.	20,709,000	14,662,000	250.1	280.99	7.06	39.8
Apr.[p]	20,448,000	14,398,000	252.3	278.95	7.08	39.4
May[p]	20,256,000	14,175,000	254.3	280.53	7.12	39.4

Personal Consumption Expenditures for the U.S.

Source: Bureau of Economic Analysis, U.S. Commerce Department (millions of dollars)

Product	1950	1955	1960	1965	1970	1975	1978	1979
Food and tobacco	58,120	72,236	87,979	106,966	147,140	224,319	289,581	321,263
Clothing accessories and jewelry	23,709	27,982	32,219	40,304	55,619	81,971	107,642	117,479
Personal care	2,438	3,162	5,242	7,617	10,920	14,228	18,569	20,264
Housing	21,286	34,339	48,117	65,469	93,986	150,151	212,153	241,463
Household operation	29,086	36,890	46,126	61,322	87,793	142,265	195,022	219,466
Medical care	9,104	13,206	20,002	30,053	49,853	89,155	131,026	146,837
Personal business	6,556	9,524	14,233	18,049	31,336	51,558	71,097	82,223
Transportation	25,415	34,583	42,391	58,205	78,032	125,493	191,327	212,221
Recreation	11,147	14,979	17,855	25,907	40,999	66,527	91,244	101,046
Private educ. and research	1,685	2,677	3,746	5,684	9,874	15,459	20,770	23,546
Religious and welfare activities	2,340	3,323	4,872	6,055	8,539	12,979	17,157	19,221
Foreign travel and other—net	655	1,619	2,121	2,858	4,705	4,965	5,177	4,770
Total personal consumption expenditures	**191,966**	**253,665**	**324,903**	**430,154**	**618,796**	**979,070**	**1,350,765**	**1,509,799**

General Manufacturing Statistics for States

Source: Bureau of the Census, U.S. Commerce Department

1978 States	All employees		Production workers			Value added by mfr. (millions)	Value of shipments (millions)	Capital expend. (millions)
	Number (1,000)	Payroll (millions)	Number (1,000)	Man-hrs. (millions)	Wages (millions)			
U.S. total	**20,508.9**	**$299,142.6**	**14,231.0**	**27,681.8**	**$176,446.6**	**$657,245.8**	**$1,523,429.9**	**$55,243.9**
Alabama	346.7	4,233.8	277.0	541.4	3,018.0	9,745.9	23,351.3	1,610.9
Alaska	10.7	170.8	8.9	16.2	127.7	546.8	1,464.6	65.0
Arizona	123.2	1,739.4	79.6	155.6	923.8	3,959.6	8,051.9	318.2
Arkansas	205.5	2,186.2	166.1	322.0	1,580.2	5,500.0	13,963.1	606.1
California	1,903.1	28,486.4	1,240.0	2,376.8	15,112.2	62,510.4	135,765.2	4,493.1
Colorado	163.0	2,442.6	102.3	197.4	1,287.4	5,237.7	11,765.5	550.7
Connecticut	432.2	6,581.5	264.0	528.2	3,218.4	12,290.7	21,957.9	679.0
Delaware	66.8	1,308.7	33.3	67.2	466.8	2,011.6	6,427.3	186.1
District of Columbia	17.7	201.3	7.8	14.2	109.8	668.2	1,047.3	17.5
Florida	396.5	4,877.6	276.8	533.5	2,755.8	11,266.2	24,991.4	1,081.1
Georgia	511.6	5,819.3	392.9	770.4	3,830.8	13,944.6	35,812.2	1,459.7
Hawaii	23.7	285.2	17.4	30.9	173.0	782.9	2,063.1	46.0
Idaho	56.9	729.4	43.4	82.7	499.4	1,843.5	4,485.6	194.7
Illinois	1,310.7	20,613.4	870.0	1,705.1	11,899.8	44,854.4	103,858.1	2,975.8
Indiana	735.2	11,754.9	541.7	1,058.6	7,922.9	25,699.9	58,934.7	2,166.8
Iowa	246.6	3,725.4	175.6	338.5	2,430.5	9,846.1	26,547.5	840.3
Kansas	185.6	2,528.1	132.3	267.4	1,635.2	6,153.9	18,671.5	413.7
Kentucky	288.9	3,890.0	215.6	409.6	2,590.1	10,845.1	25,716.5	799.8
Louisiana	200.7	3,008.8	149.0	299.1	1,997.7	10,056.5	31,852.7	2,103.8
Maine	107.2	1,226.8	88.3	170.5	876.8	2,691.1	5,866.7	424.3
Maryland	252.6	3,786.5	169.7	327.0	2,218.8	7,739.2	17,780.3	508.6
Massachusetts	640.4	8,797.6	426.1	823.0	4,734.2	18,632.0	34,450.4	1,170.3
Michigan	1,180.7	22,892.8	822.7	1,671.5	14,240.9	41,804.6	104,920.7	4,742.7
Minnesota	365.5	5,385.2	228.2	438.2	2,785.0	10,908.1	25,838.6	788.2
Mississippi	221.7	2,276.8	178.7	344.2	1,628.6	5,986.6	13,863.9	512.6
Missouri	453.4	6,549.1	308.2	590.4	3,787.0	15,031.3	37,489.7	965.5
Montana	25.3	361.0	19.4	37.4	266.3	850.6	3,070.5	130.6
Nebraska	92.5	1,231.6	66.9	132.9	786.5	3,249.7	10,572.1	219.5
Nevada	17.6	233.1	12.5	23.7	141.1	660.1	1,216.2	68.2
New Hampshire	103.9	1,220.2	78.4	149.5	773.3	2,764.2	5,055.4	196.2
New Jersey	798.1	12,025.2	493.4	956.0	5,922.5	24,725.4	54,748.0	1,639.7
New Mexico	28.1	326.8	20.1	37.1	197.7	794.9	2,126.0	56.6
New York	1,537.5	22,886.1	964.8	1,845.3	11,261.3	48,309.8	94,296.5	2,917.9
North Carolina	789.1	8,430.4	626.1	1,213.8	5,655.1	20,616.6	45,259.2	1,513.2
North Dakota	14.1	181.3	9.7	19.6	110.7	485.1	1,376.0	58.6
Ohio	1,362.4	22,703.2	937.9	1,868.3	14,252.6	47,641.4	106,487.8	3,292.6
Oklahoma	172.5	2,381.1	115.9	224.6	1,353.1	5,237.3	14,011.8	445.0
Oregon	222.4	3,323.6	165.6	311.3	2,221.6	7,166.6	16,753.0	659.1
Pennsylvania	1,350.8	20,017.8	944.1	1,801.4	12,070.2	40,550.5	88,924.8	2,557.2
Rhode Island	129.5	1,479.2	98.4	184.7	904.2	2,998.0	5,987.9	217.3
South Carolina	387.1	4,251.6	308.1	607.0	2,942.9	9,476.8	21,124.6	978.7
South Dakota	23.9	301.3	17.7	35.1	203.5	726.1	2,154.2	40.1
Tennessee	509.9	5,863.3	389.0	743.2	3,884.8	14,045.8	31,750.2	1,156.2
Texas	960.4	13,719.4	647.2	1,287.1	7,736.2	36,496.4	104,646.8	4,601.7
Utah	79.8	1,037.5	56.2	105.8	633.8	2,380.2	5,935.9	248.2
Vermont	45.0	615.8	31.5	63.1	354.2	1,382.7	2,562.5	133.4
Virginia	406.2	4,929.0	309.2	597.9	3,231.8	11,961.1	27,069.5	1,040.1
Washington	286.0	4,873.2	195.8	365.9	2,847.2	10,424.6	25,604.1	943.3
West Virginia	123.9	1,910.0	91.9	176.4	1,275.4	4,426.8	9,743.7	512.0
Wisconsin	561.8	8,457.9	399.2	780.0	5,392.4	18,813.9	43,712.1	1,408.1
Wyoming	8.6	123.8	6.1	11.7	80.8	425.6	1,402.6	53.5

Employees in Non-Agricultural Establishments

Source: Bureau of Labor Statistics, U.S. Labor Department

(thousands)

Annual Average by Industry Division

Year	Total	Mining	Contr./ construc- tion	Manu- factur- ing	Trans. and public utilities	Whole., retail trade	Finance, insur., real estate	Service, miscel- laneous	Govern- ment
1955	50,641	792	2,839	16,882	4,141	10,535	2,298	6,240	6,914
1960	54,189	712	2,926	16,796	4,004	11,391	2,629	7,378	8,353
1965	60,765	632	3,232	18,062	4,036	12,716	2,977	9,036	10,074
1970	70,880	623	3,588	19,367	4,515	15,040	3,645	11,548	12,554
1975	76,945	752	3,525	18,323	4,542	17,060	4,165	13,892	14,686
1976	79,382	779	3,576	18,997	4,582	17,755	4,271	14,551	14,871
1977	82,471	813	3,851	19,682	4,713	18,516	4,467	15,303	15,127
1978	86,697	851	4,229	20,505	4,923	19,542	4,724	16,252	15,672
1979	89,886	960	4,483	21,062	5,141	20,269	4,974	17,078	15,920

Sales and Profits of Manufacturing Corporations by Industry Groups

Source: Federal Trade Commission

Industry Group (Amounts estimated in millions of dollars)	Sales			Net profits after taxes		
	1Q 1979	1Q 1980	1Q 1981	1Q 1979	1Q 1980	1Q 1981
All manufacturing corporations	406,567	464,964	503,472	22,666	24,703	23,586
Nondurable manufacturing corporations	199,087	245,125	274,465	11,232	15,023	13,770
Food and kindred products	51,715	57,057	61,607	1,456	1,697	1,861
Tobacco manufactures	3,648	4,003	4,640	401	523	580
Textile mill products	9,496	11,142	11,317	246	314	255
Paper and allied products	12,997	14,682	14,402	867	795	758
Printing and publishing	13,572	15,401	16,920	769	794	808
Chemicals and allied products	34,772	39,657	43,583	2,746	3,160	3,164
Industrial chemicals and synthetics	17,337	19,956	21,573	1,272	1,361	1,399
Drugs	4,874	5,580	6,229	660	784	646
Petroleum and coal products.	50,715	79,802	97,609	3,976	7,200	5,586
Rubber and miscellaneous plastics products	10,517	10,369	10,615	438	247	387
Other nondurable manufacturing corporations	11,654	13,011	13,771	333	293	371
Durable manufacturing corporations . .	207,480	219,839	229,008	11,434	9,680	9,816
Stone, clay and glass products . . .	8,783	9,619	9,808	287	237	228
Primary metal industries	29,288	32,720	33,183	1,223	1,768	1,470
Iron and steel	19,511	20,655	21,488	617	810	836
Nonferrous metals	9,777	12,065	11,695	607	959	633
Fabricated metal products	22,561	23,552	24,713	1,017	1,167	1,035
Machinery, except electrical	38,018	42,520	45,931	2,682	2,563	2,813
Electrical and electronic equipment .	30,943	35,619	37,210	1,808	1,830	2,129
Transportation equipment.	51,569	46,731	48,477	2,830	568	624
Motor vehicles and equipment . . .	35,250	28,633	28,550	2,164	-217	-386
Aircraft, guided missiles and parts	12,090	13,993	15,952	557	633	903
Instruments and related products . .	8,769	10,194	10,863	776	863	1,082
Other durable manufacturing corporations	17,548	18,883	18,822	810	684	435
All mining corporations.	10,230	12,846	15,665	695	1,048	1,887
All retail trade corporations	170,941	192,213	N/A	2,813	2,174	NA
All wholesale trade corporations	185,187	241,065	263,454	3,795	4,043	3,959

Annual Rates of Profit on Stockholders' Equity

Source: Federal Trade Commission

By Industry after taxes: by percent	1Q 1979	2Q 1979	3Q 1979	4Q 1979	1Q 1980	2Q 1980	3Q 1980	4Q 1980	1Q 1981
All manufacturing corporations	15.7	18.1	16.3	15.7	15.4	13.6	12.5	14.1	13.4
Nondurable manufacturing corporations	15.3	17.8	18.4	17.9	18.0	16.4	15.6	15.4	14.9
Food and kindred products	12.2	15.6	17.2	13.8	12.8	13.5	15.2	17.4	12.6
Tobacco manufacturers	18.5	18.4	21.6	18.4	21.3	20.3	22.3	15.3	21.2
Textile mill products	9.0	12.8	13.4	12.5	11.0	7.9	6.6	8.6	8.8
Paper and allied products	16.3	16.8	20.5	13.4	13.1	13.0	10.6	11.6	12.5
Printing and publishing	16.1	19.3	20.1	16.8	15.0	16.5	17.2	16.7	13.6
Chemicals and allied products.	17.5	18.2	15.9	15.3	18.0	15.3	15.0	13.3	16.3
Industrial chemicals and synthetics	16.8	17.2	13.3	13.6	16.0	12.3	9.6	9.7	14.9
Drugs	20.8	20.2	18.4	17.9	21.6	18.3	22.6	16.9	16.4
Petroleum and coal products	15.8	20.1	21.1	24.6	23.7	21.1	17.8	17.5	16.5
Rubber and miscellaneous plastics products . .	14.1	13.4	8.8	5.6	7.3	4.9	5.4	9.2	12.0
Other nondurable manufacturing corporations .	12.6	12.7	19.0	14.3	11.4	11.4	16.3	14.6	11.5
Durable manufacturing corporations.	16.2	18.4	14.0	13.4	12.6	10.6	9.1	12.7	11.8
Stone, clay and glass products	7.8	19.6	19.4	13.9	5.9	11.5	14.4	11.5	5.3
Primary metal industries	12.7	17.2	13.3	5.7	16.8	11.8	5.6	12.5	12.8
Iron and steel	10.2	15.6	11.7	-2.3	12.8	8.2	3.4	11.7	12.2
Nonferrous metals	17.0	20.0	15.8	18.2	22.8	17.1	8.8	13.6	13.6
Fabricated metal products	15.6	18.9	15.8	15.4	16.6	13.3	12.3	13.5	13.6
Machinery, except electrical	16.4	17.8	16.0	17.2	14.1	15.4	13.7	16.6	13.8
Electrical and electronic equipment	17.2	18.6	16.4	17.6	16.0	14.8	14.1	15.6	16.2
Transportation equipment	20.0	19.1	5.2	7.9	3.8	-3.6	-6.2	3.4	4.3
Motor vehicles and equipment	21.8	18.7	-0.5	3.5	-2.1	-14.0	-18.0	-3.0	-4.3
Aircraft, guided missiles and parts	17.0	20.4	17.9	18.3	16.6	16.6	15.4	15.5	20.4
Instruments and related products	16.7	17.4	16.2	17.0	16.3	17.8	17.8	17.9	17.9
Other durable manufacturing corporations	16.3	19.3	19.7	15.7	12.3	8.8	12.0	11.2	7.4
All mining corporations	12.2	15.7	21.0	20.3	14.3	18.0	21.7	22.9	20.3
All retail trade corporations.	12.2	18.4	17.9	21.4	8.5	11.7	12.6	20.2	NA
All wholesale trade corporations	19.0	22.6	22.3	18.2	16.4	17.6	18.8	16.5	15.1

Retail Store Sales

Source: Bureau of the Census, U.S. Commerce Department (millions of dollars)

Kind of business	1979	1980	Kind of business	1979	1980
All retail stores	**894,343**	**956,655**	**Nondurable goods stores**	**589,534**	**658,729**
Durable goods stores	**304,809**	**297,926**	Apparel group	42,375	44,487
Automotive group	177,251	167,017	Men's and boys' wear stores	7,830	8,025
Motor vehicle, other			Women's apparel, accessory		
automotive dealers	150,753	148,799	stores	16,248	16,991
Auto and home supply stores	16,141	18,218	Shoe stores	7,418	8,040
Furniture and appliance group	41,868	43,918	Food group	195,826	217,511
Furniture, home furnishings			Grocery stores	182,365	202,065
stores	25,692	26,228	General merchandise group		
Household appliance, radio			with stores	109,740	116,287
TV stores	12,428	13,190	Department stores	88,520	94,185
Bldg. matl., hardware, garden supply, and			Variety stores	8,385	8,858
mobile home dealers	50,272	48,210	Eating and drinking places	79,576	86,612
Building matl. and supply stores	35,255	41,425	Gasoline service stations	73,202	94,470
Hardware stores	7,838	7,743	Drug and proprietary stores	28,107	31,557
(1) After Feb. 1979, includes some mail order.			Liquor stores	15,294	16,556

Total retail stores sales (millions of dollars) — (1955) 183,851; (1958) 200,353; (1959) 215,413; (1960) 219,529; (1961) 218,992; (1962) 235,563; (1963) 246,666; (1964) 261,870; (1965) 284,128; (1966) 303,956; (1967) 292,956; (1968) 324,358; (1969) 346,717; (1970) 368,403; (1971) 406,234; (1972) 449,069; (1973) 509,538; (1974) 540,988; (1975) 588,146; (1976) 657,375; (1977) 725,220; (1978) 804,684.

Cotton, Wool, Silk, and Man-Made Fibers Production

Source: Economics, Statistics, and Cooperatives Service, U.S. Agriculture Department

Cotton and wool from reports of the Agriculture Department; silk, rayon, and non-cellulosic man-made fibers from Textile Organon, a publication of the Textile Economics Bureau, Inc.

Year	Cotton[1] U.S. (million bales)[5]	World	Wool[2] U.S. (million pounds)	World	Silk World (mil. lbs.)	Man-made fibers[3] Cellulosic U.S. (million pounds)	World	Non-cellulosic[4] U.S.[4] (million pounds)	World[6]
1940	12.6	31.2	434.0	4,180	130	471.2	2,485.3	4.6	4.6
1950	10.0	30.6	249.3	4,000	42	1,259.4	3,552.8	145.9	177.4
1960	14.2	46.2	298.9	5,615	68	1,028.5	5,749.1	854.2	1,779.1
1965	15.0	55.0	224.8	5,731	72	1,527.0	7,359.4	2,062.4	4,928.9
1970	10.2	53.6	176.8	6,107	90	1,373.2	7,573.9	4,053.5	10,361.7
1971	10.5	59.8	172.2	5,972	90	1,390.9	7,617.1	4,761.0	12,366.0
1972	13.7	62.9	168.2	5,560	93	1,394.3	7,846.0	5,927.3	14,057.8
1973	13.0	63.3	151.7	5,474	95	1,357.0	8,069.4	6,997.4	16,842.0
1974	11.5	64.3	137.1	5,769	99	1,198.8	7,786.7	6,906.5	16,505.2
1975	8.3	54.0	125.5	5,911	104	749.0	6,523.2	6,432.2	16,209.6
1976	10.6	57.4	116.0	5,827	123	840.9	7,075.9	6,730.3	18,962.7
1977	14.4	63.9	109.8	5,838	108	887.7	7,232.7	7,482.8	20,170.7
1978	10.9	60.0	103.9	5,983	113	904.5	7,314.4	8,018.3	22,121.3
1979	14.6	65.0	105.8	6,168	121	929.8	7,451.7	7,430.5	23,387.2
1980	11.1	65.4	106.5	6,285	123	806.0	7,150.6	8,014.6	23.118.3

(1) Year beginning Aug. 1. (2) Grease basis. (3) Includes filament yarn and staple and tow fiber. (4) Includes textile glass fiber. (5) 480-pound net weight bales, U.S. beginning 1960 and world beginning 1965. (6) 1966 to date, excludes Olefin.

Work Stoppages (Strikes) in the U.S.

Source: Bureau of Labor Statistics, U.S. Labor Department

	Number stoppages	Workers involved (thousands)	Man days idle (thousands)		Number stoppages	Workers involved (thousands)	Man days idle (thousands)
Average 1935-1939	2,862	1,130	16,900	1965	3,963	1,550	23,300
War Period				1966	4,405	1,960	25,400
Dec. 8, 1941-Aug.				1967	4,595	2,870	42,100
14, 1945	14,371	6,744	36,300	1968	5,045	2,649	49,018
Year				1969	5,700	2,481	42,869
1950	4,843	2,410	38,800	1970	5,716	3,305	66,414
1952	5,117	3,540	59,100	1971	5,138	3,280	47,589
1953	5,091	2,400	28,300	1972	5,010	1,714	27,066
1954	3,468	1,530	22,600	1973	5,353	2,251	27,948
1955	4,320	2,650	28,200	1974	6,074	2,778	47,991
1956	3,825	1,900	33,100	1975	5,031	1,746	31,237
1957	3,673	1,390	16,500	1976	5,648	2,420	37,859
1958	3,694	2,060	23,900	1977	5,506	2,040	35,822
1959	3,708	1,880	69,000	1978	4,230	1,623	36,922
1960	3,333	1,320	19,100	1979[p]	4,951	1,840	32,776
1961	3,367	1,450	16,300	1980 Jan.[p]	352	207	3,142
1962	3,614	1,230	18,600	Feb.[p]	354	114	3,025
1963	3,362	941	16,100	Mar.[p]	396	123	2,705
1964	3,655	1,640	22,900	Apr.[p]	425	116	2,786
				May[p]	505	139	2,464

(p) Preliminary

Employment Status of Civilian Labor Force

Source: Bureau of Labor Statistics, U.S. Labor Department (thousands)

Employment status	Annual average 1978	Annual average 1979	1979 Nov.	Dec.	Jan.	Feb.	1980 Mar.	Apr.	May
Total noninstitutional population	161,058	163,620	164,682	164,898	165,101	165,298	165,506	165,693	166,105
Total labor force	102,537	104,996	105,744	106,088	106,310	106,346	106,184	106,511	106,634
Civilian noninstitutional population	158,941	161,532	162,589	162,809	163,020	163,211	163,416	163,601	164,013
Civilian labor force	100,420	102,908	103,652	103,999	104,229	104,260	104,094	104,419	104,542
Employed	94,373	96,945	97,608	97,912	97,804	97,953	97,656	97,154	96,537
Agriculture	3,342	3,297	3,385	3,359	3,270	3,326	3,358	3,242	3,191
Nonagricultural industries	91,031	93,648	94,223	94,553	94,534	94,626	94,298	93,912	93,346
Unemployed	6,047	5,963	6,044	6,087	6,425	6,307	6,438	7,265	8,006
Unemployment rate	6.0	5.8	5.8	5.9	6.2	6.0	6.2	7.0	7.7
Not in labor force	58,521	58,623	58,937	58,810	58,791	58,951	59,322	59,182	59,471
Men, 20 years and over									
Civilian noninstitutional population	67,006	68,293	68,804	68,940	69,047	69,140	69,238	69,329	69,532
Civilian labor force	53,464	54,486	54,709	54,781	54,855	55,038	54,996	55,114	55,220
Employed	51,212	52,264	52,374	52,478	52,279	52,531	52,300	51,868	51,510
Agriculture	2,361	2,350	2,438	2,427	2,387	2,435	2,394	2,320	2,270
Nonagricultural industries	48,852	49,913	49,936	50,051	49,892	50,096	49,906	49,548	49,240
Unemployed	2,252	2,223	2,335	2,303	2,577	2,507	2,696	3,246	3,710
Unemployment rate	4.2	4.1	4.3	4.2	4.7	4.6	4.9	5.9	6.7
Not in labor force	13,541	13,807	14,095	14,159	14,192	14,102	14,242	14,215	14,312
Women, 20 years and over									
Civilian noninstitutional population	75,489	76,860	77,426	77,542	77,656	77,766	77,876	77,981	78,211
Civilian labor force	37,416	38,910	39,445	39,559	39,678	39,857	39,751	40,137	40,125
Employed	35,180	36,698	37,248	37,402	37,574	37,604	37,496	37,602	37,530
Agriculture	586	591	612	582	540	567	582	552	541
Nonagricultural industries	34,593	36,107	36,636	36,820	37,034	37,037	36,914	37,051	36,989
Unemployed	2,236	2,213	2,197	2,257	2,304	2,254	2,255	2,534	2,596
Unemployment rate	6.0	5.7	5.6	5.7	5.8	5.7	5.7	6.3	6.5
Not in labor force	38,073	37,949	37,981	37,883	37,778	37,909	38,125	37,844	38,086

Industrial Minerals: Distribution, Resources, Reserves

Source: Organization for Economic Cooperation and Development

(Resource and reserve figures are based on average conservative estimates.)

Minerals	Distribution of reserves, 1974 (% of world total)	Resources[1] 1975/76 (million metric tons)	Reserves[2] 1975/76	Ratio of reserves to 1975 demand in years[3]	Ratio of reserves to total demand 1974-2000[4]
Iron	USSR(31.1) Brazil(16.6) Canada(11.7) Australia(10.2) India(6.4)	195,000	90,500	177	4.5
Copper	U.S.(18.4) Chile(18.4) USSR(7.9) Canada(6.8) Peru(6.5) Zambia(6.3) Zaire(5.6)	1,500	408.2	62	1.3
Lead	U.S.(35.6) Canada(11.5) USSR(10.9) Australia(10.9) Mexico(3.0)	300	150.0	49	1.2
Tin	China(23.6) Thailand(15.0) Malaysia(12.2) Bolivia(9.9) Indonesia(8.3) Brazil(6.0)	37	10.2	44	1.3
Zinc	Canada(22.8) U.S.(20.1) Australia(12.1) USSR(8.1) Ireland(5.4)	245	135.0	41	1.1
Aluminum	Australia(26.0) Guinea(26.0) Brazil(15.6) Jamaica(6.1) Greece(4.4) Cameroon(3.9)	5,700	3,483	over 200	4.0
Titanium	Brazil(65.9) India(21.7) Australia(5.4) U.S.(3.5) Sierra Leone(1.7) Canada(1.6)	1,234	340.1	over 300	4.4
Chromium	S. Africa(73.9) Rhodesia(19.7) USSR(2.9) Finland(1.2) India(0.5) Madagascar(0.4) Philippines(0.4) Turkey(0.4) Brazil(0.3)	1,049	523.2	over 200	5.7
Cobalt	Zaire(27.7) New Caledonia(27.1) Zambia(14.2) Cuba(13.8) USSR(8.3)	4.3	2.4	78	2.1
Niobium	Brazil(75.8) Canada(7.6) USSR(6.3) Zaire(3.8) Uganda(2.9) Nigeria(2.7)	14.6	10.0	over 800	over 10
Manganese	S. Africa(45.0) USSR(37.5) Australia(8.0) Gabon(5.0) Brazil(2.2)	3,265	1,814	197	4.9
Molybdenum	U.S.(49.5) USSR(15.2) Canada(14.4) Chile(13.6) China(3.8)	28.6	6.0	65	1.4
Nickel	New Caledonia(43.7) Canada(16.1) USSR(9.6) Australia(9.2) Indonesia(8.4) Cuba(5.7)	129.7	55.3	77	2.1
Tantulum	Zaire(55.0) Nigeria(11.0) USSR(6.7) Thailand(6.7) Malaysia(5.4) Canada(4.8) Brazil(4.4)	0.26	0.07	49	1.1
Tungsten	China(53.6) Canada(12.1) USSR(8.9) N. Korea(6.4) U.S.(6.1)	5.2	1.8	46	1.2
Vanadium	USSR(74.7) S. Africa(18.7) Australia(1.4) Chile(1.4) U.S.(1.1)	56.2	9.7	over 300	7.5
Bismuth	Japan(25.6) Australia(19.5) U.S.(13.3) Mexico(6.2) Peru(5.1)	0.13	0.06	22	0.5
Mercury	Spain(40.6) USSR(10.1) Yugoslavia(10.1) China(10.1) U.S.(9.1) Italy(8.1)	17,510	4,930	21	0.7
Silver	USSR(26.7) U.S.(25.0) Mexico(13.3) Canada(11.7) Peru(10.0) Australia(3.3)	0.70	0.19	16	0.4
Platinum	S. Africa(71.3) USSR(26.7) Canada(1.8) U.S.(0.2) Colombia(0.2)	0.026	0.009	110	3.1
Asbestos	Canada(45.2) USSR(24.8) S. Africa(6.9) Australia(3.6) U.S.(3.0)	249.4	145.1	35	0.9

(1) Seabed deposits not included; these are (in million metric tons): cobalt, 583; manganese, 36,425; nickel, 1,305; molybdenum, 78; vanadium, 107. Other minerals for which resource estimates are considerably increased if seabed deposits are included are titanium, aluminum, lead, copper, and to a smaller extent zinc, iron, and chromium. (2) Reserves are defined as that portion of the identified resources from which useable material can be economically and legally extracted at the time of determination. (3) Ie., iron will last 177 years if used at the 1975 rate. (4) Ie., there is 4.5 times more iron than total estimated demand between 1974 and 2000.

U.S. Nonfuel Mineral Production

Source: Bureau of Mines, U.S. Interior Department

Production as measured by mine shipments, sales, or marketable production (including consumption by producers)

Metals	1979 Quantity	1979 Value (thousands)	1980[p] Quantity	1980[p] Value (thousands)
Antinomy ore and concentrate . . . . . short tons, antimony content	W	W	343	W
Bauxite . . . . thousand metric tons, dried equivalent	1,821	$24,875	1,559	$22,353
Copper (recoverable content of ores, etc.) . . . . metric tons	[r]1,443,556	[r]2,960,675	1,168,311	2,638,020
Gold (recoverable content of ores, etc.). . . . . troy ounces	[r]969,920	[r]298,250	951,348	582,758
Iron ore, usable (excluding iron sinter) . thousand long tons, gr. wgt.	86,130	2,811,574	69,562	2,543,484
Iron oxide pigments, crude . . . . short tons	74,548	2,578	62,642	4,043
Lead (recoverable content of ores, etc.) . . . . metric tons	525,569	609,929	549,484	514,363
Manganiferous ore (5% to 35%Mn) . . . . . short tons, gross weight	240,696	2,902	173,887	2,444
Mercury . . . . 76-pound flasks	29,519	8,299	30,657	11,939
Molybdenum (content of concentrate). . . . . thousand pounds	143,504	871,067	149,311	1,344,181
Nickel (content of ore and concentration) . . . . short tons	15,065	W	14,653	W
Silver (recoverable content of ores, etc.) . . . . . thousand troy oz.	[r]38,087	[r]422,386	31,327	646,585
Titanium concentrate:				
Ilmenite . . . . short tons, gross weight	646,399	32,965	593,704	32,041
Tungsten ore and concentrate . . . . . thousand pounds contain W	6,646	55,785	6,036	50,575
Vanadium (recoverable in ore and concentrate) . . . . . short tons	5,520	73,892	4,806	64,370
Zinc (recoverable content of ores, etc.) . . . . metric tons	267,341	219,841	334,862	276,325
Combined value of beryllium, magnesium chloride for magnesium metal, platinum-group metals (1980), rare-earth metals, tin, titanium (rutile), zircon concentrate, and values indicated by symbol W	XX	144,962	XX	141,492
Total metals	XX	[r]8,540,000	XX	8,875,000

Nonmetals (Except Fuels)

	1979 Quantity	1979 Value	1980 Quantity	1980 Value
Abrasive stones[2] . . . . short tons	[r]2,094	[r]2,064	2,131	2,233
Abestos . . . . do	102,903	28,925	88,271	30,599
Asphalt and related bitumens, native:				
Bituminous Limestone, sandstone, gilsonite . thousand short tons	1,614	25,622	1,252	25,030
Barite . . . . do	[r]2,113	[r]53,581	2,245	65,957
Boron minerals . . . . do	1,590	310,211	1,545	366,760
Bromine . . . . thousand pounds	[r]497,000	[r]114,500	381,600	92,600
Calcium chloride . . . . short tons	719,709	51,884	581,012	47,950
Carbon dioxide, natural . . . . thousand cubic feet	2,028,045	3,243	1,628,424	2,561
Cement:				
Portland. . . . . thousand short tons	78,978	3,650,436	71,612	3,613,332
Masonry. . . . . do	3,748	204,797	3,040	188,456
Clays . . . . do	54,689	846,089	48,790	898,947
Diatomite. . . . . do	717	90,323	689	100,610
Emery . . . . short tons	10,005	204	7,284	153
Feldspar. . . . . short tons	740,472	21,474	710,000	23,200
Fluorspar . . . . do	109,299	12,162	92,635	12,611
Garnet (abrasive) . . . . do	21,240	[r]3,746	26,909	3,957
Gem stones(e)	NA	8,230	NA	6,930
Gypsum . . . . thousand short tons	14,630	99,868	12,376	103,061
Helium:				
Crude. . . . . million cubic feet	[r]537	[r]6,444	299	3,588
High-purity . . . . do	[r]1,080	[r]24,840	1,159	26,657
Lime . . . . thousand short tons	20,945	862,459	19,010	842,922
Mica:				
Scrap . . . . do	[r]134	[r]7,708	117	5,296
Peat . . . . do	798	15,517	788	16,190
Perlite . . . . short tons	660,000	16,435	638,000	16,500
Phosphate rock . . . . thousand metric tons	51,611	1,045,655	54,415	1,256,947
Potassium salts . . . . thousand metric tons, K₂0 equivalent	2,388	279,199	2,217	353,862
Pumice. . . . . thousand short tons	[r]4,411	[r]15,509	3,755	15,484
Pyrites . . . . thousand metric tons	1,049	17,087	847	13,812
Salt . . . . thousand short tons)	45,793	538,352	40,352	656,164
Sand and gravel . . . . do	979,000	2,427,000	794,400	2,302,000
Sodium carbonate (natural) . . . . do	W	W	W	W
Sodium sulfate (natural) . . . . do	533	29,689	583	33,389
Stone[3] . . . . do	[r]1,097,621	[r]3,388,058	981,620	3,393,478
Sulfur, Frasch process . . . . thousand metric tons	7,507	449,433	7,400	720,511
Talc, soapstone, pyrophyllite . . . . thousand short tons	1,453	20,364	1,473	25,626
Tripoli . . . . short tons	116,009	6,279	121,233	676
Vermiculite . . . . thousand short tons	346	21,955	337	23,483
Combined value of aplite, emery (1978), graphite, iodine, kyanite, lithium, minerals, magnesite, magnesium compounds, greensand marl, olivine, staurolite, wollastonite, and values indicated by symbol W	XX	[r]740,271	XX	941,112
Total nonmetals	XX	[r]15,440,000	XX	16,233,000
Grand total	XX	[r]23,980,000	XX	25,108,000

(e) Estimate. (r) Revised. (NA) Not available. (W) Withheld to avoid disclosing company proprietary data; included in "Combined value" figures. (XX) Not applicable.
(1) Production as measured by mine shipments, sales, or marketable production (including consumption by producers).
(2) Grindstones, pulpstones, grinding pebbles, sharpening stones, and tube mill liners.
(3) Excludes abrasive stone, bituminous limestone, bituminous sandstone, and soapstones, all included elsewhere in table.

U.S. Nonfuel Mineral Production—Leading States

Source: Bureau of Mines, U.S. Interior Department

State	1980	Value (thousands)	Percent of U.S. total	Principal minerals, in order of value
Arizona		$2,425,714	9.66	Copper, molybdenum, cement, silver.
California		1,885,695	7.51	Cement, sand and gravel, boron, stone.
Minnesota.		1,782,310	7.10	Iron, ore, sand and gravel, stone, lime.
Texas		1,734,651	6.91	Cement, sulfur, stone, sand and gravel.
Florida.		1,508,754	6.01	Phosphate rock, stone, cement, sand and gravel.
Michigan		1,485,450	5.92	Iron ore, cement, magnesium compounds, salt.
Colorado		1,264,515	5.04	Molybdenum, cement, sand and gravel, silver.
Missouri		1,056,756	4.21	Lead, cement, stone, lime.
Georgia		770,688	3.07	Clay, stone, cement, sand and gravel.
New Mexico		765,211	3.05	Copper, potassium salts, molybdenum, silver.

Value of U.S. Mineral Production

(millons of dollars)

Production as measured by mine shipments sales or marketable production.

Year[1]	Fuels	Nonmetallic	Metals	Total[2]	Year[1]	Fuels	Nonmetallic	Metals	Total[2]
1930 . . .	2,500	973	501	3,980	1973 . . .	24,949	7,476	4,362	36,787
1940 . . .	2,662	784	752	4,198	1974 . . .	40,889	8,687	5,501	55,077
1950 . . .	8,689	1,882	1,351	11,862	1975 . . .	47,505	9,570	5,191	62,266
1960 . . .	12,142	3,868	2,022	18,032	1976 . . .	52,484	10,616	6,086	69,186
1965 . . .	14,047	4,933	2,544	21,524	1977 . . .	59,575	11,701	5,810	77,086
1970 . . .	20,152	5,712	3,928	29,792	1978 . . .	NA	13,524	6,296	NA
1971 . . .	21,247	6,058	3,406	30,711	1979 . . .	NA	15,440	8,540	NA
1972 . . .	22,061	6,482	3,642	32,185	1980 . . .	NA	16,233	8,875	NA

(1) Excludes Alaska and Hawaii, 1930-53. (2) Data may not add to total because of rounding figures. (P) Preliminary.

U.S. Pig Iron and Steel Output

Source: American Iron and Steel Institute (net tons)

Year	Total pig iron	Pig iron and ferro-alloys	Raw steel	Year	Total pig iron	Pig iron and ferro-alloys	Raw steel
1940	46,071,666	47,398,529	66,982,686	1974	95,909,000	98,332,000	145,720,000
1945	53,223,169	54,919,029	79,701,648	1975	101,208,000	103,345,000	116,642,000
1950	64,586,907	66,400,311	96,836,075	1976	86,870,000	88,780,000	128,000,000
1955	76,857,417	79,263,865	117,036,085	1977	81,328,000	83,082,000	125,333,000
1960	66,480,648	68,566,384	99,281,601	1978	87,679,000	89,351,000	137,031,000
1965	88,184,901	90,918,040	131,461,601	1979	87,003,000	88,906,000	136,341,000
1970	91,435,000	93,851,000	131,514,000	1980	68,721,000	70,329,000	111,835,000

Steel figures include only that portion of the capacity and production of steel for castings used by foundries which were operated by companies producing steel ingots.

Raw Steel Production

(thousands of net tons)

State	1978	1979	1980	State	1978	1979	1980
New York	4,203	4,035	2,675	Michigan	10,789	10,922	7,877
Pennsylvania	28,070	28,213	23,517	Minn., Mo., Okla., Texas	7,845	8,260	8,642
R.I., Conn., N.J., Del., Md.	6,350	6,638	5,161	Ariz., Colo., Utah, Wash., Ore.,			
Va., W.Va., Ga., Fla., N.C., S.C.,	6,444	6,788	6,066	Ha.	4,968	5,165	4,795
Kentucky	2,523	2,438	2,141	California.	3,472	3,672	2,628
Ala., Tenn., Miss., Ark.	4,305	4,487	3,452				
Ohio	21,268	21,082	16,100	Total	137,031	136,341	111,835
Indiana	24,351	22,912	19,820				
Illinois	12,443	11,729	8,961				

U.S. Copper, Lead, and Zinc Production

Source: Bureau of Mines, U.S. Interior Department

Year	Copper Mil. lbs.	Copper $1,000	Lead[1] Short tons	Lead[1] $1,000	Zinc Short tons	Zinc Mil. dol.	Year	Copper Mil. lbs.	Copper $1,000	Lead[1] Metric tons	Lead[1] $1,000	Zinc Metric tons	Zinc Mil. dol.
1950	1,823	379,122	418,809	113,078	591,454	167	1977	3,008	2,009,297	537,499	363,789	407,889	309
1960	2,286	733,708	228,899	53,562	334,101	87	1978	2,993	1,990,323	529,661	393,516	302,669	207
1965	2,703	957,028	301,147	93,959	611,153	178	1979	3,182	2,960,675	525,569	609,929	267,341	220
1970	3,439	1,984,484	571,767	178,609	534,136	164	1980	2,576	2,638,020	549,484	514,363	334,862	276
1975	2,827	1,814,763	563,783	267,230	425,792	366	(1) Production from domestic ores.						

Labor Union Directory

Source: Bureau of Labor Statistics; World Almanac Questionnaire
(*) Independent union; all others affiliated with AFL-CIO.

Actors and Artistes of America, Associated (AAAA), 165 W. 46th St., New York, NY 10036; founded 1919; Frederick O'-Neal, Pres. (since 1971); no individual members, 9 affiliates.

Actors' Equity Association, 164 W. 46th St., New York, NY 10036; founded 1913; Theodore Bikel, Pres.; 30,000 members.

Air Line Pilots Association, 1625 Massachusetts Ave. NW, Washington, DC 20036. John J. O'Donnell, Pres.; 33,000 members.

Aluminum Workers International Union (AWIU), 3362 Hollenberg Drive, Bridgeton, MO 63044; founded 1953; Lawrence A. Holly, Pres. (since 1977); 35,000 members, 100 locals.

*Automobile, Aerospace & Agricultural Implement Workers of America, International Union, United (UAW), 8000 E. Jefferson Ave., Detroit, MI 48214; founded 1935; Douglas Fraser, Pres. (since 1977); 1,800,000 members, 1,611 locals.

Bakery, Confectionery & Tobacco Workers International Union (BC&T), 10401 Connecticut Ave., Kensington, MD 20795; founded 1886; John DeConcini, Pres. (since 1978); 170,000 members, 234 locals.

Barbers, Beauticians, and Allied Industries, International Association, 7050 West Washington St., Indianapolis, IN 46214; Richard Plumb, Pres.; 41,000 members, 702 locals.

Boilermakers, Iron Shipbuilders, Blacksmiths, Forgers and Helpers, International Brotherhood of (BSF), 570 New Brotherhood Bldg., Kansas City, KS 66101; founded 1880; Harold J. Buoy, Pres. (since 1973); 150,000 members, 400 locals.

Bricklayers and Allied Craftsmen, International Union of, 815 15th St. NW, Washington, DC 20005; Thomas F. Murphy, Pres.; 147,715 members, 758 locals.

Carpenters and Joiners of America, United Brotherhood of, 101 Constitution Ave. NW, Washington, DC 20001; William Konyha, Pres.; 820,000 members, 2,301 locals.

Cement, Lime Gypsum and Allied Workers International Union, United (U.C.L.G.A.W.I.U.), 7830 West Lawrence Ave., Norridge, IL 60656; founded 1939; Thomas F. Miechur, Pres. (since 1970); 35,367 members, 318 locals.

Chemical Workers Union, International (ICWU), 1655 West Market St., Akron, OH 44313; founded 1944; Frank D. Martino, Pres. (since 1975); 70,000 members, 400 locals.

Clothing and Textile Workers Union, Amalgamated (ACTWU), 15 Union Square, New York, NY 10003; founded 1914; Murray H. Finley, Pres. (since 1972); 510,000 members, 900 locals.

Communications Workers of America, 1925 K St. NW, Washington, DC 20006; Glenn E. Watts, Pres.; 600,000 members, 900 locals.

Distillery, Wine & Allied Workers International Union (DWU), 66 Grand Ave., Englewood, NJ 07631; founded 1940; George J. Oneto, Pres. (since 1974); 28,000 members, 73 locals.

*Distributive Workers of America, 13 Astor Place, New York, NY 10003; Cleveland Robinson, Pres.; 50,000 members, 40 locals.

*Education Association, National, 1201 16th St. NW, Washington, DC 20036; Willard H. McGuire, Pres.; 1,700,000 members, 12,000 affiliates.

Electrical, Radio and Machine Workers, International Union of (IUE), 1126 16th St. NW, Washington, DC 20036; founded 1949; David J. Fitzmaurice, Pres. (since 1976); 250,000 members, 640 locals.

*Electrical, Radio & Machine Workers of America, United (UE), 11 E. 51st St. New York, NY 10022; founded 1936; Denis Glavin, Gen. Pres. (since 1978); 165,000 members, 200 locals.

Electrical Workers, International Brotherhood of (IBEW), 1125 15th St., NW, Washington, DC 20005; founded 1891; Charles H. Pillard, Pres. (since 1970); 1,000,000 members, 1,479 locals.

Farm Workers of America, United (UFW), La Paz, Keene, CA 93531; founded 1962; Cesar E. Chavez, Pres. (since 1973); 100,000 members.

*Federal Employees, National Federation of (NFFE), 1016 16th St. NW, Washington, DC 20036; founded 1917; James M. Peirce Jr., Pres. (since 1976); 150,000 members, 600 locals.

Fire Fighters, International Association of, 1750 New York Ave. NW, Washington, DC 20006; William McClennan, Pres.; 171,674 members, 1,798 locals.

Firemen and Oilers, International Brotherhood of, VFW

Bldg., 200 Maryland Ave. NE, Washington, DC 20002; George J. Francisco, Pres.; 40,000 members.

Food and Commercial Workers International Union, United, 1775 K St., NW, Washington, DC 20006; William H. Wynn, Pres.; 1.3 million members, 1,002 locals.

Furniture Workers of America, United, 700 Broadway, New York, NY 10003; Carl Scarbrough, Pres.; 29,967 members, 106 locals.

Garment Workers of America, United (UGWA), 200 Park Ave. So., New York, NY 10003; founded 1891; William O'Donnell, Gen. Pres. (since 1977); 25,000 members, 155 locals.

Glass Bottle Blowers Association (GBBA), 608 E. Baltimore Pike, Media, PA 19063; founded 1842; James Hatfield, Pres.; 85,000 members, 253 locals.

Glass and Ceramic Workers of North America, United, 556 E. Town St., Columbus, OH 43215; Joseph Roman, Pres.; 30,000 members, 181 locals.

Glass Workers Union, American Flint (AFGWU), 1440 So. Byrne Rd., Toledo, OH 43614; founded 1878; George M. Parker, Pres. (since 1961); 31,000 members, 238 locals.

Government Employees, American Federation of (AFGE), 1325 Massachusetts Ave. NW, Washington, DC 20005; founded 1932; Kenneth T. Blaylock, Natl. Pres. (since 1976); 300,000 members, 1,500 locals.

Grain Millers, American Federation of (AFGM), 4949 Olson Memorial Hwy., Minneapolis, MN 55422; founded 1948; Frank Hoese, Gen. Pres. (since 1979); 35,000 members, 204 locals.

Graphic Arts International Union (GAIU), 1900 L St., NW, Washington, DC 20036; founded 1882; Kenneth J. Brown, Pres. (since 1959); 120,000 members, 220 locals.

Hotel and Restaurant Employees and Bartenders International Union, 120 E. 4th St., Cincinnati, OH 45202; Edward T. Hanley, Pres.; 451,989 members, 386 locals.

Industrial Workers of America, International Union, Allied (AIW), 3520 W. Oklahoma Ave., Milwaukee, WI 53215; founded 1935; Dominick D'Ambrosio, Intl. Pres. (since 1975); 85,000 members, 430 locals.

Iron Workers, International Association of Bridge and Structural, 1750 New York Ave. NW, Washington, DC 20006; John H. Lyons, Pres.; 181, 647 members, 322 locals.

Laborers' International Union of North America (LIUNA), 905 16th St. NW, Washington, DC 20006; founded 1903; Angelo Fosco, Gen. Pres. (since 1976); 650,000 members, 820 locals.

Ladies Garment Workers Union, International (ILGWU), 1710 Broadway, New York, NY 10019; founded 1900; Sol C. Chaikin, Pres. (since 1975); 322,505 members, 447 locals.

Leather Goods, Plastic and Novelty Workers' Union, International, 265 W. 14th St., New York, NY 10011; Frank Casale, Pres.; 40,000 members, 97 locals.

Letter Carriers, National Association of (NALC), 100 Indiana Ave. NW, Washington, DC 20001; founded 1889; Vincent R. Sombrotto, Pres. (since 1980); 233,000 members, 4,800 locals.

*Locomotive Engineers, Brotherhood of (BLE), 1365 Ontario Ave., Cleveland, OH 44114; founded 1863; John F. Sytsma, Pres. (since 1976); 62,888 members, 727 divisions.

Longshoremen's Association, International, 17 Battery Pl., New York, NY 10004; Thomas W. Gleason, Pres.; 76,579 members, 367 locals.

*Longshoremen's & Warehousemen's Union, International (ILWU), 1188 Franklin St., San Francisco, CA 94109; founded 1937; James R. Herman, Pres. (since 1977); 58,000 members, 78 locals.

Machinists and Aerospace Workers, International Association of, 1300 Connecticut Ave. NW, Washington, DC 20036; William W. Winpisinger, Pres.; 943,280 members, 1,904 locals.

Maintenance of Way Employes, Brotherhood of, 12050 Woodward Ave., Detroit, MI 48203; O. M. Berge, Pres.; 186,346 members, 987 locals.

Marine & Shipbuilding Workers of America, Industrial Union of (IUMSWA), 8121 Georgia Ave., Silver Springs, MD 20910; founded 1934; Frank Derwin, Pres. (since 1971); 25,000 members, 40 locals.

Maritime Union of America, National, 346 W. 17th St., New York NY 10011; Shannon Wall, Pres.; 35,000 members.

Mechanics Educational Society of America, 1421 First National Bldg., Detroit, MI 48226; Alfred J. Smith, Pres.; 25,000 members, 29 locals.

*Mine Workers of America, United (UMWA), 900 15th St.

NW, Washington, DC 20005; founded 1890; Sam Church Jr., Pres.; 250,000 members, 866 locals.

Molders' and Allied Workers' Union, International, 1225 E. McMillan St., Cincinnati, OH 45206; Carl W. Studenroth, Pres.; 75,000 members, 247 locals.

Musicians of the United States and Canada, American Federation of (AF of M), 1500 Broadway, New York, NY 10036; founded 1896; Victor W. Fuentealba, Pres. (since 1978); 280,000 members, 600 locals.

Newspaper Guild, The (TNG), 1125 15th St. NW, Washington, DC; founded 1933; Charles A. Perlik Jr., Pres. (since 1969); 32,000 members, 81 locals.

***Nurses Association, American,** 2420 Pershing Rd., Kansas City, MO 64108; Barbara Nichols, Pres.; 170,000 members, 53 affiliates.

Office and Professional Employees International Union, 265 W. 14th St., New York, NY 10011; John Kelly, Pres.; 125,000 members, 275 locals.

Oil, Chemical and Atomic Workers International Union, PO Box 2812, 1636 Champa St., Denver, CO 80201, A.F. Grospiron, Pres.; 177,433 members, 617 locals.

Operating Engineers, International Union of (IUOE), 1125 17th St. NW, Washington, DC 20036; founded 1896; J.C. Turner, Gen. Pres.; 420,000 members, 210 locals.

Painters and Allied Trades, International Brotherhood of (IBPAT), 1750 New York Ave. NW, Washington, DC 20006; founded 1887; S. Frank Raftery, Gen. Pres. (since 1965); 192,170 members, 809 locals.

Paperworkers International Union, United (UPIU), 163-03 Horace Harding Expressway, Flushing, NY 11365; founded 1884; Wayne E. Glenn, Pres. (since 1978); 324,842 members, 1,347 locals.

***Plant Guard Workers of America, International Union, United (UPGWA),** 25510 Kelly Rd., Roseville, MI 48066; founded 1948; James C. McGahey, Pres. (since 1948); 29,243 members, 162 locals.

Plasterers' and Cement Mason's International Association of the United States & Canada; Operative, 1125 17th St. NW, Washington, DC 20036; Melvin H. Roots, Pres.; 65,000 members, 365 locals.

Plumbing and Pipe Fitting Industry of the United States and Canada, United Association of Journeymen and Apprentices of the, 901 Massachusetts Ave. NW, Washington, DC 20001; Martin Ward, Pres.; 350,000 members.

***Police, Fraternal Order of,** G-3136 W. Pasadena Ave., Flint, MI 48504; Robert H. Stark, Pres.; 147,000 members, 1,036 affiliates.

***Postal Supervisors, National Association of,** L'Enfant Plaza East, SW, Washington, DC 20024; Donald N. Ledbetter, Pres.; 34,000 members, 450 locals.

Postal Workers Union, American (APWU), 817 14th St. NW, Washington, DC 20005; founded 1971; Moe Biller, Gen. Pres. (since 1980); 260,000 members, 5,000 locals.

Printing and Graphic Communications Union, International, 1730 Rhode Island Ave. NW, Washington, DC 20036; Sol Fishko, Pres.; 128,714 members, 785 locals.

Railway, Airline and Steamship Clerks, Freight Handlers, Express and Station Employees; Brotherhood of, 3 Research Place, Rockville, MD 20850; Fred J. Kroll, Pres.; 235,000 members, 980 locals.

Railway Carmen of the United States and Canada, Brotherhood, 4929 Main St., Kansas City, MO 64112; founded 1890; O.W. Jacobson, Gen. Pres.; 96,500 members, 621 locals.

Retail, Wholesale and Department Store Union, 30 E. 29th St., New York, NY 10016; Alvin E. Heaps, Pres.; 200,000 members, 315 locals.

Roofers, Damp and Waterproof Workers Association, United Slate, Tile and Composition, 1125 17th St. NW, Washington, DC 20036; Roy Johnson, Pres.; 28,000 members, 205 locals.

Rubber, Cork, Linoleum and Plastic Workers of America, United, 87 South High St., Akron, OH 44308; Peter Bommarito, Pres.; 140,000 members, 530 locals.

***Rural Letter Carriers' Association, National,** 1750 Pennsylvania Ave. NW, Washington, DC 20006; Dean King, Pres.; 64,000 members.

Seafarers International Union of North America (SIUNA), 675 4th Ave., Brooklyn, NY 11232; founded 1938; Frank Drozak, Pres. (act.); 90,000 members.

Service Employees International Union (SEIU), 2020 K St. NW, Washington, DC 20006; founded 1921; John J. Sweeney, Pres. (since 1980); 650,000 members, 328 locals.

Sheet Metal Workers' International Association (SMWIA), 1750 New York Ave. NW, Washington, DC 20006; founded 1888; Edward J. Carlough, Gen. Pres. (since 1970); 160,000 members, 380 locals.

Shoe Workers of America, United, 120 Boylston St., Boston,

MA 02116; George O. Fecteau, Pres.; 35,000 members, 125 locals.

State, County and Municipal Employees, American Federation of, 1625 L St. NW, Washington, DC 20036; Jerry Wurf, Pres.; 648,160 members, 2,570 locals.

Steelworkers of America, United (USWA), 5 Gateway Center, Pittsburgh, PA 15222; founded 1936; Lloyd McBride, Pres. (since 1977); 1,400,000 members, 5,200 locals.

Teachers, American Federation of (AFT), 11 Dupont Circle NW, Washington, DC 20036; founded 1916; Albert Shanker, Pres. (since 1974); 550,000 members, 2,010 locals.

***Teamsters, Chauffeurs, Warehousemen and Helpers of America, International Brotherhood of (IBT),** 25 Louisiana Ave. NW, Washington, DC 20001; founded 1903; Roy L. Williams, Gen. Pres. (since 1981); 2,000,000 members, 745 locals.

Television and Radio Artists, American Federation of, 1350 Ave. of the Americas, New York, NY; founded 1937; Bill Hillman, Pres.; 55,000 members, 43 locals.

Textile Workers of America, United (UTWA), 420 Common St., Lawrence, MA 01840; founded 1901; Francis Schaufenbil, Intl. Pres. (since 1972); 50,000 members, 221 locals.

Theatrical Stage Employees and Moving Picture Operators of the United States and Canada, International Alliance of, 1515 Broadway, New York, NY 10036; Walter Diehl, Pres.; 61,471 members, 870 locals.

Toys, Playthings, Novelties and Allied Products of the United States and Canada, International Union of Dolls, 147 E. 26th St., New York, NY 10010; Julius Isaacson, Pres.; 31,000 members, 23 locals.

Transit Union, Amalgamated (ATU), 5025 Wisconsin Ave. NW, Washington, DC 20016; founded 1892; Dan V. Maroney Jr., Intl. Pres. (since 1973); 160,000 members, 354 locals.

Transport Workers Union of America, 1980 Broadway, New York, NY 10023; Matthew Guinan, Pres.; 150,000 members, 105 locals.

Transportation Union, United (UTU), 14600 Detroit Ave., Cleveland, OH 44107; founded 1969; Fred A. Hardin, Pres. (since 1979); 245,000 members.

***Treasury Employees Union, National (NTEU),** 1730 K St. NW, Washington, DC 20006; founded 1938; Vincent L. Connery, Natl. Pres. (since 1966); 115,000 members, 201 chapters.

Typographical Union, International (ITU), PO Box 157, Colorado Springs, CO 80901; founded 1852; Joe Bingel, Pres. (since 1978); 88,200 members, 520 locals.

***University Professors, American Association of (AAUP),** 1 Dupont Circle, Washington, DC 20036; founded 1915; Henry T. Yost, Pres.; 75,000 members, 1,300 locals.

Upholsterers' International Union of North America (UIU), 25 N. 4th St., Philadelphia, PA 19106; founded 1882; Sal B. Hoffmann, Pres. (since 1937); 41,349 members, 145 locals.

Utility Workers Union of America (UWUA), 815 16th St. NW, Washington, DC 20006; founded 1946; James Joy Jr., Natl. Pres. (since 1980); 60,000 members, 220 locals.

Woodworkers of America, International (IWA), 1622 N. Lombard St., Portland, OR 97217; founded 1937; Keith Johnson, Intl. Pres. (since 1973); 120,000 members, 207 locals.

Canadian Unions

Source: Labour Canada

Independent Unions (1980)

Nurses' Association, Ontario	27,000
Quebec Govt. Employees' Union	45,000
Teachers' Association, Alberta	27,542
Teachers' Association of Ontario, Fed. of Women	32,290
Teachers' Federation, British Columbia	32,282
Teachers' Federation, Ontario Secondary School	35,627
Teaching Congress, Quebec	81,033
Teamsters, Chauffeurs, Warehousemen and Helpers of America, International Brotherhood of	92,000

Canadian Labor Congress (CLC) (1980)

Automobile, Aerospace and Agricultural Implement Workers of America, International Union, United	134,000
Communication Workers of Canada	28,000
Energy and Chemical Workers Union	30,000
Govt. Employees, National Union of Provincial	210,000
Paperworkers Union, Canadian	61,500
Postal Workers, Canadian Union of	24,000
Public Employees, Canadian Union of	267,407
Public Service Alliance of Canada	154,743
Railway, Transport and General Workers, Canadian Brotherhood of	38,500

ENERGY

Nuclear Power Reactors in U.S.

Source: Technical Information Center, U.S. Energy Department
as of Dec. 31, 1980

State	Site	Plant name	Capacity (kilowatts)	Utility	Commercial operation
Alabama	Decatur	Browns Ferry Unit 1	1,065,000	Tennessee Valley Authority	1974
	Decatur	Browns Ferry Unit 2	1,065,000	Tennessee Valley Authority	1975
	Decatur	Browns Ferry Unit 3	1,065,000	Tennessee Valley Authority	1977
	Dothan	Joseph M. Farley Unit 1	829,000	Alabama Power Co.	1977
Arkansas	Russellville	Arkansas Unit 1	850,000	Ark. Power & Light Co.	1974
	Russellville	Arkansas Unit 2	912,000	Ark. Power & Light Co.	1980
California	Eureka	Humboldt Bay Unit 3	63,000	Pacific Gas & Electric Co.	1963
	San Clemente	San Onofre Unit 1	430,000	So. Calif. Ed. & San Diego Gas & El. Co.	1968
	Diablo Canyon	Diablo Canyon Unit 1	1,084,000	Pacific Gas & Electric Co.	1981
	Clay Station	Rancho Seco Station	918,000	Sacramento Munic. Utility District.	1975
Colorado	Platteville	Ft. St. Vrain Station	330,000	Public Service Co. of Colorado	1978
Connecticut	Haddam Neck	Haddam Neck	575,000	Conn. Yankee Atomic Power Co.	1968
	Waterford	Millstone Unit 1	660,000	Northeast Nuclear Energy Co.	1971
	Waterford	Millstone Unit 2	870,000	Northeast Nuclear Energy Co.	1975
Florida	Florida City	Turkey Point Unit 3	693,000	Fla. Power & Light Co.	1972
	Florida City	Turkey Point Unit 4	693,000	Fla. Power & Light Co.	1973
	Red Level	Crystal River Unit 3	825,000	Florida Power Corp.	1977
	Ft. Pierce	St. Lucie Unit 1	802,000	Fla. Power & Light Co.	1976
Georgia	Baxley	Edwin I. Hatch Unit 1	787,000	Georgia Power Co.	1975
	Baxley	Edwin I. Hatch Unit 2	784,000	Georgia Power Co.	1978
Illinois	Morris	Dresden Unit 1	200,000	Commonwealth Edison Co.	1960
	Morris	Dresden Unit 2	794,000	Commonwealth Edison Co.	1970
	Morris	Dresden Unit 3	794,000	Commonwealth Edison Co.	1971
	Zion	Zion Unit 1	1,040,000	Commonwealth Edison Co.	1973
	Zion	Zion Unit 2	1,040,000	Commonwealth Edison Co.	1974
	Cordova	Quad-Cities Unit 1	789,000	Comm. Ed. Co.-la.-Ill. Gas & Elec. Co.	1973
	Cordova	Quad-Cities Unit 2	789,000	Comm. Ed. Co.-la.-Ill. Gas & Elec. Co.	1973
Iowa	Palo	Duane Arnold Unit 1	538,000	Iowa Electric Light and Power Co.	1975
Maine	Wiscasset	Maine Yankee	790,000	Me. Yankee Atomic Power Co.	1972
Maryland	Lusby	Calvert Cliffs Unit 1	845,000	Baltimore Gas & Electric Co.	1975
	Lusby	Calvert Cliffs Unit 2	845,000	Baltimore Gas & Electric Co.	1977
Massachusetts	Rowe	Yankee Station	175,000	Yankee Atomic Electric Co.	1961
	Plymouth	Pilgrim Unit 1	655,000	Boston Edison Co.	1972
Michigan	Big Rock Point	Big Rock Point	72,000	Consumers Power Co.	1963
	South Haven	Palisades Station	805,000	Consumers Power Co.	1971
	Bridgman	Donald C. Cook Unit 1	1,054,000	Ind. & Michigan Electric Co.	1975
	Bridgman	Donald C. Cook Unit 2	1,100,000	Ind. & Michigan Electric Co.	1978
Minnesota	Monticello	Monticello	545,000	Northern States Power Co.	1971
	Red Wing	Prairie Island Unit 1	530,000	Northern States Power Co.	1973
	Red Wing	Prairie Island Unit 2	530,000	Northern States Power Co.	1974
Nebraska	Fort Calhoun	Ft. Calhoun Unit 1	457,000	Omaha Public Power District	1973
	Brownville	Cooper Station	778,000	Neb. Pub. Power Dist.-la. Power & Light Co.	1974
New Jersey	Toms River	Oyster Creek Unit 1	650,000	Jersey Central Power & Light Co.	1969
	Salem	Salem Unit 1	1,090,000	Public Service Electric & Gas, N.J.	1977
	Salem	Salem Unit 2	1,115,000	Public Service Electric & Gas, N.J.	1980
New York	Buchanan	Indian Point Unit 2	873,000	Consolidated Edison Co.	1973
	Buchanan	Indian Point Unit 3	965,000	Power Authority of State of N.Y.	1976
	Ontario	R.E. Ginna Unit 1	470,000	Rochester Gas & Electric Co.	1970
	Scriba	9-Mile Point Unit 1	620,000	Niagra Mohawk Power.	1969
	Scriba	James A. FitzPatrick	821,000	Power Authority of State of N.Y.	1975
North Carolina	Southport	Brunswick Steam Unit 1	821,000	Carolina Power & Light Co.	1977
	Southport	Brunswick Steam Unit 2	821,000	Carolina Power & Light Co.	1975
	Cowans Ford Dam.	Wm. B. McGuire Unit 1	1,180,000	Duke Power Co.	1981
Ohio	Oak Harbor	Davis-Besse Unit 1	906,000	Toledo Edison-Cleveland El. Illum. Co.	1977
Oregon	Prescott	Trojan Unit 1	1,130,000	Portland Gen. Electric Co.	1976
Pennsylvania	Peach Bottom	Peach Bottom Unit 2	1,065,000	Philadelphia Electric Co.	1974
	Peach Bottom	Peach Bottom Unit 3	1,065,000	Philadelphia Electric Co.	1974
	Shippingport	Shippingport Station	60,000	Duquesne Light Co.	1957
	Shippingport	Beaver Valley Unit 1	852,000	Duquesne Light Co.-Ohio Edison Co.	1976
	Middletown	Three Mile Island Unit 1	819,000	Metropolitan Edison Co.	1974
	Middletown	Three Mile Island Unit 2	906,000	Jersey Central Power & Light Co.	1979
South Carolina	Hartsville	H. B. Robinson Unit 2	700,000	Carolina Power & Light Co.	1971
	Seneca	Oconee Unit 1	887,000	Duke Power Co.	1973
	Seneca	Oconee Unit 2	887,000	Duke Power Co.	1974
	Seneca	Oconee Unit 3	887,000	Duke Power Co.	1974
Tennessee	Daisy	Sequoyah Unit 1	1,148,000	Tennessee Valley Authority	1981
Vermont	Vernon	Vermont Yankee Station	514,000	Vt. Yankee Nuclear Power Corp.	1972
Virginia	Gravel Neck	Surry Unit 1	822,000	Va. Electric & Power Co.	1972
	Gravel Neck	Surry Unit 2	822,000	Va. Electric & Power Co.	1973
	Mineral	North Anna Unit 1	907,000	Va. Electric & Power Co.	1979
	Mineral	North Anna Unit 2	907,000	Va. Electric & Power Co.	1980
Washington	Richland	N-Reactor/WPPSS Steam	850,000	U.S. Energy Department.	1966
Wisconsin	La Crosse	Genoa Station	50,000	Dairyland Power Cooperative.	1969
	Two Creeks	Point Beach Unit 1	497,000	Wis. Mich. Power Co.	1970
	Two Creeks	Point Beach Unit 2	497,000	Wis. Mich. Power Co.	1972
	Carlton	Kewaunee Unit 1	535,000	Wis. Public Service Corp.	1974

Nuclear plant capacity (kilowatts): operable 74,000,000; being built 84,000,000; planned 15,000,000; Total 173,000,000.

World Nuclear Power

Source: Energy Information Agency, U.S. Energy Department

Country	Operational reactors	Capacity[1]	Generation[2] 1980	Country	Operational reactors	Capacity[1]	Generation[2] 1980
Argentina	1	360	2.3	Netherlands	2	520	4.2
Belgium	3	1,740	12.5	Pakistan	1	140	0.1
Canada	8	5,590	40.4	South Korea	1	590	3.5
Finland	2	1,150	7.0	Spain	3	1,120	5.2
France	15	7,800	61.2	Sweden	6	3,850	26.7
Germany, W.	10	7,050	43.7	Switzerland	3	1,060	14.3
Great Britain	33	9,040	37.2	Taiwan	2	1,270	8.2
India	3	620	2.9	U.S.	71	54,180	265.3
Italy	4	1,490	2.2	Total[3]	189	110,410[4]	619.7
Japan	20	12,840	82.8				

(1) Thousand kilowatts. (2) Billion kilowatt hours. (3) Non-Communist countries. (4) Total may not equal sum of components due to independent rounding.

World Electricity Production

Source: UN Monthly Bulletin of Statistics, July 1981 (1980 production, in million kilowatt-hours.)

U.S.	2,106,440	Italy	185,019	E. Germany	95,952	Netherlands	64,810
USSR[1]	1,294,900	Poland	121,862	S. Africa	90,929	Mexico[5]	59,412
Japan	519,347	China[2]	120,000	Sweden	90,874	Yugoslavia[6]	59,339
W. Germany	368,773	Spain	110,194	Norway	83,985	Belgium	53,643
Canada	366,677	India	107,847	Czechoslovakia	72,825	Switzerland	46,626
United Kingdom	285,048	Brazil[3]	99,864	Romania[4]	64,932	Austria	41,950
France	243,282	Australia	98,068				

(1) Estimated figure for December. (2) 1975 estimate. (3) 1977. (4) 1978. (5) 1979 est. (6) 1980 est.

Production of Electricity in the U.S. by Source

Source: Energy Information Administration, U.S. Energy Department
Amounts include both privately-owned and publicly-owned utilities.

Calendar Year	Net production million kwh	Percentage produced by source						Fuel Consumption		
		Coal	Oil	Gas	Nuclear	Hydro	Other[1]	Coal 1,000 sht. tns.	Oil 1,000 bbls.	Gas million cu. ft.
1971	1,612,593	44.3	13.6	23.2	2.4	16.5	0.05	327,887	396,468	3,975,971
1974	1,867,103	44.5	16.0	17.2	6.1	16.1	0.1	392,423	536,245	3,443,293
1976	2,037,775	46.4	15.7	14.4	9.4	13.9	0.2	448,456	555,937	3,081,286
1977	2,124,580	46.4	16.8	14.4	11.8	10.4	0.2	477,229	623,742	3,191,948
1978	2,206,515	44.2	16.5	13.8	12.5	12.7	0.2	481,254	635,600	3,188,306
1979	2,247,372	47.8	13.5	14.7	11.4	12.4	0.2	527,051	523,565	3,490,523
1980	2,286,439	50.8	10.7	15.1	10.9	12.0	0.2	569,274	420,214	3,681,495

(1) Includes electricity produced from geothermal power, wood, and waste.

U.S. Petroleum Imports by Source

Source: Department of Energy
(in thousands of barrels per day)

Nation	1976	1977	1978	1979	1980
Algeria	438.3	565.2	632.1	630.5	483
Indonesia	569.4	576.2	538.2	416.9	341
Iran	546.5	786.4	544.7	303.2	8
Libya	529.3	837.7	641.1	654.0	552
Nigeria	1,119.2	1,229.6	904.7	1,077.6	847
Saudi Arabia	1,365.8	1,523.8	1,137.2	1,346.8	1,257
United Arab Emirates	323.2	446.3	378.4	279.7	179
Venezuela	972.2	908.8	633.5	691.1	463
Other OPEC[1]	216.0	378.1	224.0	212.2	121
Total OPEC	6,079.9	7,252.2	5,636.9	5,612.0	4,251
Arab OPEC Members	2,773.0	3,636.5	2,920.8	3,037.4	2,541
Bahamas	116.5	168.0	158.4	147.7	78
Canada	599.3	502.8	468.6	532.5	446
Neth'lands Antilles	274.6	218.3	317.8	231.3	226
Puerto Rico	88.1	102.8	230.1	91.8	85
Trinidad/Tobago	272.6	286.0	89.4	186.3	176
Virgin Islands	422.3	468.7	251.0	431.5	383
Mexico	87.1	179.3	426.8	434.1	530
Other non-OPEC	373.5	657.1	649.9	744.0	656
Total non-OPEC	2,234.0	2,583.0	2,591.5	2,799.1	2,580
Total imports (avg.)	7,313.0	8,714.0	10,843.7	NA	5,177

(1) Ecuador, Gabon, Iraq, Kuwait, Qatar. (2) Imports do not add to totals because OPEC figures include petroleum transshipped through, and usually refined in, other countries and counted again as imports from those countries. NA-Not available.

U.S. Dependence on Petroleum Imports

Source: Department of Energy
(million barrels per day average)

Source	1975	1976	1977	1978	1979	1980	1981 Jan.-Mar.
Arab nations	1.38	2.42	3.18	2.96	3.04	2.54	2.44
All OPEC	3.60	5.07	6.19	5.64	5.61	4.25	3.78
All nations	6.06	7.31	8.81	8.23	8.41	5.17	4.46
U.S. production	16.32	17.46	18.43	18.82	18.43	8.60	8.55

World Production of Crude Oil

Leading Nations

(thousands of barrels)
Source: Energy Information Administration, U.S. Energy Dept.
Monthly Energy Review, June, 1981

	1979			1980	
Nation	Production	% of total production	Nation	Production	% of total production
1. USSR	4,186,550	18.6%			
2. Saudi Arabia	3,374,425	14.7	1. USSR	4,277,800	19.7%
3. United States[1]	3,111,625	13.7	2. Saudi Arabia	3,613,500	16.7
4. Iraq	1,253,775	5.5	3. United States[1]	947,905	4.3
5. Iran	1,107,775	5.0	4. Iraq	917,610	4.2
6. Venezuela	859,575	3.8	5. Venezuela	790,955	3.6
7. Nigeria	841,325	3.7	6. China	771,610	3.6
8. Kuwait	808,475	3.5	7. Nigeria	750,075	3.5
9. People's Republic of China	773,800	3.4	8. Mexico	707,005	3.3
			9. Libya	652,255	3.0
10. Libya	753,725	3.3	10. United Arab Emirates	623,785	2.9
11. United Arab Emirates	669,775	2.9	11. Iran	606,630	2.8
12. Indonesia	580,350	2.5	12. Kuwait	604,440	2.8
13. United Kingdom	573,050	2.5	13. United Kingdom	592,030	2.7
14. Canada[1]	545,675	2.4	14. Indonesia	575,605	2.7
15. Mexico[1]	532,900	2.3	15. Canada[1]	519,760	2.4
16. Algeria[1]	414,275	1.8	16. Algeria[1]	369,380	1.7
17. Neutral Zone	206,225	0.9	17. Qatar	172,280	0.8
Total	20,593,300		Total	21,701,075	

(1) Includes lease condensate

World Oil Supply and Demand Projections

Source: Central Intelligence Agency
(million barrels per day)

	1976	1977	1978	1979	1980	1985
Demand (non-Communist)	48.4	49.8-50.5	51.2-52.2	52.5-54.1	54.9-56.7	68.3-72.6
United States	16.7	17.8-18.3	18.2-19.0	18.4-19.7	19.3-20.7	22.2-25.6
West Europe	13.6	13.9-14.3	13.8-14.2	13.7-14.4	13.7-14.7	15.8-18.2
Japan	5.2	5.3-5.4	5.5-5.8	5.9-6.2	6.2-6.6	8.1-8.8
Canada	2.0	2.0-2.1	2.1-2.2	2.2-2.3	2.2-2.4	2.9-3.5
Other developed[1]	1.2	1.2	1.3	1.3	1.4	1.9
Non-OPEC LDCs[2]	6.7	7.1	7.5	7.8	8.5	12.0
OPEC[3] countries	2.1	2.3	2.5	2.8	3.0	4.0
Other demand[4]	0.9	0	0	0	0	0
Non-OPEC supply[5]	17.5	18.5	20.1	21.2	22.0	20.4-22.4
United States	9.7	9.6	10.2	10.2	10.0	10.0-11.0
West Europe	0.9	1.8	2.5	3.1	3.7	4.0-5.0
Japan	0	0	0	0	0	0.1
Canada	1.6	1.6	1.5	1.5	1.5	1.3-1.5
Other developed[1]	0.5	0.5	0.5	0.5	0.5	0.4
Non-OPEC LDCs	3.7	4.1	4.6	5.3	6.1	8.0-9.0
Net Communist trade[6]						
USSR-East Europe	0.9	0.7	0.5	0.2	− 0.3	− 3.5−4.5
China	0.2	0.2	0.3	0.4	0.5	0
Required OPEC production[7]	30.9	31.3-32.0	31.1-32.1	31.3-32.9	32.9-34.7	46.7-51.2

(1) Australia, Israel, New Zealand, South Africa. (2) LDCs: less developed countries. (3) OPEC: Organization of Petroleum Exporting Countries. (4) Including stock changes and statistical discrepancy. (5) Including natural gas liquids. (6) Difference of Communist countries' exports and imports; minus sign indicates net Communist imports. (7) OPEC production capacity will reach 27.5-29.4 million barrels per day by 1985, exclusive of Saudi Arabia; Saudi projections are uncertain.

U.S. Energy Consumption per GNP Dollar

Source: Department of Energy
(Average thousand Btu per 1972 constant dollar)

1973	59.4	1978/1st qtr	63.1	1979/1st qtr	60.8	1980/1st qtr	57.2
1974	58.3	2nd qtr	52.4	2nd qtr	49.4	2nd qtr	48.3
1975	57.3	3rd qtr	52.1	3rd qtr	48.9	3rd qtr	47.6
1976	57.3	4th qtr	56.1	4th qtr	53.5	4th qtr	52.7
1977	55.6	Average	54.4	Average	53.2	Average	51.5

U.S. Crude Oil Reserves

Source: American Petroleum Institute

Estimates of proved reserves, which can be recovered under present economic relationships and known technology. Improved technology or higher world prices would increase estimates of reserves. Cumulative production for all years through Dec. 31, 1978 was 117,766,214 thousand barrels.

(thousands of 42-gallon barrels)

Year	Discoveries, revisions, extensions	Production	Proved reserves at end of year	Change from previous year[1]	Year	Discoveries, revisions, extensions	Production	Proved reserves at end of year	Change from previous year[1]
1947	2,464,570	1,850,445	21,487,685	614,125	1963	2,174,110	2,593,343	30,969,990	(419,233)
1948	3,795,207	2,002,448	23,280,444	1,792,759	1964	2,664,767	2,644,247	30,990,510	20,520
1949	3,187,845	1,818,800	24,649,489	1,369,045	1965	3,048,079	2,686,198	31,352,391	361,881
1950	2,562,685	1,943,776	25,268,398	618,909	1966	2,963,978	2,864,242	31,452,127	99,736
1951	4,413,954	2,214,321	27,468,031	2,199,633	1967	2,962,122	3,037,579	31,376,670	(75,457)
1952	2,749,288	2,256,765	27,960,554	492,523	1968	2,454,635	3,124,188	30,707,117	(669,553)
1953	3,296,130	2,311,856	28,944,828	984,274	1969	2,120,036	3,195,291	29,631,862	(1,075,255)
1954	2,873,037	2,257,119	29,560,746	615,918	1970	12,688,918	3,319,445	39,001,335	9,369,473
1955	2,870,724	2,419,300	30,012,170	451,424	1971	2,317,732	3,256,110	38,062,957	(938,378)
1956	2,974,336	2,551,857	30,434,649	422,479	1972	1,557,848	3,281,397	36,339,408	(1,723,549)
1957	2,424,800	2,559,044	30,300,405	(134,244)	1973	2,145,831	3,185,400	35,299,839	(1,039,569)
1958	2,608,242	2,372,730	30,535,917	235,512	1974	1,993,573	3,043,456	34,249,956	(1,049,883)
1959	3,666,745	2,483,315	31,719,347	1,183,430	1975	1,318,463	2,886,292	32,682,127	(1,567,829)
1960	2,365,328	2,471,464	31,613,211	(106,136)	1976	1,085,291	2,825,252	30,942,166	(1,739,961)
1961	2,657,567	2,512,273	31,758,505	145,294	1977	1,403,780	2,859,544	29,486,402	(1,455,764)
1962	2,180,896	2,550,178	31,389,223	(369,282)	1978	1,347,265	3,029,898	27,803,760	(1,682,642)
					1979	2,205,673	2,958,144	27,051,289	(752,471)

(1) Parenthesis indicate decline.

U.S. Crude Petroleum Production by Chief States

Source: Energy Information Administration, U.S. Energy Department (thousands of 42-gallon barrels)

Year	Alas.	Cal.	Col.	Fla.	Kan.	La.	Miss.	N.M.	Okla.	Tex.	Wyo.
1950	0	327,607	23,303	487	107,586	208,965	38,236	47,367	164,599	829,874	61,631
1960	559	305,352	47,469	369	113,453	400,832	51,673	107,380	192,913	927,479	133,910
1965	11,128	316,428	33,511	1,462	104,733	594,853	56,183	119,166	203,441	1,000,749	138,314
1970	83,616	372,191	24,723	12,999	84,853	906,907	65,119	128,184	223,574	1,249,697	160,345
1975	69,834	322,199	38,089	41,877	59,106	650,840	46,614	95,063	163,123	1,221,929	135,943
1976	63,398	326,021	38,992	44,460	58,714	606,501	46,072	92,130	161,426	1,189,523	134,149
1977	169,201	349,609	39,460	46,641	57,496	562,905	43,022	87,223	156,382	1,137,880	136,472
1978	448,620	347,181	36,797	47,536	56,586	532,740	39,494	83,365	150,456	1,074,050	137,385
1979	511,538	352,465	32,251	47,170	56,995	494,462	38,286	79,379	143,642	1,013,255	124,553
1980	591,684	356,644	29,565	42,846	60,152	466,964	36,533	75,456	151,960	975,239	214,161

Other chief states in 1980 were N. Dakota, 40,014; Michigan, 32,753; and Montana, 29,566.

U.S. Petroleum and Natural Gas Production

Source: Energy Information Administration, U.S. Energy Department

Year	Crude oil Production 1,000 bbls.	Crude oil Value $1,000	Natural gas liquids Production 1,000 bbls.	Natural gas liquids Value $1,000	Total oil & N.G.L. 1,000 bbls.	Natural gas Marketed mil. cu. ft.	Natural gas Value $1,000
1945	1,713,655	2,094,250	112,004	187,564	1,828,539	3,944,021	191,006
1950	1,973,574	4,963,380	181,961	419,605	2,155,693	6,282,060	408,521
1955	2,484,428	6,870,380	281,371	619,006	2,766,325	9,405,351	978,357
1960	2,574,933	7,420,181	340,157	808,385	2,915,365	12,771,038	1,789,970
1965	2,848,514	8,158,298	441,556	911,603	3,290,083	16,042,753	2,494,542
1970	3,517,450	11,173,726	605,916	1,275,112	4,123,366	21,920,642	3,745,680
1975	3,056,779	23,116,059	595,958	2,772,588	3,652,737	20,108,661	8,945,062
1976	2,976,180	24,229,540	587,045	3,284,089	3,563,225	19,952,438	11,571,776
1977	2,986,710	25,397,307	584,900	4,386,750	3,571,610	19,924,671	15,522,658
1978	3,178,216	28,476,815	572,320	NA	3,578,892	19,690,000	18,095,009
1979	3,121,480	39,051,332	578,160	NA	3,086,440	20,471,000	24,113,634

Average Consumer Cost of Fuels

Source: Department of Energy
(1972 constant dollars)

Fuel	1974	1975	1976	1977	1978	1979	1980
Leaded regular gasoline (cent/gal)	44.8	43.7	43.1	43.2	41.0	49.8	119.1
Residential heating oil (cent/gal)	29.4	29.3	30.2	31.2	31.7	40.8	97.8
Residential natural gas (cent/Mcf)	123.4	132.8	145.4	162.2	163.5	185.3	391.5
Residential electricity (cent/kWh)	2.63	2.73	2.77	2.81	2.76	2.66	5.36

Mcf=million cubic feet; kwh=million kilowatt hours.

U.S. Total Fuel Supply and Demand

Source: Energy Information Administration, U.S. Energy Department

(thousands of 42-gallon barrels)

Year	Gasoline[1] Production	Gasoline[1] Total demand	Kerosene[2] Production	Kerosene[2] Total demand	Distillate fuel oil Production	Distillate fuel oil Total demand	Residual fuel oil Production	Residual fuel oil Total demand
1950[3]	1,024,181	1,019,011	118,512	119,922	398,912	75,435	425,217	570,021
1960	1,522,497	1,525,126	136,842	133,188	667,050	695,165	332,147	577,934
1965	1,733,258	1,756,419	201,788	219,932	765,430	779,644	268,567	601,893
1970	2,135,838	2,165,598	313,544	358,146	897,097	928,109	257,510	824,073
1971	2,231,157	2,246,025	306,847	365,308	912,097	974,077	274,684	851,262
1972	2,352,310	2,384,734	313,554	379,984	963,625	1,067,321	292,519	937,707
1974	2,371,004	2,436,681	290,780	346,706	974,025	1,076,771	390,491	968,185
1975	2,420,962	2,479,857	308,034	347,399	968,650	1,040,838	450,957	903,914
1976	2,549,627	2,597,305	323,114	350,565	1,070,209	1,146,695	503,953	1,025,148
1977	2,565,950	2,625,080	355,145	376,680	1,192,090	1,213,990	635,100	1,111,425
1978	2,612,670	2,702,095	354,415	386,900	1,153,765	1,242,825	615,390	1,103,395
1979	2,494,655	2,566,128	368,707	391,650	1,148,778	1,207,278	614,806	1,029,913
1980	2,369,580	2,567,410	369,380	392,740	971,995	1,208,515	575,605	1,031,490

Demand usually exceeds the production; the difference is made up by dipping into stocks or by imports. (1) Includes special naphtha production. (2) Includes kerosene type jet fuel. (3) 1950 figures are on a 48-state basis.

U.S. Natural Gas Reserves

Source: American Gas Association

Estimates of proved reserves, which can be recovered under existing economic and operating conditions.

Year	Natural gas (millions of cu. ft.) Discoveries, revisions and extensions	Change in underground storage[1]	Production[4]	Proved reserves at end of year	Natural gas liquids (1,000 42-gallon barrels) Discoveries, revisions and extensions	Production[4]	Proved reserves at end of year
1946	17,632,864	(2)	4,915,774	159,703,813	(2)	129,262	3,163,219
1947	10,921,187	(2)	5,599,235	165,025,765	251,538	160,782	3,253,975
1948	13,823,090	51,202	5,975,001	172,925,056	470,557	183,749	3,540,783
1949	12,605,615	82,146	6,211,124	179,401,693	386,776	198,547	3,729,012
1950	11,985,361	52,935	6,855,244	184,584,745	766,062	227,411	4,267,663
1951	15,965,808	132,030	7,923,673	192,758,910	723,991	267,052	4,724,602
1952	14,267,606	197,766	8,592,716	198,631,566	556,838	284,789	4,996,651
1953	20,341,933	513,629[3]	9,188,365	210,298,763	743,969	302,698	5,437,922
1954	9,547,074	90,408	9,375,314	210,560,931	107,350	300,815	5,244,457
1955	21,897,616	87,164	10,063,167	222,482,544	514,508	320,400	5,438,565
1956	24,716,115	133,241	10,848,685	236,483,215	809,820	346,053	5,902,332
1957	20,008,051	178,761	11,439,890	245,230,137	137,392	352,364	5,687,360
1958	18,896,724	57,582	11,422,651	252,761,792	858,206	341,548	6,204,018
1959	20,621,249	160,453	12,373,063	261,170,431	703,444	385,154	6,522,308
1960	13,893,978	281,273	13,019,356	262,326,326	725,130	431,379	6,816,059
1961	17,166,421	159,544	13,378,649	266,273,642	694,686	461,649	7,049,096
1962	19,483,958	159,231	13,637,973	272,278,858	732,549	470,128	7,311,517
1963	18,164,667	253,733	14,546,025	276,151,233	878,120	515,659	7,673,978
1964	20,252,139	195,110	15,347,028	281,251,454	608,744	536,090	7,746,632
1965	21,319,279	150,483	16,252,293	286,468,923	832,312	555,410	8,023,534
1966	20,220,432	134,523	17,491,073	289,332,805	894,116	588,684	8,328,966
1967	21,804,333	151,403	18,380,838	292,907,703	929,758	644,493	8,614,231
1968	13,697,008	118,568	19,373,427	287,349,852	685,659	701,782	8,598,108
1969	8,375,004	107,169	20,723,190	275,108,835	281,028	735,962	8,143,174
1970	37,196,359	402,018	21,960,804	290,746,408	307,579	747,812	7,702,941
1971	9,825,421	310,301	22,076,512	278,805,618	347,720	746,434	7,304,227
1972	9,634,563	156,563	22,511,898	266,084,846	238,273	755,941	6,786,559
1973	6,825,049	(354,282)	22,605,406	249,950,207	408,979	740,831	6,454,707
1974	8,679,184	(178,424)	21,318,470	237,132,497	619,841	724,099	6,350,449
1975	10,483,688	302,561	19,718,570	228,200,176	618,504	701,123	6,267,830
1976	7,555,468	(187,550)	19,542,020	216,026,074	834,766	700,629	6,401,967
1977	11,851,924	446,930	19,447,050	208,877,878	291,171	698,773	5,994,365
1978	10,586,144	148,733	19,311,048	200,301,707	595,666	664,179	5,925,852
1979	14,285,947	293,323	19,910,353	194,916,624	389,805	660,334	5,655,323

(1) Parentheses indicate decline. (2) Not estimated. (3) All native gas in storage reservoirs formerly classified as proved reserves is included in this figure. (4) Preliminary net production.

U.S. Passenger Car Efficiency

Source: Department of Energy

	Average fuel consumed per car Gal.	Index	Average miles traveled per car Miles	Index	Average miles per gallon Miles	Index		Average fuel consumed per car Gal.	Index	Average miles traveled per car Miles	Index	Average miles per gallon Miles	Index
1968	698	102.0	9,627	101.0	13.79	99.0	1974	704	102.9	9,448	99.1	13.43	96.4
1969	718	105.0	9,782	102.6	13.63	97.8	1975	712	104.1	9,634	101.1	13.53	97.1
1970	735	107.5	9,978	104.7	13.57	97.4	1977	706	103.2	9,839	103.2	13.94	100.1
1971	746	109.1	10,121	106.2	13.57	97.4	1978	715	104.5	10,046	105.4	14.06	100.9
1973	763	111.5	9,992	104.8	13.10	94.0	1979	664	97.1	9,485	99.5	14.29	102.6

U.S. Motor Fuel Supply and Demand

Source: Energy Information Administration, U.S. Energy Department

(thousands of 42-gallon barrels)

Year	Supply Production	Daily average	Demand Domestic	Export	Year	Supply Production	Daily average	Demand Domestic	Export
1945....	793,431	2,174	696,333	88,059	1974....	2,371,004	6,496	2,434,368	2,313
1950....	1,024,481	2,806	994,290	24,721	1975....	2,420,962	6,633	2,477,786	2,071
1955....	1,373,950	3,764	1,329,788	34,521	1976....	2,549,627	6,966	2,597,305	3,807
1960[2]...	1,522,497	4,171	1,511,670	13,456	1977....	2,566,315	7,031	2,619,605	2,155
1965....	1,733,258	4,749	1,750,028	6,391	1978....	2,615,955	7,167	2,706,840	1,250
1970....	2,135,838	5,852	2,162,642	2,956	1979....	2,513,937	6,837	2,580,080	500
1971....	2,231,157	6,113	2,242,921	3,104	1980....	2,844,007	6,492	2,401,335	1,000
1972....	2,352,310	6,445	2,382,569	2,165					
1973....	2,434,943	6,671	2,484,262	3,318					

(1) Includes special naphtha. (2) Beginning with 1960 Alaska and Hawaii are included.

Coal and Coke Production in the U.S.

Source: Energy Information Administration, U.S. Energy Department

Year	Penn. anthracite Production 1,000 net tons	Value $1,000	Bituminous Production 1,000 net tons	Value $1,000	Year	Penn. anthracite Production 1,000 net tons	Value $1,000	Bituminous Production 1,000 net tons	Value $1,000
1945	54,934	323,944	577,617	1,768,204	1970	9,729	105,341	602,932	3,772,662
1950	44,077	392,398	516,311	2,500,374	1971	8,727	103,469	552,192	3,901,496
1955	26,205	206,097	464,633	2,092,383	1972	7,106	85,251	595,386	4,561,983
1960	18,817	147,116	415,512	1,950,421	1973	6,830	90,260	591,738	5,049,612
1962	16,894	134,094	422,149	1,891,555	1974	6,617	144,695	603,406	9,502,347
1963	18,267	153,503	458,928	2,013,390	1975	6,203	198,481	648,438	12,472,486
1964	17,184	140,640	400,990	2,105,582	1976	6,228	209,234	678,685	13,189,481
1965	14,866	122,021	512,088	2,276,022	1977	5,861	202,373	691,300	13,700,000
1966	12,941	100,663	533,881	2,421,293	1978	5,370	352,260	665,127	14,500,000
1967	12,256	96,160	552,026	2,555,377	1979	4,395	180,458	621,751	16,980,001
1968	11,461	97,245	545,245	2,546,340					
1969	10,473	100,769	560,505	2,795,509					

Coke production (1,000 net tons—value in $1,000)—(1968) 63,653, $1,157,359; (1969) 64,757, $1,355,260; (1970) 66,525, $1,849,160; (1971) 57,436, $1,745,693; (1972) 60,507, $2,012,486; (1973) 64,325, $2,442,151; (1974) 61,581, $4,510,150; (1975) 57,207, $4,835,654; (1976) 58,333, $5,021,616; (1977) 53,510, $4,652,776; (1978) 49,010, $5,634,847; (1979) 52,943, $5,458,568.
Coke exports (short tons)—(1968) 791,909; (1969) 1,629,000; (1970) 2,478,338; (1971) 1,508,639; (1972) 1,231,633; (1973) 1,394,980; (1974) 1,277,681; (1975) 1,272,906; (1976) 1,314,725; (1977) 1,240,577; (1978) 693,000; (1979) 1,440,000. **Imports** —(1968) 94,085; (1969) 173,052; (1970) 152,879; (1971) 173,914; (1972) 185,023; (1973) 1,077,737; (1974) 3,540,326; (1975) 1,818,981; (1976) 1,311,472; (1977) 1,829,000; (1978) 5,722,000; (1979) 3,974,000.
Anthracite exports (net tons)—(1966) 766,025; (1967) 594,797; (1968) 518,159; (1969) 627,492; (1970) 789,499; (1971) 671,024; (1972) 743,451; (1973) 716,546; (1974) 735,173; (1975) 639,601; (1976) 615,167; (1977) 624,908; (1978) 866,000; (1979) 1,233,000.

Production of Energy by Type

Source: Energy Information Administration, U.S. Energy Department

	Coal[1]	Crude oil[2]	NGPL[3]	Natural gas (dry)	Hydro-electric power[4]	Nuclear electric power	Other[5]	Total energy produced
				Quadrillion (10[15]) Btu				
1973 Total	14.366	19.493	2.569	22.187	2.861	0.910	0.046	62.433
1974	14.468	18.575	2.471	21.210	3.177	1.272	0.056	61.229
1975	15.189	17.729	2.374	19.640	3.155	1.900	0.072	60.059
1976	15.853	17.262	2.327	19.480	2.976	2.111	0.081	60.091
1977	15.829	17.454	2.327	19.565	2.333	2.702	0.082	60.293
1978	15.037	18.434	2.245	19.485	2.958	2.977	0.068	61.204
1979	17.651	18.104	2.286	20.076	2.954	2.748	0.089	63.907
1980	18.877	18.250	2.263	19.754	2.913	2.704	0.114	64.876

Geographic coverage: the 50 United States and District of Columbia. Totals may not equal sum of components due to independent rounding. (1) Includes bituminous coal, lignite, and anthracite. (2) Includes lease condensate. (3) Natural gas plant liquids. (4) Includes industrial and utility production of hydropower. (5) Includes geothermal power and electricity produced from wood and waste. R=Revised data.

Consumption of Energy by Type

	Coal[1]	Natural gas (dry)	Petroleum	Hydro-electric power[2]	Nuclear electric power	Net imports of coal coke[3]	Other[4]	Total energy consumed
				Quadrillion (10[15]) Btu				
1973 Total	13.300	22.512	34.840	3.010	0.910	(0.008)	0.046	74.609
1974	12.876	21.732	33.455	3.309	1.272	0.059	0.056	72.759
1975	12.823	19.948	32.731	3.219	1.900	0.014	0.072	70.707
1976	13.733	20.345	35.175	3.066	2.111	0.000	0.081	74.510
1977	13.965	19.931	37.122	2.515	2.702	0.015	0.082	76.332
1978	13.846	20.000	37.965	3.164	2.977	0.131	0.068	78.150
1979	15.109	20.666	37.123	3.166	2.748	0.066	0.089	78.968
1980	15.603	20.495	34.196	3.125	2.704	(0.037)	0.114	76.201

Geographic coverage: the 50 United States and District of Columbia. Totals may not equal sum of components due to independent rounding. (1) Includes bituminous coal, lignite, and anthracite. (2) Includes industrial and utility production, and net imports of electricity. (3) Parentheses indicate exports are greater than imports. (4) Includes geothermal power and electricity produced from wood and waste. R—Revised data.

World's Largest Hydroelectric Generating Plants

Ranked in Order of Existing and Planned Rated Capacity
Source: T.W. Mermel, Water Power & Dam Construction

Rank order	Name	Present megawatts	Ultimate megawatts	Year of initial operation
1	Itaipu, Brazil/Paraguay	—	12600	(1983)
2	Grand Coulee, USA	7460	10830	1942
3	Guri (final stage), (Raul Leoni), Venezuela	2800	10060	1968
4	Tucurui, Brazil	—	6480	(1983)
5	Sayan-Shushensk, USSR	—	6400	1980
6	Corpus Christi, Argentina/Paraguay	—	6000	(1990)
7	Krasnoyarsk, USSR	6000	6000	1968
8	La Grande 2, Canada	—	5328	(1982)
9	Churchill Falls, Canada	5225	—	1971
10	Bratsk, USSR	4600	4600	1964
11	Ust-Ilim, USSR	3675	4500	1974
12	Yacyretá-Apipe, Argentina/Paraguay	—	4050	(1986)
13	Cabora Bassa, Mozambique	2000	4000	1975
14	Chief Joseph, USA	1500	3669	1956
15	Oak Creek, USA	—	3600	(1985)
16	Rogun, USSR	—	3600	(1985)
17	Pati, Argentina	3300	—	(1990)
18	Paulo Afonso, Brazil	1524	3409	1955
19	Ilha Solteira, Brazil	3200	3200	1973
20	Brumley Gap, USA	—	3000	(1985)
21	Powell Mountain, USA	—	3000	(1985)
22	John Day, USA	2160	2700	1969
23	Nurek, USSR	900	2700	1976
24	Revelstoke, Canada	—	2700	(1983)
25	Gezhouba, China	—	2700	(1986)
26	Sao-Simao, Brazil	2680	2680	1979
27	Mica, Canada	1736	2610	1976
28	Volgograd 22nd Congress, USSR	2530	2530	1958
29	Itaparica, Brazil	—	2500	(1985)
30	Bennett W.A.C. (Portage Mt.), Canada	2416	2416	1968
31	Chicoasén, Mexico	—	2400	1980
32	Atatürk, Turkey	—	2400	(1987)
33	Volga-V.I. Lenin (Kuibyshev, USSR	2300	2300	1955
34	Chapeton, Argentina	2300	2300	(1987)
35	Iron Gates, Romania/Yugoslavia	—	2300	1970
36	La Grande 3, Canada	—	2300	(1982)
37	Foz do Areia, Brazil	—	2250	(1983)
38	Bath County, USA	—	2100	(1985)
39	High Aswan, Egypt	2100	2100	1967
40	Tarbela, Pakistan	1400	2100	1977
41	Piedra de Aquila, Argentina	—	2100	(1989)
42	Itumbiara, Brazil	—	2080	(1982)
43	La Grande 4, Canada	—	2032	(1984)
44	Salto Santiago, Brazil	—	2000	1980
45	Tehri, India	—	2000	(1990)
46	Robert Moses Niagara, USA	1950	1950	1961
47	Salto Grande, Argentina/Uruguay	—	1890	1979
48	Dinorwic, Great Britain	—	1800	(1982)
49	Ludington, USA	1872	1872	1973
50	Saunders-Moses, Canada/USA	1824	1824	1958

Non-Federal Hydroelectric Plants in U.S.

Capacities of 150,000 Kilowatts or More as of Jan 1, 1981
Source: Energy Information Administration, U.S. Energy Department
Auxiliary and pumped storage units are not included in hydroelectric capacities.

Plant	State	Owner	Kilowatts
Robert Moses, (Niagara)	New York	Power Authority State of New York	1,950,000
Rocky Reach	Washington	Chelan County PUD[1]	1,213,950
Robert Moses, (Massena)	New York	Power Authority State of New York	912,000
Wanapum	Washington	Grant County PUD No. 2	831,250
Priest Rapids	Washington	Grant County PUD No. 2	788,500
Wells	Washington	Douglas County PUD No. 1	774,300
Boundary	Washington	Seattle Department of Lighting	634,600
Rock Island	Washington	Chelan County PUD No. 1	212,100
Brownlee	Idaho	Idaho Power Company	585,400
Conowingo	Maryland	Susquehanna Pow. Co., Phila. Elec. Pow. Co.	474,480
Smith Mt.	Virginia	Appalachian Power Company	432,250
Noxon Rapids	Montana	The Washington Water Power Company	396,880
Hells Canyon	Oregon	Idaho Power Company	391,500
Ross	Washington	Seattle Department of Lighting Company	360,000
Cowans Ford	North Carolina	Duke Power Company	350,000
Mossyrock	Washington	City of Tacoma	300,000
New Colgate	California	Yuba County Water Agency	284,400
Round Butte	Oregon	Portland General Electric Company	247,050
Safe Harbor	Pennsylvania	Safe Harbor Water Power Corporation	230,000
Walter Bouldin[1]	Alabama	Alabama Power Company	225,000
Swift No. 1	Washington	Pacific Power and Light Company	204,000
Cabinet Gorge	Idaho	The Washington Water Power Company	200,000
Saluda	South Carolina	South Carolina Electric and Gas Company	197,500
Oxbow	Oregon	Idaho Power Company	190,000
White Rock	California	Sacramento Municipal Utility District	190,000
Gaston	North Carolina	Virginia Electric and Power Company	177,920
Lay Dam	Alabama	Alabama Power Company	177,000
Osage	Missouri	Union Electric Company of Missouri	172,000
Kerr	Montana	The Montana Power Company	168,000
James B. Black	California	Pacific Gas and Electric Company	154,800
Martin Dam	Alabama	Alabama Power Company	154,200

(1) Public utility district.

TRADE AND TRANSPORTATION

Notable Steamships and Motorships

Source: Lloyd's Register of Shipping as of July 23, 1981

Gross tonnage is a measurement of enclosed space (1 gross ton = 100 cu. ft.) Deadweight tonnage is the weight (long tons) of cargo, fuel, etc., which a vessel is designed to carry safely.

Name, registry	Dwght. ton.	Lgth. ft.	Bdth. ft.
Oil Tankers			
Seawise Giant, Liber.	564,763	1504.0	209.0
Pierre Guillaumat, Fr.	555,051	1359.0	206.0
Prairial, Fr.	554,974	1359.0	206.0
Bellamya, Fr.	553,662	1359.0	206.0
Batillus, Fr.	553,662	1358.0	206.0
Esso Atlantic, Liber.	516,893	1333.0	233.0
Esso Pacific, Liber.	516,423	1333.0	233.0
Nanny, Swed.	491,120	1194.0	259.0
Nissei Maru, Jap.	484,337	1243.0	203.0
Globtik London, Liber.	483,933	1243.0	203.0
Globtik Tokyo, Liber.	483,662	1243.0	203.0
Burmah Enterprise, U.K.	457,927	1241.0	224.0
Burmah Endeavour, U.K.	457,841	1241.0	223.0
Robinson, Liber.	431,232	1236.0	226.0
Coraggio, It.	423,798	1240.0	226.0
Berge Empress, Nor.	423,700	1252.0	223.0
Berge Emperor, Nor.	423,700	1285.0	223.0
Hilda Knudsen, Nor.	423,639	1240.0	226.0
Esso Deutschland, W. Ger.	421,681	1240.0	226.0
Jinko Maru, Jap.	413,549	1200.0	229.0
David Packard, Liber.	413,115	1200.0	229.0
Aiko Maru, Jap.	413,012	1200.0	229.0
Chevron South America, Liber.	412,612	1200.0	229.0
Chevron No. Amer., Liber.	412,612	1200.0	229.0
World Petrobras, Liber.	411,508	1187.0	229.0
Nai Superba, It.	409,400	1253.0	207.0
Nai Genova, It.	409,400	1253.0	207.0
Al Rekkah, Kuw.	407,822	1200.0	229.0
Esso Japan, Liber.	406,640	1187.0	229.0
Esso Tokyo, Liber.	406,258	1187.0	229.0
U.S.T. Atlantic, U.S.	404,531	1188.0	228.0
Bulk, Ore, Bulk Oil, & Ore Oil Carriers			
World Gala, Liber.	282,462	1109.0	179.0
Weser Ore, Liber.	278,734	1099.0	170.0
Docecanyon, Liber.	275,589	1113.0	180.0
Jose Bonifacio Braz.	270,355	1106.0	179.0
Licorne Pacifique, Fr.	269,007	1111.0	176.0
Usa Maru, Jap.	268,767	1105.0	179.0
Cast Narwhal, Liber.	268,728	1101.0	176.0
Rhine Ore, Pan.	264,999	1099.0	170.0
Mary R. Koch, Liber.	264,999	1099.0	170.0
Lauderdale, U.K.	264,591	1101.0	176.0
Licorne Atlantique, Fr.	262,411	1101.0	176.0
Hoegh Hood, Nor.	249,259	1069.0	170.0
Hoegh Hill, Nor.	249,259	1069.0	170.0
World Truth, Liber.	249,223	1069.0	170.0
Seiko Maru, Jap.	248,228	1069.0	170.0
Konkar Dinos, Gr.	234,752	1075.0	160.0
World Recovery, Liber.	231,054	1075.0	161.0
Rimula, U.K.	231,048	1091.0	149.0
Berge Brioni, Nor.	227,558	1030.0	165.0
Berge Adria, Nor.	227,558	1030.0	164.0
Andros Antares, Liber.	227,480	1061.0	158.0
Rapana, U.K.	227,408	1091.0	149.0
Ruhr Ore, Liber.	227,086	1096.0	149.0
Alva Bay, U.K.	225,898	1091.0	149.0
Konkar Theodoros, Gr.	225,162	1091.0	164.0
Alva Sea U.K.	225,010	1090.0	149.0
Andros Atlas, Gr.	224,074	1061.0	158.0
Andros Aries, Gr.	223,605	1061.0	158.0
World Lady, Liber.	219,080	1075.0	164.0
World Era, Liber.	218,957	1075.0	164.0
Tantalus, U.K.	218,035	1075.0	164.0
Atsuta Maru, Jap.	271,451	1075.0	164.0
Tsurumi Maru, Jap.	217,273	1075.0	164.0
World's Largest Passenger Ships			
Norway, Nor.	70,202	1035.0	110.0
Queen Elizabeth 2, U.K.	67,140	963.0	105.0
Canberra, U.K.	44,807	818.0	102.0
Oriana, U.K.	41,920	804.0	97.0
United States, U.S.	38,216	990.0	101.0
Rotterdam, Neth. Ant.	37,783	748.0	94.0
Leonardo Da Vinci, It.	33,340	767.0	92.0
Eugenio C., It.	30,567	713.0	96.0

Name, registry	Dwght. ton.	Lgth. ft.	Bdth. ft.
Container, Liquefied Gas, Misc. Ships			
Hoegh Gandria, Nor.	95,683	943.0	142.0
Golar Freeze, Liber.	85,158	943.0	142.0
Khannur, Liber.	84,855	963.0	136.0
Gimi, Liber.	84,855	963.0	136.0
Hilli, Liber.	84,855	961.0	136.0
Lake Charles, U.S.	83,744	936.0	149.0
Louisiana, U.S.	83,729	936.0	149.0
LNG Libra, U.S.	83,729	936.0	149.0
LNG Taurus, U.S.	83,729	936.0	149.0
LNG Virgo, U.S.	83,729	936.0	149.0
LNG Capricorn, U.S.	83,608	936.0	149.0
LNG Gemini, U.S.	83,608	936.0	149.0
LNG Leo, U.S.	83,601	936.0	149.0
LNG Aries, U.S.	83,102	936.0	149.0
LNG Aquarius, U.S.	83,102	936.0	143.0
Mostefa Ben-Boulaid, Alger.	82,243	914.0	134.0
Bachir Chihani, Alger.	80,328	924.0	136.0
Larbi Ben M'Hidi, Alger.	80,328	924.0	136.0
Ben Franklin, Fr.	80,071	894.0	134.0
Nestor, Ber.	78,915	902.0	138.0
Methania, Belg.	78,511	918.0	136.0
Edouard L.D., Fr.	78,212	920.0	136.0
Pollenger, U.K.	76,496	857.0	131.0
Norman Lady, U.K.	76,416	818.0	131.0
Mourad Didouche, Alger.	74,741	900.0	137.0
El Paso Savannah, U.S.	72,000	931.0	140.0
El Paso Southern, U.S.	69,472	948.0	135.0
El Paso Howard Boyd, U.S.	69,472	948.0	135.0
El Paso Arzew, U.S.	69,472	948.0	135.0
Gastor, Pan.	68,247	902.0	138.0
El Paso Consolidated, Liber.	66,808	920.0	136.0
El Paso Sonatrach, Liber.	66,807	920.0	136.0
El Paso Paul Kayser, Liber.	66,807	920.0	136.0
Tenaga Empat, Malays.	66,800	924.0	136.0
Palace Tokyo, Jap.	64,378	807.0	131.0
Kurama Maru, Jap.	59,294	898.0	105.0
Cardigan Bay, U.K.	58,899	950.0	106.0
Tokyo Bay, U.K.	58,496	950.0	106.0
Liverpool Bay, U.K.	58,496	950.0	106.0
Benavon, U.K.	58,440	950.0	106.0
Kasuga Maru, Jap.	58,440	948.0	105.0
City of Edinburgh, U.K.	58,284	950.0	106.0
Benalder, U.K.	58,283	950.0	106.0
Hamburg Express, W. Ger.	58,088	943.0	106.0
Tokio Express, W. Ger.	58,082	943.0	106.0
Bremen Express, W. Ger.	57,535	941.0	106.0
Hongkong Express, W. Ger.	57,525	941.0	106.0
Korrigan, Fr.	57,249	946.0	105.0
Esso Fuji, Pan.	55,896	807.0	131.0
Esso Westernport, Liber.	54,057	838.0	116.0
City of Durban, U.K.	53,790	848.0	106.0
Barcelona, U.K.	53,784	848.0	106.0
Geomitra, U.K.	53,128	849.0	114.0
Genota, U.K.	53,128	849.0	113.0
S.A. Waterberg, So. Afr.	53,050	848.0	106.0
S.A. Winterberg, So. Afr.	53,050	848.0	106.0
S.A. Sederberg So. Afr.	53,023	848.0	106.0
S.A. Helderberg So. Afr.	53,023	848.0	106.0
Transvaal, W. Germ.	52,608	848.0	106.0
Largs Bay, Neth.	52,562	848.0	106.0
Nedlloyd Hoorn, Neth.	52,553	848.0	106.0
Ortelius, Belg.	52,444	848.0	106.0
Toyama, Nor.	52,196	902.0	106.0
Elbe Maru, Jap.	51,623	882.0	105.0
Kitano Maru, Jap.	51,269	856.0	105.0
Kamakura Maru, Jap.	51,139	856.0	105.0
Rhine Maru, Jap.	51,040	856.0	105.0
Nuclear Powered Merchant Ships			
Arktika, USSR	18,172	485.0	98.0
Otto Hahn, W. Ger.	16,871	564.0	76.0
Savannah, U.S.	15,585	595.0	78.0
Lenin, USSR	13,366	439.0	90.0
Mutsu, Jap.	8,214	428.0	62.0

Merchant Fleets of the World

Source: Maritime Administration, U.S. Commerce Department

Oceangoing steam and motor ships of 1,000 gross tons and over as of Dec. 31, 1979, excludes ships operating exclusively on the Great Lakes and inland waterways and special types such as channel ships, icebreakers, cable ships, etc., and merchant ships owned by any military force. Tonnage is in thousands. Gross tonnage is a volume measurement; each cargo gross ton represents 100 cubic ft. of enclosed space. Deadweight tonnage is the carrying capacity of a ship in long tons (2,240 lbs.).

Country of registry	Total no.	Gross tons	Dwt. tons	Bulk carriers No.	Dwt.	Freighters No.	Dwt.	Tankers No.	Dwt.
Total-All Countries	24,798	382,649	650,902	4,714	182,319	14,329	120,494	5,260	345,880
United States[1]	865	15,564	23,589	21	621	469	6,723	307	15,784
Privately-Owned . . .	569	12,967	20,540	21	621	257	4,406	285	15,462
Government-Owned .	296	2,596	3,049	—	—	212	2,316	22	322
Algeria	69	1,198	1,814	6	126	39	293	24	1,394
Argentina.	201	2,167	3,280	29	1,041	111	1,069	59	1,167
Australia	76	1,412	2,193	29	1,323	33	365	14	505
Bangladesh	29	251	363	1	93	23	221	4	43
Belgium.	69	1,639	2,589	26	1,467	29	430	13	677
Brazil	294	3,935	6,556	39	2,405	190	1,568	61	2,578
British Colonies	216	3,312	5,272	63	2,575	122	853	28	1,837
*Bulgaria.	114	1,147	1,685	39	738	53	375	20	571
Canada.	101	593	909	14	401	35	167	46	336
Chile	49	533	846	9	377	34	353	6	116
*China (People's Rep.) .	645	6,227	9,372	85	2,839	462	4,665	81	1,800
China (Taiwan)	170	1,859	2,937	33	1,197	119	1,037	13	655
Colombia.	44	282	368	—	—	37	295	4	46
*Cuba	87	664	897	7	83	66	686	11	110
Cyprus	457	2,053	2,991	24	355	404	2,302	21	314
*Czechoslovakia	17	155	232	5	163	12	70	—	—
Denmark.	290	4,801	8,090	36	1,142	175	1,510	72	5,429
Ecuador	29	231	311	—	—	16	148	11	150
Egypt	89	461	624	—	—	63	352	16	220
Finland	179	2,221	3,591	41	888	93	504	36	2,175
France	359	11,196	19,884	50	2,869	183	2,048	124	14,961
*German Dem. Republic	157	1,307	1,808	20	401	127	1,000	8	400
Germany (Fed. Rep.) . .	502	7,735	12,485	49	2,886	386	3,946	64	5,644
Ghana	26	148	198	—	—	26	198	—	—
Greece	2,876	37,359	63,542	857	26,280	1,564	15,042	395	22,002
Honduras.	40	185	223	—	—	34	198	5	16
India	363	5,598	9,100	105	4,462	221	2,599	30	1,999
Indonesia.	239	968	1,343	9	131	191	989	28	162
Iran	54	1,000	1,658	—	—	14	116	14	1,143
Iraq	35	1,217	2,245	—	—	14	116	21	2,129
Ireland	26	141	211	6	159	16	39	4	14
Israel	37	416	558	11	331	26	227	—	—
Italy	624	10,941	18,489	149	7,508	220	1,554	234	9,323
Ivory Coast.	18	165	214	—	—	18	214	—	—
Japan.	1,751	35,980	61,192	500	21,814	756	6,838	487	32,506
*Korea (People's Dem.)	23	136	202	2	52	16	99	4	50
Korea (Republic of) . . .	362	3,748	6,218	99	2,183	206	1,404	57	2,632
Kuwait	99	2,484	4,158	2	18	76	1,451	20	2,687
Lebanon	73	201	267	1	6	71	254	—	—
Liberia	2,380	81,559	158,702	920	44,729	567	6,357	887	107,569
Libya	27	836	1,530	—	—	13	46	14	1,484
Malaysia	62	573	848	11	476	44	274	4	91
Maldives	31	103	134	—	—	30	129	—	—
Malta	25	109	159	4	65	16	77	4	15
Mexico	63	806	1,236	6	189	21	167	36	880
Morocco	44	324	536	3	99	24	103	17	334
Netherlands	450	4,999	8,165	27	1,054	357	2,481	62	4,611
New Zealand	26	208	255	7	33	16	141	3	82
Nigeria	28	381	575	—	—	27	310	1	265
Norway	632	22,068	39,494	163	10,779	192	1,944	254	26,703
Pakistan	48	424	570	1	17	41	500	—	—
Panama	2,347	21,590	35,257	369	9,350	1,666	12,766	273	12,894
Peru	46	478	753	11	352	26	277	8	119
Philippines	200	1,400	2,166	21	839	135	802	33	501
Poland	303	3,119	4,631	78	2,048	208	1,607	13	965
Portugal	81	1,198	2,020	4	116	53	410	22	1,483
*Romania	184	1,673	2,498	43	1,138	132	782	8	577
Saudi Arabia	73	1,371	2,397	4	184	32	177	35	2,031
Singapore	667	7,505	12,341	82	2,683	458	4,042	116	5,564
South Africa	33	614	775	6	282	25	433	2	61
Spain	506	7,134	12,656	68	2,261	304	1,426	122	8,925
Sweden	233	4,112	6,899	31	1,320	135	1,353	65	4,220
Switzerland	26	240	364	6	207	17	149	3	9
Thailand	62	337	506	1	2	43	312	18	193
Tunisia	21	112	161	2	32	14	63	5	66
Turkey	168	1,259	1,931	21	764	108	561	28	580
United Arab Emirates. .	12	109	197	—	—	9	49	2	138
United Kingdom	1,110	25,330	41,937	236	11,459	514	5,387	348	25,018
U.S.S.R.[2]	2,512	16,333	21,590	156	3,106	1,828	10,996	470	7,349
Uruguay	17	169	271	1	22	11	80	5	169
Venezuela	71	700	1,029	5	87	51	458	15	484
Vietnam	35	173	264	3	38	28	175	4	50
Yugoslavia	253	2,315	3,540	49	1,502	183	1,649	13	352
Zaire	8	77	116	—	—	7	101	—	—

*Source material limited. (1) Excludes 59 non-merchant ships currently in the National Defense Reserve Fleet. (2) Includes U.S. Government-owned ships transferred to USSR under lend-lease agreements and still under that registry.

U.S. Foreign Trade with Leading Countries

Source: Office of Planning and Research, U.S. Commerce Department

(millions of dollars)

Exports from the U.S. to the following areas and countries and imports into the U.S. from those areas and countries:	Exports			Imports		
	1978	1979	1980	1978	1979	1980
Total	$143,663	$181,816	$220,705	$171,978	$206,256	$240,834
Western Hemisphere	50,394	61,555	74,114	56,473	68,509	78,489
Canada	28,374	33,096	35,395	33,525	38,046	41,455
20 Latin American Republics	20,185	26,259	36,030	18,556	24,767	29,851
Central American Common Market	1,571	1,655	1,951	1,478	1,895	1,849
Dominican Republic	473	610	795	537	665	786
Panama	438	528	699	153	191	330
Bahamas	284	334	396	977	1,587	1,382
Jamaica	313	292	305	390	375	383
Netherlands Antilles	377	412	448	1,262	1,830	2,564
Trinidad and Tobago	330	462	680	1,425	1,559	2,378
Europe	43,608	60,026	71,372	37,985	43,547	47,849
OECD countries (excludes depend. and Yugo.)	39,405	53,514	66,654	36,072	41,272	45,952
Western Europe	39,929	54,342	67,512	36,483	41,681	46,416
European Economic Community	32,048	42,592	53,679	29,006	33,293	35,958
Belgium and Luxembourg	3,653	5,187	6,661	1,762	1,741	1,914
Denmark	585	732	863	694	707	725
France	4,166	5,587	7,485	4,051	4,768	5,247
Germany, Federal Republic of	6,957	8,478	10,960	9,962	10,955	11,681
Ireland	527	695	836	320	323	411
Italy	3,361	4,362	5,511	4,102	4,918	4,313
Netherlands	5,683	6,917	8,669	1,602	1,853	1,910
United Kingdom	7,116	10,635	12,694	6,514	8,028	9,755
European Free Trade Association	...	...	...			
Austria	260	312	448	407	379	388
Finland	215	337	505	368	449	439
Iceland	39	48	79	174	226	200
Norway	558	688	843	1,190	1,267	2,632
Portugal	525	691	911	180	244	256
Sweden	1,091	1,515	1,767	1,328	1,652	1,617
Switzerland	1,728	3,660	3,781	1,820	2,076	2,787
Greece	699	812	922	167	183	292
Spain	1,884	2,506	3,179	1,257	1,303	1,209
Turkey	358	354	540	175	201	175
Yugoslavia	475	757	756	395	389	446
Eastern Europe	3,679	5,684	3,860	1,502	1,866	1,433
USSR	2,252	3,607	1,513	539	874	453
Asia	39,630	48,771	60,168	58,264	66,739	78,848
Near East	12,412	11,030	11,900	11,814	14,989	17,280
Iran	3,684	1,021	23	2,877	2,784	339
Iraq	317	442	724	243	618	352
Israel	1,925	1,855	2,045	720	750	943
Jordan	235	334	407	1	4	3
Kuwait	745	765	886	50	87	472
Lebanon	142	227	303	15	15	33
Saudi Arabia	4,370	4,875	5,769	5,307	7,983	12,509
Syria	143	229	239	37	165	26
Japan	12,885	17,581	20,790	24,458	26,248	30,701
East and South Asia	14,331	20,160	27,478	21,999	25,502	30,867
Bangladesh	170	204	292	79	88	85
China, People's Republic of	822	1,724	3,755	324	592	1,054
China, Republic of	2,342	3,272	4,337	5,170	5,902	6,850
Hong Kong	1,625	2,083	2,686	3,474	3,995	4,736
India	948	1,167	1,689	979	1,038	1,098
Indonesia	751	982	1,545	3,607	3,621	5,183
Korea, Republic of	3,160	4,190	4,685	3,746	4,047	4,147
Malaysia	728	932	1,337	1,519	2,146	2,577
Pakistan	496	529	642	84	120	128
Philippines	1,041	1,570	1,999	1,207	1,490	1,730
Singapore	1,462	2,330	3,033	1,068	1,467	1,920
Thailand	629	961	1,263	439	600	816
Oceania	3,464	4,319	4,876	2,350	3,072	3,392
Australia	2,912	3,617	4,093	1,659	2,164	2,509
New Zealand and Samoa	409	534	599	528	709	703
Africa	5,886	6,299	9,060	16,904	24,382	32,251
Algeria	374	404	542	3,482	4,943	6,577
Canary Islands	91	113	158	12	8	6
Egypt	1,134	1,433	1,874	105	381	458
Gabon	97	33	48	184	322	278
Ghana	126	91	127	215	225	206
Ivory Coast	93	128	185	415	363	288
Kenya	138	61	141	51	50	54
Liberia	108	108	113	133	136	128
Libya	425	468	509	3,779	5,256	7,124
Morocco	406	271	344	44	40	35
Nigeria	985	632	1,150	4,709	8,162	10,905
South Africa, Rep. of	1,080	1,413	2,464	2,259	2,616	3,321
Sudan	157	103	143	14	16	17
Tunisia	83	175	174	21	95	60
Zaire	83	113	155	225	286	361

U.S. Exports and Imports of Leading Commodities

Source: Office of Planning and Research, U.S. Commerce Department (millions of dollars)

Commodity	Exports 1978	Exports 1979	Exports 1980	Imports 1978	Imports 1979	Imports 1980
Food and live animals	**18,311**	**22,251**	**27,744**	**13,522**	**15,170**	**15,763**
Cattle, except for breeding	...	...	...	250	236	228
Meat and preparations	958	1,127	1,293	1,856	2,539	2,346
Cheese	...	...	...	270	293	NA
Dairy products and eggs	190	161	255	...	304	318
Fish	837	1,029	915	2,212	2,639	2,612
Grains and preparations	11,634	14,454	18,079	155	178	NA
Wheat, including flour	4,532	5,492	6,586	...	...	...
Rice	929	850	1,285	...	...	...
Grains and animal feed	1,921	2,318	2,878	92	298	331
Fruits and nuts	1,335	} 2,130	2,930 {	1,126	859	859
Vegetables	554			711	1,203	1,188
Sugar	...	...	...	723	974	1,988
Coffee, green	...	...	...	3,728	3,820	3,872
Cocoa or cacao beans	...	...	...	667	555	395
Tea	...	...	...	115	126	131
Spices	...	...	...	144	139	NA
Beverages and Tobacco	**2,293**	**2,337**	**2,663**	**2,221**	**2,565**	**2,772**
Alcoholic beverages	...	...	...	1,744	2,013	2,220
Tobacco and manufactures	2,107	2,092	2,390	396	436	422
Beverages and other tobacco	186	245	273	81	117	NA
Crude materials, inedible, except fuels	**15,555**	**20,756**	**23,791**	**9,294**	**10,653**	**10,496**
Hides and skins	695	992	694	248	139	88
Soybeans, oilseeds, peanuts	5,864	5,708	5,883	...	...	...
Synthetic rubber	369	579	695	...	...	...
Rubber, including latex	...	...	...	840	897	816
Lumber and rough wood	1,828	2,797	2,675	2,736	2,913	2,134
Wood pulp and pulpwood	817	1,644	2,454	1,125	1,506	1,725
Textile fibers and wastes	2,302	2,198	2,864	248	231	242
Ores and metal scrap	1,839	3,324	4,518	2,813	3,249	3,696
Mineral fuels and related mat'ls	**3,881**	**5,621**	**7,982**	**42,096**	**59,998**	**79,058**
Coal	2,046	3,328	4,523	...	...	...
Petroleum and products	1,564	1,918	2,833	39,104	56,036	73,771
Natural gas	194	180	NA	2,000	3,526	5,155
Animal and vegetable oils and fats	**1,521**	**1,845**	**1,946**	**511**	**740**	**533**
Chemicals	**12,623**	**17,308**	**20,740**	**6,430**	**7,479**	**8,583**
Medicines and pharmaceuticals	1,404	1,591	1,932	449	441	508
Fertilizers, manufactured	1,091	1,404	2,265	869	976	1,104
Plastic materials and resins	2,088	3,241	3,884	518	626	NA
Machinery and transport equip.	**59,268**	**70,495**	**84,629**	**47,590**	**53,677**	**60,546**
Machinery	38,105	44,745	55,790	24,752	28,044	31,904
Aircraft engines and parts	1,142	1,423	1,915	285	328	NA
Auto engines and parts	1,364	1,631	1,688	2,090	1,949	NA
Agricultural machinery	844	2,636	3,104	489	711	682
Tractors and parts	493	1,547	1,809	848	1,205	NA
Office machines and computers	5,006	6,475	8,709	2,254	2,500	2,929
Transport equipment	21,163	25,750	28,839	22,838	25,634	28,642
Road motor vehicles and parts	12,148	15,077	14,590	20,579	22,075	24,134
Aircraft and parts except engines	8,203	9,719	12,816	602	1,078	1,885
Other manufactured goods	**22,644**	**32,100**	**42,714**	**46,296**	**51,069**	**55,900**
Tires and tubes	280	353	511	923	1,136	1,143
Wood and manufactures, exc. furniture	356	2,797	2,675	1,219	855	632
Paper and manufactures	1,597	1,967	2,831	2,923	3,357	3,587
Glassware and pottery	574	...	...	1,048	1,097	1,224
Diamonds, excl. industrial	457	...	...	1,973	1,862	2,252
Nonmetallic mineral manuf.	1,597	1,948	2,209	...	...	...
Metals and manufactures	5,856	3,432	4,205	15,712	17,458	18,718
Pig iron and ferroalloys	...	2,342	3,123	573	702	NA
Iron and steel-mill products	1,646	2,227	2,998	6,681	6,764	6,686
Platinum group metals	...	...	...	430	800	NA
Nonferrous base metals	1,048	1,609	2,964	4,367	6,320	7,623
Other manuf. of metals	3,107	3,432	4,205	3,333	3,671	3,731
Textiles, other than clothing	2,225	3,189	3,632	2,200	2,216	2,493
Clothing	650	931	1,203	5,657	5,874	6,427
Footwear	...	...	...	2,585	2,861	2,808
Furniture	348	385	521	875	1,035	NA
Scientific and photo equip., photo supplies	4,350	5,514	6,763	1,739	1,912	NA
Printed matter	812	956	1,097	479	529	613
Clocks and watches	...	138	133	947	946	1,097
Toys, games, sporting goods	669	882	1,012	1,274	1,665	1,914
Artworks and antiques	...	...	...	1,312	1,487	2,672
Other transactions	**5,030**	**9,103**	**8,496**	**4,018**	**4,905**	**7,183**
Total	**143,663**	**181,816**	**220,705**	**171,978**	**206,256**	**240,834**

U.S. Merchandise Exports and Imports, by Continent

Source: Office of Planning and Research, U.S. Commerce Department (millions of dollars)

	Exports				General imports			
Year	Western Hemis.	Europe	Asia & Oceania	Africa	Western Hemis.	Europe	Asia & Oceania	Africa
1965	9,932	9,397	7,129	1,071	9,257	6,292	4,999	867
1970	15,611	14,817	11,294	1,502	16,928	11,395	10,515	1,090
1974	35,746	30,070	28,937	3,204	40,332	24,410	28,943	6,551
1975	38,843	32,732	31,246	4,266	37,773	21,465	28,590	8,277
1976	41,074	35,900	33,229	4,396	43,356	23,645	41,131	12,522
1977	43,751	37,304	35,295	4,564	50,697	28,801	51,210	16,950
1978	50,394	43,608	44,228	4,752	56,473	37,985	60,719	16,799
1979	61,555	60,026	53,090	6,299	68,509	43,547	69,811	24,382
1980	74,114	71,371	65,044	9,060	78,489	47,850	82,240	32,251

Value of U.S. Exports, Imports, and Merchandise Balance

(millions of dollars)

	Principal Census trade totals					Other Census totals		
Year	U.S. exports and reexports excluding military grant-aid	U.S. general imports f.a.s. transaction values[1]	U.S. merchandise balance f.a.s.[1]	U.S. general imports c.i.f.	U.S. balance exports f.a.s. imports c.i.f.	Military grant-aid shipments	Exports of domestic merchandise	Re-exports
1950	9,997	8,954	1,043	—	—	282	10,146	133
1955	14,298	11,566	2,732	—	—	1,256	15,426	128
1960	19,659	15,073	4,586	—	—	949	20,408	201
1965	26,742	21,427	5,315	—	—	773	27,178	343
1970[2]	42,664	40,114	2,550	42,591	73	565	42,590	634
1975[2]	107,589	96,570	11,019	103,843	3,746	461	106,561	1,489
1979[2]	181,651	206,256	−24,605	218,858	−37,208	165	178,406	3,225
1980[2]	220,549	240,034	−20,200	252,004	−32,255	150	210,430	4,113

Note: Export values include both commercially-financed shipments and shipments under government-financed programs such as AID and PL-480. (1) Prior to 1974, imports are customs values, i.e. generally at prices in principal foreign markets. (2) Beginning 1970, includes nonmonetary gold valued as follows in millions of dollars in 1970-79 respectively: Exports - 4, 24, 28, 50, 89, 459, 348, 1,079, 1,123, 4,929, and 3,705; imports - 162, 221, 358, 356, 397, 457, 331, 649, 898, 1,461, and 2,713.

U.S. Foreign Trade, by Economic Classes

(millions of dollars)

Economic class	1965	1970	1975	1977	1978	1979	1980
Exports, total	29,128	45,114	106,102	117,966	141,065	178,436	216,434
Excluding military grant-aid	...	...	105,641	117,899	140,980	178,271	216,278
Crude foods	2,587	2,748	11,804	9,438	12,723	15,787	19,362
Manufactured foods	1,590	1,921	4,221	5,356	6,648	7,581	9,516
Crude materials	2,887	4,492	10,883	13,976	15,654	20,088	23,765
Agricultural	1,942	2,524	5,747	8,804	10,470	11,893	12,779
Semimanufactures	4,114	6,866	12,815	14,107	18,907	30,983	37,638
Finished manufactures	16,008	26,563	66,379	75,084	87,133	103,997	126,152
Excluding military grant-aid	...	...	65,918	75,022	87,048	103,832	125,996
Imports, total[1]	22,293	40,748	96,902	147,848	173,276	207,086	241,297
Crude foods	2,008	2,579	3,642	7,065	7,240	7,689	7,735
Manufactured foods	1,877	3,519	5,953	6,755	8,128	9,624	10,245
Crude materials	3,709	4,126	23,570	40,822	40,123	56,003	76,135
Agricultural	864	797	1,280	1,732	1,971	2,339	2,307
Semimanufactures	4,964	7,263	17,326	24,182	29,171	34,298	33,865
Finished manufactures	8,871	22,464	46,411	69,025	88,614	99,473	111,963

(1) Customs values are shown for imports.

Total Exports and Exports Financed by Foreign Aid

(millions of dollars)

	1965	1970	1975	1977	1978	1979	1980
Exports, total	27,530	43,224	107,592	120,163	143,663	181,816	220,705
Agricultural commodities	6,306	7,349	22,097	24,234	29,777	35,212	41,757
Nonagricultural commodities	20,445	35,310	85,094	95,867	113,801	146,602	178,948
Manufactured goods (domestic)	17,439	29,343	70,950	80,453	94,535	116,678	143,971
Military grant—aid	779	565	461	62	85	165	156
Export financed under P.L.-480	1,323	1,021	1,181	1,074	1,144	1,239	1,094
Sales for foreign currency	899	276	—	—	—	—	—
Donations, including disaster relief	253	255	257	368	350	418	329
Long-term dollar credit sales	152	490	924	706	794	821	765
AID expend. for U.S. goods for export	—	—	665	802	988	710	673

Value of Principal Agricultural Exports

(millions of dollars)

Commodity	Avg. 1961-65	Avg. 1966-70	1965	1970	1975	1978	1979	1980
Wheat and wheat products	1,268	1,197	1,214	1,144	5,292	4,602	5,586	6,660
Feed grains	841	1,082	1,162	1,099	5,492	5,853	7,739	9,759
Rice	178	311	244	314	858	932	854	1,288
Fodders and feeds	179	386	278	496	987	609	838	1,126
Oilseeds and products	774	1,182	1,029	1,642	NA	8,175	8,886	9,393
Cotton, raw	630	408	495	377	991	1,740	2,198	2,864

Shortest Navigable Distances Between Ports

Source: Distances Between Ports. Defense Mapping Agency Hydrographic/Topographic Center

Distances shown are in nautical miles (1,852 meters or about 6,076.115 feet) To get statute miles, multiply by 1.15.

TO / FROM	New York	Montreal	Colon[1]
Algiers, Algeria	3,617	3,600	4,745
Amsterdam, Netherlands	3,438	3,162	4,825
Baltimore, Md.	417	1,769	1,901
Barcelona, Spain	3,714	3,697	4,842
Boston, Mass.	386	1,308	2,157
Buenos Aires, Argentina	5,817	6,455	5,472
Cape Town, S. Africa[2]	6,786	7,118	6,494
Cherbourg, France	3,154	2,878	4,541
Cobh, Ireland	2,901	2,603	4,308
Copenhagen, Denmark	3,846	3,570	5,233
Dakar, Senegal	3,335	3,566	3,694
Galveston, Tex.	1,882	3,165	1,492
Gibraltar[3]	3,204	3,187	4,332
Glasgow, Scotland	3,086	2,691	4,508
Halifax, N.S.	600	895	2,295
Hamburg, W. Germany	3,674	3,398	5,061
Hamilton, Bermuda	697	1,572	1,659
Havana, Cuba	1,186	2,473	998
Helsinki, Finland	4,309	4,033	5,696
Istanbul, Turkey	5,001	4,984	6,129
Kingston, Jamaica	1,474	2,690	551
Lagos, Nigeria	4,883	5,130	5,049
Lisbon, Portugal	2,972	2,943	4,152
Marseille, France	3,891	3,874	5,019
Montreal, Quebec	1,460		3,126
Naples, Italy	4,181	4,164	5,309
Nassau, Bahamas	962	2,274	1,166
New Orleans, La.	1,708	2,991	1,389
New York, N.Y.		1,460	1,974
Norfolk, Va.	294	1,700	1,779
Oslo, Norway	3,827	3,165	5,053
Piraeus, Greece	4,688	4,671	5,816
Port Said, Egypt	5,123	5,106	6,251
Rio de Janeiro, Brazil	4,770	5,354	4,367
St. John's, Nfld.	1,093	1,043	2,695
San Juan, Puerto Rico	1,399	2,445	993
Southampton, England	3,189	2,913	4,576

TO / FROM	San. Fran.	Vancouver	Panama[1]
Acapulco, Mexico	1,833	2,613	1,426
Anchorage, Alas.	1,872	1,444	5,093
Bombay, India	9,794	9,578	12,962
Calcutta, India	8,991	8,728	12,154
Colon, Panama[1]	3,298	4,076	44
Jakarta, Indonesia	7,641	7,360	10,637
Haiphong, Vietnam	6,496	6,231	9,673
Hong Kong	6,044	5,777	9,195
Honolulu, Hawaii	2,091	2,423	4,685
Los Angeles, Cal.	371	1,161	2,913
Manila, Philippines	6,221	5,976	9,347
Melbourne, Australia	6,970	7,343	7,928
Pusan, S. Korea	4,914	4,623	8,074
Ho Chi Min City, Vietnam	6,878	6,664	10,017
San Francisco, Cal.		812	3,245
Seattle, Wash.	807	126	4,020
Shanghai, China	5,396	5,110	8,566
Singapore	7,353	7,078	10,505
Suva, Fiji	4,749	5,183	6,325
Valparaiso, Chile	5,140	5,915	2,616
Vancouver, B.C.	812		4,032
Vladivostok, USSR	4,563	4,378	7,741
Yokohama, Japan	4,536	4,262	7,682

TO / FROM	Port Said	Cape Town[2]	Singapore
Bombay, India	3,049	4,616	2,441
Calcutta, India	4,695	5,638	1,649
Dar es Salaam, Tanzania	3,238	2,365	4,042
Jakarta, Indonesia	5,293	5,276	525
Hong Kong	6,462	7,006	1,454
Kuwait	3,360	5,176	3,833
Manila, Philippines	6,348	6,777	1,330
Melbourne, Australia	7,842	5,963	3,844
Ho Chi Min City, Vietnam	5,667	6,263	649
Singapore	5,018	5,614	
Yokohama, Japan	7,907	8,503	2,889

(1) Colon on the Atlantic is 44 nautical miles from Panama (port) on the Pacific. (2) Cape Town is 35 nautical miles northwest of the Cape of Good Hope. (3) Gibraltar (port) is 24 nautical miles east of the Strait of Gibraltar.

Notable Ocean Passages by Ships

Compiled by N.R.P. Bonsor

Sailing Vessels

Date	Ship		From	To	Nautical miles	Time D. H. M	Speed (knots)
1846	Yorkshire		Liverpool	New York	3150	16. 0. 0	8.46†
1853	Northern Light		San Francisco	Boston	—	76. 6. 0	—
1854	James Baines		Boston Light	Light Rock	—	12. 6. 0	—
1854	Flying Cloud		New York	San Francisco	15091	89. 0. 0	7.07†
1868-9	Thermopylae		Liverpool	Melbourne	—	63.18.15	—
—	Red Jacket		New York	Liverpool	3150	13. 1.25	10.05†
—	Starr King		50 S. Lat	Golden Gate	—	36. 0. 0	—
—	Golden Fleece		Equator	San Francisco	—	12.12. 0	—
1905	Atlantic		Sandy Hook	England	3013	12. 4. 0	10.32
Atlantic Crossing by Passenger Steamships							
1819 (5/22 - 6/20)	Savannah (a)	US	Savannah	Liverpool	—	29. 4. 0	—
1838 (5/7 - 5/22)	Great Western	Br	New York	Avonmouth	3218	14.15.59	9.14
1840 (8/4 - 8/14)	Britannia	Br	Halifax	Liverpool	2610	9.21.44	10.98†
1854 (6/28 - 7/7)	Baltic	US	Liverpool	New York	3037	9.16.52	13.04
1856 (8/6 - 8/15)	Persia	Br	Sandy Hook	Liverpool	3046	8.23.19	14.15†
1876 (12/16-12/24)	Britannic	Br	Sandy Hook	Queenstown	2882	7.12.41	15.94
1895 (5/18 - 5/24)	Lucania	Br	Sandy Hook	Queenstown	2897	5.11.40	22.00
1898 (3/30 - 4/5)	Kaiser Wilhelm der Grosse	Ger	Needles	Sandy Hook	3120	5.20. 0	22.29
1901 (7/10 - 7/17)	Deutschland	Ger	Sandy Hook	Eddystone	3082	5.11. 5	23.51
1907 (10/6 - 10/10)	Lusitania	Br	Queenstown	Sandy Hook	2780	4.19.52	23.99
1924 (8/20 - 8/25)	Mauretania	Br	Ambrose	Cherbourg	3198	5. 1.49	26.25
1929 (7/17 - 7/22)	Bremen*	Ger	Cherbourg	Ambrose	3164	4.17.42	27.83
1933 (6/27 - 7/2)	Europa	Ger	Cherbourg	Ambrose	3149	4.16.48	27.92
1933 (8/11 - 8/16)	Rex	It	Gibraltar	Ambrose	3181	4.13.58	28.92
1935 (5/30 - 6/3)	Normandie*	Fr	Bishop Rock	Ambrose	2971	4. 3. 2	29.98
1938 (8/10 - 8/14)	Queen Mary	Br	Ambrose	Bishop Rock	2938	3.20.42	31.69
1952 (7/11 - 7/15)	United States	US	Bishop Rock	Ambrose	2906	3.12.12	34.51
1952 (7/3 - 7/7)	United States* (e)	US	Ambrose	Bishop Rock	2942	3.10.40	35.59
Other Ocean Passages							
1928 (June)	USS Lexington		San Pedro	Honolulu	2226	3. 0.36	30.66
1944 (Jul-Sep)	St. Roch (c) (Can)		Halifax	Vancouver	7295	86. 0. 0	—
1945 (7/16-7/19)	USS Indianapolis (d)		San Francisco	Oahu, Hawaii	2091	3. 2.20	28.07
1945 (11/26)	USS Lake Champlain		Gibraltar	Newport News	3360	4. 8.51	32.04
1950 (Jul-Aug)	USS Boxer		Japan	San Francisco	5000	7.18.36	26.80†

Date	Ship	From	To	Nautical miles	Time D. H. M	Speed (knots)
1951 (6/1-6/9)	USS Philippine Sea	Yokohama	Alameda	5000	7.13. 0	27.62†
1958 (2/25-3/4)	USS Skate (f)	Nantucket	Portland, Eng	3161	8.11. 0	15.57
1958 (3/23-3/29)	USS Skate (f)	Lizard, Eng	Nantucket	—	7. 5. 0	—
1958 (7/23-8/7)	USS Nautilus (g)	Pearl Harbor	Iceland (via N. Pole)	—	15. 0. 0	—
1960 (2/16-5/10)	USS Triton (h)	New London	Rehoboth, Del	41500	84. 0. 0	20.59†
1960 (8/15-8/20)	USS Seadragon (i)	Baffin Bay	NW Passage, Pac	850	6. 0. 0	—
1962 (10/30-11/11)	African Comet* (US)	New York	Cape Town	6786	12.16.22	22.03
1973 (8/20)	Sea-Land Exchange (k) (US)	Bishop Rock	Ambrose	2912	3.11.24	34.92
1973 (8/24)	Sea-Land Trade (US)	Kobe	Race Rock, BC	4126	5. 6. 0	32.75

† The time taken and/or distance covered is approximate and so, therefore, is the average speed.

* Maiden voyage. (a) The Savannah, a fully rigged sailing vessel with steam auxiliary (over 300 tons, 98.5 ft. long, beam 25.8 ft., depth 12.9 ft.) was launched in the East River in 1818. It was the first ship to use steam in crossing any ocean. It was supplied with engines and detachable iron paddle wheels. On its famous voyage it used steam 105 hours. (b) First Cunard liner. (c) First ship to complete NW Passage in one season. (d) Carried Hiroshima atomic bomb in World War II. (e) Set world speed record; average speed eastbound on maiden voyage 35.59 knots (about 41 m.p.h.). (f) First atomic submarine to cross Atlantic both ways submerged. (g) World's first atomic submarine also first to make undersea voyage under polar ice cap, 1,830 mi. from Point Barrow, Alaska, to Atlantic Ocean, Aug. 1-4, 1958, reaching North Pole Aug. 3. Second undersea transit of the North Pole made by submarine USS Skate Aug. 11, 1958, during trip from New London, Conn., and return. (h) World's largest submarine. Nuclear-powered Triton was submerged during nearly all its voyage around the globe. It duplicated the route of Ferdinand Magellan's circuit (1519-1522) 30,708 mi., starting from St. Paul Rocks off the NE coast of Brazil, Feb. 24-Apr. 25, 1960, then sailed to Cadiz, Spain, before returning home. (i) First underwater transit of Northwest Passage. (k) Fastest freighter crossing of Atlantic.

Commerce at Principal North American Ports
Handling 2,000,000 tons or more per year
Source: Corps of Engineers, Department of the Army; Statistics Canada. 1979 (short tons)

Port	Tons	Port	Tons
New Orleans, La.	167,135,226	Silver Bay, Minn.	9,330,372
New York, N.Y. and N.J.	163,620,900	Galveston Channel, Tex.	8,982,285
Houston Ship Channel, Tex.	117,550,908	Buffalo, N.Y.	8,840,496
Baton Rouge, La.	76,703,422	Camden-Gloucester, N.J.	8,835,762
Valdez Harbor, Alaska	65,452,418	Providence River and Harbor, R.I.	8,579,917
Beaumont, Tex. (Neches River)	58,136,896	Longview, Wash.	8,500,070
Philadelphia Harbor, Pa.	54,865,960	Gray Harbor, Ind.	8,274,812
Baltimore Harbor and Channels, Md.	51,444,637	Presque Isle Harbor, Mich.	8,121,748
Norfolk Harbor, Va.	48,650,778	Honolulu Harbor, Oahu, Hawaii	7,463,663
Tampa Harbor, Fla.	47,884,590	Coos Bay, Oreg.	7,050,873
Duluth-Superior Harbor, Minn. and Wis.	47,725,075	Oakland Harbor, Calif.	6,840,202
Corpus Christi, Tex.	46,422,792	Barbers Point Harbor, Oahu, Hawaii	6,154,541
Pittsburgh, Pa.	40,881,073	Sandusky Harbor, Ohio	5,972,652
Chicago, Ill.	38,692,988	Port Angeles Harbor, Wash.	5,844,270
Texas City Channel, Tex.	35,954,301	Grays Harbor and Chehalis River, Wash.	5,130,743
Lake Charles Deep Water Channel, La.	35,951,037	Lorain Harbor, Ohio	4,833,011
Mobile Harbor, Ala.	35,265,204	Fall River Harbor, Mass.	4,798,674
Long Beach Harbor, Calif.	33,347,303	Milwaukee Harbor, Wis.	4,679,800
Port Arthur, Tex.	32,773,346	Matagorda Ship Channel, Tex.	4,562,702
Marcus Hook, Pa., and vicinity	32,699,711	Mount Vernon, Ind.	4,256,382
Los Angeles Harbor, Calif.	31,749,483	Port Jefferson Harbor, N.Y.	4,231,607
Portland, Oreg.	29,146,461	Port Inland, Mich.	3,892,989
Toledo Harbor, Ohio	26,256,355	Vicksburg, Miss.	3,838,205
Boston, Mass.	26,242,672	Port Dolomite, Mich.	3,834,698
Pascagoula Harbor, Miss.	25,289,493	Miami Harbor, Fla.	3,576,771
Detroit, Mich.	24,995,987	Morehead City Harbor, N.C.	3,568,907
Paulsboro, N.J. and Vicinity	24,061,473	Portsmouth Harbor, N.H.	3,519,926
St. Louis (metropolitan)	21,644,333	Canaveral Harbor, Fla.	3,473,243
Connsaut Harbor, Ohio	21,478,061	Huron Harbor, Ohio	3,457,764
Seattle Harbor, Wash.	20,038,550	Penn Manor, Pa. and Vicinity	3,411,974
Freeport Harbor, Tex.	19,983,837	Greenville, Miss.	3,329,698
Cleveland Harbor, Ohio	19,470,349	St. Clair, Mich.	3,286,404
Richmond Harbor, Calif.	18,978,302	Wilmington Harbor, Del.	3,252,629
Indiana Harbor, Ind.	18,418,640	Bridgeport Harbor, Conn.	3,243,301
Huntington, W. Va.	16,502,610	Vancouver, Wash.	3,226,532
Jacksonville Harbor, Fla.	15,278,008	New London Harbor, Conn.	3,157,705
Tacoma Harbor, Wash.	15,193,551	Alpena, Mich.	2,942,149
New Castle, Del. and Vicinity	14,751,390	Green Bay Harbor, Wis.	2,839,326
Ashtabula Harbor, Ohio	14,602,645	Channel to Victoria, Tex.	2,807,135
Savannah Harbor, Ga.	13,527,771	Ludington Harbor, Mich.	2,764,888
Escanaba, Mich.	13,452,749	Nashville, Tenn.	2,671,506
Portland Harbor, Maine	13,262,431	Hempstead Harbor, N.Y.	2,621,631
Port Everglades Harbor, Fla.	13,030,616	Helena, Ark.	2,551,946
Memphis, Tenn.	12,346,022	Brownsville, Tex.	2,508,076
Cincinnati, Ohio	12,010,905	Minneapolis, Minn.	2,488,910
Two Harbors (Agate Bay), Minn.	11,932,715	Pensacola Harbor, Fla.	2,456,708
Taconite Harbor, Minn.	11,533,434	Astoria, Oreg.	2,437,137
Newport News, Va.	11,508,735	San Diego Harbor, Calif.	2,401,349
St. Paul, Minn.	11,248,111	Fairport Harbor, Ohio.	2,391,800
New Haven Harbor, Conn.	10,622,395	San Francisco Harbor, Calif.	2,353,799
Calcite, Mich.	10,319,551	Ketchikan Harbor, Alaska	2,202,032
San Juan Harbor, P.R.	10,122,084	Richmond, Va.	2,194,520
Charleston Harbor, S.C.	10,055,566	Bellingham Bay and Harbor, Wash.	2,131,654
Albany, N.Y.	9,658,112	Drummond Island, Mich.	2,047,047
Anacortes Harbor, Wash.	9,599,065		
Wilmington, N.C.	9,576,644		
Louisville, Ky.	9,537,268	**Commerce at Principal Canadian Ports**	
Harbor Island, Tex.	9,384,532	Vancouver, B.C.	46,802,549
Stoneport, Mich.	9,357,044	Sept-Isles, Que.	29,475,729
		Port Cartier, Que.	27,539,463

St. John, N.B.	15,417,850	Levis, Que.	4,503,037
Montreal, Que.	14,551,765	New Westminster, B.C.	3,678,811
Hamilton, Ont.	8,728,825	Port Alfred, Que.	3,498,411
Baie Comeau, Que.	8,223,111	Prince Rupert, B.C.	3,260,796
Quebec, Que.	6,621,085	Sorel, Que.	2,791,613
Sault Ste. Marie, Ont.	6,411,407	Trois Rivieres, Que.	2,761,825
Sarnia, Ont.	6,366,675	Windsor, Ont.	2,557,258
Halifax, N.S.	6,264,159	Contrecoeur, Que.	2,409,868
Port Hawkesbury, N.S.	5,561,448	Nanaimo, B.C.	2,379,148
Thunder Bay, Ont.	5,323,413	Pointe Noire, Que.	2,227,171

Commerce on U.S. Inland Waterways

Source: Corps of Engineers, Department of the Army 1979

Mississippi River System and Gulf Intracoastal Waterway

Waterway	Tons
Mississippi River, Minneapolis to the Gulf	430,170,679
Mississippi River, Minneapolis to St. Louis	68,604,662
Mississippi River, St. Louis to Cairo	80,435,159
Mississippi River, Cairo to Baton Rouge	137,009,630
Mississippi River, Baton Rouge to New Orleans.	314,174,557
Mississippi River, New Orleans to Gulf	285,407,808
Gulf Intracoastal Waterway	97,272,038
Mississippi River System	582,928,724

Ton-Mileage of Freight Carried on Inland Waterways

System	Ton-miles
Atlantic Coast waterways	31,929,470
Gulf Coast waterways	38,052,138
Pacific Coast waterways	14,144,892
Mississippi River System, including Ohio River and tributaries	218,776,279
Great Lakes system, U.S. commerce only	121,666,371
Total:	**420,154,863**

Important Waterways and Canals

The St. Lawrence & Great Lakes Waterway, the largest inland navigation system on the continent, extends from the Atlantic Ocean to Duluth at the western end of Lake Superior, a distance of 2,342 miles. With the deepening of channels and locks to 27 ft., ocean carriers are able to penetrate to ports in the Canadian interior and the American midwest.

The major canals are those of the St. Lawrence Great Lakes waterway — the 3 new canals of the St. Lawrence Seaway, with their 7 locks, providing navigation for vessels of 26-foot draught from Montreal to Lake Ontario; the Welland Ship Canal by-passing the Niagara River between Lake Ontario and Lake Erie with its 8 locks, and the Sault Ste. Marie Canal and lock between Lake Huron and Lake Superior. These 16 locks overcome a drop of 580 ft. from the head of the lakes to Montreal. From Montreal to Lake Ontario the former bottleneck of narrow, shallow canals and of slow passage through 22 locks has been overcome, giving faster and safer movement for larger vessels. The new locks and linking channels now accommodate all but the largest ocean-going vessels and the upper St. Lawrence and Great

Lakes are open to 80% of the world's saltwater fleet.

Subsidiary Canadian canals or branches include the St. Peters Canal between Bras d'Or Lakes and the Atlantic Ocean in Nova Scotia; the St. Ours and Chambly Canals on the Richelieu River, Quebec; the Ste. Anne and Carillon Canals on the Ottawa River; the Rideau Canal between the Ottawa River and Lake Ontario, the Trent and Murrary Canals between Lake Ontario and Georgian Bay in Ontario and the St. Andrew's Canal on the Red River. The commercial value of these canals is not great but they are maintained to control water levels and permit the passage of small vessels and pleasure craft. The Canso Canal, completed 1957, permits shipping to pass through the causeway connecting Cape Breton Island with the Nova Scotia mainland.

The Welland Canal overcomes the 326-ft. drop of Niagara Falls and the rapids of the Niagara River. It has 8 locks, each 859 ft. long, 80 ft. wide and 30 ft. deep. Regulations permit ships of 730-ft. length and 75-ft. beam to transit.

Fastest Scheduled Train Runs in U.S. and Canada

Source: Donald M. Steffee, figures are based on 1981 timetables

Passenger—(75 mph and over)

Railroad	Train	From	To	Dis. miles	Time min.	Speed mph.
Amtrak	Four trains	Rensselear	Hudson	28.0	20	84.0
Via Rail Canada	Turbotrain	Guildwood	Dorval	310.9	223	83.6
Via Rail Canada	Turbotrain	Dorval	Guildwood	310.9	224	83.2
Amtrak	Southwest Limited	Garden City	Lamar	99.9	73	82.1
Amtrak	Bankers	Wilmington	Baltimore	68.4	50	82.1
Amtrak	Colonial	Metro Park	Trenton	33.9	25	81.4
Amtrak	Seven trains	Wilmington[1]	Baltimore	68.4	51	80.5
Amtrak	Palmetto	New Brunswick	Trenton	25.4	19	80.2
Amtrak	Metroliners(2)	Newark	Trenton	48.1	36	80.2
Amtrak	Minute Man	Wilmington	Aberdeen	38.7	29	80.1
Amtrak	Southwest Limited	Dodge City	Hutchinson	120.1	90	80.1
Conrail	Jersey Arrow	Princeton Jct.	Newark	38.4	29	79.4
Amtrak	Seventeen trains	Wilmington[1]	Baltimore	68.4	52	78.9
Amtrak	Four trains	Metro Park[1]	Trenton	33.9	26	78.2
Amtrak	Merchants Limited	Newark	Trenton	48.1	37	78.0
Amtrak	Southwest Limited	Lamar	Garden City	99.9	77	77.8
Amtrak	Three trains	Wilmington	Baltimore	68.4	53	77.4
Amtrak	San Francisco Zephyr	Akron	McCook	142.9	111	77.2
Via Rail Canada	Rapido	Guildwood	Kingston	145.1	113	77.0
Via Rail Canada	Rapido	Dorval	Kingston	165.8	130	76.8
Via Rail Canada	Rapido	Kingston	Cornwall	107.9	85	76.2
Via Rail Canada	Rapido	Guildwood	Kingston	145.1	114	76.2
Amtrak	Liberty Express	Metro Park	Princeton Jct.	24.1	19	76.1
Amtrak	Eight trains	Trenton[1]	No. Philadelphia	27.9	22	76.1
Amtrak	Six trains	Wilmington	Baltimore	68.4	54	76.0
Amtrak	Three trains	Newark	Trenton	48.1	38	75.9
Amtrak	Palmetto	Trenton	Metro Park	33.9	27	75.3

(1) Runs listed in both directions

Freight — (62 mph and over)

Union Pacific	BASV	North Platte	Cheyenne	225.4	205	66.0
Union Pacific	Super Van	North Platte	Cheyenne	225.4	215	62.9
Santa Fe	Six trains	Gallup	Winslow	125.8	120	62.9
Santa Fe	No. 199	Seligman	Kingman	88.1	85	62.2

Fastest Scheduled Passenger Train Runs in Japan and European Countries

Country	Train	From	To	Dis. miles	Time min.	Speed mph.
France	TGV train	Macon	Monchanin	39.4	20	117.6
Japan	Hikari train	Nagoya	Yokohama	196.5	105	112.3
West Germany	Three trains	Hamm	Bielefeld	41.7	24	104.2
Great Britain	High Speed trains(3)	London	Bristol Parkway	111.7	65½	102.3
Italy	Rapido(2)	Rome¹	Chiusi	91.9	65	84.8
Sweden	No. 142	Skvode	Laxa	52.2	41	77.4

(1) Runs listed in both directions.

New High Speed Railroad Opened in France.

On September 27, 1981, the southern part (St. Florient to the outskirts of Lyons) of the new Paris-Lyons high speed rail line was opened to traffic. As a result, the distance between the two cities is shortened to 280.3 miles and train time is cut to 2hr., 40 min.—more than an hour faster than via the old route through Dijon. Overall average speed is 105.1 mph. On a trial run, February 26, 1981, one of the new trains attained a world's record speed of 237 mph. When the line is fully completed in another year or so, train time will be 2 hours, calling for a speed of over 130 mph.

Passenger Car Production, U.S. Plants

Source: Motor Vehicle Manufacturers Association of the U.S., Inc.

	1979	1980	1981 6 mos.		1979	1980	1981 6 mos.
American Motors Corp.				Versailles	11,864	1,866	—
Spirit/AMX (Gremlin)	64,363	54,223	20,510	Total Lincoln-Mercury	661,410	377,321	242,822
Concord	88,580	68,344	23,200	Total Ford Motor Co.	2,043,014	1,306,948	762,170
Pacer	5,729	—	—	**General Motors Corp.**			
Eagle (Matador)	25,964	42,158	14,774	Chevrolet	447,343	134,909	95,741
Total American Motors Corp.	184,636	164,725	58,484	Corvette	48,568	44,190	15,233
Chrysler Corp.				Monte Carlo	227,043	125,474	80,798
Horizon	169,981	145,036	84,672	Malibu	322,764	231,594	126,822
Reliant (Voyager)	6,312	75,822	130,858	Camaro	257,872	118,211	79,168
Volare	183,486	51,735	—	Citation	343,821	459,388	195,156
Caravelle	9,213	6,277	2,139	Cavalier/Monza	157,979	150,544	25,297
Gran Fury (Fury)	5,412	14,472	7,448	Chevette	413,648	454,068	174,265
Total Plymouth	374,404	293,342	225,117	Acadian	17,133	18,958	12,456
LeBaron	103,678	62,592	17,236	**Total Chevrolet**	2,236,171	1,737,336	805,436
Chrysler	77,749	19,871	4,862	Pontiac	144,486	50,512	8,050
Total Chrysler-Plymouth	555,831	375,805	247,215	Grand Prix	93,158	76,030	57,107
Omni	148,125	121,703	67,014	LeMans	88,652	64,870	35,048
Aries (Sportsman)	23,124	60,666	103,855	Firebird	194,033	79,568	38,411
Aspen	132,610	36,881	—	Phoenix	88,184	136,210	62,896
Diplomat	50,610	30,733	12,644	J-2000 Sunbird	105,998	149,239	22,937
St. Regis	25,846	13,186	3,682	T-1000			38,269
Total Dodge	380,315	263,169	187,195	**Total Pontiac**	714,511	556,429	262,718
Total Chrysler Corp.	936,146	638,974	434,410	Oldsmobile	365,327	233,845	152,959
Ford Motor Co.				Toronado	53,552	37,923	26,605
LTD (Ford)	167,170	91,135	40,886	Cutlass	509,726	395,784	253,130
LTD II	22,667	—	—	Omega	58,032	115,673	81,408
Thunderbird	264,451	117,856	37,314	Starfire	21,609	—	—
Escort	—	68,179	194,973	**Total Oldsmobile**	1,008,246	783,225	514,102
Granada	139,402	113,281	44,612	Buick	252,220	149,668	88,365
Fairmont	213,761	198,219	111,693	Riviera	58,029	44,525	31,424
Pinto	172,619	68,179	—	Century/Regal	330,560	370,880	234,817
Mustang	365,357	232,507	89,870	Skylark	121,625	218,502	134,452
Total Ford	1,381,604	929,627	519,348	Skyhawk	24,715	—	—
Marquis (Mercury)	100,937	55,524	33,073	**Total Buick**	787,149	783,575	489,058
Cougar XR-7	133,479	42,927	16,305	Cadillac	230,958	115,424	95,615
Cougar/Monarch	51,729	41,264	23,089	Eldorado	66,565	54,267	35,330
Zephyr	62,837	66,657	24,485	Seville	48,308	34,300	14,472
Lynx	—	37,641	67,806	Cimarron			4,607
Bobcat	43,374	12,445	—	**Total Cadillac**	345,831	203,991	150,024
Capri	107,094	68,070	31,767	**Total General Motors Corp.**	5,091,908	4,064,556	2,221,338
Lincoln	71,783	22,781	17,699	**Checker Motors Corp.**	4,765	3,197	1,070
Mark	68,313	28,146	18,598	**Volkswagen of America**	173,192	197,106	94,180
				Total Passenger Cars	8,433,662	6,375,506	3,571,652

Automobile Factory Sales

Source: Motor Vehicle Manufacturers Association, Detroit, Mich.—wholesale values

Year	Passenger cars		Motor trucks, buses		Total	
	Number	Value	Number	Value	Number	Value
1900	4,192	$4,899,433	...	...	4,190	$4,899,443
1910	181,000	215,340,000	6,000	9,660,000	187,000	225,000,000
1920	1,905,560	1,809,170,963	321,789	423,249,410	2,227,349	2,232,420,373
1930	2,787,456	1,644,083,152	575,364	390,752,061	3,362,820	2,034,853,213
1940	3,717,385	2,370,654,083	754,901	567,820,414	4,472,286	2,938,474,497
1950	6,665,863	8,468,137,000	1,337,193	1,707,748,000	8,003,056	10,175,885,000
1960	6,674,796	12,164,234,000	1,194,475	2,350,680,000	7,869,271	14,514,914,000
1970	6,546,817	14,630,217,000	1,692,440	4,819,752,000	8,239,257	19,449,969,000
1980	6,400,026	NA	1,667,283	NA	8,067,309	NA

After July 1, 1964 all tactical vehicles are excluded. Federal excise taxes are excluded in all years.

Motor Vehicle Registrations, Taxes, Motor Fuel, Drivers' Ages

Source: Federal Highway Adm.

State, 1980	Driver's age Jan. 1, 1981 (1) Regular	(2) Juvenile	Minimum age for purchase alcoholic beverage	Licensed drivers (1,000)	Registered autos, buses & trucks (1,000)	State gas tax per gal. cents	Motor fuel adjusted net total tax receipts $1,000	Motor fuel consumption Highway 1,000 gallons	Nonhighway 1,000 gallons
Alabama	16		19	2,248	2,954	7	195,019	2,214,082	46,940
Alaska	16		19	221	255	8	18,010	221,253	45,335
Arizona	16		17	1,836	1,866	8	121,904	1,518,107	49,549
Arkansas	16		21	1,452	1,553	9.5	120,301	1,385,347	82,287
California	16/18	14	21	15,635	16,801	7	782,156	11,529,427	290,082
Colorado	21	16	21	2,052	2,395	7	106,000	1,567,938	57,061
Connecticut	16/18		18	2,148	2,240	11	149,108	1,361,839	26,905
Delaware	16/18		20	414	404	9	29,114	305,726	5,449
Dist. of Col.	18	16	21	349	257	10	16,428	205,636	3,630
Florida	16/18		19	7,509	7,911	8	382,825	4,926,335	138,384
Georgia	16		19	3,333	3,865	7.5	242,726	3,221,313	52,843
Hawaii	15		18	539	580	8.5	27,682	320,991	13,793
Idaho	16	14	19	644	810	9.5	52,712	571,340	38,200
Illinois	16/18		21	7,013	8,779	7.5	388,663	5,429,770	207,408
Indiana	16/18		21	3,658	3,922	8	251,014	3,166,524	80,998
Iowa	16/18	14	19	2,175	2,380	10	143,163	1,867,509	157,802
Kansas	16	14	21	1,885	2,354	8	122,482	1,481,397	108,838
Kentucky	16		21	2,099	2,660	9	178,655	1,939,371	30,529
Louisiana	15/17	15	18	2,328	2,792	8	181,252	2,246,826	52,535
Maine	15/17	15	20	720	722	9	49,342	554,155	11,412
Maryland	16/18	15 3/4	21	2,670	2,872	9	173,843	1,931,379	22,929
Massachusetts	17/18	16 1/2	20	3,770	3,802	8.5	216,532	2,372,821	34,572
Michigan	16/18	14	21	6,452	6,563	11	3,739	4,727,609	160,217
Minnesota	16/18	15	19	2,332	3,471	9	238,726	2,308,765	161,557
Mississippi	15		21	1,596	1,547	9	126,430	1,372,149	25,903
Missouri	16		21	3,275	3,324	7	201,570	2,925,112	124,328
Montana	15/16		19	588	958	9	47,198	564,980	41,840
Nebraska	16	14	20	1,095	1,246	10.5	110,110	983,120	85,654
Nevada	16	16	21	585	578	6	31,930	530,485	18,437
New Hampshire	16/18	16	20	661	655	11	40,543	421,267	6,628
New Jersey	17	16	19	4,421	4,835	8	286,069	3,456,197	67,133
New Mexico	15/16		21	867	1,061	7	66,805	890,733	15,201
New York	17/18	16	18	9,287	8,216	8	467,306	5,789,222	191,632
North Carolina	16/18	16	21	3,794	4,662	9	290,566	3,261,121	74,160
North Dakota	16	14	21	424	630	8	36,761	479,034	90,545
Ohio	16/18	14	21	7,573	7,510	7	387,604	5,676,689	133,561
Oklahoma	16	-	21	1,902	2,759	6.5	128,756	2,027,657	51,667
Oregon	16	14	21	1,873	2,155	7	103,962	1,516,590	47,757
Pennsylvania	17/18	16	21	7,415	6,895	11	485,443	5,413,663	127,007
Rhode Island	16/18		20	587	592	10	39,582	384,071	14,968
South Carolina	16	15	21	1,962	2,016	10	177,678	1,733,444	34,007
South Dakota	16	14	21	480	606	9	55,004	501,837	77,305
Tennessee	16	14	19	2,814	3,103	7	192,212	2,722,158	52,479
Texas	16/18	15	19	9,259	10,219	5	461,004	9,141,458	180,920
Utah	16/18		21	812	1,009	9	58,790	772,537	26,527
Vermont	18	16	18	344	339	9	22,475	272,461	5,710
Virginia	16/18		21	3,404	3,581	9	259,267	2,844,894	52,185
Washington	16/18		21	2,637	3,261	12	284,489	2,055,154	59,570
West Virginia	16/18	16	18	1,482	1,365	10.5	86,893	916,010	10,353
Wisconsin	16/18	14	18	3,012	3,208	7	205,551	2,464,641	96,835
Wyoming	16	14	19	341	491	8	36,410	451,732	38,310
Total				**145,972**	**159,029**		**9,294,804**	**116,943,876**	**3,629,877**

(1) Unrestricted operation of private passenger car. When 2 ages are shown, license is issued at lower age upon completion of approved driver education course. (2) Juvenile license issued with consent of parent or guardian.

Auto Registrations, Taxes, Motor Fuel, Drivers' Ages in Canada

Source: Statistics Canada

Province	Driver's age Minimum (1979)	Minor (1979)	Registered[1] road motor vehicles (1979)	Provincial gas tax per gal. (1979)[2]	Fuel consumption on roads and highways 1979[3] Gasoline 1,000 gallons	Diesel 1,000 gallons	Liquified petroleum 1,000 gallons
Newfoundland	17	—	197,670	.27	136,622	24,089	210
Prince Edward Island	16	—	68,361	.21	42,622	2,850	16
Nova Scotia	16	—	457,905	.21	264,464	36,439	283
New Brunswick	18	16	356,267	.20	243,918	37,010	85
Quebec	18	16	3,150,580	.19	1,907,878	342,332	720
Ontario	16	—	4,645,706	.21	2,864,371	455,221	758
Manitoba	16	—	645,552	.18	314,440	39,978	265
Saskatchewan	16	—	682,881	.19	335,686	55,565	769
Alberta	16	14	1,530,118	—	n.a.	n.a.	n.a.
British Columbia	19	16	1,569,866	.17	876,472	130,032	1,285
Yukon	16	—	17,665	.14	11,438	9,172	15
Northwest Territories	16	—	16,129	.14	7,400	4,978	4,406
Total			**13,338,700**		**7,005,312**	**1,137,667**	**4,406**

(1) Registrations include: passenger automobiles (including taxis and for-hire cars) 9,985,146; trucks and truck tractors 2,854,217; buses 52,927; motorcycles 332,933; registered mopeds 56,124; other road vehicles (ambulances, fire trucks, etc.) 57,353. (2) As of July. (3) Based on road-use tax figures; no figures are available for Alberta, the road-use tax was removed there in April, 1978.

Memorable Manned Space Flights

Sources: National Aeronautics and Space Administration and The World Almanac.

Crew, date	Mission name	Orbits[1]	Duration	Remarks
Yuri A. Gagarin (4/12/61)	Vostok 1	1	1h 48m	First manned orbital flight.
Alan B. Shepard Jr. (5/5/61)	Mercury-Redstone 3	(2)	15m 22s . .	First American in space.
Virgil I. Grissom (7/21/61)	Mercury-Redstone 4	(2)	15m 37s . .	Spacecraft sank. Grissom rescued.
Gherman S. Titov (8/6-7/61)	Vostok 2	16	25h 18m	First space flight of more than 24 hrs.
John H. Glenn Jr. (2/20/62)	Mercury-Atlas 6	3	4h 55m 23s . .	First American in orbit.
M. Scott Carpenter (5/24/62)	Mercury-Atlas 7	3	4h 56m 05s . .	Manual retrofire error caused 250 mi. landing overshoot.
Andrian G. Nikolayev (8/11-15/62)	Vostok 3	64	94h 22m	Vostok 3 and 4 made first group flight.
Pavel R. Popovich (8/12-15/62)	Vostok 4	48	70h 57m	On first orbit it came within 3 miles of Vostok 3.
Walter M. Schirra Jr. (10/3/62)	Mercury-Atlas 8	6	9h 13m 11s . .	Closest splashdown to target to date (4.5 mi.).
L. Gordon Cooper (5/15-16/63)	Mercury-Atlas 9	22	34h 19m 49s . .	First U.S. evaluation of effects on man of one day in space.
Valery F. Bykovsky (6/14-6/19/63)	Vostok 5	81	119h 06m	Vostok 5 and 6 made 2d group flight.
Valentina V. Tereshkova (6/16-19/63)	Vostok 6	48	70h 50m	First woman in space.
Vladimir M. Komarov, Konstantin P. Feoktistov, Boris B. Yegorov (10/12/64)	Voskhod 1	16	24h 17m	First 3-man orbital flight: first without space suits.
Pavel I. Belyayev, Aleksei A. Leonov (3/18/65)	Voskhod 2	17	26h 02m	Leonov made first "space walk" (10 min.)
Virgil I. Grissom, John W. Young (3/23/65)	Gemini-Titan 3	3	4h 53m 00s . .	First manned spacecraft to change its orbital path.
James A. McDivitt, Edward H. White 2d, (6/3-7/65)	Gemini-Titan 4	62	97h 56m 11s . .	White was first American to "walk in space" (20 min.).
L. Gordon Cooper Jr., Charles Conrad Jr. (8/21-29/65)	Gemini-Titan 5	120	190h 55m 14s . .	First use of fuel cells for electric power; evaluated guidance and navigation system.
Frank Borman, James A. Lovell Jr. (12/4-18/65) . .	Gemini-Titan 7	206	330h 35m 31s . .	Longest duration Gemini flight
Walter M. Schirra Jr., Thomas P. Stafford (12/15-16/65)	Gemini-Titan 6-A	16	25h 51m 24s . .	Completed world's first space rendezvous with Gemini 7.
Neil A. Armstrong, David R. Scott (3/16-17/66)	Gemini-Titan 8	6.5	10h 41m 26s . .	First docking of one space vehicle with another; mission aborted, control malfunction.
John W. Young, Michael Collins (7/18-21/66)	Gemini-Titan 10	43	70h 46m 39s . .	First use of Agena target vehicle's propulsion systems; rendezvoused with Gemini 8.
Charles Conrad Jr., Richard F. Gordon Jr. (9/12-15/66)	Gemini-Titan 11	44	71h 17m 08s . .	Docked, made 2 revolutions of earth tethered; set Gemini altitude record (739.2 mi.).
James A. Lovell Jr., Edwin E. Aldrin Jr. (11/11-15/66)	Gemini-Titan 12	59	94h 34m 31s . .	Final Gemini mission; record 5½ hrs. of extravehicular activity.
Vladimir M. Komarov (4/23/67)	Soyuz 1	17	26h 40m	Crashed after re-entry killing Komarov.
Walter M. Schirra Jr., Donn F. Eisele, R. Walter Cunningham (10/11-22/68)	Apollo-Saturn 7	163	260h 09m 03s . .	First manned flight of Apollo spacecraft command-service module only.
Georgi T. Beregovoi (10/26-30/68)	Soyuz 3	64	94h 51m	Made rendezvous with unmanned Soyuz 2.
Frank Borman, James A. Lovell Jr., William A. Anders (12/21-27/68) .	Apollo-Saturn 8	10[3]	147h 00m 42s	First flight to moon (command-service module only); views of lunar surface televised to earth.
Vladimir A. Shatalov (1/14-17/69)	Soyuz 4	45	71h 14m	Docked with Soyuz 5.
Boris V. Volyanov, Aleksei S. Yeliseyev, Yevgeny V. Khrunov (1/15-18/69)	Soyuz 5	46	72h 46m	Docked with Soyuz 4; Yeliseyev and Khrunov transferred to Soyuz 4.
James A. McDivitt, David R. Scott, Russell L. Schweickart (3/3-13/69) .	Apollo-Saturn 9	151	241h 00m 54s . .	First manned flight of lunar module.

(continued)

Crew, date	Mission name	Orbits[1]	Duration	Remarks
Thomas P. Stafford, Eugene A. Cernan, John W. Young (5/18-26/69)	Apollo-Saturn 10	31[4]	192h 03m 23s	First lunar module orbit of moon.
Neil A. Armstrong, Edwin E. Aldrin Jr., Michael Collins (7/16-24/69)	Apollo-Saturn 11	30[3]	195h 18m 35s	First lunar landing made by Armstrong and Aldrin; collected 48.5 lbs. of soil, rock samples; lunar stay time 21 h, 36m, 21 s.
Georgi S. Shonin, Valery N. Kubasov (10/11-16/69)	Soyuz 6	79	118h 42m	First welding of metals in space.
Anatoly V. Filipchenko, Vladislav N. Volkov, Viktor V. Gorbatko (10/12-17/69)	Soyuz 7	79	118h 41m	Space lab construction tests made; Soyuz 6, 7 and 8 — first time 3 spacecraft crew orbited earth at once.
Charles Conrad Jr., Richard F. Gordon, Alan L. Bean (11/14-24/69)	Apollo-Saturn 12	45[3]	244h 36m 25s	Conrad and Bean made 2d moon landing; collected 74.7 lbs. of samples, lunar stay time 31 h, 31 m.
James A. Lovell Jr., Fred W. Haise Jr., John L. Swigart Jr. (4/11-17/70)	Apollo-Saturn 13	...	142h 54m 41s	Aborted after service module oxygen tank ruptured; crew returned safely using lunar module oxygen and power.
Alan B. Shepard Jr., Stuart A. Roosa, Edgar D. Mitchell (1/31-2/9/71)	Apollo-Saturn 14	34[3]	216h 01m 57s	Shepard and Mitchell made 3d moon landing, collected 96 lbs. of lunar samples; lunar stay 33 h, 31 m.
Vladimir A. Shatalov, Aleksei S. Yeliseyev, Nikolai Rukavishnikov (4/22-24/71)	Soyuz 10	32	47h 46m	Docked with prototype Salyut orbiting space station for 5½ hrs. then mission was aborted.
Georgi T. Dobrovolsky, Vladislav N. Volkov, Viktor I. Patsayev (6/6-30/71)	Soyuz 11	360	569h 40m	Docked with Salyut space station; and orbited in Salyut for 23 days; crew died during re-entry from loss of pressurization.
David R. Scott, Alfred M. Worden, James B. Irwin (7/26-8/7/71)	Apollo-Saturn 15	74[3]	295h 11m 53s	Scott and Irwin made 4th moon landing; first lunar rover use; first deep space walk; 170 lbs. of samples; 66 h, 55 m, stay.
Charles M. Duke Jr., Thomas K. Mattingly, John W. Young (4/16-27/72)	Apollo-Saturn 16	64[3]	265h 51m 05s	Young and Duke made 5th moon landing; collected 213 lbs. of lunar samples; lunar stay time. 71 h, 2 m.
Eugene A. Cernan, Ronald E. Evans, Harrison H. Schmitt (12/7-19/72)	Apollo-Saturn 17	75[3]	301h 51m 59s	Cernan and Schmitt made 6th manned lunar landing; collected 243 lbs. of samples; record lunar stay of 75 h.
Charles Conrad Jr., Joseph P. Kerwin, Paul J. Weitz (5/25-6/22/73)	Skylab 2	...	672h 49m 49s	First American manned orbiting space station; made long-flights tests, crew repaired damage caused during boost.
Alan L. Bean, Jack R. Lousma, Owen K. Garriott (7/28-9/25/73)	Skylab 3	...	1,427h 09m 04s	Crew systems and operational tests, exceeded pre-mission plans for scientific activities; space walk total 13h, 44 m.
Gerald P. Carr, Edward G. Gibson, William Pogue (11/16/73-2/8/74)	Skylab 4	...	2,017h 16m 30s	Final Skylab mission; record space walk of 7 h, 1 m., record space walks total for a mission 22 h, 21 m.
Alexi Leonov, Valeri Kubason (7/15-7/21/75)	Soyuz 19	96	143h 31m	
Vance Brand, Thomas P. Stafford, Donald K. Slayton (7/15-7/24/75)	Apollo 18	136	217h 30m	U.S.-USSR joint flight. Crews linked-up in space, conducted experiments, shared meals, and held a joint news conference.
Boris Yolynov, Vitaly Zhobovov (7/26-8/24/76)	Soyuz 21	...	50 days	Conducted experiments aboard Salyut 5.
Viktor Gorbatko, Yuri Glazkov (2/7-2/25/77)	Soyuz 24	...	18 days	Docked with Salyut 5.
Georgi Grechko, Yuri Romanenko (12/10/77-3/16/78)	Soyuz 26	...	96 days	Docked with Salyut 6. Conducted scientific experiments. Docked with Salyut 6.
Vladimir Lyakhov, Varery Ryumin (2/26/-8/19/79)	Soyuz 32, 34	...	175 days	Set new space endurance record.
Robert L. Crippen, John W. Young (4/12-14/81)	Columbia	36	54h 22m	First demonstration of re-usable winged spaceship.

(1) The U.S. measures orbital flights in revolutions while the Soviets use "orbits." (2) Suborbital. (3) Moon orbits in command module. (4) Moon orbits.

Fire aboard spacecraft Apollo I on the ground at Cape Kennedy, Fla. killed Virgil I. Grissom, Edward H. White and Roger B. Chaffee on Jan. 27, 1967. They were the only U.S. astronauts killed in space tests.

Notable Ocean and Intercontinental Flights

(Certified by the Federation Aeronautique Internationale as of Jan., 1981)

	From	To	Miles	Time	Date
		Dirigible Balloons			
British R-34(1)	East Fortune, Scot.	Mineola, N.Y.	.....	108 hrs.	July 2-6, 1919
	Mineola, N.Y.	Pulham, Eng.	.....	75 hrs.	July 9-13, 1919
Amundsen-Ellsworth-Nobile expedition	Spitsbergen	Teller, Alas.	.....	80 hrs.	May 11-14, 1926
Graf Zeppelin	Friedrichshafen	Lakehurst, N.J.	6,630	4d 15h 46m	Oct. 11-15, 1928
Hindenburg Zeppelin	Germany	Lakehurst, N.J.	.....	51h 17m	June 30-July 2, 1936
	Lakehurst, N.J.	Frankfort, Ger.	.....	42h 53m	Aug. 9-11, 1936
USN ZPG-2 Blimp	S. Weymouth, Mass.	Africa			
	Africa	Key West, Fla.	7,000	275h	Mar. 4-16, 1957

	From	To	Miles	Time	Date
		Airplanes			
USN NC-4	Rockaway, N.Y.	Lisbon, Port.	.....	....	May 8-27, 1919
John Alcock-A.W. Brown (2)	St. John's, Nfld.	Clifden, Ireland	1,960	16h 12m	June 14-15, 1919
Richard E. Byrd (3)	Spitsbergen	North Pole	1,545	15h 30m	May 9, 1926
Charles Lindbergh (4)	Mineola, N.Y.	Paris	3,610	33h 29m 30s	May 20-21, 1927
C. Levin-C. Chamberlin (5)	Roosevelt Field, N.Y. Mineola, N.Y.	Isleben, Germany	3,911	42h 31m	June 4-6, 1927
Baron G. von Huenefeld, crew (6)	Dublin	Greenly Isl., Lab.	.....	37 hrs.	Apr. 12-13, 1928
Sir Hubert Wilkins (9)	Point Barrow, Alaska	Spitsbergen	.....	....	Apr. 16, 1928
Sir Chas. Kingsford-Smith, crew (7)	Oakland, Cal.	Brisbane, Aust.	.....	....	May 31-June 8, 1928
Amelia Earhart Putnam, W. Stultz, L. Gordon	Trepassy, Nfld.	Burry Port, Wales	.....	20h 40m	June 17-18, 1928
Richard E. Byrd (8)	Bay of Whales	South Pole	.....	....	Nov. 28-29, 1929
D. Coste-M. Bellonte	Paris	Valley Stream, N.Y.	4,100	37h 18m 30s	Sept. 1-2, 1930
Wiley Post-Harold Gatty	Harbor Grace, Nfld.	England	2,200	16h 17m	June 23-24, 1931
Clyde Pangborn-Hugh Herndon Jr. (10)	Tokyo	Wenatchee, Wash.	4,458	41h 34m	Oct. 3-5, 1931
Amelia Earhart Putnam (11)	Harbor Grace, Nfld.	Ireland	2,026	14h 56m	May 20-21, 1932
James A. Mollison (12)	Portmarnock, Ire.	Pennfield, N.B.	.....	....	Aug. 18, 1932
China Clipper (Pan Am. Airways) (13)	San Francisco	Manila, P.I.	.....	....	Nov. 22-28, 1935
	Manila, P.I.	San Francisco	.....	....	Dec. 1-6, 1935
Gromoff, Yumasheff, Danilin (USSR)	Moscow, USSR	San Jacinto, Cal.	6,262	62h 02m	July 12-14, 1937
Douglas C. Corrigan	New York	Dublin, Ire.	.....	28h 13m	July 17-18, 1938
B-29 (C.J. Miller)	Honolulu	Washington, D.C.	4,640	17h 21m	Sept. 1, 1945
C-54 (Maj. G.E. Cain)	Tokyo	Washington, D.C.	.....	31h 24m	Sept. 3, 1945
Col. David C. Schilling, USAF (14)	England	Limestone, Me.	3,300	10h 01m	Sept. 22, 1950
Chas. F. Blair Jr.	New York	London	3,500	7h 48m	Jan 31, 1951
Chas. F. Blair Jr. (15)	Bardufoss, Norway	Fairbanks, Alas.	3,300	10h 29m	May 29, 1951
Chas. F. Blair Jr.	Fairbanks, Alaska	New York	3,450	9h 31m	May 30, 1951
Canberra Bomber	England	Australia	.....	20h 20m	Mar. 16, 1952
Two U.S. S-55 Helicopters (16)	Westover AFB, Mass.	Prestwick, Scotland	3,410	42h 30m	July 15-31, 1952
Canberra Bomber (17)	Aldergrove, N.Ire.	Gander, Nfld.	2,073	4h 34m	Aug. 26, 1952
	Gander, Nfld.	Aldergrove, N.Ire.	2,073	3h 25m	Aug. 26, 1952
British Comet	London-Tokyo	Tokyo-London	20,400	74h 52m	Apr. 3-7, 1953
British Comet	London	Rio de Janeiro	6,000	12h 30m	Sept. 13-14, 1953
Max Conrad (solo)	New York	Paris	.....	22h 23m	Nov. 7, 1954
Canberra Bomber	London (round trip)	New York	6,920	14h 21m 45.4s	Aug. 23, 1955
Capt. William F. Judd	New York	Paris	.....	24h 11m	Jan. 29-30, 1956
Three USAF F-100Cs	London	Los Angeles	6,710	14h 5m	May 13, 1957
Spirit of St. Louis II (USAF F-100F jet)	McGuire AFB, N.J.	Le Bourget, Paris	.....	6h 38m	May 21, 1957
USAF KC-135	Tokyo	Lajes AFB, Azores	10,230	18h 48m	Apr. 7-8, 1958
Max Conrad (solo)	New York	Palermo, Sicily	4,440	32h 55m	June 22-23, 1958
USAF KC-135	Yokota AB, Japan	Washington, D.C.	7,100	12h 28m	Sept. 12, 1958
Max Conrad (solo)	Chicago	Rome	5,000	34h 3m	Mar. 5-6, 1959
Max Conrad (solo)	Casablanca, Mor.	Los Angeles	7,700	58h 36m	June 2-4, 1959
USSR TU-114 (18)	Moscow	New York	5,092	11h 6m	June 28, 1959
Boeing 707 airliner	San Francisco	Sydney, Australia	7,630	16h 10m	July 2, 1959
Boeing 707-320	New York	Moscow	c.5,090	8h 54m	July 23, 1959
Max Conrad (solo)	Casablanca, Mor.	El Paso, Tex.	6,911	56h 26m	Nov. 22-26, 1959
Col. J.B. Swindal	Washington, D.C.	Moscow	5,004	8h 39m 02.2s	May 19, 1963
Concorde GB	London	Washington, D.C.	1,023 mph	3h 34m 48s	May 29, 1976
Concorde	Paris	Washington, D.C.	1,071.86 mph	3h 35m 15s	Aug. 18, 1978
Concorde	Paris	New York	1,037.50 mph	3h 30m 11s	Aug. 22, 1978

Notable first flights: (1) Atlantic aerial round trip. (2) Non-stop transatlantic flight. (3) Polar flight. (4) Solo transatlantic flight in the Ryan monoplane the "Spirit of St. Louis." (5) Transatlantic passenger flight. (6) East-West transatlantic crossing. (7) U.S. to Australia flight. (8) South Pole flight. (9) Trans-Arctic flight. (10) Non-stop Pacific flight. (11) Woman's transoceanic solo flight. (12) Westbound transatlantic solo flight. (13) Pacific airmail and U.S. to Philippines crossing. (14) Non-stop jet transatlantic flight. (15) Solo across North Pole. (16) Transatlantic helicopter flight. (17) Transatlantic round trip on same day. (18) Non-stop between Moscow and New York.

International Aeronautical Records

Source: The National Aeronautic Association, 806 15th St. NW, Washington, DC 20005, representative in the United States of the Federation Aeronautique Internationale, certifying agency for world aviation and space records. The International Aeronautical Federation was formed in 1905 by representatives from Belgium, France, Germany, Great Britain, Spain, Italy, Switzerland, and the United States, with headquarters in Paris. Regulations for the control of official records were signed Oct. 14, 1905. World records are defined as maximum performance, regardless of class or type of aircraft used. Records to July, 1981.

World Air Records—Maximum Performance in Any Class

Speed over a straight course — 3,529.56 kph. (2,193.16 mph) — Capt. Elden W. Joersz, USAF, Lockheed SR-71; Beale AFB, Cal., July 28, 1976.
Speed over a closed circuit — 3,367.221 kph. (2,092.294 mph) — Maj. Adolphus H. Bledsoe Jr., USAF, Lockheed SR-71; Beale AFB, Cal., July 27, 1976.
Distance in a straight line — 20,168.78 kms (12,532.28 mi.) — Maj. Clyde P. Evely, USAF, Boeing B52-H; Kadena, Okinawa to Madrid, Spain, Jan. 11, 1962.
Distance over a closed circuit — 18,245.05 kms (11,336.92 mi.) — Capt. William Stevenson, USAF, Boeing B52-H; Seymour-Johnson, N.C., June 6-7, 1962.
Altitude — 37,650 meters (123,523.58 feet) — Alexander Fedotov, USSR, E-266M; Podmoskovnoye, USSR, Aug. 31, 1977.
Altitude in horizontal flight — 25,929.031 meters (85,068.997 ft.) — Capt. Robert C. Helt, USAF, Lockheed SR-71; Beale AFB, Cal., July 28, 1976.

Manned Space Craft

Duration — 175 days — Vladimir Lyakhov & Valery Ryumin, USSR, Salyut 6, Feb. 26—Aug. 19, 1979.
Altitude — 377,668.9 kms (234,672.5 mi.) — Frank Borman, James A. Lovell Jr., William Anders, Apollo 8; Dec. 21-27, 1968.
Greatest mass lifted — 127,980 kgs. (282,197 lbs.) — Frank Borman, James S. Lovell Jr., William Anders, Apollo 8; Dec. 21-27, 1968.
Distance — 92,941,650 kms. (57,751,264.59 mi.) — Vladimir Kovalyonok, Alexandre Ivan Chenkov, USSR; Soyuz 29, Salyut 6, Soyuz 31; June 15-Nov. 2, 1978.

World "Class" Records

All other records, international in scope, are termed World "Class" records and are divided into classes: airships, free balloons, airplanes, seaplanes, amphibians, gliders, and rotorplanes. Airplanes (Class C) are sub-divided into four groups: Group I — piston engine aircraft, Group II — turboprop aircraft, Group III — jet aircraft, Group IV — rocket powered aircraft. A partial listing of world records follows:

Airplanes (Class C, Group I—piston engine)

Distance, closed circuit — 14,441.26 kms (8,974 mi.) — James R. Bede, U.S.; BD-2, Columbus, Oh. to Kansas City course, Nov. 7-9, 1969.
Distance, straight line — 18,081.99 kms (11,235.6 miles) — Cmdr. Thomas D. Davies, USN; Cmdr. Eugene P. Rankin, USN; Cmdr. Walter S. Reid, USN, and Lt. Cmdr. Ray A. Tabeling, USN; Lockheed P2V-1; from Pearce Field, Perth, Australia, to Port Columbus, Oh., Sept. 29-Oct. 1, 1946.
Speed over 3-kilometer measured course — 803.138 kph. (499.04 mph) — Steve Hinton; P-51D; Tonopah, Nev., Aug. 14, 1979.
Speed for 100 kilometers (62.137 miles) without payload — 755.668 kph. (469.549 mph.) — Jacqueline Cochran, U.S.; North American P-51; Coachella Valley, Cal., Dec. 10, 1947.
Speed for 1,000 kilometers (621.369 miles) without payload — 693.78 kph. (431.09 mph.) — Jacqueline Cochran, U.S.; North American P-51; Santa Rosasummit, Cal. — Flagstaff, Ariz. course, May 24, 1948.
Speed for 5,000 kilometers (3,106.849 miles) without payload — 544.59 kph. (338.39 mph.) — Capt. James Bauer, USAF, Boeing B-29; Dayton, Oh., June 28, 1946.
Speed around the world — 327.73 kph (203.64 mph) — D.N. Dalton, Australia; Beechcraft Duke; Brisbane, Aust., July 20-25, 1975. Time: 5 days, 2 hours, 19 min., 57 sec.

Light Airplanes—(Class C-1.d)

Distance in a straight line — 12,341.26 kms. (7,668.48 miles) — Max Conrad, U.S.; Piper Comanche; Casablanca, Morocco to Los Angeles, June 2-4, 1959.
Speed for 100 kilometers — (62,137 miles) in a closed circuit — 519.480 kph. (322.780 mph.) — Ms. R. M. Sharpe, Great Britain; Vickers Supermarine Spitfire 5-B; Wolverhampton, June 17, 1950.

Helicopters (Class E-1)

Distance in a straight line — 3,561.55 kms. (2,213.04 miles) — Robert G. Ferry, U.S.; Hughes YOH-6A helicopter; Culver City, Cal., to Ormond Beach, Fla., Apr. 6-7, 1966.
Speed over 3-km. course — 348.971 kph. (216.839 mph.) — Byron Graham, U.S.; Sikorsky S-67 helicopter; Windsor Locks, Conn., Dec. 14, 1970.

Gliders (Class D—single place)

Distance, straight line — 1,460.8 kms. (907.7 miles) — Hans Werner Grosse, West Germany; ASK12 sailplane; Luebeck to Biarritz, Apr. 25, 1972.
Altitude above sea level — 14,102 meters (46,267 feet) — Paul F. Bikle, U.S.; Sailplane Schweizer SGS-123-E; Mojave, Lancaster, Cal., Feb. 25, 1961.

Airplanes (Class C, Group II—Turboprop)

Distance in a straight line — 14,052.95 kms. (8,732.09 miles) — Lt. Col. Edgar L. Allison Jr., USAF, Lockheed HC-130 Hercules aircraft; Taiwan to Scott AFB, Ill.; Feb. 20, 1972.
Altitude — 15,549 meters (51,014 ft.) — Donald R. Wilson, U.S.; LTV L450F aircraft; Greenville, Tex., Mar. 27, 1972.
Speed for 1,000 kilometers (621.369 miles) without payload — 871.38 kph. (541.449 mph.) — Ivan Soukhomline, USSR; TU-114 aircraft; Sternberg, USSR; Mar. 24, 1960.
Speed for 5,000 kilometers (3,106.849 miles) without payload — 877.212 kph. (545.072 mph.) — Ivan Soukhomline, USSR; TU-114 aircraft, Sternberg, USSR; Apr. 9, 1960.

Airplanes (Class C-1, Group III—Jet-powered)

Distance in a straight line — 20,168.78 kms. (12,532.28 mi.) — Maj. Clyde P. Evely, USAF, Boeing B-52-H, Kadena, Okinawa, to Madrid, Spain, Jan. 10-11, 1962.
Distance in a closed circuit — 18,245.05 kms. (11,336.92 miles) — Capt. William Stevenson, USAF, Boeing B-52-H, Seymour-Johnson,

N.C., June 6-7, 1962.
  Altitude — 36,650 meters (123,523.58 ft.) — Alexander Fedotov, USSR; E-226M airplane; Podmoskovnoye, USSR, Aug. 31, 1977.
  Speed over a 3-kilometer course — 1,590.45 kph (988.26 mph) — Darryl G. Greenamyer, U.S.; F-104; Tonopah, Nev., Oct. 24, 1977.
  Speed for 100 kilometers in a closed circuit — 2,605 kph. (1,618.7 mph.) — Alexander Fedotov, USSR; E-266 airplane, Apr. 8, 1973.
  Speed for 500 kilometers in a closed circuit — 2,981.5 kph. (1,852.61 mph.) — Mikhail Komarov, USSR; E-266 airplane, Oct. 5, 1967.
  Speed for 1,000 kilometers in a closed circuit — 3,367.221 kph (2,092.294 mph) — Maj. Adolphus H. Bledsoe Jr., USAF; Lockheed SR-71; Beale AFB, Cal., July 27, 1976.
  Speed for 2,000 kilometers in closed circuit — 1,708.817 kph. (1,061.808 mph.) — Maj. H. J. Deutschendorf Jr., U.S.; Convair B-58 Hustler Bomber; Edwards AFB, Cal., Jan. 12, 1961.

Free Balloons (Sub-Class A-10, over 4,000 cubic meters)

  Altitude — 34,668 meters (113,739.9 feet) — Cmdr. Malcolm D. Ross, USNR; Lee Lewis Memorial Winzen Research Balloon; Gulf of Mexico, May 4, 1961.

  Duration —137 hr., 5 min., 50 sec. — Ben Abruzzo and Maxie Anderson; Double Eagle II; Presque Isle, Maine to Miserey, France (3,107.61 mi.); Aug. 12-17, 1978.

FAI Course Records

  Los Angeles to New York — 1,954.79 kph (1,214.65 mph) — Capt. Robert G. Sowers, USAF; Convair B-58 Hustler; elapsed time: 2 hrs. 58.71 sec., Mar. 5, 1962.
  New York to Los Angeles — 1,741 kph (1,081.80 mph) — Capt. Robert G. Sowers, USAF; Convair B-58 Hustler; elapsed time: 2 hrs. 15 min. 50.08 sec., Mar. 5, 1962.
  New York to Paris — 1,753.068 kph (1,089.36 mph) — Maj. W. R. Payne, U.S.; Convair B-58 Hustler; elapsed time: 3 hrs 19 min. 44 sec., May 26, 1961.
  London to New York — 945.423 kph (587.457 mph) — Maj. Burl Davenport, USAF; Boeing KC-135; elapsed time: 5 hrs. 53 min. 12.77 sec.; June 27, 1958.
  Baltimore to Moscow, USSR — 906.64 kph (563.36 mph) — Col. James B. Swindal, USAF; Boeing VC-137 (707); elapsed time: 8 hrs. 33 min. 45.4 sec., May 19, 1963.
  Belfast to Gander, Newfoundland — 774.25 kph (481.099 mph) — Wing Commander R. P. Beamont, Great Britain; Canberra bomber, Aug. 31, 1951; elapsed time: 4 hrs. 18 min. 24.4 sec.
  New York to London — 2,908.026 kph (1,806.964 mph) — Maj. James V. Sullivan, USAF; Lockheed SR-71; elapsed 1 hr. 54 min. 56.4 sec., Sept. 1, 1974.
  London to Los Angeles — 2,310.353 kph (1,435.587 mph) — Capt. Harold B. Adams, USAF; Lockheed SR-71; elapsed time: 3 hrs. 47 min. 39 sec., Sept. 13, 1974.

Aviation Hall of Fame

The Aviation Hall of Fame at Dayton, Oh., is dedicated to honoring aviation's outstanding pioneers.

Allen, William M.	Earhart, (Putnam), Amelia	Lear, William P. Sr.	Rickenbacker, Edward V.
Armstrong, Neil A.			
Arnold, Henry "Hap"	Ellyson, Theodore G.	LeMay, Curtis E.	Rodgers, Calbraith P.
Balchen, Bernt	Ely, Eugene B.	LeVier, Anthony W.	Rogers, "Will"
	Fairchild, Sherman M.	Lindbergh, Anne M.	
Baldwin, Thomas S.	Fleet, Reuben H.	Lindbergh, Charles A.	Ryan, T. Claude
	Fokker, Anthony H.G.		Schriever, Bernard A.
Beachey, Lincoln	Foulois, Benjamin D.	Link, Edwin A.	Selfridge, Thomas E.
Beech, Walter H.	Gabreski, Francis S.	Loening, Grover	Shepard Jr., Alan B.
Bell, Alexander Graham	Glenn Jr., John H.	Luke Jr., Frank	Sikorsky, Igor I.
			Six, Robert F.
Bell, Lawrence D.	Goddard, George W.	Macready, John A.	Smith, C.R.
Boeing, William E.	Goddard, Robert H.	Martin, Glenn L.	Spaatz, Carl A.
Byrd, Richard E.	Gross, Robert E.	McDonnell, James S.	Sperry Sr., Elmer A.
Cessna, Clyde V.	Grumman, Leroy R.	Mitchell, William "Billy"	Taylor, Charles E.
Chamberlin, Clarence D.	Guggenheim, Harry F.	Montgomery, John J.	Towers, John H.
Chanute, Octave	Hegenberger, Albert F.	Moss, Sanford A.	Trippe, Juan T.
Chennault, Claire L.	Hughes, Howard R.	Northrop, John K.	Turner, Roscoe
Conrad Jr., Charles			
Cunningham, Alfred A.	Johnson, Clarence L.	Odlum, Jacqueline Cochran	Twining, Nathan F.
Curtiss, Glenn H.	Kenney, George C.	Patterson, William A.	Wade, Leigh
	Kettering, Charles F.	Piper Sr., William T.	
deSeversky, Alexander P.	Kindelberger, James H.	Post, Wiley H.	Walden, Henry W.
Doolittle, James H.	Knabenshue, A. Roy	Read, Albert C.	Wright, Orville
Douglas, Donald W.	Lahm, Frank P.	Reeve, Robert C.	Wright, Wilbur
Eaker, Ira C.	Langley, Samuel P.	Richardson, Holden C.	Yeager, Charles E.

The Busiest Airports, 1980

(Total take-offs and landings)

United States		Canada	
Source: Federal Aviation Administration		Source: Aviation Statistics Centre, Statistics Canada	
Chicago O'Hare	722,777	St. Hubert, Que.	289,121
Atlanta International	612,523	Pitt Meadows, B.C.	279,964
Long Beach	606,323	Vancouver International, B.C.	267,972
Van Nuys	540,560	Toronto International, Ont.	254,886
Santa Ana	524,750	Calgary International, Alta.	235,525
Los Angeles International	523,937	Springbank, Alta.	227,700
Oakland International	483,528	St. Andrews, Man.	224,182
Denver Stapleton	480,578	Buttonville, Ont.	215,910
Dallas Ft. Worth	463,834	Ottawa International, Ont.	209,502
Tamiami, Fla.	419,243	Hamilton City, Ont.	207,267
Opa Locka (Miami, Fla.)	412,833	Langley, B.C.	203,667
Seattle-Boeing	410,866	Toronto Island, Ont.	190,189

Notable Trips Around the World

(Certified by Federation Aeronautique Internationale as of Jan., 1981)

Fast circuits of the earth have been a subject of wide interest since Jules Verne, French novelist, described an imaginary trip by Phileas Fogg in Around the World in 80 Days, assertedly occurring Oct. 2 to Dec. 20, 1872.

	Terminal	Miles	Time	Date
Nellie Bly	New York, N.Y.		72d 06h 11m	1889
George Francis Train	New York, N.Y.		67d 12h 03m	1890
Charles Fitzmorris.	Chicago		60d 13h 29m	1901
J. W. Willis Sayre	Seattle		54d 09h 42m	1903
Col. Burnlay-Campbell			40d 19h 30m	1907
Andre Jaeger-Schmidt.			39d 19h 42m 38s	1911
John Henry Mears.			35d 21h 36m	1913
Two U.S. Army airplanes	Seattle (57 hops, 21 countries).	26,103	35d 01h 11m	1924
Edward S. Evans and Linton				June 16-
Wells (New York World) (1).	New York	18,400	28d 14h 36m 05s	July 14, 1926
John H. Mears and Capt.				June 29-
C.B.D. Collyer	New York		23d 15h 21m 03s	July 22, 1928
Graf Zeppelin	Friedrichshafen, Ger. via Tokyo,			Aug. 14-
	Los Angeles, Lakehurst, N.J.	21,700	20d 04h	Sept. 4, 1929
Wiley Post and Harold Gatty	Roosevelt Field, N.Y. via Arctic			June 23-
(Monoplane Winnie Mae)	Circle.	15,474	8d 15h 51m	July 1, 1931
Wiley Post (Monoplane Winnie	Floyd Bennett Field, N.Y. via Arctic			
Mae) (2)	Circle.	15,596	115h 36m 30s	July 15-22, 1933
H. R. Ekins (Scripps-Howard				
Newspapers in race) (Zeppelin				Sept. 30-
Hindenburg to Germany air	Lakehurst, N.J., via Frankfurt,			Oct. 19, 1936
planes from-Frankfurt).	Germany.	25,654	18d 11h 14m 33s	
Howard Hughes and 4 assistants	New York, Paris, Moscow, Si-			
	beria, Fairbanks.	14,824	3d 19h 08m 10s	July 10-13, 1938
Mrs. Clara Adams (Pan Ameri-	Port Washington, N.Y., return			June 28-
can Clipper).	Newark, N.J.		16d 19h 04m	July 15, 1939
Globester, U.S. Air Transport				Sept. 28-
Command.	Washington, D.C.	23,279	149h 44m	Oct. 4, 1945
Capt. William P. Odom (A-26	New York, via Paris, Cairo,			
Reynolds Bombshell)	Tokyo, Alaska.	20,000	78h 55m 12s	Apr. 12-16, 1947
America, Pan American 4-engine				
Lockheed Constellation (3).	New York	22,219	101h 32m	June 17-30, 1947
Col. Edward Eagan	New York	20,559	147h 15m	Dec. 13, 1948
USAF B-50 Lucky Lady II				Feb. 26-
(Capt. James Gallagher) (4)	Fort Worth, Tex.	23,452	94h 01m	Mar. 2, 1949
Jean-Marie Audibert	Paris		4d 19h 38m	Dec. 11-15, 1952
Pamela Martin	Midway Airport, Chicago		90h 59m	Dec. 5-8, 1953
Three USAF B-52 Stratofort-	Merced, Cal., via			
resses (5).	Nfld., Morocco, Saudi Arabia,			
	India, Ceylon, P.I., Guam.	24,325	45h 19m	Jan. 15-18, 1957
Joseph Cavoli	Cleveland, Oh.		89h 13m 37s	Jan. 31-Feb. 4,
				1958
Peter Gluckmann (solo).	San Francisco	22,800	29d	Aug. 22-
				Sept. 20, 1959
Milton Reynolds.	San Francisco		51h 45m 22s	Jan. 12-14, 1960
Sue Snyder.	Chicago	21,219	62h 59m	June 22-24, 1960
Max Conrad (solo)	Miami, Fla.	25,946	8d 18h 35m 57s	Feb. 28-
				Mar. 8, 1961
Sam Miller & Louis Fodor	New York		46h 28m	Aug. 3-4, 1963
Robert & Joan Wallick	Manila, Philippines	23,129	5d 6h 17m 10s	June 2-7, 1966
Arthur Godfrey, Richard Merrill				
Fred Austin, Karl Keller	New York	23,333	86h 9m 01s	June 4-7, 1966
Trevor K. Brougham	Darwin, Australia	24,800	5d 05h 57m	Aug. 5-10, 1972
Walter H. Mullikin, Albert Frink,				
Lyman Watt, Frank Cassaniti,				
Edward Shields	New York	23,137	1d 22h 50s	May 1-3,1976
Arnold Palmer.	Denver, Col.	22,985	57h 25m 42s	May 17-19, 1976
Boeing 747 (6)	San Francisco	26,382	54h 7m 12s	Oct. 28-31, 1977

(1) Mileage by train and auto, 4,110; by plane, 6,300; by steamship, 8,000. (2) First to fly solo around northern circumference of the world, also first to fly twice around the world. (3) Inception of regular commercial global air service. (4) First non-stop round-the-world flight, refueled 4 times in flight. (5) First non-stop global flight by jet planes; refueled in flight by KC-97 aerial tankers; average speed approx. 525 mph. (6) Speed record around the world over both the earth's poles.

U.S. Scheduled Airline Traffic

Source: Air Transport Association of America (thousands)

	1978	1979	1980
Passenger traffic			
Revenue passengers enplaned	274,716	316,683	296,749
Revenue passenger miles	226,781,182	262,023,375	254,179,944
Available seat miles	368,750,719	416,126,429	431,166,439
Cargo traffic (ton miles)	6,987,425	7,188,610	7,069,063
Freight	5,763,214	5,907,731	5,676,593
Express	56,494	56,194	55,949
U.S. Mail	1,167,717	1,206,298	1,312,910
Overall traffic and service			
Nonscheduled traffic—total ton miles	1,415,774	1,160,801	1,079,139
Total revenue ton miles—all services	31,095,184	34,550,922	33,566,303
Total available ton miles—all services	56,869,894	62,545,447	64,390,203

Air Distances Between Selected World Cities in Statute Miles

Point-to-point measurements are usually from City Hall

	Bangkok	Berlin	Cairo	Cape Town	Caracas	Chicago	Hong Kong	Hono-lulu	Lima	London
Bangkok......	....	5,352	4,523	6,300	10,555	8,570	1,077	6,609	12,244	5,944
Berlin	5,352	....	1,797	5,961	5,238	4,414	5,443	7,320	6,896	583
⋆Cairo........	4,523	1,797	....	4,480	6,342	6,141	5,066	8,848	7,726	2,185
Cape Town	6,300	5,961	4,480	....	6,366	8,491	7,376	11,535	6,072	5,989
Caracas......	10,555	5,238	6,342	6,366	....	2,495	10,165	6,021	1,707	4,655
Chicago	8,570	4,414	6,141	8,491	2,495	....	7,797	4,256	3,775	3,958
Hong Kong	1,077	5,443	5,066	7,376	10,165	7,797	....	5,556	11,418	5,990
Honolulu.....	6,609	7,320	8,848	11,535	6,021	4,256	5,556	....	5,947	7,240
London	5,944	583	2,185	5,989	4,655	3,958	5,990	7,240	6,316	....
Los Angeles. ...	7,637	5,782	7,520	9,969	3,632	1,745	7,240	2,557	4,171	5,439
Madrid.......	6,337	1,165	2,087	5,308	4,346	4,189	6,558	7,872	5,907	785
Melbourne.....	4,568	9,918	8,675	6,425	9,717	9,673	4,595	5,505	8,059	10,500
Mexico City ...	9,793	6,056	7,700	8,519	2,234	1,690	8,788	3,789	2,639	5,558
Montreal......	8,338	3,740	5,427	7,922	2,438	745	7,736	4,918	3,970	3,254
Moscow	4,389	1,006	1,803	6,279	6,177	4,987	4,437	7,047	7,862	1,564
New York	8,669	3,979	5,619	7,803	2,120	714	8,060	4,969	3,639	3,469
Paris	5,877	548	1,998	5,786	4,732	4,143	5,990	7,449	6,370	214
Peking	2,046	4,584	4,698	8,044	8,950	6,604	1,217	5,077	10,349	5,074
Rio de Janeiro ..	9,994	6,209	6,143	3,781	2,804	5,282	11,009	8,288	2,342	5,750
Rome	5,494	737	1,326	5,231	5,195	4,824	5,774	8,040	6,750	895
San Francisco ..	7,931	5,672	7,466	10,248	3,902	1,859	6,905	2,398	4,518	5,367
Singapore	883	6,164	5,137	6,008	11,402	9,372	1,605	6,726	11,689	6,747
Stockholm.....	5,089	528	2,096	6,423	5,471	4,331	5,063	6,875	7,166	942
Tokyo	2,865	5,557	5,958	9,154	8,808	6,314	1,791	3,859	9,631	5,959
Warsaw	5,033	322	1,619	5,935	5,559	4,679	5,147	7,366	7,215	905
Washington, D.C..	8,807	4,181	5,822	7,895	2,047	596	8,155	4,838	3,509	3,674

	Los Angeles	Madrid	Mel-Bourne	Mexico City	Mon-treal	Mos-cow	New Delhi	New York	Paris	Peking
Bangkok......	7,637	6,337	4,568	9,793	8,338	4,389	1,813	8,669	5,877	2,046
Berlin	5,782	1,165	9,918	6,056	3,740	1,006	3,598	3,979	548	4,584
Cairo........	7,520	2,087	8,675	7,700	5,427	1,803	2,758	5,619	1,998	4,698
Cape Town	9,969	5,308	6,425	8,519	7,922	6,279	5,769	7,803	5,786	8,044
Caracas......	3,632	4,346	9,717	2,234	2,438	6,177	8,833	2,120	4,732	8,950
Chicago	1,745	4,189	9,673	1,690	745	4,987	7,486	714	4,143	6,604
Hong Kong	7,240	6,558	4,595	8,788	7,736	4,437	2,339	8,060	5,990	1,217
Honolulu.....	2,557	7,872	5,505	3,789	4,918	7,047	7,412	4,969	7,449	5,077
London	5,439	785	10,500	5,558	3,254	1,564	4,181	3,469	214	5,074
Los Angeles. ...	....	5,848	7,931	1,542	2,427	6,068	7,011	2,451	5,601	6,250
Madrid.......	5,848	....	10,758	5,643	3,448	2,147	4,530	3,593	655	5,745
Melbourne.....	7,931	10,758	....	8,426	10,395	8,950	6,329	10,359	10,430	5,643
Mexico City ...	1,542	5,643	8,426	....	2,317	6,676	9,120	2,090	5,725	7,753
Montreal......	2,427	3,448	10,395	2,317	....	4,401	7,012	331	3,432	6,519
Moscow	6,068	2,147	8,950	6,676	4,401	....	2,698	4,683	1,554	3,607
New York	2,451	3,593	10,359	2,090	331	4,683	7,318	....	3,636	6,844
Paris	5,601	655	10,430	5,725	3,432	1,554	4,102	3,636	....	5,120
Peking	6,250	5,745	5,643	7,753	6,519	3,607	2,353	6,844	5,120	....
Rio de Janeiro ..	6,330	5,045	8,226	4,764	5,078	7,170	8,753	4,801	5,684	10,768
Rome	6,326	851	9,929	6,377	4,104	1,483	3,684	4,293	690	5,063
San Francisco ..	347	5,803	7,856	1,887	2,543	5,885	7,691	2,572	5,577	5,918
Singapore	8,767	7,080	3,759	10,327	9,203	5,228	2,571	9,534	6,673	2,771
Stockholm.....	5,454	1,653	9,630	6,012	3,714	716	3,414	3,986	1,003	4,133
Tokyo	5,470	6,706	5,062	7,035	6,471	4,660	3,638	6,757	6,053	1,307
Warsaw	5,922	1,427	9,598	6,337	4,022	721	3,277	4,270	852	4,325
Washington, D.C..	2,300	3,792	10,180	1,885	489	4,876	7,500	205	3,840	6,942

	Rio de Janiero	Rome	San Fran-cisco	Singa-pore	Stock holm	Teheran	Tokyo	Vienna	Warsaw	Wash., D.C.
Bangkok......	9,994	5,494	7,931	883	5,089	3,391	2,865	5,252	5,033	8,807
Berlin	6,209	737	5,672	6,164	528	2,185	5,557	326	322	4,181
Cairo........	6,143	1,326	7,466	5,137	2,096	1,234	5,958	1,481	1,619	5,822
Cape Town	3,781	5,231	10,248	6,008	6,423	5,241	9,154	5,656	5,935	7,895
Caracas......	2,804	5,195	3,902	11,402	5,471	7,320	8,808	5,372	5,559	2,047
Chicago	5,282	4,824	1,859	9,372	4,331	6,502	6,314	4,698	4,679	596
Hong Kong	11,009	5,774	6,905	1,605	5,063	3,843	1,791	5,431	5,147	8,155
Honolulu.....	8,288	8,040	2,398	6,726	6,875	8,070	3,859	7,632	7,366	4,838
London	5,750	895	5,367	6,747	942	2,743	5,959	771	905	3,674
Los Angeles. ...	6,330	6,326	347	8,767	5,454	7,682	5,470	6,108	5,922	2,300
Madrid.......	5,045	851	5,803	7,080	1,653	2,978	6,706	1,128	1,427	3,792
Melbourne.....	8,226	9,929	7,856	3,759	9,630	7,826	5,062	9,790	9,598	10,180
Mexico City ...	4,764	6,377	1,887	10,327	6,012	8,184	7,035	6,320	6,337	1,885
Montreal......	5,078	4,104	2,543	9,203	3,714	5,880	6,471	4,009	4,022	489
Moscow	7,170	1,483	5,885	5,228	716	1,532	4,660	1,043	721	4,876
New York	4,801	4,293	2,572	9,534	3,986	6,141	6,757	4,234	4,270	205
Paris	5,684	690	5,577	6,673	1,003	2,625	6,053	645	852	3,840
Peking	10,768	5,063	5,918	2,771	4,133	3,490	1,307	4,648	4,325	6,942
Rio de Janeiro ..	....	5,707	6,613	9,785	6,683	7,374	11,532	6,127	6,455	4,779
Rome	5,707	....	6,259	6,229	1,245	2,127	6,142	477	820	4,497
San Francisco ..	6,613	6,259	....	8,448	5,399	7,362	5,150	5,994	5,854	2,441
Singapore	9,785	6,229	8,448	....	5,936	4,103	3,300	6,035	5,843	9,662
Stockholm.....	6,683	1,245	5,399	5,936	....	2,173	5,053	780	494	4,183
Tokyo	11,532	6,142	5,150	3,300	5,053	4,775	....	5,689	5,347	6,791
Warsaw	6,455	820	5,854	5,843	494	1,879	5,689	347	....	4,472
Washington, D.C..	4,779	4,497	2,441	9,662	4,183	6,341	6,791	4,438	4,472	....

AGRICULTURE

World and Regional Food Production, 1975 to 1980

Source: UN Food and Agriculture Organization

| | (1969-71 = 100) | | | | | | Change 1979 to 1980 | Annual rate of change |
Region	1975	1976	1977	1978	1979	1980[1]	1980	1971-80
Food Production								
Developing market economies[2] . . .	115	118	122	127	127	132	+ 5	3.3
Africa	118	111	109	113	114	118	+ 4	1.7
Far East	115	115	124	128	125	132	+ 7	3.5
Latin America	116	123	127	133	136	141	+ 5	3.9
Near East.	121	128	125	131	132	136	+ 4	3.4
Asian centrally planned economies.	118	122	122	129	137	137	0	3.4
Total Developing Countries. . . .	116	119	122	128	130	134	+ 4	3.3
Developed market economies[2] . . .	112	112	116	119	122	120	− 2	2.0
North America	114	117	122	123	127	124	− 2	2.4
Oceania	119	128	124	142	136	122	− 14	2.9
Western Europe	110	108	111	116	120	123	+ 3	1.9
Eastern Europe and the USSR . . .	112	115	117	125	119	118	− 1	1.6
Total Developed Countries	112	113	116	121	121	120	− 1	1.9
World	114	116	119	124	125	126	+ 1	2.5

Note: Food production covers crops and livestock only. (1) Preliminary. (2) Including countries in other regions not specified.

Food Production Per Capita in Developing Regions, 1975-80

Source: UN Food and Agriculture Organization

| | (1969-71 = 100) | | | | | | Change 1979 to 1980 | Annual rate of change |
Region	1975	1976	1977[2]	1978	1979	1980[1]	1980	1971-80
Developing market economies[2] .	100	100	101	105	102	103	+ 1.4	+ 0.7
Africa	93	93	89	90	88	89	+ 0.5	− 1.2
Far East	101	99	103	108	103	105	+ 2.7	+ 1.0
Latin America	101	101	103	107	107	108	+ 0.5	+ 1.2
Near East	104	107	102	106	105	104	− 0.1	+ 0.6
Total developing countries . .	103	103	103	107	107	108	+ 0.4	+ 1.1

(1) Preliminary. (2) Including countries in other regions not specified.

Food Intake Below Critical Minimum Limit in Developing Regions

Source: UN Food and Agriculture Organization
(Estimated)
The critical minimum limit for food intake is 1.2 times the Basal Metabolic Rate (BMR).

| | Total Population (millions) | | Percentage below 1.2 BMR | | Total number below 1.2 BMR (millions) | |
Region	1969-71	1972-74	1969-71	1972-74	1969-71	1972-74
Africa	278	301	25	28	70	83
Far East	968	1,042	25	29	256	297
Latin America	279	302	16	15	44	46
Near East	167	182	18	16	31	29
MSA[1]	954	1,027	27	30	255	307
Other developing market economies	738	800	20	18	146	148
Total developing market economies	1,692	1,827	24	25	401	455

(1) Countries most severely affected by food shortages.

World Daily Dietary Energy Supply in Relation to Requirements

Source: UN Food and Agriculture Organization

| | Dietary energy[1] | | | | Supply as percent of requirement[2] | | | |
Region	1966-68	1969-71	1972-74	1975-77	1966-68	1969-71	1972-74	1975-77
Developing market economies	2,122	2,206	2,193	2,219	81	85	84	85
Africa	2,136	2,194	2,174	2,208	82	84	84	85
Latin America	2,511	2,531	2,518	2,552	97	97	97	98
Near East	2,413	2,431	2,498	2,657	93	94	96	102
Far East	1,959	2,079	2,053	2,053	75	80	80	80
Others	2,268	2,326	2,371	2,345	87	89	91	90
Asian centrally planned econ.	2,087	2,224	2,317	2,420	80	86	89	93
Total developing countries	2,110	2,211	2,233	2,282	81	85	86	88
Developed market economies	3,200	3,275	3,323	3,329	123	126	128	128
North America	3,384	3,467	3,493	3,519	130	133	134	135
Western Europe	3,256	3,333	3,389	3,378	125	128	130	130
Oceania	3,288	3,360	3,365	3,418	126	129	129	131
Others	2,701	2,769	2,852	2,872	104	107	110	110
Eastern Europe and the U.S.S.R.	3,300	3,379	3,413	3,465	127	130	131	133
Total developed countries	3,232	3,309	3,353	3,373	124	127	129	130
World	2,457	2,541	2,559	2,590	95	98	98	99

(1) Calories per capita per day. (2) Daily calorie requirement is 3,000 for men, 2,200 for women.

Agricultural Products — U.S. and World Production and Exports

Source: Foreign Agricultural Service, U.S. Agriculture Department

1980/81 Commodity	Unit	Production			Exports[6]		
		U.S.	World	% U.S.	U.S.	World	% U.S.
Wheat	MMT	[1] 65	[2] 439	15	[3] 42	[3] 94	45
Oats	MMT	[1] 7	[2] 44	16	[1] .189	[2] 1	19
Corn	MMT	[4] 169	[2] 402	42	[4] 64	[2] 80	80
Barley	MMT	[1] 8	[2] 162	5	[1] 2	[2] 16	13
Rice[5]	MMT	7	369	2	[5] 3	[7] 13	23
Soybeans	MMT	49	[8] 82	60	20	26	77
Lard	1,000 MT	500	3,956	13	[9] 42	[9] 221	19
Tallow & Grease	1,000 MT	3,175	5,550	57	[9] 1,516	[9] 2,807	54
Tobacco, unmfd.[9]	1,000 MT	[10] 805	[10] 5,060	16	273	1,304	21
Edible, Veg. Oils	MMT	10	40	25	[8,11] 5.7	[8] 10.8	53
Cotton[5,12]	Mil. Bales	11	65	17	6	20	30

(1) Year beginning June 1. (2) Year beginning July 1. (3) Includes wheat flour in grain. (4) Year beginning October 1. (5) Year beginning August 1. (6) Preliminary. (7) Calendar Year 1981. (8) Year beginning September 1. (9) Calendar Year 1980. (10) Farm sales weight basis. (11) Includes oil equivalent of exported oilseed. (12) Bales of 480 lbs. net weight.

Grain, Hay, Potato, Cotton, Soybean, Tobacco Production

Source: Economic Research Service, U.S. Agriculture Department

1980 State	Barley 1,000 bushels	Corn, grain 1,000 bushels	Cotton lint 1,000 bales[1]	All hay 1,000 tons	Oats 1,000 bushels	Potatoes 1,000 cwt.	Soybeans 1,000 bushels	Tobacco 1,000 pounds	All wheat 1,000 bushels
Alabama	—	14,580	275	1,031	1,260	1,105	31,500	816	5,758
Alaska	—	—	—	—	—	—	—	—	—
Arizona	3,950	4,000	1,413	1,260	—	1,276	—	—	17,200
Arkansas	—	1,036	450	1,221	2,079	—	69,600	—	31,160
California	44,144	36,450	3,150	7,736	4,340	18,692	—	—	85,500
Colorado	15,925	89,680	—	3,276	1,683	12,545	—	—	109,900
Connecticut[2]	—	—	—	168	—	405	—	5,475	—
Delaware	1,225	12,744	—	40	—	969	5,200	—	1,080
Florida	—	15,416	8	552	—	5,304	10,120	20,291	—
Georgia	—	54,600	86	736	3,445	—	25,680	110,550	19,800
Hawaii	—	—	—	—	—	—	—	—	—
Idaho	58,960	4,700	—	4,395	2,990	78,455	—	—	96,030
Illinois	258	1,065,780	—	3,558	14,030	414	309,875	—	75,360
Indiana	—	602,880	—	2,208	5,850	966	157,680	15,300	53,900
Iowa	—	1,463,000	—	8,037	62,000	322	322,530	—	3,496
Kansas	2,419	116,560	—	4,230	4,560	—	23,925	—	420,000
Kentucky	1,595	103,600	—	2,970	240	—	36,800	409,222	13,825
Louisiana	—	1,380	455	612	—	—	70,350	56	1,876
Maine[2]	—	—	—	362	2,436	24,960	—	—	—
Maryland	3,640	46,080	—	564	1,121	306	9,360	22,575	3,686
Massachusetts[2]	—	—	—	258	—	748	—	2,058	—
Michigan	1,113	247,000	—	3,844	20,100	9,022	30,400	—	35,200
Minnesota	34,638	610,130	—	7,115	82,650	111,486	152,320	—	102,556
Mississippi	—	2,464	1,150	1,040	—	—	61,600	—	7,750
Missouri	—	109,710	178	4,470	1,978	—	138,250	5,125	89,010
Montana	44,100	592	—	4,170	3,212	1,725	—	—	119,800
Nebraska	950	603,500	—	7,083	15,170	2,136	53,100	—	112,100
Nevada	1,960	—	1.2	1,095	—	4,420	—	—	1,800
New Hampshire[2]	—	—	—	187	—	—	—	—	—
New Jersey	795	7,725	—	255	275	1,968	3,492	—	1,849
New Mexico	1,995	7,225	110	1,144	—	540	—	—	10,500
New York	517	67,890	—	5,787	17,920	10,668	456	—	6,000
North Carolina	2,880	103,800	51	592	3,900	2,227	35,705	763,665	10,500
North Dakota	48,000	16,820	—	2,519	13,500	15,680	3,500	—	179,650
Ohio	416	440,700	—	3,588	19,430	2,234	135,360	20,510	67,130
Oklahoma	1,650	5,250	216	2,315	3,900	—	3,000	—	195,000
Oregon	10,075	1,166	—	2,893	4,140	19,745	—	—	77,400
Pennsylvania	3,750	96,000	—	4,182	19,040	4,180	2,524	22,750	9,250
Rhode Island[2]	—	—	—	18	—	736	—	—	—
South Carolina	1,012	24,720	76	354	1,960	—	22,400	125,125	6,912
South Dakota	13,860	121,900	—	5,359	66,000	1,072	20,020	—	62,425
Tennessee	168	28,800	200	1,764	552	196	48,450	112,544	13,300
Texas	1,080	117,000	3,305	5,515	12,580	2,306	13,860	—	130,000
Utah	10,804	1,500	—	2,058	915	1,144	—	—	8,942
Vermont[2]	—	—	—	886	—	120	—	—	—
Virginia	4,590	32,725	0.2	1,626	900	1,540	9,150	108,919	10,582
Washington	31,500	11,280	—	2,625	1,860	43,935	—	—	160,220
West Virginia	396	5,162	—	977	539	—	—	2,720	342
Wisconsin	1,534	348,400	—	12,545	58,743	16,000	10,890	24,300	4,365
Wyoming	8,645	3,589	—	1,850	2,295	1,340	—	—	8,512
Total U.S.	358,544	6,647,534	11,125	131,070	457,593	301,006	1,817,097	1,772,001	2,369,666

(1) Equiv. to 480 lbs. (2) All harvested corn acreage is for silage.

Production of Chief U.S. Crops
Source: Economics, Statistics, and Cooperatives Service: U.S. Agriculture Department

Year	Corn for grain 1,000 bushels	Oats 1,000 bushels	Barley 1,000 bushels	Sorghums for grain 1,000 bushels	All wheat 1,000 bushels	Rye 1,000 bushels	Flaxseed 1,000 bushels	Cotton lint 1,000 bales	Cotton seed 1,000 tons
1970	4,152,243	915,236	416,091	683,179	1,351,558	36,840	29,416	10,192	4,068
1974	4,701,402	600,655	298,669	622,711	1,781,918	17,506	14,083	11,540	4,510
1975	5,828,961	642,042	374,386	753,046	2,122,459	15,958	15,553	8,302	3,218
1977	6,425,457	750,901	420,159	792,983	2,036,318	17,312	15,105	14,389	5,521
1978	7,267,927	581,657	454,759	731,270	1,775,524	24,065	8,614	10,855	4,269
1979	7,938,819	526,551	382,798	808,862	2,134,060	22,389	12,014	14,629	5,778
1980	6,647,534	457,593	358,544	587,997	2,369,666	16,265	8,128	11,124	4,359

Year	Tobacco 1,000 lbs.	All hay 1,000 tons	Beans dry edible 1,000 cwt.	Peas dry edible 1,000 cwt.	Peanuts 1,000 lbs.	Soybeans 1,000 bushels	Potatoes 1,000 cwt.	Sweet potatoes 1,000 cwt.
1970	1,906,453	126,969	17,399	3,315	2,983,121	1,127,100	325,716	13,164
1974	1,989,728	126,384	20,330	3,228	3,667,604	1,216,287	342,395	13,339
1975	2,181,775	132,210	17,442	2,731	3,857,122	1,547,383	322,254	13,225
1977	1,912,759	131,313	16,610	1,023	3,726,015	1,761,755	354,576	12,395
1978	2,024,820	143,817	18,935	3,601	3,952,384	1,868,754	366,314	13,115
1979	1,526,549	147,847	20,476	2,039	3,968,485	2,267,901	342,497	13,370
1980	1,772,001	131,070	26,100	3,285	2,296,250	1,817,097	301,006	10,948

Year	Five seed crops* 1,000 lbs.	Sugar and seed 1,000 tons	Sugar beets 1,000 tons	Pecans 1,000 tons	Almonds 1,000 tons	Walnuts 1,000 tons	Filberts 1,000 tons	Oranges and tangerines** 1,000 boxes	Grapefruit** 1,000 boxes
1970	251,934	23,996	26,378	77.6	124.0	111.8	9.3	189,970	53,910
1974	179,918	25,140	22,123	68.7	189.0	156.5	6.7	221,050	65,500
1975	161,609	28,344	29,704	124.2	160.0	199.3	12.1	243,060	61,610
1977	139,101	26,830	25,007	118.3	156.5	192.5	11.8	248,720	74,600
1978	143,817	25,997	25,788	249.9	82.1	160	14.1	225,320	74,660
1979	147,847	26,532	21,996	210.6	170.6	208	13.0	216,000	67,380
1980	131,070	28,235	23,275	200.7	147.4	198	15.0	280,130	73,200

*Five seed crops include alfalfa, red clover, ladino clover, lespedeza, and timothy. ** Crop year ending in year cited.

Production of Principal Field Crops in Canada
Source: Statistics Canada

1980	Wheats 1,000 bushels	Oats 1,000 bushels	Barley 1,000 bushels	Ryes 1,000 bushels	Flaxseed 1,000 bushels
Canada[1]	702,949	196,317	507,104	17,644	18,300
Prince Edward Island	429	2,964	2,295	—	—
Nova Scotia	266	1,051	273	—	—
New Brunswick	336	1,716	440	—	—
Quebec	5,666	23,544	5,727	244	—
Ontario	27,002	23,142	24,269	2,550	—
Manitoba	70,000	18,000	69,000	2,940	8,500
Saskatchewan	397,000	40,000	126,000	4,250	6,500
Alberta	196,000	82,000	269,000	7,300	3,300
British Columbia	6,250	3,900	10,100	360	—

	Mixed grains 1,000 bushels	Corn grains 1,000 bushels	Soybeans 1,000 bushels	Rapeseed 1,000 bushels	Potatoes 1,000 c.w.t.
Canada(1)	80,778	215,043	26,204	110,500	55,622
Prince Edward Island	3,612	—	—	—	13,216
Nova Scotia	353	—	—	—	728
New Brunswick	320	—	—	—	11,700
Quebec	6,193	21,562	—	—	8,498
Ontario	51,160	185,411	26,204	—	8,820
Manitoba	4,300	7,500	—	14,600	6,240
Saskatchewan	3,700	—	—	44,000	323
Alberta	11,000	570	—	50,000	4,096
British Columbia	140	—	—	2,500	1,920

	Mustard seed 1,000 pounds	Sunflower seed 1,000 pounds	Tame hay 1,000 tons	Fodder corn 1,000 tons	Sugar beets 1,000 tons
Canada(1)	215,000	366,000	26,179	15,529	943
Prince Edward Island	—	—	296	108	—
Nova Scotia	—	—	398	135	—
New Brunswick	—	—	354	82	—
Quebec	—	—	5,610	3,678	156
Ontario	—	—	8,041	10,076	—
Manitoba	36,000	350,000	1,500	420	258
Saskatchewan	123,000	16,000	1,400	—	—
Alberta	56,000	—	6,500	480	578
British Columbia	—	—	2,080	550	—

(1) Excluding Newfoundland.

U.S. Farms by State—Number, Acreage, and Value

Source: Census of Agriculture, U.S. Bureau of the Census

State	Farms (Number)		Average size of farm (acres)		Value of land and buildings (per acre)		Percent of land area in farms	
	1974	1978	1974	1978	1974	1978	1974	1978
Alabama	56,678	57,503	209	201	$ 364	639	36.5	35.6
Alaska	291	383	5,612	3,359	42	109	0.5	0.4
Arizona	5,803	7,660	6,539	5,047	111	199	52.3	53.3
Arkansas	50,959	58,959	287	265	419	770	44.0	46.9
California	67,674	81,706	493	405	653	1,186	33.4	33.1
Colorado	25,501	29,633	1,408	1,197	188	322	54.1	53.4
Connecticut	3,421	4,560	129	110	1,525	2,227	14.1	16.1
Delaware	3,400	3,632	185	187	971	1,500	49.7	53.5
Florida	32,466	44,068	407	302	685	1,149	38.1	38.4
Georgia	54,911	58,648	253	234	474	777	37.3	37.0
Hawaii	3,020	4,310	702	461	485	897	51.5	48.3
Idaho	23,680	26,478	603	562	339	585	27.0	28.1
Illinois	111,049	109,924	262	270	846	1,858	81.5	83.3
Indiana	87,915	88,427	191	193	720	1,589	72.7	73.7
Iowa	126,104	126,456	262	266	719	1,550	92.3	93.8
Kansas	79,188	77,129	605	619	296	501	91.6	91.2
Kentucky	102,053	109,980	141	137	427	861	56.9	59.3
Louisiana	33,240	38,923	275	247	512	1,001	31.7	33.4
Maine	6,436	8,158	237	197	341	538	7.7	8.1
Maryland	15,163	18,727	174	145	1,060	1,800	39.1	41.6
Massachusetts	4,497	5,891	134	115	961	1,443	12.0	13.6
Michigan	64,094	68,237	169	168	553	975	29.8	31.5
Minnesota	98,537	102,963	280	279	429	901	54.4	56.5
Mississippi	53,620	54,182	267	256	379	681	47.2	45.8
Missouri	115,711	121,955	258	253	396	726	67.5	69.9
Montana	23,324	24,469	2,665	2,545	112	196	66.7	66.8
Nebraska	67,597	65,916	683	702	282	525	94.3	94.5
Nevada	2,076	2,877	5,209	3,641	85	191	15.4	14.9
New Hampshire	2,412	3,288	210	164	564	919	8.8	9.4
New Jersey	7,409	9,895	130	106	1,807	2,701	20.0	21.8
New Mexico	11,282	14,253	4,170	3,389	78	143	60.5	62.2
New York	43,682	49,273	215	201	510	670	30.7	32.4
North Carolina	91,280	89,367	123	127	590	1,051	36.0	36.3
North Dakota	42,710	41,169	992	1,021	195	347	95.6	94.8
Ohio	92,158	95,937	170	168	706	1,483	59.7	61.3
Oklahoma	69,719	79,388	475	433	302	512	75.2	78.0
Oregon	26,753	34,642	682	532	250	504	29.6	29.9
Pennsylvania	53,171	59,942	154	146	734	1,273	28.4	30.4
Rhode Island	597	866	102	86	1,500	2,370	9.1	11.1
South Carolina	29,275	33,430	211	189	467	773	31.9	32.7
South Dakota	42,825	39,665	1,074	1,123	145	256	94.6	91.6
Tennessee	93,659	97,036	140	136	467	860	49.5	49.7
Texas	174,068	194,253	771	708	243	386	80.0	82.0
Utah	12,184	13,833	871	760	188	400	20.2	20.0
Vermont	5,906	7,273	282	241	462	660	28.1	29.6
Virginia	52,699	56,869	184	175	558	930	38.0	39.1
Washington	29,410	37,730	567	451	350	692	39.1	39.9
West Virginia	16,909	20,532	207	188	300	592	22.7	25.1
Wisconsin	89,479	89,945	197	201	434	856	50.6	51.9
Wyoming	8,018	8,495	4,274	3,969	80	144	55.1	54.2
Total	**2,314,013**	**2,478,642**	**440**	**415**	**336**	**628**	**44.9**	**45.4**

Livestock on Farms in the U.S.

Source: Economics, Statistics, and Cooperatives Service: U.S. Agriculture Department (thousands)

Year (On Jan. 1)	All cattle	Milk cows	All sheep	Hogs	Horses* and mules	Year (On Jan. 1)	All cattle	Milk cows	All sheep	Hogs
1890....	60,014	15,000	44,518	48,130	18,054	1965......	109,000	²15,380	25,127	57,030
1900....	59,739	16,544	48,105	51,055	21,004	1970......	112,369	12,091	20,423	³57,046
1910....	58,993	19,450	50,239	48,072	24,211	1971......	114,578	11,909	19,731	³67,285
1920....	70,400	21,455	40,743	60,159	25,742	1972......	117,862	11,776	18,739	³62,412
1925....	63,373	22,575	38,543	55,770	22,569	1973......	121,539	11,622	17,641	³59,017
1930....	61,003	23,032	51,565	55,705	19,124	1974......	127,788	11,297	16,310	³60,614
1935....	68,846	26,082	51,808	39,066	16,683	1975......	132,028	11,220	14,515	³54,693
1940....	68,039	24,940	52,107	61,165	14,478	1976......	127,980	11,071	13,311	³49,267
1945....	85,573	27,770	46,520	59,373	11,950	1977......	122,810	10,998	12,722	³54,934
1950....	77,963	23,853	29,826	58,937	7,781	1978......	116,375	10,896	12,421	³56,539
1955....	96,592	23,462	31,582	50,474	4,309	1979......	110,864	10,790	12,365	³60,356
1960....	96,236	19,527	33,170	59,026	3,089	1980......	111,192	10,779	12,687	³67,353
						1981¹......	115,013	10,869	12,942	³64,520

*Discontinued in 1960. (1) Total estimated value on farms as of Jan. 1, 1981, was as follows (avg. value per head in parentheses): cattle and calves $54,359,000 ($473); sheep and lambs $904,488,000 ($69.90); hogs and pigs $4,822,265,000 ($74.70). (2) New series, milk cows and heifers that have calved, beginning 1965. (3) As of Dec. 1 of preceding year.

Harvested Acreage of Principal U.S. Crops

Source: Economics, Statistics, and Cooperatives Service: U.S. Agriculture Department (thousands of acres)

State	1978	1979	1980	State	1978	1979	1980
Alabama	3,841	5,156	4,045	Nebraska	17,560	18,213	19,025
Arizona	1,066	1,083	1,214	Nevada	547	562	571
Arkansas	8,100	7,313	8,343	New Hampshire	114	116	118
California	6,296	6,455	6,640	New Jersey	532	549	525
Colorado	6,016	6,262	6,938	New Mexico	1,230	1,323	1,383
Connecticut	148	144	145	New York	4,273	4,311	4,334
Delaware	499	519	526	North Carolina	4,980	5,263	5,408
Florida	1,499	1,537	1,521	North Dakota	20,234	20,726	18,435
Georgia	4,902	5,374	5,622	Ohio	10,764	11,023	11,040
Hawaii	106	108	108	Oklahoma	9,135	9,630	9,904
Idaho	4,693	4,594	4,681	Oregon	2,692	2,646	2,738
Illinois	23,151	23,827	24,002	Pennsylvania	4,374	4,496	4,564
Indiana	12,397	12,553	12,878	Rhode Island	19	18	18
Iowa	24,568	25,342	25,646	South Carolina	2,710	2,858	2,884
Kansas	20,136	20,858	21,995	South Dakota	14,730	15,121	14,858
Kentucky	4,995	5,223	5,447	Tennessee	5,033	5,211	5,291
Louisiana	4,926	5,129	5,273	Texas	21,113	22,750	22,450
Maine	420	411	405	Utah	1,146	1,149	1,144
Maryland	1,541	1,562	1,591	Vermont	546	544	549
Massachusetts	165	162	164	Virginia	2,783	2,849	3,012
Michigan	6,689	6,909	7,076	Washington	4,648	4,556	4,838
Minnesota	20,987	21,653	21,830	West Virginia	719	714	722
Mississippi	6,192	6,404	6,358	Wisconsin	9,431	9,476	9,559
Missouri	13,357	14,338	14,669	Wyoming	1,871	1,853	1,854
Montana	8,892	8,813	8,564	**Total U.S.**	326,766	337,686	340,905

Crop acreages included are corn, sorghum, oats, barley, wheat, rice, rye, soybeans, flaxseed, peanuts, sunflower, popcorn, cotton, all hay, dry edible beans, dry edible peas, potatoes, sweet potatoes, tobacco, sugarcane and sugar beets.

Harvested Acreage of Principal Canadian Crops

Source: Statistics Canada (thousands of acres)

Province	1977	1978	1979	1980	Province	1977	1978	1979	1980
Prince Edward Island	372	376	382	386	Manitoba	9,545	10,036	9,959	9,694
Nova Scotia	230	228	233	233	Saskatchewan	26,228	27,350	27,298	26,525
New Brunswick	306	311	308	306	Alberta	17,741	18,581	18,972	19,212
Quebec	3,890	4,003	4,073	4,141	British Columbia	1,130	1,186	1,251	1,296
Ontario	8,186	8,296	8,433	8,483	**Total**	67,627	70,667[1]	70,909[1]	70,276[1]

Crops included are winter wheat, spring wheat, oats, barley, fall rye, spring rye, flaxseed, mixed grains, corn for grain, buckwheat, peas, dry beans, soybeans, rapeseed, potatoes, mustard seed, sunflower seed, tame hay, fodder corn, and sugar beets. (1) Totals include Newfoundland potatoes (1978) 1,120 acres, (1979) 940 acres, (1980) 880 acres.

Wool Production

Source: Economic Research Service: U.S. Agriculture Department

	Sheep shorn (1,000)	Shorn wool (1,000 lbs.)	Value ($1,000)	Price per lb. (cents)	Pulled wool (1,000 lbs.)	Total wool (1,000 lbs)
1970	19,163	161,587	57,162	35.4	15,200	176,787
1974	15,956	131,382	77,788	59.2	5,700	137,082
1975	14,403	119,535	53,505	44.8	6,000	125,535
1976	13,536	111,100	73,332	66.0	4,850	115,950
1977	13,217	107,328	77,276	72.0	2,450	109,778
1978	12,719	102,942	76,690	74.5	1,000	103,942
1979	13,068	104,860	90,531	86.3	900	105,760
1980	13,249	105,452	92,862	88.1	1,050	106,502

U.S. Egg Production

Source: Economic Research Service: U.S. Agriculture Department (millions of eggs)

State	1977	1978	1979	1980	State	1977	1978	1979	1980	State	1977	1978	1979	1980
Ala.	3,183	3,329	3,300	3,354	Me.	1,849	1,912	1,913	1,793	Ore.	525	563	616	638
Alas.	6.2	4.7	6.7	4.4	Md.	324	344	356	381	Pa.	2,960	3,436	3,836	4,251
Ariz.	140	135	139	113	Mass.	355	341	339	326	R.I.	50.7	51.0	59.2	84
Ark.	3,812	4,002	4,123	4,153	Mich.	1,530	1,497	1,491	1,459	S.C.	1,249	1,411	1,561	1,679
Cal.	8,345	8,412	8,713	8,796	Minn.	2,120	2,189	2,183	2,223	S.D.	561	526	476	464
Col.	508	534	484	464	Miss.	1,775	1,696	1,653	1,584	Tenn.	993	974	999	962
Conn.	863	897	938	1,004	Mo.	1,199	1,320	1,376	1,460	Tex.	2,436	2,630	2,795	3,092
Del.	128	129	132	138	Mont.	179	193	178	170	Ut.	335	395	385	416
Fla.	2,998	2,954	3,189	3,044	Neb.	739	780	802	847	Vt.	117	110	99	100
Ga.	5,468	5,662	6,067	5,637	Nev.	3.1	2.3	1.8	1.8	Va.	819	885	939	913
Ha.	218	218	229	222	N.H.	210	222	218	182	Wash.	1,063	1,121	1,172	1,295
Ida.	192	206	192	202	N.J.	446	375	342	279	W.Vir.	192	154	178	149
Ill.	1,389	1,380	1,347	1,267	N.M.	288	359	368	378	Wis.	981	973	911	946
Ind.	3,128	3,447	3,536	3,697	N.Y.	1,805	1,845	1,767	1,776	Wyo.	19.9	14.4	10.8	10.5
Ia.	2,004	1,914	1,849	1,784	N.C.	2,846	3,081	3,155	3,174	**Total**				
Kan.	548	511	483	427	N.D.	110	115	111	82	**U.S.**	64,602	67,157	69,209	69,683
Ky.	566	553	583	536	Oh.	1,941	2,140	2,253	2,333					
La.	598	603	601	553	Okla.	487	612	754	839					

Note: The egg and chicken production year runs from Dec. 1 of the previous year through Nov. 30. (1) Included are eggs destroyed because of possible PCB contamination.

Egg Production in Canada
Source: Statistics Canada
(thousand dozens)

Province	1978	1979	1980	Province	1978	1979	1980
Newfoundland	7,115	7,222	7,399	Manitoba	49,377	48,358	51,358
Prince Edward Island	2,645	2,716	2,794	Saskatchewan	20,851	20,566	21,203
Nova Scotia	16,330	16,687	18,778	Alberta	41,646	43,924	46,593
New Brunswick	8,768	8,964	9,380	British Columbia	58,280	59,077	62,501
Quebec	73,800	74,867	78,803	**Total**	**459,203**	**462,631**	**488,059**
Ontario	180,381	180,250	189,250				

Gross farm value of eggs (1977) $313,398,000; (1978) $317,613,000; (1979) $354,069,000; (1980) $410,178,000. Average price per dozen of eggs sold for consumption (1977) $.65; (1978) $.64; (1979) $.72; (1980) $.84. Number and value of chicken and fowl (1977) 259,556,000 - $365,480,000; (1978) 277,434,000 - $415,504,000; (1979) 309,331,000 - $501,278,000; (1980) 304,125,000 - $516,486,000. Gross farm income from eggs, chicken and fowl (1977) $678,878,000; (1978) $733,117,000; (1979) $855,347,000; (1980) $926,664,000.

Grain Receipts at U.S. Grain Centers
Source: Chicago Board of Trade (thousands bushels)

1980	Wheat	Corn	Oats	Rye	Barley	Soybeans	Total
Chicago	10,173	85,060	39	—	—	16,671	111,892
Duluth	140,716	38,593	468	6,923	49,398	1,259	241,569
Enid	78,262	—	—	—	—	—	78,262
Hutchinson	24,852	2	1	—	—	—	24,855
Kansas City*	—	—	—	—	—	—	—
Milwaukee	604,923	60,654	89,703	—	5,828	856,634	1,917,742
Minneapolis	147,987	42,840	27,017	5,035	89,770	1,477	314,126
Omaha	17,823	7,374	86	18	—	533	25,834
Peoria	42	12,481	—	—	—	78	12,601
Sioux City	.69	301	763	—	—	15	1,148
St. Joseph	1,481	11,180	477	—	—	1,656	14,794
St. Louis	3,648	657	17	—	2,244	—	6,566
Toledo	27,985	135,017	2,313	—	—	55,184	220,499
Wichita	18,043	7	2	—	—	3,092	21,144
Total	**1,076,004**	**394,166**	**125,097**	**11,976**	**144,996**	**936,599**	**2,990,999**

*Not available.

Grain Storage Capacity at Principal Grain Centers in U.S.
Source: Chicago Board of Trade
(bushels)

Cities	Capacity	Cities	Capacity
Atlantic Coast	36,800,000	Texas High Plains	76,800,000
Great Lakes		Enid	66,100,000
Toledo	4,330,000	Gulf Points	
Buffalo	8,200,000	South Mississippi	43,600,000
Chicago	48,835,000	North Texas Gulf	28,200,000
Milwaukee	9,100,000	South Texas Gulf	14,000,000
Duluth	75,800,000	Plains	
River Points		Wichita	60,300,000
Minneapolis	124,200,000	Topeka	61,600,000
Peoria	6,600,000	Salina	45,000,000
St. Louis	25,500,000	Hutchinson	42,000,000
Sioux City	11,600,000	Hastings-Grand Island	24,100,000
Omaha-Council Bluffs	35,300,000	Lincoln	39,600,000
Atchison	24,500,000	Pacific N.W.	
St. Joseph	20,600,000	Puget Sound	9,500,000
Kansas City	72,400,000	Portland	24,900,000
Southwest		California Ports	14,300,000
Fort Worth	57,600,000		

Atlantic Coast — Albany, N.Y., Philadelphia, Pa., Baltimore, Md., Norfolk, Va. **Gulf Points** — New Orleans, Baton Rouge, Ama. Belle Chase, La., Mobile, Ala. **North Texas Gulf** — Houston, Galveston, Beaumont, Port Arthur, Texas. **South Texas Gulf** — Corpus Christi, Brownsville, Texas. **Pacific N.W.** — Seattle, Tacoma, Wash., Portland, Oreg., Columbia River Calif. **Ports** — San Francisco, Stockton, Sacramento, Los Angeles. **Texas High Plains** — Amarillo, Lubbock, Hereford, Plainview, Texas.

U.S. Meat and Lard Production and Consumption
Source: Economic Research Service: U.S. Agriculture Department (million lbs.)

Year	Beef Production	Beef Consumption	Veal Production	Veal Consumption	Lamb and mutton Production	Lamb and mutton Consumption	Pork (exclud. lard) Production	Pork (exclud. lard) Consumption	All meats Production	All meats Consumption	Lard Production	Lard Consumption
1940	7,175	7,257	981	981	876	873	10,044	9,701	19,076	18,812	2,288	1,901
1950	9,534	9,529	1,230	1,206	597	596	10,714	10,390	22,075	21,721	2,631	1,891
1960	14,753	15,147	1,109	1,093	768	852	13,905	13,838	30,535	30,930	2,562	1,358
1965	18,727	19,060	1,020	992	651	716	12,781	12,870	33,179	33,638	2,045	1,225
1970	21,685	22,926	588	581	551	657	14,699	14,661	37,523	38,825	1,913	939
1975	23,976	25,398	873	876	410	430	11,779	11,852	37,038	38,556	1,012	615
1980	21,664	23,321	400	412	318	350	16,615	16,562	38,977	40,645	1,202	540

Net Income per Farm by States

Source: Economic Research Service, U.S. Agriculture Department (dollars)

State	1978	1979	1980	State	1978	1979	1980
Alabama	9,563	10,115	4,426	Nebraska	9,409	14,098	1,987
Alaska	7,249	4,261	-4,680	Nevada	6,923	16,078	14,266
Arizona	54,894	64,644	56,180	New Hampshire	4,736	3,552	618
Arkansas	16,304	17,726	8,697	New Jersey	8,962	8,400	3,634
California	35,805	45,464	42,335	New Mexico	14,893	17,093	12,137
Colorado	12,801	18,509	15,302	New York	7,962	9,702	7,909
Connecticut	16,573	11,593	10,049	North Carolina	12,856	12,221	11,170
Delaware	29,105	28,492	13,708	North Dakota	12,102	9,448	2,215
Florida	34,174	37,653	28,636	Ohio	6,000	8,605	4,755
Georgia	10,286	11,454	705	Oklahoma	4,279	11,036	4,989
Hawaii	35,533	38,334	33,431	Oregon	6,291	9,025	7,259
Idaho	15,041	14,374	18,780	Pennsylvania	8,827	12,192	9,204
Illinois	11,011	17,906	1,951	Rhode Island	10,468	6,704	4,521
Indiana	8,304	11,411	6,355	South Carolina	2,691	8,028	1,097
Iowa	15,831	13,106	4,659	South Dakota	10,685	13,480	4,980
Kansas	9,274	16,655	7,165	Tenneesse	3,219	3,888	968
Kentucky	7,453	9,194	7,462	Texas	6,564	12,070	6,712
Louisiana	10,856	14,183	8,415	Utah	7,152	7,577	5,266
Maine	12,935	11,211	1,578	Vermont	14,499	15,478	12,288
Maryland	11,440	12,170	5,633	Virginia	5,886	6,170	3,750
Massachusetts	15,721	13,279	10,012	Washington	20,245	16,781	19,147
Michigan	7,556	8,903	7,810	West Virginia	866	1,623	1,440
Minnesota	13,660	13,820	11,120	Wisconsin	10,688	15,465	14,554
Mississippi	10,368	12,416	4,934	Wyoming	6,212	8,531	2,177
Missouri	7,028	10,118	2,553	Total. U.S.	10,860	13,456	8,180
Montana	11,190	4,209	4,595				

Note: Data based on the 1974 Census of Agriculture definition of a farm (sales of $1,000 or more).

Farm Income—Cash Receipts from Marketings

Source: Economic Research Service: U.S. Agriculture Department
($1,000)

1980 State	Crops	Live-stock	Gov't pay'ts	Total	1980 State	Crops	Live-stock	Gov't pay'ts	Total
Alabama	695,798	1,140,519	23,029	1,859,346	Nebraska	2,504,407	3,570,282	82,918	6,157,607
Alaska	7,458	4,076	194	11,728	Nevada	75,276	157,791	1,340	234,407
Arizona	937,500	782,704	5,081	1,725,285	New Hampshire	26,112	72,344	702	99,158
Arkansas	1,531,155	1,457,023	34,514	3,022,692	New Jersey	309,375	122,311	869	432,555
California	9,390,368	4,148,593	14,109	13,553,070	New Mexico	268,671	875,878	20,888	1,165,437
Colorado	965,204	2,219,922	18,012	3,203,138	New York	713,747	1,703,910	5,821	2,423,478
Connecticut	123,819	172,410	941	297,170	North Carolina	2,185,070	1,436,249	13,187	3,634,506
Delaware	96,620	236,505	1,035	334,160	North Dakota	1,604,961	781,422	116,634	2,503,017
Florida	2,848,338	955,937	7,043	3,811,318	Ohio	2,381,219	1,356,110	9,403	3,746,732
Georgia	1,173,405	1,503,310	28,866	2,705,581	Oklahoma	1,083,962	2,147,030	34,890	3,265,882
Hawaii	358,023	81,320	711	440,054	Oregon	1,074,480	537,334	5,897	1,617,711
Idaho	1,155,912	851,513	7,901	2,015,326	Pennsylvania	746,937	1,919,557	8,333	2,674,827
Illinois	5,578,766	2,312,430	35,734	7,926,930	Rhode Island	19,191	13,318	95	32,604
Indiana	2,846,269	1,661,756	15,024	4,523,049	South Carolina	655,354	413,215	13,431	1,082,000
Iowa	4,552,616	5,487,358	44,563	10,084,537	South Dakota	755,580	1,790,038	65,272	2,610,890
Kansas	2,524,929	3,361,761	13,251	5,899,941	Tennessee	852,453	884,681	18,681	1,755,815
Kentucky	1,332,073	1,344,850	10,757	2,687,680	Texas	3,766,373	5,188,052	231,840	9,186,265
Louisiana	1,194,789	458,079	19,229	1,672,097	Utah	140,067	383,946	5,090	529,103
Maine	124,654	299,914	3,443	428,011	Vermont	25,592	352,885	1,322	379,799
Maryland	288,146	614,612	3,514	906,272	Virginia	510,004	949,459	13,302	1,472,765
Massachusetts	182,952	125,572	743	309,267	Washington	1,858,498	846,883	9,458	2,714,839
Michigan	1,574,749	1,118,819	10,666	2,704,234	West Virginia	64,373	172,371	2,489	239,233
Minnesota	2,988,358	3,303,966	69,593	6,361,917	Wisconsin	968,307	3,743,216	12,373	4,723,896
Mississippi	1,252,940	891,797	18,770	2,163,507	Wyoming	126,361	524,327	7,323	658,011
Missouri	1,924,162	2,181,302	78,907	4,184,371	U.S.	69,025,823	67,405,497	1,285,672	137,716,992
Montana	660,450	746,840	58,484	1,465,774					

Average Farm Wages

Source: Economic Research Service, U.S. Agriculture Department
(dollars per hour)

Method of pay:	1978	1979	1980		1978	1979	1980
All hired farm workers	3.09	3.39	3.66	Packinghouse workers	3.18	3.39	3.63
Paid by piece-rate	3.76	4.07	4.61	Machine operators	3.13	3.44	3.70
Paid by other than piece-rate	3.04	3.34	3.59	Supervisors	4.95	5.22	5.59
Paid by hour only[1]	3.08	3.38	3.63	Other agricultural workers	3.60	3.82	4.06
Paid cash wages only[2]	3.22	3.58	3.82				
Paid by hour cash wages only[3]	3.10	3.41	3.67	Indexes[4]			
Type of work performed:				(1910-14 = 100)	2,044	2,242	2,421
Field and livestock workers	2.81	3.11	3.45	(1967 = 100)	241	265	286

(1) May include perquisites such as room and board, includes only those paid by the hour. (2) Does not include perquisites, includes all methods of pay. (3) Does not include perquisites, includes only those paid by the hour. (4) Indexes are based on all hired farm workers and are adjusted for seasonal variation.

Average Prices Received by U.S. Farmers

Source: Economic Research Service: U.S. Agriculture Department

The figures represent dollars per 100 lbs. for hogs, beef cattle, veal calves, sheep, lamb, and milk (wholesale), dollars per head for milk cows; cents per lb. for milk fat (in cream), chickens, broilers, turkeys, and wool; cents for eggs per dozen.

Weighted calendar year prices for livestock and livestock products other than wool. 1943 through to 1963, wool prices are weighted on marketing year basis. The marketing year has been changed (1964) from a calendar year to a Dec.-Nov. basis for hogs, chickens, broilers and eggs.

Year	Hogs	Cattle (beef)	Calves (veal)	Sheep	Lambs	Cows (milk)	All Milk	Milk fat (in cream)	Chickens (excl. broilers)	Broilers	Turkeys	Eggs	Wool
1930	8.84	7.71	9.68	4.74	7.76	74	2.21	34.5	...	...	20.2	23.7	19.5
1940	5.39	7.56	8.83	3.95	8.10	61	1.82	28.0	13.0	17.3	15.2	18.0	28.4
1950	18.00	23.30	26.30	11.60	25.10	198	3.89	62.0	22.0	27.4	32.9	36.3	62.1
1960	15.30	20.40	22.90	5.61	17.90	223	4.21	60.5	12.2	16.9	25.4	36.1	42.0
1970	22.70	27.10	34.50	7.51	26.40	332	5.71	70.0	9.1	13.6	22.6	39.1	35.5
1975	46.10	32.20	27.20	11.30	42.10	412	8.75	71.0	9.9	26.3	34.8	52.5	44.7
1978	46.60	48.50	59.10	21.80	62.80	675	10.60	102.0	12.4	26.3	43.6	52.2	74.5
1979	41.80	66.10	88.70	26.30	66.70	1,040	12.00	119.0	14.4	25.9	41.1	58.3	86.3
1980	38.00	62.40	76.80	21.10	63.60	1,190	13.00	—	11.0	27.7	41.3	56.3	88.1

The figures represent cents per lb. for cotton, apples, and peanuts; dollars per bushel for oats, wheat, corn, barley, and soybeans; dollars per 100 lbs. for rice, sorghum, and potatoes; dollars per ton for cottonseed and baled hay.

Weighted crop year prices. Crop years are as follows: apples, June-May; wheat, oats, barley, hay and potatoes, July-June; cotton, rice, peanuts and cottonseed, August-July; soybeans, September-August; and corn and sorghum grain, October-September.

Crop year	Corn	Wheat	Upland cotton[1]	Oats	Barley	Rice	Soybeans	Sorghum	Peanuts	Cotton-seed	Hay	Potatoes	Apples
1930	.663	.550	9.46	0.31	.420	1.74	1.34	1.02	3.46	22.00	11.00	1.47	...
1940	.674	.601	9.83	0.30	.393	1.80	.892	.873	3.33	21.70	9.78	.850	...
1950	2.00	1.52	39.90	0.79	1.19	5.09	2.47	1.88	10.9	86.60	21.10	1.50	...
1960	1.74	.997	30.08	0.60	.838	4.55	2.13	1.49	10.0	42.50	21.70	2.00	4.79
1970	1.33	1.33	22.81	0.62	.973	5.17	2.85	2.04	12.8	56.50	26.10	1.21	6.97
1975	2.54	3.55	51.10	1.45	2.42	8.35	4.92	4.21	19.6	97.00	52.10	4.48	8.80
1978	2.25	2.97	58.10	1.20	1.92	8.16	6.66	3.59	21.1	114.00	49.80	3.38	13.90
1979	2.52	3.78	62.10	1.36	2.29	10.50	6.28	4.18	20.6	121.00	59.50	3.48	15.40
1980	3.27	3.96	76.10	1.82	2.91	12.00	7.61	5.39	24.0	129.00	70.90	5.73	15.40

(1) Beginning 1964, 480 lb. net weight bales. (2) Series discontinued in 1980.

Index Numbers of Prices Received by Farmers

Source: Economics, Statistics, and Cooperatives Service; U.S. Agriculture Department (index 1910-14 = 100 per cent)

Year	All farm products	All crops	Livestock	Food grains	Feed grains and hay	Cotton	Tobacco	Oil-bearing crops	Fruit	Commercial vegetables	Potatoes sweetpot.	Meat animals	Dairy products	Poultry and eggs		Ratio of prices[2] received to prices paid by farmers Year	ratio
1910	104	105	102	109	96	118	84	120	100	...	83	101	100	104		1968	79
1920	211	235	190	249	202	262	233	208	188		294	171	202	222		1969	79
1930	125	115	134	93	106	104	140	111	149	128	162	133	142	128		1970	77
1940	100	90	109	84	85	83	134	103	81	122	89	108	120	98		1971	75
1950	258	233	280	224	193	282	402	276	194	211	166	340	249	186		1972	79
1960	239	222	253	203	152	254	500	214	244	230	203	296	259	160		1973	94
1965	245	230	260	163	174	245	513	265	240	262	293	315	260	144		1974	87
1970	274	225	325	162	179	183	604	265	217	292	218	405	350	147		1975	76
1975	463	452	474	426	400	348	899	529	313	458	400	567	537	235		1978	72
1980	615	541	691	452	417	602	1,219	664	469	562	465		798	255		1980	65

(1) Including dry edible beans. (2) Ratio of the index prices received by farmers, adjusted to reflect government payments to the index of prices paid, for commodities and services, interest, taxes and wage rates.

Food Stamps—Costs and Benefits

Fiscal year	Average persons participating per month	Value per year		Avg. bonus per participant per month	
		Total purchase	Bonus	Current $	1967 $
1962	142,817	$ 35,202,266	$ 13,152,695	7.67	8.47
1965	424,652	85,471,989	32,505,096	6.38	6.75
1970	4,340,030	1,089,960,761	549,663,811	10.55	9.07
1975	17,064,196	7,265,641,706	4,385,501,248	21.41	13.62
1977	17,077,149	8,351,112,000	5,066,969,000	24.73	—
1978	16,043,861	8,310,918,000	5,165,228,000	26.83	—
1979	17,669,985	7,223,375,000	6,478,066,000	30.55	—
1980(p)	21,084,952	8,690,165,000	8,690,165,000	34.35	—

(p) preliminary. The Food Stamp Program enables low-income families to buy more food of greater variety to improve their diets. If a household meets eligibility requirements it receives food stamps based on its net income and the number of people in the household. Major reform measures went into effect Jan. 1, 1979, to lower the net income eligibility standards to the official poverty level ($6,500 for a family of four for fiscal year 1978); change the allowable deductions; eliminate the food stamp purchase requirement; streamline administration; and reduce the potential for fraud or abuse. County and city welfare departments administer the program locally.

Government Payments by Programs, by States

Source: Economic Research Service: U.S. Agriculture Department ($1,000)

1980 State	Conservation[1]	Feed grain program	Wheat program	Cotton program	Rice program	Drought & flood program	Misc. program[3]	Total
Alabama	10,174	4,430	358	2,726	—	—	5,341	23,029
Alaska	173	14	—	—	—	—	7	194
Arizona	3,157	242	14	863	—	—	805	5,081
Arkansas	3,982	6,216	732	14,659	197	0	8,728	34,514
California	6,584	1,195	1,891	332	51	93	3,963	14,109
Colorado	5,159	3,357	2,128	—	—	—	7,368	18,012
Connecticut	470	2	—	—	—	—	469	941
Delaware	251	719	19	—	—	—	46	1,035
Florida	3,730	1,637	315	3	—	—	1,358	7,043
Georgia	5,012	10,664	123	4,985	—	4	8,078	28,866
Hawaii	700	—	—	—	—	—	11	711
Idaho	2,898	912	874	—	—	—	3,217	7,901
Illinois	6,982	20,875	118	—	—	—	7,759	35,734
Indiana	5,625	6,576	86	—	—	—	2,737	15,024
Iowa	7,615	6,319	96	—	—	7	30,526	44,563
Kansas	5,750	63,941	13,430	—	—	27	10,103	93,251
Kentucky	5,004	4,672	50	—	753	—	278	10,757
Louisiana	3,564	248	269	12,432	—	—	2,716	19,229
Maine	2,096	4	—	—	—	—	1,343	3,443
Maryland	1,028	2,114	37	—	—	—	335	3,514
Massachusetts	538	22	—	—	—	—	183	743
Michigan	4,074	3,428	242	—	—	3	2,919	10,666
Minnesota	5,867	10,683	20,818	—	—	4	32,221	69,593
Mississippi	5,290	946	369	10,527	30	—	1,608	18,770
Missouri	7,590	46,860	696	4,031	2	—	19,728	78,907
Montana	5,478	4,562	36,979	—	—	41	11,424	58,484
Nebraska	5,221	33,585	2,864	—	—	—	41,248	82,918
Nevada	838	9	1	—	—	—	492	1,340
New Hampshire	584	6	—	—	—	—	112	702
New Jersey	568	248	1	—	—	—	52	869
New Mexico	2,693	7,014	3,575	2,708	—	—	4,898	20,888
New York	4,266	171	17	—	—	—	1,367	5,821
North Carolina	4,313	6,267	67	625	0	—	1,915	13,187
North Dakota	4,312	19,200	74,582	—	—	—	18,540	116,634
Ohio	4,759	2,807	257	—	—	—	1,580	9,403
Oklahoma	5,061	6,256	8,686	8,112	9	—	6,766	34,890
Oregon	3,417	37	100	—	—	1	2,342	5,897
Pennsylvania	4,170	3,534	29	—	—	—	600	8,333
Rhode Island	79	—	—	—	—	—	16	95
South Carolina	2,680	4,966	57	2,578	—	—	3,150	13,431
South Dakota	3,732	24,573	18,810	—	—	—	18,157	65,272
Tennessee	5,052	8,148	148	3,454	13	14	1,852	18,681
Texas	16,315	54,926	20,886	103,723	893	61	35,036	231,840
Utah	2,753	106	211	—	—	—	2,020	5,090
Vermont	1,127	2	0	—	—	—	193	1,322
Virginia	3,139	7,576	42	4	—	—	2,541	13,302
Washington	5,869	128	609	—	—	—	2,852	9,458
West Virginia	2,097	9	0	—	—	—	383	2,489
Wisconsin	4,708	1,678	60	—	—	18	5,909	12,373
Wyoming	1,735	177	698	—	—	3	4,710	7,323
Total	198,279	382,061	211,344	171,762	1,948	1,276	320,002	1,285,672

(1) Includes amounts paid under Agricultural and Conservation Programs. (2) Includes Sugar Act, National Wool Act, Milk Indemnity Program, Beekeepers Indemnity Program, Hay and Cattle Transportation Program, Cropland Adjustment Program, Forest Incentive Program, Water Bank Program, Emergency Livestock Feed Program, Great Plains and other miscellaneous programs.

Farm Employment—Annual Averages

Source: Economic Research Service: U.S. Agriculture Department (Index 1910-14 = 100 per cent)

Year	Total Aver. no. (1,000)	Index %	Family Aver. no. (1,000)	Index %	Hired Aver. no. (1,000)	Index %	Year	Total Aver. no. (1,000)	Index %	Family Aver. no. (1,000)	Index %	Hired Aver. no. (1,000)	Index %
1920	13,432	99	10,041	99	3,391	100	1960	7,057	52	5,172	52	1,885	55
1930	12,497	92	9,307	92	3,190	94	1970	4,523	34	3,348	33	1,175	35
1940	10,979	82	8,300	81	2,679	79	1979	3,774	28	2,501	25	1,273	37
1950	9,926	75	7,597	73	2,329	69	1980	3,705	27	2,402	24	1,303	35

Canadian Farm Cash Receipts by Province

Source: Statistics Canada
(thousands of Canadian dollars)

Province	1975	1976	1977	1978	1979	1980
Prince Edward Island	86,119	104,005	91,039	101,066	121,439	143,124
Nova Scotia	114,126	126,508	133,373	156,609	174,571	203,481
New Brunswick	98,993	113,145	109,814	123,104	136,713	154,684
Quebec	1,342,362	1,371,590	1,422,497	1,716,886	1,975,195	2,257,670
Ontario	2,696,311	2,791,900	2,865,736	3,417,018	4,022,342	4,326,190
Manitoba	942,413	895,017	899,282	1,132,132	1,309,252	1,446,565
Saskatchewan	2,510,371	2,326,301	2,163,204	2,500,168	3,033,132	3,218,562
Alberta	1,898,470	1,858,629	1,989,243	2,286,876	2,823,382	3,132,510
British Columbia	422,976	481,076	516,157	582,788	655,171	754,792
Total	10,112,141	10,068,171	10,190,345	12,016,647	14,251,197	15,637,578

Canadian Farm Cash Receipts

Source: Statistics Canada
(millions of Canadian Dollars)
Cash receipts from farming operations excluding supplementary payments. Excludes Newfoundland

Crops

Year	Total cash receipts	Total crops	Wheat	Barley	C.W.B. advance pay-ments[1]	Deferred grain receipts	Other grains[2]	Pota-toes	Fruits	Vege-tables	Flori-culture and nursery	Tobacco	Other crops[3]
1976	10,068.2	4,672.5	1,642.8	451.3	526.4	149.2	639.5	199.6	147.1	243.7	170.4	233.8	268.7
1977	10,190.3	4,435.2	1,650.3	319.8	252.9	112.2	834.9	173.8	164.3	238.5	184.4	182.1	322.0
1978	12,016.6	5,046.6	1,674.7	398.2	349.6	83.8	1,100.4	151.8	207.2	281.8	201.2	267.5	330.4
1979	14,251.1	6,121.5	1,908.3	493.8	711.2	−55.3	1,354.4	160.1	219.1	306.9	237.8	289.7	495.5
1980	15,637.5	6,899.7	2,744.3	542.8	459.4	−242.7	1,544.0	203.5	242.8	347.2	256.6	213.8	588.0

Livestock and Products

Year	Total	Cattle and calves	Hogs	Dairy products	Poultry	Eggs	Other products[4]	Forest and maple products	Provincial income stabilization payments	Dairy Supple-mentary payments	Deficiency[5] payments
1976	5,395.7	1,940.9	829.1	1,331.3	477.2	295.6	100.8	54.2	82.9	258.9	24.8
1977	5,755.1	2,101.5	837.9	1,413.8	484.5	299.1	125.4	55.3	119.5	269.4	48.7
1978	6,970.0	2,868.8	1,155.8	1,559.6	536.7	303.5	154.8	63.5	31.6	253.1	42.6
1979	8,129.6	3,512.0	1,302.6	1,753.9	653.4	339.6	171.7	84.0	9.7	246.1	56.6
1980	8,737.8	3,600.1	1,402.5	2,061.3	663.0	395.0	195.8	81.5	46.9	255.1	36.6

(1) Represents participation payments made by the Canadian Wheat Board direct to producers, net cash advances and Western Grain Stabilization payments. (2) Includes oats, rye, flaxseed, rapeseed, soybeans and corn. (3) Includes sugar beets, clover and grass seed, hay, clover, mustard seed, sunflower seed, dry beans and dry peas, net non-grain cash advances, crop insurance payments and miscellaneous products. (4) Including sheep and lambs. (5) Made under the authority of the Agricultural Stabilization Act.

Federal Food Program Costs

Source: Food and Nutrition Service, U.S. Agriculture Department (millions of dollars)

Calendar year	Food stamps Total value	Bonus[1]	WIC[2]	Food distribution[3] Needy persons[4]	Schools	Institu-tions	Child nutrition School lunch	School bkfst.	Child care	Summer food	Special milk	Total costs
1971	3,105	1,699[1]	—	331	296	26	647	22	14	20	92	3,147
1975	8,325	5,073[1]	119	37	364	15	1,385	99	57	65	133	7,347
1976	8,613	5,262[1]	177	41	407	16	1,543	113	94	140	150	7,943
1977	8,272	5,014	289	50	503	19	1,700	154	117	122	151	8,119
1978	8,347	5,260	346	43	576	34	1,864	186	—	114	138	8,561
1979	6,478	6,478	480	90	682	50	2,001	224	183	112	141	10,441
1980	8,685	8,690	598	107	858	63	2,292	281	230	131	154	13,404

(1) Includes Food Certificate Program. (2) Special Supplemental Food Program for Women, Infants, and Children. (3) Cost of food delivered to state distribution centers. (4) Represents cost of the Needy Family Program, Supplemental Food Program, and the Nutrition Program for the Elderly.

Civilian Consumption of Major Food Commodities per Person

Source: Economic Research Service; U.S. Agriculture Department

Commodity[1]	1960	1970	1980[2]	Commodity[1]	1960	1970	1980[2]
Meats	134.1	151.4	151.1	Processed:			
Beef	64.3	84.1	78.1	Canned fruit	22.6	23.3	18.0
Veal	5.2	2.4	1.6	Canned juice	12.9	14.5	17.3
Lamb and mutton	4.3	2.9	1.4	Frozen (including juices)	9.2	9.3	12.6
Pork	60.3	62.0	69.1	Chilled citrus juices	2.1	4.7	5.9
Fish (edible weight)	10.3	11.8	13.2	Dried	3.1	2.7	3.0
Poultry products:				**Vegetables:**			
Eggs	42.4	39.5	35.4	Fresh[3]	96.0	91.1	100.2
Chicken (ready-to-cook)	27.8	40.5	51.2	Canned (excluding potatoes and			
Turkey (ready-to-cook)	6.2	8.0	10.6	sweet potatoes)	43.4	51.1	47.9
Dairy products:				Frozen (excluding potatoes)	7.0	9.6	10.7
Cheese	8.3	11.5	17.6	Potatoes[4]	105.0	115.2	103.8
Condensed and evaporated milk	13.7	7.1	3.8	Sweet potatoes[4]	6.5	5.3	5.6
Fluid milk and cream (product weight)	302	277	250	**Grains:**			
Ice cream (product weight)	18.3	17.7	17.6	Wheat flour[5]	118	110	120
Fats and Oils—Total fat content	45.3	53.0	55.6	Rice	6.1	6.7	9.5
Butter (actual weight)	7.5	5.3	4.6	**Other:**			
Margarine (actual weight)	9.4	11.0	11.2	Coffee	11.6	10.4	8.1
Lard	7.6	4.7	2.5	Tea	.6	.7	.8
Shortening	12.6	17.3	18.3	Cocoa	2.9	3.1	2.5
Other edible fats and oils	11.5	17.9	22.7	Peanuts (shelled)	4.9	5.9	NA
Fruits:				Dry edible beans	7.3	5.9	5.9
Fresh	90.0	79.4	84.0	Melons	23.2	21.2	18.1
Citrus	32.5	28.0	27.8	Sugar (refined)	97.3	101.8	85.6
Noncitrus	57.5	51.4	56.2				

(1) Quantity in pounds, retail weight unless otherwise shown. Data on calendar year basis except for dried fruits, fresh citrus fruits, peanuts, and rice which are on a crop-year basis. (2) Preliminary. (3) Commercial production for sale as fresh produce. (4) Including fresh equivalent of processed. (5) White, whole wheat, and semolina flour including use in bakery products. NA—Not available.

Farm-Real Estate Debt Outstanding by Lender Groups

Source: Economic Research Service, U.S. Agriculture Department

Jan. 1	Total farm-real estate debt[1]	Federal land banks[1]	Amounts held by principal lender groups			
			Farmers Home Administration[2]	Life insurance companies[3]	All commercial banks	Other[4]
	$1,000	$1,000	$1,000	$1,000	$1,000	$1,000
1953	7,240,937	1,095,257	330,087	1,716,022	1,069,398	3,030,173
1954	7,930,931	1,187,046	352,199	1,892,773	1,091,949	3,215,964
1955	8,245,278	1,279,787	378,108	2,051,784	1,161,308	3,374,291
1956	9,012,016	1,480,204	412,670	2,271,784	1,275,429	3,571,929
1957	9,821,525	1,722,381	462,942	2,476,543	1,298,113	3,861,546
1958	10,382,475	1,897,187	540,762	2,578,958	1,315,530	4,050,038
1959	11,091,390	2,065,372	608,101	2,661,229	1,407,548	4,349,140
1960	12,082,409	2,335,124	676,224	2,819,542	1,523,051	4,728,468
1961	12,820,304	2,539,044	722,870	2,974,609	1,591,762	4,992,019
1962	13,899,105	2,803,103	948,346	3,161,757	1,640,790	5,345,109
1963	15,167,821	3,024,013	1,057,923	3,391,183	1,870,216	5,824,486
1964	16,803,505	3,281,797	1,171,373	3,780,537	2,136,571	6,433,227
1965	18,894,240	3,686,755	1,284,913	4,287,671	2,416,634	7,218,267
1966	21,186,886	4,240,227	1,497,313	4,801,677	2,607,404	8,040,265
1967	23,077,186	4,914,522	1,663,067	5,213,587	2,770,010	8,516,000
1968	25,142,401	5,563,204	1,844,046	5,539,600	3,060,551	9,135,000
1969	27,397,370	6,081,229	2,054,382	5,763,500	3,333,259	10,165,000
1970	29,182,766	6,671,222	2,279,620	5,733,900	3,545,024	10,953,000
1971	30,346,083	7,145,363	2,440,043	5,610,300	3,772,377	11,378,000
1972	32,207,666	6,879,753	2,618,131	5,564,300	4,218,482	11,927,000
1973	35,757,754	9,050,067	2,835,202	5,643,300	4,792,185	13,437,000
1974	41,252,870	10,901,352	3,013,440	5,964,800	5,458,278	15,915,000
1975	46,288,419	13,402,441	3,214,657	6,297,400	5,966,282	17,407,639
1976	51,068,946	15,949,720	3,368,747	6,726,000	6,296,286	18,728,193
1977	56,559,645	18,454,578	3,657,467	7,400,200	6,781,410	20,265,990
1978	63,641,566	21,391,162	3,982,054	8,819,400	7,780,261	21,668,689
1979	70,832,679	24,619,184	4,121,038	10,478,200	8,556,542	23,057,715
1980	82,677,505	29,641,784	7,110,613	12,165,300	8,623,281	25,136,527
1981	92,017,878	35,944,492	7,714,928	12,927,800	8,745,242	26,685,416

(1) Includes data for joint stock land banks and Federal Farm Mortgage Corporations. (2) Includes loans made directly by FmHA for farm ownership, soil and water loans to individuals, recreation loans to individuals, Indian tribe land acquisition, grazing associations, and irrigation drainage and soil conservation associations. Also includes loans for rural housing on farm tracts and labor housing. (3) Taken from Life Insurance Institute Tally sheet. (4) Estimated by ERS, USDA.

Giant Trees of the U.S.

Source: The American Forestry Association

There are approximately 1,180 different species of trees native to the continental U.S., including a few imports that have become naturalized to the extent of reproducing themselves in the wild state.

The oldest living trees in the world are reputed to be the bristlecone pines, the majority of which are found growing on the arid crags of California's White Mts. Some of them are estimated to be more than 4,600 years old. The largest known bristlecone pine is the "Patriarch," believed to be 1,500 years old. The oldest known redwoods are about 3,500 years old.

Recognition as the National Champion of each species is determined by total mass of each tree, based on this formula: the circumference in inches as measured at a point 4 1/2 feet above the ground plus the total height of the tree, plus 1/4 of the average crown spread in feet. Trunk circumference is the most significant factor and in case of a tie the champion is determined on the basis of circumference. The Giant Sequoia champion has the largest circumference, 83 ft. 2 in., Gallberry Holly the smallest, 5 in. Following is a small selection of the 661 trees registered with the American Forestry Assn.

(Figure in parentheses is year of most recent measurement)

Species	Height (ft.)	Location
Acacia, Koa (1969)	140	Kau, Ha.
Ailanthus, Tree-of-Heaven (1972)	60	Long Island, N.Y.
Alder, European (1974)	68	Princeton, Ill.
Apple, Southern Crab (1981)	35.5	Swannanoa, N.C.
Ash, Blue (1970)	86	Danville, Ky.
Aspen, Bigtooth (1979)	92	Rocky, Md.
Bald Cypress, Common (1981)	83	St. Francisville, La.
Basswood, American (1971)	115	Grand Traverse Co. Mich.
Bayberry, Pacific (1972)	38	Siuslaw Natl. Forest, Ore.
Beech, American (1976)	161	Three Oaks, Mich.
Birch, River (1974)	95	Cumberland Par., Va.
Birch, Yellow (1978)	107	Huron Mtn. Club, Mich.
Birch, Yellow (1973)	114	Gould City, Mich.
Blackbead, Catclaw (1976)	88	Sarasota, Fla.
Blackhaw, Rusty (1961)	25	nr. Washington, Ark.
Bladdernut, American (1972)	36	nr. Utica, Mich.
Boxelder (1976)	110	Lenawee Co., Mich.

Species	Height (ft.)	Location
Buckeye, Painted (1972)	144	Union County, Ga.
Buckthorn, Cascara (1977)	37	Seaside, Ore.
Buckwheat tree (1967)	30	nr. Crooked Creek, Fla.
Buffaloberry, Silver (1975)	22	Malheur Co., Ore.
Bumelia, Gum (1977)	80	Robertson Co., Tex.
Butternut (1973)	102	Portland, Ore.
Buttonbush, Common (1977)	23	nr. High Springs, Fla.
Cajeput (1975)	66	Sarasota, Fla.
Camphor-tree (1977)	72	Hardee Co., Fla.
Casuarina, Horsetail (1968)	89	Olowalo, Maui, Ha.
Catalpa, Northern (1972)	94	Lansing, Mich.
Cedar, Port-Orford (1972)	219	Siskiyou Natl. Forest, Ore.
Cercocarpus, Birchleaf (1972)	34	Central Point, Ore.
Cherry, Black (1980)	132	Washtenow Co., Mich.
Chestnut, American (1979)	82	Oregon City, Ore.
Chinaberry (1967)	75	Koahe, So. Kuona, Ha.
Chinkapin, Golden (1979)	75	Cottage Grove, Ore.
Chokecherry, Common (1972)	66	Ada, Mich.
Coconut (1979)	92.5	Hilo, Ha.
Coffeetree, Kentucky (1976)	110	Van Buren Co., Mich.

Species	Height (ft.)	Location
Cottonwood, Black (1969) .	147	Unionvalle, Ore.
Cypress, Monterey (1975) .	97	Brookings, Ore.
Dahoon (1975)	72	Osceola For., Fla.
Desert Willow (1976)	56	Gila Co., Ariz.
Devil's-walkingstick (1976) .	51	San Felasco Hammock, Fla.
Devilwood (1972)	37	Mayo, Fla.
Dogwood, Pacific (1975) . .	50	nr. Clatskanie, Ore.
Douglas Fir (1972)	221	Olympic Natl. Pk., Wash.
Doveplum (1965)	45	Miami, Fla.
Elder, Blackbead (1972) . .	42	nr. Prescott, Ore.
False-Mastic (1975)	70	Lignumvitae Key, Fla.
Fig, Florida Strangler (1973)	80	Old Cutler Hammock, Fla.
Fir, Noble (1972)	278	Gifford Pinchot Natl. Forest, Wash.
Gumbo-limbo (1973)	50	Homestead, Fla.
Hackberry, Common (1972)	118	Allegany Co., Mich.
Hawthorn, Scarlet, (1967) .	50	Glenview, Ill.
Hemlock, Western (1979). .	195	Tillamock, Ore.
Hercules-club (1961)	38	Little Rock, Ark.
Hickory, Pignut (1972). . . .	125	nr. Brunswick, Ga.
Holly, American (1979) . . .	99	Congaree Swamp, S.C.
Honeylocust, Thornless (1976)	130	Washtenaw Co., Mich.
Hophornbeam, Eastern (1976).	73	Traverse Co., Mich.
Hoptree, Common (1972). .	31	Ada, Mich.
Hornbeam, American (1975)	65	Milton, N.Y.
Joshua-tree (1967)	32	San Bernardino Natl. Forest, Cal.
Juniper, Western (1954) . .	87	Stanislaus Natl. Forest, Cal.
Larch, Western (1980) . . .	175	Libby, Mont.
Laurelcherry, Carolina (1972)	44	Dellwood, Fla.
Lebbek (1968)	65	Lahaina, Maui, Ha.
Loblolly-Bay (1972)	84	Ocala Natl. Forest, Fla.
Locust, Black (1974)	96	Dansville, N.Y.
Lysiloma, Bahama (1973). .	79	Homestead, Fla.
Madrone, Pacific (1974). . .	79	Humboldt Co., Cal.
Magnolia, Cucumber tree (1979)	94	North Canton, Oh.
Mangrove, Red (1975) . . .	75	Everglades Natl. Pk., Fla.
Maple, Red (1972).	125	nr. Armada, Mich.
Mesquite, Velvet (1952). . .	55	Coronado Natl. Forest, Ariz.
Mountain-Ash, Showy (1972)	58	nr. Gould City, Mich.
Mountain-Laurel (1972) . . .	20	Chattahoochee Natl. Forest, Ga.
Mulberry, White (1976) . . .	82	Battle Creek, Mich.
Oak, Pin (1979)	134	Smithland, Ky.
Oak, Scarlet (1979)	150	Maud, Ala.
Osage-Orange (1972). . . .	51	Charlotte Co., Va.

Species	Height (ft.)	Location
Palmetto, Cabbage (1978)	90	Highlands Hammock State Pk., Fla.
Paloverde, Blue (1976) . . .	53	Riverside Co., Cal.
Paulownia, Royal (1969) . .	105	Philadelphia, Pa.
Pawpaw, Common (1972) .	41	nr. Smith Mills, Ky.
Pear (1976).	57	Clawson, Mich.
Pecan (1980).	143	Cocke Co., Tenn.
Peppertree (1973).	47	San Juan Capistrano, Cal.
Pinckneya (1972)	21	nr. Mt. Pleasant, Fla.
Pine, Ponderosa (1974). . .	223	Plumas, Cal.
Plum, American (1972) . . .	35	Oakland Co., Mich.
Poison Sumac (1972)	20	Robin's Island, N.Y.
Pondcypress (1972).	135	nr. Newton, Ga.
Poplar, Balsam (1976) . . .	128	Champion, Mich.
Possumhaw (1976)	30	Congaree Swamp, S.C.
Redbay (1972).	58	Randolph Co., Ga.
Redwood, Coast (1972). . .	362	Humboldt Redwoods State Park, Cal.
Royalpalm, Florida (1973) .	80	Homestead, Fla.
Sassafras (1972)	100	Owensboro, Ky.
Seagrape (1972).	57	Miami, Fla.
Sequoia, Giant (1975) . . .	275	Sequoia Natl. Pk., Cal.
Serviceberry, Downy (1975)	50	New Philadelphia, Oh.
Silktree (1971)	41	Gilmer, Tex.
Silverbell, Two-wing (1971).	55	Tallahassee, Fla.
Smoketree, American (1974)	47	Lewiston, Ida.
Soapberry, Western (1972).	67	Newton County, Tex.
Sourwood (1972)	118	nr. Robbinsville, N.C.
Sparkleberry Tree (1977). .	30	Pensacola, Fla.
Spruce, Sitka (1973)	216	Seaside, Ore.
Sugarberry (1976).	78	Society Hill, S.C.
Sumac, Shining (1974) . . .	55	Grenada Co., Miss.
Sweetleaf, Common (1972)	55	Tallahassee, Fla.
Sycamore, Cal. (1945) . . .	116	nr. Santa Barbara, Cal.
Tamarack (1972)	95	Jay, Me.
Tamarisk, Five-Stamen (1981). . . .	33.5	Socorro Co., N.M.
Tesota (1972)	32	nr. Quartzsite, Ariz.
Torreya, Cal. (1945).	141	nr. Mendocino, Cal.
Trifoliate-Orange (1968) . .	26	Harrisburg, Pa.
Tupelo, Black (1969)	117	Harrison Co., Tex.
(1969)	139	nr. Houston, Tex.
Walnut, Cal. (1973)	116	nr. Chico, Cal.
Willow, Crack (1972)	112	nr. Utica, Mich.
Winterberry, Common (1971).	40	Wildwood, Fla.
Witch Hazel, Common (1976).	43	Muskegon, Mich.
Yaupon (1972)	45	nr. Devers, Tex.
Yellow-Poplar (1972)	124	Bedford, Va.
Yellowwood (1967)	58	Morrisville, Pa.
Yew, Pacific (1969)	60	nr. Mineral, Wash.
Yucca, Aloe (1972)	15	Lakeland, Fla.

Giant Trees of Canada

Source: Native Trees of Canada by R.C. Hosie; Canadian Forestry Service, Dept. of Environment

There are nearly 140 species of trees native to Canada on which information is easily available. A "native" tree is defined as a single-stemmed perennial woody plant growing to a height of more than 10 feet, and which is indigenous to Canada. Most of the "giant" trees in Canada are to be found in the forest regions. These regions reflect differences caused by terrain, soil, and climate. The 9 forest regions are: The Grassland, Boreal, Great Lakes-St. Lawrence, Columbia, Deciduous, Coast, Subalpine, Acadian, and Montane.

It is difficult to obtain precise records of single trees of outstanding heights. Given below are several common species of trees native to Canada showing the usual or normal height of the species. But many exceptions have been noted. For example, the Douglas Fir, whose average range in height is given at 150 to 200 ft. with diameters of up to 9 ft., occasionally may attain heights above 300 ft. and diameters of 15 ft. or more. The Sitka Spruce is also known to have reached heights of at least 280 ft., and the Western White Pine is recorded as having attained 200 ft.

Species	Height (ft.)	Forest region
Alpine Fir	65-100	Subalpine; N. W. Boreal
Amabilis Fir	80-125	Coast & coastal parts of Subalpine
Balsam Poplar	60-80	Boreal, Great Lakes-St. Lawrence & Acadian
Black Cottonwood . . .	80-125	Throughout B.C. and western Alberta
Black Maple	80-90	Ontario to Montreal Is.
Douglas Fir	150-200	Coast
Eastern Cottonwood . .	75-100	Gt. Lakes-St. Lawrence
Eastern White Pine. . .	100-175	Through east Canada
Engelmann Spruce. . .	100-120	Southern Subalpine
Grand Fir	100-125	S. Coast & Columbia
Mockernut Hickory . . .	75-90	Deciduous
Silver Maple	80-90	S.E. parts of G. Lakes-St. Lawrence

Species	Height (ft.)	Forest region
Sitka Spruce	125-175	Coast
Sugar Maple	80-90	Gt. Lakes-St. Lawrence
Sycamore	Up to 150	Deciduous
Western Hemlock . . .	120-160	Coast & Columbia
Western Larch	100-180	Southern part of Columbia & Montane, B.C.
Western Red Cedar . .	150-200	Coast & Columbia
Western White Pine . .	90-110	S. Coast & Columbia
White Birch	Med.-80	Throughout Canada
White Elm	60-80	G. Lakes-St. Lawrence & Acadian
White Oak	Med.-100	Southern Ontario
White Spruce	80-120	Boreal
Yellow Cypress	60-80	Coast & in coastal parts of Subalpine

The Principal Languages of the World

Source: Sidney S. Culbert, Guthrie Hall NI — University of Washington

Total number of speakers of languages spoken by at least one million persons (midyear 1981)

Language	Millions	Language	Millions	Language	Millions
Achinese (Indonesia)	2	Ilocano (Philippines)	4	Pedi (see Sotho, Northern)	
Afrikaans (S. Africa)	8	Iloko (see Ilocano)		Persian (Iran, Afghanistan)	28
Albanian	4	Indonesian (see Malay-Indonesian)		Polish	38
Amharic (Ethiopia)	10	Italian	61	Portuguese	148
Arabic	151			Provencal (Southern France)	5
Armenian	4	Japanese	118	Punjabi[1] (India; Pakistan)	64
Assamese[1] (India)	14	Javanese	48	Pushtu (mainly Afghanistan)	18
Aymara (Bolivia; Peru)	1				
Azerbaijani (USSR; Iran)	8	Kamba (E. Africa)	1	Quechua (S. America)	7
		Kanarese (see Kannada)			
Bahasa (see Malay-Indonesian)		Kannada[1] (India)	31	Rajasthani (India)	12
Balinese	3	Kanuri (W. and Central Africa)	3	Romanian	23
Baluchi (Pakistan; Iran)	3	Kashmiri[1]	3	Ruanda (S. Central Africa)	7
Batak (Indonesia)	2	Kazakh (USSR)	6	Rundi (S. Central Africa)	4
Bemba (S. Central Africa)	2	Khalkha (Mongolia)	2	Russian (Great Russian only)	270
Bengali[1] (Bangladesh; India)	148	Khmer (Kampuchea)	6		
Berber[2] (N. Africa)		Kikongo (see Kongo)		Samar-Leyte (Philippines)	2
Bhili (India)	4	Kikuyu (or Gekoyo)(Kenya)	3	Sango (Central Africa)	2
Bihari (India)	13	Kimbundu (see Mbundu-Kimbundu)		Santali (India)	4
Bikol (Philippines)	2	Kirghiz (USSR)	2	Sepedi (see Sotho, Northern)	
Bisaya (see Cebuano, Panay-Hiligaynon,		Kituba (Congo River)	3	Serbo-Croatian (Yugoslavia)	19
and Samar-Leyte)		Kongo (Congo River)	2	Shan (Burma)	2
Bugi (Indonesia)	2	Konkani (India)	2	Shona (S.E. Africa)	5
Bulgarian	9	Korean	59	Siamese (see Thai)	
Burmese	26	Kurdish (S.W. of Caspian Sea)	7	Sindhi[1] (India; Pakistan)	10
Byelorussian (mainly USSR)	9	Kurukh (or Oraon)(India)	1	Sinhalese (Sri Lanka)	11
				Slovak	5
Cambodian (see Khmer)		Lao[5] (Laos, Asia)	3	Slovene (Yugoslavia)	2
Canarese (see Kannada)		Latvian (or Lettish)	2	Somali (E. Africa)	5
Cantonese (China)	54	Lingala (see Ngala)		Sotho, Northern (S. Africa)	2
Catalan (Spain; France; Andorra)	6	Lithuanian	3	Sotho, Southern (S. Africa)	3
Cebuano (Philippines)	9	Luba-Lulua (Zaire)	3	Spanish	251
Chinese[3]		Luganda (see Ganda)		Sundanese (Indonesia)	16
Chuang[7] (China)		Luhya (or Luhia)(Kenya)	1	Swahili (E. Africa)	30
Chuvash (USSR)	2	Luo (Kenya)	2	Swedish	10
Czech	11	Luri (Iran)	2		
				Tagalog (Philippines)	25
Danish	5	Macedonian (Yugoslavia)	2	Tajiki (USSR)	3
Dayak (Borneo)	1	Madurese (Indonesia)	8	Tamil[1] (India; Sri Lanka)	58
Dutch (see Netherlandish)		Makua (S.E. Africa)	3	Tatar (or Kazan-Turkic)(USSR)	7
		Malagasy (Madagascar)	8	Telugu[1] (India)	59
Edo (W. Africa)	1	Malay-Indonesian	112	Thai[5]	38
Efik	3	Malayalam[1] (India)	30	Thonga (S.E. Africa)	1
English	391	Malinke-Bambara-Dyula (Africa)	7	Tibetan	6
Esperanto	1	Mandarin (China)	713	Tigrinya (Ethiopia)	4
Estonian	1	Marathi[1] (India)	56	Tiv (E. Central Nigeria)	2
Ewe (W. Africa)	3	Mazandarani (Iran)	2	Tswana (S. Africa)	3
		Mbundu (Umbundu group)(S.Angola)	3	Tulu (India)	1
Fang-Bulu (W. Africa)	2	Mbundu (Kimbundu group)(Angola)	2	Turkish	44
Finnish	5	Mende (Sierra Leone)	1	Turkoman (USSR)	2
Flemish (see Netherlandish)		Meo (see Miao)		Twi-Fante (or Akan)(W.Africa)	5
French	105	Miao (and Meo)(S.E.Asia)	3		
Fula (W. Africa)	10	Min (China)	42	Uighur (Sinkiang, China)	5
		Minankabau (Indonesia)	4	Ukrainian (mainly USSR)	42
Galician (Spain)	3	Moldavian (inc. with Romanian)		Umbundu (see Mbundu-Umbundu)	
Galla (see Oromo)		Mongolian (see Khalkha)		Urdu[1] (Pakistan; India)	70
Ganda (or Luganda)(E. Africa)	3	Mordvin (USSR)	1	Uzbek (USSR)	10
Georgian (USSR)	4	Morê (see Mossi)			
German	119	Mossi (or Morê)(W. Africa)	3	Vietnamese	44
Gilaki (Iran)	2			Visayan (see Cebuano, Panay-	
Gondi (India)	2	Ndongo (see Mbundu-Kimbundu)		Hiligaynon, and Samar-Leyte)	
Greek	10	Nepali (Nepal; India)	11		
Guarani (mainly Paraguay)	3	Netherlandish (Dutch and Flemish)	20	White Russian (see Byelorussian)	
Gujarati[1] (India)	33	Ngala (or Lingala)(Africa)	3	Wolof (W. Africa)	3
		Norwegian	5	Wu (China)	49
Hakka (China)	23	Nyamwezi-Sukuma (S.E. Africa)	2		
Hausa (W. and Central Africa)	22	Nyanja (S.E. Africa)	3	Xhosa (S. Africa)	5
Hebrew	3				
Hindi[1,4]	245	Oraon (see Kurukh)		Yi (China)	4
Hindustani[4]		Oriya[1] (India)	26	Yiddish[6]	3
Hungarian (or Magyar)	13	Oromo (Ethiopia)	8	Yoruba (W. Africa)	14
Ibibio (see Efik)		Panay-Hiligaynon (Philippines)	4	Zhuang[7] (China)	
Ibo (or Igbo)(W. Africa)	11	Panjabi (see Punjabi)		Zulu (S. Africa)	6
Ijaw (W. Africa)	2	Pashto (see Pushtu)			

(1) One of the fifteen languages of the Constitution of India. (2) Here considered a group of dialects. (3) See Mandarin, Cantonese, Wu, Min and Hakka. The "national language" (Guoyu) or "common speech" (Putonghua) is a standardized form of Mandarin as spoken in the area of Peking. (4) Hindi and Urdu are essentially the same language, Hindustani. As the official language of India it is written in the Devanagari script and called Hindi. As the official language of Pakistan it is written in a modified Arabic script and called Urdu. (5) Thai includes Central, Southwestern, Northern and Northeastern Thai. The distinction between Northeastern Thai and Lao is political rather than linguistic. (6) Yiddish is usually considered a variant of German, though it has its own standard grammar, dictionaries, a highly developed literature, and is written in Hebrew characters. (7) A group of Thai-like dialects with about 9 million speakers.

EDUCATION

American Colleges and Universities

Student and Faculty Figures for Spring Term, 1981

Source: World Almanac questionnaires and U.S. Office of Education

(For Canadian Colleges and Universities, see Index)

All coeducational unless followed by (M) for men only, or (W) for women only. Even though marked (M) or (W) some are coeducational at graduate level and in evening and summer divisions. Asterisk (•) denotes landgrant college.

Governing official is president unless otherwise designated. Year is that of founding. The word college is part of the name unless another designation is given.

Affiliation: IP-Independent (Private), IR (Independent-Religions affiliation), Pf-Public (federal), Ps-Public (state), Pl-Public (local), Psl-Public (state and local), Psr-Public (state related).

Highest Degree Offered: A-Associate's (2 yrs.), B-Bachelor's (4 yrs.), 1P-First Professional, M-Master's, S-Specialist, D-Doctorate.

Each institution listed has an enrollment of at least 200 students of college grade. Number of teachers is the total number of individuals on teaching staff. Enrollment and faculty in italics includes all full-time and part-time students and teachers on all branches and campuses.

(A) Designates colleges that have not provided up-to-date information.

(See Index for typical tuition fees)

Name, address	Year	Governing official, affiliation, and highest degree offered		Students	Teachers
Abilene Christian, Abilene, TX 79699	1906	John C. Stevens	IP-M	4,500	211
Abraham Baldwin Agric. (A) Tifton, GA 31794	1908	Stanley R. Anderson	Ps-A	2,372	101
Adams, State, Alamosa, CO 81102	1923	William Fulkerson	Ps-M	2,000	115
Adelphi Univ., Garden City, NY 11530	1896	Timothy Costello	IP-D	11,819	360
Adirondack Community (A), Glens Falls, NY 12801	1960	Charles R. Eisenhart	Psl-A	2,037	65
Adrian (A), Adrian, MI 49221	1859	Donald S. Stanton	IR-M	945	61
Aeronautics, Academy of, Flushing, NY 11371	1932	Walter M. Hartung	IP-A	1,875	65
Agnes Scott (W) (A), Decatur, GA 30030	1889	Marvin Perry Jr.	IP-B	561	67
Aims Comm. (A), Greeley, CO 80632	1967	Jerry Kiefer, Act.	Pl-A	4,850	89
Akron, Univ. of (A), Akron, OH 44325	1870	Dominic J. Guzzetta	Ps-D	23,400	674
Alabama A&M Univ, Normal, AL 35762	1875	Richard D. Morrison	Ps-S	4,379	321
Alabama Christian, Montgomery, AL 36193	1942	George S. Benson	IP-B	1,770	87
Alabama State Univ. (A), Montgomery, AL 36101	1874	Levi Watkins	Ps-M	4,096	202
Alabama, Univ. of, University, AL 35486	1831	Joab Thomas	Ps-D	17,918	994
at Birmingham (A), Birmingham, AL 35294	1966	S.R. Hill Jr.	Ps-D	13,799	1,411
at Huntsville, Huntsville, AL 35899	1960	John C. Wright	Ps-S	5,006	224
Alameda, Coll. of (A), Alameda, CA 94501	1970	Jeanette Poore	Psl-A	7,337	241
Alaska, Univ. of•, Fairbanks, AK 99701	1922	Vacant	Ps-D	3,531	1,293
Albany Coll. of Pharmacy, Albany, NY 12208	1881	Walter Singer	IP-B	569	35
Albany Junior, Albany, GA 31707	1966	B.R. Tilley	Ps-A	1,999	86
Albany State (A), Albany, GA 31705	1903	Charles Hays	Ps-B	2,000	135
Albany, Junior Coll. of, Albany, NY 12208	1957	William Kahl	IP-A	1,021	78
Albemarle, Coll. of the (A), Elizabeth City, NC 27909	1960	J.P. Chesson Jr.	Ps-A	1,118	43
Albertus Magnus (W), New Haven, CT 06511	1925	Sister Francis Heffernan	IR-B	565	70
Albion, Albion, MI 49224	1835	Bernard Tagg Lomas	IR-B	1,851	119
Albright, Reading, PA 19603	1856	David G. Ruffer	IP-B	1,952	134
Albuquerque, Univ. of (A), Albuquerque, NM 87140	1920	Clifford Smith	IP-B	2,000	75
Alcorn State Univ., Lorman, MS 39096	1871	Walter Washington	Ps-M	2,341	152
Alderson-Broaddus, Philippi, WV 26416	1871	Richard E. Shearer	IR-B	811	64
Alexander City State Jr., Alexander City, AL 35010	1965	W. Byron Causey	Ps-A	1,133	70
Alfred Univ., Alfred, NY 14802	1836	Howard R. Neville	IP-D	2,265	147
Allan Hancock, Santa Maria, CA 93454	1920	Gary R. Edelbrock	Psl	10,500	130
Allegheny, Meadville, PA 16335	1815	David B. Harned	IP-M	1,936	150
Allegany Community, Cumberland, MD 21502	1961	Donald Alexander	Psl-A	1,755	100
Allegheny Comm. Coll. of Pittsburgh (A), PA 15668	1966	Lawrence V. Lauth	Pl-A	71,420	349
Allen Co. Comm. Jr. (A), Iola, KS 66749	1923	Bill R. Spencer	Psl-A	985	28
Allen Univ., Columbia, SC 29204	1870	David W. Williams	IP-B	410	33
Alice Lloyd, Pippa Passes, KY 41844	1923	Jerry C. Davis	IP-B	395	22
Alma, Alma, MI 48801	1886	Oscar E. Remick	IP-B	1,202	100
Alpena Community (A), Alpena, MI 49707	1952	Charles Donnelly	Pl-A	1,659	50
Alvernia, Reading, PA 19607	1967	Sister Mary Victorine	IR-B	606	76
Alverno (W) (A), Milwaukee, WI 53215	1936	Sister Joel Read	IR-B	1,364	111
Alvin Comm., Alvin, TX 77511	1949	A.R. Allbright	Psl-A	3,083	176
Amarillo, Amarillo, TX 79178	1929	John C. Mundt	Ps-M	27,000	150
American Academy of Art, Chicago, IL 60604	1923	I. Shapiro	IP-A	1,000	20
American Cons. of Music, Chicago, IL 60603	1886	Charles Moore	IP-D	400	130
Amer. Inst. of Business, Des Moines, IA 50321	1921	Keith Fenton	Pl-A	900	45
American International, Springfield, MA 01109	1885	Harry J. Courniotes	IP-M	2,254	110
American River, Sacramento, CA 95841	1955	Robert D. Jensen	Pl-A	22,025	641
American Univ., Washington DC 20016	1893	Richard Berendzen	IP-D	12,500	1,050
Amherst (A), Amherst, MA 01002	1821	John William Ward	IP-B	1,475	150
Anderson, Anderson, IN 46011	1920	Robert H. Reardon	IR-M	2,000	101
Anderson, Anderson, SC 29621	1911	Ray P. Rust	IR-A	1,077	67
Andrew, Cuthbert, GA 31740	1854	William T. Greer	IR-A	350	25
Andrews Univ., Berrien Springs, MI 49104	1874	Joseph Smoot	IR-D	3,018	228
Angelina, Lufkin, TX 75901	1966	Jack W. Hudgins	Psl-A	2,069	120
Angelo State Univ. (A), San Angelo, TX 76901	1928	Lloyd Vincent	Ps-M	5,637	187
Anna Maria, Paxton, MA 01612	1946	Bernadette Madore	IR-M	1,574	143
Anne Arundel Comm. (A), Arnold, MD 21012	1961	Thomas E. Florestano	Psl-A	6,600	180
Annhurst, Woodstock (A), CT 06281	1940	Paul Buchanan	IR-B	300	30
Anoka-Ramsey Comm. (A), Coon Rapids, MN 55433	1965	Neil Christenson	Ps-A	3,645	92
Anson Tech. Inst., Ansonville, NC 28007	1962	H.B. Monroe	Psl-A	530	50
Antelope Valley, Lancaster, CA 93534	1929	Clinton Stine	Psl-A	7,000	247
Antioch, Yellow Spgs., OH 45387	1852	William M. Birenbaum	IP-M	4,057	421
Appalachian Bible, Bradley, WV 25818	1950	Lester E. Pipkin	IR-B	243	19

Name, address	Year	Governing official, affiliation, and highest degree offered	Students	Teachers
Appalachian State Univ., Boone, NC 28608	1899	John E. Thomas	Ps-S	10,484	584
Aquinas (A), Grand Rapids, MI 49506	1922	Norbert J. Hruby	IR-M	2,172	78
Aquinas Junior, (W) Milton, MA 02186	1956	Sr. Mary Morgan	IR-A	400	30
Aquinas Junior, Nashville, TN 37205	1961	Sister Robert Ann Britton	IR-S	293	38
Arapahoe Community, Littleton, CO 80120	1965	Norman Lloyd	Ps-A	6,220	235
Arizona, State Univ., Tempe, AZ 85281	1885	J. Russell Nelson	Ps-D	36,159	1,566
Arizona, Univ. of *, Tucson, AZ 85721	1885	John Paul Schaefer	Ps-D	34,559	1,774
Arizona Western, Yuma, AZ 85364	1962	Kenneth E. Borland	Psl-A	4,268	203
Arkansas, Batesville, AR 72501	1872	Dan C. West	IR-B	537	52
Arkansas, Baptist, Little Rock, AR 72202	1884	J.C. Oliver	IR-B	271	26
Arkansas Tech (A), Russellville, AR 72801	1909	Kenneth Kersh	Ps-M	3,000	146
Arkansas State Univ., State Univ., AR 72467	1909	Ray Thornton	Ps-S	7,615	360
Arkansas, Univ. of *, Fayetteville, AR 72701	1871	James E. Martin	Ps-D	32,078	1,809
at Little Rock, Little Rock, AR 72204	1927	G. Robert Ross	Ps-M	10,038	406
at Pine Bluff, Pine Bluff, AR 71601	1873	Walter L. Littlejohn	Ps-A	2,997	191
Armstrong, Berkeley, CA 94704	1918	John E. Armstrong	IP-M	452	52
Armstrong State (A), Savannah, GA 31406	1937	Henry L. Ashmore	Ps-M	2,873	117
Art Center Coll. of Design, Pasadena, CA 91103	1930	Donald R. Kubly	IP-M	1,436	175
Art Inst. of Chicago, Chicago, IL 60603	1866	Donald Irving	IP-M	1,832	170
Asbury, Wilmore, KY 40390	1890	Dennis F. Kinlaw	IP-A	1,117	114
Asheville Buncombe Tech. (A), Asheville, NC 28801	1959	Harvey L. Haynes	Psl-A	2,500	130
Ashland, Ashland, OH 44805	1878	Joseph R. Schultz	IR-S	2,652	149
Ashland Community, Ashland, KY 41101	1957	Robert L. Goodpaster	Ps-B	1,354	75
Assumption (A), Worcester, MA 01609	1904	Joseph H. Hagan	IR-M	1,700	75
Athens State (A), Athens AL 35611	1822	Sidney Sandridge	Ps-B	1,350	48
Atlanta College of Art (A), Atlanta, GA 30309	1928	William Voos	IP-B	471	23
Atlantic Christian, Wilson, NC 27893	1902	Harold C. Doster	IR-B	1,620	113
Atlantic Comm. (A), Mays Landing, NJ 08330	1964	L.R. Winchell Jr.	Psl-A	3,767	120
Atlantic Union, So. Lancaster, MA 01561	1882	Larry Lewis	IR-B	630	90
Auburn Univ.*, Auburn, AL 36849	1856	H. Hanley Funderburk	Ps-D	18,603	1,463
Augsburg (A), Minneapolis, MN 55454	1869	Oscar A. Anderson	IR-B	1,625	85
Augusta (A), Augusta, GA 30904	1925	George A. Christenberry	Ps-M	3,719	156
Augustana, Rock Island, IL 61201	1860	J. Thomas Tredway	IP-M	2,434	156
Augustana, Sioux Falls, SD 57197	1860	William C. Nelson	IR-M	2,124	186
Aurora, Aurora, IL 60507	1893	Alan J. Stone	IR-M	1,250	89
Austin, Sherman, TX 75090	1849	Dr. Harry E. Smith	IR-M	1,190	114
Austin Comm., Austin, MN 55912	1940	Arlan Burmeister	Ps-A	900	55
Austin Peay State Univ., Clarksville, TN 37040	1927	Robert O. Riggs	PS-S	5,386	235
Averett, Danville, VA 24541	1859	Howard W. Lee	IR-M	1,028	62
Avila, Kansas City, MO 64145	1916	Sister Olive Louise Dallavis	IR-M	2,038	240
Azusa Pacific, Azusa CA 91702	1899	Paul E. Sago	IR-M	2,046	134
Babson (A), Babson Park, MA 02157	1919	Ralph Z. Sorenson	IP-M	2,800	89
Bacone (A), Muskogee, OK 74401	1880	Dean Chavers	IP-A	453	44
Baker Jr. Col. of Business, Flint, MI 48507	1911	Robert Jowell	IP-A	1,400	52
Baker Univ., Baldwin City, KS 66006	1858	Ralph Tanner	IP-M	841	61
Bakersfield, Bakersfield, CA 93305	1913	John H. Collins	PI-A	11,639	525
Baldwin-Wallace, Berea, OH 44017	1845	A.B. Bonds Jr.	IR-M	3,401	160
Ball State Univ., Muncie, IN 47306	1918	Robert Bell	Ps-S	19,968	850
Baltimore, Univ. of Baltimore, MD 21201	1925	H. Melbane Turner	Pf-M	5,350	261
Baltimore, Comm. Col. of, Baltimore, MD 21215	1947	Rafael L. Cortada	Psl-A	11,490	584
Baptist Bible, Springfield, MO 65802	1950	William E. Dowell	IR-B	1,686	65
Baptist Bible College of Pa., Clarks Summit, PA 18411	1932	Mark Jackson	IR-M	911	50
Baptist Coll. at Charleston, Charleston, SC 29411	1960	John Hamrick	IR-M	2,500	105
Barat (W), Lake Forest, IL 60045	1858	Sister Judith Cagney	IP-B	743	79
Barber-Scotia, Concord, NC 28025	1867	Mable McLean	IR-B	321	27
Bard, Annandale-on-Hudson, NY 12504	1860	Leon Botstein	IP-B	737	84
Barnard (W)(A), New York, NY 10027	1889	Ellen Futter	IP-B	2,441	165
Barrington (A), Barrington, RI 02806	1900	David G. Horner	IP-B	455	25
Barry, Miami Shores, FL 33161	1940	Sister Jeanne O'Laughlin	IR-M	2,197	155
Barstow, Barstow, CA 92311	1962	Vacant	Ps-A	1,500	70
Barton County Comm., Great Bend, KS 67530	1965	Jimmie Downing	Psl-A	3,290	252
Bates, Lewiston, ME 04240	1855	Thomas H. Reynolds	IP-B	1,425	127
Bay de Noc Comm., Escanaba, MI 49829	1963	Edwin E. Wuehle	Psl-A	1,531	92
Baylor Univ., Waco, TX 76798	1845	Abner V. McCall	IP-D	10,125	476
Bay Path Junior (W), Longmeadow, MA 01106	1897	Jeanette T. Wright	IP-A	677	26
Beal, Bangor, ME 04401	1891	David Tibbetts	IP-A	550	50
Beaufort Co. Comm. Washington, NC 27889	1967	James P. Blanton	Ps-A	912	78
Beaver, Glenside, PA 19038	1853	Edward D. Gates	IP-M	2,040	137
Beaver Co., Comm. Col. of Monaca, PA 15061	1966	Terry L. DiCianna	Psr-A	2,100	92
Becker Junior, Worcester, MA 01609	1784	Lloyd H. Van Buskirk	IP-A	1,174	54
Beckley, Beckley, WV 25801	1933	John Saunders	IP-A	1,191	58
Bee County, Beeville TX 78102	1965	Grady C. Hogue	Psl-A	2,143	106
Belhaven, Jackson, MS 39202	1883	Verne R. Kennedy	IR-B	929	40
Bellarmine, Louisville, KY 40205	1950	Eugene Petrik	IR-M	2,388	108
Belleville Area, Belleville, IL 62221	1946	Bruce R. Wissore	Psl-A	12,245	691
Bellevue, Bellevue, NE 68005	1966	Richard Winchell	IP-B	2,380	90
Bellevue Community (A), Bellevue, WA 98007	1966	Thos. O'Connell	Ps-A	10,582	114
Belmont, Nashville, TN 37203	1951	Herbert C. Gabhart	IR-B	1,706	149
Belmont Abbey, Belmont, NC 28012	1876	Rev. Neil W. Tobin	IR-B	855	60
Belmont Technical (A), St. Clairsville, OH 43950	1969	Paul R. Ohm	Ps-A	563	20
Beloit, Beloit, WI 53511	1846	Rogert Hull	IP-M	1,058	106
Bemidji State, Bemidji, NM 56601	1919	Rebecca Stafford	Ps-M	5,787	195
Benedict, Columbia, SC 29204	1870	Henry Ponder	IP-B	1,379	120
Benedictine (A), Atchison KS 66002	1858	Rev. Gerard Senecal	IR-M	1,100	90
Bennett (W), Greensboro, NC 27420	1873	Isaac H. Miller	IR-A	600	62
Bennington, Bennington, VT 05201	1925	Joseph S. Murphy	IP-M	594	77
Bentley, Waltham, MA 02154	1917	Gregory Adamian	IP-M	7,000	120
Berea, Berea, KY 40404	1855	W.D. Weatherford	IP-B	1,514	140
Bergen Community, Paramus, NJ 07652	1965	Alban E. Reid	Psl-A	11,533	519
Berkeley School, The, Little Falls, NJ 07424	1931	Larry L. Luing	IP-A	540	23
Berkshire Community, Pittsfield, MA 01201	1960	Jonathan M. Daube	Ps-A	2,896	180
Berry, Mount Berry, GA 30149	1902	Gloria M. Shatto	IP-M	1,473	108
Bethany, Lindsborg, KS 67456	1881	Arvin Hahn	IR-B	799	81
Bethany, Bethany, WV 26032	1840	Todd H. Bullard	IR-B	853	75
Bethany Bible, Santa Cruz, Ca 95060	1919	Richard B. Foth	IR-B	645	42
Bethany Nazarene, Bethany, OK 73008	1899	John Knight	IR-M	1,378	83
Bethel (A), McKenzie, TN 38201	1842	William L. Odom	IR-B	360	20
Bethel, Mishawaka, IN 46544	1947	Albert J. Beutler	IP-M	501	32

Name, address	Year	Governing official, affiliation, and highest degree offered	Stu-dents	Teach-ers
Bethel, North Newton, KS 67117	1887	Harold Schultz	IP-B	755	42
Bethel, St. Paul, MN 55112	1931	Carl Lundquist	IR-B	2,079	201
Bethune-Cookman, Daytona Beach, FL 32015	1904	O.P. Bronson	IP-B	1,626	110
Big Bend Community, Moses Lake, WA 98837	1962	Peter DeVries	Ps-A	3,045	105
Biola, La Mirada, CA 90639	1908	J. Richard Chase	IP-D	3,200	250
Birmingham-Southern, Birmingham, AL 35254	1856	Neal R. Berte	IR-B	1,443	79
Biscayne, Miami, FL 33054	1952	Rev. Patrick H. O'Neill	IR-M	3,000	200
Bishop, Dallas, TX 75241	1881	Harry S. Wright	IP-B	985	60
Bismarck Junior, Bismarck, ND 58501	1939	Kermit Lidstrom	Psl-A	2,273	89
Black Hawk, Moline, IL 61265	1946	Richard J. Puffer	Psl-A	7,450	286
Blackhawk Technical Inst. (A), Janesville, WI 53545	1968	O.L. Johnson (Dir.)	Psl-A	1,886	85
Black Hills State, Spearfish, SD 57783	1883	J. Gilbert Hause	Ps-M	5,000	217
Blackburn, Carlinville, IL 62626	1837	John Alberti	IR-B	539	50
Bladen Tech. Coll., Dublin, NC 28332	1967	Geo. Resseguie	Ps	396	30
Blinn, Brenham, TX 77833	1883	James H. Atkinson	Psl-A	2,441	125
Bliss, Columbus, OH 43214	1899	James D. Tussing	IP-A	400	15
Bloomfield, Bloomfield, NJ 07003	1868	Merle F. Allshouse	IR-B	2,150	151
Bloomsburg State, Bloomsburg, PA 17815	1839	James McCormick	Ps-M	6,503	316
Blue Mountain (W), Blue Mountain, MS 38610	1873	E. Harold Fisher	IR-B	472	32
Blue Mountain Comm., Pendleton, OR 97801	1962	Ronald L. Daniels	Ps-A	2,700	150
Bluefield, Bluefield, VA 24605	1922	Charles Tyer	IR-A	428	37
Bluefield State, Bluefield, WV 24701	1895	Jerold O. Dugger	Ps-B	2,338	115
Blue Ridge Comm., Weyers Cave, VA 24486	1965	James A. Armstrong	Ps-A	2,350	103
Bluffton, Bluffton, OH 45817	1899	Elmer Neufeld	IR-B	662	55
Bob Jones Univ., Greenville, SC 29614	1927	Bob Jones III	IP-S	6,186	395
Boca Raton, Coll. of, Boca Raton, FL 33431	1963	Donald E. Ross	IP-A	524	38
Boise State, Boise, ID 83725	1932	John Keiser	Ps	11,513	650
Boston, Chestnut Hill, MA 02167	1863	Rev. Donald J. Monan	IR-S	14,445	912
Boston State (A), Boston, MA 02115	1852	Kermit C. Morrissey	Ps-M	11,000	328
Boston Conserv. of Music, Boston, MA 02215	1867	Dale A. DuVall	IP-M	400	100
Boston Univ., Boston, MA 02215	1839	John Silber	IP-D	26,869	2,342
Bowdoin, Brunswick, ME 04011	1794	Arthur LeRoy Greason, Jr.	IP-B	1,385	100
Bowie State (A), Bowie, MD 20715	1865	Rufus L. Barfield	Ps-M	2,664	137
Bowling Green State Univ., Bowling Green, OH 43403	1910	Michael Ferrari	Ps-D	18,124	737
Bradford, Bradford, MA 01830	1803	Inge Heckel	IP-B	378	45
Bradley Univ., Peoria, IL 61625	1897	Martin G. Abegg	IP-M	5,600	400
Brainerd Comm. (A), Brainerd, MN 56401	1938	Curtis Murton Jr.	Ps-A	700	29
Brandeis Univ., Waltham, MA 02254	1948	Marver Bernstein	IP-D	3,498	441
Brandywine, Wilmington, DE 19803	1965	Robert J. Bruce	IP-A	891	43
Brazosport, Lake Jackson, TX 77566	1948	W.A. Bass	Psl-A	3,529	98
Brenau, Gainesville, GA 30501	1878	James T. Rogers	IP-M	1,406	75
Brescia, Owensboro, KY 42301	1950	Sr. George Ann Cecil	IP-B	860	75
Brevard, Brevard, NC 28712	1953	J.C. Martinson Jr.	IR-A	750	67
Brevard, Comm., Cocoa, FL 32922	1960	Maxwell King	Ps-A	10,934	600
Brewton-Parker, Mt. Vernon, GA 30445	1904	William S. Miller	IR-A	930	115
Briar Cliff, Sioux City, IA 51104	1930	Charles Bensman	IP-B	1,086	60
Bridgeport Engineering Inst., Bridgeport, CT 06606	1924	William J. Owens	IP-B	765	95
Bridgeport, Univ. of, Bridgeport, CT 06602	1927	Leland Miles	IP-D	6,805	539
Bridgewater, Bridgewater, VA 22812	1880	Wayne F. Geisert	IP-B	950	77
Bridgewater State, Bridgewater, MA 02324	1840	Adrian Rondileau	Ps-M	4,472	297
Brigham Young Univ., Provo, UT 84602	1875	Jeffrey R. Holland	IR-D	29,866	1,459
Brigham Young Univ., Laie, HI 96762	1955	J. Elliott Cameron	IR-B	1,736	78
Bristol College, Bristol, TN 37620	1895	Jack O. Anderson	IP-B	260	10
Bristol Community, Falls River, MA 02720	1966	Eileen T. Farley	Ps-A	2,205	130
Brookdale Comm (A), Lincroft NJ 07738	1967	Donald H. Smith	Ps-A	9,791	140
Brooks Inst., Santa Barbara, CA 93108	1945	Ernest Brooks II	IR-M	756	31
Broome Community (A), Binghamton, NY 13902	1946	Vacant	Psl-A	5,556	155
Broward Community, Ft. Lauderdale, FL 33301	1960	Alfred H. Adams	Ps-A	28,079	275
Brown Univ., Providence, RI 02912	1764	Howard R. Swearer	IP-D	6,943	494
Brunswick Junior, Brunswick, GA 31520	1961	John W. Teel	Ps-A	1,200	59
Bryan, Dayton, TN 37321	1930	Theodore Mercer	IP-B	543	43
Bryant, Smithfield RI 02917	1863	William O'Hara	IP-M	5,586	238
Bryant & Stratton Business Inst., Rochester, NY 14604	1973	Francis J. Gustina	IP-A	636	30
Bryn Mawr (W), Bryn Mawr, PA 19010	1885	Mary Patterson McPherson	IP-D	1,784	150
Bucknell Univ., Lewisburg, PA 17837	1846	Dennis O'Brien	IP-M	3,359	229
Bucks County Comm. (A), Newtown, PA 18940	1964	Charles Rollins	Pl-A	8,100	190
Buena Vista, Storm Lake, IA 50588	1891	Keith G. Briscoe	IR-B	1,365	100
Butler County Comm., Butler, PA 16001	1965	Thomas Ten Hoeve Jr.	Pl-A	1,500	85
Butler County Comm., El Dorado, KS 67042	1927	Carl Heinrich	Ps-A	2,195	102
Butler Univ., Indianapolis, IN 46208	1855	John G. Johnson	IP-S	3,764	318
Butte Community, Oroville, CA 95965	1967	Wendell Lee Reeder	Psl-A	10,500	520
Cabrillo Comm. Coll. (A), Aptos, CA 95003	1959	John C. Petersen	Psl-A	8,720	158
Cabrini, Wayne, PA 19087	1957	Sr. Mary Sullivan	IR-B	498	60
Caldwell, Caldwell, NJ 07006	1939	Sr. Edith Magdalen Visic	IR-B	681	80
Caldwell Comm. Coll. (A) & Tech. Inst. (A), Lenoir, NC 28645	1964	H. Edwin Beam	Psl-A	1,300	120
California Baptist, Riverside, CA 92504	1950	James R. Staples	IR-B	681	62
Cal. Coll. of Arts and Crafts, Oakland, CA 94618	1907	Harry Xavier Ford	IP-M	1,472	170
Cal. College of Podiatric Med., San Francisco, CA 94120	1914	Homi Jamshed	IP-D	400	195
Cal. Inst. of the Arts, Valencia, CA 91355	1962	Robert Fitzpatrick	IP-M	800	114
Cal. Inst. of Tech., Pasadena, CA 91125	1891	Marvin L. Goldberger	IP-D	1,710	302
Cal. Lutheran, Thousand Oaks, CA 91360	1959	Jerry H. Miller	IP-M	2,636	291
Cal. Maritime Academy, Vallejo, CA 94590	1929	R. Adm. Joseph Rizza	Ps-B	500	35
Cal. Polytechnic State Univ. (A), San Luis Obispo, CA 93407	1901	Warren J. Baker	Ps-M	16,000	850
Cal. State, Bakersfield CA 93309	1970	Jacob Frankel	Ps-M	3,154	205
Cal. State (A), California, PA 15419	1852	John P. Watkins	Ps-M	4,900	305
Cal. State Univ. (A), Dominguez Hills, CA 90747	1960	Donald Gerth	Ps-M	7,000	300
Cal. State, San Bernardino, CA 92407	1962	John Pfau	Ps-M	4,387	277
Cal. State Stanislaus, Turlock, CA 95380	1957	Walter Olson	Ps-M	4,033	NA
Cal. State Polytechnic Univ., Pomona, CA 91768	1938	Hugh La Bounty Jr	Ps-M	15,912	800
Cal. State Univ. (A), Chico, CA 95929	1887	Stanford Cazier	Ps-M	13,135	665
Cal. State Univ., Fresno, CA 93740	1911	Harold H. Haak	Ps-M	15,900	916
Cal. State Univ. (A), Fullerton, CA 92634	1959	L. Donald Shields	Ps-M	21,272	800
Cal. State Univ., Hayward, CA 94542	1957	Ellis McCune	Ps-M	10,666	608
Cal. State Univ., Long Beach, CA 90840	1949	Stephen Horn	Ps-M	30,100	2,000
Cal. State Univ. (A), Los Angeles, CA 90032	1947	James M. Rosser	Ps-D	25,000	895
Cal. State Univ., Northridge, CA 91330	1958	James W. Cleary	Ps-M	28,441	1,500
Cal. State Univ., Sacramento, CA 95819	1947	Dr. W. Lloyd Johns	Ps-M	22,190	1,268
Cal. State Univ., San Francisco, CA 94132	1899	Paul F. Romberg	Ps-D	24,120	1,812

Name, address	Year	Governing official, affiliation, and highest degree offered	Students	Teachers
Cal. Univ. of* (A), Berkeley, CA 94720	1868	David S. Saxon	Ps-D	128,478	7,000
Berkeley Campus (A), Berkeley, CA 94720	1873	Ira Michael Heyman	Ps-D	30,445	1,494
Davis Campus, Davis, CA 95616	1906	James Meyer	Psl-S	18,500	1,400
Irvine Campus, Irvine, CA 92717	1960	D.G. Aldrich	Ps-D	10,222	793
Los Angeles Campus, Los Angeles, CA 90024	1919	Charles Young	Ps-D	32,742	3,000
Riverside Campus, Riverside, CA 92502	1954	Tomas Rivera	Ps-D	4,700	416
San Diego Campus, La Jolla, CA 92093	1912	Richard C. Atkinson	Ps-M	11,410	825
San Francisco Campus, San Francisco, CA 94122	1899	Paul F. Romberg	Ps-D	28,820	1,812
Santa Barbara Campus (A), Santa Barbara, CA 93106	1898	Robert A. Huttenback	Ps-D	14,231	1,051
Santa Cruz Campus, Santa Cruz, CA 95064	1965	R.L. Sinsheimer	Ps-D	6,472	347
Calvary Bible Coll., Kansas City, MO	1932	Leslie P. Madison	IR-M	492	38
Calumet (A), Whiting, IN 46394	1951	Rev. James McCabe	IR-B	1,392	47
Calvin, Grand Rapids, MI 49506	1876	Anthony Dickema	IR-M	4,108	247
Camden County (A), Blackwood, NJ 08012	1967	Otto R. Mauke	Psl-A	7,466	335
Cameron, Lawton, OK 73505	1927	Don Davis	Ps-B	4,901	175
Campbell, Buies Creek, NC 27506	1887	Norman A. Wiggins	IR-JD	2,839	125
Campbellsville, Campbellsville, KY 42718	1906	William R. Davenport	IR-B	667	59
Canada, Redwood City, CA 94061	1968	Samuel Ferguson	Psl-A	9,200	240
Canisius (A), Buffalo, NY 14208	1870	Rev. James Demske	IP-M	3,071	155
Canyons, Coll. of the, Valencia, CA 91355	1969	L.B. Newcomer	Psl-A	3,900	85
Cape Cod Comm., W. Barnstable, MA 02668	1960	James F. Hall	Ps-A	1,625	125
Cape Fear Tech. Inst. (A), Wilmington, NC 28401	1959	M.J. McLeod	Psl-A	1,450	61
Capital City Jr, Little Rock, AR 72204	1927	Perry Turnbull	IP-A	469	22
Capital Univ., Columbus, OH 43209	1850	Harvey A. Stegemoeller	IP-M	2,507	192
Capitol Inst. of Tech., Kensington, MD 20795	1964	G.W. Troxler	IP-B	715	38
Cardinal Stritch, Milwaukee, WI 53217	1937	Sister M. Kliebhan	IR-M	1,136	109
Carl Albert Junior (A), Poteau, OK 74953	1934	Joe E. White	Ps-A	1,710	60
Carl Sandburg, Galesburg, IL 61401	1965	William Anderson	Ps-A	3,940	200
Carleton, Northfield, MN 55057	1866	Robert Edwards	IP-B	1,735	175
Carlow (W), Pittsburgh, PA 15213	1929	Sister Jane Scully	IR-B	977	96
Carnegie-Mellon (A), Univ., Pittsburgh, PA 15213	1900	Richard M. Cyert	IP-D	4,772	417
Carroll, Helena, MT 59601	1909	Francis Kerins	IR-B	1,362	100
Carroll, Waukesha, WI 53186	1846	Robert V. Cramer	IR-B	1,343	119
Carson-Newman (A), Jefferson City, TN 37760	1851	J. Cordell Maddox	IR-B	1,616	91
Carteret Tech. Inst., Morehead City, NC 28557	1968	Donald Bryant	Ps-A	969	66
Carthage, Kenosha, WI 53141	1847	Erno Dahl	IP-M	1,565	96
Case Western Reserve Univ., Cleveland OH 44106	1826	David V. Ragone	IP-D	7,935	1,450
Casper, Casper, WY 82601	1945	Lloyd H. Loftin	Ps-A	3,530	201
Castleton State, Castleton, VT 05735	1787	Thomas K. Meier	Ps-M	2,200	150
Catawba, Salisbury, NC 28144	1851	Stephen H. Wurster	IR-B	988	65
Catawba Valley Tech. Inst. (A), Hickory, NC 28601	1957	Robert E. Paap	Psl-A	2,084	69
Cathedral (A)(M), Douglaston, NY 11362	1914	Rev. Thomas Gradilone	IR-B	135	31
Catholic Univ. of America (A), Washington, DC 20064	1887	Dr. Edmund D. Pellegrino	IR-D	7,749	386
Cath. Univ. of Puerto Rico (A), Ponce, PR 00731	1948	F.J. Carreras	IR-M	8,959	380
Catonsville Comm. (A), Baltimore, MD 21228	1957	Robert Barringer	PI-A	10,000	200
Cayuga Co. Comm., Auburn, NY 13021	1953	John Anthony	Psl-A	2,829	84
Cazenovia (W), Cazenovia, NY 13035	1824	Stephen Schneeweiss	I-A	547	47
Cecil Community, North East, MD 21901	1968	Robert L. Gell	Psl-A	1,206	65
Cedar Crest, Allentown, PA 18104	1867	Dr. Gene S. Cesari	IR-B	1,125	88
Cedarville, Cedarville, OH 45314	1887	James Jeremiah	IP-A	1,500	87
Centenary (W), Hackettstown, NJ 07840	1873	Charles Dick	IP-B	593	80
Centenary Coll. of La, Shreveport, LA 71104	1825	Donald Webb	IR-M	1,014	118
Central, McPherson, KS 67460	1853	Dorsey Brause	IR-A	268	24
Central, Pella, IA 50219	1853	Kenneth J. Weller	IR-B	1,541	107
Central Arizona, Coolidge, AZ 85228	1969	Mel Everingham	PI-A	6,749	NA
Central Bible, Springfield, MO 65802	1922	H. Maurice Lednicky	IR-B	1,054	51
Central Carolina Tech. Inst., Sanford, NC 27330	1962	James F. Hockaday	Ps-A	2,069	135
Central Connecticut State, New Britain, CT 06050	1849	F. Don James	Ps-M	12,250	680
Central Florida, Univ. of, Orlando, FL 32816	1963	Trevor Colbourn	Ps-D	12,820	459
Central Florida Comm., Ocala, FL 32670	1957	Henry E. Goodlett	Ps-A	8,242	364
Centralia, Centralia, WA 98531	1925	Dale Miller	Ps-A	4,281	359
Central Methodist, Fayette, MO 65248	1854	Dr. Joe Howell	IR-B	648	60
Central Mich. Univ., Mt. Pleasant, MI 48859	1892	Harold Abel	Ps-D	18,088	791
Central Missouri St. Univ., Warrensburg, MO 64093	1871	James Horner	Ps-S	9,989	477
Central Nebr. Tech. Comm. (A), Grand Island, NE 68801	1966	Chester Guasman	Psl-A	16,072	132
Central New England, Worcester, MA 01610	1971	Edward Mattar III	IP-B	500	75
Central Ohio Tech. Coll., Newark, OH 43055	1971	Vacant	Ps-A	1,167	91
Central Oregon Comm. (A), Bend, OR 97701	1949	Frederick Boyle	PI-A	1,896	69
Central Piedmont Comm., Charlotte, NC 28204	1963	Richard H. Hagemeyer	Psl-A	54,394	NA
Central State Univ., Edmond, OK 73034	1890	Bill Lillard	Ps-M	11,723	429
Central State Univ. (A), Wilberforce, OH 45384	1887	Lionel H. Newsom	Ps-B	2,414	110
Central Tech. Comm., Grand Is., NE 68802	1966	Chester H. Gausman	PI-A	11,525	127
Central Texas (A), Killeen, TX 76541	1967	L.M. Morton Jr.	PI-A	5,000	125
Central Virginia Comm., Lynchburg, VA 24502	1967	Donald Puyear	Ps-A	3,200	150
Central Washington State, Ellensburg, WA 98926	1891	Donald L. Garrity	Ps-M	7,409	321
Central Wesleyan, Central, SC 29630	1906	John Newby	IR-B	414	41
Central Wyoming, Riverton, WY 82501	1976	Richard St. Pierre	Psl-A	1,158	67
Central YMCA Comm. (A), Chicago, IL 60606	1960	Ralph H. Lee	IP-A	3,189	83
Centre Coll. of Ky., Danville, KY 40422	1819	Thomas A. Spragens	IP-B	749	75
Cerritos, Norwalk, CA 90650	1956	Wilford Michael	Ps-A	20,996	700
Cerro Coso Comm., Ridgecrest, CA 93555	1973	Raymond A. McCue	Ps-A	4,426	134
Chabot, Hayward, CA 94545	1961	Reed L. Buffington	PI-A	18,896	900
Chadron State, Chadron, NE 69337	1911	Edwin Nelson	Ps-S	2,084	108
Chaffey (A), Alta Loma, CA 91701	1883	K.C. Hinrichsen	Psl-A	11,644	461
Chaminade Univ. of Honolulu, Honolulu, HI 96816	1955	Rev. D. Schuyler	IP-M	2,305	170
Champlain, Burlington, VT 05401	1878	Robert A. Skiff	IP-A	1,011	58
Chapman, Orange, CA 92666	1861	G.T. Smith	IR-M	4,830	346
Charles Co. Comm., La Plata, MD 20646	1958	J.N. Carsey	Psl-A	4,358	218
Charles S. Mott Comm. (A), Flint, MI 48503	1923	Charles Pappas	PI-A	8,457	220
Charleston, Coll. of, Charleston, SC 29424	1770	Edward M. Collins Jr.	Ps-M	4,214	185
Charleston, Univ. of, Charleston, WV 25304	1881	Thomas G. Voss	I-M	NA	93
Chatham (W), Pittsburgh, PA 15232	1869	Alberta Arthurs	IP-B	721	86
Chattanooga St. Tech. Comm. (A), Chattanooga, TN 37406	1963	Charles W. Branch	Ps-A	4,602	164
Chemeketa Comm., Salem, OR 97303	1969	Arthur A. Binnie	Psl	12,053	750
Chesapeake (A), Wye Mills, MD 21679	1967	Robert Schleiger	Psl-A	2,564	30
Chestnut Hill (W), Philadelphia, PA 19118	1924	Sister Matthew Anita McDonald	IR-M	785	98
Cheyney State (A), Cheyney, PA 19319	1837	Wade Wilson	Ps-M	2,262	202
Chicago, City Colleges of, Chicago, IL 60601	1911	Oscar Shabat	Psl-A	114,381	1,450
Chicago City-Wide, Chicago, IL 60601	1975	Salvatore G. Rotella	Psl-A	14,898	70

Name, address	Year	Governing official, affiliation, and highest degree offered		Students	Teachers
Daley, Chicago, IL 60652	1960	William P. Conway	Psl-A	7,388	125
Kennedy-King, Chicago, IL 60621	1934	Ewen Akin	Psl-A	9,444	225
Loop, Chicago, IL 60601	1962	Salvatore G. Rotella	Psl-A	7,428	200
Malcolm X, Chicago, IL 60612	1911	James C. Griggs	Psl-A	7,627	175
Olive-Harvey, Chicago, IL 60628	1957	Eugene T. Speller	Psl-A	7,659	175
Truman, Chicago, IL 60640	1956	Wallace B. Appelson	Psl-A	11,504	225
Wright, Chicago, IL 60634	1934	Ernest Clements	Psl-A	9,183	225
Chicago, Univ. of (A), Chicago, IL 60637	1890	Hanna Gray	IP-D	9,236	1,035
Chicago Coll. of Osteopathic, Chicago, IL 60615	1900	Thaddeus Kawalek	IP-D	391	270
Chicago State Univ., Chicago, IL 60628	1869	Benjamin Alexander	Ps-M	7,012	390
Chicago Urban Skills Inst., Chicago, IL 60609	1970	Peyton S. Hutchison	Psl-A	39,250	550
Chipola Junior, Marianna, FL 32446	1947	Raymond M. Deming	IP-A	1,150	60
Chowan (A), Murfreesboro, NC 27855	1848	Bruce E. Whitaker	IR-A	1,124	55
Christian Brothers, Memphis, TN 38104	1871	Bro. Theodore Drahmann	IR-B	1,104	150
Christopher Newport, Newport News, Va 23606	1960	John E. Anderson	Ps-B	3,900	111
Cincinnati, Univ. of, Cincinnati, OH 45221	1819	Henry Winkler	Ps-D	33,772	2,132
Cisco Junior, Cisco, TX 76437	1909	Norman Wallace	Psl-A	1,450	85
Citadel, The (A), Charleston, SC 29409	1843	V. Adm. James Stockdale	Ps-M	3,277	155
Citrus, Azusa, CA 91702	1915	Robert Haugh	Psl-A	9,284	341
City, Seattle, WA 98104	NA	Michael A. Pastore	IP-M	2,137	150
Clackamas Comm., Oregon City, OR 97045	1967	John Hakanson	Psl-A	5,547	500
Claflin, Orangeburg, SC 29115	1869	Hubert V. Manning	IR-B	739	62
Claremont Men's, Claremont, CA 91711	1946	Jack Lee Stark	IR-B	802	100
Claremore, Claremore, OK 74017	1902	Richard Mosier	Psr-A	1,872	81
Clarendon, Clarendon, TX 79226	1898	Kenneth D. Vaughan	Psl	956	45
Clarion State, Clarion, PA 16214	1867	Thomas Bond	Ps-M	4,512	309
Clark (A), Atlanta, GA 30314	1869	Elias Blake Jr.	IR-B	1,876	116
Clark, Vancouver, WA 98663	1933	Richard A. Jones	Ps-A	4,500	416
Clark Co. Comm., N. Las Vegas, NV 89030	1971	Judith Eaton	Ps-A	10,650	674
Clark Tech., Springfield, OH 45501	1962	Richard Brinkman	Ps-A	2,670	170
Clark Univ., Worcester, MA 01610	1887	Mortimer Appley	IP-D	2,495	135
Clarke, Dubuque, IA 52001	1843	Meneve Dunham	IR-M	763	80
Clarke, Newton, MS 39345	1908	A.C. Johson	IR-A	201	20
Clarkson, Potsdam, NY 13676	1896	Robert A. Plane	IP-D	3,830	233
Clatsop Community, Astoria, OR 97103	1958	Philip Bainer	Psl-A	2,830	181
Clayton Junior, Morrow, GA 30260	1969	Harry S. Downs	Ps-A	2,977	88
Cleary, Ypsilanti, MI 48197	1883	Gilbert Bursley	I-B	700	48
Clemson Univ.*, Clemson, SC 29631	1889	Bill Lee Atchley	Ps-D	11,579	868
Cleveland Inst. of Art, Cleveland, OH 44106	1882	Joseph McCullough	IP-B	535	70
Cleveland Inst. of Music, Cleveland, OH 44106	1920	Grant Johannesen	IP-D	262	79
Cleveland State Comm. (A), Cleveland, TN 37311	1967	L. Quentin Lane	Ps-A	4,260	93
Cleveland State Univ., Cleveland, OH 44115	1964	Walter Waetjen	Ps-S	19,250	773
Cleveland Tech. (A), Shelby, NC 28150	1965	James Petty	Psl-A	1,050	51
Clinton Community, Clinton, IA 52732	1946	Michael Crawford	Ps-A	840	60
Clinton Community (A), Plattsburgh, NY 12901	1966	Albert B. Light	Psl-A	1,400	31
Cloud County Comm., Concordia, KS 66901	1965	James P. Ihrig	Pl-A	2,736	237
Coahoma Junior (A), Clarksdale, MS 38614	1949	McKinley C. Martin	Psl-A	1,521	64
Coastal Carolina Comm. (A), Jacksonville, NC 28540	1965	James Henderson Jr.	Psl-A	2,157	70
Cochise (A), Douglas, AZ 85607	1962	Vacant	Pl-A	4,209	68
Coe, Cedar Rapids, IA 52402	1851	Leo Nussbaum	IP-B	1,342	101
Coffeyville Comm. Jr., Coffeyville, KS 67337	1923	Russell Graham	Pl-A	1,600	51
Coker, Hartsville, SC 29550	1908	James Daniels	IP-B	325	45
Colby (A), Waterville, ME 04901	1813	William R. Cotter	IP-B	1,625	140
Colby Comm., Colby, KS 67701	1964	James Tangeman	Psl-A	800	60
Colby-Sawyer (A), New London, NH 03257	1837	H. Nicholas Muller	IP-B	700	69
Coleman, La Mesa, CA 92041	1963	Maurice Egan	IP-B	681	40
Colgate Univ., Hamilton, NY 13346	1819	George D. Langdon, Jr.	IP-M	2,445	219
Colorado, Colo. Spgs., CO 80903	1874	Lloyd E. Worner	IP-M	1,954	206
Colorado Mountain, Glenwood Spgs., CO 81601	1962	F. Dean Lillie	Ps-A	718	68
Colorado Northwestern Comm., Rangely, CO 81648	1962	James H. Bos	Psl-A	1,187	70
Colorado Sch. of Mines (A), Golden, CO 80401	1876	Guy McBride Jr.	Ps-D	2,543	176
Colorado State Univ. *, Fort Collins, CO 80523	1870	Ralph E. Christofferson	Ps-S	20,720	1,200
Colorado, Univ. of (A), Boulder, CO 80302	1876	Arnold Weber	Ps-D	20,167	950
Colorado Springs, Colorado Springs, CO 80907	1965	Donald Schwartz, Chan	Ps-M	4,827	167
Colorado Women's (W), Denver, CO 80220	1888	Sherry Manning	IP-B	509	42
Columbia (W), Columbia, SC 29203	1854	Ralph Mirse	IR-B	959	87
Columbia, Columbia, MO 65216	1851	Bruce B. Kelly	IR-B	2,450	151
Columbia Basin (A), Pasco, WA 99301	1955	Fred L. Esvelt	Ps-A	10,000	382
Columbia Bible, Columbia, SC 29230	1923	J. Robertson McQuilkin	IP-B	528	27
Columbia Greene Comm. (A), Hudson, NY 12534	1966	Edward J. Owen	Psl-A	1,218	37
Columbia Jr., Columbia, CA 95310	1968	W. Dean Cunningham	Pl-A	3,800	140
Columbia Jr., Columbia, SC 29202	1935	Michael Gorman	IP-A	900	35
Columbia State Comm. (A), Columbia, TN 38401	1966	Harold S. Pryor	Ps-A	2,201	61
Columbia Union, Takoma Park, MD 20012	1904	William Loveлen	IR-A	892	80
Columbia Univ. (A), New York, NY 10027	1754	Michael I. Sovern	IP-D	17,861	1,666
Teachers College (A), New York, NY 10027	1887	L.A. Cremin	IP-D	4,500	300
Columbus, Columbus, GA 31907	1958	Francis J. Brook	Ps-M	4,573	238
Columbus Coll. of Art & Design, Columbus, OH 43215	1879	Joseph Canzani	IP-B	915	62
Columbus Tech. Inst. (A), Columbus, OH 43215	1963	Clarence Schauer	Ps-A	4,966	264
Compton Comm., Compton, CA 90221	1927	Abel B. Sykes Jr.	Psl-A	7,000	316
Concord, Athens, WV 24712	1872	Meredith Freeman	Ps-B	2,174	116
Concordia, Ann Arbor, MI 48105	1963	M.S. Pohl	IR-B	525	51
Concordia, Bronxville, NY 10708	1881	Ralph Schultz	IR-B	389	57
Concordia Lutheran Coll., Austin, TX 78705	1926	Ray F. Martens	IR-B	360	26
Concordia, Milwaukee, WI 53208	1881	R.J. Buuck	IR-B	505	44
Concordia, Moorhead, MN 56560	1891	Paul Dovre	IR-B	2,625	192
Concordia, Portland, OR 97211	1905	E.P. Weber	IR-A	317	37
Concordia, River Forest, IL 60305	1864	Paul A. Zimmerman	IR-M	1,200	100
Concordia, St. Paul, MN 55104	1893	Gerhardt Hyatt	IR-B	661	65
Concordia Teachers, Seward, NE 68434	1894	M.J. Stelmachowicz	IR-M	1,087	81
Concordia Theological Seminary, Ft. Wayne, IN 46825	1846	Robert Preus	IR-D	571	35
Connecticut, New London, CT 06320	1911	Oakes Ames	IP-M	1,974	199
Connecticut, Univ. of (A), Storrs, CT 06268	1881	Edward V. Gant, Act.	Ps-D	21,349	1,157
Connors State (A), Warner, OK 74469	1908	Melvin Self	Ps-A	1,800	64
Cosumnes River College, Sacramento, CA 95823	1970	Vincent P. Padilla	Psl-A	6,000	121
Contra Costa, San Pablo, CA 94806	1950	H. Rex Craig	Pl-A	10,400	366
Converse (W), Spartanburg, SC 29302	1889	Robert T. Coleman, Jr.	IP-M	1,003	85
Cooke County, Gainesville, TX 76240	1924	Alton Laird	Psl-A	1,530	91
Cooper Union, New York, NY 10003	1859	Bill N. Lacy	IP-M	827	161

Name, address	Year	Governing official, affiliation, and highest degree offered	Stu-dents	Teach-ers
Coplah-Lincoln Junior, Wesson, MS 39191	1928	Billy Thames	Isl-A	1,500	NA
Coppin State (A), Baltimore, MD 21216	1900	Calvin Burnett	Ps-M	2,873	137
Cornell, Mt. Vernon, IA 51314	1853	Philip Secor	IP-B	933	85
Cornell Univ., Ithaca, NY 14853	1865	Frank Rhodes	IP-D	19,120	1,900
Corning Community (A), Corning, NY 14830	1957	Donald H. Hangen	Psl-A	3,068	104
Cottey (A) (W), Nevada, MO 64772	1884	Evelyn Milam	IP-A	327	30
Covenant, Lookout Mt., TN 37350	1955	Martin Essenburg	IR-B	522	40
Cowley County Comm., Arkansas City, KS 67005	1922	Gwen Nelson	Pfs-A	1,720	92
Crafton Hills, Yucaipa, CA 92399	1972	Wm. Moore	Psl-A	4,050	170
Craven Comm., New Bern, NC 28560	1965	Thurman E. Brock	Psl-A	1,550	125
Creighton Univ., Omaha, NE 68178	1878	Rev. Matthew E. Creighton	IP-D	5,614	964
Crowder, Neosho, MO 64850	1964	Dell Reed	P-A	1,257	70
Cuesta, San Luis Obispo, CA 93406	1964	Frank Martinez	Psl-A	6,420	138
Culver-Stockton, Canton, MO 63435	1853	Robert W. Brown	IR-B	586	44
Cumberland, Lebanon, TN 37087	1842	Ernest Stockton	IP-A	501	26
Cumberland, Williamsburg, KY 40769	1889	Jim Taylor	IR-B	2,029	95
Cumberland County (A), Vineland, NJ 08360	1965	Philip Phelan	Psl-A	2,013	51
Curry, Milton, MA 02186	1879	William Boyle	IP-1P	868	89
Cuyahoga Community (A), Cleveland, OH 44115	1962	Nolen Ellison, Chan.	Psl-A	25,594	420
Cypress, Cypress, CA 90630	1966	Jack A. Scott	Psl-A	13,170	210
Dabney S. Lancaster, Comm., Clifton Forge, VA 24422	1964	John F. Backels	Ps-A	1,151	70
Daemen, Amherst, NY 14226	1947	R.S. Marshall	IP-B	1,372	132
Dakota State (A), Madison, SD 57042	1881	Carleton M. Opgaard	Ps-B	895	47
Dakota Wesleyan Univ. (A), Mitchell, SD 57301	1885	Donald E. Messer	IR-B	526	60
Dallas Baptist (A), Dallas, TX 75211	1963	W. Marvin Watson	IR-B	931	44
Dallas Univ., Irving, TX 75061	1956	Robert F. Sasseen	IR-D	2,688	181
Dallas Co. Comm. Col. System (A), Dallas, TX 75202	1965	Bill J. Priest	Psl-A	32,790	2,412
Dalton Jr., Dalton, GA 30720	1963	Derrell Roberts	Ps-A	1,428	60
Dana (A), Blair, NE 68008	1884	James Kallas	IR-B	503	33
Daniel Webster (A), Nashua, NH 03063	1965	Louis D'Allesandro	IP-B	900	15
Danville Junior (A), Danville, IL 61832	1946	Joseph A. Borgen	Psl-A	3,200	80
Dartmouth, Hanover, NH 03755	1769	John George Kemeny	IP-D	4,115	291
Davenport Coll. of Business, Grand Rapids, MI 49502	1866	Donald W. Maine	IP-A	3,047	170
David Lipscomb, Nashville, TN 37203	1891	G. Williard Collins	IP-B	2,113	136
Davidson County Comm., Lexington, NC 27292	1958	Grady Love	Psl-A	2,347	104
Davidson, Davidson, NC 28036	1837	Samuel R. Spencer Jr.	IP-B	1,403	112
Davis & Elkins, Elkins, WV 26241	1904	Gordon E. Hermanson	IR-B	980	81
Davis Jr. Coll. of Business (A), Toledo, OH 43604	1858	Ruth L. Davis	IP-A	450	35
Dawson Comm. (A), Glendive, MT 59330	1940	James Hoffman	Psl-A	730	43
Dayton, Univ. of, Dayton, OH 45469	1850	Bro. Raymond Fitz	IR-D	10,189	885
Daytona Beach Comm., Daytona Beach, FL 32015	1958	Charles Polk	Pl-A	8,245	750
Dean Junior, Franklin (A) MA 02038	1865	Richard Crockford	IP-A	1,606	51
DeAnza Comm., Cupertino, CA 95014	1967	A. Robert DeHart	Pl-A	29,484	808
Defiance, Defiance, OH 43512	1850	Marvin J. Ludwig	IP-B	765	62
DeKalb Community (A), Clarkston, GA 30021	1964	W.W. Scott	Pl-A	18,333	280
Delaware, Univ. of, Newark, DE 19711	1833	E.A. Trabant	Psr-D	18,949	870
Delaware State*, Dover, DE 19901	1891	Luna I. Mishoe	Ps-B	1,617	147
Delaware County Comm. of (A), Media, PA 19063	1967	Richard D. DeCosmo	Psl-A	5,880	100
Delaware Tech. and Comm. (A), Dover, DE 19901	1967	John R. Kotula	Ps-A	7,022	195
Del. Valley Coll. of S&A, Doylestown, PA 18901	1896	Joshua Feldstein	P-B	1,715	101
Delgado (A), New Orleans, LA 70122	1921	Harry J. Bayer	Psl-A	8,771	178
Del Mar (A), Corpus Christi, TX 78404	1935	Jean Richardson	Pl-A	13,155	309
Delta, University Ctr., MI 48640	1958	Donald Carlyon	Psl-A	9,800	480
Delta State Univ. (A), Cleveland, MS 38733	1924	Kent Wyatt	Ps-M	2,693	150
Denison Univ., Granville, OH 43023	1831	Robert C. Good	IP-B	2,128	188
Denver, Univ. of, Denver, CO 80208	1864	Ross Pritchard	IP-D	8,059	647
Denver, Comm. Coll. of (A), Denver, Co 80218	1968	Robert E. Lahti	Ps-A	14,308	304
DePaul Univ. (A), Chicago, IL 60604	1898	Rev. J.R. Cortelyou	IR-D	12,857	365
DePauw Univ., Greencastle, IN 46135	1837	Richard Rosser	IR-M	2,511	201
Desert, Coll. of the (A), Palm Desert (A), CA 92260	1958	F.D. Stout	Psl-A	10,000	103
Des Moines Area Comm., Ankeny, IA 50021	1966	Paul Lowery	Ps-A	5,600	300
Detroit Coll. of Business, Dearborn, MI 48126	1936	Frank Paone	IP-B	2,368	139
Detroit Coll. of Law, Detroit, MI 48201	1891	Ellsworth G. Reynolds	IP-1P	870	65
Detroit Inst. of Tech. (A), Detroit, MI 48201	1877	H. Thompson	IP-B	1,443	31
Detroit, Univ. of (A), Detroit, MI 48221	1877	Rev. M. Carron	IP-D	8,091	284
Diablo Valley (A), Pleasant Hill, CA 94523	1949	William P. Niland	Psl-A	18,742	580
Dickinson, Carlisle, PA 17013	1773	Samuel Banks	P-B	1,743	141
Dickinson School of Law, Carlisle, PA 17013	1834	Dale F. Shughart	IP-D	500	39
Dickinson State (A), Dickinson, ND 58601	1918	R.C. Gillund	Ps-B	1,100	70
Dillard Univ., New Orleans, LA 70122	1869	Samuel Cook	IR-B	1,208	92
District of Columbia, Univ. of (A), Washington, DC 20009	1851	Wendell Russell	Pl-M	1,310	132
Van Ness Campus (A), Washington, DC 20008	1977	Lisle C. Carter, Jr.	Pl-M	13,647	851
District One Tech. Ins., Eau Claire, WI 54701	1912	Norbert Wurtzel	P-A	3,700	150
Dixie, St. George, UT 84770	1911	Alton L. Wade	P-F	1,790	75
Doane, Crete, NE 68333	1872	Philip R. Heckman	IP-B	624	61
Dr. Martin Luther, New Ulm, MN 56073	1884	Lloyd O. Huebner	IR-B	756	72
Dodge City Community, Dodge City, KS 67801	1935	Charles M. Barnes	Pl-A	1,300	100
Dominican Coll. of Blauvelt, Blauvelt, NY 10962	1952	Sr. Eileen O'Brien	IP-B	1,343	78
Dominican Coll. of San Rafael, San Rafael, CA 94901	1890	Barbara Bundy	IR-M	680	108
Donnelly (A), Kansas City, KS 66102	1949	Rev. Raymond Davern	IR-A	978	35
Dordt (A), Sioux Center, IA 51250	1955	B.J. Haan	IR-B	990	50
Dowling, Oakdale, NY 11769	1968	V.P. Meskill	IP-M	2,179	153
Drake Univ., Des Moines, IA 50311	1881	Wilbur C. Miller	IP-D	6,592	408
Drew Univ., Madison, NJ 07940	1866	Paul Hardin	IR-D	2,559	178
Drexel Univ., Philadelphia, PA 19104	1891	William W. Hagerty	IP-D	11,953	679
Drury, Springfield, MO 65802	1873	Norman C. Crawford, Jr.	IP-M	2,923	211
Dubuque, Univ. of, Dubuque, IA 52001	1852	Walter F. Peterson	IR-1P	1,130	69
Duke Univ. (A), Durham, NC 27706	1838	Terry Sanford	IP-D	9,900	1,385
Dundalk Community, Baltimore, MD 21222	1970	John E. Ravekes	Pl-A	2,213	131
Du Page, Coll. of, Glen Ellyn, IL 60137	1967	Harold D. McAninch	Ps-A	19,307	1,100
Duquesne Univ., Pittsburgh, PA 15282	1878	Rev. Donald S. Nesti	IR-D	6,500	471
Durham Tech. Inst. (A), Durham, NC 27703	1965	John Crumpton Jr.	PsP-A	2,000	130
Dutchess Community (A), Poughkeepsie, NY 12601	1957	John J. Connolly	Psl-A	5,975	132
Dyersburg State Comm., Dyersburg, TN 38024	1969	Edward Eller	Ps-A	1,040	67
Dyke, Cleveland, OH 44114	1848	John Corfias	IP-B	1,435	75
D'Youville, Buffalo, NY 14201	1908	Sister Denise Roche	IP-B	1,528	116
Earlham, Richmond, IN 47374	1847	Franklin Wallin	IR-M	1,047	96

Name, address	Year	Governing official, affiliation, and highest degree offered	Students	Teachers
East Carolina Univ., Greenville, NC 27834	1907	Dr. Thomas B. Brewer, Chan.	Ps-D	12,309	775
East Central Junior, Decatur, MS 39327	1928	Charles V. Wright	Psl-A	785	50
East Central Junior, Union, MO 63084	1968	Donald D. Shook	Pl-A	2,064	108
East Central Oklahoma St. Univ., Ada, OK 74820	1909	Stanley Wagner	Ps-M	3,973	149
East Los Angeles, Monterey Park, CA 91754	1945	Arthur D. Avila, Act.	Psl-A	15,652	680
East Mississippi Jr. (A), Scooba, MS 39358	1927	C. Cheatham	Psl-A	1,554	47
East Stroudsburg State, E. Stroudsburg, PA 18301	1893	Dennis Bell	Ps-M	3,940	222
East Tennessee State Univ., Johnson City, TN 37614	1911	Ronald E. Beller	Ps-D	9,153	530
East Texas Baptist (A), Marshall, TX 75670	1912	Jerry Dawson	IR-B	858	44
East Texas State Univ. (A), Commerce, TX 75428	1889	F.H. McDowell	Ps-D	8,752	347
Eastern, St. Davids, PA 19087	1952	Daniel E. Weiss	IR-B	700	72
Eastern Arizona, Thatcher, AZ 85552	1888	W.M. McGrath	Psl-A	3,823	180
Eastern Conn. State, Willimantic, CT 06226	1889	Charles Richard Webb	Ps-M	2,950	239
Eastern Illinois Univ., Charleston, IL 61920	1895	Daniel Marvin, Jr.	Ps-S	10,774	663
Eastern Iowa Comm. (A), Davenport, IA 52803	1966	Michael E. Crawford, Supt.	Ps-A	2,900	155
Eastern Kentucky Univ. (A), Richmond, KY 40475	1906	Julius Powell	Ps-M	13,714	650
Eastern Maine Voc. Tech. Inst., Bangor, ME 04401	1966	Alan R. Campbell, Dir.	Pf-A	1,600	150
Eastern Mennonite, Harrisonburg, VA 22801	1917	Richard C. Detweiler	IR-M	990	90
Eastern Michigan Univ., Ypsilanti, MI 48197	1849	John W. Porter	Ps-S	20,000	650
Eastern Montana, Billings, MT 59101	1927	J. Van de Wetering	Ps-M	3,779	200
Eastern Nazarene, Quincy, MA 02170	1918	Stephen W. Nease	IR-M	832	56
Eastern New Mexico Univ., Portales, NM 88130	1934	Warren Armstrong	Ps-S	3,701	181
Eastern Oklahoma State (A), Wilburton, OK 74578	1909	James Miller	Ps-A	1,622	69
Eastern Oregon State, LaGrande, OR 97850	1929	Rodney A. Briggs	Ps-M	1,770	192
Eastern Utah (A), Coll. Of, Price, UT 84501	1937	Dean McDonald	Ps-A	1,250	35
Eastern Washington State, Cheney, WA 99004	1882	H.G. Frederickson	Ps-M	8,333	479
Eastern Wyoming, Torrington, WY 82240	1948	Charles Rogers	Psl-A	1,000	64
Eastfield, Mesquite, TX 75150	1970	Eleanor Ott	Psl-A	8,259	337
Eckerd, St. Petersburg, FL 33733	1958	Peter Armacost	IP-B	1,034	70
Edgecliff (A), Cincinnati, OH 45206	1935	Sr. M. Molitor	IR-B	841	42
Edgecombe Tech. Inst., Tarboro, NC 27886	1968	Charles McIntyre	Ps-A	1,050	128
Edgewood, Madison, WI 53711	1927	Sister Alice O'Rourke	IR-B	680	80
Edinboro State, Edinboro, PA 16444	1857	Foster F. Diebold	Ps-M	5,646	379
Edison Community, Ft. Myers, FL 33907	1962	David G. Robinson	Pf-A	5,066	273
Edmonds Community (A), Lynnwood, WA 98036	1967	Thomas C. Nielsen	Ps-A	8,011	84
Edmondson Junior, Chattanooga, TN 37411	1914	F. Jack Henderson, Jr	IP-A	412	26
Edward Waters (A), Jacksonville, FL 32209	1866	Cecil Wayne Cone	IR-B	703	35
Edward Williams (A), Hackensack, NJ 07601	1964	Jerome Pollack	IP-A	398	9
El Camino (A), Torrance, CA 90506	1947	Stuart E. Marsee	Psl-A	27,624	637
El Centro, Dallas, TX 75202	1966	Ruby H. Herd	Ps-A	6,721	310
El Paso County Community, El Paso, TX 79998	1969	Robert E. Shepack	Pl-A	11,018	424
El Reno Jr., El Reno, OK 73036	1938	Bill S. Cole	Ps-A	1,400	112
Elgin Community, Elgin, IL 60120	1949	Mark L. Hopkins	Psl-A	9,529	285
Elizabeth City State Univ. (A), Eliz. City, NC 27909	1891	Marion Thorpe, Chan.	Ps-B	1,560	114
Elizabeth Seton (A), Yonkers, NY 10701	1960	Sr. Mary Ellen Brosnan	IP-A	989	81
Elizabethtown (A), Elizabethtown, PA 17022	1899	Mark C. Ebersole	IR-B	1,423	98
Elizabethtown Comm., Elizabethtown, KY 42701	1964	James Owen, Dir.	Ps-A	1,939	88
Ellsworth Comm., Iowa Falls, IA 50126	1890	Duane R. Lloyd, Dean	Ps-A	960	55
Elmhurst (A), Elmhurst, IL 60126	1871	Ivan Frick	IR-B	3,031	95
Elmira, Elmira, NY 14901	1855	Leonart Grant	IP-M	2,709	165
Elon, Elon College, NC 27244	1889	J.F. Young	IR-B	2,577	84
Embry Riddle Aero. Univ., Bunnell, FL 32010	1926	Jack R. Hunt	IP-M	10,651	703
Emerson, Boston, MA 02116	1880	Allan Koenig	IP-M	2,121	140
Emmanuel (W), Boston, MA 02115	1919	Sister Janet Eisner	IR-M	1,080	116
Emmanuel, Franklin Springs, GA 30639	1919	C.Y. Melton	IR-A	379	29
Emory & Henry, Emory, VA 24327	1836	Thomas F. Chilcote	IR-B	792	60
Emory Univ., Atlanta, GA 30322	1836	James T. Laney	IR-D	7,584	1,200
Emporia State, Emporia, KS 66801	1863	John Visser	Ps-S	6,422	232
Endicott (W), Beverly, MA 01915	1939	Carol A. Hawkes	IP-A	837	70
Enterprise State Junior (A), Enterprise, AL 36331	1965	Benjamin A. Forrester	Ps-A	1,525	43
Erie Community (A), Buffalo, NY 14221	1946	Oscar Smuckler, Act.	Psl-A	10,296	325
Erskine, Due West, SC 29639	1829	J.A. Knight, Act.	IR-B	739	51
Essex Community, Baltimore, MD 21237	1957	Vernon Wanty	Psl-A	8,715	450
Essex County, Newark, NJ 07102	1968	A. Zachary Yamba	Pfsl-A	6,813	312
Eureka, Eureka, IL 61530	1855	Daniel Gilbert	IR-B	461	36
Evangel, Springfield, MO 65802	1955	Robert Spence	IR-B	1,851	126
Evansville, Univ. of, Evansville, IN 47702	1854	Wallace B. Graves	IR-M	5,180	335
Everett Comm., Everett, WA 98201	1941	Nina Haynes	Ps-A	10,179	312
Evergreen State (A), Olympia, WA 98505	1967	Daniel Evans	Ps-B	2,514	130
Fairfield Univ., Fairfield, CT 06430	1942	Rev. Aloysius P. Kelly	IR-M	5,062	299
Fairleigh Dickinson Univ. (A), Rutherford, NJ 07070	1942	Jerome Pollack	IP-D	19,796	1,574
Fairmount State, Fairmount, WV 26554	1867	Wendell G. Hardway	Ps-B	5,251	272
Faith Baptist Bible, Ankeny, IA 50021	1921	Gordon L. Shipp	IR-B	440	24
Fashion Inst. of Tech. (A), New York, NY 10001	1944	Marvin J. Feldman	Psl-B	8,444	164
Faulkner State Jr., Bay Minette, Al 36507	1965	L. Sibert	Ps-A	1,147	33
Fayetteville St. Univ., Fayetteville, NC 28301	1867	Charles Lyons Jr.	Ps-M	3,000	204
Fayetteville Tech. Inst., Fayetteville, NC 28303	1961	Howard Boudreau	Psl-A	29,288	250
Feather River, Quincy, CA 95971	1968	Donald R. Hongisto	Ps-A	1,761	80
Felician (A), Lodi, NJ 07644	1942	Sr. M. Hiltrude Koba	IR-B	659	52
Fergus Falls Comm., Fergus Falls, MN 56537	1960	W.A. Waage	Ps-A	722	42
Ferris State (A), Big Rapids, MI 49507	1884	Robert Ewigleben	Ps-1P	9,934	535
Ferrum, Ferrum, VA 24088	1913	Joseph T. Hart	IR-B	1,502	101
Findlay, Findlay, OH 45840	1882	Glen R. Rasmussen	IR-B	1,062	73
Finger Lakes, Comm. Coll. of (A), Canandaigua, NY 14424	1965	Charles Meder	Psl-A	2,800	85
Fisher Junior (A), Boston, MA 02116	1903	Scott Fisher	IP-A	2,115	97
Fisk Univ., Nashville, TN 37203	1865	Walter Leonard	IP-M	915	83
Fitchburg State (A), Fitchburg, MA 01420	1894	Vincent J. Mara	Ps-M	5,896	208
Flagler, St. Augustine, FL 32084	1967	William L. Proctor	IP-B	839	68
Flathead Valley Comm., Kalispell, MT 59901	1967	Norbert J. Berning, act.	Psl-A	1,720	65
Florida, Temple Terrace, FL 33617	1946	James R. Cope	IP-A	450	35
Florida A.&M. Univ.*, Tallahassee, FL 32307	1887	Walter L. Smith	Ps-1P	5,017	372
Florida Atlantic Univ., Boca Raton, FL 33431	1961	Glenwood L. Creech	Ps-S	7,612	426
Florida Inst. of Tech. (A), Melbourne, FL 32901	1958	Jerome P. Keuper	IP-D	3,899	180
Florida Jr. (A), Jacksonville, FL 32202	1966	Benjamin R. Wygal	Pl-A	38,524	335
Florida Keys Comm., Key West, FL 33040	1965	William A. Seeker	Ps-A	1,918	91
Florida Memorial, Miami, FL 33054	1879	Willie Robinson	IP-B	820	40
Florida Southern, Lakeland, FL 33802	1885	Robert Davis	IP-B	2,821	150
Florida State Univ., Tallahassee, FL 32306	1857	Bernard R. Sliger	Ps-D	22,424	1,300

Name, address	Year	Governing official, affiliation, and highest degree offered	Students	Teachers
Florida Tech. Univ. (A), Orlando, FL 32816	1963	Trevor Colbourn	Ps-M	10,605	397
Florida Univ. of*, Gainesville, FL 32611	1845	Robert Q. Marston	Ps-D	33,232	2,529
Floyd Junior (A), Rome, GA 30161	1970	David McCorkle	Ps-A	1,445	55
Fontbonne, St. Louis, MO 63105	1917	Sister Jane Hassett	IR-M	866	62
Foothill, Los Altos Hills, CA 94022	1958	James S. Fitzgerald	Psl-A	19,000	550
Fordham Univ., Bronx, NY 10458	1841	Rev. James C. Finlay	IP-D	14,653	499
Forsyth Sch. for Dental Hygienists (A), Boston, MA 02115	1916	Ralph R. Lobene, Dean	IP-A	201	11
Forsyth Tech. Inst., Winston-Salem, NC 27103	1963	Harley Affeldt	Psl-A	2,679	104
Ft. Hays State, Hays, KS 67601	1902	Gerald W. Tomanek	Ps-S	5,863	316
Ft. Lauderdale, Ft. Lauderdale, FL 33301	1940	Douglas Devaux	IP-B	1,480	45
Fort Lewis, Durango, CO 81301	1912	Rexer Berndt	IP-B	3,260	146
Ft. Scott Comm. Junior (A), Ft. Scott, KS 66701	1912	Wayne McElroy	Psl-A	1,181	31
Ft. Steilacoom Comm., Tacoma, WA 98498	1967	Robert H. Stauffer	Ps-B	10,000	400
Fort Valley State*, Fort Valley, GA 31030	1895	Cleveland W. Pettigrew	Ps-M	1,748	142
Fort Wayne Bible, Fort Wayne, IN 46807	1904	Harvey R. Bostrum	IP-B	487	37
Fort Wright, Spokane, WA 99204	1907	Sister Sheila McEvoy	IR-M	413	72
Fox Valley Tech. Inst., Appleton, WI 54913	1967	William Sirek	Psl-A	4,782	240
Framingham State, Framingham, MA 01701	1839	D. Justin McCarthy	Ps-M	3,082	200
Francis Marion, Florence, SC 29501	1970	Walter D. Smith	Ps-M	2,974	136
Franklin, Franklin, IN 46131	1834	Edwin A. Penn	IR-B	606	65
Franklin Inst., Boston, MA 02116	1908	Michael C. Mazzola	IP-A	862	78
Franklin Univ., Columbus, OH 43215	1902	Frederick J. Bunte	IP-B	4,011	209
Franklin and Marshall, Lancaster, PA 17604	1787	Keith Spalding	IP-B	1,994	132
Franklin Pierce, Rindge, NH 03461	1962	Walter Peterson	IP-B	991	150
Freed-Hardeman, Henderson, TN 38340	1870	E. Claude Gardner	IR-A	1,306	90
Free Will Baptist Bible (A), Nashville, TN 37205	1942	Charles A. Thigpen	IR-B	600	26
Fresno City, Fresno, CA 93741	1910	Clyde C. McCully	Ps-A	15,737	456
Fresno Pacific, (A) Fresno, CA 93702	1944	Edmund Janzen	IR-M	727	44
Friends Univ., Wichita, KS 67213	1898	Richard Felix	IP-B	837	60
Frostburg State, Frostburg, MD 21532	1898	Nelson Guild	Ps-M	3,398	203
Fullerton, Fullerton, CA 92634	1913	Philip W. Borst	Ps-A	19,062	567
Fulton-Montgomery Comm. (A), Johnstown, NY 12095	1963	Hadley S. DePuy	Psl-A	1,565	57
Furman Univ., Greenville, SC 29613	1826	John Edwin Johns	IR-M	2,547	159
Gadsden State Junior, Gadsden, AL 35999	1965	Arthur W. Dennis	Ps-A	3,441	203
Gainesville Junior, Gainesville, GA 30503	1964	Hugh M. Mills Jr.	Ps-A	1,514	59
Gallaudet (A), Washington, DC 20002	1864	Edward C. Merrill Jr.	IP-D	943	126
Galveston (A), Galveston, TX 77550	1967	Melvin M. Plexco	Ps-A	2,203	80
Gannon, Erie, PA 16541	1933	Joseph P. Scottino	IR-M	3,500	125
Garden City Comm., Garden City, KS 67846	1920	Thomas F. Saffell	Pl-A	1,800	90
Gardner-Webb, Boiling Springs, NC 28017	1905	Dr. Craven E. Williams	IR-B	1,450	80
Gaston, Dallas, NC 28034	1963	W. Wayne Scott	Psl-A	2,613	154
Gateway Tech. Inst., Kenosha, WI 53141	1911	Keith Stoehr	Psl-A	20,000	785
Gavilan (A), Gilroy, CA 95020	1963	Rudy Melone	Psl-A	2,400	83
General Motors Inst., Flint, MI 48502	1919	William B. Cottingham	IP-B	2,327	148
Genesee Community (A), Batavia, NY 14020	1966	Stuart Steiner	Psl-A	2,069	72
Geneva, Beaver Falls, PA 15010	1848	Donald W. Felker	IR-B	1,204	70
George C. Wallace St. Comm., Dothan, AL 36303	1947	Nathan L. Hodges	Ps-A	3,050	115
George Fox, Newberg, OR 97132	1891	David Le Shana	IR-B	734	73
George Mason Univ., Fairfax, VA 22030	1957	George W. Johnson	Ps-D	13,293	761
George Washington Univ., Washington, DC 20052	1821	Lloyd H. Elliott	IP-D	20,844	2,981
George Williams, Downers Grove, IL 60515	1890	Richard E. Hamlin	IP-M	1,351	100
Georgetown, Georgetown, KY 40324	1829	Ben M. Elrod	IR-M	1,369	95
Georgetown Univ., Washington, DC 20057	1789	Rev. Timothy Healy	IR-D	11,559	602
Georgia, Milledgeville, GA 31061	1889	J. Whitney Bunting	Ps-S	3,360	145
Georgia Inst. Of Tech.*, Atlanta, GA 30332	1885	Joseph M. Pettit	Ps-D	11,261	685
Georgia Southern, Statesboro, GA 30460	1906	Dale W. Lick	Ps-S	6,403	319
Georgia Southwestern, Americus, GA 31709	1906	William H. Capitan	Ps-M	2,101	114
Georgia State Univ. (A), Atlanta, GA 30303	1913	Noah N. Langdale Jr.	Ps-D	20,338	856
Georgia, Univ. of*, Athens, GA 30602	1785	Fred C. Davison	Ps-D	21,759	1,918
Georgian Court, Lakewood, NJ 08701	1908	Sister Barbara Williams	IR-M	1,358	111
Germanna Comm., Locust Grove, VA 22508	1969	William P. Briley	Ps-A	1,225	60
Gettysburg, Gettysburg, PA 18325	1832	Charles E. Glassick	IR-B	1,937	132
Glassboro State, Glassboro, NJ 08028	1923	Mark M. Chamberlain	Ps-S	9,664	565
Glendale Comm. (A), Glendale, AZ 85032	1965	John Waltrip	Pl-A	12,291	180
Glendale Comm., Glendale, CA 91208	1927	John Grande	Pl-A	10,970	413
Glen Oaks Comm. (A), Centreville, MI 49032	1965	Justus Sundermann	Pl-A	900	66
Glenville State, Glenville, WV 26351	1872	William Simmons	Pl-B	1,889	90
Gloucester County (A), Sewell, NJ 08080	1966	William Apetz	Pl-A	2,500	114
Goddard (A), Plainfield, VT 05667	1938	John Hall	IP-B	1,400	53
Gogebic Community (A), Ironwood, MI 49938	1932	R. Ernest Dear	Pl-A	1,300	50
Golden Gate Univ., San Francisco, CA 94105	1901	Otto W. Butz	IP-D	10,500	450
Golden West, Huntgtn. Bch., CA 92647	1965	Lee A. Stevens	Psl-A	22,727	763
Goldey Beacom, Wilmington, DE 19808	1886	William R. Baldt	IP-B	1,460	100
Gonzaga Univ., Spokane, WA 99258	1887	Rev. Bernard Coughlin	IR-D	3,435	238
Gordon, Wenham, MA 01984	1889	Richard Gross	IR-B	1,072	80
Gordon Junior (A), Barnesville, GA 30204	1852	Jerry M. Williamson	Ps-A	1,506	40
Goshen, Goshen, IN 46526	1894	J. Lawrence Burkholder	IR-B	1,291	95
Goucher (W), Towson, MD 21204	1885	Rhoda M. Dorsey	IP-M	1,086	130
Governors State Univ., Park Forest South, IL 60466	1969	L. Goodman-Malamuth I	Ps-M	4,853	339
Grace (A), Winona Lake, IN 46590	1948	Homer Kent	IR-B	804	34
Grace Coll. of the Bible, Omaha, NE 68108	1943	Robert W. Benton	IP-B	434	26
Graceland, Lamoni, IA 50140	1895	Joe E. Hanna	IR-A	1,306	86
Grahm Junior (A), Boston, MA 02215	1950	Robert B. Vail	IP-A	541	59
Grambling State Univ., Grambling, LA 71245	1901	Joseph B. Johnson	Ps-M	3,549	203
Grand Canyon, Phoenix, AZ 85061	1949	Bill Williams	IR-B	1,173	74
Grand Rapids Junior (A), Grand Rapids, MI 49502	1914	Richard Calkins	Pl-A	7,301	230
Grand Valley State, Allendale, MI 49401	1963	Arend D. Lubbers	Ps-M	6,563	220
Grand View, Des Moines, IA 50316	1896	Karl F. Langrock	IR-B	1,183	70
Grays Harbor, Aberdeen, WA 98520	1930	Joseph A. Malik	Ps-A	3,604	225
Grayson County Junior, Denison, TX 75020	1964	Truman Wester	Psl-A	4,037	160
Greater Hartford Comm., Hartford, CT 06105	1967	Arthur C. Banks Jr.	Ps-A	2,875	100
Great Falls, Coll. of, Great Falls, MT 59405	1932	William A. Shields	IR-M	1,253	83
Green Mountain, Poultney, VT 05764	1834	James M. Pollock	IP-B	470	60
Green River Comm., Auburn, WA 98002	1967	James P. Chadbourne	Ps-A	7,793	348
Greenfield Comm., Greenfield, MA 01301	1962	Nancy L. Goodwin	Ps-A	1,461	99
Greensboro, Greensboro, NC 27420	1838	H.C. Wilkinson	IR-B	639	70
Greenville, Greenville, IL 62246	1892	W. Richard Stephens	IR-A	858	65
Greenville Tech. (A), Greenville, SC 29606	1962	Thomas Barton Jr.	Ps-A	23,369	460

Name, address	Year	Governing official, affiliation, and highest degree offered		Students	Teachers
Grinnell, Grinnell, IA 50112	1846	George A. Drake	IP-B	1,213	125
Grossmont, El Cajon, CA 92020	1961	Ivan Jones	Psl-A	14,800	600
Grove City, Grove City, PA 16127	1876	Charles S. MacKenzie	IP-B	2,153	120
Guilford, Greensboro, NC 27410	1837	William R. Rogers	IR-B	1,645	115
Guilford Tech. Inst., Jamestown, NC 27282	1958	Raymond Needham	Psl-A	4,190	114
Gulf Coast Bible (A), Houston, TX 77008	1953	John W. Conley	IR-B	351	19
Gulf Coast Comm., Panama City, FL 32401	1957	Lawrence W. Tyree	Ps-A	4,117	180
Gustavus Adolphus, St. Peter, MN 56082	1862	John Kendall	IR-B	2,315	183
Gwynedd-Mercy, Gwynedd Valley, PA 19437	1948	Sister Isabelle Keiss	IP-B	1,880	115
Hagerstown Junior, Hagerstown, MD 21740	1946	Atlee Kepler	PI-A	2,141	135
Hahnemann Medical, Philadelphia, PA 19102	1848	William Likoff	IP-D	1,800	645
Halifax Comm., Weldon, NC 27890	1967	Phillip W. Taylor	Psl-A	794	61
Hamilton (A), Clinton, NY 13323	1812	J.M. Carovano	IP-B	1,600	145
Hamline Univ., St. Paul, MN 55104	1854	Jerry E. Hudson	IR-1P	1,803	140
Hampden-Sydney (M), Hampden-Sydney, VA 23943	1776	Josiah Bunting III	IR-A	731	65
Hampton Institute, Hampton, VA 23668	1868	William R. Harvey	IP-M	3,220	235
Hanover, Hanover, IN 47243	1827	John E. Horner	IR-B	1,012	71
Harcum Junior, Bryn Mawr, PA 19010	1915	Michael A. Duzy	IP-A	930	71
Hardbarger Jr. of Bus., Raleigh NC 27602		James W. Burnette	IP-A	750	33
Hardin-Simmons Univ., Abilene, TX 79698	1891	Dr. Jesse C. Fletcher	IR-M	1,969	138
Harding Univ., Searcy, AR 72143	1924	Clifton L. Ganus	IP-M	3,084	180
Harford Community (A), Bel Air, MD 21014	1957	A.C. O'Connell	Ps-A	6,700	282
Harris-Stowe State, St. Louis, MO 63103	1857	Henry Givens	Ps-B	1,175	55
Harrisburg Area Comm., Harrisburg, PA 17110	1964	James Odom Jr.	Psl-A	5,521	240
Hartford, Univ. of, W. Hartford, CT 06117	1877	Stephen Trachtenberg	IP-D	9,836	621
Hartford State Tech., Hartford, CT 06106	1948	L. Barrell	Psl-A	1,423	46
Hartnell, Salinas, CA 93901	1920	Gibb R. Madsen	Psl-A	9,120	325
Hartwick, Oneonta, NY 13820	1928	Philip S. Wilder Jr	IP-A	1,447	118
Harvard Univ.**, Cambridge, MA 02139	1636	Derek Curtis Bok	IP-D	16,132	3,019
Harvey Mudd, Claremont, CA 91711	1955	D. Kenneth Baker	IP-B	495	82
Haskell Indian Junior, Lawrence, KS 66044	1884	Gerald E. Gipp	Pf-A	1,028	65
Hastings, Hastings, NE 68901	1882	Clyde B. Matters	IR-B	832	63
Haverford, Haverford, PA 19041	1833	Robert B. Stevens	IP-B	1,049	106
Hawaii, Univ. of (A), Honolulu, HI 96822	1907	Durwood Long, Chan.	Ps-D	67,000	4,742
Hawkeye Inst. of Tech., Waterloo, IA 50704	1966	John I Lawse	Ps-A	2,116	147
Haywood Tech. Inst. (A), Clyde, NC 28721	1964	J.H. Nanney	Ps-A	1,600	160
Hazard Community, Hazard, KY 41701	1968	J. Marvin Jolly	Ps-A	315	12
Heidelberg, Tiffin, OH 44883	1850	William C. Cossell	IP-B	780	82
Henderson Community, Henderson, KY 42420	1960	Marshall Arnold	Ps-A	843	30
Henderson County, Athens, TX 75751	1946	William J. Campion	Psl-A	2,753	126
Henderson State Univ., Arkadelphia, AR 71923	1890	Martin B. Garrison	Ps-M	2,941	175
Hendrix, Conway, AR 72032	1876	Roy Schilling, Jr.	IR-B	1,037	63
Henry Ford Comm. (A), Dearborn, MI 48128	1938	Stuart M. Bundy	PI-A	14,856	609
Herkimer Co. Comm. (A), Herkimer, NY 13350	1966	Robert McLaughlin	Psl-A	2,059	95
Hesston, Hesston, KS 67062	1909	Kirk Alliman	IR-A	653	80
Hibbing Comm., Hibbing, MN 55746	1916	Gilbert M. Staupe	Ps-A	647	48
Highland Comm. (A), Freeport, IL 61032	1961	Howard Sims	PI-A	1,630	47
Highland Comm., Highland, KS 66035	1858	Jack D. Nutt	Psl-A	781	73
Highland Park Comm. (A), Highland Park, MI 48203	1918	Comer Heath III	Ps-A	2440	78
Highline Comm., Midway, WA 98031	1961	Shirley B. Gordon	Ps-A	10,034	381
High Point, High Point, NC 27262	1924	David W. Cole	IR-B	1,442	64
Hilbert, Hamburg, NY 14075	1957	Sister Edmunette Paczesny	IP-A	663	58
Hill Junior, Hillsboro, TX 76645	1923	Eblert C. Hutchins	PI-A	1,100	45
Hillsborough Comm. (A), Tampa, FL 33622	1968	F. Scaglione	Ps-A	11,556	196
Hillsdale (A), Hillsdale, MI 49242	1844	George C. Roche III	IP-B	1,000	70
Hinds Junior, Raymond, MS 39154	1917	Clyde Muse	Psl-A	7,219	350
Hiram, Hiram, OH 44234	1850	Elmer Jagow	IP-B	887	75
Hiwassee (A), Madisonville, TN 37354	1849	Horace N. Barker	PI-A	574	34
Hobart & William Smith, Geneva, NY 14456	1822	Allan A. Kuusisto	IP-B	1,800	145
Hocking Technical, Nelsonville, OH 45764	1968	John J. Light	Psl-A	3,000	140
Hofstra Univ., Hempstead, NY 11550	1935	James M. Shuart	IP-D	11,000	672
Hollins (W), Hollins Coll., VA 24020	1842	Paula P. Brownlee	IP-M	920	87
Holmes Junior, Goodman, MS 39079	1925	M. R. Thorne	IP-B	1,458	55
Holy Cross, Coll. of the, Worcester, MA 01610	1843	Rev. John Brooks	IR-M	2,663	219
Holy Cross Jr., Notre Dame, IN 46556	1966	Brother John Driscoll	IR-A	254	20
Holy Family, Philadelphia, PA 19114	1954	Sister Mary Lillian	IR-B	1,281	113
Holy Names, Oakland, CA 94619	1868	Sister Irene Woodward	IR-M	639	86
Holyoke Community (A), Holyoke, MA 01040	1946	David Bartley	Ps-A	4,900	250
Honolulu Comm. (A), Honolulu, HI 96817	1968	C. Yoshioka	Ps-A	4,600	220
Hood, Frederick, MD 21701	1893	Martha Church	IP-M	1,730	150
Hope, Holland, MI 49423	1866	Gordon J. Van Wylen	IR-B	2,464	140
Hopkinsville Comm. (A), Hopkinsville, KY 42240	1965	Thomas Riley	Psl-A	1,345	65
Horry-Georgetown Tech. (A), Conway, SC 29526	1966	W.F. Anderson	Psl-A	1,350	47
Houghton, Houghton, NY 14744	1883	D.R. Chamberlain	IR-B	1,264	80
Housatonic Comm. (A), Bridgeport, CT 06608	1966	Vincent Darnowski	Ps-A	2,693	60
Houston Comm. Coll. (A), Houston, TX 77007	1971	J.B. Whiteley	PI-A	30,011	265
Houston Baptist Univ. (A), Houston, TX 77074	1960	William Hinton	IR-M	1,875	95
Houston, Univ. of (A), Houston, TX 77004	1927	Philip G. Hoffman	Ps-D	40,500	1,652
Downtown College, Houston, TX 77002	1974	Alexander F. Schilt	Ps-B	4,927	253
Howard (A), Big Spring, TX 79720	1945	Charles Hays	Psl-A	1,047	33
Howard Community, Columbia, MD 21044	1966	Alfred Smith Jr	Psl-A	3,042	152
Howard Payne Univ., Brownwood, TX 76801	1889	Ralph Phelps Jr	IR-B	1,201	85
Howard Univ. (A), Washington, DC 20059	1867	James E. Cheek	IP-D	10,709	1,098
Hudson Valley Comm. (A), Troy, NY 12180	1953	J. Fitzgibbons	Ps-A	6,932	240
Humboldt State Univ. (A), Arcata, CA 95521	1913	Alistair McCrone	Ps-B	7,500	400
Humphreys (A), Stockton, CA 95207	1896	Robert G. Humphreys	IP-A	300	26
Huntingdon, Montgomery, AL 36106	1854	Allen K. Jackson	IR-B	629	58
Huntington, Huntington, IN 46750	1897	E. DeWitt Baker	IR-M	559	63
Huron, Huron, SD 57350	1883	Wendell L. Jahnke	IR-B	315	34
Husson, Bangor, ME 04401	1898	Delmont N. Merrill	IP-M	1,500	115
Huston-Tillotson, Austin, TX	1876	John Q. Taylor King	IR-B	682	50
Hutchinson Comm., Hutchinson, KS 67501	1928	James Stringer	PI-A	2,865	254
Idaho, Coll. of, Caldwell, ID 83605	1891	Arthur H. DeRosier Jr.	IP-M	735	47
Idaho State Univ. (A), Pocatello, ID 83209	1901	Myron Coulter	Ps-D	9,843	499
Idaho, Univ. of*, Moscow, ID 83843	1889	Richard D. Gibb	Pf-D	8,869	656
Illinois, Jacksonville, IL 62650	1829	Donald Mundinger	IR-B	800	52

** Oldest college in the United States

Name, address	Year	Governing official, affiliation, and highest degree offered		Stu-dents	Teach-ers
Illinois, Univ. of*, Urbana, IL 61801	1867	Stanley Ikenberry	Ps-D	62,703	8,497
Chicago Circle* (A), Chicago, IL 60680	1965	Donald Riddle	Ps-D	20,285	1,500
Medical Center* (A), Chicago, IL 60680	1896	Joseph Begando	Ps-D	4,923	729
Urbana-Champaign*, Urbana, IL 61801	1867	John E. Cribbet	Ps-D	36,199	5,386
Illinois Benedictine (A), Lisle, IL 60532	1887	Richard Becker	IR-B	1,663	85
Illinois Central, E. Peoria, IL 61635	1967	Leon Perley	PI-A	12,050	84
Illinois Coll. of Optometry, Chicago, IL 60616	1955	Alfred Rosenbloom	IP-S	598	65
Illinois Coll. of Pod. Med., Chicago, IL 60610	1912	John F. Briggs	IP-S	646	90
Illinois Eastern Comm., Olney, IL 62450	1962	Charles R. Novak	Ps-D	6,425	1,043
Illinois Inst. of Technology, Chicago, IL 60616	1892	Thomas L. Martin Jr.	IP-D	7,254	535
Illinois State Univ., Normal, IL 61761	1857	Lloyd I. Watkins	Ps-D	19,396	1,134
Illinois Valley Comm. (A), Oglesby, IL 61348	1924	Alfred Wisgoski	PI-A	3,100	143
Illinois Wesleyan Univ., Bloomington, IL 61701	1851	Robert Eckley	IP-B	1,700	131
Immaculata, Immaculata, PA 19345	1920	Sister Marie Antoine	IR-B	1,303	99
Immaculate Heart (A), Los Angeles, CA 90027	1916	Nancy Heer	IR-B	701	40
Imperial Valley, Imperial, CA 92251	1922	Dan Angel	Psl-A	5,076	275
Incarnate Word, San Antonio, TX 78209	1881	Sister Margaret Slattery	IR-M	1,573	112
Independence Comm., Independence, KS 67301	1925	M. Leon Foster	PI-A	912	92
Indiana Central Univ., Indianapolis, IN 46227	1902	Gene Sease	IR-M	2,650	182
Indiana Inst. of Techn., Ft. Wayne, IN	1930	Thomas F. Scully	IP-B	764	38
Indiana State Univ., Terre Haute, IN 47809	1865	Richard Landini	Ps-D	12,362	731
Indiana Univ. (A), Bloomington, IN 47401	1820	John W. Ryan	Ps-D	76,394	3,267
Indiana Vocational Tech., Indianapolis, IN 46206	1963	Myron E. Eicher	Ps-A	23,661	1,474
Indiana Univ. of Pa., Indiana, PA 15705	1875	John Worthen	Ps-D	12,278	675
Indian Hills Comm., Ottumwa, IA 52501	1966	Lyle A. Hellyer	Ps-A	7,305	283
Indian Hills Comm. (A), Centerville, IA 52544	1930	Lyle Hellyer	Psl-A	1,228	96
Indian River Comm., Ft. Pierce, FL 33450	1959	Herman Heise	Ps-A	6,300	367
Indian Valley, Novato, CA 94947	1971	Ervin L. Harlacher	Psl-A	3,660	126
Insurance, Coll. of., New York, NY 10038	1962	A. Leslie Leonard	IP-M	1,750	270
Inter Amer. Univ. of P.R., San Juan, PR 00753	1912	Ramon A. Cruz	IP-M	32,396	1,558
Internatl., L.A., CA 90024	1970	Robert D. Fitzgerald	IP-D	350	127
Internatl. Fine Arts, Miami, FL	1965	Edward Porter	IP-A	265	24
International Business (A), Ft. Wayne, IN 46804	1889	Anthony Conti	IP-A	600	25
Inver Hills Comm., (A), Inver Grove Hts., MN 55075	1970	Wallace A. Simpson	Psl-A	3,500	64
Iona (A), New Rochelle, NY 10801	1940	John Driscoll	IP-M	4,926	256
Iowa, Univ. of, Iowa City, IA 52242	1847	Willard L. Boyd	Ps-D	25,100	1,577
Iowa State Univ.*, Ames, IA 50011	1858	W. Robert Parks	Ps-D	24,268	2,013
Iowa Central Comm., Ft. Dodge, IA 50501	1966	Edwin Barbour	Psl-A	2,187	85
Iowa Lakes Comm. (A), Estherville, IA 51334	1967	Richard Blacker	Psl-A	1,605	85
Iowa Wesleyan, Mt. Pleasant, IA 52641	1842	Louis Haselmayer	IR-B	670	60
Iowa Western Comm., Council Bluffs, IA 51501	1966	Robert Looft	Psl-A	3,509	160
Isothermal Comm., Spindale, NC 28160	1965	Ben E. Fountain Jr.	Psl-A	2,250	84
Itasca Comm. (A), Grand Rapids, MN 55744	1922	Philip J. Anderson	Ps-A	1,046	35
Itawamba Junior, (A), Fulton, MS 38843	1948	W.O. Benjamin	PI-A	3,710	123
Ithaca, Ithaca, NY 14850	1892	James J. Whalen	IP-M	4,975	365
Jackson Comm., Jackson, MI 49201	1928	Harold Sheffer	Psl-A	9,837	107
Jackson State Comm., Jackson, TN 38301	1969	W.L. Nelms	Psl-A	2,651	124
Jackson State Univ., Jackson, MS 39217	1877	John A. Peoples Jr.	Ps-S	6,699	364
Jacksonville State Univ., Jacksonville, AL 36265	1883	Ernest Stone	Ps-M	6,724	340
Jacksonville Univ., Jacksonville, FL 32211	1934	Frances Bartlett Kinne	IP-M	2,478	189
James Madison Univ., Harrisonburg, VA 22807	1908	Ronald Carrier	Ps-S	8,817	441
Jamestown, Jamestown, ND 58401	1884	J.N. Anderson	IP-B	637	59
Jamestown Community (A), Jamestown, NY 14701	1950	David W. Petty, Act.	Ps-A	3,607	105
Jarvis Christian, Hawkins, TX 75765	1912	C.A. Berry	IR-B	555	48
Jefferson, Hillsboro, MO 63050	1963	Ray Henry	PI-A	5,000	125
Jefferson Community, Louisville, KY 40201	1968	Ronald Horvath	Pf-A	6,000	250
Jefferson Community (A), Watertown, NY 13601	1961	John Henderson	Psl-A	1,578	93
Jefferson Davis State Jr., Brewton, AL 36426	1965	George McCormick	Ps-A	846	24
Jefferson State Jr., Birmingham, AL 35215	1965	Judy Merritt	Ps-A	5,230	256
Jersey City State, Jersey City, NJ 07305	1927	William Maxwell	Ps-B	9,044	298
John A. Logan (A), Carterville, IL 62918	1967	Robert Tarvin	Psl-A	1,800	48
John Brown Univ., Siloam Springs, AR 72761	1919	John E. Brown	IR-B	803	52
John Carroll Univ. (A), Cleveland, OH 44118	1886	Rev. Thomas P. O'Malley	IP-M	4,170	174
John C. Calhoun St. Comm., Decatur, AL 35602	1965	J.R. Chasteen	Ps-A	5,264	240
John F. Kennedy Univ., Orinda, CA 94563	1964	Robert Fisher	IP-M	1,430	400
John Marshall Law School, Chicago, IL 60604	1899	Fred F. Herzog	IP-D	1,606	104
John Tyler Comm., Chester, VA 23831	1967	Freddie W. Nicholas	Psl-A	4,400	152
John Wesley (A), Owosso, MI 48867	1909	William H. Reid	IP-B	204	16
Johns Hopkins Univ., Baltimore, MD 21218	1876	Steven Muller	IP-D	9,423	2,307
Johnson County Comm., Overland Park, KS 66210	1967	Charles J. Carlsen	PI-A	6,377	290
Johnson C. Smith Univ., Charlotte, NC 28216	1867	Wilbert Greenfield	IR-B	1,482	107
Johnson State, Johnson, VT 05656	1827	Edward Elmendorf	Ps-M	1,341	96
Johnson & Wales (A), Providence, RI 02903	1914	Morris J. Gaebe	IR-B	6,000	75
Joliet Junior (A), Joliet, IL 60436	1901	Derek N. Nunney	PI-A	2,160	279
Jones, Jacksonville, FL 32211	1918	Donald C. Jones	IP-B	1,334	70
at Orlando (A), Orlando, FL 32803	1953	Donald C. Jones	IP-B	1,332	35
Jones County Junior (A), Ellisville, MS 39437	1927	Thos. Terrell Tisdale	Psl-A	2,231	119
Judson, Elgin, IL 60120	1963	Harm A. Weber	IR-B	451	46
Judson (A), Marion, AL 36756	1838	N. McCrummen	IR-B	413	28
Juilliard School, The (A), New York, NY 10023	1905	Peter Mennin	IP-D	1,000	300
Juniata, Huntingdon, PA 16652	1876	Frederick M. Binder	IP-B	1,301	91
Kalamazoo, Kalamazoo, MI 49007	1833	George N. Rainsford	IP-B	1,452	91
Kalamazoo Valley Comm., Kalamazoo, MI 49009	1968	Dale B. Lake	Psl-A	7,000	150
Kankakee Comm., Kankakee, IL 60901	1966	Lilburn H. Horton	Psl-A	2,805	150
Kan. City Art Inst. (A), Kansas City, MO 64111	1885	John W. Lottes	1P-B	600	47
Kan. City Coll. of Osteop. Med. (A), Kansas City, MO 64124	1916	Rudolph Bremen	IP-1P	617	57
Kan. City Kan. Comm., Kansas City, KS 66112	1923	Alton L. Davies	Psl-A	3,606	150
Kansas Newman, Wichita, KS 67213	1933	Rev. Romans R. Galiardi	IP-B	678	50
Kansas State Univ.*, Manhattan, KS 66506	1863	Duane Acker	Ps-D	19,547	1,950
Kansas, Univ. of, Lawrence, KS 66045	1866	Gene Budig, Chan.	Ps-D	26,745	1,800
Kansas Wesleyan, Salina, KS 67401	1886	Daniel Bratton	IR-B	490	49
Kapiolani Comm. (A), Honolulu, HI 96814	1965	J.S. Tsunoda, Prov.	Psl-A	4,160	102
Kaskaskia, Centralia, IL 62801	1939	Paul Blowers	PI-A	3,185	175
Katharine Gibbs School (A), New York, NY 10017	1917	Edith Foster	IP-B	1,000	25
Kauai Community, Lihue, HI 96766	1965	LeRoy J. King	Ps-A	1,069	51
Kean Coll. of New Jersey (A), Union, NJ 07083	1855	Nathan Weiss	Ps-B	13,800	370
Kearney State, Kearney, NE 68847	1903	Brendan McDonald	Ps-S	7,312	236

Name, address	Year	Governing official, affiliation, and highest degree offered		Stu-dents	Teach-ers
Keene State, Keene, NH 03431	1909	Barbara J. Seelye	Ps-M	2,648	188
Kellogg Community (A), Battle Creek, MI 49016	1956	Richard F. Whitmore	Psl-A	8,000	96
Kendall, Evanston, IL 60201	1934	Andrew Cothran	IR-A	434	34
Kennesaw, Marietta, GA 30061	1965	Eugene Huck	Pf-B	3,909	201
Kent State Univ., Kent, OH 44242	1910	Brage Golding	Ps-D	25,903	1,193
Kentucky, Univ. of*, Lexington, KY 40506	1865	Otis A. Singletary	Ps-D	23,013	1,437
Kentucky Jr., of Business, Lexington, KY 40576	1941	Joseph E. Flurn	IP-A	475	63
Kentucky State Univ.*, Frankfort, KY 40601	1886	W.A. Butts	Ps-M	2,342	172
Kentucky Wesleyan (A), Owensboro, KY 42301	1858	Luther A. White III	IR-B	916	50
Kenyon, Gambier, OH 43022	1824	Philip Jordan, Jr.	IP-B	1,458	123
Kettering Coll. of Med. Arts, Kettering, OH 45429	1967	Winton Beaven	IR-A	397	67
Keuka (W), Keuka Park, NY 14478	1890	Elizabeth Woods Shaw	IP-B	544	57
Keystone Junior, La Plume, PA 18440	1868	John B. Hibbard	IP-A	876	72
Kilgore, Kilgore, TX 75662	1935	Stewart McLaurin	Psl-A	4,095	173
King, Bristol, TN 37620	1867	Donald R. Mitchell	IR-B	294	40
King's, Briarcliff Manor, NY 10510	1938	Robert A. Cook	IP-B	790	66
King's (A), Charlotte, NC 28204	1901	Richard Poyner	IP-A	375	14
King's, Wilkes-Barre, PA 18711	1946	Rev. James Lackenmier	IR-B	2,120	150
King's River Comm., Reedley, CA 93654	1926	Ray A. Cattani	Psl-A	3,330	138
Kirksville Coll. of Osteop. Med., Kirksville, MO 63501	1892	H. Charles Moore	IP-1P	511	85
Kirkwood Comm., Cedar Rapids, IA 52406	1966	Bill F. Stewart	Psl-A	3,938	222
Kirtland Comm., Roscommon, MI 48653	1966	Raymond D. Horner	Ps-A	1,700	107
Kishwaukee, Malta, IL 60150	1967	Norman Jenkins	Psl-A	4,200	250
Knox, Galesburg, IL 61401	1837	E. Inman Fox	IP-B	956	92
Knoxville, Knoxville, TN 37921	1875	Clinton M. Marsh	IR-B	432	42
Kutztown State (A), Kutztown, PA 19530	1966	Lawrence M. Stratton	Ps-M	5,169	265
Labette Comm., Parsons, KS 67357	1923	Jerry L. Gallentine	PI-A	2,350	98
Lackawanna Jr., Scranton, PA 18503	1894	John X. McConkey	IP-A	766	97
Lafayette, Easton, PA 18042	1826	David W. Ellis	IP-B	2,335	170
LaGrange, LaGrange, GA 30240	1831	Walter Y. Murphy	IR-M	947	50
Lake City Comm., Lake City, FL 32055	1947	Herbert E. Phillips	Ps-A	3,000	103
Lake County, Coll. of, Grayslake, IL 60030	1967	John O. Hunter	Psl-A	11,266	466
Lake Erie, Painesville, OH 44077	1856	Charles E.P. Simmons	IP-B	1,050	96
Lake Forest, Lake Forest, IL 60045	1857	Eugene Hotchkiss III	IP-M	1,074	94
Lake Land (A), Mattoon, IL 61938	1966	Robert D. Webb	Psl-A	3,500	94
Lakeland, Lakeland, FL 33802	1927	Eugene L. Roberts	IP-A	210	10
Lakeland, Sheboygan, WI 53081	1862	Richard E. Hill	IR-B	676	53
Lakeland Comm. (A), Mentor, OH 44060	1967	Wayne Rodehorst	Psl-A	6,158	100
Lake Michigan, Benton Harbor, MI 49022	1946	Walter Browe	Pf-A	3,352	254
Lake Region Jr., Devils Lake, ND 58301	1941	Dennis Michaelis	PI-A	569	43
Lake-Sumter Comm., Leesburg, FL 32748	1962	Robert S. Palinchak	Ps-A	1,965	80
Lake Superior State, Sault Ste. Marie, MI 49783	1946	Kenneth Shouldice	Ps-B	2,501	104
Lakeshore Tech Inst. (A), Cleveland, WI 53015	1912	Frederick Nierode	Psl-A	3,000	108
Lakewood Comm. (A), White Bear Lake, MN 55110	1967	N. Christenson, Act.	Ps-A	2,474	93
Lamar Community, Lamar, CO 81052	1937	Gordon Snowbarger	IP-A	870	60
Lamar Univ., Beaumont, TX 77710	1923	C. Robert Kemble	Ps-D	13,600	650
Lambuth, Jackson, TN 38301	1843	Harry W. Gilmer	IR-B	719	53
Lander, Greenwood, SC 29646	1872	Larry Jackson	Ps-B	1,604	98
Lane, Jackson, TN 38301	1882	Herman Stone Jr.	IP-B	757	42
Lane Community, Eugene, OR 97405	1964	Eldon G. Schafer	PI-A	8,100	280
Laney (A), Oakland, CA 94607	1953	Lawrence A. Davis	Psl-A	12,500	220
Langston Univ.*, Langston, OK 73050	1897	Ernest L. Holloway	Ps-B	1,322	101
Lansing Community, Lansing, MI 48901	1957	Philip Gannon	Psl-A	19,524	1,108
Laramie County Comm. (A), Cheyenne, WY 82001	1969	Harlan L. Heglar	Psl-A	4,295	96
Laredo Junior, Laredo, TX 78040	1946	Domingo Arechiga	Psl-A	3,120	130
LaRoche, Pittsburgh, PA 15237	1963	Sr. Margaret Huber	IP-M	1,440	110
La Salle (A), Philadelphia, PA 19141	1863	Bro. Patrick Ellis	IR-M	7,000	195
Lasell Junior (W) (A), Newton, MA 02166	1851	Arthur Griffin	IP-A	650	44
Lassen Comm. (A), Susanville, CA 96130	1925	Robert Theiler	PI-A	3,100	215
Latter-Day Saints Bus., Salt Lake City, UT 84111	1886	R.F. Kirkham	IR-A	843	31
La Verne, La Verne, CA 91750	1891	Armen Sarafian	IP-D	4,500	360
Lawson State Comm. (A), Birmingham, AL 35020	1949	Jesse Lewis	Ps-A	1,740	84
Lawrence Inst. of Tech., Southfield, MI 48075	1932	Richard E. Marburger	IP-1P	5,260	250
Lawrence Univ., Appleton, WI 54912	1847	Richard Warch	IP-B	1,150	112
Lebanon Valley, Annville, PA 17003	1866	Frederick P. Sample	IR-A	1,300	108
Lee, Baytown, TX 77520	1934	Robert Cloud	Ps-A	4,813	198
Lee, Cleveland, TN 37311	1918	Charles Conn	IR-B	1,262	55
Lees Junior (A), Jackson, KY 41339	1883	Troy R. Eslinger	IP-A	260	22
Lees-McRae, Banner Elk, NC 28604	1900	H.C. Evans Jr.	IP-A	730	38
Lehigh County Comm., Schnecksville, PA 18078	1966	John G. Berrier	Psl-A	3,312	130
Lehigh Univ., Bethlehem, PA 18015	1865	W. Deming Lewis	IP-D	6,413	401
Leicester Jr. (A), Leicester, MA 01524	1784	L. Van Burkirk	IP-A	209	26
Le Moyne (A), Syracuse, NY 13214	1946	W. O'Halloran	IR-B	1,838	100
Le Moyne-Owen, Memphis, TN 38126	1870	Walter L. Walker	IR-B	930	77
Lenoir Comm. (A), Kinston, NC 28501	1958	Jesse L. McDaniel	Psl-A	1,817	70
Lenoir-Rhyne, Hickory, NC 28601	1891	Albert Anderson	IR-M	1,386	104
Lesley (W), Cambridge, MA 02238	1909	Don A. Orton	IP-M	1,870	325
LeTourneau, Longview, TX 75607	1946	Richard H. LeTourneau	IP-B	1,039	65
Lewis & Clark, Portland, OR 97219	1867	John R. Howard	IP-M	3,188	160
Lewis and Clark Comm., Godfrey, IL 62035	1970	Wilbur R.L. Trimpe	Psl-A	5,709	249
Lewis Univ., Romeoville, IL 60441	1930	Vacant	IR-M	2,813	126
Lexington Technical Inst. (A), Lexington, KY 40506	1965	William Price	Ps-A	2,074	60
Lima Technical (A), Lima, OH 45804	1971	James S. Biddle	Psl-A	1,493	50
Limestone, Gaffney, SC 29340	1845	William J. Briggs	IP-B	1,418	113
Lincoln, Lincoln, IL 62656	1865	Dale Brummet	IP-A	530	50
Lincoln Christian, Lincoln, IL 62656	1944	John P. Hasty	IP-M	611	35
Lincoln Land Comm., Springfield, IL 62708	1967	Robert L. Poorman	Psl-A	6,467	390
Lincoln Memorial Univ., Harrogate, TN 37752	1897	Frank W. Welch	IP-B	1,215	65
Lincoln Trail, Robinson, IL 62454	1969	Richard Sanders	Psl-A	2,200	110
Lincoln Univ., Jefferson City, MO 65101	1866	James Frank	Ps-M	2,643	143
Lincoln Univ.*, Lincoln Univ., PA 19352	1854	Herman Branson	Psr-M	1,200	115
Lincoln Univ., San Francisco, CA 94118	1919	E. Barbara Jorss	IP-M	650	35
Lindenwood, St. Charles, MO 63301	1827	Robert Johns	IP-M	1,969	135
Lindsey Wilson Coll., Columbia, KY 42728	1903	John B. Besley	IR-A	408	24
Linfield (A), McMinnville, OR 97128	1849	Charles Walker	IP-M	1,109	72
Linn Benton Comm. (A), Albany, OR 97321	1968	Raymond J. Needham	PI-A	13,500	150
Livingston Univ., Livingston, AL 35470	1835	Asa Green	Ps-M	1,100	84
Livingstone, Salisbury, NC 28144	1879	F. George Shipman	IR-B	879	77

Name, address	Year	Governing official, affiliation, and highest degree offered		Stu-dents	Teach-ers
Lock Haven State, Lock Haven, PA 17745	1870	Francis Hamblin	Ps-B	2,394	170
Loma Linda Univ., Loma Linda, CA 92354	1905	V. Norskov Olsen	IR-D	5,351	1,722
Lon Morris, Jacksonville, TX 75766	1854	Faulk W. Landrum	IR-A	300	33
Long Beach City, Long Beach, CA 90808	1927	John McCuen	Ps-A	30,303	1,250
Long Island Univ., Brooklyn, NY 11201	1926	Edward Clark	IP-D	6,851	456
C.W. Post (A), Greenvale, NY 11548	1954	Edward Cook	IP-M	10,803	331
Longview Community (A), Lee's Summit, MO 64063	1969	Aldo Leker	PI-A	4,027	60
Longwood, Farmville, VA 23901	1839	Janet D. Greenwood	Ps-M	2,398	178
Loop, Chicago, IL 60601	1962	Salvatore G. Rotella	Psl-A	7,151	365
Lorain County Comm., Elyria, OH 44035	1963	Omar Olson	Psl-A	6,300	220
Loras (A), Dubuque, IA 52001	1839	P. Di Pasquale Jr.	IR-B	1,771	137
Loretto Heights, Denver, CO 80236	1918	Adele Phelan	IP-B	920	100
Los Angeles Baptist, Newhall, CA 91322	1927	John Dunkin	IR-A	326	45
Los Angeles City (A), Los Angeles, CA 90029	1929	Stelle Feuers	PI-A	20,000	800
Los Angeles Harbor, Wilmington, CA 90744	1949	Leslie Koltai	Psl-A	11,000	200
Los Angeles Pierce, Woodland Hills, CA 91364	1947	Herbert Ravetch	PI-A	21,000	634
Los Angeles Southwest, Los Angeles, CA 90047	1967	Leslie Koltai	Ps-A	7,052	125
L.A. Trade Technical, Los Angeles, CA 90015	1949	Thomas L. Stevens Jr.	PI-A	18,705	600
Los Angeles Valley, Van Nuys, CA 91401	1949	Alice Thurston	Psl-A	24,000	700
Louisburg (A), Louisburg, NC 27549	1787	J. Allen Norris Jr.	IR-A	576	39
Louisiana, Pineville, LA 71360	1906	Robert Lynn	IR-B	1,085	89
Louisiana St. Univ.* (A), Baton Rouge, LA 70803	1860	Martin Woodin	Ps-D	48,049	2,241
A & M, Baton Rouge, LA 70803	1860	Paul Murrill	Ps-D	25,000	900
at Alexandria, Alexandria, LA 71301	1960	Sam H. Frank	Ps-A	1,489	96
at Eunice, Eunice, LA 70535	1966	Anthony Mumphrey	Ps-A	1,430	71
Law Center (A), Baton Rouge, LA 70803	1906	Dr. William D. Hawkland, Chan.	Ps-D	876	27
Medical Center, New Orleans, LA 70112	1931	Allen Copping	Ps-D	2,576	2,000
New Orleans Campus (A), New Orleans, LA 70122	1956	Homer L. Hitt, Chan.	Ps-D	14,161	461
Shreveport Campus, Shreveport, LA 71115	1967	E. Grady Bogue	Ps-M	3,463	147
Louisiana Tech. Univ., Ruston, LA 71272	1894	F. Jay Taylor	Ps-D	10,092	425
Louisville, Univ. of, Louisville, KY 40929	1798	Donald C. Swain	IR-D	20,386	1,278
Lowell, Univ. of, Lowell, MA 01854	1894	John B. Duff	Ps-D	13,000	550
Lower Columbia, Longview, WA 98632	1934	Vernon R. Pickett	Psl-A	5,037	94
Loyola, Baltimore, MD 21210	1852	Rev. J.A. Sellinger	IR-M	5,996	284
Loyola Marymount Univ., Los Angeles, CA 90045	1911	Rev. D.P. Merrifield	IR-M	45,624	360
Loyola Univ., Chicago, IL 60611	1870	Rev. R.C. Baumhart	IR-D	14,748	1,034
Loyola Univ. (A), New Orleans, LA 70118	1904	Rev. James Carter	IR-M	4,535	291
Lubbock Christian, Lubbock, TX 79407	1957	H.M. Pruitt	IR-B	1,238	91
Lurleen B. Wallace St. Jr., Andalusia, AL 36420	1969	W.H. McWhorter	Ps-A	875	60
Luther, Decorah, IA 52101	1861	Elwin D. Farwell	IR-B	2,007	160
Luzerne County Comm., Nanticoke, PA 18634	1966	Thomas J. Moran	Psl-A	3,274	209
Lycoming, Williamsport, PA 17701	1812	F. Blumer	IR-B	1,130	75
Lynchburg, Lynchburg, VA 24501	1903	Carey Brewer	IR-S	2,400	157
Lyndon State (A), Lyndonville, VT 05851	1911	Janet Gorman Murphy	Ps-B	1,025	59
Macalester, St. Paul, MN 55105	1874	John B. Davis Jr.	IR-B	1,633	170
MacCormac Junior, Chicago, IL 60604	1904	Gordon Borchardt	IP-B	420	46
MacMurray, Jacksonville, IL 62650	1846	B.G. Stephens	IP-B	673	65
Macomb County Comm., Warren, MI 48093	1954	Albert L. Lorenzo	PI-A	28,429	711
Macon Junior, Macon, GA 31206	1968	William Wright	Psl-A	2,382	77
Madison Area Technical, Madison, WI 53703	1912	Norman P. Mitby, Dir.	PI-A	42,700	325
Madison Business, Madison, WI 53703	1856	Stuart E. Sears	IP-A	302	14
Madonna, Livonia, MI 48150	1947	Sr. Mary Francilene	IP-B	3,213	166
Maine Maritime Academy, Castine, ME 04421	1941	E.A. Rodgers, Supt.	Ps-B	650	55
Maine System, Univ. of* (A), Bangor, ME 04401	1865	P. McCarthy, Chan.	Ps-M	26,750	1,136
at Augusta, Augusta, ME 04330	1965	Hilton Power, Act.	Ps-B	3,420	185
at Farmington (A), Farmington, ME 04938	1863	Einar Olsen	Ps-B	2,100	83
at Ft. Kent (A), Ft. Kent, ME 04743	1878	Richard J. Spath	Ps-B	650	30
at Machias (A), Machias, ME 04654	1909	Arthur Buswell	Ps-B	729	35
at Orono* (A), Orono, ME 04469	1865	Kenneth W. Allen, Act.	Ps-D	11,574	611
at Portland-Gorham (A), Portland, ME 04103	1878	N.E. Miller	Ps-M	7,602	544
at Presque Isle, Presque Isle, ME 04769	1903	Constance Carlson, Act.	Ps-B	1,416	71
Mainland, Coll. of the, Texas City, TX	1967	Donald F. Mortvedt, Act.	Psl-A	1,200	197
Malcolm X (A), Chicago, IL 60612	1911	Samuel Huffman	Ps-A	6,830	215
Malone, Canton, OH 44709	1892	Lon D. Randall	IR-A	776	50
Manatee Junior, Bradenton, FL 33507	1958	Stephen Korcheck	Ps-A	5,900	250
Manchester, N. Manchester, IN 46962	1889	Alfred B. Helman	IR-M	1,253	110
Manchester Comm. (A), Manchester, CT 06040	1963	Ronald Denison	Psl-A	5,000	110
Manhattan, Riverdale, NY 10471	1853	Brother J.S. Sullivan	IP-M	4,905	354
Manhattan Sch. of Music, New York, NY 10027	1917	John O. Crosby	IP-D	870	171
Manhattanville, Purchase, NY 10577	1841	Barbara K. Debs	IP-M	1,334	128
Mankato State Univ., Mankato, MN 56001	1867	Dr. Margaret R. Preska	Ps-S	11,616	496
Mannes Coll. of Music (A), New York, NY 10021	1916	Charles Kaufman	IP-D	550	110
Manor Junior, Jenkintown, PA 19046	1947	Sr. Miriam Clare Kowal	IR-A	400	43
Mansfield State, Mansfield, PA 16933	1857	Janet L. Travis	Pf-M	2,500	210
Maple Woods Comm., Kansas City, MO 64156	1969	Stephen R. Brainard	Psl-A	2,300	125
Maria, Albany, NY 12208	1958	Sr. L. Fitzgerald	IP-A	640	56
Maria Regina, Syracuse, NY 13208	1963	Sr. Stella M. Zuccolillo	IR-A	416	42
Marian, Indianapolis, IN 46222	1951	Louis C. Gatto	IP-B	880	85
Marian Coll. of Fond du Lac, Fond du Lac, WI 54935	1936	Leo V. Krzywkowski	IR-B	525	70
Maricopa Tech. Comm., Phoenix AZ 85004	1968	Charles A. Green.	Psl-A	3,211	160
Marietta, Marietta, OH 45750	1835	Sherrill Cleland	IP-M	1,475	135
Marin, Coll. of (A), Kentfield, CA 94904	1926	I.P. Diamond	Ps-A	6,950	162
Marion, Marion, IN 46952	1920	Robert Luckey	IR-M	1,097	91
Marion Institute (A), Marion, AL 36756	1842	Maj. Gen. Barfield	IP-A	220	19
Marist (A), Poughkeepsie, NY 12601	1946	Dennis J. Murray	IP-B	2,400	80
Marlboro (A), Marlboro, VT 05344	1946	B. Ragle	IP-B	222	35
Marquette Univ., Milwaukee, WI 53233	1881	Rev. J.P. Raynor	IR-D	13,879	911
Mars Hill, Mars Hill, NC 28754	1856	Fred Blake Bentley	IR-B	1,862	151
Marshall Univ., Huntington, WV 25701	1837	Robert B. Hayes	Ps-M	11,883	530
Marshalltown Comm., Marshalltown, IA 50158	1927	Paul Kegel	Pf-A	1,300	75
Martin, Pulaski, TN 38478	1870	Bill Starnes	IR-A	293	21
Martin Comm., Williamston, NC 27892	1968	C. Neill McLeod	Ps-A	760	50
Martin Tech. Inst. (A) Williamston, NC 27892	1968	Joseph B. Carter	Psl-A	1,250	65
Mary Baldwin, Staunton, VA 24401	1842	Virginia Lester	IR-B	785	72
Mary Hardin Baylor, Univ. of, Belton, TX 76513	1845	Bobby E. Parker	IR-B	1,037	65
Mary Holmes, West Point, MS 39773	1892	Joseph A. Gore	IP-A	399	24
Mary Washington (A), Fredericksburg, VA 22401	1908	Prince B. Woodard	Ps-B	2,292	130
Marycrest, Davenport, IA 52804	1939	A. Lynn Bryant	IP-M	1,196	90

Name, address	Year	Governing official, affiliation, and highest degree offered		Students	Teachers
Marygrove, Detroit, MI 48221	1910	John E. Shay, Jr.	IR-M	1,059	51
Maryland Inst. of Art (A), Baltimore, MD 21217	1826	Fred Lazarus IV	IP-M	1,650	169
Maryland, Univ. of*, Adelphi, MD 20783	1807	John S. Toll	Ps-D	81,538	2,886
Eastern Shore, Princess Anne, MD 21853	1886	William P. Hytche, Chan.	Ps-M	1,027	91
Marylhurst (A), Marylhurst, OR 97036	1893	Sr. V.A. Baxter	IR-B	740	22
Marymount (W), Tarrytown, NY 10591	1919	Sr. Brigid Driscoll	IP-B	1,254	150
Marymount Coll. of Ks., Salina, KS 67401	1922	John P. Murry	IR-B	844	72
Marymount Coll. of Va., Arlington, VA 22207	1950	Sr. M. Majella Berg	IP-M	1,250	85
Marymount Manhattan, New York, NY 10021	1961	Colette Mahoney	IP-B	2,251	202
Marymount Palos Verdes, Rancho Palos Verdes, CA 90274	1932	Thomas D. Wood	IR-A	385	43
Maryville, Maryville, TN 37801	1819	Wayne Anderson	IR-B	603	63
Maryville (A), St. Louis, MO 63141	1872	C. Pritchard	IR-M	1,351	58
Marywood (W), Scranton, PA 18509	1915	Sister M. Coleman Nee	IR-M	3,020	252
Mass. Bay Comm. (A), Watertown, MA 02181	1961	John McKenzie	Ps-A	4,096	248
Massachusetts Coll. Of Art, Boston, MA 02215	1873	John Nolan	Ps-M	1,123	64
Mass. Coll. of Pharmacy (A), Boston, MA 02115.	1823	Raymond A. Gosselin	IP-D	1,250	77
Mass. Institute of Tech.* (A), Cambridge, MA 02139	1861	Jerome Wiesner	IP-D	7,972	972
Mass. Maritime Academy, Buzzards Bay, MA 02532	1892	Rr. Adm. John Aylmer	Ps-B	906	55
Massachusetts, Univ. of*, Boston, MA 02135	1863	David C. Knapp	Ps-S	34,000	2,000
Amherst Campus, Amherst, MA 01003	1863	Henry Koffler, Chan.	Ps-D	24,737	1,274
Harbor Campus (A), Boston, MA 02125	1965	Robert A. Corrigan, Chan.	Ps-D	6,600	500
Massasoit Comm. (A), Brockton, MA 02402	1966	George E. Ayers	Ps-A	5,642	207
Mater Dei, Ogdensburg, NY 13669	1960	John T. Burns	IR-A	310	30
Mattatuck Comm., Waterbury, CT 06708	1967	N.P. Yarborough	Ps-A	3,571	145
Maui Community, Kahului, HI 96732	1966	Alma Cooper, Provost	Ps-A	1,900	95
Mayland Technical (A), Spruce Pine, NC 28777	1971	O.M. Blake Jr.	Psl-A	572	25
Maysville Comm., Maysville, KY 41056	1968	James C. Shires, Dir.	Ps-A	513	41
Mayville State, Mayville, ND 58257	1889	James Schobel	Ps-B	652	57
McCook Comm., McCook, NE 69001	1926	Elmer Kuntz	Psl-A	650	32
McDowell Tech. Inst., Marion, NC 28752	1964	John Price	Psl-A	568	40
McHenry County, Crystal Lake, IL 60014.	1968	Robert C. Bartlett	Pl-A	3,533	135
McKendree, Lebanon, IL 62254	1828	Gerrit J. TenBrink	IR-B	620	37
McLennan Comm., Waco, TX 76708	1965	Wilbur Ball	Psl-A	4,146	200
McMurry, Abilene, TX 79697	1923	Tom K. Kim	IR-B	1,397	115
McNeese State Univ., Lake Charles, LA 70609	1939	Jack V. Doland	Ps-S	5,560	271
McPherson (A), McPherson, KS 67460	1887	Paul Hoffman	IP-B	480	37
Medaille, Buffalo, NY 14214	1875	Dr. Leo R. Downey	IP-M	690	73
Medical Coll. of Ga., Augusta, GA 30912	1828	William Moretz	Ps-D	2,310	578
Medical Coll. of Pa. (A), Philadelphia, PA 19129	1850	Robert J. Slater	IP-D	836	423
Medical Univ. of S.C., Charleston, SC 29425.	1824	William H. Knisely	Pf-S	2,564	1,529
Med. & Dentistry of NJ, Newark, NJ 07103.	1956	S.S. Bergen Jr.	Ps-D	2,819	925
Meharry Medical (A), Nashville, TN 37208	1876	Lloyd C. Elam	IP-D	1,038	335
Memphis Acad. of Arts (A), Memphis, TN 38112.	1936	Jameson M. Jones	IP-D	219	17
Memphis State Univ., Memphis, TN 38152	1912	Thomas Carpenter	Ps-D	20,784	798
Menlo, Menlo Park, CA 94025	1927	Richard O'Brien	Ip-B	614	65
Meramec Community (A), St. Louis, MO 63122	1962	Glynn E. Clark	Pl-A	7,070	378
Merced, Merced, CA 95340	1963	W.C. Martineson	Psl-A	8,577	425
Mercer County Comm., Trenton, NJ 08690	1966	John P. Hanley	Pl-A	7,293	125
Mercer Univ., Macon, GA 31207	1833	R. Kirby Godsey	IR-D	4,955	250
Mercy, Dobbs Ferry, NY 10522	1950	Donald Grunewald	IP-B	9,458	673
Mercy Coll. of Detroit, Detroit, MI 48219	1941	Sister Agnes Mary Mansour	IR-M	2,518	221
Mercyhurst, Erie, PA 16546	1926	William P. Garvey	IR-M	1,400	140
Meredith (W) Raleigh, NC 27611	1891	John Edgar Weems	IR-B	1,578	107
Meridian Jr., Meridian, MS 39301	1937	William F. Scaggs	Pl-A	2,880	154
Merrimack, No. Andover, MA 01845.	1947	Rev. John E. Deegan	IR-B	3,510	173
Merritt Comm., Oakland, CA 94619	1953	John B. Greene.	P-A	10,500	250
Mesa, Grand Junction, CO 81501	1925	John Tomlinson	Pf-A	4,283	184
Mesa Comm. (A), Mesa, AZ 85202	1965	Theo Heap	Pl-A	12,169	187
Mesabi Comm., Virginia, MN 55792	1918	Gilbert Staupe	Ps-A	949	40
Messiah, Grantham, PA 17027	1909	D. Ray Hostetter	IR-B	1,350	90
Methodist, Fayetteville, NC 28301	1956	Richard Pearce	IR-B	951	52
Metropolitan Comm. (A), Minneapolis, MN 55403	1965	Curtis W. Johnson	Ps-A	2,450	66
Metropolitan Comm. (A), Kansas City, MO 64111.	1964	William D. Hatley, Chan.	Ps-A	11,750	241
Metropolitan State, Denver, CO 80204	1965	Donald J. MacIntyre	Ps-B	15,605	635
Miami, Univ. of, Coral Gables, FL 33124	1926	Edward T. Foote	IP-D	15,970	1,798
Miami-Dade Comm. (A), Miami, FL 33176	1960	Robert H. McCabe, Act.	Pl-A	43,822	909
Miami-Jacobs Jr. Coll. of Bus., Dayton, OH 45401	1860	Charles P. Harbottle	IP-A	738	62
Miami Univ., Oxford, OH 45056	1809	Paul Pearson	Ps-D	17,137	875
Michael J. Owens Tech. (A), Perrysburg, OH 43551	1967	Jacob H. See	Ps-A	2,991	63
Michigan Christian, Rochester, MI 48063	1959	Milton B. Fletcher	IR-B	353	24
Michigan State Univ., East Lansing, MI 48824	1855	Cecil Mackey	Ps-D	44,576	3,514
Michigan Tech Univ., Houghton, MI 49931	1885	Dale F. Stein	Ps-D	7,865	507
Michigan, Univ. of, Ann Arbor, MI 48109	1817	Harold T. Shapiro	Ps-D	47,081	3,437
Mid-America Nazarene, Olathe, KS 66061	1966	R. Curtis Smith	IP-B	1,354	67
Middle Georgia, Cochran, GA 31014	1887	Louis C. Alderman Jr.	Ps-A	1,478	110
Middle Tenn. State Univ., Murfreesboro, TN 37132	1911	Sam H. Ingram	Ps-D	11,275	450
Middlebury, Middlebury, VT 05753.	1800	Olin Robinson	IP-B	1,900	168
Middlesex Comm., Middletown, CT 06457	1966	Robert A. Chapman	Psl-A	3,307	98
Middlesex County, Edison, NJ 08818	1966	Rose M. Channing	Psl-A	11,020	292
Midland, Midland, TX 79701		Al G. Langford	Psl-A	2,599	165
Midland Lutheran, Fremont, NE 68025	1883	L. Dale Lund	IR-B	894	75
Midlands Tech., Columbia, SC 29202	1973	Robert Grigsby Jr.	Psl-A	5,341	187
Midway, Midway, KY 40347	1847	Nelsen M. Hoffman	Psl-A	316	57
Mid Michigan Comm. (A), Harrison, MI 48625	1965	Eugene W. Gillaspy	Psl-A	2,800	81
Mid-Plains Comm., No. Platte, NE 69101	1974	Kenneth L. Aten	Psl-A	1,630	60
Mid-State Tech. Inst., Wis. Rapids, WI 54494	1967	Earl F. Jaeger	Ps-A	2,200	150
Midwestern State Univ., Wichita Falls, TX 76308.	1922	Louis J. Rodriguez	Ps-M	4,400	144
Miles, Birmingham, AL 35208	1905	Clyde W. Williams	IR-B	1,265	97
Miles Comm., Miles City, MT 59301	1939	Judson H. Flower.	Psl-A	908	35
Millersville State (A), Millersville, PA 17551.	1855	William Duncan.	Ps-B	4,400	350
Milligan, Milligan Coll, TN 37682	1881	Jess W. Johnson	IR-B	754	51
Millikin Univ., Decatur, IL 62522	1901	J. Roger Miller	IP-B	1,606	158
Mills (W) (A), Oakland, CA 94613	1852	Barbara White	IP-B	973	87
Millsaps, Jackson, MS 39210	1890	George M. Harmon	IR-B	1,099	93
Milton, Milton, WI 53563.	1844	Ronald J. Dickman.	IP-B	431	35
Milwaukee Area Tech. (A), Milwaukee, WI 53203	1912	William Ramsey	Pl-A	68,863	662
Milwaukee Sch. of Eng. (A), Milwaukee, WI 53201	1903	Robert R. Spitzer.	IP-M	2,564	133
Mineral Area, Flat River, MO 63601	1922	Richard Castor	Psl-A	1,408	93

Name, address	Year	Governing official, affiliation, and highest degree offered		Students	Teachers
Minneapolis Comm., Minneapolis, MN 55403.	1965	Earl Bowman	Ps-A	3,005	100
Mpls. Coll. of Art. & Design, Minneapolis, MN 55404	1886	Jerome J. Hausman	IP-B	540	47
Minnesota, Univ. of* (A), Minneapolis, MN 55414	1851	C.P. Magrath	Ps-D	74,203	9,386
Duluth Campus* (A), Duluth, MN 55812	1902	Robt. Heller (Prov.)	Ps-M	9,060	575
Morris Campus*, Morris, MN 56267	1960	John Imholte (Prov.)	Ps-B	1,946	109
Minot State (A), Minot, ND 58701	1913	Gordon Olson.	Ps-B	2,100	110
Mira Costa (A), Oceanside, CA 92054	1934	John MacDonald	Ps-A	5,400	190
Misericordia, Dallas, PA 18612.	1924	Joseph R. Fink	IP-B	1,114	102
Mississippi, Clinton, MS 39058	1826	Lewis Nobles	IP-D	3,055	200
Mississippi Delta Jr., Moorhead, MS 38761	1926	J.T. Hall	Ps-A	2,600	115
Mississippi Gulf Coast Jr. (A), Perkinston, MS 39573	1925	J.J. Hayden Jr.	Psl-A	5,789	267
Mississippi Industrial (A), Holly Springs, MS 38635	1905	E.E. Rankin	IR-B	400	24
Miss. Univ. for Women (W), Columbus, MS 39701.	1884	James Strobel	Ps-S	2,070	206
Mississippi State Univ.*, Miss. State, MS 39762	1878	James McComas.	Pf-D	12,749	754
Mississippi, Univ. of, University, MS 38677	1848	P.L. Fortune Jr., Chan.	Ps-D	9,607	520
Mississippi Valley State Univ., Itta Bena, MS 38941	1950	E.A. Boykins	Ps-M	2,774	140
Missouri Baptist, St. Louis, MO 63141.	1963	R. Sutherland	IR-B	460	40
Missouri Inst. of Tech. (A), Kansas City, MO 64114	1931	C.R. LeValley.	IP-B	953	19
Missouri Southern State, Joplin, MO 64801	1965	Donald C. Darnton	Ps-B	4,013	196
Missouri, Univ. of* (A), Columbia, MO 65211.	1839	James Olson	Ps-D	51,829	2,183
at Columbia*, Columbia, MO 65211	1859	Barbara Uehling, Chan.	Pf-D	24,306	1,065
at Kansas City*, Kansas City, MO 64110	1929	George Russell, Chan..	Ps-S	11,416	1,000
at Rolla* (A), Rolla, MO 65401	1870	James M. Marchello, Chan.	Ps-D	6,689	382
at St. Louis*, St. Louis, MO 63121	1963	A. Grobman, Chan..	Ps-D	11,380	410
Missouri Valley, Marshall, MO 65340	1889	Robert J. Glass.	IR-B	497	45
Missouri Western State, St. Joseph, MO 64507	1967	Marvin Looney	Ps-B	4,065	179
Mitchell, New London, CT 06320	1939	Robert C. Weller.	IP-A	943	51
Mitchell Comm., Statesville, NC 28677	1852	Charles Poindexter.	Ps-A	4,500	250
Moberly Junior (A), Moberly, MO 65270	1927	Andrew Komar Jr.	Ps-A	851	25
Mobile, Mobile, AL 36613.	1961	William K. Weaver Jr.	IR-B	1,026	70
Modesto Junior (A), Modesto, CA 95350	1921	Kenneth Griffin	Psl-A	15,038	221
Mohawk Valley Comm. (A), Utica, NY 13501.	1946	G.H. Robertson.	Ps-A	6,800	175
Mohegan Comm., Norwich, CT 06360	1969	Robert N. Rue	Pf-A	1,861	66
Molloy (W), Rockville Ctre, NY 11570.	1955	Sister Janet Fitzgerald.	IR-1P	1,501	173
Monmouth, Monmouth, IL 61462.	1853	Bruce Haywood	IR-B	655	80
Monmouth (A), W. Long Branch, NJ 07764.	1933	Samuel H. Magill.	IP-M	2,848	200
Monroe Comm. (A), Rochester, NY 14623	1961	Moses Koch.	Psl-A	10,234	285
Monroe County Comm., Monroe, MI 48161.	1964	Ronald Campbell.	Pl-A	2,151	148
Montana Coll. of Mineral Science & Tech., Butte, MT 59701	1893	Fred W. DeMoney	Ps-M	1,732	85
Montana State Univ., Bozeman, MT 59717	1893	Wm. Tietz Jr.	Pf-D	10,745	700
Montana, Univ. of (A), Missoula, MT 59812.	1893	Richard Bowers	Ps-M	8,574	400
Montcalm Comm., Sidney, MI 48885	1965	Herbert N. Stoutenburg	Psl-A	1,500	57
Montclair State, Upper Montclair, NJ 07043	1908	David W.D. Dickson	Ps-M	15,743	759
Monterey Inst. of International Studies, Monterey, CA 93940.	1955	William Craig	Ps-A	400	65
Monterey Peninsula, Monterey, CA 93940	1947	Max Tadlock	Ps-A	10,000	350
Montevallo, Univ. of, Montevallo, AL 35115.	1896	James Vickrey	Ps-M	2,812	194
Montgomery Comm., Rockville, MD 20850	1947	Robert E. Parilla	Psl-A	17,300	841
Montgomery Co. Comm. (A), Blue Bell, PA 19422.	1964	Leroy Brendlinger	Pl-A	7,200	150
Montreat-Anderson, Montreat, NC 28757.	1916	Silas M. Vaughn	IR-A	431	31
Moody Bible Institute, Chicago, IL 60610	1886	George Sweeting.	IR-B	1,347	88
Moore Coll. of Art (W), Philadelphia, PA 19103	1844	H.J. Burger.	IP-B	674	73
Moorhead State, Moorhead, MN 56560.	1885	Roland Dille	Ps-M	8,004	336
Moorpark, Moorpark, CA 93021.	1967	W. Ray Hearon.	Pl-A	9,161	400
Morame Valley Comm. (A), Palos Hills, IL 60465	1968	James Koeller	Psl-A	10,516	379
Moravian, Bethlehem, PA 18018.	1742	Herman E. Collier Jr.	IR-B	1,814	125
Morehead State Univ., Morehead, KY 40351.	1922	Morris Norfleet	Ps-S	7,163	384
Morehouse (M) (A), Atlanta, GA 30314	1867	Hugh Gloster	IP-B	1,678	105
Morgan Comm., Ft. Morgan, CO 80701.	1970	Robert F. Datteri	Ps-A	813	84
Morgan State, Baltimore, MD 21239	1867	Andrew Billingsley	Ps-D	5,151	352
Morningside, Sioux City, IA 51106	1894	Miles Tommeraasen	IR-M	1,297	120
Morris, Sumter, SC 29150	1908	Luns C. Richardson	IP-B	626	49
Morris, County Coll. of, Randolph, NJ 07869	1965	Sherman H. Masten	Psl-A	10,480	486
Morris Brown, Atlanta, GA 30314	1881	Robert Threatt	IP-B	1,611	113
Morris Harvey (A), Charleston, WV 25304	1888	Thomas Voss	IP-B	2,156	80
Morton, Cicero, IL 60650	1924	Robert V. Moritary	Psl-A	4,000	200
Motlow State Comm., Tullahoma, TN 37388	1969	Harry D. Wagner	Ps-A	2,179	100
Mt. Aloysius Junior, Cresson, PA 16630	1939	J.P. Gallagher.	IR-B	525	45
Mount Holyoke (W), S. Hadley, MA 01075	1837	Elizabeth Kennan.	IP-M	2,002	206
Mountain View (A), Dallas, TX 75211	1970	David Sims	Psl-A	6,500	250
Mt. Hood Comm., Gresham, OR 97030.	1965	R.S. Nicholson	Pl-A	9,110	450
Mt. Ida Junior (A), Newton Centre, MA 02159	1899	B.E. Carlson	IP-A	1,000	75
Mt. Marty, Yankton, SD 57078.	1936	William Tucker	IR-A	568	66
Mt. Mary (W) (A), Milwaukee, WI 53222	1913	Sister Ellen Lorenz.	IR-B	1,126	80
Mt. Mercy, Cedar Rapids, IA 52402	1928	Thomas R. Feld	IR-B	1,066	90
Mt. Olive, Mt. Olive, NC 28365.	1951	Williams B. Raper	IR-B	678	55
Mt. St. Clare, Clinton, IA 52732	1928	Dan C. Johnson	IR-B	392	36
Mt. St. Joseph (W) (A), Mt. St. Joseph, OH 45051.	1920	Jean Patrice Harrington	IR-B	1,355	55
Mt. St. Mary, Newburgh, NY 12550	1959	Sr. Ann Sakac	IP-B	1,079	83
Mt. St. Mary's (A), Los Angeles, CA 90049.	1925	Sr. Magdalen Coughlin	IR-M	1,108	74
Mt. St. Mary's, Emmitsburg, MD 21727	1808	Robert Wickenheiser	IR-M	1,615	93
Mt. St. Vincent, Coll. of, Riverdale, NY 10471	1847	Sister Doris Smith	IP-B	1,250	85
Mt. San Antonio, Walnut, CA 91789	1945	John D. Randall	Psl-A	20,707	632
Mt. San Jacinto, San Jacinto, CA 92383	1963	Dennis Mayer.	IP-B	3,450	72
Mt. Senario, Ladysmith, WI 54848.	1962	Vacant.	IP-B	513	50
Mt. Union, Alliance, OH 44601.	1846	G. Benjamin Lantz Jr.	IP-B	1,074	93
Mt. Vernon (W), Washington, DC 20007	1875	Jane Evans	IP-B	525	55
Mt. Vernon Nazarene (A), Mount Vernon, OH 43050	1968	L. Guy Nees.	IR-B	1,005	51
Mt. Wachusett Comm., Gardner, MA 01440	1963	Arthur F. Haley	Ps-A	1,476	105
Muhlenberg (A), Allentown, PA 18104.	1848	John H. Morey	IP-B	1,940	150
Multnomah Sch. of the Bible, Portland, OR 97220.	1936	Joseph C. Aldrich	IP-M	758	52
Mundelein, Chicago, IL 60660	1930	Sr. Susan Rink	IP-M	1,500	139
Murray State (A), Tishomingo, OK 73460.	1908	Clyde Kindell	Ps-A	1,357	49
Murray State Univ. (A), Murray, KY 42071	1923	C. Curris.	Ps-M	8,158	360
Muskegon Business, Muskegon, MI 49442	1885	Robert Jewell.	IP-A	1,125	45
Muskegon Comm. (A), Muskegon, MI 49442	1926	J.G. Thompson.	Pl-A	4,762	200
Muskingum, New Concord, OH 43762	1837	Arthur J. DeJong	IR-B	1,013	83
Napa, (A), Napa, CA 94558	1941	Andrew J. Fox	Psl-A	5,532	82
Nash Tech. Inst., Rocky Mount, NC 27801	1968	J. Reid Parrott Jr.	Psl-A	1,250	75

Name, address	Year	Governing official, affiliation, and highest degree offered	Stu-dents	Teach-ers
Nassau Community (A), Garden City, NY 11530	1959	George Chambers	Psl-A	17,595	474
Nasson, Springvale, ME 04083	1912	William Cole	IP-B	550	41
Nathanial Hawthorne (A), Antrim, NH 03440	1962	Kenneth F. McLaughlin	IP-B	1,200	50
National Buiness College, Roanoke, VA 24011	1886	Francis H. Birchfield	IP-A	750	75
National Coll., Rapid City, SD 57709	1941	John Hauer	IP-B	1,277	68
National Coll. of Chiropractic, Lombard, IL 60148	1906	Joseph Janse	IP-1P	976	73
National Coll. of Education (A), Evanston, IL 60201	1886	Orley R. Herron	IP-M	3,524	57
Navarro (A), Corsicana, TX 75110	1946	Kenneth Walker	Pl-A	1,500	50
Nazareth Coll., Nazareth, MI 49074	1924	John E. Hopkins	IR-B	541	62
Nazareth Coll. of Rochester, Rochester, NY 14610	1924	Robert Kidera	IP-M	1,778	186
Nebraska, Univ. of* (A), Lincoln, NE 68583	1869	Roy A. Young, Chan.	Ps-D	22,755	1,250
at Omaha, Omaha, NE 68182	1908	D. Weber, Chan.	Ps-S	15,254	700
Nebraska Wesleyan Univ., Lincoln, NE 68504	1887	John White Jr.	IP-B	1,156	119
Nebraska Western, Scottsbluff, NE 69361	1926	John Harms.	Psl-A	1,367	88
Neosho County Comm. Jr. (A), Chanute, KS 66720	1936	J.C. Sanders	Pl-A	851	28
Neumann College, Aston, PA 19014	1965	Sr. M. Marie Cunningham	IR-B	766	60
Nevada, Univ. of*, Reno, NV 89557	1874	Joseph Crowley	Ps-D	8,557	332
at Las Vegas, Las Vegas, NV 89154	1957	Leonard E. Goodall	Ps-P	9,164	294
Newberry, Newberry, SC 29108	1856	Glen E. Whitesides	IR-B	775	78
New England, Henniker, NH 03242	1948	J.K. Cummiskey	IP-M	1,650	125
New England, Univ. of, Biddeford, ME 04005	1943	Jack S. Ketchum	IP-1P	443	NA
New England Cons. of Music (A), Boston, MA 02115	1867	J.S. Ballinger	IP-M	750	145
New Hampshire, Manchester, NH 03104	1932	Edward Shapiro	IP-M	5,086	245
New Hampshire, Univ. of*, Durham, NH 03824	1865	Evelyn E. Handler	P-D	12,735	597
New Hampshire Tech. Inst., Concord, NH 03301	1965	D. Larrabee Sr.	Ps-A	1,233	125
New Hampshire Voc. Tech. (A), Portsmouth, NH 03102	1943	R.E. Mandeville, Dir.	Ps-A	850	48
New Haven, Univ. of*, New Haven, CT 06516	1920	Phillip Kaplan	IP-M	7,531	446
New Jersey Inst. of Tech. (A), Newark, NJ 07102	1881	Saul K. Fenster	Psl-D	6,021	270
New Mexico Junior, Hobbs, NM 88240	1966	Robert A. Anderson	Psl-A	1,764	96
New Mexico Highlands Univ. (A), Las Vegas, NM 87701	1893	John Aragon	Ps-M	2,000	150
N. Mexico Inst. of Min. & Tech., Socorro, NM 87801	1889	Kenneth Ford	Ps-D	1,334	101
New Mexico Military Inst., Roswell, NM 88201	1893	Maj. Gen. G. Childress.	Ps-A	1,200	87
New Mexico State Univ.*, Las Cruces, NM 88003	1888	Gerald W. Thomas	Ps-D	16,789	1,022
New Mexico, Univ. of*, Albuquerque, NM 87131	1889	William Davis	Ps-D	24,482	1,511
New Orleans, Univ. of, New Orleans, LA 70122	1958	Leon J.V. Richelle, Chan.	Pf-D	16,186	627
Newport-Salve Regina (A), Newport, RI 02840	1947	Lucille McKillop	IR-M	1,700	120
New River Community, Dublin, VA 24084	1969	H.R. Edwards.	Ps-A	3,047	137
New Rochelle, Coll. of (W)(A), New Rochelle, NY 10801	1904	Sister Dorothy Ann Kelly	IP-M	4,613	90
New School for Soc. Research, New York, NY 10011	1919	John R. Everett	IP-D	25,000	1,500
New York City, Univ. of, New York, NY 10021	1847	Robert J. Kibbee, Chan.	Psl-B	172,616	11,650
Bernard M. Baruch, New York, NY 10010	1919	Joel Segall	Psl-I	14,592	665
Bronx Comm., Bronx, NY 10453	1957	Roscoe C. Brown Jr.	Psl-A	6,818	500
Brooklyn, Brooklyn, NY 11210	1930	Robert L. Hess	Psl-D	16,691	1,465
City, New York, NY 10031	1847	Bernard Harleston	Psl-M	12,341	1,112
Medgar Evers, Brooklyn, NY 11225	1969	Richard D. Trent	Psl-B	2,708	345
Herbert H. Lehman, Bronx, NY 10468	1931	Leonard Lief	Psl-D	9,248	633
Hostos Comm., Bronx, NY 10451	1968	Flora Mancuso Edwards.	Ps-A	2,673	254
Hunter, New York, NY 10021	1870	Donna E. Shalala	Psl-M	17,509	1,110
John Jay Coll. of Criminal Just., New York, NY 10019	1964	Gerald Lynch	Ps-D	6,172	382
Kingsborough Comm., Brooklyn, NY 11235	1963	Israel Glasser, Act.	Psl-A	8,450	540
LaGuardia Comm., Long Is. City, NY 11101	1968	Joseph Shenker	Psl-A	6,563	540
Manhattan Comm., New York, NY 10019	1963	Joshua Smith	Psl-A	8,355	590
Mt. Sinai School of Med., New York, NY 10029	1963	Thomas C. Chalmers	IP-1P	454	NA
New York City Tech. Comm., Brooklyn, NY 11201	1947	Ursula Schwerin	Psl-B	13,147	958
Queens, Flushing, NY 11367	1937	Saul B. Cohen	Psl-M	18,127	1,322
Queensborough Comm., Bayside, NY 11364	1958	Kurt R. Schmeller	Psl-A	11,643	966
Staten Island, Staten Island, NY 10301	1976	Edmond Volpe	Psl-M	10,608	634
York, Jamaica, NY 11451	1966	Milton G. Bassin	Psl-B	3,801	268
N.Y. Inst. of Technology, Old Westbury, NY 11568	1957	Alexander Schure	IP-M	10,639	660
New York Law School, New York, NY 10013	1891	E. Donald Shapiro, Dean	IP-1P	1,342	150
New York Medical (A), Valhalla, NY 10590	1860	Joseph A. Cimino.	IP-D	756	560
New York, State Univ. of (A), Albany, NY 12210	1948	C.R. Wharton Jr., Chan.	Ps-D	348,361	14,138
Agric. & Tech. Inst. (A), Alfred, NY 14802	1908	David H. Huntington	Ps-A	4,138	221
" " " (A), Canton, NY 13617	1907	Earl MacArthur	Ps-A	2,329	302
" " " (A), Cobleskill, NY 12043	1911	Walton A. Brown	Ps-A	2,683	145
" " " (A), Delhi, NY 13753	1913	Seldon M. Kruger	Ps-A	2,381	137
" " " (A), Farmingdale, NY 11735	1912	F.A. Cipriani	Ps-A	13,049	314
" " " (A), Morrisville, NY 13408	1908	Royson N. Whipple	Ps-A	2,997	144
State Univ. (A), Albany, NY 12222	1844	V.J. O'Leary	Ps-D	15,391	654
" " Buffalo, NY 14260	1846	Robert Ketter	Ps-D	27,000	1,838
" " Binghamton, NY 13901	1950	Clifford D. Clark	Ps-D	11,280	642
" " Stony Brook, NY 11794	1957	John H. Marburger	Ps-D	16,346	1,281
State Univ. Colleges, Brockport, NY 14420	1867	Albert W. Brown	Ps-S	9,530	481
" " Buffalo, NY 14260	1867	D. Bruce Johnstone	Ps-M	11,749	549
" " Cortland, NY 13045	1868	James M. Clark.	Ps-M	6,080	362
" " Empire State, Saratoga Spgs., NY 12866	1971	James Hall	Ps-B	4,769	195
" " (A), Fredonia, NY 14063	1867	Dallas K. Beal.	Ps-M	5,262	264
" " Geneseo, NY 14454	1867	E.B. Jakubauskas	Ps-M	5,571	309
" " (A), New Paltz, NY 12561	1885	Alice Chandler	Ps-M	4,982	350
" " Oneonta, NY 13820	1889	Clifford Craven	Ps-M	6,066	375
" " Oswego, NY 13126	1861	Virginia Radley	Ps-M	7,554	409
" " (A), Old Westbury, NY 11568	1965	John Maguire	Ps-B	2,850	125
" " Plattsburgh, NY 12901	1889	Joseph C. Burke	Ps-M	6,320	375
" " Potsdam, NY 13676	1816	James H. Young	Ps-M	4,672	289
" " Purchase, NY 10577	1967	Henrik N. Dullea, Act.	Ps-B	3,661	186
" " College of Tech., Utica/Rome, NY 13502	1966	William Kunsela.	Ps-B	3,500	164
Agri. & Tech. Coll. (A), Farmingdale, NY 11735	1948	Frank A. Cipriani	Ps-A	13,591	400
Buffalo Health Sciences Ctr. (A), Buffalo, NY 14214	1846	F.C. Pannill, V.P.	Ps-D	2,968	354
Env'm't'l. Sci. & Forestry, Syracuse, NY 13210	1911	Edward Palmer	Ps-D	1,750	201
Downstate Medical Center, Brooklyn, NY 11203	1860	Dr. Donald J. Scherl	Ps-D	1,432	650
Health Sciences Center (A), Stony Brook, NY 11790	1957	James H. Oaks, V.P.	Ps-D	1,329	175
Maritime, Bronx, NY 10465	1874	Sheldon Kinney	Ps-M	1,070	70
Upstate Medical Center, Syracuse, NY 13210	1834	Richard P. Schmidt.	Ps-D	937	300
New York Univ. (A), New York, NY 10012	1831	John Sawhill	IP-D	32,537	5,300
Niagara County Comm. (A), Sanborn, NY 14132	1962	Jack C. Watson.	Psl-A	3,835	123
Niagara Univ., Niagara Univ., NY 14109	1856	V. Rev. G. Mahoney	IR-M	3,831	262
Nicholls State Univ. (A), Thibodaux, LA 70301	1948	Vernon Galliano	Ps-D	7,016	226
Nichols, Dudley, MA 01570	1815	Lowell Smith	IP-M	1,076	50
Norfolk State, Norfolk, VA 23504	1935	Harrison B. Wilson	Ps-M	7,286	421

Name, address	Year	Governing official, affiliation, and highest degree offered		Students	Teachers
Normandale Comm., Bloomington, MN 55431	1968	Dale A. Lorenz	Ps-A	4,953	250
Northampton Co. Area Comm., Bethlehem, PA 18017	1966	Robert J. Kopecek	P-A	3,728	234
North Adams State, North Adams, MA 01247	1894	William P. Hass	Ps-M	2,400	115
North Carolina Central U., Durham, NC 27707	1910	A. Whiting, Chan.	P-1P	4,910	359
North Carolina, Univ. of, Chapel Hill, NC 27514	1972	William Friday			
A&T State Univ., Greensboro, NC 27411.	1891	Cleon Thompson, Act. Chan.	Pf-M	5,130	360
at Asheville, Asheville, NC 28814	1927	William Highsmith, Chan.	Pf-B	2,178	137
at Chapel Hill, Chapel Hill, NC 27514.	1789	Christopher C. Fordham III, Chan.	Ps-D	21,465	2,027
at Charlotte, Charlotte, NC 28223.	1946	E.K. Fretwell, Jr., Chan.	Ps-M	9,383	617
at Greensboro, Greensboro, NC 27412	1892	William E. Moran, Chan.	Ps-M	10,390	609
at Wilmington, Wilmington, NC 28406.	1947	Wm. H. Wagoner, Chan.	Ps-M	4,696	269
N.C. School of the Arts, Winston-Salem, NC 27107	1965	R. Suderburg, Chan.	Ps-B	651	98
N.C. State Univ. at Raleigh (A), NC 27650	1887	Joab Thomas	Ps-D	18,300	1,235
North Carolina Wesleyan, Rocky Mount, NC 27801	1956	S. Bruce Petteway	IR-A	867	49
North Central (A), Naperville, IL 60540	1861	Gael D. Swing	IR-B	1,111	52
North Central Bible, Minneapolis, MN 55404	1930	Don Argue	IR-B	697	26
North Central Michigan, Petoskey, MI 49770	1958	A.D. Shankland	Ps-A	1,826	93
North Central Tech. Inst. (A), Wausau, WI 54401	1912	Dwight E. Davis	PI-A	14,000	135
North County Comm. (A), Saranac Lake, NY 12983	1967	P.J. Cayan	Psl-A	1,376	48
N. Dak. St. Sch. of Science, Wahpeton, ND 58075	1903	Clair T. Blikre	Ps-A	3,394	181
North Dakota State Univ., Fargo, ND 58105	1890	L.D. Loftsgard.	Ps-D	12,148	577
North Dakota, Univ. of* (A), Grand Forks, ND 58202	1883	Thomas Clifford	Ps-D	9,708	584
Northeast Alabama State Jr., Rainsville, AL 35986	1964	E.R. Knox	Ps-A	913	57
Northeastern Illinois Univ., Chicago, IL 60625	1961	Ronald Williams	Ps-M	10,346	449
Northeastern Junior (A), Sterling, CO 80751	1941	Marvin W. Weiss	PI-A	2,111	69
Northeastern Okla. A&M, Miami, OK 74354	1919	D.D. Creech.	Ps-A	2,862	149
Northeastern State, Tahlequah, OK 74464	1909	W. Roger Webb	Ps-M	6,100	250
Northeastern Univ. (A), Boston, MA 02115	1898	Kenneth Ryder	IP-D	42,437	739
Northeast Louisiana Univ., Monroe, LA 71209	1931	Dwight Vines	Ps-D	10,037	415
Northeast Miss. Junior, Booneville, MS 38829	1948	Harold T. White.	Psl-A	1,980	134
Northeast Missouri State Univ., Kirksville, MO 63501	1867	Charles T. McClain.	Ps-S	6,400	350
Northeast Neb. Tech. Comm. (A), Norfolk, NE 68701	1973	Robert P. Cox.	Ps-A	1,500	110
Northeast Wisc. Tech. Inst. (A), Green Bay, WI 54303	1916	K.W. Hanbenschild, Dir.	Psl-A	3,050	650
Northern Arizona Univ. (A), Flagstaff, AZ 86011	1899	Eugene M. Hughes.	Ps-D	12,300	520
Northern Colorado, Univ. of, Greeley, CO 80639	1890	Richard R. Bond	Ps-D	10,269	618
Northern Essex Comm., Haverhill, MA 01830	1961	J.R. Dimitry	Ps-A	7,754	369
Northern Illinois Univ. (A), DeKalb, IL 60115	1899	Wm. Monat	Ps-D	25,259	1,011
Northern Iowa, Univ. of (A), Cedar Falls, IA 50613.	1876	John Kamerick	Ps-S	11,056	569
Northern Kentucky Univ., Highland Hts., KY 41076	1968	A.D. Albright	Ps-M	8,372	404
Northern Michigan Univ., Marquette, MI 49855.	1899	John X. Jamrich	Ps-S	9,376	350
Northern Montana, Havre, MT 59501	1929	James H.M. Erickson	Ps-M	1,473	82
Northern Oklahoma, Tonkawa, OK 74653	1901	Edwin Vineyard.	Ps-A	1,600	90
Northern State, Aberdeen, SD 57401	1901	Joseph McFadden	Ps-M	2,603	114
Northern Virginia Comm., Annandale, VA 22003.	1965	Richard Ernst	Ps-A	33,899	1,300
North Florida, Univ. of (A), Jacksonville, FL 32216.	1965	Thos. Carpenter	Ps-M	4,039	205
North Florida Junior, Madison, FL 32340	1958	Gary P. Sims	Psl-A	850	37
North Georgia, Dahlonega, GA 30597	1873	John H. Owen	Ps-B	1,837	102
North Greenville, Tigerville, SC 29688	1892	Herbert A. Slerk, Act.	IR-A	636	58
North Harris County, Houston, TX 77073	1973	W.W. Thorne	Psl-A	6,300	295
North Hennepin Comm., Brooklyn Pk., MN 55445	1966	John F. Helling	Ps-A	4,101	180
North Idaho, Coeur d'Alene, ID 83814	1939	Barry Schuler	Psl-A	2,216	139
North Iowa Area Comm., Mason City, IA 50401	1918	Dave Buettner	PI-A	1,900	110
Northland, Ashland, WI 54806	1893	Malcolm McLean	IP-B	650	56
Northland Comm. (A), Thief River Falls, MN 56701	1965	Alex Easton.	Ps-A	560	19
North Park (A), Chicago, IL 60625	1891	Lloyd Ahlem	IR-1P	1,092	77
North Shore Community (A), Beverly, MA 01915	1965	George Traicoff.	Ps-A	2,321	110
North Texas State Univ., Denton, TX 76203	1890	Frank E. Vandiver	Ps-D	17,158	812
Northrop Univ., Inglewood, CA 90306	1942	B.J. Shell	IP-1P	1,452	123
Northwest Bible, Minot, ND 58701	1934	Edward L. Williams.	IR-B	252	11
Northwest Christian, Eugene, OR 97401	1895	William E. Hays.	IR-B	325	21
Northwest Col. of the Assemblies of God (A), Kirkland, WA 98033.	1934	D.V. Hurst.	IR-B	787	21
Northwest Community, Powell, WY 82435	1946	Sinclair Orendorff	Psl-A	1,720	85
Northwestern, Orange City, IA 51041	1882	Friedhelm Radandt.	IR-B	955	85
Northwestern Conn. Comm., Winsted, CT 06098	1965	Regina Duffy	Ps-A	2,468	58
Northwestern Michigan, Traverse City, MI 49684	1951*	William J. Yankee	Psl-A	3,400	115
Northwestern State Univ., Natchitoches, LA 71457	1884	René Bienvenu	Ps-D	5,443	283
Northwestern Okla. St. Univ. (A), Alva, OK 73717.	1897	Joe Struckle	Ps-M	2,160	76
Northwestern Univ. (A), Evanston, IL 60201	1851	Robert Henry Strotz	IP-D	15,117	1,309
Northwest Miss. Junior (A), Senotobia, MS 38668	1927	Henry B. Koon	Ps-A	2,743	130
Northwest Missouri State Univ., Maryville, MO 64468.	1905	B.D. Owens	Pf-S	4,976	230
Northwest Nazarene, Nampa, ID 83651.	1913	Kenneth Pearsall	IR-M	1,320	84
Norwalk State Tech., Norwalk, CT 06854.	1961	William M. Krummel	IP-B	1,481	44
Norwich Univ. (A), Northfield, VT 05663.	1819	Loring Hart	IP-D	1,913	57
Northwood Inst., Midland, MI 48640	1959	T.J. Brown.	IP-B	2,465	92
Notre Dame, Coll. of, Belmont, CA 94002	1851	Sr. Veronica Skillin	IR-M	1,410	138
Notre Dame (W), Manchester, NH 03104.	1950	Sr. Jeannette Vezeau	IR-M	770	68
Notre Dame Coll. of Oh. (W), Cleveland, OH 44121	1922	Sister Mary Marthe.	IR-B	679	73
Notre Dame of Maryland, Baltimore, MD 21210	1873	Sister Kathleen Feeley.	IR-B	1,488	85
Notre Dame, Univ. of, Notre Dame, IN 46556	1842	Rev. T.M. Hesburgh	IP-D	8,925	695
Nova Univ. (A), Ft. Lauderdale, FL 33314.	1964	Abraham Fischler	IP-D	8,171	125
Nyack, Nyack, NY 10960	1882	Thomas Bailey	IR-M	846	68
Oakland City (A), Oakland City, IN 47660	1885	J.W. Murray.	IR-B	520	30
Oakland Comm., Bloomfield Hills, MI 48013	1965	Robert F. Roelofs	Psl-A	22,762	500
Oakland Univ., Rochester, MI 48063	1957	Joseph Champagne	Ps-D	11,519	367
Oakton Comm. (A), Morton Grove, IL 60053	1969	William Koehnline	PI-A	5,795	144
Oakwood, Huntsville, AL 35806	1896	C.B. Rock	IR-B	1,175	115
Oberlin, Oberlin, OH 44074	1833	Emil Danenberg	IP-M	2,771	244
Occidental, Los Angeles, CA 90041.	1887	Richard C. Gilman	IP-M	1,710	125
Ocean County, Toms River, NJ 08753	1964	George Silver.	Psl-A	5,587	175
Odessa, Odessa, TX 79762	1945	Philip Speegle	IP-A	4,000	235
Oglethorpe Univ., Atlanta, GA 30319	1835	Manning Pattillo Jr.	IP-M	1,100	50
Ohio Dominican, Columbus, OH 43219	1911	Sister M. Andrew Matesich	IR-B	919	76
Ohio Coll. of Podiatric Med. (A), Cleveland, OH 44106	1916	Abe Rubin	IP-B	585	28
Ohio Inst. of Technology, Columbus, OH 43209	1952	Richard A Czerniak	IP-B	2,718	50
Ohio Northern Univ., Ada, OH 45810	1871	DeBow Freed.	IR-1P	2,768	164
Ohio State Univ.* (A), Columbus, OH 43210.	1870	Edward H. Jennings	Ps-D	54,579	3,533

Name, address	Year	Governing official, affiliation, and highest degree offered		Stu-dents	Teach-ers
Ohio Univ., Athens, OH 45701	1804	Charles J. Ping	Ps-D	20,142	1,137
Ohio Wesleyan Univ., Delaware, OH 43015	1842	Thomas Wenzlau	IR-B	2,392	160
Ohlone, Fremont, CA 94538	1966	Peter Blomerly	Psl-A	8,350	376
Okaloosa-Walton Jr., Niceville, Fl 32578	1963	J.E. McCracken	Psl-A	3,801	172
Oklahoma Baptist Univ., Shawnee, OK 74801	1910	E. Eugene Hall	IR-B	1,524	132
Oklahoma Christian, Oklahoma City, OK 73111	1950	J. Johnson	IR-B	1,657	70
Oklahoma City Southwestern (A), Oklahoma City, OK 73127	1946	Scott T. Muse, Jr.	IR-A	693	25
Oklahoma City Univ. (A), Oklahoma City, OK 73106	1904	Jerald C. Walker	IR-M	2,335	86
Oklahoma Panhandle St. Univ. (A), Goodwell, OK 73939	1909	Thomas L. Palmer	Ps-B	1,115	74
Oklahoma Sch. of Business, Acctg. Law & Finance (A), Tulsa, OK 74103	1919	H. Everett Pope Jr.	IP-A	287	5
Oklahoma State Univ.*, Stillwater OK 74078	1890	Lawrence Boger	PI-S	28,228	1,362
Oklahoma, Univ. of, Norman, OK 73019	1890	William S. Banowsky	Ps-D	22,978	798
Okla. Univ. of Science & Arts, Chickasha, OK 73018	1908	Roy Troutt	Ps-B	1,362	70
Old Dominion Univ., Norfolk, VA 23508	1930	A.B. Rollins Jr.	Ps-D	16,353	796
Olivet, Olivet, MI 49076	1844	Donald A. Morris	IR-M	600	50
Olivet Nazarene, Kankakee, IL 60901	1907	Leslie Parrott	IR-M	2,140	110
Olney Central, Olney, IL 62450	1963	James Spencer	Psl-A	2,306	186
Olympic, Bremerton, WA 98310	1946	Henry Milander	Ps-A	8,175	328
Onondaga Comm. (A), Syracuse, NY 13215	1962	A. Paloumpis	PI-A	7,000	212
Oral Roberts Univ. (A), Tulsa, OK 74171	1963	Granville Oral Roberts	IR-M	3,800	300
Orangeburg-Calhoun Tech (A), Orangeburg, SC 29115	1968	M. Rudy Groomes	Ps-A	1,400	51
Orange Coast, Costa Mesa, CA 92626	1947	Robert Moore	Ps-A	29,756	500
Orange County Comm. (A), Middletown, NY 10940	1950	Robert T. Novak	Ps-A	4,988	138
Oregon College of Educ. (A), Monmouth, OR 97361	1856	G. Leinwand	Ps-M	3,200	175
Oregon Inst. of Tech., Klamath Falls, OR 97601	1947	Kenneth Light	Ps-B	2,434	160
Oregon State Univ.* (A), Corvallis, OR 97331	1868	R. MacVicar	Ps-D	16,666	1,582
Oregon, Univ. of, Eugene, OR 97403	1876	Paul Olum	Ps-D	17,058	1,509
Oscar Rose Junior (A), Midwest City, OK 73110	1970	Joe Packnett. Act.	Ps-A	7,841	148
Osteopathic Med. & Sur., Coll. of, Des Moines, IA 50312	1898	J.L. Azneer	IP-S	544	90
Otero Junior, La Junta, CO 81050	1941	William L. McDivitt	Ps-A	839	53
Otis Art Inst., Los Angeles, CA 90057	1918	Neil Hoffman	IP-M	305	60
Ottawa Univ. (A), Ottawa, KS 66067	1865	Robert Shaw	IR-B	535	52
Otterbein, Westerville, OH 43081	1847	Thomas Jefferson Kerr	IR-B	1,677	106
Ottumwa Heights (A), Ottumwa, IA 52501	1925	Sr. Bernadine Pieper	IR-A	310	27
Ouachita Baptist Univ., Arkadelphia, AR 71923	1886	Daniel R. Grant	IR-M	1,655	105
Our Lady of Elms, Col. of (W), Chicopee, MA 01013	1928	Sr. Mary Dooley	IR-B	635	78
Our Lady of the Lake Univ., San Antonio, TX 78285	1911	Sr. Eliz. Sueltenfuss	IR-M	1,768	100
Owensburg Jr. Coll. of Business, Owensburg, KY 42301		Tony Austin Payne	IP-A	397	37
Ozarks, Coll. of the, Clarksville, AR 72830	1834	John Burhorn	IR-A	687	44
Ozarks, School of the, Pt. Lookout, MO 65726	1906	James Spainhower	IP-B	1,200	82
Pace, Univ. (A), New York, NY 10038	1906	Edward J. Mortola	IP-B	21,523	373
Pacific Christian, Fullerton, CA 92631	1928	Medford Jones	IR-M	702	45
Pacific Lutheran Univ., Tacoma, WA 98447	1890	William Rieke	IR-M	3,475	254
Pacific States Univ. (A), Los Angeles, CA 90006	1928	Steven Kase	Ps-B	700	25
Pacific Union (A), Angwin, CA 94508	1882	J.W. Cassel, Jr.	IR-M	2,000	126
Pacific Univ., Forest Grove, OR 97116	1851	James Miller	IR-M	1,101	112
Pacific, Univ. of the, Stockton, CA 95211	1851	Stanley McCaffrey	IP-D	5,861	472
Paducah Comm., Paducah, KY 42201	1932	Donald J. Clemens, Dir.	Ps-A	1,869	96
Paine, Augusta, GA 30910	1882	J.S. Scott Jr.	IR-B	757	62
Palm Beach Atlantic (A), W. Palm Beach, FL 33401	1968	George Borders	IR-B	576	28
Palm Beach Junior, Lake Worth, FL 33461	1933	Edward M. Eissey	Ps-A	10,000	500
Palomar Comm. (A), San Marcos, CA 92060	1946	Omar H. Scheidt	Ps-A	15,241	243
Palo Verde Comm., Blythe, CA 92225	1947	Dan Radakovich	PI-A	680	40
Pan American Univ. (A), Edinburg, TX 78539	1927	Ralph Schilling	Ps-M	7,183	321
Panola Junior, Carthage, TX 75633	1947	Arthur Johnson	PI-A	973	41
Park, Parkville, MO 64152	1875	Harold Condit	IR-A	2,215	248
Paris Junior (A), Paris, TX 75460	1924	Louis B. Williams	Ps-A	2,042	79
Parkersburg Comm. (A), Parkersburg, WV 26101	1971	Byron N. McClenney	Ps-A	3,288	80
Parkland, Champaign, IL 61820	1967	William M. Staerkel	Psr-A	8,143	525
Parsons School of Design (A), New York, NY 10011	1896	John R. Everett	IP-M	3,000	250
Pasadena City (A), Pasadena, CA 91106	1924	Richard S. Meyers	Ps-A	19,115	408
Pasco-Hernando Comm. (A), Dade City, FL 33525	1972	Milton O. Jones	Ps-A	1,700	174
Passaic Co. Comm., Paterson, NJ 07509	1970	Gustavo Mellander	PI-A	4,113	34
Patrick Henry State Jr. (A), Monroeville, AL 36460	1965	Cecil Murphy	Ps-A	596	26
Paul D. Camp Comm., Franklin, VA 23851	1971	Johnnie E. Merritt.	Ps-A	1,096	50
Paul Smith's Coll. of Arts & Sci., Paul Smiths, NY 12970	1937	T.N. Stainback	IP-A	1,224	89
Paul Quinn (A), Waco, TX 76704	1872	William D. Watley	IR-B	381	31
Peabody Cons. of Music, Baltimore, MD 21202	1857	Elliott W. Galkin	IP-D	419	97
Peace (W), Raleigh, NC 27604	1857	S. David Frazier	IR-A	477	32
Pearl River Junior, Poplarville, MS 39470	1909	M.R. White	Psl-A	2,450	107
Peirce Junior (A), Philadelphia, PA 19102	1865	Thomas M. Peirce III	IP-A	1,407	71
Pembroke St. Univ. (A), Pembroke, NC 28372	1887	English E. Jones	Ps-M	2,158	125
Peninsula (A), Port Angeles, WA 98362	1961	Paul G. Cornaby	Ps-A	1,200	60
Pennsylvania, Univ. of (A), Philadelphia, PA 19104	1740	Martin Meyerson	IP-D	18,500	3,000
Penn Col. of Optometry, Philadelphia, PA 19141	1919	Melvin Wolfberg	IP-1P	586	98
Penn. Coll. of Podiatric Med. (A), Phila., PA 19107	1963	James Bates	IP-S	451	34
Penn., Medical Coll. of, Philadelphia, PA 19129	1850	Maurice Clifford	IP-S	456	620
Penn. State Univ.* (A), University Park, PA 16802	1855	John W. Oswald	Ps-D	59,541	2,613
Penn Valley Comm. (A), Kansas City, MO 64111	1915	Dorothy M. Wright	PI-A	5,033	105
Pensacola Jr., Pensacola, FL 32504	1948	Horace Hartsell.	Ps-A	11,000	450
Pepperdine Univ., Malibu, CA 90265	1937	Howard A. White	IR-D	6,104	481
Peralta Comm., Oakland, CA 94610	1964	Donald Godbold	PI-A	40,756	1,406
Peru State, Peru, NE 68421	1867	Larry Tangeman	Ps-B	912	47
Pfeiffer, Misenheimer, NC 28109	1885	Cameron West	IR-B	814	71
Philadelphia, Comm., Coll. of, Philadelphia, PA 19107	1964	Allen T. Bonnell	Psl-A	12,500	900
Phila. College of Art, Philadelphia, PA 19102	1886	Thomas Schutte	IP-M	1,260	150
Phila. Coll. of Bible (A), Langhorne PA 19047	1913	W. Sherrill Babb	IP-B	526	29
Phila. Coll. of Osteopathic Med., Philadelphia, PA 19131	1899	Thomas Rowland Jr.	IP-S	821	231
Phila. Coll. of Pharm. & Science, Philadelphia, PA 19104	1821	William Thawley	IP-D	1,100	80
Phila. Coll. of Textiles & Science, Philadelphia, PA 19144	1884	D.B. Partridge.	IP-M	1,562	87
Philander Smith (A), Little Rock, AR 72203	1877	Walter Hazzard.	IR-B	631	38
Phillips County Comm. (A), Helena, AR 72342	1965	John Easley.	Psl-A	2,415	61
Phillips Univ., Enid, OK 73701	1909	Joe R. Jones	IP-M	1,299	102
Phoenix, AZ 85013	1920	William Berry	PI-A	13,495	190
Piedmont, Demorest, GA 30535	1897	James E. Walker	IP-B	374	30
Piedmont Bible, Winston-Salem, NC 27101	1945	Donald Drake.	IP-B	468	29
Piedmont Tech., Greenwood, SC 29646	1966	Lex Walters	Psl-A	1,773	231

Name, address	Year	Governing official, affiliation, and highest degree offered	Stu-dents	Teach-ers
Piedmont Tech. Inst. (A), Roxboro, NC 27573	1970	Edward W. Cox	Ps-A	877	59
Piedmont Virginia Comm., Charlotte, VA 22901	1972	George B. Vaughan	Ps-A	3,811	200
Pikes Peak Comm., Colorado Springs, CO 80906	1968	Donald McInnis	Ps-A	5,439	300
Pikeville, Pikeville, KY 41501	1889	Jackson Hall	IR-B	729	45
Pima Comm. (A), Tucson, AZ 85709	1970	Irwin Spector	Ps-A	19,996	998
Pine Manor (W)(A), Chestnut Hill, MA 02167	1911	Rosemary Ashby	IP-B	516	30
Pine Manor Junior (W)(A), Chestnut Hill, MA 02167	1911	Rosemary Ashby	IP-A	377	47
Pitt Comm., Greenville, NC 27834	1964	W.E. Fulford Jr.	Ps-A	2,455	148
Pittsburgh, Univ. of, Pittsburgh, PA 15260	1787	Wesley W. Posvar	IP-D	29,315	2,333
Pittsburgh State U., Pittsburgh, KS 66762	1903	James Appleberry	Ps-S	5,120	560
Pitzer, Claremont, CA 91711	1963	Frank Ellsworth	IP-B	700	65
Plymouth State, Plymouth, NH 03264	1871	Kasper Marking	Ps-M	3,261	165
Point Loma, San Diego, CA 92106	1902	Bill D. Draper	IR-M	1,806	133
Point Park (A), Pittsburgh, PA 15222	1960	John Hopkins	IP-B	2,077	147
Polk Comm. (A), Winter Haven, FL 33880	1964	Frederick T. Lenfestey	Ps-A	5,600	150
Polytechnic Institute, Brooklyn, NY 11201	1854	George Bugliarello	IP-D	4,560	357
Pomona, Claremont, CA 91711	1887	David Alexander	IP-B	1,358	152
Porterville, Porterville, CA 93257	1927	Paul D. Alcantra	Ps-A	2,304	110
Portland Comm., Portland, OR 97219	1961	John Anthony	Ps-A	34,771	2,390
Portland State Univ., Portland, OR 97207	1955	Joseph Blumel	Ps-D	16,730	508
Portland, Univ. of, Portland, OR 97203	1901	Bro. Raphael Wilson	IR-M	2,703	109
Post Junior, Waterbury, CT 06708	1890	Douglas Picht	IP-A	1,069	63
Potomac State (A), Keyser, WV 26726	1902	J.L. McBee, Exec. Dean	Ps-A	1,007	40
Prairie State (A), Chicago Hts., IL 60411	1958	Richard Creal	Ps-A	5,434	98
Prairie View A & M Univ. (A), Prairie View, TX 77445	1878	Alvin Thomas	Ps-M	5,125	306
Pratt Community, Pratt, KS 67124	1938	Norman Myers	Psl-A	422	30
Pratt Institute (A), Brooklyn, NY 11205	1887	Richardson Pratt Jr.	IP-B	4,422	295
Presbyterian, Clinton, SC 29325	1880	Kenneth B. Orr	IR-B	946	73
Presentation, Aberdeen, SD 57401	1951	Sr. Lynn Marie Welbig	IP-A	300	39
Prestonburg Comm. (A), Prestonburg, KY	1964	Henry A. Campbell	Ps-A	623	27
Prince George's Comm. (A), Largo, MD 20870	1958	Robert Bickford	PI-A	11,830	569
Princeton Univ. (A), Princeton, NJ 08540	1746	William G. Bowen	IP-D	5,931	810
Principia, Elsah, IL 62028	1898	Arthur F. Schulz Jr.	IP-B	884	96
Providence, Providence, RI 02918	1917	Rev. T.R. Peterson	IR-D	3,493	240
Puerto Rico, Univ. of*, San Juan, PR 00931	1903	Ismael Almodovar	Ps-S	23,000	1,300
Puerto Rico Jr. (A), Rio Piedras, PR 00928	1949	Federico J. Modesto	IP-A	5,691	218
Puget Sound, Univ. of, Tacoma, WA 98416	1888	Philip M. Phibbs	IP-M	5,378	294
Purdue Univ.*, W. Lafayette, IN 47907	1869	Arthur G. Hansen	Ps-D	46,470	2,960
Queens (W), Charlotte, NC 28274	1857	Billy Wireman	IR-M	909	77
Quincy, Quincy, IL 62301	1860	Rev. G. Brinkman	IR-B	983	96
Quincy Jr., Quincy, MA 02169	1959	Edward Pierce	PI-A	3,860	50
Quinebaug Valley Comm. (A), Danielson, CT 06239	1971	Robert E. Miller	Ps-A	900	11
Quinnipiac (A), Hamden, CT 06518	1929	Richard A. Terry	IP-B	3,778	158
Quinsigamond Comm. (A), Worcester, MA 01606	1963	Donald J. Donato	Ps-A	5,094	86
Radcliffe (W) (A), Cambridge MA 02138	1879	Matina Souretia Horner	IP-D	2,161	(a)
Radford (A), Radford, VA 24142	1910	Donald N. Dedman	Ps-M	5,693	300
Ramapo Coll. of N.J. (A), Mahwah, NJ 07430	1969	George T. Potter	Ps-B	4,300	210
Randolph-Macon, Ashland, VA 23005	1830	Ladell Payne	IP-B	899	75
Randolph-Macon Woman's (W), Lynchburg, VA 24503	1891	Robert Spivey	IR-B	757	80
Randolph Tech., Asheboro, NC 27203	1962	M.H. Branson	Ps-A	1,013	35
Ranger Junior (A), Ranger TX 76470	1926	Jack Elsom	Ps-A	722	32
Reading Area Comm. (A), Reading, PA 19603	1971	Lewis Ogle	Psl-A	887	74
Redlands, Univ. of, Redlands, CA 92373	1907	Douglas R. Moore	IP-M	2,750	272
Redwoods, Coll. of the, Eureka, CA 95501	1964	Donald Weichert	PI-A	9,600	500
Reed (A), Portland, OR 97202	1909	Paul Bragdon	IP-M	1,156	78
Regis, Denver, CO 80221	1877	Rev. David M. Clarke	IR-M	1,052	79
Regis (W), Weston, MA 02193	1927	Sister Therese Higgins	IR-M	1,277	104
Reinhardt, Waleska, GA 30183	1883	Allen O. Jernigan	IR-A	509	42
Rend Lake, Ina, IL 62846	1967	Harry J. Braun	Psl-A	3,114	65
Rensselaer Poly. Inst. (A), Troy, NY 12181	1824	George M. Low	IP-D	6,031	355
Rhode Island, Providence, RI 02908	1854	David E. Sweet	Ps-M	9,648	380
Rhode Island, Comm. Coll. of, Warwick, RI 02886	1964	Edward J. Liston	Ps-A	12,000	300
R.I. School of Design, Providence, RI 0203	1877	Lee Hall	IP-M	1,788	172
Rhode Island, Univ. of*, Kingston, RI 02881	1892	Frank Newman	Ps-D	13,797	900
Rice Univ., Houston, TX 77001	1891	Norman Hackerman	IP-D	3,020	450
Richland, Dallas, TX 75243	1972	Stephen Mittlestet	PI-A	11,600	500
Richland Comm., Decatur, IL 62523	1972	John Kirk	Psl-A	3,200	153
Richmond Tech. Inst., Hamlet, NC 28345	1964	R. Kenneth Meliun	Ps-A	985	79
Richmond, Univ. of, Richmond, VA 23173	1830	E. Bruce Heilman	IR-M	4,200	329
Ricks, Rexburg, ID 83440	1888	Bruce C. Hafen	IR-A	6,495	273
Rider (A), Lawrenceville, NJ 08648	1865	Frank N. Elliott	IP-M	5,583	188
(a) Radcliffe students are taught by the Harvard faculty.					
Rio Grande, Rio Grande, OH 45674	1876	Paul Hayes	IP-B	1,225	96
Rio Hondo Comm. (A), Whittier, CA 90608	1960	L.A. Grandy	Psl-A	13,656	555
Ripon, Ripon, WI 54971	1851	Bernard S. Adams	IP-B	930	100
Riverside City (A), Riverside, CA 92506	1916	Charles A. Kane	Psl-A	13,589	191
Rivier, Nashua, NH 03060	1933	Sister Jeanne Perreault	IR-M	1,750	118
Roanoke, Salem, VA 24153	1842	Norman Fintel	IR-B	1,250	74
Roanoke-Chowan Tech. Inst., Ahoskie, NC 27910	1961	Edward Wilson	Ps-A	1,850	29
Robert Morris (A), Coraopolis, PA 15108	1921	Charles Sewall	IP-A	4,133	88
Robert Morris, Carthage, IL 62321	1965	J.R. McCartan	IP-A	1,370	67
Roberts Wesleyan, Rochester, NY 14624	1966	William C. Crothers	IR-D	617	65
Robeson Tech. Inst., Lumberton, NC 28358	1965	R. Craig Allen	Ps-A	2,011	89
Rochester Comm., Rochester, MN 55901	1915	Charles Hill	Ps-A	3,113	145
Rochester Inst. of Tech., Rochester, NY 14623	1829	M. Richard Rose	IP-M	15,704	1,166
Rochester, Univ. of, Rochester, NY 14627	1850	Robert Sproull	IP-D	8,865	1,028
Rockford, Rockford, IL 61101	1847	Norman L. Stewart	IP-M	1,233	106
Rockhurst, Kansas City, MO 64110	1910	Rev. Robert Weiss	IR-M	4,157	200
Rockingham Comm., Wentworth, NC 27375	1966	Gerald B. James	Psl-A	4,323	140
Rockland Comm. (A), Suffern, NY 10901	1959	Seymour Eskow	Psl-A	7,456	125
Rock Valley, Rockford, IL 61101	1964	Karl Jacobs	Psl-A	11,253	525
Rocky Mountain, Billings, MT 59102	1878	B. Alton	IR-A	439	40
Roger Williams, Bristol, RI 02809	1948	Wm. Rizzini	IP-B	3,750	267
Rogue Comm. (A), Grants Pass, OR 97526	1970	Henry O. Pete	PI-A	3,000	60
Rollins (A), Winter Park, FL 32789	1885	Thaddeus Seymour	IP-M	1,233	96
Roosevelt Univ. (A), Chicago, IL 60605	1945	Rolf A. Weil	IP-M	6,782	248
Rosary, River Forest, IL 60305	1901	Sister Candida Lund	IR-M	1,590	128

Name, address	Year	Governing official, affiliation, and highest degree offered	Students	Teachers
Rose-Hulman Inst. of Tech. (A), (M) Terre Haute, IN 47803	1874	S.F. Hulbert	IP-M	1,170	70
Rosemont, Rosemont, PA 19010	1921	Dorothy Brown	IR-B	603	82
Rush Univ., Chicago, IL 60612	1972	James A. Campbell	IP-D	1,152	1,885
Russell Sage (A), Troy, NY 12180	1916	Willam Kahl	IP-M	2,400	165
Rust, Holly Spgs., MS 38635	1866	W.A. McMillan	IP-B	647	40
Rutgers Univ.*, New Brunswick, NJ 08903	1766	Edward J. Bloustein	Ps-D	48,444	2,781
Rutledge Coll., Spartanburg, SC 29303	NA	Eugene Spiess	IP-A	300	15
Rutledge Coll., Winston-Salem, NC 27101	1962	John R. Middleton	IP-A	310	25
Rutledge Coll., Charlotte, NC 28202	1977	Carl Settle	IP-A	314	16
Sacramento City (A), Sacramento, CA 95822	1916	Douglas Burris	PI-A	13,080	450
Sacred Heart, Univ. of the, Santurce, PR 00914	1935	Pedro Gonzalez-Ramos	IR-B	6,238	302
Sacred Heart Univ., Bridgeport, CT 06606	1963	Thomas Melady	IP-M	4,081	279
Saddleback Comm., Mission Viejo, CA 92674	1967	R.A. Lombardi	PI-A	30,160	731
Saginaw Valley State, Univ. Center, MI 48710	1963	Jack Ryder	Ps-M	4,331	110
St. Ambrose, Davenport, LA 52803	1882	William Bakrow	IP-M	1,993	150
St. Andrews Presbyterian, Laurinburg, NC 28352	1061	A.P. Perkinson Jr.	IR-A	754	56
St. Anselm's, Manchester, NH 03102	1889	Rev. Joseph Gerry	IR-B	1,936	142
St. Augustine's, Raleigh, NC 27610	1867	Prezell R. Robinson	IP-B	1,761	82
St. Benedict, Coll. of (W), St. Joseph, MN 56374	1913	Sr. Emanuel Renner	IR-B	2,177	132
St. Bonaventure Univ., St. Bonaventure, NY 14778	1854	V. Rev. Mathias Doyle	IP-M	2,388	149
St. Catherine, Coll. of (W), St. Paul, MN 55105	1905	Catherine McNamee	IR-B	2,200	216
St. Clair County Comm., Pt. Huron, MI 48060	1923	Richard Norris	PsI-A	3,549	200
St. Cloud State Univ. (A), St. Cloud, MN 56301	1869	Charles J. Graham	Ps-M	11,591	600
St. Edward's Univ., Austin, TX 78704	1885	Stephen Walsh	IR-M	2,355	133
St. Elizabeth, Coll. of (W), Convent Station, NJ 07961	1899	Sister Jacqueline Burns	IR-B	851	92
St. Francis, Fort Wayne, IN 46808	1890	Sister M. Jo Ellen Scheetz	IR-M	1,279	83
St. Francis, Brooklyn, NY 11201	1884	Bro. Donald Sullivan	IR-B	2,882	145
St. Francis, Loretto, PA 15940	1847	Rev. Christian Oravec	IR-M	1,519	89
St. Francis, Coll. of, Joliet, IL 60435	1930	John Orr	IR-M	3,251	184
St. Gregory's (A), Shawnee, OK 74801	1875	Rev. Michael Roethier	IP-A	313	12
St. John Fisher, Rochester, NY 14618	1948	Rev. Patrick Braden	IP-M	2,335	150
St. John's, Annapolis, MD 21404	1784	Edwin J. Delattre	IP-B	375	46
St. John's (A), Winfield, KS 67156	1893	Gordon Beckler	IR-A	249	21
St. John's River Comm., Palatka, FL 32077	1958	Robert L. McLendon Jr.	PsI-A	1,500	88
St. John's Univ., Collegeville, MN 56321	1857	Rev. Michael Blecker	IR-M	2,063	160
St. John's Univ., Jamaica, NY 11439	1870	V. Rev. Joseph T. Cahill	IR-D	17,945	828
St. Joseph, West Hartford, CT 06117	1932	Sr. Mary O'Connor	IR-1P	1,334	101
St. Joseph's, Rensselaer, IN 47978	1889	Rev. Charles Banet	IP-M	1,004	73
St. Joseph's, Brooklyn, NY 11205	1916	Sr. G.A. O'Connor	IP-B	2,324	210
St. Joseph's, North Windham, ME 04062	1912	Anthony Santoro	IP-A	500	55
St. Joseph's, Philadelphia, PA 19131	1851	Rev. Donald MacLean	IR-M	5,250	314
St. Lawrence Univ., Canton, NY 13617	1856	Vacant	IP-M	2,250	150
St. Leo, St. Leo, FL 33574	1965	Thomas Southard	IP-B	1,000	55
St. Louis Coll. of Pharmacy, St. Louis, MO 63110	1864	Charles C. Rabe	IP-B	684	42
St. Louis Community, St. Louis, MO 63110	1962	Richard Greenfield, Chan.	PI-A	27,110	1,384
at Florissant Valley, St. Louis, MO 63135	1962	David Harris	Ps-A	11,210	500
at Forest Park, St. Louis, MO 63110	1962	Vernon Crawley	PI-A	7,383	332
at Meramec (A), St. Louis, MO 63122	1962	Glynn Clark	PI-A	9,040	433
St. Louis Univ., St. Louis, MO 63103	1818	Rev. Thomas J. Fitzgerald	IP-D	10,088	2,533
Parks, Cahokia, IL 62206	1927	Leon Z. Seltzer	IP-B	1,044	59
St. Martin's (A), Lacey, WA 98503	1895	Fr. John C. Scott	IR-B	655	32
St. Mary, Coll. of, Omaha, NE 68124	1923	John Richert	IR-B	751	95
St. Mary (W), Leavenworth, KS 66048	1923	Sr. Mary J. McGilley	IR-B	850	82
St. Mary of the Plains Coll. (A), Dodge City, KS 67801	1952	Michael McCarthy	IR-B	661	48
St. Mary-of-the-Woods (W), St. Mary-of-the-Woods, IN 47876	1840	Sister Jeanne Knoerle	IR-B	858	80
St. Mary's (W), Notre Dame, IN 46556	1844	John Duggan	IR-B	1,764	201
St. Mary's (W) (A), Raleigh, NC 27611	1842	John T. Rice	IR-A	510	32
St. Mary's (A), Winona, MN 55987	1912	Peter Clifford	IR-M	1,354	71
St. Mary's Jr. (A), Minneapolis, MN 55454	1964	Sr. Anne Joachim Moore	IR-A	770	100
St. Mary's, Moraga, CA 94575	1863	Bro. Mel Anderson	IR-M	2,417	244
St. Mary's Coll. of Maryland, St. Mary's City, MD 20686	1839	J. Renwick Jackson Jr.	Ps-B	1,349	102
St. Mary's Dominican (W), New Orleans, LA 70118	1910	Sr. Mary Gerald Shea	IR-B	800	91
St. Mary's Univ. (A), San Antonio, TX 78284	1852	Rev. James Young	IR-M	3,072	150
St. Michael's, Winooski, VT 05404	1904	Edward L. Henry	IR-M	2,119	120
St. Norbert, DePere, WI 54115	1898	Neil Webb	IR-B	1,686	90
St. Olaf, Northfield, MN 55057	1874	Harlan Foss	IR-B	3,148	250
St. Paul Bible, Bible College, MN 55375	1916	L.J. Eagen	IR-B	661	35
St. Paul's, Lawrenceville, VA 23868	1888	S. Dallas Simmons	IP-A	693	47
St. Peter's, Jersey City, NJ 07306	1872	Rev. Edward Glynn	IR-M	4,090	357
St. Petersburg Junior, St. Petersburg, FL 33733	1927	Carl M. Kuttler, Jr.	PI-A	15,430	660
St. Rose, Coll. of, Albany, NY 12203	1920	Thomas Manion	IP-M	2,916	182
St. Scholastica, Coll. of, Duluth, MN 55811	1912	Bruce Stender	IR-M	1,115	125
St. Teresa, Coll. of (W), Winona, MN 55987	1907	Thomas Hamilton	IR-B	650	65
St. Thomas Aquinas, Sparkill, NY 10976	1952	Donald McNeils	IP-B	1,500	75
St. Thomas, Coll. of, St. Paul, MN 55105	1885	Msgr. Terrence Murphy	IP-S	4,681	295
St. Thomas, Univ. of, Houston, TX 77006	1947	Rev. William J. Young	IR-M	1,834	126
St. Vincent (M), Latrobe, PA 15650	1846	Rev. Leopold Krul	IR-B	820	80
St. Xavier (M), Chicago, IL 60655	1846	Sr. M. Chekouras.	IR-M	2,100	107
Salem (W) (A), Winston-Salem, NC 27108	1772	Richard Morrill	IR-B	528	60
Salem, Salem, WV 26426	1888	James C. Stam	IP-A	1,150	94
Salem Community (A), Penns Grove, NJ 08069	1972	William Bryan	PI-A	1,172	35
Salem State (A), Salem, MA 01970	1854	James T. Amsler	Ps-B	8,821	443
Salisbury State, Salisbury, MD 21801	1925	Thomas Bellavance	Ps-M	3,971	153
Sam Houston State Univ., Huntsville, TX 77341	1879	E.T. Bowers	Ps-S	9,532	464
Samford Univ. (A), Birmingham, AL 35209	1841	Leslie S. Wright	IR-M	3,674	218
Sampson Tech. Inst., Clinton, NC 28328	1965	C.W. Paderick	PsI-A	4,244	180
San Antonio, San Antonio, TX 78284	1925	Bob Barringer, Act.	PsI-A	21,038	978
San Bernardino Valley, San Bernardino, CA 92410	1926	Raymond F. Ellerman, Chan.	PsI-A	15,000	605
San Diego, Mesa, San Diego, CA 92111	1963	Allen Brooks	PsI-A	23,400	930
San Diego, Univ. of (A), San Diego, CA 92110	1949	Author E. Hughes	IR-D	3,750	175
San Diego City, San Diego, CA 92101	1914	Allen Repashy	PsI-A	4,436	1,212
San Diego State Univ., San Diego, CA 92182	1897	Thomas Day	Ps-D	33,151	2,650
San Francisco, City Coll. of, San Francisco, CA 94112	1935	K.S. Washington	PsI-A	25,386	1,000
San Francisco Art Inst. (A), San Francisco, CA 94133	1874	Stephen Goldstine	IP-M	480	30
San Francisco, Univ. of, San Francisco, CA 94117	1855	Rev. J. LoSchiavo	IR-D	6,120	451
Sangamon State Univ., Springfield, IL 62708	1970	Alex B. Lacy	Ps-M	3,683	210
San Jacinto (A), Pasadena, TX 77505	1961	Thomas M. Spencer	Ps-A	12,000	300

Name, address	Year	Governing official, affiliation, and highest degree offered	Students	Teachers
San Joaquin Delta Comm. (A), Stockton, CA 95207	1935	Dale Parnell	Psl-A	20,710	549
San Jose City, San Jose, CA 95128	1921	Richard Goff	Pl-A	12,400	1,150
San Jose State Univ., San Jose, CA 95192	1857	Gail P. Fullerton	Pl-M	31,000	2,100
San Luis Obispo Co. Comm. (A), San Luis Obispo, CA 93406	1965	Merlin Eisenbise	Pl-A	5,504	200
San Mateo, Coll. of (A), San Mateo, CA 94402	1923	Lois A. Callahan	Psl-A	14,616	666
Sandhills Comm., Carthage, NC 28327	1963	Raymond A. Stone	Psl-A	1,700	130
Santa Ana, Santa Ana, CA 92706	1915	William Wenrich	Ps-A	20,232	600
Santa Barbara City (A), Santa Barbara, CA 93109	1908	Glenn Gooder	Psl-A	8,613	243
Santa Clara, Univ. of, Santa Clara, CA 95053	1851	William Rewak	IR-D	7,025	320
Santa Fe, Coll. of, Santa Fe, NM 87501	1947	Bro. Cyprian Luke	IR-B	1,117	75
Santa Fe Community (A), Gainesville, FL 32602	1965	Alan Robertson	Ps-A	6,056	326
Santa Monica, Santa Monica, CA 90405	1929	Richard Moore	Ps-A	22,034	653
Santa Rosa Junior (A), Santa Rosa, CA 95401	1928	Roy Mikalson	Pl-A	18,788	188
Sarah Lawrence, Bronxville, NY 10708	1926	Charles DeCarlo	IP-M	1,060	120
Sauk Valley, Dixon, IL 61021	1965	Dr. Garner	Psl-A	4,600	225
Savannah State, Savannah, GA 31404	1891	Wendell G. Rayburn	Ps-M	1,987	166
Schenectady Co. Comm. (A), Schenectady, NY 12305	1968	Karl Zopf	Ps-A	2,120	69
Schoolcraft, Livonia, MI 48152	1962	Vacant	Psl-A	8,077	331
Schreiner, Kerrville, TX 78028	1923	Sam Junkin	IR-A	500	31
Scott Community, Bettendorf, IA 52722	1966	Joseph Conte	Psl-A	2,000	100
Scottsdale Comm., Scottsdale, AZ 85253	1969	Arthur W. DeCabooter	Psl-A	6,787	294
Scranton, Univ. of, Scranton, PA 18510	1888	Rev. William Byron	IP-M	4,216	203
Scripps (W), Claremont, CA 91711	1926	John Chandler	IP-B	575	79
S.D. Bishop State Jr. (A), Mobile, AL 36603	1965	Sanford Bishop	Ps-A	1,650	75
Seattle Central Comm., Seattle, WA 98122	1966	Donald Phelps	Ps-A	9,167	452
Seattle Pacific Univ., Seattle, WA 98119	1891	David L. McKenna	IR-M	2,532	199
Seattle Univ., Seattle, WA 98122	1891	Rev. William Sullivan	IR-D	4,343	175
Selma Univ., Selma, AL 36701	1878	M.C. Cleveland Jr.	IR-B	500	32
Seminole Comm., Sanford, FL 32771	1965	E.S. Weldon	Psl-A	4,673	393
Sequoias, Coll. of the (A), Visalia, CA 93277	1925	Ivan Crookshanks	Pl-A	6,592	331
Seton Hall Univ., S. Orange, NJ 07079	1856	E.R. D'Alessio	IR-D	9,557	647
Seton Hill (W), Greensburg, PA 15601	1883	Eileen Farrell	IR-A	968	81
Seward County Comm. (A), Liberal, KS 67901	1967	James Hooper	Psl-A	1,402	32
Shasta, Redding, CA 96099	1949	Dale Miller	Ps-A	13,260	415
Shaw Coll. at Detroit (A), Detroit, MI 48202	1936	Romaulus Murphy	IP-B	895	41
Shaw Univ. (A), Raleigh, NC 27611	1865	Stanley Smith	IP-B	1,389	57
Shelby State Comm., Memphis, TN 38104	1970	Jess Parrish	Ps-A	5,585	300
Sheldon Jackson, Sitka, AK 99835	1878	Hugh H. Holloway	IR-B	200	22
Shenandoah Coll. of Music, Winchester, VA 22601	1875	Robert P. Parker	PR-M	900	120
Shepherd, Shepherdstown, WV 25443	1871	James Butcher	Ps-A	3,001	125
Sheridan, Sheridan, WY 82801	1948	Gordon Ward	Pl-A	3,001	123
Shippensburg State, Shippensburg, PA 17257	1871	H.E. Shaar, Act.	Pf-M	5,959	266
Shoreline Comm., Seattle, WA 98133	1964	Ronald Bell	Ps-A	8,177	360
Shorter, Rome, GA 30161	1873	Randall H. Minor	IR-B	809	64
Siena, Loudonville, NY 12211	1937	Rev. Hugh F. Hines	IP-B	2,961	180
Siena Heights, Adrian, MI 49221	1919	Louis Vaccaro	IP-M	1,800	120
Sierra, Rocklin, CA 95677	1914	G.C. Angove	Psl-A	9,544	421
Simmons (W) (A), Boston, MA 02115	1899	William J. Holmes	IP-D	1,800	250
Simpson, Indianola, IA 50125	1860	Robert McBride	IR-B	854	69
Simpson, San Francisco, CA 94134	1921	Mark W. Lee	IR-M	275	28
Sinclair Comm., Dayton, OH 45402	1887	David Ponitz	Psl-A	17,090	840
Sinte Gleska, Rosebud, SD 57570	1971	Lionel Bordeaux	Psl-B	380	50
Sioux Falls, Sioux Falls, SD 57101	1883	Owen Halleen	IR-M	849	60
Siskiyous, Coll. of the, Weed, CA 96094	1957	Ivan Crookshanks	Psl-A	7,556	310
Skagit Valley, Mt. Vernon, WA 98273	1926	James Ford	Ps-A	7,600	368
Skidmore, Saratoga Spgs., NY 12866	1911	Joseph C. Palamountian Jr.	IP-B	2,164	180
Skyline, San Bruno, CA 94066	1969	James C. Wyatt	Pl-A	7,256	321
Slippery Rock State, Slippery Rock, PA 16057	1889	Herb Reinhard Jr.	Ps-M	5,690	335
Smith (W) (A), Northampton, MA 01060	1875	Jill Kerr Conway	IP-D	2,518	240
Snead State Jr., Boaz, AL 35957	1935	William H. Osborn	Ps-A	1,032	50
Snow, Ephraim, UT 84627	1888	J.M. Higbee	Pf-A	1,283	69
Solano Comm., Suisun City, CA 94585	1945	William Wilson	Psl-A	10,700	352
Somerset Comm., Somerset, KY 42501	1965	Roscoe Kelley	Psl-A	1,059	76
Somerset County, Somerville, NJ 08876	1968	Charles Irace	Ps-A	4,500	198
Sonoma State Univ., Rohnert Park, CA 94928	1961	Peter Diamandopoulos	Pl-M	5,600	550
South, Univ. of the (A), Sewanee, TN 37375	1857	Robert Ayres Jr.	IR-1P	1,278	136
South Alabama, Univ. of, Mobile, AL 36688	1963	Frederick Whiddon	Ps-1P	8,005	349
South Carolina St.*, Orangeburg, SC 29115	1896	M.M. Nance Jr.	Ps-M	4,010	218
South Carolina, Univ. of*, Columbia, SC 29208	1801	James B. Holderman	Ps-D	36,058	1,931
S.D. Sch. of Mines & Tech., Rapid City, SD 57701	1885	Richard Schleusener	Ps-D	2,393	114
South Dakota State Univ.*, Brookings, SD 57007	1881	Sherwood Berg	Ps-D	6,843	700
South Dakota, Univ. of (A), Vermillion, SD 57069	1862	Charles D. Lein	Ps-D	5,936	522
Southeast Comm., Fairbury, NE 68352	1941	Daniel Gerber	Psl-A	475	24
Southeast Comm. (A), Cumberland, KY 40823	1960	Larry Stanley	Ps-A	600	21
South Florida, Univ. of, Tampa, FL 33620	1956	John Lott Brown	Ps-D	25,054	1,265
South Florida Jr. (A), Avon Park, FL 33825	1965	William Stallard	Ps-A	938	28
South Georgia, Douglas, GA 31533	1906	Denton Coker	Ps-A	1,152	59
South Oklahoma City, Oklahoma City, OK 73159	1970	Dale L. Gibson	Ps-A	7,934	263
South Plains, Levelland, TX 79336	1957	Marvin L. Baker	Ps-A	2,793	150
South Texas Coll. of Law, Houston, TX 77002	1923	G.R. Walker	IP-1P	1,198	44
Southeast Missouri St. Univ., Cape Girardeau, MO 63701	1873	Bill Stacy	Ps-M	9,061	422
Southeastern (A), Lakeland, FL 33801	1935	Cyril Homer	IR-B	1,208	41
Southeastern Comm. (A), Burlington, IA 52655	1966	C.A. Callison, Supt.	Ps-A	2,068	92
Southeastern Comm., Keokuk, IA 52632	1950	C.A. Callison	Ps-A	394	25
Southeastern Comm., Whiteville, NC 28472	1965	W.R. McCarter	Ps-A	1,803	147
Southeastern Illinois (A), Harrisburg, IL 62946	1960	Harry Abell	Ps-A	2,400	65
Southeastern Louisiana Univ., Hammond, LA 70402	1925	J. Larry Crain	Ps-S	7,707	351
Southeastern Mass. Univ., N. Dartmouth, MA 02747	1895	Donald E. Walker	Ps-M	5,691	342
Southeastern Okla. St. Univ., Durant, OK 74701	1909	Leon Hibbs	Ps-M	4,510	193
Southeastern Univ., Washington, DC 20024	1879	Harry Miller	IP-M	1,800	160
Southern Arkansas Univ., Magnolia, AR 71753	1909	Harold Brinson	Ps-M	1,987	100
Southern Baptist (A), Walnut Ridge, AR 72476	1941	D.J. Nicholas	Psl-A	550	25
Southern California (A), Costa Mesa, CA 92626	1920	Wayne Kraiss	IR-B	660	30
Southern Cal., Univ. of, Los Angeles, CA 90007	1880	James Zumberge	IP-D	28,129	3,684
Southern Coll. of Optometry, Memphis, TN 38104	1932	Spurgeon B. Eure	IP-1P	586	50
Southern Colorado, Univ. of (A), Pueblo, CO 81001	1933	Richard Pesqueira	Ps-B	6,000	285
Southern Conn. State (A), New Haven, CT 06515	1893	Manson Van B. Jennings	Ps-M	11,720	396
Southern Idaho, Coll. of, Twin Falls, ID 83301	1965	James L. Taylor	Psl-A	3,700	109
Southern Illinois Univ., Edwardsville, IL 62026	1965	Earl Lazerson	Ps-D	9,832	650

Name, address	Year	Governing official, affiliation, and highest degree offered		Students	Teachers
Southern Illinois Univ., Carbondale, IL 62901	1869	Kenneth Shaw	Ps-D	22,700	3,000
Southern Maine, Univ. of, Gorham, ME 04038	1878	Robert L. Woodbury	Ps-M	8,203	502
Southern Methodist Univ., Dallas, TX 75275	1911	L. Donald Shields	IR-D	9,112	589
Southern Missionary, Collegedale, TN 37315	1892	Frank Knittel	IR-B	2,100	125
Southern Miss., Univ. of, Hattiesburg, MS 39401	1910	Aubrey Lucas	Pf-S	10,210	650
Southern Ohio (A), Cincinnati, OH 45202	1927	H.W. Nagel	IP-A	1,600	60
Southern Oregon State, Ashland, OR 97520	1926	Natale Sicuro	Ps-M	4,705	250
Southern Seminary Jr. (A), Buena Vista, VA 24416	1867	Bill J. Elkins	IR-A	705	20
Southern Tech. Inst., Marietta, GA 30060	1948	Stephen Cheshier	Ps-A	2,500	120
Southern Univ., Baton Rouge, LA 70813	1880	Jesse Stone Jr.	Psl-M	8,404	403
Southern Union State Jr. (A), Wadley, AL 36276	1922	Ray Jones	Ps-A	1,413	31
Southern Utah State, Cedar City, UT 84720	1897	Orville D. Carnahan	Ps-B	1,843	119
Southern Vermont, Bennington, VT 05201	1926	Thomas Gee	Ps-B	660	35
Southwest Baptist Univ., Bolivar, MO 65613	1878	James L. Sells	IR-B	1,470	101
Southwestern, Chula Vista, CA 92010	1961	C.S. DeVore	Psl-1P	12,941	538
Southwestern, Winfield, KS 67156	1885	Robert P. Sessions	IR-B	562	68
Southwestern Adventist, Keene, TX 76059	1894	Donald McAdams	IR-B	668	47
Southwestern Comm., Creston, IA 50801	1966	John A. Smith	Ps-A	569	55
Southwestern La., Univ. of, Lafayette, LA 70504	1898	Ray Authement	PS-B	13,865	601
Southwestern at Memphis, Memphis, TN 38112	1848	James Daughdrill Jr.	PI-B	1,040	105
Southwestern Michigan, Dowagiac, MI 49047	1964	David Briegel	Psl-A	2,655	145
Southwestern Okla. St. Univ., Weatherford, OK 73096	1901	Leonard Campbell	Ps-M	4,800	245
Southwestern Oregon Comm., Coos Bay, OR 97420	1961	Jack E. Brookins	Psl-A	5,000	250
Southwestern Univ., Georgetown, TX 78626	1840	Roy B. Shilling Jr.	IR-B	1,026	81
Southwest Mississippi Jr., Summit, MS 39666	1918	Horace Holmes	Psl-A	1,135	56
Southwest Mo. St. Univ., Springfield, MO 65802	1905	Duane Meyer	Ps-S	15,137	666
Southwest St. Univ., Marshall, MN 56208	1963	Jon Wefald	Ps-B	2,131	107
Southwest Texas Junior, Uvalde, TX 78801	1946	Wayne Matthews	Psl-A	2,234	141
Southwest Texas St. Univ. (A), San Marcos, TX 78666	1903	Lee Smith	Ps-B	15,924	564
Southwest Virginia Comm., Richlands, VA 24641	1968	Charles King	Ps-A	3,500	200
Spalding, Louisville, KY 40203	1814	Sister Eileen Egan	IR-S	1,048	95
Spartanburg Methodist (A), Spartanburg, SC 29301	1911	George D. Fields, Jr.	PI-A	1,035	40
Spartanburg Tech. (A), Spartanburg, SC 29303	1963	Joe D. Gault	Ps-A	3,097	217
Spelman (W), Atlanta, GA 30314	1881	Donald Stewart	IP-B	1,367	117
Spokane Comm., Spokane, WA 99207	1963	Raymond F. LaGrandeur	Ps-A	5,132	206
Spokane Falls Comm., Spokane, WA 99204	1970	Gerald Saling	Ps-A	5,574	253
Spoon River (A), Canton, IL 61520	1959	Paul C. Gianini, Jr.	PI-A	2,200	40
Spring Arbor, Spring Arbor, MI 49283	1873	Kenneth Coffman	IR-B	1,050	90
Spring Garden, Philadelphia, PA 19118	1851	Daniel DeLucca	IP-B	1,188	88
Spring Hill, Mobile, AL 36608	1830	Rev. Paul S. Tipton	IR-B	1,018	80
Springfield (A), Springfield, MA 01109	1885	Wilbert Locklin	IP-D	2,365	131
Springfield Tech. Comm., Springfield, MA 01105	1967	Robert Geitz	Ps-A	3,865	207
Springfield Coll. in Illinois, Springfield, IL 62702	1929	Sr. Francis M. Thrailkill	IR-A	438	39
Stanford Univ., Stanford, CA 94305	1885	Donald Kennedy	Psl-D	12,866	1,692
State Fair Comm., Sedalia, MO 65301	1966	Fred E. Davis	Ps-A	1,631	93
State Tech. Inst., Memphis, TN 38134	1967	Charles Whitehead	Ps-A	5,046	552
Stephen F. Austin State Univ. (A), Nacogdoches, TX 75962	1923	William Johnson	Ps-B	9,472	415
Stephens (W) (A), Columbia, MO 65243	1833	Arland Christ-Janer	IR-B	1,450	118
Sterling, Sterling, KS 67579	1887	Charles Schoenherr	IR-B	469	57
Stetson Univ. (A), De Land, FL 32720	1883	Pope A. Duncan	IR-M	2,839	100
Steubenville, Coll. of, Steubenville, OH 43952	1946	Rev. M. Scanlon	IP-B	1,230	68
Stevens Inst. of Tech., Hoboken, NJ 07030	1870	Kenneth C. Rogers	IP-D	2,830	210
Stillman, Tuscaloosa, AL 35403	1876	B.B. Hardy, Act.	IR-B	565	35
Stockton State (A), Pomona, NJ 08240	1966	Peter Mitchell	Ps-B	4,600	163
Stonehill, N. Easton, MA 02356	1948	Rev. Bartley MacPhaidin	IR-B	2,700	200
Strayer (A), Washington, DC 20005	1904	Murray Donoho III	IP-B	1,800	50
Sue Bennett, London, KY 40741	1897	Earl F. Hays	IP-A	273	34
Suffolk County Comm. (A), Selden, NY 11784	1960	Albert M. Ammerman	Ps-A	21,000	600
Suffolk Univ. (A), Boston, MA 02114	1906	Thomas Fulham	IP-1P	4,607	257
Sullivan County Comm., Loch Sheldrake, NY 12759	1962	Richard F. Grego	Ps-A	1,740	71
Sul Ross State Univ., Alpine, TX 79830	1920	C.R. Richardson	Pf-M	2,143	94
Sumter Area Tech., Sumter, SC 29150	1963	James Hudgins	Ps-A	3,306	69
Suomi, Hancock, MI 49930	1896	Ralph J. Jalkanen	IR-A	494	40
Surry Community, Dobson, NC 27017	1964	Swanson Richards	Psl-A	2,551	62
Susquehanna Univ., Selinsgrove, PA 17870	1858	Jonathan Messerli	IR-A	1,839	125
Swarthmore, Swarthmore, PA 19081	1864	Theodore Friend	IP-B	1,316	150
Sweet Briar, Sweet Briar, VA 24595	1901	Harold B. Whiteman Jr.	IP-B	682	84
Syracuse Univ., Syracuse, NY 13210	1870	M.A. Eggers	IP-D	20,719	899
Tabor, Hillsboro, KS 67063	1908	Vernon Janzen	IR-B	478	45
Tacoma Comm. (A), Tacoma, WA 98465	1965	Larry P. Stevens	Ps-A	7,114	84
Taft, Taft, CA 93268	1922	David Cothrun	IP-A	1,211	74
Talladega (A), Talladega, AL 35160	1867	Joseph Gayles	IP-B	698	46
Tallahassee Comm. (A), Tallahassee, FL 32304	1965	Marm Harris	PI-A	3,303	126
Tampa, Tampa, FL 33609	1890	Donald C. Jones	IP-B	1,834	72
Tampa, Univ. of, Tampa, FL 33606	1931	Richard Cheshire	IP-M	2,068	146
Tarkio (A), Tarkio, MO 64491	1883	Frank Bretz	IR-B	610	62
Tarleton State Univ., Stephenville, TX 76402	1899	W.O. Trogdon	Ps-M	3,592	160
Tarrant County Junior, Ft. Worth, TX 76102	1965	Joe B. Rushing	Pf-A	20,798	757
Taylor Univ., Upland, IN 46989	1846	Gregg Lehman	IR-B	1,489	100
Technical Career Inst., New York, NY 10001	1909	Samuel Steinman	IP-A	2,000	100
Tech. Inst. of Alamance, Burlington, NC 27215	1959	William Taylor.	Ps-A	11,672	449
Temple Junior, Temple, TX 76501	1929	Marvin Felder	Psl-A	2,447	112
Temple Univ., Philadelphia, PA 19122	1884	Marvin Wachman	Psr-D	33,153	3,000
Tennessee State Univ.* (A), Nashville, TN 37203	1912	F. Humphries	Ps-M	5,545	270
Tennessee System, Univ., of*, Knoxville, TN 37916	1794	Edward Boling	Psl-D	45,402	3,392
Ctr. for Health Sci.*, Memphis, TN 38103	1911	T. Farmer, Chan.	Ps-D	2,187	1,170
at Chattanooga*, Chattanooga, TN 37401	1886	Charles Temple	Ps-M	7,596	313
at Knoxville*, Knoxville, TN 37916	1794	Jack Reese	Ps-D	30,282	1,683
at Martin*, Martin, TN 38238	1927	Charles Smith	Ps-M	5,375	238
at Nashville* (A), Nashville, TN 37203	1947	Vacant.	Ps-M	5,419	120
Tennessee Tech. Univ., Cookeville, TN 38501	1915	Arliss Roaden	Ps-D	7,306	504
Tennessee Temple, Chattanooga, TN 37404	1946	Lee Roberson.	IR-M	3,949	143
Tennessee Wesleyan, Athens, TN 37303	1857	George Naff Jr.	IR-B	533	46
Texarkana Comm., Texarkana, TX 75501	1927	Carl M. Nelson	Psl-A	3,028	197
Texas (A), Tyler, TX 75701	1894	Allen C. Hancock	IR-B	592	37
Texas A & I Univ., Kingsville, TX 78363	1925	Duane Leach	Ps-D	5,138	274
Texas A & M Univ.*, College Station, TX 77843	1876	Charles Samson, Act.	Ps-D	33,499	2,764
Texas Christian Univ., Fort Worth, TX 76129	1873	William Tucker	IR-D	6,283	422

Name, address	Year	Governing official, affiliation, and highest degree offered	Students	Teachers
Texas Eastern Univ. (A), Tyler, TX 75701	1971	James Stewart Jr.	Ps-M	1,938	78
Texas Lutheran, Seguin, TX 78155	1891	Charles Oestreich	IP-B	1,703	94
Texas Southern Univ. (A), Houston, TX 77004	1947	Granville Sawyer	Ps-D	9,147	453
Texas Southmost, Brownsville, TX 78520	1926	Albert A. Besteiro	Pl-A	4,141	182
Texas System, Univ. of, Austin, TX 78701	1881	E. Don Walker			
at Arlington (A), Arlington, TX 76019	1895	Wendell Nedderman	Ps-D	19,135	829
at Austin, Austin, TX 78712	1883	Peter Flawn	Ps-D	46,183	3,000
at Dallas, Richardson, TX 75080	1969	Bryce Jordan	Ps-D	6,082	275
at El Paso, El Paso, TX 79968	1904	Haskell Monroe	Ps-D	15,750	653
Health Science Center, Dallas, TX 75235	1943	Charles Sprague	Ps-D	1,321	897
at Houston, Houston, TX 77025	1967	Roger J. Bulger	Ps-D	575	90
at San Antonio, San Antonio, TX 78284	1959	Frank Harrison	Ps-S	2,212	505
Medical Branch, Galveston, TX 77550	1881	William Levin	Pf-1P	1,586	660
at Permian Basin, Odessa, TX 79762	1973	V.R. Cardozier	Ps-B	1,602	106
at San Antonio, San Antonio, TX 78285	1969	James Wagener	Ps-M	9,378	416
at Tyler, Tyler, TX 75701	1971	James Stewart	Ps-M	1,921	76
Texas Tech. Univ. (A), Lubbock, TX 79409	1925	Lauro Cavazos	Ps-D	21,155	1,463
Texas Wesleyan (A), Fort Worth, TX 76105	1891	Jon Fleming	IR-B	1,667	112
Texas Woman's Univ. (W), Denton, TX 76204	1901	Mary B. Huey	Ps-D	7,956	485
Thames Valley State Tech., Norwich, CT 06360	1963	Donald Welter	Ps-A	1,823	100
Thiel, Greenville, PA 16125	1866	Louis Almen	IR-B	936	83
Thomas, Waterville, ME 04901	1894	Paul G. Jenson	IP-M	1,046	53
Thomas A. Edison State, Trenton, NJ 08608	1972	Larraine Matusak	Ps-B	4,500	NA
Thomas Jefferson Univ., Philadelphia, PA 19107	1824	Lewis Bluemle	IP-D	1,469	1,912
Thomas More (A), Ft. Mitchell, KY 41017	1921	Robert J. Giroux	IR-B	1,350	85
Thomas Nelson Comm., Hampton, VA 23670	1967	Thomas Kubala	Ps-A	6,379	283
Thornton Comm., So. Holland, IL 60473	1927	Nathan A. Ivey	Pl-A	11,200	325
Three Rivers Comm. (A), Poplar Bluff, MO 63901	1966	J.L. Bottenfield	Ps-A	1,520	54
Tidewater Comm., Portsmouth, VA 23703	1968	George Pass	Ps-A	14,968	750
Tiffin Univ., Tiffin, OH 44883	1918	George Kidd Jr.	IP-B	485	33
Tift, Forsyth, GA 31029	1847	Robert W. Jackson	IR-B	NA	65
Toccoa Falls, Toccoa Falls, GA 30598	1907	Paul L. Alford	IP-B	619	47
Toledo, Univ. of, Toledo, OH 43606	1872	Glen R. Driscoll	Ps-D	20,270	1,228
Tomkins-Courtland Comm. (A), Groton, NY 13053	1967	Hushang Bahar	Ps-A	2,793	48
Tougaloo, Tougaloo, MS 39174	1869	George A. Owens	IR-B	886	76
Towson State Univ., Baltimore, MD 21204	1866	Hoke Smith	Ps-M	15,528	957
Transylvania Univ., Lexington, KY 40508	1780	William Kelly	IR-B	825	68
Treasure Valley Comm., Ontario, OR 97914	1962	Emery Skinner	Psl-A	2,000	110
Trenton State, Trenton, NJ 08625	1855	Harold Eickhoff	Pf-M	7,287	380
Trevecca Nazarene, Nashville, TN 37210	1901	Homer Adams	IR-B	920	70
Tri-County Tech., Pendleton, SC 29670	1961	Don Garrison	Ps-A	2,356	143
Trident Tech (A), Charleston, SC 29405	1964	Charles F. Ward	Ps-A	5,400	170
Trinidad State Junior (A), Trinidad, CO 81082	1925	Thomas Sullivan	Ps-A	1,200	121
Trinity (A), Hartford, CT 06106	1823	Theodore Lockwood	IP-M	1,885	135
Trinity (A), Deerfield, IL 60015	1897	Harry Evans	IP-B	805	38
Trinity, Burlington, VT 05401	1925	Janice Ryan	IR-B	783	72
Trinity, Washington, DC 20017	1897	Sr. Rose Anne Fleming	IR-M	1,000	82
Trinity Univ., San Antonio, TX 78284	1869	Robert Calgaard	IR-M	3,063	299
Tri-State Univ., Angola, IN 46703	1884	Carl Elliott	IP-B	1,263	84
Triton, River Grove, IL 60171	1965	Brent Knight	Psl-A	21,871	988
Trocaire (A), Buffalo, NY 14220	1958	Sr. M. Carmina Coppola	IP-A	911	35
Troy State Univ. System, Troy, AL 36082	1887	Ralph W. Adams	Ps-M	12,805	635
Truett McConnell, Cleveland, GA 30528	1946	Ronald Weitman	IR-A	650	58
Tufts Univ. (A), Medford, MA 02155	1852	Jean Mayer	IP-D	6,830	505
Tulane Univ., New Orleans, LA 70118	1834	Eamon Kelly	IP-D	10,040	920
Tulsa, Univ. of (A), Tulsa, OK 74104	1894	J. Paschal Twyman	IP-D	6,000	300
Tulsa Junior (A), Tulsa, OK 74119	1969	A.M. Philips	Ps-A	10,505	146
Tunxis Comm., Farmington, CT 06032	1971	Benjamin G. Davis	Ps-A	2,433	135
Tusculum, Greenville, TN 37743	1794	Earl R. Mezoff	IP-S	353	36
Tuskegee Institute, Tuskegee Inst., AL 36088	1881	Luther H. Foster	IP-S	3,721	325
Tyler Junior, Tyler, TX 75711	1926	Raymond Hawkins	Psl-A	6,794	333
Ulster County Comm. (A), Stone Ridge, NY 12484	1961	Robert T. Brown	Ps-A	2,681	87
Umpqua Comm. (A), Roseburg, OR 97470	1964	I.S. Hakanson	Ps-A	1,730	60
Union, Barbourville, KY 40906	1879	Mahlon A. Miller	IR-M	1,124	57
Union, Cranford, NJ 07016	1933	Saul Orkin	IP-A	6,200	230
Union, Lincoln, NE 68516	1891	Dean L. Hubbard	IR-B	888	84
Union (A), Schenectady, NY 12308	1795	John Morris	IP-B	3,318	140
Union County Voc.-Tech. (A), Scotch Plains, NJ 07076	1960	Myron Corman, Act.	Pl-A	1,760	94
Union Univ., Jackson, TN 38301	1825	Robert E. Craig	IR-B	1,199	80
U.S. Air Force Academy, Col. Springs, CO 80840	1954	Maj. Gen. Robert Kelley, Supt.	Pf-B	4,544	540
U.S. Coast Guard Acad., New London, CT 06320	1876	R. Adm. Charles Larkin, Supt.	Pf-B	866	116
U.S. International Univ. (A), San Diego, CA 92131	1952	William Rust	IP-D	2,893	91
U.S. Merchant Marine Acad., Kings Point, NY 11024	1938	Rear Adm. Thomas King, Supt.	Pf-B	1,150	83
U.S. Military Academy (A), West Point, NY 10996	1802	Lt. Gen. A. Goodpaster	Pf-B	4,067	636
U.S. Naval Academy, Annapolis, MD 21402	1845	V. Adm. William Lawrence, Supt.	Pf-B	4,500	550
Unity, Unity, ME 04988	1966	Louis Wilcox Jr.	IP-B	340	28
Upper Iowa Univ., Fayette, IA 52142	1857	Darcy C. Coyle	IP-B	2,199	44
Upsala, E. Orange, NJ 07019	1893	Rodney Felder	IP-M	1,738	126
Urbana, Urbana, OH 43078	1850	A. Perry Whitmore	IP-B	727	123
Ursinus, Collegeville, PA 19426	1869	Richard Richter	IP-B	1,159	101
Ursuline, Cleveland, OH 44124	1871	Sister M. Kenan Dulzer	IR-M	1,030	88
Utah State Univ.*, Logan, UT 84322	1888	Stanford Cazier	Ps-D	9,939	462
Utah, Univ. of, Salt Lake City, UT 84112	1850	David P. Gardner	Ps-D	22,982	1,433
Utica Junior (A), Utica, MS 39175	1903	J. Louis Stokes	Ps-A	950	61
Valdosta State (A), Valdosta, GA 31601	1906	Hugh C. Bailey	Ps-M	4,862	250
Valencia Comm. (A), Orlando, FL 32802	1967	James F. Gollattscheck	Ps-A	5,101	145
Valley City State, Valley City, ND 58072	1890	Ted De Vries	Ps-B	1,217	70
Valparaiso Univ., Valparaiso, IN 46383	1859	Robert V. Schnabel	IR-M	4,530	340
Vanderbilt Univ., Nashville, TN 37240	1873	Alexander Heard	IP-D	8,874	2,120
Vassar (A), Poughkeepsie, NY 12601	1861	Virginia Smith	IP-M	2,260	189
Ventura (A), Ventura, CA 93003	1925	Richard A. Glenn	Ps-A	12,612	178
Vermillion Comm., Ely, MN 55731	1922	Ralph R. Doty	Ps-A	575	30
Vermont, Comm. Coll. of (A), Montpelier, VT 05602	1970	Myrna R. Miller	Psr-A	2,220	455
Vermont, Univ. of*, Burlington, VT 05405	1791	Lattie Coor	Ps-D	10,988	1,144
Vermont Technical, Randolph Center, VT 05061	1962	James Todd	Ps-A	793	60
Victor Valley (A), Victorville, CA 92392	1961	B.W. Wadsworth	Pl-A	3,024	72
Victoria, Victoria, TX 77901	1925	Roland E. Bing	Pl-A	2,231	114

Name, address	Year	Governing official, affiliation, and highest degree offered		Students	Teachers
Villa Julie, Stevenson, MD 21153	1952	Carolyn Manuszak	Pl-A	808	90
Villa Maria (W)(A), Erie, PA 16505	1925	Sr. M. Lawrence Antoun	IR-B	545	52
Villanova Univ., Villanova, PA 19085	1811	Rev. John M. Driscoll	IP-D	10,341	538
Vincennes Univ. (A), Vincennes, IN 47591	1806	Isaac K. Beckes	Ps-A	4,445	203
Virgin Islands, Coll. of the, St. Thomas, VI 00801	1962	Arthur A. Richards	Ps-M	2,531	179
Virginia, Univ. of, Charlottesville, VA 22903	1819	Frank Hereford Jr.	Ps-D	16,452	1,429
Virginia Commonwealth Univ., Richmond, VA 23284	1838	Edmund Ackell	Ps-D	18,332	2,500
Virginia Highlands Comm. (A), Abingdon, VA 24210	1967	Emma Schulken	Ps-A	1,445	50
Virginia Intermont, Bristol, VA 24201	1884	Kenneth Glass	IR-B	196	56
Virginia Military Inst. (M), Lexington, VA 24450	1839	Lt. Gen. Richard Irby	Ps-B	1,319	130
Virginia Poly. Inst. & State Univ.*, Blacksburg, VA 24061	1872	William Lavery	Ps-D	22,729	2,795
Virginia State* (A), Petersburg, VA 23803	1882	Thomas Law	Ps-M	4,310	236
Virginia Union Univ., Richmond, VA 23220	1865	David Shannon	IR-B	1,189	137
Virginia Western Comm. (A), Roanoke, VA 24015	1966	Harold H. Hopper	Ps-A	4,167	134
Virginia Wesleyan, Norfolk, VA 23502	1961	Lambuth M. Clarke	IR-B	834	73
Viterbo, La Crosse, WI 54601	1890	Robert Gibbons	IR-B	1,025	110
Voorhees, Denmark, SC 29042	1897	George B. Thomas	IR-B	651	47
Wabash (M) (A), Crawfordsville, IN 47933	1832	Lewis S. Salter	IP-B	800	73
Wabash Valley (A), Mt. Carmel, IL 62863	1959	John Gwaltney	Psl-A	1,500	59
Wake Forest Univ., Winston-Salem, NC 27109	1834	James R. Scales	IR-D	4,787	1,048
Wake Tech. Inst. (A), Raleigh, NC 27603	1963	Robert LeMay Jr.	Psl-A	1,164	89
Waldorf, Forest City, IA 50436	1903	Arndt Braaten	IR-A	403	40
Walker (A), Jasper, AL 35501	1938	David J. Rowland	IP-A	719	45
Walla Walla, College Place, WA 99324	1892	Clifford Sorensen	IR-M	1,967	163
Walla Walla Comm. (A), Walla Walla, WA 99362	1967	Eldon Dietrich	IR-M	2,693	105
Walsh (A), North Canton, OH 44720	1958	Francis Blovin	IR-B	732	27
Walsh Coll. of Accountancy, Troy, MI 48084	1922	Jeffrey Barry	IP-M	1,500	75
Walters State Comm., Morristown, TN 37814	1970	Jack E. Campbell	Ps-A	4,009	187
Warner Pacific, Portland, OR 97215	1935	Marshall K. Christensen	IR-M	480	35
Warren Wilson, Swannanoa, NC 28778	1894	Reuben A. Holden	IR-A	500	131
Wartburg, Waverly, IA 50677	1852	Robert Vogel	IR-B	1,110	87
Washburn Univ. of Topeka, Topeka, KS 66621	1865	John W. Henderson	Pl-D	6,031	310
Washington, Chestertown, MD 21620	1782	Joseph McLain	IP-M	799	72
Washington and Jefferson, Washington, PA 15301	1781	Howard J. Burnett	IP-B	1,077	104
Washington and Lee Univ., Lexington, VA 24450	1749	Robert Huntley	IP-1P	1,634	168
Washington State Comm. (A), Spokane, WA 92207	1963	Max M. Synder	Ps-A	26,729	378
Washington State Univ., Pullman, WA 99164	1890	Glenn Terrell	Ps-D	17,468	1,108
Washington Univ., St. Louis, MO 63130	1853	W.H. Danforth, Chan.	IP-D	11,000	2,213
Washington, Univ. of* (A), Seattle, WA 98195	1861	John R. Hogness	Ps-D	36,249	2,154
Washtenaw Comm., Ann Arbor, MI 48106	1965	Gunder Myran	Psl-A	8,367	354
Waterbury State Tech, Waterbury, CT 06708	1964	Charles A. Ekstrom	Ps-A	1,715	101
Waubonsee Comm. (A), Sugar Grove, IL 60554	1966	F.D. Etheredge	Pl-A	4,910	250
Waukesha Co. Tech. Inst. (A), Pewaukee, WI 53072	1920	R. Anderson, Dist. Dir.	Psl-A	30,000	125
Wayland Baptist, Plainview, TX 79072	1908	David L. Jester	IR-B	1,468	59
Wayne Community, Goldsboro, NC 27530	1957	Clyde Erwin Jr.	Ps-A	2,082	105
Wayne County Comm., Detroit, MI 48226	1967	Richard Simons Jr.	Ps-A	21,000	904
Wayne State, Wayne, NE 68787	1910	Lyle Seymour	Ps-M	2,420	102
Wayne State Univ., Detroit, MI 48202	1868	Thomas N. Bonner	Ps-D	33,408	2,200
Waynesburg, Waynesburg, PA 15370	1849	Joseph Marsh	IP-B	871	73
Weatherford Jr. (A), Weatherford, TX 76086	1869	E.W. Mince	Pl-A	1,453	74
Weber State, Ogden, UT 84408	1889	Rodney H. Brady	Ps-B	10,065	434
Webster (A), St. Louis, MO 63119	1915	Leigh Gerdine	IP-M	3,658	588
Wellesley (W), Wellesley, MA 02181	1870	Nannerl O. Keohane	IP-B	2,168	297
Wells (W), Aurora, NY 13026	1868	Patti McGill Peterson	IP-B	527	59
Wenatchee Valley (A), Wenatchee, WA 98801	1939	James R. Daivs	Ps-A	3,939	92
Wentworth Institue of Technology (A), Boston, MA 02115	1904	Edward I. Kirkpatrick	IP-B	2,250	137
Wesley, Dover, DE 19901	1873	R.J. Cooke	IR-B	1,167	71
Wesleyan (W)(A), Macon, GA 31201	1836	Fred Hicks	IR-B	423	67
Wesleyan Univ., Middletown, CT 06457	1831	Colin G. Campbell	IP-D	2,600	275
Westbrook, Portland, ME 04103	1834	Thomas B. Courtice	IP-B	920	88
Westchester Comm. (A), Valhalla, NY 10595	1946	Joseph N. Hankin	Psl-A	7,000	300
West Chester State, West Chester, PA 19380	1871	Charles Mayo	Ps-M	8,900	503
West Coast Univ. (A), Los Angeles, CA 90020	1909	Victor Elconin	IP-M	1,400	250
West Florida, Univ. of (A), Pensacola, FL 32504	1967	James Robinson	Ps-M	5,150	256
West Georgia, Carrollton, GA 30118	1933	Maurice Townsend	Ps-S	4,865	264
West Hills Comm., Coalinga, CA 93210	1932	Robert A. Annand	Psl-A	2,420	150
West Liberty State, West Liberty, WV 26074	1837	James L. Chapman	Ps-B	2,603	148
West Los Angeles (A), Culver City, CA 90230	1968	M. Fujimoto	Ps-A	10,041	400
West Oahu, Aica, HI 96701	1976	Ralph M. Miwa	Pf-B	306	32
West Texas State Univ., Canyon, TX 79016	1909	Max Sherman	Ps-M	6,559	357
West Valley, Saratoga, CA 95070	1964	Frank Pearce, Supt.	Ps-A	15,918	500
W. Va. Inst. of Tech., Montgomery, WV 25136	1895	Leonard C. Nelson	Ps-M	3,343	190
West Virginia North, Comm. (A), Wheeling, WV 26003	1972	Daniel B. Crowder	Ps-A	3,946	63
West Virginia State (A), Institute, WV 25112	1890	Harold M. McNeill	Ps-B	4,000	135
West Virginia Univ.*, Morgantown, WV 26506	1867	Vacant.	Ps-D	21,220	2,000
W. Virginia Wesleyan, Buckhannon, WV 26201	1890	Hugh A. Latimer	IP-M	1,746	128
Western Baptist (A), Salem, OR 97302	1935	W.T. Younger	IR-B	436	20
Western Carolina Univ., Cullowhee, NC 28723	1889	H.F. Robinson, Chan.	Ps-M	6,459	322
Western Conn. State (A), Danbury, CT 06810	1903	Robert Bersi	Ps-M	5,454	168
Western Illinois Univ., Macomb, IL 61455	1899	L.F. Malpass	Ps-S	13,352	702
Western Iowa Tech. Comm., Sioux City, IA 51102	1967	Robert Kiser	Pf-A	1,161	75
Western Kentucky Univ., Bowling Green, KY 42101	1906	Donald Zacharias	Ps-S	13,533	708
Western Maryland, Westminster, MD 21157	1867	Ralph C. John	IP-M	1,947	131
Western Mich. Univ., Kalamazoo, MI 49008	1903	John T. Bernhard	Ps-D	20,835	1,149
Western Montana, Dillon, MT 59725	1893	Robert Thomas	Ps-M	960	41
Western New England, Springfield, MA 01119	1919	Beverly Miller	IP-M	5,378	323
Western New Mexico Univ. (A), Silver City, NM 88061	1893	John Snedeker	Ps-M	1,567	95
Western Okla. State, Altus, OK 73521	1926	W.C. Burris	Psr-A	2,028	76
Western Oregon State, Monmouth, OR 97361	1856	Gerald Leinwand	Ps-M	3,120	261
Western Piedmont Comm., Morganton, NC 28655	1964	Wilmon H. Droze	Ps-A	1,726	75
Western State Col. of Colo., Gunnison, CO 81230	1911	John Mellon.	Pf-M	3,268	165
Western Texas, Synder, TX 79549	1971	Don Newbury	Psl-A	1,295	88
Western Washington Univ., Bellingham, WA 98225	1899	Paul Olscamp.	Ps-M	10,616	497
Western Wisc. Tech. Inst., LaCrosse, WI 54601	1912	Charles Richardson, Dir	Psl-A	4,936	185
Westfield State, Westfield, MA 01085	1838	Francis J. Pilecki	Ps-M	4,386	217
Westmar, Le Mars, IA 51031	1890	John F. Courter.	IR-B	652	55

Name, address	Year	Governing official, affiliation, and highest degree offered		Students	Teachers
Westminster, Fulton, MO 65251	1851	J.H. Saunders	IP-B	746	59
Westminster, New Wilmington, PA 16142	1852	Earland I. Carlson	IR-M	742	126
Westminster (A), Salt Lake City, UT 84105	1875	C. David Cornell	IP-M	1,176	53
Westminster Choir, Princeton, NJ 08540	1926	Ray E. Robinson	IP-M	438	65
Westmont, Santa Barbara, CA 93101	1940	David Winter	IR-B	1,077	60
Wharton County Junior, Wharton, TX 77488	1946	Theodore Nicksick Jr.	Psl-A	2,056	112
Wheaton, Wheaton, IL 60187	1860	Hudson T. Armerding	IP-M	2,353	230
Wheaton (W), (A), Norton, MA 02766	1834	Alice F. Emerson	IP-B	1,140	84
Wheeling, Wheeling, WV 26003	1954	Rev. Charles Currie	IP-M	1,026	84
Wheelock (A), Boston, MA 02215	1888	Gordon L. Marshall	IP-M	1,001	44
White Plains, Coll. of (A), White Plains, NY 10603	1928	Edward Mortola	IP-B	800	55
Whitman, Walla Walla, WA 99362	1859	Robert Skotheim	IP-B	1,169	109
Whittier (A), Whittier, CA 90608	1901	Eugene Mills	IP-D	1,450	95
Whitworth, Spokane, WA 99251	1890	Robert Mounce	IR-M	1,768	110
Wichita State Univ., Wichita, KS 67208	1895	Clark Ahlberg	Ps-D	16,621	828
Widener, Chester, PA 19013	1821	Clarence R. Moll, Chan.	IP-M	2,275	136
Wilberforce Univ., Wilberforce, OH 45385	1856	Charles Taylor	IR-B	1,082	75
Wiley (A), Marshall, TX 75670	1873	Robert Hayes Sr.	IR-B	603	34
Wilkes, Wilkes-Barre, PA 18766	1933	Robert Capin	IP-M	3,139	181
Wilkes Community, Wilkesboro, NC 28697	1965	David E. Daniel	Psl-A	2,006	53
Willamette Univ., Salem, OR 97301	1842	Jerry E. Hudson	IP-1P	1,886	183
William Carey, Hattiesburg, MS 39401	1906	J. Ralph Noonkester	IR-S	1,703	126
William Jewell (A), Liberty, MO 64068	1849	J. Gordon Kingsley	IR-B	1,601	85
Wm. and Mary, Coll. of, Williamsburg, VA 23185	1693	Thomas A. Graves Jr.	Ps-D	6,465	467
Wm. Mitchell Coll. of Law (A), St. Paul, MN 55105	1900	Bruce Barton, Dean	IP-1P	1,127	26
Wm. Paterson (A), Wayne, NJ 07470	1855	Seymour C. Hyman	Ps-M	12,555	379
William Penn, Oskaloosa, IA 52577	1873	Gus Turbeville	IR-B	571	42
William Rainey Harper (A), Palatine, IL 60067	1965	Robert E. Lahti	Psl-A	19,575	933
William Woods (W), Fulton, MO 65251	1870	John M. Bartholomew	IP-B	1,047	75
Williams, Williamstown, MA 01267	1793	John W. Chandler	IP-M	2,000	160
Williamsburg Tech., Kingstree, SC 29556	1970	John T. Wynn	Ps-A	429	45
Williamsport Area Comm., Williamsport, PA 17701	1965	Robert Breuder	Ps-A	3,198	250
Willmar Comm., Willmar, NM 56201	1962	John Torgelson	Ps-A	868	60
Wilmington, New Castle, DE 19720	1967	Audrey K. Doberstein	IP-M	900	60
Wilmington, Wilmington, OH 45177	1870	Robert E. Lucas	IR-B	690	75
Wilson (W), Chambersburg, PA 17201	1869	Donald Bletz	IR-B	180	50
Wilson Co. Tech. Inst., Wilson, NC 27893	1958	Ernest B. Parry	Ps-A	1,297	43
Wingate, Wingate, NC 28174	1896	Thomas Corts	IR-B	1,534	63
Winona State Univ., Winona, MN 55987	1858	Robert A. Hanson	Pf-S	5,355	225
Winston-Salem St. Univ. (A), Winston-Salem, NC 27102	1892	H. Douglas Covington	Ps-B	2,224	155
Winthrop, Rock Hill, SC 29733	1886	Charles Vail	Ps-S	5,040	306
Wisconsin, Univ. of (A), Madison, WI 53706	1971	Edwin Young	Ps-D	150,629	7,036
Eau Claire (A), Eau Claire, WI 54701	1916	Leonard Haas	Ps-M	10,494	499
Green Bay (A), Green Bay, WI 54302	1969	Edward W. Weidner, Chan.	Ps-M	3,641	160
La Crosse, La Crosse, WI 54601	1909	Noel Richards, Chan.	Ps-M	9,016	533
Madison (A), Madison, WI 53706	1849	Irving Shain, Chan.	Ps-D	39,000	2,300
Milwaukee (A), Milwaukee, WI 53201	1885	Werner Baum, Chan.	Ps-D	24,686	846
Oshkosh (A), Oshkosh, WI 54901	1971	Edward Penson, Chan.	Ps-M	10,368	550
Parkside (A), Kenosha, WI 53141	1969	Alan Guskin, Chan.	Ps-E	5,300	180
Platteville, Platteville, WI 53818	1866	Warren Carrier, Chan.	Ps-M	5,150	400
River Falls, River Falls, WI 54022	1874	George Field, Chan.	Ps-M	5,339	300
Stevens Point (A), Stevens Point, WI 54481	1894	Philip R. Marshall, Chan.	Ps-M	8,942	430
Stout, Menomonie, WI 54751	1893	Robert Swanson, Chan.	Ps-S	7,400	550
Superior, Superior, WI 54880	1893	Karl W. Myer, Chan.	Ps-S	2,323	132
Whitewater, Whitewater, WI 53190	1868	James Connor, Chan.	Ps-M	10,006	487
Wisconsin Center, Univ of	1972	Edward Fort	Ps-A	9,302	534
at Baraboo, Baraboo, WI 53913	1968	Edward Fort, Chan.	Ps-A	399	28
at Barron, Rice Lake, WI 54868	1966	John Meggers, Dean	Ps-A	334	26
at Fond du Lac, Fond du Lac, WI 54935	1968	Willard J. Henken, Dean	Ps-A	555	42
at Fox Valley, Menasha, WI 54952	1960	Rue C. Johnson	Ps-A	1,052	50
at Manitowoc, Manitowoc, WI 54220	1933	C. Natunewicz, Dean	Ps-A	395	30
at Marathon (A), Wausau, WI 54401	1947	W.R. Peters, Dean	Ps-A	840	35
at Marinette, Marinette, WI 54143	1946	William Schmidtke, Dean	Ps-A	386	20
at Marshfield/Wood, Marshfield, WI 54449	1963	Norbert Koopman, Dean	Ps-A	598	34
at Medford (A), Medford, WI 54451	1968	Darwin A. Slocum, Dean	Ps-A	138	17
at Richland (A), Richland Ctr., WI 53581	1967	Marjorie Wallace, Dean	Ps-A	326	9
at Rock County, Janesville, WI 53545	1965	Thomas Walterman, Dean	Ps-A	807	44
at Sheboygan (A), Sheboygan, WI 53081	1933	K.M. Bailey, Dean	Ps-A	616	35
at Waukesha (A), Waukesha, WI 53186	1966	Kenneth D. Oliver, Dean	Ps-A	1,700	90
at Washington, West Bend, WI 53095	1967	R.O. Thompson, Dean	Ps-A	617	38
Wittenberg Univ., Springfield, OH 45501	1845	W.A. Kinnison	IR-M	2,308	148
Wofford, Spartanburg, SC 29301	1854	J.M. Lesesne Jr.	IP-B	1,036	76
Woodbury (A), Los Angeles, CA 90017	1884	Wayne Miller	IP-M	1,435	61
Wood Junior, Mathiston, MS 39752	1886	Felix Sutphin	IR-A	540	37
Wooster, Coll. of, Wooster, OH 44691	1866	Henry Copeland	IP-B	1,850	135
Wooster Business, Wooster, OH 44691	1886	Steven K. Knox	IP-A	125	7
Worcester, Worcester, MA 01610	1888	E.P. Mattar III	IP-A	1,100	75
Worcester Polytechnic Inst., Worcester, MA 01609	1865	Edmund T. Cranch	IP-D	3,400	181
Worcester State, Worcester, MA 01602	1874	Joseph Orze	Ps-M	6,318	216
Worthington Comm., Worthington, MN 56187	1936	Frederick A. Voda	Ps-A	1,280	60
Wright State Univ., Dayton, OH 45435	1967	R.J. Kegerreis	Ps-D	15,635	995
Wyoming, Univ. of (A), Laramie, WY 82071	1886	Edward H. Jennings	Ps-D	9,000	850
Xavier Univ. of La. (A), New Orleans, LA 70125	1925	Norman C. Francis	IR-M	1,700	158
Xavier Univ., Cincinnati, OH 45232	1831	Rev. Robert Mulligan	IR-M	7,209	350
Yakima Valley, Yakima, WA 98907	1928	William Russell	Ps-A	7,226	375
Yale Univ. (A), New Haven, CT 06520	1701	A.B. Giamatti	IP-D	9,526	1,580
Yankton, Yankton, SD 57078	1881	Orlan Mitchell	IR-B	254	50
Yavapai, Prescott, AZ 86301	1966	Joseph Russo	Ps-A	4,892	311
Yeshiva Univ., New York, NY 10033	1886	Norman Lamm	IP-D	6,881	1,761
York, York, NE 68567	1890	Gary Bartholomew	IR-A	360	26
York College of Pa., York, PA 17405	1776	R.V. Iosue	IP-M	3,827	186
York Technical (A), Rock Hill, SC 29730	1964	Baxter Hood	Ps-A	1,504	64
Young Harris, Young Harris, GA 30582	1876	Ray Farley	IP-A	528	35
Youngstown State Univ., Youngstown, OH 44555	1908	John J. Coffelt	Ps-M	15,784	807
Yuba Comm., Marysville, CA 95901	1927	Daniel G. Walker	Psl-A	9,755	300

Canadian Colleges and Universities

Source: Statistics Canada

Each institution listed has an enrollment of at least 200 students of college grade. Enrollment and faculty include all branches and campuses for the 1979-80 academic year. Number of full-time teachers is the total number of individuals on teaching staff. Governing official is the president unless otherwise designated. All institutions are co-educational.

Name	Location	Established	Governing official	Students	Teachers
Acadia Univ.	Wolfville, N.S.	1838	A.M. Sinclair	2,570	202
Alberta, Univ. of	Edmonton, Alta.	1906	M. Horowitz	17,850	1,556
Bishop's Univ.	Lennoxville, Que.	1843	Christopher Nicholl	760	73(1)
Brandon Univ.	Brandon, Man.	1899	H.J. Perkins	960	126
British Columbia, Univ. of	Vancouver, B.C.	1908	Douglas T. Kenny	19,470	2,034
Brock Univ.	St. Catharines, Ont.	1964	A.J. Earp	1,960	220
Calgary, Univ. of	Calgary, Alta.	1945	Norman E. Wagner	10,740	1,078
Carleton Univ.	Ottawa, Ont.	1942	William Beckel	8,280	625
Concordia Univ.	Montreal, Que.	1974	John O'Brien, Rector	10,720	690(1)
Dalhousie Univ.	Halifax, N.S.	1818	Henry D. Hicks	6,960	794
Guelph, Univ. of	Guelph, Ont.	1964	Donald F. Forster	9,190	768
King's Coll., Univ. of	Halifax, N.S.	1789	John F. Godfrey	370	11
Lakehead Univ.	Thunder Bay, Ont.	1965	G.A. Harrower	2,530	251
Laurentian Univ.	Sudbury, Ont.	1960	Henry B.M. Best	2,210	263
Laval Universite	Quebec, Que.	1852	Jean-Guy Paquet, Rector	17,940	1,458(1)
Lethbridge, Univ. of	Lethbridge, Alta.	1967	John Woods	1,420	162
Manitoba, Univ. of	Winnipeg, Man.	1877	Ralph Campbell	12,490	1,264
McGill Univ.	Montreal, Que.	1821	David Johnston	16,320	1,328(1)
McMaster Univ.	Hamilton, Ont.	1887	A.N. Bourns	9,850	903
Mem. Univ. of Newfoundland	St. John's, Nfld.	1925	M.O. Morgan	6,040	810
Moncton, Univ. de	Moncton, N.B.	1963	Jean Cadieux, Rector	2,340	295
Montreal, Univ. de	Montreal, Que.	1920	Paul Lacoste, Rector	14,390	1,738(1)
Mount Allison Univ.	Sackville, N.B.	1840	W.S.H. Crawford	1,450	135
Mount St. Vincent Univ.	Halifax, N.S.	1925	Margaret Fulton	1,540	103
New Brunswick, Univ. of	Fredericton, N.B.	1785	T.J. Condon	5,860	571
Nova Scotia Coll. of Arts & Design.	Halifax, N.S.	1887	Garry Neill Kennedy	420	45
Nova Scotia Technical	Halifax, N.S.	1907	J.C. Callaghan	790	68
Ontario Inst. for Studies in Education	Toronto, Ont.	1965	Clifford C. Pitt	630	153
Ottawa, Univ. of	Ottawa, Ont.	1848	Roger Guindon	11,530	944
Prince Edward Island, Univ. of	Charlottetown, P.E.I.	1969	Peter Meincke	1,330	120
Quebec, Univ. of	Ste-Foy, Que.	1969	Gilles Boulet	16,540	1,394(1)
Queen's Univ.	Kingston, Ont.	1841	R.L. Watts	10,270	879
Regina, Univ. of	Regina, Sask.	1974	Lloyd I. Barber	2,910	353
Royal Military Coll. of Can.	Kingston, Ont.	1876	Donald Tilley	680	146
Royal Roads Military Coll.	Victoria, B.C.	1942	E.S. Graham	228	35
Ryerson Polytechnical Inst.	Toronto, Ont.	1948	Walter G. Pitman	9,200	650
Saint Paul Univ.	Ottawa, Ont.	1000	Rev. Henri Goudreault	220	44
St. Francis Xavier Univ.	Antigonish, N.S.	1853	Rev. G.A. MacKinnon	2,020	154
St. Mary's Univ.	Halifax, N.S.	1802	Kenneth L. Ozmon	2,100	182(1)
Saskatchewan, Univ. of	Saskatoon, Sask.	1907	R.W. Begg	9,500	1,028
Sherbrooke, Univ. of	Sherbrooke, Que.	1954	Yves Martin	6,970	633(1)
Simon Fraser Univ.	Burnaby, B.C.	1965	George Pederson	5,050	473
Toronto, Univ. of	Toronto, Ont.	1827	James M. Ham	32,000	2,639
Trent Univ.	Peterborough, Ont.	1963	T.E.W. Nind	2,130	179
Victoria, Univ. of	Victoria, B.C.	1963	H.E. Petch	5,470	517
Waterloo, Univ. of	Waterloo, Ont.	1957	B.C. Mathews	13,820	747
Western Ontario, Univ. of	London, Ont.	1878	George E. Connell	14,480	1,298
Wilfrid Laurier Univ.	Waterloo, Ont.	1973	N.H. Tayler	3,430	146
Windsor, Univ. of	Windsor, Ont.	1857	Mervyn Franklin	6,190	496
Winnipeg, Univ. of	Winnipeg, Man.	1871	Henry E. Duckworth	2,340	191
York Univ.	Downsview, Ont.	1959	H. Ian MacDonald	10,300	1,014

(1) Estimate.

Typical Tuition Fees at Canadian Colleges and Universities

Source: Statistics Canada

Undergraduate tuition fees at universities and colleges with enrollment of 5,000 full day-time students or more. Fee is for 1980-81 academic year.

Institution	Tuition	Institution	Tuition
Alberta, University of	$605-908	Ottawa, University of	$773-952
British Columbia, Univ. of	590-920	Queen's University	845-1,020
Calgary, University of	606-1,210	Québec, Université du	500
Carleton University, Ottawa	806-880	Ryerson Polytechnical Institute	590
Concordia University	450-540	Saskatchewan, University of	690-990
Dalhousie University	915-1,035	Sherbrooke, University of	466(1)-650
Guelph, University of	780-920	Simon Fraser University	585
Laval Université	450-600	Toronto, University of	167(2)-1,089
Manitoba, University of	615-1,120	Victoria, University of	585-713
Montréal, Université de	380-740	Waterloo, University of	818-1,027
Memorial University of Newfoundland	630-945	Western Ontario, University of	806-1,040
McGill University	570-718	Windsor, University of	800-860
McMaster University	810-1,034	York University	915
New Brunswick, University of	850		

(1) Excludes an additional $50 a session for students in co-op program. (2) Per course.

Tuition Fees at Selected U.S. Colleges and Universities

Source: World Almanac Questionnaire

The College Entrance Examination Board has estimated that the average tuition per year in a 4-year private college in the fall of 1980 was $3,300. The tuition at a 4-year public college averaged $700.

Fees for tuition charged per year by colleges and universities for courses, use of libraries, laboratories and other facilities are a major part of student expenses. Tuition varies considerably, depending on the type of institution, its control and location. The lowest tuition fees are those of state-controlled or other public-controlled institutions for residents of their state, city, etc. Students from other states or areas have to pay more. In the following list, such state or other public institutions are shown with two figures. The lower one is the tuition fee for residents, the higher one the tuition fee for students from other states or areas.

(Tuition does not include room, board, or other expenses.)

School	Tuition	School	Tuition	School	Tuition
Abilene Christian	$2,240	Daemen	3,250	New Orleans, Univ. of	624-1,654
Adams State	524-2,822	Davidson	4,100	North Carolina State	325-1,250
Adelphi Univ.	4,170	Dayton, Univ. of	3,044	Oberlin	6,640
Alabama A&M	560	Delaware, Univ. of	940-2,540	Occidental	6,050
Alabama, Univ. of	994-2,119	Denver, Univ. of	5,670	Ohio Univ.	1,206-2,781
Alaska, Univ. of	572-1,352	DePauw	5,482	Oklahoma, Univ. of	643-1,712
Albion	4,716	Drake	5,990	Old Dominion Univ.	922-1,618
Albright	4,245	East Carolina Univ.	578-1,444	Pacific, Univ. of	6,364
Allegheny	4,300	East Arizona	280-2,537	Paine	2,175
Alma	4,144	Eastern New Mexico Univ.	678-1,793	Peru State	630-1,020
American Univ.	5,240	Fairfield Univ.	4,450	Pfeiffer	2,580
Appalachian State Univ.	614-2,334	Fordham Univ.	4,250	Pittsburgh, Univ. of	1,790-3,580
Arizona, Univ. of	650-2,950	Fort Lewis	483-2,123	Portland State Univ.	947-3,233
Arkansas, Univ. of	600-1,430	Framingham State	600-2,100	Purdue	1,008-2,600
Auburn	720-1,440	Georgetown Univ.	5,750	Quincy	1,800
Austin Peay State Univ.	666-2,172	George Washington Univ.	3,400	Randolph-Macon	4,450
Avila	2,500	Goucher	5,400	Redlands, Univ. of	5,650
Baldwin-Wallace	4,545	Green Mountain	4,230	Rhode Island, Univ. of	934-2,181
Ball State	1,116-2,460	Hastings	2,850	Richmond, Univ. of	845
Barry	4,050	Haverford	7,150	Ripon	5,316
Bates	6,960	Hope	4,490	Rochester, Univ. of	550-1,100
Baylor	2,560	Idaho, College of	3,980	St. Bonaventure Univ.	3,300
Bemidji State Univ.	748-1,325	Indiana State Univ.	1,008-2,248	St. Louis Univ.	4,200
Blue Mountain	1,640	Iowa State Univ.	950-2,350	St. Olaf	3,925
Bob Jones	1,593	Ithaca	4,584	St. Paul Bible	2,048
Boston	5,180	Jacksonville State Univ.	700-1,050	Selma Univ.	1,500
Bowdoin	6,800	John Brown Univ.	2,300	Southern Methodist Univ.	4,350
Brandeis Univ.	6,700	Johns Hopkins	5,075	Tabor	2,560
Brown	7,120	Kalamazoo	5,465	Tampa, Univ. of	2,178
Bryan	2,500	Kansas, Univ. of	900-2,200	Temple Univ.	2,068-3,854
Bucknell	6,400	Kentucky, Univ. of	682-2,032	Tennessee, Univ. of	624-1,221
Buena Vista	4,270	Knox	5,500	Tiffin Univ.	1,980
Cabrini	3,500	Lock Haven State	1,250-2,190	Utah, Univ. of	732-1,911
Cal. Inst. of Tech.	6,249	Lowell, Univ. of	842-2,900	Vanderbilt Univ.	4,700
Cal. Lutheran	6,100-7,000	Marquette Univ.	3,620	Vermont, Univ. of	1,650-4,560
Cameron Univ.	500-1,150	Memphis State Univ.	556-1,224	Virginia, Univ. of	1,044-2,404
Cardinal Stritch	3,200	Miami Univ.	1,750-3,650	Washington Univ.	6,250
Carleton	5,704	Montclair State	800-1,440	West Virginia Inst. of Tech.	372-1,313
Case Western Reserve Univ.	5,400	Montana State	672-2,042	Williams	5,950
Centenary	3,450-6,200	Muskingum	4,337	Worcester State	725-2,375
Charleston, Univ. of	2,700	Nazareth	4,240	Yale, Univ.	7,150
Chicago State Univ.	788-2,168	Nebr. Wesleyan Univ.	1,808	Yankton	3,580
Clemson Univ.	1,210-2,488	New England	4,680		
Connecticut	6,850	New Mexico, Univ. of	720-2,732		

Federal Funds for Education, 1981

Source: National Center for Education Statistics, U.S. Department of Education

Includes grants, loans, and directly administered services. Estimated. (thousands of dollars)

Type of support, level, and program area		
Elementary-secondary education	**$7,737,276**	
School asst.—federally affected areas	553,942	
Educationally deprived/Economic Opportunity Programs	5,186,820	
Supporting services	393,096	
Teacher corps	14,638	
Vocational education	461,013	
Dependents' schools abroad	421,274	
Public lands revenue for schools	373,482	
Assistance in special areas	54,457	
Emergency school asst.	226,698	
Other	51,856	
Higher education	**9,827,596**	
Basic research	3,001,600	
Research facilities	400,700	
Training grants, fellowships, and traineeships	1,003,724	
Facilities and equipment	86,424	
Other institutional support	585,000	
Other student assistance	4,750,148	
Vocational-tech. and continuing ed.	**7,710,096**	
Vocational-technical education	$7,230,264	
Veterans' education	264,804	
General continuing education	171,561	
Training, federal, state, and local personnel	43,467	
Grants, total	**25,274,968**	
Loans, total	**1,495,607**	
Student loan program, Nat. Def. Ed. Act.	1,474,970	
College facilities loans	20,637	
Total grants and loans	**26,770,575**	
Other federal funds, total	**9,263,686**	
Applied research and development	3,288,500	
School lunch and milk programs	3,288,600	
Training of federal personnel, military	1,299,594	
Library services	**474,107**	
Grants to public libraries	67,550	
National library services	406,557	
International education	**85,871**	
Educational exchange program	NA	
AID projects	84,893	
ACTION (previously Peace Corps)	NA	
Other international educ. and training	978	
Other	**911,906**	
Agricultural extension service	264,468	
Educational television facilities	167,900	
Other education; property transfers	395,624	

Fall Enrollment and Teachers in Full-time Day Schools
Elementary and Secondary Day Schools, Fall 1979
Source: National Center for Education Statistics, U.S. Education Dept.

State	Local school districts			Enrollment			Classroom teachers
	Total	Operating	Nonoperating	Total	Elementary	Secondary	
United States	15,929	15,625	304	41,578,665	27,884,432	13,694,233	2,450,504
Alabama	127	127	—	754,181	519,077	235,104	35,617
Alaska	52	52	—	88,573	61,065	27,508	5,430
Arizona	226	212	14	509,252	353,408	155,844	28,305
Arkansas	373	373	—	453,125	312,011	141,114	25,050
California	1,033	1,033	—	4,047,550	2,729,523	1,318,027	218,037
Colorado	181	181	—	550,527	369,928	180,599	32,175
Connecticut	165	165	—	566,634	377,762	188,872	41,075
Delaware	16	16	—	104,035	65,134	38,901	7,221
Florida	67	67	—	1,508,337	1,031,452	476,885	83,653
Georgia	187	187	—	1,078,462	745,910	332,552	57,392
Hawaii	1	1	—	168,660	111,693	56,967	9,057
Idaho	115	115	—	202,758	141,193	61,565	10,047
Illinois	1,013	1,011	2	2,043,239	1,367,133	676,106	124,211
Indiana	305	304	1	1,083,826	723,064	360,762	58,826
Iowa	445	445	—	548,317	357,588	190,729	36,111
Kansas	307	307	—	422,924	287,619	135,305	27,984
Kentucky	181	181	—	677,123	466,201	210,922	36,559
Louisiana	66	66	—	800,435	555,095	245,340	52,688
Maine	283	227	56	227,823	155,882	71,941	11,998
Maryland	24	24	—	777,725	510,259	267,466	48,238
Massachusetts	396	354	42	1,035,724	684,910	350,814	78,213
Michigan	573	573	—	1,860,498	1,222,830	637,668	96,650
Minnesota	440	439	1	778,056	496,170	281,886	48,949
Mississippi	152	152	—	482,039	325,650	156,389	28,806
Missouri	554	554	—	872,933	579,470	293,463	55,655
Montana	580	558	22	158,208	105,735	52,473	10,071
Nebraska	1,089	1,035	54	287,288	189,646	97,642	20,525
Nevada	17	17	—	147,734	97,819	49,915	8,386
New Hampshire	168	157	11	170,546	111,989	58,557	9,725
New Jersey	606	588	18	1,287,809	847,766	440,043	89,729
New Mexico	88	88	—	275,572	186,215	89,357	15,344
New York	722	716	6	2,969,216	1,905,387	1,063,829	190,621
North Carolina	144	144	—	1,150,053	796,033	354,020	60,169
North Dakota	338	303	35	117,688	75,542	42,146	8,210
Ohio	615	615	—	2,025,256	1,351,413	673,843	114,182
Oklahoma	620	620	—	583,458	398,695	184,763	34,360
Oregon	313	311	2	467,128	317,045	150,083	26,230
Pennsylvania	504	504	—	1,968,801	1,233,009	735,792	132,615
Rhode Island	40	40	—	154,098	99,082	55,016	10,855
South Carolina	92	92	—	624,795	428,924	195,871	33,211
South Dakota	195	187	8	133,840	88,400	45,440	9,022
Tennessee	148	148	—	866,117	610,435	255,682	45,378
Texas	1,079	1,077	2	2,872,719	2,004,224	868,495	162,426
Utah	40	40	—	333,049	237,872	95,177	12,835
Vermont	271	245	26	98,338	67,755	30,583	7,328
Virginia	139	135	4	1,031,403	714,954	316,449	61,868
Washington	300	300	—	764,879	515,258	249,621	38,698
West Virginia	55	55	—	388,398	265,645	122,753	21,001
Wisconsin	434	434	—	857,855	543,581	314,274	56,764
Wyoming	49	49	—	95,505	66,801	28,704	5,508
District of Columbia	1	1	—	106,156	75,180	30,976	7,496

Public School Attendance, Teachers, Expenditures

Source: National Center for Education Statistics, U.S. Education Department

School year	Pop. 5 to 17 yrs.	Pupils		Teachers[1]				Total expend.
		Enrolled	Av. daily attend.	Male	Female	Total	Salary[2]	
1900	21,404,322	15,503,110	10,632,772	126,588	296,474	423,062	$325	$214,964,618
1910	24,239,948	17,813,852	12,827,307	110,481	412,729	523,210	485	426,250,434
1920	27,728,788	21,578,316	16,150,035	95,654	583,648	679,302	871	1,036,151,209
1930	31,571,322	25,678,015	21,264,886	141,771	712,492	854,263	1,420	2,316,790,384
1940	29,805,259	25,433,542	22,042,151	194,725	680,752	875,477	1,441	2,344,048,927
1950	30,788,000	25,111,427	22,283,845	194,968	718,703	913,671	3,010	5,837,643,000
1960	43,881,000	36,086,771	32,477,440	392,700	962,300	1,355,000	5,174	15,613,255,000
1970 (Fall) .	52,435,000	45,909,088	42,495,346	649,250	1,411,865	2,061,115	9,570	44,423,865,000
1971 (Fall) .	52,133,000	46,081,000	42,544,000	668,000	1,395,000	2,063,000	10,100	48,513,986,000
1972 (Fall) .	51,637,000	45,744,000	42,408,000	702,000	1,400,000	2,102,000	10,608	51,905,025,000
1974 (Fall) .	51,485,000	46,441,189	41,438,054	722,868	1,432,580	2,155,448	11,185	56,970,355,000
1975 (Fall) .	50,372,000	44,790,946	41,269,720	741,000	1,455,000	2,196,000	*12,448	70,629,000,000
1976 (Fall) .	49,853,000	44,317,000	40,832,000	*741,000	*1,445,000	2,186,000	*13,397	75,014,000,000
1977 (Fall) .	49,010,000	43,576,906	40,080,000	*746,500	*1,462,070	2,208,570	*14,244	80,844,366,000
1978 (Fall) .	48,046,000	42,611,000	39,065,000	*745,000	*1,454,000	2,199,000	*14,970	86,711,615,000

* Estimated. (1) Prior to 1954 includes other nonsupervisory instructional staff (librarians and guidance and psychological personnel). (2) Average annual salary per member of instructional staff, including supervisors and principals. Beginning in 1975, data are for classroom teachers only.

Canadian Fall Enrollment, Teachers, Expenditures in Day Schools
Full-time Public Elementary and Secondary Day Schools—1979-80
Source: Statistics Canada

	Enrollment			Teachers			School Board expenditure per pupil[1] 1978 (calendar year) (e)
	Elementary Kdgn.- Gr. 8	Secondary Gr. 9 and up	Total	Elementary Kdgn.- Gr. 8	Secondary Gr. 9 and up	Total	
Canada......	3,356,742	1,578,667	4,935,409	164,791[e]	102,535[e]	267,326[e]	2,078
Nfld.........	115,216	35,166	150,382	5,926	1,866	7,792	1,533
P.E.I........	18,115	9,162	27,277	978	409	1,387	1,683
N.S.........	131,585	57,640	189,225	7,551	3,131	10,682	1,572
N.B.........	103,988	52,397	156,385	4,984	2,782	7,766	1,459
Que........	818,457	346,793	1,165,250	41,500[e]	33,500[e]	75,000[e]	2,253
Ont........	1,232,642	633,465	1,866,107	57,270	35,707	92,977	2,174
Man........	143,629	65,141	208,770	7,853	3,522	11,375	1,963
Sask.......	142,260	65,749	208,009	7,191	3,585	10,776	1,931
Alta........	293,536	140,847	434,383	16,377	6,182	22,559	2,011
B.C........	342,454	169,217	511,671	14,377	11,643	26,020	2,029
Yukon......	3,821	1,301	5,122	189	74	263	2,582
N.W.T......	11,039	1,789	12,828	595	134	729	2,811

(e) estimate. (1) Includes provincial expenditures made on behalf of school boards.

Cost per Pupil by State

Source: National Center for Education Statistics, U. S. Education Department
Expenditures per pupil in average daily attendance in public elementary and secondary day schools, 1978-79.

State	Expenditure per pupil				State	Expenditure per pupil			
	Total[1]	Current[2]	Capital outlay[3]	Interest on school debt		Total[1]	Current[2]	Capital outlay[3]	Interest on school debt
United States ..	$2,210	$2,021	$139	$50	Nevada........	2,124	1,811	219	94
Alabama.......	1,700	1,563	124	14	New Hampshire..	1,860	1,671	123	67
Alaska........	4,522	4,112	148	261	New Jersey	2,818	2,728	[4]45	[4]47
Arizona........	2,06[6]	1,720	284	60	New Mexico....	1,942	1,796	126	20
Arkansas	1,...	1,348	[4]112	[4]32	New York	3,180	3,025	70	84
California......	2,173	2,052	99	22	North Carolina ...	1,712	1,591	108	[5]12
Colorado.......	2,517	2,205	246	66	North Dakota ...	1,977	1,805	150	22
Connecticut	2,231	2,136	47	47	Ohio..........	1,917	1,789	92	36
Delaware	2,570	2,368	104	97	Oklahoma......	1,941	1,729	194	18
District of Columbia.	2,951	2,841	110	—	Oregon........	2,487	2,418	12	56
Florida........	1,847	1,657	153	36	Pennsylvania ...	2,524	2,250	113	161
Georgia	1,683	1,485	149	49	Rhode Island ...	2,450	2,387	8	54
Hawaii	2,276	2,133	140	3	South Carolina ...	1,692	1,508	151	33
Idaho.........	1,739	1,517	188	35	South Dakota ...	1,699	1,677	2	20
Illinois........	2,399	2,202	139	57	Tennessee......	1,548	1,383	154	11
Indiana........	1,859	1,690	122	47	Texas.........	2,073	1,691	[4]315	[6]68
Iowa.........	2,264	2,107	123	34	Utah..........	2,114	1,676	390	48
Kansas.......	2,137	1,978	124	36	Vermont.......	1,976	1,820	130	26
Kentucky......	1,643	1,502	94	47	Virginia........	1,870	1,671	148	51
Louisiana	1,771	1,604	125	42	Washington	2,575	2,173	358	44
Maine	1,731	1,609	78	43	West Virginia ...	1,905	1,671	214	19
Maryland	2,550	2,349	160	41	Wisconsin	2,400	2,223	132	45
Massachusetts ...	2,629	2,553	63	13	Wyoming.......	2,759	2,179	488	92
Michigan.......	2,682	2,446	161	75					
Minnesota	2,368	2,147	161	61					
Mississippi	1,610	1,507	102	1					
Missouri	1,856	1,725	96	35					
Montana	2,215	2,178	—	37					
Nebraska	2,198	1,967	176	56					

(1) Includes current expenditures for day schools, capital outlay, and interest on school debt. (2) Includes expenditures for day schools only; excludes adult education, community colleges, and community services. (3) Includes capital outlay by State and local schoolhousing authorities. (4) Data are for school year 1977-78. (5) Data are for school year 1975-76. (6) Estimated.

109 Years of Public Schools

Pupils and teachers (thousands) .	1869-70	1899-1900	1909-10	1919-20	1929-30	1939-40	1949-50	1959-60	1969-70	1977-78
Total U.S. population	39,818	75,995	90,492	104,512	121,770	130,880	148,665	179,323	203,212	216,400
Population 5-17 years of age	12,055	21,573	24,009	27,556	31,417	30,150	30,168	43,881	52,490	49,010
Percent aged 5-17 years.	30.3	28.4	26.5	26.4	25.8	23.0	20.3	24.5	25.8	22.6
Enrollment (thousands)										
Elementary and secondary	6,872	15,503	17,814	21,578	25,678	25,434	25,111	36,087	45,619	43,577
Percent pop. 5-17 enrolled	57.0	71.9	74.2	78.3	81.7	84.4	83.2	82.2	86.9	88.9
Percent in high schools	1.2	3.3	5.1	10.2	17.1	26.0	22.7	23.5	28.5	32.7
High school graduates.	....	62	111	231	592	1,143	1,063	1,627	2,589	2,825
Average school term (in days)....	132.2	144.3	157.5	161.9	172.7	175.0	177.9	178.0	178.9	....
Total instructional staff	....	....	....	678	880	912	962	1,464	2,253	2,492[4]
Teachers, librarians: Men	78	127	110	93	140	195	195	402	691	795[4]
Women ...	123	296	413	565	703	681	719	985	1,440	1,557[4]
Percent men	38.7	29.9	21.1	14.1	16.6	22.2	21.3	29.0	33.4	33.8[4]
Revenue & expenditures (millions)										
Total revenue	....	$219	$433	$970	$2,088	$2,260	$5,437	$14,746	$40,267	$81,443
Total expenditures	$63	214	426	1,036	2,316	2,344	5,837	15,613[1]	40,683	80,844
Current elem. and secondary....	....	179	356	861	1,843	1,941	4,687	12,329	34,218	73,058
Capital outlay.............	....	35	69	153	370	257	1,014	2,661	4,659	5,245
Interest on school debt ..... /	....	....	....	18	92	130	100	489	1,171	1,952
Other	....	....	....	3	9	13	35	132	636	589
Salaries and pupil cost			(Data in unadjusted dollars)							
Average annual teacher salary[2] ...	$189	$325	$485	$2,130	$3,869	$3,894	$5,928	$8,213	$10,917	$14,700[4]
Expenditure per capita total pop. .	1.59	2.83	4.71	24.24	51.85	48.40	77.34	138.21	247.23	374.00
Current expenditure per pupil ADA[3].	....	16.67	27.85	130.41	236.25	238.05	411.29	595.50	1,007.65	2,021.00

(1) Because of a modification of the scope, "current expenditures for elementary and secondary schools" data for 1959-60 and later years are not entirely comparable with data for prior years. (2) Includes supervisors, principals, teachers and other nonsupervisory instructional staff. (3) "ADA" means average daily attendance in elementary and secondary day schools. (4) Estimated.

Educational Attainment by Age, Race, and Sex

Source: U.S. Bureau of the Census (Number of persons in thousands)

Race, age, and sex	Years of school completed					Percent				
	All persons	Less than high school, 4 years	High school, 4 years	College, 1 to 3 years	College, 4 years or more	All persons	Less than high school, 4 years	High school, 4 years	College, 1 to 3 years	College, 4 years or more
March 1979										
All races										
18 to 24 years.	28,050	6,226	12,875	7,012	1,936	100.0	22.2	45.9	25.0	6.9
25 years and over	125,295	40,408	45,915	18,392	20,579	100.0	32.3	36.6	14.7	16.4
25 to 34 years	34,053	5,203	13,338	7,414	8,096	100.0	15.3	39.2	21.8	23.8
35 to 44 years	24,611	5,632	10,344	3,822	4,813	100.0	22.9	42.0	15.5	19.6
45 to 54 years	22,826	7,424	9,145	2,833	3,424	100.0	32.5	40.1	12.4	15.0
55 to 64 years	20,631	8,263	7,693	2,398	2,277	100.0	40.1	37.3	11.6	11.0
65 years and over	23,175	13,886	5,395	1,925	1,968	100.0	59.9	23.3	8.3	8.5
Male, 25 years and over . . .	58,986	18,610	19,250	9,099	12,025	100.0	31.5	32.6	15.4	20.4
Female, 25 years and over .	66,309	21,799	26,665	9,293	8,554	100.0	32.9	40.2	14.0	12.9
White										
18 to 24 years.	23,984	4,945	11,141	6,129	1,768	100.0	20.6	46.5	25.6	7.4
25 years and over	110,798	33,531	41,612	16,632	19,023	100.0	30.3	37.6	15.0	17.2
25 to 34 years	29,573	4,102	11,564	6,557	7,350	100.0	13.9	39.1	22.2	24.9
35 to 44 years	21,534	4,500	9,221	3,386	4,427	100.0	20.9	42.8	15.7	20.6
45 to 54 years	20,145	5,974	8,427	2,554	3,189	100.0	29.7	41.8	12.7	15.8
55 to 64 years	18,595	6,869	7,263	2,300	2,163	100.0	36.9	39.1	12.4	11.6
65 years and over	20,950	12,085	5,136	1,834	1,894	100.0	57.7	24.5	8.8	9.0
Male, 25 years and over . . .	52,504	15,576	17,382	8,295	11,250	100.0	29.7	33.1	15.8	21.4
Female, 25 years and over .	58,294	17,954	24,230	9,337	7,773	100.0	30.8	41.6	14.3	13.3
Black										
18 to 24 years.	3,500	1,183	1,485	708	124	100.0	33.8	42.4	20.2	3.5
25 years and over	12,227	6,190	3,670	1,404	964	100.0	50.6	30.0	11.5	7.9
25 to 34 years	3,644	970	1,534	674	466	100.0	26.6	42.1	18.5	12.8
35 to 44 years	2,577	1,026	982	362	206	100.0	39.8	38.1	14.0	8.0
45 to 54 years	2,277	1,305	589	219	164	100.0	57.3	25.9	9.6	7.2
55 to 64 years	1,776	1,267	346	83	80	100.0	71.3	19.5	4.7	4.5
65 years and over	1,954	1,621	219	66	48	100.0	83.0	11.2	3.4	2.5
Male, 25 years and over . . .	5,393	2,741	1,590	613	450	100.0	50.8	29.5	11.4	8.3
Female, 25 years and over .	6,834	3,449	2,080	791	514	100.0	50.5	30.4	11.6	7.5
Spanish Origin[1]										
18 to 24 years.	1,699	727	653	278	40	100.0	42.8	38.4	16.4	2.4
25 years and over	5,367	3,112	1,374	521	359	100.0	58.0	25.6	9.7	6.7
25 to 34 years	1,926	878	600	294	151	100.0	45.6	31.2	15.3	7.8
35 to 44 years	1,367	759	387	118	104	100.0	55.5	28.3	8.6	7.6
45 to 54 years	961	609	239	60	52	100.0	63.4	24.9	6.2	5.4
55 to 64 years	574	412	100	32	30	100.0	71.8	17.4	5.6	5.2
65 years and over	539	454	48	17	20	100.0	84.2	8.9	3.2	3.7
Male, 25 years and over . . .	2,534	1,462	581	283	208	100.0	57.7	22.9	11.2	8.2
Female, 25 years and over .	2,833	1,652	793	238	151	100.0	58.3	28.0	8.4	5.3
March 1970										
All races										
18 to 24 years.	22,494	5,732	9,996	5,392	1,374	100.0	25.5	44.4	24.0	6.1
25 years and over	109,310	48,948	37,134	11,164	12,063	100.0	44.8	34.0	10.2	11.0
25 to 34 years	24,865	6,517	10,929	3,491	3,926	100.0	26.2	44.0	14.0	15.8
35 to 44 years	23,021	8,216	9,325	2,523	2,958	100.0	35.7	40.5	11.0	12.8
45 to 54 years	23,298	9,735	8,875	2,352	2,336	100.0	41.8	38.1	10.1	10.0
55 to 64 years	18,413	10,347	4,905	1,567	1,594	100.0	56.2	26.6	8.5	8.7
65 years and over	19,713	14,134	3,100	1,230	1,249	100.0	71.7	15.7	6.2	6.3
Male, 25 years and over . . .	51,784	23,311	15,571	5,580	7,321	100.0	45.0	30.1	10.8	14.1
Female, 25 years and over .	57,527	25,638	21,563	5,584	4,743	100.0	44.6	37.5	9.7	8.2
White										
18 to 24 years.	19,536	4,496	8,865	4,886	1,289	100.0	23.0	45.4	25.0	6.6
25 years and over	98,112	41,789	34,493	10,452	11,380	100.0	42.6	35.2	10.7	11.6
25 to 34 years	21,887	5,222	9,828	3,204	3,633	100.0	23.9	44.9	14.6	16.6
35 to 44 years	20,392	6,756	8,541	2,319	2,776	100.0	33.1	41.9	11.4	13.6
45 to 54 years	20,961	8,134	8,392	2,209	2,227	100.0	38.8	40.0	10.5	10.6
55 to 64 years	16,731	8,960	4,719	1,526	1,527	100.0	53.6	28.2	9.1	9.1
65 years and over	18,141	12,716	3,013	1,193	1,218	100.0	70.1	16.6	6.6	6.7
Male, 25 years and over . . .	46,606	19,963	14,410	5,259	6,972	100.0	42.8	30.9	11.3	15.0
Female, 25 years and over .	51,506	21,825	20,083	5,191	4,408	100.0	42.4	39.0	10.1	8.6
Black										
18 to 24 years.	2,713	1,158	1,076	419	61	100.0	42.7	39.7	15.4	2.2
25 years and over	10,089	6,686	2,358	592	452	100.0	66.3	23.4	5.9	4.5
25 to 34 years	2,651	1,237	1,018	237	161	100.0	46.7	38.4	8.9	6.1
35 to 44 years	2,347	1,372	690	164	122	100.0	58.5	29.4	7.0	5.2
45 to 54 years	2,128	1,509	422	117	81	100.0	70.9	19.8	5.5	3.8
55 to 64 years	1,545	1,284	165	38	59	100.0	83.1	10.7	2.5	3.8
65 years and over	1,417	1,290	64	35	28	100.0	91.0	4.5	2.5	2.0
Male, 25 years and over . . .	4,619	3,120	1,025	261	212	100.0	67.5	22.2	5.7	4.6
Female, 25 years and over .	5,470	3,565	1,333	330	240	100.0	65.2	24.4	6.0	4.4

(1) Persons of Spanish origin may be of any race.

Public Libraries in Selected North American Cities

Source: World Almanac questionnaire (1981)

First figure in parentheses denotes number of branches-2d figure indicates number of bookmobiles. (*) indicates county library system; (†) indicates state library system; (C) Canadian dollars; (A) library has not provided up-to-date information.

City	No. bound volumes	Circulation	Cost of operation	City	No. bound volumes	Circulation	Cost of operation
Akron, Oh.* (18-3)	939,208	2,038,842	$ 4,304,433	Newark, N.J. (13-1) (A)	1,187,479	1,767,083	4,353,280
Atlanta Ga.* (27-3)	1,054,996	3,037,409	6,480,519	New Haven, Conn. (8-0)	564,386	447,334	(A)
Austin, Tex. (15-0)	652,007	1,919,884	4,334,592	New Orleans, La. (11-0)	747,135	1,143,420	3,428,398
Baltimore, Md.† (33-2)	2,157,077	2,214,845	10,188,821	New York City (research)	5,027,455	none	23,192,000
Birmingham, Ala. (18-2)	1,010,237	2,041,084	4,113,000	N.Y.C. branches (82-2)	3,572,056	8,600,017	29,948,000
Boston, Mass. (25-2)	4,829,050	1,950,492	9,291,500	Brooklyn* (57-0)	3,708,531	6,983,217	16,013,365
Buffalo, N.Y.* (42-4)	3,267,472	5,671,596	11,376,311	Queens* (58-0)	4,116,109	5,829,145	18,200,000
Calgary, Alta. (14-3)	793,053	3,739,560	8,145,777	Norfolk, Va. (11-2)	656,867	1,043,663	2,286,296
Charlotte, N.C.* (16-0)	715,580	1,837,038	3,862,243	Oakland, Cal. (18-3)	792,291	1,591,632	4,009,944
Chicago, Ill. (88-0)	4,198,162	7,229,063	28,649,000	Okla. City, Okla.* (10-5)	597,235	1,732,101	2,414,088
Cincinnati, Oh.* (3-2)	3,265,163	5,845,093	9,619,890	Omaha, Neb. (9-0)	555,527	1,735,235	2,563,283
Cleveland, Oh. (33-2)	2,541,876	3,118,006	17,819,262	Ottawa, Ont. (7-2)	613,575	2,091,956	5,640,510
Columbus, OH.* (20-3)	1,233,587	3,307,731	7,000,000+	Philadelphia, Pa. (51-0)	2,930,607	4,903,301	21,052,760
Dallas, Tex. (18-0)	1,912,317	3,743,104	8,794,444	Phoenix, Ariz. (9-1)	1,177,889	3,369,231	5,500,000
Dayton, Oh.* (19-1)	1,381,400	4,598,334	5,147,457	Pittsburgh, Pa. (21-5)	1,963,207	2,908,157	8,454,615
Denver, Col. (22-1)	1,728,648	2,922,046	7,914,500	Portland, Ore. (16-3)	1,129,743	3,042,654	4,753,707
Detroit, Mich. (26-4)	2,512,917	1,921,921	14,755,850	Richmond, Va. (6-2)	632,095	1,082,516	1,727,738
Edmonton, Alta. (11-3)	828,850	3,884,322	C10,211,000	Rochester, N.Y. (10-2)	931,458	1,567,594	5,100,100
El Paso, Tex. (8-4)	650,000	1,400,000	2,230,000	Sacramento, Cal.* (26-3)	1,057,000	3,428,680	6,700,000
Ft. Worth, Tex. (7-2) (A)	759,351	2,259,338	2,517,510	St. Catharines, Ont. (3-0)	312,352	942,574	C1,967,143
Hamilton, Ont. (9-2)	783,230	1,826,696	C8,359,000	St. Louis, Mo.* (13-22)	1,599,013	7,521,921	6,779,443
Hartford, Conn. (9-1)	486,000	432,000	2,103,800	St. Paul, Minn. (10-1)	759,286	1,754,795	3,518,690
Honolulu, Ha.† (47-8)	2,025,200	5,042,682	9,694,608	St. Petersburg, Fla. (4-1)	431,706	1,164,877	1,383,000
Houston, Tex. (30-3)	2,446,943	5,753,205	13,459,276	San Antonio, Tex. (9-7)	1,065,347	2,244,943	2,770,203
Indianapolis, Ind.* (23-2)	1,367,307	3,855,992	7,098,815	San Diego, Cal. (29-1)	1,645,912	4,102,386	5,684,811
Jacksonville, Fla.* (11-1)	942,996	2,177,556	3,196,235	San Francisco, Cal.* (26-1)	1,690,636	2,304,102	8,400,000
Kansas City, Mo. (17-0)	1,222,644	767,842	4,051,502	San Jose, Cal. (16-1)	1,082,742	2,015,020	4,786,000
Kitchener, Ont. (2-4)	406,000	1,258,405	C2,034,189	Saskatoon, Sask. (5-3) (A)	353,828	1,221,588	C2,558,712
London, Ont. (1-2)	547,123	1,836,267	4,194,828	Seattle, Wash. (22-3)	1,525,636	4,465,128	8,618,988
Long Beach, Cal. (13-0)	717,820	2,044,544	6,080,759	Syracuse, N.Y. (8-1)	911,374	1,116,000	4,920,227
Los Angeles, Cal. (66-5) (A)	5,364,882	12,009,014	17,543,199	Tampa, Fla.* (13-1)	645,648	2,048,563	4,352,269
Los Angeles, Cal.* (91-7) (A)	4,700,000	10,500,500	21,700,000	Toledo, Oh.* (17-2)	1,127,200	3,435,811	6,449,134
Louisville, Ky. (20-3)	1,009,220	2,214,707	5,196,670	Toronto, Ont. (27-1)	1,286,953	4,729,448	C12,710,186
Memphis, Tenn.* (2-3)	1,313,073	2,546,824	6,794,352	Tucson, Ariz.* (15-2)	745,000	3,400,000	5,340,500
Miami, Fla.* (24-4)	1,735,070	3,487,533	14,250,000	Tulsa, Okla.* (20-2)	800,000	1,695,987	5,510,314
Milwaukee, Wis. (12-3)	2,296,784	3,303,140	9,877,720	Vancouver, B.C. (18-1)	901,342	4,564,606	C8,238,937
Minneapolis, Minn. (14-1)	1,578,166	2,396,398	8,150,165	Washington, D.C.* (27-0)	1,425,820	1,466,623	11,200,000
Montreal, Que. (20-1)	1,244,613	3,075,370	C6,918,309	Wichita, Kan. (11-0)	431,110	1,202,542	2,608,728
Nashville, Tenn.* (13-3)	523,000	1,821,800	3,840,000	Windsor, Ont.(7-0)	482,300	1,070,000	C3,443,000
				Winnipeg, Man. (20-5) (A)	1,187,128	3,038,261	C4,306,321

Major U.S. Academic Libraries

Source: World Almanac questionnaire (1981)

(A) library has not provided up-to-date information.

Institution	No. bound volumes	Microfilm units	Enrollment	Staff Prof.	Staff Total	Annual acquisition expense
U. of California, Berkeley (A)	5,597,154	1,440,011	29,115	141	602	$3,164,447
U. of California, Los Angeles	4,108,682	1,806,105	31,300	140	584	4,989,891
U. of Chicago	4,310,824	743,893	7,889	70	287	1,935,783
U. of Colorado, Boulder	1,852,904	1,983,890	21,878	42	174	1,099,847
Columbia U.	5,100,000	2,300,000	17,000	141	516	3,200,000
Cornell U.	4,216,915	2,239,135	16,475	138	507	2,420,000
Duke U.	3,022,839	739,291	12,115	86	328	2,145,950
U. of Florida	2,162,982	1,657,092	33,242	83	368	2,844,301
Harvard U.	10,082,633	2,101,575	17,482	285	943	5,001,716
U. of Illinois, Urbana-Champaign	5,936,823	1,552,446	34,792	139	507	3,372,321
Indiana U., Bloomington (A)	3,735,523	898,879	76,394	121	471	2,433,500
U. of Iowa	2,295,266	1,502,000	24,518	74	247	2,525,400
Johns Hopkins U.	2,300,000	1,100,000	8,000	46	153	1,700,000
U. of Kansas	1,900,000	809,000	22,000	55	160	1,600,000
U. of Michigan, Ann Arbor (A)	5,049,501	1,403,096	35,824	155	576	2,212,803
Michigan State U.	2,613,447	1,117,363	41,374	77	303	1,739,402
U. of Minnesota (A)	3,702,599	1,126,011	47,000	129	434	2,250,000
U. of Missouri, Columbia	2,016,647	2,209,010	24,169	58	216	1,821,059
New York U.	2,869,122	1,456,577	30,073	80	329	1,823,388
U. of No. Carolina, Chapel Hill	2,604,404	1,447,865	21,060	82	286	2,825,763
Northwestern U.	2,806,320	944,804	16,619	94	343	2,065,770
Ohio State U.	3,446,729	1,602,962	55,152	101	322	2,670,029
U. of Pennsylvania (A)	2,900,000	1,400,000	21,900	88	242	1,471,368
U. of Pittsburgh	2,465,340	1,251,221	29,315	150	320	1,643,812
Princeton U.	3,260,396	1,396,298	5,877	94	394	2,588,531
Rutgers U.	2,216,843	1,512,086	35,297	106	362	2,542,699
Stanford U.	4,645,963	2,678,740	12,866	140	551	4,044,000
Syracuse U.	1,888,312	1,849,080	15,745	59	270	1,167,923
U. of Texas, Austin	4,547,508	2,211,079	46,148	126	533	2,880,062
Tulane U.	1,372,405	918,497	(A)	45	192	1,295,566
U. of Virginia	2,431,322	2,487,650	15,029	81	327	3,031,146
U. of Washington, Seattle	3,877,328	3,019,186	35,000	120	481	2,802,809
U. of Wisconsin, Madison	3,631,669	1,829,367	41,242	122	482	2,797,166
Yale U.	7,401,953	1,295,656	10,019	170	593	3,114,825

UNITED STATES POPULATION
1980 Census Records 226.5 Million Americans

During the past decade, the pace of population growth in the United States slowed to its lowest rate since the Great Depression.

A total of 226,504,825 Americans were counted in the 1980 census, an 11.4 percent increase since 1970. But the Census Bureau expects a downward rate of population growth—less than 10 percent—in this decade, and about 7 percent by the end of the century.

This is in sharp contrast to the 18.5 percent growth rate between 1950 and 1960, and the 13.3 percent increase in the 1960-70 decade.

A continuing decline in the rate of childbearing, which is now barely high enough to replace naturally a generation, helped accelerate the drop in the rate of population growth over the years.

1980 Census: Portrait of the Nation

Statistics tabulated thus far from the 1980 census reflect the condition of the nation at a point in time. They help direct our attention toward changes that reflect new challenges, new opportunities. For example: We're still a nation on the move. About 90 percent of the country's net population growth since 1970 occurred in the South and West. Those regions grew by 21.4 percent, while the Northeast and North Central regions grew by little more than 2 percent. More than half the population—52.3 percent—now lives in the South and West.

This population movement has major political implications. The final census numbers show that 17 seats in the U.S. House of Representatives have shifted from northern states to southern and western states. Beginning with the 98th Congress, a majority of the House will be elected from the South and West for the first time. Population changes within the congressional districts also are significant, ranging from a gain of 94 percent in 2 Florida districts to a loss of 50 percent in one district in New York.

Americans are showing a growing preference for living in less-settled areas. The 1980 census confirms that the nation has experienced a historic reversal in the metropolitan and nonmetropolitan growth rates. During the 1970s, nonmetropolitan areas grew by 15 percent, considerably more than the metropolitan rate of 9.5 percent.

This is a dramatic contrast to the 1960s when metro areas grew by 17 percent and the rest of the nation by just 4 percent. Before 1970, metropolitan areas had outpaced the growth rate of nonmetropolitan areas for at least 150 years.

A number of implications can be drawn from this new living pattern. On the one hand, it means that more and more people are showing a preference for living in small communities and in areas considered more attractive. This provides fresh economic opportunities for some of the less densely populated areas.

On the other hand, the trend creates new problems for both rural and urban areas. For growing nonmetropolitan areas it means added pressure for products and services, and it could reorder the social fabric. For metropolitan areas, and especially the central cities, the rural trend probably means a decrease in the tax base and curtailment of a wide range of social and economic services. It may force a reordering of many priorities.

Overall Drop in Metro Population

Many suburban cities and towns that boomed in the 1950s and 1960s now are experiencing stable and even declining populations. During the past decade the numerical shift toward the Sun Belt has been felt in both metropolitan and nonmetropolitan areas, negatively in the Northeast and Midwest, positively in the Sun Belt. All 25 of the fastest growing metropolitan areas, the census shows, were in the south and west; 10 of them in Florida and 5 in Texas. Fort Myers-Cape Coral in Florida nearly doubled in population, and 16 others increased by at least 50 percent. The biggest numerical gainer was Houston, with 900,000 additional people between 1970 and 1980. Nine other metro areas in Florida and Texas grew by at least 400,000.

The New York metropolitan area sustained the greatest loss, the population dropping by just over 850,000. But that area is still the nation's largest at more than 9 million. Like the New York metro area, the Buffalo, Cleveland, and Jersey City areas declined—by about 8 percent. In all, 32 metropolitan areas lost population during the decade, and all except 2 were in the Northeast and North Central states.

Despite the increased growth rate of nonmetropolitan areas, 3 of every 4 Americans lived in metropolitan areas on Census Day.

That total stands at about 170 million, an increase of 20 million since 1970. The total includes 323 metropolitan areas—318 in the United States and five in Puerto Rico. Thirty-six of the metro areas were just recently so designated.

Overall, the nation's cities lost population between 1970 and 1980, although the loss was only half of one percent. Most of the significant losses occurred in large northern cities, but some southern and west central cities had only modest gains.

There are 6 cities with more than a million people, and 4 of them—New York, Chicago, Philadelphia, and Detroit—lost population. The other 2, Los Angeles and Houston, have grown since 1970.

The number of cities between half a million and a million dropped from 20 to 16. Five major cities dropped below half a million, and they are St. Louis, Seattle, Pittsburgh, Denver, and Kansas City. Only San Jose moved above that level.

Almost no change in the ratio of males to females has occurred since 1970. On Census Day 1980, the total number of females had grown to about 116.5 million compared with 110 million men, a change of only one-tenth of a percent, in favor of women. On the other hand, there was rapid growth among the nation's minority populations.

Minority Groups Continue to Grow

Numerically, the Spanish origin population grew more rapidly than any other minority group, increasing by 61 percent since 1970 to a total of 14.6 million. This rapid rise is attributed to a relatively high birth rate and younger age distribution, greatly increased immigration, and improvements in census taking.

More than 60 percent of the Spanish origin population were living in three states on Census Day—California, New York and Texas. Hispanics have increased in numbers in some large cities to the extent that they outnumber blacks, or are close to it, in cities like New York, Los Angeles, San Diego, Phoenix, San Francisco, and Denver. They now make up the majority of the population in San Antonio.

The black population also showed a substantial gain in numbers and now totals 26.5 million—a 17 percent increase from the 1970 count of 22.6 million. About 53 percent of the nation's blacks were living in the South on Census Day.

Surveys of the 1970s show that about as many blacks moved to the South as left it during the decade, halting many decades of net migration to the North and West. Blacks currently make up at least 20 percent of the population in 7 southern states. Twelve states now have black populations of at least one million, up by 4 states since 1970, and half of them are in the South.

Asians and Pacific Islanders number 3.5 million, a substantial increase over the 1970 total of 1.5 million. Most of the increase came from immigration, including people who escaped the backwash of the Vietnam War. On Census Day nearly 60 percent of all Asians and Pacific Islanders were living on the Pacific Coast and in Hawaii, down from 71 percent in 1970.

American Indians, Eskimos and Aleuts numbered 1.4 million in 1980, a 71 percent increase since 1970. Much of this growth was due to natural increase but, again, improved census procedures helped produce a more complete count. One-third of this combined group lived in 3 states—California, Oklahoma, and Arizona. The count of American Indians passed the million mark for the first time since the Census Bureau began enumerating them.

Average American is Older

We're becoming older; some call it the graying of America. Since 1970, the median age of Americans has moved up to 30 years from 28. Expressed another way, half the population is 30 or older, half is younger. Even slight shifts in the median age are significant because these tend to be relatively stable numbers and change slowly over the years.

Three underlying factors influence this aging of the population: the decline in the fertility rate since 1970, the aging of the baby boom generation, and increasing longevity.

On Census Day 1980, the white population was the oldest at 31.3 years, followed by Asians and Pacific Islanders at 28.6. Then there was a sharp drop. The median age of blacks was 24.9; the Spanish origin population was 23.2, and the combination of American Indians, Eskimos, and Aleuts was slightly younger at exactly 23 years. Among Hispanics, nearly one-third were under 15 years old while only about 5 percent were 65 or older.

The lowest median age was in Utah, at 24.2 years, followed by

Alaska at 26.1 and Wyoming at 27.1. Four other states had a median age younger than 28. They are Idaho, Louisiana, Mississippi, and New Mexico. The latter state still remains one of the youngest even though it aged the most between censuses.

To no one's surprise, Florida continued to have the highest median age at 34.7 years. Florida was followed by New Jersey at 32.2 and Pennsylvania at 32.1. Four Northeast states—Connecticut, Massachusetts, New York and Rhode Island—had a median age between 31 and 32.

Dramatic Decrease in Household Size

The number of American households grew to 80,376,609, a substantial gain of 27 percent over 1970. But at the same time the number of people in households increased by only 12 percent. The result is a decline in the average household size from 3.11 persons in 1970 to 2.75 in 1980. This is considered a major demographic phenomenon.

California had the largest number of households in 1980, followed by New York and Texas. Utah had the largest average household size at 3.20 followed by Hawaii at 3.15. The District of Columbia recorded the smallest at 2.39, followed by Florida at 2.55.

Americans have witnessed important demographic, social and economic changes in the decades since World War II. None are more dramatic than the decade we have just left.

Population of the U.S., 1970-1980

Region, division, and state	1980 Census	1970 Census	Pct. + or –	1980			Rank	
				Urban	Rural	Pct. urban	1980	1970
United States.	226,504,825	203,235,298	11.5	166,965,380	59,539,445	73.7	. . .	. . .
Regions:								
Northeast	49,136,667	49,050,525	0.2	38,904,486	10,232,181	79.2	. . .	. . .
North Central	58,853,804	56,577,067	4.0	41,465,803	17,388,011	70.6	. . .	. . .
South.	75,349,155	62,798,347	20.0	50,382,409	24,966,746	66.9	. . .	. . .
West	43,165,199	34,809,359	24.0	36,212,682	6,952,517	83.9	. . .	. . .
New England	12,348,493	11,847,186	4.2	9,269,249	3,079,244	75.1	. . .	. . .
Maine.	1,124,660	993,663	15.2	534,072	590,588	47.5	38	38
New Hampshire.	920,610	737,681	24.8	480,325	440,285	52.2	42	41
Vermont.	511,456	444,732	15.0	172,735	338,721	33.8	48	48
Massachusetts	5,737,037	5,689,170	0.8	4,808,339	928,698	83.8	11	10
Rhode Island	947,154	949,723	-0.3	824,004	123,150	87.0	40	39
Connecticut	3,107,576	3,032,217	2.5	2,449,774	657,802	78.8	25	24
Middle Atlantic	36,788,174	37,203,339	-1.1	29,635,237	7,152,937	80.6	. . .	. . .
New York	17,557,288	18,241,266	-3.8	14,857,202	2,700,086	84.6	2	2
New Jersey	7,364,158	7,168,164	2.7	6,556,697	807,461	89.0	9	8
Pennsylvania	11,866,728	11,793,909	0.6	8,221,338	3,645,390	69.3	4	3
East North Central.	41,669,738	40,252,678	3.5	30,483,799	11,185,939	73.1	. . .	. . .
Ohio	10,797,419	10,652,017	1.3	7,916,181	2,881,238	73.3	6	6
Indiana	5,490,179	5,195,392	5.7	3,524,578	1,965,601	64.2	12	11
Illinois.	11,418,461	11,113,976	2.8	9,474,939	1,943,522	83.0	5	5
Michigan	9,258,344	8,875,083	4.2	6,547,842	2,710,502	70.7	8	7
Wisconsin	4,705,335	4,417,933	6.5	3,020,259	1,685,076	64.2	16	16
West North Central	17,184,066	16,324,389	5.3	10,982,904	6,202,062	63.9	. . .	. . .
Minnesota	4,077,148	3,805,069	7.1	2,725,270	1,351,878	66.8	21	19
Iowa	2,913,387	2,825,041	3.1	1,707,872	1,205,515	58.6	27	25
Missouri	4,917,444	4,677,399	5.1	3,350,746	1,566,698	68.1	15	13
North Dakota	652,695	617,761	5.6	318,263	334,432	48.8	46	45
South Dakota	690,178	666,257	3.6	320,223	369,955	46.4	45	44
Nebraska	1,570,006	1,483,791	5.7	983,731	586,275	62.7	35	35
Kansas	2,363,208	2,249,071	5.1	1,575,899	787,309	66.7	32	28
South Atlantic	36,943,139	30,671,337	20.4	24,798,027	12,145,112	67.1	. . .	. . .
Delaware	595,225	548,104	8.6	420,706	174,519	70.7	47	46
Maryland.	4,216,446	3,922,399	7.5	3,386,026	830,420	80.3	18	18
District of Columbia.	637,651	756,510	-15.7	637,651	—	100.0	. . .	. . .
Virginia	5,346,279	4,648,494	14.9	3,529,301	1,816,978	66.0	14	14
West Virginia	1,949,644	1,744,237	11.8	705,319	1,244,325	36.2	34	34
North Carolina.	5,874,429	5,082,059	15.5	2,818,794	3,055,635	48.0	10	12
South Carolina.	3,119,208	2,590,516	20.4	1,686,135	1,433,073	54.1	24	26
Georgia	5,464,265	4,589,575	19.1	3,406,171	2,058,094	62.3	13	15
Florida	9,739,992	6,789,443	43.4	8,207,924	1,532,068	84.3	7	9
East South Central.	14,662,882	12,804,552	14.5	8,157,600	6,505,282	55.6	. . .	. . .
Kentucky	3,661,433	3,219,311	13.7	1,859,478	1,801,955	50.8	23	23
Tennessee.	4,590,750	3,924,164	16.9	2,772,513	1,818,237	60.4	17	17
Alabama.	3,890,061	3,444,165	12.9	2,332,804	1,557,257	60.0	22	21
Mississippi	2,520,638	2,216,912	13.7	1,192,805	1,327,833	47.3	31	29
West South Central	23,743,134	19,322,458	22.9	17,426,782	6,316,352	73.4	. . .	. . .
Arkansas	2,285,513	1,923,295	18.8	1,179,079	1,106,434	51.6	33	32
Louisiana	4,203,972	3,643,180	15.3	2,885,535	1,318,437	68.6	19	20
Oklahoma	3,025,266	2,559,253	18.2	2,035,009	990,257	67.3	26	27
Texas.	14,228,383	11,196,730	27.1	11,327,159	2,901,224	79.6	3	4
Mountain	11,368,330	8,283,585	37.2	8,682,880	2,685,450	76.4	. . .	. . .
Montana	786,690	694,409	13.3	416,402	370,288	52.9	44	43
Idaho	943,935	713,008	32.4	509,702	434,233	54.0	41	42
Wyoming.	470,816	332,416	41.6	295,898	174,918	62.8	49	49
Colorado.	2,888,834	2,207,259	30.7	2,328,876	559,958	80.6	28	30
New Mexico	1,299,968	1,016,000	27.8	939,223	360,745	72.2	37	37
Arizona.	2,717,866	1,772,482	53.1	2,278,189	439,677	83.8	29	33
Utah	1,461,037	1,059,273	37.9	1,232,908	228,129	84.4	36	36
Nevada.	799,184	488,738	63.5	681,682	117,502	85.3	43	47
Pacific	31,796,869	26,525,774	19.9	27,529,802	4,267,067	86.6	. . .	. . .
Washington	4,130,163	3,409,169	21.0	3,037,765	1,092,398	73.6	20	22
Oregon.	2,632,663	2,091,385	25.9	1,787,912	844,751	67.9	30	31
California.	23,668,562	19,953,134	18.5	21,611,033	2,057,529	91.3	1	1
Alaska	400,481	302,173	32.4	258,191	142,290	64.5	50	50
Hawaii	965,000	769,913	25.3	834,901	130,099	86.5	39	40
Puerto Rico	3,196,520	2,712,083	17.9	2,134,365	1,062,155	66.8	. . .	. . .

Congressional Apportionment

	1980	1970		1980	1970		1980	1970		1980	1970		1980	1970
Ala..	7	7	Ida...	2	2	Minn..	8	8	N. D..	1	1	Vt...	1	1
Alas.	1	1	Ill...	22	24	Miss..	5	5	Oh. ,.	21	23	Va....	10	10
Ariz.	5	4	Ind...	10	11	Mo...	9	10	Okla..	6	6	Wash..	8	7
Ark..	4	4	Ia....	6	6	Mon...	2	2	Ore...	5	4	W. Va.	4	4
Cal..	45	43	Kan..	5	5	Neb...	3	3	Pa...	23	25	Wis...	9	9
Col..	6	5	Ky...	7	7	Nev...	2	1	R. I..	2	2	Wy...	1	1
Conn..	6	6	La...	8	8	N. H..	2	2	S. C..	6	6			
Del..	1	1	Me...	2	2	N. J...	14	15	S. D..	1	2	Totals.	435	435
Fla..	19	15	Md...	8	8	N. M..	3	2	Tenn..	9	8			
Ga..	10	10	Mass..	11	12	N. Y...	34	39	Tex...	27	24			
Ha..	2	2	Mich..	18	19	N. C...	11	11	Ut....	3	2			

The chief reason the Constitution provided for a census of the population every 10 years was to give a basis for apportionment of representatives among the states. This apportionment largely determines the number of electoral votes allotted to each state.

The number of representatives of each state in Congress is determined by the state's population, but each state is entitled to one representative regardless of population. A Congressional apportionment has been made after each decennial census except that of 1920.

Under provisions of a law that became effective Nov. 15, 1941, apportionment of representatives is made by the method of equal proportions. In the application of this method, the apportionment is made so that the average population per representative has the least possible variation between one state and any other. The first House of Representatives, in 1790, had 65 members, or one representative for each 30,000 of the estimated population, as provided by the Constitution. As the population grew, the number of representatives was increased but the total membership has been fixed at 435 since 1912.

U.S. Area and Population: 1790 to 1970

Source: U.S. Bureau of the Census

Area figures represent area on indicated date including in some cases considerable areas not then organized or settled, and not covered by the census. Area figures have been adjusted to bring them into agreement with remeasurements made in 1940.

	Area (square miles)			Population			
Census date	Gross	Land	Water	Number	Per sq. mile of land	Increase over preceding census Number	%
1790 (Aug. 2)	888,811	864,746	24,065	3,929,214	4.5	(X)	(X)
1800 (Aug. 4)	888,811	864,746	24,065	5,308,483	6.1	1,379,269	35.1
1810 (Aug. 6)	1,716,003	1,681,828	34,175	7,239,881	4.3	1,931,398	36.4
1820 (Aug. 7)	1,788,006	1,749,462	38,544	9,638,453	5.5	2,398,572	33.1
1830 (June 1)	1,788,006	1,749,462	38,544	12,866,020	7.4	3,227,567	33.5
1840 (June 1)	1,788,006	1,749,462	38,544	17,069,453	9.8	4,203,433	32.7
1850 (June 1)	2,992,747	2,940,042	52,705	23,191,876	7.9	6,122,423	35.9
1860 (June 1)	3,022,387	2,969,640	52,747	31,443,321	10.6	8,251,445	35.6
1870 (June 1)	3,022,387	2,969,640	52,747	'39,818,449	'13.4	8,375,128	26.6
1880 (June 1)	3,022,387	2,969,640	52,747	50,155,783	16.9	10,337,334	26.0
1890 (June 1)	3,022,387	2,969,640	52,747	62,947,714	21.2	12,791,931	25.5
1900 (June 1)	3,022,387	2,969,834	52,553	75,994,575	25.6	13,046,861	20.7
1910 (Apr. 15)	3,022,387	2,969,565	52,822	91,972,266	31.0	15,977,691	21.0
1920 (Jan. 1)	3,022,387	2,969,451	52,936	105,710,620	35.6	13,738,354	14.9
1930 (Apr. 1)	3,022,387	2,977,128	45,259	122,775,046	41.2	17,064,426	16.1
1940 (Apr. 1)	3,022,387	2,977,128	45,259	131,669,275	44.2	8,894,229	7.2
1950 (Apr. 1)[2]	3,615,211	3,552,206	63,005	151,325,798	42.6	19,161,229	14.5
1960 (Apr. 1)[2]	3,615,123	3,540,911	74,212	179,323,175	50.6	27,997,377	18.5
1970 (Apr. 1)[2]	³3,618,467	³3,540,023	³78,444	⁴203,211,926	57.4	23,888,751	13.3

(X) Not applicable. (1) Revised to include adjustments for underenumeration in Southern States; unrevised number is 38,558,371. (2) Includes Alaska and Hawaii. (3) Figures corrected after final reports were issued. (4) The official 1970 resident population count is 203,235,298; the difference of 23,372 is due to errors found after tabulations were completed.

Black and Hispanic Population by States

Source: U.S. Bureau of the Census (provisional, 1980)

	Black	Hispanic		Black	Hispanic		Black	Hispanic
Ala.	995,623	33,100	La.	1,237,263	99,105	Okla.	204,658	57,413
Alas.	13,619	9,497	Me.	3,128	5,005	Ore.	37,059	65,833
Ariz.	75,034	440,915	Md.	958,050	64,740	Pa.	1,047,609	154,004
Ark.	373,192	17,873	Mass.	221,279	141,043	R.I.	27,584	19,707
Cal.	1,819,282	4,543,770	Mich.	1,198,710	162,388	S.C.	948,146	33,414
Col.	101,702	339,300	Minn.	53,342	32,124	S.D.	2,144	4,028
Conn. . . .	217,433	124,499	Miss.	887,206	24,731	Tenn.	725,949	34,081
Del.	95,971	9,671	Mo.	514,274	51,667	Tex.	1,710,250	2,985,643
D.C.	448,229	17,652	Mon.	1,786	9,974	Ut.	9,225	60,302
Fla.	1,342,478	857,898	Neb.	48,389	28,020	Vt.	1,135	3,304
Ga.	1,465,457	61,261	Nev.	50,791	53,786	Va.	1,008,311	79,873
Ha.	17,352	71,479	N.H.	3,990	5,587	Wash. . . .	105,544	119,986
Ida.	2,716	36,615	N.J.	924,786	491,867	W.Va. . . .	65,051	12,707
Ill.	1,675,229	635,525	N.M.	24,042	476,089	Wis.	182,593	62,981
Ind.	414,732	87,020	N.Y.	2,401,842	1,659,245	Wy.	3,364	24,499
Ia.	41,700	25,536	N.C.	1,316,050	56,607	Total	26,488,218	14,605,883
Kan.	126,127	63,333	N.D.	2,568	3,903			
Ky.	259,490	27,403	Oh.	1,076,734	119,880			

U.S. Population by Official

(Members of the Armed Forces overseas or

State	1790	1800	1810	1820	1830	1840	1850	1860	1870	1880
Ala...	....	1,250	9,046	127,901	309,527	590,756	771,623	964,201	996,992	1,262,505
Alas...	....	....	....	....	....	....	....	....		
Ariz...	....	....	....	....	....	....	....	....	9,658	40,440
Ark...	....	....	1,062	14,273	30,388	97,574	209,897	435,450	484,471	802,525
Cal...	....	....	....	....	....	....	92,597	379,994	560,247	864,694
Col...	....	....	....	....	....	....	....	34,277	39,864	194,327
Conn...	237,946	251,002	261,942	275,248	297,675	309,978	370,792	460,147	537,454	622,700
Del...	59,096	64,273	72,674	72,749	76,748	78,085	91,532	112,216	125,015	146,608
D.C...	....	14,023	24,023	33,039	39,834	43,712	51,687	75,080	131,700	177,624
Fla...	....	....	....	....	34,730	54,477	87,445	140,424	187,748	269,493
Ga...	82,548	162,686	252,433	340,989	516,823	691,392	906,185	1,057,286	1,184,109	1,542,180
Ha...	....	....	....	....	....	....	....	....		
Ida...	....	....	....	....	....	....	....	....	14,999	32,610
Ill...	....	....	12,282	55,211	157,445	476,183	851,470	1,711,951	2,539,891	3,077,871
Ind...	....	5,641	24,520	147,178	343,031	685,866	988,416	1,350,428	1,680,637	1,978,301
Ia...	....	....	....	....	....	43,112	192,214	674,913	1,194,020	1,624,615
Kan...	....	....	....	....	....	....	....	107,206	364,399	996,096
Ky...	73,677	220,955	406,511	564,317	687,917	779,828	982,405	1,155,684	1,321,011	1,648,690
La...	....	....	76,556	153,407	215,739	352,411	517,762	708,002	726,915	939,946
Me...	96,540	151,719	228,705	298,335	399,455	501,793	583,169	628,279	626,915	648,936
Md...	319,728	341,548	380,546	407,350	447,040	470,019	583,034	687,049	780,894	934,943
Mass..	378,787	422,845	472,040	523,287	610,408	737,699	994,514	1,231,066	1,457,351	1,783,085
Mich..	....	....	4,762	8,896	31,639	212,267	397,654	749,113	1,184,059	1,636,937
Minn..	....	....	....	....	....	....	6,077	172,023	439,706	780,773
Miss...	....	8,850	40,352	75,448	136,621	375,651	606,526	791,305	827,922	1,131,597
Mo...	....	....	19,783	66,586	140,455	383,702	682,044	1,182,012	1,721,295	2,168,380
Mon...	....	....	....	....	....	....	....	....	20,595	39,159
Neb...	....	....	....	....	....	....	....	28,841	122,993	452,402
Nev...	....	....	....	....	....	....	....	6,857	42,491	62,266
N.H...	141,885	183,858	214,460	244,161	269,328	284,574	317,976	326,073	318,300	346,991
N.J...	184,139	211,149	245,562	277,575	320,823	373,306	489,555	672,035	906,096	1,131,116
N.M...	....	....	....	....	....	....	61,547	93,516	91,874	119,565
N.Y...	340,120	589,051	959,049	1,372,812	1,918,608	2,428,921	3,097,394	3,880,735	4,382,759	5,082,871
N.C...	393,751	478,103	555,500	638,829	737,987	753,419	869,039	992,622	1,071,361	1,399,750
N.D...	....	....	....	....	....	....	....	....	*2,405	36,909
Oh...	....	45,365	230,760	581,434	937,903	1,519,467	1,980,329	2,339,511	2,665,260	3,198,062
Okla...	....	....	....	....	....	....	....	....		
Ore...	....	....	....	....	....	....	13,294	52,465	90,923	174,768
Pa...	434,373	602,365	810,091	1,049,458	1,348,233	1,724,033	2,311,786	2,906,215	3,521,951	4,282,891
R.I...	68,825	69,122	76,931	83,059	97,199	108,830	147,545	174,620	217,353	276,531
S.C...	249,073	345,591	415,115	502,741	581,185	594,398	668,507	703,708	705,606	995,577
S.D...	....	....	....	....	....	....	....	*4,837	*11,776	98,268
Tenn...	35,691	105,602	261,727	422,823	681,904	829,210	1,002,717	1,109,801	1,258,520	1,542,359
Tex...	....	....	....	....	....	....	212,592	604,215	818,579	1,591,749
Ut...	....	....	....	....	....	....	11,380	40,273	86,786	143,963
Vt...	85,425	154,465	217,895	235,981	280,652	291,948	314,120	315,098	330,551	332,286
Va...	821,287	880,200	974,600	1,065,366	1,211,405	1,239,797	1,421,661	1,596,318	1,225,163	1,512,565
Wash..	....	....	....	....	....	....	....	1,201	11,594	23,955	75,116
W. Va..	....	....	....	....	....	....	....	....	442,014	618,457
Wis...	....	....	....	....	....	30,945	305,391	775,881	1,054,670	1,315,497
Wy...	....	....	....	....	....	....	....	....	9,118	20,789
U.S...	3,929,214	5,308,483	7,239,881	9,638,453	12,866,020	17,069,453	23,191,876	31,443,321	38,558,371	50,155,783

*1860 figure is for Dakota Territory; 1870 figures are for parts of Dakota Territory. (1) U.S. total includes persons (5,318 in 1830 and 6,100 in 1840) on public ships in the service of the United States not credited to any region, division, or state.

Density of Population by States

(Per square mile, land area only)

State	1920	1960	1970	1980	State	1920	1960	1970	1980	State	1920	1960	1970	1980
Ala...	45.8	64.2	67.9	76.7	La...	39.6	72.2	81.0	93.6	Okla...	29.2	33.8	37.2	44.0
Alas.*	0.1	0.4	0.5	0.7	Me...	25.7	31.3	32.1	36.4	Ore...	8.2	18.4	21.7	27.4
Ariz...	2.9	11.5	15.6	24.0	Md...	145.8	313.5	396.6	426.3	Pa...	194.5	251.4	262.3	263.9
Ark...	33.4	34.2	37.0	44.0	Mass...	479.2	657.3	727.0	733.1	R.I...	566.4	819.3	905.5	902.9
Cal...	22.0	100.4	127.6	151.4	Mich...	63.8	137.6	156.2	163.0	S.C...	55.2	78.7	85.7	103.2
Col...	9.1	16.9	21.3	27.8	Minn...	29.5	43.0	48.0	51.4	S.D...	8.3	9.0	8.8	9.1
Conn...	286.4	520.6	623.7	639.2	Miss...	38.6	46.0	46.9	53.3	Tenn...	56.1	86.2	94.9	111.1
Del...	113.5	225.2	276.5	300.3	Mo...	49.5	62.6	67.8	71.3	Tex...	17.8	36.4	42.7	54.3
D. C...	7,292.9	12,523.9	12,401.8	10,453.3	Mon...	3.8	4.6	4.8	5.4	Ut...	5.5	10.8	12.9	17.8
Fla...	17.7	91.5	125.5	176.8	Neb...	16.9	18.4	19.4	20.5	Vt...	38.6	42.0	47.9	55.2
Ga...	49.3	67.8	79.0	94.1	Nev...	.7	2.6	4.4	7.3	Va...	57.4	99.5	116.9	134.4
Ha.*	39.9	98.5	119.8	150.2	N. H...	49.1	67.2	81.7	102.0	Wash...	20.3	42.8	51.2	62.0
Ida...	5.2	8.1	8.6	11.4	N. J...	420.0	805.5	953.1	979.1	W. Va...	60.9	77.2	72.5	81.0
Ill...	115.7	180.4	199.4	204.8	N. M...	2.9	7.8	8.4	10.7	Wis...	47.6	72.6	81.1	86.4
Ind...	81.3	128.8	143.9	152.1	N. Y...	217.9	350.6	381.3	367.1	Wy...	2.0	3.4	3.4	4.8
Ia...	43.2	49.2	50.5	52.1	N. C...	52.5	93.2	104.1	120.4	U.S..	*29.9	50.6	57.5	64.0
Kan...	21.6	26.6	27.5	28.9	N. D...	9.2	9.1	8.9	- 9.4					
Ky...	60.1	76.2	81.2	92.3	Oh...	141.4	236.6	260.0	263.5					

*For purposes of comparison, Alaska and Hawaii included in above tabulation for 1920, even though not states then.

Census from 1790 to 1980

other U.S. nationals overseas are not included.)

1890	1900	1910	1920	1930	1940	1950	1960	1970	1980
1,513,401	1,828,697	2,138,093	2,348,174	2,646,248	2,832,961	3,061,743	3,266,740	3,444,354	3,890,061
......	......	......					226,167	302,583	400,481
88,243	122,931	204,354	334,162	435,573	499,261	749,587	1,302,161	1,775,399	2,717,866
1,128,211	1,311,564	1,574,449	1,752,204	1,854,482	1,949,387	1,909,511	1,786,272	1,923,322	2,285,513
1,213,398	1,485,053	2,377,549	3,426,861	5,677,251	6,907,387	10,586,223	15,717,204	19,971,069	23,668,562
413,249	539,700	799,024	939,629	1,035,791	1,123,296	1,325,089	1,753,947	2,209,596	2,888,834
746,258	908,420	1,114,756	1,380,631	1,606,903	1,709,242	2,007,280	2,535,234	3,032,217	3,107,576
168,493	184,735	202,322	223,003	238,380	266,505	318,085	446,292	548,104	595,225
230,392	278,718	331,069	437,571	486,869	663,091	802,178	763,956	756,668	637,651
391,422	528,542	752,619	968,470	1,468,211	1,897,414	2,771,305	4,951,560	6,791,418	9,739,992
1,837,353	2,216,331	2,609,121	2,895,832	2,908,506	3,123,723	3,444,578	3,943,116	4,587,930	5,464,265
......	......	......					632,772	769,913	965,000
88,548	161,772	325,594	431,866	445,032	524,873	588,637	667,191	713,015	943,935
3,826,352	4,821,550	5,638,591	6,485,280	7,630,654	7,897,241	8,712,176	10,081,158	11,110,285	11,418,461
2,192,404	2,516,462	2,700,876	2,930,390	3,238,503	3,427,796	3,934,224	4,662,498	5,195,392	5,490,179
1,912,297	2,231,853	2,224,771	2,404,021	2,470,939	2,538,268	2,621,073	2,757,537	2,825,368	2,913,387
1,428,108	1,470,495	1,690,949	1,769,257	1,880,999	1,801,028	1,905,299	2,178,611	2,249,071	2,363,208
1,858,635	2,147,174	2,289,905	2,416,630	2,614,589	2,845,627	2,944,806	3,038,156	3,220,711	3,661,433
1,118,588	1,381,625	1,656,388	1,798,509	2,101,593	2,363,880	2,683,516	3,257,022	3,644,637	4,203,972
661,086	694,466	742,371	768,014	797,423	847,226	913,774	969,265	993,722	1,124,660
1,042,390	1,188,044	1,295,346	1,449,661	1,631,526	1,821,244	2,343,001	3,100,689	3,923,897	4,216,446
2,238,947	2,805,346	3,366,416	3,852,356	4,249,614	4,316,721	4,690,514	5,148,578	5,689,170	5,737,037
2,093,890	2,420,982	2,810,173	3,668,412	4,842,325	5,256,106	6,371,766	7,823,194	8,881,826	9,258,344
1,310,283	1,751,394	2,075,708	2,387,125	2,563,953	2,792,300	2,982,483	3,413,864	3,806,103	4,077,148
1,289,600	1,551,270	1,797,114	1,790,618	2,009,821	2,183,796	2,178,914	2,178,141	2,216,994	2,520,638
2,679,185	3,106,665	3,293,335	3,404,055	3,629,367	3,784,664	3,954,653	4,319,813	4,677,623	4,917,444
142,924	243,329	376,053	548,889	537,606	559,456	591,024	674,767	694,409	786,690
1,062,656	1,066,300	1,192,214	1,296,372	1,377,963	1,315,834	1,325,510	1,411,330	1,485,333	1,570,006
47,355	42,335	81,875	77,407	91,058	110,247	160,083	285,278	488,738	799,184
376,530	411,588	430,572	443,083	465,293	491,524	533,242	606,921	737,681	920,610
1,444,933	1,883,669	2,537,167	3,155,900	4,041,334	4,160,165	4,835,329	6,066,782	7,171,112	7,364,158
160,282	195,310	327,301	360,350	423,317	531,818	681,187	951,023	1,017,055	1,299,968
6,003,174	7,268,894	9,113,614	10,385,227	12,588,066	13,479,142	14,830,192	16,782,304	18,241,391	17,557,288
1,617,949	1,893,810	2,206,287	2,559,123	3,170,276	3,571,623	4,061,929	4,556,155	5,084,411	5,874,429
190,983	319,146	577,056	646,872	680,845	641,935	619,636	632,446	617,792	652,695
3,672,329	4,157,545	4,767,121	5,759,394	6,646,697	6,907,612	7,946,627	9,706,397	10,657,423	10,797,419
258,657	790,391	1,657,155	2,028,283	2,396,040	2,336,434	2,233,351	2,328,284	2,559,463	3,025,266
317,704	413,536	672,765	783,389	953,786	1,089,684	1,521,341	1,768,687	2,091,533	2,632,663
5,258,113	6,302,115	7,665,111	8,720,017	9,631,350	9,900,180	10,498,012	11,319,366	11,800,766	11,866,728
345,506	428,556	542,610	604,397	687,497	713,346	791,896	859,488	949,723	947,154
1,151,149	1,340,316	1,515,400	1,683,724	1,738,765	1,899,804	2,117,027	2,382,594	2,590,713	3,119,208
348,600	401,570	583,888	636,547	692,849	642,961	652,740	680,514	666,257	690,178
1,767,518	2,020,616	2,184,789	2,337,885	2,616,556	2,915,841	3,291,718	3,567,089	3,926,018	4,590,750
2,235,527	3,048,710	3,896,542	4,663,228	5,824,715	6,414,824	7,711,194	9,579,677	11,198,655	14,228,383
210,779	276,749	373,351	449,396	507,847	550,310	688,862	890,627	1,059,273	1,461,037
332,422	343,641	355,956	352,428	359,611	359,231	377,747	389,881	444,732	511,456
1,655,980	1,854,184	2,061,612	2,309,187	2,421,851	2,677,773	3,318,680	3,966,949	4,651,448	5,346,279
357,232	518,103	1,141,990	1,356,621	1,563,396	1,736,191	2,378,963	2,853,214	3,413,244	4,130,163
762,794	958,800	1,221,119	1,463,701	1,729,205	1,901,974	2,005,552	1,860,421	1,744,237	1,949,644
1,693,330	2,069,042	2,333,860	2,632,067	2,939,006	3,137,587	3,434,575	3,951,777	4,417,821	4,705,335
62,555	92,531	145,965	194,402	225,565	250,742	290,529	330,066	332,416	470,816
62,947,714	75,994,575	91,972,266	105,710,620	122,775,046	131,669,275	150,697,361	179,323,175	203,302,031	226,504,825

U.S. Center of Population, 1790-1980

Center of Population is that point which may be considered as center of population gravity of the U.S. or that point upon which the U.S. would balance if it were a rigid plane without weight and the population distributed thereon with each individual being assumed to have equal weight and to exert an influence on a central point proportional to his distance from that point.

Year	N. Lat. °	'	"	W. Long. °	'	"	Approximate location
1790	39	16	30	76	11	12	23 miles east of Baltimore, Md.
1800	39	16	6	76	56	30	18 miles west of Baltimore, Md.
1810	39	11	30	77	37	12	40 miles northwest by west of Washington, D.C. (in Va.)
1820	39	5	42	78	33	0	16 miles east of Moorefield, W. Va.[1]
1830	38	57	54	79	16	54	19 miles west-southwest of Moorefield, W. Va.[1]
1840	39	2	0	80	18	0	16 miles south of Clarksburg, W. Va.[1]
1850	38	59	0	81	19	0	23 miles southeast of Parkersburg, W. Va.[1]
1860	39	0	24	82	48	48	20 miles south by east of Chillicothe, Oh.
1870	39	12	0	83	35	42	48 miles east by north of Cincinnati, Oh.
1880	39	4	8	84	39	40	8 miles west by south of Cincinnati, Oh. (in Ky.)
1890	39	11	56	85	32	53	20 miles east of Columbus, Ind.
1900	39	9	36	85	48	54	6 miles southeast of Columbus, Ind.
1910	39	10	12	86	32	20	In the city of Bloomington, Ind.
1920	39	10	21	86	43	15	8 miles south-southeast of Spencer, Owen County, Ind.
1930	39	3	45	87	8	6	3 miles northeast of Linton, Greene County, Ind.
1940	38	56	54	87	22	35	2 miles southeast by east of Carlisle, Sullivan County, Ind.
1950 (Inc. Alaska & Hawaii)	38	48	15	88	22	8	3 miles northeast of Louisville, Clay County, Ill.
1960	38	35	58	89	12	35	6 1/2 miles northwest of Centralia, Ill.
1970	38	27	47	89	42	22	5 miles east southeast of Mascoutah, St. Clair County, Ill.
1980	38	8	13	90	34	26	near DeSoto, Mo.

(1) West Virginia was set off from Virginia Dec. 31, 1862, and admitted as a state June 20, 1863.

Rankings of U.S. Standard Metropolitan Statistical Areas

Source: U.S. Bureau of the Census

Metropolitan areas are ranked by 1980 provisional population size based on new SMSA definitions and compared with a ranking of areas as defined in the 1970 census. Included are the Standard Metropolitan Statistical Areas (SMSAs) as defined through June 30, 1980 by the Office of Federal Statistical Policy and Standards, excluding 4 areas in Puerto Rico not covered in the report.

SMSA	1980(P) Rank	Pop.	1970 Rank	Pop.
New York, NY-NJ	1	9,080,777	1	9,973,716
Los Angeles-Long Beach, CA.	2	7,445,721	2	7,041,980
Chicago, IL	3	7,057,853	3	6,974,755
Philadelphia, PA-NJ	4	4,700,996	4	4,824,110
Detroit, MI	5	4,344,139	5	4,435,051
San Francisco-Oakland, CA.	6	3,226,867	6	3,109,249
Washington, DC-MD-VA	7	3,045,399	7	2,910,111
Dallas-Fort Worth, TX	8	2,964,342	12	2,377,623
Houston, TX	9	2,891,146	16	1,999,316
Boston, MA	10	2,759,800	8	2,899,101
Nassau-Suffolk, NY	11	2,603,817	9	2,555,868
St. Louis, MO-IL	12	2,344,912	10	2,410,884
Pittsburgh, PA.	13	2,260,919	11	2,401,362
Baltimore, MD.	14	2,166,308	13	2,071,016
Minneapolis-St. Paul, MN-WI	15	2,109,207	17	1,965,391
Atlanta, GA	16	2,010,368	18	1,595,517
Newark, NJ	17	1,963,600	15	2,057,468
Anaheim-Santa Ana-Garden Grove, CA	18	1,925,840	20	1,421,233
Cleveland, OH	19	1,895,997	14	2,063,729
San Diego, CA	20	1,859,623	23	1,357,854
Denver-Boulder, CO	21	1,615,442	27	1,239,545
Seattle-Everett, WA	22	1,600,944	19	1,424,605
Miami, FL	23	1,573,817	26	1,267,792
Tampa-St. Petersburg, FL.	24	1,550,035	30	1,088,549
Riverside-San Bernardino-Ontario, CA.	25	1,538,066	28	1,139,149
Phoenix, AZ	26	1,511,552	35	971,228
Milwaukee, WI	27	1,392,872	21	1,403,884
Cincinnati, OH-KY-IN.	28	1,392,394	22	1,387,207
Kansas City, MO-KS	29	1,322,156	25	1,273,926
San Jose, CA	30	1,290,487	31	1,065,313
Buffalo, NY	31	1,241,434	24	1,349,211
Portland, OR-WA.	32	1,236,294	34	1,007,130
New Orleans, LA	33	1,183,606	32	1,046,470
Indianapolis, IN	34	1,161,539	29	1,111,352
Columbus, OH	35	1,088,973	33	1,017,847
San Antonio, TX	36	1,070,245	38	888,179
Sacramento, CA	37	1,010,989	42	803,793
Fort Lauderdale-Hollywood, FL	38	1,005,507	58	620,100
Rochester, NY	39	970,313	36	961,516
Salt Lake City-Ogden, UT.	40	935,280	49	705,458
Providence-Warwick-Pawtucket, RI-MA.	41	917,962	37	908,887
Memphis, TN-AR-MS	42	909,767	41	834,103
Louisville, KY-IN	43	901,970	39	867,330
Birmingham, AL	44	834,067	44	767,230
Oklahoma City, OK	45	829,584	51	699,092
Nashville-Davidson, TN	46	828,540	50	699,271
Dayton, OH	47	826,891	40	852,531
Greensboro-Winston-Salem-High Point, NC	48	823,285	47	724,129
Norfolk-Virginia Beach-Portsmouth, VA-NC	49	799,853	46	732,600
Albany-Schenectady-Troy, NY	50	794,298	43	777,977
Toledo, OH-MI	51	791,137	45	762,658
Honolulu, HI	52	762,020	55	630,528
Jacksonville, FL	53	736,343	57	621,827
Hartford, CT.	54	726,036	48	720,581
Orlando, FL	55	694,645	74	453,270
Tulsa, OK	56	678,627	63	549,154
Akron, OH.	57	660,233	52	679,239
Syracuse, NY	58	642,547	53	636,596
Gary, IN	59	638,945	54	633,367
Allentown-Bethlehem-Easton, PA-NJ.	60	637,109	60	594,382
Charlotte-Gastonia, NC	61	632,083	62	557,785
Richmond, VA.	62	630,965	64	547,542
Northeast Pennsylvania	63	629,912	56	621,882
Grand Rapids, MI	64	601,106	67	539,225
New Brunswick-Perth Amboy-Sayreville, NJ	65	594,984	61	583,813
Omaha, NE-IA	66	566,140	65	542,646
Greenville-Spartanburg, SC.	67	562,934	71	473,454
Jersey City, NJ	68	555,483	59	607,839
West Palm Beach, FL	69	551,961	96	348,993
Austin, TX	70	532,811	93	360,463
Tucson, AZ	71	531,896	95	351,667
Springfield-Chicopee-Holyoke, MA.	72	530,373	66	541,752
Youngstown-Warren, OH	73	529,887	68	537,124
Oxnard-Simi Valley-Ventura, CA.	74	529,425	85	378,497
Raleigh-Durham, NC	75	525,059	76	419,254
Wilmington, DE-NJ-MD	76	523,386	70	499,493
Flint, MI	77	521,541	69	508,664
Fresno, CA	78	507,005	77	413,329
Long Branch-Asbury Park, NJ	79	496,313	72	461,849
Baton Rouge, LA	80	495,888	87	375,628
Tacoma, WA	81	482,692	78	412,344
El Paso, TX	82	479,448	94	359,291
Knoxville, TN	83	475,109	81	409,409
Lansing, MI	84	467,584	75	424,271
Las Vegas, NV	85	462,218	123	273,288
Albuquerque, NM.	86	448,798	102	333,266
Paterson-Clifton-Passaic, NJ	87	447,785	73	460,782
Harrisburg, PA	88	446,308	80	410,505
Mobile, AL.	89	439,941	86	376,690
Johnson City-Kingsport-Bristol, TN-VA.	90	433,204	88	373,591
Chattanooga, TN-GA.	91	420,873	90	370,857
New Haven, CT.	92	416,053	79	411,287
Charleston-North Charleston, SC.	93	416,012	100	336,125
Wichita, KS	94	410,121	84	389,352
Canton, OH.	95	403,847	83	393,789
Bakersfield, CA.	96	401,540	104	330,234
Columbia, SC.	97	395,775	107	322,880
Bridgeport, CT	98	395,056	82	401,752
Little Rock, AR	99	393,781	106	323,296
Davenport-Rock I.-Moline, IA-IL	100	383,017	91	362,638
York, PA.	101	380,604	105	329,540
Fort Wayne, IN	102	380,439	92	361,984
Shreveport, LA	103	376,704	101	336,000
Beaumont-Port Arthur-Orange, TX.	104	374,809	97	347,568
Worcester, MA	105	371,784	89	372,144
Peoria, IL	106	363,872	98	341,979
Newport News-Hampton, VA	107	363,817	103	333,140
Lancaster, PA.	108	361,998	108	320,079
Stockton, CA	109	347,312	113	291,073
Spokane, WA	110	341,058	115	287,487
Des Moines, IA	111	337,814	109	313,562
Vallejo-Fairfield, Napa, CA	112	327,589	135	251,129
Corpus Christi, TX	113	324,245	118	284,832
Madison, WI	114	323,109	114	290,272
Lakeland-Winter Haven, FL.	115	321,919	143	228,515
Augusta, GA-SC	116	320,574	122	275,787
Utica-Rome, NY	117	319,344	99	340,477
Colorado Springs, CO	118	317,584	139	239,288
Jackson, MS	119	316,252	130	258,906
Lexington-Fayette, KY	120	316,098	125	266,701
Reading, PA.	121	312,543	112	296,382
Huntington-Ashland, WV-KY-OH.	122	309,731	116	286,935
Huntsville, AL.	123	308,277	119	282,450
Evansville, IN-KY.	124	307,103	117	284,959
Trenton, NJ	125	305,678	110	304,116
Binghamton, NY	126	300,884	111	302,672
Santa Barbara-Santa Maria-Lompoc, CA	127	297,722	127	264,324
Santa Rosa, CA	128	292,275	156	204,885
Appleton-Oshkosh, WI	129	291,074	121	276,948
Salinas-Seaside-Monterey, CA	130	289,301	136	247,450

SMSA	1980 (P) Rank	Pop.	1970 Rank	Pop.
Pensacola, FL.	131	284,408	137	243,075
Lawrence-Haverhill, MA-NH .	132	281,283	131	258,564
McAllen-Pharr-Edinburg, TX. .	133	279,857	162	181,535
Erie, PA	134	279,290	128	263,654
Rockford, IL	135	278,841	124	272,063
Kalamazoo-Portage, MI	136	278,762	132	257,723
South Bend, IN	137	278,109	120	279,813
Lorain-Elyria, OH	138	273,980	134	256,843
Montgomery, AL	139	273,154	146	225,911
Eugene-Springfield, OR	140	273,114	151	215,401
Melbourne-Titusville-Cocoa, FL	141	270,481	142	230,006
Modesto, CA	142	265,671	158	194,506
Duluth-Superior, MN-WI . . .	143	265,430	126	265,350
Johnstown, PA	144	264,241	129	262,822
Ann Arbor, MI	145	261,345	141	234,103
Charleston, WV	146	260,637	133	257,140
Hamilton-Middletown, OH . .	147	258,380	145	226,207
Macon, GA	148	251,736	144	226,782
Daytona Beach, FL	149	250,924	174	169,487
Salem, OR	150	249,655	160	186,658
New London-Norwich, CT . . .	151	248,550	138	241,862
Fayetteville, NC	152	246,522	152	212,042
Poughkeepsie, NY	153	244,141	147	222,295
Columbus, GA-AL	154	238,593	140	238,584
Lowell, MA	155	232,859	149	218,268
Saginaw, MI	156	227,289	148	219,743
Waterbury, CT	157	226,164	150	216,808
Savannah, GA	158	225,581	154	207,987
Roanoke, VA	159	223,578	157	203,153
Lima, OH	160	217,989	153	210,074
Provo-Orem, UT	161	217,281	196	137,776
Killeen-Temple, TX	162	214,093	184	159,794
Lubbock, TX.	163	211,861	165	179,295
Brownsville-Harlingen-San Benito, TX.	164	208,222	194	140,368
Springfield, MO	165	207,830	175	168,053
Fort Myers-Cape Coral, FL . .	166	204,314	238	105,216
Fort Smith, AR-OK	167	202,367	182	160,421
Sarasota, FL.	168	201,731	218	120,413
Stamford, CT	169	196,956	155	206,340
Galveston-Texas City, TX . . .	170	194,704	172	169,812
Reno, NV	171	193,870	216	121,068
Lincoln, NE	172	192,779	176	167,972
Biloxi-Gulfport, MS	173	191,574	183	160,070
Atlantic City, NJ.	174	189,326	168	175,043
Santa Cruz, CA	175	186,873	213	123,790
Battle Creek, MI	176	186,677	164	180,129
Springfield, IL	177	186,104	169	171,020
Topeka, KS	178	185,369	163	180,619
Wheeling, WV-OH	179	185,240	161	181,954
Portland, ME	180	183,457	171	170,081
Springfield, OH	181	183,223	159	187,606
Muskegon-Norton Shores- Muskegon Hgts, MI	182	178,991	166	175,410
Asheville, NC	183	177,056	181	161,059
Fayetteville-Springdale, AR . .	184	177,013	208	127,846
Fall River, MA.	185	176,419	173	169,549
Terre Haute, IN	186	175,852	167	175,143
Green Bay, WI	187	175,470	185	158,244
Anchorage, AK	188	173,992	211	126,385
Amarillo, TX	189	173,550	192	144,396
Racine, WI.	190	172,865	170	170,838
Boise City, ID	191	172,843	232	112,230
Yakima, WA.	192	170,767	191	145,212
Waco, TX	193	170,605	188	147,553
Cedar Rapids, IA	194	169,720	179	163,213
New Bedford, MA.	195	169,422	180	161,288
Brockton, MA	196	169,195	186	150,416
Lake Charles, LA	197	167,334	189	145,415
Champaign-Urbana-Rantoul, IL	198	167,104	178	163,281
St. Cloud, MN	199	162,823	198	134,585
Steubenville-Weirton, OH-WV	200	161,612	177	166,385
Parkersburg-Marietta, WV-OH	201	160,900	187	148,132
Manchester, NH	202	160,443	201	132,512
Tallahassee, FL.	203	157,076	235	109,355
Lynchburg, VA	204	153,348	199	133,258
Jackson, MI	205	151,324	193	143,274
Alexandria, LA	206	151,304	203	131,749
Longview-Marshall, TX.	207	150,093	217	120,770
Clarksville-Hopkinsville, TN-KY	208	149,331	220	118,945

SMSA	1980(P) Rank	Pop.	1970 Rank	Pop.
Fort Collins, CO	209	149,278	258	89,900
Lafayette, LA	210	148,654	233	111,643
Gainesville, FL	211	146,534	239	104,764
Bradenton, FL.	212	146,048	247	97,115
Danbury, CT	213	144,010	227	115,538
Richland-Kennewick-Pasco, WA	214	143,287	255	93,356
New Britain, CT.	215	141,991	190	145,269
Abilene, TX	216	139,085	214	122,164
Anderson, IN	217	138,969	195	138,522
Janesville-Beloit, WI	218	138,751	202	131,970
Wilmington, NC	219	138,698	237	107,219
Waterloo-Cedar Falls, IA . . .	220	137,518	200	132,916
Monroe, LA	221	137,516	228	115,387
Fargo-Moorhead, ND-MN . . .	222	137,493	219	120,261
Elkhart, IN	223	136,686	210	126,529
Tuscaloosa, AL	224	136,501	226	116,029
Altoona, PA	225	136,447	197	135,356
Florence, AL	226	134,732	223	117,743
Vineland-Millville-Bridgeton, NJ	227	132,278	215	121,374
Mansfield, OH.	228	131,217	204	129,997
Eau Claire, WI.	229	130,789	229	114,936
Decatur, IL	230	130,622	212	125,010
Wichita Falls, TX	231	129,933	207	128,642
Petersburg-Colonial Heights- Hopewell, VA.	232	128,782	206	128,809
Muncie, IN.	233	127,455	205	129,219
Tyler, TX.	234	127,395	248	97,096
Texarkana, TX-Texarkana, AR	235	126,531	230	113,488
Pueblo, CO	236	125,753	221	118,238
Norwalk, CT.	237	125,227	209	127,595
Kenosha, WI.	238	123,393	222	117,917
Greeley, CO	239	122,916	259	89,297
Lafayette-West Lafayette, IN .	240	120,534	234	109,378
Bay City, MI	241	119,888	224	117,339
Anniston, AL.	242	119,803	241	103,092
Bloomington-Normal, IL	243	119,125	240	104,389
Williamsport, PA	244	118,548	231	113,296
Pascagoula-Moss Point, MS .	245	118,057	260	87,975
Sioux City, IA-NE	246	117,117	225	116,189
Odessa, TX	247	115,204	256	92,660
Nashua, NH	248	114,148	262	86,280
Albany, GA	249	112,257	250	96,683
Lawton, OK	250	111,973	236	108,144
Sioux Falls, SD	251	110,029	253	95,209
Billings, MT	252	107,661	261	87,367
Kokomo, IN	253	103,473	243	99,848
Gadsden, AL	254	102,789	254	94,144
Kankakee, IL	255	102,520	245	97,250
St. Joseph, MO-KS.	256	101,747	244	98,828
Grand Forks, ND-MN	257	100,653	252	95,537
Columbia, MO	258	100,240	268	80,935
Fitchburg-Leominster, MA. . .	259	99,446	246	97,164
Laredo, TX	260	99,064	273	72,859
Burlington, NC	261	98,923	251	96,502
Bloomington, IN.	262	97,599	264	85,221
Elmira, NY.	263	97,586	242	101,537
Panama City, FL	264	97,175	272	75,283
Las Cruces, NM	265	95,995	278	69,773
Dubuque, IA	266	93,634	257	90,609
Bryan-College Station, TX. . .	267	93,487	281	57,978
Rochester, MN	268	91,793	265	84,104
Rapid City, SD	269	90,937	271	76,369
Pine Bluff, AR	270	90,761	263	85,329
Pittsfield, MA	271	90,509	249	96,817
La Crosse, WI.	272	90,094	269	80,468
Sherman-Denison, TX	273	89,199	266	83,225
Owensboro, KY.	274	85,702	270	79,486
San Angelo, TX	275	84,701	276	71,047
Midland, TX.	276	82,311	279	65,433
Iowa City, IA.	277	81,549	275	72,127
Great Falls, MT	278	80,639	267	81,804
Bismarck, ND	279	79,908	280	61,024
Bristol, CT	280	73,570	277	69,878
Lewiston-Auburn, ME	281	72,445	274	72,474
Lawrence, KS.	282	66,949	282	57,932
Enid, OK.	283	62,681	283	56,343
Meriden, CT.	284	56,506	284	55,959

Cities—Growth and Decline

Source: U.S. Bureau of the Census (cities over 100,000 ranked by 1980 population)

Rank	City	1980	1970	1960	1950	1900	1850	1790
1	New York, N.Y.	7,071,030	7,895,563	7,781,984	7,891,957	3,437,202	¹696,115	¹49,401
2	Chicago, Ill.	3,005,072	3,369,357	3,550,404	3,620,962	1,698,575	29,963	...
3	Los Angeles, Cal.	2,966,763	2,811,801	2,479,015	1,970,358	102,479	1,610	...
4	Philadelphia, Pa.	1,688,210	1,949,996	2,002,512	2,071,605	1,293,697	121,376	28,522
5	Houston, Tex.	1,594,086	1,233,535	938,219	596,163	44,633	2,396	...
6	Detroit, Mich.	1,203,339	1,514,063	1,670,144	1,849,568	285,704	21,019	...
7	Dallas, Tex.	904,078	844,401	679,684	434,462	42,638	...	...
8	San Diego, Cal.	875,504	697,471	573,224	334,387	17,700	...	...
9	Baltimore, Md.	786,775	905,787	939,024	949,708	508,957	169,054	13,503
10	San Antonio, Tex.	785,410	654,153	587,718	408,442	53,321	3,488	...
11	Phoenix, Ariz.	764,911	584,303	439,170	106,818	5,544	...	...
12	Honolulu Co., Ha.	762,874	630,528	294,194	248,034	39,306	...	...
13	Indianapolis, Ind.	700,807	736,856	476,258	427,173	169,164	8,091	...
14	San Francisco, Cal.	678,974	715,674	740,316	775,357	342,782	²34,776	...
15	Memphis, Tenn.	646,356	623,988	497,524	396,000	102,320	8,841	...
16	Washington, D.C.	637,651	756,668	763,956	802,178	278,718	40,001	...
17	San Jose, Cal.	636,550	459,913	204,196	95,280	21,500	...	...
18	Milwaukee, Wis.	636,212	717,372	741,324	637,392	285,315	20,061	...
19	Cleveland, Oh.	573,822	750,879	876,050	914,808	381,768	17,034	...
20	Columbus, Oh.	564,871	540,025	471,316	375,901	125,560	17,882	...
21	Boston, Mass.	562,994	641,071	697,197	801,444	560,892	136,881	18,320
22	New Orleans, La.	557,482	593,471	627,525	570,445	287,104	116,375	...
23	Jacksonville, Fla.	540,898	504,265	201,030	204,517	28,429	1,045	...
24	Seattle, Wash.	493,846	530,831	557,087	467,591	80,671	...	...
25	Denver, Col.	491,396	514,678	493,887	415,786	133,859	...	...
26	Nashville-Davidson, Tenn.³	455,651	426,029	170,874	174,307	80,865	10,165	...
27	St. Louis, Mo.	453,085	622,236	750,026	856,796	575,238	77,860	...
28	Kansas City, Mo.	448,159	507,330	475,539	456,622	163,752	...	...
29	El Paso, Tex.	425,259	322,261	276,687	130,485	15,906	...	...
30	Atlanta, Ga.	425,022	495,039	487,455	331,314	89,872	2,572	...
31	Pittsburgh, Pa.	423,938	520,089	604,332	676,806	321,616	46,601	...
32	Oklahoma City, Okla.	403,213	368,164	324,253	243,504	10,037	...	...
33	Cincinnati, Oh.	385,457	453,514	502,550	503,998	325,902	115,435	...
34	Fort Worth, Tex.	385,141	393,455	356,268	278,778	26,688	...	...
35	Minneapolis, Minn.	370,951	434,400	482,872	521,718	202,718	...	...
36	Portland, Ore.	366,383	379,967	372,676	373,628	90,426	...	...
37	Long Beach, Cal.	361,334	358,879	344,168	250,767	2,252	...	...
38	Tulsa, Okla.	360,919	330,350	261,685	182,740	1,390	...	...
39	Buffalo, N.Y.	357,870	462,768	532,759	580,132	352,387	42,261	...
40	Toledo, Oh.	354,635	383,062	318,003	303,616	131,822	3,829	...
41	Miami, Fla.	346,931	334,859	291,688	249,276	1,681	...	...
42	Austin, Tex.	345,496	253,539	186,545	132,459	22,258	629	...
43	Oakland, Cal.	339,288	361,561	367,548	384,575	66,960	...	...
44	Albuquerque, N.M.	331,767	244,501	201,189	96,815	6,238	...	...
45	Tucson, Ariz.	330,537	262,933	212,892	45,454	7,531	...	...
46	Newark, N.J.	329,248	381,930	405,220	438,776	246,070	38,894	...
47	Charlotte, N.C.	314,447	241,420	201,564	134,042	18,091	1,065	...
48	Omaha, Neb.	311,681	346,929	301,598	251,117	102,555	...	...
49	Louisville, Ky.	298,451	361,706	390,639	369,129	204,731	43,194	200
50	Birmingham, Ala.	284,413	300,910	340,887	326,037	38,415	...	...
51	Wichita, Kan.	279,272	276,554	254,698	168,279	24,671	...	...
52	Sacramento, Cal.	275,741	257,105	191,667	137,572	29,282	6,820	...
53	Tampa, Fla.	271,523	277,714	274,970	124,681	15,839	...	...
54	St. Paul, Minn.	270,230	309,866	313,411	311,349	163,065	1,112	...
55	Norfolk, Va.	266,979	307,951	304,869	213,513	46,624	14,326	2,959
56	Virginia Beach, Va.	262,199	172,106	8,091	5,390	...	...	...
57	Rochester, N.Y.	241,741	295,011	318,611	332,488	162,608	36,403	...
58	Akron, Oh.	237,177	275,425	290,351	274,605	42,728	3,266	...
59	St. Petersburg, Fla.	236,893	216,159	181,298	96,738	1,575	...	...
60	Corpus Christi, Tex.	231,999	204,525	167,690	108,287	4,703	...	...
61	Jersey City, N.J.	223,532	260,350	276,101	299,017	206,433	6,856	...
62	Anaheim, Cal.	221,847	166,408	104,184	14,556	1,456	...	...
63	Baton Rouge, La.	219,486	165,921	152,419	125,629	11,269	3,905	...
64	Richmond, Va.	219,214	249,332	219,958	230,310	85,050	27,570	3,761
65	Fresno, Cal.	218,202	165,655	133,929	91,669	12,470	...	...
66	Colorado Springs, Col.	215,150	135,517	70,194	45,472	21,085	...	...
67	Shreveport, La.	205,815	182,064	164,372	127,206	16,013	1,728	...
68	Lexington-Fayette, Ky.⁵	204,165	108,137	62,810	55,534	26,369	8,159	834
69	Santa Ana, Cal.	203,713	155,710	100,350	45,533	4,933	...	...
70	Dayton, Oh.	203,588	243,023	262,332	243,872	85,333	10,977	...
71	Jackson, Miss.	202,895	153,968	144,422	98,271	7,816	1,881	...
72	Mobile, Ala.	200,452	190,026	194,856	129,009	38,469	20,515	...
73	Yonkers, N.Y.	195,351	204,297	190,634	152,798	47,931	...	...
74	Des Moines, Ia.	191,000	201,404	208,982	177,965	62,139	...	...
75	Knoxville, Tenn.	183,139	174,587	111,827	124,769	32,637	2,076	...
76	Grand Rapids, Mich.	181,843	197,649	177,313	176,515	87,565	2,686	...
77	Montgomery, Ala.	178,157	133,386	134,393	106,525	30,346	8,728	...
78	Lubbock, Tex.	173,979	149,101	126,691	71,747	...	...	...
79	Anchorage, Alas.	173,017	48,081	44,237	11,254	...	...	...
80	Fort Wayne, Ind.	172,196	178,269	161,776	133,607	45,115	4,282	...
81	Lincoln, Neb.	171,932	149,518	128,521	98,884	40,169	...	...
82	Spokane, Wash.	171,300	170,516	181,608	161,721	36,848	...	...
83	Riverside, Cal.	170,876	140,089	84,332	46,764	7,973	...	...
84	Madison, Wis.	170,616	171,809	126,706	96,056	19,164	1,525	...
85	Huntington Beach, Cal.	170,505	115,960	11,492	5,237	...	...	...
86	Syracuse, N.Y.	170,105	197,297	216,038	220,583	108,374	22,271	...

Rank	City	1980	1970	1960	1950	1900	1850	1790
87	Chattanooga, Tenn..........	169,565	119,923	130,009	131,041	30,154	...	...
88	Columbus, Ga.............	169,441	155,028	116,779	79,611	17,614	5,942	...
89	Las Vegas, Nev...........	164,674	125,787	64,405	24,624	...	...	...
90	Salt Lake City, Ut........	163,033	175,885	189,454	182,121	53,531	...	...
91	Worcester, Mass..........	161,799	176,572	186,587	203,486	118,421	17,049	2,095
92	Warren, Mich.............	161,134	179,260	89,246	727	350	...	...
93	Kansas City, Mo..........	161,087	168,213	121,901	129,553	51,418	...	...
94	Arlington, Tex...........	160,123	90,229	44,775	7,692	1,079	...	...
95	Flint, Mich..............	159,611	193,317	196,940	163,143	13,103	...	...
96	Aurora, Col..............	158,588	74,974	48,548	11,241	202	...	...
97	Tacoma, Wash............	158,501	154,407	147,979	143,673	37,714	...	...
98	Little Rock, Ark..........	158,461	132,483	107,813	102,213	38,307	2,167	...
99	Providence, R.I...........	156,804	179,116	207,498	248,674	175,597	41,513	6,380
100	Greensboro, N.C..........	155,642	144,076	119,574	74,389	10,035	...	...
101	Fort Lauderdale, Fla.......	153,256	139,590	83,648	36,328	...	...	...
102	Mesa, Ariz..............	152,453	63,049	33,772	16,790	...	...	...
103	Springfield, Mass.........	152,319	163,905	174,463	162,399	62,059	11,766	1,574
104	Gary, Ind...............	151,953	175,415	178,320	133,911	...	...	...
105	Stockton, Cal............	149,779	109,963	86,321	70,853	17,506	...	...
106	Raleigh, N.C............	149,771	122,830	93,931	65,679	13,643	4,518	...
107	Amarillo, Tex............	149,230	127,010	137,969	74,246	1,442	...	...
108	Hialeah, Fla.............	145,254	102,452	66,972	19,676	...	...	...
109	Newport News, Va.........	144,903	138,177	113,662	42,358	19,635	...	...
110	Bridgeport, Conn.........	142,546	156,542	156,748	158,709	70,996	6,080	...
111	Huntsville, Ala...........	142,513	139,282	72,365	16,437	8,068	2,863	...
112	Savannah, Ga............	141,634	118,349	149,245	119,638	54,244	15,312	...
113	Rockford, Ill............	139,712	147,370	126,706	92,927	31,051	...	...
114	Glendale, Cal...........	139,060	132,664	119,442	95,702	...	...	...
115	Garland, Tex............	138,857	81,437	38,501	10,571	819	...	...
116	Paterson, N.J............	137,970	144,824	143,663	139,336	105,171	11,334	...
117	Hartford, Conn...........	136,392	158,017	162,178	177,397	72,850	13,555	2,683
118	Springfield, Mo..........	133,116	120,096	95,865	66,731	23,267	415	...
119	Fremont, Cal............	131,945	100,869	43,790	...	...	...	...
120	Winston-Salem, N.C.[4]	131,885	133,683	111,135	87,811	13,650	...	...
121	Torrance, Cal...........	131,497	134,968	100,991	22,241	...	...	...
122	Evansville, Ind...........	130,496	138,764	141,543	128,636	59,007	3,235	...
123	Lansing, Mich...........	130,414	131,403	107,807	92,129	16,485	...	...
124	Orlando, Fla............	128,394	99,006	88,135	52,367	2,481	...	...
125	New Haven, Conn.........	126,109	137,707	152,048	164,443	108,027	20,345	4,487
126	Peoria, Ill..............	124,160	126,963	103,162	111,856	56,100	5,095	...
127	Garden Grove, Cal........	123,351	121,155	84,238	...	...	...	...
128	Hampton, Va............	122,617	120,779	89,258	5,966	2,764	...	...
129	Pasadena, Cal...........	119,374	112,951	116,407	104,577	9,117	...	...
130	Erie, Pa...............	119,123	129,265	138,440	130,803	52,733	5,858	...
131	Beaumont, Tex...........	118,102	117,548	119,175	94,014	9,427	...	...
132	San Bernardino, Cal.......	118,057	106,869	91,922	63,058	6,150	...	...
133	Hollywood, Fla...........	117,188	106,873	35,237	14,351	...	...	...
134	Macon, Ga..............	116,860	122,423	69,764	70,252	23,272	5,720	...
135	Youngstown, Oh..........	115,436	140,909	166,689	168,330	44,885	...	...
136	Topeka, Kan............	115,266	125,011	119,484	78,791	33,608	...	...
137	Chesapeake, Va..........	114,226	89,580	73,637	110,371	...	...	...
138	Lakewood, Col...........	112,848	92,743	19,338	...	...	...	...
139	Pasadena, Tex...........	112,560	89,957	58,737	22,483	...	...	...
140	Independence, Mo.........	111,806	111,630	62,328	36,963	6,974	...	...
141	Cedar Rapids, Ia..........	110,243	110,642	92,035	72,296	25,656	...	...
142	Irving, Tex..............	109,943	97,260	45,985	2,621	...	...	...
143	South Bend, Ind..........	109,727	125,580	132,445	115,911	35,999	1,652	...
144	Sterling Heights, Mich......	108,999	61,365	...	...	...	...	...
145	Oxnard, Cal.............	108,195	71,225	40,265	21,567	...	...	...
146	Ann Arbor, Mich..........	107,316	100,035	67,340	48,251	14,509	...	...
147	Tempe, Ariz.............	106,743	63,550	24,897	7,684	...	...	...
148	Sunnyvale, Cal..........	106,618	95,976	52,898	9,829	...	...	...
149	Elizabeth, N.J...........	106,201	112,654	107,698	112,817	52,130	5,583	...
150	Modesto, Cal............	106,105	61,712	36,585	17,389	...	...	...
151	Eugene, Ore............	105,624	79,028	50,977	35,879	3,236	...	...
152	Bakersfield, Cal..........	105,611	69,515	56,848	34,784	...	...	...
153	Livonia, Mich...........	104,814	110,109	66,702	17,534	...	...	...
154	Portsmouth, Va..........	104,577	110,963	114,773	80,039	17,427	8,626	...
155	Allentown, Pa...........	103,758	109,871	108,347	106,756	35,416	3,779	...
156	Berkeley, Cal...........	103,328	114,091	111,268	113,805	13,214	...	...
157	Waterbury, Conn.........	103,266	108,033	107,130	104,477	45,859	...	...
158	Davenport, Ia...........	103,264	98,469	88,981	74,549	...	...	...
159	Concord, Cal............	103,251	85,164	36,208	6,953	...	...	...
160	Alexandria, Va...........	103,217	110,927	91,023	61,787	14,528	8,734	2,748
161	Stamford, Conn..........	102,453	108,798	92,713	74,293	15,997	...	...
162	Boise City, Ida..........	102,451	74,990	34,481	34,393	...	...	...
163	Fullerton, Cal...........	102,034	85,987	56,180	13,958	...	...	...
164	Albany, N.Y.............	101,727	115,781	129,726	134,995	94,151	50,763	3,498
165	Pueblo, Col.............	101,686	97,774	91,181	63,685	28,157	...	...
166	Waco, Tex..............	101,261	95,326	97,808	84,706	...	...	...
167	Durham, N.C............	100,831	95,438	78,302	71,311	6,679	...	...
168	Reno, Nev..............	100,756	72,863	51,470	32,497	...	...	...
169	Roanoke, Va............	100,427	92,115	97,110	91,921	...	...	...

(1) Population shown for years prior to 1900 is for New York and its boroughs as constituted under the act of consolidation in 1898. (2) Population shown is for 1952 as given in State census for that year; 1850 returns for San Francisco were destroyed by fire. (3) Figure for 1970 and 1980 is for the Metropolitan Government of Nashville and Davidson County (consolidated 1963); figures for previous years are for Nashville city. (4) Winston city and Salem town consolidated as Winston-Salem city between 1910 and 1920. Figure for 1900 represents combined population of Winston and Salem. (5) Lexington city and Fayette county governments consolidated in 1974. Figure for 1970 and 1980 is for combined populations; figures for previous years are for Lexington city.

Jewish Population by Countries and Cities

Source: American Jewish Year Book

Europe (including Asiatic USSR and Turkey) . . .	4,102,350	Australia and New Zealand	72,000
America, North, Central, and South	6,839,560	**Total**	**14,527,150**
Asia	3,339,810		
Africa	173,430		

Europe

Albania	300
Austria	13,000
Belgium	41,000
Bulgaria	7,000
Czechoslovakia	12,000
Denmark	7,500
Finland	1,000
France	650,000
Germany	38,000
Gibraltar	600
Great Britain	410,000
Greece	6,000
Hungary	80,000
Ireland	1,900
Italy	41,000
Luxembourg	1,000
Malta	50
Netherlands	30,000
Norway	900
Poland	6,000
Portugal	600
Romania	45,000
Spain	12,000
Sweden	17,000
Switzerland	21,000
Turkey	24,000
USSR	2,630,000
Yugoslavia	5,500

North America

Canada	305,000
Mexico	37,500
United States	5,920,890
(P.R. 1,800; VI, 510)	

Central America and West Indies

Barbados	70
Costa Rica	2,500
Cuba	1,500
Curacao	700
Dominican Republic . . .	200
El Salvador	350
Guatemala	2,000
Haiti	150
Honduras	200
Jamaica	350
Nicaragua	200
Panama	2,000
Trinidad	300

South America

Argentina	300,000
Bolivia	750
Brazil	150,000
Chile	30,000
Colombia	12,000
Ecuador	1,000
Paraguay	1,200
Peru	5,200
Surinam	500
Uruguay	50,000
Venezuela	15,000

Asia

Afghanistan	200
Burma	50
China	30
Cyprus	30
Hong Kong	250
India	8,000
Indonesia	100
Iran	70,000
Iraq	450
Israel	3,254,000
Japan	400

Lebanon	400
Pakistan	250
Philippines	200
Singapore	450
Syria	4,500
Yemen	500

Australia and New Zealand

Australia	67,000
New Zealand	5,000

Africa

Algeria	1,000
Egypt	400
Ethiopia	22,000
Kenya	450
Libya	20
Morocco	22,000
Rep. of South Africa. . .	118,000
Tunisia	7,000
Zaire.	200
Zambia	400
Zimbabwe	1,960

World Cities

Adelaide	1,600
Amsterdam	15,000
Antwerp	13,000
Athens	2,800
Auckland	1,500
Basel	2,300
Belgrade	1,500
Berlin (both sectors) . .	6,000
Bogota	5,500
Bombay (and district) . .	6,970
Bordeaux	6,400
Brisbane	1,200
Brussels	24,500
Bucharest	40,000
Budapest	65,000
Cape Town	25,650
Copenhagen	7,000
Durban	5,990

Geneva	3,250
Glasgow	13,000
Goteborg	1,600
Guatemala City	1,500
Haifa	210,000
Istanbul	20,000
Izmir	2,500
Jerusalem	290,000
Johannesburg	57,500
Kiev	170,000
Leeds	18,000
Leningrad	165,000
Lima	5,000
Liverpool	6,500
London (greater)	260,000
Lyons	20,000
Madrid	3,000
Malmo	1,930

Manchester (greater) . .	35,000
Marseilles	65,000
Melbourne	32,000
Mexico, D. F.	32,500
Milan	9,000
Montevideo	48,000
Montreal	100,000
Moscow	285,000
Nice	20,000
Ottawa	6,500
Paris	300,000
Perth	3,200
Porto Alegre	12,000
Prague	3,000
Rabat	2,500
Recife	3,000
Rio de Janeiro	55,000
Rome	10,000

Salisbury	1,100
San Jose	2,500
Santiago	28,000
Sao Paulo	75,000
Sofia	4,000
Stockholm	5,000
Strasbourg	12,000
Sydney	26,500
Teheran	50,000
Tel Aviv-Jaffa	394,000
Toronto	120,000
Toulouse	18,000
Vancouver	14,000
Valparaiso	4,000
Vienna	9,000
Warsaw	4,500
Winnipeg	18,000
Zurich	6,150

U.S. Cities and Counties

Alameda and Contra Costa Co., Cal. . .	28,000
Albany, NY	13,500
Alexandria, Va. (area) . .	20,000
Atlanta, Ga.	27,500
Atlantic City, NJ	11,800
Baltimore, Md.	92,000
Bergen Co., NJ.	100,000
Boston (inc. Brockton) . .	170,000
Bridgeport, Conn.	18,500
Buffalo, NY	21,000
Camden, NJ	26,000
Chicago Metro Area. . . .	253,000
Cincinnati, Oh.	21,500
Cleveland, Oh.	75,000
Columbus, Oh.	13,000
Dallas, Tex.	20,000
Denver, Col.	30,000

Detroit, Mich.	75,000
Essex Co., NJ	95,000
Fort Lauderdale, Fla. . .	75,000
Framingham, Mass.	16,000
Hartford (inc. New Britain). . .	23,500
Hollywood, Fla.	55,000
Houston, Tex.	28,000
Indianapolis, Ind. . . .	11,000
Kansas City, Mo.	20,000
Las Vegas, Nev.	16,000
Long Beach, Cal.	13,500
Los Angeles Metro	503,000
Lynn, Mass.	19,000
Miami, Fla.	225,000
Milwaukee, Wis.	23,900
Minneapolis, Minn. . . .	23,200
Montgomery Co., Md. . .	70,000

Monmouth Co., NJ. . . .	32,000
Morris-Sussex Cos. NJ .	15,000
New Haven, Conn.	20,000
New Orleans, La.	10,600
New York, (greater) . . .	1,998,000
New York City	1,228,000
Manhattan	171,000
Brooklyn	514,000
Bronx	143,000
Queens	379,000
Staten Island.	21,000
Nassau-Suffolk	605,000
Westchester	165,000
Ocean Co., NJ	12,000
Orange Co., Cal.	40,000
Palm Beach Co., Fla. . . (excl. Boca Raton)	35,000
Philadelphia Metro. . . .	295,000
Phoenix, Ariz.	29,000

Pittsburgh, Pa.	50,000
Prince George's Co., Md.	20,000
Raritan Valley, NJ . . .	18,000
Richmond, Va.	10,000
Rochester, NY	21,500
Rockland Co., NY	25,000
San Diego, Cal.	32,500
San Francisco, Cal. . . .	75,000
San Jose, Cal.	15,000
Seattle, Wash.	16,000
Springfield, Mass. . . .	10,000
Stamford, Conn.	12,000
St. Louis, Mo.	60,000
Syracuse, NY	11,000
Union Co., NJ	39,500
Washington, DC (greater)	160,000
Worcester, Mass.	10,000

Population, Urban and Rural, by Race: 1960 and 1970

Source: U.S. Bureau of the Census

An urbanized area comprises at least one city of 50,000 inhabitants (central city) plus contiguous, closely settled areas (urban fringe). (thousands)

Year and area	1960			1970		
	Total	White	Negro and other	Total	White	Negro and other
Population, total.	179,323	158,832	20,491	203,212	177,749	25,463
Urban	125,269	110,428	14,840	149,325	128,773	20,552
Inside urbanized areas.	95,848	83,770	12,070	118,447	100,952	17,495
Central cities	57,975	47,627	10,348	63,922	49,547	14,375
Urban fringe	37,873	36,143	1,731	54,525	51,405	3,120
Outside urbanized areas.	29,420	26,658	2,762	30,878	27,822	3,057
Rural.	54,054	48,403	5,651	53,887	48,976	4,911

City Population by Race and Spanish Origin

Source: U.S. Bureau of the Census

This table presents a summary of the final 1980 census population counts for cities over 200,000, classified by race and Spanish origin. Counts of the population by race as well as Spanish origin in this table are provisional.

	Total	White	Black	Am. Indian Eskimo & Aleut.	Asian & Pacific Islander	Other	Spanish origin[1]
Akron, Oh.	237,177	182,114	52,719	368	858	1,118	1,534
Albuquerque, NM	331,767	268,731	8,361	7,341	3,162	44,172	112,084
Anaheim, CA	221,847	190,679	2,557	1,686	8,913	18,012	38,015
Atlanta, GA	425,022	137,878	282,912	422	2,000	1,810	5,842
Austin, TX	345,496	261,166	42,118	1,003	3,642	37,567	64,766
Baltimore, MD	786,775	345,113	431,151	2,108	4,949	3,454	7,641
Baton Rouge, LA	219,486	135,766	80,119	288	1,603	1,710	3,985
Birmingham, LA	284,413	124,730	158,223	185	793	402	2,227
Boston, MA	562,994	393,937	126,229	1,302	15,150	26,376	36,068
Buffalo, NY	357,870	252,365	95,116	2,383	1,322	6,684	9,499
Charlotte, NC	314,447	211,980	97,627	1,039	2,367	1,434	3,418
Chicago, IL	3,005,072	1,490,217	1,197,000	6,072	69,191	242,592	422,061
Cincinnati, OH	385,457	251,144	130,467	425	2,216	1,205	2,988
Cleveland, OH	573,822	307,264	251,347	1,094	3,384	10,733	17,772
Colorado Springs, CO	215,150	189,113	11,961	1,100	3,144	9,832	18,268
Columbus, OH	564,871	430,678	124,880	924	4,714	3,675	4,651
Corpus Christi, TX	231,999	188,279	11,089	662	1,277	29,892	108,175
Dallas, TX	904,078	555,270	265,594	3,732	7,678	71,804	111,082
Dayton, OH	203,588	126,389	75,031	300	869	999	1,748
Denver, CO	491,396	367,344	59,252	3,847	7,007	53,946	91,937
Detroit, MI	1,203,339	413,730	758,939	3,420	6,621	20,629	28,970
El Paso, TX	425,259	249,214	13,466	1,251	3,544	157,784	265,819
Fort Worth, TX	385,141	265,428	87,723	1,227	2,340	28,423	48,696
Fresno, CA	218,202	156,501	20,665	2,097	6,111	32,828	51,489
Honolulu, HI (county)	762,874	252,293	16,831	2,182	456,873	34,695	54,777
Houston, TX	1,594,086	977,530	440,257	3,228	32,898	140,173	281,224
Indianapolis, IN	700,807	540,294	152,626	994	3,792	3,101	6,145
Jackson, MS	202,895	106,285	95,357	142	621	490	1,508
Jacksonville, FL	540,898	394,734	137,324	1,198	5,240	2,402	9,775
Jersey City, NJ	223,532	127,699	61,954	261	9,793	23,825	41,672
Kansas City, MO	448,159	312,836	122,699	1,622	3,499	7,503	14,703
Lexington-Fayette, KY	204,165	174,605	27,121	225	1,360	854	1,488
Long Beach, CA	361,334	269,953	40,732	2,982	19,609	28,058	50,700
Los Angeles, CA	2,966,763	1,816,683	505,208	16,595	196,024	432,253	815,989
Louisville, KY	298,451	212,102	84,080	336	931	1,002	2,005
Memphis, TN	646,356	333,789	307,702	530	2,701	1,634	5,225
Miami, FL	346,931	231,069	87,110	329	1,861	26,562	194,087
Milwaukee, WI	636,212	466,620	146,940	5,018	3,600	14,034	26,111
Minneapolis, MN	370,951	323,832	38,433	8,932	4,104	5,650	4,684
Mobile, AL	200,452	125,786	72,568	368	972	758	2,265
Nashville-Davidson, TN	455,651	344,886	105,942	529	2,202	2,092	3,627
New Orleans, LA	557,482	236,967	308,136	524	7,332	4,523	19,219
New York, NY	7,071,030	4,293,695	1,784,124	11,824	231,505	749,882	1,405,957
Newark, NJ	329,248	101,417	191,743	551	2,366	33,171	61,254
Norfolk, VA	266,979	162,300	93,987	885	7,149	2,658	6,074
Oakland, CA	339,288	129,690	159,234	2,199	26,341	21,824	32,491
Oklahoma City, OK	403,213	322,374	58,702	10,405	4,167	7,565	11,295
Omaha, NE	311,681	266,070	37,852	1,792	1,734	4,233	7,304
Philadelphia, PA	1,688,210	983,084	638,878	2,325	17,764	46,159	63,570
Phoenix, AZ	764,911	642,059	37,682	10,771	6,979	67,420	115,572
Pittsburgh, PA	423,938	316,694	101,813	482	2,596	2,353	3,196
Portland, OR	366,383	316,993	27,734	3,526	10,636	7,494	7,807
Richmond, VA	219,214	104,743	112,357	357	976	781	2,210
Rochester, NY	241,741	168,102	62,332	1,014	1,536	8,757	13,153
Sacramento, CA	275,741	186,477	36,866	3,322	24,017	25,059	39,160
St. Louis, MO	453,085	242,576	206,386	642	1,696	1,785	5,531
St. Paul, MN	270,230	243,226	13,305	2,538	2,695	8,466	7,864
St. Petersburg, FL	236,893	193,277	41,000	331	1,272	1,013	4,210
San Antonio, TX	785,410	617,636	57,654	1,782	5,086	103,252	421,774
San Diego, CA	875,504	666,829	77,700	5,065	57,207	68,703	130,610
San Francisco, CA	678,974	395,082	86,414	3,548	147,426	46,504	83,373
San Jose, CA	636,550	470,013	29,157	4,826	52,448	80,106	140,574
Santa Ana, CA	203,713	132,072	8,232	1,627	10,631	51,151	90,646
Seattle, WA	493,846	392,766	46,755	6,253	36,613	11,459	12,646
Shreveport, LA	205,815	119,529	84,627	292	773	594	2,769
Tampa, FL	271,523	200,741	63,835	545	1,903	4,499	35,982
Toledo, OH	354,635	283,920	61,750	661	1,653	6,651	10,667
Tucson, AZ	330,537	270,188	12,301	4,341	3,523	40,184	82,189
Tulsa, OK	360,919	298,114	42,594	13,740	2,813	3,658	6,189
Virginia Beach, VA	262,199	226,788	26,291	633	6,570	1,917	5,160
Washington, DC	637,651	171,796	448,229	1,031	6,635	9,960	17,652
Wichita, KA	279,272	235,818	30,200	2,579	3,895	6,780	9,902

1) persons of spanish origin may be of any race

Immigration by Country of Last Residence 1820-1979

Source: U.S. Immigration and Naturalization Service (thousands)

Country	1820-1979, total	1951-1960, total	1961-1970, total	1975	1976	1977	1978	1979	Percent 1820-1979	Percent 1961-1970	Percent 1971-1979
All countries*	49,023	2,515.5	3,321.7	386.2	398.6	462.3	601.4	460.3	100.0	100.0	100.0
Europe	36,248	1,325.6	1,123.4	72.8	73.0	74.0	76.2	64.2	73.9	33.8	17.7
Austria[1] .... }	4,316	{67.1	20.6	0.5	0.5	0.5	0.5	0.5}	8.8	{0.6	0.2
Hungary .... }		{36.6	5.4	0.6	0.6	0.5	0.6	0.5}		{0.2	0.1
Belgium	204	18.6	9.2	0.4	0.5	0.5	0.6	0.6	0.4	0.3	0.1
Czechoslovakia	138	0.9	3.3	0.3	0.3	0.3	0.4	0.5	0.3	0.1	0.1
Denmark	364	11.0	9.2	0.3	0.4	0.4	0.4	0.4	0.7	0.3	0.1
Finland	33	4.9	4.2	0.2	0.2	0.2	0.3	0.3	0.1	0.1	0.1
France	753	51.1	45.2	1.8	2.0	2.7	2.7	2.9	1.5	1.4	0.6
Germany[1]	6,983	477.8	190.8	5.9	6.6	7.4	7.6	7.2	14.2	5.7	1.6
Great Britain[2]	4,911	195.5	210.0	12.2	13.0	14.0	16.4	15.5	10.0	6.3	3.0
Greece	659	47.6	86.0	9.8	8.6	7.8	7.0	5.9	1.3	2.6	2.0
Ireland[3]	4,731	57.3	37.5	1.1	1.0	1.0	0.9	0.8	9.7	1.1	0.3
Italy	5,298	185.5	214.1	11.0	8.0	7.4	7.0	6.0	10.8	6.4	2.8
Netherlands	360	52.3	30.6	0.8	0.9	1.0	1.2	1.2	0.7	0.9	0.2
Norway..........	856	22.9	15.5	0.4	0.3	0.3	0.4	0.4	1.7	0.5	0.1
Poland[1]	519	10.0	53.5	3.5	3.2	3.3	4.5	3.9	1.1	1.6	0.9
Portugal	450	19.6	76.1	11.3	11.0	10.0	10.5	7.1	0.9	2.3	2.3
Spain	261	7.9	44.7	2.6	2.8	5.6	4.3	3.3	0.5	1.3	0.9
Sweden	1,273	21.7	17.1	0.5	0.6	0.6	0.6	0.8	2.6	0.5	0.1
Switzerland	350	17.7	18.5	0.7	0.8	0.8	0.9	0.8	0.7	0.6	0.2
USSR[1,4]..........	3,374	0.6	2.3	4.7	7.4	5.4	4.7	1.9	6.9	0.1	0.8
Yugoslavia	115	8.2	20.4	2.9	2.3	2.3	2.2	1.7	0.2	0.6	0.7
Other Europe	308	10.8	9.2	1.3	2.0	2.0	2.5	2.0	0.6	0.3	0.4
Asia............	3,000	153.3	427.8	129.2	146.7	150.8	243.6	183.0	6.1	12.9	34.9
China[5]	536	9.7	34.8	9.2	9.9	12.5	14.5	12.3	1.1	1.0	2.5
Hong Kong........	[6]197	15.5	75.0	12.5	13.7	12.3	11.1	16.8	0.4	2.3	2.8
India	178	2.0	27.2	14.3	16.1	16.8	19.1	18.6	0.4	0.8	3.6
Iran	[6]47	3.4	10.3	2.2	2.6	4.2	5.9	8.3	0.1	0.3	0.9
Israel	[6]88	25.5	29.6	3.5	5.2	4.4	4.5	4.3	0.2	0.9	0.9
Japan..........	410	46.3	40.0	4.8	4.8	4.5	4.5	4.5	0.8	1.2	1.1
Jordan	[6]40	5.8	11.7	2.3	2.4	2.9	3.2	3.1	0.1	0.3	0.6
Korea..........	[6]269	6.2	34.5	28.1	30.6	30.7	28.8	28.7	0.5	1.0	6.2
Lebanon	[6]56	4.5	15.2	4.0	5.0	5.5	4.8	4.8	0.1	0.5	0.9
Philippines	[7]421	19.3	98.4	31.3	36.8	38.5	36.6	40.8	0.9	3.0	7.9
Turkey	386	3.5	10.1	1.1	1.0	1.0	1.0	1.3	0.8	0.3	0.3
Vietnam	[8]133	2.7	4.2	2.7	2.4	3.4	87.6	19.1	0.3	0.1	3.6
Other Asia........	240	9.0	36.7	13.2	16.2	14.1	22.0	20.4	0.5	1.2	3.6
America	9,203	996.9	1,716.4	174.7	169.2	223.2	266.5	197.1	18.8	51.7	44.8
Argentina.........	[9]96	19.5	49.7	2.8	2.7	3.1	4.1	3.1	0.2	1.5	0.7
Brazil.........	[9]59	13.8	29.3	1.4	1.4	1.9	2.2	1.8	0.1	0.9	0.4
Canada..........	4,121	378.0	413.3	11.2	11.4	18.0	23.5	20.2	8.4	12.4	3.7
Colombia.........	[9]155	18.0	72.0	6.4	5.7	8.2	10.9	10.5	0.3	2.2	1.7
Cuba..........	[10]532	78.9	208.5	25.6	28.4	66.1	27.5	14.0	1.1	6.3	6.3
Dominican Rep.....	[9]230	9.9	93.3	14.1	12.5	11.6	19.5	17.5	0.5	2.8	3.3
Ecuador	[9]90	9.8	36.8	4.7	4.5	5.2	5.7	4.4	0.2	1.1	1.1
El Salvador	[9]49	5.9	15.0	2.4	2.4	4.4	5.9	4.5	0.1	0.4	0.7
Guatemala........	[9]43	4.7	15.9	1.9	2.0	3.7	4.1	2.6	0.1	0.5	0.6
Haiti...........	[10]88	4.4	34.5	5.0	5.3	5.2	6.1	6.1	0.2	1.0	1.2
Honduras	[9]37	6.0	15.7	1.4	1.3	1.6	2.7	2.5	0.1	0.5	0.4
Mexico	2,160	299.8	453.9	62.6	58.4	44.6	92.7	52.5	4.4	13.7	14.8
Panama	[9]50	11.7	19.4	1.7	1.8	2.5	3.3	3.5	0.1	0.6	0.5
Peru	[9]51	7.4	19.1	2.3	2.6	3.9	5.1	4.0	0.1	0.6	0.7
West Indies	744	29.8	133.9	22.3	19.6	27.1	34.6	24.8	1.5	4.0	5.7
Other America.....	701	99.2	106.2	8.9	9.2	16.1	18.6	25.0	1.4	3.2	3.0
Africa............	142	14.1	29.0	5.9	5.7	9.6	10.3	11.2	0.3	0.9	1.7
Australia and New Zealand	122	11.5	19.6	1.8	2.1	2.5	2.7	2.5	0.2	0.6	0.5
Other Oceania	308	14.0	5.7	1.8	1.8	2.1	2.2	2.4	0.6	0.2	0.4

* Figures may not add to total due to rounding. (1) 1938-1945, Austria included with Germany; 1899-1919, Poland included with Austria-Hungary, Germany, and USSR. (2) Beginning 1952, includes data for United Kingdom not specified, formerly included with "Other Europe". (3) Comprises Eire and Northern Ireland. (4) Europe and Asia. (5) Beginning 1957, includes Taiwan. (6) Prior to 1951 included with "Other Asia". (7) Prior to 1951, Philippines included with "All other". (8) Prior to 1953, data for Vietnam not available. (9) Prior to 1951, included with "Other America". (10) Prior to 1951, included with "West Indies".

U.S. Places of 5,000 or More Population—With ZIP and Area Codes

Source: U.S. Bureau of the Census; U.S. Postal Service; N.Y. Telephone Co.

The listings below show the official urban population of the United States. "Urban population" is defined as all persons living in (a) places of 5,000 inhabitants or more, incorporated as cities, villages, boroughs (except Alaska), and towns (except in New England, New York, New Jersey, Pennsylvania and Wisconsin), but excluding those persons living in the rural portions of extended cities; (b) unincorporated places of 5,000 inhabitants or more; and (c) other territory, incorporated or unincorporated, included in urbanized areas.

The non-urban portion of an extended city contains one or more areas, each at least 5 square miles in extent and with a population density of less than 100 persons per square mile. The area or areas constitute at least 25 percent of the legal city's land area of a total of 25 square miles or more.

In New England, New York, New Jersey, Pennsylvania, and Wisconsin, minor civil divisions called "towns" often include rural areas and one or more urban areas. Only the urban areas of these "towns" are included here, except in the case of New England where entire town populations, which may include some rural population, are shown; these towns are indicated by italics. Boroughs in Alaska may contain one or more urban areas which are included here. Population in Hawaii is counted by county subdivisions.

(u) means place is unincorporated.

The ZIP Code of each place appears before the name of that place, if it is obtainable. Telephone Area Code appears in parentheses after the name of the state or, if a state has more than one number, after the name of the place.

CAUTION—Where an asterisk (*) appears before the ZIP Code, ask your local postmaster for the correct ZIP Code for a specific address within the place listed.

ZIP code	Place	1980	1970
	Alabama (205)		
35007	Alabaster	7,079	2,642
35950	Albertville	12,039	9,963
35010	Alexander City	13,807	12,358
36420	Andalusia	10,415	10,092
36201	Anniston	29,523	31,533
....	Anniston Northwest(u)	NA	6,609
35016	Arab	5,967	4,399
35611	Athens	14,558	14,360
36502	Atmore	8,709	8,293
35954	Attalla	7,737	7,510
36830	Auburn	28,471	22,767
36507	Bay Minette	7,455	6,727
35020	Bessemer	31,729	33,428
*35203	Birmingham	284,413	300,910
35226	Bluff Park(u)	NA	12,372
35957	Boaz	7,151	5,635
36426	Brewton	6,680	6,747
35020	Brighton	5,308	2,277
35215	Center Point(u)	NA	15,675
36611	Chickasaw	7,402	8,447
35044	Childersburg	5,084	4,831
35045	Clanton	5,832	5,868
35055	Cullman	13,084	12,601
35601	Decatur	42,002	38,044
36732	Demopolis	7,678	7,651
36301	Dothan	48,750	36,733
36330	Enterprise	18,033	15,591
36027	Eufaula	12,097	9,102
35064	Fairfield	13,040	14,369
36532	Fairhope	7,286	5,720
35555	Fayette	5,287	4,568
35630	Florence	37,029	34,031
35214	Forestdale(u)	NA	6,091
36201	Fort McClellan(u)	NA	5,334
35967	Fort Payne	11,485	8,435
36360	Fort Rucker(u)	NA	14,242
35068	Fultondale	6,217	5,163
*35901	Gadsden	47,565	53,928
35071	Gardendale	7,928	6,537
36037	Greenville	7,807	8,033
35976	Guntersville	7,041	6,491
35565	Haleyville	5,306	4,190
35640	Hartselle	8,858	7,355
35209	Homewood	21,271	21,245
35226	Hoover	15,064	688
35020	Hueytown	13,309	7,095
*35804	Huntsville	142,513	139,282
35210	Irondale	6,521	3,166
36545	Jackson	6,073	5,957
36265	Jacksonville	9,735	7,715
35501	Jasper	11,894	10,798
36863	Lanett	6,897	6,908
35094	Leeds	8,638	6,991
35228	Midfield	6,536	6,621
*36601	Mobile	200,452	190,026
36460	Monroeville	5,674	4,846
*36104	Montgomery	178,157	133,386
35223	Mountain Brook	17,400	19,474
35660	Muscle Shoals	8,911	6,907
35476	Northport	14,291	9,435
36801	Opelika	21,896	19,027
36467	Opp	7,204	6,493
36203	Oxford	8,939	4,361
36360	Ozark	13,188	13,555
35124	Pelham	6,759	931
35125	Pell City	6,616	5,602
36867	Phenix City	26,928	25,281
36272	Piedmont	5,544	5,063
35127	Pleasant Grove	7,102	5,090
36067	Prattville	18,647	13,116
36610	Prichard	39,541	41,578
35901	Rainbow City	6,299	3,099
36274	Roanoke	5,896	5,251
35653	Russellville	8,195	7,814
36571	Saraland	9,833	7,840
35768	Scottsboro	14,758	9,324
36701	Selma	26,684	27,379
35660	Sheffield	11,903	13,115
35150	Sylacauga	12,708	12,255
35160	Talladega	19,128	17,662
35217	Tarrant City	8,148	6,835
36081	Troy	12,587	11,482
35401	Tuscaloosa	75,143	65,773
35674	Tuscumbia	9,137	8,828
36083	Tuskegee	12,716	11,028
35216	Vestavia Hills	15,733	12,250
36201	West End-Cobb(u)	NA	5,515
	Alaska (907)		
*99502	Anchorage	173,017	48,081
99702	Eielson(u)	NA	6,149
99506	Elmendorf(u)	NA	6,018
99701	Fairbanks	22,645	14,771
99505	Fort Richardson(u)	NA	8,960
99703	Fort Wainwright(u)	NA	9,097
99801	Juneau	19,528	6,050
99611	Kenai Peninsula borough	25,282	16,586
99901	Ketchikan	7,198	6,994
99835	Sitka	7,803	3,370
99503	Spenard(u)	NA	18,089
	Arizona (602)		
85321	Ajo(u)	NA	5,881
85220	Apache Junction	9,935	2,443
85323	Avondale	8,134	6,626
85603	Bisbee	7,154	8,328
85222	Casa Grande	14,971	10,536
85224	Chandler	29,673	13,763
85228	Coolidge	6,851	5,314
85607	Douglas	13,058	12,462
85231	Eloy	6,240	5,381
86001	Flagstaff	34,641	26,117
85613	Fort Huachuca(u)	NA	6,659
85234	Gilbert	5,717	1,971
*85301	Glendale	96,988	36,228
85501	Globe	6,708	7,333
86025	Holbrook	5,785	4,759
86401	Kingman	9,257	7,312
86403	Lake Havasu City	15,737	4,111
85301	Luke(u)	NA	5,047
*85201	Mesa	152,453	63,049
85621	Nogales	15,683	8,946
86040	Page(u)	NA	1,439
85253	Paradise Valley	10,832	6,637
85345	Peoria	12,251	4,792
*85026	Phoenix	764,911	584,303
85301	Prescott	20,055	13,631
85546	Safford	7,010	5,493
*85251	Scottsdale	88,364	67,823
85635	Sierra Vista	25,968	6,689
85350	Somerton	5,761	2,225
85713	South Tucson	6,554	6,220
85351	Sun City(u)	NA	13,670
*85282	Tempe	106,743	63,550
*85726	Tucson	330,537	262,933
85364	West Yuma(u)	NA	5,552
86047	Winslow	7,921	8,066
85364	Yuma	42,433	29,007

ZIP code	Place	1980	1970
	Arkansas (501)		
71923	Arkadelphia	10,005	9,841
72501	Batesville	8,263	7,209
72015	Benton	17,437	16,499
72712	Bentonville	8,756	5,508
72315	Blytheville	24,314	24,752
71701	Camden	15,356	15,147
72830	Clarksville	5,237	4,616
72032	Conway	20,375	15,510
71635	Crossett	6,706	6,191
71639	Dumas	6,091	4,600
71730	El Dorado	26,685	25,283
72701	Fayetteville	36,604	30,729
71742	Fordyce	5,175	4,837
72335	Forrest City	13,803	12,521
72901	Fort Smith	71,384	62,802
72601	Harrison	9,567	7,239
72342	Helena	9,598	10,415
71801	Hope	10,290	8,830
71901	Hot Springs	35,166	35,631
72076	Jacksonville	27,589	19,832
72401	Jonesboro	31,530	27,050
*72201	Little Rock	158,461	132,483
71753	Magnolia	11,909	11,303
72104	Malvern	10,163	8,739
72360	Marianna	6,220	6,196
71654	McGehee	5,671	4,683
71953	Mena	5,154	4,530
71655	Monticello	8,259	5,085
72110	Morrilton	7,355	6,814
72653	Mountain Home	7,447	3,936
72112	Newport	8,339	7,725
*72114	North Little Rock	64,419	60,040
72370	Osceola	8,861	7,892
72450	Paragould	15,214	10,639
71601	Pine Bluff	56,576	57,389
72455	Pocahontas	5,995	4,544
72756	Rogers	17,429	11,050
72801	Russellville	14,000	11,750
72143	Searcy	13,612	9,040
72116	Sherwood	10,586	2,754
72761	Siloam Springs	7,940	6,009
72204	Southwest Little Rock(u)	NA	13,231
72764	Springdale	23,458	16,783
72160	Stuttgart	10,941	10,477
75501	Texarkana	21,459	21,682
72472	Trumann	6,044	6,023
72956	Van Buren	12,020	8,373
71671	Warren	7,646	6,433
72390	West Helena	11,367	11,007
72301	West Memphis	28,138	26,070
72396	Wynne	7,805	6,696
	California		
94501	Alameda	(415)	63,852	70,968
94507	Alamo-Danville(u)	(415)	15,101	14,059
94706	Albany	(415)	15,130	15,561
*91802	Alhambra	(213)	64,615	62,125
90249	Alondra Park(u)	(213)	NA	12,193
91001	Altadena(u)	(213)	NA	42,415
95116	Alum Rock(u)	(408)	NA	18,355
*92803	Anaheim	(714)	221,847	166,408
96007	Anderson	(916)	7,381	5,492
94509	Antioch	(415)	43,559	28,060
92307	Apple Valley(u)	(714)	NA	6,702
95003	Aptos(u)	(408)	NA	6,704
91008	Arcadia	(213)	45,994	45,138
95521	Arcata	(707)	12,338	8,985
95825	Arden-Arcade(u)	(916)	NA	82,492
93420	Arroyo Grande	(805)	11,290	7,454
90701	Artesia	(213)	14,301	14,757
93203	Arvin	(805)	6,863	5,199
94577	Ashland(u)	(415)	NA	14,810
93422	Atascadero	(805)	15,930	10,290
94025	Atherton	(415)	7,797	8,085
95301	Atwater	(209)	17,530	11,640
95603	Auburn	(916)	7,540	6,570
92505	August School Area(u)	(209)	NA	6,293
91746	Avocado Heights(u).	(213)	NA	9,810
91702	Azusa	(213)	29,380	25,217
*93302	Bakersfield	(805)	105,611	69,515
91706	Baldwin Park	(213)	50,554	47,285
92220	Banning	(714)	14,020	12,034
92311	Barstow	(714)	17,690	17,442
95903	Beale East(u)	(916)	NA	7,029
92223	Beaumont	(714)	6,818	5,484
90201	Bell	(213)	25,450	21,836
90706	Bellflower	(213)	53,441	52,334
90201	Bell Gardens	(213)	34,117	29,308
94002	Belmont	(415)	24,505	23,538
94510	Benicia	(707)	15,376	7,349
*94704	Berkeley	(415)	103,328	114,091
*90213	Beverly Hills	(213)	32,367	33,416
92314	Big Bear(u)	(714)	NA	5,268
92316	Bloomington(u)	(714)	NA	11,957
92225	Blythe	(714)	6,805	7,047
92227	Brawley	(714)	14,946	13,746
92621	Brea	(714)	27,913	18,447

ZIP code	Place		1980	1970
95605	Broderick-Bryte(u)	(916)	NA	12,782
*90620	Buena Park	(714)	64,165	63,646
*91505	Burbank	(213)	84,625	88,871
94010	Burlingame	(415)	26,173	27,320
92231	Calexico	(714)	14,412	10,625
93010	Camarillo	(805)	37,732	19,219
93010	Camarillo Heights(u)	(805)	NA	5,892
95124	Cambrian Park(u)	(408)	NA	5,316
95008	Campbell	(408)	27,067	23,797
95010	Capitola	(408)	9,095	5,080
92007	Cardiff-by-the-Sea(u)	(714)	NA	5,724
92008	Carlsbad	(714)	35,490	14,944
95608	Carmichael(u)	(916)	NA	37,625
93013	Carpinteria	(805)	10,835	6,982
90744	Carson	(213)	81,221	71,150
94546	Castro Valley(u)	(415)	NA	44,760
95307	Ceres	(209)	13,281	6,029
90701	Cerritos	(213)	52,756	15,856
94541	Cherryland(u)	(415)	NA	9,969
95926	Chico	(916)	26,601	19,580
95926	Chico North(u)	(916)	NA	6,656
93555	China Lake(u)	(714)	NA	11,105
91710	Chino	(714)	40,165	20,411
93610	Chowchilla	(209)	5,122	4,349
*92010	Chula Vista	(714)	83,927	67,901
95610	Citrus Heights(u)	(916)	NA	21,760
91711	Claremont	(714)	30,950	24,776
93612	Clovis	(209)	33,021	13,856
92236	Coachella	(714)	9,129	8,353
93210	Coalinga	(209)	6,593	6,161
92324	Colton	(714)	27,419	20,016
90022	Commerce	(213)	10,509	10,635
*90220	Compton	(213)	81,286	78,547
94520	Concord	(415)	103,251	85,164
93212	Corcoran	(209)	6,454	5,249
91720	Corona	(714)	37,791	27,519
92118	Coronado	(714)	16,859	20,020
94925	Corte Madera	(415)	8,074	8,464
*92626	Costa Mesa	(714)	82,291	72,660
*91722	Covina	(213)	33,751	30,395
91730	Cucamonga(u)	(714)	NA	5,796
90201	Cudahy	(213)	17,984	16,998
90230	Culver City	(213)	38,139	34,451
95014	Cupertino	(408)	25,770	17,895
90630	Cypress	(714)	40,391	31,569
*94017	Daly City	(415)	78,519	66,922
95616	Davis	(916)	36,640	23,488
90250	Del Aire(u)	(213)	NA	11,930
93215	Delano	(805)	16,491	14,559
92014	Del Mar	(714)	5,017	3,956
92240	Desert Hot Springs	(714)	5,941	2,738
91765	Diamond Bar(u)	(714)	NA	10,576
93618	Dinuba	(209)	9,907	7,917
95620	Dixon	(916)	7,541	4,432
90810	Dominguez(u)	(213)	NA	5,980
*90241	Downey	(213)	82,602	88,573
91010	Duarte	(213)	16,766	14,981
94566	Dublin(u)	(415)	NA	13,641
90220	East Compton(u)	(213)	NA	5,853
90638	East La Mirada(u)	(213)	NA	12,339
90022	East Los Angeles(u)	(213)	NA	104,881
94303	East Palo Alto(u)	(415)	NA	18,727
93523	Edwards(u)	(805)	NA	10,331
*92020	El Cajon	(714)	73,892	52,273
92243	El Centro	(714)	23,996	19,272
94530	El Cerrito	(415)	22,731	25,190
93017	El Encanto Heights(u)	(213)	NA	6,225
*91734	El Monte	(213)	79,494	69,892
93446	El Paso de Robles	(213)	9,163	7,168
93030	El Rio(u)	(805)	NA	6,173
90245	El Segundo	(213)	13,752	15,620
92630	El Toro(u)	(714)	NA	8,654
92709	El Toro Station(u)	(714)	NA	6,970
92024	Encinitas(u)	(714)	NA	5,375
96001	Enterprise(u)	(916)	NA	11,486
*92025	Escondido	(714)	62,480	36,792
95501	Eureka	(707)	24,153	24,337
93221	Exeter	(209)	5,619	4,475
94930	Fairfax	(415)	7,391	7,661
94533	Fairfield	(707)	58,099	44,146
95628	Fair Oaks(u)	(916)	NA	11,256
92028	Fallbrook(u)	(714)	NA	6,945
93223	Farmersville	(209)	5,544	3,456
93015	Fillmore	(805)	9,602	6,285
90001	Florence-Graham(u)	(213)	NA	42,900
95628	Florin(u)	(916)	NA	9,646
95630	Folsom	(916)	11,003	5,810
92335	Fontana	(714)	37,109	20,673
95437	Fort Bragg	(707)	5,019	4,455
95540	Fortuna	(707)	7,591	4,203
94404	Foster City	(415)	23,287	9,522
92708	Fountain Valley	(714)	55,080	31,886
95019	Freedom(u)	(408)	NA	5,563
*94536	Fremont	(415)	131,945	100,869
*93706	Fresno	(209)	218,202	165,655
*92631	Fullerton	(714)	102,034	85,987
95632	Galt	(209)	5,514	3,200
*90247	Gardena	(213)	45,165	41,021
95205	Garden Acres(u)	(213)	NA	7,870
*92640	Garden Grove	(714)	123,351	121,155
92392	George(u)	(714)	NA	7,404

ZIP code	Place		1980	1970
95020	Gilroy	(408)	21,641	12,684
92509	Glen Avon(u)	(714)	NA	5,759
*91209	Glendale	(213)	139,060	132,664
91740	Glendora	(213)	38,654	32,143
92324	Grand Terrace	(714)	8,498	5,901
95945	Grass Valley	(916)	6,697	5,149
92041	Grossmont-Mt.Helix(u)	(714)	NA	8,723
93433	Grover City	(805)	8,827	5,939
91745	Hacienda Heights	(213)	NA	35,969
94019	Half Moon Bay	(415)	7,282	4,023
93230	Hanford	(209)	20,958	15,179
90716	Hawaiian Gardens	(213)	10,548	9,052
90250	Hawthorne	(213)	56,447	53,304
*94544	Hayward	(415)	94,167	93,058
95448	Healdsburg	(707)	7,217	5,438
92343	Hemet	(714)	23,211	12,252
92343	Hemet East(u)	(714)	NA	8,598
94547	Hercules	(415)	5,963	252
90254	Hermosa Beach	(213)	18,070	17,412
92346	Highland(u)	(714)	NA	12,669
94010	Hillsborough	(415)	10,451	8,753
95023	Hollister	(408)	11,488	7,663
91720	Home Gardens(u)	(714)	NA	5,116
*92647	Huntington Beach	(714)	170,505	115,960
90255	Huntington Park	(213)	46,223	33,744
92032	Imperial Beach	(714)	22,689	20,244
92201	Indio	(714)	21,611	14,459
*90306	Inglewood	(213)	94,245	89,985
*92711	Irvine	(714)	62,134	7,381
93017	Isla Vista(u)	(408)	NA	13,441
94707	Kensington(u)	(415)	NA	5,823
93930	King City	(408)	5,495	3,717
93631	Kingsburg	(209)	5,115	3,843
91011	La Canada-Flintridge	(213)	20,153	20,714
91214	La Crescenta-Montrose(u)	(213)	NA	19,620
90045	Ladera Heights(u)	(213)	NA	6,079
94549	Lafayette	(415)	20,879	20,484
*92651	Laguna Beach	(714)	17,860	14,550
92653	Laguna Hills(u)	(714)	NA	13,676
90631	La Habra	(213)	45,232	41,350
92040	Lakeside(u)	(714)	NA	11,991
92330	Lake Elsinore	(714)	5,982	3,530
*90714	Lakewood	(213)	74,654	83,025
92041	La Mesa	(714)	50,342	39,178
90638	La Mirada	(714)	40,986	30,808
93241	Lamont(u)	(805)	NA	7,007
93534	Lancaster	(805)	48,027	32,728
90624	La Palma	(714)	15,663	9,687
91747	La Puente	(213)	30,882	31,092
94939	Larkspur	(415)	11,064	10,487
91750	La Verne	(714)	23,508	12,965
90260	Lawndale	(213)	23,460	24,825
92045	Lemon Grove	(209)	20,780	19,794
93245	Lemoore	(209)	8,832	4,219
93245	Lemoore Station(u)	(209)	NA	9,210
90304	Lennox(u)	(213)	NA	16,121
95207	Lincoln Village(u)	(916)	NA	6,112
95901	Linda(u)	(916)	NA	7,112
93247	Lindsay	(209)	6,924	5,206
95062	Live Oak(u) (Santa Cruz)	(408)	NA	6,443
94550	Livermore	(415)	48,349	37,703
95334	Livingston	(209)	5,326	2,588
95240	Lodi	(209)	35,221	28,691
92354	Loma Linda	(714)	10,694	7,651
90717	Lomita	(213)	17,191	19,784
93436	Lompoc	(805)	26,267	25,284
*90801	Long Beach	(213)	361,334	358,879
90720	Los Alamitos	(213)	11,529	11,346
94022	Los Altos	(415)	25,769	25,062
94022	Los Altos Hills	(415)	7,421	6,871
*90052	Los Angeles	(213)	2,966,763	2,811,801
93635	Los Banos	(209)	10,341	9,188
95030	Los Gatos	(408)	26,593	22,613
90262	Lynwood	(213)	48,548	43,354
93637	Madera	(209)	21,732	16,044
90266	Manhattan Beach	(213)	31,542	35,352
95336	Manteca	(209)	24,925	13,845
93933	Marina	(408)	20,647	8,343
94553	Martinez	(415)	22,582	16,506
95901	Marysville	(916)	9,898	9,353
95655	Mather(u)	(916)	NA	7,027
90270	Maywood	(213)	21,810	16,996
93250	Mc Farland	(805)	5,151	4,177
93023	Meiners Oaks-Mira Monte(u)	(805)	NA	7,025
93640	Mendota	(209)	5,038	2,705
94025	Menlo Park	(415)	25,673	26,826
95340	Merced	(209)	36,499	22,670
94030	Millbrae	(415)	20,058	20,920
94941	Mill Valley	(415)	12,967	12,942
95035	Milpitas	(408)	37,820	26,561
91752	Mira Loma(u)	(714)	NA	8,482
92675	Mission Viejo(u)	(714)	NA	11,933
*95350	Modesto	(209)	106,105	61,712
91016	Monrovia	(213)	30,531	30,562
91763	Montclair	(714)	22,628	22,546
90640	Montebello	(213)	52,929	42,807
93940	Monterey	(408)	27,558	26,302
91754	Monterey Park	(213)	54,338	49,166
94556	Moraga	(415)	15,014	14,205

ZIP code	Place		1980	1970
95037	Morgan Hill	(408)	17,060	5,579
93442	Morro Bay	(805)	9,064	7,109
*94042	Mountain View	(415)	58,655	54,132
92405	Muscoy(u)	(714)	NA	7,091
94558	Napa	(707)	50,879	36,103
92050	National City	(714)	48,772	43,184
94560	Newark	(415)	32,126	27,153
91321	Newhall(u)	(805)	NA	9,651
*92660	Newport Beach	(714)	63,475	49,582
91760	Norco	(714)	21,126	14,511
94025	North Fair Oaks(u)	(415)	NA	9,740
95660	North Highlands(u)	(916)	NA	31,854
92135	North Island(u)	(714)	NA	6,892
90650	Norwalk	(213)	85,232	90,164
94947	Novato	(415)	43,916	31,006
95361	Oakdale	(209)	8,474	6,594
*94615	Oakland	(415)	339,288	361,561
92054	Oceanside	(714)	76,698	40,494
93308	Oildale(u)	(805)	NA	20,879
93023	Ojai	(805)	6,816	5,591
95961	Olivehurst(u)	(916)	NA	8,100
*91761	Ontario	(714)	88,820	64,118
95060	Opal Cliffs(u)	(408)	NA	5,425
*92667	Orange	(714)	91,788	77,365
95662	Orangevale(u)	(916)	NA	16,493
93454	Orcutt(u)	(805)	NA	8,500
94563	Orinda Village	(415)	NA	6,790
95965	Oroville	(916)	8,683	7,536
92010	Otay-Castle Park(u)	(714)	NA	15,445
93030	Oxnard	(805)	108,195	71,225
94044	Pacifica	(415)	36,866	36,020
93950	Pacific Grove	(408)	15,755	13,505
93550	Palmdale	(805)	12,277	8,511
92260	Palm Desert	(714)	11,801	6,171
92262	Palm Springs	(714)	32,271	20,936
94302	Palo Alto	(415)	55,225	56,040
90274	Palos Verdes Estates	(213)	14,376	13,631
95969	Paradise	(916)	22,571	14,539
90723	Paramount	(213)	36,407	34,734
95823	Parkway-Sacramento So.(u)	(916)	NA	28,574
*91109	Pasadena	(213)	119,374	112,951
92055	Pendleton North(u)	(714)	NA	11,803
92055	Pendleton South(u)	(714)	NA	13,692
92370	Perris	(714)	6,740	4,228
94952	Petaluma	(707)	33,834	24,870
90660	Pico Rivera	(213)	53,459	54,170
94611	Piedmont	(415)	10,498	10,917
94564	Pinole	(415)	14,253	13,266
93449	Pismo Beach	(805)	5,364	4,043
94565	Pittsburg	(415)	33,034	21,423
92670	Placentia	(714)	35,041	21,948
95667	Placerville	(916)	6,739	5,416
94523	Pleasant Hill	(415)	25,124	24,610
94566	Pleasanton	(415)	35,160	18,328
91766	Pomona	(714)	92,742	87,384
93257	Porterville	(209)	19,707	12,602
93257	Porterville West(u)	(209)	NA	6,200
93041	Port Hueneme	(805)	17,803	14,295
92064	Poway(u)	(714)	NA	9,422
95670	Rancho Cordova(u)	(916)	NA	30,451
91730	Rancho Cucamonga	(714)	55,250	19,484
92270	Rancho Mirage	(714)	6,281	2,767
90274	Rancho Palos Verdes	(213)	35,227	33,285
95014	Rancho Rinconada(u)	(408)	NA	5,149
96080	Red Bluff	(916)	9,490	7,676
96001	Redding	(916)	41,995	16,659
92373	Redlands	(714)	43,619	36,355
*90277	Redondo Beach	(213)	57,102	57,451
*94064	Redwood City	(415)	54,965	55,686
93654	Reedley	(209)	11,071	8,131
92376	Rialto	(714)	35,615	28,370
*94802	Richmond	(415)	74,676	79,043
93555	Ridgecrest	(714)	15,929	7,629
95673	Rio Linda(u)	(916)	NA	7,524
95367	Riverbank	(209)	5,695	3,949
*92502	Riverside	(714)	170,876	140,089
95677	Rocklin	(916)	7,344	3,939
94572	Rodeo(u)	(415)	NA	5,356
94928	Rohnert Park	(707)	22,965	6,133
90274	Rolling Hills Estates	(213)	9,412	6,735
95401	Roseland(u)	(707)	NA	5,105
91770	Rosemead	(213)	42,604	40,972
95678	Roseville	(916)	24,347	18,221
90720	Rossmoor(u)	(213)	NA	12,922
91745	Rowland Heights(u)	(213)	NA	16,881
92509	Rubidoux(u)	(714)	NA	13,969
*95813	Sacramento	(916)	275,741	257,105
93901	Salinas	(408)	80,479	58,896
94960	San Anselmo	(415)	11,927	13,031
*92403	San Bernardino	(714)	118,057	106,869
94066	San Bruno	(415)	35,417	36,254
	San Buenaventura (see Ventura)	(805)		
94070	San Carlos	(415)	24,710	26,053
92672	San Clemente	(714)	27,325	17,063
*92109	San Diego	(714)	875,504	697,471
91773	San Dimas	(714)	24,014	15,692
*91340	San Fernando	(213)	17,731	16,571
*94101	San Francisco	(415)	678,974	715,674
91776	San Gabriel	(213)	30,072	29,336
93657	Sanger	(209)	12,558	10,088
92383	San Jacinto	(714)	7,098	4,385

ZIP code	Place		1980	1970
95101	San Jose	(408)	636,550	459,913
92375	San Juan Capistrano	(714)	18,959	3,781
94577	San Leandro	(415)	63,952	68,698
94580	San Lorenzo(u)	(415)	NA	24,633
93401	San Luis Obispo	(805)	34,252	28,036
92069	San Marcos	(714)	17,479	3,896
91108	San Marino	(213)	13,307	14,177
*94402	San Mateo	(415)	77,561	78,991
94806	San Pablo	(415)	19,750	21,461
*94901	San Rafael	(415)	44,700	38,977
*92711	Santa Ana	(714)	203,713	155,710
*93102	Santa Barbara	(805)	74,542	70,215
*95050	Santa Clara	(408)	87,746	86,118
95060	Santa Cruz	(408)	41,483	32,076
90670	Santa Fe Springs	(213)	14,559	14,750
93454	Santa Maria	(805)	39,685	32,749
93454	Santa Maria South(u)	(805)	NA	7,129
*90406	Santa Monica	(213)	88,314	88,289
93060	Santa Paula	(805)	20,552	18,001
*95402	Santa Rosa	(707)	83,205	50,006
92071	Santee(u)	(714)	NA	21,107
95070	Saratoga	(408)	29,261	26,810
94965	Sausalito	(415)	7,090	6,158
95066	Scotts Valley	(408)	6,891	3,621
90740	Seal Beach	(213)	25,975	24,441
93955	Seaside	(408)	36,567	36,883
95472	Sebastopol	(707)	5,500	3,993
93662	Selma	(209)	10,942	7,459
93263	Shafter	(805)	7,010	5,327
91024	Sierra Madre	(213)	10,837	12,140
90806	Signal Hill	(213)	5,734	5,588
93065	Simi Valley	(805)	77,500	59,832
92075	Solana Beach(u)	(714)	NA	5,023
93960	Soledad	(408)	5,928	4,222
95476	Sonoma	(707)	6,054	4,259
95073	Soquel(u)	(408)	NA	5,795
91733	South El Monte	(213)	16,623	13,443
90280	South Gate	(213)	66,784	56,909
95705	South Lake Tahoe	(916)	20,681	12,921
95350	South Modesto(u)	(209)	NA	7,889
91030	South Pasadena	(213)	22,681	22,979
94080	South San Francisco	(415)	49,393	46,646
91770	South San Gabriel(u)	(213)	NA	5,051
91744	South San Jose Hills(u)	(213)	NA	12,366
90605	South Whittier(u)	(213)	NA	46,641
95991	South Yuba(u)	(916)	NA	5,352
*92077	Spring Valley(u)	(714)	NA	29,742
94305	Stanford(u)	(415)	NA	8,691
90680	Stanton	(714)	21,144	18,186
*95204	Stockton	(209)	149,779	109,963
94585	Suisun City	(707)	11,087	2,917
92381	Sun City	(714)	NA	5,519
92388	Sunnymead(u)	(714)	NA	6,708
*94086	Sunnyvale	(408)	106,618	95,976
96130	Susanville	(916)	6,520	6,608
93268	Taft	(805)	5,316	4,285
91780	Temple City	(213)	28,972	31,034
*91360	Thousand Oaks	(805)	77,797	35,873
94920	Tiburon	(415)	6,685	6,209
*90510	Torrance	(213)	131,497	134,968
95396	Tracy	(209)	18,428	14,724
93274	Tulare	(209)	22,475	16,235
95380	Turlock	(209)	26,291	13,992
92680	Tustin	(714)	32,073	22,313
92705	Tustin-Foothills(u)	(714)	NA	26,699
92277	Twentynine Palms(u)	(714)	NA	5,667
92278	Twentynine Palms Base(u)	(714)	NA	5,647
95482	Ukiah	(707)	12,035	10,095
94587	Union City	(415)	39,406	14,724
91786	Upland	(714)	47,647	32,551
95688	Vacaville	(707)	43,367	21,690
91744	Valinda(u)	(213)	NA	18,837
94590	Vallejo	(707)	80,188	71,710
93437	Vandenburg(u)	(805)	NA	13,193
*93001	Ventura	(805)	74,474	57,964
92392	Victorville	(714)	14,220	10,845
90043	View Park-Windsor Hills(u)	(213)	NA	12,268
92667	Villa Park	(714)	7,137	2,723
93277	Visalia	(209)	49,729	27,130
92083	Vista	(714)	35,834	24,688
91789	Walnut	(714)	9,978	5,992
*94596	Walnut Creek	(415)	53,643	39,844
94596	Walnut Creek West(u)	(415)	49,704	8,330
90255	Walnut Park(u)	(213)	NA	8,925
93280	Wasco	(805)	9,613	8,269
95076	Watsonville	(408)	23,543	14,719
90044	West Athens(u)	(213)	NA	13,311
90502	West Carson(u)	(213)	NA	15,501
90247	West Compton(u)	(213)	NA	5,748
*91793	West Covina	(213)	80,094	68,034
90069	West Hollywood(u)	(213)	NA	34,622
92683	Westminster	(714)	71,133	60,076
95351	West Modesto(u)	(209)	NA	6,135
90047	Westmont(u)	(213)	NA	29,310
94565	West Pittsburg(u)	(415)	NA	5,969
91746	West Puente Valley(u)	(213)	NA	20,733
95691	West Sacramento(u)	(916)	NA	12,002
*90606	West Whittier-Los Nietos(u)	(213)	NA	20,845
*90605	Whittier	(213)	68,872	72,863

ZIP code	Place		1980	1970
90222	Willowbrook(u)	(213)	NA	28,705
93286	Woodlake	(209)	5,375	3,371
95695	Woodland	(916)	30,235	20,677
94062	Woodside	(415)	5,291	4,734
92686	Yorba Linda	(714)	28,254	11,856
96097	Yreka City	(916)	5,916	5,394
95991	Yuba City	(916)	18,736	13,986
92399	Yucaipa(u)	(714)	NA	19,284

Colorado (303)

ZIP code	Place	1980	1970
81101	Alamosa	6,830	6,985
80401	Applewood(u)	NA	8,214
*80001	Arvada	84,576	49,844
80010	Aurora	158,588	74,974
*80302	Boulder	76,685	66,870
80601	Brighton	12,773	8,309
80020	Broomfield	20,730	7,261
81212	Canon City	13,037	9,206
80110	Cherry Hills Village	5,127	4,605
*80901	Colorado Springs	215,150	135,517
80022	Commerce City	16,234	17,407
81321	Cortez	7,095	6,032
81625	Craig	8,133	4,205
*80202	Denver	491,396	514,678
80022	Derby(u)	NA	10,206
81301	Durango	11,426	10,333
80214	Edgewater	5,714	4,910
80110	Englewood	30,021	33,695
80620	Evans	5,063	2,570
80221	Federal Heights	7,846	1,502
80913	Fort Carson(u)	NA	19,399
80521	Fort Collins	64,632	43,337
80701	Fort Morgan	8,768	7,594
80017	Fountain	8,324	3,515
80401	Golden	12,237	9,817
81501	Grand Junction	28,144	20,170
80631	Greeley	53,006	38,902
80110	Greenwood Village	5,729	3,095
81230	Gunnison	5,785	4,613
80026	Lafayette	8,985	3,498
81050	La Junta	8,338	8,205
80215	Lakewood	112,848	92,743
81052	Lamar	7,713	7,797
80120	Littleton	28,631	26,466
80120	Littleton Southeast(u)	33,029	22,899
80501	Longmont	42,942	23,209
80027	Louisville	5,593	2,409
80537	Loveland	30,244	16,220
81401	Montrose	8,722	6,496
80233	Northglenn	29,847	27,785
81501	Orchard Mesa(u)	NA	5,824
*81003	Pueblo	101,686	97,774
80911	Security-Widefield(u)	NA	15,297
80110	Sheridan	5,377	4,787
80221	Sherrelwood(u)	NA	18,868
80477	Steamboat Springs	5,098	2,340
80751	Sterling	11,385	10,636
80906	Stratton Meadows(u)	NA	6,223
80229	Thornton	40,343	13,326
81082	Trinidad	9,663	9,901
80229	Welby(u)	NA	6,875
80030	Westminster	50,211	19,512
80221	Westminster East(u)	NA	7,576
80033	Wheat Ridge	30,293	29,778

Connecticut (203)

See Note on Page 207

ZIP code	Place	1980	1970
06401	Ansonia	19,039	21,160
06001	Avon	11,201	8,352
06037	Berlin	15,121	14,149
06801	Bethel	16,004	10,945
06002	Bloomfield	18,608	18,301
06405	Branford	23,363	20,444
*06602	Bridgeport	142,546	156,542
06010	Bristol	57,370	55,487
06804	Brookfield	12,872	9,688
06013	Burlington	5,660	4,070
06234	Brooklyn	5,691	4,965
06019	Canton	7,635	6,868
06410	Cheshire	21,788	19,051
06413	Clinton	11,195	10,267
06413	Clinton Center(u)	NA	5,957
06415	Colchester	7,761	6,603
06340	Conning Towers-Nautilus Park(u)	NA	9,791
06238	Coventry	8,895	8,140
06416	Cromwell	10,265	7,400
06810	Danbury	60,470	50,781
06820	Darien	18,892	20,336
06418	Derby	12,346	12,599
06422	Durham	5,143	4,489
06423	East Haddam	5,621	4,676
06424	East Hampton	8,572	7,078
06108	East Hartford	52,563	57,583
06512	East Haven	25,028	25,120
06333	East Lyme	13,870	11,399
06425	Easton	5,962	4,885
06016	East Windsor	8,925	8,513
06029	Ellington	9,711	7,707
06082	Enfield	42,695	46,189
06426	Essex	5,078	4,911
06430	Fairfield	54,849	56,487

ZIP code	Place	1980	1970
06032	Farmington	16,407	14,390
06033	Glastonbury	24,327	20,651
06035	Granby	7,956	6,150
06830	Greenwich	59,578	59,755
06351	Griswold	8,967	7,763
06340	Groton	41,062	38,244
06340	Groton Borough	10,086	8,933
06437	Guilford	17,375	12,033
06438	Haddam	6,383	4,934
06514	Hamden	51,071	49,357
*06101	Hartford	136,392	158,017
06248	Hebron	5,453	3,815
06239	Killingly	14,519	13,573
06339	Ledyard	13,735	14,837
06759	Litchfield	7,605	7,399
06443	Madison	14,031	9,768
06040	Manchester	49,761	47,994
06250	Mansfield	20,634	19,994
06450	Meriden	57,118	55,959
06762	Middlebury	5,995	5,542
06457	Middletown	39,040	36,924
06460	Milford	50,898	50,858
06468	Monroe	14,010	12,047
06353	Montville	16,455	15,662
06770	Naugatuck	26,456	23,034
*06050	New Britain	73,840	83,441
06840	New Canaan	17,931	17,451
06810	New Fairfield	11,260	6,991
*06510	New Haven	126,109	137,707
06111	Newington	28,841	26,037
06320	New London	28,842	31,630
06776	New Milford	19,420	14,601
06470	Newtown	19,107	16,942
06471	North Branford	11,554	10,778
06473	North Haven	22,080	22,194
06856	Norwalk	77,767	79,288
06360	Norwich	38,074	41,739
06371	Old Lyme	6,159	4,964
06475	Old Saybrook	9,287	8,468
06477	Orange	13,237	13,524
06483	Oxford	6,634	4,480
02891	Pawcatuck(u)	NA	5,255
06374	Plainfield	12,774	11,957
06062	Plainville	16,401	16,733
06782	Plymouth	10,732	10,321
06480	Portland	8,383	8,812
06712	Prospect	6,807	6,543
06260	Putnam	6,855	6,918
.....	Putnam	8,580	8,598
06875	Redding	7,272	5,590
06877	Ridgefield Center(u)	NA	5,878
.....	Ridgefield	20,120	18,188
06067	Rocky Hill	14,559	11,103
06483	Seymour	13,434	12,776
06484	Shelton	31,314	27,165
06070	Simsbury	21,161	17,475
06071	Somers	8,473	6,893
06488	Southbury	14,156	7,852
06489	Southington	36,879	30,946
06074	South Windsor	17,198	15,553
06082	Stafford	9,268	8,680
*06904	Stamford	102,453	108,798
06378	Stonington	16,220	15,940
06268	Storrs(u)	NA	10,691
06497	Stratford	50,541	49,775
06078	Suffield	9,294	8,634
06787	Thomaston	6,272	6,233
06277	Thompson	8,141	7,580
06084	Tolland	9,694	7,857
06790	Torrington	30,987	31,952
06611	Trumbull	32,989	31,394
06060	Vernon	27,974	27,237
06492	Wallingford	37,274	35,714
*06701	Waterbury	103,266	108,033
06385	Waterford	17,843	17,227
06795	Watertown	19,489	18,610
06498	Westbrook	5,216	3,820
06107	West Hartford	61,301	68,031
06516	West Haven	53,184	52,851
06880	Weston	8,284	7,417
06880	Westport	25,290	27,318
06109	Wethersfield	26,013	26,662
06226	Willimantic	14,652	14,402
06897	Wilton	15,351	13,572
06094	Winchester	10,841	11,106
06280	Windham	21,062	19,626
06095	Windsor	25,204	22,502
06096	Windsor Locks	12,190	15,080
06098	Winsted	NA	8,954
06716	Wolcott	13,008	12,495
06525	Woodbridge	7,761	7,673
06798	Woodbury	6,942	5,869
06281	Woodstock	5,117	4,311

Delaware (302)

19711	Brookside Park(u)	NA	7,856
19703	Claymont(u)	NA	6,584
19901	Dover	23,512	17,488
19901	Dover Base(u)	NA	8,106

19805	Elsmere	6,493	8,415
19963	Milford	5,356	5,314
19711	Newark	25,247	21,298
19973	Seaford	5,256	5,537
19899	Wilmington	70,195	80,386
19720	Wilmington Manor —Chelsea—Leedom	NA	10,134

District of Columbia (202)

*20013	Washington	637,651	756,668

Florida

32701	Altamonte Springs	(305)	22,028	4,391
32703	Apopka	(305)	6,019	4,045
33821	Arcadia	(813)	6,002	5,658
32233	Atlantic Beach	(904)	7,847	6,132
33823	Auburndale	(813)	6,501	5,386
33825	Avon Park	(813)	8,026	6,712
32807	Azalea Park(u)	(305)	NA	7,367
33830	Bartow	(813)	14,780	12,891
33505	Bayshore Gardens(u)	(813)	NA	9,255
33430	Belle Glade	(305)	16,535	15,949
33432	Boca Raton	(305)	49,505	28,506
33435	Boynton Beach	(305)	35,624	18,115
*33506	Bradenton	(813)	30,170	21,040
33511	Brandon(u)	(813)	NA	12,749
33314	Broadview Park-Rock Hill(u)	(305)	NA	6,049
33512	Brooksville	(904)	5,582	4,060
33311	Browardale(u)	(305)	NA	17,444
33142	Browns Village(u)	(305)	NA	23,442
33054	Bunche Park(u)	(305)	NA	5,773
32401	Callaway	(904)	7,154	3,240
32920	Cape Canaveral	(305)	5,733	4,258
33904	Cape Coral	(813)	32,103	11,470
33055	Carol City(u)	(305)	NA	27,361
33023	Carver Ranch Estates(u)	(305)	NA	5,515
32707	Casselberry	(305)	15,247	9,438
33505	Cedar Hammock-Bradenton South(u)	(813)	NA	10,820
32324	Chattahoochee	(904)	5,332	7,944
*33515	Clearwater	(813)	85,450	52,074
32711	Clermont	(904)	5,461	3,661
33440	Clewiston	(813)	5,219	3,896
32922	Cocoa	(305)	16,096	16,110
32931	Cocoa Beach	(305)	10,926	9,952
32922	Cocoa West(u)	(305)	NA	5,779
33060	Coconut Creek	(305)	6,288	1,359
33064	Collier Manor-Cresthaven(u)	(305)	NA	7,202
32809	Conway(u)	(305)	NA	8,642
33314	Cooper City	(305)	10,140	2,535
33134	Coral Gables	(305)	43,241	42,494
33065	Coral Springs	(305)	37,349	1,489
32536	Crestview	(904)	7,617	7,952
33157	Cutler Ridge(u)	(305)	NA	17,441
33004	Dania	(305)	11,811	9,013
33314	Davie	(305)	20,877	5,859
*32015	Daytona Beach	(904)	54,176	45,327
33441	Deerfield Beach	(305)	39,193	16,662
32433	DeFuniak Springs	(904)	5,563	4,966
32720	De Land	(904)	15,354	11,641
33444	Delray Beach	(305)	34,325	19,915
33528	Dunedin	(813)	30,203	17,639
33610	East Lake-Orient Park (u)	(813)	NA	5,697
33940	East Naples(u)	(813)	NA	6,152
32032	Edgewater	(904)	6,726	3,348
32542	Eglin(u)	(904)	NA	7,769
33614	Egypt Lake(u)	(813)	NA	7,556
33533	Englewood(u)	(813)	NA	5,108
32726	Eustis	(904)	9,453	6,722
32034	Fernandina Beach	(904)	7,224	6,955
33030	Florida City	(305)	6,174	5,133
*33310	Fort Lauderdale	(305)	153,256	139,590
33841	Fort Meade	(813)	5,546	4,374
*33920	Fort Myers	(813)	36,638	27,351
33901	Fort Myers Southwest(u)	(813)	NA	5,086
33450	Fort Pierce	(305)	33,802	29,721
32548	Fort Walton Beach	(904)	20,829	19,994
*32601	Gainesville	(904)	81,371	64,510
32960	Gifford(u)	(305)	NA	5,772
33170	Goulds(u)	(305)	NA	6,690
33463	Greenacres City	(305)	8,843	1,731
32561	Gulf Breeze	(904)	5,478	4,190
33581	Gulf Gate Estates(u)	(813)	NA	5,874
33737	Gulfport	(813)	11,180	9,976
33844	Haines City	(813)	10,799	8,956
33009	Hallandale	(305)	36,517	23,849
*33010	Hialeah	(305)	145,254	102,452
32805	Holden Heights(u)	(305)	NA	6,206
32017	Holly Hill	(904)	9,953	8,191
*33022	Hollywood	(305)	117,188	106,873
33030	Homestead	(305)	20,668	13,674
33030	Homestead Base(u)	(305)	NA	8,257
32937	Indian Harbour Beach	(305)	5,967	5,371
*32201	Jacksonville	(904)	540,898	504,265
33250	Jacksonville Beach	(904)	15,462	12,779
33458	Jupiter	(305)	9,868	3,136
33156	Kendall(u)	(305)	NA	35,497
33040	Key West	(305)	24,292	29,312
32741	Kissimmee	(305)	15,487	7,119
33618	Lake Carroll(u)	(813)	NA	5,577
32055	Lake City	(904)	9,257	10,575
32208	Lake Forest(u)	(904)	NA	6,216

ZIP code	Place		1980	1970
33803	Lake Holloway(u)	(305)	NA	6,227
*33802	Lakeland	(813)	47,406	42,803
33612	Lake Magdalene(u)	(813)	NA	9,266
33403	Lake Park	(305)	6,909	6,993
33853	Lake Wales	(813)	8,466	8,240
33460	Lake Worth	(305)	27,048	23,714
33460	Lantana	(305)	8,048	7,126
33540	Largo	(813)	58,977	24,230
33313	Lauderdale Lakes	(305)	25,426	10,577
33313	Lauderhill	(305)	37,271	8,465
32748	Leesburg	(904)	13,191	11,869
33614	Leto(u)	(904)	NA	8,458
33064	Lighthouse Point	(305)	11,488	9,071
32060	Live Oak	(904)	6,732	6,830
32810	Lockhart(u)	(305)	NA	5,809
33548	Longboat Key	(813)	8,221	2,850
32750	Longwood	(305)	10,029	3,203
32444	Lynn Haven	(904)	6,239	4,044
32751	Maitland	(305)	8,763	7,157
33063	Margate	(305)	36,044	8,867
32446	Marianna	(904)	7,074	7,282
*32901	Melbourne	(305)	46,536	40,236
33314	Melrose Park(u)	(904)	NA	6,111
32952	Merritt Island(u)	(305)	NA	29,233
*33152	Miami	(305)	346,931	334,859
33139	Miami Beach	(305)	96,298	87,072
33153	Miami Shores	(305)	9,244	9,425
33166	Miami Springs	(305)	12,350	13,279
32570	Milton	(904)	7,206	5,360
32754	Mims(u)	(305)	NA	8,309
33023	Miramar	(305)	32,813	23,997
32757	Mount Dora	(904)	5,883	4,646
32506	Myrtle Grove(u)	(904)	NA	16,186
33940	Naples	(813)	17,581	12,042
32233	Neptune Beach	(904)	5,248	4,281
33552	New Port Richey	(813)	11,196	6,098
32069	New Smyrna Beach	(904)	13,557	10,580
32578	Niceville	(904)	8,543	4,155
33308	North Andrews Terrace(u)	(305)	NA	7,082
33903	North Fort Myers(u)	(813)	NA	8,798
33314	North Lauderdale	(305)	18,479	1,213
33161	North Miami	(305)	42,566	34,767
33160	North Miami Beach	(305)	36,481	30,544
33408	North Palm Beach	(305)	11,344	9,035
33596	North Port	(813)	6,205	2,244
33169	Norwood(u)	(305)	NA	14,973
33308	Oakland Park	(305)	21,939	16,261
32670	Ocala	(904)	37,170	22,583
32548	Ocean City(u)	(904)	NA	5,267
32761	Ocoee	(813)	7,803	3,937
33054	Opa-Locka	(305)	14,460	11,902
32073	Orange Park	(904)	8,766	5,019
*32802	Orlando	(305)	128,394	99,006
32074	Ormond Beach	(904)	21,378	14,063
32074	Ormond By-The-Sea(u)	(904)	NA	6,002
33476	Pahokee	(305)	6,346	5,663
32077	Palatka	(904)	10,175	9,444
32905	Palm Bay	(305)	18,560	7,176
33480	Palm Beach	(305)	9,729	9,086
33403	Palm Beach Gardens	(305)	14,407	6,102
33561	Palmetto	(813)	8,637	7,422
33619	Palm River-Clair Mel(u)	(813)	NA	8,536
33460	Palm Springs	(305)	8,166	4,340
32401	Panama City	(904)	33,346	32,096
33023	Pembroke Pines	(305)	35,776	15,496
32502	Pensacola	(904)	57,619	59,507
33157	Perrine(u)	(305)	NA	10,257
32347	Perry	(904)	8,254	7,701
32808	Pine Hills(u)	(305)	NA	13,882
33565	Pinellas Park	(813)	32,811	22,287
33566	Plant City	(813)	19,270	15,451
33314	Plantation	(813)	48,501	23,523
*33060	Pompano Beach	(305)	52,618	38,587
33064	Pompano Beach Highlands(u)	(305)	NA	5,014
33950	Port Charlotte(u)	(813)	NA	10,769
32019	Port Orange	(904)	18,756	3,781
33452	Port St. Lucie	(305)	14,690	330
*33950	Punta Gorda	(813)	6,797	3,879
32351	Quincy	(904)	8,591	8,334
33156	Richmond Heights(u)	(305)	NA	6,663
33312	Riverland Vil.-Lauderdale Is.(u)	(305)	NA	5,512
33404	Riviera Beach	(305)	26,596	21,401
32955	Rockledge	(305)	11,877	10,523
33572	Safety Harbor	(813)	6,461	3,103
32084	St. Augustine	(904)	11,985	12,352
32769	St. Cloud	(305)	7,840	5,041
*33730	St. Petersburg	(813)	236,893	216,159
33706	St. Petersburg Beach	(813)	9,354	8,024
32771	Sanford	(305)	23,176	17,393
*33578	Sarasota	(813)	48,868	40,237
33579	Sarasota Southeast(u)	(813)	NA	6,885
32937	Satellite Beach	(305)	9,163	6,558
33870	Sebring	(813)	8,736	7,223
32021	South Daytona	(904)	9,608	4,979
33143	South Miami	(305)	10,884	11,780
33157	South Miami Heights(u)	(305)	NA	10,395
32937	South Patrick Shores(u)	(305)	NA	10,313
32401	Springfield	(904)	7,220	5,949
32091	Starke	(904)	5,306	4,848
33494	Stuart	(305)	9,467	4,820
33304	Sunrise	(305)	39,681	7,403
33144	Sweetwater	(305)	8,251	3,357
33614	Sweetwater Creek(u)	(813)	NA	19,453
*32303	Tallahassee	(904)	81,548	72,624
33313	Tamarac	(305)	29,142	5,193
*33602	Tampa	(813)	271,523	277,714
33589	Tarpon Springs	(813)	13,251	7,118
33617	Temple Terrace	(813)	11,097	7,347
33905	Tice(u)	(813)	NA	7,254
32780	Titusville	(305)	31,910	30,515
33740	Treasure Island	(813)	6,316	6,120
33620	University (Hillsborough)(u)	(813)	NA	10,039
32580	Valparaiso	(904)	6,142	6,504
33595	Venice	(813)	12,153	6,648
32960	Vero Beach	(305)	16,176	11,908
32960	Vero Beach South(u)	(305)	NA	7,330
32507	Warrington(u)	(904)	NA	15,848
33505	West Bradenton(u)	(813)	NA	6,162
32446	West End(u)	(904)	NA	5,289
32901	West Melbourne	(305)	5,078	3,050
33144	West Miami	(305)	6,076	5,494
*33401	West Palm Beach	(305)	62,530	57,375
32505	West Pensacola(u)	(904)	NA	20,924
33880	West Winter Haven(u)	(813)	NA	7,716
33165	Westwood Lakes(u)	(305)	NA	12,811
33305	Wilton Manors	(305)	12,742	10,948
32787	Winter Garden	(305)	6,789	5,153
33880	Winter Haven	(813)	21,119	16,136
32789	Winter Park	(305)	22,314	21,895
32707	Winter Springs	(305)	10,475	1,161
33599	Zephyrhills	(813)	5,742	3,369

Georgia

ZIP code	Place		1980	1970
31620	Adel	(912)	5,592	4,972
*31701	Albany	(912)	73,934	72,623
31709	Americus	(912)	16,120	16,091
*30601	Athens	(404)	42,549	44,342
*30304	Atlanta	(404)	425,022	495,039
*30901	Augusta	(404)	47,532	59,864
31717	Bainbridge	(912)	10,553	10,887
31723	Blakely	(912)	5,880	5,267
31520	Brunswick	(912)	17,605	19,585
30518	Buford	(404)	6,697	4,640
31728	Cairo	(912)	8,777	8,061
30701	Calhoun	(404)	5,335	4,748
31730	Camilla	(912)	5,414	4,987
30117	Carrollton	(404)	14,078	13,520
30120	Cartersville	(404)	9,508	10,138
30125	Cedartown	(404)	8,619	9,253
30341	Chamblee	(404)	7,137	9,127
31014	Cochran	(912)	5,121	5,161
30337	College Park	(404)	24,632	18,203
*31902	Columbus	(404)	169,441	155,028
30207	Conyers	(404)	6,567	4,809
31015	Cordele	(912)	10,914	10,733
30209	Covington	(404)	10,586	10,267
30720	Dalton	(404)	20,743	18,872
31742	Dawson	(912)	5,699	5,383
*30030	Decatur	(404)	18,404	21,943
31520	Dock Junction(u)	(912)	NA	6,009
30340	Doraville	(404)	7,414	9,157
31533	Douglas	(912)	10,980	10,195
30134	Douglasville	(404)	7,641	5,472
31021	Dublin	(912)	16,083	15,143
31023	Eastman	(912)	5,330	5,416
30344	East Point	(404)	37,486	39,315
30635	Elberton	(404)	5,686	6,438
31750	Fitzgerald	(912)	10,187	8,187
30050	Forest Park	(404)	18,782	19,994
31905	Fort Benning(u)	(404)	NA	27,495
30905	Fort Gordon(u)	(404)	NA	15,589
30741	Fort Oglethorpe	(404)	5,443	3,869
31030	Fort Valley	(912)	9,000	9,251
30501	Gainesville	(404)	15,280	15,459
31408	Garden City	(404)	6,895	5,790
30223	Griffin	(404)	20,728	22,734
30354	Hapeville	(404)	6,166	9,567
31313	Hinesville	(912)	11,309	4,115
31545	Jesup	(912)	9,418	9,091
30144	Kennesaw	(404)	5,095	3,548
30728	La Fayette	(404)	6,517	6,044
30240	La Grange	(404)	24,204	23,301
30245	Lawrenceville	(404)	8,928	5,207
*31201	Macon	(912)	116,860	122,423
30060	Marietta	(404)	30,805	27,216
31034	Midway-Hardwick(u)	(912)	NA	14,047
31061	Milledgeville	(912)	12,176	11,601
30655	Monroe	(404)	8,854	8,071
31768	Moultrie	(912)	15,708	14,400
30263	Newnan	(404)	11,449	11,205
30269	Peachtree City	(404)	6,429	793
31069	Perry	(912)	9,453	7,771
31643	Quitman	(912)	5,188	4,818
*30274	Riverdale	(404)	7,121	2,521
30161	Rome	(404)	29,654	30,759
30075	Roswell	(404)	23,337	5,430
31522	St. Simons(u)	(912)	NA	5,346
31082	Sandersville	(912)	6,137	5,546
*31401	Savannah	(912)	141,634	118,349
30080	Smyrna	(404)	20,312	19,157

ZIP code	Place	1980	1970
30278	Snellville............ (404)	8,514	1,990
30458	Statesboro............ (912)	14,866	14,616
30401	Swainsboro............ (912)	7,602	7,325
31791	Sylvester............ (912)	5,860	4,226
30286	Thomaston............ (404)	9,682	10,024
31792	Thomasville............ (912)	18,463	18,155
30824	Thomson............ (404)	7,001	6,503
31794	Tifton............ (912)	13,749	12,179
30577	Toccoa............ (404)	9,104	6,971
31601	Valdosta............ (912)	37,596	32,303
30474	Vidalia............ (912)	10,393	9,507
31093	Warner Robins........ (912)	39,893	33,491
31501	Waycross............ (912)	19,371	18,996
30830	Waynesboro............ (404)	5,760	5,530
30680	Winder............ (404)	6,705	6,605
31406	Windsor Forest(u)........ (912)	NA	7,288

Hawaii (808)
See Note on Page 207

ZIP code	Place	1980	1970
.....	Ewa............	190,037	132,299
.....	Hilo............	37,017	28,412
.....	Honolulu............	365,048	324,871
.....	Kahului............	13,026	8,287
.....	Keaau-Mountain View	7,055	3,802
.....	Kekaha-Waimea	5,256	4,159
.....	Kihei	6,035	1,636
.....	Koolauloa	14,195	10,562
.....	Koolaupoko	109,373	92,219
.....	Kula.	5,077	2,124
.....	Lahaina.	10,284	5,524
.....	Makawao-Paia	10,361	5,788
.....	North Kona.	13,748	4,832
.....	Papaikou-Wailea	5,261	5,503
.....	South Kona	5,914	4,004
.....	Wahiawa	41,562	37,329
.....	Waialua	9,849	9,171
.....	Waianae	32,810	24,077
.....	Wailua-Anahola	6,030	3,599
.....	Wailuku.	10,674	9,084

Idaho (208)

ZIP code	Place	1980	1970
83221	Blackfoot.	10,065	8,716
*83708	Boise City	102,451	74,990
83318	Burley.	8,761	8,279
83605	Caldwell.	17,699	14,219
83201	Chubbuck	7,052	2,924
83814	Coeur D'Alene.	20,054	16,228
83401	Idaho Falls.	39,590	35,776
83338	Jerome.	6,891	4,183
83501	Lewiston.	27,986	26,068
83642	Meridian.	6,658	2,616
83843	Moscow.	16,513	14,146
83647	Mountain Home.	7,540	6,451
83648	Mountain Home Base(u)	NA	6,038
83651	Nampa.	25,112	20,768
83661	Payette.	5,448	4,521
83201	Pocatello.	46,340	40,036
83854	Post Falls.	5,736	2,371
83440	Rexburg.	11,559	8,272
83350	Rupert.	5,476	4,563
83301	Twin Falls.	26,209	21,914

Illinois

ZIP code	Place	1980	1970
60101	Addison............ (312)	28,836	24,482
60102	Algonquin............ (312)	5,834	3,515
60658	Alsip............ (312)	17,134	11,608
62002	Alton............ (618)	34,171	39,700
62906	Anna............ (618)	5,408	4,766
*60004	Arlington Heights........ (312)	66,116	65,058
*60507	Aurora............ (312)	81,293	74,389
60010	Barrington............ (312)	9,029	8,581
60103	Bartlett............ (312)	13,254	3,501
61607	Bartonville............ (309)	6,110	7,221
60510	Batavia............ (312)	12,574	9,060
62618	Beardstown............ (217)	6,338	6,222
*62220	Belleville............ (618)	42,150	41,223
60104	Bellwood............ (312)	19,811	22,096
61008	Belvidere............ (815)	15,176	14,061
60106	Bensenville............ (312)	16,124	12,956
62812	Benton............ (618)	7,778	6,833
60162	Berkeley............ (312)	5,467	6,152
60402	Berwyn............ (312)	46,849	52,502
62010	Bethalto............ (618)	8,630	7,074
60108	Bloomingdale............ (312)	12,659	2,974
61701	Bloomington............ (309)	44,189	39,992
60406	Blue Island............ (312)	21,855	22,629
60439	Bolingbrook............ (312)	37,261	7,651
60914	Bourbonnais............ (815)	13,280	5,909
60915	Bradley............ (815)	11,008	9,881
60455	Bridgeview............ (312)	14,155	12,506
60153	Broadview............ (312)	8,618	9,623
60513	Brookfield............ (312)	19,395	20,284
60090	Buffalo Grove............ (312)	22,230	12,333
60459	Burbank............ (312)	28,462	26,726
62206	Cahokia............ (618)	18,904	20,649
62914	Cairo............ (618)	5,931	6,277
60409	Calumet City............ (312)	39,673	33,107
60643	Calumet Park............ (312)	8,788	10,069
61520	Canton............ (309)	14,626	14,217
62901	Carbondale.......... (815)	27,194	22,816
62626	Carlinville.......... (217)	5,439	5,675
62821	Carmi.......... (618)	6,264	6,033
60187	Carol Stream.......... (312)	15,472	4,434
60110	Carpentersville.......... (312)	23,272	24,059
60013	Cary.......... (312)	6,640	4,358
62801	Centralia.......... (618)	15,126	15,966
62206	Centreville.......... (618)	9,747	11,378
61820	Champaign.......... (217)	58,133	56,837
62901	Charleston.......... (217)	19,355	16,421
62629	Chatham.......... (217)	5,597	2,788
62233	Chester.......... (618)	8,027	5,310
*60607	Chicago.......... (312)	3,005,072	3,369,357
60411	Chicago Heights.......... (312)	37,026	40,900
60415	Chicago Ridge.......... (312)	13,473	9,187
61523	Chillicothe.......... (309)	6,176	6,052
60650	Cicero.......... (312)	61,232	67,058
61727	Clinton.......... (217)	8,014	7,581
62234	Collinsville.......... (618)	19,613	18,224
60477	Country Club Hills.......... (312)	14,676	6,920
60525	Countryside.......... (312)	6,538	2,864
60435	Crest Hill.......... (815)	9,252	7,460
60445	Crestwood.......... (312)	10,712	5,770
60417	Crete.......... (312)	5,417	4,656
61611	Creve Coeur.......... (309)	6,851	6,440
60014	Crystal Lake.......... (815)	18,590	14,541
61832	Danville.......... (217)	38,985	42,570
60559	Darien.......... (312)	14,968	7,789
*62521	Decatur.......... (217)	94,081	90,397
60015	Deerfield.......... (312)	17,430	18,876
60115	De Kalb.......... (815)	33,099	32,949
*60016	Des Plaines.......... (312)	53,568	57,239
61021	Dixon.......... (815)	15,659	18,147
60419	Dolton.......... (312)	24,766	25,990
60515	Downers Grove.......... (312)	39,274	32,544
62832	Du Quoin.......... (618)	6,594	6,691
62024	East Alton.......... (618)	7,123	7,309
60411	East Chicago Heights.......... (312)	5,347	5,000
61244	East Moline.......... (309)	20,907	20,956
61611	East Peoria.......... (309)	22,385	18,671
*62201	East St. Louis.......... (618)	55,200	70,169
62025	Edwardsville.......... (618)	12,460	11,070
62401	Effingham.......... (217)	11,270	9,458
62930	Eldorado.......... (618)	5,198	3,876
60120	Elgin.......... (312)	63,798	55,691
60007	Elk Grove Village.......... (312)	28,907	20,346
60126	Elmhurst.......... (312)	44,251	46,392
60635	Elmwood Park.......... (312)	24,016	26,160
*60204	Evanston.......... (312)	73,706	80,113
60642	Evergreen Park.......... (312)	22,260	25,921
62837	Fairfield.......... (618)	5,954	5,897
62208	Fairview Heights.......... (618)	12,414	10,050
62839	Flora.......... (618)	5,379	5,283
60422	Flossmoor.......... (312)	8,423	7,846
60130	Forest Park.......... (312)	15,177	15,472
60020	Fox Lake.......... (312)	6,831	4,511
60131	Franklin Park.......... (312)	17,507	20,348
61032	Freeport.......... (815)	26,406	27,736
60030	Gages Lake-Wildwood(u).......... (312)	NA	5,337
61401	Galesburg.......... (309)	35,305	36,290
61254	Geneseo.......... (309)	6,373	5,840
60134	Geneva.......... (312)	9,881	9,049
62034	Glen Carbon.......... (618)	5,197	1,897
60022	Glencoe.......... (312)	9,200	10,542
60137	Glendale Heights.......... (618)	23,163	11,406
60137	Glen Ellyn.......... (312)	23,649	21,909
60025	Glenview.......... (312)	30,842	24,880
60425	Glenwood.......... (312)	10,538	7,416
62040	Granite City.......... (618)	36,815	40,685
60030	Grayslake.......... (312)	5,260	4,907
62246	Greenville.......... (618)	5,271	4,631
60031	Gurnee.......... (312)	7,179	2,738
60103	Hanover Park.......... (312)	28,850	11,735
62946	Harrisburg.......... (618)	9,322	9,535
60033	Harvard.......... (815)	5,126	5,177
60426	Harvey.......... (312)	35,810	34,636
60656	Harwood Heights.......... (312)	8,228	9,060
60429	Hazel Crest.......... (312)	13,973	10,329
62948	Herrin.......... (618)	10,040	9,623
60457	Hickory Hills.......... (312)	13,778	13,176
62249	Highland.......... (618)	7,122	5,981
60035	Highland Park.......... (312)	30,611	32,263
60040	Highwood.......... (312)	5,452	4,973
60162	Hillside.......... (312)	8,279	8,888
60521	Hinsdale.......... (312)	16,726	15,918
60172	Hoffman Estates.......... (312)	38,258	22,238
60456	Hometown.......... (312)	5,324	6,729
60430	Homewood.......... (312)	19,724	18,871
60942	Hoopeston.......... (217)	6,411	6,461
60143	Itasca.......... (312)	7,948	4,638
62650	Jacksonville.......... (217)	20,284	20,553
62052	Jerseyville.......... (618)	7,505	7,446
*60431	Joliet.......... (815)	77,956	78,827
60458	Justice.......... (312)	10,552	9,473
60901	Kankakee.......... (815)	30,141	30,944
61109	Ken Rock(u).......... (815)	NA	5,945
61443	Kewanee.......... (309)	14,508	15,762
60525	La Grange.......... (312)	15,681	17,814
60525	La Grange Highlands(u).......... (312)	NA	6,842
60525	La Grange Park.......... (312)	13,359	15,459

ZIP code	Place		1980	1970
60045	Lake Forest	(312)	15,245	15,642
60102	Lake in the Hills	(312)	5,651	3,240
60047	Lake Zurich	(312)	8,225	4,082
60438	Lansing	(312)	29,039	25,805
61301	La Salle	(815)	10,347	10,736
62439	Lawrenceville	(618)	5,652	5,863
60439	Lemont	(312)	5,640	5,080
60048	Libertyville	(312)	16,520	11,684
62656	Lincoln	(217)	16,327	17,582
60645	Lincolnwood	(312)	11,921	12,929
60046	Lindenhurst	(312)	6,220	3,141
60532	Lisle	(312)	13,625	5,329
62056	Litchfield	(217)	7,204	7,190
60441	Lockport	(815)	9,017	9,861
60148	Lombard	(312)	37,295	34,043
61111	Loves Park	(815)	13,192	12,390
60534	Lyons	(312)	9,925	11,124
61455	Macomb	(309)	19,632	19,643
62060	Madison	(618)	5,915	7,042
62959	Marion	(618)	14,031	11,724
60426	Markham	(312)	15,172	15,987
60443	Matteson	(312)	10,223	4,741
61938	Mattoon	(217)	19,787	19,681
60153	Maywood	(312)	27,998	29,019
60050	McHenry	(815)	10,908	6,772
*60160	Melrose Park	(312)	20,735	22,716
61342	Mendota	(815)	7,134	6,902
62960	Metropolis	(618)	7,171	6,940
60445	Midlothian	(312)	14,274	14,422
61264	Milan	(309)	6,264	4,873
61265	Moline	(309)	45,709	46,237
61462	Monmouth	(309)	10,706	11,022
60450	Morris	(815)	8,833	8,194
61550	Morton	(309)	14,178	10,811
60053	Morton Grove	(312)	23,747	26,369
62863	Mount Carmel	(618)	8,908	8,096
60056	Mount Prospect	(312)	52,634	34,995
62864	Mount Vernon	(618)	16,995	16,270
60060	Mundelein	(312)	17,053	16,128
62966	Murphysboro	(618)	9,866	10,013
60540	Naperville	(312)	42,330	22,794
60451	New Lenox	(815)	5,792	2,855
60648	Niles	(312)	30,363	31,432
61761	Normal	(309)	35,672	26,396
60656	Norridge	(312)	16,483	17,113
60542	North Aurora	(312)	5,205	4,833
60062	Northbrook	(312)	30,735	25,422
60064	North Chicago	(312)	38,774	47,275
60093	Northfield	(312)	5,807	5,010
60164	Northlake	(312)	12,166	14,191
61111	North Park(u)	(815)	NA	15,679
60546	North Riverside	(312)	6,764	8,097
60521	Oak Brook	(312)	6,641	4,164
60452	Oak Forest	(312)	26,096	19,271
*60454	Oak Lawn	(312)	60,590	60,305
*60301	Oak Park	(312)	54,887	62,511
62269	O'Fallon	(618)	10,217	7,268
62450	Olney	(618)	9,026	8,974
60462	Orland Park	(312)	23,045	6,391
61350	Ottawa	(815)	18,166	18,716
60067	Palatine	(312)	32,166	26,050
60463	Palos Heights	(312)	11,096	8,544
60465	Palos Hills	(312)	16,654	6,629
62557	Pana	(217)	6,040	6,326
61944	Paris	(217)	9,885	9,971
60466	Park Forest	(312)	26,222	30,638
60466	Park Forest South	(312)	6,245	1,748
60068	Park Ridge	(312)	38,704	42,614
61554	Pekin	(309)	33,967	31,375
*61601	Peoria	(309)	124,160	126,963
61614	Peoria Heights	(309)	7,453	7,943
61354	Peru	(815)	10,886	11,772
61764	Pontiac	(815)	11,227	10,595
61356	Princeton	(815)	7,342	6,959
60070	Prospect Heights	(312)	11,808	13,333
62301	Quincy	(217)	42,352	45,288
61866	Rantoul	(217)	20,161	25,562
60471	Richton Park	(312)	9,403	2,558
60627	Riverdale	(312)	13,233	15,806
60305	River Forest	(312)	12,392	13,402
60171	River Grove	(312)	10,368	11,465
60546	Riverside	(312)	9,236	10,357
60472	Robbins	(312)	8,119	9,641
62454	Robinson	(618)	7,285	7,178
61068	Rochelle	(815)	8,982	8,594
61071	Rock Falls	(815)	10,624	10,287
*61125	Rockford	(815)	139,712	147,370
61201	Rock Island	(309)	47,036	50,166
60008	Rolling Meadows	(312)	20,167	19,178
60441	Romeoville	(312)	15,519	12,888
60172	Roselle	(312)	16,948	6,207
60073	Round Lake Beach	(312)	12,921	5,717
60174	St. Charles	(312)	17,492	12,945
62881	Salem	(618)	7,813	6,187
60411	Sauk Village	(312)	10,906	7,479
60172	Schaumburg	(312)	52,319	18,531
60176	Schiller Park	(312)	11,458	12,712
62225	Scott(u)	(618)	NA	7,871
62565	Shelbyville	(217)	5,259	4,887
61282	Silvis	(309)	7,130	5,907
60076	Skokie	(312)	60,278	68,322
60177	South Elgin	(312)	6,218	4,289
60473	South Holland	(312)	24,977	23,931
60459	South Stickney(u) (see Burbank)	(312)	NA	
*62703	Springfield	(217)	99,637	91,753
61362	Spring Valley	(815)	5,822	5,605
60475	Steger	(312)	9,269	8,104
61081	Sterling	(815)	16,273	16,113
60402	Stickney	(312)	5,893	6,601
60103	Streamwood	(312)	23,456	18,176
61364	Streator	(815)	14,769	15,600
60501	Summit	(312)	10,110	11,569
62221	Swansea	(618)	5,347	5,432
60178	Sycamore	(815)	9,219	7,843
62568	Taylorville	(217)	11,386	10,644
60477	Tinley Park	(312)	26,171	12,572
61801	Urbana	(217)	35,978	33,976
62471	Vandalia	(618)	5,338	5,160
60061	Vernon Hills	(312)	9,827	1,056
60181	Villa Park	(312)	23,185	25,891
60555	Warrenville	(312)	7,519	3,281
61571	Washington	(309)	10,364	6,790
62204	Washington Park	(618)	8,223	9,524
60970	Watseka	(815)	5,543	5,294
60084	Wauconda	(312)	5,688	5,460
60085	Waukegan	(312)	67,653	65,134
60153	Westchester	(312)	17,730	20,033
60185	West Chicago	(312)	12,550	9,988
61120	West End(u)	(815)	NA	7,554
60558	Western Springs	(312)	12,876	13,029
62896	West Frankfort	(618)	9,437	8,854
60559	Westmont	(312)	16,718	8,832
61604	West Peoria(u)	(309)	NA	6,873
60187	Wheaton	(312)	43,043	31,138
60090	Wheeling	(312)	23,266	13,243
60091	Wilmette	(312)	28,229	32,134
60093	Winnetka	(312)	12,772	14,131
60096	Winthrop Harbor	(312)	5,438	4,794
60191	Wood Dale	(312)	11,251	8,831
60515	Woodridge	(312)	22,322	11,028
62095	Wood River	(618)	12,449	13,186
60098	Woodstock	(815)	11,725	10,226
60482	Worth	(312)	11,592	11,999
60099	Zion	(312)	17,861	17,268

Indiana

ZIP code	Place		1980	1970
46001	Alexandria	(317)	6,028	5,600
46011	Anderson	(317)	64,695	70,787
46703	Angola	(219)	5,486	5,117
46706	Auburn	(219)	8,122	7,388
47421	Bedford	(812)	14,410	13,087
46107	Beech Grove	(317)	13,196	13,559
46408	Black Oak(u)	(219)	NA	9,624
47401	Bloomington	(812)	51,646	43,262
46714	Bluffton	(219)	8,705	8,297
47601	Boonville	(812)	6,300	5,736
47834	Brazil	(812)	7,852	8,163
46112	Brownsburg	(317)	6,242	5,751
46032	Carmel	(317)	18,272	6,691
46303	Cedar Lake	(219)	8,754	7,589
47111	Charlestown	(812)	5,596	5,933
46304	Chesterton	(219)	8,531	6,177
47130	Clarksville	(812)	15,164	13,298
47842	Clinton	(317)	5,267	5,340
46725	Columbia City	(219)	5,457	4,911
47201	Columbus	(812)	30,292	26,457
47331	Connersville	(317)	17,023	17,604
47933	Crawfordsville	(317)	13,325	13,842
46307	Crown Point	(219)	16,455	10,931
46733	Decatur	(219)	8,649	8,445
46311	Dyer	(219)	9,555	4,906
46312	East Chicago	(219)	39,786	46,982
46405	East Gary	(219)	NA	9,858
46514	Elkhart	(219)	41,305	43,152
46036	Elwood	(317)	10,867	11,196
*47708	Evansville	(812)	130,496	138,764
*46802	Fort Wayne	(219)	172,196	178,269
46041	Frankfort	(317)	15,168	14,956
46131	Franklin	(317)	11,563	11,477
*46401	Gary	(219)	151,953	175,415
46933	Gas City	(317)	6,370	5,742
46526	Goshen	(219)	19,665	17,871
46135	Greencastle	(317)	8,403	8,852
46140	Greenfield	(317)	11,439	9,986
47240	Greensburg	(812)	9,254	8,620
46142	Greenwood	(317)	19,327	11,869
46319	Griffith	(219)	17,026	18,168
*46320	Hammond	(219)	93,714	107,983
47348	Hartford City	(317)	7,622	8,207
46322	Highland	(219)	25,935	24,947
46342	Hobart	(219)	22,987	21,485
47542	Huntingburg	(812)	5,376	4,794
46750	Huntington	(219)	16,202	16,217
*46206	Indianapolis	(317)	700,807	736,856
47546	Jasper	(812)	9,097	8,641
47130	Jeffersonville	(812)	21,220	20,008
46755	Kendallville	(219)	7,299	6,838
46901	Kokomo	(317)	47,808	44,042
*47901	Lafayette	(317)	43,011	44,955

ZIP code	Place	1980	1970
46405	Lake Station ... (219)	14,294	9,858
46350	La Porte ... (219)	21,796	22,140
46226	Lawrence ... (317)	25,591	16,353
46052	Lebanon ... (317)	11,456	9,766
47441	Linton ... (812)	6,315	5,450
46947	Logansport ... (219)	17,899	19,255
46356	Lowell ... (219)	5,827	3,839
47250	Madison ... (812)	12,472	13,081
46952	Marion ... (317)	35,874	39,607
46151	Martinsville ... (317)	11,311	9,723
46410	Merrillville ... (219)	27,677	15,918
46360	Michigan City ... (219)	36,850	39,369
46544	Mishawaka ... (219)	40,224	36,060
47960	Monticello ... (219)	5,162	4,869
46158	Mooresville ... (317)	5,349	5,800
47620	Mount Vernon ... (812)	7,656	6,770
*47302	Muncie ... (317)	77,216	69,082
46321	Munster ... (219)	20,671	16,514
47150	New Albany ... (812)	37,103	38,402
47362	New Castle ... (317)	20,056	21,215
46774	New Haven ... (219)	6,714	5,346
46060	Noblesville ... (317)	12,056	7,548
46962	North Manchester ... (219)	5,998	5,791
47265	North Vernon ... (812)	5,768	4,582
46970	Peru ... (317)	13,764	14,139
46168	Plainfield ... (317)	9,191	8,211
46563	Plymouth ... (219)	7,693	7,661
46368	Portage ... (219)	27,409	19,127
47371	Portland ... (219)	7,074	7,115
47670	Princeton ... (812)	8,976	7,431
47374	Richmond ... (317)	41,349	43,999
46975	Rochester ... (219)	5,050	4,631
46173	Rushville ... (317)	6,113	6,686
47167	Salem ... (812)	5,290	5,041
46375	Schererville ... (219)	13,209	3,663
47170	Scottsburg ... (812)	5,068	4,791
47274	Seymour ... (812)	15,050	13,352
46176	Shelbyville ... (317)	14,989	15,094
*46624	South Bend ... (219)	109,727	125,580
46224	Speedway ... (317)	12,641	14,523
47586	Tell City ... (812)	8,704	7,933
*47808	Terre Haute ... (812)	61,125	70,335
46072	Tipton ... (317)	5,004	5,313
46383	Valparaiso ... (219)	22,247	20,020
47591	Vincennes ... (812)	20,857	19,867
46992	Wabash ... (219)	12,985	13,379
46580	Warsaw ... (219)	10,647	7,506
47501	Washington ... (812)	11,325	11,358
46408	West Glen Park(u) ... (219)	NA	5,940
47906	West Lafayette ... (317)	21,247	19,157
46394	Whiting ... (219)	5,630	7,054
47394	Winchester ... (317)	5,659	5,493

Iowa

ZIP code	Place	1980	1970
50511	Algona ... (515)	6,289	6,032
50009	Altoona ... (515)	5,764	2,883
50010	Ames ... (515)	45,775	39,505
50021	Ankeny ... (515)	15,429	9,151
50022	Atlantic ... (712)	7,789	7,306
52722	Bettendorf ... (319)	27,381	22,126
50036	Boone ... (515)	12,602	12,468
52601	Burlington ... (319)	29,529	32,366
51401	Carroll ... (712)	9,705	8,716
50613	Cedar Falls ... (319)	36,322	29,597
*52401	Cedar Rapids ... (319)	110,243	110,642
52544	Centerville ... (515)	6,558	6,531
50616	Charles City ... (515)	8,778	9,268
51012	Cherokee ... (712)	7,004	7,272
51632	Clarinda ... (712)	5,458	5,420
50428	Clear Lake City ... (515)	7,458	6,430
52732	Clinton ... (319)	32,828	34,719
50053	Clive ... (515)	5,906	3,005
52240	Coralville ... (319)	7,687	6,130
51501	Council Bluffs ... (712)	56,449	60,348
50801	Creston ... (515)	8,429	8,234
*52802	Davenport ... (319)	103,264	98,469
52101	Decorah ... (319)	7,991	7,237
51442	Denison ... (712)	6,675	6,218
*50318	Des Moines ... (515)	191,003	201,404
52001	Dubuque ... (319)	62,321	62,309
51334	Estherville ... (712)	7,518	8,108
52556	Fairfield ... (515)	9,428	8,715
50501	Fort Dodge ... (515)	29,423	31,263
52627	Fort Madison ... (319)	13,520	13,996
51534	Glenwood ... (712)	5,280	4,421
50112	Grinnell ... (515)	8,868	8,402
51537	Harlan ... (712)	5,357	5,049
50644	Independence ... (319)	6,392	5,910
50125	Indianola ... (515)	10,843	8,852
52240	Iowa City ... (319)	50,508	46,850
50126	Iowa Falls ... (515)	6,174	6,454
52632	Keokuk ... (319)	13,536	14,631
50138	Knoxville ... (515)	8,143	7,755
51031	Le Mars ... (712)	8,276	8,159
52060	Maquoketa ... (319)	6,313	5,677
52302	Marion ... (319)	19,474	18,028
50158	Marshalltown ... (515)	26,938	26,219
50401	Mason City ... (515)	30,144	30,379
52641	Mount Pleasant ... (319)	7,322	7,007
52761	Muscatine ... (319)	23,467	22,405
50201	Nevada ... (515)	5,912	4,952
50208	Newton ... (515)	15,292	15,619
50662	Oelwein ... (319)	7,564	7,735
52577	Oskaloosa ... (515)	10,629	11,224
52501	Ottumwa ... (515)	27,381	29,610
50219	Pella ... (515)	8,349	6,668
50220	Perry ... (515)	7,053	6,906
51566	Red Oak ... (712)	6,810	6,210
51201	Sheldon ... (712)	5,003	4,535
51601	Shenandoah ... (712)	6,274	5,968
*51101	Sioux City ... (712)	82,003	85,925
51301	Spencer ... ? (712)	11,726	10,278
50588	Storm Lake ... (712)	8,814	8,591
50322	Urbandale ... (515)	17,869	14,434
52349	Vinton ... (319)	5,040	4,845
52353	Washington ... (319)	6,584	6,317
*50701	Waterloo ... (319)	75,985	75,533
50677	Waverly ... (319)	8,444	7,205
50595	Webster City ... (515)	8,572	8,488
50265	West Des Moines ... (515)	21,894	16,441
50311	Windsor Heights ... (515)	5,632	6,303

Kansas

ZIP code	Place	1980	1970
67410	Abilene ... (913)	6,572	6,661
67005	Arkansas City ... (316)	13,201	13,216
66002	Atchison ... (913)	11,407	12,565
67010	Augusta ... (316)	6,968	5,977
66012	Bonner Springs ... (913)	6,266	3,884
66720	Chanute ... (316)	10,506	10,341
67337	Coffeyville ... (316)	15,185	15,116
67701	Colby ... (913)	5,544	4,658
66901	Concordia ... (913)	6,847	7,221
67037	Derby ... (316)	9,786	7,947
67801	Dodge City ... (316)	18,001	14,127
67042	El Dorado ... (316)	10,510	12,308
66801	Emporia ... (316)	25,287	23,327
66027	Fort Leavenworth(u) ... (913)	NA	8,060
66701	Fort Scott ... (316)	8,893	8,967
67846	Garden City ... (316)	18,256	14,790
67735	Goodland ... (913)	5,708	5,510
67530	Great Bend ... (316)	16,608	16,133
67601	Hays ... (913)	16,301	15,396
67060	Haysville ... (316)	8,006	6,531
67501	Hutchinson ... (316)	40,284	36,885
67301	Independence ... (316)	10,598	10,347
66749	Iola ... (316)	6,938	6,493
66441	Junction City ... (913)	19,305	19,018
*66110	Kansas City ... (913)	161,087	168,213
66043	Lansing ... (913)	5,307	3,797
66044	Lawrence ... (913)	52,738	45,698
66048	Leavenworth ... (913)	33,656	25,147
66206	Leawood ... (913)	13,360	10,645
66215	Lenexa ... (913)	18,639	5,549
67901	Liberal ... (316)	14,911	13,862
67460	McPherson ... (316)	11,753	10,851
66502	Manhattan ... (913)	32,644	27,575
66203	Merriam ... (913)	10,794	10,955
66222	Mission ... (913)	8,643	8,125
67114	Newton ... (316)	16,332	15,439
66442	North Fort Riley(u) ... (913)	NA	12,469
66061	Olathe ... (913)	37,258	17,917
66067	Ottawa ... (913)	11,016	11,036
66204	Overland Park ... (913)	81,784	77,934
67357	Parsons ... (316)	12,898	13,015
66762	Pittsburg ... (316)	18,770	20,171
66208	Prairie Village ... (913)	24,657	28,378
67124	Pratt ... (316)	6,885	6,736
66203	Roeland Park ... (913)	7,962	9,760
67665	Russell ... (913)	5,427	5,371
67401	Salina ... (913)	41,843	37,714
*66203	Shawnee ... (913)	29,653	20,946
*66603	Topeka ... (913)	115,266	125,011
67152	Wellington ... (316)	8,212	8,072
*67202	Wichita ... (316)	279,272	276,554
67156	Winfield ... (316)	10,736	11,405

Kentucky

ZIP code	Place	1980	1970
41101	Ashland ... (606)	27,064	29,245
40004	Bardstown ... (502)	6,155	5,816
41073	Bellevue ... (606)	7,678	8,847
40403	Berea ... (606)	8,226	6,956
42101	Bowling Green ... (502)	40,450	36,705
40218	Buechel(u) ... (502)	NA	5,359
42718	Campbellsville ... (502)	8,715	7,598
42330	Central City ... (502)	5,250	5,450
40701	Corbin ... (606)	8,075	7,474
*41011	Covington ... (606)	49,013	52,535
41031	Cynthiana ... (606)	5,881	6,356
40422	Danville ... (606)	12,942	11,542
41074	Dayton ... (606)	6,979	8,751
41017	Edgewood ... (606)	7,230	4,139
42701	Elizabethtown ... (502)	15,380	11,748
41018	Elsmere ... (606)	7,203	5,161
41018	Erlanger ... (606)	14,433	12,676
41139	Flatwoods ... (606)	8,354	7,380
41042	Florence ... (606)	15,586	11,661
42223	Fort Campbell North(u) ... (502)	NA	13,616
40121	Fort Knox(u) ... (502)	NA	37,608
41017	Fort Mitchell ... (606)	7,297	6,982
41075	Fort Thomas ... (606)	16,012	16,338
40601	Frankfort ... (502)	25,973	21,902

ZIP code	Place		1980	1970
42134	Franklin	(502)	7,738	6,553
40326	Georgetown	(502)	10,972	8,629
42141	Glasgow	(502)	12,958	11,301
40330	Harrodsburg	(606)	7,265	6,741
41701	Hazard	(606)	5,429	5,459
42420	Henderson	(502)	24,834	22,976
40229	Hillview	(502)	5,196	....
42240	Hopkinsville	(502)	27,318	21,395
41051	Independence	(606)	7,998	1,715
40299	Jeffersontown	(502)	15,795	9,701
40342	Lawrenceburg	(502)	5,167	3,579
40033	Lebanon	(502)	6,590	5,528
*40511	Lexington-Fayette	(606)	204,165	108,137
*40201	Louisville	(502)	298,451	361,706
42431	Madisonville	(502)	16,979	15,332
42066	Mayfield	(502)	10,705	10,724
41056	Maysville	(606)	7,983	7,411
40965	Middlesborough	(606)	12,251	11,878
42633	Monticello	(606)	5,677	3,618
40351	Morehead	(606)	7,789	7,191
40353	Mount Sterling	(606)	5,820	5,083
42071	Murray	(502)	14,248	13,537
*41071	Newport	(606)	21,587	25,998
40356	Nicholasville	(606)	10,400	5,829
40219	Okolona(u)	(502)	NA	17,643
42301	Owensboro	(502)	54,450	50,329
42001	Paducah	(502)	29,315	31,627
40361	Paris	(606)	7,935	7,823
40258	Pleasure Ridge Park(u)	(502)	NA	28,566
42445	Princeton	(502)	7,073	6,292
40160	Radcliff	(502)	14,519	8,426
40475	Richmond	(606)	21,705	16,861
42276	Russellville	(502)	7,520	6,456
40207	St. Matthews	(502)	13,354	13,152
40065	Shelbyville	(502)	5,308	4,182
40216	Shively	(502)	16,819	19,139
42501	Somerset	(606)	10,649	10,436
40272	Valley Station(u)	(502)	NA	24,471
40383	Versailles	(606)	6,427	5,679
40769	Williamsburg	(606)	5,560	3,687
40391	Winchester	(606)	15,216	13,402

Louisiana

ZIP code	Place		1980	1970
70510	Abbeville	(318)	12,391	10,996
71301	Alexandria	(318)	51,565	41,811
70714	Baker	(504)	12,865	8,281
71220	Bastrop	(318)	15,527	14,713
*70821	Baton Rouge	(504)	219,486	165,921
70360	Bayou Cane(u)	(504)	NA	9,077
70380	Bayou Vista(u)	(504)	NA	5,121
70427	Bogalusa	(504)	16,976	18,412
71010	Bossier City	(318)	49,969	43,769
70517	Breaux Bridge	(318)	5,922	4,942
71322	Bunkie	(318)	5,364	5,395
71101	Cooper Road(u)	(318)	NA	9,034
70433	Covington	(504)	7,892	7,170
70526	Crowley	(318)	16,036	16,104
70726	Denham Springs	(504)	8,412	6,752
70634	De Ridder	(318)	11,057	8,030
70346	Donaldsonville	(504)	7,901	7,367
70535	Eunice	(318)	12,479	11,390
70538	Franklin	(318)	9,584	9,325
70737	Gonzales	(504)	7,287	4,512
70053	Gretna	(504)	20,615	24,875
70401	Hammond	(504)	15,043	12,487
70123	Harahan	(504)	11,384	13,037
70058	Harvey(u)	(504)	NA	6,347
70360	Houma	(504)	32,602	30,922
70544	Jeanerette	(318)	6,511	6,322
70121	Jefferson Heights(u)	(504)	NA	16,489
70546	Jennings	(318)	12,401	11,783
71251	Jonesboro	(318)	5,061	5,072
70548	Kaplan	(318)	5,016	5,540
70062	Kenner	(504)	66,382	29,858
70501	Lafayette	(318)	81,961	68,908
70601	Lake Charles	(318)	75,051	77,998
71254	Lake Providence	(318)	6,361	6,183
70068	Laplace(u)	(504)	NA	5,953
71446	Leesville	(318)	9,054	8,928
70123	Little Farms(u)	(504)	NA	15,713
70448	Mandeville	(504)	6,076	2,571
71052	Mansfield	(318)	6,485	6,432
71351	Marksville	(318)	5,113	4,519
70072	Marrero(u)	(504)	NA	29,015
*70004	Metairie(u)	(504)	NA	136,477
71055	Minden	(318)	15,074	13,996
71201	Monroe	(318)	57,597	56,374
70380	Morgan City	(504)	16,114	16,586
71457	Natchitoches	(318)	16,664	15,974
70560	New Iberia	(318)	32,766	30,147
*70113	New Orleans	(504)	557,482	593,471
71459	North Fort Polk(u)	(318)	NA	7,955
71463	Oakdale	(318)	7,155	7,301
70570	Opelousas	(318)	18,903	20,387
71360	Pineville	(318)	12,034	8,951
70764	Plaquemine	(504)	7,521	7,739
70454	Ponchatoula	(504)	5,469	4,545
70767	Port Allen	(504)	6,114	5,728
70578	Rayne	(318)	9,066	9,510
70084	Reserve(u)	(504)	NA	6,381
71270	Ruston	(318)	20,585	17,365
70582	St. Martinville	(318)	7,965	7,153
70807	Scotlandville(u)	(504)	NA	22,589
*71102	Shreveport	(318)	205,815	182,064
70458	Slidell	(504)	26,718	16,101
71459	South Fort Polk(u)	(318)	NA	15,600
71075	Springhill	(318)	6,516	6,496
70663	Sulphur	(318)	19,709	14,959
71282	Tallulah	(318)	10,392	9,643
71285	Terry(u)	(318)	NA	13,382
70301	Thibodaux	(504)	15,810	15,028
71373	Vidalia	(318)	5,936	5,538
70586	Ville Platte	(318)	9,201	9,692
70669	Westlake	(318)	5,246	4,082
71291	West Monroe	(318)	14,993	14,868
70094	Westwego	(504)	12,663	11,402
71483	Winnfield	(318)	7,311	7,142
71295	Winnsboro	(318)	5,921	5,349
70791	Zachary	(318)	5,340	4,964

Maine (207)
See Note Page 207

ZIP code	Place	1980	1970
04210	Auburn	23,128	24,151
04330	Augusta	21,819	21,945
04401	Bangor	31,643	33,168
04530	Bath	10,246	9,679
04915	Belfast	6,243	5,957
04005	Biddeford	19,638	19,983
04412	Brewer	9,017	9,300
04011	Brunswick Center(u)	NA	10,867
04011	Brunswick	17,366	16,195
04093	Buxton	5,775	3,135
04107	Cape Elizabeth	7,838	7,873
04736	Caribou	9,916	10,419
04021	Cumberland	5,284	4,096
04605	Ellsworth	5,179	4,603
04937	Fairfield	6,113	5,684
04105	Falmouth	6,853	6,291
04938	Farmington	6,730	5,657
04032	Freeport	5,863	4,781
04345	Gardiner	6,485	6,685
04038	Gorham	10,101	7,839
04444	Hampden	5,250	4,693
04730	Houlton Center(u)	NA	6,760
04730	Houlton	6,766	8,111
04239	Jay	5,080	3,954
04043	Kennebunk	6,621	5,646
03904	Kittery Center(u)	NA	7,363
03904	Kittery	9,314	11,028
04240	Lewiston	40,481	41,779
04750	Limestone	8,719	10,360
04457	Lincoln	5,066	4,759
04250	Lisbon	8,769	6,544
04750	Loring(u)	NA	7,881
04756	Madawaska	5,282	5,585
04462	Millinocket Center(u)	NA	7,558
04462	Millinocket	7,567	7,742
04963	Oakland	5,162	3,535
04064	Old Orchard Beach Ctr.(u)	NA	5,273
04064	Old Orchard Beach	6,291	5,404
04468	Old Town	8,422	8,741
04473	Orono Center(u)	NA	9,146
04473	Orono	10,578	9,989
*04101	Portland	61,572	65,116
04769	Presque Isle	11,172	11,452
04841	Rockland	7,919	8,505
04276	Rumford Compact(u)	NA	6,198
04276	Rumford	8,240	9,363
04072	Saco	12,921	11,678
04073	Sanford Center(u)	NA	10,457
04073	Sanford	18,020	15,812
04074	Scarborough	11,347	7,845
04976	Skowhegan Center(u)	NA	6,571
04976	Skowhegan	8,098	7,601
04106	South Portland	22,712	23,267
04084	Standish	5,946	3,122
04086	Topsham	6,431	5,022
04901	Waterville	17,779	18,192
04090	Wells	8,211	4,448
04092	Westbrook	14,976	14,444
04082	Windham	11,282	6,593
04901	Winslow Center(u)	NA	5,389
04901	Winslow	8,057	7,299
04364	Winthrop	5,889	4,335
04096	Yarmouth	6,585	4,854
03909	York	8,465	5,690

Maryland (301)

ZIP code	Place	1980	1970
21001	Aberdeen	11,533	7,403
21005	Aberdeen Proving Ground(u)	NA	7,403
20331	Andrews(u)	NA	6,418
*21401	Annapolis	31,740	30,095
21227	Arbutus(u)	NA	22,745
20853	Aspen Hill(u)	NA	16,887
20783	Avenel-Hillandale(u)	NA	19,520
21905	Bainbridge Center(u)	NA	5,257
*21233	Baltimore	786,775	905,787
21014	Bel Air	7,814	6,307
20705	Beltsville(u)	NA	8,912
20014	Bethesda(u)	NA	71,621
20021	Birchwood City(u)	NA	13,514
20710	Bladensburg	7,691	7,977

ZIP code	Place	1980	1970
20715	Bowie	33,695	35,028
21225	Brooklyn(u)	NA	13,896
20705	Calverton(u)	NA	6,543
21613	Cambridge	11,703	11,595
20031	Camp Springs(u)	NA	22,776
20027	Carmody Hills-Pepper Mill(u)	NA	6,245
21228	Catonsville(u)	NA	54,812
20027	Chapel Oaks-Cedar Heights(u)	NA	6,049
20785	Cheverly	5,751	6,808
20015	Chevy Chase(u)	NA	16,424
20783	Chillum(u)	NA	35,656
20904	Colesville(u)	NA	9,455
20740	College Park	23,614	26,156
21043	Columbia(u)	NA	8,815
20027	Coral Hills(u)	NA	9,058
21502	Cumberland	25,933	29,724
21222	Defense Heights(u)	NA	6,775
20028	District Heights	6,799	7,846
21222	Dundalk(u)	NA	85,377
21601	Easton	7,536	6,809
21219	Edgemere(u)	NA	10,352
21040	Edgewood	NA	8,551
21921	Elkton	6,468	5,362
*21043	Ellicott(u)	NA	9,435
21221	Essex(u)	NA	38,193
21061	Ferndale(u)	NA	9,929
20028	Forestville(u)	NA	16,188
20755	Fort Meade(u)	NA	16,699
21701	Frederick	27,557	23,641
21532	Frostburg	7,715	7,327
20760	Gaithersburg	26,424	8,344
21061	Glen Burnie(u)	NA	38,608
20801	Good Luck(u)	NA	10,584
20770	Greenbelt	16,000	18,199
21740	Hagerstown	34,132	35,862
21740	Halfway(u)	NA	6,106
20852	Halpine(u)	NA	6,118
21078	Havre De Grace	8,763	9,791
20031	Hillcrest Heights	NA	24,037
*20780	Hyattsville	12,709	14,998
21085	Joppatowne(u)	NA	9,092
20904	Kemp Mill(u)	NA	10,037
20785	Kentland(u)	NA	9,649
20785	Landover(u)	NA	5,597
20787	Langley Park(u)	NA	11,564
20801	Lanham-Seabrook(u)	NA	13,244
21227	Lansdowne-Baltimore Highlands(u)	NA	17,770
20810	Laurel	12,103	10,525
20653	Lexington Pk.-Patuxent R.(u)	NA	9,136
21090	Linthicum(u)	NA	9,775
21093	Lutherville-Timonium(u)	NA	24,055
20810	Maryland City(u)	NA	7,102
21220	Middle River(u)	NA	19,935
20852	Montrose(u)	NA	5,902
20822	Mount Rainier	7,361	8,180
20784	New Carrollton	12,632	14,870
20854	North Potomac(u)	NA	12,784
20012	North Takoma Park(u)	NA	7,373
21113	Odenton(u)	NA	5,989
21206	Overlea(u)	NA	13,124
21117	Owings Mills(u)	NA	7,360
20021	Oxon Hill(u)	NA	11,974
20785	Palmer Park(u)	NA	8,172
21234	Parkville	NA	33,589
21128	Perry Hall(u)	NA	5,446
21208	Pikesville(u)	NA	25,395
20016	Potomac Valley(u)	NA	5,122
21227	Pumphrey(u)	NA	6,425
21133	Randallstown(u)	NA	33,683
20853	Randolph(u)	NA	13,215
21136	Reisterstown(u)	NA	12,568
20840	Riverdale Hgts.-E. Pines(u)	NA	8,941
21122	Riviera Beach(u)	NA	7,464
*20850	Rockville	43,811	42,739
21237	Rosedale(u)	NA	19,417
21801	Salisbury	16,429	15,252
20027	Seat Pleasant	5,217	7,217
21146	Severna Park	NA	16,358
*20907	Silver Spring(u)	NA	77,411
21061	South Gate(u)	NA	9,356
20795	South Kensington(u)	NA	10,289
20810	South Laurel(u)	NA	13,345
20023	Suitland-Silver Hills(u)	NA	30,355
20012	Takoma Park	16,231	18,507
21204	Towson(u)	NA	77,768
20601	Waldorf(u)	NA	7,368
20028	Walker Mill(u)	NA	7,103
21157	Westminster	8,808	7,207
20902	Wheaton(u)	NA	66,280
20903	White Oak(u)	NA	19,769
21207	Woodlawn-Woodmoor(u)	NA	28,821

Massachusetts

See Note on Page 207

ZIP code	Place		1980	1970
02351	Abington	(617)	13,517	12,334
01720	Acton	(617)	17,544	14,770
02743	Acushnet	(617)	8,704	7,767
01220	Adams Center(u)	(413)	NA	11,256
.....	Adams	(413)	10,381	11,772
01001	Agawam	(413)	26,271	21,717
01913	Amesbury Center(u)	(617)	NA	10,088
.....	Amesbury	(617)	13,971	11,388
01002	Amherst Center	(413)	NA	17,926
.....	Amherst	(413)	33,229	26,331
01810	Andover	(617)	26,370	23,695
02174	Arlington	(617)	48,219	53,524
01721	Ashland	(617)	9,165	8,882
01331	Athol Center(u)	(617)	NA	9,723
.....	Athol	(617)	10,634	11,185
02703	Attleboro	(617)	34,196	32,907
01501	Auburn	(617)	14,845	15,347
02322	Avon	(617)	5,026	5,295
*01432	Ayer	(617)	6,993	8,325
02630	Barnstable	(617)	30,898	19,842
01730	Bedford	(617)	13,067	13,513
01007	Belchertown	(413)	8,339	5,936
02019	Bellingham	(617)	14,300	13,967
02178	Belmont	(617)	26,100	28,285
01915	Beverly	(617)	37,655	38,348
01821	Billerica	(617)	36,727	31,648
01504	Blackstone	(617)	6,570	6,566
*02109	Boston	(617)	562,994	641,071
02532	Bourne	(617)	13,874	12,636
01921	Boxford	(617)	5,374	4,032
02184	Braintree	(617)	36,337	35,050
02631	Brewster	(617)	5,226	1,790
02324	Bridgewater	(617)	17,202	12,911
*02403	Brockton	(617)	95,172	89,040
02145	Brookline	(617)	55,062	58,689
01803	Burlington	(617)	23,486	21,980
*02138	Cambridge	(617)	95,322	100,361
02021	Canton	(617)	18,182	17,100
02330	Carver	(617)	6,988	2,420
01507	Charlton	(617)	6,719	4,654
02633	Chatham	(617)	6,071	4,554
01824	Chelmsford	(617)	31,174	31,432
02150	Chelsea	(617)	25,431	30,625
*01021	Chicopee	(413)	55,112	66,676
01510	Clinton	(617)	12,771	13,383
02025	Cohasset	(617)	7,174	6,954
01742	Concord	(617)	16,293	16,148
01226	Dalton	(413)	6,797	7,505
01923	Danvers	(617)	24,100	26,151
02714	Dartmouth	(617)	23,966	18,800
02026	Dedham	(617)	25,298	26,938
02638	Dennis	(617)	12,360	6,454
02715	Dighton	(617)	5,352	4,667
01826	Dracut	(617)	21,249	18,214
01570	Dudley	(617)	8,717	8,087
02332	Duxbury	(617)	11,807	7,636
02333	East Bridgewater	(617)	9,945	8,347
01027	Easthampton	(413)	15,580	13,012
01028	East Longmeadow	(413)	12,905	13,029
02334	Easton	(617)	16,623	12,157
01249	Everett	(617)	37,195	42,485
02719	Fairhaven	(617)	15,759	16,332
*02722	Fall River	(617)	92,574	96,898
*02540	Falmouth Center(u)	(617)	NA	5,806
.....	Falmouth	(617)	23,640	15,942
01420	Fitchburg	(617)	39,580	43,343
01433	Fort Devens(u)	(617)	NA	12,915
02035	Foxborough	(617)	14,148	14,218
01701	Framingham	(617)	65,113	64,048
02038	Franklin Center(u)	(617)	NA	8,863
.....	Franklin	(617)	18,217	17,830
02702	Freetown	(617)	7,058	4,270
01440	Gardner	(617)	17,900	19,748
01833	Georgetown	(617)	5,687	5,290
01930	Gloucester	(617)	27,768	27,941
01519	Grafton	(617)	11,238	11,659
01033	Granby	(413)	5,380	5,473
01230	Great Barrington	(413)	7,405	7,537
01301	Greenfield Center(u)	(413)	NA	14,642
.....	Greenfield	(413)	18,436	18,116
01450	Groton	(617)	6,154	5,109
01834	Groveland	(617)	5,040	5,382
02338	Halifax	(617)	5,513	3,537
01936	Hamilton	(617)	6,960	6,373
02339	Hanover	(617)	11,358	10,107
02341	Hanson	(617)	8,617	7,148
01451	Harvard	(617)	12,170	12,494
02645	Harwich	(617)	6,971	5,892
01830	Haverhill	(617)	46,865	46,120
02043	Hingham	(617)	20,339	18,845
02343	Holbrook	(617)	11,140	11,775
01520	Holden	(617)	13,336	12,564
01746	Holliston	(617)	12,622	12,069
01040	Holyoke	(413)	44,678	50,112
01748	Hopkinton	(617)	7,114	5,981
01749	Hudson Center(u)	(617)	NA	14,283
.....	Hudson	(617)	16,408	16,084
02045	Hull	(617)	9,714	9,961
02601	Hyannis(u)	(617)	NA	6,847
01938	Ipswich(u)	(617)	NA	5,022
.....	Ipswich	(617)	11,158	10,750
02364	Kingston	(617)	7,362	5,999
02346	Lakeville	(617)	5,931	4,376
01523	Lancaster	(617)	6,334	6,095
*01842	Lawrence	(617)	63,175	66,915
01238	Lee	(413)	6,247	6,426

ZIP code	Place		1980	1970
01524	Leicester	(617)	9,446	9,140
01240	Lenox	(413)	6,523	5,804
01453	Leominster	(617)	34,508	32,939
01273	Lexington	(617)	29,479	31,886
01773	Lincoln	(617)	7,098	7,567
01460	Littleton	(617)	6,970	6,380
01106	Longmeadow	(413)	16,301	15,630
*01853	Lowell	(617)	92,418	94,239
01056	Ludlow	(413)	18,150	17,580
01462	Lunenburg	(617)	8,405	7,419
*01901	Lynn	(617)	78,471	90,294
01940	Lynnfield	(617)	11,267	10,826
02148	Malden	(617)	53,386	56,127
01944	Manchester	(617)	5,424	5,151
02048	Mansfield	(617)	13,453	9,939
01945	Marblehead	(617)	20,126	21,295
01752	Marlborough	(617)	30,617	27,936
02050	Marshfield	(617)	20,916	15,223
02739	Mattapoisett	(617)	5,597	4,500
01754	Maynard	(617)	9,590	9,710
02052	Medfield	(617)	10,220	9,821
02155	Medford	(617)	58,076	64,397
02053	Medway	(617)	8,447	7,938
02176	Melrose	(617)	30,055	33,180
01844	Methuen	(617)	36,701	35,456
02346	Middleborough Center(u)	(617)	NA	6,259
.....	Middleborough	(617)	16,404	13,607
01757	Milford Center(u)	(617)	NA	13,740
.....	Milford	(617)	23,390	19,352
01527	Millbury	(617)	11,808	11,987
02054	Millis	(617)	6,908	5,686
02186	Milton	(617)	25,860	27,190
01057	Monson	(413)	7,315	7,355
01351	Montague	(413)	8,011	8,451
02554	Nantucket	(617)	5,087	3,774
01760	Natick	(617)	29,461	31,057
02192	Needham	(617)	27,901	29,748
*02741	New Bedford	(617)	98,478	101,777
01950	Newburyport	(617)	15,900	15,807
02158	Newton	(617)	83,622	91,263
02056	Norfolk	(617)	6,363	4,656
01247	North Adams	(413)	18,063	19,195
01060	Northampton	(413)	29,286	29,664
01845	North Andover	(617)	20,129	16,284
*02760	North Attleborough	(617)	21,095	18,665
01532	Northborough	(617)	10,568	9,218
01534	Northbridge	(617)	12,246	11,795
01864	North Reading	(617)	11,455	11,264
02060	North Scituate(u)	(617)	NA	5,507
02766	Norton	(617)	12,690	9,487
02061	Norwell	(617)	9,182	7,796
02062	Norwood	(617)	29,711	30,815
01364	Orange	(617)	6,844	6,104
02653	Orleans	(617)	5,306	3,055
01253	Otis(u)	(413)	NA	5,596
01540	Oxford Center(u)	(617)	NA	6,109
.....	Oxford	(617)	11,680	10,345
01069	Palmer	(413)	11,389	11,680
01960	Peabody	(617)	45,976	48,080
02359	Pembroke	(617)	13,487	11,193
01463	Pepperell	(617)	8,061	5,887
01201	Pittsfield	(413)	51,974	57,020
02762	Plainville	(617)	5,857	4,953
*02360	Plymouth Center(u)	(617)	NA	6,940
.....	Plymouth	(617)	35,913	18,606
02169	Quincy	(617)	84,743	87,966
02368	Randolph	(617)	28,218	27,035
02767	Raynham	(617)	9,085	6,705
01867	Reading	(617)	22,678	22,539
02769	Rehoboth	(617)	7,570	6,512
02151	Revere	(617)	42,423	43,159
02370	Rockland	(617)	15,695	15,674
01966	Rockport	(617)	6,345	5,636
01970	Salem	(617)	38,220	40,556
01950	Salisbury	(617)	5,973	4,179
02563	Sandwich	(617)	8,727	5,239
01906	Saugus	(617)	24,746	25,110
02066	Scituate	(617)	17,317	16,973
02771	Seekonk	(617)	12,269	11,116
02067	Sharon	(617)	13,601	12,367
01464	Shirley	(617)	5,124	4,909
01545	Shrewsbury	(617)	22,674	19,196
02725	Somerset	(617)	18,813	18,088
02143	Somerville	(617)	77,372	88,779
01772	Southborough	(617)	6,193	5,798
01550	Southbridge Center(u)	(617)	NA	14,261
.....	Southbridge	(617)	16,665	17,057
01075	South Hadley	(413)	16,399	17,033
01077	Southwick	(413)	7,382	6,330
02664	South Yarmouth(u)	(617)	NA	5,380
01562	Spencer Center	(617)	NA	5,895
.....	Spencer	(617)	10,774	8,779
*01101	Springfield	(413)	152,319	163,905
01564	Sterling	(617)	5,440	4,247
02180	Stoneham	(617)	21,424	20,725
02072	Stoughton	(617)	26,710	23,459
01775	Stow	(617)	5,144	3,984
01566	Sturbridge	(617)	5,976	4,878
01776	Sudbury	(617)	14,027	13,506
01527	Sutton	(617)	5,855	4,590
01907	Swampscott	(617)	13,837	13,578
02777	Swansea	(617)	15,461	12,640
02780	Taunton	(617)	45,001	43,756
01468	Templeton	(617)	6,070	5,863
01876	Tewksbury	(617)	24,635	22,755
01983	Topsfield	(617)	5,709	5,225
01469	Townsend	(617)	7,201	4,281
01376	Turners Falls(u)	(413)	NA	5,168
01879	Tyngsborough	(617)	5,683	4,204
01569	Uxbridge	(617)	8,374	8,253
01880	Wakefield	(617)	24,895	25,402
02081	Walpole	(617)	18,859	18,149
02154	Waltham	(617)	58,200	61,582
01082	Ware Center(u)	(413)	NA	6,509
.....	Ware	(413)	8,953	8,187
02571	Wareham	(617)	18,457	11,492
02172	Watertown	(617)	34,384	39,307
01778	Wayland	(617)	12,170	13,461
01570	Webster Center(u)	(617)	NA	12,432
.....	Webster	(617)	14,480	14,917
02181	Wellesley	(617)	27,209	28,051
01581	Westborough	(617)	13,619	12,594
01583	West Boylston	(617)	6,204	6,369
02379	West Bridgewater	(617)	6,359	6,070
01085	Westfield	(413)	36,465	31,433
01886	Westford	(617)	13,434	10,368
01473	Westminster	(617)	5,139	4,273
02193	Weston	(617)	11,169	10,870
02790	Westport	(617)	13,763	9,791
01089	West Springfield	(413)	27,042	28,461
02090	Westwood	(617)	13,212	12,570
02188	Weymouth	(617)	55,601	54,610
01588	Whitinsville(u)	(617)	NA	5,210
02382	Whitman	(617)	13,534	13,059
01095	Wilbraham	(413)	12,053	11,984
01267	Williamstown	(413)	8,741	8,454
01887	Wilmington	(617)	17,471	17,102
01475	Winchendon	(617)	7,019	6,635
01890	Winchester	(617)	20,701	22,269
02152	Winthrop	(617)	19,294	20,335
01801	Woburn	(617)	36,626	37,406
*01613	Worcester	(617)	161,799	176,572
02093	Wrentham	(617)	7,580	7,315
02675	Yarmouth	(617)	18,449	12,033

Michigan

ZIP code	Place		1980	1970
49221	Adrian	(517)	21,186	20,382
49224	Albion	(517)	11,059	12,112
48101	Allen Park	(313)	34,196	40,747
48801	Alma	(517)	9,652	9,611
49707	Alpena	(517)	12,214	13,805
*48106	Ann Arbor	(313)	107,316	100,035
*49016	Battle Creek	(616)	35,724	38,931
48706	Bay City	(517)	41,593	49,449
49508	Belding	(616)	5,634	5,121
49022	Benton Central(u)	(616)	NA	8,067
49022	Benton Harbor	(616)	14,707	16,481
48072	Berkley	(313)	18,637	21,879
48009	Beverly Hills	(616)	11,598	13,598
49307	Big Rapids	(616)	14,361	11,995
*48012	Birmingham	(616)	21,689	26,170
49107	Buchanan	(616)	5,142	4,645
*48502	Burton	(616)	29,976	32,540
49601	Cadillac	(517)	10,199	9,990
48724	Carrollton(u)	(517)	NA	7,300
48015	Center Line	(313)	9,293	10,379
48813	Charlotte	(517)	8,251	8,244
49721	Cheboygan	(616)	5,106	5,553
48017	Clawson	(313)	15,103	17,617
49036	Coldwater	(517)	9,461	9,155
49041	Comstock(u)	(616)	NA	5,003
49321	Comstock Park(u)	(616)	NA	5,766
49508	Cutlerville(u)	(616)	NA	6,267
48423	Davison	(313)	6,087	5,259
*48120	Dearborn	(313)	90,660	104,199
48127	Dearborn Heights	(313)	67,706	80,069
*48233	Detroit	(313)	1,203,339	1,514,063
49047	Dowagiac	(616)	6,307	6,583
48020	Drayton Plains(u)	(313)	NA	16,462
48021	East Detroit	(313)	38,280	45,920
49506	East Grand Rapids	(616)	10,914	12,565
48823	East Lansing	(517)	48,309	47,540
49001	Eastwood(u)	(517)	NA	9,682
48229	Ecorse	(313)	14,447	17,515
49829	Escanaba	(906)	14,355	15,368
48024	Farmington	(313)	11,022	10,329
48024	Farmington Hills	(313)	58,056	48,694
48430	Fenton	(313)	8,098	8,284
48220	Ferndale	(313)	26,227	30,850
48134	Flat Rock	(313)	6,853	5,643
*48502	Flint	(313)	159,611	193,317
48433	Flushing	(313)	8,624	7,190
48026	Fraser	(313)	14,560	11,868
48135	Garden City	(313)	35,640	41,864
48439	Grand Blanc	(313)	6,848	5,132
49417	Grand Haven	(616)	11,763	11,844
48837	Grand Ledge	(517)	6,920	6,032
*49501	Grand Rapids	(616)	181,843	197,649
49418	Grandville	(616)	12,412	10,764
48838	Greenville	(616)	8,019	7,493

ZIP code	Place		1980	1970
48138	Grosse Ile(u).	(313)	NA	8,306
48236	Grosse Pointe	(313)	5,901	6,637
48236	Grosse Pointe Farms	(313)	10,551	11,701
48236	Grosse Pointe Park	(313)	13,639	15,641
48236	Grosse Pointe Woods	(313)	18,886	21,878
48212	Hamtramck	(313)	21,300	26,783
49930	Hancock	(906)	5,122	4,820
48236	Harper Woods	(313)	16,361	20,186
49058	Hastings	(616)	6,418	6,501
48030	Hazel Park	(313)	20,914	23,784
48203	Highland Park	(313)	27,909	35,444
49242	Hillsdale	(517)	7,432	7,728
49423	Holland	(616)	26,281	26,479
48842	Holt(u)	(517)	NA	6,980
49931	Houghton	(906)	7,512	6,067
48843	Howell	(517)	6,976	5,224
48070	Huntington Woods	(313)	6,937	8,536
48141	Inkster	(313)	35,190	38,595
48846	Ionia	(616)	5,920	6,361
49801	Iron Mountain	(906)	8,341	8,702
49938	Ironwood	(906)	7,741	8,711
49849	Ishpeming	(906)	7,538	8,245
*49201	Jackson	(517)	39,739	45,484
49428	Jenison(u)	(616)	NA	11,266
*49001	Kalamazoo	(616)	79,722	85,555
49508	Kentwood	(616)	30,438	20,310
49788	Kincheloe(u)	(906)	NA	6,331
49801	Kingsford	(906)	5,290	5,276
49843	K.I. Sawyer(u)	(906)	NA	8,224
49015	Lakeview(u)	(517)	NA	11,391
48144	Lambertville(u)	(313)	NA	5,711
*48924	Lansing	(517)	130,414	131,403
48446	Lapeer	(313)	6,225	6,314
48503	Lapeer Heights(u)	(313)	NA	7,130
48146	Lincoln Park	(313)	45,105	52,984
*48150	Livonia	(313)	104,814	110,109
49431	Ludington	(616)	8,937	9,021
48071	Madison Heights	(313)	35,375	38,599
49660	Manistee	(616)	7,566	7,723
49855	Marquette	(906)	23,288	21,967
49068	Marshall	(616)	7,201	7,253
48040	Marysville	(313)	7,345	5,610
48854	Mason	(517)	6,019	5,468
48122	Melvindale	(313)	12,322	13,862
49858	Menominee	(906)	10,099	10,748
48640	Midland	(517)	37,250	35,176
48042	Milford	(313)	5,041	4,699
48161	Monroe	(313)	23,531	23,894
48043	Mount Clemens	(313)	18,806	20,476
48858	Mount Pleasant	(517)	23,746	20,524
*49440	Muskegon	(616)	40,823	44,631
49444	Muskegon Heights	(616)	14,611	17,304
49866	Negaunee	(906)	5,189	5,248
48047	New Baltimore	(313)	5,439	4,132
49120	Niles	(616)	13,115	12,988
48167	Northville	(313)	5,698	5,400
49441	Norton Shores	(616)	22,025	22,271
48050	Novi	(313)	22,525	9,668
48237	Oak Park	(313)	31,537	36,762
48864	Okemos(u)	(517)	NA	7,770
48867	Owosso	(517)	16,455	17,179
49770	Petoskey	(616)	6,097	6,342
48170	Plymouth	(313)	9,986	11,758
*48053	Pontiac	(313)	76,715	85,279
49081	Portage	(616)	38,157	33,590
48060	Port Huron	(313)	33,981	35,794
48024	Quakertown North(u)	(313)	NA	7,101
48218	River Rouge	(313)	12,912	15,947
48192	Riverview	(313)	14,569	11,342
48063	Rochester	(313)	7,203	7,054
48174	Romulus	(313)	24,857	22,879
48066	Roseville	(313)	54,311	60,529
*48068	Royal Oak	(313)	70,893	86,238
*48605	Saginaw	(517)	77,508	91,849
*48083	St. Clair Shores	(313)	76,210	88,093
48879	St. Johns	(517)	7,376	6,672
49085	St. Joseph	(616)	9,622	11,042
48176	Saline	(313)	6,483	4,811
49783	Sault Ste. Marie	(906)	14,448	15,136
*48075	Southfield	(313)	75,568	69,285
48198	Southgate	(313)	32,058	33,909
49090	South Haven	(616)	5,943	6,471
48178	South Lyon	(313)	5,214	2,675
49015	Springfield	(616)	5,917	3,994
*48078	Sterling Heights	(313)	108,999	61,365
49091	Sturgis	(616)	9,468	9,295
48473	Swartz Creek	(313)	5,013	4,928
48180	Taylor	(313)	77,568	70,020
49286	Tecumseh	(517)	7,015	7,120
49093	Three Rivers	(616)	7,355	7,355
49684	Traverse City	(616)	15,516	18,048
48183	Trenton	(313)	22,762	24,127
48084	Troy	(313)	67,102	39,419
48087	Utica	(313)	5,282	3,504
49504	Walker	(616)	15,088	11,492
*48089	Warren	(313)	161,134	179,260
48184	Wayne	(313)	21,159	21,054
48185	Westland	(313)	84,603	86,749
49007	Westwood(u)	(616)	41,343	9,143
48096	Wixom	(313)	6,705	2,010
48183	Woodhaven	(313)	10,902	3,566
48753	Wurtsmith(u)	(517)	NA	6,932
*48192	Wyandotte	(313)	34,006	41,061
49509	Wyoming	(616)	59,616	56,560
48197	Ypsilanti	(313)	24,031	29,538

Minnesota

ZIP code	Place		1980	1970
56007	Albert Lea	(507)	19,190	19,418
56308	Alexandria	(612)	7,608	6,973
55303	Andover	(612)	9,387	----
55303	Anoka	(612)	15,634	13,298
55068	Apple Valley	(612)	21,818	8,502
55112	Arden Hills	(612)	8,012	5,149
55912	Austin	(507)	23,020	26,210
56601	Bemidji	(218)	10,949	11,490
55433	Blaine	(612)	28,558	20,573
55420	Bloomington	(612)	81,831	81,970
56401	Brainerd	(218)	11,489	11,667
55429	Brooklyn Center	(612)	31,230	35,173
55429	Brooklyn Park	(612)	43,332	26,230
55337	Burnsville	(612)	35,674	19,940
55316	Champlin	(612)	9,006	2,275
55317	Chanhassen	(612)	6,359	4,879
55318	Chaska	(612)	8,346	4,352
55719	Chisholm	(218)	5,930	5,913
55720	Cloquet	(218)	11,142	8,699
55421	Columbia Heights	(612)	20,029	23,997
55433	Coon Rapids	(612)	35,826	30,505
55016	Cottage Grove	(612)	18,994	13,419
56716	Crookston	(218)	8,628	8,312
55428	Crystal	(612)	25,543	30,925
56501	Detroit Lakes	(218)	7,106	5,797
*55806	Duluth	(218)	92,811	100,578
55121	Eagan	(612)	20,532	10,398
55005	East Bethel	(612)	6,626	2,586
56721	East Grand Forks	(218)	8,537	7,607
55343	Eden Prairie	(612)	16,263	6,938
55424	Edina	(612)	46,073	44,046
55330	Elk River	(612)	6,785	2,252
55734	Eveleth	(218)	5,042	4,721
56031	Fairmont	(507)	11,506	10,751
55113	Falcon Heights	(612)	5,291	5,530
55021	Faribault	(507)	16,241	16,595
56537	Fergus Falls	(218)	12,519	12,443
55421	Fridley	(612)	30,228	29,233
55427	Golden Valley	(612)	22,775	24,246
55744	Grand Rapids	(218)	7,934	7,247
55303	Ham Lake	(612)	7,832	3,327
55033	Hastings	(612)	12,827	12,195
55811	Hermantown	(218)	6,759	----
55746	Hibbing	(218)	21,193	16,104
55343	Hopkins	(612)	15,336	13,428
55350	Hutchinson	(612)	9,244	8,031
56649	International Falls	(218)	5,611	6,439
55075	Inver Grove Heights	(612)	17,171	12,148
55042	Lake Elmo	(612)	5,296	3,565
55044	Lakeville	(612)	14,790	7,556
55355	Litchfield	(612)	5,904	5,262
55110	Little Canada	(612)	7,102	3,481
56345	Little Falls	(612)	7,250	7,467
56001	Mankato	(507)	28,651	30,895
55369	Maple Grove	(612)	20,525	6,275
55109	Maplewood	(612)	26,990	25,186
56258	Marshall	(507)	11,161	9,886
55120	Mendota Heights	(612)	7,288	6,565
*55401	Minneapolis	(612)	370,951	434,400
55343	Minnetonka	(612)	38,683	35,776
56265	Montevideo	(612)	5,845	5,661
56560	Moorhead	(218)	29,998	29,687
56267	Morris	(612)	5,367	5,366
55364	Mound	(612)	9,280	7,572
55112	Mounds View	(612)	12,593	10,599
55112	New Brighton	(612)	23,269	19,507
55428	New Hope	(612)	23,087	23,180
56073	New Ulm	(507)	13,755	13,051
55057	Northfield	(507)	12,562	10,235
56001	North Mankato	(507)	9,145	7,347
55109	North St. Paul	(612)	11,921	11,950
55119	Oakdale	(612)	12,123	7,795
55323	Orono	(612)	6,845	6,787
55060	Owatonna	(507)	18,632	15,341
55427	Plymouth	(612)	31,615	18,077
55372	Prior Lake	(612)	7,284	1,114
55303	Ramsey	(612)	10,093	----
55066	Red Wing	(612)	13,736	10,441
56283	Redwood Falls	(507)	5,210	4,774
55423	Richfield	(612)	37,851	47,231
55422	Robbinsdale	(612)	14,422	16,845
55901	Rochester	(507)	57,855	53,766
55068	Rosemount	(612)	5,083	1,337
55113	Roseville	(612)	35,820	34,438
55418	St. Anthony	(612)	7,981	9,239
56301	St. Cloud	(612)	42,566	39,691
55426	St. Louis Park	(612)	42,931	48,883
*55101	St. Paul	(612)	270,230	309,866
56082	St. Peter	(507)	9,056	8,339
55379	Sauk Rapids	(612)	5,793	5,051
55379	Shakopee	(612)	9,941	6,876
55112	Shoreview	(612)	17,300	10,978
55075	South St. Paul	(612)	21,235	25,016
55432	Spring Lake Park	(612)	6,477	6,417

ZIP code	Place		1980	1970
55082	Stillwater	(612)	12,290	10,191
56701	Thief River Falls	(218)	9,105	8,618
55110	Vadnais Heights	(612)	5,111	3,411
55792	Virginia	(218)	11,056	12,450
56093	Waseca	(507)	8,219	6,789
55118	West St. Paul	(612)	18,527	18,802
55110	White Bear Lake	(612)	22,538	23,313
56201	Willmar	(612)	15,895	12,869
55987	Winona	(507)	25,075	26,438
55119	Woodbury	(612)	10,297	6,184
56187	Worthington	(507)	10,243	9,916

Mississippi (601)

ZIP code	Place	1980	1970
39730	Aberdeen	7,184	6,507
38821	Amory	7,307	7,236
39520	Bay St. Louis	7,891	6,752
*39530	Biloxi	49,311	48,486
38829	Booneville	6,199	5,895
39042	Brandon	9,626	2,685
39601	Brookhaven	10,800	10,700
39046	Canton	11,116	10,503
38614	Clarksdale	21,137	21,673
38732	Cleveland	14,524	13,327
39056	Clinton	14,660	7,289
39429	Columbia	7,733	7,587
39701	Columbus	27,383	25,795
38834	Corinth	13,839	11,581
39532	D'Iberville(u)	NA	7,288
39074	Forest	5,229	4,065
38701	Greenville	40,613	39,648
38930	Greenwood	20,115	22,400
38901	Grenada	12,641	9,944
39501	Gulfport	39,676	40,791
39401	Hattiesburg	40,829	38,277
38635	Holly Springs	7,285	5,728
38751	Indianola	8,221	8,947
*39205	Jackson	202,895	153,968
39090	Kosciusko	7,415	7,266
39440	Laurel	21,897	24,145
38756	Leland	6,667	6,000
39560	Long Beach	7,967	6,170
39339	Louisville	7,323	6,626
39648	McComb	12,331	11,851
39301	Meridian	46,577	45,083
39563	Moss Point	18,998	19,321
39120	Natchez	22,015	19,704
38652	New Albany	7,072	6,426
39564	Ocean Springs	14,504	19,160
38655	Oxford	9,882	8,519
39567	Pascagoula	29,318	27,264
39571	Pass Christian	5,014	2,979
39208	Pearl	20,778	9,623
39465	Petal	8,476	6,986
39350	Philadelphia	6,434	6,274
39466	Picayune	10,361	9,760
39157	Ridgeland	5,461	1,650
38668	Senatobia	5,013	4,247
38671	Southaven(u)	NA	8,931
39759	Starkville	15,169	11,369
38801	Tupelo	23,905	20,471
39180	Vicksburg	25,434	25,478
39367	Waynesboro	5,349	4,368
39501	West Gulfport(u)	NA	6,996
39773	West Point	8,811	8,714
38967	Winona	6,177	5,521
39194	Yazoo City	12,426	11,688

Missouri

ZIP code	Place		1980	1970
63123	Affton(u)	(314)	NA	24,264
63010	Arnold	(314)	19,141	17,381
65605	Aurora	(417)	6,437	5,359
63011	Ballwin	(314)	12,750	10,656
63137	Bellefontaine Neighbors	(314)	12,082	14,084
64012	Belton	(816)	12,708	12,270
63134	Berkeley	(314)	16,146	19,743
63031	Black Jack	(314)	5,293	4,145
64015	Blue Springs	(816)	25,927	6,779
65613	Bolivar	(417)	5,919	4,769
65233	Boonville	(816)	6,959	7,514
63114	Breckenridge Hills	(314)	5,666	7,011
63144	Brentwood	(314)	8,209	11,248
63044	Bridgeton	(314)	18,445	19,992
64628	Brookfield	(816)	5,555	5,491
63701	Cape Girardeau	(314)	34,361	31,282
64836	Carthage	(417)	11,104	11,035
63830	Caruthersville	(314)	7,958	7,350
63834	Charleston	(314)	5,230	5,131
64601	Chillicothe	(816)	9,089	9,519
63105	Clayton	(314)	14,219	16,100
64735	Clinton	(816)	8,366	7,504
65201	Columbia	(314)	62,061	58,812
63128	Concord(u)	(314)	NA	21,217
63126	Crestwood	(314)	12,815	15,123
63141	Creve Coeur	(314)	12,694	8,967
63136	Dellwood	(314)	6,200	7,137
63020	De Soto	(314)	5,993	5,984
63131	Des Peres	(314)	8,254	5,333
63841	Dexter	(314)	7,043	6,024
63011	Ellisville	(314)	6,233	4,681

ZIP code	Place		1980	1970
64024	Excelsior Springs	(816)	10,424	9,411
63640	Farmington	(314)	8,270	6,590
63135	Ferguson	(314)	24,740	28,759
63028	Festus	(314)	7,574	7,530
*63033	Florissant	(314)	55,372	65,908
65473	Fort Leonard Wood(u)	(314)	NA	33,799
65251	Fulton	(314)	11,046	12,248
64118	Gladstone	(816)	24,990	23,422
63122	Glendale	(314)	6,035	6,981
64030	Grandview	(816)	24,502	17,456
63401	Hannibal	(314)	18,811	18,609
64701	Harrisonville	(816)	6,372	5,052
*63042	Hazelwood	(314)	12,935	14,082
*64051	Independence	(816)	111,806	111,630
63755	Jackson	(314)	7,827	5,896
65101	Jefferson City	(314)	33,619	32,407
63136	Jennings	(314)	17,026	19,379
64801	Joplin	(417)	38,893	39,256
*64108	Kansas City	(816)	448,159	507,330
63857	Kennett	(314)	10,145	10,090
63501	Kirksville	(816)	17,167	15,560
63122	Kirkwood	(314)	27,987	31,679
63124	Ladue	(314)	9,376	10,306
65536	Lebanon	(417)	9,507	8,616
64063	Lee's Summit	(816)	28,741	16,230
63125	Lemay(u)	(314)	NA	40,529
64067	Lexington	(816)	5,063	5,388
64068	Liberty	(816)	16,251	13,704
63552	Macon	(816)	5,680	5,301
63863	Malden	(314)	6,096	5,374
63011	Manchester	(314)	6,191	5,031
63143	Maplewood	(314)	10,960	12,785
65340	Marshall	(816)	12,781	12,051
63043	Maryland Heights(u)	(314)	NA	8,805
64468	Maryville	(816)	9,558	9,970
65265	Mexico	(314)	12,276	11,807
65270	Moberly	(816)	13,418	12,988
65708	Monett	(417)	6,148	5,937
64850	Neosho	(417)	9,493	7,517
64772	Nevada	(417)	9,044	9,736
63121	Normandy	(314)	5,174	6,236
63121	Northwoods	(314)	5,831	4,607
63366	O'Fallon	(314)	8,654	7,018
63124	Olivette	(314)	8,039	9,156
63114	Overland	(314)	19,620	24,819
63775	Perryville	(314)	7,343	5,149
63120	Pine Lawn	(314)	6,662	5,745
63901	Poplar Bluff	(314)	17,139	16,653
64133	Raytown	(816)	31,759	33,306
64085	Richmond	(816)	5,499	4,948
63117	Richmond Heights	(314)	11,516	13,802
63124	Rock Hill	(314)	5,702	6,815
65401	Rolla	(314)	13,303	13,571
63074	St. Ann	(314)	15,523	18,215
63301	St. Charles	(314)	37,379	31,834
63114	St. John	(314)	7,854	8,960
*64501	St. Joseph	(816)	76,691	72,748
*63155	St. Louis	(314)	453,085	622,236
63376	St. Peters	(314)	15,700	486
63126	Sappington(u)	(314)	NA	10,603
65301	Sedalia	(816)	20,927	22,847
63119	Shrewsbury	(314)	5,077	5,896
63801	Sikeston	(314)	17,431	14,699
63138	Spanish Lake(u)	(314)	NA	15,647
*65801	Springfield	(417)	133,116	120,096
63080	Sullivan	(314)	5,461	5,111
64683	Trenton	(816)	6,811	6,063
63084	Union	(314)	5,506	5,183
63130	University City	(314)	42,738	47,527
64093	Warrensburg	(816)	13,807	13,125
63090	Washington	(314)	9,251	8,499
64870	Webb City	(417)	7,309	6,923
63119	Webster Groves	(314)	23,097	27,457
65775	West Plains	(417)	7,741	6,893

Montana (406)

ZIP code	Place	1980	1970
59711	Anaconda-Deer Lodge County	12,518	9,771
*59101	Billings	66,798	61,581
59715	Bozeman	21,645	18,670
59701	Butte-Silver Bow	37,205	23,368
59701	Floral Park(u)	NA	5,113
59330	Glendive	5,978	6,305
*59401	Great Falls	56,725	60,091
59501	Havre	10,891	10,558
59601	Helena	23,938	22,730
59901	Kalispell	10,648	10,526
59044	Laurel	5,481	4,454
59457	Lewistown	7,104	6,437
59047	Livingston	6,994	6,883
59402	Malmstrom(u)	NA	6,374
59301	Miles City	9,602	9,023
59801	Missoula	33,388	29,497
59801	Missoula West(u)	NA	9,148
59270	Sidney	5,726	4,543

Nebraska

ZIP code	Place		1980	1970
69301	Alliance	(308)	9,869	6,862
68310	Beatrice	(402)	12,891	12,339
68005	Bellevue	(402)	21,813	21,953
68008	Blair	(402)	6,418	6,106
69337	Chadron	(308)	5,933	5,921
68601	Columbus	(402)	17,328	15,471

ZIP code	Place		1980	1970
68355	Falls City	(402)	5,374	5,444
68025	Fremont	(402)	23,979	22,962
69341	Gering	(308)	7,760	5,639
68801	Grand Island	(308)	33,180	32,358
68901	Hastings	(402)	23,045	23,580
68949	Holdrege	(308)	5,624	5,635
68847	Kearney	(308)	21,158	19,181
68128	La Vista	(402)	9,588	4,858
68850	Lexington	(308)	6,898	5,654
*68501	Lincoln	(402)	171,932	149,518
69001	McCook	(308)	8,404	8,285
68410	Nebraska City	(402)	7,127	7,441
68701	Norfolk	(402)	19,449	16,607
69101	North Platte	(308)	24,479	19,447
68113	Offutt East(u)	(402)	NA	5,195
68113	Offutt West(u)	(402)	NA	8,445
69153	Ogallala	(308)	5,638	4,976
*68108	Omaha	(402)	311,681	346,929
68046	Papillion	(402)	6,399	5,606
68048	Plattsmouth	(402)	6,295	6,371
68127	Ralston	(402)	5,143	4,731
69361	Scottsbluff	(308)	14,156	14,507
68434	Seward	(402)	5,713	5,294
69162	Sidney	(308)	6,010	6,403
68776	South Sioux City	(402)	9,339	7,920
68787	Wayne	(402)	5,240	5,379
68467	York	(402)	7,723	6,778

Nevada (702)

89005	Boulder City		9,590	5,223
89701	Carson City		32,022	15,468
89112	East Las Vegas(u)		NA	6,501
89801	Elko		8,758	7,621
89015	Henderson		24,363	16,395
*89114	Las Vegas		164,674	125,787
89110	Nellis(u)		NA	6,449
89030	North Las Vegas		42,739	46,067
89109	Paradise(u)		NA	24,477
*89501	Reno		100,756	72,863
89431	Sparks		40,780	24,187
89110	Sunrise Manor(u)		NA	9,684
89109	Vegas Creek(u)		NA	8,970
89101	Winchester(u)		NA	13,981

New Hampshire (603)

See note on page 207

03102	Bedford		9,481	5,859
03570	Berlin		13,084	15,256
03743	Claremont		14,557	14,221
03301	Concord		30,400	30,022
03038	Derry Compact(u)		NA	6,090
......	Derry		18,875	11,712
03820	Dover		22,377	20,850
03824	Durham Compact(u)		NA	7,221
......	Durham		10,652	8,869
03833	Exeter Compact(u)		NA	6,439
......	Exeter		11,024	8,892
03235	Franklin		7,901	7,292
03045	Goffstown		11,315	9,284
03842	Hampton Compact(u)		NA	5,407
......	Hampton		10,493	8,011
03755	Hanover Compact(u)		NA	6,147
......	Hanover		9,119	8,494
03106	Hooksett		7,303	5,564
03061	Hudson		14,022	10,638
03431	Keene		21,449	20,467
03246	Laconia		15,575	14,888
03766	Lebanon		11,134	9,725
03516	Littleton		5,558	5,290
03053	Londonderry		13,598	5,346
*03101	Manchester		90,936	87,754
03054	Merrimack		15,406	8,595
03055	Milford		8,685	6,622
03060	Nashua		67,865	55,820
03773	Newport		6,229	5,899
03076	Pelham		8,090	5,408
03801	Portsmouth		26,254	25,717
03867	Rochester		21,560	17,938
03079	Salem		24,124	20,142
03874	Seabrook		5,917	3,053
03878	Somersworth		10,350	9,026

New Jersey

08201	Absecon	(609)	6,859	6,094
07401	Allendale	(201)	5,901	6,240
07712	Asbury Park	(201)	17,015	16,533
*08401	Atlantic City	(609)	40,199	47,859
08106	Audubon	(609)	9,533	10,802
08007	Barrington	(609)	7,418	8,409
07002	Bayonne	(201)	65,047	72,743
07109	Belleville	(201)	35,367	37,629
08030	Bellmawr	(609)	13,721	15,618
07719	Belmar	(201)	6,771	5,782
07621	Bergenfield	(201)	25,568	29,000
07922	Berkeley Hts. Twp.	(201)	12,549	13,078
08009	Berlin	(609)	5,786	4,997
07924	Bernardsville	(201)	6,715	6,652
07003	Bloomfield	(201)	47,792	52,029
07403	Bloomingdale	(201)	7,867	7,797
07603	Bogota	(201)	8,344	8,960
07005	Boonton	(201)	8,620	9,261
08805	Bound Brook	(201)	9,710	10,450
08723	Brick Twp.	(201)	53,629	35,057
08302	Bridgeton	(609)	18,795	20,435
08203	Brigantine	(609)	8,318	6,741
08015	Browns Mills(u)	(609)	NA	7,144
08016	Burlington	(609)	10,246	12,010
07405	Butler	(201)	7,616	7,051
07006	Caldwell	(201)	7,624	8,677
*08101	Camden	(609)	84,910	102,551
08701	Candlewood(u)	(201)	NA	5,629
07072	Carlstadt	(201)	6,166	6,724
07008	Carteret	(201)	20,598	23,137
07009	Cedar Grove Twp.	(201)	12,600	15,582
07928	Chatham	(201)	8,537	9,566
*08002	Cherry Hill Twp.	(609)	68,785	64,395
08077	Cinaminson Twp.	(609)	16,072	16,962
07066	Clark Twp.	(201)	16,699	18,829
08312	Clayton	(609)	6,013	5,193
08021	Clementon	(609)	5,764	4,492
07010	Cliffside Park	(201)	21,464	18,891
07721	Cliffwood-Cliffwood Beach(u)	(201)	NA	7,056
*07015	Clifton	(201)	74,388	82,437
07624	Closter	(201)	8,164	8,604
08108	Collingswood	(609)	15,838	17,422
07016	Cranford Twp.	(201)	24,573	27,391
07626	Cresskill	(201)	7,609	8,298
08075	Delran Twp.	(609)	14,811	10,065
07834	Denville Twp.	(201)	14,380	14,045
08096	Deptford Twp.	(609)	23,473	24,232
07801	Dover	(201)	14,681	15,039
07628	Dumont	(201)	18,334	20,155
08812	Dunellen	(201)	6,593	7,072
08816	East Brunswick Twp.	(201)	37,711	34,166
*07019	East Orange	(201)	77,025	75,471
07073	East Rutherford	(201)	7,849	8,536
08520	East Windsor Twp.	(609)	21,041	11,736
07724	Eatontown	(201)	12,703	14,619
08817	Edison Twp.	(201)	70,193	67,120
*07201	Elizabeth	(201)	106,201	112,654
07407	Elmwood Park	(201)	18,377	20,511
07630	Emerson	(201)	7,793	8,428
*07631	Englewood	(201)	23,701	24,985
07632	Englewood Cliffs	(201)	5,698	5,938
08053	Evesham Twp.	(609)	21,659	13,477
08618	Ewing Twp.	(201)	34,842	32,831
07701	Fair Haven	(201)	5,679	6,142
07410	Fair Lawn	(201)	32,229	38,040
07022	Fairview	(201)	10,519	10,698
07023	Fanwood	(201)	7,767	8,920
08518	Florence-Roebling(u)	(609)	NA	7,551
07932	Florham Park	(201)	9,359	9,373
08640	Fort Dix(u)	(609)	NA	26,290
07024	Fort Lee	(201)	32,449	30,631
07417	Franklin Lakes	(201)	8,769	7,550
07728	Freehold	(201)	10,020	10,545
07026	Garfield	(201)	26,803	30,797
08028	Glassboro	(609)	14,574	12,938
07028	Glen Ridge	(201)	7,855	8,518
07452	Glen Rock	(201)	11,497	13,011
08030	Gloucester City	(609)	13,121	14,707
07093	Guttenberg	(201)	7,340	5,754
*07602	Hackensack	(201)	36,039	36,008
07840	Hackettstown	(201)	8,850	9,472
08108	Haddon Twp.	(609)	15,875	18,192
08033	Haddonfield	(609)	12,337	13,118
08035	Haddon Heights	(609)	8,361	9,365
07508	Haledon	(201)	6,607	6,767
08037	Hammonton	(609)	12,298	11,464
07981	Hanover Twp.	(201)	11,846	10,700
07029	Harrison	(201)	12,242	11,811
07604	Hasbrouck Heights	(201)	12,166	13,651
07506	Hawthorne	(201)	18,200	19,173
07730	Hazlet Twp.	(201)	23,013	22,239
08904	Highland Park	(609)	13,396	14,385
07732	Highlands	(201)	5,187	3,916
07642	Hillsdale	(201)	10,495	11,768
07205	Hillside Twp.	(201)	21,440	21,636
07030	Hoboken	(201)	42,460	45,380
07843	Hopatcong	(201)	15,531	9,052
08560	Hopewell Twp. (Mercer)	(609)	10,893	10,030
07111	Irvington	(201)	61,493	59,743
08527	Jackson Twp.	(201)	25,644	18,276
*07303	Jersey City	(201)	223,532	260,350
07734	Keansburg	(201)	10,613	9,720
07032	Kearny	(201)	35,735	37,585
08824	Kendall Park(u)	(201)	NA	7,412
07033	Kenilworth	(201)	8,221	9,165
07735	Keyport	(201)	7,413	7,205
07405	Kinnelon	(201)	7,770	7,600
07034	Lake Hiawatha(u)	(201)	NA	11,389
07871	Lake Mohawk(u)	(201)	NA	6,262
07054	Lake Parsippany(u)	(201)	NA	7,488
08701	Lakewood(u)	(201)	NA	17,874
08879	Laurence Harbor(u)	(201)	NA	6,715
07605	Leonia	(201)	8,027	8,847
07035	Lincoln Park	(201)	8,806	9,034
07036	Linden	(201)	37,836	41,409
08021	Lindenwold	(609)	18,196	12,199

ZIP code	Place		1980	1970
08221	Linwood	(609)	6,144	6,159
07424	Little Falls Twp.	(201)	11,496	11,727
07643	Little Ferry	(201)	9,399	9,064
07739	Little Silver.	(201)	5,548	6,010
07039	Livingston Twp.	(201)	28,040	30,127
07644	Lodi.	(201)	23,956	25,163
07740	Long Branch.	(201)	29,819	31,774
07071	Lyndhurst Twp.	(201)	20,326	22,729
07940	Madison	(201)	15,357	16,710
07430	Mahwah Twp.	(201)	12,127	10,800
08736	Manasquan	(201)	5,354	4,971
08835	Manville	(201)	11,278	13,029
08052	Maple Shade Twp.	(609)	20,525	16,464
07040	Maplewood Twp.	(201)	22,950	24,932
08402	Margate City.	(609)	9,179	10,576
07746	Marlboro Twp.	(201)	17,560	12,273
08053	Marlton(u)	(609)	NA	10,180
07747	Matawan.	(201)	8,837	9,136
07607	Maywood	(201)	9,895	11,087
07641	McGuire(u).	(201)	NA	10,933
08619	Mercerville-Hamilton Sq.(u)	(609)	NA	24,465
08840	Metuchen	(201)	13,762	16,031
08846	Middlesex	(201)	13,480	15,038
08748	Middletown Twp.	(201)	62,574	54,623
07432	Midland park.	(201)	7,381	8,159
07041	Milburn Twp.	(201)	19,543	21,089
08850	Milltown	(201)	7,136	6,470
08332	Millville	(609)	24,815	21,366
07434	Monroe Twp. (Gloucester) .	(201)	21,639	14,071
*07042	Montclair.	(201)	38,321	44,043
07645	Montvale	(201)	7,318	7,327
07045	Montville Twp.	(201)	14,290	11,846
08057	Moorestown-Lenola(u)	(609)	NA	14,179
07950	Morris Plains.	(201)	5,305	5,540
07960	Morristown.	(201)	16,614	17,662
07092	Mountainside	(201)	7,118	7,520
08060	Mount Holly Twp.	(609)	10,818	12,713
07753	Neptune Twp.	(201)	28,366	27,863
07753	Neptune City	(201)	5,276	5,502
*07102	Newark.	(201)	329,248	381,930
*08901	New Brunswick	(201)	41,442	41,885
08511	New Hanover	(201)	14,248	27,410
07646	New Milford	(201)	16,876	19,149
07974	New Providence.	(201)	12,426	13,796
07860	Newton.	(201)	7,748	7,297
07032	North Arlington	(201)	16,587	18,096
07047	North Bergen Twp.	(201)	47,019	47,751
08902	North Brunswick Twp.	(201)	22,220	16,691
07006	North Caldwell	(201)	5,832	6,733
08225	Northfield	(609)	7,795	8,646
07508	North Haledon	(201)	8,177	7,614
07060	North Plainfield	(201)	19,108	21,796
07647	Northvale	(201)	5,046	5,177
07110	Nutley.	(201)	28,998	31,913
07755	Oakhurst(u)	(201)	NA	5,558
07436	Oakland	(201)	13,443	14,420
08226	Ocean City	(609)	13,949	10,575
07757	Oceanport	(201)	5,888	7,503
08857	Old Bridge Twp	(201)	51,515	48,715
07649	Oradell.	(201)	8,658	8,903
*07050	Orange.	(201)	31,136	32,566
07650	Palisades Park	(201)	13,732	13,351
08065	Palmyra	(609)	7,085	6,969
07652	Paramus	(201)	26,474	28,381
07656	Park Ridge.	(201)	8,515	8,709
*07055	Passaic.	(201)	52,463	55,124
*07510	Paterson.	(201)	137,970	144,824
08066	Paulsboro	(609)	6,944	8,084
08110	Pennsauken Twp.	(609)	33,775	36,394
08069	Penns Grove	(609)	5,760	5,727
08070	Pennsville Center(u)	(609)	NA	11,014
07440	Pequannock Twp.	(201)	13,776	14,350
*08861	Perth Amboy	(201)	38,951	38,798
08865	Phillipsburg	(201)	16,647	17,849
08021	Pine Hill	(609)	8,684	5,132
08854	Piscataway Twp.	(201)	42,223	36,418
08071	Pitman	(609)	9,744	10,257
*07061	Plainfield	(201)	45,555	46,862
.08232	Pleasantville	(609)	13,435	14,007
08742	Point Pleasant.	(201)	17,747	15,968
08742	Point Pleasant Beach.	(201)	5,415	4,882
07442	Pompton Lakes	(201)	10,660	11,397
08540	Princeton.	(609)	12,035	12,311
08540	Princeton North(u)	(609)	NA	5,488
07508	Prospect Park	(201)	5,142	5,176
*07065	Rahway	(201)	26,723	29,114
08057	Ramblewood(u).	(609)	NA	5,556
07446	Ramsey	(201)	12,899	12,571
07970	Randolph Twp.	(201)	17,828	13,296
08869	Raritan	(201)	6,128	6,691
07701	Red Bank	(201)	12,031	12,847
07657	Ridgefield	(201)	10,294	11,308
07660	Ridgefield Park	(201)	12,738	13,990
*07451	Ridgewood.	(201)	25,208	27,547
07456	Ringwood	(201)	12,625	10,393
07661	River Edge.	(201)	11,111	12,850
08075	Riverside Twp.	(609)	7,941	8,591
07662	Rochell Park Twp.	(201)	5,603	6,380
07866	Rockaway	(201)	6,852	6,383
07068	Roseland.	(201)	5,330	4,453
07203	Roselle.	(201)	20,641	22,585
07204	Roselle Park.	(201)	13,377	14,277
07760	Rumson.	(201)	7,623	7,421
08078	Runnemede.	(609)	9,461	10,475
*07070	Rutherford.	(201)	19,068	20,802
07662	Saddle Brook Twp.	(201)	14,084	15,910
08079	Salem.	(609)	6,959	7,648
08872	Sayreville.	(201)	29,969	32,508
07076	Scotch Plains Twp.	(201)	20,774	22,279
07094	Secaucus.	(201)	13,719	13,228
08083	Somerdale.	(609)	5,900	6,510
08244	Somers Point.	(609)	10,330	7,919
08876	Somerville.	(201)	11,973	13,652
08879	South Amboy.	(201)	8,322	9,338
07079	South Orange Vill. Twp.	(201)	15,864	
07080	South Plainfield.	(201)	20,521	21,142
08882	South River.	(201)	14,361	15,428
07871	Sparta Twp.	(201)	13,333	10,819
08884	Spotswood.	(201)	7,840	7,891
07081	Springfield Twp.	(201)	13,955	15,740
07762	Spring Lake Heights.	(201)	5,424	4,602
08084	Stratford.	(609)	8,005	9,801
07747	Strathmore(u)	(609)	NA	7,674
07901	Summit.	(201)	21,071	23,620
07666	Teaneck Twp.	(201)	39,007	42,355
07670	Tenafly.	(201)	13,552	14,827
07724	Tinton Falls	(201)	7,740	8,395
08753	Toms River.	(201)	NA	7,303
07512	Totowa.	(201)	11,448	11,580
*08608	Trenton.	(609)	92,124	104,786
07083	Union Twp.	(201)	50,184	53,077
07735	Union Beach.	(201)	6,354	6,472
07087	Union City	(201)	55,593	57,305
07458	Upper Saddle River.	(201)	7,958	7,949
08406	Ventnor City	(609)	11,704	10,385
07044	Verona.	(201)	14,166	15,067
08360	Vineland.	(609)	53,753	47,399
07463	Waldwick	(201)	10,802	12,313
07057	Wallington	(201)	10,741	10,284
07465	Wanaque.	(201)	10,025	8,636
07882	Washington	(201)	6,429	5,943
07675	Washington Twp. (Bergen)	(201)	9,550	10,577
07060	Watchung	(201)	5,290	4,750
07470	Wayne Twp.	(201)	46,474	49,141
07087	Weehawken Twp.	(201)	13,168	13,383
07006	West Caldwell	(201)	11,407	11,913
*07091	Westfield.	(201)	30,447	33,720
07764	West Long Branch	(201)	7,380	6,845
07480	West Milford Twp..	(201)	22,750	17,304
07093	West New York	(201)	39,194	40,627
07052	West Orange	(201)	39,510	43,715
07424	West Paterson	(201)	11,293	11,692
07675	Westwood	(201)	10,714	11,105
07885	Wharton	(201)	5,485	5,535
08610	White Horse-Yardville(u).	(609)	NA	18,680
07886	White Meadow Lake(u).	(201)	NA	8,499
08046	Willingboro Twp.	(609)	39,912	43,386
08095	Winslow Twp.	(609)	20,034	11,202
07095	Woodbridge Twp.	(201)	90,074	98,944
08096	Woodbury.	(609)	10,353	12,408
07675	Woodcliff Lake	(201)	5,644	5,506
07075	Wood-Ridge.	(201)	7,929	8,311
07481	Wyckoff Twp.	(201)	15,500	16,039

New Mexico (505)

ZIP code	Place		1980	1970
88310	Alamogordo.		24,024	23,035
*87101	Albuquerque.		331,767	244,501
88210	Artesia.		10,385	10,315
87410	Aztec.		5,512	3,354
87002	Belen.		5,617	4,823
88101	Cannon(u)		NA	5,461
88220	Carlsbad.		25,496	21,297
88101	Clovis.		31,194	28,495
88030	Deming.		9,964	8,343
87532	Espanola.		6,803	4,528
87401	Farmington.		30,729	21,979
87301	Gallup.		18,161	14,596
87020	Grants.		11,451	8,768
88240	Hobbs.		28,794	26,025
88330	Holloman(u).		NA	8,001
88001	Las Cruces.		45,086	37,857
87701	Las Vegas.		14,322	7,528
87544	Los Alamos(u).		NA	11,310
88260	Lovington.		9,727	8,915
87107	North Valley(u)		NA	10,366
88130	Portales.		9,940	10,554
87740	Raton.		8,225	6,962
88201	Roswell.		39,676	33,908
87115	Sandia(u).		NA	6,867
87501	Santa Fe.		48,899	41,167
88061	Silver City.		9,887	8,557
87801	Socorro.		7,576	5,849
87105	South Valley(u)		NA	29,389
87901	Truth or Consequences.		5,219	4,656
88401	Tucumcari.		6,765	7,189

New York

ZIP code	Place		1980	1970
*12207	Albany.	(518)	101,727	115,781
11507	Albertson(u).	(516)	NA	6,825
11701	Amityville.	(516)	9,076	9,794

ZIP code	Place		1980	1970
12010	Amsterdam	(518)	21,872	25,524
12603	Arlington(u)	(914)	NA	11,203
13021	Auburn	(315)	32,548	34,599
*11702	Babylon	(516)	12,388	12,897
11510	Baldwin(u)	(516)	NA	34,525
13027	Baldwinsville	(315)	6,446	6,298
14020	Batavia	(716)	16,703	17,338
14810	Bath	(607)	6,042	6,053
11705	Bayport(u)	(516)	NA	8,232
11706	Bay Shore(u)	(516)	NA	11,119
11709	Bayville	(516)	7,034	6,147
12508	Beacon	(914)	12,937	13,255
11710	Bellmore(u)	(516)	NA	18,431
11714	Bethpage(u)	(516)	NA	18,555
*13902	Binghamton	(607)	55,860	64,123
10913	Blauvelt(u)	(914)	NA	5,426
11716	Bohemia(u)	(516)	NA	8,926
11717	Brentwood(u)	(516)	NA	28,327
10510	Briarcliff Manor	(914)	7,115	6,521
14420	Brockport	(716)	9,776	7,878
10708	Bronxville	(914)	6,267	6,674
*14240	Buffalo	(716)	357,870	462,768
14424	Canandaigua	(716)	10,419	10,488
13617	Canton	(315)	7,055	6,398
11514	Carle Place(u)	(516)	NA	6,326
11516	Cedarhurst	(516)	6,162	6,941
11720	Centereach(u)	(516)	NA	9,427
11722	Central Islip(u)	(516)	NA	36,391
12065	Clifton Knolls(u)	(518)	NA	5,771
12043	Cobleskill	(518)	5,272	4,368
12047	Cohoes	(518)	18,144	18,653
12205	Colonie	(518)	8,869	8,701
11725	Commack(u)	(516)	NA	24,138
10920	Congers(u)	(914)	NA	5,928
11726	Copiague(u)	(516)	NA	19,632
14830	Corning	(607)	12,953	15,792
13045	Cortland	(607)	20,138	19,621
10520	Croton-on-Hudson	(914)	6,889	7,523
11729	Deer Park(u)	(516)	NA	32,274
14043	Depew	(716)	19,819	22,158
13214	DeWitt(u)	(315)	NA	10,032
11746	Dix Hills(u)	(516)	NA	10,050
10522	Dobbs Ferry	(914)	10,053	10,353
14048	Dunkirk	(716)	15,310	16,855
14052	East Aurora	(716)	6,803	7,033
10709	Eastchester(u)	(914)	NA	23,750
12302	East Glenville(u)	(518)	NA	5,898
11746	East Half Hollow Hills(u)	(516)	NA	9,691
11576	East Hills	(516)	7,160	8,624
11730	East Islip(u)	(516)	NA	6,861
11758	East Massapequa(u)	(516)	NA	15,926
11554	East Meadow(u)	(516)	NA	46,290
11743	East Neck(u)	(516)	NA	5,221
11731	East Northport(u)	(516)	NA	12,392
11772	East Patchogue(u)	(516)	NA	8,092
14445	East Rochester	(716)	7,596	8,347
11518	East Rockaway	(516)	10,917	11,795
13902	East Vestal(u)	(607)	NA	10,472
*14901	Elmira	(607)	35,327	39,945
11003	Elmont(u)	(516)	NA	29,363
11731	Elwood(u)	(516)	NA	15,031
13760	Endicott	(607)	14,457	16,556
13760	Endwell(u)	(607)	NA	15,999
13219	Fairmount(u)	(315)	NA	15,317
14450	Fairport	(716)	5,970	6,474
12601	Fairview(u)	(914)	NA	8,511
11735	Farmingdale	(516)	7,946	9,297
*11001	Floral Park	(516)	16,805	18,466
11010	Franklin Square(u)	(516)	NA	32,156
14063	Fredonia	(716)	11,126	10,326
11520	Freeport	(516)	38,272	40,374
13069	Fulton	(315)	13,312	14,003
11530	Garden City	(516)	22,927	25,373
11040	Garden City Park(u)	(516)	NA	7,488
14454	Geneseo	(716)	6,746	5,714
*14456	Geneva	(315)	15,133	16,793
11542	Glen Cove	(516)	24,618	25,770
12801	Glens Falls	(518)	15,897	17,222
12078	Gloversville	(518)	17,836	19,677
*11022	Great Neck	(516)	9,168	10,798
11020	Great Neck Plaza	(516)	5,604	6,043
11740	Greenlawn(u)	(516)	NA	8,493
11746	Half Hollow Hills(u)	(516)	NA	12,081
14075	Hamburg	(716)	10,582	10,215
10528	Harrison	(914)	23,046	21,544
10530	Hartsdale(u)	(914)	NA	12,226
10706	Hastings-on-Hudson	(914)	8,573	9,479
11787	Hauppauge(u)	(516)	NA	13,957
10927	Haverstraw	(914)	8,800	8,198
*11551	Hempstead	(516)	40,404	39,411
13350	Herkimer	(315)	8,383	8,960
11040	Herricks(u)	(516)	NA	9,112
11557	Hewlett(u)	(516)	NA	6,796
*11802	Hicksville(u)	(516)	NA	49,820
10977	Hillcrest(u)	(914)	NA	5,357
11741	Holbrook-Holtsville(u)	(516)	NA	12,103
14843	Hornell	(607)	10,234	12,144
14845	Horseheads	(607)	7,348	7,989
12534	Hudson	(518)	7,986	8,940

ZIP code	Place		1980	1970
12839	Hudson Falls	(518)	7,419	7,917
11743	Huntington(u)	(516)	NA	12,601
11746	Huntington Station(u)	(516)	NA	28,817
13357	Ilion	(315)	9,190	9,808
11696	Inwood(u)	(516)	NA	8,433
10533	Irvington	(914)	5,774	5,878
11751	Islip(u)	(516)	NA	7,692
14850	Ithaca	(607)	28,732	26,226
14701	Jamestown	(716)	35,775	39,795
10535	Jefferson Valley-Yorktown(u)	(914)	NA	9,008
11753	Jericho(u)	(516)	NA	14,010
13790	Johnson City	(607)	17,126	18,025
12095	Johnstown	(518)	9,360	10,045
14217	Kenmore	(716)	18,474	20,980
11754	Kings Park(u)	(516)	NA	5,555
11024	Kings Point	(516)	5,234	5,614
12401	Kingston	(914)	24,481	25,544
14218	Lackawanna	(716)	22,701	28,657
11755	Lake Grove	(516)	9,692	8,133
14086	Lancaster	(716)	13,056	13,365
10538	Larchmont	(914)	6,308	7,203
12110	Latham(u)	(914)	NA	9,661
11559	Lawrence	(516)	6,175	6,566
11756	Levittown(u)	(516)	NA	65,440
11757	Lindenhurst	(516)	26,919	28,359
13365	Little Falls	(315)	6,156	7,629
14094	Lockport	(716)	24,844	25,399
11791	Locust Grove(u)	(516)	NA	11,626
11561	Long Beach	(516)	34,073	33,127
12211	Loudonville(u)	(518)	NA	9,299
11563	Lynbrook	(516)	20,431	23,151
10541	Mahopac(u)	(914)	NA	5,265
12953	Malone	(518)	7,668	8,048
11565	Malverne	(516)	9,262	10,036
10543	Mamaroneck	(914)	17,616	18,909
11030	Manhasset(u)	(516)	NA	8,541
13104	Manlius	(315)	5,241	4,295
11050	Manorhaven(u)	(516)	5,384	5,488
11758	Massapequa(u)	(516)	NA	26,821
11762	Massapequa Park	(516)	19,779	22,112
13662	Massena	(315)	12,851	14,042
13211	Mattydale(u)	(315)	NA	8,292
12118	Mechanicville	(518)	5,500	6,247
14103	Medina	(716)	6,392	6,415
11746	Melville(u)	(516)	NA	6,641
11566	Merrick(u)	(516)	NA	25,904
10940	Middletown	(914)	21,454	22,607
11501	Mineola	(516)	20,757	21,845
10950	Monroe	(914)	5,996	4,439
10952	Monsey(u)	(914)	NA	8,797
12701	Monticello	(914)	6,306	5,991
10549	Mt. Kisco	(914)	8,025	8,172
*10551	Mount Vernon	(914)	66,713	72,788
10954	Nanuet(u)	(914)	NA	10,447
11767	Nesconset(u)	(516)	NA	10,048
14513	Newark	(315)	10,017	11,644
12550	Newburgh	(914)	23,438	26,219
11590	New Cassel(u)	(516)	NA	8,721
10956	New City(u)	(914)	NA	27,344
11040	New Hyde Park	(516)	9,801	10,116
*10802	New Rochelle	(914)	70,794	75,385
*12550	New Windsor Center(u)	(914)	NA	8,803
*10001	New York	(212)	7,071,030	7,895,563
*10451	Bronx	(212)	1,169,115	1,471,701
*11201	Brooklyn	(212)	2,230,936	2,602,102
*10001	Manhattan	(212)	1,427,533	1,539,233
*(Q)	Queens	(212)	1,891,325	1,987,174

(u) There are 4 P.O.s for Queens: 11101 for L.I. City; 11690 Far Rockaway; 11351 Flushing; and 11431 Jamaica.

ZIP code	Place		1980	1970
*10314	Staten Island	(212)	352,121	295,443
*14302	Niagara Falls	(716)	71,384	85,615
13745	Nimmonsburg-Chenango Br.(u)	(607)	NA	5,059
12309	Niskayuna(u)	(518)	NA	6,186
11701	North Amityville(u)	(516)	NA	11,936
11703	North Babylon(u)	(516)	NA	39,526
11710	North Bellmore(u)	(516)	NA	22,893
11713	North Bellport(u)	(516)	NA	5,903
11752	North Great River(u)	(516)	NA	12,080
11757	North Lindenhurst(u)	(516)	NA	11,117
11758	North Massapequa(u)	(516)	NA	23,123
11566	North Merrick(u)	(516)	NA	13,650
11040	North New Hyde Park(u)	(516)	NA	18,154
11772	North Patchogue(u)	(516)	NA	5,232
11768	Northport	(516)	7,651	7,494
13212	North Syracuse	(315)	7,970	8,687
10591	North Tarrytown(u)	(914)	7,994	8,334
14120	North Tonawanda	(716)	35,760	36,012
11580	North Valley Stream(u)	(516)	NA	14,881
11793	North Wantagh(u)	(516)	NA	15,053
13815	Norwich	(607)	8,082	8,843
10960	Nyack	(914)	6,428	6,659
11769	Oakdale(u)	(516)	NA	7,334
11572	Oceanside(u)	(516)	NA	35,372
13669	Ogdensburg	(315)	12,375	14,554
11804	Old Bethpage(u)	(516)	NA	7,084
14760	Olean	(716)	18,207	19,169
13421	Oneida	(315)	10,810	11,658
13820	Oneonta	(607)	14,933	16,030
10562	Ossining	(914)	20,196	21,659
13126	Oswego	(315)	19,793	20,913

ZIP code	Place		1980	1970
11771	Oyster Bay(u)	(516)	NA	6,822
11772	Patchogue	(516)	11,291	11,582
10965	Pearl River(u)	(914)	NA	17,146
10566	Peekskill	(914)	18,236	19,283
10803	Pelham	(914)	6,848	2,076
10803	Pelham Manor	(914)	6,130	6,673
14527	Penn Yan	(315)	5,242	5,293
11714	Plainedge(u)	(516)	NA	10,759
11803	Plainview(u)	(516)	NA	31,695
12901	Plattsburg	(518)	21,057	18,715
12903	Plattsburgh Base(u)	(518)	NA	7,078
10570	Pleasantville	(914)	6,749	7,110
10573	Port Chester	(914)	23,565	25,803
11777	Port Jefferson	(516)	6,731	5,515
11776	Port Jefferson Station(u)	(516)	NA	7,403
12771	Port Jervis	(914)	8,699	8,852
11050	Port Washington(u)	(516)	NA	15,923
13676	Potsdam	(315)	10,635	10,303
*12601	Poughkeepsie	(914)	29,757	32,029
12144	Rensselaer	(518)	9,047	10,136
11901	Riverhead(u)	(516)	NA	7,585
*14603	Rochester	(716)	241,741	295,011
*11570	Rockville Centre	(516)	25,405	27,444
12205	Roessleville(u)	(518)	NA	5,476
13440	Rome	(315)	43,826	50,148
11779	Ronkonkoma(u)	(516)	NA	7,284
11575	Roosevelt(u)	(516)	NA	15,008
11577	Roslyn Heights(u)	(516)	NA	7,242
12303	Rotterdam(u)	(518)	NA	25,214
10580	Rye	(914)	15,083	15,869
11780	St. James(u)	(516)	NA	10,500
14779	Salamanca	(716)	6,890	7,877
11754	San Remo(u)	(516)	NA	8,302
12983	Saranac Lake	(518)	5,578	6,086
12866	Saratoga Springs	(518)	23,906	18,845
11782	Sayville(u)	(516)	NA	11,680
10583	Scarsdale	(914)	17,650	19,229
*12301	Schenectady	(518)	67,972	77,958
12302	Scotia	(518)	7,280	7,370
11579	Sea Cliff	(516)	5,364	5,890
11783	Seaford(u)	(516)	NA	17,379
11784	Selden(u)	(516)	NA	11,613
13148	Seneca Falls	(315)	7,466	7,794
11733	Setauket-South Setauket(u)	(516)	NA	6,857
11967	Shirley(u)	(516)	NA	6,280
13209	Solvay	(315)	7,140	8,280
11735	South Farmingdale(u)	(516)	NA	20,464
11741	South Holbrook(u)	(516)	NA	6,700
11746	South Huntington(u)	(516)	NA	9,115
14904	Southport(u)	(607)	NA	8,685
11790	South Stony Brook(u)	(516)	NA	15,329
11581	South Valley Stream(u)	(516)	NA	6,595
11590	South Westbury(u)	(516)	NA	10,978
10977	Spring Valley	(914)	20,537	18,112
11790	Stony Brook(u)	(516)	NA	6,391
10980	Stony Point(u)	(914)	NA	8,270
10901	Suffern(u)	(914)	10,794	8,273
11791	Syosset(u)	(516)	NA	10,084
*13201	Syracuse	(315)	170,105	197,297
10983	Tappan(u)	(914)	NA	7,424
10591	Tarrytown	(914)	10,648	11,115
10594	Thornwood(u)	(914)	NA	6,874
14150	Tonawanda	(716)	18,693	21,898
*12180	Troy	(518)	56,638	62,918
10707	Tuckahoe	(914)	6,076	6,236
11553	Uniondale(u)	(516)	NA	22,077
*13503	Utica	(315)	75,632	91,373
10989	Valley Cottage(u)	(914)	NA	6,007
*11580	Valley Stream	(516)	35,769	40,413
11731	Vernon Valley(u)	(516)	NA	7,925
13850	Vestal-Twin Orchards(u)	(607)	NA	8,303
10901	Viola(u)	(914)	NA	5,136
12586	Walden	(914)	5,659	5,277
11793	Wantagh(u)	(516)	NA	21,783
12590	Wappingers Falls	(914)	5,110	5,607
13165	Waterloo	(315)	5,303	5,418
13601	Watertown	(315)	27,861	30,787
12189	Watervliet	(518)	11,354	12,404
14580	Webster	(716)	5,499	5,037
14895	Wellsville	(716)	5,769	5,815
11758	West Amityville(u)	(516)	NA	6,424
11704	West Babylon(u)	(516)	NA	12,893
11590	Westbury	(516)	13,871	15,362
14905	West Elmira(u)	(607)	NA	5,901
10993	West Haverstraw	(914)	9,181	8,558
11552	West Hempstead(u)	(516)	NA	20,375
11795	West Islip(u)	(516)	NA	17,374
12203	Westmere(u)	(518)	NA	6,364
10994	West Nyack(u)	(914)	NA	5,510
11796	West Sayville(u)	(516)	NA	7,386
13219	Westvale(u)	(315)	NA	7,253
*10602	White Plains	(914)	46,999	50,346
14221	Williamsville	(716)	6,017	6,878
11596	Williston Park	(516)	8,216	9,154
11598	Woodmere(u)	(516)	NA	19,831
11798	Wyandach(u)	(516)	NA	15,716
11980	Yaphank(u)	(516)	NA	5,460
*10701	Yonkers	(914)	195,351	204,297
10598	Yorktown Heights(u)	(914)	NA	6,805

North Carolina

ZIP code	Place		1980	1970
28001	Albemarle	(704)	15,110	11,126
27263	Archdale	(919)	5,305	4,874
27203	Asheboro	(919)	15,252	10,797
*28801	Asheville	(704)	53,281	57,820
28607	Boone	(704)	10,191	8,754
28712	Brevard	(704)	5,323	5,243
27215	Burlington	(919)	37,266	35,930
28542	Camp Le Jeune Central(u)	(919)	NA	34,549
27510	Carrboro	(919)	7,517	5,058
27511	Cary	(919)	21,612	7,640
27514	Chapel Hill	(919)	32,421	26,199
*28202	Charlotte	(704)	314,447	241,420
28533	Cherry Point(u)	(919)	NA	12,029
28328	Clinton	(919)	7,552	7,157
28025	Concord	(704)	16,942	18,464
28334	Dunn	(919)	8,962	8,302
*27702	Durham	(919)	100,831	95,438
27288	Eden	(919)	15,672	15,871
27932	Edenton	(919)	5,264	4,956
27909	Elizabeth City	(919)	13,784	14,381
*28302	Fayetteville	(919)	59,507	53,510
28043	Forest City	(704)	7,688	7,179
28307	Fort Bragg(u)	(919)	NA	46,995
27529	Garner	(919)	9,556	4,923
28052	Gastonia	(704)	47,333	47,322
27530	Goldsboro	(919)	31,871	26,960
27253	Graham	(919)	8,415	8,172
*27420	Greensboro	(919)	155,642	144,076
27834	Greenville	(919)	35,740	29,063
28532	Havelock	(919)	17,718	3,012
27536	Henderson	(919)	13,522	13,896
28739	Hendersonville	(704)	6,862	6,443
28601	Hickory	(704)	20,757	20,569
*27260	High Point	(919)	64,107	63,229
28348	Hope Mills	(919)	5,412	1,866
28540	Jacksonville	(919)	17,056	16,289
28081	Kannapolis(u)	(704)	NA	36,293
27284	Kernersville	(919)	6,802	4,815
28086	Kings Mountain	(704)	9,080	8,465
28501	Kinston	(919)	25,234	23,020
28352	Laurinburg	(919)	11,480	8,859
28645	Lenoir	(704)	13,748	14,705
27292	Lexington	(704)	15,711	17,205
28358	Lumberton	(919)	18,340	16,961
28212	Mint Hill	(704)	9,830	
28110	Monroe	(704)	12,639	11,282
28115	Mooresville	(704)	8,575	8,808
28655	Morganton	(704)	13,763	13,625
27030	Mount Airy	(919)	6,862	7,325
28560	New Bern	(919)	14,557	14,660
28540	New River Gieger(u)	(919)	NA	8,699
28658	Newton	(704)	7,624	7,857
28012	North Belmont(u)	(704)	NA	10,672
27565	Oxford	(919)	7,580	7,178
*27601	Raleigh	(919)	149,771	122,830
27320	Reidsville	(919)	12,492	13,636
27870	Roanoke Rapids	(919)	14,702	13,508
28379	Rockingham	(919)	8,300	5,852
27801	Rocky Mount	(919)	41,283	34,284
27573	Roxboro	(919)	7,532	5,370
28144	Salisbury	(704)	22,677	22,515
27330	Sanford	(919)	14,773	11,716
27530	Seymour-Johnson(u)	(919)	NA	8,172
28150	Shelby	(704)	15,310	16,328
27577	Smithfield	(919)	7,288	6,677
28387	Southern Pines	(919)	8,620	5,937
28390	Spring Lake	(919)	6,273	3,968
28677	Statesville	(704)	18,622	20,007
27886	Tarboro	(919)	8,634	9,425
27360	Thomasville	(919)	14,144	15,230
27889	Washington	(919)	8,418	8,961
28786	Waynesville	(704)	6,765	6,488
28025	West Concord(u)	(704)	NA	5,347
28472	Whiteville	(919)	5,565	4,195
27892	Williamston	(919)	6,159	6,570
28401	Wilmington	(919)	44,000	46,169
27893	Wilson	(919)	34,424	29,347
*27102	Winston-Salem	(919)	131,885	133,683

North Dakota (701)

ZIP code	Place	1980	1970
58501	Bismarck	44,485	34,703
58301	Devils Lake	7,442	7,078
58601	Dickinson	15,924	12,405
58102	Fargo	61,308	53,365
58237	Grafton	5,293	5,946
58201	Grand Forks(u)	43,765	39,008
58201	Grand Forks Base(u)	NA	10,474
58401	Jamestown	16,280	15,385
58554	Mandan	15,513	11,093
58701	Minot	32,843	32,290
58701	Minot Base(u)	NA	12,077
58072	Valley City	7,774	7,843
58075	Wahpeton	9,064	7,076
58078	West Fargo	10,099	5,161
58801	Williston	13,336	11,280

Ohio

ZIP code	Place		1980	1970
45810	Ada	(419)	5,669	5,309
*44309	Akron	(216)	237,177	275,425
44601	Alliance	(216)	24,315	26,547

ZIP code	Place		1980	1970
44001	Amherst	(216)	10,638	9,902
44805	Ashland	(419)	20,326	19,872
44004	Ashtabula	(216)	23,449	24,313
45701	Athens	(614)	19,743	24,168
44202	Aurora	(216)	8,177	6,549
44515	Austintown(u)	(216)	NA	29,393
44011	Avon	(216)	7,241	7,214
45404	Avondale(u)	(513)	NA	5,240
44012	Avon Lake	(216)	13,222	12,261
44203	Barberton	(216)	29,751	33,052
44140	Bay Village	(216)	17,846	18,163
44122	Beachwood	(216)	9,983	9,631
45385	Beavercreek	(513)	31,589	...
44146	Bedford	(216)	15,056	17,552
44146	Bedford Heights	(216)	13,214	13,063
43906	Bellaire	(614)	8,241	9,655
45305	Bellbrook	(513)	5,174	1,268
43311	Bellefontaine	(513)	11,888	11,255
44811	Bellevue	(419)	8,187	8,604
45714	Belpre	(614)	7,193	7,189
44017	Berea	(216)	19,567	22,465
43209	Bexley	(614)	13,405	14,888
43004	Blacklick Estates(u)	(614)	NA	8,351
45242	Blue Ash	(513)	9,506	8,324
44512	Boardman(u)	(216)	NA	30,852
43402	Bowling Green	(419)	25,728	14,656
44141	Brecksville	(216)	10,132	9,137
45211	Bridgetown(u)	(513)	NA	13,352
44141	Broadview Heights	(216)	10,920	11,463
44144	Brooklyn	(216)	12,342	13,142
44142	Brook Park	(216)	26,195	30,774
44212	Brunswick	(216)	27,689	15,852
43506	Bryan	(419)	7,879	7,008
44820	Bucyrus	(419)	13,433	13,111
43725	Cambridge	(614)	13,573	13,656
44405	Campbell	(216)	11,619	12,577
44406	Canfield	(216)	5,535	4,997
*44711	Canton	(216)	94,730	110,053
45822	Celina	(419)	9,137	8,072
45459	Centerville	(513)	18,886	10,333
45211	Cheviot	(513)	9,888	11,135
45601	Chillicothe	(614)	23,420	24,842
44505	Churchill(u)	(216)	NA	7,457
*45234	Cincinnati	(513)	385,457	453,514
43113	Circleville	(614)	11,700	11,687
*44101	Cleveland	(216)	573,822	750,879
44118	Cleveland Heights	(216)	56,438	60,767
43410	Clyde	(419)	5,489	5,503
*43216	Columbus	(614)	564,871	540,025
44030	Conneaut	(216)	13,835	14,552
44410	Cortland	(216)	5,011	2,525
43812	Coshocton	(614)	13,405	13,747
45238	Covedale(u)	(513)	NA	6,639
44827	Crestline	(419)	5,406	5,965
45341	Crystal Lakes(u)	(513)	NA	5,851
*44222	Cuyahoga Falls	(216)	43,710	49,815
*45401	Dayton	(513)	203,588	243,023
45236	Deer Park	(513)	6,745	7,415
43512	Defiance	(419)	16,810	16,281
43015	Delaware	(614)	18,780	15,008
45833	Delphos	(419)	7,314	7,608
44622	Dover	(216)	11,526	11,516
44112	East Cleveland	(216)	36,957	39,600
44094	Eastlake	(216)	22,104	19,690
43920	East Liverpool	(216)	16,687	20,020
43920	East Liverpool North(u)	(216)	NA	6,223
44413	East Palestine	(216)	5,306	5,604
45320	Eaton	(513)	6,839	6,020
*44035	Elyria	(216)	57,504	53,427
45322	Englewood	(513)	11,329	7,885
44117	Euclid	(216)	59,999	71,552
45324	Fairborn	(513)	29,702	32,267
45014	Fairfield	(513)	30,777	14,680
44313	Fairlawn	(216)	6,100	6,102
44126	Fairview Park	(216)	19,311	21,699
45840	Findlay	(419)	35,594	35,800
45405	Forest Park	(513)	18,675	15,139
45426	Fort McKinley(u)	(513)	NA	11,536
44830	Fostoria	(419)	15,743	16,037
45005	Franklin	(513)	10,711	10,075
43420	Fremont	(419)	17,834	18,490
43230	Gahanna	(614)	18,001	12,400
44833	Galion	(419)	12,391	13,123
45631	Gallipolis	(614)	5,576	7,490
44125	Garfield Heights	(216)	33,380	41,417
44041	Geneva	(216)	6,655	6,449
45327	Germantown	(513)	5,015	4,088
44420	Girard	(216)	12,517	14,119
43212	Grandview Heights	(614)	7,420	8,460
45123	Greenfield	(513)	5,034	4,780
45331	Greenville	(513)	12,999	12,380
43123	Grove City	(614)	16,793	13,911
*45012	Hamilton	(513)	63,189	67,865
45030	Harrison	(513)	5,855	4,408
43055	Heath	(614)	6,969	6,768
44124	Highland Heights	(216)	5,739	5,926
43026	Hilliard	(614)	8,008	8,369
45133	Hillsboro	(513)	6,356	5,584
44425	Hubbard	(216)	9,245	8,583

ZIP code	Place		1980	1970
45424	Huber Heights(u)	(513)	NA	18,943
44839	Huron	(419)	7,123	6,896
44131	Independence	(216)	8,165	7,034
45638	Ironton	(614)	14,290	15,030
45640	Jackson	(614)	6,675	6,843
44240	Kent	(216)	26,164	28,183
43326	Kenton	(419)	8,605	8,315
45236	Kenwood(u)	(513)	NA	15,789
45429	Kettering	(513)	61,186	71,864
44094	Kirtland	(216)	5,969	5,530
45432	Knollwood(u)	(513)	NA	5,353
44107	Lakewood	(216)	61,963	70,173
43130	Lancaster	(614)	34,953	32,911
45036	Lebanon	(513)	9,636	7,934
*45802	Lima	(419)	47,381	53,734
45215	Lincoln Heights	(513)	5,259	6,099
43228	Lincoln Village(u)	(614)	NA	11,215
43138	Logan	(614)	6,557	6,269
43140	London	(614)	6,958	6,481
*44052	Lorain	(216)	75,416	78,185
44641	Louisville	(216)	7,873	6,298
45140	Loveland	(513)	9,106	7,126
44124	Lyndhurst	(216)	18,092	19,749
44056	Macedonia	(216)	6,571	6,375
45243	Madeira	(513)	9,341	6,713
44057	Madison North(u)	(216)	NA	6,882
*44901	Mansfield	(419)	53,927	55,047
44137	Maple Heights	(216)	29,735	34,093
45750	Marietta	(614)	16,467	16,861
43302	Marion	(614)	37,040	38,646
43935	Martins Ferry	(614)	9,331	10,757
43040	Marysville	(513)	7,414	5,744
45040	Mason	(513)	8,692	5,677
44646	Massillon	(216)	30,557	32,539
43537	Maumee	(419)	15,747	15,937
44124	Mayfield Heights	(216)	21,550	22,139
44256	Medina	(216)	15,268	10,913
44060	Mentor	(216)	42,065	36,912
44060	Mentor-on-the-Lake	(216)	7,919	6,517
45342	Miamisburg	(513)	15,304	14,797
44130	Middleburg Heights	(216)	16,218	12,367
45042	Middletown	(513)	43,719	48,767
45150	Milford	(513)	5,232	4,828
45242	Montgomery	(513)	10,088	5,683
45439	Moraine	(513)	5,325	4,898
45231	Mount Healthy	(513)	7,562	7,446
43050	Mount Vernon	(614)	14,380	13,373
43545	Napoleon	(419)	8,614	7,791
43055	Newark	(614)	41,200	41,836
45344	New Carlisle	(513)	6,498	6,112
43764	New Lexington	(614)	5,179	4,921
44663	New Philadelphia	(216)	16,883	15,184
44446	Niles	(216)	23,088	21,581
44720	North Canton	(216)	14,228	15,228
45239	North College Hill	(513)	10,990	12,363
44070	North Olmsted	(216)	36,486	34,861
45414	Northridge(u)	(513)	NA	10,084
44039	North Ridgeville	(216)	21,522	13,152
44133	North Royalton	(216)	17,671	12,807
43619	Northwood	(419)	5,495	4,222
44203	Norton	(216)	12,242	12,308
44857	Norwalk	(419)	14,358	13,386
45212	Norwood	(513)	26,342	30,420
45419	Oakwood	(513)	9,372	10,095
44074	Oberlin	(216)	8,660	8,761
44138	Olmsted Falls	(216)	5,868	2,504
43616	Oregon	(419)	18,675	16,563
44667	Orrville	(216)	7,511	7,408
45431	Overlook-Page Manor(u)	(513)	NA	19,719
45056	Oxford	(513)	17,655	15,868
44077	Painesville	(216)	16,391	16,536
44077	Painesville Southwest(u)	(216)	NA	5,461
44129	Parma	(216)	92,548	100,216
44130	Parma Heights	(216)	23,112	27,192
44124	Pepper Pike	(216)	6,177	5,382
43551	Perrysburg	(419)	10,215	7,693
45356	Piqua	(513)	20,480	20,741
43452	Port Clinton	(419)	7,223	7,202
45662	Portsmouth	(614)	25,943	27,633
44266	Ravenna	(216)	11,987	11,780
45215	Reading	(513)	12,879	14,617
43068	Reynoldsburg	(614)	20,661	13,921
44143	Richmond Heights	(216)	10,095	9,220
43217	Rickenbacker Base(u)	(614)	NA	5,623
44270	Rittman	(216)	6,063	6,308
44116	Rocky River	(216)	21,084	22,958
43460	Rossford	(419)	5,978	5,302
45217	St. Bernard	(513)	5,396	6,131
43950	St. Clairsville	(614)	5,452	4,754
45885	St. Marys	(419)	8,414	7,699
44460	Salem	(216)	12,869	14,186
44870	Sandusky	(419)	31,360	32,674
44870	Sandusky South(u)	(419)	NA	8,501
44672	Sebring	(216)	5,078	4,954
44131	Seven Hills	(216)	13,650	12,700
44120	Shaker Heights	(216)	32,487	36,306
45241	Sharonville	(513)	10,108	11,393
44054	Sheffield Lake	(216)	10,484	8,734
44875	Shelby	(419)	9,645	9,847
45415	Shiloh(u)	(419)	NA	11,368
45365	Sidney	(513)	17,657	16,332

ZIP code	Place	1980	1970
45236	Silverton (513)	6,172	6,588
44139	Solon (216)	14,341	11,147
44121	South Euclid (216)	25,713	29,579
45246	Springdale (216)	10,111	8,127
*45501	Springfield (513)	72,563	81,941
43952	Steubenville (614)	26,400	30,771
44224	Stow (216)	25,303	20,061
44240	Streetsboro (216)	9,055	7,966
44136	Strongsville (216)	28,577	15,182
44471	Struthers (216)	13,624	15,343
43560	Sylvania (419)	15,527	12,031
44278	Tallmadge (216)	15,269	15,274
45243	The Village of Indian Hill (513)	5,521	5,651
44883	Tiffin (419)	19,549	21,596
45371	Tipp City (513)	5,595	5,090
*43601	Toledo (419)	354,635	383,062
43964	Toronto (614)	6,934	7,705
45067	Trenton (513)	6,401	5,278
45426	Trotwood (513)	7,802	6,997
45373	Troy (513)	19,086	17,186
44087	Twinsburg (216)	7,632	6,432
44683	Uhrichsville (614)	6,130	5,731
45322	Union (513)	5,219	3,654
44118	University Heights (216)	15,401	17,055
43221	Upper Arlington (614)	35,648	38,727
43351	Upper Sandusky (419)	5,967	5,645
43078	Urbana (513)	10,762	11,237
45377	Vandalia (513)	13,161	10,796
45891	Van Wert (419)	11,035	11,320
44089	Vermilion (216)	11,012	9,872
44281	Wadsworth (216)	15,166	13,142
45895	Wapakoneta (419)	8,402	7,324
*44481	Warren (216)	56,629	63,494
44122	Warrensville Heights (216)	16,565	18,925
43160	Washington (513)	12,682	12,495
43567	Wauseon (419)	6,173	4,932
45692	Wellston (614)	6,016	5,410
43968	Wellsville (216)	5,095	5,891
45449	West Carrollton (513)	13,148	10,748
43081	Westerville (614)	23,414	12,530
44145	Westlake (216)	19,483	15,689
43213	Whitehall (614)	21,299	25,263
44092	Wickliffe (216)	16,790	20,632
44890	Willard (419)	5,674	5,510
44094	Willoughby (216)	19,329	18,634
44094	Willoughby Hills (216)	8,612	5,969
44094	Willowick (216)	17,834	21,237
45177	Wilmington (513)	10,431	10,051
44691	Wooster (216)	19,289	18,703
43085	Worthington (614)	15,016	15,326
45433	Wright-Patterson(u) (513)	NA	10,151
45215	Wyoming (513)	8,282	9,089
45385	Xenia (513)	24,653	25,373
*44501	Youngstown (216)	115,436	140,909
43701	Zanesville (614)	28,655	33,045

Oklahoma

ZIP code	Place	1980	1970
74820	Ada (405)	15,902	14,859
73521	Altus (405)	23,101	23,302
73717	Alva (405)	6,416	7,440
73005	Anadarko (405)	6,378	6,682
73401	Ardmore (405)	23,689	20,881
74003	Bartlesville (918)	34,568	29,683
73008	Bethany (405)	22,130	22,694
74008	Bixby (918)	6,969	3,973
74631	Blackwell (405)	8,400	8,645
74012	Broken Arrow (918)	35,761	11,018
73018	Chickasha (405)	15,828	14,194
73020	Choctaw (405)	7,520	4,750
74017	Claremore (918)	12,085	9,084
73601	Clinton (405)	8,796	8,513
74023	Cushing (918)	7,720	7,529
73115	Del City (405)	28,424	27,133
73533	Duncan (405)	22,517	19,718
74701	Durant (405)	11,972	11,118
73034	Edmond (405)	34,637	16,633
73644	Elk City (405)	9,579	7,323
73036	El Reno (405)	15,486	14,510
73701	Enid (405)	50,363	44,986
73503	Fort Sill(u) (405)	NA	21,217
73542	Frederick (405)	6,153	6,132
73044	Guthrie (405)	10,312	9,575
73942	Guymon (405)	8,492	7,674
74437	Henryetta (918)	6,432	6,430
74848	Holdenville (405)	5,469	5,181
74743	Hugo (405)	7,172	6,585
74745	Idabel (405)	7,622	5,946
74037	Jenks (918)	5,876	2,685
73501	Lawton (405)	80,054	74,470
73055	Marlow (405)	5,017	3,995
74501	McAlester (918)	17,255	18,802
74354	Miami (918)	14,237	13,880
73110	Midwest City (405)	49,559	48,212
73060	Moore (405)	35,063	18,761
74401	Muskogee (918)	40,011	37,331
73064	Mustang (405)	7,496	2,637
73069	Norman (405)	68,020	52,117
*73125	Oklahoma City (405)	403,213	368,164
74447	Okmulgee (918)	16,263	15,180
74055	Owasso (918)	6,149	3,491
73075	Pauls Valley (405)	5,664	5,769
73077	Perry (405)	5,796	5,341
74601	Ponca City (405)	26,238	25,940
74953	Poteau (918)	7,089	5,500
74361	Pryor Creek (918)	8,483	7,057
74955	Sallisaw (918)	6,403	4,888
74063	Sand Springs (918)	13,246	10,565
74066	Sapulpa (918)	15,853	15,159
74868	Seminole (405)	8,590	7,878
74801	Shawnee (405)	26,506	25,075
74074	Stillwater (405)	38,268	31,126
73086	Sulphur (405)	5,516	5,158
74464	Tahlequah (918)	9,708	9,254
74873	Tecumseh (405)	5,123	4,451
73120	The Village (405)	11,049	13,695
*74101	Tulsa (918)	360,919	330,350
74301	Vinita (918)	6,740	5,847
74467	Wagoner (918)	6,191	4,959
73132	Warr Acres (405)	9,940	9,887
73096	Weatherford (405)	9,640	7,959
74884	Wewoka (405)	5,480	5,284
73801	Woodward (405)	13,610	9,563
73099	Yukon (405)	17,112	8,411

Oregon (503)

ZIP code	Place	1980	1970
97321	Albany	26,546	18,181
97601	Altamont(u)	NA	15,746
97520	Ashland	14,943	12,342
97103	Astoria	9,998	10,244
97814	Baker	9,471	9,354
97005	Beaverton	30,582	18,577
97701	Bend	17,263	13,710
97013	Canby	7,659	3,813
97502	Central Point	6,357	4,004
97420	Coos Bay	14,424	13,466
97330	Corvallis	40,960	35,056
97424	Cottage Grove	7,148	6,004
97338	Dallas	8,530	6,361
*97401	Eugene	105,624	79,028
97116	Forest Grove	11,499	8,275
97301	Four Corners(u)	NA	5,823
97027	Gladstone	9,500	6,254
97526	Grants Pass	14,997	12,455
97030	Gresham	33,005	10,030
97303	Hayesville(u)	NA	5,518
97838	Hermiston	9,408	4,893
97123	Hillsboro	27,664	14,675
97303	Keizer(u)	NA	11,405
97601	Klamath Falls	16,661	15,775
97850	La Grande	11,354	9,645
97034	Lake Oswego	22,868	14,615
97355	Lebanon	10,413	6,636
97367	Lincoln City	5,469	4,198
97128	McMinnville	14,080	10,125
97501	Medford	39,603	28,973
97862	Milton-Freewater	5,086	4,105
97222	Milwaukie	17,931	16,444
97361	Monmouth	5,594	5,237
97132	Newberg	10,394	6,507
97365	Newport	7,519	5,188
97459	North Bend	9,779	8,553
97914	Ontario	8,814	6,523
97045	Oregon City	14,673	9,176
97801	Pendleton	14,521	13,197
*97208	Portland	366,383	379,967
97754	Prineville	5,276	4,101
97756	Redmond	6,452	3,721
97470	Roseburg	16,644	14,461
97051	St. Helens	7,064	6,212
*97301	Salem	89,233	68,725
97138	Seaside	5,193	4,402
97381	Silverton	5,168	4,301
97477	Springfield	41,621	26,874
97386	Sweet Home	6,921	3,799
97058	The Dalles	10,820	10,423
97223	Tigard	14,286	6,499
97060	Troutdale	5,908	1,661
97062	Tualatin	7,348	750
97068	West Linn	12,956	7,091
97071	Woodburn	11,196	7,495

Pennsylvania

ZIP code	Place	1980	1970
19001	Abington(u) (215)	NA	8,391
15001	Aliquippa (412)	17,094	22,277
*18101	Allentown (215)	103,758	109,871
*16603	Altoona (814)	57,078	63,115
19002	Ambler (215)	6,628	7,800
15003	Ambridge (412)	9,575	11,324
18403	Archbald (717)	6,295	6,118
19003	Ardmore(u) (215)	NA	5,131
15068	Arnold (412)	6,853	8,174
15202	Avalon (412)	6,240	7,010
15005	Baden (412)	5,318	5,536
19004	Bala-Cynwyd(u) (215)	NA	6,483
15234	Baldwin (412)	24,598	26,729
18013	Bangor (215)	5,006	5,425
15009	Beaver (412)	5,441	6,100
15010	Beaver Falls (412)	12,525	14,635
16823	Bellefonte (814)	6,300	6,828
15202	Bellevue (412)	10,128	11,586
18603	Berwick (717)	12,189	12,274

ZIP code	Place	1980	1970
15102	Bethel Park (412)	34,755	34,758
*18016	Bethlehem (215)	70,419	72,686
18447	Blakely (717)	7,438	6,391
17815	Bloomsburg (717)	11,717	11,652
15104	Braddock (412)	5,634	8,795
16701	Bradford (814)	11,211	12,672
19406	Brandywine Village(u) (215)	NA	11,411
15227	Brentwood (412)	11,907	13,732
15017	Bridgeville (412)	6,154	6,717
19007	Bristol (215)	10,867	12,085
19015	Brookhaven (215)	7,912	7,370
19010	Bryn Mawr(u) (215)	NA	5,815
16001	Butler (412)	17,026	18,691
15419	California (412)	5,703	6,635
17011	Camp Hill (717)	8,422	9,931
15317	Canonsburg (412)	10,459	11,439
18407	Carbondale (717)	11,255	12,478
17013	Carlisle (717)	18,314	18,079
15106	Carnegie (412)	10,099	10,864
15108	Carnot-Moon(u) (412)	NA	13,093
15234	Castle Shannon (412)	10,164	12,036
18032	Catasauqua (215)	7,944	5,702
19095	Cedarbrook-Melrose Park(u) (215)	NA	9,990
19428	Cedar Heights(u) (215)	NA	6,326
17201	Chambersburg (717)	16,174	17,315
15022	Charleroi (412)	5,717	6,723
19380	Chatwood(u) (215)	NA	7,168
*19003	Chester (215)	45,794	56,331
15025	Clairton (412)	12,188	15,051
16214	Clarion (814)	6,664	6,095
18411	Clarks Summit (717)	5,272	5,376
16830	Clearfield (814)	7,580	8,176
19018	Clifton Heights (215)	7,320	8,348
19320	Coatesville (215)	10,698	12,331
19023	Collingdale (215)	9,539	10,605
17512	Columbia (717)	10,466	11,237
15425	Connellsville (412)	10,319	11,643
19428	Conshohocken (215)	8,475	10,195
15108	Coraopolis (412)	7,308	8,435
16407	Corry (814)	7,149	7,435
15205	Crafton (412)	7,623	8,233
17821	Danville (717)	5,239	6,176
19023	Darby (215)	11,513	13,729
18519	Dickson City (717)	6,699	7,698
15033	Donora (412)	7,524	8,825
15216	Dormont (412)	11,275	12,856
19335	Downingtown (215)	7,650	7,437
18901	Doylestown (215)	8,717	8,270
15801	Du Bois (814)	9,290	10,112
18512	Dunmore (717)	16,781	18,168
15110	Duquesne (412)	10,094	11,410
18642	Duryea (717)	5,415	5,264
18042	Easton (215)	26,027	29,450
18301	East Stroudsburg (717)	8,039	7,894
15005	Economy (412)	9,538	7,176
16412	Edinboro (814)	6,324	4,871
18704	Edwardsville (717)	5,729	5,633
17022	Elizabethtown (717)	8,233	8,072
16117	Ellwood City (412)	9,998	10,857
18049	Emmaus (215)	11,001	11,511
17522	Ephrata (717)	11,095	9,662
*16501	Erie (814)	119,123	129,265
18643	Exeter (717)	5,493	4,670
16121	Farrell (412)	8,645	11,000
19031	Flourtown(u) (215)	NA	9,149
19032	Folcroft (215)	8,231	9,810
15221	Forest Hills (412)	8,198	9,561
18704	Forty Fort (717)	5,590	6,114
15238	Fox Chapel (412)	5,049	4,684
17931	Frackville (215)	5,308	5,445
16323	Franklin (814)	8,146	8,629
15143	Franklin Park (412)	6,135	5,310
18052	Fullerton(u) (215)	NA	7,908
19004	General Wayne(u) (215)	NA	5,368
17325	Gettysburg (717)	7,194	7,275
15045	Glassport (412)	6,242	7,450
19036	Glenolden (215)	7,633	8,697
19038	Glenside(u) (215)	NA	17,353
15601	Greensburg (412)	17,558	17,077
15220	Green Tree (412)	5,722	6,441
16125	Greenville (412)	7,730	8,704
16127	Grove City (412)	8,162	8,312
17331	Hanover (717)	14,890	15,623
*17105	Harrisburg (717)	53,264	68,061
19040	Hatboro (215)	7,579	8,880
19044	Hatboro West(u) (215)	NA	14,278
18201	Hazleton (717)	27,318	30,426
18055	Hellertown (215)	6,025	6,615
17033	Hershey(u) (717)	NA	7,407
18042	Highland Park (Northampton)(u) (717)	NA	5,500
16648	Hollidaysburg (814)	5,892	6,262
16001	Homeacre-Lyndora(u) (412)	NA	8,415
15120	Homestead (412)	5,092	6,309
18431	Honesdale (717)	5,128	5,224
17036	Hummelstown (717)	6,159	4,723
16552	Huntingdon (814)	7,042	6,987
15701	Indiana (412)	16,051	16,100
15644	Jeannette (412)	13,106	15,209
15344	Jefferson (412)	8,643	8,512
19401	Jefferson-Trooper(u) (215)	NA	13,901
18229	Jim Thorpe (717)	5,263	5,456
*15901	Johnstown (814)	35,496	42,476
18704	Kingston (717)	15,681	18,325
16201	Kittanning (412)	5,432	6,231
19444	Lafayette Hills-Plymouth Meeting(u) (215)	NA	8,275
*17604	Lancaster (717)	54,725	57,690
19446	Lansdale (215)	16,526	18,451
19050	Lansdowne (215)	11,891	14,090
15650	Latrobe (412)	10,799	11,749
17042	Lebanon (717)	25,711	28,572
18235	Lehighton (215)	5,826	6,095
17837	Lewisburg (717)	5,407	5,718
17044	Lewistown (717)	9,830	11,098
17543	Lititz (717)	7,590	7,072
17745	Lock Haven (717)	9,617	11,427
15068	Lower Burrell (412)	13,200	13,654
15237	McCandless (412)	NA	22,404
*15134	McKeesport (412)	31,012	37,977
15136	McKees Rocks (412)	8,742	11,901
17948	Mahanoy City (717)	6,167	7,257
17545	Manheim (717)	5,015	5,434
16335	Meadville (814)	15,544	16,573
17055	Mechanicsburg (717)	9,487	9,385
*19063	Media (215)	6,119	6,444
19066	Merion(u) (215)	NA	5,686
17057	Middletown (717)	10,122	9,080
17551	Millersville (717)	7,668	6,396
17847	Milton (717)	6,730	7,723
17954	Minersville (717)	5,635	6,012
15061	Monaca (412)	7,661	7,486
15062	Monessen (412)	11,928	15,216
15063	Monongahela (412)	5,950	7,113
15146	Monroeville (412)	30,977	29,011
17754	Montoursville (717)	5,403	5,985
10507	Moosic (717)	6,068	4,646
19067	Morrisville (215)	9,845	11,309
17851	Mount Carmel (717)	8,190	9,317
17552	Mount Joy (717)	5,680	5,041
15666	Mount Pleasant (412)	5,354	5,895
15120	Munhall (412)	14,532	16,574
15668	Murrysville (412)	16,036	12,661
18634	Nanticoke (717)	13,044	14,638
18064	Nazareth (215)	5,443	5,815
15066	New Brighton (412)	7,364	7,637
*16101	New Castle (412)	33,621	38,559
17070	New Cumberland (717)	8,051	9,803
15068	New Kensington (412)	17,660	20,312
*19401	Norristown (215)	34,684	38,169
18067	Northampton (215)	8,240	8,389
19003	North Ardmore(u) (215)	NA	5,856
15104	North Braddock (412)	8,711	10,838
19038	North Hills-Ardsley(u) (215)	NA	13,096
19074	Norwood (215)	6,647	7,229
19126	Oak Lane(u) (215)	NA	6,182
15139	Oakmont (412)	7,039	7,550
19117	Ogontz(u) (215)	NA	5,242
16301	Oil City (814)	13,881	15,033
18518	Old Forge (717)	9,304	9,522
18447	Olyphant (717)	5,204	5,422
19075	Oreland(u) (215)	NA	9,349
18071	Palmerton (215)	5,455	5,620
17078	Palmyra (717)	7,228	7,615
19301	Paoli(u) (215)	NA	5,835
17331	Parkville(u) (717)	NA	5,120
19004	Pencoyd(u) (215)	NA	6,650
19401	Penn Sq.-Plymouth Valley(u) (215)	NA	20,255
19151	Penn Wynne(u) (215)	NA	6,038
18944	Perkasie (215)	5,241	5,451
*19104	Philadelphia (215)	1,688,210	1,949,996
19460	Phoenixville (215)	14,165	14,823
*15219	Pittsburgh (412)	423,938	520,089
18640	Pittston (717)	9,930	11,113
18705	Plains(u) (717)	NA	6,606
15236	Pleasant Hills (412)	9,676	10,409
*15239	Plum (412)	25,390	21,932
16651	Plymouth (717)	7,605	9,536
15133	Port Vue (412)	5,316	5,862
19464	Pottstown (215)	22,729	25,355
17901	Pottsville (717)	18,195	19,715
19076	Prospect Park (215)	6,593	7,250
15767	Punxsutawney (814)	7,479	7,792
18951	Quakertown (215)	8,867	7,276
*19603	Reading (215)	78,686	87,643
17356	Red Lion (717)	5,824	5,645
15853	Ridgway (814)	5,604	6,022
19078	Ridley Park (215)	7,889	9,025
19001	Roslyn(u) (215)	NA	18,811
19046	Rydal(u) (215)	NA	5,826
15857	St. Marys (814)	6,417	7,470
18840	Sayre (717)	6,951	7,473
17972	Schuylkill Haven (717)	5,977	6,125
15683	Scottdale (412)	5,833	5,818
*18503	Scranton (717)	88,117	102,696
17870	Selinsgrove (717)	5,227	5,116
17872	Shamokin (717)	10,357	11,719
16146	Sharon (412)	19,057	22,653
19079	Sharon Hill (215)	6,221	7,464
16150	Sharpsville (412)	5,375	6,126

ZIP code	Place	1980	1970
17976	Shenandoah . . . . (717)	7,589	8,287
19607	Shillington . . . . (215)	5,601	6,249
17257	Shippensburg . . . . (717)	5,261	6,536
15501	Somerset . . . . (814)	6,474	6,269
18964	Souderton . . . . (215)	6,657	6,366
17701	South Williamsport	6,581	7,153
16801	State College . . . . . . (814)	36,130	32,833
17113	Steelton . . . . (717)	6,484	8,556
18360	Stroudsburg . . . . (717)	5,148	5,451
16323	Sugar Creek . . . . (814)	5,954	5,944
17801	Sunbury . . . . (717)	12,292	13,025
19081	Swarthmore . . . . (215)	5,950	6,156
15218	Swissvale . . . . (412)	11,345	13,819
18704	Swoyersville . . . . (717)	5,795	6,786
18252	Tamaqua. . . . . (717)	8,843	9,246
15084	Tarentum . . . . (412)	6,419	7,379
18517	Taylor . . . . (717)	7,246	6,977
16354	Titusville . . . . (814)	6,884	7,331
15145	Turtle Creek . . . . (412)	6,959	8,308
16686	Tyrone . . . . (814)	6,346	7,072
15401	Uniontown . . . . (814)	14,510	16,282
15690	Vandergrift . . . . (412)	6,823	7,889
16365	Warren . . . . (814)	12,146	12,998
15301	Washington . . . . (412)	18,363	19,827
17268	Waynesboro . . . . (717)	9,726	10,011
19380	West Chester . . . . . . (215)	17,435	19,301
15122	West Mifflin . . . . (412)	26,279	28,070
15905	Westmont . . . . (814)	6,113	6,673
18643	West Pittston . . . . . . (717)	5,980	7,074
15229	West View . . . . (412)	7,648	8,312
18052	Whitehall . . . . (412)	15,206	16,450
15131	White Oak . . . . (717)	9,480	9,304
*18701	Wilkes-Barre. . . . . . . (717)	51,551	58,856
15221	Wilkinsburg . . . . (412)	23,669	26,780
17701	Williamsport . . . . (717)	33,401	37,918
19090	Willow Grove(u) . . . . . (717)	NA	16,194
15025	Wilson . . . . (412)	7,564	8,406
15963	Windber . . . . (814)	5,585	6,332
19610	Wyomissing . . . . (215)	6,551	7,136
19050	Yeadon . . . . (215)	11,727	12,136
*17405	York . . . . (717)	44,619	50,335

Rhode Island (401)
See Note on Page 207

ZIP code	Place	1980	1970
02806	Barrington	16,174	17,554
02809	Bristol.	20,128	17,860
02830	Burrillville	13,164	10,087
02863	Central Falls	16,995	18,716
02816	Coventry	27,065	22,947
02910	Cranston	71,992	74,287
02864	Cumberland	27,069	26,605
02818	East Greenwich	10,211	9,577
02914	East Providence	50,980	48,207
02814	Glocester	7,550	5,160
02833	Hopkinton	6,406	5,392
02919	Johnston	24,907	22,037
02881	Kingston(u).	NA	5,601
02865	Lincoln	16,949	16,182
02840	Middletown.	17,216	29,290
02882	Narragansett	12,088	7,138
02840	Newport	29,259	34,562
02843	Newport East(u).	NA	10,285
02852	North Kingstown.	21,938	29,793
02908	North Providence	29,188	24,337
02876	North Smithfield.	9,972	9,349
*02860	Pawtucket	71,204	76,984
02871	Portsmouth	14,257	12,521
*02904	Providence.	156,804	179,116
02857	Scituate	8,405	7,489
02917	Smithfield	16,886	13,468
02879	South Kingstown	20,414	16,913
02878	Tiverton	13,526	12,559
*02880	Wakefield-Peacedale(u) . .	NA	6,331
02885	Warren	10,640	10,523
*02887	Warwick	87,123	83,694
02891	Westerly	18,580	17,248
02891	Westerly Center(u)	NA	13,654
02893	West Warwick	27,026	24,323
02895	Woonsocket	45,914	46,820

South Carolina (803)

ZIP code	Place	1980	1970
29620	Abbeville	5,863	5,515
29801	Aiken	14,978	13,436
29621	Anderson	27,313	27,556
29407	Avondale-Moorland(u) . . .	NA	5,236
29812	Barnwell	5,572	4,439
29902	Beaufort	8,634	9,434
29627	Belton	5,312	5,257
29512	Bennettsville	8,774	7,468
29611	Berea(u)	NA	7,186
29020	Camden	7,462	8,532
29033	Cayce	11,701	9,967
*29401	Charleston	69,510	66,945
29404	Charleston Base(u)	NA	6,238
29408	Charleston Yard(u)	NA	13,565
29520	Cheraw.	5,654	5,627
29706	Chester	6,820	7,045
29631	Clemson	8,118	6,690
29325	Clinton	8,596	8,138

ZIP code	Place	1980	1970
*29201	Columbia.	99,296	113,542
29526	Conway	10,240	8,151
29532	Darlington	7,989	6,990
29536	Dillon	7,042	6,391
29640	Easley	14,264	11,175
29501	Florence	30,062	25,997
29206	Forest Acres.	6,033	6,808
29340	Gaffney	13,453	13,131
29605	Gantt(u)	NA	11,386
29440	Georgetown	10,144	10,449
29445	Goose Creek	17,811	3,825
*29602	Greenville	58,242	61,436
29646	Greenwood	21,613	21,069
29651	Greer	10,525	10,642
29410	Hanahan	13,224	9,118
29550	Hartsville	7,631	8,017
29560	Lake City.	5,636	6,247
29720	Lancaster	9,603	9,186
29360	Laurens	10,587	10,298
29571	Marion	7,700	7,435
29662	Mauldin	8,245	3,797
29464	Mount Pleasant	13,838	6,879
29574	Mullins	6,068	6,006
29577	Myrtle Beach	18,758	9,035
29108	Newberry	9,866	9,218
29841	North Augusta.	13,593	12,883
29406	North Charleston	65,630	21,211
29115	Orangeburg	14,933	13,252
29905	Parris Island(u)	NA	8,868
29730	Rock Hill	35,344	33,846
29407	St. Andrews(u)	NA	9,202
29678	Seneca	7,436	6,573
29150	Shannontown(u).	NA	7,41
29152	Shaw(u)	NA	5,819
29681	Simpsonville	9,037	3,308
*29301	Spartanburg	43,968	44,546
29483	Summerville	6,368	3,839
29150	Sumter	24,890	24,555
29687	Taylors(u)	NA	6,831
29379	Union	10,523	10,775
29607	Wade-Hampton(u)	NA	17,152
29488	Walterboro.	6,036	6,257
29169	West Columbia	10,409	7,838
29388	Woodruff	5,171	4,690
29745	York	6,412	5,081

South Dakota (605)

ZIP code	Place	1980	1970
57401	Aberdeen	25,956	26,476
57006	Brookings	14,951	13,717
57706	Ellsworth(u)	NA	6,207
57350	Huron	13,000	14,299
57042	Madison	6,210	6,315
57301	Mitchell	13,916	13,425
57501	Pierre.	11,973	9,699
57701	Rapid City	46,492	43,836
*57101	Sioux Falls	81,343	72,488
57785	Sturgis	5,184	4,536
57069	Vermillion	9,582	9,128
57201	Watertown	15,649	13,388
57078	Yankton	12,011	11,919

Tennessee

ZIP code	Place	1980	1970
37701	Alcoa . . . . (615)	6,870	7,739
37303	Athens . . . . (615)	12,080	11,790
38134	Bartlett . . . . (901)	17,170	1,150
38008	Bolivar . . . . (901)	6,597	6,674
37027	Brentwood . . . . (615)	9,431	4,099
37620	Bristol . . . . (615)	23,986	20,064
38012	Brownsville . . . . (901)	9,307	7,011
*37401	Chattanooga. . . . . . . (615)	169,565	119,923
37040	Clarksville . . . . (615)	54,777	31,719
37311	Cleveland . . . . (615)	26,415	21,446
37716	Clinton . . . . (615)	5,245	4,794
38017	Collierville . . . . (901)	7,839	3,651
38401	Columbia. . . . . (615)	25,767	21,471
38501	Cookeville . . . . (615)	20,350	14,403
38019	Covington . . . . (901)	6,065	5,801
38555	Crossville . . . . (615)	6,394	5,381
37321	Dayton . . . . (615)	5,913	4,361
37055	Dickson . . . . (615)	7,040	5,665
38024	Dyersburg . . . . (901)	15,856	14,523
37801	Eagleton Village(u) . . . . (615)	NA	5,345
37412	East Ridge . . . . (615)	21,236	21,799
37643	Elizabethton . . . . . . (615)	12,431	12,269
37334	Fayetteville . . . . (615)	7,559	7,691
42223	Fort Campbell South(u) . . (615)	NA	9,279
37064	Franklin . . . . (615)	12,407	9,497
37066	Gallatin . . . . (615)	17,191	13,253
38138	Germantown. . . . . . . (901)	20,459	3,474
37072	Goodlettsville . . . . . . (615)	8,327	6,168
37075	Greater Hendersonville(u) . (615)	25,029	11,996
37743	Greeneville . . . . (615)	14,097	13,722
37748	Harriman . . . . (615)	8,303	8,734
37075	Hendersonville . . . . . (615)	26,561	412
37343	Hixson(u). . . . . (615)	NA	6,188
38343	Humboldt . . . . (901)	10,209	10,066
38301	Jackson . . . . (901)	49,131	39,996
37760	Jefferson City . . . . . . (615)	5,612	5,124
37601	Johnson City. . . . . . . (615)	39,753	33,770
*37662	Kingsport. . . . . (615)	32,027	31,938
37665	Kingsport North(u) . . . . (615)	NA	13,118
*37901	Knoxville . . . . (615)	183,139	174,587

ZIP code	Place		1980	1970
37766	La Follette	(615)	8,176	6,902
37416	Lake Hills-Murray Hills(u)	(615)	NA	7,806
37086	LaVergne	(615)	5,495	5,220
38464	Lawrenceburg	(615)	10,175	8,889
37087	Lebanon	(615)	11,872	12,492
37771	Lenoir City	(615)	5,446	5,324
37091	Lewisburg	(615)	8,760	7,207
38351	Lexington	(901)	5,934	5,024
38201	McKenzie	(901)	5,405	4,873
37110	McMinnville	(615)	10,683	10,662
37355	Manchester	(615)	7,250	5,208
38237	Martin	(901)	8,898	7,781
37801	Maryville	(615)	17,480	13,808
*38101	Memphis	(901)	646,356	623,988
38358	Milan	(901)	8,083	7,313
38053	Millington	(901)	20,236	21,177
37814	Morristown	(615)	19,683	20,318
37130	Murfreesboro	(615)	32,845	26,360
*37202	Nashville-Davidson	(615)	455,651	**426,029
37821	Newport	(615)	7,580	7,328
37830	Oak Ridge	(615)	27,662	28,319
38242	Paris	(901)	10,728	9,892
38478	Pulaski	(615)	7,184	6,989
37415	Red Bank White Oak	(615)	13,297	12,715
38063	Ripley	(901)	6,366	4,794
37854	Rockwood	(615)	5,767	5,259
38372	Savannah	(901)	6,992	5,576
37160	Shelbyville	(615)	13,530	12,262
37377	Signal Mountain	(615)	5,818	4,839
37167	Smyrna	(615)	8,839	5,698
37379	Soddy-Daisy	(615)	8,388	7,569
37172	Springfield	(615)	10,814	9,720
37388	Tullahoma	(615)	15,800	15,311
38261	Union City	(901)	10,436	11,925
37398	Winchester	(615)	5,821	5,256

**Comprises the Metropolitan Government of Nashville and Davidson County.

Texas

ZIP code	Place		1980	1970
*79604	Abilene	(915)	98,315	89,653
75001	Addison	(214)	5,553	593
78516	Alamo	(512)	5,831	4,291
78209	Alamo Heights	(512)	6,252	6,933
78332	Alice	(512)	20,961	20,121
75002	Allen	(214)	8,314	1,940
79830	Alpine	(915)	5,465	5,971
77511	Alvin	(713)	16,515	10,671
*79105	Amarillo	(806)	149,230	127,010
79714	Andrews	(915)	11,061	8,625
77515	Angleton	(713)	13,929	9,906
78336	Aransas Pass	(512)	7,173	5,813
*76010	Arlington	(817)	160,123	90,229
75751	Athens	(214)	10,197	9,582
75551	Atlanta	(214)	6,272	5,007
*78710	Austin	(512)	345,496	253,539
76020	Azle	(817)	5,822	4,493
75149	Balch Springs	(214)	13,746	10,464
77414	Bay City	(713)	17,837	13,445
77520	Baytown	(713)	56,923	43,980
*77704	Beaumont	(713)	118,102	117,548
76021	Bedford	(817)	20,821	10,049
78102	Beeville	(512)	14,574	13,506
77401	Bellaire	(713)	14,950	19,009
76704	Bellmead	(817)	7,569	7,698
76513	Belton	(817)	10,660	8,696
76126	Benbrook	(817)	13,579	8,169
79720	Big Spring	(915)	24,804	28,735
75418	Bonham	(214)	7,338	7,698
79007	Borger	(806)	15,837	14,195
76230	Bowie	(817)	5,610	5,185
76825	Brady	(915)	5,969	5,557
76024	Breckenridge	(817)	6,921	5,944
77833	Brenham	(713)	10,966	8,922
77611	Bridge City	(713)	7,667	8,164
79316	Brownfield	(806)	10,387	9,647
78520	Brownsville	(512)	84,997	52,522
76801	Brownwood	(915)	19,203	17,368
77801	Bryan	(713)	44,337	33,719
76354	Burkburnett	(817)	10,668	9,230
76028	Burleson	(817)	11,734	7,713
76520	Cameron	(817)	5,721	5,546
79015	Canyon	(806)	10,724	8,333
78834	Carrizo Springs	(512)	6,886	5,374
75006	Carrollton	(214)	40,591	13,855
75633	Carthage	(214)	6,447	5,392
75104	Cedar Hill	(214)	6,849	2,610
75935	Center	(713)	5,827	4,989
79201	Childress	(817)	5,817	5,408
76031	Cleburne	(817)	19,218	16,015
77327	Cleveland	(713)	5,977	5,627
77531	Clute	(713)	9,577	6,023
76834	Coleman	(915)	5,960	5,608
77840	College Station	(713)	37,272	17,676
76034	Colleyville	(817)	6,700	3,342
79512	Colorado City	(915)	5,405	5,227
75428	Commerce	(214)	8,136	9,534
77301	Conroe	(713)	18,034	11,969
76522	Copperas Cove	(817)	19,469	10,818
*78408	Corpus Christi	(512)	231,999	204,525
75110	Corsicana	(214)	21,712	19,972
75835	Crockett	(713)	7,405	6,616
76036	Crowley	(817)	5,852	2,662
78839	Crystal City	(512)	8,334	8,104
77954	Cuero	(512)	7,124	6,956
79022	Dalhart	(806)	6,854	5,705
*75260	Dallas	(214)	904,078	844,401
77536	Deer Park	(713)	22,648	12,773
78840	Del Rio	(512)	30,034	21,330
75020	Denison	(214)	23,884	24,923
76201	Denton	(817)	48,063	39,874
75115	De Soto	(214)	15,538	6,617
75941	Diboll	(713)	5,227	3,557
77539	Dickinson	(713)	7,505	10,776
79027	Dimmitt	(806)	5,019	4,327
78537	Donna	(512)	9,952	7,365
79029	Dumas	(806)	12,194	9,771
75116	Duncanville	(214)	27,781	14,105
78852	Eagle Pass	(512)	21,407	15,364
78539	Edinburg	(512)	24,075	17,163
77957	Edna	(512)	5,650	5,332
77437	El Campo	(713)	10,462	9,332
79910	El Paso	(915)	425,259	322,261
78543	Elsa	(512)	5,061	4,400
75119	Ennis	(214)	12,110	11,046
76039	Euless	(817)	24,002	19,316
76140	Everman	(817)	5,387	4,570
78355	Falfurrias	(512)	6,103	6,355
75234	Farmers Branch	(214)	24,863	27,492
76119	Forest Hill	(817)	11,684	8,236
79906	Fort Bliss(u)	(915)	NA	13,288
76544	Fort Hood(u)	(817)	NA	32,597
78234	Fort Sam Houston(u)	(512)	NA	10,553
79735	Fort Stockton	(915)	8,688	8,283
76101	Fort Worth	(817)	385,141	393,455
78624	Fredericksburg	(512)	6,412	5,326
77541	Freeport	(713)	13,444	11,997
77546	Friendswood	(713)	10,719	5,675
76240	Gainesville	(817)	14,081	13,830
77547	Galena Park	(713)	9,879	10,479
77550	Galveston	(713)	61,902	61,809
*75040	Garland	(214)	138,857	81,437
76528	Gatesville	(817)	6,260	4,683
78626	Georgetown	(512)	9,468	6,395
75644	Gilmer	(214)	5,167	4,196
75647	Gladewater	(214)	6,548	5,574
78629	Gonzales	(512)	7,152	5,854
76046	Graham	(817)	9,055	7,477
75050	Grand Prairie	(214)	71,462	50,904
76051	Grapevine	(817)	11,801	7,049
76401	Greenville	(214)	22,161	22,043
77619	Groves	(713)	17,090	18,067
76117	Haltom City	(817)	29,014	28,127
76541	Harker Heights	(817)	7,345	4,216
78550	Harlingen	(512)	43,543	33,503
77859	Hearne	(713)	5,418	4,982
75652	Henderson	(214)	11,473	10,187
79045	Hereford	(806)	15,853	13,414
76643	Hewitt	(817)	5,247	569
75205	Highland Park	(214)	8,909	10,133
76645	Hillsboro	(817)	7,397	7,224
77563	Hitchcock	(713)	6,655	5,565
78861	Hondo	(512)	6,057	5,487
*77013	Houston	(713)	1,594,086	1,233,535
77338	Humble	(713)	6,729	3,272
77340	Huntsville	(713)	23,936	17,610
76053	Hurst	(817)	31,420	27,215
78362	Ingleside	(512)	5,436	3,763
76367	Iowa Park	(817)	6,184	5,796
*75061	Irving	(214)	109,943	97,260
77029	Jacinto City	(713)	8,953	9,563
75766	Jacksonville	(214)	12,264	9,734
75951	Jasper	(713)	6,959	6,251
77450	Katy	(713)	5,660	2,923
79745	Kermit	(915)	8,015	7,884
78028	Kerrville	(512)	15,276	12,672
75662	Kilgore	(214)	10,968	9,495
76541	Killeen	(817)	46,296	35,507
78363	Kingsville	(512)	28,808	28,915
78219	Kirby	(512)	6,385	3,238
78236	Lackland(u)	(512)	NA	19,141
77566	Lake Jackson	(713)	19,102	13,376
77568	La Marque	(713)	15,372	16,131
79631	Lamesa	(806)	11,790	11,559
76550	Lampasas	(512)	6,165	5,922
75146	Lancaster	(214)	14,807	10,522
77571	La Porte	(713)	14,062	7,149
78040	Laredo	(512)	91,449	69,024
77573	League City	(713)	16,578	10,818
78238	Leon Valley	(512)	8,951	2,487
79336	Levelland	(806)	13,809	11,445
75067	Lewisville	(214)	24,273	9,264
77575	Liberty	(713)	7,945	5,591
79339	Littlefield	(806)	7,409	6,738
78233	Live Oak	(512)	8,183	2,779
78644	Lockhart	(512)	7,953	6,489
75601	Longview	(214)	62,762	45,547
*79408	Lubbock	(806)	173,979	149,101
77901	Lufkin	(713)	28,562	23,049
78648	Luling	(512)	5,039	4,719
78501	McAllen	(512)	67,042	37,636

ZIP code	Place		1980	1970
75069	McKinney	(214)	16,249	15,193
76063	Mansfield	(817)	8,092	3,658
76661	Marlin	(817)	7,099	6,351
75670	Marshall	(214)	24,921	22,937
78368	Mathis	(512)	5,667	5,351
78570	Mercedes	(512)	11,851	9,355
75149	Mesquite	(214)	67,053	55,131
76667	Mexia	(214)	7,094	5,943
79701	Midland	(915)	70,525	59,463
76067	Mineral Wells	(817)	14,468	18,411
78572	Mission	(512)	22,589	13,043
77459	Missouri City	(713)	24,533	4,136
79756	Monahans	(915)	8,397	8,333
75455	Mount Pleasant	(214)	11,003	9,459
75961	Nacogdoches	(713)	27,149	22,544
77868	Navasota	(713)	5,971	5,111
77627	Nederland	(713)	16,855	16,810
78130	New Braunfels	(512)	22,402	17,859
76118	North Richland Hills	(817)	30,592	16,514
*79760	Odessa	(915)	90,027	78,380
77630	Orange	(713)	23,628	24,457
75801	Palestine	(214)	15,948	14,525
79065	Pampa	(806)	21,396	21,726
75460	Paris	(214)	25,498	23,441
*77501	Pasadena	(713)	112,560	89,957
77581	Pearland	(713)	13,248	6,444
78061	Pearsall	(512)	7,383	5,545
79772	Pecos	(915)	12,855	12,682
79070	Perryton	(806)	7,991	7,810
78577	Pharr	(512)	21,381	15,829
79072	Plainview	(806)	22,187	19,096
75074	Plano	(214)	72,331	17,872
78064	Pleasanton	(512)	6,346	5,407
77640	Port Arthur	(713)	61,195	57,371
78374	Portland	(512)	12,023	7,302
77979	Port Lavaca	(512)	10,911	10,491
77651	Port Neches	(713)	13,944	10,894
78580	Raymondville	(512)	9,493	7,987
75080	Richardson	(214)	72,496	48,405
76118	Richland Hills	(817)	7,977	8,865
77469	Richmond	(713)	9,692	5,777
78582	Rio Grande City(u)	(512)	NA	5,676
77019	River Oaks	(817)	6,890	8,193
76701	Robinson	(817)	6,074	3,807
78380	Robstown	(512)	12,100	11,217
76567	Rockdale	(512)	5,611	4,655
75087	Rockwall	(214)	5,939	3,121
77471	Rosenberg	(713)	17,995	12,098
78664	Round Rock	(512)	11,812	2,811
75088	Rowlett	(214)	7,522	2,243
76179	Saginaw	(817)	5,736	2,382
76901	San Angelo	(915)	73,240	63,884
*78284	San Antonio	(512)	785,410	654,153
78586	San Benito	(512)	17,988	15,176
78384	San Diego	(512)	5,225	4,490
78589	San Juan	(512)	7,608	5,070
78666	San Marcos	(512)	23,420	18,860
77550	Santa Fe	(713)	5,413	...
78154	Schertz	(512)	7,262	4,061
75159	Seagoville	(214)	7,304	4,390
78155	Seguin	(512)	17,854	15,934
79360	Seminole	(915)	6,080	5,007
75090	Sherman	(214)	30,413	29,061
77656	Silsbee	(713)	7,684	7,271
78387	Sinton	(512)	6,044	5,563
79364	Slaton	(806)	6,804	6,583
79549	Snyder	(915)	12,705	11,171
77587	South Houston	(713)	13,293	11,527
76401	Stephenville	(214)	11,881	9,277
77478	Sugar Land	(713)	8,826	3,318
75482	Sulphur Springs	(214)	12,804	10,642
79556	Sweetwater	(915)	12,242	12,020
76574	Taylor	(512)	10,619	9,616
76501	Temple	(817)	42,483	33,431
75160	Terrell	(214)	13,225	14,182
75501	Texarkana	(214)	31,271	30,497
77590	Texas City	(713)	41,403	38,908
...	The Colony	(817)	11,586	...
79088	Tulia	(806)	5,033	5,294
75701	Tyler	(214)	70,508	57,770
78148	Universal City	(512)	10,720	7,613
76308	University Park	(214)	22,254	23,498
78801	Uvalde	(512)	14,178	10,764
76384	Vernon	(817)	12,695	11,454
77901	Victoria	(512)	50,695	41,349
77662	Vidor	(713)	12,117	9,738
*76701	Waco	(817)	101,261	95,326
76148	Watauga	(817)	10,284	3,778
75165	Waxahachie	(214)	14,624	13,452
76086	Weatherford	(817)	12,049	11,750
78596	Weslaco	(512)	19,331	15,313
77005	West University Place	(713)	12,010	13,317
77488	Wharton	(713)	9,033	7,881
76108	White Settlement	(817)	13,508	13,449
*76307	Wichita Falls	(817)	94,201	96,265
78239	Windcrest	(512)	5,332	3,371
76710	Woodway	(817)	7,091	4,819
77995	Yoakum	(512)	6,148	5,755

Utah (801)

ZIP code	Place	1980	1970
84003	American Fork	12,417	7,713
84010	Bountiful	32,877	27,751
84302	Brigham City	15,596	14,007
84720	Cedar City	10,972	8,946
84014	Centerville	8,069	3,268
84015	Clearfield	17,982	13,316
84015	Clinton	5,777	1,768
84121	Cottonwood(u)	NA	8,431
84020	Draper	5,530	...
84109	East Millcreek(u)	NA	26,579
84119	Granger-Hunter(u)	NA	9,029
84106	Granite Park(u)	NA	9,573
84117	Holladay(u)	NA	23,014
84037	Kaysville	9,811	6,192
84118	Kearns(u)	NA	17,247
84041	Layton	22,862	13,603
84043	Lehi	6,848	4,659
84321	Logan	26,844	22,333
84044	Magna(u)	NA	5,509
84047	Midvale	10,144	7,840
84532	Moab	5,333	4,793
84117	Mount Olympus(u)	NA	5,909
84107	Murray	25,750	21,206
84404	North Ogden	9,309	5,257
84054	North Salt Lake	5,548	2,143
*84401	Ogden	64,407	69,478
84057	Orem	52,399	25,729
84651	Payson	8,246	4,501
84062	Pleasant Grove	10,669	5,327
84501	Price	9,086	6,218
84601	Provo	73,907	53,131
84701	Richfield	5,482	4,471
84065	Riverton	7,293	2,820
84067	Roy	19,694	14,356
84770	St. George	11,350	7,097
*84101	Salt Lake City	163,033	175,885
84070	Sandy City	51,022	6,438
84065	South Jordan	7,492	2,942
84403	South Ogden	11,366	9,991
84115	South Salt Lake	10,561	7,810
84660	Spanish Fork	9,825	7,284
84663	Springville	12,101	8,790
84015	Sunset	5,733	6,268
84074	Tooele	14,335	12,539
84078	Vernal	6,600	3,908
84403	Washington Terrace	8,212	7,241
84084	West Jordan	26,794	4,221
74070	White City(u)	NA	6,402

Vermont (802)

See Note on Page 207

ZIP code	Place	1980	1970
05641	Barre	9,824	10,209
.....	*Barre*	7,090	6,509
05201	*Bennington*	15,815	14,586
.....	Bennington	NA	7,950
05301	Brattleboro Center(u)	NA	9,055
.....	*Brattleboro*	11,886	12,239
05401	Burlington	37,712	38,633
05446	*Colchester*	12,629	8,776
05451	*Essex*	14,392	10,951
05452	Essex Junction	7,033	6,511
05047	*Hartford*	NA	6,477
05753	*Middlebury*	7,574	6,532
05602	Montpelier	8,241	8,609
05701	Rutland	18,436	19,293
05478	St. Albans	7,308	8,082
05819	*St. Johnsbury*	7,938	8,409
05401	*South Burlington*	10,679	10,032
05156	Springfield Center(u)	NA	5,632
.....	*Springfield*	10,190	10,063
05404	Winooski	6,318	7,309

Virginia

ZIP code	Place		1980	1970
*22313	Alexandria	(703)	103,217	110,927
22003	Annandale(u)	(703)	NA	27,405
*22210	Arlington(u)	(703)	NA	174,284
22041	Bailey's Crossroads(u)	(703)	NA	7,295
24523	Bedford	(703)	5,991	6,011
22307	Belleview(u)	(703)	NA	8,299
24060	Blacksburg	(703)	30,638	9,384
24605	Bluefield	(703)	5,946	5,286
23235	Bon Air(u)	(804)	NA	10,771
24201	Bristol	(703)	19,042	14,857
24416	Buena Vista	(703)	6,717	6,425
*22906	Charlottesville	(804)	45,010	38,880
*23320	Chesapeake	(804)	114,226	89,580
23831	Chester(u)	(804)	NA	5,556
24073	Christiansburg	(703)	10,345	7,857
24422	Clifton Forge	(703)	5,046	5,501
24078	Collinsville(u)	(703)	NA	6,015
23834	Colonial Heights	(804)	16,509	15,097
24426	Covington	(703)	9,063	10,060
22701	Culpeper	(703)	6,621	6,056
22191	Dale City(u)	(703)	NA	13,857
24541	Danville	(804)	45,642	46,391
22030	Fairfax	(703)	19,390	22,727
*22046	Falls Church	(703)	9,515	10,772
23901	Farmville	(804)	6,067	4,331
22060	Fort Belvoir(u)	(703)	NA	14,591

ZIP code	Place		1980	1970
22308	Fort Hunt(u)	(703)	NA	10,415
23801	Fort Lee(u)	(804)	NA	12,435
23851	Franklin	(804)	7,308	6,880
22401	Fredericksburg	(703)	15,322	14,450
22630	Front Royal	(703)	11,126	8,211
24333	Galax	(703)	6,524	6,278
22306	Groveton(u)	(703)	NA	11,761
*23360	Hampton	(804)	122,617	120,779
22801	Harrisonburg	(703)	19,671	14,605
22070	Herndon	(703)	11,449	4,301
23075	Highland Springs(u)	(804)	NA	7,345
23860	Hopewell	(804)	23,397	23,471
22303	Huntington(u)	(703)	NA	5,559
22042	Jefferson(u)	(804)	NA	25,432
22041	Lake Barcroft(u)	(703)	NA	11,605
23228	Lakeside(u)	(804)	NA	11,137
22075	Leesburg	(703)	8,357	4,821
24450	Lexington	(703)	7,292	7,597
22312	Lincoln(u)	(703)	NA	10,761
22030	Long Branch(u)	(703)	NA	21,634
*24505	Lynchburg	(804)	66,743	54,083
22110	Manassas	(703)	15,438	9,164
22110	Manassas Park	(703)	6,524	6,844
22030	Mantua(u)	(703)	NA	6,911
24354	Marion	(703)	7,029	8,158
24112	Martinsville	(703)	18,149	19,653
22101	McLean(u)	(703)	NA	17,698
23111	Merchanicsville(u)	(804)	NA	5,189
*23607	Newport News	(804)	144,903	138,177
23501	Norfolk	(804)	266,979	307,951
22151	North Springfield(u)	(703)	NA	8,631
23803	Petersburg	(804)	41,055	36,103
23662	Poquoson	(804)	8,726	5,441
*23705	Portsmouth	(804)	104,577	110,963
24301	Pulaski	(703)	10,106	10,279
22134	Quantico Station(u)	(703)	NA	6,213
24141	Radford	(703)	13,225	11,596
22070	Reston(u)	(703)	NA	5,723
24641	Richlands	(703)	5,796	4,843
*23232	Richmond	(804)	219,214	249,332
*24001	Roanoke	(703)	100,427	92,115
22310	Rose Hill(u)	(703)	NA	14,492
24153	Salem	(703)	23,958	21,982
22044	Seven Corners(u)	(703)	NA	5,590
24592	South Boston	(804)	7,093	6,889
*22150	Springfield	(703)	NA	11,613
24401	Staunton	(703)	21,857	24,504
22170	Sterling Park(u)	(703)	NA	8,321
23434	Suffolk	(804)	47,621	9,858
22180	Vienna	(703)	15,469	17,146
24179	Vinton	(703)	8,027	6,347
*23458	Virginia Beach	(804)	262,199	172,106
22980	Waynesboro	(703)	15,329	16,707
22152	West Springfield(u)	(703)	NA	14,143
23185	Williamsburg	(804)	9,870	9,069
22601	Winchester	(703)	20,217	14,643
22191	Woodbridge-Marumsco(u)	(703)	NA	25,412
24382	Wytheville	(703)	7,135	6,069

Washington

ZIP code	Place		1980	1970
98520	Aberdeen	(206)	18,739	18,489
98221	Anacortes	(206)	9,013	7,701
98002	Auburn	(206)	26,417	21,653
*98009	Bellevue	(206)	73,903	61,196
98225	Bellingham	(206)	45,794	39,375
98390	Bonney Lake	(206)	5,328	2,700
98011	Bothell	(206)	7,943	5,420
98310	Bremerton	(206)	36,208	35,307
98607	Camas	(206)	5,681	5,790
98531	Centralia	(206)	10,809	10,054
98532	Chehalis	(206)	6,100	5,727
99004	Cheney	(509)	7,630	6,358
99403	Clarkston	(509)	6,903	6,312
99324	College Place	(509)	5,771	4,510
98188	Des Moines	(206)	7,378	3,951
99213	Dishman(u)	(509)	NA	9,079
98020	Edmonds	(206)	27,526	23,684
98926	Ellensburg	(509)	11,752	13,568
98022	Enumclaw	(206)	5,427	4,703
*98823	Ephrata	(509)	5,359	5,255
*98201	Everett	(206)	54,413	53,622
99011	Fairchild(u)	(509)	NA	6,754
98466	Fircrest	(206)	5,477	5,651
98433	Fort Lewis(u)	(206)	NA	38,054
98930	Grandview	(509)	5,615	3,605
98550	Hoquiam	(206)	9,719	10,466
98027	Issaquah	(206)	5,536	4,313
98626	Kelso	(206)	11,129	10,296
99336	Kennewick	(509)	34,397	15,212
98031	Kent	(206)	23,152	17,711
98033	Kirkland	(206)	18,779	14,970
98503	Lacey	(206)	13,940	9,696
98499	Lakes District(u)	(206)	NA	48,195
98632	Longview	(206)	31,052	28,373
98036	Lynnwood	(206)	21,937	17,381
98270	Marysville	(206)	5,080	4,343
98438	McChord(u)	(206)	NA	6,515
98040	Mercer Island	(206)	21,522	19,047
98837	Moses Lake	(509)	10,629	10,310
98043	Mountlake Terrace	(206)	16,534	16,600
98273	Mount Vernon	(206)	13,009	6,804
98277	Oak Harbor	(206)	12,271	9,167
*98501	Olympia	(206)	27,447	23,296
99214	Opportunity(u)	(509)	NA	16,604
98444	Parkland(u)	(206)	NA	21,012
99301	Pasco	(509)	17,944	13,920
98362	Port Angeles	(206)	17,311	16,367
98368	Port Townsend	(206)	6,067	5,241
99163	Pullman	(509)	23,579	20,509
98371	Puyallup	(206)	18,251	14,742
98052	Redmond	(206)	23,318	11,020
98055	Renton	(206)	30,612	25,878
99352	Richland	(509)	33,578	26,290
*98109	Seattle	(206)	493,846	530,831
98284	Sedro Woolley	(206)	6,110	4,598
98584	Shelton	(206)	7,629	6,515
98290	Snohomish	(206)	5,294	5,174
98387	Spanaway(u)	(206)	NA	5,768
*99210	Spokane	(509)	171,300	170,516
98944	Sunnyside	(509)	9,225	6,751
*98402	Tacoma	(206)	158,501	154,407
98948	Toppenish	(509)	6,517	5,744
99268	Town and Country(u)	(509)	NA	6,484
98502	Tumwater	(206)	6,705	5,373
98406	University Place(u)	(206)	NA	13,230
*98660	Vancouver	(206)	42,834	41,859
99362	Walla Walla	(509)	25,618	23,619
98801	Wenatchee	(509)	17,257	16,912
*98901	Yakima	(509)	49,826	45,588

West Virginia (304)

ZIP code	Place	1980	1970
25801	Beckley	20,492	19,884
24701	Bluefield	16,060	15,921
26330	Bridgeport	6,604	4,777
26201	Buckhannon	6,820	7,261
*25301	Charleston	63,968	71,505
26301	Clarksburg	22,371	24,864
25064	Dunbar	9,285	9,151
26241	Elkins	8,536	8,287
26554	Fairmont	23,863	26,093
26354	Grafton	6,845	6,433
*25701	Huntington	63,684	74,315
26726	Keyser	6,569	6,586
25401	Martinsburg	13,063	14,626
26505	Morgantown	27,605	29,431
26041	Moundsville	12,419	13,560
26155	New Martinsville	7,109	6,528
25143	Nitro	8,074	8,019
25901	Oak Hill	7,120	4,738
26101	Parkersburg	39,967	44,208
25550	Point Pleasant	5,682	6,122
24740	Princeton	7,493	7,253
25177	St. Albans	12,402	14,356
25303	South Charleston	15,968	16,333
26105	Vienna	11,618	11,549
26062	Weirton	24,736	27,131
26452	Weston	6,250	7,323
26003	Wheeling	43,070	48,188
25661	Williamson	5,219	5,831

Wisconsin

ZIP code	Place		1980	1970
54301	Allouez(u)	(414)	NA	13,753
54409	Antigo	(715)	8,653	9,005
54911	Appleton	(414)	59,032	56,377
54806	Ashland	(715)	9,115	9,615
54304	Ashwaubenon	(414)	14,486	9,323
53913	Baraboo	(608)	8,081	7,931
53916	Beaver Dam	(414)	14,149	14,265
53511	Beloit	(608)	35,207	35,729
54923	Berlin	(414)	5,478	5,338
53005	Brookfield	(414)	34,035	31,761
53209	Brown Deer	(414)	12,921	12,582
53105	Burlington	(414)	8,385	7,479
53012	Cedarburg	(414)	9,005	7,697
54729	Chippewa Falls	(715)	11,845	12,351
53110	Cudahy	(414)	19,547	22,078
53115	Delavan	(414)	5,684	5,526
54115	De Pere	(414)	14,892	13,309
54701	Eau Claire	(715)	51,509	44,619
53122	Elm Grove	(414)	6,735	7,201
54935	Fond Du Lac	(414)	35,863	35,515
53538	Fort Atkinson	(414)	9,785	9,164
53217	Fox Point	(414)	7,649	7,939
53132	Franklin	(414)	16,871	12,247
53022	Germantown	(414)	10,729	6,974
53209	Glendale	(414)	13,882	13,426
53024	Grafton	(414)	8,381	5,998
*54305	Green Bay	(414)	87,899	87,809
53129	Greendale	(414)	16,928	15,089
53220	Greenfield	(414)	31,467	24,424
53130	Hales Corners	(414)	7,110	7,771
53027	Hartford	(414)	7,046	6,499
53029	Hartland	(414)	5,559	2,763
54303	Howard	(414)	8,240	4,911
54016	Hudson	(715)	5,434	5,049
53545	Janesville	(608)	51,071	46,426
53549	Jefferson	(414)	5,647	5,429
54130	Kaukauna	(414)	11,310	11,308
53140	Kenosha	(414)	77,685	78,805
54136	Kimberly	(414)	5,881	6,131
54601	La Crosse	(608)	48,347	50,286

ZIP code	Place		1980	1970
53147	Lake Geneva	(414)	5,607	4,890
54140	Little Chute	(414)	7,907	5,522
*53701	Madison	(608)	170,616	171,809
54220	Manitowoc	(414)	32,547	33,430
54143	Marinette	(715)	11,965	12,696
54449	Marshfield	(715)	18,290	15,619
54952	Menasha	(414)	14,728	14,836
53051	Menomonee Falls	(414)	27,845	31,697
54751	Menomonie	(414)	12,769	11,112
53092	Mequon	(414)	16,193	12,150
54452	Merrill	(715)	9,578	9,502
53562	Middleton	(608)	11,779	8,246
*53203	Milwaukee	(414)	636,212	717,372
53716	Monona	(608)	8,809	10,420
53566	Monroe	(608)	10,027	8,654
53150	Muskego	(414)	15,277	11,573
54956	Neenah	(414)	23,272	22,902
53151	New Berlin	(414)	30,529	26,910
54961	New London	(414)	6,210	5,801
53154	Oak Creek	(414)	16,932	13,928
53066	Oconomowoc	(414)	9,909	8,741
54650	Onalaska	(608)	9,249	4,909
54901	Oshkosh	(414)	49,678	53,082
53511	Perry Go Place(u)	(608)	NA	5,912
53818	Platteville	(608)	9,580	9,599
54467	Plover	(715)	5,310	—
53073	Plymouth	(414)	6,027	5,810
53901	Portage	(608)	7,896	7,821
53074	Port Washington	(414)	8,612	8,752
53821	Prairie du Chien	(608)	5,859	5,540
*53401	Racine	(414)	85,725	95,162
53959	Reedsburg	(608)	5,038	4,585
54501	Rhinelander	(715)	7,873	8,218
54868	Rice Lake	(715)	7,691	7,278
54971	Ripon	(414)	7,111	7,053
54022	River Falls	(715)	9,036	7,238
53207	St. Francis	(414)	10,066	10,489
54166	Shawano	(715)	7,013	6,488
53081	Sheboygan	(414)	48,085	48,484
53085	Sheboygan Falls	(414)	5,253	4,771
53211	Shorewood	(414)	14,327	15,576
53172	South Milwaukee	(414)	21,069	23,297
54656	Sparta	(608)	6,934	6,258
54481	Stevens Point	(715)	22,970	23,479
53589	Stoughton	(608)	7,589	6,096
54235	Sturgeon Bay	(414)	8,847	6,776
53590	Sun Prairie	(608)	12,931	9,935
54880	Superior	(715)	29,571	32,237
54660	Tomah	(608)	7,204	5,647
54241	Two Rivers	(414)	13,354	13,732
53094	Watertown	(414)	18,113	15,683
53186	Waukesha	(414)	50,319	39,695
53963	Waupun	(414)	8,132	7,946
54401	Wausau	(715)	32,426	32,806
54401	Wausau West(u)	(715)	NA	6,399
53213	Wauwatosa	(414)	51,308	58,676
53214	West Allis	(414)	63,982	71,649
53095	West Bend	(414)	21,484	16,555
53217	Whitefish Bay	(414)	14,930	17,402
53190	Whitewater	(414)	11,520	12,038
54494	Wisconsin Rapids	(715)	17,995	18,587

Wyoming (307)

82601	Casper		51,016	39,361
82001	Cheyenne		47,283	41,254
82414	Cody		6,790	5,161
82633	Douglas		6,030	2,677
82930	Evanston		6,421	4,462
82716	Gillette		12,134	7,194
82335	Green River		12,807	4,196
82520	Lander		9,126	7,125
82070	Laramie		24,410	23,143
82435	Powell		5,310	4,807
82301	Rawlins		11,547	7,855
82501	Riverton		9,588	7,995
82901	Rock Springs		19,458	11,657
82801	Sheridan		15,146	10,856
82240	Torrington		5,441	4,237
82201	Wheatland		5,816	2,498
82401	Worland		6,391	5,055

Census and Areas of Counties and States

Source: U.S. Bureau of the Census
With names of county seats or court houses

Population figures listed below are final counts in the 1980 census, conducted on Apr. 1, 1980, for all counties and states. Figures are subject to change pending the outcome of various lawsuits dealing with the census counts.

County	Pop.	County Seat or court house	Land area sq. mi.
		Alabama	
	(67 counties, 50,708 sq. mi. land; pop., 3,890,061)		
Autauga	32,259	Prattville	599
Baldwin	78,440	Bay Minette	1,578
Barbour	24,756	Clayton	891
Bibb	15,723	Centreville	625
Blount	36,459	Oneonta	639
Bullock	10,596	Union Springs	615
Butler	21,680	Greenville	773
Calhoun	116,936	Anniston	611
Chambers	39,191	Lafayete	597
Cherokee	18,760	Centre	556
Chilton	30,612	Clanton	699
Choctaw	16,839	Butler	911
Clarke	27,702	Grove Hill	1,232
Clay	13,703	Ashland	603
Cleburne	12,595	Heflin	574
Coffee	38,533	Elba	677
Colbert	54,519	Tuscumbia	596
Conecuh	15,884	Evergreen	850
Coosa	11,377	Rockford	650
Covington	36,850	Andalusia	984
Crenshaw	14,110	Luverne	611
Cullman	61,642	Cullman	730
Dale	47,821	Ozark	559
Dallas	53,981	Selma	976
De Kalb	53,658	Fort Payne	778
Elmore	43,390	Wetumpka	624
Escambia	38,392	Brewton	962
Etowah	103,057	Gadsden	555
Fayette	18,809	Fayette	627
Franklin	28,350	Russellville	644
Geneva	24,253	Geneva	577
Greene	11,021	Eutaw	627
Hale	15,604	Greensboro	662
Henry	15,302	Abbeville	554
Houston	74,632	Dothan	575
Jackson	51,407	Scottsboro	1,079
Jefferson	671,197	Birmingham	1,115
Lamar	16,453	Vernon	605
Lauderdale	80,504	Florence	662
Lawrence	30,170	Moulton	685
Lee	76,283	Opelika	612
Limestone	46,005	Athens	546
Lowndes	13,253	Hayneville	715
Macon	26,829	Tuskegee	616
Madison	196,966	Huntsville	803
Marengo	25,047	Linden	978
Marion	30,041	Hamilton	743
Marshall	65,622	Guntersville	571
Mobile	364,379	Mobile	1,240
Monroe	22,651	Monroeville	1,032
Montgomery	197,038	Montgomery	790
Morgan	90,231	Decatur	570
Perry	15,012	Marion	734
Pickens	21,481	Carrollton	887
Pike	28,050	Troy	673
Randolph	20,075	Wedowee	581
Russell	47,356	Phenix City	627
St. Clair	41,205	Ashville & Pell City	640
Shelby	66,298	Columbiana	798
Sumter	16,908	Livingston	915
Talladega	73,826	Talladega	750
Tallapoosa	38,676	Dadeville	704
Tuscaloosa	137,473	Tuscaloosa	1,333
Walker	68,660	Jasper	805
Washington	16,821	Chatom	1,066
Wilcox	14,755	Camden	899
Winston	21,953	Double Springs	615

Alaska

(23 divisions, 566,432 sq. mi. land; pop., 400,481)

Census area	Pop.	Land area sq. mi.
Aleutian Islands	7,768	14,583
Anchorage Borough	173,017	927
Census division		
Bethel	10,999	19,642
Bristol Bay Borough	1,094	531
Dillingham	4,616	—
Fairbanks North Star Borough	53,983	7,074
Haines Borough	1,680	2,128
Juneau Borough	19,528	1,286
Kenai Peninsula Borough	25,282	12,474
Ketchikan Gateway Borough	11,316	1,345
Kobuk	4,831	42,978
Kodiak Island Borough	9,939	5,375
Matanuska-Susitna Borough	17,766	25,730
Nome	6,537	24,968
North Slope Borough	4,199	———
Prince of Wales-Outer Ketchikan	3,822	7,247
Sitka Borough	7,803	2,296
Skagway-Yakutat-Angoon	3,478	11,471
Southeast Fairbanks	5,770	17,713
Valdez Cordova	8,348	18,619

Census division	Pop.	Land area sq. mi.
Wade Hampton	4,665	16,770
Wrangell-Petersburg	6,167	6,178
Yukon-Koyukuk	7,873	73,053

Arizona

(14 counties, 113,417 sq. mi. land; pop. 2,717,866)

County	Pop.	County seat or court house	Land area sq. mi.
Apache	52,083	Saint Johns	11,171
Cochise	86,717	Bisbee	6,256
Coconino	74,947	Flagstaff	18,540
Gila	37,080	Globe	4,748
Graham	22,862	Safford	4,618
Greenlee	11,406	Clifton	1,879
Maricopa	1,508,030	Phoenix	9,155
Mohave	55,693	Kingman	13,217
Navajo	67,709	Holbrook	9,910
Pima	531,263	Tucson	9,240
Pinal	90,918	Florence	5,364
Santa Cruz	20,459	Nogales	1,246
Yavapai	68,145	Prescott	8,091
Yuma	90,554	Yuma	9,983

Arkansas

(75 counties, 51,945 sq. mi. land; pop. 2,285,513)

County	Pop.	County seat	Land area sq. mi.
Arkansas	24,175	DeWitt & Stuttgart	1,015
Ashley	26,538	Hamburg	928
Baxter	27,409	Mountain Home	537
Benton	78,115	Bentonville	851
Boone	26,067	Harrison	586
Bradley	13,803	Warren	651
Calhoun	6,079	Hampton	629
Carroll	16,203	Berryville and Eureka Sp.	626
Chicot	17,793	Lake Village	643
Clark	23,326	Arkadelphia	878
Clay	20,616	Corning; Piggott	639
Cleburne	16,909	Heber Springs	554
Cleveland	7,868	Rison	601
Columbia	26,644	Magnolia	768
Conway	19,505	Morrilton	561
Craighead	63,218	Jonesboro and Lake City	716
Crawford	36,892	Van Buren	596
Crittenden	49,097	Marion	608
Cross	20,434	Wynne	625
Dallas	10,515	Fordyce	672
Desha	19,760	Arkansas City	736
Drew	17,910	Monticello	832
Faulkner	46,192	Conway	641
Franklin	14,705	Charleston and Ozark	613
Fulton	9,975	Salem	608
Garland	69,916	Hot Spgs. Nat'l Pk.	658
Grant	13,008	Sheridan	631
Greene	30,744	Paragould	579
Hempstead	23,635	Hope	726
Hot Spring	26,819	Malvern	621
Howard	13,459	Nashville	569
Independence	30,147	Batesville	752
Izard	10,768	Melbourne	574
Jackson	21,646	Newport	629
Jefferson	90,718	Pine Bluff	873
Johnson	17,423	Clarksville	673
Lafayette	10,213	Lewisville	523
Lawrence	18,447	Walnut Ridge	590
Lee	15,539	Marianna	608
Lincoln	13,369	Star City	563
Little River	13,952	Ashdown	486
Logan	20,144	Booneville & Paris	718
Lonoke	34,518	Lonoke	796
Madison	11,373	Huntsville	832
Marion	11,334	Yellville	584
Miller	37,766	Texarkana	623
Mississippi	59,517	Blytheville and Osceola	904
Monroe	14,052	Clarendon	607
Montgomery	7,771	Mount Ida	775
Nevada	11,097	Prescott	616
Newton	7,756	Jasper	822
Ouachita	30,541	Camden	736
Perry	7,266	Perryville	551
Phillips	34,772	Helena	686
Pike	10,373	Murfreesboro	600
Poinsett	27,032	Harrisburg	760
Polk	17,007	Mena	859
Pope	39,003	Russellville	812
Prairie	10,140	Des Arc and De Valls Bluff	661
Pulaski	340,613	Little Rock	765
Randolph	16,834	Pocahontas	647
St. Francis	30,858	Forrest City	635
Saline	52,881	Benton	724
Scott	9,685	Waldron	898
Searcy	8,847	Marshall	664
Sebastian	94,930	Fort Smith; Greenwood	527
Sevier	14,060	De Queen	522
Sharp	14,607	Ash Flat	581
Stone	9,022	Mountain View	608
Union	49,988	El Dorado	1,050
Van Buren	13,357	Clinton	699

Washington	99,735	Fayetteville	958
White	50,835	Searcy	1,041
Woodruff	11,222	Augusta	591
Yell	17,026	Danville and Dardanelle	929

California

(58 counties, 156,361 sq. mi. land; pop. 23,668,562)

County	Pop.	County seat	Land area sq. mi.
Alameda	1,105,379	Oakland	733
Alpine	1,097	Markleeville	727
Amador	19,314	Jackson	583
Butte	143,851	Oroville	1,645
Calaveras	20,710	San Andreas	1,024
Colusa	12,791	Colusa	1,152
Contra Costa	657,252	Martinez	735
Del Norte	18,217	Crescent City	1,007
El Dorado	85,812	Placerville	1,715
Fresno	515,013	Fresno	5,966
Glenn	21,350	Willows	1,314
Humboldt	108,024	Eureka	3,586
Imperial	92,110	El Centro	4,241
Inyo	17,895	Independence	10,130
Kern	403,089	Bakersfield	8,152
Kings	73,738	Hanford	1,396
Lake	36,366	Lakeport	1,261
Lassen	21,661	Susanville	4,561
Los Angeles	7,477,657	Los Angeles	4,069
Madera	63,116	Madera	2,145
Marin	222,952	San Rafael	520
Mariposa	11,108	Mariposa	1,453
Mendocino	66,738	Ukiah	3,511
Merced	134,560	Merced	1,958
Modoc	8,610	Alturas	4,097
Mono	8,577	Bridgeport	3,027
Monterey	290,444	Salinas	3,324
Napa	99,199	Napa	787
Nevada	51,645	Nevada City	973
Orange	1,931,570	Santa Ana	782
Placer	117,247	Auburn	1,431
Plumas	17,340	Quincy	2,566
Riverside	663,923	Riverside	7,176
Sacramento	783,381	Sacramento	975
San Benito	25,005	Hollister	1,396
San Bernardino	893,157	San Bernardino	20,117
San Diego	1,861,846	San Diego	4,261
San Francisco	678,974	San Francisco	45
San Joaquin	347,342	Stockton	1,412
San Luis Obispo	155,345	San Luis Obispo	3,183
San Mateo	588,164	Redwood City	447
Santa Barbara	298,660	Santa Barbara	2,737
Santa Clara	1,295,071	San Jose	1,300
Santa Cruz	188,141	Santa Cruz	440
Shasta	115,715	Redding	3,788
Sierra	3,073	Downieville	958
Siskiyou	39,732	Yreka	6,262
Solano	235,203	Fairfield	823
Sonoma	299,827	Santa Rosa	1,604
Stanislaus	265,902	Modesto	1,511
Sutter	52,246	Yuba City	603
Tehama	38,888	Red Bluff	2,982
Trinity	11,858	Weaverville	3,173
Tulare	245,751	Visalia	4,812
Tuolumne	33,920	Sonora	2,252
Ventura	529,899	Ventura	1,863
Yolo	113,374	Woodland	1,028
Yuba	49,733	Marysville	639

Colorado

(63 counties, 103,766 sq. mi. land; pop. 2,888,834)

County	Pop.	County seat	Land area sq. mi.
Adams	245,944	Brighton	1,237
Alamosa	11,799	Alamosa	719
Arapahoe	293,621	Littleton	797
Archuleta	3,664	Pagosa Springs	1,364
Baca	5,419	Springfield	2,563
Bent	5,945	Las Animas	1,519
Boulder	189,625	Boulder	748
Chaffee	13,227	Salida	1,038
Cheyenne	2,153	Cheyenne Wells	1,772
Clear Creek	7,308	Georgetown	394
Conejos	7,794	Conejos	1,268
Costilla	3,071	San Luis	1,213
Crowley	2,988	Ordway	802
Custer	1,528	Westcliffe	737
Delta	21,225	Delta	1,154
Denver	491,396	Denver	95
Dolores	1,658	Dove Creek	1,026
Douglas	25,153	Castle Rock	843
Eagle	13,171	Eagle	1,681
Elbert	6,850	Kiowa	1,864
El Paso	309,424	Colorado Springs	2,157
Fremont	28,676	Canon City	1,561
Garfield	22,514	Glenwood Springs	2,996
Gilpin	2,441	Central City	148
Grand	7,475	Hot Sulphur Springs	1,854
Gunnison	10,689	Gunnison	3,220
Hinsdale	408	Lake City	1,054
Huerfano	6,440	Walsenburg	1,574
Jackson	1,863	Walden	1,622
Jefferson	371,741	Golden	783
Kiowa	1,936	Eads	1,767
Kit Carson	7,599	Burlington	2,171

County	Pop.	County seat or court house	Land area sq. mi.
Lake	8,830	Leadville	379
La Plata	27,424	Durango	1,683
Larimer	149,184	Fort Collins	2,611
Las Animas	14,897	Trinidad	4,794
Lincoln	4,663	Hugo	2,593
Logan	19,800	Sterling	1,822
Mesa	81,530	Grand Junction	3,301
Mineral	804	Creede	921
Moffat	13,133	Craig	4,743
Montezuma	16,510	Cortez	2,094
Montrose	24,352	Montrose	2,238
Morgan	22,513	Fort Morgan	1,278
Otero	22,567	LaJunta	1,254
Ouray	1,925	Ouray	540
Park	5,333	Fairplay	2,162
Phillips	4,542	Holyoke	680
Pitkin	10,338	Aspen	973
Prowers	13,070	Lamar	1,621
Pueblo	125,972	Pueblo	2,405
Rio Blanco	6,255	Meeker	3,263
Rio Grande	10,511	Del Norte	915
Routt	13,404	Steamboat Springs	2,330
Saguache	3,935	Saguache	3,144
San Juan	833	Silverton	391
San Miguel	3,192	Telluride	1,283
Sedgwick	3,266	Julesburg	544
Summit	8,848	Breckenridge	604
Teller	8,034	Cripple Creek	553
Washington	5,304	Akron	2,526
Weld	123,438	Greeley	4,002
Yuma	9,682	Wray	2,379

Connecticut

(8 counties, 4,862 sq. mi. land; pop. 3,107,576)

County	Pop.	County seat	Land area
Fairfield	807,143	Bridgeport	626
Hartford	807,766	Hartford	739
Litchfield	156,769	Litchfield	925
Middlesex	129,017	Middletown	372
New Haven	761,337	New Haven	604
New London	238,409	Norwich	667
Tolland	114,823	Rockville	416
Windham	92,312	Putnam	514

Delaware

(3 counties, 1,982 sq. mi. land; pop. 595,225)

County	Pop.	County seat	Land area
Kent	98,219	Dover	594
New Castle	399,002	Wilmington	438
Sussex	98,004	Georgetown	950

District of Columbia

(61 sq. mi. land; pop. 637,651)

Florida

(67 counties, 54,090 sq. mi. land; pop. 9,739,992)

County	Pop.	County seat	Land area
Alachua	151,348	Gainesville	916
Baker	15,289	Macclenny	585
Bay	97,740	Panama City	747
Bradford	20,023	Starke	294
Brevard	272,959	Titusville	1,011
Broward	1,014,043	Fort Lauderdale	1,219
Calhoun	9,294	Blountstown	561
Charlotte	59,115	Punta Gorda	703
Citrus	54,703	Inverness	560
Clay	67,052	Green Cove Spgs.	593
Collier	85,791	Naples	2,006
Columbia	35,399	Lake City	784
Dade	1,625,979	Miami	2,042
De Soto	19,039	Arcadia	648
Dixie	7,751	Cross City	692
Duval	570,981	Jacksonville	766
Escambia	233,794	Pensacola	665
Flagler	10,913	Bunnell	487
Franklin	7,661	Apalachicola	536
Gadsden	41,565	Quincy	512
Gilchrist	5,767	Trenton	346
Glades	5,992	Moore Haven	753
Gulf	10,658	Port St. Joe	565
Hamilton	8,761	Jasper	514
Hardee	19,379	Wauchula	629
Hendry	18,599	La Belle	1,187
Hernando	44,469	Brooksville	484
Highlands	47,526	Sebring	997
Hillsborough	646,960	Tampa	1,038
Holmes	14,723	Bonifay	482
Indian River	59,896	Vero Beach	506
Jackson	39,154	Marianna	935
Jefferson	10,703	Monticello	605
Lafayette	4,035	Mayo	549
Lake	104,870	Tavares	961
Lee	205,266	Fort Myers	785
Leon	148,655	Tallahassee	670
Levy	19,870	Bronson	1,083
Liberty	4,260	Bristol	839
Madison	14,894	Madison	703
Manatee	148,442	Bradenton	743
Marion	122,488	Ocala	1,600
Martin	64,014	Stuart	556
Monroe	63,098	Key West	1,034
Nassau	32,894	Fernandina Beach	650
Okaloosa	109,920	Crestview	944
Okeechobee	20,264	Okeechobee	777
Orange	471,660	Orlando	910
Osceola	49,287	Kissimmee	1,313
Palm Beach	573,125	West Palm Beach	2,023
Pasco	194,123	Dade City	742
Pinellas	728,409	Clearwater	265
Polk	321,652	Bartow	1,858
Putnam	50,549	Palatka	779
St. Johns	51,303	Saint Augustine	605
St. Lucie	87,182	Fort Pierce	584
Santa Rosa	55,988	Milton	1,032
Sarasota	202,251	Sarasota	587
Seminole	179,752	Sanford	305
Sumter	24,272	Bushnell	555
Suwannee	22,287	Live Oak	686
Taylor	16,532	Perry	1,051
Union	10,166	Lake Butler	241
Volusia	258,762	De Land	1,062
Wakulla	10,887	Crawfordville	601
Walton	21,300	De Funiak Springs	1,053
Washington	14,509	Chipley	585

Georgia

(159 counties, 58,073 sq. mi. land; pop. 5,464,265)

County	Pop.	County seat	Land area
Appling	15,565	Baxley	513
Atkinson	6,141	Pearson	318
Bacon	9,379	Alma	293
Baker	3,808	Newton	355
Baldwin	34,686	Milledgeville	255
Banks	8,702	Homer	231
Barrow	21,293	Winder	171
Bartow	40,760	Cartersville	461
Ben Hill	16,000	Fitzgerald	255
Berrien	13,525	Nashville	468
Bibb	151,085	Macon	254
Bleckley	10,767	Cochran	219
Brantley	8,701	Nahunta	447
Brooks	15,255	Quitman	491
Bryan	10,175	Pembroke	443
Bulloch	35,785	Statesboro	685
Burke	19,349	Waynesboro	831
Butts	13,665	Jackson	185
Calhoun	5,717	Morgan	289
Camden	13,371	Woodbine	653
Candler	7,518	Metter	250
Carroll	56,346	Carrollton	495
Catoosa	36,991	Ringgold	167
Charlton	7,343	Folkston	796
Chatham	202,226	Savannah	445
Chattahoochee	21,732	Cusseta	253
Chattooga	21,856	Summerville	317
Cherokee	51,699	Canton	415
Clarke	74,498	Athens	116
Clay	3,553	Fort Gaines	200
Clayton	150,357	Jonesboro	149
Clinch	6,660	Homerville	797
Cobb	297,694	Marietta	343
Coffee	26,894	Douglas	612
Colquitt	35,376	Moultrie	563
Columbia	40,118	Appling	290
Cook	13,490	Adel	233
Coweta	39,268	Newnan	442
Crawford	7,684	Knoxville	315
Crisp	19,489	Cordele	292
Dade	12,318	Trenton	168
Dawson	4,774	Dawsonville	211
Decatur	25,495	Bainbridge	575
De Kalb	483,024	Decatur	269
Dodge	16,955	Eastman	498
Dooly	10,826	Vienna	395
Dougherty	100,978	Albany	324
Douglas	54,573	Douglasville	202
Early	13,158	Blakely	524
Echols	2,297	Statenville	425
Effingham	18,327	Springfield	480
Elbert	18,758	Elberton	358
Emanuel	20,795	Swainsboro	686
Evans	8,428	Claxton	186
Fannin	14,748	Blue Ridge	394
Fayette	29,043	Fayetteville	199
Floyd	79,800	Rome	514
Forsyth	27,958	Cumming	219
Franklin	15,185	Carnesville	263
Fulton	589,904	Atlanta	530
Gilmer	11,110	Ellijay	439
Glascock	2,382	Gibson	143
Glynn	54,981	Brunswick	412
Gordon	30,070	Calhoun	358
Grady	19,845	Cairo	466
Greene	11,391	Greensboro	403
Gwinnett	166,903	Lawrenceville	437
Habersham	25,020	Clarkesville	282
Hall	75,649	Gainesville	378
Hancock	9,466	Sparta	478
Haralson	18,422	Buchanan	285
Harris	15,464	Hamilton	465
Hart	18,585	Hartwell	231

County	Pop.	County seat or court house	Land area sq. mi.
Heard	6,520	Franklin	297
Henry	36,309	McDonough	331
Houston	77,605	Perry	380
Irwin	8,988	Ocilla	372
Jackson	25,343	Jefferson	346
Jasper	7,553	Monticello	373
Jeff Davis	11,473	Hazlehurst	331
Jefferson	18,403	Louisville	530
Jenkins	8,841	Millen	351
Johnson	8,660	Wrightsville	313
Jones	16,579	Gray	402
Lamar	12,215	Barnesville	181
Lanier	5,654	Lakeland	177
Laurens	36,990	Dublin	810
Lee	11,684	Leesburg	355
Liberty	37,583	Hinesville	514
Lincoln	6,949	Lincolnton	193
Long	4,524	Ludowici	402
Lowndes	67,972	Valdosta	508
Lumpkin	10,762	Dahlonega	292
McDuffie	18,546	Thomson	253
McIntosh	8,046	Darien	426
Macon	14,003	Oglethorpe	403
Madison	17,747	Danielsville	281
Marion	5,297	Buena Vista	365
Meriwether	21,229	Greenville	499
Miller	7,038	Colquitt	287
Mitchell	21,114	Camilla	510
Monroe	14,610	Forsyth	398
Montgomery	7,011	Mount Vernon	237
Morgan	11,572	Madison	356
Murray	19,685	Chatsworth	342
Muscogee	170,108	Columbus	220
Newton	34,489	Covington	271
Oconee	12,427	Watkinsville	186
Oglethorpe	8,929	Lexington	435
Paulding	26,042	Dallas	318
Peach	19,151	Fort Valley	151
Pickens	11,652	Jasper	225
Pierce	11,897	Blackshear	342
Pike	8,937	Zebulon	230
Polk	32,386	Cedartown	312
Pulaski	8,950	Hawkinsville	253
Putnam	10,295	Eatonton	339
Quitman	2,357	Georgetown	156
Rabun	10,466	Clayton	368
Randolph	9,599	Cuthbert	436
Richmond	181,629	Augusta	323
Rockdale	36,747	Conyers	128
Schley	3,433	Ellaville	162
Screven	14,043	Sylvania	651
Seminole	9,057	Donalsonville	246
Spalding	47,899	Griffin	201
Stephens	21,763	Toccoa	173
Stewart	5,896	Lumpkin	452
Sumter	29,360	Americus	488
Talbot	6,536	Talbotton	390
Taliaferro	2,032	Crawfordville	195
Tattnall	18,134	Reidsville	490
Taylor	7,902	Butler	403
Telfair	11,445	McRae	440
Terrell	12,017	Dawson	329
Thomas	38,098	Thomasville	541
Tift	32,862	Tifton	266
Toombs	22,592	Lyons	368
Towns	5,638	Hiawassee	166
Treutlen	6,087	Soperton	194
Troup	50,003	La Grange	415
Turner	9,510	Ashburn	293
Twiggs	9,354	Jeffersonville	364
Union	9,390	Blairsville	309
Upson	25,998	Thomaston	334
Walker	56,470	La Fayette	445
Walton	31,211	Monroe	330
Ware	37,180	Waycross	912
Warren	6,583	Warrenton	284
Washington	18,842	Sandersville	674
Wayne	20,750	Jesup	645
Webster	2,341	Preston	195
Wheeler	5,155	Alamo	306
White	10,120	Cleveland	243
Whitfield	65,780	Dalton	281
Wilcox	7,682	Abbeville	383
Wilkes	10,951	Washington	468
Wilkinson	10,368	Irwinton	458
Worth	18,064	Sylvester	579

Hawaii

(4 counties, 6,425 sq. mi. land; pop. 965,000)

Hawaii	92,053	Hilo	4,037
Honolulu	762,874	Honolulu	596
Kauai	39,082	Lihue	619
Maui*	70,991	Wailuku	1,173

*Includes population of Kalawao County (146).

Idaho

(44 counties, 82,677 sq. mi. land; pop. 943,935)

Ada	173,036	Boise	1,043
Adams	3,347	Council	1,371
Bannock	65,421	Pocatello	1,122
Bear Lake	6,931	Paris	984
Benewah	8,292	Saint Maries	788
Bingham	36,489	Blackfoot	2,084
Blaine	9,841	Hailey	2,647
Boise	2,999	Idaho City	1,910
Bonner	24,163	Sandpoint	1,733
Bonneville	65,980	Idaho Falls	1,836
Boundary	7,289	Bonners Ferry	1,275
Butte	3,342	Arco	2,239
Camas	818	Fairfield	1,054
Canyon	83,756	Caldwell	578
Caribou	8,695	Soda Springs	1,746
Cassia	19,427	Burley	2,544
Clark	798	Dubois	1,751
Clearwater	10,390	Orofino	2,521
Custer	3,385	Challis	4,929
Elmore	21,565	Mountain Home	3,048
Franklin	8,895	Preston	664
Fremont	10,813	Saint Anthony	1,864
Gem	11,972	Emmett	555
Gooding	11,874	Gooding	720
Idaho	14,769	Grangeville	8,516
Jefferson	15,304	Rigby	1,096
Jerome	14,840	Jerome	595
Kootenai	59,770	Coeur d'Alene	1,249
Latah	28,749	Moscow	1,090
Lemhi	7,460	Salmon	4,580
Lewis	4,118	Nezperce	476
Lincoln	3,436	Shoshone	1,203
Madison	19,480	Rexberg	473
Minidoka	19,718	Rupert	750
Nez Perce	33,220	Lewiston	844
Oneida	3,258	Malad City	1,191
Owyhee	8,272	Murphy	7,641
Payette	15,722	Payette	402
Power	6,844	American Falls	1,413
Shoshone	19,226	Wallace	2,609
Teton	2,897	Driggs	457
Twin Falls	52,927	Twin Falls	1,947
Valley	5,604	Cascade	3,676
Washington	8,803	Weiser	1,462

Illinois

(102 counties, 55,748 sq. mi. land; pop. 11,418,461)

Adams	71,622	Quincy	862
Alexander	12,264	Cairo	229
Bond	16,224	Greenville	378
Boone	28,630	Belvidere	283
Brown	5,411	Mount Sterling	306
Bureau	39,114	Princeton	866
Calhoun	5,867	Hardin	247
Carroll	18,779	Mount Carroll	456
Cass	15,084	Virginia	371
Champaign	168,392	Urbana	1,000
Christian	36,446	Taylorville	709
Clark	16,913	Marshall	505
Clay	15,283	Louisville	464
Clinton	32,617	Carlyle	434
Coles	52,992	Charleston	506
Cook	5,253,190	Chicago	954
Crawford	20,818	Robinson	443
Cumberland	11,062	Toledo	347
De Kalb	74,624	Sycamore	636
De Witt	18,108	Clinton	399
Douglas	19,774	Tuscola	420
Du Page	658,177	Wheaton	331
Edgar	21,725	Paris	628
Edwards	7,961	Albion	225
Effingham	30,944	Effingham	481
Fayette	22,167	Vandalia	703
Ford	15,265	Paxton	488
Franklin	43,201	Benton	434
Fulton	43,687	Lewiston	877
Gallatin	7,590	Shawneetown	328
Greene	16,661	Carrollton	543
Grundy	30,582	Morris	432
Hamilton	9,172	McLeansboro	435
Hancock	23,877	Carthage	797
Hardin	5,383	Elizabethtown	183
Henderson	9,114	Oquawka	376
Henry	57,968	Cambridge	826
Iroquois	32,976	Watseka	1,122
Jackson	61,522	Murphysboro	605
Jasper	11,318	Newton	495
Jefferson	36,354	Mount Vernon	573
Jersey	20,538	Jerseyville	376
Jo Daviess	23,520	Galena	606
Johnson	9,624	Vienna	345
Kane	278,405	Geneva	520
Kankakee	102,926	Kankakee	678
Kendall	37,202	Yorkville	320
Knox	61,607	Galesburg	728
Lake	440,372	Waukegan	457
La Salle	109,139	Ottawa	1,150
Lawrence	17,807	Lawrenceville	374

County	Pop.	County seat or court house	Land area sq. mi.
Lee	36,328	Dixon	728
Livingston	41,381	Pontiac	1,043
Logan	31,802	Lincoln	622
McDonough	37,236	Macomb	582
McHenry	147,724	Woodstock	610
McLean	119,149	Bloomington	1,173
Macon	131,375	Decatur	578
Macoupin	49,384	Carlinville	872
Madison	247,671	Edwardsville	733
Marion	43,523	Salem	579
Marshall	14,479	Lacon	391
Mason	19,492	Havana	541
Massac	14,990	Metropolis	245
Menard	11,700	Petersburg	312
Mercer	19,286	Aledo	556
Monroe	20,117	Waterloo	382
Montgomery	31,686	Hillsboro	705
Morgan	37,502	Jacksonville	561
Moultrie	14,546	Sullivan	326
Ogle	46,338	Oregon	758
Peoria	200,466	Peoria	623
Perry	21,714	Pinckneyville	439
Piatt	16,581	Monticello	437
Pike	18,896	Pittsfield	828
Pope	4,404	Golconda	381
Pulaski	8,840	Mound City	204
Putnam	6,085	Hennepin	160
Randolph	35,566	Chester	594
Richland	17,587	Olney	364
Rock Island	165,968	Rock Island	424
St. Clair	265,469	Belleville	673
Saline	27,360	Harrisburg	383
Sangamon	176,089	Springfield	879
Schuyler	8,365	Rushville	434
Scott	6,142	Winchester	251
Shelby	23,923	Shelbyville	752
Stark	7,389	Toulon	291
Stephenson	49,536	Freeport	568
Tazewell	132,078	Pekin	652
Union	16,851	Jonesboro	416
Vermilion	95,222	Danville	899
Wabash	13,713	Mt. Carmel	222
Warren	21,943	Monmouth	541
Washington	15,472	Nashville	564
Wayne	18,059	Fairfield	715
White	17,864	Carmi	502
Whiteside	65,970	Morrison	687
Will	324,460	Joliet	847
Williamson	56,538	Marion	429
Winnebago	250,884	Rockford	519
Woodford	33,320	Eureka	528

Indiana

(92 counties; 36,097 sq. mi. land; pop. 5,490,179)

County	Pop.	County seat or court house	Land area sq. mi.
Adams	29,619	Decatur	345
Allen	294,335	Fort Wayne	671
Bartholomew	65,088	Columbus	402
Benton	10,218	Fowler	409
Blackford	15,570	Hartford City	167
Boone	36,446	Lebanon	427
Brown	12,377	Nashville	319
Carroll	19,722	Delphi	374
Cass	40,936	Logansport	415
Clark	88,838	Jeffersonville	384
Clay	24,862	Brazil	364
Clinton	31,545	Frankfort	407
Crawford	9,820	English	312
Daviess	27,836	Washington	430
Dearborn	34,291	Lawrenceburg	306
Decatur	23,841	Greensburg	370
DeKalb	33,606	Auburn	366
Delaware	128,587	Muncie	396
Dubois	34,238	Jasper	433
Elkhart	137,330	Goshen	468
Fayette	28,272	Connersville	215
Floyd	61,169	New Albany	149
Fountain	19,033	Covington	397
Franklin	19,612	Brookville	394
Fulton	19,335	Rochester	368
Gibson	33,156	Princeton	498
Grant	80,934	Marion	421
Greene	30,416	Bloomfield	549
Hamilton	82,381	Noblesville	401
Hancock	43,939	Greenfield	305
Harrison	27,276	Corydon	479
Hendricks	69,804	Danville	417
Henry	53,336	New Castle	400
Howard	86,896	Kokomo	293
Huntington	35,596	Huntington	369
Jackson	36,523	Brownstown	520
Jasper	26,138	Rensselaer	562
Jay	23,239	Portland	386
Jefferson	30,419	Madison	366
Jennings	22,854	Vernon	377
Johnson	77,240	Franklin	315
Knox	41,838	Vincennes	516
Kosciusko	59,555	Warsaw	540
Lagrange	25,550	Lagrange	381
Lake	522,965	Crown Point	513
La Porte	108,632	La Porte	607
Lawrence	42,472	Bedford	459
Madison	139,336	Anderson	453
Marion	765,233	Indianapolis	392
Marshall	39,155	Plymouth	443
Martin	11,001	Shoals	345
Miami	39,820	Peru	377
Monroe	98,387	Bloomington	386
Montgomery	35,501	Crawfordsville	507
Morgan	51,999	Martinsville	406
Newton	14,844	Kentland	413
Noble	35,443	Albion	412
Ohio	5,114	Rising Sun	87
Orange	18,677	Paoli	405
Owen	15,840	Spencer	390
Parke	16,372	Rockville	445
Perry	19,346	Cannelton	384
Pike	13,465	Petersburg	335
Porter	119,816	Valparaiso	425
Posey	26,414	Mount Vernon	412
Pulaski	13,258	Winamac	433
Putnam	29,163	Greencastle	490
Randolph	29,997	Winchester	457
Ripley	24,398	Versailles	442
Rush	19,604	Rushville	409
St. Joseph	241,617	South Bend	466
Scott	20,422	Scottsburg	193
Shelby	39,887	Shelbyville	409
Spencer	19,361	Rockport	396
Starke	21,997	Knox	310
Steuben	24,694	Angola	309
Sullivan	21,107	Sullivan	457
Switzerland	7,153	Vevay	221
Tippecanoe	121,702	Lafayette	500
Tipton	16,819	Tipton	261
Union	6,860	Liberty	168
Vanderburgh	167,515	Evansville	241
Vermillion	18,229	Newport	263
Vigo	112,385	Terre Haute	415
Wabash	36,640	Wabash	398
Warren	8,976	Williamsport	368
Warrick	41,474	Boonville	391
Washington	21,932	Salem	516
Wayne	76,058	Richmond	405
Wells	25,401	Bluffton	368
White	23,867	Monticello	497
Whitley	26,215	Columbia City	337

Iowa

(99 counties; 55,941 sq. mi. land; pop. 2,913,387)

County	Pop.	County seat or court house	Land area sq. mi.
Adair	9,509	Greenfield	569
Adams	5,731	Corning	426
Allamakee	15,108	Waukon	636
Appanoose	15,511	Centerville	523
Audubon	8,559	Audubon	448
Benton	23,649	Vinton	718
Black Hawk	137,961	Waterloo	568
Boone	26,184	Boone	573
Bremer	24,820	Waverly	439
Buchanan	22,900	Independence	568
Buena Vista	20,774	Storm Lake	572
Butler	17,668	Allison	582
Calhoun	13,542	Rockwell City	571
Carroll	22,951	Carroll	574
Cass	16,932	Atlantic	559
Cedar	18,635	Tipton	585
Cerro Gordo	48,458	Mason City	575
Cherokee	16,238	Cherokee	573
Chickasaw	15,437	New Hampton	505
Clarke	8,612	Osceola	429
Clay	19,576	Spencer	580
Clayton	21,098	Elkader	779
Clinton	57,122	Clinton	693
Crawford	18,935	Denison	716
Dallas	29,513	Adel	597
Davis	9,104	Bloomfield	509
Decatur	9,794	Leon	530
Delaware	18,933	Manchester	572
Des Moines	46,203	Burlington	408
Dickinson	15,629	Spirit Lake	380
Dubuque	93,745	Dubuque	612
Emmet	13,336	Estherville	394
Fayette	25,488	West Union	728
Floyd	19,597	Charles City	503
Franklin	13,036	Hampton	586
Fremont	9,401	Sidney	524
Greene	12,119	Jefferson	569
Grundy	14,366	Grundy Center	501
Guthrie	11,983	Guthrie Center	596
Hamilton	17,862	Webster City	577
Hancock	13,833	Garner	570
Hardin	21,776	Eldora	574
Harrison	16,348	Logan	696
Henry	18,890	Mount Pleasant	440
Howard	11,114	Cresco	471
Humboldt	12,246	Dakota City	435
Ida	8,908	Ida Grove	431
Iowa	15,429	Marengo	584
Jackson	22,503	Maquoketa	644
Jasper	36,425	Newton	731

County	Pop.	County seat or court house	Land area sq. mi.
Jefferson	16,316	Fairfield	436
Johnson	81,717	Iowa City	619
Jones	20,401	Anamosa	585
Keokuk	12,921	Sigourney	579
Kossuth	21,891	Algona	979
Lee	43,106	Fort Madison and Keokuk	527
Linn	169,775	Cedar Rapids	717
Louisa	12,055	Wapello	403
Lucas	10,313	Chariton	434
Lyon	12,896	Rock Rapids	588
Madison	12,597	Winterset	564
Mahaska	22,507	Oskaloosa	572
Marion	29,669	Knoxville	498
Marshall	41,652	Marshalltown	574
Mills	13,406	Glenwood	447
Mitchell	12,329	Osage	467
Monona	11,692	Onawa	699
Monroe	9,209	Albia	435
Montgomery	13,413	Red Oak	422
Muscatine	40,436	Muscatine	443
O'Brien	16,972	Primghar	575
Osceola	8,371	Sibley	398
Page	19,063	Clarinda	535
Palo Alto	12,721	Emmetsburg	561
Plymouth	24,743	Le Mars	863
Pocahontas	11,369	Pocahontas	581
Polk	303,170	Des Moines	578
Pottawattamie	86,500	Council Bluffs	963
Poweshiek	19,306	Montezuma	589
Ringgold	6,112	Mount Ayr	538
Sac	14,118	Sac City	578
Scott	160,022	Davenport	454
Shelby	15,043	Harlan	587
Sioux	30,813	Orange City	766
Story	72,326	Nevada	568
Tama	19,533	Toledo	720
Taylor	8,353	Bedford	528
Union	13,858	Creston	425
Van Buren	8,626	Keosauqua	487
Wapello	40,241	Ottumwa	437
Warren	34,878	Indianola	558
Washington	20,141	Washington	568
Wayne	8,199	Corydon	532
Webster	45,953	Fort Dodge	718
Winnebago	13,010	Forest City	401
Winneshiek	21,876	Decorah	688
Woodbury	100,884	Sioux City	871
Worth	9,075	Northwood	400
Wright	16,319	Clarion	577

Kansas

(105 counties, 81,787 sq. mi. land; pop. 2,363,208)

County	Pop.	County seat or court house	Land area sq. mi.
Allen	15,654	Iola	505
Anderson	8,749	Garnett	577
Atchison	18,397	Atchison	427
Barber	6,548	Medicine Lodge	1,146
Barton	31,343	Great Bend	894
Bourbon	15,969	Fort Scott	639
Brown	11,955	Hiawatha	577
Butler	44,782	El Dorado	1,442
Chase	3,309	Cottonwood Falls	774
Chautauqua	5,016	Sedan	647
Cherokee	22,304	Columbus	586
Cheyenne	3,678	Saint Francis	1,027
Clark	2,599	Ashland	983
Clay	9,802	Clay Center	635
Cloud	12,494	Concordia	711
Coffey	9,370	Burlington	617
Comanche	2,554	Coldwater	800
Cowley	36,824	Winfield	1,136
Crawford	37,916	Girard	598
Decatur	4,509	Oberlin	899
Dickinson	20,175	Abilene	855
Doniphan	9,268	Troy	388
Douglas	67,640	Lawrence	471
Edwards	4,271	Kinsley	617
Elk	3,918	Howard	647
Ellis	26,098	Hays	900
Ellsworth	6,640	Ellsworth	717
Finney	23,825	Garden City	1,301
Ford	24,315	Dodge City	1,091
Franklin	21,813	Ottawa	577
Geary	29,852	Junction City	374
Gove	3,726	Gove	1,070
Graham	3,995	Hill City	891
Grant	6,977	Ulysses	571
Gray	5,138	Cimarron	872
Greeley	1,845	Tribune	783
Greenwood	8,764	Eureka	1,133
Hamilton	2,514	Syracuse	992
Harper	7,778	Anthony	801
Harvey	30,531	Newton	540
Haskell	3,814	Sublette	580
Hodgeman	2,269	Jetmore	860
Jackson	11,644	Holton	656
Jefferson	15,207	Oskaloosa	510
Jewell	5,241	Mankato	910
Johnson	270,269	Olathe	476
Kearny	3,435	Lakin	855
Kingman	8,960	Kingman	864
Kiowa	4,046	Greensburg	720
Labette	25,682	Oswego	654
Lane	2,472	Dighton	720
Leavenworth	54,809	Leavenworth	466
Lincoln	4,145	Lincoln	725
Linn	8,234	Mound City	606
Logan	3,478	Oakley	1,073
Lyon	35,108	Emporia	841
McPherson	26,855	McPherson	896
Marion	13,522	Marion	945
Marshall	12,720	Marysville	883
Meade	4,788	Meade	979
Miami	21,618	Paola	592
Mitchell	8,117	Beloit	714
Montgomery	42,281	Independence	628
Morris	6,419	Council Grove	697
Morton	3,454	Elkhart	728
Nemaha	11,211	Seneca	708
Neosho	18,967	Erie	587
Ness	4,498	Ness City	1,081
Norton	6,689	Norton	872
Osage	15,319	Lyndon	707
Osborne	5,959	Osborne	886
Ottawa	5,971	Minneapolis	723
Pawnee	8,065	Larned	755
Phillips	7,406	Phillipsburg	897
Pottawatomie	14,782	Westmoreland	820
Pratt	10,275	Pratt	729
Rawlins	4,105	Atwood	1,078
Reno	64,983	Hutchinson	1,260
Republic	7,569	Belleville	718
Rice	11,900	Lyons	725
Riley	63,505	Manhattan	597
Rooks	7,006	Stockton	886
Rush	4,516	LaCrosse	724
Russell	8,868	Russell	867
Saline	48,905	Salina	720
Scott	5,782	Scott City	724
Sedgwick	366,531	Wichita	1,007
Seward	17,071	Liberal	646
Shawnee	154,916	Topeka	548
Sheridan	3,544	Hoxie	893
Sherman	7,759	Goodland	1,055
Smith	5,947	Smith Center	893
Stafford	5,539	Saint John	795
Stanton	2,339	Johnson	676
Stevens	4,736	Hugoton	731
Sumner	24,928	Wellington	1,186
Thomas	8,451	Colby	1,070
Trego	4,165	Wakeeney	901
Wabaunsee	6,867	Alma	792
Wallace	2,045	Sharon Springs	911
Washington	8,543	Washington	891
Wichita	3,041	Leoti	724
Wilson	12,128	Fredonia	574
Woodson	4,600	Yates Center	497
Wyandotte	172,335	Kansas City	152

Kentucky

(120 counties, 39,650 sq. mi. land; pop. 3,661,433)

County	Pop.	County seat or court house	Land area sq. mi.
Adair	15,233	Columbia	370
Allen	14,128	Scottsville	351
Anderson	12,567	Lawrenceburg	206
Ballard	8,798	Wickliffe	259
Barren	34,009	Glasgow	468
Bath	10,025	Owingsville	287
Bell	34,330	Pineville	370
Boone	45,842	Burlington	249
Bourbon	19,405	Paris	300
Boyd	55,513	Catlettsburg	159
Boyle	25,066	Danville	183
Bracken	7,738	Brooksville	204
Breathitt	17,004	Jackson	494
Breckinridge	16,861	Hardinsburg	554
Bullitt	43,346	Shepherdsville	300
Butler	11,064	Morgantown	443
Caldwell	13,473	Princeton	357
Calloway	30,031	Murray	384
Campbell	83,317	Alexandria	149
Carlisle	5,487	Bardwell	195
Carroll	9,270	Carrollton	130
Carter	25,060	Grayson	397
Casey	14,818	Liberty	435
Christian	66,878	Hopkinsville	725
Clark	28,322	Winchester	259
Clay	22,752	Manchester	474
Clinton	9,321	Albany	190
Crittenden	9,207	Marion	365
Cumberland	7,289	Burkesville	310
Daviess	85,949	Owensboro	462
Edmonson	9,962	Brownsville	298
Elliott	6,908	Sandy Hook	240
Estill	14,495	Irvine	260
Fayette	204,165	Lexington	280
Fleming	12,323	Flemingsburg	350
Floyd	48,764	Prestonsburg	399
Franklin	41,830	Frankfort	211
Fulton	8,971	Hickman	203
Gallatin	4,842	Warsaw	100

County	Pop.	County seat or court house	Land area sq. mi.
Garrard	10,853	Lancaster	236
Grant	13,308	Williamstown	249
Graves	34,049	Mayfield	60
Grayson	20,854	Leitchfield	496
Green	11,043	Greensburg	282
Greenup	39,132	Greenup	351
Hancock	7,742	Hawesville	187
Hardin	88,917	Elizabeth	616
Harlan	41,889	Harlan	469
Harrison	15,166	Cynthiana	308
Hart	15,402	Munfordville	420
Henderson	40,849	Henderson	433
Henry	12,740	New Castle	289
Hickman	6,065	Clinton	246
Hopkins	46,174	Madisonville	553
Jackson	11,996	McKee	337
Jefferson	684,793	Louisville	375
Jessamine	26,653	Nicholasville	177
Johnson	24,432	Paintsville	264
Kenton	137,058	Independence	165
Knott	17,940	Hindman	356
Knox	30,239	Barbourville	373
Larue	11,983	Hodgenville	260
Laurel	38,982	London	446
Lawrence	14,121	Louisa	425
Lee	7,754	Beattyville	210
Leslie	14,882	Hyden	409
Letcher	30,687	Whitesburg	339
Lewis	14,545	Vanceburg	486
Lincoln	19,053	Stanford	340
Livingston	9,219	Smithland	311
Logan	24,138	Russellville	563
Lyon	6,490	Eddyville	216
McCracken	61,310	Paducah	250
McCreary	15,634	Whitley City	418
McLean	10,090	Calhoun	257
Madison	53,352	Richmond	446
Magoffin	13,515	Salyersville	303
Marion	17,910	Lebanon	343
Marshall	25,637	Benton	303
Martin	13,925	Inez	231
Mason	17,760	Maysville	238
Meade	22,854	Brandenburg	305
Menifee	5,117	Frenchburg	210
Mercer	19,011	Harrodsburg	256
Metcalfe	9,484	Edmonton	296
Monroe	12,353	Tompkinsville	334
Montgomery	20,046	Mount Sterling	204
Morgan	12,103	West Liberty	369
Muhlenberg	32,238	Greenville	481
Nelson	27,584	Bardstown	437
Nicholas	7,157	Carlisle	204
Ohio	21,765	Hartford	596
Oldham	28,094	La Grange	184
Owen	8,924	Owenton	351
Owsley	5,709	Booneville	197
Pendleton	10,989	Falmouth	279
Perry	33,763	Hazard	341
Pike	81,123	Pikeville	782
Powell	11,101	Stanton	173
Pulaski	45,803	Somerset	653
Robertson	2,270	Mount Olivet	101
Rockcastle	13,973	Mount Vernon	311
Rowan	19,049	Morehead	290
Russell	13,708	Jamestown	238
Scott	21,813	Georgetown	284
Shelby	23,328	Shelbyville	383
Simpson	14,673	Franklin	239
Spencer	5,929	Taylorsville	193
Taylor	21,178	Campbellsville	277
Todd	11,874	Elkton	376
Trigg	9,384	Cadiz	408
Trimble	6,253	Bedford	146
Union	17,821	Morganfield	340
Warren	71,828	Bowling Green	546
Washington	10,764	Springfield	307
Wayne	17,022	Monticello	440
Webster	14,832	Dixon	339
Whitley	33,396	Williamsburg	459
Wolfe	6,698	Campton	227
Woodford	17,778	Versailles	193

Louisiana

(64 parishes, 44,930 sq. mi. land; pop. 4,203,972)

Parish	Pop.	Seat	Area
Acadia	56,427	Crowley	663
Allen	21,390	Oberlin	774
Ascension	50,068	Donaldsville	301
Assumption	22,084	Napoleonville	356
Avoyelles	41,393	Marksville	832
Beauregard	29,692	De Ridder	1,101
Bienville	16,387	Arcadia	832
Bossier	80,721	Benton	849
Caddo	252,294	Shreveport	899
Calcasieu	167,048	Lake Charles	1,105
Caldwell	10,761	Columbia	551
Cameron	9,336	Cameron	1,441
Catahoula	12,287	Harrisonburg	742
Claiborne	17,095	Homer	763
Concordia	22,981	Vidalia	718
De Soto	25,664	Mansfield	894
East Baton Rouge	366,164	Baton Rouge	459
East Carroll	11,772	Lake Providence	436
East Feliciana	19,015	Clinton	454
Evangeline	33,343	Ville Platte	669
Franklin	24,141	Winnsboro	648
Grant	16,703	Colfax	670
Iberia	63,752	New Iberia	589
Iberville	32,159	Plaquemine	627
Jackson	17,321	Jonesboro	582
Jefferson	454,592	Gretna	369
Jefferson Davis	32,168	Jennings	658
Lafayette	150,017	Lafayette	283
Lafourche	82,483	Thibodaux	1,141
La Salle	17,004	Jena	643
Lincoln	39,763	Ruston	469
Livingston	58,655	Livingston	654
Madison	14,733	Tallulah	661
Morehouse	34,803	Bastrop	804
Natchitoches	39,863	Natchitoches	1,292
Orleans	557,482	New Orleans	197
Ouachita	139,241	Monroe	638
Plaquemines	26,049	Pointe a la Hache	1,030
Pointe Coupee	24,045	New Roads	563
Rapides	135,282	Alexandria	1,318
Red River	10,433	Coushatta	406
Richland	22,187	Rayville	576
Sabine	25,280	Many	873
St. Bernard	64,097	Chalmette	514
St. Charles	37,259	Hahnville	294
St. Helena	9,827	Greensburg	420
St. James	21,495	Convent	253
St. John The Baptist	31,924	Edgard	227
St. Landry	84,128	Opelousas	932
St. Martin	40,214	Saint Martinville	736
St. Mary	64,395	Franklin	624
St. Tammany	110,554	Covington	887
Tangipahoa	80,698	Amite	808
Tensas	8,525	Saint Joseph	626
Terrebonne	94,393	Houma	1,368
Union	21,167	Farmerville	885
Vermilion	48,458	Abbeville	1,205
Vernon	53,475	Leesville	1,351
Washington	44,207	Franklinton	665
Webster	43,631	Minden	615
West Baton Rouge	19,086	Port Allen	203
West Carroll	12,922	Oak Grove	356
West Feliciana	12,186	Saint Francisville	405
Winn	17,253	Winnfield	950

Maine

(16 counties, 30,920 sq. mi. land; pop. 1,124,660)

County	Pop.	Seat	Area
Androscoggin	99,657	Auburn	474
Aroostook	91,331	Houlton	6,821
Cumberland	215,789	Portland	879
Franklin	27,098	Farmington	1,709
Hancock	41,781	Ellsworth	1,536
Kennebec	109,889	Augusta	872
Knox	32,941	Rockland	369
Lincoln	25,691	Wiscasset	454
Oxford	48,968	South Paris	2,080
Penobscot	137,015	Bangor	3,390
Piscataquis	17,634	Dover-Foxcroft	3,892
Sagadahoc	28,795	Bath	257
Somerset	45,028	Skowhegan	3,894
Waldo	28,414	Belfast	737
Washington	34,963	Machias	2,554
York	139,666	Alfred	1,001

Maryland

(23 cos., 1 ind. city, 9,891 sq. mi. land; pop. 4,216,446)

County	Pop.	Seat	Area
Allegany	80,548	Cumberland	428
Anne Arundel	370,775	Annapolis	423
Baltimore	655,615	Towson	598
Calvert	34,638	Prince Frederick	217
Caroline	23,143	Denton	321
Carroll	96,356	Westminster	456
Cecil	60,430	Elkton	362
Charles	72,751	La Plata	459
Dorchester	30,623	Cambridge	594
Frederick	114,263	Frederick	665
Garrett	26,498	Oakland	659
Harford	145,930	Bel Air	453
Howard	118,572	Ellicott City	251
Kent	16,695	Chestertown	281
Montgomery	579,053	Rockville	495
Prince George's	665,071	Upper Marlboro	485
Queen Anne's	25,508	Centreville	375
St. Mary's	59,895	Leonardtown	373
Somerset	19,188	Princess Anne	339
Talbot	25,604	Easton	261
Washington	113,086	Hagerstown	459
Wicomico	64,540	Salisbury	381
Worcester	30,889	Snow Hill	479
Independent City			
Baltimore	786,775	.....	78

Massachusetts

(14 counties; 7,826 sq. mi. land; pop. 5,737,037)

County	Pop.	County seat or court house	Land area sq. mi.
Barnstable	147,925	Barnstable	393
Berkshire	145,110	Pittsfield	941
Bristol	474,641	Taunton	554
Dukes	8,942	Edgartown	104
Essex	633,632	Salem	494
Franklin	64,317	Greenfield	708
Hampden	443,018	Springfield	619
Hampshire	138,813	Northampton	529
Middlesex	1,367,034	Cambridge	825
Nantucket	5,087	Nantucket	46
Norfolk	606,587	Dedham	394
Plymouth	405,437	Plymouth	654
Suffolk	650,142	Boston	56
Worcester	646,352	Worcester	1,509

Michigan

(83 counties; 56,817 sq. mi. land; pop. 9,258,344)

County	Pop.	County seat or court house	Land area sq. mi.
Alcona	9,740	Harrisville	678
Alger	9,225	Munising	905
Allegan	81,555	Allegan	826
Alpena	32,315	Alpena	565
Antrim	16,194	Bellaire	476
Arenac	14,706	Standish	367
Baraga	8,484	L'Anse	901
Barry	45,781	Hastings	554
Bay	119,881	Bay City	447
Benzie	11,205	Beulah	316
Berrien	171,276	Saint Joseph	580
Branch	40,188	Coldwater	508
Calhoun	141,557	Marshall	709
Cass	49,499	Cassopolis	491
Charlevoix	19,907	Charlevoix	414
Cheboygan	20,649	Cheboygan	721
Chippewa	29,029	Sault Sainte Marie	1,590
Clare	23,822	Harrison	571
Clinton	55,893	Saint Johns	572
Crawford	9,465	Grayling	561
Delta	38,947	Escanaba	1,177
Dickinson	25,341	Iron Mountain	757
Eaton	88,337	Charlotte	571
Emmet	22,992	Petoskey	461
Genesee	450,449	Flint	642
Gladwin	19,957	Gladwin	503
Gogebic	19,686	Bessemer	1,107
Grand Traverse	54,899	City	462
Gratiot	40,448	Ithaca	566
Hillsdale	42,071	Hillsdale	600
Houghton	37,872	Houghton	1,017
Huron	36,459	Bad Axe	819
Ingham	272,437	Mason	559
Ionia	51,815	Ionia	575
Iosco	28,349	Tawas City	544
Iron	13,635	Crystal Falls	1,171
Isabella	54,110	Mount Pleasant	572
Jackson	151,495	Jackson	698
Kalamazoo	212,378	Kalamazoo	562
Kalkaska	10,952	Kalkaska	566
Kent	444,506	Grand Rapids	857
Keweenaw	1,963	Eagle River	538
Lake	7,711	Baldwin	571
Lapeer	70,038	Lapeer	658
Leelanau	14,007	Leland	345
Lenawee	89,948	Adrian	753
Livingston	100,289	Howell	572
Luce	6,659	Newberry	906
Mackinac	10,178	Saint Ignace	1,014
Macomb	694,600	Mount Clemens	480
Manistee	23,019	Manistee	553
Marquette	74,101	Marquette	1,828
Mason	26,365	Ludington	490
Mecosta	36,961	Big Rapids	560
Menominee	26,201	Menominee	1,038
Midland	73,578	Midland	520
Missaukee	10,009	Lake City	565
Monroe	134,659	Monroe	557
Montcalm	47,555	Stanton	712
Montmorency	7,492	Atlanta	555
Muskegon	157,589	Muskegon	501
Newaygo	34,917	White Cloud	849
Oakland	1,011,793	Pontiac	867
Oceana	22,002	Hart	536
Ogemaw	16,436	West Branch	571
Ontonagon	9,861	Ontonagon	1,316
Osceola	18,928	Reed City	581
Oscoda	6,858	Mio	563
Otsego	14,993	Gaylord	527
Ottawa	157,174	Grand Haven	563
Presque Isle	14,267	Rogers City	648
Roscommon	16,374	Roscommon	521
Saginaw	228,059	Saginaw	814
St. Clair	138,802	Port Huron	734
St. Joseph	56,083	Centreville	506
Sanilac	40,789	Sandusky	961
Schoolcraft	8,575	Manistique	1,181
Shiawassee	71,140	Corunna	540
Tuscola	56,961	Caro	815
Van Buren	66,814	Paw Paw	603
Washtenaw	264,748	Ann Arbor	711
Wayne	2,337,240	Detroit	605
Wexford	25,102	Cadillac	559

Minnesota

(87 counties; 79,289 sq. mi. land; pop., 4,077,148)

County	Pop.	County seat or court house	Land area sq. mi.
Aitkin	13,404	Aitkin	1,828
Anoka	195,998	Anoka	424
Becker	29,336	Detroit Lakes	1,297
Beltrami	30,982	Bemidji	2,507
Benton	25,187	Foley	402
Big Stone	7,716	Ortonville	490
Blue Earth	52,314	Mankato	737
Brown	28,645	New Ulm	610
Carlton	29,936	Carlton	862
Carver	37,046	Chaska	359
Cass	21,050	Walker	1,998
Chippewa	14,941	Montevideo	582
Chisago	25,717	Center City	419
Clay	49,327	Moorhead	1,045
Clearwater	8,761	Bagley	1,000
Cook	4,092	Grand Marais	1,346
Cottonwood	14,854	Windom	636
Crow Wing	41,722	Brainerd	995
Dakota	194,111	Hastings	576
Dodge	14,773	Mantorville	435
Douglas	27,839	Alexandria	647
Faribault	19,714	Blue Earth	711
Fillmore	21,930	Preston	859
Freeborn	36,329	Albert Lea	701
Goodhue	38,749	Red Wing	753
Grant	7,171	Elbow Lake	546
Hennepin	941,411	Minneapolis	567
Houston	19,617	Caledonia	565
Hubbard	14,098	Park Rapids	932
Isanti	23,600	Cambridge	438
Itasca	43,006	Grand Rapids	2,633
Jackson	13,690	Jackson	696
Kanabec	12,161	Mora	524
Kandiyohi	36,763	Willmar	783
Kittson	6,672	Hallock	1,123
Koochiching	17,571	International Falls	3,127
Lac qui Parle	10,592	Madison	768
Lake	13,043	Two Harbors	2,062
Lake of the Woods	3,764	Baudette	1,311
Le Sueur	23,434	Le Center	440
Lincoln	8,207	Ivanhoe	531
Lyon	25,207	Marshall	709
McLeod	29,657	Glencoe	488
Mahnomen	5,535	Mahnomen	563
Marshall	13,027	Warren	1,789
Martin	24,687	Fairmont	703
Meeker	20,594	Litchfield	619
Mille Lacs	18,430	Milaca	571
Morrison	29,311	Falls	1,127
Mower	40,390	Austin	703
Murray	11,507	Slayton	703
Nicollet	26,929	Saint Peter	432
Nobles	21,840	Worthington	712
Norman	9,379	Ada	885
Olmsted	91,971	Rochester	656
Otter Tail	51,937	Fergus Falls	1,962
Pennington	15,258	Thief River Falls	622
Pine	19,871	Pine City	1,414
Pipestone	11,690	Pipestone	464
Polk	34,844	Crookston	2,013
Pope	11,657	Glenwood	669
Ramsey	459,784	Saint Paul	155
Red Lake	5,471	Red Lake Falls	432
Redwood	19,341	Redwood Falls	874
Renville	20,401	Olivia	979
Rice	46,087	Faribault	496
Rock	10,703	Luverne	485
Roseau	12,574	Roseau	1,676
St. Louis	222,229	Duluth	6,092
Scott	43,784	Shakopee	353
Sherburne	29,908	Elk River	431
Sibley	15,448	Gaylord	583
Stearns	108,161	Saint Cloud	1,342
Steele	30,328	Owatonna	425
Stevens	11,322	Morris	558
Swift	12,920	Benson	739
Todd	24,991	Long Prairie	942
Traverse	5,542	Wheaton	568
Wabasha	19,335	Wabasha	522
Wadena	14,192	Wadena	536
Waseca	18,448	Waseca	415
Washington	113,571	Stillwater	386
Watonwan	12,361	Saint James	433
Wilkin	8,382	Breckenridge	752
Winona	46,256	Winona	620
Wright	58,962	Buffalo	674
Yellow Medicine	13,653	Granite Falls	753

Mississippi

(82 counties, 47,296 sq. mi. land; pop. 2,520,638)

County	Pop.	County seat or court house	Land area sq. mi.
Adams	38,035	Natchez	449
Alcorn	33,036	Corinth	405
Amite	13,369	Liberty	729
Attala	19,865	Kosciusko	724
Benton	8,153	Ashland	412
Bolivar	45,965	Cleveland & Rosedale	923
Calhoun	15,664	Pittsboro	575
Carroll	9,776	Carrollton & Vaiden	637
Chickasaw	17,853	Houston & Okolona	506
Choctaw	8,996	Ackerman	417
Claiborne	12,279	Port Gibson	489
Clarke	16,945	Quitman	697
Clay	21,082	West Point	414
Coahoma	36,918	Clarksdale	569
Copiah	26,503	Hazlehurst	780
Covington	15,927	Collins	416
De Soto	53,930	Hernando	476
Forrest	66,018	Hattiesburg	468
Franklin	8,208	Meadville	568
George	15,297	Lucedale	481
Greene	9,827	Leakesville	728
Grenada	21,043	Grenada	431
Hancock	24,537	Bay Saint Louis	482
Harrison	157,665	Gulfport	585
Hinds	250,998	Jackson & Raymond	876
Holmes	22,970	Lexington	769
Humphreys	13,931	Belzoni	421
Issaquena	2,513	Mayersville	414
Itawamba	20,518	Fulton	541
Jackson	118,015	Pascagoula	736
Jasper	17,265	Bat Springs & Paulding	683
Jefferson	9,181	Fayette	521
Jefferson Davis	13,846	Prentiss	414
Jones	61,912	Ellisville & Laurel	702
Kemper	10,148	De Kalb	757
Lafayette	31,030	Oxford	668
Lamar	23,821	Purvis	500
Lauderdale	77,285	Meridian	708
Lawrence	12,518	Monticello	433
Leake	18,790	Carthage	586
Lee	57,061	Tupelo	455
Leflore	41,525	Greenwood	592
Lincoln	30,174	Brookhaven	586
Lowndes	57,304	Columbus	508
Madison	41,613	Canton	727
Marion	25,708	Columbia	550
Marshall	29,296	Holly Springs	710
Monroe	36,404	Aberdeen	769
Montgomery	13,366	Winona	403
Neshoba	23,789	Philadelphia	568
Newton	19,944	Decatur	580
Noxubee	13,212	Macon	695
Oktibbeha	36,018	Starkville	454
Panola	28,164	Batesville & Sardis	693
Pearl River	33,795	Poplarville	828
Perry	9,864	New Augusta	653
Pike	36,173	Magnolia	409
Pontotoc	20,918	Pontotoc	501
Prentiss	24,025	Booneville	418
Quitman	12,636	Marks	412
Rankin	69,427	Brandon	775
Scott	24,556	Forest	615
Sharkey	7,964	Rolling Fork	436
Simpson	23,441	Mendenhall	587
Smith	15,077	Raleigh	642
Stone	9,716	Wiggins	448
Sunflower	34,844	Indianola	694
Tallahatchie	17,157	Charleston & Sumner	644
Tate	20,119	Senatobia	405
Tippah	18,739	Ripley	464
Tishomingo	18,434	Iuka	443
Tunica	9,652	Tunica	458
Union	21,741	New Albany	422
Walthall	13,761	Tylertown	403
Warren	51,627	Vicksburg	581
Washington	72,344	Greenville	734
Wayne	19,135	Waynesboro	827
Webster	10,300	Walthall	416
Wilkinson	10,021	Woodville	674
Winston	19,474	Louisville	606
Yalobusha	13,139	Coffeeville & Water Valley	488
Yazoo	27,349	Yazoo City	938

Missouri

(114 cos., 1 ind. city, 68,995 sq. mi. land; pop. 4,917,444)

County	Pop.	County seat or court house	Land area sq. mi.
Adair	24,870	Kirksville	572
Andrew	13,980	Savannah	436
Atchison	8,605	Rockport	549
Audrain	26,458	Mexico	692
Barry	24,408	Cassville	783
Barton	11,292	Lamar	594
Bates	15,873	Butler	841
Benton	12,183	Warsaw	735
Bollinger	10,301	Marble Hill	621
Boone	100,376	Columbia	685
Buchanan	87,888	Saint Joseph	404
Butler	37,693	Poplar Buff	715
Caldwell	8,660	Kingston	430
Callaway	32,252	Fulton	835
Camden	19,963	Camdenton	640
Cape Girardeau	58,837	Jackson	574
Carroll	12,131	Carrollton	697
Carter	5,428	Van Buren	506
Cass	51,029	Harrisonville	698
Cedar	11,894	Stockton	496
Chariton	10,489	Keytesville	754
Christian	22,402	Ozark	567
Clark	8,493	Kahoka	506
Clay	136,488	Liberty	412
Clinton	15,916	Plattsburg	420
Cole	56,663	Jefferson City	384
Cooper	14,643	Boonville	566
Crawford	18,300	Steelville	566
Dade	7,383	Greenfield	504
Dallas	12,096	Buffalo	537
Daviess	8,905	Gallatin	563
De Kalb	8,222	Maysville	423
Dent	14,517	Salem	756
Douglas	11,594	Ava	809
Dunklin	36,324	Kennett	543
Franklin	71,233	Union	934
Gasconade	13,181	Hermann	519
Gentry	7,887	Albany	488
Greene	185,302	Springfield	677
Grundy	11,959	Trenton	435
Harrison	9,890	Bethany	720
Henry	19,672	Clinton	734
Hickory	6,367	Hermitage	377
Holt	6,882	Oregon	458
Howard	10,008	Fayette	472
Howell	28,807	West Plains	920
Iron	11,084	Ironton	554
Jackson	629,180	Independence	603
Jasper	86,958	Carthage	642
Jefferson	146,814	Hillsboro	668
Johnson	39,059	Warrensburg	826
Knox	5,508	Edina	512
Laclede	24,323	Lebanon	770
Lafayette	29,925	Lexington	632
Lawrence	28,973	Mount Vernon	619
Lewis	10,901	Monticello	508
Lincoln	22,193	Troy	625
Linn	15,495	Linneus	622
Livingston	15,739	Chillicothe	530
McDonald	14,917	Pineville	540
Macon	16,313	Macon	798
Madison	10,725	Fredericktown	496
Maries	7,551	Vienna	525
Marion	28,638	Palmyra	438
Mercer	4,685	Princeton	455
Miller	18,532	Tuscumbia	600
Mississippi	15,726	Charleston	415
Moniteau	12,068	California	419
Monroe	9,716	Paris	669
Montgomery	11,537	Montgomery City	534
Morgan	13,807	Versailles	592
New Madrid	22,945	New Madrid	679
Newton	40,555	Neosho	629
Nodaway	21,996	Maryville	877
Oregon	10,238	Alton	784
Osage	12,014	Linn	608
Ozark	7,961	Gainesville	732
Pemiscot	24,987	Caruthersville	493
Perry	16,784	Perryville	471
Pettis	36,378	Sedalia	679
Phelps	33,633	Rolla	677
Pike	17,568	Bowling Green	681
Platte	46,341	Platte City	427
Polk	18,822	Bolivar	637
Pulaski	42,011	Waynesville	551
Putnam	6,092	Unionville	518
Ralls	8,911	New London	478
Randolph	25,460	Huntsville	473
Ray	21,378	Richmond	573
Reynolds	7,230	Centerville	817
Ripley	12,458	Doniphan	639
St. Charles	143,455	St. Charles	551
St. Clair	8,622	Osceola	697
St. Francois	42,600	Farmington	457
St. Louis	974,815	Clayton	499
Ste. Genevieve	15,180	Ste. Genevieve	499
Saline	24,919	Marshall	757
Schuyler	4,979	Lancaster	306
Scotland	5,415	Memphis	441
Scott	39,647	Benton	421
Shannon	7,885	Eminence	999
Shelby	7,826	Shelbyville	501
Stoddard	29,009	Bloomfield	823
Stone	15,587	Galena	449
Sullivan	7,434	Milan	654
Taney	20,467	Forsyth	615
Texas	21,070	Houston	1,183
Vernon	19,806	Nevada	838
Warren	14,900	Warrenton	426
Washington	17,983	Potosi	760

County	Pop.	County seat or court house	Land area sq. mi.
Wayne	11,277	Greenville	766
Webster	20,414	Marshfield	590
Worth	3,008	Grant City	267
Wright	16,188	Hartville	684
Independent City			
St. Louis	453,085		61

Montana

(57 counties, 145,587 sq. mi. land; pop., 786,690)

County	Pop.	County seat	Land area sq. mi.
Beaverhead	8,186	Dillon	5,551
Big Horn	11,096	Hardin	5,023
Blaine	6,999	Chinook	4,275
Broadwater	3,267	Townsend	1,193
Carbon	8,099	Red Lodge	2,066
Carter	1,799	Ekalaka	3,313
Cascade	80,696	Great Falls	2,661
Chouteau	6,092	Fort Benton	3,927
Custer	13,109	Miles City	3,756
Daniels	2,835	Scobey	1,443
Dawson	11,805	Glendive	2,370
Deer Lodge	12,518	Anaconda	740
Fallon	3,763	Baker	1,633
Fergus	13,076	Lewistown	4,242
Flathead	51,966	Kalispell	5,137
Gallatin	42,865	Bozeman	2,517
Garfield	1,656	Jordan	4,455
Glacier	10,628	Cut Bank	2,964
Golden Valley	1,026	Ryegate	1,176
Granite	2,700	Philipsburg	1,733
Hill	17,985	Havre	2,927
Jefferson	7,029	Boulder	1,652
Judith Basin	2,646	Stanford	1,880
Lake	19,056	Polson	1,494
Lewis & Clark	43,039	Helena	3,476
Liberty	2,329	Chester	1,430
Lincoln	17,752	Libby	3,714
McCone	2,702	Circle	2,607
Madison	5,448	Virginia City	3,528
Meagher	2,154	White Sulphur Springs	2,354
Mineral	3,675	Superior	1,222
Missoula	76,016	Missoula	2,612
Musselshell	4,428	Roundup	1,887
Park	12,660	Livingston	2,626
Petroleum	655	Winnett	1,655
Phillips	5,367	Malta	5,213
Pondera	6,731	Conrad	1,645
Powder River	2,520	Broadus	3,288
Powell	6,958	Deer Lodge	2,336
Prairie	1,836	Terry	1,730
Ravalli	22,493	Hamilton	2,382
Richland	12,243	Sidney	2,079
Roosevelt	10,467	Wolf Point	2,385
Rosebud	9,899	Forsyth	5,037
Sanders	8,675	Thompson Falls	2,778
Sheridan	5,414	Plentywood	1,694
Silver Bow	38,092	Butte	715
Stillwater	5,598	Columbus	1,794
Sweet Grass	3,216	Big Timber	1,840
Teton	6,491	Choteau	2,294
Toole	5,559	Shelby	1,950
Treasure	981	Hysham	985
Valley	10,250	Glasgow	4,974
Wheatland	2,359	Harlowton	1,420
Wibaux	1,476	Wibaux	890
Yellowstone	108,035	Billings	2,642
Yellowstone Nat. Park	275		269

Nebraska

(93 counties, 76,483 sq. mi. land; pop., 1,570,006)

County	Pop.	County seat	Land area sq. mi.
Adams	30,656	Hastings	562
Antelope	8,675	Neligh	853
Arthur	513	Arthur	704
Banner	918	Harrisburg	738
Blaine	867	Brewster	710
Boone	7,391	Albion	683
Box Butte	13,696	Alliance	1,065
Boyd	3,331	Butte	538
Brown	4,377	Ainsworth	1,216
Buffalo	34,797	Kearney	949
Burt	8,813	Tekamah	483
Butler	9,330	David City	582
Cass	20,297	Plattsmouth	555
Cedar	10,852	Hartington	742
Chase	4,758	Imperial	890
Cherry	6,758	Valentine	5,966
Cheyenne	10,057	Sidney	1,186
Clay	8,106	Clay Center	570
Colfax	9,890	Schuyler	406
Cuming	11,664	West Point	571
Custer	13,877	Broken Bow	2,558
Dakota	16,573	Dakota City	255
Dawes	9,609	Chadron	1,386
Dawson	22,162	Lexington	975
Deuel	2,462	Chappell	436
Dixon	7,137	Ponca	475
Dodge	35,847	Fremont	528
Douglas	397,884	Omaha	335
Dundy	2,861	Benkelman	921
Fillmore	7,920	Geneva	577
Franklin	4,377	Franklin	578
Frontier	3,647	Stockville	962
Furnas	6,486	Beaver City	722
Gage	24,456	Beatrice	858
Garden	2,802	Oshkosh	1,678
Garfield	2,363	Burwell	569
Gosper	2,140	Elwood	464
Grant	877	Hyannis	764
Greeley	3,462	Greeley	570
Hall	47,690	Grand Island	537
Hamilton	9,301	Aurora	537
Harlan	4,292	Alma	556
Hayes	1,356	Hayes Center	711
Hitchcock	4,079	Trenton	712
Holt	13,552	O'Neil	2,405
Hooker	990	Mullen	722
Howard	6,773	Saint Paul	564
Jefferson	9,817	Fairbury	577
Johnson	5,285	Tecumseh	377
Kearney	7,053	Minden	512
Keith	9,364	Ogallala	1,032
Keya Paha	1,301	Springview	768
Kimball	4,882	Kimball	953
Knox	11,457	Center	1,107
Lancaster	192,884	Lincoln	845
Lincoln	36,455	North Platte	2,522
Logan	983	Stapleton	570
Loup	859	Taylor	574
McPherson	593	Tryon	856
Madison	31,382	Madison	572
Merrick	8,945	Central City	480
Morrill	6,085	Bridgeport	1,402
Nance	4,740	Fullerton	439
Nemaha	8,367	Auburn	400
Nuckolls	6,726	Nelson	579
Otoe	15,183	Nebraska City	619
Pawnee	3,937	Pawnee City	433
Perkins	3,637	Grant	885
Phelps	9,769	Holdrege	544
Pierce	8,481	Pierce	573
Platte	28,852	Columbus	667
Polk	6,320	Osceola	432
Red Willow	12,615	McCook	686
Richardson	11,315	Falls City	550
Rock	2,383	Bassett	1,009
Saline	13,131	Wilber	575
Sarpy	86,015	Papillion	239
Saunders	18,716	Wahoo	759
Scotts Bluff	38,344	Gering	726
Seward	15,789	Seward	571
Sheridan	7,544	Rushville	2,462
Sherman	4,226	Loup City	567
Sioux	1,845	Harrison	2,063
Stanton	6,549	Stanton	431
Thayer	7,582	Hebron	577
Thomas	973	Thedford	716
Thurston	7,186	Pender	388
Valley	5,633	Ord	569
Washington	15,508	Blair	389
Wayne	9,858	Wayne	443
Webster	4,858	Red Cloud	575
Wheeler	1,060	Bartlett	576
York	14,798	York	577

Nevada

(16 cos., 1 ind. city, 109,889 sq. mi. land; pop., 799,184)

County	Pop.	County seat	Land area sq. mi.
Churchill	13,917	Fallon	4,883
Clark	461,816	Las Vegas	7,874
Douglas	19,421	Minden	703
Elko	17,269	Elko	17,162
Esmeralda	777	Goldfield	3,570
Eureka	1,198	Eureka	4,182
Humboldt	9,434	Winnemucca	9,702
Lander	4,082	Austin	5,621
Lincoln	3,732	Pioche	10,649
Lyon	13,594	Yerington	2,030
Mineral	6,217	Hawthorne	3,765
Nye	9,048	Tonopah	18,064
Pershing	3,408	Lovelock	6,001
Storey	1,459	Virginia City	262
Washoe	193,623	Reno	6,366
White Pine	8,167	Ely	8,904
Independent City			
Carson City	32,022	Carson City	150

New Hampshire

(10 counties, 9,027 sq. mi. land; pop., 920,610)

County	Pop.	County seat	Land area sq. mi.
Belknap	42,884	Laconia	400
Carroll	27,931	Ossipee	938
Cheshire	62,116	Keene	715
Coos	35,147	Lancaster	1,820
Grafton	65,806	Woodsville	1,732
Hillsborough	276,608	Nashua	887
Merrimack	98,302	Concord	930
Rockingham	190,345	Exeter	691
Strafford	85,408	Dover	376
Sullivan	36,063	Newport	539

New Jersey

(21 counties, 7,521 sq. mi. land; pop., 7,364,158)

Parish	Pop.	Parish seat or court house	Land area sq. mi.
Atlantic	194,119	Mays Landing	569
Bergen	845,385	Hackensack	234
Burlington	362,542	Mount Holly	819
Camden	471,650	Camden	221
Cape May	82,266	Cape May Court House	267
Cumberland	132,866	Bridgeton	500
Essex	850,451	Newark	130
Gloucester	199,917	Woodbury	329
Hudson	556,972	Jersey City	47
Hunterdon	87,361	Flemington	423
Mercer	307,863	Trenton	228
Middlesex	595,893	New Brunswick	312
Monmouth	503,173	Freehold	476
Morris	407,630	Morristown	468
Ocean	346,038	Toms River	642
Passaic	447,585	Paterson	192
Salem	64,676	Salem	365
Somerset	203,129	Somerville	307
Sussex	116,119	Newton	527
Union	504,094	Elizabeth	103
Warren	84,429	Belvidere	362

New Mexico

(32 counties, 121,412 sq. mi. land; pop., 1,299,968)

County	Pop.	Seat	Land area
Bernalillo	419,700	Albuquerque	1,169
Catron	2,720	Reserve	6,897
Chaves	51,103	Roswell	6,084
Colfax	13,706	Raton	3,764
Curry	42,019	Clovis	1,403
De Baca	2,454	Fort Sumner	2,356
Dona Ana	96,340	Las Cruces	3,804
Eddy	47,855	Carlsbad	4,167
Grant	26,204	Silver City	3,970
Guadalupe	4,496	Santa Rosa	2,998
Harding	1,090	Mosquero	2,134
Hidalgo	6,049	Lordsburg	3,447
Lea	55,634	Lovington	4,393
Lincoln	10,997	Carrizozo	4,858
Los Alamos	17,599	Los Alamos	108
Luna	15,585	Deming	2,957
McKinley	54,950	Gallup	5,454
Mora	4,205	Mora	1,940
Otero	44,665	Alamogordo	6,638
Quay	10,577	Tucumcari	2,875
Rio Arriba	29,282	Tierra Amarilla	5,843
Roosevelt	15,695	Portales	2,454
Sandoval	34,799	Bernalillo	3,714
San Juan	80,833	Aztec	5,500
San Miguel	22,751	Las Vegas	4,741
Santa Fe	75,306	Santa Fe	1,902
Sierra	8,454	Truth or Consequences	4,166
Socorro	12,969	Socorro	6,603
Taos	18,862	Taos	2,256
Torrance	7,491	Estancia	3,346
Union	4,725	Clayton	3,816
Valencia	60,853	Los Lunas	5,656

New York

(62 counties, 47,831 sq. mi. land; pop., 17,557,288)

County	Pop.	Seat	Land area
Albany	285,909	Albany	526
Allegany	51,742	Belmon	1,047
Bronx	1,169,115	Bronx	41
Broome	213,648	Binghamton	714
Cattaraugus	85,697	Little Valley	1,318
Cayuga	79,894	Auburn	698
Chautauqua	146,925	Mayville	1,081
Chemung	97,656	Elmira	415
Chenango	49,344	Norwich	903
Clinton	80,750	Plattsburgh	1,059
Columbia	59,487	Hudson	645
Cortland	48,820	Cortland	502
Delaware	46,931	Delhi	1,443
Dutchess	245,055	Poughkeepsie	813
Erie	1,015,472	Buffalo	1,058
Essex	36,176	Elizabethtown	1,823
Franklin	44,929	Malone	1,674
Fulton	55,153	Johnstown	498
Genesee	59,400	Batavia	501
Greene	40,861	Catskill	653
Hamilton	5,034	Lake Pleasant	1,735
Herkimer	66,714	Herkimer	1,435
Jefferson	88,151	Watertown	1,294
Kings	2,230,936	Brooklyn	70
Lewis	25,035	Lowville	1,291
Livingston	57,006	Geneseo	638
Madison	65,150	Wampsville	661
Monroe	702,230	Rochester	675
Montgomery	53,439	Fonda	408
Nassau	1,321,582	Mineola	289
New York	1,427,533	New York	23
Niagara	227,101	Lockport	532
Oneida	253,466	Utica	1,223
Onondaga	463,324	Syracuse	794
Ontario	88,909	Canandaigua	651
Orange	259,603	Goshen	833
Orleans	38,496	Albion	396
Oswego	113,901	Oswego	964
Otsego	59,075	Cooperstown	1,013
Putnam	77,193	Carmel	231
Queens	1,891,325	Jamaica	108
Rensselaer	151,966	Troy	665
Richmond	352,121	Saint George	58
Rockland	259,530	New City	176
St. Lawrence	114,254	Canton	2,768
Saratoga	153,759	Ballston Spa	818
Schenectady	149,946	Schenectady	207
Schoharie	29,710	Schoharie	624
Schuyler	17,686	Watkins Glen	330
Seneca	33,733	Ovid & Waterloo	330
Steuben	99,135	Bath	1,410
Suffolk	1,284,231	Riverhead	929
Sullivan	65,155	Monticello	980
Tioga	49,812	Owego	524
Tompkins	87,085	Ithaca	482
Ulster	158,158	Kingston	1,141
Warren	54,854	Lake George	887
Washington	54,795	Hudson Falls	836
Wayne	85,230	Lyons	606
Westchester	866,599	White Plains	443
Wyoming	39,895	Warsaw	598
Yates	21,459	Penn Yan	343

North Carolina

(100 counties, 48,798 sq. mi. land; pop., 5,874,429)

County	Pop.	Seat	Land area
Alamance	99,136	Graham	428
Alexander	24,999	Taylorsville	259
Alleghany	9,587	Sparta	225
Anson	25,562	Wadesboro	533
Ashe	22,325	Jefferson	426
Avery	14,409	Newland	245
Beaufort	40,266	Washington	826
Bertie	21,024	Windsor	698
Bladen	30,448	Elizabethtown	883
Brunswick	35,767	Southport	856
Buncombe	160,934	Asheville	657
Burke	72,504	Morganton	511
Cabarrus	85,895	Concord	363
Caldwell	67,746	Lenoir	469
Camden	5,829	Camden	239
Carteret	41,092	Beaufort	536
Caswell	20,705	Yanceyville	428
Catawba	105,208	Newton	394
Chatham	33,415	Pittsboro	709
Cherokee	18,933	Murphy	452
Chowan	12,558	Edenton	173
Clay	6,619	Hayesville	208
Cleveland	83,435	Shelby	468
Columbus	51,037	Whiteville	945
Craven	71,043	New Bern	699
Cumberland	247,160	Fayetteville	654
Currituck	11,089	Currituck	246
Dare	13,377	Manteo	391
Davidson	113,162	Lexington	549
Davie	24,599	Mocksville	265
Duplin	40,952	Kenansville	815
Durham	152,785	Durham	295
Edgecombe	55,988	Tarboro	510
Forsyth	243,683	Winston-Salem	419
Franklin	30,055	Louisburg	491
Gaston	162,568	Gastonia	356
Gates	8,875	Gatesville	337
Graham	7,217	Robbinsville	292
Granville	33,995	Oxford	537
Greene	16,117	Snow Hill	267
Guilford	317,154	Greensboro	655
Halifax	55,286	Halifax	734
Harnett	59,570	Lillington	603
Haywood	46,495	Waynesville	551
Henderson	58,580	Hendersonville	378
Hertford	23,368	Winton	353
Hoke	20,383	Raeford	319
Hyde	5,873	Swanquarter	613
Iredell	82,538	Statesville	572
Jackson	25,811	Sylva	491
Johnston	70,599	Smithfield	797
Jones	9,705	Trenton	467
Lee	36,718	Sanford	256
Lenoir	59,819	Kinston	400
Lincoln	42,372	Lincolnton	297
McDowell	35,135	Marion	436
Macon	20,178	Franklin	513
Madison	16,827	Marshall	450
Martin	25,948	Williamston	455
Mecklenburg	404,270	Charlotte	530
Mitchell	14,428	Bakersville	215
Montgomery	22,469	Troy	488
Moore	50,505	Carthage	704
Nash	67,153	Nashville	544
New Hanover	103,471	Wilmington	185
Northampton	22,584	Jackson	536
Onslow	112,784	Jacksonville	765
Orange	77,055	Hillsboro	400
Pamlico	10,398	Bayboro	338

County	Pop.	County seat or court house	Land area sq. mi.
Pasquotank	28,462	Elizabeth City	228
Pender	22,215	Burgaw	871
Perquimans	9,486	Hertford	246
Person	29,164	Roxboro	401
Pitt	83,651	Greenville	655
Polk	12,984	Columbus	239
Randolph	91,861	Asheboro	798
Richmond	45,481	Rockingham	475
Robeson	101,577	Lumberton	949
Rockingham	83,426	Wentworth	569
Rowan	99,186	Salisbury	523
Rutherford	53,787	Rutherfordton	563
Sampson	49,687	Clinton	945
Scotland	32,273	Laurinburg	319
Stanly	48,517	Albemarle	398
Stokes	33,086	Danbury	457
Surry	59,449	Dobson	536
Swain	10,283	Bryson City	524
Transylvania	23,417	Brevard	382
Tyrrell	3,975	Columbia	390
Union	70,380	Monroe	639
Vance	36,748	Henderson	249
Wake	300,833	Raleigh	858
Warren	16,232	Warrenton	424
Washington	14,801	Plymouth	343
Watauga	31,678	Boone	317
Wayne	97,054	Goldsboro	557
Wilkes	58,657	Wilkesboro	757
Wilson	63,132	Wilson	375
Yadkin	28,439	Yadkinville	336
Yancey	14,934	Burnsville	312

North Dakota

(53 counties, 69,273 sq. mi. land; pop., 652,695)

County	Pop.	County seat	Land area sq. mi.
Adams	3,584	Hettinger	989
Barnes	13,960	Valley City	1,479
Benson	7,944	Minnewaukan	1,403
Billings	1,138	Medora	1,139
Bottineau	9,338	Bottineau	1,677
Bowman	4,229	Bowman	1,170
Burke	3,822	Bowbells	1,119
Burleigh	54,811	Bismarck	1,625
Cass	88,247	Fargo	1,749
Cavalier	7,636	Langdon	1,512
Dickey	7,207	Ellendale	1,143
Divide	3,494	Crosby	1,300
Dunn	4,627	Manning	1,992
Eddy	3,554	New Rockford	635
Emmons	5,877	Linton	1,503
Foster	4,611	Carrington	645
Golden Valley	2,391	Beach	1,014
Grand Forks	66,100	Grand Forks	1,438
Grant	4,274	Carson	1,666
Griggs	3,714	Cooperstown	710
Hettinger	4,275	Mott	1,134
Kidder	3,833	Steele	1,358
La Moure	6,473	La Moure	1,136
Logan	3,493	Napoleon	1,001
McHenry	7,858	Towner	1,879
McIntosh	4,800	Ashley	992
McKenzie	7,132	Watford City	2,735
McLean	12,288	Washburn	2,065
Mercer	9,378	Stanton	1,042
Morton	25,177	Mandan	1,920
Mountrail	7,679	Stanley	1,819
Nelson	5,233	Lakota	995
Oliver	2,495	Center	721
Pembina	10,399	Cavalier	1,124
Pierce	6,166	Rugby	1,038
Ramsey	13,048	Devils Lake	1,248
Ransom	6,698	Lisbon	861
Renville	3,608	Mohall	886
Richland	19,207	Wahpeton	1,449
Rolette	12,177	Rolla	913
Sargent	5,512	Forman	853
Sheridan	2,819	McClusky	989
Sioux	3,620	Fort Yates	1,103
Slope	1,157	Amidon	1,225
Stark	23,697	Dickinson	1,316
Steele	3,106	Finley	710
Stutsman	24,154	Jamestown	2,264
Towner	4,052	Cando	1,043
Traill	9,624	Hillsboro	861
Walsh	15,371	Grafton	1,286
Ward	58,392	Minot	2,044
Wells	6,979	Fessenden	1,299
Williams	22,237	Williston	2,064

Ohio

(88 counties, 40,975 sq. mi. land; pop., 10,797,419)

County	Pop.	County seat	Land area sq. mi.
Adams	24,328	West Union	587
Allen	112,241	Lima	410
Ashland	46,178	Ashland	424
Ashtabula	104,215	Jefferson	700
Athens	56,399	Athens	504
Auglaize	42,554	Wapakoneta	400
Belmont	82,569	Saint Clairsville	534
Brown	31,920	Georgetown	490
Butler	258,787	Hamilton	471
Carroll	25,598	Carrollton	390
Champaign	33,649	Urbana	432
Clark	150,236	Springfield	402
Clermont	128,483	Batavia	458
Clinton	34,603	Wilmington	410
Columbiana	113,572	Lisbon	534
Coshocton	36,024	Coshocton	562
Crawford	50,075	Bucyrus	404
Cuyahoga	1,498,295	Cleveland	456
Darke	55,096	Greenville	605
Defiance	39,987	Defiance	412
Delaware	53,840	Delaware	450
Erie	79,655	Sandusky	264
Fairfield	93,678	Lancaster	505
Fayette	27,467	Washington C. H.	404
Franklin	869,109	Columbus	538
Fulton	37,751	Wauseon	407
Gallia	30,098	Gallipolis	471
Geauga	74,474	Chardon	407
Greene	129,769	Xenia	415
Guernsey	42,024	Cambridge	528
Hamilton	873,136	Cincinnati	414
Hancock	64,581	Findlay	532
Hardin	32,719	Kenton	467
Harrison	18,152	Cadiz	401
Henry	28,383	Napoleon	416
Highland	33,477	Hillsboro	549
Hocking	24,304	Logan	421
Holmes	29,416	Millersburg	424
Huron	54,608	Norwalk	497
Jackson	30,592	Jackson	419
Jefferson	91,564	Steubenville	411
Knox	46,309	Mount Vernon	531
Lake	212,801	Painesville	231
Lawrence	63,849	Ironton	456
Licking	120,981	Newark	686
Logan	39,155	Bellefontaine	460
Lorain	274,909	Elyria	495
Lucas	471,741	Toledo	343
Madison	33,004	London	463
Mahoning	289,487	Youngstown	415
Marion	67,974	Marion	405
Medina	113,150	Medina	425
Meigs	23,641	Pomeroy	436
Mercer	38,334	Celina	444
Miami	90,381	Troy	407
Monroe	17,382	Woodsfield	456
Montgomery	571,697	Dayton	459
Morgan	14,241	McConnelsville	420
Morrow	26,480	Mount Gilead	403
Muskingum	83,340	Zanesville	651
Noble	11,310	Caldwell	398
Ottawa	40,076	Port Clinton	261
Paulding	21,302	Paulding	417
Perry	31,032	New Lexington	410
Pickaway	43,662	Circleville	504
Pike	22,802	Waverly	443
Portage	135,856	Ravenna	495
Preble	38,223	Eaton	427
Putnam	32,991	Ottawa	486
Richland	131,205	Mansfield	496
Ross	65,004	Chillicothe	687
Sandusky	63,267	Fremont	409
Scioto	84,545	Portsmouth	608
Seneca	61,901	Tiffin	551
Shelby	43,089	Sidney	408
Stark	378,823	Canton	576
Summit	524,472	Akron	408
Trumbull	241,863	Warren	608
Tuscarawas	84,614	New Philadelphia	569
Union	29,536	Marysville	434
Van Wert	30,458	Van Wert	409
Vinton	11,584	McArthur	411
Warren	99,276	Lebanon	408
Washington	64,266	Marietta	641
Wayne	97,408	Wooster	561
Williams	36,369	Bryan	421
Wood	107,372	Bowling Green	619
Wyandot	22,651	Upper Sandusky	406

Oklahoma

(77 counties, 68,782 sq. mi. land; pop., 3,025,266)

County	Pop.	County seat	Land area sq. mi.
Adair	18,575	Stillwell	570
Alfalfa	7,077	Cherokee	868
Atoka	12,748	Atoka	991
Beaver	6,806	Beaver	1,790
Beckham	19,243	Sayre	907
Blaine	13,443	Watonga	917
Bryan	30,535	Durant	889
Caddo	30,905	Anadarko	1,272
Canadian	56,452	El Reno	897
Carter	43,610	Ardmore	830
Cherokee	30,684	Tahlequah	756
Choctaw	17,203	Hugo	778
Cimarron	3,648	Boise City	1,843
Cleveland	133,173	Norman	527
Coal	6,041	Coalgate	526

County	Pop.	County seat or court house	Land area sq. mi.
Comanche	112,456	Lawton	1,084
Cotton	7,338	Walters	651
Craig	15,014	Vinita	764
Creek	59,210	Sapulpa	936
Custer	25,995	Arapaho	980
Delaware	23,946	Jay	707
Dewey	5,922	Taloga	1,018
Ellis	5,596	Arnett	1,242
Garfield	62,820	Enid	1,054
Garvin	27,856	Pauls Valley	814
Grady	39,490	Chickasha	1,096
Grant	6,518	Medford	1,007
Greer	6,877	Mangum	633
Harmon	4,519	Hollis	545
Harper	4,715	Buffalo	1,041
Haskell	11,010	Stigler	602
Hughes	14,338	Holdenville	807
Jackson	30,356	Altus	810
Jefferson	8,183	Waurika	780
Johnston	10,356	Tishomingo	638
Kay	49,852	Newkirk	950
Kingfisher	14,187	Kingfisher	904
Kiowa	12,711	Hobart	1,027
Latimer	9,840	Wilburton	737
Le Flore	40,698	Poteau	1,560
Lincoln	26,601	Chandler	973
Logan	26,881	Guthrie	751
Love	7,469	Marietta	513
McClain	20,291	Purcell	573
McCurtain	36,151	Idabel	1,800
McIntosh	15,495	Eufaula	608
Major	8,772	Fairview	963
Marshall	10,550	Madill	366
Mayes	32,261	Pryor	648
Murray	12,147	Sulphur	423
Muskogee	66,939	Muskogee	818
Noble	11,573	Perry	743
Nowata	11,486	Nowata	537
Okfuskee	11,125	Okemah	637
Oklahoma	568,933	Oklahoma City	700
Okmulgee	39,169	Okmulgee	700
Osage	39,327	Pawhuska	2,272
Ottawa	32,870	Miami	464
Pawnee	15,310	Pawnee	61
Payne	62,435	Stillwater	694
Pittsburg	40,524	McAlester	1,241
Pontotoc	32,598	Ada	714
Pottawatomie	55,239	Shawnee	794
Pushmataha	11,773	Antlers	1,420
Roger Mills	4,799	Cheyenne	1,140
Rogers	46,436	Claremore	685
Seminole	27,473	Wewoka	630
Sequoyah	30,749	Sallisaw	696
Stephens	43,419	Duncan	891
Texas	17,727	Guymon	2,062
Tillman	12,398	Frederick	901
Tulsa	470,593	Tulsa	573
Wagoner	41,801	Wagoner	563
Washington	48,113	Bartlesville	424
Washita	13,798	Cordell	1,009
Woods	10,923	Alva	1,298
Woodward	21,172	Woodward	1,251

Oregon

(36 counties, 96,184 sq. mi. land; pop., 2,632,663)

County	Pop.	County seat	Land area sq. mi.
Baker	16,134	Baker	3,068
Benton	68,211	Corvallis	668
Clackamas	241,919	Oregon City	1,884
Clatsop	32,489	Astoria	805
Columbia	35,646	Saint Helens	639
Coos	64,047	Coquille	1,604
Crook	13,091	Prineville	2,975
Curry	16,992	Gold Beach	1,627
Deschutes	62,142	Bend	3,031
Douglas	93,748	Roseburg	5,063
Gilliam	2,057	Condon	1,208
Grant	8,210	Canyon City	4,530
Harney	8,314	Burns	10,166
Hood River	15,835	Hood River	523
Jackson	132,456	Medford	2,812
Jefferson	11,599	Madras	1,793
Josephine	58,820	Grants Pass	1,625
Klamath	59,117	Klamath Falls	5,970
Lake	7,532	Lakeview	8,231
Lane	275,226	Eugene	4,552
Lincoln	35,264	Newport	986
Linn	89,495	Albany	2,283
Malheur	26,896	Vale	9,859
Marion	204,692	Salem	1,166
Morrow	7,519	Heppner	2,060
Multnomah	562,640	Portland	423
Polk	45,203	Dallas	736
Sherman	2,172	Moro	830
Tillamook	21,164	Tillamook	1,115
Umatilla	58,861	Pendleton	3,227
Union	23,921	La Grande	2,032
Wallowa	7,273	Enterprise	3,178
Wasco	21,732	The Dalles	2,381
Washington	245,401	Hillsboro	716
Wheeler	1,513	Fossil	1,707
Yamhill	55,332	McMinnville	711

Pennsylvania

(67 counties, 44,966 sq. mi. land; pop., 11,866,728)

County	Pop.	County seat	Land area sq. mi.
Adams	68,292	Gettysburg	526
Allegheny	1,450,085	Pittsburgh	728
Armstrong	77,768	Kittanning	652
Beaver	204,441	Beaver	440
Bedford	46,784	Bedford	1,018
Berks	312,509	Reading	862
Blair	136,621	Hollidaysburg	530
Bradford	62,919	Towanda	1,148
Bucks	479,211	Doylestown	614
Butler	147,912	Butler	794
Cambria	183,263	Ebensburg	692
Cameron	6,674	Emporium	401
Carbon	53,285	Jim Thorpe	404
Centre	112,760	Bellefonte	1,115
Chester	316,660	West Chester	761
Clarion	43,362	Clarion	597
Clearfield	83,578	Clearfield	1,139
Clinton	38,971	Lock Haven	899
Columbia	61,967	Bloomsburg	484
Crawford	88,869	Meadville	1,012
Cumberland	178,037	Carlisle	555
Dauphin	232,317	Harrisburg	518
Delaware	555,007	Media	184
Elk	38,338	Ridgeway	807
Erie	279,780	Erie	813
Fayette	160,395	Uniontown	802
Forest	5,072	Tionesta	419
Franklin	113,629	Chambersburg	754
Fulton	12,842	McConnellsburg	435
Greene	40,355	Waynesburg	578
Huntingdon	42,253	Huntingdon	895
Indiana	92,281	Indiana	825
Jefferson	48,303	Brookville	652
Juniata	19,188	Mifflintown	386
Lackawanna	227,908	Scranton	454
Lancaster	362,346	Lancaster	946
Lawrence	107,150	New Castle	367
Lebanon	109,829	Lebanon	363
Lehigh	273,582	Allentown	348
Luzerne	343,079	Wilkes-Barre	886
Lycoming	118,416	Williamsport	1,216
McKean	50,635	Smethport	992
Mercer	128,299	Mercer	670
Mifflin	46,908	Lewistown	431
Monroe	69,409	Stroudsburg	611
Montgomery	643,621	Norristown	496
Montour	16,675	Danville	130
Northampton	225,418	Easton	376
Northumberland	100,381	Sunbury	453
Perry	35,718	New Bloomfield	551
Philadelphia	1,688,210	Philadelphia	129
Pike	18,271	Milford	542
Potter	17,726	Coudersport	1,092
Schuylkill	160,630	Pottsville	784
Snyder	33,584	Middleburg	327
Somerset	81,243	Somerset	1,078
Sullivan	6,349	Laporte	478
Susquehanna	37,876	Montrose	833
Tioga	40,973	Wellsboro	1,146
Union	32,870	Lewisburg	318
Venango	64,444	Franklin	678
Warren	47,449	Warren	905
Washington	217,074	Washington	857
Wayne	35,237	Honesdale	741
Westmoreland	392,294	Greensburg	1,024
Wyoming	26,433	Tunkhannock	398
York	312,963	York	909

Rhode Island

(5 counties, 1,049 sq. mi. land; pop., 947,154)

County	Pop.	County seat	Land area sq. mi.
Bristol	46,942	Bristol	25
Kent	154,163	East Greenwich	173
Newport	81,383	Newport	115
Providence	571,349	Providence	416
Washington	93,317	West Kingston	321

South Carolina

(46 counties, 30,225 sq. mi. land; pop., 3,119,208)

County	Pop.	County seat	Land area sq. mi.
Abbeville	22,627	Abbeville	506
Aiken	105,625	Aiken	1,087
Allendale	10,700	Allendale	418
Anderson	133,235	Anderson	749

County	Pop.	County seat or court house	Land area sq. mi.
Bamberg	18,118	Bamberg	395
Barnwell	19,868	Barnwell	553
Beaufort	65,364	Beaufort	579
Berkeley	94,727	Moncks Corner	1,110
Calhoun	12,206	Saint Matthews	377
Charleston	277,308	Charleston	939
Cherokee	40,983	Gaffney	394
Chester	30,148	Chester	584
Chesterfield	38,161	Chesterfield	790
Clarendon	27,464	Manning	599
Colleton	31,676	Walterboro	1,049
Darlington	62,717	Darlington	543
Dillon	31,083	Dillon	407
Dorchester	58,266	Saint George	569
Edgefield	17,528	Edgefield	482
Fairfield	20,700	Winnsboro	696
Florence	110,163	Florence	805
Georgetown	42,461	Georgetown	812
Greenville	287,913	Greenville	792
Greenwood	57,847	Greenwood	446
Hampton	18,159	Hampton	562
Horry	101,419	Conway	1,154
Jasper	14,504	Ridgeland	652
Kershaw	39,015	Camden	781
Lancaster	53,361	Lancaster	502
Laurens	52,214	Laurens	711
Lee	18,929	Bishopville	409
Lexington	140,353	Lexington	717
McCormick	7,797	McCormick	360
Marion	34,179	Marion	487
Marlboro	31,634	Bennettsville	483
Newberry	31,111	Newberry	635
Oconee	48,611	Walhalla	654
Orangeburg	82,276	Orangeburg	1,106
Pickens	79,292	Pickens	492
Richland	267,823	Columbia	748
Saluda	16,150	Saluda	458
Spartanburg	201,553	Spartanburg	831
Sumter	88,243	Sumter	672
Union	30,751	Union	514
Williamsburg	38,226	Kingstree	935
York	106,720	York	684

South Dakota

(67 counties, 75,955 sq. mi. land; pop., 690,178)

County	Pop.	County seat or court house	Land area sq. mi.
Aurora	3,628	Plankinton	709
Beadle	19,195	Huron	1,259
Bennett	3,236	Martin	1,181
Bon Homme	8,059	Tyndall	560
Brookings	24,332	Brookings	1,674
Brown	36,962	Aberdeen	1,818
Brule	5,245	Chamberlain	818
Buffalo	1,795	Gannvalley	482
Butte	8,372	Belle Fourche	2,250
Campbell	2,243	Mound City	732
Charles Mix	9,680	Lake Andes	1,097
Clark	4,894	Clark	964
Clay	13,135	Vermillion	405
Codington	20,885	Watertown	687
Corson	5,196	McIntosh	2,470
Custer	6,000	Custer	1,557
Davison	17,820	Mitchell	432
Day	8,133	Webster	1,030
Deuel	5,289	Clear Lake	639
Dewey	5,366	Timber Lake	2,351
Douglas	4,181	Armour	435
Edmunds	5,159	Ipswich	1,154
Fall River	8,439	Hot Springs	1,743
Faulk	3,327	Faulkton	996
Grant	9,013	Milbank	681
Gregory	6,015	Burke	997
Haakon	2,794	Philip	1,816
Hamlin	5,261	Hayti	511
Hand	4,948	Miller	1,432
Hanson	3,415	Alexandria	430
Harding	1,700	Buffalo	2,682
Hughes	14,220	Pierre	748
Hutchinson	9,350	Olivet	815
Hyde	2,069	Highmore	863
Jackson	3,437	Kadoka	808
Jerauld	2,929	Wessington Spgs.	527
Jones	1,463	Murdo	973
Kingsbury	6,679	De Smet	818
Lake	10,724	Madison	567
Lawrence	18,339	Deadwood	800
Lincoln	13,942	Canton	576
Lyman	3,864	Kennebec	1,683
McCook	6,444	Salem	575
McPherson	4,027	Leola	1,147
Marshall	5,404	Britton	848
Meade	20,717	Sturgis	3,465
Mellette	2,249	White River	1,306
Miner	3,739	Howard	570
Minnehaha	109,435	Sioux Falls	813
Moody	6,692	Flandreau	523
Pennington	70,133	Rapid City	2,779
Perkins	4,700	Bison	2,860
Potter	3,674	Gettysburg	869
Roberts	10,911	Sisseton	1,108
Sanborn	3,213	Woonsocket	570
Shannon	11,323	(Attached to Fall River)	2,100
Spink	9,201	Redfield	1,505
Stanley	2,533	Fort Pierre	1,414
Sully	1,990	Onida	1,004
Todd	7,328	(Attached to Tripp)	1,388
Tripp	7,268	Winner	1,620
Turner	9,255	Parker	612
Union	10,938	Elk Point	452
Walworth	7,011	Selby	718
Washabaugh	—	(Attached to Jackson)	1,061
Yankton	18,952	Yankton	519
Zeibach	2,308	Dupree	1,981

Tennessee

(95 counties, 41,328 sq. mi. land; pop., 4,500,750)

County	Pop.	County seat or court house	Land area sq. mi.
Anderson	67,346	Clinton	335
Bedford	27,916	Shelbyville	482
Benton	14,901	Camden	392
Bledsoe	9,478	Pikeville	404
Blount	77,770	Maryville	575
Bradley	67,547	Cleveland	334
Campbell	34,841	Jacksboro	451
Cannon	10,234	Woodbury	271
Carroll	28,285	Huntingdon	596
Carter	50,205	Elizabethton	348
Cheatham	21,616	Ashland City	305
Chester	12,727	Henderson	285
Claiborne	24,595	Tazewell	444
Clay	7,676	Celina	233
Cocke	28,792	Newport	424
Coffee	38,311	Manchester	434
Crockett	14,941	Alamo	269
Cumberland	28,676	Crossville	678
Davidson	477,811	Nashville	508
Decatur	10,857	Decaturville	337
De Kalb	13,589	Smithville	278
Dickson	30,037	Charlotte	485
Dyer	34,663	Dyersburg	529
Fayette	25,305	Somerville	704
Fentress	14,826	Jamestown	498
Franklin	31,983	Winchester	553
Gibson	49,467	Trenton	607
Giles	24,625	Pulaski	619
Grainger	16,751	Rutledge	282
Greene	54,406	Greeneville	613
Grundy	13,787	Altamont	358
Hamblen	49,300	Morristown	155
Hamilton	287,740	Chattanooga	550
Hancock	6,887	Sneedville	230
Hardeman	23,873	Bolivar	656
Hardin	22,280	Savannah	587
Hawkins	43,751	Rogersville	480
Haywood	20,318	Brownsville	519
Henderson	21,390	Lexington	515
Henry	28,656	Paris	567
Hickman	15,151	Centerville	610
Houston	6,871	Erin	201
Humphreys	15,957	Waverly	530
Jackson	9,398	Gainesboro	323
Jefferson	31,284	Dandridge	274
Johnson	13,745	Mountain City	293
Knox	319,694	Knoxville	508
Lake	7,455	Tiptonville	167
Lauderdale	24,555	Ripley	477
Lawrence	34,110	Lawrenceburg	634
Lewis	9,700	Hohenwald	285
Lincoln	26,483	Fayetteville	580
Loudon	28,553	Loudon	237
McMinn	41,878	Athens	432
McNairy	22,525	Selmer	569
Macon	15,700	Lafayette	304
Madison	74,546	Jackson	560
Marion	24,416	Jasper	506
Marshall	19,698	Lewisburg	377
Maury	51,095	Columbia	614
Meigs	7,431	Decatur	191
Monroe	28,700	Madisonville	660
Montgomery	83,342	Clarksville	539
Moore	4,510	Lynchburg	124
Morgan	16,604	Wartburg	539
Obion	32,781	Union City	556
Overton	17,575	Livingston	441
Perry	6,111	Linden	411
Pickett	4,358	Byrdstown	158
Polk	13,602	Benton	434
Putnam	47,601	Cookeville	405
Rhea	24,235	Dayton	312
Roane	48,425	Kingston	350
Robertson	37,021	Springfield	476
Rutherford	84,058	Murfreesboro	612
Scott	19,259	Huntsville	544
Sequatchie	8,605	Dunlap	273
Sevier	41,418	Sevierville	597
Shelby	777,113	Memphis	755
Smith	14,935	Carthage	323
Stewart	8,665	Dover	470

County	Pop.	County seat or court house	Land area sq. mi.
Sullivan	143,968	Blountville	413
Sumner	85,790	Gallatin	534
Tipton	32,747	Covington	459
Trousdale	6,137	Hartsville	114
Unicoi	16,362	Erwin	185
Union	11,707	Maynardville	212
Van Buren	4,728	Spencer	254
Warren	32,653	McMinnville	439
Washington	88,755	Jonesboro	323
Wayne	13,946	Waynesboro	739
Weakley	32,896	Dresden	576
White	19,567	Sparta	382
Williamson	58,108	Franklin	593
Wilson	56,064	Lebanon	567

Texas

(254 counties, 262,134 sq. mi. land; pop., 14,228,383)

County	Pop.	County seat or court house	Land area sq. mi.
Anderson	38,381	Palestine	1,072
Andrews	13,323	Andrews	1,504
Angelina	64,172	Lufkin	738
Aransas	14,260	Rockport	275
Archer	7,266	Archer City	913
Armstrong	1,994	Claude	907
Atascosa	25,055	Jourdanton	1,206
Austin	17,726	Bellville	663
Bailey	8,168	Muleshoe	835
Bandera	7,084	Bandera	763
Bastrop	24,726	Bastrop	890
Baylor	4,919	Seymour	845
Bee	26,030	Beeville	842
Bell	157,889	Belton	1,047
Bexar	988,800	San Antonio	1,246
Blanco	4,681	Johnson City	719
Borden	859	Gail	907
Bosque	13,401	Meridian	990
Bowie	75,301	Boston	891
Brazoria	169,587	Angleton	1,423
Brazos	93,588	Bryan	586
Brewster	7,573	Alpine	6,204
Briscoe	2,579	Silverton	874
Brooks	8,428	Falfurrias	904
Brown	33,057	Brownwood	938
Burleson	12,313	Caldwell	670
Burnet	17,803	Burnet	996
Caldwell	23,637	Lockhart	544
Calhoun	19,574	Port Lavaca	527
Callahan	10,992	Baird	856
Cameron	209,680	Brownsville	896
Camp	9,275	Pittsburg	192
Carson	6,672	Panhandle	900
Cass	29,430	Linden	941
Castro	10,556	Dimmitt	880
Chambers	18,538	Anahuac	616
Cherokee	38,127	Rusk	1,049
Childress	6,950	Childress	699
Clay	9,582	Henrietta	1,102
Cochran	4,825	Morton	783
Coke	3,196	Robert Lee	911
Coleman	10,439	Coleman	1,280
Collin	144,490	McKinney	836
Collingsworth	4,648	Wellington	894
Colorado	18,823	Columbus	949
Comal	36,446	New Braunfels	567
Comanche	12,617	Comanche	944
Concho	2,915	Paint Rock	1,004
Cooke	27,656	Gainesville	985
Coryell	56,767	Gatesville	1,043
Cottle	2,947	Paducah	900
Crane	4,600	Crane	795
Crockett	4,608	4,588 Ozona	2,794
Crosby	8,859	Crosbyton	911
Culberson	3,315	Van Horn	3,851
Dallam	6,531	Dalhart	1,494
Dallas	1,556,549	Dallas	859
Dawson	16,184	Lamesa	902
Deaf Smith	21,165	Hereford	1,510
Delta	4,839	Cooper	276
Denton	143,126	Denton	911
Dewitt	18,903	Cuero	910
Dickens	3,539	Dickens	931
Dimmit	11,367	Carrizo Springs	1,344
Donley	4,075	Clarendon	905
Duval	12,517	San Diego	1,814
Eastland	19,480	Eastland	952
Ector	115,374	Odessa	907
Edwards	2,033	Rocksprings	2,076
Ellis	59,743	Waxahachie	940
El Paso	479,899	El Paso	1,057
Erath	22,560	Stephenville	1,085
Falls	17,946	Marlin	764
Fannin	24,285	Bonham	905
Fayette	18,832	La Grange	934
Fisher	5,891	Roby	904
Floyd	9,834	Floydada	993
Foard	2,158	Crowell	676
Fort Bend	130,846	Richmond	869
Franklin	6,893	Mount Vernon	293
Freestone	14,830	Fairfield	865
Frio	13,785	13,100 Pearsall	1,116
Gaines	13,150	Seminole	1,489
Galveston	195,940	Galveston	399
Garza	5,336	Post	914
Gillespie	13,532	Fredericksburg	1,055
Glasscock	1,304	Garden City	863
Goliad	5,193	Goliad	871
Gonzales	16,883	Gonzales	1,056
Gray	26,386	Pampa	934
Grayson	89,796	Sherman	940
Gregg	99,487	Longview	282
Grimes	13,580	Anderson	801
Guadalupe	46,708	Seguin	714
Hale	37,592	Plainview	979
Hall	5,594	Memphis	885
Hamilton	8,297	Hamilton	844
Hansford	6,209	Spearman	907
Hardeman	6,368	Quanah	687
Hardin	40,721	Kountze	897
Harris	2,409,544	Houston	1,723
Harrison	52,265	Marshall	894
Hartley	3,987	Channing	1,488
Haskell	7,725	Haskell	877
Hays	40,594	San Marcos	650
Hemphill	5,304	Canadian	904
Henderson	42,606	Athens	943
Hidalgo	283,229	Edinburg	1,543
Hill	25,024	Hillsboro	1,010
Hockley	23,230	Leveland	908
Hood	17,714	Granbury	426
Hopkins	25,247	Sulphur Springs	793
Houston	22,299	Crockett	1,237
Howard	33,142	Big Spring	911
Hudspeth	2,728	Sierra Blanca	4,554
Hunt	55,248	Greenville	826
Hutchinson	26,304	Stinnett	875
Irion	1,386	Mertzon	1,073
Jack	7,408	Jacksboro	945
Jackson	13,352	Edna	850
Jasper	30,781	Jasper	907
Jeff Davis	1,647	Fort Davis	2,259
Jefferson	250,938	Beaumont	951
Jim Hogg	5,168	Hebbronville	1,143
Jim Wells	36,498	Alice	845
Johnson	67,649	Cleburne	740
Jones	17,268	Anson	956
Karnes	13,593	Karnes City	758
Kaufman	39,015	Kaufman	815
Kendall	10,635	Boerne	670
Kenedy	543	Sarita	1,394
Kent	1,145	Jayton	880
Kerr	28,780	Kerrville	1,101
Kimble	4,063	Junction	1,274
King	425	Guthrie	944
Kinney	2,279	Brackettville	1,393
Kleberg	33,358	Kingsville	851
Knox	5,329	Benjamin	851
Lamar	42,156	Paris	984
Lamb	18,669	Littlefield	1,022
Lampasas	12,005	Lampasas	726
La Salle	5,514	Cotulla	1,500
Lavaca	19,004	Hallettsville	975
Lee	10,952	Giddings	637
Leon	9,594	Centerville	1,102
Liberty	47,088	Liberty	1,180
Limestone	20,224	Groesbeck	931
Lipscomb	3,766	Lipscomb	934
Live Oak	9,606	George West	1,055
Llano	10,144	Llano	941
Loving	91	Mentone	648
Lubbock	211,651	Lubbock	893
Lynn	8,605	Tahoka	915
McCulloch	8,735	Brady	1,066
McLennan	170,755	Waco	1,000
McMullen	789	Tilden	1,159
Madison	10,649	Madisonville	480
Marion	10,360	Jefferson	380
Martin	4,684	Staton	911
Mason	3,683	Mason	935
Matagorda	37,828	Bay City	1,157
Maverick	31,398	Eagle Pass	1,289
Medina	23,164	Hondo	1,352
Menard	2,346	Menard	914
Midland	82,636	Midland	939
Milam	22,732	Cameron	1,028
Mills	4,477	Goldthwaite	734
Mitchell	9,088	Colorado City	920
Montague	17,410	Montague	932
Montgomery	128,487	Conroe	1,090
Moore	16,575	Dumas	909
Morris	14,629	Daingerfield	260
Motley	1,950	Matador	980
Nacogdoches	46,786	Nacogdoches	902
Navarro	35,323	Corsicana	1,070
Newton	13,254	Newton	949
Nolan	17,359	Sweetwater	922
Nueces	268,215	Corpus Christi	841
Ochiltree	9,588	Perryton	907
Oldham	2,283	Vega	1,478

County	Pop.	County seat or court house	Land area sq. mi.
Orange	83,838	Orange	359
Palo Pinto	24,062	Palo Pinto	948
Panola	20,724	Carthage	869
Parker	44,609	Weatherford	903
Parmer	11,038	Farwell	859
Pecos	14,618	Fort Stockton	4,740
Polk	24,407	Livingston	1,100
Potter	98,637	Amarillo	898
Presidio	5,188	Marfa	3,892
Rains	4,839	Emory	210
Randall	75,062	Canyon	914
Reagan	4,135	Big Lake	1,132
Real	2,469	Leakey	622
Red River	16,101	Clarksville	1,033
Reeves	15,801	Pecos	2,608
Refugio	9,289	Refugio	774
Roberts	1,187	Miami	899
Robertson	14,653	Franklin	877
Rockwall	14,528	Rockwall	147
Runnels	11,872	Ballinger	1,058
Rusk	41,382	Henderson	939
Sabine	8,702	Hemphill	456
San Augustine	8,785	San Augustine	473
San Jacinto	11,434	Coldspring	624
San Patricio	58,013	Sinton	685
San Saba	5,693	San Saba	1,120
Schleicher	2,820	Eldorado	1,331
Scurry	18,192	Snyder	904
Shackelford	3,915	Albany	887
Shelby	23,084	Center	778
Sherman	3,174	Stratford	916
Smith	128,366	Tyler	934
Somervell	4,154	Glen Rose	197
Starr	27,266	Rio Grande City	1,211
Stephens	9,926	Breckenridge	899
Sterling	1,206	Sterling City	914
Stonewall	2,406	Aspermont	926
Sutton	5,130	Sonora	1,493
Swisher	9,723	Tulia	896
Tarrant	860,880	Fort Worth	861
Taylor	110,932	Abilene	912
Terrell	1,595	Sanderson	2,391
Terry	14,581	Brownfield	899
Throckmorton	2,053	Throckmorton	920
Titus	21,442	Mount Pleasant	418
Tom Green	84,784	San Angelo	1,500
Travis	419,335	Austin	1,012
Trinity	9,450	Groveton	707
Tyler	16,223	Woodville	919
Upshur	28,595	Gilmer	584
Upton	4,619	Rankin	1,312
Uvalde	22,441	Uvalde	1,588
Val Verde	35,910	Del Rio	3,241
Van Zandt	31,426	Canton	845
Victoria	68,807	Victoria	892
Walker	41,789	Huntsville	790
Waller	19,798	Hempstead	509
Ward	13,976	Monahans	827
Washington	21,998	Brenham	594
Webb	99,258	Laredo	3,306
Wharton	40,242	Wharton	1,076
Wheeler	7,137	Wheeler	914
Wichita	121,082	Wichita Falls	611
Wilbarger	15,931	Vernon	952
Willacy	17,495	Raymondville	591
Williamson	76,521	Georgetown	1,104
Wilson	16,756	Floresville	802
Winkler	9,944	Kermit	887
Wise	26,525	Decatur	922
Wood	24,697	Quitman	721
Yoakum	8,299	Plains	830
Young	19,001	Graham	888
Zapata	6,628	Zapata	957
Zavala	11,666	Crystal City	1,291

Utah

(29 counties, 82,096 sq. mi. land; pop. 1,461,037

County	Pop.	County seat	Land area sq. mi.
Beaver	4,378	Beaver	2,584
Box Elder	33,222	Brigham City	5,603
Cache	57,176	Logan	1,174
Carbon	22,179	Price	1,476
Daggett	769	Manila	682
Davis	146,540	Farmington	297
Duchesne	12,565	Duchesne	3,255
Emery	11,451	Castle Dale	4,439
Garfield	3,673	Panguitch	5,158
Grand	8,241	Moab	3,682
Iron	17,349	Parowan	3,300
Juab	5,530	Nephi	3,412
Kane	4,024	Kanab	3,904
Millard	8,970	Fillmore	6,793
Morgan	4,917	Morgan	603
Piute	1,329	Junction	754
Rich	2,100	Randolph	1,023
Salt Lake	619,066	Salt Lake City	764
San Juan	12,253	Monticello	7,707

Sanpete	14,620	Manti	1,597
Sevier	14,727	Richfield	1,929
Summit	10,198	Coalville	1,849
Tooele	26,033	Tooele	6,923
Uintah	20,506	Vernal	4,487
Utah	218,106	Provo	2,014
Wasatch	8,523	Heber City	1,191
Washington	26,065	Saint George	2,427
Wayne	1,911	Loa	2,486
Weber	144,616	Ogden	581

Vermont

(14 counties, 9,267 sq. mi. land; pop. 511,456)

County	Pop.	County seat	Land area sq. mi.
Addison	29,406	Middlebury	784
Bennington	33,345	Bennington	672
Caledonia	25,808	Saint Johnsbury	612
Chittenden	115,534	Burlington	533
Essex	6,313	Guildhall	663
Franklin	34,788	Saint Albans	660
Grand Isle	4,613	North Hero	83
Lamoille	16,767	Hyde Park	474
Orange	22,739	Chelsea	690
Orleans	23,440	Newport	715
Rutland	58,347	Rutland	927
Washington	52,393	Montpelier	707
Windham	36,933	Newfane	784
Windsor	51,030	Woodstock	962

Virginia

(95 cos., 41 ind. cities, 39,780 sq. mi. land; pop. 5,346,279)

County	Pop.	County seat	Land area sq. mi.
Accomack	31,268	Accomac	476
Albemarle	50,689	Charlottesville	740
Alleghany	14,333	Covington	444
Amelia	8,405	Amelia, C.H.	366
Amherst	29,122	Amherst	470
Appomattox	11,971	Appomattox	345
Arlington	152,599	Arlington	26
Augusta	53,732	Staunton	986
Bath	5,860	Warm Springs	540
Bedford	34,927	Bedford	727
Bland	6,349	Bland	369
Botetourt	23,270	Fincastle	548
Brunswick	15,632	Lawrenceville	579
Buchanan	37,989	Grundy	508
Buckingham	11,751	Buckingham	582
Campbell	45,424	Rustburg	529
Caroline	17,904	Bowling Green	545
Carroll	27,270	Hillsville	494
Charles City	6,692	Charles City	181
Charlotte	12,266	Charlotte Courthouse	470
Chesterfield	141,372	Chesterfield	442
Clarke	9,965	Berryville	174
Craig	3,948	New Castle	336
Culpeper	22,620	Culpeper	389
Cumberland	7,881	Cumberland	291
Dickenson	19,806	Clintwood	332
Dinwiddie	22,602	Dinwiddie	507
Essex	8,864	Tappahannock	250
Fairfax	596,901	Fairfax	399
Fauquier	35,889	Warrenton	660
Floyd	11,563	Floyd	383
Fluvanna	10,244	Palmyra	288
Franklin	35,740	Rocky Mount	716
Frederick	34,150	Winchester	405
Giles	17,810	Pearisburg	363
Gloucester	20,107	Gloucester	228
Goochland	11,761	Goochland	289
Grayson	16,579	Independence	452
Greene	7,625	Stanardsville	153
Greensville	10,903	Emporia	299
Halifax	30,418	Halifax	796
Hanover	50,398	Hanover	465
Henrico	180,735	Richmond	229
Henry	57,654	Martinsville	381
Highland	2,937	Monterey	416
Isle of Wight	21,603	Isle of Wight	317
James City	22,763	Williamsburg	152
King and Queen	5,968	King and Queen	318
King George	10,543	King George	176
King William	9,327	King William	278
Lancaster	10,129	Lancaster	137
Lee	25,956	Jonesville	438
Loudoun	57,427	Leesburg	517
Louisa	17,825	Louisa	517
Lunenburg	12,124	Lunenburg	442
Madison	10,232	Madison	327
Mathews	7,995	Mathews	89
Mecklenburg	29,444	Boydton	612
Middlesex	7,719	Saluda	130
Montgomery	63,516	Christiansburg	394
Nelson	12,204	Lovingston	471
New Kent	8,781	New Kent	210
Northampton	14,625	Eastville	220
Northumberland	9,828	Heathsville	190
Nottoway	14,666	Nottoway	308
Orange	17,827	Orange	355
Page	19,401	Luray	316

County	Pop.	County seat or court house	Land area sq. mi.
Patrick	17,585	Stuart	464
Pittsylvania	66,147	Chatham	1,001
Powhatan	13,062	Powhatan	269
Prince Edward	16,456	Farmville	357
Prince George	25,733	Prince George	276
Prince William	144,703	Manassas	347
Pulaski	35,229	Pulaski	328
Rappahannock	6,093	Washington	267
Richmond	6,952	Warsaw	190
Roanoke	72,945	Salem	262
Rockbridge	17,911	Lexington	601
Rockingham	57,038	Harrisonburg	865
Russell	31,761	Lebanon	483
Scott	25,068	Gate City	539
Shenandoah	27,559	Woodstock	507
Smyth	33,366	Marion	435
Southampton	18,731	Courtland	602
Spotsylvania	34,435	Spotsylvania	409
Stafford	40,470	Stafford	270
Surry	6,046	Surry	277
Sussex	10,874	Sussex	494
Tazewell	50,511	Tazewell	522
Warren	21,200	Front Royal	219
Washington	46,487	Abingdon	574
Westmoreland	14,041	Montross	229
Wise	43,863	Wise	412
Wythe	25,522	Wytheville	460
York	35,463	Yorktown	129

Independent cities

City	Pop.	Land area sq. mi.
Alexandria	103,217	15
Bedford	5,991	7
Bristol	19,042	4
Buena Vista	6,717	3
Charlottesville	45,010	10
Chesapeake	114,226	341
Clifton Forge	5,046	4
Colonial Heights	16,509	8
Covington	9,063	4
Danville	45,642	17
Emporia	4,840	2
Fairfax	19,390	6
Falls Church	9,515	2
Franklin	7,308	4
Fredericksburg	15,322	6
Galax	6,524	7
Hampton	122,617	55
Harrisonburg	19,671	6
Hopewell	23,397	9
Lexington	7,292	3
Lynchburg	66,743	25
Manassas	15,438	—
Manassas Park	6,524	—
Martinsville	18,149	11
Newport News	144,903	69
Norfolk	266,979	53
Norton	4,757	4
Petersburg	41,055	8
Poquoson	8,726	—
Portsmouth	104,577	29
Radford	13,225	5
Richmond	219,214	60
Roanoke	100,427	27
Salem	23,958	14
South Boston	7,093	5
Staunton	21,857	9
Suffolk	47,621	2
Virginia Beach	262,199	259
Waynesboro	15,329	7
Williamsburg	9,870	5
Winchester	20,217	3

Washington

(39 counties, 66,570 sq. mi. land; pop., 4,130,163)

County	Pop.	County seat or court house	Land area sq. mi.
Adams	13,267	Ritzville	1,894
Asotin	16,823	Asotin	633
Benton	109,444	Prosser	1,722
Chelan	45,061	Wenatchee	2,918
Clallam	51,648	Port Angeles	1,753
Clark	192,227	Vancouver	627
Columbia	4,057	Dayton	853
Cowlitz	79,548	Kelso	1,144
Douglas	22,144	Waterville	1,831
Ferry	5,811	Republic	2,202
Franklin	35,025	Pasco	1,253
Garfield	2,468	Pomeroy	709
Grant	48,522	Ephrata	2,675
Grays Harbor	66,314	Montesano	1,910
Island	44,048	Coupeville	212
Jefferson	15,965	Port Townsend	1,805
King	1,269,749	Seattle	2,128
Kitsap	146,609	Port Orchard	393
Kittitas	24,877	Ellensburg	2,317
Klickitat	15,822	Goldendale	1,908
Lewis	55,279	Chehalis	2,423
Lincoln	9,604	Davenport	2,306
Mason	31,184	Shelton	962
Okanogan	30,639	Okanogan	5,301
Pacific	17,237	South Bend	908
Pend Oreille	8,580	Newport	1,402
Pierce	485,643	Tacoma	1,676
San Juan	7,838	Friday Harbor	179
Skagit	64,138	Mount Vernon	1,735
Skamania	7,919	Stevenson	1,672
Snohomish	337,016	Everett	2,098
Spokane	341,835	Spokane	1,758
Stevens	28,979	Colville	2,481
Thurston	124,264	Olympia	714
Wahkiakum	3,832	Cathlamet	261
Walla Walla	47,435	Walla Walla	1,262
Whatcom	106,701	Bellingham	2,126
Whitman	40,103	Colfax	2,153
Yakima	172,508	Yakima	4,268

West Virginia

(55 counties, 24,070 sq. mi. land; pop., 1,949,644)

County	Pop.	County seat or court house	Land area sq. mi.
Barbour	16,639	Philippi	341
Berkeley	46,775	Martinsburg	316
Boone	30,447	Madison	501
Braxton	13,894	Sutton	511
Brooke	31,117	Wellsburg	88
Cabell	106,835	Huntington	279
Calhoun	8,250	Grantsville	281
Clay	11,265	Clay	343
Doddridge	7,433	West Union	319
Fayette	57,863	Fayetteville	663
Gilmer	8,334	Glenville	339
Grant	10,210	Petersburg	478
Greenbrier	37,665	Lewisburg	1,026
Hampshire	14,867	Romney	639
Hancock	40,418	New Cumberland	83
Hardy	10,030	Moorefield	585
Harrison	77,710	Clarksburg	418
Jackson	25,794	Ripley	461
Jefferson	30,302	Charles Town	211
Kanawha	231,414	Charleston	907
Lewis	18,813	Weston	392
Lincoln	23,675	Hamlin	438
Logan	50,679	Logan	456
McDowell	49,899	Welch	533
Marion	65,789	Fairmont	311
Marshall	41,608	Moundsville	304
Mason	27,045	Point Pleasant	433
Mercer	73,942	Princeton	417
Mineral	27,234	Keyser	330
Mingo	37,336	Williamson	423
Monongalia	75,024	Morgantown	365
Monroe	12,873	Union	473
Morgan	10,711	Berkeley Springs	233
Nicholas	28,126	Summersville	642
Ohio	61,389	Wheeling	106
Pendleton	7,910	Franklin	695
Pleasants	8,236	St. Marys	129
Pocahontas	9,919	Marlinton	943
Preston	30,460	Kingwood	645
Putnam	38,181	Winfield	348
Raleigh	86,821	Beckley	605
Randolph	28,734	Elkins	1,036
Ritchie	11,442	Harrisville	452
Roane	15,952	Spencer	486
Summers	15,875	Hinton	350
Taylor	16,584	Grafton	174
Tucker	8,675	Parsons	421
Tyler	11,320	Middlebourne	256
Upshur	23,427	Buckhannon	352
Wayne	46,021	Wayne	513
Webster	12,245	Webster Springs	551
Wetzel	21,874	New Martinsville	363
Wirt	4,922	Elizabeth	235
Wood	93,648	Parkersburg	368
Wyoming	35,993	Pineville	504

Wisconsin

(72 counties, 54,464 sq. mi. land; pop., 4,705,335)

County	Pop.	County seat or court house	Land area sq. mi.
Adams	13,457	Friendship	646
Ashland	16,783	Ashland	1,038
Barron	38,730	Barron	864
Bayfield	13,822	Washburn	1,460
Brown	175,280	Green Bay	524
Buffalo	14,309	Alma	711
Burnett	12,340	Grantsburg	840
Calumet	30,867	Chilton	322
Chippewa	51,702	Chippewa Falls	1,018
Clark	32,910	Neillsville	1,221
Columbia	43,222	Portage	776
Crawford	16,556	Prairie du Chien	568
Dane	323,545	Madison	1,198
Dodge	74,747	Juneau	889
Door	25,029	Sturgeon Bay	492
Douglas	44,421	Superior	1,305
Dunn	34,314	Menomonie	853
Eau Claire	78,805	Eau Claire	647
Florence	4,172	Florence	487
Fond Du Lac	88,952	Fond du Lac	725
Forest	9,044	Crandon	1,007

County	Pop.	County seat or court house	Land area sq. mi.
Grant	51,736	Lancaster	1,147
Green	30,012	Monroe	585
Green Lake	18,370	Green Lake	354
Iowa	19,802	Dodgeville	762
Iron	6,730	Hurley	747
Jackson	16,831	Black River Falls	999
Jefferson	66,152	Jefferson	564
Juneau	21,039	Mauston	774
Kenosha	123,137	Kenosha	272
Kewaunee	19,539	Kewaunee	330
La Crosse	91,056	La Crosse	451
Lafayette	17,412	Darlington	643
Langlade	19,978	Antigo	856
Lincoln	26,311	Merrill	892
Manitowoc	82,918	Manitowoc	590
Marathon	111,270	Wausau	1,586
Marinette	39,314	Marinette	1,378
Marquette	11,672	Montello	455
Menominee	3,373	Keshena	360
Milwaukee	964,988	Milwaukee	237
Monroe	35,074	Sparta	915
Oconto	28,947	Oconto	1,001
Oneida	31,216	Rhinelander	1,112
Outagamie	128,726	Appleton	634
Ozaukee	66,981	Port Washington	236
Pepin	7,477	Durand	235
Pierce	31,149	Ellsworth	590
Polk	32,351	Balsam Lake	931
Portage	57,420	Stevens Point	806
Price	15,788	Phillips	1,260
Racine	173,132	Racine	337
Richland	17,476	Richland Center	583
Rock	139,420	Janesville	721
Rusk	15,589	Ladysmith	906
St. Croix	43,872	Hudson	734
Sauk	43,469	Baraboo	841
Sawyer	12,843	Hayward	1,259
Shawano	35,928	Shawano	919

Sheboygan	100,935	Sheboygan	505
Taylor	18,817	Medford	975
Trempealeau	26,158	Whitehall	735
Vernon	25,642	Viroqua	802
Vilas	16,535	Eagle River	867
Walworth	71,507	Elkhorn	557
Washburn	13,174	Shell Lake	817
Washington	84,848	West Bend	429
Waukesha	280,326	Waukesha	554
Waupaca	42,831	Waupaca	751
Waushara	18,526	Wautoma	627
Winnebago	131,732	Oshkosh	448
Wood	72,799	Wisconsin Rapids	807

Wyoming

(23 counties, 97,203 sq. mi. land; pop., 470,816)

Albany	29,062	Laramie	4,248
Big Horn	11,896	Basin	3,157
Campbell	24,367	Gillette	4,756
Carbon	21,896	Rawlins	7,905
Converse	14,069	Douglas	4,281
Crook	5,308	Sundance	2,882
Fremont	40,251	Lander	9,106
Goshen	12,040	Torrington	2,228
Hot Springs	5,710	Thermopolis	2,022
Johnson	6,700	Buffalo	4,175
Laramie	68,649	Cheyenne	2,703
Lincoln	12,177	Kemmerer	4,085
Natrona	71,856	Casper	5,342
Niobrara	2,924	Lusk	2,614
Park	21,639	Cody	6,959
Platte	11,975	Wheatland	2,086
Sheridan	25,048	Sheridan	2,532
Sublette	4,548	Pinedale	4,851
Sweetwater	41,723	Green River	10,429
Teton	9,355	Jackson	4,000
Uinta	13,021	Evanston	2,086
Washakie	9,496	Worland	2,262
Weston	7,106	Newcastle	2,407

Population of Outlying Areas

Source: U.S. Bureau of the Census

Population figures are preliminary figures from the 1980 census conducted on Apr. 1, 1980.

Puerto Rico

ZIP code	Municipios	Pop.	Land area sq. mile	ZIP code	Municipios	Pop.	Land area sq. mile	ZIP code	Municipios	Pop.	Land area sq. mile
00601	Adjuntas	18,617	66	00650	Florida	7,193	10	00720	Orocovis	19,304	63
00602	Aguada	31,521	30	00653	Guanica	18,784	37	00723	Patillas	17,820	48
00603	Aguadilla	52,627	36	00654	Guayama	40,137	65	00724	Penuelas	18,489	44
00607	Aguas Buenas	22,431	30	00656	Guayanilla	21,012	42	00731	Ponce	188,219	116
00609	Aibonito	22,230	31	00657	Guaynabo	80,857	27	00742	Quebradillas	19,775	23
00610	Anasco	22,945	40	00658	Gurabo	23,576	28	00743	Rincon	11,770	14
00612	Arecibo	86,660	127	00659	Hatillo	28,973	42	00745	Rio Grande	34,326	61
00615	Arroyo	17,055	15	00660	Hormigueros	13,983	11	00747	Sabana Grande	20,164	37
00617	Barceloneta	18,869	24	00661	Humacao	45,916	45	00751	Salinas	26,494	69
00618	Barranquitas	21,690	33	00662	Isabela	37,451	56	00753	San German	32,941	54
00619	Bayamon	195,965	44	00664	Jayuya	14,720	39	*00936	San Juan	432,973	47
00623	Cabo Rojo	33,909	72	00665	Juana Diaz	43,464	61	00754	San Lorenzo	32,333	53
00625	Caguas	118,020	58	00666	Juncos	25,433	26	00755	San Sebastian	35,877	71
00627	Camuy	24,886	46	00667	Lajas	21,190	60	00757	Santa Isabel	19,832	34
00629	Canovanas	31,934	28	00669	Lares	26,742	62	00758	Toa Alta	31,946	27
00630	Carolina	165,207	48	00670	Las Marias	8,606	44	00759	Toa Baja	78,119	24
00632	Catano	26,318	5	00671	Las Piedras	22,425	33	00760	Trujillo Alto	51,389	21
00633	Cayey	40,927	50	00672	Loiza	20,902	25	00761	Utuado	34,384	115
00635	Ceiba	14,781	27	00673	Luquillo	14,924	26	00762	Vega Alta	28,225	28
00638	Ciales	16,014	66	00701	Manati	36,480	46	00763	Vega Baja	46,841	47
00639	Cidra	28,135	36	00706	Maricao	6,617	37	00765	Vieques	7,628	52
00640	Coamo	30,752	77	00707	Maunabo	11,785	21	00766	Villalba	20,737	37
00642	Comerio	18,212	28	00708	Mayaguez	95,886	77	00767	Yabucoa	30,589	55
00643	Corozal	28,218	42	00716	Moca	29,309	51	00768	Yauco	37,682	68
00645	Culebra	1,265	10	00717	Morovis	21,145	39		Total	3,187,570	3,421
00646	Dorado	25,515	23	00718	Naguabo	20,633	52				
00648	Fajardo	32,011	31	00719	Naranjito	23,613	28				

ZIP code	Area	Pop.	Land area sq. mile	ZIP code	Area	Pop.	Land area sq. mile	ZIP code	Area	Pop.	Land area sq. mile
	American Samoa			96916	Merizo	1,658	6		St. Thomas	44,218	32
96799	American				Mongmong-Too-Maite			00801	Charlotte Amalie	NA	
	Samoa	32,395	76			5,230	2	00820	Christiansted	NA	
	Guam				Piti	1,518	7	00840	Frederiksted	NA	
				96915	Santa Rita	10,408	17		Total	95,591	132
	Guam	105,821	209		Sinajana	2,471	1				
96910	Agana	881	1		Talofofo	2,016	17		**Trust Territory of**		
	Agana Hts	3,284	1	96911	Tamuning	13,537	6		**Pacific Islands**		
96915	Agat	3,979	10		Umatac	732	6				
	Asan	2,024	6	96914	Yigo	10,435	35		Mariana district	NA	184
96913	Barrigada	7,762	9		Yona	4,233	20		Marshall district	NA	70
	Chalan-Pago-Ordot	3,135	6						Palau district	NA	192
96912	Dededo	23,646	30		**Virgin Islands**				Ponape district	NA	176
96916	Inarajan	2,062	19						Truk district	NA	49
	Mangilao	6,810	10		St. Croix	49,013	80		Yap district	NA	46
					St. John	2,360	20		Total	NA	717

Poverty by Family Status, Sex, and Race

Source: U.S. Bureau of the Census
(In 1979, according to poverty level defined in table below. Thousands)

	1979 No.	1979 %*	1978 No.	1978 %*	1977 No.	1977 %*	1976 No.	1976 %*
Total poor	25,349	11.6	24,497	11.4	24,720	11.6	24,975	11.8
In families	19,392	10.1	19,062	10.0	19,505	10.2	19,632	10.3
Head	5,320	9.1	5,280	9.1	5,311	9.3	5,311	9.4
Related children	9,738	16.0	9,722	15.7	10,028	16.0	10,081	15.8
Other relatives	4,336	6.0	4,059	5.7	4,165	5.9	4,240	6.0
Unrelated individuals	5,600	21.9	5,435	22.1	5,216	22.6	5,344	24.9
In male-head families	10,252	6.2	9,793	5.9	10,300	6.2	10,603	6.4
Head	2,745	5.5	2,626	5.3	2,701	5.5	2,768	5.6
Related children	4,224	8.5	4,035	7.9	4,371	8.5	4,497	8.5
Other relatives	3,282	5.0	3,131	4.8	3,228	5.0	3,337	5.2
Unrelated male individuals	1,930	16.9	1,824	17.1	1,796	18.0	1,787	19.7
In female-head families	9,142	34.8	9,269	35.6	9,205	36.2	9,029	37.3
Head	2,575	30.2	2,654	31.4	2,610	31.7	2,543	33.0
Related children	5,513	48.6	5,687	50.6	5,658	50.3	5,583	52.0
Other relatives	1,054	16.4	928	14.6	938	15.8	903	15.7
Unrelated female individuals	3,669	26.0	3,611	26.0	3,419	26.1	3,557	28.7
Total white poor	16,823	8.9	16,259	8.7	16,416	8.9	16,713	9.1
In families	12,213	7.4	12,050	7.3	12,364	7.5	12,500	7.5
Head	3,515	6.8	3,523	6.9	3,540	7.0	3,560	7.1
Female	1,328	22.3	1,391	23.5	1,400	24.0	1,379	25.2
Related children	5,759	11.4	5,674	11.0	5,943	11.4	6,034	11.3
Other relatives	2,939	4.6	2,852	4.5	2,882	4.6	2,906	4.7
Unrelated individuals	4,351	19.7	4,209	19.8	4,051	20.4	4,213	22.7
Total black poor	7,838	30.9	7,625	30.6	7,726	31.3	7,595	31.1
In families	6,614	29.9	6,493	29.5	6,667	30.5	6,576	30.1
Head	1,666	27.6	1,622	27.5	1,637	28.2	1,617	27.9
Female	1,195	49.2	1,208	50.6	1,162	51.0	1,122	52.2
Related children	3,695	40.7	3,781	41.2	3,850	41.6	3,758	40.4
Other relatives	1,252	17.9	1,094	15.7	1,181	17.4	1,201	17.8
Unrelated individuals	1,143	36.8	1,132	38.6	1,059	37.0	1,019	39.8

*Percent of total population in that general category who fell below poverty level. For example, of all black female heads of households in 1978, 50.6% were poor.

Estimated Poverty Level, 1980, by Family Size and Sex of Head

Number of family members	Total	Non-Farm Total	Non-Farm Male	Non-Farm Female	Farm Total	Farm Male	Farm Female
1 member	$4,180	$4,190	$4,380	$4,040	$3,560	$3,670	$3,410
Under 65 yrs.	4,280	4,290	4,440	4,110	3,690	3,770	3,490
65 yrs. and over	3,940	3,950	3,990	3,940	3,360	3,390	3,350
2 members	5,340	5,360	5,380	5,300	4,530	4,530	4,450
Head under 65 yrs	5,510	5,540	5,570	5,410	4,720	4,730	4,570
Head 65 yrs. and over	4,950	4,980	4,990	4,950	4,230	4,240	4,180
3 members	6,540	6,570	6,610	6,390	5,580	5,590	5,310
4 members	8,380	8,410	8,420	8,380	7,180	7,190	7,110
5 members	9,920	9,960	9,970	9,870	8,510	8,510	8,520
6 members	11,180	11,250	11,260	11,170	9,560	9,570	9,430
7 members or more	13,860	13,940	13,990	13,660	11,960	11,970	11,550

Poverty Level, 1979

Numbers of family members	Total	Non-Farm Total	Non-Farm Male	Non-Farm Female	Farm Total	Farm Male	Farm Female
1 member	$3,683	$3,689	$3,855	$3,556	$3,138	$3,236	$3,001
Under 65 yrs.	3,773	3,778	3,912	3,619	3,254	3,324	3,076
65 years and over	3,472	3,479	3,515	3,469	2,963	2,988	2,948
2 members	4,702	4,725	4,737	4,669	3,987	3,991	3,917
Head under 65 yrs	4,858	4,878	4,905	4,762	4,156	4,163	4,027
Head 65 years and over	4,364	4,390	4,394	4,362	3,730	3,732	3,686
3 members	5,763	5,784	5,820	5,624	4,917	4,928	4,680
4 members	7,386	7,412	7,416	7,381	6,329	6,332	6,261
5 members	8,736	8,775	8,785	8,690	7,492	7,492	7,509
6 members	9,849	9,914	9,922	9,843	8,424	8,428	8,309
7 members or more	12,212	12,280	12,322	12,037	10,533	10,547	10,178

Income Distribution by Population Fifths

Families, 1979	Top income of each fifth Lowest	Second	Third	Fourth	Average Top 5%	Lowest fifth	Second fifth	Third fifth	Fourth fifth	Highest fifth	Top 5%
Total	$9,853	$16,250	$23,000	$31,605	$50,328	5.3	11.6	17.5	24.1	46.1	15.7
White	10,700	17,230	23,750	32,484	51,593	5.7	12.0	17.5	23.8	41.0	15.5
Black and other	5,332	9,921	15,824	24,847	39,000	4.2	9.5	15.9	25.3	45.1	16.3
Black	5,058	9,070	14,644	23,000	36,000	4.3	9.6	16.0	25.4	44.7	15.6

Aid to Families with Dependent Children

Source: Office of Research and Statistics, Social Security Administration

December, 1980 State	No. of families	Number of recipients Total[1]	Children	Payments to recipients Total amount	Average per family	recipient	% change from Dec., 1979 No. of recip.	Amount
Alabama	63,246	178,322	127,684	$6,967,928	$110.17	$39.07	-.4	.9
Alaska	6,606	15,931	10,882	2,590,514	392.15	162.61	5.5	31.3
Arizona	21,573	59,809	43,589	3,809,666	176.59	63.70	19.7	26.8
Arkansas	29,822	85,008	61,667	4,360,856	146.23	51.30	.4	3.1
California	511,486	1,498,216	996,054	220,451,580	431.00	147.14	10.1	27.8
Colorado	29,467	81,031	55,415	7,591,646	257.63	93.69	8.9	17.8
Connecticut	49,407	139,685	96,240	18,308,524	370.57	131.07	2.9	14.7
Delaware	12,404	34,243	23,555	2,817,520	227.15	82.28	5.1	5.9
Dist. of Columbia	30,278	81,985	56,556	7,661,257	253.03	93.45	-5.1	-4.4
Florida	103,315	279,392	199,015	18,229,236	176.44	65.25	12.8	16.0
Georgia	89,912	233,730	168,813	12,591,009	140.04	53.87	8.5	23.4
Guam	1,492	5,311	3,877	316,333	212.02	59.56	12.4	15.6
Hawaii	20,046	61,342	40,802	7,731,955	385.71	126.05	2.2	3.7
Idaho	7,503	20,326	13,845	2,064,949	275.22	101.59	-.9	3.0
Illinois	222,937	691,434	482,773	62,903,873	282.16	90.98	4.6	8.4
Indiana	60,229	170,239	119,431	12,351,154	205.07	72.55	11.8	23.5
Iowa	40,476	111,287	73,907	12,553,542	310.15	112.80	13.6	15.3
Kansas	27,720	71,956	50,828	7,817,479	282.02	108.64	11.3	19.3
Kentucky	67,159	175,071	122,437	12,478,662	185.81	71.28	6.7	22.5
Louisiana	72,163	218,966	160,212	11,254,465	155.96	51.40	4.1	19.1
Maine	21,466	57,700	39,504	4,954,190	230.79	85.86	-5.1	-.9
Maryland	80,823	220,316	148,989	19,304,624	238.85	87.62	5.0	17.5
Massachusetts	125,232	347,830	226,570	43,793,572	349.70	125.91	-1.2	7.2
Michigan	246,648	752,578	494,459	96,243,119	390.20	127.88	16.4	21.3
Minnesota	53,856	145,634	96,383	18,582,462	345.04	127.60	11.9	20.0
Mississippi	59,814	176,253	129,704	5,257,257	87.89	29.83	2.8	5.8
Missouri	73,506	215,682	144,865	16,795,310	228.49	77.87	12.9	24.1
Montana	7,136	19,883	13,621	1,646,790	230.77	82.82	8.7	12.0
Nebraska	13,573	37,541	25,900	3,890,757	286.65	103.64	10.6	24.8
Nevada	5,114	13,827	9,524	1,096,034	214.32	79.27	23.9	35.7
New Hampshire	8,647	23,648	15,636	2,377,068	274.90	100.52	9.7	17.2
New Jersey	152,383	469,010	322,034	49,908,100	327.52	106.41	2.8	13.1
New Mexico	19,550	56,157	38,857	3,705,145	189.52	65.98	7.8	21.9
New York	367,628	1,109,601	762,672	136,745,976	371.97	123.24	1.3	1.9
North Carolina	80,074	201,828	142,638	13,014,235	162.53	64.48	4.3	5.5
North Dakota	4,859	13,111	9,045	1,413,489	290.90	107.81	3.2	9.9
Ohio	200,243	572,347	380,365	50,348,940	251.44	87.97	16.9	16.9
Oklahoma	31,543	91,984	66,752	7,880,651	249.84	85.67	5.5	6.4
Oregon	35,440	93,993	60,731	9,315,930	262.86	99.11	-4.3	-23.5
Pennsylvania	218,713	637,387	435,408	64,712,837	295.88	101.53	2.6	9.1
Puerto Rico	40,245	169,697	118,368	2,812,545	60.82	16.57	-2.9	14.9
Rhode Island	18,772	53,950	36,563	7,613,825	405.59	141.13	7.3	8.7
South Carolina	57,643	156,080	110,573	6,685,505	115.98	42.83	4.5	21.8
South Dakota	6,946	18,753	13,120	1,555,186	223.90	82.93	-7.1	-1.8
Tennessee	65,958	173,854	122,637	7,448,916	112.93	42.85	10.2	10.7
Texas	106,104	320,002	232,384	11,490,205	108.29	35.91	4.5	4.6
Utah	13,954	43,710	27,335	4,504,653	322.82	103.06	25.9	33.8
Vermont	8,129	24,251	15,379	2,839,074	349.25	117.07	14.7	21.2
Virgin Islands	1,165	3,441	2,721	228,534	196.17	66.41	13.3	57.6
Virginia	65,272	175,927	121,821	14,487,213	221.95	82.35	7.8	19.1
Washington	61,639	173,339	108,234	23,434,682	380.19	135.20	20.9	27.2
West Virginia	28,026	79,971	60,820	4,970,373	177.35	62.15	3.8	5.6
Wisconsin	85,129	231,979	154,465	32,026,663	376.21	138.06	15.2	26.7
Wyoming	2,737	7,008	4,996	720,012	263.07	102.74	6.5	8.3
Total	3,841,208	11,101,556	7,600,455	$1,106,656,020	$288.10	$99.68	7.0	14.8

(e) Estimated. (1) Includes as recipients the children and one or both parents or one caretaker relative other than a parent in families in which the requirements of such adults were concerned in determining the amount of assistance. (2) Incomplete. Data for foster care not reported by Puerto Rico and the Virgin Islands.

Welfare Recipients and Payments, 1955-1980

Category		1955, Dec.	1965, Dec.	1970, Dec. (b)	1975, Dec. (b)	1978, Dec.	1979, Dec.	1980, Dec.
Old age:	Recipients	2,538,000	2,087,000	2,082,000	2,333,685	1,967,900	1,871,716	1,807,776
	Total amt.	$127,003,000	$131,674,000	$161,642,000	$217,002,000	$197,630,000	$229,613,000	$221,303,000
	Avg. amt.	$50.05	$63.10	$77.65	$92.99	$100.43	$122.67	$128.20
	(a)Avg. real $	$62.41	$66.75	$66.78	$57.65	$49.47	$53.50	$49.61
AFDC:	Recipients	2,192,000	4,396,000	9,659,000	11,389,000	10,325,000	10,378,679	11,101,556
	Total amt.	$51,472,000	$144,355,000	$485,877,000	$824,648,000	$891,399,000	$963,929,242	$1,106,656,000
	Avg. amt.	$23.50	$32.85	$50.30	$72.40	$86.33	$92.88	$99.68
	(a)Avg. real $	$29.30	$34.76	$43.26	$44.89	$46.49	$45.58	$38.58
Blind:	Recipients	104,000	85,100	81,000	75,315	77,135	77,250	78,401
	Total amt.	$5,803,000	$6,922,000	$8,446,000	$11,220,000	$12,681,000	$16,398,000	$16,381,000
	Avg. amt.	$55.55	$81.35	$104.35	$148.97	$164.40	$212.27	$213.23
	(a)Avg. real $	$69.27	$86.07	$89.74	$92.36	$88.34	$92.25	$82.52
Disabled:	Recipients	241,000	557,000	935,000	1,950,625	2,171,890	2,200,609	2,255,840
	Total amt.	$11,750,000	$37,035,000	$91,325,000	$279,073,000	$336,256,000	$399,879,000	$444,322,000
	Avg. amt.	$48.75	$66.50	$97.65	$143.07	$154.82	$181.71	$197.90
	(a)Avg. real $	$60.79	$70.36	$83.98	$88.70	$83.19	$79.35	$76.59

(a) Dollar amounts adjusted to represent actual purchasing power in terms of average value of dollar during 1967. (b) Administration of the public assistance programs of Old-age Assistance, Aid to the Blind, and Aid to the Disabled was transferred to the Social Security Administration by Public Law 92-603 effective 1/1/74.

Women 1981: A Total Disaster?

by June Foley

Last year's World Almanac termed 1980 a "discouraging" year for women. How, then, to describe 1981?

"A total disaster." That's how Joyce Miller, president of the Coalition of Labor Union Women, characterized the effect of the election of Ronald Reagan and a more conservative Congress on women's rights issues. The Republican platform had dropped its 40-year-old endorsement of the Equal Rights Amendment, and had included an endorsement of a constitutional amendment prohibiting abortion; the new president was personally opposed to the ERA and favored the anti-abortion amendment. In opposing Reagan's election, the National Organization for Women had referred to his position on women's issues as "medieval."

Phyllis Schlafly, leader of the Stop-ERA movement, called the election "a decisive defeat for the ERA and for the feminist movement." However, Eleanor Smeal, president of NOW, argued against this interpretation. Smeal maintained that the election was a "protest vote" against inflation, unemployment, and the Carter administration foreign policy. "Not only do I think it was not a vote on the social policies of the women's movement, I don't think it was even a vote on the social policies of the right wing," Smeal said. John Dolan, chairman of the National Conservative Political Action Committee, agreed that women's issues were "largely irrelevant" in the campaign.

Whatever accounted for it, the Republican sweep eliminated a president who supported at least some feminist goals; it also eliminated some of the strongest supporters of those goals in the Senate, the House of Representatives, and state legislatures.

The single female Senatorial candidate to win election was Paula Hawkins, a Florida Republican who opposed the ERA and favored passage of the amendment banning abortion. She was the first woman to win a Senate seat without the benefit of a politically prominent male relative.

In all, the major parties had nominated 52 women for House races and 5 for Senate races. The election gave women 19 seats in the House and 2 in the Senate. Eleanor Smeal commented, "The bottom line is that these are just token increases, and essentially women are still not represented. At this rate it will take women 217 years to reach parity, a prospect which does not give you solace."

Nor could supporters of the women's movement derive solace from a number of the early actions of the Reagan administration. During its first 3 months in office, the administration filled more than half of some 400 top federal positions requiring Senate confirmation. Among those appointees were only 18 women. As of July 13, only 42 were women. Only one—Jeane J. Kirkpatrick, the chief U.S. delegate to the U.N.—held cabinet rank. Of the 52 senior positions on the White House staff, ranging upward from the level of special assistant to the president, just 6 were filled by women, including the president's personal secretary.

One step forward, however, was the president's nomination of Sandra Day O'Connor, a 51-year-old judge on the Arizona Court of Appeals, to be the first woman to serve on the Supreme Court. Most women's rights advocates could hardly fail to approve of the idea of a woman on the Supreme Court; such a woman could be an important, inspiring role model for future generations. It remained to be seen, though, whether Judge O'Connor, a conservative Republican, was any more liberal on women's rights issues than was her moderate-to-conservative predecessor, Justice Potter Stewart.

Anti-Abortion Activity

With the inauguration of the new administration, anti-abortion forces gathered strength. In March, Sen. Jesse Helms (R., N.C.) and Rep. Henry Hyde (R., Ill.) introduced a bill that would seem to make an anti-abortion constitutional amendment unnecessary. The proposed Helms-Hyde bill declared that human life "shall be deemed to exist from conception." According to President Reagan, "Once you have determined this, the Constitution already protects the rights of human life. . .there really isn't any need for an amendment."

Impassioned arguments before the Judiciary Committee's Subcommittee on the Separation of Powers followed. Sarah Weddington, former assistant to Pres. Jimmy Carter, and one of the lawyers who argued the 1973 Supreme Court case that legalized abortion, was key witness for 75 national organizations with 34 million members opposing the bill. Weddington maintained that the bill "blatantly disregards the integrity of the constitutional process, the separation of powers, the religious liberty of our citizens, the will of the people, and sound practice of medicine and the desperate needs of women facing problem pregnancies." She added that any attempt to ban abortion "will not reduce the number of abortions because you will not have eliminated the reasons that women feel compelled to seek abortions."

Speaking in favor of the bill, Rep. Hyde called abortion "a sort of humane holocaust of the unborn." Dr. Carolyn F. Gerster, a Scottsdale, Ariz., physician and former president of the National Right to Life Committee, said, "If one is prepared to give the woman the unrestricted right to kill her unborn daughter, one had better be prepared to someday give the daughter the unrestricted right to kill the aged mother. Euthanasia has followed abortion as the night follows the day." The final bill was expected to reach the Senate floor in late Fall.

ERA Status

To many ERA-activists, the prospects for ratification of the Equal Rights Amendment seemed bleak. Supporters had only until June 30, 1982, to lobby 3 more state legislatures to approve the amendment and reach the total of 38 needed for ratification. No state had passed the amendment since 1977 and 5 state legislatures had voted to withdraw approval. However, NOW leaders expressed encouragement when the number of new memberships per month more than doubled—to 7,500 a month—after the November elections. Moreover, the public continued to support the ERA—by a 52% to 46% margin in a December 1980 Harris poll. NOW planned to mount a nationwide grass-roots campaign, raise $15 million, recruit 2 million volunteers, and focus on 7 targets—Florida, Georgia, Illinois, Missouri, No. Carolina, Oklahoma, and Virginia.

The Poorest of the Poor

On the economic front, the new year brought a series of blows to supporters of women's rights, beginning with the president's budget proposals. The proposals were attacked, Mar. 26, by a coalition of women's groups, including student, child-welfare, civil rights, political, and service organizations. The coalition especially protested budget cutbacks that would adversely affect the poor. Women are "the poorest of the poor," according to the coalition's statement, "since more than 67% of those living below the poverty line are women, since one out of every 3 households is now headed by a woman, and since the bulk of those with an income of less than half the poverty level are women." The statement continued: "We are deeply concerned about a national fiscal policy that will lock women into the cycle of poverty and offer no relief for the future."

Among the specific proposals "bound to impact disproportionately and harshly on women," the coalition listed: reductions in federal assistance for child-care facilities, cutbacks in food and nutrition programs, reductions in job training, limits in the civil right enforcement program, and cuts in the availability of family planning services.

Another source of concern for advocates of women's rights was the president's proposals to cut some Social Security benefits to keep the retirement system solvent. At a hearing by the Task Force on Social Security and Women of the House Select Committee on Aging, the proposals were criticized by Rep. Patricia Schroeder (D., Col.), co-chairwoman of the Congresswomen's Caucus, as particularly threatening to women. Among the statistics, compiled by the Women's Bureau of the Department of Labor, that were cited: one out of every 4 women working today can expect to be poor in her old age, because Social Security is tied to wages, and women earn only about 60% of what men earn; in 1979, the median Social Security benefit for all women over age 65 was $2,813 compared to $5,479 for men over age 65. The majority of single women receiving Social Security had no other major source of income. Some 81 percent of women 65 and over, not residing with relatives, lived below the poverty line. Rep. Mary Oakar (D., Oh.) remarked that "the failure of the Social Security system to meet the most basic needs of women" was "nothing less than a national scandal."

Many feminists considered it a severe blow when the Reagan administration announced that new regulations would enable almost three-fourths of the companies doing business with the federal government to eliminate affirmative action paperwork. The proposals affect regulations covering 200,000 contractors and nearly 300 million workers. Under the current rules, contractors with 50 or more employees and federal contracts worth $50,000 are required to file documents saying that they are taking "affirmative action steps," i.e., recruiting and instituting goals and timetables to increase the number of minority group members and women, if their numbers are below the level of the area workforce. Under the new proposals, only federal contractors with 250 or more employees and a contract worth $1 million would have to file.

In support of the new proposals, Labor Secretary Raymond J. Donovan argued that they would retain affirmative action protection for nearly 77% of workers who are women or minority group members. But William E. Pollard, director of the department of civil rights of the A.F.L.-C.I.O., said, "This is really a kind of backsliding by the government. Affirmative action is an effort to eliminate discrimination against minorities and women. No president until now has tried to weaken them. . . . The government ought to lead the way against discrimination, not the retreat."

Gender-Distinction Decisions

Many feminists also found onimous a number of Supreme Court decisions based on gender-distinctions. One such decision upheld the constitutionality of the all-male draft. The court based this decision on its deference to the authority of Congress about national defense issues. In 1948, Congress had barred women from the draft, and in 1980 women were barred from registering for the draft. These prohibitions were based on the idea that the draft's major function was to provide troops for combat, but federal law and military policy both kept women from combat. David Landau of the American Civil Liberties Union called the Supreme Court's decision "a devastating loss for women's rights and civil rights generally."

A second decision regarding gender-distinction rejected a constitutional challenge to statutory rape laws that punished only men for having sex with an under-age partner.

The decisions of other courts were foreboding, as well: A federal judge in Detroit ruled that educational institutions receiving federal funds did not have to provide equal athletic programs for men and women. U.S. District Judge Charles F. Joiner noted that Title IX of the 1974 Higher Education Act extended "only to those educational programs or activities which receive direct federal financial assistance." Since federal money rarely went directly into financing sports in public schools or colleges, the judge reasoned that Title IX did not apply to athletics. The ruling was called "a major attack on women and women's education programs" by Janet Wells of the National Coalition for Women and Girls in Education.

Summarizing 1981 as a total disaster for women's rights issues might be considered too strong a statement by many activists. But most would probably agree with the prediction made by Sarah Weddington after the November, 1980 elections: "It's going to take a major effort not to go backward in the next four years, let alone try to move ahead."

America's 25 Most Influential Women in 1981

The following women were chosen by The World Almanac co-sponsoring newspapers. This year, for the first time, the winners were ranked by the number of votes they received. Tied for first place as America's Most Influential Women are Katharine Graham, 64, chairman of The Washington Post Co., who has been on every list of the most influential women since the initial list in 1977; and Billie Jean King, 38, tennis veteran and feminist who makes her first appearance on the list since 1977.

Arts

Beverly Sills, general director of the New York City Opera.
Lillian Hellman, author and playwright whose *The Little Foxes* was revived on Broadway in 1981.

Business

Katharine Graham, chairman of the board and chief executive officer of the Washington Post Co., which owns the newspaper, *Newsweek* magazine, and radio and TV stations.
Gloria Vanderbilt, fashion designer, who appeared in ads for her bluejeans in 1981.

Education, Scholarship, Science

Barbara Jordan, professor at the Lyndon B. Johnson School of Public Affairs, University of Texas at Austin.
Jane Bryant Quinn, journalist, writes financial column for *Newsweek.*

Entertainment

Jane Fonda, political activist, actress; starred in movie about secretaries, *9-to-5*, in 1981.
Katharine Hepburn, veteran actress, appeared in theater, movies, and on TV in 1981.
Dolly Parton, country and pop singer; made debut as actress in *9-to-5* in 1981.
Mary Tyler Moore, TV actress nominated for Oscar for movie *Ordinary People* in 1981.

Government

Jane Byrne, mayor of Chicago, is first woman to hold that office.

Nancy Reagan, First Lady, former movie actress.
Jeane J. Kirkpatrick, chief U.S. delegate to the United Nations.
Shirley Chisholm, U.S. congresswoman from Brooklyn, spokeswoman for the rights of the poor.

Media

Ellen Goodman, Boston Globe columnist, won Pulitzer Prize for commentary.
Barbara Walters, broadcast journalist at ABC-TV, was first woman to anchor the news.
Ann Landers, nationally-syndicated personal advice columnist.
Abigail Van Buren, author of syndicated column "Dear Abby."
Erma Bombeck, syndicated columnist, author of bestselling humorous books.

Social Action

Phyllis Schlafly, leader of Stop-ERA movement.
Coretta Scott King, civil rights leader, widow of assassinated Martin Luther King.
Gloria Steinem, feminist, journalist, editor of Ms. magazine.

Sports

Billie Jean King, veteran tennis player, spearhead of "Women's Lob" for women's tennis association, bigger purses.
Nancy Lopez-Melton, golfer who won unprecedented 5 consecutive tournaments on LPGA circuits.
Chris Evert-Lloyd, tennis player, 1981 Wimbledon champ.

Presidential Election Statistics

Popular and Electoral Vote, 1976 and 1980

Source: Clerk of the House of Representatives

States	1976 Electoral Vote Carter	Ford	Democrat Carter	Republican Ford	1980 Electoral Vote Carter	Reagan	Democrat Carter	Republican Reagan	Indep. Anderson
Ala. . . .	9		659,170	504,070	0	9	636,730	654,192	16,481
Alas. . .		3	44,058	71,555	0	3	41,842	86,112	11,155
Ariz. . .		6	295,602	418,642	0	6	246,843	529,688	76,952
Ark. . . .	6		498,604	267,903	0	6	398,041	403,164	22,468
Cal. . . .		45	3,742,284	3,882,244	0	45	3,082,943	4,522,994	739,618
Col. . . .		7	460,353	584,367	0	7	368,009	652,264	130,633
Conn. . .		8	647,895	719,261	0	8	541,732	677,210	171,807
Del. . . .	3		122,596	109,831	0	3	105,754	111,252	16,288
D.C. . . .	3		137,818	27,873	3	0	130,231	23,313	16,131
Fla. . . .	17		1,636,000	1,469,531	0	17	1,419,475	2,046,951	189,692
Ga. . . .	12		979,409	483,743	12	0	890,955	654,168	36,055
Ha. . . .	4		147,375	140,003	4	0	135,879	130,112	32,021
Ida. . . .		4	126,549	204,151	0	4	110,192	290,699	27,058
Ill.		26	2,271,295	2,364,269	0	26	1,981,413	2,358,049	346,754
Ind. . . .		13	1,014,714	1,185,958	0	13	844,197	1,255,656	111,639
Ia.		8	619,931	632,863	0	8	508,672	676,026	115,633
Kan. . .		7	430,421	502,752	0	7	326,150	566,812	68,231
Ky. . . .	9		615,717	531,852	0	9	617,417	635,274	31,127
La. . . .	10		661,365	587,446	0	10	708,453	792,853	26,345
Me. . . .		4	232,279	236,320	0	4	220,974	238,522	53,327
Md. . . .	10		759,612	672,661	10	0	726,161	680,606	119,537
Mass. . .	14		1,429,475	1,030,276	0	14	1,053,802	1,057,631	382,539
Mich. . .		21	1,696,714	1,893,742	0	21	1,661,532	1,915,225	275,223
Minn. . .	10		1,070,440	819,395	10	0	954,173	873,268	174,997
Miss. . .	7		381,309	366,846	0	7	429,281	441,089	12,036
Mo. . . .	12		999,163	928,808	0	12	931,182	1,074,181	77,920
Mon. . .		4	149,259	173,703	0	4	118,032	206,814	29,281
Neb. . .		5	233,287	359,219	0	5	166,424	419,214	44,854
Nev. . .		3	92,479	101,273	0	3	66,666	155,017	17,651
N.H. . . .		4	147,645	185,935	0	4	108,864	221,705	49,693
N.J. . . .		17	1,444,653	1,509,688	0	17	1,147,364	1,546,557	234,632
N.M. . .		4	201,148	211,419	0	4	167,826	250,779	29,459
N.Y. . . .	41		3,389,558	3,100,791	0	41	2,728,372	2,893,831	467,801
N.C. . .	13		927,365	741,960	0	13	875,635	915,018	52,800
N.D. . . .		3	136,078	153,470	0	3	79,189	193,695	23,640
Oh. . . .	25		2,011,621	2,000,505	0	25	1,752,414	2,206,545	254,472
Okla. . .		8	532,442	545,708	0	8	402,026	695,570	38,284
Ore. . . .		6	490,407	492,120	0	6	456,890	571,044	112,389
Pa. . . .	27		2,328,677	2,205,604	0	27	1,937,540	2,261,872	292,921
R.I. . . .	4		227,636	181,249	4	0	198,342	154,793	59,819
S.C. . . .	8		450,807	346,149	0	8	428,220	439,277	13,868
S.D. . . .		4	147,068	151,505	0	4	103,855	198,343	21,431
Tenn. . .	10		825,879	633,969	0	10	783,051	787,761	35,991
Tex. . . .	26		2,082,319	1,953,300	0	26	1,881,147	2,510,705	111,613
Ut. . . .		4	182,110	337,908	0	4	124,266	439,687	30,284
Vt.		3	78,789	100,387	0	3	81,952	94,628	31,761
Va. . . .		12	813,896	836,554	0	12	752,174	989,609	95,418
Wash. .		8*	717,323	777,732	0	9	650,193	865,244	185,073
W.Va. . .	6		435,864	314,726	6	0	367,462	334,206	31,691
Wis. . . .	11		1,040,232	1,004,987	0	11	981,584	1,088,845	160,657
Wyo. . .		3	62,239	92,717	0	3	49,427	110,700	12,072
Total . .	**297**	**240**	**40,828,929**	**39,148,940**	**49**	**489**	**35,480,948**	**43,898,770**	**5,719,222**

*One elector in Washington for Reagan. In 1976, McCarthy (Independent) received 739,256 votes; McBride (Libertarian) received 171,818 votes.

Presidential Election Returns by Counties
Compiled from official state returns by The World Almanac.

Alabama

County	1976 Carter (D)	Ford (R)	1980 Carter (D)	Reagan (R)	Anderson (I)
Autauga	4,640	4,512	4,295	6,292	125
Baldwin	9,191	13,256	8,448	18,652	414
Barbour	4,730	3,758	4,458	4,171	65
Bibb	2,850	1,591	3,097	2,491	22
Blount	6,645	4,233	5,656	6,819	75
Bullock	3,536	1,482	3,960	1,446	29
Butler	4,271	2,909	4,156	3,810	59
Calhoun	20,466	11,763	17,017	17,475	433
Chambers	6,164	5,488	6,649	4,864	122
Cherokee	4,668	1,492	3,764	2,482	63
Chilton	5,550	4,725	4,706	6,615	60
Choctaw	3,911	3,033	3,680	2,859	22
Clarke	4,737	4,126	5,249	5,059	55
Clay	2,946	1,883	2,858	2,764	34
Cleburne	2,490	1,436	2,050	2,389	34
Coffee	7,844	4,683	6,140	6,760	189
Colbert	11,996	4,471	12,550	6,619	209
Conecuh	3,086	1,812	3,102	2,948	29
Coosa	2,533	1,196	2,383	1,714	19
Covington	7,081	4,977	6,305	7,014	110
Crenshaw	3,372	1,801	2,704	2,478	39
Cullman	12,961	6,899	11,525	10,212	228
Dale	6,346	4,996	4,936	7,247	134
Dallas	8,866	7,144	9,770	7,647	131
DeKalb	9,759	6,597	8,820	9,673	107
Elmore	6,646	6,551	5,947	8,688	171
Escambia	5,957	4,934	5,148	6,513	87
Etowah	25,020	10,333	20,790	16,177	358
Fayette	4,076	2,165	3,389	3,315	47
Franklin	6,279	3,345	6,136	4,448	51
Geneva	5,983	2,663	4,703	4,747	67
Greene	2,900	903	3,474	1,034	16
Hale	3,236	2,034	3,583	2,074	56
Henry	3,144	2,052	2,973	2,813	18
Houston	8,787	10,672	7,848	14,884	184
Jackson	10,989	3,913	8,776	4,897	156
Jefferson	99,531	113,590	113,069	132,612	3,509
Lamar	3,860	1,739	3,366	2,778	16
Lauderdale	15,549	7,226	15,379	10,467	431
Lawrence	6,810	1,415	6,112	2,456	64
Lee	8,427	9,884	9,606	10,982	643
Limestone	8,803	2,997	8,180	4,574	183
Lowndes	3,732	1,621	3,577	1,524	15
Macon	5,915	1,387	7,028	1,250	36
Madison	35,497	20,959	30,469	30,604	2,246
Marengo	4,731	3,841	5,178	4,048	35
Marion	6,244	3,036	5,450	5,182	61
Marshall	13,696	6,006	10,854	8,159	283
Mobile	50,264	53,835	46,180	67,515	1,333
Monroe	3,669	3,476	4,262	4,615	43
Montgomery	24,641	29,360	28,018	35,745	985
Morgan	16,547	9,058	14,703	13,214	457
Perry	4,486	2,164	4,208	2,262	28
Pickens	3,776	2,969	4,504	3,582	61
Pike	5,387	4,363	4,417	5,220	83
Randolph	3,539	2,286	3,378	3,279	58
Russell	8,077	4,150	8,123	4,485	137
St. Claire	5,653	4,877	5,236	7,768	121
Shelby	7,197	9,035	7,396	14,957	407
Sumter	3,457	2,191	5,015	2,104	45
Talladega	10,577	6,425	10,159	9,902	140
Tallapoosa	7,614	5,237	7,260	5,958	96
Tuscaloosa	20,275	16,021	19,103	19,750	789
Walker	16,232	7,389	13,616	8,795	82
Washington	3,471	2,171	3,520	3,045	24
Wilcox	3,723	1,824	4,951	2,280	13
Winston	4,134	3,710	3,368	4,981	39
Totals	**659,170**	**504,070**	**636,730**	**654,192**	**16,481**

Alabama Vote Since 1932

1932 (Pres.), Roosevelt, Dem., 207,910; Hoover, Rep., 34,675; Foster, Com., 406; Thomas, Soc. 2,030; Upshaw, Proh., 13.

1936 (Pres.), Roosevelt, Dem., 238,195; Landon, Rep., 35,358; Colvin, Proh., 719; Browder, Com., 679; Lemke, Union, 549; Thomas, Soc., 242.

1940 (Pres.), Roosevelt, Dem., 250,726; Willkie, Rep., 42,174; Babson, Proh., 698; Browder, Com., 509; Thomas, Soc., 100.

1944 (Pres.), Roosevelt, Dem., 198,918; Dewey, Rep., 44,540; Watson, Proh., 1,095; Thomas, Soc., 190.

1948 (Pres.), Thurmond, States' Rights, 171,443; Dewey, Rep., 40,930; Wallace, Prog., 1,522; Watson, Proh., 1,085.

1952 (Pres.), Eisenhower, Rep., 149,231; Stevenson, Dem., 275,075; Hamblen, Proh., 1,814.

1956 (Pres.), Stevenson, Dem., 290,844; Eisenhower, Rep. 195,694; Independent electors, 20,323.·

1960 (Pres.), Kennedy, Dem., 324,050; Nixon, Rep., 237,981; Faubus, States' Rights, 4,367; Decker, Proh., 2,106; King, Afro-Americans, 1,485; scattering, 236.

1964 (Pres.), Dem. 209,848 (electors unpledged); Goldwater, Rep., 479,085; scattering, 105.

1968 (Pres.), Nixon, Rep., 146,923; Humphrey, Dem., 196,579; Wallace, 3d party, 691,425; Munn, Proh., 4,022.

1972 (Pres.), Nixon, Rep., 728,701; McGovern, Dem., 219,108 plus 37,815 Natl. Demo. Party of Alabama; Schmitz, Conservative, 11,918; Munn., Proh., 8,551.

1976 (Pres.), Carter, Dem., 659,170; Ford, Rep., 504,070; Maddox, Am. Ind., 9,198; Bubar, Proh., 6,669; Hall, Com., 1,954; MacBride, Libertarian, 1,481.

1980 (Pres.), Reagan, Rep., 654,192; Carter, Dem., 636,730; Anderson, Libertarian, 16,481; Rarick, Amer. Ind., 15,010; Clark, Libertarian, 13,318; Bubar, Statesman, 1,743; Hall, Com., 1,629; DeBerry, Soc. Work., 1,303; McReynolds, Socialist, 1,006; Commoner, Citizens, 517.

Alaska

Election District	1976 Carter (D)	Ford (R)	1980 Carter (D)	Reagan (R)	Anderson (I)
No. 1	1,983	2,994	1,772	3,473	440
No. 2	1,022	1,423	1,256	1,612	329
No. 3	1,152	1,710	1,354	2,019	346
No. 4	3,214	5,252	3,899	5,345	1,282
No. 5	1,307	2,071	973	2,847	288
No. 6	1,486	2,882	1,316	5,008	402
No. 7	2,935	4,105	2,620	4,311	676
No. 8	3,368	5,412	2,860	7,432	737
No. 9	1,726	2,561	1,164	2,363	342
No. 10	2,839	6,837	2,778	7,859	849
No. 11	3,568	6,588	3,306	9,741	1,016
No. 12	2,706	6,381	2,456	7,450	829
No. 13	2,090	4,07	1,806	6,170	479
No. 14	856	1,380	844	1,473	254
No. 15	538	746	710	832	213
No. 16	876	1,063	1,083	869	204
No. 17	1,149	1,074	1,623	720	280
No. 18	804	942	1,327	769	193
No. 19	1,415	1,893	1,188	2,255	207
No. 20	6,706	10,306	5,310	11,573	1,304
No. 21	1,229	749	1,022	1,010	223
No. 22	1,086	1,129	1,193	1,081	202
Totals	**44,058**	**71,555**	**41,842**	**86,112**	**11,155**

Alaska Vote Since 1960

1960 (Pres.), Kennedy, Dem., 29,809; Nixon, Rep. 30,953.

1964 (Pres.), Johnson, Dem., 44,329; Goldwater, Rep., 22,930.

1968 (Pres.), Nixon, Rep., 37,600; Humphrey, Dem., 35,411; Wallace, 3d party, 10,024.

1972 (Pres.), Nixon, Rep., 55,349; McGovern, Dem., 32,967; Schmitz, American, 6,906.

1976 (Pres.), Carter, Dem., 44,058; Ford, Rep., 71,555; MacBride, Libertarian, 6,785.

1980 (Pres.), Reagan, Rep., 86,112; Carter, Dem., 41,842; Clark, Libertarian, 18,479; Anderson, Ind., 11,155; Write-in, 857.

Arizona

County	1976 Carter (D)	Ford (R)	1980 Carter (D)	Reagan (R)	Anderson (I)
Apache	6,583	3,447	3,917	5,991	495
Cochise	9,281	9,921	7,028	13,351	1,656
Coconino	9,450	11,036	7,832	14,613	2,815
Gila	6,440	5,136	5,068	7,405	656
Graham	3,050	3,659	2,801	4,765	268
Greenlee	2,601	1,532	2,043	1,537	150
Maricopa	144,613	258,262	119,752	316,287	38,975
Mohave	6,504	7,601	4,900	13,809	978
Navajo	7,323	6,796	5,110	10,790	710
Pima	71,214	77,264	64,418	93,055	25,294
Pinal	10,595	9,354	9,207	12,195	1,346
Santa Cruz	2,265	2,312	2,089	2,674	482
Yavapai	7,685	12,998	6,664	19,823	1,754
Yuma	7,998	9,324	6,014	13,393	1,373
Totals	**295,602**	**418,642**	**246,843**	**529,688**	**76,952**

Arizona Vote Since 1932

1932 (Pres.), Roosevelt, Dem., 79,264; Hoover, Rep., 36,104; Thomas, Soc., 2,030; Foster, Com., 406.

1936 (Pres.), Roosevelt, Dem., 86,722; Landon, Rep., 33,433; Lemke, Union, 3,307; Colvin, Proh., 384; Thomas, Soc., 317.

1940 (Pres.), Roosevelt, Dem., 95,267; Willkie, Rep., 54,030; Babson, Proh., 742.

1944 (Pres.), Roosevelt, Dem., 80,826; Dewey, Rep., 56,287; Watson, Proh., 421.

1948 (Pres.), Truman, Dem., 95,251; Dewey, Rep., 77,597; Wallace, Prog., 3,310; Watson, Proh., 786; Teichert, Soc. Labor, 121.

1952 (Pres.), Eisenhower, Rep., 152,042; Stevenson, Dem., 108,528.

1956 (Pres.), Eisenhower, Rep., 176,990; Stevenson, Dem., 112,880; Andrews, Ind. 303.

1960 (Pres.), Kennedy, Dem., 176,781; Nixon, Rep., 221,241; Hass, Soc. Labor, 469.

1964 (Pres.), Johnson, Dem., 237,753; Goldwater, Rep., 242,535; Hass, Soc. Labor, 482.

1968 (Pres.), Nixon, Rep., 266,721; Humphrey, Dem., 170,514; Wallace, 3d party, 46,573; McCarthy, New Party, 2,751; Halstead, Soc. Worker, 85; Cleaver, Peace and Freedom, 217; Blomen, Soc. Labor, 75.

1972 (Pres.), Nixon, Rep., 402,812; McGovern, Dem., 198,540; Schmitz, Amer., 21,208; Soc. Workers, 30,945. (Due to ballot peculiarities in 3 counties (particularly Pima), thousands of voters cast ballots for the Socialist Workers Party and one of the major candidates. Court ordered both votes counted as official.

1976 (Pres.), Carter, Dem., 295,602; Ford, Rep., 418,642; McCarthy, Ind., 19,229; MacBride, Libertarian, 7,647; Camejo, Soc. Workers, 928; Anderson, Amer., 564; Maddox, Am. Ind., 85.

1980 (Pres.), Reagan, Rep., 529,688; Carter, Dem., 246,843; Anderson, Ind., 76,952; Clark, Libertarian, 18,784; De Berry, Soc. Workers, 1,100; Commoner, Citizens, 551; Hall, Com., 25; Griswold, Workers World, 2.

Arkansas

County	1976 Carter (D)	Ford (R)	1980 Carter (D)	Reagan (R)	Anderson (I)
Arkansas	5,640	2,480	4,303	3,409	193
Ashley	5,253	3,092	4,552	3,960	130
Baxter	5,766	5,885	4,789	9,684	494
Benton	11,289	12,670	9,231	18,830	1,018
Boone	5,388	3,959	4,576	6,778	429
Bradley	3,567	1,134	3,139	1,650	66
Calhoun	2,014	495	1,438	896	52
Carroll	3,791	2,804	2,977	4,273	298
Chicot	3,868	1,621	3,445	2,239	26
Clark	6,641	1,816	6,122	2,743	215
Clay	5,664	1,893	3,985	3,091	121
Cleburne	5,726	1,992	4,021	4,042	204
Cleveland	2,320	646	1,856	1,124	36
Columbia	4,708	4,287	4,445	5,259	107
Conway	6,443	2,177	4,698	4,145	232
Craighead	13,840	6,213	9,231	11,010	708
Crawford	5,946	4,764	3,948	8,542	245
Crittenden	8,249	5,202	7,022	6,248	185
Cross	4,198	1,909	3,471	2,895	89
Dallas	3,266	1,012	2,838	1,596	74
Desha	4,228	1,372	3,748	2,057	77
Drew	3,750	1,730	3,757	2,272	117
Faulkner	11,423	3,904	8,528	7,544	769
Franklin	3,703	1,973	2,716	3,448	197
Fulton	2,670	1,038	2,037	2,101	83
Garland	15,707	10,394	12,515	15,739	1,042
Grant	3,797	1,047	3,078	2,007	102
Greene	7,495	2,690	5,996	4,514	219
Hempstead	5,397	2,859	4,671	3,852	72
Hot Spring	7,809	2,187	6,897	3,561	244
Howard	3,207	1,575	2,564	2,386	63
Independence	7,116	2,878	5,683	5,076	276
Izard	3,328	1,394	2,750	2,266	160
Jackson	6,456	1,783	4,651	3,191	174
Jefferson	21,001	8,034	17,292	10,697	802
Johnson	5,044	2,173	3,709	3,619	187
Lafayette	2,342	1,467	1,947	1,756	47
Lawrence	5,167	1,708	3,547	3,245	117
Lee	3,463	1,574	3,103	1,711	47
Lincoln	3,045	699	2,517	1,243	56
Little River	3,142	1,431	2,631	2,272	41
Logan	5,313	2,909	4,098	4,511	166
Lonoke	7,761	2,522	5,605	5,619	246
Madison	2,926	2,502	2,434	3,180	126

Marion	2,979	2,045	2,046	3,059	160
Miller	6,821	4,737	5,996	6,770	105
Mississippi	10,292	6,009	8,908	7,170	234
Monroe	3,556	1,285	2,686	2,027	82
Montgomery	2,420	924	1,878	1,585	86
Nevada	3,101	1,163	2,631	1,697	50
Newton	1,840	1,641	1,436	2,423	100
Ouachita	8,946	2,753	7,152	4,329	248
Perry	2,310	832	1,606	1,459	73
Phillips	7,774	3,342	6,642	4,270	163
Pike	2,822	1,234	2,094	1,916	58
Poinsett	6,835	2,726	4,894	4,040	153
Polk	3,505	2,432	2,617	3,993	139
Pope	8,355	4,348	6,364	7,217	471
Prairie	2,836	813	1,928	1,855	64
Pulaski	63,541	37,690	54,839	52,125	4,657
Randolph	4,551	1,571	3,070	2,579	125
St. Francis	6,851	3,639	5,816	4,485	132
Saline	12,008	4,123	10,368	8,330	643
Scott	2,880	1,427	2,236	2,228	92
Searcy	2,067	1,767	1,536	2,459	101
Sebastian	15,698	17,665	10,141	23,403	1,023
Sevier	3,391	1,468	2,854	2,502	97
Sharp	3,532	2,151	2,774	3,420	160
Stone	2,718	1,014	1,968	1,793	133
Union	8,257	7,918	6,852	9,401	313
Van Buren	4,004	1,624	2,968	3,090	153
Washington	15,610	14,132	12,276	20,788	1,737
White	11,412	4,756	8,750	8,079	309
Woodruff	3,040	848	2,452	1,204	74
Yell	5,785	1,932	3,702	3,187	181
Totals	**498,604**	**267,903**	**398,041**	**403,164**	**22,468**

Arkansas Vote Since 1932

1932 (Pres.), Roosevelt, Dem., 189,602; Hoover, Rep., 28,467; Thomas, Soc., 1,269; Harvey, Ind., 1,049; Foster, Com., 175.

1936 (Pres.), Roosevelt, Dem. 146,765; Landon, Rep., 32,039; Thomas, Soc., 446; Browder, Com., 164; Lemke, Union, 4.

1940 (Pres.), Roosevelt, Dem., 158,622; Willkie, Rep., 42,121; Babson, Proh., 793; Thomas, Soc., 305.

1944 (Pres.), Roosevelt, Dem., 148,965; Dewey, Rep., 63,551; Thomas, Soc. 438.

1948 (Pres.), Truman, Dem., 149,659; Dewey, Rep., 50,959; Thurmond, States' Rights, 40,068; Thomas, Soc., 1,037; Wallace, Prog., 751; Watson, Proh., 1.

1952 (Pres.), Eisenhower, Rep., 177,155; Stevenson, Dem., 226,300; Hamblen, Proh., 886; MacArthur, Christian Nationalist, 458; Hass, Soc. Labor, 1.

1956 (Pres.), Stevenson, Dem., 213,277; Eisenhower, Rep., 186,287; Andrews, Ind., 7,008.

1960 (Pres.), Kennedy, Dem., 215,049; Nixon, Rep., 184,508; Nat'l. States' Rights, 28,952.

1964 (Pres.), Johnson, Dem., 314,197; Goldwater, Rep., 243,264; Kasper, Nat'l. States Rights, 2,965.

1968 (Pres.), Nixon, Rep., 189,062; Humphrey, Dem., 184,901; Wallace, 3d party, 235,627.

1972 (Pres.), Nixon, Rep., 445,751; McGovern, Dem., 198,899; Schmitz, Amer. , 3,016.

1976 (Pres.), Carter, Dem., 498,604; Ford, Rep., 267,903; McCarthy, Ind., 639; Anderson, Amer., 389.

1980 (Pres.), Reagan, Rep., 403,164; Carter, Dem., 398,041; Anderson, Ind., 22,468; Clark, Libertarian, 8,970; Commoner, Citizens, 2,345; Bubar, Statesman, 1,350; Hall, Comm., 1,244.

California

County	1976 Carter (D)	Ford (R)	1980 Carter (D)	Reagan (R)	Anderson (I)
Alameda	235,988	155,280	201,720	158,531	40,834
Alpine	189	255	133	254	50
Amador	4,037	3,699	3,191	5,401	788
Butte	24,203	28,400	19,520	38,188	6,108
Calaveras	3,607	3,695	3,076	6,054	776
Colusa	2,340	2,733	1,605	2,897	325
Contra Costa	123,742	126,598	107,398	144,112	28,209
Del Norte	2,789	2,481	2,338	4,016	486
El Dorado	12,763	12,472	10,765	21,238	3,287
Fresno	74,858	72,533	65,254	82,515	10,727
Glenn	3,501	4,094	2,227	5,386	537
Humboldt	23,500	18,034	17,113	24,047	5,440
Imperial	10,244	10,618	7,961	12,068	1,203
Inyo	2,635	3,905	2,080	5,201	515
Kern	50,567	58,023	41,097	72,842	5,799
Kings	8,061	8,263	7,299	10,531	901
Lake	6,374	5,462	5,978	8,934	1,157
Lassen	3,801	3,007	2,941	4,464	543
Los Angeles	1,221,893	1,174,926	979,830	1,224,533	175,882

	1976 (D)	(R)	1980 (D)	(R)	(I)
Madera	7,625	6,844	7,783	10,599	1,013
Marin	43,590	53,425	39,231	49,678	13,805
Mariposa	2,093	2,012	1,889	3,082	458
Mendocino	10,653	9,784	10,784	12,432	2,747
Merced	16,637	14,842	15,886	18,043	2,316
Modoc	1,733	1,917	1,046	2,579	293
Mono	1,025	1,600	865	2,132	302
Monterey	36,849	40,896	29,086	47,452	8,008
Napa	18,048	20,839	14,898	23,632	4,218
Nevada	7,926	8,170	7,605	15,207	2,235
Orange	232,246	408,632	176,704	529,797	55,299
Placer	21,026	18,154	17,311	28,179	4,356
Plumas	3,429	2,884	2,911	4,182	783
Riverside	96,228	97,774	76,650	145,642	16,362
Sacramento	144,203	123,110	130,031	153,721	29,655
San Benito	3,122	3,398	2,749	4,054	552
San Bernardino	109,636	113,265	91,790	172,957	19,106
San Diego	263,654	353,302	195,410	435,910	67,491
San Francisco	133,733	103,561	133,184	80,967	29,365
San Joaquin	48,733	50,277	41,551	64,718	8,416
San Luis Obispo	24,926	27,785	20,508	38,631	8,407
San Mateo	102,896	117,338	87,335	116,491	27,985
Santa Barbara	55,018	60,922	40,650	69,629	14,786
Santa Clara	208,023	219,188	166,995	229,048	65,481
Santa Cruz	37,772	31,872	32,346	37,347	10,590
Shasta	19,200	17,273	15,364	27,547	3,220
Sierra	841	680	651	855	156
Siskiyou	7,060	7,070	5,664	9,331	1,269
Solano	33,682	26,136	30,952	40,919	6,713
Sonoma	50,353	50,555	45,596	60,722	14,099
Stanislaus	38,448	32,937	33,683	41,595	7,134
Sutter	6,966	8,745	5,103	11,778	1,089
Tehama	6,990	6,110	4,832	9,140	1,014
Trinity	2,172	1,989	1,734	3,048	506
Tulare	25,551	31,864	25,155	41,917	3,244
Tuolumne	6,492	6,104	5,449	8,810	1,380
Ventura	68,529	82,670	56,311	114,930	14,887
Yolo	23,533	18,376	21,527	19,603	6,669
Yuba	6,451	5,496	4,896	7,942	878
Totals	3,742,284	3,882,244	3,083,661	4,524,858	739,833

California Vote Since 1932

1932 (Pres.), Roosevelt, Dem., 1,324,157; Hoover, Rep., 847,902; Thomas, Soc., 63,299; Upshaw, Proh., 20,637; Harvey, Liberty, 9,827; Foster, Com., 1,023.

1936 (Pres.), Roosevelt, Dem., 1,766,836; Landon, Rep., 836,431; Colvin, Proh., 12,917; Thomas, Soc., 11,325; Browder, Com., 10,877.

1940 (Pres.), Roosevelt, Dem., 1,877,618; Willkie, Rep., 1,351,419; Thomas, Prog., 16,506; Browder, Com., 13,586; Babson, Proh., 9,400.

1944 (Pres.), Roosevelt, Dem., 1,988,564; Dewey, Rep., 1,512,965; Watson, Proh., 14,770; Thomas, Soc., 3,923; Teichert, Soc. Labor, 327.

1948 (Pres.), Truman, Dem., 1,913,134; Dewey, Rep., 1,895,269; Wallace, Prog., 190,381; Watson, Proh., 16,926; Thomas, Soc., 3,459; Thurmond, States' Rights, 1,228; Teichert, Soc. Labor, 195; Dobbs, Soc. Workers, 133.

1952 (Pres.), Eisenhower, Rep., 2,897,310; Stevenson, Dem., 2,197,548; Hallinan, Prog., 24,106; Hamblen, Proh., 15,653; MacArthur, (Tenny Ticket), 3,326; (Kellems Ticket) 178; Hass, Soc. Labor, 273; Hoopes, Soc., 206; scattered, 3,249.

1956 (Pres.), Eisenhower, Rep., 3,027,668; Stevenson, Dem., 2,420,136; Holtwick, Proh., 11,119; Andrews, Constitution, 6,087; Hass, Soc. Labor, 300; Hoopes, Soc., 123; Dobbs, Soc. Workers, 96; Smith, Christian Nat'l., 8.

1960 (Pres.), Kennedy, Dem., 3,224,099; Nixon, Rep., 3,259,722; Decker, Proh., 21,706; Hass, Soc. Labor, 1,051.

1964 (Pres.), Johnson, Dem., 4,171,877; Goldwater, Rep., 2,879,108; Hass, Soc. Labor, 489; DeBerry, Soc. Worker, 378; Munn, Proh., 305; Hensley, Universal, 19.

1968 (Pres.), Nixon, Rep., 3,467,664; Humphrey, Dem., 3,244,318; Wallace, 3d party, 487,270; Peace and Freedom party, 27,707; McCarthy, Alternative, 20,721; Gregory, write-in, 3,230; Mitchell, Com., 260; Munn, Proh., 59; Blomen, Soc. Labor, 341; Soeters, Defense, 17.

1972 (Pres.), Nixon, Rep., 4,602,096; McGovern, Dem., 3,475,847; Schmitz, Amer., 232,554; Spock, Peace and Freedom, 55,167; Hall, Com., 373; Hospers, Libertarian, 980; Munn, Proh., 53; Fisher, Soc. Labor, 197; Jenness, Soc. Workers, 574; Green, Universal, 21.

1976 (Pres.), Carter, Dem., 3,742,284; Ford, Rep., 3,882,244; MacBride, Libertarian, 56,388; Maddox, Am. Ind., 51,098; Wright, People's, 41,731; Camejo, Soc.

Workers, 17,259; Hall, Com., 12,766; write-in, McCarthy, 58,412; other write-in, 4,935.

1980 (Pres.) Reagan, Rep. 4,524,858; Carter, Dem., 3,083,661; Anderson, Ind., 739,833; Clark, Libertarian, 148,434; Commoner, Ind. 61,063; Smith, Peace & Freedom, 18,116; Rarick, Amer. Ind., 9,856.

Colorado

County	1976 Carter (D)	Ford (R)	1980 Carter (D)	Reagan (R)	Anderson (I)
Adams	40,551	35,392	31,357	42,916	8,342
Alamosa	2,052	2,599	1,821	2,601	289
Arapahoe	33,685	63,154	30,148	79,594	15,329
Archuleta	632	768	532	1,252	83
Baca	1,164	1,303	551	1,999	106
Bent	1,268	1,156	894	1,206	164
Boulder	33,284	42,830	28,422	40,698	13,712
Chaffee	2,064	2,925	1,583	3,327	432
Cheyenne	625	610	322	816	76
Clear Creek	1,069	1,477	837	1,784	402
Conejos	1,698	1,426	1,503	1,597	90
Costilla	1,033	392	1,036	489	38
Crowley	667	834	472	926	57
Custer	259	491	231	674	59
Delta	3,232	4,980	2,348	6,179	455
Denver	112,229	105,960	85,903	88,398	28,610
Dolores	374	343	157	615	32
Douglas	2,459	5,078	2,108	8,126	1,058
Eagle	1,502	2,961	1,608	3,061	906
Elbert	1,068	1,279	698	2,107	238
El Paso	32,911	50,929	27,463	66,199	7,886
Fremont	4,886	5,647	3,952	7,162	731
Garfield	2,852	4,699	2,639	5,416	978
Gilpin	563	451	441	694	175
Grand	910	1,703	820	2,133	413
Gunnison	1,250	2,568	1,297	2,756	704
Hinsdale	83	189	76	232	13
Huerfano	1,932	1,182	1,574	1,258	146
Jackson	279	455	283	673	80
Jefferson	52,782	87,080	41,525	97,006	19,530
Kiowa	529	598	331	754	61
Kit Carson	1,647	1,888	790	2,622	185
Lake	1,549	1,575	1,213	1,375	289
La Plata	3,843	6,228	3,034	7,291	1,537
Larimer	19,005	32,169	17,072	36,240	8,887
Las Animas	4,459	2,615	4,117	2,917	278
Lincoln	1,059	1,276	602	1,535	175
Logan	3,543	4,256	2,332	5,238	588
Mesa	8,807	17,924	7,549	22,686	2,004
Mineral	167	235	125	271	41
Moffat	1,451	2,099	1,079	3,344	329
Montezuma	1,993	3,002	1,467	4,120	275
Montrose	3,164	4,838	2,232	6,685	635
Morgan	3,798	4,603	2,246	5,209	693
Otero	4,118	4,597	3,294	4,801	572
Ouray	333	647	237	813	129
Park	741	1,034	674	1,623	293
Philips	1,173	1,142	640	1,488	193
Pitkin	2,194	2,955	1,760	2,153	1,128
Prowers	2,861	2,578	1,669	3,115	340
Pueblo	25,841	18,518	21,874	20,770	3,102
Rio Blanco	627	1,439	462	1,971	143
Rio Grande	1,475	2,627	1,370	2,844	185
Routt	2,130	2,822	1,944	3,574	920
Saguache	1,059	1,094	893	1,124	71
San Juan	167	221	146	268	94
San Miguel	674	622	651	774	297
Sedgwick	773	902	438	1,151	100
Summit	1,087	1,826	1,285	2,027	845
Teller	986	1,410	802	2,457	322
Washington	1,211	1,440	568	2,007	160
Weld	16,501	21,976	11,433	23,901	4,309
Yuma	2,025	2,350	1,043	3,220	319
Total	460,353	58,367	367,973	652,264	130,633

Colorado Vote Since 1932

1932 (Pres.), Roosevelt, Dem., 250,877; Hoover, Rep., 189,617; Thomas, Soc., 14,018; Upshaw, Proh., 1,928

1936 (Pres.), Roosevelt, Dem., 295,081; Landon, Rep., 181,267; Lemke, Union, 9,962; Thomas, Soc., 1,593; Browder, Com., 497; Aiken, Soc. Labor, 336.

1940 (Pres.), Roosevelt, Dem., 265,554; Willkie, Rep., 279,576; Thomas, Soc., 1,899; Babson, Proh., 1,597; Browder, Com., 378.

1944 (Pres.), Roosevelt, Dem., 234,331; Dewey, Rep., 268,731; Thomas, Soc., 1,977.

1948 (Pres.), Truman, Dem., 267,288; Dewey, Rep., 239,714; Wallace, Prog., 6,115; Thomas, Soc., 1,678; Dobbs, Soc. Workers, 228; Teichert, Soc. Labor, 214.

1952 (Pres.), Eisenhower, Rep., 379,782; Stevenson, Dem., 245,504; MacArthur, Constitution, 2,181; Hallinan, Prog., 1,919; Hoopes, Soc., 365; Hass, Soc. Labor, 352.

1956 (Pres.), Eisenhower, Rep., 394,479; Stevenson, Dem., 263,997; Hass, Soc. Lab., 3,308; Andrews, Ind., 759; Hoopes, Soc., 531.

1960 (Pres.), Kennedy, Dem., 330,629; Nixon, Rep., 402,242; Hass, Soc. Labor, 2,803; Dobbs, Soc. Workers, 572.

1964 (Pres.), Johnson, Dem., 476,024; Goldwater, Rep., 296,767; Hass, Soc. Labor, 302; DeBerry, Soc. Worker, 2,537; Munn, Proh., 1,356.

1968 (Pres.), Nixon, Rep., 409,345; Humphrey, Dem., 335,174; Wallace, 3d party, 60,813; Blomen, Soc. Labor, 3,016; Gregory, New-party, 1,393; Munn, Proh., 275; Halstead, Soc. Worker, 235.

1972 (Pres.), Nixon, Rep., 597,189; McGovern, Dem., 329,980; Fisher, Soc. Labor, 4,361; Hospers, Libertarian, 1,111; Hall, Com., 432; Jenness, Soc. Workers, 555; Munn, Proh., 467; Schmitz, Amer., 17,269; Spock, Peoples, 2,403.

1976 (Pres.), Carter, Dem., 460,353; Ford, Rep., 584,367; McCarthy, Ind., 26,107; MacBride, Libertarian, 5,330; Bubar, Proh., 2,882.

1980 (Pres.), Reagan, Rep., 652,264; Carter, Dem., 367,973; Anderson, Ind., 130,633; Clark, Libertarian, 25,744; Commoner, Citizens, 5,614; Bubar, Statesman, 1,180; Pulley, Socialist, 520; Hall, Com., 487.

Connecticut

County	1976 Carter (D)	Ford (R)	1980 Carter (D)	Reagan (R)	Anderson (I)
Fairfield	148,353	209,458	124,074	201,997	38,363
Hartford	191,257	175,064	164,643	150,265	52,856
Litchfield	32,419	40,705	26,705	38,725	10,027
Middlesex	29,097	31,115	24,768	28,989	9,062
New Haven	157,402	174,342	130,913	169,038	34,450
New London	45,908	47,231	36,628	47,217	13,577
Tolland	23,079	23,703	18,557	22,127	8,908
Windham	20,380	17,643	15,444	18,852	4,564
Totals	647,895	719,261	541,732	677,210	171,807

Connecticut Vote Since 1932

1932 (Pres.), Roosevelt, Dem., 281,632; Hoover, Rep., 288,420; Thomas, Soc., 22,767.

1936 (Pres.), Roosevelt, Dem., 382,129; Landon, Rep., 278,685; Lemke, Union, 21,805; Thomas, Soc., 5,683; Browder, Com., 1,193.

1940 (Pres.), Roosevelt, Dem., 417,621; Willkie, Rep., 361,021; Browder, Com., 1,091; Aiken, Soc. Labor, 971; Willkie, Union, 798.

1944 (Pres.), Roosevelt, Dem., 435,146; Dewey, Rep., 390,527; Thomas, Soc., 5,097; Teichert, Soc. Labor, 1,220.

1948 (Pres.), Truman, Dem., 423,297; Dewey, Rep., 437,754; Wallace, Prog., 13,713; Thomas, Soc., 6,964; Teichert, Soc. Labor, 1,184; Dobbs, Soc. Workers, 606.

1952 (Pres.), Eisenhower, Rep., 611,012; Stevenson, Dem., 481,649; Hoopes, Soc., 2,244; Hallinan, Peoples, 1,466; Hass, Soc. Labor, 535; write-in, 5.

1956 (Pres.), Eisenhower, Rep., 711,837; Stevenson, Dem., 405,079; scattered, 205.

1960 (Pres.), Kennedy, Dem., 657,055; Nixon, Rep., 565,813.

1964 (Pres.), Johnson, Dem., 826,269; Goldwater, Rep., 390,996; scattered, 1,313.

1968 (Pres.), Nixon, Rep., 556,721; Humphrey, Dem., 621,561; Wallace, 3d party, 76,650; scattered, 1,300.

1972 (Pres.), Nixon, Rep., 810,763; McGovern, Dem., 555,498; Schmitz, Amer., 17,239; scattered, 777.

1976 (Pres.), Carter, Dem., 647,895; Ford, Rep., 719,261; Maddox, George Wallace Party, 7,101; LaRouche, U.S. Labor, 1,789.

1980 (Pres.), Reagan, Rep., 677,210; Carter, Dem., 541,732; Anderson, Ind., 171,807; Clark, Libertarian, 8,570; Commoner, Citizens, 6,130; scattered, 836.

Delaware

County	1976 Carter (D)	Ford (R)	1980 Carter (D)	Reagan (R)	Anderson (I)
Kent	16,523	12,604	12,884	14,882	1,831
New Castle	87,521	80,074	76,897	76,898	12,828
Sussex	18,552	17,153	15,973	19,472	1,629
Totals	122,596	109,831	105,754	111,252	16,288

Delaware Vote Since 1932

1932 (Pres.), Hoover, Rep., 57,074; Roosevelt, Dem., 54,319; Thomas, Soc., 1,376; Foster, Com., 133.

1936 (Pres.), Roosevelt, Dem., 69,702; Landon, Rep. 54,014; Lemke, Union, 442; Thomas, Soc., 179; Browder, Com., 52.

1940 (Pres.), Roosevelt, Dem., 74,559; Willkie, Rep., 61,440; Babson, Proh., 220; Thomas, Soc., 115.

1944 (Pres.), Roosevelt, Dem., 68,166; Dewey, Rep., 56,747; Watson, Proh., 294; Thomas, Soc., 154.

1948 (Pres.), Truman, Dem., 67,813; Dewey, Rep., 69,688; Wallace, Prog., 1,050; Watson, Proh., 343; Thomas, Soc., 250; Teichert, Soc. Labor, 29.

1952 (Pres.), Eisenhower, Rep., 90,059; Stevenson, Dem., 83,315; Hass, Soc. Labor, 242; Hamblen, Proh., 234; Hallinan, Prog., 155; Hoopes, Soc., 20.

1956 (Pres.), Eisenhower, Rep., 98,057; Stevenson, Dem., 79,421; Oltwick, Proh., 400; Hass, Soc. Labor, 110.

1960 (Pres.), Kennedy, Dem., 99,590; Nixon, Rep., 96,373; Faubus, States' Rights, 354; Decker, Proh., 284; Hass, Soc. Labor, 82.

1964 (Pres.), Johnson, Dem., 122,704; Goldwater, Rep., 78,078; Hass, Soc. Labor, 113; Munn, Proh., 425.

1968 (Pres.), Nixon, Rep., 96,714; Humphrey, Dem., 89,194; Wallace, 3d party, 28,459.

1972 (Pres.), Nixon, Rep., 140,357; McGovern, Dem., 92,283; Schmitz, Amer., 2,638; Munn, Proh., 238.

1976 (Pres.), Carter, Dem., 122,596; Ford, Rep., 109,831; McCarthy, non-partisan, 2,437; Anderson, Amer., 645; LaRouche, U.S. Labor, 136; Bubar, Proh., 103; Levin, Soc. Labor, 86.

1980 (Pres.), Reagan, Rep., 111,252; Carter, Dem., 105,754; Anderson, Ind., 16,288; Clark, Libertarian, 1,974; Greaves, American, 400.

District of Columbia

County	1976 Carter (D)	Ford (R)	1980 Carter (D)	Reagan (R)	Anderson (I)
Totals	137,818	27,873	130,231	23,313	16,131

District of Columbia Vote Since 1964

1964 (Pres.), Johnson, Dem., 169,796; Goldwater, Rep., 28,801.

1968 (Pres.), Nixon, Rep., 31,012; Humphrey, Dem., 139,566.

1972 (Pres.), Nixon, Rep., 35,226; McGovern, Dem., 127,627; Reed, Soc. Workers, 316; Hall, Com., 252.

1976 (Pres.), Carter, Dem., 137,818; Ford, Rep., 27,873; Camejo, Soc. Workers, 545; MacBride, Libertarian, 274; Hall, Com., 219; LaRouche, U.S. Labor, 157.

1980 (Pres.), Reagan, Rep., 23,313; Carter, Dem., 130,231; Anderson, Ind., 16,131; Commoner, Citizens, 1,826; Clark, Libertarian, 1,104; Hall, Com., 369; De Berry, Soc. Work., 173; Griswold, Workers World, 52; write-ins, 690.

Florida

County	1976 Carter (D)	Ford (R)	1980 Carter (D)	Reagan (R)	Anderson (I)
Alachua	27,895	15,546	26,817	19,771	4,167
Baker	2,985	1,058	2,606	2,271	56
Bay	14,858	14,208	12,338	20,815	720
Bradford	3,868	1,680	3,340	2,771	89
Brevard	46,421	44,470	38,915	69,228	5,820
Broward	176,491	161,411	146,322	229,693	31,553
Calhoun	2,487	1,153	2,295	1,504	52
Charlotte	10,300	12,703	9,750	20,433	1,204
Citrus	9,438	7,973	9,148	14,276	784
Clay	8,410	8,468	7,589	15,497	679
Collier	8,764	14,643	7,735	23,878	1,675
Columbia	6,683	3,947	5,677	5,638	246
Dade	303,047	211,148	210,683	265,550	44,723
De Soto	2,715	2,000	2,709	3,340	155
Dixie	2,169	558	2,007	1,098	45
Duval	105,912	74,997	90,330	98,389	5,153
Escambia	38,279	41,471	33,378	51,443	2,595
Flagler	2,086	1,262	2,494	2,876	153
Franklin	1,859	1,054	1,772	1,500	53

	1976 (D)	(R)	1980 (D)	(R)	(I)
Gadsden	6,798	3,531	8,207	3,708	201
Gilchrist	1,807	528	1,625	1,089	55
Glades	1,311	624	1,203	1,096	61
Gulf	2,641	1,584	2,680	2,116	56
Hamilton	2,053	794	1,921	1,301	40
Hardee	2,670	2,189	2,597	2,595	83
Hendry	2,337	1,843	2,540	2,696	130
Hernando	7,717	5,793	8,835	12,099	852
Highlands	7,218	8,317	6,685	11,914	531
Hillsborough	94,589	78,504	88,221	106,080	8,939
Holmes	3,256	1,850	2,767	3,208	68
Indian River	3,316	9,818	7,748	15,545	1,184
Jackson	7,687	4,795	7,549	6,331	158
Jefferson	2,310	1,361	2,366	1,621	96
Lafayette	1,126	523	1,034	795	22
Lake	14,369	19,976	13,121	26,775	1,240
Lee	30,567	38,038	26,007	60,717	4,191
Leon	28,729	23,739	28,420	24,840	3,181
Levy	4,025	1,965	4,170	3,203	175
Liberty	1,137	620	1,111	895	24
Madison	3,218	1,761	3,129	2,275	65
Manatee	24,342	29,300	21,660	40,506	2,921
Marion	16,963	16,163	15,362	23,668	1,173
Martin	8,785	11,682	8,078	20,493	1,317
Monroe	11,079	8,232	7,875	11,546	1,914
Nassau	5,896	3,136	5,051	5,414	178
Okaloosa	14,210	18,598	10,738	27,665	1,080
Okeechobee	3,184	1,598	3,226	2,778	156
Orange	58,442	70,451	48,732	87,375	5,389
Osceola	6,893	7,062	6,594	10,839	560
Palm Beach	96,705	98,236	91,932	143,491	15,178
Pasco	33,710	28,306	34,045	50,080	3,565
Pinellas	141,879	150,003	138,307	185,482	17,789
Polk	47,286	44,238	43,291	59,600	2,618
Putnam	9,597	5,040	8,898	8,258	410
St. Johns	7,412	6,660	6,879	11,179	546
St. Lucie	12,386	11,502	10,341	18,107	1,109
Santa Rosa	8,020	9,122	6,964	13,802	606
Sarasota	26,293	44,157	25,557	67,946	4,773
Seminole	19,609	26,655	17,431	39,970	2,451
Sumter	4,721	2,212	4,378	3,666	141
Suwannee	4,718	2,405	4,345	3,894	135
Taylor	3,370	1,983	2,955	2,772	78
Union	1,480	544	1,235	1,120	45
Volusia	49,161	37,523	44,476	52,598	3,296
Wakulla	2,353	1,580	2,078	2,014	111
Walton	5,196	2,927	4,323	4,651	194
Washington	3,566	2,313	3,095	3,222	92
Absentees			1,788	3,945	593
Totals	**1,636,000**	**1,469,531**	**1,419,475**	**2,046,951**	**189,692**

Florida Vote Since 1932

1932 (Pres.), Roosevelt, Dem., 206,307; Hoover, Rep., 69,170; Thomas, Soc., 775.

1936 (Pres.), Roosevelt, Dem., 249,117; Landon, Rep., 78,248.

1940 (Pres.), Roosevelt, Dem., 359,334; Willkie, Rep., 126,158.

1944 (Pres.), Roosevelt, Dem., 339,377; Dewey, Rep., 143,215.

1948 (Pres.), Truman, Dem., 281,988; Dewey, Rep., 194,280; Thurmond, States' Rights, 89,755; Wallace, Prog., 11,620.

1952 (Pres.), Eisenhower, Rep., 544,036; Stevenson, Dem., 444,950; scattered, 351.

1956 (Pres.), Eisenhower, Rep., 643,849; Stevenson, Dem., 480,371.

1960 (Pres.), Kennedy, Dem., 748,700; Nixon, Rep., 795,476.

1964 (Pres.), Johnson, Dem., 948,540; Goldwater, Rep., 905,941.

1968 (Pres.), Nixon, Rep., 886,804; Humphrey, Dem., 676,794; Wallace, 3d party, 624,207.

1972 (Pres.), Nixon, Rep., 1,857,759; McGovern, Dem., 718,117; scattered, 7,407.

1976 (Pres.), Carter, Dem., 1,636,000; Ford, Rep., 1,469,531; McCarthy, Ind., 23,643; Anderson, Amer., 21,325.

1980 (Pres.), Reagan, Rep., 2,046,951; Carter, Dem., 1,419,475; Anderson, Ind., 189,692; Clark, Libertarian, 30,524; write-ins, 285.

Georgia

County	1976 Carter (D)	Ford (R)	1980 Carter (D)	Reagan (R)	Anderson (I)
Appling	3,585	961	2,985	1,961	41
Atkinson	1,560	347	1,449	747	16
Bacon	2,395	594	1,622	1,427	32
Baker	1,162	305	1,035	510	11
Baldwin	4,674	3,612	4,368	3,639	230
Banks	2,387	330	2,091	746	18
Barrow	4,756	1,364	3,876	2,284	99
Bartow	8,166	1,876	7,490	3,135	135
Ben Hill	2,449	814	2,544	1,459	41
Berrien	3,394	555	2,869	1,487	24
Bibb	31,902	12,819	31,770	15,175	848
Bleckley	2,605	972	2,014	1,261	47
Brantley	2,294	358	2,066	882	17
Brooks	2,653	1,102	2,230	1,546	39
Bryan	2,045	761	1,966	1,212	51
Bulloch	5,199	3,156	4,921	3,750	160
Burke	3,014	1,565	3,047	1,871	56
Butts	2,898	819	2,574	1,210	38
Calhoun	1,394	436	1,414	652	16
Camden	2,962	995	2,924	1,439	62
Candler	1,388	646	1,358	1,030	24
Carroll	10,050	3,640	8,202	5,815	294
Catoosa	6,020	3,799	4,921	5,962	121
Charlton	1,750	452	1,469	779	26
Chatham	32,075	24,160	28,635	26,499	1,244
Chattahoochee	506	178	476	256	16
Chattooga	4,686	1,087	4,279	1,946	61
Cherokee	6,539	2,609	6,020	5,250	230
Clarke	11,342	6,610	10,519	8,094	1,060
Clay	947	295	909	316	9
Clayton	21,432	12,905	17,540	19,160	923
Clinch	1,414	383	1,325	513	18
Cobb	45,002	34,324	39,157	51,977	3,229
Coffee	4,601	1,417	4,038	2,499	58
Colquitt	6,928	2,181	5,353	3,593	80
Columbia	4,674	3,423	5,335	6,293	248
Cook	2,882	670	2,461	1,188	25
Coweta	6,195	3,044	5,697	4,480	161
Crawford	1,842	378	1,673	642	35
Crisp	3,747	1,328	3,403	1,861	54
Dade	2,263	1,388	1,735	2,114	62
Dawson	1,384	370	1,072	729	23
Decatur	3,736	2,500	3,242	2,919	54
DeKalb	86,872	67,160	82,743	74,904	7,241
Dodge	5,267	848	4,635	1,719	56
Dooly	2,441	655	2,364	1,083	31
Dougherty	11,461	9,337	13,430	12,726	326
Douglas	7,805	3,959	6,807	6,945	304
Early	2,405	1,157	2,110	1,538	23
Echols	585	111	515	259	8
Effingham	2,906	1,654	2,783	2,528	38
Elbert	4,730	961	4,014	1,967	50
Emanuel	4,603	1,493	3,971	2,199	45
Evans	1,631	746	1,456	1,090	20
Fannin	3,402	2,646	2,526	3,196	61
Fayette	3,718	2,837	3,790	6,351	272
Floyd	15,151	7,713	13,710	9,220	398
Forsyth	4,693	1,443	4,325	3,157	160
Franklin	4,192	687	3,528	1,387	30
Fulton	129,849	61,552	118,748	64,909	6,738
Gilmer	2,499	1,261	2,246	2,170	72
Glascock	704	371	614	510	7
Glynn	9,459	5,403	7,540	7,214	296
Gordon	6,052	1,698	5,199	3,107	141
Grady	3,758	1,209	3,023	2,018	56
Greene	2,534	652	2,571	961	29
Gwinnett	20,838	13,912	21,958	27,185	1,497
Habersham	5,120	1,315	4,394	2,224	100
Hall	12,804	5,093	12,124	7,760	463
Hancock	2,117	651	2,205	573	23
Haralson	4,550	1,301	3,606	2,229	71
Harris	2,861	1,544	2,807	2,001	100
Hart	4,605	860	4,539	1,577	59
Heard	1,593	433	1,348	875	35
Henry	5,717	2,622	5,635	5,326	165
Houston	13,164	5,404	10,915	9,005	536
Irwin	2,012	561	1,155	1,056	11
Jackson	5,931	1,239	4,591	2,209	107
Jasper	1,852	689	1,546	879	38
Jeff Davis	2,405	622	2,059	1,191	40
Jefferson	3,115	1,309	3,305	1,605	44
Jenkins	1,820	563	1,632	824	24
Johnson	2,210	698	1,854	1,123	29
Jones	3,471	1,317	3,239	1,828	112
Lamar	2,785	847	2,453	1,298	42
Lanier	1,269	207	1,116	470	9
Laurens	8,617	3,281	7,860	4,392	147
Lee	1,727	1,110	1,670	1,942	26
Liberty	3,328	979	3,099	1,507	49
Lincoln	1,583	576	1,617	806	10
Long	1,243	222	1,202	514	23
Lowndes	8,830	4,512	5,989	6,622	214
Lumpkin	2,301	547	1,951	1,024	83
Macon	3,013	638	3,025	894	39
Madison	3,367	1,115	2,980	2,330	59
Marion	1,314	291	1,174	567	16
McDuffie	3,024	1,694	2,667	1,928	59
McIntosh	1,978	535	2,104	876	38
Meriwether	4,830	1,450	3,876	1,838	59
Miller	1,536	476	1,127	900	19
Mitchell	4,495	1,572	3,566	2,231	40
Monroe	2,962	1,078	2,542	1,242	43
Montgomery	1,610	626	1,663	948	23

	1976 (D)	(R)	1980 (D)	(R)	(I)
Morgan	2,274	904	2,276	1,323	57
Murray	3,511	889	3,094	1,538	42
Muscogee	24,092	13,496	23,272	15,203	811
Newton	6,294	2,137	5,611	3,206	150
Oconee	2,228	1,184	2,141	2,065	106
Oglethorpe	1,854	811	1,611	1,187	44
Paulding	5,420	1,432	4,686	2,845	97
Peach	3,989	1,163	3,415	1,642	68
Pickens	2,571	973	2,358	1,612	73
Pierce	2,628	544	1,918	1,027	21
Pike	1,903	776	1,755	1,271	45
Polk	6,115	1,944	5,421	2,949	116
Pulaski	2,318	485	1,997	1,153	54
Putnam	2,040	835	1,951	1,166	35
Quitman	677	313	589	240	2
Rabun	2,398	591	2,327	1,070	67
Randolph	2,186	747	1,861	879	1
Richmond	24,042	17,893	24,104	19,619	887
Rockdale	4,640	2,974	4,395	5,300	219
Schley	783	268	613	453	9
Screven	2,168	1,176	2,117	1,490	36
Seminole	2,074	681	1,794	1,117	16
Spalding	7,593	3,739	7,176	4,809	248
Stephens	5,560	1,340	4,529	2,045	69
Stewart	1,632	433	1,440	611	23
Sumter	5,328	2,053	4,956	2,957	103
Talbot	1,634	459	1,635	572	20
Taliaferro	748	236	670	270	8
Tattnall	3,556	1,326	2,864	2,082	37
Taylor	1,962	510	1,845	815	19
Telfair	3,534	637	2,700	1,173	41
Terrell	2,348	1,168	2,010	1,378	21
Thomas	6,147	3,263	5,695	4,294	117
Tift	5,185	2,162	4,572	3,280	99
Toombs	4,047	2,126	3,255	2,835	68
Towns	1,786	1,175	1,510	1,475	57
Treutlen	1,567	465	1,307	668	21
Troup	7,699	4,422	7,716	5,398	191
Turner	2,265	416	1,990	898	16
Twiggs	2,515	513	2,213	747	8
Union	2,795	1,154	1,700	1,546	43
Upson	4,219	2,897	4,713	2,788	77
Walker	8,007	4,807	6,809	7,088	171
Walton	5,402	1,687	4,525	2,618	112
Ware	7,719	2,661	6,307	3,715	77
Warren	1,335	720	1,517	779	20
Washington	3,865	1,657	3,452	1,822	60
Wayne	4,489	1,499	3,843	2,213	52
Webster	622	165	608	312	8
Wheeler	1,378	344	1,599	550	28
White	2,125	625	2,017	1,175	58
Whitfield	10,475	4,498	9,691	6,404	229
Wilcox	2,153	346	1,780	827	13
Wilkes	2,461	1,067	2,350	1,212	31
Wilkinson	2,652	837	2,365	1,116	31
Worth	2,790	1,156	2,567	2,076	35
Totals	**979,409**	**483,743**	**890,955**	**654,168**	**36,055**

Georgia Vote Since 1932

1932 (Pres.), Roosevelt, Dem., 234,118; Hoover, Rep., 19,863; Upshaw, Proh., 1,125; Thomas, Soc., 461; Foster, Com., 23.

1936 (Pres.), Roosevelt, Dem., 255,364; Landon, Rep., 36,942; Colvin, Proh., 660; Lemke, Union, 141; Thomas, Soc., 68.

1940 (Pres.), Roosevelt, Dem., 265,194; Willkie, Rep., 23,934; Ind. Dem., 22,428; total, 46,362; Babson, Proh., 983.

1944 (Pres.), Roosevelt, Dem., 268,187; Dewey, Rep., 56,506; Watson, Proh., 36.

1948 (Pres.), Truman, Dem., 254,646; Dewey, Rep., 76,691; Thurmond, States' Rights, 85,055; Wallace, Prog., 1,636; Watson, Proh., 732.

1952 (Pres.), Eisenhower, Rep., 198,979; Stevenson, Dem., 456,823; Liberty Party, 1.

1956 (Pres.), Stevenson, Dem., 444,388; Eisenhower, Rep., 222,778; Andrews, Ind., write-in, 1,754.

1960 (Pres.), Kennedy, Dem., 458,638; Nixon, Rep., 274,472; write-in, 239.

1964 (Pres.), Johnson, Dem., 522,557; Goldwater, Rep., 616,600.

1968 (Pres.), Nixon, Rep., 380,111; Humphrey, Dem., 334,440; Wallace, 3d party, 535,550; write-in, 162.

1972 (Pres.), Nixon, Rep., 881,496; McGovern, Dem., 289,529; Schmitz, Amer., 2,288; scattered.

1976 (Pres.), Carter, Dem., 979,409; Ford, Rep., 483,743; write-in, 4,306.

1980 (Pres.), Reagan, Rep., 654,168; Carter, Dem., 890,955; Anderson, Ind., 36,055; Clark, Libertarian, 15,627.

Hawaii

	1976		1980		
County	Carter (D)	Ford (R)	Carter (D)	Reagan (R)	Anderson (I)
Hawaii	091	15,960	17,630	14,247	3,091
Oahu	111,389	108,041	96,472	99,596	25,331
Kauai	8,105	6,278	9,081	5,883	1,352
Maui	11,921	10,318	12,674	10,359	2,237
Absentees			22	27	10
Totals	**147,375**	**140,003**	**135,879**	**130,112**	**32,021**

Hawaii Vote Since 1960

1960 (Pres.), Kennedy, Dem., 92,410; Nixon, Rep., 92,295.

1964 (Pres.), Johnson, Dem., 163,249; Goldwater, Rep., 44,022.

1968 (Pres.), Nixon, Rep., 91,425; Humphrey, Dem., 141,324; Wallace, 3d party, 3,469.

1972 (Pres.), Nixon, Rep., 168,865; McGovern, Dem., 101,409.

1976 (Pres.), Carter, Dem., 147,375; Ford, Rep., 140,003; MacBride, Libertarian, 3,923.

1980 (Pres.), Reagan, Rep., 130,112; Carter, Dem., 135,879; Anderson, Ind., 32,021; Clark, Libertarian, 3,269; Commoner, Citizens, 1,548; Hall, Com., 458.

Idaho

	1976		1980		
County	Carter (D)	Ford (R)	Carter (D)	Reagan (R)	Anderson (I)
Ada	21,125	41,135	21,324	55,205	7,987
Adams	639	809	590	1,189	88
Bannock	10,261	13,172	8,639	18,477	1,896
Bear Lake	960	2,094	508	2,941	63
Benewah	1,549	1,458	1,361	2,111	286
Bingham	4,347	7,327	2,933	11,781	489
Blaine	1,604	2,176	1,840	2,716	775
Boise	433	684	518	1,134	86
Bonner	4,065	4,549	4,060	6,727	880
Bonneville	7,230	15,793	5,052	24,715	1,355
Boundary	1,217	1,458	1,087	2,088	225
Butte	663	751	424	1,275	35
Camas	160	288	145	360	16
Canyon	9,460	17,263	9,172	24,375	1,798
Caribou	1,110	2,253	481	3,234	106
Cassia	1,881	4,575	1,369	6,511	212
Clark	169	334	87	379	11
Clearwater	1,752	1,469	1,699	2,178	291
Custer	516	850	398	1,398	64
Elmore	2,164	2,808	1,760	3,994	311
Franklin	1,157	2,720	511	3,669	61
Fremont	1,445	2,581	926	4,167	108
Gem	1,978	2,401	1,613	3,766	218
Gooding	1,923	2,909	1,481	3,897	218
Idaho	2,323	3,185	2,078	4,425	409
Jefferson	1,745	3,599	833	5,860	135
Jerome	1,800	3,188	1,368	4,962	178
Kootenai	7,225	10,493	7,521	17,022	1,808
Latah	5,314	6,846	5,037	6,967	2,465
Lemhi	1,159	1,685	794	2,646	167
Lewis	898	824	774	1,088	160
Lincoln	615	909	462	1,294	83
Madison	1,320	4,190	728	6,555	64
Minidoka	2,441	3,600	1,689	6,035	260
Nez Perce	6,324	6,151	6,565	7,495	1,344
Oneida	637	1,065	434	1,461	50
Owyhee	1,054	1,519	732	2,257	93
Payette	2,195	3,115	1,828	4,508	253
Power	1,286	1,374	727	2,235	119
Shoshone	3,216	3,570	3,102	3,994	407
Teton	514	904	360	1,227	67
Twin Falls	6,085	12,659	4,835	17,425	976
Valley	897	1,374	926	2,041	245
Washington	1,693	2,044	1,421	2,915	172
Totals	**126,549**	**204,151**	**110,192**	**290,699**	**27,058**

Idaho Vote Since 1932

1932 (Pres.), Roosevelt, Dem., 109,479; Hoover, Rep., 71,312; Harvey, Lib., 4,712; Thomas, Soc., 526; Foster, Com., 491.

1936 (Pres.), Roosevelt, Dem., 125,683; Landon, Rep., 66,256; Lemke, Union, 7,684.

1940 (Pres.), Roosevelt, Dem., 127,842; Willkie, Rep., 106,553; Thomas, Soc., 497; Browder, Com., 276.

1944 (Pres.), Roosevelt, Dem., 107,399; Dewey, Rep., 100,137; Watson, Proh., 503; Thomas, Soc., 282.

1948 (Pres.), Truman, Dem., 107,370; Dewey, Rep., 101,514; Wallace, Prog., 4,972; Watson, Proh., 628; Thomas, Soc., 332.

1952 (Pres.), Eisenhower, Rep., 180,707; Stevenson, Dem.,

95,081; Hallinan, Prog., 443; write-in, 23.
1956 (Pres.), Eisenhower, Rep., 166,979; Stevenson, Dem., 105,868; Andrews, Ind., 126; write-in, 16.
1960 (Pres.), Kennedy, Dem., 138,853; Nixon, Rep., 161,597.
1964 (Pres.), Johnson, Dem., 148,920; Goldwater, Rep., 143,557.
1968 (Pres.), Nixon, Rep., 165,369; Humphrey, Dem., 89,273; Wallace, 3d party, 36,541.
1972 (Pres.), Nixon, Rep., 199,384; McGovern, Dem., 80,826; Schmitz, Amer., 28,869; Spock, Peoples, 903.
1976 (Pres.), Carter, Dem., 126,549; Ford, Rep., 204,151; Maddox, Amer., 5,935; MacBride, Libertarian, 3,558; LaRouche, U.S. Labor, 739.
1980 (Pres.), Reagan, Rep., 290,699; Carter, Dem., 110,192; Anderson, Ind., 27,058; Clark, Libertarian, 8,425; Rarick, Amer., 1,057.

Illinois

| | 1976 | | 1980 | | |
County	Carter (D)	Ford (R)	Carter (D)	Reagan (R)	Anderson (I)
Adams	11,926	18,189	10,606	19,842	1,202
Alexander	3,246	2,349	2,925	2,650	74
Bond	3,682	3,716	2,834	4,398	244
Boone	4,458	6,470	3,175	6,697	1,578
Brown	1,533	1,519	950	1,660	59
Bureau	7,566	10,854	5,753	11,484	1,093
Calhoun	1,549	1,364	1,208	1,591	76
Carroll	3,372	5,059	2,154	5,084	705
Cass	3,589	3,524	2,543	3,965	199
Champaign	26,858	34,546	21,017	33,329	9,972
Christian	9,306	7,445	6,625	8,770	499
Clark	4,071	4,506	2,855	5,476	243
Clay	3,837	3,860	2,587	4,447	187
Clinton	6,275	7,245	4,470	8,500	528
Coles	8,639	11,021	6,743	11,994	1,726
Cook	1,180,814	987,498	1,124,584	856,574	149,712
Crawford	5,007	5,522	3,372	5,894	341
Cumberland	2,752	2,518	1,892	3,159	190
DeKalb	11,535	18,193	8,913	16,370	4,526
DeWitt	3,477	4,137	2,262	4,648	368
Douglas	3,826	4,635	2,564	5,330	344
DuPage	72,137	175,055	68,990	182,308	29,810
Edgar	5,058	5,842	3,394	6,639	400
Edwards	1,648	2,379	1,041	2,556	118
Effingham	5,952	7,194	4,229	9,104	393
Fayette	383	6,523	3,614	6,523	229
Ford	2,690	4,801	1,803	5,024	328
Franklin	12,818	7,420	9,425	9,731	558
Fulton	9,314	9,588	7,481	10,316	838
Gallatin	2,611	1,499	1,678	1,700	78
Greene	4,057	3,706	2,607	4,224	220
Grundy	5,534	7,581	3,970	8,397	701
Hamilton	3,036	2,433	1,990	3,254	171
Hancock	4,730	6,043	3,522	6,597	383
Hardin	1,602	1,393	1,314	1,721	56
Henderson	2,152	2,210	1,609	2,443	143
Henry	9,822	12,849	7,977	14,506	1,440
Iroquois	5,167	10,129	3,362	11,247	592
Jackson	12,940	10,152	10,291	10,505	2,526
Jasper	2,772	2,794	1,846	3,548	157
Jefferson	8,989	7,422	6,761	8,972	506
Jersey	4,625	4,273	3,324	5,266	314
JoDaviess	3,979	5,478	2,678	5,186	983
Johnson	2,182	2,417	1,568	3,201	84
Kane	34,057	59,275	29,015	64,106	9,179
Kankakee	18,394	23,003	14,626	23,810	1,802
Kendall	4,202	9,011	3,143	10,028	979
Knox	11,525	14,123	8,749	14,907	2,069
Lake	57,741	92,231	48,287	96,350	17,726
LaSalle	23,105	25,114	16,818	27,323	3,041
Lawrence	4,044	4,345	3,030	4,453	293
Lee	6,076	8,674	3,170	11,373	781
Livingston	5,174	10,097	4,111	11,544	980
Logan	5,686	8,623	3,916	9,681	650
Macon	28,243	24,893	22,325	28,298	2,804
Macoupin	11,910	10,242	9,116	12,131	901
Madison	56,457	44,183	43,860	51,160	4,206
Marion	9,834	8,729	6,990	10,969	567
Marshall	2,570	4,017	1,903	4,349	336
Mason	3,947	3,847	2,680	4,644	267
Massac	3,666	3,226	2,821	4,284	124
McDonough	5,464	9,683	4,093	8,995	1,230
McHenry	16,799	37,115	14,540	40,045	5,871
McLean	16,601	28,493	13,587	30,096	4,961
Menard	2,301	3,137	1,589	3,622	274
Mercer	4,090	4,816	3,361	5,144	540
Monroe	3,984	5,602	3,121	6,315	405
Montgomery	8,322	7,379	5,721	8,947	611
Morgan	7,403	8,885	5,483	10,406	900
Moultrie	3,332	2,803	2,332	3,495	280
Ogle	6,463	11,073	4,067	12,533	2,042
Peoria	34,606	46,526	28,276	47,815	6,169
Perry	5,976	5,286	4,337	5,888	319

County					
Piatt	3,509	4,442	2,421	4,867	447
Pike	5,006	4,975	3,695	5,301	303
Pope	1,070	1,187	880	1,501	58
Pulaski	2,489	1,836	1,955	2,083	49
Putnam	1,344	1,572	1,158	1,959	235
Randolph	8,693	8,190	6,052	8,810	514
Richland	3,485	4,434	2,463	5,241	358
Rock Island	35,994	34,007	30,045	34,788	5,818
St. Clair	59,177	40,333	50,046	46,063	3,879
Saline	7,472	5,970	5,683	7,157	321
Sangamon	38,017	43,309	29,354	49,372	5,439
Schuyler	2,014	5,234	1,445	2,799	155
Scott	1,424	1,789	941	1,990	80
Shelby	61,172	2,191	3,988	6,441	381
Stark	1,146	2,191	806	2,358	147
Stephenson	7,192	11,678	6,195	10,779	3,145
Tazewell	22,821	28,951	16,924	35,481	3,206
Union	5,003	3,531	3,781	4,289	291
Vermilion	18,438	19,751	14,498	22,579	2,110
Wabash	2,781	3,388	1,975	3,571	230
Warren	3,808	5,822	2,756	5,667	489
Washington	3,222	4,485	2,158	5,354	205
Wayne	4,303	5,211	3,258	6,013	222
White	5,306	4,600	3,463	5,279	274
Whiteside	11,255	14,308	7,191	17,389	1,242
Will	51,103	61,784	41,975	69,310	7,855
Williamson	13,600	10,703	10,779	14,451	793
Winnebago	42,399	52,736	32,384	48,825	22,596
Woodford	4,819	8,899	3,552	10,791	711
Totals	**2,271,295**	**2,364,269**	**1,981,413**	**2,358,049**	**346,754**

Illinois Vote Since 1932

1932 (Pres.), Roosevelt, Dem., 1,882,304; Hoover, Rep., 1,432,756; Thomas, Soc., 67,258; Foster, Com., 15,582; Upshaw, Proh., 6,388; Reynolds, Soc. Labor, 3,638.
1936 (Pres.), Roosevelt, Dem., 2,282,999; Landon, Rep., 1,570,393; Lemke, Union, 89,439; Thomas, Soc., 7,530; Colvin, Proh., 3,439; Aiken, Soc. Labor, 1,921.
1940 (Pres.), Roosevelt, Dem., 2,149,934; Willkie, Rep., 2,047,240; Thomas, Soc., 10,914; Babson, Proh., 9,190.
1944 (Pres.), Roosevelt, Dem., 2,079,479; Dewey, Rep., 1,939,314; Teichert, Soc. Labor, 9,677; Watson, Proh., 7,411; Thomas, Soc., 180.
1948 (Pres.), Truman, Dem., 1,994,715; Dewey, Rep., 1,961,103; Watson, Proh., 11,959; Thomas, Soc., 11,522; Teichert, Soc. Labor, 3,118.
1952 (Pres.), Eisenhower, Rep., 2,457,327; Stevenson, Dem., 2,013,920; Hass, Soc. Labor, 9,363; write-in, 448.
1956 (Pres.), Eisenhower, Rep., 2,623,327; Stevenson, Dem., 1,775,682; Hass, Soc. Labor, 8,342; write-in, 56.
1960 (Pres.), Kennedy, Dem., 2,377,846; Nixon, Rep., 2,368,988; Hass, Soc. Labor, 10,560; write-in, 15.
1964 (Pres.), Johnson, Dem., 2,796,833; Goldwater, Rep., 1,905,946; write-in, 62.
1968 (Pres.), Nixon, Rep., 2,174,774; Humphrey, Dem., 2,039,814; Wallace, 3d party, 390,958; Blomen, Soc. Labor, 13,878; write-in, 325.
1972 (Pres.), Nixon, Rep. 2,788,179; McGovern, Dem., 1,913,472; Fisher, Soc. Labor, 12,344; Schmitz, Amer., 2,471; Hall, Com., 4,541; others, 2,229.
1976 (Pres.), Carter, Dem., 2,271,295; Ford, Rep., 2,364,269; McCarthy, Ind., 55,939; Hall, Com., 9,250; MacBride, Libertarian, 8,057; Camejo, Soc. Workers, 3,615; Levin, Soc. Labor, 2,422; LaRouche, U.S. Labor, 2,018; write-in, 1,968.
1980 (Pres.), Reagan, Rep., 2,358,049; Carter, Dem., 1,981,413; Anderson, Ind., 346,754; Clark, Libertarian, 38,939; Commoner, Citizens, 10,692; Hall, Com., 9,711; Griswold, Workers World, 2,257; DeBerry, Socialist Workers, 1,302; write-ins, 604.

Indiana

| | 1976 | | 1980 | | |
County	Carter (D)	Ford (R)	Carter (D)	Reagan (R)	Anderson (I)
Adams	4,908	6,280	4,673	6,368	767
Allen	44,744	71,321	37,765	68,524	10,368
Bartholomew	11,203	14,771	9,260	15,801	1,604
Benton	2,071	3,093	1,520	3,189	187
Blackford	3,174	2,886	2,431	3,168	258
Boone	5,686	9,214	4,535	10,484	681
Brown	2,381	2,466	2,014	2,884	237
Carroll	3,606	4,797	2,966	5,262	338
Cass	7,610	10,342	5,838	11,500	696
Clark	16,670	12,732	14,137	15,508	1,102
Clay	5,433	5,674	4,363	6,960	311
Clinton	6,662	8,199	5,258	8,158	427
Crawford	2,721	2,181	2,130	2,554	124

	1976 (D)	(R)	1980 (D)	(R)	(I)
Daviess	4,952	6,829	4,057	7,022	345
Dearborn	6,348	6,176	5,135	7,467	464
Decatur	4,365	5,555	3,646	5,819	377
Dekalb	6,151	7,860	4,911	7,886	883
Delaware	25,151	26,417	20,923	28,342	2,743
Dubois	7,385	6,383	6,700	6,775	578
Elkhart	17,581	27,291	14,883	30,081	3,256
Fayette	5,519	5,704	4,304	6,004	293
Floyd	12,744	11,259	11,543	12,456	1,047
Fountain	4,089	4,903	2,845	5,289	280
Franklin	3,234	3,557	2,834	4,551	234
Fulton	3,488	5,083	2,788	5,458	349
Gibson	8,430	7,105	6,834	7,643	591
Grant	13,468	16,847	10,390	19,078	1,043
Greene	7,263	6,442	6,027	7,452	299
Hamilton	7,857	21,828	7,038	26,218	1,736
Hancock	6,191	10,072	5,124	12,093	746
Harrison	5,685	4,911	4,865	6,287	341
Hendricks	9,066	16,725	7,412	19,366	1,048
Henry	10,137	11,620	7,626	12,724	562
Howard	14,815	19,571	12,916	21,272	1,325
Huntington	6,515	9,182	5,415	9,497	824
Jackson	7,610	7,615	6,425	8,903	430
Jasper	3,286	5,398	2,544	6,316	283
Jay	4,124	4,606	3,256	5,351	484
Jefferson	6,139	5,573	5,496	6,831	477
Jennings	4,430	4,505	3,931	5,498	281
Johnson	10,075	16,414	8,445	20,018	1,348
Knox	9,612	9,100	7,829	10,083	617
Kosciusko	7,328	14,505	5,684	15,633	1,164
LaGrange	2,835	3,876	2,095	4,259	377
Lake	120,700	90,119	101,145	95,408	8,275
LaPorte	18,217	21,989	15,387	22,424	2,080
Lawrence	7,908	9,278	5,826	10,846	380
Madison	29,811	32,437	23,554	35,582	2,389
Marion	145,274	177,767	126,103	168,680	15,709
Marshall	6,424	9,707	5,113	10,209	836
Martin	2,827	2,702	2,479	3,082	149
Miami	6,257	8,263	4,927	8,672	508
Monroe	16,609	18,938	13,316	18,233	3,921
Montgomery	5,320	9,509	4,158	9,936	622
Morgan	7,181	10,983	5,439	13,321	498
Newton	2,236	3,204	1,649	3,850	194
Noble	5,875	6,885	4,721	7,624	749
Ohio	1,300	1,027	1,074	1,264	57
Orange	4,031	4,399	3,228	5,073	181
Owen	3,103	2,896	2,325	3,632	188
Parke	3,158	3,929	2,432	4,595	194
Perry	5,620	4,088	4,540	4,350	448
Pike	3,938	3,138	3,346	3,343	190
Porter	16,468	25,489	12,869	30,055	3,061
Posey	5,298	5,136	4,465	6,096	667
Pulaski	2,813	3,586	2,092	3,916	175
Putnam	5,116	6,063	3,996	7,090	501
Randolph	5,330	6,891	4,025	7,762	426
Ripley	4,792	5,293	4,022	5,770	303
Rush	3,052	4,723	2,388	4,829	224
St. Joseph	49,156	50,358	44,218	50,607	6,962
Scott	4,229	2,657	3,694	3,432	139
Shelby	7,098	8,918	5,861	10,496	614
Spencer	4,796	4,166	4,153	5,284	196
Starke	4,753	4,354	3,615	5,035	297
Steuben	3,323	5,079	2,606	5,670	602
Sullivan	5,198	3,747	4,335	4,465	212
Switzerland	2,150	1,329	1,704	1,584	38
Tippecanoe	17,850	29,186	14,636	27,589	5,141
Tipton	3,428	4,776	2,547	5,150	285
Union	1,160	1,631	898	1,766	92
Vanderburgh	34,911	37,975	29,930	36,248	4,150
Vermillion	4,791	3,674	3,793	4,195	269
Vigo	24,684	23,555	19,261	24,133	2,484
Wabash	5,704	8,534	4,620	8,738	797
Warren	1,906	2,377	1,287	2,665	145
Warrick	7,804	7,200	6,845	8,681	890
Washington	4,409	3,794	3,663	5,234	191
Wayne	12,306	16,697	9,599	16,981	1,174
Wells	4,250	5,596	3,760	5,864	717
White	3,963	6,287	3,247	6,999	466
Whitley	5,445	6,761	4,497	7,146	928
Totals	1,014,714	1,185,958	844,197	1,255,856	111,639

Indiana Vote Since 1932

1932 (Pres.), Roosevelt, Dem., 862,054; Hoover, Rep., 677,184; Thomas, Soc., 21,388; Upshaw, Proh., 10,399; Foster, Com., 2,187; Reynolds, Soc. Labor, 2,070.

1936 (Pres.), Roosevelt, Dem., 943,974; Landon, Rep., 691,570; Lemke, Union, 19,407; Thomas, Soc., 3,856; Browder, Com., 1,090.

1940 (Pres.), Roosevelt, Dem., 874,063; Willkie, Rep., 899,466; Babson, Proh., 6,437; Thomas, Soc., 2,075; Aiken, Soc. Labor, 706.

1944 (Pres.), Roosevelt, Dem., 781,403; Dewey, Rep., 875,891; Watson, Proh., 12,574; Thomas, Soc., 2,223.

1948 (Pres.), Truman, Dem., 807,833; Dewey, Rep., 821,079; Watson, Proh., 14,711; Wallace, Prog., 9,649;

Thomas, Soc., 2,179; Teichert, Soc. Labor, 763.

1952 (Pres.), Eisenhower, Rep., 1,136,259; Stevenson, Dem., 801,530; Hamblen, Proh., 15,335; Hallinan, Prog., 1,222; Hass, Soc. Labor, 979.

1956 (Pres.), Eisenhower, Rep., 1,182,811; Stevenson, Dem., 783,908; Holtwick, Proh., 6,554; Hass, Soc. Labor, 1,334.

1960 (Pres.), Kennedy, Dem., 952,358; Nixon, Rep., 1,175,120; Decker, Proh., 6,746; Hass, Soc. Labor, 1,136.

1964 (Pres.), Johnson, Dem. 1,170,848; Goldwater, Rep., 911,118; Munn, Proh., 8,266; Hass, Soc. Labor, 1,374.

1968 (Pres.), Nixon, Rep., 1,067,885; Humphrey, Dem., 806,659; Wallace, 3d party, 243,108; Munn, Proh., 4,616; Halstead, Soc. Worker, 1,293; Gregory, write-in, 36.

1972 (Pres.), Nixon, Rep., 1,405,154; McGovern, Dem., 708,568; Reed, Soc. Workers, 5,575; Fisher, Soc. Labor, 1,688; Spock, Peace & Freedom, 4,544.

1976 (Pres.), Carter, Dem., 1,014,714; Ford, Rep., 1,185,958; Anderson, Amer., 14,048; Camejo, Soc. Workers, 5,695; LaRouche, U.S. Labor, 1,947.

1980 (Pres.) Reagan, Rep., 1,255,656; Carter, Dem., 844,197; Anderson, Ind., 111,639; Clark, Libertarian, 19,627; Commoner, Citizens, 4,852; Greaves, American, 4,750; Hall, Com., 702; DeBerry, Soc., 610.

Iowa

County	1976 Carter (D)	Ford (R)	1980 Carter (D)	Reagan (R)	Anderson (I)
Adair	2,294	2,326	1,454	2,821	356
Adams	1,507	1,388	940	1,779	214
Allamakee	2,568	3,648	2,170	4,000	343
Appanoose	3,424	3,036	2,769	3,544	353
Audubon	2,104	1,978	1,546	2,523	251
Benton	5,514	5,014	4,223	5,329	948
Black Hawk	29,508	30,994	27,443	29,627	5,847
Boone	6,595	5,413	5,126	5,732	1,081
Bremer	4,203	6,252	3,527	6,706	970
Buchanan	4,258	4,794	3,605	5,041	689
Buena Vista	4,227	5,126	3,468	5,272	771
Butler	2,503	4,207	1,990	4,730	392
Calhoun	3,001	3,215	2,150	3,633	407
Carroll	5,333	4,094	3,885	5,017	736
Cass	2,866	4,589	2,176	5,391	475
Cedar	3,354	4,308	2,589	4,398	697
Cerro Gordo	11,189	10,604	9,363	11,189	2,024
Cherokee	3,358	3,993	2,719	4,087	599
Chickasaw	3,503	3,432	2,935	3,929	500
Clarke	2,333	1,737	1,614	2,417	310
Clay	3,776	4,548	3,179	4,479	991
Clayton	3,804	4,826	3,297	5,115	669
Clinton	11,746	12,401	9,698	13,025	2,140
Crawford	3,903	3,879	2,500	4,883	509
Dallas	6,722	5,308	5,310	6,296	1,200
Davis	2,426	1,631	1,689	2,003	200
Decatur	2,698	1,932	2,048	2,212	318
Delaware	3,168	4,161	2,671	4,316	727
Des Moines	11,268	9,023	9,977	9,158	1,041
Dickinson	3,074	3,795	2,620	4,028	687
Dubuque	20,548	17,459	18,689	18,649	3,708
Emmet	2,720	2,872	2,153	3,062	446
Fayette	5,220	6,618	4,377	6,374	647
Floyd	4,646	4,361	3,634	4,665	728
Franklin	2,682	3,056	1,920	3,290	406
Fremont	1,964	2,163	1,203	2,693	191
Greene	3,094	2,811	2,210	3,154	510
Grundy	2,410	4,173	1,869	4,644	440
Guthrie	2,873	2,644	1,866	3,214	384
Hamilton	3,953	3,932	2,741	4,745	679
Hancock	2,975	3,127	1,918	3,681	462
Hardin	4,479	4,682	3,757	5,329	730
Harrison	3,228	3,489	2,152	4,502	311
Henry	3,882	3,848	3,317	4,430	629
Howard	2,917	2,618	2,214	2,975	336
Humboldt	2,677	3,075	1,840	3,575	394
Ida	1,868	2,590	1,235	2,825	254
Iowa	3,367	3,926	2,604	4,153	667
Jackson	4,467	4,221	3,518	4,479	622
Jasper	8,783	7,758	7,258	8,266	1,221
Jefferson	3,377	3,746	2,577	4,099	505
Johnson	20,208	16,090	20,172	13,642	8,101
Jones	4,245	4,463	3,521	4,506	756
Keokuk	3,482	2,920	2,390	3,145	366
Kossuth	5,190	4,653	3,810	5,568	777
Lee	9,017	8,195	8,204	8,793	1,047
Linn	38,252	36,513	31,950	36,254	8,773
Louisa	2,089	2,284	1,700	2,530	29
Lucas	2,733	2,071	1,989	2,593	29
Lyon	1,870	3,558	1,431	4,349	375
Madison	3,109	2,681	2,496	3,320	505
Mahaska	4,838	5,267	3,968	5,650	603
Marion	6,226	5,429	5,490	6,665	1,232
Marshall	8,695	9,562	7,114	10,707	1,54
Mills	1,908	2,722	1,244	3,581	28

	1976 (D)	(R)	1980 (D)	(R)	(I)
Mitchell	2,906	2,887	2,040	3,401	361
Monona	2,661	2,636	1,660	3,268	275
Monroe	2,360	1,581	1,866	2,003	216
Montgomery	2,229	3,673	1,556	4,115	301
Muscatine	6,567	7,697	5,597	7,829	1,522
O'Brien	2,732	4,643	2,210	4,937	536
Osceola	1,309	1,955	1,051	2,177	234
Page	2,865	5,343	1,772	5,618	356
Palo Alto	3,182	2,623	2,463	3,025	412
Plymouth	4,284	5,590	2,965	6,515	756
Pocahontas	3,055	2,700	1,959	3,194	397
Polk	71,917	62,316	61,984	64,156	15,819
Pottawattamie	14,754	17,264	10,709	20,222	1,870
Poweshiek	4,360	4,194	3,529	4,598	821
Ringgold	1,739	1,543	1,150	1,884	191
Sac	2,996	3,347	1,976	3,725	467
Scott	29,771	35,021	26,391	34,701	5,760
Shelby	2,851	3,301	1,892	4,147	372
Sioux	3,322	9,448	2,698	10,768	610
Story	15,717	18,394	13,529	15,829	7,252
Tama	4,580	4,379	3,049	4,840	593
Taylor	1,947	2,059	1,226	2,715	240
Union	2,955	2,873	2,182	3,372	368
Van Buren	1,807	1,804	1,311	2,142	183
Wapello	10,249	6,786	8,923	7,475	1,050
Warren	7,653	6,099	6,610	7,360	1,369
Washington	3,448	4,218	2,877	3,967	703
Wayne	2,145	1,781	1,627	2,221	218
Webster	10,543	9,068	9,001	10,438	1,386
Winnebago	2,950	3,315	2,208	3,808	417
Winneshiek	4,158	4,765	3,201	5,033	938
Woodbury	19,664	22,853	15,930	23,553	3,184
Worth	2,399	1,964	1,721	2,247	301
Wright	3,637	3,544	2,645	3,936	497
Total	**619,931**	**632,863**	**508,672**	**676,026**	**115,633**

Iowa Vote Since 1932

1932 (Pres.), Roosevelt, Dem., 598,019; Hoover, Rep., 414,433; Thomas, Soc., 20,467; Upshaw, Proh., 2,111; Coxey, Farm-Lab., 1,094; Foster, Com., 559.

1936 (Pres.), Roosevelt, Dem., 621,756; Landon, Rep., 487,977; Lemke, Union, 29,687; Thomas, Soc., 1,373; Colvin, Proh., 1,182; Browder, Com., 506; Aiken, Soc. Labor, 252.

1940 (Pres.), Roosevelt, Dem., 578,800; Willkie, Rep., 632,370; Babson, Proh., 2,284; Browder, Com., 1,524; Aiken, Soc. Labor, 452.

1944 (Pres.), Roosevelt, Dem., 499,876; Dewey, Rep., 547,267; Watson, Proh., 3,752; Thomas, Soc., 1,511; Teichert, Soc. Labor, 193.

1948 (Pres.), Truman, Dem., 522,380; Dewey, Rep., 494,018; Wallace, Prog., 12,125; Teichert, Soc. Labor, 4,274; Watson, Proh., 3,382; Thomas, Soc., 1,829; Dobbs, Soc. Workers, 26.

1952 (Pres.), Eisenhower, Rep., 808,906; Stevenson, Dem., 451,513; Hallinan, Prog., 5,085; Hamblen, Proh., 2,882; Hoopes, Soc., 219; Hass, Soc. Labor, 139; scattering 29.

1956 (Pres.), Eisenhower, Rep., 729,187; Stevenson, Dem., 501,858; Andrews (A.C.P. of Iowa), 3,202; Hoopes, Soc., 192; Hass, Soc. Labor, 125.

1960 (Pres.), Kennedy, Dem., 550,565; Nixon, Rep., 722,381; Hass, Soc. Labor, 230; write-in, 634.

1964 (Pres.), Johnson, Dem., 733,030; Goldwater, Rep., 449,148; Hass, Soc. Labor, 182; DeBerry, Soc. Worker, 159; Munn, Proh., 1,902.

1968 (Pres.), Nixon, Rep., 619,106; Humphrey, Dem., 476,699; Wallace, 3d party, 66,422; Munn, Proh., 362; Halstead, Soc. Worker, 3,377; Cleaver, Peace and Freedom, 1,332; Blomen, Soc. Labor, 241.

1972 (Pres.), Nixon, Rep., 706,207; McGovern, Dem., 496,206; Schmitz, Amer., 22,056; Jenness, Soc. Workers, 488; Fisher, Soc. Labor, 195; Hall, Com. 272; Green, Universal, 199; scattered, 321.

1976 (Pres.), Carter, Dem., 619,931; Ford, Rep., 632,863; McCarthy, Ind., 20,051; Anderson, Amer., 3,040; MacBride, Libertarian, 1,452.

1980 (Pres.), Reagan, Rep., 676,026; Carter, Dem., 508,672; Anderson, Ind., 115,633; Clark, Libertarian, 13,123; Commoner, Citizens, 2,273; McReynolds, Socialist, 534; Hall Com., 298; DeBerry, Soc. Work., 244; Greaves, American, 189; Bubar, Statesman, 150; scattering, 519.

Kansas

County	1976 Carter (D)	Ford (R)	1980 Carter (D)	Reagan (R)	Anderson (I)
Allen	2,746	3,269	2,009	3,811	380
Anderson	1,886	1,872	1,170	2,363	184
Atchison	4,108	4,030	3,063	4,084	345
Barber	1,494	1,568	914	1,872	168
Barton	5,497	7,311	3,663	9,147	793
Bourbon	3,237	3,589	2,605	4,263	251
Brown	1,745	3,407	1,370	3,598	286
Butler	8,540	8,390	6,875	10,210	1,015
Chase	643	922	413	1,073	92
Chautauqua	866	1,159	543	1,566	57
Cherokee	5,154	3,957	3,969	5,296	282
Cheyenne	758	1,008	358	1,330	81
Clark	680	761	430	901	67
Clay	1,610	3,085	932	3,449	217
Cloud	2,976	2,954	1,793	3,581	344
Coffey	1,549	2,145	938	2,491	126
Comanche	630	719	393	877	50
Cowley	7,095	7,513	5,474	8,749	866
Crawford	9,021	7,225	7,658	8,058	847
Decatur	1,011	1,232	443	1,642	125
Dickinson	3,672	4,759	2,108	5,654	469
Doniphan	1,428	2,649	1,001	2,523	146
Douglas	11,922	14,277	9,200	14,106	4,770
Edwards	1,204	1,001	616	1,409	127
Elk	865	1,087	482	1,280	54
Ellis	6,280	4,719	3,940	5,634	923
Ellsworth	1,573	1,618	886	2,155	167
Finney	3,813	3,711	2,689	4,831	531
Ford	4,934	4,679	3,194	5,686	622
Franklin	3,607	4,760	2,726	5,525	432
Geary	2,843	3,230	2,357	3,534	332
Gove	848	860	396	1,263	91
Graham	936	1,112	473	1,450	98
Grant	1,151	1,226	683	1,711	150
Gray	1,111	837	583	1,310	123
Greeley	479	389	235	600	85
Greenwood	1,737	2,319	1,241	2,685	170
Hamilton	746	560	402	889	66
Harper	1,681	1,777	990	2,254	182
Harvey	6,003	6,624	4,173	7,045	1,356
Haskell	676	761	374	1,014	84
Hodgeman	697	576	339	831	69
Jackson	2,129	2,725	1,537	3,211	234
Jefferson	2,470	3,225	1,776	4,046	364
Jewell	1,111	1,592	578	2,074	153
Johnson	35,605	75,798	33,210	78,048	10,947
Kearny	658	674	375	924	62
Kingman	2,142	1,839	1,133	2,610	286
Kiowa	764	1,180	438	1,433	88
Labette	5,294	4,640	3,947	5,244	588
Lane	646	651	321	924	100
Leavenworth	8,022	8,407	6,354	9,157	955
Lincoln	985	1,225	528	1,685	96
Linn	1,681	1,873	1,157	2,407	103
Logan	694	957	358	1,261	66
Lyon	5,634	7,062	4,680	8,431	1,216
Marion	2,483	3,519	1,569	3,960	488
Marshall	3,004	3,226	1,555	4,127	330
McPherson	5,366	6,187	3,340	6,843	1,222
Meade	526	983	482	1,618	121
Miami	4,000	3,999	3,071	4,740	368
Mitchell	1,700	2,095	876	2,821	197
Montgomery	7,157	8,864	5,282	10,856	488
Morris	1,337	1,698	810	1,933	166
Morton	735	738	414	1,157	71
Nemaha	2,586	2,759	1,600	3,546	243
Neosho	3,842	4,038	2,923	4,613	432
Ness	1,106	1,016	616	1,657	136
Norton	1,337	2,201	666	2,625	151
Osage	2,755	2,945	2,088	3,817	330
Osborne	1,190	1,574	620	2,188	125
Ottawa	1,393	1,629	630	2,118	150
Pawnee	1,959	1,982	1,184	2,731	143
Phillips	1,264	2,317	748	2,731	143
Pottawatomie	2,316	3,483	1,724	3,895	444
Pratt	2,307	2,427	1,369	2,866	329
Rawlins	903	1,148	427	1,524	87
Reno	14,620	11,212	9,615	13,804	2,225
Republic	1,617	2,294	850	3,031	183
Rice	3,056	2,584	1,847	3,211	426
Riley	6,540	9,518	5,224	8,904	2,443
Rooks	1,412	1,664	725	2,275	144
Rush	1,359	1,170	557	1,840	144
Russell	1,453	3,165	910	3,241	229
Saline	8,476	11,218	6,382	12,758	1,706
Scott	919	1,195	456	1,829	99
Sedgwick	63,989	69,828	55,105	75,317	10,222
Seward	1,907	3,643	1,460	4,385	250
Shawnee	28,578	37,101	24,852	36,290	5,524
Sheridan	793	838	391	1,202	68
Sherman	1,573	1,671	779	2,315	215
Smith	1,333	2,009	719	2,415	183
Stafford	1,659	1,430	872	1,865	184
Stanton	489	510	231	672	62
Stevens	901	1,262	478	1,502	67
Summer	5,385	4,645	3,761	6,038	486

	1976 (D)	1976 (R)	1980 (D)	1980 (R)	1980 (I)
Thomas	1,802	2,246	1,045	2,789	269
Trego	1,003	1,025	523	1,340	138
Wabaunsee	1,354	1,921	853	2,255	173
Wallace	486	600	167	811	36
Washington	1,564	2,543	784	3,058	195
Wichita	614	593	303	880	60
Wilson	2,047	2,682	1,205	3,328	208
Woodson	904	1,104	646	1,435	89
Wyandotte	37,478	23,141	32,763	23,012	3,018
Totals	430,421	502,752	326,150	566,812	68,231

Kansas Vote Since 1932

1932 (Pres.), Roosevelt, Dem., 424,204; Hoover, Rep., 349,498; Thomas, Soc., 18,276.

1936 (Pres.), Roosevelt, Dem., 464,520; Landon, Rep., 397,727; Thomas, Soc., 2,766; Lemke, Union, 494.

1940 (Pres.), Roosevelt, Dem., 364,725; Willkie, Rep., 489,169; Babson, Proh., 4,056; Thomas, Soc., 2,347.

1944 (Pres.), Roosevelt, Dem., 287,458; Dewey, Rep., 442,096; Watson, Proh., 2,609; Thomas, Soc., 1,613.

1948 (Pres.), Truman, Dem., 351,902; Dewey, Rep., 423,039; Watson, Proh., 6,468; Wallace, Prog., 4,603; Thomas, Soc., 2,807.

1952 (Pres.), Eisenhower, Rep., 616,302; Stevenson, Dem., 273,296; Hamblen, Proh., 6,038; Hoopes, Soc., 530.

1956 (Pres.), Eisenhower, Rep., 566,878; Stevenson, Dem., 296,317; Holtwick, Proh., 3,048.

1960 (Pres.), Kennedy, Dem., 363,213; Nixon, Rep., 561,474; Decker, Proh., 4,138.

1964 (Pres.), Johnson, Dem., 464,028; Goldwater, Rep., 386,579; Munn, Proh., 5,393; Hass, Soc. Labor, 1,901.

1968 (Pres.), Nixon, Rep., 478,674; Humphrey, Dem., 302,996; Wallace, 3d, 88,921; Munn, Proh., 2,192.

1972 (Pres.), Nixon, Rep., 619,812; McGovern, Dem., 270,287; Schmitz, Cons., 21,808; Munn, Proh., 4,188.

1976 (Pres.), Carter, Dem., 430,421; Ford, Rep., 502,752; McCarthy, Ind., 13,185; Anderson, Amer., 4,724; MacBride, Libertarian, 3,242; Maddox, Cons., 2,118; Bubar, Proh., 1,403.

1980 (Pres.), Reagan, Rep., 566,812; Carter, Dem., 326,150; Anderson, Ind., 68,231; Clark, Libertarian, 14,470; Shelton, American, 1,555; Hall, Com., 967; Bubar, Statesman, 821; Rarick, Conservative, 789.

Kentucky

	1976 Carter (D)	1976 Ford (R)	1980 Carter (D)	1980 Reagan (R)	1980 Anderson (I)
County					
Adair	2,366	3,201	2,285	4,051	53
Allen	2,231	2,508	2,010	3,186	54
Anderson	2,388	1,682	2,567	2,052	90
Ballard	2,794	649	2,583	1,190	23
Barren	5,878	3,797	5,285	6,405	164
Bath	2,113	938	2,174	1,463	47
Bell	5,284	5,035	6,362	5,433	150
Boone	5,602	5,602	5,374	8,263	383
Bourbon	3,504	2,260	3,641	2,475	153
Boyd	11,150	9,106	10,702	10,367	496
Boyle	4,095	3,511	4,429	3,848	254
Bracken	1,577	879	1,420	1,154	36
Breathitt	3,544	1,014	3,916	1,532	68
Breckinridge	3,347	2,698	3,163	3,629	72
Bullitt	5,623	3,639	5,884	6,364	202
Butler	1,588	2,363	1,274	3,129	28
Caldwell	3,016	1,808	2,924	2,609	66
Calloway	8,141	3,171	6,809	4,498	318
Campbell	12,423	15,798	11,059	16,743	943
Carlisle	1,985	435	1,542	975	8
Carroll	2,251	815	2,127	1,076	82
Carter	3,915	3,185	3,782	3,934	86
Casey	1,602	3,379	1,298	4,239	38
Christian	7,845	4,964	7,048	8,209	190
Clark	4,575	3,114	5,071	4,302	242
Clay	1,674	3,652	2,121	4,594	37
Clinton	987	2,354	1,000	3,539	34
Crittenden	1,715	1,596	1,508	2,219	28
Cumberland	853	1,653	821	2,216	27
Daviess	14,114	12,826	14,902	14,643	752
Edmonson	1,418	1,976	1,252	2,913	28
Elliott	1,987	455	1,668	551	15
Estill	2,034	2,250	1,965	2,818	45
Fayette	28,012	35,170	30,511	35,349	4,933
Fleming	2,317	1,647	2,051	2,189	54
Floyd	10,151	3,108	10,975	4,179	171
Franklin	10,475	5,536	11,193	6,455	610
Fulton	2,370	1,060	2,016	1,462	31
Gallatin	1,164	436	988	684	20

Garrard	1,887	2,045	1,774	2,585	62
Grant	2,336	1,212	2,272	1,779	76
Graves	8,982	3,195	6,999	6,556	135
Grayson	3,064	3,658	2,788	5,084	78
Green	2,085	2,397	1,758	2,775	39
Greenup	6,880	5,062	7,126	6,857	220
Hancock	1,562	1,124	1,530	1,367	52
Hardin	7,977	6,965	8,339	9,779	452
Harlan	7,300	4,624	8,798	5,460	131
Harrison	3,582	1,911	3,319	2,184	107
Hart	3,189	2,013	3,005	3,129	42
Henderson	7,916	4,053	8,082	5,074	354
Henry	2,985	1,192	2,999	1,723	69
Hickman	2,035	585	1,456	1,143	28
Hopkins	7,749	5,115	8,810	6,238	213
Jackson	680	2,766	702	3,379	29
Jefferson	122,731	130,262	125,844	127,254	9,686
Jessamine	2,795	3,081	3,310	4,809	278
Johnson	3,683	4,891	3,142	5,039	96
Kenton	18,833	22,087	17,907	25,965	1,583
Knott	4,762	962	5,405	1,602	25
Knox	3,642	4,931	3,543	5,539	113
Larue	2,207	1,409	2,183	2,000	43
Laurel	3,813	6,186	3,969	8,868	114
Lawrence	2,402	1,838	2,362	2,564	32
Lee	1,091	1,449	1,017	1,650	41
Leslie	1,478	3,770	1,327	3,536	40
Letcher	4,590	3,122	4,280	3,426	78
Lewis	1,929	2,383	1,543	2,802	34
Lincoln	3,198	2,694	2,991	3,034	58
Livingston	2,497	878	2,287	1,670	30
Logan	4,850	2,430	4,264	3,366	85
Lyon	1,606	585	1,496	968	26
McCracken	14,956	6,997	13,365	10,281	369
McCreary	1,827	3,272	1,377	3,786	40
McLean	2,346	1,212	2,147	1,497	44
Madison	7,299	6,581	8,208	8,437	739
Magoffin	2,451	1,793	2,986	2,265	25
Marion	3,520	1,723	3,577	2,126	67
Marshall	6,906	2,578	6,231	4,403	96
Martin	1,267	2,120	1,567	2,793	51
Mason	3,397	2,529	3,181	2,926	127
Meade	3,030	1,755	3,205	2,740	90
Menifee	1,041	304	966	547	11
Mercer	3,411	2,451	3,528	3,275	92
Metcalfe	1,877	1,356	1,628	2,013	39
Monroe	1,412	3,352	1,156	4,592	47
Montgomery	3,141	2,032	3,391	2,869	117
Morgan	2,897	973	2,698	1,450	31
Muhlenberg	7,058	4,292	6,616	4,893	148
Nelson	4,454	2,804	5,514	3,349	162
Nicholas	1,582	738	1,349	915	56
Ohio	3,508	3,764	3,486	5,272	103
Oldham	2,819	3,695	3,487	5,586	351
Owen	2,332	676	2,323	944	43
Owsley	305	1,053	437	1,250	7
Pendleton	2,147	1,230	1,992	1,757	69
Perry	5,633	4,434	6,031	4,226	72
Pike	14,320	9,178	14,878	10,550	204
Powell	1,859	1,148	2,006	1,716	33
Pulaski	5,752	9,226	6,570	12,970	257
Robertson	546	275	562	416	14
Rockcastle	1,408	2,583	1,345	3,543	37
Rowen	3,541	2,244	2,975	2,758	191
Russell	1,803	2,882	1,693	3,804	29
Scott	3,118	2,408	3,531	2,868	197
Shelby	3,841	2,916	4,429	3,423	178
Simpson	2,782	1,481	2,713	2,020	59
Spencer	1,209	742	1,216	935	27
Taylor	3,456	3,337	3,400	4,243	84
Todd	2,436	1,095	1,956	1,945	44
Trigg	2,727	991	2,619	1,913	56
Trimble	1,568	517	1,478	824	49
Union	3,540	1,716	3,479	1,847	68
Warren	9,657	9,439	9,643	12,184	602
Washington	2,376	1,765	2,147	2,008	43
Wayne	2,537	3,243	2,673	3,972	50
Webster	3,523	1,402	3,506	1,939	52
Whitley	4,212	6,100	3,889	7,007	125
Wolfe	1,777	659	1,814	951	19
Woodford	2,689	2,646	3,122	3,105	213
Totals	615,717	531,852	616,417	635,274	31,127

Kentucky Vote Since 1932

1932 (Pres.), Roosevelt, Dem., 580,574; Hoover, Rep., 394,716; Upshaw, Proh., 2,252; Thomas, Soc., 3,853; Reynolds, Soc. Labor, 1,396; Foster, Com., 272.

1936 (Pres.), Roosevelt, Dem., 541,944; Landon, Rep., 369,702; Lemke, Union, 12,501; Colvin, Proh., 929; Thomas, Soc., 627; Aiken, Soc. Labor, 294; Browder, Com., 204.

1940 (Pres.), Roosevelt, Dem., 557,222; Willkie, Rep., 410,384; Babson, Proh., 1,443; Thomas, Soc., 1,014.

1944 (Pres.), Roosevelt, Dem., 472,589; Dewey, Rep., 392,448; Watson, Proh., 2,023; Thomas, Soc., 535; Teichert, Soc. Labor, 326.

1948 (Pres.), Truman, Dem., 466,756; Dewey, Rep.

341,210; Thurmond, States' Rights, 10,411; Wallace, Prog., 1,567; Thomas, Soc., 1,284; Watson, Proh., 1,245; Teichert, Soc. Labor, 185.

1952 (Pres.), Eisenhower, Rep., 495,029; Stevenson, Dem., 495,729; Hamblen, Proh., 1,161; Hass, Soc. Labor, 893; Hallinan, Proh., 336.

1956 (Pres.), Eisenhower, Rep., 572,192; Stevenson, Dem., 476,453; Byrd, States' Rights, 2,657; Holtwick, Proh., 2,145; Hass, Soc. Labor, 358.

1960 (Pres.), Kennedy, Dem., 521,855; Nixon, Rep., 602,607.

1964 (Pres.), Johnson, Dem., 669,659; Goldwater, Rep., 372,977; John Kasper, Nat'l. States Rights, 3,469.

1968 (Pres.), Nixon, Rep., 462,411; Humphrey, Dem., 397,547; Wallace, 3d p., 193,098; Halstead, Soc. Worker, 2,843.

1972 (Pres.), Nixon, Rep., 676,446; McGovern, Dem., 371,159; Schmitz, Amer., 17,627; Jenness, Soc. Workers, 685; Hall, Com., 464; Spock, Peoples, 1,118.

1976 (Pres.), Carter, Dem., 615,717; Ford, Rep., 531,852; Anderson, Amer., 8,308; McCarthy, Ind., 6,837; Maddox, Amer. Ind., 2,328; MacBride, Libertarian, 814.

1980 (Pres.), Reagan, Rep., 635,274; Carter, Dem., 616,417; Anderson, Ind., 31,127; Clark, Libertarian, 5,531; McCormack, Respect For Life, 4,233; Commoner, Citizens, 1,304; Pulley, Socialist, 393; Hall, Com., 348.

Louisiana

Parish	1976 Carter (D)	Ford (R)	1980 Carter (D)	Reagan (R)	Anderson (I)
Acadia	10,814	6,296	9,948	11,533	416
Allen	5,373	2,080	6,057	3,328	110
Ascension	9,100	4,435	12,381	7,238	286
Assumption	4,401	3,117	4,679	4,001	153
Avoyelles	8,104	4,574	7,174	8,216	190
Beauregard	5,322	3,196	5,556	5,250	163
Bienville	3,402	2,499	4,123	3,508	51
Bossier	8,062	12,132	9,377	16,515	327
Caddo	30,593	42,627	36,422	51,202	1,128
Calcasieu	33,980	17,485	35,446	27,600	1,259
Caldwell	1,830	1,890	1,786	2,653	43
Cameron	2,432	819	2,221	1,449	82
Catahoula	2,547	2,086	2,414	2,942	38
Claiborne	2,891	3,216	3,443	3,538	53
Concordia	3,892	3,840	3,956	4,933	52
DeSoto	4,630	3,601	5,861	4,349	49
E. Baton Rouge	49,956	51,655	57,442	71,063	3,312
East Carroll	2,367	1,681	2,283	1,867	24
East Feliciana	3,485	1,668	4,033	2,650	53
Evangeline	7,578	3,715	6,722	7,412	160
Franklin	3,824	3,947	4,177	5,301	65
Grant	3,670	2,280	3,290	3,611	77
Iberia	9,984	10,392	9,681	14,273	410
Iberville	7,254	3,822	9,361	4,463	172
Jackson	3,605	3,310	3,609	3,923	56
Jefferson	53,257	71,787	50,870	99,403	3,578
Jefferson Davis	6,376	3,603	6,140	5,667	201
Lafayette	19,918	22,805	19,694	31,429	1,263
Lafourche	14,131	11,434	14,222	14,951	675
LaSalle	2,961	3,161	2,665	3,792	61
Lincoln	4,971	6,828	5,598	7,515	177
Livingston	9,875	5,555	11,319	10,666	287
Madison	4,933	2,096	3,264	2,531	16
Morehouse	4,017	5,418	4,856	7,254	65
Natchitoches	6,892	5,248	7,102	6,568	158
Orleans	93,130	70,925	106,858	74,302	4,246
Ouachita	15,738	24,082	16,306	29,799	495
Plaquemines	2,614	6,052	4,318	5,489	154
Pointe Coupee	5,147	2,567	6,395	3,667	105
Rapides	20,851	17,766	19,436	25,576	530
Red River	1,906	1,728	2,776	2,147	29
Richland	3,495	3,630	3,745	4,772	48
Sabine	4,555	3,531	5,100	4,265	74
St. Bernard	12,969	12,707	11,367	19,410	616
St. Charles	6,872	4,270	7,898	6,779	283
St. Helen	2,622	1,046	3,183	1,531	42
St. James	4,531	2,751	6,206	3,429	113
St. John	5,700	3,597	7,647	5,819	261
St. Landry	15,631	9,956	17,125	14,940	332
St. Martin	7,992	4,112	7,760	6,701	281
St. Mary	9,401	8,919	10,506	10,378	339
St. Tammany	14,691	15,822	14,161	27,214	872
Tangipahoa	14,432	9,242	15,272	15,187	491
Tensas	2,081	1,553	2,046	1,645	25
Terrebonne	10,627	12,895	10,804	16,644	559
Union	3,600	4,139	3,841	5,130	60
Vermilion	11,246	6,133	9,743	10,481	473
Vernon	6,202	3,970	7,198	5,869	167
Washington	10,000	5,677	10,413	8,681	170
Webster	7,286	7,550	8,568	8,865	118
W. Baton Rouge	3,809	1,913	4,739	2,828	117

	1976		1980		
	Carter (D)	Ford (R)	Carter (D)	Reagan (R)	Anderson (I)
West Carroll	2,595	2,407	2,118	3,430	38
West Feliciana	1,890	990	2,341	1,237	40
Winn	3,543	3,209	3,411	3,944	57
Totals	661,365	587,446	708,453	792,853	26,345

Louisiana Vote Since 1932

1932 (Pres.), Roosevelt, Dem., 249,418; Hoover, Rep., 18,863.

1936 (Pres.), Roosevelt, Dem., 292,894; Landon, Rep., 36,791.

1940 (Pres.), Roosevelt, Dem., 319,751; Willkie, Rep., 52,446.

1944 (Pres.), Roosevelt, Dem., 281,564; Dewey, Rep., 67,750.

1948 (Pres.), Thurmond, States' Rights, 204,290; Truman, Dem., 136,344; Dewey, Rep., 72,657; Wallace, Prog., 3,035.

1952 (Pres.), Eisenhower, Rep., 306,925, Stevenson, Dem., 345,027.

1956 (Pres.), Eisenhower, Rep., 329,047; Stevenson, Dem., 243,977; Andrews, States' Rights, 44,520.

1960 (Pres.), Kennedy, Dem., 407,339; Nixon, Rep., 230,890; States' Rights (unpledged) 169,572.

1964 (Pres.), Johnson, Dem., 387,068; Goldwater, Rep., 509,225.

1968 (Pres.), Nixon, Rep., 257,535; Humphrey, Dem., 309,615; Wallace, 3d party, 530,300.

1972 (Pres.), Nixon, Rep., 686,852; McGovern, Dem., 298,142; Schmitz, Amer., 52,099; Jenness, Soc. Workers, 14,398.

1976 (Pres.), Carter, Dem., 661,365; Ford, Rep., 587,446; Maddox, Amer., 10,058; Hall, Com., 7,417; McCarthy, Ind., 6,588; MacBride, Libertarian, 3,325.

1980 (Pres.), Reagan, Rep., 792,853; Carter, Dem., 708,453; Anderson, Ind., 26,345; Rarick, Amer. Ind., 10,333; Clark, Libertarian, 8,240; Commoner, Citizens, 1,584; DeBerry, Soc. Work., 783.

Maine

County	1976 Carter (D)	Ford (R)	1980 Carter (D)	Reagan (R)	Anderson (I)
Androscoggin	26,484	16,330	22,715	18,399	4,300
Aroostook	15,484	15,550	14,492	16,343	2,528
Cumberland	47,007	48,959	47,337	45,820	12,214
Franklin	5,140	5,799	4,979	5,680	1,205
Hancock	6,725	12,064	7,027	11,435	2,300
Kennebec	23,473	22,534	20,943	21,517	5,553
Knox	5,922	8,315	5,732	7,631	1,842
Lincoln	4,818	7,554	4,776	7,434	1,556
Oxford	10,340	10,551	9,914	11,041	2,063
Penobscot	24,672	29,016	26,519	28,869	6,287
Piscataquis	3,727	4,084	3,550	4,015	781
Sagadahoc	5,529	5,988	5,663	5,946	1,252
Somerset	9,465	8,868	8,115	9,286	1,673
Waldo	4,853	6,289	4,883	6,514	1,304
Washington	6,644	7,039	6,050	7,180	1,301
York	31,996	27,380	28,279	31,412	7,168
Totals	232,279	236,320	220,974	238,522	53,327

Maine Vote Since 1932

1932 (Pres.), Roosevelt, Dem., 128,907; Hoover, Rep., 166,631; Thomas, Soc., 2,439; Reynolds, Soc. Labor, 255; Foster, Com., 162.

1936 (Pres.), Landon, Rep., 168,823; Roosevelt, Dem., 126,333; Lemke, Union, 7,581; Thomas, Soc., 783; Colvin, Proh., 334; Browder, Com., 257; Aiken, Soc. Labor, 129.

1940 (Pres.), Roosevelt, Dem., 156,478; Willkie, Rep., 165,951; Browder, Com., 411.

1944 (Pres.), Roosevelt, Dem., 140,631; Dewey, Rep., 155,434; Teichert, Soc. Labor, 335.

1948 (Pres.), Truman, Dem., 111,916; Dewey, Rep., 150,234; Wallace, Prog., 1,884; Thomas, Soc., 547; Teichert, Soc. Labor, 206.

1952 (Pres.), Eisenhower, Rep., 232,353; Stevenson, Dem., 118,806; Hallinan, Prog., 332; Hass, Soc. Labor, 156; Hoopes, Soc., 138; scattered, 1.

1956 (Pres.), Eisenhower, Rep., 249,238; Stevenson, Dem., 102,468.

1960 (Pres.), Kennedy, Dem., 181,159; Nixon, Rep., 240,608.

1964 (Pres.), Johnson, Dem., 262,264; Goldwater, Rep., 118,701.

1968 (Pres.), Nixon, Rep., 169,254; Humphrey, Dem., 217,312; Wallace, 3d party, 6,370.

1972 (Pres.), Nixon, Rep., 256,458; McGovern, Dem., 160,584; scattered, 229.

1976 (Pres.), Carter, Dem., 232,279; Ford, Rep., 236,320; McCarthy, Ind., 10,874; Bubar, Proh., 3,495.

1980 (Pres.), Reagan, Rep., 238,522; Carter, Dem., 220,974; Anderson, Ind., 53,327; Clark, Libertarian, 5,119; Commoner, Citizens, 4,394; Hall, Com., 591; write-ins, 84.

Maryland

| | 1976 | | 1980 | | |
County	Carter (D)	Ford (R)	Carter (D)	Reagan (R)	Anderson (I)
Allegany	15,967	15,435	12,167	17,512	1,486
Anne Arundel	54,351	61,353	50,780	69,443	10,020
Baltimore	118,505	143,293	121,280	132,490	23,096
Calvert	4,626	3,439	4,745	5,440	590
Caroline	3,017	3,114	2,833	3,582	291
Carroll	9,940	15,661	10,393	19,859	2,243
Cecil	8,950	7,833	7,937	9,673	1,037
Charles	9,525	7,792	8,887	11,807	1,153
Dorchester	4,528	4,768	4,908	5,160	360
Frederick	14,542	17,941	13,629	22,033	2,891
Garrett	3,332	4,640	2,708	5,475	270
Harford	19,890	24,309	20,042	26,713	3,761
Howard	20,533	21,200	20,702	24,272	6,028
Kent	3,211	2,821	2,986	2,889	371
Montgomery	131,098	122,674	105,822	125,515	32,730
Prince George	111,743	81,027	98,757	78,977	14,574
Queen Anne	3,457	3,479	3,820	4,749	480
St. Mary's	7,227	5,640	6,773	8,267	892
Somerset	3,472	3,254	3,342	3,312	215
Talbot	3,715	5,848	3,995	6,044	570
Washington	15,902	20,194	14,118	22,901	1,689
Wicomico	9,412	10,537	9,431	11,229	1,092
Worcester	4,076	4,647	4,195	5,362	586
BALTIMORE CITY	178,593	81,762	191,911	57,902	13,112
Totals	759,612	672,661	726,161	680,606	119,537

Maryland Vote Since 1932

1932 (Pres.), Roosevelt, Dem., 314,314; Hoover, Rep., 184,184; Thomas, Soc., 10,489; Reynolds,· Soc. Labor, 1,036; Foster, Com., 1,031.

1936 (Pres.), Roosevelt, Dem., 389,612; Landon, Rep., 231,435; Thomas, Soc., 1,629; Aiken, Soc. Labor, 1,305; Browder, Com., 915.

1940 (Pres.), Roosevelt, Dem., 384,546; Willkie, Rep., 269,534; Thomas, Soc., 4,093; Browder, Com., 1,274; Aiken, Soc. Labor, 657.

1944 (Pres.), Roosevelt, Dem., 315,490; Dewey, Rep., 292,949.

1948 (Pres.), Truman, Dem., 286,521; Dewey, Rep., 294,814; Wallace, Prog., 9,983; Thomas, Soc., 2,941; Thurmond, States' Rights, 2,476; Wright, write-in, 2,294.

1952 (Pres.), Eisenhower, Rep., 499,424; Stevenson, Dem., 395,337; Hallinan, Prog., 7,313.

1956 (Pres.), Eisenhower, Rep., 559,738; Stevenson, Dem., 372,613.

1960 (Pres.), Kennedy, Dem., 565,800; Nixon, Rep., 489,538.

1964 (Pres.), Johnson, Dem., 730,912; Goldwater, Rep., 385,495; write-in, 50.

1968 (Pres.), Nixon, Rep., 517,995; Humphrey, Dem., 538,310; Wallace, 3d party, 178,734.

1972 (Pres.), Nixon, Rep., 829,305; McGovern, Dem., 505,781; Schmitz, Amer., 18,726.

1976 (Pres.), Carter, Dem., 759,612; Ford, Rep., 672,661.

1980 (Pres.), Reagan, Rep., 680,606; Carter, Dem., 726,161; Anderson, Ind., 119,537; Clark, Libertarian, 14,192.

Massachusetts

| | 1976 | | 1980 | | |
County	Carter (D)	Ford (R)	Carter (D)	Reagan (R)	Anderson (I)
Barnstable	31,268	39,295	23,952	41,493	15,951
Berkshire	39,337	27,462	29,458	27,063	10,575
Bristol	116,318	69,957	83,460	77,545	25,423
Dukes	2,513	2,365	2,370	1,809	1,127
Essex	165,710	125,538	116,173	130,252	47,670
Franklin	14,985	14,837	11,830	12,528	5,162
Hampden	110,028	70,008	80,369	72,528	24,765
Hampshire	34,947	22,219	27,611	21,117	10,119
Middlesex	359,919	260,044	270,751	256,999	102,180
Nantucket	1,115	1,399	1,040	1,149	614
Norfolk	155,342	136,628	117,274	136,184	47,076
Plymouth	83,663	74,684	58,772	85,593	26,510
Suffolk	142,010	80,623	113,416	73,271	26,988
Worcester	172,320	105,217	117,326	120,100	38,379
Totals	1,429,475	1,030,276	1,053,802	1,057,631	382,539

Massachusetts Vote Since 1932

1932 (Pres.), Roosevelt, Dem., 800,148; Hoover, Rep., 736,959; Thomas, Soc., 34,305; Foster, Com., 4,821; Reynolds, Soc. Labor, 2,668; Upshaw, Proh., 1,142.

1936 (Pres.), Roosevelt, Dem., 942,716; Landon, Rep., 768,613; Lemke, Union, 118,639; Thomas, Soc., 5,111; Browder, Com., 2,930; Aiken, Soc. Labor, 1,305; Colvin, Proh., 1,032.

1940 (Pres.), Roosevelt, Dem., 1,076,522; Willkie, Rep., 939,700; Thomas, Soc., 4,091; Browder, Com., 3,806; Aiken, Soc. Labor, 1,492; Babson, Proh., 1,370.

1944 (Pres.), Roosevelt, Dem., 1,035,296; Dewey, Rep., 921,350; Teichert, Soc. Labor, 2,780; Watson, Proh., 973.

1948 (Pres.), Truman, Dem., 1,151,788; Dewey, Rep., 909,370; Wallace, Prog., 38,157; Teichert, Soc. Labor, 5,535; Watson, Proh., 1,663.

1952 (Pres.), Eisenhower, Rep., 1,292,325; Stevenson, Dem., 1,083,525; Hallinan, Prog., 4,636; Hass, Soc. Labor, 1,957; Hamblen, Proh., 886; scattered, 69; blanks, 41,150.

1956 (Pres.), Eisenhower, Rep., 1,393,197; Stevenson, Dem., 948,190; Hass, Soc. Labor, 5,573; Holtwick, Proh., 1,205; others, 341.

1960 (Pres.), Kennedy, Dem., 1,487,174; Nixon, Rep., 976,750; Hass, Soc. Labor, 3,892; Decker, Proh., 1,633; others, 31; blank and void, 26,024.

1964 (Pres.), Johnson, Dem., 1,786,422; Goldwater, Rep., 549,727; Hass, Soc. Labor, 4,755; Munn, Proh., 3,735; scattered, 159; blank, 48,104.

1968 (Pres.), Nixon, Rep., 766,844; Humphrey, Dem., 1,469,218; Wallace, 3d party, 87,088; Blomen, Soc. Labor, 6,180; Munn, Proh., 2,369; scattered, 53; blanks, 25,394.

1972 (Pres.), Nixon, Rep., 1,112,078; McGovern, Dem., 1,332,540; Jenness, Soc. Workers, 10,600; Fisher, Soc. Labor, 129; Schmitz, Amer., 2,877; Spock, Peoples, 101; Hall, Com., 46; Hospers, Libertarian, 43; scattered, 342.

1976 (Pres.), Carter, Dem., 1,429,475; Ford, Rep., 1,030,276; McCarthy, Ind., 65,637; Camejo, Soc. Workers, 8,138; Anderson, Amer., 7,555; La Rouche, U.S. Labor, 4,922; MacBride, Libertarian, 135.

1980 (Pres.), Reagan, Rep., 1,057,631; Carter, Dem., 1,053,802; Anderson, Ind., 382,539; Clark, Libertarian, 22,038; DeBerry, Soc. Workers, 3,735; Commoner, Citizens, 2,056; McReynolds, Socialist, 62; Bubar, Statesman, 34; Griswold, Workers World, 19; scattered, 2,382.

Michigan

| | 1976 | | 1980 | | |
County	Carter (D)	Ford (R)	Carter (D)	Reagan (R)	Anderson (I)
Alcona	2,038	2,328	1,857	2,905	247
Alger	2,379	1,722	2,242	2,059	263
Allegan	9,794	19,330	9,877	20,560	1,984
Alpena	6,310	6,380	5,834	6,901	913
Antrim	3,032	4,369	2,909	4,706	602
Arenac	2,695	2,687	2,547	3,436	333
Baraga	1,778	1,788	1,609	2,046	201
Barry	6,967	11,178	6,857	12,006	1,399
Bay	25,958	23,174	24,517	25,331	3,886
Benzie	1,891	3,085	1,842	3,054	455
Berrien	25,163	40,835	22,152	41,458	3,422
Branch	6,301	8,251	4,635	10,224	1,102
Calhoun	25,229	30,390	23,022	30,912	4,468
Cass	7,843	9,893	7,058	11,206	1,156
Charlevoix	3,953	5,145	3,741	5,053	816
Cheboygan	3,880	4,894	3,938	5,221	638
Chippewa	6,022	7,025	5,268	7,059	951
Clare	4,150	4,879	4,164	5,719	663
Clinton	7,549	13,475	7,539	14,968	1,736
Crawford	1,889	2,359	1,826	2,652	390
Delta	9,027	7,809	8,475	8,146	849
Dickinson	6,134	5,922	5,694	6,614	596
Eaton	12,083	22,120	12,742	22,927	3,533
Emmet	4,013	5,910	3,724	5,930	1,134
Genesee	88,967	80,004	90,393	78,572	12,274
Gladwin	3,719	3,794	3,733	4,509	463

	1976 (D)	(R)	1980 (D)	(R)	(I)
Gogebic	6,341	3,953	5,254	4,388	493
Grand Traverse	7,263	13,506	7,150	14,484	2,568
Gratiot	5,429	9,526	4,916	9,294	1,193
Hillsdale	5,427	9,307	4,375	10,951	882
Houghton	7,352	8,049	6,858	7,926	1,423
Huron	5,721	9,297	4,434	10,553	976
Ingham	47,890	66,729	48,278	56,777	17,139
Ionia	6,820	11,737	7,038	12,040	1,539
Iosco	4,875	5,500	4,255	6,680	739
Iron	4,401	3,224	3,742	3,507	371
Isabella	7,281	10,577	7,293	10,407	2,511
Jackson	24,726	32,873	23,685	33,749	4,165
Kalamazoo	33,411	51,462	34,528	48,669	10,833
Kalkaska	1,957	2,280	1,807	2,802	260
Kent	59,000	126,805	72,790	112,604	17,913
Keweenaw	658	606	570	583	87
Lake	2,179	1,598	2,041	1,730	187
Lapeer	9,503	12,349	9,671	15,996	1,868
Leelanau	2,437	4,240	2,348	4,585	839
Lenawee	14,610	18,397	12,935	20,366	2,230
Livingston	12,415	19,437	12,626	25,012	3,247
Luce	1,099	1,379	992	1,659	177
Mackinac	2,452	3,107	2,262	3,021	415
Macomb	121,176	132,499	120,125	154,155	18,975
Manistee	4,479	5,532	4,164	5,662	699
Marquette	12,837	12,984	13,312	13,181	2,481
Mason	4,541	6,812	4,134	7,137	825
Mecosta	4,725	7,287	5,228	7,754	1,322
Menominee	5,596	5,633	4,962	6,170	452
Midland	11,959	17,631	12,019	17,828	3,152
Missaukee	1,688	2,943	1,563	3,221	230
Monroe	23,290	20,676	20,578	25,612	3,111
Montcalm	6,684	10,439	6,706	10,822	1,309
Montmorency	1,684	1,882	1,654	2,400	195
Muskegon	27,013	35,548	26,645	36,512	4,094
Nowaygo	5,622	8,258	5,236	8,918	850
Oakland	164,266	244,271	164,869	253,211	38,273
Oceana	3,427	5,236	3,386	5,465	570
Ogemaw	3,545	3,212	3,426	4,169	425
Ontonagon	3,104	2,462	2,375	2,569	237
Osceola	2,603	4,467	2,650	4,902	466
Oscoda	1,108	1,541	1,325	1,915	183
Otsego	2,724	3,155	2,666	3,771	493
Ottawa	16,381	49,196	18,435	51,217	4,903
Presque Isle	3,334	3,545	2,952	3,486	382
Roscommon	3,691	4,608	3,763	5,280	508
Saginaw	36,280	46,765	41,650	45,233	5,677
St. Clair	22,734	26,311	20,410	31,021	3,592
St. Joseph	7,306	11,784	6,318	13,631	1,283
Sanilac	6,042	10,597	4,898	12,158	863
Schoolcraft	2,158	1,933	1,964	2,097	243
Shiawassee	12,202	15,113	11,985	15,756	2,121
Tuscola	7,932	12,059	7,632	13,306	1,266
Van Buren	10,366	13,615	9,248	14,451	1,691
Washtenaw	50,917	56,807	51,013	48,699	13,463
Wayne	548,767	348,588	522,024	315,532	43,608
Wexford	4,519	5,670	4,519	6,027	752
Totals	**1,696,714**	**1,893,742**	**1,661,532**	**1,915,225**	**275,223**

Michigan Vote Since 1932

1932 (Pres.), Roosevelt, Dem., 871,700; Hoover, Rep., 739,894; Thomas, Soc., 39,025; Foster, Com., 9,318; Upshaw, Proh., 2,893; Reynolds, Soc. Labor, 1,041; Harvey, Lib., 217.

1936 (Pres.), Roosevelt, Dem., 1,016,794; Landon, Rep., 699,733; Lemke, Union, 75,795; Thomas, Soc., 8,208; Browder, Com., 3,384; Aiken, Soc. Labor, 600; Colvin, Proh., 579.

1940 (Pres.), Roosevelt, Dem., 1,032,991; Willkie, Rep., 1,039,917; Thomas, Soc., 7,593; Browder, Com., 2,834; Babson, Proh., 1,795; Aiken, Soc. Labor, 795.

1944 (Pres.), Roosevelt, Dem., 1,106,899; Dewey, Rep., 1,084,423; Watson, Proh., 6,503; Thomas, Soc., 4,598; Smith, America First, 1,530; Teichert, Soc. Labor, 1,264.

1948 (Pres.), Truman, Dem., 1,003,448; Dewey, Rep., 1,038,595; Wallace, Prog., 46,515; Watson, Proh., 13,052; Thomas, Soc. 6,063; Teichert, Soc. Labor, 1,263; Dobbs, Soc. Workers, 672.

1952 (Pres.), Eisenhower, Rep., 1,551,529; Stevenson, Dem., 1,230,657; Hamblen, Proh., 10,331; Hallinan, Prog., 3,922; Hass, Soc. Labor, 1,495; Dobbs, Soc. Workers, 655; scattered, 3.

1956 (Pres.), Eisenhower, Rep., 1,713,647; Stevenson, Dem., 1,359,898; Holtwick, Proh., 6,923.

1960 (Pres.), Kennedy, Dem., 1,687,269; Nixon, Rep., 1,620,428; Dobbs, Soc. Workers, 4,347; Decker, Proh., 2,029; Daly, Tax Cut, 1,767; Hass, Soc. Labor, 1,718; Ind. American, 539.

1964 (Pres.), Johnson, Dem., 2,136,615; Goldwater, Rep.,

1,060,152; DeBerry, Soc. Workers, 3,817; Hass, Soc. Labor, 1,704; Proh. (no candidate listed), 699, scattering, 145.

1968 (Pres.), Nixon, Rep., 1,370,665; Humphrey, Dem., 1,593,082; Wallace, 3d party, 331,968; Halstead, Soc. Worker, 4,099; Blomen, Soc. Labor, 1,762; Cleaver, New Politics, 4,585; Munn, Proh., 60; scattering, 29.

1972 (Pres.), Nixon, Rep., 1,961,721; McGovern, Dem., 1,459,435; Schmitz, Amer., 63,321; Fisher, Soc. Labor, 2,437; Jenness, Soc. Workers, 1,603; Hall, Com., 1,210.

1976 (Pres.), Carter, Dem., 1,696,714; Ford, Rep., 1,893,742; McCarthy, Ind., 47,905; MacBride, Libertarian, 5,406; Wright, People's, 3,504, Camejo, Soc. Workers, 1,804; LaRouche, U.S. Labor, 1,366; Levin, Soc. Labor, 1,148; scattering, 2,160.

1980 (Pres.), Reagan, Rep., 1,915,225; Carter, Dem., 1,661,532; Anderson, Ind., 275,223; Clark, Libertarian, 41,597; Commoner, Citizens, 11,930; Hall, Com., 3,262; Griswold, Workers World, 30; Greaves, American, 21; Bubar, Statesman, 9.

Minnesota

County	1976 Carter (D)	Ford (R)	1980 Carter (D)	Reagan (R)	Anderson (I)
Aitkin	4,308	2,476	3,677	3,396	380
Anoka	48,173	27,863	45,532	33,100	6,828
Becker	6,597	5,611	5,221	6,848	866
Beltrami	7,540	5,214	7,432	6,481	1,254
Benton	6,235	4,099	5,272	5,513	646
Big Stone	2,581	1,332	1,814	1,950	249
Blue Earth	12,930	11,998	10,930	11,966	2,698
Brown	5,792	7,479	4,915	8,051	842
Carlton	9,247	4,371	8,822	4,760	883
Carver	7,574	8,199	6,621	9,909	1,496
Cass	5,424	4,443	4,717	6,119	434
Chippewa	4,648	3,254	3,164	4,252	532
Chisago	6,625	3,874	6,240	5,017	939
Clay	10,876	10,317	8,940	10,447	2,773
Clearwater	2,437	1,374	1,955	1,919	185
Cook	1,018	1,034	871	1,174	182
Cottonwood	3,813	3,906	2,958	4,258	535
Crow Wing	10,653	8,072	9,323	10,844	1,046
Dakota	44,253	37,542	43,433	40,708	8,588
Dodge	3,009	3,446	2,698	3,900	367
Douglas	7,097	5,910	5,530	7,778	664
Faribault	5,049	5,577	3,620	6,206	525
Fillmore	4,758	5,984	4,010	6,452	650
Freeborn	9,470	8,220	8,212	8,475	808
Goodhue	8,926	9,967	8,566	9,329	1,964
Grant	2,624	1,635	1,822	2,054	333
Hennepin	257,380	211,892	239,592	194,998	56,390
Houston	3,861	4,853	3,218	5,582	477
Hubbard	3,196	2,985	2,840	4,172	365
Isanti	6,013	3,159	5,457	4,480	641
Itasca	12,979	6,646	12,138	8,368	1,080
Jackson	4,311	2,870	3,062	3,391	463
Kanabec	3,188	1,943	2,654	2,500	269
Kandiyohi	9,992	6,664	8,038	8,480	1,244
Kittson	2,008	1,555	1,407	1,875	243
Koochiching	4,846	2,893	4,181	3,433	496
LacQuiParle	3,647	2,292	2,457	2,981	496
Lake	3,973	2,313	3,864	2,414	443
Lake O'Woods	1,105	757	763	1,052	128
Le Sueur	6,556	4,565	5,161	5,478	731
Lincoln	2,594	1,599	1,640	2,122	295
Lyon	7,122	5,036	5,626	5,852	1,129
McLeod	6,249	6,519	4,987	7,819	852
Mahnomen	1,590	905	1,175	1,275	153
Marshall	3,744	2,605	2,636	3,638	397
Martin	5,672	6,484	4,301	7,057	751
Meeker	5,295	4,097	4,238	5,032	668
Mille Lacs	5,172	3,212	4,443	3,860	550
Morrison	8,176	4,590	6,930	6,296	559
Mower	12,837	8,163	10,538	7,908	1,465
Murray	3,685	2,605	2,714	3,004	359
Nicollet	5,777	6,071	5,400	6,436	1,519
Nobles	6,034	4,503	4,703	4,706	657
Norman	2,946	1,983	2,253	2,192	369
Olmsted	14,676	24,030	13,983	22,704	3,638
Otter Tail	11,881	12,113	9,108	15,091	1,538
Pennington	3,787	3,023	3,101	3,715	472
Pine	5,442	3,057	5,121	3,899	467
Pipestone	3,272	3,018	2,392	3,207	561
Polk	9,078	6,522	7,151	9,036	1,207
Pope	3,746	2,251	2,527	3,159	393
Ramsey	133,682	86,480	124,774	78,860	23,222
Red Lake	1,748	737	1,318	1,223	116
Redwood	4,525	4,926	2,952	5,993	548
Renville	5,762	4,482	4,058	5,544	653
Rice	10,590	8,311	9,531	8,168	2,414
Rock	2,769	2,892	2,089	3,164	397
Roseau	3,215	2,382	2,616	3,358	259
St. Louis	75,040	35,331	69,403	33,407	8,719

	1976 (D)	(R)	1980 (D)	(R)	(I)
Scott	9,912	7,154	9,115	9,018	1,475
Sherburne	6,678	4,361	6,229	6,035	985
Sibley	3,752	3,871	2,521	4,460	509
Stearns	25,027	19,574	21,862	24,888	3,555
Steele	6,263	7,053	5,095	7,805	1,087
Stevens	3,171	2,484	2,559	3,283	524
Swift	4,428	2,190	3,245	2,943	511
Todd	6,530	4,278	4,975	6,451	451
Traverse	2,020	1,130	1,258	1,574	159
Wabasha	4,286	4,484	3,712	4,886	549
Wadena	3,164	3,048	2,635	4,089	265
Waseca	4,002	4,582	3,535	4,801	777
Washington	26,454	20,716	25,634	22,718	5,050
Watonwan	3,177	3,351	2,442	3,629	415
Wilkin	2,103	1,882	1,496	2,224	318
Winona	10,939	10,436	9,814	10,332	1,780
Wright	13,379	9,314	12,383	12,293	1,692
Yellow Med	4,337	2,946	2,833	4,004	456
Totals	**1,070,440**	**819,395**	**954,173**	**873,268**	**174,997**

Minnesota Vote Since 1932

1932 (Pres.), Roosevelt, Dem., 600,806; Hoover, Rep., 363,959; Thomas, Soc., 25,476; Foster, Com., 6,101; Coxey, Farm.-Lab., 5,731; Reynolds, Ind., 770.

1936 (Pres.), Roosevelt, Dem., 698,811; Landon, Rep., 350,461; Lemke, Union, 74,296; Thomas, Soc., 2,872; Browder, Com., 2,574; Aiken, Soc. Labor, 961.

1940 (Pres.), Roosevelt, Dem., 644,196; Willkie, Rep., 596,274; Thomas, Soc., 5,454; Browder, Com., 2,711; Aiken, Ind., 2,553.

1944 (Pres.), Roosevelt, Dem., 589,864; Dewey, Rep., 527,416; Thomas, Soc., 5,073; Teichert, Ind. Gov't., 3,176.

1948 (Pres.), Truman, Dem., 692,966; Dewey, Rep., 483,617; Wallace, Prog., 27,866; Thomas, Soc., 4,646; Teichert, Soc. Labor, 2,525; Dobbs, Soc. Workers, 606.

1952 (Pres.), Eisenhower, Rep., 763,211; Stevenson, Dem., 608,458; Hallinan, Prog., 2,666; Hass, Soc. Labor, 2,383; Hamblen, Proh., 2,147; Dobbs, Soc. Workers, 618.

1956 (Pres.), Eisenhower, Rep., 719,302; Stevenson, Dem., 617,525; Hass, Soc. Labor (Ind. Gov.), 2,080; Dobbs, Soc. Workers, 1,098.

1960 (Pres.), Kennedy, Dem., 779,933; Nixon, Rep., 757,915; Dobbs, Soc. Workers, 3,077; Industrial Gov., 962.

1964 (Pres.), Johnson, Dem., 991,117; Goldwater, Rep., 559,624; DeBerry, Soc. Workers, 1,177; Hass, Industrial Gov., 2,544.

1968 (Pres.), Nixon, Rep., 658,643; Humphrey, Dem., 857,738; Wallace, 3d party, 68,931; scattered, 2,443; Halstead, Soc. Worker, 808; Blomen, Ind. Gov't., 285; Mitchell, Com., 415; Cleaver, Peace, 935; McCarthy, write-in, 585; scattered, 170.

1972 (Pres.), Nixon, Rep., 898,269; McGovern, Dem., 802,346; Schmitz, Amer., 31,407; Spock, Peoples, 2,805; Fisher, Soc. Labor, 4,261; Jenness, Soc. Workers, 940; Hall, Com., 662; scattered, 962.

1976 (Pres.), Carter, Dem., 1,070,440; Ford, Rep., 819,395; McCarthy, Ind., 35,490; Anderson, Amer., 13,592; Camejo, Soc. Workers, 4,149; MacBride, Libertarian, 3,529; Hall, Com., 1,092.

1980 (Pres.), Reagan, Rep., 873,268; Carter, Dem., 954,173; Anderson, Ind., 174,997; Clark, Libertarian, 31,593; Commoner, Citizens, 8,406; Hall, Com., 1,117; DeBerry, Soc. Workers, 711; Griswold, Workers World, 698; McReynolds, Socialist, 536; write-ins, 281.

Mississippi

County	1976 Carter (D)	Ford (R)	1980 Carter (D)	Reagan (R)	Anderson (I)
Adams	6,619	6,431	7,228	7,523	151
Alcorn	6,995	3,430	6,242	5,196	898
Amite	2,574	2,256	3,229	2,653	43
Attala	4,068	3,146	4,117	3,975	71
Benton	2,375	790	2,094	1,254	35
Bolivar	7,561	5,136	8,839	5,148	280
Calhoun	2,724	1,892	3,295	2,579	64
Carroll	1,566	1,561	2,037	2,153	22
Chickasaw	2,891	2,581	3,622	2,540	71
Choctaw	1,520	1,562	1,729	1,927	26
Claiborne	2,657	1,078	3,032	1,129	22
Clarke	2,816	2,935	3,303	3,303	41
Clay	3,514	3,017	4,275	3,439	124
Coahoma	6,412	4,269	7,030	4,592	256
Copiah	4,267	4,108	5,517	4,461	76
Covington	2,862	2,591	2,956	3,471	39
DeSoto	7,756	6,240	6,344	9,655	237
Forrest	7,914	10,770	8,274	12,656	275
Franklin	1,578	1,719	2,040	2,026	23
George	3,072	1,957	2,757	3,052	64
Greene	2,127	1,538	1,740	1,772	23
Grenada	3,263	3,589	4,182	3,993	59
Hancock	3,855	3,765	3,544	5,088	159
Harrison	16,569	19,207	16,318	25,175	822
Hinds	28,748	45,803	39,369	48,135	1,414
Holmes	4,616	2,438	5,463	2,693	57
Humphreys	2,172	1,445	2,970	1,841	68
Issaquena	567	325	598	349	5
Itawamba	4,480	2,153	4,852	2,906	57
Jackson	12,533	17,177	12,226	22,498	653
Jasper	3,109	2,356	3,813	2,781	34
Jefferson	2,562	782	2,871	751	41
Jefferson Davis	2,747	1,868	3,831	2,280	24
Jones	10,139	11,098	11,117	12,900	155
Kemper	2,436	1,680	2,601	1,822	12
Lafayette	4,375	3,735	4,887	4,366	243
Lamar	3,109	4,056	3,005	5,395	84
Lauderdale	9,813	14,273	9,918	14,727	784
Lawrence	2,242	2,109	2,692	2,781	49
Leake	3,415	2,952	4,033	3,624	40
Lee	8,504	7,366	10,047	8,326	321
Leflore	6,135	5,872	7,498	5,798	166
Lincoln	4,043	6,084	5,213	7,286	75
Lowndes	6,181	8,003	6,187	9,973	140
Madison	6,240	4,838	7,621	6,024	276
Marion	5,283	5,300	5,366	5,218	62
Marshall	6,769	2,242	7,153	3,455	121
Monroe	6,097	4,737	6,998	4,793	177
Montgomery	2,410	2,278	2,730	2,479	42
Neshoba	3,891	3,859	3,872	5,165	72
Newton	2,741	3,813	3,455	4,317	86
Noxubee	2,121	1,860	3,434	1,970	47
Oktibbeha	4,339	5,194	6,039	6,300	258
Panola	5,517	3,341	6,179	4,219	149
Pearl River	5,024	4,332	5,028	6,822	161
Perry	1,965	1,527	1,957	2,255	25
Pike	5,749	5,659	6,694	6,661	129
Pontotoc	4,066	2,245	4,499	3,198	58
Prentiss	4,431	2,362	4,832	3,264	40
Quitman	2,621	1,287	2,926	1,691	83
Rankin	6,937	11,507	8,047	16,650	296
Scott	3,643	3,649	4,043	4,645	72
Sharkey	1,283	1,024	1,957	996	28
Simpson	3,600	4,291	4,015	5,190	70
Smith	2,434	3,147	2,474	3,772	46
Stone	1,648	1,575	1,821	1,888	53
Sunflower	4,322	3,456	5,035	3,726	82
Tallahatchie	2,991	2,146	3,467	2,183	45
Tate	3,747	2,497	3,892	3,343	80
Tippah	4,260	1,887	3,678	3,338	116
Tishomingo	3,734	1,969	4,595	2,489	79
Tunica	1,695	951	2,198	954	24
Union	5,021	2,507	5,001	3,545	94
Walthall	2,650	2,110	2,960	2,703	34
Warren	6,299	8,699	7,489	10,151	274
Washington	9,650	7,474	10,722	8,978	186
Wayne	3,306	3,022	3,494	3,844	26
Webster	2,218	1,943	2,178	2,386	75
Wilkinson	2,514	1,273	2,981	1,442	25
Winston	3,956	3,659	4,416	3,998	65
Yalobusha	2,603	1,808	3,432	2,224	78
Yazoo	4,053	4,255	5,468	4,819	99
Totals	**381,309**	**366,846**	**429,281**	**441,089**	**12,036**

Mississippi Vote Since 1932

1932 (Pres.), Roosevelt, Dem., 140,168; Hoover, Rep., 5,180; Thomas, Soc., 686.

1936 (Pres.), Roosevelt, Dem., 157,318; Landon, Rep., Howard faction, 2,760; Rowlands faction, 1,675 total 4,435; Thomas, Soc., 329.

1940 (Pres.), Roosevelt, Dem., 168,252; Willkie, Ind. Rep., 4,550; Rep., 2,814; total, 7,364; Thomas, Soc., 103.

1944 (Pres.), Roosevelt, Dem., 158,515; Dewey, Rep., 3,742; Reg. Dem., 9,964; Ind. Rep., 7,859.

1948 (Pres.), Thurmond, States' Rights, 167,538; Truman, Dem., 19,384; Dewey, Rep., 5,043; Wallace, Prog., 225.*

1952 (Pres.), Eisenhower, Ind. vote pledged to Rep. candidate, 112,966; Stevenson, Dem., 172,566.

1956 (Pres.), Stevenson, Dem., 144,498; Eisenhower, Rep., 56,372; Black and Tan Grand Old Party, 4,313; total, 60,685; Byrd, Ind., 42,966.

1960 (Pres.), Democratic unpledged electors, 116,248; Kennedy, Dem., 108,362; Nixon, Rep., 73,561. Mississippi's victorious slate of 8 unpledged Democratic electors cast their votes for Sen. Harry F. Byrd (D-Va.).

1964 (Pres.), Johnson, Dem., 52,618; Goldwater, Rep.,

356,528.

1968 (Pres.), Nixon, Rep., 88,516; Humphrey, Dem., 150,644; Wallace, 3d party, 415,349.

1972 (Pres.), Nixon, Rep., 505,125; McGovern, Dem., 126,782; Schmitz, Amer., 11,598; Jenness, Soc. Workers, 2,458.

1976 (Pres.), Carter, Dem., 381,309; Ford, Rep., 366,846; Anderson, Amer., 6,678; McCarthy, Ind., 4,074; Maddox, Ind., 4,049; Camejo, Soc. Workers, 2,805; MacBride, Libertarian, 2,609.

1980 (Pres.), Reagan, Rep., 441,089; Carter, Dem., 429,281; Anderson, Ind., 12,036; Clark, Libertarian, 5,465; Griswold, Workers World, 2,402; Pulley, Soc. Worker, 2,347.

Missouri

	1976		1980		
County	Carter (D)	Ford (R)	Carter (D)	Reagan (R)	Anderson (I)
Adair	3,684	5,249	3,507	5,513	414
Andrew	3,042	3,130	2,575	3,690	245
Atchison	1,126	1,960	1,273	2,096	151
Audrain	5,600	5,378	5,168	6,347	233
Barry	5,046	5,053	4,193	7,038	150
Barton	2,326	2,708	1,901	3,337	115
Bates	4,288	3,350	3,297	4,061	114
Benton	2,684	2,875	2,241	3,451	126
Bollinger	2,740	2,113	2,160	2,863	35
Boone	17,674	16,373	18,527	16,313	3,519
Buchanan	17,427	16,446	16,967	16,551	1,301
Butler	6,759	5,669	5,605	8,342	181
Caldwell	2,113	2,094	1,541	2,551	108
Callaway	4,843	5,115	5,560	6,755	420
Camden	3,975	4,469	3,416	6,541	218
Cape Girardeau	10,440	12,607	8,625	14,961	873
Carroll	3,114	2,936	2,130	3,291	130
Carter	1,154	842	1,087	1,218	37
Cass	9,008	7,182	8,198	10,105	667
Cedar	2,192	2,752	1,703	3,469	86
Chariton	3,055	2,128	2,250	2,641	63
Christian	3,830	4,553	3,502	6,487	205
Clark	1,679	1,582	1,494	2,042	56
Clay	26,609	24,962	24,250	28,521	2,782
Clinton	3,424	2,807	3,001	3,599	184
Cole	7,949	14,370	9,210	16,373	691
Cooper	3,047	3,694	2,687	3,996	130
Crawford	3,565	3,224	2,710	4,081	170
Dade	1,681	2,015	1,283	2,410	61
Dallas	2,453	2,430	2,011	3,297	114
Daviess	2,250	1,919	1,770	2,125	61
DeKalb	2,023	1,739	1,677	2,062	111
Dent	2,931	2,433	2,528	3,477	86
Douglas	1,981	2,652	1,677	3,440	93
Dunklin	7,107	3,314	6,120	5,253	128
Franklin	11,695	12,242	10,480	15,210	863
Gasconade	1,702	3,925	1,550	4,481	136
Gentry	2,249	1,772	1,720	2,005	117
Greene	33,824	37,691	30,498	43,116	3,261
Grundy	2,597	2,646	2,064	2,890	110
Harrison	2,304	2,478	1,732	2,734	140
Henry	5,282	4,168	4,648	4,807	238
Hickory	1,398	1,403	1,248	1,893	52
Holt	1,529	1,777	1,119	1,993	59
Howard	2,769	1,690	2,243	2,179	114
Howell	5,265	4,692	4,472	7,149	211
Iron	2,646	1,765	2,226	2,205	94
Jackson	130,120	101,401	135,805	106,156	12,260
Jasper	14,910	17,086	11,953	21,664	785
Jefferson	25,159	18,261	24,042	28,546	1,753
Johnson	5,551	5,513	5,441	6,449	571
Knox	1,319	1,216	1,187	1,475	36
Laclede	4,381	4,067	3,443	5,642	153
Lafayette	6,410	6,823	5,792	7,271	339
Lawrence	5,315	5,784	4,670	7,921	184
Lewis	2,486	1,983	2,314	2,350	102
Lincoln	4,473	3,581	4,110	4,963	182
Linn	4,092	3,114	3,467	3,585	139
Livingston	3,819	3,010	3,368	3,654	205
McDonald	3,111	2,949	2,485	4,114	124
Macon	4,296	3,360	3,578	4,430	135
Madison	2,229	1,739	2,231	2,618	70
Maries	1,796	1,485	1,732	1,985	39
Marion	6,124	5,501	5,890	6,036	192
Mercer	1,177	1,025	821	1,266	54
Miller	2,739	4,095	2,469	5,560	115
Mississippi	3,366	1,733	3,040	2,459	64
Moniteau	2,462	3,077	2,284	3,430	98
Monroe	3,039	1,585	2,445	2,026	53
Montgomery	2,535	2,665	2,007	3,061	124
Morgan	2,738	2,831	2,460	3,577	114
New Madrid	5,319	2,798	4,171	4,041	64
Newton	7,045	7,142	5,621	10,515	341
Nodaway	4,875	4,558	4,257	4,544	414
Oregon	2,564	1,122	2,326	1,523	26
Osage	2,015	3,224	2,045	3,679	72
Ozark	1,341	1,754	1,242	2,434	63
Pemiscot	4,681	2,541	4,140	3,519	52
Perry	2,801	4,086	2,416	5,053	178
Pettis	7,887	7,344	6,475	8,833	435
Phelps	6,261	6,153	5,470	7,366	620
Pike	3,770	3,355	3,454	3,932	158
Platte	8,651	8,103	7,342	10,092	1,107
Polk	3,663	3,893	3,336	4,842	135
Pulaski	4,370	2,865	3,707	3,998	128
Putnam	1,097	1,444	871	1,722	44
Ralls	2,318	1,334	2,069	1,968	75
Randolph	5,839	3,594	4,884	5,141	213
Ray	5,535	2,853	4,518	4,064	215
Reynolds	2,143	879	1,919	1,271	44
Ripley	2,577	1,640	2,156	2,524	61
St. Charles	22,063	26,105	20,668	36,050	2,494
St. Clair	2,271	1,808	1,706	2,419	60
St. Francois	8,852	7,002	7,495	8,914	397
Ste. Genevieve	3,091	2,241	3,324	2,768	151
St. Louis	196,915	246,988	192,796	263,518	25,032
Saline	5,890	4,883	4,943	5,218	353
Schuyler	1,417	1,193	1,114	1,386	48
Scotland	1,449	1,286	1,200	1,592	63
Scott	8,075	5,473	6,854	8,227	203
Shannon	1,960	989	1,818	1,523	44
Shelby	2,227	1,453	1,849	2,151	60
Stoddard	6,097	3,989	5,128	6,199	132
Stone	2,358	3,457	2,210	4,780	180
Sullivan	2,313	2,141	1,824	2,412	76
Taney	3,626	4,696	3,389	6,230	195
Texas	4,638	3,338	4,261	4,879	125
Vernon	4,921	3,715	3,704	4,391	285
Warren	2,164	3,213	2,132	4,366	192
Washington	3,543	2,526	2,873	3,439	89
Wayne	2,987	1,963	2,549	2,823	44
Webster	3,759	3,510	3,409	5,121	149
Worth	969	771	760	833	47
Wright	2,781	3,397	2,182	4,451	56
ST. LOUIS CITY	118,703	58,367	113,697	50,333	5,656
Write-in Vote			1,576	1,365	
Totals	**999,163**	**928,808**	**931,182**	**1,074,181**	**77,920**

Missouri Vote Since 1932

1932 (Pres.), Roosevelt, Dem., 1,025,406; Hoover, Rep., 564,713; Thomas, Soc., 16,374; Upshaw, Proh., 2,429; Foster, Com., 568; Reynolds, Soc. Labor, 404.

1936 (Pres.), Roosevelt, Dem., 1,111,403; Landon, Rep., 697,891; Lemke, Union, 14,630; Thomas, Soc., 3,454; Colvin, Proh., 908; Browder, Com., 417; Aiken, Soc. Labor, 292.

1940 (Pres.), Roosevelt, Dem., 958,476; Willkie, Rep., 871,009; Thomas, Soc., 2,226; Babson, Proh., 1,809; Aiken, Soc. Labor, 209.

1944 (Pres.), Roosevelt, Dem., 807,357; Dewey, Rep., 761,175; Thomas, Soc., 1,750; Watson, Proh., 1,175; Teichert, Soc. Labor, 221.

1948 (Pres.), Truman, Dem., 917,315; Dewey, Rep., 655,039; Wallace, Prog., 3,998; Thomas, Soc., 2,222.

1952 (Pres.), Eisenhower, Rep., 959,429; Stevenson, Dem., 929,830; Hallinan, Prog., 987; Hamblen, Proh., 885; MacArthur, Christian Nationalist, 302; America First, 233; Hoopes, Soc., 227; Hass, Soc. Labor, 169.

1956 (Pres.), Stevenson, Dem., 918,273; Eisenhower, Rep., 914,299.

1960 (Pres.), Kennedy, Dem., 972,201; Nixon, Rep., 962,221.

1964 (Pres.), Johnson, Dem., 1,164,344; Goldwater, Rep., 653,535.

1968 (Pres.), Nixon, Rep., 811,932; Humphrey, Dem., 791,444; Wallace, 3d party, 206,126.

1972 (Pres.), Nixon, Rep., 1,154,058; McGovern, Dem., 698,531.

1976 (Pres.), Carter, Dem., 999,163; Ford, Rep., 928,808; McCarthy, Ind., 24,329.

1980 (Pres.), Reagan, Rep., 1,074,181; Carter, Dem., 931,182; Anderson, Ind., 77,920; Clark, Libertarian, 14,422; DeBerry, Soc. Workers, 1,515; Commoner, Citizens, 573; write-ins, 31.

Montana

	1976		1980		
County	Carter (D)	Ford (R)	Carter (D)	Reagan (R)	Anderson (I)
Beaverhead	1,013	2,461	842	2,955	205
Big Horn	1,962	1,615	1,644	1,730	308
Blaine	1,356	1,349	1,107	1,686	163
Broadwater	557	820	401	1,052	69
Carbon	1,853	2,121	1,468	2,471	331
Carter	344	558	237	766	37

	1976 (D)	(R)	1980 (D)	(R)	(I)
Cascade	14,678	15,289	11,105	17,664	2,655
Chouteau	1,568	1,814	853	2,448	216
Custer	2,425	3,120	1,822	3,533	369
Daniels	797	816	483	1,086	77
Dawson	2,201	2,639	1,543	3,045	424
Deer Lodge	3,859	2,197	3,077	1,905	474
Fallon	847	934	512	1,286	94
Fergus	2,470	3,556	1,840	4,455	388
Flathead	7,827	10,494	6,349	15,102	1,621
Gallatin	6,215	11,062	5,747	12,738	2,432
Garfield	273	625	169	760	29
Glacier	1,755	1,892	1,394	2,283	297
Golden Valley	255	302	155	362	28
Granite	509	746	439	811	76
Hill	3,878	3,274	2,875	4,448	604
Jefferson	1,210	1,387	1,055	1,841	216
Judith Basin	772	809	480	1,030	93
Lake	3,253	3,809	2,615	5,083	573
Lewis & Clark	8,118	10,155	6,815	12,128	1,793
Liberty	506	638	283	872	71
Lincoln	3,146	3,017	2,422	4,202	485
Madison	870	1,688	676	2,220	174
McCone	749	730	349	1,000	86
Meagher	364	565	247	689	41
Mineral	819	679	660	800	138
Missoula	15,099	16,350	13,115	16,161	3,847
Musselshell	922	1,117	784	1,279	106
Park	2,364	3,281	1,663	3,929	459
Petroleum	110	211	90	225	15
Phillips	1,117	1,347	745	1,723	146
Pondera	1,413	1,666	897	2,270	207
Powder River	429	683	336	985	94
Powell	1,302	1,610	883	1,770	198
Prairie	415	597	283	580	57
Ravalli	3,504	4,894	3,063	7,268	743
Richland	1,961	2,189	1,252	3,348	343
Roosevelt	2,061	1,822	1,504	2,298	304
Rosebud	1,413	1,538	1,167	1,875	265
Sanders	1,725	1,738	1,395	2,194	291
Sheridan	1,560	1,114	955	1,658	247
Silver Bow	11,377	7,506	9,721	7,301	1,752
Stillwater	1,143	1,446	919	1,828	181
Sweet Grass	502	1,135	440	1,169	98
Teton	1,506	1,730	902	2,415	186
Toole	1,080	1,469	634	2,000	154
Treasure	239	315	181	321	34
Valley	2,352	2,520	1,567	3,242	264
Wheatland	535	755	381	742	88
Wibaux	352	308	219	450	45
Yellowstone	18,329	25,201	15,272	27,332	4,590
Totals	**149,259**	**173,703**	**118,032**	**206,814**	**29,281**

Montana Vote Since 1932

1932 (Pres.), Roosevelt, Dem., 127,286; Hoover, Rep., 78,078; Thomas, Soc., 7,891; Foster, Com., 1,775; Harvey, Lib., 1,449.

1936 (Pres.), Roosevelt, Dem., 159,690; Landon, Rep., 63,598; Lemke, Union, 5,549; Thomas, Soc., 1,066; Browder, Com., 385; Colvin, Proh., 224.

1940 (Pres.), Roosevelt, Dem., 145,698; Willkie, Rep., 99,579; Thomas, Soc., 1,443; Babson, Proh., 664; Browder, Com., 489.

1944 (Pres.), Roosevelt, Dem., 112,556; Dewey, Rep., 93,163; Thomas, Soc., 1,296; Watson, Proh., 340.

1948 (Pres.), Truman, Dem., 119,071; Dewey, Rep., 96,770; Wallace, Prog., 7,313; Thomas, Soc., 695; Watson, Proh., 429.

1952 (Pres.), Eisenhower, Rep., 157,394; Stevenson, Dem., 106,213; Hallinan, Prog., 723; Hamblen, Proh., 548; Hoopes, Soc., 159.

1956 (Pres.), Eisenhower, Rep., 154,933; Stevenson, Dem., 116,238.

1960 (Pres.), Kennedy, Dem., 134,891; Nixon, Rep., 141,841; Decker, Proh., 456; Dobbs, Soc. Workers, 391.

1964 (Pres.), Johnson, Dem., 164,246; Goldwater, Rep., 113,032; Kasper, Nat'l States Rights, 519; Munn, Proh., 499; DeBerry, Soc. Worker, 332.

1968 (Pres.), Nixon, Rep., 138,835; Humphrey, Dem., 114,117; Wallace, 3d party, 20,015; Halstead, Soc. Worker, 457; Munn, Proh., 510; Caton, New Reform, 470.

1972 (Pres.), Nixon, Rep., 183,976; McGovern, Dem., 120,197; Schmitz, Amer., 13,430.

1976 (Pres.), Carter, Dem., 149,259; Ford, Rep., 173,703; Anderson, Amer., 5,772.

1980 (Pres.), Reagan, Rep., 206,814; Carter, Dem., 118,032; Anderson, Ind., 29,281; Clark, Libertarian, 9,825.

Nebraska

	1976 Carter (D)	Ford (R)	1980 Carter (D)	Reagan (R)	Anderson (I)
County					
Adams	4,949	7,612	3,361	8,469	879
Antelope	1,325	2,488	659	3,192	150
Arthur	64	193	55	242	9
Banner	210	281	33	481	14
Blaine	133	281	63	361	15
Boone	1,329	2,035	769	2,598	176
Box Butte	1,516	2,956	1,206	3,898	307
Boyd	792	1,004	376	1,261	62
Brown	557	1,239	341	1,614	105
Buffalo	4,296	8,083	3,162	9,764	1,028
Burt	1,373	2,507	814	2,806	232
Butler	2,336	1,808	1,112	2,596	159
Cass	3,202	3,800	2,007	5,180	487
Cedar	2,225	2,415	1,265	3,257	273
Chase	724	1,146	324	1,593	91
Cherry	906	2,197	489	2,517	105
Cheyenne	1,663	2,285	776	3,073	196
Clay	1,369	2,254	840	2,739	190
Colfax	1,666	2,363	892	3,259	230
Cuming	1,367	3,298	803	3,999	266
Custer	1,985	3,935	1,011	4,562	285
Dakota	2,290	2,629	1,928	3,165	317
Dawes	1,278	2,435	703	3,281	228
Dawson	2,393	5,411	1,462	6,687	357
Deuel	398	775	192	943	63
Dixon	1,205	1,981	822	2,328	200
Dodge	5,276	8,972	3,556	9,514	988
Douglas	61,692	92,980	51,504	96,741	13,198
Dundy	457	774	192	1,135	55
Fillmore	1,483	2,098	1,025	2,435	221
Franklin	941	1,170	441	1,672	109
Frontier	588	994	259	1,345	84
Furnas	1,126	1,884	536	2,483	113
Gage	4,506	5,199	2,258	6,072	722
Garden	445	928	202	1,297	63
Garfield	343	726	238	611	42
Gosper	332	654	181	783	47
Grant	116	313	76	373	13
Greeley	877	787	495	1,028	78
Hall	6,077	10,931	4,391	12,083	981
Hamilton	1,337	2,737	777	3,199	245
Harlan	879	1,325	486	1,690	109
Hayes	267	411	82	617	21
Hitchcock	786	898	328	1,471	115
Holt	1,751	3,389	1,016	4,488	243
Hooker	98	326	63	386	18
Howard	1,316	1,362	788	1,969	170
Jefferson	2,067	2,628	1,125	3,090	297
Johnson	1,115	1,298	623	1,716	180
Kearney	1,218	1,827	726	2,510	227
Keith	1,139	2,485	710	3,373	199
Keya Paha	245	405	130	524	27
Kimball	696	1,257	385	1,615	97
Knox	1,922	2,610	1,057	3,404	245
Lancaster	28,193	38,937	27,040	38,630	9,221
Lincoln	5,352	7,074	3,762	9,631	841
Logan	195	283	71	442	17
Loup	140	299	74	368	21
McPherson	104	221	49	285	5
Madison	3,433	7,844	1,924	9,715	552
Merrick	1,360	2,229	712	2,710	212
Morrill	971	1,351	512	1,887	96
Nance	936	1,119	561	1,439	100
Nemaha	1,404	2,092	929	2,693	221
Nuckolls	1,424	1,752	899	2,180	159
Otoe	2,436	3,715	1,471	4,611	391
Pawnee	845	990	431	1,418	122
Perkins	622	981	313	1,338	81
Phelps	1,166	3,209	734	3,465	192
Pierce	1,004	2,172	517	2,935	155
Platte	3,681	7,206	2,385	8,781	546
Polk	1,190	1,795	538	2,206	149
Red Willow	1,722	2,978	892	4,019	254
Richardson	2,415	3,117	1,350	3,634	264
Rock	255	732	145	855	39
Saline	3,205	2,330	1,908	2,934	480
Sarpy	7,384	11,912	5,678	15,523	1,685
Saunders	3,504	3,840	2,034	5,222	516
Scotts Bluff	4,297	6,885	2,851	9,485	677
Seward	2,609	3,215	1,799	3,525	533
Sheridan	810	2,003	369	2,747	121
Sherman	1,078	935	576	1,253	116
Sioux	329	532	120	759	32
Stanton	763	1,462	361	1,942	118
Thayer	1,315	1,994	925	2,514	178
Thomas	103	343	65	306	26
Thurston	1,020	1,290	724	1,454	140
Valley	1,042	1,587	654	2,100	124
Washington	2,233	3,792	1,445	4,560	356
Wayne	1,089	2,521	733	2,844	300
Webster	1,130	1,267	547	1,676	138
Wheeler	146	274	93	371	22
York	1,655	4,202	1,118	5,065	323
Totals	**233,287**	**359,219**	**166,424**	**419,214**	**44,854**

Nebraska Vote Since 1932

1932 (Pres.), Roosevelt, Dem., 359,082; Hoover, Rep., 201,177; Thomas, Soc., 9,876.

1936 (Pres.), Roosevelt, Dem., 347,454; Landon, Rep., 248,731; Lemke, Union, 12,847.

1940 (Pres.), Roosevelt, Dem., 263,677; Willkie, Rep., 352,201.

1944 (Pres.), Roosevelt, Dem., 233,246; Dewey, Rep., 329,880.

1948 (Pres.), Truman, Dem., 224,165; Dewey, Rep., 264,774.

1952 (Pres.), Eisenhower, Rep., 421,603; Stevenson Dem., 188,057.

1956 (Pres.), Eisenhower, Rep., 378,108; Stevenson, Dem., 199,029.

1960 (Pres.), Kennedy, Dem., 232,542; Nixon, Rep., 380,553.

1964 (Pres.), Johnson, Dem., 307,307; Goldwater, Rep., 276,847.

1968 (Pres.), Nixon, Rep., 321,163; Humphrey, Dem., 170,784; Wallace, 3d party, 44,904.

1972 (Pres.), Nixon, Rep., 406,298; McGovern, Dem., 169,991; scattered 817.

1976 (Pres.), Carter, Dem., 233,287; Ford, Rep., 359,219; McCarthy, Ind., 9,383; Maddox, Amer. Ind., 3,378; MacBride, Libertarian, 1,476.

1980 (Pres.), Reagan, Rep., 419,214; Carter, Dem., 166,424; Anderson, Ind., 44,854; Clark, Libertarian, 9,041.

Nevada

County	1976 Carter (D)	Ford (R)	1980 Carter (D)	Reagan (R)	Anderson (I)
Churchill	1,800	2,358	1,055	3,841	257
Clark	51,178	48,236	38,313	76,194	8,702
Douglas	1,934	3,095	1,352	5,254	511
Elko	1,955	3,293	1,296	4,393	301
Esmeralda	214	181	110	311	29
Eureka	163	272	103	430	13
Humboldt	1,074	1,380	684	1,950	128
Lander	518	561	361	935	64
Lincoln	642	700	396	1,087	38
Lyon	1,866	2,068	1,288	3,709	271
Mineral	1,361	1,104	631	1,628	147
Nye	1,261	1,027	973	2,387	204
Pershing	633	635	311	877	60
Storey	310	274	222	460	62
Washoe	21,687	29,264	15,621	41,276	5,705
White Pine	2,009	1,543	1,181	1,896	195
CARSON CITY	3,874	5,282	2,769	8,389	964
Totals	92,479	101,273	66,666	155,017	17,651

Nevada Vote Since 1932

1932 (Pres.), Roosevelt, Dem., 28,756; Hoover, Rep., 12,674.

1936 (Pres.), Roosevelt, Dem., 31,925; Landon, Rep., 11,923.

1940 (Pres.), Roosevelt, Dem., 31,945; Willkie, Rep., 21,229.

1944 (Pres.), Roosevelt, Dem., 29,623; Dewey, Rep., 24,611.

1948 (Pres.), Truman, Dem., 31,291; Dewey, Rep., 29,357; Wallace, Prog., 1,469.

1952 (Pres.), Eisenhower, Rep., 50,502; Stevenson, Dem., 31,688.

1956 (Pres.), Eisenhower, Rep., 56,049; Stevenson, Dem., 40,640.

1960 (Pres.), Kennedy, Dem., 54,880; Nixon, Rep., 52,387.

1964 (Pres.), Johnson, Dem., 79,339; Goldwater, Rep., 56,094.

1968 (Pres.), Nixon, Rep., 73,188; Humphrey, Dem., 60,598; Wallace, 3d party, 20,432.

1972 (Pres.), Nixon, Rep., 115,750; McGovern, Dem. 66,016.

1976 (Pres.), Carter Dem., 92,479; Ford, Rep., 101,273; MacBride, Libertarian, 1,519; Maddox, Amer. Ind., 1,497; scattered 5,108.

1980 (Pres.), Reagan, Rep., 155,017; Carter, Dem., 66,666; Anderson, Ind., 17,651; Clark, Libertarian, 4,358.

New Hampshire

County	1976 Carter (D)	Ford (R)	1980 Carter (D)	Reagan (R)	Anderson (I)
Belknap	6,143	9,876	4,365	12,077	1,996
Carroll	3,374	8,561	3,119	9,980	1,584
Cheshire	10,388	12,554	7,835	13,242	4,090
Coos	7,385	7,094	4,749	8,724	941
Grafton	8,996	14,430	7,282	15,273	4,279
Hillsborough	45,554	53,581	31,789	68,994	13,613
Merrimack	14,865	21,853	12,083	23,584	5,894
Rockingham	30,051	36,738	21,712	45,960	10,974
Strafford	14,566	14,569	11,041	16,399	4,700
Sullivan	6,323	6,679	4,889	7,472	1,622
Totals	147,645	185,935	108,864	221,705	49,693

New Hampshire Vote Since 1932

1932 (Pres.), Roosevelt, Dem., 100,680; Hoover, Rep., 103,629; Thomas, Soc., 947; Foster, Com., 264.

1936 (Pres.), Roosevelt, Dem., 108,640; Landon, Rep., 104,642; Lemke, Union, 4,819; Browder, Com., 193.

1940 (Pres.), Roosevelt, Dem., 125,292; Willkie, Rep., 110,127.

1944 (Pres.), Roosevelt, Dem., 119,663; Dewey, Rep., 109,916; Thomas, Soc., 46.

1948 (Pres.), Truman, Dem., 107,995; Dewey, Rep., 121,299; Wallace, Prog., 1,970; Thomas, Soc., 86; Teichert, Soc. Labor, 83; Thurmond, States' Rights, 7.

1952 (Pres.), Eisenhower, Rep., 166,287; Stevenson, Dem., 106,663.

1956 (Pres.), Eisenhower, Rep., 176,519; Stevenson, Dem., 90,364; Andrews, Const., 111.

1960 (Pres.), Kennedy, Dem., 137,772; Nixon, Rep., 157,989.

1964 (Pres.), Johnson, Dem., 182,065; Goldwater, Rep., 104,029.

1968 (Pres.), Nixon, Rep., 154,903; Humphrey, Dem., 130,589; Wallace, 3d party, 11,173; New Party, 421; Halstead, Soc. Worker, 104.

1972 (Pres.), Nixon, Rep., 213,724; McGovern, Dem., 116,435; Schmitz, Amer., 3,386; Jenness, Soc. Workers, 368; scattered, 142.

1976 (Pres.), Carter, Dem., 147,645; Ford, Rep., 185,935; McCarthy, Ind., 4,095; MacBride, Libertarian, 936; Reagan, write-in, 388; La Rouche, U.S. Labor, 186; Camejo, Soc. Workers, 161, Levin, Soc. Labor, 66; scattered, 215.

1980 (Pres.), Reagan, Rep., 221,705; Carter, Dem., 108,864; Anderson, Ind., 49,693; Clark, Libertarian, 2,067; Commoner, Citizens, 1,325; Hall, Com., 129; Griswold, Workers World, 76; DeBerry, Soc. Workers, 72; scattered, 68.

New Jersey

County	1976 Carter (D)	Ford (R)	1980 Carter (D)	Reagan (R)	Anderson (I)
Atlantic	41,965	36,733	31,286	37,973	5,582
Bergen	180,738	237,331	139,474	232,043	38,242
Burlington	63,309	60,960	50,083	68,415	11,314
Camden	108,854	82,801	80,033	87,939	16,125
Cape May	16,489	19,498	12,708	22,729	2,550
Cumberland	29,165	20,535	19,356	23,242	3,253
Essex	174,434	133,911	145,281	117,222	21,271
Gloucester	38,726	34,888	29,804	40,306	7,533
Hudson	116,241	92,636	95,622	91,207	8,941
Hunterdon	12,592	19,616	10,029	21,403	3,610
Mercer	69,621	58,453	60,883	53,450	12,117
Middlesex	122,859	113,539	97,304	122,354	17,463
Monmouth	88,956	110,104	71,323	120,173	17,444
Morris	63,749	105,921	48,965	105,260	17,181
Ocean	56,413	77,875	46,923	98,433	10,073
Passaic	76,194	85,102	61,486	82,531	9,385
Salem	12,826	11,639	10,209	13,000	1,800
Somerset	36,258	51,260	29,470	52,591	8,346
Sussex	14,759	23,613	10,531	27,063	3,988
Union	106,267	118,019	86,074	112,288	15,586
Warren	14,238	15,254	10,510	16,935	2,828
Totals	1,444,653	1,509,688	1,147,364	1,546,557	234,632

New Jersey Vote Since 1932

1932 (Pres.), Roosevelt, Dem., 806,630; Hoover, Rep., 775,684; Thomas, Soc., 42,998; Foster, Com., 2,915; Reynolds, Soc. Labor, 1,062; Upshaw, Proh., 774.

1936 (Pres.), Roosevelt, Dem., 1,083,549; Landon, Rep., 719,421; Lemke, Union, 9,405; Thomas, Soc., 3,895; Browder, Com., 1,590; Colvin, Proh., 916; Aiken, Soc. Labor, 346.

1940 (Pres.), Roosevelt, Dem., 1,016,404; Willkie, Rep., 944,876; Browder, Com., 8,814; Thomas, Soc., 2,823; Babson, Proh., 851; Aiken, Soc. Labor, 446.

1944 (Pres.), Roosevelt, Dem., 987,874; Dewey, Rep., 961,335; Teichert, Soc. Labor, 6,939; Watson, Nat'l. Proh., 4,255; Thomas, Soc., 3,385.

1948 (Pres.), Truman, Dem., 895,455; Dewey, Rep., 981,124; Wallace, Prog., 42,683; Watson, Proh., 10,593; Thomas, Soc., 10,521; Dobbs, Soc. Workers, 5,825; Teichert, Soc. Labor, 3,354.

1952 (Pres.), Eisenhower, Rep., 1,373,613; Stevenson, Dem., 1,015,902; Hoopes, Soc., 8,593; Hass, Soc. Labor, 5,815; Hallinan, Prog., 5,589; Krajewski, Poor Man's, 4,203; Dobbs, Soc. Workers, 3,850; Hamblen, Proh., 989.

1956 (Pres.), Eisenhower, Rep., 1,606,942; Stevenson Dem., 850,337; Holtwick, Proh., 9,147; Hass, Soc. Labor, 6,736; Andrews, Conservative, 5,317; Dobbs, Soc. Workers, 4,004; Krajewski, American Third Party, 1,829.

1960 (Pres.), Kennedy, Dem., 1,385,415; Nixon, Rep., 1,363,324; Dobbs, Soc. Workers, 11,402; Lee, Conservative, 8,708; Hass, Soc. Labor, 4,262.

1964 (Pres.), Johnson, Dem., 1,867,671; Goldwater, Rep., 963,843; DeBerry, Soc. Workers, 8,181; Hass, Soc. Labor, 7,075.

1968 (Pres.), Nixon, Rep., 1,325,467; Humphrey, Dem., 1,264,206; Wallace, 3d party, 262,187; Halstead, Soc. Worker, 8,667; Gregory, Peace Freedom, 8,084; Blomen, Soc. Labor, 6,784.

1972 (Pres.), Nixon, Rep., 1,845,502; McGovern, Dem., 1,102,211; Schmitz, Amer., 34,378; Spock, Peoples, 5,355; Fisher, Soc. Labor, 4,544; Jenness, Soc. Workers, 2,233; Mahalchik, Amer. First, 1,743; Hall, Com., 1,263.

1976 (Pres.), Carter, Dem., 1,444,653; Ford, Rep., 1,509,688; McCarthy, Ind., 32,717; MacBride, Libertarian, 9,449; Maddox, Amer., 7,716; Levin, Soc. Labor, 3,686; Hall, Com., 1,662; LaRouche, U.S. Labor, 1,650; Camejo, Soc. Workers, 1,184; Wright, People's, 1,044; Bubar, Proh., 554; Zeidler, Soc., 469.

1980 (Pres.), Reagan, Rep., 1,546,557; Carter, Dem., 1,147,364; Anderson, Ind., 234,632; Clark, Libertarian, 20,652; Commoner, Citizens, 8,203; McCormack, Right to Life, 3,927; Lynen, Middle Class, 3,694; Hall, Com., 2,555; Pulley, Soc. Workers, 2,198; McReynolds, Soc., 1,973; Gahres, Down With Lawyers, 1,718; Griswold, Workers World, 1,288; Wendelken, Ind., 923.

County	Carter (D) 1976	Ford (R) 1976	Carter (D) 1980	Reagan (R) 1980	Anderson (I) 1980
Union	975	1,146	675	1,407	32
Valencia	8,566	7,851	6,886	11,177	825
Totals	**201,148**	**211,419**	**167,826**	**250,779**	**29,459**

New Mexico Vote Since 1932

1932 (Pres.), Roosevelt, Dem., 95,089; Hoover, Rep., 54,217; Thomas, Soc., 11,776; Harvey, Lib., 389; Foster, Com., 135.

1936 (Pres.), Roosevelt, Dem., 105,838; Landon, Rep., 61,710; Lemke, Union, 942; Thomas, Soc., 343; Browder, Com., 43.

1940 (Pres.), Roosevelt, Dem., 103,699; Willkie, Rep., 79,315.

1944 (Pres.), Roosevelt, Dem., 81,389; Dewey, Rep., 70,688; Watson, Proh., 148.

1948 (Pres.), Truman, Dem., 105,464; Dewey, Rep., 80,303; Wallace, Prog., 1,037; Watson, Proh., 127; Thomas, Soc., 83; Teichert, Soc. Labor, 49.

1952 (Pres.), Eisenhower, Rep., 132,170; Stevenson, Dem., 105,661; Hamblen, Proh., 297; Hallinan, Ind. Prog., 225; MacArthur, Christian National, 220; Hass, Soc. Labor, 35.

1956 (Pres.), Eisenhower, Rep., 146,788; Stevenson, Dem., 106,098; Holtwick, Proh., 607; Andrews, Ind., 364; Hass, Soc. Labor, 69.

1960 (Pres.), Kennedy, Dem., 156,027; Nixon, Rep., 153,733; Decker, Proh., 777; Hass, Soc. Labor, 570.

1964 (Pres.), Johnson, Dem., 194,017; Goldwater, Rep., 131,838; Hass, Soc. Labor, 1,217; Munn, Proh., 543.

1968 (Pres.), Nixon, Rep., 169,692; Humphrey, Dem., 130,081; Wallace, 3d party, 25,737; Chavez, 1,519; Halstead, Soc. Worker, 252.

1972 (Pres.), Nixon, Rep., 235,606; McGovern, Dem., 141,084; Schmitz, Amer., 8,767; Jenness, Soc. Workers, 474.

1976 (Pres.), Carter, Dem., 201,148; Ford, Rep., 211,419; Camejo, Soc. Workers, 2,462; MacBride, Libertarian, 1,110; Zeidler, Soc., 240; Bubar, Proh., 211.

1980 (Pres.), Reagan, Rep., 250,779; Carter, Dem., 167,826; Anderson, Ind., 29,459; Clark, Libertarian, 4,365; Commoner, Citizens, 2,202; Bubar, Statesman, 1,281; Pulley, Soc. Worker, 325.

New Mexico

County	Carter (D) 1976	Ford (R) 1976	Carter (D) 1980	Reagan (R) 1980	Anderson (I) 1980
Bernalillo	63,949	76,614	54,841	83,956	15,118
Catron	517	602	466	906	40
Chaves	7,139	10,631	5,350	12,502	543
Colfax	2,718	2,259	2,266	2,537	199
Curry	5,004	6,232	3,622	8,132	183
De Baca	597	556	484	655	14
Dona Ana	12,036	13,888	10,839	15,539	1,863
Eddy	9,073	7,698	7,028	9,817	326
Grant	5,176	4,095	4,600	4,628	349
Guadalupe	1,379	1,047	980	1,065	58
Harding	285	387	225	356	14
Hidalgo	938	891	840	1,059	59
Lea	6,533	8,773	5,006	10,727	298
Lincoln	1,415	2,320	1,127	3,009	172
Los Alamos	2,890	5,383	2,368	5,460	1,388
Luna	2,872	2,966	2,443	3,636	157
McKinley	6,856	4,617	4,869	7,329	498
Mora	1,438	904	1,274	1,037	44
Otero	5,333	5,914	4,111	7,210	478
Quay	2,095	2,059	1,422	2,499	58
Rio Arriba	7,125	3,213	6,245	3,794	379
Roosevelt	3,111	3,269	2,240	3,950	208
Sandoval	5,072	4,110	4,740	6,762	789
San Juan	8,615	10,852	6,705	15,579	741
San Miguel	5,204	3,542	4,514	3,292	416
Santa Fe	14,127	11,576	12,658	12,361	3,123
Sierra	1,564	1,665	1,169	2,222	117
Socorro	2,606	2,265	2,226	2,685	387
Taos	4,414	3,012	4,346	3,584	482
Torrance	1,526	1,462	1,261	1,907	101

New York

County	Carter (D-L*) 1976	Ford (R-C**) 1976	Carter (D) 1980	Reagan (R-C**) 1980	Anderson (L) 1980
Albany	71,616	69,592	74,429	52,354	14,563
Allegany	6,134	11,769	5,879	10,423	973
Broome	39,827	50,340	37,013	39,275	11,388
Cattaraugus	13,768	19,469	12,917	17,222	1,848
Cayuga	13,348	19,775	11,708	17,945	2,539
Chautauqua	27,447	33,730	22,871	30,081	4,699
Chemung	17,207	20,640	14,565	19,674	2,465
Chenango	7,356	12,384	6,917	10,400	1,908
Clinton	11,555	15,433	11,498	13,120	1,904
Columbia	10,514	15,871	9,500	13,946	2,204
Cortland	6,947	11,222	6,176	9,885	1,603
Delaware	7,254	12,443	6,333	10,609	1,865
Dutchess	37,531	51,312	28,616	53,616	8,824
Erie	229,397	220,310	215,283	169,209	29,580
Essex	6,556	10,194	6,443	9,025	1,213
Franklin	7,248	8,846	7,281	7,620	1,182
Fulton	9,323	12,161	8,105	11,448	1,566
Genesee	10,803	14,567	10,677	11,650	1,651
Greene	7,740	11,370	6,488	11,286	1,338
Hamilton	1,052	2,306	925	2,038	176
Herkimer	12,875	15,362	11,497	14,105	1,830
Jefferson	13,503	20,401	13,271	16,455	2,834
Lewis	3,764	5,840	3,973	4,937	716
Livingston	9,629	14,044	9,030	11,193	1,694
Madison	8,822	15,674	7,843	13,369	2,122
Monroe	134,739	167,303	142,423	128,615	29,118
Montgomery	11,271	13,281	9,645	11,917	2,080
Niagara	43,667	46,101	40,405	38,760	6,014
Oneida	47,779	57,655	44,292	51,968	6,929
Onondaga	76,097	115,474	73,453	97,887	18,805
Ontario	14,044	21,118	14,477	17,036	3,147
Orange	40,362	49,685	30,022	51,268	7,656
Orleans	5,927	8,994	5,767	7,536	977
Oswego	16,332	23,949	15,343	22,816	3,333
Otsego	9,787	14,796	8,795	11,814	2,874
Putnam	11,963	18,523	8,691	20,193	2,340
Rensselaer	28,979	40,229	29,880	32,005	6,443

	1976 (D)	(R)	1980 (D)	(R)	(I)
Rockland	48,673	52,087	35,277	59,068	8,709
St. Lawrence	17,503	16,173	17,006	18,437	3,544
Saratoga	23,768	38,296	23,641	34,184	6,201
Schenectady	31,838	40,789	29,932	32,003	7,146
Schoharie	5,250	7,154	4,715	6,382	940
Schuyler	2,885	4,267	2,514	3,838	476
Seneca	5,745	7,659	5,010	7,174	1,205
Steuben	14,685	23,164	12,826	22,418	2,257
Sullivan	14,189	13,709	9,553	15,089	2,095
Tioga	6,969	11,824	6,690	10,291	1,851
Tompkins	12,808	15,463	11,970	12,448	4,081
Ulster	30,190	35,353	22,179	36,709	5,995
Warren	7,264	14,548	6,971	13,264	1,766
Washington	7,262	13,946	7,144	12,835	1,501
Wayne	12,061	19,324	12,590	16,498	2,623
Wyoming	5,737	9,726	5,234	8,108	855
Yates	2,903	5,796	2,828	4,694	690
Outside N.Y. Metro Area	1,281,893	1,607,517	1,188,511	1,386,140	244,336
Nassau	302,869	329,176	207,602	333,567	44,758
Suffolk	208,263	248,908	149,945	256,294	34,743
Westchester	173,153	208,527	130,136	198,552	30,119
N.Y. Suburban	648,285	786,611	487,683	788,413	109,620
Bronx	238,786	96,842	181,090	86,843	11,286
Kings	419,382	190,728	288,893	200,306	24,341
New York	337,438	117,702	275,742	115,911	38,597
Queens	379,907	244,396	269,147	251,333	32,566
Richmond	47,867	56,995	37,306	64,885	7,055
N.Y. City	1,423,380	706,663	1,052,178	719,278	113,845
N.Y. Metro Area	2,107,665	1,493,274	1,539,861	1,507,691	223,465
D/R Total	3,244,165	2,825,913	2,728,372	2,637,700	-
2d party (Con)	145,393	274,878	-	256,131	-
Totals	3,389,558	3,100,791	2,728,372	2,893,831	467,801

*Democratic and Liberal **Republican and Conservative

New York Vote Since 1932

1932 (Pres.), Roosevelt, Dem., 2,534,959; Hoover, Rep., 1,937,963; Thomas, Soc., 177,397; Foster, Com., 27,956; Reynolds, Soc. Labor, 10,339.

1936 (Pres.), Roosevelt, Dem., 3,018,298; American Lab., 274,924; total 3,293,222; Landon, Rep., 2,180,670; Thomas, Soc., 86,879; Browder, Com., 35,609.

1940 (Pres.), Roosevelt, Dem., 2,834,500; American Lab., 417,418; total, 3,251,918; Willkie, Rep., 3,027,478; Thomas, Soc., 18,950; Babson, Proh., 3,250.

1944 (Pres.), Roosevelt, Dem., 2,478,598; American Lab., 496,405; Liberal, 329,325; total, 3,304,238; Dewey, Rep., 2,987,647; Teichert, Ind. Gov't., 14,352; Thomas, Soc., 10,553.

1948 (Pres.), Truman, Dem., 2,557,642; Liberal, 222,562; total, 2,780,204; Dewey, Rep., 2,841,163; Wallace, Amer. Lab., 509,559; Thomas, Soc., 40,879; Teichert, Ind. Gov't., 2,729; Dobbs, Soc. Workers, 2,675.

1952 (Pres.), Eisenhower, Rep., 3,952,815; Stevenson, Dem., 2,687,890, Liberal, 416,711; total, 3,104,601; Hallinan, American Lab., 64,211; Hoopes, Soc., 2,664; Dobbs, Soc. Workers, 2,212; Hass, Ind. Gov't., 1,560; scattering, 178; blank and void, 87,813.

1956 (Pres.), Eisenhower, Rep., 4,340,340; Stevenson, Dem., 2,458,212; Liberal, 292,557; total, 2,750,769; write-in votes for Andrews, 1,027; Werdel, 492; Hass, 150; Hoopes, 82; others, 476.

1960 (Pres.), Kennedy, Dem., 3,423,909; Liberal, 406,176; total, 3,830,085; Nixon, Rep., 3,446,419; Dobbs, Soc. Workers, 14,319; scattering, 256; blank and void, 88,896.

1964 (Pres.), Johnson, Dem., 4,913,156; Goldwater, Rep., 2,243,559; Hass, Soc. Labor, 6,085; DeBerry, Soc. Workers, 3,215; scattering, 268; blank and void, 151,383.

1968 (Pres.), Nixon, Rep., 3,007,932; Humphrey, Dem., 3,378,470; Wallace, 3d party, 358,864; Blomen, Soc. Labor, 8,432; Halstead, Soc. Worker, 11,851; Gregory, Freedom and Peace, 24,517; blank, void, and scattering, 171,624.

1972 (Pres.), Nixon, Rep., 3,824,642; Conservative, 368,136; McGovern, Dem., 2,767,956; Liberal, 183,128; Reed, Soc. Workers, 7,797; Fisher, Soc. Labor, 4,530; Hall, Com., 5,641; blank, void, or scattered, 161,641.

1976 (Pres.), Carter, Dem., 3,389,558; Ford, Rep., 3,100,791; MacBride, Libertarian, 12,197; Hall, Com., 10,270; Camejo, Soc. Workers, 6,996; LaRouche, U.S. Labor, 5,413; blank, void, or scattered, 143,037.

1980 (Pres.), Reagan, Rep., 2,893,831; Carter, Dem., 2,728,372; Anderson, Lib., 467,801; Clark, Libertarian, 52,648; McCormack, Right To Life, 24,159; Commoner, Citizens, 23,186; Hall, Com., 7,414; DeBerry, Soc. Workers, 2,068; Griswold, Workers World, 1,416; scattering, 1,064.

North Carolina

County	1976 Carter (D)	Ford (R)	1980 Carter (D)	Reagan (R)	Anderson (I)
Alamance	17,371	12,680	15,042	18,077	760
Alexander	5,287	4,661	4,546	6,376	137
Alleghany	2,550	1,532	2,198	1,995	91
Anson	4,796	1,608	4,973	1,968	111
Ashe	5,193	4,937	4,461	5,643	154
Avery	1,869	3,085	1,527	3,480	147
Beaufort	5,728	4,677	6,024	6,773	186
Bertie	4,117	1,332	3,863	1,695	45
Bladen	6,009	1,546	6,104	2,745	64
Brunswick	7,377	3,636	6,761	5,897	265
Buncombe	26,633	22,461	24,837	26,124	2,153
Burke	14,254	10,070	11,680	12,956	558
Cabarrus	12,049	12,455	9,768	15,143	562
Caldwell	11,894	9,872	8,738	12,965	440
Camden	1,231	562	1,212	813	45
Carteret	7,080	5,786	6,485	7,733	460
Caswell	3,707	1,761	3,529	2,156	66
Catawba	16,862	18,696	13,873	22,873	866
Chatham	6,397	4,279	7,144	5,414	481
Cherokee	3,571	3,210	3,114	3,849	80
Chowan	1,862	1,019	2,146	1,424	71
Clay	1,569	1,428	1,324	2,136	53
Cleveland	14,406	8,106	12,219	10,828	333
Columbus	11,148	3,184	10,212	5,522	148
Craven	7,553	5,881	7,781	8,554	356
Cumberland	24,297	14,226	22,073	21,540	1,261
Currituck	1,999	954	1,980	1,668	97
Dare	2,191	1,680	2,497	2,794	260
Davidson	17,859	18,813	14,579	22,794	679
Davie	3,635	4,772	3,289	6,302	223
Duplin	7,696	3,912	7,524	5,403	109
Durham	22,425	18,945	24,969	19,276	3,052
Edgecombe	8,001	4,850	7,945	5,916	148
Forsyth	39,561	38,886	38,870	42,389	2,897
Franklin	5,405	2,630	5,427	3,508	104
Gaston	22,878	19,727	19,016	25,139	823
Gates	2,291	722	2,435	957	61
Graham	1,791	1,621	1,608	1,961	36
Granville	5,244	2,955	5,556	3,513	133
Greene	2,740	1,356	2,835	2,221	34
Guilford	46,826	45,441	44,516	53,291	4,019
Halifax	7,892	5,257	8,364	6,033	180
Harnett	8,992	5,935	8,791	7,284	165
Haywood	10,692	5,885	9,814	7,217	349
Henderson	8,155	10,830	7,578	13,573	901
Hertford	3,986	1,517	4,102	1,854	80
Hoke	3,186	920	3,376	1,168	56
Hyde	1,084	623	1,221	807	37
Iredell	13,295	11,573	12,067	14,926	624
Jackson	5,223	3,536	4,857	4,140	246
Johnston	10,901	8,511	9,601	10,444	271
Jones	2,016	948	2,198	1,401	18
Lee	5,104	3,691	5,426	4,847	251
Lenoir	7,650	7,715	7,546	9,832	263
Lincoln	9,462	6,682	7,796	9,009	299
Macon	4,405	3,673	4,105	4,727	153
Madison	3,433	2,446	3,202	2,629	108
Martin	4,518	1,931	4,750	2,564	81
McDowell	6,246	4,450	4,703	5,680	175
Mecklenburg	63,198	61,715	66,995	68,384	6,560
Mitchell	2,031	3,728	1,765	4,322	146
Montgomery	4,308	2,872	4,129	3,587	99
Moore	7,373	7,577	8,084	10,158	563
Nash	8,937	8,477	8,184	11,043	293
New Hanover	14,504	13,687	13,670	17,243	1,114
Northampton	5,118	1,238	4,933	1,847	62
Onslow	7,954	5,953	7,371	8,861	400
Orange	15,755	9,302	15,226	9,261	3,364
Pamlico	2,113	1,068	2,224	1,504	48
Pasquotank	4,302	2,651	4,128	3,340	179
Pender	4,422	2,063	4,382	3,018	103
Perquimans	1,666	909	1,560	1,210	63
Person	3,977	3,038	4,111	3,281	104
Pitt	11,636	9,532	12,590	12,816	827
Polk	3,155	2,605	2,375	3,021	160
Randolph	12,714	14,337	10,107	19,881	563
Richmond	8,793	2,848	7,416	3,911	224
Robeson	20,695	4,907	17,618	6,982	331
Rockingham	13,413	9,362	11,708	11,205	463
Rowan	15,363	14,644	11,671	18,566	707
Rutherford	10,361	6,718	8,315	8,363	203

	1976 (D)	(R)	1980 (D)	(R)	(I)
Sampson	8,869	6,968	9,090	8,097	308
Scotland	4,430	1,932	4,446	2,133	155
Stanly	9,262	8,845	7,784	9,734	248
Stokes	6,647	6,029	5,764	7,275	151
Surry	10,024	7,403	8,987	10,065	256
Swain	2,141	1,606	1,987	1,457	70
Transylvania	4,636	4,089	4,008	4,826	274
Tyrrell	900	403	887	466	14
Union	10,578	6,184	10,073	9,012	487
Vance	5,620	3,813	5,415	4,217	101
Wake	44,005	44,291	49,003	49,768	5,455
Warren	3,185	1,427	3,750	1,582	74
Washington	2,840	1,486	3,008	1,943	68
Watauga	5,358	5,400	5,022	6,149	645
Wayne	9,265	9,607	9,586	12,860	322
Wilkes	10,176	11,768	8,184	14,462	282
Wilson	8,209	6,795	8,042	8,329	243
Yadkin	4,497	5,916	3,850	7,530	136
Yancey	3,932	2,688	4,010	3,363	110
Totals	927,365	741,960	875,635	915,018	52,800

North Carolina Vote Since 1932

1932 (Pres.), Roosevelt, Dem., 497,566; Hoover, Rep., 208,344; Thomas, Soc., 5,591.

1936 (Pres.), Roosevelt, Dem., 616,141; Landon, Rep., 223,283; Thomas, Soc., 21; Browder, Com., 11; Lemke, Union 2.

1940 (Pres.), Roosevelt, Dem., 609,015; Willkie, Rep., 213,633.

1944 (Pres.), Roosevelt, Dem., 527,399; Dewey, Rep., 263,155.

1948 (Pres.), Truman, Dem., 459,070; Dewey, Rep., 258,572; Thurmond, States' Rights, 69,652; Wallace, Prog., 3,915.

1952 (Pres.), Eisenhower, Rep., 558,107; Stevenson, Dem., 652,803.

1956 (Pres.), Eisenhower, Rep., 575,062; Stevenson, Dem., 590,530.

1960 (Pres.), Kennedy, Dem., 713,136; Nixon, Rep., 655,420.

1964 (Pres.), Johnson, Dem., 800,139; Goldwater Rep., 624,844.

1968 (Pres.), Nixon, Rep., 627,192; Humphrey, Dem., 464,113; Wallace, 3d party, 496,188.

1972 (Pres.), Nixon, Rep., 1,054,889; McGovern, Dem., 438,705; Schmitz, Amer., 25,018.

1976 (Pres.), Dem., 927,365; Ford, Rep., 741,960; Anderson, Amer., 5,607; MacBride, Libertarian, 2,219; LaRouche, U.S. Labor, 755.

1980 (Pres.), Reagan, Rep., 915,018; Carter, Dem., 875,635; Anderson, Ind., 52,800; Clark, Libertarian, 9,677; Commoner, Citizens, 2,287; DeBerry, Soc. Workers, 416.

North Dakota

	1976 Carter (D)	Ford (R)	1980 Carter (D)	Reagan (R)	Anderson (I)
County					
Adams	959	940	470	1,334	107
Barnes	3,321	4,011	2,128	4,392	705
Benson	1,973	1,689	1,119	2,149	262
Billings	285	351	122	524	33
Bottineau	1,987	2,638	1,090	3,394	267
Bowman	911	1,033	454	1,507	142
Burke	899	1,087	418	1,442	82
Burleigh	9,188	13,680	6,129	18,437	2,109
Cass	17,879	22,583	13,562	23,886	5,421
Cavalier	2,178	2,046	1,105	2,582	238
Dickey	1,612	2,027	917	2,455	161
Divide	1,057	881	509	1,267	109
Dunn	1,051	1,041	532	1,706	115
Eddy	1,123	890	539	1,153	145
Emmons	1,459	1,370	502	2,369	132
Foster	1,147	1,120	586	1,534	152
Golden Valley	479	663	259	1,006	62
Grand Forks	11,545	13,820	6,997	14,257	2,932
Grant	952	1,205	317	1,891	110
Griggs	1,122	1,086	636	1,342	158
Hettinger	1,095	1,135	434	1,699	104
Kidder	936	954	326	1,474	85
La Moure	1,718	1,735	850	2,136	254
Logan	809	944	283	1,474	69
McHenry	1,994	2,043	939	2,922	190
McIntosh	912	1,785	308	2,471	72
McKenzie	1,335	1,595	867	2,265	182
McLean	2,815	2,729	1,613	4,234	318

	1976		1980		
Mercer	1,298	1,982	1,209	3,224	204
Morton	5,241	4,921	2,861	7,659	742
Mountrail	2,189	1,430	1,183	2,165	182
Nelson	1,610	1,336	726	1,611	226
Oliver	529	575	270	966	55
Pembina	2,274	2,810	1,239	3,110	303
Pierce	1,434	1,396	517	2,273	168
Ramsey	3,096	3,293	1,607	4,078	514
Ransom	1,715	1,696	974	1,883	237
Renville	1,008	812	570	1,154	98
Richland	4,592	4,891	2,696	5,711	750
Rolette	2,531	1,094	1,660	1,599	265
Sargent	1,644	1,344	1,048	1,565	174
Sheridan	569	935	208	1,326	65
Sioux	697	354	383	620	72
Slope	347	355	128	462	45
Stark	4,076	4,374	2,016	6,312	512
Steele	1,066	835	617	997	229
Stutsman	4,883	5,653	2,573	6,545	960
Towner	1,216	993	568	1,375	152
Traill	2,352	2,800	1,428	3,092	512
Walsh	3,555	3,518	1,850	4,488	485
Ward	9,484	12,751	5,554	14,997	1,234
Wells	1,742	1,941	746	2,660	148
Williams	4,189	4,230	2,545	6,530	592
Totals	136,078	153,470	79,189	193,695	23,640

North Dakota Vote Since 1932

1932 (Pres.), Roosevelt, Dem., 178,350; Hoover, Rep., 71,772; Harvey, Lib., 1,817; Thomas, Soc., 3,521; Foster, Com., 830.

1936 (Pres.), Roosevelt, Dem., 163,148; Landon, Rep., 72,751; Lemke, Union, 36,708; Thomas, Soc., 552; Browder, Com., 360; Colvin, Proh., 197.

1940 (Pres.), Roosevelt, Dem., 124,036; Willkie, Rep., 154,590; Thomas, Soc., 1,279; Knutson, Com., 545; Babson, Proh., 325.

1944 (Pres.), Roosevelt, Dem., 100,144; Dewey, Rep., 118,535; Thomas, Soc., 943, Watson, Proh., 549.

1948 (Pres.), Truman, Dem., 95,812; Dewey, Rep., 115,139; Wallace, Prog., 8,391; Thomas, Soc., 1,000, Thurmond, States' Rights, 374.

1952 (Pres.), Eisenhower, Rep., 191,712; Stevenson, Dem., 76,694; MacArthur, Christian Nationalist, 1,075; Hallinan, Prog., 344; Hamblen, Proh., 302.

1956 (Pres.), Eisenhower, Rep., 156,766; Stevenson, Dem., 96,742; Andrews, Amer., 483.

1960 (Pres.), Kennedy, Dem., 123,963; Nixon, Rep., 154,310; Dobbs, Soc. Workers, 158.

1964 (Pres.), Johnson, Dem., 149,784; Goldwater, Rep., 108,207; DeBerry, Soc. Worker, 224; Munn, Proh., 174.

1968 (Pres.), Nixon, Rep., 138,669; Humphrey, Dem., 94,769; Wallace, 3d party, 14,244; Halstead, Soc. Worker, 128; Munn, Prohibition, 38; Troxell, Ind., 34.

1972 (Pres.), Nixon, Rep., 174,109; McGovern, Dem., 100,384; Jenness, Soc. Workers, 288; Hall, Com., 87; Schmitz, Amer., 5,646.

1976 (Pres.), Carter, Dem., 136,078; Ford, Rep., 153,470; Anderson, Amer., 3,698; McCarthy, Ind., 2,952; Maddox, Amer. Ind., 269; MacBride, Libertarian, 256; scattering, 371.

1980 (Pres.), Reagan, Rep., 193,695; Carter, Dem., 79,189; Anderson, Ind., 23,640; Clark, Libertarian, 3,743; Commoner, Libertarian, 429; McLain, Nat'l People's League, 296; Greaves, American, 235; Hall, Com., 93; DeBerry, Soc. Workers, 89; McReynolds, Soc., 82; Bubar, Statesman, 54.

Ohio

	1976 Carter (D)	Ford (R)	1980 Carter (D)	Reagan (R)	Anderson (I)
County					
Adams	4,450	4,197	4,161	5,336	303
Allen	14,627	23,721	13,140	29,070	1,439
Ashland	7,205	9,761	5,142	11,691	1,128
Ashtabula	20,883	16,885	17,363	19,847	2,481
Athens	9,896	8,387	9,514	8,170	1,544
Auglaize	5,840	9,772	5,022	11,537	785
Belmont	21,132	13,550	16,653	13,601	1,432
Brown	5,432	4,549	4,706	6,065	339
Butler	35,123	49,625	31,796	61,231	4,717
Carroll	5,006	5,091	3,476	5,806	406
Champaign	4,748	6,526	4,109	7,356	596
Clark	26,135	26,745	22,630	27,237	3,414

	1976 (D)	(R)	1980 (D)	(R)	(I)
Clermont	14,850	19,616	13,199	26,674	1,697
Clinton	4,959	6,597	3,967	7,675	608
Columbiana	23,096	22,318	17,459	20,798	2,320
Coshocton	5,827	6,361	4,725	8,359	525
Crawford	7,553	10,801	6,058	12,424	915
Cuyahoga	349,186	255,594	307,448	254,883	40,750
Darke	9,901	11,580	7,635	12,773	1,198
Defiance	5,850	7,526	5,096	9,358	896
Delaware	7,058	12,285	6,417	14,740	1,278
Erie	13,843	14,742	12,343	15,628	1,908
Fairfield	13,361	19,098	13,144	24,096	1,689
Fayette	4,477	5,719	2,810	5,827	327
Franklin	141,624	189,645	143,932	200,948	21,269
Fulton	4,850	7,891	3,972	9,519	1,026
Gallia	4,971	5,198	4,406	6,469	401
Geauga	10,449	15,004	9,542	17,762	2,359
Greene	20,245	22,598	20,068	24,922	3,160
Guernsey	7,573	7,746	5,121	8,180	604
Hamilton	135,605	211,267	129,114	206,979	17,898
Hancock	8,548	15,983	6,843	18,264	1,467
Hardin	4,650	6,076	3,863	7,457	528
Harrison	4,070	3,509	2,848	3,639	331
Henry	4,592	7,856	3,059	7,584	691
Highland	6,327	6,853	4,363	7,309	454
Hocking	5,126	4,114	3,765	4,588	312
Holmes	2,242	2,870	2,094	3,860	329
Huron	7,742	9,386	6,537	11,173	1,110
Jackson	6,699	5,987	4,409	5,902	274
Jefferson	22,318	14,839	20,382	15,777	1,797
Knox	7,361	9,290	6,586	10,384	987
Lake	40,734	36,390	35,246	43,485	5,925
Lawrence	12,072	10,668	11,366	13,799	813
Licking	19,247	23,518	17,208	28,425	2,419
Logan	5,949	9,092	4,319	9,727	718
Lorain	52,387	39,459	40,919	51,034	7,324
Lucas	103,658	76,069	85,341	86,653	16,636
Madison	4,885	7,074	3,565	7,166	438
Mahoning	75,837	46,314	63,677	50,153	9,490
Marion	10,962	13,141	9,419	14,605	1,255
Medina	16,251	19,066	13,573	24,723	2,965
Meigs	5,262	4,942	3,827	4,911	294
Mercer	6,724	7,678	5,506	8,673	941
Miami	13,074	18,666	12,893	19,928	2,429
Monroe	4,296	2,728	3,166	2,870	266
Montgomery	106,468	100,223	105,110	101,443	13,817
Morgan	2,727	2,971	1,875	3,236	156
Morrow	4,870	5,814	3,239	6,179	383
Muskingum	14,178	15,358	12,584	17,921	1,329
Noble	2,612	3,007	1,944	3,025	208
Ottawa	9,846	8,241	6,753	8,641	1,281
Paulding	3,229	3,593	2,778	4,971	550
Perry	6,268	5,637	4,383	5,725	369
Pickaway	5,907	7,695	5,052	9,289	515
Pike	5,734	3,729	4,938	4,426	257
Portage	24,417	17,927	20,570	22,829	3,798
Preble	5,850	6,654	5,416	8,376	687
Putnam	5,035	7,332	3,742	9,752	533
Richland	23,065	24,310	18,253	29,213	2,586
Ross	10,743	11,477	9,355	13,251	812
Sandusky	11,202	13,074	8,482	13,420	1,851
Scioto	18,019	13,021	15,552	15,881	816
Seneca	10,074	11,730	7,303	14,172	1,415
Shelby	6,414	8,011	6,425	8,988	895
Stark	70,012	72,607	59,005	87,769	8,030
Summit	123,711	80,415	102,459	92,299	15,002
Trumbull	53,828	36,469	44,366	41,056	6,261
Tuscarawas	16,880	14,279	12,117	15,708	1,779
Union	4,377	7,464	3,038	7,576	421
Van Wert	5,689	8,344	4,070	7,866	741
Vinton	2,629	2,148	2,381	2,484	138
Warren	13,349	16,115	11,306	22,430	1,348
Washington	8,914	11,513	7,936	14,310	1,121
Wayne	13,087	16,976	12,129	18,962	2,313
Williams	4,920	7,596	4,015	9,146	872
Wood	16,926	19,331	14,139	23,315	4,156
Wyandot	4,043	5,661	2,757	5,786	407
Totals	**2,011,621**	**2,000,505**	**1,752,414**	**2,206,545**	**254,472**

Ohio Vote Since 1932

1932 (Pres.), Roosevelt, Dem., 1,301,695; Hoover, Rep., 1,227,679; Thomas, Soc., 64,094; Upshaw, Proh., 7,421; Foster, Com., 7,221; Reynolds, Soc. Labor, 1,968.

1936 (Pres.), Roosevelt, Dem., 1,747,122; Landon, Rep., 1,127,709; Lemke, Union, 132,212; Browder, Com., 5,251; Thomas, Soc., 117; Aiken, Soc. Labor, 14.

1940 (Pres.), Roosevelt, Dem., 1,733,139; Willkie, Rep., 1,586,773.

1944 (Pres.), Roosevelt, Dem., 1,570,763; Dewey, Rep., 1,582,293.

1948 (Pres.), Truman, Dem., 1,452,791; Dewey, Rep., 1,445,684; Wallace, Prog., 37,596.

1952 (Pres.), Eisenhower, Rep., 2,100,391; Stevenson, Dem.,

1,600,367.

1956 (Pres.), Eisenhower, Rep., 2,262,610; Stevenson, Dem., 1,439,655.

1960 (Pres.), Kennedy, Dem., 1,944,248; Nixon, Rep., 2,217,611.

1964 (Pres.), Johnson, Dem., 2,498,331; Goldwater, Rep., 1,470,865.

1968 (Pres.), Nixon, Rep., 1,791,014; Humphrey, Dem., 1,700,586; Wallace, 3d party, 467,495; Gregory, 372; Munn, Proh., 19; Blomen, Soc. Labor, 120; Halstead, Soc. Worker, 69; Mitchell, Com., 23.

1972 (Pres.), Nixon, Rep., 2,441,827; McGovern, Dem., 1,558,889; Fisher, Soc. Labor, 7,107; Hall, Com., 6,437; Schmitz, Amer., 80,067; Wallace, Ind., 460.

1976 (Pres.), Carter, Dem., 2,011,621; Ford, Rep., 2,000,505; McCarthy, Ind., 58,258; Maddox, Amer. Ind., 15,529; MacBride, Libertarian, 8,961; Hall, Com., 7,817; Camejo, Soc. Workers, 4,717; LaRouche, U.S. Labor, 4,335; scattered, 130.

1980 (Pres.), Reagan, Rep., 2,206,545; Carter, Dem., 1,752,414; Anderson, Ind., 254,472; Clark, Libertarian, 49,033; Commoner, Citizens, 8,564; Hall, Com., 4,729; Congress, Ind. 4,029; Griswold, Workers World, 3,790; Bubar, Statesman, 27.

Oklahoma

County	1976 Carter (D)	Ford (R)	1980 Carter (D)	Reagan (R)	Anderson (I)
Adair	3,183	3,013	2,761	3,429	107
Alfalfa	1,725	2,113	899	2,628	86
Atoka	3,276	1,098	2,505	1,613	66
Beaver	1,213	1,801	696	2,430	58
Beckham	4,530	2,351	3,298	3,637	123
Blaine	2,297	2,682	1,399	3,708	103
Bryan	7,410	2,848	6,410	3,980	129
Caddo	7,382	3,854	4,695	5,945	232
Canadian	7,288	9,766	4,889	15,272	642
Carter	8,319	6,668	6,509	9,262	258
Cherokee	6,006	4,443	5,215	5,594	362
Choctaw	4,269	1,821	3,507	2,394	73
Cimarron	962	872	373	1,404	23
Cleveland	20,054	22,098	14,536	31,178	3,910
Coal	1,774	769	1,442	926	47
Comanche	12,910	13,163	9,972	16,609	1000
Cotton	1,911	1,127	1,410	1,702	63
Craig	3,577	2,540	2,801	2,956	156
Creek	8,964	8,458	7,339	11,749	460
Custer	4,597	4,847	3,008	6,469	290
Delaware	4,924	3,642	4,244	5,302	177
Dewey	1,540	1,230	826	1,943	70
Ellis	1,256	1,429	561	1,908	54
Garfield	8,969	14,202	5,718	17,989	846
Garvin	6,797	3,905	5,033	5,520	210
Grady	7,155	4,686	5,330	8,131	351
Grant	1,853	1,685	927	2,411	84
Greer	2,113	1,164	1,492	1,535	48
Harmon	1,371	666	961	676	21
Harper	978	1,303	517	1,652	40
Haskell	3,388	1,401	2,874	2,024	65
Hughes	4,185	1,715	3,211	2,170	85
Jackson	4,914	3,189	4,031	4,327	144
Jefferson	2,303	956	1,812	1,440	55
Johnston	2,765	1,127	2,066	1,701	57
Kay	9,371	12,441	6,449	15,004	665
Kingfisher	2,372	3,443	1,282	4,962	122
Kiowa	3,403	1,971	2,372	2,636	88
Latimer	2,661	1,312	2,105	1,737	71
Le Flore	8,033	4,907	6,668	6,807	174
Lincoln	4,988	4,429	3,231	6,064	204
Logan	4,594	4,382	3,246	6,311	259
Love	1,923	846	1,578	1,449	31
McClain	4,048	2,444	2,990	4,284	185
McCurtain	7,560	3,423	5,953	5,189	149
McIntosh	4,145	1,822	3,654	2,925	118
Major	1,357	2,282	584	3,059	62
Marshall	2,939	1,358	2,157	1,961	52
Mayes	6,298	5,040	5,344	6,633	256
Murray	2,932	1,563	2,384	2,494	126
Muskogee	14,678	10,287	13,341	11,511	633
Noble	2,278	2,624	1,398	3,663	124
Nowata	2,195	2,077	1,694	2,640	75
Okfuskee	2,663	1,630	2,177	2,126	58
Oklahoma	87,185	119,120	58,765	139,538	9,190
Okmulgee	8,449	5,333	7,236	6,652	286
Osage	6,832	6,398	5,687	8,044	363
Ottawa	7,446	4,985	6,143	6,362	317
Pawnee	3,031	3,111	2,020	3,902	161
Payne	9,987	13,481	7,466	15,955	1,812
Pittsburg	10,743	4,807	8,292	7,062	339

	1976		1980		
	(D)	(R)	(D)	(R)	(I)
Pontotoc	7,466	4,895	5,942	6,232	335
Pottawatomie	11,255	9,090	8,526	12,466	625
Pushmataha	2,987	1,360	2,666	1,989	65
Roger Mills	1,346	873	877	1,221	50
Rogers	7,368	7,318	6,399	11,581	461
Seminole	5,874	4,237	4,726	5,067	224
Sequoyah	5,873	3,938	4,983	5,987	178
Stephens	9,795	7,099	7,191	10,199	310
Texas	2,591	3,919	1,451	5,503	93
Tillman	2,852	1,802	2,144	2,450	69
Tulsa	65,298	108,653	53,438	124,643	7,802
Wagoner	5,879	5,071	5,235	8,969	369
Washington	6,898	14,560	5,854	16,563	851
Washita	3,304	2,165	2,044	3,206	71
Woods	2,530	2,788	1,364	3,592	191
Woodward	2,807	3,782	1,703	5,318	175
Totals	**532,442**	**545,708**	**402,026**	**695,570**	**38,284**

Oklahoma Vote Since 1932

1932 (Pres.), Roosevelt, Dem., 516,468; Hoover, Rep., 188,165.

1936 (Pres.), Roosevelt, Dem., 501,069; Landon, Rep., 245,122; Thomas, Soc., 2,221; Colvin, Proh., 1,328.

1940 (Pres.), Roosevelt, Dem., 474,313; Willkie, Rep., 348,872; Babson, Proh., 3,027.

1944 (Pres.), Roosevelt, Dem., 401,549; Dewey, Rep., 319,424; Watson, Proh., 1,663.

1948 (Pres.), Truman, Dem., 452,782; Dewey, Rep., 268,817.

1952 (Pres.), Eisenhower, Rep., 518,045; Stevenson, Dem., 430,939.

1956 (Pres.), Eisenhower, Rep., 473,769; Stevenson, Dem., 385,581.

1960 (Pres.), Kennedy, Dem., 370,111; Nixon, Rep., 533,039.

1964 (Pres.), Johnson, Dem., 519,834; Goldwater, Rep. 412,665.

1968 (Pres.), Nixon, Rep., 449,697; Humphrey, Dem., 301,658; Wallace, 3d party, 191,731.

1972 (Pres.), Nixon, Rep. 759,025; McGovern, Dem., 247,147; Schmitz, Amer., 23,728.

1976 (Pres.), Carter, Dem., 532,442; Ford, Rep., 545,708; McCarthy, Ind., 14,101.

1980 (Pres.), Reagan, Rep., 695,570; Carter, Dem., 402,026; Anderson, Ind., 38,284; Clark, Libertarian, 13,828.

Oregon

	1976		1980		
	Carter	Ford	Carter	Reagan	Anderson
County	(D)	(R)	(D)	(R)	(I)
Baker	3,306	3,340	2,515	4,747	487
Benton	11,887	15,555	13,150	14,982	4,950
Clackamas	42,504	47,671	40,462	54,111	11,386
Clatsop	6,690	6,178	6,482	6,124	1,854
Columbia	8,005	5,226	7,124	6,623	1,158
Coos	14,168	9,481	11,817	13,041	2,428
Crook	2,536	2,093	2,162	3,113	435
Curry	3,227	2,962	2,656	4,910	652
Deschutes	9,480	9,054	9,641	15,186	2,909
Douglas	14,965	16,500	12,564	23,101	2,529
Gilliam	508	612	394	622	85
Grant	1,393	1,640	1,274	2,519	273
Harney	1,567	1,652	1,110	2,313	255
Hood River	3,114	3,210	2,924	3,450	530
Jackson	23,384	24,237	19,903	32,879	4,019
Jefferson	1,769	1,810	1,654	2,523	431
Josephine	9,061	10,726	7,116	16,827	1,401
Klamath	9,659	11,649	7,371	16,060	1,427
Lake	1,381	1,575	1,147	2,234	201
Lane	56,479	46,245	52,240	54,750	12,076
Lincoln	6,685	5,755	7,009	7,637	1,637
Linn	15,776	14,128	13,516	18,943	2,823
Malheur	3,507	5,682	2,937	7,705	472
Marion	33,781	35,497	32,134	42,191	8,755
Morrow	1,162	1,091	1,077	1,728	239
Multnomah	129,060	112,400	120,487	101,606	27,572
Polk	8,141	8,528	7,833	10,006	2,026
Sherman	491	567	389	677	62
Tillamook	4,456	4,033	4,521	4,123	931
Umatilla	7,985	9,345	7,382	12,950	1,531
Union	4,280	5,111	3,677	6,514	763
Wallowa	1,310	1,693	995	2,485	218
Wasco	4,560	4,258	4,336	4,703	819
Washington	34,847	52,376	37,915	57,165	13,076
Wheeler	402	355	282	442	62

	1976		1980		
Yamhill	8,881	9,885	8,694	12,054	1,919
Totals	**490,407**	**492,120**	**456,890**	**571,044**	**112,389**

Oregon Vote Since 1932

1932 (Pres.), Roosevelt, Dem., 213,871; Hoover, Rep., 136,019; Thomas, Soc., 15,450; Reynolds, Soc. Labor, 1,730; Foster, Com., 1,681.

1936 (Pres.), Roosevelt, Dem., 266,733; Landon, Rep., 122,706; Lemke, Union, 21,831; Thomas, Soc., 2,143; Aiken, Soc. Labor, 500; Browder, Com., 104; Colvin, Proh., 4.

1940 (Pres.), Roosevelt, Dem., 258,415; Willkie, Rep., 219,555; Aiken, Soc. Labor, 2,487; Thomas, Soc., 398; Browder, Com., 191; Babson, Proh., 154.

1944 (Pres.), Roosevelt, Dem., 248,635; Dewey, Rep., 225,365; Thomas, Soc., 3,785; Watson, Proh., 2,362.

1948 (Pres.), Truman, Dem., 243,147; Dewey, Rep., 260,904; Wallace, Prog., 14,978; Thomas, Soc., 5,051.

1952 (Pres.), Eisenhower, Rep., 420,815; Stevenson, Dem., 270,579; Hallinan, Ind., 3,665.

1956 (Pres.), Eisenhower, Rep., 406,393; Stevenson, Dem., 329,204.

1960 (Pres.), Kennedy, Dem., 367,402; Nixon, Rep., 408,060.

1964 (Pres.), Johnson, Dem., 501,017; Goldwater, Rep., 282,779; write-in, 2,509.

1968 (Pres.), Nixon, Rep., 408,433; Humphrey, Dem., 358,866; Wallace, 3d party, 49,683; write-in, McCarthy, 1,496; N. Rockefeller, Rep.; others, 1,075.

1972 (Pres.), Nixon, Rep., 486,686; McGovern, Dem., 392,760, Schmitz, Amer., 46,211; write-in, 2,289.

1976 (Pres.), Carter, Dem., 490,407; Ford, Rep., 492,120; McCarthy, Ind., 40,207; write-in, 7,142.

1980 (Pres.), Reagan, Rep., 571,044; Carter, Dem., 456,890; Anderson, Ind., 112,389; Clark, Libertarian, 25,838; Commoner, Citizens, 13,642; scattered, 1,713.

Pennsylvania

	1976		1980		
	Carter	Ford	Carter	Reagan	Anderson
County	(D)	(R)	(D)	(R)	(I)
Adams	8,771	12,133	7,266	13,760	1,139
Allegheny	328,343	303,127	297,464	271,850	38,710
Armstrong	15,179	13,378	12,718	12,955	1,153
Beaver	46,117	33,593	43,955	30,496	4,549
Bedford	6,652	9,355	4,950	10,930	416
Berks	50,994	54,452	36,449	60,576	8,863
Blair	18,397	28,290	15,014	28,931	2,011
Bradford	7,913	12,851	6,439	13,139	1,068
Bucks	79,838	85,628	59,120	100,536	18,107
Butler	22,611	26,366	19,711	28,821	3,453
Cambria	38,797	32,469	36,121	33,072	2,398
Cameron	1,319	1,616	1,112	1,795	92
Carbon	10,791	8,883	8,009	10,042	956
Centre	17,867	21,177	15,987	20,605	5,247
Chester	42,712	67,686	34,307	73,046	10,911
Clarion	6,585	8,360	5,472	8,812	678
Clearfield	13,714	13,626	11,647	15,299	944
Clinton	6,532	5,858	4,842	6,288	733
Columbia	12,051	11,508	9,449	12,426	1,197
Crawford	14,712	15,301	11,778	16,552	2,095
Cumberland	23,008	39,950	19,789	41,152	5,437
Dauphin	34,342	46,819	27,252	44,039	6,034
Delaware	117,252	148,679	88,314	143,282	20,907
Elk	6,713	6,159	5,898	7,175	472
Erie	55,385	49,641	45,946	48,918	6,349
Fayette	32,232	20,021	27,969	19,952	1,348
Forest	1,017	1,135	819	1,206	93
Franklin	14,643	20,009	12,061	22,716	1,724
Fulton	1,737	2,219	1,342	2,740	107
Greene	8,769	5,293	8,193	5,336	450
Huntingdon	5,410	7,843	5,094	8,140	567
Indiana	14,650	15,786	13,828	15,607	1,708
Jefferson	7,456	9,437	6,296	9,628	687
Juniata	3,105	3,991	2,696	4,139	280
Lackawanna	57,685	43,354	45,257	44,242	4,209
Lancaster	35,533	72,106	30,026	79,963	7,442
Lawrence	23,337	18,546	19,506	18,404	1,908
Lebanon	11,785	20,880	8,281	24,495	2,314
Lehigh	46,620	46,895	34,827	50,782	8,977
Luzerne	74,655	60,058	59,976	67,822	4,947
Lycoming	18,635	22,648	14,609	23,415	2,034
McKean	6,424	10,305	5,064	9,229	661
Mercer	25,041	22,469	19,716	22,372	3,247
Mifflin	6,210	7,698	5,226	7,541	578
Monroe	9,544	10,228	7,551	12,357	1,967

	1976		1980		
	(D)	(R)	(D)	(R)	(I)
Montgomery....	112,644	155,480	84,289	156,996	26,133
Montour	2,727	3,259	2,272	3,399	375
Northampton....	42,514	32,926	31,920	35,787	6,823
Northumberland..	18,939	19,283	13,750	20,608	1,515
Perry........	4,605	7,454	3,681	8,026	717
Philadelphia	494,579	239,000	421,253	244,108	42,967
Pike.........	2,775	4,241	2,132	5,249	452
Potter........	2,983	3,828	2,299	4,073	225
Schuykill	33,905	31,944	24,968	36,273	3,079
Snyder.......	3,097	6,557	2,418	7,634	451
Somerset......	13,452	15,960	11,695	17,729	815
Sullivan.......	1,347	1,584	1,074	1,676	130
Susquehanna ...	6,075	8,331	4,660	8,994	786
Tioga	5,795	8,417	4,273	8,770	664
Union	3,405	6,309	2,687	6,798	628
Venango	8,653	12,270	7,800	11,547	1,015
Warren	7,412	8,508	5,560	9,165	922
Washington	49,317	32,827	45,295	32,532	3,413
Wayne	4,244	7,811	3,375	8,468	496
Westmoreland...	74,271	59,172	68,627	63,140	5,985
Wyoming.....	3,628	5,705	2,766	5,919	384
York.........	41,281	56,912	33,406	61,098	5,779
Totals	2,328,677	2,205,604	1,937,540	2,261,872	292,921

Pennsylvania Vote Since 1932

1932 (Pres.), Roosevelt, Dem., 1,295,948; Hoover, Rep., 1,453,540; Thomas, Soc., 91,119; Upshaw, Proh., 11,319; Foster, Com., 5,658; Cox, Jobless, 725; Reynolds, Indust., 659.

1936 (Pres.), Roosevelt, Dem., 2,353,788; Landon, Rep., 1,690,300; Lemke, Royal Oak, 67,467; Thomas, Soc., 14,375; Colvin, Proh., 6,691; Browder, Com., 4,060; Aiken, Ind. Lab., 1,424.

1940 (Pres.), Roosevelt, Dem., 2,171,035; Willkie, Rep., 1,889,848; Thomas, Soc., 10,967; Browder, Com., 4,519; Aiken, Ind. Gov., 1,518.

1944 (Pres.), Roosevelt, Dem., 1,940,479; Dewey, Rep., 1,835,054; Thomas, Soc., 11,721; Watson, Proh., 5,750; Teichert, Ind. Gov., 1,789.

1948 (Pres.), Truman, Dem., 1,752,426; Dewey, Rep., 1,902,197; Wallace, Prog., 55,161; Thomas, Soc., 11,325; Watson, Proh., 10,338; Dobbs, Militant Workers, 2,133; Teichert, Ind. Gov., 1,461.

1952 (Pres.), Eisenhower, Rep., 2,415,789; Stevenson, Dem., 2,146,269; Hamblen, Proh., 8,771; Hallinan, Prog., 4,200; Hoopes, Soc., 2,684; Dobbs, Militant Workers, 1,502; Hass, Ind. Gov., 1,347; scattered, 155.

1956 (Pres.), Eisenhower, Rep., 2,585,252; Stevenson, Dem., 1,981,769; Hass, Soc. Labor, 7,447; Dobbs, Militant Workers, 2,035.

1960 (Pres.), Kennedy, Dem., 2,556,282; Nixon, Rep., 2,439,956; Hass, Soc. Labor, 7,185; Dobbs, Soc. Workers, 2,678; scattering, 440.

1964 (Pres.), Johnson, Dem., 3,130,954; Goldwater, Rep., 1,673,657; DeBerry, Soc. Workers, 10,456; Hass, Soc. Labor, 5,092; scattering, 2,531.

1968 (Pres.), Nixon, Rep., 2,090,017; Humphrey, Dem., 2,259,405; Wallace, 3d party, 378,582; Blomen, Soc. Labor, 4,977; Halstead, Soc. Workers, 4,862; Gregory, 7,821; others, 2,264.

1972 (Pres.), Nixon, Rep., 2,714,521; McGovern, Dem., 1,796,951; Schmitz, Amer., 70,593; Jenness, Soc. Workers, 4,639; Hall, Com., 2,686; others, 2,715.

1976 (Pres.), Carter, Dem., 2,328,677; Ford, Rep., 2,205,604; McCarthy, Ind., 50,584; Maddox, Constitution, 25,344; Camejo, Soc. Workers, 3,009; LaRouche, U.S. Labor, 2,744; Hall, Com., 1,891; others, 2,934.

1980 (Pres.), Reagan, Rep., 2,261,872; Carter, Dem., 1,937,540; Anderson, Ind., 292,921; Clark, Libertarian, 33,263; DeBerry, Soc. Workers, 20,291; Commoner, Consumer, 10,430; Hall, Com., 5,184.

Rhode Island

	1976		1980		
	Carter	Ford	Carter	Reagan	Anderson
County	(D)	(R)	(D)	(R)	(I)
Bristol........	11,228	10,131	9,651	6,508	3,358
Kent.........	35,855	34,131	31,350	28,331	10,793
Newport	17,768	15,155	13,904	14,555	5,575
Providence.....	144,805	103,976	126,808	86,467	32,994

Washington	17,980	17,856	16,429	16,932	7,099
Totals	227,636	181,249	198,342	154,793	59,819

Rhode Island Vote Since 1932

1932 (Pres.), Roosevelt, Dem., 146,604; Hoover, Rep., 115,266; Thomas, Soc., 3,138; Foster, Com., 546; Reynolds, Soc. Labor, 433; Upshaw, Proh., 183.

1936 (Pres.), Roosevelt, Dem., 165,238; Landon, Rep., 125,031; Lemke, Union, 19,569; Aiken, Soc. Labor, 929; Browder, Com., 411.

1940 (Pres.), Roosevelt, Dem., 182,182; Willkie, Rep., 138,653; Browder, Com., 239; Babson, Proh., 74.

1944 (Pres.), Roosevelt, Dem., 175,356; Dewey, Rep., 123,487; Watson, Proh., 433.

1948 (Pres.), Truman, Dem., 188,736; Dewey, Rep., 135,787; Wallace, Prog., 2,619; Thomas, Soc., 429; Teichert, Soc. Labor, 131.

1952 (Pres.), Eisenhower, Rep., 210,935; Stevenson, Dem., 203,293; Hallinan, Prog., 187; Hass, Soc. Labor, 83.

1956 (Pres.), Eisenhower, Rep., 225,819; Stevenson, Dem., 161,790.

1960 (Pres.), Kennedy, Dem., 258,032; Nixon, Rep., 147,502.

1964 (Pres.), Johnson, Dem., 315,463; Goldwater, Rep., 74,615.

1968 (Pres.), Nixon, Rep., 122,359; Humphrey, Dem., 246,518; Wallace, 3d party, 15,678; Halstead, Soc. Worker, 383.

1972 (Pres.), Nixon, Rep. 220,383; McGovern, Dem., 194,645; Jenness, Soc. Workers, 729.

1976 (Pres.), Carter, Dem., 227,636; Ford, Rep., 181,249; MacBride, Libertarian, 715; Camejo, Soc. Workers, 462; Hall, Com., 334; Levin, Soc. Labor, 188.

1980 (Pres.), Reagan, Rep., 154,793; Carter, Dem., 198,342; Anderson, Ind., 59,819; Clark, Libertarian, 2,458; Hall, Com., 218; McReynolds, Socialist, 170; DeBerry, Soc. Worker, 90; Griswold, Workers World, 77.

South Carolina

	1976		1980		
	Carter	Ford	Carter	Reagan	Anderson
County	(D)	(R)	(D)	(R)	(I)
Abbeville	4,700	1,791	4,049	2,261	111
Aiken	14,927	16,011	13,014	18,568	601
Allendale	2,634	1,064	2,775	1,181	18
Anderson......	19,002	9,496	18,796	15,666	474
Bamberg	3,330	1,849	3,294	2,098	18
Barnwell	4,083	2,569	3,399	3,228	64
Beaufort	6,049	5,935	7,415	8,620	513
Berkeley	9,741	6,981	9,850	12,790	17
Calhoun	2,055	1,382	2,043	1,767	31
Charleston	34,328	34,010	32,744	44,006	2,213
Cherokee......	7,765	3,931	6,891	5,378	86
Chester.......	5,200	2,982	5,145	3,104	87
Chesterfield	7,687	2,537	6,393	3,477	65
Clarendon	5,489	3,040	5,980	4,158	28
Colleton	5,134	3,324	5,745	4,719	58
Darlington	10,165	6,678	9,009	8,289	219
Dillon	5,089	2,527	4,518	3,384	59
Dorchester.....	8,046	6,695	7,237	10,893	140
Edgefield	3,216	1,878	3,465	2,415	30
Fairfield......	4,155	1,817	4,153	2,098	37
Florence	16,294	13,539	16,391	17,069	348
Georgetown	7,169	4,068	6,701	5,151	148
Greenville	35,923	39,099	32,135	46,168	1,600
Greenwood	9,976	5,974	9,283	7,287	230
Hampton	3,923	1,773	4,329	2,217	35
Horry	15,720	9,339	13,885	14,322	530
Jasper	2,903	1,221	3,316	1,617	33
Kershaw	6,211	6,126	5,103	6,652	145
Lancaster......	8,324	4,997	8,282	6,409	331
Laurens	7,440	5,300	7,368	6,034	129
Lee	3,869	2,357	4,816	2,952	18
Lexington	14,339	21,442	12,334	28,313	762
Marion	5,927	3,076	1,774	797	22
Marlboro	5,409	1,961	5,377	3,318	80
585	1,774	640	5,378	2,585	52
Newberry......	5,034	4,931	4,825	5,568	80
Oconee.......	8,447	3,805	7,677	5,652	188
Orangeburg	13,652	8,794	16,178	11,313	141
Pickens.......	8,505	8,029	7,789	9,574	402
Richland	36,855	32,727	33,298	35,843	1,808
Saluda	2,715	2,085	2,649	2,451	38
Spartanburg ...	27,925	20,456	27,238	28,820	933
Sumter	10,471	9,332	9,205	10,655	250
Union	6,363	3,463	6,274	4,035	93

	1976 (D)	(R)	1980 (D)	(R)	(I)
Williamsburg....	8,745	5,275	8,135	5,110	64
York.	14,099	9,843	12,075	11,265	539
Totals	**450,807**	**346,149**	**428,220**	**439,277**	**13,868**

	(D)	(R)	(D)	(R)	(I)
Lyman	831	892	486	1,256	106
Marshall	1,721	1,233	1,120	1,710	147
McCook	1,822	1,744	1,223	2,014	269
McPherson	693	1,662	287	2,056	54
Meade	2,478	3,096	1,721	5,349	342
Mellette	429	508	279	624	46
Miner	1,289	839	833	1,172	148
Minnehaha	22,068	23,286	20,008	26,256	4,658
Moody	1,942	1,475	1,364	1,807	279
Pennington	10,058	13,352	7,121	18,900	1,650
Perkins	1,262	1,298	595	1,931	93
Potter	908	1,136	436	1,633	81
Roberts	2,890	1,915	1,829	2,904	235
Sanborn	1,025	881	628	1,178	107
Shannon	756	301	1,132	438	91
Spink	2,650	2,003	1,572	2,915	294
Stanley	548	637	339	892	55
Sully	505	630	220	852	60
Todd	826	583	972	803	112
Tripp	1,822	1,980	947	2,669	130
Turner	1,906	2,694	1,369	3,343	281
Union	2,540	2,297	1,830	2,788	359
Walworth	1,516	2,187	753	2,675	139
Washabaugh	276	229			
Yankton	3,987	4,029	2,698	5,355	553
Ziebach	370	369	246	523	30
Totals	**147,068**	**151,505**	**103,855**	**198,343**	**21,431**

South Carolina Vote Since 1932

1932 (Pres.), Roosevelt, Dem., 102,347; Hoover, Rep., 1,978; Thomas, Soc., 82.

1936 (Pres.), Roosevelt, Dem., 113,791; Landon, Rep., Tolbert faction 953, Hambright faction 693, total, 1,646.

1940 (Pres.), Roosevelt, Dem., 95,470; Willkie, Rep., 1,727.

1944 (Pres.), Roosevelt, Dem., 90,601; Dewey, Rep., 4,547; Southern Democrats, 7,799; Watson, Proh., 365; Rep. Tolbert faction, 63.

1948 (Pres.), Thurmond, States' Rights, 102,607; Truman, Dem., 34,423; Dewey, Rep., 5,386; Wallace, Prog., 154; Thomas, Soc., 1.

1952 (Pres.), Eisenhower ran on two tickets. Under state law vote cast for two Eisenhower slates of electors could not be combined. Eisenhower, Ind., 158,289; Rep., 9,793; total, 168,082; Stevenson, Dem., 173,004; Hamblen, Proh., 1.

1956 (Pres.), Stevenson, Dem., 136,372; Byrd, Ind., 88,509; Eisenhower, Rep., 75,700; Andrews, Ind., 2.

1960 (Pres.), Kennedy, Dem., 198,129; Nixon, Rep., 188,558; write-in, 1.

1964 (Pres.), Johnson, Dem., 215,700; Goldwater, Rep., 309,048; write-ins: Nixon, 1, Wallace, 5; Powell, 1; Thurmond, 1.

1968 (Pres.), Nixon, Rep., 254,062; Humphrey, Dem., 197,486; Wallace, 3d party, 215,430.

1972 (Pres.), Nixon, Rep., 477,044; McGovern, Dem., 184,559, United Citizens, 2,265; Schmitz, Amer., 10,075; write-in, 17.

1976 (Pres.), Carter, Dem., 450,807; Ford, Rep., 346,149; Anderson, Amer., 2,996; Maddox, Amer. Ind., 1,950; write-in, 681.

1980 (Pres.), Reagan, Rep., 439,277; Carter, Dem., 428,220; Anderson, Ind., 13,868; Clark, Libertarian, 4,807; Rarick, Amer. Ind., 2,086.

South Dakota

County	1976 Carter (D)	Ford (R)	1980 Carter (D)	Reagan (R)	Anderson (I)
Aurora	1,269	831	709	1,251	125
Beadle	4,846	4,758	3,521	5,921	545
Bennett	481	610	350	919	42
Bon Homme	2,154	1,897	1,191	2,794	214
Brookings	4,685	5,278	3,934	5,727	1,169
Brown	8,888	7,609	6,050	10,550	1,143
Brule	1,534	1,175	925	1,674	153
Buffalo	240	194	147	272	26
Butte	1,366	2,055	843	2,850	150
Campbell	489	897	182	1,271	39
Chas. Mix	2,593	1,779	1,741	2,608	203
Clark	1,376	1,449	774	1,963	151
Clay	2,593	2,647	2,271	3,004	906
Codington	4,680	4,504	3,353	5,903	638
Corson	967	846	522	1,233	82
Custer	995	1,373	708	2,057	129
Davison	4,510	3,688	3,107	4,743	568
Day	2,610	1,617	1,720	2,507	259
Deuel	1,465	1,177	891	1,657	169
Dewey	706	820	600	1,045	109
Douglas	975	1,315	508	1,855	91
Edmunds	1,629	1,294	883	1,881	125
Fall River	1,537	2,046	982	2,831	184
Faulk	1,063	868	520	1,300	110
Grant	2,398	2,051	1,602	2,691	254
Gregory	1,858	1,475	883	2,293	121
Haakon	477	812	255	1,162	38
Hamlin	1,402	1,452	903	1,885	197
Hand	1,477	1,510	803	2,066	159
Hanson	1,005	693	598	1,015	93
Harding	459	470	205	727	28
Hughes	2,506	3,997	1,751	4,652	554
Hutchinson	2,062	2,822	1,145	3,789	228
Hyde	572	687	273	864	60
Jackson	313	532	354	929	50
Jerauld	845	821	595	1,018	103
Jones	374	515	189	689	37
Kingsbury	1,762	1,844	1,132	2,376	258
Lake	2,930	2,530	2,207	3,093	504
Lawrence	3,102	4,206	2,259	5,306	574
Lincoln	2,957	3,105	2,261	3,848	524

South Dakota Vote Since 1932

1932 (Pres.), Roosevelt, Dem., 183,515; Hoover, Rep., 99,212; Harvey, Lib., 3,333; Thomas, Soc., 1,551; Upshaw, Proh., 463; Foster, Com., 364.

1936 (Pres.), Roosevelt, Dem., 160,137; Landon, Rep., 125,977; Lemke, Union, 10,338.

1940 (Pres.), Roosevelt, Dem., 131,862; Willkie, Rep., 177,065.

1944 (Pres.), Roosevelt, Dem., 96,711; Dewey, Rep., 135,365.

1948 (Pres.), Truman, Dem., 117,653; Dewey, Rep., 129,651; Wallace, Prog., 2,801.

1952 (Pres.), Eisenhower, Rep., 203,857; Stevenson, Dem., 90,426.

1956 (Pres.), Eisenhower, Rep., 171,569; Stevenson, Dem., 122,288.

1960 (Pres.), Kennedy, Dem., 128,070; Nixon, Rep., 178,417.

1964 (Pres.), Johnson, Dem., 163,010; Goldwater, Rep., 130,108.

1968 (Pres.), Nixon, Rep., 149,841; Humphrey, Dem., 118,023; Wallace, 3d party, 13,400.

1972 (Pres.), Nixon, Rep., 166,476; McGovern, Dem., 139,945; Jenness, Soc. Workers, 994.

1976 (Pres.), Carter, Dem., 147,068; Ford, Rep., 151,505; MacBride, Libertarian, 1,619; Hall, Com., 318; Camejo, Soc. Workers, 168.

1980 (Pres.), Reagan, Rep., 198,343; Carter, Dem., 103,855; Anderson, Ind., 21,431; Clark, Libertarian, 3,824; Pulley, Soc. Workers, 250.

Tennessee

County	1976 Carter (D)	Ford (R)	1980 Carter (D)	Reagan (R)	Anderson (I)
Anderson	13,455	10,494	10,194	14,235	1,161
Bedford	7,228	3,023	5,987	3,377	159
Benton	4,088	1,678	3,811	2,281	71
Bledsoe	1,757	1,620	1,585	1,970	26
Blount	12,096	13,851	9,412	17,959	620
Bradley	8,776	9,136	7,638	11,869	316
Campbell	5,206	4,277	4,752	5,537	120
Cannon	2,463	908	2,351	1,403	41
Carroll	5,581	4,031	5,277	5,681	125
Carter	7,443	8,934	6,006	11,648	326
Cheatham	4,225	1,376	3,771	2,296	90
Chester	2,532	1,949	2,123	2,751	52
Claiborne	3,461	3,227	2,844	4,289	94
Clay	1,671	982	1,376	1,344	27
Cocke	3,141	5,004	2,139	6,802	139
Coffee	8,017	3,848	7,612	5,454	239
Crockett	2,963	1,694	2,422	2,117	27
Cumberland	4,543	4,119	3,775	6,354	227
Davidson	99,007	60,662	103,741	65,772	4,834
Decatur	2,432	1,637	2,139	2,095	45
De Kalb	3,222	1,443	2,948	1,841	48
Dickson	6,551	2,285	6,622	3,636	157
Dyer	5,937	4,391	5,713	5,475	158
Fayette	3,853	2,133	4,141	2,944	75
Fentress	1,953	1,767	1,543	2,493	49
Franklin	6,788	2,619	6,760	3,995	251
Gibson	10,356	5,563	9,829	6,792	227

	1976 (D)	1976 (R)	1980 (D)	1980 (R)	1980 (I)
Giles	5,225	1,952	4,653	2,757	85
Grainger	2,018	2,805	1,495	3,254	66
Greene	7,070	8,664	5,822	10,704	338
Grundy	2,850	850	2,837	1,139	33
Hamblen	7,504	6,989	5,890	9,741	336
Hamilton	45,348	47,969	41,913	57,575	2,087
Hancock	764	1,309	704	1,734	32
Hardeman	3,934	2,254	4,155	2,931	73
Hardin	3,438	3,362	3,164	4,152	76
Hawkins	5,931	6,407	5,283	7,836	310
Haywood	3,681	1,952	3,445	2,435	49
Henderson	3,366	4,152	2,702	5,108	78
Henry	7,162	2,585	6,601	4,299	200
Hickman	3,590	1,154	3,225	1,903	78
Houston	1,990	407	1,757	738	31
Humphreys	4,021	1,338	3,974	1,897	74
Jackson	2,959	591	2,480	995	27
Jefferson	3,995	5,459	3,180	6,944	201
Johnson	1,464	2,986	1,141	3,716	66
Knox	53,034	56,013	45,634	66,153	4,801
Lake	1,933	591	1,718	823	11
Lauderdale	4,747	2,105	4,318	2,818	73
Lawrence	7,140	4,967	6,082	6,532	212
Lewis	2,391	617	2,190	1,076	33
Lincoln	5,732	1,724	5,387	2,856	119
Loudon	4,683	4,458	3,699	6,382	235
McMinn	7,020	6,638	5,460	7,825	200
McNairy	4,293	3,388	3,801	4,603	76
Macon	1,951	2,063	1,947	2,925	65
Madison	12,989	11,364	12,986	13,667	363
Marion	4,615	2,965	4,623	3,902	93
Marshall	4,457	1,674	4,277	2,282	78
Maury	8,747	5,327	7,957	6,637	225
Meigs	1,254	975	999	1,278	31
Monroe	5,368	5,335	4,612	6,246	125
Montgomery	12,310	5,923	11,573	8,503	490
Moore	1,101	331	993	551	34
Morgan	2,953	1,949	2,094	2,823	70
Obion	7,204	2,986	5,766	5,397	138
Overton	3,897	1,115	3,343	1,869	38
Perry	1,660	520	1,401	783	32
Pickett	948	986	758	1,319	12
Polk	3,284	1,835	2,470	2,414	45
Putnam	8,485	4,079	8,084	6,235	342
Rhea	3,735	3,449	3,070	4,689	93
Roane	9,216	7,121	6,473	11,096	481
Robertson	7,547	2,505	7,381	3,560	127
Rutherford	14,854	7,921	15,213	11,208	703
Scott	2,260	2,432	1,724	3,014	63
Sequatchie	1,733	1,065	1,509	1,512	23
Sevier	3,993	7,608	3,450	10,576	338
Shelby	147,893	128,646	159,240	140,157	7,180
Smith	3,753	1,332	3,674	1,755	69
Stewart	2,442	510	2,274	985	42
Sullivan	23,353	22,087	22,341	25,963	1,874
Sumner	13,848	7,946	14,150	11,876	540
Tipton	5,667	3,329	4,934	4,339	109
Trousdale	1,385	332	1,674	629	30
Unicoi	2,526	3,211	1,880	3,828	97
Union	1,631	1,801	1,435	2,453	45
Van Buren	1,085	346	886	499	11
Warren	6,666	2,364	6,021	3,680	148
Washington	13,951	14,770	11,599	17,457	934
Wayne	1,891	2,597	1,633	3,418	78
Weakley	6,605	2,875	5,910	5,668	136
White	3,874	1,382	3,415	2,100	64
Williamson	8,183	7,880	8,815	11,597	551
Wilson	10,537	4,696	11,248	7,535	380
Totals	825,879	633,969	783,051	787,761	35,991

Tennessee Vote Since 1932

1932 (Pres.), Roosevelt, Dem., 259,817; Hoover, Rep., 126,806; Upshaw, Proh., 1,995; Thomas, Soc., 1,786; Foster, Com., 234.

1936 (Pres.), Roosevelt, Dem., 327,083; Landon, Rep., 146,516; Thomas, Soc., 685; Colvin, Proh., 632; Browder, Com., 319; Lemke, Union, 463.

1940 (Pres.), Roosevelt, Dem., 351,601; Willkie, Rep., 169,153; Babson, Proh., 1,606; Thomas, Soc., 463.

1944 (Pres.), Roosevelt, Dem., 308,707; Dewey, Rep., 200,311; Watson, Proh., 882; Thomas, Soc., 892.

1948 (Pres.), Truman, Dem., 270,402; Dewey, Rep., 202,914; Thurmond, States' Rights, 73,815; Wallace, Prog., 1,864; Thomas, Soc., 1,288.

1952 (Pres.), Eisenhower, Rep., 446,147; Stevenson, Dem., 443,710; Hamblen, Proh., 1,432; Hallinan, Prog., 885; MacArthur, Christian Nationalist, 379.

1956 (Pres.), Eisenhower, Rep., 462,288; Stevenson, Dem., 456,507; Andrews, Ind., 19,820; Holtwick, Proh., 789.

1960 (Pres.), Kennedy, Dem., 481,453; Nixon, Rep., 556,577; Faubus, States' Rights, 11,304; Decker, Proh., 2,458.

1964 (Pres.), Johnson, Dem. 635,047; Goldwater, Rep., 508,965; write-in, 34.

1968 (Pres.), Nixon, Rep., 472,592; Humphrey, Dem., 351,233; Wallace, 3d party, 424,792.

1972 (Pres.), Nixon, Rep., 813,147; McGovern, Dem., 357,293; Schmitz, Amer., 30,373; write-in, 369.

1976 (Pres.), Carter, Dem., 825,879; Ford, Rep., 633,969; Anderson, Amer., 5,769; McCarthy, Ind., 5,004; Maddox, Am. Ind., 2,303; MacBride, Libertarian, 1,375; Hall, Com., 547; LaRouche, U.S. Labor, 512; Bubar, Proh., 442; Miller, Ind., 316; write-in, 230.

1980 (Pres.), Reagan, Rep., 787,761; Carter, Dem., 783,051; Anderson, Ind., 35,991; Clark, Libertarian, 7,116; Commoner, Citizens, 1,112; Bubar, Statesman, 521; McReynolds, Socialist, 519; Hall, Com., 503; DeBerry, Soc. Worker, 490; Griswold, Workers World, 400; write-ins, 152.

Texas

County	1976 Carter (D)	1976 Ford (R)	1980 Carter (D)	1980 Reagan (R)	1980 Anderson (I)
Anderson	5,499	4,172	5,163	5,970	137
Andrews	1,777	2,127	1,155	2,800	39
Angelina	9,750	7,223	10,140	9,900	232
Aransas	2,136	1,985	1,800	3,081	134
Archer	1,577	966	1,444	1,804	30
Armstrong	513	506	333	709	9
Atascosa	4,565	2,415	3,980	4,364	93
Austin	2,313	2,686	1,893	3,734	87
Bailey	1,356	1,255	800	1,809	26
Bandera	1,183	1,554	894	2,373	64
Bastrop	4,788	2,383	4,716	3,768	205
Baylor	1,335	783	1,183	1,098	14
Bee	3,690	2,953	3,606	4,171	125
Bell	17,499	15,126	15,823	20,729	934
Bexar	146,581	121,176	137,729	159,578	9,467
Blanco	923	1,015	794	1,434	52
Borden	234	150	131	279	3
Bosque	2,954	1,912	2,431	2,908	62
Bowie	12,445	9,590	11,339	13,942	244
Brazoria	21,711	19,475	18,253	27,614	1,205
Brazos	10,628	15,685	9,856	17,798	1,453
Brewster	1,227	1,368	1,271	1,496	89
Briscoe	823	285	561	562	13
Brooks	2,782	641	2,488	780	43
Brown	5,577	4,483	4,867	6,515	102
Burleson	2,924	1,142	2,615	1,943	33
Burnet	3,816	2,777	3,711	4,033	132
Caldwell	3,647	2,235	3,155	2,879	112
Calhoun	3,642	2,377	3,034	3,312	130
Callahan	2,241	1,581	2,002	2,284	29
Cameron	25,310	16,448	23,200	22,041	801
Camp	2,146	1,133	2,052	1,531	19
Carson	1,542	1,269	1,006	1,888	26
Cass	5,134	3,712	5,578	4,993	60
Castro	2,033	1,007	1,199	1,955	44
Chambers	2,927	1,835	2,517	3,140	96
Cherokee	6,509	3,921	5,726	5,629	92
Childress	1,578	1,043	1,222	1,443	33
Clay	2,568	1,200	2,233	1,824	40
Cochran	1,031	701	513	1,064	23
Coke	844	517	838	708	10
Coleman	2,224	1,669	1,719	2,228	33
Collin	14,039	21,608	15,187	36,559	1,559
Collingsworth	1,169	629	798	1,020	18
Colorado	3,028	2,991	2,377	3,520	58
Comal	4,068	6,377	3,554	9,758	324
Comanche	3,414	2,527	2,550	1,977	40
Concho	715	474	702	700	8
Cooke	4,483	4,804	3,842	6,760	129
Coryell	4,710	4,140	4,097	5,494	228
Cottle	1,047	311	732	511	9
Crane	664	963	607	1,310	23
Crockett	804	802	595	885	10
Crosby	2,176	897	1,408	1,361	17
Culberson	407	373	423	541	7
Dallam	1,029	936	632	965	33
Dallas	196,303	263,081	190,459	306,682	14,271
Dawson	2,162	2,474	1,867	3,267	55
Deaf Smith	2,613	2,776	1,666	4,073	77
Delta	1,563	421	1,347	767	18
Denton	18,887	20,440	17,381	29,908	1,953
DeWitt	2,540	2,754	2,044	3,450	66
Dickens	1,222	343	912	554	13
Dimmit	1,721	890	2,102	1,173	25
Donley	1,095	704	751	1,106	22
Duval	4,267	661	3,706	1,012	28
Eastland	4,320	2,340	3,346	3,442	37
Ector	10,802	18,973	9,069	26,188	636
Edwards	258	412	237	575	11
Ellis	9,991	6,996	9,219	10,046	214
El Paso	45,477	42,697	40,062	53,276	5,096
Erath	4,821	2,925	4,156	3,981	92
Falls	4,277	2,261	3,328	2,606	51

	1976 (D)	1976 (R)	1980 (D)	1980 (R)	1980 (I)
Fannin	5,845	2,102	5,284	3,196	74
Fayette	3,428	3,030	2,590	4,104	77
Fisher	1,993	573	1,564	838	23
Floyd	1,991	1,402	1,477	2,043	24
Foard	706	240	617	349	7
Fort Bend	11,264	17,354	11,583	25,366	1,005
Franklin	1,636	758	1,487	1,105	14
Freestone	2,679	1,674	2,739	2,468	33
Frio	2,598	1,280	2,849	1,753	47
Gaines	1,880	1,643	1,182	2,390	46
Galveston	37,873	25,251	30,778	29,527	1,955
Garza	957	755	677	1,188	22
Gillespie	1,260	3,541	1,170	4,736	90
Glasscock	190	218	116	416	2
Goliad	875	846	1,081	1,170	22
Gonzales	3,219	1,789	2,896	2,931	61
Gray	3,872	6,010	2,786	7,187	103
Grayson	17,015	11,981	13,807	16,811	532
Gregg	9,827	17,582	10,219	23,399	311
Grimes	2,656	1,473	2,440	2,087	42
Guadalupe	6,054	6,766	5,049	9,901	407
Hale	5,580	5,390	3,610	7,277	123
Hall	1,633	671	1,057	1,141	13
Hamilton	1,981	1,176	1,526	1,683	30
Hansford	983	1,401	518	2,046	17
Hardeman	1,403	805	1,174	1,056	28
Hardin	6,558	4,046	7,358	6,087	200
Harris	321,897	357,336	274,061	416,655	22,917
Harrison	7,796	7,787	7,746	9,328	125
Hartley	774	811	470	1,248	28
Haskell	2,512	838	1,951	1,447	22
Hays	7,005	5,714	6,013	6,517	590
Hemphill	707	858	592	1,152	21
Henderson	8,245	4,658	8,199	7,903	134
Hidalgo	35,021	19,199	34,542	25,808	1,063
Hill	5,327	2,680	4,688	4,113	73
Hockley	3,949	3,137	2,447	4,599	90
Hood	3,181	1,857	3,001	3,755	109
Hopkins	4,992	2,556	4,344	3,834	93
Houston	3,179	2,229	4,181	2,889	47
Howard	6,984	4,899	4,451	6,658	158
Hudspeth	479	395	394	471	14
Hunt	8,543	6,676	8,773	9,283	327
Hutchinson	3,691	6,137	2,935	7,439	170
Irion	297	302	239	427	2
Jack	1,814	1,049	1,349	1,482	29
Jackson	2,524	1,884	1,826	2,540	66
Jasper	5,422	3,167	5,707	4,396	98
Jeff Davis	309	288	300	409	10
Jefferson	47,581	32,451	45,642	36,763	1,664
Jim Hogg	1,645	429	1,437	535	23
Jim Wells	7,961	3,547	7,267	4,606	102
Johnson	10,864	7,194	10,542	11,411	333
Jones	3,318	2,072	3,043	2,765	45
Karnes	2,996	1,675	2,284	2,719	52
Kaufman	6,302	3,867	6,266	5,852	110
Kendall	1,190	2,543	1,075	3,890	88
Kenedy	139	65	106	76	2
Kent	474	171	351	339	0
Kerr	3,767	6,021	3,387	9,090	259
Kimble	759	846	608	1,011	22
King	100	96	55	144	5
Kinney	516	318	472	543	23
Kleberg	5,803	3,771	5,125	4,608	231
Knox	1,498	551	1,163	783	17
Lamar	8,601	4,443	7,178	6,094	148
Lamb	3,374	2,413	2,132	3,723	51
Lampasas	2,376	1,563	1,979	2,323	56
LaSalle	1,294	677	1,442	773	19
Lavaca	3,458	2,466	2,678	3,254	54
Lee	1,937	1,348	1,581	1,803	59
Leon	2,085	1,161	2,190	1,821	19
Liberty	7,086	4,552	6,810	6,470	163
Limestone	3,825	2,045	3,403	2,835	45
Lipscomb	644	911	338	1,343	28
Live Oak	1,656	1,287	1,380	2,193	32
Llano	2,361	1,947	2,130	2,866	72
Loving	35	47	22	64	0
Lubbock	24,797	38,478	18,732	46,711	1,952
Lynn	1,575	1,166	1,236	1,603	28
Madison	1,885	1,062	1,583	1,389	32
Marion	1,860	1,291	2,015	1,666	28
Martin	907	698	605	1,093	15
Mason	814	805	630	966	17
Matagorda	4,971	3,679	4,585	5,545	146
Maverick	2,840	924	2,932	1,370	39
McCulloch	1,888	1,300	1,750	1,572	24
McLennan	30,091	25,370	26,305	31,968	964
McMullen	194	217	122	271	4
Medina	3,681	3,252	3,034	4,742	84
Menard	543	441	489	548	11
Midland	7,725	19,178	6,839	25,027	586
Milam	4,871	2,404	4,230	3,251	111
Mills	1,012	684	1,028	985	24
Mitchell	1,730	1,058	1,446	1,455	12
Montague	4,087	2,182	3,233	3,143	59
Montgomery	13,718	15,739	12,593	26,237	819
Moore	2,767	2,759	1,743	3,736	67
Morris	3,071	1,843	3,105	2,133	27
Motley	522	428	341	573	7
Nacogdoches	6,697	7,315	5,981	8,626	422
Navarro	6,995	4,012	6,988	5,400	126
Newton	3,468	1,011	3,284	1,379	24
Nolan	3,094	2,431	2,796	2,781	87
Nueces	52,755	32,797	43,424	40,586	2,045
Ochiltree	1,084	2,471	594	3,032	52
Oldham	554	354	290	557	9
Orange	15,177	9,147	14,928	12,389	395
Palo Pinto	5,170	2,684	4,244	4,068	98
Panola	3,731	3,218	3,637	4,022	58
Parker	8,186	4,692	7,336	8,505	189
Parmer	1,914	1,487	707	2,640	30
Pecos	1,971	2,234	1,602	2,723	37
Polk	4,384	2,529	4,213	3,771	80
Potter	11,917	13,819	9,633	16,327	545
Presidio	1,232	687	1,039	723	22
Rains	1,339	510	1,174	813	18
Randall	9,074	17,115	7,323	23,136	677
Reagan	563	666	414	917	14
Real	510	448	603	832	14
Red River	3,670	1,852	3,501	2,225	31
Reeves	2,613	1,711	2,138	2,315	52
Refugio	2,218	1,537	2,224	1,944	57
Roberts	202	350	150	482	4
Robertson	3,741	1,244	3,572	1,661	33
Rockwall	1,828	2,087	1,985	4,036	113
Runnels	2,068	2,203	1,648	2,532	36
Rusk	6,063	6,800	5,582	8,705	116
Sabine	2,391	904	1,983	1,387	15
San Augustine	1,817	1,047	1,674	1,397	14
San Jacinto	2,406	1,094	2,376	1,726	42
San Patricio	9,469	5,853	8,627	8,326	280
San Saba	1,408	582	1,405	948	23
Schleicher	468	516	444	672	6
Scurry	2,639	2,797	2,003	3,745	53
Shackelford	764	748	606	959	9
Shelby	4,680	2,695	4,215	3,500	71
Sherman	718	679	286	1,128	28
Smith	16,856	22,238	14,838	28,236	414
Somervell	1,054	332	1,015	792	21
Starr	4,646	664	4,782	1,389	50
Stephens	1,796	1,621	1,372	2,161	34
Sterling	174	202	218	364	2
Stonewall	812	252	719	488	6
Sutton	768	831	485	1,000	13
Swisher	2,811	753	1,854	1,450	50
Tarrant	122,287	124,433	121,068	173,466	7,818
Taylor	14,453	19,822	13,245	22,961	620
Terrell	321	317	260	411	14
Terry	2,859	2,113	1,945	3,178	45
Throckmorton	658	356	455	444	7
Titus	4,205	2,603	3,872	3,747	44
Tom Green	11,064	12,316	9,892	16,555	661
Travis	78,585	71,031	75,028	73,151	9,796
Trinity	2,100	1,042	2,510	1,503	32
Tyler	3,322	1,965	3,540	2,545	70
Upshur	4,902	3,272	4,894	4,836	78
Upton	686	869	485	1,169	13
Uvalde	2,299	3,103	2,402	3,887	62
Val Verde	4,603	3,476	4,116	5,055	145
Van Zandt	6,449	3,385	5,707	5,495	78
Victoria	7,326	9,594	7,382	13,392	347
Walker	5,105	4,974	4,869	5,657	274
Waller	2,828	1,992	3,329	3,019	76
Ward	2,046	2,123	1,405	2,912	50
Washington	2,635	3,820	2,518	4,821	95
Webb	10,362	4,222	11,856	5,421	242
Wharton	5,914	4,682	5,138	6,598	160
Wheeler	1,598	1,273	1,090	1,626	16
Wichita	22,017	19,024	17,657	22,884	847
Wilbarger	3,280	2,145	2,347	3,031	53
Willacy	2,984	1,542	3,047	1,995	38
Williamson	9,355	7,481	10,408	15,035	946
Wilson	3,973	1,926	3,097	3,443	73
Winkler	1,382	1,842	1,021	2,160	35
Wise	5,133	2,856	4,674	4,350	108
Wood	4,107	3,076	4,033	4,515	74
Yoakum	1,181	1,477	715	1,937	28
Young	3,473	2,652	2,740	4,153	84
Zapata	1,216	462	1,218	874	19
Zavala	1,822	735	2,621	831	69
Totals	**2,082,319**	**1,953,300**	**1,881,147**	**2,510,705**	**111,613**

Texas Vote Since 1932

1932 (Pres.), Roosevelt, Dem., 760,348; Hoover, Rep., 97,959; Thomas, Soc., 4,450; Harvey, Lib., 324; Foster, Com., 207; Jackson Party, 104.

1936 (Pres.), Roosevelt, Dem., 734,485; Landon, Rep., 103,874; Lemke, Union, 3,281; Thomas, Soc., 1,075; Colvin, Proh., 514; Browder, Com., 253.

1940 (Pres.), Roosevelt, Dem., 840,151; Willkie, Rep., 199,152; Babson, Proh., 925; Thomas, Soc., 728; Browder, Com., 212.

1944 (Pres.), Roosevelt, Dem., 821,605; Dewey, Rep., 191,425; Texas Regulars, 135,439; Watson, Proh., 1,017; Thomas, Soc., 594; America First, 250.

1948 (Pres.), Truman, Dem., 750,700; Dewey, Rep., 282,240; Thurmond, States' Rights, 106,909; Wallace, Prog., 3,764; Watson, Proh., 2,758; Thomas, Soc., 874.

1952 (Pres.), Eisenhower, Rep., 1,102,878; Stevenson, Dem., 969,228; Hamblen, Proh., 1,983; MacArthur, Christian Nationalist, 833; MacArthur, Constitution, 730; Hallinan, Prog., 294.

1956 (Pres.), Eisenhower, Rep., 1,080,619; Stevenson, Dem., 859,958; Andrews, Ind., 14,591.

1960 (Pres.), Kennedy, Dem., 1,167,932; Nixon, Rep., 1,121,699; Sullivan, Constitution, 18,169; Decker, Proh., 3,870; write-in, 15.

1964 (Pres.), Johnson, Dem., 1,663,185; Goldwater, Rep., 958,566; Lightburn, Constitution, 5,060.

1968 (Pres.), Nixon, Rep., 1,227,844; Humphrey, Dem., 1,266,804; Wallace, 3d party, 584,269; write-in, 489.

1972 (Pres.), Nixon, Rep., 2,298,896; McGovern, Dem., 1,154,289; Schmitz, Amer., 6,039; Jenness, Soc. Workers, 8,664; others, 3,393.

1976 (Pres.), Carter, Dem., 2,082,319; Ford, Rep., 1,953,300; McCarthy, Ind., 20,118; Anderson, Amer., 11,442; Camejo, Soc. Workers, 1,723; write-in, 2,982.

1980 (Pres.), Reagan, Rep., 2,510,705; Carter, Dem., 1,881,147; Anderson, Ind., 111,613; Clark, Libertarian, 37,643; write-in, 528.

Utah

County	1976 Carter (D)	1976 Ford (R)	1980 Carter (D)	1980 Reagan (R)	1980 Anderson (I)
Beaver	963	1,088	621	1,477	43
Box Elder	3,353	9,319	2,142	12,500	306
Cache	5,430	16,636	3,639	20,251	1,494
Carbon	5,157	3,360	4,317	4,320	309
Daggett	131	217	109	290	10
Davis	14,084	31,216	9,065	45,695	2,253
Duchesne	1,110	2,619	854	3,827	87
Emery	1,771	1,717	1,315	3,076	90
Garfield	539	1,163	375	1,578	50
Grand	931	1,781	703	2,362	205
Iron	1,700	4,757	1,242	6,207	240
Juab	1,091	1,290	720	1,872	51
Kane	330	1,094	256	1,492	59
Millard	1,224	2,484	795	3,620	72
Morgan	701	1,356	373	1,985	42
Piute	265	377	157	551	3
Rich	248	541	143	762	18
Salt Lake	86,659	144,100	58,472	169,411	19,547
San Juan	1,182	1,856	763	2,774	72
Sanpete	1,925	3,683	1,260	5,143	112
Sevier	1,564	3,686	1,112	5,614	117
Summit	1,282	2,316	1,184	3,330	480
Tooele	4,371	4,657	3,132	6,024	391
Uintah	1,342	4,017	1,049	6,045	155
Utah	18,327	49,328	12,166	71,859	1,264
Wasatch	1,092	1,940	994	2,799	113
Washington	1,893	5,944	1,678	10,181	185
Wayne	334	555	226	835	15
Weber	23,111	34,811	15,404	43,807	2,501
Totals	182,110	337,908	124,266	439,687	30,284

Utah Vote Since 1932

1932 (Pres.), Roosevelt, Dem., 116,750; Hoover, Rep., 84,795; Thomas, Soc., 4,087; Foster, Com., 947.

1936 (Pres.), Roosevelt, Dem., 150,246; Landon, Rep., 64,555; Lemke, Union, 1,121; Thomas, Soc., 432; Browder, Com., 280; Colvin, Proh., 43.

1940 (Pres.), Roosevelt, Dem., 154,277; Willkie, Rep., 93,151; Thomas, Soc., 200; Browder, Com., 191.

1944 (Pres.), Roosevelt, Dem., 150,088; Dewey, Rep., 97,891; Thomas, Soc., 340.

1948 (Pres.), Truman, Dem., 149,151; Dewey, Rep., 124,402; Wallace, Prog., 2,679; Dobbs, Soc. Workers, 73.

1952 (Pres.), Eisenhower, Rep., 194,190; Stevenson, Dem., 135,364.

1956 (Pres.), Eisenhower, Rep., 215,631; Stevenson, Dem., 118,364.

1960 (Pres.), Kennedy, Dem., 169,248; Nixon, Rep., 205,361; Dobbs, Soc. Workers, 100.

1964 (Pres.), Johnson, Dem., 219,628; Goldwater, Rep., 181,785.

1968 (Pres.), Nixon, Rep., 238,728; Humphrey, Dem., 156,665; Wallace, 3d party, 26,906; Halstead, Soc. Worker, 89; Peace and Freedom, 180.

1972 (Pres.), Nixon, Rep., 323,643; McGovern, Dem.,

126,284; Schmitz, Amer., 28,549.

1976 (Pres.), Carter, Dem., 182,110; Ford, Rep., 337,908; Anderson, Amer., 13,304; McCarthy, Ind., 3,907; Mac-Bride, Libertarian, 2,438; Maddox, Am. Ind., 1,162; Camejo, Soc. Workers, 268; Hall, Com., 121.

1980 (Pres.), Reagan, Rep., 439,687; Carter, Dem., 124,266; Anderson, Ind., 30,284; Clark, Libertarian, 7,226; Commoner, Citizens, 1,009; Greaves, American, 965; Rarick, Amer. Ind., 522; Hall, Com., 139; DeBerry, Soc. Worker, 124.

Vermont

County	1976 Carter (D)	1976 Ford (R)	1980 Carter (D)	1980 Reagan (R)	1980 Anderson (I)
Addison	4,164	5,726	4,351	5,216	1,751
Bennington	5,443	6,712	5,361	6,091	1,978
Caledonia	3,511	5,488	3,284	5,986	1,068
Chittenden	17,992	22,013	18,967	18,310	8,409
Essex	1,002	1,161	799	1,305	148
Franklin	5,610	6,190	5,914	5,998	1,350
Grand Isle	866	1,004	999	947	260
Lamoille	2,016	3,535	2,414	3,228	1,048
Orange	3,171	4,768	3,079	4,656	1,371
Orleans	3,561	4,075	3,671	4,473	865
Rutland	7,613	9,867	9,596	11,142	3,174
Washington	8,764	10,919	9,559	9,714	3,256
Windham	6,794	7,928	5,830	7,062	3,167
Windsor	8,282	11,001	8,067	10,470	3,915
Totals	78,789	100,387	81,891	94,598	31,760

Vermont Vote Since 1932

1932 (Pres.), Roosevelt, Dem., 56,266; Hoover, Rep., 78,984; Thomas, Soc., 1,533; Foster, Com., 195.

1936 (Pres.), Landon, Rep., 81,023; Roosevelt, Dem., 62,124; Browder, Com., 405.

1940 (Pres.), Roosevelt, Dem., 64,269; Willkie, Rep., 78,371; Browder, Com., 411.

1944 (Pres.), Roosevelt, Dem., 53,820; Dewey, Rep., 71,527.

1948 (Pres.), Truman, Dem., 45,557; Dewey, Rep., 75,926; Wallace, Prog., 1,279; Thomas, Soc., 585.

1952 (Pres.), Eisenhower, Rep., 109,717; Stevenson, Dem., 43,355; Hallinan, Prog., 282; Hoopes, Soc., 185.

1956 (Pres.), Eisenhower, Rep., 110,390; Stevenson, Dem., 42,549; scattered, 39.

1960 (Pres.), Kennedy, Dem., 69,186; Nixon, Rep., 98,131.

1964 (Pres.), Johnson, Dem., 107,674; Goldwater, Rep., 54,868.

1968 (Pres.), Nixon, Rep., 85,142; Humphrey, Dem., 70,255; Wallace, 3d party, 5,104; Halstead, Soc. Worker, 295; Gregory, New Party, 579.

1972 (Pres.), Nixon, Rep., 117,149; McGovern, Dem., 68,174; Spock, Liberty Union, 1,010; Jenness, Soc. Workers, 296; scattered, 318.

1976 (Pres.), Carter, Dem., 77,798; Carter, Ind. Vermonter, 991; Ford, Rep., 100,387; McCarthy, Ind., 4,001; Camejo, Soc. Workers, 430; LaRouche, U.S. Labor, 196; scattered, 99.

1980 (Pres.), Reagan, Rep., 94,598; Carter, Dem., 81,891; Anderson, Ind., 31,760; Commoner, Citizens, 2,316; Clark, Libertarian, 1,900; McReynolds, Liberty Union, 136; Hall, Com. 118; DeBerry, Soc. Worker, 75; scattering, 413.

Virginia

County	1976 Carter (D)	1976 Ford (R)	1980 Carter (D)	1980 Reagan (R)	1980 Anderson (I)
Accomack	4,807	4,494	4,872	5,371	292
Albemarle	7,310	9,084	7,293	10,424	1,435
Alleghany	2,462	1,756	2,411	2,185	116
Amelia	1,715	1,634	1,643	1,969	52
Amherst	3,675	3,956	3,476	5,088	208
Appomattox	1,702	1,964	1,492	2,548	85
Arlington	32,536	30,972	26,502	30,854	8,042
Augusta	5,626	8,452	5,202	11,011	539
Bath	1,029	888	999	921	70
Bedford	4,766	4,189	4,721	6,608	336
Bland	961	1,047	1,002	1,278	35
Botetourt	4,021	3,343	3,698	4,408	329
Brunswick	3,071	2,387	3,430	2,310	70
Buchanan	5,791	3,850	5,768	4,554	95
Buckingham	2,179	1,487	1,933	1,864	77
Campbell	4,354	7,442	4,473	9,592	396
Caroline	3,064	1,648	2,924	2,071	116
Carroll	4,010	4,820	3,437	5,905	183
Charles City	1,455	439	1,564	506	39

	1976		1980		
	(D)	(R)	(D)	(R)	(I)
Charlotte	2,312	2,023	2,108	2,322	59
Chesterfield	14,126	27,812	13,060	37,908	2,182
Clarke	1,276	1,440	1,156	1,876	177
Craig	1,103	546	946	768	41
Culpeper	2,892	3,659	2,519	4,312	231
Cumberland	1,302	1,284	1,355	1,515	51
Dickenson	4,583	3,471	4,177	3,687	77
Dinwiddie	3,873	2,413	3,475	3,369	107
Essex	1,306	1,380	1,280	1,581	76
Fairfax	92,037	110,424	73,734	137,620	24,605
Fauquier	4,002	4,715	4,119	6,782	548
Floyd	1,728	2,071	1,642	2,447	131
Fluvanna	1,415	1,296	1,424	1,605	108
Franklin	6,439	3,532	5,685	4,993	304
Frederick	3,389	5,162	2,948	7,293	455
Giles	3,779	2,731	3,627	2,978	211
Gloucester	3,156	3,025	3,138	4,261	354
Goochland	2,259	2,104	2,290	2,423	113
Grayson	3,146	3,021	2,875	3,494	106
Greene	895	1,095	925	1,702	105
Greensville	2,413	1,137	2,142	1,583	39
Halifax	4,352	4,045	4,528	5,088	125
Hanover	6,069	11,559	5,383	14,262	589
Henrico	21,729	45,405	21,023	50,505	2,956
Henry	9,680	5,612	8,800	8,258	355
Highland	493	629	487	751	25
Isle of Wight	4,145	2,718	3,951	3,526	197
James City	3,000	3,186	3,068	4,289	551
King George	1,513	1,383	1,318	1,784	185
King and Queen	1,111	778	1,128	949	43
King William	1,501	1,597	1,446	2,036	80
Lancaster	1,581	2,381	1,567	2,780	106
Lee	5,415	4,679	4,758	4,417	137
Loudoun	7,995	9,192	6,694	12,076	1,312
Louisa	2,857	2,151	2,809	2,633	160
Lunenburg	1,739	1,816	1,958	2,045	59
Madison	1,466	1,710	1,351	1,959	156
Mathews	1,309	1,908	1,300	2,204	148
Mecklenburg	4,076	4,423	3,790	4,853	142
Middlesex	1,312	1,608	1,395	1,810	90
Montgomery	7,539	7,971	7,455	8,222	1,400
Nelson	2,426	1,516	2,410	1,866	143
New Kent	1,338	1,259	1,204	1,739	68
Northampton	2,459	2,043	2,363	2,165	114
Northumberland	1,814	2,167	1,551	2,598	109
Nottoway	2,558	2,486	2,593	2,813	113
Orange	2,309	2,549	2,420	3,381	241
Page	3,401	3,780	2,607	4,297	161
Patrick	2,740	2,349	2,382	3,436	105
Pittsylvania	7,929	9,173	7,653	12,022	250
Powhatan	1,528	2,010	1,484	2,933	98
Prince Edward	2,448	2,734	2,553	2,774	137
Prince George	2,630	2,254	2,310	3,389	130
Prince William	15,215	15,446	12,787	23,061	2,676
Pulaski	5,546	4,764	5,769	5,747	343
Rappahannock	1,071	881	1,055	1,179	99
Richmond	864	1,391	854	1,567	49
Roanoke	13,120	13,587	12,114	17,182	1,286
Rockbridge	2,525	2,157	2,475	2,784	296
Rockingham	5,349	9,768	5,294	11,397	771
Russell	6,014	4,287	5,764	4,778	125
Scott	4,496	4,313	4,314	4,744	153
Shenandoah	3,364	6,296	3,137	7,517	385
Smyth	5,246	5,032	5,335	6,033	224
Southampton	3,399	2,366	3,347	2,997	163
Spotsylvania	4,210	3,210	4,039	5,385	464
Stafford	4,900	4,451	4,211	7,106	623
Surry	1,829	929	1,756	962	63
Sussex	2,497	1,360	2,447	1,664	86
Tazewell	7,565	5,565	7,003	7,021	225
Warren	3,221	2,985	2,597	3,861	297
Washington	6,547	6,865	6,390	8,402	382
Westmoreland	2,355	1,909	2,271	2,510	133
Wise	7,134	5,691	6,779	5,767	258
Wythe	3,578	4,231	3,677	4,758	164
York	4,736	5,603	4,532	6,744	723
Total	**489,208**	**540,351**	**445,151**	**665,012**	**63,068**
CITIES					
Alexandria	19,858	16,880	17,134	17,865	4,546
Bedford	1,122	1,043	1,149	1,145	75
Bristol	3,343	2,943	2,889	3,432	160
Buena Vista	993	771	1,031	942	59
Charlottesville	6,846	6,673	6,866	5,907	1,377
Chesapeake	17,651	12,851	17,155	17,888	1,189
Clifton Forge	993	770	1,012	716	68
Colonial Heights	2,409	4,291	1,692	5,012	219
Covington	1,820	1,173	1,813	1,187	101
Danville	6,425	10,235	6,138	10,665	296
Emporia	899	1,055	855	988	41
Fairfax	3,464	4,174	2,614	4,475	800
Falls Church	2,202	2,323	1,703	2,485	497
Franklin	1,116	1,127	1,324	1,045	62
Fredericksburg	2,550	2,527	2,174	2,502	245
Galax	1,218	1,128	1,061	1,188	31
Hampton	19,202	15,021	18,517	17,023	1,598
Harrisonburg	1,803	3,376	1,896	3,388	403
Hopewell	3,691	3,764	3,102	4,423	178
Lexington	945	1,027	963	956	129
Lynchburg	8,227	14,564	7,783	15,245	854

	1976		1980		
Manassas	1,646	1,992	1,565	3,009	318
Manassas Park	709	444	447	729	52
Martinsville	3,491	3,147	3,337	3,433	162
Newport News	23,058	20,914	22,066	22,423	2,068
Norfolk	39,295	28,099	35,118	27,506	3,333
Norton	811	577	762	572	42
Petersburg	7,852	5,041	7,931	5,001	254
Poquoson	1,140	1,461	877	2,338	158
Portsmouth	22,837	12,872	20,900	13,660	1,124
Radford	2,240	1,844	2,225	1,964	233
Richmond	44,687	37,176	47,975	34,629	3,502
Roanoke	20,696	14,738	18,139	15,164	1,350
Salem	4,404	4,196	4,091	4,862	359
South Boston	1,001	1,389	971	1,615	51
Staunton	2,951	4,681	2,658	4,819	311
Suffolk	9,246	6,066	9,064	7,179	360
Virginia Beach	25,824	34,593	24,895	47,936	4,830
Waynesboro	2,209	3,528	1,926	3,697	255
Williamsburg	1,468	1,654	1,199	1,344	340
Winchester	2,346	4,075	2,006	4,240	320
Total	**324,688**	**296,203**	**307,023**	**324,597**	**32,350**
Aggregate	**813,896**	**836,554**	**752,174**	**989,609**	**95,418**

Virginia Vote Since 1932

1932 (Pres.), Roosevelt, Dem., 203,979; Hoover, Rep., 89,637; Thomas, Soc., 2,382; Upshaw, Proh., 1,843; Foster, Com., 86; Cox, Ind. 15.

1936 (Pres.), Roosevelt, Dem., 234,980; Landon, Rep., 98,366; Colvin, Proh., 594; Thomas, Soc., 313; Lemke, Union, 233; Browder, Com., 98.

1940 (Pres.), Roosevelt, Dem., 235,961; Willkie, Rep., 109,363; Babson, Proh., 882; Thomas, Soc., 282; Browder, Com., 71; Aiken, Soc. Labor, 48.

1944 (Pres.), Roosevelt, Dem., 242,276; Dewey, Rep., 145,243; Watson, Proh., 459; Thomas, Soc., 417; Teichert, Soc. Labor, 90.

1948 (Pres.), Truman, Dem., 200,786; Dewey, Rep., 172,070; Thurmond, States' Rights, 43,393; Wallace, Prog., 2,047; Thomas, Soc., 726; Teichert, Soc. Labor, 234.

1952 (Pres.), Eisenhower, Rep., 349,037; Stevenson, Dem., 268,677; Hass, Soc. Labor, 1,160; Hoopes, Social Dem., 504; Hallinan, Prog., 311.

1956 (Pres.), Eisenhower, Rep., 386,459; Stevenson, Dem., 267,760; Andrews, States' Rights, 42,964; Hoopes, Soc. Dem., 444; Hass, Soc. Labor, 351.

1960 (Pres.), Kennedy, Dem., 362,327; Nixon, Rep., 404,521; Coiner, Conservative, 4,204; Hass, Soc. Labor, 397.

1964 (Pres.), Johnson, Dem., 558,038; Goldwater, Rep., 481,334; Hass, Soc. Labor, 2,895.

1968 (Pres.), Nixon, Rep., 590,319; Humphrey, Dem., 442,387; Wallace, 3d party, *320,272; Blomen, Soc. Labor, 4,671; Munn, Proh., 601; Gregory, Peace and Freedom, 1,680.

*10,561 votes for Wallace were omitted in the count.

1972 (Pres.), Nixon, Rep., 988,493; McGovern, Dem., 438,887; Schmitz, Amer., 19,721; Fisher, Soc. Labor, 9,918.

1976 (Pres.), Carter, Dem., 813,896; Ford, Rep., 836,554; Camejo, Soc. Workers, 17,802; Anderson, Amer., 16,686; LaRouche, U.S. Labor, 7,508; MacBride, Libertarian, 4,648.

1980 (Pres.), Reagan, Rep., 989,609; Carter, Dem., 752,174; Anderson, Ind., 95,418; Commoner, Citizens, 14,024; Clark, Libertarian, 12,821; DeBerry, Soc. Worker, 1,986.

Washington

	1976		1980		
County	Carter (D)	Ford (R)	Carter (D)	Reagan (R)	Anderson (I)
Adams	1,790	2,795	1,223	3,248	255
Asotin	2,898	2,752	2,724	3,275	539
Benton	11,306	22,135	11,561	28,728	3,301
Chelan	7,623	10,492	6,483	11,299	1,608
Clallam	8,268	9,132	8,029	11,515	2,172
Clark	31,080	27,938	30,584	33,223	6,445
Columbia	829	1,153	587	1,349	119
Cowlitz	14,958	12,531	12,560	13,154	2,336
Douglas	3,809	4,547	2,833	5,171	564
Ferry	814	776	802	1,108	127
Franklin	4,369	5,671	3,719	7,327	699
Garfield	616	892	509	875	122
Grant	7,777	9,192	5,673	11,152	1,091
Grays Harbor	13,478	9,464	11,290	10,226	3,267
Island	5,859	7,804	5,422	10,926	1,800
Jefferson	2,913	2,794	3,279	3,645	876

	1976		1980		
	(D)	(R)	(D)	(R)	(I)
King	248,743	279,382	235,046	272,567	76,119
Kitsap	25,701	23,124	20,893	29,420	8,525
Kittitas	4,858	4,765	4,075	5,359	1,066
Klickitat	2,890	2,573	2,596	3,113	423
Lewis	9,026	10,933	6,962	13,636	1,603
Lincoln	1,978	2,925	1,597	3,324	357
Mason	6,060	4,758	5,241	6,745	1,353
Okanogan	5,543	5,455	4,634	6,460	1,030
Pacific	4,278	2,781	3,727	3,132	945
Pend Oreille	1,533	1,516	1,399	2,136	221
Pierce	78,238	74,668	64,444	90,247	18,345
San Juan	1,467	1,998	1,666	2,363	728
Skagit	12,718	13,060	11,299	15,520	2,854
Skamania	1,436	1,102	1,373	1,416	218
Snohomish	55,623	55,375	52,003	66,153	14,465
Spokane	55,660	68,290	49,263	78,096	11,258
Stevens	3,824	4,719	3,584	7,094	601
Thurston	21,247	21,000	20,508	26,369	5,993
Wahkiakum	942	704	751	828	148
Walla Walla	7,012	10,883	5,825	11,223	1,591
Whatcom	19,739	20,007	18,430	21,371	4,906
Whitman	6,197	8,168	5,726	8,636	2,331
Yakima	24,223	29,478	21,873	33,815	4,672
Totals	717,323	777,732	650,193	865,244	185,073

Washington Vote Since 1932

1932 (Pres.), Roosevelt, Dem., 353,260; Hoover, Rep., 208,645; Harvey, Lib., 30,308; Thomas, Soc., 17,080; Foster, Com., 2,972; Upshaw, Proh., 1,540; Reynolds, Soc. Labor, 1,009.

1936 (Pres.), Roosevelt, Dem., 459,579; Landon, Rep., 206,892; Lemke, Union, 17,463; Thomas, Soc., 3,496; Browder, Com., 1,907; Pellsy, Christian, 1,598; Colvin, Proh., 1,041; Aiken, Soc. Labor, 362.

1940 (Pres.), Roosevelt, Dem., 462,145; Willkie, Rep., 322,123; Thomas, Soc., 4,586; Browder, Com., 2,626; Babson, Proh., 1,686; Aiken, Soc. Labor, 667.

1944 (Pres.), Roosevelt, Dem., 486,774; Dewey, Rep., 361,689; Thomas, Soc., 3,824; Watson, Proh., 2,396; Teichert, Soc. Labor, 1,645.

1948 (Pres.), Truman, Dem., 476,165; Dewey, Rep., 386,315; Wallace, Prog., 31,692; Watson, Proh., 6,117; Thomas, Soc., 3,534; Teichert, Soc. Labor, 1,133; Dobbs, Soc. Workers, 103.

1952 (Pres.), Eisenhower, Rep., 599,107; Stevenson, Dem., 492,845; MacArthur, Christian Nationalist, 7,290; Hallinan, Prog., 2,460; Hass, Soc. Labor, 633; Hoopes, Soc., 254; Dobbs, Soc. Workers, 103.

1956 (Pres.), Eisenhower, Rep., 620,430; Stevenson, Dem., 523,002; Hass, Soc. Labor, 7,457.

1960 (Pres.), Kennedy, Dem., 599,298; Nixon, Rep., 629,273; Hass, Soc. Labor, 10,895; Curtis, Constitution, 1,401; Dobbs, Soc. Workers, 705.

1964 (Pres.), Johnson, Dem., 779,699; Goldwater, Rep., 470,366; Hass, Soc. Labor, 7,772; DeBerry, Freedom Soc., 537.

1968 (Pres.), Nixon, Rep., 588,510; Humphrey, Dem., 616,037; Wallace, 3d party, 96,990; Blomen, Soc. Labor, 488; Cleaver, Peace and Freedom, 1,609; Halstead, Soc. Worker, 270; Mitchell, Free Ballot, 377.

1972 (Pres.), Nixon, Rep., 837,135; McGovern, Dem., 568,334; Schmitz, Amer., 58,906; Spock, Ind., 2,644; Fisher, Soc. Labor, 1,102; Jenness, Soc. Worker, 623; Hall, Com., 566; Hospers, Libertarian, 1,537.

1976 (Pres.), Carter, Dem., 717,323; Ford, Rep., 777,732; McCarthy, Ind., 36,986; Maddox, Amer. Ind., 8,585; Anderson, Amer., 5,046; MacBride, Libertarian, 5,042; Wright, People's, 1,124; Camejo, Soc. Workers, 905; LaRouche, U.S. Labor, 903; Hall, Com., 817; Levin, Soc. Labor, 713; Zeidler, Soc., 358.

1980 (Pres.), Reagan, Rep., 865,244; Carter, Dem., 650,193; Anderson, Ind., 185,073; Clark, Libertarian, 29,213; Commoner, Citizens, 9,403; DeBerry, Soc. Worker, 1,137; McReynolds, Socialist, 956; Hall, Com., 834; Griswold, Workers World, 341.

	1976 Carter (D)	Ford (R)	1980 Carter (D)	Reagan (R)	Anderson (I)
Braxton	4,012	1,912	3,795	2,403	173
Brooke	8,197	4,792	6,430	4,622	634
Cabell	20,811	19,644	17,732	19,482	2,146
Calhoun	2,173	1,283	1,717	1,606	92
Clay	2,662	1,282	2,185	1,452	102
Doddridge	1,245	1,804	1,043	1,888	120
Fayette	15,496	5,459	13,175	5,784	725
Gilmer	2,245	1,371	1,854	1,452	153
Grant	1,323	2,976	1,041	3,452	87
Greenbrier	8,291	5,862	7,128	6,221	546
Hampshire	3,104	2,097	2,522	2,879	157
Hancock	10,627	6,771	8,784	6,610	917
Hardy	2,993	1,858	2,050	2,329	99
Harrison	21,467	15,172	18,813	14,251	1,339
Jackson	5,334	5,360	4,120	6,041	352
Jefferson	5,166	3,864	4,679	4,454	572
Kanawha	53,602	42,213	42,829	42,604	5,838
Lewis	3,960	3,736	3,455	3,747	359
Lincoln	5,260	2,997	5,317	4,009	128
Logan	13,122	4,021	12,024	4,945	381
Marion	17,800	10,391	14,189	10,952	1,171
Marshall	8,641	6,705	7,832	7,252	725
Mason	6,769	5,205	5,683	6,040	312
McDowell	10,557	4,107	9,822	3,862	216
Mercer	14,761	10,791	11,804	12,273	563
Mineral	5,898	5,130	4,671	6,125	386
Mingo	8,655	3,010	9,328	3,716	208
Monongalia	16,163	11,827	12,883	11,972	2,745
Monroe	3,297	2,750	2,877	2,999	166
Morgan	1,929	2,369	1,594	2,833	172
Nicholas	6,235	3,462	5,265	3,885	322
Ohio	11,817	12,476	10,973	11,414	1,334
Pendleton	2,104	1,554	1,724	1,677	80
Pleasants	1,699	1,608	1,494	1,852	84
Pocahontas	2,330	1,740	2,170	2,011	150
Preston	5,595	5,719	4,317	5,828	515
Putnam	8,226	6,334	6,409	7,561	632
Raleigh	19,768	10,637	16,955	10,713	1,046
Randolph	7,265	4,822	5,937	4,374	518
Ritchie	1,941	2,874	1,450	3,081	128
Roane	3,519	3,216	2,498	3,219	184
Summers	3,943	2,254	3,114	2,456	201
Taylor	3,905	2,891	3,216	3,010	233
Tucker	2,323	1,396	1,862	1,798	153
Tyler	1,817	2,514	1,482	2,707	163
Upshur	3,513	4,789	2,867	4,751	415
Wayne	9,958	6,009	8,687	7,541	441
Webster	2,931	971	2,578	1,262	117
Wetzel	5,042	3,793	4,035	3,588	327
Wirt	1,182	1,031	1,058	1,176	44
Wood	17,025	18,348	13,622	20,080	1,536
Wyoming	7,775	4,286	6,624	4,537	299
Totals	435,864	314,726	367,462	334,206	31,691

West Virginia Vote Since 1932

1932 (Pres.), Roosevelt, Dem., 405,124; Hoover, Rep., 330,731; Thomas, Soc., 5,133; Upshaw, Proh., 2,342; Foster, Com., 444.

1936 (Pres.), Roosevelt, Dem., 502,582; Landon, Rep., 325,358; Colvin, Prog., 1,173; Thomas, Soc., 832.

1940 (Pres.), Roosevelt, Dem., 495,662; Willkie, Rep., 372,414.

1944 (Pres.), Roosevelt, Dem., 392,777; Dewey, Rep., 322,819.

1948 (Pres.), Truman, Dem., 429,188; Dewey, Rep., 316,251; Wallace, Prog., 3,311.

1952 (Pres.), Eisenhower, Rep., 419,970; Stevenson, Dem., 453,578.

1956 (Pres.), Eisenhower, Rep., 449,297; Stevenson, Dem., 381,534.

1960 (Pres.), Kennedy, Dem., 441,786; Nixon, Rep., 395,995.

1964 (Pres.), Johnson, Dem., 538,087; Goldwater, Rep., 253,953.

1968 (Pres.), Nixon, Rep., 307,555; Humphrey, Dem., 374,091; Wallace, 3d party, 72,560.

1972 (Pres.), Nixon, Rep., 484,964; McGovern, Dem., 277,435.

1976 (Pres.), Carter, Dem., 435,864; Ford, Rep., 314,726.

1980 (Pres.), Reagan, Rep., 334,206; Carter, Dem., 367,462; Anderson, Ind., 31,691; Clark, Libertarian, 4,356.

West Virginia

	1976 Carter (D)	Ford (R)	1980 Carter (D)	Reagan (R)	Anderson (I)
Barbour	3,647	3,235	3,451	3,311	292
Berkeley	8,216	8,935	6,783	9,955	625
Boone	8,528	3,072	7,515	4,164	268

Wisconsin

	1976 Carter (D)	Ford (R)	1980 Carter (D)	Reagan (R)	Anderson (I)
Adams	3,069	2,377	2,773	3,304	318
Ashland	4,688	3,045	4,469	3,262	685
Barron	8,678	7,393	8,654	8,791	883
Bayfield	3,885	2,624	3,705	3,278	554
Brown	33,572	36,571	29,796	47,067	4,680

	1976		1980		
	(D)	(R)	(D)	(R)	(I)
Buffalo	3,448	2,844	3,276	3,569	404
Burnett	3,720	2,573	3,200	3,027	393
Calumet	6,241	6,589	5,036	7,885	1,064
Chippewa	11,538	8,137	9,836	10,531	1,160
Clark	7,238	6,095	6,091	7,921	679
Columbia	9,457	10,075	8,715	10,478	1,373
Crawford	3,629	3,393	3,392	3,934	371
Dane	82,321	63,466	85,609	57,545	19,772
Dodge	13,643	17,335	11,966	19,435	1,709
Door	4,553	6,557	4,961	7,170	655
Douglas	13,478	6,999	11,703	7,258	1,728
Dunn	7,882	6,751	7,743	7,428	1,565
Eau Claire	18,263	16,388	17,602	17,304	3,486
Florence	965	922	943	1,187	86
Fond duLac	16,571	22,226	15,293	24,196	2,191
Forest	2,574	1,604	2,402	2,070	141
Grant	9,639	12,016	8,406	13,298	1,690
Green	5,832	7,085	5,336	7,714	947
Green Lake	3,411	5,020	2,851	5,868	368
Iowa	4,252	4,195	4,154	4,068	546
Iron	2,399	1,340	1,941	1,811	219
Jackson	3,735	3,406	3,629	4,327	413
Jefferson	12,577	15,528	11,335	16,174	1,925
Juneau	4,512	4,242	3,884	5,591	463
Kenosha	27,585	22,349	26,738	24,481	3,802
Kewaunee	4,607	4,447	3,706	5,577	318
La Crosse	16,674	24,188	17,304	23,427	3,652
La Fayette	3,839	4,131	3,598	4,421	450
Langlade	4,134	4,630	4,498	4,866	369
Lincoln	5,800	5,672	5,438	6,473	630
Manitowoc	19,819	16,039	17,330	18,591	2,014
Marathon	24,934	21,898	23,281	25,868	3,257
Marinette	8,482	8,591	7,718	10,444	683
Marquette	2,516	2,607	2,180	3,166	270
Menominee	766	324	544	302	57
Milwaukee	249,739	192,008	240,174	183,450	34,281
Monroe	6,465	7,242	6,521	8,136	780
Oconto	6,541	6,232	5,352	8,292	440
Oneida	7,216	7,347	7,008	8,602	832
Outagamie	23,079	28,363	21,284	31,500	5,735
Ozaukee	11,271	19,817	10,779	21,371	2,463
Pepin	1,955	1,312	1,673	1,541	183
Pierce	8,039	5,676	7,312	6,209	1,752
Polk	8,485	6,159	7,607	7,207	1,102
Portage	15,912	9,520	16,443	10,465	2,851
Price	4,028	3,204	3,595	4,028	394
Racine	36,740	37,088	33,565	39,683	5,167
Richland	3,634	4,466	3,413	4,601	413
Rock	28,048	28,325	24,740	30,960	4,408
Rusk	4,050	2,724	3,584	3,704	340
St. Croix	10,203	7,685	10,203	9,265	1,867
Sauk	9,204	9,577	8,456	9,992	1,405
Sawyer	3,055	2,720	3,065	3,548	323
Shawano	6,751	8,505	5,410	9,922	652
Sheboygan	24,226	22,332	20,974	23,036	3,859
Taylor	4,101	3,591	3,739	4,596	403
Trempealeau	6,218	5,341	5,390	5,992	558
Vernon	5,534	6,132	5,501	6,528	494
Vilas	3,209	4,929	3,293	6,034	421
Walworth	12,418	18,091	11,344	19,194	2,581
Washburn	3,503	2,787	3,172	3,193	355
Washington	14,422	18,798	12,944	23,213	2,654
Waukesha	47,487	70,418	46,612	81,059	9,778
Waupaca	6,857	10,849	6,401	12,568	1,072
Waushara	3,485	4,449	2,987	5,576	335
Winnebago	24,485	32,149	24,203	34,286	4,779
Wood	14,728	15,479	13,804	17,987	2,010
Totals	1,040,232	1,004,987	981,584	1,088,845	160,657

Wisconsin Vote Since 1932

1932 (Pres.), Roosevelt, Dem., 707,410; Hoover, Rep., 347,741; Thomas, Soc. 53,379; Foster, Com., 3,112; Upshaw Proh., 2,672; Reynolds, Soc. Labor, 494.

1936 (Pres.), Roosevelt, Dem., 802,984; Landon, Rep., 380,828; Lemke, Union, 60,297; Thomas, Soc., 10,626; Browder, Com., 2,197; Colvin, Proh., 1,071; Aiken, Soc. Labor, 557.

1940 (Pres.), Roosevelt, Dem., 704,821; Willkie, Rep., 679,260; Thomas, Soc., 15,071; Browder, Com., 2,394; Babson, Proh., 2,148; Aiken, Soc. Labor, 1,882.

1944 (Pres.), Roosevelt, Dem., 650,413; Dewey, Rep., 674,532; Thomas, Soc., 13,205; Teichert, Soc. Labor, 1,002.

1948 (Pres.), Truman, Dem., 647,310; Dewey, Rep., 590,959; Wallace, Prog., 25,282; Thomas, Soc., 12,547; Teichert, Soc. Labor, 399; Dobbs, Soc. Workers, 303.

1952 (Pres.), Eisenhower, Rep., 979,744; Stevenson, Dem., 622,175; Hallinan, Ind., 2,174; Dobbs, Ind., 1,350; Hoopes, Ind., 1,157; Hass, Ind., 770.

1956 (Pres.), Eisenhower, Rep., 954,844; Stevenson, Dem., 586,768; Andrews, Ind., 6,918; Hoopes, Soc., 754; Hass, Soc. Labor, 710; Dobbs, Soc. Workers, 564.

1960 (Pres.), Kennedy, Dem., 830,805; Nixon, Rep., 895,175; Dobbs, Soc. Workers, 1,792; Hass, Soc. Labor, 1,310.

1964 (Pres.), Johnson, Dem., 1,050,424; Goldwater, Rep., 638,495; DeBerry, Soc. Worker, 1,692; Hass, Soc. Labor, 1,204.

1968 (Pres.), Nixon, Rep., 809,997; Humphrey, Dem., 748,804; Wallace, 3d party, 127,835; Blomen, Soc. Labor, 1,338; Halstead, Soc. Worker, 1,222; scattered, 2,342.

1972 (Pres.) Nixon, Rep., 989,430; McGovern, Dem., 810,174; Schmitz, Amer., 47,525; Spock, Ind., 2,701; Fisher, Soc. Labor, 998; Hall, Com., 663; Reed, Ind., 506; scattered, 893.

1976 (Pres.), Carter, Dem., 1,040,232; Ford, Rep., 1,004,987; McCarthy, Ind., 34,943; Maddox, Amer. Ind., 8,552; Zeidler, Soc., 4,298; MacBride, Libertarian, 3,814; Camejo, Soc. Workers, 1,691; Wright, People's, 943; Hall, Com., 749; LaRouche, U.S. Lab., 738; Levin, Soc. Labor, 389; scattered, 2,839.

1980 (Pres.), Reagan, Rep., 1,088,845; Carter, Dem., 981,584; Anderson, Ind., 160,657; Clark, Libertarian, 29,135; Commoner, Citizens, 7,767; Rarick, Constitution, 1,519; McReynolds, Socialist, 808; Hall, Com., 772; Griswold, Workers World, 414; DeBerry, Soc. Workers, 383; scattering, 1,337.

Wyoming

	1976		1980		
County	Carter (D)	Ford (R)	Carter (D)	Reagan (R)	Anderson (I)
Albany	4,663	6,734	3,772	5,830	1,630
Big Horn	1,618	3,117	1,212	3,709	209
Campbell	1,620	3,306	1,400	5,613	460
Carbon	3,010	3,556	2,272	4,337	493
Converse	1,150	2,188	922	2,987	215
Crook	653	1,438	413	1,909	70
Fremont	4,423	6,584	3,307	9,077	731
Goshen	2,262	2,764	1,373	3,572	269
Hot Springs	958	1,413	745	1,602	136
Johnson	797	2,042	635	2,291	139
Laramie	12,040	14,061	9,512	15,361	2,225
Lincoln	1,555	2,464	1,063	3,412	120
Natrona	8,640	13,761	7,111	16,801	1,768
Niobrara	427	1,042	270	1,075	38
Park	2,656	5,878	1,718	6,435	496
Platte	1,593	1,844	1,555	2,642	262
Sheridan	3,206	5,382	3,034	5,649	641
Sublette	528	1,284	357	1,538	139
Sweetwater	5,575	4,937	4,728	6,265	826
Teton	1,204	2,667	1,361	3,004	664
Uinta	1,559	2,124	1,138	2,738	189
Washakie	1,168	2,361	945	2,634	230
Weston	934	1,770	584	2,219	122
Totals	62,239	92,717	49,427	110,700	12,072

Wyoming Vote Since 1932

1932 (Pres.), Roosevelt, Dem., 54,370; Hoover, Rep., 39,583; Thomas, Soc. 2,829; Foster, Com., 180.

1936 (Pres.), Roosevelt, Dem., 62,624; Landon, Rep., 38,739; Lemke, Union, 1,653; Thomas, Soc., 200; Browder, Com., 91; Colvin, Proh., 75.

1940 (Pres.), Roosevelt, Dem., 59,287; Willkie, Rep., 52,633; Babson, Proh., 172; Thomas, Soc., 148.

1944 (Pres.), Roosevelt, Dem., 49,419; Dewey, Rep., 51,921.

1948 (Pres.), Truman, Dem., 52,354; Dewey, Rep., 47,947; Wallace, Prog., 931; Thomas, Soc., 137; Teichert, Soc. Labor, 56.

1952 (Pres.), Eisenhower, Rep., 81,047; Stevenson, Dem., 47,934; Hamblen, Proh., 194; Hoopes, Soc., 40; Haas, Soc. Labor, 36.

1956 (Pres.), Eisenhower, Rep., 74,573; Stevenson, Dem., 49,554.

1960 (Pres.), Kennedy, Dem., 63,331; Nixon, Rep., 77,451.

1964 (Pres.), Johnson, Dem., 80,718; Goldwater, Rep., 61,998.

1968 (Pres.), Nixon, Rep., 70,927; Humphrey, Dem., 45,173; Wallace, 3d party, 11,105.

1972 (Pres.), Nixon, Rep., 100,464; McGovern, Dem., 44,358; Schmitz, Amer., 748.

1976 (Pres.), Carter, Dem., 62,239; Ford, Rep., 92,717; McCarthy, Ind., 624; Reagan, Ind., 307; Anderson, Amer., 290; MacBride, Libertarian, 89; Brown, Ind., 47; Maddox, Amer. Ind., 30.

1980 (Pres.), Reagan, Rep., 110,700; Carter, Dem., 49,427; Anderson, Ind., 12,072; Clark, Libertarian, 4,514.

Major Parties' Popular and Electoral Vote for President

(F) Federalist; (D) Democrat; (R) Republican; (DR) Democrat Republican; (NR) National Republican;
(W) Whig; (P) People's; (PR) Progressive; (SR) States' Rights; (LR) Liberal Republican; Asterisk (*)—See notes.

Year	President elected	Popular	Elec.	Losing candidate	Popular	Elec.
1789	George Washington (F)	Unknown	69	No opposition		
1792	George Washington (F)	Unknown	132	No opposition		
1796	John Adams (F)	Unknown	71	Thomas Jefferson (DR)	Unknown	68
1800*	Thomas Jefferson (DR)	Unknown	73	Aaron Burr (DR)	Unknown	73
1804	Thomas Jefferson (DR)	Unknown	162	Charles Pinckney (F)	Unknown	14
1808	James Madison (DR)	Unknown	122	Charles Pinckney (F)	Unknown	47
1812	James Madison (DR)	Unknown	128	DeWitt Clinton (F)	Unknown	89
1816	James Monroe (DR)	Unknown	183	Rufus King (F)	Unknown	34
1820	James Monroe (DR)	Unknown	231	John Quincy Adams (DR)	Unknown	1
1824*	John Quincy Adams (DR) . . .	105,321	84	Andrew Jackson (DR)	155,872	99
				Henry Clay (DR)	46,587	37
				William H. Crawford (DR)	44,282	41
1828	Andrew Jackson (D)	647,231	178	John Quincy Adams (NR)	509,097	83
1832	Andrew Jackson (D)	687,502	219	Henry Clay (NR)	530,189	49
1836	Martin Van Buren (D)	762,678	170	William H. Harrison (W)	548,007	73
1840	William H. Harrison (W)	1,275,017	234	Martin Van Buren (D)	1,128,702	60
1844	James K. Polk (D)	1,337,243	170	Henry Clay (W)	1,299,068	105
1848	Zachary Taylor (W)	1,360,101	163	Lewis Cass (D)	1,220,544	127
1852	Franklin Pierce (D)	1,601,474	254	Winfield Scott (W)	1,386,578	42
1856	James C. Buchanan (D)	1,927,995	174	John C. Fremont (R)	1,391,555	114
1860	Abraham Lincoln (R)	1,866,352	180	Stephen A. Douglas (D)	1,375,157	12
				John C. Breckinridge (D)	845,763	72
				John Bell (Const. Union)	589,581	39
1864	Abraham Lincoln (R)	2,216,067	212	George McClellan (D)	1,808,725	21
1868	Ulysses S. Grant (R)	3,015,071	214	Horatio Seymour (D)	2,709,615	80
1872*	Ulysses S. Grant (R)	3,597,070	286	Horace Greeley (D-LR)	2,834,079	. . .
1876*	Rutherford B. Hayes (R)	4,033,950	185	Samuel J. Tilden (D)	4,284,757	184
1880	James A. Garfield (R)	4,449,053	214	Winfield S. Hancock (D)	4,442,030	155
1884	Grover Cleveland (D)	4,911,017	219	James G. Blaine (R)	4,848,334	182
1888*	Benjamin Harrison (R)	5,444,337	233	Grover Cleveland (D)	5,540,050	168
1892	Grover Cleveland (D)	5,554,414	277	Benjamin Harrison (R)	5,190,802	145
				James Weaver (P)	1,027,329	22
1896	William McKinley (R)	7,035,638	271	William J. Bryan (D-P)	6,467,946	176
1900	William McKinley (R)	7,219,530	292	William J. Bryan (D)	6,358,071	155
1904	Theodore Roosevelt (R)	7,628,834	336	Alton B. Parker (D)	5,084,491	140
1908	William H. Taft (R)	7,679,006	321	William J. Bryan (D)	6,409,106	162
1912	Woodrow Wilson (D)	6,286,214	435	Theodore Roosevelt (PR)	4,216,020	88
				William H. Taft (R)	3,483,922	8
1916	Woodrow Wilson (D)	9,129,606	277	Charles E. Hughes (R)	8,538,221	254
1920	Warren G. Harding (R)	16,152,200	404	James M. Cox (D)	9,147,353	127
1924	Calvin Coolidge (R)	15,725,016	382	John W. Davis (D)	8,385,586	136
				Robert M. LaFollette (PR)	4,822,856	13
1928	Herbert Hoover (R)	21,392,190	444	Alfred E. Smith (D)	15,016,443	87
1932	Franklin D. Roosevelt (D) . . .	22,821,857	472	Herbert Hoover (R)	15,761,841	59
				Norman Thomas (Socialist) . . .	884,781	. . .
1936	Franklin D. Roosevelt (D) . . .	27,751,597	523	Alfred Landon (R)	16,679,583	8
1940	Franklin D. Roosevelt (D) . . .	27,243,466	449	Wendell Willkie (R)	22,304,755	82
1944	Franklin D. Roosevelt (D) . . .	25,602,505	432	Thomas E. Dewey (R)	22,006,278	99
1948	Harry S. Truman (D)	24,105,812	303	Thomas E. Dewey (R)	21,970,065	189
				J. Strom Thurmond (SR)	1,169,021	39
				Henry A. Wallace (PR)	1,157,172	. . .
1952	Dwight D. Eisenhower (R) . . .	33,936,252	442	Adlai E. Stevenson (D)	27,314,992	89
1956*	Dwight D. Eisenhower (R) . . .	35,585,316	457	Adlai E. Stevenson (D)	26,031,322	73
1960*	John F. Kennedy (D)	34,227,096	303	Richard M. Nixon (R)	34,108,546	219
1964	Lyndon B. Johnson (D)	43,126,506	486	Barry M. Goldwater (R)	27,176,799	52
1968	Richard M. Nixon (R)	31,785,480	301	Hubert H. Humphrey (D)	31,275,166	191
				George C. Wallace (3d party) .	9,906,473	46
1972*	Richard M. Nixon (R)	47,165,234	520	George S. McGovern (D)	29,170,774	17
1976*	Jimmy Carter (D)	40,828,929	297	Gerald R. Ford (R)	39,148,940	240
1980	Ronald Reagan (R)	43,899,248	489	Jimmy Carter (D)	35,481,435	49
				John B. Anderson (independent)	5,719,437	. . .

1800—Elected by House of Representatives because of tied electoral vote.
1824—Elected by House of Representatives. No candidate polled a majority. In 1824, the Democrat Republicans had become a loose coalition of competing political groups. By 1828, the supporters of Jackson were known as Democrats, and the J.Q. Adams and Henry Clay supporters as National Republicans.
1872—Greeley died Nov. 29, 1872. His electoral votes were split among 4 individuals.
1876—Fla., La., Ore., and S. C. election returns were disputed. Congress in joint session (Mar. 2, 1877) declared Hayes and Wheeler elected President and Vice-President.
1888—Cleveland had more votes than Harrison but the 233 electoral votes cast for Harrison against the 168 for Cleveland elected Harrison president.
1956—Democrats elected 74 electors but one from Alabama refused to vote for Stevenson.
1960—Sen. Harry F. Byrd (D-Va.) received 15 electoral votes.
1972—John Hospers of Cal. and Theodora Nathan of Ore. received one vote from an elector of Virginia.
1976—Ronald Reagan of Cal. received one vote from an elector of Washington.

Electoral Votes for President, 1964-80

The Constitution, Article 2, Section 1 (consult index), provides for the appointment of electors, the counting of the electoral ballots and the procedure in the event of a tie. (see *Electoral College*.)

State	1964 R.	1964 D.	1968 R.	1968 D.	1968 3d	1972 R.	1972 D.	1976 R.	1976 D.	1980 R.	1980 D.
Ala.	....	10	...	...	10	9	...	...	9	9	...
Alas.	3	3	...	...		3	...	3	...	3	...
Ariz.	5	...	5	...	...	6	...	6	...	6	...
Ark.	6	...	...	6	6	...	...	6	6	...	
Cal.	...	40	40	...	...	45	...	45	...	45	...
Col.	6	6	...	...		7	...	7	...	7	...
Conn.	...	8	...	8		8	...	8	...	8	...
Del.	3	3	...	...		3	...	...	3	3	...
D.C.	...	3	...	3		...	3	...	3	...	3
Fla.	14	14	...	...		17	...	17	17	...	
Ga.	12	...	...	12	12	...	12	...	12	...	
Ha.	4	...	4	...	...	4	...	...	4	4	...
Ida.	4	4	...	...		4	...	4	...	4	...
Ill.	...	26	26	...	...	26	...	26	...	26	...
Ind.	13	13	...	...		13	...	13	...	13	...
Ia.	9	9	...	...		8	...	8	...	8	...
Kan.	7	7	...	...		7	...	7	...	7	...
Ky.	9	9	...	...		9	...	...	9	9	...
La.	....	10	...	10	10	...	...	10	10	...	
Me.	4	...	4	...	...	4	...	4	...	4	...
Md.	...	10	...	10		...	10	...	10	10	
Mass.	...	14	...	14		...	14	14	...	14	...
Mich.	...	21	21	...		21	...	21	...	21	...
Minn.	...	10	...	10		...	10	...	10	10	
Miss.	7	...	...	...	7	7	...	...	7	7	...
Mo.	...	12	12	...		12	...	...	12	12	...
Mon.	4	4	...	...		4	...	4	...	4	...

State	1964 R.	1964 D.	1968 R.	1968 D.	1968 3d	1972 R.	1972 D.	1976 R.	1976 D.	1980 R.	1980 D.
Neb.	...	5	5	...	...	5	...	5	...	5	...
Nev.	3	3	...	...		3	...	3	...	3	...
N.H.	4	...	4	...	...	4	...	4	...	4	...
N.J.	...	17	17	...		17	...	17	...	17	...
N.M.	4	...	4	...	...	4	...	4	...	4	...
N.Y.	...	43	...	43		...	41	...	41	41	
N.C.	13	12	...	(1)	13	...	...	13	13	...	
N.D.	4	4	...	...		3	...	3	...	3	...
Oh.	...	26	26	...		25	...	...	25	25	...
Okla.	8	8	...	...		8	...	8	...	8	...
Ore.	6	6	...	...		6	...	6	...	6	...
Pa.	...	29	...	29		27	...	...	27	27	...
R.I.	...	4	...	4		...	4	...	4	...	4
S.C.	8	...	...	8	8	...	...	8	8	...	
S.D.	4	4	...	...		4	...	4	...	4	...
Tenn.	11	11	...	...		10	...	...	10	10	...
Tex.	...	25	...	25		26	...	...	26	26	...
Ut.	4	4	...	...		4	...	4	...	4	...
Vt.	3	3	...	...		3	...	3	...	3	...
Va.	12	12	...	11(2)	12	...	...	12	12	...	
Wash.	9	...	9	...	9	9	8(3)	...	9	...	
W.Va.	...	7	...	7		6	...	...	6	6	
Wis.	12	12	...	...		11	...	11	11	...	
Wy.	3	3	...	...		3	...	3	...	3	...
Totals	52	486	301	191	46	520	17	240	297	489	49
Plurality	...	434	110	(1)	...	503	(2)	...(3)	57	440	...

(1) In 1968 in N. C. one Rep. elector cast his ballot for Wallace. (2) In 1972 one Rep. elector in Va. cast his ballot for John Hospers. (3) In 1976 one Rep. elector in Wash. cast his ballot for Reagan.

Voter Turnout in Presidential Elections
Source: Committee for the Study of the American Electorate

National average of voting age population voting: 1960—62.8; 1964—61.9; 1968—60.6; 1972—55.5; 1976—54.3; 1980—53.9. The sharp drop in 1972 reflects the expansion of eligibility with the enfranchisement of 18 to 21 year olds.

	1980 Registered voters voting	1980 Voting age population voting	1976 Voting age population voting		1980 Registered voters voting	1980 Voting age population voting	1976 Voting age population voting		1980 Registered voters voting	1980 Voting age population voting	1976 Voting age population voting
Ala.	62.9%	49.7%	47.2%	Ky.	71.0	51.2	49.1	N.D.	n/a	64.3	67.2
Alas.	60.7	61.3	48.3	La.	76.8	55.7	49.8	Oh.	72.8	55.6	55.4
Ariz.	78.0	49.1	48.6	Me.	68.8	66.2	65	Okla.	78.2	54.0	55.6
Ark.	70.6	53.6	52.2	Md.	74.6	50.7	49.9	Ore.	75.3	61.9	62.1
Cal.	75.6	50.6	51.3	Mass.	80.1	58.7	61.6	Pa.	79.3	52.7	54.7
Col.	82.6	57.8	60.4	Mich.	68.3	59.6	58.7	R.I.	78.4	60.5	61.5
Conn.	82.4	60.6	62.4	Minn.	86.9	69.2	71.4	S.C.	71.9	42.9	41.7
Del.	78.4	56.1	58.4	Miss.	60.2	54.1	49.5	S.D.	73.2	67.6	63.8
D.C.	60.2	36.6	33.3	Mo.	73.9	58.8	57.7	Tenn.	75.3	50.5	49.6
Fla.	76.7	53.6	51.5	Mon.	73.3	65.0	63.7	Tex.	68.4	47.1	47.3
Ga.	n/a	43.6	43.3	Neb.	74.7	56.2	56.1	Ut.	77.3	67.1	69.4
Ha.	75.3	46.2	48.1	Nev.	81.7	45.7	47.5	Vt.	68.4	59.4	56.9
Ida.	75.3	69.0	61.6	N.H.	73.5	58.4	58.8	Va.	81.0	48.9	47.7
Ill.	76.2	59.0	60.6	N.J.	79.0	55.1	58.1	Wash.	79.8	62.3	61.1
Ind.	n/a	58.2	61.6	N.M.	69.9	52.5	54.6	W.Va.	71.0	54.4	58.1
Ia.	76.7	63.0	63.7	N.Y.	n/a	48.1	50.8	Wis.	n/a	66.0	65.9
Kan.	75.9	55.8	58.4	N.C.	66.9	45.8	44.1	Wy.	80.5	52.8	58.1

n/a—not available.

Party Nominees for President and Vice President
Asterisk (*) denotes winning ticket

Year	Democratic President	Democratic Vice President	Republican President	Republican Vice President
1916	Woodrow Wilson*	Thomas R. Marshall	Charles E. Hughes	Charles W. Fairbanks
1920	James M. Cox	Franklin D. Roosevelt	Warren G. Harding*	Calvin Coolidge
1924	John W. Davis	Charles W. Bryan	Calvin Coolidge*	Charles G. Dawes
1928	Alfred E. Smith	Joseph T. Robinson	Herbert Hoover*	Charles Curtis
1932	Franklin D. Roosevelt*	John N. Garner	Herbert Hoover	Charles Curtis
1936	Franklin D. Roosevelt*	John N. Garner	Alfred M. Landon	Frank Knox
1940	Franklin D. Roosevelt*	Henry A. Wallace	Wendell L. Willkie	Charles McNary
1944	Franklin D. Roosevelt*	Harry S. Truman	Thomas E. Dewey	John W. Bricker
1948	Harry S. Truman*	Alben W. Barkley	Thomas E. Dewey	Earl Warren
1952	Adlai E. Stevenson	John J. Sparkman	Dwight D. Eisenhower*	Richard M. Nixon
1956	Adlai E. Stevenson	Estes Kefauver	Dwight D. Eisenhower*	Richard M. Nixon
1960	John F. Kennedy*	Lyndon B. Johnson	Richard M. Nixon	Henry Cabot Lodge
1964	Lyndon B. Johnson*	Hubert H. Humphrey	Barry M. Goldwater	William E. Miller
1968	Hubert H. Humphrey	Edmund S. Muskie	Richard M. Nixon*	Spiro T. Agnew
1972	George S. McGovern	R. Sargent Shriver Jr.	Richard M. Nixon*	Spiro T. Agnew
1976	Jimmy Carter*	Walter F. Mondale	Gerald R. Ford	Robert J. Dole
1980	Jimmy Carter	Walter F. Mondale	Ronald Reagan*	George Bush

Presidents of the U.S.

No.	Name	Politics	Born	in	Inaug. at age	Died . . . . at age
1	George Washington	Fed.	1732, Feb. 22	Va.	1789 . . . 57	1799, Dec. 14 67
2	John Adams	Fed.	1735, Oct. 30	Mass.	1797 . . . 61	1826, July 4 90
3	Thomas Jefferson	Dem.-Rep.	1743, Apr. 13	Va.	1801 . . . 57	1826, July 4 83
4	James Madison	Dem.-Rep.	1751, Mar. 16	Va.	1809 . . . 57	1836, June 28 85
5	James Monroe	Dem.-Rep.	1758, Apr. 28	Va.	1817 . . . 58	1831, July 4 73
6	John Quincy Adams	Dem.-Rep.	1767, July 11	Mass.	1825 . . . 57	1848, Feb. 23 . . . 80
7	Andrew Jackson	Dem.	1767, Mar. 15	S.C.	1829 . . . 61	1845, June 8 78
8	Martin Van Buren	Dem.	1782, Dec. 5	N.Y.	1837 . . . 54	1862, July 24 79
9	William Henry Harrison	Whig	1773, Feb. 9	Va.	1841 . . . 68	1841, Apr. 4 68
10	John Tyler	Whig	1790, Mar. 29	Va.	1841 . . . 51	1862, Jan. 18 71
11	James Knox Polk	Dem.	1795, Nov. 2	N.C.	1845 . . . 49	1849, June 15 . . . 53
12	Zachary Taylor	Whig	1784, Nov. 24	Va.	1849 . . . 64	1850, July 9 65
13	Millard Fillmore	Whig	1800, Jan. 7	N.Y.	1850 . . . 50	1874, Mar. 8 74
14	Franklin Pierce	Dem.	1804, Nov. 23	N.H.	1853 . . . 48	1869, Oct. 8 64
15	James Buchanan	Dem.	1791, Apr. 23	Pa.	1857 . . . 65	1868, June 1 77
16	Abraham Lincoln	Rep.	1809, Feb. 12	Ky.	1861 . . . 52	1865, Apr. 15 . . . 56
17	Andrew Johnson	(1)	1808, Dec. 29	N.C.	1865 . . . 56	1875, July 31 66
18	Ulysses Simpson Grant	Rep.	1822, Apr. 27	Oh.	1869 . . . 46	1885, July 23 . . . 63
19	Rutherford Birchard Hayes	Rep.	1822, Oct. 4	Oh.	1877 . . . 54	1893, Jan. 17 70
20	James Abram Garfield	Rep.	1831, Nov. 19	Oh.	1881 . . . 49	1881, Sept. 19 . . . 49
21	Chester Alan Arthur	Rep.	1829, Oct. 5	Vt.	1881 . . . 50	1886, Nov. 18 . . . 57
22	Grover Cleveland	Dem.	1837, Mar. 18	N.J.	1885 . . . 47	1908, June 24 . . . 71
23	Benjamin Harrison	Rep.	1833, Aug. 20	Oh.	1889 . . . 55	1901, Mar. 13 . . . 67
24	Grover Cleveland	Dem.	1837, Mar. 18	N.J.	1893 . . . 55	1908, June 24 . . . 71
25	William McKinley	Rep.	1843, Jan. 29	Oh.	1897 . . . 54	1901, Sept. 14 . . . 58
26	Theodore Roosevelt	Rep.	1858, Oct. 27	N.Y.	1901 . . . 42	1919, Jan. 6 60
27	William Howard Taft	Rep.	1857, Sept. 15	Oh.	1909 . . . 51	1930, Mar. 8 72
28	Woodrow Wilson	Dem.	1856, Dec. 28	Va.	1913 . . . 56	1924, Feb. 3 67
29	Warren Gamaliel Harding	Rep.	1865, Nov. 2	Oh.	1921 . . . 55	1923, Aug. 2 57
30	Calvin Coolidge	Rep.	1872, July 4	Vt.	1923 . . . 51	1933, Jan. 5 60
31	Herbert Clark Hoover	Rep.	1874, Aug. 10	Ia.	1929 . . . 54	1964, Oct. 20 . . . 90
32	Franklin Delano Roosevelt	Dem.	1882, Jan. 30	N.Y.	1933 . . . 51	1945, Apr. 12 . . . 63
33	Harry S. Truman	Dem.	1884, May 8	Mo.	1945 . . . 60	1972, Dec. 26 . . . 88
34	Dwight David Eisenhower	Rep.	1890, Oct. 14	Tex.	1953 . . . 62	1969, Mar. 28 . . . 78
35	John Fitzgerald Kennedy	Dem.	1917, May 29	Mass.	1961 . . . 43	1963, Nov. 22 . . . 46
36	Lyndon Baines Johnson	Dem.	1908, Aug. 27	Tex.	1963 . . . 55	1973, Jan. 22 64
37	Richard Milhous Nixon (2)	Rep.	1913, Jan. 9	Cal.	1969 . . . 56	
38	Gerald Rudolph Ford	Rep.	1913, July 14	Neb.	1974 . . . 61	
39	Jimmy (James Earl) Carter	Dem.	1924, Oct. 1	Ga.	1977 . . . 52	

(1) Andrew Johnson — a Democrat, nominated vice president by Republicans and elected with Lincoln on National Union ticket. (2) Resigned Aug. 9, 1974.

Presidents, Vice Presidents, Congresses

President	Service	Vice President	Congress
1 George Washington	Apr. 30, 1789—Mar. 3, 1797	1 John Adams	1, 2, 3, 4
2 John Adams	Mar. 4, 1797—Mar. 3, 1801	2 Thomas Jefferson	5, 6
3 Thomas Jefferson	Mar. 4, 1801—Mar. 3, 1805	3 Aaron Burr	7, 8
"	Mar. 4, 1805—Mar. 3, 1809	4 George Clinton	9, 10
4 James Madison	Mar. 4, 1809—Mar. 3, 1813	"(1)	11, 12
"	Mar. 4, 1813—Mar. 3, 1817	5 Elbridge Gerry (2)	13, 14
5 James Monroe	Mar. 4, 1817—Mar. 3, 1825	6 Daniel D. Tompkins	15, 16, 17, 18
6 John Quincy Adams	Mar. 4, 1825—Mar. 3, 1829	7 John C. Calhoun	19, 20
7 Andrew Jackson	Mar. 4, 1829—Mar. 3, 1833	"(3)	21, 22
"	Mar. 4, 1833—Mar. 3, 1837	8 Martin Van Buren	23, 24
8 Martin Van Buren	Mar. 4, 1837—Mar. 3, 1841	9 Richard M. Johnson	25, 26
9 William Henry Harrison (4)	Mar. 4, 1841—Apr. 4, 1841	10 John Tyler	27
10 John Tyler	Apr. 6, 1841—Mar. 3, 1845		27, 28
11 James K. Polk	Mar. 4, 1845—Mar. 3, 1849	11 George M. Dallas	29, 30
12 Zachary Taylor (4)	Mar. 5, 1849—July 9, 1850	12 Millard Fillmore	31
13 Millard Fillmore	July 10, 1850—Mar. 3, 1853		31, 32
14 Franklin Pierce	Mar. 4, 1853—Mar. 3, 1857	13 William R. King (5)	33, 34
15 James Buchanan	Mar. 4, 1857—Mar. 3, 1861	14 John C. Breckinridge	35, 36
16 Abraham Lincoln	Mar. 4, 1861—Mar. 3, 1865	15 Hannibal Hamlin	37, 38
"	Mar. 4, 1865—Apr. 15, 1865	16 Andrew Johnson	39
17 Andrew Johnson	Apr. 15, 1865—Mar. 3, 1869		39, 40
18 Ulysses S. Grant	Mar. 4, 1869—Mar. 3, 1873	17 Schuyler Colfax	41, 42
"	Mar. 4, 1873—Mar. 3, 1877	18 Henry Wilson (6)	43, 44
19 Rutherford B. Hayes	Mar. 4, 1877—Mar. 3, 1881	19 William A. Wheeler	45, 46
20 James A. Garfield (4)	Mar. 4, 1881—Sept. 19, 1881	20 Chester A. Arthur	47
21 Chester A. Arthur	Sept. 20, 1881—Mar. 3, 1885		47, 48
22 Grover Cleveland (7)	Mar. 4, 1885—Mar. 3, 1889	21 Thomas A. Hendricks (8)	49, 50
23 Benjamin Harrison	Mar. 4, 1889—Mar. 3, 1893	22 Levi P. Morton	51, 52
24 Grover Cleveland (7)	Mar. 4, 1893—Mar. 3, 1897	23 Adlai E. Stevenson	53, 54
25 William McKinley	Mar. 4, 1897—Mar. 3, 1901	24 Garret A. Hobart (9)	55, 56
" (4)	Mar. 4, 1901—Sept. 14, 1901	25 Theodore Roosevelt	57
26 Theodore Roosevelt	Sept. 14, 1901—Mar. 3, 1905		57, 58
"	Mar. 4, 1905—Mar. 3, 1909	26 Charles W. Fairbanks	59, 60

President	Service	Vice President	Congress
27 William H. Taft	Mar. 4, 1909—Mar. 3, 1913	27 James S. Sherman (10).	61, 62
28 Woodrow Wilson	Mar. 4, 1913—Mar. 3, 1921	28 Thomas R. Marshall	63, 64, 65, 66
29 Warren G. Harding (4)	Mar. 4, 1921—Aug. 2, 1923	29 Calvin Coolidge	67
30 Calvin Coolidge	Aug. 3, 1923—Mar. 3, 1925		68
"	Mar. 4, 1925—Mar. 3, 1929	30 Charles G. Dawes	69, 70
31 Herbert C. Hoover	Mar. 4, 1929—Mar. 3, 1933	31 Charles Curtis	71, 72
32 Franklin D. Roosevelt (16)	Mar. 4, 1933—Jan. 20, 1941	32 John N. Garner	73, 74, 75, 76
"	Jan. 20, 1941—Jan. 20, 1945	33 Henry A. Wallace	77, 78
"(4)	Jan. 20, 1945—Apr. 12, 1945	34 Harry S. Truman	79
33 Harry S. Truman	Apr. 12, 1945—Jan. 20, 1949		79, 80
	Jan. 20, 1949—Jan. 20, 1953	35 Alben W. Barkley	81, 82
34 Dwight D. Eisenhower	Jan. 20, 1953—Jan. 20, 1961	36 Richard M. Nixon.	83, 84, 85, 86
35 John F. Kennedy (4)	Jan. 20, 1961—Nov. 22, 1963	37 Lyndon B. Johnson	87, 88
36 Lyndon B. Johnson	Nov. 22, 1963—Jan. 20, 1965		88
"	Jan. 20, 1965—Jan. 20, 1969	38 Hubert H. Humphrey	89, 90
37 Richard M. Nixon.	Jan. 20, 1969—Jan. 20, 1973	39 Spiro T. Agnew (11)	91, 92, 93
"(12)	Jan. 20, 1973—Aug. 9, 1974	40 Gerald R. Ford (13)	93
38 Gerald R. Ford (14).	Aug. 9, 1974—Jan. 20, 1977	41 Nelson A. Rockefeller (15)	93, 94
39 Jimmy (James Earl) Carter	Jan. 20, 1977—Jan. 20, 1981	42 Walter F. Mondale	95, 96
40 Ronald Reagan . . . . :	Jan. 20, 1981—	43 George Bush	97

(1) Died Apr. 20, 1812. (2) Died Nov. 23, 1814. (3) Resigned Dec. 28, 1832, to become U.S. Senator. (4) Died in office. (5) Died Apr. 18, 1853. (6) Died Nov. 22, 1875. (7) Terms not consecutive. (8) Died Nov. 25, 1885. (9) Died Nov. 21, 1899. (10) Died Oct. 30, 1912. (11) Resigned Oct. 10, 1973. (12) Resigned Aug. 9, 1974. (13) First non-elected vice president, chosen under 25th Amendment procedure. (14) First non-elected president. (15) 2d non-elected vice president. (16) First president to be inaugurated under 20th Amendment, Jan. 20, 1937.

Vice Presidents of the U.S.

The numerals given vice presidents do not coincide with those given presidents, because some presidents had none and some had more than one.

Name	Birthplace	Year	Home	Inaug.	Politics	Place of death	Year	Age
1 John Adams	Quincy, Mass.	1735	Mass. . .	1789	Fed. . . .	Quincy, Mass.	1826	90
2 Thomas Jefferson . . .	Shadwell, Va.	1743	Va. . .	1797	Dem.-Rep.	Monticello, Va.	1826	83
3 Aaron Burr	Newark, N.J.	1756	N.Y. . .	1801	Dem.-Rep.	Staten Island, N.Y. . . .	1836	80
4 George Clinton	Ulster Co., N.Y. . . .	1739	N.Y. . . .	1805	Dem.-Rep.	Washington, D.C. . . .	1812	73
5 Elbridge Gerry	Marblehead, Mass. . .	1744	Mass. . .	1813	Dem.-Rep.	Washington, D.C. . . .	1814	70
6 Daniel D. Tompkins . .	Scarsdale, N.Y. . .	1774	N.Y. . . .	1817	Dem.-Rep.	Staten Island, N.Y. . .	1825	51
7 John C. Calhoun (1) . .	Abbeville, S.C. . . .	1782	S.C. . . .	1825	Dem.-Rep.	Washington, D.C. . . .	1850	68
8 Martin Van Buren	Kinderhook, N.Y. . .	1782	N.Y. . .	1833	Dem. . . .	Kinderhook, N.Y. . . .	1862	79
9 Richard M. Johnson . .	Louisville, Ky.	1780	Ky. . . .	1837	Dem. . . .	Frankfort, Ky.	1850	70
10 John Tyler	Greenway, Va.	1790	Va. . .	1841	Whig . . .	Richmond, Va.	1862	71
11 George M. Dallas . . .	Philadelphia, Pa. . . .	1792	Pa. . .	1845	Dem. . . .	Philadelphia, Pa. . . .	1864	72
12 Millard Fillmore	Summerhill, N.Y. . . .	1800	N.Y. . .	1849	Whig . . .	Buffalo, N.Y.	1874	74
13 William R. King	Sampson Co., N.C.	1786	Ala. . . .	1853	Dem. . . .	Dallas Co., Ala.	1853	67
14 John C. Breckinridge . .	Lexington, Ky. . . .	1821	Ky. . . .	1857	Dem. . . .	Lexington, Ky.	1875	54
15 Hannibal Hamlin	Paris, Me.	1809	Me. . . .	1861	Rep. . . .	Bangor, Me.	1891	81
16 Andrew Johnson	Raleigh, N.C.	1808	Tenn. . .	1865	(2). . . .	Carter Co., Tenn. . . .	1875	66
17 Schuyler Colfax	New York, N.Y. . . .	1823	Ind. . .	1869	Rep. . . .	Mankato, Minn.	1885	62
18 Henry Wilson	Farmington, N.H. . . .	1812	Mass. . .	1873	Rep. . . .	Washington, D.C. . . .	1875	63
19 William A. Wheeler. . . .	Malone, N.Y.	1819	N.Y. . . .	1877	Rep. . . .	Malone, N.Y.	1887	68
20 Chester A. Arthur . . .	Fairfield, Vt.	1829	N.Y. . . .	1881	Rep. . . .	New York, N.Y.	1886	56
21 Thomas A. Hendricks . .	Muskingum Co., Oh. .	1819	Ind. . . .	1885	Dem. . . .	Indianapolis, Ind. . . .	1885	66
22 Levi P. Morton	Shoreham, Vt.	1824	N.Y. . . .	1889	Rep. . . .	Rhinebeck, N.Y.	1920	96
23 Adlai E. Stevenson (3). .	Christian Co., Ky. . .	1835	Ill. . . .	1893	Dem. . . .	Chicago, Ill.	1914	78
24 Garret A. Hobart	Long Branch, N.J. . .	1844	N.J. . .	1897	Rep. . . .	Paterson, N.J.	1899	55
25 Theodore Roosevelt . .	New York, N.Y. . . .	1858	N.Y. . . .	1901	Rep. . . .	Oyster Bay, N.Y. . . .	1919	60
26 Charles W. Fairbanks . .	Unionville Centre, Oh.	1852	Ind. . . .	1905	Rep. . . .	Indianapolis, Ind. . . .	1918	66
27 James S. Sherman . .	Utica, N.Y.	1855	N.Y. . . .	1909	Rep. . . .	Utica, N.Y.	1912	57
28 Thomas R. Marshall . . .	N. Manchester, Ind. .	1854	Ind. . .	1913	Dem. . . .	Washington, D.C. . . .	1925	71
29 Calvin Coolidge	Plymouth, Vt.	1872	Mass. . .	1921	Rep. . . .	Northampton, Mass. . .	1933	60
30 Charles G. Dawes . . .	Marietta, Oh.	1865	Ill. . . .	1925	Rep. . . .	Evanston, Ill.	1951	85
31 Charles Curtis	Topeka, Kan.	1860	Kan. . .	1929	Rep. . . .	Washington, D.C. . . .	1936	76
32 John Nance Garner . . .	Red River Co., Tex. .	1868	Tex. . .	1933	Dem. . . .	Uvalde, Tex.	1967	98
33 Henry Agard Wallace . .	Adair County, Ia. . . .	1888	Iowa	1941	Dem. . . .	Danbury, Conn.	1965	77
34 Harry S. Truman	Lamar, Mo.	1884	Mo. . .	1945	Dem. . . .	Kansas City, Mo. . . .	1972	88
35 Alben W. Barkley	Graves County, Ky. . .	1877	Ky. . . .	1949	Dem. . . .	Lexington, Va.	1956	78
36 Richard M. Nixon.	Yorba Linda, Cal. . .	1913	Cal. . . .	1953	Rep.			
37 Lyndon B. Johnson . . .	Johnson City, Tex. . .	1908	Tex. . . .	1961	Dem. . . .	San Antonio, Tex. . . .	1973	64
38 Hubert H. Humphrey . . .	Wallace, S.D.	1911	Minn. . .	1965	Dem. . . .	Waverly, Minn.	1978	66
39 Spiro T. Agnew	Baltimore, Md.	1918	Md. . .	1969	Rep.			
40 Gerald R. Ford	Omaha, Neb.	1913	Mich. . .	1973	Rep.			
41 Nelson A. Rockefeller . .	Bar Harbor, Me. . . .	1908	N.Y. . . .	1974	Rep. . . .	New York, N.Y.	1979	70
42 Walter F. Mondale	Ceylon, Minn.	1928	Minn. . .	1977	Dem.			
43 George Bush	Milton, Mass.	1924	Tex. . .	1981	Rep.			

(1) John C. Calhoun resigned Dec. 28, 1832, having been elected to the Senate to fill a vacancy. (2) Andrew Johnson — Democrat nominated by Republicans and elected with Lincoln on the National Union Ticket. (3) Adlai E. Stevenson, 23 vice president, was grandfather of Democratic candidate for president, 1952 and 1956.

The Continental Congress: Meetings, Presidents

Meeting places	Dates of meetings	Congress presidents	Date elected
Philadelphia	Sept. 5 to Oct. 26, 1774	Peyton Randolph, Va. (1)	Sept. 5, 1774
"	"	Henry Middleton, S.C.	Oct. 22, 1774
Philadelphia	May 10, 1775 to Dec. 12, 1776	Peyton Randolph, Va.	May 10, 1775
		John Hancock, Mass.	May 24, 1775
Baltimore	Dec. 20, 1776 to Mar. 4, 1777	"	
Philadelphia	Mar. 5 to Sept. 18, 1777		
Lancaster, Pa.	Sept. 27, 1777 (one day)		
York, Pa.	Sept. 30, 1777 to June 27, 1778	Henry Laurens, S.C.	Nov. 1, 1777(4)
Philadelphia	July 2, 1778 to June 21, 1783	John Jay, N.Y.	Dec. 10, 1778
		Samuel Huntington, Conn..	Sept. 28, 1779
"	"	Thomas McKean, Del..	July 10, 1781
"	"	John Hanson, Md. (2)	Nov. 5, 1781
"	"	Elias Boudinot, N.J..	Nov. 4, 1782
Princeton, N.J.	June 30 to Nov. 4, 1783	Thomas Mifflin, Pa..	Nov. 3, 1783
Annapolis, Md.	Nov. 26, 1783 to June 3, 1784		
Trenton, N.J.	Nov. 1 to Dec. 24, 1784	Richard Henry Lee, Va.	Nov. 30, 1784
New York City	Jan. 11 to Nov. 4, 1785		
"	Nov. 7, 1785 to Nov. 3, 1786	John Hancock, Mass. (3)	Nov. 23, 1785
		Nathaniel Gorman, Mass.	June 6, 1786
"	Nov. 6, 1786 to Oct. 30, 1787	Arthur St. Clair, Pa.	Feb. 2, 1787
"	Nov. 5, 1787 to Oct. 21, 1788	Cyrus Griffin, Va..	Jan. 22, 1788
"	Nov. 3, 1788 to Mar. 2, 1789	"	

(1) Resigned Oct. 22, 1774. (2) Titled "President of the United States in Congress Assembled," John Hanson is considered by some to be the first U.S. President as he was the first to serve under the Articles of Confederation. He was, however, little more than presiding officer of the Congress, which retained full executive power. He could be considered the head of government, but not head of state. (3) Resigned May 29, 1786, without serving, because of illness. (4) Articles of Confederation agreed upon, Nov. 15, 1777; last ratification from Maryland, Mar. 1, 1781.

Cabinets of the U. S.

Secretaries of State

The Department of Foreign Affairs was created by act of Congress July 27, 1789, and the name changed to Department of State on Sept. 15.

President	Secretary	Home	Apptd.	President	Secretary	Home	Apptd.
Washington	Thomas Jefferson.	Va.	1789	Cleveland . . .	"	"	1885
"	Edmund Randolph	"	1794	"	Thomas F. Bayard	Del. . . .	1885
"	Timothy Pickering	Pa.	1795	Harrison, B. . .	"	"	1889
Adams, J. . . .	"	"	1797	"	James G. Blaine.	Me.	1889
"	John Marshall	Va.	1800	"	John W. Foster	Ind.	1892
Jefferson	James Madison	"	1801	Cleveland . .	Walter Q. Gresham. . . .	Ill.	1893
Madison	Robert Smith	Md. . .	1809	"	Richard Olney.	Mass. . .	1895
"	James Monroe	Va. . . .	1811	McKinley	"	"	1897
Monroe	John Quincy Adams . .	Mass. . .	1817	"	John Sherman	Oh. . . .	1897
Adams, J.Q. . .	Henry Clay	Ky. . . .	1825	"	William R. Day.	"	1898
Jackson	Martin Van Buren	N.Y. . . .	1829	"	John Hay.	D.C. . . .	1898
"	Edward Livingston	La. . . .	1831	Roosevelt, T.. .	"	"	1901
"	Louis McLane	Del. . . .	1833	"	Elihu Root	N.Y. . . .	1905
"	John Forsyth	Ga. . . .	1834	"	Robert Bacon	"	1909
Van Buren . . .	"	"	1837	Taft	"	"	1909
Harrison, W.H.	Daniel Webster	Mass. . .	1841	"	Philander C. Knox	Pa. . . .	1909
Tyler	"	"	1841	Wilson	"	"	1913
"	Abel P. Upshur	Va. . . .	1843	"	William J. Bryan	Neb. . . .	1913
"	John C. Calhoun	S.C. . . .	1844	"	Robert Lansing	N.Y. . . .	1915
Polk.	"	"	1845	"	Bainbridge Colby	"	1920
"	James Buchanan	Pa. . . .	1845	Harding	Charles E. Hughes	"	1921
Taylor.	"	"	1849	Coolidge	"	"	1923
"	John M. Clayton.	Del. . . .	1849	"	Frank B. Kellogg	Minn. . .	1925
Fillmore.	"	"	1850	Hoover	"	"	1929
"	Daniel Webster	Mass. . .	1850	"	Henry L. Stimson	N.Y. . . .	1929
"	Edward Everett	"	1852	Roosevelt, F.D.	Cordell Hull	Tenn. . .	1933
Pierce.	William L. Marcy	N.Y. . .	1853	"	E.R. Stettinius Jr.	Va. . . .	1944
Buchanan . . .	"	"	1857	Truman.	"	"	1945
"	Lewis Cass	Mich. . .	1857	"	James F. Byrnes	S.C. . . .	1945
"	Jeremiah S. Black . . .	Pa. . . .	1860	"	George C. Marshall. . . .	Pa. . . .	1947
Lincoln	"	"	1861	"	Dean G. Acheson	Conn. . .	1949
"	William H. Seward	N.Y. . . .	1861	Eisenhower . .	John Foster Dulles	N.Y. . . .	1953
Johnson, A. . .	"	"	1865	"	Christian A. Herter	Mass. . .	1959
Grant	Elihu B. Washburne. . . .	Ill.	1869	Kennedy	Dean Rusk	N.Y. . . .	1961
"	Hamilton Fish	N.Y. . . .	1869	Johnson, L.B.	"	"	1963
Hayes.	"	"	1877	Nixon	William P. Rogers	N.Y. . . .	1969
"	William M. Evarts	"	1877	"	Henry A. Kissinger	D.C. . . .	1973
Garfield.	"	"	1881	Ford.	"	"	1974
"	James G. Blaine	Me. . . .	1881	Carter.	Cyrus R. Vance	N.Y. . . .	1977
Arthur.	"	"	1881	"	Edmund S. Muskie	Me. . . .	1980
"	F.T. Frelinghuysen	N.J. . . .	1881	Reagan.	Alexander M. Haig Jr. . . .	Conn. . .	1981

Secretaries of the Treasury

The Treasury Department was organized by act of Congress Sept. 2, 1789.

President	Secretary	Home	Apptd.	President	Secretary	Home	Apptd.
Washington	Alexander Hamilton	N.Y.	1789	Arthur	Charles J. Folger	N.Y.	1881
"	Oliver Wolcott	Conn.	1795	"	Walter Q. Gresham	Ind.	1884
Adams, J.	"	"	1797	"	Hugh McCulloch	"	1884
"	Samuel Dexter	Mass.	1801	Cleveland	Daniel Manning	N.Y.	1885
Jefferson	"	"	1801	Cleveland	Charles S. Fairchild	"	1887
"	Albert Gallatin	Pa.	1801	Harrison, B.	William Windom	Minn.	1889
Madison	"	Pa	1809	"	Charles Foster	Oh.	1891
"	George W. Campbell	Tenn.	1814	Cleveland	John G. Carlisle	Ky.	1893
"	Alexander J. Dallas	Pa.	1814	McKinley	Lyman J. Gage	Ill.	1897
"	William H. Crawford	Ga.	1816	Roosevelt, T.	"	"	1901
Monroe	"	"	1817	"	Leslie M. Shaw	Ia.	1902
Adams, J.Q.	Richard Rush	Pa.	1825	"	George B. Cortelyou	N.Y.	1907
Jackson	Samuel D. Ingham	Pa.	1829	Taft	Franklin MacVeagh	Ill.	1909
"	Louis McLane	Del.	1831	Wilson	William G. McAdoo	N.Y.	1913
"	William J. Duane	Pa.	1833	"	Carter Glass	Va.	1918
"	Roger B. Taney	Md.	1833	"	David F. Houston	Mo.	1920
"	Levi Woodbury	N.H.	1834	Harding	Andrew W. Mellon	Pa.	1921
Van Buren	"	"	1837	Coolidge	"	"	1923
Harrison, W.H.	Thomas Ewing	Oh.	1841	Hoover	"	"	1929
Tyler	"	"	1841	"	Ogden L. Mills	N.Y.	1932
"	Walter Forward	Pa.	1841	Roosevelt, F.D.	William H. Woodin	"	1933
"	John C. Spencer	N.Y.	1843	"	Henry Morgenthau, Jr.	"	1934
Tyler	George M. Bibb	Ky.	1844	Truman	Fred M. Vinson	Ky.	1945
Polk	Robert J. Walker	Miss.	1845	"	John W. Snyder	Mo.	1946
Taylor	William M. Meredith	Pa.	1849	Eisenhower	George M. Humphrey	Oh.	1953
Fillmore	Thomas Corwin	Oh.	1850	"	Robert B. Anderson	Conn.	1957
Pierce	James Guthrie	Ky.	1853	Kennedy	C. Douglas Dillon	N.J.	1961
Buchanan	Howell Cobb	Ga.	1857	Johnson, L.B.	"	"	1963
"	Phillip F. Thomas	Md.	1860	"	Henry H. Fowler	Va.	1965
"	John A. Dix	N.Y.	1861	"	Joseph W. Barr	Ind.	1968
Lincoln	Salmon P. Chase	Oh.	1861	Nixon	David M. Kennedy	Ill.	1969
"	William P. Fessenden	Me.	1864	"	John B. Connally	Tex.	1971
"	Hugh McCulloch	Ind.	1865	"	George P. Shultz	Ill.	1972
Johnson, A.	"	"	1865	"	William E. Simon	N.J.	1974
Grant	George S. Boutwell	Mass.	1869	Ford	"	"	1974
"	William A. Richardson	Mass.	1873	Carter	W. Michael Blumenthal	Mich.	1977
"	Benjamin H. Bristow	Ky.	1874	"	G. William Miller	R.I.	1979
"	Lot M. Morrill	Me.	1876	Reagan	Donald T. Regan	N.Y.	1981
Hayes	John Sherman	Oh.	1877				
Garfield	William Windom	Minn.	1881				

Secretaries of Defense

The Department of Defense, originally designated the National Military Establishment, was created Sept. 18, 1947. It is headed by the secretary of defense, who is a member of the president's cabinet.

The departments of the army, of the navy, and of the air force function within the Department of Defense, and their respective secretaries are no longer members of the president's cabinet.

President	Secretary	Home	Apptd.	President	Secretary	Home	Apptd.
Truman	James V. Forrestal	N.Y.	1947	"	Clark M. Clifford	Md.	1968
"	Louis A. Johnson	W.Va.	1949	Nixon	Melvin R. Laird	Wis.	1969
"	George C. Marshall	Pa.	1950	"	Elliot L. Richardson	Mass.	1973
"	Robert A. Lovett	N.Y.	1951	"	James R. Schlesinger	Va.	1973
Eisenhower	Charles E. Wilson	Mich.	1953	Ford	"	"	1974
"	Neil H. McElroy	Oh.	1957	"	Donald H. Rumsfeld	Ill.	1975
"	Thomas S. Gates Jr.	Pa.	1959	Carter	Harold Brown	Cal.	1977
Kennedy	Robert S. McNamara	Mich.	1961	Reagan	Caspar W. Weinberger	Cal.	1981
Johnson, L.B.	Robert S. McNamara	Mich.	1963				

Secretaries of the Armed Services

Not members of the president's Cabinet

The Department of Defense; created Sept. 18, 1947, consolidated the navy, army, air force into a single department.

Secretary of the Air Force	Appointed
W. Stuart Symington	1947
Thomas K. Finletter	1950
Harold E. Talbot	1953
Donald A. Quarles	1965
James H. Douglas	1957
Dudley C. Sharpe	1959
Eugene M. Zuckert	1961
Dr. Harold Brown	1965
Robert C. Seamans Jr.	1969
John L. McLucas	1973
Thomas C. Reed	1976
John C. Stetson	1977
Hans M. Mark	1979
Verne Orr	1981

Secretary of the Army	Appointed
Kenneth C. Royall	1947

Gordon Gray*	1949
Frank Pace Jr.	1950
Earl D. Johnson (acting)	1953
Robert T. Stevens	1953
Wilber M. Brucker	1955
Elvis J. Stahr Jr.	1961
Cyrus R. Vance	1962
Stephen Ailes	1964
Stanley R. Resor	1965
Robert F. Froehlke	1971
Howard H. Callaway	1973
Norman R. Augustine (acting)	1975
Martin R. Hoffman	1975
Clifford L. Alexander Jr.	1977
John O. Marsh Jr.	1981

*In addition, Gordon Gray was acting secretary of the army from Apr. 28, 1949, and under secretary from May 25, 1949, until June 20, 1949.

Secretary of the Navy	Appointed
John L. Sullivan	1947
Francis P. Matthews	1949
Dan A. Kimball	195
Robert B. Anderson	195
Charles S. Thomas	195
Thomas S. Gates Jr.	195
William B. Franke	195
John B. Connally Jr.	196
Fred Korth	196
Paul H. Nitze	196
John T. McNaughton	196
Paul R. Ignatius	196

John H. Chafee	1969	J. William Middendorf 2d	1974	Edward Hidalgo	1979
John W. Warner	1972	W. Graham Claytor Jr.	1977	John F. Lehman Jr.	1981

Secretaries of War

The War (and Navy) Department was created by act of Congress Aug. 7, 1789, and Gen. Henry Knox was commissioned secretary of war under that act Sept. 12, 1789.

President	Secretary	Home	Apptd.	President	Secretary	Home	Apptd.
Washington	Henry Knox	Mass.	1789	Grant	John A. Rawlins	Ill.	1869
"	Timothy Pickering	Pa.	1795	"	William T. Sherman	Oh.	1869
"	James McHenry	Md.	1796	"	William W. Belknap	Ia.	1869
Adams, J.	"	"	1797	"	Alphonso Taft	Oh.	1876
"	Samuel Dexter	Mass.	1800	Grant	James D. Cameron	Pa.	1876
Jefferson	Henry Dearborn	"	1801	Hayes	George W. McCrary	Ia.	1877
Madison	William Eustis	Mass.	1809	"	Alexander Ramsey	Minn.	1879
"	John Armstrong	N.Y.	1813	Garfield	Robert T. Lincoln	Ill.	1881
Madison	James Monroe	Va.	1814	Arthur	"	"	1881
"	William H. Crawford	Ga.	1815	Cleveland	William C. Endicott	Mass.	1885
Monroe	John C. Calhoun	S.C.	1817	Harrison, B.	Redfield Proctor	Vt.	1889
Adams, J.Q.	James Barbour	Va.	1825	"	Stephen B. Elkins	W.Va.	1891
"	Peter B. Porter	N.Y.	1828	Cleveland	Daniel S. Lamont	N.Y.	1893
Jackson	John H. Eaton	Tenn.	1829	McKinley	Russel A. Alger	Mich.	1897
"	Lewis Cass	Oh.	1831	"	Elihu Root	N.Y.	1899
"	Benjamin F. Butler	N.Y.	1837	Roosevelt, T.	"	"	1901
Van Buren	Joel R. Poinsett	S.C.	1837	"	William H. Taft	Oh.	1904
Harrison, W.H.	John Bell	Tenn.	1841	"	Luke E. Wright	Tenn.	1908
Tyler	"	"	1841	Taft	Jacob M. Dickinson	"	1909
Tyler	John C. Spencer	N.Y.	1841	"	Henry L. Stimson	N.Y.	1911
"	James M. Porter	Pa.	1843	Wilson	Lindley M. Garrison	N.J.	1913
"	William Wilkins	"	1844	"	Newton D. Baker	Oh.	1916
Polk	William L. Marcy	N.Y.	1845	Harding	John W. Weeks	Mass.	1921
Taylor	George W. Crawford	Ga.	1849	Coolidge	"	"	1923
Fillmore	Charles M. Conrad	La.	1850	"	Dwight F. Davis	Mo.	1925
Pierce	Jefferson Davis	Miss.	1853	Hoover	James W. Good	Ill.	1929
Buchanan	John B. Floyd	Va.	1857	Hoover	Patrick J. Hurley	Okla.	1929
"	Joseph Holt	Ky.	1861	Roosevelt, F.D.	George H. Dern	Ut.	1933
Lincoln	Simon Cameron	Pa.	1861	"	Harry H. Woodring	Kan.	1937
"	Edwin M. Stanton	Pa.	1862	Roosevelt, F.D.	Henry L. Stimson	N.Y.	1940
Johnson, A.	"	"	1865	Truman	Robert P. Patterson	N.Y.	1945
"	John M. Schofield	Ill.	1868	"	*Kenneth C. Royall	N.C.	1947

Secretaries of the Navy

The Navy Department was created by act of Congress Apr. 30, 1798.

President	Secretary	Home	Apptd.	President	Secretary	Home	Apptd.
Adams, J.	Benjamin Stoddert	Md.	1798	Lincoln	Gideon Welles	Conn.	1861
Jefferson	"	"	1801	Johnson, A.	"	"	1865
"	Robert Smith	"	1801	Grant	Adolph E. Borie	Pa.	1869
Madison	Paul Hamilton	S.C.	1809	"	George M. Robeson	N.J.	1869
"	William Jones	Pa.	1813	Hayes	Richard W. Thompson	Ind.	1877
"	Benjamin Williams Crowninshield	Mass.	1814	"	Nathan Goff Jr.	W.Va.	1881
Monroe	"	"	1817	Garfield	William H. Hunt	La.	1881
"	Smith Thompson	N.Y.	1818	Arthur	William E. Chandler	N.H.	1882
"	Samuel L. Southard	N.J.	1823	Cleveland	William C. Whitney	N.Y.	1885
Adams, J.Q.	"	"	1825	Harrison, B.	Benjamin F. Tracy	N.Y.	1889
Jackson	John Branch	N.C.	1829	Cleveland	Hilary A. Herbert	Ala.	1893
"	Levi Woodbury	N.H.	1831	McKinley	John D. Long	Mass.	1897
"	Mahlon Dickerson	N.J.	1834	Roosevelt, T.	"	"	1901
Van Buren	"	"	1837	"	William H. Moody	"	1902
"	James K. Paulding	N.Y.	1838	"	Paul Morton	Ill.	1904
Harrison, W.H.	George E. Badger	N.C.	1841	"	Charles J. Bonaparte	Md.	1905
Tyler	"	"	1841	"	Victor H. Metcalf	Cal.	1906
"	Abel P. Upshur	Va.	1841	"	Truman H. Newberry	Mich.	1908
"	David Henshaw	Mass.	1843	Taft	George von L. Meyer	Mass.	1909
"	Thomas W. Gilmer	Va.	1844	Wilson	Josephus Daniels	N.C.	1913
"	John Y. Mason	"	1844	Harding	Edwin Denby	Mich.	1921
Polk	George Bancroft	Mass.	1845	Coolidge	"	"	1923
"	John Y. Mason	Va.	1846	"	Curtis D. Wilbur	Cal.	1924
Taylor	William B. Preston	"	1849	Hoover	Charles Francis Adams	Mass.	1929
Fillmore	William A. Graham	N.C.	1850	Roosevelt, F.D.	Claude A. Swanson	Va.	1933
"	John P. Kennedy	Md.	1852	"	Charles Edison	N.J.	1940
Pierce	James C. Dobbin	N.C.	1853	"	Frank Knox	Ill.	1940
Buchanan	Isaac Toucey	Conn.	1857	"	*James V. Forrestal	N.Y.	1944
				Truman	"	"	1945

*Last members of Cabinet. The War Department became the Department of the Army and it and the Navy Department became branches of the Department of Defense, created Sept. 18, 1947.

Attorneys General

The office of attorney general was organized by act of Congress Sept. 24, 1789. The Department of Justice was created June 22, 1870.

President	Attorney General	Home	Apptd.	President	Attorney General	Home	Apptd.
Washington	Edmund Randolph	Va.	1789	Jefferson	Caesar A. Rodney	Del.	1807
"	William Bradford	Pa.	1794	Madison	"	"	1809
"	Charles Lee	Va.	1795	"	William Pinkney	Md.	1811
Adams, J.	"	"	1797	"	Richard Rush	Pa.	1814
Jefferson	Levi Lincoln	Mass.	1801	Monroe	"	"	1817
"	John Breckenridge	Ky.	1805	"	William Wirt	Va.	1817

President	Attorney General	Home	Apptd.
Adams, J.Q.	"	"	1825
Jackson	John M. Berrien	Ga.	1829
"	Roger B. Taney	Md.	1831
"	Benjamin F. Butler	N.Y.	1833
Van Buren	"	"	1837
"	Felix Grundy	Tenn.	1838
"	Henry D. Gilpin	Pa.	1840
Harrison, W.H.	John J. Crittenden	Ky.	1841
Tyler	"	"	1841
"	Hugh S. Legare	S.C.	1841
"	John Nelson	Md.	1843
Polk	John Y. Mason	Va.	1845
"	Nathan Clifford	Me.	1846
"	Isaac Toucey	Conn.	1848
Taylor	Reverdy Johnson	Md.	1849
Fillmore	John J. Crittenden	Ky.	1850
Pierce	Caleb Cushing	Mass.	1853
Buchanan	Jeremiah S. Black	Pa.	1857
"	Edwin M. Stanton	Pa.	1860
Lincoln	Edward Bates	Mo.	1861
"	James Speed	Ky.	1864
Johnson, A.	"	"	1865
"	Henry Stanbery	Oh.	1866
"	William M. Evarts	N.Y.	1868
Grant	Ebenezer R. Hoar	Mass.	1869
"	Amos T. Akerman	Ga.	1870
"	George H. Williams	Ore.	1871
"	Edwards Pierrepont	N.Y.	1875
"	Alphonso Taft	Oh.	1876
Hayes	Charles Devens	Mass.	1877
Garfield	Wayne MacVeagh	Pa.	1881
Arthur	Benjamin H. Brewster	"	1881
Cleveland	Augustus Garland	Ark.	1885
Harrison, B.	William H. H. Miller	Ind.	1889
Cleveland	Richard Olney	Mass.	1893
"	Judson Harmon	Oh.	1895
McKinley	Joseph McKenna	Cal.	1897
"	John W. Griggs	N.J.	1898
"	Philander C. Knox	Pa.	1901
Roosevelt, T.	"	"	1901
"	William H. Moody	Mass.	1904
"	Charles J. Bonaparte	Md.	1906
Taft	George W. Wickersham	N.Y.	1909
Wilson	J.C. McReynolds	Tenn.	1913
"	Thomas W. Gregory	Tex.	1914
"	A. Mitchell Palmer	Pa.	1919
Harding	Harry M. Daugherty	Oh.	1921
Coolidge	"	"	1923
"	Harlan F. Stone	N.Y.	1924
"	John G. Sargent	Vt.	1925
Hoover	William D. Mitchell	Minn.	1929
Roosevelt, F.D.	Homer S. Cummings	Conn.	1933
"	Frank Murphy	Mich.	1939
"	Robert H. Jackson	N.Y.	1940
"	Francis Biddle	Pa.	1941
Truman	Thomas C. Clark	Tex.	1945
"	J. Howard McGrath	R.I.	1949
"	J.P. McGranery	Pa.	1952
Eisenhower	Herbert Brownell Jr.	N.Y.	1953
"	William P. Rogers	Md.	1957
Kennedy	Robert F. Kennedy	Mass.	1961
Johnson, L.B.	"	"	1963
"	N. de B. Katzenbach	Ill.	1964
"	Ramsey Clark	Tex.	1967
Nixon	John N. Mitchell	N.Y.	1969
"	Richard G. Kleindienst	Ariz.	1972
"	Elliot L. Richardson	Mass.	1973
"	William B. Saxbe	Oh.	1974
Ford	"	"	1974
"	Edward H. Levi	Ill.	1975
Carter	Griffin B. Bell	Ga.	1977
"	Benjamin R. Civiletti	Md.	1979
Reagan	William French Smith	Cal.	1981

Secretaries of the Interior

The Department of Interior was created by act of Congress Mar. 3, 1849

President	Secretary	Home	Apptd.
Taylor	Thomas Ewing	Oh.	1849
Fillmore	Thomas M. T. McKennan	Pa.	1850
Fillmore	Alex H. H. Stuart	Va.	1850
Pierce	Robert McClelland	Mich.	1853
Buchanan	Jacob Thompson	Miss.	1857
Lincoln	Caleb B. Smith	Ind.	1861
"	John P. Usher	"	1863
Johnson, A.	"	"	1865
"	James Harlan	Ia.	1865
"	Orville H. Browning	Ill.	1866
Grant	Jacob D. Cox	Oh.	1869
"	Columbus Delano	"	1870
"	Zachariah Chandler	Mich.	1875
Hayes	Carl Schurz	Mo.	1877
Garfield	Samuel J. Kirkwood	Ia.	1881
Arthur	Henry M. Teller	Col.	1882
Cleveland	Lucius Q.C. Lamar	Miss.	1885
"	William F. Vilas	Wis.	1888
Harrison, B.	John W. Noble	Mo.	1889
Cleveland	Hoke Smith	Ga.	1893
"	David R. Francis	Mo.	1896
McKinley	Cornelius N. Bliss	N.Y.	1897
"	Ethan A. Hitchcock	Mo.	1898
Roosevelt, T.	"	"	1901
"	James R. Garfield	Oh.	1907
Taft	Richard A. Ballinger	Wash.	1909
"	Walter L. Fisher	Ill.	1911
Wilson	Franklin K. Lane	Cal.	1913
"	John B. Payne	Ill.	1920
Harding	Albert B. Fall	N.M.	1921
"	Hubert Work	Col.	1923
Coolidge	"	"	1923
"	Roy O. West	Ill.	1929
Hoover	Ray Lyman Wilbur	Cal.	1929
Roosevelt, F.D.	Harold L. Ickes	Ill.	1933
Truman	"	"	1945
"	Julius A. Krug	Wis.	1946
"	Oscar L. Chapman	Col.	1949
Eisenhower	Douglas McKay	Ore.	1953
"	Fred A Seaton	Neb.	1956
Kennedy	Stewart L. Udall	Ariz.	1961
Johnson, L.B.	"	"	1963
Nixon	Walter J. Hickel	Alas.	1969
"	Rogers C.B. Morton	Md.	1971
Ford	"	"	1974
"	Stanley K. Hathaway	Wyo.	1975
"	Thomas S. Kleppe	N.D.	1975
Carter	Cecil D. Andrus	Ida.	1977
Reagan	James G. Watt	Cal.	1981

Secretaries of Agriculture

The Department of Agriculture was created by act of Congress May 15, 1862. On Feb. 8, 1889, its commissioner was renamed secretary of agriculture and became a member of the cabinet.

President	Secretary	Home	Apptd.
Cleveland	Norman J. Colman	Mo.	1889
Harrison, B.	Jeremiah M. Rusk	Wis.	1889
Cleveland	J. Sterling Morton	Neb.	1893
McKinley	James Wilson	Ia.	1897
Roosevelt, T.	"	"	1901
Taft	"	"	1909
Wilson	David F. Houston	Mo.	1913
"	Edwin T. Meredith	Ia.	1920
Harding	Henry C. Wallace	Ia.	1921
Coolidge	"	"	1923
"	Howard M. Gore	W.Va.	1924
"	William M. Jardine	Kan.	1925
Hoover	Arthur M. Hyde	Mo.	1929
Roosevelt, F.D.	Henry A. Wallace	Ia.	1933
"	Claude R. Wickard	Ind.	1940
Truman	Clinton P. Anderson	N.M.	1945
"	Charles F. Brannan	Col.	1948
Eisenhower	Ezra Taft Benson	Ut.	1953
Kennedy	Orville L. Freeman	Minn.	1961
Johnson, L.B.	"	"	1963
Nixon	Clifford M. Hardin	Ind.	1969
"	Earl L. Butz	Ind.	1971
Ford	"	"	1974
"	John A. Knebel	Va.	1976
Carter	Bob Bergland	Minn.	1977
Reagan	John R. Block	Ill.	1981

Secretaries of Commerce and Labor

The Department of Commerce and Labor, created by Congress Feb. 14, 1903, was divided by Congress Mar. 4, 1913, into separate departments of Commerce and Labor. The secretary of each was made a cabinet member.

President	Secretary	Home	Apptd.	President	Secretary	Home	Apptd.
Secretaries of Commerce and Labor				Harding	Herbert C. Hoover	Cal.	1921
Roosevelt, T.	George B. Cortelyou	N.Y.	1903	Coolidge	"	"	1923
"	Victor H. Metcalf	Cal.	1904	"	William F. Whiting	Mass.	1928
"	Oscar S. Straus	N.Y.	1906	Hoover	Robert P. Lamont	Ill.	1929
Taft	Charles Nagel	Mo.	1909	"	Roy D. Chapin	Mich.	1932
Secretaries of Labor				Roosevelt, F.D.	Daniel C. Roper	S.C.	1933
Wilson	William B. Wilson	Pa.	1913	"	Harry L. Hopkins	N.Y.	1939
Harding	James J. Davis	Pa.	1921	"	Jesse Jones	Tex.	1940
Coolidge	"	"	1923	"	Henry A. Wallace	Ia.	1945
Hoover	"	"	1929	Truman	"	"	1945
"	William N. Doak	Va.	1930	"	W. Averell Harriman	N.Y.	1947
Roosevelt, F.D.	Frances Perkins	N.Y.	1933	"	Charles Sawyer	Oh.	1948
Truman	L.B. Schwellenbach	Wash.	1945	Eisenhower	Sinclair Weeks	Mass.	1953
"	Maurice J. Tobin	Mass.	1949	"	Lewis L. Strauss	N.Y.	1958
Eisenhower	Martin P. Durkin	Ill.	1953	"	Frederick H. Mueller	Mich.	1959
"	James P. Mitchell	N.J.	1953	Kennedy	Luther H. Hodges	N.C.	1961
				Johnson, L.B.	"	"	1963
Kennedy	Arthur J. Goldberg	Ill.	1961	"	John T. Connor	N.J.	1965
"	W. Willard Wirtz	Ill.	1962	"	Alex B. Trowbridge	N.J.	1967
Johnson, L.B.	"	Ill.	1963	"	Cyrus R. Smith	N.Y.	1968
Nixon	George P. Shultz	Ill.	1969	Nixon	Maurice H. Stans	Minn.	1969
"	James D. Hodgson	Cal.	1970	"	Peter G. Peterson	Ill.	1972
"	Peter J. Brennan	N.Y.	1973	"	Frederick B. Dent	S.C.	1973
Ford	"	"	1974	Ford	"	"	1974
"	John T. Dunlop	Cal.	1975	"	Rogers C.B. Morton	Md.	1975
"	W.J. Usery Jr.	Ga.	1976	"	Elliot L. Richardson	Mass.	1975
Carter	F. Ray Marshall	Tex.	1977	Carter	Juanita M. Kreps	N.C.	1977
Reagan	Raymond J. Donovan	N.J.	1981				
Secretaries of Commerce				"	Philip M. Klutznick	Ill.	1979
Wilson	William C. Redfield	N.Y.	1913	Reagan	Malcolm Baldrige	Conn.	1981
"	Joshua W. Alexander	Mo.	1919				

Secretaries of Education, and Health and Human Services

The Department of Health, Education and Welfare, created by Congress Apr. 11, 1953, was divided by Congress Sept. 27, 1979, into separate departments of Education, and Health and Human Services. The secretary of each is a cabinet member.

President	Secretary	Home	Apptd.	President	Secretary	Home	Apptd.
Secretaries of Health, Education, and Welfare				"	Caspar W. Weinberger	Cal.	1973
Eisenhower	Oveta Culp Hobby	Tex.	1953	Ford	"	"	1974
"	Marion B. Folsom	N.Y.	1955	"	Forrest D. Mathews	Ala.	1975
"	Arthur S. Flemming	Oh.	1958	Carter	Joseph A. Califano, Jr.	D.C.	1977
Kennedy	Abraham A. Ribicoff	Conn.	1961	"	Patricia Roberts Harris	D.C.	1979
"	Anthony J. Celebrezze	Oh.	1962	**Secretaries of Health and Human Services**			
Johnson, L.B.	"	"	1963	Carter	Patricia Roberts Harris	D.C.	1979
"	John W. Gardner	N.Y.	1965	Reagan	Richard S. Schweiker	Pa.	1981
Johnson, L.B.	Wilbur J. Cohen	Mich.	1968	**Secretaries of Education**			
Nixon	Robert H. Finch	Cal.	1969	Carter	Shirley Hufstedler	Cal.	1979
"	Elliot L. Richardson	Mass.	1970	Reagan	Terrel Bell	Ut.	1981

Secretaries of Housing and Urban Development

The Department of Housing and Urban Development was created by act of Congress Sept. 9, 1965.

President	Secretary	Home	Apptd.	President	Secretary	Home	Apptd.
Johnson, L.B.	Robert C. Weaver	Wash.	1966	"	Carla Anderson Hills	Cal.	1975
"	Robert C. Wood	Mass.	1969	Carter	Patricia Roberts Harris	D.C.	1977
Nixon	George W. Romney	Mich.	1969	"	Moon Landrieu	La.	1979
"	James T. Lynn	Oh.	1973	Reagan	Samuel R. Pierce Jr.	N.Y.	1981
Ford	"		1974				

Secretaries of Transportation

The Department of Transportation was created by act of Congress Oct. 15, 1966.

President	Secretary	Home	Apptd.	President	Secretary	Home	Apptd.
Johnson, L.B.	Alan S. Boyd	Fla.	1966	Carter	Brock Adams	Wash.	1977
Nixon	John A. Volpe	Mass.	1969	"	Neil E. Goldschmidt	Ore.	1979
"	Claude S. Brinegar	Cal.	1973	Reagan	Andrew L. Lewis Jr.	Pa.	1981
Ford	Claude S. Brinegar	Cal.	1974				
"	William T. Coleman Jr.	Pa.	1975				

Secretaries of Energy

The Department of Energy was created by federal law Aug. 4, 1977.

President	Secretary	Home	Apptd.	President	Secretary	Home	Apptd.
Carter	James R. Schlesinger	Va.	1977	"	Robert W. Duncan Jr.	Wyo.	1979
				Reagan	James B. Edwards	S.C.	1981

Postmasters General

Congress established the Post Office Department as a branch of the Treasury Sept. 22, 1789. The postmaster general was made a member of the Cabinet Mar. 9, 1829. The Postal Reorganization Act of 1970 replaced the department with the U.S. Postal Service, an independent federal agency. Its head, the postmaster general, is not a member of the Cabinet.

President	Postmaster General	Home	Apptd.	President	Postmaster General	Home	Apptd.
Washington	Samuel Osgood	Mass.	1789	Garfield	Thomas L. James	N.Y.	1881
"	Timothy Pickering	Pa.	1791	Arthur	Timothy O. Howe	Wis.	1881
"	Joseph Habersham	Ga.	1795	"	Walter Q. Gresham	Ind.	1883
Adams, J.	"	"	1797	"	Frank Hatton	Ia.	1884
Jefferson	"	"	1801	Cleveland	William F. Vilas	Wis.	1885
"	Gideon Granger	Conn.	1801	"	Don M. Dickinson	Mich.	1888
Madison	"	"	1809	Harrison, B.	John Wanamaker	Pa.	1889
"	Return J. Meigs Jr.	Ohio	1814	Cleveland	Wilson S. Bissel	N.Y.	1893
Monroe	"	"	1817	"	William L. Wilson	W.Va.	1895
"	John McLean	"	1823	McKinley	James A. Gary	Md.	1897
Adams, J.Q.	"	"	1825	"	Charles E. Smith	Pa.	1898
Jackson	William T. Barry	Ky.	1829	Roosevelt, T.	"	"	1901
"	Amos Kendall	"	1835	"	Henry C. Payne	Wis.	1902
Van Buren	"	"	1837	"	Robert J. Wynne	Pa.	1904
"	John M. Niles	Conn.	1840	"	George B. Cortelyou	N.Y.	1905
Harrison, W.H.	Francis Granger	N.Y.	1841	"	George von L. Meyer	Mass.	1907
Tyler	"	N.Y.	1841	Taft	Frank H. Hitchcock	"	1909
"	Charles A. Wickliffe	Ky.	1841	Wilson	Albert S. Burleson	Tex.	1913
Polk	Cave Johnson	Tenn.	1845	Harding	Will H. Hays	Ind.	1921
Taylor	Jacob Collamer	Vt.	1849	"	Hubert Work	Col.	1922
Fillmore	Nathan K. Hall	N.Y.	1850	"	Harry S. New	Ind.	1923
"	Samuel D. Hubbard	Conn.	1852	Coolidge	"	"	1923
Pierce	James Campbell	Pa.	1853	Hoover	Walter F. Brown	Oh.	1929
Buchanan	Aaron V. Brown	Tenn.	1857	Roosevelt, F.D.	James A. Farley	N.Y.	1933
"	Joseph Holt	Ky.	1859	"	Frank C. Walker	Pa.	1940
"	Horatio King	Me.	1861	Truman	Robert E. Hannegan	Mo.	1945
Lincoln	Montgomery Blair	D.C.	1861	"	Jesse M. Donaldson	Mo.	1947
"	William Dennison	Oh.	1864	Eisenhower	A.E. Summerfield	Mich.	1953
Johnson, A.	"	"	1865	Kennedy	J. Edward Day	Cal.	1961
"	Alex W. Randall	Wis.	1866	"	John A. Gronouski	Wis.	1963
Grant	John A.J. Creswell	Md.	1869	Johnson, L.B.	"	"	1963
"	James W. Marshall	Va.	1874	"	Lawrence F. O'Brien	Mass.	1965
"	Marshall Jewell	Conn.	1874	"	W. Marvin Watson	Tex.	1968
"	James N. Tyner	Ind.	1876	Nixon	Winton M. Blount	Ala.	1969
Hayes	David McK. Key	Tenn.	1877				
"	Horace Maynard	Tenn.	1880				

Law on Succession to the Presidency

If by reason of death, resignation, removal from office, inability, or failure to qualify there is neither a president nor vice president to discharge the powers and duties of the office of president, then the speaker of the House of Representatives shall upon his resignation as speaker and as representative, act as president. The same rule shall apply in the case of the death, resignation, removal from office, or inability of an individual acting as president.

If at the time when a speaker is to begin the discharge of the powers and duties of the office of president there is no speaker, or the speaker fails to qualify as acting president, then the president pro tempore of the Senate, upon his resignation as president pro tempore and as senator, shall act as president.

An individual acting as president shall continue to act until the expiration of the then current presidential term, except that (1) if his discharge of the powers and duties of the office is founded in whole or in part in the failure of both the president-elect and the vice president-elect to qualify, then

he shall act only until a president or vice president qualifies, and (2) if his discharge of the powers and duties of the office is founded in whole or in part on the inability of the president or vice president, then he shall act only until the removal of the disability of one of such individuals.

If, by reason of death, resignation, removal from office, or failure to qualify, there is no president pro tempore to act as president, then the officer of the United States who is highest on the following list, and who is not under disability to discharge the powers and duties of president, shall act as president; the secretaries of state, treasury, defense, attorney general; secretaries of interior, agriculture, commerce, labor, health and human services, housing and urban development, transportation, energy, education.

(Legislation approved July 18, 1947; amended Sept. 9, 1965, Oct. 15, 1966, Aug. 4, 1977, and Sept. 27, 1979. (See also Constitutional Amendment XXV.)

Burial Places of the Presidents

Washington	Mt. Vernon, Va.
J. Adams	Quincy, Mass.
Jefferson	Charlottesville, Va.
Madison	Montpelier Station, Va.
Monroe	Richmond, Va.
J.Q. Adams	Quincy, Mass.
Jackson	Nashville, Tenn.
Van Buren	Kinderhook, N.Y.
W.H. Harrison	North Bend, Oh.
Tyler	Richmond, Va.
Polk	Nashville, Tenn.
Taylor	Louisville, Ky.

Fillmore	Buffalo, N.Y.
Pierce	Concord, N.H.
Buchanan	Lancaster, Pa.
Lincoln	Springfield, Ill.
A. Johnson	Greeneville, Tenn.
Grant	New York City
Hayes	Fremont, Oh.
Garfield	Cleveland, Oh.
Arthur	Albany, N.Y.
Cleveland	Princeton, N.J.
B. Harrison	Indianapolis, Ind.
McKinley	Canton, Oh.

T. Roosevelt	Oyster Bay, N.Y.
Taft	Arlington Nat'l. Cem'y.
Wilson	Washington Cathedral
Harding	Marion, Oh.
Coolidge	Plymouth, Vt.
Hoover	West Branch, Ia.
F.D. Roosevelt	Hyde Park, N.Y.
Truman	Independence, Mo.
Eisenhower	Abilene, Kan.
Kennedy	Arlington Nat'l. Cem'y.
L.B. Johnson	Stonewall, Tex.

BIOGRAPHIES OF U.S. PRESIDENTS

George Washington

George Washington, first president, was born Feb. 22, 1732 (Feb. 11, 1731, old style), the son of Augustine Washington and Mary Ball, at Wakefield on Pope's Creek, Westmoreland Co., Va. His early childhood was spent on the Ferry farm, near Fredericksburg. His father died when George was 11. He studied mathematics and surveying and when 16 went to live with his half brother Lawrence, who built and named Mount Vernon. George surveyed the lands of William Fairfax in the Shenandoah Valley, keeping a diary. He accompanied Lawrence to Barbados, West Indies, contracted small pox, and was deeply scarred. Lawrence died in 1752 and George acquired his property by inheritance. He valued land and when he died owned 70,000 acres in Virginia and 40,000 acres in what is now West Virginia.

Washington's military service began in 1753 when Gov. Dinwiddie of Virginia sent him on missions deep into Ohio country. He clashed with the French and had to surrender Fort Necessity July 3, 1754. He was an aide to Braddock and at his side when the army was ambushed and defeated on a march to Ft. Duquesne, July 9, 1755. He helped take Fort Duquesne from the French in 1758.

After his marriage to Martha Dandridge Custis, a widow, in 1759, Washington managed his family estate at Mount Vernon. Although not at first for independence, he opposed British exactions and took charge of the Virginia troops before war broke out. He was made commander-in-chief by the Continental Congress June 15, 1775.

The successful issue of a war filled with hardships was due to his leadership. He was resourceful, a stern disciplinarian, and the one strong, dependable force for unity. He favored a federal government and became chairman of the Constitutional Convention of 1787. He helped get the Constitution ratified and was unanimously elected president by the electoral college and inaugurated, Apr. 30, 1789, on the balcony of New York's Federal Hall.

He was reelected 1792, but refused to consider a 3d term and retired to Mount Vernon. He suffered acute laryngitis after a ride in snow and rain around his estate, was bled profusely, and died Dec. 14, 1799.

John Adams

John Adams, 2d president, Federalist, was born in Braintree (Quincy), Mass., Oct. 30, 1735 (Oct. 19, o. s.), the son of John Adams, a farmer, and Susanna Boylston. He was a great-grandson of Henry Adams who came from England in 1636. He was graduated from Harvard, 1755, taught school, studied law. In 1765 he argued against taxation without representation before the royal governor. In 1770 he defended the British soldiers who fired on civilians in the "Boston Massacre." He was a delegate to the first Continental Congress, and signed the Declaration of Independence. He was a commissioner to France, 1778, with Benjamin Franklin and Arthur Lee; won recognition of the U.S. by The Hague, 1782; was first American minister to England, 1785-1788, and was elected vice president, 1788 and 1792.

In 1796 Adams was chosen president by the electors. Intense antagonism to America by France caused agitation for war, led by Alexander Hamilton. Adams, breaking with Hamilton, opposed war.

To fight undue influence and muzzle criticism Adams supported the Alien and Sedition laws of 1798, which led to his defeat for reelection. He died July 4, 1826, on the same day as Jefferson (the 50th anniversary of the Declaration of Independence).

Thomas Jefferson

Thomas Jefferson, 3d president, was born Apr. 13, 1743 (Apr. 2, o. s.), at Shadwell, Va., the son of Peter Jefferson, a civil engineer of Welsh descent who raised tobacco, and Jane Randolph. His father died when he was 14, leaving him 2,750 acres and his slaves. Jefferson attended the College of William and Mary, 1760-1762, read classics in Greek and Latin and played the violin. In 1769 he was elected to the House of Burgesses. In 1770 he began building Monticello, near Charlottesville. He was a member of the Virginia Committee of Correspondence and the Continental Congress. Named a member of the committee to draw up a Declaration of Independence, he wrote the basic draft. He was a member of the Virginia House of Delegates, 1776-79, elected governor to succeed Patrick Henry, 1779, reelected 1780, resigned June 1781, amid charges of ineffectual military preparation. During his term he wrote the statute on religious freedom. In the Continental Congress, 1783, he drew up an ordinance for the Northwest Territory, forbidding slavery after 1800; its terms were put into the Ordinance of 1787. He was sent to Paris with Benjamin Franklin and John Adams to negotiate commercial treaties, 1784; made minister to France, 1785.

Washington appointed him secretary of state, 1789. Jefferson's strong faith in the consent of the governed, as opposed to executive control favored by Hamilton, secretary of the treasury, often led to conflict: Dec. 31, 1793, he resigned. He was the Republican candidate for president in 1796; beaten by John Adams, he became vice president. In 1800, Jefferson and Aaron Burr received equal electoral college votes for president. The House of Representatives elected Jefferson. Major events of his administration were the Louisiana Purchase, 1803, and the Lewis and Clark Expedition. He established the Univ. of Virginia and designed its buildings. He died July 4, 1826, on the same day as John Adams.

James Madison

James Madison, 4th president, Republican, was born Mar. 16, 1751 (Mar. 5, 1750, o. s.) at Port Conway, King George Co., Va., eldest son of James Madison and Eleanor Rose Conway. Madison was graduated from Princeton, 1771; studied theology, 1772; sat in the Virginia Constitutional Convention, 1776. He was a member of the Continental Congress. He was chief recorder at the Constitutional Convention in 1787, and supported ratification in the Federalist Papers, written with Alexander Hamilton and John Jay. He was elected to the House of Representatives in 1789, helped frame the Bill of Rights and fought the Alien and Sedition Acts. He became Jefferson's secretary of state, 1801.

Elected president in 1808, Madison was a "strict constructionist," opposed to the free interpretation of the Constitution by the Federalists. He was reelected in 1812 by the votes of the agrarian South and recently admitted western states. Caught between British and French maritime restrictions, the U.S. drifted into war, declared June 18, 1812. The war ended in a stalemate. He retired in 1817 to his estate at Montpelier. There he edited his famous papers on the Constitutional Convention. He became rector of the Univ. of Virginia, 1826. He died June 28, 1836.

James Monroe

James Monroe, 5th president, Republican, was born Apr. 28, 1758, in Westmoreland Co., Va., the son of Spence Monroe and Eliza Jones, who were of Scottish and Welsh descent, respectively. He attended the College of William and Mary, fought in the 3d Virginia Regiment at White Plains, Brandywine, Monmouth, and was wounded at Trenton. He studied law with Thomas Jefferson, 1780, was a member of the Virginia House of Delegates and of Congress, 1783-86. He opposed ratification of the Constitution because it lacked a bill of rights; was U.S. senator, 1790; minister to France, 1794-96; governor of Virginia, 1799-1802, and 1811. Jefferson sent him to France as minister, 1803. He helped R. Livingston negotiate the Louisiana Purchase, 1803. He ran against Madison for president in 1808. He was elected to the Virginia Assembly, 1810-1811; was secretary of state under Madison, 1811-1817.

In 1816 Monroe was elected president; in 1820 reelected

with all but one electoral college vote. Monroe's administration became the "Era of Good Feeling." He obtained Florida from Spain; settled boundaries with Canada, and eliminated border forts. He supported the anti-slavery position that led to the Missouri Compromise. His most significant contribution was the "Monroe Doctrine," which became a cornerstone of U.S. foreign policy. Monroe retired to Oak Hill, Va. Financial problems forced him to sell his property. He moved to New York City to live with a daughter. He died there July 4, 1831.

John Quincy Adams

John Quincy Adams, 6th president, independent Federalist, was born July 11, 1767, at Braintree (Quincy), Mass., the son of John and Abigail Adams. His father was the 2d president. He was educated in Paris, Leyden, and Harvard, graduating in 1787. He served as American minister in various European capitals, and helped draft the War of 1812 peace treaty. He was U.S. Senator, 1803-08. President Monroe made him secretary of state, 1817, and he negotiated the cession of the Floridas from Spain, supported exclusion of slavery in the Missouri Compromise, and helped formulate the Monroe Doctrine. In 1824 he was elected president by the House after he failed to win an electoral college majority. His expansion of executive powers was strongly opposed and he was beaten in 1828 by Jackson. In 1831 he entered Congress and served 17 years with distinction. He opposed slavery, the annexation of Texas, and the Mexican War. He helped establish the Smithsonian Institution. He had a stroke in the House and died in the Speaker's Room, Feb. 23, 1848.

Andrew Jackson

Andrew Jackson, 7th president, was a Jeffersonian-Republican, later a Democrat. He was born in the Waxhaws district, New Lancaster Co., S.C., Mar. 15, 1767, the posthumous son of Andrew Jackson and Elizabeth Hutchinson, who were Irish immigrants. At 13, he joined the militia in the Revolution and was captured.

He read law in Salisbury, N.C., moved to Nashville, Tenn., speculated in land, married, and practiced law. In 1796 he helped draft the constitution of Tennessee and for a year occupied its one seat in Congress. He was in the Senate in 1797, and again in 1823. He defeated the Creek Indians at Horseshoe Bend, Ala., 1814. With 6,000 backwoods fighters he defeated Packenham's 12,000 British troops at the Chalmette, outside New Orleans, Jan. 8, 1815. In 1818 he briefly invaded Spanish Florida to quell Seminoles and outlaws who harassed frontier settlements. In 1824 he ran for president against John Quincy Adams and had the most popular and electoral votes but not a majority; the election was decided by the House, which chose Adams. In 1828 he defeated Adams, carrying the West and South. He was a noisy debater and a duelist and introduced rotation in office called the "spoils system." Suspicious of privilege, he ruined the Bank of the United States by depositing federal funds with state banks. Though "Let the people rule" was his slogan, he at times supported strict constructionist policies against the expansionist West. He killed the Congressional caucus for nominating presidential candidates and substituted the national convention, 1832. When South Carolina refused to collect imports under his protective tariff he ordered army and naval forces to Charleston. Jackson recognized the Republic of Texas, 1836. He died at the Hermitage, June 8, 1845.

Martin Van Buren

Martin Van Buren, 8th president, Democrat, was born Dec. 5, 1782, at Kinderhook, N.Y., the son of Abraham Van Buren, a Dutch farmer, and Mary Hoes. He was surrogate of Columbia County, N.Y., state senator and attorney general. He was U.S. senator 1821, reelected, 1827, elected governor of New York, 1828. He helped swing eastern support to Jackson in 1828 and was his secretary of state 1829-31. In 1832 he was elected vice president. He was a

consummate politician, known as "the little magician," and influenced Jackson's policies. In 1836 he defeated William Henry Harrison for president and took office as the Panic of 1837 initiated a 5-year nationwide depression. He inaugurated the independent treasury system. His refusal to spend land revenues led to his defeat by Harrison in 1840. He lost the Democratic nomination of 1844 to Polk. In 1848 he ran for president on the Free Soil ticket and lost. He died July 24, 1862, at Kinderhook.

William Henry Harrison

William Henry Harrison, 9th president, Whig, who served only 31 days, was born in Berkeley, Charles City Co., Va., Feb. 9, 1773, the 3d son of Benjamin Harrison, signer of the Declaration of Independence. He attended Hampden Sydney College. He was secretary of the Northwest Territory, 1798; its delegate in Congress, 1799; first governor of Indiana Territory, 1800; and superintendent of Indian affairs. With 900 men he routed Tecumseh's Indians at Tippecanoe, Nov. 7, 1811. A major general, he defeated British and Indians at Battle of the Thames, Oct. 5, 1813. He served in Congress, 1816-19; Senate, 1825-28. In 1840, when 68, he was elected president with a "log cabin and hard cider" slogan. He caught pneumonia during the inauguration and died Apr. 4, 1841.

John Tyler

John Tyler, 10th president, independent Whig, was born Mar. 29, 1790, in Greenway, Charles City Co., Va., son of John Tyler and Mary Armistead. His father was governor of Virginia, 1808-11. Tyler was graduated from William and Mary, 1807; member of the House of Delegates, 1811; in congress, 1816-21; in Virginia legislature, 1823-25; governor of Virginia, 1825-26; U.S. senator, 1827-36. In 1840 he was elected vice president and, on Harrison's death, succeeded him. He favored pre-emption, allowing settlers to get government land; rejected a national bank bill and thus alienated most Whig supporters; refused to honor the spoils system. He signed the resolution annexing Texas, Mar. 1, 1845. He accepted renomination, 1844, but withdrew before election. In 1861, he chaired an unsuccessful Washington conference called to avert civil war. After its failure he supported secession, sat in the provisional Confederate Congress, became a member of the Confederate House, but died, Jan. 18, 1862, before it met.

James Knox Polk

James Knox Polk, 11th president, Democrat, was born in Mecklenburg Co., N.C., Nov. 2, 1795, the son of Samuel Polk, farmer and surveyor of Scotch-Irish descent, and Jane Knox. He graduated from the Univ. of North Carolina, 1818; member of the Tennessee state legislature, 1823-25. He served in Congress 1825-39 and as speaker 1835-39. He was governor of Tennessee 1839-41, but was defeated 1841 and 1843. In 1844, when both Clay and Van Buren announced opposition to annexing Texas, the Democrats made Polk the first dark horse nominee because he demanded control of all Oregon and annexation of Texas. Polk reestablished the independent treasury system originated by Van Buren. His expansionist policy was opposed by Clay, Webster, Calhoun; he sent troops under Zachary Taylor to the Mexican border and, when Mexicans attacked, declared war existed. The Mexican war ended with the annexation of California and much of the Southwest as part of America's "manifest destiny." He compromised on the Oregon boundary ("54-40 or fight!") by accepting the 49th parallel and giving Vancouver to the British. Polk died in Nashville, June 15, 1849.

Zachary Taylor

Zachary Taylor, 12th president, Whig, who served only 16 months, was born Nov. 24, 1784, in Orange Co., Va., the son of Richard Taylor, later collector of the port of Louisville, Ky., and Sarah Strother. Taylor was commissioned first lieutenant, 1808; fought in the War of 1812; the Black

Hawk War, 1832; and the second Seminole War, 1837. He was called Old Rough and Ready. He settled on a plantation near Baton Rouge, La. In 1845 Polk sent him with an army to the Rio Grande. When the Mexicans attacked him, Polk declared war. Taylor was successful at Palo Alto and Resaca de la Palma, 1846; occupied Monterey. Polk made him major general but sent many of his troops to Gen. Winfield Scott. Outnumbered 4-1, he defeated Santa Anna at Buena Vista, 1847. A national hero, he received the Whig nomination in 1848, and was elected president. He resumed the spoils system and though once a slave-holder worked to have California admitted as a free state. He died in office July 9, 1850.

Millard Fillmore

Millard Fillmore, 13th president, Whig, was born Jan. 7, 1800, in Cayuga Co., N.Y., the son of Nathaniel Fillmore and Phoebe Miller. He taught school and studied law; admitted to the bar, 1823. He was a member of the state assembly, 1829-32; in Congress, 1833-35 and again 1837-43. He opposed the entrance of Texas as slave territory and voted for a protective tariff. In 1844 he was defeated for governor of New York. In 1848 he was elected vice president and succeeded as president July 10, 1850, after Taylor's death. Fillmore favored the Compromise of 1850 and signed the Fugitive Slave Law. His policies pleased neither expansionists nor slave-holders and he was not renominated in 1852. In 1856 he was nominated by the American (Know-Nothing) party and accepted by the Whigs, but defeated by Buchanan. He died in Buffalo, Mar. 8, 1874.

Franklin Pierce

Franklin Pierce, 14th president, Democrat, was born in Hillsboro, N. H., Nov. 23, 1804, the son of Benjamin Pierce, veteran of the Revolution and governor of New Hampshire, 1827. He graduated from Bowdoin, 1824. A lawyer, he served in the state legislature 1829-33; in Congress, supporting Jackson, 1833-37; U.S. senator, 1837-42. He enlisted in the Mexican War, became brigadier general under Gen. Winfield Scott. In 1852 Pierce was nominated on the 49th ballot over Lewis Cass, Stephen A. Douglas, and James Buchanan, and defeated Gen. Scott, Whig. Though against slavery, Pierce was influenced by Southern pro-slavery men. He ignored the Ostend Manifesto that the U.S. either buy or take Cuba. He approved the Kansas-Nebraska Act, leaving slavery to popular vote ("squatter sovereignty"), 1854. He signed a reciprocity treaty with Canada and approved the Gadsden Purchase from Mexico, 1853. Denied renomination by the Democrats, he spent most of his remaining years in Concord, N.H., where he died Oct. 8, 1869.

James Buchanan

James Buchanan, 15th president, Federalist, later Democrat, was born of Scottish descent near Mercersburg, Pa., Apr. 23, 1791. He graduated Dickinson, 1809; was a volunteer in the War of 1812; member, Pennsylvania legislature, 1814-16, Congress, 1820-31; Jackson's minister to Russia, 1831-33; U.S. senator 1834-45. As Polk's secretary of state, 1845-49, he ended the Oregon dispute with Britain, supported the Mexican War and annexation of Texas. As minister to Britain, 1853, he signed the Ostend Manifesto. Nominated by Democrats, he was elected, 1856, over John C. Fremont (Republican) and Millard Fillmore (American Know-Nothing and Whig tickets). On slavery he favored popular sovereignty and choice by state constitutions; he accepted the pro-slavery Dred Scott decision as binding. He denied the right of states to secede. A strict constructionist, he desired to keep peace and found no authority for using force. He died at Wheatland, near Lancaster, Pa., June 1, 1868.

Abraham Lincoln

Abraham Lincoln, 16th president, Republican, was born Feb. 12, 1809, in a log cabin on a farm then in Hardin Co., Ky., now in Larue. He was the son of Thomas Lincoln, a carpenter, and Nancy Hanks.

The Lincolns moved to Spencer Co., Ind., near Gentryville, when Abe was 7. Nancy died 1818, and his father married Mrs. Sarah Bush Johnston, 1819; she had a favorable influence on Abe. In 1830 the family moved to Macon Co., Ill. Lincoln lost election to the Illinois General Assembly, 1832, but later won 4 times, beginning in 1834. He enlisted in the militia for the Black Hawk War, 1832. In New Salem he ran a store, surveyed land, and was postmaster.

In 1837 Lincoln was admitted to the bar and became partner in a Springfield, Ill., law office. He was elected to Congress, 1847-49. He opposed the Mexican War. He supported Zachary Taylor, 1848. He opposed the Kansas-Nebraska Act and extension of slavery, 1854. He failed, in his bid for the Senate, 1855. He supported John C. Fremont, 1856.

In 1858 Lincoln had Republican support in the Illinois legislature for the Senate but was defeated by Stephen A. Douglas, Dem., who had sponsored the Kansas-Nebraska Act.

Lincoln was nominated for president by the Republican party on an anti-slavery platform, 1860. He ran against Douglas, a northern Democrat; John C. Breckinridge, southern pro-slavery Democrat; John Bell, Constitutional Union party. When he won the election, South Carolina seceded from the Union Dec. 20, 1860, followed in 1861 by 10 Southern states.

The Civil War erupted when Fort Sumter was attacked Apr. 12, 1861. On Sept. 22, 1862, 5 days after the battle of Antietam, he announced that slaves in territory then in rebellion would be free Jan. 1, 1863, date of the Emancipation Proclamation. His speeches, including his Gettysburg and Inaugural addresses, are remembered for their eloquence.

Lincoln was reelected, 1864, over Gen. George B. McClellan, Democrat. Lee surrendered Apr. 9, 1865. On Apr. 14, Lincoln was shot by actor John Wilkes Booth in Ford's Theatre, Washington. He died the next day.

Andrew Johnson

Andrew Johnson, 17th president, Democrat, was born in Raleigh, N.C., Dec. 29, 1808, the son of Jacob Johnson, porter at an inn and church sexton, and Mary McDonough. He was apprenticed to a tailor but ran away and eventually settled in Greeneville, Tenn. He became an alderman, 1828; mayor, 1830; state representative and senator, 1835-43; member of Congress, 1843-53; governor of Tennessee, 1853-57; U.S. senator, 1857-62. He supported John C. Breckinridge against Lincoln in 1860. He had held slaves, but opposed secession and tried to prevent his home state, Tennessee, from seceding. In Mar. 1862, Lincoln appointed him military governor of occupied Tennessee. In 1864 he was nominated for vice president with Lincoln on the National Union ticket to win Democratic support. He succeeded Lincoln as president April 15, 1865. In a controversy with Congress over the president's power over the South, he proclaimed, May 26, 1865, an amnesty to all Confederates except certain leaders if they would ratify the 13th Amendment abolishing slavery. States doing so added anti-Negro provisions that enraged Congress, which restored military control over the South. When Johnson removed Edwin M. Stanton, secretary of war, without notifying the Senate, thus repudiating the Tenure of Office Act, the House impeached him for this and other reasons. He was tried by the Senate, and acquitted by only one vote, May 26, 1868. He returned to the Senate in 1875. Johnson died July 31, 1875.

Ulysses Simpson Grant

Ulysses S. Grant, 18th president, Republican, was born at Point Pleasant, Oh., Apr. 27, 1822, son of Jesse R. Grant, a tanner, and Hannah Simpson. The next year the family moved to Georgetown, Oh. Grant was named Hiram Ulysses, but on entering West Point, 1839, his name was entered as Ulysses Simpson and he adopted it. he was graduated in 1843; served under Gens. Taylor and Scott in the Mexican War; resigned, 1854; worked in St. Louis until 1860, then went to Galena, Ill. With the start of the Civil War, he was named colonel of the 21st Illinois Vols., 1861, then brigadier general; took Forts Henry and Donelson; fought at Shiloh, took Vicksburg. After his victory at Chattanooga, Lincoln placed him in command of the Union Armies. He accepted Lee's surrender at Appomattox, Apr., 1865. President Johnson appointed Grant secretary of war when he suspended Stanton, but Grant was not confirmed. He was nominated for president by the Republicans and elected over Horatio Seymour, Democrat. The 15th Amendment, amnesty bill, and civil service reform were events of his administration. The Liberal Republicans and Democrats opposed him with Horace Greeley, 1872, but he was reelected. An attempt by the Stalwarts (Old Guard) to nominate him in 1880 failed. In 1884 the collapse of Grant & Ward, investment house, left him penniless. He wrote his personal memoirs while ill with cancer and completed them 4 days before his death at Mt. McGregor, N.Y., July 23, 1885. The book realized over $450,000.

Rutherford Birchard Hayes

Rutherford B. Hayes, 19th president, Republican, was born in Delaware, Oh., Oct. 4, 1822, the posthumous son of Rutherford Hayes, a farmer, and Sophia Birchard. He was raised by his uncle Sardis Birchard. He graduated from Kenyon College, 1842, and Harvard Law School, 1845. He practiced law in Lower Sandusky, Oh., now Fremont; was city solicitor of Cincinnati, 1858-61. In the Civil War, he was major of the 23d Ohio Vols., was wounded several times, and rose to the rank of brevet major general, 1864. He served in Congress 1864-67, supporting Reconstruction and Johnson's impeachment. He was elected governor of Ohio, 1867 and 1869; beaten in the race for Congress, 1872; reelected governor, 1875. In 1876 he was nominated for president and believed he had lost the election to Samuel J. Tilden, Democrat. But a few Southern states submitted 2 different sets of electoral votes and the result was in dispute. An electoral commission, appointed by Congress, 8 Republicans and 7 Democrats, awarded all disputed votes to Hayes allowing him to become president by one electoral vote. Hayes, keeping a promise to southerners, withdrew troops from areas still occupied in the South, ending the era of Reconstruction. He proceeded to reform the civil service, alienating political spoilsmen. He advocated repeal of the Tenure of Office Act. He supported sound money and specie payments. Hayes died in Fremont, Oh., Jan. 17, 1893.

James Abram Garfield

James A. Garfield, 20th president, Republican, was born Nov. 19, 1831, in Orange, Cuyahoga Co., Oh., the son of Abram Garfield and Eliza Ballou. His father died in 1833. He worked as a canal bargeman, farmer, and carpenter; attended Western Reserve Eclectic, later Hiram College, and was graduated from Williams in 1856. He taught at Hiram, and later became principal. He was in the Ohio senate in 1859. Anti-slavery and anti-secession, he volunteered for the war, became colonel of the 42d Ohio Infantry and brigadier in 1862. He fought at Shiloh, was chief of staff for Rosecrans and was made major general for gallantry at Chickamauga. He entered Congress as a radical Republican in 1863; supported specie payment as against paper money (greenbacks). On the electoral commission in 1876 he voted for Hayes against Tilden on strict party lines. He was senator-elect in 1880 when he became the Republican nominee for president. He was chosen as a compromise over Gen. Grant, James G. Blaine, and John Sherman. This alienated the Grant following but Garfield was elected. On July 2, 1881, Garfield was shot by mentally disturbed office-seeker, Charles J. Guiteau, while entering a railroad station in Washington. He died Sept. 19, 1881, at Elberon, N.J.

Chester Alan Arthur

Chester A. Arthur, 21st president, Republican, was born at Fairfield, Vt., Oct. 5, 1829, the son of the Rev. William Arthur, from County Antrim, Ireland, and Malvina Stone. He graduated Union College, 1848, taught school at Pownall, Vt., studied law in New York. In 1853 he argued in a

fugitive slave case that slaves transported through N.Y. State were thereby freed; in 1885 he obtained a ruling that Negroes were to be treated the same as whites on street cars. He was made collector of the Port of New York, 1871. President Hayes, reforming the civil service, forced Arthur to resign, 1879. This made the New York machine stalwarts enemies of Hayes. Arthur and the stalwarts tried to nominate Grant for a 3d term in 1880. When Garfield was nominated, Arthur received 2d place in the interests of harmony. When Garfield died, Arthur became president. He supported civil service reform and the tariff of 1883. He was defeated for renomination by James G. Blaine. He died in New York City Nov. 18, 1886.

Grover Cleveland

(According to a ruling of the State Dept., Grover Cleveland is both the 22d and the 24th president, because his 2 terms were not consecutive. By individuals, he is only the 22d.)

Grover Cleveland, 22d and 24th president, Democrat, was born in Caldwell, N.J. Mar. 18, 1837, the son of Richard F. Cleveland, a Presbyterian minister, and Ann Neale. He was named Stephen Grover, but dropped the Stephen. He clerked in Clinton and Buffalo, N.Y., taught at the N.Y. City Institution for the Blind; was admitted to the bar in Buffalo, 1859; became assistant district attorney, 1863; sheriff, 1871; mayor, 1881; governor of New York, 1882. He was an independent, honest administrator who hated corruption. He was nominated for president over Tammany Hall opposition, 1884, and defeated Republican James G. Blaine. He enlarged the civil service, vetoed many pension raids on the Treasury. In 1888 he was defeated by Benjamin Harrison, although his popular vote was larger. Reelected over Harrison in 1892, he faced a money crisis brought about by lowering of the gold reserve, circulation of paper and exorbitant silver purchases under the Sherman Act; obtained a repeal of the latter and a reduced tariff. A severe depression and labor troubles racked his administration but he refused to interfere in business matters and rejected Jacob Coxey's demand for unemployment relief. He broke the Pullman strike, 1894. In 1896, the Democrats repudiated his administration and chose silverite William Jennings Bryan as their candidate. Cleveland died in Princeton, N.J., June 24, 1908.

Benjamin Harrison

Benjamin Harrison, 23d president, Republican, was born at North Bend, Oh., Aug. 20, 1833. His great-grandfather, Benjamin Harrison, was a signer of the Declaration of Independence; his grandfather, William Henry Harrison, was 9th President; his father, John Scott Harrison, was a member of Congress. His mother was Elizabeth F. Irwin. He attended school on his father's farm; graduated from Miami Univ. at Oxford, Oh., 1852; admitted to the bar, 1853, and practiced in Indianapolis. In the Civil War, he rose to the rank of brevet brigadier general, fought at Kennesaw Mountain, Peachtree Creek, Nashville, and in the Atlanta campaign. He failed to be elected governor of Indiana, 1876; but became senator, 1881, and worked for the G. A. R. pensions vetoed by Cleveland. In 1888 he defeated Cleveland for president despite having fewer popular votes. He expanded the pension list; signed the McKinley high tariff bill and the Sherman Silver Purchase Act. During his administration, 6 states were admitted to the union. He was defeated for reelection, 1892. He represented Venezuela in a boundary arbitration with Great Britain in Paris, 1899. He died at Indianapolis, Mar. 13, 1901.

William McKinley

William McKinley, 25th president, Republican, was born in Niles, Oh., Jan. 29, 1843, the son of William McKinley, an ironmaker, and Nancy Allison. McKinley attended school in Poland, Oh., and Allegheny College, Meadville, Pa., and enlisted for the Civil War at 18 in the 23d Ohio, in which Rutherford B. Hayes was a major. He rose to captain and in 1865 was made brevet major. He studied law in Albany, N.Y., law school; opened an office in Canton, Oh., in 1867, and campaigned for Grant and Hayes. He served in the House of Representatives, 1877-83, 1885-91, and led the fight for passage of the McKinley Tarriff, 1890. Defeated for reelection on the issue in 1890, he was governor of Ohio, 1892-96. He had support for president in the convention that nominated Benjamin Harrison in 1892. In 1896 he was elected president on a protective tariff, sound money (gold standard) platform over William Jennings Bryan, Democratic proponent of free silver. McKinley was reluctant to intervene in Cuba but the loss of the battleship Maine at Havana crystallized opinion. He demanded Spain's withdrawal from Cuba; Spain made some concessions but Congress announced state of war as of Apr. 21. He was reelected in the 1900 campaign, defeating Bryan's anti-imperialist arguments with the promise of a "full dinner pail." McKinley was respected for his conciliatory nature, but conservative on business issues. On Sept. 6, 1901, while welcoming citizens at the Pan-American Exposition, Buffalo, N.Y., he was shot by Leon Czolgosz, an anarchist. He died Sept. 14.

Theodore Roosevelt

Theodore Roosevelt, 26th president, Republican, was born in N.Y. City, Oct. 27, 1858, the son of Theodore Roosevelt, a glass importer, and Martha Bulloch. He was a 5th cousin of Franklin D. Roosevelt and an uncle of Mrs. Eleanor Roosevelt. Roosevelt graduated from Harvard, 1880; attended Columbia Law School briefly; sat in the N.Y. State Assembly, 1882-84; ranched in North Dakota, 1884-86; failed election as mayor of N.Y. City, 1886; member of U.S. Civil Service Commission, 1889; president, N.Y. Police Board, 1895, supporting the merit system; assistant secretary of the Navy under McKinley, 1897-98. In the war with Spain, he organized the 1st U.S. Volunteer Cavalry (Rough Riders) as lieutenant colonel; led the charge up Kettle Hill at San Juan. Elected New York governor, 1898-1900, he fought the spoils system and achieved taxation of corporation franchises. Nominated for vice president, 1900, he became nation's youngest president when McKinley died. As president he fought corruption of politics by big business; dissolved Northern Securities Co. and others for violating, anti-trust laws; intervened in coal strike on behalf of the public, 1902; obtained Elkins Law forbidding rebates to favored corporations, 1903; Hepburn Law regulating railroad rates, 1906; Pure Food and Drugs Act, 1906, Reclamation Act and employers' liability laws. He organized conservation, mediated the peace between Japan and Russia, 1905; won the Nobel Peace Prize. He was the first to use the Hague Court of International Arbitration. By recognizing the new Republic of Panama he made Panama Canal possible. He was reelected in 1904.

In 1908 he obtained the nomination of William H. Taft, who was elected. Feeling that Taft had abandoned his policies, Roosevelt unsuccessfully sought the nomination in 1912. He bolted the party and ran on the Progressive "Bull Moose", ticket against Taft and Woodrow Wilson, splitting the Republicans and insuring Wilson's election. He was shot during the campaign but recovered. In 1916 he supported Charles E. Hughes, Republican. A strong friend of Britain, he fought American isolation in World War I. He wrote some 40 books on many topics; his Winning of the West is best known. He died Jan. 6, 1919, at Sagamore Hill, Oyster Bay, N.Y.

William Howard Taft

William Howard Taft, 27th president, Republican, was born in Cincinnati, Oh., Sept. 15, 1857, the son of Alphonso Taft and Louisa Maria Torrey. His father was secretary of war and attorney general in Grant's cabinet; minister to Austria and Russia under Arthur. Taft was graduated from Yale, 1878; Cincinnati Law School, 1880; became law reporter for Cincinnati newspapers; was assistant prosecuting attorney, 1881-83; assistant county solicitor, 1885; judge, superior court, 1887; U.S. solicitor-general, 1890; federal circuit judge, 1892. In 1900 he became head of the U.S. Philippines Commission and was first civil governor of the Philippines, 1901-04; secretary of war, 1904; provisional governor of Cuba, 1906. He was groomed for president by Roosevelt and elected over Bryan, 1908. His administration dissolved Standard Oil and tobacco trusts; instituted Dept. of Labor; drafted direct election of senators and income tax amend-

ments. His tariff and conservation policies angered progressives; though renominated he was opposed by Roosevelt; the result was Democrat Woodrow Wilson's election. Taft, with some reservations, supported the League of Nations. He was professor of constitutional law, Yale, 1913-21; chief justice of the U.S., 1921-30; illness forced him to resign. He died in Washington, Mar. 8, 1930.

Woodrow Wilson

Woodrow Wilson, 28th president, Democrat, was born at Staunton, Va., Dec. 28, 1856, as Thomas Woodrow Wilson, son of a Presbyterian minister, the Rev. Joseph Ruggles Wilson and Janet (Jessie) Woodrow. In his youth Wilson lived in Augusta, Ga., Columbia, S.C., and Wilmington, N.C. He attended Davidson College, 1873-74; was graduated from Princeton, A.B., 1879; A.M., 1882; read law at the Univ. of Virginia, 1881; practiced law, Atlanta, 1882-83; Ph.D., Johns Hopkins, 1886. He taught at Bryn Mawr, 1885-88; at Wesleyan, 1888-90; was professor of jurisprudence and political economy at Princeton, 1890-1910; president of Princeton, 1902-1910; governor of New Jersey, 1911-13. In 1912 he was nominated for president with the aid of William Jennings Bryan, who sought to block James "Champ" Clark and Tammany Hall. Wilson won the election because the Republican vote for Taft was split by the Progressives under Roosevelt.

Wilson protected American interests in revolutionary Mexico and fought for American rights on the high seas. His sharp warnings to Germany led to the resignation of his secretary of state, Bryan, a pacifist. In 1916 he was reelected by a slim margin with the slogan, "He kept us out of war." Wilson's attempts to mediate in the war failed. After 4 American ships had been sunk by the Germans, he secured a declaration of war against Germany on Apr. 6, 1917.

Wilson proposed peace Jan. 8, 1918, on the basis of his "Fourteen Points," a state paper with worldwide influence. His doctrine of self-determination continues to play a major role in territorial disputes. The Germans accepted his terms and an armistice, Nov. 11.

Wilson went to Paris to help negotiate the peace treaty, the crux of which he considered the League of Nations. The Senate demanded reservations that would not make the U.S. subordinate to the votes of other nations in case of war. Wilson refused to consider any reservations and toured the country to get support. He suffered a stroke, Oct., 1919. An invalid for months, he clung to his executive powers while his wife and doctor sought to shield him from affairs which would tire him.

He was awarded the 1919 Nobel Peace Prize, but the treaty embodying the League of Nations was rejected by the Senate, 1920. He died Feb. 3, 1924.

Warren Gamaliel Harding

Warren Gamaliel Harding, 29th president, Republican, was born near Corsica, now Blooming Grove, Oh., Nov. 2, 1865, the son of Dr. George Tyron Harding, a physician, and Phoebe Elizabeth Dickerson. He attended Ohio Central College. He was state senator, 1900-04; lieutenant governor, 1904-06; defeated for governor, 1910; chosen U.S. senator, 1915. He supported Taft, opposed federal control of food and fuel; voted for anti-strike legislation, woman's suffrage, and the Volstead prohibition enforcement act over President Wilson's veto; and opposed the League of Nations. In 1920 he was nominated for president and defeated James M. Cox in the election. The Republicans capitalized on war weariness and fear that Wilson's League of Nations would curtail U.S. sovereignty. Harding stressed a return to "normalcy"; worked for tariff revision and repeal of excess profits law and high income taxes. Two Harding appointees, Albert B. Fall (interior) and Harry Daugherty (attorney general), became involved in the Teapot Dome scandal that embittered Harding's last days. He called the International Conference on Limitation of Armaments, 1921-22. Returning from a trip to Alaska he became ill and died in San Francisco, Aug. 2, 1923.

Calvin Coolidge

Calvin Coolidge, 30th president, Republican, was born in Plymouth, Vt., July 4, 1872, the son of John Calvin Coolidge, a storekeeper, and Victoria J. Moor, and named John

Calvin Coolidge. Coolidge graduated from Amherst in 1895. He entered Republican state politics and served as mayor of Northampton, Mass., state senator, lieutenant governor, and, in 1919, governor. In Sept., 1919, Coolidge attained national prominence by calling out the state guard in the Boston police strike. He declared: "There is no right to strike against the public safety by anybody, anywhere, anytime." This brought his name before the Republican convention of 1920, where he was nominated for vice president. He succeeded to the presidency on Harding's death. He opposed the League of Nations; approved the World Court; vetoed the soldiers' bonus bill, which was passed over his veto. In 1924 he was reelected by a huge majority. He reduced the national debt by $2 billion in 3 years. He twice provided relief to financially hard-pressed farmers. With Republicans eager to renominate him he announced, Aug. 2, 1927: "I do not choose to run for president in 1928." He died in Northampton, Jan. 5, 1933.

Herbert Hoover

Herbert C. Hoover, 31st president, Republican, was born at West Branch, Ia., Aug. 10, 1874, son of Jesse Clark Hoover, a blacksmith, and Hulda Randall Minthorn. Hoover grew up in Indian Territory (now Oklahoma) and Oregon; won his A.B. in engineering at Stanford, 1891. He worked briefly with U.S. Geological Survey and western mines; then was a mining engineer in Australia, Asia, Europe, Africa, America. While chief engineer, imperial mines, China, he directed food relief for victims of Boxer Rebellion, 1900. He directed American Relief Committee, London, 1914-15; U.S. Comm. for Relief in Belgium, 1915-1919; was U.S. Food Administrator, 1917-1919; American Relief Administrator, 1918-1923, feeding children in defeated nations; Russian Relief, 1918-1923. He was secy. of commerce, 1921-28. He was elected president over Alfred E. Smith, 1928. In 1929 the stock market crashed and the economy collapsed. During the depression, Hoover opposed federal aid to the unemployed. He was defeated in the 1932 election by Franklin D. Roosevelt. President Truman made him coordinator of European Food Program, 1947, chairman of the Commission for Reorganization of the Executive Branch, 1947-49. He founded the Hoover Institution on War, Revolution, and Peace at Stanford Univ. He died in N.Y. City, Oct. 20, 1964.

Franklin Delano Roosevelt

Franklin D. Roosevelt, 32d president, Democrat, was born near Hyde Park, N.Y., Jan. 30, 1882, the son of James Roosevelt and Sara Delano. He graduated Harvard, 1904; attended Columbia Law School; was admitted to the bar. He went to the N.Y. Senate, 1910 and 1913. In 1913 President Wilson made him assistant secretary of the navy.

Roosevelt ran for vice president, 1920, with James Cox and was defeated. From 1920 to 1928 he was a N.Y. lawyer and vice president of Fidelity & Deposit Co. In Aug., 1921, polio paralyzed his legs. He learned to walk with leg braces and a cane.

Roosevelt was elected governor of New York, 1928 and 1930. In 1932, W. G. McAdoo, pledged to John N. Garner, threw his votes to Roosevelt, who was nominated. The depression and the promise to repeal prohibition insured his election. He asked emergency powers, proclaimed the New Deal, and put into effect a vast number of administrative changes. Foremost was the use of public funds for relief and public works, resulting in deficit financing. He greatly expanded the controls of the central government over business, and by an excess profits tax and progressive income taxes produced a redistribution of earnings on an unprecedented scale. The Wagner Act gave labor many advantages in organizing and collective bargaining. He was the last president inaugurated on Mar. 4 (1933) and the first inaugurated on Jan. 20 (1937).

Roosevelt was the first president to use radio for "fireside chats." When the Supreme Court nullified some New Deal laws, he sought power to "pack" the court with additional justices, but Congress refused to give him the authority. He was the first president to break the "no 3d term" tradition (1940) and was elected to a 4th term, 1944, despite failing health. He was openly hostile to fascist governments before

World War II and launched a lend-lease program on behalf of the Allies. He wrote the principles of fair dealing into the Atlantic Charter, Aug. 14, 1941 (with Winston Churchill), and urged the Four Freedoms (freedom of speech, of worship, from want, from fear) Jan. 6, 1941. When Japan attacked Pearl Harbor, Dec. 7, 1941, the U.S. entered the war. He conferred with allied heads of state at Casablanca, Jan., 1943; Quebec, Aug., 1943; Teheran, Nov.-Dec., 1943; Cairo, Dec., 1943; Yalta, Feb., 1945. He died at Warm Springs, Ga., Apr. 12, 1945.

Harry S. Truman

Harry S. Truman, 33d president, Democrat, was born at Lamar, Mo., May 8, 1884, the son of John Anderson Truman and Martha Ellen Young. A family disagreement on whether his middle name was Shippe or Solomon, after names of 2 grandfathers, resulted in his using only the middle initial S. He attended public schools in Independence, Mo., worked for the Kansas City Star, 1901, and as railroad timekeeper, and helper in Kansas City banks up to 1905. He ran his family's farm, 1906-17. He was commissioned a first lieutenant and took part in the Vosges, Meuse-Argonne, and St. Mihiel actions in World War I. After the war he ran a haberdashery, became judge of Jackson Co. Court, 1922-24; attended Kansas City School of Law, 1923-25.

Truman was elected U.S. senator in 1934; reelected 1940. In 1944 with Roosevelt's backing he was nominated for vice president and elected. On Roosevelt's death Truman became president. In 1948 he was elected president.

Truman authorized the first uses of the atomic bomb (Hiroshima and Nagasaki, Aug. 6 and 9, 1945), bringing World War II to a rapid end. He was responsible for creating NATO, the Marshall Plan, and what came to be called the Truman Doctrine (to aid nations such as Greece and Turkey, threatened by Russian or other communist takeover). He broke a Russian blockade of West Berlin with a massive airlift, 1948-49. When communist North Korea invaded South Korea, June, 1950, he won UN approval for a "police action" and sent in forces under Gen. Douglas MacArthur. When MacArthur sought to pursue North Koreans into China, Truman removed him from command.

On the domestic front, Truman was responsible for higher minimum-wage, increased social-security, and aid-for-housing laws. Truman died Dec. 26, 1972, in Independence, Mo.

Dwight David Eisenhower

Dwight D. Eisenhower, 34th president, Republican, was born Oct. 14, 1890, at Denison, Tex., the son of David Jacob Eisenhower and Ida Elizabeth Stover. The next year, the family moved to Abilene, Kan. He graduated from West Point, 1915. He was on the American military mission to the Philippines, 1935-39 and during 4 of those years on the staff of Gen. Douglas MacArthur. He was made commander of Allied forces landing in North Africa, 1942, full general, 1943. He became supreme Allied commander in Europe, 1943, and as such led the Normandy invasion June 6, 1944. He was given the rank of general of the army Dec. 20, 1944, made permanent in 1946. On May 7, 1945, he received the surrender of the Germans at Rheims. He returned to the U.S. to serve as chief of staff, 1945-1948. In 1948, Eisenhower published Crusade in Europe, his war memoirs, which quickly became a best seller. From 1948 to 1953, he was president of Columbia Univ., but took leave of absence in 1950, to command NATO forces.

Eisenhower resigned from the army and was nominated for president by the Republicans, 1952. He defeated Adlai E. Stevenson in the election. He again defeated Stevenson, 1956. He called himself a moderate, favored "free market system" vs. government price and wage controls; kept government out of labor disputes; reorganized defense establishment; promoted missile programs. He continued foreign aid; sped end of Korean fighting; endorsed Taiwan and SE Asia defense treaties; backed UN in condemning Anglo-French raid on Egypt; advocated "open skies" policy of mutual inspection to USSR. He sent U.S. troops into Little Rock, Ark., Sept., 1957, during the segregation crisis and ordered Marines into Lebanon July-Aug., 1958.

During his retirement at his farm near Gettysburg, Pa., Eisenhower took up the role of elder statesman, counseling, his 3 successors in the White House. He died Mar. 28, 1969, in Washington.

John Fitzgerald Kennedy

John F. Kennedy, 35th president, Democrat, was born May 29, 1917, in Brookline, Mass., the son of Joseph P. Kennedy, financier, who later became ambassador to Great Britain, and Rose Fitzgerald. He entered Harvard, attended the London School of Economics briefly in 1935, received a B.S., from Harvard, 1940. He served in the Navy, 1941-1945, commanded a PT boat in the Solomons and won the Navy and Marine Corps Medal. He wrote *Profiles in Courage*, which won a Pulitzer prize. He served as representative in Congress, 1947-1953; was elected to the Senate in 1952, reelected 1958. He nearly won the vice presidential nomination in 1956.

In 1960, Kennedy won the Democratic nomination for president and defeated Richard M. Nixon, Republican. He was the first Roman Catholic president.

Kennedy's most important act was his successful demand Oct. 22, 1962, that the Soviet Union dismantle its missile bases in Cuba. He established a quarantine of arms shipments to Cuba and continued surveillance by air. He defied Soviet attempts to force the Allies out of Berlin. He made the steel industry rescind a price rise. He backed civil rights, a mental health program, arbitration of railroad disputes, and expanded medical care for the aged. Astronaut flights and satellite orbiting were greatly developed during his administration.

On Nov. 22, 1963, Kennedy was assassinated in Dallas, Tex.

Lyndon Baines Johnson

Lyndon B. Johnson, 36th president, Democrat, was born near Stonewall, Tex., Aug. 27, 1908, son of Sam Ealy Johnson and Rebekah Baines. He received a B.S. degree at Southwest Texas State Teachers College, 1930, attended Georgetown Univ. Law School, Washington, 1935. He taught public speaking in Houston, 1930-32; served as secretary to Rep. R. M. Kleberg, 1932-35. In 1937 Johnson won a contest to fill the vacancy caused by the death of a representative and in 1938 was elected to the full term, after which he returned for 4 terms. He was elected U.S. senator in 1948 and reelected in 1954. He became Democratic leader, 1953. Johnson was Texas' favorite son for the Democratic presidential nomination in 1956 and had strong support in the 1960 convention, where the nominee, John F. Kennedy, asked him to run for vice president. His campaigning helped overcome religious bias against Kennedy in the South.

Johnson became president on the death of Kennedy. Johnson worked hard for welfare legislation, signed civil rights, anti-proverty, and tax reduction laws, and averted strikes on railroads. He was elected to a full term, 1964. The war in Vietnam overshadowed other developments, 1965-68.

In face of increasing division in the nation and his own party over his handling of the war, Johnson announced that he would not seek another term, Mar. 31, 1968.

Retiring to his ranch near Johnson City, Tex., Johnson wrote his memoirs and oversaw the construction of the Lyndon Baines Johnson Library on the campus of the Univ. of Texas at Austin. He died Jan. 22, 1973.

Richard Milhous Nixon

Richard M. Nixon, 37th president, Republican, was the only president to resign without completing an elected term. He was born in Yorba Linda, Cal., Jan. 9, 1913, the son of Francis Anthony Nixon and Hannah Milhous. Nixon graduated from Whittier College, 1934; Duke Univ. Law School, 1937. After practicing law in Whittier and serving briefly in the Office of Price Administration in 1942, he entered the navy, serving in the South Pacific, and was discharged as a lieutenant commander.

Nixon was elected to the House of Representatives in 1946 and 1948. He achieved prominence as the House Un-American Activities Committee member who forced the showdown that resulted in the Alger Hiss perjury conviction. In 1950 Nixon moved to the Senate.

He was elected vice president in the Eisenhower landslides of 1952 and 1956. With Eisenhower's endorsement, Nixon won the Republican nomination in 1960. He was defeated by Democract John F. Kennedy, returned to Cal. and was defeated in his race for governor, 1962.

In 1968, he won the presidential nomination and went on to defeat Democrat Hubert H. Humphrey.

Nixon became the first U.S. president to visit China and Russia (1972). He and his foreign affairs advisor, Henry A. Kissinger, achieved a detente with China. Nixon appointed 4 new Supreme Court justices, including the chief justice, thus altering the court's balance in favor of a more conservative view.

Reelected 1972, Nixon secured a cease-fire agreement in Vietnam and completed the withdrawal of U.S. troops.

Nixon's 2d term was cut short by a series of scandals beginning with the burglary of Democratic party national headquarters in the Watergate office complex on June 17, 1972. Nixon denied any White House involvement in the Watergate break-in. On July 16, 1973, a White House aide, under questioning by a Senate committee, revealed that most of Nixon's office conversations and phone calls had been recorded. Nixon claimed executive privilege to keep the tapes secret and the courts and Congress sought the tapes for criminal proceedings against former White House aides and for a House inquiry into possible impeachment.

On Oct. 10, 1973, Nixon fired the Watergate special prosecutor and the attorney general resigned in protest. The public outcry which followed caused Nixon to appoint a new special prosecutor and to turn over to the courts a number of subpoenaed tape recordings. Public reaction also brought the initiation of a formal inquiry into impeachment.

On July 24, 1974, the Supreme Court ruled that Nixon's claim of executive privilege must fall before the special prosecutor's subpoenas of tapes relevant to criminal trial proceedings. That same day, the House Judiciary Committee opened debate on impeachment. On July 30, the committee recommended House adoption of 3 articles of impeachment charging Nixon with obstruction of justice, abuse of power, and contempt of Congress.

On Aug. 5, Nixon released transcripts of conversations held 6 days after the Watergate break-in showing that Nixon had known of, approved, and directed Watergate cover-up activities. Nixon resigned from office Aug. 9.

Gerald Rudolph Ford

Gerald R. Ford, 38th president, Republican, was born July 14, 1913, in Omaha, Neb., son of Leslie King and Dorothy Gardner, and was named Leslie Jr. When he was 2, his parents were divorced and his mother moved with the boy to Grand Rapids, Mich. There she met and married Gerald R. Ford, who formally adopted the boy and gave him his own name.

He graduated from the Univ. of Michigan, 1935 and Yale Law School, 1941.

He began practicing law in Grand Rapids, but in 1942 joined the navy and served in the Pacific, leaving the service in 1946 as a lieutenant commander.

He entered congress in 1948 and continued to win elections, spending 25 years in the House, 8 of them as Republican leader.

On Oct. 12, 1973, after Vice President Spiro T. Agnew resigned, Ford was nominated by President Nixon to replace him. It was the first use of the procedures set out in the 25th Amendment.

When Nixon resigned Aug. 9, 1974, Ford became president, the first to serve without being chosen in a national election. On Sept. 8 he pardoned Nixon for any federal crimes he might have committed as president. Ford vetoed 48 bills in his first 21 months in office, saying most would prove too costly. He visited China. In 1976, he was defeated in the election by Democrat Jimmy Carter.

Jimmy (James Earl) Carter

Jimmy (James Earl) Carter, 39th president, Democrat, was the first president from the Deep South since before the Civil War. He was born Oct. 1, 1924, at Plains, Ga., where his parents, James and Lillian Gordy Carter, had a farm and several businesses.

After studying at Georgia Tech, he entered the Naval Academy at Annapolis. On graduating, he entered the Navy's nuclear submarine program as an aide to Adm. Hyman Rickover, and also studied nuclear physics at Union College, Schenectady.

His father died in 1953 and Carter left the Navy to take over the family businesses — peanut-raising, warehousing, and cotton-ginning. He became a Baptist Church deacon, a Sunday school teacher, and public school board member, was elected to the Georgia state senate, was defeated for governor, 1966, but elected in 1970.

Carter won the Democratic nomination and defeated President Gerald R. Ford in the election of 1976.

As president, Carter launched a campaign on behalf of worldwide human rights, calling in his inaugural address, for people in all nations to join the U.S. in an effort to achieve human freedom and dignity.

In 1979, Carter played a major role in the peace negotiations between Israel and Egypt. In Nov., Iranian student militants attacked the U.S. embassy in Teheran and held members of the embassy staff hostage.

During 1980, Carter was widely criticized for the poor state of the economy and high inflation. He was also viewed as weak in his handling of foreign policy. He reacted to the Soviet invasion of Afghanistan by imposing a grain embargo and boycotting the Moscow Olympic games. His failure to obtain the release of the remaining 52 hostages held in Iran, whose first anniversary of capture fell on Election Day, plagued Carter to the end of his term. He was defeated by Ronald Reagan in the election. Carter finally succeeded in obtaining the release of the hostages on Inauguration Day, the new president was taking the oath of office.

Ronald Wilson Reagan

Ronald Wilson Reagan, 40th president, Republican, was born Feb. 6, 1911, in Tampico, Ill., the son of John Edward Reagan and Nellie Wilson. Reagan graduated from Eureka (Ill.) College in 1932. Following his graduation, he worked for 5 years as a sports announcer in Des Moines, Ia.

Reagan began a successful career as a film actor in 1937, and starred in numerous movies, and later television, until the 1960s. He was a captain in the Army Air Force during World War II.

He served as president of the Screen Actors Guild from 1947 to 1952, and in 1959.

Once a liberal Democrat, Reagan became active in Republican politics during the 1964 presidential campaign of Barry Goldwater. He was elected governor of California in 1966, and reelected in 1970.

Following his retirement as governor, Reagan became the leading spokesman for the conservative wing of the Republican Party, and made a strong bid for the party's 1976 presidential nomination.

In 1980, he gained the Republican nomination and won a landslide victory over Jimmy Carter.

As president, he proposed massive reductions in government spending and substantial tax cuts to revive the economy and reduce inflation. He also called for increased military spending.

Wives and Children of the Presidents

Listed in order of presidential administrations.

Name	State	Born	Married	Died	Sons	Daughters
Martha Dandridge Custis Washington	Va.	1732	1759	1802	...	...
Abigail Smith Adams	Mass.	1744	1764	1818	3	2
Martha Wayles Skelton Jefferson	Va.	1748	1772	1782	1	5
Dorothea "Dolley" Payne Todd Madison	N.C.	1768	1794	1849	...	...
Elizabeth Kortright Monroe	N.Y.	1768	1786	1830	... (1)	2
Louise Catherine Johnson Adams	Md. (2)	1775	1797	1852	3	1
Rachel Donelson Robards Jackson	Va.	1767	1791	1828	...	...
Hannah Hoes Van Buren	N.Y.	1783	1807	1819	4	...
Anna Symmes Harrison	N.J.	1775	1795	1864	6	4
Letitia Christian Tyler	Va.	1790	1813	1842	3	4
Julia Gardiner Tyler	N.Y.	1820	1844	1889	5	2
Sarah Childress Polk	Tenn.	1803	1824	1891	...	...
Margaret Smith Taylor	Md.	1788	1810	1852	1	5
Abigail Powers Fillmore	N.Y.	1798	1826	1853	1	1
Caroline Carmichael McIntosh Fillmore	N.J.	1813	1858	1881	...	...
Jane Means Appleton Pierce	N.H.	1806	1834	1863	3	...
Mary Todd Lincoln	Ky.	1818	1842	1882	4	...
Eliza McCardle Johnson	Tenn.	1810	1827	1876	3	2
Julia Dent Grant	Mo.	1826	1848	1902	3	1
Lucy Ware Webb Hayes	Oh.	1831	1852	1889	7	1
Lucretia Rudolph Garfield	Oh.	1832	1858	1918	4	1
Ellen Lewis Herndon Arthur	Va.	1837	1859	1880	2	1
Frances Folsom Cleveland	N.Y.	1864	1886	1947	2	3
Caroline Lavinia Scott Harrison	Oh.	1832	1853	1892	1	1
Mary Scott Lord Dimmick Harrison	Pa.	1858	1896	1948	...	1
Ida Saxton McKinley	Oh.	1847	1871	1907	...	2
Alice Hathaway Lee Roosevelt	Mass.	1861	1880	1884	...	1
Edith Kermit Carow Roosevelt	Conn.	1861	1886	1948	4	1
Helen Herron Taft	Oh.	1861	1886	1943	2	1
Ellen Louise Axson Wilson	Ga.	1860	1885	1914	...	3
Edith Bolling Galt Wilson	Va.	1872	1915	1961	...	...
Florence Kling De Wolfe Harding	Oh.	1860	1891	1924	...	...
Grace Anna Goodhue Coolidge	Vt.	1879	1905	1957	2	...
Lou Henry Hoover	Ia.	1875	1899	1944	2	...
Anna Eleanor Roosevelt Roosevelt	N.Y.	1884	1905	1962	4 (1)	1
Bess Wallace Truman	Mo.	1885	1919	...	...	1
Mamie Geneva Doud Eisenhower	Ia.	1896	1916	1979	1 (1)	...
Jacqueline Lee Bouvier Kennedy	N.Y.	1929	1953	...	1 (1)	1
Claudia "Lady Bird" Alta Taylor Johnson	Tex.	1912	1934	...	...	2
Thelma Catherine Patricia Ryan Nixon	Nev.	1912	1940	...	...	2
Elizabeth Bloomer Warren Ford	Ill.	1918	1948	...	3	1
Rosalynn Smith Carter	Ga.	1927	1946	...	3	1
Anne Frances "Nancy" Robbins Davis Reagan	N.Y.	1923	1952	...	1 (3)	1(3)

James Buchanan, 15th president, was unmarried. (1) plus one infant, deceased. (2) Born London, father a Md. citizen. (3) President Reagan has a son and daughter from a former marriage.

Presidents Pro Tempore of the Senate

Until 1890, presidents "pro tem" were named "for the occasion only." Beginning with that year, they have served "until the Senate otherwise ordered." Sen. John J. Ingalls, chosen under the old rule in 1887, was again elected, under the new rule, in 1890. Party designations are D, Democrat; R, Republican.

Name	Party	State	Elected	Name	Party	State	Elected
John J. Ingalls	R	Kan.	Apr. 3, 1890	Key Pittman	D	Nev.	Mar. 9, 1933
Charles F. Manderson	R	Neb.	Mar. 2, 1891	William H. King	D	Ut.	Nov. 19, 1940
Isham G. Harris	D	Tenn.	Mar. 22, 1893	Pat Harrison	D	Miss.	Jan. 6, 1941
Matt W. Ransom	D	N.C.	Jan. 7, 1895	Carter Glass	D	Va.	July 10, 1941
Isham G. Harris	D	Tenn.	Jan. 10, 1895	Kenneth McKellar	D	Tenn.	Jan. 6, 1945
William P. Frye	R	Me.	Feb. 7, 1896	Arthur H. Vandenberg	R	Mich.	Jan. 4, 1947
Charles Curtis	R	Kan.	Dec. 4, 1911	Kenneth McKellar	D	Tenn.	Jan. 3, 1949
Augustus O. Bacon	D	Ga.	Jan. 15, 1912	Styles Bridges	R	N.H.	Jan. 3, 1953
Jacob H. Gallinger	R	N.H.	Feb. 12, 1912	Walter F. George	D	Ga.	Jan. 5, 1955
Henry Cabot Lodge	R	Mass.	Mar. 25, 1912	Carl Hayden	D	Ariz.	Jan. 3, 1957
Frank R. Brandegee	R	Conn.	May 25, 1912	Richard B. Russell	D	Ga.	Jan. 3, 1969
James P. Clarke	D	Ark.	Mar. 23, 1915	Allen J. Ellender	D	La.	Jan. 22, 1971
Willard Saulsbury	D	Del.	Dec. 14, 1916	James O. Eastland	D	Miss.	July 28, 1972
Albert B. Cummins	R	Ia.	May 19, 1919	Warren G. Magnuson	D	Wash.	Jan. 23, 1979
George H. Moses	R	N.H.	Mar. 6, 1925	Strom Thurmond	R	S.C.	Jan. 5, 1981

Speakers of the House of Representatives

Party designations: A, American; D, Democratic; DR, Democratic Republican; F, Federalist; R, Republican; W, Whig. *Served only one day.

Name	Party	State	Tenure	Name	Party	State	Tenure
Frederick Muhlenberg	F	Pa.	1789-1791	Schuyler Colfax	R	Ind.	1863-1869
Jonathan Trumbull	F	Conn.	1791-1793	*Theodore M. Pomeroy	R	N.Y.	1869-1869
Frederick Muhlenberg	F	Pa.	1793-1795	James G. Blaine	R	Mo.	1009-1875
Jonathan Dayton	F	N.J.	1795-1799	Michael C. Kerr	D	Ind.	1875-1876
Theodore Sedgwick	F	Mass.	1799-1801	Samuel J. Randall	D	Pa.	1876-1881
Nathaniel Macon	DR	N.C.	1801-1807	Joseph W. Keifer	R	Oh.	1881-1883
Joseph B. Varnum	DR	Mass.	1807-1811	John G. Carlisle	D	Ky.	1883-1889
Henry Clay	DR	Ky.	1811-1814	Thomas B. Reed	R	Me.	1889-1891
Langdon Cheves	DR	S.C.	1814-1815	Charles F. Crisp	D	Ga.	1891-1895
Henry Clay	DR	Ky.	1815-1820	Thomas B. Reed	R	Me.	1895-1899
John W. Taylor	DR	N.Y.	1820-1821	David B. Henderson	R	Ia.	1899-1903
Philip P. Barbour	DR	Va.	1821-1823	Joseph G. Cannon	R	Ill.	1903-1911
Henry Clay	DR	Ky.	1823-1825	Champ Clark	D	Mo.	1911-1919
John W. Taylor	D	N.Y.	1825-1827	Frederick H. Gillett	R	Mass.	1919-1925
Andrew Stevenson	D	Va.	1827-1834	Nicholas Longworth	R	Oh.	1925-1931
John Bell	D	Tenn.	1834-1835	John N. Garner	D	Tex.	1931-1933
James K. Polk	D	Tenn.	1835-1839	Henry T. Rainey	D	Ill.	1933-1935
Robert M. T. Hunter	D	Va.	1839-1841	Joseph W. Byrns	D	Tenn.	1935-1936
John White	W	Ky.	1841-1843	William B. Bankhead	D	Ala.	1936-1940
John W. Jones	D	Va.	1843-1845	Sam Rayburn	D	Tex.	1940-1947
John W. Davis	D	Ind.	1845-1847	Joseph W. Martin Jr.	R	Mass.	1947-1949
Robert C. Winthrop	W	Mass.	1847-1849	Sam Rayburn	D	Tex.	1949-1953
Howell Cobb	D	Ga.	1849-1851	Joseph W. Martin Jr.	R	Mass.	1953-1955
Linn Boyd	D	Ky.	1851-1855	Sam Rayburn	D	Tex.	1955-1961
Nathaniel P. Banks	A	Mass.	1856-1857	John W. McCormack	D	Mass.	1962-1971
James L. Orr	D	S.C.	1857-1859	Carl Albert	D	Okla.	1971-1977
William Pennington	R	N.J.	1860-1861	Thomas P. O'Neill Jr.	D	Mass.	1977-
Galusha A. Grow	R	Pa.	1861-1863				

National Political Parties

As of Mid-1981

Republican Party

National Headquarters—310 First St., SE, Washington, DC 20003.

Chairman—Richard Richards
Co-Chairman—Betty Heitman
Deputy Chairmen—Chuck Bailey, Fred Biebel.
Vice Chairmen—Ranny Riecker, Clarke Reed, Bernard M. Shanley, Paula F. Hawkins, Bruce B. Melchert, Shelia Roberge, Dennis Dunn, Edith Holm.
Secretary—Jean G. Birch.
Treasurer—Wm. J. McManus.

General Counsel—Roger Allan Moore.

Democratic Party

National Headquarters—1625 Massachusetts Ave., NW, Washington, DC 20036.

Chairman—Charles T. Manatt.
Vice Chairpersons—Richard Hatcher, Polly Baca Barragan, Lynn Culter.
Secretary—Dorothy V. Bush.
Treasurer—Charles Curry.
Finance Chairman—Peter G. Kelly.

Other Major Political Organizations

Americans For Democratic Action
(1411 K St. NW, Washington, DC 20005)
President—Patsy T. Mink.
National Director—Leon Shull.
Chairperson Exec. Comm.—Winn Newman.

Comm. on Political Education, AFL-CIO
(AFL-CIO Building, 815 16th St., Wash., DC 20006)

Chairman—Lane Kirkland.
Secretary-Treasurer—Thomas R. Donahue.

Communist Party U.S.A.
(235 W. 23d St., New York, NY 10011)
National Chairman—Henry Winston.
General Secretary—Gus Hall.

Conservative Party of the State of N.Y.
(45 E. 29th St., New York, NY 10016)
Chairman—J. Daniel Mahoney.
Executive Director—Serphin R. Maltese.
Secretary—Wilson G. Price.
Treasurer—James E. O'Doherty.

Liberal Party of New York State
(1560 Broadway, New York, NY 10036)
Chairman—Donald S. Harrington.
First Vice Chairman—Nicholas Gyory.
Treasurer—Bernice Benedick.
Secretary & Executive Director—James F. Notaro.

Libertarian National Committee
(2300 Wisconsin Ave. NW, Washington, DC 20007)
Chair—David P. Bergland.
Vice-Chair—Mary Louise Hanson.
Secretary—Sylvia Sanders.
Treasurer—Dallas Cooley.
National Director—Eric O'Keefe.

National States' Rights Party
(P.O. Box 1211, Marietta, GA 30061)
Chairman—J.B. Stoner.

Secretary—Edward R. Fields.
Treasurer—Peter Xavier.

Prohibition National Committee
(P.O. Box 2635, Denver, CO 80201)
National Chairman—Earl F. Dodge.
National Secretary—Rayford G. Feather.

Socialist Labor Party
In Minnesota: Industrial Gov't. Party
(914 Industrial Ave., Palo Alto, CA 94303)
National Secretary—Robert Bills.
Financial Secretary—Nathan Karp.

Socialist Party, U.S.A.
(135 W. Wells St., Milwaukee, WI 53203)
National Chairperson—Frank P. Ziedler.

Socialist Workers Party
(14 Charles Lane, New York, NY 10014)
National Secretary—Jack Barnes.
National Co-Chairpersons—Malik Miah, Barry Sheppard, Mary-Alice Waters.

America's Third Parties

Since 1860, there have been only 4 presidential elections in which all third parties together polled more than 10% of the vote: the Populists (James Baird Weaver) in 1892, the National Progressives (Theodore Roosevelt) in 1912, the La Follette Progressives in 1924, and George Wallace's American Party in 1968. In 1948, the combined third parties (Henry Wallace's Progressives, Strom Thurmond's States'

Rights party or Dixiecrats, Prohibition, Socialists, and others) received only 5.75% of the vote. In most elections since 1860, fewer than one vote in 20 has been cast for a third party. The only successful third party in American history was the Republican Party in the election of Abraham Lincoln in 1860.

Major Third Parties

Party	Presidential nominee	Election	Issues	Strength in
Anti-Masonic	William Wirt	1832	Against secret societies and oaths	Pa., Vt.
Free Soil	Martin Van Buren	1848	Anti-slavery	New York, Ohio
American (Know Nothing)	Millard Fillmore	1856	Anti-immigrant	Northeast, South
Greenback	Peter Cooper	1876	For "cheap money,"	
Greenback	James B. Weaver	1880	labor rights	National
Prohibition	(numerous)	1872	Anti-liquor	National
Populist	James B. Weaver	1892	For "cheap money," end of national banks	South, West
Socialist	Eugene V. Debs	1900-20	For public ownership	National
Socialist	Norman Thomas	1928-48	Liberal reforms	National
Progressive (Bull Moose)	Theodore Roosevelt	1912	Against high tariffs	Midwest, West
Union	William Lemke	1936	Anti "New Deal"	National
Progressive	Robert M. LaFollette	1924	Farmer & labor rights	Midwest, West
States' Rights	Strom Thurmond	1948	For segregation	South
Progressive	Henry Wallace	1948	Anti-cold war	New York, California
American	George Wallace	1968	For states' rights	South
American	John G. Schmitz	1972	For "law and order"	Far West, Oh., La.
None (Independent)	John B. Anderson	1980	A 3d choice	National

The Electoral College

The president and the vice president of the United States are the only elective federal officials not elected by direct vote of the people. They are elected by the members of the Electoral College, an institution that has survived since the founding of the nation despite repeated attempts in Congress to alter or abolish it. In the elections of 1824, 1876 and 1888 the presidential candidate receiving the largest popular vote failed to win a majority of the electoral votes.

On presidential election day, the first Tuesday after the first Monday in November of every 4th year, each state chooses as many electors as it has senators and representatives in Congress. In 1964, for the first time, as provided by the 23d Amendment to the Constitution, the District of Columbia voted for 3 electors. Thus, with 100 senators and 435 representatives, there are 538 members of the Electoral College, with a majority of 270 electoral votes needed to elect the president and vice president.

Political parties customarily nominate their lists of electors at their respective state conventions. An elector cannot be a member of Congress or any person holding federal office.

Some states print the names of the candidates for president and vice president at the top of the November ballot

while others list only the names of the electors. In either case, the electors of the party receiving the highest vote are elected. The electors meet on the first Monday after the 2d Wednesday in December in their respective state capitals or in some other place prescribed by state legislatures. By long-established custom they vote for their party nominees, although the Constitution does not require them to do so. All of the state's electoral votes are then awarded to the winners. The only Constitutional requirement is that at least one of the persons each elector votes for shall not be an inhabitant of that elector's home state.

Certified and sealed lists of the votes of the electors in each state are mailed to the president of the U.S. Senate. He opens them in the presence of the members of the Senate and House of Representatives in a joint session held on Jan. 6 (the next day if that falls on a Sunday), and the electoral votes of all the states are then counted. If no candidate for president has a majority, the House of Representatives chooses a president from among the 3 highest candidates, with all representatives from each state combining to cast one vote for that state. If no candidate for vice president has a majority, the Senate chooses from the top 2, with the senators voting as individuals.

The Ninety-Seventh Congress
With 1980 Election Results
The Senate

Terms are for 6 years and end Jan. 3 of the year preceding name. Annual salary $60,662.50. To be eligible for the U.S. Senate a person must be at least 30 years of age, a citizen of the United States for at least 9 years, and a resident of the state from which he is chosen. The Congress must meet annually on Jan. 3, unless it has, by law, appointed a different day.

Address: Washington, DC 20510

Senate officials (97th Congress): President Pro Tempore Strom Thurmond; Majority Leader Howard H. Baker Jr.; Majority Whip Ted Stevens; Minority Leader Robert C. Byrd; Minority Whip Alan Cranston.

Rep., 53; Dem., 46; Indep., 1; Total, 100. *Designates senior senator.
Official returns.

Term ends	Senator (Party, home)	1980 Election	Term ends	Senator (Party, home)	1980 Election
	Alabama			**Idaho**	
1985	Howell Heflin* (D, Tuscumbia)		1985	James A. McClure* (R, Payette)	
1987	Jeremiah Denton (R, Mobile)	650,362	1987	Steven D. Symms (R, Boise)	218,701
	Jim Folsom Jr. (D, Cullman)	610,195		Frank Church (D, Boise)	214,439
	Alaska			**Illinois**	
1985	Ted Stevens* (R, Anchorage)		1985	Charles H. Percy* (R, Wilmette)	
1987	Frank H. Murkowski (R, Anchorage)	84,159	1987	Alan J. Dixon (D, Belleville)	2,565,302
	Clark S. Gruening (D, Anchorage)	72,007		Dave C. O'Neal (R, Belleville)	1,946,296
	Arizona			**Indiana**	
1983	Dennis DeConcini (D, Tucson)		1983	Richard G. Lugar* (R, Indianapolis)	
1987	Barry M. Goldwater* (R, Scottsdale)	432,371	1987	Dan Quayle (R, Huntington)	1,182,414
	Bill Schulz (D, Scottsdale)	422,972		Birch Bayh (D, W. Terre Haute)	1,015,962
	Arkansas			**Iowa**	
1985	David Pryor (D, Little Rock)		1985	Roger W. Jepsen* (R, Davenport)	
1987	Dale Bumpers* (D, Charleston)	477,905	1987	Charles E. Grassley (R, New Hartford)	683,014
	Bill Clark (R, Little Rock)	330,576		John C. Culver (D, Cedar Rapids)	581,545
	California			**Kansas**	
1983	S.I. (Sam) Hayakawa (R, Mill Valley)		1985	Nancy Landon Kassebaum (R, Wichita)	
1987	Alan Cranston* (D, Palm Springs)	4,705,399	1987	Robert J. Dole* (R, Russell)	598,686
	Paul Gann (R, Carmichael)	3,093,426		John Simpson (D, Salina)	340,271
	Colorado			**Kentucky**	
1985	William L. Armstrong (R, Aurora)		1985	Walter D. Huddleston* (D, Elizabethtown)	
1987	Gary Hart* (D, Denver)	590,501	1987	Wendell H. Ford (D, Owensboro)	720,861
	Mary Estill Buchanan (R, Boulder)	571,295		Mary Louise Foust (R, Shelbyville)	386,029
	Connecticut			**Louisiana**	
1983	Lowell P. Weicker Jr.* (R, Greenwich)		1985	J. Bennett Johnston (D, Shreveport)	
1987	Christopher J. Dodd (D, Norwich)	763,969	1987	Russell B. Long* (D, Baton Rouge)	484,770
	James L. Buckley (R, Sharon)	581,884		Louis Woody Jenkins (D, Baton Rouge)	352,922
	Delaware			**Maine**	
1983	William V. Roth Jr.* (R, Wilmington)		1983	George J. Mitchell (D, Waterville)	
1985	Joseph R. Biden Jr. (D, Wilmington)		1985	William S. Cohen* (R, Bangor)	
	Florida			**Maryland**	
1983	Lawton Chiles* (D, Lakeland)		1983	Paul S. Sarbanes (D, Baltimore)	
1987	Paula Hawkins (R, Winter Park)	1,822,460	1987	Charles McC. Mathias Jr.* (R, Frederick)	850,970
	Bill Gunter (D, Tallahassee)	1,705,409		Edward T. Conroy (D, Bowie)	435,118
	Georgia			**Massachusetts**	
1985	Sam Nunn (D, Perry)		1983	Edward M. Kennedy* (D, Boston)	
1987	Mack Mattingly (R, St. Simons Is.)	803,686	1985	Paul E. Tsongas (D, Lowell)	
	Herman E. Talmadge* (D, Lovejoy)	776,143			
	Hawaii				
1983	Spark M. Matsunaga (D, Honolulu)				
1987	Daniel K. Inouye (D, Honolulu)	224,485			
	Cooper Brown (R, Honolulu)	53,068			

Term ends	Senator (Party, home)	1980 Election
	Michigan	
1983	Donald W. Riegle Jr.* (D, Flint)	
1985	Carl Levin (D, Detroit)	
	Minnesota	
1983	David Durenberger* (R, Minneapolis)	
1985	Rudolph E. Boschwitz (R, Wayzata)	
	Mississippi	
1983	John C. Stennis* (D, DeKalb)	
1985	Thad Cochran (R, Jackson)	
	Missouri	
1983	John C. Danforth (R, Jefferson City)	
1987	Thomas F. Eagleton* (D, St. Louis) . .	1,074,859
	Gene McNary (R, Sunset Hills)	985,399
	Montana	
1983	John Melcher* (D, Forsyth)	
1985	Max Baucus (D, Missoula)	
	Nebraska	
1983	Edward Zorinsky* (D, Omaha)	
1985	J. James Exon (D, Lincoln)	
	Nevada	
1983	Howard W. Cannon* (D, Las Vegas)	
1987	Paul Laxalt (R, Carson City)	144,224
	Mary Gojack (D, Reno)	92,129
	New Hampshire	
1985	Gordon J. Humphrey* (R, Swapee)	
1987	Warren Rudman (R, Nashua)	195,559
	John A. Durkin (D, Manchester). . . .	179,455
	New Jersey	
1983	Harrison A. Williams Jr.* (D, Bedminster)	
1985	Bill Bradley (D, Denville)	
	New Mexico	
1983	Harrison "Jack" Schmitt (R, Silver City)	
1985	Pete V. Domenici* (R, Albuquerque)	
	New York	
1983	Daniel Patrick Moynihan* (D, New York)	
1987	Alphonse M. D'Amato (R, C, RTL, Island Park).	2,699,652
	Elizabeth Holtzman (D, Brooklyn). . .	2,618,661
	Jacob K. Javits (L, New York).	664,544
	North Carolina	
1985	Jesse A. Helms* (R, Raleigh)	
1987	John P. East (R, Greenville)	898,064
	Robert Morgan (D, Lillington)	887,653
	North Dakota	
1983	Quentin N. Burdick* (D, Fargo)	
1987	Mark Andrews (R, Mapleton)	210,347
	Kent Johanneson (D, Bismarck). . . .	86,658
	Ohio	
1983	Howard M. Metzenbaum (D, Shaker Heights)	
1987	John Glenn* (D, Grandview Hts.) . . .	2,770,786
	James E. Betts (R, Rocky River) . . .	1,137,695

Term ends	Senator (Party, home)	1980 Election
	Oklahoma	
1985	David Lyle Boren* (D, Okla. City)	
1987	Don Nickles (R, Ponca City)	587,252
	Andy Coats (D, Okla. City)	478,283
	Oregon	
1985	Mark O. Hatfield* (R, Salem)	
1987	Bob Packwood (R, Lake Oswego) . .	594,290
	Ted Kulongoski (D, Eugene).	501,963
	Pennsylvania	
1983	John Heinz* (R, Pittsburgh)	
1987	Arlen Specter (R, Philadelphia)	2,230,404
	Peter Flaherty (D, Pittsburgh)	2,122,391
	Rhode Island	
1983	John H. Chafee (R, Warwick)	
1985	Claiborne Pell* (D, Newport)	
	South Carolina	
1985	Strom Thurmond* (R, Aiken)	
1987	Ernest Fritz Hollings (D, Columbia) . .	612,554
	Marshall T. Mays (R, Greenwood) . .	257,946
	South Dakota	
1985	Larry Pressler* (R, Humboldt)	
1987	James Abdnor (R, Mitchell)	190,594
	George McGovern (D, Mitchell)	129,018
	Tennessee	
1983	James R. Sasser (D, Nashville)	
1985	Howard H. Baker Jr.* (R, Huntsville)	
	Texas	
1983	Lloyd Bentsen (D, Houston)	
1985	John G. Tower* (R, Wichita Falls)	
	Utah	
1983	Orrin G. Hatch (R, Salt Lake City)	
1987	Jake Garn* (R, Salt Lake City)	437,675
	Dan Berman (D, Salt Lake City). . . .	151,454
	Vermont	
1983	Robert T. Stafford* (R, Rutland)	
1987	Patrick J. Leahy (D, Burlington)	104,176
	Stewart Ledbetter (R, Montpelier) . .	101,421
	Virginia	
1983	Harry F. Byrd Jr.* (I, Winchester)	
1985	John William Warner (R, Middleburg)	
	Washington	
1983	Henry M. Jackson* (D, Everett)	
1987	Slade Gorton (R, Olympia)	936,317
	Warren G. Magnuson (D, Seattle) . .	792,052
	West Virginia	
1983	Robert C. Byrd* (D, Sophia)	
1985	Jennings Randolph (D, Charleston)	
	Wisconsin	
1983	William Proxmire* (D, Madison)	
1987	Robert W. Kasten Jr. (R, Thiensville) .	1,106,311
	Gaylord A. Nelson (D, Madison) . . .	1,065,487
	Wyoming	
1983	Malcolm Wallop* (R, Big Horn)	
1985	Alan Kooi Simpson (R, Cody)	

The House of Representatives

Members' terms to Jan. 3, 1983. Annual salary $60,662.50; house speaker $79,125. To be eligible for membership, a person must be at least 25, a U.S. citizen for at least 7 years, and a resident of the state from which he is chosen.

Address: Washington, DC 20515

House Officials (97th Congress): Speaker Thomas P. O'Neill; Majority Leader James Wright; Majority Whip Thomas S. Foley; Minority Leader Robert H. Michel; Minority Whip Trent Lott.

C-Conservative; D-Democratic; DFL-Democrat Farmer-Labor; I-Independent; L-Liberal; Libert-Libertarian; R-Republican; S-Statesmen's Party; U-Unopposed; RTL-Right to Life.

Democrats, 242, Republicans, 190, vacant, 3. Total 435.

(Those marked * served in the 96th Congress.)

Bold face denotes the winner.

Official returns.

Dist.	Representative (Party, Home)	1980 Election	Dist.	Representative (Party, Home)	1980 Election
	Alabama		9.	**Fortney H. (Pete) Stark*** (D, Oakland)	**90,504**
1.	**Jack Edwards*** (R, Mobile)	**111,089**		William J. Kennedy (R, Pleasanton)	67,265
	Steve Smith (Libert, Birmingham)	6,130	10.	**Don Edwards*** (D, San Jose)	**102,231**
2.	**William L. Dickinson*** (R, Montgomery)	**104,796**		John M. Lutton (R, San Jose)	45,987
	Cecil Wyatt (D, Ramer)	63,447	11.	**Tom Lantos** (D, Hillsborough)	**85,823**
3.	**Bill Nichols*** (D, Sylacauga)	**107,654U**		Bill Royer* (R, Redwood City)	80,100
4.	**Tom Bevill*** (D, Jasper)	**129,365**	12.	**Paul N. McCloskey Jr.*** (R, Menlo Park)	**143,817**
	A.J. Killingsworth (S, Leeds)	2,721		Kirsten Olsen (D, Atherton)	37,009
5.	**Ronnie G. Flippo*** (D, Florence)	**117,626**	13.	**Norman Y. Mineta*** (D, San Jose)	**132,246**
	Betty T. Benson (Libert, Madison)	7,341		W. E. (Ted) Gagne (R, Saratoga)	79,766
6.	**Albert Lee Smith Jr.** (R, Birmingham)	**95,019**	14.	**Norman D. Shumway*** (R, Stockton)	**133,979**
	W. B. (Pete) Clifford (D, Birmingham)	87,536		Ann Cerney (D, Lodi)	79,883
7.	**Richard C. Shelby*** (D, Woodstock)	**122,505**	15.	**Tony Coelho*** (D, Merced)	**108,072**
	James E. "Jim" Bacon (R, Hueytown)	43,320		Ron Schwartz (R, Fresno)	37,895
			16.	**Leon E. Panetta*** (D, Carmel Valley)	**158,360**
	Alaska At Large			W. A. (Jack) Roth (R, Pacific Grove)	54,675
	Don Young* (R, Fort Yukon)	**114,089**	17.	**Charles Pashayan Jr.*** (R, Fresno)	**129,159**
	Kevin "Pat" Parnell (D, Anchorage)	39,922		Willard H. Johnson (D, Selma)	53,780
			18.	**William M. Thomas*** (R, Bakersfield)	**126,046**
	Arizona			Mary "Pat" Timmermans (D, Bakersfield)	51,415
1.	**John J. Rhodes*** (R, Mesa)	**136,961**	19.	**Robert J. Lagomarsino*** (R, Ojai)	**162,854**
	Steve Jancek (D, Mesa)	40,045		Carmen Lodise (D, Isla Vista)	36,990
2.	**Morris K. Udall*** (D, Tucson)	**127,736**	20.	**Barry M. Goldwater Jr.*** (R, Woodland Hills)	**199,681**
	Richard H. Huff (R, Tucson)	88,653		Matt Miller (D, Camarillo)	43,025
3.	**Bob Stump*** (D, Tolleson)	**141,448**	21.	**Bobbi Fiedler** (R, Northridge)	**74,843**
	Bob Croft (R, Munds Park)	65,845		James C. Corman* (D, Van Nuys)	74,091
	Sharon Hayse (write-in) (Libert, Sedona)	12,529	22.	**Carlos J. Moorhead*** (R, Glendale)	**115,241**
4.	**Eldon Rudd*** (R, Scottsdale)	**142,565**		Pierce O'Donnell (D, Altadena)	57,477
	Les Miller (D, Phoenix)	85,046	23.	**Anthony C. Beilenson*** (D, Los Angeles)	**126,020**
				Robert Winckler (R, Woodland Hills)	62,742
	Arkansas		24.	**Henry A. Waxman*** (D, Los Angeles)	**93,569**
1.	**Bill Alexander*** (D, Osceola)	**Unopposed**		Roland Cayard (R, Los Angeles)	39,744
2.	**Ed Bethune*** (R, Searcy)	**159,148**	25.	**Edward R. Roybal*** (D, Los Angeles)	**49,080**
	James G. (Jim) Reid (D, Jacksonville)	42,278		Richard E. Ferraro Jr. (R, Los Angeles)	21,116
3.	**John Paul Hammerschmidt*** (R, Harrison)	**Unopposed**	26.	**John H. Rousselot*** (R, San Marino)	**116,715**
4.	**Beryl Anthony Jr.*** (D, El Dorado)	**Unopposed**		Joseph L. Lisoni (D, Arcadia)	40,099
According to Arkansas law, it is not required to tabulate votes for unopposed candidates.			27.	**Robert K. Dornan*** (R, Los Angeles)	**109,807**
				Carey Peck (D, Santa Monica)	100,061
	California		28.	**Julian C. Dixon*** (D, Los Angeles)	**108,725**
1.	**Gene Chappie** (R, Roseville)	**145,585**		Robert Reid (D, Culver City)	23,179
	Harold T. Johnson* (D, Roseville)	107,993	29.	**Augustus F. Hawkins*** (D, Los Angeles)	**80,095**
2.	**Don H. Clausen*** (R, Crescent City)	**141,698**		Michael A. Hirt (R, Los Angeles)	10,282
	Norma K. Bork (D, Angwin)	109,789	30.	**George E. Danielson*** (D, Monterey Park)	**74,119**
3.	**Robert T. Matsui*** (D, Sacramento)	**170,670**		J. Arthur Platten (R, El Monte)	24,136
	Joseph Murphy (R, Sacramento)	64,215	31.	**Mervyn M. Dymally** (D, Compton)	**69,146**
4.	**Vic Fazio*** (D, Sacramento)	**133,853**		Don Grimshaw (R, Lawndale)	38,203
	Albert Dehr (R, Sacramento)	60,935	32.	**Glenn M. Anderson*** (D, Harbor City)	**84,057**
5.	**John L. Burton*** (D, San Francisco)	**101,105**		John R. Adler (R, Torrance)	39,260
	Dennis McQuaid (R, Novato)	89,624	33.	**Wayne Grisham*** (R, La Mirada)	**122,439**
6.	**Phillip Burton*** (D, San Francisco)	**93,400**		Fred L. Anderson (D, Whittier)	50,365
	Tom Spinosa (R, San Francisco)	34,500	34.	**Dan Lungren*** (R, Long Beach)	**138,024**
7.	**George Miller*** (D, Martinez)	**142,044**			
	Giles St. Clair (R, Alaino)	70,479			
8.	**Ronald V. Dellums*** (D, Berkeley)	**108,380**			
	Charles V. Hughes (R, Berkeley)	76,580			

Dist.	Representative (Party, Home)	1980 Election

Simone (D, Los Alamitos) 46,351
35. **David Dreier** (R, La Verne) **100,743**
Jim Lloyd* (D, West Covina) 88,279
36. **George E. Brown Jr.*** (D, Colton) . . **88,634**
John Paul Stark (R, San Bernardino). 73,252
37. **Jerry Lewis*** (R, Highland) **166,640**
Donald M. Rusk (D, Redlands) 58,462
38. **Jerry M. Patterson*** (D, Santa Ana) **91,880**
Art Jacobson (R, Los Alamitos). . . . 66,256
39. **William E. Dannemeyer*** (R, Fuller-
ton) **175,228**
Leonard L. Lahtinen (D, Anaheim) . . 54,504
40. **Robert E. Badham*** (R, Newport
Beach) **213,999**
Michael F. Dow (D, Balboa Island) . . 66,512
41. **Bill Lowery** (R, San Diego) **123,187**
Bob Wilson (D, La Mesa) 101,101
42. **Duncan Hunter** (R, San Diego) . . . **79,713**
Lionel Van Deerlin* (D, Chula Vista) . 69,936
43. **Clair W. Burgener*** (R, Rancho
Santa Fe) **299,037**
Tom Metgzer (D, Fallbrook) 46,383

Colorado
1. **Patricia Schroeder*** (D, Denver) . . **107,364**
Naomi Bradford (R, Denver) 67,804
2. **Timothy E. Wirth*** (D, Denver) . . . **153,550**
John McElderry (R, Wheatridge) . . . 111,868
3. **Ray Kogovsek*** (D, Pueblo) **105,820**
Harold L. "Mack" McCormick (R,
Canon City) 84,292
4. **Hank Brown** (R, Greeley) **178,221**
Polly Baca Barragan (D, Thornton) . . 76,849
5. **Ken Kramer*** (R, Colorado Springs). **177,319**
Ed Scheiber (D, Greenwood Village) . 62,003

Connecticut
1. **William R. Cotter*** (D, Hartford) . . . **137,849**
Marjorie D. Anderson (R, West Hart-
ford) 80,816
2. **Samuel Gejdenson** (D, Bozrah) . . . **119,176**
Tony Guglielmo (R, Stafford Springs) 104,107
3. **Lawrence J. DeNardis** (R, Hamden) **117,024**
Joseph I. Lieberman (D, New Haven) 103,903
4. **Stewart B. McKinney*** (R, Fairfield). **124,285**
John A. Phillips (D, Norwalk) 74,326
5. **William R. Ratchford** (D, Danbury) **117,316**
Edward M. Donahue (R, Shelton). . . 115,614
6. **Anthony Toby Moffett*** (D, Union-
ville) **142,685**
Nicholas Schaus (R, Farmington) . . . 98,331

Delaware At Large
Thomas B. Evans Jr.* (R, Wilming-
ton) **133,842**
Robert L. Maxwell (D, Wilmington) . . 81,227

Florida
1. **Earl Hutto*** (D, Panama City). **119,829**
Warren Briggs (R, Pensacola) 75,939
2. **Don Fuqua*** (D, Altha) **138,252**
John R. LaCapra (R, Tallahassee) . . 57,588
3. **Charles E. Bennett*** (D, Jackson-
ville) **104,672**
Harry Radcliff (R, Jacksonville) 31,208
4. **Bill Chappell*** (D, Ocala) **147,775**
Barney E. Dillard Jr. (R, Altoona) . . . 76,924
5. **Bill McCollum** (R, Altamonte Springs) **177,603**
David Best (D, Crystal River) 140,903
6. **C. W. Bill Young** (R, St. Petersburg). **Unopposed**
7. **Sam Gibbons*** (D, Tampa). **132,529**
Charles P. Jones (R, Tampa) 52,138
8. **Andy Ireland*** (D, Winter Haven) . . **151,613**
Scott Nicholson (R, Bradenton). . . . 61,820
9. **Bill Nelson*** (D, Melbourne) **139,468**
Stan Dowiat (R, Melbourne Beach). . 58,734
10. **L. A. (Skip) Bafalis*** (R, Fort Myers
Beach) **272,393**
Richard D. Sparkman (D, Naples) . . . 72,646
11. **Dan Mica*** (D, West Palm Beach) . . **201,713**
Al Coogler (R, West Palm Beach) . . . 137,520

Dist.	Representative (Party, Home)	1980 Election

12. **E. Clay Shaw** (R, Ft. Lauderdale) . . **128,561**
Alan S. Becker (D, Plantation 107,164
13. **William Lehman*** (D, N. Miami
Beach) **127,828**
Alvin E. Entin (R, Miami) 42,830
14. **Claude Pepper*** (D, Miami) **95,820**
Evelio S. Estrella (R, Miami) 32,027
15. **Dante B. Fascell*** (D, Miami) **132,952**
Herbert J. Hoodwin (R, Miami) 70,433
According to Florida law, it is not required to tabulate votes for unopposed candidates.

Georgia
1. **Bo Ginn*** (D, Millen) **82,145U**
2. **Charles Hatcher** (D, Albany) . . . **92,264**
Jack E. Harrell Jr. (R, Quitman) 33,107
3. **Jack Brinkley*** (D, Columbus) **89,040U**
4. **Elliot H. Levitas** (D, Atlanta) **117,091**
Barry E. Billington (R, Decatur) 51,546
5. **Wyche Fowler Jr.*** (D, Atlanta) . . . **101,646**
F. William Dowda (R, Atlanta). 35,640
6. **Newt Gingrich*** (R, Carrollton) . . . **96,071**
Dock H. Davis (D, Franklin 66,606
7. **Larry P. McDonald*** (D, Marietta) . . **115,892**
Richard L. Castellucis (R, Marietta) 54,242
8. **Billy Lee Evans*** (D, Macon) **91,103**
Darwin Carter (R, Alma) 31,033
9. **Ed Jenkins*** (D, Jasper) **115,576**
David G. Ashworth (R, Canton) 54,341
10. **Doug Barnard Jr.*** (D, Augusta) . . . **102,177**
Bruce J. Neubauer (R, Athens) 25,194

Hawaii
1. **Cecil (Cec) Heftel*** (D, Honolulu) . . **98,256**
Aloma Keen Noble (R, Honolulu) . . . 19,819
2. **Daniel K. Akaka*** (D, Honolulu) . . . **141,477**
Don G. Smith (Libert, Kaneohe). . . . 15,903

Idaho
1. **Larry E. Craig** (R, Midvale) **116,845**
Glenn W. Nichols (D, Boise). 100,697
2. **George Hansen*** (R, Pocatello) . . . **116,196**
Diane Bilyeu (D, Pocatello) 81,364

Illinois
1. **Harold Washington** (D, Chicago) . . **119,562**
George Williams (R, Chicago) 5,660
2. **Gus Savage** (D, Chicago) **129,771**
Marsha A. Harris (R, Chicago) 17,428
3. **Marty Russo*** (D, South Holland) . . **137,283**
Lawrence C. Sarsoun (R, Midlothian) 61,955
4. **Edward J. Derwinski*** (R, Floss-
moor) **152,377**
Richard S. Jalovec (D, Burr Ridge) . . 71,814
5. **John G. Fary*** (D, Chicago) **106,142**
Robert V. Kotowski (R, Chicago) . . . 27,136
6. **Henry J. Hyde*** (R, Bensenville) . . . **123,593**
Mario Raymond Reda (D, River For-
est) 60,951
7. **Cardiss Collins*** (D, Chicago) **80,056**
Ruth R. Hooper (R, Chicago) 14,041
8. **Dan Rostenkowski*** (D, Chicago) . . **98,524**
Walter F. Zilke (R, Chicago). 17,854
9. **Sidney R. Yates*** (D, Chicago) **106,543**
John D. Andrica (D, Chicago) 39,244
10. **John E. Porter** (R, Evanston) **137,707**
Robert A. Weinberger (D, Glencoe) . 89,008
11. **Frank Annunzio*** (D, Chicago) **121,166**
Michael R. Zanillo (R, Chicago) 52,417
12. **Philip M. Crane*** (R, Mt. Prospect) . **185,080**
David McCartney (D, Kildeer) 64,729
13. **Robert McClory*** (R, Lake Bluff) . . **131,448**
Michael Reese (D, Elgin) 52,000
14. **John N. Erienborn*** (R, Glen Ellyn) . **202,583**
LeRoy E. Kennel (D, Lombard) 61,224
15. **Tom Corcoran*** (R, Ottowa) **150,898**
John P. Quillin (D, Seneca) 45,721
16. **Lynn Martin** (R, Rockford) **132,905**
Douglas R. Aurand (D, Rockford). . . 64,224
17. **George M. O'Brien*** (R, Joliet). . . . **125,806**

Dist.	Representative (Party, Home)	1980 Election
	Michael A. Murer (D, Joliet)	65,305
18.	**Robert H. Michel*** (R, Peoria)	**125,561**
	John L. Knuppel (D, Havana)	76,471
19.	**Tom Railsback*** (R, Moline)	**142,616**
	Thomas J. Hand (D, Fulton)	51,753
20.	**Paul Findley*** (R, Pittsfield)	**123,427**
	David L. Robinson (D, Springfield) . .	96,950
21.	**Edward R. Madigan*** (R, Lincoln) . .	**132,186**
	Penny L. Severns (D, Decator)	63,476
22.	**Daniel B. Crane*** (R, Danville) . . .	**146,014**
	Peter M. Voelz (D, Paris)	66,065
23.	**Melvin Price*** (D, East St. Louis) . .	**107,786**
	Ronald L. Davinroy (R, O'Fallon) . . .	59,644
24.	**Paul Simon*** (D, Carbondale)	**112,134**
	John T. Anderson (R, Marion)	110,176

Indiana

Dist.	Representative (Party, Home)	1980 Election
1.	**Adam Benjamin Jr.*** (D, Hobart) . .	**112,016**
	Joseph Douglas Harkin (R, Highland)	43,537
2.	**Floyd J. Fithian*** (D, Lafayette) . . .	**122,326**
	Ernest Niemeyer (R, Lowell)	103,957
3.	**John Patrick Hiler** (R, LaPorte) . . .	**103,972**
	John Brademas* (D, South Bend) . .	85,136
4.	**Dan R. Coats** (R, Fort Wayne)	**120,055**
	John D. Walda (D, Fort Wayne)	77,542
5.	**Elwood Hillis*** (R, Kokomo)	**129,474**
	Nels J. Ackerson (D, Noblesville) . . .	80,378
6.	**Dave Evans*** (D, Indianapolis)	**99,089**
	David G. Crane (R, Martinsville)	98,302
7.	**John T. Myers*** (R, Covington) . . .	**137,604**
	Patrick D. Carroll (R, Bloomington) . .	69,051
8.	**Joel Deckard** (R, Evansville)	**119,415**
	Kenneth C. Snider (D, Decker)	97,059
9.	**Lee H. Hamilton*** (D, Columbus) . .	**136,574**
	George Meyer Jr. (R, Jeffersonville) .	75,601
10.	**Philip R. Sharp*** (D, Muncie)	**103,083**
	William G. Frazier (R, Muncie)	90,051
11.	**Andrew Jacobs Jr.*** (D, Indianapolis)	**105,468**
	Sheila Suess (R, Indianapolis)	78,743

Iowa

Dist.	Representative (Party, Home)	1980 Election
1.	**Jim Leach*** (R, Davenport)	**133,349**
	Jim Larew (D, Iowa City)	72,602
2.	**Thomas J. Tauke** (R, Dubuque) . . .	**111,587**
	Steve Sovern (D, Marion)	93,175
3.	**Cooper Evans** (R, Grundy Center) . .	**107,869**
	Lynn G. Cutler (D, Waterloo)	101,735
4.	**Neal Smith*** (D, Altoona)	**117,896**
	Donald C. Young (R, Des Moines) . .	100,335
5.	**Tom Harkin*** (D, Ames)	**127,895**
	Cal Hultman (R, Red Oak)	84,472
6.	**Berkley Bedell*** (D, Spirit Lake) . . .	**129,460**
	Clarence S. Carney (R, Sioux City) .	71,866

Kansas

Dist.	Representative (Party, Home)	1980 Election
1.	**Pat Roberts** (R, Dodge City)	**121,545**
	Phil Martin (D, Larned)	73,586
2.	**Jim Jeffries*** (R, Atchison)	**92,107**
	Sam Keys (D, Manhattan)	78,859
3.	**Larry Winn Jr.** (R, Overland Park) . .	**109,294**
	Dan Watkins (D, Lawrence)	82,414
4.	**Dan Glickman*** (D, Wichita)	**124,014**
	Clay Hunter (R, Wichita)	55,899
5.	**Bob Whittaker** (R, Augusta)	**141,029**
	David L. Miller (D, Parsons)	45,676

Kentucky

Dist.	Representative (Party, Home)	1980 Election
1.	**Carroll Hubbard Jr.*** (D, Mayfield) .	**118,565U**
2.	**William H. Natcher*** (D, Bowling Green)	**99,670**
	Mark T. Watson (R, Elizabethtown) . .	52,110
3.	**Romano L. Mazzoli*** (D, Louisville) .	**85,873**
	Richard Cesler (R, Louisville)	46,681
4.	**Gene Snyder*** (R, Brownsboro Farms)	**126,049**
	Phil M. McGary (D, Louisville)	62,138
5.	**Harold Rogers** (R, Somerset)	**112,093**
	Ted R. Marcum (D, Richmond)	54,027
6.	**Larry J. Hopkins** (R, Lexington) . . .	**105,376**
	Tom Easterly (D, Frankfort)	72,473
7.	**Carl D. Perkins*** (D, Hindman)	**117,665U**

Dist.	Representative (Party, Home)	1980 Election
	Louisiana	
1.	**Bob Livingston*** (R, New Orleans) .	**81,777**
	Michael J. Musmeci Sr. (D, Chalmette) .	8,277
2.	**Lindy (Mrs. Hale) Boggs*** (D, New Orleans) .	**45,091**
	Rob Couhig (R, New Orleans)	25,521
3.	**W.J. "Billy" Tauzin** (D, Thibodaux) .	**80,455**
	Bob Namer (D, Metairie)	14,074
4.	**Buddy Roemer** (D, Bossier City) . .	**103,625**
	Claude "Buddy" Leach (D, Leesville)	58,705
5.	**Jerry Huckaby*** (D, Ringgold)	**93,519**
	L.D. (None of the Above) Knox (D, Winnsboro) .	11,748
6.	**W. Henson Moore*** (R, Baton Rouge) .	**118,540**
	Alice Brooks (D, Springfield)	12,149
7.	**John B. Breaux*** (D, Crowley)	**Unopposed**
8.	**Gillis W. Long*** (D, Alexandria) . . .	**75,433**
	Clyde C. Holloway (R, Forest Hill) . .	27,816
	Robert H. Mitchell (R, Forest Hill) . .	6,243

According to Louisiana law, it is not required to tabulate votes for unopposed candidates.

Maine

Dist.	Representative (Party, Home)	1980 Election
1.	**David F. Emery*** (R, Rockland) . . .	**188,667**
	Harold C. Pachios (D, Cape Elizabeth)	86,819
2.	**Olympia J. Snowe*** (R, Auburn) . . .	**186,406**
	Harold L. Silverman (D, Calais)	51,026

Maryland

Dist.	Representative (Party, Home)	1980 Election
1.	**Roy Dyson** (D, Great Mills)	**97,743**
	Robert E. Bauman* (R, Easton)	91,143
2.	**Clarence D. Long*** (D, Towson) . . .	**121,017**
	Helen D. Bentley (R, Lutherville) . . .	89,961
3.	**Barbara A. Mikulski*** (D, Baltimore) .	**102,293**
	Russell T. Schaffer (R, Towson) . . .	32,074
4.	**Majorie S. Holt*** (R, Severna Park) .	**120,985**
	James J. Riley (D, Severna Park) . . .	47,375
5.	**Steny H. Hoyer** (D, Berkshire) a . .	**42,573**
	Audrey Scott (R, Bowie)	33,708
6.	**Beverly B. Byron*** (D, Frederick) . .	**146,101**
	Raymond E. Beck (R, Westminster) .	62,913
7.	**Parren J. Mitchell*** (D, Baltimore) .	**97,104**
	Victor Clark Jr. (R, Baltimore)	12,650
8.	**Michael D. Barnes*** (D, Kensington)	**148,301**
	Newton I. Steers Jr. (R, Bethesda) . .	101,659

(a) Vacancy declared, Feb. 24, 1981, due to incapacitation of Gladys Noon Spellman; Hoyer elected in special election, May 19, 1981.

Massachusetts

Dist.	Representative (Party, Home)	1980 Election
1.	**Silvio O. Conte*** (R, Pittsfield)	**156,514**
	Helen Poppy Doyle (D, Ashfield) . . .	52,457
2.	**Edward P. Boland*** (D, Springfield) .	**120,711**
	Thomas P. Swank (R, West Brookfield) .	38,672
3.	**Joseph D. Early*** (D, Worcester) . .	**141,560**
	David G. Skehan (R, Milford)	54,213
4.	**Barney Frank** (D, Newton)	**103,466**
	Richard A. Jones (R, Harvard)	95,898
5.	**James M. Shannon** (D, Lawrence) . .	**136,758**
	William C. Sawyer (R, Acton)	70,547
6.	**Nicholas Mavroules** (D, Peabody) .	**111,393**
	Thomas H. Trimarco (R, Beverly) . . .	103,192
7.	**Edward J. Markey*** (D, Malden) . . .	**155,759U**
8.	**Thomas P. O'Neill Jr.*** (D, Cambridge) .	**128,689**
	William A. Barnstead (R, Arlington) . .	35,477
9.	**Joe Moakley*** (D, Boston)	**104,010U**
10.	**Margaret M. Heckler*** (R, Wellseley)	**131,794**
	Robert E. McCarthy (D, East Bridgewater) .	85,629
11.	**Brian J. Donnelly*** (D, Dorchester) .	**137,066U**
12.	**Gerry E. Studds*** (D, Cohasset) . . .	**195,791**
	Paul V. Doane (R, Harwich)	71,620

Michigan

Dist.	Representative (Party, Home)	1980 Election
1.	**John Conyers Jr.*** (D, Detroit) . . .	**123,286**
	William M. Bell (R, Detroit)	6,244
2.	**Carl D. Pursell*** (R, Plymouth) . . .	**115,562**

Dist.	Representative (Party, Home)	1980 Election
	Kathleen F. O'Reilly (D, Plymouth) . .	83,550
3.	**Howard Wolpe*** (D, Lansing)	**113,080**
	James S. Gilmore (R, Kalamazoo) . .	102,591
4.	**Mark D. Siljander** (R, Three Rivers)(b)	**36,046**
	Johnie Rodebush (D, Niles)	12,461
5.	**Howard S. Sawyer*** (R, Rockford) .	**118,061**
	Dale R. Sprik (D, Grand Rapids) . . .	101,737
6.	**Jim Dunn** (R, East Lansing)	**111,272**
	Bob Carr* (D, East Lansing)	108,548
7.	**Dale E. Kildee*** (D, Flint)	**147,280**
	Dennis L. Berry (L, Burton)	11,507
8.	**Bob Traxler*** (D, Bay City)	**124,155**
	Norman R. Hughes (R, Metamora) . .	77,009
9.	**Guy Vander Jagt*** (R, Luther) . . .	**168,713**
	Marshall A. Tufts (Am I, Fruitport) . .	5,985
10.	**Donald Joseph Albosta*** (D, St. Charles)	**126,962**
	Richard J. Allen (R, Ithaca)	111,496
11.	**Robert W. Davis*** (R, Gaylord) . .	**146,205**
	Dan Dorrity (D, Saulte Ste. Marie) . .	75,515
12.	**David E. Bonior*** (D, Mt. Clemens) .	**112,698**
	Kirk Walsh (R, St. Clair Shores) . . .	90,931
13.	**George W. Crockett Jr.*** (D, Detroit) .	**79,719**
	M. Michael Hurd (R, Detroit)	6,473
14.	**Dennis M. Hertel** (D, Detroit)	**90,362**
	Vic Caputo (R, Grosse Pointe)	78,395
15.	**William D. Ford*** (D, Taylor)	**113,492**
	Gerald R. Carlson (R, Dearborn) . . .	53,046
16.	**John D. Dingell*** (D, Trenton) . . .	**105,844**
	Pamella A. Seay (R, Trenton)	42,735
17.	**William M. Brodhead*** (D, Detroit) .	**127,525**
	Alfred L. Patterson (R, Detroit)	44,313
18.	**James J. Blanchard*** (D, Pleasant Ridge)	**135,705**
	Betty J. Suida (R, Royal Oak)	68,575
19.	**William S. Broomfield*** (R, Birmingham)	**168,530**
	Wayne E. Daniels (D, Union Lake) . .	60,100

Siljander elected Apr. 21, 1981 to fill vacancy due to resignation of Dave Stockman, Jan. 27, 1981.

Minnesota

Dist.	Representative (Party, Home)	1980 Election
1.	**Arlen Erdahl*** (R, West St. Paul) .	**171,099**
	Russell V. Smith (D, Rochester) . . .	67,279
2.	**Tom Hagedorn*** (R, Truman) . . .	**158,082**
	Harold J. Bergquist (D, Burnsville) . .	102,586
3.	**Bill Frenzel*** (R, Golden Valley) . .	**179,393**
	Joel A. Saliterman (D, St. Louis Park) .	57,868
4.	**Bruce F. Vento*** (D, St. Paul) . . .	**119,182**
	John Berg (R, St. Paul)	82,537
5.	**Martin Olav Sabo*** (D, Minneapolis) .	**126,451**
	John Doherty (R, Minneapolis)	48,200
6.	**Vin Weber** (R, St. Cloud)	**140,402**
	Archie Baumann (D, Redwood Falls) .	126,173
7.	**Arlan Stangeland*** (R, Barnesville) .	**135,084**
	Gene Wenstrom (D, Elbow Lake) . . .	124,026
8.	**James L. Oberstar*** (D, Chisholm) .	**182,228**
	Edward Fiore (R, Anoka)	72,350

Mississippi

Dist.	Representative (Party, Home)	1980 Election
1.	**Jamie L. Whitten*** (D, Charleston) .	**104,269**
	Terrill K. Moffett (R, Oxford)	61,292
2.	**David R. Bowen*** (D, Cleveland) . .	**96,750**
	Frank Drake (R, Durant)	42,300
3.	**G. V. (Sonny) Montgomery*** (D, Meridian)	**128,035**
4.	**Jon Hinson*** (R, Tylertown)(c)	**69,321**
	Britt R. Singletary (D, Jackson) . . .	52,303
	Leslie B. McLemore (I, Jackson) . . .	52,959
5.	**Trent Lott*** (R, Pascagoula) . . .	**131,559**
	Jimmy McVeay (D, Ocean Springs) . .	46,416

(c) Vacancy due to the resignation of Jon Hinson, Apr. 13, 1981.

Missouri

Dist.	Representative (Party, Home)	1980 Election
1.	**William (Bill) Clay*** (D, St. Louis) . .	**91,272**
	Bill White (R, Rock Hill)	38,667
2.	**Robert A. Young*** (D, Maryland Heights)	**148,227**

Dist.	Representative (Party, Home)	1980 Election
	John O. Shields (R, St. Louis)	81,762
3.	**Richard A. Gephardt*** (D, St. Louis)	**143,132**
	Robert A. Cedarburg (R, St. Louis) . .	41,277
4.	**Ike Skelton*** (D, Lexington)	**151,459**
	Bill Baker (R, Lee's Summit)	71,869
5.	**Richard Bolling*** (D, Kansas City) . .	**110,957**
	Vincent E. Baker (R, Kansas City) . .	47,309
6.	**E. Thomas Coleman*** (R, Kansas City)	**149,281**
	Vernon King (D, Excelsior Springs) . .	62,048
7.	**Gene Taylor*** (R, Sarcoxie)	**161,668**
	Ken Young (D, Point Lookout)	76,844
8.	**Wendell Bailey*** (R, Willow Springs) .	**127,675**
	Steve Gardner (D, Ellisville)	95,751
9.	**Harold L. Volkmer*** (D, Hannibal) . .	**135,905**
	John W. Turner (R, St. Louis)	104,835
10.	**Bill Emerson** (R, DeSoto)	**116,167**
	Bill D. Burlison* (D, Cape Girardeau) .	94,465

Montana

Dist.	Representative (Party, Home)	1980 Election
1.	**Pat Williams*** (D, Helena)	**112,866**
	John K. McDonald (R, Lakeside) . . .	70,874
2.	**Ron Marlenee*** (R, Scobey)	**91,431**
	Tom Monahan (D, Billings)	63,370

Nebraska

Dist.	Representative (Party, Home)	1980 Election
1.	**Douglas K. Bereuter*** (R, Utica). . .	**160,705**
	Rex S. Story (D, Lincoln)	43,605
2.	**Hal Daub** (R, Omaha)	**107,736**
	Richard M. Fellman (D, Omaha) . . .	88,843
3.	**Virginia Smith*** (R, Chappell) . . .	**182,887**
	Stan Ditus (D, McCook)	32,967

Nevada At Large

Dist.	Representative (Party, Home)	1980 Election
	Jim Santini* (D, Las Vegas) . . .	**165,107**
	Vince Saunders (R, Las Vegas)	63,163

New Hampshire

Dist.	Representative (Party, Home)	1980 Election
1.	**Norman E. D'Amours*** (D, Manchester)	**114,061**
	Marshall W. Cobleigh (R, Manchester)	73,565
2.	**Judd Gregg** (R, Greenfield)	**113,304**
	Maurice L. Arel (D, Nashua)	63,350

New Jersey

Dist.	Representative (Party, Home)	1980 Election
1.	**James J. Florio*** (D, Camden) . . .	**147,352**
	Scott L. Sibert (R, Woodbury)	42,154
2.	**William J. Hughes*** (D, Ocean City).	**135,437**
	Beech N. Fox (R, Cape May Courthouse)	97,072
3.	**James J. Howard*** (D, Spring Lake Heights)	**106,269**
	Marie Sheehan Muhler (R, Marlboro) .	104,184
4.	**Christopher H. Smith** (R, Old Bridge)	**95,447**
	Frank Thompson Jr.* (D, Trenton) . .	68,480
5.	**Millicent Fenwick*** (R, Bernardsville)	**156,016**
	Kieran E. Pillion Jr. (D, Millington) . .	41,269
6.	**Edwin B. Forsythe*** (R, Moorestown)	**125,792**
	Lewis M. Weinstein (D, Cherry Hill) . .	92,227
7.	**Marge Roukema** (R, Ridgewood) . .	**108,760**
	Andrew Maguire* (D, Ridgewood) . .	99,737
8.	**Robert A. Roe*** (D, Wayne)	**95,493**
	William R. Cleveland (R, Pompton Lakes)	44,625
9.	**Harold C. Hollenbeck*** (R, East Rutherford)	**116,128**
	Gabriel Ambrosio (D, Lyndhurst) . . .	75,321
10.	**Peter W. Rodino Jr.*** (D, Newark) . .	**76,154**
	Everett J. Jennings (R, East Orange) .	11,778
11.	**Joseph G. Minish*** (D, West Orange)	**106,155**
	Robert A. Davis (R, Verona)	57,772
12.	**Matthew J. Rinaldo*** (R, Union) . . .	**134,973**
	Rose Zeidwerg Monyek (D, Rahway) .	36,577
13.	**James A. Courter*** (R, Hackettstown)	**152,862**
	Dave Stickle (D, Pompton Plains) . . .	56,251
14.	**Frank J. Guarini*** (D, Jersey City) . .	**86,921**
	Dennis E. Teti (R, Weehawken)	45,606
15.	**Bernard J. Dwyer** (D, Edison) . . .	**92,457**
	William J. O'Sullivan Jr. (R, Sayreville)	75,812

Dist.	Representative (Party, Home)	1980 Election
	New Mexico	
1.	**Manuel Lujan Jr.*** (R, Albuquerque).	**125,910**
	Bill Richardson (D, Santa Fe)	120,903
2.	**Joe Skeen** (R, Picacho).	**61,564**
	David King (D, Pie Town)	55,085
	Dorothy Runnels (Un, Lovington) . . .	45,343
	New York	
1.	**William Carney*** (R, C, RTL Hauppauge) .	**115,213**
	Thomas A. Twomey (D, East Hampton).	85,629
2.	**Thomas J. Downey*** (D, W. Islip) .	**84,035**
	Louis J. Modica (R, C, RTL, Brightwaters)	65,106
3.	**Gregory W. Carman** (R, C, Farmingdale).	**87,952**
	Jerome A. Ambro* (D, RTL, East Northport)	83,389
4.	**Norman F. Lent** (R, C, RTL, Baldwin)	**117,455**
	Charles F. Brennan (D, L, Baldwin) .	58,270
5.	**Raymond J. McGrath** (R, C, RTL, Valley Stream)	**105,140**
	Karen S. Burstein (D, L, Woodmere) .	77,228
6.	**John LeBoutillier** (R, C, RTL, Westbury).	**89,762**
	Lester L. Wolff* (D, L, Great Neck). .	80,209
7.	**Joseph P. Addabbo*** (D, R, L, Ozone Park)	**96,137**
	Francis A. Lees (C, RTL, East Meadow)	4,703
8.	**Benjamin S. Rosenthal*** (D, L, Flushing)	**84,273**
	Albert Lemishow (R, C, RTL, Flushing)	27,156
9.	**Geraldine A. Ferraro*** (D, Forest Hills).	**63,796**
	Vito P. Battista (R, C, RTL, Brooklyn)	44,473
10.	**Mario Biaggi*** (D, R, L, Bronx)	**95,322**
	Joseph P. Cavanna (C, Bronx)	3,942
11.	**James H. Scheuer*** (D, L, Neponsit)	**72,798**
	Andrew E. Carlan (R, C, RTL, Nassau)	25,424
12.	**Shirley Chisholm*** (D, L, Brooklyn) .	**35,446**
	Charles Gibbs (R, Brooklyn).	3,372
13.	**Stephen J. Solarz** (D, L, Brooklyn) .	**81,954**
	Harry DeMell (R, C, Brooklyn)	19,536
14.	**Frederick W. Richmond*** (D, L, Brooklyn)	**45,029**
	Christopher Lovell (R, C, Brooklyn) .	8,257
15.	**Leo C. Zeferetti*** (D, Brooklyn) . . .	**49,684**
	Paul M. Atanasio (R, C, RTL, Brooklyn)	46,467
16.	**Charles E. Schumer** (D, L, Brooklyn)	**67,343**
	Theodore Silverman (R, C, Brooklyn) .	17,050
17.	**Guy V. Molinari** (R, C, Staten Island)	**69,573**
	John M. Murphy* (D, RTL, Staten Island).	50,954
18.	**Bill Green** (R, I, New York)	**91,341**
	Mark J. Green* (D, L, New York) . . .	68,786
19.	**Charles B. Rangel*** (D, R, L, New York)	**84,062**
	Marjorie Garvey (C, RTL, New York) .	2,622
20.	**Theodore Weiss*** (D, L, New York) .	**86,454**
	James E. Greene (R, New York) . . .	15,350
21.	**Robert Garcia*** (D, R, L, Bronx) . . .	**32,173**
	Gina A. Aceto (C, Bronx)	272
22.	**Jonathan B. Bingham*** (D, L, Bronx)	**66,301**
	Robert S. Black (R, Bronx)	9,943
23.	**Peter A. Peyser*** (D, Irvington) . . .	**85,749**
	Andrew Albanese (R, C, Scarsdale) .	66,771
24.	**Richard L. Ottinger*** (D, Pleasantville)	**100,182**
	Joseph W. Christiana (R, C, RTL, Mt. Vernon)	66,689
25.	**Hamilton Fish Jr.*** (R, C, Millbrook) .	**158,936**
	Gunars Ozols (D, Wappingers)	37,369
26.	**Benjamin A. Gilman*** (R, Middletown)	**137,159**
	Eugene Victor (D, L, Goshen)	37,475

Dist.	Representative (Party, Home)	1980 Election
27.	**Matthew F. McHugh*** (D, Ithaca) . .	**103,863**
	Neil T. Wallace (R, C, Ithaca)	83,096
28.	**Samuel S. Stratton*** (D, Amsterdam)	**164,088**
	Frank Wicks (R, Schenectady)	37,504
29.	**Gerald B. H. Solomon*** (R, C, RTL, Glenn Falls).	**141,631**
	Roger L. Hurley (D, L, Granville) . . .	70,697
30.	**David O'B. Martin** (R, C, Canton) . .	**111,008**
	Mary Anne Krupsak (D, L, Canajoharie).	54,896
31.	**Donald J. Mitchell*** (R, RTL, Herkimer)	**135,976**
	Irving A. Schwartz (D, L, Utica)	39,589
32.	**George C. Wortley** (R, C, Fayetteville)	**108,128**
	Jeffery S. Brooks (D, L, Green)	56,535
33.	**Gary A. Lee*** (R, C, Ithaca)	**132,831**
	Dolores M. Reed (D, L, Syracuse) . .	39,542
34.	**Frank Horton*** (R, Rochester)	**133,278**
	James Toole (D, Rochester)	37,883
35.	**Barber B. Conable Jr.** (R, Alexander)	**127,623**
	John M. Owens (D, C, Rochester) . .	44,754
36.	**John J. LaFalce*** (D, L, Kenmore) . .	**122,929**
	H. William Feder (R, C, RTL, Niagara Falls)	48,428
37.	**Henry J. Nowak*** (D, L, Buffalo) . . .	**94,890**
	Roger Heymanowski (R, C, Buffalo) .	16,560
38.	**Jack F. Kemp*** (R, C, RTL, Hamburg)	**167,434**
	Gale A. Denn (D, L, Eden)	37,875
39.	**Stanley N. Lundine*** (D, Jamestown)	**93,839**
	James Abdella (R, C, Jamestown) . . .	75,039
	North Carolina	
1.	**Walter B. Jones*** (D, Farmville) . . .	**108,738U**
2.	**L. H. Fountain*** (D, Tarboro)	**99,297**
	Barry L. Gardner (R, Rocky Mount) .	35,946
3.	**Charles O. Whitley*** (D, Mt. Olive) .	**84,862**
	Larry J. Parker (R, Erwin)	39,393
4.	**Ike Andrews*** (D, Siler City)	**97,167**
	Thurman Hogan (R, Asheboro)	84,631
5.	**Stephen L. Neal*** (D, Winston-Salem)	**99,117**
	Anne Bagnal (R, Winston-Salem) . .	94,894
6.	**Eugene Johnston** (R, Greensboro) .	**80,275**
	Richardson Preyer (D, Greensboro) .	76,957
7.	**Charles Rose*** (D, Fayetteville) . . .	**88,564**
	Vivian S. Wright (R, Wilmington) . . .	40,270
8.	**W. G. (Bill) Hefner*** (D, Concord) . .	**95,013**
	L. E. (Larry) Harris (R, Kannapolis) . .	67,317
9.	**James G. Martin*** (R, Charlotte) . . .	**101,156**
	Randall R. Kincaid (D, Davidson) . .	71,504
10.	**James T. Broyhill*** (R, Lenoir)	**120,777**
	James O. Icenhour (D, Hickory)	52,485
11.	**William M. (Bill) Hendon** (R, Asheville)	**104,485**
	Lamar Gudger* (D, Asheville).	90,789
	North Dakota At Large	
	Byron L. Dorgan (D, Bismarck) . . .	**166,437**
	Jim Smykowski (R, Cayuga)	124,707
	Ohio	
1.	**Willis D. Gradison Jr.*** (R, Cincinnati)	**124,080**
	Donald J. Zwick (D, Cincinnati)	38,529
2.	**Thomas A. Luken*** (D, Cincinnati) . .	**103,423**
	Tom Atkins (R, Cincinnati)	72,693
3.	**Tony P. Hall*** (D, Dayton).	**95,558**
	Albert H. Sealy (R, Dayton).	66,698
4.	**Tennyson Guyer*** (R, Findlay) (d). . .	**133,795**
	Geraldine Tebben (D, Lima	51,150
5.	**Delbert L. Latta** (R, Bowling Green) .	**137,003**
	James R. Sherck (D, Fremont	57,704
6.	**Bob McEwen** (R, Hillsboro).	**101,288**
	Ted Strickland (D, Lucasville)	84,235
7.	**Clarence J. Brown*** (R, Urbana) . . .	**124,137**
	Donald Hollister (D, Yellow Springs) .	38,952

Dist. Representative (Party, Home)	1980 Election
8. **Thomas N. Kindness*** (R, Hamilton)	**139,590**
John W. Griffen (D, Miamisburg) . . .	44,162
9. **Ed Weber** (R, Toledo)	**96,927**
Thomas Ludlow Ashley* (D, Maumee)	68,728
10. **Clarence E. Miller*** (R, Lancaster). .	**143,403**
Jack E. Stecker (D, Zanesville)	49,433
11. **J. William Stanton*** (R, Painesville)	**128,507**
Patrick J. Donlin (D, Hubbard)	51,224
12. **Bob Shamansky** (D, Columbus) . . .	**108,690**
Samuel L. Devine* (R, Columbus) . . .	98,110
13. **Donald J. Pease*** (D, Oberlin)	**113,439**
David Earl Armstrong (R, North Ridgeville)	64,296
14. **John F. Seiberling*** (D, Akron) . . .	**103,336**
Louis A. Mangels (R, Akron)	55,962
15. **Chalmers P. Wylie*** (R, Worthington)	**129,025**
Terry Freeman (D, Columbus)	48,708
16. **Ralph Regula*** R, Navarre)	**149,960**
Larry V. Slagle (D, Massillon)	39,219
17. **John M. Ashbrook*** (R, Johnstown)	**128,870**
Donald E. Yunker (D, Galion)	47,900
18. **Douglas Applegate*** (D, Steubenville)	**134,835**
Gary L. Hammersley (R, Bolivar) . . .	42,354
19. **Lyle Williams*** (R, Lordstown) . . .	**107,032**
Harry Meshel (D, Youngstown)	77,272
20. **Mary Rose Oakar*** (D, Cleveland). .	**96,217U**
21. **Louis Stokes*** (D, Cleveland). . . .	**83,188**
Robert L. Woodall (R, Cleveland). . .	11,103
22. **Dennis E. Eckart** (D, Euclid)	**108,137**
Joseph J. Nahra (R, Cleveland Heights)	80,836
23. **Ronald M. Mottl*** (D, Parma).	**144,371U**

(d) Vacancy due to the death of Tennyson Guyer, Apr. 12, 1981.

Oklahoma

Dist. Representative (Party, Home)	1980 Election
1. **James R. Jones*** (D, Tulsa)	**115,381**
Richard C. Freeman (R, Tulsa)	82,293
2. **Mike Synar*** (D, Muskogee)	**101,516**
Gary Richardson (R, Muskogee) . . .	86,544
3. **Wes Watkins*** (D, Ada).	**Unopposed**
4. **Dave McCurdy** (D, Norman)	**74,245**
Howard Rutledge (R, Norman)	71,339
5. **Mickey Edwards*** (R, Oklahoma City)	**90,053**
David C. Hood (D, Oklahoma City) . .	36,815
6. **Glenn English*** (D, Cordell)	**111,694**
Carol McCurley (R, Oklahoma City) .	60,980

According to Oklahoma law, it is not required to tabulate votes for unopposed candidates.

Oregon

Dist. Representative (Party, Home)	1980 Election
1. **Les AuCoin*** (D, Forest Grove) . . .	**203,532**
Lynn Engdahl (R, Portland)	105,083
2. **Denny Smith** (R, Salem)	**141,854**
Al Ullman* (D, Baker)	138,089
3. **Ron Wyden** (D, Portland)	**156,371**
Darrell R. Conger (R, Portland)	60,940
4. **James Weaver*** (D, Eugene)	**158,745**
Michael Fitzgerald (R, Brookings) . .	130,861

Pennsylvania

Dist. Representative (Party, Home)	1980 Election
1. **Thomas M. Foglietta** (I, Philadelphia)	**58,737**
Michael (Ozzie) Meyers (D, Philadelphia)	52,956
Robert R. Burke (R, Philadelphia) . .	37,893
2. **William H. Gray III*** (D, Philadelphia)	**127,106**
James L. Buckman (I, Philadelphia) .	2,396
Garland Dempsey (Cnsmr, Philadelphia).	2,396
3. **Raymond F. Lederer*** (D, Philadelphia) (e)	**67,942**
William J. Phillips (R, Philadelphia) . .	40,866
4. **Charles F. Dougherty*** (R, Philadelphia).	**127,475**
Thomas J. Magrann (D, Philadelphia)	73,895
5. **Richard T. Schulze*** (R, Malvern) . .	**148,898**
Grady G. Brickhouse (R, (D, Spring) .	47,092

Dist. Representative (Party, Home)	1980 Election
6. **Gus Yatron*** (D, Reading)	**117,965**
George Hulshart (R, Laureldale) . . .	57,844
7. **Bob Edgar*** (D, Broomall)	**99,381**
Dennis J. Rochford (R, Springfield). .	87,643
8. **James K. Coyne** (R, Washington's Crossing)	**103,585**
Peter H. Kostmayer* (D, New Hope).	99,593
9. **Bud Shuster*** (R, D, Everett).	**157,241U**
10. **Joseph M. McDade*** (R, Scranton) .	**145,703**
Gene Bosalyga (D, Olyphant).	43,152
11. **James L. Nelligan** (R, Forty-Fort) .	**93,621**
Raphael Musto* (D, Pittston)	86,703
12. **John P. Murtha*** (D, Johnstown). . .	**106,750**
Charles A. Getty (R, Johnstown) . . .	72,999
13. **Lawrence Coughlin*** (R, Villanova) .	**138,212**
Peter Slawek (D, Lafayette Hill) . . .	57,745
14. **William J. Coyne** (D, Pittsburgh) . .	**102,545**
Stan Thomas (R, Pittsburgh)	44,071
15. **Don Ritter*** R, Coopersburg)	**99,874**
Jeanette Reibman (D, Easton)	66,626
16. **Robert S. Walker** (R, E. Petersburg)	**129,765**
James A. Woodcock (D, Lancaster). .	38,891
17. **Allen E. Ertel*** (D, Montoursville). . .	**97,995**
Daniel S. Seiverling (R, Hershey). . .	63,790
18. **Doug Walgren*** (D, Pittsburgh) . . .	**127,641**
Steven R. Snyder (R, Sewickley) . . .	58,821
19. **William F. Goodling*** (R, Jacoby) .	**136,873**
Richard P. Noll (D, York)	41,584
20. **Joseph M. Gaydos*** (D, McKeesport)	**122,100**
Kathleen M. Meyer (R, Pittsburgh) . .	46,313
21. **Don Bailey*** (D, Greensburg).	**112,427**
Dirk Matson (R, Ligonier)	51,821
22. **Austin J. Murphy** (D, Monongahela)	**118,084**
Marilyn C. Ecoff (R, Pittsburgh). . . .	50,020
23. **William F. Clinger Jr.*** (R, Warren) .	**122,855**
Peter Atigan (D, Kane).	41,033
24. **Marc L. Marks*** (R, Sharon)	**86,687**
David C. DiCarlo (R, Erie)	86,567
25. **Eugene V. Atkinson*** (D, Aliquippa).	**119,817**
Robert H. Morris (R, New Castle) . .	58,768

(e) Vacancy due to resignation of Raymond F. Lederer, May 5, 1981.

Rhode Island

Dist. Representative (Party, Home)	1980 Election
1. **Fernand J. St Germain*** (D, Woonsocket)	**120,756**
William P. Montgomery (R, Central Falls)	57,844
2. **Claudine Schneider** (R, Narragansett)	**115,057**
Edward P. Beard* (D, Cranston) . . .	92,970

South Carolina

Dist. Representative (Party, Home)	1980 Election
1. **Thomas F. Hartnett** (R, Charleston)	**81,988**
Charles D. (Pug) Ravenel (D, Charleston).	76,743
2. **Floyd Spence** (R, Lexington).	**92,306**
Tom Turnipseed (D, Columbia)	73,353
3. **Butler Derrick*** (D, Edgefield)	**87,680**
Marshall Parker (R, Clemson)	57,840
4. **Carroll A. Campbell Jr.*** (R, Fountain Inn)	**90,941**
Thomas Waldenfels (LIBERT, Landrum)	6,984
5. **Ken Holland*** (D, Rock Hill)	**99,773**
Thomas Campbell (LIBERT, Blacksburg)	14,252
6. **John L. Napier** (R, Bennettsville) . .	**75,964**
John W. Jenrette Jr. (D, N. Myrtle Beach)	70,747

South Dakota

Dist. Representative (Party, Home)	1980 Election
1. **Thomas A. Daschle*** (D, Aberdeen)	**109,910**
Bart Kull (R, Sioux Falls).	57,155
2. **Clint Roberts** (R, Presho).	**88,991**
Kenneth D. Stofferahn (D, Pierre). . .	63,447

Tennessee

Dist. Representative (Party, Home)	1980 Election
1. **James H. Quillen*** (R, Kingsport) . .	**130,296U**

Dist.	Representative (Party, Home)	1980 Election
2.	**John J. Duncan** (R, Knoxville)	147,947
	David H. (Dave) Dunnaway (D, La Follette)	46,578
3.	**Marilyn Lloyd Bouquard*** (D, Chattanooga)	117,355
	Glen Byers (R, Cleveland)	74,761
4.	**Albert Gore Jr.*** (D, Carthage)	137,612
	James Beau Seigneur (R, Shelbyville)	35,954
5.	**Bill Boner*** (D, Nashville)	118,506
	Mike Adams (R, Nashville)	62,746
6.	**Robin L. Beard Jr.*** (R, Memphis) . .	127,945U
7.	**Ed Jones*** (D, Yorkville)	133,606
	Daniel Campbell (R, Memphis)	39,227
8.	**Harold E. Ford*** (D, Memphis)	110,139U

Texas

1.	**Sam B. Hall Jr.*** (D, Marshall)	137,665
2.	**Charles Wilson*** (D, Lufkin)	142,496
	F. H. Pannill Sr. (R, Huntsville)	60,742
3.	**James M. Collins*** (R, Dallas)	218,228
	Earle S. Porter (R, Dallas)	49,667
4.	**Ralph M. Hall** (D, Rockwall)	102,787
	John H. Wright (R, Tyler)	93,915
5.	**Jim Mattox*** (D, Dallas)	70,892
	Tom Pauken (R, Mesquite)	67,848
6.	**Phil Gramm** (D, College Station) . .	144,816
	Dave (Buster) Haskins (R, Fort Worth)	59,503
7.	**Bill Archer*** (R, Houston)	242,810
	Robert L. Hutchings (D, Houston) . .	48,504
8.	**Jack Fields** (R, Humble)	72,856
	Bob Eckhardt* (D, Houston)	67,921
9.	**Jack Brooks*** (D, Beaumont)	103,225U
10.	**J. J. "Jake" Pickle** (D, Austin) . . .	135,618
	John Biggar (R, Austin)	88,940
11.	**Marvin Leath** (D, Marlin)	128,520U
12.	**Jim Wright*** (D, Fort Worth)	99,104
	Jim Bradshaw (R, Fort Worth)	65,005
13.	**Jack Hightower*** (D, Vernon)	98,779
	Ron Slover (R, Amarillo)	80,819
14.	**William N. "Bill" Patman** (D, Ganacio)	93,884
	Charles L. Concklin (R, Corpus Christi)	71,495
15.	**E. "Kika" de la Garza*** (D, Mission) .	105,325
	Lendy McDonald (R, Pt. Isabel)	45,090
16.	**Richard C. "Dick" White*** (D, Bethesda)	104,734
	Catherine A. McDivitt (Libert, El Paso)	19,010
17.	**Charles W. Stenholm*** (D, Stamford)	130,465U
18.	**Mickey Leland** (D, Houston)	71,985
	C. L. Kennedy (R, Houston)	16,128
19.	**Kent Hance*** (D, Lubbock)	126,632
	J. D. Webster (Libert, Midland)	8,792
20.	**Henry B. Gonzalez*** (D, San Antonio)	84,113
	Merle W. Nash (R, San Antonio)	17,725
21.	**Tom Loeffler** (R, Hunt)	196,424
	Joe Sullivan (D, San Antonio)	54,425
22.	**Ron Paul** (R, Lake Jackson)	106,797
	Mike Andrews (D, Houston)	101,094
23.	**Abraham "Chick" Kazen Jr.*** (D, Laredo)	104,595
	Bobby Locke (R, San Antonio)	45,139
24.	**Martin Frost** (D, Dallas)	93,690
	Clay Smothers (R, Fort Worth)	59,172

Utah

1.	**James V. Hansen** (R, Farmington) .	157,111
	Gunn McKay* (D, Huntsville)	144,459
2.	**Dan Marriott*** (R, Salt Lake City) . .	194,885
	Arthur L. Monson (D, Salt Lake City) .	87,967

Vermont At Large

1.	**James M. Jeffords*** (R, Montpelier) .	154,274
	Robin Lloyd (Cit, Burlington)	24,758

Virginia

1.	**Paul S. Trible Jr.*** (R, Tappahannock)	130,130
	Sharon D. Grant (I, Newport News) .	13,688

Dist.	Representative (Party, Home)	1980 Election
2.	**G. William Whitehurst*** (R, Virginia Beach)	97,319
	Kenneth P. Morrison (I, Norfolk). . . .	11,003
3.	**Thomas J. Bliley Jr.** (R, Richmond) .	96,524
	John A. Mapp (D, Richmond)	60,962
4.	**Robert W. Daniel Jr.*** (R, Spring Grove)	92,557
	Cecil Y. Jenkins Jr.* (D, Chesapeake	59,930
5.	**Dan Daniel*** (D, Danville)	112,143U
6.	**M. Caldwell Butler*** (R, Roanoke). .	123,125U
7.	**J. Kenneth Robinson*** (R, Winchester).	139,957U
8.	**Stan Parris** (R, Woodbridge)	95,624
	Herbert E. Harris II* (D, Alexandria) .	94,530
9.	**William C. Wampler*** (R, Bristol). . .	119,196
	Roosevelt C. Ferguson (D, Lebanon)	52,636
10.	**Frank R. Wolf** (R, Vienna).	110,840
	Joseph L. Fisher* (D, Arlington)	105,883

Washington

1.	**Joel Pritchard*** (R, Seattle)	180,475
	Robin Drake (D, Seattle).	41,830
2.	**Al Swift** (D, Bellingham)	162,002
	Neal Snider (R, Bellingham)	82,639
3.	**Don Bonker*** (D, Olympia)	155,906
	Rod Culp (R, Montesano)	92,872
4.	**Sid Morrison** (R, Zillah)	134,691
	Mike McCormack* D, Richland	100,114
5.	**Thomas S. Foley*** (D, Spokane). . .	120,530
	John Sonneland (R, Spokane)	111,705
6.	**Norman D. Dicks*** (D, Bremerton). .	122,903
	Jim Beaver (R, Tacoma).	106,236
7.	**Mike Lowry*** (D, Mercer Island) . . .	112,848
	Ron Dunlap (R, Bellevue)	84,218

West Virginia

1.	**Robert H. Mollohan*** (D, Fairmont) .	107,471
	Joe Bartlett (R, Lost Creek)	61,438
2.	**Cleve Benedict** (R, Lewisburg)	102,805
	Pat R. Hamilton (D, Oak Hill)	80,940
3.	**Mick Staton** (R, South Charleston) . .	94,583
	John G. Hutchinson* (D, Charleston).	84,980
4.	**Nick J. Rahall*** (D, Beckley)	117,595
	Winton B. Covey Jr. (R, Lerona) . . .	36,020

Wisconsin

1.	**Les Aspin*** (D, East Troy)	126,222
	Kathryn H. Canary (R, Delavan)	96,047
2.	**Robert Kastenmeier*** (D, Sun Prairie)	142,037
	James A. Wright (R, Baraboo)	119,514
3.	**Steven Gunderson** (R, Osseo)	132,001
	Alvin Baldus* (D, Menomonie)	126,859
4.	**Clement J. Zablocki*** (D, Milwaukee)	146,437
	Elroy C. Honadel (R, Oak Creek). . .	61,027
5.	**Henry S. Reuss*** (D, Milwaukee) . .	129,574
	David Bathke (R, Milwaukee)	37,267
6.	**Thomas E. Petri** (R, Fond du Lac) . .	143,980
	Gary R. Goyke (D, Oshkosh)	98,628
7.	**David Obey*** (D, Wausau)	164,340
	Vinton A. Vesta* (R, Hayward)	89,745
8.	**Toby Roth** (R, Appleton)	169,664
	Michael R. Monfils (D, Green Bay) . .	81,043
9.	**F. James Sensenbrenner Jr.** (R, Shorewood)	206,227
	Gary C. Benedict (D, New Berlin). . .	56,838

Wyoming At Large

	Richard B. Cheney* (R, Casper) . . .	116,361
	Jim Rogers (D, Lyman)	53,338

Non-Voting Delegates
District of Columbia

	Walter E. Fauntroy* (D, D.C.)	111,631
	Robert J. Roehr (R, D.C.)	21,021

Guam

	Antonio Borja Won Pat* (D, Agana) .	14,834
	Antonio M. Palomo (R, Agana)	10,622

Virgin Islands

	Ron deLugo (D, St. Thomas)	10,027
	Melvin H. Evans (R, St. Croix)	8,876

Political Divisions of the U.S. Senate and House of Representatives
From 1857 (35th Cong.) to 1981-1983 (97th Cong.)

Source: Clerk of the House of Representatives

All figures reflect immediate result of elections.

Congress	Years	Number of Senators	Democrats	Republicans	Other parties	Vacant	Number of Representatives	Democrats	Republicans	Other parties	Vacant
35th....	1857-59	64	39	20	5		237	131	92	14	
36th....	1859-61	66	38	26	2		237	101	113	23	
37th....	1861-63	50	11	31	7	1	178	42	106	28	2
38th....	1863-65	51	12	39			183	80	103		
39th....	1865-67	52	10	42			191	46	145		
40th....	1867-69	53	11	42			193	49	143		1
41st....	1869-71	74	11	61		2	243	73	170		
42d....	1871-73	74	17	57			243	104	139		
43d....	1873-75	74	19	54		1	293	88	203		2
44th....	1875-77	76	29	46		1	293	181	107	3	2
45th....	1877-79	76	36	39	1		293	156	137		
46th....	1879-81	76	43	33			293	150	128	14	1
47th....	1881-83	76	37	37	2		293	130	152	11	
48th....	1883-85	76	36	40			325	200	119	6	
49th....	1885-87	76	34	41		1	325	182	140	2	1
50th....	1887-89	76	37	39			325	170	151	4	
51st....	1889-91	84	37	47			330	156	173	1	
52d....	1891-93	88	39	47	2		333	231	88	14	
53d....	1893-95	88	44	38	3	3	356	220	126	10	
54th....	1895-97	88	39	44	5		357	104	246	7	
55th....	1897-99	90	34	46	10		357	134	206	16	1
56th....	1899-1901	90	26	53	11		357	163	185	9	
57th....	1901-03	90	29	56	3	2	357	153	198	5	1
58th....	1903-05	90	32	58			386	178	207		1
59th....	1905-07	90	32	58			386	136	250		
60th....	1907-09	92	29	61		2	386	164	222		
61st....	1909-11	92	32	59		1	391	172	219		
62d....	1911-13	92	42	49		1	391	228	162	1	
63d....	1913-15	96	51	44	1		435	290	127	18	
64th....	1915-17	96	56	39	1		435	231	193	8	3
65th....	1917-19	96	53	42	1		435	210	216	9	
66th....	1919-21	96	47	48	1		435	191	237	7	
67th....	1921-23	96	37	59			435	132	300	1	2
68th....	1923-25	96	43	51	2		435	207	225	3	
69th....	1925-27	96	40	54	1	1	435	183	247	5	
70th....	1927-29	96	47	48	1		435	195	237	3	
71st....	1929-31	96	39	56	1		435	163	267	1	4
72d....	1931-33	96	47	48	1		435	216	218	1	
73d....	1933-35	96	59	36	1		435	313	117	5	
74th....	1935-37	96	69	25	2		435	322	103	10	
75th....	1937-39	96	75	17	4		435	333	89	13	
76th....	1939-41	96	69	23	4		435	262	169	4	
77th....	1941-43	96	66	28	2		435	267	162	6	
78th....	1943-45	96	57	38	1		435	222	209	4	
79th....	1945-47	96	57	38	1		435	243	190	2	
80th....	1947-49	96	45	51			435	188	246	1	
81st....	1949-51	96	54	42			435	263	171	1	
82d....	1951-53	96	48	47	1		435	234	199	2	
83d....	1953-55	96	46	48	2		435	213	221	1	
84th....	1955-57	96	48	47	1		435	232	203		
85th....	1957-59	96	49	47			435	234	201		
86th....	1959-61	98	64	34			[3]436	283	153		
87th....	1961-63	100	64	36			[4]437	262	175		
88th....	1963-65	100	67	33			435	258	176		1
89th....	1965-67	100	68	32			435	295	140		
90th....	1967-69	100	64	36			435	248	187		
91st....	1969-71	100	58	42			435	243	192		
92d....	1971-73	100	54	44	2		435	255	180		
93d....	1973-75	100	56	42	2		435	242	192	1	
94th....	1975-77	100	61	37	2		435	291	144		
95th....	1977-79	100	61	38	1		435	292	143		
96th....	1979-81	100	58	41	1		435	277	158		
97th....	1981-83	100	46	53	1		435	242	190		3

(1) Democrats organized House with help of other parties. (2) Democrats organized House due to Republican deaths. (3) Proclamation declaring Alaska a State issued Jan. 3, 1959. (4) Proclamation declaring Hawaii a State issued Aug. 21, 1959.

UNITED STATES GOVERNMENT

The Reagan Administration

As of mid-1981

Terms of office of the president and vice president, from Jan. 20, 1981 to Jan. 20, 1985. No person may be elected president of the United States for more than two 4-year terms.

President — Ronald Reagan of California receives salary of $200,000 a year taxable; in addition an expense allowance of $50,000 to assist in defraying expenses resulting from his official duties. Also there may be expended not exceeding $100,000, nontaxable, a year for travel expenses and $12,000 for official entertainment available for allocation within the Executive Office of the President. Congress has provided lifetime pensions of $69,630 a year, free mailing privileges, free office space, and up to $96,000 a year for office help for former Presidents except for the first 30 month period during which a former President is entitled to staff assistance for which an amount up to $150,000 a year may be paid, and $20,000 annually for their widows.

Vice President — George Bush of Texas receives salary of $79,125 a year and $10,000 for expenses, all of which is taxable.

For succession to presidency, see Succession in Index.

The Cabinet

(Salary: $69,630 per annum)

Secretary of State — Alexander M. Haig Jr., Conn.
Secretary of Treasury — Donald T. Regan, N.Y.
Secretary of Defense — Caspar W. Weinberger, Cal.
Attorney General — William French Smith, Cal.
Secretary of Interior — James G. Watt, Col.
Secretary of Agriculture — John R. Block, Ill.
Secretary of Commerce — Malcolm Baldrige, Conn.
Secretary of Labor — Raymond J. Donovan, N.J.
Secretary of Health and Human Services — Richard S. Schweiker, Pa.
Secretary of Housing and Urban Development — Samuel R. Pierce Jr., N.Y.
Secretary of Transportation — Andrew L. Lewis Jr., Pa.
Secretary of Energy — James B. Edwards, S.C.
Secretary of Education — Terrel Bell, Ut.

The White House Staff

1600 Pennsylvania Ave. NW 20500

Counsellor to the President — Edwin Meese 3d.
Chief of Staff — James A. Baker 3d.
Deputy Chief of Staff — Michael K. Deaver.
Press Secretary to the President — James S. Brady.
Counsel to the President — Fred F. Fielding.
Assistant to the President — Edwin L. Harper.
Presidential Assistants — Martin Anderson (Policy Development); Elizabeth Hanford-Dole (Public Liaison); Max L. Freidersdorf (Legislative Affairs); David R. Gergen (Staff Director); E. Pendleton James (Presidential Personnel); Franklyn C. Nofziger (Political Affairs); Richard Salisbury Williamson (Intergovernmental Affairs).
Director of Staff for the First Lady — Peter McCoy.

Executive Agencies

National Security Council — Assistant to the President for Natl. Security Affairs — Richard V. Allen.
Council of Economic Advisers — Murray L. Weidenbaum, chmn.
Central Intelligence Agency — William J. Casey, dir.
Office of Management and Budget — David A. Stockman, dir.
U.S. Trade Representative — William E. Brock.
Office of Administration — John F. W. Rogers, act. dir.

Department of State

2201 C St. NW 20520

Secretary of State — Alexander M. Haig Jr.

Deputy Secretary — William P. Clark.
Under Sec. for Political Affairs — Walter J. Stoessel.
Under Sec. for Security Assistance, Science and Technology — James L. Buckley.
Under Sec. for Economic Affairs — Myer Rashish.
Under Secretary for Management — Richard T. Kennedy.
Counselor — Robert C. McFarlane.
Legal Advisor — vacant.
Assistant Secretaries for:
  Administration — Thomas M. Tracy.
  African Affairs — Chester Crocker.
  Congressional Relations — Richard Fairbanks.
  Economic Affairs — Robert D. Hormats.
  European Affairs — Lawrence C. Eagleburger.
  Human Rights & Humanitarian Affairs — vacant.
  Inter-American Affairs — Thomas Enders.
  International Organization Affairs — Elliott Abrams.
  Near-Eastern & S. Asian Affairs — Nicholas Veliotes.
  Public Affairs — Dean Fischer.
  Oceans & International Environmental & Scientific Affairs — James L. Malone.
Consular Affairs — Diego Asencio, act.
Chief of Protocol — Leonore Annenberg.
Dir. General, Foreign Service & Dir. of Personnel — Joan M. Clark.
Dir. of Intelligence & Research — vacant.
Dir. of Politico-Military Affairs — Richard Burt.
Office of Inspector General — Robert Lyle Brown.
Policy Planning Staff — Paul Wolfowitz.
Agency for International Development — M. Peter McPherson.
U.S. Rep. to the UN — Jeane Kirkpatrick.

Treasury Department

1500 Pennsylvania Ave. NW 20220

Secretary of the Treasury — Donald T. Regan.
Deputy Sec. of the Treasury — R. Tim McNamar.
Under Sec. for Monetary Affairs — Dr. Beryl Sprinkel.
Under Sec. for Tax and Economic Affairs — Dr. Norman Ture.
General Counsel — vacant.
Assistant Secretaries: — Marc Leland, John Walker, Dennis Thomas, Roger Mehle, John Kelly, Craig Roberts, John Chapoton, Ann McLaughlin, Cora Beebe.
Bureaus:
  Alcohol, Tobacco, and Firearms — G. R. Dickerson, dir.
  Comptroller of the Currency — John G. Heimann.
  Customs — vacant.
  Engraving & Printing — Harry R. Clements, dir.
  Government Financial Operations — William E. Douglas, comm.
  Internal Revenue Service — Roscoe Egger, comm.
  Mint — Donna Pope, dir.
  Public Debt — H. J. Hintgen, comm.
  Treasurer of the U.S. — Angela Buchanan.
  U.S. Secret Service — H. Stuart Knight, dir.

Department of Defense

The Pentagon 20301

Secretary of Defense — Caspar Weinberger.
Deputy Secretary — Frank C. Carlucci.
Special Asst. to the Secretary and Deputy Secretary of Defense — vacant.
Under Secretaries of Defense:
  Policy — Fred C. Ikle.

Policy and International Security Affairs — Francis J. West Jr.
Policy Planning — Walter Slocombe.
Policy Review — Daniel J. Murphy.
Research and Engineering — Richard DeLauer.
Research and Engineering and Communications, Command, Control and Intelligence — vacant.
Assistant Secretaries of Defense:
    Atomic Energy — James P. Wade Jr.
    Comptroller — Jack Borsting.
    Health Affairs — John Moxley 3d.
    Manpower, Reserve Affairs and Logistics — Lawrence J. Korb.
    Program Analysis and Evaluation — Russell Murray 2d.
    Public Affairs — Henry Catto Jr.
    Legislative Affairs — vacant.
Inspector General for Defense Intelligence — Werner E. Michel.
Chairman, Joint Chiefs of Staff — Gen. David C. Jones, USAF.
NATO Affairs: — Gen. Richard H. Groves.
General Counsel — William Howard Taft IV.

Department of the Army
The Pentagon 20301
Secretary of the Army — John O. Marsh Jr.
Under Secretary — vacant.
Assistant Secretaries for:
    Civil Works — vacant.
    Installations, Logistics and Financial Management — vacant.
    Research, Development and Acquisition — Percy A. Pierre.
    Manpower & Reserve Affairs — vacant.
Chief of Public Affairs — Maj. Gen. Robert A. Sullivan.
Chief of Staff — Gen. Edward C. Meyer.
General Counsel — Sara Lister.
Comptroller of the Army — Lt. Gen. Richard L. West.
Surgeon General — Lt. Gen. Charles C. Pixley.
Adjutant General — Brig. Gen. Robert M. Joyce.
Inspector General — Lt. Gen. Richard G. Trefry.
Judge Advocate General — Maj. Gen. Alton Harvey.
Deputy Chiefs of Staff:
    Logistics — Lt. Gen. Arthur J. Gregg.
    Operations & Plans — Lt. Gen. Glenn T. Otis.
    Research, Development, Acquisition — Lt. Gen. Donald R. Keith.
    Personnel — Lt. Gen. Robert G. Yerks.
Ass't. Chief of Staff, Intelligence — Maj. Gen. Edmund R. Thompson.
Commanders:
    U.S. Army Material Development and Readiness Command — Gen. John R. Guthrie.
    U.S. Army Forces Command — Gen. Robert M. Shoemaker.
    U.S. Army Training and Doctrine Command — Gen. Donn A. Starry.
    First U.S. Army — Lt. Gen. John C. Forrest.
    Fifth U.S. Army — Lt. Gen. John R. McGiffert.
    Sixth U.S. Army — Lt. Gen. Charles M. Hall.
    Military Dist. of Washington — Maj. Gen. Robert Arter.

Department of the Navy
The Pentagon 20350
Secretary of the Navy — John Lehman.
Under Secretary — vacant.
Assistant Secretaries for:
    Financial Management — vacant.
    Manpower, Reserve Affairs, & Logistics — vacant.
    Research, Engineering, & Systems — vacant.
Judge Advocate General — RADM John S. Jenkins.
Chief of Naval Operations — Adm. Thomas B. Hayward.
Chief of Naval Material — Adm. A. J. Whittle Jr.

Chief of Information — RADM Bruce Newell.
Surgeon General/Chief, Bureau of Medicine & Surgery — VADM J. William Cox.
Naval Military Personnel Command — RADM Robert F. Dunn.
Military Sealift Command — RADM Bruce Keener 3d.
Chief of Naval Personnel — VADM Lando W. Zech Jr.
Commandants, Naval Bases:
    Philadelphia — RADM C. A. Brettschneider.
    Norfolk — RADM Joseph F. Frick.
    Charleston — RADM Robert B. McClinton.
    San Diego and San Francisco — RADM J. E. Langille 3d.
    Seattle — RADM James D. Williams.
    Pearl Harbor — RADM Stanley J. Anderson.
Commandant, Naval District Washington — RADM Karl J. Bernstein.

U.S. Marine Corps: (zip code: 20380)
Commandant — Gen. Robert H. Barrow, USMC
Chief of Staff — vacant.

Department of the Air Force
The Pentagon 20330
Secretary of the Air Force — Verne Orr.
Under Secretary — vacant.
Assistant Secretaries for:
    Financial Management — Willard Mitchell, act.
    Research, Development & Logistics — Robert J. Hermann.
    Manpower, Reserve Affairs & Installations — Tidal W. McCoy.
General Counsel — Stuart R. Reichart.
Public Affairs — Richard Abel.
Director of Space Systems — Jimmie D. Hill.
Chief of Staff — Gen. Lew Allen Jr.
Surgeon General — Lt. Gen. Paul W. Myers.
Judge Advocate — Maj. Gen. Thomas B. Bruton.
Inspector General — Maj. Gen. Howard W. Leaf.
Deputy Chiefs of Staff:
    Logistics & Engineering — Lt. Gen. Billy M. Minter.
    Programs & Evaluation — Lt. Gen. Charles C. Blanton.
    Manpower & Personnel — Lt. Gen. Andrew P. Iosue.
    Research, Development & Acquisition — Lt. Gen. Kelly H. Burke.
    Operations, Plans & Readiness — Lt. Gen. Jerome F. O'Malley.
Major Air Commands:
    AF Logistics Command — Gen. Bryce Poe 2d.
    AF Systems Command — Gen. Robert T. Marsh.
    Air Training Command — Gen. Bennie L. Davis.
    Military Airlift Command — Gen. Robert E. Huyser.
    Strategic Air Command — Gen. Richard H. Ellis.
    Tactical Air Command — Gen. Wilbur L. Creech.
    Alaskan Air Command — Lt. Gen. Lynwood E. Clark.
    Pacific Air Forces — Lt. Gen. Arnold W. Braswell.
    USAF Europe — Gen. Charles A. Gabriel.
    Electronic Security Command — Maj. Gen. Doyle E. Larson.
    AF Communications Command — Maj. Gen. Robert T. Herres.

Department of Justice
Constitution Ave. & 10th St. NW 20530
Attorney General — William French Smith.
Deputy Attorney General — Edward C. Schmults.
Legal Policy — Jonathan C. Rose.
Legal Counsel — Theodore B. Olsen.
Intelligence Policy & Review — Richard C. Willard.
Professional Responsibility — Michael E. Shaheen Jr.
Solicitor General — Rex E. Lee.
Associate Attorney General — Rudolph W. Giuliani.
    Antitrust Division — William F. Baxter.

Civil Division — vacant.
Civil Rights Division — Bradford Reynolds.
Criminal Division — D. Lowell Jensen.
Drug Enforcement Admin. — Peter B. Bensinger.
Justice Management Division — Kevin D. Rooney.
Land & Natural Resources Division — Carol E. Dinkins.
Office of Legislative Affairs — Robert A. McConnel.
Tax Division — vacant.
Fed. Bureau of Investigation — William H. Webster, dir.
Board of Immigration Appeals — David L. Milhollan, chmn.
Bureau of Prisons — Norman A. Carlson, dir.
Office of Public Affairs — Thomas P. DeCair.
Immigration and Naturalization Service — Doris Meissner, act. comm.
Pardon Attorney — D. C. Stephenson, act.
U.S. Parole Commission — Cecil C. McCall, chmn.
U.S. Marshalls Service — William E. Hall.

Department of the Interior

C St. between 18th & 19th Sts. NW 20240
Secretary of the Interior — James G. Watt.
Under Secretary — Don Hodel.
Assistant Secretaries for:
Fish, Wildlife and Parks — G. Ray Arnett.
Energy & Minerals — Dan Miller.
Land and Water Resources — Garrey E. Carruthers.
Policy, Budget, and Administration — vacant.
Indian Affairs — Kenneth L. Smith.
Bureau of Land Management — Bob Burford, dir.
Bureau of Mines — vacant.
Bureau of Reclamation — Robert Broadbent, comm.
Fish & Wildlife Service — Lynn Greenwalt.
Geological Survey — H. W. Menard Jr., dir.
National Park Service — Russell Dickenson.
Public Affairs — Douglas Baldwin.
Office of Water Research and Technology — Gary D. Cobb, dir.
Office of Congressional and Legislative Affairs — Stanley W. Hulett.
Solicitor — William H. Coldiron.

Department of Agriculture

The Mall, 12th & 14th Sts. 20250
Secretary of Agriculture — John R. Block.
Deputy Secretary — Raymond E. Lyng.
Executive Assistant — Ray Lett.
Administration — Joan S. Wallace.
Internat. Affairs & Commodity Programs — Seely Lodwick.
Food & Consumer Services — Mary C. Jarratt.
Marketing Services & Transportation — C. W. McMillan.
Small Community Rural Development — Frank Naylor.
Economics, Policy Analysis and Budget — William Gene Lesher.
Governmental & Public Affairs — Claude Gifford, act.
Natural Resources & Environment — John B. Crowell.
General Counsel — A. James Barnes.
Science & Education Admin. — Anson R. Bertrand, dir.

Department of Commerce

14th St. between Constitution & E St. NW 20230
Secretary of Commerce — Malcolm Baldridge.
Deputy Secretary — Joseph W. Wright Jr.
Asst. Secy. for Trade Development — William H. Morris Jr.
General Counsel — Sherman E. Unger.
Maritime Affairs — Samuel B. Nemirow.
Off. of Productivity, Technology & Innovation — Robert Ellert, act.
Administration — Arlene Triplett.
Bureau of the Census — Daniel B. Levine, act.
Bureau of Economic Analysis — George Jaszi.
Office of East-West Trade — Kempton Jenkins.

International Trade — Lionel H. Olmer
Under Secy. for Asst. Secy. for Econ. Affairs — Robert Dederick.
Natl. Oceanic & Atmospheric Admin. — James Walsh, act.
Natl. Technical Info. Service — Melvin Day, dir.
Economic Develop. Admin. — Harold W. Williams, act.
Natl. Bureau of Standards — Ernest Ambler.
Minority Business Development Agency — Victor M. Rivera.
Office of Product Standards — Howard I. Forman.
Natl. Telecomm & Information Admin. — Dale Hatfield, act.
Tourism — Frederick Morris Bush.
Bureau of Industrial Economics — Beatrice N. Vaccaro.

Department of Labor

200 Constitution Ave. NW 20210
Secretary of Labor — Raymond J. Donovan.
Under Secretary — vacant.
Executive Assistant-Counselor — James L. Hooley.
Assistant Secretaries for:
Administration and Management — Alfred M. Zuck.
Employment and Training — Albert Angrisani.
Mine Safety & Health — vacant.
Occupational Safety & Health — Thorne G. Auchter.
Policy, Evaluation and Research — vacant.
Labor Management Relations — Donald Dotson.
Solicitor of Labor — T. Timothy Ryan.
Comm. of Labor Statistics — Janet Norwood.
Dep. Under Secy. for Employment Standards — Robert B. Collyer.
Dep. Under Secy. for Internatl. Affairs — vacant.
Dep. Under Secy. for Legislation & Intergovernmental Relations — Don Shasteen.
Office of Information, Publications & Reports — John W. Leslie.
Dir. of Women's Bureau — vacant.

Department of Health and Human Services

200 Independence Ave. SW 20201
Secretary of HEW — Richard S. Schweiker.
Under Secretary — David Swoat.
Assistant Secretaries for:
Management and Budget — Alair Towsend.
Public Affairs — Pamila Bailey.
Health — Edward Brandt.
Planning and Evaluation — Gerald Britten.
Human Development — Dorcas Hardy.
Legislation — Dale Sopper.
Personnel Administration — Thomas McFee.
General Counsel — Juan Del Real.
Civil Rights — Paul Kretchmar.
Health Care Financing Admin. — Carolyn Davis, adm.
Social Security — John Svahn, comm.

Department of Housing and Urban Development

451 7th St. SW 20410
Secretary of Housing & Urban Development — Samuel R. Pierce Jr.
Under Secretary — Donald I. Hovde.
Assistant Secretaries for:
Administration — Judith L. Tardy.
Community Planning & Development — Stephen Bollinger.
Fair Housing & Equal Opportunity — Antonio Monroig.
Housing & Federal Housing Commissioner — Philip Winn.
Legislation & Intergovernmental Relations — Steve May.
Neighborhoods, Voluntary Assns. & Consumer Protection — vacant.
Policy Development & Research — E. S. Savas.
President, Govt. Natl. Mortgage Assn. — vacant.
Public Affairs — Leonard Burchman.

International Affairs — Theodore Britton Jr., act.
Labor Relations — vacant.
General Counsel — John J. Knapp.
Inspector General — Charles L. Dempsey.

Department of Transportation

400 7th St. SW 20590

Secretary of Transportation — Andrew L. Lewis.
Deputy Secretary — Darrell T. Trent.
Assistant Secretaries — Judith T. Connor (Policy and International Affairs); Donald Derman (Budget and Programs); Robert Fairman, act. (Administration); Lee L. Verstandig (Governmental Affairs).
General Counsel — John M. Fowler.
National Highway Traffic Safety Admin. — Raymond A. Peck Jr.
U. S. Coast Guard Commandant — John B. Hayes.
Federal Aviation Admin. — J. Lynn Helms.
Federal Highway Admin. — Ray Barnhart.
Federal Railroad Admin. — Robert W. Blanchette.
Urban Mass Transportation Admin. — Arthur E. Teele Jr.
Research & Special Programs Admin. — Howard Duqoff.
Saint Lawrence Seaway Development Corp. Admin. — David W. Oberlin.

Department of Energy

1000 Independence Ave. SW 20585

Secretary of Energy — James B. Edwards.
Deputy Secy. — W. Kenneth Davis.

Under Secy. — Raymond Romatowski, act.
Federal Energy Regulatory Comm. — Charles M. Butler 3d, chmn.
Off. of Hearings & Appeals — George Breznay, dir.
Inspector General — James R. Richards.
Economic Regulatory Admin. — Barton R. House, act.
International Affairs — Peter C. Borre, act.
Conservation & Renewable Energy — Joseph J. Tribble.
Energy Information Adm. — J. Erich Evered.
Office of Energy Research — Alvin Trivelpiece, dir.

Department of Education

Wash., D.C. 20202

Secretary of Education — Terrel H. Bell.
Under Secretary — William C. Clohan Jr.
Deputy Under Secretaries — Gary Jones, Kent Lloyd, John Rodriguez.
General Counsel — Dan Oliver.
Assistant Secretaries:
Legislation & Public Affairs — Anne Graham.
Elementary and Secondary Education — Vincent Reed.
Postsecondary Education — Thomas P. Melady.
Educational Research and Improvement — Donald J. Senese.
Vocational & Adult Education — Robert Worthington.
Special Education and Rehabilitative Services — Jean Tufts.
Civil Rights — Clarence Thomas.

Judiciary of the U.S.

Data as of July, 1981

Justices of the United States Supreme Court

The Supreme Court comprises the chief justice of the United States and 8 associate justices, all appointed by the president with advice and consent of the Senate. Salaries: chief justice $84,675 annually, associate justice $81,288.

Name; apptd from Chief Justices in italics	Service Term	Yrs.	Born	Died
John Jay, N.Y.	1789-1795	5	1745	1829
John Rutledge, S. C.	1789-1791	1	1739	1800
William Cushing, Mass.	1789-1810	20	1732	1810
James Wilson, Pa.	1789-1798	8	1742	1798
John Blair, Va.	1789-1796	6	1732	1800
James Iredell, N. C.	1790-1799	9	1751	1799
Thomas Johnson, Md.	1791-1793	1	1732	1819
William Paterson, N. J.	1793-1806	13	1745	1806
John Rutledge, S.C.	1795(a)	—	1739	1800
Samuel Chase, Md.	1796-1811	15	1741	1811
Oliver Ellsworth, Conn.	1796-1800	4	1745	1807
Bushrod Washington, Va.	1798-1829	31	1762	1829
Alfred Moore, N. C.	1799-1804	4	1755	1810
John Marshall, Va.	1801-1835	34	1755	1835
William Johnson, S. C.	1804-1834	30	1771	1834
Henry B. Livingston, N.Y.	1806-1823	16	1757	1823
Thomas Todd, Ky.	1807-1826	18	1765	1826
Joseph Story, Mass.	1811-1845	33	1779	1845
Gabriel Duval, Md.	1811-1835	22	1752	1844
Smith Thompson, N. Y.	1823-1843	20	1768	1843
Robert Trimble, Ky.	1826-1828	2	1777	1828
John McLean, Oh.	1829-1861	32	1785	1861
Henry Baldwin, Pa.	1830-1844	14	1780	1844
James M. Wayne, Ga.	1835-1867	32	1790	1867
Roger B. Taney, Md.	1836-1864	28	1777	1864
Philip P. Barbour, Va.	1836-1841	4	1783	1841
John Catron, Tenn.	1837-1865	28	1786	1865
John McKinley, Ala.	1837-1852	15	1780	1852
Peter V. Daniel, Va.	1841-1860	19	1784	1860
Samuel Nelson, N. Y.	1845-1872	27	1792	1873
Levi Woodbury, N. H.	1845-1851	5	1789	1851
Robert C. Grier, Pa.	1846-1870	23	1794	1870
Benjamin R. Curtis, Mass.	1851-1857	6	1809	1874
John A. Campbell, Ala.	1853-1861	8	1811	1889
Nathan Clifford, Me.	1858-1881	23	1803	1881
Noah H. Swayne, Oh.	1862-1881	18	1804	1884
Samuel F. Miller, Ia.	1862-1890	28	1816	1890
David Davis, Ill.	1862-1877	14	1815	1886
Stephen J. Field, Cal.	1863-1897	34	1816	1899
Salmon P. Chase, Oh.	1864-1873	8	1808	1873
William Strong, Pa.	1870-1880	10	1808	1895
Joseph P. Bradley, N. J.	1870-1892	21	1813	1892
Ward Hunt, N. Y.	1872-1882	9	1810	1886
Morrison R. Waite, Oh.	1874-1888	14	1816	1888
John M. Harlan, Ky.	1877-1911	34	1833	1911
William B. Woods, Ga.	1880-1887	6	1824	1887
Stanley Matthews, Oh.	1881-1889	7	1824	1889
Horace Gray, Mass.	1881-1902	20	1828	1902
Samuel Blatchford, N. Y.	1882-1893	11	1820	1893
Lucius Q. C. Lamar, Miss.	1888-1893	5	1825	1893
Melville W. Fuller, Ill.	1888-1910	21	1833	1910
David J. Brewer, Kan.	1889-1910	20	1837	1910
Henry B. Brown, Mich.	1890-1906	15	1836	1913
George Shiras Jr., Pa.	1892-1903	10	1832	1924
Howell E. Jackson, Tenn.	1893-1895	2	1832	1895
Edward D. White, La.	1894-1910	16	1845	1921
Rufus W. Peckham, N. Y.	1895-1909	13	1838	1909
Joseph McKenna, Cal.	1898-1925	26	1843	1926
Oliver W. Holmes, Mass.	1902-1932	29	1841	1935
William R. Day, Oh.	1903-1922	19	1849	1923
William H. Moody, Mass.	1906-1910	3	1853	1917
Horace H. Lurton, Tenn.	1909-1914	4	1844	1914
Charles E. Hughes, N. Y.	1910-1916	5	1862	1948
Willis Van Devanter, Wy.	1910-1937	26	1859	1941
Joseph R. Lamar, Ga.	1910-1916	5	1857	1916
Edward D. White, La.	1910-1921	10	1845	1921
Mahlon Pitney, N. J.	1912-1922	10	1858	1924
James C. McReynolds, Tenn.	1914-1941	26	1862	1946
Louis D. Brandeis, Mass.	1916-1939	22	1856	1941
John H. Clarke, Oh.	1916-1922	5	1857	1945
William H. Taft, Conn.	1921-1930	8	1857	1930
George Sutherland, Ut.	1922-1938	15	1862	1942
Pierce Butler, Minn.	1922-1939	16	1866	1939
Edward T. Sanford, Tenn.	1923-1930	7	1865	1930
Harlan F. Stone, N. Y.	1925-1941	16	1872	1946
Charles E. Hughes, N. Y.	1930-1941	11	1862	1948
Owen J. Roberts, Pa.	1930-1945	15	1875	1955
Benjamin N. Cardozo, N.Y.	1932-1938	6	1870	1938
Hugo L. Black, Ala.	1937-1971	34	1886	1971

Name; apptd from	Service Term	Yrs.	Born	Died
Stanley F. Reed, Ky.	1938-1957	19	1884	1980
Felix Frankfurter, Mass. . .	1939-1962	23	1882	1965
William O. Douglas,				
Conn.	1939-1975	36	1898	1980
Frank Murphy, Mich.	1940-1949	9	1890	1949
Harlan F. Stone, N. Y. . . .	1941-1946	5	1872	1946
James F. Byrnes, S. C. . . .	1941-1942	1	1879	1972
Robert H. Jackson, N. Y. . .	1941-1954	12	1892	1954
Wiley B. Rutledge, Ia.	1943-1949	6	1894	1949
Harold H. Burton, Oh. . . .	1945-1958	13	1888	1964
Fred M. Vinson, Ky.	1946-1953	7	1890	1953
Tom C. Clark, Tex.	1949-1967	18	1899	1977
Sherman Minton, Ind.	1949-1956	7	1890	1965
Earl Warren, Cal.	1953-1969	16	1891	1974
John Marshall Harlan,				
N. Y.	1955-1971	16	1899	1971
William J. Brennan Jr.,				
N. J.	1956 ——	——	1906	——

Name; apptd from	Service Term	Yrs.	Born	Died
Charles E. Whittaker,				
Mo.	1957-1962	5	1901	1973
Potter Stewart, Oh.	1958-1981	23	1915	——
Byron R. White, Col.	1962 ——	——	1917	——
Arthur J. Goldberg, Ill. . . .	1962-1965	3	1908	——
Abe Fortas, Tenn.	1965-1969	4	1910	——
Thurgood Marshall, N.Y. . .	1967 ——	——	1908	——
Warren E. Burger, Va. . . .	1969 ——	——	1907	——
Harry A. Blackmun,				
Minn.	1970 ——	——	1908	——
Lewis F. Powell Jr., Va. . .	1972 ——	——	1907	——
William H. Rehnquist,				
Ariz.	1972 ——	——	1924	——
John Paul Stevens, Ill. . . .	1975 ——	——	1920	——
Sandra Day O'Connor,				
Ariz.	1981 ——	——	1930	——
(a) Rejected Dec. 15, 1795.				

U.S. Court of Customs and Patent Appeals

Washington, DC 20439 (Salaries, $65,000)
Chief Judge — Howard T. Markey.
Associate Judges — Giles S. Rich, Phillip B. Baldwin, Jack B. Miller, Helen W. Niles.

U.S. Court of International Trade

New York, NY 10007 (Salaries, $61,500)
Chief Judge — Edward D. Re.
Judges — Paul P. Rao, Morgan Ford, Scovel Richardson, Frederick Landis, James L. Watson, Herbert N. Maletz, Bernard Newman, Nils A. Boe.

U.S. Court of Claims

Washington, DC 20005 (Salaries, $65,000)
Chief Judge — Daniel M. Friedman
Associate Judges — Oscar H. Davis, Shiro Kashiwa, Robert L. Kunzig, Marion T. Bennett, Philip Nichols Jr., Edward S. Smith.

U.S. Tax Court

Washington DC 20217 (Salaries, $61,500)
Chief Judge — C. Moxley Featherston.
Judges — Irene F. Scott, William M. Fay, Howard A. Dawson Jr., Theodore Tannenwald Jr., Charles R. Simpson, Leo H. Irwin, Samuel B. Sterrett, William A. Goffe, Cynthia H. Hall, Darrell D. Wiles, Richard C. Wilbur, Herbert L. Chabot, Sheldon V. Ekman, Arthur L. Nims 3d, Edna G. Parker.

U.S. Courts of Appeals

(Salaries, $65,000. CJ means Chief Judge)

District of Columbia — Carl McGowen, CJ; J. Skelly Wright, Edward Allen Tamm, Spottswood W. Robinson III, Roger Robb, George E. MacKinnon, Malcolm Richard Wilkey, Patricia M. Wald, Abner J. Mikva, Harry T. Edwards, Ruth Bader Ginsburg; Clerk's Office, Washington, DC 20001.
First Circuit (Me., Mass., N.H., R.I., Puerto Rico) — Frank M. Coffin, CJ; Levin H. Campbell, Hugh H. Bownes, Stephen Breyer; Clerk's Office, Boston, MA 02109.
Second Circuit (Conn., N.Y., Vt.) — Wilfred Feinberg, CJ; Irving R. Kaufman, Walter R. Mansfield, William H. Mulligan, James L. Oakes, William H. Timbers, Ellsworth Van Graafeiland, Thomas J. Meskill, Jon O. Newman, Amalya Lyle Kearse; Clerk's Office, New York, NY 10007.
Third Circuit (Del., N.J., Pa., Virgin Is.) — Collins J. Seitz, CJ; Ruggero J. Aldisert, Arlin M. Adams, John J. Gibbons, James Hunter 3d, Joseph F. Weis Jr., Leonard I. Garth, A. Leon Higginbotham Jr., Dolores K. Sloviter; Clerk's Office, Philadelphia, PA 19106.
Fourth Circuit (Md., N.C., S.C., Va., W.Va.) — Clement F. Haynsworth Jr., CJ; Harrison L. Winter, Kenneth K. Hall, John D. Butzner Jr., Donald Stuart Russell, H. Emory Widener Jr., James D. Phillips Jr., Francis D. Murnaghan Jr., James M. Sprouse, Sam J. Ervin 3d; Clerk's Office, Richmond, VA 23219.
Fifth Circuit (Ala., Fla., Ga., La., Miss., Tex., Canal Zone) — James P. Coleman, CJ; John R. Brown, Robert A. Ainsworth Jr., John C. Godbold, Charles Clark, Thomas G. Gee, Paul H. Roney, Gerald B. Tjoflat, James C. Hill, Peter T. Fay, Alvin B. Rubin, Reynaldo G. Garza, Albert J. Henderson Jr., Thomas M. Reavley, Joseph W. Hatchett, Henry A. Politz, R. Lanier Anderson, Carolyn D. Randall, Samuel D. Johnson, Albert Tate Jr., Thomas A. Clark,

Jerre S. Williams; Clerk's Office, New Orleans, LA 70130.
Sixth Circuit (Ky., Mich., Ohio, Tenn.) — George Clifton Edwards Jr., CJ; Paul C. Weick, Albert J. Engel, Pierce Lively, Gilbert S. Merritt, Damon J. Keith, Bailey Brown, Cornelia G. Kennedy, Boyce F. Martin Jr., Nathaniel R. Jones; Clerk's Office, Cincinnati, OH 45202.
Seventh Circuit (Ill., Ind., Wis.) — Thomas E. Fairchild, CJ; Luther M. Swygert, Walter J. Cummings, Wilbur F. Pell Jr., Robert A. Sprecher, Harlington Wood Jr., William J. Bauer, Richard D. Cudahy; Clerk's Office, Chicago, IL 60604.
Eighth Circuit (Ark., Ia., Minn., Mo., Neb., N.D., S.D.) — Donald P. Lay, CJ; Gerald W. Heaney, Myron H. Bright, Donald R. Ross, Roy L. Stephenson, J. Smith Henley, Theodore McMillian, Richard S. Arnold; Clerk's Office, St. Louis, MO 63101.
Ninth Circuit (Ariz., Cal., Ida., Mont., Nev., Ore., Wash., Alaska, Ha., Guam) — James R. Browning, CJ; Eugene A. Wright, Herbert Y. C. Choy, J. Clifford Wallace, Alfred T. Goodwin, Anthony M. Kennedy, J. Blaine Anderson, Procter Hug Jr., Thomas Tang, Joseph T. Sneed, Jerome Farris, Betty B. Fletcher, Mary M. Schroeder, Otto R. Skopil Jr., Harry Pregerson, Arthur L. Alarcon, Cecil F. Poole, Warren J. Ferguson, Dorothy W. Nelson, William C. Canby Jr., Robert Boochever, William A. Norris, Stephen Reinhardt; Clerk's Office, San Francisco, CA 94101.
Tenth Circuit (Col., Kan., N.M., Okla., Ut., Wy.) — Oliver Seth, CJ; William J. Holloway Jr., Robert H. McWilliams, James E. Barrett, William E. Doyle, Monroe G. McKay, James K. Logan, Stephanie K. Seymour; Clerk's Office, Denver, CO 80294.
Temporary Emergency Court of Appeals — Edward Allen Tamm, CJ; Clerk's Office, Washington, DC 20001.

U.S. District Courts

(Salaries, $61,500. CJ means Chief Judge)

Alabama — **Northern:** Frank H. McFadden, CJ; Sam C. Pointer Jr., James Hughes Hancock, J. Foy Guin Jr., Robert B. Probst, E. B. Haltom Jr., U. W. Clemon; Clerk's Office, Birmingham 35203. **Middle:** Robert E. Varner, CJ; Truman M. Hobbs, Myron H. Thompson; Clerk's Office, Montgomery 36101. **Southern:** Virgil Pittman, CJ; William Brevard Hand; Clerk's Office, Mobile 36601.

Alaska — James A. von der Heydt, CJ; James M. Fitzgerald; Clerk's Office, Anchorage 99513.

Arizona — C. A. Muecke, CJ; William P. Copple, Mary Ann Richey, Vlademar A. Cordova, Richard M. Bilby, Charles L. Hardy, Alfredo C. Marquez, Earl H. Carroll; Clerk's Office, Phoenix 85025.

Arkansas — **Eastern:** Garnett Thomas Eisele, CJ; Elsijane Trimble Roy, William Ray Overton, Henry Woods, George Howard Jr.; Clerk's Office, Little Rock 72203. **Western:** Paul X. Williams, CJ; Elsijane Trimble Roy, George Howard Jr.; Clerk's Office, Fort Smith 72902.

California — **Northern:** Robert F. Peckham, CJ; Lloyd H. Burke, Stanley A. Weigel, Robert H. Schnacke, Samuel Conti, Spencer M. Williams, William H. Orrick Jr., William W. Schwarzer, William A. Ingram, Robert P. Aguilar, Thelton E. Henderson, Marilyn H. Patel, George B. Harris, Albert C. Wollenberg, Wiliam T. Sweigert, Alfonso Zirpoli; Clerk's Office, San Francisco 94102. **Eastern:** Philip C. Wilkins, CJ; Lawrence K. Karlton, Milton L. Schwartz, Edward Dean Price, Raul A. Ramirez; Clerk's Office, Sacramento 95814. **Central:** A. Andrew Hauk, CJ; William P. Gray, Manuel L. Real, David W. Williams, Robert J. Kelleher, Wm. Matthew Byrne Jr., Lawrence T. Lydick, Malcolm M. Lucas, Robert M. Takasugi, Laughlin E. Waters, Mariana R. Pfaelzer, Terry J. Hatter Jr., A. Wallace Tashima, Consuelo Bland Marshall, David V. Kenyon; Clerk's Office, Los

Angeles 90012. **Southern:** Edward J. Schwartz, CJ; Howard B. Turrentine, Gordon Thompson Jr., Leland C. Nielsen, William B. Enright, Judith N. Keep, Earl B. Gilliam; Clerk's Office, San Diego 92189.

Colorado — Fred M. Winner, CJ; Sherman G. Finesilver, Richard P. Matsch, John L. Kane, Jim R. Carrigan, Zita L. Weinshienk; Clerk's Office, Denver 80294.

Connecticut — T. Emmet Clarie, CJ; T. F. Gilroy Daly, Ellen B. Burns, Warren W. Eginton, Jose A. Cabranes; Clerk's Office, New Haven 06505.

Delaware — James L. Latchum, CJ; Walter K. Stapleton, Murray M. Schwartz; Clerk's Office, Wilmington 19801.

District of Columbia — William B. Bryant, CJ; Oliver Gasch, John Lewis Smith Jr., Aubrey E. Robinson Jr., Gerhard A. Gesell. John H. Pratt, June L. Green, Barrington D. Parker, Charles R. Richey, Thomas A. Flannery, Louis F. Oberdorfer, Harold H. Greene, John Garrett Penn, Joyce Hens Green, Norma H. Johnson; Clerk's Office, Washington DC 20001.

Florida — **Northern:** Winston E. Arnow, CJ; William H. Stafford Jr., Lyle C. Higby; Clerk's Office, Tallahassee 32302. **Middle:** George C. Young, CJ; Ben Krentzman, Howell W. Melton, William Terrell Hodges, John A. Reed Jr., George C. Carr, Susan H. Black, William J. Castagna; Clerk's Office, Jacksonville 32201. **Southern:** C. Clyde Atkins, CJ; Joe Eaton, James Lawrence King, Norman C. Roettger Jr.; Sidney M. Aronovitz, William H. Hoeveler, Jose A. Gonzalez, James W. Kehoe, Eugene P. Spellman, Edward B. Davis, James C. Paine, Alcee L. Hastings; Clerk's Office, Miami 33101.

Georgia — **Northern:** Charles A.Moye Jr., CJ; William C.O'Kelley, Richard C. Freeman, Newell Edenfield, Harold L. Murphy, Marvin H. Shoob, G. Ernest Tidwell, Orinda Dale Evans, Robert L. Vining Jr., Robert H. Hall, Harold T. Ward; Clerk's Office, Atlanta 30303. **Middle:** Wilbur D. Owens Jr., CJ; J. Robert Elliott; Clerk's Office, Macon 31202. **Southern:** Anthony A. Alaimo, CJ; B. Avant Edenfield, Dudley Bowen Jr.; Clerk's Office, Savannah 31402.

Hawaii — Samuel P. King, CJ; Clerk's Office, Honolulu 96850.

Idaho — Ray McNichols, CJ; Marion J. Callister; Clerk's Office, Boise 83724.

Illinois — **Northern:** James B. Parsons, CJ; Bernard M. Decker, Frank J. McGarr, Thomas R. McMillen, Prentice H. Marshall, Joel M. Flaum, John F. Grady, George N. Leighton, John Powers Crowley, Nicholas J. Bua, Stanley J. Roszkowski, James B. Moran, Marvin E. Aspen, Milton I. Shadur, Charles P. Kocoras, Susan Getzendanner; Clerk's Office, Chicago 60604. **Central** Robert D. Morgan, CJ; J. Waldo Ackerman, Harold A. Baker; Clerk's Office, Peoria 61602. **Southern:** James L. Foreman, CJ; William L. Beatty; Clerk's Office, E. St. Louis 62202.

Indiana — **Northern:** Jesse E. Eschbach, CJ; Allen Sharp, Phil M. McNagny Jr.; Clerk's Office, South Bend 46601. **Southern:** William E. Steckler, CJ; Cale J. Holder, S. Hugh Dillin, James E. Noland, Gene E. Brooks; Clerk's Office, Indianapolis 46204.

Iowa — **Northern:** Edward J. McManus, CJ; Donald E. O'Brien; Clerk's Office, Cedar Rapids 52407. **Southern:** William C. Stuart, CJ; Donald E. O'Brien, Harold D. Vietor; Clerk's Office, Des Moines 50309.

Kansas — Frank G. Theis, CJ; Earl E. O'Connor, Richard Dean Rogers, Dale E. Saffels, Patrick F. Kelly; Clerk's Office, Wichita 67201.

Kentucky — **Eastern:** Bernard T. Moynahan Jr., CJ; Howard David Hermansdorfer, Eugene E. Siler Jr., Scott Reed, William Bertelsman, G. Wix Unthank, Clerk's Office, Lexington 40501. **Western:** Charles M. Allen, CJ; Eugene E. Siler Jr., Edward H. Johnstone, Thomas A. Ballantine; Clerk's Office, Louisville 40202.

Louisiana — **Eastern:** Frederick J. R. Heebe, CJ; Edward J. Boyle Sr., Lansing L. Mitchell, Fred J. Cassibry, Jack M. Gordon, Morey L. Sear, Charles Schwartz Jr., Adrian A. Duplantier, Robert F. Collins, George Arceneaux Jr., Veronica D. Wicker, Patrick E. Carr, Peter Hill Beer; Clerk's Office, New Orleans 70130. **Middle:** John V. Parker, CJ; Frank J. Polozola; Clerk's Office, Baton Rouge 70801. **Western:** Nauman S. Scott, CJ; Tom Stagg, W. Eugene Davis, Earl Ernest Veron, John M. Shaw; Clerk's Office, Shreveport 71161,

Maine — Edward Thaxter Gignoux, CJ; Clerk's Office, Portland 04101.

Maryland — Edward S. Northrop, CJ; Frank A. Kaufman, Alexander Harvey 2d, James R. Miller Jr., Joseph H. Young, Herbert F. Murray, Shirley B. Jones, Joseph C. Howard, Norman P. Ramsey; Clerk's Office, Baltimore 21201.

Massachusetts — Andrew A. Caffrey, CJ; W. Arthur Garrity Jr., Frank H. Freedman, Joseph L. Tauro, Walter Jay Skinner, A.

David Mazzone, Robert E. Keeton, John J. McNaught, Rya W. Zobel, David S. Nelson; Clerk's Office, Boston 02109:

Michigan — **Eastern:** John Feikens, CJ; Philip Pratt, Robert E. DeMascio, Charles W. Joiner, James Harvey, James P. Churchill, Ralph B. Guy Jr., Julian A. Cook, Patricia A. Boyle, Stewart A. Newblatt, Avern Cohn, Anna Diggs Taylor, Horace W. Gilmore; Clerk's Office, Detroit 48226. **Western:** Wendell A. Miles, CJ; Douglas W. Hillman, Benjamin F. Gibson, Richard A. Enslen; Clerk's Office, Grand Rapids 49503.

Minnesota — Edward J. Devitt, CJ; Miles W. Lord, Donald D. Alsop, Harry H. MacLaughlin, Robert G. Renner, Diana Murphy, Clerk's Office, St. Paul 55101.

Mississippi — **Northern:** William C. Keady, CJ; L. T. Senter Jr.; Clerk's Office, Oxford 38655. **Southern:** Dan M. Russell Jr., CJ; William Harold Cox, Walter L. Nixon Jr.; Clerk's Office, Jackson 39205.

Missouri — **Eastern:** H. Kenneth Wangelin, CJ; John F. Nangle, Edward D. Filippine, William L. Hungate, Clyde S. Cahill Jr.; Clerk's Office, St. Louis 63101. **Western:** Russell G. Clark, CJ; Harold Sachs, Scott O. Wright; Clerk's Office, Kansas City 64106.

Montana — James F. Battin, CJ; Paul G. Hatfield; Clerk's Office, Billings 59101.

Nebraska — Warren K. Urbom, CJ; Robert V. Denney, Albert G. Schatz; Clerk's Office, Omaha 68101.

Nevada — Harry E. Claiborne, CJ; Roger D. Foley, Edward C. Reed; Clerk's Office, Las Vegas 89101.

New Hampshire — Shane Devine, CJ; Martin J. Loughlin; Clerk's Office, Concord 03301.

New Jersey — Clarkson S. Fisher, CJ; Frederick B. Lacey, Vincent P. Biunno, Herbert J. Stern, H. Curtis Meanor, John F. Gerry, Stanley S. Brotman, Anne E. Thompson, D. R. Debevoise, H. Lee Sarokin, Harold Ackerman; Clerk's Office, Trenton 08605.

New Mexico — Howard C. Bratton, CJ; Edwin L. Mechem, Santiago E. Campos, Juan G. Burciaga; Clerk's Office, Albuquerque 87103.

New York — **Northern:** Howard G. Munson, CJ; Neal P. McCurn; Clerk's Office, Albany 12201. **Eastern:** Jack B. Weinstein, CJ; Mark A. Costantino, Edward R. Neaher, Thomas C. Platt Jr., Henry Bramwell, George C. Pratt, Charles P. Sifton, Eugene H. Nickerson; Clerk's Office, Brooklyn 11201. **Southern:** Lloyd F. MacMahon, CJ; David N. Edelstein, Edward Weinfeld, Lloyd F. MacMahon, Constance Baker Motley, Milton Pollack, Morris E. Lasker, Lawrence W. Pierce, Lee P. Gagliardi, Charles L. Brieant, Whitman Knapp, Charles E. Stewart Jr., Thomas P. Griesa, Robert L. Carter, Robert J. Ward, Kevin Thomas Duffy, William C. Conner, Richard Owen, Leonard B. Sand, Mary Johnson Lowe, Henry F. Werker, Gerard L. Goettel, Charles S. Haight Jr., Vincent L. Broderick, Pierre N. Laval, Robert W. Sweet, Abraham D. Sofaer; Clerk's Office N. Y. City 10007. **Western:** John T. Curtin, CJ; Harold P. Burke, John T. Elfvin; Clerk's Office, Buffalo 14202.

North Carolina — **Eastern:** Franklin T. Dupree Jr., CJ; W. Earl Britt; Clerk's Office, Raleigh 27611. **Middle:** Eugene A. Gordon, CJ; Hiram H. Ward, Richard C. Erwin; Clerk's Office, Greensboro 27402. **Western:** Woodrow Wilson Jones, CJ; James B. McMillan; Clerk's Office, Asheville 28802.

North Dakota — Paul Benson, CJ; Bruce M. Van Sickle; Clerk's Office, Bismarck 58501.

Ohio — **Northern:** Frank J. Battisti, CJ; William K. Thomas, Thomas D. Lambros, Robert B. Krupansky, Nicholas J. Walinski, Leroy J. Contie Jr., John M. Manos, George W. White, Ann Aldrich; Clerk's Office, Cleveland 44114. **Southern:** Carl B. Rubin, CJ; Joseph P. Kinneary, Robert M. Duncan, John D. Holschuh, Walter H. Rice, S. Arthur Spiegel; Clerk's Office, Columbus 43215.

Oklahoma — **Northern:** H. Dale Cook, CJ; Frederick A. Daugherty, James O. Ellison, Thomas R. Brett; Clerk's Office, Tulsa 74103. **Eastern:** Frank H. Shey, CJ; Frederick A. Daugherty, H. Dale Cook; Clerk's Office, Muskogee 74401. **Western:** Frederick A. Daugherty, CJ; Luther B. Eubanks, H. Dale Cook, Ralph G. Thompson, Lee R. West; Clerk's Office, Oklahoma City 73102.

Oregon — James M. Burns, CJ; Robert C. Belloni, Owen M. Panner, James A. Redden, Helen J. Frye; Clerk's Office, Portland 97205.

Pennsylvania — **Eastern:** Joseph S. Lord 3d, CJ; Alfred L. Luongo, John P. Fullam, Charles R. Weiner, E. Mac Troutman, John B. Hannum, Daniel H. Huyett 3d, Donald W. VanArtsdalen, J. William Ditter Jr., Edward R. Becker, Raymond J. Broderick, Clarence C. Newcomer, Clifford Scott Green, Louis Charles Bechtle, Joseph L. McGlynn Jr., Edward N. Cahn, Louis H. Pollak, Norma L. Shapiro, James T. Giles; Clerk's Office, Philadelphia 19106. **Middle:** William J. Nealon Jr., CJ; R. Dixon Herman, Malcolm Muir, Richard P. Conaboy, Sylvia H. Rambo; Clerk's Office,

Scranton 18501. **Western:** Gerald J. Weber, CJ; William W. Knox, Hubert I. Teitelbaum, Barron P. McCune, Maurice B. Cohill Jr., Paul A. Simmons, Gustave Diamond, Donald E. Zeigler, Alan N. Bloch; Clerk's Office, Pittsburgh 15230.

Rhode Island — Raymond J. Pettine, CJ; Francis J. Boyle; Clerk's Office, Providence 02903

South Carolina — Charles E. Simons Jr., CJ; Solomon Blatt Jr., Robert F. Chapman, C. Weston Houck, Falcon B. Hawkins, Matthew J. Perry Jr., George R. Anderson Jr.; Clerk's Office, Columbia 29202.

South Dakota — Andrew A. Bogue, CJ; Donald J. Porter; Clerk's Office, Sioux Falls 57102.

Tennessee — **Eastern:** Frank W. Wilson, CJ; Robert L. Taylor, C. G. Neese; Clerk's Office, Knoxville 37901. **Middle:** L. Clure Morton, CJ, Thomas A. Wiseman Jr, John T. Nixon; Clerk's Office, Nashville 37203. **Western:** Robert M. McRae Jr., CJ; Harry W. Wellford, Odell Horton; Clerk's Office, Memphis 38103.

Texas — **Northern:** Halbert O. Woodward, CJ; Eldon B. Mahon, Robert M. Hill, Robert W. Porter, Patrick E. Higginbotham, Mary Lou Robinson, Barefoot Sanders, David O. Belew Jr., Jerry Buchmeyer; Clerks's Office, Dallas 75242. **Southern:** John V. Singleton Jr., CJ; Woodrow B. Seals, Carl O. Bue Jr., Owen D. Cox, Robert O'Conor Jr., Ross N. Sterling, Norman W. Black, James De Anda, George E. Cire, Gabrielle K. McDonald, George P. Kazen, Hugh Gibson, Filemon B. Vela; Clerk's Office, Houston 77208. **Eastern:** William Wayne Justice, CJ; Joe J. Fisher, William M. Steger, Robert Parker; Clerk's Office, Beaumont 77701. **Western:** William S. Sessions, CJ; Lucius D. Bunton 3d, Harry Lee Hudspeth, Fred Shannon, Hipolito F. Garcia; Clerk's Office, San Antonio 78206.

Utah — Aldon J. Anderson, CJ; Bruce S. Jenkins, David K. Winder; Clerk's Office, Salt Lake City 84101.

Vermont — James S. Holden, CJ; Albert W. Coffrin; Clerk's Office, Burlington 05402.

Virginia — **Eastern:** John A. MacKenzie, CJ; Robert R. Merhige Jr., Richard B. Kellam, Albert V. Bryan Jr., D. Dortch Warriner, J. Calvitt Clarke, Richard L. Williams; Clerk's Office, Norfolk 23501. **Western:** James C. Turk, CJ; Glen M. Williams, James H. Michael Jr.; Clerk's Office, Roanoke 24006.

Washington — **Eastern:** Robert J. McNichols, CJ; Justin Quackenbush; Clerk's Office, Spokane 99210. **Western:** Walter T. McGovern, CJ; Donald S. Voorhees, Jack E. Tanner, Barbara J. Rothstein; Clerk's Office, Seattle 98104.

West Virginia — **Northern:** Robert Earl Maxwell, CJ; Charles H. Haden 2d; Clerk's Office, Elkins 26241. **Southern:** Dennis Raymond Knapp, CJ; John T. Copenhaver Jr., Charles H. Haden 2d, Robert Staker, William M. Kidd; Clerk's Office Charleston 25329.

. **Wisconsin** — **Eastern:** John W. Reynolds, CJ; Myron L. Gordon, Robert W. Warren, Terence T. Evans; Clerk's Office, Milwaukee 53202. **Western:** James E. Doyle, CJ; Barbara B. Crabb; Clerk's Office, Madison 53701.

Wyoming — Clarence A. Brimmer; Clerk's Office, Cheyenne 82001.

U.S. Territorial District Courts

Canal Zone — Morey L. Sear; Clerk's Office, Balboa Heights.
Guam — Cristobal C. Duenas; Clerk's Office, P.O. Box DC, Agana 96910.
Puerto Rico — Hernan G. Pesquera, CJ; Juan R. Torruella, Juan M. Perez-Gimenez, Gilberto Gierbolini-Ortiz, Carman Consuelo Cerezo; Clerk's Office, San Juan 00904.
Virgin Islands — Almeric L. Christian, CJ; Clerk's Office, Charlotte Amalie, St. Thomas 00801.

Governors of States and Possessions

As of mid-1981

State	Capital	Governor	Party	Term years	Term expires	Annual salary
Alabama	Montgomery	Forrest "Fob" James	Dem.	4	Jan. 1983	$50,000
Alaska	Juneau	Jay S. Hammond	Rep.	4	Dec. 1982	74,196
Arizona	Phoenix	Bruce Babbitt	Dem.	4	Jan. 1983	50,000
Arkansas	Little Rock	Frank White	Rep.	2	Jan. 1983	35,000
California	Sacramento	Edmund G. Brown Jr.	Dem.	4	Jan. 1983	49,100
Colorado	Denver	Richard D. Lamm	Dem.	4	Jan. 1983	50,000
Connecticut	Hartford	William A. O'Neill	Dem.	4	Jan. 1983	42,000
Delaware	Dover	Pierre S. du Pont 4th	Rep.	4	Jan. 1985	35,000
Florida	Tallahassee	Robert Graham	Dem.	4	Jan. 1983	59,098
Georgia	Atlanta	George Busbee	Dem.	4	Jan. 1983	60,000
Hawaii	Honolulu	George R. Ariyoshi	Dem.	4	Dec. 1982	50,000
Idaho	Boise	John V. Evans	Dem.	4	Jan. 1983	40,000
Illinois	Springfield	James R. Thompson	Rep.	4	Jan. 1983	58,000
Indiana	Indianapolis	Robert D. Orr	Rep.	4	Jan. 1985	48,000
Iowa	Des Moines	Robert D. Ray	Rep.	4	Jan. 1983	55,000
Kansas	Topeka	John Carlin	Dem.	4	Jan. 1983	45,000
Kentucky	Frankfort	John Y. Brown Jr.	Dem.	4	Dec. 1983	45,000
Louisiana	Baton Rouge	David C. Treen	Rep.	4	May 1984	68,000
Maine	Augusta	Joseph E. Brennan	Dem.	4	Jan. 1983	35,000
Maryland	Annapolis	Harry Hughes	Dem.	4	Jan. 1983	60,000
Massachusetts	Boston	Edward J. King	Dem.	4	Jan. 1983	40,000
Michigan	Lansing	William G. Milliken	Rep.	4	Jan. 1983	65,000
Minnesota	St. Paul	Albert H. Quie	Rep.	4	Jan. 1983	66,500
Mississippi	Jackson	William Winter	Dem.	4	Jan. 1984	53,000
Missouri	Jefferson City	Christopher S. Bond	Rep.	4	Jan. 1985	55,000
Montana	Helena	Ted Schwinden	Dem.	4	Jan. 1985	43,360
Nebraska	Lincoln	Charles Thone	Rep.	4	Jan. 1983	40,000
Nevada	Carson City	Robert List	Rep.	4	Jan. 1983	50,000
New Hampshire	Concord	Hugh J. Gallen	Dem.	2	Jan. 1983	44,520
New Jersey	Trenton	Brendan T. Byrne	Dem.	4	Jan. 1982	65,000
New Mexico	Santa Fe	Bruce King	Dem.	4	Jan. 1983	60,000
New York	Albany	Hugh L. Carey	Dem.	4	Jan. 1983	85,000
North Carolina	Raleigh	James B. Hunt	Dem.	4	Jan. 1985	55,104
North Dakota	Bismarck	Allen I. Olson	Rep.	4	Jan. 1985	47,000
Ohio	Columbus	James A. Rhodes	Rep	4	Jan. 1983	50,000
Oklahoma	Oklahoma City	George Nigh	Dem.	4	Jan. 1983	48,000
Oregon	Salem	Victor Atiyeh	Rep.	4	Jan. 1983	55,423
Pennsylvania	Harrisburg	Richard Thornburgh	Rep.	4	Jan. 1983	66,000
Rhode Island	Providence	J. Joseph Garrahy	Dem.	2	Jan. 1983	42,500
South Carolina	Columbia	Richard W. Riley	Dem.	4	Jan. 1983	60,000
South Dakota	Pierre	William J. Janklow	Rep.	4	Jan. 1983	46,750
Tennessee	Nashville	Lamar Alexander	Rep.	4	Jan. 1983	68,226
Texas	Austin	William P. Clements Jr.	Rep.	4	Jan. 1983	71,400

State	Capital	Governor	Party	Term years	Term expires	Annual salary
Utah	Salt Lake City	Scott M. Matheson	Dem.	4	Jan. 1985	48,000
Vermont	Montpelier	Richard A. Snelling	Rep.	2	Jan. 1983	44,850
Virginia	Richmond	John N. Dalton	Rep.	4	Jan. 1982	60,000
Washington	Olympia	John Spellman	Rep.	4	Jan. 1985	63,000
West Virginia	Charleston	John D. Rockefeller 4th	Dem.	4	Jan. 1985	50,000
Wisconsin	Madison	Lee Dreyfus	Rep.	4	Jan. 1983	65,801
Wyoming	Cheyenne	Ed Herschler	Dem.	4	Jan. 1983	55,000
Possessions						
Amer. Samoa	Pago Pago	Peter Coleman	Rep.	4	Jan. 1985	—
Guam	Agana	Paul Calvo	Rep.	4	Jan. 1985	50,000
N. Mariana Isls.	Saipan	Carlos Camacho	Dem.	4	Jan. 1982	20,000
Puerto Rico	San Juan	Carlos Romero Barcelo	N.P.	4	Jan. 1985	36,200
Virgin Isls.	Charlotte Amalie	Juan Luis	Ind.	4	Jan. 1983	52,000

State Officials, Salaries, Party Membership

Compiled from data supplied by state officials, mid-1981

Alabama

Governor — Forrest "Fob" James, D., $50,000.
Lt. Gov. — George McMillan Jr. D., $65 per legislative day, plus annual salary of $400 per month.
Sec. of State — Don Siegelman, D., $25,800.
Atty. Gen. — Charles Graddick, D., $39,500.
Treasurer — Mrs. Annie Laurie Gunter, D., $25,800.
Legislature: meets annually the first Tuesday in Apr. (first year of term of office, first Tuesday in Feb. (2d and 3d years), 2d Tuesday in Jan. (4th year) at Montgomery. Members receive $400 per month, plus $65 per day during legislative sessions, and mileage of 10c per mile.
Senate — Dem., 35; Rep., 0. Total, 35.
House — Dem., 101; Rep., 4. Total, 105.

Alaska

Governor — Jay S. Hammond, R., $74,196.
Lt. Gov. — Terry Miller, R., $69,240.
Atty. General — Wilson Condon, D., $66,700.
Legislature: meets annually in January at Juneau, for as long as may be necessary. First session in odd years. Members receive $18,768 per year plus $67 per day while in session (Juneau legislators receive $50 per day). Also $4,000 for postage, personal stationery, and other expenses.
Senate — Dem., 10; Rep., 10. Total, 20.
House — Dem., 22; Rep., 16; Libertarian 2. Total, 40.

Arizona

Governor — Bruce Babbitt, D., $50,000.
Sec. of State — Rose Mofford, D., $28,000.
Atty. Gen. — Bob Corbin, R., $45,000.
Treasurer — Clark Dierks, R., $30,000.
Legislature: meets annually in January at Phoenix. Each member receives an annual salary of $15,000.
Senate — Dem., 14; Rep., 16. Total, 30.
House — Dem., 17; Rep., 43. Total, 60.

Arkansas

Governor — Frank White, R., $35,000.
Lt. Gov. — Winston Bryant, D., $14,000.
Sec. of State — Paul Riviere, D., $22,500.
Atty. Gen. — Steve Clark, D., $26,500.
Treasurer — Jimmie Lou Fisher, D., $22,500.
General Assembly: meets odd years in January at Little Rock. Members receive $7,500 per year, $45 a day while in regular session, plus 13c a mile travel expense.
Senate — Dem., 33; Rep., 1; 1 vacancy. Total, 35.
House — Dem., 92; Rep., 7; 1 vacancy. Total, 100.

California

Governor — Edmund G. Brown Jr., D., $49,100.
Lt. Gov. — Mike Curb, R., $42,500.
Sec. of State — March Fong Eu, D., $42,500.
Controller — Kenneth Cory, D., $42,500.
Atty. Gen. — George Deukmejian, R., $47,500.
Treasurer — Jesse M. Unruh, D., $42,500.
Legislature: meets at Sacramento; regular sessions commence on the first Monday in Dec. of every even-numbered year; each session lasts 2 years. Members receive $28,110 per year plus mileage and $46 per diem.
Senate — Dem., 23; Rep., 17. Total, 40.
Assembly — Dem., 49; Rep., 31. Total, 80.

Colorado

Governor — Richard D. Lamm, D., $50,000.

Lt. Gov. — Nancy Dick, D., $25,000.
Secy. of State — Mary Estill Buchanan, R., $27,500.
Atty. Gen. — J.D. MacFarlane, D., $35,000.
Treasurer — Roy Romer, D., $27,500.
General Assembly: meets annually in January at Denver. Members receive $14,000 annually, except holdover senators who receive $12,000.
Senate — Dem., 13; Rep., 22. Total, 35.
House — Dem., 25; Rep., 40. Total, 65.

Connecticut

Governor — William A. O'Neill, D., $42,000.
Lt. Gov. — Joseph J. Fauliso, D., $25,000.
Sec. of State — Barbara B. Kennelly, D., $25,000.
Treasurer — Henry E. Parker, D., $25,000.
Comptroller — J. Edward Caldwell, D., $25,000.
Atty. Gen. — Carl R. Ajello, D., $38,500.
General Assembly: meets annually odd years in January and even years in February at Hartford. Salary $17,000 per 2-year term plus $2,000 per 2-year term for expenses, plus 15c per mile travel allowance.
Senate — Dem., 23; Rep., 13. Total, 36.
House — Dem., 82; Rep., 69. Total, 151.

Delaware

Governor — Pierre S. du Pont 4th, R., $35,000.
Lt. Gov. — Michael N. Castle, R., $14,300.
Sec. of State — Glenn C. Kenton, R., $38,800.
Atty. Gen. — Richard S. Gebelein, R., $37,000.
Treasurer — Thomas R. Carper, D., $24,000.
General Assembly: meets annually at Dover from the 2d Tuesday in January to midnight June 30. Members receive $10,545 base salary.
Senate — Dem., 12; Rep., 9. Total, 21.
House — Dem., 16; Rep., 25. Total, 41.

Florida

Governor — Robert Graham, D., $59,098.
Lt. Gov. — Wayne Mixon, D., $47,279.
Sec. of State — George Firestone, D., $47,279.
Comptroller — Gerald Lewis, D., $47,279.
Atty. Gen. — Jim Smith, D., $47,279.
Treasurer — Bill Gunter, D., $47,279.
Legislature: meets annually in April at Tallahassee. Members receive $12,000 per year plus expense allowance while on official business.
Senate — Dem., 27; Rep., 13. Total, 40.
House — Dem., 81; Rep., 39. Total, 120.

Georgia

Governor — George Busbee, D., $60,000.
Lt. Gov. — Zell Miller, D., $28,846.
Sec. of State — David B. Poythress, D., $38,400.
Comptroller General — Johnnie L. Caldwell, D., $38,400.
Atty. Gen. — Arthur K. Bolton, D., $46,000.
General Assembly: meets annually at Atlanta. Members receive $7,200 per year. During session $44 per day for expenses.
Senate — Dem., 51; Rep., 5. Total, 56.
House — Dem., 156; Rep., 24. Total, 180.

Hawaii

Governor — George R. Ariyoshi, D., $50,000.
Lt. Gov. — Jean King, D., $45,000.
Dir., Budg. & Finance — Eileen Anderson, D., $42,500.
Atty. Gen. — Wayne Minami, D., $42,500.
Comptroller — Hideo Murakami, D., $42,500.

Dir., Finance & Budget — Jensen S. L. Hee, D., $42,500.
Legislature: meets annually on 3d Wednesday in January at Honolulu. Members receive $12,000 per year plus expenses.
Senate — Dem., 17. Rep., 8. Total, 25.
House — Dem., 39. Rep., 12. Total, 51.

Idaho

Governor — John V. Evans, D., $40,000.
Lt. Gov. — Philip E. Batt, R., $12,000.
Sec. of State — Pete T. Cenarrusa, R., $28,000.
Treasurer — Marjorie Ruth Moon, D., $28,000.
Atty. Gen. — David Leroy, R., $35,000.
Legislature: meets annually on the Monday after the first day in January at Boise. Members receive $4,200 per year, plus $25 per day when authorized, plus travel allowances.
Senate — Dem., 12; Rep., 23. Total, 35.
House — Dem., 14; Rep., 56. Total, 70.

Illinois

Governor — James R. Thompson, R., $58,000.
Lt. Gov. — David C. O'Neal, R., $45,500.
Sec. of State — Jim Edgar, R., $50,500.
Comptroller — Roland W. Burris, D., $48,000.
Atty. Gen. — Tyrone C. Fahner, R., $50,500.
Treasurer — Jerome A. Cosentimo, D., $48,000.
General Assembly: meets annually in January at Springfield. Members receive $28,000 per annum.
Senate — Dem., 30; Rep., 29. Total, 59.
House — Dem., 85; Rep., 91; 1 3d party. Total, 177.

Indiana

Governor — Robert D. Orr, R., $48,000 plus discretionary expenses.
Lt. Gov. — John M. Mutz, R., $34,000 plus discretionary expenses.
Sec. of State — Edwin J. Simcox, R., $34,000.
Atty. Gen. — Linley E. Pearson, R., $39,000.
Treasurer — Julian Ridlen, R., $34,000.
General Assembly: meets annually in January. Members receive $9,600 per year plus $50 per day while in session, $12.50 per day while not in session.
Senate — Dem., 15; Rep., 35. Total, 50.
House — Dem., 37; Rep., 63. Total, 100.

Iowa

Governor — Robert D. Ray, R., $55,000 plus $5,000 expenses.
Lt. Gov. — Terry Branstad, R., $18,000 plus personal expenses and travel allowances at same rate as for a senator.
Sec. of State — Mary Jane Odell, R., $30,000.
Atty. Gen. — Tom Miller, D., $40,000.
Treasurer — Maurice E. Baringer, R., $30,000.
General Assembly: meets annually in January at Des Moines. Members receive $12,000 annually plus maximum expense allowance of $30 per day for first 120 days of first session, and first 100 days of 2d session; mileage expenses at 15c a mile.
Senate — Dem., 21; Rep., 29. Total, 50.
House — Dem., 42; Rep., 58. Total, 100.

Kansas

Governor — John Carlin, D., $45,000.
Lt. Gov. — Paul V. Dugan, D., $13,500 plus expenses.
Sec. of State — Jack H. Brier, R., $27,500.
Atty. Gen. — Robert T. Stephan, R., $40,000.
Treasurer — Joan Finney, D., $27,500.
Legislature: meets annually in January at Topeka. Members receive $40 a day plus $50 a day expenses while in session, plus $400 per month while not in session.
Senate — Dem., 16; Rep., 24. Total, 40.
House — Dem., 53; Rep., 72. Total, 125.

Kentucky

Governor — John Y. Brown Jr., D., $45,000.
Lt. Gov. — Martha A. Collins, D., $38,640.
Sec. of State — Francis Jones Mills, D., $38,640.
Atty. Gen. — Steve Beshear, D., $38,640.
Treasurer — Drexel Davis, D., $38,640.
General Assembly: meets even years in January at Frankfort. Members receive $50 per day and $75 per day during session and $750 per month for expenses for interim.
Senate — Dem., 29; Rep., 9. Total, 38.
House — Dem., 75; Rep., 25. Total, 100.

Louisiana

Governor — David C. Treen, R., $68,000.
Lt. Gov. — Robert L. Freeman, D., $58,673.
Sec. of State — James H. Brown, D., $55,712.
Atty. Gen. — William J. Guste Jr., D., $55,712.
Treasurer — Mary Evelyn Parker, D., $55,712.
Legislature: meets annually for 60 legislative days commencing

on 3d Monday in April. Members receive $75 per day and mileage at 21c a mile for 8 round trips, plus $1,400 per month expense allowance.
Senate — Dem., 39; Rep., 0. Total, 39.
House — Dem., 95; Rep., 10. Total, 105.

Maine

Governor — Joseph E. Brennan, D., $35,000.
Sec. of State — Rodney Quinn, D., $25,000.
Atty. Gen. — James Tierney, D., $36,637.
Treasurer — Samuel Shapiro, D., $25,000.
Legislature: meets biennially in January at Augusta. Members receive $4,500 for regular sessions, $2,500 for special session plus expenses; presiding officers receive 50% more.
Senate — Dem., 16; Rep., 16; 1 Ind. Total, 33.
House — Dem., 84; Rep., 67. Total, 151.

Maryland

Governor — Harry Hughes, D., $60,000.
Lt. Gov. — Samuel Bogley, D., $52,500.
Comptroller — Louis L. Goldstein, D., $50,000.
Atty. Gen. — Stephen H. Sachs, D., $50,000.
Sec. of State — Fred L. Wineland, D., $36,000.
Treasurer — William S. James, D., $50,000.
General Assembly: meets 90 days annually on the 2d Wednesday in January at Annapolis. Members receive $17,600 per year.
Senate — Dem., 40; Rep., 7. Total, 47.
House — Dem., 125; Rep., 15; 1 Ind. Total, 141.

Massachusetts

Governor — Edward J. King, D., $40,000.
Lt. Gov. — Thomas P. O'Neill 3d, D., $30,000.
Sec. of the Commonwealth — Michael Joseph Connolly, D., $30,000.
Atty. Gen. — Francis X. Bellotti, D., $37,500.
Treasurer — Robert Q. Crane, D., $30,000.
Auditor — John J. Finnegan, D., $30,000.
General Court (Legislature): meets each January in Boston. Salaries $19,124 per annum.
Senate — Dem., 32; Rep., 6; 1 vacancy; 1 Ind. Total, 40.
House — Dem., 127; Rep., 31; 1 vacancy; 1 Ind. Total, 160.

Michigan

Governor — William G. Milliken, R., $65,000.
Lt. Gov. — James H. Brickley, R., $45,000.
Sec. of State — Richard H. Austin, D., $60,000.
Atty. Gen. — Frank J. Kelley, D., $60,000.
Treasurer — Loren Monroe, non-part., $54,100.
Legislature: meets annually in January at Lansing. Members receive $27,000 per year, plus $5,200 expense allowance.
Senate — Dem., 24; Rep., 14. Total, 38.
House — Dem., 64; Rep., 46. Total, 110.

Minnesota

Governor — Albert H. Quie, IR, $66,500.
Lt. Gov. — Lou Wangberg, IR, $38,000.
Sec. of State — Joan Anderson Growe, DFL., $36,000.
Atty. Gen. — Warren Spannaus, DFL., $56,000.
Treasurer — Jim Lord, DFL., $36,000.
Auditor — Arne H. Carlson, IR, $36,000.
Legislature: meets for a total of 120 days within every 2 years at St. Paul. Members receive $18,500 per year, plus expense allowance during session.
Senate — DFL., 45; IR, 22. Total, 67.
House — DFL., 70; IR, 64. Total, 134.
(DFL means Democratic-Farmer-Labor. IR means Independent Republican.)

Mississippi

Governor — William Winter, D., $53,000.
Lt. Gov. — Brad Dye, D., $34,000 per regular legislative session, plus expense allowance.
Sec. of State — Edwin Lloyd Pittman, D., $34,000.
Atty. Gen. — William A. Allain, D., $41,000.
Treasurer — William J. Cole 3d, D., $34,000.
Legislature: meets annually in January at Jackson. Members receive $8,100 per regular session plus travel allowance, and $210 per month while not in session.
Senate — Dem., 48; Rep., 4. Total, 52.
House — Dem., 116; Rep., 4; Ind., 2. Total, 122.

Missouri

Governor — Christopher S. Bond, R., $55,000.
Lt. Gov. — Kenneth J. Rothman, D., $30,000.

Sec. of State — James C. Kirkpatrick, D., $42,500.
Atty. Gen. — John Ashcroft, R., $45,000.
Treasurer — Mel Carnahan, D., $42,500.
General Assembly: meets annually in Jefferson City on the first Wednesday after first Monday in January; adjournment in odd-numbered years by June 30, in even-numbered years by May 15. Members receive $15,000 annually.
Senate — Dem., 23; Rep., 11. Total, 34.
House — Dem., 111; Rep., 52. Total, 163.

Montana

Governor — Ted Schwinden, D., $43,360.
Lt. Gov. — George Turman, D., $31,077.
Sec. of State — Jim Waltermire, R., $28,685.
Atty. Gen. — Mike Greely, D., $39,555.
Legislative Assembly: meets odd years in January at Helena. Members receive $39.50 per legislative day plus $45 per day for expenses while in session.
Senate — Dem., 21; Rep., 29. Total, 50.
House — Dem., 43; Rep., 57. Total, 100.

Nebraska

Governor — Charles Thone, R., $40,000.
Lt. Gov. — Roland Luedtke, R., $32,000.
Sec. of State — Allen J. Beermann, R., $32,000.
Atty. Gen. — Paul Douglas, R., $39,500.
Treasurer — Frank Marsh, R., $32,000.
Legislature: meets annually in January at Lincoln. Members receive salary of $4,800 annually plus travelling expenses for one round trip to and from session.
Unicameral body composed of 49 members who are elected on a nonpartisan ballot and are classed as senators.

Nevada

Governor — Robert List, R., $50,000.
Lt. Gov. — Myron E. Leavitt, D., $8,000 plus $60 per day when acting as governor and president of the Senate during legislative sessions.
Sec. of State — William D. Swackhamer, D., $32,500.
Comptroller — Wilson McGowen, R., $31,500.
Atty. Gen. — Richard H. Bryan, D., $40,500.
Treasurer — Stanton B. Colton, D., $31,500.
Legislature: meets odd years in January at Carson City. Members receive $80 per day for 60 days (20 days for special sessions), plus per diem of $40 per day for entire length of session. Travel allowance of 17c per mile.
Senate — Dem., 15; Rep., 5. Total, 20.
Assembly — Dem., 26; Rep., 14. Total, 40.

New Hampshire

Governor — Hugh J. Gallen, D., $44,520.
Sec. of State — William M. Gardner, D., $31,270.
Atty. Gen. — Gregory H. Smith, $38,690.
Comptroller — Arthur H. Fowler.
Treasurer — Robert W. Flanders, R., $31,270.
General Court (Legislature): meets odd years in January at Concord. Members receive $200; presiding officers $250.
Senate — Dem., 10; Rep., 13; 1 vacancy. Total, 24.
House — Rep., 158; Dem., 240; 2 vacancies. Total, 400.

New Jersey

Governor — Brendan T. Byrne, D., $65,000.
Sec. of State — Donald Lan, $56,000.
Atty. Gen. — John J. Degnan, $56,000.
Treasurer — Clifford Goldman, $56,000.
Legislature: meets annually in January at Trenton. Members receive $18,000 per year, except president of Senate and speaker of Assembly who receive 1/3 more.
Senate — Dem., 27; Rep., 13. Total, 40.
Assembly — Dem., 43; Rep. 37. Total, 80.

New Mexico

Governor — Bruce King, D., $60,000.
Lt. Gov. — Roberto Mondragon, D., $38,500. Acting governor, $150 per day.
Sec. of State — Shirley Hooper, D., $38,500.
Atty. Gen. — Jeff Bingaman, D., $44,000.
Treasurer — Jan Alan Hartke, D., $38,500.
Legislature: meets in January at Sante Fe; odd years for 60 days, even years for 30 days. Members receive $40 per day while in session.
Senate — Dem., 22; Rep., 20. Total, 42.
House — Dem., 41; Rep., 29. Total, 70.

New York

Governor — Hugh L. Carey, D., $85,000.
Lt. Gov. — Mario M. Cuomo, D., $60,000.
Sec. of State — Basil A. Paterson, D., $64,400.
Comptroller — Edward V. Regan, R., $60,000.
Atty. Gen. — Robert Abrams, D., $60,000.
Legislature: meets annually in January at Albany. Members receive $28,788 per year.
Senate — Dem., 25; Rep., 35. Total, 60.
Assembly — Dem., 86; Rep., 64. Total, 150.

North Carolina

Governor — James B. Hunt, D., $55,104 plus $11,500 per year expenses.
Lt. Gov. — James C. Green, D., $45,636 per year, plus $11,500 per year expense allowance.
Sec. of State — Thad Eure, D., $45,636.
Atty. Gen. — Rufus L. Edmisten, D., $51,396.
Treasurer — Harlan E. Boyles, D., $45,636.
General Assembly: meets odd years in January at Raleigh. Members receive $6,936 annual salary and $2,064 annual expense allowance, plus $50 per diem subsistence and travel allowance while in session.
Senate — Dem., 40; Rep., 10. Total, 50.
House — Dem., 96; Rep., 24. Total, 120.

North Dakota

Governor — Allen I. Olson, R., $47,000 plus $7,027 expenses.
Lt. Gov. — Ernest Sands, R., $33,500.
Sec. of State — Ben Meier, R., $33,500 plus $5,008 expenses.
Atty. Gen. — Bob Wefald, R., $38,000 plus $5,681 expenses.
Treasurer — John Lesmeister, R., $33,500 plus $5,008 expenses.
Legislative Assembly: meets odd years in January at Bismarck. Members receive $85 per day plus expenses during session and $180 per month when not in session.
Senate — Dem., 10; Rep., 40. Total, 50.
House — Dem., 27; Rep., 73. Total, 100.

Ohio

Governor — James A. Rhodes, R., $50,000.
Lt. Gov. — vacancy.
Sec. of State — Anthony J. Celebrezze Jr., D., $50,000.
Atty. Gen. — William J. Brown, D., $50,000.
Treasurer — Gertrude W. Donahey, D., $50,000.
Auditor — Thomas E. Ferguson, D., $50,000.
General Assembly: meets odd years at Columbus on first Monday in January for the 1st session, and no later than Mar. 15th of the following year for the 2d session. Members receive $22,500 per annum.
Senate — Dem., 15; Rep., 18. Total, 33.
House — Dem., 56; Rep., 43. Total, 99.

Oklahoma

Governor — George Nigh, D., $48,000.
Lt. Gov. — Spencer T. Bernard, D., $27,500.
Sec. of State — Jeannette B. Edmondson, D., $24,000.
Atty. Gen. — Jan Cartwright, D., $35,000.
Treasurer — Leo Winters, D., $30,000.
Legislature: meets annually in January at Oklahoma City. Members receive $12,948.
Senate — Dem., 40; Rep., 8. Total, 48.
House — Dem., 75; Rep., 26. Total, 101.

Oregon

Governor — Victor Atiyeh, R., $55,423, plus $1,000 monthly expenses.
Sec. of State — Norma Paulus, R., $45,619.
Atty. Gen. — David B. Frohnmayer, R., $53,308.
Treasurer — Clay Myers, R., $45,619.
Legislative Assembly: meets odd years in January at Salem. Members receive $700 monthly and $44 expenses per day while in session; $300 per month while not in session.
Senate — Dem., 22; Rep., 8. Total, 30.
House — Dem., 33; Rep., 27. Total, 60.

Pennsylvania

Governor — Richard Thornburgh, R., $66,000.
Lt. Gov. — William W. Scranton 3d, R., $49,500.
Sec. of the Commonwealth — William R. Davis, R., $38,500.
Atty. Gen. — LeRoy S. Zimmerman, R., $55,000.
Treasurer — R. Budd Dwyer, R., $48,000.
General Assembly — convenes annually in January at Harris-

burg. Members receive $25,000 per year plus $7,500 for expenses.
Senate — Dem., 23; Rep., 26; 1 vacancy. Total, 50.
House — Dem., 100; Rep., 102; 1 vacancy. Total, 203.

Rhode Island

Governor — J. Joseph Garrahy, D., $42,500.
Lt. Gov. — Thomas R. DiLuglio, D., $30,500.
Sec. of State — Robert F. Burns, D., $30,500.
Atty. Gen. — Dennis J. Roberts 2d, D., $36,875.
Treasurer — Anthony J. Solomon, D., $30,500.
General Assembly: meets annually in January at Providence.
Members receive $5 per day for 60 days, and travel allowance of 8¢
per mile.
Senate — Dem., 43; Rep., 7. Total, 50.
House — Dem., 82; Rep., 18. Total, 100.

South Carolina

Governor — Richard W. Riley, D., $60,000.
Lt. Gov. — Nancy Stevenson, D., $30,000.
Sec. of State — John T. Campbell, D., $45,000.
Comptroller Gen. — Earle E. Morris Jr., D., $45,000.
Atty. Gen. — Daniel R. McLeod, D., $45,000.
Treasurer — G.L. Patterson Jr., D., $45,000.
General Assembly: meets annually in January at Columbia.
Members receive $10,000 per year and expense allowance of $35
per day, plus travel and postage allowance.
Senate — Dem., 41; Rep., 5. Total, 46.
House — Dem. 107; Rep., 17. Total, 124.

South Dakota

Governor — William J. Janklow, R., $46,750.
Lt. Gov. — Lowell C. Hansen 2d, R., $6,500 plus $50 per day
during legislative session.
Sec. of State — Alice Kundert, R., $31,750.
Treasurer — David Volk, R., $31,750.
Atty. Gen. — Mark Meierhenry, R., $39,750.
Auditor — Vernon Larson, $31,750.
Legislature: meets annually in January at Pierre. Members re-
ceive $3,200 for 40-day session in odd-numbered years, and $2,800
for 35-day session in even-numbered years, plus $50 per legislative
day.
Senate — Dem., 10; Rep., 25. Total, 35.
House — Dem., 21; Rep., 49. Total, 70.

Tennessee

Governor — Lamar Alexander, R., $68,226.
Lt. Gov. — John S. Wilder, D., $8,308.
Sec. of State — Gentry Crowell, D., $46,524.
Comptroller — William Snodgrass, D., $51,504.
Atty. Gen. — William M. Leech, D., $64,494.
General Assembly: meets annually in January at Nashville.
Members receive $8,308 yearly plus $66.47 expenses for each day
in session, plus mileage and expense allowances.
Senate — Dem., 20; Rep., 12; Ind., 1. Total, 33.
House — Dem., 60; Rep., 38; Ind., 1. Total, 99.

Texas

Governor — William P. Clements Jr., R., $71,400.
Lt. Gov. — Bill Hobby, D., $7,200, plus living quarters. Gover-
nor's salary when acting as governor.
Sec. of State — George W. Strake Jr., R., $42,700.
Comptroller — Bob Bullock, D., $43,700.
Atty. Gen. — Mark White, D., $45,200.
Treasurer — Warren G. Harding, D., $45,200.
Legislature: meets odd years in January at Austin. Members re-
ceive annual salary not exceeding $7,200, per diem while in session,
and travel allowance.
Senate — Dem., 24; Rep., 7. Total, 31.
House — Dem., 115; Rep., 35. Total, 150.

Utah

Governor — Scott M. Matheson, D., $48,000.
Sec. of State/Lt. Gov. — David S. Monson, R., $33,500.
Atty. Gen. — David L. Wilkinson, R., $36,500.
Treasurer — Edward T. Alter, D., $33,500.
Legislature: convenes for 60 days on 2d Monday in January in
odd-numbered years; for 20 days in even-numbered years; members
receive $25 per day, $15 daily expenses, and mileage.
Senate — Dem., 7; Rep., 22. Total, 29.
House — Dem., 16; Rep., 59. Total, 75.

Vermont

Governor — Richard A. Snelling, R., $44,850.
Lt. Gov. — Madeleine M. Kunin, D., $19,200.
Sec. of State — James H. Douglas, R., $24,380.
Atty. Gen. — John J. Easton Jr., R., $31,400.
Treasurer — Emory H. Hebard, R., $24,380.
Auditor of Accounts — Alexander V. Acebo, R., $24,380.
General Assembly: meets odd years in January at Montpelier.
Members receive $250 weekly while in session, with a limit of
$7,500 for a regular session and $50 per day for special session,
plus specified expenses.
Senate — Dem., 14; Rep., 16. Total, 30.
House — Dem., 64; Rep., 83; 2 Ind.; 1 vacancy. Total, 150.

Virginia

Governor — John N. Dalton, R., $60,000.
Lt. Gov. — Charles S. Robb, D., $16,000.
Atty. Gen. — J. Marshall Coleman, R., $45,000.
Sec. of the Commonwealth — Frederick T. Gray Jr., R.,
$25,000.
Treasurer — Robert C. Watts Jr., R., $37,900.
General Assembly: meets annually in January at Richmond.
Members receive $5,475 annually plus expense and mileage allow-
ances.
Senate — Dem., 31; Rep., 9. Total, 40.
House — Dem., 74; Rep., 25; Ind., 1. Total, 100.

Washington

Governor — John Spellman, R., $63,000.
Lt. Gov. — John A. Cherberg, D., $28,600.
Sec. of State — Ralph Munro, R., $31,000.
Atty. Gen. — Ken Eikenberry, R., $47,100.
Treasurer — Robert S. O'Brien, D., $37,200.
Legislature: meets annually in January at Olympia. Members
receive $11,200 annually, plus $44 per day while in session and 10¢
per mile.
Senate — Dem., 24; Rep., 25. Total, 49.
House — Dem., 42; Rep., 56. Total, 98.

West Virginia

Governor — John D. Rockefeller 4th, D., $50,000.
Sec. of State — A. James Manchin, D., $36,000.
Atty. Gen. — Chauncey Browning Jr., D., $42,000.
Treasurer — Larrie Bailey, D., $42,000.
Comm. of Agric. — Gus R. Douglas, D., $39,000.
Auditor — Glen B. Gainer Jr., $39,000.
Legislature: meets annually in January at Charleston. Members
receive compensation fixed by citizens' commission.
Senate — Dem., 27; Rep., 7. Total, 34.
House — Dem., 78; Rep., 22. Total, 100.

Wisconsin

Governor — Lee Dreyfus, R., $65,801.
Lt. Gov. — Russell A. Olson, R., $36,151.
Sec. of State — Vel R. Phillips, D., $32,608.
Treasurer — Charles P. Smith, D., $32,608.
Atty. Gen. — Bronson C. La Follette, D., $50,780.
Superintendent of Public Instruction — Barbara Thompson,
$45,840.
Legislature: meets in January at Madison. Members receive
$22,632 annually plus $30 per day expenses.
Senate — Dem., 19; Rep., 14. Total, 33.
Assembly — Dem., 58; Rep., 40; 1 vacancy. Total, 99.

Wyoming

Governor — Ed Herschler, D., $55,000.
Sec. of State — Thyra Thomson, R., $37,500.
Atty. Gen. — Steven F. Freudental.
Treasurer — Shirley Wittler, R., $37,500.
Legislature: meets odd years in January, even years in February,
at Cheyenne. Members receive $30 per day while in session, plus
$44 per day for expenses.
Senate — Dem., 11; Rep., 19. Total, 30.
House — Dem., 23; Rep. 39. Total, 62.

Puerto Rico

Governor — Carlos Romero-Barcelo.
Secretary of State — Carlos S. Quirós.
Atty. Gen. — Miguel Gimenez-Munoz.
All officials belong to the New Progressive party.
Legislative Assembly: composed of a Senate of 27 members and
a House of Representatives of 51 members. Meets annually, in Jan-
uary at San Juan.

U.S. Government Independent Agencies

Source: General Services Administration
Address: Washington, DC. Location and ZIP codes of agencies in parentheses; as of June, 1981.

ACTION — vacancy, dir. (806 Connecticut Ave., NW, 20525).

Administrative Conference of the United States — Reuben B. Robertson, chmn. (2120 L St., NW, 20037).

American Battle Monuments Commission — Mark W. Clark, chmn. (5127 Pulaski Bldg., 20314).

Appalachian Regional Commission — Albert P. Smith Jr., federal co-chmn.; Gov. John D. Rockefeller, 4th, states co-chmn. (1666 Connecticut Ave. NW, 20235).

Arms Control & Disarmament Agency — James Malone, act. dir. (Department of State Bldg. 20451).

Board for International Broadcasting — Charles Ablard, act. chmn. (1130 15th St., 20005).

Central Intelligence Agency — William J. Casey, dir. (Wash., DC 20505).

Civil Aeronautics Board — Marvin S. Cohen, chmn. (1825 Connecticut Ave. NW, 20428).

Commission on Civil Rights — Mary Berry, chmn. (1121 Vermont Ave. NW, 20425).

Commission of Fine Arts — J. Carter Brown, chmn. (708 Jackson Pl. NW, 20006).

Commodity Futures Trading Commission — James M. Stone, chmn. (2033 K St. NW, 20581).

Community Services Administration — vacancy, dir. (1200 19th St. NW, 20506).

Consumer Product Safety Commission — Stuart M. Statler, chmn. (1111 18th St. NW, 20036).

Environmental Protection Agency — Walter J. Barber Jr., act. adm. (401 M St., SW, 20460).

Equal Employment Opportunity Commission — vacancy, chmn. (2401 E St., NW, 20506).

Export-Import Bank of the United States — John L. Moore Jr., pres. and chmn. (811 Vermont Ave. NW, 20571).

Farm Credit Administration — William Dale, chmn. (490 L'Enfant Plaza East SW, 20578).

Federal Communications Commission — Charles D. Ferris, chmn. (1919 M St. NW, 20554).

Federal Deposit Insurance Corporation — Irvine H. Sprague, chmn. (550 17th St. NW, 20429).

Federal Election Commission — John Warren McGarry, chmn. (1325 K St. NW, 20463).

Federal Emergency Management Agency — Bernard T. Gallagher, dir. (1725 I St., 20472).

Federal Home Loan Bank Board — John H. Dalton, chmn. (1700 G St. NW, 20552).

Federal Labor Relations Authority — Ronald W. Haughton, chmn. (1900 E St. NW, 20424).

Federal Maritime Commission — Leslie L. Kanuk, chmn. (1100 L St. NW, 20573).

Federal Mediation and Conciliation Service — vacancy, dir. (2100 K St. NW, 20427).

Federal Reserve System — Chairman, board of governors: Paul A. Volcker. (20th St. & Constitution Ave. NW, 20551).

Federal Trade Commission — Commissioners: David A. Clanton, act. chmn.; Paul Rand Dixon, Robert Pitofsky, Patricia P. Bailey, Michael Dertschuk. (Pennsylvania Ave. at 6th St. NW, 20580).

General Accounting Office — Comptroller general of the U.S.; Elmer B. Staats. (441 G St. NW, 20548).

General Services Administration — Ray Kline, act. adm. (18th & F Sts. NW, 20405).

Government Printing Office — Public printer: Samuel L. Saylor, act. (North Capitol and H Sts. NW, 20401).

Inter-American Foundation — Peter T. Jones, chmn. (1515 Wilson Blvd., Rosslyn, VA 22209).

International Communication Agency — Charles W. Wick, dir. (1750 Pennsylvania Ave. NW, 20547).

Interstate Commerce Commission — Marcus Alexis, chmn. (12th St. and Constitution Ave. NW, 20423).

Library of Congress — Daniel J. Boorstin, librarian (10 First St. SE, 20540).

Merit Systems Protection Board — Ruth T. Prokop, chmn. (1717 H St. NW, 20419).

National Aeronautics and Space Administration — Alan M. Lovelace, act. adm. (400 Maryland Ave., SW 20546).

National Capital Planning Commission — Helen M. Scharf, chmn. (1325 G St., 20576).

National Credit Union Administration — Lawrence Connell, adm. (1776 G St. NW, 20456).

National Foundation on the Arts and Humanities — Livingston L. Biddle Jr. chmn. (arts). Joseph D. Duffey, chmn. (arts: 2401 E St. NW, 20506; humanities: 806 15th St. NW, 20506).

National Labor Relations Board — John H. Fanning, chmn. (1717 Pennsylvania Ave. NW, 20570).

National Mediation Board — George Ives, chmn. (1425 K St. NW, 20572).

National Science Foundation — Lewis M. Branscomb, chmn. (1800 G St. NW, 20550).

National Transportation Safety Board — James B. King, chmn. (800 Independence Ave. SW, 20594).

Nuclear Regulatory Commission — Joseph M. Hendrie, chmn. (1717 H St. NW, 20555).

Occupational Safety and Health Review Commission — Timothy F. Cleary, chmn. (1825 K St. NW, 20006).

Office of Personnel Management — Donald J. Devine, dir., (1900 E St. NW, 20415).

Overseas Private Investment Corporation — Gerald T. West, pres. (1129 20th St. NW, 20527).

Panama Canal Commission — Dennis P. McAuliffe, adm. (in Panama); Michael Rhode Jr., secy. (in Washington).

Pennsylvania Avenue Development Corporation — Max N. Berry, chmn., board of directors (425 13th St. NW, 20004).

Pension Benefit Guaranty Corporation — Robert E. Nagle, exec. dir. (2020 K St. NW, 20006).

Postal Rate Commission — A. Lee Fritschler, chmn. (2000 L St. NW, 20268).

Railroad Retirement Board — William P. Adams, chmn. (Rm. 444, 425 13th St. NW, 20004), Main Office (844 Rush St., Chicago, IL 60611).

Securities and Exchange Commission — Commissioners: Harold M. Williams, chmn.; Philip Loomis Jr., John R. Evans, Stephen J. Friedman, Barbara Thomas (500 N. Capitol St., 20549).

Selective Service System — Bernard D. Rostker, dir. (600 E St. NW, 20435).

Small Business Administration — Michael Cardenas, adm. (1441 L St. NW, 20416).

Smithsonian Institution — S. Dillon Ripley, secy. (1000 Jefferson Dr. SW, 20560).

Tennessee Valley Authority — Chairman, board of directors: S. David Freeman. (400 Commerce Ave., Knoxville, TN 37902 and Woodward Bldg. 15th and H Sts. NW, Washington, D.C. 20444).

United States International Development Cooperation Agency — M. Peter McPherson, act. dir. (320 21st St., 20523).

United States International Trade Commission — Bill Alberger, chmn. (701 E St. NW, 20436).

United States Metric Board — Louis F. Polk, chmn. (1815 N. Lynn St. Arlington, Va. 22209).

United States Postal Service — William F. Bolger, postmaster general (475 L'Enfant Plaza West SW, 20260).

Veterans Administration — Rufus H. Wilson, adm. (810 Vermont Ave. NW, 20420).

NATIONAL DEFENSE

Data as of July, 1981

Chairman, Joint Chiefs of Staff
David C. Jones (USAF)

The Joint Chiefs of Staff consists of the Chairman of the Joint Chiefs of Staff; the Chief of Staff, U.S. Army; the Chief of Naval Operations; the Chief of Staff, U.S. Air Force; and the Commandant of the Marine Corps.

Army

Chief of Staff—Edward C. Meyer

Generals

	Date of Rank		
Guthrie, John R.	May	1,	1977
Kroesen, Frederick J.	Oct.	1,	1976
Meyer, Edward C.	June	22,	1979
Rogers, Bernard W.	Nov.	7,	1974
Shoemaker, Robert M.	Aug.	22,	1978
Starry, Donn A.	Jul.	1,	1977
Vessey Jr., John W.	Nov.	1,	1976
Warner, Volney F.	Aug.	1,	1979
Wickham, John A.	July	10,	1979

Air Force

Chief of Staff—Lew Allen Jr.

Generals

Allen, James R.	Aug.	1,	1977
Allen Jr., Lew	July	1,	1978
Creech, Wilbur L.	May	1,	1978
Davis, Benny L.	Apr.	1,	1979
Gabiel, Charles A.	Aug.	1,	1980
Jones, David C.	June	21,	1978
Lawson, Richard L.	July	1,	1980
Marsh, Robert T.	Feb.	1,	1981
Mathis, Robert C.	Mar.	1,	1980
Poe, Bryce, II	Feb.	2,	1978
Smith, William Y.	July	1,	1979

Navy

Chief of Naval Operations
Admiral Thomas B. Hayward (aviator)

Admirals

Crowe, William J., Jr. (submariner)	May	30,	1980
Davis, Donald C. (aviator)	May	9,	1978
Hayward, Thomas B. (aviator)	Aug.	12,	1976
Long, Robert L.J. (submariner)	July	5,	1977
Rickover, Hyman G. (retired, serving on active duty)	Nov.	16,	1973
Train, Harry D. II (surface warfare)	Oct.	1,	1978
Watkins, James D. (submariner)	Sept.	18,	1979
Whittle, Afred J. Jr. (submariner)	Aug.	1,	1978

Marine Corps

Corps Commandant, with rank of General

Robert H. Barrow	July	1,	1978

Asst. Commandant and Chief of Staff, with rank of General

Kenneth McLennan	July	1,	1979

Coast Guard

Commandant, with rank of Admiral

John B. Hayes	May	31,	1978

Vice Commandant, with rank of Vice Admiral

Robert H. Scarborough	June	30,	1978

United States Unified and Specified Commands

Atlantic Command—Admiral Harry D. Train II, USN

HQ Aerospace Defense Command—Lt. Gen. James V. Hartinger, USAF

U.S. European Command—General Bernard W. Rogers, USA

Pacific Command—Admiral Robert L. Long, USN

U.S. Southern Command—Lt. Gen. Wallace H. Nutting, USA

Strategic Air Command—General Richard H. Ellis, USAF

U.S. Readiness Command—General Volney F. Warner, USA

Military Air Lift Command—General Robert E. Huyser, USAF

Military Sea Lift Command—Rear Admiral Bruce Keener III, USN

North Atlantic Treaty Organization International Commands

Supr. Allied Commander, Europe (SACEUR)—Gen. Bernard W. Rogers, USA

Deputy SACEUR—Air Ch. Marshal Sir Peter Terry (UK), Adm. G. Luther (Germany)

C-in-C Allied Forces, Northern Europe—Gen. Sir Anthony Farrar-Hockley (UK)

C-in-C Allied Forces, Central Europe—Gen. Dr. F. von Senger and Etterlin (Germany)

C-In-C Allied Forces, Southern Europe—Adm. W.J. Crowe, USN

Supr. Allied Commander Atlantic (SACLANT)—Adm. Harry D. Train II, USN

Deputy SACLANT—V. Adm. Sir Cameron Rusby (UK)

Commander Strike Force South—V. Adm. W.N. Small, USN

Allied Commander in Chief, Channel—Adm. Sir Edward Ashmore (UK)

Principal U.S. Military Training Centers

Army

Name, P.O. address	Zip	Nearest city	Name, P.O. address	Zip	Nearest city
Aberdeen Proving Ground, MD	21005	Aberdeen	Fort Huachuca, AZ	85613	Sierra Vista
Carlisle Barracks, PA	17013	Carlisle	Fort Jackson, SC	29207	Columbia
Fort Belvoir, VA	22060	Alexandria	Fort Knox, KY	40121	Louisville
Fort Benning, GA	31905	Columbus	Fort Leavenworth, KS	66027	Leavenworth
Fort Bliss, TX	79916	El Paso	Fort Lee, VA	23801	Petersburg
Fort Bragg, NC	28307	Fayetteville	Fort McClellan, AL	36205	Anniston
Fort Devens, MA	01433	Ayer	Fort Monmouth, NJ	07703	Red Bank
Fort Dix, NJ	08640	Trenton	Fort Rucker, AL	36362	Dothan
Fort Eustis, VA	23604	Newport News	Fort Sill, OK	73503	Lawton
			Fort Leonard Wood, MO	65473	Rolla
Fort Gordon, GA	30905	Augusta	Redstone Arsenal, AL	35809	Huntsville
Fort Benjamin Harrison, IN	46216	Indianapolis	The Judge Advocate		Charlottes-
Fort Sam Houston, TX	78234	San Antonio	General School, VA	22901	ville

Navy

Name, P.O. address	Zip	Nearest city	Name, P.O. address	Zip	Nearest city
Great Lakes, IL	60088	North Chicago	Orlando, FL	32813	Orlando
San Diego, CA	92133	San Diego			

Major Marine Corps Facilities

Name, P.O. address	Zip	Nearest city	Name, P.O. address	Zip	Nearest city
MCB Camp Lejeune, NC	28542	Jacksonville	MCAS Iwakuni, Japan	FPO Seattle 98764	Iwakuni
MCB Camp Pendleton, CA	92055	Oceanside			
MCB Camp Butler, Okinawa	FPO Seattle 98773	Futenma, Okinawa	MCAS Kaneohe Bay, Oahu, HI	FPO San Francisco 96615	Kailua
MCAGCC Twentynine Palms, CA	92278	Palm Springs			
MCDEC Quantico, VA	22134	Quantico	MCAS (Helo) Futenma, Okinawa	FPO Seattle 98764	Futenma
MCRD Parris Island, SC	29905	Beaufort			
MCRD San Diego, CA	92140	San Diego			
MCAS Cherry Point, NC	28533	Cherry Point	MCAS Beaufort, SC	29902	Beaufort
MCAS El Toro (Santa Ana), CA	92709	Santa Ana	MCAS Yuma, AZ	85364	Yuma
MCAS (Helo) Tustin, CA	92780	Santa Ana	MCMWTC Bridgeport, CA	93517	Bridgeport
MCAS (Helo) New River, NC	28540	Jacksonville			

MCB = Marine Corps Base. MCDEC = Marine Corps Development & Education Command. MCAS = Marine Corps Air Station. Helo = Helicopter. MCAGCC = Marine Corps Air-Ground Combat Center. MCMWTC = Marine Corps Mountain Warfare Training Center.

Air Force

Chanute AFB, IL	61868	Rantoul	Mather AFB, CA	95655	Sacramento
Columbus AFB, MS	36701	Columbus	Maxwell AFB, AL	36112	Montgomery
Fairchild AFB, WA	99011	Spokane	Randolph AFB, TX	78148	San Antonio
Goodfellow AFB, TX	76903	San Angelo	Reese AFB, TX	79489	Lubbock
Keesler AFB, MS	39534	Biloxi	Sheppard AFB, TX	76311	Wichita Falls
Lackland AFB, TX	78236	San Antonio	Vance AFB, OK	73701	Enid
Laughlin AFB, TX	78840	Del Rio	Williams AFB, AZ	85224	Chandler
Lowry AFB, CO	80230	Denver			

Personal Salutes and Honors

The United States national salute, 21 guns, is also the salute to a national flag. The independence of the United States is commemorated by the salute to the union — one gun for each state — fired at noon on July 4 at all military posts provided with suitable artillery.

A-21-gun salute on arrival and departure, with 4 ruffles and flourishes, is rendered to the President of the United States, to an ex-President and to a President-elect. The national anthem or *Hail to the Chief*, as appropriate, is played for the President, and the national anthem for the others. A 21-gun salute on arrival and departure with 4 ruffles and flourishes, also is rendered to the sovereign or chief of state of a foreign country or a member of a reigning royal family; the national anthem of his or her country is played. The music is considered an inseparable part of the salute and will immediately follow the ruffles and flourishes without pause.

Rank	Salute—guns Arrive—Leave		Ruffles, flourishes	Music
Vice President of United States	19		4	Hail Columbia
Speaker of the House	19		4	March
American or foreign ambassador	19		4	Nat. anthem of official
Premier or prime minister	19		4	Nat. anthem of official
Secretary of Defense, Army, Navy or Air Force	19	19	4	March
Other Cabinet members, Senate President pro tempore, Governor, or Chief Justice of U.S.	19		4	March
Chairman, Joint Chiefs of Staff	19	19	4	
Army Chief of Staff, Chief of Naval Operations, Air Force Chief of Staff, Marine Commandant	19	19	4	General's or Admiral's March
General of the Army, General of the Air Force, Fleet Admiral	19	19	4	
Generals, Admirals	17	17	4	
Assistant Secretaries of Defense, Army, Navy or Air Force	17	17	4	March
Chairman of a Committee of Congress	17		4	March

Other salutes (on arrival only) include 15 guns for American envoys or ministers and foreign envoys or ministers accredited to the United States; 15 guns for a lieutenant general or vice admiral; 13 guns for a major general or rear admiral (upper half); 13 guns for American ministers resident and ministers resident accredited to the U.S.; 11 guns for a brigadier general or rear admiral (lower half); 11 guns for American charges d'affaires and like officials accredited to U.S.; and 11 guns for consuls general accredited to U.S.

Military Units, U.S. Army and Air Force

Army units. Squad. In infantry usually ten men under a staff sergeant. **Platoon.** In infantry 4 squads under a lieutenant. **Company.** Headquarters section and 4 platoons under a captain. (Company in the artillery is a battery; in the cavalry, a troop.) **Battalion.** Hdqts. and 4 or more companies under a lieutenant colonel. (Battalion size unit in the cavalry is a squadron.) **Brigade.** Hdqts. and 3 or more battalions under a colonel. **Division.** Hdqts. and 3 brigades with artillery, combat support, and combat service support units under a major general. **Army Corps.** Two or more divisions with corps troops under a lieutenant general. **Field Army.** Hdqts. and two or more corps with field Army troops under a general.

Air Force Units. Flight. Numerically designated flights are the lowest level unit in the Air Force. They are used primarily where there is a small mission elements to be incorporated into an organized unit. **Squadron.** A squadron is the basic unit in the Air Force. It is used to designate the mission units in operational commands. **Group.** The group is a flexible unit composed of two or more squadrons whose functions may be either tactical, support or administrative in nature. **Wing.** An operational wing normally has two or more assigned mission squadrons in an area such as combat, flying training or airlift. **Air Division.** The organization of the air division may be similar to that of the numbered air force, though on a much smaller scale. Functions are usually limited to operations and logistics. **Numbered Air Forces.** Normally an operationally oriented agency, the numbered air force is designed for the control of two or more air divisions or units of comparable strength. It is a flexible organization and may be of any size. Its wings may be assigned to air divisions or directly under the numbered air force. **Major Command.** A major subdivision of the Air Force that is assigned a major segment of the USAF mission.

U.S. Army Insignia and Chevrons

Source: Department of the Army

Grade	Insignia

General of the Armies

General John J. Pershing, the only person to have held this rank, was authorized to prescribe his own insignia, but never wore in excess of four stars. The rank originally was established by Congress for George Washington in 1799, and he was promoted to the rank by joint resolution of Congress, approved by Pres. Ford Oct. 19, 1976.

General of Army. . . Five silver stars fastened together in a circle and the coat of arms of the United States in gold color metal with shield and crest enameled.

General . . . . Four silver stars
Lieutenant General . . . . . Three silver stars
Major General . . . . Two silver stars
Brigadier General . . . . . . One silver star
Colonel . . . . Silver eagle
Lieutenant Colonel . . . . Silver oak leaf
Major . . . . Gold oak leaf
Captain . . . . Two silver bars
First Lieutenant . . . . . . One silver bar
Second Lieutenant . . . . . . One gold bar

Warrant officers

Grade Four—Silver bar with 4 enamel black bands.
Grade Three—Silver bar with 3 enamel black bands.
Grade Two—Silver bar with 2 enamel black bands.
Grade One—Silver bar with 1 enamel black band.

Non-commissioned Officers

Sergeant Major of the Army (E-9). Same as Command Sergeant Major (below) but with 2 stars. Also wears distinctive red and white shield on lapel.

Command Sergeant Major (E-9). Three chevrons above three arcs with a 5-pointed star with a wreath around the star between the chevrons and arcs.

Sergeant Major (E-9). Three chevrons above three arcs with a five-pointed star between the chevrons and arcs.

First Sergeant (E-8). Three chevrons above three arcs with a lozenge between the chevrons and arcs.

Master Sergeant (E-8). Three chevrons above three arcs.

Platoon Sergeant or Sergeant First Class (E-7). Three chevrons above two arcs.

Staff Sergeant (E-6). Three chevrons above one arc.

Sergeant (E-5). Three chevrons.

Corporal (E-4). Two chevrons.

Specialists

Specialist Seven (E-7). Three arcs above the eagle device.
Specialist Six (E-6). Two arcs above the eagle device.
Specialist Five (E-5). One arc above the eagle device.
Specialist Four (E-4). Eagle device only.

Other enlisted

Private First Class (E-3). One chevron above one arc.
Private (E-2). One chevron.
Private (E-1). None.

U.S. Army

Source: Department of the Army

Army Military Personnel on Active Duty[1]

June 30[2]	Total strength	Commissioned officers			Warrant officers		Enlisted personnel		
		Total	Male	Female[3]	Male[4]	Female	Total	Male	Female
1940	267,767	17,563	16,624	939	763	—	249,441	249,441	—
1942	3,074,184	203,137	190,662	12,475	3,285	—	2,867,762	2,867,762	—
1943	6,993,102	557,657	521,435	36,222	21,919	0	6,413,526	6,358,200	55,325
1944	7,992,868	740,077	692,351	47,726	36,893	10	7,215,888	7,144,601	71,287
1945	8,266,373	835,403	772,511	62,892	56,216	44	7,374,710	7,283,930	90,780
1946	1,889,690	257,300	240,643	16,657	9,826	18	1,622,546	1,605,847	16,699
1950	591,487	67,784	63,375	4,409	4,760	22	518,921	512,370	6,551
1955	1,107,606	111,347	106,173	5,174	10,552	48	985,659	977,943	7,716
1960	871,348	91,056	86,832	4,224	10,141	39	770,112	761,833	8,279
1965	967,049	101,812	98,029	3,783	10,285	23	854,929	846,409	8,520
1969	1,509,637	148,836	143,699	5,137	23,734	20	1,337,047	1,316,326	10,721
1970	1,319,735	143,704	138,469	5,235	23,005	13	1,153,013	1,141,537	11,476
1975	781,316	89,756	85,184	4,572	13,214	22	678,324	640,621	37,703
1976 (Apr. 30)	766,979	85,515	80,588	4,927	12,748	30	668,686	625,792	42,894
1977 (Mar. 31)	774,664	84,984	79,599	5,385	13,005	36	676,639	631,410	45,229
1978 (May 31)	772,202	96,553	90,749	5,804	13,160	57	662,432	614,961	47,471
1979 (May 31)	757,822	87,420	80,922	6,498	13,181	78	657,143	606,872	50,271
1980 (Mar. 31)	762,739	83,117	76,237	6,880	13,093	103	666,426	608,223	58,203
1981 (Jan.) . .	769,673	85,017	77,179	7,374	13,563	120	671,057	608,293	62,764

(1) Represents strength of the active Army, including Philippine Scouts, retired Regular Army personnel on extended active duty, and National Guard and Reserve personnel on extended active duty; excludes U.S. Military Academy cadets, contract surgeons, and National Guard and Reserve personnel not on extended active duty.

(2) Data for 1940 to 1947 include personnel in the Army Air Forces and its predecessors (Air Service and Air Corps).

(3) Includes: women doctors, dentists, and Medical Service Corps officers for 1946 and subsequent years, women in the Army Nurse Corps for all years, and the Women's Army Corps and Women's Medical Specialists Corps (dieticians, physical therapists, and occupational specialists) for 1943 and subsequent years.

(4) Act of Congress approved April 27, 1926, directed the appointment as warrant officers of field clerks still in active service. Includes flight officers as follows: 1943, 5,700; 1944, 13,615; 1945, 31,117; 1946, 2,580.

The Federal Service Academies

U.S. Military Academy, West Point, N.Y. Founded 1802. Awards B.S. degree and Army commission for a 5-year service obligation. For admissions information, write Admissions Office, USMA, West Point, NY 10996.

U.S. Naval Academy, Annapolis, Md. Founded 1845. Awards B.S. degree and Navy or Marine Corps commission for a 6-year service obligation. For admissions information, write Dean of Admissions, Naval Academy, Annapolis, MD 21402.

U.S. Air Force Academy, Colorado Springs, Colo. Founded 1954. Awards B.S. degree and Air Force commission for a 5-year service obligation. For admissions information, write Registrar, U.S. Air Force Academy, CO 80840.

U.S. Coast Guard Academy, New London, Conn. Founded 1876. Awards B.S. degree and Coast Guard commission for a 5-year service obligation. For admissions information, write Director of Admissions, Coast Guard Academy, New London, CT 06320.

U.S. Merchant Marine Academy, Kings Point, N.Y. Founded 1943. Awards B.S. degree, a license as a deck, engineer, or dual officer, and a U.S. Naval Reserve commission. Service obligations vary according to options taken by the graduate. For admissions information, write Admission Office, U.S. Merchant Marine Academy, Kings Point, NY 11024.

U.S. Navy Insignia

Source: Department of the Navy

Navy

Stripes and corps device are of gold embroidery.

Stripes

Fleet Admiral . . . . . 1 two inch with 4 one-half inch.
Admiral . . . . 1 two inch with 3 one-half inch.
Vice Admiral . . . . . 1 two inch with 2 one-half inch.
Rear Admiral . . . . . 1 two inch with 1 one-half inch.
Commodore Admiral . 1 two inch.
Captain. . . . . 4 one-half inch.
Commander . . . . . . 3 one-half inch.
Lieut. Commander . . 2 one-half inch, with 1 one-quarter inch between.
Lieutenant . . . . 2 one-half inch.
Lieutenant (j.g.) . . . . 1 one-half inch with one-quarter inch above.
Ensign . . . . 1 one-half inch.
Warrant Officers—One 1/2″ broken with 1/2″ intervals of blue as follows:
 Warrant Officer W-4—1 break
 Warrant Officer W-3—2 breaks, 2″ apart

Warrant Officer W-2—3 breaks, 2″ apart
The breaks are symmetrically centered on outer face of the sleeve.
Enlisted personnel (non-Commissioned petty officers). . .A rating badge worn on the upper left arm, consisting of a spread eagle, appropriate number of chevrons, and centered specialty mark.

Marine Corps

Marine Corps and Army officer insignia are similar. Marine Corps and Army enlisted insignia, although basically similar, differ in color, design, and fewer Marine Corps subdivisions. The Marine Corps' distinctive cap and collar ornament is a combination of the American eagle, globe, and anchor.

Coast Guard

Coast Guard insignia follow Navy custom, with certain minor changes such as the officer cap insignia. The Coast Guard shield is worn on both sleeves of officers and on the right sleeve of all enlisted men.

U.S. Navy Personnel on Active Duty

June 30	Officers[1]	Nurses	Enlisted[2]	Off. Cand.	Total
1940	13,162	442	144,824	2,569	160,997
1945	320,293	11,086	2,988,207	61,231	3,380,817
1950	42,687	1,964	331,860	5,037	381,538
1960	67,456	2,103	544,040	4,385	617,984
1970	78,488	2,273	605,899	6,000	692,660
1975	65,900	—	483,500	—	549,400
1980	63,100	—	464,100	—	527,200
1981	64,800	—	472,600	—	537,500

(1) Nurses are included after 1973. (2) Officer candidates are included after 1973.

Marine Corps Personnel On Active Duty

Yr.	Officers	Enl.	Total	Yr.	Officers	Enl.	Total	Yr.	Officers	Enl.	Total
1955 . .	18,417	186,753	205,170	1965 . . .	17,258	172,955	190,213	1975. . .	18,591	177,360	195,951
1960 . .	16,203	154,418	170,621	1970 . . .	24,941	234,796	259,737	1980. . .	18,198	170,271	188,469

Armed Services Senior Enlisted Adviser

The U.S. Army, Navy and Air Force in 1966-67 each created a new position of senior enlisted adviser whose primary job is to represent the point of view of his services' enlisted men and women on matters of welfare, morale, and any problems concerning enlisted personnel. The senior adviser will have direct access to the military chief of his branch of service and policy-making bodies.

The senior enlisted adviser for each Dept. is:
 Army-Sgt. Major of the Army William A. Connelly.
 Navy-Master Chief Petty Officer of the Navy Thomas S. Crow.
 Air Force-Chief Master Sgt. of the AF James M. McCoy.
 Marines-Sgt. Major of the Marine Corps Leland D. Crawford.

Veteran Population

Source: Veterans Administration

	March 1981
Veterans in civil life, end of month — Total	30,129,000
War Veterans — Total	25,940,000
Vietnam Era — Total (a)	9,061,000
And service in Korean Conflict	551,000
No service in Korean Conflict.	8,510,000
Korean Conflict — Total (includes line 4)	5,805,000
And service in WW II	1,158,000
No service in WW II	4,647,000
World War II (includes line 7).	12,301,000
World War I	482,000
Spanish-American War	110
Post-Vietnam Era	1,144,000
Service between Korean Conflict (January 31, 1955) and Vietnam (August 5, 1964) only (b)	3,045,000
(a) Service after Aug. 4, 1964; (b) excludes men who served on active duty for training only.	

Pension Cases and Compensation Payments

Fiscal year	Living veteran cases No.	Deceased veteran cases No.	Total cases No.	Total disbursement Dollars	Fiscal year	Living veteran cases No.	Deceased veteran cases No.	Total cases No.	Total disbursement Dollars
1890 . . .	415,654	122,290	537,944	106,093,850	1965 . . .	3,204,275	1,277,009	4,481,284	3,901,598,010
1900 . . .	752,510	241,019	993,529	138,462,130	1970 . . .	3,127,338	1,487,176	4,614,514	5,113,649,490
1910 . . .	602,622	318,461	921,083	159,974,056	1974 . . .	3,241,263	1,627,482	4,868,745	6,615,599,000
1920 . . .	419,627	349,916	769,543	316,418,029	1975 . . .	3,226,701	1,628,146	4,854,847	7,600,000,000
1930 . . .	542,610	298,223	840,833	418,432,808	1976 . . .	3,235,778	1,630,830	4,866,608	8,074,488,000
1940 . . .	610,122	239,176	849,298	429,138,465	1977 . . .	3,272,821	1,628,488	4,901,309	8,874,720,000
1950 . . .	2,368,238	658,123	3,026,361	2,009,462,298	1978 . . .	3,283,120	1,622,269	4,905,389	9,371,704,000
1955 . . .	2,668,786	808,303	3,477,089	2,634,292,537	1979 . . .	3,240,283	1,529,206	4,769,489	10,324,258,000
1960 . . .	3,008,935	950,802	3,959,737	3,314,761,383	1980 . . .	3,195,395	1,450,785	4,646,180	11,045,412,000

U.S. Air Force

Source: Department of the Air Force

The Army Air forces were started Aug. 1, 1907, as the Aeronautical Division of the Signal Corps, U.S. Army. The division consisted of one officer and two enlisted men, and it was more than a year before it carried out its first mission in an airplane of its own. When the U.S. entered World War I (April 6, 1917), the Aviation Service, as it was called then, had 55 planes and 65 officers, only 35 of whom were fliers. On the day the Japanese struck at Pearl Harbor (Dec. 7, 1941), the Army Air Forces, as they had been re-named 6 months previously, had 10,329 planes, of which only 2,846 were suited for combat service. But when the Army's air arm reached its peak during World War II (in July, 1944), it had 79,908 of all types of aircraft and (in May 1945) 43,248 combat aircraft and (in March, 1944) 2,411,294 officers and enlisted men. The Air Force was established under the Armed Services Unification Act of July 26, 1947.

USAF Personnel at Home and Overseas — Officers and Enlisted

June 30	Continental U.S.	Overseas	Total	June 30	Continental U.S.	Overseas	Total
1940	40,229	10,936	51,165	1970	531,386	255,819	787,205
1945	1,153,373	1,128,886	2,282,259	1975	457,484	150,853	608,337
1950	317,816	93,461	411,277	1979	417,196	140,660	557,856
1955	689,635	270,311	959,946	1980	434,646	118,604	553,250
1957[1]	651,674	268,161	919,835	1981	429,026	134,480	563,506
1960[2]	607,383	207,369	814,752				
1965	635,430	189,232	824,662				

(1) Since 1957 continental U.S. includes Air Force Academy Cadets as follows: (1957) 504; (1960) 1,949; (1963) 2,660; (1964) 2,838; (1965) 2,907; (1966) 3,152; (1967) 3,361; (1968) 3,652; (1969) 3,941; (1970) 4,144; (1971) 2,997; (1972) 2,885; (1973) 4,356; (1974) 4,412; (1975) 4,414; (1976) 4,415; (1977) 4,680; (1978) 4,524; (1979) 4,578; (1980) 4,000; (1981) 4,178.
(2) Since 1960 Overseas includes Alaska and Hawaii. All figures include Mobilized Personnel.

USAF Military Personnel

June 30	Officers & airmen	Male commissioned officers USAF (Reg.) & RA	USAFR & ORC	ANG & NG	AFUS & AUS	Total warrant officers
1955	959,946	23,463	105,587	984	2	3,961
1960	814,752	49,584	72,115	248	3	4,069
1965	824,662	62,076	62,537	280	54	2,532
1970	787,205	63,678	65,852	168	105	639
1975	603,317	57,854	42,131	128	28	39
1978	570,216	56,838	39,598	148	18	2
1979	557,856	55,815	39,688	142	15	1
1980	553,250	54,621	35,454	115	6	1
1981	563,506	54,628	35,000	11,384	—	0

Female Commissioned Officers, and Enlisted Personnel

June 30	Total	Female commissioned officers USAF	Nurses	WMSC	Female WO	Total	Enlisted personnel Male	Female
1960	3,858	679	3,020	159	5	685,063	679,412	5,651
1965	4,099	708	3,185	206	1	690,177	685,436	4,741
1970	4,667	1,072	3,407	188	0	657,402	648,415	8,987
1975	4,981	1,542	3,236	203	0	503,176	477,944	25,232
1979	6,698	3,061	3,128	509	0	466,774	421,016	45,758
1980	8,060	4,291	3,200	569	0	454,994	404,480	50,514
1981	9,045	5,016	3,317	712	0	460,198	406,721	53,477

Women in the Armed Forces

The Army, Navy, Air Force, Marines, and Coast Guard are all fully integrated. Expansion of military women's programs began in the Department of Defense in fiscal year 1973. The planned end strength for fiscal year 1983 is approximately 199,000, which is 11.1% of the planned strength of the active forces.

Although women are prohibited by law and directives based on law from serving in combat positions, policy changes in the department have resulted in making possible the assignment of women to almost all other career fields. Career progression for women is now comparable to that for male personnel. Women are routinely assigned to overseas locations formerly closed to female personnel. Women are in command of activities and units that have missions other than administration of women.

Admission of women to the service academies began in the fall of 1976 and will further the goal of increased numbers of women officers. The academies will provide single track education, allowing only for minor variations in the cadet program based on physiological differences between men and women.

Army — Information: Chief, Office of Public Affairs, Dept. of Army, Wash., DC 20310; 7,855 women officers, including Army Nurse Corps, and 63,190 enlisted women;

women excluded only from direct combat roles—8% of jobs.

Army Nurse Corps — Brig. Gen. Hazel Johnson, Chief Army Nurse Corps, Office of the Surgeon General, Dept. of Army, Wash., DC 20310; includes 28.3% men.

Navy — Information: Chief of Information, Dept. of Navy, Wash., DC 20350; 4,877 women officers; 29,806 enlisted women.

Navy Nurse Corps — Rear Adm. Frances T. Shea, Director, Navy Nurse Corps, Bureau of Medicine and Surgery, Dept. of Navy, Wash., DC 20372; 1,994 women officers; includes 25% men.

Air Force — Information: Office of Public Affairs, 1221 S. Fern St., Arlington, VA 22202; 8,508 women officers; 59,905 enlisted women.

Air Force Nurse Corps — Brig. Gen. Sarah P. Wells, Chief, Air Force Nurse Corps, Office of the Surgeon Gen., USAF, Bolling AFB, Wash., DC 20332; 4,092 officers; includes men.

Marines — Information: Commandant of the Marine Corps (Code M), Headquarters, Marine Corps, Wash., DC 20380; 528 women officers; 6,731 enlisted women.

Coast Guard — Information: Commandant (G-APA), U.S. Coast Guard, Wash., DC 20593; 73 women officers; 1,400 enlisted women.

Monthly Pay Scale of
Fiscal

Commissioned Officers

Pay grade	Rank or pay grade Army rank	Navy rank	Under 2	Over 2	Cumulative years of service Over 3	Over 4	Over 6	Over 8
O-10¹	General*	Admiral	$3,529.80	$3,654.00	$3,654.00	$3,654.00	$3,654.00	$3,794.10
O-9	Lieutenant General	Vice Admiral	3,128.40	3,210.60	3,278.70	3,278.70	3,278.70	3,362.40
O-8	Major General	Rear Admiral (up. half)	2,833.50	2,918.40	2,987.70	2,987.70	2,987.70	3,210.60
O-7	Brigadier General	Rear Admiral (low half)	2,354.40	2,514.60	2,514.60	2,514.60	2,627.10	2,627.10
O-6	Colonel	Captain	1,745.10	1,917.60	2,042.70	2,042.70	2,042.70	2,042.70
O-5	Lieutenant Colonel	Commander	1,395.90	1,639.20	1,752.30	1,752.30	1,752.30	1,752.30
O-4	Major	Lieutenant Comdr.	1,176.60	1,432.20	1,528.20	1,528.20	1,556.10	1,625.40
O-3	Captain	Lieutenant	1,093.50	1,222.20	1,306.50	1,445.70	1,514.70	1,569.60
O-2	First Lieutenant	Lieutenant (J.G.)	953.10	1,041.30	1,250.70	1,293.00	1,319.70	1,319.70
O-1	Second Lieutenant	Ensign	827.40	861.30	1,041.30	1,041.30	1,041.30	1,041.30
Commissioned officers with over 4 years service as enlisted members								
O-3	Captain	Lieutenant	0.00	0.00	0.00	1,445.70	1,514.70	1,569.60
O-2	First Lieutenant	Lieutenant (J.G.)	0.00	0.00	0.00	1,293.00	1,319.70	1,361.70
O-1	Second Lieutenant	Ensign	0.00	0.00	0.00	1,041.30	1,112.10	1,153.20

Warrant Officers

W-4	Chief Warrant	Comm. Warrant	1,113.90	1,194.90	1,194.90	1,222.20	1,278.00	1,334.40
W-3	Chief Warrant	Comm. Warrant	1,012.50	1,098.30	1,098.30	1,112.10	1,125.30	1,207.50
W-2	Chief Warrant	Comm. Warrant	886.30	959.10	959.10	987.00	1,041.30	1,098.30
W-1	Warrant Officer	Warrant Officer	738.90	847.20	847.20	917.70	959.10	1,000.50

Enlisted Personnel²

E-9³	Sergeant Major**	Master C.P.O.	0.00	0.00	0.00	0.00	0.00	0.00
E-8³	Master Sergeant	Senior C.P.O.	0.00	0.00	0.00	0.00	0.00	1,061.70
E-7	Sgt. 1st Class	Chief Petty Officer	741.30	800.10	829.80	858.60	888.30	916.20
E-6	Staff Sergeant	Petty Officer 1st Class	640.20	698.10	727.20	757.80	786.00	814.80
E-5	Sergeant	Petty Officer 2nd Cl.	562.20	611.70	641.40	669.30	713.10	742.20
E-4	Corporal	Petty Officer 3rd Cl.	540.30	570.60	603.90	651.00	676.80	676.80
E-3	Private 1st Class	Seaman	519.60	548.10	570.30	592.80	592.80	592.80
E-2	Private	Seaman Apprentice	500.10	500.10	500.10	500.10	500.10	500.10
E-1	Private	Seaman Recruit	448.80	448.80	448.80	448.80	448.80	448.80

The pay scale also applies to: Coast Guard and Marine Corps, National Oceanic and Atmospheric Administration, Public Health Service, National Guard, and the Organized Reserves.
*Basic pay is limited to $4,466.40 by Level V of the Executive Schedule and further limited by Sec. 101C, P.L. 96-86 to $4,176.00 max. Four star General or Admiral—personal money allowances of $2,200 per annum, or $4,000 if Chief of Staff of the Army, Chief of Staff of the Air Force, Chief of Naval Operations, Commandant of the Marine Corps, or Commandant of the Coast Guard. Three star General or Admiral—personal money allowance of $500 per annum.
**A new title of Chief Master Sergeant created in 1965 rates E-9 classification.
(1) While serving as Chairman of Joint Chiefs of Staff, Chief of Staff of the Army, Chief of Naval Operations, Chief of Staff of the Air Forces, or Commandant of the Marine Corps, basic pay for this grade is $5,114.70 regardless of years of service, limited by Executive Schedule to $3,958.20
(2) Air Force enlisted personnel pay grades, E-9, Chief Master Sergeant; E-8, Sr. Master Sergeant; E-7, Master Sergeant; E-6, Technical Sergeant; E-5, Staff Sergeant; E-4, Sergeant; E-3, Airman 1st Class; E-2, Airman; E-1, Basic Airman.
Marine Corps enlisted ranks are as follows: E-9, Sergeant Major and Master Gunnery Sergeant; E-8, First Sergeant and Master Sergeant; E-7, Gunnery Sergeant; E-6, Staff Sergeant; E-5, Sergeant; E-4, Corporal; E-3, Lance Corporal; E-2, Private, First Class Marine; E-1, Private.
Marine Corps and Air Force officer ranks are same as Army.
(3) While serving as Sergeant Major of the Army, Master Chief Petty Officer of the Navy, Chief Master Sergeant of the Air Force, or Sergeant Major of the Marine Corps, basic pay for this grade is $1,980.90 regardless of years of service.

American Military Actions, 1900-1973

1900—Occupation of Puerto Rico (ceded to U.S., 1899).
1900—500 Marines, 1,500 Army troops help relieve Peking in Boxer Rebellion.
1900-1902—Occupation of Cuba.
1900-1902—Guerrilla war in Philippines.
1903—Sailors and Marines from U.S.S. Nashville stop Colombian Army at Panama.
1904—Brief intervention in Dominican Republic.
1906-1909—Intervention in Cuba.
1909—Brief intervention in Honduras.
1910, 1912-1913—Intervention in Nicaragua.
1911—Intervention (to collect customs) in Honduras, Nicaragua, Dominican Republic.
1912-1917—Intervention in Cuba.
1914—Intervention in Dominican Republic.
1914—April 21 to Nov. 23. Marines in Vera Cruz.
1914—Navy and Marines enter Haiti, stay until 1934.
1916—Gen. John J. Pershing and 10,000 into Northern Mexico to stop raids by Pancho Villa, Mar. 15-Nov. 24.
1916-1924—Marines in Dominican Republic.

1917—Apr. 6 to Nov. 11, 1918. War with Germany, Austria-Hungary.
1918-1920—Expeditions into North Russia, Siberia.
1918-1923—Occupation of Germany.
1922-1924—Marines in Nicaragua.
1926-1933—Marines in Nicaragua.
1927—1,000 Marines in China.
1941-1945—War with Japan, Germany, Italy and allies.
1950-1953—U.S. and other UN countries aid the Republic of Korea to repel North Korean invaders; U.S. Navy protects Taiwan.
1956—U.S. Fleet evacuates U.S. nationals during Suez crisis.
1957—U.S. Fleet to Near East during Jordan crisis.
1958—Navy, Marines and Army units support Lebanon.
1960—Navy patrol in Caribbean to protect Guatemala and Nicaragua.
1961—Army units to Vietnam.
1962—Units of Navy on Cuban quarantine duty. Marines in Thailand.

the Uniformed Services
Year 1980

Commissioned Officers

Over 10	Over 12	Over 14	Over 16	Over 18	Over 20	Over 22	Over 26	Basic allowances for quarters Without dependents	With dependents
$3,794.10	$4,084.80	$4,084.80	$4,377.00*	$4,377.00*	$4,669.80*	$4,669.80*	$4,961.10*	$383.10	$479.10
3,362.40	3,501.90	3,501.90	3,794.10	3,794.10	4,084.80	4,084.80	4,377.00*	383.10	479.10
3,210.60	3,362.40	3,302.40	3,501.90	3,654.00	3,794.10	3,946.20	3,946.20	383.10	479.10
2,779.80	2,779.80	2,918.40	3,210.60	3,431.10	3,431.10	3,431.10	3,431.10	383.10	479.10
2,042.70	2,042.70	2,112.00	2,446.50	2,571.60	2,627.10	2,779.80	3,014.70	343.80	419.40
1,805.70	1,902.30	2,029.50	2,181.60	2,307.00	2,376.60	2,459.70	2,459.70	316.80	381.60
1,736.10	1,833.90	1,917.60	2,001.30	2,057.10	2,057.10	2,057.10	2,057.10	282.30	340.50
1,653.90	1,736.10	1,778.70	1,778.70	1,778.70	1,778.70	1,778.70	1,778.70	248.10	306.30
1,319.70	1,319.70	1,319.70	1,319.70	1,319.70	1,319.70	1,319.70	1,319.70	215.40	272.70
1,041.30	1,041.30	1,041.30	1,041.30	1,041.30	1,041.30	1,041.30	1,041.30	168.00	219.00
1,653.90	1,736.10	1,805.70	1,805.70	1,805.70	1,805.70	1,805.70	1,805.70	248.10	306.30
1,432.20	1,487.40	1,528.20	1,528.20	1,528.20	1,528.20	1,528.20	1,528.20	215.40	272.70
1,194.90	1,236.60	1,293.00	1,293.00	1,293.00	1,293.00	1,293.00	1,293.00	168.00	219.00

Warrant Officers

1,390.20	1,487.40	1,556.10	1,611.30	1,653.90	1,707.90	1,765.20	1,902.30	271.80	328.20
1,278.00	1,319.70	1,361.70	1,402.50	1,445.70	1,501.50	1,556.10	1,611.30	242.40	298.80
1,139.70	1,181.40	1,222.20	1,265.10	1,306.50	1,347.90	1,402.50	1,402.50	210.90	268.20
1,041.30	1,084.20	1,125.30	1,166.70	1,207.50	1,250.70	1,250.70	1,250.70	190.50	246.60

Enlisted Personnel

1,265.40	1,294.20	1,323.60	1,354.20	1,384.20	1,411.20	1,485.60	1,629.60	205.20	288.60
1,091.40	1,120.50	1,149.90	1,179.90	1,207.20	1,236.90	1,309.50	1,455.60	189.00	266.70
945.60	975.00	1,019.10	1,047.90	1,077.60	1,091.40	1,164.90	1,309.50	160.80	248.10
844.80	888.30	916.30	945.60	960.00	960.00	960.00	960.00	146.10	228.30
771.90	800.10	814.80	814.80	814.80	814.80	814.80	814.80	140.40	209.70
676.80	676.80	676.80	676.80	676.80	676.80	676.80	676.80	123.90	184.50
592.80	592.80	592.80	592.80	592.80	592.80	592.80	592.80	110.70	160.80
500.10	500.10	500.10	500.10	500.10	500.10	500.10	500.10	97.80	160.80
448.80	448.80	448.80	448.80	448.80	448.80	448.80	448.80	92.40	160.80

*Limited under existing law to $4,176.00

Basic Allowance for Subsistence

This allowance, the quarters allowance, and any other allowance are not subject to income tax.
Officers — Subsistence (food) is paid to all officers regardless of rank. . . . . $67.21 per month
Enlisted members: When on leave or authorized to mess separately. . . . . $3.21 per day
When rations in kind are not available. . . . . $3.62 per day
When assigned to duty under emergency conditions where
no government messing facilities are available . . . . $4.79 per day (maximum rate)

Family Separation Allowance

Under certain conditions of family separation of more than 30 days, a member in Pay Grades E-4 (with over 4 years' service) and above will be allowed $30 a month in addition to any other allowances to which he is entitled. When separated from family and required to maintain a home for his family and one for himself, the member is entitled to an additional monthly basic allowance for quarters at the "without dependents" rate for his grade.

1965—Navy, Marines, Army units to Dominican Republic.
1965—American commanders in Vietnam authorized to send U.S. Armed Force into combat.
1969—President Nixon announces, June 8, first phase of withdrawal of U.S. troops from Vietnam.

1970—Army units participate in Cambodian sanctuary operations, Apr. 29-June 30.
1973—Last U.S. troops leave Vietnam, U.S. Military Assistance Command deactivated, March 29.
1973—End of all U.S. bombing operations over Indochina, Aug. 15.

The Medal of Honor

The Medal of Honor is the highest military award for bravery that can be given to any individual in the United States. The first Army Medals were awarded on March 25, 1863, and the first Navy Medals went to sailors and Marines on April 3, 1863.

The Medal of Honor, established by Joint Resolution of Congress, 12 July 1862 (amended by Act of 9 July 1918 and Act of 25 July 1963) is awarded in the name of Congress to a person who, while a member of the Armed Forces, distinguishes himself conspicuously by gallantry and intrepidity at the risk of his life above and beyond the call of duty while engaged in an action against any enemy of the United States; while engaged in military operations involving conflict with an opposing foreign force; or while serving with friendly foreign forces engaged in an armed conflict against an opposing armed force in which the United States is not a belligerent party. The deed performed must have been one of

personal bravery or self-sacrifice so conspicuous as to clearly distinguish the individual above his comrades and must have involved risk of life. Incontestable proof of the performance of service is exacted and each recommendation for award of this decoration is considered on the standard of extraordinary merit.

Prior to World War I, the 2,625 Army Medal of Honor awards up to that time were reviewed to determine which past awards met new stringent criteria. The Army removed 911 names from the list, most of them former members of a volunteer infantry group during the Civil War who had been induced to extend their enlistments when they were promised the Medal.

Since that review Medals of Honor have been awarded in the following numbers:

World War I 124   Korean War 131
World War II 434   Vietnam (to date) 239

Strategic Nuclear Armaments: U.S. and USSR

Source: International Institute for Strategic Services, London

United States

Land-based missiles[1]		Range[2] (km)	Estimated warhead yield[3]	Deployed (July 1980)
ICBM	Titan 2	15,000	5-10 MT	54
	Minuteman 2	11,300	1-2 MT	450
	Minuteman 3	13,000	3x170 KT	550
Sea-based missiles				
SLBM (nuclear subs)	Polaris A3	4,600	3x200 KT	160
	Poseidon C3	4,600	10x50 KT	496
	Trident C4	7,400	8x100 KT	48

Aircraft[7]		Range[8] (km)	Weapons load (lb)	Deployed (July 1980)
Long-range	B-52D	9,900	60,000	75
	B-52G-H	14,000	70,000	241
Medium range	FB-111A	4,700	37,500	68
Strike aircraft; land-based	F-4C-E	2,250	16,000	(350)[9]
	F-111A/E	4,700	25,000	
Strike aircraft; carrier-based	A-6E	3,200	18,000	(100)[9]
	A-7E	2,800	15,000	(100)[9]
	F-4J/N	2,250	16,000	(144)[9]

Soviet Union

Land-based missiles[1]		Range[2] (km)	Estimated warhead yield[3]	Deployed (July 1980)
ICBM	SS-9 Scarp	12,000	18-25 MT[4]	—
	SS-11 Sego	10,500	1-2 MT[5]	580
	SS-13 Savage	10,000	1 MT	60
	SS-17	10,000	4x KT	150
	SS-18	9,933	15-25 MT[6]	308
	SS-19	5,750	6x KT	300
Sea-based missiles				
SLBM (nuclear subs)	SS-N-6-Sawfly	1,750	MT	469
	SS-N-8	4,800	MT	302
	SS-NX-17	5,000	MT	12
	SS-N-18	9,933	MT	160

Aircraft[7]	Range[8] (km)	Weapons load (lb)	Deployed (July 1980)
Tu-95 Bear	12,800	40,000	100
Mya-4 Bison	11,200	20,000	35
Tu-16 Badger	6,400	20,000	740
Backfire B	8,000	20,000	65
Su-7 Fitter A	1,400	4,500	165
Tu-22 Blinder	2,250	12,000	165
MiG-21 Fishbed J/K/L/N	1,100	2,000	(1,000)[9]
MiG-27 Flogger D	1,400	2,800	400
Su-17/20 Fitter C/D	1,800	5,000	640
Su-19A Fencer	1,600	8,000	370

(1) ICBM = intercontinental ballistic missile. IRBM = intermediate-range ballistic missile. MRBM = medium-range missile. SLBM = submarine-launched ballistic missile. SLCM = sub-launched cruise missile. (2) Operation range depends upon the payload carried; use of maximum payload may reduce missile range by up to 25%. (3) MT = megaton range = 1,000,000 tons of TNT equivalent or over; KT = kiloton range = 1,000 tons of TNT equivalent or more, but less than 1 MT. (4) Some SS-9 missiles carry 3 warheads of 4-5 MT each. (5) Some SS-11 missiles may carry 3xKT warheads. (6) Some SS-18 may carry 8xMT warheads. (7) All aircraft listed are dual-capable and many, especially in the categories of strike aircraft, would be more likely to carry conventional than nuclear weapons. (8) Theoretical maximum range, with internal fuel only, at optimum altitude and speed. Ranges for strike aircraft assume no weapons load. Especially in the case of strike aircraft, therefore, range falls sharply for flights at lower altitude, at higher speed, or with full weapons load. (9) Figures in parentheses are estimates of Europe-based systems only.

Debts Owed U.S. Arising from World War I

Source: U.S. Treasury Department (Dec. 31, 1980)

Country	[1]Original indebtedness	Interest thru Dec. 31, 1980	Total	Cumulative payments		Total outstanding
				Principal	Interest	
Armenia	$11,959,917	$36,662,580	$48,622,497	$32	–	$48,622,465
Austria[2]	26,843,149	12,425,458	39,268,607	862,668	–	38,405,939
Belgium	423,587,630	441,137,932	864,725,563	19,157,630	$33,033,643	812,534,290
Cuba	10,000,000	2,286,752	12,286,752	10,000,000	2,286,752	–
Czechoslovakia	185,071,023	224,609,559	409,680,582	19,829,914	304,178	389,546,490
Estonia	16,958,373	30,142,974	47,101,347	11	1,248,432	45,852,904
Finland	9,000,000	12,661,578	21,661,578	[3]9,000,000	[3]12,661,578	–
France	4,128,326,088	5,109,357,855	9,237,683,943	226,039,588	260,036,303	8,751,608,052
Germany	1,059,107,666	1,001,049,873	2,060,157,539	[11]31,539,596	[11]2,048,214	2,026,569,729
Great Britain	4,933,701,642	9,174,444,069	14,108,145,711	434,181,642	1,590,672,656	12,083,291,413
Greece	[4]34,319,844	7,144,162	41,464,005	1,949,589	6,453,141	[5]33,061,275
Hungary[6]	2,051,898	3,627,378	5,679,276	1,690,338	3,626,823	362,115
Italy	2,044,870,444	627,960,004	2,672,830,449	37,464,319	63,365,561	2,572,000,569
Latvia	7,094,654	12,706,537	19,801,191	9,200	752,349	19,039,642
Liberia	26,000	10,472	36,472	26,000	10,472	–
Lithuania	6,618,395	11,724,078	18,342,474	234,783	1,003,174	17,104,517
Nicaragua[7]	141,950	26,625	168,576	141,950	26,625	–
Poland	[8]213,506,132	382,942,971	596,449,104	1,287,297	21,359,000	573,802,806
Romania	68,359,192	93,483,188	161,842,381	[9]4,498,632	[10]8,750,312	789,986,080
Russia	192,601,297	606,135,095	798,736,392	–	636,059	116,033,958
Yugoslavia	63,577,714	55,045,017	118,622,729	1,952,713	–	–

(1) Includes capitalized interest. (2) The Federal Republic of Germany has recognized liability for securities falling due between March 12, 1938, and May 8, 1945. (3) $8,480,090 has been made available for educational exchange programs with Finland pursuant to 22 U.S.C. 2455(e). (4) Includes $13,155,921 refunded by the agreement of May 28, 1964 which was ratified by Congress Nov. 5, 1966. (5) Includes $12,190,255 on agreement of May 28, 1964. (6) Interest payment from December 15, 1932, to June 15, 1937 were paid in pengo equivalent. (7) The indebtedness of Nicaragua was canceled pursuant to the agreement of April 14, 1938. (8) Excludes claim allowance of $1,813,429 dated December 15, 1969. (9) Excludes payment of $100,000 on June 14, 1940, as a token of good faith. (10) Principally proceeds from liquidation of Russian assets in the United States. (11) Payments converted to U. S. dollars at rate applicable at the time of payment.

Casualties in Principal Wars of the U.S.

Data on Revolutionary War casualties is from **The Toll of Independence**, Howard H. Peckham, ed., U. of Chicago Press, 1974.

Data prior to World War I are based on incomplete records in many cases. Casualty data are confined to dead and wounded personnel and therefore exclude personnel captured or missing in action who were subsequently returned to military control. Dash (—) indicates information is not available.

Wars	Branch of service	Number serving	Casualties			
			Battle deaths	Other deaths	Wounds not mortal[a]	Total
Revolutionary War	Total	—	6,824	18,500	8,445	33,769
1775-1783	Army	184,000	5,992	—	7,988	13,980
	Navy &	to	—	—	—	
	Marines	250,000	832	—	457	1,289
War of 1812	Total	²286,730	2,260	—	4,505	6,765
1812-1815	Army	—	1,950	—	4,000	5,950
	Navy	—	265	—	439	704
	Marines	—	45	—	66	111
Mexican War	Total	²78,718	1,733	11,550	4,152	17,435
1846-1848	Army	—	1,721	11,500	4,102	17,373
	Navy	—	1	—	3	4
	Marines	—	11	—	47	58
Civil War	Total	²2,213,363	140,414	224,097	281,881	646,392
(Union forces only)	Army	2,128,948	138,154	221,374	280,040	639,568
1861-1865	Navy	—	2,112	2,411	1,710	6,233
	Marines	84,415	148	312	131	591
Confederate forces	Total	—	74,524	59,297	—	133,821
(estimate)¹	Army	600,000	—	—	—	—
1863-1866	Navy	to	—	—	—	—
	Marines	1,500,000	—	—	—	—
Spanish-American	Total	306,760	385	2,061	1,662	4,108
War	Army⁴	280,564	369	2,061	1,594	4,024
1898	Navy	22,875	10	0	47	57
	Marines	3,321	6	0	21	27
World War I	Total	4,743,826	53,513	63,195	204,002	320,710
April 6, 1917-	Army⁵	4,057,101	50,510	55,868	193,663	300,041
Nov. 11, 1918	Navy	599,051	431	6,856	819	8,106
	Marines	78,839	2,461	390	9,520	12,371
	Coast Gd.	8,835	111	81	—	192
World War II	Total	16,353,659	292,131	115,185	670,846	1,078,162
Dec. 7, 1941-	Army⁶	11,260,000	234,874	83,400	565,861	884,135
Dec. 31, 1946²	Navy⁷	4,183,466	36,950	25,664	37,778	100,392
	Marines	669,100	19,733	4,778	67,207	91,718
	Coast Gd.	241,093	574	1,343	—	1,917
Korean War	Total	5,764,143	33,629	20,617	103,284	157,530
June 25, 1950-	Army	2,834,000	27,704	9,429	77,596	114,729
July 27, 1953³	Navy	1,177,000	458	4,043	1,576	6,077
	Marines	424,000	4,267	1,261	23,744	29,272
	Air Force	1,285,000	1,200	5,884	368	7,452
	Coast Gd.	44,143	—	—	—	—
Vietnam (preliminary)¹⁰	Total	8,744,000	47,752	10,903	155,419	214,074
Aug. 4, 1964-	Army	4,368,000	30,839	7,242	96,811	134,892
Jan. 27, 1973	Navy	1,842,000	1,592	907	4,180	6,679
	Marines	794,000	13,053	1,682	51,399	66,134
	Air Force	1,740,000	1,708	1,072	3,029	5,809

(1) Authoritative statistics for the Confederate Forces are not available. An estimated 26,000-31,000 Confederate personnel died in Union prisons.

(2) Data are for the period Dec. 1, 1941 through Dec. 31, 1946 when hostilities were officially terminated by Presidential Proclamation, but few battle deaths or wounds not mortal were incurred after the Japanese acceptance of Allied peace terms on Aug. 14, 1945. Numbers serving from Dec. 1, 1941-Aug. 31, 1945 were: Total—14,903,213; Army—10,420,000; Navy—3,883,520; and Marine Corps—599,693.

(3) Tentative final data based upon information available as of Sept. 30, 1954, at which time 24 persons were still carried as missing in action.

(4) Number serving covers the period April 21-Aug. 13, 1898, while dead and wounded data are for the period May 1-Aug. 31, 1898. Active hostilities ceased on Aug. 13, 1898, but ratifications of the treaty of peace were not exchanged between the United States and Spain until April 11, 1899.

(5) Includes Air Service Battle deaths and wounds not mortal include casualties suffered by American forces in Northern Russia to Aug. 25, 1919 and in Siberia to April 1, 1920. Other deaths covered the period April 1, 1917-Dec. 31, 1918.

(6) Includes Army Air Forces.

(7) Battle deaths and wounds not mortal include casualties incurred in Oct. 1941 due to hostile action.

(8) Marine Corps data for World War II, the Spanish-American War and prior wars represent the number of individuals wounded, whereas all other data in this column represent the total number (incidence) of wounds.

(9) As reported by the Commissioner of Pensions in his Annual Report for Fiscal Year 1903.

(10) Number serving covers the period Aug. 4 1964-Jan. 27, 1973 (date of ceasefire). Number of casualties incurred in connection with the conflict in Vietnam from Jan. 1, 1961-Sept. 30, 1977. Includes casualties incurred in Mayaguez Incident. Wounds not mortal exclude 150,375 persons not requiring hospital care.

Major New U.S. Weapons Systems

Source: DMS, Inc., U.S. Defense Department

(As of April 1, 1981) Item	Description	Estimated total cost	Estimated unit cost	Estimated production	Major contractors	Comment
		(millions)	(thousands)			
F-14 Tomcat	Swing-wing jet fighter.	$11,957.6	$23,900	500	Grumman	In production
F-15 Eagle	Tactical jet fighter. Air Force.	14,271.1	18,655	765	McDonnell Douglas	In production; 40 for Israel, 100 for Japan, 60 for S. Arabia
F-16 Fighting Falcon	Supersonic, day-time fighter, defense. Air Force.	21,905.8	10,000	1,388	General Dynamics	In production; 348 for NATO, 75 for Israel
F-18 Hornet	All-weather fighter and attack plane. Fleet escort, Marine Corps ground support.	37,890.2	27,300	1,366 for U.S.	McDonnell Douglas; Northrop	Advanced development; several hundred more may be sold abroad
YAH-64	Attack helicopter: anti-tank, air cavalry, escort. Army.	6,598.6	12,000	536	Hughes	Advanced development
Trident	Nuclear-powered submarine carries 24 missiles with 4,000-mile range	31,731.8	Boat = 1,300,000 missile = 10,500	14 boats; 690 missiles	General Dynamics; Lockheed	Boats in production, missiles in development
CG-47 Aegis	Missile cruiser	22,551.0	820.2	21 to 24	Litton Ind.	In production
SSN-688 Los Angeles	Nuclear-powered attack submarines to destroy enemy shipping, subs.	14,356.0	473,000	34	Newport News; General Dynamics	In production
FFG-7	Guided-missile frigate; anti-sub, anti-aircraft, attack and defense.	8,790.8	207,000?	54	Bath; Todd	In production
PHM	Patrol Combatant Missile (hydrofoil boat)	413.3	66,650	6	Boeing	In production
XM-1 Abrams	Main battle tank. Army.	18,955.2	1,550	7,058	Chrysler	In production
IFV/CFV	Infantry or Cavalry fighting vehicle	13,147.3	5,500	6,882	FMC Corp., Chrysler	In production
Copperhead	Cannon-launched, laser-guided projectile; 10-12 mile range. Army.	1,274.3	25	60,000	Martin Marietta	In production
Hellfire	Missile for AH-64; may be laser-guided.	1,653.4	120	24,600	Rockwell	In development
Patriot (SAM-D)	Surface-to-air missile for field air defense.	8,323.2	45,200	103 batteries[1]	Martin Marietta; Raytheon	In engineering development
MX	Advanced ICBM to replace Minuteman.	51,700.0	(Unknown)	200	Martin Marietta	In development
GLCM	Ground-launched, surface-to-surface cruise missile.	2,723.4	1,370	1,024	General Dynamics	In development
ALCM	Air-launched, air-to-ground	6,059.5	1,135	3,418	Boeing	In development
Tomahawk SLCM	Sea-launched; strategic potential	2,924.6	689	925	Gen. Dynam.	Near production
PLSS	Strike system	1,200.0	N.A.	10?	Lockheed, IBM	In development

(1) Batteries consist of 5 launch vehicles and 2 fire control centers.
Some comparable costs: Total moon program, $30 billion, Bay Area Rapid Transit system, $1.6 billion; World Trade Center, land acquisition and construction, $1 billion; one manned moon shot, $400 million; December 1979 welfare payments to families with dependent children, $964 million; fiscal 1979 Ohio state budget outlays, $9.7 billion. 1979 Philadelphia public library operations costs, $19.3 million.

World War II Merchant Marine Casualties

Source: U.S. Coast Guard

Died from direct causes while serving on American flag ships, 845; died in prisoner-of-war camps, 37; listed as missing, 4,807; most lost at sea and presumed dead.

There were 572 released prisoners of war, and one prisoner unaccounted for. Another 500 men died while serving on foreign flag ships under U.S. control.

The number of U.S. flag ships lost was 605 of 6,000,000 deadweight tons.

ASSOCIATIONS AND SOCIETIES

Source: World Almanac questionnaire

Arranged according to **key words** in titles. Founding year of organization in parentheses; last figure after ZIP code indicates membership.

Aaron Burr Assn. (1946), R.D. #1, Route 33, Box 429, Hightstown-Freehold, Hightstown, NJ 08520; 500.

Abortion Federation, Natl. (1977), 110 E. 59th St., Suite 1011, N.Y., N.Y., NY 10022; 400.

Abortion Rights Action League, Natl. (1969), 825 15th St. NW, Wash., DC 20005; 90,000.

Accountants, Amer. Institute of Certified Public (1887), 1211 Ave. of the Americas, N.Y., NY 10036; 168,424.

Accountants, Natl. Assn. of (1919), 919 Third Ave., N.Y., NY 10022; 93,270.

Accountants, Natl. Society of Public (1945), 1717 Pennsylvania Ave., NW, Wash., DC 20006; 17,000.

Acoustical Society of America (1929), 335 E. 45 St., N.Y., NY 10017; 5,600.

Actors' Equity Assn. (1913), 165 W. 46 St., N.Y., NY 10036; 28,000.

Actors' Fund of America (1882), 1501 Broadway, N.Y., NY 10036; 4,000.

Actuaries, American Academy of (1965), 1835 K St. NW, Wash., DC 20006; 6,400.

Actuaries, Society of (1949), 208 S. La Salle St., Chicago, Il. 60604; 6,700.

Adirondack Mountain Club (1922), 172 Ridge St., Glens Falls, NY 12801; 8,000.

Adult Education Assn. of the U.S.A. (1951), 810 18th St. NW, Wash., DC 20006; 3,500.

Advertisers, Assn. of Natl. (1910), 155 E. 44th St., N.Y., NY 10017; 400 cos.

Advertising Agencies, Amer. Assn. of (1917), 666 Third Ave., N.Y., NY 10017; 520 agencies

Aeronautic Assn., Natl. (1922), 821 15th St. NW, Wash., DC 20005; 170,000.

Aeronautics and Astronautics, Amer. Institute of (1932), 1290 Ave. of the Americas, N.Y., NY 10104; 30,000.

Aerospace Industries Assn. of America (1919), 1725 De Sales St. NW, Wash., DC 20036; 59 cos.

Aerospace Medical Assn. (1929), Washington Natl. Airport, Wash., DC 20001; 3,500.

Afro-American Life and History, Assn. for the Study of (1915), 1401 14th St. NW, Wash., DC 20005; 16,289.

Aging Assn., Amer. (1970), Univ. of Nebraska Medical Center, 42d & Dewey Ave., Omaha, NE 68105; 500.

Agricultural Chemicals Assn., Natl. (1933), 1155 15th St. NW, Wash., DC 20005; 125 cos.

Agricultural Economics Assn., Amer. (1910), Univ. of Kentucky, Lexington, KY 40506; 4,500.

Agricultural Engineers, Amer. Society of (1907), 2950 Niles Rd., St. Joseph, MI 49085; 11,000.

Agricultural History Society (1919), Room 140, 500–12th St., SW, Wash., DC 20250.

Air, Citizens for Clean (1965), 32 Broad St., N.Y., NY 10004; 2,000.

Aircraft Assn., Experimental (1953), 11311 W. Forest Home Ave., Franklin, WI 53132; 70,000.

Aircraft Owners and Pilots Assn. (1939), 7315 Wisconsin Ave., Wash., DC 20014; 260,000.

Air Force Aid Society (1942), 1117 N. 19th St., Arlington, VA 22209; 24,000.

Air Force Assn. (1946), 1750 Pennsylvania Ave. NW, Wash., DC 20006; 156,000.

Air Force Sergeants Assn. (1961), 4235 28th Ave., Marlow Heights, MD 20031; 128,000.

Air Line Employees Assn. (1953), 5600 S. Central Ave., Chicago, IL 60638; 10,000.

Air Line Pilots Assn. (1931), 1625 Massachusetts Ave. NW, Wash., DC 20036; 32,000.

Air Pollution Control Assn. (1907), 211 S. Dithridge St., Pittsburgh, PA 15213; 7,192.

Airport Operators Council Intl. (1946), 1700 K St. NW, Wash., DC 20006; 178.

Air Transport Assn., Intl. (1945), 1000 Sherbrooke St. W., Montreal, Quebec, Canada H3A 2R4; 109 airlines.

Air Transport Assn. of America (1936), 1709 New York Ave. NW, Wash., DC 20006; 31 airlines.

Albert Schweitzer Center (1967), Hurlburt Rd., Great Barrington, MA 01230.

Albert Schweitzer Fellowship (1939), 866 UN Plaza, N.Y., NY 10017.

Alcohol Problems, Amer. Council on (1895), 119 Constitution Ave. NE, Wash., DC 20002; 4,000.

Alcoholics Anonymous (1935), P.O. Box 459, Grand Central Station, N.Y., NY 10163; over 1,000,000.

Alcoholism, Natl. Council on (1944), 733 Third Ave., N.Y., NY 10017; 200 affiliates.

Allergy, Amer. Academy of (1943), 611 E. Wells St., Milwaukee, WI 53202; 2,906.

Alpine Club, Amer. (1902), 113 E. 90th St., N.Y., NY 10028; 1,500.

Altrusa Intl. (1917), 332 S. Michigan Ave., Chicago, IL 60604; 19,800.

American Federation of Labor & Congress of Industrial Organizations (AFL-CIO) (1955, by merging **American Federation of Labor** estab. 1881 and **Congress of Industrial Organizations** estab. 1935), 815 16th St. NW, Wash., DC 20006; 13,600,000.

Amer. Field Service (1947), 313 E. 43d St., N.Y., NY 10017; 100,000.

Amer. Indian Affairs, Assn. on (1923), 432 Park Ave. So., N.Y., NY, 10016; 50,000.

American Legion, The (1919), 700 N. Pennsylvania St., Indianapolis, IN 46204; 2,400,000. **American Legion Auxiliary** (1919), 777 N. Meridian St., Indianapolis, IN 46204; 1,000,000.

Amer. States, Organization of (1948), General Secretariat, Wash., DC 20006; 28 countries.

Amer. Veterans of World War II, Korea & Vietnam (AMVETS), (1944), 4647 Forbes Blvd., Lanham, MD 20801; 200,000. **AMVETS Auxiliary** (1947), Saco Rd., Old Orchard Beach, ME 04064; 25,000.

Amnesty Intl. (1965), 304 W. 58th St., N.Y., NY 10019; 100,000.

Amputation Foundation, Natl. (1919), 12-45 150th St., Whitestone, NY 11357; 2,500.

Animal Ecologist Society (1978), P.O. Box 160371, Sacramento, CA 95816; 29.

Animal Protection Institute of America (1968), 5894 S. Land Park Dr., Sacramento, CA 95822; 100,000.

Animal Welfare Institute (1951), P.O. Box 3650, Wash., DC 20007; 3,858.

Animals, Amer. Society for Prevention of Cruelty to (ASPCA) (1866), 441 E. 92d St., N.Y., NY 10028; 3,000.

Animals, Friends of (1957), 11 W. 60th St., N.Y., NY 10023; 100,000.

Animals, The Fund for (1967), 140 W. 57th St., N.Y., NY 10019; 128,000.

Anthropological Assn., Amer. (1902), 1703 New Hampshire Ave. NW, Wash., DC 20009; 10,000.

Antiquarian Society, Amer. (1812), 185 Salisbury St., Worcester, MA 01609; 357.

Anti-Vivisection Society, Amer. (1883), Suite 204, Noble Plaza, 801 Old York Rd., Jenkintown, PA 19046; 10,500.

Appalachian Mountain Club (1876), 5 Joy St., Boston, MA 02108; 24,000.

Appalachian Trail Conference (1925), Box 236, Harpers Ferry, WV 25425; 12,500.

Appraisers, Amer. Society of (1936), Dulles Intl Airport, Box 17265, Wash., DC 20041; 5,000.

Arab Americans, Natl. Assn. of (1972), Suite 211, 1825 Connecticut Ave. NW, Wash., DC 20009; 3,000.

Arbitration Assn., Amer. (1926), 140 W. 51st St., N.Y., NY 10002; 5,000.

Arboriculture, Intl. Society of (1924), P.O. Box 71, 5 Lincoln Sq., Urbana, IL 61801; 4,000.

Archaeological Institute of America (1879), 53 Park Place, N.Y., NY 10007; 7,500.

Archaeology, Institute of Nautical (1972), Drawer AU, College Station, TX 77840; 429.

Archery, Assn., Natl. (1879), 1750 E. Boulder St., Colorado Springs, CO 80909; 2,850.

Architects, Amer. Institute of (1857), 1735 New York Ave. NW, Wash., DC 20006; 28,500.

Architectural Historians, Society of (1940), 1700 Walnut St., Phila., PA 19103; 4,500.

Archivists, Society of Amer. (1936), 330 S. Wells St., Suite 810, Chicago, IL 60606; 4,000.

Armed Forces Communications and Electronics Assn. (1946), 5205 Leesburg Pike, Falls Church, VA 22041; 14,800.

Army, Assn. of the United States (1950), 2425 Wilson Blvd., Arlington, VA 22201; 113,850.

Art, Natl. Assn. of Schools of (1944), 11250 Roger Bacon Dr. 5, Reston, VA 22090; 104 institutions.

Arts, Amer. Council for the (1960), 570 7th Ave., N.Y., NY 10018; 1,100.

Arts, Amer. Federation of (1909), 41 E. 65th St., N.Y., NY 10021; 1,600.

Arts, Associated Councils of the (1969), 570 Seventh Ave., N.Y., NY 10018; 2,000.

Arts, Natl. Endowment for the (1965), 2401 E. St. NW, Wash., DC 20506.

Arts and Letters, Amer. Academy and Institute of (1898), 633 W. 155th St., N.Y., NY 10032; 242.

Arts and Letters, Natl. Society of (1944), 9915 Litzsinger Rd., St. Louis, MO 63124; 1,600.

Arts & Psychology, Assn. for the (1976), P.O. Box 160371, Sacramento, CA 95816.

Arts & Sciences, Amer. Academy of (1780), Norton's Woods, 136 Irving St., Cambridge, MA 02138; 2,300.

Assistance League, Natl. (1935), 5627 Fernwood Ave., Hollywood, CA 90028; 14,000.

Astrologers, Amer. Federation of (1938), P.O. Box 22040, Tempe, AZ 85282; 4,000.

Astronautical Society, Amer. (1953), 6060 Duke St., Alexandria, VA 22304; 800.

Astronomical Society, Amer. (1899), 1816 Jefferson Pl. NW, Wash., DC 20036; 3,700.

Atheist Assn. (1925), 3024 5th Ave., San Diego, CA 92103; 400.

Atheists, Amer. (1963), 2210 Hancock Dr., Austin, TX 78756; 70,000 families.

Athletic Assn., Natl. Jr. College (1938), 12 E. 2d St., Hutchinson, KS 67501; 1,042.

Athletic Associations, Natl. Federation of State High School (1920), 11724 Plaza Circle, Box 20626, Kansas City, MO 64195; 51.

Athletic Union of the U.S., Amateur (1888), 3400 W. 86th St., Indianapolis, IN 46268; 380,000.

Athletics Congress/USA, The (1979), P.O. Box 120, 155 W. Washington St., Suite 220, Indianapolis, IN 46206; 250,000.

Audubon Society, Natl. (1905), 950 Third Ave., N.Y., NY 10022; 400,000.

Authors and Composers, Amer. Guild of (1931), 40 W. 57th St., N.Y., NY 10019; 3,000.

Authors League of America (1912), 234 W. 44th St., N.Y., NY 10036; 8,100.

Autistic Children, Natl. Society for, 1234 Massachusetts Ave. NW, Wash., DC 20005; 4,500.

Automobile Assn., Amer. (1902), 8111 Gatehouse Rd., Falls Church, VA 22047; 21 million.

Automobile Club, Natl. (1924), One Market Plaza, San Francisco, CA 94105; 400,000.

Automobile Club of America, Antique (1935), 501 W. Governor Rd., Hershey, PA 17033; 47,000.

Automobile Dealers Assn., Natl. (1917), 8400 Westpark Dr., McLean, VA 22102; 21,000.

Automobile License Plate Collectors' Assn. (1954), P.O. Box 712, Weston, W. VA 26452; 1,600.

Automotive Booster Clubs Intl. (1921), 5105 Tollview Dr., Rolling Meadows, IL 60008; 3,100.

Automotive Organization Team (1939), P.O. Box 1742, Midland, MI 48640; 3,000.

Aviation Historical Society, Amer. (1956), P.O. Box 99, Garden Grove, CA 92642; 4,200.

B-24 Liberator Club, Intl. (1968), P.O. Box 841, San Diego, CA 92112; 6,000.

Backpackers' Assn., Intl. (1973), P.O. Box 85, Lincoln Center, ME 04458; 22,861.

Badminton Assn., U.S. (1938), P.O. Box 237, Swartz Creek, MI 48473; 1,200.

Ballplayers of Amer., Assn. of Professional (1924), 12062 Valley View St., #211, Garden Grove, CA 92645; 6,000.

Bankers Assn., Amer. (1875), 1120 Connecticut Ave. NW, Wash., DC 20036; 13,200 banks.

Bankers Assn. of America, Independent (1930), 1168 S. Main St., Sauk Centre, MN 56378; 7,400 banks.

Banks, Natl. Assn. of Mutual Savings (1920), 200 Park Ave., N.Y., NY 10166; 459 banks.

Bar Assn., Amer. (1878), 1155 E. 60th St., Chicago, IL 60637; 275,000.

Bar Assn., Federal (1920), 1815 H St. NW, Wash., DC 20006; 15,000.

Barbershop Quartet Singing in America, Society for the Preservation & Encouragement of (1938), 6315 Third Ave., Kenosha, WI 53141; 36,000.

Baseball Congress, Amer. Amateur (1935), 212 Plaza Bldg., 2855 W. Market St., P.O. Box 5332, Akron, OH 44313; 6,905 teams.

Baseball Congress, Natl. (1931), 338 S. Sycamore, Wichita, KS 67213; 15,150.

Baseball Players of America, Assn. of Professional (1924), 12062 Valley View St., Suite 211, Garden Grove, CA 92645; 10,200.

Basketball Assn., Natl. (1946), 645 5th Ave., N.Y., NY 10022; 22 teams.

Baton Twirling Assn. of America & Abroad, Intl. (1967), Box 234, Waldwick, NJ 07463; 1,500.

Battleship Assn., Amer. (1963), P.O. Box 11247, San Diego, CA 92111; 2,500.

Beer Can Collectors of America (1970), 747 Merus Ct., Fenton, MO 63026; 8,500.

Beta Gamma Sigma (1907), 11500 Olive Blvd., Suite 142, St. Louis, MO 63141; 151,933.

Beta Sigma Phi (1931), 1800 W. 91st Pl., Kansas City, MO 64114; 250,000.

Bible Society, Amer. (1816), 1865 Broadway, N.Y., NY 10023; 400,000

Biblical Literature, Society of (1880), Iliff School of Theology, 2201 S. University Blvd., Denver, CO 80210; 4,981.

Bibliographical Society of America (1904), P.O. Box 397, Grand Central Sta., N.Y., NY 10163; 1,455.

Bide-A-Wee Home Assn. (1903), 410 E. 38th St., N.Y., NY 10016; 8,600.

Big Brothers/Big Sisters of America (1977), 117 S. 17th St., Suite 1200, Phila., PA 19103; 400 affiliates.

Biological Chemists, Amer. Society of (1906), 9650 Rockville Pike, Bethesda, MD 20014; 5,000.

Biological Sciences, Amer. Institute of (1947), 1401 Wilson Blvd., Arlington, VA 22209; 8,000.

Birding Assn., Amer. (1969), Box 4335, Austin, TX 78765; 4,000.

Blind, Amer. Foundation for the (1921), 15 W. 16th St., N.Y., NY 10011.

Blind, Natl. Federation of the (1940), 1629 K St., NW, Wash., DC 20006; 50,000.

Blind & Visually Handicapped, Natl. Accreditation Council for Agencies Serving the (1967), 79 Madison Ave., N.Y., NY 10016; 119 agencies and schools.

Blindness, Natl. Society to Prevent (1908), 79 Madison Ave., N.Y., NY 10016.

Blindness, Research to Prevent (1960), 598 Madison Ave., N.Y., NY 10022; 2,000.

Blizzard Club, January 12th, 1888, (1940), c/o Historian, 4827 Hillside Ave., Lincoln, NE 68506; 65.

Blood Banks, Amer. Assn. of (1947), 1828 L St. NW, Wash., DC 20036; 8,199.

Blue Cross Assn. (1948), 676 St. Clair, Chicago, IL 60611; 74 plans.

Blue Shield Plans, Natl. Assn. of (1946), 676 St. Clair, Chicago, IL 60611; 70 plans.

Blueberry Council, No. Amer. (1966), P.O. Box 38, Sewell, NJ 08086; 29 organizations.

Bluebird Society, No. Amer. (1978), Box 6295, Silver Spring, MD 20906; 2,000.

B'nai B'rith Intl. (1843), 1640 Rhode Island Ave. NW, Wash., DC 20036; 500,000.

Boat Owners Assn. of the U.S. (1966), 880 S. Pickett St., Alexandria, VA 22304; 82,000.

Booksellers Assn., Amer. (1900), 122 E. 42d St., N.Y., NY 10168; 5,000.

Botanical Gardens & Arboreta, Amer. Assn. of (1940), Dept. of Biology, 124 Botany Bldg., Univ. of Cal., Los Angeles, CA 90024; 1,250.

Bottle Clubs, Federation of Historical (1969), 5001 Queen Ave. N., Minneapolis, MN 55430; 130 clubs.

Bowling Congress, Amer. (1895), 5301 S. 76th St., Greendale, WI 53129; 4.7 million.

Boys' Brigades of America, United (1893), P.O. Box 8406, Baltimore, MD 21234; 150.

Boys' Clubs of America (1906), 771 First Ave., N.Y., NY 10017; 1,000,000+.

Boy Scouts of America (1910), P.O. Box 61030, Dallas/Ft. Worth Airport, TX; 4,200,000.

Brand Names Foundation (1943), 477 Madison Ave., N.Y., NY 10022; 400.

Bread for the World (1974), 32 Union Sq. E., N.Y., NY 10003; 31,000.

Brick Institute of America (1934), 1750 Old Meadow Rd., McLean, VA 22101; 100 cos.

Bridge, Tunnel and Turnpike Assn., Intl. (1932), 1225 Connecticut Ave. NW, Suite 307, Wash., DC 20036; 200.

Brith Sholom (1905), 1235 Chestnut St., Phila., PA 19107; 20,000.

Broadcasters, Natl. Assn. of (1922), 1771 N St. NW, Wash., DC 20036; 5,600.

Burroughs Bibliophiles, The (1960), 454 Elaine Dr., Pittsburgh, PA 15236; 290.

Bus Assn., Amer. (1926), 1025 Connecticut Ave. NW, Wash., DC 20036; 700.

Business Bureaus, Council of Better (1970), 1150 17th St. NW, Wash., DC 20036; 146.

Business Clubs, Natl. Assn. of Amer. (1922), 3315 No. Main St., High Point, NC 27262; 5,678.

Business Communication Assn., Amer. (1935), 911 S. Sixth St., Champaign, IL 61820; 1,600.

Business Communicators, Intl. Assn. of (1970), 870 Market St., Suite 928, San Francisco, CA 94102; 7,000+.

Business Education Assn., Natl. (1946), 1906 Association Dr., Reston, VA 22091; 18,000.

Business Law Assn., Amer. (1923), Georgia State Univ., University Plaza, Atlanta, GA 30303; 950.

Business-Professional Advertising Assn. (1922), 205 E. 42d St., N.Y., NY 10017; 3,445.

Button Society, Natl. (1938), 2733 Juno Pl., Akron, OH 44313; 1,516.

Byron Society, The (1971 England, 1973 in U.S.), 259 New Jersey Ave., Collingswood, NJ 08108; 300.

CARE (Cooperative For American Relief Everywhere) (1945), 660 First Ave., N.Y., NY 10016; 28 agencies.

CORE (Congress of Racial Equality) (1942), 1916-38 Park Ave., N.Y., NY 10037.

Cable Television Assn., Natl. (1952), 1724 Massachusetts Ave. NW, Wash., DC 20036.

Campers & Hikers Assn., Natl. (1954), 7172 Transit Rd., Buffalo, NY 14221; 45,000 families.

Camp Fire (1910), 4601 Madison Ave., Kansas City, MO 64112; 500,000.

Camping Assn., Amer. (1910), Bradford Woods, Martinsville, IN 46151; 6,000.

Cancer Council, United (1963), 1803 N. Meridian St., Indianapolis, IN 46202.

Cancer Society, Amer. (1913), 777 Third Ave., N.Y., NY 10017; 246.

Canners Assn., Natl. (1907), 1133 20th St. NW, Wash., DC 20036; 600 companies.

Canoe Assn., U.S. (1968), 617 South 94, Milwaukee, WI 53214; 1,700.

Captive European Nations, Assembly of (1954), 29 W. 57th St., N.Y., NY 10019; 9 national committees.

Carillonneurs in North America, Guild of (1962), 3718 Settle Rd., Cincinnati, OH 45227; 493.

Carnegie Hero Fund Commission (1904), 606 Oliver Bldg., Pittsburgh, PA 15222.

Cartoonists Society, Natl. (1946), 9 Ebony Ct., Brooklyn, NY 11229; 500.

Cat Fanciers' Assn. (1919), P.O. Box 430, 11 Globe Ct., Red Bank, NJ 07701; 550 clubs.

Catch Society of America, The (1968), Dept. of English, SUNY—Fredonia; Fredonia, NY 14063; 300.

Catholic Bishops, Natl. Conference of/U.S. Catholic Conference (1966), 1312 Massachusetts Ave. NW, Wash., DC 20015; 350.

Catholic Charities, Natl. Conference of (1910), 1346 Connecticut Ave. NW, Wash., DC 20036; 2,935.

Catholic Church Extension Society of the U.S.A. (1905), 35 E. Wacker Dr., Chicago, IL 60601; 20,000.

Catholic Daughters of America (1903), 10 W. 71st St., N.Y., NY 10023; 170,000.

Catholic Educational Assn., Natl. (1904), One Dupont Circle NW, Wash., DC 20036; 14,000.

Catholic Extension Society (1905), 35 E. Wacker Dr., Chicago, IL 60601; 60,000.

Catholic Press Assn. (1912), 119 N. Park Ave., Rockville Centre, NY 11570; 568.

Catholic Rural Life Conference, Natl. (1923), 4625 NW Beaver Dr., Des Moines, IA 50322; 2,600.

Catholic War Veterans of the U.S.A. (1935), 2 Massachusetts Ave. NW, Wash., DC 20001; 50,000.

Cemetery Assn., Amer. (1935), 5201 Leesburg Pike, Falls Church, VA 22041; 2,500.

Ceramic Society, Amer. (1899), 65 Ceramic Dr., Columbus, OH 43214; 7,500.

Cerebral Palsy Assns., United (1949), 66 E. 34th St., N.Y., NY 10016; 255 affiliates.

Chamber of Commerce of the U.S.A. (1912), 1615 H St. NW, Wash., DC 20062; 100,000+.

Chamber Music Players, Amateur (1947), P.O. Box 547, Vienna, VA 22180; 5,000.

Chaplain's Assn., Intl. (1964), U.S. Box 6005, March Air Force Base, Riverside, CA 92518; 300.

Chaplain's Assn., Natl. (1900), Gatlinburg, TN 37738; 2,500.

Chaplains Assn. of the U.S.A., Military (1925), 7758 Wisconsin Ave. NW, Wash., DC 20014; 1,785.

Chartered Life Underwriters, Amer. Society of (1928), 270 Bryn Mawr Ave., Bryn Mawr, PA 19010; 27,000.

Chartered Property & Casualty Underwriters, Society of (1944), Providence & Sugartown Rds., Malvern, PA 19355; 8,800.

Chemical Engineers, Amer. Institute of (1908), 345 E. 47th St., N.Y., NY 10017; 51,060.

Chemical Manufacturers Assn. (1872), 2501 M St. NW, Wash., DC 20037; 200 cos.

Chemical Society, Amer. (1876), 1155 16th St. NW, Wash.,

DC 20036; 120,000.

Chemistry, Amer. Assn. for Clinical (1948), 1725 K St. NW, Wash., DC 20006; 5,500.

Chemists, Amer. Institute of (1923), 7315 Wisconsin Ave., Wash., DC 20014; 5,387.

Chemists and Chemical Engineers, Assn. of Consulting (1928), 50 E. 41st St., N.Y. NY 10017; 120.

Chemists Assn., Manufacturing (1872), 1825 Connecticut Ave. NW, Wash., DC 20009; 200 cos.

Chess Federation, U.S. (1939), 186 Rte. 9W, New Windsor, NY 12550; 51,000.

Chess League of Amer., Correspondence (1898), Box 124, Algonquin, IL 60102; 1,500.

Child Welfare League of America (1920), 67 Irving Pl., N.Y., NY 10003; 387 agencies.

Childbirth Without Pain Education Assn. (1960), 20134 Snowden, Detroit, MI 48235; 2,000.

Childhood Education Intl., Assn. for (1892), 3615 Wisconsin Ave. NW, Wash., DC 20016; 20,000.

Children of the Amer. Revolution, Natl. Society (1895), 1776 D St. NW, Wash., DC 20006; 12,000.

Children's Aid Society (1853), 105 E. 22d St., N.Y., NY 10010.

Children's Book Council (1945), 67 Irving Pl., N.Y., NY 10003; 75 publishing houses.

Chiropractic Assn., Amer. (1963), 1735 De Sales St. NW, Wash., DC 20036; 17,298.

Chiropractors Assn., Intl. (1926), 1901 L St. NW, Wash., DC 20036; 5,493.

Christian Culture Society (1974), P.O. Box 325, Kokomo, IN 46901; 16,124.

Christian Endeavor, Intl. Society of (1881), 1221 E. Broad St., P.O. Box 1110, Columbus, OH 43216; 1,000,000.

Christian Laity Counseling Board (1970), 5901 Plainfield Dr., Charlotte, NC 28215; 38,000,000.

Christians and Jews, Natl. Conference of (1928), 43 W. 57th St., N.Y., NY 10019; 200,000.

Churches, U.S. Conference for the World Council of (1948), 475 Riverside Dr., Room 1062, N.Y., NY 10115; 27 churches.

Church Women United in the U.S.A. (1941), 475 Riverside Dr., N.Y., NY 10027; 2,000 units.

Cincinnati, Society of the (1783), 2118 Massachusetts Ave. NW, Wash., DC 20008; 3,000.

Circulation Managers Assn., Intl. (1898), 11600 Sunrise Valley Dr., Reston, VA 22091; 1,375.

Circus Fans Assn. of America (1926), 4 Center Dr., Camp Hill, PA 17011; 2,374.

Cities, Natl. League of (1924), 1301 Pennsylvania Ave. NW, Wash., DC 20004; 900 cities.

Citizens Band Radio Patrol (1972), 1100 NE 125th St., N. Miami, FL 33161; 32,000.

Citizens Band Radio Patrol, Amer. Law Enforcement Officers (1975), 1100 NE 125th St., N. Miami, FL 33161; 30,000.

City Management Assn., Intl. (1914), 1140 Connecticut Ave. NW, Wash., DC 20036; 7,000.

Civil Engineers, Amer. Society of (1852), 345 E. 47th St., N.Y., NY 10017; 80,000.

Civil Liberties Union, Amer. (1920), 270 Bryn Mawr Ave., Bryn Mawr, PA 19010; 27,000.

Civitan Internatl. (1920), P.O. Box 2102, Birmingham, AL 35201; 31,000.

Classical League, Amer. (1918), Miami Univ., Oxford, OH 45056; 2,850.

Clergy, Academy of Parish (1968), 12604 Britton Dr., Cleveland, OH 44120, 520.

Clinical Pastoral Education, Assn. for (1967), 475 Riverside Dr., N.Y., NY 10115; 3,246.

Clinical Pathologists, Amer. Society of (1922), 2100 W. Harrison St., Chicago, IL 60612; 28,000.

Clowns of America (1968), P.O. Box 3906, Baltimore, MD 21222; 9,300.

Coal Exporters Assn., Natl. (1945), 1130 17th St. NW, Wash., DC 20036; 27 companies.

Collectors Assn., Amer. (1939), 4040 W. 70th St., Minneapolis, MN 55435; 2,750.

College Athletic Assn., Natl. Junior (1938), 12 E. 2d, Box 1586, Hutchinson, KS 67501; 995.

College Athletic Conference, Eastern (1938), 1311 Craigville Beach Rd., P.O. Box 3, Centerville, MA 02632; 229.

College Board, The (1900), 888 Seventh Ave., N.Y., NY 10019; 2,500 institutions.

College Physical Education Assn. for Men, Natl. (1897), 108 Cooke Hall, Univ. of Minnesota, Minneapolis, MN 55455; 1,200.

College Placement Council (1956), 62 Highland Ave., Bethlehem, PA 18017; 2,500.

Colleges, Amer. Assn. of Community and Jr. (1920), One Dupont Circle, Wash., DC 20036; 910 institutions.

Colleges, Assn. of Amer. (1915), 1818 R St. NW, Wash., DC

20009; 653 institutions.

Collegiate Athletic Assn., Natl. (1906), P.O. Box 1906, Shawnee Mission, KS 66222; 880.

Collegiate Schools of Business, Amer. Assembly of (1916), 760 Office Parkway, St. Louis, MO 63141; 650 schools.

Colonial Dames of America (1890), 421 E. 61 St., N.Y., NY 10021; 2,000.

Colonial Dames XVII Century, Natl. Society (1915), 1300 New Hampshire Ave. NW, Wash., DC 20036; 15,000.

Colonial Wars, Society of (1893), 840 Woodbine Ave., Glendale, OH 45246; 4,350.

Colored Women's Clubs, Natl. Assn. of (1896), 5808 16th St. NW, Wash., DC 20011; 50,000.

Commercial Law League of America (1895), 222 W. Adams St., Chicago, IL 60606; 6,000.

Commercial Travelers of America, Order of United (1888), 632 N. Park St., Columbus, OH 43215; 219,354.

Common Cause (1970), 2030 M St. NW, Wash., DC 20036; 225,000.

Community Cultural Center Assoc., Amer. (1978), 19 Foothills Dr., Pompton Plains, NJ 07444; 11,081.

Composers/USA, Natl. Assn. of (1929), P.O. Box 49652, Barrington Sta., Los Angeles, CA 90049; 300.

Composers, Authors & Publishers, Amer. Society of (ASCAP) (1914), One Lincoln Plaza, N.Y., NY 10023; 24,000.

Computing Machinery, Assn. for (1947), 1133 Ave. of the Americas, N.Y., NY 10036; 52,000.

Concrete Institute, Amer. (1904), 22400 W. Seven Mile Rd., Detroit, MI 48219; 13,700.

Conference Board, The (1916), 845 Third Ave., N.Y., NY 10022; 4,000.

Consairway (1942), P.O. Box 1642, La Mesa, CA 92041; 490.

Conscientious Objection, Central Committee for (1948), 2208 South St., Phila., PA 19146.

Conservation Engineers, Assn. of (1961), Missouri Dept. of Conservation, P.O. Box 180, Jefferson City, MO 65101; 161.

Conservation Foundation (1948), 1717 Massachusetts Ave. NW, Wash., DC 20036.

Construction Industry Manufacturers Assn. (1903), 111 E. Wisconsin Ave., Milwaukee, WI 53202; 200 companies.

Construction Specifications Institute (1948), 1150 17th St. NW, Wash., DC 20036; 11,500.

Consumer Credit Assn., Intl. (1912), 243 N. Lindbergh, St. Louis, MO 63141; 26,958.

Consumer Federation of America (1968), 1314 14th St. NW, Wash., DC 20005; 240 organizations.

Consumer Interests, Amer. Council on (1953), 162 Stanley Hall, Univ. of Missouri, Columbia, MO 65211; 2,700.

Consumers League, Natl. (1899), 1522 K St. NW, Suite 406, Wash., DC 20005; 650.

Consumers Union of the U.S. (1936), 256 Washington St., Mount Vernon, NY 10550; 250,000.

Consumers Unions, Intl. Organization of (1960), 9 Emmastraat, The Hague, Netherlands; 111 organizations.

Contract Bridge League, Amer. (1927), 2200 Democrat Rd., Memphis, TN 38116; 200,000.

Contractors of Amer., General (1918), 1957 E St. NW, Wash., DC 20036; 30,000.

Cooperative League of the U.S.A. (1916), 1828 L St. NW, Wash., DC 20036; 176 co-ops.

Correctional Assn., Amer. (1870), 4321 Hartwick Rd., Suite L-208, College Park, MD 20740; 10,000.

Correctional Officers, Amer. Assn. of (1977), 1474 Willow Ave., Des Plaines, IL 60016; 5,000.

Cosmopolitan Intl. (1914), 7341 W. 108 Pl., Overland Park, KS 66204; 4,000.

Cotton Council of America, Natl. (1938), 1918 North Parkway, Memphis, TN 38112; 290.

Country Music Assn. (1958), 7 Music Circle No., Nashville, TN 37202; 5,500.

Creative Children and Adults, Natl. Assn. for (1974), 8080 Springvalley Dr., Cincinnati, OH 45236; 1,000.

Credit Management, Nat. Assn. of (1896), 475 Park Ave. So., N.Y., NY 10016; 43,200.

Credit Unions, Natl. Assn. of (1934), 5710 Mineral Point Rd., Madison, WI 53701; 22,069 credit unions.

Crime and Delinquency, Natl. Council on (1907), 411 Hackensack Ave., Hackensack, NJ 07601; 15,000.

Criminology, Amer. Assn. of (1953), P.O. Box 1115, North Marshfield, MA 02059; 2,500.

Criminology, Amer. Society of (1940), 1314 Kinnear Rd., Columbus, OH 43212; 1,850.

Crop Science Society of America (1955), 677 S. Segoe Rd., Madison, WI 53711; 4,035.

Cross-Examination Debate Assn. (1971), Speech Dept., Cal. State Univ., Long Beach, CA 90840; 176 institutions.

Cryptogram Assn., Amer. (1932) 9504 Forest Rd., Bethesda, MD 20014; 1,000.

Cyprus, Sovereign Order of (1192, 1964 in U.S.), 853 Seventh Ave., N.Y., NY 10019; 462.

Dairy Council, Natl. (1915), 6300 N. River Rd., Rosemont, IL 60018; 700.

Dairy and Food Industries Supply Assn. (1918), 5530 Wisconsin Ave., Wash., DC 20015; 510 organizations.

Dairylea Cooperative (1919), One Blue Hill Plaza, Pearl River, NY 10965; 4,400.

Daughters of the American Revolution, Natl. Society (1890), 1776 D St. NW, Wash., DC 20006; 208,000.

Daughters of the Confederacy, United (1894), 328 N. Blvd., Richmond, VA 23220; 35,000.

Daughters of 1812, Natl. Society, U.S. (1892), 1461 Rhode Island Ave. NW, Wash., DC 20005; 4,400.

Daughters of Union Veterans of the Civil War (1885), 503 S. Walnut St., Springfield, IL 62704; 6,500.

Deaf, Alexander Graham Bell Assn. for the (1890), 3417 Volta Pl. NW, Wash., DC 20007; 6,500.

Deaf, Natl. Assn. of the (1880), 814 Thayer Ave., Silver Spring, MD 20910; 19,700.

Defense Preparedness Assn., Amer. (1919), 1700 N. Moore St., Arlington, VA 22209; 35,000.

Delta Kappa Gamma Society Intl. (1929), P.O. Box 1589, Austin, TX 78767; 152,000+.

Deltiologists of America (1960), 3709 Gradyville Rd., Newton Square, PA 19073; 1,800.

Democratic Natl. Committee (1848), 1625 Massachusetts Ave. NW, Wash., DC 20036; 369

DeMolay, Intl. Council, Order of (1919), 201 E. Armour Blvd., Kansas City, MO 64111; 100,000.

Dental Assn., Amer. (1859), 211 E. Chicago Ave., Chicago, IL 60611; 138,000.

Descendants of the Colonial Clergy, Society of the (1933), 30 Leewood Rd., Wellesley, MA 02181; 1,400.

Descendants of the Signers of the Declaration of Independence (1907), 1300 Locust St., Phila., PA 19107; 945.

Descendants of Washington's Army at Valley Forge, Society of (1976), Valley Forge, PA 19481; 400.

Desert Protective Council (1959), Box 4294, Palm Springs, CA 92263; 400.

Diabetes Assn., Amer. (1940), 2 Park Ave., N.Y., NY 10016; 55,000.

Dialect Society, Amer. (1890), MacMurray College, Jacksonville, IL 62650; 750.

Dietetic Assn., Amer. (1917), 430 N. Michigan Ave., Chicago, IL 60611; 42,405.

Ding-A-Ling Club, Natl. (1972), Box 2188, Glen Ellyn, IL 60137; 2,050.

Direct Mail/Marketing Assn. (1916), 6 E. 43d St., N.Y., NY 10017; 3,500 companies.

Directors Guild of America (1936), 7950 Sunset Blvd., Los Angeles, CA 90046; 6,300.

Disabled Amer. Veterans (1920), 3725 Alexandria Pike, Cold Spring, KY 41076; 685,000.

Disabled Officers Assn. (1919), 927 S. Walter Reed Dr. #6, Arlington, VA 22204; 5,000.

Divorce Reform, U.S. (1961), P.O. Box 243, Kenwood, CA 95452; 6,000.

Dowsers, Amer. Society of (1961), P.O. Box 24, Danville, VT 05328; 1,875.

Dracula Society, Count (1962), 334 W. 54th St., Los Angeles, CA 90037; 500.

Dragon, Imperial Order of the (1900), P.O. Box 1707, San Francisco, CA 94101.

Drug, Chemical and Allied Trades Assn. (1890), 42-40 Bell Blvd., Suite 604, Bayside, NY 11361; 500 cos.

Drum Corps Internatl. (1971), 719 S. Main St., Lombard, IL 60148; 26.

Ducks Unlimited (1937), P.O. Box 66300, Chicago, IL 60666; 375,000.

Dulcimer Assn., Southern Appalachian (1974), Rte. 1, Box 473, Helena, AL 35080; 114.

Dutch Settlers Soc. of Albany (1924), Box 163, R.D. 2, Troy, NY 12182; 277.

Dwelling Sculpture Institute (1978), 431 Crestvale Dr., Sierra Madre, CA 91024; 30.

Earth, Friends of the (1969), 124 Spear St., San Francisco, CA 94105; 24,000.

Easter Seal Society, Natl. (1919), 2023 W. Ogden Ave., Chicago, IL 60612.

Eastern Star, Order of the (1876), 1618 New Hampshire Ave. NW, Wash., DC 20009; 2,500,000.

Economic Assn., Amer. (1885), 1313 21st Ave. So., Nashville, TN 37212; 26,000.

Economic Development, Committee for (1942), 477 Madison Ave., N.Y., NY 10022.

Edison Electric Institute (1933), 1111 19th St. NW, Wash., DC 20036; 189 cos.

Education, Amer. Council on (1918), One Dupont Circle NW, Wash., DC 20036; 1,400 schools.

Education, Council for Advancement & Support of (1974), 11 Dupont Circle NW, Wash., DC 20036; 2,200 schools.

Education, Council for Basic (1956), 725 15th St. NW, Wash., DC 20005; 8,400.

Education, Natl. Committee for Citizens in (1973), 410 Wilde Lake Village Green, Columbia, MD 21044; 352.

Education, Natl. Society for the Study of (1902), 5835 Kimbark Ave., Chicago, IL 60637; 4,500.

Education, Society for the Advancement of (1939), 1860 Broadway, N.Y., NY 10023; 3,000.

Education, Institute of Intl. (1919), 809 United Nations Plaza, N.Y., NY 10017.

Education Assn., Natl. (1857), 1201 16th St. NW, Wash., DC 20036; 1,600,000.

Education Society, Comparative and Intl. (1956), Univ. of S. California, Univ. Park, Los Angeles, CA 90007; 3,000.

Education of Young Children, Natl. Assn. for the (1926), 1834 Connecticut Ave. NW, Wash., DC 20009; 32,000.

Educational Broadcasters, Natl. Assn. of (1925), 1346 Connecticut Ave. NW, Wash., DC 20036; 2,500.

Educational Exchange, Council on Intl. (1947), 205 E. 42d St., N.Y., NY 10017; 174 organizations.

Educational Research Assn., Amer. (1916), 1230 17th St. NW, Wash., DC 20036; 14,000.

Educators for World Peace, Intl. Assn. of (1969), 5610 Ten Oaks Rd., Clarksville, MD 21029; 15,000.

Electric Railroaders Assn. (1934), Grand Central Terminal, 89 E. 42d St., N.Y., NY 10017; 1,800.

Electrical and Electronics Engineers, Institute of (1884), 345 E. 47th St., N.Y., NY 10017; 202,000.

Electrical Manufacturers Assn., Natl. (1926), 2101 L St. NW, Wash., DC 20037; 550 companies.

Electrochemical Society (1902), 10 S. Main St., Pennington, NJ 08534; 5,000.

Electronic Industries Assn. (1924), 2001 Eye St. NW, Wash., DC 20006; 350 firms.

Electronic Service Dealers Assn., Natl. (1963), 2708 W. Berry, Ft. Worth, TX 76109; 1,920.

Electronics Technicians, Intl. Society of Certified (1970), 2708 W. Berry, Ft. Worth, TX 76109; 800.

Electroplaters' Society, Amer. (1909), 1201 Louisiana Ave., Winter Park, FL 32789; 8,400.

Elks of the U.S.A., Benevolent and Protective Order of (1869), 2750 N. Lake View Ave., Chicago, IL 60614; 1,644,496.

Energy, Intl. Assn. for Hydrogen (1974), P.O. Box 24866, Coral Gables, FL 33124; 1,500.

Engine and Boat Manufacturers, Natl. Assn. of (1904), 666 Third Ave., N.Y., NY 10017; 435 firms.

Engineering, Natl. Academy of (1964), 2101 Constitution Ave. NW, Wash., DC 20418; 854.

Engineering Education, Amer. Society for (1893), One Dupont Circle, Wash., DC 20036; 10,000.

Engineering Societies, Amer. Assn. of (1979), 345 E. 47th St., N.Y., NY 10017; 38 societies.

Engineering Society of N. America, Illuminating (1906), 345 E. 47th St., N.Y., NY 10017; 9,000.

Engineering Technicians, Amer. Society of Certified (1964), 4550 W. 109th, Suite 220, Overland Park, KS 66211; 6,500.

Engineering Trustees, United (1904), 345 E. 47th St., N.Y., NY 10017.

Engineers, Amer. Society of Lubrication (1944), 838 Busse Hwy., Park Ridge, IL 60068; 3,200.

Engineers, Amer. Soc. of Plumbing (1964), 15233 Ventura Blvd., #811, Sherman Oaks, CA 91403; 4,500.

Engineers, Assn. of Energy (1977), 4025 Pleasantdale Rd., Suite 340, Atlanta, GA 30340; 3,000.

Engineers, Natl. Society of Professional (1934), 2029 K St. NW, Wash., DC 20006; 80,000.

Engineers, Institute of Transportation (1930), 525 School St. SW, Suite 410, Wash., DC 20024; 6,500.

Engineers, Soc. of American Military (1919), 607 Prince St., Alexandria, VA 22314; 22,000.

Engineers, Soc. of Manufacturing (1932), P.O. Box 930, Dearborn, MI 48128; 50,000.

English Assn., College (1939), Kean College of N.J., Union, NJ 07083; 2,000.

English-Speaking Union of the U.S. (1920), 16 E. 69th St., N.Y., NY 10021; 31,000.

Entomological Society of America (1903), 4603 Calvert Rd., P.O. Box AJ, College Park, MD 20740; 8,000.

Epigraphic Society, Inc., The (1974), P.O. Box 335, Cambridge, MA 02138; 1,000.

Esperanto League for North America (1952), P.O. Box 1129, El Cerrito, CA 94530; 700.

Euthanasia Foundation, Amer. (1972), 95 N. Birch Rd., Ft. Lauderdale, FL 33304; 40,000.

Evangelicals, Natl. Assn. of (1942), Box 28, Wheaton, IL 60187.

Evangelism Crusades, Intl. (1959), 7970 Woodman Ave., Van Nuys, CA 91402; 200,000.

Exchange Club, Natl. (1911), 3050 Central Ave., Toledo, OH 43606; 50,000.

Experiment in Internatl. Living (1932), Kipling Rd., Brattleboro, VT 05301; 64,000.

Fairs & Expositions, Intl. Assn. of (1885), P.O. Box 985, Springfield, MO 65801; 1,000.

Family Life, Natl. Alliance for, Inc. (1972), 2025 I St. NW #306, Wash., DC 20006.

Family Service Assn. of America (1911), 44 E. 23d St., N.Y., NY 10010; 260 agencies.

Farm Bureau Federation, Amer. (1920), 225 Touhy Ave., Park Ridge, IL 60068; 3,500,000 families.

Farmer Cooperatives, Natl. Council of (1929), 1800 Massachusetts Ave. NW, Wash., DC 20036; 121 co-ops.

Farmers of America, Future (1928), Box 15160, Alexandria, VA 22309; 507,108.

Farmers Educational and Co-Operative Union of America (1902), Box 117, Bailey, CO 80421; 300,000 families.

Fat Americans, Natl. Assn. to Aid (NAAFA) (1969), P.O. Box 43, Bellerose, NY 11426; 2,000.

Federal Employees, Natl. Federation of (1917), 1016 16th St. NW, Wash., DC 20036; 135,000.

Federal Employees Veterans Assn. (1954), P.O. Box 183, Merion Sta., PA 19066; 635.

Feline Society, Amer. (1938), 41 Union Sq. W., N.Y., NY 10003; 450.

Feminists for Life of America (1972), 1503 N. 47, Milwaukee, WI 53208; 1,000.

Fencers League of America, Amateur (1893), 601 Curtis St., Albany, CA 94706; 8,000.

Fiddlers Assn., Amer. Old Time (1965), 6141 Morrill Ave., Lincoln, NE 68507; 5,000.

Film Library Assn., Educational (1943), 43 W. 61st St., N.Y., NY 10023; 2,000.

Financial Analysts Federation (1947), 1633 Broadway, N.Y., NY 10019; 14,500.

Financial Executives Institute (1931), 633 Third Ave., N.Y., NY 10017; 10,600.

Fire Chiefs, Intl. Assn. of (1873), 1329 18th St. NW, Wash., DC 20036; 8,300.

Fire Fighters, Intl. Assn. of (1918), 1750 New York Ave. NW, Wash., DC 20006; 175,000.

Fire Marshals Assn. of No. America (1906), Suite 570-S., 1800 M St. NW, Wash., DC 20036; 1,000.

Fire Protection Assn., Natl. (1896), 470 Atlantic Ave., Boston MA 02210; 32,500.

Fire Protection Engineers, Society of (1950), 60 Batterymarch St., Boston, MA 02110; 2,917.

Fish Assn., Intl. Game (1939), 3000 E. Las Olas Blvd., Ft. Lauderdale, FL 33316; 15,000.

Fishing Institute, Sport (1949), 608 13th St. NW, Wash., DC 20005; 107.

Fishing Tackle Manufacturers Assn., Amer. (1933), 2625 Clearbrook Dr., Arlington Heights, IL 60005; 400 companies.

Flag Assn., Amer. (1888), P.O. Box 1121, Denver, CO 80201.

Flag Institute, The Amer. (1976), 205 E. 78th St., N.Y., NY 10021; 534.

Fluid Power Society (1958), 909 N. Mayfair Rd., Milwaukee, WI 53226; 2,600.

Food Processing Machinery and Supplies Assn. (1885), 1828 L St. NW, Wash., DC 20036; 470 organizations.

Food Processors Assn., Natl. (1907), 1133 20th St. NW, Wash., DC 20036; 700.

Football Assn., U.S. Touch and Flag (1976), 2705 Normandy Dr., Youngstown, OH 44511; 20,000.

Footwear Industries Assn., Amer. (1869), 1611 N. Kent St., Arlington, VA 22209; 260.

Foreign Policy Assn. (1918), 205 Lexington Ave., N.Y., NY 10016.

Foreign Relations, Council on (1921), 58 E. 68th St., N.Y., NY 10021; 2,031.

Foreign Student Affairs, Natl. Assn. for (1948), 1860 19th St. NW, Wash., DC 20009; 3,700.

Foreign Study, Amer. Institute for (1964), 102 Greenwich Ave., Greenwich, CT 06830; 110,000.

Foreign Trade Council, Inc., Natl. (1914), 10 Rockefeller Center, N.Y., NY 10020; 600 companies.

Forensic Sciences, Amer. Academy of (1954), 225 S. Academy Blvd., Colorado Springs, CO 80910; 2,250.

Forest Institute, Amer. (1932), 1619 Massachusetts Ave. NW, Wash., DC 20036; 60 companies.

Forest Products Assn., Natl. (1902), 1619 Massachusetts

Ave. NW, Wash., DC 20036; 41.

Forest Products Research Society (1947), 2801 Marshall Ct., Madison, WI 53705; 4,500.

Foresters, Society of Amer. (1900), 5400 Grosvenor La., Wash., DC 20014; 22,000.

Forestry Assn., Amer. (1875), 1319 18th St. NW, Wash., DC 20036; 80,000.

Fortean Organization, Intl. (1965), 7317 Baltimore Ave., College Park, MD 20740; 1,000.

Foundrymen's Society, Amer. (1896), Golf & Wolf Rds., Des Plaines, IL 60016; 17,600.

4-H Clubs (1901-1905), Extension Service, U.S. Dept of Agriculture, Wash., DC 20250; 5.8 million.

Franklin D. Roosevelt Philatelic Society (1963), 154 Laguna Ct., St. Augustine Shores, FL 32084; 363.

Freedom, Young Americans for (1960), Woodland Rd., Sterling, VA 22170; 80,000.

Freidreich's Ataxia Group in Amer. (1969), P.O. Box 11116, Oakland, CA 94611; 2,000.

French Institute (1911), 22 E. 60th St., N.Y., NY 10022; 20,000.

Friends Service Committee, Amer. (1917), 1501 Cherry St., Phila., PA 19102; 120,000.

Frisbee Assn., Intl. (1967), 900 E. El Monte, San Gabriel, CA 91776; 110,000.

Funeral and Memorial Societies, Continental Assn. of (1963), 1828 L St. NW, Wash., DC 20036; 900,000.

GASP (Group Against Smokers' Pollution) (1971), P.O. Box 632, College Park, MD 20740; 25,000.

Gamblers Anonymous (1957), 2703A W. 8th St., Los Angeles, CA 90005; 6,000.

Garden Club of America (1913), 598 Madison Ave., N.Y., NY 10022; 14,000.

Garden Clubs, Natl. Council of State (1929), 4401 Magnolia Ave., St. Louis, MO 63110; 350,524.

Garden Clubs of America, Men's (1932), 5560 Merle Hay Rd., Des Moines, IA 50323; 10,000.

Gas Appliance Manufacturers Assn. (1935), 1901 N. Ft. Myer Dr., Arlington, VA 22209; 240 companies.

Gas Assn., Amer. (1918), 1515 Wilson Blvd., Arlington, VA 22209; 300 cos.

Gay Academic Union (1974), P.O. Box 927, Los Angeles, CA 90028; 650.

Gay Task Force, Natl. (1973), 80 Fifth Ave., Suite 1601, N.Y., NY 10011; 10,000.

Genealogical Society, Natl. (1903), 1921 Sunderland Pl. NW, Wash., DC 20036; 5,000.

Genetic Assn., Amer. (1914), 818 18th St. NW, Wash., DC 20006; 1,600.

Geographers, Assn. of Amer. (1904), 1710 16th St. NW, Wash., DC 20009; 6,000.

Geographic Education, Natl. Council for (1914), 115 N. Marion St., Oak Park, IL 60301; 5,000.

Geographic Society, Natl. (1888), 1145 17th St. NW, Wash., DC 20036, 10,700,000.

Geographical Society, Amer. (1851), Broadway at 156th St., N.Y., NY 10032; 3,000.

Geolinguistics, Amer. Society of (1964), Bronx Community College, 120 E. 181st St., Bronx, NY 10453; 100.

Geological Institute, Amer. (1948), 5205 Leesburg Pike, Falls Church, VA 22041; 18 societies.

Geological Society of America (1888), 3300 Penrose Pl., Boulder, CO 80301; 12,500.

Geologists, Assn. of Engineering (1957), 8310 San Fernando Way, Dallas, TX 75218; 3,500.

Geophysicists, Society of Exploration (1930), 3707 E. 51st St., Tulsa, OK 74135; 14,000.

George Smith Patton, Jr. Historical Society (1970), 11307 Vela Dr., San Diego, CA 92106.

Geriatrics Society, Amer. (1942), 10 Columbus Circle, N.Y., NY 10019; 6,000.

Gideons Intl. (1899), 2900 Lebanon Rd., Nashville, TN 37214; 66,000.

Gifted Children, Amer. Assn. for (1946), 15 Gramercy Park, N.Y., NY 10003.

Gifted Children, Natl. Assn. for (1952), 2070 Country Rd. H, St. Paul, MN 55112; 4,468.

Girls Clubs of America (1945), 205 Lexington Ave., N.Y., NY 10016; 220,000.

Girl Scouts of the U.S.A. (1912), 830 Third Ave., N.Y., NY 10022; 2,784,000.

Gladiolus Council, No. Amer. (1945), 21 S. Drive, E. Brunswick, NJ 08316; 1,500.

Goat Assn., American Dairy (1904), 209 W. Main St., Spindale, NC 28160; 17,700.

Gold Star Mothers, Amer. (1929), 2128 Leroy Pl. NW,

Wash., DC 20008; 8,000.

Golf Association, U.S. (1894), Golf House, Far Hills, NJ 07931; 5,023 clubs.

Goose Island Bird & Girl Watching Society (1960), 301 Arthur Ave., Park Ridge, IL 60068; 924.

Gospel Music Assn. (1964), 38 Music Sq. W., Nashville, TN 37203; 2,500.

Governmental Research Assn. (1914), 4302 Airport Blvd., Austin, TX 78722; 700.

Graduate Schools in the U.S., Council of (1961), One Dupont Circle NW, Wash., DC 20036; 365 institutions.

Grandmother Clubs of America, Natl. Federation of (1938), 203 N. Wabash Ave., Chicago, IL 60601; 15,000.

Grange, Natl. (1867), 1616 H St. NW, Wash., DC 20006; 475,000.

Graphic Artists, Society of Amer. (1915), 32 Union Sq., 1214, N.Y., NY 10003; 232.

Graphic Arts, Amer. Institute of (1914), 1059 Third Ave., N.Y., NY 10021; 1,700.

Gray Panthers (1970), 3635 Chestnut, Phila., PA 19104; 50,000.

Greek-Amer. War Veterans in America, Natl. Legion (1938), 739 W. 186th St., N.Y., NY 10033; 41.

Green Mountain Club, The (1910), 43 State St., Box 889, Montpelier, VT 05602; 4,000.

Grocers, Natl. Assn. of Retail (1893), 11800 Sunrise Valley Dr., Reston, VA 22091; 40,000.

Grocery Manufacturers of America (1908), 1010 Wisconsin Ave., Wash., DC 20007; 130 cos.

Guide Dog Foundation for the Blind (1946), 109-19 72d Ave., Forest Hills, NY 11375; 35,000.

Gyro Intl. (1912), 1096 Mentor Ave., Painesville, OH 44077; 5,473.

HIAS (Hebrew Immigrant Aid Society) (1884), 200 Park Ave. S, N.Y., NY 10003; 14,000.

Hadassah, the Women's Zionist Organization of America (1912), 50 W. 58th St., N.Y., NY 10019; 370,000+.

Hairdressers and Cosmetologists Assn., Natl. (1921), 3510 Olive St., St. Louis, MO 63103; 70,000.

Handball Assn., U.S. (1951), 4101 Dempster St., Skokie, IL 60076; 12,500.

Handicapped, Federation of the (1935), 211 W. 14th St., N.Y., NY 10011; 650.

Handicapped, Natl. Assn. of the Physically (1958), 76 Elm St., London, OH 43140; 1,000.

Hang Gliding Assn., U.S. (1971), 11312 1/2 Venice Blvd., Los Angeles, CA 90066; 8,000.

Health Council, Natl. (1920), 70 W. 40th St., N.Y., NY 10018; 77 agencies.

Health Insurance Assn. of America (1956), 1750 K St. NW, Wash., DC 20006; 306 companies.

Health Insurance Institute (1956), 1850 K St. NW, Wash., DC; 325 companies.

Health, Physical Education, Recreation and Dance, Amer. Alliance for (1885), 1900 Association Dr., Reston, VA 22091; 45,000.

Hearing Aid Society, Natl. (1951), 20361 Middlebelt Rd., Livonia, MI 48152; 3,600.

Hearing and Speech Action, Natl. Assn. for (1919), 814 Thayer Ave., Silver Spring, MD 20910; 12,000.

Heart Assn., Amer. (1924), 7320 Greenville Ave., Dallas TX 75231; 144,000.

Hearts, Mended (1955), 721 Huntington Ave., Boston, MA 02115; 9,000.

Heating, Refrigerating & Air Conditioning Engineers, Amer. Society of (1895), 345 E. 47th St., N.Y., NY 10017; 36,000.

Helicopter Assn. Intl. (1948), 1110 Vermont Ave. NW, Wash., DC 20005; 840 companies.

Helicopter Society, Amer. (1943), 1325 18th St. NW, Wash., DC 144,000. 3,500.

Hemispheric Affairs, Council on (1975), 1201 16th St. NW, Wash., DC 20036.

High School Assns., Natl. Federation of State (1921), 11724 Plaza Circle, Kansas City, MO 64195; 51.

High Twelve Internatl. (1921), 3681 Lindell Blvd., St. Louis, MO 63108; 125,000.

Historians, Organization of Amer. (1907), 112 N. Bryan St. Bloomington, IN 47401; 8,391.

Historical Assn., Amer. (1884), 400 A St. SE, Wash., DC 20003; 15,000.

Historic Preservation, Natl. Trust for (1949), 1785 Massachusetts Ave. NW, Wash., DC 20036; 160,000.

Hockey Assn. of the U.S., Amateur (1937), 2997 Broadmoor Valley Rd., Colorado Springs, CO 80906; 10,490 teams.

Holiday Institute of Yonkers (1969), Box 414, Yonkers, NY 10710.

Holy Cross of Jerusalem, Order of (1965), 853 Seventh Ave., N.Y., NY 10019; 2,014.

Home Builders, Natl. Assn. of (1942), 15th & M Sts. NW, Wash., DC 20005; 120,000+ firms.

Home Economics Assn., Amer. (1909), 2010 Massachusetts Ave. NW, Wash., DC 20036; 40,000.

Home Improvement Council, Natl. (1956), 11 E. 44th St., N.Y., NY 10017; 3,200.

Homemakers of America, Future (1945), 2010 Massachusetts Ave. NW, Wash., DC 20036; 400,000.

Homemakers Council, Natl. Extension (1936), 1139 19th Ave., Longview, WA 98632; 510,428.

Horatio Alger Society (1961), 4907 Allison Dr., Lansing, MI 48910; 150.

Horse Protection Assn., Amer. (1966), 1312 18th St. NW, Wash., DC 20036; 15,000.

Horse Show Assn. of America Ltd., Natl. (1883), 527 Madison Ave., N.Y., NY 10022.

Horse Shows Assn., Amer. (1917), 598 Madison Ave., N.Y., NY 10022; 25,000.

Hospital Assn., Amer. (1899), 840 N. Lake Shore Dr., Chicago, IL 60611; 34,200.

Hospital Public Relations, Amer. Society for (1965), 840 N. Lake Shore Dr., Chicago, IL 60611; 1,069.

Hotel & Motel Assn., Amer. (1910), 888 Seventh Ave., N.Y., NY 10019; 7,742 hotels & motels.

Hot Rod Assn., Natl. (1951), 10639 Riverside Dr., N. Hollywood, CA 91602; 40,000.

Humane Legislation, Committee for (1976), 11 W. 60th St., N.Y., NY 10023; 100,000.

Humane Society of the U.S. (1954), 2100 L St. NW, Wash., DC 20037; 138,000.

Humanics Foundation, Amer. (1948), 912 Baltimore Ave., Kansas City, MO 64111; 1,400.

Humanities, Natl. Endowment for the (1965), 806 15th St. NW, Wash., DC 20506.

Human Rights and Social Justice, Americans for (1977), 109 Bentbridge Rd., Greenville, SC 29611; 1,400.

Hydrogen Energy, Intl. Assn. for (1975), P.O. Box 248266, Coral Gables, FL 33124; 2,000.

Iceland Veterans (1948), 2101 Walnut St., Phila., PA 19103; 1,600.

Identification, Intl. Assn. for (1915), P.O. Box 139, Utica, NY 13503; 2,500.

Illustrators, Society of (1901), 128 E. 63d St., N.Y., NY 10021; 800.

Indian Rights Assn. (1882), 1505 Race St., Phila., PA 19102; 1,300.

Industrial Democracy, League for (1905), 275 Seventh Ave., N.Y., NY 10001; 1,500.

Industrial Designers Society of America, 1717 N St. NW, Wash., DC 20036; 1,500.

Industrial Engineers, Amer. Institute of (1948), 25 Technology Park, Norcross, GA 30092; 35,000.

Industrial Health Foundation (1935), 5231 Centre Ave., Pittsburgh, PA 15232; 150 companies.

Industrial Management Society (1936), 570 Northwest Hwy., Des Plaines, IL 60016; 1,200.

Infant Death Syndrome (SIDS) Foundation, Natl. Sudden (1962), 310 S. Michigan Ave., Chicago, IL 60604; 69 chapters.

Information, Freedom of, Center (1958), P.O. Box 858, Columbia, MO 65205; 900.

Information Managers, Associated (1978), 316 Pennsylvania Ave. SE, Suite 502, Wash., DC 20003; 850.

Information Industry Assn. (1968), 316 Pennsylvania Ave. SE, Suite 502, Wash., DC 20003; 150 companies.

Insurance Assn., Amer. (1866), 85 John St., N.Y., NY 10038; 150 companies.

Intelligence Officers, Assn. of Former (1975), 6723 Whittier Ave., Suite 303A, McLean, VA 22101; 3,000.

Intercollegiate Athletics, Natl. Assn. of (1940), 1221 Baltimore Ave., Kansas City, MO 64105; 520 schools.

Interior Designers, Amer. Society of (1975), 730 Fifth Ave., N.Y., NY 10019; 17,000.

Inventors, Amer. Assn. of (1977), 6562 E. Curtis Rd., Bridgeport, MI 48722; 2,300.

Investment Clubs, Natl. Assn. of (1951), 1515 E. Eleven Mile Rd., Royal Oak, MI 48067; 70,000.

Iron Castings Society (1975), 20611 Center Ridge Rd., Rocky River, OH 44116; 250 firms.

Iron and Steel Engineers, Assn. of (1907), Three Gateway Center, Suite 2350, Pittsburgh, PA 15222; 13,447.

Iron and Steel Institute, Amer. (1908), 1000 16th St. NW, Wash., DC 20036; 2,500.

Italian Historical Society of America (1949), 111 Columbia Heights, Bklyn., NY 11201; 2,300.

Italy-America Chamber of Commerce (1887), 350 Fifth Ave., N.Y., NY 10118; 750.

Izaak Walton League of America, The (1922), 1800 N. Kent St., Arlington, VA 22209; 43,011.

Jamestowne Society (1936), P.O. Box 7389, Richmond, VA 23221; 2,000.

Japanese Amer. Citizens League (1929), 1765 Sutter St., San Francisco, CA 94115; 30,000.

Jaycees, U.S. (1920), 4 W. 21st St., Tulsa, OK 74121; 380,000.

Jewish Appeal, United (1939), 1290 Ave. of the Americas, N.Y., NY 10019.

Jewish Center Workers, Assn. of (1918), 15 E. 26th St., N.Y., NY 10010; 1,000.

Jewish Committee, Amer. (1906), 165 E. 56th St., N.Y., NY 10022; 40,000.

Jewish Congress, Amer. (1918), 15 E. 84th St., N.Y., NY 10028; 50,000.

Jewish Federations, Council of (1932), 575 Lexington Ave., N.Y., NY 10022; 200 agencies.

Jewish Historical Society, Amer. (1892), 2 Thornton Rd., Waltham, MA 02154; 3,450.

Jewish War Veterans of the U.S.A. (1896), 1712 New Hampshire Ave. NW, Wash., DC 20009; 73,000.

Jewish Welfare Board, Natl. (1917), 15 E. 26th St., N.Y., NY 10010; serves 1,000,000.

Jewish Women, Natl. Council of (1893), 15 E. 26th St., N.Y., NY 10010; 100,000.

Job's Daughters, Internatl. Order of (1921), 1820 Douglas, Masonic Temple, Omaha, NE 68102; 78,000.

Jockey Club (1894), 380 Madison Ave., N.Y., NY 10017; 84.

Jogging Assn., Natl. (1968), 2420 K St. NW, Wash., DC 20037, 35,000.

John Birch Society (1958), 395 Concord Ave., Belmont, MA 02178; 50,000 to 100,000.

Journalists, Society of Professional; (Sigma Delta Chi) (1909), 840 N. Lake Shore Dr., Suite 801, Chicago, IL 60611; 28,000.

Journalists and Authors, Amer. Society of (1948), 1501 Broadway, Suite 1907, N.Y., NY 10036; 575.

Judaism, Amer. Council for (1943), 307 Fifth Ave., N.Y., NY 10016.

Judicature Society, Amer. (1913), 200 W. Monroe, Suite 1606, Chicago, IL 60606; 30,000.

Juggler's Assn., Intl. (1947), P.O. Box 29, Kenmore, NY 14217; 1,300.

Junior Achievement (1919), 550 Summer St., Stamford, CT 06901; 300,000.

Junior Colleges, Amer. Assn. of Community and (1921), One Dupont Circle NW, Wash., DC 20036; 900.

Junior Leagues, Assn. of (1921), 825 Third Ave., N.Y., NY 10022; 130,000.

Kennel Club, Amer. (1884), 51 Madison Ave., N.Y., NY 10010; 413 clubs.

Key Club Intl. (1925), 101 E. Erie St., Chicago, IL 60611; 100,000.

Kitefliers Assn., Intl. (1955), 321 E. 48th St., N.Y., NY 10017; 30,000.

Kiwanis Intl. (1915), 101 E. Erie St., Chicago, IL 60611; 300,000.

Knights of Columbus (1882), One Columbus Plaza, New Haven, CT 06507; 1,342,978.

Knights Templar U.S.A., Grand Encampment (1816), 14 E. Jackson Blvd., Suite 1700, Chicago, IL 60604; 350,000.

Lacrosse Foundation (1959), Newton H. White Athletic Ctr., Homewood, Baltimore, MD 21218; 5,000.

La Leche League Intl. (1956), 9616 Minneapolis, Franklin Park, IL 60131; 60,000.

Lambs, The (1876), 3 W. 51st St., N.Y., NY 10019; 250.

Landscape Architects, Amer. Society of (1899), 1900 M St. NW, Wash., DC 20036; 4,700.

Law, Amer. Society of Intl. (1906), 2223 Massachusetts Ave. NW, Wash., DC 20008; 5,500.

Law Enforcement Officers Assn., Amer. (1975), P.O. Box 9935, Wash., DC 20015; 80,000.

Law Libraries, Amer. Assn. of (1906), 53 W. Jackson Blvd., Chicago, IL 60604; 3,000.

Law and Social Policy, Center for (1969), 1751 N St. NW, Wash., DC 20036; 500.

Learned Societies, Amer. Council of (1919), 800 Third Ave., N.Y., NY 10022; 43 societies.

Lefthanders, League of (1975), P.O. Box 89, New Milford, NJ 07646; 400.

Lefthanders Intl. (1975), 3601 SW 29th St., Topeka, KS 66614; 5,000.

Legal Secretaries, Natl. Assn. of (1949), 3005 E. Skelly Dr., Tulsa, OK 74105; 25,000.

Legion of Valor of the U.S.A. (1890), 548 Bellemeade, Gretna, LA 70053; 750.

Leprosy Missions, Amer. (1906), 1262 Broad St., Bloomfield, NJ 07003.

Leukemia Society of America (1949), 800 Second Ave., N.Y., NY 10017; 1,470 trustees.

Lewis Carroll Society of N. America (1974), 617 Rockford Rd., Silver Spring, MD 20902; 300.

Liberty Lobby (1955), 300 Independence Ave. SE, Wash., DC 20003; 27,000.

Libraries Assn., Special (1909), 235 Park Ave. So., N.Y., NY 10003; 11,500.

Library Assn., Amer. (1876), 50 E. Huron St., Chicago, IL 60611; 30,000.

Library Assn., Medical (1898), 919 N. Michigan Ave., Chicago, IL 60611; 5,300.

Life Insurance, Amer. Council of (1976), 1850 K St. NW, Wash., DC 20006; 500+ companies.

Life Office Management Assn. (1924), 100 Colony Sq., Atlanta, GA 30361; 600 companies.

Life Underwriters, Natl. Assn. of (1890), 1922 F St. NW, Wash., DC 20006; 135,000.

Lighter-Than-Air Society (1952), 1800 Triplett Blvd., Akron, OH 44306; 1,000.

Lions Clubs, Intl. Assn. of (1917), 300 22d St., Oak Brook, IL 60570; 1,300,000.

Literacy Volunteers of America (1962), 623 Midtown Plaza, 700 E. Water St., Syracuse, NY 13210; 22,000.

Little League Baseball (1939), P.O. Box 3485, Williamsport, PA 17701; 14,000 leagues.

Little People of America (1957), Box 633, San Bruno, CA 94066; 3,000.

London Club (1975), P.O. Box 4527, Topeka, KS 66604; 1,000+.

Lung Assn., Amer. (1904), 1740 Broadway, N.Y., NY 10019.

Lutheran Education Assn. (1942), 7400 Augusta St., River Forest, IL 60305; 2,850.

Lutheran World Ministries, 360 Park Ave. S., N.Y., NY 10010.

Macaroni Manufacturers Assn., Natl. (1904), 19 S. Bothwell, Box 336, Palatine, IL 60067; 93 firms.

Magazine Publishers Assn. (1919), 575 Lexington Ave., N.Y., NY 10022; 176 companies.

Magicians, Intl. Brotherhood of (1926), 28 N. Main St., Kenton, OH 43326; 11,000.

Magicians, Society of Amer. (1902), P.O. Box 272, Rocky Hill, CT 06067; 5,342.

Magicians Guild of America (1944), 20 W. 40th St., N.Y., NY 10018; 102.

Male Nurse Assn., Natl. (1971), Rush Univ., 1725 W. Harrison St., Chicago, IL 60612; 1,400.

Management Assns., Amer. (1923), 135 W. 50th St., N.Y., NY 10020; 83,000.

Management Consultants, Institute of (1968), 19 W. 44th St., N.Y., NY 10017; 825.

Management Engineers, Assn. of Consulting (1929), 230 Park Ave., N.Y., NY 10169; 57 firms.

Manufacturers, Natl. Assn. of (1895), 1776 F St. NW, Wash., DC 20006; 12,000 companies.

Manufacturers' Agents Natl. Assn. (1947), 2021 Business Center Dr., Irvine, CA 92713; 6,000.

Manuscript Society, 1206 N. Stoneman Ave., 15, Alhambra, CA 91801; 1,500.

Man Watchers (1974), 2865 State St., San Diego, CA 92103; 4,000.

March of Dimes Birth Defects Foundation (1938), 1275 Mamaroneck Ave., White Plains, NY 10605; 760 chapters.

Marijuana Laws, Natl. Organization for the Reform of (NORML) (1970), 2317 M St. NW, Wash., DC 20037; 25,000.

Marine Corps League (1923), 933 N. Kenmore St., Arlington, VA 22201; 25,000.

Marine Manufacturers Assn., Natl. (1979), 401 N. Michigan

Ave., Chicago, IL 60611; 800 companies.

Marine Surveyors, Natl. Assn. of (1960), 86 Windsor Gate Dr., N. Hills, NY 11040; 405.

Marine Technology Society (1963), 1730 M St. NW, Wash., DC 20036; 4,000.

Marketing Assn., Amer. (1937), 222 S. Riverside Plaza, Chicago, IL 60606; 30,000.

Masonic Relief Assn. of U.S. and Canada (1885), 32613 Seidel Dr., Burlington, WS 53105; 14,700.

Masonic Service Assn. of the U.S. (1919), 8120 Fenton St., Silver Spring, MD 20910; 43 Grand Lodges.

Masons, Ancient and Accepted Scottish Rite, Southern Jurisdiction, Supreme Council (1801), 1733 16th St. NW, Wash., DC 20009; 666,000.

Masons, Supreme Council 33°, Ancient and Accepted Scottish Rite, Northern Masonic Jurisdiction (1872), 33 Marrett Rd., Lexington, MA 02173; 502,114.

Masons, Royal Arch, General Grand Chapter (1797), P.O. Box 5320, Lexington, KY 40505; 375,000.

Mathematical Assn. of America (1915), 1225 Connecticut Ave. NW, Wash., DC 20036; 18,500.

Mathematical Society, Amer. (1888), Box 6248, Providence, RI 02904; 20,000.

Mathematical Statistics, Institute of (1930), 3401 Investment Blvd., 6, Hayward, CA 94545; 5,000.

Mathematics, Society for Industrial and Applied (1952), 117 S. 17th St., Phila., PA 19103; 5,500.

Mayflower Descendants, General Society of (1897), 4 Winslow St., Plymouth, MA 02360; 20,000.

Mayors, U.S. Conference of (1933), 1620 Eye St. NW, Wash., DC 20006; 500 cities.

Mechanical Engineers, Amer. Society of (1880), 345 E. 47th St., N.Y., NY 10017; 75,000.

Mechanics, Amer. Academy of (1969), 105 Hammond Bldg., Univ. Park, PA 16802; 994.

Mechanics, Assn. of Chairmen of Departments of (1969), Dept. of Theoretical and Applied Mechanics, Univ. of Ill. at Urbana-Champaign, Urbana, IL 61801; 96.

Mechanics, Junior Order of United Amer. (1853), 170 Railway Rd., Crafton, VA 23692; 3,000.

Mediaeval Academy of America (1925), 1430 Massachusetts Ave., Cambridge, MA 02138; 3,900.

Medical Assn., Amer. (1847), 535 N. Dearborn St., Chicago, IL 60610; 200,000.

Medical Assn., Natl. (1895), 1720 Massachusetts Ave. NW, Wash., DC 20036; 6,400.

Medical Record Assn., Amer. (1928), 875 N. Michigan Ave., Chicago, IL 60611; 25,000.

Medical Technologists, Amer. College of (1942), 5608 Lane, Raytown, MO 64133; 368.

Memorabilia Americana (1973), 1211 Ave. Eye, Brooklyn, NY 11230; 3,000.

Mensa, Amer. (1960), 1701 W. 3d St., Brooklyn, NY 11223; 46,500.

Mental Health, Natl. Assn. for (1950), 1800 N. Kent St., Arlington, VA 22209; 1,000,000+.

Mental Health Program Directors, Natl. Assn. of State (1963), 1001 3d St. SW, Wash., DC 20024, 54.

Merchant Marine Library Assn., Amer. (1921), One World Trade Center, Suite 2601, N.Y., NY 10048.

Merchants Assn., Natl. Retail (1911), 100 W. 31st St., N.Y., NY 10001; 35,000 stores.

Metal Finishers, Natl. Assn. of (1955), 111 E. Wacker Dr., Chicago, IL 60601; 1,100.

Metallurgy Institute, Amer. Powder (1959), P.O. Box 2054, Princeton, NJ 08540; 2,000.

Metal Powder Industries Federation, (1946), P.O. Box 2054, Princeton, NJ 08540; 225 cos.

Metals, Amer. Society for (1913), Metals Park, OH 44073; 50,000.

Meteorological Society, Amer. (1919), 45 Beacon St., Boston, MA 02108; 9,800.

Metric Assn., U.S. (1916), 10245 Andasol Ave., Northridge, CA 91325; 3,500.

Microbiology, Amer. Society for (1899), 1913 Eye St. NW, Wash. DC 20006; 31,829.

Micrographics Assn., Natl. (1942), 8719 Colesville Rd., Silver Spring, MD 20910; 9,000.

Mideast Educational and Training Services, America-, formerly Amer. Friends of the Middle East (1951), 1717 Massachusetts Ave. NW, Wash., DC 20036; 390.

Military Order of the Loyal Legion of the U.S.A. (1865), 1805 Pine St., Phila., PA 19103; 1,200.

Military Order of the Purple Heart (1782, by Gen. George Washington; reactivated Feb. 22, 1932, by President Herbert Hoover and Chief of Staff Douglas MacArthur), 1022 Wilson Blvd., Arlington, VA 22209; 10,000.

Military Order of the USA (1932), 5413-B Backlick Rd., Springfield, VA 22151; 10,000.

Military Order of the World Wars (1920), 1100 17th St. NW, Wash., DC 20036; 14,500.

Mining, Metallurgical and Petroleum Engineers, Amer. Institute of (1871), 345 E. 47th St., N.Y., NY 10017; 63,754.

Mining and Metallurgical Society of America (1908), 230 Park Ave., N.Y., NY 10017; 310.

Ministerial Assn., Amer. (1929), 446 Salem Ave., P.O. Box 1252, York, PA 17405; 18,179.

Model Railroad Assn., Natl. (1935), 7061 Twin Oaks Dr., Indianapolis, IN 46226; 29,000.

Modern Language Assn. of America (1883), 62 Fifth Ave., N.Y., NY 10011; 26,000.

Modern Language Teachers Assns., Natl. Federation of (1916), Prof. Max Kirch, Univ. of Delaware, Neward, DE 19711; 7,000.

Monopoly Assn., U.S. (1963), 1646 City National Bank Bldg., Detroit, MI 48226; 625.

Moose, Loyal Order of (1888), Mooseheart, IL 60539; 1,746,733.

Mothers Committee, Amer. (1933), Waldorf Astoria Hotel, 301 Park Ave., N.Y., NY 10022; 5,000.

Mothers-in-Law Club Intl. (1970), 420 Adelberg Ln., Cedarhurst, NY 11516; 5,000.

Mothers of Twins Clubs, Natl. Organization of (1960), 5402 Amberwood Ln., Rockville, MD 20853; 8,000.

Motion Picture Arts & Sciences, Academy of (1929), 8949 Wilshire Blvd., Beverly Hills, CA 90211; 4,225.

Motion Pictures, Natl. Board of Review of (1909), P.O. Box 589, Lenox Hill Sta., N.Y., NY 10021; 4,000.

Motion Picture & Television Engineers, Society of (1916), 862 Scarsdale Ave., Scarsdale, NY 10583; 9,442.

Motor Vehicle Administrators, Amer. Assn. of (1933), 1201 Connecticut Ave. NW, Wash., DC 20036.

Motor Vehicle Manufacturers Assn. (1913), 300 New Center Building, Detroit, MI 48202; 12 companies.

Motorcyclist Assn., Amer. (1924), P.O. Box 141, Westerville, OH 43081; 125,000.

Multiple Sclerosis Society, Natl. (1946), 205 E. 42d St., N.Y., NY 10017; 450,000.

Municipal Finance Officers Assn. (1971), 180 N. Michigan Ave., Suite 800, Chicago, IL 60601; 9,218.

Municipal League, Natl. (1894), 47 E. 68th St., N.Y., NY 10021; 6,500.

Mural Painters, Natl. Society of (1895), 41 E. 65th St., N.Y., NY 10021; 150.

Muscular Dystrophy Assn. (1950), 810 Seventh Ave., N.Y., NY 10019, 1,800,000.

Museums, Amer. Assn. of (1906), 1055 Thomas Jefferson St. NW, Wash., DC 20007; 6,166.

Music, Natl. Assn. of Schools of (1924), 11250 Roger Bacon Dr. #5, Reston, VA 22090; 519 institutions.

Music Center, Amer. (1940), 250 W. 57th St., N.Y., NY 10019; 1,000+.

Music Clubs, Natl. Federation of (1898), 310 S. Michigan Ave., Chicago, IL 60604; 500,000.

Music Conference, Amer. (1947), 1000 Skokie Blvd., Wilmette, IL 60091; 400.

Music Council, Natl. (1940), 250 W. 54th St., N.Y., NY 10019; 65 organizations.

Music Educators Natl. Conference (1907), 1902 Association Dr., Reston, VA 22091; 55,000.

Musicians, Amer. Federation of (1896), 1500 Broadway, N.Y., NY 10036; 330,000.

Musicological Society, Amer. (1934), 201 S. 34th St., Phila., PA 19104, 3,700.

Music Publishers' Assn., Natl. (1917), 110 E. 59th St., N.Y., NY 10022; 203.

Music Scholarship Assn., Amer. (1956), 1826 Carew Tower, Cincinnati, OH 45202; 1,500.

Music Teachers Natl. Assn. (1876), 2113 Carew Tower, Cincinnati, OH 45202; 19,740.

Muzzle Loading Rifle Assn., Natl. (1933), P.O. Box 67, Friendship, IN 47021; 24,000.

Mystic Seaport Museum (1929), 30 Greenmanville Ave., Mystic, CT 06355; 16,100.

NAACP (Natl. Assn. for the Advancement of Colored People (1909), 1790 Broadway, N.Y., NY 10019, 500,000.

Name Society, Amer. (1951), N. Country Community College, Saranac Lake, NY 12983; 810.

Narcolepsy and Cataplexy Foundation of Amer. (1975), 1410 York Ave., Suite 2D, N.Y. NY 10021; 3,560.

Narcolepsy Assoc., Amer. (1975), P.O. Box 5846, Stanford, CA 94305; 3,000.

National Guard Assn. of the U.S. (1878), One Massachusetts Ave. NW, Wash., DC 20001; 48,000.

Nationalities Service, Amer. Council for (1918), 20 W. 40th St., N.Y., NY 10018; 31 agencies.

Naturalists, Assn. of Interpretive (1961), 6700 Needwood Rd., Derwood, MD 20855; 1,400.

Natural Science for Youth Foundation (1961), 763 Silvermine Rd., New Canaan, CT 06840; 400.

Nature Conservancy (1951), 1800 N. Kent St., Arlington, VA 22209; 100,000.

Nature & Natural Resources, Intl. Union for Conservation of (1948), Avenue du Mont Blanc, 1196 Gland, Switzerland; 471.

Nature Study Society, Amer. (1908), 790 Ewing Ave., Franklin Lakes, NJ 07417; 1,000.

Navajo Code Talkers Assn. (1971), Red Rock State Park, P.O. Box 328, Church Rock, NM 87311; 90.

Naval Architects & Marine Engineers, Society of (1893), One World Trade Center, Suite 1369, N.Y., NY 10048; 12,500.

Naval Engineers, Amer. Society of (1888), 1012 14th St. NW, Wash., DC 20005; 5,000.

Naval Institute, U.S. (1873), U.S. Naval Academy, Annapolis, MD 21402; 72,885.

Naval Reserve Assn. (1954), 910 17th St. NW, Wash., DC 20006; 21,500.

Navigation, Institute of (1945), 815 15th St. NW, Suite 832, Wash., DC 20005; 2,500.

Navy Club of the U.S.A. Auxiliary (1941), 418 W. Pontiac St., Ft. Wayne, IN 46807; 1,000.

Navy League of the U.S. (1902); 818 18th St. NW, Wash., DC 20006; 40,000.

Needlework Guild of America (1885), 1342 E. Lincoln Hwy., Langhorne, PA 19047; 200 branches.

Negro College Fund, United (1944), 500 E. 62d St., N.Y., NY 10021; 41 institutions.

Newspaper Editors, Amer. Society of (1922), 1350 Sullivan Trail, Easton, PA 18042; 875.

Newspaper Promotion Assn., Intl. (1930), 11600 Sunrise Valley Dr., Reston, VA 22091; 1,300.

Newspaper Publishers Assn., Amer. (1887), 11600 Sunrise Valley Dr., Reston, VA 22091; 1,420 newspapers.

Ninety-Nines (Intl. Organization of Women Pilots) (1929), P.O. Box 59965; Will Rogers World Airport, Oklahoma City, OK 73159, 5,800.

Non-Commissioned Officers Assn. (1960), 10635 IH 35 No., San Antonio, TX 78233; 250,000+.

Non-Parents, Natl. Organization for (1972), 3 N. Liberty, Baltimore, MD 21201; 1,500.

Notaries, Amer. Society of (1965), 810 18th St. NW, Wash., DC 20006; 10,830.

Nuclear Society, Amer. (1954), 555 N. Kensington Ave., La Grange Park, IL 60525; 13,000.

Numismatic Assn., Amer. (1891), 818 N. Cascade Ave., Colorado Springs, CO 80901; 39,000.

Numismatic Society, Amer. (1858), Broadway at 155th St., N.Y., NY 10032; 2,065.

Nurse Education and Service, Natl. Assn. for Practical (1941), 254 W. 31st St., N.Y., NY 10001; 30,000.

Nurses, Natl. Federation of Licensed Practical (1949), 888 7th Ave., N.Y., NY 10019; 18,000.

Nurses' Assn., Amer. (1896), 2420 Pershing Rd., Kansas City, MO 64108; 180,000.

Nursing, Natl. League for (1952), 10 Columbus Circle, N.Y., NY 10019; 18,000.

Nutrition, Amer. Institute of (1928), 9650 Rockville Pike, Bethesda, MD 20014; 2,000.

ORT Federation, Amer. (Org. for Rehabilitation through Training) (1922), 817 Broadway, N.Y., NY 10013, 150,000.

Odd Fellows, Sovereign Grand Lodge Independent Order of (1819), 16 W. Chase St., Baltimore, MD 21201; 1,000,000.

Old Crows, Assn. of (1964), 2300 9th St. S., Arlington, VA 22204; 10,000.

Olympic Committee, U.S. (1920), 1750 E. Boulder St., Colorado Springs, CO 80909.

Optical Society of America (1916), 1816 Jefferson Pl. NW, Wash., DC 20036; 8,987.

Optimist Intl. (1919), 4494 Lindell Blvd., St. Louis, MO 63108; 135,000.

Optometric Assn., Amer. (1898), 243 N. Lindbergh Blvd., St. Louis, MO 63141; 16,457.

Oral and Maxillofacial Surgeons, Amer. Assn. of (1918), 211 E. Chicago Ave., Chicago, IL 60611; 3,866.

Organists, Amer. Guild of (1896), 815 Second Ave., Suite 318, N.Y., NY 10017; 18,000.

Oriental Society, Amer. (1842), 329 Sterling Memorial Library, Yale Sta., New Haven, CT 06520; 1,696.

Ornithologists' Union, Amer. (1883), c/o National Museum of Natural History, Smithsonian Institution, Wash., DC 20560; 4,000.

Osteopathic Assn., Amer. (1897), 212 E. Ohio St., Chicago, IL 60611; 14,419.

Ostomy Assn., United (1962), 2001 W. Beverly Blvd., Los Angeles, CA 90057; 43,000.

Outlaw and Lawman History, Natl. Assn. and Center for (1974), Utah State Univ., Merrill Library 104, UMC 30, Logan, Utah 84321; 400.

Overeaters Anonymous (1960), 2190 190th St., Torrance, CA 90504; 100,000.

Over-the-Counter Cos., Natl. Assn. of (1973), Box 60, Oreland, PA 19075; 225

PTA (Parent-Teacher Assn.), Natl. (1897), 700 N. Rush St., Chicago, IL 60611; 6,069,438.

Paleontological Research Institution (1932), 1259 Trumansburg Rd., Ithaca, NY 14850, 600.

Paper Converters Assn. (1976), 1000 Vermont Ave. NW, Wash., DC 20005; 120 companies.

Paper Institute, Amer. (1964), 260 Madison Ave., N.Y., NY 10016; 200 companies.

Parasitologists, Amer. Society of (1925), 1041 New Hampshire St., Box 368, Lawrence, KS 66044; 1,800.

Parenthood, Natl. Alliance for Optional (1972), 2010 Massachusetts Ave. NW, Wash., DC 20036; 1,000.

Parents Without Partners (1958), 7910 Woodmont Ave. NW, Wash., DC 20014; 182,559.

Parking Assn., Natl. (1951), 1101 17th St. NW, Wash., DC 20036; 1,000 companies.

Parkinson's Disease Foundation (1957), Wm. Black Research Bldg., 650 W. 168th St., N.Y., NY 10032.

Pathologists, Amer. Assn. of (1976), 9650 Rockville Pike, Bethesda, MD 20014; 2,100.

Patriotism, Natl. Committee for Responsible (1967), P.O. Box 665, Grand Central Sta., N.Y., NY 10163; 175.

Patriotism, Natl. Council for the Encouragement of (1968), 1502 Janice Ln., Munster, IN 46321; 2,000.

Pearl Harbor Survivors Assn. (1958), P.O. Box 205, Sperryville, VA 22740; 8,650.

P.E.N. Amer. Center (1922), 47 Fifth Ave., N.Y., NY 10003; 1,800.

Pen Women, Natl. League of Amer. (1897), 1300 17th St. NW, Wash., DC 20036; 6,200.

Pennsylvania Society (1899), Suite 594, Waldorf Astoria Hotel, 301 Park Ave., N.Y., NY 10022; 2,200.

Pension Actuaries, Amer. Society of (1966), 1700 K St. NW, Ste. 404, Wash., DC 20006; 1,800.

P.E.O (Philanthropic Educational Organization) Sisterhood (1869), 3700 Grand Ave., Des Moines, IA 50312; 215,000.

Personnel Administration, Amer. Society for (1949), 30 Park Dr., Berea, OH 44017; 28,448.

Petroleum Geologists, Amer. Assn. of (1917), Box 979, 1444 S. Boulder, Tulsa, OK 74101; 18,734.

Petroleum Institute, Amer. (1919), 2101 L St. NW, Wash., DC 20037; 7,500.

Petroleum Landmen, Amer. Assn. of (1955), 2408 Continental Life Bldg., Fort Worth, TX 76102; 6,200.

Pharmaceutical Assn., Amer. (1852), 2215 Constitution Ave. NW, Wash., DC 20037; 56,000.

Philatelic Americans, Society of (1894), P.O. Box 9041, Wilmington, DE 19809; 8,500.

Philatelic Society, Amer. (1886), P.O. Box 800, 336 S. Fraser St., State College, PA 16801; 53,000.

Philatelists of Amer., Jr. (1976), P.O. Box 116, Ashton, RI 02864; 800.

Philaticians, Society of (1972), 154 Laguna Ct., St. Augustine Shores, FL 32084; 290.

Philological Assn., Amer. (1869), 617 Hamilton Hall, Columbia Univ., N.Y., NY 10027; 2,500.

Philosophical Assn., Amer. (1900), Univ. of Delaware, Newark, DE 19711; 6,200.

Philosophical Enquiry, Intl. Society for (1974), 12 N. Church Rd., Saddle River, NJ 07458; 239.

Philosophical Society, Amer. (1743), 104 S. 5th St., Phila., PA 19106; 626.

Photographers of America, Professional (1880), 1090 Executive Way, Des Plaines, IL 60018; 1,500.

Photographic Society of Amer. (1933), 2005 Walnut St., Phila. PA 19103; 17,000.

Physical Therapy Assn., Amer. (1921), 1156 15th St. NW. Wash., DC 20005; 34,000.

Physicians, Amer. Academy of Family (1947), 1740 W. 92nd St., Kansas City, MO 64114; 50,000.

Physics, Amer. Institute of (1931), 335 E. 45th St., N.Y., NY 10017; 68,500.

Physiological Society, Amer. (1887), 9650 Rockville Pike,

Bethesda, MD 20014; 5,800.

Pilgrim Society (1820), 75 Court St., Plymouth, MA 02360; 700.

Pilgrims of the U.S. (1903), 74 Trinity Pl., N.Y., NY 10006; 1,000.

Pilot Club Intl. (1921), 244 College St., Macon, GA 31213; 20,000.

Pioneer Women, The Women's Labor Zionist Organization of America (1925), 200 Madison Ave., N.Y., NY 10016; 50,000.

Planned Parenthood Federation of America (1916), 810 Seventh Ave., N.Y., NY 10019; 189 affiliates.

Planning Assn., Amer. (1978), 1976 Massachusetts Ave. NW, Wash., DC 20036; 20,000.

Plastic Modelers Society, Intl. (1962), P.O. Box 480, Denver, CO 80201; 5,200.

Plastics Engineers, Society of (1942), 14 Fairfield Dr., Brookfield Cntr., CT 06805; 23,500.

Plastics Industry, Society of (1937), 355 Lexington Ave., N.Y., NY 10017; 1,400 companies.

Platform Assn., Intl. (1831), 2564 Berkshire Rd., Cleveland Heights, OH 44106; 5,000+.

Podiatry Assn., Amer. (1912), 20 Chevy Chase Circle NW, Wash., DC 20015; 7,000.

Poetry Day Committee, Natl. (1947), 1110 N. Venetian Dr., Miami, FL 33139; 17,000.

Poetry Society of America (1910), 15 Gramercy Park, N.Y., NY 10003; 1,050.

Poets, Academy of Amer. (1934), 177 E. 87th St., N.Y., NY 10028; 3,500.

Polar Society, Amer. (1934), c/o Secretary, 98-20 62d Dr., Apt. 7H, Rego Park, NY 11374; 2,391.

Police, Internatl. Assn. of Chiefs of (1894), 11 Firstfield Rd., Gaithersburg, MD 20760; 12,300.

Police Reserve Officers Assn., Natl. (1967), 609 W. Main St., Louisville, KY 40202; 11,000.

Polish Army Veterans Assn. of America (1921), 19 Irving Pl., N.Y., NY 10003; 9,762.

Polish Cultural Society of America (1940), 43 John St., N.Y., NY 10038; 68,591.

Polish Legion of American Veterans (1920), 3024 N. Laramie Ave., Chicago, IL 60641; 150,000.

Political Items Collectors, Amer. (1945), 1054 Sharpsburg Dr., Huntsville, AL 35803; 2,500.

Political Science, Academy of (1880), 619 W. 114th St., Suite 500, N.Y., NY 10025; 11,000.

Political Science Assn., Amer. (1903), 1527 New Hampshire Ave. NW, Wash., DC 20036; 13,075.

Political & Social Science, Amer. Academy of (1889), 3937 Chestnut St., Phila., PA 19104; 10,715.

Pollution Control, Internatl. Assn. for (1970), 1625 Eye St. NW, Wash. DC 20006; 500.

Polo Assn., U.S. (1890), 1301 W. 22d St., Oak Brook, IL 60521; 1,825.

Population Assn. of America (1931), 806 15th St. NW, Wash., DC 20005; 2,600.

Portuguese Continental Union of the U.S.A. (1925), 899 Boylston St., Boston, MA 02115; 9,000.

Postmasters of the U.S., Natl. Assn. of (1935), 1616 N. Ft. Myer Dr., Arlington, VA 22209; 28,000.

Postmasters of the U.S., Natl. League of (1903), 1023 N. Royal St., Alexandria, VA 22314; 19,500.

Poultry Science Assn. (1926), 309 W. Clark, Champaign, IL 61820; 1,676.

Power Boat Assn., Amer. (1903), 17640 E. Nine Mile Rd., E. Detroit, MI 48021; 6,000.

Precancel Collectors, Natl. Assn. of (1950), 5121 Park Blvd., Wildwood, NJ 08260; 6,000+.

Press, Associated (1848), 50 Rockefeller Plaza, N.Y., NY 10020; 1,365 newspapers & 3,600 broadcast stations.

Press Club, Natl. (1908), 529 14th St. NW, Wash., DC 20045; 4,500.

Press Intl., United (1907), 220 E. 42d St., N.Y., NY 10017.

Press and Radio Club (1948), P.O. Box 7023, Montgomery, AL 36107; 707.

Press Women, Natl. Federation of (1937), 1105 Main St., Blue Springs, MD 64015; 5,000.

Procrastinators' Club of America (1956), 1111 Broad-Locust Bldg., Phila., PA 19102; 4,000+.

Propeller Club of the U.S. (1927), 1730 M St. NW, Suite 413, Wash., DC 20036; 15,000+.

Psychiatric Assn., Amer. (1894), 1700 18th St. NW, Wash., DC 20009; 25,440.

Psychical Research, Amer. Society for (1905), 5 W. 73d St., N.Y., NY 10023; 2,500.

Psychoanalytic Assn., Amer. (1911), One E. 57th St., N.Y., NY 10022; 2,648.

Psychological Assn., Amer. (1892), 1200 17th St. NW, Wash., DC 20036; 50,000.

Psychological Assn. for Psychoanalysis, Natl. (1948), 150 W. 13th St., N.Y., NY 10011; 235.

Psychological Minorities, Society for the Aid of (1963), 42-25 Hampton St., Elmhurst, NY 11373; 653.

Psychotheatrics, Assn. for (1976), P.O. Box 160371, Sacramento, CA 95816; 121.

Psychotherapy Assn., Amer. Group (1942), 1995 Broadway, N.Y., NY 10023; 3,000.

Public Health Assn., Amer. (1872), 1015 15th St. NW, Wash., DC 20005; 30,000.

Public Relations Society of America (1947), 845 Third Ave., N.Y., NY 10022; 10,000.

Publishers, Assn. of Amer. (1970), One Park Ave., N.Y., NY 10016; 450 publishing houses.

Puppeteers of Amer. (1936), 5 Cricklewood Path, Pasadena, CA 91107; 2,500.

Quality Control, Amer. Society for (1946), 161 W. Wisconsin Ave., Milwaukee, WI 53203; 26,000.

Rabbinical Alliance of America (1945), 156 5th Ave., N.Y., NY 10010; 500.

Rabbinical Assembly (1900), 3080 Broadway, N.Y., NY 10027; 1,200.

Rabbis, Central Conference of Amer. (1889), 790 Madison Ave., N.Y., NY 10021; 1,300.

Racquetball Assn., U.S. (1973), 4101 Dempster St., Skokie, IL 60076; 45,000.

Radio Union, Intl. Amateur (1925), P.O. Box AAA, Newington, CT 06111; 113 societies.

Radio and Television Society, Intl. (1940), 420 Lexington Ave., N.Y., NY 10017; 1,300+.

Radio Relay League, Amer. (1914), 225 Main St., Newington, CT 06111; 150,000+.

Railroad Passengers, Natl. Assn. of (1967), 417 New Jersey Ave. SE, Wash., DC 20003; 10,600.

Railroads, Assn. of Amer. (1934), 1920 L St. NW, Wash., DC 20036; 67.

Railway Historical Society, Natl. (1935), P.O. Box 2051, Phila., PA 19103; 10,602.

Railway Progress Institute (1908), 801 N. Fairfax St., Alexandria, VA 22314; 145 companies.

Range Management, Society for (1948), 2760 W. 5th Ave., Denver, CO 80204; 5,000.

Real Estate Appraisers, Natl. Assn. of (1967), 853 Broadway, N.Y., NY 10003; 1,000.

Real Estate Investment Trusts, Natl. Assn. of (1960), 1101 17th St. NW, Wash., DC 20036; 141 trusts, 223 associates.

Rebekah Assemblies, Intl. Assn. of (1914), P.O. Box 153, Minneapolis, KS 67467; 338,050.

Reconciliation, Fellowship of (1915), 523 N. Broadway, Nyack, NY 10960; 26,000.

Recording Industry Assn. of America (1951), 1370 Ave. of Amer., N.Y., NY 10019; 68.

Records Managers & Administrators, Assn. of (1975), 4200 Somerset Dr., Suite 215, Prairie Village, KS 66208; 6,600.

Recreation and Park Assn., Natl. (1965), 1601 N. Kent St., Arlington, VA 22209; 16,000.

Red Cross, Amer. Natl. (1881), 17th & D Sts. NW, Wash., DC 20006; 3,108 chapters.

Red Men, Improved Order Of (1765), 1525 West Ave., P.O. Box 683, Waco, TX 76707; 51,000.

Redwoods League, Save-the- (1918), 114 Sansome St., San Francisco, CA 94104; 40,000.

Regional Plan Assn. (1929), 235 E. 45th St., N.Y., NY 10017; 3,000.

Rehabilitation Assn., Natl. (1925), 1522 K St. NW, Wash., DC 20005; 25,000.

Religion, Amer. Academy of (1909), Dept. of Religious Studies, Cal. State Univ., Chico, CA 95929; 4,200.

Renaissance Society of America (1954), 1161 Amsterdam Ave., N.Y., NY 10027; 2,900.

Reserve Officers Assn. of the U.S. (1922), One Constitution Ave., NE, Wash., DC 20002; 127,000.

Restaurant Assn., Natl. (1919), 311 First St. NW, Wash., DC 20001; 10,000 businesses.

Retarded Citizens, Natl. Assn. for (1950), P.O. Box 6109, 2709 Ave. E East, Arlington, TX 76011; 250,000.

Retired Federal Employees, Natl. Assn. of (1921), 1533 New Hampshire Ave. NW, Wash., DC 20036; 300,000.

Retired Officers Assn. (1929), 201 N. Washington St., Alexandria, VA 22314; 290,000.

Retired Persons, Amer. Assn. of (1958), 1909 K St. NW, Wash., DC 20049; 11,500,000.

Retired Teachers Assn., Natl. (1947), 1909 K St. NW, Wash., DC 20049; 540,000.

Retreads (of World War I & II) (1947), 40-07 154th St., Flushing, NY 11354; 1,400.

Revolver Assn., U.S. (1900), 59 Alvin St., Springfield, MA 01104; 1,350.

Reye's Syndrome Foundation, Natl. (1974), P.O. Box 829, Bryan, OH 43506; 8,000.

Richard III Society (1924), P.O. Box 217, Sea Cliff, NY 11579; 2,700.

Rifle Assn., Natl. (1871), 1600 Rhode Island Ave. NW, Wash., DC 20036; 1,600,000.

Road & Transportation Builders' Assn., Amer. (1902), 525 School St. SW, Wash., DC 20024; 5,800.

Rodeo Cowboys Assn., Professional (1936), 101 Pro Rodeo Dr., Colorado Springs, CO 80919; 5,000.

Roller Skating, U.S. Amateur Confederation of (1973), P.O. Box 83067, Lincoln, NE 68501; 40,000.

Roller Skating Rink Operators Assn. (1937), 7700 A St., Lincoln, NE 68510; 2,200.

Rose Society, Amer. (1898), P.O. Box 30,000, Shreveport, LA 71130; 18,500.

Rosicrucian Fraternity (1614, Germany, 1861 in U.S.), R.D. No. 3, Box 220, Quakertown, PA 18951.

Rosicrucian Order, AMORC (1915), Rosicrucian Park, San Jose, CA 95191; 220,000.

Rosicrucians, Society of (1909), 321 W. 101st St., N.Y., NY 10025.

Rotary Intl. (1905), 1600 Ridge Ave., Evanston, IL 60201; 876,000.

Ruritan Natl. (1928), Ruritan Natl. Rd., Dublin, VA 24084; 38,790.

Russian Americans, Congress of (1973), P.O. Box 5025, Long Island City, NY 11105.

Russian Orthodox Clubs, Federated (1927), 10 Downs Dr. (Plains), Wilkes-Barre, PA 18705; 3,000.

Safety Council, Natl. (1913), 444 N. Michigan Ave., Chicago, IL 60611; 17,000.

Safety Engineers, Amer. Society of (1911), 850 Busse Hwy., Park Ridge, IL 60068; 15,000.

St. Dennis of Zante, Sovereign Greek Order of (1096; 1953 in U.S.), 739 W. 186th St., N.Y., NY 10033; 950.

St. Paul, Natl. Guild of (1937), 601 Hill 'n Dale, Lexington, KY 40503; 13,652.

Salesmen, Natl. Assn. of Professional (1970), 266 Tram Rd., Columbia, SC 29210; 20,000.

Salt Institute (1914), 206 N. Washington St., Alexandria, VA 22314; 32 cos.

Samuel Butler Society (1978), Chaplain Library, Williams College, P.O. Box 426, Williamstown, MA 01267; 100.

Sane World, A Citizen's Organization for a (1957), 514 C St. NE, Wash., DC 20002; 24,000.

Savings & Loan League, Natl. (1943), 1101 15th St. NW, Wash., DC 20005; 300 associations.

School Administrators, Amer. Assn. of (1865), 1801 N. Moore St., Arlington, VA 22209; 19,000.

School Boards Assn., Natl. (1940), 1055 Thomas Jefferson St. NW, Wash., DC 20007; 16,000 boards.

School Counselor Assn., Amer. (1953), 2 Skyline Pl., Suite 400, 5203 Leesburg Pk., Falls Church, VA 22041; 10,000+.

Schools & Colleges, Amer. Council on (1927), 446 Salem Ave., P.O. Box 1252, York, PA 17405; 121 institutions.

Science, Amer. Assn. for the Advancement of (1848), 1515 Massachusetts Ave. NW, Wash., DC 20005; 128,308.

Science Club of Amer., Jr. (1978), 2505 Prestwick, Richmond, VA 23229; 116.

Science Fiction, Fantasy and Horror Films, Academy of (1972), 334 W. 54th St., Los Angeles, CA 90037; 3,000.

Sciences, Natl. Academy of (1863), 2101 Constitution Ave. NW, Wash., DC 20418; 1,300.

Science Service (1921), 1719 N St. NW, Wash., DC 20036.

Science Teachers Assn., Natl. (1944), 1742 Connecticut Ave. NW, Wash., DC 20009; 19,272.

Science Writers, Natl. Assn. of (1934), P.O. Box 294,

Greenlawn, NY 11740; 1,040.

Scientists, Federation of Amer. (1946), 307 Massachusetts Ave. NE, Wash., DC 20002; 7,000.

Screen Actors Guild (1933), 7750 Sunset Blvd., Hollywood, CA 90046; 42,000.

Sculpture Society, Natl. (1893), 15 E. 26th St., N.Y., NY 10010; 325.

Seamen's Service, United (1942), One World Trade Ctr., Suite 2601, N.Y., NY 10048.

2d Air Division Assn. (1947), 1 Jeffrey's Neck Rd., Ipswich, MA 01938; 4,186.

Secondary School Principals, Natl. Assn. of (1916), 1904 Association Dr., Reston, VA 22091; 35,000.

Secretaries, Natl. Assn. of Legal (1950), 3005 E. Skelly Dr., Tulsa, OK 74105; 23,000.

Secularists of America United (1947), 377 Vernon St., Oakland, CA 94610.

Securities Industry Assn. (1972), 20 Broad St., N.Y., NY 10005; 512 firms.

Seeing Eye, The (1929), Washington Valley Rd., Morristown, NJ 07960.

Semantics, Institute of General (1938), R.R. 1; Box 215, Lakeville, CT 06039; 464.

Separation of Church & State, Americans United for (1948), 8120 Fenton St., Silver Spring, MD 20910; 75,000.

Sertoma Internatl. (1912), 1912 E. Meyer Blvd., Kansas City, MO 64132; 35,018.

Sex Information & Education Council of the U.S. (SIECUS) (1964), 84 5th Ave., N.Y., NY 10011; 1,000.

Shakespeare Assn. of America (1972), Box 6328, Vanderbilt Sta., Nashville, TN 37235; 1,700.

Sheriff's Assn., Natl. (1940), 1250 Connecticut Ave. NW, Wash., DC 195,000. 50,000+.

Shipbuilders Council of America (1920), 600 New Hampshire Ave. NW, Wash., DC 20037; 40 companies.

Ship Society, World (1946), 3319 Sweet Dr., Lafayette, CA 94549; 4,000.

Shoe Retailers Assn., Natl. (1912), 200 Madison Ave., N.Y., NY 10016; 4,000.

Shore & Beach Preservation Assn., Amer. (1926), 412 O'Brien Hall, Univ. of California, Berkeley, CA 94720; 1,000.

Shrine, Ancient Arabic Order of the Nobles of the Mystic (1872), 2900 Rocky Pt. Dr., Tampa, FL 33607; 1,000,000.

Shut-In Day Society, Natl. (1970), 237 Franklin St., Reading, PA 19602; 1,300.

Sierra Club (1892), 530 Bush St., San Francisco, CA 94108; 195,000.

Silurians, Society of the (1924), 45 John St., N.Y., NY 10010; 740.

Skating Union of the U.S., Amateur (1928), 4423 W. Deming Pl., Chicago, IL 60639; 2,000.

Skeet Shooting Assn., Natl. (1946), P.O. Box 28188, San Antonio, TX 78228; 13,000.

Ski Assn., U.S. (1904), 1726 Champa St., Denver, CO 80202; 110,000.

Small Business, Amer. Federation of (1938), 407 S. Dearborn St., Chicago, IL 60605; 5,000.

Small Business Assn., Natl. (1937), 1604 K St. NW, Wash., DC 20006; 50,000.

Smoking & Health, Natl. Clearinghouse for (1965), Center for Disease Control, 1600 Clifton Road NE, Atlanta, GA 30333.

Soaring Society of America (1932), 3200 Airport Ave., Rm. 25, Santa Monica, CA 90405; 17,000.

Soccer Federation, U.S. (1913), 350 Fifth Ave., N.Y., NY 10001; 700,000.

Social Biology, Society for the Study of (1926), Medical Dept., Brookhaven Natl. Laboratory, Upton, NY 11973; 415.

Social Science Research Council (1924), 605 Third Ave., N.Y., NY 10016.

Social Sciences, Natl. Institute of (1899), 150 Amsterdam Ave., N.Y., NY 10023; 680.

Social Service, Intl., Amer. Branch (1925), 291 Broadway, N.Y., NY 10007.

Social Welfare, Intl. Council on (1928), 345 E. 46th St., N.Y., NY 10017; 70 natl. committees.

Social Work Education, Council on (1952), 111 8th Ave., N.Y., NY 10017; 4,500.

Social Workers, Natl. Assn. of (1955), 1425 H St. NW, Wash., DC 20005; 80,000.

Sociological Assn., Amer. (1905), 1722 N St. NW, Wash., DC 20036; 14,000.

Softball Assn. of America, Amateur (1933), 2801 N.E. 50th St., Oklahoma City, OK 73111; 1,575,000.

Softball League, Cinderella (1956), P.O. Box 1411, Corning, NY 14830; 5,000.

Soft Drink Assn., Natl. (1919), 1101 16th St. NW, Wash., DC 20036; 1,500.

Soil Conservation Society of America (1945), 7515 N.E. Ankeny Rd., Ankeny, IA 50021; 15,000.

Soil Science Society of America (1936), 677 S. Segoe Rd., Madison, WI 53711; 4,595.

Sojourners, Natl. (1921), 8301 E. Boulevard Dr., Alexandria, VA 22308; 9,516.

Soldier's, Sailor's and Airmen's Club (1919), 283 Lexington Ave., N.Y., NY 10016.

Sons of the Amer. Legion (1935), 700 N. Pennsylvania, Indianapolis, IN 46206; 40,000.

Sons of the American Revolution, Natl. Society of (1889), 1000 S. 4th, Louisville, KY 40203; 22,500.

Sons of Confederate Veterans (1896), Southern Sta., P.O. Box 5164, Hattiesburg, MS 39401; 6,000.

Sons of the Desert (1964), P.O. Box 8341, Universal City, CA 91608; 4,000.

Sons of Italy i i America, Order (1905), 1520 Locust St., Phila., PA 19102; 400,000.

Sons of Norway (1895), 1455 W. Lake St., Minneapolis, MN 55408; 105,429.

Sons of Poland, Assn. of the (1903), 665 Newark Ave., Jersey City, NJ 07306; 20,000.

Sons of St. Patrick, Society of the Friendly (1784), 80 Wall St., N.Y., NY 10005; 1,300.

Sons of Sherman's March to the Sea (1966), 1725 Farmers Ave., Tempe, AZ 85281; 414.

Sons of Union Veterans of the Civil War (1881), P.O. Box 24, Gettysburg, PA 17325; 3,100.

Soroptimist Intl. of the Americas (1921), 1616 Walnut St., Phila., PA 19103; 32,000.

Southern Christian Leadership Conference (1957), 334 Auburn Ave. NE, Atlanta, GA 30303; 1,000,000.

Southern Regional Council (1944), 75 Marietta St. NW, Atlanta, GA 30303; 120.

Space Education Assoc., U.S. (1973), 746 Turnpike Rd., Elizabethtown, PA 17022; 8 countries.

Spanish War Veterans, United (1904), P.O. Box 1915, Wash., DC 20013; 50.

Speech Communication Assn. (1914), 5105 Backlick Rd., Annandale, VA 22003; 5,000.

Speech-Language-Hearing Assn., Amer. (1925), 10801 Rockville Pike, Rockville, MD 20852; 36,000.

Speleological Society, Natl. (1941), Cave Ave., Huntsville, AL 35810; 5,200.

Sports Car Club of America (1944), 6750 S. Emporia, Englewood, CO 80112; 24,000.

Sports Club, Indoor (1930), 1145 Highland St., Napoleon, OH 43545.

Standards Institute, Amer. Natl. (1918), 1430 Broadway, N.Y., NY 10018; 1,000.

State Communities Aid Assn. (1872), 105 E. 22d St., N.Y., NY 10010; 220.

State Governments, Council of (1933), P.O. Box 11910, Iron Works Pike, Lexington, KY 40578; 50 states.

State & Local History, Amer. Assn. for (1940), 1400 8th Ave. So., Nashville, TN 37203; 7,200.

Statistical Assn., Amer. (1839), 806 15th St. NW, Wash., DC 20005; 14,000.

Steamship Historical Society of America (1935), 414 Pelton Ave., Staten Island, NY 10310; 3,033.

Steel Construction, Amer. Institute of (1921), 400 N. Michigan Ave., Chicago, IL 60611; 350.

Sterilization, Assn. for Voluntary (1943), 708 Third Ave., N.Y., NY 10017; 1,989.

Stock Car Auto Racing, Natl. Assn. for (NASCAR) (1948), 1801 Speedway Blvd., Daytona Beach, FL 32015; 17,000.

Stock Exchange, Amer. (1971), 86 Trinity Pl., N.Y., NY 10006; 611.

Stock Exchange, New York (1792), 11 Wall St., N.Y., NY 10005; 1,366.

Stock Exchange, Philadelphia (1790), 17th St., Stock Exchange Pl., Phila., PA 19103; 381.

Structural Stability Research Council (1944), Fritz Engineering Laboratory No. 13, Lehigh Univ., Bethlehem, PA 18015; 200.

Student Assn., U.S. (1947), 1220 G St. SE, Wash., DC 20024; 3,400,000.

Student Councils, Natl. Assn. of (1931), 1904 Association Dr., Reston, VA 22091; 8,000 secondary schools.

Students Consumer Protection Council, Natl. (1972), Villanova Univ., Villanova, PA 19085; 50.

Stuttering Project, Natl. (1977), 4438 Park Blvd., Oakland, CA 94602; 750.

Sugar Brokers Assn., Natl. (1903), 1 World Trade Center N.Y., NY 10047; 250.

Sunbathing Assn., Amer. (1931), 810 N. Mills Ave., Orlando, FL 32803; 25,000.

Sunday League (1933), 279 Highland Ave., Newark, NJ 07104; 25,000.

Surfing, Intl. Council for the Advancement of (1974), 2131 Kalakaua Ave., Honolulu, HI 96815; 273,000.

Surgeons, Amer. College of (1913), 55 E. Erie St., Chicago IL 60611; 42,000.

Surgeons, Intl. College of (1935), 1516 N. Lake Shore Dr., Chicago IL 60610; 12,000.

Surgeons of the U.S., Assn. of Military (1891), 10605 Concord St., Kensington, MD 20795; 14,000.

Surveying & Mapping, Amer. Congress on (1941), 210 Little Falls, Falls Church, VA 22046; 11,130.

Symphony Orchestra League, Amer. (1942), P.O. Box 669, Vienna, VA 22180; 4,131.

Systems Management, Assn. for (1947), 24587 Bagley Rd., Cleveland, OH 44138; 9,500.

Table Tennis Assn., U.S. (1933), Olympic House, 1750 E. Boulder, Colorado Springs, CO 80909; 6,000.

Tall Buildings and Urban Habitat, Council on (1969), Fritz Engineering Laboratory, Lehigh Univ., Bethlehem, PA 18015; 1,500.

Tattoo Club of America (1974), 112 W. First St., Mt. Vernon, NY 10550; 11,000.

Tax Accountants, Natl. Assn. of Enrolled Federal (1960), 6108 N. Harding Ave., Chicago, IL 60659; 500.

Tax Administrators, Federation of (1937), 444 N. Capitol St. NW, Wash., DC 20001; 50 revenue departments.

Tax Assn.-Natl. Tax Institute of America (1907), 21 E. State St., Columbus, OH 43215; 2,150.

Tax Foundation (1937), 1875 Connecticut Ave. NW, Wash., DC 20009; 1,500.

Tea Assn. of the U.S.A. (1899), 230 Park Ave., N.Y., NY 10017; 176.

Teachers of English, Natl. Council of (1911), 1111 Kenyon Rd., Urbana, IL 61801; 80,000.

Teachers of English to Speakers of Other Languages (1966), 202 DC Transit Bldg., Georgetown Univ., Wash., DC 20057, 9,500.

Teachers of French, Amer. Assn. of (1927), 57 E. Armory Ave., Champaign, IL 61820; 10,000.

Teachers of German, Amer. Assn. of (1928), 523 Bldg., Suite 201, Route 38, Cherry Hill, NJ 08034; 7,738.

Teachers of Singing, Natl. Assn. of (1944), 250 W. 57th St., N.Y., NY 10107; 3,600.

Teachers of Spanish & Portuguese, Amer. Assn. of (1917), Holy Cross Coll., Worcester, MA 01610; 12,000.

Teaching of Foreign Languages, Amer. Council on the (1967), 2 Park Ave., N.Y., NY 10016; 10,000.

Technical Communication, Society for (1958), 815 15th St. NW, Wash., DC 20005; 5,000.

Telephone Pioneers of Amer. (1911), 195 Broadway, N.Y., NY 10007; 525,926.

Television Arts & Sciences, Natl. Academy of (1947), 291 S. La Cienega Blvd., Beverly Hills, CA 90211; 11,000.

Television Bureau of Advertising (1954), 1345 Ave. of the Americas, N.Y., NY 10019; 560 stations.

Television & Radio Artists, Amer. Federation of (1937), 1350 Ave. of the Americas, N.Y., NY 10019; 48,000.

Telluride Assn. (1911), 217 West Ave., Ithaca, NY 14850; 76.

Tennis Assn., U.S. (1881), 51 E. 42d St., N.Y., NY 10017; 170,000.

Terrain Vehicle Owners Assn., Natl. All (1972), P.O. Box 574, Feasterville, PA 19047; 1,381.

Testing & Materials, Amer. Society for (1898), 1916 Race St., Phila., PA 19103; 28,500.

Textile Assn., Northern (1854), 211 Congress St., Boston, MA 02110; 150.

Textile Manufacturers Institute, Amer. (1949), 2124 Wachovia Ctr., Charlotte, NC 28285; 250 companies.

Theatre & Academy, Amer. Natl. (1935), 245 W. 52d St., N.Y., NY 10019; 1,500.

Theatre Assn., Amer. (1936), 1000 Vermont Ave. NW, Wash., DC 20005; 5,900.

Theatre Organ Society, Amer. (1955), P.O. Box 1002, Middleburg, VA 22117; 6,000 families.

Theodore Roosevelt Assn. (1919), P.O. Box 720, Oyster Bay, NY 11771; 700.

Theological Library Assn., Amer. (1947), Lutheran Theological Seminary, 7301 Germantown Ave., Phila., PA 19119; 450.

Theological Schools in the U.S. and Canada, Assn. of (1918), 42 E. Natl. Rd., P.O. Box 130, Vandalia, OH 45377; 197 schools.

Theological Seminary, Intl. (1979), 7970 Woodman Ave., Suite A, Van Nuys, CA 91402; 300.

Theosophical Society (1875), P.O. Box 270, 1926 N. Main St., Wheaton, IL 60187; 5,100.

Thoreau Society (1941), SUNY-Geneseo, Geneseo, NY 14454; 1,200.

Thoroughbred Racing Assn. of North America (1942), 8000 Marcus Ave., Lake Success, NY 11040; 53 racetracks.

Titanic Historical Society (1963), P.O. Box 53, Indian Orchard, MA 01151; 2,227.

Toastmasters Intl. (1924), 2200 N. Grand Ave., Santa Ana,, CA 92711; 80,000.

Toastmistress Clubs, Intl. (1938), 9068 E. Firestone Blvd., Downey CA 90241; 25,000.

Topical Assn., Amer. (1949), 3306 N. 50th St., Milwaukee, WI 53216; 10,000.

Torch Clubs, Internatl. Assn. of (1924), P.O. Box 30578, Lincoln, NE 68503; 4,300.

Toy Manufacturers of America (1916), 200 Fifth Ave., N.Y., NY 10010; 250.

Trade Relations Council of the U.S. (1885), 1001 Connecticut Ave. NW, Wash., DC 20036; 50 companies.

Traffic and Transportation, Amer. Society of (1946), P.O. Box 33095, Louisville, KY 40232; 2,600.

Trail Association, North Country (1979), P.O. Box 100, Lincoln Center, ME 04458; 200.

Training Corps, Amer. (1960), 107-12 Jamaica Ave., Richmond Hill, NY 11418; 125.

Training & Development, Amer. Society for (1944), P.O. Box 5307, Madison, WI 53705; 15,000.

Transit Assn., Amer. Public (1974), 1100 17th St. NW, Wash., DC 20036; 620.

Translators Assn., Amer. (1959), 109 Croton Ave., Ossining, NY 10560; 1,800+.

Transportation Assn. of America (1935), 1100 17th St. NW, Wash., DC 20036; 800 companies.

Trapshooting Assn., Amateur (1924), 601 W. National Rd. Vandalia, OH 45377; 90,000.

Travel Agents, Amer. Society of (1931), 711 Fifth Ave., N.Y., NY 10022; 16,500.

Travel Industry Assn. of America (1965), 1899 L St. NW, Wash., DC 20036; 1,600.

Travel Organizations, Discover America (1939), 1899 L St NW, Wash., DC 20036; 1,200

Travelers Protective Assn. of America (1890), 3755 Lindell Blvd., St. Louis, MO 63108; 220,000.

Trilateral Commission (1973), 345 E. 46th, N.Y., NY 10017; 300.

Trucking Assn., Amer. (1933), 1616 P St. NW, Wash., DC 20036; 51 assns.

True Sisters, United Order (1846), 150 W. 85th St., N.Y., NY 10024; 15,000.

UFOs (Unidentified Flying Objects), Natl. Investigations Commitee on (1967), 7970 Woodman Ave., Van Nuys, CA 91402; 500.

UNICEF, U.S. Committee for (1947), 331 E. 38th St., N.Y., NY 10016.

Uniformed Services, Natl. Assn. for (1968), 5535 Hempstead Way, Springfield, VA 22151; 26,000.

UNIMA (l'Union Internationale de la Marionnette)–USA (1966), 117 E. 69th St., N.Y., NY 10021; 600.

United Nations Assn. of the U.S.A. (1923, as League of Nations Assn.) 300 E. 42d St., N.Y., NY 10017; 25,000.

United Service Organizations (USO) (1941), 237 E. 52d St., N.Y., NY 10022.

U.S., Amer. Assn. for Study of in World Affairs (1948), 3813 Annandale Rd., Annandale, VA 22003; 1,000.

United Way of America (1918), 801 N. Fairfax St., Alexandria, VA 22314; 1,139.

Universities, Assn. of Amer. (1900), One Dupont Circle NW, Wash., DC 20036; 50 institutions.

Universities & Colleges, Assn. of Governing Boards of (1921), One Dupont Circle NW, Wash., DC 20036; 24,000.

University Extension Assn., Natl. (1915), One Dupont Circle, Suite 360, NW, Wash., DC 20036; 1,200.

University Foundation, Intl. (1973), 1301 S. No Land Rd., Independence, MO 64055; 6,000+.

University Professors, Amer. Assn. of (1915), One Dupont Circle, Suite 500, NW, Wash., DC 20036; 70,000.

University Professors for Academic Order (1970), 635 SW 4th St., Corvallis, OR 97330; 531.

University Women, Amer. Assn. of (1881), 2401 Virginia Ave. NW, Wash., DC 20037; 190,000.

Urban Coalition, Natl. (1968), 1201 Connecticut Ave. NW, Wash., DC 20024.

Urban League, Natl. (1910), 500 E. 62d St., N.Y., NY 10021.

Utility Commissioners, Natl. Assn. of Regulatory (1889), 1102 ICC Bldg., P.O. Box 684, Wash., DC 20044; 338.

Valley Forge, Society of the Descendants of Washington's Army at (1976), P.O. Box 608, Manhasset, NY 11030; 251.

Variety Clubs Intl. (1928), 58 W. 58th St., N.Y., NY 10019; 11,000.

VASA Order of America (1896), 3720 Daryl Dr., Landisville, PA 17538; 35,000.

Veterans Assn., Blinded (1945), 1735 DeSales St. NW, Wash., DC 20036; 3,000.

Veterans Assn., China-Burma-India (1947), 750 N. Lincoln Memorial Dr., Milwaukee, WI 53201; 3,221+.

Veterans Committee, Amer. (1944), 1346 Connecticut Ave. NW, Wash., DC 20036; 25,000.

Veterans of Foreign Wars of the U.S. (1898) **& Ladies Auxiliary** (1914), 406 W. 34th St., Kansas City, MO 64111; 1,873,474 & 643,000.

Veterans of World War I (1958), 916 Prince St., Alexandria, VA 22314; 60,000.

Veterinary Medical Assn., Amer. (1863), 930 N. Meacham Rd., Schaumburg, IL 60196; 31,686.

Victorian Society in America (1966), The Athenaeum, East Washington Sq., Phila., PA 19106; 7,000.

Vocational Assn., Amer. (1925), 2020 N. 14th St., Arlington, VA 22201; 56,000.

Volleyball Assn., U.S. (1928), 1750 E. Boulder, Colorado Springs, CO 80909; 20,000.

Walking Assn. (1976), 4113 Lee Hwy., Arlington, VA 22207; 235.

War of 1812, General Society of the (1814), 1307 New Hampshire Ave. NW, Wash., DC 20036; 1,432.

War Mothers, Amer. (1917), 2615 Woodley Pl. NW, Wash., DC 20008; 11,000.

Warrant and Warrant Officers' Assn., Chief, U.S. Coast Guard (1929), 492 L'Enfant Plaza E., SW, Wash., DC 20024; 3,397.

Watch & Clock Collectors, Natl. Assn. of (1943), 514 Poplar St., Columbia, PA 17512; 33,496.

Watercolor Society, Amer. (1866), 1083 Fifth Ave., N.Y., NY 10028; 500.

Water Pollution Control Federation (1928), 2626 Pennsylvania Ave. NW, Wash., DC 20037; 30,000.

Water Resources Assn., Amer. (1964), St. Anthony Falls Hydraulic Lab, Mississippi River at 3d Ave. SE, Minneapolis, MN 55414; 2,500.

Water Ski Assn., Amer. (1939), State Rte. 550 at Carl Floyd Rd., Winter Haven, FL 33880; 16,000.

Water Well Assn., Natl. (1948), 500 W. Wilson Bridge Rd., Worthington, OH 43085; 8,200.

Water Works Assn., Amer. (1881), 6666 W. Quincy Ave., Denver, CO 80235; 31,000.

Watts Family Assn. (1969), 12401 Burton St., N. Hollywood, CA 91605; 12 branches.

Weather Modification Assn. (1969), P.O. Box 8116, Fresno, CA 93727; 250.

Welding Society, Amer. (1919), 2501 NW 7th St., Miami, FL 33125; 30,000+.

Wheelchair Athletic Assn., Natl. (1958), Nassau Community College, Garden City, NY 11530; 2,000+.

Wilderness Society (1935), 1901 Pennsylvania Ave. NW, Wash., DC 20006; 45,000.

Wild Horse Organized Assistance (WHOA!) (1971), 140 Greenstone Dr., Reno, NV 89512; 10,000.

Wildlife, Defenders of (1925), 1244 19th St. NW, Wash., DC 20036; 50,000.

Wildlife Federation, Natl. (1936), 1412 16th St. NW, Wash., DC 20036; 4,600,000.

Wildlife Foundation, No. Amer. (1911), 1000 Vermont Ave. NW, Wash., DC 20005.

Wildlife Fund, World (1961), 1601 Connecticut Ave. NW, Wash., DC 20009; 67,000.

Wildlife Management Institute (1911), 1000 Vermont Ave. NW, Wash., DC 20005.

William Penn Assn. (1886), 429 Forbes Ave., Pittsburgh, PA 15219; 72,000+.

Wireless Pioneers, Society of (1968), 3366—15 Mendocino Ave., Santa Rosa, CA 95401; 4,688.

Wizard of Oz Club, Intl. (1957), Box 95, Kinderhook, IL 62345; 1,850.

Woman's Assn., Amer. (1914), 1271 Ave. of the Americas, N.Y., NY 10020; 250.

Woman's Christian Temperance Union, Natl. (1874), 1730 Chicago Ave., Evanston, IL 60201; 250,000.

Women, Natl. Assn. of Bank (1921), 500 No. Michigan Ave., Chicago, IL 60611; 26,500.

Women, Natl. Organization for (NOW) (1966), 425 13th St. NW, Wash., DC 20004; 120,000.

Women Artists, Natl. Assn. (1889), 41 Union Sq., N.Y., NY 10003; 650.

Women, Rural American (1977), 1522 K St. NW, Wash., DC 20005; 35,000.

Women Engineers, Society of (1950), 345 E. 47th St., N.Y., NY 10017; 9,000.

Women in Communications (1909), P.O. Box 9561, Austin, TX 78766; 9,000.

Women Geographers, Society of (1925), 1619 New Hampshire Ave. NW, Wash., DC 20009; 500.

Women Marines Assn. (1960), 2545 E. Reno Ave., Las Vegas, NV 89120; 2,300.

Women Strike for Peace (1961), 145 S. 13th St., Phila., PA 19107.

Women's Army Corps Veterans Assn. (1946), 1409 E. Euclid Ave., Arlington Heights, IL 60004; 2,400.

Women's Clubs, General Federation of (1889), 1734 N St. NW, Wash., DC 20036; 600,000.

Women's Clubs, Natl. Federation of Business & Professional (1919), 2012 Massachusetts Ave. NW, Wash., DC 20036; 160,800.

Women's Educational & Industrial Union (1877), 356 Boylston St., Boston, MA 02116; 3,200.

Women's Intl. League for Peace & Freedom (1915), 1213 Race St., Phila., PA 19107; 9,000.

Women's Overseas Service League (1921), P.O. Box 39058, Friendship Sta., Wash., DC 20016; 1,466.

Women of the U.S., Natl. Council of (1888), 777 U.N. Plaza, N.Y., NY 10017; 27 organizations.

Women Voters of the U.S., League of (1920), 1730 M St. NW, Wash., DC 20036; 122,000.

Women World War Veterans (1919), 237 Madison Ave., N.Y., NY 10016; 85,000.

Woodmen of America, Modern (1883), 1701 First Ave., Rock Island, IL 61201; 500,000.

Woodmen of the World (1890), 1450 Speer Blvd., Denver, CO 80204; 28,954.

Wool Growers Assn., Natl. (1865), 1776 F St. NW, Wash., DC 20004; 24 state assns.

Workmen's Circle (1900), 45 E. 33d St., N.Y., NY 10016; 57,204.

World Future Society (1966), 4916 St. Elmo Ave., Wash., DC 20014; 40,000.

World Health, Amer. Assn. for (1953), 2121 Virginia Ave. NW, Wash., DC 20037; 350.

World Health, U.S. Committee for (1951), 777 United Nations Plaza, N.Y., NY 10017; 2,017.

Writers of America, Western (1953), Route 1, Box 35-H, Victor, MT 59875; 441.

Writers Assn. of America, Outdoor (1927), 4141 W. Bradley Rd., Milwaukee, WI 53209; 1,500.

Writers Guild of America, West (1931), 8955 Beverly Blvd., Los Angeles, CA 90048; 5,500.

Yeoman F. Natl. (1936), 223 El Camino Real, Vallejo, CA 94590; 800.

Young Americans for Freedom (1960), Woodland Rd., Sterling, VA 22170; 55,000.

Young Men's Christian Assns. of the U.S.A., Natl. Council of (1851), 101 N. Wacker Dr., Chicago, IL 60606; 10,662,904.

YM-YWHAs of Greater New York, Associated (1957), 130 E. 59th St., N.Y., NY 10022; 70,000.

Young Women's Christian Assn. of the U.S.A. (1858), 600 Lexington Ave., N.Y., NY 10022; 2,500,000.

Young Scientists of Amer. Foundation (1959), P.O. Box 9066, Phoenix, AZ 85068; 270 school chapters.

Youth, Allied (1936), 1556 Wisconsin Ave., Wash., DC 20007; 10,000.

Youth Hostels, Amer. (1934), Natl. Campus, Delaplane, VA 22025; 80,000.

Zero Population Growth (1968), 1346 Connecticut Ave. NW, Wash., DC 20036; 10,000.

Ziegfeld Club (1936), 3 W. 51st St., N.Y., NY 10019; 300.

Zionist Organization of America (1897), 4 E. 34th St., N.Y., NY 10016; 130,000.

Zonta Intl. (1919), 35 E. Wacker Dr., Rm. 2040, Chicago, IL 60605; 30,000.

Zoological Parks & Aquariums, Amer. Assn. of (1924), Oglebay Park, Wheeling, WV 26003; 3,000.

Zoologists, Amer. Society of (1913), Box 2739, California Lutheran College, Thousand Oaks, CA 91360; 4,500.

RELIGIOUS INFORMATION

Census of Religious Groups in the U.S.

Source: World Almanac questionnaire and 1981 Yearbook of American and Canadian Churches

Membership figures in the following table are the latest available. Some denominations submitted carefully compiled data while others approached the task more casually. The number of churches is given in parentheses. Asterisk (*) indicates church declines to publish membership figures.

Group	Members
Adventist churches:	
Advent Christian Ch. (360)	30,000
Primitive Advent Christian Ch. (10)	550
Seventh-day Adventists (3,730)	571,141
American Rescue Workers (15)	**2,140**
Anglican Orthodox Church (37)	**2,630**
Baha'i Faith (7,000)	*
Baptist churches:	
Amer. Baptist Assn. (5,000)	1,500,000
Amer. Baptist Chs. in U.S.A. (5,897)	1,231,646
Baptist General Conference (701)	131,000
Baptist Missionary Assn. of America (1,487)	130,360
Conservative Baptist Assn. of America (1,126)	225,000
Duck River (and Kindred) Assn. of Baptists (85)	8,632
Free Will Baptists (2,452)	227,888
Gen. Assn. of General Baptists (894)	74,159
Gen. Assn. of Regular Baptist Chs. (1,544)	243,141
Natl. Baptist Convention of America (11,398)	2,668,799
Natl. Baptist Convention, U.S.A. (30,000)	6,300,000
Natl. Primitive Baptist Convention (606)	250,000
No. Amer. Baptist Conference (254)	42,779
Seventh Day Baptist General Conference (60)	5,181
Southern Baptist Convention (35,778)	13,600,124
United Free Will Baptists (250)	55,000
Brethren (German Baptists):	
Brethren Ch. (Ashland, Ohio) (127)	15,070
Christian Congregation (La Follette, IN) (1,266)	89,379
Ch. of the Brethren (1,063)	170,839
Fellowship of Grace Brethren Chs. (262)	39,605
Old German Baptist Brethren (50)	4,898
Brethren, River:	
Brethren in Christ Ch. (156)	11,384
Buddhist Churches of America (60)	**60,000**
Calvary Grace Christian Churches of Faith (360)	*
Calvary Grace Church of Faith, Inc. (150)	**15,000**
Christadelphians (100)	*
The Christian and Missionary Alliance (1,382)	**189,710**
Christian Catholic Church (6)	**2,500**
Christian Church (Disciples of Christ) (4,362)	**1,217,747**
Christian Churches and Churches of Christ (5,535)	**1,054,266**
Christian Nation Church U.S.A. (18)	**2,000**
Christian Union (104)	**4,590**
Churches of Christ (17,000)	**2,500,000**
Churches of Christ in Christian Union (250)	**10,700**
Churches of God:	
Chs. of God, General Conference (350)	36,374
Church of God (2,035)	75,890
Ch. of God (Anderson, Ind.) (2,271)	176,429
Ch. of God (Seventh Day), Denver, Col. (104)	8,000
Church of Christ, Scientist (3,000)	*
The Church of God by Faith (105)	**4,500**
Church of the Nazarene (4,853)	**484,276**
Church of Revelation (8)	**750**
National Council of Community Churches (200)	**190,000**
Natl. Assn. of Congregational Christian Churches (397)	**110,000**
Conservative Congregational Christian Conference (130)	**22,750**
Eastern Orthodox churches:	
Albanian Orth. Diocese of America (16)	40,000
American Carpatho-Russian Orth. Greek Catholic Ch. (70)	100,000
Antiochian Orth. Christian Archdiocese of No. Amer. (110)	152,000
Diocese of the Armenian Ch. of America (52)	150,000
Bulgarian Eastern Orth. Ch. (13)	86,000
Coptic Orthodox Ch. (26)	90,000
Greek Orth. Archdiocese of N. and S. America (550)	3,000,000
Orthodox Ch. in America (440)	1,000,000

Group	Members
Romanian Orth. Episcopate of America (43)	40,000
Patriarchal Parishes of the Russian Orth. Ch. in the U.S.A. (41)	51,500
Serbian Eastern Orth. Ch. (52)	65,000
Syrian Orth. Ch. of Antioch (Archdiocese of the U.S.A. and Canada) (14)	35,000
Ukrainian Orth. Ch. of America (Ecumenical Patriarchate) (30)	30,000
The Episcopal Church in the U.S.A. (7,022)	**2,841,350**
American Ethical Union (Ethical Culture Movement) (21)	**5,000**
Evangelical Christian Churches (137)	**54,000**
Evangelical Christian Churches, California Synod (160)	**73,761**
Evangelical Church of North America (138)	**12,210**
Evangelical Congregational Church (161)	**28,459**
The Evangelical Covenant Church of America (543)	**77,846**
Evangelical Free Church of America (621)	**100,000**
Evangelical associations:	
Apostolic Christian Chs. of America (80)	17,888
Apostolic Christian Ch. (Nazarean) (42)	4,804
Christian Congregation (1,133)	81,604
Friends:	
Evangelical Friends Alliance (247)	26,912
Friends General Conference (350)	33,000
Friends United Meeting (525)	63,682
Religious Society of Friends (Conservative) (27)	1,728
Religious Society of Friends (Unaffiliated Meetings) (87)	5,696
Independent Fundamental Churches of America (614)	**125,563**
Grace Gospel Fellowship (48)	**3,500**
Jehovah's Witnesses (7,515)	**565,309**
Jewish congregations:	
Agudath Israel of America (Orthodox) (40)	100,000
Union of Amer. Hebrew Congregations (Reformed) (750)	1,200,000
Natl. Council of Young Israel (Orthodox) (163)	185,000
Union of Orthodox Jewish Congregations of America (1,700)	1,000,000
United Synagogue of America (Conservative) (815)	221,000
Latter-day Saints:	
Ch. of Jesus Christ (Bickertonites) (60)	2,551
Ch. of Jesus Christ of Latter-day Saints (Mormon) (7,218)	4,638,000
Reorganized Ch. of Jesus Christ of Latter Day Saints (1,034)	160,101
Lutheran churches:	
American Lutheran Ch. (4,860)	2,352,431
Ch. of the Lutheran Brethren (106)	10,523
Ch. of the Lutheran Confession (72)	9,316
Assn. of Evangelical Lutheran Chs. (287)	121,000
Evangelical Lutheran Synod (109)	19,885
Assn. of Free Lutheran Congregations (133)	15,317
Latvian Evangelical Lutheran Church in America (56)	12,308
Lutheran Ch. in America (5,801)	2,925,188
Lutheran Ch.-Missouri Synod (5,937)	2,719,319
Protestant Conference (Lutheran) (9)	2,660
Wisconsin Evangelical Lutheran Synod (1,146)	407,987
Mennonite churches:	
Beachy Amish Mennonite Chs. (74)	4,762
Evangelical Mennonite Ch. (21)	3,634
General Conference of Mennonite Brethren Chs. (120)	16,042

Group	Members	Group	Members
The General Conference Mennonite Ch. (217) .	36,736	Pentecostal Assemblies of the World (150) . . .	15,000
Hutterian Brethren (35)	3,500	Pentecostal Church of Christ (50)	1,659
Mennonite Ch. (1,140)	99,511	Pentecostal Church of God (1,147)	113,405
Old Order Amish Ch. (513)	33,000	United Pentecostal Ch. (2,792)	462,000
Old Order (Wisler) Mennonite Ch. (60)	8,400	Pentecostal Free-Will Baptist Ch. (125)	3,500
Methodist churches:			
African Methodist Episcopal Ch. (3,050)	1,970,000	**Plymouth Brethren (800)**	**74,000**
African Methodist Episcopal Zion Ch. (6,020) . .	1,125,176	**Polish Natl. Catholic Church (162) . . . .**	**282,411**
Evangelical Methodist Ch. (132)	9,730	**Presbyterian churches:**	
Free Methodist Ch. of North America (1,030) . .	70,183	Associate Reformed Presbyterian Ch. (Gen.	
Fundamental Methodist Ch. (15)	745	Synod) (158)	32,139
Primitive Methodist Ch., U.S.A. (88)	10,222	Cumberland Presbyterian Ch. (827)	87,836
Reformed Methodist Union Episcopal Ch. (20) .	45,000	Orthodox Presbyterian Ch. (136)	15,806
Southern Methodist Ch. (169)	11,000	Presbyterian Ch. in America (487)	81,111
United Methodist Ch. (25,223)	9,584,771	Presbyterian Ch. in the U.S. (4,159)	844,116
Moravian churches:		Reformed Presbyterian Ch., Evangelical	
Moravian Ch. (Unitas Fratrum), Northern Prov-		Synod (195)	29,489
ince (96)	34,424	Reformed Presbyterian Ch. of No. Amer. (68) . .	4,878
Moravian Ch. in America (Unitas Fratrum),		United Presbyterian Ch. in the U.S.A. (8,507) . .	2,520,367
Southern Province (54)	21,057		
Unity of the Brethren (26)	*	**Reformed churches:**	
Muslims	**2,000,000**	Christian Reformed Ch. (626)	213,995
		Hungarian Reformed Ch. in America (29)	10,500
New Apostolic Church of North America (367) .	**26,384**	Protestant Reformed Chs. in America (21). . . .	4,040
North American Old Roman Catholic Church		Reformed Ch. in America (896)	211,000
(121)	**67,314**	Reformed Ch. in the U.S. (26)	3,790
		The Roman Catholic Church (18,695)	**49,602,035**
Old Catholic churches:			
American Catholic Ch. (Syro-Antiochean) (3) . .	501	**The Salvation Army (1,109) . . . .**	**414,659**
Christ Catholic Ch. (7)	1,365	**The Schwenkfelder Church (5) . . . .**	**2,748**
Mariavite Old Cath. Ch. Province of North		**Social Brethren (30) . . . .**	**1,784**
America (166)	358,066	**Natl. Spiritualist Assn. of Churches (164). . . . .**	**5,168**
No. Amer. Old Roman Cath. Ch. (Schweikert)		**Gen. Convention, The Swedenborgian**	
(121)	60,124	**Church (47) . . . .**	**2,640**
Pentecostal churches:			
Apostolic Faith (45)	4,100	**Unitarian Universalist Assn. (946) . . . .**	**170,352**
Assemblies of God (9,773).	1,064,490	**United Brethren:**	
Bible Church of Christ (5)	2,300	Ch. of the United Brethren in Christ (261)	27,075
Bible Way Church of Our Lord Jesus Christ		United Christian Ch. (11)	430
World Wide (350).	30,000	**United Church of Christ (6,467) . . . .**	**1,745,533**
Church of God (Cleveland, Tenn.) (5,018)	411,385	**Universal Fellowship of Metropolitan**	
Church of God of Prophecy (1,791)	65,801	**Community Chs. (135). . . . .**	**25,000**
Congregational Holiness Ch. (175)	5,925		
Gen. Conference, Christian Ch. of No. Amer.		**Vedanta Society (12) . . . .**	**1,000**
(101)	12,000	**Volunteers of America (602) . . . .**	**36,380**
Intl. Ch. of the Foursquare Gospel (883)	138,236		
Open Bible Standard Chs. (271)	46,549	**The Wesleyan Church (1,785). . . . .**	**108,243**

Religious Population of the World

Source: The 1981 Encyclopaedia Britannica Book of the Year

Religion	N. America[1]	S. America	Europe[2]	Asia[3]	Africa	Oceania[4]	Totals
Total Christian. . . .	237,096,500	175,114,000	342,630,400	95,987,240	128,617,000	18,058,500	997,503,640
Roman Catholic . .	133,489,000	162,489,000	177,087,300	55,077,000	47,024,500	4,395,500	579,562,300
Eastern Orthodox	4,750,000	516,000	55,035,600	2,428,000	13,306,000[6]	409,000	76,444,600
Protestant[5]	98,857,500	12,109,000	100,507,500	38,482,240	62,286,500[7]	13,254,000	341,496,740
Jewish	6,250,340	595,800	4,045,120	3,192,860	176,400	76,000	14,336,520
Muslim[6]	376,200	251,500	14,945,000	428,266,000	145,214,700	90,000	589,143,400
Zoroastrian	1,250	2,100	10,000	256,000	650	1000	271,000
Shinto	60,000	90,000	—	57,003,000	1,200	—	57,154,200
Taoist	16,000	10,000	—	31,260,000	—	—	31,286,000
Confucian	97,100	70,000	—	155,887,500	1,500	14,000	156,070,100
Buddhist	185,250	193,200	193,000	254,241,000	20,000	35,000	254,867,450
Hindu.	88,500	850,000	400,000	475,073,000	1,179,800	400,000	477,991,300
Totals.	244,171,140	177,176,600	362,223,520	1,501,166,600	275,211,250	18,674,500	2,578,623,610
Population[7]	369,759,000	245,067,000	750,198,000	2,557,562,000	469,361,000	22,775,000	4,414,722,000

(1) Includes Central America and West Indies. (2) Includes communist countries where it is difficult to determine religious affiliation. (3) Includes areas in which persons have traditionally enrolled in several religions, as well as China, with an official communist establishment. (4) Includes Australia, New Zealand, and islands of the South Pacific. (5) Protestant figures outside Europe usually include "full members" (adults) rather than all baptized persons and are not comparable to those of ethnic religions or churches counting all adherents. (6) According to the Islamic Center, Wash., D.C., there are 1 billion Muslims worldwide. (7) United Nations data, midyear 1979.

National Council of Churches

The National Council of the Churches of Christ in the U.S.A. is a cooperative federation of 32 Protestant and Orthodox churches which seeks to advance programs and policies of mutual interest to its members. The NCC was formed in 1950 by the merger of 12 inter-denominational agencies. The Council's member churches now have an aggregate membership totaling approximately 40 million. The NCC is not a governing body and has no control over the policies or operations of any church belonging to it. The work of the Council is divided into 3 divisions — Church and Society; Education and Ministry; Overseas Ministries — and 5 commissions — Faith and Order; Regional and Local Ecumenism; Communication; Stewardship; and Justice, Liberation, and Human Fulfillment. The chief administrative officer of the NCC is Dr. Claire Randall, 475 Riverside Drive, N.Y., NY 10115.

Headquarters, Leaders of U.S. Religious Groups

See Associations and Societies section for religious organizations. (year organized in parentheses)

Adventist churches:
Advent Christian Church (1854) — Pres., Joe Tom Tate; exec. v.p., Rev. Adrian B. Shepard, Box 23152, Charlotte, NC 28212.
Seventh-day Adventists (1863) — Pres., Neal C. Wilson; sec., G. Ralph Thompson, 6840 Eastern Ave. NW, Wash., DC 20012.

Baha'i Faith — Chpsn., Judge James E. Nelson; sec., Glenford E. Mitchell, 536 Sheridan Rd., Wilmette, IL 60091.

Baptist churches:
American Baptist Assn. (1905) — Pres., Dr. Vernon L. Barr; rec. clk., W E. Norris, 4605 N. State Line, Texarkana, TX 75501.
American Baptist Churches in the U.S.A. (1907) — Pres., Rev. Dr. William F. Keucher; gen. sec., Rev. Dr. Robert C. Campbell, Valley Forge, PA 19481.
Baptist General Conference (1879) — Gen. sec., Dr. Warren Magnuson, 2002 S. Arlington Heights Rd., Arlington Heights, IL 60005.
Baptist Missionary Assn. of America (formerly **North American Baptist Assn.**) (1950) — Pres., Rev. Gordon Renshaw, rec. sec., Rev. Ralph Cottrell, Box 2866, Texarkana, AR 75501.
Conservative Baptist Assn. of America (1947) — Gen. Dir., Dr. Russell A. Shive, Box 66, Wheaton, IL 60187.
Free Will Baptists (1727) — Mod., Rev. Bobby Jackson; exec. sec., Dr. Melvin Worthington, Box 1088, Nashville, TN 37202.
General Assn. of General Baptists (1823) — Exec. sec., Rev. Glen Spence, 100 Stinson Dr., Poplar Bluff, MO 63901.
General Assn. of Regular Baptist Churches (1932) — Chpsn., Dr. John Balyo; natl. rep., Dr. Paul N. Tassell, 1300 N. Meacham Rd., Schaumburg, IL 60195.
Natl. Baptist Convention, U.S.A. (1880) — Pres., Dr. J.H. Jackson, 405 E. 31st St., Chicago, IL 60616.
North American Baptist Conference (1865) — Mod., Dr. Peter Fehr; exec. sec., Dr. John Binder, 1 S. 210 Summit Ave., Oakbrook Terrace, IL 60181.
Southern Baptist Convention (1945) — Pres., Bailey E. Smith; exec. sec., exec. comm., Dr. Harold C. Bennett, 460 James Robertson Pkwy., Nashville, TN 37219.
United Free Will Baptist Church (1870) — Gen. Bishop, W.L. Jones; gen. fin. sec., Bishop J.E. Reddick, Kinston College, 1057 University St., Kinston, NC 28501.

Brethren in Christ Church (1798) — Mod., Bishop Harvey R. Sider, sec., Dr. Arthur M. Climenhaga, 1093 Twp. Rd. 1704, RD 4, Ashland, OH 44805.

Brethren (German Baptists):
Brethren Church (Ashland, Oh.) (1708) — Adm., Charles Beekleg, 524 College Ave., Ashland, OH 44805.
Church of the Brethren (1719) — Mod., Duane H. Ramsey; gen. sec., Robert Neff, 1451 Dundee Ave., Elgin, IL 60120.

Buddhist Churches of America (1899) — Bishop, Rt. Rev. Kenryu Tsuji, 1710 Octavia St., San Francisco, CA 94109.

Calvary Grace Christian Church of Faith (1898) — Intl. gen. supt., Col. Herman Keck Jr., P.O. Box 6005, March Air Force Base, CA 92518.

Calvary Grace Church of Faith (1874) — Intl. gen. supt., Rev. A.C. Spern, Box 333, Rillton, PA 15678.

The Christian and Missionary Alliance (1887) — Pres., Dr. Louis L. King; sec., Dr. Elwood N. Nielsen, 350 N. Highland Ave., Nyack, NY 10960.

Christian Church (Disciples of Christ) (1809) — Gen. minister and pres., Dr. Kenneth L. Teegarden, 222 S. Downey Ave., Box 1986, Indianapolis, IN 46206.

The Christian Congregation (1887) — Gen. supt., Rev. Ora Wilbert Eads, 804 W. Hemlock St., LaFollette, TN 37766.

Churches of Christ in Christian Union (1909) — Gen. supt., Rev. Robert Kline; gen. sec., Rev. Paul Dorsey, Box 30, Circleville, OH 43113.

Churches of God:
Churches of God, General Conference (1825) — Admin., Dr. Richard E. Wilkin, Box 926, Findlay, OH 45840.
Church of God (Anderson, Ind.) (1880) — Chpsn., Paul L.

Hart; exec. sec., Paul A. Tanner, Box 2420, Anderson, IN 46011.

Church of Christ, Scientist (1879) — Pres., Berthe S. Girardin; clerk, Robert H. Mitchell, Christian Science Center, Boston, MA 02115.

Church of the Nazarene (1908) — Gen. sec., B. Edgar Johnson, 6401 The Paseo, Kansas City, MO 64131.

National Association of Congregational Christian Churches (1955) — Mod., Rev. Louis B. Gerhardt; exec. sec., Rev. Erwin A. Britton, D.D., Box 1620, Oak Creek, WI 53154.

Eastern Orthodox churches:
Antiochian Orthodox Christian Archdiocese of North America (formerly **Syrian Antiochian Orthodox Church**) (1894) — Primate, Metropolitan Archbishop Philip (Saleba); aux., Archbishop Michael Shaheen, 358 Mountain Rd., Englewood, NJ 07631.
Diocese of the Armenian Church of America (1889) — Primate, His Eminence Archbishop Torkom Manoogian; sec., V. Rev. Houssig Bagdasian, 630 2d Ave., N.Y., NY 10016.
Coptic Orthodox Ch. — Correspnt., Archpriest Fr. Gabriel Abdelsayed, 427 West Side Ave., Jersey City, NJ 07304.
Greek Orthodox Archdiocese of North and South America (1864) — Primate, Archbishop Iakovos; chan., V. Rev. George Bacopulos, 8-10 E. 79th St., N.Y., NY 10021.
Orthodox Church in America (formerly **Russian Orthodox Greek Catholic Church of North America**) (1792) — Primate, Metropolitan Theodosius; sec., Serge Troubetzkoy, P.O. Box 675, Syosset, NY 11791.
Romanian Orthodox Episcopate of America (1929) — Archbishop, Valerian (D. Trifa); sec., Most Rev. Laurence C. Lazar, 2522 Grey Tower Rd., Jackson, MI 49201.
Serbian Eastern Orthodox Church for the U.S.A. and Canada — Bishops, Rt. Rev. Bishop Firmilian, Rt. Rev. Bishop Gregory; Bishop Christophor; St. Sava Monastery, Libertyville, IL 60048.
Syrian Orthodox Church of Antioch, Archdiocese of the U.S.A. and Canada (1957) — Primate, Archbishop MarAthanasius Y. Samuel; gen. sec., Rev. Fr. John Meno, 293 Hamilton Pl., Hackensack, NJ 07601.
Ukrainian Orthodox Church in America (Ecumenical Patriarchate) (1928) — Primate, Most Rev. Bishop Andrei Kuschak, 90-34 139th St., Jamaica, NY 11435.
Ukrainian Orthodox Church in the U.S.A. (1919) — Metropolitan, Most Rev. Mstyslav S. Skrypnyk, Box 495, South Bound Brook, NJ 08880.

The Episcopal Church (1789) — Presiding bishop, Rt. Rev. John M. Allin; exec. off., Rev. James R. Gundrum, 815 2d Ave., N.Y., NY 10017.

Evangelical Christian Churches (1966) — Pres., Rev. John Wahnert, 336 E. Olney Ave., Phila., PA 19120.

Evangelical Christian Churches, California Synod (1966) — Pres.-Treas., Dr. Richard W. Hart Sr., 2450 First Ave., San Bernardino, CA 92405.

The Evangelical Covenant Church of America (1885) — Pres., Dr. Milton B. Engebretson; sec., Rev. Clifford Bjorklund, 5101 N. Francisco Ave., Chicago, IL 60625.

Friends:
Evangelical Friends Alliance (1965) — Pres., Stanley Perisho, 4595 Eliot St., Denver, CO 80211.
Friends General Conference (1900) — Clk., Dorothea C. Morse; gen. sec., Dwight Spann-Wilson, 1520B Race St., Phila., PA 19102.
Friends United Meeting (formerly **Five Years Meeting of Friends**) (1902) — Presiding clerk, Walter E. Schutt, 101 Quaker Hill Dr., Richmond, IN 47374.

Independent Fundamental Churches of America (1930) — Pres., Rev. Robert L. Gray, 2105 Sunnyside, Westchester, IL 60153.

Islamic Center of Washington — 2551 Massachusetts Ave. NW, Washington, DC 20008.

Jehovah's Witnesses (1879) — Watch Tower Pres., Frederick W. Franz, 124 Columbia Heights, Brooklyn, NY 11201.

Jewish congregations:
Union of American Hebrew Congregations (Reform) —

Pres., Rabbi Alexander M. Schindler, 838 5th Ave., N.Y., NY 10021.

National Council of Young Israel (Orthodox) (1912) — Pres., Nathaniel Saperstein; exec. v.p., Rabbi Ephraim H. Sturm, 3 W. 16th St., N.Y., NY 10011.

Union of Orthodox Jewish Congregations of America — Pres., Julius Berman, 116 E. 27th St., N.Y., NY 10016.

United Synagogue of America (Conservative) — Pres., Simon Schwartz, exec. v.p., Rabbi Benjamin Z. Kreitman, 155 5th Ave., N.Y., NY 10010.

Latter-day Saints:

The Church of Jesus Christ of Latter-day Saints (Mormon) (1830) — Pres., Spencer W. Kimball, 47 E. South Temple St., Salt Lake City, UT 84150.

Reorganized Church of Jesus Christ of Latter Day Saints (1830) — Pres., Wallace B. Smith, The Auditorium, Independence, MO 64051.

Lutheran churches:

The American Lutheran Church (1961) — Pres., Dr. David W. Preus; gen. sec., Dr. A.R. Mickelson, 422 S. 5th St., Minneapolis, MN 55415.

Church of the Lutheran Brethren (1900) — Pres., Rev. Everald H. Strom; sec., Rev. George Aase, 1007 Westside Dr., Box 655, Fergus Falls, MN 56537.

Church of the Lutheran Confession (1960) — Pres., Rev. Egbert Albrecht; sec., Rev. Paul Nolting, Rt. 2, Markesan, WI 53946.

Assn. of Evangelical Lutheran Churches (1976) — Pres., Dr. William H. Kohn; exec. sec., Elwyn Ewald, 12015 Manchester Rd., St. Louis, MO 63131.

Evangelical Lutheran Synod (1853) — Pres., Rev. George Orvick; sec., Rev. Alf Merseth, 106 13th St. S., Northwood, IA 50459.

Assn. of Free Lutheran Congregations (1962) — Pres., Richard Snipstead; sec., Rev. Hubert DeBoer, 3110 E. Medicine Lake Blvd., Minneapolis, MN 55441.

Lutheran Church in America (1962) — Bishop, Rev. Dr. James R. Crumley; sec., Rev. Dr. Reuben T. Swanson, 231 Madison Ave., N.Y. NY 10016.

Lutheran Church — Missouri Synod (1847) — Pres., Dr. J.A.O. Preus; sec., Rev. Herbert A. Mueller, 500 N. Broadway, St. Louis, MO 63102.

Wisconsin Evangelical Lutheran Synod (1850) — Pres., Rev. Carl H. Mischke; 3512 W. North Ave., Milwaukee, WI 53208; sec., Heinrich J. Vogel, 11757 N. Seminary Dr., 65W, Mequon, WI 53092.

Mennonite churches:

The General Conference Mennonite Church (1860) — Pres. Jacob Tilitzky; gen. sec., Vern Preheim, 722 Main, Box 347, Newton, KS 67114.

Mennonite Church (1690) — Mod., Ross T. Bender, sec., Ivan J. Kauffmann, 528 E. Madison St., Lombard, IL 60148.

Methodist churches:

African Methodist Episcopal Zion Church (1796) — Sr. Bishop, William M. Smith; gen. sec.-aud., Rev. Earle E. Johnson; Box 32843, Charlotte, NC 28232.

Evangelical Methodist Church (1946) — Gen. supt., John F. Kunkle; gen. sec., Rev. R.D. Driggers, 3000 W. Kellogg Dr., Wichita, KS 67213.

Free Methodist Church of North America (1860) — Bishops R. Andrews, D. Bastian, W. Cryderman, E. Parsons, C. Van Valin, gen. conf. sec., C.T. Denbo, 901 College Ave., Winona Lake, IN 46590.

The United Methodist Church (1968) — Bishop H. Ellis Finger Jr.; sec., Bishop James M. Ault, 223 Fourth Ave. Pittsburgh, PA 15222.

Universal Fellowship of Metropolitan Community Churches —Mod., Rev. Troy Perry; 5300 Santa Monica Blvd., Suite 304, Los Angeles, CA 90029.

Moravian Church (Unitas Fratum) (1740) **Northern Province** — Pres., Dr. J.S. Groenfeldt, 69 W. Church St., Box 1245, Bethlehem, PA 18018. **Southern Province** — Pres., Dr. Richard E. Amos, 459 S. Church St., Winston-Salem, NC 27101.

Old Catholic churches:

Mariavite Old Catholic Church-Province of North America (1932) — Prime bishop, Most Rev. Robert R.J.M. Zaborowski O.M., D.D., 2803 10th St., Wyandotte, MI 48192.

North American Old Roman Catholic Church (1915) — Archbishop, Most Rev. J.E. Schweikert, 4200 N. Kedvale Ave., Chicago, IL 60641.

Pentecostal churches:

Assemblies of God (1914) — Gen. supt., Thomas F. Zim-

merman; gen. sec., Joseph R. Flower, 1445 Boonville Ave., Springfield, MO 65802.

Bible Way Church of Our Lord Jesus Christ World Wide (1927) — Presiding bishop, Dr. Smallwood E. Williams, 1100 New Jersey Ave. NW, Wash., DC 20001.

Gen. Council, Christian Church of No. America (1948) — Gen. overseer; Rev. Dr. Carmine Saginario; gen. sec., Rev. Richard Tedesco, Box 801, Rt. 18 & Rutledge Rd., Transfer, PA 16154.

The Church of God (1903) — Gen. overseer, Bishop Voy M. Bullen, 2504 Arrow Wood Dr. SE, Huntsville, AL 35803.

Church of God (Cleveland, Tenn.) (1886) — Gen. overseer, Dr. Ray H. Hughes; gen. sec.-treas., E. C. Thomas, Keith at 25th St. NW, Cleveland, TN 37311.

International Church of the Foursquare Gospel (1927) — Pres., Dr. Rolf K. McPherson; sec., Dr. Leland E. Edwards, 1100 Glendale Blvd., Los Angeles, CA 90026.

Open Bible Standard Churches (1919) — Gen. supt., Ray E. Smith; sec.-treas., O. Ralph Isbill, 2020 Bell Ave., Des Moines, IA 50315.

Pentecostal Church of God (1919) — Gen. supt., Rev. Roy M. Chappell; sec.-treas., Rev. Ray J. Smith, 211 Main St., Joplin, MO 64801.

United Pentecostal Church International (1945) — Gen. supt., Nathaniel A. Urshan; gen. sec., Robert L. McFarland, 8855 Dunn Rd., Hazelwood, MO 63042.

Pentecostal Free Will Baptist Church (1959) — Gen. supt., Rev. Herbert Carter; gen. sec., Rev. Don Sauls, Box 1081, Dunn, NC 28334.

Presbyterian churches:

Cumberland Presbyterian Church (1810) — Mod., Robert L. Hull; stated clerk, T.V. Warnick, 1978 Union Ave., Memphis, TN 38104.

The Orthodox Presbyterian Church (1936) — Mod. Thomas E. Tyson, stated clerk, Richard A. Barker, 7401 Old York Rd., Phila., PA 19126.

Presbyterian Church in America (1973) — Mod., Rev. Paul G. Settle; stated clerk, Rev. Morton H. Smith, Box 312, Brevard, NC 28712.

Presbyterian Church in the U.S. (1865) — Mod., Dorothy Barnard; stated clerk, James E. Andrews, 341 Ponce de Leon Ave. NE, Atlanta, GA 30365.

Reformed Presbyterian Church, Evangelical Synod (1965) — Mod., Rev. Roger B. Lambert; stated clerk, Dr. Paul R. Gilchrist, 107 Hardy Rd., Lookout Mountain, TN 37350.

United Presbyterian Church in the U.S.A. (1958) — Mod., Rev. Robert M. Davidson; stated clerk, William P. Thompson, 475 Riverside Dr., N.Y., NY 10027.

Reformed Episcopal Church (1873) — Pres., Rev. Theophilos J. Herter; sec., Rev. D. Ellsworth Raudenbush, 560 Fountain St., Havre de Grace, MD 21078.

Reformed churches:

Christian Reformed Church in North America (1857) — Stated clerk, Rev. William P. Brink, 2850 Kalamazoo Ave., SE, Grand Rapids, MI 49560.

Reformed Church in America (1628) — Pres., Rev. Jack Hascup; gen. sec., Rev. Dr. Arie R. Brouwer, 475 Riverside Dr., N.Y., NY 10115.

Roman Catholic Church — National Conference of Catholic Bishops. Pres., Archbishop John R. Roach; sec., Bishop Thomas C. Kelly, O.P., 1312 Massachusetts Ave. NW, Wash., DC 20005.

The Salvation Army (1880) — Natl. cmdr., Ernest W. Holz; natl. chief sec., Col. G. Ernest Murray, 120-130 W. 14th St., N.Y., NY 10011.

Sikh (1972) — Chief adm., Siri Singh Sahib, Harbhajan Singh Khalsa Yogiji; sec. gen., Mukhia Sardarni Sahiba, Sardarni Premka Kaur Khalsa, 1649 S. Robertson Blvd., Los Angeles, CA 90035.

Unitarian Universalist Assn. (1961) — Pres., Rev. Dr. Eugene Pickett; sec., Lori Pederson, 25 Beacon St., Boston, MA 02108.

United Brethren in Christ (1789) — Chpsn., Bishop C. Ray Miller; 302 Lake St., Box 650, Huntington, IN 46750.

United Church of Christ (1957) — Pres., Rev. Avery D. Post; sec., Rev. Joseph H. Evans, 105 Madison Ave., N.Y., NY 10016.

Volunteers of America (1896) — Cmdr.-in-chief, Gen. Ray C Tremont; natl. field sec., Maj. John A. Hood, 3939 N. Causeway Blvd., Metairies LA 70002.

The Wesleyan Church (1968) — Gen. supts., Drs. J. Abbott, F McIntyre, V. Mitchell, O.D. Emery, sec., D. Wayne Brown, Bc 2000, Marion, IN 46952.

Headquarters of Religious Groups in Canada

(year organized in parentheses)

Anglican Church of Canada (creation of General Synod 1893) - Primate, Most Rev. E.W. Scott; 600 Jarvis St., Toronto, Ont. M4Y 2J6.

Apostolic Church in Canada - H.O. 27 Castlefield Ave., Toronto, Ont. M4R 1G3; Pres., Rev. D.S. Morris, 685 Park St. South, Peterborough, Ont. K9J 3S9.

Baha'is of Canada, The National Spiritual Assembly of the (1949) - Gen. Sec. J.D. Martin, 7200 Leslie St., Thornhill, Ont. L3T 2A1.

Baptist Federation of Canada - Pres., Jerry Zeman; Gen. Sec.-Treasurer, Rev. Michael Steeves, 217 Yonge St., Toronto, Ont. M5R 2M2.

Bible Holiness Movement, The (1949) - Pres., Evangelist Wesley H. Wakefield, Box 223, Stn. A, Vancouver, B.C. V6C 2M3.

Buddhist Churches of Canada (1945) - Administrative H.O., 220 Jackson Ave., Vancouver, B.C. V6A 3B3.

Canadian Council of Churches, The (1938) - Gen. Sec., Rev. Donald W. Anderson, 40 St. Clair Ave. E., Toronto, Ont. M4T 1M9.

Christian and Missionary Alliance in Canada, The (1889) - Pres., Rev. M.P. Sylvester, Box 7900, Stn. B, Willowdale, Ont. M2K 2R3.

Christian Church (Disciples of Christ) (All Canada Committee formed 1922) - 39 Arkell Rd., R.R. 2, Guelph, Ont. N1H 6H8.

Christian Science in Canada - Mr. J.D. Fulton, 339 Bloor St. W., Ste. 214, Toronto, Ont. M5S 1W7.

Church of Jesus Christ of Latter-Day Saints (Mormons) (1830) - Pres. Calgary Stake, R.H. Walker, 930 Prospect Ave. S.W., Calgary Alta. T2T 0W5; Pres. Edmonton Stake, Warren Wilde, 5108-112 St., Edmonton, Alta. T6H 3J2; Pres. Toronto Stake, James L. Kirschbaum, 5 Edenbrook Hill, Islington, Ont. M9A 3Z5; Pres. Vancouver Stake, R.W. Komm, 1348 Chartwell Dr., West Vancouver, B.C. V7S 2R5.

Church of the Nazarene (1902) - Dist. Superintendent of Canada Central District, Rev. Lorne MacMillan, 38 Riverhead Dr., Rexdale, Ont. M9W 4G6; Chairman of Exec. Board, Rev. Alexander Ardrey, 2236 Capitol Hill Cres. N.W., Calgary, Alta. T2M 4B9.

Fellowship of Evangelical Baptist Churches in Canada (1953) - Gen. Sec. Dr. Roy W. Lawson, 74 Sheppard Ave. W., Willowdale, Ont. M2N 1M3.

Free Methodist Church in Canada (1880) - Pres., Bishop D.N. Bastian, 96 Elmbrook Cres., Etobicoke, Ont. M9C 5E2; Exec. Sec., Rev. C.A. Horton, 833-D Upper James St., Hamilton, Ont. L9C 3A3.

Greek Orthodox Church in Canada - His Grace Bishop Sotirios, 27 Teddington Park Ave., Toronto, Ont. M4N 2C4.

Jehovah's Witnesses (Branch Office estab. in Winnipeg 1918) - Branch Coordinator, Mr. Kenneth A. Little, Box 4100, Georgetown, Ont. L7J 4Y4.

Jewish Congress, Canadian (1919) - Exec. Vice-Pres., Alan Rose, 1590 Avenue Docteur Penfield, Montreal, Que. H3G 1C5.

Lutheran Council in Canada (a joint body of **The Evangelical Lutheran Church of Canada, Lutheran Church-Canada,** and **Lutheran Church in America - Canada Section**) - Pres., Rev. Val Hennig; Exec. Dir. W.A. Schultz, 500-365 Hargrave St., Winnipeg, Man. R3B 2K3.

Mennonite Brethren Churches of North America, Canadian Conference (inc. 1945) - Mod. David Redekop, 101 Lamont Blvd., Winnipeg, Man. R3P 0E7.

Mennonites in Canada, Conference of (1903) - Chairman, Jack Fransen, Smithville, Ont. L0R 2A0.

Pentecostal Assemblies of Canada, The (inc. 1919) - Gen. Supt., Rev. Robert W. Taitinger, 10 Overlea Blvd., Toronto, Ont. M4H 1A5.

Presbyterian Church in Canada, The (1875) - Mod., Dr. A.F. MacSween, 50 Wynford Dr., Don Mills, Ont. M3C 1J7.

Religious Society of Friends (Quakers), (Canadian Yearly Meeting of the Religious Society of Friends formed 1955) - Presiding Clerk, Joan Benz, 60 Lowther Ave., Toronto, Ont. M5R 1C7.

Reorganized Church of Jesus Christ of Latter-Day Saints (Canada) (1830) - Ont. Regional Pres., Donald H. Comer; Bishop of Canada and Ont. Region, Kenneth G. Fisher, 390 Speedvale Ave. E., Guelph, Ont. N1E 1N5.

Roman Catholic Church in Canada - Canadian Conference of Catholic Bishops, 90 Parent Ave., Ottawa, Ont. K1N 7B1.

Salvation Army, The (1882) - Commissioner John D. Waldron, P.O. Box 4021, Postal Station A, Toronto, Ont. M5W 2B1.

Seventh-day Adventist Church in Canada - Pres., L.L. Reile; Sec., P.F. Lemon; 1148 King St. E., Oshawa, Ont. L1H 1H8.

Ukrainian Greek Orthodox Church in Canada - Primate, Metropolitan of Winnipeg and of all Canada, His Beatitude Metropolitan Andrew (Metiuk), 9 St. Johns Ave., Winnipeg, Man. R2W 0T9.

Union of Spiritual Communities of Christ (Orthodox Doukhobors in Canada) (1938) - Honorary Chmn. of the Exec. Comm., John J. Verigin, Box 760, Grand Forks, B.C. V0H 1B0.

Unitarian Council, Canadian (1961) - Pres., Brian Reid; Admin. Sec. Mrs. Thelma Peters, 175 St. Clair Ave. W., Toronto, Ont. M4V 1P7.

United Church of Canada, The (1925) - Mod. Rt. Rev. Lois Wilson; Sec. of General Council, Rev. Donald Ray, 85 St. Clair Ave. E., Toronto, Ont. M4T 1M8.

Episcopal Church Calendar and Liturgical Colors

White—from Christmas Day through the First Sunday after Epiphany; Maundy Thursday (as an alternative to crimson at the Eucharist); from the Vigil of Easter to the Day of Pentecost (Whitsunday); Trinity Sunday; Feasts of the Lord (except Holy Cross Day); the Confession of St. Peter; the Conversion of St. Paul; St. Joseph; St. Mary Magdalene; St. Mary the Virgin; St. Michael and All Angels; All Saint's Day; St. John the Evangelist; memorials of other saints who were not martyred; Independence Day and Thanksgiving Day; weddings and funerals. **Red**—the Day of Pentecost; Holy Cross Day; feasts of apostles and evangelists (except those listed above); feasts and memorials of martyrs (including Holy Innocents' Day). **Violet**—Advent and Lent. **Crimson** (dark red)—Holy Week. **Green**—the seasons after Epiphany and after Pentecost. **Black**—optional alternative for funerals. Alternative colors used in some churches: **Blue**—Advent; **Lenten White**—Ash Wednesday to Palm Sunday.

Days, etc.	1981		1982		1983		1984		1985		1986	
Golden Number	6		7		8		9		10		11	
Sunday Letter	D		C		B		AG		F		E	
Sundays after Epiphany	8		7		6		9		6		5	
Ash Wednesday	Mar.	4	Feb.	24	Feb.	16	Mar.	7	Feb.	20	Feb.	12
First Sunday in Lent	Mar.	8	Feb.	28	Feb.	20	Mar.	11	Feb.	24	Feb.	16
Passion/Palm Sunday	Apr.	12	Apr.	4	Mar.	27	Apr.	15	Mar.	31	Mar.	23
Good Friday	Apr.	17	Apr.	9	Apr.	1	Apr.	20	Apr.	5	Mar.	28
Easter Day	Apr.	19	Apr.	11	Apr.	3	Apr.	22	Apr.	7	Mar.	30
Ascension Day	May	28	May	20	May	12	May	31	May	16	May	8
The Day of Pentecost	June	7	May	30	May	22	June	10	May	26	May	18
Trinity Sunday	June	14	June	6	May	29	June	17	June	2	May	25
Numbered Proper of 2 Pentecost	#7		#6		#5		#7		#5		#4	
First Sunday of Advent	Nov.	29	Nov.	28	Nov.	27	Dec.	2	Dec.	1	Nov.	30

In the Episcopal Church the days of fasting are Ash Wednesday and Good Friday. Other days of special devotion (abstinence) are the 40 days of Lent and all Fridays of the year, except those in Christmas and Easter seasons and any Feasts of the Lord which occur on a Friday or during Lent. Ember Days (optional) are days of prayer for the Church's ministry. They fall on the Wednesday, Friday, and Saturday after the First Sunday in Lent, the Day of Pentecost, Holy Cross Day, and the Third Sunday of Advent. Rogation Days (also optional) are the three days before Ascension Day, and are days of prayer for God's blessing on the crops, on commerce and industry, and for the conservation of the earth's resources.

Ash Wednesday and Easter Sunday

Year	Ash Wed.	Easter Sunday	Year	Ash Wed.	Easter Sunday	Year	Ash Wed.	Easter Sunday	Year	Ash Wed.	Easter Sunday
1901	Feb. 20	Apr. 7	1951	Feb. 7	Mar. 25	2001	Feb. 28	Apr. 15	2051	Feb. 15	Apr. 2
1902	Feb. 12	Mar. 30	1952	Feb. 27	Apr. 13	2002	Feb. 13	Mar. 31	2052	Mar. 6	Apr. 21
1903	Feb. 25	Apr. 12	1953	Feb. 18	Apr. 5	2003	Mar. 5	Apr. 20	2053	Feb. 19	Apr. 6
1904	Feb. 17	Apr. 3	1954	Mar. 3	Apr. 18	2004	Feb. 25	Apr. 11	2054	Feb. 11	Mar. 29
1905	Mar. 8	Apr. 23	1955	Feb. 23	Apr. 10	2005	Feb. 9	Mar. 27	2055	Mar. 3	Apr. 18
1906	Feb. 28	Apr. 15	1956	Feb. 15	Apr. 1	2006	Mar. 1	Apr. 16	2056	Feb. 16	Apr. 2
1907	Feb. 13	Mar. 31	1957	Mar. 6	Apr. 21	2007	Feb. 21	Apr. 8	2057	Mar. 7	Apr. 22
1908	Mar. 4	Apr. 19	1958	Feb. 19	Apr. 6	2008	Feb. 6	Mar. 23	2058	Feb. 27	Apr. 14
1909	Feb. 24	Apr. 11	1959	Feb. 11	Mar. 29	2009	Feb. 25	Apr. 12	2059	Feb. 12	Mar. 30
1910	Feb. 9	Mar. 27	1960	Mar. 2	Apr. 17	2010	Feb. 17	Apr. 4	2060	Mar. 3	Apr. 18
1911	Mar. 1	Apr. 16	1961	Feb. 15	Apr. 2	2011	Mar. 9	Apr. 24	2061	Feb. 23	Apr. 10
1912	Feb. 21	Apr. 7	1962	Mar. 7	Apr. 22	2012	Feb. 22	Apr. 8	2062	Feb. 8	Mar. 26
1913	Feb. 5	Mar. 23	1963	Feb. 27	Apr. 14	2013	Feb. 13	Mar. 31	2063	Feb. 28	Apr. 15
1914	Feb. 25	Apr. 12	1964	Feb. 12	Mar. 29	2014	Mar. 5	Apr. 20	2064	Feb. 20	Apr. 6
1915	Feb. 17	Apr. 4	1965	Mar. 3	Apr. 18	2015	Feb. 18	Apr. 5	2065	Feb. 11	Mar. 29
1916	Mar. 8	Apr. 23	1966	Feb. 23	Apr. 10	2016	Feb. 10	Mar. 27	2066	Feb. 24	Apr. 11
1917	Feb. 21	Apr. 8	1967	Feb. 8	Mar. 26	2017	Mar. 1	Apr. 16	2067	Feb. 16	Apr. 3
1918	Feb. 13	Mar. 31	1968	Feb. 28	Apr. 14	2018	Feb. 14	Apr. 1	2068	Mar. 7	Apr. 22
1919	Mar. 5	Apr. 20	1969	Feb. 19	Apr. 6	2019	Mar. 6	Apr. 21	2069	Feb. 27	Apr. 14
1920	Feb. 18	Apr. 4	1970	Feb. 11	Mar. 29	2020	Feb. 26	Apr. 12	2070	Feb. 12	Mar. 30
1921	Feb. 9	Mar. 27	1971	Feb. 24	Apr. 11	2021	Feb. 17	Apr. 4	2071	Mar. 4	Apr. 19
1922	Mar. 1	Apr. 16	1972	Feb. 16	Apr. 2	2022	Mar. 2	Apr. 17	2072	Feb. 24	Apr. 10
1923	Feb. 14	Apr. 1	1973	Mar. 7	Apr. 22	2023	Feb. 22	Apr. 9	2073	Mar. 8	Apr. 26
1924	Mar. 5	Apr. 20	1974	Feb. 27	Apr. 14	2024	Feb. 14	Mar. 31	2074	Feb. 28	Apr. 15
1925	Feb. 25	Apr. 12	1975	Feb. 12	Mar. 30	2025	Mar. 5	Apr. 20	2075	Feb. 20	Apr. 7
1926	Feb. 17	Apr. 4	1976	Mar. 3	Apr. 18	2026	Feb. 18	Apr. 5	2076	Mar. 4	Apr. 19
1927	Mar. 2	Apr. 17	1977	Feb. 23	Apr. 10	2027	Feb. 10	Mar. 28	2077	Feb. 24	Apr. 11
1928	Feb. 22	Apr. 8	1978	Feb. 8	Mar. 26	2028	Mar. 1	Apr. 16	2078	Feb. 16	Apr. 3
1929	Feb. 13	Mar. 31	1979	Feb. 28	Apr. 15	2029	Feb. 14	Apr. 1	2079	Mar. 8	Apr. 23
1930	Mar. 5	Apr. 20	1980	Feb. 20	Apr. 6	2030	Mar. 6	Apr. 21	2080	Feb. 21	Apr. 7
1931	Feb. 18	Apr. 5	1981	Mar. 4	Apr. 19	2031	Feb. 26	Apr. 13	2081	Feb. 12	Mar. 30
1932	Feb. 10	Mar. 27	1982	Feb. 24	Apr. 11	2032	Feb. 11	Mar. 28	2082	Mar. 4	Apr. 19
1933	Mar. 1	Apr. 16	1983	Feb. 16	Apr. 3	2033	Mar. 2	Apr. 17	2083	Feb. 17	Apr. 4
1934	Feb. 14	Apr. 1	1984	Mar. 7	Apr. 22	2034	Feb. 22	Apr. 9	2084	Mar. 9	Apr. 26
1935	Mar. 6	Apr. 21	1985	Feb. 20	Apr. 7	2035	Feb. 7	Mar. 25	2085	Feb. 28	Apr. 15
1936	Feb. 26	Apr. 12	1986	Feb. 12	Mar. 30	2036	Feb. 27	Apr. 13	2086	Feb. 13	Mar. 31
1937	Feb. 10	Mar. 28	1987	Mar. 4	Apr. 19	2037	Feb. 18	Apr. 5	2087	Mar. 5	Apr. 20
1938	Mar. 2	Apr. 17	1988	Feb. 17	Apr. 3	2038	Mar. 10	Apr. 25	2088	Feb. 25	Apr. 11
1939	Feb. 22	Apr. 9	1989	Feb. 8	Mar. 26	2039	Feb. 23	Apr. 10	2089	Feb. 16	Apr. 3
1940	Feb. 7	Mar. 24	1990	Feb. 28	Apr. 15	2040	Feb. 15	Apr. 1	2090	Mar. 1	Apr. 16
1941	Feb. 26	Apr. 13	1991	Feb. 13	Mar. 31	2041	Mar. 6	Apr. 21	2091	Feb. 21	Apr. 8
1942	Feb. 18	Apr. 5	1992	Mar. 4	Apr. 19	2042	Feb. 19	Apr. 6	2092	Feb. 13	Mar. 30
1943	Mar. 10	Apr. 25	1993	Feb. 24	Apr. 11	2043	Mar. 11	Mar. 29	2093	Feb. 25	Apr. 12
1944	Feb. 23	Apr. 9	1994	Feb. 16	Apr. 3	2044	Mar. 2	Apr. 17	2094	Feb. 17	Apr. 4
1945	Feb. 14	Apr. 1	1995	Mar. 1	Apr. 16	2045	Feb. 22	Apr. 9	2095	Mar. 9	Apr. 24
1946	Mar. 6	Apr. 21	1996	Feb. 21	Apr. 7	2046	Feb. 7	Mar. 25	2096	Feb. 29	Apr. 15
1947	Feb. 19	Apr. 6	1997	Feb. 12	Mar. 30	2047	Feb. 27	Apr. 14	2097	Feb. 13	Mar. 31
1948	Feb. 11	Mar. 28	1998	Feb. 25	Apr. 12	2048	Feb. 19	Apr. 5	2098	Mar. 5	Apr. 20
1949	Mar. 2	Apr. 17	1999	Feb. 17	Apr. 4	2049	Mar. 3	Apr. 18	2099	Feb. 25	Apr. 12
1950	Feb. 22	Apr. 9	2000	Mar. 8	Apr. 23	2050	Feb. 23	Apr. 10	2100	Feb. 10	Mar. 28

A lengthy dispute over the date for the celebration of Easter was settled by the first Council of the Christian Churches at Nicaea, in Asia Minor, in 325 A.D. The Council ruled that Easter would be observed on the first Sunday following the 14th day of the Paschal Moon, referred to as the Paschal Full Moon. The Paschal Moon is the first moon whose 14th day comes on or after March 21. Dates of the Paschal Full Moon, which are not necessarily the same as those of the real or astronomical full moon, are listed in the table below with an explanation of how to compute the date of Easter.

If the Paschal Full Moon falls on a Sunday, then Easter is the following Sunday. The earliest date on which Easter can fall is March 22; it fell on that date in 1761 and 1818 but will not do so in the 20th or 21st century. The latest possible date for Easter is April 25; it fell on that date in 1943 and will again in 2038.

For western churches Lent begins on Ash Wednesday, which comes 40 days before Easter Sunday, not counting Sundays. Originally it was a period of but 40 hours. Later it comprised 30 days of fasting, omitting all the Sundays and also all the Saturdays except one. Pope Gregory (590-604) added Ash Wednesday to the fast, together with the remainder of that week.

The last seven days of Lent constitute Holy Week, beginning with Palm Sunday. The last Thursday — Maundy Thursday — commemorates the institution of the Eucharist. The following day, Good Friday, commemorates the day of the Crucifixion.

Easter is the chief festival of the Christian year, commemorating the Resurrection of Christ. It occurs about the same time as the ancient Roman celebration of the Vernal Equinox, the arrival of spring. In the second century, A.D., Easter Day among Christians in Asia Minor was the 14th Nisan, the seventh month of the Jewish calendar. The Christians in Europe observed the nearest Sunday.

Date of Paschal Full Moon, 1900-2199

The Golden Number, used in determining the date of Easter, is greater by unity (one) than the remainder obtained upon dividing the given year by 19. For example, when dividing 1982 by 19, one obtains a remainder of 6. Adding 1 gives 7 as the Golden Number for the year 1982. From the table then the date of the Paschal Full Moon is Apr. 8, 1982. Since this is a Thursday, Easter is celebrated on the next Sunday, Apr. 11.

Golden Number	Date	Golden Number	Date	Golden Number	Date	Golden Number	Date
1	Apr. 14	6	Apr. 18	11	Mar. 25	16	Mar. 25
2	Apr. 3	7	Apr. 8	12	Apr. 13	17	Apr. 17
3	Mar. 23	8	Mar. 28	13	Apr. 2	18	Apr. 7
4	Apr. 11	9	Apr. 16	14	Mar. 22	19	Mar. 27
5	Mar. 31	10	Apr. 5	15	Apr. 10		

Jewish Holy Days, Festivals, and Fasts

Source: Synagogue Council of America

Festivals and fasts	Hebrew date		5742 (1981-1982)		5743 (1982-1983)		5744 (1983-1984)		5745 (1984-1985)	
Rosh Hashana (New Year)[1]	Tishri	1	Sept. 29	Tu	Sept. 18	Sa	Sept. 8	Th	Sept. 27	Th
Fast of Gedalia	Tishri	3	Oct. 1	Th	Sept. 20	Mo	. . . .		. . . .	
Fast of Gedalia	Tishri	4	. . . .		. . . .		Sept. 11	Su	Sept. 30	Su
Yom Kippur (Day of Atonement)	Tishri	10	Oct. 8	Th	Sept. 27	Mo	Sept. 17	Sa	Oct. 6	Sa
Sukkoth (Feast of Tabernacles), 1st Day[1]	Tishri	15	Oct. 13	Tu	Oct. 2	Sa	Sept. 22	Th	Oct. 11	Th
Sukkoth, 8th Day of Assembly (Shemini Atzereth)	Tishri	22	Oct. 20	Tu	Oct. 9	Sa	Sept. 29	Th	Oct. 18	Th
Simchat Torah (Rejoicing of the Law)	Tishri	23	Oct. 21	We	Oct. 10	Su	Sept. 30	Fr	Oct. 19	Fr
Chanukah (Feast of Lights)	Kislev	25	Dec. 21	Mo	Dec. 11	Sa	Dec. 1	Th	Dec. 19	We
Fast of Tebet[2]	Tebet	10	Jan. 5	Tu	Dec. 26	Su	Dec. 16	Fr	Jan. 3	Th
Fast of Esther[2]	Adar	13	Mar. 8	Mo	Feb. 24	Th	. . . .		Mar. 6	We
Fast of Esther[2]	Adar II	13	. . . .		. . . .		Mar. 15	Th	. . . .	
Purim (Feast of Lots)	Adar	14	Mar. 9	Tu	Feb. 27	Su	. . . .		Mar. 7	Th
Purim	Adar II	14	. . . .		. . . .		Mar. 18	Su	. . . .	
Pesach (Passover), 1st Day[1]	Nisan	15	Apr. 8	Th	Mar. 29	Tu	Apr. 17	Tu	Apr. 6	Sa
Pesach, 7th Day[1]	Nisan	21	Apr. 14	We	Apr. 4	Mo	Apr. 23	Mo	Apr. 12	Fr
Lag B'Omer	Iyar	18	May 11	Tu	May 1	Su	May 20	Su	May 9	Th
Shavuoth (Feast of Weeks)[1]	Sivan	6	May 28	Fr	May 18	We	June 6	We	May 26	Su
Fast of Tammuz[2]	Tammuz	17	July 8	Th	June 28	Tu	July 17	Tu	July 7	Su
Tisha B'Av (Fast of Av)[2]	Av	9	July 29	Th	July 19	Tu	Aug. 7	Tu	July 28	Su

The months of the Jewish year are: 1) Tishri; 2) Cheshvan (also Marcheshvan); 3) Kislev; 4) Tebet (also Tebeth); 5) Shebat (also Shebhat); 6) Adar; 6a) Adar Sheni (II) added in leap years; 7) Nisan; 8) Iyar; 9) Sivan; 10) Tammuz; 11) Av (also Abh); 12) Elul. All Jewish holy days, etc., begin at sunset on the day previous. (1) Also observed the following day. (2) Hebrew date varies to avoid conflict with Sabbath.

Greek Orthodox Church Calendar, 1982

Date		Holy Days
Jan.	1	Circumcision of Jesus Christ; feast day of St. Basil
Jan.	6	Epiphany: Baptism of Jesus Christ - Sanctification of the Waters
Jan.	7	Feast day of St. John the Baptist
Jan.	30	Feast day of the Three Hierarchs: St. Basil the Great, St. Gregory the Theologian, and St. John Chrysostom
Feb.	2	Presentation of Jesus Christ in the Temple
*Mar.	1	Easter Lent begins
*Mar.	7	Sunday of Orthodoxy (1st Sun. of Lent)
Mar.	25	Annunciation of the Virgin Mary
*Apr.	11	Palm Sunday
*Apr.	12-17	Holy Week
*Apr.	16	Holy (Good) Friday: Burial of Jesus Christ
*Apr.	18	Easter Sunday: Resurrection of Jesus Christ
*Apr.	23	Feast day of St. George
May	21	Feast day of Sts. Constantine and Helen
*May	27	Ascension of Jesus Christ

Date		Holy Days
*June	5	Sunday of Pentecost
June	29	Feast day of Sts. Peter and Paul
June	30	Feast day of the Twelve Apostles of Jesus Christ
Aug.	6	Transfiguration of Jesus Christ
Aug.	15	Dormition of the Virgin Mary
Aug.	29	Beheading of St. John the Baptist
Sept.	1	Beginning of the Church Year
Sept.	14	Adoration of the Holy Cross
Oct.	23	Feast day of St. James
Oct.	26	Feast day of St. Demetrios the Martyr
Nov.	15	Christmas Lent begins
Nov.	21	Presentation of the Virgin Mary
Nov.	30	Feast day of St. Andrew the Apostle
Dec.	6	Feast day of St. Nicholas, Bishop of Myra
Dec.	25	Christmas Day: Nativity of Jesus Christ

*Movable holy days dependent upon the date of Easter. (The feast day of St. George is normally celebrated Apr. 23. If this day arrives during Lent, it is then celebrated the day after Easter.) The Greek Orthodox Church celebrates holy days in accordance with the Gregorian Calendar. Some Eastern Orthodox Churches still adhere to the Julian Calendar and observe the holy days (with the exception of the Easter cycle) 13 days later.

Islamic (Moslem) Calendar 1981-1982

The Islamic Calendar, often referred to as Mohammedan, is a lunar reckoning from the year of the *hegira*, 622 A.D., when Muhammed moved to Medina from Mecca. It runs in cycles of 30 years, of which the 2d, 5th, 7th, 10th, 13th, 16th, 18th, 21st, 24th, 26th, and 29th are leap years; 1402 and 1403 are the 22nd and 23rd years, respectively, of the cycle. Common years have 354 days, leap years 355, the extra day being added to the last month, Zu'lhijjah. Except for this case, the 12 months beginning with Muharram have alternately 30 and 29 days.[1]

Year	Name of month	Month begins	Year	Name of Month	Month begins
1402	Muharram (New Year)	Oct. 30, 1981	1403	Muharram (New Year)	Oct. 19, 1982
1402	Safar	Nov. 30, 1981	1403	Safar	Nov. 16, 1982
1402	Rabia I	Dec. 29, 1981	1403	Rabia I	Dec. 15, 1982
1402	Rabia II	Jan. 28, 1982	1403	Rabia II	Jan. 12, 1982
1402	Jumada I	Feb. 26, 1982	1403	Jumada I	Feb. 10, 1982
1402	Jumada II	Mar. 28, 1982	1403	Jumada II	Mar. 10, 1982
1402	Rajab	Apr. 26, 1982	1403	Rajab	Apr. 9, 1982
1402	Shaban	May 26, 1982	1403	Shaban	May 8, 1982
1402	Ramadan	June 24, 1982	1403	Ramadan	June 7, 1982
1402	Shawwai	July 24, 1982	1403	Shawwai	July 7, 1982
1402	Zu'lkadah	Aug. 22, 1982	1403	Zu'lkadah	Aug. 7, 1982
402	Zu'lhijjah	Sept. 21, 1982	1403	Zu'lhijjah	Sept. 6, 1982

1) The date on which Ramadan begins may vary from the calendar date. It actually starts only after the new moon is lighted from the Naval Observatory in Cairo.

Major Christian Denominations:
Italics indicate that area which, generally speaking, most

Denomination	Origins	Organization	Authority	Special rites
Baptists	In radical Reformation objections to infant baptism, demands for church-state separation; John Smyth, English Separatist in 1609; Roger Williams, 1638, Providence, R.I.	Congregational, *i.e.*, each local church is autonomous.	Scripture; some Baptists, particularly in the South, interpret the Bible literally.	Baptism, after about age 12, by total immersion; Lord's Supper.
Church of Christ (Disciples)	Among evangelical Presbyterians in Ky. (1804) and Penn. (1809), in distress over Protestant factionalism and decline of fervor. Organized 1832.	Congregational.	*"Where the Scriptures speak, we speak; where the Scriptures are silent, we are silent."*	Adult baptism, Lord's Supper (weekly).
Episcopalians	Henry VIII separated English Catholic Church from Rome, 1534, for political reasons. Protestant Episcopal Church in U.S. founded 1789.	*Bishops, in apostolic succession, are elected by diocesan representatives; part of Anglican Communion, symbolically headed by Archbishop of Canterbury.*	Scripture as interpreted by tradition, esp. 39 Articles (1563); not dogmatic. Tri-annual convention of bishops, priests, and laymen.	Infant baptism, Holy Communion, others. Sacrament is symbolic, but has real spiritual effect.
Lutherans	Martin Luther in Wittenberg, Germany, 1517, objected to Catholic doctrine of salvation by merit and sale of indulgences; break complete by 1519.	Varies from congregational to episcopal; in U.S. a combination of regional synods and congregational polities is most common.	*Scripture, and tradition as spelled out in Augsburg Confession (1530) and other creeds. These confessions of faith are binding although interpretations vary.*	Infant baptism, Lord's Supper. Bread and wine in Supper is less than the actual body and blood of Christ, but more than simply symbolic.
Methodists	Rev. John Wesley began movement, 1738, to infuse pietist enthusiasm into Church of England formalism. First U.S. conference, 1773.	*Bishops (not a priestly order, only an office) are elected for life, appoint district superintendents and local ministers.*	Scripture as interpreted by tradition, reason, and personal insight.	Infant baptism, Lord's Supper.
Mormons	In visions of the Angel Moroni by Joseph Smith, 1827, in New York, in which he received a new revelation on golden tablets: *The Book of Mormon.*	Theocratic; all male adults are in priesthood which culminates in Council of 12 Apostles and 1st Presidency (1st President, 2 counselors).	*The Bible, Book of Mormon and other revelations to Smith, and certain pronouncements of the 1st Presidency.*	Adult baptism, laying on of hands (which grants gifts of the Spirit), Lord's Supper. Temple rites: baptism for the dead, marriage for eternity, others.
Orthodox	Original Christian proselytizing in 1st century; broke with Rome, 1054, after centuries of doctrinal disputes and diverging traditions.	Synods of bishops in autonomous, usually national, churches elect a patriarch, archbishop or metropolitan. These men, as a group, are the heads of the church.	Scripture, tradition, and the first 7 church councils up to Nicaea II in 787. Bishops in council have authority in doctrine and policy.	Seven sacraments: infant baptism and anointing, Eucharist (both bread and wine), ordination, penance, anointing of the sick, marriage.
Pentecostal	In Topeka, Kansas (1901), and Los Angeles (1906) in reaction to loss of evangelical fervor among Methodists and other denominations.	Originally a movement, not a formal organization, Pentecostalism now has a variety of organized forms and continues also as a movement.	Scripture, individual charismatic leaders, the teachings of the Holy Spirit.	*Spirit baptism, esp. as shown in "speaking in tongues"; healing and sometimes exorcism; adult baptism, Lord's Supper.*
Presbyterians	In Calvinist Reformation in 1500s; differed with Lutherans over sacraments, church government. John Knox founded Scotch Presbyterian church about 1560.	*Highly structured representational system of ministers and laypersons (presbyters) in local, regional and national bodies. (synods).*	Scripture.	Infant baptism, Lord's Supper; bread and wine symbolize Christ's spiritual presence.
Roman Catholics	Traditionally, by Jesus who named St. Peter the 1st Vicar; historically, in early Christian proselytizing and the conversion of imperial Rome in the 4th century.	Hierarchy with supreme power vested in Pope elected by cardinals. Councils of Bishops advise on matters of doctrine and policy.	*The Pope, when speaking for the whole church in matters of faith and morals, and tradition, which is partly recorded in scripture and expressed in church councils.*	Seven sacraments: baptism, contrition and penance, confirmation, Eucharist, marriage, ordination, and anointing of the sick (unction).
United Church of Christ	*By ecumenical union, 1957, of Congregationalists and Evangelical & Reformed, representing both Calvinist and Lutheran traditions.*	Congregational; a General Synod, representative of all congregations, sets general policy.	Scripture.	Infant baptism, Lord's Supper.

How Do They Differ?

distinguishes that denomination from any other.

Practice	Ethics	Doctrine	Other	Denomination
Worship style varies from staid to evangelistic. Extensive missionary activity.	Usually opposed to alcohol and tobacco; sometimes tends toward a perfectionist ethical standard.	*No creed; true church is of believers only, who are all equal.*	Since no authority can stand between the believer and God, the Baptists are strong supporters of church-state separation.	Baptists
Tries to avoid any rite or doctrine not explicitly part of the 1st century church. Some congregations may reject instrumental music.	Some tendency toward perfectionism; increasing interest in social action programs.	Simple New Testament faith; avoids any elaboration not firmly based on Scripture.	Highly tolerant in doctrinal and religious matters; strongly supportive of scholarly education.	Church of Christ (Disciples)
Formal, based on *Book of Common Prayer* (1549); services range from austerely simple to highly elaborate.	Tolerant; sometimes permissive; some social action programs.	*Apostles' Creed* is basic; otherwise, considerable variation ranges from rationalist and liberal to acceptance of most Roman Catholic dogma.	Strongly ecumenical, holding talks with all other branches of Christendom.	Episcopalians
Relatively simple formal liturgy with emphasis on the sermon.	Generally, conservative in personal and social ethics; doctrine of "2 kingdoms" (worldly and holy) supports conservatism in secular affairs.	Salvation by faith alone through grace. Lutheranism has made major contributions to Protestant theology.	Though still somewhat divided along ethnic lines (German, Swede, etc.), main divisions are between funamentalists and liberals.	Lutherans
Worship style varies; usually staid, sometimes evangelistic.	Originally pietist and perfectionist with a tendency to withdraw from secular affairs; now with strong social activist elements.	No distinctive theological development; *25 Articles,* abridged from Church of England's 39, not binding.	In 1968, the United Methodist Church was formed by the union of the major Methodist church and the 1946 union of Evangelical and United Brethren churches.	Methodists
Staid service with hymns, sermon. Secret temple ceremonies may be more elaborate. Strong missionary activity.	Temperance; strict tithing. Combine a strong work ethic with communal self-reliance.	God is a material being; he created the universe out of pre-existing matter; all persons can be saved and many will become divine. Most other beliefs are traditionally Christian.	Mormons regard mainline churches as apostate, corrupt. Reorganized Church (founded 1852) rejects most Mormon doctrine and practice except Book of Mormon.	Mormons
Elaborate liturgy, usually in the vernacular, though extremely traditional. The liturgy is the essence of Orthodoxy. Veneration of icons.	Tolerant; very little social action; divorce, remarriage permitted in some cases. Priests need not be celibate; bishops are.	Emphasis on Christ's resurrection, rather than crucifixion; the Holy Spirit proceeds from God the Father only.	Orthodox Church in America, originally under Patriarch of Moscow, was granted autonomy in 1970. Greek Orthodox do not recognize this autonomy.	Orthodox
Loosely structured service with rousing hymns and sermons, culminating in spirit baptism.	Usually, emphasis on perfectionism with varying degrees of tolerance.	Simple traditional beliefs, usually Protestant, with emphasis on the immediate presence of God in the Holy Spirit	Once confined to lower-class "holy rollers," Pentecostalism now appears in mainline churches and has established middle-class congregations.	Pentecostal
A simple, sober service in which the sermon is central.	Traditionally, a tendency toward strictness with firm church- and self-discipline; otherwise tolerant.	Emphasizes the sovereignty and justice of God; no longer doctrinaire.	While traces of belief in predestination (that God has foreordinated salvation for the "elect") remain, this idea is no longer a central element in Presbyterianism.	Presbyterians
Relatively elaborate ritual; wide variety of public and private rites, eg., rosary recitation, processions, novenas.	Theoretically very strict; tolerant in practice on most issues. Divorce and remarriage not accepted. Celibate clergy, except in Eastern rite.	Highly elaborated. Salvation by merit gained through faith. Unusual development of doctrines surrounding Mary. Dogmatic.	Roman Catholicism is presently in a period of relatively rapid change as a result of Vatican Councils I and II.	Roman Catholics
Usually simple services with emphasis on the sermon.	Tolerant; some social action emphasis.	Standard Protestant; *Statement of Faith* (1959) is not binding.	The 2 main churches in the 1957 union represented earlier unions with small groups of almost every Protestant denomination.	United Church of Christ

The Major World Religions

Buddhism

Founded: About 525 BC, reportedly near Benares, India.

Founder: Gautama Siddhartha (ca. 563-480), the Buddha, who achieved enlightenment through intense meditation.

Sacred Texts: The *Tripitaka*, a collection of the Buddha's teachings, rules of monastic life, and philosophical commentaries on the teachings; also a vast body of Buddhist teachings and commentaries, many of which are called *sutras.*

Organization: The basic institution is the *sangha* or monastic order through which the traditions are passed to each generation. Monastic life tends to be democratic and anti-authoritarian. Large lay organizations have developed in some sects.

Practice: Varies widely according to the sect and ranges from austere meditation to magical chanting and elaborate temple rites. Many practices, such as exorcism of devils, reflect pre-Buddhist beliefs.

Divisions: A wide variety of sects grouped into 3 primary branches: Therevada (sole survivor of the ancient Hinayana schools) which emphasizes the importance of pure thought and deed; Mahayana, which includes Zen and Soka-gakkai, ranges from philosophical schools to belief in the saving grace of higher beings or ritual practices, and to practical meditative disciplines; and Tantrism, an unusual combination of belief in ritual magic and sophisticated philosophy.

Location: Throughout Asia, from Ceylon to Japan. Zen and Soka-gakkai have several thousand adherents in the U.S.

Beliefs: Life is misery and decay, and there is no ultimate reality in it or behind it. The cycle of endless birth and rebirth continues because of desire and attachment to the unreal "self". Right meditation and deeds will end the cycle and achieve Nirvana, the Void, nothingness.

Hinduism

Founded: Ca. 1500 BC by Aryan invaders of India where their Vedic religion intermixed with the practices and beliefs of the natives.

Sacred texts: The *Veda,* including the *Upanishads,* a collection of rituals and mythological and philosophical commentaries; a vast number of epic stories about gods, heroes and saints, including the *Bhagavadgita,* a part of the *Mahabharata,* and the *Ramayana;* and a great variety of other literature.

Organization: None, strictly speaking. Generally, rituals should be performed or assisted by Brahmins, the priestly caste, but in practice simpler rituals can be performed by anyone. Brahmins are the final judges of ritual purity, the vital element in Hindu life. Temples and religious organizations are usually presided over by Brahmins.

Practice: A variety of private rituals, primarily passage rites (eg. initiation, marriage, death, etc.) and daily devotions, and a similar variety of public rites in temples. Of the latter, the *puja,* a ceremonial dinner for a god, is the most common.

Divisions: There is no concept of orthodoxy in Hinduism, which presents a bewildering variety of sects, most of them devoted to the worship of one of the many gods. The 3 major living traditions are those devoted to the gods Vishnu and Shiva and to the goddess Shakti; each of them divided into further sub-sects. Numerous folk beliefs and practices, often in amalgamation with the above groups, exist side-by-side with sophisticated philosophical schools and exotic cults.

Location: Confined to India, except for the missionary work of Vedanta, the Krishna Consciousness society, and individual *gurus* (teachers) in the West.

Beliefs: There is only one divine principle; the many gods are only aspects of that unity. Life in all its forms is an aspect of the divine, but it appears as a separation from the divine, a meaningless cycle of birth and rebirth (*samsara*) determined by the purity or impurity of past deeds (*karma*). To improve one's *karma* or escape *samsara* by pure acts, thought, and/or devotion is the aim of every Hindu.

Islam (submission)

Founded: 622 AD in Medina, Arabian peninsula.

Founder: Mohammed (ca. 570-632), the Prophet, as a result of visions.

Sacred texts: *Koran,* the words of God, delivered to Mohammed by the angel Gabriel; *Hadith,* collections of the sayings of the Prophet.

Organization: Theoretically the state and religious community are one, administered by a caliph. In practice, Islam is a loose collection of congregations united by a very conservative tradition. Islam is basically egalitarian and non-authoritarian.

Practice: Every Moslem is supposed to make the profession of faith ("There is no god but Allah . . ."), pray 5 times a day, give a regular portion of his goods to charity, fast during the day in the month of Ramadan, and make at least one pilgrimage to Mecca if possible. Additionally saints' days are celebrated and pilgrimages made to shrines.

Divisions: The 2 major sects of Islam are the Sunni (orthodox) and the Shi'ah. The Shi'ah believe in 12 *imams,* perfect teachers, who still guide the faithful from Paradise. Shi'ah practice tends toward the ecstatic, while the Sunni is staid and simple. The Shi'ah sect affirms man's free will; the Sunni is deterministic. The mystic tradition in Islam is Sufism. A Sufi adept believes he has acquired a special inner knowledge direct from Allah.

Location: From the west coast of Africa to the Philipines across a broad band that includes Tanzania, southern USSR and western China, India, Malaysia and Indonesia. Islam has perhaps 100,000 adherents among American blacks.

Beliefs: Strictly monotheistic. God is creator of the universe, omnipotent, just, and merciful. Man is God's highest creation, but limited and sinful. He is misled by Satan, a prideful angel. God gave the *Koran* to Mohammed to guide men to the truth. Those who repent and sincerely submit to God return to a state of sinlessness. In the end, the sinless go to Paradise, a place of physical and spiritual pleasure, and the wicked burn in Hell.

Judaism

Founded: About 1300 BC, reportedly at Mt. Sinai.

Founder: Moses, probably an historical person.

Sacred Texts: Torah, or divine teaching, found particularly in the first 5 books of the Bible; Talmud and Midrash, commentaries on Torah.

Organization: Originally theocratic, Judaism has evolved a congregational polity. The basic institution is the local synagogue, operated by the congregation and led by a rabbi of their choice. Chief Rabbis in France and Great Britain have authority only over those who accept it; in Israel, the 2 Chief Rabbis have civil authority in family law.

Practice: Among the very conservative, prayers accompany almost every action of daily life. Synagogue services center around the Torah reading. The chief annual observances are Passover, celebrating the liberation of the Israelites from Egypt and marked by the ritual Seder meal in the home, and the 10 days from Rosh Hashana (New Year) to Yom Kippur (Day of Atonement), a period of fasting and penitence.

Divisions: Judaism is an unbroken spectrum from ultra-conservative to ultra-liberal. Distinctions depend primarily on the care taken to observe the many prescribed duties and prohibitions in daily life, particularly the dietary and Sabbath regulations, and whether these are seen as binding or optional. The amount of Hebrew used in services distinguishes groups on the liberal end of the spectrum. Hasidism is a pietistic movement which emphasizes joyful devotion and the charismatic power of individual Hasidic leaders.

Location: Almost world-wide, with concentrations in Israel and the U.S.

Beliefs: Strictly monotheistic. God is the creator and absolute ruler of the universe. Men are free to choose to rebel against God's rule. God established a particular relationship with the Hebrew people: by obeying the divine law God gave them they would be a special witness to God's mercy and justice. The emphasis in Judaism is on ethical behavior (and, among the conservative, careful ritual obedience) as the true worship of God.

Roman Catholic Hierarchy

Source: Apostolic Delegation, Washington, D.C.

Supreme Pontiff

At the head of the Roman Catholic Church is the Supreme Pontiff, Pope John Paul II, Karol Wojtyla, born at Wadowice (Krakow), Poland, May 18, 1920; ordained priest Nov. 1, 1946; promoted to Archbishop of Krakow Jan. 13, 1964; proclaimed Cardinal June 26, 1967; elected pope as successor of Pope John Paul I Oct. 16, 1978; solemn commencement as pope Oct. 22, 1978.

Cardinals

Name	Office	Nationality	Born	Named
Alfrink, Bernard		Dutch	1900	1960
Antonelli, Ferdinando		Italian	1896	1973
Aponte Martinez, Luis	Archbishop of San Juan in Puerto Rico	American	1922	1973
Aramburu, Juan	Archbishop of Buenos Aires	Argentinian	1912	1976
Arns, Paulo	Archbishop of Sao Paulo	Brazilian	1921	1973
Bafile, Corrado		Italian	1903	1976
Baggio, Sebastiano	Prefect of the Sacred Congregation for the Bishops	Italian	1913	1969
Ballestrero, Anastasio A.	Archbishop of Turin	Italian	1913	1979
Baum, William	Prefect of the Sacred Congregation for Catholic Education	American	1926	1976
Benelli, Giovanni	Archbishop of Florence	Italian	1921	1977
Beras Rojas, Octavio	Archbishop of Santo Domingo	San Domingan	1906	1976
Bertoli, Paolo	Chamberlain of the Holy Roman Church	Italian	1908	1969
Brandao Vilela, Avelar	Archbishop of Sao Salvador da Bahia	Brazilian	1912	1973
Bueno y Monreal, Jose M.	Archbishop of Seville	Spanish	1904	1958
Caprio, Giuseppe	President of Administration of Patrimony of the Holy See	Italian	1914	1979
Carberry, John		American	1904	1969
Carpino, Francesco		Italian	1905	1967
Carter, Gerald E.	Archbishop of Toronto	Canadian	1912	1979
Casariego, Mario	Archbishop of Guatemala	Guatemalan	1909	1969
Casaroli, Agostino	Secretary of State of His Holiness	Italian	1914	1979
Cè, Marco	Patriarch of Venice	Italian	1925	1979
Ciappi, O.P., Mario Luigi	Pro-Theologian of Pontifical Household	Italian	1909	1977
Civardi, Ernesto		Italian	1906	1979
Cody, John P.	Archbishop of Chicago	American	1907	1967
Colombo, Giovanni		Italian	1902	1965
Confalonieri, Carlo	Dean of the Sacred College	Italian	1893	1958
Cooke, Terence	Archbishop of New York	American	1921	1969
Cooray, Thomas B.		Ceylonese	1901	1965
Cordeiro, Joseph	Archbishop of Karachi	Pakistanian	1918	1973
Corripio Ahumada, Ernesto	Archbishop of Mexico City	Mexican	1919	1979
Darmojuwono, Justinus	Archbishop of Semarang	Indonesian	1914	1967
de Araujo Sales, Eugenio	Archbishop of St. Sebastian of Rio de Janeiro	Brazilian	1920	1969
Dearden, John		American	1907	1969
de Furstenberg, Maximilian		Belgian	1904	1967
Duval, Leon-Etienne	Archbishop of Algiers	Algerian	1903	1965
Ekandem, Dominic	Bishop of Ikot Ekpene	Nigerian	1917	1976
Enrique y Tarancon, Vicente	Archbishop of Madrid	Spanish	1907	1969
Etchegaray, Roger	Archbishop of Marseilles	French	1922	1979
Felici, Pericle	President of Pontifical Commission for the Revision of Code of Canon Law, Prefect of Supreme Tribunal of Apostolic Signatura	Italian	1911	1967
Flahiff, George	Archbishop of Winnipeg	Canadian	1905	1969
Florit, Ermenegildo		Italian	1901	1965
Freeman, James	Archbishop of Sydney	Australian	1907	1973
Gantin, Bernardin	President, Pontifical Commission "Justitia et Pax"	Benin	1922	1977
Garrone, Gabriel-Marie		French	1901	1967
Gonzalez Martin, Marcelo	Archbishop of Toledo	Spanish	1918	1973
Gouyon, Paul	Archbishop of Rennes	French	1910	1969
Gray, Gordon	Archbishop of St. Andrews and Edinburgh	Scottish	1910	1969
Guerri, Sergio	Pro-President of the Pontifical Comm. for Vatican City State	Italian	1905	1969
Guyot, Jean		French	1905	1973
Hoffner, Joseph	Archbishop of Cologne	German	1906	1969
Hume, George Basil	Archbishop of Westminster	English	1923	1976
Jubany Arnau, Narciso	Archbishop of Barcelona	Spanish	1913	1973
Kim, Stephan Sou Hwan	Archbishop of Seoul	Korean	1922	1969
Knox, James	Prefect of the Sacred Congregation of the Sacraments and of Divine Worship	Australian	1914	1973
König, Franz	Archbishop of Vienna	Austrian	1905	1958
Krol, John	Archbishop of Philadelphia	American	1910	1967
Landazuri, Ricketts Juan	Archbishop of Lima	Peruvian	1913	1962
Léger, Paul		Canadian	1904	1953
Lékai, Laszlo	Archbishop of Esztergom	Hungarian	1910	1976
Lorscheider, Aloisio	Archbishop of Fortaleza	Brazilian	1924	1976

Name	Office	Nationality	Born	Named
Macharski, Franciszek	Archbishop of Cracow	Polish	1927	1979
Malula, Joseph	Archbishop of Kinshasa	Congolese	1917	1969
Manning, Timothy	Archbishop of Los Angeles	American	1909	1973
Marella, Paolo		Italian	1895	1959
Marty, Francois		French	1904	1969
Maurer, Jose	Archbishop of Sucre	Bolivian	1900	1967
McCann, Owen	Archbishop of Cape Town	S. African	1907	1965
Medeiros, Humberto	Archbishop of Boston	American	1915	1973
Miranda y Gomez, Miguel		Mexican	1895	1969
Motta, Carlos Carmelo de Vasconcellos	Archbishop of Aparecida	Brazilian	1890	1946
Mozzoni, Umberto		Italian	1904	1973
Munoz Duque, Anibal	Archbishop of Bogota	Colombian	1908	1973
Munoz Vega, Paolo	Archbishop of Quito	Ecuadorian	1903	1969
Nasalli Rocca di Corneliano, Mario		Italian	1903	1969
Nsubuga, Emmanuel	Archbishop of Kampala	Ugandan	1914	1976
O'Boyle, Patrick		American	1896	1967
Oddi, Silvio	Prefect of Sacred Congregation for the Clergy	Italian	1910	1969
O'Fiaich, Tomás	Archbishop of Armagh, Primate of all Ireland	Irish	1923	1979
Otunga, Maurice	Archbishop of Nairobi	Kenyan	1923	1973
Palazzini, Pietro	Prefect of the Sacred Congregation for the Causes of Saints	Italian	1912	1973
Pappalardo, Salvatore	Archbishop of Palermo	Italian	1918	1973
Parecattil, Joseph	Archbishop of Ernakulam	Indian	1912	1969
Parente, Pietro		Italian	1891	1967
Paupini, Giuseppe	Grand Penitentiary	Italian	1907	1969
Pellegrino, Michele		Italian	1903	1967
Philippe, Paul		French	1905	1973
Picachy, Lawrence	Archbishop of Calcutta	Indian	1916	1976
Pironio, Eduardo	Prefect of the Sacred Congregation for Religious and for Secular Institutes	Argentinian	1920	1976
Poletti, Ugo	Vicar General of His Holiness for the City of Rome	Italian	1914	1973
Poma, Antonio	Archbishop of Bologna	Italian	1910	1969
Primatesta, Raul Francisco	Archbishop of Cordoba	Argentinian	1919	1973
Quintero, Jose	Archbishop of Caracas	Venezuelan	1902	1961
Ratzinger, Joseph	Archbishop of Munich and Freising	German	1927	1977
Razafimahatratra, Victor	Archbishop of Tananarive	Madagascan	1921	1976
Renard, Alexandre	Archbishop of Lyon	French	1906	1967
Ribeiro, Antonio	Patriarch of Lisbon	Portuguese	1928	1973
Righi-Lambertini, Egano		Italian	1906	1979
Rosales, Julio	Archbishop of Cebu	Filipino	1906	1969
Rossi, Agnelo	Prefect of the Sacred Congregation for the Evangelization of Peoples	Brazilian	1913	1965
Rossi, Opilio	President of the Council for the Laity and the Committee for the Family	Italian	1910	1976
Roy, Maurice	Archbishop of Quebec	Canadian	1905	1965
Rubin, Wladyslaw	Prefect of the Sacred Congregation for the Oriental Churches	Polish	1917	1979
Rugambwa, Laurean	Archbishop of Dar-es-Salaam	Tanzanian	1912	1960
Salazar Lopez, Jose	Archbishop of Guadalajara	Mexican	1910	1973
Samore, Antonio	Librarian and Archivist of the Holy Roman Church	Italian	1905	1967
Satowaki, Joseph A.	Archbishop of Nagasaki	Japanese	1904	1979
Scherer, Alfred	Archbishop of Porto Alegre	Brazilian	1903	1969
Schroeffer, Joseph		German	1903	1976
Sensi, Giuseppe		Italian	1907	1976
Seper, Franjo	Prefect of Sacred Congregation for the Doctrine of the Faith	Yugoslav	1905	1965
Shehan, Lawrence		American	1898	1965
Sidarouss, Stephanos	Coptic Patriarch of Alexandria	Egyptian	1904	1965
Silva Henriquez, Raul	Archbishop of Santiago	Chilean	1907	1962
Sin, Jaime	Archbishop of Manila	Filipino	1928	1976
Siri, Giuseppe	Archbishop of Genoa	Italian	1906	1953
Slipyj, Josyf	Ukrainian Archbishop of Lwow	Ukrainian	1892	1965
Suenens, Leo		Belgian	1904	1962
Taofinu'u, Pio	Bishop of Samoa and Tokelau	Samoan	1923	1973
Thiandoum, Hyacinthe	Archbishop of Dakar	Senegalese	1921	1976
Tomasek, Frantisek	Archbishop of Prague	Czechoslovakian	1899	1977
Trinh Van Can, Joseph-Marie	Archbishop of Hanoi	Vietnamese	1921	1979
Ursi, Corrado	Archbishop of Naples	Italian	1908	1967
Volk, Hermann	Bishop of Mainz	German	1903	1973
Willebrands, John	President of Secretariat for the Union of Christians Archbishop of Utrecht	Dutch	1909	1969
Wyszynski, Stefan	Archbishop of Gniezno-Warsaw	Polish	1901	1953
Zoungrana, Paul	Archbishop of Ouagadougou	Upper Voltan	1917	1965

NOTED PERSONALITIES

Widely Known Americans of the Present

Statesmen, authors, military men, and other prominent persons not listed in other categories.

Name (Birthplace)	Birthdate	Name (Birthplace)	Birthdate
Abel, I. W. (Magnolia, Oh.)	8/11/08	Dole, Robert (Russell, Kan.)	7/22/23
Abernathy, Ralph (Linden, Ala.)	3/11/26	Doolittle, James H. (Alameda, Cal.)	12/14/96
Abzug, Bella (New York, N.Y.)	7/24/20	Dubinsky, David (Brest-Litovsk, Poland)	2/22/92
Agnew, Spiro (Baltimore, Md.)	11/9/18		
Albert, Carl (McAlester, Okla.)	5/10/08	Eagleton, Thomas (St. Louis, Mo.)	9/4/29
Aldrin, Edwin E. Jr. "Buzz" (Glen Ridge, N.J.)	1/20/30	Eastland, James O. (Doddsville, Miss.)	11/28/04
Alsop, Joseph W. Jr. (Avon, Conn.)	10/11/10	Ehrlichman, John (Tacoma, Wash.)	3/20/25
Anderson, Jack (Long Beach, Cal.)	10/19/22	Eisenhower, Milton S. (Abilene, Kan.)	9/15/99
Anderson, John B. (Rockford, Ill.)	2/15/22	Eizenstat, Stuart E. (Chicago, Ill.)	1943
Andrus, Cecil (Hood River, Ore.)	8/25/31	Ervin, Sam (Morganton, N.C.)	9/27/96
Armstrong, Neil (Wapakoneta, Oh.)	8/5/30		
Askew, Reubin (Muskogee, Okla.)	9/11/28	Falwell, Jerry (Lynchburg, Va.)	8/11/33
		Farmer, James (Marshall, Tex.)	1/12/20
Bailey, F. Lee (Waltham, Mass.)	6/10/33	Fischer, Bobby (Chicago, Ill.)	3/9/43
Baker, Howard (Huntsville, Tenn.)	11/15/25	Fitzsimmons, Frank (Jeannette, Pa.)	4/7/08
Baker, James A. (Houston, Tex.)	4/28/30	Flynt, Larry (Salyersville, Ky.)	11/1/42
Baker, Russell (Loudoun Co., Va.)	8/14/25	Fong, Hiram (Honolulu, Ha.)	10/1/07
Ball, George (Des Moines, Ia.)	12/21/09	Ford, Elizabeth (Mrs. Gerald) (Chicago, Ill.)	4/8/18
Bayh, Birch (Terre Haute, Ind.)	1/22/28	Ford, Gerald R. (Omaha, Neb.)	7/14/13
Bell, Griffin (Americus, Ga.)	10/31/18	Fraser, Douglas A. (Glasgow, Scotland)	12/18/16
Belli, Melvin (Sonora, Cal.)	7/29/07	Friedan, Betty (Peoria, Ill.)	2/4/21
Bentsen, Lloyd (Mission, Tex.)	2/11/21	Friedman, Milton (Brooklyn, N.Y.)	7/31/12
Blackmun, Harry (Nashville, Ill.)	11/12/08	Fulbright, J. William (Sumner, Mo.)	4/9/05
Bok, Derek (Ardmore, Pa.)	3/22/30		
Bombeck, Erma (Dauton, Oh.)	2/21/27	Galbraith, John Kenneth (Ontario, Can.)	10/15/08
Bond, Julian (Nashville, Tenn.)	1/14/40	Gardner, John (Los Angeles, Cal.)	10/8/12
Borman, Frank (Gary, Ind.)	3/14/28	Ginsberg, Allen (Paterson, N.J.)	6/3/21
Bowles, Chester (Springfield, Mass.)	4/5/01	Glenn, John (Cambridge, Oh.)	7/18/21
Bradley, Thomas (Calvert, Tex.)	12/29/17	Goheen, Robert F. (Vengurla, India)	8/15/19
Brady, James (Centralia, Ill.)	8/29/40	Goldberg, Arthur J. (Chicago, Ill.)	8/8/08
Brennan, William J. (Newark, N.J.)	4/25/06	Goldwater, Barry M. (Phoenix, Ariz.)	1/1/09
Breslin, Jimmy (Jamaica, N.Y.)	10/17/30	Graham, Billy (Charlotte, N.C.)	11/7/18
Brewster, Kingman (Longmeadow, Mass.)	6/17/19	Graham, Katharine (New York, N.Y.)	6/16/17
Brinkley, David (Wilmington, N.C.)	7/10/20	Greenspan, Alan (New York, N.Y.)	3/6/26
Brokaw, Tom (Webster, S. Dak.)	2/6/40	Griffin, Robert P. (Traverse City, Mich.)	11/6/23
Brooke, Edward (Washington, D.C.)	10/26/19		
Brown, Edmund G. Jr. (San Francisco, Cal.)	4/7/38	Haig, Alexander (Philadelphia, Pa.)	12/2/24
Brown, Harold (New York, N.Y.)	9/19/27	Hanks, Nancy (Miami Beach, Fla.)	12/31/27
Brown, Helen Gurley (Green Forest, Ark.)	2/18/22	Harriman, W. Averell (New York, N.Y.)	11/15/91
Brzezinski, Zbigniew (Warsaw, Poland)	3/28/28	Harris, Patricia Roberts (Mattoon, Ill.)	5/31/24
Buchwald, Art (Mt. Vernon, N.Y.)	10/20/25	Hartman, David (Pawtucket, R.I.)	5/19/35
Buckley, William F. (New York, N.Y.)	11/24/25	Hatfield, Mark O. (Dallas, Ore.)	7/12/22
Bundy, McGeorge (Boston, Mass.)	3/30/19	Hayakawa, S.I. (Vancouver, British Columbia)	7/18/06
Bunker, Ellsworth (Yonkers, N.Y.)	5/11/94	Hefner, Hugh (Chicago, Ill.)	4/9/26
Burger, Warren (St. Paul, Minn.)	9/17/07	Heller, Walter (Buffalo, N.Y.)	8/27/15
Burns, Arthur F. (Stanislau, Aust.)	4/27/04	Helms, Richard (St. Davids, Pa.)	3/30/13
Burton, Phillip (Cincinnati, Oh.)	6/1/26	Hershey, Lenore (New York, N.Y.)	3/20/20
Bush, George (Milton, Mass.)	6/12/24	Hesburgh, Theodore (Syracuse, N.Y.)	5/25/17
Byrd, Robert (N. Wilkesboro, N.C.)	11/20/17	Hills, Carla (Los Angeles, Cal.)	1/3/34
Byrne, Jane M. (Chicago, Ill.)	5/24/34	Hiss, Alger (Baltimore, Md.)	11/11/04
		Hollings, Ernest (Charleston, S.C.)	1/1/22
Califano, Joseph A. Jr. (Brooklyn, N.Y.)	3/15/21	Hughes, Harold (Ida Grove, Ia.)	2/10/22
Carey, Hugh (Brooklyn, N.Y.)	4/11/19		
Carter, Amy (Plains, Ga.)	10/19/67	Iacocca, Lee A. (Allentown, Pa.)	10/15/24
Carter, Billy (Plains, Ga.)	3/29/37	Inouye, Daniel (Honolulu, Ha.)	9/7/24
Carter, Jimmy (Plains, Ga.)	10/1/24		
Carter, John William "Jack" (Portsmouth, Va.)	7/3/47	Jackson, Henry (Everett, Wash.)	5/31/12
Carter, Lillian (Richland, Ga.)	8/15/98	Jackson, Jesse (Greenville, N.C.)	10/8/41
Carter, Rosalynn (Plains, Ga.)	8/18/27	Jackson, Maynard (Dallas, Tex.)	3/23/38
Case, Clifford (Franklin Park, N.J.)	4/16/04	Javits, Jacob K. (New York, N.Y.)	5/18/04
Chancellor, John (Chicago, Ill.)	7/14/27	Johnson, Lady Bird (Mrs. Lyndon) (Karnack, Tex.)	12/22/12
Chandler, Otis (Los Angles, Cal.)	11/23/27	Jones, David C. (Aberdeen, S.D.)	7/9/21
Chavez, Cesar (Yuma, Ariz.)	3/31/27	Jordan, Barbara (Houston, Tex.)	2/21/36
Chisholm, Shirley (Brooklyn, N.Y.)	11/30/24	Jordan, Hamilton (Charlotte, N.C.)	9/21/44,
Church, Frank (Boise, Ida.)	7/25/24	Jordan, Vernon (Atlanta, Ga.)	8/15/35
Civiletti, Benjamin R. (Peekskill, N.Y.)	7/17/35		
Commager, Henry Steele (Pittsburgh, Pa.)	10/25/02	Kahn, Alfred E. (Paterson, N.J.)	10/17/17
Commoner, Barry (Brooklyn, N.Y.)	5/28/17	Kemp, Jack (Los Angeles, Cal.)	7/13/35
Connally, John B. (Floresville, Tex.)	2/28/17	Kennedy, Edward M. (Brookline, Mass.)	2/22/32
Cooke, Terence Cardinal (New York, N.Y.)	3/1/21	Kennedy, Rose (Mrs. Joseph P.) (Boston, Mass.)	7/22/90
Cooney, Joan Ganz (Phoenix, Ariz.)	10/30/29	Kerr, Walter (Evanston, Ill.)	7/8/13
Cosell, Howard (Winston-Salem, N.C.)	1920	King, Coretta (Mrs. Martin L.) (Marion, Ala.)	4/27/27
Cousins, Norman (Union Hill, N.J.)	6/24/12	Kirbo, Charles (Bainbridge, Ga.)	3/15/17
Cox, Archibald (Plainfield, N.J.)	5/17/12	Kirkland, Lane (Camden, S.C.)	3/12/22
Crane, Philip (Chicago, Ill.)	11/3/30	Kissinger, Henry (Fuerth, Germany)	5/27/23
Cranston, Alan (Palo Alto, Cal.)	6/19/14	Koch, Edward I. (New York, N.Y.)	12/12/24
Crippen, Robert L. (Beaumont, Tex.)	9/11/37	Kreps, Juanita M. (Lynch, Ky.)	1/11/21
Cronkite, Walter (St. Joseph, Mo.)	11/4/16		
Curtis, Charlotte (Chicago, Ill.)	1929	Laird, Melvin (Omaha, Neb.)	9/1/22
		Lance, Thomas B. "Bert" (Young Harris, Ga.)	6/3/31
Davis, Angela (Birmingham, Ala.)	1/26/44	Landers, Ann (Sioux City, Ia.)	7/4/18
Deaver, Michael K. (Bakersfield, Cal.)	4/11/38	Landon, Alfred (West Middlesex, Pa.)	9/9/87

Name (Birthplace)	Birthdate
Landrieu, Moon (New Orleans, La.)	7/23/30
LeMay, Curtis (Ohio)	11/15/06
Lemnitzer, Lyman L. (Honesdale, Pa.)	8/29/99
Levi, Edward (Chicago, Ill.)	6/26/11
Lindbergh, Anne Morrow (Englewood, N.J.)	1906
Lipshutz, Robert J. (Atlanta, Ga.)	12/27/21
Lodge, Henry Cabot (Nahant, Mass.)	7/5/02
Long, Russell B. (Shreveport, La.)	11/3/18
Luce, Clare Boothe (New York, N.Y.)	4/10/03
Maddox, Lester (Atlanta, Ga.)	9/30/15
Mansfield, Mike (New York, N.Y.)	3/16/03
Marshall, Thurgood (Baltimore, Md.)	7/2/08
Mayer, Martin (New York, N.Y.)	1/14/28
McCarthy, Eugene (Watkins, Minn.)	3/29/16
McCloskey, Paul (San Bernardino, Cal.)	9/29/27
McGovern, George (Avon, S.D.)	7/19/22
McNamara, Robert S. (San Francisco, Cal.)	6/9/16
Meese, Edwin (Oakland, Cal.)	12/2/31
Miller, Arnold (Leewood, W. Va.)	1/05/??
Miller, G. William (Sapulpa, Okla.)	3/9/25
Milliken, William (Traverse City, Mich.)	3/26/22
Mitchell, John (Detroit, Mich.)	9/15/13
Mondale, Joan (Eugene, Ore.)	8/8/30
Mondale, Walter (Ceylon, Minn.)	1/5/28
Morgan, Marabel (Crestline, Oh.)	6/25/37
Moses, Robert (New Haven, Conn.)	12/18/88
Moynihan, Daniel P. (Tulsa, Okla.)	3/16/27
Mudd, Roger (Washington, D.C.)	2/9/28
Muskie, Edmund (Rumford, Me.)	3/28/14
Nader, Ralph (Winsted, Conn.)	2/27/34
Nixon, Julie (Mrs. David Eisenhower) (Wash., D.C.)	7/5/48
Nixon, Pat (Mrs. Richard) (Ely, Nev.)	3/16/12
Nixon, Richard (Yorba Linda, Cal.)	1/9/13
Nixon, Tricia (Mrs. Edward Cox) (Cal.)	2/21/46
Nizer, Louis (London, England)	2/6/02
Norton, Eleanor Holmes (Washington, D.C.)	6/13/37
Nunn, Sam (Perry, Ga.)	9/8/38
O'Brien, Lawrence F. (Springfield, Mass.)	7/7/17
Onassis, Jacqueline (Southampton, N.Y.)	7/28/29
O'Neill, Thomas P. (Cambridge, Mass.)	12/9/12
Paley, William S. (Chicago, Ill.)	9/28/01
Pauley, Jane (Indianapolis, Ind.)	10/31/50
Pauling, Linus (Portland, Ore.)	2/28/01
Peale, Norman Vincent (Bowersville, Oh.)	5/31/98
Percy, Charles H. (Pensacola, Fla.)	9/27/19
Powell, Jody (Cordele, Ga.)	9/30/43
Powell, Lewis F. (Suffolk, Va.)	9/19/07
Proxmire, William (Lake Forest, Ill.)	1/11/15
Rather, Dan (Wharton, Tex.)	10/31/31
Ray, Dixy Lee (Tacoma, Wash.)	9/3/14
Reagan, Nancy (New York, N.Y.)	7/6/23
Reagan, Ronald (Tampico, Ill.)	2/6/11
Reasoner, Harry (Dakota City, Ia.)	4/17/23
Regan, Donald T. (Cambridge, Mass.)	12/21/18
Rehnquist, William (Milwaukee, Wis.)	10/1/24
Reston, James (Clydebank, Scotland)	11/3/09
Rhodes, John (Council Grove, Kan.)	9/18/16
Ribicoff, Abe (New Britain, Conn.)	4/9/10
Richardson, Elliot L. (Boston, Mass.)	7/20/20
Rickover, Hyman (Makowa, Poland)	1/27/00
Rockefeller, David (New York, N.Y.)	6/12/15
Rockefeller, John D. 4th "Jay" (New York, N.Y.)	6/18/37
Rockefeller, Laurance S. (New York, N.Y.)	5/26/10
Rodino, Peter (Newark, N.J.)	6/7/09
Romney, George W. (Chihuahua, Mexico)	7/8/07
Roosevelt, Elliot (New York, N.Y.)	9/23/10
Roosevelt, Franklin D. Jr. (Canada)	8/17/14
Ruckelshaus, William (Indianapolis, Ind.)	7/24/32
Rumsfeld, Donald (Chicago, Ill.)	7/9/32
Rusk, Dean (Cherokee Co., Ga.)	2/9/09
Safer, Morley (Toronto, Ontario)	11/8/31
Safire, William (New York, N.Y.)	12/17/29
Sagan, Carl (New York, N.Y.)	11/9/34
Salk, Jonas (New York, N.Y.)	10/28/14
Samuelson, Paul A. (Gary, Ind.)	5/15/15

Name (Birthplace)	Birthdate
Savitch, Jessica (Kennett Sq., Pa.)	2/1/48
Schlafly, Phyllis (St. Louis, Mo.)	8/15/24
Schlesinger, Arthur Jr. (Columbus, Oh.)	10/15/17
Schlesinger, James R. (New York, N.Y.)	2/15/29
Schultze, Charles (Alexandria, Va.)	12/22/24
Scott, Hugh (Fredericksburg, Va.)	11/11/00
Scranton, William W. (Madison, Conn.)	7/19/17
Seaborg, Glenn T. (Ishpeming, Mich.)	4/19/12
Sevareid, Eric (Velva, N.D.)	11/26/12
Shanker, Albert (New York, N.Y.)	9/14/28
Shirer, William L. (Chicago, Ill.)	2/23/04
Shriver, R. Sargent (Westminster, Md.)	11/9/15
Shultz, George (New York, N.Y.)	12/13/20
Simon, William (Paterson, N.J.)	1927
Sirica, John J. (Waterbury, Conn.)	3/19/04
Smeal, Eleanor (Ashtabula, Oh.)	7/30/39
Smith, Howard K. (Ferriday, La.)	5/12/14
Smith, Margaret Chase (Skowhegan, Me.)	12/14/97
Smith, William French (Wilton, N.H.)	8/26/17
Snyder, Tom (Milwaukee, Wisc.)	5/12/36
Spock, Benjamin (New Haven, Conn.)	5/2/03
Stahl, Leslie (Lynn, Mass.)	12/16/41
Stassen, Harold (West St. Paul, Minn.)	4/13/07
Steinbrenner, George (Rocky River, Oh.)	7/4/30
Steinem, Gloria (Toledo, Oh.)	3/25/34
Stennis, John (Kamper City, Miss.)	8/3/01
Stevens, John Paul (Chicago, Ill.)	4/20/20
Stevenson 3d, Adlai (Chicago, Ill.)	10/10/30
Stewart, Potter (Jackson, Mich.)	1/23/15
Stockman, David (Ft. Hood, Tex.)	11/10/46
Stokes, Carl (Cleveland, Oh.)	6/21/27
Strauss, Robert S. (Lockhart, Tex.)	10/19/18
Sulzberger, Arthur Ochs (New York, N.Y.)	2/5/26
Symington, Stuart (Amherst, Mass.)	6/26/01
Taft, Robert Jr. (Cincinnati, Oh.)	2/26/17
Talmadge, Herman (Lovejoy, Ga.)	8/9/13
Taylor, Maxwell D. (Keytesville, Mo.)	8/26/01
Thomas, Helen (Winchester, Ky.)	8/4/20
Thomas, Lowell (Woodington, Oh.)	4/6/92
Thompson, James R. (Chicago, Ill.)	5/8/36
Thurmond, J. Strom (Edgefield, S.C.)	12/5/02
Tower, John (Houston, Tex.)	9/29/25
Truman, Mrs. Harry (Independence, Mo.)	2/13/85
Truman, Margaret (Mrs. Clifton Daniel) (Independence, Mo.)	2/17/24
Tuchman, Barbara (New York, N.Y.)	1/30/12
Turner, Stansfield (Chicago, Ill.)	2/1/33
Udall, Morris K. (St. Johns, Ariz.)	6/15/22
Ullman, Al (Great Falls, Mont.)	3/9/14
Van Buren, Abigail (Sioux City, Ia.)	7/4/18
Vance, Cyrus R. (Clarksburg, W. Va.)	3/27/17
Vanderbilt, Alfred G. (London, England)	9/22/12
Veeck, Bill (Chicago, Ill.)	2/9/14
Volcker, Paul A. (Cape May, N.J.)	9/5/27
Wallace, George (Clio, Ala.)	8/25/19
Wallace, Mike (Brookline, Mass.)	5/9/18
Walters, Barbara (Boston, Mass.)	9/25/31
Warnke, Paul (Webster, Mass.)	1/31/20
Washington, Walter E. (Dawson, Ga.)	4/15/15
Watt, James G. (Lusk., Wyo.)	1/31/38
Webster, William H. (St. Louis, Mo.)	3/6/24
Weicker, Lowell (Paris, France)	5/16/31
Weinberger, Caspar (San Francisco, Cal.)	8/18/17
Westmoreland, William (Spartanburg, S.C.)	3/26/14
White, Byron R. (Ft. Collins, Col.)	6/8/17
White, E.B. (Mt. Vernon, N.Y.)	7/11/99
White, Theodore (Boston, Mass.)	5/6/15
Wicker, Tom (Hamlet, N.C.)	6/18/26
Wilkins, Roy (St. Louis, Mo.)	8/30/01
Williams, Edward Bennett (Hartford, Conn.)	5/31/20
Wolfe, Tom (Richmond, Va.)	3/2/31
Woodcock, Leonard (Providence, R.I.)	2/15/11
Wright, James C. Jr. (Ft. Worth, Tex.)	12/22/22
Wriston, Walter B. (Middletown, Conn.)	8/3/19
Young, Andrew (New Orleans, La.)	3/12/32
Young, John W. (San Francisco, Cal.)	9/24/30
Zumwalt, Elmo (San Francisco, Cal.)	11/29/20

Noted Black Americans

Names of black athletes and entertainers are not included here as they are listed elsewhere in The World Almanac.

The Rev. Dr. Ralph David Abernathy, b. 1926, organizer, 1957, and president, 1968, of the Southern Christian Leadership Conference.

Crispus Attucks, c. 1723-1770, agitator led group which precip- itated the "Boston Massacre," Mar. 5, 1770.

James Baldwin, b. 1924, author, playwright; *Another Country, The Fire Next Time, Blues for Mister Charlie, Just Above My Head.*

Benjamin Banneker, 1731-1806, inventor, astronomer, mathematician, and gazeteer; served on commission which surveyed and laid out Washington, D. C.

Imamu Amiri Baraka, b. LeRoi Jones, 1934, poet, playwright.

James P. Beckwourth, 1798-c. 1867, western fur-trader, scout, after whom Beckwourth Pass in northern California is named.

Dr. Mary McCleod Bethune, 1875-1955, adviser to presidents F. D. Roosevelt and Truman; division administrator, National Youth Administration, 1935; founder, president of Bethune-Cookman College.

Henry Blair, 19th century, obtained patents (believed the first issued to a black) for a corn-planter, 1834, and for a cotton-planter, 1836.

Julian Bond, b. 1940, civil rights leader first elected to the Georgia state legislature, 1965; helped found Student Nonviolent Coordinating Committee.

Edward Bouchet, 1852-1918, first black to earn a Ph.D., Yale, 1876, at a U. S. university; first black to be elected to Phi Beta Kappa.

Thomas Bradley, b. 1917, elected mayor of Los Angeles, 1973.

Andrew F. Brimmer, b. 1926, first black member, 1966, Federal Reserve Board.

Edward W. Brooke, b. 1919, attorney general, 1962, of Massachusetts; first black elected to U. S. Senate, 1967, since 19th century Reconstruction.

Gwendolyn Brooks, b. 1917, poet, novelist; first black to win a Pulitzer Prize, 1950, for *Annie Allen.*

William Wells Brown, 1815-1884, novelist, dramatist; first American black to publish a novel.

Dr. Ralph Bunche, 1904-1971, first black to win the Nobel Peace Prize, 1950; undersecretary of the UN, 1950.

George E. Carruthers, b. 1940, physicist developed the Apollo 16 lunar surface ultraviolet camera/spectograph.

George Washington Carver, 1861-1943, botanist, chemurgist, and educator; his extensive experiments in soil building and plant diseases revolutionized the economy of the South.

Charles Waddell Chestnutt, 1858-1932, author known primarily for his short stories, including *The Conjure Woman.*

Shirley Chisholm, b. 1924, first black woman elected to House of Representatives, Brooklyn, N. Y., 1968.

Countee Cullen, 1903-1946, poet; won many literary prizes.

Lt. Gen. Benjamin O. Davis Jr. b. 1912, West Point, 1936, first black Air Force general, 1954.

Brig. Gen. Benjamin O. Davis Sr., 1877-1970, first black general, 1940, in U. S. Army.

William L. Dawson, 1886-1970, Illinois congressman, first black chairman of a major House of Representatives committee.

Isaiah Dorman, 19th century, U. S. Army interpreter, killed with Custer, 1876, at Battle of the Little Big Horn.

Aaron Douglas, 1900-1979, painter; called father of black American art.

Frederick Douglass, 1817-1895, author, editor, orator, diplomat; edited the abolitionist weekly, The North Star, in Rochester, N. Y.; U.S. minister and counsul general to Haiti.

Dr. Charles Richard Drew, 1904-1950, pioneer in development of blood banks; director of American Red Cross blood donor project in World War II.

William Edward Burghardt Du Bois, 1868-1963, historian, sociologist; a founder of the National Association for the Advancement of Colored People (NAACP), 1909, and founder of its magazine The Crisis; author, *The Souls of Black Folk.*

Paul Laurence Dunbar, 1872-1906, poet, novelist; won fame with *Lyrics of Lowly Life,* 1896.

Jean Baptiste Point du Sable, c. 1750-1818, pioneer trader and first settler of Chicago, 1779.

Ralph Ellison, b. 1914, novelist, winner of 1952 National Book Award, for *Invisible Man.*

Estevanico, explorer led Spanish expedition of 1538 into the American Southwest.

James Farmer, b. 1920, a founder of the Congress of Racial Equality, 1942; asst. secretary, Dept. of HEW, 1969.

Henry O. Flipper, 1856-1940, first black to graduate, 1877, from West Point.

Marcus Garvey, 1887-1940, founded Universal Negro Improvement Assn., 1911.

Kenneth Gibson, b. 1932, elected mayor of Newark, N.J., 1970.

Charles Gordone, b. 1925, won 1970 Pulitzer Prize in Drama, with *No Place to Be Somebody.*

Vice Adm. Samuel L. Gravely Jr. b. 1922, first black admiral, 1971, served in World War II, Korea, and Vietnam; commander, Third Fleet.

Alex Haley, b. 1921, Pulitzer Prize-winning author; *Roots, The Autobiography of Malcolm X.*

Jupiter Hammon, c. 1720-1800, poet; the first black American to have his works published, 1761.

Lorraine Hansberry, 1930-1965, playwright; won N. Y. Drama Critics Circle Award, 1959, with *Raisin in the Sun.*

Patricia Roberts Harris, b. 1924, U. S. ambassador to Luxembourg, 1965-67, secretary; Dept. of HUD, 1977-1979, Dept. of H.H.S., 1979-1981.

William H. Hastie, 1904-1976 first black federal judge, appointed 1937; governor of Virgin Islands, 1946-49; judge, U.S. Circuit Court of Appeals, 1949.

Matthew A. Henson, 1866-1955, member of Peary's 1909 expedition to the North Pole; placed U.S. flag at the Pole.

Dr. William A. Hinton, 1883-1959, developed the Hinton and Davies-Hinton tests for detection of syphilis; first black professor, 1949, at Harvard Medical School.

Benjamin L. Hooks, b. 1925, first black member, 1972-1979, Federal Communications Comm.; exec. dir., 1977, NAACP.

Langston Hughes, 1902-1967, poet; story, song lyric author.

The Rev. Jesse Jackson, b. 1941, national director, Operation Bread Basket, and major community leader in Chicago.

Maynard Jackson, b. 1938, elected mayor of Atlanta, 1973.

Gen. Daniel James Jr. 1920-1978, first black 4-star general, 1975; Commander, North American Air Defense Command.

Pvt. Henry Johnson, 1897-1929, the first American decorated by France in World War I with the Croix de Guerre.

James Weldon Johnson, 1871-1938, poet, lyricist, novelist; first black admitted to Florida bar; U.S. consul in Venezuela and Nicaragua.

Barbara Jordan, b. 1936, former congresswoman from Texas; member, House Judiciary Committee.

Vernon E. Jordan, b. 1935, exec. dir. Natl. Urban League, 1972.

Ernest E. Just, 1883-1941, marine biologist, studied egg development; author, *Biology of Cell Surfaces,* 1941.

The Rev. Dr. Martin Luther King Jr., 1929-1968, led 382-day, Montgomery, Ala., boycott which brought 1956 U.S. Supreme Court decision holding segregation on buses unconstitutional; founder, president of the Southern Christian Leadership Conference, 1957; won Nobel Peace Prize, 1964.

Lewis H. Latimer, 1848-1928, associate of Edison; supervised installation of first electric street lighting in N.Y.C.

Malcolm X, 1925-1965, leading spokesman for black pride, founded, 1963, Organization of Afro-American Unity.

Thurgood Marshall, b. 1908, first black U.S. solicitor general 1965; first black justice of the U.S. Supreme Court, 1967; as a lawyer led the legal battery that won the historic decision from the Supreme Court declaring racial segregation of public schools unconstitutional, 1954.

Jan Matzeliger, 1852-1889, invented lasting machine, patented 1883, which revolutionized the shoe industry.

Wade H. McCree Jr., b. 1920, solicitor general of the U.S.

Donald E. McHenry, b. 1936, U.S. ambassador to the United Nations, 1979-1981.

Dorie Miller, 1919-1943, Navy hero of Pearl Harbor attack; awarded the Navy Cross.

Ernest N. Morial, b. 1929, elected first black mayor of New Orleans, 1977.

Willard Motley, 1912-1965, novelist; *Knock on Any Door.*

Elijah Muhammad, 1897-1975, founded the Black Muslims, 1931.

Pedro Alonzo Nino, navigator of the Nina, one of Columbus' 3 ships on his first voyage of discovery to the New World, 1492.

Adam Clayton Powell, 1908-1972, early civil rights leader, congressman, 1945-1969; chairman, House Committee on Education and Labor, 1960-1967.

Joseph H. Rainey, 1832-1887, first black elected to House of Representatives, 1869, from South Carolina.

A. Philip Randolph, 1889-1979, organized the Brotherhood of Sleeping Car Porters, 1925; organizer of 1941 and 1963 March on Washington movements; vice president, AFL-CIO.

Charles Rangel, b. 1930, congressman from N.Y.C., 1970; chairman, Congressional Black Caucus.

Hiram R. Revels, 1822-1901, first black U.S. senator, elected in Mississippi, served 1870-1871.

Wilson C. Riles, b. 1917, elected, 1970, California State Superintendent of Public Instruction.

Norbert Rillieux, 1806-1894; invented a vacuum pan evaporator, 1846, revolutionizing the sugar-refining industry.

Carl T. Rowan, b. 1925, prize-winning journalist; director of the U.S. Information Agency, 1964, the first black to sit on the National Security Council; U. S. ambassador to Finland, 1963.

John B. Russwurm, 1799-1851, with **Samuel E. Cornish,** 1793-1858, founded, 1827, the nation's first black newspaper, Freedom's Journal, in N.Y.C.

Bayard Rustin, b. 1910, organizer of the 1963 March on Washington; executive director, A. Philip Randolph Institute.

Peter Salem, at the Battle of Bunker Hill, June 17, 1775, shot and killed British commander Maj. John Pitcairn.

Ntozake Shange, b. Paulette Williams, 1948, playwright, *For Colored Girls Who Have Considered Suicide/When the Rainbow is Enuf.*

Bishop Stephen Spottswood, 1897-1974, board chairman of NAACP from 1966.

Willard Townsend, 1895-1957, organized the United Transport Service Employees, 1935 (redcaps, etc.); vice pres. AFL-CIO.

Sojourner Truth, 1797-1883, born Isabella Baumfree; preacher, abolitonist; raised funds for Union in Civil War; worked for black educational opportunities.

Harriet Tubman, 1823-1913, Underground Railroad conductor served as nurse and spy for Union Army in the Civil War.

Nat Turner, 1800-1831, leader of the most significant of over 200 slave revolts in U.S. history, in Southampton, Va.; he and 16 others were hanged.

Booker T. Washington, 1856-1915, founder, 1881, and first president of Tuskegee Institute; author, *Up From Slavery.*

Dr. Robert C. Weaver, b. 1907, first black member of the U.S. Cabinet, secretary, Dept. of HUD, 1966.

Phillis Wheatley, c. 1753-1784, poet; 2d American woman and first black woman to have her works published, 1770.

Walter White, 1893-1955, exec. secretary, NAACP, 1931-1955.

Roy Wilkins, b. 1901, executive director, NAACP, 1955-1977.

Dr. Daniel Hale Williams, 1858-1931, performed one of first 2 open-heart operations, 1893; founded Provident, Chicago's first Negro hospital; first black elected a fellow of the American College of Surgeons.

Granville T. Woods, 1856-1910, invented the third-rail system now used in subways, a complex railway telegraph device that helped reduce train accidents, and an automatic air brake.

Dr. Carter G. Woodson, 1875-1950, historian; founded Assn. for the Study of Negro Life and History, 1915, and Journal of Negro History, 1916.

Richard Wright, 1908-1960, novelist; *Native Son, Black Boy.*

Frank Yerby, b. 1916, most successful of American black novelists; *The Foxes of Harrow, Vixen.*

Andrew Young, b. 1932, civil rights leader, congressman from Georgia, U.S. ambassador to the United Nations, 1977-79.

Whitney M. Young Jr., 1921-1971, exec. director, 1961, National Urban League; author, lecturer, newspaper columnist.

About 5,000 blacks served in the Continental Army during the **American Revolution,** mostly in integrated units, some in all-black combat units. Some 200,000 blacks served in the Union Army during the **Civil War;** 38,000 gave their lives; 22 won the Medal of Honor, the nation's highest award. Of 367,000 blacks in the armed forces during **World War I,** 100,000 served in France. More than 1,000,000 blacks served in the armed forces during **World War II;** all-black fighter and bomber AAF units and infantry divisions gave distinguished service. In 1954 the policy of all-black units was finally abolished. Of 274,937 blacks who served in the armed forces during the **Vietnam War** (1965-1974), 5,681 were killed in combat.

As of July, 1980, there were 182 black mayors, 2,356 members of municipal governing bodies, 451 county officers, 323 state legislators, and 17 U.S. representatives. There are now 4,912 blacks holding elected office in the U.S. and Virgin Islands, an increase of 6.6% over the previous year, according to a survey by the Joint Center for Political Studies, Washington, D.C.

Notable American Fiction Writers and Playwrights

Name (Birthplace)	Birthdate	Name (Birthplace)	Birthdate
Abbott, George (Forestville, N.Y.)	6/25/87	Kazan, Elia (Constantinople, Turkey)	9/7/09
Albee, Edward (Washington, D.C.)	3/12/28	Kerr, Jean (Scranton, Pa.)	7/?/23
Algren, Nelson (Detroit, Mich.)	3/28/09	Kesey, Ken (La Junta, Col.)	9/17/35
Anderson, Robert (New York, N.Y.)	4/28/17	King, Stephen (Portland, Me.)	9/21/47
Asimov, Isaac (Petrovichi, Russia)	1/2/20	Kingsley, Sidney (New York, N.Y.)	10/22/06
Auchincloss, Louis (Lawrence, N.Y.)	9/27/17	Knowles, John (Fairmont, W. Va.)	9/16/26
		Kosinski, Jerzy (Lódz, Poland)	6/14/33
Baldwin, James (New York, N.Y.)	8/2/24		
Barth, John (Cambridge, Md.)	5/27/30	L'Amour, Louis (Jamestown, N.D.)	
Barthelme, Donald (Philadelphia, Pa.)	1931	Lee, Harper (Alabama)	1926
Bellow, Saul (Quebec, Canada)	7/10/15	LeGuin, Ursula (Berkeley, Cal.)	10/21/29
Benchley, Nathaniel (Newton, Mass.)	11/13/15	Levin, Ira (New York, N.Y.)	8/27/29
Benchley, Peter (New York, N.Y.)	5/8/40	Loos, Anita (Sisson, Cal.)	4/26/93
Bishop, Jim (Jersey City, N.J.)	11/21/07	Ludlum, Robert (New York, N.Y.)	5/25/27
Blume, Judy (Elizabeth, N.J.)	2/12/38		
Bradbury, Ray (Waukegan, Ill.)	8/22/20	MacDonald, John D. (Sharon, Pa.)	7/24/16
Brooks, Gwendolyn (Topeka, Kan.)	6/7/17	MacDonald, Ross (Los Gatos, Cal.)	12/13/15
Burrows, Abe (New York, N.Y.)	12/18/10	MacInnes, Helen (Glasgow, Scotland)	10/7/07
		Mailer, Norman (Long Branch, N.J.)	1/31/23
Caldwell, Erskine (Coweta Co., Ga.)	12/17/03	Malamud, Bernard (Brooklyn, N.Y.)	4/26/14
Caldwell, Taylor (London, England)	1900	Mamet, David (Chicago, Ill.)	11/30/47
Calisher, Hortense (New York, N.Y.)	12/20/11	McCarthy, Mary (Seattle, Wash.)	6/21/12
Capote, Truman (New Orleans, La.)	9/30/24	McMurtry, Larry (Wichita Falls, Tex.)	6/3/36
Chase, Mary (Denver, Col.)	2/25/07	Michener, James A. (New York, N.Y.)	2/3/07
Chayefsky, Paddy (New York, N.Y.)	1/29/23	Miller, Arthur (New York, N.Y.)	10/17/15
Cheever, John (Quincy, Mass.)	5/27/12		
Clavell, James (England)	10/10/24	Oates, Joyce Carol (Lockport, N.Y.)	6/16/38
Crews, Harry (Alma, Ga.)	6/6/35		
Crichton, Michael (Chicago, Ill.)	10/23/42	Percy, Walker (Birmingham, Ala.)	5/28/16
		Porter, Katherine Ann (Indian Creek, Tex.)	5/15/90
De Vries, Peter (Chicago, Ill.)	2/27/10	Potok, Chaim (New York, N.Y.)	2/17/29
Dickey, James (Atlanta, Ga.)	2/2/23	Puzo, Mario (New York, N.Y.)	10/15/20
Didion, Joan (Sacramento, Cal.)	12/5/34	Pynchon, Thomas (Glen Cove, N.Y.)	5/8/37
Doctorow, E. L. (New York, N.Y.)	1/6/31		
Drury, Allen (Houston, Tex.)	9/2/18	Rand, Ayn (St. Petersburg, Russia)	1905
		Reed, Ishmael (Chattanooga, Tenn.)	2/22/38
Elkin, Stanley (New York, N.Y.)	5/11/30	Robbins, Harold (New York, N.Y.)	5/21/12
Ellison, Ralph (Oklahoma City, Okla.)	3/1/14	Roth, Henry (Austria-Hungary)	2/8/06
		Roth, Philip (Newark, N.J.)	3/19/33
Fast, Howard (New York, N.Y.)	11/11/14		
		Salinger, J. D. (New York, N.Y.)	1/1/19
Geisel, Theodore ("Dr. Seuss,"		Saroyan, William (Fresno, Cal.)	8/31/08
Springfield, Mass.)	3/2/04	Schary, Dore (Newark, N.J.)	8/31/05
Gibson, William (New York, N.Y.)	11/13/14	Schisgal, Murray (New York, N.Y.)	11/25/26
Gilroy, Frank (New York, N.Y.)	10/13/25	Schulberg, Budd (New York, N.Y.)	3/27/14
Goldman, William (Chicago, Ill.)	8/12/31	Segal, Erich (Brooklyn, N.Y.)	6/16/37
Grau, Shirley Ann (New Orleans, La.)	7/8/29	Sendak, Maurice (New York, N.Y.)	6/10/28
		Shaw, Irwin (New York, N.Y.)	2/27/13
Hailey, Arthur (Luton, England)	4/5/20	Simon, Neil (New York, N.Y.)	7/4/27
Haley, Alex (Ithaca, N.Y.)	8/11/21	Singer, Isaac Bashevis (Radzymin, Poland)	7/14/04
Hawkes, John (Stamford, Conn.)	8/17/25	Slaughter, Frank (Washington, D.C.)	2/25/08
Heinlein, Robert (Butler, Mon.)	7/7/07	Spillane, Mickey (Brooklyn, N.Y.)	3/9/18
Heller, Joseph (Brooklyn, N.Y.)	5/1/23	Stegner, Wallace (Lake Mills, Ia.)	2/18/09
Hellman, Lillian (New Orleans, La.)	6/20/07	Stone, Irving (San Francisco, Cal.)	7/14/03
Hersey, John (Tientsin, China)	6/17/14	Styron, William (Newport News, Va.)	6/11/25
Himes, Chester (Jefferson City, Mo.)	7/29/09		
		Theroux, Paul (Medford, Mass.)	4/10/41
Irving, John (Exeter, N.H.)	3/2/42	Tryon, Thomas (Hartford, Conn.)	1/14/26
		Updike, John (Shillington, Pa.)	3/18/32
Jong, Erica (New York, N.Y.)	4/26/42		

Name, (Birthplace)	Birthdate	Name (Birthplace)	Birthdate
Uris, Leon (Baltimore, Md.)	8/3/24	Welty, Eudora (Jackson, Miss.)	4/13/09
		Williams, Tennessee (Columbus, Miss.)	3/26/11
Vidal, Gore (West Point, N.Y.)	10/3/25	Wilson, Lanford (Lebanon, Mo.)	4/13/37
Vonnegut, Kurt Jr. (Indianapolis, Ind.)	11/11/22	Willingham, Calder (Atlanta, Ga.)	12/23/22
		Wouk, Herman (New York, N.Y.)	5/27/15
Wallace, Irving (Chicago, Ill.)	3/18/16	Yerby, Frank (Augusta, Ga.)	9/5/16
Wambaugh, Joseph (East Pittsburgh, Pa.)	1/22/37	Zindel, Paul (New York, N.Y.)	5/15/36
Warren, Robert Penn (Guthrie, Ky.)	4/24/05		

American Architects and Some of Their Achievements

Max Abramovitz, b. 1908, Avery Fisher Hall, Lincoln Center, N.Y.C.

Henry Bacon, 1866-1924, Lincoln Memorial.

Pietro Belluschi, b. 1899, Juilliard School of Music, Lincoln Center, N.Y.C.

Marcel Breuer, b. 1902, Whitney Museum of American Art, N.Y.C. (with Hamilton Smith).

Charles Bulfinch, 1763-1844, State House, Boston; Capitol, Wash. D.C., (part).

Daniel H. Burnham, 1846-1912, Union Station, Wash. D.C.; Flatiron, N.Y.C.

Ralph Adams Cram, 1863-1942, Cathedral of St. John the Divine, N.Y.C.; U.S. Military Academy (part).

R. Buckminster Fuller, b. 1895, U.S. Pavilion, Expo 67, Montreal (geodesic domes).

Cass Gilbert, 1859-1934, Custom House, Woolworth Bldg., N.Y.C.; Supreme Court bldg., Wash., D.C.

Bertram G. Goodhue, 1869-1924, Capitol, Lincoln, Neb.; St. Thomas, St. Bartholomew, N.Y.C.

Walter Gropius, 1883-1969, Pan Am Building, N.Y.C. (with Pietro Belluschi).

Peter Harrison, 1716-1775, Touro Synagogue, Redwood Library, Newport, R.I.

Wallace K. Harrison, b. 1895, Metropolitan Opera House, Lincoln Center, N.Y.C.

Thomas Hastings, 1860-1929, Public Library, Frick Mansion, N.Y.C.

James Hoban, 1762-1831, The White House.

William Holabird, 1854-1923, Crerar Library, City Hall, Chicago.

Raymond Hood, 1881-1934, Rockefeller Center, N.Y.C. (part); Daily News, N.Y.C.; Tribune, Chicago.

Richard M. Hunt, 1827-1895, Metropolitan Museum, N.Y.C. (part); Natl. Observatory, Wash., D.C.

William Le Baron Jenney, 1832-1907, Home Insurance, Chicago (demolished 1931).

Philip C. Johnson, b. 1906, N.Y. State Theater, Lincoln Center, N.Y.C.

Albert Kahn, 1869-1942, Athletic Club Bldg., General Motors Bldg., Detroit.

Louis Kahn, 1901-1974, Salk Laboratory, La Jolla, Cal.; Yale Art Gallery.

Christopher Grant LaFarge, 1862-1938, Roman Catholic Chapel, West Point.

Benjamin H. Latrobe, 1764-1820, U.S. Capitol (part).

William Lescaze, 1896-1969, Philadelphia Savings Fund Society; Borg-Warner Bldg., Chicago.

Charles F. McKim, 1847-1909, Public Library, Boston, Columbia Univ., N.Y.C. (part).

Charles M. McKim, b. 1920, KUHT-TV Transmitter Building, Houston; Lutheran Church of the Redeemer, Houston.

Ludwig Mies van der Rohe, 1886-1969, Seagram Building, N.Y.C. (with Philip C. Johnson); National Gallery, Berlin.

Robert Mills, 1781-1855, Washington Monument.

Richard J. Neutra, 1892-1970, Mathematics Park, Princeton; Orange Co. Courthouse, Santa Ana, Cal.

Gyo Obata, b. 1923, Natl. Air & Space Mus., Smithsonian Institution; Dallas-Ft. Worth Airport.

Frederick L. Olmsted, 1822-1903, Central Park, N.Y.C.; Fairmount Park, Philadelphia.

Ieoh Ming Pei, b. 1917, National Center for Atmospheric Research, Boulder, Col.

William Pereira, b. 1909, Cape Canaveral; Transamerica Bldg., San Francisco.

John Russell Pope, 1874-1937, National Gallery.

John Portman, b. 1924, Peachtree Center, Atlanta.

James Renwick Jr., 1818-1895, Grace Church, St. Patrick's Cathedral, N.Y.C.; Smithsonian, Corcoran Galleries, Wash., D.C.

Henry H. Richardson, 1838-1886, Trinity Church, Boston.

Kevin Roche, b. 1922, Oakland Cal. Museum; Fine Arts Center, U. of Mass.

James Gamble Rogers, 1867-1947, Columbia-Presbyterian Medical Center, N.Y.C.; Northwestern Univ., Chicago.

John Weldon Root, b. 1887, Palmolive Building, Chicago; Hotel Statler, Washington; Hotel Tamanaco, Caracas.

Paul Rudolph, b. 1918, Jewitt Art Center, Wellesley College; Art & Architecture Bldg., Yale.

Eero Saarinen, 1910-1961, Gateway to the West Arch, St. Louis; Trans World Flight Center, N.Y.C.

Louis Skidmore, 1897-1962, AEC town site, Oak Ridge, Tenn.; Terrace Plaza Hotel, Cincinnati.

Clarence S. Stein, b. 1882, Temple Emanu-El, N.Y.C.

Edward Durell Stone, 1902-1978, U.S. Embassy, New Delhi, India; (H. Hartford) Gallery of Modern Art, N.Y.C.

Louis H. Sullivan, 1856-1924, Auditorium, Chicago.

Richard Upjohn, 1802-1878, Trinity Church, N.Y.C.

Ralph T. Walker, 1889-1973, N.Y. Telephone Hdqrs., N.Y.C.; IBM Research Lab., Poughkeepsie, N.Y.

Roland A. Wank, 1898-1970, Cincinnati Union Terminal; head architect TVA, 1933-44.

Stanford White, 1853-1906, Washington Arch; first Madison Square Garden, N.Y.C.

Frank Lloyd Wright, 1867 or 1869-1959, Imperial Hotel, Tokyo; Guggenheim Museum, N.Y.C.

William Wurster, b. 1895, Ghirardelli Sq., San Francisco; Cowell College, U. Cal., Berkeley.

Minoru Yamasaki, b. 1912, World Trade Center, N.Y.C.

Noted American Cartoonists

Charles Addams, b. 1912, noted for macabre cartoons.

Peter Arno, 1904-1968, noted for urban characterizations.

George Baker, 1915-1975, The Sad Sack.

C. C. Beck, b. 1910, Captain Marvel.

Herb Block (Herblock), b. 1909, leading political cartoonist.

Clare Briggs, 1875-1930, Mr. & Mrs.

Dik Browne, b. 1917, Hi & Lois, Hagar the Horrible.

Ernie Bushmiller, b. 1905, Nancy.

Milton Caniff, b. 1907, Terry & the Pirates; Steve Canyon.

Al Capp, 1909-1979, Li'l Abner.

Roy Crane, 1901-1977, Captain Easy; Buz Sawyer.

Robert Crumb, b. 1943, "Underground" cartoonist.

Jay N. Darling (Ding), 1876-1962, political cartoonist.

Billy DeBeck, 1890-1942, Barney Google.

Rudolph Dirks, 1877-1968, The Katzenjammer Kids.

Walt Disney, 1901-1966, producer of animated cartoons created Mickey Mouse & Donald Duck.

Jules Feiffer, b. 1929, satirical *Village Voice* cartoonist.

Bud Fisher, 1884-1954, Mutt & Jeff.

Ham Fisher, 1900-1955, Joe Palooka.

James Montgomery Flagg, 1877-1960, illustrator created the famous Uncle Sam recruiting poster during WWI.

Hal Foster, b. 1892, Tarzan; Prince Valiant.

Fontaine Fox, 1884-1964, Toonerville Folks.

Rube Goldberg, 1883-1970, Boob McNutt.

Chester Gould, b. 1900, Dick Tracy.

Harold Gray, 1894-1968, Little Orphan Annie.

Johnny Hart, b. 1931, BC, Wizard of Id.

Jimmy Hatlo, 1898-1963, Little Iodine.

John Held Jr., 1889-1958, "Jazz Age" cartoonist.

George Herriman, 1881-1944, Krazy Kat.

Harry Hershfield, 1885-1974, Abie the Agent.

Burne Hogarth, b. 1911, Tarzan.

Helen Hokinson, 1900-1949, satirical drawings of clubwomen.

Walt Kelly, 1913-1973, Pogo.

Hank Ketcham, b. 1920, Dennis the Menace.

Ted Key, b. 1912 Hazel.

Frank King, 1883-1969, Gasoline Alley.

Jack Kirby, b. 1917, Captain America.

Rollin Kirby, 1875-1952, political cartoonist.

Bill Mauldin, b. 1921, depicted squalid life of the G.I. in WWII.

Winsor McCay, 1872-1934, Little Nemo.

John T. McCutcheon, 1870-1949, midwestern rural life.

George McManus, 1884-1954, Bringing Up Father (Maggie & Jiggs).

Dale Messick, b. 1906, Brenda Starr.

Bob Montana, 1920-1975, Archie.

Willard Mullin, 1902-1978, sports cartoonist created the Dodgers "Bum" and the Mets "Kid".

Thomas Nast, 1840-1902, political cartoonist instrumental in breaking the corrupt Boss Tweed ring in N.Y. Created the Democratic donkey and Republican elephant.

Frederick Burr Opper, 1857-1937, Happy Hooligan.

Richard Outcault, 1863-1928, Yellow Kid; Buster Brown.

Alex Raymond, 1909-1956, Flash Gordon; Jungle Jim.

Charles Schulz, b. 1922, Peanuts.

Elzie C. Segar, 1894-1938, Popeye.

Sydney Smith, 1887-1935, The Gumps.

Otto Soglow, 1900-1975, Little King; Canyon Kiddies.

James Swinnerton, 1875-1974, Little Jimmy.

James Thurber, 1894-1961, *New Yorker* cartoonist of the smugly childish line coupled with the sophisticated caption.

Garry Trudeau, b. 1948, Doonesbury.

Mort Walker, b. 1923, Beetle Bailey.

Russ Westover, 1887-1966, Tillie the Toiler.

Frank Willard, 1893-1958, Moon Mullins.

J. R. Williams, 1888-1957, The Willets Family; Out Our Way.

Gahan Wilson, b. 1930, cartoonist of the macabre.

Art Young, 1866-1943, political radical and satirist.

Chic Young, 1901-1973, Blondie.

Business Hall of Fame

Established and supported by Junior Achievement Inc. Laureates selected by *Fortune* board of editors.

William M. Allen	Roswell Garst	John J. McCloy	Cyrus R. Smith
William Mildred Button	Amadeo P. Giannini	Cyrus H. McCormick	Charles Clinton Spaulding
Stephen D. Bechtel Sr.	Florence Nightingale Graham	Andrew W. Mellon	Alexander T. Stewart
William Blackie	Walter Abraham Haas	Charles E. Merrill	J. Edgar Thomson
Andrew Carnegie	Joyce Clyde Hall	J. Irwin Miller	Theodore N. Vail
Willis Haviland Carrier	H.J. Heinz	George S. Moore	Cornelius Vanderbilt
Frederick Coolidge Crawford	James J. Hill	J. Pierpont Morgan	De Witt Wallace
Harry B. Cunningham	Conrad N. Hilton	David MacKenzie Ogilvy	Lila Acheson Wallace
Arthur Vining Davis	J. Erik Jonsson	John Henry Patterson	George Washington
Walter E. Disney	Henry John Kaiser	William Allan Patterson	Thomas J. Watson Jr.
Georges Frederic Doriot	Robert Justus Kleberg Sr.	James Cash Penney	George Westinghouse
Donald W. Douglas	Edwin Herbert Land	William C. Procter	Frederick W. Weyerhaeuser
Pierre S. du Pont	Albert D. Lasker	M.J. Rathbone	Eli Whitney
George Eastman	Royal Little	Donald T. Regan	Joseph C. Wilson
Thomas A. Edison	Francis Cabot Lowell	John D. Rockefeller	Robert Elkington Wood
Henry Ford	Henry R. Luce	James Wilson Rouse	Robert W. Woodruff
Benjamin Franklin	Ian Kinloch MacGregor	David Sarnoff	Owen D. Young
		Alfred P. Sloan Jr.	

Noted Political Leaders of the Past

(U.S. presidents and most vice presidents, Supreme Court justices, signers of Declaration of Independence, listed elsewhere.)

Abu Bakr, 573-634, Mohammedan leader, first caliph, chosen successor to Mohammed.

Dean Acheson, 1893-1971, (U.S.) secretary of state, chief architect of cold war foreign policy.

Samuel Adams, 1722-1803, (U.S.) patriot, Boston Tea Party firebrand.

Konrad Adenauer, 1876-1967, (G.) West German chancellor.

Emilio Aguinaldo, 1869-1964, (Philip.) revolutionary, fought against Spain and the U.S.

Akbar, 1542-1605, greatest Mogul emperor of India.

Salvador Allende Gossens, 1908-1973, (Chil.) president, advocate of democratic socialism.

Herbert H. Asquith, 1852-1928, (Br.) Liberal prime minister, instituted an advanced program of social reform.

Atahualpa, ?-1533, Inca (ruling chief) of Peru, executed by Pizarro.

Kemal Atatürk, 1881-1938, (Turk.) founded modern Turkey.

Clement Attlee, 1883-1967, (Br.) Labour party leader, prime minister, enacted national health, nationalized gas, electric, coal, iron, steel industries.

Stephen F. Austin, 1793-1836, (U.S.) led Texas colonization.

Mikhail Bakunin, 1814-1876, (R.) revolutionary, leading exponent of anarchism.

Arthur J. Balfour, 1848-1930, (Br.) as foreign secretary under Lloyd George issued Balfour Declaration expressing official British approval of Zionism.

Bernard M. Baruch, 1870-1965, (U.S.) financier, gvt. adviser.

Fulgencio Batista y Zaldívar, 1901-1973, (Cub.) dictator overthrown by Castro.

Lord Beaverbrook, 1879-1964, (Br.) financier, statesman, newspaper owner (Daily and Sunday Express, Evening Standard).

Eduard Benes, 1884-1948, (Czech.) president during interwar and post-WW II eras.

David Ben-Gurion, 1886-1973, (Isr.) first premier of Israel.

Thomas Hart Benton, 1782-1858, (U.S.) Missouri senator, championed agrarian interests and westward expansion.

Lavrenti Beria, 1899-1953, (USSR) Communist leader prominent in political purges under Stalin.

Aneurin Bevan, 1897-1960, (Br.) Labour party leader, developed socialized medicine system.

Ernest Bevin, 1881-1951, (Br.) Labour party leader, foreign minister, helped lay foundation for NATO.

Otto von Bismarck, 1815-1898, (G.) statesman known as the Iron Chancellor, uniter of Germany, 1870.

James G. Blaine, 1830-1893, (U.S.) Republican politician, diplomat, influential in launching Pan-American movement.

Léon Blum, 1872-1950, (F.) socialist leader, writer, headed first Popular Front government.

Simón Bolívar, 1783-1830, (Venez.) South American revolutionary who liberated much of the continent from Spanish rule.

William E. Borah, 1865-1940, (U.S.) isolationist senator, instrumental in blocking U.S. membership in League of Nations and the World Court.

Cesare Borgia, 1476-1507, (It.) soldier, politician, an outstanding figure of the Italian Renaissance.

Aristide Briand, 1862-1932, (F.) foreign minister, chief architect of Locarno Pact and anti-war Kellogg-Briand Pact.

William Jennings Bryan, 1860-1925, (U.S.) Democratic, populist leader, orator, 3 times lost race for presidency.

Nikolai Bukharin, 1888-1938, (USSR) communist leader.

William C. Bullitt, 1891-1967, (U.S.) diplomat, first ambassador to USSR, ambassador to France.

Ralph Bunche, 1904-1971, (U.S.) a founder and key diplomat of United Nations for more than 20 years.

John C. Calhoun, 1782-1850, (U.S.) political leader, champion of states' rights and a symbol of the Old South.

Robert Castlereagh, 1769-1822, (Br.) foreign secretary, guided Grand Alliance against Napoleon, major figure at the Congress of Vienna, 1814-15.

Camillo Benso Cavour, 1810-1861, (It.) statesman, largely responsible for uniting Italy under the House of Savoy.

Austen Chamberlain, 1863-1937, (Br.) Conservative party leader, largely responsible for Locarno Pact of 1925.

Neville Chamberlain, 1869-1940, (Br.) Conservative prime minister whose appeasement of Hitler led to Munich Pact.

Salmon P. Chase, 1808-1873, (U.S.) public official, abolitionist, jurist, 6th Supreme Court chief justice.

Chiang Kai-shek, 1887-1975, (Chin.) Nationalist Chinese president whose govt. was driven from mainland to Taiwan.

Chou En-lai, 1898-1976, (Chin.) diplomat, prime minister, a leading figure of the Chinese Communist party.

Winston Churchill, 1874-1965, (Br.) prime minister, soldier, author, guided Britain through WW II.

Galeazzo Ciano, 1903-1944, (It.) fascist foreign minister, helped create Rome-Berlin Axis, executed by Mussolini.

Henry Clay, 1777-1852, (U.S.) "The Great Compromiser," one of most influential pre-Civil War political leaders.

Georges Clemenceau, 1841-1929, (F.) twice premier, Wilson's chief antagonist at Paris Peace Conference after WW I.

DeWitt Clinton, 1769-1828, (U.S.) political leader, responsible for promoting idea of the Erie Canal.

Robert Clive, 1725-1774, (Br.) first administrator of Bengal, laid foundation for British Empire in India.

Jean Baptiste Colbert, 1619-1683, (F.) statesman, influential under Louis XIV, created the French navy.

Oliver Cromwell, 1599-1658, (Br.) Lord Protector of England, led parliamentary forces during Civil War.

Curzon of Kedleston, 1859-1925, (Br.) viceroy of India, foreign secretary, major force in dealing with post-WW I problems in Europe and Far East.

Édouard Daladier, 1884-1970, (F.) radical socialist politician, arrested by Vichy, interned by Germans until liberation in 1945.

Georges Danton, 1759-1794, (F.) a leading figure in the French Revolution.

Jefferson Davis, 1808-1889, (U.S.) president of the Confederate States of America.

Charles G. Dawes, 1865-1951, (U.S.) statesman, banker, advanced Dawes Plan to stabilize post-WW I German finances.

Alcide De Gasperi, 1881-1954, (It.) premier, founder of the Christian Democratic party.

Charles DeGaulle, 1890-1970, (F.) general, statesman, and first president of the Fifth Republic.

Thomas E. Dewey, 1902-1971, (U.S.) New York governor, twice loser in try for presidency.

Ngo Dinh Diem, 1901-1963, (Viet.) South Vietnamese president, assassinated in government take-over.

Everett M. Dirksen, 1896-1969, (U.S.) Senate Republican minority leader, orator.

Benjamin Disraeli, 1804-1881, (Br.) prime minister, considered founder of modern Conservative party.

Engelbert Dollfuss, 1892-1934, (Aus.) chancellor, assassinated by Austrian Nazis.

Andrea Doria, 1466-1560, (It.) Genoese admiral, statesman, called "Father of Peace" and "Liberator of Genoa."

Stephen A. Douglas, 1813-1861, (U.S.) Democratic leader, orator, opposed Lincoln for the presidency.

John Foster Dulles, 1888-1959, (U.S.) secretary of state under Eisenhower, cold war policy maker.

Friedrich Ebert, 1871-1925, (G.) Social Democratic movement leader, instrumental in bringing about Weimar constitution.

Sir Anthony Eden, 1897-1977, (Br.) foreign secretary, prime minister during Suez invasion of 1956.

Ludwig Erhard, 1897-1977, (G.) economist, West German chancellor, led nation's economic rise after WW II.

Hamilton Fish, 1808-1893, (U.S.) secretary of state, successfully mediated disputes with Great Britain, Latin America.

James V. Forrestal, 1892-1949, (U.S.) secretary of navy, first secretary of defense.

Francisco Franco, 1892-1975, (Sp.) leader of rebel forces during Spanish Civil War and dictator of Spain.

Benjamin Franklin, 1706-1790, (U.S.) printer, publisher, author, inventor, scientist, diplomat.

Louis de Frontenac, 1620-1698, (F.) governor of New France (Canada) where he encouraged explorations and fought Iroquois.

Hugh Gaitskell, 1906-1963, (Br.) Labour party leader, major force in reversing its stand for unilateral disarmament.

Albert Gallatin, 1761-1849, (U.S.) second secretary of treasury, instrumental in negotiating end of War of 1812.

Léon Gambetta, 1838-1882, (F.) statesman, politician, one of the founders of the Third Republic.

Mohandas K. Gandhi, 1869-1948, (Ind.) political leader, ascetic, led nationalist movement against British rule.

Giuseppe Garibaldi, 1807-1882, (It.) patriot, soldier, a leading figure in the Risorgimento, the Italian unification movement.

Genghis Khan, c. 1167-1227, brilliant Mongol conqueror, ruler of vast Asian empire.

William E. Gladstone, 1809-1898, (Br.) prime minister 4 times, dominant force of Liberal party from 1868 to 1894.

Paul Joseph Goebbels, 1897-1945, (G.) Nazi propagandist, master of mass psychology.

Klement Gottwald, 1896-1953, (Czech.) communist leader ushered communism into his country.

Che (Ernesto) Guevara, 1928-1967, (Arg.) guerilla leader, prominent in Cuban revolution, killed in Bolivia.

Haile Selassie, 1891-1975, (Eth.) emperor, maintained traditional monarchy in face of foreign invasion, occupation, and internal resistance.

Alexander Hamilton, 1755-1804, (U.S.) first treasury secretary, champion of strong central government.

Dag Hammarskjold, 1905-1961, (Swed.) statesman, UN secretary general.

John Hancock, 1737-1793, (U.S.) revolutionary leader, first signer of Declaration of Independence.

John Hay, 1838-1905, (U.S.) secretary of state, primarily associated with Open Door Policy toward China.

Patrick Henry, 1736-1799, (U.S.) major revolutionary figure, remarkable orator.

Édouard Herriot, 1872-1957, (F.) Radical Socialist leader, twice premier, president of National Assembly.

Theodor Herzl, 1860-1904, (Aus.) founder of modern Zionism.

Heinrich Himmler, 1900-1945, (G.) chief of Nazi SS and Ge-

stapo, primarily responsible for the Holocaust.

Paul von Hindenburg, 1847-1934, (G.) field marshal, president.

Adolf Hitler, 1889-1945, (G.) dictator, founder of National Socialism.

Ho Chi Minh, 1890-1969, (Viet.) North Vietnamese president, Vietnamese Communist leader, national hero.

Harry L. Hopkins, 1890-1946, (U.S.) New Deal administrator, closest adviser to FDR during WW II.

Edward M. House, 1858-1938, (U.S.) diplomat, confidential adviser to Woodrow Wilson.

Samuel Houston, 1793-1863, (U.S.) leader of struggle to win control of Texas from Mexico.

Cordell Hull, 1871-1955, (U.S.) secretary of state, initiated reciprocal trade to lower tariffs, helped organize UN.

Hubert H. Humphrey, 1911-1978, (U.S.) Minnesota Democrat, senator, vice president, spent 32 years in public service.

Ibn Saud, c. 1888-1953, (S. Arab.) founder of Saudi Arabia and its first king.

Benito Juarez, 1806-1872, (Mex.) national hero, rallied countrymen against foreign threats, sought to create democratic, federal republic.

Frank B. Kellogg, 1856-1937, (U.S.) secretary of state, negotiated Kellogg-Briand Pact to outlaw war.

Robert F. Kennedy, 1925-1968, (U.S.) attorney general, senator, assassinated while seeking presidential nomination.

Aleksandr Kerensky, 1881-1970, (R.) revolutionary, served as premier after Feb. 1917 revolution until Bolshevik overthrow.

Nikita Khrushchev, 1894-1971, (USSR) communist leader, premier, first secretary of Communist party, initiated de-Stalinization.

Lajos Kossuth, 1802-1894, (Hung.) principal figure in 1848 Hungarian revolution.

Pyotr Kropotkin, 1842-1921, (R.) anarchist, championed the peasants but opposed Bolshevism.

Kublai Khan, c. 1215-1294, Mongol emperor, founder of Yüan dynasty in China.

Béla Kun, 1886-c.1939, (Hung.) communist dictator, member of 3d International, tried to foment worldwide revolution.

Robert M. LaFollette, 1855-1925, (U.S.) Wisconsin public official, leader of progressive movement.

Pierre Laval, 1883-1945, (F.) politician, Vichy foreign minister, executed for treason.

Andrew Bonar Law, 1858-1923, (Br.) Conservative party politician, led opposition to Irish home rule.

Vladimir Ilyich Lenin (Ulyanov), 1870-1924, (USSR) revolutionary, founder of Bolshevism, Soviet leader 1917-1924.

Ferdinand de Lesseps, 1805-1894, (F.) diplomat, engineer, conceived idea of Suez Canal.

Liu Shao-ch'i, c.1898-1974, (Chin.) communist leader, fell from grace during "cultural revolution."

Maxim Litvinov, 1876-1951, (USSR), revolutionary, commissar of foreign affairs, proponent of cooperation with western powers.

David Lloyd George, 1863-1945, (Br.) Liberal party prime minister, laid foundations for the modern welfare state.

Henry Cabot Lodge, 1850-1924, (U.S.) conservative Republican senator, led opposition to participation in League of Nations.

Huey P. Long, 1893-1935, (U.S.) Louisiana political demagogue, governor, assassinated.

Rosa Luxemburg, 1871-1919, (G.) revolutionary, leader of the German Social Democratic party and Spartacus party.

J. Ramsay MacDonald, 1866-1937, (Br.) first Labour party prime minister of Great Britain.

Joseph R. McCarthy, 1908-1957, (U.S.) senator notorious for his witch hunt for communists in the government.

Makarios III, 1913-1977, (Cypr.) Greek Orthodox archbishop, first president of Cyprus.

Malcolm X (Malcolm Little), 1925-1965, (U.S.) black separatist leader, assassinated.

Mao Tse-tung, 1893-1976, (Chin.) chief Chinese Marxist theorist, soldier, lead Chinese revolution establishing his nation as an important communist state.

Jean Paul Marat, 1743-1793, (F.) revolutionary politician, identified with radical Jacobins, assassinated by Charlotte Corday.

José Marti, 1853-1895, (Cub.) patriot, poet, leader of Cuban struggle for independence.

Jan Masaryk, 1886-1948, (Czech.) foreign minister, died by mysterious suicide following communist coup.

Thomas G. Masaryk, 1850-1937, (Czech.) statesman, philosopher, first president of Czechoslovak Republic.

Jules Mazarin, 1602-1661, (F.) cardinal, statesman, prime minister under Louis XIII and queen regent Anne of Austria.

Tom Mboya, 1930-1969, (Kenyan) political leader, instrumental in securing independence for his country.

Cosimo I de' Medici, 1519-1574 (It.) Duke of Florence, grand duke of Tuscany.

Lorenzo de' Medici, the Magnificent, 1449-1492, (It.) merchant prince, a towering figure in Italian Renaissance.

Catherine de Medicis, 1519-1589, (F.) queen consort of Henry II, regent of France, influential in Catholic-Huguenot wars.

Golda Meir, 1898-1978, (Isr.) prime minister, 1969-74.

Klemens W.N.L. Metternich, 1773-1859, (Aus.) statesman, arbiter of post-Napoleonic Europe.

Anastas Mikoyan, 1895-1978, (USSR) prominent Soviet leader from 1917; president, 1964-65.

Guy Mollet, 1905-1975, (F.) socialist politician, resistance leader.

Henry Morgenthau Jr., 1891-1967, (U.S.) secretary of treasury, raised funds to finance New Deal and U.S. WW II activities.

Gouverneur Morris, 1752-1816, (U.S.) statesman, diplomat, financial expert who helped plan decimal coinage system.

Wayne Morse, 1900-1974, (U.S.) senator, long-time critic of Vietnam War.

Muhammad Ali, 1769?-1849, (Egypt), pasha, founder of dynasty that encouraged emergence of modern Egyptian state.

Benito Mussolini, 1883-1945, (It.) dictator and leader of the Italian fascist movement.

Imre Nagy, c. 1895-1958, (Hung.) communist premier, assassinated after Soviets crushed 1956 uprising.

Gamel Abdel Nasser, 1918-1970, (Egypt.) leader of Arab unification, second Egyptian president.

Jawaharlal Nehru, 1889-1964, (Ind.) prime minister, guided India through its early years of independence.

Kwame Nkrumah, 1909-1972, (Ghan.) dictatorial prime minister, deposed in 1966.

Frederick North, 1732-1792, (Br.) prime minister, his inept policies led to loss of American colonies.

Daniel O'Connell, 1775-1847, (Ir.) political leader, known as The Liberator.

Omar, c.581-644, Mohammedan leader, 2d caliph, led Islam to become an imperial power.

Ignace Paderewski, 1860-1941, (Pol.) statesman, pianist, composer, briefly prime minister, an ardent patriot.

Viscount Palmerston, 1784-1865, (Br.) Whig-Liberal prime minister, foreign minister, embodied British nationalism.

George Papandreou, 1888-1968, (Gk.) Republican politician, served three times as prime minister.

Franz von Papen, 1879-1969, (G.) politician, played major role in overthrow of Weimar Republic and rise of Hitler.

Charles Stewart Parnell, 1846-1891, (Ir.) nationalist leader, "uncrowned king of Ireland."

Lester Pearson, 1897-1972, (Can.) diplomat, Liberal party leader, prime minister.

Robert Peel, 1788-1850, (Br.) reformist prime minister, founder of the Conservative party.

Juan Perón, 1895-1974, (Arg.) president, dictator.

Joseph Pilsudski, 1867-1935, (Pol.) statesman, instrumental in re-establishing Polish state in the 20th century.

Charles Pinckney, 1757-1824, (U.S.) founding father, his Pinckney plan was largely incorporated into constitution.

William Pitt, the Elder, 1708-1778, (Br.) statesman, called the "Great Commoner," transformed Britain into imperial power.

William Pitt, the Younger, 1759-1806, (Br.) prime minister during the French Revolutionary wars.

Georgi Plekhanov, 1857-1918, (R.) revolutionary, social philosopher, called "father of Russian Marxism."

Raymond Poincaré, 1860-1934, (F.) 9th president of the Republic, advocated harsh punishment of Germany after WW I.

Georges Pompidou, 1911-1974, (F.) Gaullist political leader, president from 1969 to 1974.

Grigori Potemkin, 1739-1791, (R.) field marshal, favorite of Catherine II.

Edmund Randolph, 1753-1813, (U.S.) attorney, prominent in drafting, ratification of constitution.

John Randolph, 1773-1833, (U.S.) southern planter, strong advocate of states' rights.

Jeanette Rankin, 1880-1973, (U.S.) pacifist, first woman member of U.S. Congress.

Walter Rathenau, 1867-1922, (G.) industrialist, social theorist, statesman.

Sam Rayburn, 1882-1961, (U.S.) Democratic leader, representative for 47 years, House speaker for 17.

Paul Reynaud, 1878-1966, (F.) statesman, premier in 1940 at the time of France's defeat by Germany.

Syngman Rhee, 1875-1965, (Kor.) first president of the Republic of Korea.

Cecil Rhodes, 1853-1902, (Br.) imperialist, industrial magnate, established Rhodes scholarships in his will.

Cardinal de Richelieu, 1585-1642, (F.) statesman, known as "red eminence," chief minister to Louis XIII.

Maximilien Robespierre, 1758-1794, (F.) leading figure of French Revolution, responsible for much of Reign of Terror.

Nelson Rockefeller, 1908-1979, (U.S.) Republican whose career spanned 40 years; gov. of N.Y., 1958-73; U.S. vice president, 1974-77.

Eleanor Roosevelt, 1884-1962, (U.S.) humanitarian, United Nations diplomat.

Elihu Root, 1845-1937, (U.S.) lawyer, statesman, diplomat, leading Republican supporter of the League of Nations.

John Russell, 1792-1878, (Br.) Liberal prime minister during the Irish potato famine.

Antônio de O. Salazar, 1899-1970, (Port.) statesman, long-time dictator.

José de San Martin, 1778-1850, South American revolutionary, protector of Peru.

Eisaku Sato, 1901-1975, (Jap.) prime minister, presided over Japan's post-WW II emergence as major world power.

Philipp Scheidemann, 1865-1939, (G.) Social Democratic leader, first chancellor of the German republic.

Robert Schuman, 1886-1963, (F.) statesman, founded European Coal and Steel Community.

Carl Schurz, 1829-1906, (U.S.) German-American political leader, journalist, orator, dedicated reformer.

Kurt Schuschnigg, 1897-1977, (Aus.) chancellor, unsuccessful in stopping his country's annexation by Germany.

William H. Seward, 1801-1872, (U.S.) anti-slavery activist, as Lincoln's secretary of state purchased Alaska.

Carlo Sforza, 1872-1952, (It.) foreign minister, prominent Italian anti-fascist.

Alfred E. Smith, 1873-1944, (U.S.) New York Democratic governor, first Roman Catholic to run for presidency.

Jan C. Smuts, 1870-1950, (S.Af.) statesman, philosopher, soldier, prime minister.

Paul Henri Spaak, 1899-1972, (Belg.) statesman, socialist leader.

Joseph Stalin, 1879-1953, (USSR) Soviet dictator from 1924 to 1953.

Edwin M. Stanton, 1814-1869, (U.S.) Lincoln's secretary of war during the Civil War.

Edward R. Stettinius Jr., 1900-1949, (U.S.) industrialist, secretary of state who coordinated aid to WW II allies.

Adlai E. Stevenson, 1900-1965, (U.S.) Democratic leader, diplomat, Illinois governor, presidential candidate.

Henry L. Stimson, 1867-1950, (U.S.) statesman, served in 5 administrations, influenced foreign policy in 1930s and 1940s.

Gustav Stresemann, 1878-1929, (G.) chancellor, foreign minister, dedicated to regaining friendship for post-WW I Germany.

Sukarno, 1901-1970, (Indon.) dictatorial first president of the Indonesian republic.

Sun Yat-sen, 1866-1925, (Chin.) revolutionary, leader of Kuomintang, regarded as the father of modern China.

Robert A. Taft, 1889-1953, (U.S.) conservative Senate leader, called "Mr. Republican."

Charles de Talleyrand, 1754-1838, (F.) statesman, diplomat, the major force of the Congress of Vienna of 1814-15.

U Thant, 1909-1974, (Bur.) statesman, UN secretary-general.

Norman M. Thomas, 1884-1968, (U.S.) social reformer, 6 times unsuccessful Socialist party presidential candidate.

Josip Broz Tito, 1892-1980, (Yug.) president of Yugoslavia from 1953, World War II guerrilla chief, postwar rival of Stalin, leader of 3d world movement.

Palmiro Togliatti, 1893-1964, (It.) major leader of Italian Communist party.

Hideki Tojo, 1885-1948, (Jap.) statesman, soldier, prime minister during most of WW II.

François Toussaint L'Ouverture, c. 1744-1803, (Hait.) patriot, martyr, thwarted French colonial aims.

Leon Trotsky, 1879-1940, (USSR) revolutionary, communist leader, founded Red Army, expelled from party in conflict with Stalin.

Rafael L. Trujillo Molina, 1891-1961, (Dom.) absolute dictator, assassinated.

Moise K. Tshombe, 1919-1969, (Cong.) politician, president of secessionist Katanga, premier of Repubic of Congo (Zaire).

William M. Tweed, 1823-1878, (U.S.) politician, absolute leader of Tammany Hall, NYC's Democratic political machine.

Walter Ulbricht, 1893-1973, (G.) communist leader of German Democratic Republic.

Arthur H. Vandenberg, 1884-1951, (U.S.) senator, proponent of anti-communist bipartisan foreign policy after WW II.

Eleutherios Venizelos, 1864-1936, (Gk.) most prominent Greek statesman in early 20th century, considerably expanded Greek territory through his diplomacy.

Hendrik F. Verwoerd, 1901-1966, (S.Af.) prime minister, rigorously applied apartheid policy despite protest.

Robert Walpole, 1676-1745, (Br.) statesman, generally considered Britain's first prime minister.

Daniel Webster, 1782-1852, (U.S.) orator, politician, enthusiastic nationalist, advocate of business interests during Jacksonian agrarianism.

Chaim Weizmann, 1874-1952, Zionist leader, scientist, first Israeli president.

Wendell L. Willkie, 1892-1944, (U.S.) Republican who tried to unseat FDR when he ran for his 3d term.

Emiliano Zapata, c. 1879-1919, (Mex.) revolutionary, major influence on modern Mexico.

Notable Military and Naval Leaders of the Past

Creighton Abrams, 1914-1974, (U.S.) commanded forces in Vietnam, 1968-72.

Harold Alexander, 1891-1969, (Br.) led Allied invasion of Italy, 1943.

Ethan Allen, 1738-1789, (U.S.) headed Green Mountain Boys; captured Ft. Ticonderoga, 1775.

Edmund Allenby, 1861-1936, (Br.) in Boer War, WW1; led Egyptian expeditionary force, 1917-18.

Benedict Arnold, 1741-1801, (U.S.) victorious at Saratoga; tried to betray West Point to British.

Henry "Hap" Arnold, 1886-1950, (U.S.) commanded Army Air Force in WW2.

Petr Bagration, 1765-1812, (R.) hero of Napoleonic wars.

John Barry, 1745-1803, (U.S.) won numerous sea battles during revolution.

Pierre Beauregard, 1818-1893, (U.S.) Confederate general ordered bombardment of Ft. Sumter that began the Civil War.

Gebhard v. Blücher, 1742-1819, (G.) helped defeat Napoleon at Waterloo.

Napoleon Bonaparte, 1769-1821, (F.) defeated Russia and Austria at Austerlitz, 1805; invaded Russia, 1812; defeated at Waterloo, 1815.

Edward Braddock, 1695-1755, (Br.) commanded forces in French and Indian War.

Omar N. Bradley, 1893-1981, (U.S.) headed U.S. ground troops in Normandy invasion, 1944.

John Burgoyne, 1722-1792, (Br.) defeated at Saratoga.

Claire Chennault, 1890-1958, (U.S.) headed Flying Tigers in WW2.

Karl v. Clausewitz, 1780-1831, (G.) wrote books on military theory.

Henry Clinton, 1738-1795, (Br.) commander of forces in America, 1778-81

Lucius D. Clay, 1897-1978, (U.S.) led Berlin airlift, 1948-49.

Charles Cornwallis, 1738-1805, (Br.) victorious at Brandywine, 1777; surrendered at Yorktown.

Crazy Horse, 1849-1877, (U.S.) Sioux war chief victorious at Little Big Horn.

George A. Custer, 1839-1876, (U.S.) defeated and killed at Little Big Horn.

Stephen Decatur, 1779-1820, (U.S.) naval hero of Barbary wars, War of 1812.

Anton Denikin, 1872-1947, (R.) led White forces in Russian civil war.

George Dewey, 1837-1917, (U.S.) destroyed Spanish fleet at Manila, 1898.

Hugh C. Dowding, 1883-1970, (Br.) headed RAF, 1936-40.

Jubal Early, 1816-1894, (U.S.) Confederate general led raid on Washington, 1864.

Dwight D. Eisenhower, 1890-1969, (U.S.) commanded Allied forces in Europe, WW2.

David Farragut, 1801-1870, (U.S.) Union admiral captured New Orleans, Mobile Bay.

Ferdinand Foch, 1851-1929, (F.) headed victorious Allied armies, 1918.

Nathan Bedford Forrest, 1821-1877, (U.S.) Confederate general led cavalry raids against Union supply lines.

Frederick the Great, 1712-1786, (G.) led Prussia in The Seven Years War.

Charles G. Gordon, 1833-1885, (Br.) led forces in China; killed at Khartoum.

Horatio Gates, 1728-1806, (U.S.) commanded army at Saratoga.

Ulysses S. Grant, 1822-1885, (U.S.) headed Union army, 1864-65; forced Lee's surrender, 1865.

Heinz Guderian, 1888-1953, (G.) tank theorist led panzer forces in Poland, France, Russia.

Douglas Haig, 1861-1928, (Br.) led British armies in France, 1915-18.

William F. Halsey, 1882-1959, (U.S.) defeated Japanese fleet at Leyte Gulf, 1944.

Richard Howe, 1726-1799, (Br.) commanded navy in America, 1776-78; first of June victory against French, 1794.

William Howe, 1729-1814, (Br.) commanded forces in America, 1776-78.

Isaac Hull, 1773-1843, (U.S.) sunk British frigate Guerriere, 1812.

Thomas (Stonewall) Jackson, 1824-1863, (U.S.) Confederate general led forces in the Shenandoah Valley campaign; killed at Chancellorsville.

Joseph Joffre, 1852-1931, (F.) headed Allied armies, won Battle of the Marne, 1914.

John Paul Jones, 1747-1792, (U.S.) raided British coast; commanded Bonhomme Richard in victory over Serapis, 1779.

Stephen Kearny, 1794-1848, (U.S.) headed Army of the West in Mexican War.

Ernest J. King, 1878-1956, (U.S.) chief naval strategist in WW2.

Horatio H. Kitchener, 1850-1916, (Br.) led forces in Boer War; victorious at Khartoum; organized army in WW1.

Lavrenti Kornilov, 1870-1918, (R.) Commander-in-Chief, 1917; led counter-revolutionary march on Petrograd.

Thaddeus Kosciusko, 1746-1817, (P.) aided American cause in revolution.

Mikhail Kutuzov, 1745-1813, (R.) fought French at Borodino, 1812; abandoned Moscow; forced French retreat.

Marquis de Lafayette, 1757-1834, (F.) aided American cause in the revolution.

Thomas E. Lawrence (of Arabia), 1888-1935, (Br.) organized revolt of Arabs against Turks in WW1.

Henry (Light-Horse Harry) Lee, 1756-1818, (U.S.) cavalry officer in revolution.

Robert E. Lee, 1807-1870, (U.S.) Confederate general defeated at Gettysburg; surrendered to Grant, 1865.

James Longstreet, 1821-1904, (U.S.) aided Lee at Gettysburg.

William D. Leahy, 1875-1959, (U.S.) personal chief of staff to Roosevelt during WW2.

Douglas MacArthur, 1880-1964, (U.S.) commanded forces in SW Pacific in WW2; headed occupation forces in Japan, 1945-50; UN commander in Korean War.

Francis Marion, 1733-1795, (U.S.) led guerrilla actions in S.C. during revolution.

Duke of Marlborough, 1650-1722, (Br.) led forces against Louis XIV in War of the Spanish Sucession.

George C. Marshall, 1880-1959, (U.S.) chief of staff in WW2; authored Marshall Plan.

George B. McClellan, 1826-1885, (U.S.) Union general commanded Army of the Potomac, 1861-62.

George Meade, 1815-1872; (U.S.) commanded Union forces at Gettysburg.

Billy Mitchell, 1879-1936, (U.S.) air-power advocate; court-martialed for insubordination, later vindicated.

Helmuth v. Moltke, 1800-1891; (G.) victorious in Austro-Prussian, Franco-Prussian wars.

Louis de Montcalm, 1712-1759, (F.) headed troops in Canada; defeated at Quebec, 1759.

Bernard Law Montgomery, 1887-1976, (Br.) stopped German offensive at Alamein, 1942; helped plan Normandy invasion.

Daniel Morgan, 1736-1802, (U.S.) victorious at Cowpens, 1781.

Louis Mountbatten, 1900-1979, (Br.) Supreme Allied Commander of SE Asia, 1943-46.

Joachim Murat, 1767-1815, (F.) leader of cavalry at Marengo, 1800; Austerlitz, 1805; and Jena, 1806.

Horatio Nelson, 1758-1805, (Br.) naval commander destroyed French fleet at Trafalgar.

Michel Ney, 1769-1815, (F.) commanded forces in Switzerland, Austria, Russia; defeated at Waterloo.

Chester Nimitz, 1885-1966, (U.S.) commander of naval forces in Pacific in WW2.

George S. Patton, 1885-1945, (U.S.) led assault on Sicily, 1943; headed 3d Army invasion of German-occupied Europe.

Oliver Perry, 1785-1819, (U.S.) won Battle of Lake Erie in War of 1812.

John Pershing, 1860-1948, (U.S.) commanded Mexican border campaign, 1916; American expeditionary forces in WW1.

Henri Philippe Pétain, 1856-1951, (F.) defended Verdun, 1916; headed Vichy government in WW2.

George E. Pickett, 1825-1875, (U.S.) Confederate general famed for "charge" at Gettysburg.

Erwin Rommel, 1891-1944, (G.) headed Afrika Korps in WW2.

Karl v. Rundstedt, 1875-1953, (G.) supreme commander in West, 1943-45.

Aleksandr Samsonov, 1859-1914, (R.) led invasion of E. Prussia, defeated at Tannenberg, 1914.

Winfield Scott, 1786-1866, (U.S.) hero of War of 1812; headed forces in Mexican war, took Mexico City.

Philip Sheridan, 1831-1888, (U.S.) Union cavalry officer headed Army of the Shenandoah, 1864-65.

William T. Sherman, 1820-1891, (U.S.) Union general sacked Atlanta during "march to the sea," 1864.

Carl Spaatz, 1891-1974, (U.S.) directed strategic bombing against Germany, later Japan, in WW2.

Raymond Spruance, 1886-1969, (U.S.) victorious at Midway Island, 1942.

Joseph W. Stilwell, 1883-1946, (U.S.) headed forces in the China, Burma, India theater in WW2.

J.E.B. Stuart, 1833-1864, (U.S.) Confederate cavalry commander.

George H. Thomas, 1816-1870, (U.S.) saved Union army at Chattanooga, 1863; victorious at Nashville, 1864.

Semyon Timoshenko, 1895-1970, (USSR) defended Moscow, Stalingrad; led winter offensive, 1942-43.

Alfred v. Tirpitz, 1849-1930, (G.) responsible for submarine blockade in WW1.

Jonathan M. Wainwright, 1883-1953, (U.S.) forced to surrender on Corregidor, 1942.

George Washington, 1732-1799, (U.S.) led Continental army, 1775-83.

Archibald Wavell, 1883-1950, (Br.) commanded forces in N. and E. Africa, and SE Asia in WW2.

Anthony Wayne, 1745-1796, (U.S.) captured Stony Point, 1779; defeated Indians at Fallen Timbers, 1794.

Duke of Wellington, 1769-1852, (Br.) defeated Napoleon at Waterloo.

James Wolfe, 1727-1759, (Br.) captured Quebec from French, 1758.

Georgi Zhukov, 1895-1974, (USSR) defended Moscow, 1941; led assault on Berlin.

Noted Writers of the Past

Henry Adams, 1838-1918, (U.S.) historian, philosopher. *The Education of Henry Adams.*

George Ade, 1866-1944, (U.S.) humorist. *Fables in Slang.*

Conrad Aiken, 1889-1973, (U.S.) poet, critic. *Collected Poems.*

Louisa May Alcott, 1832-1888, (U.S.) novelist. *Little Women.*

Sholom Aleichem, 1859-1916. (R.) Yiddish writer. *Tevye's Daughter, The Great Fair.*

Horatio Alger, 1002-1899, (U.S.) author of "rags-to-riches" boys' books.

Hans Christian Anderson, 1805-1875, (Den.) author of fairy tales. *The Princess and the Pea, The Ugly Duckling.*

Maxwell Anderson, 1888-1959, (U.S.) playwright. *What Price Glory?, High Tor, Winterset, Key Largo.*

Sherwood Anderson, 1876-1941, (U.S.) author. *Winesburg, Ohio.*

Matthew Arnold, 1822-1888, (Br.) poet, critic. "Thrysis," "Dover Beach."

Jane Austen, 1775-1817, (Br.) novelist. *Pride and Prejudice, Sense and Sensibility, Emma, Mansfield Park.*

Isaac Babel, 1894-1941, (R.) short-story writer, playwright. *Odessa Tales, Red Cavalry.*

James M. Barrie, 1860-1937, (Br.) playwright, novelist. *Peter Pan, Dear Brutus, What Every Woman Knows.*

Honoré de Balzac, 1799-1850, (Fr.) novelist. *Le Père Goriot, Cousine Bette, Eugénie Grandet, The Human Comedy.*

Charles Baudelaire, 1821-1867, (Fr.) symbolist poet. *Les Fleurs du Mal.*

L. Frank Baum, 1856-1919, (U.S.) children's author. *Wizard of Oz* series.

Brendan Behan, 1923-1964, (Ir.) playwright. *The Quare Fellow, The Hostage, Borstal Boy.*

Robert Benchley, 1889-1945, (U.S.) humorist. *From Bed to Worse, My Ten Years in a Quandary.*

Stephen Vincent Benét, 1898-1943, (U.S.) poet, novelist. *John Brown's Body.*

John Berryman, 1914-1972, (U.S.) poet. *Homage to Mistress Bradstreet.*

Ambrose Bierce, 1842-1914, (U.S.) short-story writer, journalist. *In the Midst of Life, The Devil's Dictionary.*

William Blake, 1757-1827, (Br.) poet, mystic, artist. *Songs of Innocence, Songs of Experience.*

Giovanni Boccaccio, 1313-1375, (It.) poet, storyteller. *Decameron, Filostrato.*

James Boswell, 1740-1795, (Sc.) author. *The Life of Samuel Johnson.*

Anne Bradstreet, c. 1612-1672, (U.S.) poet. *The Tenth Muse Lately Sprung Up in America.*

Bertolt Brecht, 1898-1956, (G.) dramatist, poet. *The Threepenny Opera, Mother Courage and Her Children.*

Charlotte Brontë, 1816-1855, (Br.) novelist. *Jane Eyre.*

Emily Brontë, 1818-1848, (Br.) novelist. *Wuthering Heights.*

Elizabeth Barrett Browning, 1806-1861, (Br.) poet. *Sonnets from the Portuguese.*

Robert Browning, 1812-1889, (Br.) poet. "My Last Duchess," "Soliloquy of the Spanish Cloister."

Pearl Buck, 1892-1973, (U.S.) novelist. *The Good Earth.*

Mikhail Bulgakov, 1891-1940, (R.) novelist, playwright. *The Heart of a Dog, The Master and Margarita.*

John Bunyan, 1628-1688, (Br.) writer. *Pilgrim's Progress.*

Robert Burns, 1759-1796, (Sc.) poet. "Flow Gently, Sweet Afton," "My Heart's in the Highlands," "Auld Lang Syne."

Edgar Rice Burroughs, 1875-1950, (U.S.) novelist. *Tarzan of the Apes.*

George Gordon Lord Byron, 1788-1824, (Br.) poet. *Don Juan, Childe Harold.*

Albert Camus, 1913-1960, (F.) novelist. *The Plague, The Stranger, Caligula, The Fall.*

Lewis Carroll, 1832-1898, (Br.) writer, mathematician. *Alice's Adventures in Wonderland, Through the Looking Glass.*

Karel Capek, 1890-1938, (Czech.) playwright, novelist, essayist. *R.U.R. (Rossum's Universal Robots).*

Giacomo Casanova, 1725-1798, (It.) Venetian adventurer, author, world famous for his memoirs.

Willa Cather, 1876-1947, (U.S.) novelist, essayist. *O Pioneers!, My Antonia.*

Miguel de Cervantes Saavedra, 1547-1616, (Sp.) novelist, dramatist, poet. *Don Quixote de la Mancha.*

Raymond Chandler, 1888-1959, (U.S.) writer of detective fiction. *Philip Marlowe* series.

Geoffrey Chaucer, c. 1340-1400, (Br.) poet. *The Canterbury Tales.*

Anton Chekhov, 1860-1904, (R.) short-story writer, dramatist. *Uncle Vanya, The Cherry Orchard, The Three Sisters.*

G.K. Chesterton, 1874-1936, (Br.) author, *Fr. Brown* series.

Agatha Christie, 1891-1976, (Br.) mystery writer. *And Then There Were None, Murder on the Orient Express.*

Jean Cocteau, 1889-1963, (F.) writer, visual artist, filmmaker. *The Beauty and the Beast, Enfants Terribles.*

Samuel Taylor Coleridge, 1772-1834, (Br.) poet, man of letters. "Kubla Khan," "The Rime of the Ancient Mariner."

Sidonie Colette, 1873-1954, (F.) novelist. *Claudine, Gigi.*

Joseph Conrad, 1857-1924, (Br.) novelist. *Lord Jim, Heart of Darkness, The Nigger of the Narcissus.*

James Fenimore Cooper, 1789-1851, (U.S.) novelist. *Leather-Stocking Tales.*

Pierre Corneille, 1606-1684, (F.) Dramatist. *Medeé, Le Cid, Horace, Cinna, Polyeucte.*

Hart Crane, 1899-1932, (U.S.) poet. "The Bridge."

Stephen Crane, 1871-1900, (U.S.) novelist. *The Red Badge of Courage.*

e.e. cummings, 1894-1962, (U.S.) poet. *Tulips and Chimneys, Is 5, 95 Poems, The Enormous Room.*

Gabriele D'Annunzio, 1863-1938, (It.) poet, novelist, dramatist. *The Child of Pleasure, The Intruder, The Victim.*

Dante Alighieri, 1265-1321, (It.) poet. *The Divine Comedy.*

Daniel Defoe, 1660-1731, (Br.) writer. *Robinson Crusoe, Moll Flanders, Journal of the Plague Year.*

Charles Dickens, 1812-1870, (Br.) novelist. *David Copperfield, Oliver Twist, Great Expectations, The Pickwick Papers.*

Emily Dickinson, 1830-1886, (U.S.) poet.

Isak Dinesen (Karen Blixen), 1885-1962, (Dan.) author. *Out of Africa, Seven Gothic Tales, Winter's Tales.*

John Donne, 1573-1631, (Br.) poet. *Songs and Sonnets, Holy Sonnets,* "Death Be Not Proud."

John Dos Passos, 1896-1970, (U.S.) author. *U.S.A., Midcentury.*

Fyodor Dostoyevsky, 1821-1881, (R.) author. *Crime and Punishment, The Brothers Karamazov, The Possessed.*

Arthur Conan Doyle, 1859-1930, (Br.) author, created Sherlock Holmes.

Theodore Dreiser, 1871-1945, (U.S.) novelist. *An American Tragedy, Sister Carrie.*

John Dryden, 1631-1700, (Br.) poet, dramatist, critic. *Fables, Ancient and Modern.*

Alexandre Dumas, 1802-1870, (F.) novelist, dramatist. *The Three Musketeers, The Count of Monte Cristo.*

Alexandre Dumas (fils), 1824-1895, (F.) dramatist, novelist. *La Dame aux camélias, Le Demi-Monde.*

Ilya G. Ehrenburg, 1891-1967, (R.) novelist, journalist. *The Thaw.*

George Eliot, 1819-1880, (Br.) novelist. *Adam Bede, Silas Marner, The Mill on the Floss.*

T.S. Eliot, 1888-1965, (Br.) poet, critic. *The Wasteland,* "The Love Song of J. Alfred Prufrock," *Murder in the Cathedral.*

Ralph Waldo Emerson, 1803-1882, (U.S.) poet, essayist. "The Concord Hymn," "Brahma," "The Rhodora."

James T. Farrell, 1904-1979, (U.S.) novelist. *Studs Lonigan* trilogy.

William Faulkner, 1897-1962, (U.S.) novelist. *Sanctuary, Light in August, The Sound and the Fury, Absalom, Absalom!*

Edna Ferber, 1885-1968, (U.S.) novelist, dramatist. *Show Boat, Saratoga Trunk, Giant, Dinner at Eight.*

Henry Fielding, 1707-1754, (Br.) novelist. *Tom Jones.*

F. Scott Fitzgerald, 1896-1940, (U.S.) short-story writer, novelist. *The Great Gatsby, Tender is the Night.*

Gustave Flaubert, 1821-1880, (F.) novelist. *Madame Bovary.*

C.S. Forester, 1899-1966, (Br.) novelist. *Horatio Hornblower* series.

E.M. Forster, 1879-1970, (Br.) novelist. *A Passage to India, Where Angels Fear to Tread, Maurice.*

Anatole France, 1844-1924, (F.) writer. *Penguin Island, My Friend's Book, Le Crime de Sylvestre Bonnard.*

Robert Frost, 1874-1963, (U.S.) poet. "Birches," "Fire and Ice," "Stopping by Woods on a Snowy Evening."

John Galsworthy, 1867-1923, (Br.) novelist, dramatist. *The Forsyte Saga, A Modern Comedy.*

Erle Stanley Gardner, 1889-1970, (U.S.) author, lawyer.

Perry Mason series.

André Gide, 1869-1951, (F.) writer. *The Immoralist, The Pastoral Symphony, Strait is the Gate.*

Jean Giraudoux, 1882-1944, (F.) novelist, dramatist. *Electra, The Madwoman of Chaillot, Ondine, Tiger at the Gate.*

Johann W. von Goethe, 1749-1832, (G.) poet, dramatist, novelist. *Faust.*

Nikolai Gogol, 1809-1852, (R.) short-story writer, dramatist, novelist. *Dead Souls, The Inspector General.*

Oliver Goldsmith, 1730?-1774, (Br.-Ir.) writer. *The Vicar of Wakefield, She Stoops to Conquer.*

Maxim Gorky, 1868-1936, (R.) writer, founder of Soviet realism. *Mother, The Lower Depths.*

Thomas Gray, 1716-1771, (Br.) poet. "Elegy Written in a Country Churchyard."

Zane Grey, 1875-1939, (U.S.) writer of western stories.

Jakob Grimm, 1785-1863, (G.) philologist, folklorist. *German Methodology, Grimm's Fairy Tales.*

Wilhelm Grimm, 1786-1859, (G.) philologist, folklorist. *Grimm's Fairy Tales.*

Edgar A. Guest, 1881-1959, (U.S.) poet. *A Heap of Livin!*

Dashiell Hammett, 1894-1961, (U.S.) writer of detective fiction, created Sam Spade.

Thomas Hardy, 1840-1928, (Br.) novelist, poet. *The Return of the Native, Tess of the D'Urbervilles, Jude the Obscure.*

Joel Chandler Harris, 1848-1908, (U.S.) short-story writer. Uncle Remus series.

Moss Hart, 1904-1961, (U.S.) playwright. *Once in a Lifetime, You Can't Take It With You.*

Bret Harte, 1836-1902, (U.S.) short-story writer, poet. *The Luck of Roaring Camp.*

Jaroslav Hasek, 1883-1923, (Czech.) writer. *The Good Soldier Schweik.*

Nathaniel Hawthorne, 1804-1864, (U.S.) novelist, short story writer. *The Scarlet Letter, The House of the Seven Gables.*

Heinrich Heine, 1797-1856, (G.) poet. *Book of Songs.*

Ernest Hemingway, 1899-1961, (U.S.) novelist, short-story writer. *A Farewell to Arms, For Whom the Bell Tolls.*

O. Henry (W.S. Porter), 1862-1910, (U.S.) short-story writer. "The Gift of the Magi."

Hermann Hesse, 1877-1962, (G.) novelist, poet. *Death and the Lover, Steppenwolf, Siddhartha.*

Oliver Wendell Holmes, 1809-1894, (U.S.) poet, novelist. *The Autocrat of the Breakfast-Table.*

Alfred E. Housman, 1859-1936, (Br.) poet. *A Shropshire Lad.*

Langston Hughes, 1902-1967, (U.S.) poet, playwright. *The Weary Blues, One-Way Ticket, Shakespeare in Harlem.*

Victor Hugo, 1802-1885, (F.) poet, dramatist, novelist. *Notre Dame de Paris, Les Misérables.*

Aldous Huxley 1894-1963, (Br.) author. *Point Counter Point, Brave New World.*

Henrik Ibsen, 1828-1906, (Nor.) dramatist, poet. *A Doll's House, Ghosts, The Wild Duck, Hedda Gabler.*

William Inge, 1913-1973, (U.S.) playwright. *Come Back Little Sheba, Bus Stop, The Dark at the Top of the Stairs, Picnic.*

Washington Irving, 1783-1859, (U.S.) essayist, author. "Rip Van Winkle," "The Legend of Sleepy Hollow."

Shirley Jackson, 1919-1965, (U.S.) writer. *The Lottery.*

Henry James, 1843-1916, (U.S.) novelist, critic. *Washington Square, Portrait of a Lady, The American.*

Robinson Jeffers, 1887-1962, (U.S.) poet, dramatist. *Tamar and Other Poems, Medea.*

Samuel Johnson, 1709-1784, (Br.) author, scholar, critic. *Dictionary of the English Language.*

Ben Jonson, 1572-1637, (Br.) dramatist, poet. *The Alchemist, Volpone.*

James Joyce, 1882-1941, (Ir.) novelist. *Ulysses, A Portrait of the Artist as a Young Man, Finnegans Wake.*

Franz Kafka, 1883-1924, (G.) novelist, short-story writer. *The Trial, Amerika, The Castle.*

George S. Kaufman, 1889-1961, (U.S.) playwright. *The Man Who Came to Dinner, You Can't Take It With You, Stage Door.*

Nikos Kazantzakis, 1883?-1957, (Gk.) novelist. *Zorba the Greek, A Greek Passion.*

John Keats, 1795-1821, (Br.) poet. *On a Grecian Urn, La Belle Dame Sans Merci.*

Joyce Kilmer, 1886-1918, (U.S.) poet. "Trees."

Rudyard Kipling, 1865-1936, (Br.) author, poet. "The White Man's Burden," "Gunga Din," *The Jungle Book.*

Jean de la Fontaine, 1621-1695, (F.) poet. *Fables choisies.*

Pär Lagerkvist, 1891-1974, (Swed.) poet, dramatist, novelist. *Barabbas, The Sybil.*

Selma Lagerlöf, 1858-1940, (Swed.) novelist. *Jerusalem, The Ring of the Lowenskolds.*

Alphonse de Lamartine, 1790-1869, (F.) poet, novelist, statesman. *Méditations poétiques.*

Charles Lamb, 1775-1834, (Br.) essayist. *Specimens of English Dramatic Poets, Essays of Elia.*

Giuseppe di Lampedusa, 1896-1957, (It.) novelist. *The Leopard.*

Ring Lardner, 1885-1933, (U.S.) short story writer, humorist. *You Know Me, Al.*

D. H. Lawrence, 1885-1930, (Br.) novelist. *Women in Love, Lady Chatterley's Lover, Sons and Lovers.*

Mikhail Lermontov, 1814-1841, (R.) novelist, poet. "Demon," *Hero of Our Time.*

Alain-René Lesage, 1668-1747, (F.) novelist. *Gil Blas de Santillane.*

Gotthold Lessing, 1729-1781, (G.) dramatist, philosopher, critic. *Miss Sara Sampson, Minna von Barnhelm.*

Sinclair Lewis, 1885-1951, (U.S.) novelist, playwright. *Babbitt, Arrowsmith, Dodsworth, Main Street.*

Vachel Lindsay, 1879-1931, (U.S.) poet. *General William Booth Enters into Heaven, The Congo.*

Hugh Lofting, 1886-1947, (Br.) children's author. Dr. Doolittle series.

Jack London, 1876-1916, (U.S.) novelist, journalist. *Call of the Wild, The Sea-Wolf.*

Henry Wadsworth Longfellow, 1807-1882, (U.S.) poet. "The Wreck of the Hesperus," *Evangeline, The Song of Hiawatha.*

Amy Lowell, 1874-1925, (U.S.) poet, critic. *A Dome of Many-Colored Glass,* "Patterns," "Lilacs."

James Russell Lowell, 1819-1891, (U.S.) poet, editor. *Poems, The Bigelow Papers.*

Robert Lowell, 1917-1977, (U.S.) poet. "Lord Weary's Castle."

Emil Ludwig, 1881-1948, (G.) biographer. *Goethe, Beethoven, Napoleon, Bismarck.*

Niccolò Machiavelli, 1469-1527, (It.) author, statesman. *The Prince, Discourses on Livy.*

Stéphane Mallarmé, 1842-1898, (F.) poet. *The Afternoon of a Faun.*

Thomas Malory, ?-1471, (Br.) writor. *Morte d'Arthur.*

Andre Malraux, 1901-1976, (F.) novelist. *Man's Fate, The Voices of Silence.*

Osip Mandelstam, 1891-1938, (R.) Acmeist poet.

Thomas Mann, 1875-1955, (G.) novelist, essayist. *Buddenbrooks, Death in Venice, The Magic Mountain.*

Katherine Mansfield, 1888-1923, (Br.) short story writer. *Bliss, The Garden Party.*

Christopher Marlowe, 1564-1593, (Br.) dramatist, poet. *Tamburlaine the Great, Dr. Faustus, The Jew of Malta.*

John Masefield, 1878-1967, (Br.) poet. "Sea Fever," "Cargoes," *Salt Water Ballads.*

Edgar Lee Masters, 1869-1950, (U.S.) poet, biographer. *Spoon River Anthology.*

W. Somerset Maugham, 1874-1965, (Br.) author. *Of Human Bondage, The Razor's Edge, The Moon and Sixpence.*

Guy de Maupassant, 1850-1893, (F.) novelist, short-story writer. *A Life, Bel-Ami,* "The Necklace."

François Mauriac, 1885-1970, (F.) novelist, dramatist. *Viper's Tangle, The Kiss to the Leper.*

Vladimir Mayakovsky, 1893-1930, (R.) poet, dramatist. *The Cloud in Trousers.*

Carson McCullers, 1917-1967, (U.S.) novelist. *The Heart is a Lonely Hunter, Member of the Wedding.*

Herman Melville, 1819-1891, (U.S.) novelist, poet. *Moby Dick, Typee, Billy Budd, Omoo.*

H.L. Mencken, 1880-1956, (U.S.) author, critic, editor. *Prejudices, The American Language.*

George Meredith, 1828-1909, (Br.) novelist, poet. *The Ordeal of Richard Feverel, The Egoist.*

Prosper Mérimée, 1803-1870, (F.) author. *Carmen.*

Edna St. Vincent Millay, 1892-1950, (U.S.) poet. *The Harp Weaver and Other Poems, A Few Figs from Thistles.*

A.A. Milne, 1882-1956, (Br.) author. *When We Were Very Young, Winnie-the-Pooh, The House at Pooh Corner.*

John Milton, 1608-1674, (Br.) poet. *Paradise Lost, Samson Agonistes.*

Gabriela Mistral, 1889-1957, (Chil.) poet. *Sonnets of Death, Desolación, Tala, Lagar.*

Margaret Mitchell, 1900-1949, (U.S.) novelist. *Gone With the Wind.*

Jean Baptiste Molière, 1622-1673, (F.) dramatist. *Le Tartuffe, Le Misanthrope, Le Bourgeois Gentilhomme.*

Ferenc Molnár, 1878-1952, (Hung.) dramatist, novelist. *Liliom, The Guardsman, The Swan.*

Michel de Montaigne, 1533-1592, (F.) essayist. *Essais.*

Clement C. Moore, 1779-1863, (U.S.) poet, educator. "A Visit from Saint Nicholas."

Marianne Moore, 1887-1972, (U.S.) poet. *Observations, O to Be a Dragon.*

Thomas More, 1478-1535, (Br.) author. *Utopia.*

H.H. Munro (Saki), 1870-1916, (Br.) author. *Reginald, The Chronicles of Clovis, Beasts and Super-Beasts.*

Alfred de Musset, 1810-1857, (F.) poet, dramatist. *Confession d'un enfant du siècle.*

Vladimir Nabokov, 1899-1977, (U.S.) author. *Lolita, Ada.*

Ogden Nash, 1902-1971, (U.S.) poet. *Hard Lines, I'm a*

Stranger Here Myself, The Private Dining Room.

Pablo Neruda, 1904-1973, (Chil.) poet. *Twenty Love Poems and One Song of Despair, Toward the Splendid City.*

Sean O'Casey, 1884-1964, (Ir.) dramatist. *Juno and the Paycock, The Plough and the Stars.*

Flannery O'Connor, 1925-1964, (U.S.) novelist, short story writer. *Wise Blood,* "A Good Man Is Hard to Find," "Everything That Rises Must Converge."

Clifford Odets, 1906-1963, (U.S.) playwright. *Waiting for Lefty, Awake and Sing, Golden Boy, The Country Girl.*

John O'Hara, 1905-1970, (U.S.) novelist. *Butterfield 8, From the Terrace, Appointment in Samarra.*

Omar Khayyam, c. 1028-1122, (Per.) poet, mathematician. *Rubaiyat.*

Eugene O'Neill, 1888-1953, (U.S.) playwright. *Emperor Jones, Anna Christie, Long Day's Journey into Night, Desire Under the Elms, Mourning Becomes Electra.*

George Orwell, 1903-1950, (Br.) novelist, essayist. *Animal Farm, Nineteen Eighty-Four.*

Thomas (Tom) Paine, 1737-1809, (U.S.) author, political theorist. *Common Sense.*

Dorothy Parker, 1893-1967, (U.S.) poet, short-story writer. *Enough Rope, Laments for the Living.*

Boris Pasternak, 1890-1960, (R.) poet, novelist. *Doctor Zhivago, My Sister, Life.*

Samuel Pepys, 1633-1703, (Br.) public official, author of the greatest diary in the English language.

S. J. Perelman, 1904-1979, (U.S.) humorist. *The Road to Miltown, Under the Spreading Atrophy.*

Francesco Petrarca, 1304-1374, (It.) poet, humanist. *Africa, Trionfi, Canzoniere, On Solitude.*

Luigi Pirandello, 1867-1936, (It.) novelist, dramatist. *Six Characters in Search of an Author.*

Edgar Allan Poe, 1809-1849, (U.S.) poet, short-story writer, critic. "Annabel Lee," "The Raven," "The Purloined Letter."

Alexander Pope, 1688-1744, (Br.) poet. *The Rape of the Lock, An Essay on Man.*

Ezra Pound, 1885-1972, (U.S.) poet. *Cantos.*

Marcel Proust, 1871-1922, (F.) novelist. *A la recherche du temps perdu (Remembrance of Things Past).*

Aleksandr Pushkin, 1799-1837, (R.) poet, prose writer. *Boris Godunov, Eugene Onegin, The Bronze Horseman.*

François Rabelais, 1495-1553, (F.) writer, physician. Gargantua, Pantagruel.

Jean Racine, 1639-1699, (F.) dramatist. *Andromaque, Phèdre, Bérénice, Britannicus.*

Erich Maria Remarque, 1898-1970, (Ger.-U.S.) novelist. *All Quiet on the Western Front.*

Samuel Richardson, 1689-1761, (Br.) novelist. *Clarissa Harlowe, Pamela; or, Virtue Rewarded.*

James Whitcomb Riley, 1849-1916, (U.S.) poet. "When the Frost is on the Pumpkin," "Little Orphant Annie."

Rainer Maria Rilke, 1875-1926, (G.) poet. *Life and Songs, Divine Elegies, Sonnets to Orpheus.*

Arthur Rimbaud, 1854-1891, (F.) *A Season in Hell,* "Le Bateau ivre."

Edwin Arlington Robinson, 1869-1935, (U.S.) poet. "Richard Cory," "Miniver Cheevy."

Theodore Roethke, 1908-1963, (U.S.) poet. *Open House, The Waking, The Far Field.*

Romain Rolland, 1866-1944, (F.) novelist, biographer. *Jean-Christophe.*

Pierre de Ronsard, 1524-1585, (F.) poet. *Sonnets pour Hélène.*

Edmond Rostand, 1868-1918, (F.) poet, dramatist. *Cyrano de Bergerac.*

Damon Runyon, 1884-1946, (U.S.) short-story writer, journalist. *Guys and Dolls, Blue Plate Special.*

John Ruskin, 1819-1900, (Br.) critic, social theorist. *Modern Painters, The Seven Lamps of Architecture.*

Antoine de Saint-Exupery, 1900-1944, (F.) writer, aviator. *Wind, Sand and Stars, Le Petit Prince.*

George Sand, 1804-1876, (F.) novelist. *Consuelo, The Haunted Pool, Les Maitres sonneurs.*

Carl Sandburg, 1878-1967, (U.S.) poet. *Chicago Poems, Smoke and Steel, Harvest Poems.*

George Santayana, 1863-1952, (U.S.) poet, essayist, philosopher. *The Sense of Beauty, The Realms of Being.*

Friedrich von Schiller, 1759-1805, (G.) dramatist, poet, historian. *Don Carlos, Maria Stuart, Wilhelm Tell.*

Sir Walter Scott, 1771-1832, (Sc.) novelist, poet. *Ivanhoe, Rob Roy, The Bride of Lammermoor.*

William Shakespeare, 1564-1616, (Br.) dramatist, poet. *Romeo and Juliet, Hamlet, King Lear, The Merchant of Venice.*

George Bernard Shaw, 1856-1950, (Ir.) playwright, critic. *St. Joan, Pygmalion, Major Barbara, Man and Superman.*

Mary Wollstonecraft Shelley, 1797-1851, (Br.) author. *Frankenstein.*

Percy Bysshe Shelley, 1792-1822, (Br.) poet. *Prometheus Unbound, Adonais,* "Ode to the West Wind," "To a Skylark."

Richard B. Sheridan, 1751-1816, (Br.) dramatist. *The Rivals,*

School for Scandal.

Robert Sherwood, 1896-1955, (U.S.) playwright. *The Petrified Forest, Abe Lincoln in Illinois, Reunion in Vienna.*

Upton Sinclair, 1878-1968, (U.S.) novelist. *The Jungle.*

Edmund Spenser, 1552-1599, (Br.) poet. *The Faerie Queen.*

Richard Steele, 1672-1729, (Br.) essayist, playwright, began the Tatler and Spectator. *The Conscious Lovers.*

Lincoln Steffens, 1866-1936, (U.S.) editor, author. *The Shame of the Cities.*

Gertrude Stein, 1874-1946, (U.S.) author. *Three Lives.*

John Steinbeck, 1902-1968, (U.S.) novelist. *Grapes of Wrath, Of Mice and Men, Winter of Our Discontent.*

Stendhal (Marie Henri Beyle), 1783-1842, (F.) poet, novelist. *The Red and the Black, The Charterhouse of Parma.*

Laurence Sterne, 1713-1768, (Br.) novelist. *Tristram Shandy.*

Wallace Stevens, 1879-1955, (U.S.) poet. *Harmonium, The Man With the Blue Guitar, Transport to Summer.*

Robert Louis Stevenson, 1850-1894, (Br.) novelist, poet, essayist. *Treasure Island, A Child's Garden of Verses.*

Rex Stout, 1886-1975, (U.S.) mystery novelist, created Nero Wolfe.

Harriet Beecher Stowe, 1811-1896, (U.S.) novelist. *Uncle Tom's Cabin.*

Lytton Strachey, 1880-1932, (Br.) biographer, critic. *Eminent Victorians, Queen Victoria, Elizabeth and Essex.*

August Strindberg, 1849-1912, (Swed.) dramatist, novelist. *The Father, Miss Julie, The Creditors.*

Jonathan Swift, 1667-1745, (Br.) author. *Gulliver's Travels.*

Algernon C. Swinburne, 1837-1909, (Br.) poet, critic. *Songs Before Sunrise.*

John M. Synge, 1871-1909, (Ir.) poet, dramatist. *Riders to the Sea, The Playboy of the Western World.*

Rabindranath Tagore, 1861-1941, (Ind.), author, poet. *Sadhana, The Realization of Life, Gitanjali.*

Booth Tarkington, 1869-1946, (U.S.) novelist. *Seventeen, Alice Adams, Penrod.*

Sara Teasdale, 1884-1933, (U.S.) poet. *Helen of Troy and Other Poems, Rivers to the Sea, Flame and Shadow.*

Alfred Lord Tennyson, 1809-1892, (Br.) poet. *Idylls of the King, In Memoriam,* "The Charge of the Light Brigade."

William Makepeace Thackeray, 1811-1863, (Br.) novelist. *Vanity Fair.*

Dylan Thomas, 1914-1953, (Welsh) poet. *Under Milk Wood, A Child's Christmas in Wales.*

James Thurber, 1894-1961, (U.S.) humorist, artist. *The New Yorker, The Owl in the Attic, Thurber Carnival.*

J.R.R. Tolkien, 1892-1973, (Br.) author. *The Hobbit, Lord of the Rings.*

Lev Tolstoy, 1828-1910, (R.) novelist. *War and Peace, Anna Karenina.*

Anthony Trollope, 1815-1882, (Br.) novelist. *The Warden, Barchester Towers,* The Palliser novels.

Ivan Turgenev, 1818-1883, (R.) novelist, short-story writer. *Fathers and Sons, First Love, A Month in the Country.*

Mark Twain (Samuel Clemens), 1835-1910, (U.S.) novelist, humorist. *The Adventures of Huckleberry Finn, Tom Sawyer.*

Sigrid Undset, 1881-1949, (Nor.) novelist, poet. *Kristin Lavransdatter.*

Paul Valéry, 1871-1945, (F.) poet, critic. *La Jeune Parque, The Graveyard by the Sea.*

Jules Verne, 1828-1905, (F.) novelist, originator of modern science fiction. *Twenty Thousand Leagues Under the Sea.*

François Villon, 1431-1463?, (F.) poet. *Le petit et le Grand, Testament.*

Evelyn Waugh, 1903-1966, (Br.) satirist. *The Loved One.*

H.G. Wells, 1866-1946, (Br.) author. *The Time Machine, The Invisible Man, The War of the Worlds.*

Edith Wharton, 1862-1937, (U.S.) novelist. *The Age of Innocence, The House of Mirth.*

T.H. White, 1906-1964, (Br.) author. *The Once and Future King.*

Walt Whitman, 1819-1892, (U.S.) poet. *Leaves of Grass.*

John Greenleaf Whittier, 1807-1892, (U.S.) poet, journalist. *Snow-bound.*

Oscar Wilde, 1854-1900, (Ir.) author, wit, *The Picture of Dorian Gray, The Importance of Being Earnest.*

Thornton Wilder, 1897-1975, (U.S.) playwright. *Our Town, The Skin of Our Teeth, The Matchmaker.*

William Carlos Williams, 1883-1963, (U.S.) poet, physician. *Tempers, Al Que Quiere!, Paterson.*

Edmund Wilson, 1895-1972, (U.S.) author, literary and social critic. *Axel's Castle, To the Finland Station.*

P.G. Wodehouse, 1881-1975, (U.S.) dramatist. The "Jeeves" novels, *Anything Goes.*

Thomas Wolfe, 1900-1938, (U.S.) novelist. *Look Homeward, Angel, You Can't Go Home Again, Of Time and the River.*

Virginia Woolf, 1882-1941, (Br.) novelist, essayist. *Mrs. Dalloway, To the Lighthouse, The Waves.*

William Wordsworth, 1770-1850, (Br.) poet. "Tintern Abbey," "Ode: Intimations of Immortality." **William Butler Yeats,** 1865-1939, (Ir.) poet, playwright. The

Wild Swans at Coole, The Tower, Last Poems. **Émile Zola,** 1840-1902, (F.) novelist. *Nana, The Dram Shop.*

Poets Laureate of England

There is no authentic record of the origin of the office of Poet Laureate of England. According to Warton, there was a Versificator Regis, or King's Poet, in the reign of Henry III (1216-1272), and he was paid 100 shillings a year. Geoffrey Chaucer (1340-1400) assumed the title of Poet Laureate, and in 1389 got a royal grant of a yearly allowance of wine. In the reign of Edward IV (1461-1483), John Kay held the post. Under Henry VII (1485-1509), Andrew Bernard was the Poet Laureate, and was succeeded under Henry VIII (1509-1547) by John Skelton. Next came Edmund Spenser, who died in 1599; then Samuel Daniel, appointed 1599, and

then Ben Jonson, 1619. Sir William D'Avenant was appointed in 1637. He was a godson of William Shakespeare.

Others were John Dryden, 1670; Thomas Shadwell, 1688; Nahum Tate, 1692; Nicholas Rowe, 1715; the Rev. Laurence Eusden, 1718; Colley Cibber, 1730; William Whitehead, 1757, on the refusal of Gray; Rev. Thomas Warton, 1785, on the refusal of Mason; Henry J. Pye, 1790; Robert Southey, 1813, on the refusal of Sir Walter Scott; William Wordsworth, 1843; Alfred, Lord Tennyson, 1850; Alfred Austin, 1896; Robert Bridges, 1913; John Masefield, 1930; Cecil Day Lewis, 1967; Sir John Betjeman, 1972.

Noted Artists and Sculptors of the Past
Artists are painters unless otherwise indicated.

Washington Allston, 1779-1843, landscapist. Belshazzar's Feast.

Albrecht Altdorfer, 1480-1538, landscapist. Battle of Alexander.

Andrea del Sarto, 1486-1530, frescoes. Madonna of the Harpies.

Fra Angelico, c. 1400-1455, Renaissance muralist. Madonna of the Linen Drapers' Guild.

Alexsandr Archipenko, 1887-1964, sculptor. Boxing Match, Medranos.

John James Audubon, 1785-1851, Birds of America.

Hans Baldung Grien, 1484-1545, Todentanz.

Ernst Barlach, 1870-1938, Expressionist sculptor. Man Drawing a Sword.

Frederic-Auguste Bartholdi, 1834-1904, Liberty Enlightening the World, Lion of Belfort.

Fra Bartolommeo, 1472-1517, Vision of St. Bernard.

Aubrey Beardsley, 1872-1898, illustrator. Salome, Lysistrata.

Max Beckmann, 1884-1950, Expressionist. The Descent from the Cross.

Gentile Bellini, 1426-1507, Renaissance. Procession in St. Mark's Square.

Giovanni Bellini, 1428-1516, St. Francis in Ecstasy.

Jacopo Bellini, 1400-1470, Crucifixion.

George Wesley Bellows, 1882-1925, sports artist. Stag at Sharkey's.

Thomas Hart Benton, 1889-1975, American regionalist. Threshing Wheat, Arts of the West.

Gianlorenzo Bernini, 1598-1680, Baroque sculpture. The Assumption.

Albert Bierstadt, 1830-1902, landscapist. The Rocky Mountains, Mount Corcoran.

George Caleb Bingham, 1811-1879, Fur Traders Descending the Missouri.

William Blake, 1752-1827, engraver. Book of Job, Songs of Innocence, Songs of Experience.

Rosa Bonheur, 1822-1899, The Horse Fair.

Pierre Bonnard, 1867-1947, Intimist. The Breakfast Room.

Paul-Emile Borduas, 1905-1960, Abstractionist. Leeward of the Island, Enchanted Shields.

Gutzon Borglum, 1871-1941, sculptor. Mt. Rushmore Memorial.

Hieronymus Bosch, 1450-1516, religious allegories. The Crowning with Thorns.

Sandro Botticelli, 1444-1510, Renaissance. Birth of Venus.

Constantin Brancusi, 1876-1957, Nonobjective sculptor. Flying Turtle, The Kiss.

Georges Braque, 1882-1963, Cubist. Violin and Palette.

Pieter Bruegel the Elder, c. 1525-1569, The Peasant Dance.

Pieter Bruegel the Younger, 1564-1638, Village Fair, The Crucifixion.

Edward Burne-Jones, 1833-1898, Pre-Raphaelite artist-craftsman. The Mirror of Venus.

Alexander Calder, 1898-1976, sculptor. Lobster Trap and Fish Tail.

Michelangelo Merisi da Caravaggio, 1573-1610, Baroque. The Supper at Emmaus.

Emily Carr, 1871-1945, landscapist. Blunden Harbour, Big Raven.

Carlo Carra, 1881-1966, Metaphysical school. Lot's Daughters.

Mary Cassatt, 1845-1926, Impressionist. Woman Bathing.

George Catlin, 1796-1872, American Indian life. Gallery of Indians.

Benvenuto Cellini, 1500-1571, Mannerist sculptor, goldsmith. Perseus.

Paul Cezanne, 1839-1906, Card Players, Mont-Sainte-Victoire with Large Pine Trees.

Jean Simeon Chardin, 1699-1779, still lifes. The Kiss, The Grace.

Frederic Church, 1826-1900, Hudson River school. Niagara, Andes of Ecuador.

Cimabue, 1240-1302, Byzantine mosaicist. Madonna Enthroned with St. Francis.

Claude Lorrain, 1600-1682, ideal-landscapist. The Enchanted Castle.

Thomas Cole, 1801-1848, Hudson River school. The Ox-Bow.

John Constable, 1776-1837, landscapist. Salisbury Cathedral from the Bishop's Grounds.

John Singleton Copley, 1738-1815, portraitist. Samuel Adams, Watson and the Shark.

Lovis Corinth, 1858-1925, Expressionist. Apocalypse.

Jean-Baptiste-Camille Corot, 1796-1875, landscapist. Souvenir de Mortefontaine, Pastorale.

Correggio, 1494-1534, Renaissance muralist. Mystic Marriages of St. Catherine.

Gustave Courbet, 1819-1877, Realist. The Artist's Studio.

Lucas Cranach the Elder, 1472-1553, Protestant Reformation portraitist. Luther.

Nathaniel Currier, 1813-1888, and **James M. Ives,** 1824-1895, lithographers. A Midnight Race on the Mississippi.

Honore Daumier, 1808-1879, caricaturist. The Third-Class Carriage.

Jacques-Louis David, 1748-1825, Neoclassicist. The Oath of the Horatii.

Arthur Davies, 1862-1928, Romantic landscapist. Unicorns.

Edgar Degas, 1834-1917, The Ballet Class.

Eugene Delacroix, Co. 1400-1455, Romantic. Massacre at Chios.

Paul Delaroche, 1797-1856, historical themes. Children of Edward IV.

Luca Della Robbia, 1400-1482, Renaissance terracotta artist. Cantoria (singing gallery), Florence cathedral.

Donatello, 1386-1466, Renaissance sculptor. David, Gattamelata.

Raoul Dufy, 1877-1953, Fauvist. Chateau and Horses.

Asher Brown Durand, 1796-1886, Hudson River school. Kindred Spirits.

Albrecht Durer, 1471-1528, Renaissance engraver, woodcuts. St. Jerome in His Study, Melancholia I, Apocalypse.

Anthony van Dyck, 1599-1641, Baroque portraitist. Portrait of Charles I Hunting.

Thomas Eakins, 1844-1916, Realist. The Gross Clinic.

Jacob Epstein, 1880-1959, religious and allegorical sculptor. Genesis, Ecce Homo.

Jan van Eyck, 1380-1441, naturalistic panels. Adoration of the Lamb.

Anselm Feuerbach, 1829-1880, Romantic Classicism. Judgement of Paris, Iphigenia.

John Bernard Flannagan, 1895-1942, animal sculptor. Triumph of the Egg.

Jean-Honore Fragonard, 1732-1806, Rococo. The Swing.

Daniel Chester French, 1850-1931, The Minute Man of Concord; seated Lincoln, Lincoln Memorial, Washington, D.C.

Caspar David Friedrich, 1774-1840, Romantic landscapes. Man and Woman Gazing at the Moon.

Thomas Gainsborough, 1727-1788, portraitist. The Blue Boy.

Paul Gauguin, 1848-1903, Post-impressionist. The Tahitians.

Lorenzo Ghiberti, 1378-1455, Renaissance sculptor. Gates of Paradise baptistry doors, Florence.

Alberto Giacometti, 1901-1966, attenuated sculptures of solitary figures. Man Pointing.

Giorgione, c. 1477-1510, Renaissance. The Tempest.

Giotto di Bondone, 1267-1337, Renaissance. Presentation

of Christ in the Temple.

Francois Girardon, 1628-1715, Baroque sculptor of classical themes. Apollo Tended by the Nymphs.

Vincent van Gogh, 1853-1890, The Starry Night, L'Arlesienne.

Arshile Gorky, 1905-1948, Surrealist. The Liver Is the Cock's Comb.

Francisco de Goya y Lucientes, 1746-1828, The Naked Maja, The Disasters of War (etchings).

El Greco, 1541-1614, View of Toledo, Burial of the Count of Orgaz.

Horatio Greenough, 1805-1852, Neo-classical sculptor. George Washington.

Matthias Grünewald, 1480-1528, mystical religious themes. The Resurrection.

Frans Hals, c. 1580-1666, portraitist. Laughing Cavalier, Gypsy Girl.

Childe Hassam, 1859-1935, Impressionist. Southwest Wind.

Edward Hicks, 1780-1849, folk painter. The Peaceable Kingdom.

Hans Hofmann, 1000 1066, early Abstract Expressionist. Spring. The Gate.

William Hogarth, 1697-1764, caricaturist. The Rake's Progress.

Katsushika Hokusai, 1760-1849, printmaker. Crabs.

Hans Holbein the Elder, 1460-1524, late Gothic. Presentation of Christ in the Temple.

Hans Holbein the Younger, 1497-1543, portraitist. Henry VIII.

Winslow Homer, 1836-1910, marine themes. Marine Coast, High Cliff.

Edward Hopper, 1882-1967, realistic urban scenes. Sunlight in a Cafeteria.

Jean-Auguste-Dominique Ingres, 1780-1867, Classicist. Valpincon Bather.

George Inness, 1825-1894, luminous landscapist. Delaware Water Gap.

Vasily Kandinsky, 1866-1944, Abstractionist. Capricious Forms.

Paul Klee, 1879-1940, Abstractionist. Twittering Machine.

Kathe Kollwitz, 1867-1945, printmaker, social justice themes. The Peasant War.

Gaston Lachaise, 1882-1935, figurative sculptor. Standing Woman.

John La Farge, 1835-1910, muralist. Red and White Peonies.

Fernand Leger, 1881-1955, machine art. The Cyclists, Adam and Eve.

Leonardo da Vinci, 1452-1519, Mona Lisa, Last Supper, The Annunciation.

Emanuel Leutze, 1816-1868, historical themes. Washington Crossing the Delaware.

Jacques Lipchitz, 1891-1973, Cubist sculptor. Harpist.

Filippino Lippi, 1457-1504, Renaissance. The Vision of St. Bernard.

Fra Filippo Lippi, 1406-1469, Renaissance. Coronation of the Virgin.

Aristide Maillol, 1861-1944, sculptor. Night, The Mediterranean.

Edouard Manet, 1832-1883, forerunner of Impressionism. Luncheon on the Grass, Olympia.

Andrea Mantegna, 1431-1506, Renaissance frescoes. Triumph of Caesar.

Franz Marc, 1880-1916, Expressionist. Blue Horses.

John Marin, 1870-1953, expressionist seascapes. Maine Island.

Reginald Marsh, 1898-1954, satirical artist. Tattoo and Haircut.

Masaccio, 1401-1428, Renaissance. The Tribute Money.

Henri Matisse, 1869-1954, Fauvist. Woman with the Hat.

Michelangelo Buonarroti, 1475-1564, Pieta, David, Moses, The Last Judgment, Sistine Ceiling.

Carl Milles, 1875-1955, expressive rhythmic sculptor. Playing Bears.

Jean-Francois Millet, 1814-1875, painter of peasant subjects. The Gleaners, The Man with a Hoe.

David Milne, 1882-1953, landscapist. Boston Corner, Berkshire Hills.

Amedeo Modigliani, 1884-1920, Reclining Nude.

Piet Mondrian, 1872-1944, Abstractionist. Composition.

Claude Monet, 1840-1926, Impressionist. The Bridge at Argenteuil, Haystacks.

Gustave Moreau, 1826-1898, Symbolist. The Apparition, Dance of Salome.

James Wilson Morrice, 1865-1924, landscapist. The Ferry, Quebec, Venice, Looking Over the Lagoon.

Grandma Moses, 1860-1961, folk painter. Out for the Christmas Trees.

Edvard Munch, 1863-1944, Expressionist death themes. The Cry.

Bartolome Murillo, 1618-1682, Baroque religious artist. Vision of St. Anthony. The Two Trinities.

Barnett Newman, 1905-1970, Abstract Expressionist. Stations of the Cross.

Jose Clemente Orozco, 1883-1949, frescoes. House of Tears.

Charles Willson Peale, 1741-1827, American Revolutionary portraitist. Washington, Franklin, Jefferson, John Adams.

Rembrandt Peale, 1778-1860, portraitist. Thomas Jefferson.

Pietro Perugino, 1446-1523, Renaissance. Delivery of the Keys to St. Peter.

Pablo Picasso, 1881-1973, Guernica, Dove, Head of a Woman.

Piero della Francesca, c. 1415-1492, Renaissance. Duke of Urbino, Flagellation of Christ.

Camille Pissarro, 1830-1903, Impressionist. Morning Sunlight.

Jackson Pollock, 1912-1956, Abstract Expressionist. Autumn Rhythm.

Nicolas Poussin, 1594-1665, Baroque pictorial classicism. St. John on Patmos.

Maurice B. Prendergast, c. 1860-1924, Post-impressionist watercolorist. Umbrellas in the Rain

Pierre-Paul Prud'hon, 1758-1823, Romanticist. Crime pursued by Vengeance and Justice.

Pierre Cecile Puvis de Chavannes, 1824-1898, muralist. The Poor Fisherman.

Raphael Sanzio, 1483-1520, Renaissance. Disputa, School of Athens, Sistine Madonna.

Man Ray, 1890-1976, Dadaist. Observing Time, The Lovers.

Odilon Redon, 1840-1916, Symbolist lithographer. In the Dream.

Rembrandt van Rijn, 1606-1669, The Bridal Couple, The Night Watch.

Frederic Remington, 1861-1909, painter, sculptor, portrayer of the American West. Bronco Buster, Cavalry Charge on the Southern Plains.

Pierre-Auguste Renoir, 1841-1919, Impressionist. The Luncheon of the Boating Party.

Ilya Repin, 1844-1918, historical canvases. Zaporozhye Cossacks.

Joshua Reynolds, 1723-1792, portraitist. Mrs. Siddons as the Tragic Muse.

Diego Rivera, 1886-1957, frescoes. The Fecund Earth.

Auguste Rodin, 1840-1917, sculptor. The Thinker, The Burghers of Calais.

Mark Rothko, 1903-1970, Abstract Expressionist. Light, Earth and Blue.

Georges Rouault, 1871-1958, Expressionist. The Old King.

Henri Rousseau, 1844-1910, primitive exotic themes. The Snake Charmer.

Theodore Rousseau, 1812-1867, landscapist. Under the Birches, Evening.

Peter Paul Rubens, 1577-1640, Baroque. Mystic Marriage of St. Catherine.

Andrey Rublyov, 1370-1430, icon painter. Old Testament Trinity.

Jacob van Ruisdael, c. 1628-1682, landscapist. Jewish Cemetery.

Salomon van Ruysdael, c. 1600-1670, landscapist. River with Ferry-Boat.

Albert Pinkham Ryder, 1847-1917, seascapes and allegories. Toilers of the Sea.

Augustus Saint-Gaudens, 1848-1907, memorial statues. Farragut, Mrs. Henry Adams (Grief).

Andrea Sansovino, 1460-1529, Renaissance sculptor. Baptism of Christ.

Jacopo Sansovino, 1486-1570, Renaissance sculptor. St. John the Baptist.

John Singer Sargent, 1856-1925, Edwardian society portraitist. The Wyndham Sisters, Madam X.

Johann Gottfried Schadow, 1764-1850, monumental sculptor. Quadriga, Brandenburg Gate.

Georges Seurat, 1859-1891, Pointillist. Sunday Afternoon on the Island of Grande Jatte.

Gino Severini, 1883-1891, Futurist and Cubist. Dynamic Hieroglyph of the Bal Tabarin.

Ben Shahn, 1898-1969, social and political themes. Sacco and Vanzetti series, Seurat's Lunch, Handball.

Charles Sheeler, 1883-1965, Abstractionist. Upper Deck, Rolling Power.

David Alfaro Siqueiros, 1896-1974, political muralist. March of Humanity.

John F. Sloan, 1871-1951, depictions of New York City. Wake of the Ferry.

David Smith, 1906-1965, welded metal sculpture. Hudson River Landscape, Zig, Cubi series.

Gilbert Stuart, 1755-1828, portraitist. George Washington.

Thomas Sully, 1783-1872, portraitist. Col. Thomas Handasyd Perkins, The Passage of the Delaware.

Yves Tanguy, 1900-1955, Surrealist. Rose of the Four Winds.

Thomas J. Thomson, 1877-1918, landscapist. Spring Ice.
Giovanni Battista Tiepolo, 1696-1770, Rococo frescoes. The Crucifixion.
Jacopo Tintoretto, 1518-1594, Mannerist. The Last Supper.
Titian, c. 1485-1576, Renaissance. Venus and the Lute Player, The Bacchanal.
Henri de Toulouse-Lautrec, 1864-1901, At the Moulin Rouge.
John Trumbull, 1756-1843, historical themes. The Declaration of Independence.
Joseph Mallord William Turner, 1775-1851, Romantic landscapist. Snow Storm.
Paolo Uccello, 1397-1475, Gothic-Renaissance. The Rout of San Romano.
Maurice Utrillo, 1883-1955, Impressionist. Sacre-Coeur de Montmartre.
John Vanderlyn, 1775-1852, Neo-classicist. Ariadne Asleep on the Island of Naxos.
Diego Velazquez, 1599-1660, Baroque. Las Meninas, Portrait of Juan de Pareja.
Jan Vermeer, 1632-1675, interior genre subjects. Young Woman with a Water Jug.
Paolo Veronese, 1528-1588, devotional themes, vastly peopled canvases. The Temptation of St. Anthony.
Andrea del Verrocchio, 1435-1488, Florentine sculptor. Colleoni.
Maurice de Vlaminck, 1876-1958, Fauvist landscapist. The Storm.
Antoine Watteau, 1684-1721, Rococo painter of "scenes of gallantry". The Embarkation for Cythera.
George Frederic Watts, 1817-1904, painter and sculptor of grandiose allegorical themes. Hope, Physical Energy.
Benjamin West, 1738-1820, realistic historical themes. Death of General Wolfe.
James Abbott McNeill Whistler, 1834-1903, Arrangement in Grey and Black, No. 1: The Artist's Mother.
Archibald M. Willard, 1836-1918, The Spirit of '76.
Grant Wood, 1891-1942, Midwestern regionalist. American Gothic, Daughters of Revolution.
Ossip Zadkine, 1890-1967, School of Paris sculptor. The Destroyed City, Musicians, Christ.

Noted Philosophers and Religionists of the Past

Lyman Abbott, 1835-1922, (U.S.) clergyman, reformer; advocate of Christian Socialism.
Pierre Abelard, 1079-1142, (F.) philosopher, theologian, and teacher, used dialectic method to support Christian dogma.
Felix Adler, 1851-1933, (U.S.) German-born founder of the Ethical Culture Society.
St. Augustine, 354-430, Latin bishop considered the founder of formalized Christian theology.
Averroes, 1126-1198, (Sp.) Islamic philosopher.
Roger Bacon, c.1214-1294, (Br.) philosopher and scientist.
Karl Barth, 1886-1968, (Sw.) theologian, a leading force in 20th-century Protestantism.
St. Benedict, c.480-547, (It.) founded the Benedictines.
Jeremy Bentham, 1748-1832, (Br.) philosopher, reformer, founder of Utilitarianism.
Henri Bergson, 1859-1941, (F.) philosopher of evolution.
George Berkeley, 1685-1753, (Ir.) philosopher, churchman.
John Biddle, 1615-1662, (Br.) founder of English Unitarianism.
Jakob Boehme, 1575-1624, (G.) theosophist and mystic.
William Brewster, 1567-1644, (Br.) headed Pilgrims, signed Mayflower Compact.
Emil Brunner, 1889-1966, (Sw.) theologian.
Giordano Bruno, 1548-1600, (It.) philosopher.
Martin Buber, 1878-1965, (G.) Jewish philosopher, theologian, wrote *I and Thou.*
Buddha (Siddhartha Gautama), c.563-c.483 BC, (Ind.) philosopher, founded Buddhism.
John Calvin, 1509-1564, (F.) theologian, a key figure in the Protestant Reformation.
Rudolph Carnap, 1891-1970, (U.S.) German-born philosopher, a founder of logical positivism.
William Ellery Channing, 1780-1842, (U.S.) clergyman, early spokesman for Unitarianism.
Auguste Comte, 1798-1857, (F.) philosopher, the founder of positivism.
Confucius, 551-479 BC, (Chin.) founder of Confucianism.
John Cotton, 1584-1652, (Br.) Puritan theologian.
Thomas Cranmer, 1489-1556, (Br.) churchman, wrote much of the first *Book of Common Prayer;* promoter of the English Reformation.
René Descartes, 1596-1650, (F.) philosopher, mathematician.
John Dewey, 1859-1952, (U.S.) philosopher, educator; helped inaugurate the progressive education movement.
Denis Diderot, 1713-1784, (F.) philosopher, creator of first modern encyclopedia.
Mary Baker Eddy, 1821-1910, (U.S.) founder of Christian Science.
Jonathan Edwards, 1703-1758, (U.S.) preacher, theologian.
(Desiderius) Erasmus, c.1466-1536, (Du.) Renaissance humanist.
Johann Fichte, 1762-1814, (G.) philosopher, the first of the Transcendental Idealists.
George Fox, 1624-1691, (Br.) founder of Society of Friends.
St. Francis of Assisi, 1182-1226, (It.) founded the Franciscans.
al Ghazali, 1058-1111, Islamic philosopher.
Georg W. Hegel, 1770-1831, (G.) Idealist philosopher.
Martin Heidegger, 1889-1976, (G.) existentialist philosopher, affected fields ranging from physics to literary criticism.
Johann G. Herder, 1744-1803, (G.) philosopher, cultural historian; a founder of German Romanticism.
David Hume, 1711-1776, (Sc.) philosopher, historian.
Jan Hus, 1369-1415, (Czech.) religious reformer.
Edmund Husserl, 1859-1938, (G.) philosopher, founded the Phenomenological movement.
Thomas Huxley, 1825-1895, (Br.) agnostic philosopher, educator.
Ignatius of Loyola, 1491-1556, (Sp.) founder of the Jesuits.
William Inge, 1860-1954, (Br.) theologian, explored the mystic aspects of Christianity.
William James, 1842-1910, (U.S.) philosopher, psychologist; advanced theory of the pragmatic nature of truth.
Karl Jaspers, 1883-1969, (G.) existentialist philosopher.
Immanuel Kant, 1724-1804, (G.) metaphysician, preeminent founder of modern critical philosophy.
Soren Kierkegaard, 1813-1855, (Den.) philosopher, considered the father of Existentialism.
John Knox, 1505-1572, (Sc.) leader of the Protestant Reformation in Scotland.
Lao-Tzu, 604-531 BC, (Chin.) philosopher, considered the founder of the Taoist religion.
Gottfried von Leibniz, 1646-1716, (G.) philosopher, mathematician.
Martin Luther, 1483-1546, (G.) leader of the Protestant Reformation, founded Lutheran church.
Maimonides, 1135-1204, (Sp.) Jewish physician and philosopher.
Jacques Maritain, 1882-1973, (F.) Neo-Thomist philosopher.
Cotton Mather, 1663-1728, (U.S.) defender of orthodox Puritanism; founded Yale, 1703.
Aimee Semple McPherson, 1890-1944, (U.S.) evangelist.
Philipp Melanchthon, 1497-1560, (G.) theologian, humanist; an important voice in the Reformation.
Mohammed, c.570-632, Arab prophet of the religion of Islam.
Dwight Moody, 1837-1899, (U.S.) evangelist.
George E. Moore, 1873-1958, (Br.) ethical theorist.
Elijah Muhammad, 1897-1975, (U.S.) leader of the Black Muslim sect.
Heinrich Muhlenberg, 1711-1787, (G.) organized the Lutheran Church in America.
John H. Newman, 1801-1890, (Br.) Roman Catholic cardinal, led Oxford Movement.
Reinhold Niebuhr, 1892-1971, (U.S.) Protestant theologian, social and political critic.
Friedrich Nietzsche, 1844-1900, (G.) moral philosopher.
Blaise Pascal, 1623-1662, (F.) philosopher and mathematician.
St. Patrick, c.389-c.461, brought Christianity to Ireland.
St. Paul, ?-c.67, a founder of the Christian religion.
Charles S. Peirce, 1839-1914, (U.S.) philosopher, logician; originated concept of Pragmatism, 1878.
Josiah Royce 1855-1916, (U.S.) Idealist philosopher.
Charles T. Russell, 1852-1916, (U.S.) founder of Jehovah's Witnesses.
Fredrich von Schelling, 1775-1854, (G.) philosopher.
Friedrich Schleiermacher, 1768-1834, (G.) theologian, a founder of modern Protestant theology.
Arthur Schopenhauer, 1788-1860, (G.) philosopher.
Joseph Smith, 1805-1844, (U.S.) founded Latter Day Saints (Mormon) movement, 1830.
Herbert Spencer, 1820-1903, (Br.) philosopher of evolution.
Baruch Spinoza, 1632-1677, (Du.) rationalist philosopher.
Billy Sunday, 1862-1935, (U.S.) evangelist.
Daisetz Teitaro Suzuki, 1870-1966, (Jap.) Buddhist scholar.
Emanuel Swedenborg, 1688-1722, (Swed.) philosopher, mystic.
Thomas à Becket, 1118-1170, (Br.) archbishop of Canterbury, opposed Henry II.
Thomas à Kempis, c.1380-1471, (G.) theologian probably wrote *Imitation of Christ.*

Thomas Aquinas, 1225-1274, (It.) theologian and philosopher.

Paul Tillich, 1886-1965, (U.S.) German-born philosopher and theologian.

John Wesley, 1703-1791, (Br.) theologian, evangelist; founded Methodism.

Alfred North Whitehead, 1861-1947, (Br.) philosopher, mathematician.

William of Occam, c.1285-c.1349 (Br.) philosopher.

Roger Williams, c.1603-1683, (U.S.) clergyman, championed religious freedom and separation of church and state.

Ludwig Wittgenstein, 1889-1951, (Aus.) philosopher.

John Wycliffe, 1320-1384, (Br.) theologian, reformer.

Brigham Young, 1801-1877, (U.S.) Mormon leader, colonized Utah.

Huldrych Zwingli, 1484-1531, (Sw.) theologian, led Swiss Protestant Reformation.

Noted Social Reformers and Educators of the Past

Jane Addams, 1860-1935, (U.S.) co-founder of Hull House; won Nobel Peace Prize, 1931.

Susan B. Anthony, 1820-1906, (U.S.) a leader in temperance, anti-slavery, and women's suffrage movements.

Henry Barnard, 1811-1900, (U.S.) public school reformer.

Thomas Barnardo, 1845-1905, (Br.) social reformer, pioneered in the care of destitute children.

Clara Barton, 1821-1912, (U.S.) organizer of the American Red Cross.

Henry Ward Beecher, 1813-1887, (U.S.) clergyman, abolitionist.

Amelia Bloomer, 1818-1894, (U.S.) social reformer, women's rights advocate.

William Booth, 1829-1912, (Br.) founded the Salvation Army.

Nicholas Murray Butler, 1862-1947, (U.S.) educator headed Columbia Univ., 1902-45; won Nobel Peace Prize, 1931.

Frances X. (Mother) Cabrini, 1850-1917, (U.S.) Italian-born nun founded numerous charitable institutions; first American to be canonized.

Carrie Chapman Catt, 1859-1947, (U.S.) suffragette, helped win passage of the 19th amendment.

Eugene V. Debs, 1855-1926, (U.S.) labor leader, led Pullman strike, 1894; 4-time Socialist presidential candidate.

Melvil Dewey, 1851-1931, (U.S.) devised decimal system of library-book classification.

Dorothea Dix, 1802-1887, (U.S.) crusader for humane care of mentally ill.

Frederick Douglass, 1817-1895, (U.S.) abolitionist.

W.E.B. DuBois, 1868-1963, (U.S.) Negro-rights leader, educator, and writer.

William Lloyd Garrison, 1805-1879, (U.S.) abolitionist, reformer.

Giovanni Gentile, 1875-1944, (It.) philosopher, educator; reformed Italian educational system.

Samuel Gompers, 1850-1924, (U.S.) labor leader; a founder and president of AFL.

William Green, 1873-1952, (U.S.) president of AFL, 1924-52.

Sidney Hillman, 1887-1946, (U.S.) labor leader, helped organize CIO.

Samuel G. Howe, 1801-1876, (U.S.) social reformer, changed public attitudes toward the handicapped.

Helen Keller, 1880-1968, (U.S.) crusader for better treatment for the handicapped.

Martin Luther King Jr., 1929-1968, (U.S.) civil rights leader; won Nobel Peace Prize, 1964.

John L. Lewis, 1880-1969, (U.S.) labor leader, headed United Mine Workers, 1920-60.

Horace Mann, 1796-1859, (U.S.) pioneered modern public school system.

William H. McGuffey, 1800-1873, (U.S.) author of *Reader,* the mainstay of 19th century U.S. public education.

Alexander Meiklejohn, 1872-1964, (U.S.) British-born educator, championed academic freedom and experimental curricula.

Lucretia Mott, 1793-1880, (U.S.) reformer, pioneer feminist.

Philip Murray, 1886-1952, (U.S.) Scotch-born labor leader.

Florence Nightingale, 1820-1910, (Br.) founder of modern nursing.

Emmeline Pankhurst, 1858-1928, (Br.) woman suffragist.

Elizabeth P. Peabody, 1804-1894, (U.S.) education pioneer, founded 1st kindergarten in U.S., 1860.

Walter Reuther, 1907-1970, (U.S.) labor leader, headed UAW.

Jacob Riis, 1849-1914, (U.S.) crusader for urban reforms.

Margaret Sanger, 1883-1966, (U.S.) social reformer, pioneered the birth control movement.

Elizabeth Seton, 1774-1821, (U.S.) established parochial school education in U.S.

Earl of Shaftesbury (A.A. Cooper), 1801-1885, (Br.) social reformer.

Elizabeth Cady Stanton, 1815-1902, (U.S.) women's suffrage pioneer.

Lucy Stone, 1818-1893, (U.S.) feminist, abolitionist.

Harriet Tubman, c.1820-1913, (U.S.) abolitionist, ran Underground Railroad.

Booker T. Washington, 1856-1915, (U.S.) educator, reformer; championed vocational training for blacks.

Walter F. White, 1893-1955, (U.S.) headed NAACP, 1931-55.

William Wilberforce, 1759-1833, (Br.) social reformer, prominent in struggle to abolish the slave trade.

Emma Hart Willard, 1787-1870, (U.S.) pioneered higher education for women.

Frances E. Willard, 1839-1898, (U.S.) temperance, woman's rights leader.

Whitney M. Young Jr., 1921-1971, (U.S.) civil rights leader, headed National Urban League, 1961-71.

Noted Historians, Economists, and Social Scientists of the Past

Brooks Adams, 1848-1927, (U.S.) historian, political theoretician.

Francis Bacon, 1561-1626, (Br.) philosopher, essayist, and statesman.

George Bancroft, 1800-1891, (U.S.) historian, wrote 10-volume *History of the United States.*

Charles A. Beard, 1874-1948, (U.S.) historian, attacked motives of the Founding Fathers.

Bede (the Venerable), c.673-735, (Br.) scholar, historian.

Ruth Benedict, 1887-1948, (U.S.) anthropologist, studied Indian tribes of the Southwest.

Louis Blanc, 1811-1882, (F.) Socialist leader and historian whose ideas were a link between utopian and Marxist socialism.

Franz Boas, 1858-1942, (U.S.) German-born anthropologist, studied American Indians.

Van Wyck Brooks, 1886-1963, (U.S.) cultural historian, critic.

Edmund Burke, 1729-1797, (Ir.) British parliamentarian and political philosopher; influenced many Federalists.

Thomas Carlyle, 1795-1881, (Sc.) philosopher, historian, and critic.

Edward Channing, 1856-1931, (U.S.) historian wrote 6-volume *A History of the United States.*

John R. Commons, 1862-1945, (U.S.) economist, labor historian.

Benedetto Croce, 1866-1952, (It.) philosopher, statesman, and historian.

Bernard A. De Voto, 1897-1955, (U.S.) historian, won Pulitzer prize in 1948 for *Across the Wide Missouri.*

Emile Durkheim, 1858-1917, (F.) a founder of modern sociology.

Friedrich Engels, 1820-1895, (G.) political writer, with Marx

wrote the *Communist Manifesto.*

Irving Fisher, 1867-1947, (U.S.) economist, contributed to the development of modern monetary theory.

John Fiske, 1842-1901, (U.S.) historian and lecturer, popularized Darwinian theory of evolution.

Charles Fourier, 1772-1837, (F.) utopian socialist.

Henry George, 1839-1897, (U.S.) economist, reformer, led single-tax movement.

Edward Gibbon, 1737-1794, (Br.) historian, wrote *The History of the Decline and Fall of the Roman Empire.*

Francesco Guicciardini, 1483-1540, (It.) historian, wrote *Storia d'Italia,* principal historical work of the 16th-century.

Alvin Hansen, 1887-1975, (U.S.) economist.

Thomas Hobbes, 1588-1679, (Br.) social philosopher.

Richard Hofstadter, 1916-1970, (U.S.) historian, wrote *The Age of Reform.*

John Maynard Keynes, 1883-1946, (Br.) economist, principal advocate of deficit spending.

Alfred L. Kroeber, 1876-1960, (U.S.) cultural anthropologist, studied Indians of North and South America.

James L. Laughlin, 1850-1933, (U.S.) economist, helped establish Federal Reserve System.

Lucien Lévy-Bruhl, 1857-1939, (F.) philosopher, studied the psychology of primitive societies.

Kurt Lewin, 1890-1947, (U.S.) German-born psychologist, studied human motivation and group dynamics.

John Locke, 1632-1704, (Br.) political philosopher.

Thomas B. Macaulay, 1800-1859, (Br.) historian, statesman.

Bronislaw Malinowski, 1884-1942, (Pol.) anthropologist, considered the father of social anthropology.

Thomas R. Malthus, 1766-1834, (Br.) economist, famed for

Essay on the Principal of Population.

Karl Mannheim, 1893-1947, (Hung.) sociologist, historian.

Karl Marx, 1818-1883, (G.) political philosopher, proponent of modern communism.

Giuseppe Mazzini, 1805-1872, (It.) political philosopher.

George H. Mead, 1863-1931, (U.S.) philosopher and social psychologist.

James Mill, 1773-1836, (Sc.) philosopher, historian, and economist; a proponent of Utilitarianism.

John Stuart Mill, 1806-1873, (Br.) philosopher, political economist.

Perry G. Miller, 1905-1963, (U.S.) historian, interpreted 17th-century New England.

Theodor Mommsen, 1817-1903, (G.) historian, wrote *The History of Rome.*

Charles-Louis Montesquieu, 1689-1755, (F.) social philosopher.

Samuel Eliot Morison, 1887-1976, (U.S.) historian, chronicled voyages of early explorers.

Allen Nevins, 1890-1971, (U.S.) historian, biographer; twice won Pulitzer prize.

Jose Ortega y Gasset, 1883-1955, (Sp.) philosopher and humanist; advocated control by an elite.

Robert Owen, 1771-1858, (Br.) political philosopher, reformer.

Vilfredo Pareto, 1848-1923, (It.) economist, sociologist.

Francis Parkman, 1823-1893, (U.S.) historian, wrote 8-volume *France and England in North America, 1851-92.*

Marco Polo, c.1254-1324, (It.) narrated an account of his travels to China.

William Prescott, 1796-1859, (U.S.) early American historian.

Pierre Joseph Proudhon, 1809-1865, (F.) social theorist, regarded as the father of anarchism.

Francois Quesnay, 1694-1774, (F.) economic theorist, demonstrated the circular flow of economic activity throughout society.

David Ricardo, 1772-1823, (Br.) economic theorist, advocated free international trade.

James H. Robinson, 1863-1936, (U.S.) historian, educator.

Jean-Jacques Rousseau, 1712-1778, (F.) social philosopher, author.

Bertrand Russell, 1872-1970, (Br.) political philosopher, mathematician; wrote *Principia Mathematica.*

Hjalmar Schacht, 1877-1970, (G.) economist.

Joseph Schumpeter, 1883-1950, (U.S.) Czech.-born economist, championed big business, capitalism.

Albert Schweitzer, 1875-1965, (Alsatian) social philosopher, theologian, and humanitarian.

George Simmel, 1858-1918, (G.) sociologist, philosopher.

Adam Smith, 1723-1790, (Br.) economist, advocated laissez-faire economy and free trade.

Jared Sparks, 1789-1866, (U.S.) historian, among first to do research from original documents.

Oswald Spengler, 1880-1936, (G.) philosopher and historian, wrote *The Decline of the West.*

William G. Sumner, 1840-1910, (U.S.) social scientist, economist; championed laissez-faire economy, Social Darwinism.

Hippolyte Taine, 1828-1893, (F.) historian.

Frank W. Taussig, 1859-1940, (U.S.) economist, educator.

Alexis de Tocqueville, 1805-1859, (F.) political scientist, historian.

Francis E. Townsend, 1897-1960, (U.S.) author of old-age pension plan.

Arnold Toynbee, 1889-1975, (Br.) historian, wrote 10-volume *A Study of History.*

Heinrich von Treitschke, 1834-1896, (G.) historian, political writer.

George Trevelyan, 1838-1928, (Br.) historian, statesman.

Frederick J. Turner, 1861-1932, (U.S.) historian, educator.

Thorstein B. Veblen, 1857-1929, (U.S.) economist, social philosopher.

Giovanni Vico, 1668-1744, (It.) historian, philosopher.

Voltaire (F.A. Arouet), 1694-1778, (F.) philosopher, historian, and poet.

Izaak Walton, 1593-1683, (Br.) author, wrote first biographical works in English literature.

Sidney J., 1859-1947, and wife **Beatrice,** 1858-1943, **Webb** (Br.) leading figures in Fabian Society and British Labour Party.

Walter P. Webb, 1888-1963, (U.S.) historian of the West.

Max Weber, 1864-1920, (G.) sociologist.

Noted Scientists of the Past

Howard H. Aiken, 1900-1973, (U.S.) mathematician, designed world's first large-scale digital computer (Mark I) for IBM.

Albertus Magnus, 1193-1280, (G.) theologian, philosopher, scientist, established medieval Christian study of natural science.

Andre-Marie Ampère, 1775-1836, (F.) scientist known for contributions to electrodynamics.

Amedeo Avogadro, 1776-1856, (It.) chemist, physicist, advanced important theories on properties of gases.

A.C. Becquerel, 1788-1878, (F.) physicist, pioneer in electrochemical science.

A.H. Becquerel, 1852-1908, (F.) physicist, discovered radioactivity in uranium.

Alexander Graham Bell, 1847-1922, (U.S.) inventor, first to patent and commercially exploit the telephone, 1876.

Daniel Bernoulli, 1700-1782, (Swiss) mathematician, advanced kinetic theory of gases and fluids.

Jöns Jakob Berzelius, 1779-1848, (Swed.) chemist, developed modern chemical symbols and formulas.

Henry Bessemer, 1813-1898, (Br.) engineer, invented Bessemer steel-making process.

Louis Blériot, 1872-1936, (F.) engineer, pioneer aviator, invented and constructed monoplanes.

Niels Bohr, 1885-1962, (Dan.) physicist, leading figure in the development of quantum theory.

Max Born, 1882-1970, (G.) physicist known for research in quantum mechanics.

Robert Bunsen, 1811-1899, (G.) chemist, invented Bunsen burner.

Luther Burbank, 1849-1926, (U.S.) plant breeder whose work developed plant breeding into a modern science.

Vannevar Bush, 1890-1974, (U.S.) electrical engineer, developed differential analyzer, first electronic analogue computer.

Alexis Carrel, 1873-1944, (F.) surgeon, biologist, developed methods of suturing blood vessels and transplanting organs.

George Washington Carver, 1860?-1943, (U.S.) agricultural chemist, experimenter, benefactor of South, a black hero.

Henry Cavendish, 1731-1810, (Br.) chemist, physicist, discovered hydrogen.

James Chadwick, 1891-1974, (Br.) physicist, discovered the neutron.

Jean M. Charcot, 1825-1893, (F.) neurologist known for work on hysteria, hypnotism, sclerosis.

John D. Cockcroft, 1897-1967, (Br.) nuclear physicist, constructed first atomic particle accelerator with E.T.S. Walton.

William Crookes, 1832-1919, (Br.) physicist, chemist, discovered thallium, invented a cathode-ray tube, radiometer.

Marie Curie, 1867-1934, (Pol.-F.) physical chemist known for work on radium and its compounds.

Pierre Curie, 1859-1906, (F.) physical chemist known for work with his wife on radioactivity.

Gottlieb Daimler, 1834-1900, (G.) engineer, inventor, pioneer automobile manufacturer.

John Dalton, 1766-1844, (Br.) chemist, physicist, formulated atomic theory, made first table of atomic weights.

Charles Darwin, 1809-1882, (Br.) naturalist, established theory of organic evolution.

Humphry Davy, 1778-1829, (Br.) chemist, research in electrochemistry led to isolation of potassium, sodium, calcium, barium, boron, magnesium, and strontium.

Lee De Forest, 1873-1961, (U.S.) inventor, pioneer in development of wireless telegraphy, sound pictures, television.

Rudolf Diesel, 1858-1913, (G.) mechanical engineer, patented Diesel engine.

Thomas Dooley, 1927-1961, (U.S.) "jungle doctor," noted for efforts to supply medical aid to underdeveloped countries.

Christian Doppler, 1803-1853, (Aus.) physicist, demonstrated Doppler effect (change in energy wavelengths caused by motion).

Thomas A. Edison, 1847-1931, (U.S.) inventor, held over 1,000 patents, including incandescent electric lamp, phonograph.

Paul Ehrlich, 1854-1915, (G.) bacteriologist, pioneer in modern immunology and bacteriology.

Albert Einstein, 1879-1955, (U.S.) theoretical physicist, known for formulation of relativity theory.

Gabriel Fahrenheit, 1686-1736, (G.) physicist, introduced Fahrenheit scale for thermometers.

Michael Faraday, 1791-1867, (Br.) chemist, physicist, known for work in field of electricity.

Pierre de Fermat, 1601-1665, (F.) mathematician, discovered analytic geometry, founded modern theory of numbers and calculus of probabilities.

Enrico Fermi, 1901-1954, (It.) physicist, one of chief architects of the nuclear age.

Galileo Ferraris, 1847-1897, (It.) physicist, electrical engineer, discovered principle of rotary magnetic field.

Camille Flammarion, 1842-1925, (F.) astronomer, popularized study of astronomy.

Alexander Fleming, 1881-1955, (Br.) bacteriologist, discovered penicillin.

Jean B.J. Fourier, 1768-1830, (F.) mathematician, discovered theorem governing periodic oscillation.

James Franck, 1882-1964, (G.) physicist, proved value of quantum theory.

Sigmund Freud, 1856-1939, (Aus.) psychiatrist, founder of psychoanalysis.

Galileo Galilei, 1564-1642, (It.) astronomer, physicist, a founder of the experimental method.

Luigi Galvani, 1737-1798, (It.) physician, physicist, known as founder of galvanism.

Joseph Gay-Lussac, 1778-1850, (F.) chemist, physicist, investigated behavior of gases, discovered law of combining volumes.

Josiah W. Gibbs, 1839-1903, (U.S.) theoretical physicist, chemist, founded chemical thermodynamics.

George W. Goethals, 1858-1928, (U.S.) army engineer, built the Panama Canal.

William C. Gorgas, 1854-1920, (U.S.) sanitarian, U.S. army surgeon-general, his work to prevent yellow fever, malaria helped insure construction of Panama Canal.

Ernest Haeckel, 1834-1919, (G.) zoologist, evolutionist, a strong proponent of Darwin.

Otto Hahn, 1879-1968, (G.) chemist, worked on atomic fission.

J.B.C. Haldane, 1892-1964, (Sc.) scientist, known for work as geneticist and application of mathematics to science.

James Hall, 1761-1832, (Br.) geologist, chemist, founded experimental geology, geochemistry.

Edmund Halley, 1656-1742, (Br.) astronomer, calculated the orbits of many planets.

William Harvey, 1578-1657, (Br.) physician, anatomist, discovered circulation of the blood.

Hermann v. Helmholtz, 1821-1894, (G.) physicist, anatomist, physiologist, made fundamental contributions to physiology, optics, electrodynamics, mathematics, meteorology.

William Herschel, 1738-1822, (Br.) astronomer, discovered Uranus.

Heinrich Hertz, 1857-1894, (G.) physicist, his discoveries led to wireless telegraphy.

David Hilbert, 1862-1943, (G.) mathematician, formulated first satisfactory set of axioms for modern Euclidean geometry.

Edwin P. Hubble, 1889-1953, (U.S.) astronomer, produced first observational evidence of expanding universe.

Alexander v. Humboldt, 1769-1859, (G.) explorer, naturalist, propagator of earth sciences, originated ecology, geophysics.

Julian Huxley, 1887-1975, (Br.) biologist, a gifted exponent and philosopher of science.

Edward Jenner, 1749-1823, (Br.) physician, discovered vaccination.

William Jenner, 1815-1898, (Br.) physician, pathological anatomist.

Frederic Joliot-Curie, 1900-1958, (F.) physicist, with his wife continued work of Curies on radioactivity.

Irene Joliot-Curie, 1897-1956, (F.) physicist, continued work of Curies in radioactivity.

James P. Joule, 1818-1889, (Br.) physicist, determined relationship between heat and mechanical energy (conservation of energy).

Carl Jung, 1875-1961, (Sw.) psychiatrist, founder of analytical psychology.

Wm. Thomas Kelvin, 1824-1907, (Br.) mathematician, physicist, known for work on heat and electricity.

Sister Elizabeth Kenny, 1886-1952, (Austral.) nurse, developed method of treatment for polio.

Johannes Kepler, 1571-1630, (G.) astronomer, discovered important laws of planetary motion.

Joseph Lagrange, 1736-1813, (F.) geometer, astronomer, worked in all fields of analysis, and number theory, and analytical and celestial mechanics.

Jean B. Lamarck, 1744-1829, (F.) naturalist, forerunner of Darwin in evolutionary theory.

Irving Langmuir, 1881-1957, (U.S.) physical chemist, his studies of molecular films on solid and liquid surfaces opened new fields in colloid research and biochemistry.

Pierre S. Laplace, 1749-1827, (F.) astronomer, physicist, put forth nebular hypothesis of origin of solar system.

Antoine Lavoisier, 1743-1794, (F.) chemist, founder of modern chemistry.

Ernest O. Lawrence, 1901-1958, (U.S.) physicist, invented the cyclotron.

Louis Leakey, 1903-1972, (Br.) anthropologist, discovered

important fossils, remains of early hominids.

Anton van Leeuwenhoek, 1632-1723, (Du.) microscopist, father of microbiology.

Gottfried Wilhelm Leibniz, 1646-1716, (G.) mathematician, developed theories of differential and integral calculus.

Justus von Liebig, 1803-1873, (G.) chemist, established quantitative organic chemical analysis.

Percival Lowell, 1855-1916, (U.S.) astronomer, predicted the existence of Pluto.

Guglielmo Marconi, 1874-1937, (It.) physicist, known for his development of wireless telegraphy.

James Clerk Maxwell, 1831-1879, (Sc.) physicist, known especially for his work in electricity and magnetism.

Maria Goeppert Mayer, 1906-1972, (G.-U.S.) physicist, independently developed theory of structure of atomic nuclei.

Margaret Mead, 1901-1978, (U.S.) cultural anthropologist, popularized field.

Lise Meitner, 1878-1968, (Aus.) physicist whose work contributed to the development of the atomic bomb.

Gregor J. Mendel, 1822-1884, (Aus.) botanist, known for his experimental work on heredity.

Franz Mesmer, 1734-1815, (G.) physician, developed theory of animal magnetism.

Albert A. Michelson, 1852-1931, (U.S.) physicist, established speed of light as a fundamental constant.

Robert A. Millikan, 1868-1953, (U.S.) physicist, noted for study of elementary electronic charge and photoelectric effect.

Thomas Hunt Morgan, 1866-1945, (U.S.) geneticist, embryologist, established chromosome theory of heredity.

Isaac Newton, 1642-1727, (Br.) natural philosopher, mathematician, discovered law of gravitation, laws of motion.

J. Robert Oppenheimer, 1904-1967, (U.S.) physicist, director of Los Alamos during development of the atomic bomb.

Wilhelm Ostwald, 1853-1932, (G.) physical chemist, philosopher, chief founder of physical chemistry.

Louis Pasteur, 1822-1895, (F.) chemist, originated process of pasteurization.

Max Planck, 1858-1947, (G.) physicist, originated and developed quantum theory.

Henri Poincaré, 1854-1912, (F.) mathematician, physicist, influenced cosmology, relativity, and topology.

Joseph Priestley, 1733-1804, (Br.) chemist, one of the discoverers of oxygen.

Walter S. Reed, 1851-1902, (U.S.) army pathologist, bacteriologist, proved mosquitos transmit yellow fever.

Wilhelm Roentgen, 1845-1923, (G.) physicist, discovered X-rays.

Ernest Rutherford, 1871-1937, (Br.) physicist, discovered the atomic nucleus.

Giovanni Schiaparelli, 1835-1910, (It.) astronomer, hypothesized canals on the surface of Mars.

Angelo Secchi, 1818-1878, (It.) astronomer, pioneer in classifying stars by their spectra.

Harlow Shapley, 1885-1972, (U.S.) astronomer, noted for his studies of the galaxy.

Charles P. Steinmetz, 1865-1923, (U.S.) electrical engineer, developed fundamental ideas on alternating current systems.

Leo Szilard, 1898-1964, (U.S.) physicist, helped create first sustained nuclear reaction.

Rudolf Virchow, 1821-1902, (G.) pathologist, a founder of cellular pathology.

Alessandro Volta, 1745-1827, (It.) physicist, pioneer in electricity.

Alfred Russell Wallace, 1823-1913, (Br.) naturalist, proposed concept of evolution similar to Darwin.

August v. Wasserman, 1866-1925, (G.) bacteriologist, discovered reaction used as test for syphilis.

James E. Watt, 1736-1819, (Sc.) mechanical engineer, inventor, invented modern steam condensing engine.

Alfred L. Wegener, 1880-1930, (G.) meteorologist, geophysicist, postulated theory of continental drift.

Norbert Wiener, 1894-1964, (U.S.) mathematician, founder of the science of cybernetics.

Ferdinand v. Zeppelin, 1838-1917 (G.) soldier, aeronaut, airship designer.

Noted Business Leaders, Industrialists, and Philanthropists of the Past

Elizabeth Arden (F.N. Graham), 1884-1966, (U.S.) Canadian-born businesswoman founded and headed cosmetics empire.

Philip D. Armour, 1832-1901, (U.S.) industrialist, streamlined meat packing.

John Jacob Astor, 1763-1848, (U.S.) German-born fur trader, banker, real estate magnate; at death, richest in U.S.

Francis W. Ayer, 1848-1923, (U.S.) ad industry pioneer.

August Belmont, 1816-1890, (U.S.) German-born financier.

James B. (Diamond Jim) Brady, 1856-1917, (U.S.) financier, philanthropist, legendary bon vivant.

Adolphus Busch, 1839-1913, (U.S.) German-born business-

man, established brewery empire.

Asa Candler, 1851-1929, (U.S.) founded Coca-Cola Co.

Andrew Carnegie, 1835-1919, (U.S.) Scots-born industrialist, founded U.S. Steel; financed over 2,800 libraries.

William Colgate, 1783-1857, (U.S.) British-born businessman, philanthropist; founded soap-making empire.

Jay Cooke, 1821-1905, (U.S.) financier, sold $1 billion in Union bonds during Civil War.

Peter Cooper, 1791-1883, (U.S.) industrialist, inventor, philanthropist.

Ezra Cornell, 1807-1874, (U.S.) businessman, philanthropist;

headed Western Union, established univ.

Erastus Corning, 1794-1872, (U.S.) financier, headed N.Y. Central.

Charles Crocker, 1822-1888, (U.S.) railroad builder, financier.

Samuel Cunard, 1787-1865, (Can.) pioneered trans-Atlantic steam navigation.

Marcus Daly, 1841-1900, (U.S.) Irish-born copper magnate.

Walt Disney, 1901-1966, (U.S.) pioneer in cinema animation, built entertainment empire.

Herbert H. Dow, 1866-1930, (U.S.) Canadian-born founder of chemical co.

James Duke, 1856-1925, (U.S.) founded American Tobacco, Duke Univ.

Eleuthere I. du Pont, 1771-1834, (U.S.) French-born gunpowder manufacturer; founded one of world's largest business empires.

Thomas C. Durant, 1820-1885, (U.S.) railroad official, financier.

William C. Durant, 1861-1947, (U.S.) industrialist, formed General Motors.

George Eastman, 1854-1932, (U.S.) inventor, manufacturer of photographic equipment.

Marshall Field, 1834-1906, (U.S.) merchant, founded Chicago's largest department store.

Harvey Firestone, 1868-1938, (U.S.) industrialist, founded tire co.

Henry M. Flagler, 1830-1913, (U.S.) financier, helped form Standard Oil; developed Florida as resort state.

Henry Ford, 1863-1947, (U.S.) auto maker, developed first popular low-priced car.

Henry C. Frick, 1849-1919, (U.S.) industrialist, helped organize U.S. Steel.

Jakob Fugger (Jakob the Rich), 1459-1525, (G.) headed leading banking house, trading concern, in 16th-century Europe.

Alfred C. Fuller, 1885-1973, (U.S.) Canadian-born businessman, founded brush co.

Elbert H. Gary, 1846-1927, (U.S.) U.S. Steel head, 1903-27.

Amadeo P. Giannini, 1870-1949, (U.S.) founded Bank of America.

Stephen Girard, 1750-1831, (U.S.) French-born financier, philanthropist; richest man in U.S. at his death.

Jean Paul Getty, 1892-1976, (U.S.) founded oil empire.

Jay Gould, 1836-1892, (U.S.) railroad magnate, financier, speculator.

Hetty Green, 1834-1916, (U.S.) financier, the "witch of Wall St."; richest woman in U.S. in her day.

William Gregg, 1800-1867, (U.S.) launched textile industry in the South.

Meyer Guggenheim, 1828-1905, (U.S.) Swiss-born merchant, philanthropist; built merchandising, mining empires.

Edward H. Harriman, 1848-1909, (U.S.) railroad financier, administrator; headed Union Pacific.

Henry J. Heinz, 1844-1919, (U.S.) founded food empire.

James J. Hill, 1838-1916, (U.S.) Canadian-born railroad magnate, financier; founded Great Northern Railway.

Conrad N. Hilton, 1888-1979, (U.S.) intl. hotel chain founder.

Howard Hughes, 1905-1976, (U.S.) industrialist, financier, movie maker.

H.L. Hunt, 1889-1974, (U.S.) oil magnate.

Collis P. Huntington, 1821-1900, (U.S.) railroad magnate.

Henry E. Huntington, 1850-1927, (U.S.) railroad builder, philanthropist.

Howard Johnson, 1896-1972, (U.S.) founded restaurant chain.

Henry J. Kaiser, 1882-1967, (U.S.) industrialist, built empire in steel, aluminum.

Minor C. Keith, 1848-1929, (U.S.) railroad magnate; founded United Fruit Co.

Will K. Kellogg, 1860-1951, (U.S.) businessman, philanthropist, founded breakfast food co.

Richard King, 1825-1885, (U.S.) cattleman, founded half-million acre King Ranch in Texas.

William S. Knudsen, 1879-1948, (U.S.) Danish-born auto industry executive.

Samuel H. Kress, 1863-1955, (U.S.) businessman, art collector, philanthropist; founded "dime store" chain.

Alfred Krupp, 1812-1887, (G.) armaments magnate.

Albert Lasker, 1880-1952, (U.S.) businessman, philanthropist.

Thomas Lipton, 1850-1931, (Ir.) merchant, built tea empire.

James McGill, 1744-1813, (Can.) Scots-born fur trader, founded univ.

Andrew W. Mellon, 1855-1937, (U.S.) financier, industrialist; benefactor of National Gallery of Art.

Charles E. Merrill, 1885-1956, (U.S.) financier, developed firm of Merrill Lynch.

John Pierpont Morgan, 1837-1913, (U.S.) most powerful figure in finance and industry at the turn-of-the-century.

Malcolm Muir, 1885-1979, (U.S.) created *Business Week* magazine; headed *Newsweek,* 1937-61.

Samuel Newhouse, 1895-1979, (U.S.) publishing and broadcasting magnate, built communications empire.

Aristotle Onassis, 1900-1975, (Gr.) shipping magnate.

George Peabody, 1795-1869, (U.S.) merchant, financier, philanthropist.

James C. Penney, 1875-1971, (U.S.) businessman, developed department store chain.

William C. Procter, 1862-1934, (U.S.) headed soap co.

John D. Rockefeller, 1839-1937, (U.S.) industrialist, established Standard Oil; became world's wealthiest person.

John D. Rockefeller Jr., 1874-1960, (U.S.) philanthropist, established foundation; provided land for United Nations.

Meyer A. Rothschild, 1743-1812, (G.) founded international banking house.

Thomas Fortune Ryan, 1851-1928, (U.S.) financier, dominated N.Y. City public transportation; helped found American Tobacco.

Russell Sage, 1816-1906, (U.S.) financier.

David Sarnoff, 1891-1971, (U.S.) broadcasting pioneer, established first radio network, NBC.

Richard W. Sears, 1863-1914, (U.S.) founded mail-order co.

(Ernst) Werner von Siemens, 1816-1892, (G.) industrialist, inventor.

Alfred P. Sloan, 1875-1966, (U.S.) industrialist, philanthropist, headed General Motors.

A. Leland Stanford, 1824-1893, (U.S.) railroad official, philanthropist; founded univ.

Nathan Strauss, 1848-1931, (U.S.) German-born merchant, philanthropist; headed Macy's.

Levi Strauss, c.1829-1902, (U.S.) pants manufacturer.

Clement Studebaker, 1831-1901, (U.S.) wagon, carriage manufacturer.

Gustavus Swift, 1839-1903, (U.S.) pioneer meat-packer; promoted refrigerated railroad cars.

Gerard Swope, 1872-1957, (U.S.) industrialist, economist; headed General Electric.

James Walter Thompson, 1847-1928, (U.S.) ad executive.

Theodore N. Vail, 1845-1920, (U.S.) organized Bell Telephone system, headed ATT.

Cornelius Vanderbilt, 1794-1877, (U.S.) financier, established steamship, railroad empires.

Henry Villard, 1835-1900, (U.S.) German-born railroad executive, financier.

Charles R. Walgreen, 1873-1939, (U.S.) founded drugstore chain.

John Wanamaker, 1838-1922, (U.S.) pioneered department-store merchandising.

Aaron Montgomery Ward, 1843-1913, (U.S.) established first mail-order firm.

Thomas J. Watson, 1874-1956, (U.S.) headed IBM, 1924-49.

Charles E. Wilson, 1890-1961, (U.S.) auto industry executive; public official.

Frank W. Woolworth, 1852-1919, (U.S.) created 5 & 10 chain.

William Wrigley Jr., 1861-1932, (U.S.) founded chewing gum co.

Composers of the Western World

Carl Philipp Emanuel Bach, 1714-1788, (G.) Prussian and Wurtembergian Sonatas.

Johann Christian Bach, 1735-1782, (G.) Concertos; sonatas.

Johann Sebastian Bach, 1685-1750, (G.) St. Matthew Passion, The Well-Tempered Clavichord.

Samuel Barber, b. 1910, (U.S.) Adagio for Strings, Vanessa.

Bela Bartok, 1881-1945, (Hung.) Concerto for Orchestra, The Miraculous Mandarin.

Ludwig Van Beethoven, 1770-1827, (G.) Concertos (Emperor); sonatas (Moonlight, Pastorale, Pathetique); symphonies (Eroica).

Vincenzo Bellini, 1801-1835, (It.) La Sonnambula, Norma, I Puritani.

Alban Berg, 1885-1935, (Aus.) Wozzeck, Lulu.

Hector Berlioz, 1803-1869, (F.) Damnation of Faust, Symphonie Fantastique, Requiem.

Leonard Bernstein, b. 1918, (U.S.) Jeremiah, West Side Story.

Georges Bizet, 1838-1875, (F.) Carmen, Pearl Fishers.

Ernest Bloch, 1880-1959, (Swiss) Schelomo, Voice in the Wilderness, Sacred Service.

Luigi Boccherini, 1743-1805, (It.) Cello Concerto in B Flat, Symphony in C.

Alexander Borodin, 1834-1887, (R.) Prince Igor, In the Steppes of Central Asia.

Johannes Brahms, 1833-1897, (G.) Liebeslieder Waltzes,

Rhapsody in E Flat Major, Opus 119 for Piano, Academic Festival Overture; symphonies; quartets.

Benjamin Britten, 1913-1976, (Br.) Peter Grimes, Turn of the Screw, Ceremony of Carols.

Anton Bruckner, 1824-1896, (Aus.) Symphonies (Romantic), Intermezzo for String Quintet.

Ferruccio Busoni, 1866-1924, (It.) Doctor Faust, Comedy Overture.

Dietrich Buxtehude, 1637-1707, (D.) Cantatas, trio sonatas.

William Byrd, 1543-1623, (Br.) Masses, sacred songs.

Alexis Emmanuel Chabrier, 1841-1894, (Fr.) Le Roi Malgre Lui, Espana.

Gustave Charpentier, 1860-1956, (F.) Louise.

Frederic Chopin, 1810-1849, (Pol.) Concertos, Polonaise No. 6 in A Flat Major (Heroic); sonatas.

Aaron Copland, b. 1900, (U.S.) Appalachian Spring.

Claude Achille Debussy, 1862-1918, (F.) Pelleas et Melisande, La Mer, Prelude to the Afternoon of a Faun.

C.P. Leo Delibes, 1836-1891, (F.) Lakme, Coppelia, Sylvia.

Norman Dello Joio, b. 1913, (U.S.), Triumph of St. Joan, Psalm of David.

Gaetano Donizetti, 1797-1848, (It.) Elixir of Love, Lucia Di Lammermoor, Daughter of the Regiment.

Paul Dukas, 1865-1935, (Fr.) Sorcerer's Apprentice.

Antonin Dvorak, 1841-1904, (C.) Symphony in E Minor (From the New World).

Edward Elgar, 1857-1934, (Br.) Pomp and Circumstance.

Manuel de Falla, 1876-1946, (Sp.) La Vide Breve, El Amor Brujo.

Gabriel Faure, 1845-1924, (Fr.) Requiem, Ballade.

Friedrich von Flotow, 1812-1883, (G.) Martha.

Cesar Franck, 1822-1890, (Belg.) D Minor Symphony.

George Gershwin, 1898-1937, (U.S.) Rhapsody in Blue, American in Paris, Porgy and Bess.

Umberto Giordano, 1867-1948, (It.) Andrea Chenier.

Alex K. Glazunoff, 1865-1936, (R.) Symphonies, Stenka Razin.

Mikhail Glinka, 1804-1857, (R.) Ruslan and Ludmilla.

Christoph W. Gluck, 1714-1787, (G.) Alceste, Iphigenie en Tauride.

Charles Gounod, 1818-1893, (F.) Faust, Romeo and Juliet.

Edvard Grieg, 1843-1907, (Nor.) Peer Gynt Suite, Concerto in A Minor.

George Frederick Handel, 1685-1759, (G., Br.) Messiah, Xerxes, Berenice.

Howard Hanson, b. 1896, (U.S.) Symphonies No. 1 (Nordic) and 2 (Romantic).

Roy Harris, b. 1898, (U.S.) Symphonies, Amer. Portraits.

Joseph Haydn, 1732-1809, (Aus.) Symphonies (Clock); oratorios; chamber music.

Paul Hindemith, 1895-1963, (U.S.) Mathis Der Maler.

Gustav Holst, 1874-1934, (Br.) The Planets.

Arthur Honegger, 1892-1955, (Swiss) Judith, Le Roi David, Pacific 231.

Alan Hovhaness, b. 1911, (U.S.) Symphonies, Magnificat.

Engelbert Humperdinck, 1854-1921, (G.) Hansel and Gretel.

Charles Ives, 1874-1954, (U.S.) Third Symphony.

Aram Khachaturian, 1903-1978, (R.) Gayane (ballet), symphonies.

Zoltan Kodaly, 1882-1967, (Hung.) Hary Janos, Psalmus Hungaricus.

Fritz Kreisler, 1875-1962, (Aus.) Caprice Viennois, Tambourin Chinois.

Rodolphe Kreutzer, 1766-1831, (F.) 40 etudes for violin.

Edouard V.A. Lalo, 1823-1892, (F.) Symphonie Espagnole.

Ruggiero Leoncavallo, 1858-1919, (It.) I Pagliacci.

Franz Liszt, 1811-1886, (Hung.) 20 Hungarian rhapsodies; symphonic poems.

Edward MacDowell, 1861-1908, (U.S.) To a Wild Rose.

Gustav Mahler, 1860-1911, (Aus.) Lied von der Erde.

Pietro Mascagni, 1863-1945, (It.) Cavalleria Rusticana.

Jules Massenet, 1842-1912, (F.) Manon, Le Cid, Thais.

Mendelssohn-Bartholdy, 1809-1847, (G.) Midsummer Night's Dream, Songs Without Words.

Gian-Carlo Menotti, b. 1911, (It.-U.S.) The Medium, The Consul, Amahl and the Night Visitors.

Giacomo Meyerbeer, 1791-1864, (G.) Robert le Diable, Les Huguenots.

Claudio Monteverdi, 1567-1643, (It.) Opera; masses; madrigals.

Wolfgang Amadeus Mozart, 1756-1791, (Aus.) Magic Flute, Marriage of Figaro; concertos; symphonies, etc.

Modest Moussorgsky, 1835-1881, (R.) Boris Godunov, Pictures at an Exhibition.

Jacques Offenbach, 1819-1880, (F.) Tales of Hoffman.

Karl Orff, b. 1895, (G.) Carmina Burana.

Ignace Paderewski, 1860-1941, (P.) Minuet in G.

Giovanni P. da Palestrina, 1524-1594, (It.) Masses; madrigals.

Amilcare Ponchielli, 1834-1886, (It.) La Gioconda.

Francis Poulenc, 1899-1963, (F.) Dialogues des Carmelites.

Serge Prokofiev, 1891-1953, (R.) Love for Three Oranges, Lt. Kije, Peter and the Wolf.

Giacomo Puccini, 1858-1924, (It.) La Boheme, Manon Lescaut, Tosca, Madame Butterfly.

Sergei Rachmaninov, 1873-1943, (R.) Prelude in C Sharp Minor.

Maurice Ravel, 1875-1937, (Fr.) Bolero, Daphnis et Chloe, Rapsodie Espagnole.

Nikolai Rimsky-Korsakov, 1844-1908, (R.) Golden Cockerel, Capriccio Espagnol, Scheherazade, Russian Easter Overture.

Gioacchino Rossini, 1792-1868, (It.) Barber of Seville, Semiramide, William Tell.

Chas. Camille Saint-Saens, 1835-1921, (F.) Samson and Delilah, Danse Macabre.

Alessandro Scarlatti, 1659-1725, (It.) Cantatas; concertos.

Arnold Schoenberg, 1874-1951, (Aus.) Pelleas and Melisande, Transfigured Night, De Profundis.

Franz Schubert, 1797-1828, (A.) Lieder; symphonies (Unfinished); overtures (Rosamunde).

William Schuman, b. 1910, (U.S.) Credendum, New England Triptych.

Robert Schumann, 1810-1856, (G.) Symphonies, songs.

Aleksandr Scriabin, 1872-1915, (R.) Prometheus.

Dimitri Shostakovich, 1906-1975, (R.) Symphonies, Lady Macbeth of Minsk, The Nose.

Jean Sibelius, 1865-1957, (Finn.) Finlandia, Karelia.

Bedrich Smetana, 1824-1884, (Cz.) The Bartered Bride.

Karlheinz Stockhausen, b. 1928, (G.) Kontrapunkte, Kontakte.

Richard Strauss, 1864-1949, (G.) Salome, Elektra, Der Rosenkavalier, Thus Spake Zarathustra.

Igor F. Stravinsky, 1882-1971, (R.-U.S.) Oedipus Rex, Le Sacre du Printemps, Petrushka.

Peter I. Tchaikovsky, 1840-1893, (R.) Nutcracker Suite, Swan Lake, Eugene Onegin.

Ambroise Thomas, 1811-1896, (F.) Mignon.

Virgil Thomson, b. 1896, (U.S.) Opera, ballet; Four Saints in Three Acts.

Ralph Vaughan Williams, 1872-1958, (Br.) Job, London Symphony, Symphony No. 7 (Antarctica).

Giuseppe Verdi, 1813-1901, (It.) Aida, Rigoletto, Don Carlo, Il Trovatore, La Traviata, Falstaff, Macbeth.

Hector Villa-Lobos, 1887-1959, (Brazil) Choros.

Antonio Vivaldi, 1678-1741, (It.) Concerti, The Four Seasons.

Richard Wagner, 1813-1883, (G.) Rienzi, Tannhauser, Lohengrin, Tristan und Isolde.

Karl Maria von Weber, 1786-1826, (G.) Der Freischutz.

Composers of Operettas, Musicals, and Popular Music

Richard Adler, b. 1921, (U.S.) Pajama Game; Damn Yankees.

Milton Ager, 1893-1979, (U.S.) I Wonder What's Become of Sally; Hard Hearted Hannah; Ain't She Sweet?

Leroy Anderson, 1908-1975, (U.S.) Syncopated Clock; Blue Tango; Sleigh Ride.

Harold Arlen, b. 1905, (U.S.) Stormy Weather; Over the Rainbow; Blues in the Night; That Old Black Magic.

Burt Bacharach, b. 1928, (U.S.) Raindrops Keep Fallin' on My Head; Walk on By; What the World Needs Now is Love.

Ernest Ball, 1878-1927, (U.S.) Mother Machree; When Irish Eyes Are Smiling.

Irving Berlin, b. 1888, (U.S.) This is the Army; Annie Get Your Gun; Call Me Madam; God Bless America; White Christmas.

Eubie Blake, b. 1883, (U.S.) Shuffle Along; I'm Just Wild about Harry.

Jerry Bock, b. 1928, (U.S.) Mr. Wonderful; Fiorello; Fiddler on the Roof; The Rothschilds.

Carrie Jacobs Bond, 1862-1946, (U.S.) I Love You Truly.

Nacio Herb Brown, 1896-1964, (U.S.) Singing in the Rain; You Were Meant for Me; All I Do Is Dream of You.

Hoagy Carmichael, b. 1899, (U.S.) Stardust; Georgia on My Mind; Old Buttermilk Sky.

George M. Cohan, 1878-1942, (U.S.) Give My Regards to Broadway; You're A Grand Old Flag; Over There.

Noel Coward, 1899-1973 (Br.) Bitter Sweet; Mad Dogs and Englishmen; Mad About the Boy.

Walter Donaldson, 1893-1947, (U.S.) My Buddy; Carolina in the Morning; You're Driving Me Crazy; Makin' Whoopee.

Vernon Duke, 1903-1969, (U.S.) April in Paris.

Gus Edwards, 1879-1945, (U.S.) School Days; By the Light of the Silvery Moon; In My Merry Oldsmobile.

Sherman Edwards, b. 1919, (U.S.) See You in September; Wonderful! Wonderful!
Sammy Fain, b. 1902, Wedding Bells Are Breaking Up That Old Gang of Mine; Let a Smile Be Your Umbrella.
Fred Fisher, 1875-1942, (U.S.) Peg O' My Heart; Chicago; Dardanella.
Stephen Collins Foster, 1826-1864, (U.S.) My Old Kentucky Home; Old Folks At Home.
Rudolf Friml, 1879-1972, (naturalized U.S.) The Firefly; Rose Marie; Vagabond King; Bird of Paradise.
John Gay, 1685-1732, (Br.) The Beggar's Opera.
Edwin F. Goldman, 1878-1956, (U.S.) marches.
Percy Grainger, 1882-1961, (Br.) Country Gardens.
John Green, b. 1908, (U.S.) Body and Soul; Out of Nowhere; I Cover the Waterfront.
Ferde Grofe, 1892-1972, (U.S.) Grand Canyon Suite.
W. C. Handy, 1873-1958, (U.S.) St. Louis Blues.
Ray Henderson, 1896-1970, (U.S.) George White's Scandals; That Old Gang of Mine; Five Foot Two, Eyes of Blue.
Victor Herbert, 1859-1924, (Ir.-U.S.) Mlle. Modiste; Babes in Toyland; The Red Mill; Naughty Marietta; Sweethearts.
Jerry Herman, b. 1932, (U.S.) Milk and Honey; Hello Dolly; Mame; Dear World.
Al Hoffman, 1902-1960, (U.S.) Heartaches, Mairzy Doats.
Scott Joplin, 1868-1917, (U.S.) Treemonisha.
John Kander, b. 1927, (U.S.) Cabaret; Chicago; Funny Lady.
Jerome Kern, 1885-1945, (U.S.) Sally; Sunny; Show Boat; Cat and the Fiddle; Music in the Air; Roberta.
Burton Lane, b. 1912, (U.S.) Three's a Crowd; Finian's Rainbow; On A Clear Day You Can See Forever.
Franz Lehar, 1870-1948, (Hung.) Merry Widow.
Mitch Leigh, b. 1928, (U.S.) Man of La Mancha.
Frank Loesser, 1910-1969, (U.S.) Guys and Dolls; Where's Charley?; The Most Happy Fella; How to Succeed . . .
Frederick Loewe, b. 1901, (Aust.-U.S.) The Day Before Spring; Brigadoon; Paint Your Wagon; My Fair Lady; Camelot.
Henry Mancini, b. 1924, (U.S.) Moon River; Days of Wine and Roses; Pink Panther Theme.
Jimmy McHugh, 1894-1969, (U.S.) I Can't Give You Anything But Love; I Feel a Song Coming On.
Joseph Meyer, b. 1894, (U.S.) If You Knew Susie; California, Here I Come; Crazy Rhythm.
Chauncey Olcott, 1860-1932, (U.S.) Mother Machree; My Wild Irish Rose.
Cole Porter, 1893-1964, (U.S.) Anything Goes; Jubilee; Du-Barry Was a Lady; Panama Hattie; Mexican Hayride; Kiss Me Kate; Can Can; Silk Stockings.
Andre Previn, b. 1929, (U.S.) Coco.
Richard Rodgers, 1902-1979, (U.S.) Garrick Gaieties; Connecticut Yankee; America's Sweetheart; On Your Toes; Babes in Arms; The Boys from Syracuse; Oklahoma!; Carousel; South Pacific; The King and I; Flower Drum Song; The Sound of Music.
Sigmund Romberg, 1887-1951, (Hung.) Maytime; The Student Prince; Desert Song; Blossom Time.
Harold Rome, b. 1908, (U.S.) Pins and Needles; Call Me Mister; Wish You Were Here; Fanny; Destry Rides Again.
Vincent Rose, b. 1880-1944, (U.S.) Avalon; Whispering; Blueberry Hill.
Harry Ruby, 1895-1974, (U.S.) Three Little Words; Who's Sorry Now?
Arthur Schwartz, b. 1900, (U.S.) The Band Wagon; Inside U.S.A.; A Tree Grows in Brooklyn.
Stephen Sondheim, b. 1930, (U.S.) A Little Night Music; Company.
John Philip Sousa. 1854-1932, (U.S.) El Capitan; Stars and Stripes Forever.

Oskar Straus, 1870-1954, (Aus.) Chocolate Soldier.
Johann Strauss, 1825-1899, (Aus.) Gypsy Baron; Die Fledermaus; waltzes: Blue Danube, Artist's Life.
Charles Strouse, b. 1928, (U.S.) Bye Bye, Birdie; All American; Golden Boy; Applause; Annie.
Jule Styne, b. 1905, (b. London-U.S.) Gentlemen Prefer Blondes; Bells Are Ringing; Gypsy; Funny Girl.
Arthur S. Sullivan, 1842-1900, (Br.) H.M.S. Pinafore, Pirates of Penzance; The Mikado.
Deems Taylor, 1885-1966, (U.S.) Peter Ibbetson.
Egbert van Alstyne, 1882-1951, (U.S.) In the Shade of the Old Apple Tree; Memories; Pretty Baby.
James Van Heusen, b. 1913, (U.S.) Moonlight Becomes You; Swinging on a Star.
Albert von Tilzer, 1878-1956, (U.S.) I'll Be With You in Apple Blossom Time; Take Me Out to the Ball Game.
Harry von Tilzer, 1872-1946, (U.S.) Only a Bird in a Gilded Cage; On a Sunday Afternoon.
Harry Warren, b. 1893, (U.S.) You're My Everything; We're in the Money; I Only Have Eyes for You; September in the Rain.
Kurt Weill, 1900-1950, (G.-U.S.) Threepenny Opera; Lady in the Dark; Knickerbocker Holiday; One Touch of Venus.
Percy Wenrich, 1887-1952, (U.S.) When You Wore a Tulip; Moonlight Bay; Put On Your Old Gray Bonnet.
Richard A. Whiting, 1891-1938, (U.S.) Till We Meet Again; Sleepytime Gal; Beyond the Blue Horizon.
Meredith Willson, b. 1902, (U.S.) The Music Man.
Vincent Youmans, 1898-1946, (U.S.) Two Little Girls in Blue; Wildflower; No, No, Nanette; Hit the Deck; Rainbow; Smiles.

Lyricists

Sammy Cahn, b. 1913, (U.S.) High Hopes; Love and Marriage, The Second Time Around.
Betty Comden, b. 1919 (U.S.) and **Adolph Green**, b. 1915 (U.S.) The Party's Over; Just in Time; New York, New York.
Buddy De Sylva, 1895-1950, (U.S.) When Day is Done; Look for the Silver Lining; April Showers.
Hal David, b. 1921 (U.S.) What the World Needs Now Is Love.
Howard Dietz, b. 1896, (U.S.) Dancing in the Dark; You and the Night and the Music.
Al Dubin, 1891-1945, (U.S.) Tiptoe Through the Tulips; Anniversary Waltz; Lullaby of Broadway.
Dorothy Fields, 1905-1974, (U.S.) On the Sunny Side of the Street; Don't Blame Me; The Way You Look Tonight.
Ira Gershwin, b. 1896, (U.S.) The Man I Love; Fascinating Rhythm; S'Wonderful; Embraceable You.
Wm. S. Gilbert, 1836-1911, (Br.) The Mikado; H.M.S. Pinafore.
Oscar Hammerstein II, 1895-1960, (U.S.) Ol' Man River; Oklahoma; Carousel.
E. Y. (Yip) Harburg, b. 1898, (U.S.) Brother, Can You Spare a Dime; April in Paris; Over the Rainbow.
Lorenz Hart, 1895-1943, (U.S.) Isn't It Romantic; Blue Moon; Lover; Manhattan; My Funny Valentine.
DuBose Heyward, 1885-1940, (U.S.) Summertime; A Woman Is A Sometime Thing.
Gus Kahn, 1886-1941, (U.S.) Memories; Ain't We Got Fun.
Johnny Mercer, 1909-1976, (U.S.) Blues in the Night; Come Rain or Come Shine; Laura; That Old Black Magic.
Jack Norworth, 1879-1959, (U.S.) Take Me Out to the Ball Game; Shine On Harvest Moon.
Jack Yellen, b. 1892, (U.S.) Down by the O-Hi-O; Ain't She Sweet; Happy Days Are Here Again.

Noted Jazz Artists

Jazz has been called America's only completely unique contribution to Western culture. The following individuals have made major contributions in this field:

Julian "Cannonball" Adderley, 1928-1975: alto sax.
Henry "Red" Allen, 1908-1967: trumpet.
Albert Ammons, 1907-1949: boogie-woogie pianist.
Louis "Satchmo" Armstrong, 1900-1971: trumpet, singer; originated the "scat" vocal.
Mildred Bailey, 1907-1951: blues singer.
Count Basie, b. 1904: orchestra leader, piano.
Sidney Bechet, 1897-1950: early innovator, soprano sax.
Bix Beiderbecke, 1903-1931: cornet, piano, composer.
Bunny Berrigan, 1909-1942: trumpet, singer.
Barney Bigard, b. 1906: clarinet.
Art Blakey, b. 1919: drums, leader.
Jimmy Blanton, 1921-1942: bass.
Charles "Buddy" Bolden, 1868-1931: cornet; formed the first jazz band in the 1890s.
Big Bill Broonzy, 1893-1958: blues singer, guitar.

Dave Brubeck, b. 1920: piano, combo leader.
Harry Carney, 1910-1975: baritone sax.
Benny Carter, b. 1907: alto sax, trumpet, clarinet.
Sidney Catlett, 1910-1951: drums.
Charlie Christian, 1919-1942: guitar; often given credit for the term "bebop".
Kenny Clarke, b. 1914: pioneer of modern drums; founder-member Modern Jazz Quartet, 1952.
Buck Clayton, b. 1911: trumpet, arranger.
Al Cohn, b. 1925: tenor sax, composer.
Cozy Cole, 1909-1981: drums.
Ornette Coleman, b. 1930: saxophone; unorthodox style.
John Coltrane, 1926-1967: tenor sax innovator.
Eddie Condon, 1904-1973: guitar, band leader; promoter of Dixieland.
Chick Corea, b. 1941: pianist, composer.

Miles Davis, b. 1926: trumpet; pioneer of cool jazz.
Tadd Dameron, 1917-1965: piano, composer.
Wild Bill Davison, b. 1906: cornet, leader; prominent in early Chicago jazz.
Buddy De Franco, b. 1933: clarinet.
Paul Desmond, 1924-1977: alto sax.
Vic Dickenson, b. 1906: trombone, composer.
Warren "Baby" Dodds, 1898-1959: Dixieland drummer.
Johnny Dodds, 1892-1940: clarinet.
Jimmy Dorsey, 1904-1957: clarinet, alto sax; band leader.
Tommy Dorsey, 1905-1956: trombone; band leader.
Roy Eldridge, b. 1911: trumpet, drums, singer.
Duke Ellington, 1899-1974: piano, orchestra leader, composer.
Bill Evans, 1929-1980: piano.
Gil Evans, b. 1912: composer, piano.
Ella Fitzgerald, b. 1918: singer.
Erroll Garner, 1921-1977: piano, composer, "Misty."
Stan Getz, b. 1927: tenor sax.
Dizzy Gillespie, b. 1917: trumpet, composer; bop developer.
Benny Goodman, b. 1909: clarinet, band and combo leader.
Dexter Gordon, b. 1923: tenor sax; bop-derived style
Stephane Grappelli, b. 1908: violin.
Bobby Hackett, 1915-1976: trumpet, cornet.
Lionel Hampton, b. 1913: vibes, drums, piano, combo leader.
W. C. Handy, 1873-1958: composer, "St. Louis Blues."
Coleman Hawkins, 1904-1969: tenor sax; 1939 recording of "Body and Soul", a classic.
Roy Haynes, b. 1926: drums.
Fletcher Henderson, 1898-1952: orchestra leader, arranger; pioneered jazz and dance bands of the 30s.
Woody Herman, b. 1913: clarinet, alto sax, band leader.
Jay C. Higginbotham, 1906-1973: trombone.
Earl "Fatha" Hines, b. 1905: piano, songwriter.
Johnny Hodges, 1906-1971: alto sax.
Billie Holiday, 1915-1959: blues singer, "Strange Fruit."
Sam "Lightnin' " Hopkins, b. 1912: blues singer, guitar.
Mahalia Jackson, 1911-1972: gospel singer.
Milt Jackson, b. 1923: vibes, piano, guitar.
Illinois Jacquet, b. 1922: tenor sax.
Keith Jarrett, b. 1945: technically phenomenal pianist.
Blind Lemon Jefferson, 1897-1930: blues singer, guitar.
Bunk Johnson, 1879-1949: cornet, trumpet.
James P. Johnson, 1891-1955: piano, composer.
J. J. Johnson, b. 1924: trombone, composer.
Jo Jones, b. 1911: drums.
Philly Joe Jones, 1923: drums.
Quincy Jones, b. 1933: arranger.
Thad Jones, b. 1923: trumpet, cornet.
Scott Joplin, 1868-1917: composer; "Maple Leaf Rag."
Stan Kenton, 1912-1979: orchestra leader, composer, piano.
John Kirby, 1908-1952: major combo leader of the 30s.
Lee Konitz, b. 1927: alto sax.
Gene Krupa, 1909-1973: drums, band and combo leader.
Tommy Ladnier, 1900-1939: trumpet.
Scott LaFaro, 1936-1961: bass.
Eddie Lang, 1904-1933: guitar.
Huddie Ledbetter (Leadbelly), 1888-1949: blues singer, guitar.
John Lewis, b. 1920: composer, piano, combo leader.
Jimmie Lunceford, 1902-1947: band leader, sax.
Jimmy McPartland, b. 1907: trumpet.
Glenn Miller, 1904-1944: trombone, dance band leader.
Charles Mingus, 1922-1979: bass, composer, combo leader.
Thelonious Monk, b. 1920: piano, composer, combo leader; a developer of bop.
Wes Montgomery, 1925-1971: guitar.
"Jelly Roll" Morton, 1885-1941: composer, piano, singer.
Bennie Moten, 1894-1935: piano; an early organizer of large

jazz orchestras.
Gerry Mulligan, b. 1927: baritone sax, arranger, leader.
Turk Murphy, b. 1915: trombone, band leader.
Theodore "Fats" Navarro, 1923-1950: trumpet.
Red Nichols, 1905-1965: cornet, combo leader.
Jimmie Noone, 1895-1944: clarinet, leader.
Red Norvo, b. 1908: vibes, band leader.
Anita O'Day, b. 1919: singer.
King Oliver, 1885-1938: cornet, band leader; teacher of Louis Armstrong.
Kid Ory, 1886-1973: trombone, composer, "Muskrat Ramble".
Charlie "Bird" Parker, 1920-1955: alto sax, composer; rated by many as the greatest jazz improviser.
Oscar Peterson, b. 1925: piano, composer, combo leader.
Oscar Pettiford, 1922-1960: a leading bassist in the bop era.
Bud Powell, 1924-1966: piano, composer; modern jazz pioneer
Gertrude "Ma" Rainey, 1886-1939: blues singer.
Don Redman, 1900-1964: composer, arranger; pioneer in the evolution of the large orchestra.
Django Reinhardt, 1910-1953: guitar; Belgian gypsy, first European to influence American jazz.
Buddy Rich, b. 1917: drums, band leader
Max Roach, b. 1925: drums.
Shorty Rogers, b. 1924: composer, trumpet, band leader.
Sonny Rollins, b. 1929: tenor sax.
Pete Rugolo, b. 1915: composer, orchestra leader.
Jimmy Rushing, 1903-1972: blues singer.
George Russell, b. 1923: composer, piano.
Pee Wee Russell, 1906-1969: clarinet.
Artie Shaw, b. 1910: clarinet, combo leader.
George Shearing, b. 1919: piano, composer, "Lullaby of Birdland."
Horace Silver, b. 1928: piano, combo leader.
Zoot Sims, b 1925: tenor, alto sax; clarinet.
Zutty Singleton, 1898-1975: Dixieland drummer.
Bessie Smith, 1894-1937: blues singer.
Clarence "Pinetop" Smith, 1904-1929: piano, singer; pioneer of boogie woogie.
Joe Smith, 1902-1937: trumpet.
Willie "The Lion" Smith, 1897-1973: stride style pianist.
Muggsy Spanier, 1906-1967: cornet, band leader.
Billy Strayhorn, 1915-67: composer, piano.
Sonny Stitt, b. 1924: alto, tenor sax.
Art Tatum, 1910-1956: piano; technical virtuoso.
Cecil Taylor, b. 1933: avant-garde pianist, composer.
Jack Teagarden, 1905-1964: trombone, singer.
Dave Tough, 1908-1948: drums.
Lennie Tristano, 1919-1978: piano, composer.
Joe Turner, b. 1911: blues singer.
Joe Turner, b. 1907: stride piano.
McCoy Tyner, b. 1938: piano, composer.
Sarah Vaughan, b. 1924: singer.
Joe Venuti, 1904-1978: first great jazz violinist.
Thomas "Fats" Waller, 1904-1943: piano, singer, composer, "Ain't Misbehavin' ".
Dinah Washington, 1924-1963: singer.
Chick Webb, 1902-1939: band leader, drums; generally credited with laying the foundations for jazz percussion.
Paul Whiteman, 1890-1967: orchestra leader; a major figure in the introduction of jazz to a large audience.
Charles "Cootie" Williams, b. 1908: trumpet, band leader.
Mary Lou Williams, b. 1914: pianist, composer.
Teddy Wilson, b. 1912: piano, composer.
Kai Winding, b. 1922: trombone, composer.
Jimmy Yancey, 1894-1951: piano.
Lester "Pres" Young, 1909-1959: tenor sax, composer; a bop pioneer.

Popular American Songs

(m-music; w-words)

After You've Gone: Turner Layton(m); Henry Creamer(w); 1918; popularized by Al Jolson, Sophie Tucker.
Ain't She Sweet: Milton Ager(m); Jack Yellen(w); 1927; introduced by Paul Ash orch., Oriental Theater, Chicago.
Alexander's Ragtime Band: Irving Berlin(m,w); 1911.
Always (I'll Be Loving You): Irving Berlin(m,w); 1925.
April in Paris: Vernon Duke(m); E. Y. Harburg(w); 1932.
April Showers: Louis Silvers(m); Buddy De Sylva(w); 1921; introduced by Al Jolson in musical *Bombo*.
As Time Goes By: Herman Hupfeld(m,w); 1931, in musical *Everbody's Welcome*, also movie *Casablanca*, in 1942.
Baby Face: Harry Akst(m); Benny Davis(w); 1926; introduced by Jan Garber on RCA Victor record.
The Band Played On: C. B. Ward(m); J. E. Palmer(w); 1895; song owned and promoted by newspaper, New York *World*.

Beer Barrel Polka: J. Vejvoda and Lew Brown(w); 1934; music was a Czech popular song.
The Best Things in Life Are Free: Ray Henderson(m); Buddy De Sylva and Lew Brown(w); 1927; in musical *Good News*.
Beyond the Blue Horizon: R. A. Whiting(m); Leo Robin(w); 1930; introduced by Jeanette MacDonald in movie *Monte Carlo*.
Blowin' in the Wind: Bob Dylan(m,w); 1963.
Blue Skies: Irving Berlin(m,w); 1926.
Body and Soul: John Green(m); E. Heyton, R. Sour, F. Eyton(w); 1930; introduced by Gertrude Lawrence on BBC.
Bye, Bye Blackbird: R. Henderson(m); Mort Dixon(w); 1926; popularized by Eddie Cantor.
By the Beautiful Sea: Harry Carroll(m); Harold Atteridge(w); 1914; vaudeville.

By the Light of the Silvery Moon: Gus Edwards(m); Edward Madden(w); 1909; in revue *School Boys and Girls*.

Chicago: Fred Fisher(m,w); 1922; vaudeville.

California, Here I Come: Joseph Meyer(m); Al Jolson, Buddy De Sylva(w); 1923; by Al Jolson in road tour of *Bombo*.

Daisy Bell (Bicycle Built for Two): Harry Dacre(m,w); circa 1892; London tune popularized in U.S. by Tony Pastor.

Dancing in the Dark: Arthur Schwartz(m); Howard Dietz(w); 1931; in revue *The Band Wagon*.

Down by the Old Mill Stream: Tell Taylor(m,w); 1910.

Easter Parade: Irving Berlin(m,w); 1933; introduced by Clifton Webb and Marilyn Miller in musical *As Thousands Cheer*.

Feelings: Paul Evans(m); Paul Parnes(w); 1969.

For Me and My Gal: G. W. Meyer(m); Edgar Leslie, E. R. Goetz(w); 1917; sung by Jolson, Cantor, Sophie Tucker, others.

Give My Regards to Broadway: George M. Cohan(m,w); 1904; in musical *Little Johnny Jones*.

Good Night Irene: Huddie Ledbetter(m,w); 1936; found by John Lomax in Louisiana State Prison, Angola, La.

Hail, Hail, the Gang's All Here: Arthur S. Sullivan(m); T. A. Morse(w), under pseudonym. D. A. Esrom; 1917.

Happy Days Are Here Again: Milton Ager(m); Jack Yellen(w); 1929; introduced on Black Thursday (10-24-29).

Heartaches: Al Hoffman(m); John Klenner(w); 1931; popularized by Ted Weems.

Hello, Dolly: Jerry Herman(m,w); 1964; by Carol Channing in musical of same name.

Home on the Range: Daniel E. Kelly?(m); Brewster (Bruce) Higley (w,m); 1904, called Arizona Home(w) 1873; composer and author uncertain.

Hot Time in the Old Town Tonight: T. M. Metz(m); Joe Hayden(w); 1896; minstrel show.

I Can't Give You Anything But Love: Jimmy McHugh(m); Dorothy Fields(w); 1928; in revue *Delmar's Revels*.

I Could Have Danced All Night: F. Loewe(m); A. J. Lerner(w); 1956; by Julie Andrews in *My Fair Lady*.

I Don't Know Why I Love You Like I Do: F. E. Ahlert(m); Roy Turk(w); 1931.

If You Knew Susie: Bud De Sylva and Joseph Meyer(w,m); 1925; by Al Jolson in *Big Boy*.

I Got Plenty o'Nothin': G. Gershwin(m); I. Gershwin, DuBose Heyward(w); 1935; in *Porgy and Bess*.

I'll Be Seeing You: Sammy Fain(m); Irving Kahal(w); 1938; popularized by Sinatra, Hildegarde, in 1943.

I'll See You in My Dreams: Isham Jones(m); Gus Kahn(w); 1924.

I Love You Truly: Carrie Jacobs Bond(m,w); 1901; originally an art song, later picked up by vaudeville.

I'm in the Mood for Love: J. McHugh(m); Dorothy Fields(w); 1935; by Alice Faye in movie *Every Night at Eight*.

The Impossible Dream: Mitch Leigh(m); Joe Darion(w); 1966; in musical *Man of La Mancha*.

I'm Sitting on Top of the World: Ray Henderson(m); Sam M. Lewis, Joe Young(w); 1925; popularized by Jolson in 1929 movie *The Singing Fool*.

In the Good Old Summertime: George Evans(m); Ren Shields(w); 1902.

I Only Have Eyes for You: Harry Warren(m); Al Dubin(w); 1934; by Dick Powell in movie *Dames*.

It Had To Be You: Isham Jones(m); Gus Kahn(w); 1924.

It's Been a Long, Long Time: Julie Styne(m); Sammy Cahn(w); 1945.

It Was a Very Good Year: Ervin Drake(m,w); 1965; introduced by Kingston Trio on record; popularized by Sinatra.

I've Got You Under My Skin: Cole Porter(m,w); 1936.

I Want a Girl Just Like the Girl: Harry von Tilzer(m); William Dilion(w); 1911.

I Wish You Love: J.W. Stole, Del Roma(m); Arthur Altman, Norman Gimbel(w); 1963.

I Wonder Who's Kissing Her Now: J. E. Howard, H. Orlob(m); Wm. M. Hough, F. R. Adams(w); 1909.

Jeannie With the Light Brown Hair: Stephen Foster(m,w); 1854.

June is Busting Out All Over: R. Rodgers(m); O. Hammerstein II(w); 1945; in *Carousel*.

Lazy River: S. Arodin, Hoagy Carmichael(m,w); 1931; on record by Carmichael with band including both Dorseys, Teagarden, Krupa, Goodman, Venuti, and Beiderbecke.

Let Me Call You Sweetheart: Leo Friedman(m); Beth Slater Whitson(w); 1910.

Lover: R. Rodgers(m); Lorenz Hart(w); 1933; by Jeanette MacDonald in movie *Love Me Tonight*.

Lullaby of Broadway: Harry Warren(m); Al Dubin(w); 1935; in movie *Gold Diggers of 1935*.

Memories: Egbert van Alstyne(m); Gus Kahn(w); 1915.

Misty: Erroll Garner(m); Johnny Burke(w); 1955.

Moon River: Henry Mancini(m); Johnny Mercer(w); 1961; by Andy Williams under title for movie *Breakfast at Tiffany's*.

Moonlight Bay: Percy Wenrich(m); Edward Madden(w);

1912; vaudeville.

My Blue Heaven: Walter Donaldson(m); George Whiting(w); 1927; Tommy Lyman radio theme song.

Melancholy Baby: Ernie Burnett(m); George A. Norton(w); 1912; vaudeville.

My Wild Irish Rose: Chauncey Olcott(m,w); 1899; in musical *A Romance of Athlone*.

Night and Day: Cole Porter(m,w); 1932; by Fred Astaire and Claire Luce in musical *Gay Divorce*; title of Porter film biography.

Oh, What a Beautiful Mornin': R. Rodgers(m); O. Hammerstein II(w); 1943; by Alfred Drake in *Oklahoma!*

Oh! You Beautiful Doll: Nat D. Ayer(m); A. Seymour Brown(w); 1911; vaudeville.

Old Folks at Home (Swanee River): Stephen Foster(m,w); 1851; minstrel show.

Ol' Man River: Jerome Kern(m); O. Hammerstein II(w); 1927; by Jules Bledsoe in *Show Boat*.

On the Sunny Side of the Street: J. McHugh(m); Dorothy Fields(w); 1930; in *International Revue* with Gertrude Lawrence.

Over The Rainbow: Harold Arlen(m); E. Y. Harburg(w); 1939; by seventeen-year-old Judy Garland in *Wizard of Oz*.

Peg O'My Heart: Fred Fisher(m); Alfred Bryan(w); in *Ziegfeld Follies of 1913*.

Pennies From Heaven: Arthur Johnston(m); Johnny Burke(w); 1936; by Bing Crosby in movie of same name.

People: Jule Styne(m); Bob Merrill(w); 1964; by Barbra Streisand in musical *Funny Girl*.

Pretty Baby: E. van Alstyne, Tony Jackson(m); Gus Kahn(w); 1916; by Dolly Hackett in musical *The Passing Show*.

A Pretty Girl Is Like a Melody: Irving Berlin(m,w); in *Ziegfeld Follies of 1919*; became Follies theme song.

Put On Your Old Gray Bonnet: Percy Wenrich(m); Stanley Murphy(w); 1909.

Put Your Arms Around Me, Honey: Albert von Tilzer(m); Junie McCree(w); 1910; vaudeville.

Raindrops Keep Falling on My Head: Burt Bacharach(m); Hal David(w); 1969, in film *Butch Cassidy and the Sundance Kid*.

Rudolph, the Red-Nosed Reindeer: Johnny Marks(m,w); 1949; by Gene Autry on Columbia record.

School Days: Gus Edwards(m); Will D. Cobb(w); 1907; vaudeville.

September Song: Kurt Weill(m); Maxwell Anderson(w); 1938; by Walter Huston in play *Knickerbocker Holiday*.

The Shadow of Your Smile: Johnny Mandel(m); Paul Francis Webster(w); 1965; in film *The Sandpiper*.

Shine On Harvest Moon: Nora Bayes, Jack Norworth(m); Norworth(w); introduced by Nora Bayes in *Ziegfeld Follies of 1908*.

Sidewalks of New York: J. W. Blake, C. B. Lawlor(m,w); 1894; by Lottie Gilson at Old London Theatre on the Bowery.

Singing in the Rain: Nacio Herb Brown(m); Arthur Freed(w); 1929; by Cliff Edwards in movie *Hollywood Revue of 1929*.

Smoke Gets in Your Eyes: Jerome Kern(m); Otto Harbach(w); 1933; by Tamara in musical *Roberta*.

Somebody Loves Me: G. Gershwin(m); B. DeSylva, B. MacDonald(w); 1924; *George White's Scandals of 1924*.

Some Enchanted Evening: R. Rodgers(m); O. Hammerstein II(w); 1949; by Ezio Pinza in *South Pacific*.

Stardust: Hoagy Carmichael(m); Mitchell Parish(w); 1929.

Stormy Weather: Harold Arlen(m); Ted Koehler(w); 1933; popularized by Ethel Waters.

Strike Up the Band: George Gershwin(m); Ira Gershwin(w); 1930; in musical of the same name.

Summertime: George Gershwin(m); DuBose Heyward(w); 1935; by Abbie Mitchell opening *Porgy and Bess*.

Sweet Georgia Brown: Ben Bernie, M. Pinkard, K. Casey(m,w); 1925.

Sweethearts: Victor Herbert(m); R. B. Smith(w); 1913; in musical of the same name.

Take Me Out to the Ball Game: Albert von Tilzer(m); Jack Norworth(w); 1908; vaudeville.

Tea for Two: Vincent Youmans(m); Irving Caesar(w); 1920; by Louise Groody, John Barker, in *No, No, Nanette*.

Tennessee Waltz: Redd Stewart, Pee Wee King(m,w); 1948; popularized by Patti Page.

That Old Black Magic: Harold Arlen(m); Johnny Mercer(w); 1942; in movie *Star Spangled Rhythm*.

Three Little Words: Harry Ruby(m); Bert Kalmar(w); 1930; by Bing Crosby in Amos & Andy movie *Check and Double Check*.

Toot, Toot, Tootsie, Goodbye: Dan Russo(m); Gus Kahn, Ernie Erdman(w); 1922; by Jolson in *Bombo*; later in first talkie *The Jazz Singer*.

When Irish Eyes Are Smiling: Ernest R. Ball(m); C. Olcott, G. Graft(w); 1912; by Olcott in musical *Isle of Dreams*.

When Johnny Comes Marching Home: Louis Lambert(m,w); 1863; Lambert thought pen-name for Patrick S. Gilmore.

When You're Smiling: M. Fisher, J. Goodwin, L. Shay(m,w); 1928.

When You Wish Upon A Star: Leigh Harline(m); Ned Washington(w); 1940; by Cliff Edwards in animated *Pinocchio.*

When You Wore a Tulip: Percy Wenrich(m); Jack Mahoney(w); 1914; vaudeville.

Whispering: John Schonberger, Vincent Rose(m); Richard Coburn(w); 1920; introduced by Paul Whiteman.

White Christmas: Irving Berlin(m,w); 1942; by Bing Crosby in movie *Holiday Inn.*

With a Song in My Heart: R. Rodgers(m); Lorenz Hart(w);

1929; in musical *Spring Is Here.*

Without a Song: Vincent Youmans(m); Billy Rose, E. Eliscu(w); 1929; in musical *Great Day.*

Yellow Rose of Texas: nothing is known of the songwriter but initials "J. K."; 1853; minstrel show.

Yes, Sir, That's My Baby: Walter Donaldson(m); Gus Kahn(w); 1925; popularized by Eddie Cantor.

You and the Night and the Music: Arthur Schwartz(m); Howard Dietz(w); 1934; in musical play *Revenge With Music.*

You Are My Sunshine: Jimmie Davis(m); C. Mitchell(w); 1940; in Tex Ritter movie *Take Me Back to Oklahoma.* Davis governor of Louisiana, 1944-48.

You Made Me Love You: J. V. Monaco(m); Joe McCarthy(w); 1913; by Al Jolson in musical *Honeymoon Express.*

Entertainment Personalities — Where and When Born

Actors, Actresses, Dancers, Musicians, Producers, Radio-TV Performers, Singers

Name	Birthplace	Born	Name	Birthplace	Born
Abbott, George	Forestville, N.Y.	6/25/87	Arnaz, Lucie	Hollywood, Cal.	7/17/51
Abel, Walter	St. Paul, Minn.	6/6/98	Arness, James	Minneapolis, Minn.	5/26/23
Ackermann, Bettye	Cottageville, S.C.	2/28/28	Arnold, Eddy	Henderson, Tenn.	5/15/18
Acuff, Roy	Maynardville, Tenn.	9/15/03	Arrau, Claudio	Chillau, Chile	2/6/03
Adams, Don	New York, N.Y.	4/19/27	Arroyo, Martina	New York, N.Y.	1937
Adams, Edie	Kingston, Pa.	4/16/29	Arthur, Beatrice	New York, N.Y.	5/13/26
Adams, Joey	New York, N.Y.	1/6/11	Arthur, Jean	New York, N.Y.	10/17/08
Adams, Julie	Waterloo, Ia.	10/17/28	Ashley, Elizabeth	Ocala, Fla.	8/30/41
Adams, Mason	New York, N.Y.	2/26/-	Asner, Edward	Kansas City, Mo.	11/15/29
Adler, Larry	Baltimore, Md.	2/10/14	Astaire, Fred	Omaha, Neb.	5/10/99
Adler, Luther	New York, N.Y.	5/4/03	Astin, John	Baltimore, Md.	3/30/30
Agar, John	Chicago, Ill.	1/31/21	Astor, Mary	Quincy, Ill.	5/3/06
Aherne, Brian	Worcestershire, England.	5/2/02	Atkins, Chet	Luttrell, Tenn.	6/20/24
Ailey, Alvin	Rogers, Tex.	1/5/31	Attenborough, Richard	Cambridge, England	8/29/23
Aimee, Anouk	Paris, France	4/27/32	Aumont, Jean-Pierre	Paris, France	1/5/09
Akins, Claude	Nelson, Ga.	5/25/18	Autry, Gene	Tioga, Tex.	9/29/11
Albanese, Licia	Bari, Italy	7/22/13	Avalon, Frankie	Philadelphia, Pa.	9/8/40
Alberghetti, Anna Maria.	Pesaro, Italy	5/15/36	Aykroyd, Dan	Ottawa, Ont.	7/1/52
Albert, Eddie	Rock Island, Ill.	4/22/08	Ayres, Lew	Minneapolis, Minn.	12/28/08
Albert, Edward	Los Angeles, Cal.	2/20/51	Aznavour, Charles.	Paris, France	5/22/24
Albertson, Jack	Malden, Mass.	6/16/10			
Albright, Lola.	Akron, Oh.	7/20/24	Bacall, Lauren	New York, N.Y.	9/16/24
Alda, Alan	New York, N.Y.	1/28/36	Bach, Catherine	Warren, Oh.	3/1/-
Alda, Robert	New York, N.Y.	2/26/14	Backus, Jim	Cleveland, Oh.	2/25/13
Alexander, Jane	Boston, Mass.	10/28/39	Baddeley, Hermione	Shropshire, England	11/13/06
Allan, Elizabeth	England	1910	Baer, Max Jr.	Oakland, Cal.	12/4/37
Allen, Mel.	Birmingham, Ala.	2/14/13	Baez, Joan	Staten Island, N.Y.	1/9/41
Allen, Steve	New York, N.Y.	12/26/21	Bailey, Pearl	Newport News, Va.	3/29/18
Allen, Woody	Brooklyn, N.Y.	12/1/35	Bain, Barbara	Chicago, Ill.	1934
Allison, Fran	LaPorte City, Ia.	—	Bain, Conrad	Lethbridge, Alta.	2/4/23
Allyson, June.	Lucerne, N.Y.	10/7/23	Baio, Scott	Brooklyn, N.Y.	9/22/61
Alpert, Herb	Los Angeles, Cal.	3/31/35	Baird, Bil	Grand Island, Neb.	8/15/04
Altman, Robert	Kansas City, Mo.	2/20/25	Baker, Carroll	Johnstown, Pa.	5/28/31
Ameche, Don	Kenosha, Wis.	5/31/08	Baker, Diane	Hollywood, Cal.	1938
Ames, Ed.	Boston, Mass.	1929	Baker, Joe Don	Groesbeck, Tex.	2/12/36
Ames, Leon	Portland, Ind.	1/20/03	Baker, Kenny	Monrovia, Cal.	9/30/12
Amos, John	Newark, N.J.	—	Bakewell, William	Hollywood, Cal.	1908
Amsterdam, Morey	Chicago, Ill.	12/14/14	Balanchine, George	St. Petersburg, Russia	1/9/04
Anderson, Ian	Blackpool, England.	8/10/47	Ball, Lucille.	Jamestown, N.Y.	8/6/11
Anderson, Judith.	Adelaide, Australia	2/10/98	Ballard, Kaye	Cleveland, Oh.	11/20/26
Anderson, Loni.	St. Paul, Minn.	8/5/-	Balsam, Martin.	New York, N.Y.	11/4/19
Anderson, Lynn	Grand Forks, N.D.	9/26/47	Bancroft, Anne.	New York, N.Y.	9/17/31
Anderson, Marian	Philadelphia, Pa.	2/17/02	Barber, Red	Columbus, Miss.	2/17/08
Anderson, Mary	Birmingham, Ala.	1922	Bardot, Brigitte	Paris, France	1934
Anderson, Melissa Sue	Berkeley, Cal.	9/26/62	Bari, Lynn	Roanoke, Va.	1917
Anderson, Michael Jr..	London, England	1943	Barrault, Jean-Louis.	Le Vesinet, France	1910
Anderson, Richard	Long Branch, N.J.	8/8/26	Barrie, Barbara	Chicago, Ill.	5/23/31
Andersson, Bibi	Stockholm, Sweden	11/11/35	Barrie, Mona	London, England	12/18/09
Andress, Ursula	Switzerland	1936	Barris, Chuck	Philadelphia, Pa.	6/2/29
Andrews, Dana	Collins, Miss.	1/1/12	Barry, Gene	New York, N.Y.	6/4/22
Andrews, Edward	Griffin, Ga.	10/9/15	Barry, Jack.	Lindenhurst, N.Y.	3/20/18
Andrews, Julie	Walton, England	10/1/35	Bartholomew, Freddie	London, England	3/28/24
Andrews, Maxene	Minneapolis, Minn.	1918	Bartok, Eva.	Budapest, Hungary.	1929
Andrews, Patty	Minneapolis, Minn.	1920	Baryshnikov, Mikhail	Riga, Latvia	1/28/48
Angel, Heather.	Oxford, England	2/9/09	Basehart, Richard	Zanesville, Oh.	8/31/19
Anka, Paul	Ottawa, Ont.	7/30/41	Basie, Count (Wm.)	Red Bank, N.J.	8/21/04
Ann-Margret	Stockholm, Sweden	4/28/41	Bassey, Shirley	Cardiff, Wales.	1937
Annabella	Paris, France	1912	Bates, Alan.	Allestree, England	2/17/34
Ansara, Michael	Lowell, Mass.	4/15/27	Baum, Kurt.	Cologne, Germany.	1908
Arden, Eve	Mill Valley, Cal.	4/30/12	Bavier, Frances	New York, N.Y.	1905
Arkin, Alan	New York, N.Y.	3/26/34	Baxter, Anne.	Michigan City, Ind.	5/7/23
Arnaz, Desi.	Santiago, Cuba	3/2/17	Baxter-Birney, Meredith.	Los Angeles, Cal.	6/21/-
Arnaz, Desi Jr.	Los Angeles, Cal.	1/19/53	Beal, John	Joplin, Mo.	8/13/09

Name	Birthplace	Born	Name	Birthplace	Born
Bean, Orson	Burlington, Vt.	7/22/28	Brown, Les	Reinerton, Pa.	3/14/12
Beatty, Ned	Louisville, Ky.	7/6/37	Brown, Ray	Pittsburgh, Pa.	10/13/26
Beatty, Robert	Hamilton, Ont.	10/19/09	Brown, Tom	New York, N.Y.	1/6/13
Beatty, Warren	Richmond, Va.	3/30/38	Browne, Roscoe Lee	Woodbury, N.J.	1925
Bedelia, Bonnie	New York, N.Y.	3/25/48	Bruce, Carol	Great Neck, N.Y.	11/15/19
Bee Gees			Bruce, Virginia	Minneapolis, Minn.	1910
Gibb, Barry	Manchester, England.	9/1/46	Bryant, Anita	Barnsdale, Okla.	3/25/40
Gibb, Robin	" "	12/22/49	Brynner, Yul	Sakhalin, Japan.	7/11/20
Gibb, Maurice	" "	12/22/49	Buchholz, Horst	Berlin, Germany	12/4/33
Beery, Noah Jr.	New York, N.Y.	8/10/16	Bujold, Geneviève	Montreal, Que.	7/1/42
Belafonte, Harry	New York, N.Y.	3/1/27	Bumbry, Grace	St. Louis, Mo.	1/4/37
Bel Geddes, Barbara	New York, N.Y.	10/31/22	Buono, Victor	San Diego, Cal.	2/3/38
Bellamy, Ralph	Chicago, Ill.	6/17/04	Burghoff, Gary	Bristol, Conn.	5/24/-
Belmondo, Jean-Paul	Neuilly-sur-Seine, France	4/9/33	Burke, Paul	New Orleans, La.	7/21/26
Belushi, John	Chicago, Ill.	1/24/49	Burnett, Carol	San Antonio, Tex.	4/26/36
Benjamin, Richard	New York, N.Y.	5/22/38	Burns, George	New York, N.Y.	1/20/96
Bennett, Joan	Palisades, N.J.	2/27/10	Burr, Raymond	New Westminster, B.C.	5/21/17
Bennett, Michael	Buffalo, N.Y.	4/8/43	Burstyn, Ellen	Detroit, Mich.	12/7/32
Bennett, Tony	Astoria, N.Y.	8/3/26	Burton, Richard	South Wales	11/10/25
Benson, Robby	Dallas, Tex.	1957	Bushell, Anthony	Kent, England	1904
Bentley, John	Warwickshire, England.	12/2/16	Buttons, Red	New York, N.Y.	2/5/19
Bergen, Candice	Beverly Hills, Cal.	5/9/46	Buzzi, Ruth	Westerly, R.I.	7/24/36
Bergen, Polly	Knoxville, Tenn.	7/14/30			
Bergerac, Jacques	Biarritz, France	5/26/27	Caan, James	New York, N.Y.	3/26/39
Bergman, Ingmar	Uppsala, Sweden	7/14/18	Caballe, Montserrat	Barcelona, Spain	4/12/33
Bergman, Ingrid	Stockholm, Sweden	8/29/15	Caesar, Sid	Yonkers, N.Y.	9/8/22
Bergner, Elisabeth	Vienna, Austria	8/22/00	Cagney, James	New York, N.Y.	7/17/99
Berle, Milton	New York, N.Y.	7/12/08	Caine, Michael	London, England	3/14/33
Berlinger, Warren	Brooklyn, N.Y.	8/31/37	Caldwell, Sarah	Maryville, Mo.	1929
Berman, Shelley	Chicago, Ill.	2/3/26	Caldwell, Zoe	Melbourne, Australia	9/14/33
Bernardi, Herschel	New York, N.Y.	1923	Calhoun, Rory	Los Angeles, Cal.	8/8/22
Bernstein, Elmer	New York, N.Y.	4/4/22	Callan, Michael	Philadelphia, Pa.	1935
Bernstein, Leonard	Lawrence, Mass.	8/25/18	Callas, Charlie	Brooklyn, N.Y.	12/20/-
Berry, Chuck	San Jose, Cal.	1/15/26	Calloway, Cab	Rochester, N.Y.	12/25/07
Berry, Ken	Moline, Ill.	—	Calvert, Phyllis	London, England	2/18/15
Bertinelli, Valerie	Wilmington, Del.	4/23/60	Calvet, Corinne	Paris, France	4/30/26
Bessell, Ted	Flushing, N.Y.	1936	Cameron, Rod	Calgary, Canada	12/7/12
Bikel, Theodore	Vienna, Austria	5/2/24	Campbell, Glen	Billstown, Ark.	4/22/36
Birney, David	Washington, D.C.	4/23/40	Cannon, Dyan	Tacoma, Wash.	1/4/37
Bishop, Joey	Bronx, N.Y.	2/3/18	Canova, Judy	Starke, Fla.	11/20/16
Bisoglio, Val	New York, N.Y.	5/7/26	Cantinflas	Mexico City, Mex.	1917
Bisset, Jacqueline	Weybridge, England	9/13/46	Cantrell, Lana	Sydney, Australia	8/7/43
Bixby, Bill	San Francisco, Cal.	1/22/34	Capra, Frank	Palermo, Italy	5/18/97
Black, Karen	Park Ridge, Ill.	7/1/42	Cardinale, Claudia	Tunisia	1939
Blaine, Vivian	Newark, N.J.	11/21/23	Carey, Macdonald	Sioux City, Ia.	3/15/13
Blair, Linda	St. Louis, Mo.	1/22/59	Carey, Phil	Hackensack, N.J.	7/15/25
Blake, Amanda	Buffalo, N.Y.	2/20/31	Carey, Ron	Newark, N.J.	12/11/35
Blake, Robert	Nutley, N.J.	9/18/38	Carle, Frankie	Providence, R.I.	1903
Blakeley, Ronee	Idaho	1946	Carlisle, Kitty	New Orleans, La	9/3/15
Blakely, Susan	Germany	—	Carman, Eric	Cleveland, Oh.	8/11/49
Blanc, Mel	San Francisco, Cal.	5/30/08	Carmichael, Hoagy	Bloomington, Ind	11/22/99
Bloch, Ray	Alsace-Lorraine.	1902	Carmichael, Ian	Hull, England	6/18/20
Bloom, Claire	London, England	2/15/31	Carne, Judy	Northampton, England.	1939
Blyth, Ann	Mt. Kisco, N.Y.	8/16/28	Carney, Art	Mt. Vernon, N.Y.	11/4/18
Bohm, Karl	Graz, Austria	8/28/94	Carnovsky, Morris	St. Louis, Mo.	9/5/97
Bogarde, Dirk	London, England	3/28/21	Caron, Leslie	Boulogne, France.	7/1/31
Bogdanovich, Peter	Kingston, N.Y.	7/30/39	Carpenter, Karen	New Haven, Conn.	3/2/50
Bolger, Ray	Dorchester, Mass.	1/10/04	Carpenter, Richard	New Haven, Conn.	10/15/46
Bono, Sonny	Detroit, Mich.	2/16/40	Carr, Vikki	El Paso, Tex.	7/19/42
Boone, Debby	Hackensack, N.J.	9/22/56	Carradine, David	Hollywood, Cal.	8/8/40
Boone, Pat	Jacksonville, Fla.	6/1/34	Carradine, John	New York, N.Y.	2/5/06
Booth, Shirley	New York, N.Y.	8/30/07	Carradine, Keith	San Mateo, Cal.	8/8/49
Borge, Victor	Copenhagen, Denmark	1/3/09	Carreras, Jose	Barcelona, Spain	12/5/47
Borgnine, Ernest	Hamden, Conn.	1/24/17	Carroll, Diahann	Bronx, N.Y.	7/17/35
Bosley, Tom	Chicago, Ill.	10/1/27	Carroll, Madeleine	W. Bromwich, England.	2/26/06
Bottoms, Timothy	Santa Barbara, Cal.	8/30/51	Carroll, Pat	Shreveport, La.	5/5/27
Bowie, David	London, England	1/8/47	Carson, Johnny	Corning, Ia.	10/23/25
Boyle, Peter	Philadelphia, Pa.	1933	Carter, Jack	New York, N.Y.	6/24/23
Bracken, Eddie	Astoria, N.Y.	2/7/20	Carter, June	Maces Spring, Va.	6/23/29
Brand, Neville	Kewanee, Ill.	8/13/21	Carter, Lynda	Phoenix, Ariz.	7/24/-
Brando, Marlon	Omaha, Neb.	4/3/24	Casadesus, Gaby	Marseilles, France	1902
Brasselle, Keefe	Elyria, Oh.	2/7/23	Cash, Johnny	Kingsland, Ark.	2/26/32
Brazzi, Rossano	Bologna, Italy	9/18/16	Cass, Peggy	Boston, Mass.	5/21/24
Brennan, Eileen	Los Angeles, Cal.	9/3/35	Cassavetes, John	New York, N.Y.	12/9/29
Brenner, David	Philadelphia, Pa.	1945	Cassidy, David	New York, N.Y.	4/12/50
Brewer, Teresa	Toledo, Oh.	5/7/31	Cassidy, Shaun	Los Angeles, Cal.	9/27/58
Brian, David	New York, N.Y.	8/5/14	Castellano, Richard	New York, N.Y.	9/4/33
Bridges, Beau	Hollywood, Cal.	12/9/41	Caulfield, Joan	West Orange, N.J.	6/1/22
Bridges, Jeff	Los Angeles, Cal.	1950	Cavallaro, Carmen	New York, N.Y.	1913
Bridges, Lloyd	San Leandro, Cal.	1/15/13	Cavett, Dick	Gibbon, Neb.	11/19/36
Bridges, Todd	San Francisco, Cal.	5/27/65	Chamberlain, Richard	Beverly Hills, Cal.	3/31/35
Broderick, James	Charlestown, N.H.	3/7/27	Champion, Marge	Los Angeles, Cal.	9/2/23
Brolin, James	Los Angeles, Cal.	7/10/42	Channing, Carol	Seattle, Wash.	1/31/23
Bronson, Charles	Scooptown, Pa.	11/3/22	Channing, Stockard	New York, N.Y.	—
Brooks, Louise	Cherryvale, Kan.	1906	Chaplin, Geraldine	Santa Monica, Cal.	7/31/44
Brooks, Mel	New York, N.Y.	1926	Chaplin, Sydney	Beverly Hills, Cal.	3/31/26
Brooks, Stephen	Columbus, Oh.	1942	Charisse, Cyd	Amarillo, Tex.	3/8/23
Brown, James	Pulaski, Tenn.	6/17/28	Charles, Ray	Albany, Ga.	9/23/30
Brown, Jimmy	St. Simons Island, Ga.	2/17/36	Chase, Chevy	New York, N.Y.	10/8/43

Name	Birthplace	Born	Name	Birthplace	Born
Checker, Chubby	Philadelphia, Pa.	10/3/41	Dalton, Abby	Las Vegas, Nev.	1935
Cher	El Centro, Cal.	5/20/46	Daly, John	Johannesburg, S. Africa	2/20/14
Christian, Linda	Tampico, Mexico	11/13/24	Damone, Vic	Brooklyn, N.Y.	6/12/28
Christie, Julie	Chukur, India	4/14/41	Dana, Bill	Quincy, Mass.	1924
Christopher, Jordon	Youngstown, Oh.	1941	Dangerfield, Rodney	Babylon, N.Y.	1921
Christy, June	Springfield, Ill.	1925	Daniels, William	Brooklyn, N.Y.	3/31/27
Cilento, Diane	Queensland, Australia	1933	Danilova, Alexandra	Peterhof, Russia	1907
Cimino, Michael	New York, N.Y.	1943	Danner, Blythe	Philadelphia, Pa.	—
Claire, Ina	Washington, D.C.	1892	Danton, Ray	New York, N.Y.	9/19/31
Clapton, Eric	Surrey, England	3/30/45	Darby, Kim	Hollywood, Cal.	7/8/48
Clark, Dane	New York, N.Y.	2/18/15	Darcel, Denise	Paris, France	9/8/25
Clark, Dick	Mt. Vernon, N.Y.	11/30/29	Darren, James	Philadelphia, Pa.	6/8/36
Clark, Petula	Ewell, Surrey, England	11/15/34	Darrieux, Danielle	Bordeaux, France	5/1/17
Clark, Roy	Meherrin, Va.	4/15/33	Darrow, Henry	New York, N.Y.	1933
Clark, Susan	Sarnia, Ont.	3/8/44	Da Silva, Howard	Cleveland, Oh.	5/4/09
Clayburgh, Jill	New York, N.Y.	4/30/44	Dassin, Jules	Middletown, Conn.	12/18/11
Clayton, Jan	Tularosa, N.M.	—	Davidson, John	Pittsburgh, Pa.	1943
Cliburn, Van	Shreveport, La.	7/12/34	Davis, Ann B.	Schenectady, N.Y.	5/5/26
Clooney, Rosemary	Maysville, Ky.	5/23/28	Davis, Bette	Lowell, Mass.	4/5/08
Coburn, James	Laurel, Neb.	8/31/28	Davis, Clifton	Chicago, Ill.	1945
Coca, Imogene	Philadelphia, Pa.	11/18/08	Davis, Mac	Lubbock, Tex.	1/21/42
Coco, James	New York, N.Y.	3/21/30	Davis, Ossie	Cogdell, Ga.	12/18/17
Cohen, Myron	Grodno, Poland	1902	Davis, Sammy Jr.	New York, N.Y.	12/8/25
Colbert, Claudette	Paris, France	9/18/05	Dawber, Pam	Detroit, Mich.	10/18/-
Cole, Michael	Madison, Wis.	1945	Dawn, Hazel	Ogden, Ut.	1898
Cole, Natalie	Los Angeles, Cal.	2/6/50	Dawson, Richard	Hampshire, England	11/20/-
Coleman, Gary	Zion, Ill.	2/8/68	Day, Dennis	New York, N.Y.	1917
Collins, Dorothy	Windsor, Ont.	11/18/26	Day, Doris	Cincinnati, Oh.	4/3/24
Collins, Joan	London, England	5/23/36	Day, Laraine	Roosevelt, Ut.	10/13/20
Collins, Judy	Seattle, Wash.	5/1/39	Dean, Jimmy	Plainview, Tex.	8/10/28
Colonna, Jerry	Boston, Mass.	1903	De Camp, Rosemary	Prescott, Ariz.	1913
Comden, Betty	Brooklyn, N.Y.	5/3/19	DeCarlo, Yvonne	Vancouver, B.C.	9/4/22
Como, Perry	Canonsburg, Pa.	5/18/12	Dee, Frances	Los Angeles, Cal.	1907
Conner, Nadine	Compton, Cal.	1913	Dee, Joey	Passaic, N.J.	1940
Connery, Sean.	Edinburgh, Scotland	8/25/30	Dee, Ruby	Cleveland, Oh.	10/27/23
Conniff, Ray	Attleboro, Mass.	11/6/16	Dee, Sandra	Bayonne, N.J.	4/23/42
Connors, Chuck	Brooklyn, N.Y.	4/10/21	Defore, Don	Cedar Rapids, Ia.	8/25/17
Connors, Michael	Fresno, Cal.	8/15/25	DeHaven, Gloria	Los Angeles, Cal.	1925
Conrad, Robert	Chicago, Ill.	3/1/35	de Havilland, Olivia	Tokyo, Japan	7/1/16
Conrad, William	Louisville, Ky.	9/27/20	De Niro, Robert	New York, N.Y.	1945
Conried, Hans	Baltimore, Md.	4/1/15	Del Rio, Dolores	Durango, Mexico	8/3/08
Constantine, Michael	Reading, Pa.	5/22/27	Dell, Gabriel	Brooklyn, N.Y.	1921
Convy, Bert	St. Louis, Mo.	6/23/39	Della Chiesa, Vivienne	Chicago, Ill.	1920
Conway, Gary	Boston, Mass.	1938	Delon, Alain	Sceaux, France	11/8/35
Conway, Tim	Willoughby, Oh.	12/15/33	DeLuise, Dom	Brooklyn, N.Y.	8/1/33
Coogan, Jackie	Los Angeles, Cal.	10/26/14	Demarest, William	St. Paul, Minn.	2/27/92
Cook, Barbara	Atlanta, Ga.	10/25/27	De Mille, Agnes	New York, N.Y.	1905
Cooke, Alistair	England	11/20/08	Dempster, Carol	Duluth, Minn.	1905
Coolidge, Rita	Nashville, Tenn.	1944	Deneuve, Catherine	Paris, France	10/22/43
Cooper, Alice	Detroit, Mich.	2/4/48	Denning, Richard	Poughkeepsie, N.Y.	3/27/14
Cooper, Jackie	Los Angeles, Cal.	9/15/22	Dennis, Sandy	Hastings, Neb.	4/27/37
Coppola, Francis Ford	Detroit, Mich.	4/7/39	Denver, Bob	New Rochelle, N.Y.	1935
Corby, Ellen	Racine, Wis.	1913	Denver, John	Roswell, N.M.	12/31/43
Corelli, Franco	Ancona, Italy	4/8/23	Derek, Bo	Long Beach, Cal.	1956
Corey, Jeff	New York, N.Y.	8/10/14	Derek, John	Hollywood, Cal.	1926
Cosby, Bill	Philadelphia, Pa.	7/12/37	Dern, Bruce	Chicago, Ill.	6/4/36
Cotten, Joseph	Petersburg, Va.	5/15/05	Desmond, Johnny	Detroit, Mich.	11/14/21
Courtenay, Tom	Hull, England	2/25/37	Devane, William	Albany, N.Y.	9/5/37
Crabbe, Buster	Oakland, Cal.	2/07/08	DeVito, Danny	Neptune, N.J.	11/17/-
Craddock, Crash	Greensboro, N.C.	6/16/40	Dewhurst, Colleen	Montreal, Que.	6/3/26
Crain, Jeanne	Barstow, Cal.	5/25/25	DeWitt, Joyce	Wheeling, W.Va.	4/23/49
Crawford, Broderick.	Philadelphia, Pa.	12/9/11	Dey, Susan.	Pekin, Ill.	12/10/52
Crawford, Michael	Salisbury, England	1942	Diamond, Neil	Brooklyn, N.Y.	1/24/41
Crenna, Richard	Los Angeles, Cal.	11/30/27	Dickinson, Angie	Kulm, N.D.	9/30/31
Cronyn, Hume	London, Ont.	7/18/11	Dierkop, Charles.	La Crosse, Wis.	9/11/36
Crosby, Bob	Spokane, Wash.	8/23/13	Dietrich, Marlene	Berlin, Germany	1901
Crosby, David	Los Angeles, Cal.	8/14/41	Diller, Phyllis	Lima, Oh.	7/17/17
Crosby, Kathryn	Houston, Tex.	11/25/33	Dillman, Bradford	San Francisco, Cal.	4/14/30
Crosby, Mary	Los Angeles, Cal.	9/14/-	Dixon, Ivan	New York, N.Y.	4/6/31
Crosby, Norm	Boston, Mass.	1/15/-	Domingo, Placido	Madrid, Spain	1/21/41
Crowley, Pat	Scranton, Pa.	1929	Domino, Fats.	New Orleans, La.	2/26/28
Crystal, Billy	Long Beach, N.Y.	3/14/47	Donahue, Phil	Cleveland, Oh.	12/21/35
Cugat, Xavier	Barcelona, Spain	1/1/00	Donahue, Troy	New York, N.Y.	1/27/36
Cullen, Bill	Pittsburgh, Pa.	2/18/20	Donald, James	Aberdeen, Scotland	5/18/17
Cullum, John	Knoxville, Tenn.	3/2/30	Donnelly, Ruth	Trenton, N.J.	1896
Culp, Robert	Oakland, Cal.	8/16/30	Donovan	Glasgow, Scotland	5/10/46
Cummings, Constance	Seattle, Wash.	5/15/10	Dors, Diana	Swindon, England	10/23/31
Cummings, Robert	Joplin, Mo.	6/9/10	d'Orsay, Fifi	Montreal, Que.	1908
Curtin, Phyllis	Clarksburg, W.Va.	12/3/30	Douglas, Kirk	Amsterdam, N.Y.	12/9/18
Curtis, Keene	Salt Lake City, Ut.	2/15/23	Douglas, Melvyn	Macon, Ga.	4/5/01
Curtis, Ken	Lamar, Col.	7/2/16	Douglas, Michael	New Brunswick, N.J.	9/25/45
Curtis, Tony	New York, N.Y.	6/3/25	Douglas, Mike	Chicago, Ill.	8/11/25
Cusack, Cyril.	Durban, S. Africa	11/26/10	Downey, Morton	Wallingford, Conn.	11/14/01
Cushing, Peter	Surrey, England	5/26/13	Downs, Hugh	Akron, Oh.	2/14/21
			Doyle, David	Lincoln, Neb.	12/1/29
Dagmar (Egnor)	Huntington, W.Va.	1926	Dragon, Daryl	Los Angeles Cal.	8/27/42
Dahl, Arlene	Minneapolis, Minn.	8/11/28	Drake, Alfred.	Bronx, N.Y.	10/7/14
Dale, Jim	Rothwell, England	8/15/35	Drake, Betsy	Paris, France	1923
Dalrymple, Jean	Morristown, N.J.	9/2/10	Drew, Ellen.	Kansas City, Mo.	11/23/15

Name	Birthplace	Born
Dreyfuss, Richard	Brooklyn, N.Y.	10/29/47
Dru, Joanne	Logan, W.Va.	1/31/23
Drury, James	New York, N.Y.	1934
Duchin, Peter	New York, N.Y.	7/28/37
Duff, Howard	Bremerton, Wash.	11/24/17
Duffy, Patrick	Townsend, Mont.	3/17/49
Dufour, Val	New Orleans, La.	2/5/27
Duke, Patty	New York, N.Y.	12/14/46
Dullea, Keir	Cleveland, Oh.	5/30/36
Dunaway, Faye	Bascom, Fla.	1/14/41
Duncan, Sandy	Henderson, Tex.	2/20/46
Duncan, Todd	Danville, Ky.	1900
Duncan, Vivian	Los Angeles, Cal.	1902
Dunham, Katherine	Chicago, Ill.	6/22/10
Dunne, Irene	Louisville, Ky.	12/20/04
Dunnock, Mildred	Baltimore, Md.	1/25/06
Durbin, Deanna	Winnipeg, Man.	12/4/22
Dussault, Nancy	Pensacola, Fla.	6/30/36
Duvall, Robert	San Diego, Cal.	1931
Duvall, Shelley	Houston, Tex.	1949
Dylan, Bob	Duluth, Minn.	5/24/41
Eastwood, Clint	San Francisco, Cal.	5/31/30
Ebsen, Buddy	Belleville, Ill.	4/2/08
Eckstine, Billy	Pittsburgh, Pa.	7/8/14
Edelman, Herb	Brooklyn, N.Y.	11/5/33
Eden, Barbara	Tucson, Ariz.	1934
Edwards, Ralph	Merino, Col.	1913
Edwards, Vincent	Brooklyn, N.Y.	7/7/28
Egan, Richard	San Francisco, Cal.	7/29/23
Eggar, Samantha	London, England	3/5/39
Ekberg, Anita	Malmo, Sweden	9/29/31
Ekland, Britt	Stockholm, Sweden	1942
Elam, Jack	Miami, Ariz.	11/13/16
Eldridge, Florence	Brooklyn, N.Y.	9/5/01
Elgart, Larry	New London, Conn.	3/20/22
Elgart, Les	New Haven, Conn.	1918
Elliott, Bob	Boston, Mass.	1923
Emerson, Faye	Elizabeth, La.	7/8/17
Erickson, Leif	Alameda, Cal.	10/27/11
Esmond, Jill	London, England	1908
Estrada, Erik	New York, N.Y.	3/16/49
Evans, Dale	Uvalde, Tex.	10/31/12
Evans, Gene	Holbrook, Ariz.	7/11/24
Evans, Maurice	Dorchester, England	6/3/01
Evans, Robert	New York, N.Y.	6/29/30
Everett, Chad	South Bend, Ind.	6/11/37
Everly, Don	Brownie, Ky.	2/1/37
Everly, Phil	Brownie, Ky.	1/19/38
Ewell, Tom	Owensboro, Ky.	4/29/09
Fabares, Shelley	Santa Monica, Cal.	1944
Fabian (Forte)	Philadelphia, Pa.	2/6/43
Fabray, Nanette	San Diego, Cal.	10/27/20
Fadiman, Clifton	Brooklyn, N.Y.	5/15/04
Fairbanks, Douglas Jr.	New York, N.Y.	12/9/09
Falk, Peter	New York, N.Y.	9/16/27
Falkenberg, Jinx	Barcelona, Spain	1/21/19
Farber, Barry	Baltimore, Md.	1930
Farentino, James	Brooklyn, N.Y.	2/24/38
Fargo, Donna	Mt. Airy, N.C.	11/10/49
Farr, Jamie	Toledo, Oh.	7/1/36
Farrell, Charles	Onset Bay, Mass.	8/9/01
Farrell, Eileen	Willimantic, Conn.	2/13/20
Farrell, Mike	St. Paul, Minn.	2/6/42
Farrow, Mia	Los Angeles, Cal.	2/9/45
Fawcett, Farrah	Corpus Christi, Tex.	2/2/47
Faye, Alice	New York, N.Y.	5/5/15
Feld, Fritz	Berlin, Germany	10/15/00
Feldman, Marty	England	1933
Feldon, Barbara	Pittsburgh, Pa.	3/12/41
Feldshun, Tovah	New York, N.Y.	12/27/52
Feliciano, Jose	Puerto Rico	9/10/45
Fell, Norman	Philadelphia, Pa.	3/24/25
Fellini, Federico	Rimini, Italy	1/20/20
Fellows, Edith	Boston, Mass.	1923
Ferrer, Jose	Santurce, P.R.	1/8/12
Ferrer, Mel	Elberon, N.J.	8/25/17
Ferrigno, Lou	Brooklyn, N.Y.	11/9/52
Ferris, Barbara	London, England	1942
Fetchit, Stepin	Key West, Fla.	1902
Field, Sally	Pasadena, Cal.	11/6/46
Finney, Albert	Salford, England	5/9/36
Firkusny, Rudolf	Napajedla, Czechoslovakia	2/11/12
Fischer-Dieskau, Dietrich	Berlin, Germany	5/28/25
Fisher, Carrie	Beverly Hills, Cal.	10/21/56
Fisher, Eddie	Philadelphia, Pa.	8/10/28
Fitzgerald, Ella	Newport News, Va.	4/25/18
Fitzgerald, Geraldine	Dublin, Ireland	11/24/13
Fitzgerald, Pegeen	Norcatur, Kan.	1910
Fix, Paul	Dobbs Ferry, N.Y.	3/13/02
Flack, Roberta	Black Mountain, N.C.	2/10/39
Fleming, Rhonda	Hollywood, Cal.	8/10/23
Flanders, Ed	Minneapolis, Minn.	12/29/34
Fletcher, Louise	Birmingham, Ala.	1936
Foch, Nina	Leyden, Netherlands	4/20/24
Fonda, Henry	Grand Island, Neb.	5/16/05
Fonda, Jane	New York, N.Y.	12/21/37
Fonda, Peter	New York, N.Y.	2/23/39
Fontaine, Joan	Tokyo, Japan	10/22/17
Fontanne, Lynn	London, England	12/6/87
Fonteyn, Margot	Reigate, England	5/18/19
Forbes, Bryan	London, England	7/22/26
Ford (Tenn.), Ernie	Bristol, Tenn.	2/13/19
Ford, Glenn	Quebec, Canada	5/1/16
Ford, Harrison	Chicago, Ill.	7/13/42
Ford, Ruth	Hazelhurst, Miss.	1920
Forrest, Steve	Huntsville, Tex.	9/29/25
Forsythe, John	Penns Grove, N.J.	1/29/18
Fosse, Bob	Chicago, Ill.	6/23/27
Foster, Jodie	Los Angeles, Cal.	1962
Foster, Phil	Brooklyn, N.Y.	3/29/14
Fox, James	London, England	1939
Foxx, Redd	St. Louis, Mo.	12/9/22
Foy, Eddie Jr.	New Rochelle, N.Y.	2/4/05
Frampton, Peter	Kent, England	4/22/50
Francescatti, Zino	Marseilles, France	8/9/05
Franciosa, Anthony	New York, N.Y.	10/25/28
Francis, Anne	Ossining, N.Y.	9/16/32
Francis, Arlene	Boston, Mass.	10/20/08
Francis, Connie	Newark, N.J.	12/12/38
Franciscus, James	Clayton, Mo.	1/31/34
Frankenheimer, John	Malba, N.Y.	2/19/30
Franklin, Aretha	Memphis, Tenn.	3/25/42
Franklin, Bonnie	Santa Monica, Cal.	1/6/44
Franklin, Joe	New York, N.Y.	1929
Franz, Arthur	Perth Amboy, N.J.	2/29/20
Freberg, Stan	Pasadena, Cal.	8/7/26
Freed, Bert	New York, N.Y.	11/3/19
Freeman, Mona	Baltimore, Md.	1926
Frick, Mr. (G. Werner)	Basel, Switzerland	4/21/15
Frost, David	Tenterden, England	4/7/39
Frye, David	Brooklyn, N.Y.	1934
Funicello, Annette	Utica, N.Y.	1942
Funt, Allen	New York, N.Y.	9/16/14
Furness, Betty	New York, N.Y.	1/3/16
Gabel, Martin	Philadelphia, Pa.	6/19/12
Gabor, Eva	Hungary	1921
Gabor, Zsa Zsa	Hungary	1919
Gail, Max	Detroit, Mich.	4/5/43
Galloway, Don	Brooksville, Ky.	7/27/37
Galway, James	Galway, Ireland	12/8/39
Gam, Rita	Pittsburgh, Pa.	1929
Gambling, John	New York, N.Y.	1930
Garagiola, Joe	St. Louis, Mo.	2/12/26
Garbo, Greta	Stockholm, Sweden	9/18/05
Gardenia, Vincent	Naples, Italy	1/7/22
Gardner, Ava	Smithfield, N.C.	12/24/22
Garfunkel, Art	New York, N.Y.	10/13/41
Garland, Beverly	Santa Cruz, Cal.	10/17/29
Garner, James	Norman, Okla.	4/7/28
Garner, Peggy Ann	Canton, Oh.	2/3/32
Garrett, Betty	St. Joseph, Mo.	5/23/19
Garroway, Dave	Schenectady, N.Y.	7/13/13
Garson, Greer	Co. Down, N. Ireland	9/29/08
Gary, John	Watertown, N.Y.	11/29/32
Gavin, John	Los Angeles, Cal.	4/8/32
Gaye, Marvin	Washington, D.C.	4/2/39
Gayle, Crystal	Paintsville, Ky.	1951
Gaynor, Janet	Philadelphia, Pa.	10/6/06
Gaynor, Mitzi	Chicago, Ill.	9/4/30
Gazzara, Ben	New York, N.Y.	8/28/30
Gedda, Nicolai	Stockholm, Sweden	7/11/25
Gennaro, Peter	Metairie, La.	1924
Gentry, Bobbie	Chickasaw Co., Miss.	7/27/44
Gerard, Gil	Little Rock, Ark.	1/23/43
Gere, Richard	Philadelphia, Pa.	1950
Ghostley, Alice	Eve, Mo.	8/14/26
Giannini, Giancarlo	Spezia, Italy	8/1/42
Gibb, Andy	Manchester, England	3/5/58
Gibson, Henry	Germantown, Pa.	9/21/35
Gielgud, John	London, England	4/14/04
Gilbert, Melissa	Los Angeles, Cal.	5/8/64
Gilford, Jack	New York, N.Y.	7/25/07
Gillette, Anita	Baltimore, Md.	8/16/36
Gingold, Hermione	London, England	12/9/97
Ginty, Robert	New York, N.Y.	11/14/48

Name	Birthplace	Born
Gish, Lillian.	Springfield, Oh.	10/14/96
Givot, George	Omaha, Neb.	1903
Glaser, Paul Michael	Cambridge, Mass.	3/25/-
Glass, Ron	Evansville, Ind.	7/1/-
Gleason, Jackie	Brooklyn, N.Y.	2/26/16
Gobel, George	Chicago, Ill.	5/20/19
Godard, Jean Luc	Paris, France	12/3/30
Goddard, Paulette	Great Neck, N.Y.	6/3/15
Godfrey, Arthur	New York, N.Y.	8/31/03
Goldsboro, Bobby	Marianna, Fla.	1/11/41
Goodman, Benny	Chicago, Ill.	5/30/09
Goodman, Dody	Columbus, Oh.	10/28/29
Gordon, Gale	New York, N.Y.	2/2/06
Gordon, Ruth.	Wollaston, Mass.	10/30/96
Gorin, Igor	Ukraine, Russia	1909
Gorman, Cliff.	New York, N.Y.	10/13/36
Gorme, Eydie	Bronx, N.Y.	8/16/32
Gorshin, Frank	Pittsburgh, Pa.	4/5/34
Gortner, Marjoe	Long Beach, Cal.	1/14/44
Gosden, Freeman (Amos).	Richmond, Va.	5/5/99
Gossett, Louis	Brooklyn, N.Y.	5/27/36
Gould, Elliott	Brooklyn, N.Y.	8/29/38
Gould, Morton	Richmond Hill, N.Y.	12/10/13
Goulding, Ray	Lowell, Mass.	3/20/22
Goulet, Robert.	Lawrence, Mass.	11/26/33
Gowdy, Curt	Green River, Wyo.	1919
Graham, Martha.	Pittsburgh, Pa.	5/11/94
Graham, Virginia	Chicago, Ill.	7/4/12
Grahame, Gloria	Los Angeles, Cal.	11/28/29
Granger, Farley	San Jose, Cal.	7/1/25
Granger, Stewart	London, England	5/6/13
Granville, Bonita	New York, N.Y.	1923
Grant, Cary	Bristol, England	1/18/04
Grant, Lee	New York, N.Y.	10/31/31
Graves, Peter	Minneapolis, Minn.	3/18/26
Gray, Coleen	Staplehurst, Neb.	10/23/22
Gray, Dolores	Chicago, Ill.	6/7/24
Grayson, Kathryn	Winston-Salem, N.C.	2/9/23
Graziano, Rocky	New York, N.Y.	6/7/22
Greco, Buddy	Philadelphia, Pa.	8/14/26
Greco, Jose	Abruzzi, Italy	12/23/18
Green, Adolph	New York, N.Y.	12/2/15
Green, Al	Forest City, Ark.	4/13/46
Greene, Lorne	Ottawa, Ont.	2/12/15
Greene, Richard	England	1918
Greenwood, Joan	London, England	3/4/21
Greer, Jane	Washington, D.C.	9/9/24
Gregory, Dick	St. Louis, Mo.	10/12/32
Gregory, James	Bronx, N.Y.	12/23/11
Grey, Joel	Cleveland, Oh.	4/11/32
Griffin, Merv	San Mateo, Cal.	7/6/25
Griffith, Andy	Mount Airy, N.C.	6/1/26
Grimes, Gary.	San Francisco, Cal.	1955
Grimes, Tammy	Lynn, Mass.	1/30/36
Grizzard, George	Roanoke Rapids, N.C.	4/1/28
Grodin, Charles	Pittsburgh, Pa.	4/21/35
Guardino, Harry	New York, N.Y.	12/23/25
Guillaume, Robert.	St. Louis, Mo.	11/30/-
Guinness, Alec.	London, England	4/2/14
Gunn, Moses.	St. Louis, Mo.	10/2/29
Guthrie, Arlo	New York, N.Y.	7/10/47
Hackett, Buddy	Brooklyn, N.Y.	8/31/24
Hackett, Joan	New York, N.Y.	3/1/-
Hackman, Gene	San Bernardino, Cal.	1/30/30
Hagen, Uta	Gottingen, Germany	6/12/19
Haggard, Merle	Bakersfield, Cal.	4/6/37
Haggerty, Dan.	Hollywood, Cal.	11/19/41
Hagman, Larry.	Ft. Worth, Tex.	9/21/31
Hale, Barbara	DeKalb, Ill.	1922
Hall, Huntz	New York, N.Y.	1920
Hall, Monty.	Winnipeg, Man.	1925
Hall, Tom T.	Olive Hill, Ky.	5/25/36
Hamilton, George	Memphis, Tenn.	8/12/39
Hamilton, Margaret	Cleveland, Oh.	9/12/02
Hamilton, Neil	Lynn, Mass	1899
Hampshire, Susan.	London, England	5/12/42
Hampton, Lionel	Birmingham, Ala.	4/12/13
Harding, Ann.	Ft. Sam Houston, Tex.	8/7/02
Harmon, Mark	Burbank, Cal.	9/2/-
Harper, David W.	Abilene, Tex.	10/4/61
Harper, Valerie	Suffern, N.Y.	8/22/40
Harrington, Pat Jr.	New York, N.Y.	8/13/29
Harris, Barbara	Evanston, Ill.	1935
Harris, Emmy Lou	Birmingham, Ala.	1949
Harris, Julie	Grosse Pte. Park, Mich.	12/2/25
Harris, Phil	Linton, Ind.	6/24/06
Harris, Richard.	Co. Limerick, Ireland	10/1/33

Name	Birthplace	Born
Harris, Rosemary	Ashby, England	9/19/30
Harrison, George	Liverpool, England	2/25/43
Harrison, Gregory	Avalon, Cal.	5/31/50
Harrison, Rex	Huyton, England	3/5/08
Hartley, Mariette	New York, N.Y.	6/21/40
Hartman, David	Pawtucket, R.I.	5/19/35
Hasso, Signe	Stockholm, Sweden	8/15/15
Haver, June	Rock Island, Ill.	6/10/26
Havoc, June	Vancouver, B.C.	11/8/16
Hawn, Goldie	Washington, D.C.	11/21/45
Hayden, Melissa.	Toronto, Ont.	4/25/23
Hayden, Russell	Chico, Cal.	6/12/12
Hayden, Sterling.	Montclair, N.J.	3/26/16
Hayes, Helen	Washington, D.C.	10/10/00
Hayes, Isaac.	Covington, Tenn.	8/20/42
Hayes, Peter Lind	San Francisco, Cal.	6/25/15
Hayward, Louis	Johannesburg, S. Africa	1909
Hayworth, Rita.	New York, N.Y.	10/17/18
Healy, Mary	New Orleans, La.	4/14/18
Heatherton, Joey	Rockville Centre, N.Y.	9/14/44
Heckart, Eileen	Columbus, Oh.	3/29/19
Hefner, Hugh.	Chicago, Ill.	4/9/26
Heifetz, Jascha	Vilna, Lithuania	2/2/01
Helmond, Katherine	Galveston, Tex.	7/5/-
Helpmann, Robert.	Mt. Gambier, Australia	4/9/09
Hemmings, David	Guilford, England	11/2/41
Hemsley, Sherman	Philadelphia, Pa.	2/1/-
Henderson, Florence	Dale, Ind.	2/14/34
Henderson, Skitch.	Halstad, Minn.	1/27/18
Henner, Marilu.	Chicago, Ill.	4/6/-
Henning, Doug.	Ft. Garry, Man., Canada	1947
Henreid, Paul	Trieste, Austria	1/10/08
Henson, Jim	Greenville, Miss.	9/24/36
Hepburn, Audrey	Brussels, Belgium	5/4/29
Hepburn, Katharine	Hartford, Conn.	11/8/09
Herbert, Evelyn	Philadelphia, Pa.	1898
Hesseman, Howard	Lebanon, Ore.	2/27/40
Heston, Charlton	Evanston, Ill.	10/4/24
Heywood, Anne	Birmingham, England.	1937
Hickman, Darryl	Los Angeles, Cal.	1931
Hickman, Dwayne	Los Angeles, Cal.	1934
Hildegarde	Adell, Wis.	2/1/06
Hill, Arthur	Melfort, Sask.	8/1/22
Hiller, Wendy	Stockport, England	8/15/12
Hines, Earl (Fatha)	Duquesne, Pa.	12/28/05
Hines, Jerome	Hollywood, Cal.	11/8/21
Hines, Mimi.	Vancouver, B.C.	1933
Hingle, Pat	Denver, Col.	7/19/24
Hirsch, Judd	Bronx, N.Y.	3/15/35
Hirt, Al	New Orleans, La.	11/7/22
Ho, Don.	Kakaako, Oahu, Ha.	1930
Hoffman, Dustin	Los Angeles, Cal.	8/8/37
Holbrook, Hal	Cleveland, Oh.	2/17/25
Holden, William	O'Fallon, Ill.	4/17/18
Holder, Geoffrey.	Trinidad	8/1/30
Holliday, Polly	Jasper, Ala.	7/2/37
Holliman, Earl	Delhi, La.	9/11/28
Holloway, Stanley	London, England	10/1/90
Holloway, Sterling	Cedartown, Ga.	1905
Holm, Celeste	New York, N.Y.	4/29/19
Holtz, Lou	San Francisco, Cal.	1893
Homeier, Skip	Chicago, Ill.	10/5/30
Hooks, Robert.	Washington, D.C.	4/18/37
Hope, Bob	London, England	5/29/03
Hopkins, Anthony	Wales	12/31/37
Hopper, Dennis	Dodge City, Kan.	5/17/36
Horne, Lena	Brooklyn, N.Y.	6/30/17
Horne, Marilyn	Bradford, Pa.	1/16/34
Horowitz, Vladimir.	Kiev, Russia	10/1/04
Horton, Robert.	Los Angeles, Cal.	7/29/24
Houseman, John	Bucharest, Romania	9/22/02
Howard, Ken	El Centro, Cal.	3/28/44
Howard, Ron.	Duncan, Okla.	3/1/54
Howard, Trevor	Kent, England	9/29/16
Howes, Sally Ann	London, England	7/20/34
Hudson, Rock	Winnetka, Ill.	11/17/25
Hughes, Barnard	Bedford Hills, N.Y.	7/16/15
Humperdinck, Engelbert	Madras, India	5/3/36
Hunt, Lois	York, Pa.	11/26/25
Hunt, Marsha	Chicago, Ill.	10/17/17
Hunter, Kim	Detroit, Mich.	11/12/22
Hunter, Ross	Cleveland, Oh.	5/6/26
Hunter, Tab	New York, N.Y.	7/11/31
Hurt, John	Chesterfield, England	1/22/40
Hussey, Olivia	Buenos Aires, Argentina	1952
Hussey, Ruth	Providence, R.I.	10/30/17
Huston, John	Nevada, Mo.	8/5/06
Hutchinson, Josephine	Seattle, Wash.	1916
Hutton, Betty	Battle Creek, Mich.	2/26/21

Name	Birthplace	Born	Name	Birthplace	Born
Hutton, Ina Ray	Chicago, Ill.	1918	Kirkland, Gelsey	Bethlehem, Pa.	1953
Hutton, Lauren	Charleston, S.C.	1944	Kirsten, Dorothy	Montclair, N.J.	7/6/19
Hyde-White, Wilfrid	Gloucester, England	5/12/03	Kitt, Eartha	North, S.C.	1/26/28
Ian, Janis	New York, N.Y.	5/7/51	Klemperer, Werner	Cologne, Germany	3/22/20
Ingels, Marty	Brooklyn, N.Y.	3/9/36	Klein, Robert	New York, N.Y.	2/8/42
Ireland, Jill	London, England	4/24/41	Klugman, Jack	Philadelphia, Pa.	4/27/22
Ireland, John	Vancouver, B.C.	1/30/15	Knight, Gladys	Atlanta, Ga.	5/28/44
Ives, Burl	Hunt, Ill.	6/14/09	Knight, Ted	Terryville, Conn.	12/7/23
Jackson, Anne	Allegheny, Pa.	9/3/26	Knotts, Don	Morgantown, W. Va.	7/21/24
Jackson, Glenda	Cheshire, England	5/9/36	Knox, Alexander	Strathroy, Canada	1/16/07
Jackson, Kate	Birmingham, Ala.	10/29/49	Kopell, Bernard	New York, N.Y.	6/21/33
Jackson, Michael	Gary, Ind.	8/29/58	Korman, Harvey	Chicago, Ill.	2/15/27
Jaeckel, Richard	Long Beach, Cal.	10/10/26	Kramer, Stanley	New York, N.Y.	9/29/13
Jaffe, Sam	New York, N.Y.	3/10/91	Kristofferson, Kris	Brownsville, Tex.	6/22/36
Jagger, Dean	Columbus Grove, Oh.	11/7/05	Kruger, Hardy	Berlin, Germany	4/12/28
Jagger, Mick	Dartford, England	7/26/43	Kubelik, Rafael	Bychori, Czechoslovakia	6/29/14
James, Dennis	Jersey City, N.J.	8/24/17	Kubrick, Stanley	Bronx, N.Y.	7/26/28
James, Harry	Albany, Ga.	3/15/16	Kulp, Nancy	Harrisburg, Pa.	8/28/21
Janis, Conrad	New York, N.Y.	2/11/28	Kwan, Nancy	Hong Kong	1939
Jason, Rick	New York, N.Y.	5/21/26	Kyser, Kay	Rocky Mount, N.C.	6/18/05
Jeanmaire, Renee	Paris, France	4/29/24			
Jeffreys, Anne	Goldsboro, N.C.	1/26/23	Ladd, Cheryl	Huron, S.D.	7/12/51
Jeffries, Fran	San Jose, Cal.	1939	Laine, Frankie	Chicago, Ill.	3/30/13
Jeffries, Lionel	England	1926	Lamarr, Hedy	Vienna, Austria	9/11/15
Jennings, Waylon	Littlefield, Tex.	6/15/37	Lamas, Fernando	Buenos Aires, Argentina	1/9/25
Jens, Salome	Milwaukee, Wis.	5/8/35	Lamb, Gil	Minneapolis, Minn.	6/14/06
Jepson, Helen	Titusville, Pa.	1907	Lamour, Dorothy	New Orleans, La.	12/10/14
Joel, Billy	Bronx, N.Y.	5/9/49	Lancaster, Burt	New York, N.Y.	11/2/13
John, Elton	Middlesex, England	3/25/47	Lanchester, Elsa	London, England	10/28/02
Johns, Glynis	Durban, S. Africa	10/5/23	Landau, Martin	Brooklyn, N.Y.	1934
Johnson, Arte	Benton Harbor, Mich.	1/20/34	Landon, Michael	Forest Hills, N.Y.	—
Johnson, Ben	Foraker, Okla.	1918	Lane, Abbe	Brooklyn, N.Y.	1932
Johnson, Van	Newport, R.I.	8/25/16	Lane, Priscilla	Indianola, Ia.	1917
Jones, Allan	Scranton, Pa.	1907	Lange, Hope	Redding Ridge, Conn.	11/28/33
Jones, Carolyn	Amarillo, Tex.	4/28/33	Langella, Frank	Bayonne, N.J.	1/1/46
Jones, Chris	Jackson, Tenn.	1941	Langford, Frances	Lakeland, Fla.	4/4/13
Jones, Dean	Morgan City, Ala.	1/25/35	Lansbury, Angela	London, England	10/16/25
Jones, Grandpa	Niagara, Ky.	10/20/13	Lansing, Robert	San Diego, Cal.	6/5/29
Jones, Henry	Philadelphia, Pa.	8/1/12	Lanson, Snooky (Roy)	Memphis, Tenn.	1919
Jones, Jack	Hollywood, Cal.	1938	La Rosa, Julius	Brooklyn, N.Y.	1930
Jones, James Earl	Tate Co., Miss.	1/17/31	La Rue, Jack	New York, N.Y.	—
Jones, Jennifer	Tulsa, Okla.	3/2/19	Lasser, Louise	New York N.Y.	1941
Jones, Shirley	Smithton, Pa.	3/31/34	Laughlin, Tom	Minneapolis, Minn.	1938
Jones, Tom	Pontypridd, Wales	6/7/40	Laurie, Piper	Detroit, Mich.	1/22/32
Jory, Victor	Dawson, Yukon, Canada	11/23/02	Lavin, Linda	Portland, Me.	10/15/37
Jourdan, Louis	Marseilles, France	6/19/21	Lawford, Peter	London, England	9/7/23
Jurado, Katy	Guadalajara, Mexico	1927	Lawrence, Carol	Melrose Park, Ill.	9/5/34
			Lawrence, Steve	Brooklyn, N.Y.	7/8/35
Kahn, Madeline	Boston, Mass.	9/29/42	Lawrence, Vicki	Inglewood, Cal.	3/26/49
Kaplan, Gabe	Brooklyn, N.Y.	3/31/45	Leachman, Cloris	Des Moines, Ia.	4/4/26
Kaufman, Andy	New York, N.Y.	1/17/49	Lean, David	Croydon, England	3/25/08
Kavner, Judy	Los Angeles, Cal.	9/7/51	Lear, Norman	New Haven, Conn.	7/27/22
Kaye, Danny	Brooklyn, N.Y.	1/18/13	Learned, Michael	Washington, D.C.	4/9/39
Kaye, Sammy	Lakewood, Oh.	3/13/13	Lederer, Francis	Prague, Czechoslovakia	11/6/06
Kazan, Elia	Constantinople, Turkey	9/7/09	Lee, Brenda	Atlanta, Ga.	12/11/44
Kazan, Lainie	New York, N.Y.	5/15/42	Lee, Christopher	London, England	5/27/22
Keach, Stacy	Savannah, Ga.	6/2/41	Lee, Michele	Los Angeles, Cal.	1942
Keaton, Diane	Santa Ana, Cal.	1949	Lee, Peggy	Jamestown, N.D.	5/26/20
Keel, Howard	Gillespie, Ill.	4/13/19	Lee, Pinky	St. Paul, Minn.	—
Keeler, Ruby	Halifax, N.S.	8/25/10	Le Gallienne, Eva	London, England	1/11/99
Keeshan, Bob	Lynbrook, N.Y.	6/27/27	Legrand, Michel	Paris, France	1932
Keitel, Harvey	Brooklyn, N.Y.	1947	Leibman, Ron	New York, N.Y.	10/11/37
Keith, Brian	Bayonne, N.J.	11/14/21	Leigh, Janet	Merced, Cal.	7/6/27
Keller, Marthe	Basel, Switzerland	1945	Leinsdorf, Erich	Vienna, Austria	2/4/12
Kellerman, Sally	Long Beach, Cal.	6/2/37	Lembeck, Harvey	New York, N.Y.	1923
Kelley, DeForrest	Atlanta, Ga.	1/20/20	Lemmon, Jack	Boston, Mass.	2/8/25
Kelly, Gene	Pittsburgh, Pa.	8/23/12	Lennon, Dianne	Los Angeles, Cal.	1939
Kelly, Grace	Philadelphia, Pa.	11/12/29	Lennon, Janet	Culver City, Cal.	1946
Kelly, Jack	Astoria, N.Y.	1927	Lennon, Kathy	Santa Monica, Cal.	1944
Kelly, Nancy	Lowell, Mass.	3/25/21	Lennon, Peggy	Los Angeles, Cal.	1941
Kelly, Patsy	Brooklyn, N.Y.	1/12/10	Lenya, Lotte	Vienna, Austria	10/18/00
Kelsey, Linda	Minneapolis, Minn.	7/28/-	Leonard, Sheldon	New York, N.Y.	2/22/07
Kennedy, Arthur	Worcester, Mass.	2/17/14	Leontovich, Eugenie	Moscow, Russia	3/21/00
Kennedy, George	New York, N.Y.	2/18/26	LeRoy, Mervyn	San Francisco, Cal.	10/15/00
Kent, Allegra	Los Angeles, Cal.	8/11/37	Leslie, Joan	Detroit, Mich.	1/26/25
Kerr, Deborah	Helensburgh, Scotland	9/30/21	Lester, Jerry	Chicago, Ill.	1911
Kerr, John	New York, N.Y.	11/15/31	Levine, James	Cincinnati, Oh.	6/23/43
Kert, Larry	Los Angeles, Cal.	12/5/30	Lewis, Jerry	Newark, N.J.	3/16/26
Keyes, Evelyn	Port Arthur, Tex.	1925	Lewis, Jerry Lee	Ferriday, La.	9/29/35
Kidd, Michael	New York, N.Y.	8/12/25	Lewis, Monica	Chicago, Ill.	5/5/25
Kiley, Richard	Chicago, Ill.	3/31/22	Lewis, Robert Q.	New York, N.Y.	1924
King, Alan	Brooklyn, N.Y.	12/26/27	Lewis, Shari	New York, N.Y.	1/17/34
King, B. B.	Itta Bena, Miss.	9/16/25	Liberace	West Allis, Wis.	5/16/19
King, Carole	Brooklyn, N.Y.	2/9/42	Lightfoot, Gordon	Orillia, Ont.	11/17/38
King, Walter Woolf	San Francisco, Cal.	1899	Lillie, Beatrice	Toronto, Ont.	5/29/94
King, Wayne	Savannah, Ill.	1901	Linden, Hal	New York, N.Y.	3/20/31
Kirby, Durward	Covington, Ky.	8/24/12	Lindfors, Viveca	Uppsala, Sweden.	12/29/20
Kirk, Lisa	Brownsville, Pa.	1925	Lindsey, Mort	Newark, N.J.	1923
Kirk, Phyllis	Plainfield, N.J.	9/18/30	Linkletter, Art	Saskatchewan, Canada	7/17/12

Name	Birthplace	Born
Little, Cleavon	Chickasha, Okla.	6/1/39
Little, Rich	Ottawa, Ont.	11/26/38
Little Richard	Macon, Ga.	1935
Livingstone, Mary	Seattle, Wash.	1909
Lockhart, June	New York, N.Y.	6/25/25
Lockwood, Margaret	Karachi, India	9/15/16
Loder, John	London, England	1898
Logan, Joshua	Texarkana, Tex.	10/5/08
Loggins, Kenny	Everett, Wash.	1/7/48
Lollobrigida, Gina	Subiaco, Italy	7/4/28
Lom, Herbert	Prague, Czechoslovakia	1917
London, Julie	Santa Rosa, Cal.	9/26/26
Longet, Claudine	France	1/29/42
Lopez, Trini	Dallas, Tex.	5/15/37
Lord, Jack	New York, N.Y.	—
Loren, Sophia	Rome, Italy	9/20/34
Loudon, Dorothy	Boston, Mass.	9/17/33
Louise, Tina	New York, N.Y.	1934
Love, Bessie	Midland, Tex.	9/10/98
Loy, Myrna	Helena, Mon.	8/2/05
Lucas, George	Modesto, Cal.	1944
Luckinbill, Laurence	Ft. Smith, Ark.	11/21/34
Ludwig, Christa	Berlin, Germany	1928
Luke, Keye	Canton, China.	1904
Lumet, Sidney	Philadelphia, Pa.	6/25/24
Lund, John	Rochester, N.Y.	1913
Lupino, Ida	London, England	2/4/18
Lynde, Paul	Mt. Vernon, Oh.	6/13/26
Lynley, Carol	New York, N.Y.	2/13/42
Lynn, Jeffrey	Auburn, Mass.	1909
Lynn, Loretta	Butcher Hollow, Ky.	4/14/35
Lyon, Sue	Davenport, Ia.	7/10/46
Maazel, Lorin	Paris, France	3/6/30
MacArthur, James	Los Angeles, Cal.	12/8/37
MacGraw, Ali	Pound Ridge, N.Y.	4/1/39
MacKenzie, Gisele	Winnipeg, Man.	1/10/27
MacLaine, Shirley	Richmond, Va.	4/24/34
MacMurray, Fred	Kankakee, Ill.	8/30/08
MacNeil, Cornell	Minneapolis, Minn.	9/24/22
MacRae, Gordon	East Orange, N.J.	3/12/21
MacRae, Meredith	Houston, Tex.	1945
MacRae, Sheila	London, England	9/24/24
Macy, Bill	Revere, Mass.	5/18/22
Madison, Guy	Bakersfield, Cal.	1/19/22
Majors, Lee	Wyandotte, Mich.	4/23/40
Makarova, Natalia	Leningrad, USSR.	11/21/40
Malbin, Elaine	New York, N.Y.	1932
Malden, Karl	Chicago, Ill.	3/22/13
Malone, Dorothy	Chicago, Ill.	1/30/25
Manchester, Melissa	Bronx, N.Y.	2/15/51
Mancini, Henry	Cleveland, Oh.	4/16/24
Mandrell, Barbara	Houston, Tex.	12/25/48
Mangione, Chuck	Rochester, N.Y.	11/29/40
Manilow, Barry	New York, N.Y.	6/17/46
Mann, Herbie	New York, N.Y.	4/16/30
Marceau, Marcel	France	3/22/23
Marchand, Nancy	Buffalo, N.Y.	6/19/28
Margo	Mexico City, Mexico	5/10/18
Margolin, Janet	New York, N.Y.	1943
Markova, Alicia	London, England	12/1/10
Marlowe, Hugh	Philadelphia, Pa.	1/20/11
Marriner, Neville	Lincoln, England	4/15/25
Marsh, Jean	London, England	7/1/34
Marshall, E. G.	Owatonna, Minn.	6/18/10
Marshall, Penny	New York, N.Y.	10/15/43
Marshall, Peter	Huntington, W.Va.	3/30/-
Martin, Dean	Steubenville, Oh.	6/17/17
Martin, Dick	Detroit, Mich.	1/30/22
Martin, Mary	Weatherford, Tex.	12/1/13
Martin, Steve	Waco, Tex.	1945
Martin, Tony	San Francisco, Cal.	12/25/13
Martino, Al	Philadelphia, Pa.	1927
Marvin, Lee	New York, N.Y.	2/19/24
Mason, Jackie	Sheboygan, Wis.	1931
Mason, James	Huddersfield, England	5/15/09
Mason, Marsha	St. Louis, Mo.	4/3/42
Mason, Pamela	London, England	3/10/22
Massey, Raymond	Toronto, Ont.	8/30/96
Mastroianni, Marcello	Rome, Italy	9/28/24
Matheson, Tim	Glendale, Cal.	12/31/47
Mathieu, Mireille	Avignon, France	1946
Mathis, Johnny	San Francisco, Cal.	9/30/35
Matthau, Walter	New York, N.Y.	10/1/20
Mature, Victor	Louisville, Ky.	1/19/16
May, Billy	Pittsburgh, Pa.	1916
May, Elaine	Philadelphia, Pa.	4/21/32
Mayehoff, Eddie	Baltimore, Md.	7/7/14
Mayo, Virginia	St. Louis, Mo.	11/30/20

Name	Birthplace	Born
Mazurki, Mike	Austria	12/25/09
Mazursky, Paul	Brooklyn, N.Y.	4/25/30
McArdle, Andrea	Philadelphia, Pa.	11/4/63
McBride, Patricia	Teaneck, N.J.	8/23/42
McCallum, David	Glasgow, Scotland	9/19/33
McCambridge, Mercedes	Joliet, Ill.	3/17/18
McCarthy, Kevin	Seattle, Wash.	2/15/14
McCartney, Paul	Liverpool, England	6/18/42
McClure, Doug	Glendale, Cal.	5/11/38
McCord, Kent	Los Angeles, Cal.	1942
McCrary, Tex (John)	Calvert, Tex.	10/13/10
McCrea, Joel	Los Angeles, Cal.	11/5/05
McDonough, Mary	Los Angeles, Cal.	5/4/61
McDowall, Roddy	London, England	9/17/28
McDowell, Malcolm	Leeds, England	6/19/43
McEachin, James	Pennert, N.C.	1930
McFarland, George (Spanky)	Dallas, Tex.	1928
McGavin, Darren	San Joaquin, Cal.	5/7/22
McGee, Fibber	Peoria, Ill.	11/6/96
McGoohan, Patrick	New York, N.Y.	3/19/28
McGuire, Dorothy	Omaha, Neb.	6/14/19
McGuire Sisters:		
Christine	Middletown, Oh.	1928
Dorothy	Middletown, Oh.	1930
Phyllis	Middletown, Oh.	1931
McHugh, Frank	Homestead, Pa.	5/23/99
McIntire, John	Spokane, Wash.	6/27/07
McKechnie, Donna	Pontiac, Mich.	11/16/42
McKenna, Siobhan	Belfast, Ireland	5/24/23
McLean, Don	New Rochelle, N.Y.	10/2/45
McLerie, Allyn	Grand Mere, Que.	12/1/26
McLeod, Gavin	Mt. Kisco, N.Y.	2/28/-
McMahon, Ed	Detroit, Mich.	3/6/23
McNair, Barbara	Racine, Wis.	3/4/39
McNichol, Jimmy	Los Angeles, Cal.	7/2/61
McNichol, Kristy	Los Angeles, Cal.	9/11/62
McQueen, Butterfly	Tampa, Fla.	1/7/11
Meadows, Audrey	Wu Chang, China.	1924
Meadows, Jayne	Wu Chang, China.	9/27/26
Meara, Anne	New York, N.Y.	1929
Meeker, Ralph	Minneapolis, Minn.	11/21/20
Mehta, Zubin	Bombay, India	4/29/36
Melanie	New York, N.Y.	1/3/47
Menuhin, Yehudi	New York, N.Y.	4/22/16
Mercouri, Melina	Athens, Greece	10/18/25
Meredith, Burgess	Cleveland, Oh.	11/16/08
Merkel, Una	Covington, Ky.	12/10/03
Merman, Ethel	Astoria, N.Y.	1/16/09
Merrick, David	Hong Kong	11/27/12
Merrill, Dina	New York, N.Y.	12/9/25
Merrill, Gary	Hartford, Conn.	8/2/15
Merrill, Robert	Brooklyn, N.Y.	6/4/19
Messina, Jim	Maywood, Cal.	12/5/47
Middleton, Ray	Chicago, Ill.	2/8/07
Midler, Bette	Paterson, N.J.	12/1/45
Milanov, Zinka	Zagreb, Yugoslavia.	5/17/08
Miles, Sarah	Ingatestone, England.	12/31/43
Miles, Vera	near Boise City, Okla.	8/23/30
Milland, Ray	Neath, Wales	1/3/08
Miller, Ann	Houston, Tex.	4/12/23
Miller, Jason	Scranton, Pa.	4/22/39
Miller, Mitch	Rochester, N.Y.	7/4/11
Miller, Roger	Ft. Worth, Tex.	1/2/36
Mills, Hayley	London, England	4/18/46
Mills, John	Suffolk, England	2/22/08
Mills, Juliet	London, England	11/21/41
Mills Brothers:		
Mills, Herbert	Piqua, Oh.	4/12/12
Mills, Harry	Piqua, Oh.	8/19/13
Mills, Donald	Piqua, Oh.	4/29/15
Milner, Martin	Detroit, Mich.	12/28/31
Milnes, Sherrill	Downers Grove, Ill.	1/10/35
Milsap, Ronnie	Robinsville, N.C.	1/16/-
Milstein, Nathan	Odessa, Russia	12/31/04
Mimieux, Yvette	Hollywood, Cal.	1/8/42
Minnelli, Liza	Los Angeles, Cal.	3/12/46
Mitchell, Cameron	Dallastown, Pa.	11/4/18
Mitchell, Guy	Detroit, Mich.	2/22/25
Mitchell, Joni	McLeod, Alta.	11/7/43
Mitchum, Robert	Bridgeport, Conn.	8/6/17
Moffo, Anna	Wayne, Pa.	6/27/34
Molinaro, Al	Kenosha, Wis.	6/24/-
Montalban, Ricardo	Mexico City, Mexico	11/25/20
Montand, Yves	Monsummano, Italy	10/31/21
Montgomery, Elizabeth	Hollywood, Cal.	4/15/33
Montgomery, George	Brady, Mon.	8/29/16
Montgomery, Robert	Beacon, N.Y.	5/21/04

Name	Birthplace	Born
Moody, Ron	London, England	1/8/24
Moore, Clayton	Chicago, Ill.	9/14/14
Moore, Constance	Sioux City, Ia.	1/18/22
Moore, Dudley	London, England	4/19/35
Moore, Garry	Baltimore, Md.	1/31/15
Moore, Mary Tyler	Brooklyn, N.Y.	12/29/37
Moore, Melba	New York, N.Y.	10/29/45
Moore, Roger	London, England	10/14/27
Moore, Terry	Los Angeles, Cal.	1/1/32
Moran, Erin	Los Angeles, Cal.	10/18/61
Moreau, Jeanne	Paris, France	1/23/28
Moreno, Rita	Humacao, P.R.	12/11/31
Morgan, Dennis	Prentice, Wis.	1910
Morgan, Harry	Detroit, Mich.	4/10/15
Morgan, Henry	New York, N.Y.	3/31/15
Morgan, Jane	Boston, Mass.	1920
Morgan, Jaye P.	Mancos, Col.	12/3/31
Morgana, Nina	Buffalo, N.Y.	1895
Moriarty, Michael	Detroit, Mich.	4/5/41
Morini, Erika	Vienna, Austria	1/5/10
Morley, Robert	Wiltshire, England	5/26/08
Morris, Greg	Cleveland, Oh.	9/27/34
Morris, Howard	New York, N.Y.	9/4/25
Morrow, Vic	Bronx, N.Y.	2/14/32
Morse, Robert	Newton, Mass.	5/18/31
Moss, Arnold	Brooklyn, N.Y.	1/28/10
Mulhare, Edward	Ireland	1923
Mull, Martin	Chicago, Ill.	1943
Mulligan, Richard	New York, N.Y.	11/13/32
Munsel, Patrice	Spokane, Wash.	5/14/25
Murphy, George	New Haven, Conn.	7/4/02
Murphy, Michael	Los Angeles, Cal.	5/5/38
Murray, Anne	Springhill, Nova Scotia	6/20/45
Murray, Arthur	New York, N.Y.	4/4/95
Murray, Don	Hollywood, Cal.	7/31/29
Murray, Jan	New York, N.Y.	1917
Murray, Kathryn	Jersey City, N.J.	9/15/06
Murray, Ken	New York, N.Y.	7/14/03
Musante, Tony	Bridgeport, Conn.	6/30/-
Musburger, Brent	Portland, Ore.	5/26/39
Nabors, Jim	Sylacauga, Ala.	6/12/33
Natwick, Mildred	Baltimore, Md.	6/19/08
Neal, Patricia	Packard, Ky.	1/20/26
Neff, Hildegarde	Ulm, Germany	12/28/25
Negri, Pola	Lipno, Poland	1899
Nelson, Barry	San Francisco, Cal.	1920
Nelson, David	New York, N.Y.	10/24/36
Nelson, Ed	New Orleans, La.	12/21/28
Nelson, Gene	Seattle, Wash.	3/24/20
Nelson, Harriet (Hilliard)	Des Moines, Ia.	7/18/14
Nelson, Rick	Teaneck, N.J.	5/8/40
Nelson, Willie	Waco, Tex.	4/30/33
Nero, Peter	New York, N.Y.	5/22/34
Nesbit, Cathleen	Cheshire, England	11/24/89
Newhart, Bob	Oak Park, Ill.	9/5/29
Newley, Anthony	Hackney, England	9/24/31
Newman, Barry	Boston, Mass.	11/7/38
Newman, Paul	Cleveland, Oh.	1/26/25
Newman, Phyllis	Jersey City, N.J.	3/19/35
Newman, Randy	Los Angeles, Cal.	11/28/43
Newmar, Julie	Los Angeles, Cal.	1935
Newton, Wayne	Roanoke, Va.	4/3/42
Newton-John, Olivia	Cambridge, England	9/26/48
Nichols, Mike	Berlin, Germany	11/6/31
Nicholson, Jack	Neptune, N.J.	4/28/37
Nielsen, Leslie	Regina, Sask.	2/11/26
Nilsson, Birgit	Karop, Sweden	1918
Nimoy, Leonard	Boston, Mass.	3/26/31
Niven, David	Kirriemuir, Scotland	3/1/10
Nolan, Doris	New York, N.Y.	1916
Nolan, Jeannette	Los Angeles, Cal.	1911
Nolan, Kathy	St. Louis, Mo.	9/27/33
Nolan, Lloyd	San Francisco, Cal.	8/11/02
Nolte, Nick	Omaha, Neb.	1940
Norman, Jessye	Augusta, Ga.	9/15/45
North, Jay	Hollywood, Cal.	1953
North, Sheree	Los Angeles, Cal.	1/17/33
Norton-Taylor, Judy	Santa Monica, Cal.	1/29/58
Novak, Kim	Chicago, Ill.	2/18/33
Nureyev, Rudolf	Russia	3/17/38
Oakland, Simon	New York, N.Y.	1922
O'Brian, Hugh	Rochester, N.Y.	4/19/30
O'Brien, Edmond	New York, N.Y.	9/10/15
O'Brien, Margaret	San Diego, Cal.	1/15/37
O'Brien, Pat	Milwaukee, Wis.	11/11/99
O'Connell, Arthur	New York, N.Y.	3/29/08
O'Connell, Helen	Lima, Oh.	1920
O'Connor, Carroll	New York, N.Y.	8/2/24
O'Connor, Donald	Chicago, Ill.	8/28/25
Odetta	Birmingham, Ala.	12/31/30
O'Driscoll, Martha	Tulsa, Okla.	1922
O'Hara, Maureen	Dublin, Ireland	8/17/21
O'Herlihy, Dan	Wexford, Ireland	5/1/19
O'Keefe, Walter	Hartford, Conn.	1907
Olivier, Laurence	Dorking, England	5/22/07
O'Malley, J. Pat	Burnley, England	1901
O'Neal, Patrick	Ocala, Fla.	9/26/27
O'Neal, Ryan	Los Angeles, Cal.	4/20/41
O'Neal, Tatum	Los Angeles, Cal.	11/5/63
O'Neill, Jennifer	Brazil	2/20/49
Opatoshu, David	New York, N.Y.	1/30/18
Orbach, Jerry	New York, N.Y.	10/20/35
Orlando, Tony	New York, N.Y.	4/3/44
Ormandy, Eugene	Budapest, Hungary	11/18/99
Osmond, Donny	Ogden, Ut.	12/9/57
Osmond, Marie	Ogden, Ut.	10/13/59
O'Sullivan, Maureen	Boyle, Ireland	5/17/11
O'Toole, Peter	Connemara, Ireland	8/2/32
Owens, Buck	Sherman, Tex.	8/12/29
Owens, Gary	Mitchell, S.D.	5/10/36
Ozawa, Seiji	Shenyang, China	9/1/35
Paar, Jack	Canton, Oh.	5/1/18
Pacino, Al	New York, N.Y.	4/25/40
Page, Geraldine	Kirksville, Mo.	11/22/24
Page, LaWanda	Cleveland, Oh.	10/19/20
Page, Patti	Claremore, Okla.	11/8/27
Paige, Janis	Tacoma, Wash.	9/16/22
Palance, Jack	Lattimer, Pa.	2/18/20
Palmer, Betsy	East Chicago, Ind.	11/1/29
Palmer, Lilli	Posen, Germany	5/24/14
Papas, Irene	Greece	1926
Papp, Joseph	Brooklyn, N.Y.	6/22/21
Parker, Eleanor	Cedarville, Oh.	6/26/22
Parker, Fess	Ft. Worth, Tex.	8/16/25
Parker, Frank	New York, N.Y.	1906
Parker, Jean	Deer Lodge, Mon.	1916
Parker, Suzy	San Antonio, Tex.	10/28/33
Parkins, Barbara	Vancouver, B.C.	1942
Parks, Bert	Atlanta, Ga.	12/30/14
Parsons, Estelle	Lynn, Mass.	11/20/27
Parton, Dolly	Sevierville, Tenn.	1/19/46
Pasternak, Joseph	Hungary	9/19/01
Patane, Giuseppe	Napoli, Italy	1/1/32
Patterson, Neva	Nevada, Ia.	1922
Paulsen, Pat	South Bend, Wash.	—
Pavan, Marisa	Cagliari, Sardinia	6/19/32
Pavarotti, Luciano	Modena, Italy	10/12/35
Payne, John	Roanoke, Va.	1912
Pearl, Minnie	Centerville, Tenn.	10/25/12
Peck, Gregory	La Jolla, Cal.	4/5/16
Peckinpah, Sam	Fresno, Cal.	2/21/25
Peerce, Jan	New York, N.Y.	1904
Pendergrass, Teddy	Philadelphia, Pa.	3/26/50
Penn, Arthur	Philadelphia, Pa.	9/27/22
Peppard, George	Detroit, Mich.	10/1/28
Perkins, Anthony	New York, N.Y.	4/4/32
Perlman, Itzhak	Tel Aviv, Israel	10/31/45
Perrine, Valerie	Galveston, Tex.	9/3/43
Persoff, Nehemiah	Jerusalem, Palestine	8/14/20
Peters, Bernadette	Queens, N.Y.	2/28/48
Peters, Brock	New York, N.Y.	7/2/27
Peters, Jean	Canton, Oh.	10/15/26
Peters, Roberta	New York, N.Y.	5/4/30
Petit, Pascale	France	1937
Phillips, MacKenzie	Alexandria, Va.	11/10/59
Phillips, Michelle	Long Beach, Cal.	4/6/44
Piazza, Marguerite	New Orleans, La.	5/6/26
Pickens, Slim	Kingsberg, Cal.	6/29/19
Picon, Molly	New York, N.Y.	6/1/98
Pidgeon, Walter	E. St. John, N.B.	9/23/97
Pleasance, Donald	Worksop, England	10/5/21
Pleshette, Suzanne	New York, N.Y.	1/31/37
Plowright, Joan	Brigg, England	10/28/29
Plummer, Christopher	Toronto, Ont.	12/13/29
Poitier, Sidney	Miami, Fla.	2/20/27
Polanski, Roman	Paris, France	8/18/33
Ponti, Carlo	Milan, Italy	12/11/13
Poston, Tom	Columbus, Oh.	10/17/21
Powell, Eleanor	Springfield, Mass.	11/21/12
Powell, Jane	Portland, Ore.	4/1/29
Powell, William	Pittsburgh, Pa.	7/29/92
Powers, Mala	San Francisco, Cal.	1931
Powers, Stefanie	Hollywood, Cal.	11/12/42
Preminger, Otto	Vienna, Austria	12/5/06
Prentiss, Paula	San Antonio, Tex.	3/4/39
Preston, Robert	Newton, Mass.	6/8/18

Name	Birthplace	Born
Previn, Andre	Berlin, Germany	4/6/29
Price, Leontyne	Laurel, Miss.	2/10/27
Price, Ray	Perryville, Tex.	1/12/26
Price, Vincent	St. Louis, Mo.	5/27/11
Pride, Charlie	Sledge, Miss.	3/18/39
Prince, William	Nichols, N.Y.	1/26/13
Principal, Victoria	Fukuoka, Japan.	1/3/-
Provine, Dorothy	Deadwood, S.D.	1/20/37
Prowse, Juliet	Bombay, India.	9/25/37
Pryor, Richard	Peoria, Ill.	12/1/40
Pyle, Denver	Bethune, Col.	5/11/20
Qualen, John	Vancouver, B.C.	1899
Quayle, Anthony	Lancashire, England	9/7/13
Quillan, Eddie	Philadelphia, Pa.	3/31/07
Quinn, Anthony	Chihuahua, Mexico	4/21/15
Rabb, Ellis	Memphis, Tenn.	6/20/30
Rabbitt, Eddie	Brooklyn, N.Y.	11/27/41
Radner, Gilda	Detroit, Mich.	6/28/-
Rae, Charlotte	Milwaukee, Wis.	4/22/26
Raffin, Deborah	Los Angeles, Cal.	1953
Rainer, Luise	Vienna, Austria	1912
Raines, Ella	Snoqualmie Falls, Wash.	8/6/21
Raitt, John	Santa Ana, Cal.	1/19/17
Ralston, Esther	Bar Harbor, Me.	9/19/02
Ralston, Vera	Prague, Czechoslovakia	1921
Randall, Tony	Tulsa, Okla.	2/26/20
Rawls, Lou	Chicago, Ill.	12/1/35
Ray, Aldo	Pen Argyl, Pa.	9/25/26
Ray, Johnnie	Dallas, Ore.	1927
Rayburn, Gene	Christopher, Ill.	12/22/17
Raye, Martha	Butte, Mon.	8/27/16
Raymond, Gene	New York, N.Y.	8/13/08
Reddy, Helen	Melbourne, Australia	10/25/41
Redford, Robert	Santa Monica, Cal.	8/18/37
Redgrave, Lynn	London, England	3/8/43
Redgrave, Michael	Bristol, England	3/20/08
Redgrave, Vanessa	London, England	1/30/37
Reed, Donna	Denison, Ia.	1/27/21
Reed, Jerry	Atlanta, Ga.	3/20/37
Reed, Rex	Ft. Worth, Tex.	10/2/38
Reed, Robert	Highland Park, Ill.	1932
Reese, Della	Detroit, Mich.	7/6/31
Regan, Phil	Brooklyn, N.Y.	5/28/06
Reid, Kate	London, England	11/4/30
Reilly, Charles Nelson	New York, N.Y.	1/13/31
Reiner, Carl	Bronx, N.Y.	3/20/22
Reiner, Rob	Bronx, N.Y.	3/6/45
Remick, Lee	Boston, Mass.	12/14/35
Resnik, Regina	New York, N.Y.	8/30/24
Rey, Alejandro	Buenos Aires, Argentina	2/8/30
Reynolds, Burt	Waycross, Ga.	2/11/36
Reynolds, Debbie	El Paso, Tex.	4/1/32
Reynolds, Marjorie	Buhl, Ida.	8/12/21
Rhodes, Hari	Cincinnati, Oh.	1932
Rich, Charlie	Forest City, Ark.	12/14/32
Rich, Irene	Buffalo, N.Y.	10/13/97
Richardson, Ralph	Cheltenham, England	12/19/02
Richardson, Tony	Shipley, England	6/5/28
Rickles, Don	New York, N.Y.	5/8/26
Riddle, Nelson	Hackensack, N.J.	6/1/21
Rigg, Diana	Doncaster, England	7/20/38
Ritter, John	Burbank, Cal.	9/17/48
Ritz, Harry	Newark, N.J.	1908
Ritz, Jimmy	Newark, N.J.	1905
Rivera, Chita	Washington, D.C.	1/23/33
Rivers, Joan	Brooklyn, N.Y.	1937
Robards, Jason Jr.	Chicago, Ill.	7/26/22
Robbins, Jerome	New York, N.Y.	10/11/18
Robbins, Marty	Glendale, Ariz.	9/26/25
Roberts, Pernell	Waycross, Ga.	5/18/-
Robertson, Cliff	La Jolla, Cal.	9/9/25
Robertson, Dale	Oklahoma City, Okla.	7/14/23
Robson, Flora	South Shields, England	3/28/02
Rodgers, Jimmie	Camas, Wash.	1933
Rodriquez, Johnny	Sabinal, Tex.	12/10/51
Rogers, Chas. (Buddy)	Olathe, Kan.	8/13/04
Rogers, Ginger	Independence, Mo.	7/16/11
Rogers, Kenny	Houston, Tex.	8/21/38
Rogers, Roy	Cincinnati, Oh.	11/5/12
Roland, Gilbert	Juarez, Mexico	12/11/05
Rolle, Esther	Pompano Beach, Fla.	11/8/-
Roman, Ruth	Boston, Mass.	12/23/24
Romero, Cesar	New York, N.Y.	2/15/07
Ronstadt, Linda	Tucson, Ariz.	7/15/46
Rooney, Mickey	Brooklyn, N.Y.	9/23/20
Rose, George	Bicester, England.	2/19/20
Rose Marie	New York, N.Y.	—
Ross, Diana	Detroit, Mich.	3/26/44
Ross, Katharine	Hollywood, Cal.	1/29/43
Ross, Lanny	Seattle, Wash.	1/19/06
Rostropovich, Mstislav	Baku, USSR.	3/27/27
Roundtree, Richard	New Rochelle, N.Y.	7/9/42
Rowan, Dan	Beggs, Okla.	7/2/22
Rowlands, Gena	Cambria, Wis.	6/19/36
Rubin, Benny	Boston, Mass.	1899
Rubinoff, David	Grodno, Russia	1897
Rubinstein, Artur	Lodz, Poland	1/28/87
Rudolf, Max	Frankfurt, Germany	6/15/02
Rule, Janice	Norwood, Oh.	8/15/31
Rush, Barbara	Denver, Col.	1/4/30
Russell, Jane	Bemidji, Minn.	6/21/21
Russell, Ken	Southampton, England.	7/3/27
Russell, Kurt	Springfield, Mass.	3/17/51
Russell, Nipsey	Atlanta, Ga.	1924
Rutherford, Ann	Toronto, Ont.	1924
Ryan, Peggy	Long Beach, Cal.	8/28/24
Rydell, Bobby	Philadelphia, Pa.	1942
Sahl, Mort	Montreal, Que.	5/11/27
Saint, Eva Marie	Newark, N.J.	7/4/24
St. James, Susan	Los Angeles, Cal.	8/14/46
St. John, Jill	Los Angeles, Cal.	8/19/40
Sainte-Marie, Buffy	Maine	2/20/41
Saks, Gene	New York, N.Y.	11/8/21
Sales, Soupy	Franklinton, N.C.	1920
Sand, Paul	Los Angeles, Cal.	3/5/35
Sands, Tommy	Chicago, Ill.	8/27/37
Sanford, Isabel	New York, N.Y.	8/29/-
Santana, Carlos	Mexico	7/20/47
Sarnoff, Dorothy	New York, N.Y.	1919
Sarrazin, Michael	Quebec City, Que.	5/22/40
Savalas, Telly	Garden City, N.Y.	1/21/24
Saxon, John	Brooklyn, N.Y.	8/5/35
Sayao, Bidu	Rio de Janeiro, Brazil	5/11/02
Sayer, Leo	Sussex, England	5/21/48
Schallert, William	Los Angeles, Cal.	7/6/22
Scheider, Roy	Orange, N.J.	11/10/35
Schell, Maria	Vienna, Austria	1/15/26
Schell, Maximilian	Vienna, Austria	12/8/30
Schenkel, Chris	Bippus, Ind.	1924
Schnabel, Stefan	Berlin, Germany	2/2/12
Schneider, Alexander	Vilna, Poland	10/21/08
Schneider, John	Mt. Kisco, N.Y.	4/8/-
Schneider, Romy	Austria	9/23/38
Schreiber, Avery	Chicago, Ill.	1935
Schwarzkopf, Elisabeth	Jarotschin, Poland	12/9/15
Scofield, Paul	Hurst, Pierpont, England.	1/21/22
Scorsese, Martin	New York, N.Y.	11/17/42
Scott, George C.	Wise, Va.	10/18/27
Scott, Hazel	Trinidad	1920
Scott, Lizabeth	Scranton, Pa.	1923
Scott, Martha	Jamesport, Mo.	9/22/14
Scott, Randolph	Orange Co., Va.	1/23/03
Scotto, Renata	Savona, Italy	2/24/34
Scourby, Alexander	New York, N.Y.	11/13/13
Sebastian, John	New York N.Y.	3/17/44
Sedaka, Neil	New York, N.Y.	3/13/39
Seeger, Pete	New York, N.Y.	5/3/19
Segal, George	Great Neck, N.Y.	2/13/34
Segal, Vivienne	Philadelphia, Pa.	4/19/97
Segovia, Andres	Linares, Spain.	2/21/93
Selleck, Tom	Detroit, Mich.	1/29/-
Serkin, Rudolf	Eger, Austria	3/28/03
Severinsen, Doc	Arlington, Ore.	7/7/27
Seymour, Jane	England	2/15/51
Shankar, Ravi	India	4/7/20
Sharif, Omar	Alexandria, Egypt.	4/10/32
Shatner, William	Montreal, Que.	3/22/31
Shaw, Robert	Red Bluff, Cal.	4/30/16
Shawn, Dick	Buffalo, N.Y.	12/1/29
Shearer, Moira	Scotland	1/17/26
Shearer, Norma	Montreal Que.	1904
Sheen, Martin	Dayton, Oh.	8/3/40
Sheldon, Jack	Jacksonville, Fla.	1931
Shepherd, Cybill	Memphis, Tenn.	2/18/50
Shepherd, Jean	Chicago, Ill.	7/26/29
Shera, Mark	Bayonne, N.J.	7/10/49
Sherwood, Roberta	St. Louis, Mo.	1913
Shields, Brooke	New York, N.Y.	5/31/65
Shire, Talia	New York, N.Y.	4/25/46
Shirley, Ann	New York, N.Y.	1918
Shore, Dinah	Winchester, Tenn.	3/1/17
Short, Bobby	Danville, Ill.	9/15/24
Sidney, Sylvia	New York, N.Y.	8/8/10
Siepi, Cesare	Milan, Italy.	2/10/23
Signoret, Simone	Wiesbaden, Germany	3/25/21
Sills, Beverly	Brooklyn, N.Y.	5/25/29

Name	Birthplace	Born	Name	Birthplace	Born
Silvers, Phil	Brooklyn, N.Y.	5/11/12	Summer, Donna	Boston, Mass.	12/31/48
Simmons, Jean	London, England	1/31/29	Susskind, David	New York, N.Y.	12/19/20
Simon, Carly	New York, N.Y.	6/25/45	Sutherland, Donald	St. John, New Brunswick	7/17/34
Simon, Paul	Newark, N.J.	11/5/42	Sutherland, Joan	Sydney, Australia	11/7/26
Simon, Simone	Marseilles, France	4/23/14	Suzuki, Pat	Cressey, Cal	1931
Simone, Nina	Tyron, N.C.	2/21/33	Swanson, Gloria	Chicago, Ill.	3/27/99
Sinatra, Frank	Hoboken, N.J.	12/12/15	Sweet, Blanche	Chicago, Ill.	6/18/95
Sinatra, Frank Jr.	Jersey City, N.J.	1944	Swit, Loretta	Passaic, N.J.	11/4/-
Sinatra, Nancy	Jersey City, N.J.	6/8/40			
Skelton, Red (Richard)	Vincennes, Ind.	7/18/13	Talbot, Lyle	Pittsburgh, Pa.	1902
Slezak, Walter	Vienna, Austria	5/3/02	Talbot, Nita	New York, N.Y.	1930
Slick, Grace	Chicago, Ill.	10/30/39	Tallchief, Maria	Fairfax, Okla.	1/24/25
Smith, Alexis	Penticton, B.C.	6/8/21	Tamblyn, Russ	Los Angeles, Cal.	12/30/35
Smith, Bob	Buffalo, N.Y.	1917	Tandy, Jessica	London, England	6/7/09
Smith, Connie	Elkhart, Ind.	1941	Tayback, Vic	New York, N.Y.	1/6/-
Smith, Ethel	Pittsburgh, Pa.	1921	Taylor, Elizabeth	London, England	2/27/32
Smith, Jaclyn	Houston, Tex.	10/26/48	Taylor, James	Boston, Mass.	3/12/48
Smith, Kate	Greenville, Va.	5/1/07	Taylor, Kent	Nashua, Ia.	5/11/07
Smith, Keeley	Norfolk, Va.	3/9/35	Taylor, Rod	Sydney, Australia	1/11/30
Smith, Maggie	Ilford, England	12/28/34	Tebaldi, Renata	Pesaro, Italy	2/1/22
Smith, Patti	Chicago, Ill.	1946	Temple, Shirley	Santa Monica, Cal.	4/23/28
Smith, Roger	South Gate, Cal.	12/18/32	Tennille, Toni	Montgomery, Ala.	5/8/43
Smothers, Dick	New York, N.Y.	11/20/39	Terris, Norma	Columbus, Kan.	1904
Smothers, Tom	New York, N.Y.	2/2/37	Terry-Thomas	London, England	7/14/11
Snodgrass, Carrie	Park Ridge, Ill.	10/27/45	Thaxter, Phyllis	Portland, Me.	11/20/21
Snow, Hank	Nova Scotia, Canada	5/9/14	Thebom, Blanche	Monessen, Pa.	9/19/19
Snyder, Tom	Milwaukee, Wis.	5/12/36	Thibault, Conrad	Northbridge, Mass.	11/13/08
Solti, Georg	Budapest, Hungary	10/21/12	Thinnes, Roy	Chicago, Ill.	4/6/38
Somes, Michael	nr. Stroud, England	1917	Thomas, B.J.	Houston, Tex.	8/7/42
Somers, Suzanne	San Bruno, Cal.	10/16/46	Thomas, Danny	Deerfield, Mich.	1/6/14
Sommer, Elke	Berlin, Germany	11/5/41	Thomas, Lowell	Woodrington, Oh.	4/6/92
Sorvino, Paul	Brooklyn, N.Y.	1939	Thomas, Marlo	Detroit, Mich.	11/21/43
Sothern, Ann	Valley City, N.D.	1/22/12	Thomas, Richard	New York, N.Y.	6/13/51
Soul, David	Chicago, Ill.	8/28/-	Thompson, Marshall	Peoria, Ill.	11/27/26
Spacek, Sissy	Quitman, Tex.	12/25/49	Thompson, Sada	Des Moines, Ia.	9/27/29
Spewack, Bella	Hungary	1899	Thulin, Ingrid	Sweden	1/27/29
Speilberg, Stephen	Cincinnati, Oh.	12/18/47	Tiegs, Cheryl	California	—
Spivak, Lawrence	Brooklyn, N.Y.	6/11/00	Tierney, Gene	Brooklyn, N.Y.	11/20/20
Springsteen, Bruce	Freehold, N.J.	9/23/49	Tierney, Lawrence	Brooklyn, N.Y.	3/15/19
Stack, Robert	Los Angeles, Cal.	1/13/19	Tillis, Mel	Tampa, Fla.	8/8/32
Stafford, Jo	Coalinga, Cal.	1918	Tillstrom, Burr	Chicago, Ill.	10/13/17
Stallone, Sylvester	New York, N.Y.	7/6/46	Tilton, Charlene	San Diego, Cal.	12/1/-
Stamp, Terence	London, England	1940	Tiny Tim	New York, N.Y.	—
Stang, Arnold	Chelsea, Mass.	1925	Todd, Richard	Dublin, Ireland	6/11/19
Stanley, Kim	Tularosa, N.M.	2/11/25	Tomlin, Lily	Detroit, Mich.	1939
Stanwyck, Barbara	Brooklyn, N.Y.	7/16/07	Tomlinson, David	Scotland	5/7/17
Stapleton, Jean	New York, N.Y.	1/19/23	Toomey, Regis	Pittsburgh, Pa.	8/13/02
Stapleton, Maureen	Troy, N.Y.	6/21/25	Torme, Mel	Chicago, Ill.	9/13/25
Starr, Kay	Dougherty, Okla.	7/21/22	Torn, Rip	Temple, Tex.	2/6/31
Starr, Ringo	Liverpool, England	7/7/40	Tracy, Arthur	Kamenetz, Podolsk, Russia	6/25/03
Steber, Eleanor	Wheeling, W. Va.	7/17/16			
Steele, Tommy	London, England	12/17/36	Travers, Mary	Louisville, Ky.	11/9/36
Steiger, Rod	W. Hampton, N.Y.	4/14/25	Travolta, John	Englewood, N.J.	2/18/54
Steinberg, David	Winnipeg, Man.	8/9/42	Trevor, Claire	New York, N.Y.	3/8/09
Stephens, James	Mt. Kisco, N.Y.	5/18/51	Truffaut, Francois	Paris, France	2/6/32
Sterling, Jan	New York, N.Y.	4/3/23	Tucker, Forrest	Plainfield, Ind.	2/12/19
Sterling, Robert	New Castle, Pa.	11/13/17	Tucker, Tanya	Seminole, Tex.	10/10/58
Stern, Isaac	Kreminiecz, Russia	7/21/20	Tucker, Tommy	Souris, N.D.	1907
Stevens, Cat	London, England	7/21/48	Tune, Tommy	Wichita Falls, Tex.	2/28/39
Stevens, Connie	Brooklyn, N.Y.	8/8/38	Turner, Ike	Clarksdale, Miss.	11/5/31
Stevens, Kaye	Pittsburgh, Pa.	1935	Turner, Lana	Wallace, Ida.	2/8/20
Stevens, Mark	Cleveland, Oh.	12/13/22	Turner, Tina	Brownsville, Tex.	11/25/41
Stevens, Rise	New York, N.Y.	6/11/13	Tushingham, Rita	Liverpool, England	3/14/42
Stevens, Stella	Yazoo City, Miss.	10/1/36	Twiggy (Leslie Hornby)	London, England	9/19/49
Stevens, Warren	Clark's Summit, Pa.	11/2/19	Twitty, Conway	Friar's Point, Miss.	9/1/33
Stevenson, McLean	Normal, Ill.	11/14/29	Tyrell, Susan	New Canaan, Conn.	1946
Stevenson, Parker	Philadelphia, Pa.	6/4/53	Tyson, Cicely	New York, N.Y.	12/19/33
Stewart, Don	New York, N.Y.	11/14/35			
Stewart, James	Indiana, Pa.	5/20/08	Uggams, Leslie	New York, N.Y.	5/25/43
Stewart, Rod	London, England	1/10/45	Ullmann, Liv	Tokyo, Japan	12/16/39
Stickney, Dorothy	Dickinson, N.D.	6/21/00	Umeki, Miyoshi	Hokkaido, Japan	1929
Stiers, David Ogden	Peoria, Ill.	10/31/42	Ustinov, Peter	London, England	4/16/21
Stills, Stephen	Dallas, Tex.	1/3/45			
Stockwell, Dean	Hollywood, Cal.	3/5/36	Vaccaro, Brenda	Brooklyn, N.Y.	11/18/39
Stone, Ezra	New Bedford, Mass.	12/2/17	Vale, Jerry	New York, N.Y.	1931
Storch, Larry	New York, N.Y.	1/8/25	Valente, Caterina	Paris, France	1/14/32
Storm, Gale	Bloomington, Tex.	4/5/22	Valentine, Karen	Santa Rosa, Cal.	1947
Storrs, Suzanne	Salt Lake City, Ut.	1934	Vallee, Rudy	Island Pond, Vt.	7/28/01
Straight, Beatrice	Old Westbury, N.Y.	8/2/18	Valli, Alida	Pola, Italy	5/31/21
Strasberg, Susan	New York, N.Y.	5/22/38	Valli, Frankie	Newark, N.J.	5/3/37
Stratas, Teresa	Toronto, Ont.	5/26/39	Van Cleef, Lee	Somerville, N.J.	1/9/25
Strauss, Peter	New York, N.Y.	1947	Van Devere, Trish	Tenafly, N.J.	1945
Streep, Meryl	Summit, N.J.	1949	Van Doren, Mamie	Rowena, S.D.	2/6/33
Streisand, Barbra	Brooklyn, N.Y.	4/24/42	Van Dyke, Dick	West Plains, Mo.	12/13/25
Stritch, Elaine	Detroit, Mich.	2/2/26	Van Dyke, Jerry	Danville, Ill.	1932
Strode, Woody	Los Angeles, Cal.	1914	Van Fleet, Jo	Oakland, Cal.	1922
Struthers, Sally	Portland, Ore.	7/28/48	Van Patten, Dick	New York, N.Y.	12/9/28
Sullivan, Barry	New York, N.Y.	8/29/12	Van Vooren, Monique	Brussels, Belgium	4/17/33
Sumac, Yma	Ichocan, Peru	9/10/27	Varnay, Astrid	Stockholm, Sweden	4/25/18
			Vaughan, Sarah	Newark, N.J.	3/27/24

Name	Birthplace	Born	Name	Birthplace	Born
Vaughn, Robert	New York, N.Y.	11/22/32	Wilcoxon, Henry	British West Indies	1905
Venuta, Benay	San Francisco, Cal.	1/27/11	Wilde, Cornel	New York, N.Y.	10/13/18
Vera-Ellen	Cincinnati, Oh.	2/16/26	Wilder, Billy	Vienna, Austria	6/22/06
Verdon, Gene	Los Angeles, Cal.	1/13/25	Wilder, Gene	Milwaukee, Wis.	6/11/35
Vereen, Ben	Miami, Fla.	10/10/46	Williams, Andy	Wall Lake, Ia.	12/3/30
Vernon, Jackie	New York, N.Y.	1929	Williams, Cindy	Van Nuys, Cal.	8/22/47
Vickers, Jon	Prince Albert, Sask.	10/26/26	Williams, Clarence	New York, N.Y.	8/21/39
Vidor, King Wallis	Galveston, Tex.	2/8/95	Williams, Emlyn	Mostyn, Wales	11/26/05
Vigoda, Abe	New York, N.Y.	2/24/21	Williams, Esther	Los Angeles, Cal.	8/8/23
Villella, Edward	Long Island, N.Y.	10/1/36	Williams Jr., Hank	Shreveport, La.	5/26/49
Vincent, Jan-Michael	Ventura, Cal.	7/15/44	Williams, Joe	Cordele, Ga.	1918
Vinson, Helen	Beaumont, Tex.	1907	Williams, Paul	Omaha, Neb.	9/19/40
Vinton, Bobby	Canonsburg, Pa.	4/16/35	Williams, Robin	Chicago, Ill.	7/21/52
Voight, Jon	Yonkers, N.Y.	12/29/38	Williams, Roger	Omaha, Neb.	1926
Von Furstenberg, Betsy	Neihern Heusen, Germany	8/16/31	Williamson, Nicol	Hamilton, Scotland	9/14/38
Von Sydow, Max	Lund, Sweden.	4/10/29	Wilson, Demond	Valdosta, Ga.	—
Von Zell, Harry	Indianapolis, Ind.	7/11/06	Wilson, Dolores	Philadelphia, Pa.	1929
Voorhees, Donald	Allentown, Pa.	7/26/03	Wilson, Don	Lincoln, Neb.	1900
			Wilson, Flip	Jersey City, N.J.	12/8/33
			Wilson, Nancy	Chillicothe, Oh.	2/20/07
Waggoner, Lyle	Kansas City, Kan.	4/13/35	Winchell, Paul	New York, N.Y.	12/21/22
Wagner, Lindsay	Los Angeles, Cal.	6/22/49	Windom, William	New York, N.Y.	9/28/23
Wagner, Robert	Detroit, Mich.	2/10/30	Winkler, Henry	New York, N.Y.	10/30/45
Wagoner, Porter	West Plains, Mo.	8/12/27	Winters, Jonathan	Dayton, Oh.	11/11/25
Wain, Bea	Bronx, N.Y.	1917	Winters, Shelley	St. Louis, Mo.	8/18/22
Waite, Ralph	White Plains, N.Y.	6/22/29	Winwood, Estelle	Lee, England	1884
Waldon, Robert	New York, N.Y.	9/25/43	Wiseman, Joseph	Montreal, Que.	5/15/18
Walker, Clint	Hartford, Ill.	5/30/27	Withers, Jane	Atlanta, Ga.	1927
Walker, Jimmy	New York, N.Y.		Wonder, Stevie	Saginaw, Mich.	5/13/50
Walker, Nancy	Philadelphia, Pa.	5/10/21	Wood, Natalie	San Francisco, Cal.	7/20/38
Wallach, Eli	Brooklyn, N.Y.	12/7/15	Woodward, Joanne	Thomasville, Ga.	2/27/30
Wallenstein, Alfred	Chicago, Ill.	10/7/98	Worley, Jo Anne	Lowell, Ind.	9/6/37
Wallis, Hal	Chicago, Ill.	9/14/99	Worth, Irene	Nebraska	6/23/16
Ward, Simon	London, England	10/19/41	Wray, Fay	Alberta, Canada	9/10/07
Warden, Jack	Newark, N.J.	9/18/20	Wright, Martha	Seattle, Wash.	1926
Warfield, William	W. Helena, Ark.	1/22/20	Wright, Teresa	New York, N.Y.	10/27/18
Warhol, Andy	Pittsburgh, Pa.	8/6/27	Wrightson, Earl	Baltimore, Md.	1916
Waring, Fred	Tyrone, Pa.	6/9/00	Wyatt, Jane	Campgaw, N.J.	8/12/12
Warwick, Dionne	E. Orange, N.J.	12/12/41	Wyler, William	Mulhouse, France	7/1/02
Waters, Muddy	Rolling Fork, Miss.	4/4/15	Wyman, Jane	St. Joseph, Mo.	1/4/14
Watson, Mills.	Oakland, Cal.	7/10/40	Wynette, Tammy	Red Bay, Ala.	5/5/42
Watts, Andre	Nuremberg, Germany	6/20/46	Wynn, Keenan	New York, N.Y.	7/27/16
Wayne, David	Traverse City, Mich.	1/30/14	Wynter, Dana	London, England	6/8/30
Wayne, Patrick	Los Angeles, Cal.	7/15/39			
Weaver, Dennis	Joplin, Mo.	6/4/25	Yarborough, Glenn	Milwaukee, Wis.	1930
Weaver, Fritz	Pittsburgh, Pa.	1/19/26	Yarrow, Peter	New York, N.Y.	5/31/38
Webb, Jack	Santa Monica, Cal.	4/2/20	York, Dick	Ft. Wayne, Ind.	9/4/28
Weissmuller, Johnny	Windber, Pa.	6/2/03	York, Michael	Fulmer, England	3/27/42
Welch, Raquel	Chicago, Ill.	9/5/42	York, Susannah	London, England	1/9/41
Weld, Tuesday	New York, N.Y.	8/27/43	Young, Alan	Northumberland, England	11/19/19
Welk, Lawrence	nr. Strasburg, N.D.	3/11/03	Young, Burt	New York, N.Y.	4/30/40
Welles, Orson	Kenosha, Wis.	5/6/15	Young, Loretta	Salt Lake City, Ut.	1/6/13
Wells, Kitty	Nashville, Tenn.	8/30/19	Young, Neil	Toronto, Ont.	11/12/45
Werner, Oskar	Vienna, Austria	11/13/22	Young, Robert	Chicago, Ill.	2/22/07
White, Barry	Galveston, Tex.	9/12/44	Youngman, Henny	Liverpool, England	1906
White, Betty	Oak Park, Ill.	1/17/-	Zappa, Frank	Baltimore, Md.	12/21/40
White, Jesse	Buffalo, N.Y.	1/3/19	Zeffirelli, Franco	Florence, Italy	2/12/23
Whiting, Margaret	Detroit, Mich.	7/22/24	Zimbalist, Efrem	Rostov, Russia	4/9/89
Whitman, Stuart	San Francisco, Cal.	2/1/26	Zimbalist, Efrem Jr.	New York, N.Y.	11/30/23
Whitmore, James	White Plains, N.Y.	10/1/21	Zimmer, Norma	Larsen, Ida	—
Widmark, Richard	Sunrise, Minn.	12/26/14	Zorina, Vera	Berlin, Germany	1/2/17
Wilcox, Larry	San Diego, Cal.	8/8/47	Zukerman, Pinchas	Tel Aviv, Israel	7/16/48

Entertainment Personalities of the Past

Born	Died	Name	Born	Died	Name	Born	Died	Name
1896	1974	Abbott, Bud	1885	1946	Atwill, Lionel	1890	1962	Barton, James
1872	1953	Adams, Maude	1845	1930	Auer, Leopold	1873	1951	Bauer, Harold
1931	1968	Adams, Nick	1905	1967	Auer, Mischa	1893	1951	Baxter, Warner
1855	1926	Adler, Jacob P.	1900	1972	Austin, Gene	1880	1928	Bayes, Nora
1898	1933	Adoree, Renee	1898	1940	Ayres, Agnes	1904	1965	Beatty, Clyde
1909	1964	Albertson, Frank				1904	1962	Beavers, Louise
1885	1952	Alda, Frances	1864	1922	Bacon, Frank	1884	1946	Beery, Noah
1894	1956	Allen, Fred	1903	1951	Bailey, Mildred	1889	1949	Beery, Wallace
1906	1964	Allen, Gracie	1891	1968	Bainter, Fay	1901	1970	Begley, Ed
1883	1950	Allgood, Sara	1895	1957	Baker, Belle	1854	1931	Belasco, David
1882	1971	Anderson, Gilbert (Bronco Billy)	1906	1975	Baker, Josephine	1906	1968	Benaderet, Bea
			1898	1963	Baker, Phil	1906	1964	Bendix, William
1886	1954	Anderson, John Murray	1882	1956	Bancroft, George	1904	1965	Bennett, Constance
1915	1967	Andrews, Laverne	1903	1968	Bankhead, Tallulah	1873	1944	Bennett, Richard
1933	1971	Angeli, Pier	1890	1952	Banks, Leslie	1894	1974	Benny, Jack
1876	1958	Anglin, Margaret	1890	1955	Bara, Theda	1924	1970	Benzell, Mimi
1887	1933	Arbuckle, Fatty (Roscoe)	1810	1891	Barnum, Phineas T.	1899	1966	Berg, Gertrude
1900	1976	Arlen, Richard	1912	1978	Barrie, Wendy	1903	1978	Bergen, Edgar
1868	1946	Arliss, George	1879	1959	Barrymore, Ethel	1895	1976	Berkeley, Busby
1900	1971	Armstrong, Louis	1882	1942	Barrymore, John	1863	1927	Bernard, Sam
1890	1956	Arnold, Edward	1878	1954	Barrymore, Lionel	1844	1923	Bernhardt, Sarah
1905	1974	Arquette, Cliff (Charlie Weaver)	1848	1905	Barrymore, Maurice	1893	1943	Bernie, Ben
			1897	1963	Barthelmess, Richard	1889	1967	Bickford, Charles

Born	Died	Name
1911	1960	Bjoerling, Jussi
1898	1973	Blackmer, Sidney
1882	1951	Blaney, Charles E.
1900	1943	Bledsoe, Jules
1928	1972	Blocker, Dan
1909	1979	Blondell, Joan
1888	1959	Blore, Eric
1901	1975	Blue, Ben
1899	1957	Bogart, Humphrey
1885	1965	Boland, Mary
1897	1969	Boles, John
1903	1960	Bond, Ward
1892	1981	Bondi, Beulah
1917	1981	Boone, Richard
1833	1893	Booth, Edwin
1796	1852	Booth, Junius Brutus
1894	1953	Bordoni, Irene
1888	1960	Bori, Lucrezia
1867	1943	Bosworth, Hobart
1905	1965	Bow, Clara
1874	1946	Bowes, Maj. Edward
1928	1977	Boyd, Stephen
1895	1972	Boyd, William
1899	1978	Boyer, Charles
1893	1939	Brady, Alice
1871	1936	Breese, Edmund
1898	1964	Brendel, El
1901	1948	Breneman, Tom
1894	1974	Brennan, Walter
1904	1979	Brent, George
1875	1948	Brian, Donald
1891	1951	Brice, Fanny
1891	1959	Broderick, Helen
1904	1951	Bromberg, J. Edward
1892	1973	Brown, Joe E.
1926	1966	Bruce, Lenny
1895	1953	Bruce, Nigel
1903	1979	Buchanan, Edgar
1891	1957	Buchanan, Jack
1885	1957	Buck, Gene
1885	1970	Burke, Billie
1912	1967	Burnette, Smiley
1896	1956	Burns, Bob
1902	1971	Burns, David
1882	1941	Burr, Henry
1883	1966	Bushman, Francis X.
1896	1946	Butterworth, Charles
1893	1971	Byington, Spring
1905	1972	Cabot, Bruce
1918	1977	Cabot, Sebastian
1895	1956	Calhern, Louis
1923	1977	Callas, Maria
1853	1942	Calve, Emma
1933	1976	Cambridge, Godfrey
1865	1940	Campbell, Mrs. Patrick
1892	1964	Cantor, Eddie
1878	1947	Carey, Harry
1876	1941	Carle, Richard
1880	1961	Carrillo, Leo
1892	1972	Carroll, Leo G.
1905	1965	Carroll, Nancy
1910	1963	Carson, Jack
1862	1937	Carter, Mrs. Leslie
1873	1921	Caruso, Enrico
1876	1973	Casals, Pablo
1927	1976	Cassidy, Jack
1893	1969	Castle, Irene
1887	1918	Castle, Vernon
1889	1960	Catlett, Walter
1874	1944	Cavalieri, Lina
1887	1950	Cavanaugh, Hobart
1873	1938	Chaliapin, Feodor
1921	1980	Champion, Gower
1919	1961	Chandler, Jeff
1883	1930	Chaney, Lon
1906	1973	Chaney Jr., Lon
1889	1977	Chaplin, Charles
1893	1940	Chase, Charlie
1893	1961	Chatterton, Ruth
1888	1971	Chevalier, Maurice
1888	1960	Clark, Bobby
1914	1968	Clark, Fred
1887	1950	Clayton, Lou
1920	1966	Clift, Montgomery
1932	1963	Cline, Patsy
1900	1937	Clive, Colin
1892	1967	Clyde, Andy
1911	1976	Cobb, Lee J.
1877	1961	Coburn, Charles
1887	1934	Cody, Lew
1878	1942	Cohan, George M.
1876	1916	Cohan, Josephine
1919	1965	Cole, Nat (King)
1878	1955	Collier, Constance
1890	1965	Collins, Ray
1891	1958	Colman, Ronald
1908	1934	Columbo, Russ
1907	1944	Compton, Betty
1887	1940	Connolly, Walter
1855	1909	Conried, Henrich
1918	1975	Conte, Richard
1904	1967	Conway, Tom
1901	1961	Cook, Donald
1890	1959	Cook, Joe
1893	1958	Cook, Phil
1901	1961	Cooper, Gary
1891	1971	Cooper, Gladys
1896	1973	Cooper, Melville
1914	1968	Corey, Wendell
1893	1974	Cornell, Katharine
1890	1972	Correll, Charles (Andy)
1876	1951	Cossart, Ernest
1905	1979	Costello, Dolores
1904	1957	Costello, Helene
1906	1959	Costello, Lou
1877	1950	Costello, Maurice
1899	1973	Coward, Noel
1890	1950	Cowl, Jane
1924	1973	Cox, Wally
1847	1924	Crabtree, Lotta
1875	1945	Craven, Frank
1903	1977	Crawford, Joan
1916	1944	Cregar, Laird
1880	1942	Crews, Laura Hope
1880	1974	Crisp, Donald
1942	1973	Croce, Jim
1910	1960	Cromwell, Richard
1903	1977	Crosby, Bing
1897	1975	Cross, Milton
1893	1966	Crouse, Russell
1878	1968	Currie, Finlay
1816	1876	Cushman, Charlotte
1917	1970	Dailey, Dan
1923	1965	Dandridge, Dorothy
1869	1941	Danforth, William
1894	1963	Daniell, Henry
1901	1971	Daniels, Bebe
1860	1935	Daniels, Frank
1936	1973	Darin, Bobby
1921	1965	Darnell, Linda
1879	1967	Darwell, Jane
1866	1949	Davenport, Harry
1900	1961	Davies, Marion
1908	1961	Davis, Joan
1931	1955	Dean, James
1881	1950	DeCordoba, Pedro
1905	1968	Dekker, Albert
1898	1965	Demarco, Tony
1881	1959	DeMille, Cecil B.
1891	1967	Denny, Reginald
1901	1974	DeSica, Vittorio
1878	1949	Desmond, William
1905	1977	Devine, Andy
1942	1972	De Wilde, Brandon
1907	1974	De Wolfe, Billy
1865	1950	De Wolfe, Elsie
1879	1947	Digges, Dudley
1890	1944	Dinehart, Alan
1901	1966	Disney, Walt
1895	1949	Dix, Richard
1856	1924	Dockstader, Lew
1892	1958	Dolly, Jennie
1892	1970	Dolly, Rosie
1905	1958	Donat, Robert
1903	1972	Donlevy, Brian
1907	1939	Douglas, Paul
—	1980	Dragonette, Jessica
1889	1956	Draper, Ruth
1881	1965	Dresser, Louise
1869	1934	Dressler, Marie
1820	1897	Drew, Mrs. John
1853	1927	Drew, John (son)
1909	1951	Duchin, Eddy
1890	1965	Dumont, Margaret
1878	1927	Duncan, Isadora
1905	1967	Dunn, James
1893	1980	Durante, Jimmy
1907	1968	Duryea, Dan
1858	1924	Duse, Eleanora
1894	1929	Eagels, Jeanne
1896	1930	Eames, Clare
1865	1952	Eames, Emma
1901	1967	Eddy, Nelson
1897	1971	Edwards, Cliff
1879	1945	Edwards, Gus
1899	1974	Ellington, Duke
1941	1974	Elliot, Cass
1871	1940	Elliott, Maxine
1891	1967	Elman, Mischa
1881	1951	Errol, Leon
1903	1967	Erwin, Stuart
1888	1976	Evans, Edith
1913	1967	Evelyn, Judith
1883	1939	Fairbanks, Douglas
1915	1970	Farmer, Frances
1870	1929	Farnum, Dustin
1876	1953	Farnum, William
1882	1967	Farrar, Geraldine
1904	1971	Farrell, Glenda
1868	1940	Faversham, William
1861	1939	Fawcett, George
1897	1960	Fay, Frank
1895	1962	Fazenda, Louise
1894	1979	Fiedler, Arthur
1918	1973	Field, Betty
1898	1979	Fields, Gracie
1867	1941	Fields, Lew
1880	1946	Fields, W.C.
1931	1978	Fields, Totie
1916	1977	Finch, Peter
1865	1932	Fiske, Minnie Maddern
1888	1961	Fitzgerald, Barry
1895	1962	Flagstad, Kirsten
1900	1971	Flippen, Jay C.
1909	1959	Flynn, Errol
1925	1974	Flynn, Joe
1880	1942	Fokine, Michel
1910	1968	Foley, Red
1905	1951	Forbes, Ralph
1853	1937	Forbes-Robertson, J.
1887	1970	Ford, Ed (Senator)
1895	1973	Ford, John
1901	1976	Ford, Paul
1899	1966	Ford, Wallace
1806	1872	Forrest, Edwin
1904	1970	Foster, Preston
1857	1928	Foy, Eddie
1905	1968	Francis, Kay
1893	1966	Frawley, William
1885	1938	Frederick, Pauline
1870	1955	Friganza, Trixie
1890	1958	Frisco, Joe
1860	1915	Frohman, Charles
1851	1940	Frohman, Daniel
1885	1947	Fyffe, Will
1901	1960	Gable, Clark
1889	1963	Galli-Curci, Amelita
1877	1967	Garden, Mary
1913	1952	Garfield, John
1922	1969	Garland, Judy
1893	1963	Gaxton, William
1902	1978	Geer, Will
1904	1953	George, Gladys
1879	1961	George, Grace
1892	1962	Gibson, Hoot
1890	1957	Gigli, Beniamino
1894	1971	Gilbert, Billy
1897	1936	Gilbert, John
1855	1937	Gillette, William
1867	1943	Gillmore, Frank
1879	1939	Gilpin, Charles
1898	1968	Gish, Dorothy
1886	1959	Gleason, James
1884	1938	Gluck, Alma
1874	1955	Golden, John
1884	1974	Goldwyn, Samuel
1917	1969	Gorcey, Leo
1884	1940	Gordon, C. Henry
1887	1948	Gordon, Vera
1869	1944	Gottschalk, Ferdinand
1829	1869	Gottschalk, Louis
1916	1973	Grable, Betty
1901	1959	Gray, Gilda
1879	1954	Greenstreet, Sydney
1875	1948	Griffith, David Wark

Born	Died	Name	Born	Died	Name	Born	Died	Name
1888	1956	Morgan, Ralph	1941	1967	Redding, Otis	1900	1941	Stephenson, James
1901	1970	Morris, Chester	1914	1959	Reeves, George	1883	1939	Sterling, Ford
1849	1925	Morris, Clara	1860	1916	Rehan, Ada	1882	1928	Stevens, Emily A.
1914	1959	Morris, Wayne	1893	1923	Reid, Wallace	1934	1970	Stevens, Inger
1943	1971	Morrison, Jim	1873	1943	Reinhardt, Max	1896	1961	Stewart, Anita
1915	1977	Mostel, Zero	1909	1971	Rennie, Michael	1882	1977	Stokowski, Leopold
1897	1969	Mowbray, Alan	1870	1940	Richman, Charles	1873	1959	Stone, Fred
1895	1967	Muni, Paul	1895	1972	Richman, Harry	1879	1953	Stone, Lewis
1894	1953	Munn, Frank	1872	1961	Ring, Blanche	1904	1980	Stone, Milburn
1906	1955	Munson, Ona	1888	1958	Risdon, Elizabeth	1898	1959	Sturges, Preston
1924	1971	Murphy, Audie	1897	1977	Ritchard, Cyril	1911	1960	Sullavan, Margaret
1885	1965	Murray, Mae	1907	1974	Ritter, Tex	1902	1974	Sullivan, Ed
1896	1970	Nagel, Conrad	1905	1969	Ritter, Thelma	1903	1956	Sullivan, Francis L.
1900	1973	Naish, J. Carroll	1903	1966	Ritz, Al	1892	1946	Summerville, Slim
1898	1961	Naldi, Nita	1898	1976	Robeson, Paul	1904	1969	Swarthout, Gladys
1888	1950	Nash, Florence	1878	1949	Robinson, Bill	1893	1957	Talmadge, Norma
1865	1945	Nash, George	1893	1973	Robinson, Edward G.	1900	1972	Tamiroff, Akim
1879	1945	Nazimova, Alla	1865	1942	Robson, May	1878	1947	Tanguay, Eva
1846	1905	Neilson, Ada	1905	1977	Rochester (E. Anderson)	1899	1934	Tashman, Lilyan
1848	1880	Neilson, Adelaide	1897	1933	Rodgers, Jimmy	1885	1966	Taylor, Deems
1868	1957	Neilson-Terry, Julia	1894	1958	Rodzinsky, Artur	1899	1958	Taylor, Estelle
1907	1975	Nelson, Ozzie	1879	1935	Rogers, Will	1887	1946	Taylor, Laurette
1885	1967	Nesbit, Evelyn	1897	1937	Roland, Ruth	1911	1969	Taylor, Robert
1870	1951	Nethersole, Olga	1880	1962	Rooney, Pat	1878	1938	Tearle, Conway
1905	1956	Newton, Robert	1899	1966	Rose, Billy	1884	1953	Tearle, Godfrey
1874	1948	Niblo, Fred	1910	1980	Roth, Lillian	1892	1937	Tell, Alma
1890	1950	Nijinsky, Vaslav	1882	1936	Rothafel, S. L. (Roxy)	1881	1934	Tellegen, Lou
1893	1974	Nilsson, Anna Q.	1878	1953	Ruffo, Titta	1864	1942	Tempest, Marie
1898	1930	Normand, Mabel	1892	1970	Ruggles, Charles	1910	1963	Templeton, Alec
1879	1959	Norworth, Jack	1864	1936	Russell, Annie	1847	1928	Terry, Ellen
1905	1968	Novarro, Ramon	1924	1961	Russell, Gail	1871	1940	Tetrazzini, Luisa
1893	1951	Novello, Ivor	1861	1922	Russell, Lillian	1899	1973	Thalberg, Irving
1903	1978	Oakie, Jack	1911	1976	Russell, Rosalind	1857	1914	Thomas, Brandon
1860	1926	Oakley, Annie	1892	1972	Rutherford, Margaret	1892	1960	Thomas, John Charles
1911	1979	Oberon, Merle	1902	1973	Ryan, Irene	1882	1976	Thorndike, Sybil
1898	1943	O'Connell, Hugh	1909	1973	Ryan, Robert			(Three Stooges)
1883	1959	O'Connor, Una				1902	1975	Fine, Larry
1878	1945	O'Hara, Fiske	1924	1963	Sabu (Dastagir)	1906	1952	Howard, Curly
1908	1968	O'Keefe, Dennis	1877	1968	St. Denis, Ruth	1897	1975	Howard, Moe
1880	1938	Oland, Warner	1884	1955	Sakall, S.Z.	1869	1936	Thurston, Howard
1860	1932	Olcott, Chauncey	1885	1936	Sale (Chic), Charles	1896	1960	Tibbett, Lawrence
1883	1942	Oliver, Edna May	1906	1972	Sanders, George	1887	1940	Tinney, Frank
1892	1963	Olsen, Ole	1934	1973	Sands, Diana	1909	1958	Todd, Michael
1849	1920	O'Neill, James	1896	1960	Savo, Jimmy	1906	1935	Todd, Thelma
1876	1949	Ouspenskaya, Maria	1879	1954	Scheff, Fritzi	1874	1947	Toler, Sidney
1887	1972	Owen, Reginald	1892	1930	Schenck, Joe	1906	1968	Tone, Franchot
1860	1941	Paderewski, Ignace	1895	1964	Schildkraut, Joseph	1878	1933	Torrence, Ernest
1889	1954	Pallette, Eugene	1865	1930	Schildkraut, Rudolph	1867	1957	Toscanini, Arturo
1894	1958	Pangborn, Franklin	1889	1965	Schipa, Tito	1898	1968	Tracy, Lee
1914	1975	Parks, Larry	1882	1951	Schnabel, Artur	1900	1967	Tracy, Spencer
1881	1972	Parsons, Louella	1910	1949	Schumann, Henrietta	1903	1972	Traubel, Helen
1881	1940	Pasternack, Josef A.	1861	1936	Schumann-Heink, E.	1894	1975	Treacher, Arthur
1837	1908	Pastor, Tony	1866	1945	Scott, Cyril	1853	1917	Tree, Herbert Beerbohm
1843	1919	Patti, Adelina	1914	1965	Scott, Zachary	1889	1973	Truex, Ernest
1840	1889	Patti, Carlotta	1843	1896	Scott-Siddons, Mrs.	1915	1975	Tucker, Richard
1885	1931	Pavlova, Anna	1938	1979	Seberg, Jean	1884	1966	Tucker, Sophie
1900	1973	Paxinou, Katina	1892	1974	Seeley, Blossom	1911	1970	Tufts, Sonny
1917	1966	Pearce, Alice	1902	1965	Selznick, David O.	1869	1940	Turpin, Ben
1885	1950	Pemberton, Brock	1858	1935	Sembrich, Marcella	1908	1958	Twelvetrees, Helen
1899	1967	Pendleton, Nat	1880	1960	Sennett, Mack	1894	1970	Ulric, Lenore
1905	1941	Penner, Joe	1881	1951	Shattuck, Arthur	1933	1975	Ure, Mary
1892	1937	Perkins, Osgood	1860	1929	Shaw, Mary	1895	1926	Valentino, Rudolph
1893	1956	Peters, Brandon	1927	1978	Shaw, Robert	1870	1950	Van, Billy B.
1915	1963	Piaf, Edith	1891	1972	Shawn, Ted	1912	1979	Vance, Vivian
1893	1979	Pickford, Mary	1868	1949	Shean, Al	1893	1943	Veidt, Conrad
1892	1957	Pinza, Ezio	1915	1967	Sheridan, Ann	1885	1957	Von Stroheim, Erich
1900	1963	Pitts, Zasu	1924	1973	Sherman, Allan	1887	1969	Walburn, Raymond
1904	1976	Pons, Lili	1885	1934	Sherman, Lowell	1874	1946	Waldron, Charles D.
1903	1969	Portman, Eric	1918	1970	Shriner, Herb	1904	1966	Walker, June
1904	1963	Powell, Dick	1875	1953	Shubert, Lee	1914	1951	Walker, Robert
1869	1931	Power, F. Tyrone	1755	1831	Siddons, Mrs. Sarah	1887	1980	Walsh, Raoul
1913	1958	Power, Tyrone	1882	1930	Sills, Milton	1876	1962	Walter, Bruno
1872	1935	Powers, Eugene	1914	1970	Silvera, Frank	1878	1936	Walthall, Henry B.
1935	1977	Presley, Elvis	1900	1976	Sim, Alastair	1872	1952	Ward, Fannie
1900	1964	Price, George E.	1878	1946	Sis Hopkins (Melville)	1866	1951	Warfield, David
1856	1919	Primrose, George	1891	1934	Skelly, Hal	1876	1958	Warner, H. B.
1954	1977	Prinze, Freddie	1858	1942	Skinner, Otis	1878	1964	Warwick, Robert
1879	1956	Prouty, Jed	1870	1952	Skipworth, Alison	1924	1963	Washington, Dinah
1871	1942	Pryor, Arthur	1892	1970	Skulnik, Menasha	1900	1977	Waters, Ethel
1895	1980	Raft, George	1863	1948	Smith, C. Aubrey	1867	1945	Watson, Billy
1905	1946	Ragland, John (Rags)	1917	1979	Soo, Jack	1879	1962	Watson, Lucille
1890	1967	Rains, Claude	1826	1881	Sothern, Edward A.	1890	1965	Watson, Minor
1889	1970	Rambeau, Marjorie	1859	1933	Sothern, Edward H.	1907	1979	Wayne, John
1900	1947	Rankin, Arthur	1884	1957	Sothern, Harry	1896	1966	Webb, Clifton
1892	1967	Rathbone, Basil	1854	1932	Sousa, John Philip	1867	1942	Weber, Joe
1897	1960	Ratoff, Gregory	1884	1957	Sparks, Ned	1905	1973	Webster, Margaret
1881	1953	Rawlinson, Herbert	1876	1948	Speaks, Oley	1896	1975	Wellman, William
1891	1943	Ray, Charles	1890	1970	Spitalny, Phil	1883	1953	Werrenrath, Reinald
			1873	1937	Standing, Guy			

Born	Died	Name
1892	1980	West, Mae
1879	1942	Westley, Helen
1895	1968	Wheeler, Bert
1889	1938	White, Pearl
1891	1967	Whiteman, Paul
1865	1948	Whitty, Dame May
1906	1966	Whorf, Richard
1912	1979	Wilding, Michael
1895	1948	William, Warren
1877	1922	Williams, Bert

Born	Died	Name
1867	1918	Williams, Evan
1923	1953	Williams, Hank
1902	1978	Wills, Chill
1917	1972	Wilson, Marie
1884	1969	Winninger, Charles
1904	1959	Withers, Grant
1881	1931	Wolheim, Louis
1907	1961	Wong, Anna May
1892	1978	Wood, Peggy
1888	1963	Woolley, Monty

Born	Died	Name
1889	1938	Woolsey, Robert
1881	1956	Wycherly, Margaret
1886	1966	Wynn, Ed
1906	1964	Wynyard, Diana
1890	1960	Young, Clara Kimball
1917	1978	Young, Gig
1887	1953	Young, Roland
1902	1979	Zanuck, Darryl F.
1869	1932	Ziegfeld, Florenz
1873	1976	Zukor, Adolph

Ancient Greeks and Latins

Greeks

Aeschines, orator, 389-314BC.
Aeschylus, dramatist, 525-456BC.
Aesop, fableist, c620-c560BC.
Anacreon, poet, c582-c485BC.
Anaxagoras, philosopher, c500-428BC.
Archimedes, math. c287-212BC.
Aristophanes, dramatist, c448-380BC.
Aristotle, philosopher, 384-322BC.
Athenaeus, scholar, fl.c200.
Callicrates, architect, fl.5th cent.BC.
Callimachus, poet, c305-240BC.
Democritus, philosopher, c460-370BC.
Demosthenes, orator, 384-322BC.
Diodorus, historian, fl.20BC.
Diogenes, philosopher, c372-c287BC.

Dionysius, historian, d.c7BC.
Empedocles, philosopher, c490-430BC.
Epictetus, philosopher, c55-c135.
Epicurus, philosopher, 341-270BC.
Euclid, mathematician, fl.c300BC.
Euripides, dramatist, c484-406BC.
Heraclitus, philosopher, c535-c475BC.
Herodotus, historian, c484-420BC.
Hesiod, poet, 8th cent. BC.
Hippocrates, physician, c460-377BC.
Homer, poet, believed lived c850BC.
Menander, dramatist, 342-292BC.
Pindar, poet, c518-c438BC.
Plato, philosopher, c428-c347BC.
Plutarch, biographer, c46-120.

Polybius, historian, c200-c118BC.
Pythagoras, phil., math., c580-c500BC.
Sappho, poet, c610-c580BC.
Simonides, poet, 556-c468BC.
Socrates, philosopher, c470-399BC.
Sophocles, dramatist, C496-406BC.
Strabo, geographer, c63BC-AD24.
Thales, philosopher, c634-c546BC.
Themistocles, politician, c524-c460BC.
Theocritus, poet, c310-250BC.
Theophrastus, phil. c372-c287BC.
Thucydides, historian, fl.5th cent.BC.
Timon, philosopher, c320-c230BC.
Xenophon, historian, c434-c355BC.
Zeno, philospher, c495-c430BC.

Latins

Ammianus, historian, c330-395.
Apuleius, satirist, c124-c170.
Boethius, scholar, c480-524
Caesar, Julius, general, 100-44BC.
Cato (Elder), statesman, 234-149BC.
Catullus, poet, c84-54BC.
Cicero, orator, 106-43BC.
Claudian, poet, c370-c404.
Gellius, author, c130-c165.
Horace, poet, 65-8BC.
Juvenal, satirist, c60-c127.

Livy, historian, 59BC-AD17.
Lucan, poet, 39-65.
Lucilius, poet, c180-c102BC.
Lucretius, poet, c99-c55BC.
Martial, epigrammatist, c38-c103.
Nepos, historian, c100-c25BC.
Ovid, poet, 43BC-AD17.
Persius, satirist, 34-62.
Plautus, dramatist, c254-c184BC.
Pliny, scholar, 23-79.
Pliny (Younger), author, 62-113.

Quintilian, rhetorician, c35-c97.
Sallust, historian, 86-34BC.
Seneca, philosopher, 4BC-AD65.
Silius, poet, c25-101.
Statius, poet, c45-c96.
Suetonius, biographer, c69-c122.
Tacitus, historian, c56-c120.
Terence, dramatist, 185-c159BC.
Tibullus, poet, c55-c19BC.
Virgil, poet, 70-19BC.
Vitruvius, architect, fl.1st cent.BC.

Rulers of England and Great Britain

Name	England	Began	Died	Age	Rgd
Saxons and Danes					
Egbert	King of Wessex, won allegiance of all English	829	839	—	10
Ethelwulf	Son, King of Wessex, Sussex, Kent, Essex	839	858	—	19
Ethelbald	Son of Ethelwulf, displaced father in Wessex	858	860	—	2
Ethelbert	2d son of Ethelwulf, united Kent and Wessex	860	866	—	6
Ethelred I	3d son, King of Wessex, fought Danes	866	871	—	5
Alfred	The Great, 4th son, defeated Danes, fortified London	871	899	52	28
Edward	The Elder, Alfred's son, united English, claimed Scotland	899	924	55	25
Athelstan	The Glorious, Edward's son, King of Mercia, Wessex	924	940	45	16
Edmund I	3d son of Edward, King of Wessex, Mercia	940	946	25	6
Edred	4th son of Edward	946	955	32	9
Edwy	The Fair, eldest son of Edmund, King of Wessex	955	959	18	3
Edgar	The Peaceful, 2d son of Edmund, ruled all English	959	975	32	17
Edward	The Martyr, eldest son of Edgar, murdered by stepmother	975	978	17	4
Ethelred II	The Unready, 2d son of Edgar, married Emma of Normandy	978	1016	48	37
Edmund II	Ironside, son of Ethelred II, King of London	1016	1016	27	0
Canute	The Dane, gave Wessex to Edmund, married Emma	1016	1035	40	19
Harold I	Harefoot, natural son of Canute	1035	1040	—	5
Hardecanute	Son of Canute by Emma, Danish King	1040	1042	24	2
Edward	The Confessor, son of Ethelred II (Canonized 1161)	1042	1066	62	24
Harold II	Edward's brother-in-law, last Saxon King	1066	1066	44	0
House of Normandy					
William I	The Conqueror, defeated Harold at Hastings	1066	1087	60	21
William II	Rufus, 3d son of William I, killed by arrow	1087	1100	43	13
Henry I	Beauclerc, youngest son of William I	1100	1135	67	35
House of Blois					
Stephen	Son of Adela, daughter of William I, and Count of Blois	1135	1154	50	19
House of Plantagenet					
Henry II	Son of Geoffrey Plantagenet (Angevin) by Matilda, dau. of Henry I	1154	1189	56	35
Richard I	Coeur do Lion, son of Henry II, crusader	1189	1199	42	10
John	Lackland, son of Henry II, signed Magna Carta, 1215	1199	1216	50	17
Henry III	Son of John, acceded at 9, under regency until 1227	1216	1272	65	56
Edward I	Longshanks, son of Henry III	1272	1307	68	35
Edward II	Son of Edward I, deposed by Parliament, 1327	1307	1327	43	20
Edward III	Of Windsor, son of Edward II	1327	1377	65	50
Richard II	Grandson of Edw. III, minor until 1389, deposed 1399	1377	1400	34	22
House of Lancaster					
Henry IV	Son of John of Gaunt, Duke of Lancaster, son of Edw. III	1399	1413	47	13
Henry V	Son of Henry IV, victor of Agincourt	1413	1422	34	9
Henry VI	Son of Henry V, deposed 1461, died in Tower	1422	1471	49	39

House of York

Edward IV	Great-great-grandson of Edward III, son of Duke of York	1461	1483	41	22
Edward V	Son of Edward IV, murdered in Tower of London	1483	1483	13	0
Richard III	Crookback, bro. of Edward IV, fell at Bosworth Field	1483	1485	35	2

House of Tudor

Henry VII	Son of Edmund Tudor, Earl of Richmond, whose father had married the widow of Henry V; descended from Edward III through his mother, Margaret Beaufort via John of Gaunt. By marriage with dau. of Edward IV he united Lancaster and York	1485	1509	53	24
Henry VIII	Son of Henry VII by Elizabeth, dau. of Edward IV.	1509	1547	56	38
Edward VI	Son of Henry VIII, by Jane Seymour, his 3d queen. Ruled under regents. Was forced to name Lady Jane Grey his successor. Council of State proclaimed her queen July 10, 1553. Mary Tudor won Council, was proclaimed queen July 19, 1553. Mary had Lady Jane Grey beheaded for treason, Feb., 1554	1547	1553	16	6
Mary I	Daughter of Henry VIII, by Catherine of Aragon	1553	1558	43	5
Elizabeth I	Daughter of Henry VIII, by Anne Boleyn	1558	1603	69	44

Great Britain
House of Stuart

James I	James VI of Scotland, son of Mary, Queen of Scots. *First to call himself King of Great Britain. This became official with the Act of Union, 1707*	1603	1625	59	22
Charles I	Only surviving son of James I; beheaded Jan. 30, 1649	1625	1649	48	24

Commonwealth, 1649-1660
Council of State, 1649; Protectorate, 1653

The Cromwells	Oliver Cromwell, Lord Protector	1653	1658	59	—
	Richard Cromwell, son, Lord Protector, resigned May 25, 1659	1658	1712	86	—

House of Stuart (Restored)

Charles II	Eldest son of Charles I, died without issue	1660	1685	55	25
James II	2d son of Charles I. Deposed 1688. Interregnum Dec. 11, 1688, to Feb. 13, 1689	1685	1701	68	3
William III	Son of William, Prince of Orange, by Mary, dau. of Charles I	1689	1702	51	13
and Mary II	Eldest daughter of James II and wife of William III		1694	33	6
Anne	2d daughter of James II	1702	1714	49	12

House of Hanover

George I	Son of Elector of Hanover, by Sophia, grand-dau. of James I	1714	1727	67	13
George II	Only son of George I, married Caroline of Brandenburg	1727	1760	77	33
George III	Grandson of George II, married Charlotte of Mecklenburg	1760	1820	81	59
George IV	Eldest son of George III, Prince Regent, from Feb., 1811	1820	1830	67	10
William IV	3d son of George III, married Adelaide of Saxe-Meiningen	1830	1837	71	7
Victoria	Dau. of Edward, 4th son of George III; married (1840) Prince Albert of Saxe-Coburg and Gotha, who became Prince Consort	1837	1901	81	63

House of Saxe-Coburg and Gotha

Edward VII	Eldest son of Victoria, married Alexandra, Princess of Denmark	1901	1910	68	9

House of Windsor
Name Adopted July 17, 1917

George V	2d son of Edward VII, married Princess Mary of Teck	1910	1936	70	25
Edward VIII	Eldest son of George V; acceded Jan. 20, 1936, abdicated Dec. 11	1936	1972	77	1
George VI	2d son of George V; married Lady Elizabeth Bowes-Lyon	1936	1952	56	15
Elizabeth II	Elder daughter of George VI, acceded Feb. 6, 1952	1952	—	—	—

Rulers of Scotland

Kenneth I MacAlpin was the first Scot to rule both Scots and Picts, 846 AD.

Duncan I was the first general ruler, 1034. Macbeth seized the kingdom 1040, was slain by Duncan's son, Malcolm III MacDuncan (Canmore), 1057.

Malcolm married Margaret, Saxon princess who had fled from the Normans. Queen Margaret introduced English language and English monastic customs. She was canonized, 1250. Her son Edgar, 1097, moved the court to Edinburgh. His brothers Alexander I and David I succeeded. Malcolm IV, the Maiden, 1153, grandson of David I, was followed by his brother, William the Lion, 1165, whose son was Alexander II, 1214. The latter's son, Alexander III, 1249, defeated the Norse and regained the Hebrides. When he died, 1286, his granddaughter, Margaret, child of Eric of Norway and grandniece of Edward I of England, known as the Maid of Norway, was chosen ruler, but died 1290, aged 8.

John Baliol, 1292-1296. (Interregnum, 10 years).

Robert Bruce (The Bruce), 1306-1329, victor at Bannockburn, 1314.

David II, only son of Robert Bruce, ruled 1329-1371.

Robert II, 1371-1390, grandson of Robert Bruce, son of Walter, the Steward of Scotland, was called The Steward, first of the so-called Stuart line.

Robert III, son of Robert II, 1390-1406.

James I, son of Robert III, 1406-1437.

James II, son of James I, 1437-1460.

James III, eldest son of James II, 1460-1488.

James IV, eldest son of James III, 1488-1513.

James V, eldest son of James IV, 1513-1542.

Mary, daughter of James V, born 1542, became queen when one week old; was crowned 1543. Married, 1558, Francis, son of Henry II of France, who became king 1559, died 1560. Mary ruled Scots 1561 until abdication, 1567. She also married (2) Henry Stewart, Lord Darnley, and (3) James, Earl of Bothwell. Imprisoned by Elizabeth I, Mary was beheaded 1587.

James VI, 1567-1625, son of Mary and Lord Darnley, became King of England on death of Elizabeth in 1603. Although the thrones were thus united, the legislative union of Scotland and England was not effected until the Act of Union, May 1, 1707.

Rulers of France: Kings, Queens, Presidents

Caesar to Charlemagne

Julius Caesar subdued the Gauls, native tribes of Gaul (France) 57 to 52 BC. The Romans ruled 500 years. The Franks, a Teutonic tribe, reached the Somme from the East ca. 250 AD. By the 5th century the Merovingian Franks ousted the Romans. In 451 AD, with the help of Visigoths, Burgundians and others,

they defeated Attila and the Huns at Chalons-sur-Marne.

Childeric I became leader of the Merovingians 458 AD. His son Clovis I (Chlodwig, Ludwig, Louis), crowned 481, founded the dynasty. After defeating the Alemanni (Germans) 496, he was baptized a Christian and made Paris his capital. His line ruled until Childeric III was deposed, 751.

The West Merovingians were called Neustrians, the eastern

Austrasians. Pepin of Herstal (687-714) major domus, or head of the palace, of Austrasia, took over Neustria as dux (leader) of the Franks. Pepin's son, Charles, called Martel (the Hammer) defeated the Saracens at Tours-Poitiers, 732; was succeeded by his son, Pepin the Short, 741, who deposed Childeric III and ruled as king until 768.

His son, Charlemagne, or Charles the Great (742-814) became king of the Franks, 768, with his brother Carloman, who died 771. He ruled France, Germany, parts of Italy, Spain, Austria, and enforced Christianity. Crowned Emperor of the Romans by Pope Leo III in St. Peter's, Rome, Dec. 25, 800 AD. Succeeded by son, Louis I the Pious, 814. At death, 840, Louis left empire to sons, Lothair (Roman emperor); Pepin I (king of Aquitaine); Louis II (of Germany); Charles the Bald (France). They quarreled and by the peace of Verdun, 843, divided the empire.

AD   Name, year of accession

The Carolingians

843   Charles I (the Bald), Roman Emperor, 875
877   Louis II (the Stammerer), son
879   Louis III (died 082) and Carloman, brothers
885   Charles II (the Fat), Roman Emperor, 881
888   Eudes (Odo) elected by nobles
898   Charles III (the Simple), son of Louis II; defeated by
922   Robert, brother of Eudes, killed in war
923   Rudolph (Raoul) Duke of Burgundy
936   Louis IV, son of Charles III
954   Lothair, son, aged 13, defeated by Capet
986   Louis V (the Sluggard), left no heirs

The Capets

987   Hugh Capet, son of Hugh the Great
996   Robert II (the Wise), his son
1031   Henry I, his son, last Norman
1060   Philip I (the Fair), son
1108   Louis VI (the Fat), son
1137   Louis VII (the Younger), son
1180   Philip II (Augustus), son, crowned at Reims
1223   Louis VIII (the Lion), son
1226   Louis IX, son, crusader; Louis IX (1214-1270) reigned 44 years, arbitrated disputes with English King Henry III; led crusades, 1248 (captured in Egypt 1250) and 1270, when he died of plague in Tunis. Canonized 1297 as St. Louis.
1270   Philip III (the Hardy), son
1285   Philip IV (the Fair), son, king at 17
1314   Louis X (the Headstrong), son. His posthumous son, John I, lived only 7 days
1316   Philip V (the Tall), brother of Louis X
1322   Charles IV (the Fair), brother of Louis X

House of Valois

1328   Philip VI (of Valois), grandson of Philip III
1350   John II (the Good), his son, retired to England
1364   Charles V (the Wise), son
1380   Charles VI (the Beloved), son
1422   Charles VII (the Victorious), son. In 1429 Joan of Arc (Jeanne d'Arc) promised Charles to oust the English, who occupied northern France. Joan won at Orleans and Patay and had Charles crowned at Reims July 17, 1429. Joan was captured May 24, 1430, and executed May 30, 1431, at Rouen for heresy. Charles ordered her rehabilitation, effected 1455.
1461   Louis XI (the Cruel), son, civil reformer
1483   Charles VIII (the Affable), son
1498   Louis XII, great-grandson of Charles V
1515   Francis I, of Angouleme, nephew, son-in-law. Francis I (1494-1547) reigned 32 years, fought 4 big wars, was patron of the arts, aided Cellini, del Sarto, Leonardo da Vinci, Rabelais, embellished Fontainebleau.
1547   Henry II, son, killed at a joust in a tournament. He was the husband of Catherine de Medicis (1519-1589) and the lover of Diane de Poitiers (1499-1566). Catherine was born in Florence, daughter of Lorenzo de Medicis. By her marriage to Henry II she became the mother of Francis II, Charles IX, Henry III and Queen Margaret (Reine Margot) wife of Henry IV. She persuaded Charles IX to order the massacre of Huguenots on the Feast of St. Bartholomew, Aug. 24, 1572, the day her daughter was married to Henry of Navarre.
1559   Francis II, son. In 1548, Mary, Queen of Scots since infancy, was betrothed when 6 to Francis, aged 4. They were married 1558. Francis died 1560, aged 16; Mary ruled Scotland, abdicated 1567.
1560   Charles IX, brother

1574   Henry III, brother, assassinated

House of Bourbon

1589   Henry IV, of Navarre, assassinated. Henry IV made enemies when he gave tolerance to Protestants by Edict of Nantes, 1598. He was grandson of Queen Margaret of Navarre, literary patron. He married Margaret of Valois, daughter of Henry II and Catherine de Medicis; was divorced; in 1600 married Marie de Medicis, who became Regent of France, 1610-17 for her son, Louis XIII, but was exiled by Richelieu, 1631.
1610   Louis XIII (the Just), son. Louis XIII (1601-1643) married Anne of Austria. His ministers were Cardinals Richelieu and Mazarin.
1643   Louis XIV (The Grand Monarch), son. Louis XIV was king 72 years. He exhausted a prosperous country in wars for thrones and territory. By revoking the Edict of Nantes (1685) he caused the emigration of the Huguenots. He said: "I am the state."
1715   Louis XV, great-grandson. Louis XV married a Polish princess; lost Canada to the English. His favorites, Mme. Pompadour and Mme. Du Barry, influenced policies. Noted for saying "After me, the deluge".
1774   Louis XVI, grandson; married Marie Antoinette, daughter of Empress Maria Theresa of Austria. King and queen beheaded by Revolution, 1793. Their son, called Louis XVII, died in prison, never ruled.

First Republic

1792   National Convention of the French Revolution
1795   Directory, under Barras and others
1799   Consulate, Napoleon Bonaparte, first consul. Elected consul for life, 1802.

First Empire

1804   Napoleon I, emperor. Josephine (de Beauharnais) empress, 1804-09; Marie Louise, empress, 1810-1814. Her son, Francois (1811-1832), titular King of Rome, later Duke de Reichstadt and "Napoleon II," never ruled. Napoleon abdicated 1814, died 1821.

Bourbons Restored

1814   Louis XVIII king; brother of Louis XVI.
1824   Charles X, brother; reactionary; deposed by the July Revolution, 1830.

House of Orleans

1830   Louis-Philippe, the "citizen king."

Second Republic

1848   Louis Napoleon Bonaparte, president, nephew of Napoleon I. He became:

Second Empire

1852   Napoleon III, emperor; Eugenie (de Montijo) empress. Lost Franco-Prussian war, deposed 1870. Son, Prince Imperial (1856-79), died in Zulu War. Eugenie died 1920.

Third Republic—Presidents

1871   Thiers, Louis Adolphe (1797-1877)
1873   MacMahon, Marshal Patrice M. de (1808-1893)
1879   Grevy, Paul J. (1807-1891)
1887   Sadi-Carnot, M. (1837-1894), assassinated
1894   Casimir-Perier, Jean P. P. (1847-1907)
1895   Faure, Francois Felix (1841-1899)
1899   Loubet, Emile (1838-1929)
1906   Fallieres, C. Armand (1841-1931)
1913   Poincare, Raymond (1860-1934)
1920   Deschanel, Paul (1856-1922)
1920   Millerand, Alexandre (1859-1943)
1924   Doumergue, Gaston (1863-1937)
1931   Doumer, Paul (1857-1932), assassinated
1932   Lebrun, Albert (1871-1950), resigned 1940
1940   Vichy govt. under German armistice: Henri Philippe Petain (1856-1951) Chief of State, 1940-1944.
      Provisional govt. after liberation: Charles de Gaulle (1890-1970) Oct. 1944-Jan. 21, 1946; Felix Gouin (1884-1977) Jan. 23, 1946; Georges Bidault (1899-) June 24, 1946.

Fourth Republic—Presidents

1947   Auriol, Vincent (1884-1966)
1954   Coty, Rene (1882-1962)

Fifth Republic—Presidents

1959   de Gaulle, Charles Andre J. M. (1890-1970)
1969   Pompidou, Georges (1911-1974)
1974   Giscard d'Estaing, Valery (1926-)
1981   Mitterrand, Francois (1916-)

Rulers of Middle Europe; Rise and Fall of Dynasties

Carolingian Dynasty

Charles the Great, or Charlemagne, ruled France, Italy, and

Middle Europe; established Ostmark (later Austria); crowned Roman emperor by pope in Rome, 800 AD; died 814.
     Louis I (Ludwig) the Pious, son; crowned by Charlemagne 814,

d. 840.

Louis II, the German, son; succeeded to East Francia (Germany) 843-876.

Charles the Fat, son; inherited East Francia and West Francia (France) 876, reunited empire, crowned emperor by pope, 881, deposed 887.

Arnulf, nephew, 887-899. Partition of empire.

Louis the Child, 899-911, last direct descendant of Charlemagne.

Conrad I, duke of Franconia, first elected German king, 911-918, founded House of Franconia.

Saxon Dynasty; First Reich

Henry I, the Fowler, duke of Saxony, 919-936.

Otto I, the Great, 936-973, son; crowned Holy Roman Emperor by pope, 962.

Otto II, 973-983, son; failed to oust Greeks and Arabs from Sicily.

Otto III, 983-1002, son; crowned emperor at 16.

Henry II, the Saint, duke of Bavaria, 1002-1024, greatgrandson of Otto the Great.

House of Franconia

Conrad II, 1024-1039, elected king of Germany.

Henry III, the Black, 1039-1056, son; deposed 3 popes; annexed Burgundy.

Henry IV, 1056-1106, son; regency by his mother, Agnes of Poitou. Banned by Pope Gregory VII, he did penance at Canossa.

Henry V, 1106-1125, son; last of Salic House.

Lothair, duke of Saxony, 1125-1137. Crowned emperor in Rome, 1134.

House of Hohenstaufen

Conrad III, duke of Swabia, 1138-1152. In 2d Crusade.

Frederick I, Barbarossa, 1152-1190; Conrad's nephew.

Henry VI, 1190-1196, took lower Italy from Normans. Son became king of Sicily.

Philip of Swabia, 1197-1208, brother.

Otto IV, of House of Welf, 1198-1215; deposed.

Frederick II, 1215-1250, son of Henry VI; king of Sicily; crowned king of Jerusalem; in 5th Crusade.

Conrad IV, 1250-1254, son; lost lower Italy to Charles of Anjou.

Conradin (1252-1268) son, king of Jerusalem and Sicily; beheaded. Last Hohenstaufen.

Interregnum, 1254-1273, Rise of the Electors.

Transition

Rudolph I of Hapsburg, 1273-1291, defeated King Ottocar II of Bohemia. Bequeathed duchy of Austria to eldest son, Albert.

Adolph of Nassau, 1292-1298, killed in war with Albert of Austria.

Albert I, king of Germany, 1298-1308, son of Rudolph.

Henry VII, of Luxemburg, 1308-1313, crowned emperor in Rome. Seized Bohemia, 1310.

Louis IV of Bavaria (Wittelsbach), 1314-1347. Also elected was Frederick of Austria, 1314-1330 (Hapsburg). Abolition of papal sanction for election of Holy Roman Emperor.

Charles IV, of Luxemburg, 1347-1378, grandson of Henry VII, German emperor and king of Bohemia, Lombardy, Burgundy; took Mark of Brandenburg.

Wenceslaus, 1378-1400, deposed.

Rupert, Duke of Palatine, 1400-1410.

Hungary

Stephen I, house of Arpad, 997-1038. Crowned king 1000; converted Magyars; canonized 1083. After several centuries of feuds Charles Robert of Anjou became Charles I, 1308-1342.

Louis I, the Great, son, 1342-1382; joint ruler of Poland with Casimir III, 1370. Defeated Turks.

Mary, daughter, 1382-1395, ruled with husband. Sigismund of Luxemburg, 1387-1437, also king of Bohemia. As bro. of Wenceslaus he succeeded Rupert as Holy Roman Emperor, 1410.

Albert II, 1438-1439, son-in-law of Sigismund; also Roman emperor. *(see under Hapsburg.)*

Ulaszlo I of Poland, 1440-1444.

Ladislaus V, posthumous son of Albert II, 1444-1457. John Hunyadi (Hunyadi Janos) governor (1446-1452), fought Turks, Czechs; died 1456.

Matthias I (Corvinus) son of Hunyadi, 1458-1490. Shared rule of Bohemia, captured Vienna, 1485, annexed Austria, Styria, Carinthia.

Ladislas II (king of Bohemia), 1490-1516.

Louis II, son, aged 10, 1516-1526. Wars with Suleiman, Turk.

In 1527 Hungary was split between Ferdinand I, Archduke of Austria, bro.-in-law of Louis II, and John Zapolya of Transylvania. After Turkish invasion, 1547, Hungary was split between Ferdinand, Prince John Sigismund (Transylvania) and the Turks.

House of Hapsburg

Albert V of Austria, Hapsburg, crowned king of Hungary, Jan. 1438, Roman emperor, March, 1438, as Albert II; died 1439.

Frederick III, cousin, 1440-1493. Fought Turks.

Maximilian I, son, 1493-1519. Assumed title of Holy Roman Emperor (German), 1493.

Charles V, grandson, 1519-1556. King of Spain with mother co-regent; crowned Roman emperor at Aix, 1520. Confronted Luther at Worms; attempted church reform and religious conciliation; abdicated 1556.

Ferdinand I, king of Bohemia, 1526, of Hungary, 1527; disputed. German king, 1531. Crowned Roman emperor on abdication of brother Charles V, 1556.

Maximilian II, son, 1564-1576.

Rudolph II, son, 1576-1612.

Matthias, brother, 1612-1619, king of Bohemia and Hungary.

Ferdinand II of Styria, king of Bohemia, 1617, of Hungary, 1618, Roman emperor, 1619. Bohemian Protestants deposed him, elected Frederick V of Palatine, starting Thirty Years War.

Ferdinand III, son, king of Hungary, 1625, Bohemia, 1627, Roman emperor, 1637. Peace of Westphalia, 1648, ended war. Leopold I, 1658-1705; Joseph I, 1705-1711; Charles VI, 1711-1740.

Maria Theresa, daughter, 1740-1780, Archduchess of Austria, queen of Hungary; ousted pretender, Charles VII, crowned 1742; in 1745 obtained election of her husband Francis I as Roman emperor and co-regent (d. 1765). Fought Seven Years' War with Frederick II (the Great) of Prussia. Mother of Marie Antoinette, Queen of France.

Joseph II, son 1765-1790, Roman emperor, reformer; powers restricted by Empress Maria Theresa until her death, 1780. First partition of Poland. Leopold II, 1790-1792.

Francis II, son, 1792-1835. Fought Napoleon. Proclaimed first hereditary emperor of Austria, 1804. Forced to abdicate as Roman emperor, 1806; last use of title. Ferdinand I, son, 1835-1848, abdicated during revolution.

Austro-Hungarian Monarchy

Francis Joseph I, nephew, 1848-1916, emperor of Austria, king of Hungary. Dual monarchy of Austria-Hungary formed, 1867. After assassination of heir, Archduke Francis Ferdinand, June 28, 1914, Austrian diplomacy precipitated World War I.

Charles I, grand-nephew, 1916-1918, last emperor of Austria and king of Hungary. Abdicated Nov. 11-13, 1918, died 1922.

Rulers of Prussia

Nucleus of Prussia was the Mark of Brandenburg. First margrave was Albert the Bear (Albrecht), 1134-1170. First Hohenzollern margrave was Frederick, burgrave of Nuremberg, 1417-1440.

Frederick William, 1640-1688, the Great Elector. Son, Frederick III, 1688-1713, was crowned King Frederick of Prussia, 1701.

Frederick William I, son, 1713-1740.

Frederick II, the Great, son, 1740-1786, annexed Silesia part of Austria.

Frederick William II, nephew, 1786-1797.

Frederick William III, son, 1797-1840. Napoleonic wars.

Frederick William IV, son, 1840-1861. Uprising of 1848 and first parliament and constitution.

Second and Third Reich

William I, 1861-1888, brother. Annexation of Schleswig and Hanover; Franco-Prussian war, 1870-71, proclamation of German Reich, Jan. 18, 1871, at Versailles; William, German emperor (Deutscher Kaiser), Bismarck, chancellor.

Frederick III, son, 1888.

William II, son, 1888-1918. Led Germany in World War I, abdicated as German emperor and king of Prussia, Nov. 9, 1918. Died in exile in Netherlands June 4, 1941. Minor rulers of Bavaria, Saxony, Wurttemberg also abdicated.

Germany proclaimed a republic at Weimar, July 1, 1919. Presidents: Frederick Ebert, 1919-1925, Paul von Hindenburg-Beneckendorff, 1925, reelected 1932, d. Aug. 2, 1934. Adolf Hitler, chancellor, chosen successor as Leader-Chancellor (Fuehrer & Reichskanzler) of Third Reich. Annexed Austria, March, 1938. Precipitated World War II, 1939-1945. Committed suicide April 30, 1945.

Rulers of Poland

House of Piasts

Miesko I, 962?-992; Poland Christianized 966. Expansion under 3 Boleslavs: I, 992-1025, son, crowned king 1024; II, 1058-1079, great-grandson, exiled after killing bishop Stanislav who became chief patron saint of Poland; III, 1106-1138, nephew, divided Poland among 4 sons eldest suzerain.

1138-1306, feudal division. 1226 founding in Prussia of military order Teutonic Knights. 1226 invasion by Tartars/Mongols.

Vladislav I, 1306-1333, reunited most Polish territories, crowned king 1320. Casimir III the Great, 1333-1370, son, developed economic, cultural life, foreign policy.

House of Anjou

Louis I, 1370-1382, nephew/identical with Louis I of Hungary.

Jadwiga, 1384-1399, daughter, married 1386 Jagiello, Grand Duke of Lituania.

House of Jagelloneans

Vladislav II, 1386-1434, Christianized Lituania, founded personal union between Poland & Lituania. Defeated 1410 Teutonic Knights at Grunwald.

Vladislav III, 1434-1444, son, simultaneously king of Hungary. Fought Turks, killed 1444 in battle of Varna.

Casimir IV, 1446-1492, brother, competed with Hapsburgs, put son Vladislav on throne of Bohemia, later also of Hungary.

Sigismund I, 1506-1548, brother, patronized science & arts, his & son's reign "Golden Age."

Sigismund II, 1548-1572, son, established 1569 real union of Poland and Lituania (lasted until 1795).

Elective kings

Polish nobles proclaimed 1572 Poland a Republic headed by king to be elected by whole nobility.

Stephen Balory, 1676-1586, duke of Transylvania, married Ann, sister of Sigismund II August. Fought Russians.

Sigismund III Vasa, 1587-1632, nephew of Sigismund II. 1592-1598 also king of Sweden. His generals fought Russians, Turks.

Vladislav II Vasa, 1632-1648, son. Fought Russians.

John II Casimir Vasa, 1648-1668, brother. Fought Cossacks, Swedes, Russians, Turks, Tartars (the "Deluge"). Abdicated

1668.

John III Sobieski, 1674-1696. Won Vienna from Turks, 1683.

Stanislav II, 1764-1795, last king. Encouraged reforms; 1791 1st modern Constitution in Europe. 1772, 1793, 1795 Poland partitioned among Russia, Prussia, Austria. Unsuccessful insurrection against foreign invasion 1794 under Kosciuszko, Amer-Polish gen.

1795-1918 Poland under foreign rule

1807-1815 Grand Duchy of Warsaw created by Napoleon I, Frederick August of Saxony grand duke.

1815 Congress of Vienna proclaimed part of Poland "Kingdom" in personal union with Russia.

Polish uprisings: 1830 against Russia, 1846, 1848 against Austria, 1863 against Russia—all repressed.

1918-1939 Second Republic

1918-1922 Head of State Jozef Pilsudski. Presidents: Gabriel Narutowicz 1933, assassinated. Stanislav Wojsiechowski 1922-1926, had to abdicate after Pilsudski's coup d'état. Ignacy Moscicki, 1926-1939, ruled with Pilsudski as (until 1935) virtual dictator.

1939-1945 Poland under foreign occupation

Nazi aggression Sept. 1939. Polish govt.-in-exile, first in France, then in England. Vladislav Raczkiewicz près., Gen. Vladislav Sikorski, then Stanislav Mikolajczyk, prime ministers. Polish Committee of Natl. Liberation proclaimed at Lublin July 1944, transformed into govt. Jan. 1, 1945.

Rulers of Denmark, Sweden, Norway

Denmark

Earliest rulers invaded Britain; King Canute, who ruled in London 1016-1035, was most famous. The Valdemars furnished kings until the 15th century. In 1282 the Danes won the first national assembly, Danehof, from King Erik V.

Most redoubtable medieval character was Margaret, daughter of Valdemar IV, born 1353, married at 10 to King Haakon VI of Norway. In 1376 she had her first infant son Olaf made king of Denmark. After his death, 1387, she was regent of Denmark and Norway. In 1388 Sweden accepted her as sovereign. In 1389 she made her grand-nephew, Duke Erik of Pomerania, titular king of Denmark, Sweden, and Norway, with herself as regent. In 1397 she effected the Union of Kalmar of the three kingdoms and had Erik VII crowned. In 1439 the three kingdoms deposed him and elected, 1440, Christopher of Bavaria king (Christopher III). On his death, 1448, the union broke up.

Succeeding rulers were unable to enforce their claims as rulers of Sweden until 1520, when Christian II conquered Sweden. He was thrown out 1522, and in 1523 Gustavus Vasa united Sweden. Denmark continued to dominate Norway until the Napoleonic wars, when Frederick VI, 1808-1839, joined the Napoleonic cause after Britain had destroyed the Danish fleet, 1807. In 1814 he was forced to cede Norway to Sweden and Helgoland to Britain, receiving Lauenburg. Successors Christian VIII, 1839; Frederick VII, 1848; Christian IX, 1863; Frederick VIII, 1906; Christian X, 1912; Frederick IX, 1947; Margrethe II, 1972.

Sweden

Early kings ruled at Uppsala, but did not dominate the country. Sverker, c1130-c1156, united the Swedes and Goths. In 1435 Sweden obtained the Riksdag, or parliament. After the Union of Kalmar, 1397, the Danes either ruled or harried the country until Christian II of Denmark conquered it anew, 1520. This led to a

rising under Gustavus Vasa, who ruled Sweden 1523-1560, and established an independent kingdom. Charles IX, 1599-1611, crowned 1604, conquered Moscow. Gustavus II Adolphus, 1611-1632, was called the Lion of the North. Later rulers: Christina, 1632; Charles X, Gustavus 1654; Charles XI, 1660; Charles XII (invader of Russia and Poland, defeated at Poltava, June 28, 1709), 1697; Ulrika Eleanora, sister, elected queen 1718; Frederick I (of Hesse), her husband, 1720; Adolphus Frederick, 1751; Gustavus III, 1771; Gustavus IV Adolphus, 1792; Charles XIII, 1809. (Union with Norway began 1814.) Charles XIV John, 1818. He was Jean Bernadotte, Napoleon's Prince of Ponte Corvo, elected 1810 to succeed Charles XIII. He founded the present dynasty: Oscar I, 1844, Charles XV, 1859; Oscar II, 1872; Gustavus V, 1907; Gustav VI Adolf, 1950; Carl XVI Gustaf, 1973.

Norway

Overcoming many rivals, Harald Haarfager, 872-930, conquered Norway, Orkneys, and Shetlands; Olaf I, great-grandson, 995-1000, brought Christianity into Norway, Iceland, and Greenland. In 1035 Magnus the Good also became king of Denmark. Haakon V, 1299-1319, had married his daughter to Erik of Sweden. Their son, Magnus became ruler of Norway and Sweden at 6. His son, Haakon VI, married Margaret of Denmark; their son Olaf IV became king of Norway and Denmark, followed by Margaret's regency and the Union of Kalmar, 1397.

In 1450 Norway became subservient to Denmark. Christian IV, 1588-1648, founded Christiania, now Oslo. After Napoleonic wars, when Denmark ceded Norway to Sweden, a strong nationalist movement forced recognition of Norway as an independent kingdom united with Sweden under the Swedish kings, 1814-1905. In 1905 the union was dissolved and Prince Carl of Denmark became Haakon VII. He died Sept. 21, 1957, aged 85; succeeded by son, Olav V, b. July 2, 1903.

Rulers of the Netherlands and Belgium

The Netherlands (Holland)

William Frederick, Prince of Orange, led a revolt against French rule, 1813, and was crowned King of the Netherlands, 1815. Belgium seceded Oct. 4, 1830, after a revolt, and formed a separate government. The change was ratified by the two kingdoms by treaty Apr. 19, 1839.

Succession: William II, son, 1840; William III, son, 1849; Wilhelmina, daughter of William III and his 2d wife Princess Emma of Waldeck, 1890; Wilhelmina abdicated, Sept. 4, 1948, in favor of daughter, Juliana. Juliana abdicated Apr. 30, 1980, in favor of daughter, Beatrix.

Belgium

A national congress elected Prince Leopold of Saxe-Coburg King; he took the throne July 21, 1831, as Leopold I. Succession: Leopold II, son 1865; Albert I, nephew of Leopold II, 1909; Leopold III, son of Albert, 1934; Prince Charles, Regent 1944; Leopold returned 1950, yielded powers to son Baudouin, Prince Royal, Aug. 6, 1950, abdicated July 16, 1951. Baudouin I took throne July 17, 1951.

For political history prior to 1830 see articles on the Netherlands and Belgium.

Roman Rulers

From Romulus to the end of the Empire in the West. Rulers of the Roman Empire in the East sat in Constantinople and for a brief period in Nicaea, until the capture of Constantinople by the Turks in 1453, when Byzantium was succeeded by the Ottoman Empire.

BC	Name			
	The Kingdom	534	L. Tarquinius Superbus	435	Censorship instituted

BC	Name			
	The Kingdom			
753	Romulus (Quirinus)		
716	Numa Pompilius		
673	Tullus Hostilius		
640	Ancus Marcius		
616	L. Tarquinius Priscus		
578	Servius Tullius		

BC	Name		BC	**The Republic**			
534	L. Tarquinius Superbus			**The Republic**		435	Censorship instituted
			509	Consulate established		366	Praetorship established
			509	Quaestorship instituted		366	Curule Aedileship created
			498	Dictatorship introduced		362	Military Tribunate elected
			494	Plebeian Tribunate created		326	Proconsulate introduced
			494	Plebeian Aedileship created		311	Naval Duumvirate elected
			444	Consular Tribunate organized		217	Dictatorship of Fabius Maximus
						133	Tribunate of Tiberius Gracchus

123	Tribunate of Gaius Gracchus
82	Dictatorship of Sulla
60	First Triumvirate formed
	(Caesar, Pompeius, Crassus)
46	Dictatorship of Caesar
43	Second Triumvirate formed
	(Octavianus, Antonius, Lepidus)
	The Empire
27	Augustus (Gaius Julius
	Caesar Octavianus)
AD	
14	Tiberius I
37	Gaius Caesar (Caligula)
41	Claudius I
54	Nero
68	Galba
69	Galba; Otho, Vitellius
69	Vespasianus
79	Titus
81	Domitianus
96	Nerva
98	Trajanus
117	Hadrianus
138	Antoninus Pius
161	Marcus Aurelius and Lucius Verus
169	Marcus Aurelius (alone)
180	Commodus
193	Pertinax; Julianus I
193	Septimius Severus
211	Caracalla and Geta
212	Caracalla (alone)
217	Macrinus
218	Elagabalus (Heliogabalus)
222	Alexander Severus
235	Maximinus I (the Thracian)

238	Gordianus I and Gordianus II;
	Pupienus and Balbinus
238	Gordianus III
244	Philippus (the Arabian)
249	Decius
251	Gallus and Volusianus
253	Aemilianus
253	Valerianus and Gallienus
258	Gallienus (alone)
268	Claudius II (the Goth)
270	Quintillus
270	Aurelianus
275	Tacitus
276	Florianus
276	Probus
282	Carus
283	Carinus and Numerianus
284	Diocletianus
286	Diocletianus and Maximianus
305	Galerius and Constantius I
306	Galerius, Maximinus II, Severus I
307	Galerius, Maximinus
	II, Constantinus I, Licinius,
	Maxentius
311	Maximinus II, Constantinus I,
	Licinius, Maxentius
314	Maximinus II, Constantinus I,
	Licinius
314	Constantinus I and Licinius
324	Constantinus I (the Great)
337	Constantinus II, Constans I,
	Constantius II
340	Constantius II and Constans I
350	Constantius II
361	Julianus II (the Apostate)
363	Jovianus

West (Rome) and East (Constantinople)

364	Valentinianus I (West) and Valens (East)
367	Valentinianus I with Gratianus (West) and Valens (East)
375	Gratianus with Valentinianus II (West) and Valens (East)
378	Gratianus with Valentinianus II (West) Theodosius I (East)
383	Valentinianus II (West) and Theodosius I (East)
394	Theodosius I (the Great)
395	Honorius (West) and Arcadius (East)
408	Honorius (West) and Theodosius II (East)
423	Valentinianus III (West) and Theodosius II (East)
450	Valentinianus III (West) and Marcianus (East)
455	Maximus (West), Avitus (West); Marcianus (East)
456	Avitus (West), Marcianus (East)
457	Majorianus (West), Leo I (East)
461	Severus II (West), Leo I (East)
467	Anthemius (West), Leo I (East)
472	Olybrius (West), Leo I (East)
473	Glycerius (West), Leo I (East)
474	Julius Nepos (West), Leo II (East)
475	Romulus Augustulus (West) and Zeno (East)
476	End of Empire in West; Odovacar, King, drops title of Emperor; murdered by King Theodoric of Ostrogoths 493 AD

Rulers of Modern Italy

After the fall of Napoleon in 1814, the Congress of Vienna, 1815, restored Italy as a political patchwork, comprising the Kingdom of Naples and Sicily, the Papal States, and smaller units. Piedmont and Genoa were awarded to Sardinia, ruled by King Victor Emmanuel I of Savoy.

United Italy emerged under the leadership of Camillo, Count di Cavour (1810-1861), Sardinian prime minister. Agitation was led by Giuseppe Mazzini (1805-1872) and Giuseppe Garibaldi (1807-1882), soldier, Victor Emmanuel I abdicated 1821. After a brief regency for a brother, Charles Albert was King 1831-1849, abdicating when defeated by the Austrians at Novara. Succeeded by Victor Emmanuel II, 1849-1861.

In 1859 France forced Austria to cede Lombardy to Sardinia, which gave rights to Savoy and Nice to France. In 1860 Garibaldi led 1,000 volunteers in a spectacular campaign, took Sicily and expelled the King of Naples. In 1860 the House of Savoy annexed Tuscany, Parma, Modera, Romagna, the Two Sicilies, the Marches, and Umbria. Victor Emmanuel assumed the title of King

of Italy at Turin Mar. 17, 1861. In 1866 he allied with Prussia in the Austro-Prussian War, with Prussia's victory received Venetia. On Sept. 20, 1870, his troops under Gen. Raffaele Cardorna entered Rome and took over the Papal States, ending the temporal power of the Roman Catholic Church.

Succession: Umberto I; 1878, assassinated 1900; Victor Emmanuel III, 1900, abdicated 1946, died 1947; Umberto II, 1946, ruled a month. In 1921 Benito Mussolini (1883-1945) formed the Fascist party and became prime minister Oct. 31, 1922. He made the King Emperor of Ethiopia, 1937; entered World War II as ally of Hitler. He was deposed July 25, 1943.

At a plebiscite June 2, 1946, Italy voted for a republic; Premier Alcide de Gasperi became chief of state June 13, 1946. On June 28, 1946, the Constituent Assembly elected Enrico de Nicola, Liberal, provisional president. Successive presidents: Luigi Einaudi, elected May 11, 1948, Giovanni Gronchi, Apr. 29, 1955; Antonio Segni, May 6, 1962; Giuseppe Saragat, Dec. 28, 1964; Giovanni Leone, Dec. 29, 1971; Alessandro Pertini, July 9, 1978.

Rulers of Spain

From 8th to 11th centuries Spain was dominated by the Moors (Arabs and Berbers). The Christian reconquest established small competing kingdoms of the Asturias, Aragon, Castile, Catalonia, Leon, Navarre, and Valencia. In 1474 Isabella (Isabel), b. 1451, became Queen of Castile & Leon. Her husband, Ferdinand, b. 1452, inherited Aragon 1479, with Catalonia, Valencia, and the Balearic Islands, became Ferdinand V of Castile. By Isabella's request Pope Sixtus IV established the Inquisition, 1478. Last Moorish kingdom, Granada, fell 1492. Columbus opened New World of colonies, 1492. Isabella died 1504, succeeded by her daughter, Juana "the Mad," but Ferdinand ruled until his death 1516.

Charles I, b. 1500, son of Juana and grandson of Ferdinand and Isabella, and of Maximilian I of Hapsburg; succeeded later as Holy Roman Emperor, Charles V, 1520; abdicated 1556. Philip II, son, 1556-1598, inherited only Spanish throne; conquered Portugal, fought Turks, persecuted non-Catholics, sent Armada against England. Was briefly married to Mary I of England, 1554-1558. Succession: Philip III, 1598-1621; Philip IV, 1621-1665; Charles II, 1665-1700, left Spain to Philip of Anjou, grandson of Louis XIV, who as Philip V, 1700-1746, founded Bourbon dynasty. Ferdinand VI, 1746-1759; Charles III, 1759-1788; Charles IV, 1788-1808, abdicated.

Napoleon now dominated politics and made his brother Joseph King of Spain 1808, but the Spanish ousted him finally in 1813. Ferdinand VII, 1808, 1814-1833, lost American colonies; succeeded by daughter Isabella II, aged 3, with wife Maria Christina of Na-

ples regent until 1843. Isabella deposed by revolution 1868. Elected king by the Cortes, Amadeo of Savoy, 1870; abdicated 1873. First republic, 1873-1874. Alphonso XII, son of Isabella, 1875-1885. His posthumous son was Alphonso XIII, with his mother, Queen Maria Christina regent; Spanish-American war, Spain lost Cuba, gave up Puerto Rico, Philippines, Sulu Is., Marianas. Alphonso took throne 1902, aged 16, married British Princess Victoria Eugenia of Battenberg. The dictatorship of Primo de Rivera, 1923-30, precipitated the revolution of 1931. Alphonso agreed to leave without formal abdication. The monarchy was abolished and the second republic established, with strong socialist backing. Presidents were Niceto Alcala Zamora, to 1936, when Manuel Azaña was chosen.

In July, 1936, the army in Morocco revolted against the government and General Francisco Franco led the troops into Spain. The revolution succeeded by Feb., 1939, when Anzana resigned. Franco became chief of state, with provisions that if he was incapacitated the Regency Council by two-thirds vote may propose a king to the Cortes, which must have a two-thirds majority to elect him.

Alphonso XIII died in Rome Feb. 28, 1941, aged 54. His property and citizenship had been restored.

A succession law restoring the monarchy was approved in a 1947 referendum. Prince Juan Carlos, son of the pretender to the throne, was designated by Franco and the Cortes in 1969 as the future king and chief of state. Upon Franco's death, Nov. 20, 1975, Juan Carlos was proclaimed king, Nov. 22, 1975.

Leaders in the South American Wars of Liberation

Simon Bolivar (1783-1830), Jose Francisco de San Martin (1783-1850), and Francisco Antonio Gabriel Miranda (1750-1816), are among the heroes of the early 19th century struggles of South American nations to free themselves from Spain. All three, and their contemporaries, operated in periods of intense factional strife, during which soldiers and civilians suffered.

Miranda, a Venezuelan, who had served with the French in the American Revolution and commanded parts of the French Revolutionary armies in the Netherlands, attempted to start a revolt in Venezuela in 1806 and failed. In 1810, with British and American backing, he returned and was briefly a dictator, until the British withdrew their support. In 1812 he was overcome by the royalists in Venezuela and taken prisoner, dying in a Spanish prison in 1816.

San Martin was born in Argentina and during 1789-1811 served in campaigns of the Spanish armies in Europe and Africa. He first joined the independence movement in Argentina in 1812 and then in 1817 invaded Chile with 4,000 men over the high mountain passes. Here he and General Bernardo O'Higgins (1778-1842) defeated the Spaniards at Chacabuco, 1817, and O'Higgins was named Liberator and became first director of Chile, 1817-1823. In 1821 San Martin occupied Lima and Callao, Peru, and became pro-tector of Peru.

Bolivar, the greatest leader of South American liberation from Spain, was born in Venezuela, the son of an aristocratic family. His organizing and administrative abilities were superior and he foresaw many of the political difficulties of the future. He first served under Miranda in 1812 and in 1813 captured Caracas, where he was named Liberator. Forced out next year by civil strife, he led a

campaign that captured Bogota in 1814. In 1817 he was again in control of Venezuela and was named dictator. He organized Nueva Granada with the help of General Francisco de Paula Santander (1792-1840). By joining Nueva Granada, Venezuela, and the present terrain of Panama and Ecuador, the republic of Colombia was formed with Bolivar president. After numerous setbacks he decisively defeated the Spaniards in the second battle of Carabobo, Venezuela, June 24, 1821.

In May, 1822, Gen. Antonio Jose de Sucre, Bolivar's trusted lieutenant, took Quito. Bolivar went to Guayaquil to confer with San Martin, who resigned as protector of Peru and withdrew from politics. With a new army of Colombians and Peruvians Bolivar defeated the Spaniards in a saber battle at Junín in 1824 and cleared Peru.

De Sucre organized Charcas (Upper Peru) as Republica Bolivar (now Bolivia) and acted as president in place of Bolivar, who wrote its constitution. De Sucre defeated the Spanish faction of Peru at Ayacucho, Dec. 19, 1824.

Continued civil strife finally caused the Colombian federation to break apart. Santander turned against Bolivar, but the latter defeated him and banished him. In 1828 Bolivar gave up the presidency he had held precariously for 14 years. He became ill from tuberculosis and died Dec. 17, 1830. He was honored as the great liberator and is buried in the national pantheon in Caracas.

Rulers of Russia; Premiers of the USSR

First ruler to consolidate Slavic tribes was Rurik, leader of the Russians who established himself at Novgorod, 862 A.D. He and his immediate successors had Scandinavian affiliations. They moved to Kiev after 972 AD and ruled as Dukes of Kiev. In 988 Vladimir was converted and adopted the Byzantine Greek Orthodox service, later modified by Slav influences. Important as organizer and lawgiver was Yaroslav, 1019-1054, whose daughters married kings of Norway, Hungary, and France. His grandson, Vladimir II (Monomakh), 1113-1125, was progenitor of several rulers, but in 1169 Andrew Bogolubski overthrew Kiev and began the line known as Grand Dukes of Vladimir.

Of the Grand Dukes of Vladimir, Alexander Nevsky, 1246-1263, had a son, Daniel, first to be called Duke of Muscovy (Moscow) who ruled 1294-1303. His successors became Grand Dukes of Muscovy. After Dmitri III Donskoi defeated the Tartars in 1380, they also became Grand Dukes of all Russia. Independence of the Tartars and considerable territorial expansion were achieved under Ivan III, 1462-1505.

Tsars of Muscovy—Ivan III was referred to in church ritual as Tsar. He married Sofia, niece of the last Byzantine emperor. His successor, Basil III, died in 1533 when Basil's son Ivan was only 3. He became Ivan IV, "the Terrible," crowned 1547 as Tsar of all the Russias, ruled till 1584. Under the weak rule of his son, Feodor I, 1584-1598, Boris Godunov had control. The dynasty died, and after years of tribal strife and intervention by Polish and Swedish armies, the Russians united under 17-year-old Michael Romanov, distantly related to the first wife of Ivan IV. He ruled 1613-1645 and established the Romanov line. Fourth ruler after Michael was Peter I.

Tsars, or Emperors of Russia (Romanovs)—Peter I, 1682-1725, known as Peter the Great, took title of Emperor in 1721. His successors and dates of accession were: Catherine, his widow, 1725; Peter II, his grandson, 1727-1730; Anne, Duchess of Courland,

1730, daughter of Peter the Great's brother, Tsar Ivan V; Ivan VI, 1740-1741, great-grandson of Ivan V, child, kept in prison and murdered 1764; Elizabeth, daughter of Peter I, 1741; Peter III, grandson of Peter I, 1761, deposed 1762 for his consort, Catherine II, former princess of Anhalt Zerbst (Germany) who is known as Catherine the Great, 1762-1796; Paul I, her son, 1796, killed 1801; Alexander I, son of Paul, 1801-1825, defeated Napoleon; Nicholas I, his brother, 1825; Alexander II, son of Nicholas, 1855, assassinated 1881 by terrorists; Alexander III, son, 1881-1894.

Nicholas II, son, 1894-1917, last Tsar of Russia, was forced to abdicate by the Revolution that followed losses to Germany in WWI. The Tsar, the Empress, the Tsesarevich (Crown Prince) and the Tsar's 4 daughters were murdered by the Bolsheviks in Ekaterinburg, July 16, 1918.

Provisional Government—Prince Georgi Lvov and Alexander Kerensky, premiers, 1917.

Union of Soviet Socialist Republics

Bolshevik Revolution, Nov. 7, 1917, displaced Kerensky; council of People's Commissars formed, Lenin (Vladimir Ilyich Ulyanov), premier. Lenin died Jan. 21, 1924. Aleksei Rykov (executed 1938) and V. M. Molotov held the office, but actual ruler was Joseph Stalin (Joseph Vissarionovich Djugashvili), general secretary of the Central Committee of the Communist Party. Stalin became president of the Council of Ministers (premier) May 7, 1941, died Mar. 5, 1953. Succeeded by Georgi M. Malenkov, as head of the Council and premier and Nikita S. Khrushchev, first secretary of the Central Committee. Malenkov resigned Feb. 8, 1955, became deputy premier, was dropped July 3, 1957. Marshal Nikolai A. Bulganin became premier Feb. 8, 1955; was demoted and Khrushchev became premier Mar. 27 1958. Khrushchev was ousted Oct. 14-15, 1964, replaced by Leonid I. Brezhnev as first secretary of the party and by Aleksei N. Kosygin as premier. On June 16, 1977, Brezhnev took office as president.

Governments of China

(Until 221 BC and frequently thereafter, China was not a unified state. Where dynastic dates overlap, the rulers or events referred to appeared in different areas of China.)

Hsia	c1994BC	c1523BC
Shang	c1523	c1028
Western Chou	c1027	770
Eastern Chou	770	256
Warring States	403	222
Ch'in (first unified empire)	221	206
Han	202BC	220AD
Western Han (expanded Chinese state beyond the Yellow and Yangtze River valleys)	202BC	9AD
Hsin (Wang Mang, usurper)	9AD	23AD
Eastern Han (expanded Chinese state into Indo-China and Turkestan)	25	220
Three Kingdoms (Wei, Shu, Wu)	220	265
Chin (western)	265	317
(eastern)	317	420
Northern Dynasties (followed several short-lived governments by Turks, Mongols, etc.)	386	581
Southern Dynasties (capital: Nanking)	420	589
Sui (reunified China)	581	618
Tang (a golden age of Chinese cul-ture; capital: Sian)	618	906
Five Dynasties (Yellow River basin)	902	960
Ten Kingdoms (southern China)	907	979
Liao (Khitan Mongols; capital: Peking)	947	1125
Sung	960	1279
Northern Sung (reunified central and southern China)	960	1126
Western Hsai (non-Chinese rulers in northwest)	990	1227
Chin (Tartars; drove Sung out of central China)	1115	1234
Yuan (Mongols; Kublai Khan made Peking his capital in 1267)	1271	1368
Ming (China reunified under Chinese rule; capital: Nanking, then Peking in 1420)	1368	1644
Ch'ing (Manchus, descendents of Tartars)	1644	1911
Republic (disunity; provincial rulers, warlords)	1912	1949
People's Republic of China (Nationalist China established on Taiwan)	1949	—

Chronological List of Popes

Source: Annuario Pontificio. Table lists year of accession of each Pope.

The Roman Catholic Church names the Apostle Peter as founder of the Church in Rome. He arrived there c. 42, was martyred there c. 67, and raised to sainthood.

The Pope's temporal title is: Sovereign of the State of Vatican City.

The Pope's spiritual titles are: Bishop of Rome, Vicar of Jesus Christ, Successor of St. Peter, Prince of the Apostles, Supreme Pontiff of the Universal Church, Patriarch of the West, Primate of Italy, Archbishop and Metropolitan of the Roman Province.

Anti-Popes are in *Italics*. Anti-Popes were illegitimate claimants of or pretenders to the papal throne.

Year	Name of Pope	Year	Name of Pope	Year	Name of Pope	Year	Name of Pope
See above.	St. Peter	615	St. Deusdedit	974	Benedict VII	1305	Clement V
67	St. Linus		or Adeodatus	983	John XIV	1316	John XXII
76	St. Anacletus	619	Boniface V	985	John XV	*1328*	*Nicholas V*
	or Cletus	625	Honorius I	996	Gregory V	1334	Benedict XII
88	St. Clement I	640	Severinus	*997*	*John XVI*	1342	Clement VI
97	St. Evaristus	640	John IV	999	Sylvester II	1352	Innocent VI
105	St. Alexander I	642	Theodore I	1003	John XVII	1362	Bl. Urban V
115	St. Sixtus I	649	St. Martin I, Martyr	1004	John XVIII	1370	Gregory XI
125	St. Telesphorus	654	St. Eugene I	1009	Sergius IV	1378	Urban VI
136	St. Hyginus	657	St. Vitalian	1012	Benedict VIII	*1378*	*Clement VII*
140	St. Pius I	672	Adeodatus II	*1012*	*Gregory*	1389	Boniface IX
155	St. Anicetus	676	Donus	1024	John XIX	*1394*	*Benedict XIII*
166	St. Soter	678	St. Agatho	1032	Benedict IX	1404	Innocent VII
175	St. Eleutherius	682	St. Leo II	1045	Sylvester III	1406	Gregory XII
189	St. Victor I	684	St. Benedict II	1045	Benedict IX	*1409*	*Alexander V*
199	St. Zephyrinus	685	John V	1045	Gregory VI	*1410*	*John XXIII*
217	St. Callistus I	686	Conon	1046	Clement II	1417	Martin V
217	*St. Hippolytus*	*687*	*Theodore*	1047	Benedict IX	1431	Eugene IV
222	St. Urban I	*687*	*Paschal*	1048	Damasus II	*1439*	*Felix V*
230	St. Pontian	687	St. Sergius I	1049	St. Leo IX	1447	Nicholas V
235	St. Anterus	701	John VI	1055	Victor II	1455	Callistus III
236	St. Fabian	705	John VII	1057	Stephen IX (X)	1458	Pius II
251	St. Cornelius	708	Sisinnius	*1058*	*Benedict X*	1464	Paul II
251	*Novatian*	708	Constantine	1059	Nicholas II	1471	Sixtus IV
253	St. Lucius I	715	St. Gregory II	1061	Alexander II	1484	Innocent VIII
254	St. Stephen I	731	St. Gregory III	*1061*	*Honorius II*	1492	Alexander VI
257	St. Sixtus II	741	St. Zachary	1073	St. Gregory VII	1503	Pius III
259	St. Dionysius	752	Stephen II (III)	*1080*	*Clement III*	1503	Julius II
269	St. Felix I	757	St. Paul I	1086	Bl. Victor III	1513	Leo X
275	St. Eutychian	*767*	*Constantine*	1088	Bl. Urban II	1522	Adrian VI
283	St. Caius	*768*	*Philip*	1099	Paschal II	1523	Clement VII
296	St. Marcellinus	768	Stephen III (IV)	*1100*	*Theodoric*	1534	Paul III
308	St. Marcellus I	772	Adrian I	*1102*	*Albert*	1550	Julius III
309	St. Eusebius	795	St. Leo III	*1105*	*Sylvester IV*	1555	Marcellus II
311	St. Melchiades	816	Stephen IV (V)	1118	Gelasius II	1555	Paul IV
314	St. Sylvester I	817	St. Paschal I	*1118*	*Gregory VIII*	1559	Pius IV
336	St. Marcus	824	Eugene II	1119	Callistus II	1566	St. Pius V
337	St. Julius I	827	Valentine	1124	Honorius II	1572	Gregory XIII
352	Liberius	827	Gregory IV	*1124*	*Celestine II*	1585	Sixtus V
355	*Felix II*	*844*	*John*	1130	Innocent II	1590	Urban VII
366	St. Damasus I	844	Sergius II	*1130*	*Anacletus II*	1590	Gregory XIV
366	*Ursinus*	847	St. Leo IV	*1138*	*Victor IV*	1591	Innocent IX
384	St. Siricius	855	Benedict III	1143	Celestine II	1592	Clement VIII
399	St. Anastasius I	*855*	*Anastasius*	1144	Lucius II	1605	Leo XI
401	St. Innocent I	858	St. Nicholas I	1145	Bl. Eugene III	1605	Paul V
417	St. Zosimus	867	Adrian II	1153	Anastasius IV	1621	Gregory XV
418	St. Boniface I	872	John VIII	1154	Adrian IV	1623	Urban VIII
418	*Eulalius*	882	Marinus I	1159	Alexander III	1644	Innocent X
422	St. Celestine I	884	St. Adrian III	*1159*	*Victor IV*	1655	Alexander VII
432	St. Sixtus III	885	Stephen V (VI)	*1164*	*Paschal III*	1667	Clement IX
440	St. Leo I	891	Formosus	*1168*	*Callistus III*	1670	Clement X
461	St. Hilary	896	Boniface VI	*1179*	*Innocent III*	1676	Bl. Innocent XI
468	St. Simplicius	896	Stephen VI (VII)	1181	Lucius III	1689	Alexander VIII
483	St. Felix III (II)	897	Romanus	1185	Urban III	1691	Innocent XII
492	St. Gelasius I	897	Theodore II	1187	Gregory VIII	1700	Clement XI
496	Anastasius II	898	John IX	1187	Clement III	1721	Innocent XIII
498	St. Symmachus	900	Benedict IV	1191	Celestine III	1724	Benedict XIII
498	*Lawrence*	903	Leo V	1198	Innocent III	1730	Clement XII
	(501-505)	*903*	*Christopher*	1216	Honorius III	1740	Benedict XIV
514	St. Hormisdas	904	Sergius III	1227	Gregory IX	1758	Clement XIII
523	St. John I, Martyr	911	Anastasius III	1241	Celestine IV	1769	Clement XIV
526	St. Felix IV (III)	913	Landus	1243	Innocent IV	1775	Pius VI
530	Boniface II	914	John X	1254	Alexander IV	1800	Pius VII
530	*Dioscorus*	928	Leo VI	1261	Urban IV	1823	Leo XII
533	John II	928	Stephen VII (VIII)	1265	Clement IV	1829	Pius VIII
535	St. Agapitus I	931	John XI	1271	Bl. Gregory X	1831	Gregory XVI
536	St. Silverius, Martyr	936	Leo VII	1276	Bl. Innocent V	1846	Pius IX
537	Vigilius	939	Stephen VIII (IX)	1276	Adrian V	1878	Leo XIII
556	Pelagius I	942	Marinus II	1276	John XXI	1903	St. Pius X
561	John III	946	Agapitus II	1277	Nicholas III	1914	Benedict XV
575	Benedict I	955	John XII	1281	Martin IV	1922	Pius XI
579	Pelagius II	963	Leo VIII	1285	Honorius IV	1939	Pius XII
590	St. Gregory I	964	Benedict V	1288	Nicholas IV	1958	John XXIII
604	Sabinian	965	John XIII	1294	St. Celestine V	1963	Paul VI
607	Boniface III	973	Benedict VI	1294	Boniface VIII	1978	John Paul I
608	St. Boniface IV	*974*	*Boniface VII*	1303	Bl. Benedict XI	1978	John Paul II

AWARDS — MEDALS — PRIZES

The Alfred B. Nobel Prize Winners

Alfred B. Nobel, inventor of dynamite, bequeathed $9,000,000, the interest to be distributed yearly to those who had most benefited mankind in physics, chemistry, medicine-physiology, literature, and peace. The first Nobel Memorial Prize in Economics was awarded in 1969. No awards given for years omitted. In 1980, each prize was worth approximately $212,000.

Physics

1980 James W. Cronin, Val L. Fitch, both U.S.
1979 Steven Weinberg, Sheldon L. Glashow, both U.S.; Abdus Salam, Pakistani
1978 Pyotr Kapitsa, USSR; Arno Penzias, Robert Wilson, both U.S.
1977 John H. Van Vleck, Philip W. Anderson, both U.S.; Nevill F. Mott, British
1976 Burton Richter, U.S. Samuel C. C. Ting, U.S.
1975 James Rainwater, U.S. Ben Mottelson, U.S.-Danish; Aage Bohr, Danish
1974 Martin Ryle, British Antony Hewish, British
1973 Ivar Giaever, U.S. Leo Esaki, Japan Brian D. Josephson, British
1972 John Bardeen, U.S. Leon N. Cooper, U.S. John R. Schrieffer, U.S.
1971 Dennis Gabor, British
1970 Louis Neel, French Hannes Alfven, Swedish
1969 Murray Gell-Mann, U.S.
1968 Luis W. Alvarez, U.S.
1967 Hans A. Bethe, U.S.
1966 Alfred Kastler, French
1965 Richard P. Feynman, U.S. Julian S. Schwinger, U.S. Shinichiro Tomonaga, Japanese
1964 Nikolai G. Basov, USSR Aleksander M. Prochorov, USSR Charles H. Townes, U.S.
1963 Maria Goeppert-Mayer, U.S. J. Hans D. Jensen, German Eugene P. Wigner, U.S.

1962 Lev. D. Landau, USSR
1961 Robert Hofstadter, U.S. Rudolf L. Mossbauer, German
1960 Donald A. Glaser, U.S.
1959 Owen Chamberlain, U.S. Emilio G. Segre, U.S.
1958 Pavel Cherenkov, Ilya Frank, Igor Y. Tamm, all USSR
1957 Tsung-dao Lee, Chen Ning Yang, both U.S.
1956 John Bardeen, U.S. Walter H. Brattain, U.S. William Shockley, U.S.
1955 Polykarp Kusch, U.S. Willis E. Lamb, U.S.
1954 Max Born, British Walter Bothe, German
1953 Frits Zernike, Dutch
1952 Felix Bloch, U.S. Edward M. Purcell, U.S.
1951 Sir John D. Cockroft, British Ernest T. S. Walton, Irish
1950 Cecil F. Powell, U.S.
1949 Hideki Yukawa, Japanese
1948 Patrick M. S. Blackett, British
1947 Sir Edward V. Appleton, British
1946 Percy Williams Bridgman, U.S.
1945 Wolfgang Pauli, U.S.
1944 Isidor Isaac Rabi, U.S.
1943 Otto Stern, U.S.
1939 Ernest O. Lawrence, U.S.
1938 Enrico Fermi, U.S.
1937 Clinton J. Davisson, U.S. Sir George P. Thomson, British
1936 Carl D. Anderson, U.S. Victor F. Hess, Austrian
1935 Sir James Chadwick, British
1933 Paul A. M. Dirac, British Erwin Schrodinger, Austrian

1932 Werner Heisenberg, German
1930 Sir Chandrasekhara V. Raman, Indian
1929 Prince Louis-Victor de Broglie, French
1928 Owen W. Richardson, British
1927 Arthur H. Compton, U.S. Charles T. R. Wilson, British
1926 Jean B. Perrin, French
1925 James Franck, Gustav Hertz, both German
1924 Karl M. G. Siegbahn, Swedish
1923 Robert A. Millikan, U.S.
1922 Niels Bohr, Danish
1921 Albert Einstein, Ger.-U.S.
1920 Charles E. Guillaume, French
1919 Johannes Stark, German
1918 Max K. E. L. Planck, German
1917 Charles G. Barkla, British
1915 Sir William H. Bragg, British Sir William L. Bragg, British
1914 Max von Laue, German
1913 Heike Kamerlingh-Onnes, Dutch
1912 Nils G. Dalen, Swedish
1911 Wilhelm Wien, German
1910 Johannes D. van der Waals, Dutch
1909 Carl F. Braun, German Guglielmo Marconi, Italian
1908 Gabriel Lippmann, French
1907 Albert A. Michelson, U.S.
1906 Sir Joseph J. Thomson, British
1905 Philipp E. A. von Lenard, Ger.
1904 John W. Strutt, Lord Rayleigh, British
1903 Antoine Henri Becquerel, Marie and Pierre Curie, all French
1902 Hendrik A. Lorentz, Pieter Zeeman, both Dutch
1901 Wilhelm C. Roentgen, German

Chemistry

1980 Paul Berg, U.S.; Walter Gilbert, U.S.; Frederick Sanger, U.K.
1979 Herbert C. Brown, U.S. George Wittig, German
1978 Peter Mitchell, British
1977 Ilya Prigogine, Belgian
1976 William N. Lipscomb, U.S.
1975 John Cornforth, Austral.-Brit., Vladimir Prelog, Yugo.-Switz.
1974 Paul J. Flory, U.S.
1973 Ernst Otto Fischer, W. German Geoffrey Wilkinson, British
1972 Christian B. Anfinsen, U.S. Stanford Moore, U.S. William H. Stein, U.S.
1971 Gerhard Herzberg, Canadian
1970 Luis F. Leloir, Arg.
1969 Derek H. R. Barton, British Odd Hassel, Norwegian
1968 Lars Onsager, U.S.
1967 Manfred Eigen, German Ronald G. W. Norrish, British George Porter, British
1966 Robert S. Mulliken, U.S.
1965 Robert B. Woodward, U.S.
1964 Dorothy C. Hodgkin, British
1963 Giulio Natta, Italian Karl Ziegler, German
1962 John C. Kendrew, British Max F. Perutz, British
1961 Melvin Calvin, U.S.

1960 Willard F. Libby, U.S.
1959 Jaroslav Heyrovsky, Czech
1958 Frederick Sanger, British
1957 Sir Alexander R. Todd, British
1956 Sir Cyril N. Hinshelwood, British Nikolai N. Semenov, USSR
1955 Vincent du Vigneaud, U.S.
1954 Linus C. Pauling, U.S.
1953 Hermann Staudinger, German
1952 Archer J. P. Martin, British Richard L. M. Synge, British
1951 Edwin M. McMillan, U.S. Glenn T. Seaborg, U.S.
1950 Kurt Alder, German Otto P. H. Diels, German
1949 William F. Giauque, U.S.
1948 Arne W. K. Tiselius, Swedish
1947 Sir Robert Robinson, British
1946 James B. Sumner, John H. Northrop, Wendell M. Stanley, all U.S.
1945 Artturi I. Virtanen, Finnish
1944 Otto Hahn, German
1943 Georg de Hevesy, Hungarian
1939 Adolf F. J. Butenandt, German Leopold Ruzicka, Swiss
1938 Richard Kuhn, German
1937 Walter N. Haworth, British Paul Karrer, Swiss
1936 Peter J. W. Debye, Dutch
1935 Frederic Joliot-Curie, French Irene Joliot-Curie, French

1934 Harold C. Urey, U.S.
1932 Irving Langmuir, U.S.
1931 Friedrich Bergius, German Karl Bosch, German
1930 Hans Fischer, German
1929 Sir Arthur Harden, British Hans von Euler-Chelpin, Swed.
1928 Adolf O. R. Windaus, German
1927 Heinrich O. Wieland, German
1926 Theodor Svedberg, Swedish
1925 Richard A. Zsigmondy, German
1923 Fritz Pregl, Austrian
1922 Francis W. Aston, British
1921 Frederick Soddy, British
1920 Walther H. Nernst, German
1918 Fritz Haber, German
1915 Richard M. Willstatter, German
1914 Theodore W. Richards, U.S.
1913 Alfred Werner, Swiss
1912 Victor Grignard, French Paul Sabatier, French
1911 Marie Curie, French
1910 Otto Wallach, German
1909 Wilhelm Ostwald, German
1908 Ernest Rutherford, British
1907 Eduard Buchner, German
1906 Henri Moissan, French
1905 Adolf von Baeyer, German
1904 Sir William Ramsay, British
1903 Svante A. Arrhenius, Swedish
1902 Emil Fischer, German
1901 Jacobus H. van't Hoff, Dutch

Physiology or Medicine

1980 Baruj Benacerraf, George Snell, both U.S.; Jean Dausset, France

1979 Alian M. Cormack, U.S. Geoffrey N. Hounsfield, British

1978 Daniel Nathans, Hamilton O. Smith, both U.S.; Werner Arber, Swiss

1977 Rosalyn S. Yalow, Roger C.L. Guillemin, Andrew V. Schally, all U.S.
1976 Baruch S. Blumberg, U.S. Daniel Carleton Gajdusek, U.S.
1975 David Baltimore, Howard Temin, both U.S.; Renato Dulbecco, Ital.-U.S.
1974 Albert Claude, Lux.-U.S.; George Emil Palade, Rom.-U.S.; Christian Rene de Duve, Belg.
1973 Karl von Frisch, Ger.; Konrad Lorenz, Ger.-Austrian; Nikolaas Tinbergen, Brit.
1972 Gerald M. Edelman, U.S. Rodney R. Porter, British
1971 Earl W. Sutherland Jr., U.S.
1970 Julius Axelrod, U.S. Sir Bernard Katz, British Ulf von Euler, Swedish
1969 Max Delbruck, Alfred D. Hershey, Salvador Luria, all U.S.
1968 Robert W. Holley, H. Gobind Khorana, Marshall W. Nirenberg, all U.S.
1967 Ragnar Granit, Swedish Haldan Keffer Hartline, U.S. George Wald, U.S.
1966 Charles B. Huggins, Francis Peyton Rous, both U.S.
1965 Francois Jacob, Andre Lwoff, Jacques Monod, all French
1964 Konrad E. Bloch, U.S. Feodor Lynen, German
1963 Sir John C. Eccles, Australian Alan L. Hodgkin, British Andrew F. Huxley, British
1962 Francis H. C. Crick, British James D. Watson, U.S.

Maurice H. F. Wilkins, British
1961 Georg von Bekesy, U.S.
1960 Sir F. MacFarlane Bumet, Australian Peter B. Medawar, British
1959 Arthur Kornberg, U.S. Severo Ochoa, U.S.
1958 George W. Beadle, U.S. Edward L. Tatum, U.S. Joshua Lederberg, U.S.
1957 Daniel Bovet, Italian
1956 Andre F. Cournand, U.S. Werner Forssmann, German Dickinson W. Richards, Jr., U.S.
1955 Alex H. T. Theorell, Swedish
1954 John F. Enders, Frederick C. Robbins, Thomas H. Weller, all U.S.
1953 Hans A. Krebs, British Fritz A. Lipmann, U.S.
1952 Selman A. Waksman, U.S.
1951 Max Theiler, U.S.
1950 Philip S. Hench, Edward C. Kendall, both U.S. Tadeus Reichstein, Swiss
1949 Walter R. Hess, Swiss Antonio Moniz, Portuguese
1948 Paul H. Müller, Swiss
1947 Carl F. Cori, Gerty T. Cori, both U.S. Bernardo A. Houssay, Arg.
1946 Hermann J. Muller, U.S.
1945 Ernst B. Chain, British Sir Alexander Fleming, British Sir Howard W. Florey, British
1944 Joseph Erlanger, U.S. Herbert S. Gasser, U.S.
1943 Henrik C. P. Dam, Danish Edward A. Doisy, U.S.
1939 Gerhard Domagk, German

1938 Corneille J. F. Heymans, Belg.
1937 Albert Szent-Gyorgyi, U.S.
1936 Sir Henry H. Dale, British Otto Loewi, U.S.
1935 Hans Spemann, German
1934 George R. Minot, Wm. P. Murphy, G. H. Whipple, all U.S.
1933 Thomas H. Morgan, U.S.
1932 Edgar D. Adrian, British Sir Charles S. Sherrington, Brit.
1931 Otto H. Warburg, German
1930 Karl Landsteiner, U.S.
1929 Christiaan Eijkman, Dutch Sir Frederick G. Hopkins, British
1928 Charles J. H. Nicolle, French
1927 Julius Wagner-Jauregg, Aus.
1926 Johannes A. G. Fibiger, Danish
1924 Willem Einthoven, Dutch
1923 Frederick G. Banting, Canadian John J. R. Macleod, Scottish
1922 Archibald V. Hill, British Otto F. Meyerhof, German
1920 Schack A. S. Krogh, Danish
1919 Jules Bordet, Belgian
1914 Robert Barany, Austrian
1913 Charles R. Richet, French
1912 Alexis Carrel, French
1911 Allvar Gullstrand, Swedish
1910 Albrecht Kossel, German
1909 Emil T. Kocher, Swiss
1908 Paul Ehrlich, German Elie Metchnikoff, French
1907 Charles L. A. Laveran, French
1906 Camillo Golgi, Italian Santiago Ramon y Cajal, Sp.
1905 Robert Koch, German
1904 Ivan P. Pavlov, Russian
1903 Niels R. Finsen, Danish
1902 Sir Ronald Ross, British
1901 Emil A. von Behring, German

Literature

1980 Czeslaw Milosz, Polish-U.S.
1979 Odysseus Elytis, Greek
1978 Isaac Bashevis Singer, U.S. (Yiddish)
1977 Vicente Aleixandre, Spanish
1976 Saul Bellow, U.S.
1975 Eugenio Montale, Ital.
1974 Eyvind Johnson, Harry Edmund Martinson, both Swedish
1973 Patrick White, Australian
1972 Heinrich Boll, W. German
1971 Pablo Neruda, Chilean
1970 Aleksandr I. Solzhenitsyn, Russ.
1969 Samuel Beckett, Irish
1968 Yasunari Kawabata, Japanese
1967 Miguel Angel Asturias, Guate.
1966 Samuel Joseph Agnon, Israeli Nelly Sachs, Swedish
1965 Mikhail Sholokhov, Russian
1964 Jean Paul Sartre, French (Prize declined)
1963 Giorgos Seferis, Greek
1962 John Steinbeck, U.S.
1961 Ivo Andric, Yugoslavian
1960 Saint-John Perse, French
1959 Salvatore Quasimodo, Italian
1958 Boris L. Pasternak, Russian (Prize declined)

1957 Albert Camus, French
1956 Juan Ramon Jimenez, Puerto Rican-Span.
1955 Halldor K. Laxness, Icelandic
1954 Ernest Hemingway, U.S.
1953 Sir Winston Churchill, British
1952 Francois Mauriac, French
1951 Par F. Lagerkvist, Swedish
1950 Bertrand Russell, British
1949 William Faulkner, U.S.
1947 Andre Gide, French
1946 Hermann Hesse, Swiss
1945 Gabriela Mistral, Chilean
1944 Johannes V. Jensen, Danish
1939 Frans E. Sillanpaa, Finnish
1938 Pearl S. Buck, U.S.
1937 Roger Martin du Gard, French
1936 Eugene O'Neill, U.S.
1934 Luigi Pirandello, Italian
1933 Ivan A. Bunin, French
1932 John Galsworthy, British
1931 Erik A. Karlfeldt, Swedish
1930 Sinclair Lewis, U.S.
1929 Thomas Mann, German
1928 Sigrid Undset, Norwegian
1927 Henri Bergson, French
1926 Grazia Deledda, Italian

1925 George Bernard Shaw, British
1924 Wladyslaw S. Reymont, Polish
1923 William Butler Yeats, Irish
1922 Jacinto Benavente, Spanish
1921 Anatole France, French
1920 Knut Hamsun, Norwegian
1919 Carl F. G. Spitteler, Swiss
1917 Karl A. Gjellerup, Danish Henrik Pontoppidan, Danish
1916 Verner von Heidenstam, Swod.
1915 Romain Rolland, French
1913 Rabindranath Tagore, Indian
1912 Gerhart Hauptmann, German
1911 Maurice Maeterlinck, Belgian
1910 Paul J. L. Heyse, German
1909 Selma Lagerlof, Swedish
1908 Rudolf C. Eucken, German
1907 Rudyard Kipling, British
1906 Giosue Carducci, Italian
1905 Henryk Sienkiewicz, Polish
1904 Frederic Mistral, French Jose Echegaray, Spanish
1903 Bjornsterne Bjornson, Norw.
1902 Theodor Mommsen, German
1901 Rene F. A Sully Prudhomme, French

Peace

1980 Adolfo Perez Esquivel, Argentine
1979 Mother Theresa of Calcutta, Yugoslavian-Indian
1978 Anwar Sadat, Egyptian Menachem Begin, Israeli
1977 Amnesty International
1976 Mairead Corrigan, Betty Williams, N. Irish
1975 Andrei Sakharov, USSR
1974 Eisaku Sato, Japanese, Sean MacBride, Irish
1973 Henry Kissinger, U.S. Le Duc Tho, N. Vietnamese (Tho declined)
1971 Willy Brandt, W. German
1970 Norman E. Borlaug, U.S.

1969 Intl. Labor Organization
1968 Rene Cassin, French
1965 U.N. Children's Fund (UNICEF)
1964 Martin Luther King Jr., U.S.
1963 International Red Cross, League of Red Cross Societies
1962 Linus C. Pauling, U.S.
1961 Dag Hammarskjold, Swedish
1960 Albert J. Luthuli, South African
1959 Philip J. Noel-Baker, British
1958 Georges Pire, Belgian
1957 Lester B. Pearson, Canadian
1954 Office of the UN High Commissioner for Refugees
1953 George C. Marshall, U.S.
1952 Albert Schweitzer, French

1951 Leon Jouhaux, French
1950 Ralph J. Bunche, U.S.
1949 Lord John Boyd Orr of Brechin Mearns, British
1947 Friends Service Council, Brit. Amer. Friends Service Com.
1946 Emily G. Balch, John R. Mott, both U.S.
1945 Cordell Hull, U.S.
1944 International Red Cross
1938 Nansen International Office for Refugees
1937 Viscount Cecil of Chelwood, Brit.
1936 Carlos de Saavedra Lamas, Arg.
1935 Carl von Ossietzky, German
1934 Arthur Henderson, British

1933 Sir Norman Angell, British
1931 Jane Addams, U.S.
    Nicholas Murray Butler, U.S.
1930 Nathan Soderblom, Swedish
1929 Frank B. Kellogg, U.S.
1927 Ferdinand E. Buisson, French
    Ludwig Quidde, German
1926 Aristide Briand, French
    Gustav Stresemann, German
1925 Sir J. Austen Chamberlain, Brit.
    Charles G. Dawes, U.S.
1922 Fridtjof Nansen, Norwegian
1921 Karl H. Branting, Swedish

Christian L. Lange, Norwegian
1920 Leon V.A. Bourgeois, French
1919 Woodrow Wilson, U.S.
1917 International Red Cross
1913 Henri La Fontaine, Belgian
1912 Elihu Root, U.S.
1911 Tobias M.C. Asser, Dutch
    Alfred H. Fried, Austrian
1910 Permanent International Peace
    Bureau
1909 Auguste M. F. Beernaert, Belg.
    Paul H. B. B. d'Estournelles de
    Constant, French

1908 Klas P. Arnoldson, Swedish
    Fredrik Bajer, Danish
1907 Ernesto T. Moneta, Italian
    Louis Renault, French
1906 Theodore Roosevelt, U.S.
1905 Baroness Bertha von Suttner,
    Austrian
1904 Institute of International Law
1903 Sir William R. Cremer, British
1902 Elie Ducommun,
    Charles A. Gobat, both Swiss
1901 Jean H. Dunant, Swiss
    Frederic Passy, French

Nobel Memorial Prize in Economics

1980 Lawrence R. Klein, U.S.
1979 Theodore W. Schultz, U.S.,
    Sir Arthur Lewis, British
1978 Herbert A. Simon, U.S.
1977 Bertil Ohlin, Swedish
    James E. Meade, British
1976 Milton Friedman, U.S.

1975 Tjalling Koopmans, Dutch-U.S.,
    Leonid Kantorovich, USSR
1974 Gunnar Myrdal, Swed.,
    Friedrich A. von Hayek, Austrian
1973 Wassily Leontief, U.S.
1972 Kenneth J. Arrow, U.S.
    John R. Hicks, British

1971 Simon Kuznets, U.S.
1970 Paul A. Samuelson, U.S.
1969 Ragnar Frisch, Norwegian
    Jan Tinbergen, Dutch

Pulitzer Prizes in Journalism, Letters, and Music

The Pulitzer Prizes were endowed by Joseph Pulitzer (1847-1911), publisher of The World, New York, N.Y., in a bequest to Columbia University, New York, N.Y., and are awarded annually by the president of the university on recommendation of the Pulitzer Prize Board for work done during the preceding year. The administrator is Prof. Richard T. Baker of Columbia Univ. All prizes are $1,000 (originally $500) in each category, except Meritorious Public Service for which a gold medal is given.

Journalism

Meritorious Public Service

For distinguished and meritorious public service by a United States newspaper.
1918—New York Times. Also special award to Minna Lewinson and Henry Beetle Hough.
1919—Milwaukee Journal.
1921—Boston Post.
1922—New York World.
1923—Memphis (Tenn.) Commercial Appeal.
1924—New York World.
1926—Enquirer-Sun, Columbus, Ga.
1927—Canton (Oh.) Daily News.
1928—Indianapolis Times.
1929—Evening World, New York.
1931—Atlanta (Ga.) Constitution
1932—Indianapolis (Ind.) News.
1933—New York World-Telegram.
1934—Medford (Ore.) Mail-Tribune.
1935—Sacramento (Cal.) Bee.
1936—Cedar Rapids (Ia.) Gazette.
1937—St. Louis Post-Dispatch.
1938—Bismarck (N.D.) Tribune.
1939—Miami (Fla.) Daily News.
1940—Waterbury (Conn.) Republican and American.
1941—St. Louis Post-Dispatch.
1942—Los Angeles Times.
1943—Omaha World Herald.
1944—New York Times.
1945—Detroit Free Press.
1946—Scranton (Pa.) Times.
1947—Baltimore Sun.
1948—St. Louis Post-Dispatch.
1949—Nebraska State Journal.
1950—Chicago Daily News; St. Louis Post-Dispatch.
1951—Miami (Fla.) Herald and Brooklyn Eagle.
1952—St. Louis Post-Dispatch.
1953—Whiteville (N.C.) News Reporter; Tabor City (N.C.) Tribune.
1954—Newsday (Long Island, N.Y.)
1955—Columbus (Ga.) Ledger and Sunday Ledger-Enquirer.
1956—Watsonville (Cal.) Register-Pajaronian.
1957—Chicago Daily News.
1958—Arkansas Gazette, Little Rock.
1959—Utica (N.Y.) Observer-Dispatch and Utica Daily Press.
1960—Los Angeles Times.
1961—Amarillo (Tex.) Globe-Times.
1962—Panama City (Fla.) News-Herald.
1963—Chicago Daily News.
1964—St. Petersburg (Fla.) Times.
1965—Hutchinson (Kan.) News.
1966—Boston Globe.
1967—The Louisville Courier-Journal; The Milwaukee Journal.
1968—Riverside (Cal.) Press-Enterprise.
1969—Los Angeles Times.
1970—Newsday (Long Island, N.Y.).
1971—Winston Salem (N.C.) Journal & Sentinel.
1972—New York Times.
1973—Washington Post.
1974—Newsday (Long Island, N.Y.).
1975—Boston Globe.
1976—Anchorage Daily News.
1977—Lufkin (Tex.) News.
1978—Philadelphia Inquirer.
1979—Point Reyes (Cal.) Light.

1980—Gannett News Service.
1981—Charlotte (N.C.) Observer.

Reporting

This category originally embraced all fields, local, national, and international. Later separate categories were created for the different fields of reporting.
1917—Herbert Bayard Swope, New York World.
1918—Harold A. Littledale, New York Evening Post.
1920—John J. Leary, Jr., New York World.
1921—Louis Seibold, New York World.
1922—Kirke L. Simpson, Associated Press.
1923—Alva Johnston, New York Times.
1924—Magner White, San Diego Sun.
1925—James W. Mulroy and Alvin H. Goldstein, Chicago Daily News.
1926—William Burke Miller, Louisville Courier-Journal.
1927—John T. Rogers, St. Louis Post-Dispatch.
1929—Paul Y. Anderson, St. Louis Post-Dispatch.
1930—Russell D. Owens, New York Times. Also $500 to W.O. Dapping, Auburn (N.Y.) Citizen.
1931—A.B. MacDonald, Kansas City (Mo.) Star.
1932—W.C. Richards, D.D. Martin, J.S. Pooler, F.D. Webb, J.N.W. Sloan, Detroit Free Press.
1933—Francis A. Jamieson, Associated Press.
1934—Royce Brier, San Francisco Chronicle.
1935—William H. Taylor, New York Herald Tribune.
1936—Lauren D. Lyman, New York Times.
1937—John J. O'Neill, N. Y. Herald Tribune; William L. Laurence, N.Y Times; Howard W. Blakeslee, A. P.; Gobind Behan Lal, University Service; and David Dietz, Scripps-Howard Newspapers.
1938—Raymond Sprigle, Pittsburgh Post-Gazette.
1939—Thomas L. Stokes, Scripps-Howard Newspaper Alliance.
1940—S. Burton Heath, New York World-Telegram.
1941—Westbrook Pegler, New York World-Telegram.
1942—Stanton Delaplane, San Francisco Chronicle.
1943—George Weller, Chicago Daily News.
1944—Paul Schoenstein, N.Y. Journal-American.
1945—Jack S. McDowell, San Francisco Call-Bulletin.
1946—William L. Laurence, New York Times.
1947—Frederick Woltman, N.Y. World-Telegram.
1948—George E. Goodwin, Atlanta Journal.
1949—Malcolm Johnson, New York Sun.
1950—Meyer Berger, New York Times.
1951—Edward S. Montgomery, San Francisco Examiner.
1952—Geo. de Carvalho, San Francisco Chronicle.
    (1) General or Spot; (2) Special or Investigative
1953—(1) Providence (R.I.) Journal and Evening Bulletin; (2) Edward J. Mowery, N.Y. World-Telegram & Sun.
1954—(1) Vicksburg (Miss.) Sunday Post-Herald; (2) Alvin Scott McCoy, Kansas City (Mo.) Star.
1955—(1) Mrs. Caro Brown, Alice (Tex.) Daily Echo; (2) Roland K. Towery, Cuero (Tex.) Record.
1956—(1) Lee Hills, Detroit Free Press; (2) Arthur Daley, New York Times.
1957—(1) Salt Lake Tribune, Salt Lake City, Ut.; (2) Wallace Turner and William Lambert, Portland Oregonian.
1958—(1) Fargo, (N.D.) Forum; (2) George Beveridge, Evening Star, Washington, D.C.
1959—(1) Mary Lou Werner, Washington Evening Star; (2) John Harold Brislin, Scranton (Pa.) Tribune, and The Scrantonian.
1960—(1) Jack Nelson, Atlanta Constitution; (2) Miriam Ottenberg, Washington Evening Star.
1961—(1) Sanche de Gramont, N.Y. Herald Tribune; (2) Edgar May,

Buffalo Evening News.

1962—(1) Robert D. Mullins, Deseret News, Salt Lake City; (2) George Bliss, Chicago Tribune.

1963—(1) Shared by Sylvan Fox, William Longgood, and Anthony Shannon, N.Y. World-Telegram & Sun; (2) Oscar Griffin, Jr., Pecos (Tex.) Independent and Enterprise.

(1) General Reporting; (2) Special Reporting.

1964—(1) Norman C. Miller, Wall Street Journal; (2) Shared by James V. Magee, Albert V. Gaudiosi, and Frederick A. Meyer, Philadelphia Bulletin.

1965—(1) Melvin H. Ruder, Hungry Horse News (Columbia Falls, Mon.); (2) Gene Goltz, Houston Post.

1966—(1) Los Angeles Times Staff; (2) John A. Frasca, Tampa (Fla.) Tribune.

1967—(1) Robert V. Cox, Chambersburg (Pa.) Public Opinion; (2) Gene Miller, Miami Herald.

1968—Detroit Free Press Staff; (2) J. Anthony Lukas, N.Y. Times.

1969—(1) John Fetterman, Louisville Courier-Journal and Times; (2) Albert L. Delugach, St. Louis Globe Democrat, and Denny Walsh, Life.

1970—(1) Thomas Fitzpatrick, Chicago Sun-Times; (2) Harold Eugene Martin, Montgomery Advertiser & Alabama Journal.

1971—(1) Akron Beacon Journal Staff, (2) William Hugh Jones, Chicago Tribune.

1972—(1) Richard Cooper and John Machacek, Rochester Times-Union; (2) Timothy Leland, Gerard M. O'Neill, Stephen Kurkjian and Anne De Santis, Boston Globe.

1973—(1) Chicago Tribune; (2) Sun Newspapers of Omaha.

1974—(1) Hugh F. Hough, Arthur M. Petacque, Chicago Sun-Times; (2) William Sherman, N.Y. Daily News.

1975—(1) Xenia (Oh.) Daily Gazette; (2) Indianapolis Star.

1976—(1) Gene Miller, Miami Herald; (2) Chicago Tribune.

1977—(1) Margo Huston, Milwaukee Journal; (2) Acel Moore, Wendell Rawls Jr., Philadelphia Inquirer.

1978—(1) Richard Whitt, Louisville Courier-Journal; (2) Anthony R. Dolan, Stamford (Conn.) Advocate.

1979—(1) San Diego (Cal.) Evening Tribune; (2) Gilbert M. Gaul, Elliot G. Jaspin, Pottsville (Pa.) Republican.

1980—(1) Philadelphia Inquirer; (2) Stephen A. Korkjian, Alexander B. Hawes Jr., Nils Bruzelius, Joan Vennochi, Boston Globe.

1981—(1) Longview (Wash.) Daily News staff; (2) Clark Hallas and Robert B. Lowe, Arizona Daily Star.

Criticism or Commentary

(1) Criticism; (2) Commentary

1970—(1) Ada Louise Huxtable, N.Y. Times; (2) Marquis W. Childs, St. Louis Post-Dispatch.

1971—(1) Harold C. Schonberg, N.Y. Times; (2) William A. Caldwell, The Record, Hackensack, N.J.

1972—(1) Frank Peters Jr., St. Louis Post-Dispatch; (2) Mike Royko, Chicago Daily News.

1973—(1) Ronald Powers, Chicago Sun-Times; (2) David S. Broder, Washington Post.

1974—(1) Emily Genauer, Newsday, (N.Y.); (2) Edwin A. Roberts, Jr., National Observer.

1975—(1) Roger Ebert, Chicago Sun Times; (2) Mary McGrory, Washington Star.

1976—(1) Alan M. Kriegsman, Washington Post; (2) Walter W. (Red) Smith, N.Y. Times.

1977—(1) William McPherson, Washington Post; (2) George F. Will, Wash. Post Writers Group.

1978—(1) Walter Kerr, New York Times; (2) William Safire, New York Times.

1979—(1) Paul Gapp, Chicago Tribune; (2) Russell Baker, New York Times.

1980—(1) William A. Henry III, Boston Globe; (2) Ellen Goodman, Boston Globe.

1981—(1) Jonathan Yardley, Washington Star; (2) Dave Anderson, New York Times.

National Reporting

1942—Louis Stark, New York Times.

1944—Dewey L. Fleming, Baltimore Sun.

1945—James B. Reston, New York Times.

1946—Edward A. Harris, St. Louis Post-Dispatch.

1947—Edward T. Folliard, Washington Post.

1948—Bert Andrews, New York Herald Tribune; Nat S. Finney, Minneapolis Tribune.

1949—Charles P. Trussell, New York Times.

1950—Edwin O. Guthman, Seattle Times.

1952—Anthony Leviero, New York Times.

1953—Don Whitehead, Associated Press.

1954—Richard Wilson, Cowles Newspapers.

1955—Anthony Lewis, Washington Daily News.

1956—Charles L. Bartlett, Chattanooga Times.

1957—James Reston, New York Times.

1958—Relman Morin, AP; Clark Mollenhoff, Des Moines Register & Tribune.

1959—Howard Van Smith, Miami (Fla.) News.

1960—Vance Trimble, Scripps-Howard, Washington, D.C.

1961—Edward R. Cony, Wall Street Journal.

1962—Nathan G. Caldwell and Gene S. Graham, Nashville Tennessean.

1963—Anthony Lewis, New York Times.

1964—Merriman Smith, UPI.

1965—Louis M. Kohlmeier, Wall Street Journal.

1966—Haynes Johnson, Washington Evening Star.

1967—Monroe Karmin and Stanley Penn, Wall Street Journal.

1968—Howard James, Christian Science Monitor; Nathan K. Kotz, Des Moines Register.

1969—Robert Cahn, Christian Science Monitor.

1970—William J. Eaton, Chicago Daily News.

1971—Lucinda Franks & Thomas Powers, UPI.

1972—Jack Anderson, United Features.

1973—Robert Boyd and Clark Hoyt, Knight Newspapers.

1974—James R. Polk, Washington Star-News; Jack White, Providence Journal-Bulletin.

1975—Donald L. Barlett and James B. Steele, Philadelphia Inquirer.

1976—James Risser, Des Moines Register.

1977—Walter Mears, Associated Press.

1978—Gaylord D. Shaw, Los Angeles Times.

1979—James Risser, Des Moines Register.

1980—Charles Stafford, Bette Swenson Orsini, St. Petersburg (Fla.) Times.

1981—John M. Crewdson, New York Times.

International Reporting

1942—Laurence Edmund Allen, Associated Press.

1943—Ira Wolfert, No. Am. Newspaper Alliance.

1944—Daniel DeLuce, Associated Press.

1945—Mark S. Watson, Baltimore Sun.

1946—Homer W. Bigart, New York Herald Tribune.

1947—Eddy Gilmore, Associated Press.

1948—Paul W. Ward, Baltimore Sun.

1949—Price Day, Baltimore Sun.

1950—Edmund Stevens, Christian Science Monitor.

1951—Keyes Beech and Fred Sparks, Chicago Daily News; Homer Bigart and Marguerite Higgins, New York Herald Tribune; Relman Morin and Don Whitehead, AP.

1952—John M. Hightower, Associated Press.

1953—Austin C. Wehrwein, Milwaukee Journal.

1954—Jim G. Lucas, Scripps-Howard Newspapers.

1955—Harrison Salisbury, New York Times.

1956—William Randolph Hearst, Jr., Frank Conniff, Hearst Newspapers; Kingsbury Smith, INS.

1957—Russell Jones, United Press.

1958—New York Times.

1959—Joseph Martin and Philip Santora, N.Y. News.

1960—A.M. Rosenthal, New York Times.

1961—Lynn Heinzerling, Associated Press.

1962—Walter Lippmann, N.Y. Herald Tribune Synd.

1963—Hal Hendrix, Miami (Fla.) News.

1964—Malcolm W. Browne, AP; David Halberstam, N.Y. Times.

1965—J.A. Livingston, Philadelphia Bulletin.

1966—Peter Arnett, AP.

1967—R. John Hughes, Christian Science Monitor.

1968—Alfred Friendly, Washington Post.

1969—William Tuohy, L.A. Times.

1970—Seymour M. Hersh, Dispatch News Service.

1971—Jimmie Lee Hoagland, Washington Post.

1972—Peter R. Kann, Wall Street Journal.

1973—Max Frankel, N.Y. Times.

1974—Hedrick Smith, N.Y. Times.

1975—William Mullen and Ovie Carter, Chicago Tribune.

1976—Sydney H. Schanberg, N.Y. Times.

1978—Henry Kamm, N.Y. Times.

1979—Richard Ben Cramer, Philadelphia Inquirer.

1980—Joel Brinkley, Jay Mather, Louisville (Ky.) Courier-Journal.

1981—Shirley Christian, Miami Herald.

Correspondence

For Washington or foreign correspondence. Category was merged with those in national and international reporting in 1948.

1929—Paul Scott Mowrer, Chicago Daily News.

1930—Leland Stowe, New York Herald Tribune.

1931—H.R. Knickerbocker, Philadelphia Public Ledger and New York Evening Post.

1932—Walter Duranty, New York Times, and Charles G. Ross, St. Louis Post-Dispatch.

1933—Edgar Ansel Mowrer, Chicago Daily News.

1934—Frederick T. Birchall, New York Times.

1935—Arthur Krock, New York Times.

1936—Wilfred C. Barber, Chicago Tribune.

1937—Anne O'Hare McCormick, New York Times.

1938—Arthur Krock, New York Times.

1939—Louis P. Lochner, Associated Press.

1940—Otto D. Tolischus, New York Times.

1941—Bronze plaque to commemorate work of American correspondents on war fronts.

1942—Carlos P. Romulo, Philippines Herald.

1943—Hanson W. Baldwin, New York Times.

1944—Ernest Taylor Pyle, Scripps-Howard Newspaper Alliance.

1945—Harold V. (Hal) Boyle, Associated Press.

1946—Arnaldo Cortesi, New York Times.

1947—Brooks Atkinson, New York Times.

Editorial Writing

1917—New York Tribune.

1918—Louisville (Ky.) Courier-Journal.

1920—Harvey E. Newbranch, Omaha Evening World-Herald.

1922—Frank M. O'Brien, New York Herald.

1923—William Allen White, Emporia Gazette.

1924—Frank Buxton, Boston Herald, Special Prize. Frank I. Cobb, New York World.

1925—Robert Lathan, Charleston (S.C.) News and Courier.

1926—Edward M. Kingsbury, N. Y. Times.

1927—F. Lauriston Bullard, Boston Herald.

1928—Grover C. Hall, Montgomery Advertiser.

1929—Louis Isaac Jaffe, Norfolk Virginian-Pilot.

1931—Chas. Ryckman, Fremont (Neb.) Tribune.

1933—Kansas City (Mo.) Star

1934—E. P. Chase, Atlantic (Ia.) News Telegraph.

1936—Felix Morley, Washington Post. George B. Parker, Scripps-Howard Newspapers.

1937—John W. Owens, Baltimore Sun.
1938—W.W. Waymack, Des Moines (Ia.) Register and Tribune.
1939—Ronald G. Callvert, Portland Oregonian.
1940—Bart Howard, St. Louis Post-Dispatch.
1941—Reuben Maury, Daily News, N.Y.
1942—Geoffrey Parsons, New York Herald Tribune.
1943—Forrest W. Seymour, Des Moines (Ia.) Register and Tribune.
1944—Henry J. Haskell, Kansas City (Mo.) Star.
1945—George W. Potter, Providence (R.I.) Journal-Bulletin.
1946—Hodding Carter, Greenville (Miss.) Delta Democrat-Times.
1947—William H. Grimes, Wall Street Journal.
1948—Virginius Dabney, Richmond (Va.) Times-Dispatch.
1949—John H. Crider, Boston (Mass.) Herald, Herbert Elliston, Washington Post.
1950—Carl M. Saunders, Jackson (Mich.) Citizen-Patriot.
1951—William H. Fitzpatrick, New Orleans States.
1952—Louis LaCoss, St. Louis Globe Democrat.
1953—Vermont C. Royster, Wall Street Journal.
1954—Don Murray, Boston Herald.
1955—Royce Howes, Detroit Free Press.
1956—Lauren K. Soth, Des Moines (Ia.) Register and Tribune.
1957—Buford Boone, Tuscaloosa (Ala.) News.
1958—Harry S. Ashmore, Arkansas Gazette.
1959—Ralph McGill, Atlanta Constitution.
1960—Lenoir Chambers, Norfolk Virginian-Pilot.
1961—William J. Dorvillier, San Juan (Puerto Rico) Star.
1962—Thomas M. Storke, Santa Barbara (Cal.) News-Press.
1963—Ira B. Harkey, Jr., Pascagoula (Miss.) Chronicle.
1964—Hazel Brannon Smith, Lexington (Miss.) Advertiser.
1965—John R. Harrison, The Gainesville (Fla.) Sun.
1966—Robert Lasch, St. Louis Post-Dispatch.
1967—Eugene C. Patterson, Atlanta Constitution.
1968—John S. Knight, Knight Newspapers.
1969—Paul Greenberg, Pine Bluff (Ark.) Commercial.
1970—Philip L. Geyelin, Washington Post.
1971—Horance G. Davis, Jr., Gainesville (Fla.) Sun.
1972—John Strohmeyer, Bethlehem (Pa.) Globe-Times.
1973—Roger B. Linscott, Berkshire Eagle, Pittsfield, Mass.
1974—F. Gilman Spencer, Trenton (N.J.) Trentonian.
1975—John D. Maurice, Charleston (W. Va.) Daily Mail.
1976—Philip Kerby, Los Angeles Times.
1977—Warren L. Lerude, Foster Church, and Norman F. Cardoza, Reno (Nev.) Evening Gazette and Nevada State Journal.
1978—Meg Greenfield, Washington Post.
1979—Edwin M. Yoder, Washington Star.
1980—Robert L. Bartley, Wall Street Journal.

Editorial Cartooning

1922—Rollin Kirby, New York World.
1924—Jay N. Darling, New York Herald Tribune.
1925—Rollin Kirby, New York World.
1926—D. R. Fitzpatrick, St. Louis Post-Dispatch.
1927—Nelson Harding, Brooklyn Eagle.
1928—Nelson Harding, Brooklyn Eagle.
1929—Rollin Kirby, New York World.
1930—Charles Macauley, Brooklyn Eagle.
1931—Edmund Duffy, Baltimore Sun.
1932—John T. McCutcheon, Chicago Tribune.
1933—H. M. Talburt, Washington Daily News.
1934—Edmund Duffy, Baltimore Sun.
1935—Ross A. Lewis, Milwaukee Journal.
1937—C. D. Batchelor, New York Daily News.
1938—Vaughn Shoemaker, Chicago Daily News.
1939—Charles G. Werner, Daily Oklahoman.
1940—Edmund Duffy, Baltimore Sun.
1941—Jacob Burck, Chicago Times.
1942—Herbert L. Block, Newspaper Enterprise Assn.
1943—Jay N. Darling, New York Herald Tribune.
1944—Clifford K. Berryman, Washington Star.
1945—Bill Mauldin, United Feature Syndicate.
1946—Bruce Alexander Russell, Los Angeles Times.
1947—Vaughn Shoemaker, Chicago Daily News.
1948—Reuben L. (Rube) Goldberg, N. Y. Sun.
1949—Lute Pease, Newark (N.J.) Evening News.
1950—James T. Berryman, Washington Star.
1951—Reginald W. Manning, Arizona Republic.
1952—Fred L. Packer, New York Mirror.
1953—Edward D. Kuekes, Cleveland Plain Dealer.
1954—Herbert L. Block, Washington Post & Times-Herald.
1955—Daniel R. Fitzpatrick, St. Louis Post-Dispatch.
1956—Robert York, Louisville (Ky.) Times.
1957—Tom Little, Nashville Tennessean.
1958—Bruce M. Shanks, Buffalo Evening News.
1959—Bill Mauldin, St. Louis Post-Dispatch.
1961—Carey Orr, Chicago Tribune.
1962—Edmund S. Valtman, Hartford Times.
1963—Frank Miller, Des Moines Register.
1964—Paul Conrad, Denver Post.
1966—Don Wright, Miami News.
1967—Patrick B. Oliphant, Denver Post.
1968—Eugene Gray Payne, Charlotte Observer.
1969—John Fischetti, Chicago Daily News.
1970—Thomas F. Darcy, Newsday.
1971—Paul Conrad, L. A. Times.
1972—Jeffrey K. MacNelly, Richmond News-Leader.
1974—Paul Szep, Boston Globe.
1975—Garry Trudeau, Universal Press Syndicate.
1976—Tony Auth, Philadelphia Inquirer.
1977—Paul Szep, Boston Globe.

1978—Jeffrey K. MacNelly, Richmond News Leader.
1979—Herbert L. Block, Washington Post.
1980—Don Wright, Miami (Fla.) News.
1981—Mike Peters, Dayton (Oh.) Daily News.

Spot News Photography

1942—Milton Brooks, Detroit News.
1943—Frank Noel, Associated Press.
1944—Frank Filan, AP; Earl L. Bunker, Omaha World-Herald.
1945—Joe Rosenthal, Associated Press, for photograph of planting American flag on Iwo Jima.
1947—Arnold Hardy, amateur, Atlanta, Ga.
1948—Frank Cushing, Boston Traveler.
1949—Nathaniel Fein, New York Herald Tribune.
1950—Bill Crouch, Oakland (Cal.) Tribune.
1951—Max Desfor, Associated Press.
1952—John Robinson and Don Ultang, Des Moines Register and Tribune.
1953—William M. Gallagher, Flint (Mich.) Journal.
1954—Mrs. Walter M. Schau, amateur.
1955—John L. Gaunt, Jr., Los Angeles Times.
1956—New York Daily News.
1957—Harry A. Trask, Boston Traveler.
1958—William C. Beall, Washington Daily News.
1959—William Seaman, Minneapolis Star.
1960—Andrew Lopez, UPI.
1961—Yasushi Nagao, Mainichi Newspapers, Tokyo.
1962—Paul Vathis, Associated Press.
1963—Hector Rondon, La Republica, Caracas, Venezuela.
1964—Robert H. Jackson, Dallas Times-Herald.
1965—Horst Faas, Associated Press.
1966—Kyoichi Sawada, UPI.
1967—Jack R. Thornell, Associated Press.
1968—Rocco Morabito, Jacksonville Journal.
1969—Edward Adams, AP.
1970—Steve Starr, AP.
1971—John Paul Filo, Valley Daily News & Daily Dispatch of Tarentum & New Kensington, Pa.
1972—Horst Faas and Michel Laurent, AP.
1973—Huynh Cong Ut, AP.
1974—Anthony K. Roberts, AP.
1975—Gerald H. Gay, Seattle Times.
1976—Stanley Forman, Boston Herald American.
1977—Neal Ulevich, Associated Press; Stanley Forman, Boston Herald American.
1978—Jim Schweiker, UPI.
1979—Thomas J. Kelly III, Pottstown (Pa.) Mercury.
1980—UPI.
1981—Larry C. Price, Ft. Worth (Tex.) Star-Telegram.

Feature Photography

1968—Toshio Sakai, UPI.
1969—Moneta Sleet Jr., Ebony.
1970—Dallas Kinney, Palm Beach Post.
1971—Jack Dykinga, Chicago Sun-Times.
1972—Dave Kennerly, UPI.
1973—Brian Lanker, Topeka Capitol-Journal.
1974—Slava Veder, AP.
1975—Matthew Lewis, Washington Post.
1976—Louisville Courier-Journal and Louisville Times.
1977—Robin Hood, Chattanooga News-Free Press.
1978—J. Ross Baughman, AP.
1979—Staff Photographers, Boston Herald American.
1980—Erwin H. Hagler, Dallas Times-Herald.
1981—Taro M. Yamasaki, Detroit Free Press.

Special Citation

1938—Edmonton (Alberta) Journal, bronze plaque.
1941—New York Times.
1944—Byron Price and Mrs. William Allen White. Also to Richard Rodgers and Oscar Hammerstein 2d, for musical, Oklahoma!
1945—Press cartographers for war maps.
1947—(Pulitzer centennial year.) Columbia Univ. and the Graduate School of Journalism, and St. Louis Post-Dispatch.
1948—Dr. Frank Diehl Fackenthal.
1951—Cyrus L. Sulzberger, New York Times.
1952—Max Kase, New York Journal-American.
1953—The New York Times; Lester Markel.
1957—Kenneth Roberts, for his historical novels.
1958—Walter Lippmann, New York Herald Tribune.
1960—Garrett Mattingly, for The Armada.
1961—American Heritage Picture History of the Civil War.
1964—The Gannett Newspapers.
1973—James T. Flexner, for "George Washington," a four-volume biography.
1976—John Hohenberg, for services to American journalism.
1977—Alex Haley, for Roots, $1,000.
1978—Richard Lee Strout, Christian Science Monitor and New Republic.
    —E.B. White, for his work.

Feature Writing

Category was inaugurated in 1979.
1979—Jon D. Franklin, Baltimore Evening Sun.
1980—Madeleine Blais, Miami Herald Tropic Magazine.
1981—Teresa Carpenter, Village Voice, New York City.

Letters

Fiction

For fiction in book form by an American author, preferably dealing with American life.

1918—Ernest Poole, His Family.
1919—Booth Tarkington, The Magnificent Ambersons.
1921—Edith Wharton, The Age of Innocence.
1922—Booth Tarkington, Alice Adams.
1923—Willa Cather, One of Ours.
1924—Margaret Wilson, The Able McLaughlins.
1925—Edna Ferber, So Big.
1926—Sinclair Lewis, Arrowsmith. (Refused prize.)
1927—Louis Bromfield, Early Autumn.
1928—Thornton Wilder, Bridge of San Luis Rey.
1929—Julia M. Peterkin, Scarlet Sister Mary.
1930—Oliver LaFarge, Laughing Boy.
1931—Margaret Ayer Barnes, Years of Grace.
1932—Pearl S. Buck, The Good Earth.
1933—T. S. Stribling, The Store.
1934—Caroline Miller, Lamb in His Bosom.
1935—Josephine W. Johnson, Now in November.
1936—Harold L. Davis, Honey in the Horn.
1937—Margaret Mitchell, Gone with the Wind.
1938—John P. Marquand, The Late George Apley.
1939—Marjorie Kinnan Rawlings, The Yearling.
1940—John Steinbeck, The Grapes of Wrath.
1942—Ellen Glasgow, In This Our Life.
1943—Upton Sinclair, Dragon's Teeth.
1944—Martin Flavin, Journey in the Dark.
1945—John Hersey, A Bell for Adano.
1947—Robert Penn Warren, All the King's Men.
1948—James A Michener, Tales of the South Pacific.
1949—James Gould Cozzens, Guard of Honor.
1950—A. B. Guthrie Jr., The Way West.
1951—Conrad Richter, The Town.
1952—Herman Wouk, The Caine Mutiny.
1953—Ernest Hemingway, The Old Man and the Sea.
1955—William Faulkner, A Fable.
1956—MacKinlay Kantor, Andersonville.
1958—James Agee, A Death in the Family.
1959—Robert Lewis Taylor, The Travels of Jaimie McPheeters.
1960—Allen Drury, Advise and Consent.
1961—Harper Lee, To Kill a Mockingbird.
1962—Edwin O'Connor, The Edge of Sadness.
1963—William Faulkner, The Reivers.
1965—Shirley Ann Grau, The Keepers of the House.
1966—Katherine Anne Porter, Collected Stories of Katherine Anne Porter.
1967—Bernard Malamud, The Fixer.
1968—William Styron, The Confessions of Nat Turner.
1969—N. Scott Momaday, House Made of Dawn.
1970—Jean Stafford, Collected Stories.
1972—Wallace Stegner, Angle of Repose.
1973—Eudora Welty, The Optimist's Daughter.
1975—Michael Shaara, The Killer Angels.
1976—Saul Bellow, Humboldt's Gift.
1978—James Alan McPherson, Elbow Room.
1979—John Cheever, The Stories of John Cheever.
1980—Norman Mailer, The Executioner's Song.
1981—John Kennedy Toole, A Confederacy of Dunces.

Drama

For an American play, preferably original and dealing with American life.

1918—Jesse Lynch Williams, Why Marry?
1920—Eugene O'Neill, Beyond the Horizon.
1921—Zona Gale, Miss Lulu Bett.
1922—Eugene O'Neill, Anna Christie.
1923—Owen Davis, Icebound.
1924—Hatcher Hughes, Hell-Bent for Heaven.
1925—Sidney Howard, They Knew What They Wanted.
1926—George Kelly, Craig's Wife.
1927—Paul Green, In Abraham's Bosom.
1928—Eugene O'Neill, Strange Interlude.
1929—Elmer Rice, Street Scene.
1930—Marc Connelly, The Green Pastures.
1931—Susan Glaspell, Alison's House.
1932—George S. Kaufman, Morrie Ryskind and Ira Gershwin, Of Thee I Sing.
1933—Maxwell Anderson, Both Your Houses.
1934—Sidney Kingsley, Men in White.
1935—Zoe Akins, The Old Maid.
1936—Robert E. Sherwood, Idiot's Delight.
1937—George S. Kaufman and Moss Hart, You Can't Take It With You.
1938—Thornton Wilder, Our Town.
1939—Robert E. Sherwood, Abe Lincoln in Illinois.
1940—William Saroyan, The Time of Your Life.
1941—Robert E. Sherwood, There Shall Be No Night.
1943—Thornton Wilder, The Skin of Our Teeth.
1945—Mary Chase, Harvey.
1946—Russel Crouse and Howard Lindsay, State of the Union.
1948—Tennessee Williams, A Streetcar Named Desire.

1949—Arthur Miller, Death of a Salesman.
1950—Richard Rodgers, Oscar Hammerstein 2d, and Joshua Logan, South Pacific.
1952—Joseph Kramm, The Shrike.
1953—William Inge, Picnic.
1954—John Patrick, Teahouse of the August Moon.
1955—Tennessee Williams, Cat on a Hot Tin Roof.
1956—Frances Goodrich and Albert Hackett, The Diary of Anne Frank.
1957—Eugene O'Neill, Long Day's Journey Into Night.
1958—Ketti Frings, Look Homeward, Angel.
1959—Archibald MacLeish, J. B.
1960—George Abbott, Jerome Weidman, Sheldon Harnick and Jerry Bock, Fiorello.
1961—Tad Mosel, All the Way Home.
1962—Frank Loesser and Abe Burrows, How To Succeed In Business Without Really Trying.
1965—Frank D. Gilroy, The Subject Was Roses.
1967—Edward Albee, A Delicate Balance.
1969—Howard Sackler, The Great White Hope.
1970—Charles Gordone, No Place to be Somebody.
1971—Paul Zindel, The Effect of Gamma Rays on Man-in-the-Moon Marigolds.
1973—Jason Miller, That Championship Season.
1975—Edward Albee, Seascape.
1976—Michael Bennett, James Kirkwood, Nicholas Dante, Marvin Hamlisch, Edward Kleban, A Chorus Line.
1977—Michael Cristofer, The Shadow Box.
1978—Donald L. Coburn, The Gin Game.
1979—Sam Shepard, Buried Child.
1980—Lanford Wilson, Talley's Folly.
1981—Beth Henley, Crimes of the Heart.

History

For a book on the history of the United States.

1917—J. J. Jusserand, With Americans of Past and Present Days.
1918—James Ford Rhodes, History of the Civil War.
1920—Justin H. Smith, The War with Mexico.
1921—William Sowden Sims, The Victory at Sea.
1922—James Truslow Adams, The Founding of New England.
1923—Charles Warren, The Supreme Court in United States History.
1924—Charles Howard McIlwain, The American Revolution: A Constitutional Interpretation.
1925—Frederick L. Paxton, A History of the American Frontier.
1926—Edward Channing, A History of the U.S.
1927—Samuel Flagg Bemis, Pinckney's Treaty.
1928—Vernon Louis Parrington, Main Currents in American Thought.
1929—Fred A. Shannon, The Organization and Administration of the Union Army, 1861-65.
1930—Claude H. Van Tyne, The War of Independence.
1931—Bernadotte E. Schmitt, The Coming of the War, 1914.
1932—Gen. John J. Pershing, My Experiences in the World War.
1933—Frederick J. Turner, The Significance of Sections in American History.
1934—Herbert Agar, The People's Choice.
1935—Charles McLean Andrews, The Colonial Period of American History.
1936—Andrew C. McLaughlin, The Constitutional History of the United States.
1937—Van Wyck Brooks, The Flowering of New England.
1938—Paul Herman Buck, The Road to Reunion, 1865-1900.
1939—Frank Luther Mott, A History of American Magazines.
1940—Carl Sandburg, Abraham Lincoln: The War Years.
1941—Marcus Lee Hansen, The Atlantic Migration, 1607-1860.
1942—Margaret Leech, Reveille in Washington.
1943—Esther Forbes, Paul Revere and the World He Lived In.
1944—Merle Curti, The Growth of American Thought.
1945—Stephen Bonsal, Unfinished Business.
1946—Arthur M. Schlesinger Jr., The Age of Jackson.
1947—James Phinney Baxter 3d, Scientists Against Time.
1948—Bernard De Voto, Across the Wide Missouri.
1949—Roy F. Nichols, The Disruption of American Democracy.
1950—O. W. Larkin, Art and Life in America.
1951—R. Carlyle Buley, The Old Northwest: Pioneer Period 1815-1840.
1952—Oscar Handlin, The Uprooted.
1953—George Dangerfield, The Era of Good Feelings.
1954—Bruce Catton, A Stillness at Appomattox.
1955—Paul Horgan, Great River: The Rio Grande in North American History.
1956—Richard Hofstadter, The Age of Reform.
1957—George F. Kennan, Russia Leaves the War.
1958—Bray Hammond, Banks and Politics in America—From the Revolution to the Civil War.
1959—Leonard D. White and Jean Schneider, The Republican Era; 1869-1901.
1960—Margaret Leech, In the Days of McKinley.
1961—Herbert Feis, Between War and Peace: The Potsdam Conference.
1962—Lawrence H. Gibson, The Triumphant Empire: Thunderclouds Gather in the West.
1963—Constance McLaughlin Green, Washington: Village and Capital, 1800-1878.
1964—Sumner Chilton Powell, Puritan Village: The Formation of A New England Town.
1965—Irwin Unger, The Greenback Era.

1966—Perry Miller, Life of the Mind in America.
1967—William H. Goetzmann, Exploration and Empire: the Explorer and Scientist in the Winning of the American West.
1968—Bernard Bailyn, The Ideological Origins of the American Revolution.
1969—Leonard W. Levy, Origin of the Fifth Amendment.
1970—Dean Acheson, Present at the Creation: My Years in the State Department.
1971—James McGregor Burns, Roosevelt: The Soldier of Freedom.
1972—Carl N. Degler, Neither Black Nor White.
1973—Michael Kammen, People of Paradox: An Inquiry Concerning the Origins of American Civilization.
1974—Daniel J. Boorstin, The Americans: The Democratic Experience.
1975—Dumas Malone, Jefferson and His Time.
1976—Paul Horgan, Lamy of Santa Fe.
1977—David M. Potter, The Impending Crisis.
1978—Alfred D. Chandler, Jr., The Visible Hand: The Managerial Revolution in American Business.
1979—Don E. Fehrenbacher, The Dred Scott Case: Its Significance in American Law and Politics.
1980—Leon F. Litwack, Been in the Storm So Long.
1981—Lawrence A. Cremin, American Education: The National Experience, 1783-1876.

Biography or Autobiography

For a distinguished biography or autobiography by an American author, preferably on an American subject.

1917—Laura E. Richards and Maude Howe Elliott, assisted by Florence Howe Hall, Julia Ward Howe.
1918—William Cabell Bruce, Benjamin Franklin, Self-Revealed.
1919—Henry Adams, The Education of Henry Adams.
1920—Albert J. Beveridge, The Life of John Marshall.
1921—Edward Bok, The Americanization of Edward Bok.
1922—Hamlin Garland, A Daughter of the Middle Border.
1923—Burton J. Hendrick, The Life and Letters of Walter H. Page.
1924—Michael Pupin, From Immigrant to Inventor.
1925—M. A. DeWolfe Howe, Barrett Wendell and His Letters.
1926—Harvey Cushing, Life of Sir William Osler.
1927—Emory Holloway, Whitman: An Interpretation in Narrative.
1928—Charles Edward Russell, The American Orchestra and Theodore Thomas.
1929—Burton J. Hendrick, The Training of an American: The Earlier Life and Letters of Walter H. Page.
1930—Marquis James, The Raven (Sam Houston).
1931—Henry James, Charles W. Eliot.
1932—Henry F. Pringle, Theodore Roosevelt.
1933—Allan Nevins, Grover Cleveland.
1934—Tyler Dennett, John Hay.
1935—Douglas Southall Freeman, R. E. Lee
1936—Ralph Barton Perry, The Thought and Character of William James.
1937—Allan Nevins, Hamilton Fish: The Inner History of the Grant Administration.
1938—Divided between Odell Shepard, Pedlar's Progress; Marquis James, Andrew Jackson.
1939—Carl Van Doren, Benjamin Franklin.
1940—Ray Stannard Baker, Woodrow Wilson, Life and Letters.
1941—Ola Elizabeth Winslow, Jonathan Edwards.
1942—Forrest Wilson, Crusader in Crinoline.
1943—Samuel Eliot Morison, Admiral of the Ocean Sea (Columbus).
1944—Carleton Mabee, The American Leonardo: The Life of Samuel F. B. Morse.
1945—Russell Blaine Nye, George Bancroft; Brahmin Rebel.
1946—Linny Marsh Wolfe, Son of the Wilderness.
1947—William Allen White, The Autobiography of William Allen White.
1948—Margaret Clapp, Forgotten First Citizen: John Bigelow.
1949—Robert E. Sherwood, Roosevelt and Hopkins.
1950—Samuel Flag Bemis, John Quincy Adams and the Foundations of American Foreign Policy.
1951—Margaret Louise Coit, John C. Calhoun: American Portrait.
1952—Merlo J. Pusey, Charles Evans Hughes.
1953—David J. Mays, Edmund Pendleton, 1721-1803.
1954—Charles A. Lindbergh, The Spirit of St. Louis.
1955—William S. White, The Taft Story.
1956—Talbot F. Hamlin, Benjamin Henry Latrobe.
1957—John F. Kennedy, Profiles in Courage.
1958—Douglas Southall Freeman (decd. 1953), George Washington, Vols. I-VI: John Alexander Carroll and Mary Wells Ashworth, Vol. VII.
1959—Arthur Walworth, Woodrow Wilson: American Prophet.
1960—Samuel Eliot Morison, John Paul Jones.
1961—David Donald, Charles Sumner and The Coming of the Civil War.
1963—Leon Edel, Henry James: Vol. II. The Conquest of London, 1870-1881; Vol. III, The Middle Years, 1881-1895.
1964—Walter Jackson Bate, John Keats.
1965—Ernest Samuels, Henry Adams.
1966—Arthur M. Schlesinger Jr., A Thousand Days.
1967—Justin Kaplan, Mr. Clemens and Mark Twain.
1968—George F. Kennan, Memoirs (1925-1950).
1969—B. L. Reid, The Man from New York: John Quinn and his Friends.
1970—T. Harry Williams, Huey Long.
1971—Lawrence Thompson, Robert Frost: The Years of Triumph, 1915-1938.
1972—Joseph P. Lash, Eleanor and Franklin.
1973—W. A. Swanberg, Luce and His Empire.
1974—Louis Sheaffer, O'Neill, Son and Artist.
1975—Robert A. Caro, The Power Broker: Robert Moses and the Fall of New York.

1976—R.W.B. Lewis, Edith Wharton: A Biography.
1977—John E. Mack, A Prince of Our Disorder, The Life of T.E. Lawrence.
1978—Walter Jackson Bate, Samuel Johnson.
1979—Leonard Baker, Days of Sorrow and Pain: Leo Baeck and the Berlin Jews.
1980—Edmund Morris, The Rise of Theodore Roosevelt.
1981—Robert K. Massie, Peter the Great: His Life and World.

American Poetry

Before this prize was established in 1922, awards were made from gifts provided by the Poetry Society: 1918—Love Songs, by Sara Teasdale. 1919—Old Road to Paradise, by Margaret Widemer; Corn Huskers, by Carl Sandburg.

1922—Edwin Arlington Robinson, Collected Poems.
1923—Edna St. Vincent Millay, The Ballad of the Harp-Weaver; A Few Figs from Thistles; Eight Sonnets in American Poetry, 1922; A Miscellany.
1924—Robert Frost, New Hampshire: A Poem with Notes and Grace Notes.
1925—Edwin Arlington Robinson, The Man Who Died Twice.
1926—Amy Lowell, What's O'Clock.
1927—Leonora Speyer, Fiddler's Farewell.
1928—Edwin Arlington Robinson, Tristram.
1929—Stephen Vincent Benet, John Brown's Body.
1930—Conrad Aiken, Selected Poems.
1931—Robert Frost, Collected Poems.
1932—George Dillon, The Flowering Stone.
1933—Archibald MacLeish, Conquistador.
1934—Robert Hillyer, Collected Verse.
1935—Audrey Wurdemann, Bright Ambush.
1936—Robert P. Tristram Coffin, Strange Holiness.
1937—Robert Frost, A Further Range.
1938—Marya Zaturenska, Cold Morning Sky.
1939—John Gould Fletcher, Selected Poems.
1940—Mark Van Doren, Collected Poems.
1941—Leonard Bacon, Sunderland Capture.
1942—William Rose Benet, The Dust Which Is God.
1943—Robert Frost, A Witness Tree.
1944—Stephen Vincent Benet, Western Star.
1945—Karl Shapiro, V-Letter and Other Poems.
1947—Robert Lowell, Lord Weary's Castle.
1948—W. H. Auden, The Age of Anxiety.
1949—Peter Viereck, Terror and Decorum.
1950—Gwendolyn Brooks, Annie Allen.
1951—Carl Sandburg, Complete Poems.
1952—Marianne Moore, Collected Poems.
1953—Archibald MacLeish, Collected Poems.
1954—Theodore Roethke, The Waking.
1955—Wallace Stevens, Collected Poems.
1956—Elizabeth Bishop, Poems, North and South.
1957—Richard Wilbur, Things of This World.
1958—Robert Penn Warren, Promises: Poems 1954-1956.
1959—Stanley Kunitz, Selected Poems 1928-1958.
1960—W. D. Snodgrass, Heart's Needle.
1961—Phyllis McGinley, Times Three: Selected Verse from Three Decades.
1962—Alan Dugan, Poems.
1963—William Carlos Williams, Pictures From Breughel.
1964—Louis Simpson, At the End of the Open Road.
1965—John Berryman, 77 Dream Songs.
1966—Richard Eberhart, Selected Poems.
1967—Anne Sexton, Live or Die.
1968—Anthony Hecht, The Hard Hours.
1969—George Oppen, Of Being Numerous.
1970—Richard Howard, Untitled Subjects.
1971—William S. Merwin, The Carrier of Ladders.
1972—James Wright, Collected Poems.
1973—Maxine Winokur Kumin, Up Country.
1975—Gary Snyder, Turtle Island.
1976—John Ashbery, Self-Portrait in a Convex Mirror.
1977—James Merrill, Divine Comedies.
1978—Howard Nemerov, Collected Poems.
1979—Robert Penn Warren, Now and Then: Poems 1976-1978.
1980—Donald Justice, Selected Poems.
1981—James Schuyler, The Morning of the Poem.

General Non-Fiction

For best book by an American, not eligible in any other category.
1962—Theodore H. White, The Making of the President 1960.
1963—Barbara W. Tuchman, The Guns of August.
1964—Richard Hofstadter, Anti-Intellectualism in American Life.
1965—Howard Mumford Jones, O Strange New World.
1966—Edwin Way Teale, Wandering Through Winter.
1967—David Brion Davis, The Problem of Slavery in Western Culture.
1968—Will and Ariel Durant, Rousseau and Revolution.
1969—Norman Mailer, The Armies of the Night; and Rene Jules Dubos, So Human an Animal: How We Are Shaped by Surroundings and Events.
1970—Eric H. Erikson, Gandhi's Truth.
1971—John Toland, The Rising Sun.
1972—Barbara W. Tuchman, Stilwell and the American Experience in China, 1911-1945.
1973—Frances FitzGerald, Fire in the Lake: The Vietnamese and the Americans in Vietnam; and Robert Coles, Children of Crisis, Volumes II and III.
1974—Ernest Becker, The Denial of Death.

1975—Annie Dillard, Pilgrim at Tinker Creek.
1976—Robert N. Butler, Why Survive? Being Old in America.
1977—William W. Warner, Beautiful Swimmers.
1978—Carl Sagan, The Dragons of Eden.

1979—Edward O. Wilson, On Human Nature.
1980—Douglas R. Hofstadter, Gödel, Escher, Bach: An Eternal Golden Braid.
1981—Carl E. Schorske, Fin-de-Siecle Vienna: Politics and Culture.

Music

For composition by an American (before 1977, by a composer resident in the U.S.), in the larger forms of chamber, orchestra or choral music or for an operatic work including ballet. A special posthumous award was granted in 1976 to Scott Joplin.

1943—William Schuman, Secular Cantata No. 2, A Free Song.
1944—Howard Hanson, Symphony No. 4, Op. 34.
1945—Aaron Copland, Appalachian Spring.
1946—Leo Sowerby, The Canticle of the Sun.
1947—Charles E. Ives, Symphony No. 3.
1948—Walter Piston, Symphony No. 3.
1949—Virgil Thomson, Louisiana Story.
1950—Gian-Carlo Menotti, The Consul.
1951—Douglas Moore, Giants in the Earth.
1952—Gail Kubil, Symphony Concertante.
1954—Quincy Porter, Concerto for Two Pianos and Orchestra.
1955—Gian-Carlo Menotti, The Saint of Bleecker Street.
1956—Ernest Toch, Symphony No. 3.
1957—Norman Dello Joio, Meditations on Ecclesiastes.
1958—Samuel Barber, Vanessa.

1959—John La Montaine, Concerto for Piano and Orchestra.
1960—Elliott Carter, Second String Quartet.
1961—Walter Piston, Symphony No. 7.
1962—Robert Ward, The Crucible.
1963—Samuel Barber, Piano Concerto No. 1.
1966—Leslie Bassett, Variations for Orchestra.
1967—Leon Kirchner, Quartet No. 3.
1968—George Crumb, Echoes of Time and The River.
1969—Karel Husa, String Quartet No. 3.
1970—Charles W. Wuorinen, Time's Encomium.
1971—Mario Davidovsky, Synchronisms No. 6.
1972—Jacob Druckman, Windows.
1973—Elliott Carter, String Quartet No. 3.
1974—Donald Martino, Notturno. (Special citation) Roger Sessions.
1975—Dominick Argento, From the Diary of Virginia Woolf.
1976—Ned Rorem, Air Music.
1977—Richard Wernick, Visions of Terror and Wonder.
1978—Michael Colgrass, Deja Vu for Percussion and Orchestra.
1979—Joseph Schwantner, Aftertones of Infinity.
1980—David Del Tredici, In Memory of a Summer Day.

Special Awards

Awarded in 1981 unless otherwise designated

Books, Allied Arts

Academy of American Poets Fellowship, for distinguished achievement, $10,000: Mona Van Duyn.

American Academy and Institute of Arts and Letters Awards, $5,000 each: Louise Gluck, Gail Godwin, Howard Frank Mosher, James Salter, Elizabeth Sewell, William Stafford, Hilma Wolitzer, Jay Wright; Amer. Academy in Rome Fellowship in Creative Writing, $2,000: Edwin Field; Witter Bynner Prize for Poetry, $1,350: Allen Grossman; Sue Kaufman Prize for First Fiction, $1,000: Tom Lorenz, Guys Like Us; Loines Award for Poetry, $1,000: Ben Belitt; Award of Merit Medal, $1,000: John Guare; Richard and Hinda Rosenthal Foundation Awards in literature, $3,000: Jerome Charyn, Darlin' Bill; Harold D. Vursell Memorial Award, $5,000: Edward Hoagland.

American Book Awards, by Assn. of American Publishers: National Medal for Literature, $15,000: Kenneth Burke; fiction: Plains Song, Wright Morris; paperback: The Stories of John Cheever, John Cheever; first novel: Sister Wolf, Ann Arensberg; general nonfiction: China Men, Maxine Hong Kingston; paperback: The Last Cowboy, Jane Kramer; autobiography/biography: Walt Whitman, Justin Kaplan; paperback: Samuel Beckett, Deirdre Bair; history: Christianity, Social Tolerance and Homosexuality, John Boswell; paperback: Been in the Storm So Long, Leon F. Litwack; children's fiction: The Night Swimmers, Betsy Byars; paperback: Ramona and Her Mother, Beverly Cleary; nonfiction: Oh Boy! Babies, Alison Cragin Herzig, Jane Lawrence Mali; poetry: The Need to Hold Still, Lisel Mueller; science: The Panda's Thumb, Stephen Jay Gould; paperback: The Medusa and the Snail, Lewis Thomas; translation: The Letters of Gustave Flaubert 1830-1857, Francis Steegmuller; paperback: Evening Edged in Gold, John E. Woods.

American-Scandinavian Foundation-PEN Translation Prizes, $500: poetry: Anselm Hollo, for Pentti Saarikoski; fiction: Jack Brondum, for Complete Freedom, by Tove Ditlevsen.

Bancroft Prizes, by Columbia Univ., for American history, $4,000 each: Ronald Steel, Walter Lippmann and the American Century; Jean Strouse, Alice James: A Biography.

Bollingen Prize in Poetry, by Yale Univ. Library, $5,000: Howard Nemerov, May Swenson.

Boston Globe-Horn Book Awards for children's books: fiction: Andrew Davies, Conrad's War; nonfiction: Mario Salvadori, Building: The Fight Against Gravity; illustration: Chris Van Allsburg: The Garden of Abdul Gasazi.

Randolph Caldecott Medal, by American Library Association, for children's book illustration: Arnold Lobel, Fables.

Canada Council Children's Literature Prizes (1980), $5,000 each: Christie Harris, The Trouble with Princesses;

Elizabeth Cleaver, illustration, Petrouchka; Betrand Gauthier, Hébert Lúee; illustration: Miyuki Tanobe, Les Gens de mon pays.

Canada Council Governor General's Literary Awards: English-language: fiction: George Bowering, Burning Water; poetry or drama: Stephen Scobie, McAlmon's Chinese Opera; non-fiction: Jeffrey Simpson, Discipline of Power; French-language: fiction: Pierre Turgeon, La première personne; poetry or drama: Michel Van Schendel, De l'oeil et de l'écoute; non-fiction: Maurice Champagne-Gilbert, La famille et 'homme à délivrer du pouvoir.

Goethe House-PEN Prize, $500: Joachim Neugroschel, for The Tongue Set Free: Remembrance of a European Childhood, by Elias Cennetti.

Golden Kite Awards, by Society of Children's Book Writers: fiction: Patricia MacLachlan, Arthur, for the Very First Time; non-fiction: Dorothy Hinshaw Patent, The Lives of Spiders.

Hemingway Foundation Award, $6,000: Alan Saperstein, Mom Kills Kids and Self.

Harold Morton Landon Translation Award: Saralyn R. Daly, The Book of True Love.

Iowa School of Letters Short Fiction Award, $1,000: Annabel Thomas, The Phototropic Woman.

Lamont Poetry Selection: Michael Van Walleghen, More Trouble with the Obvious.

Lucille J. Medwick Memorial Award for editing, $500: Henry Robbins.

Frederick C. Melcher Book Award, by Unitarian Universalist Association, for contribution to religious liberalism, $1,000: John Boswell, Christianity, Social Tolerance and Homosexuality.

Mystery Writers of America Edgar Allan Poe Awards: novel: Arthur Maling, The Rheingold Route; first novel: Richard North Patterson, The Lasko Tangent; paperback original novel: William L. DeAndrea, The Hog Murders; short story: Geoffrey Norman, Armed and Dangerous; fact crime book: Robert Lindsey, The Falcon and the Snowman; critical/biographical study: Ralph E. Hone, Dorothy L. Sayers, A Literary Biography; Grand Master Award: W.R. Burnett.

National Arts Club Gold Medal of Honor for Literature: Isaac Bashevis Singer.

National Book Critics Circle Awards: fiction: The Transit of Venus, Shirley Hazzard; general non-fiction: Walter Lippman and the American Century, Ronald Steel; poetry: Sunrise, Federick Seidel; criticism: Part of Nature, Part of Us: Modern American Poets, Helen Vendler.

National Jewish Book Awards, by Jewish Book Council, $500: fiction: Johanna Kaplan, *Oh My America!;* holocaust: Randolph L. Braham, *The Politics of Genocide;* history: Mark R. Cohen, *Jewish Self-Government in Medieval Egypt;* Jewish thought: Isador Twersky, *Introduction to the Code of Maimonides;* children's: Leonard Everett Fisher, *A Russian Farewell;* poetry: Louis Simpson, *Caviar at the Funeral;* visual arts: Yeshiva University.

John Newbery Medal, by American Library Association, for children's book: Katherine Paterson, *Jacob Have I Loved.*

New York Times Best Illustrated Children's Books: Edward Ardizzone, *A Child's Christmas in Wales,* by Dylan Thomas; Guy Billout, *Stone & Steel: A Look at Engineering;* M.B. Goffstein, *An Artist;* Helme Heine, *Mr. Miller the Dog;* Arnold Lobel, *The Headless Horseman Rides Tonight,* by Jack Prelutsky; David Macaulay: *Unbuilding;* Allen Say, *The Lucky Yak,* by Annetta Lawson; Binette Schroeder, *The Wonderful Travels and Adventures of Baron Munchhausen,* by Peter Nicki; William Steig, *Gorky Rises;* James Stevenson, *Howard.*

PEN/Faulkner Award for Fiction: Walter Abish, *How German Is it?*

PEN Translation Prize, $1,000: Charles Simic, for *Homage to the Lame Wolf,* by Vasco Popa.

Phi Beta Kappa Book Awards: Ralph Waldo Emerson Award: Frank E. Manuel, Fritzie P. Manuel, *Utopian Thought in the Western World;* Christian Gauss Award: Donald L. Fanger, *The Creation of Nikolai Gogol;* science award: David A. Park, *The Image of Eternity: Roots of Time in the Physical World.*

Renato Poggioli Translation Award, $3,000: Lawrence Venuti.

Present Tense Magazine Awards, by American Jewish Committee, $1,000 each: fiction: Johanna Kaplan, *Oh My America!;* history: Salo Baron, *Byzantines, Mamelukes, and Maghribians;* religious thought: Isadore Twersky, *Introduction to the Code of Maimonides;* social analysis: Amos Elon, *Flight into Egypt;* translation: Shlomo Noble, Joshua Fishman, *History of the Yiddish Language.*

Science Fiction Writers of America Nebula Awards: novel: Arthur C. Clarke, *The Fountains of Paradise;* novella: Barry B. Longyear, *Enemy Mine,* novelette. George R.R. Martin, *Sandkings;* short story, Edward Bryant, *giANTS.*

Walt Whitman Award, Academy of American Poets, $1,000: Alberto Rios, *One Night in a Familiar Room.*

Journalism Awards

Worth Bingham Prizes, for political reporting or commentary, $1,000: John Fialka, *Washington Star.*

Heywood Broun Award, for concern for the underdog (1980), $1,000: Gene Miller, Pat Malone, Carl Hiassen, William D. Montalbano, Steven Doig, John Campter, *Miami Herald.*

Maria Moors Cabot Prizes, for Inter-American journalism, by Columbia University, $1,000 each: Guido Fernandez, former editor in chief of *La Naciòn,* San Jose, Costa Rica; Penny Lernoux, freelance journalist, Los Angeles; Alan Riding, Mexico City bureau chief, *New York Times;* special posthumous citations: Bill Stewart, ABC News, Richard T. Baker, Columbia University.

Raymond Clapper Award, for reporting on governmental affairs (1980), $1,500: George P. Antham, *Des Moines* (Ia.) *Register.*

Sidney Hillman Foundation Prizes, for humanitarian causes, $750 (1980): Michael H. Brown, *Atlantic Monthly;* Deirdre Murphy, *Rochester* (N.Y.) *Democrat and Chronicle.*

Roland Michener Award, for public service journalism in Canada (1980): *Kingston Whig-Standard.*

National Magazine Awards, by American Society of Magazine Editors: general excellence: *Glamour, Business Week, Audubon, ARTnews;* public service: *Reader's Digest;* design: *Attenzione;* fiction: *North American Review;* reporting: *National Journal;* essays, criticism: *Time;* single-topic issue: *Business Week.*

National Press Club Awards, for Washington correspondence (1980): Dennis Farney, *Wall Street Journal;* Eric Planin, Finlay Lewis, *Minneapolis Tribune;* John Herbers, *New York Times;* Joseph Volz, *New York Daily News.*

Overseas Press Club Awards, for foreign reporting: Hal Boyle Award for best daily newspaper or wire service reporting: Richard Ben Cramer, *Philadelphia Inquirer;* Bob Considine Award: Guy Gugliotta, *Miami Herald;* photography: Steve McCurry, *Time;* interpretation: *Time.*

Penney-Missouri Awards, University of Missouri School of Journalism, $13,150: Paul Myhre Awards for excellence in reporting: single story: Richard S. Vonier, *Tucson* (Ariz.) *Citizen;* series: Richard Whitmire, *Rochester* (N.Y.) *Times-Union;* consumer affairs: Linda Rockey and Carol Perkins, *Seattle* (Wash.) *Post-Intelligencer;* fashion & clothing: James McBride, *Evening Journal,* Wilmington, Del.

Penney-Missouri Magazine Awards, University of Missouri School of Journalism, $6,000: contemporary living: Bonnie Ghazarbekian, *Ms.;* consumerism: George J. Church, Edward F. Magnuson, *Time;* health: Judson Gooding, *Across the Board;* personal lifestyle: Nicholas Lemann, *Texas Monthly;* expanding opportunities: Lawrence D. Maloney, George Jones, *U.S. News & World Report;* excellence, smaller magazines: Verne Jackson, *Chicago.*

Pictures of the Year Awards, by Nikon, Inc., National

Press Photographers Association, and University of Missouri (1980): newspaper photographer of the year: Bill Wax, *Gainesville* (Fla.) *Sun;* magazine photographer: David Burnett, Contact Press Images, New York; world understanding: Ethan Hoffman, Washington freelance; newspaper picture editor: Susie Eaton Hopper, *Muskegon* (Mich.) *Chronicle;* best use of photos by a newspaper: *Columbia* (Mo.) *Daily Tribune;* newspaper magazine picture editing: Rich Shulman, *Everett* (Wash.) *Herald's Panorama.*

Reuben Awards, for editorial cartoons, comic strips and panels, by National Cartoonists Society (1980): Jeff MacNelly, *Richmond* (Va.) *News Leader,* for cartoons and "Shoe"; Milton Caniff, "Steve Canyon"; Mel Lazarus, "Miss Peach"; Bob Dunn and Al Scaduto, "They'll Do It Every Time"; Frank Evers, *New York Daily News;* cartoons: Karl Hubenthal, Los Angeles Herald Examiner, comic books: Allan Jaffe, Will Eisner; gag cartoons: Jack Markow, *National Enquirer;* animation: Hilda Terry; illustration: Arnold Roth.

Scripps-Howard Foundation Awards, $24,000: Walker Stone Award, for editorial writing: Tom Dearmore, *San Francisco Examiner;* Edward Willis Scripps Award, for First Amendment reporting: *Lexington* (Ky.) *Herald;* Ernie Pyle Memorial Award, for human interest writing: Richard Ben Cramer, *Philadelphia Inquirer;* Edward J. Meeman Award, for conservation reporting: *Minneapolis Star;* Charles M. Schulz Award, for promising cartoonist: Dick Codor, freelance cartoonist; Roy W. Howard Award, for public service, *Charlotte Observer,* Charlotte, No. Carolina.

Sigma Delta Chi Awards, by Society of Professional Journalists (1980): distinguished service: *Miami Herald,* Danny Goodgame, Patrick Riordan, Morris Thompson, James Savage, Diane Carlebach; general reporting: *Miami Herald* team: Gene Miller, Carl Hiassen, Patrick Malone, William D. Montalbano; editorial: Rick Sinding, Hackensack (N.J.) *Bergen Record;* Washington correspondence: Gordon Eliot White, Salt Lake City, Ut. *Deseret News;* foreign correspondence: Karen DeYoung, *Washington Post;* photography: Eddie Adams, Associated Press; cartoons: John P. Trever, *Albuquerque* (N.M.) *Journal;* research: Lloyd Wendt, Sarasota, Fla.

Merriman Smith Award, for presidential news coverage, $750 (1980): Frank A. Van Riper, Lars-Erik Nelson, *New York Daily News;* Thomas M. DeFrank, *Newsweek.*

Edward Weintal Prize, for reporting and analysis of U.S. foreign policy, by Georgetown University School of Foreign Service (1980): Karen Elliott House, Wall Street Journal; Jonathan C. Randal, *Washington Post;* Strode Talbot, *Time;* John Wallach, Hearst newspapers.

William Allen White Citation, for service to journalism and the community, by University of Kansas (1980): Keith Fuller, Associated Press.

Broadcasting and Theater Awards

American Theater Wing Awards, $15,000: Circle in the Square; American Academy of Dramatic Arts; New York University School of the Arts; Eugene O'Neill Memorial Theater Center; Circle Repertory Theater; Playwrights Horizons; American Shakespeare Theater; Foundation for the Extension and Development of the American Professional Theater; New Dramatists; Saturday Theater for Children; Harold Clurman Theater; Performing Arts Foundation; Equity Library Theater.

Clarence Derwent Awards, $1,000: most promising actress: Mia Dillon, *Crimes of the Heart* and *Summer;* Bob Gunton, *How I Got That Story.*

Emmy Awards, by Academy of Television Arts and Sciences, for nighttime programs, 1979-80: dramatic series: *Lou Grant;* actor: Ed Asner, *Lou Grant;* actress: Barbara Bel Geddes, *Dallas;* supporting actor: Stuart Margolin, *Rockford Files;* supporting actress: Nancy Marchand, *Lou Grant;* director: Roger Grant, *Lou Grant;* writer: Seth Freeman, *Lou Grant.* Comedy series: *Taxi;* actor: Richard Mulligan, *Soap;* actress: Cathryn Damon, *Soap;* supporting actor, Harry Morgan, *M*A*S*H;* supporting actress: Loretta Swit, M*A*S*H; director: James Burrows, *Taxi;* writer: Bob Colleary, *Barney Miller.* Limited series or specials: *Edward and Mrs. Simpson;* actor: Powers Boothe, *Guyana Tragedy;* actress: Patty Duke Astin, *Miracle Worker;* supporting actor: George Grizzard, *Oldest Living Graduate;* supporting actress: Mare Winningham, *Amber Waves;* director: Marvin Chomsky, *Attica;* writer: David Chase, *Off the Minnesota Strip.* Specials: drama: *Miracle Worker;* information: *Body Human: the Magic Sense;* variety or music: *Baryshnikov on Broadway;* classical performing arts: *Live from Studio 8H: A Tribute to Toscanini.*

John F. Kennedy Center Performing Arts Awards (1980): Leonard Bernstein, James Cagney, Agnes de Mille, Lynn Fontanne, Leontyne Price.

National Opera Institute Awards, for service to American opera: Kirk Browning; New York City Opera; Mary Ellis Peltz; Jay William Fisher; Sherill Milnes.

National Society of Film Critics: film: Melvin and Howard; actor: Peter O'Toole, *The Stunt Man;* actress: Sissy Spacek, *Coal Miner's Daughter;* director: Martin Scorsese, *Raging Bull.*

New Dramatists-Playbill Award, $5,000: Wendy Kesselman, *My Sister in This House.*

Obie Award, for Off-Broadway and Off-Off-Broadway theater, $1,000: sustained achievement: Negro Ensemble Company; new play: David Henry Hwang, *FOB;* Emily Mann, *Still Life.*

Outer Critics Circle: Broadway play: *Amadeus,* Peter Shaffer; actor: Ian McKellen, *Amadeus;* actress: Swoosie Kurtz, *Fifth of July;* off-Broadway play: *March of the Falsettos,* William Finn; musical revival: *The Pirates of Penzance,* Joseph Papp; new director: Geraldine Fitzgerald, *Mass Appeal, Long Day's Journey Into Night.*

George Foster Peabody Awards, for news (1980): Roger Mudd, CBS News; Robert Trout, ABC News; WTTW-TV, Chicago; Charles Kuralt, CBS News; WMAQ-TV, Chicago; KRON-TV, San Francisco; KTVI-TV, St. Louis.

Antoinette Perry Awards (Tonys): play: *Amadeus,* Peter Shaffer; actor: Ian McKellen, *Amadeus;* actress: Jane Lapotaire, *Piaf;* director: Peter Hall, *Amadeus;* reproduction: *Pirates of Penzance;* musical: *42nd Street;* featured actress in a musical: Marilyn Cooper, *Woman of the Year;* featured actress: Swoosie Kurtz, *Fifth of July;* featured actor in a musical: Hinton Battle, *Sophisticated Ladies;* featured actor: Brian Backer, *The Floating Light Bulb;* direction of a musical: Wilford Leach, *The Pirates of Penzance;* choreography: Gower Champion, *42nd Street;* scenic design: John Bury, *Amadeus;* costume design: Willa Kim, *Sophisticated Ladies;* lighting design: John Bury, *Amadeus.*

George Polk Awards, by Long Island University: national radio reporting: National Public Radio; local radio reporting: KNOX, CBS, St. Louis, Mo.; political reporting: Bill Moyers, WNET, New York; local TV reporting: Stephen Talbot, Jonathan Dann, KQED, San Francisco; national TV reporting: Charles Kuralt, CBS News.

Richard Rodgers Production Award, American Academy and Institute of Arts and Letters: musical-comedy version of Fellini's film, *8 1/2.*

Theater Hall of Fame: Winthrop Ames, Robert Anderson, Junius Brutus Booth, John Mason Brown, Carol Channing, Lee J. Cobb, Betty Comden, Colleen Dewhurst, Howard Dietz, Alfred Drake, Jose Ferrer, Adolph Green, Uta Hagen, Jed Harris, Leslie Howard, Sidney Howard, Michael Kidd, Rouben Mamoulian, Osgood Perkins, Molly Picon, Arthur Schwartz, Oliver Smith, Maureen Stapleton, Jule Styne, Margaret Sullavan, Gwen Verdon.

Miscellaneous Awards

American Academy and Institute of Arts and Letters Awards, $5,000 each: art: John Duff, Friedel Dzubas, Mimi Gross, Leo Manso, Jane Wilson; music: Edwin Dugger, Robert Erickson, Meyer Kupferman, Ursula Mamlok; Richard and Hinda Rosenthal Foundation Awards in art, $3,000: Alan Magee; distinguished service to the arts: Joseph Papp; medal for spoken language: James Earl Jones.

American Institute of Architects Gold Medal: Jose Luis Sert.

Dance Magazine Awards: Selma Jeanne Cohen, Anton Dolin, Twyla Tharp, Stanley Williams.

Albert Einstein Peace Prize, $50,000: George F. Kennan.

Albert Lasker Medical Research Awards, $45,000 (1980): basic medical research: Paul Berg, Stanley N. Cohen, A. Dale Kaider, Herbert W. Boyer; clinical medical research: Vincent J. Freda, John Gorman, William Pollack, Sir Cyril A. Clarke, Ronald Finn; special public health award: National Heart, Lung and Blood Institute's Hypertension and Detection Follow-up Program, Robert I. Levy, Director.

Edward MacDowell Medal, to distinguished American artist: Samuel Barber.

Pritzker Architecture Prize, $100,000: James Stirling.

Scientist of the Year, by Industrial Research/Development Magazine (1980): Jacob Rabinow.

Samuel H. Scripps American Dance Festival Award, for lifetime achievement in American modern dance, $25,000: Martha Graham.

W. Eugene Smith Grant for Humanistic Photography, $10,000: Jane Evelyn Atwood.

Westinghouse Science Search: $12,000 scholarship: Amy Sue Reichel; $10,000 scholarships: Douglas A. Simons, Michael M. Dowling.

Motion Picture Academy Awards (Oscars)

1927-28
Actor: Emil Jannings, *The Way of All Flesh.*
Actress: Janet Gaynor, *Seventh Heaven.*
Picture: *Wings,* Paramount.

1928-29
Actor: Warner Baxter, *In Old Arizona.*
Actress: Mary Pickford, *Coquette.*
Picture: *Broadway Melody,* MGM.

1929-30
Actor: George Arliss, *Disraeli.*

Actress: Norma Shearer, *The Divorcee.*
Picture: *All Quiet on the Western Front,* Univ.

1930-31
Actor: Lionel Barrymore, *Free Soul.*
Actress: Marie Dressler, *Min and Bill.*
Picture: *Cimarron,* RKO.

1931-32
Actor: Fredric March, *Dr. Jekyll and Mr. Hyde;* Wallace Beery, *The Champ* (tie).
Actress: Helen Hayes, *Sin of Madelon Claudet.*

Picture: *Grand Hotel*, MGM.
Special: Walt Disney, *Mickey Mouse.*

1932-33

Actor: Charles Laughton, *Private Life of Henry VIII.*
Actress: Katharine Hepburn, *Morning Glory.*
Picture: *Cavalcade*, Fox.

1934

Actor: Clark Gable, *It Happened One Night.*
Actress: Claudette Colbert, same.
Picture: *It Happened One Night*, Columbia.

1935

Actor: Victor McLaglen, *The Informer.*
Actress: Bette Davis, *Dangerous.*
Picture: *Mutiny on the Bounty*, MGM.

1936

Actor: Paul Muni, *Story of Louis Pasteur.*
Actress: Luise Rainer, *The Great Ziegfeld.*
Picture: *The Great Ziegfeld*, MGM.

1937

Actor: Spencer Tracy, *Captains Courageous.*
Actress: Luise Rainer, *The Good Earth.*
Picture: *Life of Emile Zola*, Warner.

1938

Actor: Spencer Tracy, *Boys Town.*
Actress: Bette Davis, *Jezebel.*
Picture: *You Can't Take It With You*, Columbia.

1939

Actor: Robert Donat, *Goodbye Mr. Chips.*
Actress: Vivien Leigh, *Gone With the Wind.*
Picture: *Gone With the Wind*, Selznick International.

1940

Actor: James Stewart, *The Philadelphia Story.*
Actress: Ginger Rogers, *Kitty Foyle.*
Picture: *Rebecca*, Selznick International.

1941

Actor: Gary Cooper, *Sergeant York.*
Actress: Joan Fontaine, *Suspicion.*
Picture: *How Green Was My Valley*, 20th Cent.-Fox.

1942

Actor: James Cagney, *Yankee Doodle Dandy.*
Actress: Greer Garson, *Mrs. Miniver.*
Picture: *Mrs. Miniver*, MGM.

1943

Actor: Paul Lukas, *Watch on the Rhine.*
Actress: Jennifer Jones, *The Song of Bernadette.*
Picture: *Casablanca*, Warner.

1944

Actor: Bing Crosby, *Going My Way.*
Actress: Ingrid Bergman, *Gaslight.*
Picture: *Going My Way*, Paramount.

1945

Actor: Ray Milland, *The Lost Weekend.*
Actress: Joan Crawford, *Mildred Pierce.*
Picture: *The Lost Weekend*, Paramount.

1946

Actor: Fredric March, *Best Years of Our Lives.*
Actress: Olivia de Havilland, *To Each His Own.*
Picture: *The Best Years of Our Lives*, Goldwyn, RKO.

1947

Actor: Ronald Colman, *A Double Life.*
Actress: Loretta Young, *The Farmer's Daughter.*
Picture: *Gentleman's Agreement*, 20th Cent.-Fox.

1948

Actor: Laurence Olivier, *Hamlet.*
Actress: Jane Wyman, *Johnny Belinda.*
Picture: *Hamlet*, Two Cities Film, Universal International.

1949

Actor: Broderick Crawford. *All the King's Men.*
Actress: Olivia de Havilland, *The Heiress.*
Picture: *All the King's Men*, Columbia.

1950

Actor: Jose Ferrer, *Cyrano de Bergerac.*
Actress: Judy Holliday, *Born Yesterday.*
Picture: *All About Eve*, 20th Century-Fox.

1951

Actor: Humphrey Bogart, *The African Queen.*
Actress: Vivien Leigh, *A Streetcar Named Desire.*
Picture: *An American in Paris*, MGM.

1952

Actor: Gary Cooper, *High Noon.*
Actress: Shirley Booth, *Come Back, Little Sheba.*
Picture: *Greatest Show on Earth*, C.B. DeMille, Paramount.

1953

Actor: William Holden, *Stalag 17.*
Actress: Audrey Hepburn, *Roman Holiday.*
Picture: *From Here to Eternity*, Columbia.

1954

Actor: Marlon Brando, *On the Waterfront.*

Actress: Grace Kelly, *The Country Girl.*
Picture: *On the Waterfront*, Horizon-American, Colum.

1955

Actor: Ernest Borgnine, *Marty.*
Actress: Anna Magnani, *The Rose Tattoo.*
Picture: *Marty*, Hecht and Lancaster's Steven Prods., U.A.

1956

Actor: Yul Brynner, *The King and I.*
Actress: Ingrid Bergman, *Anastasia.*
Picture: *Around the World in 80 Days*, Michael Todd, U.A.

1957

Actor: Alec Guinness, *The Bridge on the River Kwai.*
Actress: Joanne Woodward, *The Three Faces of Eve.*
Picture: *The Bridge on the River Kwai*, Columbia.

1958

Actor: David Niven, *Separate Tables.*
Actress: Susan Hayward, *I Want to Live.*
Picture: *Gigi*, Arthur Freed Production, MGM.

1959

Actor: Charlton Heston, *Ben-Hur.*
Actress: Simone Signoret, *Room at the Top.*
Picture: *Ben-Hur*, MGM.

1960

Actor: Burt Lancaster, *Elmer Gantry.*
Actress: Elizabeth Taylor, *Butterfield 8.*
Picture: *The Apartment*, Mirisch Co., U.A.

1961

Actor: Maximilian Schell, *Judgment at Nuremberg.*
Actress: Sophia Loren, *Two Women.*
Picture: *West Side Story*, United Artists.

1962

Actor: Gregory Peck, *To Kill a Mockingbird.*
Actress: Anne Bancroft, *The Miracle Worker.*
Picture: *Lawrence of Arabia*, Columbia.

1963

Actor: Sidney Poitier, *Lilies of the Field.*
Actress: Patricia Neal, *Hud.*
Picture: *Tom Jones*, Woodfall Prod., UA-Lopert Pictures.

1964

Actor: Rex Harrison, *My Fair Lady.*
Actress: Julie Andrews, *Mary Poppins.*
Picture: *My Fair Lady*, Warner Bros.

1965

Actor: Lee Marvin, *Cat Ballou.*
Actress: Julie Christie, *Darling.*
Picture: *The Sound of Music*, 20th Century-Fox.

1966

Actor: Paul Scofield, *A Man for All Seasons.*
Actress: Elizabeth Taylor, *Who's Afraid of Virginia Woolf?*
Picture: *A Man for All Seasons*, Columbia.

1967

Actor: Rod Steiger, *In the Heat of the Night.*
Actress: Katharine Hepburn, *Guess Who's Coming to Dinner.*
Picture: *In the Heat of the Night.*

1968

Actor: Cliff Robertson, *Charly.*
Actress: Katharine Hepburn, *The Lion in Winter;* Barbra Streisand, *Funny Girl* (tie).
Picture: *Oliver.*

1969

Actor: John Wayne, *True Grit.*
Actress: Maggie Smith, *The Prime of Miss Jean Brodie.*
Picture: *Midnight Cowboy.*

1970

Actor: George C. Scott, *Patton* (refused).
Actress: Glenda Jackson, *Women in Love.*
Picture: *Patton.*

1971

Actor: Gene Hackman, *The French Connection.*
Actress: Jane Fonda, *Klute.*
Picture: *The French Connection.*

1972

Actor: Marlon Brando, *The Godfather* (refused).
Actress: Liza Minnelli, *Cabaret.*
Picture: *The Godfather.*

1973

Actor: Jack Lemmon, *Save the Tiger.*
Actress: Glenda Jackson, *A Touch of Class.*
Picture: *The Sting.*

1974

Actor: Art Carney, *Harry and Tonto.*
Actress: Ellen Burstyn, *Alice Doesn't Live Here Anymore.*
Picture: *The Godfather, Part II.*

1975
Actor: Jack Nicholson, *One Flew Over the Cuckoo's Nest.*
Actress: Louise Fletcher, same.
Picture: *One Flew Over the Cuckoo's Nest.*
1976
Actor: Peter Finch, *Network.*
Actress: Faye Dunaway, same.
Picture: *Rocky.*
1977
Actor: Richard Dreyfuss, *The Goodbye Girl.*
Actress: Diane Keaton, *Annie Hall.*
Picture: *Annie Hall.*
1978
Actor: Jon Voight, *Coming Home.*
Actress: Jane Fonda, *Coming Home.*
Picture: *The Deer Hunter.*
1979
Actor: Dustin Hoffman, *Kramer vs. Kramer.*
Actress: Sally Field, *Norma Rae.*

Picture: *Kramer vs. Kramer.*
1980
Actor: Robert De Niro, *Raging Bull.*
Actress: Sissy Spacek, *Coal Miner's Daughter.*
Picture: *Ordinary People.*
Director: Robert Redford, *Ordinary People.*
Foreign Film: *Moscow Does Not Believe in Tears.*
Supporting Actor: Timothy Hutton, *Ordinary People.*
Supporting Actress: Mary Steenburgen, *Melvin and Howard.*
Screenplay (original): Bo Goldman, Melvin and Howard;
    (adapted): Alvin Sargent, *Ordinary People.*
Editing: Thelma Schoonmaker, *Raging Bull.*
Cinematography: Geoffrey Unsworth, Ghislain Cloquet, *Tess.*
Score (original): Michael Gore, *Fame.*
Song: Michael Gore and Dean Pitchford, Fame, from *Fame.*
Art Direction: Pierre Guffroy, Jack Stephens, *Tess.*
Costumes: Anthony Powell, *Tess.*
Sound: Bill Varney, Steve Maslow, Gregg Landaker, Peter Sutton, *The Empire Strikes Back.*
Visual Effects: *The Empire Strikes Back.*

Canadian Film Awards
Source: Canadian Film Institute

1970
Actor: Doug McGrath and Paul Bradley (tied), Goin' Down the Road
Actress: Genevieve Bujold, Act of the Heart
Picture: Psychocratie
1971
Actor: Jean Duceppe, Mon oncle Antoine
Actress: Ann Knox, The Only Thing You Know
Picture: Mon oncle Antoine
1972
Actor: Gordon Pinsent, The Rowdyman
Actress: Micheline Lanctot, Vrai nature de Bernadette
Picture: Wedding in White
1973
Actor: Jacques Godin, O.K. Laliberte
Actress: Genevieve Bujold, Kamouraska
Picture: Slipstream
1974
No awards
1975
Actor: Stuart Gillard, Why Rock the Boat?
Actress: Margot Kidder, Black Christmas and A Quiet Day in Belfast

Picture: Les Ordres
Film of the Year: The Apprenticeship of Duddy Kravitz
1976
Actor: Andre Melancon, Partis pur la gloire
Actress: Marilyn Lightstone, Lies My Father Told Me
Picture: Lies My Father Told Me
1977
Actor: Len Cariou, One Man
Actress: Monique Mercure, J.A. Martin: Photographe
Picture: J.A. Martin: Photographe
1978
Actor: Richard Gabourie, Three Card Monte
Actress: Helen Shaver, In Praise of Older Women
Picture: The Silent Partner
1979
Actor: Christopher Plummer, Murder By Decree
Actress: Kate Lynch, Meatballs
Picture: The Changeling
1980
Actor: Thomas Peacocke, The Hounds of Notre Dame
Actress: Marie Tifo, Les Bons Debarras
Picture: Les Bons Debarras

The Spingarn Medal

The Spingarn Medal has been awarded annually since 1914 by the National Association for the Advancement of Colored People for the highest achievement by a black American.

1946	Dr. Percy L. Julian		Rock Nine	1969	Jacob Lawrence
1947	Channing H. Tobias	1958	Edward Kennedy (Duke) Ellington	1970	Leon Howard Sullivan
1948	Ralph J. Bunche	1959	Langston Hughes	1971	Gordon Parks
1949	Charles Hamilton Houston	1960	Kenneth B. Clark	1972	Wilson C. Riles
1950	Mabel Keaton Staupers	1961	Robert C. Weaver	1973	Damon Keith
1951	Harry T. Moore	1962	Medgar Wiley Evers	1974	Henry (Hank) Aaron
1952	Paul R. Williams	1963	Roy Wilkins	1975	Alvin Ailey
1953	Theodore K. Lawless	1964	Leontyne Price	1976	Alex Haley
1954	Carl Murphy	1965	John H. Johnson	1977	Andrew Young
1955	Jack Roosevelt Robinson	1966	Edward W. Brooke	1978	Mrs. Rosa L. Parks
1956	Martin Luther King Jr.	1967	Sammy Davis Jr.	1979	Dr. Rayford W. Logan
1957	Mrs. Daisy Bates and the Little	1968	Clarence M. Mitchell Jr.	1980	Coleman Young

The Molson Prize

The Molson Prizes are given annually for outstanding contributions in the arts, humanities or social sciences. The prizes, worth $20,000 each, are financed from an endowment established by the Molson Foundation.

1967 Arthur Erickson; Anne Hebert; Marshall McLuhan
1968 Glenn Gould; Jean Le Moyne
1969 Jean-Paul Audet; Morley Callaghan; Arnold Spohr
1970 Northrop Frye; Duncan Macpherson; Yves Pheriault
1971 Maureen Forrester; Rina Lasnier; Norman McLaren
1972 John Deutsch; Alfred Pellan; George Woodcock
1973 W.A.C.H. Dobson; Celia Franca; Jean-Paul Lemieux
1974 Alex Colville, Margaret Laurence; Pierre Dansereau

1975 Jon Vickers; Denise Pelletier; the Orford String Quartet: Andrew Dawes; Terrence Helmer; Kenneth Perkins and Marcel St-Cyr
1976 John Hirsch; Bill Reid; Jean-Louis Roux
1977 Gabrielle Roy; Jack Shadbolt; George Story
1978 Jean Duceppe; Betty Oliphant; Michael Snow
1979 Michel Brault, Lois Marshall, Robert Weaver
1980 Margaret Atwood, Marcel Trudel, John Weinzweig

ARTS AND MEDIA

Notable New York Theater Openings, 1980-81 Season

A Lesson From Aloes, drama set in South Africa; written and directed by Athol Fugard; with James Earl Jones.

A Life, drama by Hugh Leonard about a small-town civil servant; with Roy Dotrice.

Amadeus, drama by Peter Shaffer about the rivalry between Mozart and Antonio Salieri; with Ian McKellen and Tim Curry.

Brigadoon, revival of the 1947 Lerner & Loewe musical; with Martin Vidnovic and Meg Bussert.

Can-Can, revival of the 1953 Cole Porter musical; with Zizi Jeanmaire, Ron Husmann, and Avery Schreiber.

Copperfield, musical by Al Kasha and Joel Hirschhorn based on the Dicken's classic; with George S. Irving and Brian Matthews.

Division Street, play by Steve Tesich about 1960s radicals; with John Lithgow, Keene Curtis, and Justin Lord.

Fifth of July, drama by Lanford Wilson; with Christopher Reeve and Amy Wright.

Fools, comedy by Neil Simon about a mythical Ukrainian village; with John Rubinstein.

42nd Street, musical directed and choreographed by Gower Champion, based on the 1933 film; with Jerry Orbach, Tammy Grimes, and Wanda Richert.

Frankenstein, play by Victor Giaianella based on the Mary Shelley horror classic; with David Dukes and Keith Jochim.

It Had to Be You, comedy by Joseph Bologna and Renee Taylor; with Mr. Bologna and Ms. Taylor.

John Gabriel Borkman, revival of the Ibsen play of the late 1890s; with E.G. Marshall and Irene Worth.

Lena Horne: The Lady and Her Music, Ms. Horne performs her most memorable songs.

Lolita, Edward Albee's adaptation of the Vladimir Nabokov novel; with Donald Sutherland and Blanche Baker.

Lunch Hour, play by Jean Kerr; directed by Mike Nichols; with Sam Waterston and Gilda Radner.

Onward Victoria, musical comedy about the career of 19th-century suffragist Victoria Woodhull; with Jill Eikenberry.

Passione, comedy by Albert Innaurato about an Italian-American family; with Jerry Stiller and Angela Paton.

Perfectly Frank, revue featuring 60 Frank Loesser songs;

with Jo Sullivan and Debbie Shapiro.

Piaf, musical based on the life of French singer Edith Piaf; with Jane Lapotaire and Zoe Wanamaker.

Rose, play by Andrew Davies; with Glenda Jackson and Jessica Tandy.

Sophisticated Ladies, revue featuring the music of Duke Ellington; with Gregory Hines and Judith Jamison.

The American Clock, drama by Arthur Miller set in the 1930s; with William Atherton and John Randolph.

The Five O'Clock Girl, revival of the 1927 Guy Bolton-Fred Thompson musical; with Lisby Larson and Roger Rathburn.

The Floating Light Bulb, play by Woody Allen, with Beatrice Arthur, Jack Weston, Brian Backer, and Danny Aiello.

The Legendary Stardust Boys, drama by D.B. Gilles about members of a polka band; with Robert Mont.

The Little Foxes, revival of the 1939 Lillian Hellman play; with Elizabeth Taylor, Maureen Stapleton, Tom Aldredge, Dennis Christopher, and Anthony Zerbe.

The Moony Shapiro Songbook, satirical revue of the life and work of a fictitious songwriter; with Jeff Goldblum.

The Philadelphia Story, revival of the 1939 Philip Barry comedy; with Blythe Danner, Edward Herrmann, and Frank Converse.

The Pirates of Penzance, Joseph Papp's production of the Gilbert and Sullivan operetta; with Estelle Parsons, George Rose, Linda Ronstadt, Rex Smith, and Kevin Kline.

The Sea Gull, revival of the Chekhov classic; with Christopher Walken and Rosemary Harris.

Tintypes, musical revue featuring songs from pre-1914 years; with Lynne Thigpen and Carolyn Mignini.

To Grandmother's House We Go, play by Joanna M. Glass; with Eva Le Gallienne, Kim Hunter, and Shepperd Strudwick.

Tricks of the Trade, melodrama by Sidney Michaels; with George C. Scott and Trish Van Devere.

True West, drama by Sam Shepard; with Peter Boyle and Tommy Lee Jones.

Woman of the Year, musical by John Kander and Fred Ebb; with Lauren Bacall and Harry Guardino.

Record Long Run Broadway Plays *Still Running June 28, 1981

Grease	3,388	The Wiz	1,666	Angel Street	1,295
Fiddler on the Roof	3,242	Born Yesterday	1,643	Lightnin'	1,291
Life With Father	3,224	Mary, Mary	1,572	Promises, Promises	1,281
Tobacco Road	3,182	Voice of the Turtle	1,557	*Best Little Whorehouse in Texas	1,264
Hello Dolly	2,844	Barefoot in the Park	1,532	The King and I	1,246
My Fair Lady	2,717	Mame	1,508	Cactus Flower	1,234
*Chorus Line	2,443	Arsenic and Old Lace	1,444	Sleuth	1,222
Man of La Mancha	2,329	Same Time, Next Year	1,444	"1776"	1,217
Abie's Irish Rose	2,327	The Sound of Music	1,443	Equus	1,207
Oklahoma!	2,212	How To Succeed in Business		Guys and Dolls	1,200
*Oh, Calcutta (revival)	1,998	Without Really Trying	1,417	Cabaret	1,166
Pippin	1,900	Hellzapoppin	1,404	Mister Roberts	1,157
Magic Show	1,859	*Death Trap	1,393	Annie Get Your Gun	1,147
Harvey	1,775	The Music Man	1,375	Butterflies Are Free	1,128
*Annie	1,748	*Dancin'	1,359	Pins and Needles	1,108
Hair	1,742	Funny Girl	1,348	Plaza Suite	1,097
*Gemini	1,709	Oh! Calcutta!	1,316	Kiss Me Kate	1,070
South Pacific	1,694	*Ain't Misbehavin'	1,311		

Plays in London *Still running June 30, 1981

*The Mousetrap	11,880	There's a Girl in my Soup	2,547	Chu Chin Chow	2,238
Black and White Minstrels	4,354	Pyjama Tops	2,498	Charley Girl	2,202
*No Sex Please, We're British	4,204	Sound of Music	2,386	The Boy Friend	2,084
Oh! Calcutta!	3,863	Sleuth	2,359	Canterbury Tales	2,082
Jesus Christ Superstar	3,401	Salad Days	2,283	Boeing Boeing	2,035
Oliver	2,618	My Fair Lady	2,281		

Symphony Orchestras of the U.S. and Canada

Source: American Symphony Orchestra League
(as of June 29, 1981)

Classifications are based on annual incomes or budgets of orchestras.

Major Symphony Orchestras

		Conductor
Atlanta Symphony	1280 Peachtree St., NE, Atlanta, GA 30309	Robert Shaw
Baltimore Symphony	1313 St. Paul St., Baltimore, MD 21210	Sergiu Comissiona
Boston Symphony	Symphony Hall, Boston, MA 02115	Seiji Ozawa
Buffalo Philharmonic	26 Richmond Ave., Buffalo, NY 14222	Julius Rudel
Chicago Symphony	220 S. Michigan Ave., Chicago, IL 60604	Sir Georg Solti
Cincinnati Symphony	1241 Elm St., Cincinnati, OH 45210	Michael Gielen
Cleveland Orchestra	11001 Euclid Ave., Cleveland, OH 44106.	Lorin Maazel
Dallas Symphony	P.O. Box 26207, Dallas, TX 75226.	Eduardo Mata
Denver Symphony	1245 Champa St., Denver, CO 80204.	Gaetano Delogu
Detroit Symphony	20 Auditorium Dr., Detroit, MI 48226.	Antal Dorati
Honolulu Symphony	1000 Bishop St., Honolulu, HI 96813	Donald Johanos
Houston Symphony	615 Louisiana, Houston, TX 77002	Erich Bergel
Indianapolis Symphony	P.O. Box 88207, Indianapolis, IN 46208	John Nelson
Kansas City Philharmonic	200 W. 14th Street, Kansas City, MO 64105	Marc Gottlieb
Los Angeles Philharmonic	135 North Grand, Los Angeles, CA 90012	Carlo Giulini
Milwaukee Symphony	929 N. Water St., Milwaukee, WI 53202.	Lucas Foss
Minnesota Orchestra	1111 Nicollet Mall, Minneapolis, MN 55403.	Neville Marriner
Montreal Symphony	200 de Maisonneuve W., Montreal, Que. H2X 1Y9	Charles Dutoit
National Symphony	JFK Center for the Performing Arts, Wash., DC 20566	Mstislav Rostropovich
New Jersey Symphony	213 Washington St., Newark, NJ 07101.	Thomas Michalak
New Orleans Philharmonic-Symphony	203 Carondelet St., New Orleans, LA 70130.	Philippe Entremont
New York Philharmonic	Avery Fisher Hall, New York, NY 10023	Zubin Mehta
North Carolina Symphony	P.O. Box 28026, Raleigh, NC 28026.	Lawrence Smith
Philadelphia Orchestra	1420 Locust St., Philadelphia, PA 19102	Ricardo Muti
Pittsburgh Symphony	600 Penn Ave., Pittsburgh, PA 15222	Andre Previn
Rochester Philharmonic	20 Grove Pl., Rochester, NY 14605	David Zinman
St. Louis Symphony	718 N. Grand Blvd., St. Louis, MO 63103.	Leonard Slatkin
St. Paul Chamber Orchestra	315 Landmark Ctr., St. Paul, MN 55102	Pinchas Zukerman
San Antonio Symphony	109 Lexington Ave., San Antonio, TX 78205	Lawrence Smith
San Diego Symphony	P.O. Box 3175, San Diego, CA 92103.	David Atherton
San Francisco Symphony	Davies Symphony Hall, San Fran., CA 94102	Edo de Waart
Seattle Symphony	305 Harrison St., Seattle, WA 98108	Rainer Miedel
Syracuse Symphony	411 Montgomery St., Syracuse, NY 13202	Christopher Keene
Toronto Symphony	215 Victoria St., Toronto, Ont. M5B 1V1	Andrew Davis
Utah Symphony	123 W. South Temple, Salt Lake City, UT 84101	Varujan Kojian
Vancouver Symphony	873 Beatty St., Vancouver, B.C. V6B 2M6	Kazuyoshi Akiyama

Regional Orchestras

Alabama Symphony	P.O. Box 2125, N., Birmingham, AL 35201	Amerigo Marino
American Symphony	119 W. 57th St., New York, NY 10019	Sergiu Comissiona
Calgary Philharmonic	200-505 Fifth St. SW, Calgary, Alta. T2P 3J2	Arpad Joo
Charlotte Symphony	110 E. 7th Street, Charlotte, NC 28202	Leo Driehuys
Columbus Symphony	101 E. Town St., Columbus, OH 43215	Evan Whallon
Edmonton Symphony Society	11712 87 Avenue, Edmonton, Alta. T6G 0Y3.	Yuval Zaliouk
Flint Symphony	1025 E. Kearsley St., Flint, MI 48503	John Covelli
Florida Gulf Coast Symphony	3430 W. Kennedy Blvd., Tampa, FL 33609	Irwin Hoffman
Florida Philharmonic	265 Sevilla Ave., Coral Gables, FL 33134	Ranier Meidel
Florida Symphony	P.O. Box 782, Orlando, FL 32802	Pavle Despalj
Fort Worth Symphony	4401 Trail Lake Dr., Fort Worth, TX 76109	John Giordano
Grand Rapids Symphony	Exhibitors Bldg., Grand Rapids, MI 49503.	Semyon Bychkov
Hamilton Philharmonic	P.O. Box 2080, Sta. A, Hamilton, Ont. L8N 3Y7	Boris Brott
Hartford Symphony	609 Farmington, Hartford, CT 06105	Arthur Winograd
Hudson Valley Philharmonic	Box 191, Poughkeepsie, NY 12602	Imre Pallo
Jacksonville Symphony	333 Laura St., Jacksonville, FL 32202.	Willis Page
Long Beach Symphony	121 Linden Ave., Long Beach, CA 90802	Murry Sidlin
Los Angeles Chamber Orchestra	285 W. Green St., Pasadena, CA 91105	Gerard Schwarz
Louisville Orchestra	333 W. Broadway, Louisville, KY 40202.	Akira Endo
Memphis Symphony	3100 Walnut Grove Rd., Memphis, TN 38111	Vincent de Frank
Nashville Symphony	1805 West End Ave., Nashville, TN 37203	Michael Charry
Oakland Symphony	P.O. Box 1619, Oakland, CA 94604.	Calvin Simmons
Oklahoma Symphony	512 Civic Center Music Hall, Oklahoma City, OK 73102	Luis Herrera dela Fuente
Omaha Symphony	310 Aquila Ct., Omaha, NE 68102.	Thomas Briccetti
Oregon Symphony	1119 SW Park Ave., Portland, OR 97205.	James DePreist
Phoenix Symphony	6328 N. 7th St., Phoenix, AZ 85014	Theo Alcantara
Puerto Rico Symphony	Apto 41227, Minillas Sta., San Juan, PR 00940	John Barnett
Quebec Symphony	350 E. St-Cyrille Blvd., Quebec G1R 2B4	James DePreist
Richmond Symphony	15 S. Fifth St., Richmond, VA 23219.	Jacques Houtmann
Sacramento Symphony	Suite 11, 451 Parkfair Dr., Sacramento, CA 95825	Carter Nice
San Jose Symphony	170 Park Center Plaza, San Jose, CA 95113	George Cleve
St. Paul Chamber Orchestra	75 W. Fifth St., St. Paul, MN 55102	Pinchas Zukerman
Spokane Symphony	West 621 Mallon, Spokane, WA 99201	Donald Thulean
Toledo Symphony	1 Stranahan Sq., Toledo, OH 43604.	Yuval Zaliouk
Tulsa Philharmonic	2210 South Main, Tulsa, OK 74114	Joel Lazar
Victoria Symphony	631 Superior St., Victoria, B.C. V8V 1V1	Paul Freeman
Wichita Symphony	225 W. Douglas, Wichita, KS 67202.	Michael Palmer
Winnipeg Symphony	555 Main St., Winnipeg, Man. R3B 1C3.	Franz-Paul Decker

Metropolitan Orchestras

Akron Symphony	Thomas Hall, Hill & Center Sts., Akron, OH 44325	Louis Lane
Albany Symphony	19 Clinton Ave., Albany, NY 12207	Julius Hegyi

Amarillo Symphony	P.O. Box 2552, Amarillo, TX 79105	Thomas Conlin
Arkansas Symphony	P.O. Box 3295, Little Rock, AR 72202	Robert Henderson
Atlantic Symphony	5639 Spring Garden Rd., Halifax, Nova Scot. B3J 1G9	Victor Yampolsky
Austin Symphony	1101 Red River St., Austin, TX 78701	Akira Endo
B.C. Pops Orchestra	233 Main St., Vestal City, NY 13850	David L. Agard
Baton Rouge Symphony	P.O. Box 103, Baton Rouge, LA 70821	James Yestadt
Battle Creek Symphony	P.O. Box 1319, Battle Creek, MI 49016	William Stein
Boise Philharmonic	P.O. Box 2205, Boise, IA 83701	Daniel Stern
(Greater) Bridgeport Symphony	Univ. of Bridgeport, Bridgeport, CT 06602	Gustav Meier
Brooklyn Philharmonia	30 Lafayette Ave., Brooklyn, NY 11217	Lukas Foss
California Chamber Orchestra	6380 Wilshire Blvd., Los Angeles, CA 90048	Henri Temianka
Canton Symphony	1001 Market Ave. N., Canton, OH 44702	Gerhardt Zimmerman
Cedar Rapids Symphony	201 Second St. SE, Cedar Rapids, IA 52401	Vacant
Charleston Symphony	3 Chisholm St., Charleston, SC 29401	Lucien DeGroote
Charleston Symphony	P.O. Box 2292, Charleston, WV 25328	Sidney Rothstein
Chattanooga Symphony	615 Lindsay St., Chattanooga, TN 37402	Richard Cormier
Chautauqua Symphony	Chautauqua Institute, Chautauqua, NY 14722	Varujan Kojian
Clarion Music Society	1860 Broadway, New York, NY 10023	Newell Jenkins
Colorado Music Festival	1245 Pearl, No. 210, Boulder, CO 80302	Giora Bernstein
Colorado Springs Symphony	P.O. Box 1692, Colorado Springs, CO 80901	Charles Ansbacher
Concerto Soloisto of Philadelphia	1722 Spruce St., Philadelphia, PA 19103	Marc Mostovoy
Corpus Christi Symphony	P.O. Box 495, Corpus Christi, TX 78403	Cornelius Eberhardt
County Symphony of Westchester	Box 333, Scarsdale, NY 10583	Stephen Simon
Dayton Philharmonic	125 E. First St., Dayton, OH 45402	C. Wendelken-Wilson
Delaware Symphony	P.O. Box 1870, Wilmington, DE 19899	Stephen Gunzenhauser
Des Moines Symphony	411 Shops Bldg., Des Moines, IA 50309	Yuri Krasnapolsky
Duluth-Superior Symphony	506 W. Michigan St., Duluth, MN 55802	Taavo Virkhaus
Eastern Philharmonic	200 N. Davie St., Greensboro, NC 27401	Sheldon Morgenstern
Elkhart Symphony	P.O. Box 144, Elkhart, IN 46514	Michael J. Esselstrom
El Paso Symphony	P.O. Box 180, El Paso, TX 79942	Abraham Chavez Jr.
Erie Philharmonic	409 G. Daniel Baldwin Bldg., Erie, PA 16501	Walter Hendl
Evansville Philharmonic	P.O. Box 84, Evansville, IN 47701	Stewart Kershaw
Florida West Coast Symphony	709 N. Tamiami Trail, Sarasota, FL 33577	Paul C. Wolfe
Fort Lauderdale Symphony	1430 N. Federal Hwy., Fort Lauderdale, FL 33304	Emerson Buckley
Fort Wayne Philharmonic	107 S. Harrison, Fort Wayne, IN 46802	Ronald Ondrejka
Fresno Philharmonic	1382 N. Fresno St., Fresno, CA 93703	Guy Taylor
Glendale Symphony	401 N. Brand Blvd., Glendale, CA 91203	Carmen Dragon
Grant Park Symphony	425 E. McFetridge Dr., Chicago, IL 60605	Vacant
Greensboro Symphony	200 N. Davie St., Greensboro, NC 27401	Peter Paul Fuchs
Harrisburg Symphony	22 S. Third St., Harrisburg, PA 17101	Larry Newland
Hartford Chamber Orchestra	15 Lewis St., Hartford, CT 06103	Daniel Parker
Jackson Symphony	P.O. Box 4584, Jackson, MS 39216	Lewis Dalvit
Johnstown Symphony	230 Walnut St., Johnstown, PA 15901	Donald Barra
Kalamazoo Symphony	426 S. Park St., Kalamazoo, MI 49007	Yoshimi Takeda
Kingston Symphony	86 Lakeshore Blvd., Kingston, Ont. K7L 5C8	Vacant
Kitchener-Waterloo Symphony	101 Queen St. N., Kitchener, Ont., N2H 6P7	Raffi Armenian
Knoxville Symphony	618 Gay St., Knoxville, TN 37902	Zoltan Rozsnyai
Lansing Symphony	230 N. Washington Sq., Lansing, MI 48933	Gustav Meier
Lexington Philharmonic	412 Rose St., Lexington, KY 40508	George Zack
Lincoln Symphony	1315 Sharp Bldg., Lincoln, NE 68506	Robert Emile
London Symphony	520 Wellington St., London, Ont. N6A 3R2	Alexis Hauser
Long Island Philharmonic	P.O. Box 199, Huntington, NY 11743	Christopher Keene
Lubbock Symphony	1721 Broadway, Lubbock, TX 79401	William A. Harrod
Madison Symphony	211 N. Carroll St., Madison, WI 53703	Roland Johnson
Marin Symphony	P.O. Box 127, San Rafael, CA 94915	Sandor Salgo
Miami Beach Symphony	420 Lincoln Rd. Mall, Miami Beach, FL 33139	Barnett Breeskin
Midland-Odessa Symphony	P.O. Box 6266, Midland, TX 79701	Thomas Hohstadt
Monterey County Symphony	P.O. Box 3965, Carmel, CA 93921	Haymo Taeuber
Music for Westchester Symphony	Box 35, Gedney Station, White Plains, NY 10605	Siegfried Landau
National Arts Centre Orchestra	Box 1534, Sta. B, Ott., Ont. K7P 5W1	Mario Bernardi
New Haven Symphony	33 Whitney Ave., New Haven, CT 06511	Murry Sidlin
New Mexico Symphony	P.O. Box 769, Albuquerque, NM 87103	Yoshima Takeda
Niagara Symphony	P.O. Box 401, St. Catherines, Ont. L2R 6V9	Ian Spraggon
Northeastern Pennsylvania Philharmonic	P.O. Box 71, Avoca, PA 18641	Hugh H. Wolff
Northwest Chamber Orchestra	119 S. Main St., Seattle, WA 98104	Alun Francis
Ohio Chamber Orchestra	11125 Magnolia Dr., Cleveland, OH 44106	Dwight Oltman
Opera Orchestra of N.Y.	211 W. 56th St., N.Y., NY 10019	Eve Queler
Orchestra da Camera	129 East Dr., N. Massapequa, NY 11758	James Conlon
(Greater) Palm Beach Symphony	P.O. Box 2232, Palm Beach, FL 33480	John Iuele
Pasadena Symphony	300 E. Green St., Pasadena, CA 91101	Daniel Lewis
Peoria Symphony	416 Hamilton, Peoria, IL 61602	William Wilsen
Portland Symphony	30 Myrtle St., Portland, ME 04101	Bruce Hangen
Queens Symphony	99-11 Queens Blvd., Rego Park, NY 11374	David Katz
Regina Symphony	200 Lakeshore Dr., Regina, Sask. S4S 0B3	Gregory Millar
Rhode Island Philharmonic	334 Westminster Mall, Providence, RI 02903	Alvaro Cassuto
Rockford Symphony	415 N. Church St., Rockford, IL 61103	Crawford Gates
Saginaw Symphony	P.O. Box 415, Saginaw, MI 48606	Leo Najar
San Francisco Orchestra	840 Battery St., San Francisco, CA 94111	Edgar J. Braun
Santa Barbara Symphony	3 W. Carrillo, Santa Barbara, CA 93101	Frank Collura
Santa Rosa Symphony	P.O. Box 1081, Santa Rosa, CA 95402	Corrick L. Brown
Savannah Symphony	P.O. Box 9505, Savannah, GA 31412	Christian Badea
Shreveport Symphony	P.O. Box 4057, Shreveport, LA 71104	John Shenaut
Sioux City Symphony	P.O. Box 754, Sioux City, IA 51102	Tom Lewis
South Bend Symphony	215 W. North Shore Drive, South Bend, IN 46617	Herbert Butler
South Dakota Symphony	707 E. 41st St., Sioux Falls, SD 57105	Emanuel Vardi
Spokane Symphony	W. 621 Mallon, Spokane, WA 99201	Donald Thulean
Springfield (Mass.) Symphony	56 Dwight St., Springfield, MA 01103	Robert Gutter
Springfield (Ohio) Symphony	Box 1374, Springfield, OH 45501	John E. Ferritto
Stockton Symphony	Box 4273, Stockton, CA 95204	Kyung-Soo Won
Tacoma Symphony	P.O. Box 19, Tacoma, WA 98401	Edward Sefarian

Tri-City Symphony	P.O. Box 67, Davenport, IA 52805	James Dixon
Tucson Symphony	443 So. Stone Ave., Tucson, AZ 85701	Denis de Coteau
Vermont Symphony	77 College St., Burlington VT 05401	Efrain Guigui
Virginia Orchestra Group	P.O. Box 26, Norfolk, VA 23501	Richard Williams
Warren Symphony	4504 E. Nine Mile Rd., Warren, MI 48091	David Daniels
Wheeling Symphony	Hawley Bldg., Wheeling, WV 26003	Jeff Holland Cook
Winston-Salem Symphony	610 Coliseum Dr., Winston-Salem, NC 27106	Peter Perret
Youngstown Symphony	260 Federal Plaza West, Youngstown, OH 44503	Vacant

Major U.S. and Canadian Opera Companies

Source: Central Opera Service, New York, N.Y.

Arizona Opera Company (Tucson); James Sullivan, gen. dir.

Artists Internationale (Providence, R.I.); Dorothy McKenzie, exec. dir.

Asolo Opera Company (Sarasota); Philip Hall, exec. dir.

Baltimore Opera Company; Jay Holbrook, gen. mgr.

Canadian Opera Company (Toronto); Lotfi Mansouri, gen. dir.

Central City Opera (Denver); Robert Darling, art. dir.

Chautauqua Opera (N.Y.C.); Cynthia Auerbach, opera dir.

Chicago Opera Theatre; Alan Stone, art. dir.

Cincinnati Opera Assn.; James deBlasis, gen. dir.

Civic Opera of the Palm Beaches (Fla.); Paul Csonka, art. dir.

Cleveland Opera Co.; David Bamberger, gen. mgr., art. dir.

Colorado Opera Festival (Colorado Springs); Donald Jenkins, art. dir.

Columbus Opera Symphony (Oh.); Evan Whallon, mus. dir.

Connecticut Opera Assn. (Hartford); George Osborne, gen. mgr.

Dallas Civic Opera; Plato Karayanis, gen. dir.

Dayton Opera Assn.; Lester Freedman, gen. dir., art. dir.

Des Moines Metro Opera (Indianola, Iowa); Douglas Duncan, mng. dir.

Edmonton Opera Assn.; Lorin J. Moore, adm. dir.

Florentine Opera Company (Milwaukee, Wis.); John Gage.

Fort Worth Opera Assn.; Rudolf Kruger, gen. mgr., mus. dir.

Greater Miami Opera Assn.; Robert Herman, gen. mgr.

Hawaii Opera Theatre (Honolulu); Donald Johanos, art. dir.

Hidden Valley Music Seminar (Carmel Valley, Cal.); David Effron, dir.

Houston Grand Opera; David Gockley, gen. dir.

Indianapolis Opera Company; Jackson Wiley, art. dir.

Kentucky Opera Assn. (Louisville); Moritz Bomhard, dir.

Lake George Opera Company (Glens Falls, N.Y.); Paulette Haupt-Nolen, gen. dir.

Light Opera of Manhattan (N.Y.C.); William Mount-Burke, prod. dir.

L'Opera de Montreal; Jean-Paul Jeannotte, art. dir.

Lyric Opera of Chicago; Ardis Krainick, gen. mgr.

Lyric Opera of Kansas City (Mo.); Russell Patterson, gen. dir., art. dir.

Manitoba Opera Assn. (Winnipeg); Irving Guttman, art. dir.

Metropolitan Opera Assn. (N.Y.C.); Anthony A. Bliss, gen. mgr.

Michigan Opera Theatre (Detroit); David DiChiera, gen. dir.

Minnesota Opera Company (St. Paul); Charles Fullmer, gen. mgr.

Music Theatre of Wichita; John Holly, prod. dir.

National Opera Co. (Raleigh, N.C.); David Witherspoon, gen. mgr.

National Opera Touring Co. (N.Y.C.); Nancy Kelly, adm.

Nevada Opera Co. (Reno); Tedd Puffer, dir.

New Jersey State Opera (Newark); Alfredo Silipigni, art. dir.

New Orleans Opera Assn.; Arthur Cosenza, gen. dir.

New York City Opera Company; Beverly Sills, gen. dir.

Opera Company of Boston; Sarah Caldwell, art. dir.

Opera Company of Philadelphia; Margaret Everill, act. mgr.

Opera Memphis; Anne Atherton Randolph, gen. mgr.

Opera/Omaha; Norman Kaderlan, gen. dir.

Opera Orchestra of New York (N.Y.C.); Eve Queler, dir.

Opera Theatre of St. Louis; Richard Gaddes, gen. dir.

Opera Theatre of Syracuse; Robert Driver, gen. mgr., art. dir.

Ottawa Festival Opera; Andree Gingras, adm.

Pittsburgh Opera; Vincent Artz, gen. mgr.

Portland Opera Assn. (Ore.) Stefan Minde, gen. dir.

San Antonio Opera and Symphony; Nat Greenberg, mng. dir.

San Diego Opera; Tito Capobiano, gen. dir.

San Francisco Opera Assn.; Kurt Herbert Adler, gen. dir.

Santa Fe Opera/Opera Assn. of New Mexico; John Crosby, gen. dir.

Seattle Opera Assn.; Glynn Ross, gen. dir.

Skylight Opera (Milwaukee, Wis.); Colin Cabot, mng. dir.

Southern Alberta Opera Assn. (Calgary); Brian Hanson, gen. mgr.

Spoleto Festival USA (Charleston, S.C.); James Kearny, gen. mgr.

Spring Opera Theater of San Francisco; Kurt Herbert Adler, gen. dir.

Toledo Opera Assn.; Lester Freedman, gen. dir.

Tri-Cities Opera Company (Binghamton, N.Y.); Peyton Hibbitt and Carmen Savoca, art. dirs.

Tulsa Opera; Edward Purrington, gen. dir.

Utah Opera Co. (Salt Lake City); Glade Peterson, gen. dir.

Virginia Opera Assn. (Norfolk); Peter Mark, gen. dir.

Vancouver Opera Assn.; Hamilton McClymont, gen. mgr.

The Washington Opera (D.C.); Martin Feinstein, gen. dir.

Western Opera Theater (San Francisco); Earl Jay Schub, mgr.

Wolf Trap Company (Vienna, Va.); E. Craig Hanenson, exec. dir.

Grammy Awards

Source: National Academy of Recording Arts & Sciences

1958

Record: Domenico Modugno, *Nel Blu Dipinto Di Blu (Volare)*.
Album: Henry Mancini, *The Music from Peter Gunn*.
Male vocalist: Perry Como, *Catch a Falling Star*.
Female vocalist: Ella Fitzgerald, *The Irving Berlin Song Book* (album).
Group: Louis Prima & Keely Smith, *That Old Black Magic*.

1959

Record: Bobby Darin, *Mack the Knife*.
Album: Frank Sinatra, *Come Dance With Me*.
Male vocalist: Frank Sinatra, *Come Dance With Me* (album).
Female vocalist: Ella Fitzgerald, *But Not For Me*.
Group: Mormon Tabernacle Choir, *Battle Hymn of the Republic*.

1960

Record: Percy Faith, *Theme From A Summer Place*.
Album: Bob Newhart, *Button Down Mind*.
Male vocalist (single): Ray Charles, *Georgia On My Mind*.
Female vocalist (single): Ella Fitzgerald, *Mack the Knife*.
Group: Steve Lawrence & Eydie Gorme, *We Got Us*.

1961

Record: Henry Mancini, *Moon River*.
Album: Judy Garland, *Judy At Carnegie Hall*.
Male vocalist: Jack Jones, *Lollipops and Roses*.
Female vocalist: Judy Garland, *Judy at Carnegie Hall* (album).
Group: Lambert, Hendricks and Ross, *High Flying*.

1962
Record: Tony Bennett, *I Left My Heart in San Francisco.*
Album: Vaughn Meader, *The First Family.*
Male vocalist: Tony Bennett, *I Left My Heart in San Francisco.*
Female vocalist: Ella Fitzgerald, *Ella Swings Brightly with Nelson Riddle* (album).
Group: Peter, Paul and Mary, *If I Had a Hammer.*
1963
Record: Henry Mancini, *The Days of Wine and Roses.*
Album: *The Barbra Streisand Album.*
Male vocalist: Jack Jones, *Wives and Lovers.*
Female vocalist: *The Barbra Streisand Album.*
Group: Peter, Paul and Mary, *Blowin' in the Wind.*
1964
Record: Stan Getz and Astrud Gilberto, *The Girl From Ipanema.*
Album: *Getz/Gilberto.*
Male vocalist: Louis Armstrong, *Hello, Dolly!*
Female vocalist: Barbra Streisand, *People.*
Group: The Beatles, *A Hard Day's Night.*
1965
Record: Herb Alpert, *A Taste Of Honey.*
Album: Frank Sinatra, *September of My Years.*
Male vocalist: Frank Sinatra, *It Was a Very Good Year.*
Female vocalist: Barbra Streisand, *My Name is Barbra* (album).
Group: Anita Kerr Singers, *We Dig Mancini* (album).
1966
Record: Frank Sinatra, *Strangers in the Night.*
Album: Frank Sinatra, *A Man and His Music.*
Male vocalist: Frank Sinatra, *Strangers in the Night.*
Female vocalist: Eydie Gorme, *If He Walked into My Life.*
Group: Anita Kerr Singers, *A Man and A Woman.*
1967
Record: 5th Dimension, *Up, Up and Away.*
Album: The Beatles, *Sgt. Pepper's Lonely Hearts Club Band.*
Male vocalist: Glen Campbell, *By the Time I Get to Phoenix.*
Female vocalist: Bobbie Gentry, *Ode to Billie Joe.*
Group: 5th Dimension, *Up, Up and Away.*
1968
Record: Simon & Garfunkel, *Mrs. Robinson.*
Album: Glen Campbell, *By the Time I Get to Phoenix.*
Male pop vocalist: Jose Feliciano, *Light My Fire.*
Female pop vocalist: Dionne Warwick, *Do You Know the Way to San Jose.*
Pop group: Simon & Garfunkel, *Mrs. Robinson.*
1969
Record: 5th Dimension, *Aquarius/Let the Sunshine In.*
Album: *Blood, Sweat and Tears.*
Male pop vocalist: Harry Nilsson, *Everybody's Talkin'.*
Female pop vocalist: Peggy Lee, *Is That All There Is.*
Pop group: 5th Dimension, *Aquarius/Let the Sunshine In.*
1970
Record: Simon & Garfunkel, *Bridge Over Troubled Waters.*
Album: *Bridge Over Troubled Waters.*
Male pop vocalist: Ray Stevens, *Everything is Beautiful.*
Female pop vocalist: Dionne Warwick, *I'll Never Fall in Love Again.*
Pop group: The Carpenters, *Close to You.*
1971
Record: Carole King, *It's Too Late.*
Album: Carole King, *Tapestry.*
Male pop vocalist: James Taylor, *You've Got a Friend.*
Female pop vocalist: Carole King, *Tapestry (album).*
Pop group: *The Carpenters (album).*

1972
Record: Roberta Flack, *The First Time Ever I Saw Your Face.*
Album: *The Concert For Bangla Desh.*
Male pop vocalist: Harry Nilsson, *Without You.*
Female pop vocalist: Helen Reddy, *I Am Woman.*
Pop group: Roberta Flack, Donny Hathaway, *Where is the Love.*
1973
Record: Roberta Flack, *Killing Me Softly with His Song.*
Album: Stevie Wonder, *Innervisions.*
Male pop vocalist: Stevie Wonder, *You Are the Sunshine of My Life.*
Female pop vocalist: Roberta Flack, *Killing Me Softly with His Song.*
Pop group: Gladys Knight & The Pips, *Neither One of Us (Wants to Be the First to Say Goodbye).*
1974
Record: Olivia Newton-John, *I Honestly Love You.*
Album: Stevie Wonder, *Fulfullingness' First Finale.*
Male pop vocalist: Stevie Wonder, *Fulfillingness' First Finale (album).*
Female pop vocalist: Olivia Newton-John, *I Honestly Love You.*
Pop group: Paul McCartney & Wings, *Band on the Run.*
1975
Record: Captain & Tennille, *Love Will Keep Us Together.*
Album: Paul Simon, *Still Crazy After All These Years.*
Male pop vocalist: Paul Simon, *Still Crazy After All These Years (album).*
Female pop vocalist: Janis Ian, *At Seventeen.*
Pop group: Eagles, *Lyin' Eyes.*
1976
Record: George Benson, *This Masquerade.*
Album: Stevie Wonder, *Songs in the Key of Life.*
Male pop vocalist: Stevie Wonder, *Songs in the Key of Life (album).*
Female pop vocalist: Linda Ronstadt, *Hasten Down the Wind (album).*
Pop group: Chicago, *If You Leave Me Now.*
1977
Record: Eagles, *Hotel California.*
Album: Fleetwood Mac, *Rumours.*
Male pop vocalist: James Taylor, *Handy Man.*
Female pop vocalist: Barbra Streisand, *Evergreen.*
Pop group: Bee Gees, *How Deep is Your Love.*
1978
Record: Billy Joel, *Just the Way You Are.*
Album: Bee Gees, *Saturday Night Fever.*
Male pop vocalist: Barry Manilow, *Copacabana.*
Female pop vocalist: Anne Murray, *You Needed Me.*
Pop group: Bee Gees, *Saturday Night Fever (album).*
1979
Record: The Doobie Brothers, *What a Fool Believes.*
Album: Billy Joel, *52nd Street.*
Male pop vocalist: Billy Joel, *52nd Street (album).*
Female pop vocalist: Dionne Warwick, *I'll Never Love This Way Again.*
Pop group: The Doobie Brothers, *Minute by Minute (album).*
1980
Record: Christopher Cross, *Sailing.*
Album: Christopher Cross, *Christopher Cross.*
Male pop vocalist: Kenny Loggins, *This Is It.*
Female pop vocalist: Bette Midler, *The Rose.*
Pop group: Barbra Streisand & Barry Gibb, *Guilty* (album).

Recordings

The Recording Industry Association of America, Inc. confers Gold Record Awards on single records that sell one million units, Platinum Awards to those selling two million, Gold Awards to albums and their tape equivalents that sell 500,000 units, Platinum Awards to those selling one million. Platinum Album Awards, Platinum and Gold Single Awards in 1980-81 follow:

Artists and Recording Titles

Albums, Platinum

AC/DC; *Highway to Hell.*
AC/DC; *Back in Black.*
AC/DC; *Dirty Deeds Done Dirt Cheap.*
Air Supply; *Lost in Love.*
Herb Alpert; *Rise.*
Original Cast Album; *Annie.*
Bee Gees; *Bee Gees Greatest.*
Pat Benatar; *Crimes of Passion.*
Pat Benatar; *In the Heat of the Night.*
Pat Benatar; *Hit Me with Your Best Shot.*
George Benson; *Give Me the Night.*
Blondie; *The Tide Is High.*

Blondie; *Autoamerican.*
Blondie; *Eat to the Beat.*
Jackson Browne; *Hold Out.*
Kim Carnes; *Mistaken Identity.*
The Cars; *Panorama.*
Cheap Trick; *Dream Police.*
Christopher Cross; *Christopher Cross.*
Charlie Daniels Band; *Full Moon.*
John Denver & The Muppets; *A Christmas Together.*
John Denver; *John Denver's Greatest Hits, Vol. II.*
Neil Diamond; *The Jazz Singer.*
Doobie Brothers; *One Step Closer.*
Bob Dylan; *Slow Train Coming.*
The Eagles; *The Long Run.*
Electric Light Orchestra; *ELO's Greatest Hits.*

Fleetwood Mac; *Tusk.*
Dan Fogelberg; *Phoenix.*
Foreigner; *Head Games.*
Gap Band; *Gap Band III.*
Willie Nelson & Family; *Honeysuckle Rose* Original Soundtrack.
Isley Brothers; *Go All the Way.*
Jacksons; *Triumph.*
Rick James; *Street Songs.*
Billy Joel; *Glass Houses.*
Brothers Johnson; *Light Up the Night.*
Journey; *Departure.*
Kool & the Gang; *Celebrate.*
Kool & the Gang; *Ladies' Night.*
Led Zeppelin; *In Through the Out Door.*
John Lennon/Yoko Ono; *Double Fantasy.*
Gordon Lightfoot; *Summertime Dream.*
Kenny Loggins; *Celebrate Me Home.*
Barry Manilow; *One Voice.*
Barry Manilow; *Barry.*
Ronnie Milsap; *Greatest Hits.*
Mickey Mouse; *Mickey Mouse Disco.*
Molly Hatchet; *Flirtin' with Disaster.*
Molly Hatchet; *Molly Hatchet.*
Anne Murray; *Greatest Hits.*
Willie Nelson; *Willie Nelson & Family Live.*
Oak Ridge Boys; *Fancy Free.*
Pablo Cruise; *A Place in the Sun.*
Teddy Pendergrass; *TP.*
Tom Petty & The Heartbreakers; *Damn the Torpedoes.*
Pink Floyd; *The Wall.*
Police: *Zenyatta Mondatta.*
Prince; *Prince.*
Queen; *The Game.*
Eddie Rabbit; *Horizon.*
REO Speedwagon; *You Can Tune a Piano...*
REO Speedwagon; *Hi Infidelity.*
Kenny Rogers; *Kenny.*
Kenny Rogers; *Gideon.*
Kenny Rogers; *Greatest Hits.*
Rolling Stones; *Emotional Rescue.*
Linda Ronstadt; *Mad Love.*
Bette Midler; *The Rose* Original Soundtrack.
Diana Ross; *Diana.*
Rush; *2112.*
Rush; *All the World's a Stage.*
Rush; *Moving Pictures.*
Boz Scaggs; *Middle Man.*
Bob Seger & the Silver Bullet Band; *Against the Wind.*
Lynyrd Skynyrd; *Gold and Platinum.*
Bruce Springsteen; *The River.*
Steely Dan; *Gaucho.*
Rod Stewart; *Greatest Hits.*
Rod Stewart; *Foolish Behavior.*
Barbra Streisand; *Wet.*
Barbra Streisand; *Guilty.*
Donna Summer; *On the Radio, Vol I & II.*
Styx; *Cornerstone.*
Styx; *Paradise Theater.*
Various Artists; *Urban Cowboy* Original Soundtrack.
Van Halen; *Women and Children First.*
Dionne Warwick; *Dionne.*
Grover Washington, Jr.; *Winelight.*
Whispers; *The Whispers.*
Steve Winwood; *Arc of a Diver.*
Stevie Wonder; *Hotter Than July*

Olivia Newton-John & Electric Light Orchestra; *Xanadu* Original Soundtrack.
Neil Young; *Rust Never Sleeps.*

Singles, Platinum

Kool and the Gang; *Celebration.*
Lipps, Inc.; *Funkytown.*
Queen; *Another One Bites the Dust.*
S.O.S. Band; *Take Your Time (Do it Right).*

Singles, Gold

Air Supply; *All Out of Love.*
Pat Benatar; *Hit Me with Your Best Shot.*
Blondie; *Call Me.*
Blondie; *Rapture.*
Kurtis Blow; *The Breaks.*
Captain & Tennille; *Do That to Me One More Time.*
Kim Carnes; *Bette Davis Eyes.*
Teri De Sario & KC; *Yes, I'm Ready.*
Devo; *Whip It.*
Dr. Hook; *Sexy Eyes.*
Eagles; *Heartache Tonight.*
Electric Light Orchestra; *I'm Alive.*
Sheena Easton; *Morning Train.*
Barry Gibb & Barbra Streisand; *Guilty.*
Larry Graham; *One in a Million You.*
Hall & Oates; *Kiss on My List.*
Rupert Holmes; *Escape.*
Michael Jackson; *Rock with You.*
Waylon Jennings; *Theme from Dukes of Hazzard.*
Billy Joel; *It's Still Rock 'n' Roll to Me.*
Elton John; *Little Jeannie.*
Johnny Lee; *Lookin' for Love.*
John Lennon; *Starting Over.*
John Lennon; *Woman.*
Manhattans; *Shining Star.*
Paul McCartney; *Coming Up.*
Bette Midler; *The Rose.*
Stephanie Mills; *Never Knew Love Like This Before.*
Juice Newton; *Angel of the Morning.*
Olivia Newton-John; *Magic.*
Oak Ridge Boys; *Elvira.*
Dolly Parton; *9 to 5.*
Pink Floyd; *Another Brick in the Wall, Part II.*
Pointer Sisters; *He's So Shy.*
Prince; *I Wanna Be Your Lover.*
Queen; *Crazy Little Thing Called Love.*
Ray, Goodman & Brown; *Special Lady.*
Smokey Robinson; *Being with You.*
Kenny Rogers; *Coward of the County.*
Kenny Rogers; *Lady.*
Leo Sayer; *More Than I Can Say.*
Shalamar; *Second Time Around.*
Carly Simon; *Jessie.*
Frankie Smith; *Double Dutch Bus.*
Spinners; *Workin' My Way Back to You.*
Stars On; *Stars On 45.*
Barbra Streisand; *No More Tears.*
Barbra Streisand; *Woman in Love.*
Donna Summer; *No More Tears.*
Donna Summer; *On the Radio.*
Donna Summer; *The Wanderer.*
Styx; *Babe.*
Taste of Honey; *Sukiyaki.*
Whispers; *And the Beat Goes On.*
Yarbrough & Peoples; *Don't Stop the Music.*

Miss America Winners

1933	Marion Bergeron, West Haven, Connecticut
1935	Henrietta Leaver, Pittsburgh, Pennsylvania
1936	Rose Coyle, Philadelphia, Pennsylvania
1937	Bette Cooper, Bertrand Island, New Jersey
1938	Marilyn Meseke, Marion, Ohio
1939	Patricia Donnelly, Detroit, Michigan
1940	Frances Marie Burke, Philadelphia, Pennsylvania
1941	Rosemary LaPlanche, Los Angeles, California
1942	Jo-Caroll Dennison, Tyler, Texas
1943	Jean Bartel, Los Angeles, California
1944	Venus Ramey, Washington, D.C.
1945	Bess Myerson, New York City, N.Y.
1946	Marilyn Buferd, Los Angeles, California
1947	Barbara Walker, Memphis, Tennessee
1948	BeBe Shopp, Hopkins, Minnesota
1949	Jacque Mercer, Litchfield, Arizona
1951	Yolande Betbeze, Mobile, Alabama
1952	Coleen Kay Hutchins, Salt Lake City, Utah
1953	Neva Jane Langley, Macon, Georgia
1954	Evelyn Margaret Ay, Ephrata, Pennsylvania
1955	Lee Meriwether, San Francisco, California
1956	Sharon Ritchie, Denver, Colorado
1957	Marian McKnight, Manning, South Carolina
1958	Marilyn Van Derbur, Denver, Colorado
1959	Mary Ann Mobley, Brandon, Mississippi
1960	Lynda Lee Mead, Natchez, Mississippi
1961	Nancy Fleming, Montague, Michigan
1962	Maria Fletcher, Asheville, North Carolina
1963	Jacquelyn Mayer, Sandusky, Ohio
1964	Donna Axum, El Dorado, Arkansas
1965	Vonda Kay Van Dyke, Phoenix, Arizona
1966	Deborah Irene Bryant, Overland Park, Kansas
1967	Jane Anne Jayroe, Laverne, Oklahoma
1968	Debra Dene Barnes, Moran, Kansas
1969	Judith Anne Ford, Belvidere, Illinois
1970	Pamela Anne Eldred, Birmingham, Michigan
1971	Phyllis Ann George, Denton, Texas
1972	Laurie Lea Schaefer, Columbus, Ohio
1973	Terry Anne Meeuwsen, DePere, Wisconsin
1974	Rebecca Ann King, Denver, Colorado
1975	Shirley Cothran, Fort Worth, Texas
1976	Tawney Elaine Godin, Yonkers, N.Y.
1977	Dorothy Kathleen Benham, Edina, Minnesota
1978	Susan Perkins, Columbus, Ohio
1979	Kylene Baker, Galax, Virginia
1980	Cheryl Prewitt, Ackerman, Mississippi
1981	Susan Powell, Elk City, Oklahoma

Best-Selling Books of 1980-81

Listed according to frequency of citation on best seller reports from Aug. 1980 through July 1981.
Numbers in parentheses show rank on top ten list for calendar year 1980, according to *Publishers Weekly.*

Hardcover Fiction

1. Firestarter, Stephen King (5)
2. The Key to Rebecca, Ken Follett (6)
3. The Covenant, James A. Michener (1)
4. Rage of Angels, Sidney Sheldon (3)
5. Masquerade, Kit Williams
6. Gorky Park, Martin Cruz Smith
7. Noble House, James Clavell
8. Answer As a Man, Taylor Caldwell
9. The Fifth Horseman, Larry Collins & Dominique La-pierre (9)
10. Come Pour the Wine, Cynthia Freeman
11. Loon Lake, E.L. Doctorow
12. Free Fall in Crimson, John D. MacDonald
13. Brain, Robin Cook
14. Random Winds, Belva Plain (7)
15. Century, Fred Mustard Stewart
16. The Spike, Arnaud de Borchgrave & Robert Moss (10)
17. God Emperor of Dune, Frank Herbert
18. The Origin, Irving Stone
19. Reflex, Dick Francis
20. Creation, Gore Vidal
21. Unfinished Tales, J.R.R. Tolkien
22. Fanny, Erica Jong
23. Sins of the Father, Susan Howatch
24. Kane & Abel, Jeffrey Archer
25. The Bourne Identity, Robert Ludlum (2)

Hardcover Nonfiction

1. Cosmos, Carl Sagan (2)
2. Crisis Investing, Douglas R. Casey (1)
3. Never-Say-Diet Book, Richard Simmons
4. The Sky's the Limit, Wayne Dyer (6)
5. Craig Claiborne's Gourmet Diet, Craig Claiborne with Pierre Franey (8)
6. Shelley Also Known as Shirley, Shelley Winters (10)
   (tie) The Lord Made Them All, James Herriot
7. Nice Girls Do, Irene Kassorla
8. Side Effects, Woody Allen
9. Free to Choose, Milton & Rose Friedman (3)
10. Betty Crocker's International Cookbook
11. Beverly Hills Diet, Judy Mazel
12. Music for Chameleons, Truman Capote
13. Peter the Great, Robert K. Massie
14. The Last Mafiosi, Ovid Demaris

15. American Dreams, Studs Terkel
16. William E. Donahue's Complete Money Market Guide, William E. Donahue with Thomas Tilling
17. Thy Neighbor's Wife, Gay Talese (5)
18. Little Gloria...Happy at Last, Barbara Goldsmith
19. Goodbye, Darkness, William Manchester
    (tie) Ingrid Bergman: My Story, Ingrid Bergman and Alan Burgess
20. Best Evidence, David S. Lifton
    (tie) The Eagle's Gift, Carlos Casteneda
21. The Coming Currency Collapse, Jerome F. Smith
22. Paper Money, "Adam Smith"
23. You Can Negotiate Anything, Herb Cohen
24. Dr. Atkins' Nutrition Breakthrough, Robert C. Atkins, M.D.
25. Nothing Down, Robert G. Allen (9)

Mass Market Paperback

1. A Woman of Substance, Barbara Taylor Bradford
2. Princess Daisy, Judith Krantz
3. The Complete Scarsdale Medical Diet, Herman Tarnower, M.D. & Samm Sinclair Baker
4. Kane & Abel, Jeffrey Archer
5. Rage of Angels, Sidney Sheldon
6. Smiley's People, John leCarre
7. Portraits, Cynthia Freeman
8. Sophie's Choice, William Styron
9. The Devil's Alternative, Frederick Forsyth
   (tie) Random Winds, Belva Plain
10. Memories of Another Day, Harold Robbins
11. The Bourne Identity, Robert Ludlum
12. Triple, Ken Follett
13. Dead Zone, Stephen King
14. Lost Love, Last Love, Rosemary Rogers
15. If There Be Thorns, V.C. Andrews
16. Shogun, James Clavell
17. The Establishment, Howard Fast
18. Shelley Also Known as Shirley, Shelley Winters
19. Men in Love, Nancy Friday
20. Shibumi, Trevanian
21. The Brethren, Bob Woodward & Scott Armstrong
22. Donahue, Phil Donahue & Co.
23. Petals on the Wind, V.C. Andrews
24. The Books of Rachel, Joel Gross
25. Thy Neighbor's Wife, Gay Talese

Selected U.S. Daily Newspaper Circulation

Source: Audit Bureau of Circulations' FAS-FAX Report. Average paid circulation for 6 months to Mar. 31, 1981. †3 months. For the 6 months up to Sept. 30, 1980, 1,745 English language dailies in the U.S. (387 morning, 1,388 evening, 30 all day) had an average audited circulation of 62,201,840. Sunday papers included 736 with audited average circulation of 54,676,173. (m) morning; (e) evening; *Mon.-Fri. average.

Newspaper	Daily	Sunday
Akron Beacon Journal (e)	162,344	221,344
Allentown Call (m)	*118,348	155,373
Asbury Park Press (e)	109,313	149,503
Atlanta Constitution (m)	215,684	
Atlanta Journal (e)	193,916	499,341
Austin American-Statesman (m&e)	132,163	152,712
Baltimore News-American (e)	146,371	216,320
Baltimore Sun (m&e)	*348,459	375,644
Bergen Co. (N.J.) Record (e)	†149,593	†211,554
Birmingham News (e)	*167,321	214,295
Birmingham Post-Herald (m)	*67,293	
Boston Globe (m&e)	*502,920	741,614
Boston Herald American (m)	*209,128	246,298
Buffalo Courier-Express (m)	131,990	263,584
Buffalo News (e)	*268,928	177,288
Camden (N.J.) Courier-Post (e)	†119,879	†100,546
Charlotte News (e)	47,964	
Charlotte Observer (m)	167,964	246,327
Chicago Sun-Times (m)	*661,531	715,892
Chicago Tribune (m&e)	*790,475	1,150,540
Christian Science Monitor (m)	*164,311	
Cincinnati Enquirer (m)	194,469	293,710
Cincinnati Post (e)	147,018	
Cleveland Plain Dealer (m)	406,444	468,541
Cleveland Press (e)	302,410	
Columbia, S.C. State (m)	106,836	131,153
Columbia, S.C. Record (e)	31,232	
Columbus, Ga. Enquirer (m)	*30,698	63,942
Columbus, Ga. Ledger (e)	*25,209	
Columbus, O. Citizen-Journal (m)	114,899	
Columbus, O. Dispatch (e)	202,209	343,721
Dallas News (m)	286,955[1]	353,677[1]
Dallas Time Herald (e)	*249,890[1]	345,736[1]
Dayton Journal-Herald (m)	101,629	
Dayton News (e)	139,022	219,268
Denver Post (e)	*276,389	357,157
Denver: Rocky Mountain News (m)	288,410	306,627
Des Moines Register (m)	210,465	391,421
Des Moines Tribune (e)	80,114	
Detroit Free Press (m)	*613,311	737,119
Detroit News (e)	*617,879	819,992
Flint Journal (e)	†107,778	110,135
Ft. Worth Star-Telegram (m&e)	229,474	256,660
Fresno Bee (e)	134,777	152,993
Grand Rapids Press (e)	127,550	152,289
Hartford Courant (m)	212,032	290,167
Honolulu Advertiser (m)	85,137	
Honolulu Star-Bulletin (e)	116,777	202,887
Houston Chronicle (m&e)	*367,782	453,036
Houston Post (m)	*347,921	419,308
Indianapolis News (e)	†140,576	
Indianapolis Star (m)	†220,292	†363,201
Jacksonville Journal (e)	45,475	
Jacksonville: Fla. Times Union (m)	157,776	203,725
Kansas City Star (e)	*253,064	404,424
Kansas City Times (m)	297,406	
Knoxville News-Sentinel (e)	100,646	158,654
Little Rock: Ark. Gazette (m)	*128,740	154,875
Long Island, N.Y.: Newsday (e)	*503,336	573,726
Los Angeles Herald-Examiner (e)	*285,099	303,724
Los Angeles Times (m)	*1,026,092	1,271,603
Louisville Courier-Journal (m)	186,348	327,565
Louisville Times (e)	149,423	
Madison, Wis. State Journal	77,811	130,732
Memphis Commercial Appeal (m)	203,920	281,978
Memphis Press Scimitar (e)	95,553	
Miami Herald (m)	444,806	444,085
Milwaukee Journal (e)	318,203	519,365
Milwaukee Sentinel (m)	173,264	
Minneapolis Star (e)	*192,508	
Minneapolis Tribune (m)	*231,759	587,255
Nashville Banner (e)	79,556	
Nashville Tennessean (m)	132,146	244,204
Newark Star-Ledger (m)	*†403,798	†585,174
New Haven Register (e)	96,526	140,372
New Haven Journal-Courier (m)	*37,837	
New Orleans Times-Picayune/States-Item (m&e)	*†281,546	†323,731
New York News (m)	*1,491,556	1,995,702
New York Post (m&e)	732,158	
New York Times (m)	*930,546	1,479,263
Norfolk Ledger-Star (e)	†95,500	
Norfolk Virginian-Pilot (m)	†129,022	†200,680
Oakland Tribune (e)	*134,489	179,206
Oklahoma City Oklahoman (m)	*194,119	304,552
Oklahoma City Times (e)	*90,531	
Omaha World-Herald (m&e)	*229,044	281,045
Orange Co. (Cal.) Register (m&e)	*238,757	272,369
Orlando Sentinel-Star (m&e)	*207,621	248,282
Palm Beach Post (m)	*95,474	148,072
Palm Beach Times (e)	*29,296	
Peoria Journal Star (m&e)	103,097	121,374
Philadelphia Bulletin (e)	*412,268	466,409
Philadelphia Inquirer (m)	*428,862	851,376
Philadelphia News (e)	*232,190	
Phoenix Gazette (e)	†113,329	
Phoenix Republic (m)	*272,173	†411,156
Pittsburgh Post Gazette (m)	*180,375	
Pittsburgh Press (e)	*268,490	637,435
Portland, Me. Press-Herald (m)	55,939	
Portland, Me. Express (e) & Maine Sunday Telegram	30,371	120,136
Portland Oregonian (m)	247,811	420,688
Portland: Oregon Journal (e)	*109,199	
Providence Bulletin (e)	*139,305	
Providence Journal (m)	79,739	233,306
Raleigh News & Observer (m)	†129,044	†166,501
Raleigh Times (e)	†33,872	
Richmond News Leader (e)	114,412	
Richmond Times Dispatch (m)	136,385	222,273
Rochester Democrat-Chronicle (m)	128,539	233,343
Rochester Times-Union (e)	116,144	
Sacramento Bee (m)	214,021	238,854
Sacramento Union (m)	103,701	105,220
St. Louis Globe-Democrat (m)	*256,226	250,815
St. Louis Post-Dispatch (e)	*244,599	436,298
St. Paul Dispatch (e)	*118,737	
St. Paul Pioneer Press (m)	*109,199	251,320
St. Petersburg Independent (e)	41,895	
St. Petersburg Times (m)	244,226	304,039
Salt Lake City Tribune (m)	110,998	178,299
San Antonio Express (m)	*81,112	186,815
San Antonio News (e)	*73,954	
San Antonio Light (e)	*115,172	181,778
San Diego Union (m)	†207,171	†329,820
San Diego Tribune (e)	†127,271	
San Francisco Examiner (e)	*154,099	
San Francisco Chronicle (m)	*515,453	665,887
San Jose Mercury (m)	*154,750	269,351
San Jose News (e)	*65,772	
Seattle Post-Intelligencer (m)	*185,962	211,876
Seattle Times (m&e)	*261,432	344,724
South Bend Tribune (e)	106,211	126,044
Spokane Chronicle (e)	59,026	
Spokane Spokesman-Review (m)	77,818	125,898
Springfield, Ill. State Journal-Register (m&e)	*71,936	72,878
Springfield, Mass. Union (m)	72,360	
Springfield, Mass. News (e) & Sunday Republican	75,715	144,219
Syracuse Herald-Journal (e)	112,140	233,220
Syracuse Post-Standard (m)	81,696	
Tacoma News Tribune (e)	107,169	111,211
Tampa Tribune (m)	198,489	246,271
Toledo Blade (e)	167,028	211,721
Tucson Daily Star (m)	†75,452	†138,094
Tulsa Tribune (e)	†77,772	
Tulsa World (m)	†128,587	†222,755
Wall St. Journal (m) (total)	*1,948,121	
Washington, D.C. Post (m)	*618,111	845,176
Washington, D.C. Star (e)	*322,827	294,086
Wichita Eagle (m)	124,984	173,591
Winston-Salem Journal (m)	†72,106	96,852
Winston-Salem Sentinel (e)	36,646	
Youngstown Vindicator (e)	†102,319	†155,159

(1) as of March 31, 1980.

Circulation of Leading U.S. Magazines

Source: Audit Bureau of Circulations' FAS-FAX Report

General magazines, exclusive of groups and comics. Based on total average paid circulation during the 6 months prior to Dec. 31, 1980.

Magazine	Circulation	Magazine	Circulation	Magazine	Circulation
TV Guide	17,981,657	Sport	1,222,718	Harper's Bazaar	660,468
Reader's Digest	17,898,681	Bon Appetit	1,190,001	Workbench	658,537
National Geographic		Psychology Today	1,171,347	Gourmet	653,219
Magazine	10,711,886	House & Garden	1,126,114	Esquire Magazine	652,220
Better Homes & Gar	8,052,693	1001 Decorating Ideas	1,106,394	Modern Photography	636,281
Woman's Day	7,748,069	US	1,103,404	Signature	633,541
Family Circle	7,529,734	Vogue	1,101,451	Forum	619,483
McCall's	6,218,169	Mademoiselle	1,096,558	Sports Afield	610,493
Ladies' Home Journal	5,601,449	Teen	1,058,870	Road & Track	601,598
Good Housekeeping	5,290,833	Mother Earth News	1,043,774	Essence	600,254
National Enquirer	5,051,496	Family Handyman	1,018,380	Gallery	590,030
Playboy	5,011,099	Golf Digest	1,016,161	The Lutheran	582,593
Time	4,358,911	Discovery	1,004,939	Catholic Digest	574,528
Redbook	4,353,745	Travel & Leisure	957,391	National Lampoon	555,311
Penthouse	4,330,949	Hot Rod	900,208	Club	544,692
The Star	3,508,558	Self	889,999	Colonial Homes	544,054
Consumer Reports	3,000,000*	House Beautiful	869,702	Stereo Review	529,758
Newsweek	2,964,279	Popular Photography	868,556	The Saturday Evening Post	525,050
Cosmopolitan	2,837,325	Junior Scholastic	868,055	Saturday Review	511,101
American Legion	2,599,187	Omni	858,027	Girl Scout Leader	505,273
Sr. Scholastic	2,529,206	Scouting	853,991	Flower & Garden	504,928
People Weekly	2,499,573	Yankee	851,027	The New Yorker	503,124
Prevention	2,429,439	Money	835,043	Architectural Digest	500,442
Sports Illustrated	2,265,760	Apartment Life	830,231	Easyriders	488,582
U.S. News-World Report	2,055,993	Decorating & Craft Ideas	828,946	Tennis	488,151
Field & Stream	2,021,599	Business Week	824,259	Guns & Ammo	475,121
Glamour	1,935,636	Family Health	811,175	The Rotarian	470,239
Popular Science	1,933,262	Book Digest	806,541	Science 80	461,906
Smithsonian	1,904,515	Co-ed	801,985	Natural History	461,236
V.F.W. Magazine	1,844,891	Weight Watchers		New York Magazine	451,996
Globe	1,802,988	Magazine	793,351	The Sporting News	444,224
The Elks Magazine	1,651,862	Grit	791,975	Westways	442,959
Today's Education	1,651,783	Playgirl	786,761	Cycle	441,629
Mechanix Illustrated	1,626,182	Jet	766,073	Country Music	440,531
Seventeen	1,552,884	Motor Trend	754,343	Skiing Magazine	434,953
Parents	1,515,707	Oui	751,301	Cheri	430,950
The Workbasket	1,472,139	Golf	726,010	Car Craft	427,337
Boys' Life	1,462,745	Car and Driver	721,182	GQ-Gentlemen's Quarterly	426,479
True Story	1,432,900	Scientific American	712,902	World Tennis	420,601
Sunset	1,417,304	Rolling Stone	701,271	Ski	417,282
Changing Times	1,407,690	Eagle	694,316	Working Woman	414,747
Life	1,338,026	Forbes	693,945	Capper's Weekly	413,210
Ebony	1,287,670	Games	691,095	Popular Electronics	400,114
Nation's Business	1,265,555	Fortune	675,570		
New Woman	1,251,595	Soap Opera Digest	661,143		

* Circulation figure provided by publisher.

Selected Canadian Daily Newspaper Circulation

Source: Audit Bureau of Circulations' FAS-FAX Report of average paid circulation for 6 months ending Mar. 31, 1981.

For the 6 months up to Sept. 30, 1980. 119 daily newspapers in Canada (25 morning: 95 evening, 1 all day) had an average audited circulation of 5,158,368; 37 Saturday-Sunday-weekend newspapers had an average circulation of 4,853,050.

Newspaper	Daily	Saturday	Newspaper	Daily	Saturday
Calgary Sun. (m)	51,128		St. Catharines Standard (e)	†43,455	
Calgary Herald (e)	*139,244	175,684	St. John's Telegram (e)	*34,102	46,394
Edmonton Journal (e)	*178,596	244,185	Saint John Telegraph-Journal (m)	*30,539	67,463
Halifax Chronicle-Herald (m)	71,642		Saint John Times Globe (e)	*31,913	
Halifax Mail-Star (e)	57,574		Saskatoon Star-Phoenix (e)	55,001	
Hamilton Spectator (e)	†149,828		Sherbrooke: La Tribune (m)	*41,099	44,217
Kingston Whig-Standard (e)	†35,467		Sudbury Star (e)	30,082	
Kitchener-Waterloo Record (e)	†71,577		Sydney: Cape Breton Post (e)	31,437	
London Free Press (m & e)	*126,868	131,258	Toronto Globe and Mail (m)	339,193	
Montreal Gazette (m)	*211,578	283,183	Toronto Star (e)	*481,855	800,162
Montreal: La Presse (m)	*191,811	290,734	Toronto Sun (m)	*225,323	**399,799
Montreal: Le Devoir (m)	40,732¹	40,503¹	Trois Rivieres Nouvelliste (e)	*52,968	
Montreal: Le Journal de Montreal (m)	*317,213	**285,668	Vancouver Province (m)	*129,331	**151,697
Ottawa Citizen (e)	*171,278	215,958	Vancouver Sun (e)	*283,222	284,649
Ottawa: Le Droit (e)	*45,201	50,771	Victoria Times-Colonist (m & e)	79,046¹	50,568¹
Quebec: Le Journal de Quebec (m)	*105,545	95,020	Windsor Star (e)	92,244	
Quebec: Le Soleil (e)	*130,978	140,643	Winnipeg Free Press (e)	*187,867	237,055
Regina Leader Post (e)	69,078				

(m) Morning; (e) Evening; * Based on Monday to Friday average; **Sunday. (†) Indicates 3 month circulation average. (1) As of Sept. 30, 1980.

Circulation of Leading Canadian Magazines

Source: Audit Bureau of Circulations' FAS-FAX Report.

General magazines, exclusive of groups and comics. Statistics based on average paid circulation during the 6 months prior to June 30, 1981.

Magazine	Circulation	Magazine	Circulation	Magazine	Circulation
Reader's Digest (Eng.-Fr.) . .	1,629,734	Legion Magazine	494,291	T.V. Hebdo.	271,409
Chatelaine (English-French) .	1,347,499	Selection du Reader's Digest	323,934	L'Actualite	241,443
Reader's Digest (English) . .	1,305,800	Canadian Motorist.	322,757	Flare	187,561
Chatelaine (English).	1,055,215	Time Canada	320,617	Harrowsmith Magazine. . . .	153,916
TV Guide (English-French) . .	941,195	Canadian Living	302,548	Saturday Night.	129,289
MacLean's Magazine	640,558	Chatelaine (French).	292,284		

America's Favorite Television Programs

Source: A.C. Nielsen
(Percent of TV households and persons in TV households)

Network Programs (Oct. to Dec. 1980)

(Nielsen average audience estimates)

	TV House-holds	Women	Men	Teens	Chil-dren
Dallas	34.9	31.8	23.3	19.3	16.8
60 Minutes	28.3	21.7	21.8	—	—
Dukes of Hazzard	26.7	21.1	18.6	18.7	30.7
Love Boat	25.7	21.4	15.2	17.6	23.3
Alice	25.6	22.0	15.5	—	—
One Day at a Time	25.2	21.9	16.3	—	—
Jeffersons	25.2	21.9	15.8	—	—
Happy Days	24.4	18.0	—	19.6	24.7
Archie Bunker's Place	24.2	21.4	16.5	—	—
Three's Company	23.3	17.6	—	16.7	—
Laverne & Shirley	23.0	17.6	—	16.7	22.0
NBC Tues. Night Movie	22.6	—	15.9	18.3	—
Too Close for Comfort	22.1	—	—	—	—
Little House-Prairie	22.1	17.8	—	—	17.3
M*A*S*H	22.0	17.6	—	14.9	—
Fantasy Island	—	17.8	—	14.6	—
Diff'rent Strokes	—	16.6	—	19.7	—
NFL Mon. Night Football	—	—	19.8	—	—
NFL Football Game 2-NBC	—	—	18.4	—	—
That's Incredible	—	—	16.7	—	—
CBS NFL Football Game 1	—	—	16.2	—	—
Big Event	—	—	15.7	—	—
ABC Sun. Night Movie	—	—	15.3	19.8	—
Mork & Mindy	—	—	—	18.0	20.2
Disney's Wonderful World	—	—	—	16.9	29.3
Enos	—	—	—	16.3	20.5
Soap	—	—	—	16.0	—
Incredible Hulk	—	—	—	—	25.5
Richie Rich	—	—	—	—	20.3
Fonz/Happy Days Gang	—	—	—	—	19.3
Scooby & Scrappy Doo	—	—	—	—	18.5
Bugs Bunny/Road Runner 2	—	—	—	—	18.1
Bugs Bunny/Road Runner 3	—	—	—	—	17.4

Syndicated Programs (Nov. 1980)

(Average ratings for total U.S.)

	TV house-holds	Women	Men	Teens	Chil-dren
M*A*S*H	12.8	8.8	8.7	9.1	6.7
Muppets	12.0	8.3	7.4	8.3	17.1
Hee Haw	9.9	7.7	7.5	4.6	—
Family Feud PM	9.7	8.1	6.1	4.8	—
Happy Days, Again	9.3	5.0	4.1	11.7	12.3
Tic Tac Dough	8.9	7.6	5.4	—	—
Lawrence Welk	8.8	8.0	5.4	—	—
PM Magazine	8.7	6.8	6.0	—	—
Donahue Show	6.6	5.5	—	—	—
Sanford & Son	6.3	—	3.7	6.3	6.5
Joker's Wild	—	4.7	—	—	—
All in the Family	—	—	3.6	—	—
Solid Gold	—	—	—	5.9	—
Good Times	—	—	—	5.7	—
Welcome Back, Kotter	—	—	—	5.7	—
Dance Fever	—	—	—	4.7	—
Tom and Jerry	—	—	—	—	10.8
Bugs Bunny	—	—	—	—	8.4
Flintstones	—	—	—	—	7.2
Gilligan's Island	—	—	—	—	6.7
Woody Woodpecker	—	—	—	—	6.5
Sha Na Na	—	—	—	—	4.5

Total TV households — 77.8 million; in TV households; 18 + women — 81.53 million, 18 + men — 73.37 million, teens 12–17 — 22.13 million, children 2–11 — 31.71 million.

Average Television Viewing Time

Source: A.C. Nielsen estimates, Nov. 1980 (hours: minutes, per week)

		Total	Mon.-Fri. 10am-4:30pm	Mon.-Fri. 4:30pm-7:30pm	Mon.-Sun. 8-11pm	Sat. 8am-1pm	Mon.-Fri. 11:30pm-1am
Avg. all persons		29:46	4:10	4:43	9:16	:44	1:04
Women	Total 18+	33:31	6:16	5:01	10:22	:26	1:16
	18-24	28:28	5:16	4:03	8:32	:37	1:04
	55+	38:26	7:26	6:38	11:20	:22	1:12
Men	Total 18+	28:45	2:26	4:13	9:37	:28	1:20
	18-24	22:33	2:14	2:58	6:46	:33	1:13
	55+	35:39	4:02	6:18	11:22	:28	1:20
Teens	Female	22:19	3:21	4:05	7:22	:47	:41
	Male	23:40	1:40	3:37	8:31	:56	:52
Children	2-5	29:14	6:01	6:02	4:56	2:17	:05
	6-11	25:44	2:30	5:27	7:26	1:56	:08

U.S. Television Sets and Stations Received

Set Ownership
(Nielsen est. as of Jan. 1, 1981)
Total TV homes	77,800,000	100%
(98% of U.S. homes own at least one TV set)		
Homes with:		
Color TV sets	66,250,000	85%
B&W only	11,550,000	15
2 or more sets	39,800,000	51
One set	38,000,000	49
CATV (Feb. 1980)	21,260,000	26.5

Number of Stations
(FCC, May 31, 1981)
Commercial	762
Educational	269
Total	1,031

Stations Receivable
(Nielsen, Jan. 1981)
% of TV homes receiving:
1-3 stations	3%
4	6
5	10
6	10
7	10
8	7
9	11
10+	43

All-time Top Television Programs

Source: A.C. Nielsen estimates

Program	Date	Network	Households	Program	Date	Network	Households
Dallas	11/21/80	CBS	41,470,000	World Series Game 6	10/21/80	NBC	31,120,000
Roots	1/30/77	ABC	36,380,000	Dallas	11/9/80	CBS	31,120,000
Super Bowl XIV	1/20/80	CBS	35,330,000	Roots	1/29/77	ABC	30,120,000
Super Bowl XIII	1/21/79	NBC	35,090,000	Jaws	11/4/79	ABC	29,830,000
Super Bowl XII	1/15/78	CBS	34,410,000	Dallas	11/7/80	CBS	29,720,000
Gone With The Wind, Pt. 1	11/7/76	NBC	33,960,000	Super Bowl X	1/18/76	CBS	29,440,000
Gone With The Wind, Pt. 2	11/8/76	NBC	33,750,000	Super Bowl IX	1/12/75	NBC	29,040,000
				Dallas	12/5/80	CBS	29,020,000
Roots	1/28/77	ABC	32,680,000	Roots	1/23/77	ABC	28,840,000
Roots	1/27/77	ABC	32,540,000	Shogun, Pt. 3	9/17/80	NBC	28,710,000
Roots	1/25/77	ABC	31,900,000	Three's Company	3/13/79	ABC	28,610,000
Super Bowl XI	1/9/77	NBC	31,610,000	Dallas	1/23/81	CBS	28,320,000
Roots	1/24/77	ABC	31,400,000	World Series Game 7	10/17/79	ABC	28,150,000
Roots	1/26/77	ABC	31,190,000	Dallas	1/2/81	CBS	28,090,000

Estimated Advertising Expenditures in the U.S.

Source: Advertising Age; prepared by Robert J. Coen of McCann-Erickson, Inc.

Medium Newspapers	1977 Dollars (millions)	1977 Percent of total	1978 Dollars (millions)	1978 Percent of total	1979 Dollars (millions)	1979 Percent of total	1980[1] Dollars (millions)	1980[1] Percent of total	% change '80 vs. '79
Total	$ 11,132	29.4	$12,707	28.9	14,493	29.2	15,541	28.4	+7.2
National	1,677	4.4	1,787	4.1	2,085	4.2	2,353	4.3	+12.9
Local	9,455	24.9	10,920	24.8	12,408	25.0	13,188	24.1	+6.3
Magazines									
Total	2,162	5.7	2,597	5.9	2,930	5.9	3,149	5.8	+7.4
Weeklies	903	2.4	1,158	2.6	1,315	2.6	1,418	2.6	+6.9
Women's	565	1.5	672	1.5	735	1.5	782	1.4	+7.1
Monthlies	694	1.8	767	1.8	880	1.8	949	1.8	+8.5
Farm publications	90	0.1	104	0.2	120	0.2	130	0.2	+8.3
Television									
Total	7,612	20.1	8,979	20.4	10,195	20.5	11,387	20.8	+12.1
Network	3,460	9.1	3,975	9.0	4,540	9.1	5,132	9.4	+11.6
Spot	2,204	5.8	2,581	5.9	2,890	5.8	3,290	6.0	+14.5
Local	1,948	5.1	2,423	5.5	2,765	5.6	2,965	5.4	+10.6
Radio									
Total	2,634	6.9	3,052	6.9	3,385	6.8	3,827	7.0	+15.1
Network	137	0.4	147	0.3	170	0.3	180	0.3	+11.8
Spot	546	1.4	620	1.4	680	1.4	774	1.4	+16.0
Local	1,951	5.1	2,285	5.2	2,535	5.1	2,873	5.3	+15.0
Direct Mail	5,164	13.6	5,987	13.6	6,650	13.4	7,596	13.9	+14.2
Business publications	1,221	3.2	1,400	3.2	1,595	3.2	1,674	3.1	+6.3
Outdoor									
Total	418	1.1	466	1.1	535	1.1	610	1.1	+13.0
National	290	0.8	307	0.7	350	0.7	400	0.7	12.7
Local	128	0.3	159	0.4	185	0.4	210	0.4	+13.5
Miscellaneous									
Total	7,487	19.7	8,678	19.8	9,817	19.7	10,786	19.7	+10.2
National	3,899	10.3	4,485	10.2	5,060	10.2	5,672	10.4	+12.0
Local	3,588	9.5	4,193	9.6	4,757	9.5	5,114	9.3	+8.3
Total									
National	20,850	55.0	23,980	54.6	27,070	54.4	30,350	55.5	+12.1
Local	17,070	44.0	19,990	45.4	22,650	45.6	24,350	44.5	+8.2
Grand total	37,920	100.0	43,970	100.0	49,720	100.0	54,700	100.0	+10.1

(1) Preliminary figures, subject to adjustment when final 1980 FCC broadcast data are released.

Network TV Program Ratings

Source: A. C. Nielson, November, 1980

Program or type	TV Households		Audience Composition (thousands)			
	Rating %	No. (000)	Men (18+)	Women (18+)	Teens 12-17	Children 2-11
Today (7:30-8:00)	5.3	4,120	2,020	3,140	130	150
Morning (7:15-8:00)	3.1	2,410	1,080	1,700	70	360
Good Morning Amer. (7:30-8:00)	5.3	4,120	1,490	3,210	260	440
Daytime						
Drama (Soaps)	7.1	5,540	1,170	4,950	440	530
Quiz & Aud. Participation	4.6	3,560	1,160	2,890	160	450
All 10am-4:30pm	6.2	4,850	1,160	4,180	380	570
Evening						
Informational						
News Mon.-Fri.	14.1	10,970	7,100	8,260	760	1,260
General Drama	25.4	19,740	11,240	17,750	3,000	3,920
Susp. & Mystery	17.6	13,730	8,660	11,240	2,290	1,150
Sit. Comedy	21.7	16,910	9,680	14,190	3,150	4,750
Feature Film	17.2	13,350	8,890	10,550	2,440	2,200
All 7-11pm regular	19.4	15,090	9,890	11,920	2,570	3,140

Television Network Addresses

American Broadcasting Company (ABC)
1330 Avenue of Americas
New York, NY 10019

Columbia Broadcasting System (CBS)
51 W. 52nd St.
New York, NY 10019

National Broadcasting Company (NBC)
30 Rockefeller Plaza
New York, NY 10020

Westinghouse Broadcasting (Group W)
90 Park Ave.
New York, NY 10016

Metromedia
485 Lexington Ave.
New York, NY 10017

Public Broadcasting Service (PBS)
609 Fifth Ave.
New York, NY 10017

Canadian Broadcasting Corp. (CBC)
1500 Bronson Ave.
Ottawa, Ontario, Canada K1G 3J5

50 Leading U.S. Advertisers, 1979

Source: Advertising Age, Sept. 11, 1980; copyright © Crain Communications Inc. 1980.

Rank	Company	Ad Costs (000)	Sales (000)	Ads as % sales	Rank	Company	Ad Costs (000)	Sales (000)	Ads as % sales
	Appliances, TV, radio					**Retail Chains**			
24	RCA Corp.	$158,600	$ 7,454,600	2.1	3	Sears, Roebuck & Co.	379,313	17,514,000	2.1
31	General Electric	139,408	22,460,600	0.6	6	Kmart	287,095	12,731,145	2.3
					38	J.C. Penney Co.	122,000	11,274,000	1.1
	Automobiles								
4	General Motors Corp.	323,395	66,311,200	0.5		**Soaps, cleansers**			
10	Ford Motor Corp.	215,000	1,409,003	0.5	1	Procter & Gamble	614,900	10,772,186	5.7
40	Chrysler Corp.	118,000	12,000,000	1.0	23	Unilever U.S. Inc.	160,000	2,124,000	7.5
					37	Colgate-Palmolive Co.	122,500	4,949,000	2.7
	Chemicals								
34	American Cyanamid Co.	127,000	3,186,998	4.0		**Soft drinks**			
					11	PepsiCo Inc.	212,000	5,050,566	4.2
	Communications				18	Coca-Cola Co.	169,271	4,961,400	3.4
29	CBS Inc.	146,118	3,729,701	3.9					
46	Time Inc.	102,360	2,504,060	4.1		**Telephones**			
48	Transamerica Corp.	95,048	4,044,647	2.3	9	American T & T	219,756	45,408,078	0.4
					32	International T & T	132,400	17,197,423	0.8
	Drugs								
36	Richardson-Merrell	123,800	1,090,546	11.4		**Tobacco**			
43	SmithKline Corp.	107,737	1,351,145	8.0	5	Philip Morris	291,201	8,302,892	3.5
49	Sterling Drug Co.	92,000	81,180	11.2	7	R.J. Reynolds Industries	258,115	8,935,200	2.9
					41	B.A.T. Industries	116,396	1,440,000	8.1
	Food								
2	General Foods Corp.	393,000	5,959,600	6.5		**Toiletries, cosmetics**			
14	McDonald's Corp.	202,807	5,385,000	3.8	8	Warner-Lambert Co.	220,242	3,217,208	6.8
16	General Mills	190,746	4,170,287	4.6	12	Bristol-Meyers Co.	210,600	2,752,777	7.7
17	Esmark Inc.	170,547	6,771,883	2.5	13	American Home Products	206,000	3,649,476	5.6
21	Norton Simon Inc.	163,188	2,755,934	5.9	35	Gillette Co.	126,960	1,984,722	6.4
27	Beatrice Foods Co.	150,000	8,290,509	1.8	44	Chesebrough-Pond's	107,342	1,174,274	9.1
33	Pillsbury Co.	131,549	3,032,000	4.3					
39	Kraft Inc.	119,654	6,432,935	1.9		**Wine, beer, liquor**			
42	Ralston Purina Co.	108,028	4,600,000	2.3	19	Seagram Co.	168,000	2,553,096	6.6
45	Consolidated Foods Corp.	105,000	5,000,000	2.1	22	Anheuser-Busch	160,524	3,263,744	4.9
50	Kellogg Co.	91,646	1,850,000	5.0	26	Heublein Inc.	155,000	1,769,074	8.8
						Miscellaneous			
	Oil				15	Gulf & Western Industries	191,500	6,507,000	2.9
					25	Johnson & Johnson	157,700	2,372,128	6.6
					28	U.S. Government	146,121	----	---
20	Mobil Corp.	165,841	48,241,000	2.9	30	Loews Corp.	144,468	4,065,475	3.6

World Communication

Sources: UNESCO for newspapers, 1976-77; UN Statistical Year Book 1978 for radios, TVs, and film theaters.

Nation	No. of daily newspapers	Copies per 1,000 pop.	No. of Radios (thousands)	Radios per 1,000 pop.	No. of TV sets (thousands)	TV sets per 1,000 pop.	No. of film theaters	Theater seats per 1,000 pop.	Avg. visits per year pop.
Algeria	4	13	3,000	173	525	30	317	11.3	2.7
Argentina	142	149	21,000	838	4,500	180	1,415	30.5	3.2
Australia	60	310	10,500	770	4,785	351	609	N/A	N/A
Austria	31	336	2,185	291	1,772	236	576	23.9	2.8
Bahrain	N/A	N/A	100	412	31	120	10	43.2	8.2
Belgium	27	241	4,044	409	2,646	268	604	27.3	2.6
Bolivia	13	26	430	74	N/A	N/A	N/A	N/A	N/A
Brazil	299	45	16,980	158	10,525	96	3,261	10.1	2.6
Bulgaria	12	237	2,750	314	3,793	254	3,597	84.5	13.1
Canada	122	221	23,400	1,011	9,895	428	1,176	29.3	4.3
Chile	42	N/A	1,800	172	710	68	291	18.1	2.3
China (P R)	N/A	N/A	12,000	16	N/A	N/A	N/A	N/A	N/A
Colombia	42	N/A	2,860	117	1,700	70	850	N/A	4.1
Cuba	16	N/A	2,100	222	650	09	429	33.6	14.2
Czechoslovakia	29	296	3,928	263	3,793	254	3,390	64.5	5.8
Denmark	49	362	1,851	365	1,637	323	375	25.2	3.7
Ecuador	37	46	1,700	279	N/A	N/A	185	16.5	5.6
Egypt	10	79	5,250	138	N/A	17	N/A	N/A	N/A
Ethiopia	2	1	210	7	21	0.7	31	0.9	N/A
Finland	59	472	2,179	461	1,714	363	319	20.1	2.0
France	96	205	17,442	330	14,500	274	5,543	31.8	3.3
Germany, E.	39	496	6,167	367	5,180	309	1,546	20.5	4.6
Germany, W.	412	423	20,244	329	19,226	311	3,094	18.4	2.1
Ghana	4	42	1,080	105	35	3.4	9	1.4	0.1
Greece	112	80	2,750	300	1,165	127	N/A	N/A	N/A
Guinea	1	2	120	26	N/A	N/A	N/A	N/A	N/A
Hungary	27	243	2,538	241	2,495	236	3,528	53.0	7.0
Iceland	6	554	64	291	53	241	42	N/A	10.8
India	929	13	14,848	24	280	0.5	5,650	6.6	3.8
Indonesia	178	N/A	5,100	37	325	2.3	960	4.9	0.9
Iran	23	N/A	2,100	63	1,720	51	448	9.0	N/A
Iraq	7	N/A	1,252	113	425	37	N/A	N/A	N/A
Ireland	7	220	949	300	655	207	184	N/A	N/A
Israel	24	231	655	189	475	137	233	46.5	7.8
Italy	72	97	13,024	232	12,377	220	12,471	N/A	9.2
Jamaica	3	49	555	270	111	54	44	22.8	0.2
Japan	177	546	59,650	530	26,545	239	2,468	10.1	1.7
Kenya	3	11	514	37	50	3.6	48	1.8	42.5
Korea, S.	44	197	5,000	139	2,300	64	584	10.4	2.2
Kuwait	7	159	502	487	182	183	9	13.0	4.7
Lebanon	33	84	1,600	540	425	144	N/A	N/A	N/A
Liberia	3	5	265	151	8.9	5.1	N/A	N/A	N/A
Libya	2	26	110	45	10	4.1	50	12.3	9.4
Malaysia	37	75	1,450	118	555	45	410	21.0	9.1
Mexico	325	115	14,005	301	4,885	84	2,402	26.2	4.2
Morocco	10	N/A	1,500	84	522	29	222	N/A	1.8
Netherlands	67	315	3,997	290	3,774	274	419	12.3	2.1
New Zealand	39	376	2,715	865	813	259	228	39.8	3.8
Nigeria	19	8	5,100	79	105	1.6	120	0.8	0.5
Norway	82	430	1,288	320	1,087	270	451	35.6	4.6
Pakistan	103	37	1,200	17	350	4.8	578	4.7	0.3
Panama	6	79	270	157	186	108	45	26.9	4.8
Paraguay	4	80	80	66	55	20	N/A	N/A	N/A
Peru	30	51	2,068	129	600	37	276	N/A	N/A
Philippines	17	N/A	1,875	43	800	18	716	13.5	7.6
Poland	44	240	8,288	239	6,820	198	2,188	16.3	4.1
Portugal	28	54	1,525	161	723	76	459	29.9	4.1
Rhodesia	2	12	255	39	72	11	N/A	N/A	N/A
Romania	34	171	3,104	145	2,963	138	6,084	10.3	8.7
Saudi Arabia	12	8	260	28	130	14	60	N/A	0.7
Senegal	1	5	290	57	2.0	0.4	71	26.8	18.7
Singapore	10	215	356	156	294	129	N/A	N/A	N/A
S. Africa	24	66	N/A	N/A	N/A	N/A	N/A	N/A	N/A
Spain	143	128	9,300	259	6,640	185	5,267	70.9	7.0
Sri Lanka	22	49	800	58	N/A	N/A	350	13.1	4.0
Sweden	112	528	3,203	390	2,988	363	1,253	N/A	3.1
Switzerland	91	414	2,108	332	1,809	285	519	29.7	3.6
Syria	7	N/A	1,367	N/A	N/A	N/A	100	7.6	5.5
Tanzania	2	8	300	19	N/A	N/A	31	N/A	0.2
Thailand	23*	21	5,500	131	761	18	658	9.2	1.7
Tunisia	5*	18	N/A	N/A	N/A	N/A	106	9.2	2.3
Turkey	493	N/A	4,228	105	1,769	44	217	N/A	N/A
USSR	686	396	122,477	481	55,181	N/A	145,600	N/A	17.7
UK	110	410	2,108	332	1,809	285	N/A	14.8	1.9
U.S.	1,829	287	402,000	1,882	121,100	571	11,250	N/A	N/A
Uruguay	26	N/A	1,600	516	355	114	N/A	N/A	N/A
Venezuela	54	178	5,034	407	1,431	116	572	N/A	N/A
Vietnam	5	5	510	24	N/A	N/A	N/A	N/A	N/A
Yugoslavia	26	96	4,526	210	3,463	161	1,327	22.0	3.8
Zaire	6	9	N/A	N/A	7.0	0.3	91	1.0	0.1
Zambia	2	20	110	21	25	4.9	N/A	N/A	N/A

*Morning dailies only.

Major Movies of the Year (Sept. 1, 1980 to Aug. 1, 1981)

Listed below, alphabetically, are some of the major films rated by the New York Daily News star system: 4☆ is for excellent, 3½☆ very good, 3☆ good, 2½☆ fair, 2☆ mediocre, 1½☆ poor, 1☆very poor, 0☆ not worth rating.

Kathleen Carroll, N. Y. Daily News Movie Editor and Critic

Movie	Rating	Stars	Director
A Change of Seasons	2☆	Anthony Hopkins, Shirley MacLaine, Bo Derek	Richard Lang
A Second Chance	1☆	Catherine Deneuve	Claude Lelouch
Alligator	2☆	Robert Forster, Robin Riker	Lewis Teague
Any Which Way You Can	2☆	Clint Eastwood, Sondra Locke	Buddy Van Horn
Arthur	3½☆	Dudley Moore, Liza Minnelli	Steve Gordon
Back Roads	2½☆	Sally Field, Tommy Lee Jones	Ralph Bakshi
Blow Out	2½☆	John Travolta, Nancy Allen	Brian De Palma
Bustin' Loose	2☆	Richard Pryor, Cicely Tyson	Oz Scott
The Cannonball Run	2☆	Burt Reynolds, Roger Moore	Hal Needham
Cattle Annie and Little Britches	2½☆	Burt Lancaster, Rod Steiger	Lamont Johnson
Caveman	2½☆	Ringo Starr, Barbara Bach	Carl Gottlieb
Cheech and Chong's Nice Dreams	2☆	Cheech Marin, Thomas Chong	Thomas Chong
City of Women	2½☆	Marcello Mastroianni, Ettore Manni	Federico Fellini
Clash of the Titans	1½☆	Laurence Olivier, Harry Hamlin	Desmond Davis
Coast to Coast	2☆	Robert Blake, Dyan Cannon	Joseph Sargent
The Competition	2☆	Richard Dreyfuss, Amy Irving, Lee Remick	Joel Oliansky
Cutter and Bone	2☆	Jeff Bridges, John Heard	Ivan Passer
Death Hunt	2½☆	Charles Bronson, Lee Marvin	Peter Hurt
The Devil and Max Devlin	1½☆	Elliott Gould, Bill Cosby	Steven Hilliard Stern
Divine Madness	3☆	Bette Midler	Joseph Sargent
The Dogs of War	2½☆	Christopher Walken, Tom Berenger	John Irvin
Dragonslayer	2☆	Peter MacNicol, Caitlin Clarke	Matthew Robbins
The Elephant Man	3☆	Anthony Hopkins, John Hurt	David Lynch
Endless Love	2☆	Brooke Shields, Martin Hewitt	Franco Zeffirelli
Escape From New York	2☆	Kurt Russell, Lee Van Cleef	John Carpenter
Excalibur	2½☆	Nigel Terry, Nicol Williamson	John Boorman
Eye of the Needle	2½☆	Donald Sutherland, Kate Nelligan	Richard Marquand
Eyewitness	3☆	William Hurt, Sigourney Weaver	Peter Yates
The Fan	3☆	Lauren Bacall, Maureen Stapleton	Edward Bianchi
The First Deadly Sin	1☆	Frank Sinatra, Faye Dunaway	Brian Hutton
First Family	1☆	Bob Newhart, Gilda Radner, Madeline Kahn	Buck Henry
Flash Gordon	2½☆	Sam J. Jones, Max von Sydow	Mike Hodges
For Your Eyes Only	2½☆	Roger Moore, Carole Bouquet	John Glen
The Formula	2☆	Marlon Brando, George C. Scott	John G. Avildsen
Fort Apache, The Bronx	2☆	Paul Newman, Ed Asner	Daniel Petrie
The Four Seasons	2½☆	Alan Alda, Carol Burnett	Alan Alda
Gloria	2½☆	Gena Rowlands, John Adams	John Cassavetes
The Great Muppet Caper	3☆	Diana Rigg, Miss Piggy	Jim Henson
The Hand	2½☆	Michael Caine, Andrea Marcovicci	Oliver Stone
Happy Birthday To Me	2☆	Melissa Sue Anderson, Glenn Ford	J. L. Thompson
The Haunting of Julia	1½☆	Mia Farrow	Richard Loncraine
Herbie Goes Bananas	1½☆	Harvey Korman, Cloris Leachman	Vincent McEveety
History of the World—Part 1	2☆	Mel Brooks, Dom De Luise	Mel Brooks
Hopscotch	3☆	Walter Matthau, Glenda Jackson	Ronald Neame
The Howling	2½☆	Dee Wallace, Patrick Macnee	Joe Dante
The Idolmaker	2½☆	Ray Sharkey, Tovah Feldshun	Taylor Hackford
Improper Channels	1☆	Alan Arkin, Mariette Hartley	Eric Tilf
In God We Trust	1☆	Marty Feldman, Peter Boyle, Louise Lasser	Marty Feldman
The Incredible Shrinking Woman	2½☆	Lily Tomlin, Charles Grodin	Joel Schumacher
The Jazz Singer	1½☆	Neil Diamond, Laurence Olivier, Lucie Arnaz	Richard Donner
The Last Metro	3½☆	Catherine Deneuve	Francois Truffaut
The Legend of the Lone Ranger	3☆	Klinton Spilsbury, Michael Horse	William Fraker
Lion of the Desert	3☆	Anthony Quinn, Oliver Reed	Moustapha Akkad
The Mirror Crack'd	2½☆	Elizabeth Taylor, Angela Lansbury, Rock Hudson	Guy Hamilton
Nighthawks	2½☆	Sylvester Stallone, Billy Dee Williams	Bruce Malmuth
Nine to Five	3☆	Jane Fonda, Dolly Parton, Lily Tomlin	Colin Higgins
Oh, God! Book II	1☆	George Burns, Suzanne Pleshette	Gilbert Cates
One-Trick Pony	2½☆	Paul Simon, Blair Brown	Robert M. Young
Ordinary People	4☆	Mary Tyler Moore, Donald Sutherland	Robert Redford
Outland	3½☆	Sean Connery, Peter Boyle	Peter Hyams
Polyester	2☆	Divine, Tab Hunter	John Waters
Popeye	2½☆	Robin Williams, Shelley Duvall	Robert Altman
The Postman Always Rings Twice	2½☆	Jack Nicholson, Jessica Lange	Bob Rafelson
Raging Bull	3☆	Robert De Niro, Cathy Moriarty	Martin Scorsese
Raiders of the Lost Ark	3½☆	Harrison Ford, Karen Allen	Steven Spielberg
Richard's Things	3☆	Liv Ullmann	Anthony Harvey
S.O.B.	2½☆	Julie Andrews, William Holden	Blake Edwards
Second Hand Hearts	1☆	Robert Blake, Barbara Harris	Hal Ashby
Seems Like Old Times	2☆	Goldie Hawn, Chevy Chase	Jay Sandrich
Somewhere in Time	1☆	Christopher Reeve, Jane Seymour	Jeannot Szwarc
Stardust Memories	3½☆	Woody Allen, Charlotte Rampling	Woody Allen
Stir Crazy	1☆	Richard Pryor, Gene Wilder	Sidney Poitier
Stripes	1½☆	Bill Murray, Harold Ramis	Ivan Reitman
Superman II	3½☆	Christopher Reeve, Margot Kidder	Richard Lester
Tess	3☆	Nastassia Kinski, Peter Firth	Roman Polanski
Those Lips, Those Eyes	3☆	Frank Langella, Glynnis O'Connor	Michael Pressman
Tribute	2½☆	Jack Lemmon, Robby Benson, Lee Remick	Bob Clark
Victory	3☆	Sylvester Stallone, Michael Caine, Pele	John Huston
Wolfen	2½☆	Albert Finney, Diane Verona	Michael Wadleigh
Zorro, The Gay Blade	2☆	George Hamilton, Lauren Hutton	Peter Medak

WORLD FACTS

Early Explorers of the Western Hemisphere

The first men to discover the New World or Western Hemisphere are believed to have walked across a "land bridge" from Siberia to Alaska, an isthmus since broken by the Bering Strait. From Alaska, these ancestors of the Indians spread through North, Central, and South America. Anthropologists have placed these crossings at between 18,000 and 14,000 B.C.; but evidence found in 1967 near Puebla, Mex., indicates mankind reached there as early as 35,000-40,000 years ago.

At first, these people were hunters using flint weapons and tools. In Mexico, about 7000-6000 B.C., they founded farming cultures, developing corn, squash, etc. Eventually, they created complex civilizations — Olmec, Toltec, Aztec, and Maya and, in South America, Inca. Carbon-14 tests show men lived about 8000 B.C. near what are now Front Royal, Va., Kanawha, W. Va., and Dutchess Quarry, N.Y. The Hopewell Culture, based on farming, flourished about 1000 B.C.; remains of it are seen today in large mounds in Ohio and other states.

Norsemen (Norwegian Vikings) sailing out of Iceland and Greenland) are credited by most scholars with being the first Europeans to discover America, with at least 5 voyages around 1000 A.D. to areas they called Helluland, Markland, Vinland—possibly Labrador, Nova Scotia or Newfoundland, and New England.

Christopher Columbus, most famous of the explorers, was born at Genoa, Italy, but made his discoveries sailing for the Spanish rulers Ferdinand and Isabella. Dates of his voyages, places he discovered, and other information follow:

1492—First voyage. Left Palos, Spain, Aug. 3 with 88 men (est.). Discovered San Salvador (Guanahani or Watling Is., Bahamas) Oct. 12. Also Cuba, Hispaniola (Haiti-Dominican Republic); built Fort La Navidad on latter.

1493—Second voyage, first part, Sept. 25, with 17 ships, 1,500 men. Dominica (Lesser Antilles) Nov. 3; Guadeloupe, Montserrat, Antigua, San Martin, Santa Cruz, Puerto Rico, Virgin Islands. Settled Isabela on Hispaniola. **Second part** (Columbus having remained in Western Hemisphere), Jamaica, Isle of Pines, La Mona Is.

1498—Third voyage. Left Spain May 30, 1498, 6 ships. Discovered Trinidad. Saw South American continent Aug. 1, 1498, but called it Isla Sancta (Holy Island). Entered Gulf of Paria and landed, first time on continental soil. At mouth of Orinoco Aug. 14 he decided this was the mainland

1502—Fourth voyage, 4 caravels, 150 men. St. Lucia, Guanaja off Honduras; Cape Gracias a Dios, Honduras; San Juan River, Costa Rica; Almirante, Portobelo, and Laguna de Chiriqui, Panama.

Year	Explorer	Nationality and employer	Discovery or exploration
1497	John Cabot	Italian-English	Newfoundland or Nova Scotia
1498	John and Sebastian Cabot	Italian-English	Labrador to Hatteras
1499	Alonso de Ojeda	Spanish	South American coast, Venezuela
1500, Feb.	Vicente y Pinzon	Spanish	South American coast, Amazon River
1500, Apr.	Pedro Alvarez Cabral	Portuguese	Brazil (for Portugal)
1500-02	Gaspar Corte-Real	Portuguese	Labrador
1501	Rodrigo de Bastidas	Spanish	Central America
1513	Vasco Nunez de Balboa	Spanish	Pacific Ocean
1513	Juan Ponce de Leon	Spanish	Florida
1515	Juan de Solis	Spanish	Rio de la Plata
1519	Alonso de Pineda	Spanish	Mouth of Mississippi River
1519	Hernando Cortes	Spanish	Mexico
1520	Ferdinand Magellan	Portuguese-Spanish	Straits of Magellan, Tierra del Fuego
1524	Giovanni da Verrazano	Italian-French	Atlantic Coast-New York harbor
1532	Francisco Pizarro	Spanish	Peru
1534	Jacques Cartier	French	Canada, Gulf of St. Lawrence
1536	Pedro de Mendoza	Spanish	Buenos Aires
1536	A.N. Cabeza de Vaca	Spanish	Texas coast and interior
1539	Francisco de Ulloa	Spanish	California coast
1539-41	Hernando de Soto	Spanish	Mississippi River near Memphis
1539	Marcos de Niza	Italian-Spanish	Southwest (now U.S.)
1540	Francisco V. de Coronado	Spanish	Southwest (now U.S.)
1540	Hernando Alarcon	Spanish	Colorado River
1540	Garcia de L. Cardenas	Spanish	Grand Canyon of the Colorado
1541	Francisco de Orellana	Spanish	Amazon River
1542	Juan Rodriquez Cabrillo	Portuguese-Spanish	San Diego harbor
1565	Pedro Menendez	Spanish	St. Augustine
1576	Martin Frobisher	Engish	Frobisher's Bay, Canada
1577-80	Francis Drake	English	California Coast
1582	Antonio de Espejo	Spanish	Southwest (named New Mexico)
1584	Amadas & Barlow (for Raleigh)	English	Virginia
1585-87	Sir Walter Raleigh's men	English	Roanoke Is., N.C.
1595	Sir Walter Raleigh	English	Orinoco River
1603-09	Samuel de Champlain	French	Canadian interior, Lake Champlain
1607	Capt. John Smith	English	Atlantic coast
1609-10	Henry Hudson	English-Dutch	Hudson River, Hudson Bay
1634	Jean Nicolet	French	Lake Michigan; Wisconsin
1673	Jacques Marquette, Louis Jolliet	French	Mississippi S to Arkansas
1682	Sieur de La Salle	French	Mississippi S to Gulf of Mexico
1789	Alexander Mackenzie	Canadian	Canadian Northwest

Arctic Exploration

Early Explorers

1587 — John Davis (England). Davis Strait to Sanderson's Hope, 72° 12′ N.

1596 — Willem Barents and Jacob van Heemskerck (Holland). Discovered Bear Island, touched northwest tip of Spitsbergen, 79° 49′ N, rounded Novaya Zemlya, wintered at Ice Haven.

1607 — Henry Hudson (England). North along Greenland's east coast to Cape Hold-with-Hope, 73° 30′, then north of Spitsbergen to 80° 23′. Returning he discovered Hudson's Touches (Jan Mayen).

1616 — William Baffin and Robert Bylot (England). Baffin Bay to Smith Sound.

1728 — Vitus Bering (Russia). Proved Asia and America were separated by sailing through strait.

1733-40 — Great Northern Expedition (Russia). Surveyed Siberian Arctic coast.

1741 — Vitus Bering (Russia). Sighted Alaska from sea, named Mount St. Elias. His lieutenant, Chirikof, discovered coast.

1771 — Samuel Hearne (Hudson's Bay Co.). Overland from Prince of Wales Fort (Churchill) on Hudson Bay to mouth of Coppermine River.

434

1778 — James Cook (Britain). Through Bering Strait to Icy Cape, Alaska, and North Cape, Siberia.

1789 — Alexander Mackenzie (North West Co., Britain). Montreal to mouth of Mackenzie River.

1806 — William Scoresby (Britain). North of Spitsbergen to 81° 30′.

1820-3 — Ferdinand von Wrangel (Russia). Completed a survey of Siberian Arctic coast. His exploration joined that of James Cook at North Cape, confirming separation of the continents.

1845 — Sir John Franklin (Britain) was one of many to seek the Northwest Passage—an ocean route connecting the Atlantic and Pacific via the Arctic. His 2 ships (the Erebus and Terror) were last seen entering Lancaster Sound July 26.

1888 — Fridtjof Nansen (Norway) crossed Greenland's icecap, 1893-96 — Nansen in Fram drifted from New Siberian Is. to Spitsbergen; tried polar dash in 1895, reached Franz Josef Land.

1896 — Salomon A. Andree (Sweden) and companion, in June, made first attempt to reach North Pole by balloon; failed and returned in August. On July 11, 1897, Andree and 2 others started in balloon from Danes, Is., Spitsbergen, to drift across pole to America, and disappeared. Over 33 years later, Aug. 6, 1930, Dr. Gunnar Horn (Norway) found their frozen bodies on White Is., 82° 57′ N 29° 52′ E.

1903-06 — Roald Amundsen (Norway) first sailed Northwest Passage.

Discovery of North Pole

Robert E. Peary began exploring in 1886 on Greenland, when he was 30. With his hq. at McCormick Bay he explored Greenland's coast 1891-92, tried for North Pole 1893, returned with large meteorites. In 1900 he reached northern limit of Greenland and 83° 50′ N; in 1902 he reached 84° 06′ N; in 1906 he went from Ellesmere Is. to 87° 06′ N. He sailed in the Roosevelt, July, 1908, to winter off Cape Sheridan, Grant Land. The dash for the North Pole began Mar. 1 from Cape Columbia, Ellesmere Land. Peary reached the pole, 90° N, Apr. 6, 1909.

Peary had several supporting groups carrying supplies until the last group, under Capt. Robt. A. Bartlett, turned back at 87° 47′ N. Peary, Matthew Henson, and 4 eskimos proceeded with dog teams and sleds. They crossed the pole several times, finally built an igloo at 90°, remained 36 hours. Started south Apr. 7 at 4 p.m. for Cape Columbia. Eskimos were Coqueeh, Ootah, Eginwah, and Seegloo. Adm. Peary died Feb. 20, 1920. Henson, a Negro, born Aug. 8, 1866, died in New York, N.Y., Mar. 9, 1955, aged 88. Ootah, the last survivor, died near Thule, Greenland, May, 1955,

aged 80.

1914 — Donald Macmillan (U.S.). Northwest, 200 miles, from Axel Hieberg Island to seek Peary's Crocker Land.

1915-17 — Vihjalmur Stefansson (Canada) discovered Borden, Brock, Meighen, and Lougheed Islands.

1918-20 — Amundsen sailed Northeast Passage.

1925 — Roald Amundsen and Lincoln Ellsworth (U.S.) reached 87° 44′ N in attempt to fly to North Pole from Spitsbergen.

1926 — Richard E. Byrd and Floyd Bennett (U.S.) first over North Pole by air, May 9.

1926 — Amundsen, Ellsworth, and Umberto Nobile (Italy) flew from Spitsbergen over North Pole May 12, to Teller, Alaska, in dirigible Norge.

1928 — Nobile crossed North Pole in airship Italia May 24, crashed May 25. Amundsen lost while trying to effect rescue by plane.

1928 — Sir Hubert Wilkins and Eielson flew from Point Barrow to Spitsbergen, 84° N.

North Pole Exploration Records

On Aug. 3, 1958, the Nautilus, under Comdr. William R. Anderson, became the first ship to cross the North Pole beneath the Arctic ice.

On Aug. 12, 1958, the nuclear submarine Skate, Comdr. James F. Calvert, became the 2d ship to make an underwater crossing of the North Pole.

In March, 1959, the Skate returned to the Arctic and on its 3d attempt, broke through at the North Pole, the first time any ship had been on the surface at 90° N.

The nuclear-powered U.S. submarine Seadragon, Comdr. George P. Steele 2d, made the first east-west underwater transit through the Northwest Passage during August, 1960. It sailed from Portsmouth N.H., headed between Greenland and Labrador through Baffin Bay, then west through Lancaster Sound and McClure Strait to the Beaufort Sea. Traveling submerged for the most part, the submarine made 850 miles from Baffin Bay to the Beaufort Sea in 6 days.

On Aug. 16, 1977, according to press dispatches from Moscow, the Soviet nuclear icebreaker Arktika reached the North Pole and became the first surface ship to break through the Arctic ice pack to the top of the world.

On April 30, 1978, Naomi Uemura, a Japanese explorer, became the first man to reach the North Pole alone by dog sled. During the 54-day, 600-mile trek over the frozen Arctic, Uemura survived attacks by a marauding polar bear.

Antarctic Exploration

Early History

Antarctica has been approached since 1773-75, when Capt. Jas. Cook (Britain) reached 71° 10′ S. Many sea and landmarks bear names of early explorers. Bellingshausen (Russia) discovered Peter I and Alexander I Islands, 1819-21. Nathaniel Palmer (U.S.) discovered Palmer Peninsula, 60° W, 1820, without realizing that this was a continent. Jas. Weddell (Britain) found Weddell Sea, 74° 15′ S, 1823.

First to announce existence of the continent of Antarctica was Charles Wilkes (U.S.), who followed the coast for 1,500 mi., 1840. Adelie Coast, 140° E, was found by Dumont d'Urville (France), 1840. Ross Ice Shelf was found by Jas. Clark Ross (Britain), 1841-42.

1895 — Leonard Kristensen, Norwegian whaling captain, landed a party on the coast of Victoria Land in Jan. 1895. They were the first ashore on the main continental mass. C.E. Borchgrevink, a member of that party, returned in 1899 with a British expedition, first to winter on Antarctica.

1902-04 — Robert F. Scott (Britain) discovered Edward VII Peninsula. In 1902 he reached 82° 17′ S, 146° 33′ E from McMurdo Sound.

1908-09 — Ernest Shackleton, in 1908, introduced the use of Manchurian ponies in Antarctic sledging. In 1909 he reached 88° 23′ S, discovering a route on to the plateau by way of the Beardmore Glacier and pioneering the way to the pole.

Discovery of South Pole

1911 — Roald Amundsen (Norway) with 4 men and dog teams reached the pole Dec. 14, 1911.

1912 — Capt. Scott reached the pole from Ross Island Jan. 18, 1912, with 4 companions, where they found Amundsen's tent. None of Scott's party survived. They were found Nov. 12, 1912.

1928 — First man to use an airplane over Antarctica was Hubert Wilkins (Britain).

1929 — Richard E. Byrd (U.S.) established Little America on Bay of Whales. On 1600-mi. airplane flight begun Nov. 28 he crossed South Pole Nov. 29 with his pilot, a radio operator, and a photographer. Dropped U.S. flag over pole, temp. 16° below zero.

1934-35 — Richard E. Byrd (U.S.) led 2d expedition to Little America, which explored 450,000 sq. mi. Byrd wintered alone at an advance weather station in 80° 08′ S.

1934-37 — John Rymill led British Graham Land expedition of

1934-37; discovered that Palmer Peninsula is part of Antarctic mainland.

1935 — Lincoln Ellsworth (U.S.) flew south along Palmer Peninsula's east coast, then crossed continent to Little America, making 4 landings on unprepared terrain in bad weather.

1939-41 — U.S. Antarctic Service built West Base on Ross Ice Shelf under Paul Siple, and East Base on Palmer Peninsula under Richard Black. U.S. Navy plane flights discovered about 150,000 sq. miles of new land.

1940 — Richard E. Byrd (U.S.) charted most of coast between Ross Sea and Palmer Peninsula.

1946-47 — U.S. Navy undertook Operation High-jump under Rear Admiral Byrd. Expedition included 13 ships and 4,000 men. Twenty-nine land-based flights from Little America and 35 by seaplanes from tenders photomapped coastline and penetrated beyond pole.

1946-48 — Ronne Antarctic Research Expedition, Comdr. Finn Ronne, USNR, determined the Antarctic to be only one continent with no strait between Weddell Sea and Ross Sea; discovered 250,000 sq. miles of land by flights to 79° S Lat., and made 14,000 aerial photographs over 450,000 sq. miles of land. Mrs. Ronne and Mrs. H. Darlington, who accompanied their husbands, were the first women to winter on Antarctica.

1955-57 — U.S. Navy's Operation Deep Freeze led by Adm. Richard E. Byrd. Supporting U.S. scientific efforts for the International Geophysical Year, the operation was commanded by Rear Adm. George Dufek. It established 5 coastal stations fronting the Indian, Pacific, and Atlantic Oceans and also 3 interior stations; explored more than 1,000,000 sq. miles in Wilkes Land. Seven Navy men under Adm. Dufek landed by plane at the Pole Oct. 31, 1956, and landed radar reflectors.

1957-58 — During the International Geophysical year, July, 1957, through Dec. 1958, scientists from 12 countries conducted ambitious programs of Antarctic research. A network of some 60 stations on the continent and sub-Arctic islands studied oceanography, glaciology, meteorology, seismology, geomagnetism, the ionosphere, cosmic rays, aurora, and airglow. A party from Ellsworth IGY station (U.S.) south of Weddell Sea under the direction of Captain Finn Ronne explored beyond 1947 flight and delineated Berkner Island imbedded in the Filchner Ice Shelf.

Dr. V.E. Fuchs led a 12-man Trans-Antarctic Expedition on the first land crossing of Antarctica. Starting from the Weddell Sea, they reached Scott Station Mar. 2, 1958, after traveling 2,158 miles in 98 days.

1958 — A group of 5 U.S. scientists led by Edward C. Thiel, seismologist, moving by tractor from Ellsworth Station on Weddell Sea, identified a huge mountain range, 5,000 ft. above the ice sheet and 9,000 ft. above sea level. The range, originally seen by a Navy plane, was named the Dufek Massif, for Rear Adm. George Dufek.

1959 — Twelve nations — Argentina, Australia, Belgium, Chile, France, Japan, New Zealand, Norway, South Africa, the Soviet Union, the United Kingdom, and the U.S. — signed a treaty suspending any territorial claims for 30 years and reserving the continent for research.

1961-62 — Scientists discovered a trough, the Bentley Trench, running from Ross Ice Shelf, Pacific, into Marie Byrd Land, around the end of the Ellsworth Mtns., toward the Weddell Sea, which may be the long-suspected link between the Atlantic and Pacific Oceans.

1962 — First nuclear power plant began operation at McMurdo Sound.

1963 — On Feb. 22 a U.S. plane made the longest nonstop flight ever made in the S. Pole area, covering 3,600 miles in 10 hours. The flight was from McMurdo Station south past the geographical S. Pole to Shackleton Mtns., southeast to the "Area of Inaccessibility" and back to McMurdo Station.

1963 — Three turbine-powered helicopters made the first copter landings on the S. Pole.

1964 — A British survey team was landed by helicopter on Cook Island, the first recorded visit since its discovery in 1775.

1964 — New Zealanders completed one of the last and most important surveys when they mapped the mountain area from Cape Adare west some 400 miles to Pennell Glacier.

1966-67 — Fifteen Antarctic areas set aside as Specially Protected Areas for the conservation of flora and fauna.

Notable Volcanoes of the World

Year of last eruption in parentheses.

More than 75 per cent of the world's 850 active volcanoes lie within the "Ring of Fire," a zone running along the west coast of the Americas from Chile to Alaska and down the east coast of Asia from Siberia to New Zealand. Twenty per cent of these volcanoes are located in Indonesia. Other prominent groupings are located in Japan, the Aleutian Islands, and Central America. Almost all active regions are found at the boundaries of the large moving plates which comprise the earth's surface. The "Ring of Fire" marks the boundary between the plates underlying the Pacific Ocean and those underlying the surrounding continents. Other active regions, such as the Mediterranean Sea and Iceland, are located on plate boundaries.

Major Historical Eruptions

Approximately 7,000 years ago, Mazama, a 9,900-feet-high volcano in southern Oregon, erupted violently, ejecting ash and lava. The ash spread over the entire northwestern United States and as far away as Saskatchewan, Canada. During the eruption, the top of the mountain collapsed, leaving a caldera 6 miles across and about a half mile deep, which filled with rain water to form what is now called Crater Lake.

In 79 A.D., Vesuvio, or Vesuvius, a 4,190 feet volcano overlooking Naples Bay became active after several centuries of quiescence. On Aug. 24 of that year, a heated mud and ash flow swept down the mountain engulfing the cities of Pompeii, Herculaneum, and Stabiae with debris over 60 feet deep. About 10 percent of the population of the 3 towns was killed.

The largest eruptions in recent centuries have been in Indonesia. In 1883, an eruption similar to the Mazama eruption occurred on the island of Krakatau. On August 27, the 2,640-feet-high peak of the volcano collapsed to 1,000 feet below sea level, leaving only a small portion of the island standing above the sea. Ash from the eruption colored sunsets around the world for 2 years. A tsunami ("tidal wave") generated by the collapse killed 36,000 people in nearby Java and Sumatra and eventually reached England. A similar, but even more powerful, eruption had taken place 68 years earlier at Tambora volcano on the Indonesian island of Sumbawa.

Events in 1980-81

Mt. St. Helen in the Cascade Mountains of southwest Washington erupted May 18 in a blast that hurled a plume of ash and steam some 60,000 feet into the sky, set off mudslides and floods, and ignited lightning storms and forest fires.

Authorities reported that 25 persons had been killed by the eruption and that at least 40 others were missing and presumed dead. The economic damage to the southern Washington and northern Oregon region was set at $2.7 billion.

Smaller eruptions occurred on May 25, June 12, July 22, and Aug. 7, as well as a series of eruptions Oct. 16-18. The volcano, which had been dormant for 123 years, continued to extrude lava in 1981.

Mt. Etna in Sicily continued to be active. An eruption in March, 1981, extruded lava from several fissures on the NNW flank and caused an estimated $10 million damage. Of the volcano's 90 historic eruptions, it was only the third on the NW or NNW flank.

Japan's Sakurazima volcano, which has been active since 1955, erupted 11 times in March, 1981. Krafla volcano in Iceland, Langila volcano in New Britain, Suwanosezima volcano in Japan, and White Island volcano in New Zealand were especially active in 1980 and 1981.

Name	Location	Feet	Name	Location	Feet
Africa			Slamet (1967)	Java	11,247
Kilimanjaro	Tanzania	19,340	Raung (1945)	Java	10,932
Cameroon	Cameroons	13,354	Shiveluch (1964)	USSR	10,771
Teide (Tenerife) (1909)	Canary Is.	12,198	Dempo (1940)	Sumatra	10,364
Nyirangongo (1977)	Zaire	11,400	Ardjuno-Welirang	Java	10,354
Nyamuragira (1980)	Zaire	10,028	Agung (1964)	Bali	10,308
Fogo (1951)	Cape Verde Is.	9,281	Sundoro (1906)	Java	10,285
Karthala (1977)	Comoro Is.	8,000	Tjiremai (1938)	Java	10,098
Piton de la Fournaise (1981)	Reunion Is.	5,981	On-Take (1980)	Japan	10,049
Erta-Ale (1973)	Ethiopia	1,650	Mayon (1978)	Philippines	9,991
Antarctica			Papandajan (1925)	Java	9,802
Erebus (1979)	Ross Island	12,450	Gede (1949)	Java	9,705
Big Ben (1960)	Heard Island	9,007	Zhupanovsky (1959)	USSR	9,705
Melbourne	Victoria Land	8,500	Apo	Philippines	9,690
Deception Island (1970)	South Shetland Islands	1,890	Merapi (1976)	Java	9,551
Asia-Oceania			Bezymianny (1979)	USSR	9,514
Klyuchevskaya (1974)	USSR	15,584	Marapi (1981)	Sumatra	9,485
Kerintji (1968)	Sumatra	12,467	Tambora (1913)	Indonesia	9,353
Fuji	Japan	12,388	Ruapehu (1980)	New Zealand	9,175
Rindjani (1966)	Indonesia	12,224	Peuetsagoe (1921)	Sumatra	9,121
Tolbachik (1941)	USSR	12,080	Avachinskaya (1945)	USSR	9,026
Semeru (1981)	Java	12,060	Balbi	Solomon Is.	9,000
Ichinskaya	USSR	11,880	Geureudong	Sumatra	8,497
Kronotskaya (1923)	USSR	11,575	Asama (1973)	Japan	8,300
Koryakskaya (1957)	USSR	11,339	Sumbing (1921)	Sumatra	8,225
			Tandikat (1914)	Sumatra	8,166

Name	Location	Feet
Niigata Yakeyama (1974)	Japan	8,111
Yake Dake (1963)	Japan	8,064
Canlaon	Philippines	8,015
Sinabung	Sumatra	7,913
Bromo (1950)	Java	7,848
Idjen (1936)	Java	7,828
Alaid (1972)	Kuril Is.	7,662
Ulawun (1980)	New Britain	7,532
Ngauruhoe (1975)	New Zealand	7,515
Guntur	Java	7,379
Bamus	New Britain	7,338
Chokai (1974)	Japan	7,300
Galunggung (1918)	Java	7,113
Amburombu (1969)	Indonesia	7,051
Sorikmerapi (1917)	Sumatra	7,037
Butak Petarangan (1939)	Java	6,890
Sibajak	Sumatra	6,870
Tokachi (1962)	Japan	6,813
Azuma (1978)	Japan	6,700
Tangkuban Prahu (1967)	Java	6,637
Tongariro	New Zealand	6,458
Zheltovskaya (1923)	USSR	6,401
Catarman (1952)	Philippines	6,371
Kaba (1941)	Sumatra	6,358
Sangeang Api (1966)	Indonesia	6,351
Nasu (1977)	Japan	6,210
Tiatia (1973)	Kuril Islands	6,013
Manam (1981)	Papua New Guinea	6,000
Soputan (1968)	Celebes	5,994
Siau (1976)	Indonesia	5,853
Kelud (1967)	Java	5,679
Batur (1968)	Bali	5,636
Ternate (1963)	Indonesia	5,627
Lewotobi (1935)	Indonesia	5,591
Kirisima (1979)	Japan	5,577
Lamongan	Java	5,482
Keli Mutu (1968)	Indonesia	5,460
Akita Komaga take (1970)	Japan	5,449
Lli Boleng (1950)	Indonesia	5,443
Gamkunoro (1949)	Indonesia	5,364
Aso (1980)	Japan	5,223
Lewotobi Laki-Laki (1968)	Indonesia	5,217
Lokon-Empung (1970)	Celebes	5,187
Bulusan (1980)	Philippines	5,115
Sarycheva (1976)	Kuril Islands	4,960
Me-akan (1966)	Japan	4,931
Ibu (1911)	Indonesia	4,921
Karkar (1981)	Papua New Guinea	4,920
Karymskaya (1976)	USSR	4,869
Lopevi (1960)	New Hebrides	4,755
Ambrym (1979)	New Hebrides	4,376
Mahawu	Celebes	4,367
Awu (1968)	Indonesia	4,350
Ili Lewotolo (1920)	Indonesia	4,348
Tongkoko	Celebes	3,770
Ili Werung (1948)	Indonesia	3,678
Komaga take (1942)	Japan	3,669
Sakurazima (1981)	Japan	3,668
Langila (1981)	New Britain	3,586
Dukono (1971)	Indonesia	3,566
Lamington (1952)	Papua New Guinea	3,500
Lolobau (1905)	New Britain	3,058
Suwanosezima (1981)	Japan	2,640
O-Sima (1977)	Japan	2,550
Usu (1978)	Japan	2,400
White Island (1981)	New Zealand	1,075
Taal (1977)	Philippines	984

Central America—Caribbean

Name	Location	Feet
Tajumulco	Guatemala	13,845
Tacana	Guatemala	13,428
Acatenango (1972)	Guatemala	12,992
Fuego (1980)	Guatemala	12,582
Santiaguito (Santa Maria) (1981)	Guatemala	12,362
Atitlan	Guatemala	11,565
Irazu (1967)	Costa Rica	11,260
San Pedro	Guatamala	9,921
Poas (1981)	Costa Rica	8,930
Pacaya (1981)	Guatemala	8,346
Izalco (1966)	El Salvador	7,749
San Miguel (1976)	El Salvador	6,994
Rincon de la Vieja (1968)	Costa Rica	6,234
El Viejo (San Cristobal) (1981)	Nicaragua	5,840
Ometepe (Concepcion) (1978)	Nicaragua	5,106

Name	Location	Feet
Arenal (1981)	Costa Rica	5,092
La Soufrière	Guadeloupe	4,813
Pelée (1932)	Martinique	4,583
Momotombo (1952)	Nicaragua	4,199
Conchagua (1947)	El Salvador	4,100
Soufriere (1979)	St. Vincent	4,048
Telica (1981)	Nicaragua	3,409

South America

Name	Location	Feet
Guallatiri (1960)	Chile	19,882
Lascar (1968)	Chile	19,652
Cotopaxi (1975)	Ecuador	19,347
El Misti	Peru	19,098
Tupungatito (1980)	Chile	18,504
Tolima (1943)	Colombia	18,002
Sangay (1976)	Ecuador	17,159
Tungurahua (1944)	Ecuador	16,512
Cotopachi (1955)	Ecuador	16,204
Pichincha	Ecuador	15,696
Purace (1977)	Colombia	15,604
Lautaro (1960)	Chile	11,098
Llaima (1979)	Chile	10,239
Villarrica (1980)	Chile	9,318
Hudson (1973)	Chile	8,580
Shoshuenco (1960)	Chile	7,743
Puyehue (1960)	Chile	7,349
Caibuco (1961)	Chile	6,611
Alcedo (1970)	Galapagos Is.	3,599

Mid-Pacific

Name	Location	Feet
Mauna Kea	Hawaii	13,796
Mauna Loa (1978)	Hawaii	13,680
Kilauea (1980)	Hawaii	4,077

Mid-Atlantic Ridge

Name	Location	Feet
Beerenberg (1970)	Jan Mayen Is.	7,470
Tristan da Cunha (1962)	Tristan da Cunha Is.	6,760
Askja (1961)	Iceland	4,954
Hekla (1981)	Iceland	4,892
Katla (1918)	Iceland	3,182
Leirhnukur (1975)	Iceland	2,145
Krafla (1981)	Iceland	2,145
Surtsey (1967)	Iceland	568

Europe

Name	Location	Feet
Etna (1981)	Italy	11,053
Vesuvius (1944)	Italy	4,190
Stromboli (1975)	Italy	3,038
Thera (1956)	Greece	1,824
Vulcano	Italy	1,637

North America

Name	Location	Feet
Citlaltepec	Mexico	18,700
Popocatepetl (1920)	Mexico	17,887
Rainier	Washington	14,410
Wrangell	Alaska	14,163
Colima (1975)	Mexico	14,003
Torbert (1953)	Alaska	11,413
Spurr (1953)	Alaska	11,069
Baker	Washington	10,779
Lassen (1915)	California	10,457
Redoubt (1966)	Alaska	10,197
Iliamna (1978)	Alaska	10,092
Mt. St. Helens (1981)	Washington	9,677
Shishaldin (1979)	Aleutian Is.	9,387
Veniaminof	Alaska	8,225
Pavlof (1980)	Aleutian Is.	8,215
Griggs	Alaska	7,600
Paricutin (1952)	Mexico	7,451
Mageik (1912)	Alaska	7,244
Douglas	Alaska	7,064
Chiginagak	Alaska	7,031
Katmai (1962)	Alaska	6,715
Kukak	Alaska	6,700
Makushin (1980)	Aleutian Is.	6,680
Pogromni (1964)	Aleutian Is.	6,568
Martin (1960)	Alaska	6,050
Trident (1963)	Alaska	6,010
Tanaga	Aleutian Is.	5,925
Great Sitkin (1974)	Aleutian Is.	5,710
Cleveland (1951)	Aleutian Is.	5,675
Gareloi (1980)	Aleutian Is.	5,334
Korovin	Aleutian Is.	4,852
Kanaga	Aleutian Is.	4,416
Aniakchak	Alaska	4,400
Akutan (1980)	Aleutian Is.	4,275
Kiska (1969)	Aleutian Is.	4,275
Augustine (1976)	Alaska	3,927
Little Sitkin	Aleutian Is.	3,897
Okmok (1958)	Aleutian Is.	3,519
Seguam (1977)	Alaska	3,458

Continental Drift: Lithospheric

(Illustrations adapted from U.S.

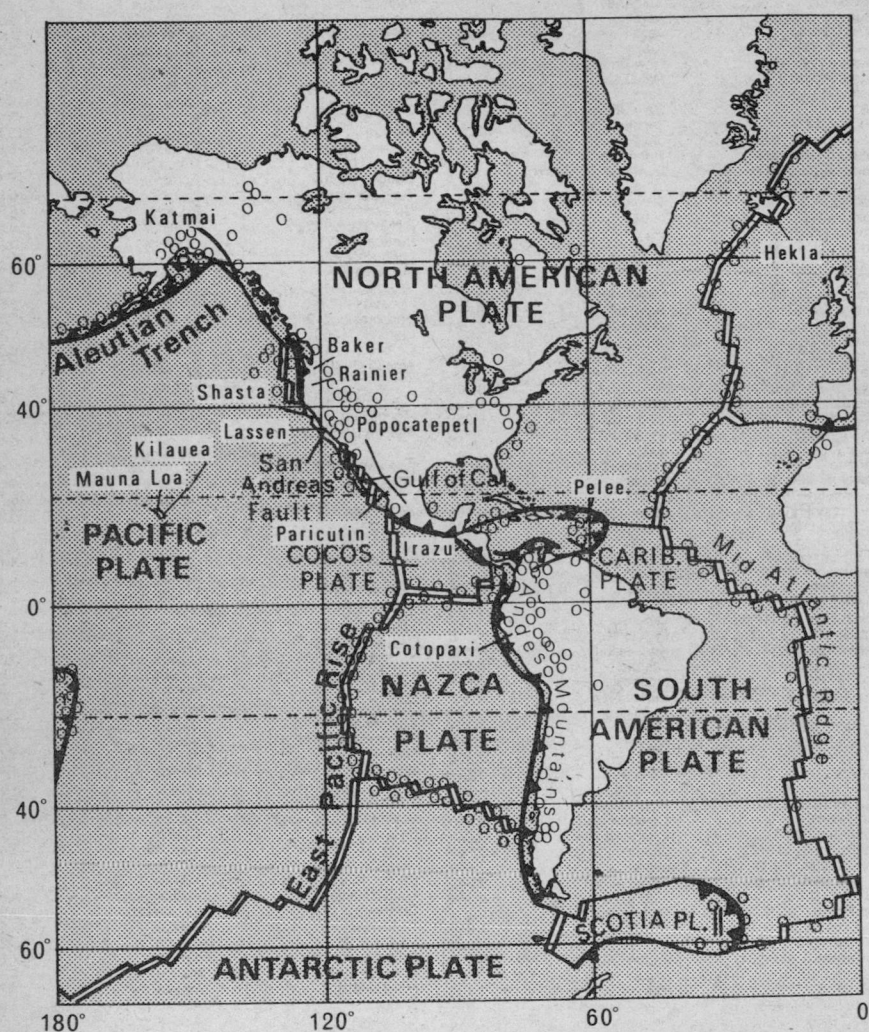

Map Symbols

The earth's crust is broken into moving plates of "lithosphere" (lith**ō**=rock). There are 7 major plates and at least 12 minor ones (not all of which are shown above). Each plate is more than 50 miles thick and has at least 2 levels. On top, a relatively shallow part can be deformed by brittle breaking or by bending. The deeper bottom part yields to pressure like firm clay. The plates rest on and slide over a layer of viscous material.

Map Symbols

The plate boundaries shown above are those that are presently active. The *double line* indicates a zone of spreading where plates are moving away from each other. A *single line* represents a slip-strike fault, along which plates are sliding by each other (the San Andreas fault in California and the long line stretching from the western Himalayas toward Africa). A *barbed line* marks a subduction zone, an area where one plate is being pushed down under another; the barbs show the direction of motion of the underriding plate.

Volcanoes and earthquakes tend to occur along plate boundaries, although there are notable exceptions such as the volcanoes of Hawaii. The *white circles* in the maps indicate areas of strong earthquakes, while 20 volcanoes are indicated by name.

Earthquakes are caused by the grinding of the lithospheric plates against each other and by the extensive deformations of the earth's surface that can occur thousands of miles away from a zone where one plate is riding over another. Volcanoes are caused by the upwelling of material from deep within the lithosphere which breaks through the thinner plate material of the ocean floor or

Plates, Earthquakes and Volcanoes

Geological Survey Annual Report 1976).

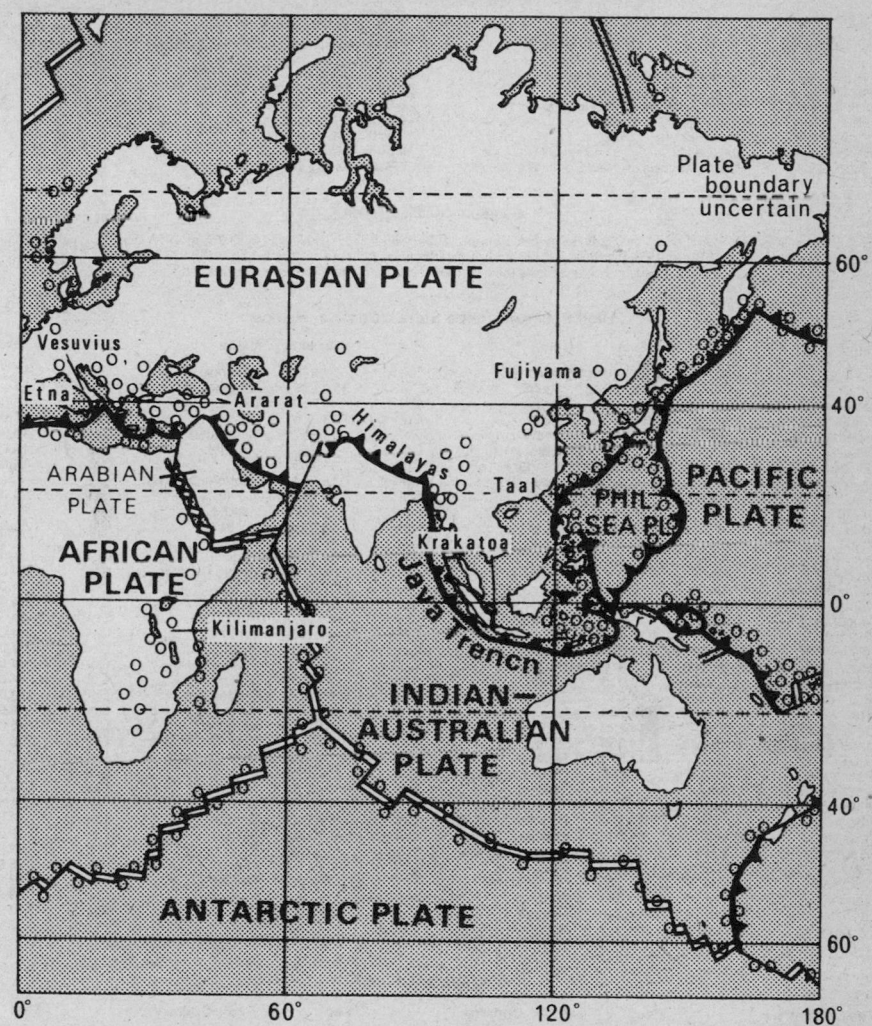

through weakened plates along the overriding edge of subduction zones.

Undersea volcanic activity along the Mid-Atlantic Ridge and East Pacific Rise has broken the once solid lithosphere into plates and is pushing the plates apart at rates estimated at one-half inch to as much as 8 inches a year. In Hawaii, volcanic activity has not been strong enough or widespread enough to break the lithosphere into separate plates.

Wegener's Hypothesis

The theory of continental drift was first systematically proposed early in the 20th century, although laymen and scientists, noting the close fit between the bulge of South America and the bight of west Africa, had suggested the idea as early as 1620. In 1912, a German meteorologist and astronomer, Alfred Wegener, postulated that all the earth's continents had once formed a single large land mass that began to break up about 40 million years ago (the breakup is now dated to 190 million years ago).

Wegener's hypothesis was roundly attacked from all sides, particularly because no force was known to be strong enough to break up the original continent and set its pieces adrift. After some 15 years of bitter controversy, Wegener's idea was disregarded by most scientists. Then in the 1960s new data, particularly oceanographic studies that confirmed sea-floor spreading along the Mid-Atlantic Ridge, brought strong support to the theory. Today the idea of continental drift is widely accepted because of a variety of convincing evidence, even though the nature of the powerful forces that cause the drift has yet to be understood.

Highest and Lowest Continental Altitudes

Source: National Geographic Society, Washington, D.C.

Continent	Highest point	Feet elevation	Lowest point	Feet below sea level
Asia	Mount Everest, Nepal-Tibet	29,028	Dead Sea, Israel-Jordan	1,312
South America	Mount Aconcagua, Argentina	22,834	Valdes Peninsula, Argentina	131
North America	Mount McKinley, Alaska	20,320	Death Valley, California	282
Africa	Kilimanjaro, Tanzania	19,340	Lake Assal, Djibouti	512
Europe	Mount El'brus, USSR	18,510	Caspian Sea, USSR	92
Antarctica	Vinson Massif	16,864	Unknown	...
Australia	Mount Kosciusko, New South Wales	7,310	Lake Eyre, South Australia	52

Height of Mount Everest

Mt. Everest was considered to be 29,002 ft. tall when Edmund Hillary and Tenzing Norgay scaled it in 1953. This triangulation figure had been accepted since 1850. In 1954 the Surveyor General of the Republic of India set the height at 29,028 ft., plus or minus 10 ft. because of snow. The National Geographic Society accepts the new figure, but many mountaineering groups still use 29,002 ft.

High Peaks in United States, Canada, Mexico

Name	Place	Feet	Name	Place	Feet	Name	Place	Feet
McKinley	Alas	20,320	Crestone	Col	14,294	Columbia	Col	14,073
Logan	Can	19,850	Lincoln	Col	14,286	Augusta	Alas-Can	14,070
Citlaltepec (Orizaba)	Mexico	18,700	Grays	Col	14,270	Missouri	Col	14,067
St. Elias	Alas-Can	18,008	Antero	Col	14,269	Humboldt	Col	14,064
Popocatepetl	Mexico	17,887	Torreys	Col	14,267	Bierstadt	Col	14,060
Foraker	Alas	17,400	Castle	Col	14,265	Sunlight	Col	14,059
Iztaccihuatl	Mexico	17,343	Quandary	Col	14,265	Split	Cal	14,058
Lucania	Can	17,147	Evans	Col	14,264	Nauhcampatepetl		
King	Can	16,971	Longs	Col	14,256	(Cofre de Perote)	Mexico	14,049
Steele	Can	16,644	McArthur	Can	14,253	Handies	Col	14,048
Bona	Alas	16,550	Wilson	Col	14,246	Culebra	Col	14,047
Blackburn	Alas	16,390	White	Cal	14,246	Langley	Cal	14,042
Kennedy	Alas	16,286	North Palisade	Cal	14,242	Lindsey	Col	14,042
Sanford	Alas	16,237	Shavano	Col	14,229	Middle Palisade	Cal	14,040
South Buttress	Alas	15,885	Belford	Col	14,197	Little Bear	Col	14,037
Wood	Can	15,885	Princeton	Col	14,197	Sherman	Col	14,036
Vancouver	Alas-Can	15,700	Crestone Needle	Col	14,197	Redcloud	Col	14,034
Churchill	Alas	15,638	Yale	Col	14,196	Tyndall	Cal	14,018
Fairweather	Alas-Can	15,300	Bross	Col	14,172	Pyramid	Col	14,018
Zinantecatl (Toluca)	Mexico	15,016	Kit Carson	Col	14,165	Wilson Peak	Col	14,017
Hubbard	Alas-Can	15,015	Wrangell	Alas	14,163	Muir	Cal	14,015
Bear	Alas	14,831	Shasta	Cal	14,162	Wetterhorn	Col	14,015
Walsh	Can	14,780	Sill	Cal	14,162	North Maroon	Col	14,014
East Buttress	Alas	14,730	El Diente	Col	14,159	San Luis	Col	14,014
Matlalcueyetl	Mexico	14,636	Maroon	Col	14,156	Huron	Col	14,005
Hunter	Alas	14,573	Tabeguache	Col	14,155	Holy Cross	Col	14,005
Alverstone	Alas-Can	14,565	Oxford	Col	14,153	Colima	Mexico	14,003
Browne Tower	Alas	14,530	Sneffels	Col	14,150	Sunshine	Col	14,001
Whitney	Cal	14,494	Point Success	Wash	14,150	Grizzly	Col	14,000
Elbert	Col	14,433	Democrat	Col	14,148	Barnard	Cal	13,990
Massive	Col	14,421	Capitol	Col	14,130	Stewart	Cal	13,980
Harvard	Col	14,420	Liberty Cap	Wash	14,112	Keith	Cal	13,977
Rainier	Wash	14,410	Pikes Peak	Col	14,110	Ouray	Col	13,971
Williamson	Cal	14,375	Snowmass	Col	14,092	Le Conte	Cal	13,960
Blanca	Col	14,345	Windom	Col	14,087	Meeker	Col	13,911
La Plata	Col	14,336	Russell	Cal	14,086	Kennedy	Can	13,905
Uncompahgre	Col	14,309	Eolus	Col	14,084			

South America

Peak, Country	Feet	Peak, Country	Feet	Peak, Country	Feet
Aconcagua, Argentina	22,834	Laudo, Argentina	20,997	Polleras, Argentina	20,456
Ojos del Salado, Arg.-Chile	22,572	Ancohuma, Bolivia	20,958	Pular, Chile	20,423
Bonete, Argentina	22,546	Ausangate, Peru	20,945	Chani, Argentina	20,341
Tupungato, Argentina-Chile	22,310	Toro, Argentina-Chile	20,932	Aucanquilcha, Chile	20,295
Pissis, Argentina	22,241	Illampu, Bolivia	20,873	Juncal, Argentina-Chile	20,276
Mercedario, Argentina	22,211	Tres Cruces, Argentina-Chile	20,853	Negro, Argentina	20,184
Huascaran, Peru	22,205	Huandoy, Peru	20,852	Quela, Argentina	20,128
Llullaillaco, Argentina-Chile	22,057	Parinacota, Bolivia-Chile	20,768	Condoriri, Bolivia	20,095
El Libertador, Argentina	22,047	Tortolas, Argentina-Chile	20,745	Palermo, Argentina	20,079
Cachi, Argentina	22,047	Ampato, Peru	20,702	Solimana, Peru	20,068
Yerupaja, Peru	21,709	Condor, Argentina	20,669	San Juan, Argentina-Chile	20,049
Galan, Argentina	21,654	Salcantay, Peru	20,574	Sierra Nevada, Arg.-Chile	20,023
El Muerto, Argentina-Chile	21,457	Chimborazo, Ecuador	20,561	Antofalla, Argentina	20,013
Sajama, Bolivia	21,391	Huancarhuas, Peru	20,531	Marmolejo, Argentina-Chile	20,013
Nacimiento, Argentina	21,302	Famatina, Argentina	20,505	Chachani, Peru	19,931
Illimani, Bolivia	21,201	Pumasillo, Peru	20,492	Licancabur, Argentina-Chile	19,425
Coropuna, Peru	21,083	Solo, Argentina	20,492		

The highest point in the West Indies is in the Dominican Republic, Pico Duarte (10,417 ft.).

Africa, Australia, and Oceania

Peak, country	Feet	Peak, country	Feet	Peak, country	Feet
Kilimanjaro, Tanzania	19,340	Meru, Tanzania	14,979	Toubkal, Morocco	13,665
Kenya, Kenya	17,058	Wilhelm, New Guinea	14,793	Kinabalu, Malaysia	13,455
Margherita Pk., Uganda-Zaire	16,763	Karisimbi, Zaire-Rwanda	14,787	Kerinci, Sumatra	12,467
Jaja, New Guinea	16,500	Elgon, Kenya-Uganda	14,178	Cook, New Zealand	12,349
Trikora, New Guinea	15,585	Batu, Ethiopia	14,131	Teide, Canary Islands	12,198
Mandala, New Guinea	15,420	Guna, Ethiopia	13,881	Semeru, Java	12,060
Ras Dashan, Ethiopia	15,158	Gughe, Ethiopia	13,780	Kosciusko, Australia	7,310

Europe

Peak, country	Feet	Peak, county	Feet	Peak, country	Feet
Alps		Breithorn, It., Switz.	13,665	Scerscen, Switz.	13,028
		Bishorn, Switz.	13,645	Eiger, Switz.	13,025
Mont Blanc, Fr. It.	15,771	Jungfrau, Switz.	13,642	Jagerhorn, Switz.	13,024
Monte Rosa (high-		Ecrins, Fr.	13,461	Rottalhorn, Switz.	13,022
est peak of group), Switz.	15,203	Monch, Switz.	13,448		
Dom, Switz.	14,911	Pollux, Switz.	13,422	**Pyrenees**	
Liskamm, It., Switz.	14,852	Schreckhorn, Switz.	13,379		
Weisshorn, Switz.	14,780	Ober Gabelhorn, Switz.	13,330	Aneto, Sp.	11,168
Taschhorn, Switz.	14,733	Gran Paradiso, It.	13,323	Posets, Sp.	11,073
Matterhorn, It., Switz.	14,690	Bernina, It., Switz.	13,284	Perdido, Sp.	11,007
Dent Blanche, Switz.	14,293	Fiescherhorn, Switz.	13,283	Vignemale, Fr., Sp.	10,820
Nadelhorn, Switz.	14,196	Grunhorn, Switz.	13,266	Long, Sp.	10,479
Grand Combin, Switz.	14,154	Lauteraarhorn, Switz.	13,261	Estats, Sp.	10,304
Lonzpitze, Switz.	14,088	Durrenhorn, Switz.	13,238	Montcalm, Sp.	10,105
Finsteraarhorn, Switz.	14,022	Allalinhorn, Switz.	13,213		
Castor, Switz.	13,865	Weissmies, Switz.	13,199	**Caucasus (Europe-Asia)**	
Zinalrothorn, Switz.	13,849	Lagginhorn, Switz.	13,156		
Hohberghorn, Switz.	13,842	Zupo, Switz.	13,120	El'brus, USSR	18,510
Alphubel, Switz.	13,799	Fletschhorn, Switz.	13,110	Shkara, USSR	17,064
Rimpfischhorn, Switz.	13,776	Adlerhorn, Switz.	13,081	Dykh Tau, USSR	17,054
Aletschorn, Switz.	13,763	Gletscherhorn, Switz.	13,068	Kashtan Tau, USSR	16,877
Strahlhorn, Switz.	13,747	Schalihorn, Switz.	13,040	Dzhangi Tau, USSR	16,565
Dent D'Herens, Switz.	13,686			Kazbek, USSR	16,558

Asia

Peak	Country	Feet	Peak	Country	Feet	Peak	Country	Feet
Everest	Nepal-Tibet	29,028	Kungur	Sinkiang	25,325	Badrinath	India	23,420
K2 (Godwin Aus-			Tirich Mir	Pakistan	25,230	Nunkun	Kashmir	23,410
ten)	Kashmir	28,250	Makalu II	Nepal-Tibet	25,120	Lenina Peak	USSR	23,405
Kanchenjunga	India-Nepal	28,208	Minya Konka	China	24,900	Pyramid	India-Nepal	23,400
Lhotse I (Everest)	Nepal-Tibet	27,923	Kula Gangri	Bhutan-Tibet	24,784	Api	Nepal	23,399
Makalu I	Nepal-Tibet	27,824	Changtzu			Pauhunri	India-Tibet	23,385
Lhotse II (Everest)	Nepal-Tibet	27,560	(Everest)	Nepal-Tibet	24,780	Trisul	India	23,360
Dhaulagiri	Nepal	26,810	Muz Tagh Ata	Sinkiang	24,757	Kangto	India-Tibet	23,260
Manaslu I	Nepal	26,760	Skyang Kangri	Kashmir	24,750	Nyenchhen		
Cho Oyu	Nepal-Tibet	26,750	Communism Peak	USSR	24,590	Thanglha	Tibet	23,255
Nanga Parbat	Kashmir	26,660	Jongsang Peak	India-Nepal	24,472	Trisuli	India	23,210
Annapurna I	Nepal	26,504	Pobedy Peak	Sinkiang-		Pumori	Nepal-Tibet	23,190
Gasherbrum	Kashmir	26,470		USSR	24,406	Dunagiri	India	23,184
Broad	Kashmir	26,400	Sia Kangri	Kashmir	24,350	Lombo Kangra	Tibet	23,165
Gosainthan	Tibet	26,287	Haramosh Peak	Pakistan	24,270	Saipal	Nepal	23,100
Annapurna II	Nepal	26,041	Istoro Nal	Pakistan	24,240	Macha Pucchare	Nepal	22,958
Gyachung Kang	Nepal-Tibet	25,910	Tent Peak	India-Nepal	24,165	Numbar	Nepal	22,817
Disteghil Sar	Kashmir	25,868	Chomo Lhari	Bhutan-Tibet	24,040	Kanjiroba	Nepal	22,580
Himalchuli	Nepal	25,801	Chamlang	Nepal	24,012	Ama Dablam	Nepal	22,350
Nuptse (Everest)	Nepal-Tibet	25,726	Kabru	India-Nepal	24,002	Cho Polu	Nepal	22,093
Masherbrum	Kashmir	25,660	Alung Gangri	Tibet	24,000	Lingtren	Nepal-Tibet	21,972
Nanda Devi	India	25,645	Baltoro Kangri	Kashmir	23,990	Khumbutse	Nepal-Tibet	21,785
Rakaposhi	Kashmir	25,550	Mussu Shan	Sinkiang	23,890	Hlako Gangri	Tibet	21,266
Kamet	India-Tibet	25,447	Mana	India	23,860	Mt. Grosvenor	China	21,190
Namcha Barwa	Tibet	25,445	Baruntse	Nepal	23,688	Thagchhab Gangri	Tibet	20,970
Gurla Mandhata	Tibet	25,355	Nepal Peak	India-Nepal	23,500	Damavand	Iran	18,606
Ulugh Muz Tagh	Sinkiang-		Amne Machin	China	23,490	Ararat	Turkey	16,854
	Tibet	25,340	Gauri Sankar	Nepal-Tibet	23,440			

Antarctica

Peak	Feet	Peak	Feet	Peak	Feet	Peak	Feet
Vinson Massif	16,860	Andrew Jackson	13,750	Shear	13,100	Campbell	12,434
Tyree	16,290	Sidley	13,720	Odishaw	13,008	Don Pedro Christo-	
Shinn	15,750	Ostenso	13,710	Donaldson	12,894	phersen	12,355
Gardner	15,375	Minto	13,668	Ray	12,808	Lysaght	12,326
Epperly	15,100	Miller	13,650	Sellery	12,779	Huggins	12,247
Kirkpatrick	14,855	Long Gables	13,620	Waterman	12,730	Sabine	12,200
Elizabeth	14,698	Dickerson	13,517	Anne	12,703	Astor	12,175
Markham	14,290	Giovinetto	13,412	Press	12,566	Mohl	12,172
Bell	14,117	Wade	13,400	Falla	12,549	Frankes	12,064
Mackellar	14,098	Fisher	13,386	Rucker	12,520	Jones	12,040
Anderson	13,957	Fridtjof Nansen	13,350	Goldthwait	12,510	Gjelsvik	12,008
Bentley	13,934	Wexler	13,202	Morris	12,500	Coman	12,000
Kaplan	13,878	Lister	13,200	Erebus	12,450		

How Deep Is the Ocean?

Principal ocean depths. **Source:** Defense Mapping Agency Hydrographic/Topographic Center

Name of area	Location		Meters	Depth Fathoms	Feet
Pacific Ocean					
Mariana Trench	11°25'N	142°10'E	11,776	6,439	38,635
Philippine Trench	09°49'N	126°52'E	11,497	6,287	37,720
Tonga Trench	23°16'S	174°45'W	11,313	6,186	37,116
Izu Trench	30°45'N	142°30'E	11,232	6,142	36,850
Kermadec Trench	31°45'S	176°59'W	10,585	5,788	34,728
Kuril Trench	44°11'N	150°32'E	10,570	5,780	34,678
New Britain Trench	06°35'S	153°52'E	9,649	5,276	31,657
Bonin Trench	23°52'N	143°55'E	9,088	4,969	29,816
Japan Trench	38°13'N	144°31'E	8,887	4,859	29,157
Palau Trench	07°42'N	135°12'E	8,526	4,662	27,972
Peru-Chile Trench	23°28'S	71°23'W	8,439	4,615	27,687
Yap Trench	08°37'N	138°03'E	8,398	4,592	27,552
Aleutian Trench	51°08'N	174°48'E	8,161	4,462	26,775
New Hebrides Trench	20°36'S	100°07'E	7,916	4,329	25,971
Ryukyu Trench	24°30'N	127°11'E	7,802	4,266	25,597
Mid. America Trench	13°57'N	93°35'W	6,796	3,716	22,297
Atlantic Ocean					
Puerto Rico Trench	19°46'N	68°03'W	9,460	5,173	31,037
So. Sandwich Trench	55°43'S	25°59'W	8,658	4,734	28,406
Romanche Gap	0°13'S	18°31'W	8,090	4,424	26,542
Cayman Trench	18°50'N	81°38'W	8,083	4,420	26,519
Brazil Basin	03°31'S	22°47'W	6,789	3,712	22,274
Indian Ocean					
Java Trench	10°15'S	109°50'E	7,542	4,124	24,744
Diamantina Trench	34°56'S	102°32'E	7,391	4,041	24,249
Ob' Trench	09°45'S	67°18'E	6,640	3,631	21,785
Vema Trench	32°47'S	98°44'E	5,938	3,247	19,482
Agulhas Basin	45°20'S	26°50'E	5,907	3,230	19,380
Arctic Ocean					
Eurasia Basin	78°16'N	04°W	4,914	2,687	16,122
Mediterranean Sea					
Ionian Basin	36°32'N	21°23'E	5,275	2,884	17,306

Ocean Areas and Average Depths

Four major bodies of water are recognized by geographers and mapmakers. They are: the Pacific, Atlantic, Indian, and Arctic oceans. The Atlantic and Pacific oceans are considered divided at the equator into the No. and So. Atlantic; the No. and So. Pacific. The Arctic Ocean is the name for waters north of the continental land masses in the region of the Arctic Circle.

	Sq. miles	Avg. depth in feet		Sq. miles	Avg. depth in feet
Pacific Ocean	64,186,300	13,739	Hudson Bay	281,900	305
Atlantic Ocean	33,420,000	12,257	East China Sea	256,600	620
Indian Ocean	28,350,500	12,704	Andaman Sea	218,100	3,667
Arctic Ocean	5,105,700	4,362	Black Sea	196,100	3,906
South China Sea	1,148,500	4,802	Red Sea	174,900	1,764
Caribbean Sea	971,400	8,448	North Sea	164,900	308
Mediterranean Sea	969,100	4,926	Baltic Sea	147,500	180
Bering Sea	873,000	4,893	Yellow Sea	113,500	121
Gulf of Mexico	582,100	5,297	Persian Gulf	88,800	328
Sea of Okhotsk	537,500	3,192	Gulf of California	59,100	2,375
Sea of Japan	391,100	5,468			

The Malayan Sea is not considered a geographical entity but a term used for convenience for waters between the South Pacific and the Indian Ocean.

Continental Statistics

Source: National Geographic Society, Washington, D.C.

Continents	Area (sq. mi.)	% of Earth	Population (est.)	% World total	Highest point (in feet)	Lowest point
Asia	16,999,000	29.7	2,637,100,000	58.7	Everest, 29,028	Dead Sea, −1,312
Africa	11,688,000	20.4	486,000,000	10.8	Kilimanjaro, 19,340	Lake Assal, −512
North America	9,366,000	16.3	377,000,000	8.4	McKinley, 20,320	Death Valley, −282
South America	6,881,000	12.0	243,000,000	5.4	Aconcagua, 22,834	Valdes Penin., −131
Europe	4,017,000	7.0	686,700,000	15.3	El'brus, 18,510	Caspian Sea, −92
Australia	2,966,000	5.2	14,800,000	0.3	Kosciusko, 7,310	Lake Eyre, −52
Antarctica	5,100,000	8.9	—	—	Vinson Massif, 16,864	Not Known
Est. World Population			4,492,000,000			

Important Islands and Their Areas

Source: National Geographic Society, Washington, D.C.

Figure in parentheses shows rank among the world's 10 largest islands; some islands have not been surveyed accurately; in such cases estimated areas are shown.

Location-Ownership
Area in square miles

Arctic Ocean

Canadian

Axel Heiberg	16,671
Baffin (5)	195,928
Banks	27,038
Bathurst	6,194
Devon	21,331
Ellesmere (10)	75,767
Melville	10,274
Prince of Wales	12,872
Somerset	9,570
Southampton	15,913
Victoria (9)	83,896

USSR

Franz Josef Land	8,000
Novaya Zemlya (two is.)	35,000
Wrangel	2,800

Norwegian

Svalbard	23,940
Nordaustlandet	5,410
Spitsbergen	15,060

Atlantic Ocean

Anticosti, Canada	3,066
Ascension, UK	34
Azores, Portugal	902
Faial	67
Sao Miguel	291
Bahamas	5,380
Bermuda Is., UK	20
Block, Rhode Island	10
Canary Is., Spain	2,808
Fuerteventura	668
Gran Canaria	592
Tenerife	795
Cape Breton, Canada	3,981
Cape Verde Is.	1,750
Faeroe Is., Denmark	540
Falkland Is., UK	4,700
Fernando de Noronha Archipelago, Brazil	7
Greenland, Denmark (1)	840,000
Iceland	39,769
Long Island, N. Y.	1,396
Bioko Is. Equatorial Guinea	785
Madeira Is., Portugal	307
Marajo, Brazil	15,528
Martha's Vineyard, Mass.	91
Mount Desert, Me.	108
Nantucket, Mass.	46
Newfoundland, Canada	42,030
Prince Edward, Canada	2,184
St. Helena, UK	47
South Georgia, UK	1,450
Tierra del Fuego, Chile and Argentina	18,800
Tristan da Cunha, UK	40

British Isles

Great Britain, mainland (8)	84,200
Channel Islands	75
Guernsey	24
Jersey	45
Sark	2
Hebrides	2,744
Ireland	32,599
Irish Republic	27,136
Northern Ireland	5,463
Man	227

Orkney Is.	390
Scilly Is.	6
Shetland Is.	567
Skye	670
Wight	147

Baltic Sea

Aland Is., Finland	581
Bornholm, Denmark	227
Gotland, Sweden	1,164

Caribbean Sea

Antigua	108
Aruba, Netherlands	75
Barbados	166
Cuba	44,218
Isle of Pines	1,182
Curacao, Netherlands	171
Dominica	290
Guadeloupe, France	687
Hispaniola, Haiti and Dominican Republic	29,530
Jamaica	4,244
Martinique, France	425
Puerto Rico, U.S.	3,435
Tobago	116
Trinidad	1,864
Virgin Is., UK	59
Virgin Is., U.S.	133

Indian Ocean

Andaman Is., India	2,500
Madagascar (4)	226,658
Mauritius	720
Pemba, Tanzania	380
Reunion, France	969
Seychelles	171
Sri Lanka	25,332
Zanzibar, Tanzania	640

Persian Gulf

Bahrain	258

Mediterranean Sea

Balearic Is., Spain	1,936
Corfu, Greece	229
Corsica, France	3,365
Crete, Greece	3,186
Cyprus	3,572
Elba, Italy	86
Euboea, Greece	1,409
Malta	122
Rhodes, Greece	542
Sardinia, Italy	9,262
Sicily, Italy	9,822

Pacific Ocean

Aleutian Is., U.S.	6,821
Adak	289
Amchitka	121
Attu	388
Kanaga	135
Kiska	110
Tanaga	209
Umnak	675
Unalaska	1,064
Unimak	1,600
Canton, Kiribati*	
Caroline Is., U.S. trust terr.	472
Christmas, Kiribati*	94

Diomede, Big, USSR	11
Diomede, Little, U.S.	2
Easter, Chile	69
Fiji	7,056
Vanua Levi	2,242
Viti Levu	4,109
Funafuti, Tuvalu*	2
Galapagos Is., Ecuador	3,043
Guadalcanal, UK	2,500
Hainan, China	13,000
Hawaiian Is., U.S.	6,450
Hawaii	4,037
Oahu	593
Hong Kong, UK	29
Japan	145,809
Hokkaido	30,144
Honshu (7)	87,805
Iwo Jima	8
Kyushu	14,114
Okinawa	459
Shikoku	7,049
Kodiak, U.S.	3,670
Mariana Is., U.S. trust terr. excluding Guam	185
Guam, U.S.	212
Marquesas Is., France	492
Marshall Is., U.S. trust terr.	70
Bikini*	2
Nauru	8
New Caledonia, France	6,530
New Guinea (2)	306,000
New Zealand	103,883
Chatham	372
North	44,035
South	58,305
Stewart	674
Philippines	115,831
Leyte	2,787
Luzon	40,880
Mindanao	36,775
Mindoro	3,790
Negros	4,907
Palawan	4,554
Panay	4,446
Samar	5,050
Quemoy	56
Sakhalin, USSR	29,500
Samoa Is.	1,177
American Samoa	76
Tutuila	52
Samoa (Western)	1,101
Savaii	670
Upolu	429
Santa Catalina, U.S.	72
Tahiti, France	402
Taiwan	13,812
Tasmania, Australia	26,178
Tonga Is.	270
Vancouver, Canada	12,079
Vanuatu	5,700

East Indies

Bali, Indonesia	2,147
Borneo, Indonesia-Malaysia, UK (3)	280,100
Celebes, Indonesia	69,000
Java, Indonesia	48,900
Madura, Indonesia	2,113
Moluccas, Indonesia	28,766
New Britain, Papua New Guinea	14,050
New Ireland, Papua New Guinea	2,700
Sumatra, Indonesia (6)	165,000
Timor	11,570

*Atolls: Bikini (lagoon area, 230 sq. mi., land area 2 sq. mi.), U.S. Trust Territory of the Pacific Islands; Canton (lagoon 20 sq. mi., land 4 sq. mi.), Kiribati; Christmas (lagoon 140 sq. mi., land 94 sq. mi.), Kiribati; Funafuti (lagoon 84 sq. mi., land 2 sq. mi.), Tuvalu.

Australia, often called an island, is a continent. Its mainland area is 2,939,975 sq. mi.

Islands in minor waters: Manhattan (23 sq mi.) Staten (58 sq. mi.) and Governors (173 acres), all in New York Harbor, U.S.; Isle Royale (209 sq. mi.), Lake Superior, U.S.; Manitoulin (1,068 sq. mi.), Lake Huron, Canada; Pinang (110 sq. mi.), Strait of Malacca, Malaysia; Singapore (239 sq. mi.), Singapore Strait, Singapore.

Major Rivers in North America

Source: U.S. Geological Survey

River	Source or Upper Limit of Length	Outflow	Miles
Alabama	Gilmer County, Ga.	Mobile River	735
Albany	Lake St. Joseph, Ont., Can.	James Bay	610
Allegheny	Potter County, Pa.	Ohio River	325
Altamaha-Ocmulgee	Junction of Yellow and South Rivers, Newton County, Ga.	Atlantic Ocean	392
Apalachicola-Chattahoochee	Towns County, Ga.	Gulf of Mexico, Fla.	524
Arkansas	Lake County, Col.	Mississippi River, Ark.	1,459
Assiniboine	Eastern Saskatchewan	Red River	450
Attawapiskat	Attawapiskat, Ont., Can.	James Bay	465
Big Black (Miss.)	Webster County, Miss.	Mississippi River	330
Big Horn	Junction of Wind and Popo Agie Rivers, Fremont County, Wyo.	Yellowstone River, Mon.	336
Black (N.W.T.)	Contwoyto Lake	Chantrey Inlet	600
Brazos	Junction of Salt and Double Mountain Forks, Stonewall County, Tex.	Gulf of Mexico	870
Canadian	Las Animas County, Col.	Arkansas River, Okla.	906
Cedar (Iowa)	Dodge County, Minn.	Iowa River, Ia.	329
Cheyenne	Junction of Antelope Creek and Dry Fork, Converse County, Wyo.	Missouri River	290
Churchill	Methy Lake	Hudson Bay	1,000
Cimarron	Colfax County, N.M.	Arkansas River, Okla.	600
Clark Fork-Pend Oreille	Silver Bow County, Mon.	Columbia River, B.C.	505
Colorado (Ariz.)	Rocky Mountain National Park, Col. (90 miles in Mexico)	Gulf of Cal., Mexico	1,450
Colorado (Texas)	West Texas	Matagorda Bay	840
Columbia	Columbia Lake, British Columbia	Pacific Ocean, bet. Ore. and Wash.	1,243
Columbia, Upper	Columbia Lake, British Columbia	To mouth of Snake River	890
Connecticut	Third Connecticut Lake, N.H.	L.I. Sound, Conn.	407
Coppermine (N.W.T.)	Lac de Gras	Coronation Gulf (Atlantic Ocean)	525
Cumberland	Letcher County, Ky.	Ohio River	720
Delaware	Schoharie County, N.Y.	Liston Point, Delaware Bay	390
Fraser	Near Mount Robson (on Continental Divide)	Strait of Georgia	850
Gila	Catron County, N.M.	Colorado River, Ariz.	630
Green (Ut.-Wyo.)	Junction of Wells and Trail Creeks, Sublette County, Wyo.	Colorado River, Ut.	730
Hamilton (Lab.)	Lake Ashuanipi	Atlantic Ocean	600
Hudson	Henderson Lake, Essex County, N.Y.	Upper N.Y. Bay, N.Y.,-N.J.	306
Illinois	St. Joseph County, Ind.	Mississippi River	420
James (N.D.-S.D.)	Wells County, N.D.	Missouri River, S.D.	710
James (Va.)	Junction of Jackson and Cowpasture Rivers, Botetourt County, Va.	Hampton Roads	340
Kanawha-New	Junction of North and South Forks of New River, N.C.	Ohio River	352
Kentucky	Junction of North and Middle Forks, Lee County, Ky.	Ohio River	259
Klamath	Lake Ewauna, Klamath Falls, Ore.	Pacific Ocean	250
Koyukuk	Endicott Mountains, Alaska	Yukon River	470
Kuskokwim	Alaska Range	Kuskokwim Bay	680
Liard	Southern Yukon, Alaska	Mackenzie River	693
Little Missouri	Crook County, Wyo.	Missouri River	560
Mackenzie	Great Slave Lake	Arctic Ocean	900
Milk	Junction of North and South Forks, Alberta Province	Missouri River, Mon.	625
Minnesota	Big Stone Lake, Minn.	Mississippi River, St. Paul, Minn.	332
Mississippi	Lake Itasca, Minn.	Mouth of Southwest Pass	2,348
Mississippi, Upper	Lake Itasca, Minn.	To mouth of Missouri R.	1,171
Mississippi-Missouri-Red Rock	Source of Red Rock, Beaverhead Co., Mon.	Mouth of Southwest Pass	3,710
Missouri	Junction of Jefferson, Madison, and Gallatin Rivers, Madison County, Mon.	Mississippi River	2,315
Missouri-Red Rock	Source of Red Rock, Beaverhead Co., Mon.	Mississippi River	2,533
Mobile-Alabama-Coosa	Gilmer County, Ga.	Mobile Bay	780
Nelson (Manitoba)	Lake Winnipeg	Hudson Bay	410
Neosho	Morris County, Kan.	Arkansas River, Okla.	460
Niobrara	Niobrara County, Wyo.	Missouri River, Neb.	431
North Canadian	Union County, N.M.	Canadian River, Okla.	760
North Platte	Junction of Grizzly and Little Grizzly Creeks, Jackson County, Col.	Platte River, Neb.	618
Ohio	Junction of Allegheny and Monongahela Rivers, Pittsburgh, Pa.	Mississippi River, Ill.-Ky.	981
Ohio-Allegheny	Potter County, Pa.	Mississippi River	1,306
Osage	East-central Kansas	Missouri River, Mo.	500
Ottawa	Lake Capimitchigama	St. Lawrence	790
Ouachita	Polk County, Ark.	Red River, La.	605
Peace	Stikine Mountains, B.C.	Slave River	1,195
Pearl	Neshoba County, Miss.	Gulf of Mexico, Miss.-La.	411
Pecos	Mora County, N.M.	Rio Grande, Tex.	735
Pee Dee-Yadkin	Watauga County, N.C.	Winyah Bay, S.C.	435
Pend Oreille	Near Butte, Mon.	Columbia River	490
Platte	Junction of North and South Platte Rivers, Neb.	Missouri River, Neb.	310
Porcupine	Ogilvie Mountains, Alaska	Yukon River, Alaska	460
Potomac	Garrett County, Md.	Chesapeake Bay	383
Powder	Junction of South and Middle Forks, Wyo.	Yellowstone River, Mon.	375

River	Source or Upper Limit of Length	Outflow	Miles
Red (Okla.-Tex.-La.)	Curry County, N.M.	Mississippi River	1,270
Red River of the North	Junction of Otter Tail and Bois de Sioux Rivers, Wilkin County, Minn.	Lake Winnipeg, Manitoba	545
Republican	Junction of North Fork and Arikaree River, Neb.	Kansas River, Kan.	445
Rio Grande	San Juan County, Col.	Gulf of Mexico	1,885
Roanoke	Junction of North and South Forks, Montgomery County, Va.	Albemarle Sound, N.C.	380
Rock (Ill.-Wis.)	Dodge County, Wis.	Mississippi River, Ill.	300
Sabine	Junction of South and Caddo Forks, Hunt County, Tex.	Sabine Lake, Tex.-La.	380
Sacramento	Siskiyou County, Cal.	Suisun Bay	377
St. Francis	Iron County, Mo.	Mississippi River, Ark.	425
St. Lawrence	Lake Ontario	Gulf of St. Lawrence (Atlantic Ocean)	800
Salmon (Idaho)	Custer County, Ida.	Snake River, Ida.	420
San Joaquin	Junction of South and Middle Forks, Madera County, Cal.	Suisun Bay	350
San Juan	Silver Lake, Archuleta County, Col.	Colorado River, Ut.	360
Santee-Wateree-Catawba	McDowell County, N.C.	Atlantic Ocean, S.C.	538
Saskatchewan, North	Rocky Mountains	Lake Winnipeg	1,100
Saskatchewan, South	Rocky Mountains	Lake Winnipeg	1,205
Savannah	Junction of Seneca and Tugaloo Rivers, Anderson County, S.C.	Atlantic Ocean, Ga.-S.C.	314
Severn (Ontario)	Sandy Lake	Hudson Bay	610
Smoky Hill	Cheyenne County, Col.	Kansas River, Kan.	540
Snake	Teton County, Wyo.	Columbia River, Wash.	1,038
South Platte	Junction of South and Middle Forks, Park County, Col.	Platte River, Neb.	424
Susitna	Alaska Range	Cook Inlet	300
Susquehanna	Otsego Lake, Otsego County, N.Y.	Chesapeake Bay, Md.	444
Tallahatchie	Tippah County, Miss.	Yazoo River, Miss.	301
Tanana	Wrangell Mountains	Yukon River, Alaska	620
Tennessee	Junction of French Broad and Holston Rivers	Ohio River, Ky.	652
Tennessee-French Broad	Bland County, Va.	Ohio River	900
Tombigbee	Prentiss County, Miss.	Mobile River, Ala.	525
Trinity	North of Dallas, Tex.	Galveston Bay, Tex.	360
Wabash	Darke County, Oh.	Ohio River, Ill.-Ind.	529
Washita	Hemphill County, Tex.	Red River, Okla.	500
White (Ark.-Mo.)	Madison County, Ark.	Mississippi River	720
Willamette	Douglas County, Ore.	Columbia River	270
Wisconsin	LeVieux Desert, Vilas County, Wis.	Mississippi River	430
Yellowstone	Park County, Wyo.	Missouri River, N.D.	671
Yukon	Junction of Lewes and Pelly Rivers, Yukon	Bering Sea, Alaska	1,770

Flows of Largest U.S. Rivers

Source: U.S. Geological Survey (average discharges for the period 1941-70). Ranked according to average discharge in cubic feet per second (cfs) at mouth.

Rank	River	Average discharge	Length[a] (miles)	Drainage area	Most distant source	Maximum discharge at gauging station farthest downstream	Date
1	Mississippi	[b]640,000	[c]3,710	[d]1,247,300	Beaverhead Co., Mont.	2,080,000	2-17-37
2	Columbia	262,000	1,243	258,000	Columbia Lake, B.C.	1,240,000	June 1894
3	Ohio	258,000	1,306	203,900	Potter Co., Pa.	1,850,000	2-1-37
4	St. Lawrence	[e]243,000		[e]302,000		[f]350,000	July 1973
5	Yukon	[g]240,000	1,770	327,600	Coast Mountains, B.C.	1,030,000	6-22-64
6	[h]Atchafalaya	183,000	135	95,105	Curry Co., N. Mex.		
7	Missouri	76,300	2,533	529,400	Beaverhead Co., Mont.	892,000	June 1844
8	Tennessee	[m]64,000	900	40,910	Bland Co., Va.	500,000	2-17-48
9	Red	[i]62,300	1,270	93,244	Curry Co., N. Mex.	233,000	4-17-45
10	Kuskokwim	62,000	680	49,000	Alaska Range, Alas.	392,000	6-5-64
11	Mobile	61,400	780	43,800	Gilmer, Co., Ga.		
12	Snake	50,000	1,038	109,000	Teton Co., Wyo.	409,000	June 1894
13	Arkansas	45,100	1,459	160,600	Lake Co., Col.	536,000	5-27-43
14	Copper	[j]43,000	280	24,000	Alaska Range, Alas.	265,000	7-15-71
15	Tanana	[k]41,000	620	44,000	Wrangell Mtn., Alas.	186,000	8-18-67
16	Susitna	[l]40,000	300	20,000	Alaska Range, Alas.	197,000	6-16-77
17	Susquehanna	37,190	444	27,570	Otsego Co., N.Y.	1,080,000	6-23-72
18	Willamette	35,660	270	11,200	Douglas Co., Ore.	500,000	12-4-1861
19	Alabama	32,400	735	22,600	Gilmer Co., Ga.	267,000	3-7-61
20	White	32,100	720	28,000	Madison Co., Ark.	343,000	4-17-45
21	Wabash	30,400	529	33,150	Darke Co., Oh.	428,000	3-30-13
22	Pend Oreille	29,900	490	25,820	Near Butte, Mont.	171,300	6-13-48
23	Tombigbee	27,300	525	20,100	Prentiss Co., Miss.	286,000	4-22-79
24	Cumberland	[m]26,900	720	18,080	Letcher Co., Ky.	209,000	3-16-75
25	Stikine	[n]26,000	310	20,000	Stikine Range, B.C.	219,000	8-12-76
26	Sacramento		377	27,100	Siskiyou Co., Cal.	[o]322,000	12-25-64
27	Apalachicola	24,700	524	19,600	Towns Co., Ga.	293,000	3-20-29
28	Illinois	22,800	420	27,900	St. Joseph Co., Ind.	123,000	May 1943
29	Koyukuk	[p]22,000	470	32,400	Endicott Mtns., Alas.	266,000	6-6-64
30	Porcupine	[q]20,000	460	45,000	Ogilvie Mtns., Alas.	299,000	5-24-73
31	Hudson	19,500	306	13,370	Essex Co., N.Y.	215,000	3-19-36
32	Allegheny	19,290	325	11,700	Potter Co., Pa.	365,000	3-18-36
33	Delaware	[r]17,200	390	11,440	Schoharie Co., N.Y.	329,000	8-20-55

(a) Because river lengths and methods of measurement may change from time to time, the length figures given are subject to revision; (b) about 25 percent of flow occurs in the Atchafalaya River; (c) the length from mouth to source of the Mississippi River in Minnesota is 2,348 miles; (d) at Baptiste Collete Bayou, Louisiana; (e) at international boundary lat. 45°; (f) maximum monthly discharge; (g) period

1957-70; (h) continuation of Red River; (i) flow of Ouachita River added; (j) period 1956-69; (k) period 1962-69; (l) based on records of Chulitna, Talkeetna, and Yetna rivers; (m) period 1931-60; (n) period 1954-63; summer records only; (o) discharge of American River not included (p) period 1960-69; (q) period 1964-69; (r) at Liston Point on Delaware Bay.

Large Rivers in Canada

Source: "Inland Waters Directorate," Department of Fisheries and the Environment.
(Ranked according to average discharge in cubic feet per second (cfs). Figures indicate discharge and drainage to river mouths.

Rank	River	Average discharge	Length (miles	Drainage area (sq. mi.)
1	St. Lawrence (to Nicolet)	355,000	1,900	396,000[1]
2	Mackenzie	350,000	2,635	690,000
3	Fraser	128,000	850	89,900[2]
4	Columbia (International Boundary)	102,000	498	59,700[3]
5	Nelson	100,000	1,600	437,000[4]
6	Kokosak	85,500	543	51,500
7	Yukon (International Boundary)	83,000	714	115,000[5]
8	Ottawa	70,500	790	56,500
9	Saguenay (to head of Peribonea)	62,200	434	34,000
10	Skeena	62,100	300	21,200

(1) Including 195,000 sq. mi. in U.S. (2) Including diversion. (3) Including 20,000 sq. mi. in U.S. (4) Including 69,500 sq. mi. in U.S. (5) Including 9,000 sq. mi. in U.S.

Principal World Rivers

Source: National Geographic Society, Washington, D.C. (length in miles)

River	Outflow	Lgth	River	Outflow	Lgth	River	Outflow	Lgth
Albany	James Bay	610	Indus	Arabian Sea	1,800	Red River of N.	Lake Winnipeg	545
Amazon	Atlantic Ocean	4,000	Irrawaddy	Bay of Bengal	1,300	Rhine	North Sea	820
Amu	Aral Sea	1,578	Japura	Amazon River	1,750	Rhone	Gulf of Lions	505
Amur	Tatar Strait	2,744	Jordan	Dead Sea	200	Rio de la Plata	Atlantic Ocean	150
Angara	Yenisey River	1,151	Kootenay	Columbia River	485	Rio Grande	Gulf of Mexico	1,885
Arkansas	Mississippi	1,459	Lena	Laptev Sea	2,734	Rio Roosevelt	Aripuana	400
Back	Arctic Ocean	605	Loire	Bay of Biscay	634	Saguenay	St. Lawrence R.	434
Brahmaputra	Bay of Bengal	1,800	Mackenzie	Arctic Ocean	2,635	St. John	Bay of Fundy	418
Bug, Southern	Dnieper River	532	Madeira	Amazon River	2,013	St. Lawrence	Gulf of St. Law.	800
Bug, Western	Wisla River	481	Magdalena	Caribbean Sea	956	Salween	Andaman Sea	1,500
Canadian	Arkansas River	906	Marne	Seine River	326	Sao Francisco	Atlantic Ocean	1,988
Chang	E. China Sea	3,964	Mekong	S. China Sea	2,600	Saskatchewan	Lake Winnipeg	1,205
Churchill, Man.	Hudson Bay	1,000	Meuse	North Sea	580	Seine	English Chan.	482
Churchill, Que.	Atlantic Ocean	532	Mississippi	Gulf of Mexico	2,348	Shannon	Atlantic Ocean	230
Colorado	Gulf of Calif.	1,450	Missouri	Mississippi	2,533	Snake	Columbia River	1,038
Columbia	Pacific Ocean	1,243	Murray-Darling	Indian Ocean	2,310	Sungari	Amur River	1,150
Congo	Atlantic Ocean	2,900	Negro	Amazon	1,400	Syr	Aral Sea	1,370
Danube	Black Sea	1,776	Nelson	Hudson Bay	1,600	Tajo, Tagus	Atlantic Ocean	626
Dnieper	Black Sea	1,420	Niger	Gulf of Guinea	2,590	Tennessee	Ohio River	652
Dniester	Black Sea	877	Nile	Mediterranean	4,145	Thames	North Sea	215
Don	Sea of Azov	1,224	Ob-Irtysh	Gulf of Ob	3,362	Tiber	Tyrrhenian Sea	252
Drava	Danube River	447	Oder	Baltic Sea	567	Tigris	Shatt al-Arab	1,180
Dvina, North	White Sea	824	Ohio	Mississippi	975	Tisza	Danube River	600
Dvina, West	Gulf of Riga	634	Orange	Atlantic Ocean	1,300	Tocantins	Para River	1,677
Ebro	Mediterranean	565	Orinoco	Atlantic Ocean	1,600	Ural	Caspian Sea	1,575
Elbe	North Sea	724	Ottawa	St. Lawrence R.	790	Uruguay	Rio de la Plata	1,000
Euphrates	Shatt al-Arab	1,700	Paraguay	Parana River	1,584	Volga	Caspian Sea	2,194
Fraser	Str. of Georgia	850	Parana	Rio de la Plata	2,485	Weser	North Sea	454
Gambia	Atlantic Ocean	700	Peace	Slave River	1,195	Wisla	Bay of Danzig	675
Ganges	Bay of Bengal	1,560	Pilcomayo	Paraguay River	1,000	Yellow (See Huang)		
Garonne	Bay of Biscay	357	Po	Adriatic Sea	405	Yenisey	Kara Sea	2,543
Hsi	S. China Sea	1,200	Purus	Amazon River	2,100	Yukon	Bering Sea	1,070
Huang	Yellow Sea	2,903	Red	Mississippi	1,270	Zambezi	Indian Ocean	1,700

Famous Waterfalls

Source: National Geographic Society, Washington, D.C.

The earth has thousands of waterfalls, some of considerable magnitude. Their importance is determined not only by height but volume of flow, steadiness of flow, crest width, whether the water drops sheerly or over a sloping surface, and in one leap or a succession of leaps. A series of low falls flowing over a considerable distance is known as a cascade.

Sete Quedas or Guaira is the world's greatest waterfall when its mean annual flow (estimated at 470,000 cusecs, cubic feet per second) is combined with height. A greater volume of water passes over Boyoma Falls (Stanley Falls), though not one of its seven cataracts, spread over nearly 60 miles of the Congo River, exceeds 10 feet.

Estimated mean annual flow, in cusecs, of other major waterfalls are: Niagara, 212,200; Paulo Afonso, 100,000; Urubupunga, 97,000; Iguazu, 61,000; Patos-Maribondo, 53,000; Victoria, 38,400; and Kaieteur, 23,400.

Height = total drop in feet in one or more leaps. † = falls of more than one leap; * = falls that diminish greatly seasonally; ** = falls that reduce to a trickle or are dry for part of each year. If river names not shown, they are same as the falls. R. = river; L. = lake; (C) = cascade type.

Name and location	Ht.	Name and location	Ht.	Name and location	Ht.
Africa		Tesissat, Blue Nile R.	140	**Tanzania-Zambia**	
		Lesotho		*Kalambo	726
Angola		*Maletsunyane	630	**Uganda**	
Duque de Braganca,		**Zimbabwe-Zambia**		Kabalega (Murchison) Victoria	
Lucala R.	344	*Victoria, Zambezi R.	343	Nile R.	130
Ruacana, Cuene R.	406	**South Africa**			
Ethiopia		*Augrabies, Orange R.	480	**Asia**	
Dal Verme,		Howick, Umgeni R.	364	India—*Cauvery	330
Dorya R.	98	† Tugela	2,014	*Gokak, Ghataprabha R.	170
Fincha	508	Highest fall	597	*Jog (Gersoppa), Sharavathi R.	830

Name and location	Ht.	Name and location	Ht.	Name and location	Ht.
Japan		Handegg, Aare R.	150	New Jersey	
*Kegon, Daiya R.	330	Iffigen	120	Passaic	70
Laos		Pissevache, Salanfe R.	213	New York	
Khon Cataracts,		† Reichenbach	656	*Taughannock	215
Mekong R. (C)	70	Rhine	79	Oregon	
		† Simmen	459	† Multnomah	620
Australasia		Staubbach.	984	Highest fall	542
Australia		† Trummelbach	1,312	Tennessee	
New South Wales				Fall Creek	256
† Wentworth.	614	**North America**		Washington	
Highest fall	360			Mt. Rainier Natl. Park	
Wollomombi.	1,100	**Canada**		Narada, Paradise R.	168
Queensland		Alberta		Sluiskin, Paradise R.	300
Coomera	210	Panther, Nigel Cr..	600	Palouse	197
Tully	885	British Columbia		**Snoqualmie	268
† Wallaman, Stony Cr..	1,137	† Della.	1,443	Wisconsin	
Highest fall.	937	† Takakkaw, Daly Glacier	1,200	*Big Manitou, Black R. (C).	165
New Zealand		Northwest Territories		Wyoming	
Bowen	540	Virginia, S. Nahanni R.	294	Yellowstone Natl. Pk. Tower	132
Helena.	890	Quebec		*Yellowstone (upper).	109
Stirling	505	Montmorency	274	*Yellowstone (lower).	308
† Sutherland, Arthur R.	1,904	**Canada—United States**		**Mexico**	
Highest fall	815	Niagara: American	182	El Salto	218
		Horseshoe	173	**Juanacatlan, Santiago R.	72
Europe		**United States**			
Austria—† Gastein	492	California		**South America**	
Highest fall	280	*Feather, Fall R.	640	**Argentina-Brazil**	
† *Golling, Schwarzbach R.	250	Yosemite National Park		Iguazu	230
† Krimml.	1,312	*Bridalveil	620	**Brazil**	
France—*Gavarnie	1,385	*Illilouette	370	Glass	1,325
Great Britain—Scotland		*Nevada, Merced R.	594	Patos-Maribondo, Grande R.	115
Glomach.	370	**Ribbon.	1,612	Paulo Afonso, Sao Francisco R.	275
Wales		**Silver Strand, Meadow Br.	1,170	Urubupunga, Parana R.	40
Cain	150	*Vernal, Merced R.	317	**Brazil-Paraguay**	
Rhaiadr	240	† **Yosemite	2,425	Sete Qeudas	
Iceland—Detti	144	Yosemite (upper).	1,430	Parana R.	130
† Gull, Hvita R.	105	Yosemite (lower)	320	**Colombia**	
Italy—Frua, Toce R. (C).	470	Yosemite (middle) (C)	675	Catarata de Candelas,	
Norway		Colorado		Cusiana R.	984
Mardalsfossen (Northern)	1,535	† Seven, South Cheyenne Cr..	300	*Tequendama, Bogota R.	427
† Mardalsfossen (Southern).	2,149	Hawaii		**Ecuador**	
† **Skjeggedal, Nybuai R.	1,378	Akaka, Kolekole Str.	442	*Agoyan, Pastaza R..	200
**Skykje.	984	Idaho		**Guyana**	
Vetti, Morka-Koldedola R.	900	**Shoshone, Snake R.	212	Kaieteur, Potaro R.	741
Voring, Bjoreio R..	597	Twin, Snake R.	120	Great, Kamarang R.	1,600
Sweden		Kentucky		† Marina, Ipobe R.	500
† Handol.	427	Cumberland.	68	Highest fall	300
† Tannforsen, Are R.	120	Maryland		**Venezuela—**	
Switzerland		*Great, Potomac R. (C)	71	† *Angel.	3,212
† Diesbach	394	Minnesota		Highest fall	2,648
Giessbach (C)	984	**Minnehaha	53	Cuquenan.	2,000

Notable Deserts of the World

Arabian (Eastern), 70,000 sq. mi. in Egypt between the Nile river and Red Sea, extending southward into Sudan.

Atacama, 600 mi. long area rich in nitrate and copper deposits in N. Chile.

Black Rock, 1,000 sq. mi. barren plain in NW Nev.

Death Valley, 2,936 sq. mi. in E. Cal. and SW Nev. Contains lowest point below sea level (282 ft.) in western hemisphere.

Gibson, 250,000 sq. mi. in the interior of W. Australia.

Gobi, 500,000 sq. mi. in Mongolia and China.

Great Sandy, 150,000 sq. mi. in W. Australia.

Great Victoria, 250,000 sq. mi. in W. and S. Australia.

Kalahari, 225,000 sq. mi. in southern Africa.

Kara-Kum, 120,000 sq. mi. in Turkmen, SSR.

Kavir (Dasht-e-Kavir), great salt waste in central Iran some 400 mi. long.

Kyzyl-Kum, 100,000 sq. mi. in Kazakh and Uzbek; SSRs.

Libyan, 600,000 sq. mi. in the Sahara extending from Lybia through SW Egypt into Sudan.

Lut (Dasht-e-Lut), 20,000 sq. mi. in E. Iran.

Mojave, 15,000 sq. mi. in S. Cal.

Nafud (An Nafud), 50,000 sq. mi. near Jawf in Saudi Arabia.

Namib, long narrow area extending 800 miles along SW coast of Africa.

Nubian, 120,000 sq. mi. in the Sahara in NE Sudan.

Painted Desert, section of high plateau in N. Ariz. extending 150 mi.

Rub al-Khali (Empty Quarter), 250,000 sq. mi. in the south Arabian Peninsula. World's largest continuous sand area.

Sahara, 3,320,000 sq. mi. in N. Africa extending westward to the Atlantic. Largest tropical and climatic desert in the world.

Simpson, 120,000 sq. mi. in central Australia.

Sonoran, 120,000 sq. mi. in SW Ariz. and SE Cal. extending into Mexico.

Syrian, 100,000 sq. mi. arid wasteland extending over much of N. Saudi Arabia, E. Jordan, S. Syria, and W. Iraq.

Taklamakan, 125,000 sq. mi. in Sinkiang Province, China.

Thar (Great Indian), 100,000 sq. mi. arid area extending 400 mi. along India-Pakistan border.

The Great Lakes

Source: National Ocean Survey, U.S. Commerce Department

The Great Lakes form the largest body of fresh water in the world and with their connecting waterways are the largest inland water transportation unit. Draining the great North Central basin of the U.S., they enable shipping to reach the Atlantic via their outlet, the St. Lawrence R., and also the Gulf of Mexico via the Illinois Waterway, from Lake Michigan to the Mississippi R. A third outlet connects with the Hudson R. and thence the Atlantic via the N. Y. State Barge Canal System. Traffic on the Illinois Waterway and the N.Y. State Barge Canal System is limited to recreational boating and small shipping vessels.

Only one of the lakes, Lake Michigan, is wholly in the United States; the others are shared with Canada. Ships carrying grain, lumber and iron ore move from the shores of Lake Superior to Whitefish Bay at the east end of the lake, thence through the Soo (Sault Ste. Marie) locks, through the St. Mary's River and into Lake Huron. To reach the steel mills at Gary, and Port of Indiana and South Chicago, Ill., ore ships move west from Lake Huron to Lake Michigan through the Straits of Mackinac.

Lake Huron discharges its waters into Lake Erie through a narrow waterway, the St. Clair R., Lake St. Clair (both included in the drainage basin figures) and the Detroit R. Lake St. Clair, a marshy basin, is 26 miles long and 24 miles wide at its maximum. A ship channel has been dredged through the lake.

Lake Superior is 600 feet above mean water level at Point-au-Pere, Quebec, on the International Great Lakes Datum (1955). From Duluth, Minn., to the eastern end of Lake Ontario is 1,156 mi.

	Superior	Michigan	Huron	Erie	Ontario
Length in miles	350	307	206	241	193
Breadth in miles	160	118	183	57	53
Deepest soundings in feet	1,330	923	750	210	802
Volume of water in cubic miles	2,900	1,180	850	116	393
Area (sq. miles) water surface—U.S.	20,600	22,300	9,100	4,980	3,560
Canada	11,100	.....	13,900	4,930	3,990
Area (sq. miles) entire drainage basin—U.S.	16,900	45,600	16,200	18,000	15,200
Canada	32,400	.....	35,500	4,720	12,100
Total Area (sq. miles) U.S. and Canada	81,000	67,900	74,700	32,630	34,850
Mean surface above mean water level at Point-au-Pere, Quebec, aver. level in feet (1900-1980)	600.58	578.22	578.22	570.37	244.70
Latitude, North	46° 25' / 49° 00'	41° 37' / 46° 06'	43° 00' / 46° 17'	41° 23' / 42° 52'	43° 11' / 44° 15'
Longitude, West	84° 22' / 92° 06'	84° 45' / 88° 02'	79° 43' / 84° 45'	78° 51' / 83° 29'	76° 03' / 79° 53'
National boundary line in miles	282.8	None	260.8	251.5	174.6
United States shore line (mainland only) miles	863	1,400	580	431	300

Largest Lake in Each Province and Territory of Canada

Source: "Inland Waters Directorate", Environment Canada.

Province	Largest within:	Largest partly in:	Shared with:	Origin	Area (sq. miles)	Ft. above sea level
Alberta	Claire			Natural	555	700
		Athabasca	Saskatchewan	Natural	3,066	700
British Columbia	Williston			Manmade	640	2,180
Manitoba	Winnipeg			Natural	9,417	713
Newfoundland	Smallwood Reservoir			Manmade	2,520	S.L.
New Brunswick	Grand			Natural	70	4
Northwest Territories	Great Bear			Natural	12,096	512
Nova Scotia	Bras d'Or			Natural	424	Tidal
Ontario	Nipigon			Natural	1,872	1,050
		Huron	U.S.	Natural	15,241	580
Prince Edward Island	Forest Hill Pond			Manmade	.7	50
Quebec	Mistassini			Natural	902	1,230
Saskatchewan	Reindeer			Natural	2,560	1,106
		Athabasca	Alberta	Natural	3,066	700
Yukon Territory	Kluane			Natural	158	2,563

Lakes of the World

Source: National Geographic Society, Washington, D.C.

A lake is a body of water surrounded by land. Although some lakes are called seas, they are lakes by definition. The Caspian Sea is bounded by the Soviet Union and Iran and is fed by eight rivers.

Name	Continent	Area sq. mi.	Length mi.	Depth feet	Elev. feet
Caspian Sea	Asia-Europe	143,244	760	3,363	-92
Superior	North America	31,700	350	1,333	600
Victoria	Africa	26,828	250	270	3,720
Aral Sea	Asia	24,904	280	220	174
Huron	North America	23,000	206	750	579
Michigan	North America	22,300	307	923	579
Tanganyika	Africa	12,700	420	4,823	2,534
Baykal	Asia	12,162	395	5,315	1,493
Great Bear	North America	12,096	192	1,463	512
Malawi	Africa	11,150	360	2,280	1,550
Great Slave	North America	11,031	298	2,015	513
Erie	North America	9,910	241	210	570
Winnipeg	North America	9,417	266	60	713
Ontario	North America	7,550	193	802	245
Ladoga	Europe	6,835	124	738	13
Balkhash	Asia	7,115	376	85	1,115
Chad	Africa	6,300	175	24	787
Maracaibo	South America	5,217	133	115	Sea level
Onega	Europe	3,710	145	328	108
Volta	Africa	3,276	250	....	....
Titicaca	South America	3,200	122	922	12,500
Athabasca	North America	3,064	208	407	700
Nicaragua	North America	3,100	102	230	102
Eyre	Australia	3,600	90	4	-52
Rudolf	Africa	2,473	154	240	1,230
Reindeer	North America	2,568	143	720	1,106
Issyk Kul	Asia	2,355	115	2,303	5,279
Torrens	Australia	2,230	130	....	92
Vanern	Europe	2,156	91	328	144
Winnipegosis	North America	2,075	141	38	830
Albert	Africa	2,075	100	168	2,030
Kariba	Africa	2,050	175	390	1,590
Nettilling	North America	2,140	67	Sea level	95
Nipigon	North America	1,872	72	540	1,050
Gairdner	Australia	1,840	90	....	112
Manitoba	North America	1,799	140	12	813
Urmia	Asia	1,815	90	49	4,180

Largest Lake in Each State of the U.S.

Source: National Geographic Society, Washington, D.C.
*indicates reservoir

State	Largest entirely within state	Largest partly in another state	Shared with	Origin	Total area (square miles)	Feet above sea level	Maximum depth (feet)	Shoreline length (miles)
Ala.. .	Guntersville			Man-made ..	108	595	94	962
		Walter F. George	Ga.	Man-made ..	71	190	90	640
Alas. .	Iliamna			Natural	1,150	150	1,289	230
Ariz. .	Theodore Roosevelt			Man-made .	27	2,136	280	88
		Powell	Ut.	Man-made .	252	3,700	580	1,800
Ark. .	Ouachita			Man-made .	63	578	179	690
		Bull Shoals	Mo.	Man-made .	71	654	175	740
Cal. .	Salton Sea			Natural	360	-235	48	—
		Tahoe	Nev.	Natural	192	6,229	1,644	71
Col. .	Blue Mesa*			Man-made	14	7,519	325	95
		Navajo*	N.M.	Man-made	24	6,085	382	150
Conn. .	Candlewood			Man-made .	8	429	85	75
Del. .	Lum's Pond			Man-made .	.34	44	22	5
Fla. .	Okeechobee			Natural	700	14	15	96
Ga. .	Sidney Lanier			Man-made .	59	1,070	156	540
		Clark Hill	S.C.	Man-made .	109	330	150	1,200
Ha. .	Waita*				.66	242	—	4
Ida. .	Pend Oreille			Natural	136	2,063	1,200	127
Ill. .	Carlyle*			Man-made	41	445	40	83
		Michigan	Wis., Ind., Mich	Natural	22,300	579	923	1,660
Ind. .	Monroe*			Man-made	29	556	75	100
		Michigan	Wis., Ill., Mich.	Natural	22,300	579	923	1,660
Ia. .	Rathbun*			Man-made .	18	904	55	180
Kan. .	Tuttle Creek*			Man-made .	25	1,079	90	112
Ky. .	Cumberland			Man-made .	79	760	183	1,255
		Kentucky	Tenn.	Man-made .	250	359	90	2,380
La. .	Pontchartrain			Natural	621	sea lev.	18	112
Me. .	Moosehead			Natural	117	1,042	246	190
Md. .	Deep Creek			Man-made .	6	2,462	72	62
		Conowingo*	Pa.	Man-made .	13	109	110	38
Mass. .	Quabbin*			Man-made .	39	524	150	104
Mich. .	Houghton			Natural	31	1,138	20	30
		Superior	Wis., Minn., Ont.	Natural	31,700	600	1,333	2,980
Minn. .	Red			Natural	452	1,172	—	—
		Superior	Wis., Mich., Ont.	Natural	31,700	600	1,333	2,980
Miss. .	Grenada			Man-made .	100	231	102	282
Mo. .	Lake of the Ozarks			Man-made .	93	659	148	1,300
Mon. .	Fort Peck*			Man-made .	375	2,246	220	1,540
Neb. .	McConaughy			Man-made .	50	3,260	130	105
Nev. .	Pyramid			Man-made .	169	3,789	330	66
		Mead	Ariz.	Man-made .	247	1,221	432	550
N.H. .	Winnipesaukee			Natural	70	504	169	240
N.J. .	Hopatcong			Natural	4	924	58	32
N.M. .	Elephant Butte*			Man-made .	57	4,450	176	201
N.Y. .	Oneida			Natural	80	369	55	63
		Erie	Mich., Pa., Ont., Oh.	Natural	9,910	570	210	856
N.C. .	Mattamuskeet			Natural	67	3	5	—
		John H. Kerr*	Va.	Man-made .	76	300	99	800
N.D. .	Sakakawea			Man-made .	575	1,850	180	1,600
		Oahe*	S.D.	Man-made .	556	1,617	200	2,250
Oh. .	Grand			Man-made .	17	869	10	60
		Erie	Mich., Pa., N.Y., Ont.	Natural	9,910	570	210	856
Okla. .	Eufaula			Man-made .	160	585	87	600
Ore. .	Upper Klamath			Natural	143	4,143	50	165
		Goose Lake	Cal.	Natural	194	4,716	24	90
Pa. .	Raystown*			Man-made .	13	786	185	110
		Erie	Mich., N.Y., Oh., Ont.	Natural	9,910	570	210	856
R.I. .	Scituate			Man-made .	5	284	94	38
S.C. .	Marion			Man-made .	173	75	55	300
S.D. .	Francis Case			Man-made .	159	1,375	140	540
		Oahe*	N.D.	Man-made .	556	1,617	200	2,250
Tenn. .	Watts Bar			Man-made .	61	741	75	783
		Kentucky	Ky.	Man-made .	250	359	90	2,380
Tex. .	Sam Rayburn*			Man-made .	179	164	74	—
		Toledo Bend*	La.	Man-made .	284	172	92	—
Ut. .	Great Salt Lake			Natural	1,438	4,200	36	334
Vt. .	Bornoseen			Natural	4	413	—	—
		Champlain	N.Y., Que.	Natural	437	95	400	379
Va. .	Smith Mountain			Man-made .	31	795	200	500
		John H. Kerr*	N.C.	Man-made .	76	300	99	800
Wash. .	F.D. Roosevelt			Man-made .	123	1,288	375	325
W. Va. .	Summersville			Man-made .	4	1,652	267	65
Wis. .	Winnebago			Natural	215	747	21	78
		Superior	Minn., Mich., Ont.	Natural	31,700	600	1,333	2,980
Wyo. .	Yellowstone			Natural	137	7,733	309	110
		Flaming Gorge*	Utah	Man-made .	—	6,040	437	—

Notable Bridges in North America

Source: State Highway Engineers: Canadian Civil Engineering — ASCE

Asterisk (*) designates railroad bridge. Span of a bridge is distance (in feet) between its supports.

Suspension

Year	Bridge	Location	Longest span
1964	Verrazano-Narrows	New York, N.Y.	4,260
1937	Golden Gate	San Fran. Bay, Cal.	4,200
1957	Mackinac	Sts. of Mackinac	3,800
1931	Geo. Washington	Hudson River	3,500
1952	Tacoma	Washington	2,800
1936	¹Transbay	San Fran. Bay, Cal.	2,310
1939	Bronx-Whitestone	East R., N.Y.C.	2,300
1970	Pierre Laporte	Quebec	2,190
1951	Del. Memorial	Wilmington, Del.	2,150
1968	Del. Mem. (new)	Wilmington, Del.	2,150
1957	Walt Whitman	Phila., Pa.	2,000
1929	Ambassador	Detroit-Canada	1,850
1961	Throgs Neck	Long Is. Sound	1,800
1926	Benjamin Franklin	Philadelphia	1,750
1924	Bear Mt., N.Y.	Hudson River	1,632
1952	²Wm. Preston Lane Mem.	Sandy Point, Md.	1,600
1903	Williamsburg	East R., N.Y.C.	1,600
1969	Newport	Narragansett Bay, R.I.	1,600
1883	Brooklyn	East R., N.Y.C.	1,595
1939	Lions Gate	Burrard Inlet, B.C.	1,550
1930	Mid-Hudson, N.Y.	Poughkeepsie	1,500
1964	Vincent Thomas	Los Angeles Harbor	1,500
1909	Manhattan	East R., N.Y.C.	1,470
1936	Triborough	East R., N.Y.C.	1,380
1931	St. Johns	Portland, Ore.	1,207
1929	Mount Hope	Rhode Island	1,200
1939	Deer Isle	Maine.	1,080
1931	Maysville (Ky.)	Ohio River	1,060
1867	Cincinnati	Ohio River	1,057
1971	Dent.	Clearwater Co., Ida.	1,050
1900	Miampimi	Mexico	1,030
1849	Wheeling, W. Va.	Ohio River	1,010

Cantilever

Year	Bridge	Location	Longest span
1917	Quebec	Quebec	1,800
1970	Commodore Barry	Chester, Pa.	1,644
1958	New Orleans, La.	Mississippi R.	1,575
1936	Transbay	San Fran. Bay	1,400
1968	Baton Rouge, La.	Mississippi R.	1,235
1955	Nyack-Tarrytown	Hudson River	1,212
1930	Longview, Wash.	Columbia River	1,200
1909	Queensboro	East R., N.Y.C.	1,182
1927	Carquinez Strait	California.	1,100
1958	Parallel Span	"	1,100
1930	Jacques Cartier	Montreal, P.Q.	1,097
1968	Isaiah D. Hart	Jacksonville, Fla.	1,088
1957	³Richmond	San Fran. Bay, Cal.	1,070
1929	Grace Memorial	Charleston, S.C.	1,050
1963	Newburgh-Beacon	Hudson, R., N.Y.	1,000
1975	Caruthersville, Mo.	Mississippi R.	920
1977	Saint Marys	Saint Marys, W. Va.	900
1969	Silver Memorial	Pt. Pleasant, W. Va.	900
1940	Natchez	Mississippi R.	875
1938	Blue Water	Pt. Huron, Mich.	871
1972	Vicksburg	Mississippi River.	870
1954	Sunshine Skyway	St. Petersburg, Fla.	864
1940	*Baton Rouge	Mississippi R.	848
1899	*Cornwall	St. Lawrence R.	843
1940	Greenville	Mississippi R.	840
1961	Helena, Ark.	Mississippi R.	840
1963	Brent Spence	Covington, Ky.	831
1963	Cincinnati, Oh.	Ohio River	830
1956	Earl C. Clements	Ohio R., Ill-Ky.	825⁵
1930	*Vicksburg	Mississippi R.	825
1929	Louisville	Ohio River	820
1961	Campbellton-Cross Point	New Brunswick-Quebec	815
1943	Jeff'rson Barr'ks., Mo.	Mississippi R.	804
1950	Maurice J. Tobin	Boston, Mass.	800
1935	Rip Van Winkle	Catskill, N.Y.	800
1938	Cairo	Ohio River, Ill-Ky.	800
1940	Ludlow Ferry.	Potomac R.	800
1932	Washington Mem.	Seattle, Wash.	800
1936	McCullough	Coos Bay, Ore.	793
1935	⁴Huey P Long	New Orleans	790
1916	*Memphis (Harahan)	Mississippi R.	790
1892	*Memphis	Mississippi R.	790
1949	Memphis-Arkansas	Mississippi R.	790
1904	*Mingo Jct., W. Va.	Ohio River	769

Simple Truss

Year	Bridge	Location	Longest span
1910	*Beaver, Pa.	Ohio River	767
1966	⁵S.N. Pearman	Charleston, S.C.	760
1940	Owensboro.	Ohio River	750
1911	Sewickley, Pa.	Ohio River	750
1928	Outerbridge, N.Y.-N.J.	Arthur Kill	750
1964	Sunshine, Don'ville	Mississippi, La.	750

Simple Truss

Year	Bridge	Location	Longest span
1977	Chester.	Chester, W. Va.	746
1917	*Metropolis.	Ohio River	720
1929	Irvin S. Cobb.	Ohio River-Ill.-Ky.	716
1922	*Tanana River	Nenana, Alaska	700
1933	*Henderson	Ohio River-Ind.-Ky.	665
1967	I-77, Ohio River	Marietta, Oh.	650
1917	MacArthur, Ill.-Mo.	St. Louis	647
1919	Louisville	Ohio River	644
1933	Atchafalaya	Morgan City, La.	608
1924	*Castleton	Hudson River	598
1889	*Cincinnati	Ohio River	542
1951	Allegheny River	Allegheny Co., Pa.	533
1914	Pittsburgh	Allegheny R.	531
1930	*Martinez.	California.	528
1967	Tanana River	Alaska	500
1974	Fort Hill, I-64.	Charleston, W. Va.	465

Steel Truss

Year	Bridge	Location	Longest span
1940	Gov. Nice Mem.	Potomac River, Md.	800
1975	I-24	Tenn R., Ky.	720
1938	US-62, Ky.	Green River	700
1952	US-62, Ky.	Cumberland River.	700
1940	Jamestown.	Jamestown, R.I.	640
1940	Greenville	Mississippi R., Ark.	640
1949	Memphis	Mississippi R., Ark.	621
1938	US-22.	Delaware River, N.J.	540
1972	Mississippi River	Muscatine, Ia.	512
1896	Newport	Ohio River, Ky.	511
1931	US-60.	Cumberland R., Ky.	500
1958	Lake Oahe	Mobridge, S.D.	500
1958	Lake Oahe.	Gettysburg, S.D.	500
1910	McKinley, St. Louis	Mississippi River.	500
1963	Millard E. Tydings	Susquehanna R., Md.	490
1955	Four Bears	Missouri R., N.D.	475
1930	Lake Champlain	Lake Champlain, N.Y.	434
1947	Mayo	Suwanee R., Fla.	420
1929	Clarendon	White River, Ark.	400
1931	US-60.	Tennessee R., Ky.	400

Continuous Truss

Year	Bridge	Location	Longest span
1966	Astoria, Ore.	Columbia R.	1,232
1966	Marquam.	Willamette R., Ore.	1,044
1969	Miss. R.	Dyersburg, Tenn.	900
1969	Irondequoit Bay	Rochester, N.Y.	891
1943	Dubuque, Ia.	Mississippi R.	845
1953	John E. Mathews	Jacksonville, Fla.	810
1957	Kingston-Rhinecliff	Hudson R., N.Y.	800
1918	*Sciotoville.	Ohio River	775
1974	Betsy Ross.	Philadelphia, Pa.	729
1929	Madison-Milton	Ohio River	727
1966	Matthew E. Welsh	Mauckport	707⁶
1962	Champlain.	Montreal, P.Q.	707
1975	Girard Point	Philadelphia, Pa.	700
1929	Chain of Rocks	Mississippi R.	699
1966	Braga.	Taunton R., Mass.	682
1938	Port Arthur-Orange	Texas.	680
1929	*Cincinnati	Ohio River	675
1928	Cape Girardeau, Mo.	Mississippi R.	672
1946	Chester, Ill.	Mississippi R.	670
1930	Quincy, Ill.	Mississippi R.	628
1959	US 181, over harbor	Corpus Christi, Tex.	620
1934	Bourne	Cape Cod Canal	616
1935	Sagamore.	Cape Cod Canal	616
1965	Clarion River.	Clarion Co., Pa.	612
1957	Blatnik.	Duluth, Minn.	600
1965	Rio Grande Gorge.	Taos, N.M.	600
1941	Columbia River	Kettle Falls, Wash.	600
1954	Columbia River	Umatilla, Ore.	600
1954	Columbia River	The Dalles, Ore.	576
1962	W. Br. Feather River	Oroville, Cal.	576
1936	Meredosia	Illinois River	567
1936	Mark Twain Mem.	Hannibal, Mo.	562
1957	Mackinac	Mackinac Straits, Mich.	560
1937	Homestead.	Pittsburgh	553
1961	Ship Canal	Seattle, Wash.	552

Year	Bridge	Location	Longest span
1932	Pulaski Skyway	Passaic R., N.J.	550
1973	I-95, Thames River ...	New London, Conn...	540
1927	Ross Island........	Portland, Ore......	535
1958	Interstate.........	Portland, Ore......	531
1936	South Omaha	Missouri R, Neb.-Ia...	525
1932	Savanna, Ill.-Sabula. .	Mississippi R......	520
1962	Columbia River	Beebe, Wash......	520
1970	Snake River	Central Ferry, Wash..	520

Continuous Box and Plate Girder

Year	Bridge	Location	Longest span
1967	San Mateo-Hayward No. 2......	San Fran. Bay, Cal...	750
1963	Gunnison River	Gunnison, Col......	720
1969	San Diego-Coronado ..	San Diego Bay, Cal. .	660[7]
1973	Ship Channel	Houston, Tex.....	630
1967	Poplar St..........	St. Louis, Mo.....	600
1977	US-64, Tennessee R.. .	Savannah, Tenn. ...	525
1965	McDonald-Cartier ...	Ottawa, Ont.	520
1971	Lake Koocanusa.....	Lincoln Co., Mon....	500
1972	Sitka Harbor.......	Sitka, Alaska	450
1974	I-430	Arkansas R........	430
1972	I-635, Kansas City....	Missouri R., Kan.-Mo..	425
1967	Chattanooga.......	Tennessee R., Tenn..	420
1978	Snake River	Clarkston, Wash...	420
1975	Yukon River	North Slope Road, Alas.	410
1972	I-75, Tennessee River..	Loudon, Co., Tenn ...	400
1941	Susquehanna	Susquehanna R., Md..	400
1963	Lake Charles B'Pass ..	Louisiana.......	399
1957	Conn. Turnpike	Quinnipiac R.	387
1960	Route 34	New Haven, Conn. ..	379
1971	S.H. No. 1	Pendleton, Ark....	377
1960	Tennessee River	Chattanooga, Tenn..	375
1966	I-80, LeClaire, Ia.....	Mississippi	370
1971	Sacramento R.......	Bryte, Cal.......	370
1963	I-40, Tennessee River..	Benton Co., Tenn....	365
1967	San Mateo Creek	Hillsborough, Cal...	360
1950	US-62, Kentucky Dam .	Tennessee R., Ky....	350
1961	Whiskey Creek	Trinity Co., Cal....	350
1972	Franklin Falls.......	Snoq'lmie Pass, Wash.	350
1971	Don Pedro Reserv ...	Tuolumne Co., Cal. ..	350

Continuous Plate

Year	Bridge	Location	Longest span
1965	New Chain of Rocks ..	Mississippi R., Ill. ...	5,411[9]
1973	Great Congress Gty. ..	Schenectady, N.Y. ..	1,870
1971	Congress St........	Troy, N.Y.	1,420
1967	Mississippi River	LaCrescent, Minn....	450
1966	I-480	Missouri R., Ia.-Neb..	425
1970	I-435	Missouri R., Mo.....	425
1972	I-80	Missouri R., Ia.-Neb..	425
1971	St. Croix River	Hudson, Minn.....	390
1968	Lafayette St........	St. Paul, Minn.....	362
1970	Green River	Hendersonville, N.C..	350
1974	Mississippi R.......	Praire du Chien, Wisc.	350
1969	Fort Smith	Arkansas River ...	340
1964	Lexington Ave......	St. Paul, Minn....	340

I-Beam Girder

Year	Bridge	Location	Longest span
1941	US-31E...........	Rolling Fork R., Ky..	340
1948	US-27............	Licking River, Ky....	316
1947	US-31E...........	Green River, Ky. ...	316
1941	US-62............	Rolling Fork, Ky....	240
1942	Licking River	Owingsville, Ky....	240
1954	Fuller Warren	Jacksonville, Fla. ...	224

Steel Arch

Year	Bridge	Location	Longest span
1977	New River Gorge	Fayetteville, W. Va...	1,700
1931	Bayonne, N.J.	Kill Van Kull	1,652
1972	Fremont	Portland, Ore......	1,255
1964	Port Mann	British Columbia. . .	1,200
1967	Trois-Rivieres	St. Lawrence R., P.Q.	1,100
1959	Glen Canyon.......	Colorado River	1,028
1962	Lewiston-Queenston .	Niagara River, Ont. ..	1,000
1976	Perrine	Twin Falls, Ida. ...	993
1917	*Hell Gate	East R., N.Y.C.	977
1941	Rainbow	Niagara Falls	950
1972	I-40, Mississippi R....	Memphis, Tenn....	900[10]
1970	Lake Quinsigamond..	Worcester, Mass. ..	849
1966	Charles Braga	Somerset, Mass. ...	840
1967	Lincoln Trail	Ohio R., Ind.-Ky....	825
1961	Sherman Minton	Louisville, Ky.	800
1936	Henry Hudson	Harlem River	800
1936	French King	Conn. R. (Rt. 2, Mass.)	782
1931	West End..........	Pittsburgh	778
1972	Piscataqua R.......	I-95, Maine......	756

Year	Bridge	Location	Longest span
1979	SR 156, Tennessee R. .	So. Pittsburgh, Tenn..	750
1963	Cold Spring Canyon...	Santa Barbara, Cal...	700
1973	I-24, Paducah, Ky.....	Ohio River	700

Concrete Arch

Year	Bridge	Location	Longest span
1971	Selah Creek (twin) ...	Selah, Wash......	549
1968	Cowlitz River.......	Mossyrock, Wash. ..	520
1931	Westinghouse	Pittsburgh	425
1923	Cappelen..........	Minneapolis	400
1930	Jack's Run	Pittsburgh	400
1973	Elwha River	Port Angeles, Wash. .	380
1931	Bixby Creek	Monterey Coast, Cal..	330
1953	Arroyo Seco	Pasadena, Cal. ...	320
1927	Mendota	Ft. Snelling, Minn....	304

Twin Concrete Trestle

Year	Bridge	Location	Longest span
1963	Slidell, La.........	L. Pontchartrain	28,547[9]

Concrete Slab Dam

Year	Bridge	Location	Longest span
1927	Conowingo Dam....	Maryland........	4,611
1952	John H. Kerr Dam....	Roanoke River, Va...	2,785
1936	Hoover Dam	Boulder City, Nev...	1,324

Drawbridges
Vertical Lift

Year	Bridge	Location	Longest span
1959	*Arthur Kill	N.Y.-N.J.......	558
1935	*Cape Cod Canal....	Massachusetts ...	544
1960	*Delair, N.J.	Delaware River ...	542
1937	Marine Parkway	New York City....	540
1931	Burlington, N.J......	Delaware R.......	534
1912	*A-S-B Fratt	Kansas City	428
1945	*Harry S. Truman	Kansas City	427
1932	*M-K-T R.R.	Missouri R.......	414
1969	Wilm'gtn Mem......	Wilmington, N.C....	408
1930	Aerial	Duluth, Minn.....	386
1941	Main St...........	Jacksonville, Fla. ..	386
1962	Burlington	Ontario	370
1922	*Cincinnati	Ohio River	365
1967	Benj. Harrison Mem. ..	James River, Va....	363
1961	Corpus Christi Harbor. .	Corpus Christi, Tex...	344[4]
1962	Sand Island Access...	Oahu, Hawaii	340
1941	U.S. 1&9, Passaic R. ..	Newark, N.J......	332
1929	Carlton	Bath-Woolwich, Me...	328
1930	*Martinez.........	California	328
1960	St. Andrews Bay.....	Panama City, Fla....	327
1929	*Penn-Lehigh	Newark Bay	322
1920	*Chattanooga	Tennessee R......	310
1936	Triboro, N.Y.C.......	Harlem River	310
1936	Hardin	Illinois River	309
1960	Sacramento River....	Rio Vista, Cal.....	306
1957	Claiborne Ave.......	New Orleans	305
1927	Cochrane..........	Mobile, Ala.	300
1928	James River	Newport News ...	300
1929	San Mateo.........	California	300
1926	*Missouri Pacific.....	Kragen, Ark......	300

Bascule

Year	Bridge	Location	Longest span
1926	Fort Madison	Mississippi R......	525[4]
1969	Pearl River	Slidell, La.......	482
1916	Keokui Municipal	Mississippi R., Ia. ...	377
1917	SR-8, Tennessee River.	Chattanooga, Tenn...	306
1940	Lorain, Ohio........	Black River	300
1958	Morrison	Portland, Ore.....	285
1969	Elizabeth River......	Chesapeake, Va. ...	281
1957	Craig Memorial	I-280, Toledo, Oh....	245
1952	Downtown	Norfolk, Va.	230

Swing Bridges

Year	Bridge	Location	Longest span
1950	Douglass Memorial ...	Anac'tia R., Wash. D.C.	386
1945	Lord Delaware......	Mattaponi River, Va. .	252
1957	Eltham	Pamunkey River, Va..	237
1939	Chickahominy River..	Route 5, Va......	222
1930	Nansemond River....	Route 125, Va.	200

Swing Span

Year	Bridge	Location	Longest span
1908	*Willamette R.......	Portland, Ore.....	521
1903	*East Omaha	Missouri R.......	519
1952	Yorktown	York River, Va. ...	500
1897	*Duluth, Minn.......	St. Louis Bay	486
1899	*C.M.&N.R.R.	Chicago	474
1897	Sioux City, Ia.	Missouri R. (Nebr.-Ia.)	470
1914	*Coos Bay	Oregon........	458

Floating Pontoon

Year	Bridge	Location	Longest span
1963	Evergreen Pt........	Seattle, Wash.....	7,518
1940	Lacey V. Murrow ...	Seattle........	6,561
1961	Hood Canal	Pt. Gamble, Wash. ..	6,471

(1) The Transbay Bridge has 2 spans of 2,310 ft. each. (2) A second bridge in parallel will be completed. (3) The Richmond Bridge has twin spans 1,070 ft. each. (4) Railroad and vehicular bridge. (5) Two spans each 760 ft. (6) Two spans each 707 ft. (7) Two spans each 660 ft. (8) Two spans each 825 ft. (9) Total length of bridge: (10) Two spans each 900 ft.

Construction Details of Large and Unusual Bridges

Verrazano-Narrows Bridge, between Staten Island and Brooklyn, N.Y., has a suspension span of 4,260 ft., exceeding the Golden Gate Bridge, San Francisco, by 60 ft. One level in use Nov., 1964, second opened Jun. 28, 1969. The name is a compromise; it spans the Narrows and commemorates a visit to New York Harbor in Apr., 1524, deduced from certain notes left by Giovanni da Verrazano, Italian navigator sailing for Francis I of France.

Allegheny River Bridge (Interstate 80) near Emlenton, Pa., 270 ft. above the water, tallest in eastern U.S., a continuous truss, 688 ft. long, 1968.

Angostura, suspension type, span 2,336 feet, 1967 at Ciudad Bolivar, Venezuela. Total length; 5,507.

Charles Braga Bridge over Taunton River between Fall River and Somerset, Mass. It is 5,780 feet long.

Bendorf Bridge on the Rhine River, 5 mi. n. of Coblenz, completed 1965, is a 3-span cement girder bridge, 3,378 ft. overall length, 101 ft. wide, with the main span 682 ft.

Burro Creek Bridge with 4 spans over Burro Creek on highway 93 near Kingman, Ariz. Main span steel truss 680 ft. Others plate girder, 110 and 2 of 85 ft. 1966.

Champlain Bridge at Montreal crossing the St. Lawrence River was opened 1962. It is 4 miles long.

Chesapeake Bay Bridge-Tunnel, opened Apr. 15, 1964 on US-13, connects Virginia Beach-Norfolk with the Eastern Shore of Virginia. Shore to shore, 17.6 miles. Twelve miles of trestles, 4 man-made islands, 2 mile-long tunnels, and 2 bridges.

Cross Bay Parkway Bridge (N.Y.), 3,000 feet long with 6 traffic lanes, 11 eight foot wide precast, prestressed concrete T girders to support spans 130 feet long each with main span 275 feet.

Delaware Memorial Bridge over Delaware River near Wilmington. A twin suspension bridge paralleling the original 250 ft. upstream has a 2,150 ft. main span suspended from 440-ft. towers.

Eads Bridge across the Mississippi R. between St. Louis and E. St. Louis, built in 1874 has 4 main spans 1,520 ft., 2,502 ft., and 1,118 ft. crossing Miss. R., a railroad and a road.

Evergreen Point Bridge, Wash. consists of 33 floating concrete pontoons weighing 4,700 tons each, held in place by 77 ton crete anchors. Pontoon structure is 6,561 ft. long; with approaches bridge is 12,596 ft. long.

Fremont Bridge. Part of Stadium Freeway, Portland, Ore., crossing Willamette R. 1,255 ft. steel arch span with two 452 ft. flanking steel arch spans. 1971.

Frontenac Bridge, Quebec, suspension, span 2,190 ft., open 1970.

Gladesville Bridge at Sydney, Australia, has the longest concrete arch in the world (1,000 ft. span).

George Washington Bridge, New York City, 4th longest suspension bridge in the world, spans the Hudson River between W. 178th St., Manhattan, and Ft. Lee, N.J.; 4,760 ft. between anchorages, two levels, 14 traffic lanes. Triborough Bridge connects Manhattan, the Bronx, and Queens; project comprises a suspension bridge, a vertical lift bridge, and a fixed bridge, all connected by long viaducts. The famous Brooklyn Bridge over the East River, connecting Manhattan and Brooklyn, was completed in 1883, breaking all previous records by spanning 1,595 ft.

Golden Gate Bridge, crossing San Francisco Bay, has the second longest single span, 4,200 ft.

Hampton Roads Bridge-Tunnel, Va. A crossing completed in 1957 consisting of 2 man-made islands, 2 concrete trestle bridges, and one tunnel, under Hampton Roads with a length of 7,479 ft. A parallel facility with a 7,315 ft. tunnel is now open to traffic.

Hood Canal Floating Bridge, Wash., 23 floating concrete pontoons, 4,980 tons each. Roadway is supported on crete T-beam sections mounted on pontoons 20 feet above canal. Floating section is 6,471 ft. long, overall 7,866 ft. Closed Feb. 13, 1979; severe storm damage.

Humber Bridge, with a suspension span of 4,626 ft., the longest in the world, crosses the Humber estuary 5 miles west of the city of Kingston upon Hull, England. Unique in a large suspension bridge are the towers of reinforced concrete instead of steel.

International Bridge, a series of 8 arch and truss bridges crossing St. Mary's and the Soo Locks between Mich. and Ontario. Two-mile toll completed 1962.

Lacy V. Murrow Floating Bridge, Wash., 25 floating pontoons of 4,558 tons each. Bridge with approaches is 8,583 ft.

Lake Pontchartrain Twin Causeway, a twin-span crete trestle bridge and 24-mile link within metropolitan New Orleans that connects the north and south shore. First span opened 1956, second 1969.

Lavaca Bay Causeway, Tex., 2.2 miles long, consisting of one 260 ft. continuous plate girder unit and 194 precast, prestressed concrete spans of 60 ft. length. 1961.

Newport Bridge between Newport and Jamestown, R.I. Total length 11,248 ft., a main suspension span of 1,600 feet, 2 side spans each 688 feet long. It has U.S.A.'s first prefabricated wire strands.

New York City bridges, see Verrazano-Narrows Bridge and George Washington Bridge above.

Ogdensburg-Prescott Internat'l Bridge across the St. Lawrence River from Ogdensburg, N.Y., to Johnston, Ont., opened 1970, is 13,510 ft. long with approaches and 7,260 ft. between abutments.

Oland Island Bridge in Sweden was completed in 1972. It is 19,882 feet long, Europe's longest.

Oosterscheldebrug, opened Dec. 15, 1965, is a 3.125-mile causeway for automobiles over a sea arm in Zeeland, the Netherlands. It completes a direct connection between Flushing and Rotterdam.

Poplar St. Bridge over the Mississippi at St. Louis, a 5-span continuous orthotropic deck plate girder bridge, longest span 600 ft. Eight lanes, 2,165 ft. long.

Quebec Road, suspension, span 2,190 feet, 1969, Quebec, Canada.

Rio-Niterói, Guanabara Bay, Brazil, under construction, will be world's longest continuous box and plate girder bridge, 8 miles, 3,363 feet long, with a center span of 984 feet and a span on each side of 656 feet.

Robert Opie Norris Bridge, Rappahannock R. between Greys Pt. and White Stone, Va. 9,989 ft. long. Main spans are two 144 foot cantilever truss spans with a 360 foot truss span suspended between them.

Rockville Bridge, world's longest 4-track stone arch bridge, 3,810 ft., with 48 arches. Part of the Consolidated Rail Corp. system west of Harrisburg, Pa. It contains 440 million lbs. of stone, 100,000 cubic yds. of masonry and crosses the Susquehanna Riv. to Rockville, Pa.

Royal Gorge Bridge, 1,053 ft. above the Arkansas River in Colorado, is the highest bridge above water. Opened Dec. 8, 1929, it is 1,260 ft. long with a main span of 880 ft., width 18 ft.

San Mateo-Hayward Bridge across San Francisco Bay is first major orthotropic bridge in U.S. It is 6.7 miles long, 4.9 mile low-level concrete trestle and 1.8 miles high-level steel bridge.

Seven Mile Bridge is the longest of an expanse of bridges connecting the Florida Keys. It was built by the Florida East Coast Railway between 1904 and 1916, now a state highway.

Shenandoah River Bridges, one spans the south fork, 1,924 ft. long, the other the north fork, 1,090 ft. long. Warren County, Va.

Straits of Mackinac Bridge, completed in 1957, is the longest suspension bridge between anchorages and with approaches extends nearly 5 mi. between Mackinaw City and St. Ignace, Mich.

Sunshine Skyway, a 15-mile-long bridge-causeway with twin roadbeds that crosses Tampa Bay at St. Petersburg, Fla., a system of twin bridges 864 feet long and 4 smaller bridges with 6 causeways. The main span of the south bound bridge was torn away May 9, 1980, when support tower was hit by a cargo ship.

Tagus River Bridge near Lisbon, Portugal, longest suspension bridge outside the United States, has a 3,323-ft. main span. Opened Aug. 6, 1966, it was named Salazar Bridge for the former premier.

Thomas A. Edison Memorial Bridge (causeway) across Sandusky Bay between Martin Point and Danbury, Oh., is 2.67 miles long. The main bridge is 2,044 feet long.

Thousand Island Bridge, St. Lawrence River. American span 800 ft.; Canadian 750 ft.

Union St. Bridge in Woodstock, Vt., a timber lattice truss with a span of 122 feet built in 1969 using old time procedure of hand drilled holes and wooden pegs.

Vancouver Bridge, Canada's longest railway lift span connecting Vancouver and North Vancouver over Burrard Inlet. It is in 3 sections, the longest 493 ft. Spans are part of a project that includes a 2-mile tunnel under Vancouver Hts.

Woodrow Wilson Memorial Bridge across the Potomac River at Alexandria, Va., is over a mile long.

Zoo Bridge across the Rhine at Cologne, with steel box girders, has a main span of 850 ft.

The Interstate Highway 610 crossing of the Houston Ship Channel in Texas is 6,300 feet in length and consists of various lengths of prestressed concrete beam and slab approach spans and a 1,233 foot main unit of two 471'6" plate girder units and one 290 ft. simple span.

Underwater Vehicular Tunnels in North America

(3,000 feet in length or more)

Name	Location	Waterway	Lgth. Ft.
Bart Trans-Bay Tubes (Rapid Transit)	San Francisco, Cal.	S.F. Bay	3.6 miles
Brooklyn-Battery	New York, N.Y.	East River	9,117
Holland Tunnel	New York, N.Y.	Hudson River	8,557
Lincoln Tunnel	New York, N.Y.	Hudson River	8,216
Baltimore Harbor Tunnel	Baltimore, Md.	Patapsco River	7,650
Hampton Roads	Norfolk, Va.	Hampton Roads	7,479
Queens Midtown	New York, N.Y.	East River	6,414
Thimble Shoal Channel	Cape Henry, Va.	Chesapeake Bay	5,738
Sumner Tunnel	Boston, Mass.	Boston Harbor	5,650
Chesapeake Channel	Cape Charles, Va.	Chesapeake Bay	5,450
Louis-Hippolyte Lafontaine Tunnel	Montreal, Que.	St. Lawrence River	5,280
Detroit-Windsor	Detroit, Mich.	Detroit River	5,135
Callahan Tunnel	Boston, Mass.	Boston Harbor	5,046
Midtown Tunnel	Norfolk, Va.	Elizabeth River	4,194
Baytown Tunnel	Baytown, Tex.	Houston Ship Channel	4,111
Posey Tube	Oakland, Cal.	Oakland Estuary	3,500
Downtown Tunnel	Norfolk, Va.	Elizabeth River	3,350
Webster St.	Alameda, Cal.	Oakland Estuary	3,350
Bankhead Tunnel	Mobile, Ala.	Mobile River	3,109
I-10 Twin Tunnel	Mobile, Ala.	Mobile River	3,000

Land Vehicular Tunnels in U.S.

(over 1,200 feet in length.)

Name	Location	Lgth. Ft.	Name	Location	Lgth. Ft.
Eisenhower Memorial	Route 70, Col.	8,941	F.D. Roosevelt Dr.	81-89 Sts. N.Y.C.	2,400
Copperfield	Copperfield, Ut.	6,989	Dewey Sq.	Boston, Mass.	2,400
Allegheny (twin)	Penna. Turnpike	6,070	Battery Park	N.Y.C.	2,300
Liberty Tubes	Pittsburgh, Pa.	5,920	Battery St.	Seattle, Wash.	2,140
Zion Natl. Park	Rte. 9, Utah.	5,766	Big Oak Flat	Yosemite Natl. Park	2,083
East River Mt. (twin)	Interstate 77, W. Va.-Va.	5,661	Carlin	I-80, Nev.	1,993
Tuscarora (twin)	Penna. Turnpike	5,326	Prudential	Boston, Mass.	1,980
Kittatinny (twin)	Penna. Turnpike	4,727	Internatl. Underpass	Los Angeles, Cal.	1,910
Lehigh	Penna. Turnpike	4,379	Street-Car	Providence, R.I.	1,793
Blue Mountain (twin)	Penna. Turnpike	4,339	Broadway	San Francisco, Cal.	1,616
Wawona	Yosemite Natl. Park	4,233	9th Street Expy.	Washington, D.C.	1,610
Squirrel Hill	Pittsburgh, Pa.	4,225	F.D. Roosevelt Dr.	42-48 Sts. N.Y.C.	1,600
Big Walker Mt.	Route I-77, Va.	4,200	Lowry Hill	Minneapolis.	1,496
Fort Pitt	Pittsburgh, Pa.	3,560	Wheeling	Interstate 70, W. Va.	1,490
Mall Tunnel	Dist. of Columbia.	3,400	Mt. Baker Ridge (3)	Seattle, Wash.	1,466
Caldecott	Oakland, Cal.	3,371	Knowls Creek	Lane County, Ore.	1,430
Cody No. 1	U.S. 14, 16, 20, Wyo.	3,224	Mule Pass.	Near Bisbee, Ariz.	1,400
Kalihi.	Honolulu, Ha.	2,780	Arch Cape	Oregon Coast Hwy. 9	1,228
Memorial	W. Va. Tpke. (I-77).	2,669	Queen Creek	Superior, Ariz.	1,200
Cross-Town.	178 St. N.Y.C.	2,414	West Rock	New Haven, Conn.	1,200

World's Longest Railway Tunnels

Source: Railway Directory & Year Book 1980. Tunnels over 4.9 miles in length.

Tunnel	Date	Miles	Yds	Operating railway	Country
Dai-shimizu	1979	13	1,384	Japanese National	Japan
Simplon No. 1 and 2	1906, 1922	12	546	Swiss Fed. & Italian St.	Switz.-Italy
Kanmon	1975	11	1,093	Japanese National	Japan
Apennine	1934	11	881	Italian State.	Italy
Rokko	1972	10	158	Japanese National.	Japan
Gotthard	1882	9	552	Swiss Federal	Switzerland
Lotschberg	1913	9	130	Bern-Lotschberg-Simplon.	Switzerland
Hokuriku	1962	8	1,079	Japanese National.	Japan
Mont Cenis (Frejus)	1871	8	847	Italian State.	France-Italy
Shin-Shimizu	1961	8	675	Japanese National.	Japan
Aki	1975	8	161	Japanese National.	Japan
Cascade	1929	7	1,388	Burlington Northern	U.S.
Flathead	1970	7	1,319	Great Northern.	U.S.
Keijo	1970	7	88	Japanese National.	Japan
Lierasen	1973	6	1,135	Norwegian State.	Norway
Santa Lucia	1977	6	656	Italian State.	Italy
Arlberg	1884	6	643	Austrian Federal	Austria
Moffat	1928	6	366	Denver & Rio Grande Western.	U.S.
Shimizu	1931	6	44	Japanese National.	Japan
Kvineshei	1943	5	1,107	Norwegian State.	Norway
Bigo	1975	5	927	Japanese National.	Japan
Rimutaka	1955	5	816	New Zealand Gov.	New Zealand
Ricken	1910	5	603	Swiss Federal	Switzerland
Kaimai	1978	5	873	New Zealand Gov.	New Zealand
Grenchenberg	1915	5	575	Swiss Federal	Switzerland
Otira	1923	5	559	New Zealand Gov.	New Zealand
Tauern	1909	5	546	Austrian Federal	Austria
Haegebostad	1943	5	462	Norwegian State.	Norway
Ronco	1889	5	272	Italian State.	Italy
Hauenstein (Lower).	1916	5	90	Swiss Federal	Switzerland
Connaught.	1916	5	34	Canadian Pacific.	Canada
Karawanken	1906	4	1,677	Austrian Federal	Austria-Yugo.
Kobe	1972	4	1,671	Japanese National.	Japan
New Tanna	1964	4	1,658	Japanese National.	Japan

Major World Dams

Source: Bureau of Reclamation, U.S. Interior Department. *Replaces existing dam.
Volume in cubic yards. Capacity (gross) in acre feet. Year of completion. U.C. under construction.
Type: A—Arch. B—Buttress. E—Earthfill. G—Gravity. R—Rockfill. MA—Multi-arch.

Name of dam	Type	Year	River and basin	Country	Height Feet	Crest Length Feet	Volume (1,000 C.Y.)	Res. cap. (1,000 A.F.)
Afsluitdijk	E	1932	Zuider Zee	Netherlands	62	105,000	82,927	4,864
Akosombo-Main	R	1965	Volta	Ghana	463	2,100	10,440	120,000
Almendra	A	1970	Turmes-Douro	Spain	662	1,860	2,188	2,148
Alpe Gera	G	1965	Comor-Adda-Po	Italy	584	1,710	2,252	53
Bagdad Tailings	E	1973	Maroney Gulch	U.S.	121	2,601	37,304	40
Beas	G	1975	Beas-Indus	India	435	6,400	45,800	6,600
W.A.C. Bennett*	E	1967	Peace-Mackenzie	Canada	600	6,700	57,203	57,006
Bhakra	G	1963	Sutlend-Indus	India	742	1,700	5,400	8,000
Bratsk	GE	1964	Angara	USSR	410	16,864	18,283	137,220
Brouwershavense Gat	E	1972		Netherlands	118	20,341	35,316	466
Castaic	E	1973	Castaic Cr.	U.S.	340	5,200	44,000	432
Charvak	E	1970	Chirchik-Sir Darya	USSR	551	2,483	24,983	1,620
Chirkey	A	1975	Sulak-Caspian Sea	USSR	764	1,109	1,602	2,252
Chivor	R	1975	Bata	Colombia	778	919	14,126	661
Cochiti	E	1975	Rio Grande	U.S.	253	26,891	64,631	513
Copper Cities Tailing 2	E	1973	Tinhorn Wash.	U.S.	325	7,598	30,003	4
Cougar	R	1964	S.F. McKenzie	U.S.	519	1,600	13,000	219
Dartmouth	R	1978	Mitta-Mitta	Australia	591	2,200	18,312	3,202
Dneprodzerzhinsk	GE	1964	Dnieper	USSR	112	118,090	28,503	1,994
Don Pedro*	R	1971	Tuolume-San Joaquin	U.S.	585	1,900	16,760	2,030
Dworshak	G	1974	N. Fork Clearwater	U.S.	717	3,287	6,500	3,453
El Chocon	E	1974	Limay	Argentina	282	7,546	17,004	17,025
Emosson	A	1974	Barberine	Switz.	590	1,818	1,426	184
Esperanza Tailings	E	1973	Santa Cruz	U.S.	121	10,600	39,704	5
Fort Peck	E	1940	Missouri	U.S.	250	21,026	125,612	19,133
Fort Randall	E	1956	Missouri	U.S.	165	10,700	50,205	5,701
Gardiner*	E	1968	South Saskatchewan	Canada	223	16,700	85,743	8,000
Garrison	E	1956	Missouri	U.S.	203	11,300	66,506	24,321
Gepatsch	R	1965	Faggenbach-Inn	Austria	500	1,908	9,810	113
Glen Canyon	A	1964	Colorado	U.S.	710	1,560	4,901	27,000
Goscheneralp	E	1960	Goschener	Switz.	508	1,771	12,230	62
Grand Coulee	G	1942	Columbia	U.S.	550	4,173	10,585	9,724
Grande Dixence	G	1962	Dixence-Rhone	Switz.	935	2,280	7,792	325
Guri	GE	1968	Caroni-Orinoco	Venezuela	348	2,264	4,917	14,349
Haringvliet	E	1970	Haringvliet	Netherlands	79	18,044	26,160	527
High Aswan (Sadd-El-Aali)	ER	1970	Nile	Egypt	364	12,565	57,203	137,000
Hirakud	GE	1956	Mahandi	India	202	15,748	25,100	6,600
Hoover	AG	1936	Colorado	U.S.	726	1,244	4,400	29,755
Hungry Horse	AG	1953	S. Fork Flathead	U.S.	564	2,115	3,086	3,468
Ilha Solteira	EG	1973	Parana Rio de la Plata	Brazil	295	20,308	29,454	27,730
Irkutsk	GE	1956	Angara	USSR	144	8,989	16,219	37,290
Iroquois	G	1958	St. Lawrence	Canada	76	2,665	175	24,298
Ivankova	EG	1937	Volga-Caspian S.	USSR	98	31,398	20,207	908
Jari	E	1967	Jari	Pakistan	234	5,700	42,400	400
Daniel Johnson*	MA	1968	Manicougan-St. Lawrence	Canada	703	4,311	2,950	115,000
Kakhovka	EG	1955	Dnieper	USSR	121	5,380	46,617	14,755
Kanev	E	1974	Dnieper	USSR	82	52,950	49,520	2,125
Kapchagay	E	1970	Ili	USSR	164	1,542	5,078	22,813
Kariba	A	1959	Zambesi	Rhodesia-Zambia	420	2,025	1,350	130,000
Keban	ERG	1974	First (Euphrates)	Turkey	679	3,881	20,900	25,110
Kiev	E	1964	Dnieper	USSR	72	177,448	57,552	3,021
King Paul (Kremasta)	ER	1965	Acheloos	Greece	541	1,510	10,686	3,850
Kremenchug	EG	1961	Dnieper	USSR	108	39,844	41,192	10,945
Kurobegawa No. 4	A	1964	Kurobe	Japan	610	1,603	1,782	162
Lauwerszee	E	1969	Lauwerszee	Netherlands	75	42,650	46,532	40
Ludington	E	1973	Lake Michigan	U.S.	170	29,301	37,703	83
Luzzone	A	1963	Brenno di Luzzone	Switz.	682	1,738	1,739	71
Mangla	E	1967	Jhelum	Pakistan	380	11,000	85,872	5,150
Marimbondo	E	1975	Grande	Brazil	315	12,297	24,328	5,184
Mauvoisin	A	1957	Drance de Bagnes	Switz	777	1,706	2,655	148
Mica	E	1974	Columbia	Canada	794	2,000	42,000	20,025
Mingechaur	E	1953	Kura	USSR	262	5,085	20,400	12,970
Navajo	E	1963	San Juan	U.S.	407	3,648	26,841	1,709
New Bullards Bar	A	1970	North Yuba-Sacramento	U.S.	637	2,200	2,700	960
New Cornelia Tailings	E	1973	Ten Mile Wash, Ariz.	U.S.	98	35,600	274,026	20
New Melones	R	1975	Stanislaus-San Joaquin	U.S.	625	1,600	15,970	2,400
Oahe	E	1963	Missouri	U.S.	245	9,300	92,008	23,590
Okutadami	G	1961	Tadami	Japan	515	1,575	2,145	48
Oroville	E	1968	Feather-Sacramento	U.S.	770	6,920	78,008	3,530
Owen Falls	G	1954	Lake Victoria-Nile	Uganda	100	2,725		166,000
Place Moulin	AG	1965	Buthier-Dora Baltea	Italy	502	2,181	1,962	8
Reza Shah Kabir	A	1975	Karoun	Iran	656	1,247	1,570	2,350
Rybinsk	GE	1941	Volga-Caspian S.	USSR	98	2,060	3,329	20,590
Sakuma	G	1956	Tenryu	Japan	510	963	1,465	26
San Luis	E	1967	San Luis-San Joaquin	U.S.	382	18,600	77,666	2,030
Saratov	E	1967	Volga-Caspian S.	USSR	131	37,204	52,843	10,450
Shasta	AG	1945	Sacramento	U.S.	602	3,460	8,711	4,550
Swift	E	1958	Lewis-Columbia	U.S.	610	2,100	15,800	75
Tabka	E	1975	Euphrates	Syria	197	14,764	60,168	11,350
Talbingo	R	1971	Tamut	Australia	530	2,300	18,950	74
Tarbela	ER	1975	Indus	Pakistan	486	9,000	158,268	11,110
Trinity	E	1962	Trinity-Klamath	U.S.	537	2,600	29,252	2,440
Tsimlyansk	EG	1952	Don	USSR	128	43,411	44,323	17,710
Tuttle Creek	E	1962	Big Blue-Missouri	U.S.	154	7,500	22,937	41
Twin Buttes	E	1963	Concho-Colorado, Texas	U.S.	134	42,463	21,442	64
Twin Buttes Tailings	E	1973	Santa Cruz	U.S.	239	11,299	38,604	24
Vilyui	ER	1967	Vilyui	USSR	246	2,297	3,793	29,140
Volga-22d congress USSR	ERG	1958	Volga-Caspian S.	USSR	144	13,108	33,020	27,130
Volga-V. I. Lenin	EG	1955	Volga-Caspian S.	USSR	148	12,405	44,298	47,020
Yellowtail	A	1966	Bighorn-Missouri	U.S.	525	1,480	1,456	1,375
Zeya	G	1975	Zeya	USSR	369	2,343	3,139	55,460

Major U.S. Public and Private Dams and Reservoirs

Source: Corps of Engineers, U.S. Army
Heights over 350 feet.

Height—Difference in elevation in feet, between lowest point in foundation and top of dam, exclusive of parapet or other projections. **Length**—Overall length of barrier in feet, main dam and its integral features as located between natural abutments. **Volume**—Total volume in cubic yards of all material in main dam and its appurtenant works. **Year**—Date structure was originally completed for use. (UC) Under construction subject to revision. **River**—Mainstream. **Purpose**—I-Irrigation; C-Flood Control; H-Hydroelectric; N-Navigation; S-Water Supply; R-Recreation; D-Debris Control; O-Other. **Parentheses** after name indicate type of dam as follows: (RE)-Earth; (PG)-Gravity; (ER)-Rockfill; (CB)-Buttress; (VA)-Arch; (MV)-Multi-arch; (OT)-Other. †Replacing existing dam.

Name of dam	State	River	Ht.	Lgth.	Vol. (1,000)	Purpose	Year
Oroville (RE)	Cal.	Feather River	756	6800	78000	IR	1968
Hoover (VA)	Nev.	Colorado River	726	1242	4400	IHCO	1936
Dworshak (PG)	Ida.	North Fork of Clearwater	717	3287	6450	HCR	1973
Glen Canyon (VA)	Ariz.	Colorado River	710	1560	4901	HCSR	1966
New Bullards Bar (VA)	Cal.	North Yuba River	635	2200	2600	SD	1970
New Melones (ER)	Cal.	Stanislaus River	625	1560	16000	IH	1979
Swift Dam (RE)	Wash.	North Fork Lewis River	610	2100	15400	HR	1958
Mossyrock Dam (VA)	Wash.	Cowlitz River	606	1648	1270	HCR	1968
Shasta (PG)	Cal.	Sacramento River	602	3460	8711	ISHN	1945
Yankee Doodle Tailings (ER)	Mon.	Yankee Doodle and Silver Bow Cr.	570	13200	200000	O	1972
Don Pedro (RE)	Cal.	Tuolumne River	568	1800	16000	HI	1971
Hungry Horse (VA)	Mon.	South Fork of Flathead River	564	2115	3086	IHCN	1953
Grand Coulee (PG)	Wash.	Columbia River	550	4173	10585	IHCN	1942
Ross Dam (VA)	Wash.	Skagit River	540	1300	919	HR	1949
Trinity (RE)	Cal.	Trinity River	537	2600	29410	IHCR	1962
John's Branch No. 2 (OT)	W.Va.	John's Branch of Toney Fork	534	2250	8218	O	1963
Yellowtail (VA)	Mon.	Bighorn River	525	1360	146	ICHR	1966
Cougar (ER)	Ore.	South Fork McKenzie River	519	1600	13000	HCIR	1964
Flaming Gorge (VA)	Ut.	Green River	502	1285	987	HCSR	1964
Stirrat No. 15 Waste Embank. (OT)	W.Va.	Rockhouse Br. of Island Cr.	500	1800	11000	O	1977
Fontana Dam (PG)	N.C.	Little Tennessee River	480	2365	3576	H	1944
New Exchequer (ER)	Cal.	Merced River	479	1240	5169	HI	1926
Wyco No. 2 Refuse Embank. (OT)	W.Va.	Guyandot River	469	1500	6453	O	1978
Morrow Point (VA)	Col.	Gunnison River	468	741	365	HCRO	1968
Dry Fork Slurry Impound (OT)	W.Va.	Trib. Dry Fork of Tug Fork	465	2100	14406	O	1960
Mill Branch Coal Refuse Dam (OT)	W.Va.	Crane Fork of Clear Fork	465	1584	4000	O	1963
Carters Main Dam (ER,RE)	Ga.	Coosawattee River	464	1950	15000	OHR	1974
Detroit (PG)	Ore.	North Santiam River	463	1580	1500	HCRI	1953
Anderson Ranch (RE)	Ida.	South Fork Boise River	456	1350	9653	IHCR	1950
Union Valley (RE)	Cal.	Silver Creek	453	1800	10000	SH	1963
Round Butte Dam (RE,ER)	Ore.	Deschutes River	440	1450	9600	HR	1964
Pine Flat Lake (PG)	Cal.	Kings River	440	1840	2400	CIRH	1954
Jocassee (ER)	S.C.	Keowee River	435	1800	11600	H	1973
O'Shaughnessy (PG)	Cal.	Moccasin Creek	430	900	663	H	1923
Mud Mountain Dam (ER)	Wash.	White River	425	700	2300	C	1948
Libby Dam (PG)	Mon.	Kootenai River	422	2890	375	HC	1973
Pacoima (VA)	Cal.	Pacoima Creek	420	640	226	C	1929
Owyhee Dam (VA)	Ore.	Owyhee River	417	833	538	ICR	1932
Lower Hell Hole (ER)	Cal.	Rubicon River	410	1550	8315	SD	1966
Castaic (RE)	Cal.	Castaic Creek	410	5200	44000	IR	1973
Mammoth Pool (RE)	Cal.	San Joaquin River	406	820	5355	HS	1960
Navajo (RE)	N.M.	San Juan River	402	3648	26840	IR	1963
Little Blue Run Dam (RE)	Pa.	Little Blue Run of Ohio River	400	2100	13000	O	1977
No name (RE)	S.C.	Jocassee River	400	1000		H	1972
Pyramid (ER)	Cal.	Piru Creek	400	1080	6952	IR	1973
Rockhouse Branch Refuse Bank	W.Va.	Rockhouse Br. of Cow Ck.	400	1350	11200	O	1973
Brownlee Dam (ER)	Ida.	Snake River	395	1380	6000	H	1958
Summersville Dam (ER)	W.Va.	Gauley River	390	2280	13565	CRSO	1965
Blue Mesa (RE)	Col.	Gunnison River	390	785	3093	HCRO	1966
Diablo Dam (VA)	Wash.	Skagit River	386	1180	350	HR	1929
San Luis (RE)	Cal.	San Luis Creek	382	18600	77664	ISHR	1967
Green Peter (PG)	Ore.	Middle Santiam River	378	1517	1142	CHRI	1967
Merriman Dam (RE)	N.Y.	Roundout Creek	375	2400	5800	S	1945
Jenkins Refuse Dam (OT)	Ky.	Elkhorn Creek	363	1700	12229	D	1974
San Gabriel No. 1 (ER)	Cal.	San Gabriel River	360	1520	10600	C	1938
Spruce Lick Fork Refuse Disp. (OT)	W.Va.	Spruce Lick Fk. of West Pond	360	400	17736	O	1977
Steel Trap Br. Refuse Dam (OT)	Ky.	Steel Trap Br. of Phillips Fk.	358	650	4250	O	1979
Abiquiu Dam (RE)	N.M.	Rio Chama	354	1540	11793	CD	1963
Arrowrock	Ida.	Boise River	350	1150	636	IDCR	1915

World's Largest Dams

Source: Bureau of Reclamation, U.S. Interior Department

Based on total volume of structure. All dams listed are predominantly earthfill or rockfill and may contain concrete section.

Name of dam	Cubic yards	Completed	Name of dam	Cubic yards	Completed
New Cornelia Tailings, U.S.	274,026,000	1973	W.A.C. Bennett, Canada	57,203,000	1967
Tarbela, Pakistan	158,268,000	1975	High Aswan Sadd-El-Aili, Egypt	57,203,000	1970
Fort Peck, U.S.	125,612,000	1940	Dantiwada Left Earthenbank, India	53,680,000	1965
Oahe, U.S.	92,000,000	1963	Saratov, U.S.S.R.	52,843,000	1967
Mangla, Pakistan	85,872,000	1967	Mission Tailings, No. 2, U.S.	52,435,000	1973
Gardiner, Canada	85,596,000	1968	Fort Randall, U.S.	50,205,000	1956
Afsluitdijk, Netherlands	82,927,000	1932	Kanev, USSR	49,520,000	1974
Oroville, U.S.	78,008,000	1968	Kakhovka, USSR	46,617,000	1955
San Luis, U.S.	77,666,000	1967	Lauwerszee, Netherlands.	46,532,000	1969
Garrison, U.S.	66,506,000	1956	Beas, India	45,800,000	1975
Cochiti, U.S.	64,631,000	1975	Volga, V.I. Lenin, USSR	44,298,000	1955
Tabka, Syria	60,168,000	1975	Castaic, U.S.	44,000,000	1971
Kiev, USSR	57,552,000	1964	Jari, Pakistan	42,900,000	1967

Superlative U.S. Statistics

Source: National Geographic Society, Washington, D.C.

Area for 50 states	Total	3,618,467 sq. mi.
	Land 3,540,023 sq. mi.—Water 78,444 sq. mi.	
Largest state	Alaska	589,757 sq. mi.
Smallest state	Rhode Island	1,214 sq. mi.
Largest county	San Bernardino County, California	20,119 sq. mi.
Smallest county	New York, New York	23 sq. mi.
Northernmost city	Barrow, Alaska	71°17′N.
Northernmost point	Point Barrow, Alaska	71°23′N.
Southernmost city	Hilo, Island of Hawaii	19°43′N.
Southernmost town	Naalehu, Island of Hawaii	19°03′N.
Southernmost point	Ka Lae (South Cape), Island of Hawaii	18°56′N. (155°41′W.)
Easternmost city	Eastport, Maine	66°59′02″W.
Easternmost town	Lubec, Maine	66°58′49″W.
Easternmost point	West Quoddy Head, Maine	66°57′W.
Westernmost city	Lihue, Island of Kauai, Hawaii	159°22′W.
Westernmost town	Adak, Aleutians, Alaska	176°45′W.
Westernmost point	Cape Wrangell, Attu Island, Aleutians, Alaska	172°27′E.
Highest city	Leadville, Colorado	10,200 ft.
Lowest town	Calipatria, California	−184 ft.
Highest point on Atlantic coast	Cadillac Mountain, Mount Desert Is., Maine	1,530 ft.
Largest and oldest national park	Yellowstone National Park (1872), Wyoming, Montana, Idaho	3,468 sq. mi.
Largest national monument	Wrangell-St. Elias, Alaska	18,630 sq. mi.
Highest waterfall	Yosemite Falls—Total in three sections	2,425 ft.
	Upper Yosemite Fall	1,430 ft.
	Cascades in middle section	675 ft.
	Lower Yosemite Fall	320 ft.
Longest river	Mississippi-Missouri	3,710 mi.
Highest mountain	Mount McKinley, Alaska	20,320 ft.
Lowest point	Death Valley, California	−282 ft.
Deepest lake	Crater Lake, Oregon	1,932 ft.
Rainiest spot	Mt. Waialeale, Hawaii	Annual aver. rainfall 460 inches
Largest gorge	Grand Canyon, Colorado River, Arizona	277 miles long, 600 ft. to 18 miles wide, 1 mile deep
Deepest gorge	Hell's Canyon, Snake River, Idaho-Oregon	7,900 ft.
Strongest surface wind	Mount Washington, New Hampshire recorded 1934	231 mph
Biggest dam	New Cornelia Tailings, Ten Mile Wash, Arizona	274,026,000 cu. yds. material used
Tallest building	Sears Tower, Chicago, Illinois	1,454 ft.
Largest building	Boeing 747 Manufacturing Plant, Everett, Washington	205,600,000 cu. ft.; covers 47 acres.
Tallest structure	TV tower, Blanchard, North Dakota	2,063 ft.
Longest bridge span	Verrazano-Narrows, New York	4,260 ft.
Highest bridge	Royal Gorge, Colorado	1,053 ft. above water
Deepest well	Gas well, Washita County, Oklahoma	31,441 ft.

The 49 States, Including Alaska

Area for 49 states	Total	3,612,017 sq. mi.
	Land 3,533,598 sq. mi.—Water 78,419 sq. mi.	

The 48 Contiguous States

Area for 48 states	Total	3,022,260 sq. mi.
	Land 2,963,998 sq. mi.—Water 58,262 sq. mi.	
Largest state	Texas	267,338 sq. mi
Northernmost town	Angle Inlet, Minnesota	49°22′N.
Northernmost point	Northwest Angle, Minnesota	49°23′N.
Southernmost city	Key West, Florida	24°33′N.
Southernmost mainland city	Florida City, Florida	25°27′N.
Southernmost point	Key West, Florida	24°33′N.
Westernmost town	La Push, Washington	124°38′W.
Westernmost point	Cape Alava, Washington	124°44′W.
Highest mountain	Mount Whitney, California	14,494 ft.

Note to users: The distinction between cities and towns varies from state to state. In this table the U.S. Bureau of the Census usage was followed.

Geodetic Datum Point of North America

The geodetic datum point of the U.S. is the National Ocean Survey's triangulation station Meades Ranch in Osborne County, Kansas, at latitude 39° 13′26″. 686 N and longitude 98° 32′30″. 506 W. This geodetic datum point is a fundamental point from which all latitude and longitude computations originate for North America and Central America.

Statistical Information about the U.S.

In the *Statistical Abstract of the United States* the Bureau of the Census, U.S. Dept. of Commerce, annually publishes a summary of social, political, and economic information. A book of more than 1,000 pages, it presents in 34 sections comprehensive data on population, housing, health, education, employment, income, prices, business, banking, energy, science, defense, trade, government finance, foreign country comparison, and other subjects. Special features include an appendix on statistical methodology and reliability. The book is prepared under the direction of Glenn W. King, Chief, Statistical Compendia Staff, Bureau of the Census. Supplements to the *Statistical Abstract* are *Pocket Data Book USA, 1979; County and City Data Book, 1977; Congressional District Data Book, 93rd Congress with supplements for the 3 states redistricted for the 94th Congress; Historical Statistics of the United States, Colonial Times to 1970;* and *State and Metropolitan Area Data Book, 1979.* Information concerning these and other publications may be obtained from the Supt. of Documents, Government Printing Office, Wash., D.C. 20402, or from the U.S. Bureau of the Census, Data User Services Division, Wash., D.C. 20233.

Highest and Lowest Altitudes in the U.S. and Territories

Source: Geological Survey, U.S. Interior Department. (Minus sign means below sea level; elevations are in feet.)

State	Highest Point Name	County	Elev.	Lowest Point Name	County	Elev.
Alabama	Cheaha Mountain	Cleburne	2,407	Gulf of Mexico		Sea level
Alaska	Mount McKinley		20,320	Pacific Ocean		Sea level
Arizona	Humphreys Peak	Coconino	12,633	Colorado R.	Yuma	70
Arkansas	Magazine Mountain	Logan	2,753	Ouachita R.	Ashley Union	55
California	Mount Whitney	Inyo-Tulare	14,494	Death Valley	Inyo	−282
Colorado	Mount Elbert	Lake	14,433	Arkansas R.	Prowers	3,350
Connecticut	Mount Frissell	Litchfield	2,380	L.I. Sound		Sea level
Delaware	On Ebright Road	New Castle	442	Atlantic Ocean		Sea level
Dist. of Col.	Tenleytown	N. W. part	410	Potomac R.		1
Florida	Sec. 30, T 6N, R 20W	Walton	345	Atlantic Ocean		Sea level
Georgia	Brasstown Bald	Towns-Union	4,784	Atlantic Ocean		Sea level
Guam	Mount Lamlam	Agat District	1,329	Pacific Ocean		Sea level
Hawaii	Mauna Kea	Hawaii	13,796	Pacific Ocean		Sea level
Idaho	Borah Peak	Custer	12,662	Snake R.	Nez Perce	710
Illinois	Charles Mound	Jo Daviess	1,235	Mississippi R.	Alexander	279
Indiana	Franklin Township	Wayne	1,257	Ohio R.	Posey	320
Iowa	Sec. 29, T 100N, R 41W	Osceola	1,670	Mississippi R.	Lee	480
Kansas	Mount Sunflower	Wallace	4,039	Verdigris R.	Montgomery	680
Kentucky	Black Mountain	Harlan	4,145	Mississippi R.	Fulton	257
Louisiana	Driskill Mountain	Bienville	535	New Orleans	Orleans	−5
Maine	Mount Katahdin	Piscataquis	5,268	Atlantic Ocean		Sea level
Maryland	Backbone Mountain	Garrett	3,360	Atlantic Ocean		Sea level
Massachusetts	Mount Greylock	Berkshire	3,491	Atlantic Ocean		Sea level
Michigan	Mount Curwood	Baraga	1,980	Lake Erie		572
Minnesota	Eagle Mountain	Cook	2,301	Lake Superior		602
Mississippi	Woodall Mountain	Tishomingo	806	Gulf of Mexico		Sea level
Missouri	Taum Sauk Mt.	Iron	1,772	St. Francis R.	Dunklin	230
Montana	Granite Peak	Park	12,799	Kootenai R.	Lincoln	1,800
Nebraska	Johnson Township	Kimball	5,426	S.E. cor. State	Richardson	840
Nevada	Boundary Peak	Esmeralda	13,143	Colorado R.	Clark	470
New Hamp.	Mt. Washington	Coos	6,288	Atlantic Ocean		Sea level
New Jersey	High Point	Sussex	1,803	Atlantic Ocean		Sea level
New Mexico	Wheeler Peak	Taos	13,161	Red Bluff Res.	Eddy	2,817
New York	Mount Marcy	Essex	5,344	Atlantic Ocean		Sea level
North Carolina	Mount Mitchell	Yancey	6,684	Atlantic Ocean		Sea level
North Dakota	White Butte	Slope	3,506	Red R.	Pembina	750
Ohio	Campbell Hill	Logan	1,550	Ohio R.	Hamilton	433
Oklahoma	Black Mesa	Cimarron	4,973	Little R.	McCurtain	287
Oregon	Mount Hood	Clackamas-Hood R.	11,239	Pacific Ocean		Sea level
Pennsylvania	Mt. Davis	Somerset	3,213	Delaware R.	Delaware	Sea level
Puerto Rico	Cerro de Punta	Ponce	4,389	Atlantic Ocean		Sea level
Rhode Island	Jerimoth Hill	Providence	812	Atlantic Ocean		Sea level
Samoa	Lata Mountain	Tau Island	3,160	Pacific Ocean		Sea level
South Carolina	Sassafras Mountain	Pickens	3,560	Atlantic Ocean		Sea level
South Dakota	Harney Peak	Pennington	7,242	Big Stone Lake	Roberts	962
Tennessee	Clingmans Dome	Sevier	6,643	Mississippi R.	Shelby	182
Texas	Guadalupe Peak	Culberson	8,749	Gulf of Mexico		Sea level
Utah	Kings Peak	Duchesne	13,528	Beaverdam Cr.	Washington	2,000
Vermont	Mount Mansfield	Lamoille	4,393	Lake Champlain	Franklin	95
Virginia	Mount Rogers	Grayson-Smyth	5,729	Atlantic Ocean		Sea level
Virgin Islands	Crown Mountain	Is. St. Thomas	1,556	Atlantic Ocean		Sea level
Washington	Mount Rainier	Pierce	14,410	Pacific Ocean		Sea level
West Virginia	Spruce Knob	Pendleton	4,863	Potomac R.	Jefferson	240
Wisconsin	Timms Hill	Price	1,951	Lake Michigan		581
Wyoming	Gannett Peak	Fremont	13,804	B. Fourche R.	Crook	3,100

U.S. Coastline by States

Source: NOAA, U.S. Commerce Department
(statute miles)

State	Coastline[1]	Shoreline[2]	State	Coastline[1]	Shoreline[2]
Atlantic coast	**2,069**	**28,673**	Virginia	112	3,315
Connecticut	0	618	**Gulf coast**	**1,631**	**17,141**
Delaware	28	381	Alabama	53	607
Florida	580	3,331	Florida	770	5,095
Georgia	100	2,344	Louisiana	397	7,721
Maine	228	3,478	Mississippi	44	359
Maryland	31	3,190	Texas	367	3,359
Massachusetts	192	1,519	**Pacific coast**	**7,623**	**40,298**
New Hampshire	13	131	Alaska	5,580	31,383
New Jersey	130	1,792	California	840	3,427
New York	127	1,850	Hawaii	750	1,052
North Carolina	301	3,375	Oregon	296	1,410
Pennsylvania	0	89	Washington	157	3,026
Rhode Island	40	384	**Arctic coast, Alaska**	**1,060**	**2,521**
South Carolina	187	2,876	**United States**	**12,383**	**88,633**

(1) Figures are lengths of general outline of seacoast. Measurements were made with a unit measure of 30 minutes of latitude on charts as near the scale of 1:1,200,000 as possible. Coastline of sounds and bays is included to a point where they narrow to width of unit measure, and includes the distance across at such point. (2) Figures obtained in 1939-40 with a recording instrument on the largest-scale charts and maps then available. Shoreline of outer coast, offshore islands, sounds, bays, rivers, and creeks is included to the head of tidewater or to a point where tidal waters narrow to a width of 100 feet.

States: Settled, Capitals, Entry into Union, Area, Rank

The original 13 states—The 13 colonies that seceded from Great Britain and fought the War of Independence (American Revolution) became the 13 original states. They were: Delaware, Pennsylvania, New Jersey, Georgia, Connecticut, Massachusetts, Maryland, South Carolina, New Hampshire, Virginia, New York, North Carolina, and Rhode Island. The order for the original 13 states is the order in which they ratified the Constitution.

State	Set-tled*	Capital	Entered Union Date	Order	Extent in miles Long (approx. mean)	Wide	Area in square miles Land	Inland water	Total	Rank in area
Ala. . .	1702 . .	Montgomery . .	Dec.	14, 1819	22	330	190	50,708	901	51,609	29
Alas. .	1784 . .	Juneau	Jan.	3, 1959	49	(a)1,480	810	569,600	20,157	589,757	1
Ariz. .	1776 . .	Phoenix	Feb.	14, 1912	48	400	310	113,417	492	113,909	6
Ark. . .	1686 . .	Little Rock . . .	June	15, 1836	25	260	240	51,945	1,159	53,104	27
Cal. . .	1769 . .	Sacramento . .	Sept.	9, 1850	31	770	250	156,361	2,332	158,693	3
Col. . .	1858 . .	Denver	Aug.	1, 1876	38	380	280	103,766	481	104,247	8
Conn. .	1634 . .	Hartford. . . .	Jan.	9, 1788	5	110	70	4,862	147	5,009	48
Del. . .	1638 . .	Dover	Dec.	7, 1787	1	100	30	1,982	75	2,057	49
D.C. . .	. . . . .	Washington. . .				. . .	. . .	61	6	67	51
Fla. . .	1565 . .	Tallahassee . .	Mar.	3, 1845	27	500	160	54,090	4,470	58,560	22
Ga. . .	1733 . .	Atlanta	Jan.	2, 1788	4	300	230	58,073	803	58,876	21
Ha. . .	1820 . .	Honolulu	Aug.	21, 1959	50	. . .	. . .	6,425	25	6,450	47
Ida. . .	1842 . .	Boise	July	3, 1890	43	570	300	82,677	880	83,557	13
Ill. . . .	1720 . .	Springfield . .	Dec.	3, 1818	21	390	210	55,748	652	56,400	24
Ind. . .	1733 . .	Indianapolis. . .	Dec.	11, 1816	19	270	140	36,097	194	36,291	38
Ia. . . .	1788 . .	Des Moines . .	Dec.	28, 1846	29	310	200	55,941	349	56,290	25
Kan. . .	1727 . .	Topeka	Jan.	29, 1861	34	400	210	81,787	477	82,264	14
Ky. . .	1774 . .	Frankfort	June	1, 1792	15	380	140	39,650	745	40,395	37
La. . .	1699 . .	Baton Rouge . .	Apr.	30, 1812	18	380	130	44,930	3,593	48,523	31
Me. . .	1624 . .	Augusta. . . .	Mar.	15, 1820	23	320	190	30,920	2,295	33,215	39
Md. . .	1634 . .	Annapolis. . . .	Apr.	28, 1788	7	250	90	9,891	686	10,577	42
Mass. .	1620 . .	Boston	Feb.	6, 1788	6	190	50	7,826	431	8,257	45
Mich. .	1668 . .	Lansing	Jan.	26, 1837	26	490	240	56,817	1,399	58,216	23
Minn. .	1805 . .	St. Paul	May	11, 1858	32	400	250	79,289	4,779	84,068	12
Miss. .	1699 . .	Jackson.	Dec.	10, 1817	20	340	170	47,296	420	47,716	32
Mo. . .	1735 . .	Jefferson City . .	Aug.	10, 1821	24	300	240	68,995	691	69,686	19
Mon. .	1809 . .	Helena	Nov.	8, 1889	41	630	280	145,587	1,551	147,138	4
Neb. . .	1823 . .	Lincoln	Mar.	1, 1867	37	430	210	76,483	744	77,227	15
Nev. . .	1849 . .	Carson City . .	Oct.	31, 1864	36	490	320	109,889	651	110,540	7
N.H. . .	1623 . .	Concord	June	21, 1788	9	190	70	9,027	277	9,304	44
N.J. . .	1664 . .	Trenton	Dec.	18, 1787	3	150	70	7,521	315	7,836	46
N.M. . .	1610 . .	Santa Fe . . .	Jan.	6, 1912	47	370	343	121,412	254	121,666	5
N.Y. . .	1614 . .	Albany	July	26, 1788	11	330	283	47,831	1,745	49,576	30
N.C. . .	1660 . .	Raleigh	Nov.	21, 1789	12	500	150	48,798	3,788	52,586	28
N.D. . .	1812 . .	Bismarck	Nov.	2, 1889	39	340	211	69,273	1,392	70,665	17
Oh. . .	1788 . .	Columbus . . .	Mar.	1, 1803	17	220	220	40,975	247	41,222	35
Okla. .	1889 . .	Oklahoma City .	Nov.	16, 1907	46	400	220	68,782	1,137	69,919	18
Ore. . .	1811 . .	Salem.	Feb.	14, 1859	33	360	261	96,184	797	96,981	10
Pa. . .	1682 . .	Harrisburg . . .	Dec.	12, 1787	2	283	160	44,966	367	45,333	33
R.I. . .	1636 . .	Providence . . .	May	29, 1790	13	40	30	1,049	165	1,214	50
S.C. . .	1670 . .	Columbia	May	23, 1788	8	260	200	30,225	830	31,055	40
S.D. . .	1859 . .	Pierre	Nov.	2, 1889	40	380	210	75,955	1,092	77,047	16
Tenn. .	1769 . .	Nashville	June	1, 1796	16	440	120	41,328	916	42,244	34
Tex. . .	1692 . .	Austin.	Dec.	29, 1845	28	790	660	262,134	5,204	267,338	2
Ut. . . .	1847 . .	Salt Lake City . .	Jan.	4, 1896	45	350	270	82,096	2,820	84,916	11
Vt. . . .	1724 . .	Montpelier . . .	Mar.	4, 1791	14	160	80	9,267	342	9,609	43
Va. . . .	1607 . .	Richmond. . . .	June	25, 1788	10	430	200	39,780	1,037	40,817	36
Wash. .	1811 . .	Olympia	Nov.	11, 1889	42	360	240	66,570	1,622	68,192	20
W.Va. .	1727 . .	Charleston . . .	June	20, 1863	35	240	130	24,070	111	24,181	41
Wis. . .	1766 . .	Madison	May	29, 1848	30	310	260	54,464	1,690	56,154	26
Wy. . .	1834 . .	Cheyenne . . .	July	10, 1890	44	360	280	97,203	711	97,914	9

*First European permanent settlement. (a) Aleutian Islands and Alexander Archipelago are not considered in these lengths.

The Continental Divide
Source: Geological Survey, U.S. Interior Department

The Continental Divide: watershed, created by mountain ranges or table-lands of the Rocky Mountains, from which the drainage is easterly or westerly; the easterly flowing waters reaching the Atlantic Ocean chiefly through the Gulf of Mexico, and the westerly flowing waters reaching the Pacific Ocean through the Columbia River, or through the Colorado River, which flows into the Gulf of California.

The location and route of the Continental Divide across the United States may briefly be described as follows:

Beginning at point of crossing the United States-Mexican boundary, near long. 108°45'W., the Divide, in a northerly direction, crosses New Mexico along the western edge of the Rio Grande drainage basin, entering Colorado near long. 106°41'W.

Thence by a very irregular route northerly across Colorado along the western summits of the Rio Grande and of the Arkansas, the South Platte, and the North Platte River basins, and across Rocky Mountain National Park, entering Wyoming near long. 106°52'W.

Thence in a northwesterly direction, forming the western rims of the North Platte, Big Horn, and Yellowstone River basins, crossing the southwestern portion of Yellowstone National Park.

Thence in a westerly and then a northerly direction forming the common boundary of Idaho and Montana, to a point on said boundary near long. 114°00'W.

Thence northeasterly and northwesterly through Montana and the Glacier National Park, entering Canada near long. 114°04'W.

Chronological List of Territories

Source: National Archives and Records Service

Name of territory	Date of Organic Act	Organic Act effective	Admission as state	Yrs. terr.
Northwest Territory(a)	July 13, 1787	No fixed date	Mar. 1, 1803(b)	16
Territory southwest of River Ohio	May 26, 1790	No fixed date	June 1, 1796(c)	6
Mississippi	Apr. 7, 1798	When president acted	Dec. 10, 1817	19
Indiana	May 7, 1800	July 4, 1800	Dec. 11, 1816	16
Orleans	Mar. 26, 1804	Oct. 1, 1804	Apr. 30, 1812(d)	7
Michigan	Jan. 11, 1805	June 30, 1805	Jan. 26, 1837	31
Louisiana-Missouri(e)	Mar. 3, 1805	July 4, 1805	Aug. 10, 1821	16
Illinois	Feb. 3, 1809	Mar. 1, 1809	Dec. 3, 1818	9
Alabama	Mar. 3, 1817	When Miss. became a state	Dec. 14, 1819	2
Arkansas	Mar. 2, 1819	July 4, 1819	June 15, 1836	17
Florida	Mar. 30, 1822	No fixed date	Mar. 3, 1845	23
Wisconsin	Apr. 20, 1836	July 3, 1836	May 29, 1848	12
Iowa	June 12, 1838	July 3, 1838	Dec. 28, 1846	7
Oregon	Aug. 14, 1848	Date of act	Feb. 14, 1859	10
Minnesota	Mar. 3, 1849	Date of act	May 11, 1858	9
New Mexico	Sept. 9, 1850	On president's proclamation	Jan. 6, 1912	61
Utah	Sept. 9, 1850	Date of act	Jan. 4, 1896	44
Washington	Mar. 2, 1853	Date of act	Nov. 11, 1889	36
Nebraska	May 30, 1854	Date of act	Mar. 1, 1867	12
Kansas	May 30, 1854	Date of act	Jan. 29, 1861	6
Colorado	Feb. 28, 1861	Date of act	Aug. 1, 1876	15
Nevada	Mar. 2, 1861	Date of act	Oct. 31, 1864	3
Dakota	Mar. 2, 1861	Date of act	Nov. 2, 1889	28
Arizona	Feb. 24, 1863	Date of act	Feb. 14, 1912	49
Idaho	Mar. 3, 1863	Date of act	July 3, 1890	27
Montana	May 26, 1864	Date of act	Nov. 8, 1889	25
Wyoming	July 25, 1868	When officers were qualified	July 10, 1890	22
Alaska(f)	May 17, 1884	No fixed date	Jan. 3, 1959	75
Oklahoma	May 2, 1890	Date of act	Nov. 16, 1907	17
Hawaii	Apr. 30, 1900	June 14, 1900	Aug. 21, 1959	59

(a) Included Ohio, Indiana, Illinois, Michigan, Wisconsin, eastern Minnesota; (b) as the state of Ohio; (c) as the state of Tennessee; (d) as the state of Louisiana; (e) organic act for Missouri Territory of June 4, 1812, became effective Dec. 7, 1812; (f) Although the May 17, 1884 act actually constituted Alaska as a district, it was often referred to as a territory, and unofficially administered as such. The Territory of Alaska was legally and formally organized by an act of Aug. 24, 1912.

Geographic Centers, U.S. and Each State

Source: Geological Survey, U.S. Interior Department

United States, including Alaska and Hawaii — South Dakota; Butte County, 17 miles W of Castle Rock, 14 miles E of junction of borders of South Dakota, Montana, and Wyoming. Approx. lat. 44°58′N. long. 103°46′W.

Contiguous U. S. (48 states) — Near Lebanon, Smith Co., Kansas, lat. 39°50′N. long. 98°35′W.

North American continent — The geographic center is in Pierce County, North Dakota, 6 miles W of Balta, latitude 48°10′, longitude 100°10′W.

State—county, locality

Alabama—Chilton, 12 miles SW of Clanton.
Alaska—lat. 63°50′N. long. 152°W. Approx. 60 mi. NW of Mt. McKinley.
Arizona—Yavapai, 55 miles ESE of Prescott.
Arkansas—Pulaski, 12 miles NW of Little Rock.
California—Madera, 38 miles E of Madera.
Colorado—Park, 30 miles NW of Pikes Peak.
Connecticut—Hartford, at East Berlin.
Delaware—Kent, 11 miles S of Dover.
District of Columbia—Near 4th St. and New York Ave., NW.
Florida—Hernando, 12 miles NNW of Brooksville.
Georgia—Twiggs, 18 miles SE of Macon.
Hawaii—Hawaii, 20°15′N, 156°20′W, off Maui Island.
Idaho—Custer, at Custer, SW of Challis.
Illinois—Logan, 28 miles NE of Springfield.
Indiana—Boone, 14 miles NNW of Indianapolis.
Iowa—Story, 5 miles NE of Ames.
Kansas—Barton, 15 miles NE of Great Bend.
Kentucky—Marion, 3 miles NNW of Lebanon.
Louisiana—Avoyelles, 3 miles SE of Marksville.
Maine—Piscataquis, 18 miles north of Dover.

Maryland—Prince Georges, 4.5 miles NW of Davidsonville.
Massachusetts—Worcester, north part of city.
Michigan—Wexford, 5 miles NNW of Cadillac.
Minnesota—Crow Wing, 10 miles SW of Brainerd.
Mississippi—Leake, 9 miles WNW of Carthage.
Missouri—Miller, 20 miles SW of Jefferson City.
Montana—Fergus, 12 miles west of Lewistown.
Nebraska—Custer, 10 miles NW of Broken Bow.
Nevada—Lander, 26 miles SE of Austin.
New Hampshire—Belknap, 3 miles E of Ashland.
New Jersey—Mercer, 5 miles SE of Trenton.
New Mexico—Torrance, 12 miles SSW of Willard.
New York—Madison, 12 miles S of Oneida and 26 miles SW of Utica.
North Carolina—Chatham, 10 miles NW of Sanford.
North Dakota—Sheridan, 5 miles SW of McClusky.
Ohio—Delaware, 25 miles NNE of Columbus.
Oklahoma—Oklahoma, 8 miles N of Oklahoma City.
Oregon—Crook, 25 miles SE of Prineville.
Pennsylvania—Centre, 2.5 miles SW of Bellefonte.
Rhode Island—Kent, 1 mile SSW of Crompton.
South Carolina—Richland, 13 miles SE of Columbia.
South Dakota—Hughes, 8 miles NE of Pierre.
Tennessee—Rutherford, 5 mi. NE of Murfreesboro.
Texas—McCulloch, 15 miles NE of Brady.
Utah—Sanpete, 3 miles N of Manti.
Vermont—Washington, 3 miles E of Roxbury.
Virginia—Buckingham, 5 miles SW of Buckingham.
Washington—Chelan, 10 mi. WSW of Wenatchee.
West Virginia—Braxton, 4 miles E of Sutton.
Wisconsin—Wood, 9 miles SE of Marshfield.
Wyoming—Fremont, 58 miles ENE of Lander.

There is no generally accepted definition of geographic center, and no satisfactory method for determining it. The geographic center of an area may be defined as the center of gravity of the surface, or that point on which the surface of the area would balance if it were a plane of uniform thickness.

No marked or monumented point has been established by any government agency as the geographic center of either the 50 states, the contiguous United States, or the North American continent. A monument was erected in Lebanon, Kan., contiguous U.S. center, by a group of citizens.

International Boundary Lines of the U.S.

The length of the northern boundary of the contiguous U.S. — the U.S.-Canadian border, excluding Alaska — is 3,987 miles according to the U.S. Geological Survey, Dept. of the Interior. The length of the Alaskan-Canadian border is 1,538 miles. The length of the U.S.-Mexican border, from the Gulf of Mexico to the Pacific Ocean, is approximately 1,933 miles (1963 boundary agreement).

Origin of the Names of U.S. States

Source: State officials, the Smithsonian Institution, and the Topographic Division, U.S. Geological Survey.

Alabama—Indian for tribal town, later a tribe (Alabamas or Alibamons) of the Creek confederacy.

Alaska—Russian version of Aleutian (Eskimo) word, alakshak, for "peninsula," "great lands," or "land that is not an island."

Arizona—Spanish version of Pima Indian word for "little spring place," or Aztec arizuma, meaning "silver-bearing."

Arkansas—French variant of Kansas, a Sioux Indian name for "south wind people."

California—Bestowed by the Spanish conquistadors (possibly by Cortez). It was the name of an imaginary island, an earthly paradise, in "Las Serges de Esplandian," a Spanish romance written by Montalvo in 1510. Baja California (Lower California, in Mexico) was first visited by Spanish in 1533. The present U.S. state was called Alta (Upper) California.

Colorado—Spanish, red, first applied to Colorado River.

Connecticut—From Mohican and other Algonquin words meaning "long river place."

Delaware—Named for Lord De La Warr, early governor of Virginia; first applied to river, then to Indian tribe (Lenni-Lenape), and the state.

District of Columbia—For Columbus, 1791.

Florida—Named by Ponce de Leon on Pascua Florida, "Flowery Easter," on Easter Sunday, 1513.

Georgia—For King George II of England by James Oglethorpe, colonial administrator, 1732.

Hawaii—Possibly derived from native world for homeland, Hawaiki or Owhyhee.

Idaho—A coined name with an invented Indian meaning: "gem of the mountains;" originally suggested for the Pike's Peak mining territory (Colorado), then applied to the new mining territory of the Pacific Northwest. Another theory suggests Idaho may be a Kiowa Apache term for the Comanche.

Illinois—French for Illini or land of Illini, Algonquin word meaning men or warriors.

Indiana—Means "land of the Indians."

Iowa—Indian word variously translated as "one who puts to sleep" or "beautiful land."

Kansas—Sioux word for "south wind people."

Kentucky—Indian word variously translated as "dark and bloody ground," "meadow land" and "land of tomorrow."

Louisiana—Part of territory called Louisiana by Sieur de La Salle for French King Louis XIV.

Maine—From Maine, ancient French province. Also: descriptive, referring to the mainland in distinction to the many coastal islands.

Maryland—For Queen Henrietta Maria, wife of Charles I of England.

Massachusetts—From Indian tribe named after "large hill place" identified by Capt. John Smith as near Milton, Mass.

Michigan—From Chippewa words mici gama meaning "great water," after the lake of the same name.

Minnesota—From Dakota Sioux word meaning "cloudy water" or "sky-tinted water" of the Minnesota River.

Mississippi—Probably Chippewa; mici zibi, "great river" or "gathering-in of all the waters." Also: Algonquin word, "Messipi."

Missouri—Algonquin Indian tribe named after Missouri River, meaning "muddy water."

Montana—Latin or Spanish for "mountainous."

Nebraska—From Omaha or Otos Indian word meaning "broad water" or "flat river," describing the Platte River.

Nevada—Spanish, meaning snow-clad.

New Hampshire—Named 1629 by Capt. John Mason of Plymouth Council for his home county in England.

New Jersey—The Duke of York, 1664, gave a patent to John

Berkeley and Sir George Carteret to be called Nova Caesaria, or New Jersey, after England's Isle of Jersey.

New Mexico—Spaniards in Mexico applied term to land north and west of Rio Grande in the 16th century.

New York—For Duke of York and Albany who received patent to New Netherland from his brother Charles II and sent an expedition to capture it, 1664.

North Carolina—In 1619 Charles I gave a large patent to Sir Robert Heath to be called Province of Carolana, from Carolus, Latin name for Charles. A new patent was granted by Charles II to Earl of Clarendon and others. Divided into North and South Carolina, 1710.

North Dakota—Dakota is Sioux for friend or ally.

Ohio—Iroquois word for "fine or good river."

Oklahoma—Choctaw coined word meaning red man, proposed by Rev. Allen Wright, Choctaw-speaking Indian.

Oregon—Origin unknown. One theory holds that the name may have been derived from that of the Wisconsin River shown on a 1715 French map as "Ouaricon-sint."

Pennsylvania—William Penn, the Quaker, who was made full proprietor by King Charles II in 1681, suggested Sylvania, or woodland, for his tract. The king's government owed Penn's father, Admiral William Penn, £16,000, and the land being granted in part settlement, the king added the Penn to Sylvania, against the desires of the modest proprietor, in honor of the admiral.

Puerto Rico—Spanish for Rich Port.

Rhode Island—Exact origin is unknown. One theory notes that Giovanni de Verrazano recorded an island about the size of Rhodes in the Mediterranean in 1524, but others believe the state was named Roode Eylandt by Adriaen Block, Dutch explorer, because of its red clay.

South Carolina—See North Carolina.

South Dakota—See North Dakota.

Tennessee—Tanasi was the name of Cherokee villages on the Little Tennessee River. From 1784 to 1788 this was the State of Franklin, or Frankland.

Texas—Variant of word used by Caddo and other Indians meaning friends or allies, and applied to them by the Spanish in eastern Texas. Also written texias, tejas, teysas.

Utah—From a Navajo word meaning upper, or higher up, as applied to a Shoshone tribe called Ute. Spanish form is Yutta, English Uta or Utah. Proposed name Deseret, "land of honeybees," from Book of Mormon, was rejected by Congress.

Vermont—From French words vert, green, and mont, mountain. The Green Mountains were said to have been named by Samuel de Champlain. The Green Mountain Boys were Gen. Stark's men in the Revolution. When the state was formed, 1777, Dr. Thomas Young suggested combining vert and mont into Vermont.

Virginia—Named by Sir Walter Raleigh, who fitted out the expedition of 1584, in honor of Queen Elizabeth, the Virgin Queen of England.

Washington—Named after George Washington. When the bill creating the Territory of Columbia was introduced in the 32d Congress, the name was changed to Washington because of the existence of the District of Columbia.

West Virginia—So named when western counties of Virginia refused to secede from the United States, 1863.

Wisconsin—An Indian name, spelled Ouisconsin and Mesconsing by early chroniclers. Believed to mean "grassy place" in Chippewa. Congress made it Wisconsin.

Wyoming—The word was taken from Wyoming Valley, Pa., which was the site of an Indian massacre and became widely known by Campbell's poem, "Gertrude of Wyoming." In Algonquin it means "large prairie place."

Accession of Territory by the U.S.

Source: Statistical Abstract of the United States

Division	Year	Sq. mi.[1]	Division	Year	Sq. mi.[1]	Division	Year	Sq. mi.[1]
Total U.S.	1970	3,630,854	Oregon	1846	285,580	American Samoa	1900	76
50 states & D.C.		3,618,467	Mexican Cession	1848	529,017	Corn Islands[4]	1914	4
Territory in 1790[2]		888,685	Gadsden Purchase	1853	29,640	Virgin Islands, U.S.	1917	133
Louisiana Purchase	1803	827,192	Alaska	1867	589,757	Trust Territory of		
By treaty with Spain:			Hawaii	1898	6,450	the Pacific Is.	1947	8,489
Florida	1819	58,560	The Philippines[3]	1898	115,600	All other[5]		42
Other areas	1819	13,443	Puerto Rico	1899	3,435			
Texas	1845	390,143	Guam	1899	212			

(1) Gross area (land and water). (2) Includes drainage basin of Red River on the north, south of 49th parallel, sometimes considered a part of the Louisiana Purchase. (3) Area not included in total; became Republic of the Philippines July 4, 1946. (4) Leased from Nicaragua for 99 years but returned Apr. 25, 1971; area not included in total. (5) See index for Outlying Areas, U.S.

Public Lands of the U. S.

Source: Bureau of Land Management, U.S. Interior Department

Acquisition of the Public Domain 1781-1867

Acquisition	Area* (acres)	Land	Water	Total	Cost[1]
State Cessions (1781-1802)		233,415,680	3,409,920	236,825,600	*$6,200,000
Louisiana Purchase (1803)[3]		523,446,400	6,465,280	529,911,680	23,213,568
Red River Basin[4]		29,066,880	535,040	29,601,920	
Cession from Spain (1819)		43,342,720	2,801,920	46,144,640	6,674,057
Oregon Compromise (1846)		180,644,480	2,741,760	183,386,240	
Mexican Cession (1848)		334,479,360	4,201,600	338,680,960	16,295,149
Purchase from Texas (1850)		78,842,880	83,840	78,926,720	15,496,448
Gadsden Purchase (1853)		18,961,920	26,880	18,988,800	10,000,000
Alaska Purchase (1867)		362,516,480	12,787,200	375,303,680	7,200,000
Total		**1,804,716,800**	**33,053,440**	**1,837,770,240**	**$85,079,222**

*All areas except Alaska were computed in 1912, and have not been adjusted for the recomputation of the area of the United States which was made for the 1950 Decennial Census. (1) Cost data for all except "State Cessions" obtained from U.S. Geological Survey. (2) Paid by federal government for Georgia cession, 1802 (56,689,920 acres). (3) Excludes areas eliminated by Treaty of 1819 with Spain. (4) Basin of the Red River of the North, south of the 49th parallel.

Disposition of Public Lands 1781 to 1970

Disposition by methods not elsewhere classified[1]	Acres	Granted to states for:	Acres
Granted or sold to homesteaders	303,500,000	Support of common schools	77,600,000
Granted to railroad corporations	287,500,000	Reclamation of swampland	64,900,000
Granted to veterans as military bounties	94,300,000	Construction of railroads	37,100,000
Confirmed as private land claims[2]	61,100,000	Support of misc. institutions[6]	21,700,000
Sold under timber and stone law[3]	34,000,000	Purposes not elsewhere classified[7]	117,600,000
Granted or sold under timber culture law[4]	13,900,000	Canals and rivers	6,100,000
Sold under desert land law[5]	10,900,000	Construction of wagon roads	3,400,000
	10,700,000	**Total granted to states**	**328,300,000**

(1) Chiefly public, private, and preemption sales, but includes mineral entries, script locations, sales of townsites and townlots. (2) The Government has confirmed title to lands claimed under valid grants made by foreign governments prior to the acquisition of the public domain by the United States. (3) The law provided for the sale of lands valuable for timber or stone and unfit for cultivation. (4) The law provided for the granting of public lands to settlers on condition that they plant and cultivate trees on the lands granted. (5) The law provided for the sale of arid agricultural public lands to settlers who irrigate them and bring them under cultivation. (6) Universities, hospitals, asylums, etc. (7) For construction of various public improvements (individual items not specified in the granting act) reclamation of desert lands, construction of water reservoirs, etc.

Public Lands Administered by Federal Agencies

Agency (Acres, June 30, 1979)	Public domain	Acquired	Total
Bureau of Land Management	395,155,546	2,367,290	397,522,836
Forest Service	160,002,140	27,506,087	187,508,227
Fish and Wildlife Service	38,686,170	4,364,420	43,050,590
National Park Service	61,547,223	6,716,663	68,263,886
U.S. Army	6,616,134	4,041,741	10,657,875
U.S. Air Force	6,923,551	1,352,686	8,276,237
Corps of Engineers	658,984	7,575,499	8,234,483
U.S. Navy	1,976,128	1,182,494	3,158,622
Water and Power Resources Services	4,684,992	1,930,826	6,615,818
Energy Research and Development Admin.	627,182	701,727	1,328,909
Others	980,196	2,057,536	3,037,732
Total	**677,858,246**	**59,796,969**	**737,655,215**
		Grand Total	**1,144,300,000**

National Parks, Other Areas Administered by Nat'l Park Service

Figures given are date area was set aside by Congress or proclaimed by president, and gross area in acres Dec. 31, 1980.

National Parks

Acadia, Me. (1916) 38,971. Includes Mount Desert Island, half of Isle au Haut, Schoodic Point on mainland. Highest elevation on Eastern seaboard.

Arches, Ut. (1929) 73,379. Contains giant red sandstone arches and other products of erosion. Renamed national park in 1978.

Badlands, S.D. (1929) 243,302; eroded prairie, bison, bighorn and antelope. Renamed national park in 1978.

Big Bend, Tex. (1935) 708,118. Rio Grande, Chisos Mts.

Biscayne, Fla. (1968) 180,128. Nat'l monument redesignated acquatic nat'l park by 1980 act.

Bryce Canyon, Ut. (1923) 35,835. Spectacularly colorful and unusual display of erosion effects.

Canyonlands, Ut. (1964) 337,570. At junction of Colorado and Green rivers, extensive evidence of prehistoric Indians.

Capitol Reef, Ut. (1937) 241,904. A 70-mile uplift of sandstone cliffs dissected by high-walled gorges.

Carlsbad Caverns, N.M. (1923) 46,755. Largest known caverns; not yet fully explored.

Channel Islands, Cal. (1938) 249,354. Park absorbed national monument in 1980 park act.

Crater Lake, Ore. (1902) 160,290. Extraordinary blue lake in crater of extinct volcano encircled by lava walls 500 to 2,000 feet high.

Denali, Alas. (1917) 4,065,593. Name changed from Mt. McKinley NP Dec. 2, 1980. Contains highest mountain in U.S., wildlife.

Everglades, Fla. (1934) 1,398,800. Largest remaining subtropical wilderness in Continental U.S.

Gates of the Arctic, Alas. (1978) 7,052,000. Vast wilderness in north central region. Park status: Dec. 2, 1980.

Glacier, Mon. (1910) 1,013,595. Superb Rocky Mountain scenery, numerous glaciers and glacial lakes. Part of Waterton-Glacier International Peace Park established by U.S. and Canada in 1932.

Glacier Bay, Alas. (1925) 3,878,269. Nat'l monument popular for its glaciers became nat'l park Dec. 2, 1980.

Grand Canyon, Ariz. (1908) 1,218,375. Most spectacular part of Colorado River's greatest canyon.

Grand Teton, Wy. (1929) 310,516. Most impressive part of the Teton Mountains, winter feeding ground of largest American elk herd.

Great Smoky Mountains, N.C.-Tenn. (1926) 520,269. Largest eastern mountain range, magnificent forests.

Guadalupe Mountains, Tex. (1966) 76,293. Extensive Permian limestone fossil reef; tremendous earth fault.

Haleakala, Ha. (1960) 28,655. 10,023 foot dormant volcano on Maui.

Hawaii Volcanoes, Ha. (1916) 229,177. Contains Kilauea and Mauna Loa, active volcanoes.

Hot Springs, Ark. (1832) 5,826. Government supervised bath houses use waters of 45 of the 47 natural hot springs.

Isle Royale, Mich. (1931) 571,796. Largest island in Lake Superior, noted for its wilderness area and wildlife.

Katmai, Alas. (1918) 4,430,125. Nat'l monument famous for brown bear and salmon upgraded to park Dec. 2, 1980.

Kenai Fjords, Alas. (1978) 572,000. Abundant mountain goats, marine mammals, birdlife. Park status Dec. 2, 1980.

Kings Canyon, Cal. (1890) 460,136. Mountain wilderness, dominated by Kings River Canyons and High Sierra; contains giant sequoias.

Kobuk Valley, Alas. (1978) 1,764,000. Broad river is core of native culture. Park status Dec. 2, 1980.

Lake Clark, Alas. (1978) 2,439,000. Across Cook Inlet from Anchorage. A scenic wilderness rich in fish and wildlife. Park status Dec. 2, 1980.

Lassen Volcanic, Cal. (1907) 106,372. Contains Lassen Peak, recently active volcano, and other volcanic phenomena.

Mammoth Cave, Ky. (1926) 52,452. 144 miles of surveyed underground passages, beautiful natural formations, river 360 feet below surface.

Mesa Verde, Col. (1906) 52,085. Most notable and best preserved prehistoric cliff dwellings in the United States.

Mount Rainier, Wash. (1899) 235,404. Greatest single-peak glacial system in the lower 48 states.

North Cascades, Wash. (1968) 504,781. Spectacular mountainous region with many glaciers, lakes.

Olympic, Wash. (1909) 914,890. Mountain wilderness containing finest remnant of Pacific Northwest rain forest, active glaciers, Pacific shoreline, rare elk.

Petrified Forest, Ariz. (1906) 93,493. Extensive petrified wood and Indian artifacts. Contains part of Painted Desert.

Redwood, Cal. (1968) 109,391. Forty miles of Pacific coastline, groves of ancient redwoods and world's tallest trees.

Rocky Mountain, Col. (1915) 263,809. On the continental divide, includes 107 named peaks over 11,000 feet.

Sequoia, Cal. (1890) 402,488. Groves of giant sequoias, highest mountain in contiguous United States — Mount Whitney (14,494 feet). World's largest tree.

Shenandoah, Va. (1926) 194,826. Portion of the Blue Ridge Mountains; overlooks Shenandoah Valley; Skyline Drive.

Theodore Roosevelt, N.D. (1947) 70,416; contains part of T.R.'s ranch and scenic badlands. National park in 1978.

Virgin Islands, V.I. (1956) 14,695. Covers 75% of St. John Island, lush growth, lovely beaches, Indian relics, evidence of colonial Danes.

Voyageurs, Minn. (1971) 219,128. Abundant lakes, forests, wildlife, canoeing, boating.

Wind Cave, S.D. (1903) 28,292. Limestone Caverns in Black Hills. Extensive wildlife includes a herd of bison.

Wrangell-St. Elias, Alas. (1978) 8,147,000. Largest area in parks system, most peaks over 16,000 feet, abundant wildlife; day's drive east of Anchorage.

Yellowstone, Ida.-Mon., Wy., (1872) 2,219,823. Oldest national park. World's greatest geyser area has about 3,000 geysers and hot springs; spectacular falls and impressive canyons of the Yellowstone River; grizzly bear, moose, bison, other wildlife are major attractions.

Yosemite, Cal. (1890) 760,917. Yosemite Valley, the nation's highest waterfall, 3 groves of sequoias, and mountainous.

Zion, Ut. (1909) 146,551. Unusual shapes and landscapes have resulted from erosion and faulting; Zion Canyon, with sheer walls ranging up to 2,500 feet, is readily accessible.

National Historical Parks

Appomattox Court House, Va. (1930) 1,319. Where Lee surrendered to Grant.

Boston, Mass. (1974) 41. Includes Faneuil Hall, Old North Church, Bunker Hill, Paul Revere House.

Chaco Culture, N.M. (1907) 33,189. Enlarged and redesignated in 1980 from nat'l monument status.

Chesapeake and Ohio Canal, Md.-W.Va.-D.C. (1961) 20,781. 185 mile historic canal; D.C. to Cumberland, Md.

Colonial, Va. (1930) 9,462. Includes most of Jamestown Island, site of first successful English colony; Yorktown, site of Cornwallis' surrender to George Washington; and the Colonial Parkway.

Cumberland Gap, Ky.-Tenn.-Va. (1940) 20,351. Mountain pass of the Wilderness Road which carried the first great migration of pioneers into America's interior.

George Rogers Clark, Vincennes, Ind. (1966) 24. Commemorates American defeat of British in west during Revolution.

Harpers Ferry, Md., W. Va. (1944) 2,280. At the confluence of the Shenandoah and Potomac rivers, the site of John Brown's 1859 raid on the Army arsenal. Scene of several Civil War maneuvers.

Independence, Pa. (1948) 45. Contains several properties in Philadelphia associated with the Revolutionary War and the founding of the U.S.

Jean Laffite (and preserve), La. (1978) 20,000. Includes Chalmette, site of 1814 Battle of New Orleans; French Quarter.

Kalaupapa, Ha. (1980) 5,000. Molokai's former leper colony site and other historic areas.

Kaloko-Honokohau, Ha. (1978) 1,250. Culture center has 234 historic features and grave of first king, Kamehameha.

Klondike Gold Rush, Alas.-Wash. (1976) 13,270. Skagway, Alaskan Trails in 1898 Gold Rush. Museum in Seattle.

Lowell, Mass. (1978) 137. Seven mills, canal, 19th C. structures, park to show planned city of Industrial Revolution.

Lyndon B. Johnson, Tex. (1969) 236. Redesignated from nat'l historic site in 1980. President's birthplace, boyhood home, ranch.

Minute Man, Mass. (1959) 752. Where the colonial Minute Men battled the British, April 19, 1775. Also contains Nathaniel Hawthorne's home.

Morristown, N.J. (1933) 1,678. Sites of important military encampments during the Revolutionary War; Washington's headquarters 1777, 1779-80.

Nez Perce, Ida. (1965) 2,109. Illustrates the history and culture of the Nez Perce Indian country. 22 separate sites.

Pu'uhonua o Honaunau, Ha. (1955) 182. Until 1819, a sanctuary for Hawaiians vanquished in battle, and those guilty of crimes or breaking taboos.

San Antonio Missions, Tex. (1978) 2,500. Four of finest Spanish missions in U.S., 18th C. irrigation system.

San Juan Island, Wash. (1966) 1,752. Commemorates peaceful relations of the U.S., Canada and Great Britain since the 1872 boundary disputes.

Saratoga, N.Y. (1938) 2,602. Scene of a major battle which became a turning point in the War of Independence.

Sitka, Alas. (1910) 108. Scene of last major resistance of the Tlingit Indians to the Russians, 1804.

Valley Forge, Pa. (1976) 3,300. Continental Army campsite in 1777-78 winter.

War in the Pacific, Guam (1978) 1,920. Scenic park memorial for WWII combatants in Pacific.

Women's Rights, N.Y. (1980) 2.45. Seneca Falls site where Susan B. Anthony, Elizabeth Cady Stanton began rights movement in 1848.

National Battlefields

Antietam, Md. (1890) 3,246. Battle ended first Confederate invasion of North, Sept. 17, 1862.

Big Hole, Mon. (1910) 656. Site of major battle with Nez Perce Indians.

Cowpens, S.C. (1929) 841. Revolutionary War battlefield.

Fort Necessity, Pa. (1931) 903. First battle of French and Indian War.

Monocacy, Md. (1976) 1,220. Civil War battle in defense of Wash., D.C., July 9, 1864.

Moores Creek, N.C. (1926) 87. Pre-Revolutionary War battle.

Petersburg, Va. (1926) 1,536. Scene of 10-month Union campaign 1864-65.

Stones River, Tenn. (1927) 331. Civil War battle leading to Sherman's "March to the Sea."

Tupelo, Miss. (1929) 1. Crucial battle over Sherman's supply line.

Wilson's Creek, Mo. (1960) 1,750. Civil War battle for control of Missouri.

National Battlefield Parks

Kennesaw Mountain, Ga. (1917) 2,884. Two major battles of Atlanta campaign in Civil War.

Manassas, Va. (1940) 3,047 Two early Civil War battles.

Richmond, Va. (1936) 769. Site of battles defending Confederate capital.

National Battlefield Site

Brices Cross Roads, Miss. (1929) 1. Civil War battlefield.

National Military Parks

Chickamauga and Chattanooga, Ga.-Tenn. (1890) 8,104. Four Civil War battlefields.

Fort Donelson, Tenn. (1928) 536. Site of first major Union victory.

Fredericksburg and Spotsylvania County, Va. (1927) 5,909. Sites of several major Civil War battles and campaigns.

Gettysburg, Pa. (1895) 3,862. Site of decisive Confederate defeat in North. Gettysburg Address.

Guilford Courthouse, N.C. (1917) 220. Revolutionary War battle site.

Horseshoe Bend, Ala. (1956) 2,040. On Tallapoosa River, where Gen. Andrew Jackson broke the power of the Creek Indian Confederacy.

Kings Mountain, S.C. (1931) 3,945. Revolutionary War battle.

Pea Ridge, Ark. (1956) 4,300. Civil War battle.

Shiloh, Tenn. (1894) 3,838. Major Civil War battle; site includes some well-preserved Indian burial mounds.

Vicksburg, Miss. (1899) 1,741. Union victory gave North control of the Mississippi and split the Confederacy in two.

National Memorials

Arkansas Post, Ark. (1960) 389. First permanent French settlement in the lower Mississippi River valley.

Arlington House, the Robert E. Lee Memorial, Va. (1925) 28. Lee's home overlooking the Potomac.

Chamizal, El Paso, Tex. (1966) 55. Commemorates 1963 settlement of 99-year border dispute with Mexico.

Coronado, Ariz. (1952) 4,977. Commemorates first European exploration of the Southwest.

DeSoto, Fla. (1948) 27. Commemorates 16th-century Spanish explorations.

Federal Hall, N.Y. (1939) 0.45. First seat of U.S. government under the Constitution.

Fort Caroline, Fla. (1950) 139. On St. Johns River, overlooks site of second attempt by French Huguenots to colonize North America.

Fort Clatsop, Ore. (1958) 130. Lewis and Clark encampment 1805-06.

General Grant, N.Y. (1958) 0.76. Tombs of Pres. and wife.

Hamilton Grange, N.Y. (1962) 0.71. Home of Alexander Hamilton.

John F. Kennedy Center for the Performing Arts, D.C. (1972) 18.

Johnstown Flood, Pa. (1964) 163. Commemorates tragic flood of 1889.

Lincoln Boyhood, Ind. (1962) 198. Lincoln grew up here.

Lincoln Memorial, D.C. (1911) 164.

Lyndon B. Johnson Grove on the Potomac, D.C. (1973) 17.

Mount Rushmore, S.D. (1925) 1,278. World famous sculpture of 4 presidents.

Roger Williams, R.I. (1965) 5. Memorial to founder of Rhode Island.

Thaddeus Kosciuszko, Pa. (1972) 0.02. Memorial to Polish hero of American Revolution.

Theodore Roosevelt Island, D.C. (1947) 89.

Thomas Jefferson Memorial, D.C. (1943) 18.

USS Arizona, Ha. (1980) 14. Memorializes American losses at Pearl Harbor.

Washington Monument, D.C. (1848) 106.

Wright Brothers, N.C. (1927) 431. Site of first powered flight.

National Historic Sites

Abraham Lincoln Birthplace, Hodgenville, Ky. (1916) 117.

Adams, Quincy, Mass. (1946) 9. Home of Presidents John Adams, John Quincy Adams, and celebrated descendants.

Allegheny Portage Railroad, Pa. (1964) 1,135. Part of the Pennsylvania Canal system.

Andersonville, Andersonville, Ga. (1970) 476. Noted Civil War prison.

Andrew Johnson, Greeneville, Tenn. (1935) 17. Home of the President.

Bent's Old Fort, Col. (1960) 800. Old West fur-trading post.

Boston African American, Mass. (1980). Pre-Civil War free African community.

Carl Sandburg Home, N.C. (1968) 264. Poet's farm home.

Christiansted, St. Croix; V.I. (1952) 27. Commemorates Danish colony.

Clara Barton, Md. (1974) 9. Home of founder of American Red Cross.

Edgar Allan Poe, Pa. (1978) 0.52. Poet's home.

Edison, West Orange, N.J. (1955) 21. Home and laboratory.

Eisenhower, Gettysburg, Pa. (1967) 690. Home of 34th president. Not open to public.

Eleanor Roosevelt, Hyde Park, N.Y. (1977) 180.

Eugene O'Neill, Danville, Cal. (1980) 14. Playwright's home.

Ford's Theatre, Washington, D.C. (1866) 0.29. Includes theater, now restored, where Lincoln was assassinated, house where he died, and Lincoln Museum.

Fort Bowie, Ariz. (1964) 1,000. Focal point of operations against Geronimo and the Apaches.

Fort Davis, Tex. (1961) 460. Frontier outpost battled Comanches and Apaches.

Fort Laramie, Wy. (1938) 836. Military post on Oregon Trail.

Fort Larned, Kan. (1964) 718. Military post on Santa Fe Trail.

Fort Point, San Francisco, Cal. (1970) 29. Largest West Coast fortification.

Fort Raleigh, N.C. (1941) 157. First English settlement.

Fort Scott, Kan. (1978) 17. Commemorates events of Civil War period.

Fort Smith, Ark. (1961) 63. Active post from 1817 to 1890.

Fort Union Trading Post, Mon., N.D. (1966) 436. Principal fur-trading post on upper Missouri, 1828-1867.

Fort Vancouver, Wash. (1948) 209. Hdqts. for Hudson's Bay Company in 1825. Early military and political seat.

Frederick Law Olmsted, Mass. (1979) 1.75. Home of famous park planner (1822-1903).

Friendship Hill, Pa. (1978) 675. Home of Alfred Gallatin, Jefferson's Sec'y of Treasury.

Georgia O'Keeffe, Abiquiu, N.M. (1980) 3.5. Artist's home, studio.

Golden Spike, Utah (1957) 2,203. Commemorates completion of first transcontinental railroad in 1869.

Grant-Kohrs Ranch, Mon. (1972) 1,528. Ranch house and part of 19th century ranch.

Hampton, Md. (1948) 59. 18th-century Georgian mansion.

Herbert Hoover, West Branch, Ia. (1965) 187. Birthplace and boyhood home of 31st president.

Home of Franklin D. Roosevelt, Hyde Park, N.Y. (1944) 264. Birthplace, home and "Summer White House".

Hopewell Village, Pa. (1938) 848. 19th-century iron making village.

Hubbell Trading Post, Ariz. (1965) 160. Indian trading post.

James A. Garfield, Mentor, Oh. (1980) 7.6. President's home.

Jefferson National Expansion Memorial, St. Louis, Mo. (1935) 91. Commemorates westward expansion with park and memorial arch.

John Fitzgerald Kennedy, Brookline, Mass. (1967) .09. Birthplace and childhood home of the President.

John Muir, Martinez, Cal. (1964) 9. Home of early conservationist and writer.

Knife River Indian Villages, N.D. (1974) 1,293. Remnants of 5 Hidatsa villages.

Lincoln Home, Springfield, Ill. (1971) 12. Lincoln's residence when he was elected President, 1860.

Longfellow, Cambridge, Mass. (1972) 2. Longfellow's home, 1837-82, and Washington's hq. during Boston Siege, 1775-76. **No federal facilities.**

Maggie L. Walker, Va. (1978) 1.29. Richmond home of black leader and 1903 founder of bank.

Martin Luther King, Jr., Atlanta, Ga. (1980) 23.5. Birthplace, grave.

Martin Van Buren, N.Y. (1974) 40. Lindenwald, home of 8th president, near Kinderhook.

Ninety Six, S.C. (1976) 1,115. Colonial trading village.

Palo Alto Battlefield, Tex. (1978) 50. One of 2 Mexican War battles fought in U.S.

Puukohola Heiau, Ha. (1972) 77. Ruins of temple built by King Kamehameha.

Sagamore Hill, Oyster Bay, N.Y. (1962) 78. Home of President Theodore Roosevelt from 1885 until his death in 1919.

Saint-Gaudens, Cornish, N.H. (1964) 148. Home, studio and gardens of American sculptor Augustus Saint-Gaudens.

Salem Maritime, Mass. (1938) 9. Only port never seized from the patriots by the British. Major fishing and whaling port.

San Juan, P.R. (1949) 53. 16th-century Spanish fortifications.

Saugus Iron Works, Mass. (1968) 9. Reconstructed 17th-century colonial ironworks.

Sewall-Belmont House, D.C. (1974) 0.35. National Women's Party headquarters 1929-74.

Springfield Armory, Mass. (1974) 55. Small arms manufacturing center for nearly 200 years.

Theodore Roosevelt Birthplace, N.Y., N.Y. (1962) 0.11.

Theodore Roosevelt Inaugural, Buffalo, N.Y. (1966) 1. Wilcox House where he took oath of office, 1901.

Thomas Stone, Md. (1978) 328. Home of signer of Declaration, built in 1771.

Tuskegee Institute, Ala. (1974) 74. College founded by Booker T. Washington in 1881 for blacks, includes student-made brick buildings.

Vanderbilt Mansion, Hyde Park, N.Y. (1940) 212. Mansion of 19th-century financier.

Whitman Mission, Wash. (1936) 98. Site where Dr. and Mrs. Marcus Whitman ministered to the Indians until slain by them in 1847.

William Howard Taft, Cincinnati, Oh. (1969) 4. Birthplace and early home of the 27th president.

National Capital Parks

District of Columbia — Maryland — Virginia (1790) 6,469. Comprises 346 units.

White House

Washington, D.C. (1792) 18. Presidential residence since November 1800.

National Monuments

Name	State	Year	Acreage
Agate Fossil Beds	Neb.	1965	3,055
Alibates Flint Quarries	N.M.-Tex.	1965	1,333
Aniakchak	Alas.	1978	138,000
Aztec Ruins	N.M.	1923	27
Bandelier	N.M.	1916	36,971
Black Canyon of the Gunnison	Col.	1933	13,672
Booker T. Washington	Va.	1956	224
Buck Island Reef	V.I.	1961	880
Cabrillo	Cal.	1913	144
Canyon de Chelly	Ariz.	1931	83,840
Cape Krusenstern	Alas.	1978	560,000
Capulin Mountain	N.M.	1916	775
Casa Grande Ruins	Ariz.	1892	473
Castillo de San Marcos	Fla.	1924	20
Castle Clinton	N.Y.	1946	1
Cedar Breaks	Ut.	1933	6,155
Chiricahua	Ariz.	1924	11,088
Colorado	Col.	1911	20,457
Congaree Swamp	S.C.	1976	15,200
Craters of the Moon	Ida.	1924	53,545
Custer Battlefield	Mon.	1879	765

Name	State	Year	Acreage
Death Valley	Cal.-Nev.	1933	2,067,628
Devils Postpile	Cal.	1911	798
Devils Tower	Wy.	1906	1,347
Dinosaur	Col.-Ut.	1915	211,058
Effigy Mounds	Ia.	1949	1,475
El Morro	N.M.	1906	1,279
Florissant Fossil Beds**	Col.	1969	5,998
Fort Frederica	Ga.	1936	214
Fort Jefferson	Fla.	1935	47,125
Fort Matanzas	Fla.	1924	299
Fort McHenry National Monument and Historic Shrine	Md.	1925	43
Fort Pulaski	Ga.	1924	5,616
Fort Stanwix	N.Y.	1935	16
Fort Sumter	S.C.	1948	67
Fort Union	N.M.	1954	721
Fossil Butte	Wy.	1972	8,198
G. Washington Birthplace	Va.	1930	538
George Washington Carver	Mo.	1940	210
Gila Cliff Dwellings	N.M.	1907	533
Grand Portage	Minn.	1951	710
Great Sand Dunes	Col.	1932	38,952
Hohokam Pima*	Ariz.	1972	1,690
Homestead Nat'l. Monument of America	Neb.	1936	195
Hovenweep	Col.-Ut.	1923	785
Jewel Cave	S.D.	1908	1,275
John Day Fossil Beds	Ore.	1974	14,012
Joshua Tree	Cal.	1936	559,960
Lava Beds	Cal.	1925	46,821
Lehman Caves	Nev.	1922	640
Montezuma Castle	Ariz.	1906	858
Mound City Group	Oh.	1923	68
Muir Woods	Cal.	1908	554
Natural Bridges	Ut.	1908	7,779
Navajo	Ariz.	1909	360
Ocmulgee	Ga.	1934	683
Oregon Caves	Ore.	1909	474
Organ Pipe Cactus	Ariz.	1937	330,689
Pecos	N.M.	1965	365
Pinnacles	Cal.	1908	16,222
Pipe Spring	Ariz.	1923	40
Pipestone	Minn.	1937	282
Rainbow Bridge	Ut.	1910	160
Russell Cave	Ala.	1961	310
Saguaro	Ariz.	1933	83,576
Saint Croix Island**	Me.	1949	35
Salinas	N.M.	1900	1,113
Scotts Bluff	Neb.	1919	2,997
Statue of Liberty	N.J.-N.Y.	1924	58
Sunset Crater	Ariz.	1930	3,040
Timpanogos Cave	Ut.	1922	250
Tonto	Ariz.	1907	1,120
Tumacacori	Ariz.	1908	17
Tuzigoot	Ariz.	1939	849
Walnut Canyon	Ariz.	1915	2,249
White Sands	N.M.	1933	144,458
Wupatki	Ariz.	1924	35,253
Yucca House*	Col.	1919	10

National Preserves

Aniakchak	Alas.	1978	364,000
Bering Land Bridge	Alas.	1978	2,848,000
Big Cypress	Fla.	1974	570,000
Big Thicket	Tex.	1974	85,858
Denali	Alas.	1978	1,330,000
Gates of the Arctic	Alas.	1978	900,000
Glacier Bay	Alas.	1978	57,000
Katmai	Alas.	1978	308,000
Lake Clark	Alas.	1978	1,214,000
Noatak	Alas.	1978	5,800,000
Wrangell-St. Elias	Alas.	1978	4,171,000
Yukon-Charley Rivers	Alas.	1978	2,520,000

National Seashores

Assateague Island	Md.-Va.	1965	39,631
Canaveral	Fla.	1975	57,627
Cape Cod	Mass.	1961	44,596
Cape Hatteras	N.C.	1937	30,319
Cape Lookout**	N.C.	1966	29,081
Cumberland Island	Ga.	1972	36,978
Fire Island	N.Y.	1964	19,579
Gulf Islands	Fla.-Miss.	1971	139,775
Padre Island	Tex.	1962	133,919
Point Reyes	Cal.	1962	67,265

National Parkways

Blue Ridge	Va.-N.C.	1936	82,329
George Washington Memorial	Va.-Md.	1930	7,142
John D. Rockefeller Jr. Mem.	Wy.	1972	23,777
Natchez Trace	Ala.-Miss.-Tenn.	1938	48,375

National Lakeshores

Apostle Islands	Wis.	1970	42,000
Indiana Dunes	Ind.	1966	12,535
Pictured Rocks	Mich.	1966	70,757
Sleeping Bear Dunes	Mich.	1970	71,105

National Rivers

Big South Fork	Ky.-Tenn.	1976	122,960
Buffalo	Ark.	1972	94,146
New River Gorge	W.Va.	1978	62,024

National Scenic Rivers and Riverways

Delaware	N.Y.-N.J.-Pa.	1978	1,973
Lower Saint Croix	Minn.-Wis.	1972	9,389
Obed Wild	Tenn.	1976	5,250
Ozark	Mo.	1964	81,216
Rio Grande	Tex.	1978	9,600
Saint Croix	Minn.-Wis.	1968	62,701
Upper Delaware	N.Y.-N.J.	1978	75,000

Parks (no other classification)

Arlington House, The Robert E. Lee Memorial	Va.	1925	28
Catoctin Mountain	Md.	1954	5,769
Fort Benton	Mon.	1976	...
Fort Washington	Md.	1930	341
Frederick Douglass Home	D.C.	1962	8
Greenbelt	Md.	1933	1,176
Perry's Victory	Oh.	1936	26
Piscataway	Md.	1961	4,251
Prince William Forest	Va.	1948	18,572
Rock Creek	D.C.	1890	1,754
Wolf Trap Farm Park for the Performing Arts	Va.	1966	130

National Recreation Areas

Amistad	Tex.	1965	62,452
Bighorn Canyon	Mon.-Wy.	1964	120,280
Chattahoochee R.	Ga.	1978	8,515
Chickasaw	Okla.	1976	9,500
Coulee Dam	Wash.	1946	100,059
Curecanti	Col.	1965	42,114
Cuyahoga Valley	Oh.	1974	32,460
Delaware Water Gap	N.J.-Pa.	1965	71,000
Gateway	N.Y.-N.J.	1972	26,172
Glen Canyon	Ariz.-Ut.	1958	1,236,880
Golden Gate	Cal.	1972	38,677
Lake Chelan	Wash.	1968	61,890
Lake Mead	Ariz.-Nev.	1936	1,496,601
Lake Meredith	Tex.	1965	44,994
Ross Lake	Wash.	1968	117,574
Santa Monica Mts.	Cal.	1978	150,000
Whiskeytown	Cal.	1962	42,503

National Mall

National Mall	D.C.	1933	146
National Visitor Center	D.C.	1968	...

National Scenic Trail

Appalachian	Me. to Ga.	1968	52,034

*Not open to the public **No federal facilities

National Recreation Areas Administered by Forest Service

Name	State	Year	Acreage
Arapaho	Col.	1978	36,235
Flaming Gorge	Ut.-Wyo.	1968	201,114
Hell's Canyon	Ida.-Ore.	1975	647,500
Mount Rogers	Va.	1966	154,000
Oregon Dunes	Ore.	1972	32,348
Rattlesnake	Mon.	1980	60,000
Sawtooth	Ida.	1972	754,999
Shasta-Trinity	Cal.	1965	153,200
Spruce Knob-Seneca Rocks	W. Va.	1965	100,000

The Homestead Act; Sale of Public Land

On October 21, 1976 Congress repealed the Homestead Act of 1862 for all states except Alaska. At the present time the exception for Alaska has little meaning since homesteading along with all disposal laws had been suspended from operation by the Alaska Native Claims Settlement Act. The suspension which was first imposed by Secretarial order in 1969, will remain in effect until all claims for Federal land by Alaska's native Eskimos, Indians and Aleuts have been satisfied. The Homestead Act is scheduled to expire in Alaska in 1986.

The Homestead Act was repealed because there was no longer any land in the public domain suitable for cultivation. The law had been in effect for 114 years. During that time it had exerted a profound influence on the settlement of the west. Under the authority of the Homestead Act more than 1.6 million settlers claimed more than 270 million acres of public lands. The influx of settlers into the west made such states as Oklahoma, Kansas, Nebraska, and North and South Dakota a reality and brought substantial numbers of settlers into many other western states.

Federal Indian Reservations[1]

Source: Bureau of Indian Affairs, U.S. Interior Department (data as of 1979)

State	No. of reser.	Tribally-owned acreage[2]	Allotted acreage[2]	No. of tribes[3]	No. of persons[4]	Avg. (%) unemp. rate[5]	Major tribes and/or natives
Alaska	1[6]	86,741	299,400	6	72,664	51	Aleut, Eskimo, Athapascan[7], Haida, Tlingit, Tsimpshian
Arizona	20	19,554,391	252,972	13	145,258	21	Navajo, Apache, Papago, Hopi, Yavapai, Pima
California	78	500,036	73,014	—[8]	11,608	35	Huupa, Paiute, Yurok, Karok, Mission Bands
Colorado.	2	752,017	3,878	1	2,285	57	Ute
Florida	3	79,015	—	1	1,567	31	Seminole, Miccosukee[9]
Idaho	4	459,756	334,475		5,847	30	Shoshone, Bannock, Nez Perce
Iowa	1	4,164	0		649	34	Sac and Fox[10]
Kansas.	4	5,504	22,522		2,225	17	Potawatomi, Kickapoo, Iowa
Louisiana	2	374	—		554	7	Chitimacha, Coushatta
Maine	3	71,568	—		1,247	20	Passamaquoddy, Penobscot, Maliseet
Michigan	5	12,039	9,247		3,354	50	Chippewa, Potawatomi, Ottawa
Minnesota	14	712,125	50,750		16,476	50	Chippewa, Sioux
Mississippi	1	17,478	18		4,490	18	Choctaw
Montana	7	2,170,265	3,051,321		16,483	27	Blackfeet, Crow, Sioux, Assiniboine, Cheyenne
Nebraska	3	22,275	42,531		3,318	42	Omaha, Winnebago, Santee Sioux
Nevada	23	1,067,674	78,388		6,281	30	Paiute, Shoshone, Washoe
New Mexico . . .	24	6,462,826	677,845		104,153	20	Zuni, Apache, Navajo
New York	6	—	—		8,753	23	Seneca, Mohawk, Onondaga, Oneida[11]
North Carolina .	1	56,460	—		5,925	17	Cherokee
North Dakota . .	5	200,683	650,481		18,386	31	Sioux, Chippewa, Mandan, Arikara, Hidatsa
Oklahoma	—[12]	85,566	1,145,871		126,213	15	Cherokee, Creek, Choctaw, Chickasaw, Osage, Cheyenne, Arapahoe, Kiowa, Comanche
Oregon		615,692	11,293		3,873	20	Warm Springs, Wasco, Paiute, Umatilla, Siletz
S. Dakota	9	2,572,817	2,516,505		42,439	34	Sioux
Utah	6	2,249,068	34,525		8,755	20	Ute, Goshute, Southern Paiute
Washington . . .	26	1,996,018	497,219		34,940	35	Yakima, Lummi, Quinault
Wisconsin	15	328,437	80,886		16,544	34	Chippewa, Oneida, Winnebago
Wyoming	1	1,791,808	94,927		6,926	37	Shoshone, Arapahoe

(1) As of 1979 the federal government recognized and acknowledged that it had a special relationship with, and a trust responsibility for, 496 Federally recognized Indian entities in the U.S., including Alaska. The term "Indian entities" encompasses Indian tribes, bands, villages, groups, pueblos, Eskimos, and Aleuts, eligible for federal services and classified in the following 3 categories: (a) Officially approved Indian organizations pursuant to federal statutory authority (Indian Reorganization Act; Oklahoma Indian Welfare Act and Alaska Native Act.) (b) Officially approved Indian organizations outside of specified federal statutory authority. (c) Traditional Indian organizations recognized without formal federal approval of organizational structure.

(2) The acreages refer only to Indian lands which are either owned by the tribes or individual Indians, and held in trust by the U.S. government.

(3) "Tribe" among the North American Indians originally meant a body of persons bound together by blood ties who were socially, politically, and religiously organized, and who lived together, occupying a definite territory and having a common language or dialect. With the relegation of Indians to reservations, the word "tribe" developed a number of different meanings. Today, it can be a distinct group within an Indian village or community, the entire community, a large number of communities, several different groups or villages speaking different languages but sharing a common government, or a widely scattered number of villages with a common language but no common government.

(4) Number of Indians living on or adjacent to federally recognized reservations comprising the BIA service population.

(5) Unemployment rate of Indian work force consisting of all those 16 years old and over who are able and actively seeking work.

(6) Alaskan Indian Affairs are carried out under the Alaska Native Claims Settlement Act (Dec. 18, 1971). The Act provided for the establishment of regional and village corporations to conduct business for profit and non-profit purposes. There are 13 such regional corporations, each one with organized village corporations. The Metlakatla Reservation remains the only federally recognized reservation in Alaska in the sense of specific reservation boundaries, trust lands, etc.

(7) Aleuts and Eskimos are racially and linguistically related. Athapascans are related to the Navaho and Apache Indians.

(8) Some 62 distinct tribes are known to have lived in or wandered through what is now California at some time in the past. Many of these were village groups and are historically associated with bands which settled near Spanish missions where much of the traditional culture was destroyed. Many of these bands, however, still retain some of their Indian language and customs. Excluding the 30 mission bands, who are primarily of the Cahuilla, Diegueno, or Luiseno, there are some 22 tribes represented on the California reservations.

(9) "Seminole" means "runaways" and these Indians from various tribes were originally refugees from whites in the Carolinas and Georgia. Later joined by escaping slaves, the Seminole were united by their hostility to the United States. Formal peace with the Seminoles in Florida was not achieved until 1934. The Miccosukee are a branch of the Seminole; they retain their Indian religion and have not made formal peace with the United States.

(10) Once two tribes, the Sac and Fox formed a political alliance in 1734.

(11) These 4 tribes along with the Cayuga and Tuscarora made up the Iroquois League, which ruled large portions of New York, New England and Pennsylvania and ranged into the Midwest and South. The Onondaga, who traditionally provide the president of the league, maintain that they are a foreign nation within New York and the United States.

(12) Indian land status in Oklahoma is unique and there are no reservations in the sense that the term is used elsewhere in the U.S. Likewise, many of the Oklahoma tribes are unique in their high degree of assimilation to the white culture.

Declaration of Independence

The Declaration of Independence was adopted by the Continental Congress in Philadelphia, on July 4, 1776. John Hancock was president of the Congress and Charles Thomson was secretary. A copy of the Declaration, engrossed on parchment, was signed by members of Congress on and after Aug. 2, 1776. On Jan. 18, 1777, Congress ordered that "an authenticated copy, with the names of the members of Congress subscribing the same, be sent to each of the United States, and that they be desired to have the same put upon record." Authenticated copies were printed in broadside form in Baltimore, where the Continental Congress was then in session. The following text is that of the original printed by John Dunlap at Philadelphia for the Continental Congress.

IN CONGRESS, July 4, 1776.

A DECLARATION

By the REPRESENTATIVES of the

UNITED STATES OF AMERICA,

In GENERAL CONGRESS assembled

When in the Course of human Events, it becomes necessary for one People to dissolve the Political Bands which have connected them with another, and to assume among the Powers of the Earth, the separate and equal Station to which the Laws of Nature and of Nature's God entitle them, a decent Respect to the Opinions of Mankind requires that they should declare the causes which impel them to the Separation.

We hold these Truths to be self-evident, that all Men are created equal, that they are endowed by their Creator with certain unalienable Rights, that among these are Life, Liberty, and the Pursuit of Happiness—That to secure these Rights, Governments are instituted among Men, deriving their just Powers from the Consent of the Governed, that whenever any Form of Government becomes destructive of these Ends, it is the Right of the People to alter or to abolish it, and to institute new Government, laying its Foundation on such Principles, and organizing its Powers in such Form, as to them shall seem most likely to effect their Safety and Happiness. Prudence, indeed, will dictate that Governments long established should not be changed for light and transient Causes; and accordingly all Experience hath shewn, that Mankind are more disposed to suffer, while Evils are sufferable, than to right themselves by abolishing the Forms to which they are accustomed. But when a long Train of Abuses and Usurpations, pursuing invariably the same Object, evinces a Design to reduce them under absolute Despotism, it is their Right, it is their Duty, to throw off such Government, and to provide new Guards for their future Security. Such has been the patient Sufferance of these Colonies; and such is now the Necessity which constrains them to alter their former Systems of Government. The History of the present King of Great-Britain is a History of repeated Injuries and Usurpations, all having in direct Object the Establishment of an absolute Tyranny over these States. To prove this, let Facts be submitted to a candid World.

He has refused his Assent to Laws, the most wholesome and necessary for the public Good.

He has forbidden his Governors to pass Laws of immediate and pressing Importance, unless suspended in their Operation till his Assent should be obtained; and when so suspended, he has utterly neglected to attend to them.

He has refused to pass other Laws for the Accommodation of large Districts of People, unless those People would relinquish the Right of Representation in the Legislature, a Right inestimable to them, and formidable to Tyrants only.

He has called together Legislative Bodies at Places unusual, uncomfortable, and distant from the Depository of their Public Records, for the sole Purpose of fatiguing them into Compliance with his Measures.

He has dissolved Representative Houses repeatedly, for opposing with manly Firmness his Invasions on the Rights of the People.

He has refused for a long Time, after such Dissolutions, to cause others to be elected; whereby the Legislative Powers, incapable of Annihilation, have returned to the People at large for their exercise; the State remaining in the mean time exposed to all the Dangers of Invasion from without, and Convulsions within.

He has endeavoured to prevent the Population of these States; for that Purpose obstructing the Laws for Naturalization of Foreigners; refusing to pass others to encourage their Migrations hither, and raising the Conditions of new Appropriations of Lands.

He has obstructed the Administration of Justice, by refusing his Assent to Laws for establishing Judiciary Powers.

He has made Judges dependent on his Will alone, for the Tenure of their Offices, and the Amount and payment of their Salaries.

He has erected a Multitude of new Offices, and sent hither Swarms of Officers to harrass our People, and eat out their Substance.

He has kept among us, in Times of Peace, Standing Armies, without the consent of our Legislatures.

He has affected to render the Military independent of, and superior to the Civil Power.

He has combined with others to subject us to a Jurisdiction foreign to our Constitution, and unacknowledged by our Laws; giving his Assent to their Acts of pretended Legislation:

For quartering large Bodies of Armed Troops among us:

For protecting them, by a mock Trial, from Punishment for any Murders which they should commit on the Inhabitants of these States:

For cutting off our Trade with all Parts of the World:

For imposing Taxes on us without our Consent:

For depriving us, in many Cases, of the Benefits of Trial by Jury:

For transporting us beyond Seas to be tried for pretended Offences:

For abolishing the free System of English Laws in a neighbouring Province, establishing therein an arbitrary Government, and enlarging its Boundaries, so as to render it at once an Example and fit Instrument for introducing the same absolute Rule into these Colonies:

For taking away our Charters, abolishing our most valuable Laws, and altering fundamentally the Forms of our Governments:

For suspending our own Legislatures, and declaring themselves invested with Power to legislate for us in all Cases whatsoever.

He has abdicated Government here, by declaring us out of his Protection and waging War against us.

He has plundered our Seas, ravaged our Coasts, burnt our towns, and destroyed the Lives of our People.

He is, at this Time, transporting large Armies of foreign Mercenaries to compleat the works of Death, Desolation, and Tyranny, already begun with circumstances of Cruelty and Perfidy, scarcely paralleled in the most barbarous Ages, and totally unworthy the Head of a civilized Nation.

He has constrained our fellow Citizens taken Captive on the high Seas to bear Arms against their Country, to become the Executioners of their Friends and Brethren, or to fall themselves by their Hands.

He has excited domestic Insurrections amongst us, and has endeavoured to bring on the Inhabitants of our Frontiers, the merciless Indian Savages, whose known Rule of Warfare, is an undistinguished Destruction, of all Ages, Sexes and Conditions.

In every stage of these Oppressions we have Petitioned for Redress in the most humble Terms: Our repeated Petitions have been answered only by repeated Injury. A Prince, whose Character is thus marked by every act which may define a Tyrant, is unfit to be the Ruler of a free People.

Nor have we been wanting in Attentions to our British Brethren. We have warned them from Time to Time of Attempts by their Legislature to extend an unwarrantable Jurisdiction over us. We have reminded them of the Circumstances of our Emigration and Settlement here. We have appealed to their native Justice and Magnanimity, and we have conjured them by the Ties of our common Kindred to disavow these Usurpations, which, would inevitably interrupt our Connections and Correspondence. They too have been deaf to the Voice of Justice and of Consanguinity. We must, therefore, acquiesce in the Necessity, which denounces our Separation, and hold them, as we hold the rest of Mankind, Enemies in War, in Peace, Friends.

We, therefore, the Representatives of the UNITED STATES OF AMERICA, in General Congress, Assembled, appealing to the Supreme Judge of the World for the Rectitude of our Intentions, do, in the Name, and by Authority of the good People of these Colonies, solemnly Publish and Declare, That these United Colonies are, and of Right ought to be, Free and Independent States; that they are absolved from all Allegiance to the British Crown, and that all political Connection between them and the State of Great-Britain, is and ought to be totally dissolved; and that as Free and Independent States, they have full Power to levy War, conclude Peace, contract Alliances, establish Commerce, and to do all other Acts and Things which Independent States may of right do. And for the support of this declaration, with a firm Reliance on the Protection of divine Providence, we mutually pledge to each other our lives, our Fortunes, and our sacred Honor.

JOHN HANCOCK, President

Attest.
CHARLES THOMSON, Secretary.

Signers of the Declaration of Independence

Delegate and state	Vocation	Birthplace	Born	Died
Adams, John (Mass.)	Lawyer	Braintree (Quincy), Mass.	Oct. 30, 1735	July 4, 1826
Adams, Samuel (Mass.)	Political leader	Boston, Mass.	Sept. 27, 1722	Oct. 2, 1803
Bartlett, Josiah (N.H.)	Physician, judge	Amesbury, Mass.	Nov. 21, 1729	May 19, 1795
Braxton, Carter (Va.)	Farmer	Newington Plantation, Va.	Sept. 10, 1736	Oct. 10, 1797
Carroll, Chas. of Carrollton (Md.)	Lawyer	Annapolis, Md.	Sept. 19, 1737	Nov. 14, 1832
Chase, Samuel (Md.)	Judge	Princess Anne, Md.	Apr. 17, 1741	June 19, 1811
Clark, Abraham (N.J.)	Surveyor	Roselle, N.J.	Feb. 15, 1726	Sept. 15, 1794
Clymer, George (Pa.)	Merchant	Philadelphia, Pa.	Mar. 16, 1739	Jan. 23, 1813
Ellery, William (R.I.)	Lawyer	Newport, R.I.	Dec. 22, 1727	Feb. 15, 1820
Floyd, William (N.Y.)	Soldier	Brookhaven, N.Y.	Dec. 17, 1734	Aug. 4, 1821
Franklin, Benjamin (Pa.)	Printer, publisher	Boston, Mass.	Jan. 17, 1706	Apr. 17, 1790
Gerry, Elbridge (Mass.)	Merchant	Marblehead, Mass.	July 17, 1744	Nov. 23, 1814
Gwinnett, Button (Ga.)	Merchant	Down Hatherly, England.	c. 1735	May 19, 1777
Hall, Lyman (Ga.)	Physician	Wallingford, Conn.	Apr. 12, 1724	Oct. 19, 1790
Hancock, John (Mass.)	Merchant	Braintree (Quincy), Mass.	Jan. 12, 1737	Oct. 8, 1793
Harrison, Benjamin (Va.)	Farmer	Berkeley, Va.	Apr. 5, 1726	Apr. 24, 1791
Hart, John (N.J.)	Farmer	Stonington, Conn.	c. 1711	May 11, 1779
Hewes, Joseph (N.C.)	Merchant	Princeton, N.J.	Jan. 23, 1730	Nov. 10, 1779
Heyward, Thos. Jr. (S.C.)	Lawyer, farmer	St. Luke's Parish, S.C.	July 28, 1746	Mar. 6, 1809
Hooper, William (N.C.)	Lawyer	Boston, Mass.	June 28, 1742	Oct. 14, 1790
Hopkins, Stephen (R.I.)	Judge, educator	Providence, R.I.	Mar. 7, 1707	July 13, 1785
Hopkinson, Francis (N.J.)	Judge, author	Philadelphia, Pa.	Sept. 21, 1737	May 9, 1791
Huntington, Samuel (Conn.)	Judge	Windham County, Conn.	July 3, 1731	Jan. 5, 1796
Jefferson, Thomas (Va.)	Lawyer	Shadwell, Va.	Apr. 13, 1743	July 4, 1826
Lee, Francis Lightfoot (Va.)	Farmer	Westmoreland County, Va.	Oct. 14, 1734	Jan. 11, 1797
Lee, Richard Henry (Va.)	Farmer	Westmoreland County, Va.	Jan. 20, 1732	June 19, 1794
Lewis, Francis (N.Y.)	Merchant	Llandaff, Wales	Mar., 1713	Dec. 31, 1802
Livingston, Philip (N.Y.)	Merchant	Albany, N.Y.	Jan. 15, 1716	June 12, 1778
Lynch, Thomas Jr. (S.C.)	Farmer	Winyah, S.C.	Aug. 5, 1749	(at sea) 1779
McKean, Thomas (Del.)	Lawyer	New London, Pa.	Mar. 19, 1734	June 24, 1817
Middleton, Arthur (S.C.)	Farmer	Charleston, S.C.	June 26, 1742	Jan. 1, 1787
Morris, Lewis (N.Y.)	Farmer	Morrisania (Bronx County), N.Y.	Apr. 8, 1726	Jan. 22, 1798
Morris, Robert (Pa.)	Merchant	Liverpool, England	Jan. 20, 1734	May 9, 1806
Morton, John (Pa.)	Judge	Ridley, Pa.	1724	Apr., 1777
Nelson, Thos. Jr. (Va.)	Farmer	Yorktown, Va.	Dec. 26, 1738	Jan. 4, 1789
Paca, William (Md.)	Judge	Abingdon, Md.	Oct. 31, 1740	Oct. 23, 1799
Paine, Robert Treat (Mass.)	Judge	Boston, Mass.	Mar. 11, 1731	May 12, 1814
Penn, John (N.C.)	Lawyer	Near Port Royal, Va.	May 17, 1741	Sept. 14, 1788
Read, George (Del.)	Judge	Near North East, Md.	Sept. 18, 1733	Sept. 21, 1798
Rodney, Caesar (Del.)	Judge	Dover, Del.	Oct. 7, 1728	June 29, 1784
Ross, George (Pa.)	Judge	New Castle, Del.	May 10, 1730	July 14, 1779
Rush, Benjamin (Pa.)	Physician	Byberry, Pa. (Philadelphia)	Dec. 24, 1745	Apr. 19, 1813
Rutledge, Edward (S.C.)	Lawyer	Charleston, S.C.	Nov. 23, 1749	Jan. 23, 1800
Sherman, Roger (Conn.)	Lawyer	Newton, Mass.	Apr. 19, 1721	July 23, 1793
Smith, James (Pa.)	Lawyer	Dublin, Ireland	c. 1719	July 11, 1806
Stockton, Richard (N.J.)	Lawyer	Near Princeton, N.J.	Oct. 1, 1730	Feb. 28, 1781
Stone, Thomas (Md.)	Lawyer	Charles County, Md.	1743	Oct. 5, 1787
Taylor, George (Pa.)	Ironmaster	Ireland	1716	Feb. 23, 1781
Thornton, Matthew (N.H.)	Physician	Ireland	1714	June 24, 1803
Walton, George (Ga.)	Judge	Prince Edward County, Va.	1741	Feb. 2, 1804
Whipple, William (N.H.)	Merchant, judge	Kittery, Me.	Jan. 14, 1730	Nov. 28, 1785
Williams, William (Conn.)	Merchant	Lebanon, Conn.	Apr. 23, 1731	Aug. 2, 1811
Wilson, James (Pa.)	Judge	Carskerdo, Scotland	Sept. 14, 1742	Aug. 28, 1798
Witherspoon, John (N.J.)	Educator	Gifford, Scotland	Feb. 5, 1723	Nov. 15, 1794
Wolcott, Oliver (Conn.)	Judge	Windsor, Conn.	Dec. 1, 1726	Dec. 1, 1797
Wythe, George (Va.)	Lawyer	Elizabeth City Co. (Hampton), Va.	1726	June 8, 1806

Constitution of the United States
The Original 7 Articles

PREAMBLE

We, the people of the United States, in order to form a more perfect Union, establish justice, insure domestic tranquility, provide for the common defense, promote the general welfare, and secure the blessings of liberty to ourselves and our posterity do ordain and establish this Constitution for the United States of America.

ARTICLE I.

Section 1—Legislative powers; in whom vested:

All legislative powers herein granted shall be vested in a Congress of the United States, which shall consist of a Senate and House of Representatives.

Section 2—House of Representatives, how and by whom chosen. Qualifications of a Representative. Representatives and direct taxes, how apportioned. Enumeration. Vacancies to be filled. Power of choosing officers, and of impeachment.

1. The House of Representatives shall be composed of members chosen every second year by the people of the several States, and the electors in each State shall have the qualifications requisite for electors of the most numerous branch of the State Legislature.

2. No person shall be a Representative who shall not have attained to the age of twenty-five years, and been seven years a citizen of the United States, and who shall not, when elected, be an inhabitant of that State in which he shall be chosen.

3. *(Representatives and direct taxes shall be apportioned among the several States which may be included within this Union, according to their respective numbers, which shall be determined by adding to the whole number of free persons, including those bound to service for a term of years, and excluding Indians not taxed, three-fifths of all other persons.) (The previous sentence was superseded by Amendment XIV, section 2.)* The actual enumeration shall be made within three years after the first meeting of the Congress of the United States, and within every subsequent term of ten years, in such manner as they shall by law direct. The number of Representatives shall not exceed one for every thirty thousand, but each State shall have at least one Representative; and until such enumeration shall be made, the State of New Hampshire shall be entitled to choose three, Massachusetts eight, Rhode Island and Providence Plantations one, Connecticut five, New York six, New Jersey four, Pennsylvania eight, Delaware one, Maryland six, Virginia ten, North Carolina five, South Carolina five, and Georgia three.

4. When vacancies happen in the representation from any State, the Executive Authority thereof shall issue writs of election to fill such vacancies.

5. The House of Representatives shall choose their Speaker and other officers; and shall have the sole power of impeachment.

Section 3—Senators, how and by whom chosen. How classified. Qualifications of a Senator. President of the Senate, his right to vote. President pro tem., and other officers of the Senate, how chosen. Power to try impeachments. When President is tried, Chief Justice to preside. Sentence.

1. The Senate of the United States shall be composed of two Senators from each State, *(chosen by the Legislature thereof), (The preceding five words were superseded by Amendment XVII, section 1.)* for six years; and each Senator shall have one vote.

2. Immediately after they shall be assembled in consequence of the first election, they shall be divided as equally as may be into three classes. The seats of the Senators of the first class shall be vacated at the expiration of the second year, of the second class at the expiration of the fourth year, and of the third class at the expiration of the sixth year, so that one-third may be chosen every second year; *(and if vacancies happen by resignation, or otherwise, during the recess of the Legislature of any State, the Executive thereof may make temporary appointments until the next meeting of the Legislature, which shall then fill such vacancies.) (The words*

in parentheses were superseded by Amendment XVII, section 2.)

3. No person shall be a Senator who shall not have attained to the age of thirty years, and been nine years a citizen of the United States, and who shall not, when elected, be an inhabitant of that State for which he shall be chosen.

4. The Vice President of the United States shall be President of the Senate, but shall have no vote, unless they be equally divided.

5. The Senate shall choose their other officers, and also a President pro tempore, in the absence of the Vice President, or when he shall exercise the office of President of the United States.

6. The Senate shall have the sole power to try all impeachments. When sitting for that purpose, they shall be on oath or affirmation. When the President of the United States is tried, the Chief Justice shall preside: and no person shall be convicted without the concurrence of two-thirds of the members present.

7. Judgment in cases of impeachment shall not extend further than to removal from office, and disqualification to hold and enjoy any office of honor, trust or profit under the United States: but the party convicted shall nevertheless be liable and subject to indictment, trial, judgment and punishment, according to law.

Section 4—Times, etc., of holding elections, how prescribed. One session each year.

1. The times, places and manner of holding elections for Senators and Representatives, shall be prescribed in each State by the Legislature thereof; but the Congress may at any time by law make or alter such regulations, except as to the places of choosing Senators.

2. The Congress shall assemble at least once in every year, and such meeting shall *(be on the first Monday in December,) (The words in parentheses were superseded by Amendment XX, section 2).* unless they shall by law appoint a different day.

Section 5—Membership, quorum, adjournments, rules. Power to punish or expel. Journal. Time of adjournments, how limited, etc.

1. Each House shall be the judge of the elections, returns and qualifications of its own members, and a majority of each shall constitute a quorum to do business; but a smaller number may adjourn from day to day, and may be authorized to compel the attendance of absent members, in such manner, and under such penalties as each House may provide.

2. Each House may determine the rules of its proceedings, punish its members for disorderly behavior, and, with the concurrence of two-thirds, expel a member.

3. Each House shall keep a journal of its proceedings, and from time to time publish the same, excepting such parts as may in their judgment require secrecy; and the yeas and nays of the members of either House on any question shall, at the desire of one-fifth of those present, be entered on the journal.

4. Neither House, during the session of Congress, shall, without the consent of the other, adjourn for more than three days, nor to any other place than that in which the two Houses shall be sitting.

Section 6—Compensation, privileges, disqualifications in certain cases.

1. The Senators and Representatives shall receive a compensation for their services, to be ascertained by law, and paid out of the Treasury of the United States. They shall in all cases, except treason, felony and breach of the peace, be privileged from arrest during their attendance at the session of their respective Houses, and in going to and returning from the same; and for any speech or debate in either House, they shall not be questioned in any other place.

2. No Senator or Representative shall, during the time for which he was elected, be appointed to any civil office under the authority of the United States, which shall have been created, or the emoluments whereof shall have been increased during such time; and no person holding any office under the United States, shall be a member of either House

during his continuance in office.

Section 7—House to originate all revenue bills. Veto. Bill may be passed by two-thirds of each House, notwithstanding, etc. Bill, not returned in ten days, to become a law. Provisions as to orders, concurrent resolutions, etc.

1. All bills for raising revenue shall originate in the House of Representatives; but the Senate may propose or concur with amendments as on other bills.

2. Every bill which shall have passed the House of Representatives and the Senate, shall, before it becomes a law, be presented to the President of the United States; if he approves he shall sign it, but if not he shall return it, with his objections to that House in which it shall have originated, who shall enter the objections at large on their journal, and proceed to reconsider it. If after such reconsideration two-thirds of that House shall agree to pass the bill, it shall be sent, together with the objections, to the other House, by which it shall likewise be reconsidered, and if approved by two-thirds of that House, it shall become a law. But in all such cases the votes of both Houses shall be determined by yeas and nays, and the names of the persons voting for and against the bill shall be entered on the journal of each House respectively. If any bill shall not be returned by the President within ten days (Sundays excepted) after it shall have been presented to him, the same shall be a law, in like manner as if he had signed it, unless the Congress by their adjournment prevent its return, in which case it shall not be a law.

3. Every order, resolution, or vote to which the concurrence of the Senate and House of Representatives may be necessary (except on a question of adjournment) shall be presented to the President of the United States; and before the same shall take effect, shall be approved by him, or being disapproved by him, shall be repassed by two-thirds of the Senate and House of Representatives, according to the rules and limitations prescribed in the case of a bill.

Section 8—Powers of Congress.

The Congress shall have power

1. To lay and collect taxes, duties, imposts and excises, to pay the debts and provide for the common defense and general welfare of the United States; but all duties, imposts and excises shall be uniform throughout the United States;

2. To borrow money on the credit of the United States;

3. To regulate commerce with foreign nations, and among the several States, and with the Indian tribes;

4. To establish a uniform rule of naturalization, and uniform laws on the subject of bankruptcies throughout the United States;

5. To coin money, regulate the value thereof, and of foreign coin, and fix the standard of weights and measures;

6. To provide for the punishment of counterfeiting the securities and current coin of the United States;

7. To establish post-offices and post-roads;

8. To promote the progress of science and useful arts, by securing for limited times to authors and inventors the exclusive right to their respective writings and discoveries;

9. To constitute tribunals inferior to the Supreme Court;

10. To define and punish piracies and felonies committed on the high seas, and offenses against the law of nations;

11. To declare war, grant letters of marque and reprisal, and make rules concerning captures on land and water;

12. To raise and support armies, but no appropriation of money to that use shall be for a longer term than two years;

13. To provide and maintain a navy;

14. To make rules for the government and regulation of the land and naval forces;

15. To provide for calling forth the militia to execute the laws of the Union, suppress insurrections and repel invasions;

16. To provide for organizing, arming, and disciplining the militia, and for governing such part of them as may be employed in the service of the United States, reserving to the States respectively, the appointment of the officers, and the authority of training and militia according to the discipline prescribed by Congress;

17. To exercise exclusive legislation in all cases whatsoever, over such district (not exceeding ten miles square) as

may, by cession of particular States, and the acceptance of Congress, become the seat of the Government of the United States, and to exercise like authority over all places purchased by the consent of the Legislature of the State in which the same shall be, for the erection of forts, magazines, arsenals, dockyards, and other needful buildings;—And

18. To make all laws which shall be necessary and proper for carrying into execution the foregoing powers, and all other powers vested by this Constitution in the Government of the United States, or in any department or officer thereof.

Section 9—Provision as to migration or importation of certain persons. Habeas corpus, bills of attainder, etc. Taxes, how apportioned. No export duty. No commercial preference. Money, how drawn from Treasury, etc. No titular nobility. Officers not to receive presents, etc.

1. The migration or importation of such persons as any of the States now existing shall think proper to admit, shall not be prohibited by the Congress prior to the year one thousand eight hundred and eight, but a tax or duty may be imposed on such importation, not exceeding ten dollars for each person.

2. The privilege of the writ of habeas corpus shall not be suspended, unless when in cases of rebellion or invasion the public safety may require it.

3. No bill of attainder or ex post facto law shall be passed.

4. No capitation, or other direct, tax shall be laid, unless in proportion to the census or enumeration herein before directed to be taken. *(Modified by Amendment XVI.)*

5. No tax or duty shall be laid on articles exported from any State.

6. No preference shall be given by any regulation of commerce or revenue to the ports of one State over those of another: nor shall vessels bound to, or from, one State, be obliged to enter, clear, or pay duties in another.

7. No money shall be drawn from the Treasury, but in consequence of appropriations made by law; and a regular statement and account of the receipts and expenditures of all public money shall be published from time to time.

8. No title of nobility shall be granted by the United States: and no person holding any office of profit or trust under them, shall, without the consent of the Congress, accept of any present, emolument, office, or title, of any kind whatever, from any king, prince, or foreign state.

Section 10—States prohibited from the exercise of certain powers.

1. No State shall enter into any treaty, alliance, or confederation; grant letters of marque and reprisal; coin money; emit bills of credit; make anything but gold and silver coin a tender in payment of debts; pass any bill of attainder, ex post facto law, or law impairing the obligation of contracts, or grant any title of nobility.

2. No State shall, without the consent of the Congress, lay any imposts or duties on imports or exports, except what may be absolutely necessary for executing its inspection laws: and the net produce of all duties and imposts, laid by any State on imports or exports, shall be for the use of the Treasury of the United States; and all such laws shall be subject to the revision and control of the Congress.

3. No State shall, without the consent of Congress, lay any duty of tonnage, keep troops, or ships of war in time of peace, enter into any agreement or compact with another State, or with a foreign power, or engage in war, unless actually invaded, or in such imminent danger as will not admit of delay.

ARTICLE II.

Section 1—President: his term of office. Electors of President; number and how appointed. Electors to vote on same day. Qualification of President. On whom his duties devolve in case of his removal, death, etc. President's compensation. His oath of office.

1. The Executive power shall be vested in a President of the United States of America. He shall hold his office during the term of four years, and together with the Vice President, chosen for the same term, be elected as follows

2. Each State shall appoint, in such manner as the Legis-

lature thereof may direct, a number of electors, equal to the whole number of Senators and Representatives to which the State may be entitled in the Congress: but no Senator or Representative, or person holding an office of trust or profit under the United States, shall be appointed an elector.

(The electors shall meet in their respective States, and vote by ballot for two persons, of whom one at least shall not be an inhabitant of the same State with themselves. And they shall make a list of all the persons voted for, and of the number of votes for each; which list they shall sign and certify, and transmit sealed to the seat of the Government of the United States, directed to the President of the Senate. The President of the Senate shall, in the presence of the Senate and House of Representatives, open all the certificates, and the votes shall then be counted. The person having the greatest number of votes shall be the President, if such number be a majority of the whole number of electors appointed; and if there be more than one who have such majority, and have an equal number of votes, then the House of Representatives shall immediately choose by ballot one of them for President; and if no person have a majority, then from the five highest on the list the said House shall in like manner choose the President. But in choosing the President, the votes shall be taken by States, the representation from each State having one vote; a quorum for this purpose shall consist of a member or members from two-thirds of the States, and a majority of all the States shall be necessary to a choice. In every case, after the choice of the President, the person having the greatest number of votes of the electors shall be the Vice President. But if there should remain two or more who have equal votes, the Senate shall choose from them by ballot the Vice President.)

(This clause was superseded by Amendment XII.)

3. The Congress may determine the time of choosing the electors, and the day on which they shall give their votes; which day shall be the same throughout the United States.

4. No person except a natural born citizen, or a citizen of the United States, at the time of the adoption of this Constitution, shall be eligible to the office of President; neither shall any person be eligible to that office who shall not have attained to the age of thirty-five years, and been fourteen years a resident within the United States.

(For qualification of the Vice President, see Amendment XII.)

5. In case of the removal of the President from office, or of his death, resignation, or inability to discharge the powers and duties of the said office, the same shall devolve on the Vice President, and the Congress may by law provide for the case of removal, death, resignation or inability, both of the President and Vice President, declaring what officer shall then act as President, and such officer shall act accordingly, until the disability be removed, or a President shall be elected.

(This clause has been modified by Amendments XX and XXV.)

6. The President shall, at stated times, receive for his services, a compensation, which shall neither be increased nor diminished during the period for which he shall have been elected, and he shall not receive within that period any other emolument from the United States, or any of them.

7. Before he enter on the execution of his office, he shall take the following oath or affirmation:

"I do solemnly swear (or affirm) that I will faithfully execute the office of President of the United States, and will to the best of my ability, preserve, protect and defend the Constitution of the United States."

Section 2—President to be Commander-in-Chief. He may require opinions of cabinet officers, etc., may pardon. Treaty-making power. Nomination of certain officers. When President may fill vacancies.

1. The President shall be Commander-in-Chief of the Army and Navy of the United States, and of the militia of the several States, when called into the actual service of the United States; he may require the opinion, in writing, of the principal officer in each of the executive departments, upon any subject relating to the duties of their respective offices, and he shall have power to grant reprieves and pardons for offenses against the United States, except in cases of impeachment.

2. He shall have power, by and with the advice and consent of the Senate, to make treaties, provided two-thirds of the Senators present concur; and he shall nominate, and by and with the advice and consent of the Senate, shall appoint ambassadors, other public ministers and consuls, judges of the Supreme Court, and all other officers of the United States, whose appointments are not herein otherwise provided for, and which shall be established by law: but the Congress may by law vest the appointment of such inferior officers, as they think proper, in the President alone, in the courts of law, or in the heads of departments.

3. The President shall have power to fill up all vacancies that may happen during the recess of the Senate, by granting commissions, which shall expire at the end of their next session.

Section 3—President shall communicate to Congress. He may convene and adjourn Congress, in case of disagreement, etc. Shall receive ambassadors, execute laws, and commission officers.

He shall from time to time give to the Congress information of the state of the Union, and recommend to their consideration such measures as he shall judge necessary and expedient; he may, on extraordinary occasions, convene both Houses, or either of them, and in case of disagreement between them, with respect to the time of adjournment, he may adjourn them to such time as he shall think proper; he shall receive ambassadors and other public ministers; he shall take care that the laws be faithfully executed, and shall commission all the officers of the United States.

Section 4—All civil offices forfeited for certain crimes.

The President, Vice President, and all civil officers of the United States, shall be removed from office on impeachment for, and conviction of, treason, bribery, or other high crimes and misdemeanors.

ARTICLE III.

Section 1—Judicial powers, Tenure. Compensation.

The judicial power of the United States, shall be vested in one Supreme Court, and in such inferior courts as the Congress may from time to time ordain and establish. The judges, both of the Supreme and inferior courts, shall hold their offices during good behavior, and shall at stated times, receive for their services, a compensation, which shall not be diminished during their continuance in office.

Section 2—Judicial power; to what cases it extends. Original jurisdiction of Supreme Court; appellate jurisdiction. Trial by jury, etc. Trial, where.

1. The judicial power shall extend to all cases, in law and equity, arising under this Constitution, the laws of the United States, and treaties made, or which shall be made, under their authority; to all cases affecting ambassadors, other public ministers and consuls; to all cases of admiralty and maritime jurisdiction; to controversies to which the United States shall be a party; to controversies between two or more States; between a State and citizens of another State; between citizens of different States, between citizens of the same State claiming lands under grants of different States, and between a State, or the citizens thereof, and foreign states, citizens or subjects.

(This section is modified by Amendment XI.)

2. In all cases affecting ambassadors, other public ministers and consuls, and those in which a State shall be party, the Supreme Court shall have original jurisdiction. In all the other cases before mentioned, the Supreme Court shall have appellate jurisdiction, both as to law and fact, with such exceptions, and under such regulations as the Congress shall make.

3. The trial of all crimes, except in cases of impeachment, shall be by jury; and such trial shall be held in the State where the said crimes shall have been committed; but when not committed within any State, the trial shall be at such place or places as the Congress may by law have directed.

Section 3—Treason Defined, Proof of, Punishment of.

1. Treason against the United States, shall consist only in levying war against them, or in adhering to their enemies,

giving them aid and comfort. No person shall be convicted of treason unless on the testimony of two witnesses to the same overt act, or on confession in open court.

2. The Congress shall have power to declare the punishment of treason, but no attainder of treason shall work corruption of blood, or forfeiture except during the life of the person attainted.

ARTICLE IV.

Section 1—Each State to give credit to the public acts, etc., of every other State.

Full faith and credit shall be given in each State to the public acts, records, and judicial proceedings of every other State. And the Congress may by general laws prescribe the manner in which such acts, records and proceedings shall be proved, and the effect thereof.

Section 2—Privileges of citizens of each State. Fugitives from justice to be delivered up. Persons held to service having escaped, to be delivered up.

1. The citizens of each State shall be entitled to all privileges and immunities of citizens in the several States.

2. A person charged in any State with treason, felony, or other crime, who shall flee from justice, and be found in another State, shall on demand of the Executive authority of the State from which he fled, be delivered up, to be removed to the State having jurisdiction of the crime.

(3. No person held to service or labor in one State, under the laws thereof, escaping into another, shall in consequence of any law or regulation therein, be discharged from such service or labor, but shall be delivered up on claim of the party to whom such service or labor may be due.) (This clause was superseded by Amendment XIII.)

Section 3—Admission of new States. Power of Congress over territory and other property.

1. New States may be admitted by the Congress into this Union; but no new State shall be formed or erected within the jurisdiction of any other State; nor any State be formed by the junction of two or more States, or parts of States, without the consent of the Legislatures of the States concerned as well as of the Congress.

2. The Congress shall have power to dispose of and make all needful rules and regulations respecting the territory or other property belonging to the United States; and nothing in this Constitution shall be so construed as to prejudice any claims of the United States, or of any particular State.

Section 4—Republican form of government guaranteed. Each state to be protected.

The United States shall guarantee to every State in this Union a Republican form of government, and shall protect each of them against invasion; and on application of the Legislature, or of the Executive (when the Legislature cannot be convened) against domestic violence.

ARTICLE V.

Constitution: how amended; proviso.

The Congress, whenever two-thirds of both Houses shall deem it necessary, shall propose amendments to this Constitution, or, on the application of the Legislatures of two-thirds of the several States, shall call a convention for proposing amendments, which, in either case, shall be valid to all intents and purposes, as part of this Constitution, when ratified by the Legislatures of three-fourths of the several States, or by conventions in three-fourths thereof, as the one

or the other mode of ratification may be proposed by the Congress; provided that no amendment which may be made prior to the year one thousand eight hundred and eight shall in any manner affect the first and fourth clauses in the Ninth Section of the First Article; and that no State, without its consent, shall be deprived of its equal suffrage in the Senate.

ARTICLE VI.

Certain debts, etc., declared valid. Supremacy of Constitution, treaties, and laws of the United States. Oath to support Constitution, by whom taken. No religious test.

1. All debts contracted and engagements entered into, before the adoption of this Constitution, shall be as valid against the United States under this Constitution, as under the Confederation.

2. This Constitution, and the laws of the United States which shall be made in pursuance thereof; and all treaties made, or which shall be made, under the authority of the United States, shall be the supreme law of the land; and the judges in every State shall be bound thereby, any thing in the Constitution or laws of any State to the contrary notwithstanding.

3. The Senators and Representatives before mentioned, and the members of the several State Legislatures, and all executive and judicial officers, both of the United States and of the several States, shall be bound by oath or affirmation, to support this Constitution; but no religious test shall ever be required as a qualification to any office or public trust under the United States.

ARTICLE VII.

What ratification shall establish Constitution.

The ratification of the Conventions of nine States, shall be sufficient for the establishment of this Constitution between the States so ratifying the same.

Done in convention by the unanimous consent of the States present the Seventeenth day of September in the year of our Lord one thousand seven hundred and eighty seven, and of the independence of the United States of America the Twelfth. In witness whereof we have hereunto subscribed our names.

George Washington, President and deputy from Virginia.
New Hampshire—John Langdon, Nicholas Gilman.
Massachusetts—Nathaniel Gorham, Rufus King.
Connecticut—Wm. Saml. Johnson, Roger Sherman.
New York—Alexander Hamilton.
New Jersey—Wil: Livingston, David Brearley, Wm. Paterson, Jona: Dayton.
Pennsylvania—B. Franklin, Thomas Mifflin, Robt. Morris, Geo. Clymer, Thos. FitzSimons, Jared Ingersoll, James Wilson, Gouv. Morris.
Delaware—Geo: Read, Gunning Bedford Jun., John Dickinson, Richard Bassett, Jaco: Broom.
Maryland—James McHenry, Daniel of Saint Thomas' Jenifer, Danl. Carroll.
Virginia—John Blair, James Madison Jr.
North Carolina—Wm. Blount, Rich'd. Dobbs Spaight, Hugh Williamson.
South Carolina—J. Rutledge, Charles Cotesworth Pinckney, Charles Pinckney, Pierce Butler.
Georgia—William Few, Abr. Baldwin.
Attest: William Jackson, Secretary.

Ten Original Amendments: The Bill of Rights
In force Dec. 15, 1791

(The First Congress, at its first session in the City of New York, Sept. 25, 1789, submitted to the states 12 amendments to clarify certain individual and state rights not named in the Constitution. They are generally called the Bill of Rights.

(Influential in framing these amendments was the Declaration of Rights of Virginia, written by George Mason (1725-1792) in 1776. Mason, a Virginia delegate to the Constitutional Convention, did not sign the Constitution and opposed its ratification on the ground that it did not sufficiently oppose slavery or safeguard individual rights.

(In the preamble to the resolution offering the proposed amendments, Congress said: "The conventions of a number of the States having at the time of their adopting the Constitution, expressed a desire, in order to prevent misconstruction or abuse of its powers, that further declaratory and restrictive clauses should be added, and as extending the ground of public confidence in the government will best insure the beneficent ends of its institution, be it resolved," etc.

(Ten of these amendments now commonly known as one to 10 inclusive, but originally 3 to 12 inclusive, were ratified by the states as follows: New Jersey, Nov. 20, 1789; Maryland, Dec. 19, 1789; North Carolina, Dec. 22, 1789; South Carolina, Jan. 19, 1790; New Hampshire, Jan 25, 1790; Delaware, Jan 28, 1790; New York, Feb. 24, 1790; Pennsylvania, Mar. 10, 1790; Rhode

Island, June 7, 1790; Vermont, Nov 3, 1791; Virginia, Dec. 15, 1791; Massachusetts, Mar. 2, 1939; Georgia, Mar. 18, 1939; Connecticut, Apr. 19, 1939. These original 10 ratified amendments follow as Amendments I to X inclusive.

(Of the two original proposed amendments which were not ratified by the necessary number of states, the first related to apportionment of Representatives; the second, to compensation of members.)

AMENDMENT I.
Religious establishment prohibited. Freedom of speech, of the press, and right to petition.

Congress shall make no law respecting an establishment of religion, or prohibiting the free exercise thereof; or abridging the freedom of speech, or of the press; or the right of the people peaceably to assemble, and to petition the Government for a redress of grievances.

AMENDMENT II.
Right to keep and bear arms.

A well-regulated militia, being necessary to the security of a free State, the right of the people to keep and bear arms, shall not be infringed.

AMENDMENT III.
Conditions for quarters for soldiers.

No soldier shall, in time of peace be quartered in any house, without the consent of the owner, nor in time of war, but in a manner to be prescribed by law.

AMENDMENT IV.
Right of search and seizure regulated.

The right of the people to be secure in their persons, houses, papers, and effects, against unreasonable searches and seizures, shall not be violated, and no warrants shall issue, but upon probable cause, supported by oath or affirmation, and particularly describing the place to be searched, and the persons or things to be seized.

AMENDMENT V.
Provisions concerning prosecution. Trial and punishment—private property not to be taken for public use without compensation.

No person shall be held to answer for a capital, or otherwise infamous crime, unless on a presentment or indictment of a Grand Jury, except in cases arising in the land or naval forces, or in the militia, when in actual service in time of war or public danger; nor shall any person be subject for the same offense to be twice put in jeopardy of life or limb; nor

shall be compelled in any criminal case to be a witness against himself, nor be deprived of life, liberty, or property, without due process of law; nor shall private property be taken for public use without just compensation.

AMENDMENT VI.
Right to speedy trial, witnesses, etc.

In all criminal prosecutions, the accused shall enjoy the right to a speedy and public trial, by an impartial jury of the State and district wherein the crime shall have been committed, which district shall have been previously ascertained by law, and to be informed of the nature and cause of the accusation; to be confronted with the witnesses against him; to have compulsory process for obtaining witnesses in his favor, and to have the assistance of counsel for his defense.

AMENDMENT VII.
Right of trial by jury.

In suits at common law, where the value in controversy shall exceed twenty dollars, the right of trial by jury shall be preserved, and no fact tried by a jury shall be otherwise reexamined in any court of the United States, than according to the rules of the common law.

AMENDMENT VIII.
Excessive bail or fines and cruel punishment prohibited.

Excessive bail shall not be required, nor excessive fines imposed, nor cruel and unusual punishments inflicted.

AMENDMENT IX.
Rule of construction of Constitution.

The enumeration in the Constitution, of certain rights, shall not be construed to deny or disparage others retained by the people.

AMENDMENT X.
Rights of States under Constitution.

The powers not delegated to the United States by the Constitution, nor prohibited by it to the States, are reserved to the States respectively, or to the people.

Amendments Since the Bill of Rights

AMENDMENT XI.
Judicial powers construed.

The judicial power of the United States shall not be construed to extend to any suit in law or equity, commenced or prosecuted against one of the United States by citizens of another State, or by citizens or subjects of any foreign state.

(This amendment was proposed to the Legislatures of the several States by the Third Congress on March 4, 1794, and was declared to have been ratified in a message from the President to Congress, dated Jan. 8, 1798.

(It was on Jan 5, 1798, that Secretary of State Pickering received from 12 of the States authenticated ratifications, and informed President John Adams of that fact.

(As a result of later research in the Department of State, it is now established that Amendment XI became part of the Constitution on Feb. 7, 1795, for on that date it had been ratified by 12 States as follows:

(1. New York, Mar. 27, 1794. 2. Rhode Island, Mar. 31, 1794. 3. Connecticut, May 8, 1794. 4. New Hampshire, June 16, 1794. 5. Massachusetts, June 26, 1794. 6. Vermont, between Oct 9, 1794, and Nov. 9, 1794. 7. Virginia, Nov. 18, 1794. 8. Georgia, Nov. 29, 1794. 9. Kentucky, Dec. 7, 1794. 10. Maryland, Dec. 26, 1794. 11. Delaware, Jan 23, 1795. 12. North Carolina, Feb. 7, 1795.

(On June 1, 1796, more than a year after Amendment XI had become a part of the Constitution (but before anyone was officially aware of this), Tennessee had been admitted as a State; but not until Oct. 16, 1797, was a certified copy of the resolution of Congress proposing the amendment sent to the Governor of Tennessee (John Sevier) by Secretary of State Pickering, whose office was then at Trenton, New Jersey, because

of the epidemic of yellow fever at Philadelphia; it seems, however, that the Legislature of Tennessee took no action on Amendment XI, owing doubtless to the fact that public announcement of its adoption was made soon thereafter.

(Besides the necessary 12 States, one other, South Carolina, ratified Amendment XI, but this action was not taken until Dec. 4, 1797; the two remaining States, New Jersey and Pennsylvania, failed to ratify.)

AMENDMENT XII.
Manner of choosing President and Vice-President.

(Proposed by Congress Dec. 9, 1803; ratification completed June 15, 1804.)

The Electors shall meet in their respective States and vote by ballot for President and Vice-President, one of whom, at least, shall not be an inhabitant of the same State with themselves; they shall name in their ballots the person voted for as President, and in distinct ballots the person voted for as Vice-President, and they shall make distinct lists of all persons voted for as President, and of all persons voted for as Vice-President, and of the number of votes for each, which lists they shall sign and certify, and transmit sealed to the seat of the Government of the United States, directed to the President of the Senate; the President of the Senate shall, in the presence of the Senate and House of Representatives, open all the certificates and the votes shall then be counted;—The person having the greatest number of votes for President, shall be the President, if such number be a majority of the whole number of Electors appointed; and if no person have such majority, then from the persons having the highest numbers not exceeding three on the list of those voted for as President, the House of Representatives shall choose immediately, by ballot, the President. But in choosing the President, the votes shall be taken by States, the representation from each State having one vote; a quorum for this purpose shall consist of a member or members from two-thirds of the States, and a majority of all the States shall be necessary to a choice. *(And if the House of Representatives shall not choose a President whenever the right of choice shall devolve upon them, before the fourth day of March next following, then the Vice-President shall act as President, as in the case of the death or other constitutional disability of the President.) (The words in parentheses were superseded by Amendment XX, section 3.)* The person having the greatest number of votes as Vice-President, shall be the Vice-President, if such number be a majority of the whole number of Electors appointed, and if no person have a majority, then from the two highest numbers on the list, the Senate shall choose the Vice-President; a quorum for the purpose shall consist of two-thirds of the whole number of Senators, and a majority of the whole number shall be necessary to a choice. But no person constitutionally ineligible to the office of President shall be eligible to that of Vice-President of the United States.

THE RECONSTRUCTION AMENDMENTS

(Amendments XIII, XIV, and XV are commonly known as the Reconstruction Amendments, inasmuch as they followed the Civil War, and were drafted by Republicans who were bent on imposing their own policy of reconstruction on the South. Post-bellum legislatures there—Mississippi, South Carolina, Georgia, for example—had set up laws which, it was charged, were contrived to perpetuate Negro slavery under other names.)

AMENDMENT XIII.

Slavery abolished.

(Proposed by Congress Jan. 31, 1865; ratification completed Dec. 18, 1865. The amendment, when first proposed by a resolution in Congress, was passed by the Senate, 38 to 6, on Apr. 8, 1864, but was defeated in the House, 95 to 66 on June 15, 1864. On reconsideration by the House, on Jan. 31, 1865, the resolution passed, 119 to 56. It was approved by President Lincoln on Feb. 1, 1865, although the Supreme Court had decided in 1798 that the President has nothing to do with the proposing of amendments to the Constitution, or their adoption.)

1. Neither slavery nor involuntary servitude, except as a punishment for crime whereof the party shall have been duly convicted, shall exist within the United States or any place subject to their jurisdiction.

2. Congress shall have power to enforce this article by appropriate legislation.

AMENDMENT XIV.

Citizenship rights not to be abridged.

(The following amendment was proposed to the Legislatures of the several states by the 39th Congress, June 13, 1866, and was declared to have been ratified in a proclamation by the Secretary of State, July 28, 1868.

(The 14th amendment was adopted only by virtue of ratification subsequent to earlier rejections. Newly constituted legislatures in both North Carolina and South Carolina (respectively July 4 and 9, 1868), ratified the proposed amendment, although earlier legislatures had rejected the proposal. The Secretary of State issued a proclamation, which, though doubtful as to the effect of attempted withdrawals by Ohio and New Jersey, entertained no doubt as to the validity of the ratification by North and South Carolina. The following day (July 21, 1868), Congress passed a resolution which declared the 14th Amendment to be a part of the Constitution and directed the Secretary of State so to promulgate it. The Secretary waited, however, until the newly constituted Legislature of Georgia had ratified the amendment, subsequent to an earlier rejection, before the promulgation of the ratification of the new amendment.)

1. All persons born or naturalized in the United States, and subject to the jurisdiction thereof, are citizens of the United States and of the State wherein they reside. No State shall make or enforce any law which shall abridge the privileges or immunities of citizens of the United States; nor shall any State deprive any person of life, liberty, or property, without due process of law; nor deny to any person within its jurisdiction the equal protection of the laws.

2. Representatives shall be apportioned among the several States according to their respective numbers, counting the whole number of persons in each State, excluding Indians not taxed. But when the right to vote at any election for the choice of Electors for President and Vice-President of the United States, Representatives in Congress, the executive and judicial officers of a State, or the members of the Legislature thereof, is denied to any of the male inhabitants of such State, being twenty-one years of age, and citizens of the United States, or in any way abridged, except for participation in rebellion, or other crime, the basis of representation therein shall be reduced in the proportion which the number of such male citizens shall bear to the whole number of male citizens twenty-one years of age in such State.

3. No person shall be a Senator or Representative in Congress, or Elector of President and Vice-President, or hold any office, civil or military, under the United States, or under any State, who, having previously taken an oath, as a member of Congress, or as an officer of the United States, or as a member of any State Legislature, or as an executive or judicial officer of any State, to support the Constitution of the United States, shall have engaged in insurrection or rebellion against the same, or given aid or comfort to the enemies thereof. But Congress may by a vote of two-thirds of each House, remove such disability.

4. The validity of the public debt of the United States, authorized by law, including debts incurred for payment of pensions and bounties for services in suppressing insurrection or rebellion, shall not be questioned. But neither the United States nor any State shall assume or pay any debt or obligation incurred in aid of insurrection or rebellion against the United States, or any claim for the loss or emancipation of any slave; but all such debts, obligations and claims, shall be held illegal and void.

5. The Congress shall have power to enforce, by appropriate legislation, the provisions of this article.

AMENDMENT XV.

Race no bar to voting rights.

(The following amendment was proposed to the legislatures of the several States by the 40th Congress, Feb. 26, 1869, and was declared to have been ratified in a proclamation by the Secretary of State, Mar. 30, 1870.)

1. The right of citizens of the United States to vote shall not be denied or abridged by the United States or by any State on account of race, color, or previous condition of servitude.

2. The Congress shall have power to enforce this article by appropriate legislation.

AMENDMENT XVI.

Income taxes authorized.

(Proposed by Congress July 12, 1909; ratification declared by the Secretary of State Feb. 25, 1913.)

The Congress shall have power to lay and collect taxes on incomes, from whatever source derived, without apportionment among the several States, and without regard to any census or enumeration.

AMENDMENT XVII.

United States Senators to be elected by direct popular vote.

(Proposed by Congress May 13, 1912; ratification declared by the Secretary of State May 31, 1913.)

1. The Senate of the United States shall be composed of two Senators from each State, elected by the people thereof, for six years; and each Senator shall have one vote. The electors in each State shall have the qualifications requisite for electors of the most numerous branch of the State Legislatures.

2. When vacancies happen in the representation of any State in the Senate, the executive authority of such State shall issue writs of election to fill such vacancies: Provided, That the Legislature of any State may empower the Executive thereof to make temporary appointments until the peo-

ple fill the vacancies by election as the Legislature may direct.

3. This amendment shall not be so construed as to affect the election or term of any Senator chosen before it becomes valid as part of the Constitution.

AMENDMENT XVIII.

Liquor prohibition amendment.

(Proposed by Congress Dec. 18, 1917; ratification completed Jan. 16, 1919. Repealed by Amendment XXI, effective Dec. 5, 1933.)

(1. After one year from the ratification of this article the manufacture, sale, or transportation of intoxicating liquors within, the importation thereof into, or the exportation thereof from the United States and all territory subject to the jurisdiction thereof for beverage purposes is hereby prohibited.

(2. The Congress and the several States shall have concurrent power to enforce this article by appropriate legislation.

(3. This article shall be inoperative unless it shall have been ratified as an amendment to the Constitution by the Legislatures of the several States, as provided in the Constitution, within seven years from the date of the submission hereof to the States by the Congress.)

(The total vote in the Senates of the various States was 1,310 for, 237 against—84.6% dry. In the lower houses of the States the vote was 3,782 for, 1,035 against—78.5% dry.

(The amendment ultimately was adopted by all the States except Connecticut and Rhode Island.)

AMENDMENT XIX.

Giving nationwide suffrage to women.

(Proposed by Congress June 4, 1919; ratification certified by Secretary of State Aug. 26, 1920.)

1. The right of citizens of the United States to vote shall not be denied or abridged by the United States or by any State on account of sex.

2. Congress shall have power to enforce this Article by appropriate legislation.

AMENDMENT XX.

Terms of President and Vice President to begin on Jan. 20; those of Senators, Representatives, Jan. 3.

(Proposed by Congress Mar. 2, 1932; ratification completed Jan. 23, 1933.)

1. The terms of the President and Vice President shall end at noon on the 20th day of January, and the terms of Senators and Representatives at noon on the 3rd day of January, of the years in which such terms would have ended if this article had not been ratified; and the terms of their successors shall then begin.

2. The Congress shall assemble at least once in every year, and such meeting shall begin at noon on the 3rd day of January, unless they shall by law appoint a different day.

3. If, at the time fixed for the beginning of the term of the President, the President elect shall have died, the Vice President elect shall become President. If a President shall not have been chosen before the time fixed for the beginning of his term, or if the President elect shall have failed to qualify, then the Vice President elect shall act as President until a President shall have qualified; and the Congress may by law provide for the case wherein neither a President elect nor a Vice President elect shall have qualified, declaring who shall then act as President, or the manner in which one who is to act shall be selected, and such person shall act accordingly until a President or Vice President shall have qualified.

4. The Congress may by law provide for the case of the death of any of the persons from whom the House of Representatives may choose a President whenever the right of choice shall have devolved upon them, and for the case of the death of any of the persons from whom the Senate may choose a Vice President whenever the right of choice shall have devolved upon them.

5. Sections 1 and 2 shall take effect on the 15th day of October following the ratification of this article (Oct., 1933).

6. This article shall be inoperative unless it shall have been ratified as an amendment to the Constitution by the Legislatures of three-fourths of the several States within

seven years from the date of its submission.

AMENDMENT XXI.

Repeal of Amendment XVIII.

(Proposed by Congress Feb. 20, 1933; ratification completed Dec. 5, 1933.)

1. The eighteenth article of amendment to the Constitution of the United States is hereby repealed.

2. The transportation or importation into any State, Territory, or Possession of the United States for delivery or use therein of intoxicating liquors, in violation of the laws thereof, is hereby prohibited.

3. This article shall be inoperative unless it shall have been ratified as an amendment to the Constitution by conventions in the several States, as provided in the Constitution, within seven years from the date of the submission hereof to the States by the Congress.

AMENDMENT XXII.

Limiting Presidential terms of office.

(Proposed by Congress Mar. 24, 1947; ratification completed Feb. 27, 1951.)

1. No person shall be elected to the office of the President more than twice, and no person who has held the office of President, or acted as President, for more than two years of a term to which some other person was elected President shall be elected to the office of the President more than once. But this Article shall not apply to any person holding the office of President when this Article was proposed by the Congress, and shall not prevent any person who may be holding the office of President, or acting as President, during the term within which this Article becomes operative from holding the office of President or acting as President during the remainder of such term.

2. This article shall be inoperative unless it shall have been ratified as an amendment to the Constitution by the Legislatures of three-fourths of the several States within seven years from the date of its submission to the States by the Congress.

AMENDMENT XXIII.

Presidential vote for District of Columbia.

(Proposed by Congress June 16, 1960; ratification completed Mar. 29, 1961.)

1. The District constituting the seat of Government of the United States shall appoint in such manner as the Congress may direct:

A number of electors of President and Vice President equal to the whole number of Senators and Representatives in Congress to which the District would be entitled if it were a State, but in no event more than the least populous State; they shall be in addition to those appointed by the States, but they shall be considered, for the purposes of the election of President and Vice President, to be electors appointed by a State; and they shall meet in the District and perform such duties as provided by the twelfth article of amendment.

2. The Congress shall have power to enforce this article by appropriate legislation.

AMENDMENT XXIV.

Barring poll tax in federal elections.

(Proposed by Congress Aug. 27, 1962; ratification completed Jan. 23, 1964.)

1. The right of citizens of the United States to vote in any primary or other election for President or Vice President, for electors for President or Vice President, or for Senator or Representative in Congress, shall not be denied or abridged by the United States or any State by reason of failure to pay any poll tax or other tax.

2. The Congress shall have power to enforce this article by appropriate legislation.

AMENDMENT XXV.

Presidential disability and succession.

(Proposed by Congress July 6, 1965; ratification completed Feb. 10, 1967.)

1. In case of the removal of the President from office or of

his death or resignation, the Vice President shall become President.

2. Whenever there is a vacancy in the office of the Vice President, the President shall nominate a Vice President who shall take office upon confirmation by a majority vote of both houses of Congress.

3. Whenever the President transmits to the President pro tempore of the Senate and the Speaker of the House of Representatives his written declaration that he is unable to discharge the powers and duties of his office, and until he transmits to them a written declaration to the contrary, such powers and duties shall be discharged by the Vice President as Acting President.

4. Whenever the Vice President and a majority of either the principal officers of the executive departments or of such other body as Congress may by law provide, transmit to the President pro tempore of the Senate and the Speaker of the House of Representatives their written declaration that the President is unable to discharge the powers and duties of his office, the Vice President shall immediately assume the powers and duties of the office as Acting President.

Thereafter, when the President transmits to the President pro tempore of the Senate and the Speaker of the House of Representatives his written declaration that no inability exists, he shall resume the powers and duties of his office unless the Vice President and a majority of either the principal officers of the executive department or of such other body as Congress may by law provide, transmit within four days to the President pro tempore of the Senate and the Speaker of the House of Representatives their written declaration that the President is unable to discharge the powers and duties of his office. Thereupon Congress shall decide the issue, assembling within forty-eight hours for that purpose if not in session. If the Congress, within twenty-one days after receipt of the latter written declaration, or, if Congress is not in session, within twenty-one days after Congress is required to assemble, determines by two-thirds vote of both houses that the President is unable to discharge the powers and duties of his office, the Vice President shall continue to discharge the same as Acting President; otherwise, the President shall resume the powers and duties of his office.

AMENDMENT XXVI.
Lowering voting age to 18 years.
(Proposed by Congress Mar. 8, 1971; ratification completed July 1, 1971.)

1. The right of citizens of the United States, who are 18 years of age or older, to vote shall not be denied or abridged by the United States or any state on account of age.

2. The Congress shall have the power to enforce this article by appropriate legislation.

PROPOSED EQUAL RIGHTS AMENDMENT
(Proposed by Congress Mar. 22, 1972; ratified, as of mid-1980, by 35 states: 5 voted later to rescind their approval. Total of 38 needed for approval before deadline, originally Mar. 22, 1979; extended to June 30, 1982, by Senate action Oct. 6, 1978.)

1. Equality of rights under the law shall not be denied or abridged by the United States or by any State on account of sex.

2. The Congress shall have the power to enforce, by appropriate legislation, the provisions of this article.

3. This amendment shall take effect two years after the date of ratification.

PROPOSED D.C. REPRESENTATION AMENDMENT
(Proposed by Congress Aug. 22, 1978; ratified, as of mid-1980, by 8 states.)

1. For purposes of representation in the Congress, election of the President and Vice President, and article V of this Constitution, the District constituting the seat of government of the United States shall be treated as though it were a State.

2. The exercise of the rights and powers conferred under this article shall be by the people of the District constituting the seat of government, and as shall be provided by the Congress.

3. The twenty-third article of amendment to the Constitution of the United States is hereby repealed.

4. This article shall be inoperative, unless it shall have been ratified as an amendment to the Constitution by the legislatures of three-fourths of the several States within seven years from the date of its submission.

Origin of the Constitution

The War of Independence was conducted by delegates from the original 13 states, called the Congress of the United States of America and generally known as the Continental Congress. In 1777 the Congress submitted to the legislatures of the states the Articles of Confederation and Perpetual Union, which were ratified by New Hampshire, Massachusetts, Rhode Island, Connecticut, New York, New Jersey, Pennsylvania, Delaware, Virginia, North Carolina, South Carolina, and Georgia, and finally, in 1781, by Maryland.

The first article of the instrument read: "The stile of this confederacy shall be the United States of America." This did not signify a sovereign nation, because the states delegated only those powers they could not handle individually, such as power to wage war, establish a uniform currency, make treaties with foreign nations and contract debts for general expenses (such as paying the army). Taxes for the payment of such debts were levied by the individual states. The president under the Articles signed himself "President of the United States in Congress assembled," but here the United States were considered in the plural, a cooperating group. Canada was invited to join the union on equal terms but did not act.

When the war was won it became evident that a stronger federal union was needed to protect the mutual interests of the states. The Congress left the initiative to the legislatures. Virginia in Jan. 1786 appointed commissioners to meet with representatives of other states, with the result that delegates from Virginia, Delaware, New York, New Jersey, and Pennsylvania met at Annapolis. Alexander Hamilton prepared for their call by asking delegates from all states to meet in Philadelphia in May 1787 "to render the Constitution of the Federal government adequate to the exigencies of the union." Congress endorsed the plan Feb. 21, 1787. Delegates

were appointed by all states except Rhode Island.

The convention met May 14, 1787. George Washington was chosen president (presiding officer). The states certified 65 delegates, but 10 did not attend. The work was done by 55, not all of whom were present at all sessions. Of the 55 attending delegates, 16 failed to sign, and 39 actually signed Sept. 17, 1787, some with reservations. Some historians have said 74 delegates (9 more than the 65 actually certified) were named and 19 failed to attend. These 9 additional persons refused the appointment, were never delegates and never counted as absentees. Washington sent the Constitution to Congress with a covering letter and that body, Sept. 28, 1787, ordered it sent to the legislatures, "in order to be submitted to a convention of delegates chosen in each state by the people thereof."

The Constitution was ratified by votes of state conventions as follows: Delaware, Dec. 7, 1787, unanimous; Pennsylvania, Dec. 12, 1787, 43 to 23; New Jersey, Dec. 18, 1787, unanimous; Georgia, Jan 2, 1788, unanimous; Connecticut, Jan. 9, 1788, 128 to 40; Massachusetts, Feb. 6, 1788, 187 to 168; Maryland, Apr. 28, 1788, 63 to 11; South Carolina, May 23, 1788, 149 to 73; New Hampshire, June 21, 1788, 57 to 46; Virginia, June 26, 1788, 89 to 79; New York, July 26, 1788, 30 to 27. Nine states were needed to establish the operation of the Constitution "between the states so ratifying the same" and New Hampshire was the 9th state. The government did not declare the Constitution in effect until the first Wednesday in Mar. 1789 which was Mar. 4. After that North Carolina ratified it Nov. 21, 1789, 194 to 77; and Rhode Island, May 29, 1790, 34 to 32. Vermont in convention ratified it Jan. 10, 1791, and by act of Congress approved Feb. 18, 1791, was admitted into the Union as the 14th state, Mar. 4, 1791.

How the Declaration of Independence Was Adopted

On June 7, 1776, Richard Henry Lee, who had issued the first call for a congress of the colonies, introduced in the Continental Congress at Philadelphia a resolution declaring "that these United Colonies are, and of right ought to be, free and independent states, that they are absolved from all allegiance to the British Crown, and that all political connection between them and the state of Great Britain is, and ought to be, totally dissolved."

The resolution, seconded by John Adams on behalf of the Massachusetts delegation, came up again June 10 when a committee of 5, headed by Thomas Jefferson, was appointed to express the purpose of the resolution in a declaration of independence. The others on the committee were John Adams, Benjamin Franklin, Robert R. Livingston, and Roger Sherman.

Drafting the Declaration was assigned to Jefferson, who worked on a portable desk of his own construction in a room at Market and 7th Sts. The committee reported the result June 28, 1776. The members of the Congress suggested a number of changes, which Jefferson called "deplorable." They didn't approve Jefferson's arraignment of the British people and King George III for encouraging and fostering the slave trade, which Jefferson called "an execrable commerce." They made 86 changes, eliminating 480 words and leaving 1,337. In the final form capitalization was erratic. Jefferson had written that men were endowed with "inalienable" rights; in the final copy it came out as "unalienable" and has been thus ever since.

The Lee-Adams resolution of independence was adopted by 12 yeas July 2 — the actual date of the act of independence. The Declaration, which explains the act, was adopted July 4, in the evening.

After the Declaration was adopted, July 4, 1776, it was turned over to John Dunlap, printer, to be printed on broadsides. The original copy was lost and one of his broadsides

was attached to a page in the journal of the Congress. It was read aloud July 8 in Philadelphia, Easton, Pa., and Trenton, N.J. On July 9 at 6 p.m. it was read by order of Gen. George Washington to the troops assembled on the Common in New York City (City Hall Park).

The Continental Congress of July 19, 1776, adopted the following resolution:

"Resolved, That the Declaration passed on the 4th, be fairly engrossed on parchment with the title and stile of 'The Unanimous Declaration of the thirteen United States of America' and that the same, when engrossed, be signed by every member of Congress."

Not all delegates who signed the engrossed Declaration were present on July 4. Robert Morris (Pa.), William Williams (Conn.) and Samuel Chase (Md.) signed on Aug. 2, Oliver Wolcott (Conn.), George Wythe (Va.), Richard Henry Lee (Va.) and Elbridge Gerry (Mass.) signed in August and September, Matthew Thornton (N. H.) joined the Congress Nov. 4 and signed later. Thomas McKean (Del.) rejoined Washington's Army before signing and said later that he signed in 1781.

Charles Carroll of Carrollton was appointed a delegate by Maryland on July 4, 1776, presented his credentials July 18, and signed the engrossed Declaration Aug. 2. Born Sept. 19, 1737, he was 95 years old and the last surviving signer when he died Nov. 14, 1832.

Two Pennsylvania delegates who did not support the Declaration on July 4 were replaced.

The 4 New York delegates did not have authority from their state to vote on July 4. On July 9 the New York state convention authorized its delegates to approve the Declaration and the Congress was so notified on July 15, 1776. The 4 signed the Declaration on Aug. 2.

The original engrossed Declaration is preserved in the National Archives Building in Washington.

The Liberty Bell: Its History and Significance

The Liberty Bell, in Independence Hall, Philadelphia, is an object of great reverence to Americans because of its association with the historic events of the War of Independence.

The original Province bell, ordered to commemorate the 50th anniversary of the Commonwealth of Pennsylvania, was cast by Thomas Lister, Whitechapel, London, and reached Philadelphia in Aug. 1752. It bore an inscription from Leviticus XXV, 10: "Proclaim liberty throughout all the land unto all the inhabitants thereof."

The bell was cracked by a stroke of its clapper in Sept. 1752 while it hung on a truss in the State House yard for testing. Pass & Stow, Philadelphia founders, recast the bell, adding 1 1/2 ounces of copper to a pound of the original metal to reduce brittleness. It was found that the bell contained too much copper, injuring its tone, so Pass & Stow recast it again, this time successfully.

In June 1753 the bell was hung in the wooden steeple of the State House, erected on top of the brick tower. In use while the Continental Congress was in session in the State House, it rang out in defiance of British tax and trade restrictions, and proclaimed the Boston Tea Party and the first public reading of the Declaration of Independence.

On Sept. 18, 1777, when the British Army was about to occupy Philadelphia, the bell was moved in a baggage train of the American Army to Allentown, Pa. where it was hidden in the Zion Reformed Church until June 27, 1778. It was moved back to Philadelphia after the British left.

In July 1781 the wooden steeple became insecure and had to be taken down. The bell was lowered into the brick section of the tower. Here it was hanging in July, 1835, when it cracked while tolling for the funeral of John Marshall, chief justice of the United States. Because of its association with the War of Independence it was not recast but remained mute in this location until 1846, the year of the Mexican War, when it was placed on exhibition in the Declaration Chamber of Independence Hall.

In 1876, when many thousands of Americans visited Philadelphia for the Centennial Exposition, it was placed in its old walnut frame in the tower hallway. In 1877 it was hung from the ceiling of the tower by a chain of 13 links. It was returned again to the Declaration Chamber and in 1896 taken back to the tower hall, where it occupied a glass case. In 1915 the case was removed so that the public might touch it. On Jan. 1, 1976, just after midnight to mark the opening of the Bicentennial Year, the bell was moved to a new glass and steel pavilion behind Independence Hall for easier viewing by the larger number of visitors expected during the year.

The measurements of the bell follow: circumference around the lip, 12 ft.; circumference around the crown, 7 ft. 6 in.; lip to the crown, 3 ft.; height over the crown, 2 ft. in.; thickness at lip, 3 in.; thickness at crown, 1 1/4 in; weight, 2080 lbs.; length of clapper, 3 ft. 2 in.; cost, £60 14s 5d.

Confederate States and Secession

The American Civil War, 1861-65, grew out of sectional disputes over the continued existence of slavery in the South and the contention of Southern legislators that the states retained many sovereign rights, including the right to secede from the Union.

The war was not fought by state against state but by one

federal regime against another, the Confederate government in Richmond assuming control over the economic, political and military life of the South, under protest from Georgia and South Carolina.

South Carolina voted an ordinance of secession from the Union, repealing its 1788 ratification of the U.S. Constit

tion on Dec. 20, 1860, to take effect Dec. 24. Other states seceded in 1861. Their votes in conventions were: Mississippi, Jan. 9, 84-15; Florida, Jan. 10, 62-7; Alabama, Jan. 11, 61-39; Georgia, Jan. 19, 208-89; Louisiana, Jan. 26, 113-17; Texas, Feb. 1, 166-7, ratified by popular vote Feb. 23 (for 34,794, against 11,325); Virginia, Apr. 17, 88-55, ratified by popular vote May 23 (for 128,884; against 32,134); Arkansas, May 6, 69-1; Tennessee, May 7, ratified by popular vote June 8 (for 104,019, against 47,238); North Carolina, May 21.

Missouri Unionists stopped secession in conventions Feb. 28 and Mar. 9. The legislature condemned secession Mar. 7. Under the protection of Confederate troops, secessionist members of the legislature adopted a resolution of secession at Neosho, Oct. 31. The Confederate Congress seated the secessionists' representatives.

Kentucky did not secede and its government remained Unionist. In a part occupied by Confederate troops, Kentuckians approved secession and the Confederate Congress admitted their representatives.

The Maryland legislature voted against secession Apr. 27, 53-13. Delaware did not secede. Western Virginia held conventions at Wheeling, named a pro-Union governor June 11, 1861; admitted to Union as West Virginia June 30, 1863; its constitution provided for gradual abolition of slavery.

Confederate Government

Forty-two delegates from South Carolina, Georgia, Alabama, Mississippi, Louisiana, and Florida met in convention at Montgomery, Ala., Feb. 4, 1861. They adopted a provisional constitution of the Confederate States of America, and elected Jefferson Davis (Miss.) provisional president, and Alexander H. Stephens (Ga.) provisional vice president.

A permanent constitution was adopted Mar. 11; it abolished the African slave trade. The Congress moved to Richmond, Va. July 20. Davis was elected president in October, and was inaugurated Feb. 22, 1862.

The Congress adopted a flag, consisting of a red field with a white stripe, and a blue jack with a circle of white stars. Later the more popular flag was the red field with blue diagonal cross bars that held 13 white stars. The stars represented the 11 states actually in the Confederacy plus Kentucky and Missouri.

(*See also Civil War, U.S., in Index*)

Lincoln's Address at Gettysburg, 1863

Fourscore and seven years ago our fathers brought forth on this continent a new nation, conceived in liberty and dedicated to the proposition that all men are created equal.

Now we are engaged in a great civil war, testing whether that nation or any nation so conceived and so dedicated can long endure. We are met on a great battle field of that war. We have come to dedicate a portion of that field, as a final resting-place for those who here gave their lives that that nation might live. It is altogether fitting and proper that we should do this.

But, in a larger sense, we can not dedicate — we can not consecrate — we can not hallow — this ground. The brave men, living and dead, who struggled here, have consecrated it, far above our poor power to add or detract. The world will little note, nor long remember, what we say here, but it can never forget what they did here. It is for us the living, rather, to be dedicated here to the unfinished work which they who fought here have thus far so nobly advanced. It is rather for us to be here dedicated to the great task remaining before us — that from these honored dead we take increased devotion to that cause for which they gave the last full measure of devotion — that we here highly resolve that these dead shall not have died in vain — that this nation, under God, shall have a new birth of freedom — and that government of the people, by the people, for the people, shall not perish from the earth.

History of the Address

President Lincoln delivered his address at the dedication of the military cemetery at Gettysburg, Pa., Nov. 19, 1863. The battle had been fought July 1-3, 1863. He was preceded by Edward Everett, former president of Harvard, secretary of state and senator from Massachusetts, then 69 and one of the nation's great orators. Everett gave a full resume of the battle, Lincoln's speech was so short that the photographer did not get his camera adjusted in time. The report that newspapers ignored Lincoln's address is not entirely accurate; Everett's address swamped their columns, but the greatness of Lincoln's speech was immediately recognized. Everett wrote him: "I should be glad if I could flatter myself that I came as near the central idea of the occasion in 2 hours as you did in 2 minutes."

Five copies of the Gettysburg address in Lincoln's hand are extant. The first and 2d drafts, prepared in Washington and Gettysburg just before delivery, are in the Library of Congress. The 3d draft, written at the request of Everett to be sold at a fair in New York for the benefit of soldiers, was given the Illinois State Historical Library by popular subscription.

The 4th copy was written out by Lincoln for George Bancroft, the historian, and remained in custody of the Bancroft family until 1929, when it was acquired by Mrs. Nicholas H. Noyes, of Indianapolis, Ind. In 1949 Mrs. Noyes presented this copy to the Cornell University Library, Ithaca, N.Y. The 5th copy, usually described as the clearest and best, was also written by Lincoln for George Bancroft. It is in the Lincoln Room of the White House, where it was placed in Mar. 1959. Lincoln's spelling of battle field and can not as separated words in that version is reproduced above.

The National Anthem — The Star-Spangled Banner

The Star-Spangled Banner was ordered played by the military and naval services by President Woodrow Wilson in 1916. It was designated the National Anthem by Act of Congress, Mar. 3, 1931. It was written by Francis Scott Key, of Georgetown, D. C., during the bombardment of Fort McHenry, Baltimore, Md., Sept. 13-14, 1814. Key was lawyer, a graduate of St. John's College, Annapolis, and a volunteer in a light artillery company. When a friend, Dr. Beanes, a physician of Upper Marlborough, Md., was taken aboard Admiral Cockburn's British squadron for interfering with ground troops, Key and J. S. Skinner, carrying a note from President Madison, went to the fleet under a flag of truce on a cartel ship to ask Beanes' release. Admiral Cockburn consented, but as the fleet was about to sail up the Patapsco to bombard Fort McHenry he detained them, first on M. S. Surprise, and then on a supply ship.

Key witnessed the bombardment from his own vessel. It began at 7 a.m., Sept. 13, 1814, and lasted, with intermissions, for 25 hours. The British fired over 1,500 shells, each weighing as much as 220 lbs. They were unable to approach closely because the Americans had sunk 22 vessels in the channel. Only four Americans were killed and 24 wounded. A British bomb-ship was disabled.

During the bombardment Key wrote a stanza on the back of an envelope. Next day at Indian Queen Inn, Baltimore, he wrote out the poem and gave it to his brother-in-law, Judge J. H. Nicholson. Nicholson suggested the tune, Anacreon in Heaven, and had the poem printed on broadsides, of which two survive. On Sept. 20 it appeared in the "Baltimore American." Later Key made 3 copies; one is in the Library of Congress and one in the Pennsylvania Historical Society.

The copy that Key wrote in his hotel Sept. 14, 1814, remained in the Nicholson family for 93 years. In 1907 it was sold to Henry Walters of Baltimore. In 1934 it was bought at auction in New York from the Walters estate by the Walters Art Gallery, Baltimore, for $26,400. The Walters Gallery in 1953 sold the manuscript to the Maryland Historical Society for the same price.

The flag that Key saw during the bombardment is preserved in the Smithsonian Institution, Washington. It is 30 by 42 ft., and has 15 alternate red and white stripes and 15 stars, for the original 13 states plus Kentucky and Vermont.

It was made by Mary Young Pickersgill. The Baltimore Flag House, a museum, occupies her premises, which were restored in 1953.

The Star-Spangled Banner

I

Oh, say can you see by the dawn's early light
  What so proudly we hailed at the twilight's last gleaming?
Whose broad stripes and bright stars thru the perilous fight,
  O'er the ramparts we watched were so gallantly streaming?
And the rocket's red glare, the bomb bursting in air,
  Gave proof through the night that our flag was still there.
Oh, say does that star-spangled banner yet wave
  O'er the land of the free and the home of the brave?

II

On the shore, dimly seen through the mists of the deep,
  Where the foe's haughty host in dread silence reposes,
What is that which the breeze, o'er the towering steep,
  As it fitfully blows, half conceals, half discloses?
Now it catches the gleam of the morning's first beam,
  In full glory reflected now shines in the stream:

'Tis the star-spangled banner! Oh long may it wave
  O'er the land of the free and the home of the brave!

III

And where is that band who so vauntingly swore
  That the havoc of war and the battle's confusion,
A home and a country should leave us no more!
  Their blood has washed out their foul footsteps' pollution.
No refuge could save the hireling and slave
  From the terror of flight, or the gloom of the grave:
And the star-spangled banner in triumph doth wave
  O'er the land of the free and the home of the brave!

IV

Oh! thus be it ever, when freemen shall stand
  Between their loved home and the war's desolation!
Blest with victory and peace, may the heav'n rescued land
  Praise the Power that hath made and preserved us a nation.
Then conquer we must, when our cause it is just,
  And this be our motto: "In God is our trust."
And the star-spangled banner in triumph shall wave
  O'er the land of the free and the home of the brave!

Statue of Liberty National Monument

Since 1886, the Statue of Liberty Enlightening the World has stood as a symbol of freedom in New York harbor. It also commemorates French-American friendship for it was given by the people of France, designed by Frederic Auguste Bartholdi (1834-1904). A $2.5 million building housing the American Museum of Immigration was opened by Pres. Nixon Sept. 26, 1972, at the base of the statue. It houses a permanent exhibition of photos, posters, and artifacts tracing the history of American immigration. In addition, there is a small immigration library. The Monument is administered by the National Park Service.

Nearby Ellis Island, gateway to America for more than 12 million immigrants between 1892 and 1954, was proclaimed part of the National Monument in 1965 by Pres. Johnson. It can be visited between May and October.

Edouard de Laboulaye, French historian and admirer of American political institutions, suggested that the French present a monument to the United States, the latter to provide pedestal and site. Bartholdi visualized a colossal statue at the entrance of New York harbor, welcoming the peoples of the world with the torch of liberty.

The French approved the idea and formed the Franco-American Union to raise funds, which eventually reached $250,000. Bartholdi began work about 1874 in Paris.

On Washington's birthday, Feb. 22, 1877, Congress approved the use of a site on Bedloe's Island suggested by Bartholdi. This island of 12 acres had been owned in the 17th century by a Walloon named Isaac Bedloe. It was called Bedloe's until Aug. 3, 1956, when Pres. Eisenhower approved a resolution of Congress changing the name to Liberty Island.

The statue was finished May 21, 1884, and formally presented to U.S. Minister Morton July 4, 1884, by Ferdinand de Lesseps, head of the Franco-American Union, promoter of the Panama Canal, and builder of the Suez Canal.

On Aug. 5, 1884, the Americans laid the cornerstone for the pedestal. This was to be built on the foundations of Fort Wood, which had been erected by the Government in 1811. The American committee had raised $125,000, but this was found to be inadequate. Joseph Pulitzer, owner of the New York World, appealed on Mar. 16, 1885, for general donations. By Aug. 11, 1885, he had raised $100,000.

The statue arrived dismantled, in 214 packing cases, from Rouen, France, in June, 1885. The last rivet of the statue was driven Oct. 28, 1886, when Pres. Grover Cleveland dedicated the monument.

The statue weighs 450,000 lbs. or 225 tons. The copper sheeting weighs 200,000 lbs. There are 167 steps from the land level to the top of the pedestal, 168 steps inside the statue to the head, and 54 rungs on the ladder leading to the arm that holds the torch.

Dimensions of the Statue	Ft.	In.
Height from base to torch (45.3 meters)	151	1
Foundation of pedestal to torch (91.5 meters). . .	305	1
Heel to top of head	111	1
Length of hand	16	5
Index finger	8	0
Circumference at second joint.	3	6
Size of finger nail . . . . 13x10 in.		
Head from chin to cranium.	17	3
Head thickness from ear to ear	10	0
Distance across the eye	2	6
Length of nose	4	6
Right arm, length	42	
Right arm, greatest thickness	12	
Thickness of waist	35	
Width of mouth	3	
Tablet, length	23	
Tablet, width	13	
Tablet, thickness	2	

Emma Lazarus' Famous Poem

A poem by Emma Lazarus is graven on a tablet with the pedestal on which the statue stands.

The New Colossus

Not like the brazen giant of Greek fame,
With conquering limbs astride from land to land;
Here at our sea-washed, sunset gates shall stand
A mighty woman with a torch, whose flame
Is the imprisoned lightning, and her name
Mother of Exiles. From her beacon-hand
Glows world-wide welcome; her mild eyes command
The air-bridged harbor that twin cities frame.
"Keep ancient lands, your storied pomp!" cries she
With silent lips. "Give me your tired, your poor,
Your huddled masses yearning to breathe free,
The wretched refuse of your teeming shore.
Send these, the homeless, tempest-tost to me,
I lift my lamp beside the golden door!"

Forms of Address for Persons of Rank and Public Office

In these examples John Smith is used as a representative American name. The salutation Dear Sir or Dear Madam is ways permissible when addressing a person not known to the writer.

President of the United States

Address: The President, The White House, Washington, DC 20500. Also, The President and Mrs. ____.

Salutation: Dear Sir or Mr. President or Dear Mr. President. More intimately: My dear Mr. President. Also: Dear Mr. President and Mrs. ____

The vice president takes the same forms.

Cabinet Officers

Address: Mr. John Smith, Secretary of State, Washing D.C. or The Hon. John Smith. Similar addresses for o members of the cabinet. Also: Secretary and Mrs. Smith.

Salutation: Dear Sir, or Dear Mr. Secretary. Also: Dear Mr. and Mrs. Smith.

The Bench

Address: The Hon. John Smith, Chief Justice of the United States. The Hon. John Smith, Associate Justice of the Supreme Court of the United States. The Hon. John Smith, Associate Judge, U.S. District Court.

Salutation: Dear Sir, or Dear Mr. Chief Justice. Dear Mr. Justice. Dear Judge Smith.

Members of Congress

Address: The Hon. John Smith, United States Senate, Washington, DC 20510, or Sen. John Smith, etc. Also The Hon. John Smith, House of Representatives, Washington, DC 20515, or Rep. John Smith, etc.

Salutation: Dear Mr. Senator, or Dear Mr. Smith; for Representative, Dear Mr. Smith.

Officers of Armed Forces

Address: Careful attention should be given to the precise rank, thus: General of the Army John Smith, Fleet Admiral John Smith. The rules for Air Force are same as Army.

Salutation: Dear Sir, or Dear General. All general officers, whatever rank, are entitled to be addressed as generals. Likewise a lieutenant colonel is addressed as colonel and first and second lieutenants are addressed as lieutenant.

Warrant officers and flight officers are addressed as Mister. Chaplains are addressed as Chaplain. A Catholic chaplain may be addressed as Father. Cadets of the United States Military Academy and Air Force Academy are addressed as Cadet. Noncommissioned officers are addressed by their titles. In the U. S. Navy all men from midshipman at Annapolis up to and including lieutenant commander are addressed as Mister.

Ambassador, Governor, Mayor

Address: The Hon. John Smith, followed by his or her title. They can be addressed either at their embassy, or at the Department of State, Washington, D.C. An ambassador from a foreign nation may be addressed as His or Her Excellency. An American is not to be so addressed.

Salutation: Dear Mr. or Madam Ambassador. An ambassador from a foreign nation may be called Your Excellency.

Governors and mayors are often addressed as The Hon. Jane Smith, Governor of _____, or The Hon. John Smith, Mayor of _____; also Governor John Smith, State House, Albany, N.Y., or Mayor Jane Smith, City Hall, Erie, Pa.

The Clergy

Address: His Holiness, the Pope, or His Holiness Pope (name), State of Vatican City, Italy.

Salutation: Your Holiness or Most Holy Father.

Also: His Eminence, John, Cardinal Smith; salutation: Your Eminence. An archbishop or a bishop is addressed The Most Reverend, and the salutation is Your Excellency. A monsignor who is a papal chamberlain is The Very Reverend Monsignor and the salutation is Dear Sir or Very Reverend Monsignor; a monsignor who is a domestic prelate is The Right Reverend Monsignor and salutation is Right Reverend Monsignor. A priest is addressed Reverend John Smith. A brother of an order is addressed Brother —. A sister takes the same form.

A bishop of the Protestant Episcopal Church is The Right Reverend John Smith; salutation is Right Reverend Sir, or Dear Bishop Smith. If a clergyman is a doctor of divinity, he is addressed: The Reverend John Smith, D.D., and the salutation is Reverend Sir, or Dear Dr. Smith. When a clergyman does not have the degree the salutation is Dear Mr. Smith.

A bishop of the Methodist Church is addressed Bishop John Smith with titles following.

Royalty and Nobility

An emperor is to be addressed in a letter as Sir, or Your Imperial Majesty.

A king or queen is addressed as His Majesty (Name), King of (Name), or Her Majesty (Name), Queen of (Name), Salutation: Sir, or Madam, or May it please Your Majesty.

Princes and princesses and other persons of royal blood are addressed as His (or Her) Royal Highness, and saluted with May it please Your Royal Highness.

A duke or marquis is My Lord Duke (or Marquis), a duke is His (or Your) Grace.

Code of Etiquette for Display and Use of the U.S. Flag

Although the Stars and Stripes originated in 1777, it was not until 146 years later that there was a serious attempt to establish a uniform code of etiquette for the U.S. flag. The War Department issued Feb. 15, 1923, a circular on the rules of flag usage. These were adopted almost in their entirety June 14, 1923, by a conference of 68 patriotic organizations in Washington. Finally, on June 22, 1942, a joint resolution of Congress, amended by Public Law 94-344 July 7, 1976, codified "existing rules and customs pertaining to the display and use of the flag. . ."

When to Display the Flag—The flag should be displayed on all days, especially on legal holidays and other special occasions, on official buildings when in use, in or near polling places on election days, and in or near schools when in session. A citizen may fly the flag at any time he wishes. It is customary to display the flag only from sunrise to sunset on buildings and on stationary flagstaffs in the open. However, it may be displayed at night on special occasions, preferably lighted. In Washington, the flag now flies over the White House both day and night. It flies over the Senate wing of the Capitol when the Senate is in session and over the House wing when that body is in session. It flies day and night over the east and west fronts of the Capitol, without floodlights at night but receiving light from the illuminated Capitol Dome. It flies 24 hours a day at several other places, including the Fort McHenry Nat'l Monument in Baltimore, where it inspired Francis Scott Key to write The Star Spangled Banner.

How to Fly the Flag—The flag should be hoisted briskly and lowered ceremoniously, and should never be allowed to touch the ground or the floor. When hung over a sidewalk from a rope extending from a building to a pole, the union should be away from the building. When hung over the center of a street it should have the union to the north in an east-west street and to the east in a north-south street. No other flag may be flown above or, if on the same level, to the right of the U.S. flag, except that at the United Nations Headquarters the UN flag may be placed above flags of all member nations and other national flags may be flown with equal prominence or honor with the flag of the U.S. At services by Navy chaplains at sea, the church pennant may be flown above the flag.

When two flags are placed against a wall with crossed staffs, the U.S. flag should be at right—its own right, and its staff should be in front of the staff of the other flag; when a number of flags are grouped and displayed from staffs, it should be at the center and highest point of the group.

Church and Platform Use—In an auditorium, the flag may be displayed flat, above and behind the speaker. When displayed from a staff in a church or public auditorium, the flag should hold the position of superior prominence, in advance of the audience, and in the position of honor at the clergyman's or speaker's right as he faces the audience. Any other flag so displayed should be placed on the left of the clergyman or speaker or to the right of the audience.

When the flag is displayed horizontally or vertically against a wall, the stars should be uppermost and at the observer's left.

When to Salute the Flag—All persons present should face the flag, stand at attention and salute on the following occasions: (1) When the flag is passing in a parade or in a review, (2) During the ceremony of hoisting or lowering, (3) When the National Anthem is played, and (4) During the Pledge of Allegiance. Those present in uniform should render the military salute. When not in uniform, men should remove the hat with the right hand holding it at the left shoulder, the hand being over the heart. Men without hats should salute in the same manner. Aliens should stand at attention. Women should salute by placing the right hand over the heart.

On Memorial Day, the flag should fly at half-staff until noon, then be raised to the peak.

As provided by Presidential proclamation the flag should fly at half-staff for 30 days from the day of death of a president or former president; for 10 days from the day of death of a vice president, chief justice or retired chief justice of the U.S., or speaker of the House of Representatives; from day of death until burial of an associate justice of the Supreme Court, cabinet member, former vice president, or Senate president pro tempore, majority or minority Senate leader, or majority or minority House leader; for a U.S. senator, representative, territorial delegate, or the resident commissioner of Puerto Rico, on day of death and the following day within the metropolitan area of the District of Columbia and from day of death until burial within the decedent's state, congressional district, territory or commonwealth; and for the death of the governor of a state, territory, or possession of the U.S., from day of death until burial within that state, territory, or possession.

When used to cover a casket, the flag should be placed so that the union is at the head and over the left shoulder. It should not be lowered into the grave nor touch the ground.

Prohibited Uses of the Flag—The flag should never be dipped to any person or thing. It should never be displayed with the union down save as a distress signal. It should never be carried flat or horizontally, but always aloft and free.

It should not be displayed on a float, motor car or boat except from a staff.

It should never be used as a covering for a ceiling, nor have placed upon it any word, design, or drawing. It should never be used as a receptacle for carrying anything. It should not be used to cover a statue or a monument.

The flag should never be used for advertising purposes, nor be embroidered on such articles as cushions or hankerchiefs, printed or otherwise impressed on boxes or used as a costume or athletic uniform. Advertising signs should not be fastened to its staff or halyard.

The flag should never be used as drapery of any sort, never festooned, drawn back, nor up, in folds, but always allowed to fall free. Bunting of blue, white and red always arranged with the blue above and the white in the middle, should be used for covering a speaker's desk, draping the front of a platform, and for decoration in general.

An Act of Congress approved Feb. 8, 1917, provided certain penalties for the desecration, mutilation or improper use of the flag within the District of Columbia. A 1968 federal law provided penalties of up to a year's imprisonment or a $1,000 fine or both, for publicly burning or otherwise desecrating any flag of the United States. In addition, many states have laws against flag desecration.

How to Dispose of Worn Flags—The flag, when it is in such condition that it is no longer a fitting emblem for display, should be destroyed in a dignified way, preferably by burning in private.

Pledge of Allegiance to the Flag

I pledge allegiance to the flag of the United States of America and to the republic for which it stands, one nation under God, indivisible, with liberty and justice for all.

This, the current official version of the Pledge of Allegiance, has developed from the original pledge, which was first published in the Sept. 8, 1892, issue of the Youth's Companion, a weekly magazine then published in Boston. The original pledge contained the phrase "my flag," which was changed more than 30 years later to "flag of the United States of America." An act of Congress in 1954 added the words "under God."

The authorship of the pledge has been in dispute for many years. The Youth's Companion stated in 1917 that the original draft was written by James B. Upham, an executive of the magazine who died in 1910. A leaflet circulated by the magazine later named Upham as the originator of the draft "afterwards condensed and perfected by him and his associates of the Companion force."

Francis Bellamy, a former member of the Youth's Companion editorial staff, publicly claimed authorship of the pledge in 1923. The United States Flag Assn., acting on the advice of a committee named to study the controversy, upheld in 1939 the claim of Bellamy, who had died 8 years earlier. The Library of Congress issued in 1957 a report attributing the authorship to Bellamy.

The Flag of the U.S.—The Stars and Stripes

The 50-star flag of the United States was raised for the first time officially at 12:01 a.m. on July 4, 1960, at Fort McHenry National Monument in Baltimore, Md. The 50th star had been added for Hawaii; a year earlier the 49th, for Alaska. Before that, no star had been added since 1912, when N.M. and Ariz. were admitted to the Union.

History of the Flag

The true history of the Stars and Stripes has become so cluttered by a volume of myth and tradition that the facts are difficult, and in some cases impossible, to establish. For example, it is not certain who designed the Stars and Stripes, who made the first such flag, or even whether it ever flew in any sea fight or land battle of the American Revolution.

One thing all agree on is that the Stars and Stripes originated as the result of a resolution offered by the Marine Committee of the Second Continental Congress at Philadelphia and adopted June 14, 1777. It read:

Resolved: that the flag of the United States be thirteen stripes, alternate red and white; that the union be thirteen stars, white in a blue field, representing a new constellation.

Congress gave no hint as to the designer of the flag, no instructions as to the arrangement of the stars, and no information on its appropriate uses. Historians have been unable to find the original flag law.

The resolution establishing the flag was not even published until Sept. 2, 1777. Despite repeated requests, Washington did not get the flags until 1783, after the Revolutionary War was over. And there is no certainty that they were the Stars and Stripes.

Early Flags

Although it was never officially adopted by the Continental Congress, many historians consider the first flag of the United States to have been the Grand Union (sometimes called Great Union) flag. This was a modification of the British Meteor flag, which had the red cross of St. George and the white cross of St. Andrew combined in the blue canton. For the Grand Union flag, 13 horizontal stripes were imposed on the red field, dividing it into 13 alternate red and white stripes. On Jan. 1, 1776, when the Continental Army came into formal existence, this flag was unfurled on Prospect Hill, Somerville, Mass. Washington wrote that "we hoisted the Union Flag in compliment to the United Colonies."

One of several flags about which controversy has raged for years is at Easton, Pa. Containing the devices of the national flag in reversed order, this has been in the public library at Easton for over 150 years. Some contend that this flag was actually the first Stars and Stripes, first displayed on July 8, 1776. This flag has 13 red and white stripes in the canton, 13 white stars centered in a blue field.

A flag was hastily improvised from garments by the defenders of Fort Schuyler at Rome, N.Y., Aug. 3-22, 1777. Historians believe it was the Grand Union Flag.

The Sons of Liberty had a flag of 9 red and white stripes, to signify 9 colonies, when they met in New York in 1765 to oppose the Stamp Tax. By 1775, the flag had grown to 13 red and white stripes, with a rattlesnake on it.

At Concord, Apr. 19, 1775, the minute men from Bedford, Mass., are said to have carried a flag having a silver arm with sword on a red field.

At Cambridge, Mass., the Sons of Liberty used a plain red flag with a green pine tree on it.

In June 1775, Washington went from Philadelphia to Boston to take command of the army, escorted to New York by the Philadelphia Light Horse Troop. It carried a yellow flag which had an elaborate coat of arms — the shield charged with 13 knots, the motto "For These We Strive" — and a canton of 13 blue and silver stripes.

In Feb., 1776, Col. Christopher Gadsden, member of the Continental Congress, gave the South Carolina Provincial Congress a flag "such as is to be used by the commander-in-chief of the American Navy." It had a yellow field, with a rattlesnake about to strike and the words "Don't Tread on Me."

At the battle of Bennington, Aug. 16, 1777, patriots used a flag of 7 white and 6 red stripes with a blue canton extending down 9 stripes and showing an arch of 11 white stars over the figure 76 and a star in each of the upper corners. The stars are seven-pointed. This flag is preserved in the Historical Museum at Bennington, Vt.

At the Battle of Cowpens, Jan. 17, 1781, the 3d Maryland Regt. is said to have carried a flag of 13 red and white stripes, with a blue canton containing 12 stars in a circle around one star.

Legends about the Flag

Who Designed the Flag? No one knows for a certainty. Francis Hopkinson, designer of a naval flag, declared he also had designed the flag and in 1781 asked Congress to reimburse him for his services. Congress did not do so. Dumas Malone of Columbia Univ. wrote: "This talented man . . . designed the American flag."

Who Called the Flag Old Glory? — The flag is said to have been named Old Glory by William Driver, a sea captain of Salem, Mass. One legend has it that when he raised the flag on his brig, the Charles Doggett, in 1824, he said: "I name thee Old Glory." But his daughter, who presented the flag to the Smithsonian Institution, said he named it at his 21st birthday celebration Mar. 17, 1824, when his mother presented the homemade flag to him.

The Betsy Ross Legend — The widely publicized legend that Mrs. Betsy Ross made the first Stars and Stripes in June 1776, at the request of a committee composed of George Washington, Robert Morris, and George Ross, an uncle, was first made public in 1870, by a grandson of Mrs. Ross. Historians have been unable to find a historical record of such a meeting or committee.

Adding New Stars

The flag of 1777 was used until 1795. Then, on the admission of Vermont and Kentucky to the Union, Congress passed and Pres. Washington signed an act that after May 1, 1795, the flag should have 15 stripes, alternate red and white, and 15 white stars on a blue field in the union.

When new states were admitted it became evident that the flag would become burdened with stripes. Congress thereupon ordered that after July 4, 1818, the flag should have 13 stripes, symbolizing the 13 original states; that the union have 20 stars, and that whenever a new state was admitted a new star should be added on the July 4 following admission. No law designates the permanent arrangement of the stars. However, since 1912 when a new state has been admitted, the new design has been announced by executive order. No star is specifically identified with any state.

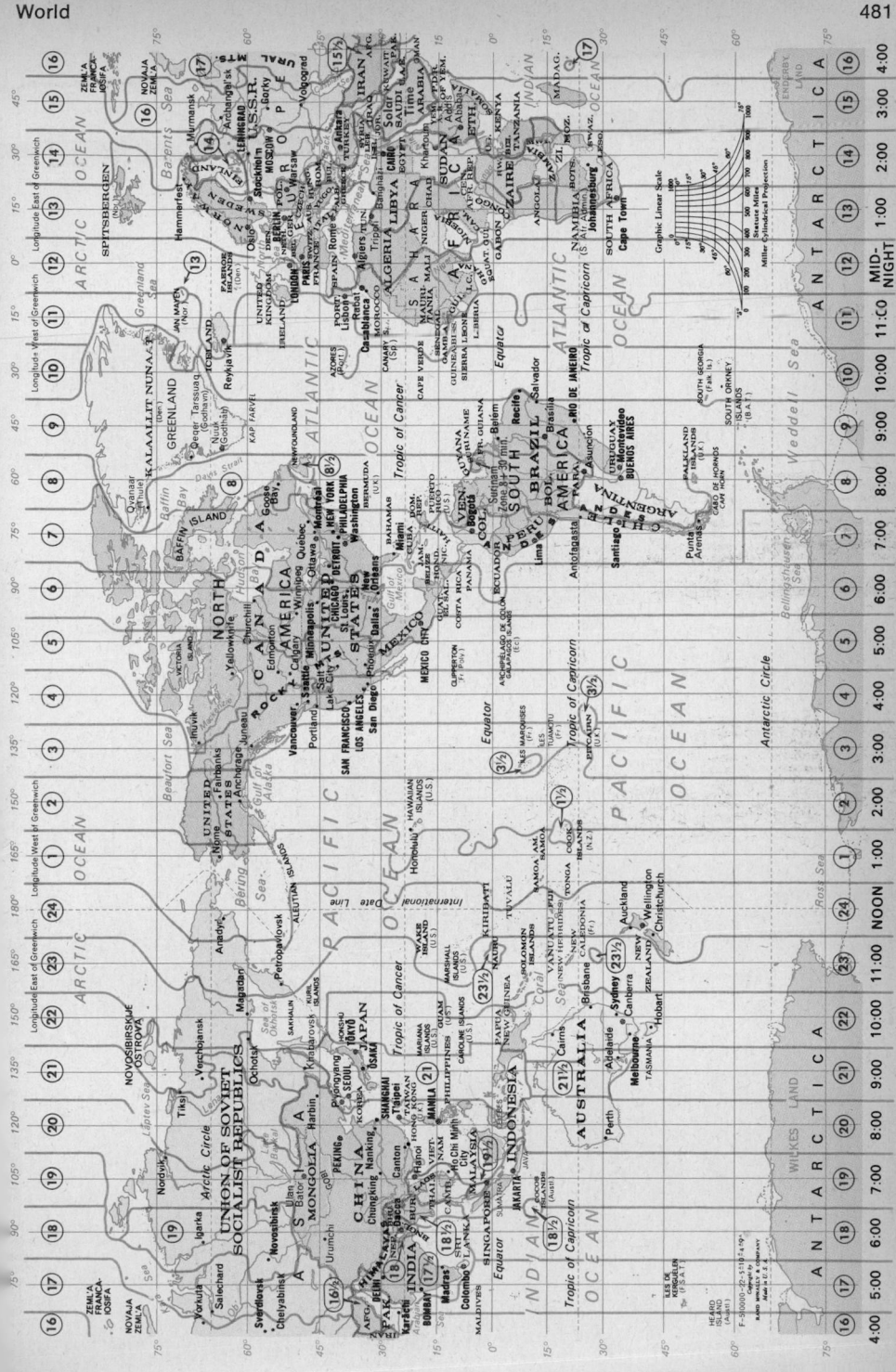

Map of Asia, with portions of Europe and Africa.

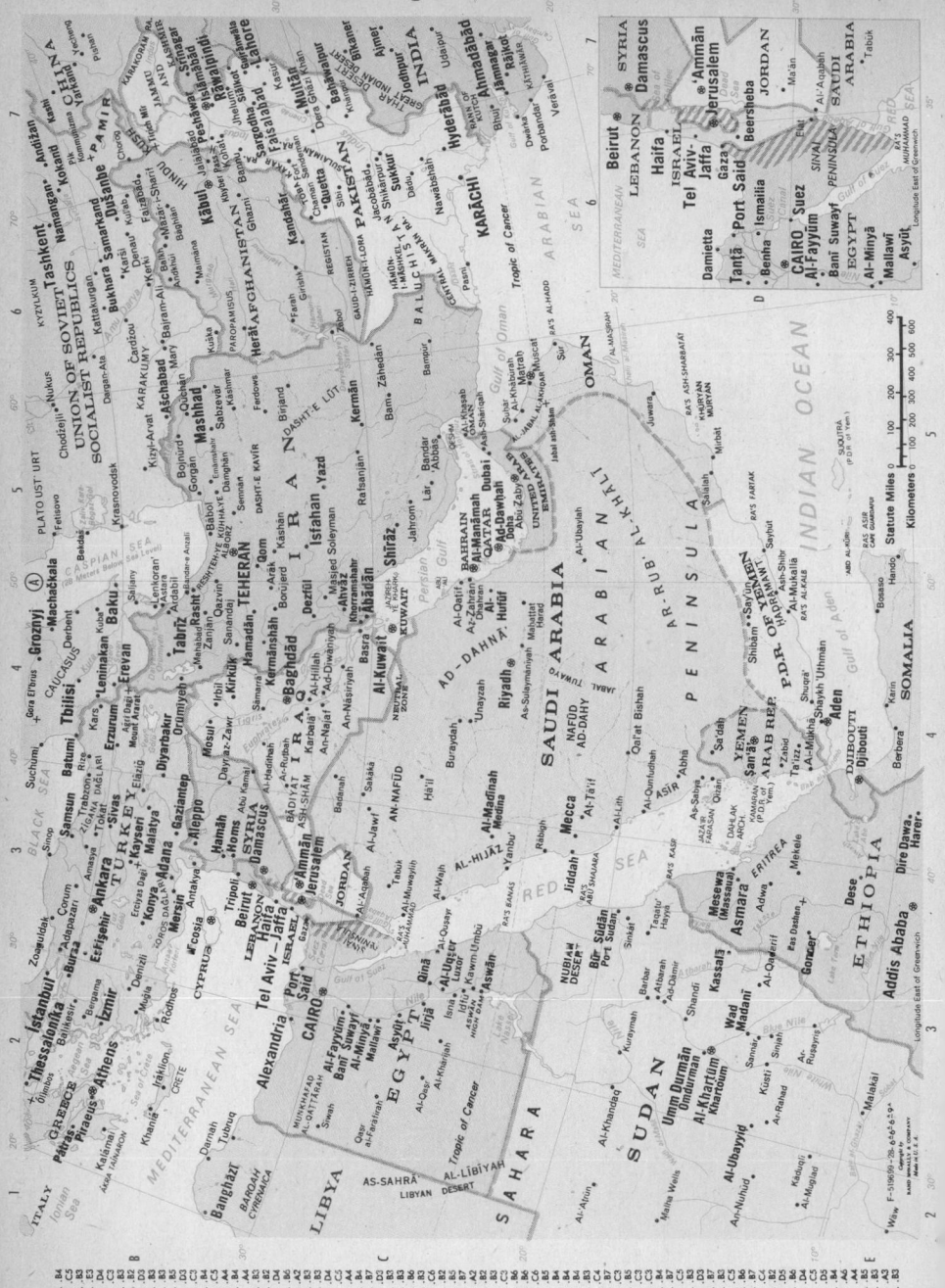

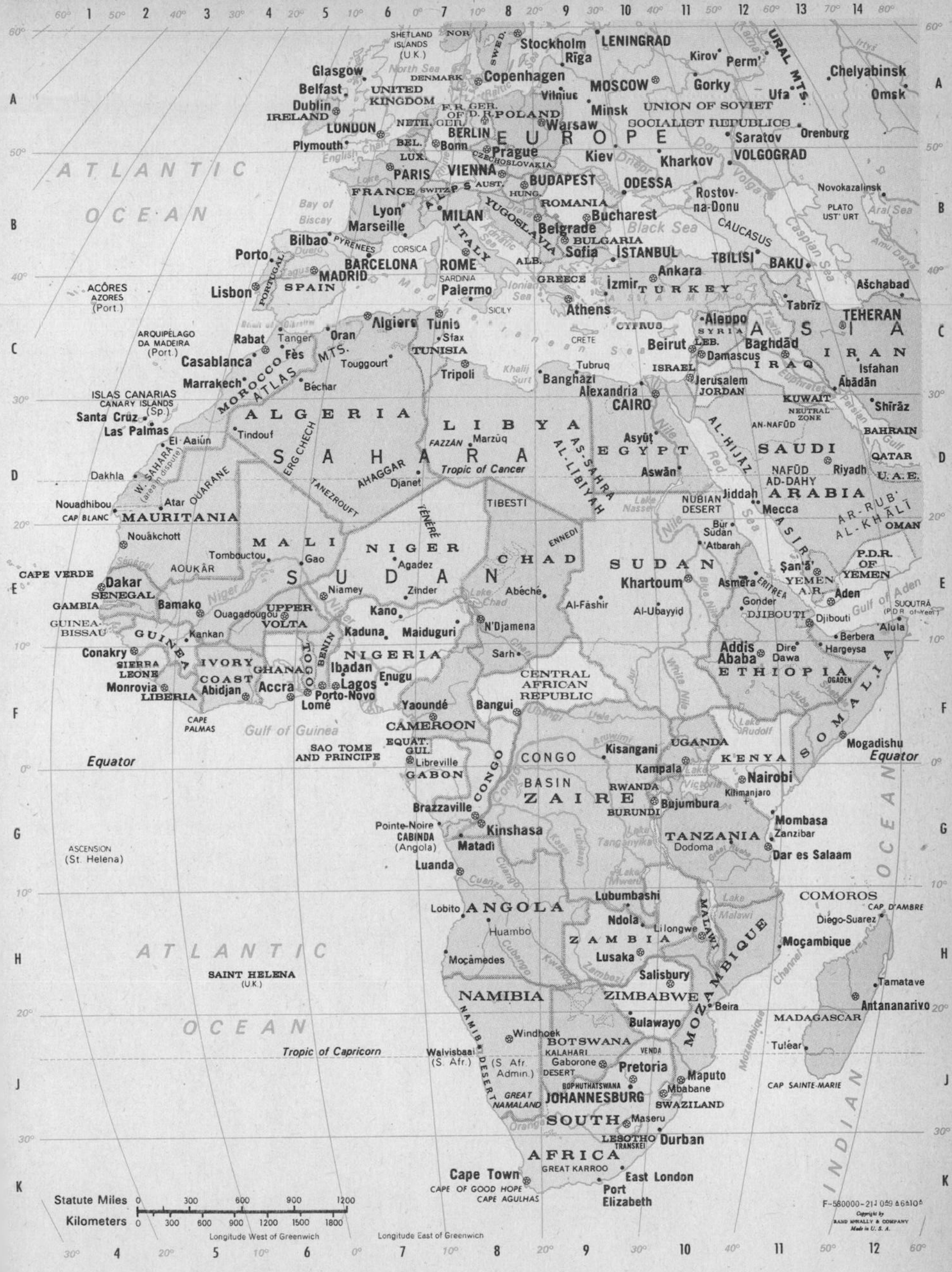

Map of Africa with major cities, countries, and geographic features including the Atlantic Ocean, Indian Ocean, Mediterranean Sea, Sahara, Sudan, the Equator, Tropic of Cancer, and Tropic of Capricorn.

Scale:
Statute Miles 0 300 600 900 1200
Kilometers 0 300 600 900 1200 1500 1800

Longitude West of Greenwich — Longitude East of Greenwich

F-580000-217 089 AGA1Q5
Copyright by
RAND McNALLY & COMPANY
Made in U. S. A.

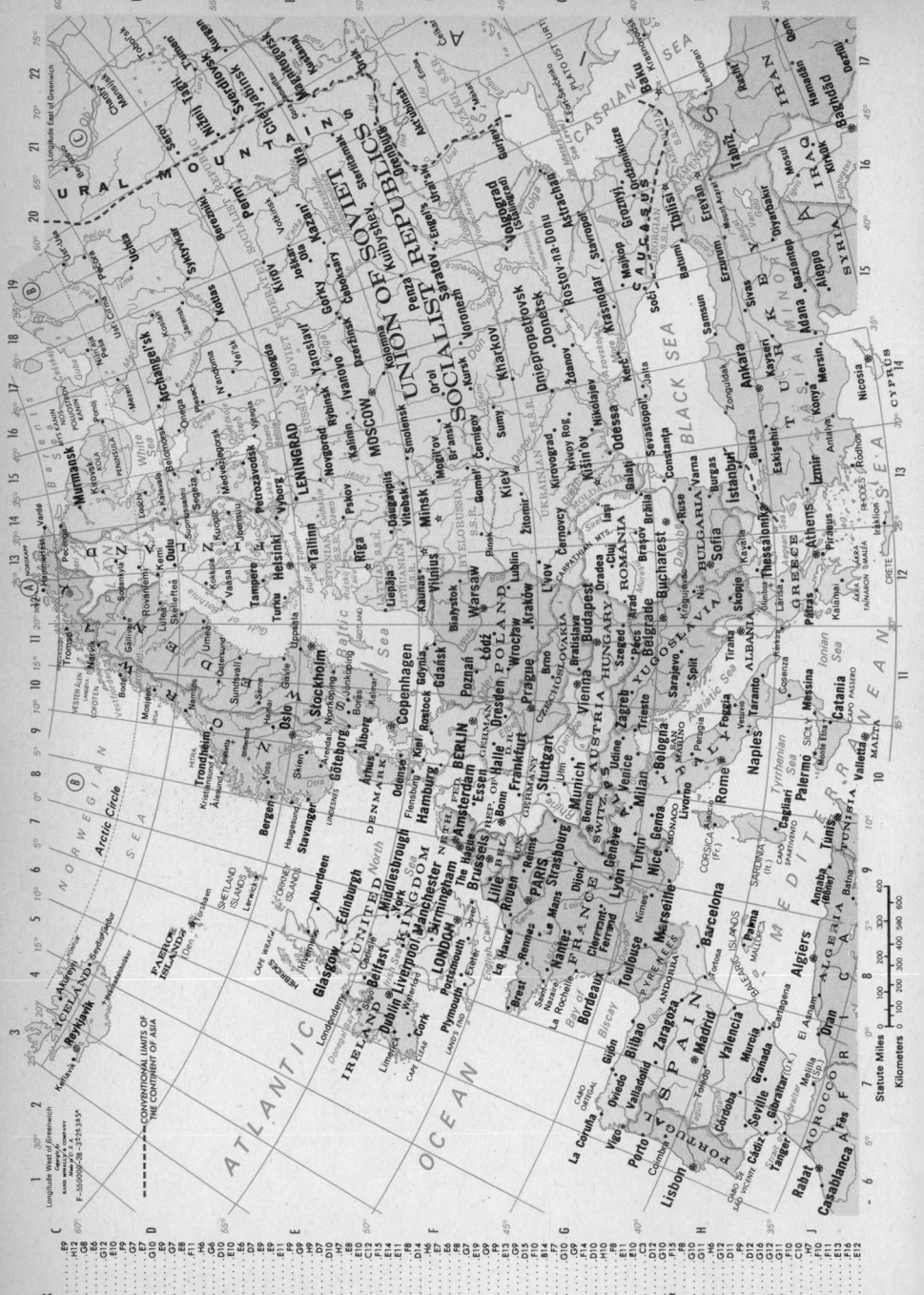

INDEX

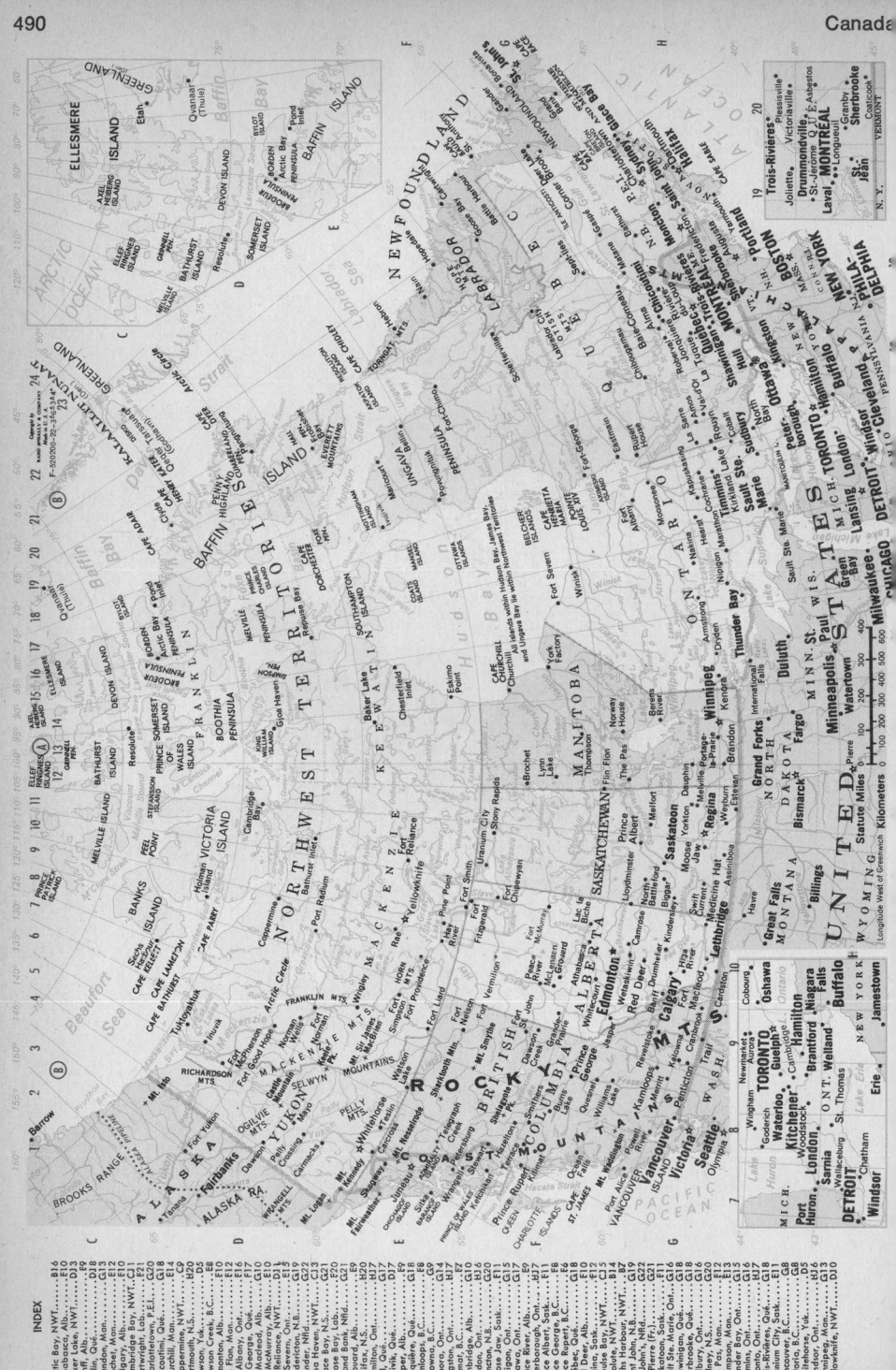

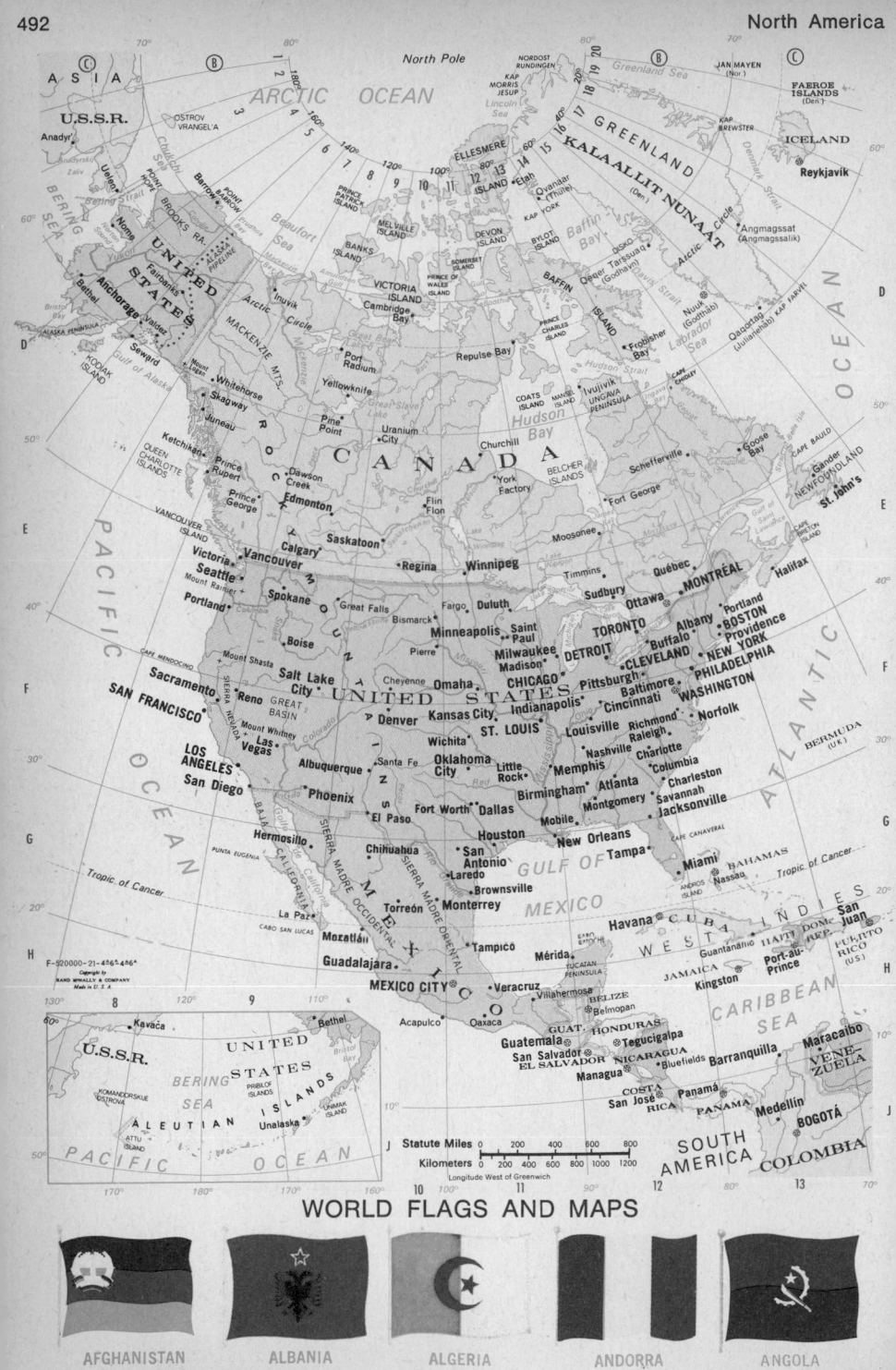

North Pole

ARCTIC OCEAN

ASIA
U.S.S.R.
Anadyr'

BERING SEA

GREENLAND
KALAALLIT NUNAAT (Den.)

Greenland Sea
JAN MAYEN (Nor.)
FAEROE ISLANDS (Den.)
ICELAND
Reykjavik

Barrow
UNITED STATES
Anchorage
Seward
Valdez
KODIAK ISLAND
ALASKA PENINSULA

Whitehorse
Skagway
Juneau
Ketchikan
Prince Rupert

CANADA

ELLESMERE ISLAND
Elah
Qaanaaq (Thule)
KAP YORK

BAFFIN BAY
Baffin Island

Labrador Sea

Inuvik
MACKENZIE MTS.
Yellowknife

Port Radium
Uranium City
Great Slave Lake

Churchill
York Factory

Hudson Bay

Nuuk (Godthåb)
Qaqortoq (Julianehåb)
Angmagssat (Angmagssalik)

NEWFOUNDLAND
St. John's
Gander
CAPE BAULD

PACIFIC OCEAN

Vancouver
Victoria
Seattle
Portland

Calgary
Saskatoon
Regina
Winnipeg

Edmonton
Prince George
Dawson Creek

Timmins
Sudbury
Ottawa
MONTRÉAL
Québec
Halifax

ATLANTIC OCEAN

Sacramento
SAN FRANCISCO
LOS ANGELES
San Diego

Salt Lake City
Reno
Las Vegas
GREAT BASIN

UNITED STATES

Spokane
Boise
Great Falls
Bismarck
Fargo
Pierre
Cheyenne
Denver

Minneapolis
Saint Paul
Madison
Milwaukee
CHICAGO
Omaha
Kansas City
Wichita

Duluth
TORONTO
DETROIT
CLEVELAND
Buffalo
Pittsburgh
Cincinnati
Indianapolis
ST. LOUIS
Louisville

Albany
BOSTON
Providence
NEW YORK
PHILADELPHIA
WASHINGTON
Baltimore
Richmond
Raleigh
Norfolk

BERMUDA (U.K.)

Phoenix
Albuquerque
Santa Fe
Oklahoma City
Little Rock
Memphis
Nashville
Charlotte
Columbia
Charleston

El Paso
Fort Worth
Dallas
Birmingham
Atlanta
Montgomery
Savannah
Jacksonville

Chihuahua
San Antonio
Laredo
Houston
New Orleans
Mobile
Tampa
Miami

BAHAMAS
Nassau

Hermosillo
Monterrey
Torreón
Brownsville

GULF OF MEXICO

La Paz
Mazatlán
Tampico
Mérida
YUCATAN PENINSULA

Havana
CUBA
HAITI
DOMINICAN REP.
San Juan
PUERTO RICO (U.S.)
JAMAICA
Kingston

WEST INDIES

CARIBBEAN SEA

Guadalajara
MEXICO CITY
Veracruz
Villahermosa
Acapulco
Oaxaca

BELIZE
Belmopan
GUATEMALA
Guatemala
San Salvador
EL SALVADOR
HONDURAS
Tegucigalpa
NICARAGUA
Managua
Bluefields
COSTA RICA
San José
PANAMA
Panama

Barranquilla
Maracaibo
VENEZUELA
Medellín
BOGOTÁ
COLOMBIA

SOUTH AMERICA

Tropic of Cancer

Statute Miles 0 200 400 600 800
Kilometers 0 200 400 600 800 1000 1200
Longitude West of Greenwich

U.S.S.R.
BERING SEA
UNITED STATES
ALEUTIAN ISLANDS
PACIFIC OCEAN
Kavaca
Bethel
Unalaska

WORLD FLAGS AND MAPS

AFGHANISTAN   ALBANIA   ALGERIA   ANDORRA   ANGOLA

Flags shown are *national* flags in common use and vary slightly from official *state* flags, most particularly by omitting coats of arms in some cases.

493

ARGENTINA

AUSTRALIA

AUSTRIA

BAHAMAS

BAHRAIN

BANGLADESH

BARBADOS

BELGIUM

BENIN

BHUTAN

BOLIVIA

BOTSWANA

BRAZIL

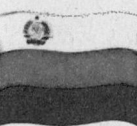
BULGARIA

BURMA

BURUNDI

CAMBODIA

CAMEROON

CANADA

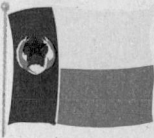
CAPE VERDE

CENTRAL AFRICAN
REPUBLIC

CHAD

CHILE

CHINA (MAINLAND)

CHINA (TAIWAN)

COLOMBIA

COMOROS

CONGO

COSTA RICA

CUBA

CYPRUS

CZECHOSLOVAKIA

DENMARK

DJIBOUTI

DOMINICA

MINICAN REPUBLIC

ECUADOR

EGYPT

EL SALVADOR

EQUATORIAL GUINEA

ETHIOPIA	FIJI	FINLAND	FRANCE	GABON
GAMBIA	GERMAN DEM. REP.	GERMANY, FED. REP. OF	GHANA	GREECE
GRENADA	GUATEMALA	GUINEA	GUINEA-BISSAU	GUYANA
HAITI	HONDURAS	HUNGARY	ICELAND	INDIA
INDONESIA	IRAN	IRAQ	IRELAND	ISRAEL
ITALY	IVORY COAST	JAMAICA	JAPAN	JORDAN
KENYA	KIRIBATI	KOREA, NORTH	KOREA, SOUTH	KUWAIT
LAOS	LEBANON	LESOTHO	LIBERIA	LIBYA

 LIECHTENSTEIN
 LUXEMBOURG
 MADAGASCAR
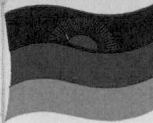 MALAWI
 MALAYSIA

 MALDIVES
 MALI
 MALTA
 MAURITANIA
 MAURITIUS

 MEXICO
 MONACO
 MONGOLIA
 MOROCCO
 MOZAMBIQUE

 NAURU
 NEPAL
 NETHERLANDS
 NEW ZEALAND
 NICARAGUA

 NIGER
 NIGERIA
 NORWAY
 OMAN
 PAKISTAN

 PANAMA
 PAPUA NEW GUINEA
 PARAGUAY
 PERU
 PHILIPPINES

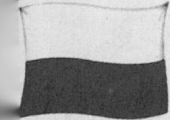 POLAND
 PORTUGAL
 QATAR
 ROMANIA
 RWANDA

 SAINT LUCIA
 ST. VINCENT/ GRENADINES
 SAMOA
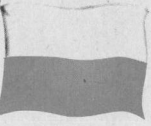 SAN MARINO
 SAO TOME & PRINCIPE

SAUDI ARABIA	 SENEGAL	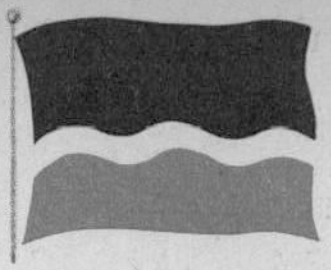 SEYCHELLES	 SIERRA LEONE	 SINGAPORE
 SOLOMON ISLANDS	 SOMALIA	 SOUTH AFRICA	 SPAIN	 SRI LANKA
 SUDAN	 SURINAME	 SWAZILAND	 SWEDEN	 SWITZERLAND
 SYRIA	 TANZANIA	 THAILAND	 TOGO	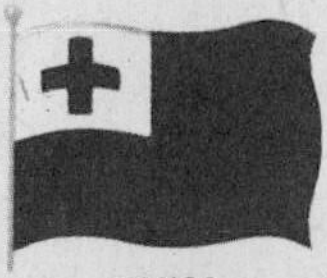 TONGA
 TRINIDAD & TOBAGO	 TUNISIA	 TURKEY	 TUVALU	 UGANDA
 U.S.S.R.	 UNITED ARAB EMIRATES	 UNITED KINGDOM	 UNITED STATES	 UPPER VOLTA
 URUGUAY	 VATICAN CITY	 VENEZUELA	 VIETNAM	 YEMEN

YEMEN, P.D.R. OF	YUGOSLAVIA	ZAIRE	ZAMBIA	ZIMBABWE

CANADA

See Index for Calgary, Edmonton, Halifax, Hamilton, Kitchener-Waterloo, Lethbridge, Montreal, Ottawa, Quebec, Regina, Saskatoon, Toronto, Vancouver, Windsor, Winnipeg.

Capital: Ottawa. Area: 3,849,670 sq. mi. Population (Govt. est., Jan. 1981): 24,088,700. Monetary unit: Canadian dollar.

The Land

The world's second largest country in land size, Canada stretches 3,223 miles from east to west and extends southward from the North Pole to the U.S. border. Its seacoast includes 36,356 miles of mainland and 115,133 miles of islands, including the Arctic islands almost from Greenland to near the Alaskan border.

Canada's continental climate, while generally temperate, varies from freezing winter cold to blistering summer heat - a range beyond 100 degrees Fahrenheit.

Major cities, industrial centres, agricultural regions, and the vast majority of the population are situated along a thin, southern fringe bordering the United States. To the north lie vast expanses of varied, virgin land. The remote north, due to extreme cold, is virtually uninhabitable.

Fragmented by history, geography, and economic factors, the country is as diverse as it is large. Regionally, Canada's 10 provinces can be put into 5 groups: the industrially-poor Atlantic Provinces of New Brunswick, Newfoundland, Nova Scotia, and Prince Edward Island; predominantly French-speaking Quebec; Ontario, financial and governmental heartland of the nation; the Prairies, including Manitoba, Saskatchewan, and oil-rich Alberta; and British Columbia, separated from the rest of the country by the Rocky Mountains.

Despite continuing problems of regional disparity in political, economic, and cultural outlook, Canada has survived as a nation by accepting the need to recognize and tolerate differences. Unlike the U.S., Canada has never been a melting pot, nor has it strived to become one.

History

French explorer Jacques Cartier, who discovered the Gulf of St. Lawrence in 1534, is generally regarded as the founder of Canada. But English seaman John Cabot sighted Newfoundland 37 years earlier, in 1497, and Vikings are believed to have reached the Atlantic coast centuries before either explorer.

Canadian settlement was pioneered by the French who established Quebec City (1608) and Montreal (1642) and declared New France a colony in 1663.

Britain, as part of its American expansion, acquired Acadia (later Nova Scotia) in 1717 and, through military victory over French forces in Canada (an extension of a European conflict between the 2 powers), captured Quebec (1759) and obtained control of the rest of New France in 1763. The French, through the Quebec Act of 1774, retained the rights to their own language, religion, and civil law.

The British presence in Canada increased during the American Revolution when many colonials, proudly calling themselves United Empire Loyalists, moved north to Canada.

Fur traders and explorers led Canadians westward across the continent. Sir Alexander Mackenzie reached the Pacific in 1793 and scrawled on a rock by the ocean, "from Canada by land."

In Upper and Lower Canada (later called Ontario and Quebec) and in the Maritimes, legislative assemblies appeared in the 18th century and reformers called for responsible government. But the War of 1812 intervened. The war, a conflict between Great Britain and the United States fought mainly in Upper Canada, ended in a stalemate in 1814.

In 1837 political agitation for more democratic government culminated in rebellions in Upper and Lower Canada. Britain sent Lord Durham to investigate and, in a famous report (1839), he recommended union of the 2 parts into one colony called Canada. The union lasted until Confederation, July 1, 1867, when proclamation of the British North America (BNA) Act launched the Dominion of Canada, consisting of Ontario, Quebec, and the former colonies of Nova Scotia and New Brunswick.

Since 1840 the Canadian colonies had held the right to internal self-government. The BNA act, which became the country's written constitution, established a federal system of government on the model of a British parliament and cabinet structure under the crown. Canada was proclaimed a self-governing Dominion within the British Empire in 1931. Empire has given way to Commonwealth, of which Canada is an independent member.

The Government

Canada is a constitutional monarchy with a parliamentary system of government. It is also a federal state. Official head of state remains England's Queen Elizabeth, represented by a resident governor-general. But in practice the nation is governed by the Prime Minister, leader of the party able to command the support of a majority of members of the House of Commons, dominant chamber of Canada's bicameral Parliament.

The Commons' 282 members are elected at least every 5 years - sooner if the Prime Minister so chooses or if the government is defeated in Parliament. This can occur either through passage of a motion of nonconfidence in the government or by defeat of a major piece of government legislation.

The upper house of Canada's Parliament is the Senate, comprised of 104 members traditionally appointed by party patronage and serving to age 75.

Legislation becomes law by receiving 3 "readings" in the Commons, passing in the Senate and obtaining assent from the governor-general. The latter 2 steps are, in practice, mere formality.

The Prime Minister heads the executive branch of government composed of the cabinet and governor-general. The cabinet is chosen by the Prime Minister, almost always from among members of his party holding seats in the House of Commons.

Provincial governments follow a modified version of the Ottawa pattern, with a unicameral legislature and an executive head usually referred to as the Premier.

Politics

Continued disagreement between the federal and provincial governments has dominated Canadian politics in recent years. A succession of federal-provincial conferences held to resolve differences on such matters as ownership of resources and the "patriation" (bringing home from Britain) of Canada's constitution—the outmoded British North America Act—have failed to make any progress. After a September 1980 conference involving Prime Minister Pierre Trudeau and the 10 provincial premiers failed to achieve consensus on any one of a dozen issues, the Trudeau government announced its intention to move ahead with constitutional reform without provincial support. Trudeau's plan to patriate the constitution with an amending formula and a new charter of rights was opposed by 8 of the 10 provinces (all except Ontario and New Brunswick) which challenged the federal government action before the Supreme Court of Canada. The Court had not yet made a ruling by midsummer of 1981.

The increased political fragmentation of Canada is reflected in the results of the 1980 federal election in which the voting was split along regional and linguistic lines. The Liberal Party, with Trudeau as leader, formed a majority government by capturing 74 of 75 seats in predominantly French-speaking Quebec but won only 2 of 80 seats west of Ontario. The Progressive Conservative Party, led by Joe Clark, won only one seat in Quebec but 51 in western Canada—an area of increasing political importance because of the westward shift of economic power, especially to oil-rich Alberta. The election results and voting pattern increased the alienation that some western Canadians feel toward the central government.

Despite repeated negotiations during 1980 and the first half of 1981, Alberta and Ottawa were unable to reach agreement on an oil pricing policy. Alberta wants higher prices for the oil it produces and sells within Canada; Ottawa has agreed to edge closer to the world price, but not as quickly as Alberta would like. The world price is more than double the domestic price of Canadian oil. Ottawa's policy is to provide a single low (by world standards) price for oil in all provinces by subsidizing the cost of imported oil to refineries in Quebec and the Maritime provinces. In the spring of 1981, Alberta protested the existing pricing arrangement by cutting back oil production—forcing Canada to import more expensive foreign oil at an added cost of about $1.5 million daily. The federal government passed this cost on to the consumer through an increased tax on gasoline and heating oil.

In Quebec, the separatist Parti Quebecois was returned to power by a wide margin in April 1981. The PQ won 82 of 124 seats—bouncing back from a political setback a year earlier when 60% of the Quebec electorate voted against giving the PQ government of Premier Rene Levesque a mandate to negotiate "sovereignty association"—a watered down form of independence by which the province would retain economic links with Canada. During the 1981 campaign and again after victory, Levesque promised not to hold another separatist referendum during the PQ's present term which could last until 1986. But Levesque stated at a party meeting in June of 1981 that independence is still the PQ's "fundamental goal" for the future.

The Economy

The Canadian economy was plagued by combined problems of high inflation, a devalued currency, and slow growth through the first half of 1981.

Inflation, as measured by the Consumer Price Index, reached 12.8% in June—the highest in more than 30 years. Interest rates topped 20% in midsummer, following the lead set by the U.S. tight money policy. Canada must stay close to U.S. interest rates or face a strongly devalued dollar as investors transfer funds south of the border. A devalued currency, the government believes, fuels inflation by increasing the cost of imported goods.

Despite the Bank of Canada's efforts to prop up the Canadian dollar, it dropped to a 48-year low of less than .82 U.S. (although it rose during the first half of 1981 in relation to most world currencies). The dollar's poor performance reflected investors' concern over the lack of an oil pricing agreement between the federal government and Alberta, high inflation, the transfer of funds out of the country by Canadian firms purchasing foreign oil companies, and a sluggish economy.

Real growth in the Gross National Product (a measure of all goods and services produced in the country and considered the best barometer of economic activity) was zero in

1980—down from 2.9% in 1979. During the first quarter of 1981 the GNP rose by 1%.

Principal Canadian industries are motor vehicle manufacturing, petroleum refining, pulp and paper production, slaughtering and meat processing, iron and steel production, the manufacture of miscellaneous machinery and equipment, saw and planing mill industries, and smelting and refining.

In Canada, an historical tradition of state aid necessitated by a harsh climate and sparse population has fostered development of a mixed economic system in which publicly-owned corporations exist alongside—and sometimes compete with—private enterprise. Most hydroelectric and many transportation and communication enterprises are government-owned. Air Canada and the Canadian National Railways, both large federal crown corporations, compete with the privately-owned Canadian Pacific Ltd. whose 1980 operating revenue was the largest of any company in Canada.

Foreign Policy

Canada's major foreign ally and trading partner remains the United States with whom she shares a broad range of mutually beneficial ties. Canada supported U.S. actions to protest the Soviet invasion of Afghanistan. In 1980, the friendship between the 2 nations was highlighted by the Canadian rescue of 6 U.S. embassy personnel in Iran. U.S. President Ronald Reagan met with Prime Minister Pierre Trudeau in Ottawa in March 1981—Reagan's first state visit after taking office.

At the same time, Canada-U.S. relations have been strained by prolonged maritime boundary and fish catch quota disputes, concern over "acid rain" pollution of Canadian lakes from U.S. industrial emissions, and U.S. annoyance at Canadian government encouragement of the purchase by Canadian firms of foreign oil companies operating in Canada. In March 1981, Reagan withdrew from the U.S. Senate an East Coast fisheries treaty agreed to by both nations in 1979 but never ratified by the Senate foreign relations committee. The unilateral U.S. move was described by Canadian External Affairs Minister Mark MacGuigan as "disturbing, distressing, and profoundly disappointing." At the same time Reagan proposed that the maritime boundary issue, for which a tentative settlement had also been reached 2 years earlier, go to the World Court for arbitration.

A major Canadian foreign policy thrust in 1981 was the promotion of a North-South dialogue to eliminate the economic gap between the developed nations of the northern hemisphere and the under-developed ones below the Equator. In a foreign policy speech to the House of Commons in July 1981, Trudeau called for "a major assault on world poverty" in the interests of justice and world security. At a summit meeting in Ottawa a month later, leaders of the major western powers agreed to consider "global negotiations" involving poorer nations. Earlier in the year, Canada committed itself to increased foreign aid, to be directed mainly to the poorest African and South American nations.

The promotion of North-South relations is also seen by the Canadian government as a means of extending economic links and improving trade with such nations as Venezuela and Mexico—major suppliers of imported oil—as well as Brazil, Algeria, Saudi Arabia, Nigeria, and several Asian nations including China. Canadian exports to developing countries rose to 11.6% of total exports in 1980—up from 9.7% in 1979. Exports to Brazil and Mexico more than doubled.

Canada's Native Peoples

Canada's native population consists of 3 groups, the Indian, Inuit (Eskimo), and Metis. The Indian and Inuit are thought to have crossed from Asia via the Bering Sea several thousand years before the arrival of Europeans in North America. Metis are of mixed native Indian and non-Indian ancestry.

There are approximately 303,000 "status" Indians - those registered under the federal Indian Act - most of whom belong to one of 575 Indian bands. About 65% live on one of the 2,240 federal reserves or on other government lands set aside for their use. Only Newfoundland had no registered Indians. The majority (82%) live in Ontario and the 4 western provinces. In addition, there are an estimated one million non-registered Indians and Metis.

The number of Inuit (meaning "the people" in their language, Inuktitut; Eskimo is an Indian word adopted by European settlers) in Canada is approximately 23,000. More than 75% live in the Northwest Territories, the remainder in Arctic Quebec and northern Labrador.

Due to the remoteness of their settlements close to the northern coasts where sea mammals provided the chief source of food, fuel and clothing, the Inuit lifestyle was affected later and less directly than that of the Indian by the encroachment of western civilization. Many Inuit still live by their traditional skills of hunting, trapping and fishing as well as through the production and sale of artwork. But increasing numbers now find work outside their communities, particularly since the search for oil, gas and minerals has brought more jobs to the north.

Both Inuit and status Indians are entitled to/a broad range of government benefits administered through the federal Dept. of Indian and Northern Affairs as well as through provincial and territorial governments. Indian people living on reserves are eligible for direct federal assistance in such areas as education, housing, social services, and community development.

In addition, approximately half the registered Indians in Canada (mainly those living in Ontario and the 3 Prairie provinces) are entitled to payments as a result of treaties between their ancestors and the federal government during the early 19th and early 20th centuries. In remote northern areas, however, no such legal settlements were made, and recently Indian and Inuit groups have pressed claims to aboriginal rights to vast areas of land in northern British Columbia, the Yukon and Northwest Territories, and northern Quebec and Labrador.

In 1973 the federal government agreed to consider native claims. Thus far 2 settlements have been reached: In 1975 the Inuit, Cree living in northern Quebec surrendered claim to 400,000 sq. mi. in return for $225 million and a range of rights and privileges. In October, 1978, the government reached a tentative settlement with the Inuit, of the western Arctic (the Inuvialuit) providing payment of $118 million over 14 years. The agreement would also give the Inuvialuit a clear grant to 37,000 sq. mi. of land.

Inuit cultural and legal interests are represented in Ottawa by the Inuit Tapirisat (Brotherhood), founded in 1971. The National Indian Brotherhood, incorporated in 1970, performs a similar role for status Indians. The Metis and non-status Indians are represented by the Native Council of Canada.

Provinces of Canada

Alberta

People. Population (Jan. 1981: 2,135,900; **rank:** 4. **Pop. density:** 8.6 per sq. mi. **Urban** (1976) 75%. **Ethnic distrib.** (1976): English 80.7%; German 4.3%; Ukrainian 3.5%; French 2.4%. **Net migration** (1979-80) +42,597.

Geography. Total area: 255,290 sq. mi.; **rank:** 4. **Land area:** 248,800 sq. mi. **Acres forested land:** 68,341,000. **Location:** Canada's 2d most westerly province, bounded to the W by British Columbia, to the E by Saskatchewan, to the N by the Northwest Territories, and to the S by Montana. **Climate:** great variance in temperatures between regions and seasons; summer highs can range between 16°C and 32°C; winter temperatures can drop as low as −45°C; mean Jan. temperature in Edmonton is −14°C. **Topography:** ranges from the Rocky Mountains in the SW to flat prairie in the SE; the far north is a wilderness of forest and muskeg.

Economy. Principal industries: mining, oil production, agriculture, manufacturing, construction. **Principal manufactured goods:** foods and beverages, wood products, fabricated metal, transportation equipment, refined petroleum. **Value added by manufacture** (1978): $2.5 billion. **Gross Domestic Product** (1979): $33.9 billion. **Agriculture: Chief crops:** wheat, barley, rapeseed, sugar beets, flaxseed. **Livestock** (1981): 3,695,000 cattle; 1,280,000 pigs; 114,000 sheep. **Forestry production** (1978): $31.7 million. **Mineral production** (1979): total value, $12.9 billion; fuels, $12.6 billion (87% of national production of petroleum, 91% of natural gas); structural materials, $174 million. **Commercial fishing** (1978): $1.3 million. **Value of construction** (1980): $10.7 billion. **Employment distribution** (1980): 28% services; 18% trade; 10% construction; 9% manufacturing; 8% agriculture; 6% public administration. **Per capita income** (1979): $9,717. **Unemployment** (1980): 3.7%.

Finance: No. banks: 772; **No. credit unions, caisses populaires:** 302.

International airports: Edmonton, Calgary.

Federal government: No. federal employees (Dec. 1980). 29,485; **Federal payroll** (1980): $511 million.

Energy. Electricity production, by mwh, (1980): mineral, 20,210,417; hydroelectric, 1,699,250.

Education. No schools: 1,387 elementary; 166 secondary; 23 higher education. **Avg. salary, public school teachers** (1979-80): $22,208.

Provincial data. Motto: none. **Flower:** The Wild Rose.

Bird: Great horned owl. **Date entered Confederation:** 1905. **Capital:** Edmonton.

Politics. Premier: Peter Lougheed (Progressive Conservative). **Leaders, opposition parties:** Ray Speaker (Social Credit), Grant Notley (New Democratic). **Composition of legislature** (June, 1980): PC 73; SC 4; NDP 1; Independent 1. **Date of last general election:** Mar. 14, 1979.

Tourist attractions: Banff, Jasper, and Waterton Lakes national parks; resorts at Banff, Jasper and Lake Louise; spectacular skiing, hiking, trail riding and camping in the Canadian Rockies; the Badlands near Drumheller; Elk Island National Park.

British Columbia

People. Population (Jan. 1981): 2,687,000; **rank:** 3. **Pop. density:** 7.5 per sq. mi. **Urban** (1976) 76.9%. **Ethnic distrib.** (1976): English 82.6%; German 3.3%; Chinese 1.9%; French 1.6%; Italian 1.1%. **Net migration** (1979-80): +49,598.

Geography. Total area: 365,950 sq. mi.; **rank:** 3. **Land area:** 358,970 sq. mi. **Acres forested land:** 134,652,000. **Location:** bounded to the N by the Yukon and Northwest Territories, to the NW by the Alaskan panhandle, to the W by the Pacific Ocean, to the E by Alberta, and to the S by Washington, Idaho and Montana. **Climate:** maritime with mild termperatures and abundant rainfall in the coastal areas; continental climate with temperature extremes in the interior and northeast. **Topography:** mostly mountainous except for the NE corner which is an extension of the Great Plains.

Economy. Principal industries: forestry, mining, tourism, agriculture, fishing, manufacturing. **Principal manufactured goods:** wood products, paper and allied products, food and beverages, petroleum and coal products, primary metals, transportation equipment. **Value added by manufacture** (1978): $5.6 billion. **Gross Domestic Product** (1979): $32.6 billion (including GDP for Yukon and NWT). **Agriculture: Chief crops:** fruits and vegetables, barley, oats. **Livestock** (1981): 654,000 cattle; 245,000 pigs; 34,000 sheep. **Forestry production** (1978): $849.3 million. **Mineral production** (1979): total value, $2.7 billion; metals, $1.4 billion; fuels, $1 billion; structural materials, $185 million. **Commercial fishing** (1978): $252.2 million. **Value of construction** (1980):

$6.6 billion. **Employment distribution** (1980): 31% services; 19% trade; 15% manufacturing; 7% construction; 7% public administration; 1.9% agriculture. **Per capita income** (1979): $9,821. **Unemployment** (1980): 6.8%.
Finance: No. banks: 855; **No. credit unions, caisses populaires:** 335.
International airports: Vancouver, Victoria.
Federal government: No. federal employees (Dec. 1980). 42,898. **Federal payroll** (1980): $751 million.
Energy. Electricity production, by mwh, (1980): mineral, 738,959, hydroelectric, 29,726,684.
Education. No schools: 1,540 elementary; 330 secondary; 26 higher education. **Avg. salary, public school teachers** (1979-80): $21,765.
Provincial data. Motto: Splendor Sine Occasu (Spendor Without Diminishment). **Flower:** Dogwood. **Bird:** None. **Date entered Confederation:** 1871. **Capital:** Victoria.
Politics. Premier: William R. Bennett (Social Credit).
Leaders, opposition parties: Dave Barrett (New Democratic), Shirley McLoughlin (Liberal), Brian Westwood (Progressive Conservative). **Composition of legislature** (June 1981): SC 31; NDP 26. **Date of last general election:** May 10, 1979.

Tourist attractions. Victoria: Butchart Gardens, Crystal Garden, Provincial Museum; Vancouver: Stanley Park Zoo, Capilano Canyon, Gastown, Public Aquarium, Grouse Mountain, Planetarium; also Pacific Rim National Park, the Gulf Islands, Okanagan Valley, Yellowhead Highway, Totem Triangle Tour.

Manitoba

People. Population (Jan. 1981): 1,027,000; **rank:** 5. **Pop. density:** 4.8 per sq. mi. **Urban** (1976) 69.9%. **Ethnic distrib.** (1976): English 71.2%; German 7.2%; Ukrainian 5.9%; French 5.4%; Native Indians 2.4%. **Net migration** (1979-80): —11,016.
Geography. Total area: 250,950 sq. mi.; **rank:** 6. **Land area:** 211,720 sq. mi. **Acres forested land:** 33,476,000.
Location: bounded to the N by the Northwest Territories, to the S by Minnesota and North Dakota, to the E by Ontario and Hudson Bay, to the W by Saskatchewan. **Climate:** continental, with seasonal extremes: Winnipeg avg. Jan. low —23°C, avg. July high 26°C. **Topography:** the land rises gradually S and W from Hudson Bay; most of the province is between 500 and 1,000 feet above sea level.
Economy. Principal industries: manufacturing, agriculture, slaughtering and meat processing, mining. **Principal manufactured goods:** agricultural implements, processed food, machinery, transportation equipment, clothing. **Value added by manufacture** (1978): $1.3 billion. **Gross Domestic Product** (1979): $10.2 billion. **Agriculture:** Chief crops: cereal grains, mustard seed, sunflower seeds, rape, flax. **Livestock** (1981): 1,060,000 cattle; 826,300 pigs; 13,400 sheep; **Forestry production** (1978): $15.6 million. **Mineral production** (1979): total value, $653 million; metals, $510 million; structural materials, $86 million; fuels, $48 million. **Commercial fishing:** (1978) $10.5 million. **Value of construction** (1980): $1.5 billion. **Employment distribution** (1980): 29% services; 17% trade; 14% manufacturing; 9% agriculture; 7% public administration; 5% construction. **Per capita income** (1979): $8,198. **Unemployment** (1980): 5.5%
Finance: No. banks: 362; **No. credit unions, caisses populaires:** 213.
International airports: Winnipeg.
Federal Government: No. federal employees (Dec. 1980): 19,366. **Federal payroll** (1980): $347 million.
Energy. Electricity production, by mwh, (1980): mineral, 279,105; hydroelectric, 19,095,643.
Education. No. schools: 701 elementary; 117 secondary; 14 higher education. **Avg. salary, public school teachers** (1979-80): $20,855.
Provincial data. Motto: None. **Flower:** Prairie crocus. **Bird:** none. **Date entered Confederation:** July 15, 1870. **Capital:** Winnipeg.
Politics. Premier: Sterling Lyon (Progressive Conservative). **Leaders, opposition parties:** Howard Pawley

(New Democratic). Sidney Green (Progressive); Doug Lauchlan (Liberal). **Composition of legislature:** (June 1981): PC 33; NDP 20; Prog. 3; Lib. 1. **Date of last general election:** Sept. 11, 1977.

Tourist attractions. Museum of Man and Nature (Winnipeg), Lower Fort Garry (near Lockport), Red River cruises, Riding Mountain National Park, canoeing, fishing and camping on northern lakes.

New Brunswick

People. Population (Jan. 1981): 709,100; **rank:** 8. **Pop. density:** 25.5 per sq. mi. **Urban** (1976) 52.3%. **Ethnic distrib.** (1976): English 64.4%; French 33%. **Net migration** (1979-80): +908.
Geography. Total area: 28,360 sq. mi.; **rank:** 8. **Land area:** 27,840 sq. mi. **Acres forested land:** 15,594,000.
Location: bounded by Quebec to the N, Nova Scotia and the Bay of Fundy to the S, the Gulf of St. Lawrence and Northumberland Strait to the E, and Maine to the W. **Climate:** humid continental climate except along the shores where there is a marked maritime effect; avg. Jan. low in Fredericton is —14°C, avg. July high 22°C. **Topography:** upland, lowland and plateau regions throughout the province.
Economy. Principal industries: manufacturing, mining, forestry, pulp and paper. **Principal manufactured goods:** paper and allied products, wood products, fish products, semi-processed mineral products. **Value added by manufacture** (1978): $782.6 million. **Gross Domestic Product** (1979): $4.9 billion. **Agriculture:** Chief crops: potatoes, apples, blueberries, oats. **Livestock** (1981): 103,000 cattle; 61,000 pigs; 8,700 sheep. **Forestry production** (1978): $88 million. **Mineral production** (1979): total value, $480 million; metals, $419 million; structural materials, $39 million; fuels, $10 million. **Commercial fishing** (1978): $50 million. **Value of construction** (1980): $1.03 billion. **Employment distribution** (1980): 29% services; 18% trade; 15% manufacturing; 8% public administration; 8% construction; 2.4% agriculture. **Per capita income** (1979): $6,472. **Unemployment** (1980) 11.1%.
Finance: No. banks: 247; **No. credit unions, caisses populaires:** 124.
International airports: none.
Federal Government: No. federal employees (Dec. 1980): 14,217. **Federal payroll** (1980): $246.7 million.
Energy. Electricity production, by mwh, (1980): mineral, 5,960,554; hydroelectric, 2,592,528.
Education. No. schools: 418 elementary; 65 secondary; 13 higher education. **Avg. salary, public school teachers** (1979-80): $18,004.
Provincial Data. Motto: Spem Reduxit (Hope Restored). **Flower:** Purple violet. **Bird:** none. **Date entered Confederation:** 1867. **Capital:** Fredericton.
Politics. Premier: Richard Hatfield (Progressive Conservative). **Leaders, opposition parties:** Joseph Daigle (Liberal). **Composition of legislature** (June, 1981): P.C. 30; Lib. 27; 1 independent. **Date of last general election:** Oct. 23, 1978.

Tourist attractions: Roosevelt-Campobello International Memorial Park; the tidal bore at Chignacto Bay (Moncton); Magnetic Hill (Moncton); sport salmon fishing in the Miramichi River; 108 covered bridges including the world's longest at Hartland.

Newfoundland

People. Population (Jan. 1981): 583,600; **rank:** 9. **Pop. density:** 4 per sq. mi. **Urban** (1976) 58.9%. **Ethnic distrib.** (1976): English 98%. **Net migration** (1979-80): —1,358.
Geography. Total area: 156,650 sq. mi.; **rank:** 7. **Land area:** 143,510 sq. mi. **Acres forested land:** 31,504,000.
Location: 2 parts: a 43,010 sq. mi. Atlantic island and 100,500 sq. mi. mainland Labrador, bordered to the E by northern Quebec and to the W by the Atlantic Ocean. **Climate:** ranges from subarctic in Labrador and northern tip

of island to humid continental with cool summers and heavy precipitation. **Topography:** highlands of the Long Range (max. elev. 2,673 ft.) along the western coast; central plateau contains uplands descending to lowlands towards the northeast; interior barren and rocky with many lakes and bogs; Labrador is part of the Canadian Shield.

Economy. Principal industries: mining, manufacturing, fishing, pulp and paper, electricity production. **Principal manufactured goods:** fish products, paper products. **Value added by manufacture** (1978): $394.8 million. **Gross Domestic Product** (1979): $3.6 billion. **Agriculture:** Forestry production (1978): $37 million. **Mineral production** (1979): total value, $1.1 billion; metals, $1 billion; asbestos, $36 million; structural materials, $26 million. **Commercial fishing:** (1978): $118 million. **Value of construction** (1980): $831.9 million. **Employment distribution** (1980): 27% services; 17% trade; 15% manufacturing; 8.5% construction; 8.5% public administration. **Per capita income** (1979): $5,862. **Unemployment** (1980): 13.5%.

Finance: No. banks: 151; **no. credit unions, caisses populaires:** 17.

International airports: Gander.

Federal Government: No. federal employees (Dec. 1980): 8,601. **Federal payroll** (1980): $146.3 million.

Energy. Electricity production, by mwh, (1980): mineral, 1,358,602; hydroelectric, 44,375,858.

Education. No. schools: 534 elementary; 141 secondary; 7 higher education. **Avg. salary, public school teachers** (1979-80): $21,409.

Provincial data. Motto: Quaerite prime regnum Dei (Seek ye first the kingdom of God). **Flower:** Pitcher plant. **Bird:** none. **Date entered Confederation:** 1949. **Capital:** St. John's.

Politics. Premier: Brian Peckford (Progressive Conservative). **Leaders, opposition parties:** Len Stirling, (Liberal) Fonse Faour, (New Democratic). **Composition of legislature** (June, (1981): PC 33: Lib. 19; **Date of last general election:** June 18, 1979.

Tourist attractions: numerous picturesque "outport" fishing villages; Signal Hill National Historical Park (St. John's); the Aviation Museum at Gander International Airport; Witless Bay Island Seabird Sanctuary.

Nova Scotia

People. Population (Jan. 1981): 856,100; **rank:** 7. **Pop. density:** 42 per sq. mi. **Urban** (1976) 55.8%. **Ethnic distrib.** (1976): English 92.7%; French 4.4%. **Net migration** (1979-80): −730.

Geography. Total area: 21,420 sq. mi.; **rank:** 9. **Land area:** 20,400 sq. mi. **Acres forested land:** 10,762,000. **Location:** connected to New Brunswick by a 17-mi. isthmus, otherwise surrounded by water - the Gulf of St. Lawrence, Atlantic Ocean and Bay of Fundy. **Climate:** humid continental, with some moderating effects due to the province's maritime location; avg. July temperature high in Halifax is 23°C, avg. Jan. low −10°C. **Topography:** the Atlantic Uplands in the southern half of the province descend to lowlands in the northern portion; 6,479 mi. of coastline, 3,000 lakes, hundreds of rivers.

Economy. Principal industries: manufacturing, fishing, mining, tourism, agriculture, petroleum refining. **Principal manufactured goods:** paper and allied products, petroleum and coal products, fish products. **Value added by manufacture** (1978): $961.4 million. **Gross Domestic Product** (1979): $6.3 billion. **Agriculture: Chief crops:** apples, blueberrries, strawberries, oats, potatoes. **Livestock** (1981): 127,000 cattle; 110,000 pigs; 28,000 sheep. **Forestry production** (1978): $26.6 million. **Mineral production** (1979): total value, $210 million; fuels, $100 million (all from coal); structural materials, $58 million; gypsum, $26 million. **Commercial fishing** (1978): $195.4 million. **Value of construction** (1980): $602.6 million. **Employment distribution** (1980): 29% services; 19% trade; 15% manufacturing; 8% construction; 8% public administration; 2.2% agriculture. **Per capita income** (1979): $7,088. **Unemployment** (1980): 9.8%.

Finance: No. banks: 180; **No. credit unions, caisses populaires:** 138.

International airports: Halifax.

Federal Government: No. federal employees (Dec. 1980): 35,626. **Federal payroll** (1980): $621 million.

Energy. Electricity production, by mwh, (1980): mineral, 5,512,203; hydroelectric, 863,707.

Education. No. schools: 532 elementary; 78 secondary; 24 higher education. **Avg. salary, public school teachers** (1979-80): $21,496.

Provincial Data. Motto: Munit Haec et Altera Vincit (One Defends and the Other Conquers). **Flower:** Trailing arbutus. **Bird:** None. **Date entered Confederation:** 1867. **Capital:** Halifax.

Politics. Premier: John M. Buchanan (Progressive conservative). **Leaders, opposition parties:** A.M. "Sandy" Cameron (Liberal); Alexa McDonough (New Democratic). **Composition of legislature** (June, 1981): P.C. 31; Lib 15; NDP 2; 1 independent. **Date of last general election:** Sept. 19, 1978.

Tourist attractions: Cabot Trail around Cape Breton Island; Fortress Louisbourg; Peggy's Cove; Alexander Graham Bell Museum (Baddeck); the Miners' Museum (Glace Bay); Nova Scotia Museum (Halifax); Citadel Hill (Halifax).

Ontario

People. Population (Jan. 1981); 8,600,500; **rank:** 1. **Pop. density:** 25 per sq. mi. **Urban** (1976) 81.2% **Ethnic distrib.** (1976): English 78.1%; French 5.6%; Italian 4.8%; German 1.9%; Portuguese 1%. **Net migration** (1979-80) +7,349.

Geography. Total area: 412,580 sq. mi.; **rank:** 2. **Land area:** 344,090 sq. mi. **Acres forested land:** 106,806,000. **Location:** Canada's most centrally-situated province, with Quebec on the E and Manitoba to the W; extends N to shores of James and Hudson Bays; southern boundary with New York, Michigan, Minnesota, and 4 Great Lakes. **Climate:** ranges from humid continental in southern regions to subarctic in the far north, westerly winds bring winter storms; the Great Lakes moderate winter temperatures. **Topography:** 2/3 of province is Precambrian rock of the Canadian Shield; lowland areas lie along the shores of Hudson Bay, the St. Lawrence River and the southern Great Lakes region.

Economy. Principal industries: manufacturing, construction, tourism, agriculture, mining, forestry, fisheries and wildlife. **Principal manufactured goods:** motor vehicles, iron and steel, motor vehicle parts and accessories, foods and beverages, paper and allied products. **Value added by manufacture** (1978): $27.8 billion. **Gross Domestic Product** (1979): $101.6 billion. **Agriculture: Chief crops:** corn, wheat, oats, barley, soybeans, tobacco, tree fruits. **Livestock** (1981): 3,030,000 cattle; 3,155,000 pigs; 162,000 sheep. **Forestry production** (1978): $253.7 million. **Mineral production** (1979): total value, $3.3 billion; metals, $2.5 billion; structural materials, $584 million; fuels, $30 million. **Commercial fishing** (1978): $17.2 million. **Value of construction** (1980): $12.3 billion. **Employment distribution** (1980): 28% services; 25% manufacturing; 16% trade; 6% construction; 6% public administration; 3.5% agriculture. **Per capita income:** (1979): $9,608. **Unemployment** (1980): 6.9%

Finance: No. banks: 2,856; **No credit unions, caisses populaires:** 1,100

International airports: Toronto, Ottawa.

Federal Government: No. federal employees (Dec. 1980): 166,110. **Federal payroll** (1980): $3.2 billion.

Energy. Electricity production, by mwh, (1980): mineral, 31,329,854; hydroelectric, 38,388,238; nuclear, 35,879,600.

Education. No. schools: 4,389 elementary; 815 secondary; 51 higher education. **Avg. salary, public school teachers** (1979-80): $23,260.

Provincial data. Motto: Ut Incepit Fidelis Sic Permanet (Loyal she began, loyal she remains). **Flower:** White trillium. **Bird:** none. **Date entered Confederation:** 1867. **Capital:** Toronto.

Politics. Premier: William (Bill) Davis (Progressive Conservative), **Leaders, opposition parties:** Dr. Stuart Smith (Liberal) Michael Cassidy (New Democratic). **Composition of legislature** (June 1981): PC 70; Lib. 34; NDP 21. **Date of last general election:** March 19, 1981.

Tourist attractions. Toronto C.N. Tower, Ontario Science Centre, Ontario Place, Metro Toronto Zoo, McLaughlin Planetarium, Black Creek Pioneer Village, Canadian Nation Exhibition (mid Aug. to Labor Day); Ottawa's Parliament buildings; Niagara Falls; Polar Bear Express and Agawa Canyon train rides into northern Ontario.

Prince Edward Island

People. Population (Jan. 1981): 124,100; **rank:** 10. **Pop. density:** 56.9 per sq. mi. **Urban** (1976) 37.1% **Ethnic distrib.** (1976): English 92.7%; French 5.5%. **Net migration** (1979-80): +462.

Geography. Total area: 2,180 sq. mi.; **rank:** 10. **Land area:** 2,180 sq. mi. **Acres forested land:** 619,000. **Location:** an island 140 mi. long, between 40 and 140 mi. wide, situated in the Gulf of St. Lawrence approx. 10 mi. from the coasts of Nova Scotia and New Brunswick. **Climate:** humid continental with temperatures moderated by maritime location; avg. Jan. low in Charlottetown is −11°C, avg. July high 23°C. **Topography:** gently rolling hills; sharply indented coastline; many streams but only small rivers and lakes.

Economy. Principal industries: agriculture, tourism, fisheries, light manufacturing. **Principal manufactured goods:** paint, farm vehicles, metal products, electronic equipment. **Value added by manufacture** (1978): $63 million. **Gross Domestic Product** (1979): $709 million. **Agriculture: Chief crops:** potatoes, mixed grains, oats, barley. **Livestock** (1981): 99,000 cattle; 101,500 pigs; 5,000 sheep. **Mineral production** (1979): total value, $2 million, all from sand and gravel. **Commercial fishing:** (1978) $23.4 million. **Value of construction** 1980): $179.2 million. **Employment distribution** (1980): 30% services; 15% trade; 13% agriculture; 11% manufacturing; 9% public administration 7% construction. **Per capita income** (1979): $6,057. **Unemployment** (1980): 10.8%.

Finance: No. banks: 33; **No. credit unions, caisses populaires:** 13.

International airports: none.

Federal Government: No. federal employees (Dec. 1980): 2,703. **Federal payroll:** (1980): $49.3 million.

Energy. Electricity production, by mwh, (1980): mineral, 126,675.

Education. No. schools: 58 elementary; 13 secondary; 3 higher education. **Avg. salary, public school teachers** (1979-80): $20,471.

Provincial Data. Motto: Parva Sub Ingenti (The small under the protection of the large). **Flower:** Lady's slipper. **Bird:** Blue jay. **Date entered Confederation:** 1873. **Capital:** Charlottetown.

Politics. Premier: Angus MacLean (Progressive Conservative). **Leaders, opposition parties:** Gilbert Clements (Liberal), Douglas Murray (New Democratic). **Composition of legislature** (June, 1981): P.C. 21; Lib. 10; 1 vacant. **Date of last general election:** Apr. 23, 1979.

Tourist attractions: P.E.I. National Park; beaches all along the coastline; 9 golf courses; 70 campgrounds; Summerside Lobster Carnival, 3d wk. in July; Charlottetown Old Home Week, 3d wk. in Aug.; Charlottetown Confederation Centre; Woodleigh Replicas (Burlington).

Quebec

People. Population (Jan. 1981): 6,325,200; **rank:** 2. **Pop. density:** 12 per sq. mi. **Urban** (1976) 79.1%. **Ethnic distrib.** (1976): French 80%; English 12.8%; Italian 2%. **Net migration** (1979-80): −30,790. **Geography. Total area:** 594,860 sq. mi.; **rank:** 1. **Land area:** 523,860 sq. mi. **Acres forested land:** 171,998,000. **Location:** borders Ontario on the W and Labrador and New Brunswick on the E; extends N to Hudson Strait and NW to James and

Hudson Bays; the southern border touches New York, Vermont, New Hampshire and Maine. **Climate:** varies from subarctic in the northern half of the province to continental in the southern populated regions; avg. Jan. low in Montreal is −14°C, avg. Jan. High 26°C. **Topography:** half a million sq. mi. of Quebec consists of the Laurentian Uplands, part of the Canadian Shield; Appalachian Highlands are in southeastern Quebec; lowlands form a small area along the shore of the St. Lawrence River.

Economy. Principal industries: manufacturing, agriculture, electrical production, mining, meat processing, petroleum refining. **Principal manufactured goods:** foods and beverages, clothing, textiles, paper and paper products, furniture. **Value added by manufacture** (1979): $14.6 billion. **Gross Domestic Product** (1979): $62.1 billion. **Agriculture: Chief crops:** oats, corn grains, potatoes, mixed grains, tame hay, apples. **Livestock** (1981): 1,605,000 cattle; 3,150,000 pigs; 58,000 sheep. **Forestry production** (1978): $324 million. **Mineral production** (1979): total value, $2.2 billion; metals, $1 billion; asbestos, $506 million; structural materials, $442 million. **Commercial fishing** (1978): $30.2 million. **Value of construction** (1980): $9.8 billion. **Employment distribution** (1980): 30% services; 23% manufacturing; 17% trade; 7% public administration; 5% construction; 2.8% agriculture. **Per capita income** (1979): $8,341. **Unemployment** (1980): 9.9%.

Finance: No. banks: 1,493; **no. credit unions, caisses populaires:** 1,850.

International airports: Dorval, Mirabel (both near Montreal).

Federal Government: No. federal employees (Dec. 1980): 79,995. **Federal payroll** (1980): $1.5 billion.

Energy. Electricity production, by mwh, (1980): mineral, 121,090; hydroelectric, 80,558,646.

Education. No. schools: 1,945 elementary; 706 secondary; 90 higher education. **Avg. salary, public school teachers** (1978-79): $n.a.

Provincial Data. Motto Je me souviens (I remember). **Flower:** Fleur de Lys. **Birds:** Alouette (lark). **Date entered Confederation:** 1867. **Capital:** Quebec City.

Politics. Premier: Rene Levesque (Parti Quebecois). **Leaders, opposition parties:** Claude Ryan (Liberal); vacant (Union Nationale); **Composition of legislature** (June, 1981): PQ 82; Lib. 42. **Date of last general election:** April 13, 1981.

Tourist attractions: Quebec City, often described as North America's "most European city", and sophisticated Montreal each offer numerous attractions; the north shore of the St. Lawrence River and the Gaspé Peninsula are picturesque.

Saskatchewan

People. Population (Jan. 1981): 975,700; **rank:** 6. **Pop. density:** 4.4 per sq. mi. **Urban** (1976) 55.5% **Ethnic distrib.** (1976): English 77.7%; German 6.6%; Ukrainian 5%; French 2.9%; Native Indian 2.3% **Net migration** (1979-80): +1,473.

Geography. Total area: 251,870 sq. mi.; **rank:** 5. **Land area:** 220,350 sq. mi. **Acres forested land:** 31,678,000. **Location:** borders on the Northwest Territories to the N, Manitoba to the E, Alberta to the W, and Montana and North Dakota to the S. **Climate:** continental, with cold winters (Jan. avg. low in Regina is −23°C) and hot summers (July avg. high in Regina is 26°C). **Topography:** southern 2/3ds of province are plains and grassland; northern 3d is Canadian Shield.

Economy. Principal industries: agriculture, mining of potash, meat processing, electricity production, petroleum refining. **Principal manufactured goods:** foods and beverages, agricultural implements, fabricated metals, nonmetallic mineral products. **Value added by manufacture** (1978): $568 million. **Gross Domestic product** (1979): $11.1 billion. **Agriculture: Chief crops:** wheat (57% of national total), barley, oats, mustard seed, rapeseed, flax. **Livestock** (1981): 2,095,000 cattle; 625,000 pigs; 65,000 sheep. **Forestry production** (1978): $21.2 million. **Mineral production** (1979): total value, $1.9 billion; fuels,

$787 million; potash, $735 million; metals, $266 million; structural materials, $51 million. **Commercial fishing** (1978): $3.2 million. **Value of construction** (1980): $2.3 billion. Employment distribution (1980): 26% services; 20% agriculture; 18% trade; 8% public administration; 7% construction; 5% manufacturing. **Per capita income** (1979): $8,335. **Unemployment** (1980): 4.4%.
Finance: No. banks: 389; **No. credit unions, caisses populaires:** 339.
International airports: none.
Federal Government: No. Federal employees (Dec. 1980): 13,347. **Federal payroll** (1980): $236 million.
Energy. Electricity production, by mwh, (1980): mineral, 6,317,575; hydroelectric, 2,456,569.
Education. No. schools: 916 elementary; 145 second-

ary; 6 higher education. **Avg. salary, public school teachers** (1979-80); $20,194.
Provincial Data. Motto: none. **Flower:** Red prairie lily. **Bird:** Prairie sharp-tailed grouse. **Date entered Confederation:** 1905. **Capital:** Regina.
Politics. Premier: Allan Blakeney (New Democratic). **Leaders, opposition parties:** Grant Devine (Progressive Conservative); Dick Colver (Unionest). **Composition of legislature** (June, 1981): NDP 44; PC 15; Unst. 2. **Date of last general election:** Oct. 18, 1978.

Tourist attractions. Regina: RCMP Museum, Museum of Natural History, Wascana Centre; Western Development Museums located at Saskatoon, Yorkton, North Battleford, Moose Jaw.

Territories of Canada

In addition to its 10 provinces, Canada contains the Yukon and Northwest Territories making up more than a third of the nation's land area but less than .3% of its population. Each territory is administered by a resident commissioner appointed by the federal government which retains control over natural resources excluding wildlife. An elected legislative assembly in each territory exercises jurisdiction over such matters as education, housing, social services and renewable resources. The Commissioner of the Northwest Territories serves as chairman of and acts on the advice of a 9-

member executive committee, 7 of them appointed from a 22-member elected assembly. The Yukon commissioner acts on the advice of a 5-member executive council, all of whom are appointed on the recommendation of the leader of the majority party in the assembly.
The NWT elects 2 members to the federal parliament, the Yukon one member. Each territory has one Senate representative. There is strong support in both territories for increased autonomy or provincial status.

The Yukon

*Data applies to both Territories.

People. Population (Jan. 1981): 21,500; **Pop. density:** 0.1 per sq. mi. **Urban** (1976) 61%. **Ethnic distrib. by mother tongue** (1976): English 86.7%; French 2.4%; Native Indian 2.3%; German 1.9%. (Using other criteria Native Indians make up 19% of the population). **Net migration** (1979-80): −654.
Geography. Total area: 186,660 sq. mi. **Land area:** 184,930 sq. mi. **Acres forested land:** 57,417,000. **Location:** extreme northwestern area of mainland Canada; bounded on the N by the Beaufort Sea, on the S by British Columbia, on the E by the Mackenzie District of the Northwest Territories, and on the W by Alaska. **Climate:** great variance in temperatures; warm summers, very cold winters; low precipitation. **Topography:** main feature is the Yukon plateau with 21 peaks exceeding 10,000 ft.; open tundra in the far north.

Economy. Principal industries: mining, tourism. **Principal manufactured goods:** small amounts of cement, explosives, forest products, and outdoor recreation equipment. **Value added by manufacture** (1978) $8.1 million*.

Gross domestic product (1979): $787 million*. **Agriculture:** hay, oats, vegetable gardens for local use. **Mineral production** (1979): total value, $300 million. **Commercial fishing:** (1978) $500,000*. **Per capita income** (1979): $8,569.* **No. of banks:** 14.

Federal Government: No. federal employees (Dec. 1880): 1,323. **Federal payroll** (1980): $23 million.

Energy. Electricity production, by mwh, (1980): minerals, 62,715; hydroelectric, 321,658.

Education. No. schools: 21 elementary; 1 secondary; 0 higher education. **Avg. salary, public school teachers** (1979-80): $26,679.

Territorial Data. Flower: Fireweed. **Date established:** June 13, 1898. **Capital:** Whitehorse. **Commissioner:** Doug Bell. **Party leaders:** Chris Pearson (Progressive Conservative), Ron Veale (Liberal), Tony Penikett (New Democratic). **Composition of assembly** (June 1981): P.C. 11; Lib. 2; NDP 1; 2 Independent. **Date of last election:** Nov. 20, 1978.

Tourist attractions: Historic sites from the Gold Rush period in Whitehorse and Dawson City; Miles Canyon;

Kluane National Park.

The Northwest Territories

People. Population (Jan. 1981): 42,800; **Pop. density:** 0.03 per sq. mi. **Urban** (1976) 49.7% **Ethnic distrib. by mother tongue** (1976): English 54.2%; Native Indian 9.7%; French 2.6%. (Using other criteria the Inuit make up 34% of the population, Native Indians 18%.) **Net migration** (1979-80): −1,401.
Geography. Total area: 1,322,900 sq. mi. **Land area:** 1,271,440 sq. mi. **Acres forested land:** 135,194,000 **Location:** all land north of the 60th parallel between the Yukon Territory and Hudson Bay and all northern islands east to Greenland; land area bounded by the Yukon Territory to the W, Hudson Bay to the E, the Beaufort Sea to the N and B.C, Alta., Sask. and Man. to S. **Climate:** extreme temperatures and low precipitation; Arctic and sub-Arctic. **Topography:** mostly tundra plains formed on the rocks of the Canadian Shield; the Mackenzie Lowland is a continuation of the Great Plains; the Mackenzie River Valley is forested.

Economy. Principal industries: mining, mineral and hydrocarbon exploration; oil refining. **Value added by manufacture** (1978): see Yukon. **Gross domestic product** (1979): see Yukon. **Agriculture:** scattered market gardening in the southern Mackenzie district only. **Mineral production** (1979): total value, $435 million; metals, $383 million; fuels, $52 million. **Commercial fishing:** (1978): see Yukon. **Per capita income** (1979): see Yukon. **No. of banks** 17.

Federal Government: No. federal employees (Dec. 1980): 2,482. **Federal payroll** (1980); $46 million.

Energy. Electricity production, by mwh, (1980): mineral, 162,765; hydroelectric, 268,034.

Education. No. schools: 64 elementary; 6 secondary; 0 higher education. **Avg. salary, public school teachers** (1979-80): $26,679.

Territorial Data. Flower: Mountain avens. **Date Established:** June 22, 1869. **Capital:** Yellowknife. **Commissioner:** John H. Parker. **Council:** 22 independent elected representatives.

Tourist attractions: Wood Buffalo, Auyuittuq, and Nahanni National Parks; Mackenzie River and Delta; annual Midnight Golf Tournament in Yellowknife July 21.

Head of State and Cabinet

Canada's official head of state, Queen Elizabeth of England, who succeeded to the throne in 1952, is represented by Governor-General Rt. Hon. Edward Schreyer, appointed in 1979. Titles: Minister unless otherwise stated or *Minister of State.

(listed according to precedence) (March 3, 1980)

Prime Minister — Pierre Elliott Trudeau
Deputy Prime Minister and Minister of Finance — Allan J. MacEachen
Government House Leader and President of the Privy Council — Yvon Pinard
*Department of Finance — Pierre Bussieres
Secretary of State for External Affairs — Mark R. MacGuigan
Energy, Mines and Resources — Marc Lalonde
Leader of the Government in the Senate — Senator Ray Perrault
President of the Treasury Board — Donald Johnston
National Health and Welfare — Monique Begin
Industry, Trade and Commerce — Herb Gray
*Trade — Ed Lumley
*Economic Development, Senate House Leader — Senator H.A. (Bud) Olson
Employment and Immigration, *Status of Women — Lloyd Axworthy
Justice, Attorney-General, *Social Development — Jean Chretien

Transport — Jean-Luc Pepin
Communications, Secretary of State — Francis Fox
National Defence — Gilles Lamontagne
National Revenue — William Rompkey
Labor, *Sports — Gerald Regan
Indian Affairs and Northern Development — John Munro
Agriculture — Eugene Whelan
Supply and Services — Jean-Jacques Blais
Solicitor-General — Robert Kaplan
Consumer and Corporate Affairs, Postmaster-General — Andre Oullet
Regional Economic Expansion — Pierre De Bane
Fisheries and Oceans — Romeo LeBlanc
Veterans Affairs — Daniel MacDonald
Public Works with Responsibility for the Canada Mortgage and Housing Corp. — Paul Cosgrove
*Multiculturalism — Jim Fleming
*Small Business — Charles Lapointe
Environment, *Science and Technology — John Roberts
*Canadian Wheat Board — Senator Hazen Argue
*Mines — Judy Erola

Governors-General of Canada Since Confederation, 1867

Name	Term	Name	Term
The Viscount Monck of Ballytrammon	1867-1868	General The Baron Byng of Vimy	1921-1926
The Baron Lisgar of Lisgar and Bailieborough	1869-1872	The Viscount Willingdon of Ratton	1926-1931
The Earl of Dufferin	1872-1878	The Earl of Bessborough	1931-1935
The Marquis of Lorne	1878-1883	The Baron Tweedsmuir of Elsfield	1935-1940
The Marquis of Lansdowne	1883-1888	Major General The Earl of Athlone	1940-1946
The Baron Stanley of Preston	1888-1893	Field Marshall The Viscount Alexander of Tunis	1946-1952
The Earl of Aberdeen	1893-1898	The Right Hon. Vincent Massey	1952-1959
The Earl of Minto	1898-1904	General The Right Hon. Georges P. Vanier	1959-1967
The Earl Grey	1904-1911	The Right Hon. Roland Michener	1967-1974
Field Marshall H.R.H. The Duke of Connaught	1911-1916	The Right Hon. Jules Leger	1974-1979
The Duke of Devonshire	1916-1921	The Right Hon. Edward Schreyer	1979-

Fathers of Confederation

Union of the British North American colonies into the Dominion of Canada was discussed and its terms negotiated at 3 confederation conferences held at Charlottetown (C), Sept. 1, 1864; Quebec (Q), Oct. 10, 1864; and London (L), Dec. 4, 1866. The names of delegates are followed by the provinces they represented. Canada refers to what are now the provinces of Ontario and Quebec.

Adams G. Archibald, N.S.	(C,Q,L)	Hector L. Langevin, Canada	(C,Q,L)
George Brown, Canada	(C,Q)	Jonathan McCully, N.S.	(C,Q,L)
Alexander Campbell, Canada	(C,Q)	A.A. Macdonald, P.E.I.	(C,Q)
Frederick B.T. Carter, Nfld.	(Q)	John A. Macdonald, Canada	(C,Q,L)
George-Etienne Cartier, Canada	(C,Q,L)	William McDougall, Canada	(C,Q,L)
Edward B. Chandler, N.B.	(C,Q)	Thomas D'Arcy McGee, Canada	(C,Q)
Jean-Charles Chapais, Canada	(Q)	Peter Mitchell, N.B.	(Q,L)
James Cockburn, Canada	(Q)	Oliver Mowat, Canada	(Q)
George H. Coles, P.E.I.	(C,Q)	Edward Palmer, P.E.I.	(C,Q)
Robert B. Dickey, N.S.	(Q)	William H. Pope, P.E.I.	(C,Q)
Charles Fisher, N.B.	(Q,L)	John W. Ritchie, N.S.	(L)
Alexander T. Galt, Canada	(C,Q,L)	J. Ambrose Shea, Nfld.	(Q)
John Hamilton Gray, N.B.	(C,Q)	William H. Steeves, N.B.	(C,Q)
John Hamilton Gray, P.E.I.	(C,Q)	Sir Etienne-Paschal Tache, Canada	(Q)
Thomas Heath Haviland, P.E.I.	(Q)	Samuel Leonard Tilley, N.B.	(C,Q,L)
William A. Henry, N.S.	(C,Q,L)	Charles Tupper, N.S.	(C,Q,L)
William P. Howland, Canada	(L)	Edward Whelan, P.E.I.	(Q)
John M. Johnson, N.B.	(C,Q,L)	R.D. Wilmot, N.B.	(L)

The Political Parties

Canadian parties, from whatever point in the political spectrum they begin, gravitate towards the middle of the road where most of the votes lie. Despite variations in outlook and policy, all 3 official parties tend to adopt a practical rather than dogmatic line on most issues.

Progressive Conservatives — Canada's oldest party and theoretically the furthest to the right, the Conservatives have

nevertheless endorsed an extension of social welfare. Though their support is based in western Canada, the Conservatives were the only party to elect at least one representative from each province in the 1980 election. The party has held office only briefly since 1962, and then only with minority governments, mainly due to a failure to gain support in Quebec.
Leader: Joe Clark.

Liberals — Though politically situated between the Conservatives to the right and the New Democrats on the left, the Liberals are flexible enough to lean in either direction depending on specific issues and political situations. In 1975 they belatedly adopted a Conservative proposal for wage and price controls; in 1979 they sided with the NDP to oppose Conservative plans to return some government-owned corporations to the private sector. Most of their traditional electoral support comes from middle and upper class urban residents, from ethnic voters, and among French-speaking Canadians. **Leader:** Pierre Trudeau.

New Democratic Party — Successor to the Cooperative Commonwealth Federation, which combined the agrarian protest movement in western Canada with a democratic socialism of the British Labor Party variety, the NDP was founded in 1961. It now attempts to attract the vote of middle-class Canadians and fuse it with the party's labor support. **Leader:** Ed Broadbent.

Political power in Canada has been dominated by the Conservative and Liberal parties. Of 32 federal elections since Confederation, the Conservatives have won 13, holding power for 47 years; the Liberals have gained office 19 times, governing for 66 years. As a measure of Liberal strength, all of the party's 20th century leaders have been elected Prime Minister—though not always on the first attempt.

Despite the dominance of the Liberals and Conservatives, third parties have played an important role under Canada's parliamentary system in which a governing party holding less than half the seats in the House of Commons can remain in office and pass legislation only with the support of a minor party. A minority Conservative Government lost power in 1979 when none of the opposition parties supported its proposed budget.

The NDP has been the most influential of the third parties, consistently winning between 15% and 20% of the popular vote—though its proportion of elected members is always less. NDP pressure from the left has influenced policy decisions by both major parties. The Social Credit Party, once a strong political force with federal support in Quebec and the western provinces, has declined in stature over the past 2 decades and in 1980 failed to elect any members to Parliament.

Prime Ministers of Canada

Name	Party	Term	Name	Party	Term
Sir John A. MacDonald	Conservative	1867-1873	W.L.M. King.	Liberal	1921-1926
		1878-1891			1926-1930
Alexander Mackenzie	Liberal	1873-1878			1935-1948
Sir John J. C. Abbott	Conservative	1891-1892	R. B. Bennett.	Conservative	1930-1935
Sir John S. D. Thompson . . .	Conservative	1892-1894	Louis St. Laurent	Liberal	1948-1957
Sir Mackenzie Bowell	Conservative	1894-1896	John G. Diefenbaker.	Prog. Cons.	1957-1963
Sir Charles Tupper.	Conservative	1896	Lester B. Pearson	Liberal	1963-1968
Sir Wilfrid Laurier.	Liberal	1896-1911	Pierre Elliott Trudeau	Liberal	1968-1979
Sir Robert L. Borden	Conservative	1911-1920	Joe Clark	Prog. Cons.	1979-1980
	Unionist		Pierre Elliott Trudeau	Liberal	1980-
Arthur Meighen	Cons. Union.	1920-1921			

Election Results by Province and Party, May 22, 1980

Province	Total Valid Votes	Liberal	Conservative	New Dem.	Soc. Cred.	Other
Alberta	794,946	176,565	515,639	81,732	8,162	12,848
British Columbia.	1,209,453	268,069	501,921	426,857	1,709	10,897
Manitoba	476,001	133,353	179,607	159,432	—	3,609
New Brunswick	335,702	168,316	109,053	54,481	—	3,852
Newfoundland.	203,045	95,354	72,999	33,943	—	749
Nova Scotia	422,281	168,303	163,436	88,115	—	2,427
Ontario	4,000,162	1,675,164	1,420,263	874,092	804	29,839
Prince Edward Island.	66,174	31,055	30,576	4,335	—	208
Quebec	2,957,120	2,017,067	373,233	268,677	174,282	123,861
Saskatchewan	455,709	110,501	177,338	165,294	178	2,398
N.W. Territories.	16,195	5,801	4,000	6,214	—	180
Yukon	9,669	3,825	3,926	1,918	—	—
TOTAL.	**10,946,457**	**4,853,373**	**3,551,991**	**2,165,090**	**185,135**	**190,868**
Percent.	100	44.34	32.45	19.78	1.69	1.71
Seats.	282	147	103	32	0	0

Party Representation by Regions, 1949-1980

Canada	1949	1953	1957	1958	1962	1963	1965	1968	1972	1974	1979	1980
Liberal.	193	171	105	48	100	129	131	155	109	141	114	147
Conservative	41	51	112	208	116	95	97	72	107	95	136	103
New Democratic[1]	13	23	25	8	19	17	21	22	31	16	26	32
Social Credit	10	15	19	—	30	24	14	14	15	11	6	0
Other	5	5	4	1	—	—	2	1	2	1	0	0
Ontario												
Liberal.	56	51	21	14	44	52	51	64	36	55	32	52
Conservative	25	33	61	67	35	27	25	17	40	25	57	38
New Democratic[1]	1	1	3	3	6	6	9	6	11	8	6	5
Quebec												
Liberal.	68	66	62	25	35	47	56	56	56	60	67	74
Conservative	2	4	9	50	14	8	8	4	2	3	2	1
Social Credit	—	—	—	—	26	20	9	14	15	11	6	—
Atlantic												
Liberal.	26	27	12	8	14	20	15	7	10	13	12	19
Conservative	7	5	21	25	18	13	18	25	22	17	18	13
New Democratic[1]	1	1	—	—	1	—	—	—	—	1	2	—
Western[2]												
Liberal.	43	27	10	1	7	10	9	28	7	13	3	2
Conservative	7	9	21	66	49	47	46	26	43	50	59	51
New Democratic[1]	11	21	22	5	12	11	12	16	20	7	18	27
Social Credit	10	15	19	—	4	4	5	—	—	—	—	—

(1) Prior to 1962 election was known as the Cooperative Commonwealth Federation.
(2) Includes the Yukon and Northwest Territories.

Canadian Armed Forces

In Feb., 1968, Canada carried out the unification of its traditionally separate services: the Royal Canadian Navy, the Canadian Army, and the Royal Canadian Air Force. The first step towards a unified force was taken in 1964 when the 3 services were brought together under one control with common logistics and supply and training systems, but retaining their separate legal entities. The positions of Chairman of the Chiefs of Staff and Chiefs of the Navy, Army, and Air Force were abolished and replaced by the Chief of the Defense Staff. On Feb. 1, 1968, the 3 services ceased to exist. They were unified into the Canadian Armed Forces in which all officers, men, and women are managed within a single body, with a common uniform.

Chief of the Defense Staff: Gen. R.M. Withers
Vice Chief of the Defense Staff: Lieut. Gen. G.C.E. Theriault

Maritime Command — Vice Admiral J.A. Fulton
Mobile Command — Lieut. Gen. C. H. Belzile
Air Command — Lieut. Gen. K.E. Lewis

Communications Command — Brig. Gen. D. P. Harrison
Canadian Forces Europe — Maj. Gen. Francois Richard

Regular Forces Strength

(as of March 31)

Year	Navy	Army	Air Force	Total	Year	Total	Year	Total	Year	Total
1945	92,529	494,258	174,254	761,041	1970	91,433	1976	78,394	1979	78,974
1955	19,207	49,409	49,461	118,077	1974	80,639	1977	78,091	1980	79,909
1965	19,756	46,264	48,144	114,164	1975	78,448	1978	79,656	1981	79,549

Canadian Military Participation in Major Conflicts

Northwest Rebellion (1885)[1]
Participants—3,323
Killed—38
Last veteran died at the age of 104 in 1971.
South African War (1899-1902)
Participants—7,368[2]
Killed—89
Living Veterans—less than 30
First World War (1914-1918)
Participants—626,636[3]

Killed—61,332[4]
Living Veterans—42,222[5]

Second World War (1939-1945)
Participants—1,086,343 (inc. 45,423 women)
Killed—32,714 (inc. 8 women)
Living Veterans—747,365[5][6]

Korean War (1950-1953)
Participants—25,583
Killed—314

(1) First battle in history to be fought entirely by Canadian troops. (2) Includes Canadians in the South African constabulary and 8 nursing sisters. (3) Includes 2,854 nursing sisters. (4) Includes 21 nursing sisters and 1,563 airmen serving with the British air forces. (5) 1980 est. based on mortality rates applied to 1971 census data. (6) Includes Korean War veterans.

Canadian World War II Winners of the Victoria Cross

The Victoria Cross is Britain's highest military honor. It has been accorded to 94 Canadians since its inception in 1856. The cross was originally cast from metal of a Russian cannon captured during the Crimean War.

Name	Unit	Theater of war, date
Sgt. J. R. Osborn	Winnipeg Grenadiers	Hong Kong, Dec. 19, 1941
Lt. Col. C. E. Merritt	S. Sask. Regiment	Dieppe, Aug. 19, 1942
Capt. J. W. Foote	Royal Hamilton Light Infantry	Dieppe, Aug. 19, 1942
Capt. F. T. Peters	Royal Navy	Oran, North Africa, Nov. 8, 1942
Capt. Paul Triquet	Royal 22d Regiment	Casa Berardi, Dec. 14, 1943
Maj. C. F. Hoey	Lincolnshire Regiment	Burma, Feb. 16, 1944
Maj. John K. Mahoney	Westminster Regiment	Melfa River, May 24, 1944
P.O.A.C. Mynarksi	RCAF	Camria, France, June 12, 1944
Flt. Lieut. D. E. Hornell	RCAF	"Northern waters", June 25, 1944
Sqd. Ldr. Ian Bazalgette	RAF	Trossy St. Maximin, Aug. 4, 1944
Maj. D. V. Currie	South Alberta Regiment	Normandy, Aug. 20, 1944
Pvt. E. A. Smith	Seaforth Highlanders	Savio River, Italy, Oct. 22, 1944
Sgt. Aubrey Cosens	Queen's Own Rifles	Holland, Feb. 26, 1945
Maj. F. A. Tilston	Essex Scottish	Hochwald Forest, Mar. 1, 1945
Cpl. F. G. Topham	1st Canadian Parachute Battalion	Germany, Mar. 24, 1945
Lt. R. H. Gray	Royal Canadian Navy	Pacific, Aug. 9, 1945

Canadian Peacekeeping Operations

Canada has played a major role in the United Nations' efforts to preserve peace and promote international security, participating in almost all UN peacekeeping operations to date - in Egypt, Israel, Syria, Lebanon, Cyprus, Korea, India, Pakistan, West New Guinea, the Congo, Yemen and Nigeria.

Nearly 900 Canadian soldiers served in the Gaza Strip following the Israeli-Egyptian crisis of 1956 until the peacekeeping force there was disbanded in 1967. Another 850 Canadians served with the United Nations Emergency Force in the Middle East from 1973 until it was disbanded in Nov., 1979.

In the Congo, a 300-man signals unit provided communications for the UN force from 1960 to 1964.

Canadian participation in the International Commission for Control and Supervision in Vietnam and Laos began in 1954, and, at its height following U.S. military withdrawal from Vietnam in 1973, involved 245 Canadian Forces personnel. The Canadian Vietnam supervisory contingent was withdrawn in July 1973, the Laos mission in 1974.

Canadian peacekeeping operations in 1981:
—some 515 Canadians in the UN Peacekeeping Force in Cyprus where Canadian participation began in 1964 and was augmented in 1974.
—250 Canadians, mostly logistics troops, with the UN Disengagement Observer Force in the Middle East.
—20 Canadian combat arms officers with the UN Truce Supervisory Organization, Israel.

Population and Area of Canada by Provinces

Source: Statistics Canada

Province, territory	Capital	Area in square miles			Population		
		Land	Fresh water	Total	1966 census	1976 census	Jan. 1980 estimate
Newfoundland	St. John's	143,510	13,140	156,650	493,396	557,725	583,600
Prince Edward Island	Charlottetown	2,180	. . .	2,180	108,645	118,229	124,100
Nova Scotia	Halifax	20,400	1,020	21,420	756,039	828,571	856,100
New Brunswick	Fredericton	27,840	520	28,360	616,788	677,250	709,100
Quebec	Quebec	523,860	71,000	594,860	5,780,845	6,234,445	6,325,200
Ontario	Toronto	344,090	68,490	412,580	6,960,870	8,264,465	8,600,500
Manitoba	Winnipeg	211,720	39,230	250,950	963,066	1,021,506	1,027,000
Saskatchewan	Regina	220,350	31,520	251,870	955,344	921,323	975,700
Alberta	Edmonton	248,800	6,490	255,290	1,463,203	1,838,037	2,135,900
British Columbia	Victoria	358,970	6,980	365,950	1,837,674	2,466,608	2,687,000
Yukon Territory	Whitehorse	184,930	1,730	186,660	14,382	21,836	21,500
Northwest Territories	Yellowknife	1,271,440	51,460	1,322,900	28,738	42,609	42,800
Total		3,558,090	291,580	3,849,670	20,014,880	22,992,604	24,088,700

Canadian Cities with Metropolitan Populations Over 100,000

Source: Statistics Canada

Census Metropolitan Areas. All figures shown are for the 1976 Census.

	Metro Area	City		Metro Area	City
Toronto, Ontario	2,803,101(1)	633,318	Halifax, Nova Scotia	267,991	117,882
Montreal, Quebec	2,802,485	1,080,546	Windsor, Ontario	247,582	196,526
Vancouver, British Columbia	1,166,348	410,188	Victoria, British Columbia	218,250	62,551
Ottawa-Hull, Ontario, Quebec	693,288	304,462	Sudbury, Ontario	157,030	97,604
Winnipeg, Manitoba	578,217	560,874	Regina, Saskatchewan	151,191	149,593
Edmonton, Alberta	554,228	461,361	St. John's, Newfoundland	143,390	86,576
Quebec, Quebec	542,158	177,082	Oshawa, Ontario	135,196	107,023
Hamilton, Ontario	529,371	312,003	Saskatoon, Saskatchewan	133,750	133,750
Calgary, Alberta	469,917	469,917	Chicoutimi-Jonquiere, Quebec	128,643	57,737
St. Catharines-Niagara, Ontario	301,921	123,351	Thunder Bay, Ontario	119,253	111,476
Kitchener, Ontario	272,158	131,870	Saint John, New Brunswick	112,974	85,956
London, Ontario	270,383	240,392			

(1) Includes North York, pop. 563,000, given city status within metro Feb., 1979, and the city of Mississauga, 1976 pop. 230,073.

Immigration to Canada, by Province of Intended Destination

Source: Canadian Statistical Review, May 1981

Year	Canada	Nfld.	P.E.I.	N.S.	N.B.	Que.	Ont.	Man.	Sask.	Alta.	B.C.	N.W.T. Yukon
1974	218,465	1,036	311	2,601	2,207	33,458	120,115	7,423	2,244	14,289	34,481	300
1975	187,881	1,106	235	2,124	2,093	28,042	98,471	7,134	2,837	16,277	29,272	290
1976	149,429	725	235	1,942	1,752	29,282	72,031	5,509	2,323	14,896	20,484	250
1977	114,914	583	192	1,587	1,158	19,248	56,594	5,058	2,231	12,694	15,395	174
1978	86,313	374	145	980	661	14,290	42,397	3,574	1,564	9,826	12,331	171
1979	112,096	553	289	1,338	1,145	19,534	51,979	4,906	2,762	12,786	16,596	208
1980	142,439	541	190	1,615	1,204	22,333	61,968	7,656	3,596	18,775	24,373	188

Superlative Canadian Statistics

Source: Statistics Canada; Dept. of Energy, Mines and Resources

Area	Total: Land 3,539,462 sq. mi.; Water 291,571 sq. mi.	3,831,033 sq. mi.
Largest city in area	Timmins, Ont.	1,230 sq. mi.
Smallest city in area (east)	Vanier, Ont.	1.1 sq. mi.
Smallest city in area (west)	Chilliwack, B.C.	1.6 sq. mi.
Northernmost point	Cape Columbia, Ellesmere Island, N.W.T.	83°07'30"N.
Northernmost settlement	Alert, Ellesmere Island, N.W.T.	82°30'N.
Southernmost point	Middle Island (Lake Erie), Ont.	41°41'N.
Southernmost settlement	Pelee Island South, Essex Co., Ont.	41°45'N.
Easternmost point	Cape Spear, Nfld.	52°37'28"W.
Easternmost settlement	Blackhead, St. John's, Nfld.	52°39'W.
Westernmost point	Mount St. Elias, Yukon (at Alaskan border)	141°W.
Westernmost settlement	Beaver Creek, Yukon	140°52'W.
Highest city	Rossland, B.C. at R.R. Stn. (49°05'N,117°47'W)	3,465 ft.
Highest town	Lake Louise, Alta.	5,051 ft.
Highest waterfall	Takakkaw Falls (Daly Glacier), B.C. (51°30'N,116°29'W)	1,650 ft.
Longest river	Mackenzie (from head of Finlay R.)	2,635 mi.

(continued)

Highest mountain . . . . Mt. Logan (Yukon) . . . . 19,524 ft.
Rainiest spot . . . . Henderson Lake, Vancouver Is. yrly. avg. rainfall . . . . 262 inches
Highest lake . . . . Chilco Lake (51°20'N,124°05'W) 75.1 sq. mi . . . . 3,842 ft.

Immigration to Canada by Country of Last Permanent Residence

Source: Canadian Statistical Review, May 1981

Year	Total	UK and Ireland	France	Germany	Netherlands	Greece	Italy
1976	149,429	22,187	3,251	2,672	1,359	2,487	4,530
1977	114,914	18,568	2,757	2,254	1,247	1,960	3,411
1978	86,313	12,270	1,754	1,471	1,237	1,474	2,976
1979	112,096	13,406	1,900	1,323	1,479	1,247	1,996
1980	142,439	18,890	1,890	1,642	1,864	1,091	1,544

Year	Portugal	Other Europe	Asia	Australasia	United States	West Indies	All Other
1976	5,344	8,078	44,328	1,886	17,315	14,723	21,269
1977	3,579	6,972	31,368	1,545	12,888	12,022	16,343
1978	1,898	6,995	24,007	1,233	9,945	8,231	12,822
1979	3,723	7,784	50,540	1,395	9,617	6,262	11,424
1980	4,219	9,713	71,453	1,555	9,900	7,187	11,491

Canadian Population by Mother Tongue, 1976

Source: Statistics Canada

Province	English	French	Italian	German	Ukrainian	Indian, Eskimo	Chinese	Portuguese	Other
Newfoundland	545,340	2,760	170	450	40	1,555	535	210	6,665
Prince Edward Island	109,745	6,545	30	145	30	70	55	—	1,610
Nova Scotia	768,070	36,870	1,135	1,555	570	2,340	800	185	17,045
New Brunswick	435,975	223,780	550	1,020	170	1,695	495	110	13,455
Quebec	800,680	4,989,245	124,575	22,630	10,975	18,375	10,680	19,150	238,135
Ontario	6,457,645	462,070	309,810	154,625	76,035	21,285	51,660	88,495	642,840
Manitoba	727,240	54,745	5,875	73,375	60,250	24,855	3,705	5,455	66,010
Saskatchewan	715,685	26,710	1,260	61,250	45,920	20,860	3,390	220	46,030
Alberta	1,482,725	44,440	13,745	79,925	64,960	17,690	14,430	3,445	116,680
British Columbia	2,037,645	38,430	26,715	80,970	22,775	8,245	46,655	9,245	195,930
Yukon	18,940	525	45	405	140	510	45	—	1,230
Northwest Territories	23,085	1,095	135	365	195	15,525	120	25	2,066
Total	14,122,770	5,887,205	484,050	476,715	282,060	133,005	132,560	126,535	1,347,696

Population by Religious Denomination

Source: Statistics Canada

Denomination	1961	1971	Denomination	1961	1971
Adventist	25,999	28,590	Lutheran	662,744	715,740
Anglican	2,409,068	2,543,180	Mennonite(2)	152,452	168,150
Baptist	593,553	667,245	Mormon	50,016	66,635
Buddhist	11,611	16,175	Orthodox(3)	239,766	316,605
Chr. & Miss'nary Alliance	18,006	23,630	Pentecostal	143,877	220,390
Christian Reformed	62,257	83,990	Presbyterian	818,588	872,335
Ch. of Christ, Disciples	19,512	16,405	Roman Catholic	8,342,826	9,974,895
Confucian	5,089	2,165	Salvation Army	92,054	119,665
Doukhobor	13,234	9,107	Ukrainian Catholic(4)	189,653	227,730
Free Methodist	14,245	19,125	Unitarian	15,062	20,995
Hutterite	(1)	13,650	United Church	3,664,008	3,768,800
Jehovah's Witnesses	68,018	174,810	Other	277,508	293,240
Jewish	254,368	276,025	No religion	94,763	929,575

(1) Included with Mennonite. (2) Includes Hutterites in 1961. (3) Those churches which observe the Eastern Orthodox rite, including Greek, Russian, Ukrainian, and Syrian Orthodox. (4) Includes other "Greek Catholic."

Births and Deaths in Canada by Province

Source: Statistics Canada

Province	Births 1979	Births 1980	Deaths 1979	Deaths 1980	Province	Births 1979	Births 1980	Deaths 1979	Deaths 1980
Newfoundland	10,650	10,870	3,170	3,220	Saskatchewan	16,130	16,470	7,290	7,590
Prince Edward Island	1,930	1,970	1,020	1,000	Alberta	34,860	37,610	12,020	12,340
Nova Scotia	12,250	12,480	6,800	7,030	British Columbia . . .	37,100	38,490	20,090	20,150
New Brunswick	10,680	10,860	5,420	5,500	Yukon	470	480	110	130
Quebec	93,510	96,780	43,360	43,410	Northwest Territories	1,200	1,120	190	210
Ontario	123,070	124,520	62,550	62,750					
Manitoba	15,740	16,380	8,560	8,750	Total	357,590	368,030	170,580	172,080

Marriages, Divorces in Canada

Source: Statistics Canada
(Rates per 1,000 population)

Year	Marriages No.	Rate	Divorces No.	Rate	Year	Marriages No.	Rate	Divorces No.	Rate
1940. . . .	125,709	10.8	2,416	0.21	1975. . . .	197,585	8.7	50,611	2.22
1950. . . .	125,083	9.1	5,386	0.39	1977. . . .	187,344	8.0	55,370	2.38
1960. . . .	130,338	7.3	6,980	0.39	1978. . . .	185,523	7.9	57,155	2.43
1970. . . .	188,428	8.8	29,775	1.39	1979. . . .	187,811	7.9	59,574	2.51

Canadian Legal or Public Holidays, 1982

Legal public holidays in all provinces are: New Year's Day, Good Friday, Easter Monday, Victoria Day, Dominion Day, Labor Day, Remembrance Day and Christmas Day. Additional holidays may be proclaimed provincially by the Lieutenant-Governor or in the municipalities by an order of the local council. For some holidays, government and business closing practices vary. In most provinces the provincial Ministry or Department of Labor can provide details of holiday closings.

Chief Legal or Public Holidays

Jan. 1 (Friday) - New Year's Day. All provinces.

Apr. 9 - Good Friday. All provinces.

Apr. 12 - Easter Monday. Que. (businesses remain open in other provinces)

May 24 (the Monday preceding May 25) - Victoria Day. All provinces.

July 1 (Thursday) - Dominion Day. All provinces.

Aug. 2 (1st Monday in Aug.) - Civic Holiday. Alb. B.C. Man. N.B. NWT Ont. Sask.

Sept. 6 (1st Monday in Sept.) - Labor Day. All provinces.

Oct. 11 (2d Monday in Oct.) - Thanksgiving. All provinces.

Nov. 11 (Thursday) - Remembrance Day. Observed in all provinces but most businesses remain open.

Dec. 25 (Saturday) - Christmas Day. All provinces.

Dec. 26 (Sunday) - Boxing Day. All provinces except Que.

Other Legal or Public Holidays

Jan. 11 (Monday) - Sir John A. MacDonald's Birthday. Schools closed in some provinces.

March 15 (Monday) - St. Patrick's Day. Nfld.

April 26 (Monday) - St. George's Day. Nfld.

June 21 (Monday) - Discovery Day. Nfld.

June 24 (Thursday) - St. John the Baptist's Day. Que.

July 12 (Monday) - Orangemen's Day. Nfld.

Aug. 16 (3d Monday in Aug.) - Discovery Day. Yukon.

Widely Known Canadians of the Present

Statesmen, authors, performers, artists, industrialists, and other prominent persons. (Canadians widely known in the North American entertainment industry are found on pages 386–400; some sports personalities can be found on pages 841–843.)

Name (Birthplace)	Birthdate	Name (Birthplace)	Birthdate
Amiel, Barbara (Watford, England)	12/4/40	Douglas, Tommy (Falkirk, Scotland)	10/20/04
Anderson, Doris (Calgary, Alta.)	11/10/25	Drapeau, Jean (Montreal, Que.)	2/18/16
Atwood, Margaret (Ottawa, Ont.)	11/18/39		
Augustyn, Frank (Hamilton, Ont.)	1/27/53	Forrester, Maureen (Montreal, Que.)	7/25/30
Axworthy, Lloyd (Winnipeg, Man.)	12/21/39	Fotheringham, Allan (Hearne, Sask.)	8/31/32
		Fox, Francis (Montreal, Que.)	12/2/39
Ballard, Harold (Toronto, Ont.)	7/30/03	Frum, Barbara (Niagara Falls, Ont.)	9/8/38
Bennett, William (Kelowna, B.C.)	4/14/32	Frye, Northrop (Sherbrooke, Que.)	7/14/12
Berton, Pierre (Whitehorse, Yukon)	7/12/20	Fulford, Robert (Ottawa, Ont.)	7/13/32
Birney, Earle (Calgary, Alta.)	5/13/04		
Black, Conrad (Montreal, Que.)	8/25/44	Gagnon, Andre (St.-Pacome, Que.)	8/2/37
Blakeney, Allan (Bridgewater, N.S.)	9/7/25	Gordon, Walter (Toronto, Ont.)	1/27/06
Blaikie, Peter (Shawinigan, Que.)	5/10/37	Gould, Glenn (Toronto, Ont.)	9/25/32
Bouey, Gerald (Axford, Sask.)	5/2/20	Gray, Herb (Windsor, Ont.)	5/25/31
Broadbent, Ed (Oshawa, Ont.)	3/21/36	Gzowski, Peter (Toronto, Ont.)	7/13/34
Bronfman, Charles (Montreal, Que.)	6/27/31		
Bronfman, Edgar (Montreal, Que.)	6/20/29	Harron, Don (Toronto, Ont.)	9/19/24
Buchanan, John M. (Sydney, N.S.)	4/22/31	Hatfield, Richard (Hartland, N.B.)	4/9/31
Bulloch, John (Toronto, Ont.)	8/24/33	Herzberg, Gerhard (Hamburg, Germany)	12/25/04
		Hewitt, Foster (Toronto, Ont.)	11/21/03
Callaghan, Morley (Toronto, Ont.)	2/22/03	Hill, Dan (Toronto, Ont.)	6/3/54
Camp, Dalton (Woodstock, N.B.)	9/11/20	Horner, Jack (Blain Lake, Sask.)	7/20/27
Carrier, Roch (Ste.-Justine-de-Dorchester, Que.)	5/13/37	Hurtig, Mel (Edmonton, Alta.)	6/24/32
Chretien, Jean (Shawinigan, Que.)	1/11/34		
Clark, Joe (High River, Alta.)	6/5/39	Irving, K.C. (Buctouche, N.B.)	1899
Cohen, Leonard (Montreal, Que.)	9/21/34		
Colville, Alex (Toronto, Ont.)	8/24/20	Jewison, Norman (Toronto, Ont.)	7/21/26
Connors, Stompin' Tom (Skinner's Pond, P.E.I.)	2/9/36	Kain, Karen (Hamilton, Ont.)	3/28/51
Cranston, Toller (Kirkland Lake, Ont.)	4/20/49	Karsh, Yousuf (Armenia-in-Turkey)	12/23/08
Crombie, David (Toronto, Ont.)	4/24/36		
Crosbie, John (St. John's, Nfld.)	1/30/31	Lalonde, Marc (Ile Perrot, Que.)	7/26/29
Cummings, Burton (Winnipeg, Man.)	12/31/47	Lapierre, Laurier (Lac Megantic, Que.)	11/21/29
		Laskin, Bora (Fort William, Ont.)	10/5/12
Danby, Ken (Sault Ste. Marie, Ont.)	3/16/40	Laurence, Margaret (Neopawa, Man.)	7/18/26
Davies, Robertson (Thamesville, Ont.)	8/28/13	Layton, Irving (Neamtz, Romania)	3/12/12
Davey, Keith (Toronto, Ont.)	4/21/26	Levesque, Rene (New Carlisle, Que.)	8/24/22
Davis, Bill (Brampton, Ont.)	7/30/29	Lightfoot, Gordon (Orillia, Ont.)	11/17/38
Desmarais, Paul (Sudbury, Ont.)	1/4/27	Lougheed, Peter (Calgary, Alta.)	7/26/28

Name (Birthplace)	Birthdate
Lyon, Sterling (Windsor, Ont.)	1/30/27
MacDonald, Donald (Ottawa, Ont.)	3/1/32
Macdonald, Flora (North Sydney, N.S.)	6/3/26
MacEachen, Allan (Inverness, N.S.)	7/6/21
MacGuigan, Mark (Charlottetown, P.E.I.)	2/17/31
Mackassey, Bryce (Quebec City, Que.)	8/25/27
MacLean, J. Angus (Lewis, Belle River, P.E.I.)	5/15/14
Maloney, Arthur (Eganville, Ont.)	11/26/19
McDermott, Dennis (Portsmouth, England)	11/3/22
McLauchlan, Murray (Paisley, Scotland)	6/30/48
McLennon, Hugh (Glace Bay, N.S.)	3/20/07
McTeer, Maureen (Ottawa, Ont.)	2/27/52
Mitchell, W.O. (Weyburn, Sask.)	3/13/14
Morin, Claude (Montmorency, Que.)	1929
Mowat, Farley (Belleville, Ont.)	5/12/21
Mulroney, Brian (Baie Comeau, Que.)	3/20/39
Munro, Alice (Wingham, Ont.)	7/10/31
Nash, Knowlton (Toronto, Ont.)	11/18/27
Newman, Peter C. (Vienna, Austria)	5/10/29
Parizeau, Jacques (Montreal, Que.)	8/9/30
Peckford, Brian (Whitbourne, Nfld.)	8/27/42
Pepin, Jean-Luc (Drummondville, Que.)	11/1/24
Podborski, Steve (Toronto, Ont.)	7/25/57
Pratt, Christopher (St. John's, Nfld.)	12/9/35
Rae, Bob (Ottawa Ont.)	8/2/48
Regan, Gerald (Windsor, N.S.)	2/13/28
Richler, Mordecai (Montreal, Que.)	1/27/31

Name (Birthplace)	Birthdate
Robarts, John (Banff, Alta.)	1/11/17
Rohmer, Richard (Hamilton, Ont.)	1/24/24
Roy, Gabrielle (St. Boniface, Man.)	3/22/09
Ryan, Claude (Montreal, Que.)	1/26/25
Russell, Craig (Toronto, Ont.)	1/10/48
Sauve, Jeanne (Prud'Homme, Sask.)	4/26/22
Schreyer, Edward (Beausejour, Man.)	12/21/35
Selye, Hans (Vienna, Austria)	1/26/07
Shulman, Morton (Toronto, Ont.)	4/2/25
Simmonds, Robert H. (Hafford, Sask.)	4/6/26
Sinclair, Gordon (Toronto, Ont.)	6/3/00
Skalbania, Nelson (Regina, Sask.)	2/12/38
Smallwood, Joey (Gambo, Nfld.)	12/24/00
Stanfield, Robert (Truro, N.S.)	4/11/14
Stevens, Sinclair (Esquesing Twp., Ont.)	2/11/27
Suzuki, David (Vancouver, B.C.)	3/24/36
Taylor, E.P. (Ottawa, Ont.)	1/29/01
Taylor, Ken (Calgary, Alta.)	10/5/34
Templeton, Charles (Toronto, Ont.)	10/7/15
Thomson, Ken (Toronto, Ont.)	9/1/23
Trudeau, Margaret (Vancouver, B.C.)	9/10/48
Trudeau, Pierre (Montreal, Que.)	10/18/19
Turner, John (Richmond, England)	6/7/29
Vigneault, Gilles (Natashquan, Que.)	11/27/28
Wainman, Tracey (Kirkland Lake, Ont.)	5/27/67
Weston, Galen (England)	10/26/40
Whelan, Eugene (Amherstburg, Ont.)	7/11/24

Noted Canadian Personalities of the Past

Name	Born	Died
Statesmen		
Aberhart, William	1878	1943
Baldwin, Robert	1804	1858
Bennett, Richard B.	1870	1957
Blake, Edward	1833	1912
Borden, Robert	1854	1937
Bowell, Mackenzie	1823	1917
Brown, George	1818	1880
Cartier, Georges	1814	1873
Diefenbaker, John	1895	1979
Howe, Joseph	1804	1873
King, W. Mackenzie	1874	1950
Laurier, Wilfrid	1841	1919
Macdonald, John A.	1815	1891
Mackenzie, Alexander	1822	1892
Mackenzie, Wm. Lyon	1795	1861
Massey, Vincent	1887	1967
McGee, Thomas D'Arcy	1825	1868
Meighen, Arthur	1874	1960
Mowat, Oliver	1820	1903
Papineau, Louis-Joseph	1786	1871
Pearson, Lester B.	1897	1972
Riel, Louis	1844	1885
Tilley, Samuel Leonard	1818	1896
Tupper, Charles H.	1855	1927
Woodsworth, James S.	1874	1942
Scientists, Industrialists		
Aitken, William M.	1879	1964
(Lord Beaverbrook)		
Allan, Hugh	1810	1882
Banting, Fredk. G.	1891	1941
Beatty, Edward W.	1877	1943
Best, Charles H.	1910	1978
Bethune, Norman	1890	1939
Bronfman, Samuel	1891	1971
Eaton, Timothy	1834	1907
Eddy, Ezra Butler	1827	1906

Name	Born	Died
Fleming, Sandford	1827	1915
Hilton, Hugh G.	1889	1966
Macleod, John J.R.	1876	1935
McDougald, John (Bud)	1908	1978
McLaughlin, R. Sam	1871	1972
Osler, William	1849	1919
Penfield, Wilder	1891	1976
Thomson, Roy	1894	1976
(Lord Thomson of Fleet)		
Van Horne, William	1843	1915
Weston, Garfield	1898	1978
Authors		
Belaney, George S.	1888	1938
(Grey Owl)		
Bourassa, Henri	1868	1952
Buchan, John	1875	1940
(Baron Tweedsmuir)		
Campbell, W. Wilfred	1861	1918
Carman, W. Bliss	1861	1929
Clark, Gregory	1892	1977
Cremazie, Octave	1827	1879
Creighton, Donald	1902	1979
Dafoe, John Wesley	1866	1944
Dawson, R. MacGregor	1895	1958
De Mille, James	1836	1880
Doughty, Arthur G.	1860	1936
Duncan, Sara J.	1862	1932
Edwards, Robert (Bob)	1864	1922
Frechette, Louis H.	1839	1908
Gordon, Chas. W.	1860	1937
(Ralph Connor)		
Grove, Frederick	1871	1948
Haliburton, Thos. C.	1796	1865
Innis, H.A.	1894	1952
Kirby, William	1817	1906
Johnson, Pauline	1862	1913
Lampman, Archibald	1861	1899

Name	Born	Died
Leacock, Stephen	1869	1944
Lowry, Malcolm	1909	1957
McLuhan, Marshall	1911	1980
McClung, Nellie	1873	1951
McCrae, John	1872	1918
Montgomery, Lucy M.	1874	1942
Moodie, Susanna	1803	1885
Morin, Paul	1889	1963
Nelligan, Emile	1879	1941
Parker, Gilbert	1862	1932
Pickthall, Marjorie	1883	1922
Pratt, Edwin J.	1883	1964
Roberts, Chas. G.D.	1860	1943
Roche, Mazo de la	1885	1961
Routhier, Adolphe B.	1839	1920
Sangster, Charles	1822	1893
Scott, Duncan C.	1862	1947
Service, Robert W.	1874	1958
Anthropologists, Geologists, and Naturalists		
Adams, Frank D.	1859	1942
Anderson, Rudolph M.	1876	1961
Billings, Elkanah	1820	1876
Dionne, Charles Eusibe	1846	1925
Hill-Tout, Charles	1859	1944
Hunt, Thomas Sterry	1826	1892
Jenness, Diamond	1886	1969
Logan, William E.	1798	1875
Macoun, John	1831	1920
Miner, John T. (Jack)	1865	1944
Provancher, Leon, abbe	1820	1892
Rowan, William	1891	1957
Saunders, Charles E.	1867	1937
Saunders, William	1836	1914
Taverner, Percy A.	1875	1947
Traill, Catharine Parr	1802	1899
Tyrrell, Joseph Burr	1858	1957

Assets and Deposits of Chartered Banks in Canada

Source: Supplement to the Canada Gazette, May 4, 1981
(as of March 31, 1981 - thousands of Canadian dollars)

Bank	Assets	Deposits
Royal Bank of Canada	72,069,108	61,906,514
Canadian Imperial Bank of Commerce	58,973,291	51,101,247
Bank of Montreal	54,417,329	47,121,886
Bank of Nova Scotia	44,544,241	38,651,958
Toronto-Dominion Bank	38,370,615	32,696,984

Bank	Assets	Deposits
Banque Nationale du Canada	16,005,800	14,687,654
Mercantile Bank of Canada	4,077,073	3,729,203
Bank of British Columbia	2,626,039	2,391,153
Continental Bank of Canada	1,784,138	1,571,008
Commercial and Industrial Bank	1,083,127	937,706
Northland Bank	320,712	289,936

Canadian Government Budget

Source: Canadian Statistical Review (May 1981)
(millions of Canadian dollars)

Expenditures

Fiscal Year	National defense	Health and welfare	Agriculture	Post Office	Public works	Transport	Veterans affairs	Payments to provinces	Total expenditures
1974-75..	2,509	5,199	664	732	524	1,303	619	2,639	26,055
1975-76..	2,973	9,731	651	913	624	1,185	684	2,460	33,977
1976-77..	3,365	10,952	631	1,104	684	1,314	754	3,356	38,951
1977-78..	3,771	11,635	959	1,237	1,431	1,478	841	3,003	42,902
1978-79..	4,108	13,024	768	1,275	1,657	1,725	890	3,028	46,923
1979-80..	4,389	14,038	782	1,412	1,615	1,726	933	3,522	52,297

Revenues[1]

Fiscal year	Personal income tax	Corporation income tax	Sales tax	Other excise tax[2]	Excise duties	Customs duties	Estate taxes	Post Office	Total budgetary revenues
1974-75..	10,060	4,285	2,900	2,083	748	1,809	7	485	24,909
1975-76..	12,708	5,748	3,939	1,501	817	1,887	12	443	29,956
1976-77..	14,620	5,377	4,529	1,146	865	2,097	70	615	32,650
1977-78..	13,439	5,828	5,026	904	882	2,312	66	773	32,866
1978-79..	14,048	6,262	5,245	827	878	2,747	77	903	35,216
1979-80..	16,327	7,537	5,119	1,252	895	3,000	96	1,118	40,159

(1) This statement includes only receipts relating to revenue. Excluded are non-budgetary revenues such as Old Age Security Fund taxes, Prairie Farm Assistance Act levies, employer and employee contributions to government-held funds. (2) Beginning in Dec. 1973, this category includes oil export tax.

Canada's Largest Corporations

Source: The Financial Post 500; Toronto, Canada; June, 1981

Industrials Company (Home office)	Sales or operating revenue C$000	Assets	Foreign ownership %	Foreign owner(s)
Canadian Pacific Ltd. (Montreal Que.)	9,984,546[1]	13,038,501	35	U.S. 22%; Britain 6%; other 7%
General Motors of Canada Ltd. (Oshawa, Ont.)	9,451,307[2]	2,662,201	100	General Motors Corp., Detroit
George Weston Ltd. (Toronto, Ont.)	6,776,728	1,757,489	—	
Ford Motor Co. of Canada (Oakville, Ont.)	6,408,300[2]	2,164,500	89	Ford Motor Co., Dearborn, Mich.
Imperial Oil Ltd. (Toronto, Ont.)	6,325,000[3]	6,244,000	71	Exxon Corp., New York 70%
Alcan Aluminium Ltd. (Montreal, Que.)	6,097,378[4]	6,546,496	61	U.S. 53%; Other 8%
Bell Canada (Montreal, Que.)	6,037,084	11,449,046	4	
Gulf Canada Ltd. (Toronto, Ont.)	4,030,000[3]	3,692,000	60	Gulf Oil Corp., Pittsburgh
Shell Canada Ltd. (Toronto, Ont.)	3,962,000[3]	3,449,000	71	Royal Dutch/Shell Group
Hudson's Bay Co. (Winnipeg, Man.)	3,813,886	3,051,233	—	
Canadian National Railway (Montreal, Que.)	3,705,600	5,645,213	—	
Massey-Ferguson Ltd. (Toronto, Ont.)	3,652,968[4]	3,327,237	45	Wide distribution
Inco Ltd. (Toronto, Ont.)	3,549,807[4]	5,542,955	38	U.S. 24%; other 14%
Texaco Canada Inc. (Toronto, Ont.)	3,503,179[3]	2,603,101	91	Texaco Inc., New York
TransCanada Pipelines Ltd. (Calgary, Alta.)	3,143,382	3,399,219	—	
Seagram Co. (Montreal, Que.)	2,960,824[3]	3,240,232	—	
Simpsons-Sears Ltd. (Toronto, Ont.)	2,954,606	1,696,433	50	Sears Roebuck, Chicago
Noranda Mines Ltd. (Toronto, Ont.)	2,889,295	3,938,221	6	
Canada Packers Inc. (Toronto, Ont.)	2,842,369	n.a.	—	
Ontario Hydro (Toronto, Ont.)	2,819,215	15,593,347	—	

(1) After eliminating inter-company transactions. (2) Figures include sales to parent and affiliated companies: Ford $2,249 million (plus $1,990 overseas subsidiaries); General Motors, Chrysler unstated. (3) Excise taxes deducted. (4) Converted from $U.S. or British pounds at average rate during fiscal year; assets converted at fiscal year end rate.

Personal Expenditure on Consumer Goods and Services in Current Dollars

Source: Statistics Canada   (millions of dollars)

	1972	1973	1974	1975	1976	1977	1978	1979
Food, beverages and tobacco........	13,437	15,395	17,762	20,757	22,679	24,715	27,769	30,864
Clothing and footwear............	4,550	5,120	6,412	7,155	8,132	8,787	9,555	10,667
Gross rent, fuel and power..........	11,412	12,506	14,271	16,445	19,146	21,882	24,372	27,190
Furniture, furnishings household equipment and operation...	6,135	7,304	8,652	9,884	11,117	12,006	12,997	14,306
Medical care and health services.......	1,804	2,054	2,466	2,896	3,465	3,809	4,249	4,555
Transportation and communication......	9,030	10,551	12,161	14,292	16,390	17,963	19,586	22,380
Recreation, entertainment, education and cultural services.....	6,288	7,265	8,655	9,972	11,554	12,696	13,894	15,349
Personal goods and services.........	9,423	10,912	12,870	15,062	17,463	19,263	21,547	24,403
Total..............	62,208	71,278	83,388	96,995	110,886	122,471	135,359	150,489
Durable goods.............	9,440	11,481	13,139	15,320	17,021	18,400	20,053	22,601
Semi-durable goods.............	7,962	9,059	11,184	12,428	14,176	15,396	16,796	18,831
Non-durable goods.............	19,432	22,302	26,218	30,422	33,967	37,343	41,813	46,513
Services.............	25,374	28,436	32,847	38,825	45,722	51,332	56,697	62,544

Canadian Foreign Trade

Source: Canadian Statistical Review (May 1981)
(millions of Canadian dollars)

	Exports[1]				Imports			
Year	All countries	U.S.	Japan	UK	All other countries	All countries	U.S.	Japan	UK	All other countries
1974	32,176.7	21,325.1	2,229	1,902.9	6,719.7	31,639.3	21,305.9	1,428.1	1,126.5	6,488
1975	33,245.5	21,697.1	2,133.4	1,800.4	7,614.6	34,690.7	23,616.3	1,205.3	1,221.9	7,640.4
1976	38,396.6	25,893.9	2,396.5	1,877.9	8,228.3	37,444.4	25,751.7	1,523.9	1,149.7	9,019.1
1977	44,553.5	31,111.5	2,518.6	1,946.1	8,977.3	42,332.3	29,814.9	1,792.9	1,278.8	9,445.7
1978	53,182.8	37,371.6	3,063.2	2,006.5	10,741.5	50,101.6	35,436.3	2,276.0	1,609.5	10,779.8
1979	65,514.3	44,452.4	4,093.5	2,622.4	14,364	62,724.0	45,419.5	2,157.1	1,928.5	13,218.9
1980(p)	75,952.3	48,058.4	4,387.4	3,239.0	20,267.5	68,979.4	48,414.2	2,792.2	1,977.3	15,795.7

(1) including re-exports. p-preliminary

Canadian Shipping Traffic

Source: Statistics Canada (thousand short tons)
Total cargo handled includes cargo loaded and unloaded in foreign and coastwise shipping.

Year	Halifax	Saint John	Quebec	Montreal	Toronto	Vancouver	All Ports	Coastwise
1973	13,703	12,181	15,946	21,177	4,170	39,126	320,498	122,436
1974	13,290	9,998	12,943	19,654	4,605	36,761	302,138	118,241
1975	11,743	10,851	12,496	18,633	4,891	35,521	303,098	119,871
1976	11,547	11,121	13,405	17,159	3,098	29,244	307,605	118,790
1977	12,213	11,251	15,334	18,529	2,982	32,767	325,477	128,548
1978	12,143	13,824	15,081	17,899	2,824	43,929	330,307	133,749

Canadian Sea Fish Catch and Exports

Source: Fisheries and Oceans Canada

	Total	Landings of Sea Fish						Exports to[1]			Exports[1]	
Year	Value	Total	Nfld.	P.E.I.	N.S.	N.B.	Que.	B.C.	Total	U.S.	Other	Salmon	Lobster
		(in metric tons)							(in millions of pounds)				
1973	$296,288,000	993,559	306,586	28,531	279,144	129,774	73,165	176,359	752.6	491.6	211.1	93.1	20.1
1974	259,108,000	834,165	234,510	16,329	283,045	160,120	53,524	132,904	551.4	396.4	155.0	78.5	18.2
1975	225,423,000	688,591	86,637	13,608	263,993	121,564	48,988	114,306	558.9	397.8	191.1	51.3	19.5
1976	364,754,000	1,063,071	340,241	17,123	368,456	117,937	41,948	177,366	652.9	427.2	225.7	30.6	19.3
1977	456,130,000	1,211,408	394,148	19,801	407,368	131,937	54,292	203,862	830.6	450.7	379.9	66.6	20.0
1978	668,191,000	1,352,027	463,959	25,660	444,869	151,393	67,350	198,796	931.2	494.0	436.9	78.2	21.9
1979	840,267,000	1,393,295	569,107	31,059	421,154	137,217	79,165	155,593	938.6	514.6	424.0	69.7	28.2

(1) Exports include sea and freshwater fish and shellfish products but exclude bait, meal, oils, offal, livers, fish roe, and fishery foods and feeds.

Marketed Value of Canadian Fish Catches

Source: Fisheries and Oceans Canada (thousands of Canadian dollars)

Province	1978[1]	1979[1]	Province	1978[1]	1979[1]
Newfoundland	325,004	411,212	Manitoba	15,242	21,940
Prince Edward Island	42,548	71,935	Saskatchewan	4,521	7,255
Nova Scotia	428,697	418,311	Alberta	1,154	1,749
New Brunswick	164,300	223,066	British Columbia	517,557	565,630
Quebec	53,264	72,833	Yukon & NWT	2,333	3,222
Ontario	34,322	51,746	Total[2]	1,534,922	1,804,689

(1) Value after processing, both sea and freshwater fisheries; includes marine plants, aquatic mammals etc. (2) The sum of the provincial totals differs from the Canada total due to removal of inter-provincial shipments.

Canadian Grain Deliveries at Western Grain Centers

Source: Canadian Grain Commission
(thousands of tons)

Crop year 1979-80

Province or area	Wheat	Oats	Barley	Rye	Flaxseed	Rapeseed	Total
Western Canada	18,704	319	5,408	449	675	2,928	28,483
Manitoba	2,448	39	921	94	368	472	4,341
Saskatchewan	12,056	59	1,598	198	206	944	15,062
Alberta & B.C.	4,199	222	2,889	157	100	1,512	9,080

Crop year 1978-79

Province or area	Wheat	Oats	Barley	Rye	Flaxseed	Rapeseed	Total
Western Canada	14,473	363	5,364	247	425	2,945	23,816
Manitoba	1,914	116	1,039	42	234	473	3,818
Saskatchewan	9,646	108	1,838	110	152	1,130	12,984
Alberta & B.C.	2,913	139	2,487	94	39	1,342	7,014

Canadian Consumer Price Index

Source: Statistics Canada
(All items: 1971 = 100)

Year	Avg.	Year	Avg.	Year	Avg.	Year	Avg.
1965	80.5	1969	94.1	1973	112.7	1977	160.8
1966	83.5	1970	97.2	1974	125.0	1978	175.2
1967	86.5	1971	100.0	1975	138.5	1979	191.2
1968	90.0	1972	104.8	1976	148.9	1980	210.6

Price Indexes By Item

Source: Canadian Statistical Review, April 1981 (1971 = 100)

Year and month	All items	Food	Shelter	Clothing	Trans-portation	Health, personal	Recreation, education	Tobacco, alcohol	Total services
1976	148.9	166.2	145.7	132.0	143.3	144.3	136.2	134.3	149.6
1977	160.8	180.1	159.3	141.0	153.3	155.0	142.7	143.8	163.2
1978	175.2	208.0	170.8	146.4	162.2	166.2	148.2	155.5	174.3
1979	191.2	235.4	180.5	159.9	178.0	181.2	158.4	166.7	186.5
1980	210.6	260.6	192.4	178.7	200.7	199.3	173.5	185.3	201.8
1981 (March)	229.4	285.1	204.0	188.9	227.1	216.7	186.3	197.3	216.8

Canadian General and Allied Special Hospitals

Source: Health and Welfare Canada

1980[1]	Hospitals			Beds			Admissions[2]			Expenses[2] ($1,000)
	Public	Private	Fed.	Public	Private	Fed.	Public	Private	Fed.	Public
Newfoundland . .	47	—	—	3,323	—	—	91,962	—	—	163,675
Prince Edward Is.	10	—	1	741	—	14	26,129	—	n.a.	27,053
Nova Scotia. . . .	48	—	3	5,505	—	162	144,092	—	2,608	266,769
New Brunswick. .	33	—	1	4,250	—	10	116,392	—	n.a.	193,304
Quebec	194	39	11	48,745	2,591	1,265	701,509	5,212	1,793	2,281,844
Ontario	231	22	17	48,136	571	615	1,291,776	11,772	9,119	2,530,757
Manitoba	80	—	23	6,276	—	654	157,323	—	4,015	291,745
Saskatchewan . .	138	—	3	7,799	—	74	206,328	—	1,220	274,964
Alberta	144	—	9	14,863	—	848	366,955	—	8,816	630,685
British Columbia .	119	1	15	18,320	7	115	411,847	255	965	759,678
Yukon	—	—	6	—	—	159	—	—	3,838	—
N.W.T.	3	—	43	147	—	250	3,789	—	3,939	8,998
Canada	1,047	62	132	158,105	3,169	4,166	3,518,102	17,239	36,313	7,429,472

(1) as of March 31. (2) Preliminary data.

Canadian Active Civilian Doctors

Source: Health and Welfare Canada (Dec. 31, 1981)

Province	Number[1]	Population per physician[1]	Province	Number[1]	Population per physician[1]
Newfoundland	866	674	Saskatchewan	1,442	677
Prince Edward Island	152	816	Alberta	3,406	627
Nova Scotia	1,588	539	British Columbia	5,265	510
New Brunswick.	786	902	Yukon	28	768
Quebec.	12,160	520	Northwest Territories	40	1,070
Ontario	16,664	516			
Manitoba	1,878	547	Canada	44,275	544

(1) Includes interns and residents.

Patients in Canadian Mental Hospitals

Source: Health and Welfare Canada

Average patients per day, 1978

	Canada	Nfld.	P.E.I.	N.S.	N.B.	Que.	Ont.	Man.	Sask.	Alta.	B.C.
Public hospitals:											
Mental	9,596	319	242	273	921	465	3,952	913	275	1,023	1,213
Psychiatric	827	—	—	405	—	—	340	40	25	—	17
Other.	901	—	—	—	—	87	88	—	—	37	689
Total private	320	—	—	—	—	—	320	—	—	—	—
Total mental hospitals	11,644	319	242	678	921	552	4,700	953	300	1,060	1,919

NATIONS OF THE WORLD

The nations of the world are listed in alphabetical order. Initials in the following articles include UN (United Nations), OAS (Org. of American States), NATO (North Atlantic Treaty Org.), EC (European Communities or Common Market), OAU (Org. of African Unity). Sources: Population figures: International Demographic Data Center, U.S. Bureau of the Census; areas: U.S. State Department; crude steel production statistics: International Iron and Steel Institute, Brussels. Health and education statistics as reported in *World Military and Social Expenditures 1980*, Ruth Leger Sivard; copyright © 1980 by World Priorities Inc., Box 1003, Leesburg, VA 22075.

PQLI - Physical Quality of Life Index: a composite index of infant mortality, life expectancy at age one, and literacy (each indexed on a scale from 0 to 100), calculated by averaging the 3 indexes, giving equal weight to each. Source: *The United States and World Development: Agenda 1980*, by Martin M. McLaughlin and the Staff of the Overseas Development Council (New York: Praeger Publishers, 1980). © Overseas Development Council.

See special color section for maps and flags of all nations.

Afghanistan

Democratic Republic of Afghanistan

People: Population (1980 est.): 15,800,000. **Pop. density:** 60.77 per sq. mi. **Ethnic groups:** Pushtuns (Pathans) nearly 60%; Tajiks nearly 30%; Uzbek over 5%; Hazara, others. **Languages:** Pushtu (Iranian), Dari Persian (spoken by Tajiks, Hazaras), Uzbek (Turkic). **Religions:** Sunni Muslim (90%), Shi'a Muslim (10%).

Geography: Area: 260,000 sq. mi., slightly smaller than Texas. **Location:** Between Soviet Central Asia and the Indian subcontinent. **Neighbors:** Pakistan on E, S, Iran on W, USSR on N; the NE tip touches China. **Topography:** The country is landlocked and mountainous, much of it over 4,000 ft. above sea level. The Hindu Kush Mts. tower 16,000 ft. above Kabul and reach a height of 25,000 ft. to the E. Trade with Pakistan flows through the 35-mile long Khyber Pass. The climate is dry, with extreme temperatures, and large desert regions, though mountain rivers produce intermittent fertile valleys. **Capital:** Kabul. **Cities** (1978 est.): Kabul 800,000; Kandahar 230,000; Herat 150,000; Baghlan 110,874; Kundus 108,000; Mazir-i-Sharif 100,000.

Government: Head of state, head of government, and secy. gen., People's Democratic Party: Pres. Babrak Karmal; in office: Dec. 27, 1979. **Local divisions:** 24 provinces, each under a governor. **Armed forces:** regulars 90,000; reserves 150,000.

Economy: Industries: Textiles, carpets, cement, sheepskin coats. **Chief crops:** Cotton, oilseeds, fruits. **Minerals:** Copper, lead, gas, coal, zinc, iron, silver, asbestos. **Crude oil reserves** (1978): 284 mln. bbls. **Other resources:** Wool, hides, karacui pelts. **Per capita arable land:** 1.3 acres. **Meat prod.** (1978): beef: 66,000 metric tons; lamb: 122,000 metric tons. **Electricity prod.** (1977): 700.00 mln. kwh. **Labor force:** 53% agric., 7% commerce, 16% services.

Finance: Currency: Afghani (Apr. 1981: 44.50 = $1 US). **Gross domestic product** (1978 est.): $3.76 bln. **Per capita income** (1978): $168. **Imports** (1978): $395 mln.; partners (1976): USSR 24%, Jap. 19%, W.Ger. 12%, Ind. 12%. **Exports** (1980): $610 mln.; partners (1976): USSR 39%, Ind. 12%, Pak. 12%, W.Ger. 10%. **Tourists** (1977): 117,100; receipts: $38 mln. **International reserves less gold** (Feb. 1981): $345.99 mln. **Gold:** 965,000 oz t. **Consumer prices** (change in 1976): 0.04% **Transport: Motor vehicles:** in use (1971): 38,400 passenger cars, 26,100 comm. vehicles **Civil aviation:** 290 mln. passenger-km (1977); 13.9 mln. freight ton-km.

Communications: Radios: 115,000 in use (1976). **Telephones in use** (1978): 31,200. **Daily newspaper circ.** (1977): 77,000; 4 per 1,000 pop.

Health: Life expectancy at birth (1975): 39.9 male; 40.7 female. **Births** (per 1,000 pop. 1978): 45.2. **Deaths** (per 1,000 pop. 1978): 21.1 **Natural increase** (1978): 2.4%. **Hospital beds** (per 100,000 pop. 1977): 21. **Physicians** (per 100,000 pop. 1977): 5.

Education (1977): **Literacy:** 12% **Pop. 5-19:** in school: 13%, teachers per 1,000: 4. **PQLI:** 14.

Afghanistan, occupying a favored invasion route since antiquity, has been variously known as Ariana or Bactria (in ancient times) and Khorasan (in the Middle Ages). Foreign empires alternated rule with local emirs and kings until the 18th century, when a unified kingdom was established. In 1973, a military coup ushered in a republic.

Afghanistan has received aid from the U.S., USSR, and China.

Largest trade partner is the USSR, natural gas the chief export. Pro-Soviet leftists took power in a bloody 1978 coup, and concluded a 20-year economic and military treaty with the USSR. The U.S. cut off aid, 1979, following the Feb. 14 death of its ambassador in a shootout between government and rebel forces. Late in Dec. 1979, the USSR began a massive military airlift into Kabul. The three-month old regime of Hafizullah Amin ended with a Soviet backed coup, Dec. 27th. He was replaced by Babrak Karmal, considered a more pro-Soviet leader. Soviet troops, estimated at between 60,000-100,000, fanned out over Afghanistan, fighting rebels. Fighting continued during 1980 and 1981 as the Soviets found themselves engaged in a long, protracted guerilla war.

Albania

People's Socialist Republic of Albania

People: Population (1980 est.): 2,730,000. **Pop. density:** 245.95 per sq. mi. **Urban** (1977): 38%. **Ethnic groups:** Albanians (Gegs in N, Tosks in S) 95%, Greeks 2.5%. **Languages:** Albanian (Tosk is official dialect), Greek. **Religions:** (historically) Moslems 70%, Orthodox 20%, Roman Catholic 10%. All public worship and religious institutions were outlawed in 1967.

Geography: Area: 11,100 sq. mi., slightly larger than Maryland. **Location:** On SE coast of Adriatic Sea. **Neighbors:** Greece on S, Yugoslavia on N, E. **Topography:** Apart from a narrow coastal plain, Albania consists of hills and mountains covered with scrub forest, cut by small E-W rivers. **Capital:** Tirana. **Cities** (1973 est.): Tirana 169,300; Shkoder 49,000; Durres 80,000; Vlore 58,400.

Government: Head of state: Pres. Haxhi Lleshi; b. 1913; in office: Aug. 1, 1953. **Head of government:** Chmn. Mehmet Shehu; b. Jan. 10, 1913; in office: July 20, 1954. **Head of Communist Party:** Enver Hoxha; b. Oct. 16, 1908; in office: Nov. 8, 1941. **Local divisions:** 29 administrative districts and one independent city. **Armed forces:** regulars 43,000; reserves 60,000.

Economy: Industries: Chem. fertilizers, textiles, electric cables. **Chief crops:** Grain, corn, sugar beets, cotton, tobacco, fruits. **Minerals:** Chromium, coal, copper, bitumen, iron, oil. **Other resources:** Forests. **Per capita arable land:** 0.5 acres. **Meat prod.** (1978): beef: 20,000 metric tons; pork: 12,000 metric tons; lamb: 23,000 metric tons. **Electricity prod.** (1977): 2.15 bln. kwh. **Labor force:** 61% agric; 40% industry and commerce.

Finance: Currency: Lek (Mar. 1980: 7.00 = $1 US). **Gross domestic product** (1976 est.) $1.3 bln. **Per capita income** (1976): $490. **Imports** (1976): $250 mln.; partners (1975): China, E. Eur., It. **Exports** (1976): $200 mln.; partners (1975): China, E. Eur.

Transport: Motor vehicles: in use (1971): 38,400 passenger cars, 26,100 comm. vehicles. **Chief ports:** Durres, Vlone.

Communications: Television sets: 4,500 in use (1976). **Radios:** 180,000 in use (1976). **Daily newspaper circ.** (1976): 115,000; 45 per 1,000 pop.

Health: Life expectancy at birth (1966): 64.9 male; 67.0 female. **Births** (per 1,000 pop. 1971): 33.3. **Deaths** (per 1,000 pop. 1971): 8.1 **Natural increase** (1971): 2.5%. **Hospital beds** (per 100,000 pop. 1977): 649. **Physicians** (per 100,000 pop. 1977): 104. **Infant mortality** (per 1,000 live births 1971): 86.8.

Education (1977): **Literacy:** 75%. **Pop. 5-19:** in school: 64%, teachers per 1,000: 29. **PQLI:** 76.

Ancient Illyria was conquered by Romans, Slavs, and Turks

(15th century); the latter Islamized the population. Independent Albania was proclaimed in 1912, republic was formed in 1920. Self-styled King Zog I ruled 1925-39, until Italy invaded.

Communist partisans took over in 1944, allied Albania with USSR, then broke with USSR in 1960 over de-Stalinization. Strong political alliance with China followed, leading to several billion dollars in aid, which was curtailed after 1974. China cut off aid in 1978 when Albania attacked its policies after the 1976 death of Chinese ruler Mao Tse-tung.

In 1971, after years of mistrust, Albania resumed relations with Greece and Yugoslavia, but ties with U.S. and USSR are still rejected.

Industrialization, pressed in 1960s, slowed in 1970s. Large-scale purges of officials occurred 1973-76.

Algeria

Democratic and Popular Republic of Algeria

People: Population (1980 est.); 19,700,000. **Age distrib. (%):** 0–14: 47.2; 15–59: 46.2; 60+: 6.6. **Pop. density:** 21.45 per sq. mi. **Urban** (1974): 52.0%. **Ethnic groups:** Arabs 75%, Berbers 25%. **Languages:** Arab, Berber (indigenous language), French. **Religions:** Sunni Moslem (state religion).

Geography: Area: 918,497 sq. mi., more than 3 times the size of Texas. **Location:** In NW Africa, from Mediterranean Sea into Sahara Desert. **Neighbors:** Morocco on W, Mauritania, Mali, Niger on S, Libya, Tunisia on E. **Topography:** The Tell, located on the coast, comprises fertile plains 50-100 miles wide, with a moderate climate and adequate rain. Two major chains of the Atlas Mts., running roughly E-W, and reaching 7,000 ft., enclose a dry plateau region. Below lies the Sahara, mostly desert with major mineral resources. **Capital:** Algiers. **Cities** (1980 est.): Algiers 2,200,000; Oran 633,000; Constantine 384,000; Annaba 284,000.

Government: Head of state: Pres. Chadli Bendjedid; b. Apr. 14, 1929; in office: Feb. 9, 1979. **Head of government:** Mohammed Behahmed Abdelghani; in office: Mar. 8, 1979. **Local divisions:** 31 wilayas (states); governors are responsible to the center. **Armed forces:** regulars 88,800; reserves 100,000.

Economy: Industries: Wine, cigarettes, oil products, iron, steel, textiles, fertilizer, plastics. **Chief crops:** Grains, corn, winegrapes, potatoes, artichokes, flax, olives, tobacco, dates, figs, pomegranates. **Minerals:** Mercury, oil, iron, zinc, lead, coal, copper, natural gas, phosphates. **Crude oil reserves** (1980): 8.44 bln. bbls. **Other resources:** Cork trees. **Per capital arable land:** .9 acres. **Meat prod.** (1978): beef: 29,000 metric tons; lamb: 58,000 metric tons. **Fish catch** (1977): 43,500 metric tons. **Electricity prod.** (1978): 4.70 bln. kwh. **Crude steel prod.** (1979): 600,000 metric tons. **Labor force:** 50% agric.; 20% ind. and commerce; 10% government; 10% services.

Finance: Currency: Dinar (Apr. 1981: 4.25 = $1 US). **Gross domestic product** (1979): $29 bln. **Per capita income** (1979): $1,600. **Imports** (1980): $10.56 bln.; partners (1977); France 24%, W. Ger. 15%, It. 10%, U.S. 9%. **Exports** (1980): $12.5 bln.; partners (1977): U.S. 52%, W. Ger. 15%, France 13%, It. 5%. **Tourists** (1977): 241,700; receipts: $56 mln. **National budget** (1974): $5.68 bln. revenues; $2.99 bln. expenditures. **International reserves less gold** (Apr. 1981): $3.84 bln. **Gold:** 5.56 mln. oz t. **Consumer prices** (change in 1979): 11.5%

Transport: Railway traffic (1977): 1.51 bln. passenger-km; 1.94 bln. net ton-km. **Motor vehicles:** in use (1975): 286,100 passenger cars, 154,700 comm. vehicles; assembled (1977): 6,360 comm. vehicles. **Chief ports:** Algiers, Oran.

Communications: Television sets: 525,000 in use (1976), 54,000 manuf. (1976). **Radios:** 3.00 mln. in use (1976), 21,000 manuf. (1976). **Telephones in use** (1978): 297,689. **Daily newspaper circ.** (1977): 236,000; 13 per 1,000 pop.

Health: Life expectancy at birth (1975): 52.9 male; 55.0 female. **Births** (per 1,000 pop. 1975): 48.8. **Deaths** (per 1,000 pop. 1975): 15.4. **Natural increase** (1975): 3.3%. **Hospital beds,** (per 100,000 pop. 1977): 263. **Physicians** (per 100,000 pop. 1977): 19. **Infant mortality** (per 1,000 live births 1977): 110.

Education (1977): **Literacy:** 36%. **Pop. 5-19:** in school: 55%, teachers per 1,000: 16. **PQLI:** 45.

Earliest known inhabitants were ancestors of Berbers, followed by Phoenicians, Romans, Vandals, and, finally, Arabs; but 25% still speak Berber dialects. Turkey ruled 1518 to 1830,

when France took control.

Large-scale European immigration and French cultural inroads did not prevent an Arab nationalist movement from launching guerilla war. Peace, and French withdrawal, was negotiated with French Pres. Charles de Gaulle. One million Europeans left.

Ahmed Ben Bella was the victor of infighting, and ruled 1962-65, when an army coup installed Col. Houari Boumedienne as leader. Ben Bella remained under house arrest until 1979.

In 1967, Algeria declared war with Israel, broke with U.S., and moved toward eventual military and political ties with the USSR. French oil interests were partly seized in 1971, but relations with the West have since improved, based on oil and gas exports; U.S. ties were resumed 1974.

Algeria, strongly backing Saharan guerillas' demands for a cease fire and self-determination, encouraged Mauritania to come to terms with the Polisario Front, 1979.

The one-party Socialist regime faces endemic mass unemployment and poverty, despite land reform and industrialization attempts.

Andorra

Valleys of Andorra

People: Population (1980 est.): 35,000. **Age distrib. (%):** 0–14: 29.2; 14–59: 61.7; 60+: 9.1. **Pop. density:** 180.85 per sq. mi. **Ethnic groups:** Spanish over 60%, Andorran 30%, French 6%. **Languages:** Catalan (official), Spanish, French. **Religions:** Roman Catholic.

Geography: Area: 188 sq. mi., half the size of New York City. **Location:** In Pyrenees Mtns. **Neighbors:** Spain on S, France on N. **Topography:** High mountains and narrow valleys over the country. **Capital:** Andorra la Vella.

Government: Head of state: Co-princes are the president of France (François Mitterrand; in office: May 21, 1981) and the Roman Catholic bishop of Urgel in Spain (Joan Martí y Alanís, in office: Jan. 31, 1971). **Head of govt:** Syndic Estanislao Sangra Font, in office: Jan 1, 1979. **Local divisions:** 7 parishes.

Economy: Industries: Tourism, sheep raising. **Labor force:** 20% agric.; 80% ind. and commerce; services; government.

Finance: Currency: French franc, Spanish peseta.

Communications: Television sets: 3,000 in use (1976). **Radios:** 6,600 in use (1976). **Telephones in use** (1978): 10,361.

Health: Births (per 1,000 pop. 1976): 16.5. **Deaths** (per 1,000 pop. 1976): 5.0. **Natural increase** (1976): 1.2%.

The present political status, with joint sovereignty by France and the bishop of Urgel, dates from 1278.

Tourism, especially skiing, is the economic mainstay. A free port, allowing for an active trading center, draws more than 7 million tourists annually. The ensuing economic prosperity accompanied by Andorra's virtual law-free status, has given rise to calls for reform.

Angola

People's Republic of Angola

People: Population (1980 est.): 7,080,000. **Pop. density:** 14.70 per sq. mi. **Ethnic groups:** Ovimbundu 38%, Kimbundu 23%; Bakongo 13%, European 1%; Mesticos 2%. **Languages:** Portuguese (official), various Bantu languages. **Religions:** Animists 84%, Roman Catholic 12%, Protestant 4%.

Geography: Area: 481,351 sq. mi., larger than Texas and California combined. **Location:** In SW Africa on Atlantic coast. **Neighbors:** Namibia (SW Africa) on S, Zambia on E, Zaire on N; Cabinda, an enclave separated from rest of country by short Atlantic coast of Zaire, borders Congo Republic. **Topography:** Most of Angola consists of a plateau elevated 3,000 to 5,000 feet above sea level, rising from a narrow coastal strip. There is also a temperate highland area in the west-central region, a desert in the S, and a tropical rain forest covering Cabinda. **Capital:** Luanda. **Cities** (1970 cen.): Luanda (met.) 475,328.

Government: Head of state: Pres. Jose Eduardo dos Santos b. Aug. 28, 1942; in office: Sept. 20, 1979. **Local divisions:** 17 provinces. **Armed forces:** regulars 40,000.

Economy: Industries: Alcohol, cotton goods, fishmeal, paper, palm oil, footwear. **Chief crops:** Coffee (5% of world crop), corn, sugar, palm oil, cotton, wheat, tobacco, caeao, sisal, wax.

Minerals: Iron, diamonds (over 2 mln. carats a year), copper, manganese, sulphur, phosphates, oil. **Crude oil reserves** (1980): 1.2 bln. bbls. **Per capita arable land:** 0.5 acres. **Meat prod.** (1978): beef: 52,000 metric tons; pork: 12,000 metric tons. **Fish catch** (1977): 113,400 metric tons. **Electricity prod.** (1977): 1.36 bln. kwh. **Labor force:** 75% agric., industry, commerce, service.

Finance: Currency: Kwanza (Sept. 1979: 31.50 = $1 US). **Gross domestic product** (1976): $1.83 bln. **Per capita income** (1976): $500. **Imports** 1979): $830 mln.; partners: Port. 22%, W. Ger. 13%, U.S. 10%, S. Afr. 10%. **Exports** (1979): $1.4 bln.; partners: U.S. 38%, Port. 27%, Can. 8%, Jap. 6%. **Tourists** (1974): 995,100; receipts: bb $109 bln.

Transport: Railway traffic (1974): 418 mln. passenger-km; 5.46 bln. net ton-km. **Motor vehicles:** in use (1973): 127,300 passenger cars, 35,700 comm. vehicles. **Chief ports:** Lobito, Luanda.

Communications: Radios: 116,000 in use (1976), 38,000 manuf. (1974). **Telephones in use** (1978): 29,796. **Daily newspaper circ.** (1976): 119,000; 19 per 1,000 pop.

Health: Life expectancy at birth (1975): 37.0 male; 40.1 female. **Births** (per 1,000 pop. 1975): 48.0. **Deaths** (per 1,000 pop. 1975): 25.3. **Natural increase** (1975): 2.3%. **Hospital beds** (per 100,000 pop. 1977): 306. **Physicians** (per 100,000 pop 1977): 6. **Infant mortality** (per 1,000 live births 1979): 182.

Education (1977): **Literacy:** 12%. **Pop. 5-19:** in school: 28%, teachers per 1,000: 9. **PQLI:** 14.

From the early centuries AD to 1500, Bantu tribes penetrated most of the region. Portuguese came in 1583, allied with the Bakongo kingdom in the north, and developed the slave trade. Large-scale colonization did not begin until the 20th century, when 400,000 Portuguese immigrated.

A guerrilla war begun in 1961 lasted until 1974, when Portugal offered independence. Violence between the National Front, based in Zaire, the Soviet-backed Popular Movement, and the National Union, aided by the U.S. and S. Africa, killed thousands of blacks, drove most whites to emigrate, and completed economic ruin. Some 15,000 Cuban troops and massive Soviet aid helped the Popular Movement win most of the country after independence Nov. 11, 1975. Some units of the National Union continued to resist in 1978.

In the first such large-scale action since 1978, 3,000 S. African troops crossed the southern Angolan border June 7, killing more than 300 civilians and occupying several towns.

Russian influence, backed by 25,000 Cubans, East Germans, and Portuguese Communists, is strong in the Marxist regime.

Argentina

Argentine Republic

People: Population (1980 est.): 27,300,000. **Age distrib.** (%): 0–14: 28.5; 15–59: 59.6; 60+: 11.9 **Pop. density:** 25.46 per sq. mi. **Urban** (1977): 72%. **Ethnic groups:** Europeans 97% (Spanish, Italian), Indians, Mestizos, Arabs. **Languages:** Spanish (official), English, Italian, German, French. **Religions:** Roman Catholic 90%, Protestant 2%, Jewish 2%, other 6%.

Geography: Area: 1,072,067 sq. mi., 4 times the size of Texas, second largest in S. America. **Location:** Occupies most of southern S. America. **Neighbors:** Chile on W, Bolivia, Paraguay on N, Brazil, Uruguay on NE. **Topography:** The mountains in W: the Andean, Central, Misiones, and Southern. Aconcagua is the highest peak in the Western hemisphere, alt. 22,834 ft. E of the Andes are heavily wooded plains, called the Gran Chaco in the N, and the fertile, treeless Pampas in the central region. Patagonia, in the S, is bleak and arid. Rio de la Plata, 170 by 140 mi., is mostly fresh water, from 2,500-mi. Paranak and 1,000-mi. Uruguay rivers. **Capital:** Buenos Aires. **Cities** (1978 est.): Buenos Aires 2,982,000; Cordoba 781,565; Rosario 750,455; La Plata 391,247; San Miguel de Tucuman 321,567.

Government: Head of state: Pres. Roberto Eduardo Viola; b. Oct. 13, 1924; in office: Oct. 3, 1980. **Local divisions:** 22 provinces, 1 natl. terr. and 1 federal dist., under military governors. **Armed forces:** regulars 132,900; reserves 250,000.

Economy: Industries: Meat processing, flour milling, chemicals, textiles, machinery, autos. **Chief crops:** Cotton, grains, corn, grapes, linseed, sugar, fruit, tobacco, peanuts. Grains are exported. **Minerals:** Oil, coal, lead, zinc, iron, sulphur, silver, copper, gold. **Crude oil reserves** (1980): 2.40 bln. bbls. **Per capita arable land:** 2.3 acres. **Meat prod.** (1978): beef: 3.19 mln. metric tons; pork: 211,000 metric tons; lamb: 137,000 metric tons. **Fish catch** (1977): 392,800 metric tons. **Electricity prod.** (1978): 29.05 bln, kwh. **Crude steel prod.** (1979): 3.2 mln. metric tons. **Labor force:** 19% agric.; 36% ind. and man.; 20% services.

Finance: Currency: Peso (Apr. 1981: 3,165.0 = $1 US). **Gross domestic product** (1978 est.): $61.5 bln. **Per capita income** (1978 est.): $2,331. **Imports** (1979): $6.7 bln.; partners (1977): U.S. 19%, W. Ger. 10%, Braz. 9%, Jap. 9%. **Exports** (1979): $7.8 bln.; partners (1977): Neth. 10%, Braz. 8%, It. 8%, U.S. 7%. **Tourists** (1977): 1,350,000; receipts: $213 mln. **National budget** (1978): $4.28 bln. revenues; $6.64 bln. expenditures. **International reserves less gold** (Feb. 1981): $4.54 bln. **Gold:** 4.37 mln. oz t. **Consumer prices** (change in 1980): 100.8%.

Transport: Railway traffic (1978): 11.24 bln. passenger-km; 10.37 bln. net ton-km. **Motor vehicles:** in use (1974): 2.03 mln. passenger cars, 879,800 comm. vehicles; manuf. (1978): 135,600 passenger cars, 45,480 comm. vehicles. **Civil aviation:** 5,292 mln. passenger-km (1978); 128,568 mln. freight ton-km (1978). **Chief ports:** Buenos Aires, Bahia Blanca, La Plata.

Communications: Television sets: 4.5 mln. in use (1975), 254,000. manuf. (1977). **Radios:** 21 mln. in use (1975). **Telephones in use** (1978): 2,584,801. **Daily newspaper circ.** (1976): 2,682,000.

Health: Life expectancy at birth (1975): 65.16 male; 71.38 female. **Births** (per 1,000 pop. 1970): 22.9. **Deaths** (per 1,000 pop. 1970): 9.4. **Natural increase** (1970): 1.4%. **Hospital beds** (per 100,000 pop. 1977): 524. **Physicians** (per 100,000 pop. 1977): 192. **Infant mortality** (per 1,000 live births 1970): 59.0.

Education (1977): **Literacy:** 93%. **Pop. 5-19:** in school: 59%, teachers per 1,000: 37. **PQLI:** 85.

Nomadic Indians roamed the Pampas when Spaniards arrived, 1515-1516, led by Juan Diaz de Solis. Nearly all the Indians were killed by the late 19th century. The colonists won independence, 1810-1819, and a long period of disorders ended in a strong centralized government.

Large-scale Italian, German, and Spanish immigration in the decades after 1880 spurred modernization, making Argentina the most prosperous, educated, and industrialized of the major Latin American nations. Social reforms were enacted in the 1920s, but military coups prevailed 1930-46, until the election of Gen. Juan Peron as president.

Peron, with his wife Eva Duarte effected labor reforms, but also suppressed speech and press freedoms, closed religious schools, and ran the country into debt. A 1955 coup exiled Peron, who was followed by a series of military and civilian regimes. Peron returned in 1973, and was once more elected president. He died 10 months later, succeeded by his wife, Isabel, who had been elected vice president, and who became the first woman head of state in the Western hemisphere.

A military junta ousted Mrs. Peron in 1976 amid charges of corruption and placed her under house arrest. Under a continuing state of siege, the army battled guerrillas and leftists, killed 5,000 people, and jailed and tortured others. The government rejected a report of the Inter-American Human Rights Commission, 1980, which charged widespread killing, torture, and arbitrary detention.

A severe worsening in economic conditions placed extreme pressure on the military government of Viola. It was reported that in the first half of 1981, unemployment doubled, inflation was into triple figures and the peso was devalued by more than 200 percent. On July 6, 1981, the 50-year-old Mrs. Peron was ordered freed on parole by a federal court.

Australia

Commonwealth of Australia

People: Population (1980 est): 14,620,000. **Age distrib.** (%): 0–14: 26.6; 15–59: 60.2; 60+: 13.2. **Pop. density:** 4.93 per sq. mi. **Urban** (1976): 86%. **Ethnic groups:** British 95%, other European 3%, aborigines (including mixed) 1.5%. **Languages:** English, aboriginal languages. **Religions:** Anglican 28%, other Protestant 25%, Roman Catholic 25%.

Geography: Area: 2,965,368 sq. mi., almost as large as the 48 contiguous U.S. states. **Location:** SE of Asia, Indian O. is W and S, Pacific O. (Coral, Tasman seas) is E; they meet N of Australia in Timor and Arafura seas: Tasmania lies 150 mi. S of Victoria state, across Bass Strait. **Neighbors:** Nearest are Indonesia, Papua New Guinea on N, Solomons, Fiji, and New Zealand on E. **Topography:** An island continent. The Great Dividing Range along the E coast has Mt. Kosciusko, 7,310 ft. The W plateau rises to 2,000 ft., with arid areas in the Great Sandy and Great Victoria deserts. The NW part of Western Australia and Northern Terr. are arid and hot. The NE has heavy rainfall and Cape York Peninsula has jungles. The Murray R. rises in New South Wales and flows 1,600 mi. to the Indian O. **Capital:** Canberra. **Cities** (1978 est.): Sydney 3,474,000; Melbourne 2,994,600; Brisbane 1,101,700; Adelaide 1,035,000; Perth 925,750.

Government: Head of state: Queen Elizabeth II, represented by Gov.-Gen. Zelman Cowen; b. Oct. 7, 1919; in office: Dec. 8, 1977. **Head of government:** Prime Min. John Malcolm Fraser; b. May 21, 1930; in office: Nov. 11, 1975. **Local divisions:** 6 states, with elected governments and substantial powers; 2 territories. **Armed forces:** regulars 70,261; reserves 25,049.

Economy: Industries: Iron, steel, textiles, electrical equip., chemicals, autos, aircraft, ships, machinery. **Chief crops:** Wheat (a leading export), sugar, wine, fruit, vegetables. **Minerals:** Bauxite, antimony, coal, cobalt, copper, gold, iron, lead, manganese, nickel, silver, tin, tungsten, uranium, zinc. **Crude oil reserves** (1980): 2.13 bln. bbls. **Other resources:** Wool (30% of world output). **Per capita arable land:** 7.8 acres. **Meat prod.** (1978): beef: 2.13 mln. metric tons; pork: 197,000 metric; lamb: 516,000 metric tons. **Fish catch** (1977): 127,800 metric tons. **Electricity prod.** (1978): 88.52 bln. kwh. **Crude steel prod.** (1979): 8.1 mln. metric tons. **Labor force:** 14% agric.; 47% ind. and commerce; 37% service.

Finance: Currency: Dollar (Jun. 1981: 0.88 = $1 US). **Gross domestic product** (1980): $140 bln. **Per capita income** (1978): $7,720. **Imports** (1980): $22.33 bln; partners (1978): U.S. 22%, Jap. 19%, UK 11%, W. Ger. 7%. **Exports** (1980): $21.99 bln.; partners (1978): Jap. 30%, U.S. 11%, NZ 5%. **Tourists** (1977): 548,900; receipts: $343 mln. **National budget** (1980): $38.80 bln. revenues; $36.15 bln. expenditures. **International reserves less gold** (Apr. 1981): $2.65 bln. **Gold:** 7.93 mln. oz t. **Consumer prices** (change in 1980): 10.2%.

Transport: Railway traffic (1977): 32.03 bln. net ton-km. **Motor vehicles:** in use (1977): 5.55 mln. passenger cars, 1.33 mln. comm. vehicles; manuf. (1978): 315,600 passenger cars; 69,600 comm. vehicles. **Civil aviation:** 11,946 mln. passenger-miles (1977); 256,587 mln. freight ton-miles (1977). **Chief ports:** Sydney, Melbourne, Newcastle, Port Kembla, Fremantle, Geelong.

Communications: Television sets: 4.8 mln. licensed (1976), 525,000 manuf. (1977). **Radios:** 10.5 mln. licensed (1976), 68,000 manuf. (1977). **Telephones in use** (1978): 5,583,330. **Daily newspaper circ.** (1977): 4,365,000; 310 per 1,000 pop.

Health: Life expectancy at birth (1967): 67.63 male; 74.15 female. **Births** (per 1,000 pop. 1980): 15.4. **Deaths** (per 1,000 pop. 1980): 7.4. **Natural increase** (1978): .8%. **Hospital beds** (per 100,000 pop. 1977): 1,244. **Physicians** (per 100,000 pop. 1977): 154. **Infant mortality** (per 1,000 live births 1978): 12.5.

Education (1977): **Literacy:** 98%. **Pop. 5-19:** in school: 73%, teachers per 1,000: 44. **PQLI:** 95.

Capt. James Cook explored the E coast in 1770, when the continent was inhabited by a variety of different tribes. Within decades, Britain had claimed the entire continent, which became a penal colony until immigration increased in the 1850s. The commonwealth was proclaimed Jan. 1, 1901. Northern Terr. was granted limited self-rule July 1, 1978. Their capitals and 1979 pop.:

	Area (sq. mi.)	Population
New South Wales, Sydney	309,418	5,011,600
Victoria, Melbourne	87,854	3,818,700
Queensland, Brisbane	666,699	2,166,700
South Aust., Adelaide	379,824	1,287,600
Western Aust., Perth	974,843	1,222,100
Tasmania, Hobart	26,178	413,700
Aust. Capital Terr., Canberra	926	215,900
Northern Terr., Darwin	519,633	112,300

Australia's racially discriminatory immigration policies were abandoned in 1973, after 3 million Europeans (half British) had entered since 1945. The 500,000 aborigines and 150,000 part-aborigines are mostly detribalized, but there are several preserves in the Northern Territory. They remain economically disadvantaged.

Australia's agricultural success makes it among the top ex-

porters of beef, lamb, wool, and wheat. Major mineral deposits have been developed as well, largely for exports. Industrialization has been completed since 1945.

Australia harbors many plant and animal species not found elsewhere, including the kangaroo, koala bear, platypus, dingo (wild dog), Tasmanian devil (racoon-like marsupial), wombat (bear-like marsupial), and barking and frilled lizards.

Australian External Territories

Norfolk Is., area 13½ sq. mi., pop. (1978) 1,900, was taken over, 1914. The soil is very fertile, suitable for citrus fruits, bananas, and coffee. Many of the inhabitants are descendants of the Bounty mutineers, moved to Norfolk 1856 from Pitcairn Is. Australia offered the island limited home rule, 1978.

Coral Sea Is. Territory, 1 sq. mi., is administered from Norfolk Is.

Territory of Ashmore and Cartier Is., area 2 sq. mi., in the Indian O. came under Australian authority 1934 and are administered as part of Northern Territory. **Heard** and **McDonald Is.** are administered by the Dept. of Science.

Cocos (Keeling) Is., 27 small coral islands in the Indian O. 1,750 mi. NW of Australia. Pop. (1978) 435, area: 5½ sq. mi.

Christmas Is., 52 sq. mi., pop. 3,094 (1978), 230 mi. S of Java, was transferred by Britain in 1958. It has phosphate deposits.

Australian Antarctic Territory was claimed by Australia in 1933, including 2,472,000 sq. mi. of territory S of 60th parallel S Lat. and between 160th-45th meridians E Long.

Austria

Republic of Austria

People: Population (1980 est.): 7,510,000. **Age distrib.** (%): 0–14: 22.8; 15–59: 57.0; 60+: 20.2. **Pop. density:** 231.97 per sq. mi. **Urban** (1971): 51.9%. **Ethnic groups:** German 98%, Slovene, Croatian, Hungarian, Italian. **Languages:** German, Slovene. **Religions:** Roman Catholic 88%, Protestant 6%, none 4.5%.

Geography: Area: 32,374 sq. mi., slightly smaller than Maine. **Location:** In S Central Europe. **Neighbors:** Switzerland, Liechtenstein on W, W. Germany, Czechoslovakia on N, Hungary on E, Yugoslavia, Italy on S. **Topography:** Austria is primarily mountainous, with the Alps and foothills covering the western and southern provinces. The eastern provinces and Vienna are located in the Danube River Basin. **Capital:** Vienna. **Cities** (1978 est.): Vienna 1,592,800; Graz 250,893; Linz 208,000; Salzburg 130,000; Innsbruck 115,000.

Government: Head of state: Pres. Rudolf Kirchschlaeger; b. Mar. 20, 1915; in office: July 8, 1974. **Head of government:** Chancellor Bruno Kreisky; b. Jan. 22, 1911; in office: Apr. 21, 1970. **Local divisions:** 9 lander (states), each with a legislature. **Armed forces:** regulars 38,000; reserves 117,700.

Economy: Industries: Steel, machinery, autos, electrical and optical equip., glassware, sport goods, paper, textiles, chemicals, cement. **Chief crops:** Grains, corn, potatoes, beets, grapes. **Minerals:** Iron ore, oil, magnesite, aluminum, coal, lignite, copper, graphite. **Crude oil reserves** (1980): 140 mln. bbls. **Other resources:** Forests, hydro power. **Per capita arable land:** 0.5 acres. **Meat prod.** (1978): beef: 185,000 metric tons; pork: 317,000 metric tons. **Electricity prod.** (1978): 38.09 bln. kwh. **Crude steel prod.** (1979): 4.9 mln. metric tons. **Labor force:** 13.8% agric.; 60% manuf.; 25.5% service.

Finance: Currency: Schilling (Jun. 1981: 16.92 = $1 US). **Gross domestic product** (1980): $76.34 bln. **Per capita income** (1978): $6,739. **Imports** (1980): $24.46 bln.; partners (1978): W. Ger. 43%, It. 9%, Switz. 6%. **Exports** (1980): $17.48 bln.; partners (1978): W. Ger. 29%, It. 9%, Switz. 8%. **Tourists** (1977): 11,747,800; receipts: $3.32 bln. **National budget** (1979): $14.19 bln. revenues; $16.55 bln. expenditures. **International reserves less gold** (Apr. 1981): $4.40 bln. **Gold:** 21.11 mln. oz t. **Consumer prices** (change in 1980): 6.3%.

Transport: Railway traffic (1978): 7.31 bln. passenger-km; 9.62 bln. net ton-km. **Motor vehicles:** in use (1977): 1.87 mln. passenger cars, 472,100 comm. vehicles; manuf. (1978): 360 passenger cars; 6,240 comm. vehicles. **Civil aviation:** 1,034 mln. passenger-km (1978); 12.492 mln. freight ton-km (1978).

Communications: Television sets: 1.77 mln. licensed (1976), 429,000 manuf. (1977). **Radios:** 2.19 mln. licensed (1976), 82,000 manuf. (1972). **Telephones in use** (1978):

2,443,412. **Daily newspaper circ.** (1977): 2,529,000; 336 per 1,000 pop.

Health: Life expectancy at birth (1976): 68.07 male; 75.05 female. **Births** (per 1,000 pop. 1980): 12.0. **Deaths** (per 1,000 pop. 1980): 12.2. **Natural increase** (1978): −.1%. **Hospital beds** (per 100,000 pop. 1977): 1,128. **Physicians** (per 100,000 pop. 1977): 233. **Infant mortality** (per 1,000 live births 1978): 14.9.

Education (1977): **Literacy:** 99%. **Pop. 5-19:** in school: 65%, teachers per 1,000: 38. **PQLI:** 94.

Rome conquered Austrian lands from Celtic tribes around 15 BC. In 788 the territory was incorporated into Charlemagne's empire. By 1300, the House of Hapsburg had gained control; they added vast territories in all parts of Europe to their realm in the next few hundred years.

Austrian dominance of Germany was undermined in the 18th century and ended by Prussia by 1866. But the Congress of Vienna, 1815, confirmed Austrian control of a large empire in southeast Europe consisting of Germans, Hungarians, Slavs, Italians, and others.

The dual Austro-Hungarian monarchy was established in 1867, giving autonomy to Hungary and 50 years of peace.

World War I, started after the June 28, 1914 assassination of Archduke Ferdinand, the Hapsburg heir, by a Serbian nationalist, destroyed the empire. By 1918 Austria was reduced to a small republic, with the borders it has today.

Nazi Germany invaded Austria Mar. 13, 1938, after four years of control by right-wing dictators Dollfuss and Schuschnigg. The republic was reestablished in 1945, under Allied occupation. Full independence and neutrality were guaranteed by a 1955 treaty with the major powers.

Austria produces 85% of its food, as well as an array of industrial products. A large part of Austria's economy is controlled by state enterprises. Socialists have shared or alternated power with the conservative People's Party.

Economic agreements with the Common Market give Austria access to a free-trade area encompassing most of West Europe.

Bahamas

Commonwealth of the Bahamas

People: Population (1980 est.): 240,000. **Age distrib.** (%): 0–14: 43.6; 15–59: 50.9; 60+: 5.5. **Pop. density:** 44.61 per sq. mi. **Urban** (1970): 57.9%. **Ethnic groups:** Negro 85%, Caucasian (British, Canadian, U.S.). **Languages:** English. **Religions:** Baptist 29%, Anglican 23%, Roman Catholic 22%.

Geography: Area: 5,380 sq. mi., slightly smaller than Connecticut. **Location:** In Atlantic O., E of Florida. **Neighbors:** Nearest are U.S. on W, Cuba on S. **Topography:** Nearly 700 islands (30 inhabited) and over 2,000 islots in the western Atlantic extend 760 mi. NW to SE. **Capital:** Nassau. **Cities** (1971 cen.): Nassau 120,000; Freeport 16,000.

Government: Head of state: Queen Elizabeth II, represented by Gov.-Gen. Gerald C. Cash; b. May 28, 1917, in office: Sept. 29, 1979. **Head of government:** Prime Min. Lynden Oscar Pindling; b. Mar. 22, 1930; in office: Jan. 16, 1967. **Local divisions:** 18 districts.

Economy: Industries: Tourism, intl. banking, rum, drugs. **Chief crops:** Fruits, vegetables. **Minerals:** Salt. **Other resources:** Lobsters. **Per capita arable land:** 0.02 acres. **Electricity prod.** (1977): 650.00 mln. kwh. **Labor force:** 9% agric.; 91% ind., tourism, commerce.

Finance: Currency: Dollar (Apr. 1981: 1 = $1 US). **Gross domestic product** (1975 est.): $500 mln. **Per capita income** (1975 est): $3,310. **Imports** (1979): $3.95 bln.; partners (1977): U.S. 35%, S. Arab. 24%, Iran 10%, Nigeria 9%. **Exports** (1979): $3.49 bln.; partners (1977): U.S. 81%, S. Arab. 10%. **Tourists** (1977): 942,600; receipts: $372 mln. **National budget** (1980): $245 mln. revenues; $245 mln. expenditures. **International reserves less gold** (Apr. 1981): $113.8 mln. **Gold** (Jan. 1980): 17,000 oz t. **Consumer prices** (change in 1980): 12.1%.

Transport: Motor vehicles: in use (1976): 36,500 passenger cars, 5,300 comm. vehicles. **Chief ports:** Nassau, Freeport.

Communications: Radios: 96,000 in use (1976). **Telephones in use** (1978): 61,756. **Daily newspaper circ.** (1976): 25,000; 118 per 1,000 pop.

Health: Life expectancy at birth (1971): 64.0 male; 67.3 female. **Births** (per 1,000 pop. 1976): 24.8. **Deaths** (per 1,000 pop. 1976): 4.6. **Natural increase** (1976): 2.0%. **Infant mortality** (per 1,000 live births 1976): 24.7. **PQLI:** 88.

Christopher Columbus first set foot in the New World on San Salvador (Watling I.) in 1492, when Arawak Indians inhabited the islands. British settlement began in 1647; the islands became a British colony in 1783. Internal self-government was granted in 1964; full independence within the Commonwealth was attained July 10, 1973.

International banking and investment management has become a major industry alongside tourism, despite controversy over financial irregularities.

Bahrain

State of Bahrain

People: Population (1979 est.): 370,000. **Age distrib.** (%): 0–14: 44.3; 15–59: 51.1; 60+: 4.6. **Pop. density:** 1,471.86 per sq. mi. **Urban** (1971): 78.1%. **Ethnic groups:** Arabs 80%, Iranians 12%, Indians, Pakistanis 5%. **Languages:** Arabic (official), English, Farsi, Urdu. **Religions:** Sunni Moslem 60%, Shiite Moslem 40%.

Geography: Area: 231 sq. mi., smaller than New York City. **Location:** In Persian Gulf. **Neighbors:** Nearest are Saudi Arabia on W. Qatar on E. **Topography:** Bahrain Island, and several adjacent, smaller islands, are flat, hot and humid, with little rain. **Capital:** Manama. **Cities** (1971 cen.): Manama 88,785.

Government: Head of state: Amir Isa bin Salman Al-Khalifa; b. July 3, 1933; in office: Nov. 2, 1961. **Head of government:** Prime Min. Khalifa bin Salman Al-Khalifa; b. 1935; in office: Jan. 19, 1970. **Local divisions:** 6 towns and cities. **Armed forces:** regulars 2,300.

Economy: Industries: Oil products, aluminum smelting, shipping. **Chief crops:** Fruits, vegetables. **Minerals:** Oil, gas. **Crude oil reserves** (1980): 240 mln. bbls. **Per capita arable land:** 0.007 acres. **Electricity prod.** (1977): 896.00 mln. kwh. **Labor force:** 5% agric.; 90% ind. and commerce; 5% services; 3% gov.

Finance: Currency: Dinar (Apr. 1981: 0.38 = $1 US). **Gross domestic product** (1979 est.): $1.7 bln. **Per capita income** (1979 est.): $4,967. **Imports** (1979): $2.48 bln.; partners (1977): Sau. Ar. 43%, UK 11%, Jap. 8%, U.S. 7%. **Exports** (1980): $3.68 bln.; partners (1977): Jap. 14%, Sau. Ar. 14%, UAE 9%, U.S. 8%. **National Budget** (1978): $600 mln. revenues; $736 mln. expenditures. **International reserves less gold** (Apr. 1981): $1.27 bln. **Gold:** 150,000 oz t. **Consumer prices** (change in 1980): 3.9%.

Transport: Motor vehicles: in use (1977): 35,500 passenger cars, 13,200 comm. vehicles. **Chief ports:** Sitra.

Communications: Television sets: 31,000 in use (1976). **Radios:** 100,000 in use (1975). **Telephones in use** (1978): 38,284.

Health: Births (per 1,000 pop. 1975): 30.0. **Hospital beds** (per 100,000 pop. 1977): 303. **Physicians** (por 100,000 pop. 1977): 62.

Education (1977): **Literacy:** 40%. **Pop. 5–19:** in school: 60%, teachers per 1,000: 36. **PQLI:** 61.

Long ruled by the Khalifa family, Bahrain was a British protectorate from 1861 to 1971, when it regained independence.

Pearls, shrimp, fruits, and vegetables were the mainstays of the economy until oil was discovered in 1932. By the 1970s, oil reserves were depleted; international banking thrived.

Bahrain took part in the 1973-74 Arab oil embargo against the U.S. and other nations. The government bought controlling interest in the oil industry in 1975.

Saudi Arabia announced, Dec., 1979, that it will build a 15-mile, $1 billion causeway linking Bahrain with the Arab mainland.

Bangladesh

People's Republic of Bangladesh

People: Population (1980 est.): 88,660,000. **Age distrib.** (%): 0-14: 43.2; 15-59: 52.4; 60+: 4.4. **Pop. density:** 1,608.32 per sq. mi. **Urban** (1974): 8.8%. **Ethnic groups:** Bengali 98%,

Bihari, tribesmen. **Languages:** Bangla (official), English. **Religions:** Moslems 85%, Hindus 14%, Christian, Buddhist, animist.
Geography: Area: 55,126 sq. mi. slightly smaller than Wisconsin. **Location:** In S Asia, on N bend of Bay of Bengal. **Neighbors:** India nearly surrounds country on W, N, E; Burma on SE. **Topography:** The country is mostly a low plain cut by the Ganges and Brahmaputra rivers and their delta. The land is alluvial and marshy along the coast, with hills only in the extreme SE and NE. A tropical monsoon climate prevails, among the rainiest in the world. **Capital:** Dacca. **Cities** (1974 cen.): Dacca (met.) 1,730,253; Chittagong (met.) 889,760; Khulna (met.) 437,304.
Government: Head of state: Act. Pres. Abdus Sattar. **Head of government:** Prime Minister Shah Mohammad Azizur Rahman, b. 1925, in office: Mar. 16, 1979. **Local divisions:** 19 districts. **Armed forces:** regulars 76,500; para-military 66,000.
Economy: Industries: Cement, textiles, jute, fertilizers. **Chief crops:** Jute (most of world output), rice. **Minerals:** Natural gas, offshore oil. **Other resources:** Water. **Per capita arable land:** 0.3 acres. **Meat prod.** (1978) beef: 159,000 metric tons; lamb: 30,000 metric tons. **Fish catch** (1977): 835,000 metric tons. **Electricity prod.** (1978): 2.00 bln. kwh. **Labor force:** 70% agric.
Finance: Currency: Taka (Apr. 1981: 17.39 = $1 US). **Gross domestic product** (1980): $10.50 bln. **Per capita income** (1976): $85. **Imports** (1980): $2.42 bln.; partners: U.S. 14%, Jap. 12%, UK 9%, Can. 6%. **Exports** (1980): $758 mln.; partners: U.S. 15%, UK 9%, Pak. 8%, Jap. 6%. **Tourists** (1977): 45,300; receipts: $3 mln. **International reserves less gold** (Apr. 1981): $260.0 mln. **Gold:** 54,000 oz t. **Consumer prices** (change in 1980): 13.2%.
Transport: Railway traffic (1973): 3.33 bln. passenger-miles; 639 mln. net ton-miles. **Motor vehicles:** in use (1972): 31,700 passenger cars, 24,800 comm. vehicles. **Chief ports:** Chittagong, Chalna.
Communications: Telephones in use (1978): 89,211. **Daily newspaper circ.** (1976) 350,000.
Health: Life expectancy at birth (1974): 45.8 male; 46.6 female. **Births** (per 1,000 pop. 1975): 47.4. **Deaths** (per 1,000 pop. 1975): 20.5. **Natural increase** (1975): 2.7%. **Hospital beds** (per 100,000 pop. 1977): 22. **Physicians** (per 100,000 pop. 1977): 8.
Education (1977): **Literacy:** 29%. **Pop. 5–19:** in school: 35%, teachers per 1,000: 9. **PQLI:** 32.

Moslem invaders conquered the formerly Hindu area in the 12th century. British rule lasted from the 18th century to 1947, when East Bengal became part of Pakistan.

Charging West Pakistani domination, the Awami League, based in the East, won National Assembly control in 1971. Assembly sessions were postponed; riots broke out. Pakistani troops attacked Mar. 25; Bangladesh independence was proclaimed the next day. In the ensuing civil war, one million died amid charges of Pakistani atrocities. Ten million fled to India.

War between India and Pakistan broke out Dec. 3, 1971. Pakistan surrendered in the East Dec. 15. Sheik Mujibur Rahman became prime minister. The country moved into the Indian and Soviet orbits, in response to U.S. support of Pakistan, and much of the economy was nationalized.

In 1974, the government took emergency powers to curb widespread violence; Mujibur was assassinated and a series of coups followed.

Chronic destitution among the densely crowded population has been worsened by the decline of jute as a major world commodity.

A Ganges waterpact with India, signed 1977, was recommitted by the 2 nations, 1979. Martial law, in force since 1975, was lifted on Apr. 6, 1979, prior to the opening of the new parliament.

On May 30, 1981, Pres. Ziaur Rahman was shot and killed in an unsuccessful coup attempt by army rivals. Vice President Abdus Sattar assumed the duties of acting president.

Barbados

People: Population (1979) est.): 279,000. **Age distrib.** (%): 0–14: 31.5; 15–59: 54.9; 60+: 13.6. **Pop. density:** 1,506.02 per sq. mi. **Urban** (1970): 3.7%. **Ethnic groups:** African 80%, mixed 16%, Caucasian 4%. **Languages:** English. **Religions:** Anglican 70%, Methodist, Pentecostal, Roman Catholic.
Geography: Area: 166 sq. mi. **Location:** In Atlantic, farthest E of W. Indies. **Neighbors:** Nearest are Trinidad, Grenada on

SW. **Topography:** The island lies alone in the Atlantic almost completely surrounded by coral reefs. Highest point is Mt. Hillaby, 1,115 ft. **Capital:** Bridgetown. **Cities** (1970 cen.): Bridgetown 8,789.
Government: Head of state: Queen Elizabeth II, represented by Gov.-Gen. Deighton L. Ward; b. May 16, 1909; in office: Nov. 17, 1976. **Head of government:** Prime Min. John M.G. Adams; b. Sept. 24, 1931; in office: Sept. 2, 1976. **Local divisions:** 11 parishes, one city.
Economy: Industries: Rum, molasses, tourism. **Chief crops:** Sugar, cotton. **Minerals:** Lime. **Crude oil reserves** (1980): 1.5 mln. bbls. **Other resources:** Fish. **Per capita arable land:** 0.3 acres. **Electricity prod.** (1978): 264.00 mln. kwh. **Labor force:** 9.8% agric.; 24.6% ind. and commerce; 65.6% services and government.
Finance: Currency: Dollar (Apr 1981: 2.01 = $1 US). **Gross domestic product** (1979): $636.90 mln. **Per capita income** (1976): $1,450. **Imports** (1980): $524 mln.; partners (1977): U.S. 24%, UK 19%, Trin./Tob. 10%, Can. 7%. **Exports** (1980): $226 mln.; partners (1977): U.S. 32%, Trin./Tob. 11%, Ire. 11%, UK 8%. **Tourists** (1977): 235,000; receipts: $83 million. **National budget** (1978): $166 mln. revenues; $177 mln. expenditures. **International reserves less gold** (Apr. 1981): $85.05 mln. **Consumer prices** (change in 1980): 18.7%.
Transport: Motor vehicles: in use (1976): 24,700 passenger cars; 4,000 comm. vehicles. **Chief ports:** Bridgetown.
Communications: Television sets: 48,000 in use (1976). **Radios:** 130,000 in use (1976). **Telephones in use** (1978): 47,266. **Daily newspaper circ.** (1976): 29,000; 115 per 1,000 pop.
Health: Life expectancy at birth (1961): 62.74 male; 67.43 female. **Births** (per 1,000 pop. 1976): 18.6. **Deaths** (per 1,000 pop. 1976): 9.2. **Natural increase** (1976): .9%. **Hospitals beds** (per 100,000 pop. 1977): 833. **Physicians** (per 100,000 pop. 1977): 76. **Infant mortality** (per 1,000 live births 1976): 28.3.
Education (1977): **Literacy:** 97%. **Pop. 5–19:** in school: 75%, teachers per 1,000: 36. **PQLI:** 91.

Barbados was probably named by Portuguese sailors in reference to bearded fig trees. An English ship visited in 1605, and British settlers arrived on the uninhabited island in 1627. Slaves worked the sugar plantations, but were freed in 1834.

Self-rule came gradually, with full independence proclaimed Nov. 30, 1966. British traditions have remained.

Belgium

Kingdom of Belgium

People: Population (1980 est.): 9,920,000. **Age distrib.** (%): 0–14: 21.8; 15–59: 59.3; 60+: 18.9. **Pop. density:** 842.18 per sq. mi. **Urban** (1976): 94.6%. **Ethnic groups:** Flemings 58%, Walloons 41%. **Languages:** Flemish (Dutch) 56%, French 32%, legally bilingual 11%, German 1%. **Religions:** Roman Catholic 75%, Protestant.
Geography: Area: 11,779 sq. mi., slightly larger than Maryland. **Location:** In NW Europe, on N. Sea. **Neighbors:** France on W, S, Luxembourg on SE, W. Germany on E, Netherlands on N. **Topography:** Mostly flat, the country is trisected by the Scheldt and Meuse, major commercial rivers. The land becomes hilly and forested in the SE (Ardennes) region. **Capital:** Brussels. **Cities** (1979 est.): Antwerp 197,000; Ghent 243,000; Liege 224,000; Brugge 118,023; Brussels 1,000,000.
Government: Head of state: King Baudouin; b. Sept. 7, 1930; in office: July 17, 1951. **Head of government:** Prime Min. Wilfried Martens; b. Apr. 19, 1936; in office: Apr. 3, 1979. **Local divisions:** 9 provinces. **Armed forces:** regulars 86,800; reserves 54,400.
Economy: Industries: Steel, glassware, diamond cutting, textiles, chemicals. **Chief crops:** Grains, potatoes, sugar beets. **Minerals:** Coal. **Other resources:** Forests. **Per capita arable land** (incl. Lux.): 0.2 acres. **Meat prod.** (1978): beef: 289,000 metric tons; pork: 628,000 metric tons. **Fish catch** (1977): 44,400 metric tons. **Electricity prod.** (1978): 50.84 bln. kwh. **Crude steel prod.** (1979): 13.4 mln. metric tons. **Labor force:** 3.4% agric.; 37% manuf.
Finance: Currency: Franc (Apr. 1981: 36.03 = $1 US). **Gross domestic product** (1979): $110.9 bln. **Per capita income** (1979): $10,800. Note: the following trade and tourist data includes Luxembourg. **Imports** (1980): $71.61 bln.; partners

(1978): W. Ger. 23%, Neth. 16%, France 16%, UK 8%. **Exports** (1980): $64.46 bln.; partners (1978): W. Ger. 23%, France 19%, Neth. 16%, UK 7%. **Tourists** (1977): 7,623,300; receipts: $993 mln. **National budget** (1980): $34.62 bln. revenues; $44.90 bln. expenditures. **International reserves less gold** (Apr. 1981): $6.77 bln. **Gold:** 34.18 mln. oz t. **Consumer prices** (change in 1980): 6.7%.

Transport: Railway traffic (1978): 7.14 bln. passenger-km; 7.10 bln. net ton-km. **Motor vehicles:** in use (1977): 2.81 mln. passenger cars, 297,100 comm. vehicles; assembled (1978): 1.01 mln. passenger cars; 37,090 comm. vehicles. **Civil aviation:** 4,500 mln. passenger-km (1978); 386 mln. freight ton-km (1978). **Chief ports:** Antwerp, Zeebrugge, Ghent.

Communications: Television sets: 2.6 mln. licensed (1976), 588,000 manuf. (1977). **Radios:** 4.04 mln. licensed (1976), 1.89 mln. manuf. (1977). **Telephones in use** (1978): 3,100,109. **Daily newspaper circ.** (1977): 2,369,000; 241 per 1,000 pop.

Health: Life expectancy at birth (1972): 67.79 male; 74.21 female. **Births** (per 1,000 pop. 1980): 12.7. **Deaths** (per 1,000 pop. 1980): 11.6. **Natural increase** (1978) .07%. **Hospital beds** (per 100,000 pop. 1977): 894. **Physicians** (per 100,000 1977): 211. **Infant mortality** (per 1,000 live births 1978): 11.9.

Education (1977): **Literacy:** 99%. **Pop. 5-19:** in school: 58%, teachers per 1,000: 40. **PQLI:** 94.

Belgium derives its name from the Belgae, the first recorded inhabitants, probably Celts. The land was conquered by Julius Caesar, and was ruled for 1800 years by conquerors, including Rome, the Franks, Burgundy, Spain, Austria, and France. After 1815, Belgium was made a part of the Netherlands, but it became an independent constitutional monarchy in 1830.

Belgian neutrality was violated by Germany in both world wars. King Leopold III surrendered to Germany, May 28, 1940. After the war, he was forced by political pressure to abdicate in favor of his son, King Baudouin.

The Flemings of northern Belgium speak Dutch while French is the language of the Walloons in the south. The language difference has been a perennial source of controversy. Disagreement between the 2 groups has caused government crises twice in 2 years.

Belgium lives by its foreign trade; about 50% of its entire production is sold abroad. The poor economy, with a 7.6% unemployment rate, deteriorated public finances, and weakened balance of payments, is the prime concern of the second Martens government.

Benin

People's Republic of Benin

People: Population (1980 est.): 3,570,000. **Age distrib. (%):** 0–14: 46.1; 15–59: 48.3; 60+: 5.6. **Pop. density:** 82.10 per sq. mi. **Urban** (1978): 13.8%. **Ethnic groups:** Fons, Adjas, Baribas, Yorubas. **Languages:** French is only common language. **Religions:** Christian 15% (south), Moslem 13% (north), animist 65%.

Geography: Area: 43,483 sq. mi., slightly smaller than Pennsylvania. **Location:** In W Africa on Gulf of Guinea. **Neighbors:** Togo on W, Upper Volta, Niger on N, Nigeria on E. **Topography:** most of Benin is flat and covered with dense vegetation. The coast is hot, humid, and rainy. **Capitals:** Porto–Novo, Cotonou. **Cities** (1978 est.): Cotonou 178,000; Porto-Novo 104,000.

Government: Head of state: Pres. Mathieu Kerekou; b. Sept. 2, 1933; in office: Oct. 27, 1972. **Local divisions:** 6 departments. **Armed forces:** regulars 2,200; para-military 1,000.

Economy: Chief crops: Palm products, peanuts, cotton, kapok, coffee, tobacco. **Minerals:** Oil. **Per capita arable land:** 2.1 acres. **Fish catch** (1977): 24,900 metric tons. **Electricity prod.** (1977): 5.00 mln. kwh. **Labor force:** 90% agric.

Finance: Currency: CFA franc (Apr. 1981: 262.70 = $1 US). **Gross domestic product** (1978): $734 mln. **Per capita income** (1975): $162. **Imports** (1979): $320 mln.; partners (1977): Fr. 23%, UK 13%, W. Ger. 8%, Neth. 6%. **Exports** (1979): $26 mln.; partners (1977): Fr. 25%, Jap. 20%, Neth. 13%, W. Ger. 8%. **Tourists** (1977): 23,000; receipts b.b. $3 mln. **International reserves less gold** (Jan. 1981): $10.1 mln. **Gold:** 11,000 oz t.

Transport: Railway traffic (1978): 133.2 mln. passenger-km; 152 mln. net ton-km. **Motor vehicles:** in use (1976): 17,000 passenger cars, 9,500 comm. vehicles. **Chief ports:** Cotonou.

Communications: Radios: 150,000 in use (1976). **Daily**

newspaper circ. (1976): 1,000; 0.3 per 1,000 pop.

Health: Life expectancy at birth (1975): 44.8 male; 45.0 female. **Births** (per 1,000 pop. 1975): 49.0. **Deaths** (per 1,000 pop. 1975): 21.1. **Natural increase** (1975): 2.8%. **Hospital beds** (per 100,000 pop. 1977): 137. **Physicians** (per 100,000 pop. 1977): 3. **Infant mortality** (per 1,000 live births 1975): 109.6.

Education (1977): **Literacy:** 20%. **Pop. 5-19:** in school: 29%, teachers per 1,000: 7. **PQLI:** 26.

The Kingdom of Abomey, rising to power in wars with neighboring kingdoms in the 17th century, came under French domination in the late 19th century, and was incorporated into French West Africa by 1904.

Under the name Dahomey, the country became independent Aug. 1, 1960. The name was changed to Benin in 1975. In the fifth coup since independence Maj. Mathieu Kerekou took power in 1972; two years later he declared a socialist state with a "Marxist-Leninist" philosophy. A 3-yr. economic plan started in 1977 relies on the development of agriculturally-based industries.

Bhutan

Kingdom of Bhutan

People: Population (1980 est.): 1,300,000. **Pop. density:** 67.34 per sq. mi. **Ethnic groups:** Bhotia (Tibetan) 60%. Nepalese 25%, Lepcha (indigenous), Indians. **Languages:** Dzongkha Tibetan (official), Nepali. **Religions:** Buddhist 75%, Hindu 25%.

Geography: Area: 19,305 sq. mi., the size of Vermont and New Hampshire combined. **Location:** In eastern Himalayan Mts. **Neighbors:** India on W (Sikkim) and S, China on N. **Topography:** Bhutan is comprised of very high mountains in the N, fertile valleys in the center, and thick forests in the Duar Plain in the S. **Capital:** Thimphu. **City** (1978 est.): Thimphu 8,992.

Government: Head of state: King Jigme Singye Wangchuk; b. Nov. 11, 1955; in office: July 21, 1972. **Local divisions:** 4 regions comprised of 15 districts.

Economy: Industries: Cloth. **Chief crops:** Rice, corn, wheat, oranges, cardamon, yak butter, lac, wax. **Other resources:** Elephants, timber. **Per capita arable land:** 0.5 acres. **Labor force:** 95% agric.

Finance: Currency: Ngultrum (Oct. 1979: 1 = $0.12 US) (Indian Rupee also used). **Gross domestic product** (1976 est.): $90 mln. **Per capita income** (1976): $70. **Imports** (1976): $1.4 mln.; partners India 99%. **Exports** (1976): $1 mln.; partners India 99%.

Communications: Radios: 10,000 licensed (1976). **Telephones in use** (1978): 1,355.

Health: Life expectancy at birth (1975): 42.0 male; 40.5 female. **Births** (per 1,000 pop. 1975): 43.7. **Deaths** (per 1,000 pop. 1975): 22.3. **Natural increase** (1975): 2.5%. **Pop. per hospital bed** (1975): 1,616. **Pop. per physician** (1975): 4,264.

The region came under Tibetan rule in the 16th century. British influence grew in the 19th century. A monarchy, set up in 1907, became a British protectorate by a 1910 treaty. The country became independent in 1949, with India guiding foreign relations and supplying aid.

Links to India have been strengthened by airline service and a road network. Most of the population engages in subsistence agriculture.

Bolivia

Republic of Bolivia

People: Population (1980 est.): 5,600,000. **Age distrib. (%):** 0–14: 41.9; 15–59: 52.0; 60+: 6.4. **Pop. density:** 13.20 per sq. mi. **Ethnic groups:** Quechua 30%, Aymara 25%, Mestizo (cholo) 25-30%, European 5-15%. **Languages:** Spanish (official) 55%, Quechua, Aymara. **Religions:** Roman Catholic 95%.

Geography: Area: 424,162 sq. mi., the size of Texas and California combined. **Location:** In central Andes Mtns. **Neighbors:** Peru, Chile on W, Argentina, Paraguay on S, Brazil on E and N. **Topography:** The great central plateau, at an altitude of 12,000 ft., over 500 mi. long, lies between two great cordilleras having 3 of the highest peaks in S. America. Lake Titicaca, on Peruvian border, is highest lake in world on which steamboats ply (12,506 ft.). The E central region has semitropical forests; the llanos, or Amazon-Chaco lowlands are in E. **Capitals:** Sucre, La Paz. **Cities** (1976 cen.): La Paz 654,713; Santa Cruz 237,128; Cochabamba 194,156.

Government: Head of state: Pres. Luis Garcia Meza; in office: July 17, 1980. **Local divisions:** 9 departments headed by prefects, 94 provinces. **Armed forces:** regulars 22,500.

Economy: Chief crops: Potatoes, sugar, coffee, barley, cocoa, rice, corn, bananas, citrus. **Minerals:** Antimony, tin, tungsten, silver, copper, lead, zinc, oil, gas, bismuth, wolfram, gold, iron, cadmium, borate of lime. **Crude oil reserves** (1980): 150 mln. bbls. **Other resources:** rubber, cinchona bark. **Per capita arable land:** 1.5 acres. **Meat prod.** (1978): beef: 78,000 metric tons; pork: 29,000 metric tons; lamb: 25,000 metric tons. **Electricity prod.** (1977): 1.15 bln. kwh. **Labor force:** 67% agric.

Finance: Currency: Peso (Jun. 1981: 24.75 = $1 US). **Gross domestic product** (1980): $6.10 bln. **Per capita income** (1975): $477. **Imports** (1980): $814 mln.; partners (1977): U.S. 27%, Arg. 12%, Jap. 12%, Braz. 10%. **Exports** (1980): $942.1 mln.; partners (1977): U.S. 34%, Arg. 20%, UK 12%, Neth. 5%. **Tourist receipts** (1977): $29 mln. **National budget** (1978): $437 mln. revenues; $590 mln. expenditures. **International reserves less gold** (Apr. 1981): $137.7 mln. **Gold:** 782,000 oz t. **Consumer prices** (change in 1980): 47.2%

Transport: Railway traffic (1977): 395 mln. passenger-km; 579 mln. net ton-miles. **Motor vehicles:** in use (1977): 35,300 passenger cars, 25,400 comm. vehicles. **Civil aviation:** 347 mln. passenger-miles (1977); 17,244 freight ton-miles (1977).

Communications: Radios: 430,000 in use (1976). **Telephones in use** (1978): 101,500. **Daily newspaper circ.** (1976): 150,000; 26 per 1,000 pop.

Health: Life expectancy at birth (1975): 46.5 male; 51.1 female. **Births** (per 1,000 pop. 1975): 46.6. **Deaths** (per 1,000 pop. 1975): 18.0. **Natural increase** (1975): 2.9%. **Hospital beds** (per 100,000 pop. 1977): 228. **Physicians** (per 100,000 pop. 1977): 38. **Infant mortality** (per 1,000 live births 1975): 77.3.

Education (1977): Literacy: 50%. **Pop. 5-19:** in school: 58%, teachers per 1,000: 25. **PQLI:** 47.

The Incas conquered the region from earlier Indian inhabitants in the 13th century. Spanish rule began in the 1530s, and lasted until Aug. 6, 1825. The country is named after Simon Bolivar, independence fighter.

In a series of wars, Bolivia lost its Pacific coast to Chile, the oilbearing Chaco to Paraguay, and rubber-growing areas to Brazil, 1879-1935.

Economic unrest, especially among the militant mine workers, has contributed to continuing political instability. A reformist government under Victor Paz Estenssoro, 1951-64, nationalized tin mines and attempted to improve conditions for the Indian majority, but was overthrown by a military junta. A series of coups and countercoups continued through 1980, when military forces took control to head off the expected congressional choice of a leftist as the nation's democratically elected president.

Botswana

Republic of Botswana

People: Population (1980 est.): 820,000. **Age distrib.** (%): 0–14: 46.1; 15–59: 43.1; 60+: 7.4. **Pop. density:** 3.73 per sq. mi. **Urban** (1974): 12.3%. **Ethnic groups:** Bantus (8 main tribes), Bushmen. **Languages:** English (official), Setswana. **Religions:** Christian 15%, animist.

Geography: Area: 220,000 sq. mi., slightly smaller than Texas. **Location:** In southern Africa. **Neighbors:** Namibia (S.W. Africa) on N and W, S. Africa on S, Zimbabwe on NE; Botswana claims border with Zambia on N. **Topography:** The Kalahari Desert, supporting nomadic Bushmen and wildlife, spreads over SW; there are swamplands and farming areas in N, and rolling plains in E where livestock are grazed. **Capital:** Gaborone. **Cities** (1979 est.): Gaborone 60,000; Francistown 33,000.

Government: Head of state: Pres. Quett Masire; in office: July 13, 1980. **Local divisions:** 9 districts and 4 independent towns, all with local councils. **Armed forces:** regulars 1,000; para-military 1,260.

Economy: Industries: Tourism. **Chief crops:** Corn, sorghum, beans, peanuts. **Minerals:** Copper, coal, nickel, diamonds.

Other resources: Big game. **Per capita arable land:** 4.6 acres. **Meat prod.** (1978): beef: 40,000 metric tons; lamb: 5,000 metric tons. **Electricity prod.** (1977): 348.00 mln. kwh. **Labor force:** 75% agric.

Finance: Currency: Pula (Apr. 1981: 0.80 = $1 US). **Gross domestic product** (1978): $401 mln. **Per capita income** (1978): $544. **Imports** (1980): $672 mln.; partners (1976): S. Africa 80%. **Exports** (1980): $504 mln.; partners (1976): UK 47%, S. Africa 24%, U.S. 22%. **National budget** (1979): $260.4 mln. revenues; $279.9 mln. expenditures. **International reserves less gold** (Apr. 1981): $357.06 mln. **Consumer prices** (change in 1979): 11.7%

Transport: Railway traffic (1978): 1.04 bln. net ton km. **Motor vehicles:** in use (1977): 3,400 passenger cars, 10,800 comm. vehicles.

Communications: Radios: 60,000 in use (1976). **Daily newspaper circ.** (1977): 17,000; 24 per 1,000 pop.

Health: Life expectancy at birth (1975): 44.3 male; 47.5 female. **Births** (annual per 1,000 pop. 1975): 50.7 **Deaths** (per 1,000 pop. 1975): 19.4. **Natural increase** (1975): 3.1%. **Hospital beds** (per 100,000 pop. 1977): 303. **Physicians** (per 100,000 pop. 1977): 14.

Education (1977): Literacy: 27%. **Pop. 5-19:** in school: 49%; teachers per 1,000: 16. **PQLI:** 51.

First inhabited by bushmen, then by Bantus, the region became the British protectorate of Bechuanaland in 1886, halting encroachment by Boers and Germans from the south and southwest. The country became fully independent Sept. 30, 1966, changing its name to Botswana.

Cattle-raising and mining (diamonds, copper, nickel) have contributed to the country's rapid economic growth. Many workers are migrants in S. Africa, and much of Botswana's exports go to that country.

Brazil

Federative Republic of Brazil

People: Population (1980 est.): 123,030,000. **Age distrib.** (%): 0–14: 41.1; 15–59: 53.7; 60+: 5.2. **Pop. density:** 37.44 per sq. mi. **Urban** (1977): 61.2%. **Ethnic groups:** Portuguese, Africans, and mulattoes make up the vast majority; Italians, Germans, Japanese, Indians, Jews, Arabs. **Languages:** Portuguese. **Religions:** Roman Catholic 89%, Protestant 10%.

Geography: Area: 3,286,470 sq. mi., larger than contiguous 48 U.S. states; largest country in S. America. **Location:** Occupies eastern half of S. America. **Neighbors:** French Guiana, Suriname, Guyana, Venezuela on N, Colombia, Peru, Bolivia, Paraguay, Argentina on W, Uruguay on S. **Topography:** Brazil's Atlantic coastline stretches 4,603 miles. In N is the heavily-wooded Amazon basin covering half the country. Its network of rivers navigable for 15,814 mi. The Amazon itself flows 2,093 miles in Brazil, all navigable. The NE region is semiarid scrubland, heavily settled and poor. The S central region, favored by climate and resources, has 45% of the population, produces 75% of farm goods and 80% of industrial output. The narrow coastal belt includes most of the major cities. Almost the entire country has a tropical or semitropical climate. **Capital:** Brasilia. **Cities** (1978 est.): Sao Paulo 7,198,608; Rio de Janeiro 4,857,716; Belo Horizonte 1,557,464; Recife 1,249,821; Salvador 1,237,393; Fortaleza 1,109,839; Porto Alegre 1,043,964; Nova Iguacu 931,954; Belem 771,665; Curitiba 765,716; Brasilia 763,254.

Government: Head of state: Pres. Joao Baptista Figueiredo; b. Jan. 15, 1918; in office: Mar. 15, 1979. **Local divisions:** 22 states, with individual constitutions and elected governments; 4 territories, 1 federal district. **Armed forces:** regulars 281,000; para-military 200,000.

Economy: Industries: Textiles, steel, autos, aluminum, chemicals, drugs, plastics, ships, appliances, shoes, paper, glass, machinery. **Chief crops:** Coffee (largest grower), cotton, soybeans; sugar, cocoa, rice, corn, fruits. **Minerals:** Chromium, iron, manganese, tin, quartz crystals, beryl, sheet mica, columbium, titanium, diamonds, thorium, gold, nickel, gem stones, coal, tin, tungsten, bauxite, oil. **Crude oil reserves** (1980): 1.22 bln. bbls. **Per capita arable land:** 0.7 acres. **Meat prod.** (1978): beef: 2.25 mln. metric tons; pork: 850,000 metric tons; lamb: 48,000 metric tons. **Fish catch** (1977): 790,100 metric tons. **Electricity prod.** (1977): 99.87 bln. kwh. **Crude steel prod.** (1979): 13.9

mln. metric tons. **Labor force:** 38% agric.; 20% manuf. **Finance: Currency:** Cruzeiro (Apr. 1981: 81.35 = $1 US). **Gross domestic product** (1979): $214.58 bln. **Per capita income** (1978): $1,523. **Imports** (1980): $25.00 bln.; partners (1977): U.S. 20%, Sau. Ar. 11%, Iraq 9%, W. Ger. 9%, Jap. 7%. **Exports** (1980): $20.13 bln.; partners (1977): U.S. 18%, W. Ger. 9%, Neth. 8%, Japan 6%. **Tourists** (1977): 634,600; receipts: $55 mln. **National budget** (1979): $18.91 bln. revenues; $18.83 bln. expenditures. **International reserves less gold** (Apr. 1981): $5.29 bln. **Gold:** 1.98 mln. oz t. **Consumer prices** (change in 1980): 82.8%.

Transport: Railway traffic (1977): 11.70 bln. passenger-km; 60.72 bln. net ton-km. **Motor vehicles:** in use (1976): 5.92 mln. passenger cars, 1.4 mln. comm. vehicles; manuf. (1978): 537,600 passenger cars; 525,600 comm. vehicles. **Civil aviation:** 8,724 mln. passenger-km (1978); 478 mln. freight ton-km (1978). **Chief ports:** Santos, Rio de Janeiro, Vitoria, Salvador, Rio Grande, Recife.

Communications: Television sets: 10.53 mln. in use (1976), 1.64 mln. manuf. (1976). **Radios:** 16.98 mln. in use (1975), 759,000 manuf. (1976). **Telephones in use** (1978): 4,708,000. **Daily newspaper circ.** (1976): 4,895,000; 45 per 1,000 pop.

Health: Life expectancy at birth (1970): 57.61 male; 61.10 female. **Births** (per 1,000 pop. 1975): 37.1. **Deaths** (per 1,000 pop. 1975): 8.8. **Natural increase** (1975): 2.8%. **Hospital beds** (per 100,000 pop. 1977): 327. **Physicians** (per 100,000 pop. 1977): 59.

Education (1977): **Literacy:** 70%. **Pop. 5-19:** in school: 51%, teachers per 1,000: 25. **PQLI:** 69.

Pedro Alvares Cabral, a Portuguese navigator, is generally credited as the first European to reach Brazil, in 1500. The country was thinly settled by various Indian tribes. Only a few have survived to the present, mostly in the Amazon basin.

In the next centuries, Portuguese colonists gradually pushed inland, bringing along large numbers of African slaves. Slavery was not abolished until 1888.

The King of Portugal, fleeing before Napoleon's army, moved the seat of government to Brazil in 1808. Brazil thereupon became a kingdom under Dom Joao VI. After his return to Portugal, his son Pedro proclaimed the independence of Brazil, Sept. 7, 1822, and was acclaimed emperor. The second emperor, Dom Pedro II, was deposed in 1889, and a republic proclaimed, called the United States of Brazil. In 1967 the country was renamed the Federative Republic of Brazil.

A military junta took control in 1930; dictatorial power was assumed by Getulio Vargas, who alternated with military coups until finally forced out by the military in 1954. A democratic regime prevailed 1956-64, during which time the capital was moved from Rio de Janeiro to Brasilia in the interior.

The next 5 presidents were all military leaders. Censorship was imposed, and much of the opposition was suppressed amid charges of torture. In 1974 elections, the official opposition party made gains in the chamber of deputies; some relaxation of censorship occurred, though church liberals, labor leaders, and intellectuals continued to report cases of arrest and torture.

Since 1930, successive governments have pursued industrial and agricultural growth and the development of interior areas. Exploiting vast mineral resources, fertile soil in several regions, and a huge labor force, Brazil became the leading industrial power of Latin America by the 1970s, while agricultural output soared. The 1979 government declared an amnesty and enacted democratic reforms.

However, income maldistribution, a return of inflation (83% in 1980), a long autoworkers strike, and government land policies have all come under attack. A huge oil import bill increased the $53 bln. foreign debt.

Bulgaria

People's Republic of Bulgaria

People: Population (1980 est.): 8,860,000. **Age distrib.** (%): 0–14: 22.3; 15–59: 61.7; 60+: 16.0. **Pop. density:** 206.87 per sq. mi. **Urban** (1978): 60.5%. **Ethnic groups:** Bulgarians 85%, Turks 9%, Gypsies 2%. **Languages:** Bulgarian, Turkish, Greek. **Religions:** Orthodox 70%, Moslem 9%.

Geography: Area: 42,829 sq. mi., slightly larger than Tennessee. **Location:** In eastern Balkan Peninsula on Black Sea. **Neighbors:** Romania on N, Yugoslavia on W, Greece, Turkey

on S. **Topography:** The Stara Planina (Balkan) Mts. stretch E-W across the center of the country, with the Danubian plain on N, the Rhodope Mts. on SW, and Thracian Plain on SE. **Capital:** Sofia. **Cities** (1978 est.): Sofia 976,015; Plovdiv 307,414; Varna 257,731.

Government: Head of state: Pres. Todor Zhivkov; b. Sept. 7, 1911; in office: July 7, 1971. **Head of government:** Prime Min. Stanko Todorov; b. Dec. 10, 1920; in office: July 7, 1971. **Head of Communist Party:** First Sec. Todor Zhivkov; in office: Jan. 1954. **Local divisions:** 27 provinces, one city. **Armed forces:** regulars 150,000; reserves 240,000.

Economy: Industries: Chemicals, machinery, metals, textiles, fur, leather goods, vehicles, wine, processed food. **Chief crops:** Grains, fruit, corn, potatoes, tobacco. **Minerals:** Lead, molybdenum, coal, oil, zinc. **Per capita arable land:** 1.1 acres. **Meat prod.** (1978): beef: 118,000 metric tons; pork: 281,000 metric tons; lamb: 67,000 metric tons. **Fish catch** (1977): 138,100 metric tons. **Electricity prod.** (1978): 31.79 bln. kwh. **Crude steel prod.** (1979): 2.4 mln. metric tons. **Labor force:** 24% agric.; 32% manuf.

Finance: Currency: Lev (Mar. 1980: .85 = $1 US). **Net material product** (1978): $14.4 bln. **Per capita income** (1976): $2,100. **Imports** (1979): $8.51 bln.; partners: USSR 57%, E. Ger. 7%, W. Ger. 5%. **Exports** (1979): $8.89 bln.; partners: USSR 55%, E. Ger. 8%, Pol. 5%. **Tourists** (1977): 4,569,700; receipts (1975): $230 mln.

Transport: Railway traffic (1978): 7.14 bln. passenger-km; 17.15 bln. net ton-km. **Motor vehicles:** manuf. (1977): 15,000 passenger cars, 6,900 comm. vehicles. **Chief ports:** Burgas, Varna.

Communications: Television sets: 1.55 mln. licensed (1976), 65,000 manuf. (1977). **Radios:** 2.75 mln. licensed (1974), 147,000 manuf. (1977). **Telephones in use** (1978): 946,023. **Daily newspaper circ.** (1977): 2,083,000; 237 per 1,000 pop.

Health: Life expectancy at birth (1976): 68.68 male; 73.91 female. **Births** (per 1,000 pop. 1978): 15.5. **Deaths** (per 1,000 pop. 1978): 10.5. **Natural increase** (1977): .5%. **Hospital beds** (per 100,000 pop. 1977): 872. **Physicians** (per 100,000 pop. 1977): 226. **Infant mortality** (per 1,000 live births 1978): 21.8

Education (1977): **Literacy:** 95%. **Pop. 5-19:** in school: 57%, teachers per 1,000: 30. **PQLI:** 90.

Bulgaria was settled by Slavs in the 6th century. Turkic Bulgars arrived in the 7th century, merged with the Slavs, became Christians by the 9th century, and set up powerful empires in the 10th and 12th centuries. The Ottomans prevailed in 1396 and remained for 500 years.

A revolt in 1876 led to an independent kingdom in 1908. Bulgaria expanded after the first Balkan War but lost its Aegean coastline in World War I, when it sided with Germany. Bulgaria joined the Axis in World War II, but withdrew in 1944. Communists took power with Soviet aid; the monarchy was abolished Sept. 8, 1946.

Burma

Socialist Republic of the Union of Burma

People: Population (1979 est.): 33,590,000. **Age distrib.** (%): 0–14: 40.5; 15–59: 53.5; 60+: 6.0. **Pop. density:** 123.04 per sq. mi. **Ethnic groups:** Burmans (related to Tibetans) 72%; Karen 7%, Shan 6%, Kachin 2%, Chinese 2%, Indians 3%, others. **Languages:** Burmese (official) 80%, English, others. **Religions:** Buddhist 85%; Hinduism, Islam, Christianity, others.

Geography: Area: 261,789 sq. mi., nearly as large as Texas. **Location:** Between S. and S.E. Asia, on Bay of Bengal. **Neighbors:** Bangladesh, India on W, China, Laos, Thailand on E. **Topography:** Mountains surround Burma on W, N, and E, and dense forests cover much of the nation. N-S rivers provide habitable valleys and communications, especially the Irrawaddy, navigable for 900 miles. The country has a tropical monsoon climate. **Capital:** Rangoon. **Cities** (1978 est.): Rangoon 2,276,000; Mandalay 458,000; Karbe (73 cen.): 253,600; Moulmein 188,000.

Government: Head of state: Pres. Ne Win; b. May 24, 1911; in office: Mar. 2, 1962. **Head of government:** Prime Min. Maung Maung Kha; b. Nov. 2, 1917; in office: Mar. 29, 1977. **Local divisions:** 7 states and 7 divisions. **Armed forces:** regulars 169,500; para-military 73,000.

Economy: Chief crops: Rice, cotton, maize, tobacco. **Miner-**

als: Oil, lead, silver, tin, tungsten, zinc, rubies, sapphires, jade. **Crude oil reserves** (1980): 25 mln. bbls. **Other resources:** Rubber, teakwood. **Per capita arable land:** 0.7 acres. **Meat prod.** (1978): beef: 94,000 metric tons; pork: 74,000 metric tons; lamb: 4,000 metric tons. **Fish catch** (1977): 518,700 metric tons. **Electricity prod.** (1978): 960.00 mln. kwh. **Labor force:** 65% agric.

Finance: Currency: Kyat (Apr. 1981: 7.11 = $1 US). **Gross domestic product** (1979): $5.16 bln. **Per capita income** (1977): $113. **Imports** (1980): $354 mln.; partners (1978): Jap. 25%, Sing. 12%, UK 8%, W. Ger. 7%. **Exports** (1980): $472 mln.; partners (1978): Sing. 15%, Indon. 14%, Bang. 14%, Sri Lanka 10%. **Tourists** (1976): 18,280; receipts (1975): $3 mln. **National budget** (1978): $692 mln. revenues; $697 mln. expenditures. **International reserves less gold** (Feb. 1981): $262.2 mln. **Gold:** 251,000 oz t. **Consumer prices** (change in 1980): 0.6%.

Transport: Railway traffic (1978): 3.07 bln. passenger-km; 468 mln. net ton-km. **Motor vehicles:** in use (1977): 38,600 passenger cars, 41,300 comm. vehicles. **Civil aviation:** 101 mln. passenger-miles (1975); 745 mln. freight ton-miles (1975). **Chief ports:** Rangoon, Sittwe, Bassein, Moulmein, Tavoy.

Communications: Radios: 665,000 licensed (1976), 12,000 manuf. (1977). **Telephones in use** (1978): 32,616. **Daily newspaper circ.** (1977): 329,000; 11 per 1,000 pop.

Health: Life expectancy at birth (1975): 48.6 male; 51.5 female. **Births** (per 1,000 pop. 1975): 39.4. **Deaths** (per 1,000 pop. 1975): 15.8. **Natural increase** (1975): 2.4%. **Hospital beds** (per 100,000 pop. 1977): 89. **Physicians** (per 100,000 pop. 1977): 19. **Infant mortality** (per 1,000 live births 1975): 195-300.

Education (1977): **Literacy:** 70%. **Pop. 5-19:** in school: 40%, teachers per 1,000: 8. **PQLI:** 53.

The Burmese arrived from Tibet before the 9th century, displacing earlier cultures, and a Buddhist monarchy was established by the 11th. Burma was conquered by the Mongol dynasty of China in 1272, then ruled by Shans as a Chinese tributary, until the 16th century.

Britain subjugated Burma in 3 wars, 1824-84, and ruled the country as part of India until 1937, when it became self-governing. Independence outside the Commonwealth was achieved Jan. 4, 1948.

Gen. Ne Win has dominated politics since 1958. He led a Revolutionary Council set up in 1962, which drove Indians from the civil service and Chinese from commerce. Socialization of the economy was advanced, isolation from foreign countries enforced. Lagging production and export have begun to turn around, due to government incentives in the agriculture and petroleum sectors and receptivity to foreign investment in the economy. Phased repatriation to Burma of Moslem refugees in Bangladesh was begun, 1979.

Burundi

Republic of Burundi

People: Population (1980 est.): 4,510,000. **Age distrib. (%):** 0-14: 44.1; 15-59: 51.9; 60+: 4.1. **Pop. density:** 419.96 per sq. mi. **Urban** (1970): 2.2%. **Ethnic groups:** Hutu 85%, Tutsi 14%, Twa (pygmy) 1%. **Languages:** French and Kirundi (both official), Swahili. **Religions:** Roman Catholic 50%, Protestant 4%, others.

Geography: Area: 10,739 sq. mi., the size of Maryland. **Location:** In central Africa. **Neighbors:** Rwanda on N, Zaire on W, Tanzania on E. **Topography:** Much of the country is grassy highland, with mountains reaching 8,900 ft. The southernmost source of the White Nile is located in Burundi. Lake Tanganyika is the second deepest lake in the world. **Capital:** Bujumbura. **Cities** (1978 est.): Bujumbura (met.) 78,810.

Government: Head of state and head of government: Pres. Jean Baptiste Bagaza; b. Aug. 29, 1946; in office: Nov. 9, 1976 (govt: Oct. 1978). **Local divisions:** 8 provinces and capital city. **Armed forces:** regulars 5,000; para-military 1,500.

Economy: Chief crops: Coffee (chief export), cotton, tea. **Minerals:** Nickel. **Per capita arable land:** 0.6 acres. **Fish catch** (1977): 18,900 metric tons. **Electricity prod.** (1977): 27.00 mln. kwh. **Labor force:** 92% agric.

Finance: Currency: Franc (Apr. 1981: 90 = $1 US). **Gross domestic product** (1979 est.): $700 mln. **Per capita income**

(1979 est.) $171. **Imports** (1980): $168 mln.; partners (1978): Benelux 23%, W. Ger. 10%, France 9%, Jap. 7%. **Exports** (1980): $65.1 mln.; partners (1978): U.S. 47%, China 6%. **Tourists** (1977): 32,000; receipts (1975): $1 mln. **National budget** (1980): $127 mln. revenues; $145 mln. expenditures. **International reserves less gold** (Apr. 1981): $84.06 mln. **Gold:** 17,000 oz t. **Consumer prices** (change in 1980): 2.3%.

Transport: Motor vehicles: in use (1976): 5,100 passenger cars, 2,200 comm. vehicles.

Communications: Radios: 105,000 in use (1976). **Telephones in use** (1978): 4,995. **Daily newspaper circ.** (1970): 300; 0.1 per 1,000 pop.

Health: Life expectancy at birth (1971): 40 male; 43 female. **Births** (per 1,000 pop. 1971): 42.0. **Deaths** (per 1,000 pop. 1971): 20.4. **Natural increase** (1971): 2.2%. **Hospital beds** (per 100,000 pop. 1977): 118. **Physicians** (per 100,000 pop. 1977): 3. **Infant mortality** (per 1,000 live births 1971): 150.

Education (1977): **Literacy:** 18%. **Pop. 5-19:** in school: 10%, teachers per 1,000: 3. **PQLI:** 30.

The pygmy Twa were the first inhabitants, followed by Bantu Hutus, who were conquered in the 16th century by the tall Tutsi (Watusi), probably from Ethiopia. Under German control in 1899, the area fell to Belgium in 1916, which exercised successively a League of Nations mandate and UN trusteeship over Ruanda-Urundi (now 2 countries).

Independence came in 1962, and the monarchy was overthrown in 1966. An unsuccessful Hutu rebellion in 1972-73 left 10,000 Tutsi and 150,000 Hutu dead. Over 100,000 Hutu fled to Tanzania and Zaire. The present regime is pledged to ethnic reconciliation but, Burundi remains one of the poorest and most densely populated countries in Africa.

Cambodia

Cambodian People's Republic

People: Population (1980 est.): 8,870,000. **Pop. density:** 126.89 per sq. mi. **Ethnic groups:** Khmers 90%, Vietnamese 4%, Chinese 3%. **Languages:** Khmer (official), French. **Religions:** Theravada Buddhism, animism, atheism.

Geography: Area: 69,900 sq. mi., the size of Missouri. **Location:** In Indochina Peninsula. **Neighbors:** Thailand on W, N, Laos on NE, Vietnam on E. **Topography:** The central area, formed by the Mekong R. basin and Tonle Sap lake, is level. Hills and mountains are in SE, a long escarpment separates the country from Thailand on NW. 75% of the area is forested. **Capital:** Phnom Penh. **Cities** (1979 est.): Phnom Penh 300,000.

Government: Head of government: Pres., People's Revolutionary Council Heng Samrin; in office: Jan. 7, 1979. **Local divisions:** 5 regions and a special capital region.

Economy: Industries: Textiles, paper, plywood, oil products. **Chief crops:** Rice, corn, pepper, tobacco, cotton, oil seeds, beans, palm sugar. **Minerals:** Iron, copper, manganese, gold. **Other resources:** Forests, rubber, kapok. **Per capita arable land:** 0.8 acres. **Meat prod.** (1978): beef: 22,000 metric tons; pork: 32,000 metric tons. **Fish catch** (1977): 84,700 metric tons. **Electricity prod.** (1977): 150.00 mln. kwh.

Finance: Currency: Riel (Sept. 1980: 1,200 = $1 US). **Per capita income** (1976): $90. **Imports** (1979): $10 mln. **Exports** (1979): $10 mln. **Tourists** (1973): 16,500.

Transport: Railway traffic (1973): 33.53 mln. passenger-miles; 6.21 mln. net ton-miles. **Motor vehicles:** in use (1972): 27,200 passenger cars, (1973) 10,100 comm. vehicles. **Chief ports:** Kompong Som.

Communications: Television sets: 35,000 in use (1977). **Radios:** 110,000 in use (1975). **Telephones in use** (1977): 71,000.

Health: Life expectancy at birth (1975): 44.0 male; 46.9 female. **Births** (per 1,000 pop. 1975): 45.9. **Deaths** (per 1,000 pop. 1975): 16.9. **Natural increase** (1975): 2.9%. **Hospital beds** (per 100,000 pop. 1977): 106. **Physicians** (per 100,000 pop. 1977): 7.

Education (1977): **Literacy:** 48%. **Pop. 5-19:** (1975): in school: 40%, per teacher: 124. **PQLI:** 36.

Early kingdoms dating from that of Funan in the 1st century AD culminated in the great Khmer empire which flourished from the 9th century to the 13th, encompassing present-day Thailand, Cambodia, Laos, and southern Vietnam. The peripheral areas were lost to invading Siamese and Vietnamese, and France established a protectorate in 1863. Independence came in 1953.

Prince Norodom Sihanouk, king 1941-1955 and head of state from 1960, tried to maintain neutrality. Relations with the U.S. were broken in 1965, after South Vietnam planes attacked Vietcong forces within Cambodia. Relations were restored in 1969, after Sihanouk charged Viet communists with arming Cambodian insurgents.

In 1970, pro-U.S. premier Lon Nol seized power, demanding removal of 40,000 North Viet troops; the monarchy was abolished. Sihanouk formed a government-in-exile in Peking, and open war began between the government and Khmer Rouge. The U.S. provided heavy military and economic aid. U.S. troops fought Vietcong forces within Cambodia for 2 months in 1970.

Khmer Rouge forces captured Phnom Penh April 17, 1975. Over 100,000 people had died in 5 years of fighting. The new government evacuated all cities and towns, and shuffled the rural population, sending virtually the entire population to clear jungle, forest, and scrub, which covered half the country.

The government guarded its international isolation, but repeated reports from refugees in Thailand and Vietnam indicated that over one million people were killed in executions and enforced hardships that continued unabated through 1978.

Severe border fighting broke out with Vietnam in 1978; developed into a full-fledged Vietnamese invasion. The Vietnamese-backed Kampuchean National United Front for National Salvation, a Cambodian rebel movement, announced, Jan. 8, 1979, the formation of a government one day after the Vietnamese capture of Phnom Pehn. Civil war continued into 1980; thousands of refugees flowed into Thailand. Widespread starvation was reported; by Sept., when the UN confirmed diplomatic recognition to the ousted Pol Pot government, international food assistance was allowed to aid the famine-stricken country. In July 1981, renewed efforts to bring about a Vietnamese troop withdrawal and institute supervised elections were pursued in a UN conference on Cambodia. But prospects for a diplomatic settlement were dimmed when Vietnam and the Soviet Union boycotted the proceedings.

Cameroon
United Republic of Cameroon

People: Population (1980 est.): 8,400,000. **Age distrib.** (%): 0-14: 43.4; 15-59: 50.8; 60+: 5.8. **Pop. density:** 45.76 per sq. mi. **Urban** (1970): 20.3%. **Ethnic groups:** Some 200 tribes; largest are Bamileke 30%, Fulani 7%. **Languages:** English, French (both official), 24 others. **Religions:** Roman Catholic 20%, Protestant 15%, Islam (mostly in N) 12%, others.

Geography: Area: 183,568 sq. mi., somewhat larger than California. **Location:** Between W and central Africa. **Neighbors:** Nigeria on NW, Chad, Central African Republic on E, Congo, Gabon, Equatorial Guinea on S. **Topography:** A low coastal plain with rain forests is in S; plateaus in center lead to forested mountains in W, including Mt. Cameroon, 13,000 ft.; grasslands in N lead to marshes around Lake Chad. **Capital:** Yaounde. **Cities** (1975 est.): Douala 485,797; Yaounde 274,399.

Government: Head of state: Pres. Ahmadou Ahidjo; b. Aug. 5, 1924; in office: Jan. 1, 1960. **Head of government:** Paul Biya; b. Feb. 13, 1933; in office: June 30, 1975. **Local divisions:** 7 provinces with appointed governors. **Armed forces:** regulars 8,500; para-military 5,700.

Economy: Industries: Aluminum processing, palm products. **Chief crops:** Cocoa, coffee, peanuts, tea, bananas, cotton, tobacco. **Crude oil reserves** (1980): 140 mln. bbls. **Other resources:** Timber, rubber. **Per capita arable land:** 2.1 acres. **Meat prod.** (1978): beef: 47,000 metric tons; pork: 19,000 metric tons; lamb: 17,000 metric tons. **Fish catch** (1977): 71,600 metric tons. **Electricity prod.** (1978): 1.31 bln. kwh. **Labor force:** 75-80% agric., 10-15% ind. and commerce.

Finance: Currency: CFA franc (Apr. 1981: 262.70 = $1 US). **Gross domestic product** (1979): $5.2 bln. **Per capita income** (1979): $628. **Imports** (1979): 1.28 bln.; partners (1977): Fr. 43%, W. Ger. 7%, U.S. 7%, Jap. 6%. **Exports** (1979): $1.13 bln.; partners (1977): Fr. 27%, Neth. 26%, W. Ger. 10%, It. 8%. **Tourists** (1974): 96,100; receipts (1977): $21 mln. **National budget** (1978): $707 mln. revenues; $685 mln. expenditures. **International reserves less gold** (Dec. 1980): $188.84 mln. **Gold:** 30,000 oz t. **Consumer prices** (change in 1979): 6.6%.

Transport: Railway traffic (1978): 230.4 mln. passenger-km;

513.6 mln. net ton-km. **Motor vehicles:** in use (1976): 59,500 passenger cars, 51,200 comm. vehicles. **Chief ports:** Douala.

Communications: Radios: 603,000 in use (1975), 80,000 manuf. (1977). **Telephones in use** (1978): 14,321. **Daily newspaper circ.** (1976): 30,000; 5 per 1,000 pop.

Health: Life expectancy at birth (1975): 41.9 male; 45.1 female. **Births** (per 1,000 pop. 1975): 42.1. **Deaths** (per 1,000 pop. 1975): 21.2. **Natural increase** (1975): 2.1%. **Hospital beds** (per 100,000 pop. 1977): 269. **Physicians** (per 100,000 pop. 1977): 6.

Education (1977): **Literacy:** 20%. **Pop. 5-19:** in school: 49%, teachers per 1,000: 10. **PQLI:** 30.

Portuguese sailors were the first Europeans to reach Cameroon, in the 15th century. The European and American slave trade was very active in the area. German control lasted from 1884 to 1916, when France and Britain divided the territory, later receiving League of Nations mandates and UN trusteeships. French Cameroon became independent Jan. 1, 1960; one part of British Cameroon joined Nigeria in 1961, the other part joined Cameroon. Stability has allowed for development of roads, railways, and agriculture.

Canada

See also Canada in Index.

People: Population (1980 est.): 23,940,000. **Age distrib.** (%): 0-14: 24.9; 15-59: 62.2; 60+: 12.8. **Pop. density:** 6.10 per sq. mi. **Urban** (1976): 75.5%. **Cities** (met. 1978 est.): Montreal 2,798,000; Toronto 2,741,000; Vancouver 1,137,000; Ottawa 626,000; Winnipeg 570,000; Edmonton 529,000.

Government: Head of state: Queen Elizabeth II, represented by Gov.-Gen. Edward R. Schreyer; b. Dec. 21, 1935; in office: Jan. 22, 1979. **Head of government:** Prime Min. b. Oct. 18, 1919; in office: Mar. 3, 1980. **Local divisions:** 10 provinces, 2 territories. **Armed forces:** regulars 80,000; reserves 19,100.

Economy: Minerals: Nickel, zinc, antimony, cobalt, copper, gold, iron, lead, molybdenum, potash, silver, tungsten, uranium. **Crude oil reserves** (1980): 6.8 bln. bbls. **Per capita arable land:** 4.6 acres. **Meat prod.** (1978): beef: 1.06 mln. metric tons; pork 570,000 metric tons. **Fish catch** (1977): 1.3 mln. metric tons. **Electricity prod.** (1978): 335.71 bln. kwh. **Crude steel prod.** (1979): 16.1 mln. metric tons. **Labor force:** 5% agric.; 30% manuf.

Finance: Currency: Dollar (Jun. 1981: 1.20 = $1 US). **Gross domestic product** (1980): $245.8 bln. **Per capita income** (1980 est.) $10,296. **Imports** (1980): $62.57 bln.; partners (1978): U.S. 71%, Jap. 5%. **Exports** (1980): $67.54 bln.; partners (1978): U.S. 70%, Jap. 6%. **Tourists** (1977): 12,702,800; receipts: $1.62 bln. **National budget** (1979): 42.09 bln. revenues; $48.13 bln. expenditures. **International reserves less gold** (Apr. 1981): $2.27 bln. **Gold:** 20.91 mln. oz t. **Consumer prices** (change in 1980): 10.1%.

Transport: Railway traffic (1978). 3.07 bln. passenger-km; 215.35 bln. net ton-km. **Motor vehicles:** in use (1977): 9.02 mln. passenger cars, 2.32 mln. comm. vehicles; manuf. (1978): 1.14 mln. passenger cars; 610,800 comm. vehicles. **Civil aviation:** 26,964 mln. passenger-km (1978); 676 mln. freight ton-km (1978).

Communications: Television sets: 9.9 mln. in use (1976), 606,000 manuf. (1977). **Radios:** 23.4 mln. in use (1976), 837,000 manuf. (1976). **Telephones in use** (1978): 14,505,728. **Daily newspaper circ.** (1977): 5,150,000; 221 per 1,000 pop.

Health: Life expectancy at birth (1972): 69.34 male; 76.36 female. **Births** (per 1,000 pop. 1979): 15.5. **Deaths** (per 1,000 pop. 1979): 7.1. **Natural increase** (1977): .8%. **Hospital beds** (per 100,000 pop. 1977): 875. **Physicians** (per 100,000 pop. 1977): 178. **Infant mortality** (per 1,000 live births 1977): 12.4.

Education (1977): **Literacy:** 98%. **Pop. 5-19:** in school: 76%, teachers per 1,000: 40. **PQLI:** 95.

Cape Verde

Republic of Cape Verde

People: Population (1979 est.): 328,000. **Age distrib.** (%): 0-14: 46.9; 15-59: 44.9; 60+: 7.9. **Pop. density:** 199.10 per sq. mi. **Urban** (1970): 19.7%. **Ethnic groups:** Creole (mulatto)

70%, African 28%, European 1%. **Languages:** Portuguese (official), Crioulo. **Religions:** 65% Roman Catholic, 35% animists.
Geography: Area: 1,557 sq. mi., a bit larger than Rhode Island. **Location:** In Atlantic O., off western tip of Africa. **Neighbors:** Nearest are Mauritania, Senegal. **Topography:** Cape Verde Islands are 15 in number, volcanic in origin (active crater on Fogo). The landscape is eroded and stark, with vegetation mostly in interior valleys. **Capital:** Praia. **Cities** (1970 cen.): Mindelo 28,797; Praia 21,494.
Government: Head of state: Pres. Aristides Pereira; b. Nov. 17, 1923; in office: July 5, 1975. **Head of government:** Prime Min. Pedro Pires, b. Apr. 29, 1934; in office: July 5, 1975. **Local divisions:** 24 electoral districts.
Economy: Chief crops: Bananas, coffee, sugarcane, grain. **Minerals:** Salt. **Other resources:** Fish. **Per capita arable land:** 0.3 acres. **Electricity prod.** (1977): 7.00 mln. kwh.
Finance: Currency: Escudo (Jan. 1979: 47.22 = $1 US). **Gross domestic product** (1978 est.): $130 mln. **Per capita income** (1978): $180. **Imports** (1979): $40 mln.; partners: Port. 58%, Neth. 5%. **Exports** (1979): $4 mln.; partners: Port. 63%, Ang. 14%, UK 5%, Zaire 5%. **Consumer prices** (change in 1977): 4.8%.
Transport: Motor vehicles: in use (1977): 3,100 passenger cars, 900 comm. vehicles. **Chief ports:** Mindelo, Praia.
Communications: Radios: 36,000 licensed (1976). **Telephones in use** (1978): 1,717.
Health: Life expectancy at birth (1975): 56.3 male; 60.0 female. **Births** (per 1,000 pop. 1975): 27.6. **Deaths** (per 1,000 pop. 1975): 9.4. **Natural increase** (1975): 1.8%. **Pop. per hospital bed** (1977): 516. **Pop. per physician** (1977): 7,750. **Infant mortality** (per 1,000 live births 1975): 104.9. **PQLI:** 53.

The uninhabited Cape Verdes were discovered by the Portuguese in 1456 or 1460. The first Portuguese colonists landed in 1462; African slaves were brought soon after, and most Cape Verdeans descend from both groups. Cape Verde independence came July 5, 1975. The government backs eventual union with Guinea-Bissau. The islands have suffered from repeated extreme droughts and famines, especially 1978; the banana crop, the sole export, has declined.

Central African Republic

People: Population (1979 est.): 2,284,000. **Pop. density:** 10.82 per sq. mi. **Ethnic groups:** Banda 47%, Baya 27%, 80 other groups. **Languages:** French (official), Sangho (national). **Religions:** Protestant 40%, Roman Catholic 24%, Moslem, others.
Geography: Area: 241,313 sq. mi., slightly smaller than Texas. **Location:** In central Africa. **Neighbors:** Chad on N, Cameroon on W, Congo, Zaire on S, Sudan on E. **Topography:** Mostly rolling plateau, average altitude 2,000 ft., with rivers draining S to the Congo and N to Lake Chad. Open, well-watered savanna covers most of the area, with an arid area in NE, and tropical rainforest in SW. **Capital:** Bangui. **Cities** (1978 est.): Bangui (met.) 187,000.
Government: Head of state: Pres. David Dacko, b. Mar. 24, 1930; in office: Sept. 20, 1979. **Head of government:** Prime Min. Bernard Ayandho; in office: Sept. 26, 1979. **Local divisions:** 14 prefectures. **Armed forces:** regulars 1,200; paramilitary 1,400.
Economy: Industries: Textiles, radios. **Chief crops:** Cotton, coffee, peanuts, corn, sorghum. **Minerals:** Diamonds (chief export), uranium, iron, copper. **Other resources:** Timber. **Per capita arable land:** 5.5 acres. **Meat prod.** (1978): beef: 21,000 metric tons. **Fish catch** (1977): 13,000 metric tons. **Electricity prod.** (1977): 58.00 mln. kwh. **Labor force:** 87% agric.
Finance: Currency: CFA franc (Apr. 1981: 262.70 = $1 US). **Gross domestic product** (1979): $592 mln. **Per capita income** (1979): $257. **Imports** (1979): $70 mln.; partners (1977): Fr. 55%, W. Ger. 7%, Jap. 5%. **Exports** (1979): $79.6 mln.; partners (1977): Fr. 63%, Bel.-Lux. 16%. **Tourists** (1974): 4,100; receipts (1977): $3 mln. **International reserves less gold** (Dec. 1980): $54.98 mln. **Gold:** 11,000 oz t. **Consumer prices** (change in 1978): 11.9%.
Transport: Motor vehicles: in use (1974): 9,100 passenger cars, 3,900 comm. vehicles.
Communications: Radios: 75,000 in use (1976), 11,000 manuf. (1977).
Health: Life expectancy at birth (1960): 33 male; 36 female. **Births** (per 1,000 pop. 1975): 41.0. **Deaths** (per 1,000 pop.

1975): 20.7%. **Natural increase** (1975): 2.0%. **Hospital beds** (per 100,000 pop. 1977): 138. **Physicians** (per 100,000 pop. 1977): 5. **Infant mortality** (per 1,000 live births 1975): 190.
Education (1977): **Literacy:** 16%. **Pop. 5-19:** in school: 37%, teachers per 1,000: 7. **PQLI:** 21.

Various Bantu tribes migrated through the region for centuries before French control was asserted in the late 19th century, when the region was named Ubangi-Shari. Complete independence was attained Aug. 13, 1960.
All political parties were dissolved in 1960, and the country became a center for Chinese political influence in Africa. Relations with China were severed after 1965. Elizabeth Domitien, premier 1975-76, was the first woman to hold that post in an African country. Pres. Jean-Bedel Bokassa, who seized power in a 1965 military coup, proclaimed himself constitutional emperor of the renamed Central African Empire Dec. 1976.
Emp. Bokassa's rule was characterized by virtually unchecked ruthless and cruel authority, and human rights violations. Bokassa was ousted in a bloodless coup aided by the French government, Sept. 20, 1979, and replaced by his cousin David Dacko, former president from 1960 to 1965.

Chad
Republic of Chad

People: Population (1979 est.): 4,528,000. **Age distrib.** (%): 0-14: 40.7; 15-59: 54.9; 60+: 4.4. **Pop. density:** 8.69 per sq. mi. **Urban** (1978): 18.4%. **Ethnic groups:** Sudanese Arab 30%, Sudanic tribes 25%, Nilotic, Saharan tribes. **Languages:** French (official), Arabic, others. **Religions:** Moslems 40%, Christians 30%, others.
Geography: Area: 495,752 sq. mi., four-fifths the size of Alaska. **Location:** In central N Africa. **Neighbors:** Libya on N, Niger, Nigeria, Cameroon on W, Central African Republic on S, Sudan on E. **Topography:** Southern wooded savanna, steppe, and desert, part of the Sahara, in the N. Southern rivers flow N to Lake Chad, surrounded by marshland. **Capital:** N'Djamena. **Cities** (1978 est.): N'Djamena (met.) 179,000.
Government: Head of state: Pres. Goukouni Oueddei; in office: Aug. 21, 1979. **Local divisions:** 14 prefectures with appointed governors. **Armed forces:** regulars 5,200; para-military 6,000.
Economy: Chief crops: Cotton. **Minerals:** Uranium. **Per capita arable land:** 4.0 acres. **Meat prod.** (1978): beef: 28,000 metric tons; lamb: 16,000 metric tons. **Fish catch** (1977): 115,000 metric tons. **Electricity prod.** (1978): 62.40 mln. kwh. **Labor force:** 90% agric.
Finance: Currency: CFA franc (Apr. 1981: 262.70 = $1 US). **Gross domestic product** (1976 est.): $540 mln. **Per capita income** (1976): $73. **Imports** (1979): $140 mln.; partners (1975): Fr. 37%, Nigeria 10%, Neth. 7%, U.S. 6%. **Exports** (1975): $58 mln.; partners (1975): Nigeria 20%, Fr. 7%, Congo 5%. **Tourist receipts** (1977): $7 mln. **National budget** (1976): $63 mln. revenues; $97 mln. expenditures. **International reserves less gold** (Dec. 1980): $5.06 mln. **Gold:** 11,000 oz t. **Consumer prices** (change in 1977): 9.3%.
Transport: Motor vehicles: in use (1973): 5,800 passenger cars, 6,300 comm. vehicles.
Communications: Radios: 76,000 in use (1976). **Telephones in use** (1978): 3,850.
Health: Life expectancy at birth (1964): 29 male; 35 female. **Births** (per 1,000 pop. 1975): 43.8. **Deaths** (per 1,000 pop. 1975): 22.7. **Natural increase** (1975): 2.1%. **Hospital beds** (per 100,000 pop. 1977): 82. **Physicians** (per 100,000 pop. 1977): 2. **Infant mortality** (per 1,000 live births 1975): 160.
Education (1977): **Literacy:** 15%. **Pop. 5-19:** in school: 16%, teachers per 1,000: 2. **PQLI:** 23.

Chad was the site of paleolithic and neolithic cultures before the Sahara Desert formed. A succession of kingdoms and Arab slave traders dominated Chad until France took control around 1900. Independence came Aug. 11, 1960.
Northern Moslem rebels, reportedly aided by Libya, have fought animist and Christian southern government and French troops from 1966, despite numerous cease-fires and peace pacts.
A Libyan offensive on the uranium and iron-rich Aouzou strip in the north failed, Apr., 1979,

Chile
Republic of Chile

People: Population (1980 est.): 11,100,000. **Age distrib. (%):** 0–14: 34.4; 15–59: 57.7; 60+: 7.9. **Pop. density:** 38.76 per sq. mi. **Urban** (1978): 79.8%. **Ethnic groups:** Mestizo 66%, Spanish 25%, Indian 5%. **Languages:** Spanish. **Religions:** Roman Catholic 90%, Protestants 6%.

Geography: Area: 286,396 sq. mi., larger than Texas. **Location:** Occupies western coast of southern S. America. **Neighbors:** Peru on N, Bolivia on NE, Argentina on E. **Topography:** Andes Mtns. are on E border including some of the world's highest peaks; on W is 2,650-mile Pacific Coast. Width varies between 100 and 250 miles. In N is Atacama Desert, in center are agricultural regions, in S are forests and grazing lands. **Capital:** Santiago. **Cities** (1978 est.) Santiago 3,448,700; Vina del Mar 262,100; Valparaiso 248,200; Concepción 209,986.

Government: Head of state: Pres. Augusto Pinochet Ugarte; b. Nov. 25, 1915; in office: Sept. 11, 1973. **Local divisions:** 12 regions and Santiago region, comprised of 25 provinces. **Armed forces:** regulars 85,000; reserves 160,000.

Economy: Industries: Steel, textiles, wood products. **Chief crops:** Grain, rice, beans, potatoes, peas, fruits, grapes. **Minerals:** Copper (10% world output), molybdenum, silver, nitrates, iodine (half world output), iron, coal, oil, gas, gold, cobalt, zinc, manganese, borate, mica, mercury, salt, sulphur, marble, onyx. **Crude oil reserves** (1980): 400 mln. bbls. **Other resources:** Water, forests. **Per capita arable land:** 1.3 acres. **Meat prod.** (1978): beef: 184,000 metric tons; pork: 38,000 metric tons; lamb: 26,000 metric tons. **Fish catch** (1977): 1.3 mln. metric tons. **Electricity prod.** (1978): 10.16 bln. kwh. **Crude steel prod.** (1979): 642,000 metric tons. **Labor force:** 19% agric.; 30% manuf.; 6.5% government.

Finance: Currency: Peso (Jun. 1981: 39.0 = $1 US). **Gross domestic product** (1979): $19.8 bln. **Per capita income** (1979): $1,950. **Imports** (1980): $5.82 bln.; partners (1978): U.S. 23%, Braz. 8%, Jap. 7%, Arg. 7%. **Exports** (1980): $4.82 bln.; partners (1978): W. Ger. 14%, Braz. 13%, Jap. 12%, U.S. 12%. **Tourists** (1977): 296,900; receipts: $97 mln. **National budget** (1978): $4.95 bln. revenues; $5.23 bln. expenditures. **International reserves less gold** (Apr. 1981): $3.29 bln. **Gold:** 1.70 mln. oz. t. **Consumer prices** (change in 1980): 35.1%.

Transport: Railway traffic (1978): 2.12 bln. passenger-km; 2.04 bln. net ton-km. **Motor vehicles:** in use (1977): 297,100 passenger cars, 182,000 comm. vehicles; assembled (1977): 9,000 passenger cars; 3,200 comm. vehicles. **Civil aviation:** 1,433 mln. passenger-km (1977); 108 mln. freight ton-km (1977). **Chief ports:** Valparaiso, Arica, Antofagasta.

Communications: Television sets: 710,000 in use (1976), 139,000 manuf. (1977). **Radios:** 1.8 mln. in use (1976), 68,000 manuf. (1977). **Telephones in use** (1978): 483,225.

Health: Life expectancy at birth (1970): 60.48 male; 66.01 female. **Births** (per 1,000 pop. 1976): 23.9. **Deaths** (per 1,000 pop. 1976): 7.7. **Natural increase** (1976): 1.6%. **Hospital beds** (per 100,000 pop. 1977): 359. **Physicians** (per 100,000 pop. 1977): 62. **Infant mortality** (per 1,000 live births 1978): 39.7.

Education (1977): **Literacy:** 90%. **Pop. 5–19:** in school: 72%, teachers per 1,000: 25. **PQLI:** 79.

Northern Chile was under Inca rule before the Spanish conquest, 1536-40. The southern Araucanian Indians resisted until the late 19th century. Independence was gained 1810-18, under Jose de San Martin and Bernardo O'Higgins; the latter, as supreme director 1817-23, sought social and economic reforms until deposed. Chile defeated Peru and Bolivia in 1836-39 and 1879-84, gaining mineral-rich northern land.

Eduardo Frei Montalva came into office in 1964, instituting social programs and gradual nationalization of foreign-owned mining companies. In 1970, Salvador Allende Gossens, a Marxist, became president with a third of the national vote, despite reported attempts by the U.S. Central Intelligence Agency and the International Telephone & Telegraph Corp. to foment a military coup.

The Allende government furthered nationalizations, and improved conditions for the poor. But illegal and violent actions by extremist supporters of the government, the regime's failure to attain majority support, and poorly planned socialist economic programs led to political and financial chaos.

A military junta seized power Sept. 11, 1973, and said Allende killed himself. The junta named a mostly-military cabinet, and announced plans to "exterminate Marxism." According to a 1977 statement of the Conference of Chilean Bishops, about 900 Chilean political prisoners had disappeared since the coup.

The economy continued to deteriorate under the new regime, though inflation had been reduced to 30% by 1980. Soaring increased world copper prices, which provide more than half of Chile's foreign income, were expected to cover the higher cost of petroleum imports in 1980.

Tierra del Fuego is the largest (17,800 sq. mi.) island in the archipelago of the same name at the southern tip of South America, an area of majestic mountains, tortuous channels, and high winds. It was discovered 1520 by Magellan and named the Land of Fire because of its many Indian bonfires. Part of the island is in Chile, part in Argentina. Punta Arenas, on a mainland peninsula, is a center of sheep-raising and the world's southernmost city (pop. 67,600); Puerto Williams, pop. 949, is the southernmost settlement.

China
People's Republic of China

People: Population (1980 est.): 1,027,000,000. **Pop. density:** 278.24 per sq. mi. **Ethnic groups:** Han Chinese 94%, Mongol, Korean, Turkic groups, Manchu, others. **Languages:** Mandarin Chinese (official), Shanghai, Canton, Fukien, Hakka dialects; Tibetan, Vigus (Turkic). **Religions:** Confucianism, Buddhism, Taoism, are traditional; Moslems 5%.

Geography: Area: 3,691,502 sq. mi., slightly larger than the U.S. **Location:** Occupies most of the habitable mainland of E. Asia. **Neighbors:** Mongolia on N, USSR on NE and NW, Afghanistan, Pakistan on W, India, Nepal, Bhutan, Burma, Laos, Vietnam on S, N. Korea on NW. **Topography:** Two-thirds of the vast territory is mountainous or desert, and only one-tenth is cultivated. Rolling topography rises to high elevations in the N in the Daxinganlingshanmai separating Manchuria and Mongolia; the Tienshan in Xinjiang; the Himalayan and Kunlunshanmai in the SW and in Tibet. Length is 1,860 mi. from N to S, width E to W is more than 2,000 mi. The eastern half of China is one of the best-watered lands in the world. Three great river systems, the Changjiang, the Huanghe, and the Xijiang provide water for vast farmlands. **Capital:** Peking. **Cities** (1979 est.): Shanghai 12,000,000; Peking 8,500,000; Tianjin 7,200,000; Canton 5,200,000; Shenyang 4,800,000; Wuhan 4,400,000; (1957 est.): Chongqing 2,121,000; Harbin 1,552,000; Lushun 1,508,000; Nanjing 1,419,000; Xian 1,310,000; Qingdao 1,121,000; Chengdu 1,107,000; Taiyuan 1,020,000.

Government: Head of Yaobang; Chmn. Natl. People's Congress Ye Jianying; b. 1899; in office: Mar. 5, 1978. **Head of government:** Party Chairman Hu Yaobang, b. 1915; in office: June 29, 1981. **Effective head of government:** First Dep. Prime Min. Deng Xiaoping; b. Aug. 22, 1904; in office: July 22, 1977. **Communist Party Chmn.:** Hu Yaobang; in office: June 29, 1981. **Local divisions:** 21 provinces, 5 ethnic autonomous regions, and 3 cities. **Armed forces:** regulars 4,360,000; civil militia 7,000,000.

Economy: Industries: Textiles, steel, chemicals, cement, plastics, agriculture implements, trucks. **Chief crops:** Grain, corn, peas, soybeans in N; rice, sugar in S, abutilon, hemp, jute, ramie, flax, cotton, tea. **Minerals:** Tungsten, antimony, coal, iron, lead, manganese, mercury, molybdenum, phosphates, potash, tin. **Crude oil reserves** (1980): 20 bln. bbls. **Other resources:** Silk. **Per capita arable land:** 0.3 acres. **Meat prod.** (1978): beef: 2.24 mln. metric tons; pork: 14.06 mln. metric tons; lamb: 716,000 metric tons. **Fish catch** (1977): 6.9 mln. metric tons. **Electricity prod.** (1978): 256 bln. kwh. **Crude steel prod.** (1979 est). 34.4 mln. metric tons. **Labor force:** 85% agric.; 15% man.

Finance: Currency: Yuan (Mar. 1980): 1.51 = $1 US). **Gross domestic product** (1978 est.): $407 bln. **Per capita income** (1979): $232. **Imports** (1978): $11.1 bln.; partners (1978): Jap. 30%, W. Ger. 10%, U.S. 8%, Austral. 5%. **Exports** (1978): $10.2 bln.; partners (1978): Hong Kong 20%, Jap. 19%, N. Kor. 6%. **Foreign currency reserves** (1978): $3 bln.

Transport: Railway traffic (1971): 301 bln. net ton-km. **Motor vehicles:** in use (1977): 30,000 passenger cars, 650,000 comm. vehicles. **Chief ports:** Shanghai, Tianjin, Luda.

Communications: Television sets: over 1.2 mln. in use (1978). **Radios:** 150 mln. in use (1978).

Health: Life expectancy at birth (1975): 60.7 male; 64.4 female. **Births** (per 1,000 pop. 1975): 26.0. **Deaths** (per 1,000 pop. 1975): 9.4. **Natural increase** (1975): 1.7%. **Hospital beds**

(per 100,000 pop. 1977): 185. **Physicians** (per 100,000 pop. 1977): 33.

Education (1977): **Literacy:** 70%. **Pop. 5-19:** in school: 65%, teachers per 1,000: 18. **PQLI:** 71.

History. Remains of various man-like creatures who lived as early as several hundred thousand years ago have been found in many parts of China. Neolithic agricultural settlements dotted the Huanghe basin from about 5,000 BC. Their language, religion, and art were the sources of later Chinese civilization.

Bronze metallurgy reached a peak and Chinese pictographic writing, similar to today's, was in use in the more developed culture of the Shang Dynasty (c. 1500 BC-c. 1000 BC) which ruled much of North China.

A succession of dynasties and interdynastic warring kingdoms ruled China for the next 3,000 years. They expanded Chinese political and cultural domination to the south and west, and developed a brilliant technologically and culturally advanced society. Rule by foreigners (Mongols in the Yuan Dynasty, 1271-1368, and Manchus in the Ch'ing Dynasty, 1644-1911) did not alter the underlying culture.

A period of relative stagnation left China vulnerable to internal and external pressures in the 19th century. Rebellions left tens of millions dead, and Russia, Japan, Britain, and other powers exercised political and economic control in large parts of the country. China became a republic Jan. 1, 1912, following the Wuchang Uprising inspired by Dr. Sun Yat-sen.

For a period of 50 years, 1894-1945, China was involved in conflicts with Japan. In 1895, China ceded Korea, Taiwan, and other areas. On Sept. 18, 1931, Japan seized the Northeastern Provinces (Manchuria) and set up a puppet state called Manchukuo. The border province of Jehol was cut off as a buffer state in 1933. Japan invaded China proper July 7, 1937. After its defeat in World War II, Japan gave up all seized land.

After the war with Japan ended, Aug. 15, 1945, internal disturbances arose involving the Kuomintang, communists, and other factions. China proper came under domination of communist armies, 1949-1950. The Kuomintang government moved to Taiwan (Formosa), 90 mi. off the mainland, Dec. 8, 1949.

The People's Republic of China was proclaimed in Peking Sept. 21, 1949, by the Chinese People's Political Consultative Conference under Mao Tse-tung, communist leader.

The communist regime and the USSR signed a 30-year treaty of "friendship, alliance and mutual assistance," Feb. 15, 1950, repudiating the 1945 treaty between the Soviet Union and the Kuomintang government authorized by the Yalta Agreement. Great Britain recognized the People's Republic in 1950 and France did so in 1964. By 1975, over 100 nations had recognized the regime.

The U.S. refused recognition, and after its consular officers met with abuse, withdrew them. On Nov. 26, 1950, the People's Republic sent armies into Korea against U.S. troops and forced a stalemate.

By the 1960s, relations with the USSR deteriorated, with disagreements on borders, ideology and leadership of world communism. The USSR cancelled aid accords, and China, with Albania, launched anti-Soviet propaganda drives.

China sought to promote revolutionary movements in Africa, Asia and South America.

On Oct. 25, 1971, the UN General Assembly ousted the Taiwan government from the UN and seated Communist China in its place. The U.S. had supported the mainland's admission but opposed Taiwan's expulsion.

U.S. Pres. Nixon visited China Feb. 21-28, 1972, on invitation from Premier Chou En-lai, ending years of antipathy between the 2 nations. China and the U.S. opened liaison offices in each other's capitals, May-June 1973. The U.S., Dec. 15, 1978, formally recognized the People's Republic of China as the sole legal government of China; diplomatic relations between the 2 nations were established, Jan. 1, 1979. Trade between the two countries neared $1 billion in 1974, largely U.S. grain exports, declined in subsequent years, but was revitalized with U.S. recognition, 1979.

In a continuing "reassessment" of the policies of Mao Zedong, Mao's widow, Jiang Quing, and other Gang of Four members were convicted of "committing crimes during the 'Cultural Revolution,'" Jan. 25, 1981. The ouster of Hua Guofeng, Jun. 29, 1981, the handpicked successor of Mao, was seen as another step in China's attempt to redefine Maoist policies.

Internal developments. After an initial period of consolidation, 1949-52, industry, agriculture, and social and economic institutions were forcibly molded according to Maoist ideals. However, frequent drastic changes in policy and violent factionalism have interfered with economic development.

In 1957, Mao Tse-tung admitted an estimated 800,000 people had been executed 1949-54; opponents claimed much higher figures. Some 110,000 political prisoners seized in 1957 were released in 1978.

The Great Leap Forward, 1958-60, tried to force the pace of economic development through intensive labor on huge new rural communes, and through emphasis on ideological purity and enthusiasm. The program caused resistance and was largely abandoned. Serious food shortages developed, and the government was forced to buy grain from the West.

The Great Proletarian Cultural Revolution, 1965, was an attempt to oppose pragmatism and bureaucratic power and instruct a new generation in revolutionary principles. Massive purges took place. A program of forcibly relocating millions of urban teenagers into the countryside was launched.

By 1968 the movement had run its course; many purged officials returned to office in subsequent years, and reforms in education and industry that had placed ideology above expertise were gradually weakened.

In the mid-1970s, factional and ideological fighting increased, and emerged into the open after the 1976 deaths of Mao and Premier Chou En-lai. Chiang Ching, Mao's widow and 3 other leading leftists were purged and placed under arrest, after reportedly trying to seize power. Their opponents said the "gang of four" had used severe repression and mass torture, had sparked local fighting and had disrupted production. The new ruling group modified Maoist policies in education, culture, and industry, and sought better ties with non-communist countries.

Relations with Vietnam deteriorated in 1978 as China charged persecution of ethnic Chinese. In retaliation for Vietnam's invasion of Cambodia, China attacked 4 Vietnamese border provinces Feb. 17, 1979; heavy border fighting ensued. Peace talks between the 2 countries continued through the year.

About 800,000 people were killed in 1976 when an earthquake leveled the northern industrial city of Tangshan. Drought and transport disruptions reportedly caused food shortages.

Increased army influence was reflected by a series of nuclear test explosions in 1976. The first Chinese atomic bomb was exploded in 1964; the first hydrogen bomb in 1967. There is a growing stockpile of nuclear weapons and intermediate range missiles. Long range missiles have been tested. The Chinese navy has been built into the world's third largest. The first orbiting space satellite was launched in 1970.

Manchuria. Home of the Manchus, rulers of China 1644-1911, Manchuria has accommodated millions of Chinese settlers in the 20th century. Under Japanese rule 1931-45, the area became industrialized. China no longer uses the name Manchuria for the region, which is divided into the 3 NE provinces of Heilongjiang, Jilin, and Liaoning.

Guandong is the southernmost part of Manchuria. Russia in 1898 forced China to lease it Guandong, and built Port Arthur (Lushun) and the port of Dairen (Luda). Japan seized Port Arthur in 1905. It was turned over to the USSR by the 1945 Yalta agreement, but finally returned to China in 1950.

Inner Mongolia was organized by the People's Republic in 1947. Its boundaries have undergone frequent changes, reaching its greatest extent (and restored in 1979) in 1956, with an area of 460,000 sq. mi., allegedly in order to dilute the minority Mongol population. Chinese settlers outnumber the Mongols more than 10 to 1. Total pop., 8.5 million. Capital: Hohhot.

Xinjiang Uygur Autonomous Region, in Central Asia, is 633,802 sq. mi., pop. 11 million (75% Uygurs, a Turkic Moslem group, with a heavy Chinese increase in recent years). Capital: Urumqi. It is China's richest region in strategic minerals. Some Uygurs have fled to the USSR, claiming national oppression.

Tibet, 470,000 sq. mi., is a thinly populated region of high plateaus and massive mountains, the Himalayas on the S, the Kunluns on the N. High passes connect with India and Nepal; roads lead into China proper. Capital: Lhasa. Average altitude is 15,000 ft. Jiachan, 15,870 ft., is believed to be the highest inhabited town on earth. Agriculture is primitive. Pop. 1.7 million (of whom 500,000 are Chinese). Another 4 million Tibetans form the majority of the population of vast adjacent areas that have long been incorporated into China.

China ruled all of Tibet from the 18th century, but independence came in 1911. China reasserted control in 1951, and a communist government was installed in 1953, revising the theocratic Lamaist Buddhist rule. Serfdom was abolished, but all land remained collectivized.

A Tibetan uprising within China in 1956 spread to Tibet in 1959. The rebellion was crushed with Chinese troops, and Buddhism was almost totally suppressed. The Dalai Lama and 100,000 Tibetans fled to India.

China (Taiwan)

Republic of China

People: Population (1979 est.): 17,456,000. **Pop. density:** 1,181 per sq. mi. **Ethnic groups:** Han Chinese 98% (18% from mainland), aborigines (of Indonesian origin) 2%. **Languages:** Mandarin Chinese (official), Taiwan, Hakka dialects, Japanese, English. **Religions:** Buddhism, Taoism, Confucianism prevail, Christians 2.5%.

Geography: Area: 13,892 sq. mi., the size of Maryland and Delaware combined. **Location:** Off SE coast of China, between E. and S. China Seas. **Neighbors:** Nearest is China. **Topography:** A mountain range forms the backbone of the island; the eastern half is very steep and craggy, the western slope is flat, fertile, and well-cultivated. **Capital:** Taipei. **Cities** (1979 est.): Taipei (met.) 2,183,500; (1978) Kaohsiung 1,062,999; Taichung 578,935; Tainan 557,075.

Government: Head of state: Chiang Ching-kuo; b. Mar. 18, 1910; in office: May 20, 1978. **Head of government:** Prime Min. Sun Yun-suan; b. Nov. 11, 1913; in office: May 30, 1978. **Local divisions:** Taiwan province, Taipei Municipality. **Armed forces:** regulars 539,000; reserves 1,170,000.

Economy: Industries: Textiles, clothing, electrical and electronic equip., processed foods, chemicals, glass, machinery. **Chief crops:** Rice, bananas, pineapples, sugar cane, sweet potatoes, wheat, soybeans, peanuts. **Minerals:** Coal, gold, copper, sulphur, oil. **Crude oil reserves** (1980): 10.2 mln. bbls. **Per capita arable land:** 0.2 acres. **Meat prod.** (1977): beef: 15,798 metric tons; pork: 574,656 metric tons. **Fish catch** (1977): 854,900 metric tons. **Crude steel prod.** (1979): 4.3 mln. metric tons. **Labor force:** 34% agric.; 37.8% manuf.; 29% transportation and service.

Finance: Currency: New Taiwan dollar (Mar. 1980: 36.10 = $1 US). **Gross domestic product** (1979): $32 bln. **Per capita income** (1978): $1,300. **Imports** (1979): $14.78 bln.; partners (1978): Jap. 33%, U.S. 22%, Kuw. 7%, Saudi Ar. 6%. **Exports** (1979): $16.07 bln.; partners (1978): U.S. 40%, Jap. 12%, Hong Kong 7%. **Tourists** (1978): 1,270,977; receipts (1978): $608 mln. **National budget** (1978): $4.03 bln. revenues; $3.10 bln. expenditures. **International reserves less gold** (Mar. 1980): $1.51 bln. **Gold:** 2.49 mln. oz t. **Consumer prices** (change in 1979): 9.7%.

Transport: Motor vehicles: in use (1978): 256,000 passenger cars, 171,000 comm. vehicles; assembled (1975): 23,000 passenger cars, 6,500 comm. vehicles. **Chief ports:** Kaohsiung, Keelung, Hualien, Taichung.

Communications: Television sets: 3 mln. in use (1978). **Radios:** 3.5 mln. in use (1974). **Telephones in use** (1978): 1,685,132. **Daily newspaper circ.** (1974): 1,300,000; 83 per 1,000 pop.

Health: Life expectancy at birth (1972): 66.8 male; 72.0 female. **Births** (per 1,000 pop. 1978): 24.1. **Deaths** (per 1,000 pop. 1978): 4.7. **Natural increase** (1978): 1.90%. **Hospital beds** (per 100,000 pop. 1977): 143. **Physicians** (per 100,000 pop. 1977): 33. **Infant mortality** (per 1,000 live births 1978): 14.

Education (1977): **Literacy:** 85%. **Pop. 5-19:** in school: 65%, teachers per 1,000: 17. **PQLI:** 87.

Large-scale Chinese immigration began in the 17th century. The island came under mainland control after an interval of Dutch rule, 1620-62. Taiwan (also called Formosa) was ruled by Japan 1895-1945. Two million Kuomintang supporters fled to Taiwan in 1949. Both the Taipei and Peking governments consider Taiwan an integral part of China.

The U.S. upon its recognition of the People's Republic of China, Dec. 15, 1978, severed diplomatic ties with Taiwan. It maintains the unofficial American Institute in Taiwan, while Taiwan has established the Coordination Council for North American Affairs in Washington, D.C.

Land reform, government planning, U.S. aid and investment, and free universal education have brought huge advances in industry, agriculture, and mass living standards.

The Penghu (Pescadores), 50 sq. mi., pop. 120,000, lie be-

tween Taiwan and the mainland. **Quemoy** and **Matsu,** pop. 75,000, lie just off the mainland.

Colombia

Republic of Colombia

People: Population (1980 est.): 27,520,000. **Age distrib.** (%): 0-14: 44.6; 15-59: 50.7; 60+: 4.7. **Pop. density:** 60.44 per sq. mi. **Urban** (1973): 59.5%. **Ethnic groups:** Mestizo 58%, Caucasian 20%, Mulatto 14%, Negro 4%, Indian 1%. **Languages:** Spanish. **Religions:** Roman Catholic 95%, Protestant under 1%.

Geography: Area: 455,355 sq. mi., larger than Texas and California combined. **Location:** At the NW corner of S. America. **Neighbors:** Panama on NW, Ecuador, Peru on S, Brazil, Venezuela on E. **Topography:** Three ranges of Andes, the Western, Central, and Eastern Cordilleras, run through the country from N to S. The eastern range consists mostly of high table lands, densely populated. The Magdalena R. rises in Andes, flows N to Carribean, through a rich alluvial plain. Sparsely-settled plains in E are drained by Orinoco and Amazon systems. **Capital:** Bogota. **Cities** (1973 cen.): Bogota 2,836,361; Medellin 1,112,390; Cali 967,908; Barranquilla 690,471.

Government: Head of state: Pres. Julio Cesar Turbay Ayala; b. June 8, 1916; in office: Aug. 7, 1978. **Local divisions:** 22 departments, 9 national territories, and federal district of Bogota. **Armed forces:** regulars 67,500; reserves 500,000.

Economy: Industries: Textiles, rubber goods, hides, steel, paper, cement, chemicals. **Chief crops:** Coffee (2d in exports), rice, tobacco, cotton, cocoa, maize, potatoes, sugar, bananas. **Minerals:** Oil, gas, emeralds (95% world output), gold, silver, copper, lead, mercury, cinnabar, manganese, platinum, coal, iron, nickel, salt. **Crude oil reserves** (1980): 710 mln. bbls. **Other resources:** Rubber, balsam, dye-woods, copaiba, hydro power. **Per capita arable land:** 0.4 acres. **Meat prod.** (1978): beef: 431,000 metric tons; pork: 110,000 metric tons; lamb 7,000 metric tons. **Fish catch** (1977): 75,100 metric tons. **Electricity prod.** (1977): 15.22 bln. kwh. **Crude steel prod.** (1979): 361,000 metric tons. **Labor force:** 47% agric.; 22% man.; 18% services.

Finance: Currency: Peso (Jun. 1981: 53.27 = $1 US). **Gross domestic product** (1979 est.): $26.2 bln. **Per capita income** (1979): $986. **Imports** (1980): $4.74 bln.; partners (1977): U.S. 42%, W. Ger. 10%, Jap. 12%, Venez. 7%. **Exports** (1980): $3.92 bln.; partners (1977): U.S. 32%, W. Ger. 19%, Venez. 6%, Jap. 5%. **Tourists** (1977): 622,900; receipts: $201 mln. **National budget** (1978): $2.14 bln. revenues; $1.99 bln. expenditures. **International reserves less gold** (Apr. 1981): $4.70 bln. **Gold** 3.05 mln. oz t. **Consumer prices** (change in 1980): 26.5%.

Transport: Railway traffic (1977): 3.91 bln. passenger-km; 1.22 bln. net ton-km. **Motor vehicles:** in use (1977): 453,600 passenger cars, 104,500 comm. vehicles; assembled (1976): 26,900 passenger cars; 9,500 comm. vehicles. **Civil aviation:** 2,072 mln. passenger-miles (1977); 109.381 mln. freight ton-miles (1977). **Chief ports:** Buena Ventura, Santa Marta, Barranquilla, Cartagena.

Communications: Television sets: 1.7 in use (1976), 76,000 manuf. (1974). **Radios:** 2.9 in use (1976). **Telephones in use** (1978): 1,396,591. **Daily newspaper circ.** (1976): 1,330,000.

Health: Life expectancy at birth (1979): 65 male; 70 female. **Births** (per 1,000 pop. 1975): 34.1. **Deaths** (per 1,000 pop. 1975): 9.0. **Natural increase** (1975): 2.5%. **Hospital beds** (per 100,000 pop. 1977): 161. **Physicians** (per 100,000 pop. 1977): 51. **Infant mortality** (per 1,000 live births 1975): 46.6%.

Education (1977): **Literacy:** 80%. **Pop. 5-19:** in school: 54%, teachers per 1,000: 19. **PQLI:** 69.

Spain subdued the local Indian kingdoms (Funza, Tunja) by the 1530s, and ruled Colombia and neighboring areas as New Granada for 300 years. Independence was won by 1819. Venezuela and Ecuador broke away in 1829-30, and Panama withdrew in 1903.

One of the few functioning Latin American democracies, Colombia is nevertheless plagued by rural and urban violence, though scaled down from "La Violencia" of 1948-58, which claimed 200,000 lives. Attempts at land and social reform, and progress in industrialization have not yet succeeded in reducing massive social problems aggravated by a very high birth rate.

Comoros
Federal and Islamic Republic of the Comoros

People: Population (1979 est.): 359,000. **Age distrib. (%):** 0–14: 43.0; 15–59: 47.0; 60+: 8.0. **Pop. density:** 461.76 per sq. mi. **Ethnic groups:** Arabs, Africans, East Indians. **Languages:** Arabic, French, Swahili. **Religions:** Islam prevails.

Geography: Area: 693 sq. mi., half the size of Rhode Island. **Location:** 3 islands (Grande Comore, Anjouan, and Moheli) in the Mozambique Channel between NW Madagascar and SE Africa. **Neighbors:** Nearest are Mozambique on W, Madagascar on E. **Topography:** The islands are of volcanic origin, with an active volcano on Grand Comoro. **Capital:** Moroni. **Cities** (1978 est.): Moroni (met.) 12,000.

Government: Head of state: Pres. Ahmed Abdallah; in office: May 23, 1978. **Head of govt.:** Prime Min. Salim Ben Ali; in office: Dec. 22, 1978. **Local divisions:** each of the 3 main islands is a prefecture.

Economy: Industries: Perfume. **Chief crops:** Vanilla, copra, perfume plants, fruits. **Per capita arable land:** 0.6 acres. **Electricity prod.** (1977): 3.0 mln. kwh. **Labor force:** 87% agric.

Finance: Currency: CFA franc (Mar. 1980: 223.92 = $1 US). **Gross domestic product** (1976 est.): $51 mln. **Per capita income** (1976): $153. **Imports** (1979): $24 mln.; partners: Fr. 30%, Madag. 23%, Ken. 13%. **Exports** (1979): $15 mln.; partners: Fr. 59%, U.S. 15%, W. Ger. 10%.

Transport: Chief ports: Dzaoudzi.

Communications: Radios: 36,000 in use (1976). **Telephones in use** (1977): 1,035.

Health: Life expectancy at birth (1975): 43.4 male; 46.6 female. **Births** (per 1,000 pop. 1975): 44.4 **Deaths** (per 1,000 pop. 1975): 19.3. **Natural increase** (1975): 2.5%. **Infant mortality** (per 1,000 live births 1975): 51.7. **PQLI:** 44.

The islands were controlled by Moslem sultans until the French acquired them 1841-1909. A 1974 referendum favored independence, with only the Christian island of Mayotte preferring association with France. The French National Assembly decided to allow each of the islands to decide its own fate. The Comoro Chamber of Deputies declared independence July 6, 1975. In a referendum in 1976, Mayotte voted to remain French. A leftist regime that seized power in 1975 was deposed in a pro-French 1978 coup.

Congo
People's Republic of the Congo

People: Population (1980 est.): 1,540,000. **Pop. density:** 11.66 per sq. mi. **Ethnic groups:** Bakongo 45%, Bateke 20%, others. **Languages:** French (official), Lingala, Kikongo. **Religions:** Christians 47% (two-thirds Roman Catholic), animists 48%, Muslim 2%.

Geography: Area: 132,046 sq. mi., slightly smaller than Montana. **Location:** In western central Africa. **Neighbors:** Gabon, Cameroon on W, Central African Republic on N, Zaire on E, Angola (Cabinda) on SW. **Topography:** Much of the Congo is covered by thick forests. A coastal plain leads to the fertile Niari Valley. The center is a plateau; the Congo R. basin consists of flood plains in the lower and savanna in the upper portion. **Capital:** Brazzaville. **Cities** (1974 cen.): Brazzaville (met.) 289,700; Pointe-Noire 141,700; Loubomo 34,000.

Government: Head of state: Pres. Denis Sassou-Nguesso; b. 1943; in office: Feb. 8, 1979. **Head of government:** Prime Min. Louis Sylvain Ngoma; in office: Dec. 18, 1975. **Local divisions:** 9 regions and capital district. **Armed forces:** regulars 7,000; para-military 3,900.

Economy: Chief crops: Palm oil and kernels, cocoa, coffee, bananas, peanuts. **Minerals:** Oil, potash, lead, zinc. **Crude oil reserves** (1980): 400 mln. bbls. **Per capita arable land:** 1.1 acres. **Fish catch** (1977): 16,400 metric tons. **Electricity prod.** (1978): 97.20 mln. kwh. **Labor force:** 90% agric.

Finance: Currency: CFA franc (Apr. 1981: 267.20 = $1 US). **Gross domestic product** (1978 est.): $89 mln. **Per capita income** (1978): $500. **Imports** (1978): $261 mln.; partners (1977): Fr. 49%, W. Ger. 6%, U.S. 5%. **Exports** (1977): $185 mln.; partners (1977): Ital. 30%, Fr. 12%, U.S. 7%, Sp. 7%. **Tourist receipts** (1977): $4 mln. **International reserves less gold** (Dec. 1980): $85.90 mln. **Gold:** 11,000 oz t. **Consumer prices** (change in 1980): 7.2%.

Transport: Railway traffic (1978): 294 mln. passenger-km; 478.8 mln. net ton-km. **Motor vehicles:** in use (1976): 20,000 passenger cars, 13,000 comm. vehicles. **Chief ports:** Pointe-Noire, Brazzaville.

Communications: Television sets: 3,300 in use (1976). **Radios:** 83,000 in use (1976). **Telephones in use** (1978): 13,376.

Health: Life expectancy at birth (1975): 41.9 male; 45.1 female. **Births** (per 1,000 pop. 1975): 45.0. **Deaths** (per 1,000 pop. 1975): 20.9. **Natural increase** (1975): 2.4%. **Hospital beds** (per 100,000 pop. 1977): 499. **Physicians** (per 100,000 pop. 1977): 14. **Infant mortality** (per 1,000 live births 1978): 200.

Education (1977): **Literacy:** 40%. **Pop. 5-19:** in school: 75%, teachers per 1,000: 20. **PQLI:** 37.

The Loango Kingdom flourished in the 15th century, as did the Anzico Kingdom of the Batekes; by the late 17th century they had become weakened. France established control by 1885. Independence came Aug. 15, 1960.

After a 1963 coup sparked by trade unions, the country adopted a Marxist-Leninist stance, with the USSR and China vying for influence. Tribal divisions remain strong. France remains a dominant trade partner and source of technical assistance, and French-owned private enterprise retained a major economic role. However, the government of Pres. Sassou-Nguesso favored a strengthening of relations with the USSR, a socialist constitution was adopted, 1979, and on May 13, 1981 a treaty of friendship and cooperation was signed with the Soviets.

Costa Rica
Republic of Costa Rica

People: Population (1980 est.): 2,210,000. **Age distrib. (%):** 0–14: 44.0; 15–59: 50.4; 60+: 5.6. **Pop. density:** 112.45 per sq. mi. **Urban** (1973): 40.6%. **Ethnic groups:** Spanish (with Mestizo minority); Indians 0.4%, Jamaican Negroes 2%. **Languages:** Spanish (official), English. **Religions:** Roman Catholicism prevails.

Geography: Area: 19,653 sq. mi., smaller than W. Virginia. **Location:** In central America. **Neighbors:** Nicaragua on N, Panama on S. **Topography:** Lowlands by the Caribbean are tropical. The interior plateau, with an altitude of about 4,000 ft., is temperate. **Capital:** San Jose. **Cities** (1978 est.): San Jose 236,747; Alajuela (1979 est.) 40,000; Cartago (1979 est.) 40,000.

Government: Head of state: Pres. Rodrigo Carazo Odio; b. Dec. 27, 1926; in office May 8, 1978. **Local divisions:** 7 provinces and 80 cantons. **Armed forces:** para-military 5,000.

Economy: Industries: Fiberglass, aluminum, textiles, fertilizers, roofing, cement. **Chief crops:** Coffee (chief export), bananas, sugar, cocoa, cotton, hemp. **Minerals:** Gold, salt, sulphur, iron. **Other resources:** Fish, forests. **Per capita arable land:** 0.3 acres. **Meat prod.** (1978): beef: 63,000 metric tons; pork: 9,000 metric tons. **Fish catch** (1977): 13,000 metric tons. **Electricity prod.** (1978): 1.80 bln. kwh. **Labor force:** 34.1% agric.; 36.4% manuf.; 25% service and government.

Finance: Currency: Colone (Dec. 1980: 8.57 = $1 US). **Gross domestic product** (1979): $3.99 bln. **Per capita income** (1978): $1,512. **Imports** (1980): $1.46 bln.; partners (1977): U.S. 34%, Jap. 13%, Guat. 6%, W. Ger. 5%. **Exports** (1980): $1.0 bln.; partners (1977): U.S. 29%, W. Ger. 12%, Nic. 7%, Neth. 7%. **Tourists** (1977): 327,500; receipts: $54 mln. **National budget** (1978): $480 mln. revenues; $633 mln. expenditures. **International reserves less gold** (Apr. 1981): $103.54 mln. **Gold:** 87,000 oz t. **Consumer prices** (change in 1980): 18.1%.

Transport: Railway traffic (1974): 81 mln. passenger-km; 14 mln. net ton-km. **Motor vehicles:** in use (1976): 64,900 passenger cars, 42,400 comm. vehicles. **Civil aviation:** 360 mln. passenger-km (1978); 19 mln. freight ton-km (1978). **Chief ports:** Limon, Puntarenas.

Communications: Television sets: 155,000 in use (1976). **Radios:** 150,000 in use (1976). **Telephones in use** (1978): 145,069. **Daily newspaper circ.** (1976): 210,000; 104 per 1,000 pop.

Health: Life expectancy at birth (1974): 66.26 male; 70.49 female. **Births** (per 1,000 pop. 1977): 31.1. **Deaths** (per 1,000 pop. 1977): 4.3. **Natural increase** (1977): 2.7%. **Hospital beds** (per 100,000 pop. 1977): 345. **Physicians** (per 100,000 pop. 1977): 72. **Infant mortality** (per 1,000 live births 1977): 27.8.

Education (1977): **Literacy:** 90%. **Pop. 5–19:** in school: 58%, teachers per 1,000: 21. **PQLI:** 86.

Guaymi Indians inhabited the area when Spaniards arrived, 1502. Independence came in 1821. Costa Rica seceded from the Central American Federation in 1838. Since the civil war of 1948-49, there has been no violent social conflict, and free political institutions have been preserved.

Costa Rica, though still a largely agricultural country, has achieved a relatively high standard of living and social services, and land ownership is widespread.

Cuba

Republic of Cuba

People: Population (1980 est.): 9,980,000. **Age distrib. (%):** 0–14: 36.9; 15–59: 53.5; 60+: 9.6. **Pop. density:** 225.70 per sq. mi. **Urban** (1970): 60.3%. **Ethnic groups:** Spanish, Negro, and mixtures. **Languages:** Spanish. **Religions:** Roman Catholicism prevailed in past.

Geography: Area: 44,218 sq. mi.; nearly as large as Pennsylvania. **Location:** Westernmost of West Indies. **Neighbors:** Bahamas, U.S., on N, Mexico on W, Jamaica on S, Haiti on E. **Topography:** The coastline is about 2,500 miles. The N coast is steep and rocky, the S coast low and marshy. Low hills and fertile valleys cover more than half the country. Sierra Maestra, in the E is the highest of 3 mountain ranges. **Capital:** Havana. **Cities** (1978 est.): Havana 1,008,500; Santiago de Cuba 315,801; Camaguey 221,826.

Government: Head of state: Pres. Fidel Castro Ruz; b. Aug. 13, 1926; in office: Dec. 3, 1976 (formerly Prime Min. since Feb. 16, 1959). **Local divisions:** 14 provinces, 169 municipal assemblies. **Armed forces:** regulars 189,000; reserves 90,000.

Economy: Industries: Texiles, wood products, cement, chemicals, cigars. **Chief crops:** Sugar cane (80% of exports), tobacco, coffee, pineapples, bananas, citrus fruit, coconuts. **Minerals:** Cobalt, nickel, iron, copper, manganese, salt. **Other resources:** Forests. **Per capita arable land:** 0.6 acres. **Meat prod.** (1978): beef: 143,000 metric tons; pork: 63,000 metric tons. **Fish catch** (1977): 185,200 metric tons. **Electricity prod.** (1977): 7.70 bln. kwh. **Crude steel prod.** (1979 est.): 300,000 metric tons. **Labor force:** 34% agric.

Finance: Currency: Peso (Mar. 1980: .72 = $1 US). **Net material product** (1974): $6.1 bln. **Per capita income** (1977): $840. **Imports** (1979): $5.1 bln.; partners (1975): USSR 40%, Jap. 12%, Sp. 5%, W. Ger. 5%. **Exports** (1979): $5.3 bln.; partners (1975): USSR 56%, Spain 8%, Jap. 8%.

Transport: Railway traffic (1976): 767 mln. passenger-km; 1.85 bln. net ton-km. **Motor vehicles:** in use (1976): 80,000 passenger cars, 40,000 comm. vehicles. **Chief ports:** Havana, Matanzas, Cienfuegos, Santiago de Cuba.

Communications: Television sets: 650,000 in use (1976). **Radios:** 2.1 mln. in use (1976), 120,000 manuf. (1977). **Telephones in use** (1978): 321,054.

Health: Life expectancy at birth: (1970): 68.5 male; 71.8 female. **Births** (per 1,000 pop. 1977): 17.6 **Deaths** (per 1,000 pop. 1977): 5.8 **Natural increase** (1977): 1.2%. **Hospital beds** (per 100,000 pop. 1977): 413. **Physicians** (per 100,000 pop. 1977): 94. **Infant mortality** (per 1,000 live births 1977): 24.8.

Education (1977): **Literacy:** 94%. **Pop. 5–19:** in school: 75% teachers per 1,000: 43. **PQLI:** 92.

Some 50,000 Indians lived in Cuba when it was discovered by Columbus in 1492. Its name derives from the Indian Cubanacan. Except for British occupation of Havana, 1762-63, Cuba remained Spanish until 1898. A slave-based sugar plantation economy developed from the 18th century, aided by early mechanization of milling. Sugar remains the chief product and chief export despite government attempts to diversify.

A ten-year uprising ended in 1878 with guarantees of rights by Spain, which Spain failed to carry out. A full-scale movement under Jose Marti began Feb. 24, 1895.

The U.S. declared war on Spain in April, 1898, after the sinking of the U.S.S. Maine in Havana harbor, and defeated it in the short Spanish-American War. Spain gave up all claims to Cuba. U.S. troops withdrew in 1902, but under 1903 and 1934 agreements, the U.S. leases a site at Guantanamo Bay in the SE as a naval base. U.S. and other foreign investments acquired a dominant role in the economy.

In 1952, former president Fulgencio Batista seized control and

established a dictatorship, which grew increasingly harsh and corrupt. Former student leader Fidel Castro assembled a rebel band in 1956; guerrilla fighting intensified in 1958. Batista fled Jan. 1, 1959, and in the resulting political vacuum Castro took power, becoming premier Feb. 16.

The government, quickly dominated by extreme leftists, began a program of sweeping economic and social changes, without restoring promised liberties. Opponents were imprisoned and some were executed. Some 700,000 Cubans emigrated in the years after the Castro takeover, mostly to the U.S.

Cattle and tobacco lands were nationalized, while a system of cooperatives was instituted. By the end of 1960 all banks and industrial companies had been nationalized, including over $1 billion worth of U.S.-owned properties, mostly without compensation.

Soviet, Chinese, and Eastern European economic penetration was extended by trade and credit agreements. Cuba is a member of Comecon, the Soviet economic union.

Poor sugar crops resulted in collectivization of farms, stringent labor controls, and rationing, despite continued aid from the USSR and other Communist countries.

The U.S. cut back Cuba's sugar quota in 1960, and imposed a partial export embargo, which became total in 1962, severely damaging the economy. In 1961, some 1,400 Cubans, trained and backed by the U.S. Central Intelligence Agency, unsuccessfully tried to invade and overthrow the regime. It was revealed in 1975 that CIA agents had plotted to kill Castro in 1959 or 1960.

In the fall of 1962, the U.S. learned that the USSR had brought nuclear missiles to Cuba. After an Oct. 22 warning from Pres. Kennedy, the missiles were removed.

In 1973, Cuba and the U.S. signed an agreement providing for extradition or punishment of hijackers of planes or vessels, and for each nation to bar activity from its territory against the other. In 1977, the 2 countries signed agreements to exchange diplomats, without restoring full ties, and to regulate offshore fishing. In 1978, and again in 1980, the U.S. agreed to accept political prisoners released by Cuba.

But relations were, and continue to be strained by ongoing Cuban military involvement abroad. In 1975-78, Cuba sent over 20,000 troops to aid one faction in the Angola Civil War. Some 20,000 other Cuban troops or advisers were reported in the Congo, Ethiopia (where they fought Somali and Eritrean insurgents), Equatorial Guinea, Guinea, Guinea-Bissau, Somalia, and Mozambique, and, in a widely disputed "white paper", the U.S. charged, Feb. 23, 1981, that covert deliveries of arms were being funneled through Cuba to aid guerrilla forces in El Salvador.

Cyprus

Republic of Cyprus

People: Population (1980 est.): 630,000. **Age distrib. (%):** 0–14: 25.0; 15–59: 61.0; 60+: 14.0. **Pop. density:** 176.37 per sq. mi. **Urban** (1974): 42.2%. **Ethnic groups:** Greeks 75%, Turks 20%, Armenians, Maronites. **Languages:** Greek, Turkish. **Religions:** Orthodox 76%, Moslems 20%.

Geography: Area: 3,572 sq. mi., smaller than Connecticut. **Location:** In eastern Mediterranean Sea, off Turkish coast. **Neighbors:** Nearest are Turkey on N, Syria, Lebanon on E. **Topography:** Two mountain ranges run E-W, separated by a wide, fertile plain. **Capital:** Nicosia. **Cities** (1973 cen.): Nicosia (met. 115,700.

Government: Head of state: Pres. Spyros Kyprianou; b. Oct. 28, 1932; in office: Aug. 3, 1977. **Local divisions:** 6 districts. **Armed forces:** Greek: regulars 10,000; reserves 20,000; Turkish: 5,000.

Economy: Industries: Wine, clothing, shoes, tourism. **Chief crops:** Grains, grapes, carobs, citrus fruits, potatoes, olives. **Minerals:** Copper, iron, asbetos, gypsum, chrome, umber. **Per capita arable land:** 1.5 acres. **Meat prod.** (1978): pork: 16,000 metric tons; lamb: 10,000 metric tons. **Electricity prod.** (1978): 924.00 mln. kwh. **Labor force:** 36% agric.; 47% manuf.

Finance: Currency: Pound (Apr. 1981: 0.41 = $1 US). **Gross domestic product** (1980): $2.12 bln. **Per capita income** (1978): $2,200. **Imports** (1980): $1.21 bln.; partners (1978): UK 22%, It. 12%, W. Ger. 7%, Gr. 6%. **Exports** (1980): $536 mln.; partners (1978): UK 23%, Leb. 9%, Sau. Ar. 9%, Syria 5%. **Tourists** (1977): 178,200; receipts: $60 mln. **National budget** (1978): $268 mln. revenues; $344 mln. expenditures. **International reserves less gold** (Apr. 1981): $285.6 mln.

Gold (Jan. 1980): 459,000 oz. t. **Consumer prices** (change in 1980): 13.6%.
Transport: Motor vehicles: in use (1977): 74,500 passenger cars, 18,600 comm. vehicles. **Civil aviation:** 524 mln. passenger-km (1978); 21 mln. freight ton-km (1978). **Chief ports:** Famagusta, Limassol.
Communications: Television sets: 57,000 licensed (1976). **Radios:** 200,000 licensed (1976). **Telephones in use** (1978): 82,800. **Daily newspaper circ.** (1976): 72,000; (1975) 107 per 1,000 pop.
Health: Life expectancy at birth (1973): 70.0 male; 72.9 female. **Births** (per 1,000 pop. 1975): 18.4. **Deaths** (per 1,000 pop. 1975): 9.8. **Natural increase** (1975): .9%. **Hospital beds** (per 100,000 pop. 1977): 538. **Physicians** (per 100,000 pop. 1977): 82. **Infant mortality** (per 1,000 live births 1975): 17.5.
Education (1977): Literacy: 86%. **Pop. 5-19:** in school: 54%, teachers per 1,000: 22. **PQLI:** 85.

Agitation for enosis (union) with Greece increased after World War II, with the Turkish minority opposed, and broke into violence in 1955-56. In 1959, Britain, Greece, Turkey, and Cypriot leaders approved a plan for an independent republic, with constitutional guarantees for the Turkish minority and permanent division of offices on an ethnic basis. Greek and Turkish Communal Chambers dealt with religion, education, and other matters.
Archbishop Makarios, formerly the leader of the enosis movement, was elected president, and full independence became final Aug. 16, 1960. Makarios was re-elected in 1968 and 1973.
Further communal strife led the United Nations to send a peace-keeping force in 1964; its mandate has been repeatedly renewed.
The Cypriot National Guard, led by officers from the army of Greece, seized the government July 15, 1974, and named Nikos Sampson, an advocate of union with Greece, president. Makarios fled the country. On July 20, Turkey invaded the island; Greece mobilized its forces but did not intervene. A cease-fire was arranged July 22. On the 23d, Sampson turned over the presidency to Glafkos Clerides (on the same day, Greece's military junta resigned). A peace conference collapsed Aug. 14; fighting resumed. By Aug. 16 Turkish forces had occupied the NE 40% of the island, despite the presence of UN peace forces. Makarios resumed the presidency in Dec., until his death, 1977.
Turkish Cypriots voted overwhelmingly, June 8, 1975, to form a separate Turkish Cypriot federated state. A president and assembly were elected in 1976. Some 200,000 Greeks had left the Turkish-controlled area, replaced by thousands of Turks, some from the mainland.

Czechoslovakia

Czechoslovak Socialist Republic

People: Population (1980 est.): 15,320,000. **Age distrib.** (%): 0-14: 23.4; 15-59: 52.5; 60+: 17.4. **Pop. density:** 310.30 per sq. mi. **Urban** (1974): 66.7%. **Ethnic groups:** Czechs 65%, Slovaks 30%, Hungarians 4%, Germans, Poles, Ukrainians. **Languages:** Czech, Slovak, Hungarian. **Religions:** Roman Catholics were majority, Lutherans, Orthodox.
Geography: Area: 49,371 sq. mi., the size of New York. **Location:** In E central Europe. **Neighbors:** Poland, E. Germany on N, W. Germany on W. Austria, Hungary on S, USSR on E. **Topography:** Bohemia, in W, is a plateau surrounded by mountains; Moravia is hilly, Slovakia, in E, has mountains (Carpathians) in N, fertile Danube plain in S. Vltava (Moldau) and Labe (Elbe) rivers flow N from Bohemia to G. **Capital:** Prague. **Cities** (1978 est.): Prague 1,173,031; Brno 361,561; Bratislava 345,515; Ostrava 302,111.
Government: Head of state: Pres. Gustav Husak; b. Jan 10, 1913; in office: May 29, 1975; **Head of government:** Prime Min. Lubomir Strougal; b. Oct. 19, 1924; in office: Jan. 28, 1970. **Head of Communist Party:** First Sec. Gustav Husak; in office: Apr. 17, 1969. **Local divisions:** Czech and Slovak republics each have an assembly. **Armed forces:** regulars 194,000; reserves 350,000.
Economy: Industries: Machinery, oil products, weapons, steel, glass, chemicals, aircraft, textiles, shoes. **Chief crops:** Wheat, sugar beets, potatoes, rye, hops. **Minerals:** Mercury, coal, iron. Jachymor has Europe's greatest pitchblende (for uranium and radium) deposits. **Per capita arable land:** 0.8 acres. **Meat prod.** (1978): beef: 393,000 metric tons; pork: 815,000 metric tons; lamb 6,000 metric tons. **Fish catch** (1977): 18,300

metric tons. **Electricity prod.** (1978): 69.06 bln. kwh. **Crude steel prod.** (1979): 14.8 mln. metric tons. **Labor force:** 14% agric.; manuf. 39%.
Finance: Currency: Koruna (Mar. 1980: 10.44 = $1 US). **Net material product** (1978): $40.6 bln. **Per capita income** (1976): $3,985. **Imports** (1979): $14.3 bln.; partners (1977): USSR 34%, E. Ger. 11%, Pol. 8%, W. Ger. 6%. **Exports** (1979): $13.2 bln.; partners (1977): USSR 33%, E. Ger. 12%, Pol. 9%, Hung. 6%. **Tourists** (1977): 6,982,700; receipts $184 mln. **Consumer prices** (change in 1979): 3.7%.
Transport: Railway traffic (1978): 18.64 bln. passenger-km; 72.34 bln. net ton-km. **Motor vehicles:** in use (1977): 1.83 mln. passenger cars, 289,800 comm. vehicles; manuf. (1978): 175,200 passenger cars; (1977): 80,400 comm. vehicles. **Civil aviation:** 1,584 mln. passenger-km (1978); 18 mln. freight ton-km (1978).
Communications: Television sets: 3.8 mln. licensed (1976), 461,000 manuf. (1977). **Radios:** 3.93 mln. licensed (1976), 235,000 manuf. (1977). **Telephones in use** (1978): 2,863,307. **Daily newspaper circ.** (1977): 4,453,000; 296 per 1,000 pop.
Health: Life expectancy at birth (1976): 66.99 male; 74.05 female. **Births** (per 1,000 pop. 1980): 16.4 **Deaths** (per 1,000 pop. 1980): 12.1. **Natural increase** (1978): .7%. **Hospital beds** (per 100,000 pop. 1977): 1,229. **Physicians** (per 100,000 pop. 1977): 254. **Infant mortality** (per 1,000 live births 1978): 18.7.
Education (1977): **Literacy:** 99%. **Pop. 5–19:** in school: 60%, teachers per 1,000: 30. **PQLI:** 92.

Bohemia, Moravia and Slovakia were part of the Great Moravian Empire in the 9th century. Later, Slovakia was overrun by Magyars, while Bohemia and Moravia became part of the Holy Roman Empire. Under the kings of Bohemia, Prague in the 14th century was the cultural center of Central Europe. Bohemia and Hungary became part of Austria-Hungary.
In 1914-1918 Thomas G. Masaryk and Eduard Benes formed a provisional government with the support of Slovak leaders including Milan Stefanik. They proclaimed the Republic of Czechoslovakia Oct. 30, 1918.
By 1938 Nazi Germany had worked up disaffection among German-speaking citizens in Sudetenland and demanded its cession. Prime Min. Neville Chamberlain of Britain, with the acquiescence of France, signed with Hitler at Munich, Sept. 30, 1938, an agreement to the cession, with a guarantee of peace by Hitler and Mussolini. Germany occupied Sudetenland Oct. 1-2.
Hitler on Mar. 15, 1939, dissolved Czechoslovakia, made protectorates of Bohemia and Moravia, and supported the autonomy of Slovakia, which was proclaimed independent Mar. 14, 1939, with Josef Tiso president.
Soviet troops with some Czechoslovak contingents entered eastern Czechoslovakia in 1944 and reached Prague in May 1945; Benes returned as president. In May 1946 elections, the Communist Party won 38% of the votes, and Benes accepted Klement Gottwald, a Communist, as prime minister. Tiso was executed in 1947.
In February, 1948, the Communists seized power in advance of scheduled elections. In May 1948 a new constitution was approved. Benes refused to sign it. On May 30 the voters were offered a one-slate ballot and the Communists won full control. Benes resigned June 7. Gottwald became president and Benes died Sept. 3. A harsh Stalinist period followed, with complete and violent suppression of all opposition.
In Jan. 1968 a liberalization movement spread explosively through Czechoslovakia. Antonin Novotny, long the Stalinist boss of the nation, was deposed as party leader and succeeded by Alexander Dubcek, a Slovak, who declared he intended to make communism democratic. On Mar. 22 Novotny resigned as president and was succeeded by Gen. Ludvik Svoboda. On Apr. 6, Premier Joseph Lenart resigned and was succeeded by Oldrich Cernik, whose new cabinet was pledged to carry out democratization and economic reforms.
In July 1968 the USSR and 4 hard-core Warsaw Pact nations demanded an end to liberalization. On Aug. 20, the Russian, Polish, East German, Hungarian, and Bulgarian armies invaded Czechoslovakia.
Despite demonstrations and riots by students and workers, press censorship was imposed, liberal leaders were ousted from office and promises of loyalty to Soviet policies were made by some old-line Communist Party leaders.
On Apr. 17, 1969, Dubcek resigned as leader of the Communist Party and was succeeded by Gustav Husak. In Jan. 1970,

Premier Cernik was ousted. Censorship was tightened and the Communist Party expelled a third of its members. In 1972, more than 40 liberals were jailed on subversion charges. In 1973, amnesty was offered to some of the 40,000 who fled the country after the 1968 invasion, but repressive policies remained in force through 1976.

More than 700 leading Czechoslovak intellectuals and former party leaders signed a human rights manifesto in 1977, called Charter 77, prompting a renewed crackdown by the regime.

Czechoslovakia has long been an industrial and technological leader of the eastern European countries, though its relative standing has declined in recent years.

Denmark

Kingdom of Denmark

People: Population (1980 est.): 5,120,000. **Age distrib.** (%): 0–14: 22.4 15–59: 58.7; 60+: 18.9. **Pop. density:** 300.68 per sq. mi. **Urban** (1970): 66.9%. **Ethnic groups:** Almost all Scandinavian. **Languages:** Danish. **Religions:** Lutherans 97%.

Geography: Area: 17,028 sq. mi., the size of Massachusetts and New Hampshire combined. **Location:** In northern Europe, separating the North and Baltic seas. **Neighbors:** W. Germany on S., Norway on NW, Sweden on NE. **Topography:** Denmark consists of the Jutland Peninsula and about 500 islands, 100 inhabited. The land is flat or gently rolling, and is almost all in productive use. **Capital:** Copenhagen. **Cities** (1978 est.): Copenhagen 699,300; Arhus 246,111.

Government: Head of state: Queen Margrethe II; b. Apr. 16, 1940; in office: Jan. 14, 1972. **Head of government:** Prime Min. Anker Joergensen; b. July 13, 1922; in office: Feb. 13, 1975. **Local divisions:** 14 counties and one city (Copenhagen). **Armed forces:** regulars 34,650; reserves 154,260.

Economy: Industries: Machinery, ships, textiles, furniture, steel. **Chief crops:** Dairy products, grains, potatoes. **Crude oil reserves** (1980): 375 mln. bbls. **Per capita arable land:** 1.2 acres. **Meat prod.** (1978): beef: 240,000 metric tons; pork: 790,000 metric tons. **Fish catch** (1977): 1.81 mln. metric tons. **Electricity prod.** (1978): 20.52 bln. kwh. **Crude steel prod.** (1979): 804,000 metric tons. **Labor force:** 8.5% agric.; 44% manuf.

Finance: Currency: Krone (Apr. 1981: 6.98 = $1 US). **Gross domestic product** (1980): $66.40 bln. **Per capita income** (1978): $9,869. **Imports** (1980): $19.34 bln.; partners (1978): W. Ger. 21% Swed. 13%, UK 11%, Neth. 6%. **Exports** (1980): $16.71 bln.; partners (1978): W. Ger. 17%, UK 14%, Swed. 13%, Nor. 7%. **Tourists** (1976): 16,231,900; receipts: $805 mln. **National budget** (1975): $11.87 bln. revenues; $13.79 bln. expenditures. **International reserves less gold** (Apr. 1981): $2.78 bln. **Gold:** 1.63 mln. oz t. **Consumer prices** (change in 1980): 12.3%.

Transport: Railway traffic (1978): 3.08 bln. passenger-km; 1.76 bln. net ton-km. **Motor vehicles:** in use (1977): 1.38 mln. passenger cars, 274,900 comm. vehicles; assembled (1975): 1,000 passenger cars; (1977): 900 comm. vehicles. **Civil aviation:** 2,832 mln. passenger-km (1978); 136 mln. freight ton-km (1978). **Chief ports:** Copenhagen, Alborg, Arhus, Odense.

Communications: Television sets: 1.64 mln. licensed (1976), 77,000 manuf. (1977). **Radios:** 1.85 mln. licensed (1976), 161,000 manuf. (1977). **Telephones in use** (1978): 2,743,758. **Daily newspaper circ.** (1977): 1,840,000; 362 per 1,000 pop.

Health: Life expectancy at birth (1976): 71.1 male; 76.8 female. **Births** (per 1,000 pop. 1980): 11.2. **Deaths** (per 1,000 pop. 1980): 10.9. **Natural increase** (1978): .2%. **Hospital beds** (per 100,000 pop. 1977): 853. **Physicians** (per 100,000 pop. 1977): 204. **Infant mortality** (per 1,000 live births 1978): 8.9.

Education (1977): **Literacy:** 99%. **Pop. 5–19:** in school: 70%, teachers per 1,000; 51. **PQLI:** 97.

The origin of Copenhagen dates back to ancient times, when the fishing and trading place named Havn (port) grew up on a cluster of islets, but Bishop Absalon (1128-1201) is regarded as the actual founder of the city.

Danes formed a large component of the Viking raiders in the early Middle Ages. The Danish kingdom was a major north European power until the 17th century, when it lost its land in southern Sweden. Norway was separated in 1815, and Schleswig-Holstein in 1864. Northern Schleswig was returned in 1920.

The **Faeroe Islands** in the N. Atlantic, about 300 mi. NE of the Shetlands, and 850 mi. from Denmark proper, 18 inhabited, have an area of 540 sq. mi. and pop. (1979) of 43,000. They are self-governing in most matters.

Greenland
(Kalâtdlit Nunât)

Greenland, a huge island between the N. Atlantic and the Polar Sea, is separated from the North American continent by Davis Strait and Baffin Bay. Its total area is 840,000 sq. mi., 705,234 of which are ice-capped. Most of the island is a lofty plateau 9,000 to 10,000 ft. in altitude. The average thickness of the cap is 1,000 ft. The population (1979 est.) is 49,300. Under the 1953 Danish constitution the colony became an integral part of the realm with representatives in the Folketing. The Danish parliament, 1978, approved home rule for Greenland, effective May 1, 1979. Accepting home rule the islanders elected a socialist-dominated legislature, Apr. 4th. With home rule, Greenlandic place names came into official use. The technically-correct name for Greenland is now Kalâtdlit Nunât; its capital is Nuuk, rather than Gothab. Fish and fur are exported.

Djibouti

Republic of Djibouti

People: Population (1979 est.): 386,000. **Pop. density:** 12.23 per sq. mi. **Ethnic groups:** Issa (Somali) 47%; Afar 37%; European 8%; Arab 6%. **Languages:** Somali, Afar, French, Arabic. **Religions:** Most are Moslems; Europeans are Roman Catholic.

Geography: Area: 8,996 sq. mi., about the size of Massachusetts. **Location:** On E coast of Africa, separated from Arabian Peninsula by the strategically vital strait of Bab el-Mandeb. **Neighbors:** Ethiopia on N (Eritrea) and W, Somalia on S. **Topography:** The territory, divided into a low coastal plain, mountains behind, and an interior plateau, is arid, sandy, and desolate. The climate is generally hot and dry. **Capital:** Djibouti. **Cities** (1978 est): Djibouti (met.) 62,000; Dikhil; Ali-Sabieh; Obock.

Government: Head of state: Pres. Hassan Gouled Aptidon b. 1916; in office: June 24, 1977; **Head of government:** Prem. Barkat Gourad Hamadou; in office: Sept. 30, 1978. **Local divisions:** 5 cercles (districts). **Armed forces:** regulars 3,000; paramilitary 10,000.

Economy: Minerals: Salt. **Electricity prod.** (1977): 62 mln. kwh.

Finance: Currency: Franc (1976: 166=$1 US). **Per capita income** (1976): $1,000. **Imports** (1979): $140 mln.; partners (1973): Fr. 49%, Eth. 12%, Jap. 6%, UK 6%. **Exports** (1979): $20 mln.; partners (1973): Fr. 84%.

Transport: Motor vehicles: in use (1977): 11,800 passenger cars, 3,300 commercial vehicles. **Chief ports:** Djibouti.

Communications: Television sets: 3,500 in use (1976). **Radios:** 15,000 in use (1976). **Telephones in use** (1978): 3,675.

Health: Births (per 1,000 pop. 1970): 42.0. **Deaths** (per 1,000 pop. 1970): 7.6. **Natural increase** (1970): 3.4%.

France gained control of the territory in stages between 1862 and 1900.

Ethiopia and Somalia have renounced their claims to the area, but each has accused the other of trying to gain control. There were clashes between Afars (ethnically related to Ethiopians) and Issas (related to Somalis) in 1976. Immigrants from both countries continued to enter the country up to independence, which came June 27, 1977.

Unemployment is about 80%. There are few natural resources; trade is the main contributor to domestic product. French aid is the mainstay of the economy and 7,000 French troops are present.

Dominica

Commonwealth of Dominica

People: Population (1980 est.): 80,000. **Pop. density:** 275.86 per sq. mi. **Ethnic groups:** nearly all African or mulatto, Caribs. **Languages:** English, French patois. **Religions:** mainly Roman Catholic.

Geography: Area: 290 sq. mi., about one-fourth the size of Rhode Island. **Location:** In Eastern Caribbean, most northerly Windward Is. **Neighbors:** Guadeloupe to N, Martinique to S. **Topography:** Mountainous, a central ridge running from N to S terminating in cliffs; volcanic in origin, with numerous thermal springs; rich deep topsoil on leeward side, red tropical clay on windward coast. **Capital** (1976 est.) Roseau 16,800.

Government: Head of state: Pres. Aurelius Marie; in office: 1980. **Head of government:** Prime Min. Mary Eugenia Charles; elected to office: July 21, 1980. **Local divisions:** 25 village councils and 2 town councils.

Economy: Industries: Agriculture, tourism. **Chief crops:** Bananas, citrus fruits, coconuts. **Minerals:** Pumice. **Other resources:** Forests. **Per capita arable land:** 0.2 acres. **Electricity prod.** (1977): 16 mln. kwh.

Finance: Currency: East Caribbean dollar (Mar. 1980: 2.70 = $1 US). **Gross domestic product** (1977): $33.48 mln. **Per capita income** (1976): $460. **Imports** (1975): $16.70 mln.; partners (1975): UK 30%, U.S. 10%, Can. 10%. **Exports** (1975): $8.81 mln.; partners (1975): UK 78%. **Tourists** (1977): 31,000; receipts: $3 mln. **National budget** (1976): $6.29 mln. revenues; $7.51 mln. expenditures. **Consumer prices** (change in 1978): 7.7%.

Transport: Chief ports: Roseau.
Communications: Telephones in use (1978): 4,036.
Health: Life expectancy at birth (1962): 56.97 male; 59.18 female. **Births** (per 1,000 pop. 1978): 21.4. **Deaths** (per 1,000 pop. 1978): 5.3. **Natural increase** (1978): 1.6%. **Pop. per hospital bed** (1973): 234. **Pop. per physician** (1971): 5,385. **Infant mortality** (per 1,000 live births 1978): 19.6.
Education: Pop. 5–19: in school (1975): 24,113. **PQLI:** 68.

A British colony since 1805, Dominica was granted self government in 1967. Independence was achieved Nov. 3, 1978. Tourism is a small sector of the economy. France was expected to increase aid to the island.

Hurricane David struck, Aug. 30, 1979, devastating the island and destroying the banana plantations, Dominica's economic mainstay.

Dominican Republic

People: Population (1979 est.): 5,551,000. **Age distrib.** (%): 0–14: 47.5; 15–59: 47.5; 60+: 4.9. **Pop. density:** 273.74 per sq. mi. **Urban** (1978): 49.1%. **Ethnic groups:** Caucasian 16%, mulatto 73%, Negro 11%. **Languages:** Spanish. **Religions:** Roman Catholic 95%, Protestant 2%.

Geography: Area: 18,704 sq. mi., the size of Vermont and New Hampshire combined. **Location:** In West Indies, sharing I. of Hispaniola with Haiti. **Neighbors:** Haiti on W. **Topography:** The Cordillera Central range crosses the center of the country, rising to over 10,000 ft., highest in the Caribbean. The Cibao valley to the N is major agricultural area. **Capital:** Santo Domingo. **Cities** (1970 cen.): Santo Domingo 673,470; Santiago de Los Caballeros 155,000.

Government: Head of state: Pres. Antonio Guzman Fernandez; b. Feb. 12, 1911; in office Aug. 16, 1978. **Local divisions:** 26 provinces and a national district. **Armed forces:** regulars 18,500; para-military 10,000.

Economy: Industries: Molasses, rum, alcohol, cement, textiles, furniture, apparel. **Chief crops:** sugar, cocoa, coffee, tobacco, corn, peanuts, bananas. **Minerals:** Nickel, gold, copper, iron, salt, chalk, bauxite, marble, amber, kaolin. **Other resources:** Timber. **Per capita arable land:** 0.4 acres. **Meat prod.** (1978): beef: 39,000 metric tons; pork: 23,000 metric tons. **Electricity prod.** (1977): 2.67 bln. kwh. **Labor force:** 44% agric.; 8% manuf.

Finance: Currency: Peso (Apr. 1981: 1 = $1 US). **Gross domestic product** (1979): $5.50 bln. **Per capita income** (1978): $841. **Imports** (1980): $1.65 bln.; partners (1978): U.S. 43%, Venez. 15%, Jap. 9%. **Exports** (1980): $961.9 mln.; partners (1978): U.S. 55% Swit. 9%, Venez. 8%, Neth. 6%. **Tourists** (1977): 265,000; receipts: $93 mln. **National budget** (1978): $596 mln. revenues; $664 mln. expenditures. **International reserves less gold** (Apr. 1981): $169.6 mln. **Gold:** 131,000 oz t. **Consumer prices** (change in 1979): 9.2%

Transport: Motor vehicles: in use (1976): 77,300 passenger cars, 39,400 comm. vehicles. **Chief ports:** Santo Domingo, San Pedro de Macoris, Puerto Plata.

Communications: Television sets: 160,000 in use (1976). **Radios:** 120,000 in use (1976). **Telephones in use** (1978): 139,412. **Daily newspaper circ.** (1976): 208,000; 28 per 1,000 pop.

Health: Life expectancy at birth (1961): 57.15 male; 58.59 female. **Births** (per 1,000 pop. 1975): 42.0. **Deaths** (per 1,000

pop. 1975): 10.7. **Natural increase** (1975): 3.1%. **Hospital beds** (per 100,000 pop. 1977): 233. **Physicians** (per 100,000 pop. 1977): 53. **Infant mortality** (per 1,000 live births 1975): 37.2.

Education (1977): **Literacy:** 68%. **Pop. 5–19:** in school: 51%, teachers per 1,000: 12. **PQLI:** 64.

Carib and Arawak Indians inhabited the island of Hispaniola when Columbus landed in 1492. The city of Santo Domingo, founded 1496, is the oldest settlement by Europeans in the hemisphere and has the supposed ashes of Columbus in an elaborate tomb in its ancient cathedral.

The western third of the island was ceded to France in 1697. Santo Domingo itself was ceded to France in 1795. Haitian leader Toussaint L'Ouverture seized it, 1801. Spain returned intermittently 1803-21, as several native republics came and went. Haiti ruled again, 1822-44, and Spanish occupation occurred 1861-63.

The country was occupied by U.S. Marines from 1916 to 1924, when a constitutionally elected government was installed.

In 1930, Gen. Rafael Leonidas Trujillo Molina was elected president. Trujillo ruled brutally until his assassination in 1961. Pres. Joaquin Balaguer, appointed by Trujillo in 1960, resigned under pressure in 1962. Juan Bosch, elected president in the first free elections in 38 years, was overthrown in 1963.

On April 24, 1965, a revolt was launched by followers of Bosch and others, including a few communists. Four days later 405 U.S. Marines intervened against the pro-Bosch forces; their numbers grew to 21,000. Token units were later sent by 5 So. American countries as a peace-keeping force.

A provisional government supervised a June 1966 election, in which Balaguer defeated Bosch by a 3-2 margin; there were some charges of election fraud.

The Inter-American Peace Force completed its departure Sept. 20, 1966. Balaguer was reelected, 1970 and 1974, the latter time without real opposition.

In 1971, scores of leftists were reported killed by terrorists. Renewed violence occurred in 1975.

Continued depressed world prices affected the main export commodity, sugar. Hurricane David devastated the island, killing over 600, Aug. 1979.

Ecuador
Republic of Ecuador

People: Population (1980 est.): 8,350,000. **Age distrib.** (%): 0–14: 44.5; 15–59: 49.6; 60+: 6.0. **Pop. density:** 79.00 per sq. mi. **Urban** (1978): 42.8% **Ethnic groups:** Indians 40%, Mestizos 40%, Caucasians 10%, Negroes 10%. **Languages:** Spanish (official) 93%, Quechua dialects 7%. **Religions:** Roman Catholics 94%, Protestants 6%.

Geography: Area: 105,685 sq. mi., the size of Colorado. **Location:** In NW S. America, on Pacific coast, astride Equator. **Neighbors:** Colombia to N, Peru to E and S. **Topography:** Two ranges of Andes run N and S, splitting the country into 3 zones: hot, humid lowlands on the coast; temperate highlands between the ranges, and rainy, tropical lowlands to the E. **Capital:** Quito. **Cities** (1978 est.): Guayaquil 1,022,010; Quito 742,858.

Government: Head of state: Pres. Osvaldo Hurtado Larrea; in office: May 24, 1981. **Local divisions:** 20 provinces. **Armed forces:** regulars 32,800; para-military 5,800.

Economy: Industries: Cement, edible oils, textiles, sugar, chemicals, oil products, paper. **Chief crops:** Bananas (largest exporter), rice, grains, potatoes, fruits, cocoa, kapok. **Minerals:** Oil, copper, iron, lead, coal, sulphur. **Crude oil reserves** (1980): 1.1 bln. bbls. **Other resources:** Rubber, bark. **Per capita arable land:** 1.3 acres. **Meat prod.** (1978): beef: 70,000 metric tons; pork: 36,000 metric tons; lamb: 13,000 metric tons. **Fish catch** (1977): 476,000 metric tons. **Electricity prod.** (1977): 2.15 bln. kwh. **Labor force:** 54% agric.

Finance: Currency: Sucre (Apr. 1981: 25.00 = $1 US). **Gross domestic product** (1979): $9.17 bln. **Per capita income** (1977): $741. **Imports** (1980): $2.25 bln.; partners (1977): U.S. 38%, Jap. 16%, W. Ger. 8%. **Exports** (1979): $2.01 bln.; partners (1977): U.S. 36%, Pan. 10%, Peru 9%, Chile 7%. **Tourists** (1977): 201,900; receipts: $36 mln. **National budget** (1979): $922 mln. revenues; $984 mln. expenditures. **International reserves less gold** (Apr. 1981): $801.5 mln. **Gold:** 414,000 oz t. **Consumer prices** (change in 1980): 13.1%.

Transport: Railway traffic (1978) 65.3 mln. passenger-km;

34.2 mln. net ton-km. **Motor vehicles:** in use (1975): 51,300 passenger cars, 77,200 comm. vehicles. **Chief ports:** Guayaquil, Manta, Esmeraldas.
Communications: Television sets: 300,000 in use (1976), 5,000 manuf. (1975). **Radios:** 1.7 mln. in use (1970). **Telephones in use** (1978): 221,578. **Daily newspaper circ.** (1977): 350,000 46 per 1,000 pop.
Health: Life expectancy at birth (1974): 54.89 male; 58.07 female. **Births** (per 1,000 pop. 1975): 42.2. **Deaths** (per 1,000 pop. 1975): 12.1. **Natural increase** (1975): 3.0%. **Hospital beds** (per 100,000 pop.1977): 204. **Physicians** (per 100,000 pop. 1977): 64. **Infant mortality** (per 1,000 live births 1975): 65.8.
Education (1977): Literacy: 74%. **Pop. 5–19:** in school: 60%, teachers per 1,000: 20. **PQLI:** 70.

Spain conquered the region, which was the northern Inca empire, in 1533. Liberation forces defeated the Spanish May 24, 1822, near Quito. Ecuador became part of the Great Colombia Republic but seceded, May 13, 1830.

Ecuador had been ruled by civilian and military dictatorships since 1968. A peaceful transfer of power from the military junta to the democratic civilian government took place, 1979.

Since 1972, the economy has revolved around its petroleum exports. Despite this, Ecuador remains an underdeveloped country.

Ecuador and Peru have long disputed their Amazon Valley boundary.

President Jaime Roldós Aguilera (b. Nov. 5, 1940; in office: Aug. 10, 1979) was killed, May 24, 1981, in a plane crash. Vice President Larrea assumed the presidency and will serve out the remaining three years of Mr. Roldós' term.

The **Galapagos Islands,** 600 mi. to the W, are the home of hugh tortoises and other unusual animals.

Egypt

Arab Republic of Egypt

People: Population (1980 est.): 41,990,000. **Pop. density:** 115.60 per sq. mi. **Urban** (1977): 44.1%. **Ethnic groups:** Egyptians, Bedouins, Nubians. **Languages:** Arabic. **Religions:** Sunni Moslems (state religion) 92%, Christians 7% (mostly Copts).
Geography: Area: 363,250 sq. mi (excluding Sinai Peninsula, 23,622 sq. mi.) the size of Texas and Oregon combined. **Location:** NE corner of Africa. **Neighbors:** Libya on W, Sudan on S, Israel on E. **Topography:** Almost entirely desolate and barren, with hills and mountains in E and along Nile. The Nile Valley, where most of the people live, stretches 550 miles. **Capital:** Cairo. **Cities** (1976 cen.): Cairo 5,084,463; Alexandria 2,318,655; Giza 1,246,713; Subra-El Khema 393,700; El-Mahalla El-Kubra 292,853.
Government: Head of state and head of gov't.: Pres. Mohamed Anwar El-Sadat; b. Dec. 25, 1918; in office: Sept. 28, 1970 (P.M.: May 14, 1980). **Local divisions:** 25 governorates. **Armed forces:** regulars 395,000; reserves 500,000.
Economy: Industries: Textiles, chemicals, steel, cement, fertilizers, motion pictures. **Chief crops:** Cotton (one of largest producers), grains, vegetables, sugar cane, fruits. **Minerals:** Oil, phosphates, salt, iron, manganese, cement, gold, gypsum, kaolin, titanium. **Crude oil reserves** (1980): 3.1 bln. bbls. **Per capita arable land:** 0.2 acres. **Meat prod.** (1978): beef: 241,000 metric tons; lamb: 49,000 metric tons. **Fish catch** (1977): 104,500 metric tons. **Electricity prod.** (1977): 13.00 bln. kwh. **Crude steel prod.** (1979 est.): 800,000 metric tons. **Labor force:** 50% agric.
Finance: Currency: Pound (Apr. 1981: 0.70 = $1 US). **Gross domestic product** (1977): $18.76 bln. **Per capita income** (1977): $448. **Imports** (1979): $3.84 bln.; partners (1978): U.S. 16%, W. Ger. 11%, It. 8%, UK 8%. **Exports** (1979): $1.84 bln.; partners (1978): USSR 17%, It. 12%, U.S. 12%, Neth. 5%. **Tourists** (1977): 1,003,900; receipts: $658 mln. **International reserves less gold** (Dec. 1980): $1.05 bln. **Gold:** 2.43 mln. oz t.
Consumer prices (change in 1979): 9.9%
Transport: Railway traffic (1976): 8.75 bln. passenger-km; 2.20 bln. net ton-km. **Motor vehicles:** in use (1977): 283,200 passenger cars, 64,000 comm. vehicles; assembled (1978): 15,024 passenger cars; 4,080 comm. vehicles. **Civil aviation:** 2,040 mln. passenger-km (1977); 25 mln. freight ton-km (1977). **Chief ports:** Alexandria, Port Said, Suez.
Communications: Television sets: 620,000 in use (1975), 138,000 manuf. (1977). **Radios:** 5.25 mln. in use (1976),

265,000 manuf. (1977). **Telephones in use** (1977): 503,947. **Daily newspaper circ.** (1976): 3,012,000; 79 per 1,000 pop.
Health: Life expectancy at birth (1960): 51.6 male; 53.8 female. **Births** (per 1,000 pop. 1978): 37.6. **Deaths** (per 1,000 pop. 1978): 10.5. **Natural increase** (1978): 2.7%. **Hospital beds** (per 100,000 pop. 1977): 209. **Physicians** (per 100,000 pop. 1977): 92. **Infant mortality** (per 1,000 live births 1978): 89.2.
Education (1977): **Literacy:** 44%. **Pop. 5-19:** in school: 44%, teachers per 1,000: 13. **PQLI:** 52.

Archeological records of ancient Egyptian civilization date back to 4000 BC. A unified kingdom arose around 3200 BC, and extended its way south into Nubia and north as far as Syria. A high culture of rulers and priests was built on an economic base of serfdom, fertile soil, and annual flooding of the Nile banks.

Imperial decline facilitated conquest by Asian invaders (Hyksos, Assyrians). The last native dynasty fell in 341 BC to the Persians, who were in turn replaced by Greeks (Alexander and the Ptolemies), Romans, Byzantines, and Arabs, who introduced Islam and the Arabic language. The ancient Egyptian language is preserved only in the liturgy of the Coptic Christians.

Egypt was ruled as part of larger Islamic empires for several centuries. The Mamluks, a military caste of Caucasian origin, ruled Egypt from 1250 until defeat by the Ottoman Turks in 1517. Under Turkish sultans the khedive as hereditary viceroy had wide authority. Britain intervened in 1882 and took control of administration, though nominal allegiance to the Ottoman Empire continued until 1914.

The country was a British protectorate from 1914 to 1922. A 1936 treaty strengthened Egyptian autonomy, but Britain retained bases in Egypt and a condominium over the Sudan. Britain fought German and Italian armies from Egypt, 1940-42, but Egypt did not declare war against Germany until 1945. In 1951 Egypt abrogated the 1936 treaty. The Sudan became independent in 1956.

The uprising of July 23, 1952, led by the Society of Free Officers, named Maj. Gen. Mohammed Naguib commander in chief and forced King Farouk to abdicate. When the republic was proclaimed June 18, 1953, Naguib became its first president and premier. Lt. Col. Gamal Abdel Nasser removed Naguib and became premier in 1954. In 1956, he was voted president. Nasser died in 1970 and was replaced by Vice Pres. Anwar Sadat.

A series of decrees in July, 1961, nationalized about 90% of industry. Economic liberalization was begun, 1974, with more emphasis on private domestic and foreign investment.

In July, 1956, the U. S. and UK withdrew support for loans to start the Aswan High Dam. Nasser obtained credits and technicians from the USSR to build the dam. The billion-dollar Aswan High Dam project, begun 1960, completed 1971, provided irrigation for more than a million acres of land and a potential of 10 billion kwh of electricity per year. Artesian wells, drilled in the Western Desert, reclaimed 43,000 acres, 1960-66.

When the state of Israel was proclaimed in 1948, Egypt joined other Arab nations invading Israel and was defeated.

After terrorist raids across its border, Israel invaded Egypt's Sinai Peninsula, Oct. 29, 1956. Egypt rejected a cease-fire demand by Britain and France; on Oct. 31 the 2 nations dropped bombs and on Nov. 5-6 landed forces. Egypt and Israel accepted a UN cease-fire; fighting ended Nov. 7.

A UN Emergency Force guarded the 117-mile long border between Egypt and Israel until May 19, 1967, when it was withdrawn at Nasser's demand. Egyptian troops entered the Gaza Strip and the heights of Sharm el Sheikh and 3 days later closed the Strait of Tiran to all Israeli shipping. Full-scale war broke out June 5 and before it ended under a UN cease-fire June 10, Israel had captured Gaza and the Sinai Peninsula, controlled the east bank of the Suez Canal and reopened the gulf.

Sporadic fighting with Israel broke out late in 1968 and continued almost daily, 1969-70. Military and economic aid was received from the USSR; it was est. in 1971 there were 19,000 or more Soviet military personnel in Egypt. Israel and Egypt agreed, Aug. 7, 1970, to a cease-fire and peace negotiations proposed by the U.S. Negotiations failed to achieve results, but the cease-fire continued into 1973.

In July 1972 Sadat ordered most of the 20,000 Soviet military advisers and personnel to leave Egypt; they complied. Some Soviet military shipments have continued.

In a surprise attack Oct. 6, 1973, Egyptian forces crossed the Suez Canal into the Sinai. (At the same time, Syrian forces attacked Israelis on the Golan Heights.) Egypt was supplied by a

USSR military airlift; the U.S. responded with an airlift to Israel. Israel counter-attacked, crossed the canal, surrounded Suez City. A UN cease-fire took effect Oct. 24.

A disengagement agreement was signed Jan. 18, 1974. Under it, Israeli forces withdrew from the canal's W bank; limited numbers of Egyptian forces occupied a strip along the E bank. A second accord was signed in 1975, with Israel yielding Sinai oil fields. Pres. Sadat's surprise visit to Jerusalem, Nov. 1977, opened the prospect of peace with Israel, but worsened relations with Libya (border clashes, July 1977). On Mar. 26, 1979, Egypt and Israel signed a formal peace treaty, ending 30 years of war, and establishing diplomatic relations. Negotiations concerning the West Bank and Gaza Strip elections opened, amid Arab World reprisals against Egypt.

The U.S. and Egypt resumed, in Feb. 1974, diplomatic relations severed by Egypt after the 1967 war.

The **Suez Canal**, 103 mi. long, links the Mediterranean and Red seas. It was built by a French corporation 1859-69, but Britain obtained controlling interest in 1875. The last British troops were removed June 13, 1956. On July 26, Egypt nationalized the canal. French and British stockholders eventually received some compensation.

Egypt had barred Israeli ships and cargoes destined for Israel since 1948, and closed the canal to all shipping after the 1967 Arab-Israeli War. The canal was reopened in 1975; Egypt agreed to allow passage to Israeli cargo in third party ships. By 1979, annual tolls, at $700 million, had once more become a major source of government revenue. A $1.3 billion expansion project will enable the canal to accomodate larger tankers.

El Salvador
Republic of El Salvador

People: Population (1980 est.): 4,810,000. **Age distrib.** (%): 0–14: 46.2; 15–59: 48.4; 60+: 5.4. **Pop. density:** 582.32 per sq. mi. **Urban** (1974): 38.8%. **Ethnic groups:** Mestizos 89%, Indians 10%, Caucasians 1%. **Languages:** Spanish, Nahuatl (among some Indians). **Religions:** Roman Catholicism prevails.

Geography: Area: 8,260 sq. mi., the size of Massachusetts. **Location:** In Central America. **Neighbors:** Guatemala on W, Honduras on N. **Topography:** A hot Pacific coastal plain in the south rises to a cooler plateau and valley region, densely populated. The N is mountainous, including many volcanoes. **Capital:** San Salvador. **Cities** (1979 est.): San Salvador 400,000.

Government: Pres. of military-civilian junta, José Napoleón Duarte. **Local divisions:** 14 departments; pres. appoints governors. **Armed forces:** regulars 6,930; para-military 3,000.

Economy: Industries: Cement, textiles, refined sugar. **Chief crops:** Coffee, cotton, rice, maize, cacao, tobacco, indigo, sugar. **Other resources:** Rubber, forests. **Per capita arable land:** 0.3 acres. **Meat prod.** (1978): beef: 34,000 metric tons; pork: 14,000 metric tons. **Electricity prod.** (1978): 1.45 bln. kwh. **Labor force:** 47% agric.; 8% man.; 14% services.

Finance: Currency: Colon (Apr. 1981: 2.50 = $1 US). **Gross domestic product** (1978): $3.77 bln. **Per capita income** (1978): $639. **Imports** (1979): $1.02 bln.; partners (1977): U.S. 29%, Guat. 13%, Jap. 11%, Venez. 9%. **Exports** (1979): $1.13 bln.; partners (1977): U.S. 33%, W. Ger. 19%, Guat. 13%, Neth. 9%. **Tourists** (1976): 277,900; receipts (1977): $23 mln. **National budget** (1980): $412 mln. revenues; $569 mln. expenditures. **International reserves less gold** (Apr. 1981): $88.2 mln. **Gold:** 516,000 oz t. **Consumer prices** (change in 1980): 17.4%.

Transport: Motor vehicles: in use (1974): 41,000 passenger cars, 19,100 comm. vehicles. **Chief ports:** La Union, Acajutla.

Communications: Television sets: 136,000 in use (1976), 109,000 (includes radios) manuf. (1977). **Radios:** 1.4 mln. in use (1976). **Telephones in use** (1978): 70,400. **Daily newspaper** circ. (1976): 331,000.

Health: Life expectancy at birth (1961): 56.56 male; 60.42 female. **Births** (per 1,000 pop. 1980): 34.7. **Deaths** (per 1,000 pop. 1980): 7.9. **Natural increase** (1977): 3.4%. **Hospital beds** (per 100,000 pop. 1977): 161. **Physicians** (per 100,000 pop. 1977): 27. **Infant mortality** (per 1,000 live births 1979): 60.0. **Education** (1977): **Literacy:** 63%. **Pop. 5–19:** in school: 50%; teachers per 1,000: 11. **PQLI:** 66.

El Salvador became independent of Spain in 1821, and of the Central American Federation in 1839.

A fight with Honduras in 1969 over the presence of 300,000 Salvadorean workers left 2,000 dead. Clashes were renewed 1970 and 1974.

A military coup overthrew the Romero government, 1979, but the ruling military-civilian junta has failed to quell the extremist violence and unrest that contines to undermine the economy. The prognosis for El Salvador appears to be one of a long and protracted guerrilla war between leftist rebels and Salvadoran armed forces. Political assassinations and atrocities have dimmed any faint hope for a negotiated settlement in the near future.

Equatorial Guinea
Republic of Equatorial Guinea

People: Population (1980 est.): 360,000. **Age distrib.** (%): 0–14: 35.2; 15–59: 57.1; 60+: 7.7. **Pop. density:** 33.23 per sq. mi. **Ethnic groups:** Fangs 75%, several other groups. **Languages:** Spanish (official), Fang, English. **Religions:** Roman Catholicm 90%, Protestants, others.

Geography: Area: 10,832 sq. mi., the size of Maryland. **Location:** Bioko Is. off W. Africa coast in Gulf of Guinea, and Rio Muni, mainland enclave. **Neighbors:** Gabon on S, Cameroon on E, N. **Topography:** Bioko Is. consists of 2 volcanic mountains and a connecting valley. Rio Muni, with over 90% of the area, has a coastal plain and low hills beyond. **Capital:** Malabo. **Cities** (1973 est.): Bata 50,000; Malabo 23,000.

Government: Head of state: Pres., Supreme Military Council Teodoro Obiang Nguema Mbasogo; b. June 5, 1942; in office: Oct. 10, 1979. **Local divisions:** 2 provinces.

Economy: Chief crops: Cocoa, coffee, bananas, palm oil. **Other resources:** Timber. **Per capita arable land:** 0.9 acres. **Electricity prod.** (1977): 23 mln. kwh. **Labor force:** 95% agric.

Finance: Currency: Ekuele (Sept. 1979: 69 = $1 US). **Gross domestic product** (1976 est.): $112 mln. **Per capita income** (1975): $342. **Imports** (1976): $13.5 mln.; partner (1970): Spain 80%. **Exports** (1976): $42 mln.; partner (1970): Spain 91%.

Transport: Chief ports: Malabo, Bata.

Communications: Radios: 80,000 in use (1976).

Health: Life expectancy at birth (1975): 41.9 male; 45.1 female. **Births** (per 1,000 pop. 1975): 42.1. **Deaths** (per 1,000 pop. 1975): 21.2. **Natural increase** (1975): 2.1% **Hospital beds** (per 100,000 pop. 1977): 704. **Physicians** (per 100,000 pop. 1977): 2. **Infant mortality** (per 1,000 live births 1975): 53.2. **Education** (1977): **Literacy:** 20%. **Pop. 5–19:** in school: 45%, teachers per 1,000: 9.

Fernando Po (now Bioko) Island was discovered by Portugal in the late 15th century and ceded to Spain in 1778. Independence came Oct. 12, 1968. Riots occurred in 1969 over disputes between the island and the more backward Rio Muni province on the mainland. Masie Nguema Biyogo, himself from the mainland, became president for life in 1972.

Masie's 11-year reign was described as one of the most brutal in Africa, resulting in a bankrupted nation. Most of the nation's 7,000 Europeans emigrated. In 1976, 45,000 Nigerian workers were evacuated amid charges of a reign of terror. According to reports, slavery had been revived and as many as 50,000 people were murdered by government forces. Masie was ousted in a military coup, Aug., 1979.

Ethiopia

People: Population (1980 est.): 32,600,000. **Age distrib.** (%): 0–14: 43.1; 15–59: 52.5; 60+: 4.4. **Pop. density:** 71.31 per sq. mi. **Urban** (1974): 12.9%. **Ethnic groups:** Galla 33%, Amhara 25%, Tigre 12%, Somali, Afar, Sidama. **Languages:** Amharic, Tigre (Semitic languages); Galla (Hamitic), Arabic, others. **Religions:** Orthodox Christian 40%, Moslem 40%.

Geography: Area: 457,142 sq. mi., four-fifths the size of Alaska. **Location:** In E. Africa. **Neighbors:** Sudan on W, Kenya on S. Somalia, Djibouti on E. **Topography:** A high central plateau, between 6,000 and 10,000 ft. high, rises to higher mountains near the Great Rift Valley, cutting in from the SW. The Blue Nile and other rivers cross the plateau, which descends to plains on both W and SE. **Capital:** Addis Ababa. **Cities** (1978 est.): Addis Ababa 1,196,300; Asmara 393,800.

Government: Head of state and head of gov't.: Chmn. of Provisional Military Administrative Council Mengistu Haile Mariam; b. 1937; in office: Feb. 11, 1977. **Local divisions:** 14 provinces. **Armed forces:** regulars 221,600; reserves 20,000; paramilitary 169,000.

Economy: Industries: Food processing, cement, shoes, textiles. **Chief crops:** Coffee (50% export earnings), grains, tobacco, sugar. **Minerals:** Coal, iron, platinum, gold, silver, manganese, tin, copper, asbestos, potash, sulphur, mica, cement, salt. **Other resources:** Hydro power potential. **Per capita arable land:** 1.1 acres. **Meat prod.** (1978): beef: 212,000 metric tons; lamb: 131,000 metric tons. **Fish catch** (1977): 26,800 metric tons. **Electricity prod.** (1978): 696 mln. kwh. **Labor force:** 86% agric.

Finance: Currency: Birr (Apr. 1981: 2.07 = $1 US). **Gross domestic product** (1980): $4.07 bln. **Per capita income** (1975): $91. **Imports** (1979): $555 mln.; partners (1977): Jap. 16%, Saud. Ar. 10%, Ital. 10%, U.S. 9%. **Exports** (1979): $424 mln.; partners (1977): U.S. 26%, E. Ger. 15%, W. Ger. 9%, Saud. Ar. 8%. **Tourists** (1976): 36,900; receipts (1977): $3 mln. **National budget** (1977): $490 mln. revenues; $638 mln. expenditures. **International reserves less gold** (Apr. 1981): $63.9 mln. **Gold:** 260,000 oz t. **Consumer prices** (change in 1980): 4.5%.

Transport: Railway traffic (1976): 132 mln. passenger-km; 260 mln. net ton-km. **Motor vehicles:** in use (1976): 52,500 passenger cars, 13,100 comm. vehicles. **Civil aviation:** 512 mln. passenger-km (1978); 26 mln. freight ton-km (1978). **Chief ports:** Masewa, Aseb.

Communications: Television sets: 21,000 in use (1976), **Radios:** 210,000 in use (1976). **Telephones in use** (1978): 73,691. **Daily newspaper circ.** (1977): 35,000; 1 per 1,000 pop.

Health: Life expectancy at birth (1975): 37.0 male; 40.1 female. **Births** (per 1,000 pop. 1975): 49.9. **Deaths** (per 1,000 pop. 1975): 25.4. **Natural increase** (1975): .3%. **Hospital beds** (per 100,000 pop. 1977): 29. **Physicians** (per 100,000 pop. 1977): 1. **Infant mortality** (per 1,000 live births 1975): 84.2.

Education (1977): **Literacy:** 7%. **Pop 5-19:** in school: 12%, teachers per 1,000: 3. **PQLI:** 21.

Ethiopian culture was influenced by Egypt and Greece. The ancient monarchy was invaded by Italy in 1880, but maintained its independence until another Italian invasion in 1936. British forces freed the country in 1941.

The last emperor, Haile Selassie I, established a parliament and judiciary system in 1931, but barred all political parties.

A series of droughts since 1972 have killed hundreds of thousands. An army mutiny, strikes, and student demonstrations led to the dethronement of Selassie in 1974. The ruling junta pledged to form a one-party socialist state, and instituted a successful land reform; opposition was violently suppressed. The influence of the Coptic Church, embraced in 330 AD, was curbed, and the monarchy was abolished in 1975. A new famine and a locust plague threatened 1.5 million people in 1978.

The regime, torn by bloody coups, faced uprisings by tribal and political groups in part aided by Sudan and Somalia. Ties with the U.S., once a major arms and aid source, deteriorated, while cooperation accords were signed with the USSR in 1977. In 1978, Soviet advisors and 20,000 Cuban troops helped defeat Somali rebels & Somalia forces.

Eritrea, an Italian colony since 1890, reverted to Ethiopia in 1952 in accordance with a UN General Assembly vote.

Fiji

Dominion of Fiji

People: Population (1980 est.): 620,000. **Age distrib.** (%): 0–14: 41.1; 15–59: 54.7; 60+: 4.0. **Pop. density:** 87.87 per sq. mi. **Urban** (1976): 37.2%. **Ethnic groups:** Indian 50%, Fijians (Melanesian-Polynesian) 42%, Europeans 2%. **Languages:** English (official), Fijian, Hindi. **Religions:** Most Fijians are Methodist, most Indians are Hindu.

Geography: Area: 7,056 sq. mi., the size of New Jersey. **Location:** In western S. Pacific O. **Neighbors:** Nearest are Solomons on NW, Tonga on E. **Topography:** 840 islands (106 inhabited), many mountainous, with tropical forests and large fertile areas. Viti Levu, the largest island, has over half the total land area. **Capital:** Suva. **Cities** (1978): Suva 66,018.

Government: Head of state: Queen Elizabeth II, represented by Gov. Gen. George Cakobau; b. Nov. 6, 1912; in office: Jan. 13, 1973. **Head of government:** Prime Min. Kamisese Mara; b. May 13, 1920; in office: Oct. 10, 1970. **Local divisions:** 4 administrative divisions. **Armed forces:** regulars 870; para-military: 900.

Economy: Industries: Cement, shipyards, light industry, molasses, tourism. **Chief crops:** Sugar, coconut products, ginger.

Minerals: Gold. **Other resources:** Timber. **Per capita arable land:** 0.6 acres. **Electricity prod.** (1977): 290.00 mln. kwh. **Labor force:** 44% agric.

Finance: Currency: Dollar (Apr. 1981: 0.83 = $1 US). **Gross domestic product** (1978): $937 mln. **Per capita income** (1978): $1,440. **Imports** (1980): $561 mln.; partners (1978): Austral. 30%, Jap. 16%, N.Z. 15%, UK 9%. **Exports** (1980): $362 mln.; partners (1978): UK 40%, Austral. 11%, U.S. 10%, N.Z. 9%. **Tourists** (1977): 173,000; receipts $87 mln. **National budget** (1979): $226 mln. revenues; $269 mln. expenditures. **International reserves less gold** (Apr. 1981): $139.16 mln. **Gold:** 11,000 oz t. **Consumer prices** (change in 1980): 14.5%.

Transport: Motor vehicles: in use (1977): 19,300 passenger cars, 11,000 comm. vehicles. **Chief ports:** Suva, Lautoka.

Communications: Radios: 300,000 in use (1976). **Telephones in use** (1978): 32,721. **Daily newspaper circ.** (1976): 38,000; 66 per 1,000 pop.

Health: Life expectancy at birth (1975): 68.5 male; 71.7 female. **Births** (per 1,000 pop. 1975): 29.1. **Deaths** (per 1,000 pop. 1975): 4.4. **Natural increase** (1975): 2.5%. **Hospital beds** (per 100,000 pop. 1977): 264. **Physicians** (per 100,000 pop. 1977): 50. **Infant mortality** (per 1,000 live births 1975): 14.5.

Education (1977): **Literacy:** 75%. **Pop. 5-19:** in school: 74%, teachers per 1,000 27. **PQLI:** 79.

A British colony since 1874, Fiji became an independent parliamentary democracy Oct. 10, 1970.

Cultural differences between the majority Indian community, descendants of contract laborers brought to the islands in the 19th century, and the less modernized native Fijians, who by law own 83% of the land in communal villages, have led to political polarization.

The discovery of copper on Viti Levu, and favorable off-shore oil prospects, along with an expected all-time high in sugar production bode well for the economy.

Finland

Republic of Finland

People: Population (1980 est.): 4,780,000. **Age distrib.** (%): 0–14: 21.7; 15–59: 62.6; 60+: 15.7. **Pop. density:** 36.74 per sq. mi. **Urban** (1976): 59.0%. **Ethnic groups:** Finns, Swedes. **Languages:** Finnish 93.5%, Swedish 6.5% (both official). **Religions:** Lutheran 92%, Russian Orthodox 1.3%.

Geography: Area: 130,119 sq. mi., slightly smaller than Montana. **Location:** In northern Baltic region of Europe. **Neighbors:** Norway on N, Sweden on W, USSR on E. **Topography:** South and central Finland are mostly flat areas with low hills and many lakes. The N has mountainous areas, 3,000-4,000 ft. **Capital:** Helsinki. **Cities** (1978 est.): Helsinki 496,263; Tampere 166,177; Turku 164,344.

Government: Head of state: Pres. Urho K. Kekkonen; b. Sept. 3, 1900; in office: March 1, 1956. **Head of government:** Prime Min. Mauno Koivisto, b. Nov. 25, 1923; in office: May 26, 1979. **Local divisions:** 12 laanit (provinces). **Armed forces:** regulars 39,900; reserves 700,000.

Economy: Industries: Machinery, metal, shipbuilding, textiles, leather, chemicals, tourism. **Chief crops:** Grains, potatoes. **Minerals:** Chromium, cobalt, mercury, copper, iron, zinc, lead. **Other resources:** Forests (55% of exports). **Per capita arable land:** 1.3 acres. **Meat prod.** (1978): beef: 105,000 metric tons pork: 148,000 metric tons. **Fish catch** (1977): 117,000 metric tons. **Electricity prod.** (1978): 34.20 bln. kwh. **Crude steel prod.** (1979): 2.5 mln. metric tons. **Labor force:** 6% agric.; 38% manuf.

Finance: Currency: Markkaa (Apr. 1981: 4.20 = $1 US). **Gross domestic product** (1979): $41.28 bln. **Per capita income** (1978): $6,090. **Imports** (1980): $15.63 bln.; partners (1978): USSR 19%, Swed. 14%, W. Ger. 13%, UK 9%. **Exports** (1980): $14.17 bln.; partners (1978): USSR 18%, Swed. 15%, UK 13%, W. Ger. 10%. **Tourists** (1977): 259,000. **National budget** (1980): $11.67 bln. revenues; $12.03 bln. expenditures. **International reserves less gold** (Apr. 1981): $1.85 bln. **Gold** 986,000 oz t. **Consumer prices** (change in 1980): 11.6%.

Transport: Railway traffic (1978): 2.99 bln. passenger-km; 6.32 bln. net ton-km. **Motor vehicles:** in use (1977): 1.08 mln. passenger cars, 145,000 comm. vehicles; manuf. (1976): 27,300 passenger cars. **Civil aviation:** 1,644 mln. passenger-km (1978); 42 mln. freight ton-km (1978). **Chief ports:** Helsink, Turku.

Communications: Television sets: 1.71 mln. licensed (1976), 275,000 manuf. (1976). **Radios:** 2.18 licensed (1976), 185,000 manuf. (1976). **Telephones in use** (1978): 2,032,280. **Daily newspaper circ.** (1977): 2,235,000; 472 per 1,000 pop.

Health: Life expectancy at birth (1975): 67.38 male; 75.93 female. **Births** (per 1,000 pop. 1980): 13.1. **Deaths** (per 1,000 pop. 1980): 9.4. **Natural increase** (1978): .4%. **Hospital beds** (per 100,000 pop. 1977): 1,531. **Physicians** (per 100,000 pop. 1977): 160. **Infant mortality** (per 1,000 live births 1978): 12.0.

Education (1977): **Literacy:** 99%. **Pop. 5–19:** in school: 71%, teachers per 1,000: 41. **PQLI:** 95.

The early Finns probably migrated from the Ural area at about the beginning of the Christian era. Swedish settlers brought the country into Sweden, 1154 to 1809, when Finland became an autonomous grand duchy of the Russian Empire. Russian exactions created a strong national spirit; on Dec. 6, 1917, Finland declared its independence and in 1919 became a republic. On Nov. 30, 1939, the Soviet Union invaded, and the Finns were forced to cede 16,173 sq. mi., including the Karelian Isthmus, Viipuri, and an area on Lake Ladoga. After World War II, in which Finland tried to recover its lost territory, further cessions were exacted. In 1948, Finland signed a treaty of mutual assistance with the USSR. In 1956 Russia returned Porkkala, which had been ceded as a military base.

Finland is oriented toward the West in trade and culture; it is an integral member of the Nordic group of five countries and also maintains good relations with the Soviet Union. The governing coalition usually includes the Communist Party.

Aland, constituting an autonomous department, is a group of small islands, 572 sq. mi., in the Gulf of Bothnia, 25 mi. from Sweden, 15 mi. from Finland. Mariehamn is the principal port.

France

French Republic

People: Population (1980 est.): 53,710,000. **Age distrib.** (%): 0–14: 23.1; 15–59: 59.4; 60+: 17.5. **Pop. density:** 252.19 per sq. mi. **Urban** (1975): 73.0%. **Ethnic groups:** A mixture of various European and Mediterranean groups. **Languages:** French; minorities speak Breton, Alsatian German, Flemish, Italian, Basque, Catalan. **Religions:** Roman Catholic 90%, Protestant 1%, Jewish 1%, Moslems 1%.

Geography: Area: 212,973 sq. mi., four-fifths the size of Texas. **Location:** In western Europe, between Atlantic O. and Mediterranean Sea. **Neighbors:** Spain on S, Italy, Switzerland, W. Germany on E, Luxembourg, Belgium on N. **Topography:** A wide plain covers more than half of the country, in N and W, drained to W by Seine, Loire, Garonne rivers. The Massif Central is a mountainous plateau in center. In E are Alps (Mt. Blanc is tallest in W. Europe, 15,771 ft.), the lower Jura range, and the forested Vosges. The Rhone flows from Lake Geneva to Mediterranean. Pyrenees are in SW, on border with Spain. **Capital:** Paris. **Cities** (1975 cen.): Paris 2,296,945; Marseille 912,130; Lyon 457,410; Toulouse 371,835; Nice 344,040; Nantes 255,700; Strasbourg 253,355; Bordeaux 223,845.

Government: Head of state: Pres. François Mitterrand; b. Oct. 26, 1916; in office: May 21, 1981. **Head of government:** Prime Min. Pierre Mauroy; in office: May 21, 1980. **Local divisions:** 96 departments. **Armed forces:** regulars 509,300; reserves 350,000.

Economy: Industries: Steel, chemicals, autos, textiles, wine, perfume, aircraft, ships, instruments, plastics, electronic equipment. **Chief crops:** Grains, corn, rice, fruits, vegetables. France is largest food producer, exporter, in W. Eur. **Minerals:** Bauxite, iron, potash, silver, uranium, cobalt, nickel, coal, asphalt, rock salt. **Crude oil reserves** (1980): 50 mln. bbls. **Other resources:** Forests. **Per capita arable land:** 0.8 acres. **Meat prod.** (1978): beef: 1.68 mln. metric tons; pork: 1.67 mln. metric tons; lamb: 160,000 metric tons. **Fish catch** (1977): 760,300 metric tons. **Electricity prod.** (1978): 222.55 bln. kwh. **Crude steel prod.** (1979): 23.4 mln. metric tons. **Labor force:** 11.5% agric.; 37.5 manuf.; 47% services.

Finance: Currency: Franc (Apr. 1981: 5.25 = $1 US). **Gross domestic product** (1979): $571.30 bln. **Per capita income** (1978): $7,908. **Imports** (1980): $134.87 bln.; partners (1978): W. Ger. 19%, It. 10%, Belg. 9%, U.S. 7%. **Exports** (1980): $116.1 bln.; partners (1978): W. Ger. 17%, It. 11%, Belg. 10%, UK 7%. **Tourists** (1977) 26,265,000; receipts: $4.38 bln. **National budget** (1978): $97.80 bln. revenues; $101.59 bln. ex-

penditures. **International reserves less gold** (Apr. 1981): $30.05 bln. **Gold:** 81.85 mln. oz t. **Consumer prices** (change in 1980): 13.3%.

Transport: Railway traffic (1978): 53.51 bln. passenger-km; 68.69 bln. net ton-km. **Motor vehicles:** in use (1977): 16.7 mln. passenger cars, 2.6 mln. comm. vehicles; manuf. (1978): 3.62 mln. passenger cars; 456,000 comm. vehicles. **Civil aviation:** 30,216 mln. passenger-km (1978); 1,810 mln. freight ton-km (1978). **Chief ports:** Marseille, LeHavre, Nantes, Bordeaux, Rouen.

Communications: Television sets: 14.5 mln. licensed (1976), 1.91 mln. manuf. (1977). **Radios:** 17.4 mln. licensed (1976), 3.57 mln. manuf. (1977). **Telephones in use** (1978): 17,518,813. **Daily newspaper circ.** (1977): 10,863,000; 205 per 1,000 pop.

Health: Life expectancy at birth (1976): 69.2 male; 77.2 female. **Births** (per 1,000 pop. 1980): 14.8. **Deaths** (per 1,000 pop. 1980): 10.1. **Natural increase** (1977): .4%. **Hospital beds** (per 100,000 pop. 1977): 1,125. **Physicians** (per 100,000 pop. 1977): 164. **Infant mortality** (per 1,000 live births 1977): 11.4.

Education (1977): **Literacy:** 99%. **Pop. 5-19:** in school: 68%, teachers per 1,000: 41. **PQLI:** 96.

Celtic Gaul was conquered by Julius Caesar 58-51 BC; Romans ruled for 500 years. Under Charlemagne, Frankish rule extended over much of Europe. After his death France emerged as one of the successor kingdoms.

The monarchy was overthrown by the French Revolution (1789-93) and succeeded by the First Republic; followed by the First Empire under Napoleon (1804-15), a monarchy (1814-48), the Second Republic (1848-52), the Second Empire (1852-70), the Third Republic (1871-1946), the Fourth Republic (1946-58), and the Fifth Republic (1958 to present).

France suffered severe losses in manpower and wealth in the first World War, 1914-18, when it was invaded by Germany. By the Treaty of Versailles, France exacted return of Alsace and Lorraine, French provinces seized by Germany in 1871. Germany invaded France again in May, 1940, and signed an armistice with a government based in Vichy. After France was liberated by the Allies Sept. 1944, Gen. Charles de Gaulle became head of the provisional government, serving until 1946.

De Gaulle again became premier in 1958, during a crisis over Algeria, and obtained voter approval for a new constitution, ushering in the Fifth Republic. Using strong executive powers, he promoted French economic and technological advances in the context of the European Economic Community, and guarded French foreign policy independence.

France had withdrawn from Indochina in 1954, and from Morocco and Tunisia in 1956. Most of its remaining African territories were freed 1958-62, but France retained strong economic and political ties.

France tested atomic bombs in the Sahara beginning in 1960. Land-based and submarine launched strategic missiles were also developed. In 1966, France withdrew all its troops from the integrated military command of NATO, though 60,000 remained stationed in Germany. France continued to attend political meetings of NATO.

In May 1968 rebellious students in Paris and other centers rioted, battled police, and were joined by workers who launched nationwide strikes. The government awarded pay increases to the strikers May 26. In elections to the Assembly in June, de Gaulle's backers won a landslide victory. Nevertheless, he resigned from office in April, 1969, after losing a nationwide referendum on constitutional reform. De Gaulle's policies were largely continued after his death in 1970.

On May 10, 1981, France elected François Mitterand, a Socialist candidate, president in a stunning victory over Valéry Giscard d'Estaing.

The island of **Corsica,** in the Mediterranean W of Italy and N of Sardinia, is an official region of France comprising 2 departments. Area: 3,369 sq. mi.; pop. (1975 cen.): 289,842. The capital is Ajaccio, birthplace of Napoleon. A militant separatist movement led to violence after 1975.

Overseas Departments

French Guiana is on the NE coast of South America with Suriname on the W and Brazil on the E and S. Its area is 35,135 sq. mi.; pop. (1979 est.): 63,000. Guiana sends one senator and one deputy to the French Parliament. Guiana is administered by a prefect and has a Council General of 16 elected members; capital is Cayenne.

The famous penal colony, Devil's Island, was phased out between 1938 and 1951.

Immense forests of rich timber cover 90% of the land. Placer gold mining is the most important industry. Exports are cocoa, bananas, wood, gold, fish glue, rum and brandy, rosewood essence, shrimp, and hides.

Guadeloupe, in the West Indies' Leeward Islands, consists of 2 large islands, Basse-Terre and Grande-Terre, separated by the Salt River, plus Marie Galante and the Saintes group to the S and, to the N, Desirade, St. Barthelemy, and over half of St. Martin (the Netherlands portion is St. Maarten). A French possession since 1635, the department is represented in the French Parliament by 2 senators and 2 deputies; administration consists of a prefect (governor) and an elected General Council.

Area of the islands is 686 sq. mi.; pop. (1979 est.) 312,000, mainly descendants of slaves; capital is Basse-Terre on Basse-Terre Is. The land is fertile; sugar, rum, and bananas are exported; tourism is an important industry.

Martinique, one of the Windward Islands, in the West Indies, has been a possession since 1635, and a department since March, 1946. It is represented in the French Parliament by 2 senators and 3 deputies. The island was the birthplace of Napoleon's Empress Josephine.

It has an area of 431 sq. mi.; pop. (1979 est.) 310,000, mostly descendants of slaves. The capital is Fort-de-France. It is a popular tourist stop. The chief exports are sugar, rum, bananas, pineapples, and cocoa.

Mayotte, formerly part of Comoros, voted in 1976 to become an overseas department of France. An island NW of Madagascar, area is 144 sq. mi., pop. (1978 est.) 51,800.

Reunion is a volcanic island in the Indian O. about 420 mi. E of Madagascar, and has belonged to France since 1665. Area, 970 sq. mi.; pop. (1979 est.) 503,000, 30% of French extraction. Capital: Saint-Denis. The chief products are sugar, rum, corn, perfume essences, vanilla, and spices. It elects 3 deputies, 2 senators to the French Parliament.

St. Pierre and Miquelon, formerly an Overseas Territory, made the transition to department status in 1976. It consists of 2 groups of rocky islands near the SW coast of Newfoundland, inhabited by fishermen. The exports are chiefly fish products. The St. Pierre group has an area of 10 sq. mi.; Miquelon, 83 sq. mi. Total pop. (1979 est.), 6,000. The capital is St. Pierre. A deputy and a senator are elected to the French Parliament.

Overseas Territories

French Polynesia Overseas Territory, comprises 130 islands widely scattered among 5 archipelagos in the South Pacific; administered by a governor. Territorial Assembly and a Council with headquarters at Papeete, Tahiti, one of the **Society Islands** (which include the **Windward** and **Leeward** islands). A deputy and a senator are elected to the French Parliament.

Other groups are the **Marquesas Islands,** the **Tuamotu Archipelago,** including the **Gambier Islands,** and the **Austral Islands.**

Total area of the islands administered from Tahiti is 1,544 sq. mi.; pop. (1979 est.), 144,000, more than half on Tahiti. Tahiti is picturesque and mountainous with a productive coastline bearing coconut, banana and orange trees, sugar cane and vanilla.

Tahiti was visited by Capt. James Cook in 1769 and by Capt. Bligh in the Bounty, 1788-89. Its beauty impressed Herman Melville, Paul Gauguin, and Charles Darwin; Robert Louis Stevenson, buried there, called Tahitians "God's sweetest works."

French Southern and Antarctic Lands Overseas Territory, comprises **Adelie Land,** on Antarctica, and 4 island groups in the Indian O. Adelie, discovered 1840, has a research station, a coastline of 185 mi. and tapers 1,240 mi. inland to the South Pole. The U.S. does not recognize national claims in Antarctica. There are 2 huge glaciers, Ninnis, 22 mi. wide, 99 mi. long, and Mentz, 11 mi. wide, 140 mi. long. The Indian O. groups are:

Kerguelen Archipelago, discovered 1772, one large and 300 small islands. The chief is 87 mi. long, 74 mi. wide, and has Mt. Ross, 6,429 ft. tall. Principal research station is Port-aux-Francais. Seals often weigh 2 tons; there are blue whales, coal, peat, semi-precious stones. **Crozet Archipelago,** discovered 1772, covers 195 sq. mi. Eastern Island rises to 6,560 ft. **Saint Paul,** in southern Indian O., has warm springs with earth at places heating to 120° to 390° F. **Amsterdam** is nearby; both produce cod and rock lobster.

New Caledonia and its dependencies, an overseas territory, are a group of islands in the Pacific O. about 1,115 mi. E of Australia and approx. the same distance NW of New Zealand. Dependencies are the **Loyalty Islands,** the **Isle of Pines, Huon**

Islands and the **Chesterfield Islands.**

New Caledonia, the largest, has 6,530 sq. mi. Total area of the territory is 8,548 sq. mi.; population (1979 est.) 136,000. The group was acquired by France in 1853.

The territory is administered by a governor and government council. There is a popularly elected Territorial Assembly. A deputy and a senator are elected to the French Parliament. Capital: Noumea.

Mining is the chief industry. New Caledonia is the world's 3d largest nickel producer. Other minerals found are chrome, iron, cobalt, manganese, silver, gold, lead, and copper. Agricultural products include coffee, copra, cotton, manioc (cassava), corn, tobacco, bananas and pineapples.

Wallis and Futuna Islands, 2 archipelagos raised to status of overseas territory July 29, 1961, are in the SW Pacific S of the Equator between Fiji and Samoa. The islands have a total area of 106 sq. mi. and population (1979 est.) of 10,000. **Alofi,** attached to Futuna, is uninhabited. Capital: Mata-Utu. Chief products are copra, yams, taro roots, bananas. A senator and a deputy are elected to the French Parliament.

Gabon

Gabonese Republic

People: Population (1980 est.): 585,000. **Pop. density:** 5.72 per sq. mi. **Urban** (1970): 32.0%. **Ethnic groups:** Fangs 25%, Bapounon 10%, others. **Languages:** French (official), Fang, Bantu languages. **Religions:** Roman Catholics 25%, Protestants 10%, others.

Geography: Area: 102,317 sq. mi., the size of Colorado. **Location:** On Atlantic coast of central Africa. **Neighbors:** Equatorial Guinea, Cameroon on N, Congo on E, S. **Topography:** Heavily forested, the country consists of coastal lowlands plateaus in N, E, and S, mountains in N, SE, and center. The Ogooue R. system covers most of Gabon. **Capital:** Libreville. **Cities** (1974 est.): Libreville 251,400; Port-Gentil 77,111.

Government: Head of state: Pres. El Hadj Omar Bongo; b. Dec. 30, 1935; in office: Dec. 2, 1967. **Head of government:** Prime Min. Leon Mebiame, b. Sept. 1, 1934; in office: Apr. 16, 1975. **Local divisions:** 9 provinces. **Armed forces:** regulars 1,300; para-military 1,600.

Economy: Industries: Oil products. **Chief crops:** Cocoa, coffee, rice, peanuts, palm products, cassava, bananas. **Minerals:** Manganese, uranium, oil, iron, gas. **Crude oil reserves** (1980): 500 mln. bbls. **Other resources:** Timber. **Per capita arable land:** 1.2 acres. **Electricity prod.** (1978): 324.00 mln. kwh. **Labor force:** 65% agric.; 30% man.; 2.5% services.

Finance: Currency: CFA franc (Apr. 1981: 262.70 = $1 US). **Gross domestic product** (1979) $2.9 bln. **Per capita income** (1979): $4,487. **Imports** (1980): $835 mln.; partners (1976): Fr. 69%, U.S. 6%. **Exports** (1979): $1.48 bln.; partners (1976): Fr. 42%, U.S. 17%, UK 10%, Bah. 10%. **Tourists receipts** (1977): $17 mln. **National budget** (1976): $971 mln. revenues; $1.42 bln. expenditures. **International reserves less gold** (Dec. 1980): $107.50 mln. **Gold:** ¹³,000 oz t. **Consumer prices** (change in 1979): 7.9%.

Transport: Motor vehicles: in use (1974): 10,100 passenger cars, 7,300 comm. vehicles. **Chief ports:** Libreville, Port-Gentil. **Communications: Television sets:** 8,500 licensed (1976). **Radios:** 93,000 licensed (1976).

Health: Life expectancy at birth (1961): 25 male; 45 female. **Births** (per 1,000 pop. 1975): 31.4. **Deaths** (per 1,000 pop. 1975): 23.2 **Natural increase** (1975): .8%. **Hospital beds** (per 100,000 pop. 1977): 736. **Physicians** (per 100,000 pop. 1977): 32. **Infant mortality** (per 1,000 live births 1979): 178.

Education (1977): **Literacy:** 40%. **Pop. 5-19:** in school: 74%, teachers per 1,000: 26. **PQLI:** 21.

France established control over the region in the second half of the 19th century. Gabon became independent Aug. 17, 1960. It is one of the most prosperous black African countries, thanks to abundant natural resources, foreign private investment, and government development programs.

The Gambia

Republic of The Gambia

People: Population (1980 est.): 600,000. **Age distrib.** (%) 0–14: 45.9; 15–59: 54.4; 60+: 3.8. **Pop. density:** 149.89 per sq.

Urban (1973): 15.9%. **Ethnic groups:** Mandinka 37.7%, Fula 16.2%, Wolof 14%, others. **Languages:** English (official), Mandinka, Wolof. **Religions:** Moslems 85%, Christian 14%, others.

Geography: Area: 4,003 sq. mi., smaller than Connecticut. **Location:** On Atlantic coast near western tip of Africa. **Neighbors:** Surrounded on 3 sides by Senegal. **Topography:** A narrow strip of land on each side of the lower Gambia. **Capital:** Banjul. **Cities** (1978 est.): Banjul 45,604.

Government: Head of state: Pres. Dawda Kairaba Jawara; b. May 16, 1924; in office: Apr. 24, 1970 (prime min. from June 12, 1962). **Local divisions:** 5 divisions and Banjul.

Economy: Industries: Tourism. **Chief crops:** Peanuts (main export), rice. **Per capita arable land:** 1.1 acres. **Fish catch** (1977): 10,800 metric tons. **Electricity prod.** (1978): 31.40 mln. kwh. **Labor force:** 78% agric.; 15.2% man.

Finance: Currency: Dalasi (Apr. 1981: 1.85 = $1 US). **Gross domestic product** (1979): $161 mln. **Per capita income** (1979): $275. **Imports** (1980): $164 mln.; partners (1978): UK 33%, China 10%, Fr. 7%, W. Ger. 7%. **Exports** (1980): $31.9 mln.; partners (1978): Fr. 27%, UK 25%, Swit. 18%, Ghana 7%. **Tourist receipts** (1977): $8 mln. **National budget** (1978): $34 mln. revenues; $48 mln. expenditures. **International reserves less gold** (Apr. 1981): $9.95 mln. **Consumer prices** (change in 1980): 6.7%.

Transport: Motor vehicles: in use (1973): 3,000 passenger cars, (1972): 2,500 comm. vehicles. **Chief ports:** Banjul.

Communications: Radios: 61,000 in use (1976). **Telephones in use** (1978): 2,779.

Health: Life expectancy at birth (1975): 39.4 male; 42.5 female. **Births** (per 1,000 pop. 1975): 46.7. **Deaths** (per 1,000 pop. 1975): 23.1. **Natural increase** (1975): 2.4%. **Hospital beds** (per 100,000 pop. 1977): 123. **Physicians** (per 100,000 pop. 1977): 8. **Infant mortality** (per 100,000 live births 1979): 217.

Education (1977): Literacy: 12%. **Pop. 5-19:** in school: 17%, teachers per 1,000: 10. **PQLI:** 22.

The tribes of Gambia were at one time associated with the West African empires of Ghana, Mali, and Songhay. The area became Britain's first African possession in 1588.

Independence came Feb. 18, 1965; republic status within the Commonwealth was achieved in 1970. Gambia is one of the only functioning democracies in Africa. The country suffered from severe famine in 1977-78.

Germany

Now comprises 2 nations: Federal Republic of Germany (West Germany), German Democratic Republic (East Germany).

Germany, prior to World War II, was a central European nation composed of numerous states which had a common language and traditions and which had been united in one country since 1871; since World War II it has been split in 2 parts.

History and government. Germanic tribes were defeated by Julius Caesar, 55 and 53 BC, but Roman expansion N of the Rhine was stopped in 9 AD. Charlemagne, ruler of the Franks, consolidated Saxon, Bavarian, Rhenish, Frankish, and other lands; after him the eastern part became the German Empire. The Thirty Years' War, 1618-1648, split Germany into small principalities and kingdoms. After Napoleon, Austria contended with Prussia for dominance, but lost the Seven Weeks' War to Prussia, 1866. Otto von Bismarck, Prussian chancellor, formed the North German Confederation, 1867.

In 1870 Bismarck maneuvered Napoleon III into declaring war. After the quick defeat of France, Bismarck formed the German Empire and on Jan. 18, 1871, in Versailles, proclaimed King Wilhelm I of Prussia German emperor (Deutscher kaiser).

The German Empire reached its peak before World War I in 1914, with 208,780 sq. mi., plus a colonial empire. After that war Germany ceded Alsace-Lorraine to France; West Prussia and Posen (Poznan) province to Poland; part of Schleswig to Denmark; lost all of its colonies and the ports of Memel and Danzig.

Republic of Germany, 1919-1933, adopted the Weimar constitution; met reparation payments and elected Friedrich Ebert and Gen. Paul von Hindenburg presidents.

Third Reich, 1933-1945, Adolf Hitler led the National Socialist German Workers' (Nazi) party after World War I. In 1923 he at-tempted to unseat the Bavarian government and was imprisoned. Pres. von Hindenburg named Hitler chancellor Jan. 30, 1933; on Aug. 3, 1934, the day after Hindenburg's death, the cabinet joined the offices of president and chancellor and made Hitler fuehrer (leader). Hitler abolished freedom of speech and assembly, and began a long series of persecutions climaxed by the murder of millions of Jews and opponents.

Hitler repudiated the Versailles treaty and reparations agreements. He remilitarized the Rhineland 1936 and annexed Austria (Anschluss, 1938). At Munich he made an agreement with Neville Chamberlain, British prime minister, which permitted Hitler to annex part of Czechoslovakia. He signed a non-aggression treaty with the USSR, 1939. He declared war on Poland Sept. 1, 1939, precipitating World War II.

With total defeat near, Hitler committed suicide in Berlin Apr. 1945. The victorious Allies voided all acts and annexations of Hitler's Reich.

Postwar changes. The zones of occupation administered by the Allied Powers and later relinquished gave the USSR Saxony, Saxony-Anhalt, Thuringia, and Mecklenburg, and the former Prussian provinces of Saxony and Brandenburg.

The territory E of the Oder-Neisse line within 1937 boundaries comprising the provinces of Silesia, Pomerania, and the southern part of East Prussia, totaling about 41,220 sq. mi., was taken by Poland. Northern East Prussia was taken by the USSR.

The Western Allies ended the state of war with Germany in 1951. The USSR did so in 1955.

There was also created the area of Greater Berlin, within but not part of the Soviet zone, administered by the 4 occupying powers under the Allied Command. In 1948 the USSR withdrew, established its single command in East Berlin, and cut off supplies. The Allies utilized a gigantic airlift to bring food to West Berlin, 1948-1949. In Aug. 1961 the East Germans built a wall dividing Berlin, after over 3 million E. Germans had emigrated.

East Germany

German Democratic Republic

People: Population (1980 est.): 16,800,000. **Age distrib.** (%): 0–14: 20.6; 15–59: 58.7; 60+: 20.7. **Pop. density:** 413.32 per sq. mi. **Urban** (1976): 75.5%. **Ethnic groups:** Germans, Wends (0.7%). **Languages:** German. **Religions:** Protestant 80%, Roman Catholic 11%.

Geography: Area: 40,646 sq. mi., the size of Virginia. **Location:** In E. Central Europe. **Neighbors:** W. Germany on W, Czechoslovakia on S, Poland on E. **Topography:** E. Germany lies mostly on the North German plains, with lakes in N, Harz Mtns., Elbe Valley, and sandy soil of Bradenburg in center, and highlands in S. **Capital:** East Berlin. **Cities** (1978 est.): Berlin 1,111,398; Leipzig 565,178; Dresden 511,223.

Government: Head of state: Chmn. Erich Honecker; b. Aug. 25, 1912; in office: Oct. 29, 1976. **Head of government:** Prime Min. Willi Stoph; b. July 9, 1914; in office: Oct. 29, 1976. **Head of Communist Party:** Sec.-Gen. Erich Honecker; in office: May 3, 1971. **Local divisions:** 15 administrative districts. **Armed forces:** regulars 159,000; reserves 305,000.

Economy: Industries: Steel, chemicals, cement, textiles, shoes, oil products, machinery. **Chief crops:** Grains, potatoes, sugar beets. **Minerals:** Potash, lignite, uranium, cobalt, bismuth, arsenic, antimony. **Per capita arable land:** 0.7 acres. **Meat prod.** (1978): beef: 427,000 metric tons; pork: 1.17 min. metric tons; lamb: 15,000 metric tons. **Fish catch** (1977): 209,400 metric tons. **Electricity prod.** (1978): 95.95 bln. kwh. **Crude steel prod.** (1979): 7.0 min metric tons. **Labor force:** 10.9% agric.; 42.5% manuf.

Finance: Currency: Mark (Mar. 1980: 1.76 = $1 US). **Net material product** (1978): $113.4 bln. **Per capita income** (1976): $4,000. **Imports:** (1979): $16.21 bln.; partners (1977): USSR 35%, Czech. 8%, Pol. 8%, W. Ger. 7%. **Exports** (1979): $15.06 bln.; partners (1977): USSR 32%, Czech. 9%, W. Ger. 9%, Pol. 8%. **Tourists** (1977): 1,100,000.

Transport: Railway traffic (1978): 22.32 bln. passenger-km; 58.92 bln. net ton-km. **Motor vehicles:** in use (1977): 2.24 min. passenger cars, 570,000 comm. vehicles; manuf. (1978): 170,400 passenger cars; 37,200 comm. vehicles. **Chief ports:** Rostock, Wismar, Stralsund.

Communications: Television sets: 5.18 mln. licensed (1976), 525,000 manuf. (1977). **Radios:** 6.17 min. licensed (1976), 1.13 min. manuf. (1977). **Telephones in use** (1978): 2,860,069. **Daily newspaper circ.** (1977): 8,317,000; 496 per

1,000 pop.
   Health: Life expectancy at birth (1976): 68.82 male; 74.42 female. **Births** (per 1,000 pop. 1980): 14.6. **Deaths** (per 1,000 pop. 1980): 14.2. **Natural increase** (1978): 0.0%. **Hospital beds** (per 100,000 pop. 1977): 1,065. **Physicians** (per 100,000 pop. 1977): 190. **Infant mortality** (per 1,000 live births 1978): 13.2.
   Education (1977): **Literacy:** 99%. **Pop. 5-19:** in school: 66%, teachers per 1,000: 43. **PQLI:** 94.

The German Democratic Republic was proclaimed in the Soviet sector of Berlin Oct. 7, 1949. It was proclaimed fully sovereign in 1954, but 400,000 Soviet troops remain on grounds of security and the 4-power Potsdam agreement.
   Coincident with the entrance of W. Germany into the European Defense community in 1952, the East German government decreed a prohibited zone 3 miles deep along its 600-mile border with W. Germany and cut Berlin's telephone system in two. Berlin was further divided by erection of a fortified wall in 1961, but the exodus of refugees to the West continued, though on a smaller scale. By 1979, nearly 150,000 had fled to the West. Some 20,000 others held in East German jails were released upon West German payments totalling $250 million.
   E. Germany suffered severe economic problems until the mid-1960s. A "new economic system" was introduced, easing the former central planning controls and allowing factories to make profits provided they were reinvested in operations or redistributed to workers as bonuses. By the early 1970s, the economy was highly industrialized. In May 1972 the few remaining private firms were ordered sold to the government. The nation was credited with the highest standard of living among communist countries. But growth slowed in the late 1970s, due to shortages of natural resources and labor, and a huge debt to lenders in the West.

West Germany
Federal Republic of Germany

   People: Population (1980 est.): 61,560,000. **Age distrib.** (%): 0–14: 20.3; 15–59: 58.4; 60+: 19.7. **Pop. density:** 642.49 per sq. mi. **Ethnic groups:** Germans, immigrant workers from Spain, Italy, Yugoslavia, Turkey. **Languages:** German. **Religions:** Protestant 44%, Roman Catholic 45%.
   Geography: Area: 95,815 sq. mi., the size of Oregon. **Location:** In central Europe. **Neighbors:** Denmark on N, Netherlands, Belgium, Luxembourg, France on W, Switzerland, Austria on S, Czechoslovakia, E. Germany on E. **Topography:** West Germany is flat in N, hilly in center and W, and mountainous in Bavaria. Chief rivers are Elbe, Weser, Ems, Rhine, and Main, all flowing toward North Sea, and Danube, flowing toward Black Sea. **Capital:** Bonn. **Cities** (1978 est.): Berlin 1,926,826; Hamburg 1,680,340; Munich 1,313,939; Cologne 976,761; Essen 664,408; Frankfurt 632,565; Dortmund 617,590; Dusseldorf 607,560; Stuttgart 584,554.
   Government: Head of state: Pres. Karl Carstens; b. Dec. 14, 1914; in office: July 1, 1979. **Head of government:** Chan. Helmut Schmidt; b. Dec. 23, 1918; in office: May 16, 1974. **Local divisions:** West Berlin and 10 laender (states) with substantial powers: Schleswig-Holstein, Hamburg, Lower Saxony, Bremen, North Rhine-Westphalia, Hessen, Rhineland-Palatinate, Baden-Wurttemberg, Bavaria, Saarland. **Armed forces:** regulars 495,000; reserves 1,250,000.
   Economy: Industries: Steel, ships, oil products, autos, machinery, textiles, electrical and electronic equip., wine. **Chief crops:** Grains, potatoes, sugar beets, fruits, tobacco, nuts. **Minerals:** Coal, mercury, potash, lignite, iron, zinc, lead, copper, salt, oil. **Crude oil reserves** (1980): 480 mln. bbls. **Per capita arable land:** 0.3 acres. **Meat prod.** (1978): beef: 1.38 mln. metric tons; pork: 2.6 mln. metric tons; lamb: 23,000 metric tons. **Fish catch** (1977): 432,100 metric tons. **Electricity prod.** (1978): 353.41 mln. kwh. **Crude steel prod.** (1979): 46.0 mln. metric tons. **Labor force:** 6% agric.; 48% manuf.; 25% service.
   Finance: Currency: Mark (Apr. 1981: 2.21 = $1 US). **Gross domestic product** (1980): $824.61 bln. **Per capita income** (1978): 9,278. **Imports** (1980): $187.94 bln.; partners (1978): Neth. 13%, Fr. 12%, It. 10%, Belg. 8%. **Exports** (1980): $192.77 bln.; partners (1978): Fr. 12%, Neth. 10%, Belg. 8%, It. 7%. **Tourists** (1977): 7,832,300; receipts $3.83 bln. **National budget** (1980): $109.7 bln. revenues; $125.6 bln. expenditures. **International reserves less gold** (Apr. 1981): $49.65 bln.

   Gold: 95.18 mln. oz t. **Consumer prices** (change in 1980): 5.5%.
   Transport: Railway traffic (1978): 36.79 bln. passenger-km; 57.32 bln. net ton-km. **Motor vehicles:** in use (1977): 20.02 mln. passenger cars, 1.39 mln. comm. vehicles; manuf. (1978): 3.9 mln. passenger cars; 300,000 comm. vehicles. **Civil aviation:** 17,568 mln. passenger-km (1978); 1,411 mln. freight ton-km (1978). **Chief ports:** Hamburg, Bremen, Lubeck.
   Communications: Television sets: 19.23 mln. licensed (1975), 4.08 mln. manuf. (1977). **Radios:** 20.2 mln. licensed (1976) 5.59 mln. manuf. (1977). **Telephones in use** (1978): 22,931,683. **Daily newspaper circ.** (1977): 25,968,000; 423 per 1,000 pop.
   Health: Life expectancy at birth (1977): 68.61 male; 75.21 female. **Births** (per 1,000 pop. 1980): 10.0. **Deaths** (per 1,000 pop. 1980): 11.5. **Natural increase** (1978): −.3%. **Hospital beds** (per 100,000 pop. 1977): 1,178. **Physicians** (per 100,000 pop. 1977): 204. **Infant mortality** (per 1,000 live births 1978): 15.5.
   Education (1977): **Literacy:** 99%. **Pop. 5-19:** in school: 69%, teachers per 1,000: 35. **PQLI:** 94.

The Federal Republic of Germany was proclaimed May 23, 1949, in Bonn, after a constitution had been drawn up by a consultative assembly formed by representatives of the 11 laender (states) in the French, British, and American zones. Later reorganized into 9 units, the laender numbered 10 with the addition of the Saar, 1957. Berlin also was granted land (state) status, but the 1945 occupation agreements placed restrictions on it.
   The occupying powers, the U.S., Britain, and France, restored the civil status, Sept. 21, 1949. The U. S. resumed diplomatic relations July 2, 1951. The powers lifted controls and the republic became fully independent May 5, 1955.
   Dr. Konrad Adenauer, Christian Democrat, was made chancellor Sept. 15, 1949, re-elected 1953, 1957, 1961. Willy Brandt, heading a coalition of Social Democrats and Free Democrats, became chancellor Oct. 21, 1969.
   In 1970 Brandt signed friendship treaties with the USSR and Poland. In 1971, the U.S., Britain, France, and the USSR signed an agreement on Western access to West Berlin. In 1972 the Bundestag approved the USSR and Polish treaties and East and West Germany signed their first formal treaty, implementing the agreement easing access to West Berlin. In 1973 a West Germany-Czechoslovakia pact normalized relations and nullified the 1938 "Munich Agreement." In 1974 Bonn agreed to extend $350 million yearly in long-term credits to East Germany until 1981. Other credits spurred trade with the East European countries.
   In May 1974 Brandt resigned, saying he took full responsibility for "negligence" for allowing an East German spy to become a member of his staff. Helmut Schmidt, Brandt's finance minister, succeeded him.
   West Germany has experienced tremendous economic growth since the 1950s. It is the world's 4th greatest economic power. The country leads Europe in provisions for worker participation in the management of industry.
   Helgoland, an island of 130 acres in the North Sea, was taken from Denmark by a British Naval Force in 1807 and later ceded to Germany to become a part of Schleswig-Holstein province in return for rights in East Africa. The heavily fortified island was surrendered to UK, May 23, 1945, demilitarized in 1947 and returned to W. Germany, Mar 1, 1952. It is a free port.

Ghana
Republic of Ghana

   People: Population (1979 est.): 11,742,000. **Age distrib.** (%): 0–14: 46.9; 15–59: 47.7; 60+: 5.3. **Pop. density:** 127.6 per sq. mi. **Urban** (1974): 31.4%. **Ethnic groups:** Akan 44% Moshi-Dagomba 16%, Ewe 13%, Ga 8%, others. **Languages:** English (official), others. **Religions:** Protestant 29%, Roman Catholic 14%, Moslem 12%, others.
   Geography: Area: 92,010 sq. mi., slightly smaller than Oregon. **Location:** On southern coast of W. Africa. **Neighbors:** Ivory Coast on W, Upper Volta on N, Togo on E. **Topography:** Most of Ghana consists of low fertile plains and scrubland, cut by rivers and by the artificial Lake Volta. **Capital:** Accra. **Cities** (1970 cen.): Accra 564,194; Kumasi 260,286.
   Government: Head of government: Pres. Hilla Limmann; 1934; in office: Sept. 24, 1979. **Local divisions:** 9 regions. **Armed forces:** regulars 20,000; para-military 3,000.

Economy: Industries: Aluminum, light industry. **Chief crops:** Cocoa (largest producer), coffee, palm products, corn, rice, cassava, plantain, peanuts, yams, tobacco. **Minerals:** Gold, manganese, industrial diamonds, bauxite. **Crude oil reserves:** (1980): 7 mln. bbls. **Other resources:** Timber, rare woods, rubber. **Per capita arable land:** 0.2 acres. **Meat prod.** (1978): beef: 12,000 metric tons; pork: 7,000 metric tons; lamb: 10,000 metric tons. **Fish catch** (1977): 383,000 metric tons. **Electricity prod.** (1977): 4.30 bln. kwh. **Labor force:** 60% agric.; 10% man.

Finance: Currency: Cedi (Apr. 1981: 2.78 = $1 US). **Gross domestic product** (1979): $10.1 bln. **Per capita income** (1979): $380. **Imports** (1978): $937 mln.; partners (1975): U.S. 16%, UK 15%, W. Ger. 11%, Nigeria 7%. **Exports** (1978): $1.09 bln.; partners (1975): UK 15%, U.S. 11%, Neth. 10%, Swit. 8%. **Tourists** (1977): 58,900; receipts $6 mln. **National budget** (1976): $773 mln. revenues; $1.30 bln. expenditures. **International reserves less gold** (Mar. 1981): $189.3 mln. **Gold:** 270,000 oz t. **Consumer prices** (change in 1980): 50.1%.

Transport: Railway traffic (1972): 431 mln. passenger-km; 305 mln. net ton-km. **Motor vehicles:** in use (1977): 72,400 passenger cars, 49,300 comm. vehicles. **Civil aviation:** 234 mln. passenger-km (1977); 3.6 mln. freight ton-km (1977). **Chief ports:** Tema, Sekondi-Takoradi.

Communications: Television sets: 35,000 in use (1976), 2,000 manuf. (1975). **Radios:** 1.08 mln. in use (1976), 90,000 manuf. (1975). **Telephones in use** (1978): 66,405. **Daily newspaper circ.** (1976): 435,000; 42 per 1,000 pop.

Health: Life expectancy at birth (1975): 41.9 male; 45.1 female. **Births** (per 1,000 pop. 1975): 48.6. **Deaths** (per 1,000 pop. 1975): 19.1. **Natural increase** (1975): 3.0%. **Hospital beds** (per 100,000 pop. 1977): 146. **Physicians** (per 100,000 pop. 1977): 10. **Infant mortality** (per 1,000 live births 1975): 156.

Education (1977): **Literacy:** 30%. **Pop. 5–19:** in school: 45%, teachers per 1,000: 18. **PQLI:** 41.

Named for an African empire along the Niger River, 400-1240 AD, Ghana was ruled by Britain for 113 years as the Gold Coast. The UN in 1956 approved merger with the British Togoland trust territory. Independence came March 6, 1957. Republic status within the Commonwealth was attained in 1960.

Pres. Kwame Nkrumah built hospitals and schools, promoted development projects like the Volta R. hydroelectric and aluminum plants, but ran the country into debt, jailed opponents, and was accused of corruption. A 1964 referendum gave Nkrumah dictatorial powers and set up a one-party socialist state.

Nkrumah was overthrown in 1966 by a police-army coup, which expelled Chinese and East German teachers and technicians. Elections were held in 1969, but 3 further coups occurred in 1972, 1978, and 1979. The June 1979 coup, led by Flight Lieut. Jerry Rawlings, returned the government to civilian rule, Sept. The stagnant economy has further deteriorated.

Greece
Hellenic Republic

People: Population (1980 est.): 9,506,000. **Age distrib. (%):** 0–14: 23.7; 15-59: 58.9; 60+: 17.5. **Pop. density:** 188.06 per sq. mi. **Urban** (1971): 64.8%. **Ethnic groups:** Greeks 98.5%, Turks 0.9%, Pomaks 0.3%, Armenians 0.2%. **Languages:** Greek, others. **Religions:** Greek Orthodox 97%, Moslem 1.2%.

Geography: Area: 50,547 sq. mi., the size of New York State. **Location:** Occupies southern end of Balkan Peninsula in SE Europe. **Neighbors:** Albania, Yugoslavia, Bulgaria on N, Turkey on E. **Topography:** About 75% of Greece is non-arable, with mountains in all areas. Pindus Mts. run through the country N to S. The heavily indented coastline is 9,385 mi. long. Of over 2,000 islands, only 169 are inhabited, among them Crete, Rhodes, Milos, Kerkira (Corfu), Chios, Lesbos, Samos, Euboea, Delos, Mykonos. **Capital:** Athens. **Cities** (1971 cen.): Athens 867,023; Thessaloniki 345,799; Piraeus 187,362; Patras 120,847.

Government: Head of state: Pres. Constantine Karamanlis; b. Feb. 23, 1907; in office: May 15, 1980. **Head of government:** Prime Min. George Rallis; b. Dec. 26, 1918; in office: May 10, 1980. **Local divisions:** 51 prefectures. **Armed forces:** regulars 184,600; reserves 290,000.

Economy: Industries: Textiles, chemicals, aluminum, wine, food processng, cement. **Chief crops:** Grains, corn, rice, cotton, tobacco, olives, citrus fruits, raisins, figs. **Minerals:** Bauxite, iron, emery, lignite, oil, silver, manganese, chromite, nickel, baryte. **Crude oil reserves** (1980): 150 mln. bbls. **Per capita arable land:** 0.8 acres. **Meat prod.** (1978): beef: 104,000 metric tons; pork: 119,000 metric tons; lamb: 119,000 metric tons. **Fish catch** (1977): 105,600 metric tons. **Electricity prod.** (1978): 19.46 bln. kwh. **Crude steel prod.** (1979): 1 mln. metric tons. **Labor force:** 34% agric.; 26% manuf.

Finance: Currency: Drachma (Apr. 1981: 53.74 = $1 US). **Gross domestic product** (1979): $39.5 bln. **Per capita income** (1979): $3,665. **Imports** (1979): $9.70 bln.; partners (1978): W. Ger. 16%, Jap. 13%, It. 10%, Fr. 6%. **Exports** (1979): $3.89 bln.; partners (1978): W. Ger. 21%, It. 11%, Fr. 7%, Saudi Ar. 6%. **Tourists** (1979): 5,793,360; receipts $1.66 bln. **National budget** (1978): $6.60 bln. revenues; $7.78 bln. expenditures. **International reserves less gold** (Mar. 1981): $978.6 mln. **Gold:** 3.84 mln. oz t. **Consumer prices** (change in 1980): 24.9%.

Transport: Railway traffic (1978): 1.57 bln. passenger-km; 854.4 mln. net ton-km. **Motor vehicles:** in use (1979): 839,341 passenger cars, 367,188 comm. vehicles. **Civil aviation:** 4,356 mln. passenger-km (1977); 58 mln. freight ton-km (1977). **Chief ports:** Piraeus, Thessaloniki, Patrai.

Communications: Television sets: 1.17 mln. in use (1976), 187,000 manuf. (1976). **Radios:** 2.8 mln. in use (1976). **Telephones in use** (1978): 2,319,797. **Daily newspaper circ.** (1981): 676,377; 70 per 1,000 pop.

Health: Life expectancy at birth (1970): 70.13 male; 73.64 female. **Births** (per 1,000 pop. 1979): 15.9. **Deaths** (per 1,000 pop. 1979): 8.7. **Natural increase** (1977): .7%. **Hospital beds** (per 100,000 pop. 1977): 638. **Physicians** (per 100,000 pop. 1977): 221. **Infant mortality** (per 1,000 live births 1977): 20.3.

Education (1977): **Literacy:** 84%. **Pop. 5–19:** in school: 69%, teachers per 1,000: 25. **PQLI:** 90.

The achievements of ancient Greece in art, architecture, science, mathematics, philosophy, drama, literature, and democracy became legacies for succeeding ages. Greece reached the height of its glory and power, particularly in the Athenian city-state, in the 5th century BC.

Greece fell under Roman rule in the 2d and 1st centuries BC. In the 4th century AD it became part of the Byzantine Empire and, after the fall of Constantinople to the Turks in 1453, part of the Ottoman Empire.

Greece won its war of independence from Turkey 1821-1829, and became a kingdom. A republic was established 1924; the monarchy was restored, 1935, and George II, King of the Hellenes, resumed the throne. In Oct., 1940, Greece rejected an ultimatum from Italy. Nazi support resulted in its defeat and occupation by Germans, Italians, and Bulgarians. By the end of 1944 the invaders withdrew. Communist resistance forces were defeated by Royalist and British troops. A plebiscite recalled King George II. He died Apr. 1, 1947, was succeeded by his brother, Paul I.

Communists waged guerrilla war 1947-49 against the government but were defeated with the aid of the U.S. (acting under the Truman Doctrine).

A period of reconstruction and rapid development followed, mainly with conservative governments under Premier Constantine Karamanlis. The Center Union led by George Papandreou won elections in 1963 and 1964. King Constantine, who acceded in 1964, forced Papandreou to resign. A period of political maneuvers ended in the military takeover of April 21, 1967, by Col. George Papadopoulos. King Constantine tried to reverse the consolidation of the harsh dictatorship Dec. 13, 1967, but failed and fled to Italy. Papadopoulos was ousted Nov. 25, 1973, in a coup led by rightist Brig. Demetrius Ioannides.

Greek army officers serving in the National Guard of Cyprus staged a coup on the island July 15, 1974. Turkey invaded Cyprus a week later, precipitating the collapse of the Greek junta, which was implicated in the Cyprus coup.

The military turned the government over to Karamanlis, who named a civilian cabinet, freed political prisoners, and sought to solve the Cyprus crisis. In Nov. 1974 elections his party won a large parliamentary majority, reduced by socialist gains in 1977. A Dec. 1974 referendum resulted in the proclamation of a republic.

The new government promoted educational and agricultural reforms, and sought to advance from associate to full membership in the EC.

Greece was reintegrated into the military wing of NATO in October 1980, and it became the 10th full member of the European

Community on Jan. 1, 1981.

Grenada

State of Grenada

People: Population (1980 est.): 108,000. **Pop. density:** 812.03 per sq. mi. **Ethnic groups:** Negroes over 52%, whites 1%, mulattoes 43% (including some E. Indians), Carib. Indians. **Languages:** English, French-African patois. **Religions:** Roman Catholics, Anglicans.

.**Geography: Area:** 133 sq. mi., twice the size of Washington, D.C. **Location:** Southernmost of West Indies, 90 mi. N. of Venezuela. **Topography:** Main island is mountainous; country includes Carriacon and Petit Martinique islands. **Capital:** St. George's. **Cities** (1975 est.): St. George's 30,000.

Government: Head of state: Queen Elizabeth II, represented by Gov.-Gen. Paul Scoon, b. July 4, 1935; in office: Sept. 30, 1978. **Head of government:** Prime Min. Maurice Bishop, b. May 29, 1944; in office: Mar. 13, 1979. **Local divisions:** 6 parishes and one dependency.

Economy: Industries: Rum. **Chief crops:** Nutmegs, bananas, cocoa, sugar, mace. **Per capita arable land:** 0.05 acres. **Electricity prod.** (1977): 28.00 mln. kwh. **Labor force:** 31% agric.; 6% man.; 62.8% service.

Finance: Currency: East Caribbean dollar (Apr. 1981: 2.70 = $1 US). **Gross domestic product** (1977 est.): $54 mln. **Per capita income** (1977): $500. **Imports** (1979): $45 mln.; partners (1973): UK 27%, Trin./Tob. 20%, U.S. 9%, Can. 8%. **Exports** (1979): $22 mln.; partners (1973): UK 33%, W. Ger. 19%, Neth. 14%, U.S. 8%. **Tourists** (1977): 28,500; receipts (1976): $8 mln. **National budget** (1977): $12.46 mln. revenues; $12.88 mln. expenditures. **International reserves less gold** (Mar. 1980): $19.32 mln.

Transport: Motor vehicles: in use (1971): 3,800 passenger cars, 100 comm. vehicles. **Chief ports:** Saint George's.

Communications: Radios: 22,000 in use (1976). **Telephones in use** (1978): 5,217. **Daily newspaper circ.** (1970): 2,600.

Health: Life expectancy at birth (1961): 60.14 male; 65.60 female. **Births** (per 1,000 pop. 1975): 27.4. **Deaths** (per 1,000 pop. 1975): 5.9. **Natural increase** (1975): 2.2%. **Infant mortality** (per 1,000 live births 1979): 23.5. **PQLI:** 78.

Columbus sighted the island 1498. First European settlers were French, 1650. The island was held alternately by France and England until final British occupation, 1784. Grenada became fully independent Feb. 7, 1974 during a general strike. It is the smallest independent nation in the Western Hemisphere.

Guatemala

Republic of Guatemala

People: Population (1980 est.): 7,260,000. **Age distrib.** (%): 0–14: 45.1; 15–59: 50.6; 60+: 4.4. **Pop. density:** 172.68 per sq. mi. **Urban** (1975): 35.6%. **Ethnic groups:** Indians 54%, Mestizos 42%, whites 4%. **Languages:** Spanish, 18 Maya-Quiche dialects. **Religions:** Roman Catholics over 90%; Mayan religion practiced.

Geography: Area: 42,042 sq. mi., the size of Tennessee. **Location:** In Central America. **Neighbors:** Mexico N, W; El Salvador on S, Honduras, Belize on E. **Topography:** The central highland and mountain areas are bordered by the narrow Pacific coast and the lowlands and fertile river valleys on the Caribbean. There are numerous volcanoes in S, more than half a dozen over 11,000 ft. **Capital:** Guatemala City. **Cities** (1973 cen.): Guatemala City 700,504.

Government: Head of state: Pres. Romeo Lucas Garcia; b. July 4, 1924; in office: July 1, 1978. **Local divisions:** Guatemala City and 22 departments. **Armed forces:** regulars 17,960; para-military 3,000.

Economy: Industries: Shoes, textiles. **Chief crops:** Coffee (one third of exports), sugar, bananas, cotton. **Minerals:** Zinc, lead, antimony, tungsten, cadmium, silver, copper, nickel, gas. **Crude oil reserves** (1980): 16 mln. bbls. **Other resources:** Rare woods, fish, chicle. **Per capita arable land:** 0.5 acres. **Meat prod.** (1978): beef: 78,000 metric tons; pork: 12,000 metric tons. **Electricity prod.** (1977): 1.29 bln. kwh. **Labor force:** 57% agric.; 14% manuf.

Finance: Currency: Quetzal (Apr. 1981: 1.00 = $1 US).

Gross domestic product (1979): $6.89 bln. **Per capita income** (1977): $749. **Imports** (1979): $1.50 bln.; partners: U.S. 39%, Jap. 11%, W. Ger. 7%, Venez. 6%. **Exports** (1980): $1.55 bln.; partners: U.S. 32%, W. Ger. 13%, El Salv. 9%, Jap. 8%. **Tourists** (1977): 444,800; receipts: $105 mln. **National budget** (1979): $682 mln. revenues; $850 mln. expenditures. **International reserves less gold** (Apr. 1981): $389.2 mln. **Gold:** 522,000 oz t. **Consumer prices** (change in 1980): 10.7%.

Transport: Railway traffic (1976): 117 mln. net ton-km. **Motor vehicles:** in use (1976): 82,700 passenger cars, 50,100 comm. vehicles. **Civil aviation:** 153 mln. passenger-km (1978); 7 mln. freight ton-km (1978). **Chief ports:** Puerto Barrios, San Jose.

Communications: Television sets: 120,000 in use (1976). **Radios:** 265,000 in use (1976). **Telephones in use** (1978): 70,614. **Daily newspaper circ.** (1976): 214,000.

Health: Life expectancy at birth (1965): 48.29 male; 49.74 female. **Births** (per 1,000 pop. 1976): 42.6. **Deaths** (per 1,000 pop. 1976): 13.1. **Natural increase** (1976): 3.0% **Hospital beds** (per 100,000 pop. 1977): 187. **Physicians** (per 100,000 pop. 1977): 40. **Infant mortality** (per 1,000 live births 1976): 76.5.

Education (1977): **Literacy:** 47%. **Pop. 5-19:** in school: 31%, teachers per 1,000: 11. **PQLI:** 59.

The old Mayan Indian empire flourished in what is today Guatemala for over 1,000 years before the Spanish.

Guatemala was a Spanish colony 1524-1821; briefly a part of Mexico and then of the U.S. of Central America, the republic was established in 1839.

Since 1945 when a liberal government was elected to replace the long-term dictatorship of Jorge Ubico, the country has seen a swing toward socialism, an armed revolt, renewed attempts at social reform and a military coup. Assassinations and political violence from left and right plagued the country. The Guerrilla Army of the Poor, an insurgent group founded 1975, has stepped up their military offensive by attacking army posts and has succeeded in incorporating segments of the large Indian population in its struggle against the government.

Guatemala has a long-standing claim to Belize.

Guinea

People's Revolutionary Republic of Guinea

People: Population (1980 est.): 5,300,000. **Pop. density:** 55.83 per sq. mi. **Ethnic groups:** Foulah 40%, Malinké 25%, Soussous 10%, 15 other tribes. **Languages:** French (official), tribal languages. **Religions:** Muslims 71%, Christians 1%, animists 24%.

Geography: Area: 94,925 sq. mi., slightly smaller than Oregon. **Location:** On Atlantic coast of W. Africa. **Neighbors:** Guinea-Bissau, Senegal, Mali on N, Ivory Coast on E, Liberia on S. **Topography:** A narrow coastal belt leads to the mountainous middle region, the source of the Gambia, Senegal, and Niger rivers. Upper Guinea, farther inland, is a cooler upland. The SE is forested. **Capital:** Conakry. **Cities** (1980 est.): Conakry 575,000; Labe 419,000; N'Zerekore 291,000; Kankan 265,000.

Government: Head of state: Pres. Ahmed Sékou Touré; b. Jan. 9, 1922; in office: Oct. 2, 1958. **Head of government:** Prime Min. Lansana Beavogui; b. 1923; in office: Apr. 26, 1972. **Local divisions:** 33 districts. **Armed forces:** regulars 8,650; para-military 8,000.

Economy: Chief crops: Bananas, pineapples, rice, corn, palm nuts, coffee, honey. **Minerals:** Bauxite, iron, diamonds. **Per capita arable land:** 2.2 acres. **Meat prod.** (1978): beef 11,000 metric tons. **Electricity prod.** (1977) 500.00 mln. kwh. **Labor force:** 84% agric.; 9% man.

Finance: Currency: Syli (Mar. 1979: 19.2 = $1 US). **Gross domestic product** (1978 est.): $1.2 bln. **Per capita income** (1978): $140. **Imports** (1978): $276 mln.; partners (1977): Fr. 20% USSR 11%, U.S. 6% It. 6%. **Exports** (1978): $342 mln.; partners (1977): U.S. 18%, Fr. 13%, W. Ger. 12%, USSR 12%.

Transport: Motor vehicles: in use (1972): 10,200 passenger cars, 10,800 comm. vehicles. **Chief ports:** Conakry.

Communications: Radios: 120,000 in use (1976). **Daily newspaper circ.** (1976): 10,000; 2 per 1,000 pop.

Health: Life expectancy at birth (1975): 39.4 male; 42.6 female. **Births** (per 1,000 pop. 1975): 46.6. **Deaths** (per 1,000 pop. 1975): 22.9. **Natural increase** (1975): 2.4%. **Hospital beds** (per 100,000 pop. 1977): 158. **Physicians** (per 100,000 pop. 1977): 6. **Infant mortality** (per 1,000 live births 1980): 172.

Education (1977): **Literacy:** 15%. **Pop. 5-19:** in school: 18%, teachers per 1,000: 8. **PQLI:** 20.

Part of the ancient West African empires, Guinea fell under French control 1849-98. Under Sekou Toure, it opted for full independence in 1958, and France withdrew all aid.

Toure turned to communist nations for support, and set up a militant one-party state. France and Guinea restored ties in 1975, after a 10-year break. Western firms, as well as the Soviet government, have invested in Guinea's vast bauxite mines.

According to reports, thousands of opponents were jailed in the 1970s, in the aftermath of an unsuccessful Portuguese invasion. Many were tortured and killed.

Guinea-Bissau

Republic of Guinea-Bissau

People: Population (1979 est.): 638,000. **Pop. density:** 39.43 per sq. mi. **Ethnic groups:** Balanta 30%, Fula 20%, Mandyako 14%, other tribes. **Languages:** Portuguese (official), Crioulo, tribal languages. **Religions:** Moslems 30%, Christians 1%, others.

Geography: Area: 13,948 sq. mi. **Location:** On Atlantic coast of W. Africa. **Neighbors:** Senegal on N, Guinea on E, S. **Topography:** A swampy coastal plain covers most of the country; to the east is a low savanna region. **Capital:** Bissau. **Cities** (1971 est.): Bissau 65,000.

Government: Head of state: Pres. Luis de Almeida Cabral; b. 1931; in office: July 22, 1973. **Head of government:** Prime Min. Maj. Joao Bernardo Viera. **Local divisions:** 8 regions. **Armed forces:** regulars 6,100; para-military 2,000.

Economy: Chief crops: Peanuts, palm oil. **Minerals:** Bauxite, oil. **Per capita arable land:** 1.1 acres. **Electricity prod.** (1977): 24.00 mln. kwh. **Labor force:** 86% agric.

Finance: Currency: Peso (Mar. 1979: 34.19 = $1 US). **Gross domestic product** (1976 est.): $200 mln. **Per capita income** (1976): $330. **Imports** (1979): $50 mln.; partners: Port. 40%, Swed. 8%, USSR 8%, Fr. 7%. **Exports** (1979): $14 mln.; partners: Port. 59%, Egypt 18% Sen. 11%.

Communications: Radios: 11,000 licensed (1976). **Daily newspaper circ.** (1976): 6,000; 11 per 1,000 pop.

Health: Life expectancy at birth (1975): 37.0 male; 40.1 female. **Births** (per 1,000 pop. 1975): 40.1. **Deaths** (per 1,000 pop. 1975): 25.1. **Natural increase** (1975): 1.5%. **Infant mortality** (per 1,000 live births 1969): 47.1. **PQLI:** 14.

Portuguese mariners explored the area in the mid-15th century; the slave trade flourished in the 17th and 18th centuries, and colonization began in the 19th.

Beginning in the 1960s, an independence movement waged a guerrilla war and formed a government in the interior that achieved international support. Full independence came Sept. 10, 1974, after the Portuguese regime was overthrown.

Union with Cape Verde was foreseen in a number of cooperation accords signed in 1976.

Guyana

Cooperative Republic of Guyana

People: Population (1979 est.): 832,000. **Age distrib.** (%): 0-14: 43.7; 5-59: 50.7; 60+: 5.6. **Pop. density:** 9.88 per sq. mi. **Urban** (1971): 29.6%. **Ethnic groups:** East Indians 55%, Neroes 36%, others (Amerindians, Chinese, Europeans) 10%. **Languages:** English (official), Hindi, Portuguese, Chinese, Negro patois. **Religions:** Christians 57%, Hindus 33%, Moslems 9%, others.

Geography: Area: 83,000 sq. mi., the size of Idaho. **Location:** On N coast of S. America. **Neighbors:** Venezuela on W, Brazil on S, Suriname on E. **Topography:** Dense tropical forests cover much of the land, although a flat coastal area up to 40 mi. wide, where 90% of the population lives, provides rich alluvial soil for agriculture. A grassy savanna divides the 2 zones. **Capital:** Georgetown. **Cities** (1978 est.): Georgetown 72,049.

Government: Head of state and Head of government: Prime Min. and President Linden Forbes Burnham; b. Feb. 20, 1923; in office: Dec. 14, 1964. **Local divisions:** 6 regions. **Armed forces:** regulars 5,000; para-military 10,000.

Economy: Industries: Cigarettes, rum, clothing, furniture, rugs. **Chief crops:** Sugar, rice, coconuts, coffee, cocoa, citrus and other fruits. **Minerals:** Bauxite (5th largest producer), gold,

diamonds. **Other resources:** Timber, shrimp. **Per capita arable land:** 1.1 acres. **Fish catch** (1977): 21,800 metric tons. **Electricity prod.** (1977): 416.00 mln. kwh. **Labor force:** 30% agric.

Finance: Currency: Dollar (Apr. 1981: 2.55 = $1 US). **Gross domestic product** (1977). $437 mln. **Per capita income** (1977): $437. **Imports** (1979): $317 mln.; partners (1977): U.S. 27%, Trin-Tob. 23%, UK 21%. **Exports** (1980): $386 mln.; partners (1977): UK 33%, U.S. 18%, Trin-Tob. 6%. **Tourist receipts** (1977): $3 mln. **National budget** (1973): $74 mln. revenues; $141 mln. expenditures. **International reserves less gold** (Mar. 1981): $49.67 mln. **Consumer prices** (change in 1980): 14.1%.

Transport: Railway traffic (1974): 6 mln. passenger-km. **Motor vehicles:** in use (1977): 28,400 passenger cars, 14,700 comm. vehicles. **Chief ports:** Georgetown.

Communications: Radios: 275,000 in use (1976). **Telephones in use** (1978): 27,064. **Daily newspaper circ.** (1976): 50,000; 63 per 1,000 pop.

Health: Life expectancy at birth (1961): 59.03 male; 63.01 female. **Births** (per 1,000 pop. 1978): 28.3. **Deaths** (per 1,000 pop. 1978): 7.3. **Natural increase** (1978): 2.1% **Hospital beds** (per 100,000 pop. 1977): 485. **Physicians** (per 100,000 pop. 1977): 25. **Infant mortality** (per 1,000 live births 1972): 50.5.

Education (1977): **Literacy:** 85%. **Pop. 5-19:** in school: 62%, teachers per 1,000: 24. **PQLI:** 84.

Guyana became a Dutch possession in the 17th century, but sovereignty passed to Britain in 1815. Indentured servants from India soon outnumbered African slaves. Ethnic tension has affected political life.

Guyana became independent May 26, 1966. A Venezuelan claim to the western half of Guyana was suspended in 1970 for 12 years. The Suriname border is also disputed. The government has nationalized most of the economy in recent years.

The Port Kaituma ambush of U.S. Rep. Leo J. Ryan and others investigating mistreatment of American followers of the Rev. Jim Jones' People's Temple cult, triggered a mass suicide-execution of 911 cultists in the Guyana jungle, Nov. 18, 1979.

Haiti

Republic of Haiti

People: Population (1980 est.): 5,740,000. **Age distrib.** (%): 4-14: 41.2; 15-59: 52.9; 60+: 5.9. **Pop. density:** 535.75 per sq. mi. **Urban** (1978): 24.3%. **Ethnic groups:** African descent 95%, mulattoes 5%. **Languages:** French (official), Creole (majority). **Religions:** Roman Catholics 80%, Protestants 10%; Voodoo widely practiced.

Geography: Area: 10,714 sq. mi., the size of Maryland. **Location:** In West Indies, occupies western third of I. of Hispaniola. **Neighbors:** Dominican Republic on E, Cuba on W. **Topography:** About two-thirds of Haiti is mountainous. Much of the rest is semiarid. Coastal areas are warm and moist. **Capital:** Port-au-Prince. **Cities** (1978 est.): Port-au-Prince 745,700; Cap-Haitien 50,000.

Government: Head of state: Pres. Jean-Claude Duvalier; b. July 3, 1951; in office: Apr. 22, 1971. **Local divisions:** 9 departments. **Armed forces:** regulars 6,550; para-military 14,900.

Economy: Industries: Rum, molasses, tourism. **Chief crops:** Coffee, sisal, cotton, sugar, bananas, cocoa, tobacco, rice. **Minerals:** Bauxite, copper, gold, silver, cement. **Other resources:** Timber. **Per capita arable land:** 0.3 acres. **Meat prod.** (1978): beef: 18,000 metric tons; pork: 25,000 metric tons; lamb: 5,000 metric tons. **Electricity prod.** (1977): 215 mln. kwh. **Labor force:** 79% agric.; 7% man.; 14% services.

Finance: Currency: Gourde (Apr. 1981: 5.00 = $1 US). **Gross domestic product** (1978): $1.34 bln. **Per capita income** (1980): $260. **Imports** (1978): $221 mln.; partners: U.S. 56%, Neth. Ant. 7%, Jap. 6%. Can. 6%. **Exports** (1980): $185 mln.; partners (1977): U.S. 61%, Fr. 10%, It. 6%, Belg. 5%. **Tourists** (1977): 96,000; receipts $37 mln. **National budget** (1978): $269 mln. revenues; $195 mln. expenditures. **International reserves less gold** (Apr. 1981): $7.8 mln. **Gold:** 18,000 oz t. **Consumer prices** (change in 1980): 17.9%.

Transport: Motor vehicles: in use (1976): 18,700 passenger cars, 2,400 comm. vehicles. **Chief ports:** Port-au-Prince, Les Cayes.

Communications: Television sets: 14,000 in use (1976). **Radios:** 95,000 in use (1976). **Telephones in use** (1977):

17,800. **Daily newspaper circ.** (1976): 92,000; 20 per 1,000 pop.

Health: Life expectancy at birth (1975): 47.1 male; 50.0 female. **Births** (per 1,000 pop. 1975): 42.7. **Deaths** (per 1,000 pop. 1975): 17.4. **Natural increase** (1975): 2.5%. **Hospital beds** (per 100,000 pop. 1977): 72. **Physicians** (per 100,000 pop. 1977): 7.

Education (1977): **Literacy:** 22%. **Pop. 5-19:** in school: 32%, teachers per 1,000: 9. **PQLI:** 37.

Haiti, visited by Columbus, 1492, and a French colony from 1677, attained its independence, 1804, following the rebellion led by former slave Toussaint L'Ouverture. Following a period of political violence, the U.S. occupied the country 1915-34.

Dr. Francois Duvalier was voted president in 1957; in 1964 he was named president for life. Upon his death in 1971, he was succeeded by his son, Jean-Claude. Under the latter's less violent rule, foreign investment and tourism revived. But drought in 1975-77 brought famine, aggravated by erosion caused by the destruction of most trees for charcoal.

Honduras

Republic of Honduras

People: Population (1980 est.): 3,690,000. **Age distrib.** (%): 0-14: 48.1; 15-59: 47.5; 60+: 4.5. **Pop. density:** 85.26 per sq. mi. **Urban** (1974): 31.4%. **Ethnic groups:** Mestizo 90%, Caucasian, Negroes, Indians. **Languages:** Spanish, English (on N coast). **Religions:** Roman Catholics, small Protestant minority.

Geography: Area: 43,277 sq. mi., slightly larger than Tennessee. **Location:** In Central America. **Neighbors:** Guatemala on W, El Salvador, Nicaragua on S. **Topography:** The Caribbean coast is 500 mi. long. Pacific coast, on Gulf of Fonseca, is 40 mi. long. Honduras is mountainous, with wide fertile valleys and rich forests. **Capital:** Tegucigalpa. **Cities** (1974 cen.): Tegucigalpa 273,894; San Pedro Sula 150,991.

Government: President of military junta: Gen. Policarpo Paz Garcia; in office: Aug. 8, 1978. **Local divisions:** 18 departments. **Armed forces:** regulars 11,300; para-military 3,000.

Economy: Industries: Clothing, textiles, cement, chemicals. **Chief crops:** Bananas (chief export), coffee, cotton, sugar, timber, tobacco. **Minerals:** Gold, silver, copper, lead, zinc, iron, antimony, coal. **Other resources:** Timber. **Per capita arable land:** 0.5 acres. **Meat prod.** (1978): beef: 51,000 metric tons; pork: 10,000 metric tons. **Electricity prod.** (1977): 701.00 mln. kwh. **Labor force:** 56% agric.; 19% man.; 11% service.

Finance: Currency: Lempira (Apr. 1981): 2.00 = $1 US). **Gross domestic product** (1980): $2.55 bln. **Per capita income** (1978): $528. **Imports** (1980): $1.02 bln.; partners (1977): U.S. 43%, Jap. 11%, Guat. 6%, Venez. 5%. **Exports** (1980): $806 mln.; partners (1977): U.S. 49%, W. Ger. 18%, Jap. 6%, Neth. 5%. **Tourist receipts** (1977): $14 mln. **National budget** (1979): $328 mln. revenues; $368 mln. expenditures. **International reserves less gold** (Jan. 1981): $138.15 mln. **Gold:** (Feb. 1980): 16,000 oz t. **Consumer prices** (change in 1979): 9.0%.

Transport: Motor vehicles: in use (1976) 20,500 passenger cars, 30,200 comm. vehicles. **Civil aviation:** 256 mln. passenger-km (1976); 5 mln. freight ton-km (1976). **Chief ports:** Puerto Cortes, La Ceiba.

Communications: Television sets: 48,000 in use (1976). **Radios:** 161,000 in use (1976). **Telephones in use** (1977): 19,227. **Daily newspaper circ.** (1976): 140,000.

Health: Life expectancy at birth (1975): 52.4 male; 55.9 female. **Births** (per 1,000 pop. 1975): 48.6. **Deaths** (per 1,000 pop. 1975): 13.7. **Natural increase** (1975): 3.5%. **Hospital beds** (per 100,000 pop. 1977): 32. **Physicians** (per 100,000 pop. 1977): 137. **Infant mortality** (per 1,000 live births 1975): 31.4.

Education (1977): **Literacy:** 57%. **Pop. 5-19:** in school: 42%, teachers per 1,000: 14. **PQLI:** 57.

Mayan civilization flourished in Honduras in the 1st millenium AD. Columbus arrived in 1502. Honduras became independent after freeing itself from Spain, 1821 and from the Fed. of Central America, 1838.

Gen. Oswaldo Lopez Arellano, president for most of the period 1963-75 by virtue of 1 election and 2 coups, was ousted by the Army in 1975 over charges of pervasive bribery by United

Brands Co. of the U.S.

A constitutional assembly was elected, 1980; direct elections for president were scheduled for early 1981, with only civilian candidates expected to run. The government has resumed land distribution, raised minimum wages, and started a literacy campaign.

Hungary

Hungarian People's Republic

People: Population (1980 est.): 10,710,000. **Age distrib.** (%): 0-14: 21.0; 15-59: 61.5; 60+: 17.5. **Pop. density:** 297.61 per sq. mi. **Urban** (1977): 51.8%. **Ethnic groups:** Magyar 98%, German 0.5%, Slovak 0.3%, Gypsy 0.3%, Croatian 0.3%. **Languages:** Hungarian (Magyar). **Religions:** Roman Catholics 67.5%, Calvinist 20%, Lutherans 5%, Jews 1%.

Geography: Area: 35,919 sq. mi., slightly smaller than Indiana. **Location:** In East Central Europe. **Neighbors:** Czechoslovakia on N, Austria on W, Yugoslavia on S, Romania, USSR on E. **Topography:** The Danube R. forms the Czech border in the NW, then swings S to bisect the country. The eastern half of Hungary is mainly a great fertile plain, the Alfold; the W and N are hilly. **Capital:** Budapest. **Cities** (1978 est.): Budapest 2,085,615; Miskolc 205,610; Debrecen 193,958.

Government: Head of state: Pres. Pal Losonczi; b. Sept. 18, 1919; in office: Apr. 14, 1967. **Head of government:** Chmn. Gyorgy Lazar; b. Sept. 15, 1924; in office: May 15, 1975. **Head of Communist Party:** Janos Kadar; b. May 26, 1912; in office: Oct. 25, 1956. **Local divisions:** 19 counties, 5 cities with county status. **Armed forces:** regulars 104,000; reserves 143,000.

Economy: Industries: Iron and steel, machinery, chemicals, vehicles, communications equip., milling, distilling. **Chief crops:** Grains, vegetables, fruits, grapes. **Minerals:** Bauxite, natural gas. **Per capita arable land:** 1.2 acres. **Meat prod.** (1978): beef: 145,000 metric tons; pork: 880,000 metric tons. **Fish catch** (1977): 34,700 metric tons. **Electricity prod.** (1978): 25.42 bln. kwh. **Crude steel prod.** (1979): 3.9 mln. metric tons. **Labor force:** 23% agric.; 36% manuf.

Finance: Currency: Forint (Mar. 1980: 20.31 = $1 US). **Net material product** (1978): $29.1 bln. **Per capita income** (1978): $3,000. **Imports** (1979): $8.67 bln.; partners (1978): USSR 28%, W. Ger. 12%, E. Ger. 8%, Czech. 5%. **Exports** (1979): $7.94 bln.; partners (1978): USSR 30%, E. Ger. 8%, W. Ger. 8%, Czech. 7%. **Tourists** (1977): 7,194,000; receipts $320 mln. **Consumer prices** (change in 1979): 8.8%.

Transport: Railway traffic (1978): 12.6 bln. passenger-km; 23.9 bln. net ton-km. **Motor vehicles:** in use (1977): 744,700 passenger cars, 228,900 comm. vehicles; manuf. (1978): 14,880 comm. vehicles.

Communications: Television sets: 2.5 mln. licensed (1976), 423,000 manuf. (1977). **Radios:** 2.54 mln. licensed (1975), 259,000 manuf. (1977). **Telephones in use** (1978): 1,103,843. **Daily newspaper circ.** (1977): 2,585,000; 243 per 1,000 pop.

Health: Life expectancy at birth (1979): 66.54 male; 72.42 female. **Births** (per 1,000 pop. 1980): 13.9 **Deaths** (per 1,000 pop. 1980): 13.6. **Natural increase** (1978): .3%. **Hospital beds** (per 100,000 pop. 1977): 690. **Physicians** (per 100,000 pop. 1977): 230 **Infant mortality** (per 1,000 live births 1979): 24.

Education (1977): **Literacy:** 98%. **Pop. 5-19:** in school: 55%, teachers per 1,000: 27. **PQLI:** 91.

Earliest settlers, chiefly Slav and Germanic, were overrun by Huns and Magyars from the east. Stephen I (997-1038) was made king by Pope Sylvester II in 1000 AD. The country suffered repeated Turkish invasions in the 15th-17th centuries. After the defeats of the Turks, 1686-1697, Austria dominated, but Hungary obtained concessions until it regained internal independence in 1867, with the emperor of Austria as king of Hungary in a dual monarchy with a single diplomatic service. Defeated with the Central Powers in 1918, Hungary lost Transylvania to Romania, Croatia and Bacska to Yugoslavia, Slovakia and Carpatho Ruthenia to Czechoslovakia, all of which had large Hungarian minorities. A republic under Michael Karolyi and a bolshevist revolt under Bela Kun were followed by a vote for a monarchy in 1920 with Admiral Nicholas Horthy as regent.

Hungary joined Germany in World War II, and was allowed to annex most of its lost territories. Russian troops captured the country, 1944-1945. By terms of an armistice with the Allied powers Hungary agreed to give up territory acquired by the

1938 dismemberment of Czechoslovakia and to return to its borders of 1937.

A republic was declared Feb. 1, 1946; Zoltan Tildy was elected president. In 1947 the communists forced Tildy out. Premier Imre Nagy, in office since mid 1953, was ousted for his moderate policy of favoring agriculture and consumer production, April 18, 1955.

In 1956, popular demands for the ousting of Erno Gero, Communist party secretary, and for formation of a government by Nagy, resulted in the latter's appointment Oct. 23; demonstrations against communist rule developed into open revolt. Gero called in Soviet forces. On Nov. 4 Soviet forces launched a massive attack against Budapest with 200,000 troops, 2,500 tanks and armored cars.

Estimates varied from 6,500 to 32,000 dead, and thousands deported. About 200,000 persons fled the country. The U.S. received 38,248 under a refugee emergency program. In the spring of 1963 the regime freed many anti-communists and captives from the revolution in a sweeping amnesty. Nagy was executed by the Russians.

Some 40,000 Soviet troops are stationed in Hungary. Hungarian troops participated in the 1968 Warsaw Pact invasion of Czechoslovakia.

Major economic reforms were launched early in 1968, switching from a central planning system to one in which market forces and profit control much of production. Productivity and living standards have improved. By the 1970s, Hungary led the communist states in comparative tolerance for cultural freedoms and small private enterprise. Some 60,000 of the 1956 emigres have returned.

Iceland

Republic of Iceland

People: Population (1980 est.): 230,000. **Age distrib.** (%): 0–14: 29.0; 15–59: 58.0; 60+: 13.1. **Pop. density:** 5.79 per sq. mi. **Urban** (1977): 87.4% **Ethnic groups:** Homogeneous, descendants of Norwegians, Celts. **Language:** Icelandic. **Religon:** Lutherans 98%.

Geography: Area: 39,702 sq. mi., the size of Virginia. **Location:** At N end of Atlantic O. **Neighbors:** Nearest is Greenland. **Topography:** Iceland is of recent volcanic origin. Three-quarters of the surface is wasteland: glaciers, lakes, a lava desert. There are geysers and hot springs, and the climate is moderated by the Gulf Stream. **Capital:** Reykjavik. **Cities** (1978 est.): Reykjavik 83,887.

Government: Head of state: Pres. Vigdis Finnbogadottir; b. Apr. 15, 1930; in office: Aug. 1, 1980. **Head of government:** Prime Min. Gunnar Thoroddsen, b. Dec. 29, 1910; in office: Feb. 8, 1980. **Local divisions:** 18 syslur (counties); 25–30 kaupstaudr (urban municipalities.)

Economy: Industries: Fish products, aluminum, cement, chemicals. **Chief crops:** Potatoes, turnips, hay. **Per capita arable land:** 0.09 acres. **Meat prod.** (1978): lamb: 15,000 metric tons. **Fish catch** (1977): 1.4 mln. metric tons. **Electricity prod.** (1978): 2.66 bln. kwh. **Labor force:** 10% agric.; 26% manuf.; 18% fishing.

Finance: Currency: Krona (Apr. 1981: 6.72 = $1 US). **Gross domestic product** (1979): $2.47 bln. **Per capita income** (1978): $6,392. **Imports** (1980): $1.00 bln.; partners (1978): W. Ger. 11%, UK 11%, Den. 10%, Swed. 9%. **Exports** (1980): $929 mln.; partners (1978): U.S. 29%, UK 17%, W. Ger. 8%. **Tourists** (1977): 72,700; receipts: $15 mln. **National budget** (1977): $538 mln. revenues; $546 mln. expenditures. **International reserves less gold** (Apr. 1981): $205.8 mln. **Gold:** 49,000 oz t. **Consumer prices** (change in 1980): 54.6%.

Transport: Motor vehicles: in use (1977): 70,100 passenger cars, 7,900 comm. vehicles. **Civil aviation:** 2,118 mln. passenger-km (1978); 37 mln. freight ton-km (1978). **Chief ports:** Reykjavik.

Communications: Television sets: 53,000 in use (1976). **Radios:** 64,000 licensed (1976). **Telephones in use** (1978): 95,515. **Daily newspaper circ.** (1977): 123,000; 554 per 1,000 pop.

Health: Life expectancy at birth (1976): 73.0 male; 79.2 female. **Births** (per 1,000 pop. 1978): 18.6. **Deaths** (per 1,000 pop. 1978): 6.5. **Natural increase** (1978): 1.2%. **Hospital beds** (per 100,000 pop. 1977): 1,700. **Physicians** (per 100,000 pop. 1977): 180. **Infant mortality** per (1,000 live births 1978): 10.8.

Education (1977): **Literacy:** 99%. **Pop. 5-19:** in school: 70%,

teachers per 1,000: 46. **PQLI:** 98.

Iceland was an independent republic from 930 to 1262, when it joined with Norway. Its language has maintained its purity for 1,000 years. Danish rule lasted from 1380-1918; the last ties with the Danish crown were severed in 1941. The Althing, or assembly, is the world's oldest surviving parliament.

A four-year dispute with Britain ended in 1976 when the latter accepted Iceland's 200-mile territorial waters claim.

A conservative coalition won power in 1974 and stopped plans to oust U.S. NATO air and naval personnel, which totalled 2,859 in 1979.

India

Republic of India

People: Population (1979 est.): 667,326,000. **Age distrib.** (%): 0–14: 40.8; 15–59: 53.9; 60+: 5.3. **Pop. density:** 519.13 per sq. mi. **Urban** (1977): 21.2%. **Ethnic groups:** Indo-Aryan groups 72%, Dravidians 25%, Mongoloids 3%. **Languages:** 15 languages, including Hindi (official) and English (associate official). **Religions:** Hindus 84%, Moslems 10%, Christians 2.6%, Sikhs 1.9%, Buddhists 0.7%, Jains 0.5%, others.

Geography: Area: 1,229,737 sq. mi., one third the size of the U.S. **Location:** Occupies most of the Indian subcontinent in S. Asia. **Neighbors:** Pakistan on W, China, Nepal, Bhutan on N, Burma, Bangladesh on E. **Topography:** The Himalaya Mts., highest in world, stretch across India's northern borders. Below, the Ganges Plain is wide, fertile, and among the most densely populated regions of the world. The area below includes the Deccan Peninsula. Close to one quarter the area is forested. The climate varies from tropical heat in S to near-Arctic cold in N. Rajasthan Desert is in NW; NE Assam Hills get 400 in. of rain a year. **Capital:** New Delhi. **Cities** (1971 cen.): Bombay 5,970,575; Calcutta 3,148,746; Delhi 3,287,883; Madras 2,469,449; Hyderabad 1,607,396; Ahmedabad 1,585,544; Bangalore 1,540,741; Kanpur 1,154,388.

Government: Head of state: Pres. Neelam Sanjiva Reddy; b. May 19, 1913; in office: July 25, 1977. **Head of government:** Prime Min. Indira Gandhi, b. Nov. 19, 1917; in office: Jan. 14, 1980. **Local divisions:** 22 states, 9 union territories. **Armed forces:** regulars 1,096,000; reserves 200,000.

Economy: Industries: Textiles, steel, processed foods, cement, machinery, chemicals, fertilizers, consumer appliances, autos. **Chief crops:** Rice, grains, coffee, sugar cane, spices, tea, cashews, cotton, copra, coir, juta, linseed. **Minerals:** Chromium, coal, iron, manganese, mica salt, bauxite, gypsum, oil. **Crude oil reserves** (1980): 2.60 bln. bbls. **Other resources:** Rubber, timber. **Per capita arable land:** 0.6 acres. **Meat prod.** (1978): beef: 188,000 metric tons; pork: 65,000 metric tons; lamb: 393,000 metric tons. **Fish catch** (1977): 2.5 mln. metric tons. **Electricity prod.** (1978): 101.00 bln. kwh. **Crude steel prod.** (1979): 10.1 mln. metric tons. **Labor force:** 74% agric.

Finance: Currency: Rupee (Apr. 1981: 8.31 = $1 US). **Gross domestic product** (1978): $117.59 bln. **Per capita income** (1977): $150. **Imports** (1980): $12.6 bln.; partners (1978): U.S. 13%, Iran 9%, W. Ger. 9%, UK 8%. **Exports** (1980): $5.91 bln.; partners (1978): U.S. 13%, USSR 12%, UK 10%, Jap. 9%. **Tourists** (1977): 640,400; receipts: $350 mln. **National budget** (1977): $10.54 bln. revenues; $13.07 bln. expenditures. **International reserves less gold** (Jan. 1981): $6.99 bln. **Gold:** 8.59 mln. oz. t. **Consumer prices** (change in 1980): 11.5%.

Transport: Railway traffic (1977): 176.7 bln. passenger-km; (1978) 152.52 bln. net ton-km. **Motor vehicles** in use (1977): 805,400 passenger cars, 690,400 comm. vehicles; manuf. (1978): 45,600 passenger cars, 48,720 comm. vehicles. **Civil aviation:** 8,316 mln. passenger-km (1977); 304 mln. freight ton-km (1977). **Chief ports:** Calcutta, Bombay, Madras, Cochin, Vishakhapatnam.

Communications: Television sets: 280,000 licensed (1976). **Radios:** 14.85 mln. licensed (1976), 1.81 mln. manuf. (1977). **Telephones in use** (1978): 2,247,187. **Daily newspaper circ.** (1977): 10,672,000.

Health: Life expectancy at birth (1960): 41.89 male; 40.55 female. **Births** (per 1,000 pop. 1976): 34.4. **Deaths** (per 1,000 pop. 1976): 15.0. **Natural increase** (1976): 1.9%. **Hospital beds** (per 100,000 pop. 1977): 75. **Physicians** (per 100,000 pop. 1977): 26. **Infant mortality** (per 1,000 live births 1976): 122.

Education (1977): **Literacy:** 36%. **Pop. 5-19:** in school: 42%, teachers per 1,000: 13. **PQLI:** 43.

India has one of the oldest civilizations in the world. Excavations trace the Indus Valley civilization back for at least 5,000 years. Paintings in the mountain caves of Ajanta, richly carved temples, the Taj Mahal in Agra, and the Kutab Minar in Delhi are among relics of the past.

Aryan tribes, speaking Sanskrit, invaded from the NW around 1500 BC, and merged with the earlier inhabitants to create classical Indian civilization.

Asoka ruled most of the Indian subcontinent in the 3d century BC, and established Buddhism. But Hinduism revived and eventually predominated. During the Gupta kingdom, 4th-6th century AD, science, literature, and the arts enjoyed a "golden age."

Arab invaders established a Moslem foothold in the W in the 8th century, and Turkish Moslems gained control of North India by 1200. The Mogul emperors ruled 1526-1707.

Vasco de Gama established Portuguese trading posts 1498-1503. The Dutch followed. The British East India Co. sent Capt. William Hawkins, 1609, to get concessions from the Mogul emperor for spices and textiles. Operating as the East India Co. the British gained control of most of India. The British parliament assumed political direction; under Lord Bentinck, 1828-35, rule by rajahs was curbed. After the Sepoy troops mutinied, 1857-58, the British supported the native rulers.

Nationalism grew rapidly after World War I. The Indian National Congress and the Moslem League demanded constitutional reform. A leader emerged in Mohandas K. Gandhi (called Mahatma, or Great Soul), born Oct. 2, 1869, assassinated Jan. 30, 1948. He began advocating self-rule, non-violence, removal of untouchability in 1919. In 1930 he launched "civil disobedience," including boycott of British goods and rejection of taxes without representation.

In 1935 Britain gave India a constitution providing a bicameral federal congress. Mohammed Ali Jinnah, head of the Moslem League, sought creation of a Moslem nation, Pakistan.

The British government partitioned British India into the dominions of India and Pakistan. Aug. 15, 1947, was designated Indian Independence Day. India became a self-governing member of the Commonwealth and a member of the UN. It became a democratic republic, Jan. 26, 1950.

More than 12 million Hindu & Moslem refugees crossed the India-Pakistan borders in a mass transferral of some of the 2 peoples during 1947; about 200,000 were killed in communal fighting.

After Pakistan troops began attacks on Bengali separatists in East Pakistan, Mar. 25, 1971, some 10 million refugees fled into India. On Aug. 9, India and the USSR signed a 20-year friendship pact while U.S.-India relations soured. India and Pakistan went to war Dec. 3, 1971, on both the East and West fronts. Pakistan troops in the East surrendered Dec. 16; Pakistan agreed to a cease-fire in the West Dec. 17.

India and Pakistan signed a pact agreeing to withdraw troops from their borders and seek peaceful solutions, July 3, 1972. In Aug. 1973 India agreed to release 93,000 Pakistanis held prisoner since 1971; the return was completed in Apr. 1974. The 2 countries resumed full relations in 1976.

In 2 days of carnage, the Bengali population of the village of Mandai, Tripura State, 700 people, were massacred in a raid by indigenous tribal residents of the area, June 8-9, 1980. A similar year-long campaign against Bengali immigrants had been going on in Assam State.

Prime Min. Mrs. Indira Gandhi, named Jan. 19, 1966, was the 2d successor to Jawaharlal Nehru, India's prime minister from 1947 to his death, May 27, 1964.

Long the dominant power in India's politics, the Congress party lost some of its near monopoly by 1967. The party split into New and Old Congress parties in 1969. Mrs. Gandhi's New Congress party won control of the House.

Threatened with adverse court rulings in a voting law case, an opposition protest campaign and strikes, Gandhi invoked emergency provisions of the constitution June, 1975. Thousands of opponents were arrested and press censorship imposed. Measures to control prices, protect small farmers, and improve productivity were adopted.

The emergency, especially enforcement of coercive birth control measures in some areas, and the prominent extra-constitutional role of Indira Gandhi's son Sanjay, was widely resented. Opposition parties, united in the Janata coalition, scored massive victories in federal and state parliamentary elections in 1977, turning the New Congress Party from power.

Amid growing political tensions within the majority Janata party, and facing a censure vote in Parliament, Prime Min.

Morarji R. Desai resigned, July 15, 1979. He was succeeded by the coalition government of Charan Singh, which only lasted 24 days before the prime minister's resignation in the face of opposition from Indira Gandhi's New Congress Party.

With 350 candidates of her party winning seats to Parliament, Indira Gandhi became prime minister for the second time, Jan. 14, 1980.

India's 1st nuclear power plant, built with U.S. help, was dedicated in 1970 near Bombay; Canada helped India build 2 reactors. In May, 1974, India exploded a nuclear device underground, assertedly for peaceful development. Canada halted shipments of nuclear equipment and material to India. Restricted shipments from both the U.S. & Canada resumed in 1976. An Indian space satellite was launched by the USSR April 19, 1975.

Sikkim, bordered by Tibet, Bhutan, Nepal and India, formerly British protected, became a protectorate of India in 1950. Area, 2,818 sq. mi.; pop. 1977 est. 250,000; capital, Gangtok. In Sept. 1974 India's Parliament voted to make Sikkim an associate Indian state, absorbing it into India. The monarchy was abolished in an April, 1975, referendum.

Kashmir, a predominantly Moslem region in the northwest, has been in dispute between India and Pakistan since 1947. A cease-fire was negotiated by the UN Jan. 1, 1949; it gave Pakistan control of one-third of the area, in the west and northwest, and India the remaining two-thirds, the Indian state of Jammu and Kashmir, which enjoys internal autonomy. Repeated clashes broke out along the line.

There were also clashes in April 1965 along the Assam-East Pakistan border and in the **Rann** (swamp) **of Kutch** area along the West Pakistan-Gujarat border near the Arabian Sea. An international arbitration commission on Feb. 19, 1968, awarded 90% of the Rann to India, 10% to Pakistan.

France, 1952-54, peacefully yielded to India its 5 colonies, former French India, comprising Pondicherry, Karikal, Mahe, Yanaon (which became Pondicherry Union Territory, area 185 sq. mi., pop. 1971 471,707) and Chandernagor (which was incorporated into the state of West Bengal).

Goa, 1,429 sq. mi., pop., 1971, 795,120, which had been ruled by Portugal since 1505 AD, was taken by India by military action Dec. 18, 1961, together with 2 other Portuguese enclaves, Damán and Diu, located near Bombay.

Indonesia

Republic of Indonesia

People: Population (1980 est.): 151,890,000. **Age distrib.** (%): 0–14: 44.0; 15–59: 51.5; 60+: 4.5. **Pop. density:** 206.65 per sq. mi. **Urban** (1974): 18.2%. **Ethnic groups:** Javanese 45%, Sundanese 13.6%, Chinese 2.3%, others. **Languages:** Bahasa Indonesian (Malay) (official), Javanese, other Austronesian languages. **Religions:** Moslems 90%, Christians 5%, Hindus 3%.

Geography: Area: 735,268 sq. mi. **Location:** Archipelago SE of Asia along the Equator. **Neighbors:** Malaysia on N, Papua New Guinea on E. **Topography:** Indonesia comprises 13,000 islands, including Java (one of the most densely populated areas in the world with 1,500 persons to the sq. mi.), Sumatra, Kalimantan (most of Borneo), Sulawesi (Celebes), and West Irian (Irian Jaya, the W. half of New Guinea). Also: Bangka, Billiton, Madura, Bali, Timor. The mountains and plateaus on the major islands have a cooler climate than the tropical lowlands. **Capital:** Jakarta. **Cities** (1971 cen.): Jakarta 4,576,009; Surabaja 1,556,255; Bandung 1,201,730; Semarang 646,590; Medan 635,562.

Government: Head of state: Pres. Suharto; b. June 8, 1921; in office: Mar. 6, 1967. **Local divisions:** 27 provinces with elected legislatures, appointed governors. **Armed forces:** regulars 239,000; para-military 112,000.

Economy: Industries: Food processing, textiles, light industry. **Chief crops:** Rice, maize, cassava, peanuts, soybeans, tobacco, coffee, pepper, kapok, coconuts, palm oil, tea, sugar, indigo. **Minerals:** Nickel, tin, oil, coal, bauxite, manganese, copper gold, silver. **Crude oil reserves** (1980): 9.6 bln. bbls. **Other resources:** Rubber, cinchona. **Per capita arable land:** 0.3 acres. **Meat prod.** (1978): beef: 182,000 metric tons; pork: 108,000 metric tons, lamb: 38,000 metric tons. **Fish catch** (1977): 1.55 mln. metric tons. **Electricity prod.** (1977): 4.38 bln. kwh. **Crude steel prod.** (1979): 518,000 metric tons. **Labor force:** 61% agric.; 6% manuf.

Finance: Currency: Rupiah (Apr. 1981: 629 = $1 US). **Gross domestic product** (1980): $66.81 bln. **Per capita income** (1978): $304. **Imports** (1979): $7.20 bln.; partners (1978): Jap. 30%, U.S. 12%, W. Ger. 9%, Sing. 7%. **Exports** (1979): $15.59 bln · partners (1978): Jap. 29%, U.S. 26%, Sing. 11%, Trin./Tob. 5%. **Tourists** (1977): 457,000; receipts: $39 mln. **National budget** (1979): $11.26 bln. revenues; $11.52 bln. expenditures. **International reserves less gold** (Mar. 1981): $6.15 bln. **Gold:** 2.79 mln. oz t. **Consumer prices** (change in 1980): 18.5%.

Transport: Railway traffic (1978)· 4.46 bln. passenger-km; 980.4 mln. net ton-km. **Motor vehicles:** in use (1977): 479,300 passenger cars, 327,100 comm. vehicles; assembled (1977): 20,000 passenger cars, 69,400 comm. vehicles. **Civil aviation:** 3,912 mln. passenger-km (1977); 57 mln. freight ton-km (1977). **Chief ports:** Jakarta, Surabaja, Medan, Palembang, Semarang.

Communications: Television sets: 325,000 in use (1976), 482,000 manuf. (1977). **Radios:** 5.1 mln. licensed (1976), 1.0 mln. manuf. (1977). **Telephones in use** (1978): 324,546. **Daily newspaper circ.** (1976): 2,358,000.

Health: Life expectancy at birth (1960): 47.5 male; 47.5 female. **Births** (per 1,000 pop. 1975): 41.5. **Deaths** (per 1,000 pop. 1975): 16.7. **Natural increase** (1975): 2.5%. **Hospital beds** (per 100,000 pop. 1977): 60. **Physicians** (per 100,000 pop. 1977): 7. **Infant mortality** (per 1,000 live births 1975): 125.

Education (1977): **Literacy:** 62%. **Pop. 5-19:** in school: 39%, teachers per 1,000: 14. **PQLI:** 55.

Hindu and Buddhist civilization from India reached the peoples of Indonesia nearly 2,000 years ago, taking root especially in Java. Islam spread along the maritime trade routes in the 15th century, and became predominant by the 16th century. The Dutch replaced the Portuguese as the most important European trade power in the area in the 17th century. They secured territorial control over Java by 1750. The outer islands were not finally subdued until the early 20th century, when the full area of present-day Indonesia was united under one rule for the first time in history.

Following Japanese occupation, 1942-45, nationalists led by Sukarno and Hatta proclaimed a republic. The Netherlands ceded sovereignty Dec. 27, 1949, after 4 years of fighting. West Irian, on New Guinea, remained under Dutch control.

After the Dutch in 1957 rejected proposals for new negotiations over West Irian, Indonesia stepped up the seizure of Dutch property. A U.S. mediator's plan was adopted in 1962. In 1963 the UN turned the area over to Indonesia, which promised a plebiscite. In 1969, voting by tribal chiefs favored staying with Indonesia, despite an uprising and widespread opposition.

Sukarno suspended Parliament in 1960, and was named president for life in 1963. Russian-armed Indonesian troops staged raids in 1964 and 1965 into Malaysia, whose formation Sukarno had opposed. Indonesia withdrew from the UN in 1965; anti-American demonstrations were staged.

Indonesia's popular, pro-Peking Communist party tried to seize control in 1965; the army smashed the coup, later intimated that Sukarno had played a role in it. In parts of Java, Communists seized several districts before being defeated; over 300,000 Communists were executed.

Gen. Suharto, head of the army, was named president for 5 years in 1968, reelected 1973 and 1978. A coalition of his supporters won a strong majority in House elections in 1971, the first national vote in 16 years. Moslem opposition parties made gains in 1977 elections. The military retains a predominant political role.

In 1966 Indonesia and Malaysia signed an agreement ending hostility, and Indonesia reentered the UN. After ties with Peking were cut in 1967, there were riots against the economically important ethnic Chinese minority. Riots against Chinese and Japanese also occurred in 1974.

The former Portuguese Timor became Indonesia's 27th province in 1976 during a local civil war. Thousands of civilians were reportedly killed by the Indonesians.

Oil export earnings, and a decline in the high birth rate, have given hope for future improvements in very low living conditions.

Iran

Islamic Republic of Iran

People: Population (1980 est.): 38,080,000. **Age distrib. (%):** 0–14: 44.4; 15–59: 50.3; 60+: 5.2. **Pop. density:** 59.84 per

sq. mi. **Urban** (1976): 46.8%. **Ethnic groups:** Iranian groups 66%, Turkish groups 25%, Kurds 5%, Arabs 4%. **Languages:** Farsi, Turk, Kurdish, Arabic, English, French. **Religions:** Moslems 98% (Shiite [official] 93%, Sunni 5%), Christians, Jews, Zoroastrians.

Geography: Area: 636,363 sq. mi. **Location:** Between the Middle East and S. Asia. **Neighbors:** Turkey, Iraq on W, USSR of N (Armenia, Azerbaijan, Turkmenistan), Afghanistan, Pakistan on E. **Topography:** Interior highlands and plains are surrounded by high mountains, up to 18,000 ft. Large salt deserts cover much of the area, but there are many oases and forest areas. Most of the population inhabits the N and NW. **Capital:** Teheran. **Cities** (1976 cen.): Teheran 4,496,159; Isfahan 671,825; Mashhad 670,180; Tabriz 598,576.

Government: Religious head (Faghi): Ayatollah Ruhollah Khomeini, b. 1901. **Head of state:** Prime Minister Mohammed Ali Rajai; in office July 24, 1981. **Local divisions:** 21 provinces, 2 governorates. **Armed forces:** regulars 415,000; reserves 300,000.

Economy: Industries: Steel, petrochemicals, cement, auto assembly, sugar refining, carpets. **Chief crops:** Grains, rice, fruits, sugar beets, cotton, grapes. **Minerals:** Chromium, oil, gas, copper, iron, lead, manganese, zinc, barite, sulphur, coal, emeralds, turquoise. **Crude oil reserves** (1980): 58.00 bln. bbls. **Other resources:** Gums, wool, silk, caviar. **Per capita arable land:** 1.1 acres. **Meat prod.** (1978): beef: 118,000 metric tons; lamb: 243,000 metric tons. **Electricity prod.** (1977): 18.00 bln. kwh. **Crude steel prod.** (1979 est.) 1.4 mln. metric tons. **Labor force:** 37% agric.; 27% manuf.

Finance: Currency: Rial (Apr. 1981: 76.85 = $1 US). **Gross domestic product** (1977): $76.37 bln. **Per capita income** (1976): $1,986. **Imports** (1980): $10.55 bln.; partners (1978 est.): U.S. 20%, W. Ger. 19%, Jap. 15%, UK 8%. **Exports** (1980): $13.64 bln.; partners (1978 est.): Jap. 17%, U.S. 13%, W. Ger. 9%, U.S. Vir. Is. 7%. **Tourists** (1977): 690,500; receipts: $153 mln. **National budget** (1978): $22.87 bln. revenues; $29.61 bln. expenditures. **International reserves less gold** (Jun. 1980): $15.48 bln. **Gold:** 4.34 mln. oz t. **Consumer prices** (change in 1980): 20.7%.

Transport: Railway traffic (1976): 3.51 bln. passenger-km; 4.63 bln. net ton-km. **Motor vehicles:** in use (1977): 932,700 passenger cars, 204,000 comm. vehicles; assembled (1977): 103,000 passenger cars; 65,000 comm. vehicles. **Chief ports:** Khorramshahr, Bushehr, Bandar-e Shahpur, Bendar Abbas.

Communications: Television sets: 1.7 mln. in use (1976), 293,000 manuf. (1976). **Radios:** 2.1 mln. in use (1976), 151,000 manuf. (1976). **Telephones in use** (1978): 828,576. **Daily newspaper circ.** (1976): 473,000.

Health: Life expectancy at birth (1976): 57.63 male; 57.44 female. **Births** (per 1,000 pop. 1975): 42.5. **Deaths** (per 1,000 pop. 1975): 11.5. **Natural increase** (1975): 3.1%. **Hospital beds** (per 100,000 pop. 1977): 148. **Physicians** (per 100,000 pop. 1977): 39. **Infant mortality** (per 1,000 live births 1975): 108.1.

Education (1977): **Literacy:** 50% **Pop. 5-19:** in school: 51%, teachers per 100,000: 20. **PQLI:** 52.

Iran is the official name of the country long known as Persia. The Iranians, who supplanted an earlier agricultural civilization, came from the E during the 2d millenium BC; they were an Indo-European group related to the Aryans of India.

In 549 BC Cyrus the Great united the Medes and Persians in the Persian Empire, conquered Babylonia in 538 BC, restored Jerusalem to the Jews. Alexander the Great conquered Persia in 333 BC, but Persians regained their independence in the next century under the Parthians, themselves succeeded by Sassanian Persians in 226 AD. Arabs brought Islam to Persia in the 7th century, replacing the indigenous Zoroastrian faith. After Persian political and cultural autonomy was reasserted in the 9th century, the arts and sciences flourished for several centuries.

Turks and Mongols ruled Persia in turn from the 11th century to 1502, when a native dynasty reasserted full independence. The British and Russian empires vied for influence in the 19th century, and Afghanistan was severed from Iran by Britain in 1857.

The previous dynasty was founded by Reza Khan, a military leader, in 1925. He abdicated as shah in 1941, and was succeeded by his son, Mohammad Reza Pahlavi.

British and Russian forces entered Iran Aug. 25, 1941, withdrawing later. Britain and the USSR signed an agreement Jan. 29, 1942, to respect Iranian integrity and give economic aid. In 1946 a Soviet attempt to take over the Azerbaijan region in the NW was defeated when a puppet regime was ousted by force.

Parliament, under Premier Mohammed Mossadegh, nationalized the oil industry in 1951, leading to a British blockade. Mossadegh was overthrown in 1953; the shah assumed control. Under his rule, Iran underwent economic and social change. However, political opposition was not tolerated. Thousands were arrested in the 1970s, while hundreds of purported terrorists were executed.

Conservative Moslem protests led to 1978 violence. Martial law in 12 cities was declared Sept. 8. A military government was appointed Nov. 6 to deal with striking oil workers. Continued clashes with demonstrators led to greater violence; oil production fell to a 27-year low, Dec. 27. In a 3d change of government in 5 months, Prime Min. Shahpur Bakhtiar was designated by the shah to head a regency council in his absence. The shah left Iran Jan. 16, 1979.

Violence continued throughout January. Exiled religious leader Ayatollah Ruhollah Khomeini named a provisional government council in preparation for his return to Iran, Jan. 31. Clashes between Khomeini's supporters and government troops culminated in a rout of Iran's elite Imperial Guard Feb. 11, leading to the fall of Bakhtiar's government. Ayatollah Khomeini's choice for prime minister, Mehdi Bazargan, headed an interim government pledged to establish an Islamic republic, but resigned Nov. 6, 1979, conceding power to the Islamic authority of Ayatollah Khomeini.

The Iranian revolution was marked by revolts among the ethnic minorities and by a continuing struggle between the clerical forces and westernized intellectuals and liberals. The Islamic Constitution, drafted under the domination of the clergy, established final authority to be vested in a Faghi, the Ayatollah Khomeini.

Iranian militants seized the U.S. embassy, Nov. 4, 1979, and took 90 hostages including some 65 Americans. The students vowed to stay in the embassy until the deposed shah was returned to Iran to stand trial. Despite international condemnations and U.S. efforts, including an abortive Apr., 1980, rescue attempt, the crisis continued. The U.S. broke diplomatic relations with Iran, Apr. 7th. The shah died in Egypt, July 27th.

The hostage drama finally ended Jan. 21, 1981 when an accord, involving the release of frozen Iranian assets, was reached. Minutes after Ronald Reagan was sworn in as 40th president, the 52 Americans flew to freedom.

Turmoil continued in Teheran however. The ruling Islamic Party, increasingly dissatisfied with President Abolhassan Bani-Sadr, declared him unfit for office. In the weeks following Bani-Sadr's dismissal, June 22, 1981, and retreat into hiding, a new wave of executions began. 200 people, reportedly members of the Majahedeen-i-Khalq and smaller Marxist-Leninist/Maoist factions, had died before revolutionary firing squads as of July 13, 1981.

Then on June 28, 1981, a bomb destroyed the Teheran headquarters of Iran's ruling Islamic Party, killing the party's leader, Chief Justice Ayatollah Mohammed Beheshti, and 73 other high-ranking party members. (*See Index for Chronology.*)

Iraq

Republic of Iraq

People: Population (1980 est.): 13,080,000. **Age distrib. (%):** 0–14: 48.3; 15–59: 46.5; 60+: 5.3. **Pop. density:** 76.04 per sq. mi. **Urban** (1977): 65.9%. **Ethnic groups:** Arabs 78%, Kurds 18%, Persians 1.2%, Turks 1.2%, Assyrians 0.5%. **Languages:** Arabic (official), Kurdish, others. **Religions:** Moslems 95% (Shiites two-thirds, Sunnis one-third), Christians 3%.

Geography: Area: 172,000 sq. mi., larger than California. **Location:** In the Middle East, occupying most of historic Mesopotamia. **Neighbors:** Jordan, Syria on W, Turkey on N, Iran on E, Kuwait, Saudi Arabia on S. **Topography:** Mostly an alluvial plain, including the Tigris and Euphrates rivers, descending from mountains in N to desert in SW. Persian Gulf region is marshland. **Capital:** Baghdad. **Cities** (1975 est.): Baghdad (met.) 3,205,645.

Government: Head of state: Pres. Saddam Hussein, b. 1935 in office: July 16, 1979. **Local divisions:** 18 governorates. **Armed forces:** regulars 222,000; reserves 250,000.

Economy: Industries: Textiles, food processing, cigarettes, oil refining, cement. **Chief crops:** Grains, rice, dates, cotton, tobacco. **Minerals:** Oil, gas. **Crude oil reserves** (1980): 31.00 bln. bbls. **Other resources:** Wool, hides. **Per capita arable land:** 1.0 acres. **Meat prod.** (1978): beef: 50,000 metric tons; lamb: 50,000 metric tons. **Fish catch** (1977): 26,100 metric tons. **Electricity prod.** (1977): 5.00 bln. kwh. **Labor force:** 50% agric.

Finance: Currency: Dinar (Apr. 1981: 0.29 = $1 US). **Gross domestic product** (1977 est.): $19 bln. **Per capita income** (1978): $1,561. **Imports** (1980): $12.94 bln.; partners (1977): W. Ger. 18%, Jap. 18%, UK 7%, Fr. 6%. **Exports** (1980): $26.35 bln.; partners (1977): Fr. 17%, It. 16%, Braz. 9%, UK 8%. **Tourists** (1977): 721,600; receipts (1975): $84 mln. **International reserves less gold** (Dec. 1977): $6.82 bln. **Gold:** 4.14 mln. oz t. **Consumer prices** (change in 1978): 4.6%.

Transport: Railway traffic (1976): 797 mln. passenger-km; 2.25 bln. net ton-km. **Motor vehicles:** in use (1977): 150,400 passenger cars, 74,500 comm. vehicles. **Civil aviation:** 1,334 mln. passenger-km (1978); 41 mln. freight ton-km (1978). **Chief ports:** Basra.

Communications: Television sets: 425,000 in use (1976), 25,000 manuf. (1975). **Radios:** 1.25 mln. in use (1975). **Telephones in use** (1978): 319,591. **Daily newspaper circ.** (1976): 202,000.

Health: Life expectancy at birth (1975): 51.2 male; 54.3 female. **Births** (per 1,000 pop. 1975): 47.4. **Deaths** (per 1,000 pop. 1975): 14.6. **Natural increase** (1975): 3.3%. **Hospital beds** (per 100,000 pop. 1977): 199. **Physicians** (per 100,000 pop. 1977): 44. **Infant mortality** (per 1,000 live births 1977): 28.

Education (1977): **Literacy:** 30%. **Pop. 5-19:** in school: 60% teachers per 1,000: 22. **PQLI:** 45.

The Tigris-Euphrates valley, formerly called Mesopotamia was the site of one of the earliest civilizations in the world. The Sumerian city-states of 3,000 BC originated the culture later developed by the Semitic Akkadians, Babylonians, and Assyrians.

Mesopotamia ceased to be a separate entity after the conquests of the Persians, Greeks, and Arabs. The latter founded Baghdad, from where the caliph ruled a vast empire in the 8th and 9th centuries. Mongol and Turkish conquests led to a decline in population, the economy, cultural life, and the irrigation system.

Britain secured a League of Nations mandate over Iraq after World War I. Independence under a king came in 1932. A leftist pan-Arab revolution established a republic in 1958, which oriented foreign policy toward the USSR. Most industry has been nationalized, and large land holdings broken up.

A local faction of the international Baath Arab Socialist party has ruled by decree since 1968. Russia and Iraq signed an ai pact in 1972, and arms were sent along with several thousan advisers. The 1978 execution of 21 Communists and a shift o trade to the West signalled a more neutral policy, straining rela tions with the USSR. In the 1973 Arab-Israeli war Iraq ser forces to aid Syria. Relations with Syria were improving steadi to negotiations of uniting the 2 nations as a single political entit but were halted by the Hussein government, July, 1979. Within month of assuming power, Saddam Hussein instituted a blooc purge in the wake of a reported coup attempt against the ne regime.

Years of battling with the Kurdish minority resulted in total de feat for the Kurds in 1975, when Iran withdrew support. Kurdi rebels continued their war, 1979; fighting led to Iraqi bombing Kurdish villages in Iran, causing relations with Iran to deteriorat

After skirmishing intermittently for 10 months over the sove eignty of the disputed Shatt al-Arab waterway that divides th two countries, Iraq and Iran, Sept. 22, 1980, entered into ope warfare when Iraqi fighter-bombers attacked 10 Iranian airfield including Teheran airport, and Iranian planes retaliated wi strikes on 2 Iraqi bases. In the following days, there was hea ground fighting around Abadan and the adjacent port of Khi ramshahr as Iraq pressed its attack on Iran's oil-rich province Khuzistan. Fighting has continued to the present with little pro pect for a negotiated settlement. (*See Index for Chronology.*)

Ireland

Irish Republic

People: Population (1979 est.): 3,365,000. **Age distrib. (%** 0–14: 31.2; 15–59: 53.5; 60+:15.3. **Pop. density:** 121.8 per s mi. **Urban** (1971): 52.2%. **Ethnic groups:** Irish, Anglo-Irish minority. **Languages:** English predominates, Irish (Gaelic) spoken by minority. **Religions:** Roman Catholics 94%, Anglican 5%.

Geography: Area: 26,600 sq. mi. **Location:** In the Atlantic O. just W of Great Britain. **Neighbors:** United Kingdom (Northern Ireland). **Topography:** Ireland consists of a central plateau surrounded by isolated groups of hills and mountains. The coastline is heavily indented by the Atlantic O. **Capital:** Dublin. **Cities** (1971 cen.): Dublin 566,034; Cork (met.) 128,235.

Government: Head of State: Pres. Patrick J. Hillery; b. May 2, 1923; in office: Dec. 3, 1976. **Head of government:** Prime Min. Charles J. Haughey; b. Sept. 26, 1925; in office: Dec. 11, 1979. **Local divisions:** 26 counties. **Armed forces:** regulars 14,581; reserves 18,661.

Economy: Industries: Tobacco, food processing, auto assembly, metals, textiles, chemicals, brewing, electrical and nonelectrical machinery, tourism. **Chief crops:** Potatoes, grain, sugar beets, fruits, vegetables. **Minerals:** Zinc, lead, silver, gas. **Per capita arable land:** 0.8 acres. **Meat prod.** (1978): beef: 384,000 metric tons; pork: 132,000 metric tons; lamb: 40,000 metric tons. **Fish catch** (1977): 95,500 metric tons. **Electricity prod.** (1978): 9.97 bln. kwh. **Crude steel prod.** (1979): 72,000 metric tons. **Labor force:** 23% agric.; 30% manuf.

Finance: Currency: Pound (Apr. 1981: 0.60 = $1 US). **Gross domestic product** (1979): 14.89 bln. **Per capita income** (1977): $2,711. **Imports** (1980): $11.51 bln.; partners (1978): UK 49% U.S. 8%, W. Ger. 7%, Fr. 5%. **Exports** (1980): $8.50 bln.; partners (1978): UK 47%, Fr. 9%, W. Ger. 8%, U.S. 6%. **Tourists** (1977): 566,000; receipts $308 mln. **National budget** (1980): $6.70 bln. revenues; $9.35 bln. expenditures. **International reserves less gold** (Apr. 1981): $2.22 bln. **Gold:** 357,000 oz. t. **Consumer prices** (change in 1980): 18.2%.

Transport: Railway traffic (1978): 964.8 mln. passenger-km; 630 mln. net ton-km. **Motor vehicles:** in use (1979): 682,960 passenger cars, 61,540 comm. vehicles; assembled (1978): 45,492 passenger cars; 2,376 comm. vehicles. **Civil aviation:** 1,836 mln. passenger-km (1978); 86 mln. freight ton-km. (1978). **Chief ports:** Dublin, Cork.

Communications: Television sets: 655,000 licensed (1976), 112,000 manuf. (1977). **Radios:** 949,000 licensed (1975), 72,000 manuf. (1973). **Telephones in use** (1978): 519,000. **Daily newspaper circ.** (1977): 702,000; 220 per 1,000 pop.

Health: Life expectancy at birth (1972): 68.77 male; 73.52 female. **Births** (per 1,000 pop. 1979): 21.5. **Deaths** (per 1,000 pop. 1979): 9.7. **Natural increase** (1977): 1.1%. **Hospital beds** (per 100,000 pop. 1977): 1,051. **Physicians** (per 100,000 pop. 1977): 116. **Infant mortality** per 1,000 live births 1977): 15.7.

Education (1977): **Literacy:** 99%. **Pop. 5-19:** in school: 72%, teachers per 1,000: 30. **PQLI:** 93.

Celtic tribes invaded the islands about the 4th century BC; their Gaelic culture and literature flourished and spread to Scotland and elsewhere in the 5th century AD, the same century in which St. Patrick converted the Irish to Christianity. Invasions by Norsemen began in the 8th century, ended with defeat of the Danes by the Irish King Brian Boru in 1014. English invasions started in the 12th century; for over 700 years the Anglo-Irish struggle continued with bitter rebellions and savage repressions.

The Easter Monday Rebellion (1916) failed but was followed by guerrilla warfare and harsh reprisals by British troops, the "Black and Tans." The Dail Eireann, or Irish parliament, reaffirmed independence in Jan. 1919. The British offered dominion status to Ulster (6 counties) and southern Ireland (26 counties) Dec. 1921. The constitution of the Irish Free State, a British dominion, was adopted Dec. 11, 1922. Northern Ireland remained part of the United Kingdom.

A new constitution adopted by plebiscite came into operation Dec. 29, 1937. It declared the name of the state Eire in the Irish language (Ireland in the English) and declared it a sovereign democratic state.

On Dec. 21, 1948, an Irish law declared the country a republic rather than a dominion and withdrew it from the Commonwealth. The British Parliament recognized both actions, 1949, but reasserted its claim to incorporate the 6 northeastern counties in the United Kingdom. This claim has not been recognized by Ireland. *(See United Kingdom — Northern Ireland.)*

First president was William T. Cosgrave, 1922-32. Eamon de Valera, hero of the rebellion, was president 1932-37, 1959-66, 1966-73; prime minister 1937-48, 1951-54, 1957-59.

Irish governments have favored peaceful unification of all Ireland. Ireland cooperated with England against terrorist groups.

Israel
State of Israel

People: Population (1980 est.): 3,880,000. **Age distrib.** (%): 0–14: 33.2; 15–59: 63.0; 60+: 11.7. **Pop. density:** 448.96 per sq. mi. **Urban** (1977): 87.2%. **Ethnic groups:** Jews (half Ashkenazi, half Sephardi), Arabs, Druzes, Christians. **Languages:** Hebrew and Arabic (official), Yiddish, various European and West Asian languages. **Religions:** Jews 85%, Moslems 11%, Christians 2.5%, Druzes 1.2%.

Geography: Area: 8,219 sq. mi. (the size of Massachusetts), the "Green Line" border before the 1967 war; 2,986 sq. mi. occupied territory, excluding Sinai Peninsula, 23,622 sq. mi. **Location:** On eastern end of Mediterranean Sea. **Neighbors:** Lebanon on N, Syria, Jordan on E, Egypt on W. **Topography:** The Mediterranean coastal plain is fertile and well-watered. In the center is the Judean Plateau. A triangular-shaped semi-desert region, the Negev, extends from south of Beersheba to an apex at the head of the Gulf of Aqaba. The eastern border drops sharply into the Jordan Rift Valley, including Lake Tiberias (Sea of Galilee) and the Dead Sea, which is 1,296 ft. below sea level, lowest point on the earth's surface. **Capital:** Jerusalem. **Cities** (1978 est.): Jerusalem 376,000; Tel Aviv-Yafo 343,300; Haifa 227,800.

Government: Head of state: Pres. Yitzhak Navon; b. Apr. 19, 1921; in office: May 29, 1978. **Head of government:** Prime Min. Menachem Begin; b. Aug. 16, 1913; in office: June 21, 1977. **Local divisions:** 6 administrative districts. **Armed forces:** regulars 165,600; reserves 460,000.

Economy: Industries: Diamond cutting, textiles, electronics, machinery, plastics, tires, drugs, aircraft, munitions, wine. **Chief crops:** Citrus fruit, grains, olives, fruits, grapes, figs, cotton, vegetables. **Minerals:** Potash, limestone, gypsum, copper, iron, phosphates, magnesium, manganese, salt, sulphur. **Crude oil reserves** (1980): 1.0 mln. bbls. **Per capita arable land:** 0.2 acres. **Meat prod.** (1978): beef: 26,000 metric tons; pork: 10,000 metric tons. **Fish catch** (1977): 24,400 metric tons. **Electricity prod.** (1978): 11.89 bln. kwh. **Crude steel prod.** (1979): 107,000 metric tons. **Labor force:** 6.5% agric.; 25.3% manuf.

Finance: Currency: Shekel (Mar. 1981: 8.87 = $1 US). **Gross domestic product** (1980): $19.91 bln. **Per capita income** (1978): $3,332. **Imports** (1979): $8.59 bln.; partners: U.S. 19%, Switz. 11%, W. Ger. 10%, UK 9%. **Exports** (1980): $5.53 bln.; partners: U.S. 17%, W. Ger. 9%, HK 8%, UK 7%. **Tourists** (1977): 893,900; receipts $461 mln. **National budget** (1977): $7.20 bln. revenues; $8 bln. expenditures. **International reserves less gold** (Mar. 1981): $3.51 bln. **Gold:** 1.22 mln. oz t. **Consumer prices** (change in 1980): 131.0%.

Transport: Railway traffic (1978): 220.8 mln. passenger-km; 636 mln. net ton-km. **Motor vehicles:** in use (1977): 312,700 passenger cars, 107,600 comm. vehicles; assembled (1978): 2,604 passenger cars, 4,140 comm. vehicles. **Civil aviation:** 4,692 mln. passenger-km (1977); 179 mln. freight ton-km (1977). **Chief ports:** Haifa, Ashdod, Eilat.

Communications: Television sets: 475,000 in use (1976), 48,000 manuf. (1977). **Radios:** 655,000 in use (1976), 10,000 manuf. (1976). **Telephones in use** (1978): 929,837. **Daily newspaper circ.** (1976): 801,000; 231 per 1,000 pop.

Health: Life expectancy at birth (1977): 71.32 male; 74.68 female. **Births** (per 1,000 pop. 1980): 24.1. **Deaths** (per 1,000 pop. 1980): 6.7%. **Natural increase** (1977): 2.0%. **Hospital beds** (per 100,000 pop. 1977): 556. **Physicians** (per 100,000 pop. 1977): 277. **Infant mortality** (per 1,000 live births 1977): 17.8.

Education (1977): **Literacy:** 88%. **Pop. 5-19:** in school: 62%, teachers per 1,000: 50. **PQLI:** 91.

Occupying the SW corner of the ancient Fertile Crescent, Israel contains some of the oldest known evidence of agriculture and of primitive town life. A more advanced civilization emerged in the 3d millenium BC. The Hebrews probably arrived early in the 2d millenium BC. Under King David and his successors (c.1000 BC-597 BC), Judaism was developed and secured. After conquest by Babylonians, Persians, and Greeks, an independent Jewish kingdom was revived, 168 BC, but Rome took effective control in the next century, suppressed Jewish revolts in 70 AD and 135 AD, and renamed Judea Palestine, after the earlier coastal inhabitants, the Philistines.

Arab invaders conquered Palestine in 636. The Arabic language and Islam prevailed within a few centuries, but a Jewish minority remained. The land was ruled from the 11th century as a part of non-Arab empires by Seljuks, Mamluks, and Ottomans (with a crusader interval, 1098-1291).

After 4 centuries of Ottoman rule, during which the population declined to a low of 350,000 (1785), the land was taken in 1917 by Britain, which in the Balfour Declaration that year pledged to support a Jewish national homeland there, as foreseen by the Zionists. In 1920 a British Palestine Mandate was recognized; in 1922 the land east of the Jordan was detached.

Jewish immigration, begun in the late 19th century, swelled in the 1930s with refugees from the Nazis; heavy Arab immigration from Syria and Lebanon also occurred. Arab opposition to Jewish immigration turned violent in 1920, 1921, 1929, and 1936. The UN General Assembly voted in 1947 to partition Palestine into an Arab and a Jewish state. Britain withdrew in May 1948.

Israel was declared an independent state May 14, 1948; the Arabs rejected partition. Egypt, Jordan, Syria, Lebanon, Iraq, and Saudi Arabia invaded, but failed to destroy the Jewish state, which gained territory. Separate armistices with the Arab nations were signed in 1949; Jordan occupied the West Bank, Egypt occupied Gaza, but neither granted Palestinian autonomy. No peace settlement was obtained, and the Arab nations continued policies of economic boycott, blockade in the Suez Canal, and support of guerrillas. Several hundred thousand Arabs left the area of Jewish control; an equal number of Jews left the Arab countries for Israel 1949-53.

After persistent terrorist raids, Israel invaded Egypt's Sinai, Oct. 29, 1956, aided briefly by British and French forces. A UN cease-fire was arranged Nov. 6.

An uneasy truce between Israel and the Arab countries, supervised by a UN Emergency Force, prevailed until May 19, 1967, when the UN force withdrew at the demand of Egypt's Pres. Nasser. Egyptian forces reoccupied the Gaza Strip and closed the Gulf of Aqaba to Israeli shipping. In a 6-day war that started June 5, the Israelis took the Gaza Strip, occupied the Sinai Peninsula to the Suez Canal, and captured Old Jerusalem, Syria's Golan Heights, and Jordan's West Bank. The fighting was halted June 10 by UN-arranged cease-fire agreements.

Egypt and Syria attacked Israel, Oct. 6, 1973 (Yom Kippur, most solemn day on the Jewish calendar). Egypt and Syria were supplied by massive USSR military airlifts; the U.S. responded with an airlift to Israel. Israel counter-attacked, driving the Syrians back, and crossed the Suez Canal.

A cease fire took effect Oct. 24; a UN peace-keeping force went to the area. A disengagement agreement was signed Jan. 18, 1974, following negotiations by U.S. Secretary of State Henry Kissinger. Israel withdrew from the canal's W bank. A second withdrawal was completed in 1976; Israel yielded additional territory including an oil field. Some 200 unarmed American technicians were stationed to monitor the cease-fire. The U.S. agreed to provide substantial arms aid to Israel.

Israel and Syria agreed to disengage June 1; Israel completed withdrawing from its salient (and a small part of the land taken in the 1967 war) June 25. Nearly all black African nations broke relations with Israel in 1972-74, reportedly at the urging of Libya, despite Israel's technical aid programs.

In the wake of the war, Golda Meir, long Israel's premier, resigned; severe inflation gripped the nation. Palestinian guerrillas staged massacres, killing scores of civilians 1974-75. Israel conducted preventive attacks in Lebanon through 1975. Israel aided Christian forces in the 1975-76 Lebanese civil war.

Israeli forces raided Entebbe, Uganda, July 3, 1976, and rescued 103 hostages seized by Arab and German terrorists.

In 1977, the conservative opposition, led by Menachem Begin, was voted into office for the first time. Egypt Pres. Sadat's visit to Jerusalem Nov. 1977 raised peace hopes, but the issue of Arab Palestinian autonomy or independence complicated negotiations. On Mar. 26, 1979, Egypt and Israel signed a formal peace treaty, ending 30 years of war, and establishing diplomatic relations.

A massive Israeli invasion of S. Lebanon, March 1978, following a Lebanon-based terrorist attack in Israel, left over 1,000 Lebanese and Palestinians dead. Israel withdrew in favor of a 6,000-man UN force, but continued to aid Christian militiamen.

A 5-day occupation of Israeli forces in southern Lebanon took place April 1980, in retaliation to the Palestinian raid on a kibbutz earlier that month. Violence on the Israeli-occupied West Bank rose in 1980. (*See Index for Chronology.*)

Israel affirmed the entire city of Jerusalem as its capital, July, 1980, annexing the annexed Arab East Jerusalem.

Israel shot down, Apr. 28, 1981, two Syrian helicopters Israel claimed were attacking Lebanese Christian militia forces in the Beirut-Zahle area of Lebanon. Syria responded by installing Soviet-built surface-to-air missiles in Lebanon. Both the U.S. and Israel were unable to persuade Syria to withdraw the missiles, and Israel threatened to destroy them.

On June 7, 1981, Israeli jets destroyed an Iraqi atomic reactor near Baghdad that, Israel claimed, would have enabled Iraq to manufacture nuclear weapons. The attack came as a complete surprise to Israeli friends and foes alike, and brought widespread condemnation.

In a close election, June 30, 1981, Prime Min. Menachem Begin was able to assemble a narrow coalition, but his slender one-seat majority could mean new elections within a year.

Italy
Italian Republic

People: Population (1980 est.): 57,040,000. **Age distrib. (%):** 0–14: 23.7; 15–59: 58.8; 60+: 17.5. **Pop. density:** 490.44 per sq. mi. **Ethnic groups:** Italians, small minorities of Germans, Slovenes, Albanians, French, Ladins, Greeks. **Languages:** Italian. **Religions:** Roman Catholics 99%.

Geography: Area: 116,303 sq. mi., slightly larger than Arizona. **Location:** In S Europe, jutting into Mediterranean S. **Neighbors:** France on W, Switzerland, Austria on N, Yugoslavia on E. **Topography:** Occupies a long boot-shaped peninsula, extending SE from the Alps into the Mediterranean, with the islands of Sicily and Sardinia offshore. The alluvial Po Valley drains most of N. The rest of the country is rugged and mountainous, except for intermittent coastal plains, like the Campajna, S of Rome. Appenine Mts. run down through center of peninsula. **Capital:** Rome. **Cities** (1978 est.): Rome 2,897,505; Milan 1,706,268; Naples 1,225,227; Turin 1,181,567; Genoa 795,027.

Government: Head of state: Pres. Alessandro Pertini; b. Sept. 25, 1896; in office: July 9, 1978; **Head of government:** Prime Min. Giovanni Spadolini; in office: June 9, 1981. **Local divisions:** 20 regions with some autonomy, 93 provinces. **Armed forces:** regulars 365,000; reserves 738,000.

Economy: Industries: Steel, machinery, autos, textiles, shoes, machine tools, chemicals, oil products, typewriters. **Chief crops:** Grapes, olives, citrus fruits, vegetables, wheat, rice. **Minerals:** Mercury, potash, gas, marble, sulphur, coal. **Crude oil reserves** (1980): 645 mln. blns. **Per capita arable land:** 0.4 acres. **Meat prod.** (1978): beef: 1.10 mln. metric tons; pork: 920,000 metric tons; lamb: 53,000 metric tons. **Fish catch** (1977): 427,000 metric tons. **Electricity prod.** (1978): 174.77 bln. kwh. **Crude steel prod.** (1979): 24.3 mln. metric tons. **Labor force:** 15% agric.; 38% ind. and commerce; 46% services.

Finance: Currency: Lira (Apr. 1981: 1,102.00 = $1 US). **Gross domestic product** (1979): $323.60 bln. **Per capita income** (1977): $3,076. **Imports** (1980): $99.48 bln.; partners (1978): W. Ger. 17%, Fr. 15%, U.S. 7%. **Exports** (1980): $77.91 bln.; partners (1978): W. Ger. 19%, Fr. 14%, U.S. 7%, UK 6%. **Tourists** (1977): 14,836,100; receipts $4.76 bln. **National budget** (1980): $108.12 bln. revenues; $141.90 bln. expenditures. **International reserves less gold** (Mar. 1981): $17.97 bln. **Gold:** 66.67 mln. oz t. **Consumer prices** (change in 1980): 21.2%.

Transport: Railway traffic (1978): 39.2 bln. passenger-km; 16.6 bln. net ton-km. **Motor vehicles:** in use (1977): 16.4 mln. passenger cars, (1976) 1.7 comm. vehicles; manuf. (1978): 1.51 mln. passenger cars, 146,400 comm. vehicles. **Civil aviation:** 12,816 mln. passenger-km (1977); 528 mln. freight ton-km (1977). **Chief ports:** Genoa, Venice, Trieste, Taranto, Naples, La Spezia.

Communications: Television sets: 12.38 mln. licensed (1976), 1.8 mln. manuf. (1976). **Radios:** 13.02 mln. licensed (1976), 1.54 mln. manuf. (1976). **Telephones in use** (1978): 16,118,928. **Daily newspaper circ.** (1977): 5,491,000; 97 per 1,000 pop.

Health: Life expectancy at birth (1972): 68.97 male; 74.88 female. **Births** (per 1,000 pop. 1980): 11.2. **Deaths** (per 1,000 pop. 1980): 9.7. **Natural increase** (1977): .4%. **Hospital beds** (per 100,000 pop. 1977): 1,036. **Physicians** (per 100,000 pop. 1977): 208. **Infant mortality** (per 1,000 live births 1977): 17.6.

Education (1977): **Literacy:** 94%. **Pop. 5-19:** in school: 62%, teachers per 1,000: 42. **PQLI:** 94.

Rome emerged as the major power in Italy after 500 BC, dominating the more civilized Etruscans to the N and Greeks to the S. Under the Empire, which lasted until the 5th century AD, Rome ruled most of Western Europe, the Balkans, the Near

East, and North Africa.

After the Germanic invasions, lasting several centuries, a high civilization arose in the city-states of the N, culminating in the Renaissance. But German, French, Spanish, and Austrian intervention prevented the unification of the country. In 1859 Lombardy came under the crown of King Victor Emmanuel II of Sardinia. By plebiscite in 1860, Parma, Modena, Romagna, and Tuscany joined, followed by Sicily and Naples, and by the Marches and Umbria. The first Italian parliament declared Victor Emmanuel king of Italy Mar. 17, 1861. Mantua and Venetia were added in 1866 as an outcome of the Austro-Prussian war. The Papal States were taken by Italian troops Sept. 20, 1870, on the withdrawal of the French garrison. The states were annexed to the kingdom by plebiscite. Italy recognized the State of Vatican City as independent Feb. 11, 1929.

Fascism appeared in Italy Mar. 23, 1919, led by Benito Mussolini, who took over the government at the invitation of the king Oct. 28, 1922. Mussolini acquired dictatorial powers. He made war on Ethiopia and proclaimed Victor Emmanuel III emperor, defied the sanctions of the League of Nations, joined the Berlin-Tokyo axis, sent troops to fight for Franco against the Republic of Spain and joined Germany in World War II.

After Fascism was overthrown in 1943, Italy declared war on Germany and Japan and contributed to the Allied victory. It surrendered conquered lands and lost its colonies. Mussolini was killed by partisans Apr. 28, 1945.

Victor Emmanuel III abdicated May 9, 1946; his son Humbert II was king until June 10, when Italy became a republic after a referendum, June 2-3.

Reorganization of the Fascist party is forbidden. The cabinet normally represents a coalition of the Christian Democrats, largest of Italy's many parties, and one or 2 other parties. The 39th government since World War II was formed Apr. 1980, a center-left coalition that included socialists for the first time in 6 years.

The Vatican agreed in 1976 to revise its 1929 concordat with the state, depriving Roman Catholicism of its status as state religion. In 1974 Italians voted by a 3-to-2 margin to retain a 3-year-old law permitting divorce, which was opposed by the church.

Italy has enjoyed an extraordinary growth in industry and living standards since World War II, in part due to membership in the Common Market. Italy joined the European Monetary System, 1980. But in 1973-74, a fourfold increase in international oil prices helped disrupt the economy. Taxes were boosted in 1974. Western aid helped ease the crisis in 1975, but inflation and decline in confidence continued through 1980. A wave of left-wing political violence worsened in 1977 with kidnappings and assassinations and continued through 1979. Christian Dem. leader and former Prime Min. Moro was murdered May 1978 by Red Brigade terrorists.

The Cabinet of Prime Min. Arnaldo Forlani resigned, May 26, 1981, in the wake of revelations that numerous high-ranking officials were members of an illegally secret Masonic lodge.

Sicily, 9,822 sq. mi., pop. (1980) 5,000,000, is an island 180 by 120 mi., seat of a region that embraces the island of **Pantelleria,** 32 sq. mi., and the **Lipari** group, 44 sq. mi., 63 14,000, including 2 active volcanoes: **Vulcano,** 1,637 ft. and **Stromboli,** 3,038 ft. From prehistoric times Sicily has been settled by various peoples; a Greek state had its capital at Syracuse. Rome took Sicily from Carthage 215 BC. **Mt. Etna,** 10,705 ft. active volcano, is tallest peak.

Sardinia, 9,262 sq. mi., pop. (1976) 1,600,000, lies in the Mediterranean, 115 mi. W of Italy and 7-½ mi. S of Corsica. It is 160 mi. long, 68 mi. wide, and mountainous, with mining of coal, zinc, lead, copper. In 1720 Sardinia was added to the possessions of the Dukes of Savoy in Piedmont and Savoy to form the Kingdom of Sardinia. Giuseppe Garibaldi is buried on the nearby isle of Caprera. **Elba,** 86 sq. mi., lies 6 mi. W of Tuscany. Napoleon I lived in exile on Elba 1814-1815.

Trieste. An agreement, signed Oct. 5, 1954, by Italy and Yugoslavia, confirmed, Nov. 10, 1975, gave Italy provisional administration over the northern section and the seaport of Trieste, and Yugoslavia the part of Istrian peninsula it has occupied.

Ivory Coast
Republic of Ivory Coast

People: Population (1980 est.): 7,970,000. **Age distrib.** (%): 0–14: 44.6; 15–59: 52.0; 60+: 3.4. **Pop. density:** 64.01 per sq. mi. **Urban** (1975): 32.4%. **Ethnic groups:** Baule 23%, Bete 18%, Senufo 15%, Malinke 11%, over 60 tribes. **Languages:** French (official), tribal languages. **Religions:** Moslems 25%, Christians 12%, animists 63%.

Geography: Area: 124,503 sq. mi., slightly larger than New Mexico. **Location:** On S. coast of W. Africa. **Neighbors:** Liberia, Guinea on W, Mali, Upper Volta on N, Ghana on E. **Topography:** Forests cover the W half of the country, and range from a coastal strip to halfway to the N on the E. A sparse inland plain leads to low mountains in NW. **Capital:** Abidjan. **Cities** (1976 est.): Abidjan 1,388,320; Bouaké (1977 cen.) 805,356.

Government: Head of state: Pres. Felix Houphouet-Boigny; b. Oct. 18, 1905; in office: Aug. 7, 1960. **Local divisions:** 25 departments. **Armed forces:** regulars 4,950; para-military 3,000.

Economy: Chief crops: Coffee, cocoa, bananas, cotton, pineapples, rice, oil palms. **Minerals:** Diamonds, manganese. **Other resources:** Tropical woods, rubber. **Per capita arable land:** 2.6 acres. **Meat prod.** (1978): beef: 39,000 metric tons; pork: 6,000 metric tons; lamb: 12,000 metric tons. **Fish catch** (1977): 83,400 metric tons. **Electricity prod.** (1978): 1.42 bln. kwh. **Labor force:** 75% agric.; 25% ind. and commerce.

Finance: Currency: CFA franc (Apr. 1981: 262.70 = $1 US). **Gross domestic product** (1980 est.): $10.6 bln. **Per capita income** (1980): $1,293. **Imports** (1979): $2.49 bln.; partners: Fr. 39%, W. Ger. 7%, Jap. 7%, U.S. 5%. **Exports** (1979): $2.51 bln.; partners: Fr. 23%, Neth. 19%, U.S. 15%, It. 6%. **Tourists** (1976): 122,200; receipts: $26 mln. **International reserves less gold** (Jan. 1981): $26.9 mln. **Gold:** 45,000 oz t. **Consumer prices** (changed in 1980): 14.6%.

Transport: Railway traffic (1978): 1.27 bln. passenger-km; 532.8 mln. net ton-km. **Motor vehicles:** in use (1976): 84,900 passenger cars, 43,500 comm. vehicles; assembled (1976): 7,000 passenger cars. **Chief ports:** Abidjan, Sassandra.

Communications: Television sets: 257,000 in use (1976). **Radios:** 600,000 in use (1976), 80,000 manuf. (1975). **Telephones in use** (1978): 58,558. **Daily newspaper circ.** (1976): 63,000; 13 per 1,000 pop.

Health: Life expectancy at birth (1975): 41.9 male; 45.1 female. **Births** (per 1,000 pop. 1975): 49.0. **Deaths** (per 1,000 pop. 1975): 20.4. **Natural increase** (1975): 2.9%. **Hospital beds** (per 100,000 pop. 1977): 124. **Physicians** (per 100,000 pop. 1977): 4. **Infant mortality** (per 1,000 live births 1975): 138.

Education (1977): **Literacy:** 22%. **Pop. 5-19:** in school: 37%, teachers per 1,000: 9. **PQLI:** 31.

A French protectorate from 1842, Ivory Coast became independent in 1960. It is the most prosperous of tropical African nations, due to diversification of agriculture for export, close ties to France, and encouragement of foreign investment. About 20% of the population are workers from neighboring countries. Ivory Coast is a leader of the pro-Western bloc in Africa.

Jamaica

People: Population (1979 est.): 2,215,000. **Age distrib.** (%): 0–14: 45.9; 15–59: 45.7; 60+: 8.5. **Pop. density:** 501.89 per sq. mi. **Urban** (1970): 37.1%. **Ethnic groups:** Negroes 85%, mixed 10%, Chinese, Caucasians, East Indians. **Languages:** English; Jamaican Creole. **Religions:** Protestants 75%, Roman Catholics, 5%.

Geography: Area: 4,244 sq. mi., slightly smaller than Connecticut. **Location:** In West Indies. **Neighbors:** Nearest are Cuba on N, Haiti on E. **Topography:** The country is four-fifths covered by mountains. **Capital:** Kingston. **Cities** (1970 cen.): Kingston 111,879.

Government: Head of state: Queen Elizabeth II, represented by Gov.-Gen. Florizel A. Glasspole; b. Sept. 25, 1909; in office: Mar. 2, 1973. **Head of government:** Prime Min. Michael Manley; b. Dec. 10, 1924; in office: Mar. 2, 1972. **Local divisions:** 12 parishes; Kingston and St. Andrew corporate area. **Armed forces:** regulars 4,000; para-military 8,200.

Economy: Industries: Aluminum, rum, molasses, cigars, oil products, tourism. **Chief crops:** Sugar cane, coffee, bananas, coconuts, ginger, cocoa, pimento, fruits. **Minerals:** Bauxite, marble, silica, gypsum. **Per capita arable land:** 0.2 acres. **Meat prod.** (1978): beef: 12,000 metric tons; pork: 9,000 metric tons. **Fish catch** (1977): 10,100 metric tons. **Electricity prod.** (1978): 1.42 bln. kwh. **Labor force:** 28.1% agric.

Finance: Currency: Dollar (Apr. 1981: 1.78 = $1 US). **Gross domestic product** (1978): $2.70 bln. **Per capita income** (1978): $1143. **Imports** (1979): $101 bln.; partners (1977): U.S. 36%, Venez. 16%, Neth. Ant. 11%, UK 10%. **Exports** (1979): $772 mln.; partners (1977): U.S. 44%, UK 20%, Nor. 11%, Can. 9%. **Tourists** (1977): 264,900; receipts: $106 mln. **National**

budget (1978): $621 mln. revenues; $1.04 bln. expenditures. **International reserves less gold** (Feb. 1981): $96.0 mln. **Consumer prices** (change in 1979): 29.1%.

Transport: Railway traffic (1977): 83 mln. passenger-km; 186 mln. net ton-km. **Chief ports:** Kingston, Montego Bay.

Communications: Television sets: 111,000 in use (1976), 5,000 manuf. (1977). **Radios:** 555,000 in use (1976), 7,000 manuf. (1975). **Telephones in use** (1978): 111,192. **Daily newspaper circ.** (1977): 101,000; 49 per 1,000 pop.

Health: Life expectancy at birth (1961): 62.65 male; 66.63 female. **Births** (per 1,000 pop. 1976): 29.8. **Deaths** (per 1,000 pop. 1976): 7.1 **Natural increase** (1976): 2.3%. **Hospital beds** (per 100,000 pop. 1977): 369. **Physicians** (per 100,000 pop. 1977): 28. **Infant mortality** (per 1,000 live births 1976): 20.4.

Education (1977): Literacy: 86%. **Pop. 5-19:** in school: 63%, teachers per 1,000: 23. **PQLI:** 87.

Jamaica was visited by Columbus, 1494, and ruled by Spain (under whom Arawak Indians died out) until seized by Britain, 1655. Jamaica won independence Aug. 6, 1962.

In 1974 Jamaica sought an increase in taxes paid by U.S. and Canadian companies which mine bauxite on the island. The socialist government acquired 50% ownership of the companies' Jamaican interests in 1976, and was reelected that year. Rudimentary welfare state measures have been passed, but unemployment has increased. Relations with the U.S. and UK became strained, as those with Cuba and the USSR improved.

Japan

People: Population (1980 est.): 116,780,000. **Age distrib. (%):** 0–14: 24.2; 15–59: 63.6; 60+: 12.2. **Pop. density:** 810.97 per sq. mi. **Urban** (1975): 75.9%. **Ethnic groups:** Japanese 99.4%, Korean 0.5%. **Religions:** Buddhism, Shintoism shared by large majority, Christians 0.8%.

Geography: Area: 143,574 sq. mi., slightly smaller than Montana. **Location:** Archipelago off E. coast of Asia. **Neighbors:** USSR on N, S. Korea on W. **Topography:** Japan consists of 4 main islands: Honshu ("mainland"), 87,805 sq. mi.; Hokkaido, 30,144 sq. mi.; Kyushu, 14,114 sq. mi.; and Shikoku, 7,049 sq. mi. The coast, deeply indented, measures 16,654 mi. The northern islands are a continuation of the Sakhalin Mts. The Kunlun range of China continues into southern islands, the ranges meeting in the Japanese Alps. In a vast transverse fissure crossing Honshu E-W rises a group of volcanoes, mostly extinct or inactive, including 12,388 ft. Fuji-San (Fujiyama) near Tokyo. **Capital:** Tokyo. **Cities** (1978 est.): Tokyo 8,543,775; Osaka 2,723,752; Yokohama 2,684,260; Nagoya 2,083,616; Kyoto 1,464,964; Kobe 1,366,397; Sapporo 1,307,686; Kitakyushu 1,067,915; Fukuoka 1,039,286; Kawasaki 1,032,852.

Government: Head of state: Emp. Hirohito; b. Apr. 29, 1901; in office: Dec. 25, 1926. **Head of government:** Prime Min. Zenko Suzuki; b. Jan. 11, 1911; in office: July 17, 1980. **Local divisions:** 43 prefectures and 4 major municipal units. **Armed forces:** regulars 241,000; reserves 39,600.

Economy: Industries: Steel, vehicles, machinery, ships, electronics, precision instruments, chemicals, textiles, ceramics, wood products. **Chief crops:** Rice, grains, potatoes, tobacco, tea, beans, fruits. **Minerals:** Gold, molybdenum, silver, zinc, copper, lead, chromite, coal, sulphur, salt, oil. **Crude oil reserves** (1980). 55 mln. bbls. **Per capita arable land:** 0.09 acres. **Meat prod.** (1978): beef: 364,000 metric tons; pork: 1.23 mln. metric tons. **Fish catch** (1977): 10.7 mln. metric tons. **Electricity prod.** (1978): 495.18 bln. kwh. **Crude steel prod.** (1979): 111.8 mln. metric tons. **Labor force:** 12% agric.; 25% manuf.

Finance: Currency: Yen (Apr. 1981: 215.00 = $1 US). **Gross domestic product** (1980): $990 bln. **Per capita income** (1980): $8,460. **Imports** (1980): $141.29 bln.; partners (1978): U.S. 19%, Saudi Ar. 11%, Austral. 7%, Indon. 7%. **Exports** (1980): $129.58 bln.; partners (1978): U.S. 26%, S. Kor. 6%. **Tourists** (1977): 890,700; receipts: $425 mln. **National budget** (1979): $86.33 bln. revenues; $140.04 bln. expenditures. **International reserves less gold** (Apr. 1981): $26.93 bln. **Gold:** 24.23 mln. **Consumer prices** (change in 1980): 8.0%.

Transport: Railway traffic (1978): 311.2 bln. passenger-km; 40.3 bln. net ton-km. **Motor vehicles:** in use (1977): 19.83 mln. passenger cars, 11.55 mln. comm. vehicles; manuf. (1978): 5.98 mln. passenger cars; 3.26 mln. comm. vehicles. **Civil aviation:** 25,656 mln. passenger-km (1978); 1,316 mln. freight ton-km (1978). **Chief ports:** Yokohama, Tokyo, Kobe, Osaka, Nagoya, Chiba, Kawasaki, Hakodate.

Communications: Television sets: 26.55 mln. in use (1975),

15.21 mln. manuf. (1977). **Radios:** 59.65 mln. in use (1976), 19.93 mln. manuf. (1977). **Telephones in use** (1978): 50,625,589. **Daily newspaper circ.** (1977): 62,221,000; 546 per 1,000 pop.

Health: Life expectancy at birth (1976): 72.15 male; 77.35 female. **Births** (per 1,000 pop. 1980): 13.7. **Deaths** (per 1,000 pop. 1980): 6.2. **Natural increase** (1977): 1.0%. **Hospital beds** (per 100,000 pop. 1977): 1,060. **Physicians** (per. 100,000 pop. 1977): 119. **Infant mortality** (per 1,000 live births 1977): 8.9.

Education (1977): Literacy: 99%. **Pop. 5–19:** in school: 71%, teachers per 1,000: 25. **PQLI:** 97.

According to Japanese legend, the empire was founded by Emperor Jimmu, 660 BC, but earliest records of a unified Japan date from 1,000 years later. Chinese influence was strong in the formation of Japanese civilization. Buddhism was introduced before the 6th century.

A feudal system, with locally powerful noble families and their samurai warrior retainers, dominated from 1192. Central power was held by successive families of shoguns (military dictators), 1192-1867, until recovered by the Emperor Meiji, 1868. The Portuguese and Dutch had minor trade with Japan in the 16th and 17th centuries; U.S. Commodore Matthew C. Perry opened it to U.S. trade in a treaty ratified 1854. Japan fought China, 1894-95, gaining Taiwan. After war with Russia, 1904-05, Russia ceded S half of Sakhalin and gave concessions in China. Japan annexed Korea 1910. In World War I Japan ousted Germany from Shantung, took over German Pacific islands. Japan took Manchuria 1931, started war with China 1932. Japan launched war against the U.S. by attack on Pearl Harbor Dec. 7, 1941. Japan surrendered Aug. 14, 1945.

In a new constitution adopted May 3, 1947, Japan renounced the right to wage war; the emperor gave up claims to divinity; the Diet became the sole law-making authority.

The U.S. and 48 other non-communist nations signed a peace treaty and the U.S. a bilateral defense agreement with Japan, in San Francisco Sept. 8, 1951, restoring Japan's sovereignty as of April 28, 1952. Japan signed separate treaties with Nationalist China, 1952; India, 1952; a declaration with USSR ending a technical state of war, 1956. In Dec. 1965 Japan and South Korea agreed to resume diplomatic relations.

On June 26, 1968, the U.S. returned to Japanese control the Bonin Is., the Volcano Is. (including Iwo Jima) and Marcus Is. On May 15, 1972, Okinawa, the other Ryukyu Is. and the Daito Is. were returned to Japan by the U.S.; it was agreed the U.S. would continue to maintain military bases on Okinawa. Japan and the USSR have failed to resolve disputed claims of sovereignty over 4 of the Kurile Is. and over offshore fishing rights.

On Sept. 29, 1972, Japan and mainland China agreed to resume diplomatic relations; Japan and Taiwan severed diplomatic relations. A Japan-China friendship treaty was signed 1978.

Industrialization was begun in the late 19th century. After World War II, Japan emerged as the 3d most powerful economy in the world, and as a leader in technology. Huge trade surpluses caused the yen to soar in value in the late 1970s.

The Liberal Democratic (conservative) party controlled almost every post-war government, but by declining margins.

Jordan
Hashemite Kingdom of Jordan

People: Population (1980 est.): 3,190,000. **Age distrib. (%):** 0–14: 51.6; 15–59: 44.4; 60+: 4.0. **Pop. density:** 85.53 per sq. mi. **Urban** (1974): 42.0%. **Ethnic groups:** Arabs, small minorities of Circassians, Armenians, Kurds. **Languages:** Arabic is universal. **Religions:** Sunni Moslems 93.6%, Christians 6.4%.

Geography: Area: 37,297 sq. mi., slightly larger than Indiana. **Location:** In W Asia. **Neighbors:** Israel on W, Saudi Arabia on S, Iraq on E, Syria on N. **Topography:** About 88% of Jordan is arid. Fertile areas are in W. Only port is on short Aqaba Gulf coast. Country shares Dead Sea (1,296 ft. below sea level) with Israel. **Capital:** Amman. **Cities** (1978 est.): Amman 711,850 Zarka 263,400; Irbid 136,770.

Government: Head of state: King Hussein I; b. Nov. 14 1935; in office: Aug. 11, 1952. **Head of government:** Prime Min. Mudar Badran, b. 1934; in office: Aug. 28, 1980. **Local divisions:** 8 governorates. **Armed forces:** regulars 67,200; reserves 30,000.

Economy: Industries: Textiles, plastics, cement, food processing. **Chief crops:** Grains, olives, vegetables, fruits. **Minerals:** Phosphates, potash. **Per capita arable land:** 1.0 acres.

Electricity prod. (1977): 601 mln. kwh. **Labor force:** 23% agric.

Finance: Currency: Dinar (Apr. 1981: 0.33 = $1 US). **Gross domestic product** (1979): $2.11 bln. **Per capita income** (1976): $552. **Imports** (1979): $1.96 bln.; partners (1977): U.S. 15%, W. Ger. 14%, Saudi Ar. 9%, UK 7%. **Exports** (1079). $402 mln.; partners (1977): Saudi Ar. 30%, Syria 11%, Iran 9%, Iraq 6%. **Tourists** (1977): 937,100; receipts: $180 mln. **National budget** (1980): $751.59 mln. revenues; $1.68 bln. expenditures. **International reserves less gold** (Apr. 1981): $1.11 bln. **Gold:** 1,046,000 oz t. **Consumer prices** (change in 1980): 11.0%.

Transport: Motor vehicles: in use (1977): 57,000 passenger cars, 21,000 comm. vehicles. **Civil aviation:** 1,254 mln. passenger-km (1978); 52 mln. freight ton-km (1978). **Chief ports:** Aqaba.

Communications: Television sets: 125,000 licensed (1976). **Radios:** 531,000 in use (1976). **Telephones in use** (1978): 53,107. **Daily newspaper circ.** (1977): 85,000; 29 per 1,000 pop.

Health: Life expectancy at birth (1963): 52.6 male; 52.0 female. **Births** (per 1,000 pop. 1975): 47.2. **Deaths** (per 1,000 pop. 1975): 14.7. **Natural increase** (1975): 3.3%. **Hospital beds** (per 100,000 pop. 1977): 86. **Physicians** (per 100,000 pop. 1977): 37. **Infant mortality** (per 1,000 live births 1975): 14.9.

Education (1977): **Literacy:** 54%. **Pop. 5-19:** in school: 56%, teachers per 1,000: 20. **PQLI:** 56.

From ancient times to 1922 the lands to the E of the Jordan were culturally and politically united with the lands to the W. Arabs conquered the area in the 7th century; the Ottomans took control in the 16th. Britain's 1920 Palestine Mandate covered both sides of the Jordan. In 1921, Abdullah, son of the ruler of Hejaz in Arabia, was installed by Britain as emir of an autonomous Transjordan, covering two-thirds of Palestine. An independent kingdom was proclaimed, 1946.

During the 1948 Arab-Israeli war the West Bank and old city of Jerusalem were added to the kingdom, which changed its name to Jordan. All these territories were lost to Israel in the 1967 war, which swelled the number of Arab refugees on the East Bank. A 1974 Arab summit conference designated the Palestine Liberation Organization as the sole representative of Arabs on the West Bank. Jordan accepted the move, and was granted an annual subsidy by Arab oil states. The U.S. has also provided substantial economic and military support.

King Hussein actively promoted rejection of the Egyptian-Israeli peace treaty; Jordan was the first Arab country to sever diplomatic relations with Egypt, Mar. 1979. Jordan abandoned its pro-Western orientation in favor of non-alignment, 1979.

Kenya
Republic of Kenya

People: Population (1980 est.): 16,400,000. **Age distrib.** (%): 0–14: 48.4; 15–59: 46.3; 60+: 5.4. **Pop. density:** 72.90 per sq. mi. **Urban** (1969): 9.9%. **Ethnic groups:** Kikuyu 20%, Luo 15%, Luhya 14%, Balhya 13%, Kamba 11%, others, including 280,000 Asians, Arabs, Europeans. **Languages:** Swahili, English both official. **Religions:** Protestants 37%, Roman Catholics 22%, Moslems 3%, others.

Geography: Area: 224,960 sq. mi., slightly smaller than Texas. **Location:** On Indian O. coast of E. Africa. **Neighbors:** Uganda on W, Tanzania on S, Somalia on E, Ethopia, Sudan on N. **Topography:** The northern three-fifths of Kenya is arid. To the S, a low coastal area and a plateau varying from 3,000 to 10,000 ft. The Great Rift Valley enters the country N-S, flanked by high mountains. **Capital:** Nairobi. **Cities** (1978 est.): Nairobi (met.) 818,000; Mombasa (met.) 391,000.

Government: Head of state: Pres. Daniel arap Moi, b. Sept., 1924; in office: Aug. 22, 1978. **Local divisions:** Nairobi and 7 provinces. **Armed forces:** regulars 12,400; para-military 2,000.

Economy: Industries: Tourism, light industry. **Chief crops:** Coffee, tea, cereals, cotton, sisal. **Minerals:** Gold, limestone, diatomite, salt, barytes, magnesite, felspar, sapphires, fluospar, garnets. **Other resources:** Timber, hides. **Per capita arable land:** 0.3 acres. **Meat prod.** (1978): beef: 145,000 metric tons; pork: 5,000 metric tons; lamb: 31,000 metric tons. **Fish catch** (1977): 39,000 metric tons. **Electricity prod.** (1978): 1.12 bln. kwh. **Labor force:** 21% agric.; 23% ind. and commerce; 13% services.

Finance: Currency: Shilling (Mar. 1981: 8.29 = $1 US). **Gross domestic product** (1979): $6.04 bln. **Per capita income** (1978): $337. **Imports** (1980): $2.30 bln.; partners; UK 22%, W. Ger. 13%, Jap. 10%, Iran 7%. **Exports** (1980): $1.30 bln.; partners: W. Ger. 14%, UK 14%, Ugan. 10%, Neth. 6%. **Tourists** (1977): 346,500; receipts: $121 mln. **National budget** (1980): $1.69 bln. revenues; $1.87 bln. expenditures. **International reserves less gold** (Apr. 1981): $422.3 mln. **Gold:** 80,000 oz t. **Consumer prices** (change in 1980): 13.8%.

Transport: Motor vehicles: in use (1977): 114,100 passenger cars, 83,900 comm. vehicles. **Chief ports:** Mombasa.

Communications: Television sets: 50,000 in use (1976). **Radios:** 514,000 in use (1976). **Telephones in use** (1978): 143,768. **Daily newspaper circ.** (1976): 154,000; 11 per 1,000 pop.

Health: Life expectancy at birth (1969): 46.9 male; 51.2 female. **Births** (per 1,000 pop. 1975): 50.5. **Deaths** (per 1,000 pop. 1975): 14.0. **Natural increase** (1975): 3.7%. **Hospital beds** (per 100,000 pop. 1977): 128. **Physicians** (per 100,000 pop. 1977): 8. **Infant mortality** (per 1,000 live births 1979): 83.

Education (1977): **Literacy:** 40%. **Pop. 5-19:** in school: 57%, teachers per 1,000: 18. **PQLI:** 48.

Arab colonies exported spices and slaves from the Kenya coast as early as the 8th century. Britain obtained control in the 19th century. Kenya won independence Dec. 12, 1963, 4 years after the end of the violent Mau Mau uprising.

Kenya has shown steady growth in industry and agriculture under a modified private enterprise system, and has had a relatively free political life. But stability was shaken in 1974-5, with opposition charges of corruption and oppression.

In 1968 ties with Somalia were restored after 4 years of skirmishes. Tanzania closed its Kenya border in 1977 in a dispute over the collapse of the East African Community. Kenya welcomed the overthrow of Idi Amin.

The U.S. agreed in 1976 to sell several jet fighters to Kenya. A military and economic aid accord giving the U.S. access to air and naval bases was concluded, Apr. 1980.

Kiribati
Republic of Kiribati

People: Population (1980 est.): 60,000. **Pop. density:** 227.27 per sq. mi. **Ethnic groups:** nearly all Micronesian, some Polynesians, Europeans. **Languages:** Gilbertese and English. **Religions:** mainly Christian, evenly divided between Protestant and Roman Catholic.

Geography: Area: 264 sq. mi., slightly smaller than New York City. **Location:** 33 Micronesian islands (the Gilbert, Line, and Phoenix groups) in the mid-Pacific scattered in a 2-mln. sq. mi. chain around the point where the International Date Line cuts the Equator. **Neighbors:** Nearest are Nauru to SW, Tuvalu and Tokelau Is. to S. **Topography:** except Banaba (Ocean) I., all are low-lying, with soil of coral sand and rock fragments, subject to erratic rainfall. **Capital** (1979 est.): Tarawa 17,000.

Government: Head of state and of government: Pres. Ieremia T. Tabai, b. Dec. 16, 1950; in office: July 12, 1979.

Economy: Industries: Copra. **Chief crops:** Coconuts, breadfruit, pandanus, bananas, paw paw. **Other resources:** Fish. **Electricity prod.** (1977): 36.00 mln. kwh.

Finance: Currency: Australian dollar. **Imports** (1979): $15.0 mln.; partners (1976): Austral. 51%, NZ 11%, UK 9%, Jap. 6%. **Exports** (1979): $20 mln.; partners (1976): Austral. 63%, NZ 31%, UK 5%. **National budget** (1977): $16.37 mln. revenues; $14.87 mln. expenditures.

Transport: Chief port: Tarawa.

Communications: Radios: 8,200 in use (1976). **Telephones in use** (1978): 1,386.

Health: Pop. per hospital bed (1977): 200.
Education: Pop. 5–19: in school (1977): 13,679.

A British protectorate since 1892, the Gilbert and Ellice Islands colony was completed with the inclusion of the Phoenix Islands, 1937. Self-rule was granted 1971; the Ellice Islands separated from the colony 1975 and became independent Tuvalu, 1978 (see Index). Kiribati (pronounced Kiribass) independence was attained July 12, 1979. Under a Treaty of Friendship, pending ratification by the U.S. Senate, the U.S. relinquishes its claims to several of the Line and Phoenix islands, including Christmas, Canton, and Enderbury.

Tarawa Atoll was the scene of some of the bloodiest fighting in the Pacific during WW II. Banaba (Ocean) I. has been desecrated by strip mining of phosphate, now virtually exhausted.

North Korea
Democratic People's Republic of Korea

People: Population (Jan. 1980 est.): 19,000,000. **Pop. density:** 406.26 per sq. mi. **Ethnic groups:** Korean. **Languages:** Korean. **Religions:** Buddhism, Confucianism, Shamanism, Chondolsyo prevailed before 1945, repressed since.

Geography: Area: 46,768 sq. mi., slightly smaller than Mississippi. **Location:** In northern E. Asia. **Neighbors:** China, USSR on N, S. Korea on S. **Topography:** Mountains and hills cover nearly all the country, with narrow valleys and small plains in between. The N and the E coast are the most rugged areas. **Capital:** Pyongyang. **Cities** (1973 est.): Pyongyang 957,000; Hamhung 484,000; Chongjin 306,000.

Government: Head of state: Pres. Kim Il-song; b. Apr. 15, 1912; in office: Dec. 28, 1972. **Head of government:** Prime Min. Yi Chong-ok; in office: Dec. 15, 1977. **Head of Communist Party:** Gen. Sec. Kim Il-song; in office: 1945. **Local divisions:** 9 provinces, 4 municipalities, one urban district. **Armed forces:** regulars 632,000-672,000; reserves 260,000.

Economy: Industries: Textiles, fertilizers, cement. **Chief crops:** Grain, rice. **Minerals:** Coal, lead tungsten, zinc, graphite, magnesite, iron, copper, gold, phosphate, salt, fluorspar. **Per capita arable land:** 0.3 acres. **Meat prod.** (1978): beef: 27,000 metric tons; pork: 84,000 metric tons. **Fish catch** (1977): 1.6 mln. metric tons. **Crude steel prod.** (1979 est.) 5.3 mln. metric tons. **Labor force:** 48% agric.

Finance: Currency: Won (Sept. 1979): .91 = $1 US). **Gross domestic product** (1978 est.) = $10.4 bln. **Per capita income** (1978, in 1975 U.S. dollars): $570. **Imports** (1978): $1.59 bln.; partners: China 50%, USSR 18%, Jap. 13%. **Exports** (1978): $1.36 bln.; partners: USSR 25% China 40%, Jap. 9%, W.Ger. 5%.

Transport: Chief ports: Chonglin, Hamhung, Nampo.

Health: Life expectancy at birth (1975): 58.8 male; 62.5 female. **Births** (per 1,000 pop. 1975): 35.7. **Deaths** (per 1,000 pop. 1975): 9.4. **Natural increase** (1975): 2.6%. **Hospital beds** (per 100,000 pop. 1977): 59; **Physicians** (per 100,000 pop. 1977): 40.

Education (1977): Literacy: 85%. **Pop. 5-19:** in school: 61%, teachers per 1,000: 13. **PQLI:** 75.

The Democratic People's Republic of Korea was founded May 1, 1948, in the zone occupied by Russian troops after World War II. Its armies tried to conquer the south, 1950. After 3 years of fighting with Chinese and U.S. intervention, a cease-fire was proclaimed. N. Korea has maintained ties with both China and Russia. The U.S. has no diplomatic ties.

N. Korea's attempts to purchase western technology in the 1970s foundered over $1 billion in defaulted loans. Industry, begun by the Japanese during their 1910-45 occupation, and nationalized in the 1940s, had grown substantially, using N. Korea's abundant mineral and hydroelectric resources. Political life is dominated by a cult of personality around Pres. Kim Il-song.

South Korea
Republic of Korea

People: Population (1979 est.): 39,140,000. **Age distrib. (%):** 0–14: 38.1; 15–59: 56.3; 60+: 5.6. **Pop. density:** 973.42 per sq. mi. **Urban** (1975): 48.4%. **Ethnic groups:** Korean. **Languages:** Korean. **Religions:** Buddhism, Confucianism, Shamanism, Chondokyo widespread; Protestants 13%, Roman Catholics 3%.

Geography: Area: 38,031 sq. mi., slightly larger than Indiana. **Location:** In Northern E. Asia. **Neighbors:** N. Korea on N. **Topography:** The country is mountainous, with a rugged east coast. The western and southern coasts are deeply indented, with many islands and harbors. **Capital:** Seoul. **Cities** (1975 cen.): Seoul 6,879,464; Pusan 2,450,125; Taegu 1,309,131; Inchon 797,143; Kwangchu 606,468.

Government: Head of state: Pres. Chun Doo Hwan; in office: Dec. 1979. **Head of government:** Prime Min. Nam Duck Woo; approved: Sept. 22, 1980. **Local divisions:** 9 provinces, 2 special cities. **Armed forces:** regulars 619,000; reserves 1,215,000.

Economy: Industries: Electronics, ships, rubber, glass, chemicals, oil products, steel. **Chief crops:** Rice, grain, tobacco, beans. **Minerals:** Molybdenum, tungsten, coal, iron, bismuth,

fluorspar, graphite. **Per capita arable land:** 0.1 acres. **Meat prod.** (1978): beef: 81,000 metric tons; pork: 187,000 metric tons. **Fish catch:** (1977): 2.4 mln. metric tons. **Electricity prod.** (1978): 31.51 bln. kwh. **Crude steel prod.** (1979): 7.6 mln. metric tons. **Labor force:** 43% agric.; 21% manuf.

Finance: Currency: Won (Apr. 1981: 678.90 = $1 US). **Gross domestic product** (1980): $59.17 bln. **Per capita income** (1978): $1,187. **Imports** (1980): $22.30 bln.; partners (1977): Jap. 36%, U.S. 23%, Saudi Ar. 10%, Kuw. 5%. **Exports** (1980): $17.50 bln.; partners (1977): U.S. 31%, Jap. 21%, Saudi Ar. 7%, W. Ger. 5%. **Tourists** (1977): 949,700; receipts: $370 mln. **National budget** (1979): $12.90 bln. revenues; $12.26 bln. expenditures. **International reserves less gold** (Mar. 1981): $2.86 bln. **Gold:** (Mar. 1980): 299,000 oz t. **Consumer prices** (change in 1980): 28.7.

Transport: Railway traffic (1978): 20.1 bln. passenger-km; 10.7 bln. net ton-km. **Motor vehicles** in use (1977): 125,600 passenger cars, 144,900 comm. vehicles; assembled (1978): 92,328 passenger cars; 65,616 comm. vehicles. **Chief ports:** Pusan, Inchon.

Communications: Television sets: 2.3 mln. licensed (1976), 2.99 mln. manuf. (1977). **Radios:** 5 mln. in use (1976), 6.4 mln. manuf. (1977). **Telephones in use** (1978): 1,978,366. **Daily newspaper circ.** (1977): 7,169,000; 197 per 1,000 pop.

Health: Life expectancy at birth (1970): 63 male; 67 female. **Births** (per 1,000 pop. 1975): 28.8. **Deaths** (per 1,000 pop. 1975): 8.9. **Natural increase** (1975): 2.0%. **Hospital beds** (per 100,000 pop. 1977): 68. **Physicians** (per 100,000 pop. 1977): 49.

Education (1977): **Literacy:** 91%. **Pop. 5-19:** in school: 65%, teachers per 1,000: 14. **PQLI:** 83.

Korea, once called the Hermit Kingdom, has a recorded history since the 1st century BC. It was united in a kingdom under the Silla Dynasty, 668 AD. It was at times associated with the Chinese empire; the treaty that concluded the Sino-Japanese war of 1894-95 recognized Korea's complete independence. In 1910 Japan forcibly annexed Korea as Chosun.

At the Potsdam conference, July, 1945, the 38th parallel was designated as the line dividing the Soviet and the American occupation. Russian troops entered Korea Aug. 10, 1945, U.S. troops entered Sept. 8, 1945. The Soviet military organized socialists and communists and blocked efforts to let the Koreans unite their country. (See Index for Korean War.)

The South Koreans formed the Republic of Korea in May 1948 with Seoul as the capital. Dr. Syngman Rhee was chosen president July 20 but a movement spearheaded by college students forced his resignation Apr. 26, 1960.

In an army coup May 16, 1961, Gen. Park Chung Hee became chairman of the ruling junta. He was elected president, 1963; a 1972 referendum provided more presidential powers and allowed him to be reelected for 6 year terms unlimited times. Park was assassinated by the chief of the Korean CIA, Oct. 26, 1979. The calm of the new government was halted by the rise of Gen. Chon Too Hwan, head of the military intelligence, who reinstated martial law, and reverted South Korea to the police state it was under Park. (See Index for Chronology.)

North Korean raids across the border tapered off in 1971, but incidents occurred in 1973 and 1974. In July 1972 South and North Korea agreed on a common goal of reunifying the 2 nations by peaceful means. Red Cross delegates from both nations met to find ways to aid divided families.

The U.S. announced in 1977 that it would withdraw 39,000 ground troops by 1982. Some 12,000 Air Force and logistics troops would remain. Alleged Korean agents were charged in 1976-77 with giving questionable gifts to U.S. congresspersons to promote foreign aid.

Kuwait
State of Kuwait

People: Population (1980 est.): 1,370,000. **Age distrib. (%):** 0–14: 44.4; 15–59: 53.1; 60+: 2.6. **Pop. density:** 176.09 per sq. mi. **Ethnic groups:** Arabs 85%, Iranians, Indians, Pakistanis 13%. **Languages:** Arabic, others. **Religions:** Moslems (most Sunni) predominate.

Geography: Area: 7,780 sq. mi., the size of Massachusetts. **Location:** In Middle East, at N end of Persian Gulf. **Neighbors:** Iraq on N, Saudi Arabia on S. **Topography:** The country is flat, very dry, and extremely hot. **Capital:** Kuwait. **Cities** (1970 cen.): Hawalli 106,542; Kuwait City 80,405.

Government: Head of state: Amir Shaikh Jaber Al-Ahmad Al-Sabah; b. 1928; in office: Jan. 1, 1978. **Head of government:** Prime Min. Shaikh Sa'ad Abdulla Al-Sabah; in office: Feb. 8, 1978. **Local divisions:** 3 governorates. **Armed forces:** regulars 11,100; para-military 15,000.

Economy: Industries: Oil products. **Minerals:** Oil, gas. **Crude oil reserves** (1980): 65.4 bln. bbls. **Per capita arable land:** 0.002 acres. **Electricity prod.** (1978): 7.00 bln. kwh. **Labor force:** 2% agric.; 8%. manuf.

Finance: Currency: Dinar (Apr. 1981: 0.28 = $1 US). **Gross domestic product** (1979): $23.17 bln. **Per capita income** (1975): $11,431. **Imports** (1980): 65.4 bln.; partners (1977): Jap. 20%, U.S. 14%, UK 10%, W. Ger. 9%. **Exports** (1980): $19.97 bln.; partners (1977): Jap. 25%, UK 9%, Neth. 7%, It. 7%. **National budget** (1978): $11.2 bln. revenues; $6.26 bln. expenditures. **International reserves less gold** (Feb. 1981): $3.71 bln. **Gold:** 2.54 mln. oz t. **Consumer prices** (change in (1980): 7.7%.

Transport: Motor vehicles: in use (1977): 203,800 passenger cars, 95,100 comm. vehicles. **Chief ports:** Mina al-Ahmadi.

Communications: Television sets: 182,000 in use (1975). **Radios:** 506,000 in use (1976). **Telephones in use** (1978): 152,517. **Daily newspaper circ.** (1977): 180,000; 159 per 1,000 pop.

Health: Life expectancy at birth (1970): 66.4 male; 71.5 female. **Births** (per 1,000 pop. 1977): 41.5. **Deaths** (per 1,000 pop. 1977): 4.8. **Natural increase** (1977): 3.7%. **Hospital beds** (per 100,000 pop. 1977): 388. **Physicians** (per. 100,000 pop. 1977): 124. **Infant mortality** (per 1,000 live births 1977): 39.1.

Education (1977): Literacy: 60%. **Pop. 5-19:** in school: 68%, teachers per 1,000: 49. **PQLI:** 77.

Kuwait is ruled by the Al-Sabah dynasty, founded 1759. Britain ran foreign relations and defense from 1899 until independence in 1961. The majority of the population is non-Kuwaiti, with many Palestinians, and cannot vote.

Iraqi troops crossed the Kuwait border in 1973 but soon withdrew. Kuwait has ordered weapons from France and the U.S.

Oil, first exported in 1946, is the fiscal mainstay. Reserves are 15% of the world total. Oil pays for free medical care, education, and social security. There are no taxes, except customs duties.

Laos
Lao People's Democratic Republic

People: Population (1980 est.): 3,720,000. **Pop. density:** 40.69 per sq. mi. **Urban** (1973): 14.7%. **Ethnic groups:** Lao 50%, Thai 20%, Meo and Yao 15%, others. **Languages:** Lao (official), others. **Religions:** Buddhists 90%, animists, Christians 1.5%.

Geography: Area: 91,428 sq. mi., slightly larger than Utah. **Location:** In Indochina Peninsula in SE Asia. **Neighbors:** Burma, China on N, Vietnam on E, Cambodia on S, Thailand on W. **Topography:** Landlocked, dominated by jungle. High mountains along the eastern border are the source of the E-W rivers slicing across the country to the Mekong R., which defines most of the western border. **Capital:** Vientiane. **Cities** (1973 cen.): Vientiane 176,637; Savannakhet, Pakse, Thakhet.

Government: Head of state: Pres. Souphanouvong; b. July 13, 1909; in office: Dec. 2, 1975. **Head of government:** Prime Min. Kaysone Phomvihan; b. Dec. 13, 1920; in office: Dec. 2, 1975. **Head of Communist Party:** Gen. Sec. Kaysone Phomvihan; in office: 1955. **Local divisions:** 13 provinces. **Armed forces:** regulars 48,550.

Economy: Industries: Wood products. **Chief crops:** Rice, corn, tobacco, cotton, opium, citrus fruits, coffee. **Minerals:** Tin. **Other resources:** Forests. **Per capita arable land:** 0.7 acres. **Meat prod.** (1978): beef: 19,000 metric tons; pork: 26,000 metric tons. **Fish catch** (1977): 20,000 metric tons. **Electricity prod.** (1977): 250 mln. kwh. **Labor force:** 76% agric.

Finance: Currency: New kip (Nov. 1979: 16 = $1 US). **Gross domestic product** (1978 est.): $220 mln. **Per capita income** (1976 est.): $85. **Imports** (1979): $64 mln.; partners (1974): Thai. 49%, Jap. 19%, Fr. 7%, W. Ger. 7%. **Exports** (1979): $20 mln.; partners (1974): Thai. 73%, Malaysia 11%, HK 10%. **Tourists** (1973): 23,100; receipts: $3 mln. **Consumer prices** (change in 1975): 84.3%.

Transport: Motor vehicles: in use (1974): 14,100 passenger cars, 2,500 comm. vehicles.

Communications: Radios: 200,000 licensed (1976).

Health: Life expectancy at birth (1975): 39.1 male; 41.8 fe-

---

male. **Births** (per 1,000 pop. 1975): 44.6. **Deaths** (per 1,000 pop. 1975): 22.8. **Natural increase** (1975): 2.2%. **Hospital beds** (per 100,000 pop. 1977): 98. **Physicians** (per 100,000 pop. 1977): 6.

Education: (1977): **Literacy:** 28%. **Pop. 5-19:** in school: 35%, teachers per 1,000: 14. **PQLI:** 26.

Laos became a French protectorate in 1893, but regained independence as a constitutional monarchy July 19, 1949.

Conflicts among neutralist, communist and conservative factions created a chaotic political situation. Armed conflict increased after 1960.

The 3 factions formed a coalition government in June 1962, with neutralist Prince Souvanna Phouma as premier. A 14-nation conference in Geneva signed agreements, 1962, guaranteeing neutrality and independence. By 1964 the Pathet Lao had withdrawn from the coalition, and, with aid from N. Vietnamese troops, renewed sporadic attacks. U.S. planes bombed the Ho Chi Minh trail, supply line from N. Vietnam to communist forces in Laos and S. Vietnam. An estimated 2.75 million tons of bombs were dropped on Laos during the fighting.

In 1970 the U.S. stepped up air support and military aid. There were an est. 67,000 N. Vietnamese troops in Laos, and some 15,000 Thais financed by the U.S.

After Pathet Lao military gains, Souvanna Phouma in May 1975 ordered government troops to cease fighting; the Pathet Lao took control. A Lao People's Democratic Republic was proclaimed Dec. 3, 1975; it is strongly influenced by Vietnam.

While signing alliances with Cambodia and Thailand, Laos moved further away from China, 1979.

Lebanon
Republic of Lebanon

People: Population (1980 est.): 3,160,000. **Age distrib. (%):** 0–14: 42.6; 15–59: 49.6; 60+: 7.7. **Pop. density:** 787.05 per sq. mi. **Urban** (1970): 60.1%. **Ethnic groups:** Arabs 93%, Armenians 6%. **Languages:** Arabic, French, Armenian. **Religions:** Moslems (Sunni and Shiite) 57%, Christians (Maronite, Orthodox) 40%, Druze 3%.

Geography: Area: 4,015 sq. mi., smaller than Connecticut. **Location:** On Eastern end of Mediterranean Sea. **Neighbors:** Syria on E. Israel on S. **Topography:** There is a narrow coastal strip, and 2 mountain ranges running N-S enclosing the fertile Beqaa Valley. The Litani R. runs S through the valley, turning W to empty into the Mediterranean. **Capital:** Beirut. **Cities** (1978 est.): Beirut 702,000; Tripoli 175,000.

Government: Head of state: Pres. Elias Sarkis; b. July 20, 1924; in office: Sept. 23, 1976; **Head of government:** Prime Min. Shafig al-Wazan; in office: Oct. 26, 1980. **Local divisions:** 5 provinces. **Armed forces:** regulars 8,750; para-military 5,000.

Economy: Industries: Trade, food products, textiles, cement, oil products. **Chief crops:** Fruits, olives, tobacco, grapes, vegetables, grains. **Minerals:** Iron. **Per capita arable land:** 0.2 acres. **Meat prod.** (1978): beef: 10,000 metric tons; lamb: 11,000 metric tons. **Electricity prod.** (1977): 1.60 bln. kwh. **Labor force:** 18% agric.; 17% manuf.

Finance: Currency: Pound (Mar. 1981: 3.97 = $1 US). **Gross domestic product** (1973 est.): $3.0 bln. **Per capita income** (1975): $1,142. **Imports** (1980): $3.46 bln.; partners (1978): It. 12%, Fr. 9%, U.S. 7%, Saudi Ar. 7%. **Exports** (1979): $705 mln.; partners (1978): Saudi Ar. 41%, Syria 8%, Jor. 7%, Kuw. 6%. **Tourists** (1975): 1,554,900; receipts (1977): $65 mln. **International reserves less gold** (Mar. 1981): $1.44 bln. **Gold:** 9.22 mln. oz t. **Consumer prices** (change in 1975): 3.9%.

Transport: Railway traffic (1974): 2 mln. passenger-km; 42 mln. net ton-km. **Motor vehicles:** in use (1974): 220,200 passenger cars, 23,400 comm. vehicles. **Civil aviation:** 1,548 mln. passenger-km (1977); 543 mln. freight ton-km (1977). **Chief ports:** Beirut, Tripoli, Sidon.

Communications: Television sets: 425,000 in use (1976). **Radios:** 1.6 mln. in use (1976). **Daily newspaper circ.** (1976): 281,000.

Health: Life expectancy at birth (1975): 61.4 male; 65.1 female. **Births** (per 1,000 pop. 1975): 34.5. **Deaths** (per 1,000 pop. 1975): 9.5. **Natural increase** (1975): 2.5%. **Hospital beds** (per 100,000 pop. 1977): 384. **Physicians** (per 100,000 pop. 1977): 75. **Infant mortality** (per 1,000 live births 1975): 13.6.

Education: (1977): Literacy: 76%. **Pop. 5-19:** in school: 69%, teachers per 1,000: 40. **PQLI:** 72.

Formed from 5 former Turkish Empire districts, Lebanon became an independent state Sept. 1, 1920, administered under French mandate 1920-41. French troops withdrew in 1946.

Under the 1943 National Covenant, all public positions were divided among the various religious communities, with Christians in the majority. By the 1970s, Moslems became the majority, and demanded a larger political and economic role.

U.S. Marines intervened, May-Oct. 1958, during a Syrian-aided revolt. Lebanon's efforts to restrain Palestinian commandos caused armed clashes in 1969. Continued raids against Israeli civilians, 1970-75, brought Israeli attacks against guerrilla camps and villages. Israeli troops occupied S. Lebanon, March 1978, but were replaced by a UN force, and again in Apr. 1980.

An estimated 60,000 were killed and billions of dollars in damage inflicted in a 1975-76 civil war. Palestinian units and leftist Moslems fought against the Maronite militia, the Phalange, and other Christians. Several Arab countries provided political and arms support to the various factions, while Israel aided Christian forces. Up to 15,000 Syrian troops intervened in 1976, and fought Palestinian groups. Arab League troops from several nations tried to impose a cease-fire. But sporadic fighting, among Palestinian factions, among Christian factions, and between Palestinians and Christians near Israel continued in 1979.

Clashes between Syrian troops and Christian forces erupted, Apr. 1, 1981, near Zahle, Lebanon, bringing to an end the cease-fire that had been in place. By Apr. 22, fighting had broken out not only between Syrians and Christians, but also between two Moslem factions; as of Apr. 25, the total death toll in Lebanon had risen to 400.

Lesotho
Kingdom of Lesotho

People: Population (1980 est.): 1,340,000. **Age distrib. (%):** 0-14: 39.5; 15-59: 53.9; 60+: 6.6. **Pop. density:** 114.37 per sq. mi. **Ethnic groups:** Sotho 85%, Nguni 15%. **Languages:** English, Lesotho both official. **Religions:** Christians 70%, others.

Geography: Area: 11,716 sq. mi., slightly larger than Maryland. **Location:** In Southern Africa. **Neighbors:** Completely surrounded by Republic of South Africa. **Topography:** Landlocked and mountainous, with altitudes ranging from 5,000 to 11,000 ft. **Capital:** Maseru. **Cities** (1976 est.): Maseru 45,000.

Government: Head of state: King Moshoeshoe II, b. May 2, 1938; in office: Mar. 12, 1960. **Head of government:** Prime Min. Leabua Jonathan; b. Oct. 31, 1914; in office: Oct. 4, 1966. **Local divisions:** 9 districts.

Economy: Industries: Diamond polishing. **Chief crops:** Corn, grains, peas, beans. **Other resources:** Wool, mohair. **Per capita arable land:** 0.7 acres. **Electricity prod.** (1967): 5.00 mln. kwh. **Labor force:** 90% agric.; 2% ind. and commerce.

Finance: Currency: Maloti (Sept. 1980: .75 = $1 US). **Gross domestic product** (1977 est.): $240 mln. **Per capita income** (1976): $240. **Imports** (1979): $170 mln.; partners: Mostly So. Afr. **Exports** (1979): $40 mln.; partners: Mostly So. Afr. **National budget** (1978): $56.2 mln. revenues; $104.4 mln. expenditures. **Consumer prices** (change in 1978): 13%.

Transport: Motor vehicles: in use (1975): 4,600 passenger cars, 3,200 comm. vehicles.

Communications: Radios: 23,000 licensed (1976). **Daily newspaper circ.** (1976): 1,300; 1 per 1,000 pop.

Health: Life expectancy at birth (1975): 46.7 male; 48.9 female. **Births** (per 1,000 pop. 1971): 36.7. **Deaths** (per 1,000 pop. 1971): 14.5. **Natural increase** (1971): 2.2%. **Hospital beds** (per 100,000 pop. 1977): 205. **Physicians** (per 100,000 pop. 1977): 8. **Infant mortality** (per 1,000 live births 1973): 146. **Education** (1977): **Literacy:** 50%. **Pop. 5-19:** in school: 58%, teachers per 1,000: 12. **PQLI:** 52.

Lesotho (once called Basutoland) became a British protectorate in 1868 when Chief Moshesh sought protection against the Boers. Independence came Oct. 4, 1966. Elections were suspended in 1970. Over 50% of males work abroad in So. Africa. Livestock raising is the chief industry; wool and mohair are the chief exports.

Liberia
Republic of Liberia

People: Population (1980 est.): 1,860,000. **Age distrib. (%):** 0-14: 40.9; 15-59: 53.1; 60+: 5.9. **Pop. density:** 43.26 per sq. mi. **Urban** (1971): 27.6%. **Ethnic groups:** Americo-Liberians

2.5%, 16 tribes 97.5%. **Languages:** English (official), 28 tribal languages. **Religions:** Moslems 10-20%, Christians 10%, tribal religions.

Geography: Area: 43,000 sq. mi., slightly smaller than Pennsylvania. **Location:** On SW coast of W. Africa. **Neighbors:** Sierra Leone on W, Guinea on N, Ivory Coast on E. **Topography:** Marshy Atlantic coastline rises to low mountains and plateaus in the forested interior; 6 major rivers flow in parallel courses to the ocean. **Capital:** Monrovia. **Cities** (1974 cen.): Monrovia 171,680.

Government: Head of state: Pres. Samuel K. Doe; in office: Apr. 12, 1980. **Local divisions:** 9 counties. **Armed forces:** regulars 5,250; para-military 7,600.

Economy: Industries: Food processing and other light industry. **Chief crops:** Fibers, palm kernels, rice, cassava, coffee, cocoa, sugar. **Minerals:** Iron, diamonds, gold. **Other resources:** Rubber, timber. **Per capita arable land:** 0.2 acres. **Fish catch** (1977): 16,500 metric tons. **Electricity prod.** (1977): 887.00 mln. kwh. **Labor force:** 74% agric.

Finance: Currency: Dollar (Apr. 1981: 1 = $1 US). **Gross domestic product** (1979): $864.2 mln. **Per capita income** (1976): $453. **Imports** (1980): $535 mln.; partners (1977): U.S. 26%, W. Ger. 9%, Jap. 9%, Neth. 9%. **Exports** (1980): $601 mln.; partners (1977): W. Ger. 24%, U.S. 21%, It. 13%, Fr. 8%. **National budget** (1980): $202.3 mln. revenues; (1980) $313.6 mln. expenditures. **International reserves less gold** (Feb. 1981): $14.65 mln. **Consumer prices** (change in 1980): 13.8%.

Transport: Motor vehicles: in use (1974): 12,100 passenger cars, 10,000 comm. vehicles. **Chief ports:** Monrovia, Buchanan.

Communications: Television sets: 8,900 in use (1976). **Radios:** 265,000 in use (1976). **Telephones** in use (1978): 8,420. **Daily newspaper circ.** (1976): 8,000.

Health: Life expectancy at birth (1971): 45.8 male; 44.0 female. **Births** (per 1,000 pop. 1971): 49.8. **Deaths** (per 1,000 pop. 1971): 20.9. **Natural increase** (1971): 2.9%. **Hospital beds** (per 100,000 pop. 1977): 161. **Physicians** (per 100,000 pop. 1977): 12. **Infant mortality** (per 1,000 live births 1978): 159.2

Education (1977): **Literacy:** 18%. **Pop. 5-19:** in school: 33%, teachers per 1,000: 9. **PQLI:** 51.

Liberia was founded in 1822 by U.S. black freedmen who settled at Monrovia with the aid of colonization societies. It became a republic July 26, 1847, with a constitution modeled on that of the U.S. Descendants of freedmen dominated politics.

Charging rampant corruption, an Army Redemption Council of enlisted men staged a bloody predawn coup, April 12, 1980, in which Pres. Tolbert was killed and replaced as head of state by Sgt. Samuel Doe. The new regime was rebuffed by the Organization of African Unity.

Libya
Socialist People's Libyan Arab Jamahiriya

People: Population: (1980 est.): 2,980,000. **Age distrib. (%):** 0-14: 51.4; 15-59: 42.6; 60+: 5.9. **Pop. density:** 4.39 per sq. mi. **Urban** (1974): 29.8%. **Ethnic groups:** Arab-Berber 97%, Italian 1.4%, others. **Languages:** Arabic. **Religions:** Sunni Moslems 97%, Christians 2.5%.

Geography: Area: 679,536 sq. mi., larger than Alaska. **Location:** On Mediterranean coast of N. Africa. **Neighbors:** Tunisia, Algeria on W, Niger, Chad on S, Sudan, Egypt on E. **Topography:** Desert and semidesert regions cover 92% of the land, with low mountains in N, higher mountains in S, and a narrow coastal zone. **Capital:** Tripoli. **Cities** (1973 cen.): Tripoli 551,477; Benghazi 282,192.

Government: Head of state: Sec.-Gen. Abdul Ali al-Obeidi; b. 1933; in office: Mar. 1, 1979. **Head of government:** Chmn. Jadallah Azzuz al Talhi; in office: Mar. 1, 1979. **Local divisions:** 10 regions. **Armed forces:** regulars 42,000.

Economy: Industries: Carpets, textiles, shoes. **Chief crops:** Dates, olives, citrus and other fruits, grapes, tobacco. **Minerals:** Oil, gas. **Crude oil reserves** (1980): 23.5 bln. bbls. **Per capita arable land:** 2.2 acres. **Meat prod.** (1978): beef: 11,000 metric tons; lamb: 40,000 metric tons. **Electricity prod.** (1978): 1.55 bln. kwh. **Labor force:** 20% agric.

Finance: Currency: Dinar (Apr. 1981: 0.30 = $1 US). **Gross domestic product** (1978): $19.97 bln. **Per capita income** (1978): $6,335. **Imports** (1980): $9.78 bln.; partners (1977): It. 27%, W. Ger. 13%, Fr. 8%, Jap. 7%. **Exports** (1980): $22.58 bln.; partners (1977): U.S. 40%, It. 17%, W. Ger. 17%, Sp. 5%.

Tourists (1977): 125,700; receipts: $8 mln. **International reserves less gold** (Apr. 1981): $13.07 bln. **Gold**: 3.53 mln. oz t. **Consumer prices** (change in 1978): 29.3%.

Transport: Motor vehicles: in use (1975): 263,100 passenger cars, 131,300 comm. vehicles. **Chief ports:** Tripoli, Benghazi.

Communications: Television sets: 10,000 licensed (1975). **Radios:** 110,000 licensed (1976). **Daily newspaper circ.** (1976): 64,000; 26 per 1,000 pop.

Health: Life expectancy at birth (1975): 51.4 male; 54.5 female. **Births** (per 1,000 pop. 1975): 49.0 **Deaths** (per 1,000 pop. 1975): 14.8. **Natural increase** (1975): 3.4%. **Hospital beds** (per 100,000 pop. 1977): 476. **Physicians** (per 100,000 pop. 1977): 106.

Education (1977): **Literacy:** 40%. **Pop. 5-19:** in school: 79%, teachers per 1,000: 40. **PQLI:** 49.

First settled by Berbers, Libya was ruled by Carthage, Rome, and Vandals, the Ottomans, Italy from 1912, and Britain and France after WW II. It became an independent constitutional monarchy Jan. 2, 1952. In 1969 a junta lead by Col. Muammar al-Qadhafi seized power, instituting socialist policies.

In the mid-1970s, it was widely reported that Libya had armed violent revolutionary groups in Egypt and Sudan, and had aided terrorists of various nationalities including Moslem rebels in the Philippines. The USSR sold several billion dollars worth of advanced arms after 1975, and established close political ties.

Libya and Egypt fought several air and land battles along their border in July, 1977. Chad charged Libya with military occupation of its uranium-rich northern region in 1977. Libya's 1979 offensive into the Aouzou Strip was repulsed by Chadian forces.

Despite a new system of government of elected people's congresses, Qaddafi remained the nation's leader. Widespread nationalization, arrests, imposition of currency regulations and wholesale conscription of civil servants into the army, from Jan. 1980, paralysed the economy. Over half the one million Libyan work force are foreigners.

Reports have emerged that opposition to the increasingly repressive regime of Col. Muammar el-Qaddafi has grown, and defections of prominent Libyan aides are increasing.

On May 6, 1981, the U.S., citing "a wide range of Libyan provocations and misconduct," closed the Libyan mission in Wash.

Liechtenstein
Principality of Liechtenstein

People: Population (1980 est.): 30,000. **Age distrib.** (%): 0–14: 27.9; 15–59: 60.2; 60+: 11.9. **Pop. density:** 491.8 per sq. mi. **Ethnic groups:** Alemannic. **Languages:** German (official), Alemannic dialects. **Religions:** Roman Catholics 82.1%, Protestants 7%.

Geography: Area: 61 sq. mi., the size of Washington, D.C. **Location:** In the Alps. **Neighbors:** Switzerland on W, Austria on E. **Topography:** The Rhine Valley occupies one-third of the country, the Alps cover the rest. **Capital:** Vaduz. **Cities** (1977 cen.): Vaduz 4,704.

Government: Head of state: Prince Franz Josef II; b. Aug. 16, 1906; in office: Mar. 30, 1938. **Head of government:** Hans Brunhart; b. Mar. 28, 1945; in office: Apr. 26, 1978. **Local divisions:** 11 communes.

Economy: Industries: Machines, textiles, precision instruments, false teeth, drugs, ceramics. **Per capita arable land:** 0.3 acres. **Labor force:** 54.6% industry, trade and building; 41.5% services; 3.9% agric., fishing, forestry.

Finance: Currency: Swiss Franc (Feb. 1981): 1.94 = $1. **Tourists** (1977): 80,425.

Communications: Radios: 8,000 licensed (1976). **Telephones in use** (1978): 17,163. **Daily newspaper circ.** (1976): 12,000; 527 per 1,000 pop.

Health: Births (per 1,000 pop. 1977): 12.5. **Deaths** (per 1,000 pop. 1977): 6.0. **Natural increase** (1977): .7%. **Infant mortality** (per 1,000 live births 1980): 5.8.

Education: Literacy: 100%. **Pop. 5-19:** in school: 100%.

Liechtenstein became sovereign in 1866. Austria administered Liechtenstein's ports up to 1920; Switzerland has administered its postal services since 1921. Liechtenstein is united with Switzerland by a customs and monetary union. Taxes are low; many international corporations have headquarters there. Foreign workers comprise a third of the population.

Luxembourg
Grand Duchy of Luxembourg

People: Population: (1980 est.): 360,000. **Age distrib.** (%): 0–14: 20.2; 15–59: 61.4; 60+: 18.2. **Pop. density:** 360.36 per sq. mi. **Urban** (1974): 67.9%. **Ethnic groups:** Mixture of French and Germans predominate, Italians 7%. **Languages:** French, German, Luxembourgish. **Religions:** Roman Catholics 94%, Protestants 1%.

Geography: Area: 999 sq. mi., smaller than Rhode Island. **Location:** In W. Europe. **Neighbors:** Belgium on W, France on S, W. Germany on E. **Topography:** Heavy forests (Ardennes) cover N, S is a low, open plateau. **Capital:** Luxembourg. **Cities** (1978 est.): Luxembourg 78,400.

Government: Head of state: Grand Duke Jean; b. Jan. 5, 1921; in office: Nov. 12, 1964. **Head of government:** Prime Min. Pierre Werner, b. Dec. 29, 1913; in office: July 16, 1979. **Local divisions:** 3 districts, 12 cantons. **Armed forces:** regulars 660; para-military 430.

Economy: Industries: Steel (90% of exports), chemicals, beer, tires, tobacco, metal products, cement. **Chief crops:** Grain, potatoes, roses. **Minerals:** Iron. **Per capita arable land:** (see Belgium). **Electricity prod.** (1978): 1.39 bln. kwh. **Crude steel prod.** (1979): 5.0 min. metric tons. **Labor force:** 6% agric.; 46% manuf.; 48% services and gov.

Finance: Currency: Franc (Apr. 1981: 36.04 = $1 US). **Gross domestic product** (1979 est.): $3.9 bln. **Per capita income** (1978): $10,040. **Note:** trade and tourist data included in Belgian statistics. **Consumer prices** (change in 1979): 4.2%.

Transport: Railway traffic (1978): 295.2 mln. passenger-km; 649.2 mln. net ton-km. **Motor vehicles:** in use (1977): 141,400 passenger cars, 10,800 comm. vehicles. **Civil aviation:** 84 mln. passenger-miles (1974); 142,000 freight ton-miles (1974).

Communications: Television sets: 105,000 in use (1976). **Radios:** 205,000 in use (1976). **Telephones in use** (1978): 185,549. **Daily newspaper circ.** (1976): 150,000.

Health: Life expectancy at birth (1973): 67.0 male; 73.9 female. **Births** (per 1,000 pop. 1980): 11.4. **Deaths** (per 1,000 pop. 1980): 11.3. **Natural increase** (1978): −.04%. **Hospital beds** (per 100,000 pop. 1977): 978. **Physicians** (per 100,000 pop. 1977): 112. **Infant mortality** (per 1,000 live births 1978): 10.6.

Education (1977): **Literacy:** 98%. **Pop. 5–19:** in school: 59%, teachers per 1,000: 40. **PQLI:** 93.

Luxembourg, founded about 963, was ruled by Burgundy, Spain, Austria, and France from 1448 to 1815. It left the Germanic Confederation in 1866. Overrun by Germany in 2 world wars, Luxembourg ended its neutrality in 1948, when a customs union with Belgium and Netherlands was adopted.

Madagascar
Democratic Republic of Madagascar

People: Population (1980 est.): 8,740,000. **Pop. density:** 38.56 per sq. mi. **Urban** (1970): 14.1%. **Ethnic groups:** 18 Malayan-Indonesian tribes (Merina 26%), with Arab and African presence. **Languages:** Malagasy spoken in various dialects by all tribes, Merina dialect official. **Religions:** Animists 55%, Christian 40%, Muslim 5%.

Geography: Area: 226,658 sq. mi., slightly smaller than Texas. **Location:** In the Indian O., off the SE coast of Africa. **Neighbors:** Comoro Is., Mozambique (across Mozambique Channel). **Topography:** Humid coastal strip in the E, fertile valleys in the mountainous center plateau region, and a wider coastal strip on the W. **Capital:** Antananarivo. **Cities** (1978 est.): Antananarivo 400,000; Toamasina 59,100; Majunga 57,500.

Government: Head of state: Pres. Didier Ratsiraka; b. Nov. 4, 1936; in office: June 15, 1975. **Head of government:** Prime Min. Desire Rakotoarijaona; b. June 19, 1934; in office: Aug. 4, 1977. **Local divisions:** 6 provinces. **Armed forces:** regulars 10,500; para-military 7,000.

Economy: Industries: Light industry. **Chief crops:** Coffee, cloves, vanilla (80% world supply), rice, sugar, sisal, tobacco, peanuts. **Minerals:** Chromium, graphite. **Per capita arable land:** 0.7 acres. **Meat prod.** (1978): beef: 106,000 metric tons; pork: 21,000 metric tons; lamb: 6,000 metric tons. **Fish catch** (1977): 56,000 metric tons. **Electricity prod.** (1978): 300.00 mln. kwh. **Labor force:** 88% agric.; 1.5% ind. and commerce.

Finance: Currency: Franc (Apr. 1981: 262.70 = $1 US).

Gross domestic product (1978): $2.1 bln. **Per capita income** (1979 est.): $275. **Imports** (1979): $641 mln.; partners (1976): Fr. 37%, Qatar 9%, W. Ger. 9%. **Exports** (1979): $394 mln.; partners (1976): Fr. 29%, U.S. 16% Jap. 7%, W. Ger. 7%. **Tourists** (1977): 9,000; receipts: $3 mln. **National budget** (1974): $242 mln. revenues; $263 mln. expenditures. **International reserves less gold** (Mar. 1980): $1.9 mln. **Consumer prices** (change in 1980): 18.3%.

Transport: Railway traffic (1978): 296.4 mln. passenger-km; 211.2 mln. net ton-km. **Motor vehicles:** in use (1977): 57,400 passenger cars, 52,300 comm. vehicles. **Civil aviation:** 280 mln. passenger-km (1977); 8 mln. freight ton-km (1977). **Chief ports:** Tamatave, Diego-Suarez, Majunga, Tulear.

Communications: Television sets: 8,000 in use (1976). **Radios:** 609,000 in use (1976). **Telephones in use** (1978): 28,686.

Health: Life expectancy at birth (1966): 37.5 male; 38.3 female. **Births** (per 1,000 pop. 1966): 46.0. **Deaths** (per 1,000 pop. 1966): 25.0. **Natural increase** (1966): 2.1%. **Hospital beds** (per 100,000 pop. 1977): 245. **Physicians** (per 100,000 pop. 1977): 10. **Infant mortality** (per 1,000 live births 1966): 102.

Education (1977): **Literacy:** 45%. **Pop. 5-19:** in school: 48%, teachers per 1,000: 9. **PQLI:** 46.

Madagascar was settled 2,000 years ago by Malayan-Indonesian people, whose descendants still predominate. A unified kingdom ruled the 18th and 19th centuries. The island became a French protectorate, 1885, and a colony 1896. Independence came June 26, 1960.

Discontent with inflation and French domination led to a coup in 1972. The new regime nationalized French-owned financial interests, closed French bases and a U.S. space tracking station, and obtained Chinese aid. The government conducted a program of arrests, expulsion of foreigners, and repression of strikes, 1979.

Malawi
Republic of Malawi

People: Population (1980 est.): 5,970,000. **Age distrib.** (%): 0–14: 43.9; 15–59: 50.4; 60+: 5.6. **Pop. density:** 130.50 per sq. mi. **Urban** (1972): 10.1%. **Ethnic groups:** Chewa, Nyanja, Lomwe, other Bantu tribes. **Languages:** English (official), Chichewa, other Bantu languages. **Religions:** Christians 50% (half Roman Catholic, half Protestant), Moslems 30%.

Geography: Area: 45,747 sq. mi., the size of Pennsylvania. **Location:** In SE Africa. **Neighbors:** Zambia on W, Mozambique on SE, Tanzania on N. **Topography:** Malawi stretches 560 mi. N-S along Lake Malawi (Lake Nyasa), most of which belongs to Malawi. High plateaus and mountains line the Rift Valley the length of the nation. **Capital:** Lilongwe. **Cities** (1978 est.): Blantyre-Limbe (met.) 219,000; Lilongwe (met.) 75,000.

Government: Head of state: Pres. Hastings Kamuzu Banda, b. May 14, 1906; in office: July 6, 1966. **Local divisions:** 3 regions, 24 districts, 3 subdistricts. **Armed forces:** regulars 5,000; para-military 460.

Economy: Industries: Textiles, sugar, farm implements. **Chief crops:** Tea, tobacco, peanuts, cotton, sugar, soybeans, coffee. **Other resources:** Rubber. **Per capita arable land:** 1.0 acres. **Fish catch** (1977): 68,200 metric tons. **Electricity prod.** (1978): 276.00 mln. kwh. **Labor force:** 90% agric.; 10% ind. and commerce.

Finance: Currency: Kwacha (Apr. 1981: 0.87 = $1 US). **Gross domestic product** (1980): $1.53 bln. **Per capita income** (1979): $220. **Imports** (1980): $437 mln.; partners (1977): So. Afr. 37%, UK 19%, Jap. 9%, U.S. 5%. **Exports** (1980): $293 mln.; partners (1977): UK 42%, U.S. 10%, Neth. 7%, So. Afr. 7%. **Tourists** (1975): 40,500; receipts (1976): $3 mln. **National budget** (1980): $245 mln. revenues; $372 mln. expenditures. **International reserves less gold** (Apr. 1981): $20.69 mln. **Gold:** 13,000 oz t. **Consumer prices** (change in 1980): 18.9%.

Transport: Railway traffic (1978): 67.2 mln. passenger-km; 200.4 mln. net ton-km. **Motor vehicles:** in use (1976): 10,200 passenger cars, 10,600 comm. vehicles. **Civil aviation:** 138 mln. passenger-km (1978); 7 mln. freight ton-km (1978).

Communications: Radios: 130,000 in use (1976). **Telephones in use** (1978): 22,582. **Daily newspaper circ.** (1977): 18,000; 3 per 1,000 pop.

Health: Life expectancy at birth (1972): 40.9 male; 44.2 female. **Births** (per 1,000 pop. 1972): 50.5. **Deaths** (per 1,000 pop. 1972): 26.5. **Natural increase** (1972): 2.4%. **Hospital beds** (per 100,000 pop. 1977): 174. **Physicians** (per 100,000 pop. 1977): 2. **Infant mortality** (per 1,000 live births 1972): 142.1.

Education (1977): **Literacy:** 25%. **Pop. 5-19:** in school: 32%, teachers per 1,000: 6. **PQLI:** 31.

Bantus came in the 16th century, Arab slavers in the 19th. The area became the British protectorate Nyasaland, in 1891. It became independent July 6, 1964, and a republic in 1966. It has a pro-West foreign policy and cooperates economically with Zimbabwe and S. Africa.

Malaysia

People: Population (1980 est.): 13,923,215. **Age distrib.** (%): 0–14: 41.5; 15–59: 53.0; 60+: 5.4. **Pop. density:** 100.99 per sq. mi. **Urban** (1970): 20.6%. **Ethnic groups:** Malays 50%, Chinese 36%, Indians 10%, others. **Languages:** Malay (official), English, Chinese, Indian languages. **Religions:** Malays, some Indians are Moslem; Chinese, Indian, and local religions.

Geography: Area: 128,328 sq. mi., slightly larger than New Mexico. **Location:** On the SE tip of Asia, plus the N. coast of the island of Borneo. **Neighbors:** Thailand on N, Indonesia on S. **Topography:** Most of W. Malaysia is covered by tropical jungle, including the central mountain range that runs N-S through the peninsula. The western coast is marshy, the eastern, sandy. E. Malaysia has a wide, swampy coastal plain, with interior jungles and mountains. **Capital:** Kuala Lumpur. **Cities** (1970 cen.): Kuala Lumpur 451,977; George Town 269,603; Ipoh 247,953.

Government: Head of state: Paramount Ruler Ahmad Shah ibni Sultan Abu Bakar; b. Oct. 24, 1930; in office: Mar. 29, 1979. **Head of government:** Prime Min. Datuk Hussein bin Onn; b. Feb. 12, 1922; in office: Jan. 15, 1976. **Local divisions:** 13 states, each with legislature, chief minister, and titular ruler. **Armed forces:** regulars 64,500; reserves 27,000.

Economy: Industries: Rubber goods, pottery, fertilizers. **Chief crops:** Palm oil, copra, rice, tapioca, sugar, pepper. **Minerals:** Tin (35% world output), iron. **Crude oil reserves** (1980): 2.80 bln. bbls. **Other resources:** Rubber (35% world output). **Per capita arable land:** 0.6 acres. **Meat prod.** (1978): beef: 13,000 metric tons; pork: 48,000 metric tons. **Fish catch** (1977): 619,000 metric tons. **Electricity prod.** (1978): 8.20 bln. kwh. **Crude steel prod.** (1979): 233,000 metric tons. **Labor force:** 48% agric.; 32% ind. and commerce; 12% service.

Finance: Currency: Ringgit (Apr. 1981: 2.32 = $1 US). **Gross domestic product** (1979): $20.26 bln. **Per capita income** (1975): $714. **Imports** (1980): $10.82 bln.; partners: Jap. 23%, U.S. 14%, Sing. 9%, UK 7%. **Exports** (1980): $12.93 bln.; partners: Jap. 22%, U.S. 19% Sing. 16%, Neth. 6%. **Tourists** (1977): 1,289,000; receipts: $38 mln. **National budget** (1979): $4.8 bln. revenues; $5.88 bln. expenditures. **International reserves less gold** (Feb. 1981): $4.21 bln. **Gold:** 2.33 mln. oz t. **Consumer prices** (change in 1980): 6.7%.

Transport: Railway traffic (incl. Singapore) (1978): 1.27 bln. passenger-km; 1.29 bln. net ton-km. **Motor vehicles:** in use (1977): 572,100 passenger cars, 196,200 comm. vehicles; assembled (1978): 61,200 passenger cars; 11,724 comm. vehicles. **Civil aviation:** 2,532 mln. passenger-km (1978); 87 mln. freight ton-km (1978). **Chief ports:** George Town, Kelang, Melaka, Kuching.

Communications: Television sets: 555,000 in use (1976), 142,000 manuf. (1977). **Radios:** 1.45 mln. in use (1976). **Telephones in use** (1978): 374,676. **Daily newspaper circ.** (1976): 1,834,000; 75 per 1,000 pop.

Health: Life expectancy at birth (1976): 66.2 male; 71.4 female. **Births** (per 1,000 pop. 1977): 30.7. **Deaths** (per 1,000 pop. 1977): 6.3. **Natural increase** (1977): 2.4%. **Hospital beds** (per 100,000 pop. 1977): 308. **Physicians** (per 100,000 pop. 1977): 12. **Infant mortality** (per 1,000 live births 1977): 31.8.

Education (1977): **Literacy:** 60%. **Pop. 5-19:** in school: 60%, teachers per 1,000: 20. **PQLI:** 73.

European traders appeared in the 16th century; Britain established control in 1867. Malaysia was created Sept. 16, 1963. It included Malaya (which had become independent in 1957 after the suppression of Communist rebels), plus the formerly-British Singapore, Sabah (N Borneo) and Sarawak (NW Borneo). Singapore was separated in 1965, in order to end tensions between Chinese, the majority in Singapore, and Malays in control of the

Malaysian government. Chinese have charged economical and political discrimination.

A monarch is elected by a council of hereditary rulers of the Malayan states every 5 years.

Abundant natural resources have assured prosperity, and foreign investment has aided industrialization.

The influx of thousands of Vietnamese refugees reached crisis proportions, June 1979.

Maldives
Republic of Maldives

People: Population (1980 est.): 150,000. **Age distrib.** (%): 0–14: 44.9; 15–59: 51.3; 60+: 3.8. **Pop. density:** 1,217.39 per sq. mi. **Urban** (1967): 11.3%. **Ethnic groups:** Sinhalese, Dravidian, Arab mixture. **Languages:** Divehi (Sinhalese dialect). **Religions:** Sunni Moslems.

Geography: Area: 115 sq. mi., twice the size of Washington, D.C. **Location:** In the Indian O. SW of India. **Neighbors:** Nearest is India on N. **Topography:** 19 atolls with 1,087 islands, 203 inhabited. None of the islands are over 5 sq. mi. in area, and all are nearly flat. **Capital:** Male. **Cities** (1978 cen.): Male 29,555.

Government: Head of state: Pres. Maumoon Abdul Gayoom; b. Dec. 29, 1937; in office: Nov. 11, 1978. **Local divisions:** 19 atolls, each with an elected committee and a government-appointed chief.

Economy: Industries: Fish processing, tourism. **Chief crops:** Coconuts, fruit, millet. **Other resources:** Shells. **Fish catch** (1977): 26,700 metric tons. **Electricity prod.** (1977): 2.00 mln. kwh. **Labor force:** 80% fishing.

Finance: Currency: Rupee (Dec. 1979: 7.50 = $1 US). **Gross domestic product** (1978 IMF est.): $22 mln. **Per capita income** (1978 IMF est.): $150. **Imports** (1978): $9.8 mln.; partners: Jap., UK, Thai., Sri Lan. **Exports** (1978): $3.4 mln.; partners: Jap., Sri Lan., Thai. **Tourists** (1976): 15,000.

Transport: Chief ports: Male Atoll.

Communications: Radios: 3,500 licensed (1976). **Telephones in use** (1978): 556.

Health: Births (per 1,000 pop. 1977): 40.5. **Deaths** (per 1,000 pop. 1977): 11.8. **Natural increase** (1977): 2.9%. **Pop. per hospital bed** (1977): 3,500. **Pop. per physician** (1977): 15,555. **Infant morality** (per 1,000 live births 1977): 118.8.

Education (1975): **Literacy:** 36%. **Pop. 5-19:** in school: 40%, per teacher: 80.

The islands had been a British protectorate since 1887. The country became independent July 26, 1965. Long a sultanate, the Maldives became a republic in 1968. Natural resources and tourism are being developed.

A cultural and scientific agreement was signed with the USSR, 1980.

Mali
Republic of Mali

People: Population (1980 est.): 6,910,000. **Age distrib.** (%): 0–14: 47.9; 15–59: 49.1; 60+: 3.0. **Pop. density:** 14.86 per sq. mi. **Urban** (1976): 16.6%. **Ethnic groups:** Mande (Bambara, Malinke, Sarakolle) 50%, Peul 17%, Voltaic 12%, Songhai, Tuareg, Moors. **Languages:** French (official), Bambara (spoken by approx. 80% pop.), others. **Religions:** Moslems 90%, Christians 1%, others.

Geography: Area: 464,873 sq. mi., larger than Texas and California combined. **Location:** In the interior of W. Africa. **Neighbors:** Mauritania, Senegal on W, Guinea, Ivory Coast, Upper Volta on S, Niger on E, Algeria on N. **Topography:** A landlocked grassy plain in the upper basins of the Senegal and Niger rivers, extending N into the Sahara. **Capital:** Bamako. **Cities** (1976 cen.): Bamako (met.) 404,022.

Government: Head of state and head of govt.: Pres. Moussa Traore; b. Sept. 25, 1936; in office: Dec. 6, 1968 (state); Sept. 19, 1969 (govt.) **Local divisions:** 6 regions. **Armed forces:** regulars 4,450; para-military 5,700.

Economy: Chief crops: Millet, rice, peanuts, cotton. **Other resources:** Rubber. **Per capita arable land:** 3.8 acres. **Meat prod.** (1978): beef: 34,000 metric tons; lamb: 41,000 metric tons. **Fish catch** (1977): 100,000 metric tons. **Electricity prod.** (1977): 98 mln. kwh. **Labor force:** 80% agric.; 1% ind. and commerce.

Finance: Currency: Franc (Apr. 1981: 525.40 = $1 US).

Gross domestic product (1977): $603 mln. **Per capita income** (1977): $96. **Imports** (1980): $417 mln.; partners (1976): Fr. 40% Ivory Coast 14%, Sen. 10%, China 7%. **Exports** (1980): $176 mln.; partners (1976): Fr. 31%, Ivory Coast 13%, W. Ger. 11%, China 10%. **Tourists** (1977): 19,500; receipts: $8 mln. **International reserves less gold** (Apr. 1981): $16.1 mln. **Gold:** 19,000 oz t. **Consumer prices** (change in 1976): 8%.

Transport: Railway traffic (1977): 129 mln. passenger-km; 148 mln. net ton-km. **Motor vehicles:** in use (1974): 11,900 passenger cars, 7,000 comm. vehicles. **Civil aviation:** 97 mln. passenger-km (1977); 612,000 freight ton-km (1977).

Communications: Radios: 82,000 in use (1976).

Health: Life expectancy at birth (1975): 39.4 male; 42.5 female. **Births** (per 1,000 pop. 1975): 49.0. **Deaths** (per 1,000 pop. 1975): 23.2. **Natural increase** (1975): 2.6%. **Hospital beds** (per 100,000 pop. 1977): 56. **Physicians** (per 100,000 pop. 1977): 5. **Infant mortality** (per 1,000 live births 1975): 120.

Education (1977): **Literacy:** 10%. **Pop. 5-19:** in school: 14%, teachers per 1,000: 4. **PQLI:** 18.

Until the 15th century the area was part of the great Mali Empire. Timbuktu was a center of Islamic study. French rule was secured, 1898. The Sudanese Rep. and Senegal became independent as the Mali Federation June 20, 1960, but Senegal withdrew, and the Sudanese Rep. was renamed Mali.

Mali signed economic agreements with France and, in 1963, with Senegal. In 1968, a coup ended the socialist regime. Famine struck in 1973-74, killing as many as 100,000 people. Drought conditions returned 1977-78. Loss of livestock and dislocation of Tuareg nomads remained problems.

Malta

People: Population (1980 est.): 360,000. **Age distrib.** (%): 0–14: 24.6; 15–59: 63.2; 60+: 12.2. **Pop. density:** 2,950.81 per sq. mi. **Ethnic groups:** Italian, Arab, English, and Phoenician mixture. **Languages:** Maltese, English both official. **Religions:** Roman Catholics 98%.

Geography: Area: 122 sq. mi., twice the size of Washington, D.C. **Location:** In center of Mediterranean Sea. **Neighbors:** Nearest is Italy on N. **Topography:** Island of Malta is 95 sq. mi.; other islands in the group: Gozo, 26 sq. mi., Comino, 1 sq. mi. The coastline is heavily indented. Low hills cover the interior. **Capital:** Valletta. **Cities** (1979 est.): Valletta 15,000; Sliema 22,000.

Government: Head of state: Pres. Anton Buttigieg; b. Feb. 19, 1912; in office: Dec. 27, 1976. **Head of government:** Prime Min. Dom Mintoff; b. Aug. 6, 1916; in office: June 17, 1971. **Armed forces:** regulars 1,000; para-military 1,400.

Economy: Industries: Ship repair, textiles, tourism. **Chief crops:** Wheat, potatoes, onions, beans. **Per capita arable land:** 0.1 acres. **Electricity prod.** (1978): 456.00 mln. kwh. **Labor force:** 27.8% manuf.; 31.4% market services; 21.5% gov.

Finance: Currency: Pound (Apr. 1981: 0.39 = $1 US). **Gross domestic product** (1979): $979 mln. **Per capita income** (1978): $2,036. **Imports** (1979): $759 mln.; partners: UK 20%, It. 22%, W. Ger. 13%, U.S. 6%. **Exports** (1979): $425 mln.; partners: W. Ger. 33%, UK 21%, Libya 8%, China 5%. **Tourists** (1977): 361,900; receipts: $81 mln. **National budget** (1978): $325 mln. revenues; $276 mln. expenditures. **International reserves less gold** (Mar. 1981): $957.9 mln. **Gold:** 434,000 oz t. **Consumer prices** (change in 1980): 25.1%.

Transport: Motor vehicles: in use (1977): 60,700 passenger cars, 12,500 comm. vehicles. **Civil aviation:** 532 mln. passenger-km (1978); 4 mln. freight ton-km (1978). **Chief ports:** Valletta.

Communications: Television sets: 63,000 licensed (1976). **Radios:** 63,000 licensed (1976). **Telephones in use** (1978): 67,250.

Health: Life expectancy at birth (1976): 68.27 male; 73.10 female. **Births** (per 1,000 pop. 1980: 15.4. **Deaths** (per 1,000 pop. 1980): 9.1. **Natural increase** (1978): .7%. **Hospital beds** (per 100,000 pop. 1977): 1,040. **Physicians** (per 100,000 pop. 1977): 127. **Infant mortality** (per 1,000 live births 1980): 15.

Education (1977): **Literacy:** 85%. **Pop. 5-19:** in school: 69% teachers per 1,000: 36. **PQLI:** 90.

Malta was ruled by Phoenicians, Romans, Arabs, Normans, the Knights of Malta, France, and Britain (since 1814). It became independent Sept. 21, 1964, with Britain retaining a naval base. Malta became a republic in 1974. The withdrawal of the last of its sailors, Apr. 1, 1979, ended 179 years of British military presence on the island.

Maltese is a Semitic language, with Italian influences, written in the Latin alphabet. Malta is democratic but nonaligned, and receives aid from Libya and China.

Mauritania
Islamic Republic of Mauritania

People: Population (1980 est.): 1,630,000. **Age distrib. (%):** 0–14: 42.2; 15–59: 49.8; 60+: 13.4. **Pop. density:** 3.89 per sq. mi. **Urban** (1977): 22.8%. **Ethnic groups:** Arab-Berber 80%, Negroes 20%. **Languages:** French (official), Hassanya Arabic (national), Niger-Congo languages. **Religions:** Moslems 95%, others.

Geography: Area: 419,229 sq. mi., the size of Texas and California combined. **Location:** In W. Africa. **Neighbors:** Morocco on N, Algeria, Mali on E, Senegal on S. **Topography:** The fertile Senegal R. valley in the S gives way to a wide central region of sandy plains and scrub trees. The N is arid and extends into the Sahara. **Capital:** Nouakchott. **Cities** (1978 est.): Nouakchott 200,000; Nouadhibou 21,960; Kaedi 20,850.

Government: Head of state and head of govt.: Pres. Mohamed Khouna Ould Haidala, b. 1940: in office: May 31, 1979 (govt.); Jan. 4, 1980 (state). **Local divisions:** 8 regions, one district. **Armed forces:** regulars 9,450; para-military 6,000.

Economy: Chief crops: Dates, grain. **Minerals:** Iron, copper. **Per capita arable land:** 0.3 acres. **Meat prod.** (1978): beef: 16,000 metric tons; lamb: 12,000 metric tons. **Fish catch** (1977): 34,200 metric tons. **Electricity prod.** (1978): 96.00 mln. kwh. **Labor force:** 85% agric.

Finance: Currency: Ouguiya (Apr. 1981: 47.58 = $1 US). **Gross domestic product** (1978): $544 mln. **Per capita income** (1979): $376. **Imports** (1979): $259 mln.; partners (1978): Fr. 28%, Bel. 12%, W. Ger. 9%, Sp. 9%. **Exports** (1980): $194 mln.; partners (1978): Fr. 26%, It. 17%, Jap. 13%, UK 10%. **Tourists** (1975): 20,700; receipts (1976): $7 mln. **International reserves less gold** (Apr. 1981): $123.7 mln. **Gold:** 11,000 oz t. **Consumer prices** (change in 1980): 9.9%.

Transport: Railway traffic (1974): 7.81 bln. net ton-km. **Motor vehicles:** in use (1972): 4,400 passenger cars, 5,000 comm. vehicles. **Chief ports:** Nouakchott, Nouadhibou.

Communications: Radios: 95,000 in use (1976).

Health: Life expectancy at birth (1975): 39.4 male; 42.5 female. **Births** (per 1,000 pop. 1975): 49.9. **Deaths** (per 1,000 pop. 1975): 23.3. **Natural increase** (1975): 2.7%. **Hospital beds** (per 100,000 pop. 1977): 38. **Physicians** (per 100,000 pop. 1977): 7. **Infant mortality** (per 1,000 live births 1975): 187. **Education** (1977): **Literacy:** 10%. **Pop. 5-19:** in school: 15%, teachers per 1,000: 4. **PQLI:** 21.

Mauritania became independent Nov. 28, 1960. It annexed the south of former Spanish Sahara in 1976. Saharan guerrillas stepped up attacks in 1977; 8,000 Moroccan troops and French bomber raids aided the government. Mauritania signed a peace treaty with the Polsario Front, 1980, resumed diplomatic relations with Algeria while breaking a defense treaty with Morocco, and renounced sovereignty over its share of former Spanish Sahara. Morocco annexed the territory.

Famine struck in 1973-74 and again in 1977-78. France, China, and the U.S. have sent aid.

Mauritius

People: Population (1980 est.): 960,000. **Age distrib. (%):** 0–14: 36.3; 15–59: 57.2; 60+: 6.4. **Pop. density:** 1,219.82 per sq. mi. **Urban** (1976): 43.6%. **Ethnic groups:** Indo-Mauritians 67%, Creoles 28%, Sino-Mauritians 3%, Franco-Mauritians 2%. **Languages:** English (official), French, Creole, Hindi, Urdu, Chinese. **Religions:** Hindu 49%, Roman Catholic 32%, Moslems 16%, Protestants 1%.

Geography: Area: 787 sq. mi., smaller than Rhode Island. **Location:** In the Indian O., 500 mi. E of Madagascar. **Neighbors:** Nearest is Madagascar on W. **Topography:** A volcanic island nearly surrounded by coral reefs. A central plateau is encircled by mountain peaks. **Capital:** Port Louis. **Cities** (1978 est.): Port Louis 141,022.

Government: Head of state: Queen Elizabeth II, represented by Gov.-Gen. Dayendranath Burrenchobay; b. Mar. 24, 1919; in office: Mar. 23, 1978. **Head of government:** Prime Min.

Seewoosagur Ramgoolam, b. 1900; in office: 1961. **Local divisions:** 9 administrative divisions.

Economy: Industries: Tourism. **Chief crops:** Sugar cane, tea. **Per capita arable land:** 0.3 acres. **Electricity prod.** (1978): 336.00 mln. kwh. **Labor force:** 28.9% agric.; 28% ind. and commerce.

Finance: Currency: Rupee (Apr. 1981: 8.33 = $1 US). **Gross domestic product** (1979): $1.03 bln. **Per capita income** (1978 est.): $738. **Imports** (1979): $557 mln.; partners (1977): UK 18%, Fr. 11%, So. Afr. 11%, Jap. 8%. **Exports** (1979): $372 mln.; partners (1977): UK 67%, Fr. 8%, U.S. 6%. **Tourists** (1975): 74,600; receipts (1977): $32 mln. **National budget** (1978): $201 mln. revenues; $291 mln. expenditures. **International reserves less gold** (Apr. 1981): $87.8 mln. **Gold:** 38,000 oz t. **Consumer prices** (change in 1980): 42.7%.

Transport: Motor vehicles: in use (1977): 24,300 passenger cars, 13,000 comm. vehicles. **Chief ports:** Port Louis.

Communications: Television sets: 41,000 licensed (1976). **Radios:** 200,000 licensed (1976). **Telephones in use** (1978): 29,145. **Daily newspaper circ.** (1977): 85,000; 94 per 1,000 pop.

Health: Life expectancy at birth (1973): 60.68 male; 65.31 female. **Births** (per 1,000 pop. 1980): 27.0. **Deaths** (per 1,000 pop. 1980): 7.2. **Natural increase** (1978): 2.0%. **Hospital beds** (per 100,000 pop. 1977): 354. **Physicians** (per 100,000 pop. 1977): 44. **Infant mortality** (per 1,000 live births 1978): 33.8. **Education** (1977): **Literacy:** 80%. **Pop. 5-19:** in school: 63%, teachers per 1,000: 24. **PQLI:** 77.

Mauritius was uninhabited when settled in 1638 by the Dutch, who introduced sugar cane. France took over in 1721, bringing African slaves. Britain ruled from 1810 to Mar. 12, 1968, bringing Indian workers for the sugar plantations. Mauritius has a free political life and high literacy and life expectancy. The 1970s brought declining birth rates and some economic growth.

Mexico
United Mexican States

People: Population (1980 est.): 71,910,000. **Age distrib. (%):** 0–14: 46.2; 15–59: 50.0; 60+: 4.8. **Pop. density:** 94.49 per sq. mi. **Urban** (1978): 65.2%. **Ethnic groups:** Mestizo 60%, American Indian 30%, Caucasian 10%. **Languages:** Spanish, Indian languages 1.5%, bilingual 6.5%. **Religions:** Roman Catholics 97%, Protestants 2%.

Geography: Area: 761,601 sq. mi., three times the size of Texas. **Location:** In southern N. America. **Neighbors:** U.S. on N, Guatemala, Belize on S. **Topography:** The Sierra Madre Occidental Mts. run NW-SE near the west coast; the Sierra Madre Oriental Mts., run near the Gulf of Mexico. They join S of Mexico City. Between the 2 ranges lies the dry central plateau, 5,000 to 8,000 ft. alt., rising toward the S, with temperate vegetation. Coastal lowlands are tropical. About 45% of land is arid. **Capital:** Mexico City. **Cities** (1978 est.): Mexico City 8,988,230; Netzahualcoyotl 2,067,992; Guadalajara 1,813,131; Monterrey 1,054,029; Puebla de Zaragoza 677,959.

Government: Head of state: Pres. Jose Lopez Portillo; b. June 16, 1920; in office: Dec. 1, 1976. **Local divisions:** Federal district and 31 states. **Armed forces:** regulars 100,000; reserves 250,000.

Economy: Industries: Steel, chemicals, electric goods, textiles, rubber, paper, cement, shoes, glass, handicrafts, tourism. **Chief crops:** Cotton, coffee, sugar cane, tomatoes, wheat, corn, rice, tobacco, beans, cocoa, sisal (50% world supply) bananas. **Minerals:** Silver, antimony, lead, manganese, mercury, molybdenum, zinc, gold, arsenic, graphite, sulphur, coal, opal, oil, gas. **Crude oil reserves** (1980): 31.25 bln. bbls. **Per capita arable land:** 0.8 acres. **Meat prod.** (1978): beef: 562,000 metric tons; pork: 440,000 metric tons; lamb: 31,000 metric tons. **Fish catch** (1977): 670,100 metric tons. **Electricity prod.** (1978): 56.05 bln. kwh. **Crude steel prod.** (1979): 7.0 mln. metric tons. **Labor force:** 41% agric.; 18% manuf.

Finance: Currency: Peso (Apr. 1981: 23.99 = $1 US). **Gross domestic product** (1980): $128 bln. **Per capita income** (1980): $1,800. **Imports** (1980): $19.46 bln.; partners (1980): U.S. 60%, Jap. 8%, W. Ger. 7%. **Exports** (1980): $15.35 bln.; partners (1980): U.S. 63% EC, Japan. **Tourists** (1977): 3,338,000; receipts (1980): $781 mln. **National budget** (1978): $13.78 bln. revenues; $15.74 bln. expenditures. **International reserves less gold** (Nov. 1980): $2.79 bln. **Gold:** 2.07 mln. oz t. **Consumer prices (change in 1980): 26.4%.

Transport: Railway traffic (1977): 5.4 bln. passenger-km; 36.2 bln. net ton-km. **Motor vehicles:** in use (1977): 2.68 mln. passenger cars, 1.08 mln. comm. vehicles; manuf. (1978): 253,200 passenger cars, 105,600 comm. vehicles. **Civil aviation:** 8,532 mln. passenger-km (1977); 96 mln. freight ton-km (1977). **Chief ports:** Veracruz, Tampico, Mazatlan, Coatzacoalcos.

Communications: Television sets: 4.88 mln. in use (1975), 699,000 manuf. (1977). **Radios:** 17.15 mln. in use (1975), 976,000 manuf. (1977). **Telephones in use** (1978): 3,712,407. **Daily newspaper circ.** (1976): 3,994,000.

Health: Life expectancy at birth (1975): 62.76 male; 66.57 female. **Births** (per 1,000 pop. 1978): 34.0. **Deaths** (per 1,000 pop. 1978): 6.0. **Natural increase** (1975): 3.3%. **Hospital beds** (per 100,000 pop. 1977): 115. **Physicians** (per 100,000 pop. 1977). **57. Infant mortality** (per 1,000 live births 1975): 54.7.

Education (1977): **Literacy:** 80%. **Pop. 5-19:** in school: 64%, teachers per 1,000: 19. **PQLI:** 76.

Mexico was the site of advanced Indian civilizations. The Mayas, an agricultural people, moved up from Yucatan, built immense stone pyramids, invented a calendar. The Toltecs were overcome by the Aztecs, who founded Tenochtitlan 1325 AD, now Mexico City. Hernando Cortes, Spanish conquistador, destroyed the Aztec empire, 1519-1521.

After 3 centuries of Spanish rule the people rose, under Fr. Miguel Hidalgo y Costilla, 1810, Fr. Morelos y Payon, 1812, and Gen. Agustin Iturbide, who made independence effective Sept. 27, 1821, but made himself emperor as Agustin I. A republic was declared in 1823.

Mexican territory extended into the present American Southwest and California until Texas revolted and established a republic in 1836; the Mexican legislature refused recognition but was unable to enforce its authority there. After numerous clashes, the U.S.-Mexican War, 1846-48, resulted in the loss by Mexico of the lands north of the Rio Grande.

French arms supported an Austrian archduke on the throne of Mexico as Maximilian I, 1864-67, but pressure from the U.S. forced France to withdraw. A dictatorial rule by Porfirio Diaz, president 1877-80, 1884-1911, led to fighting by rival forces until the new constitution of Feb. 5, 1917 provided social reform. Since then Mexico has developed large-scale programs of social security, labor protection, and school improvement. A constitutional provision requires management to share profits with labor.

The Institutional Revolutionary Party has been dominant in politics since 1929. Radical opposition, including some guerrilla activity, has been contained by strong measures.

The presidency of Luis Echeverria, 1970-76, was marked by a more leftist foreign policy and domestic rhetoric. Some land redistribution begun in 1976 was reversed under the succeeding administration.

Gains in agriculture, industry, and social services have been achieved since 1940. The land is rich, but the rugged topography and lack of sufficient rainfall are major obstacles. Crops and farm prices are controlled, as are export and import. Large estates have been expropriated; since 1915 the government has distributed about 160 million acres to small farmers through landholding communities (ejidos), yet 4 million peasants are still without land, and 5 million others hold minimal plots. Economic prospects brightened with the discovery of vast oil reserves, perhaps the world's greatest. But half the work force is jobless or underemployed.

Monaco
Principality of Monaco

People: Population (1980 est.): 30,000. **Age distrib. (%):** 0-14: 12.7; 15-59: 56.3 60+: 30.7. **Ethnic groups:** French 58%, Italian 17%, Monegasque 15%. **Languages:** French (official), Monegasque, Italian, English. **Religions:** Roman Catholics 95%.

Geography: Area: 600 acres. **Location:** On the NW Mediterranean coast. **Neighbors:** France to W, N, E. **Topography:** Monaco-Ville sits atop a high promontory, the rest of the principality rises from the port up the hillside. **Capital:** Monaco-Ville (1979 est.): 1,700.

Government: Head of state: Prince Rainier III; b. May 31, 1923; in office: May 9, 1949. **Head of government:** Min. of State Andre Saint-Mleux; b. Sept. 25, 1920; in office: May 24, 1972.

Economy: Industries: Tourism, gambling, chemicals, precision instruments, plastics.

Finance: Currency: French franc or Monégasque franc. **Tourists** (1976): 181,000.

Transport: Chief ports: La Condamine.

Communications: Television sets: 16,000 in use (1976). **Radios:** 7,500 in use (1976). **Telephones in use** (1978): 32,000. **Daily newspaper circ.** (1977): 11,000; 420 per 1,000 pop.

Health: Births (per 1,000 pop. 1977): 7.5. **Deaths** (per 1,000 pop. 1977): 10.6. **Natural increase** (1977): −.3%. **Infant mortality** (per 1,000 live births 1970): 9.3.

An independent principality for over 300 years, Monaco has belonged to the House of Grimaldi since 1297 except during the French Revolution. It was placed under the protectorate of Sardinia in 1815, and under that of France, 1861. The Prince of Monaco was an absolute ruler until a 1911 constitution.

Monaco's fame as a tourist resort is widespread. It is noted for its mild climate and magnificent scenery. The area has been extended by land reclamation.

Mongolia
Mongolian People's Republic

People: Population (1980 est.): 1,670,000. **Pop. density:** 2.76 per sq. mi. **Urban** (1973): 46.4%. **Ethnic groups:** Khalkha Mongols 76%, other Mongols 8%, Kazakhs 5%, other Turks, Russians, Chinese. **Languages:** Khalkha Mongolian (official, written in Cyrillic letters since 1941), Turkic 7%, Russian, Chinese. **Religions:** Lama Buddhism prevailed, has been curbed.

Geography: Area: 604,247 sq. mi., more than twice the size of Texas. **Location:** In E Central Asia. **Neighbors:** USSR on N, China on S. **Topography:** Mostly a high plateau with mountains, salt lakes, and vast grasslands. Arid lands in the S are part of the Gobi Desert. **Capital:** Ulaanbaatar. **Cities** (1978 est.): Ulaanbaatar 400,000, Darhan.

Government: Head of state: Chmn. Yumjaagiyn Tsedenbal; b. Sept. 17, 1916; in office: June 11, 1974. **Head of government:** Chmn. Jambyn Batmounkh; b. Mar. 10, 1926; in office: June 11, 1974. **Head of Communist Party:** First Sec. Yumjaagiyn Tsedenbal; in office: Nov. 22, 1958. **Local divisions:** 18 provinces, 2 autonomous municipalities **Armed forces:** regulars 30,000; reserves 30,000.

Economy: Industries: Food processing, textiles, chemicals, cement. **Chief crops:** Grain. **Minerals:** Coal, tungsten, copper, molybdenum, gold, tin. **Per capita arable land:** 1.7 acres. **Meat prod.** (1978): beef: 57,000 metric tons; lamb: 96,000 metric tons. **Electricity prod.** (1977): 990 mln. kwh. **Labor force:** 52% agric.; 10% manuf.

Finance: Currency: Tugrik (Mar. 1980: 2.85 = $1 US). **Gross domestic product** (1976 est.): $1.20 bln. **Per capita income** (1976 est.): $750. **Imports** (1975): $550 mln.; partners (1976): USSR 93%. **Exports** (1975): $220 mln.; partners (1976): USSR 81%, Czech. 6%.

Transport: Railway traffic (1977): 227 mln. passenger-km; 2.54 bln. net ton-km.

Communications: Television sets: 3,600 in use (1976). **Radios:** 115,000 in use (1976). **Telephones in use** (1977): 37,792. **Daily newspaper circ.** (1976): 112,000; 75 per 1,000 pop.

Health: Life expectancy at birth (1975): 59.1 male; 62.3 female. **Births** (per 1,000 pop. 1975): 38.8. **Deaths** (per 1,000 pop. 1975): 9.6. **Natural increase** (1975): 2.9%. **Hospital beds** (per 100,000 pop. 1977): 1,067. **Physicians** (per 100,000 pop. 1977): 209.

Education (1977): **Literacy:** 95%. **Pop. 5-19:** in school: 56%, teachers per 1,000: 21. **PQLI:** 78.

One of the world's oldest countries, Mongolia reached the zenith of its power in the 13th century when Genghis Khan and his successors conquered all of China and extended their influence as far W as Hungary and Poland. In later centuries, the empire dissolved and Mongolia came under the suzerainty of China.

With the advent of the 1911 Chinese revolution, Mongolia, with Russian backing, declared its independence. A Mongolian Communist regime was established July 11, 1921.

In the early 1970s Mongolia was changing from a nomadic culture to one of settled agriculture and growing industries with aid from the USSR and East European nations.

Mongolia has sided with the Russians in the Sino-Soviet dispute. A Mongolian-Soviet mutual assistance pact was signed

Jan. 15, 1966, and thousands of Soviet troops are based in the country. Ties were expanded in a 1976 pact.

urban areas, but the Polisario Front's guerrillas move freely in the vast, sparsely populated deserts.

Morocco

Kingdom of Morocco

People: Population (1979 est.): 20,368,000. **Age distrib.** (%): 0–14: 46.4; 15–59: 49.2; 60+: 4.2. **Pop. density:** 109.97 per sq. mi. **Urban** (1974): 37.9%. **Ethnic groups:** Arabs 65%, Berbers 33%, Europeans 1%. **Languages:** Arabic (official), Berber, French. **Religions:** Sunni Moslems 99%.

Geography: Area: 171,953 sq. mi., larger than California. **Location:** on NW coast of Africa. **Neighbors:** Mauritania on S, Algeria on E. **Topography:** Consists of 5 natural regions: mountain ranges (Riff in the N, Middle Atlas, Upper Atlas, and Anti-Atlas); rich plains in the W; alluvial plains in SW; well-cultivated plateaus in the center; a pre-Sahara arid zone extending from SE. **Capital:** Rabat. **Cities** (1978 est.): Casablanca 1,371,330; Rabat-Sale 435,510; Marrakech 330,400, Tangier.

Government: Head of state: King Hassan II; b. July 9, 1929; in office: Mar. 3, 1961. **Head of government:** Prime Min. Maati Bouabid; b. Nov. 11, 1927; in office: Mar. 23, 1979. **Local divisions:** 2 urban prefectures, 33 provinces. **Armed forces:** regulars 98,000; para-military 30,000.

Economy: Industries: Carpets, clothing, leather goods, tourism. **Chief crops:** Grain, fruits, dates, grapes. **Minerals:** Antimony, cobalt, manganese, phosphate, zinc, lead, oil, coal. **Crude oil reserves** (1980): 100 mln. bbls. **Per capita arable land:** 1.0 acres. **Meat prod.** (1978): beef: 76,000 metric tons; lamb: 59,000 metric tons. **Fish catch** (1977): 260,600 metric tons. **Electricity prod.** (1978): 3.59 bln. kwh. **Labor force:** 50% agric.

Finance: Currency: Dirham (Apr. 1981: 5.03 = $1 US). **Gross domestic product** (1979): $14.95 bln. **Per capita income** (1977): $555. **Imports** (1980): $4.26 bln.; partners (1978): Fr. 26%, Sp. 10 %, U.S. 8%, W. Ger. 7%. **Exports** (1980): $2.45 bln.; partners (1978): Fr. 27%, W. Ger. 11%, Sp. 7%, It. 6%. **Tourists** (1977): 1,427,500; receipts $375 mln. **National budget** (1974): $1.68 bln. revenues; $2.00 bln. expenditures. **International reserves less gold** (Mar. 1981): $423 mln. **Gold:** 704,000 oz t. **Consumer prices** (change in 1980): 9.4%.

Transport: Railway traffic (1978): 871.2 mln. passenger-km; 3.78 bln. net ton-km. **Motor vehicles:** in use (1976): 347,400 passenger cars, 145,700 comm. vehicles; assembled (1976): 25,000 passenger cars; 6,000 comm. vehicles. **Civil aviation:** 1,227 mln. passenger-km (1976); 18 mln. freight ton-km (1976). **Chief ports:** Tangier, Casablanca, Kenitra.

Communications: Television sets: 522,000 licensed (1976). **Radios:** 1.5 mln. licensed (1976), 157,000 manuf. (1975). **Telephones in use** (1978): 210,000. **Daily newspaper circ.** (1976): 190,000.

Health: Life expectancy at birth (1975): 51.4 male; 54.5 female. **Births** (per 1,000 pop. 1975): 46.8. **Deaths** (per 1,000 pop. 1975): 15.7. **Natural increase** (1975): 3.1%. **Hospital beds** (per 100,000 pop. 1977): 123. **Physicians** (per 100,000 pop. 1977): 9. **Infant mortality** (per 1,000 live births 1975): 149.

Education (1977): **Literacy:** 24%. **Pop. 5-19:** in school: 29%; teachers per 1,000: 9. **PQLI:** 43.

Berbers were the original inhabitants, followed by Carthaginians and Romans. Arabs conquered in 683. In the 11th and 12th centuries, a Berber empire ruled all NW Africa and most of Spain from Morocco.

Part of Morocco came under Spanish rule in the 19th century; France controlled the rest in the early 20th. Tribal uprisings lasted from 1911 to 1933. The country became independent Mar. 2, 1956. Tangier, an internationalized seaport, was turned over to Morocco, 1956. Ifni, a Spanish enclave, was ceded in 1969.

Morocco annexed over 70,000 sq. mi. of phosphate-rich land Apr. 14, 1976, two-thirds of former Spanish Sahara, with the remainder annexed by Mauritania. Spain had withdrawn in February. Polisario, a guerrilla movement, proclaimed the region independent Feb. 27, and launched attacks with Algerian support. Morocco accepted U.S. military and economic aid. When Mauritania signed a treaty with the Polisario Front, and gave up its portion of the former Spanish Sahara, Morocco occupied the area, 1980. Morocco accused Algeria of instigating Polisario attacks.

After six years of bitter fighting, Morocco controls the main

Mozambique

People's Republic of Mozambique

People: Population (1980 est.): 10,470,000. **Age distrib.** (%): 0–14: 45.3; 15–59: 50.6; 60+: 4.1. **Pop. density:** 34.55 per sq. mi. **Ethnic groups:** Bantu tribes. **Languages:** Portuguese (official), others. **Religions:** Christians 20%, Moslems 10%, 65% animist.

Geography: Area: 303,073 sq. mi.; larger than Texas. **Location:** On SE coast of Africa. **Neighbors:** Tanzania on N, Malawi, Zambia, Zimbabwe on W, South Africa, Swaziland on S. **Topography:** Coastal lowlands comprise nearly half the country with plateaus rising in steps to the mountains along the western border. **Capital:** Maputo. **Cities:** (1970 cen.): Maputo 383,775.

Government: Head of state: Pres. Samora Machel; b. Sept. 29, 1933; in office: June 25, 1975. **Local divisions:** 10 provinces. **Armed forces:** regulars 24,000.

Economy: Industries: Cement, alcohol, textiles. **Chief crops:** Cashews, cotton, sugar, copra, sisal, tea. **Minerals:** Coal, tantalite, copper, iron, bauxite, gold. **Per capita arable land:** 0.7 acres. **Meat prod.** (1978): beef: 37,000 metric tons; pork: 7,000 metric tons. **Fish catch** (1977): 14,000 metric tons. **Electricity prod.** (1978): 7.68 bln. kwh. **Labor force:** 74% agric., 16% man., 10% services.

Finance: Currency: Escudo (Sept. 1979: 33 = $1 US). **Gross domestic product** (1978): $2 bln. **Per capita income** (1978 est.): $170. **Imports** (1979): $280 mln.; partners: So. Afr. 20%, W. Ger. 15%, Zimb. 13%, Port. 10%. **Exports** (1979): $100 mln.; partners: U.S. 27%, Port. 16%, UK 7%, So. Afr. 6%. **National budget** (1977): $190 mln. revenues; $292 mln. expenditures. **Consumer prices** (change in 1976): 4.5%.

Transport: Railway traffic (1973): 396 mln. passenger-km; 3.4 bln. net ton-km. **Motor vehicles:** in use (1972): 89,300 passenger cars, 21,500 comm. vehicles. **Chief ports:** Maputo, Beira, Nacala.

Communications: Radios: 225,000 licensed (1976), 24,000 manuf. (1974). **Telephones in use** (1977): 52,270. **Daily newspaper circ.** (1976): 42,000; 4 per 1,000 pop.

Health: Life expectancy at birth (1975): 41.9 male; 45.1 female. **Births** (per 1,000 pop. 1975): 45.5. **Deaths** (per 1,000 pop. 1975): 21.0. **Natural increase** (1975): 2.5%. **Hospital beds** (per 100,000 pop. 1977): 129. **Physicians** (per 100,000 pop. 1977): 6. **Infant mortality** (per 1,000 live births 1975): 19.1

Education (1977): **Literacy:** 10%. **Pop. 5-19:** in school: 20%, teachers per 1,000: 4. **PQLI:** 27.

The first Portuguese post on the Mozambique coast was established in 1505, on the trade route to the East. Mozambique became independent June 25, 1975, after a ten-year war against Portuguese colonial domination. The 1974 revolution in Portugal paved the way for the orderly transfer of power to Frelimo (Front for the Liberation of Mozambique). Frelimo took over local administration Sept. 20, 1974, over the opposition, in part violent, of some blacks and whites. The new government, led by Maoist Pres. Samora Machel, promised a gradual transition to a communist system, beginning with indoctrination to combat "individualism" and capitalist or traditionalist values. All private schools were closed. Rural collective farms were called for in a July 27, 1975, directive. All private homes were nationalized in 1976. Economic problems included the emigration of most of the country's 160,000 whites, a politically untenable economic dependence on white-ruled South Africa, and a large external debt.

Mozambique closed its border with Rhodesia in March 1976. Border clashes intensified, with Rhodesian troops attacking black Rhodesian guerrillas within Mozambique. Soviet arms were sent following a 1977 friendship treaty. But most aid comes from the West, with which most trade is conducted.

Early in 1979 the government announced that the country was in a state of war as a result of increased guerrilla activities. Incidents and reprisals continued.

Nauru

Republic of Nauru

People: Population (1979): 8,000. **Pop density:** 906.75 per sq. mi. **Ethnic groups:** Nauruans, Gilbert and Tuvalu Islanders. Chinese 15%, European 7%. **Languages:** Nauruan, English. **Religions:** Christianity nearly universal.

Geography: Area: 8 sq. mi. **Location:** In Western Pacific O. just S of Equator. **Neighbors:** Nearest are Solomon Is. **Topography:** Mostly a plateau bearing high grade phosphate deposits, surrounded by a coral cliff and a sandy shore in concentric rings. **Capital:** Yaren.

Government: Head of state: Pres. Hammer De Roburt, b. Sept. 25, 1922; in office: May 11, 1978. **Local divisions:** 14 districts.

Economy: Electricity prod. (1977): 26.00 mln. kwh.

Finance: Currency: Australian dollar. **Gross domestic product** (1976 est.): $100 mln. **Per capita income** (1976): $12,000. **Imports** (1976): $15 mln.; partners (1974): Austral. 58%, Neth. 30%. **Exports** (1976): $41 mln.; partners (1974): Austral. 51%, NZ 41%, Jap. 5%. **National budget** (1979): $46 mln. revenues; $38 mln. expenditures.

Communications: Radios: 3,600 in use (1976). **Telephones in use** (1978): 1,500.

Health: Births (per 1,000 pop. 1976): 19.8. **Deaths** (per 1,000 pop. 1976): 4.5. **Natural increase** (1976): 1.5%. **Infant mortality** (per 1,000 live births 1976): 19.0.

The island was discovered in 1798 by the British but was formally annexed to the German Empire in 1886. After World War I, Nauru became a League of Nations mandate administered by Australia. During World War II the Japanese occupied the island and shipped 1,200 Nauruans to the fortress island of Truk as slave laborers.

In 1947 Nauru was made a UN trust territory, administered by Australia. Nauru became an independent republic Jan. 31, 1968.

Phosphate exports provide one of the world's highest per capita revenues for the 4,032 native Nauruans (some 3,975 Chinese, Europeans, and Pacific Islanders also live in Nauru, many working in the phosphate industry). The deposits are expected to be nearly exhausted by 1990.

Nepal
Kingdom of Nepal

People: Population (1979 est.): 14,608,000. **Age distrib.** (%): 0–14: 40.5; 15–59: 53.9; 60+: 5.6. **Pop. density:** 246.86 per sq. mi. **Urban** (1971): 4.0%. **Ethnic groups:** The many tribes are descendants of Indian, Tibetan, and Central Asian migrants. **Languages:** Nepali (official) (an Indic language), Newari, 11 others. **Religions:** Hindus 90%, Buddhists 9%.

Geography: Area: 54,362 sq. mi., the size of North Carolina. **Location:** Astride the Himalaya Mts. **Neighbors:** China on N, India on S. **Topography:** The Himalayas stretch across the N, the hill country with its fertile valleys extends across the center, while the southern border region is part of the flat, subtropical Ganges Plain. **Capital:** Kathmandu. **Cities** (1971 cen.): Kathmandu 150,402, Pokhara, Biratnagar, Birganj.

Government: Head of state: King Birendra Bir Bikram Shah Dev; b. Dec. 28, 1945; in office: Jan. 31, 1972. **Head of government:** Prime Min. Surya Bahadur Thapa; in office: June 1, 1979. **Local divisions:** 14 zones; 75 districts. **Armed forces:** regulars 20,000; para-military 12,000.

Economy: Industries: Hides, drugs, tourism. **Chief crops:** Jute, rice, grain. **Minerals:** Quartz. **Other resources:** Forests. **Per capita arable land:** 0.4 acres. **Meat prod.** (1978): beef: 22,000 metric tons; pork: 5,000 metric tons; lamb: 18,000 metric tons. **Electricity prod.** (1977): 180 mln. kwh. **Labor force:** 94% agric.; 1% manuf.

Finance: Currency: Rupee (Apr. 1981: 12.00 = $1 US). **Gross domestic product** (1980): $1.99 bln. **Per capita income** (1975): $114. **Imports** (1980): $342 mln.; partners (1978): India 31%, Jap. 16%. **Exports** (1980): $80 mln.; partners (1978): India 48%, Jap. 8%, U.S. 5%, W. Ger. 5%. **Tourists** (1977): 129,300; receipts: $2 mln. **National budget** (1980): $144 mln. revenues; $295 mln. expenditures. **International reserves less gold** (Apr. 1981): $165.9 mln. **Gold:** 151,000 oz t. **Consumer prices** (change in 1980): 16.4%.

Communications: Radios: 150,000 in use (1976). **Telephones in use** (1978): 9,425. **Daily newspaper circ.** (1976): 96,000.

Health: Life expectancy at birth (1975): 42.2 male; 45.0 female. **Births** (per 1,000 pop. 1975): 44.4. **Deaths** (per 1,000

pop. 1975): 22.5. **Natural increase** (1975): 2.2%. **Hospital beds** (per 100,000 pop. 1977): 15. **Physicians** (per 100,000 pop. 1977): 3.

Education (1977): **Literacy:** 19%. **Pop. 5-19:** in school: 22%, teachers per 1,000: 7. **PQLI:** 29.

Nepal was originally a group of petty principalities, the inhabitants of one of which, the Gurkhas, became dominant about 1769. In 1951 King Tribhubana Bir Bikram, member of the Shah family, ended the system of rule by hereditary premiers of the Ranas family, who had kept the kings virtual prisoners, and established a cabinet system of government.

Virtually closed to the outside world for centuries, Nepal is now linked to India and Pakistan by roads and air service and to Tibet by road. Polygamy, child marriage, and the caste system were officially abolished in 1963.

India, the largest aid donor, is the chief trade partner, but Nepal has cultivated good relations with China as well.

Students and political opponents were arrested in 1974 following violent protests. A new wave of protests, 1979, led to more arrests and executions, but a change in premiers.

The promised referendum on Nepalese government was held May 2, 1980, backing the retention of the partyless form of government. Political reforms were promised by the king.

Netherlands
Kingdom of the Netherlands

People: Population (1980 est.) 14,140,000. **Age distrib.** (%): 0–14: 24.2; 15–59: 60.5; 60 + : 15.4. **Pop. density:** 1,002.62 per sq. mi. **Urban** (1976): 88.4%. **Ethnic groups:** Dutch, some Indonesian and Surinamese. **Languages:** Dutch. **Religions:** Roman Catholics 40%, Protestants 40%.

Geography: Area: 14,103 sq. mi., the size of Mass., Conn., and R.I. combined. **Location:** In NW Europe on North Sea. **Topography:** The land is flat, an average alt. of 37 ft. above sea level, with much land below sea level reclaimed and protected by 1,500 miles of dikes. Since 1927 the government has been draining the IJsselmeer, formerly the Zuider Zee. By 1972, 410,000 of a planned 550,000 acres had been drained and reclaimed. **Capital:** Amsterdam. **Cities** (1978 est.): Amsterdam 733,593; Rotterdam 595,662; Hague 467,997; Utrecht 243,001.

Government: Head of state: Queen Beatrix; b. Jan. 31, 1938; in office: Apr. 30, 1980. **Head of government:** Prime Min. Andries A.M. van Agt, b. Feb. 2, 1931; in office: Dec. 19, 1977. **Seat of govt.:** The Hague. **Local divisions:** 11 provinces. **Armed forces:** regulars 114,820; reserves 171,000.

Economy: Industries: Metals, machinery, food products, chemicals, textiles, oil refinery, diamond cutting, pottery, electronics, tourism. **Chief crops:** Grains, potatoes, sugar beets, vegetables, fruits, flowers. **Minerals:** Natural gas, oil. **Crude oil reserves** (1980): 60 mln. bbls. **Per capita arable land:** 0.1 acres. **Meat prod.** (1978): beef: 374,000 metric tons; pork: 1.05 mln. metric tons; lamb: 16,000 metric tons. **Fish catch** (1977): 313,000 metric tons. **Electricity prod.** (1978): 61.70 bln. kwh. **Crude steel prod.** (1979): 5.8 mln. metric tons. **Labor force:** 6% agric.; 30% ind. and commerce, 20% services, 15% gov.

Finance: Currency: Guilder (Apr. 1981: 2.45 = $1 US). **Gross domestic product** (1980): $161.36 bln. **Per capita income** (1979): $9,500. **Imports** (1980): $78.07 bln.; partners (1978): W. Ger. 25%, Belg. 13%, U.S. 9%, Fr. 8%. **Exports** (1980): $73.82 bln.; partners (1978): W. Ger. 31%, Belg. 15%, Fr. 11%, UK 7%. **Tourists** (1977): 2,939,400; receipts: $1.11 bln. **National budget** (1980): $58.02 bln. revenues; $63.33 bln. expenditures. **International reserves less gold** (Apr. 1981): $10.16 bln. **Gold:** 43.94 mln. oz t. **Consumer prices** (change in 1980): 6.5%.

Transport: Railway traffic (1978): 8.1 bln. passenger-km; 2.9 bln. net ton-km. **Motor vehicles:** in use (1977): 3.85 mln. passenger cars, 355,000 comm. vehicles; manuf. (1978): 62,400 passenger cars; 11,520 comm. vehicles. **Civil aviation:** 12,384 mln. passenger-km (1978); 82.3 mln. freight ton-km (1978). **Chief ports:** Rotterdam, Amsterdam, IJmuiden.

Communications: Television sets: 3.77 mln. licensed (1976). **Radios:** 4 mln. licensed (1976). **Telephones in use** (1978): 5,845,894. **Daily newspaper circ.** (1976): 4,371,000.

Health: Life expectancy at birth (1977): 72.0 male; 78.4 female. **Births** (per 1,000 pop. 1979): 12.5. **Deaths** (per 1,000 pop. 1979): 8.0. **Natural increase** (1978): .4%. **Hospital beds** (per 100,000 pop. 1977): 1,009. **Physicians** (per 100,000 pop. 1977): 172. **Infant mortality** (per 1,000 live births 1978): 9.5.

Education (1977): **Literacy:** 99%. **Pop. 5-19:** school: 63%, teachers per 1,000: 29. **PQLI:** 97.

Julius Caesar conquered the region in 55 BC, when it was inhabited by Celtic and Germanic tribes.

After the empire of Charlemagne fell apart, the Netherlands (Holland, Belgium, Flanders) split among counts, dukes and bishops, passed to Burgundy and thence to Charles V of Spain. His son, Philip II, tried to check the Dutch drive toward political freedom and Protestantism (1568-1573). William the Silent, prince of Orange, led a confederation of the northern provinces, called Estates, in the Union of Utrecht, 1579. The Estates retained individual sovereignty, but were represented jointly in the States-General, a body that had control of foreign affairs and defense. In 1581 they repudiated allegiance to Spain. The rise of the Dutch republic to naval, economic, and artistic eminence came in the 17th century.

The United Dutch Republic ended 1795 when the French formed the Batavian Republic. Napoleon made his brother Louis king of Holland, 1806; Louis abdicated 1810 when Napoleon annexed Holland. In 1813 the French were expelled. In 1815 the Congress of Vienna formed a kingdom of the Netherlands, including Belgium, under William I. In 1830, the Belgians seceded and formed a separate kingdom.

The constitution, promulgated 1814, and subsequently revised, assures a hereditary constitutional monarchy.

The Netherlands maintained its neutrality in World War I, but was invaded and brutally occupied by Germany from 1940 to 1945. After the war, neutrality was abandoned, and the country joined NATO, the Western European Union, the Benelux Union, and, in 1957, became a charter member of the Common Market.

In 1949, after several years of fighting, the Netherlands granted independence to Indonesia, where it had ruled since the 17th century. In 1963, West New Guinea was turned over to Indonesia, after five years of controversy and seizure of Dutch property in Indonesia.

Some 200,000 Indonesians emigrated to the Netherlands. Of them, 35,000 were from the South Moluccan islands. Terrorists demanding independence for South Molucca from Indonesia staged train hijackings and other incidents in the Netherlands in 1975 and 1977.

The independence of Suriname, 1975, instigated mass emigrations to the Netherlands, adding to problems of unemployment.

Though the Netherlands has been heavily industrialized, its productive small farms export large quantitites of pork and dairy foods.

Rotterdam, located along the principal mouth of the Rhine, handles the most cargo of any ocean port in the world. Canals, of which there are 3,478 miles, are important in transportation.

Citing age, Queen Juliana abdicated, Apr. 30, 1980, in favor of her eldest daughter, Princess Beatrix.

Netherlands Antilles

The **Netherlands Antilles,** constitutionally on a level of equality with the Netherlands homeland within the kingdom, consist of 2 groups of islands in the West Indies. **Curacao, Aruba,** and **Bonaire** are near the South American coast; **St. Eustatius, Saba,** and the southern part of **St. Maarten** are SE of Puerto Rico. Northern two-thirds of St. Maarten belong to French Guadeloupe; the French call the island St. Martin. Total area of the 2 groups is 385 sq. mi., including: Aruba 74, Bonaire 111, Curacao 171, St. Eustatius 11, Saba 5, St. Maarten (Dutch part) 13.

Total pop. (est. 1979) was 246,500. Willemstad, on Curacao, is the capital. Chief products are corn, pulse, salt and phosphate; principal industry is the refining of crude oil from Venezuela. Tourism is an important industry, as are electronics and shipbuilding.

New Zealand

People: Population: (1980 est.): 3,200,000. **Age distrib. (%):** 0–14: 29.0; 15–59: 57.9; 60+: 13.1. **Pop. density:** 30.80 per sq. mi. **Urban** (1976): 83.0%. **Ethnic groups:** European (mostly British) 90%, Polynesian (mostly Maori) 9%. **Languages:** English, Maori. **Religions:** Anglican 29.2%, Presbyterian 18.1%, Roman Catholics 15.3%, other 37.4%.

Geography: Area: 103,883 sq. mi., the size of Colorado. **Location:** in SW Pacific O. **Neighbors:** Nearest are Australia on W, Fiji, Tonga on N. **Topography:** Each of the 2 main islands (North and South Is.) is mainly hilly and mountainous. The east coasts consist of fertile plains, especially the broad Canterbury

Plains on South Is. A volcanic plateau is in center of North Is. South Is. has glaciers and 15 peaks over 10,000 ft. **Capital:** Wellington. **Cities** (1978 est.): Christchurch 172,400; Auckland 149,000; Manukau 142,200; Wellington 139,200.

Government: Head of state: Queen Elizabeth II, represented by Gov.-Gen. Keith Jacka Holyoake; b. Feb. 11, 1904; in office: Oct. 26, 1977. **Head of government:** Prime Min. Robert David Muldoon; b. Sept. 21, 1921; in office: Dec. 12, 1975. **Local divisions:** 96 counties, 132 boroughs, 3 towns, 4 districts. **Armed forces:** regulars 12,739; reserves 4,541.

Economy: Industries: Food processing, paper, steel, aluminum, oil products. **Chief crops:** Grain. **Minerals:** Oil, gas, gold, iron, limestone, diatomite, coal, pumice. **Crude oil reserves** (1980): 110 mln. bbls. **Other resources:** Wool, timber. **Per capita arable land:** 0.3 acres. **Meat prod.** (1978): beef: 529,000 metric tons; pork: 41,000 metric tons; lamb: 519,000 metric tons. **Fish catch** (1977): 110,500 metric tons. **Electricity prod.** (1978): 21.35 bln. kwh. **Crude steel prod.** (1979): 229,000 metric tons. **Labor force:** 14% agric.; 65% ind. and commerce, 24% services and gov.

Finance: Currency: Dollar (Apr. 1981: 1.11 = $1 US). **Gross domestic product** (1979-80): $20.9 bln. **Per capita income** (1979-80): $6,650. **Imports** (1980): $5.47 bln.; partners (1978): Austral. 22%, UK 16%, U.S. 14%, Jap. 13%. **Exports** (1980): $5.42 bln.; partners (1978): UK 18%, U.S. 15%, Jap. 14%, Austral. 12%. **Tourists** (1977): 389,500; receipts $155 mln. **National budget** (1978-79): $6.8 bln. revenues; $6.64 bln. expenditures. **International reserves less gold** (Apr. 1981): $372 mln. **Gold:** 22,000 oz t. **Consumer prices** (change in 1980): 17.1%.

Transport: Railway traffic (1978): 500 mln. passenger-km; 3.4 bln. net ton-km. **Motor vehicles** in use (1977): 1.21 mln. passenger cars; (1976): 221,700 comm. vehicles; assembled (1978): 51,828 passenger cars; 11,088 comm. vehicles. **Civil aviation:** 4,116 mln. passenger-km (1978); 146 mln. freight ton-km (1978). **Chief ports:** Auckland, Wellington, Lyttleton, Tauranga.

Communications: Television sets: 813,000 mln. licensed (1976), 119,000 manuf. (1977). **Radios:** 2.7 mln. in use (1976), 169,000 manuf. (1977). **Telephones in use** (1978): 1,715,343. **Daily newspaper circ.** (1976): 848,000.

Health: Life expectancy at birth (1979): 69.01 male; 75.45 female. **Births** (per 1,000 pop. 1979): 16.7. **Deaths** (per 1,000 pop. 1979): 8.2. **Natural increase** (1977): .9%. **Hospital beds** (per 100,000 pop. 1977): 1,022. **Physicians** (per 100,000 pop. 1977): 135. **Infant mortality** (per 1,000 live births 1980): 14.2

Education (1977): **Literacy:** 98%. **Pop. 5-19:** in school: 81%, teachers per 1,000: 35. **PQLI:** 94.

The Maoris, a Polynesian group from the eastern Pacific, reached New Zealand before and during the 14th century. The first European to sight New Zealand was Dutch navigator Abel Janszoon Tasman, but Maoris refused to allow him to land. British Capt. James Cook explored the coasts, 1769-1770.

British sovereignty was proclaimed in 1840, with organized settlement beginning in the same year. Representative institutions were granted in 1853. Maori Wars ended in 1870 with British victory. The colony became a dominion in 1907, and is an independent member of the Commonwealth.

New Zealand fought on the side of the Allies in both world wars, and signed the ANZUS Treaty of Mutual Security with the U.S. and Australia in 1951. New Zealand joined with Australia and Britain in a pact to defend Singapore and Malaysia; New Zealand units are stationed in those 2 countries.

A labor tradition in politics dates back to the 19th century. Private ownership is basic to the economy, but state ownership or regulation affects many industries. Transportation, broadcasting, mining, and forestry are largely state-owned.

The native Maoris numbered an estimated 200,000 in the early 19th century; violence and European diseases cut them to 40,000 by the end of the century. Recently they have increased at 3% annually and totaled over 250,000 in 1976. Four of 92 members of the House of Representatives are elected directly by the Maori people.

New Zealand comprises **North Island,** 44,204 sq. mi.; **South Island,** 58,304 sq. mi.; **Stewart Island,** 674 sq. mi.; **Chatham Islands,** 372 sq. mi.

In 1965, the **Cook Islands** (pop. 1976 cen., 18,112; area 93 sq. mi.) became self-governing although New Zealand retains responsibility for defense and foreign affairs. **Niue** attained the same status in 1974; it lies 400 mi. to W (pop. 1977 est., 6,000; area 100 sq. mi.). **Tokelau Is.,** (pop. 1976 cen., 1,575; area 4 sq.

mi.) are 300 mi. N of Samoa.

Ross Dependency, administered by New Zealand since 1923, comprises 160,000 sq. mi. of Antarctic territory.

Nicaragua

Republic of Nicaragua

People: Population (1980 est.): 2,740,000. **Age distrib.** (%): 0–14: 48.1; 15–59: 47.2; 60+: 4.7. **Pop. density:** 47.95 per sq. mi. **Urban** (1972): 48.6%. **Ethnic groups:** Mestizo 70%, Caucasian 17%, Negro 9%, Indian 4%. **Languages:** Spanish, English (on Caribbean coast). **Religions:** Roman Catholics 95%.

Geography: Area: 57,143 sq. mi., slightly larger than Wisconsin. **Location:** In Central America. **Neighbors:** Honduras on N, Costa Rica on S. **Topography:** Both Atlantic and Pacific coasts are over 200 mi. long. The Cordillera Mtns., with many volcanic peaks, runs NW-SE through the middle of the country. Between this and a volcanic range to the E lie Lakes Managua and Nicaragua. **Capital:** Managua. **Cities** (1971 cen.): Managua 398,514.

Government: 5-member junta, effective head: Sergio Ramirez Mercado, b. Aug 5, 1942; took power: July 20, 1979. **Local divisions:** 16 departments; one national district. **Armed forces:** regulars 8,300; para-military 4,000.

Economy: Industries: Oil refining, chemicals, textiles. **Chief crops:** Bananas, cotton, fruit, yucca, coffee, sugar, corn, beans, cocoa, rice, sesame, tobacco, wheat. **Minerals:** Gold, silver, copper, tungsten. **Other resources:** Forests, shrimp. **Per capita arable land:** 1.4 acres. **Meat prod.** (1978): beef: 85,000 metric tons; pork: 20,000 metric tons. **Fish catch:** (1977): 22,400 metric tons. **Electricity prod.** (1977): 1.18 bln. kwh. **Labor force:** 53% agric.

Finance: Currency: Cordoba (Apr. 1981: 10.05 = $1 US). **Gross domestic product** (1979): $1.45 bln. **Per capita income** (1978): $825. **Imports** (1979): $350 mln.; partners (1977): U.S. 30%, Venez. 12%, Jap. 9%, Costa Rica 8%. **Exports** (1979): $700 mln.; partners (1977): U.S. 22%, W. Ger. 13%, Jap. 11%, Costa Rica 8%. **Tourists** (1976): 207,000; receipts: $28 mln. **National budget** (1978): $228 mln. revenues; $393 mln. expenditures. **International reserves less gold** (Nov. 1979): $85.36 mln. **Gold:** 18,000 oz t. **Consumer prices** (change in 1979): 47.9%.

Transport: Railway traffic (1977): 19 mln. passenger-miles; 11 mln. net ton-miles. **Motor vehicles:** in use (1973): 32,000 passenger cars, 20,000 comm. vehicles. **Chief ports:** Corinto, Puerto Somoza, San Juan del Sur.

Communications: Television sets: 90,000 in use (1976). **Radios:** 126,000 in use (1975). **Telephones in use** (1978): 55,803. **Daily newspaper circ.** (1976): 113,000; 51 per 1,000 pop.

Health: Life expectancy at birth (1975): 51.2 male; 54.6 female. **Births** (per 1,000 pop. 1975): 48.3. **Deaths** (per 1,000 pop. 1975): 13.8. **Natural increase** (1975): 3.5%. **Hospital beds** (per 100,000 pop. 1977): 207. **Physicians** (per 100,000 pop. 1977): 60. **Infant mortality** (per 1,000 live births 1975): 37.0.

Education (1977): **Literacy:** 58%. **Pop. 5-19:** in school: 43%, teachers per 1,000: 13. **PQLI:** 54.

Nicaragua, inhabited by various Indian tribes, was conquered by Spain in 1552. After gaining independence from Spain, 1821, Nicaragua was united for a short period with Mexico, then with the United Provinces of Central America, finally becoming an independent republic, 1838.

U.S. Marines occupied the country at times in the early 20th century, the last time from 1926 to 1933.

Gen. Anastasio Somoza-Debayle was elected president 1967. He resigned 1972, but was elected president again Sept. 1, 1974. The Somozas, richest Nicaraguan family, have dominated politics for 4 decades. Martial law was imposed in Dec. 1974, after officials were kidnapped by the Marxist Sandinista guerrillas. The country's Roman Catholic bishops charged in 1977 that the government had tortured, raped, and executed civilians in its anti-guerrilla campaign. The Inter-American Commission on Human Rights made a similar report to the OAS, 1978. Violent opposition spread to nearly all classes, 1978; a nationwide strike called against the government Aug. 25 touched off a state of civil war at Matagalpa. Nicaragua rejected a U.S.-supported mediation offer to end the strife; the U.S. cut off military ties and aid.

Months of simmering civil war erupted when Sandinist guerrillas invaded Nicaragua May 29, 1979, touching off a 7-week-offensive that culminated in the resignation and exile of Somoza, July 17. Border clashes and incursions, May 1981, into Nicaragua from Honduras by anti-Sandinista Nicaraguans led to fears of armed conflict between the two nations. A 5-member provisional junta governs, modeling their own form of socialism, which includes a private sector and independent political opinion.

Niger

Republic of Niger

People: Population (1979 est.): 5,346,000. **Age distrib.** (%): 0–14: 43.0; 15–59: 52.2; 60+: 4.8. **Pop. density:** 10.2 per sq. mi. **Ethnic groups:** Hausas 50%, Djermas 23%, Fulanis 15%, Tuaregs 12%. **Languages:** French (official), Hausa, Djerma, others. **Religions:** Muslims 85%, animism, Christian.

Geography: Area: 489,206 sq. mi., almost twice the size of Texas. **Location:** In the interior of N. Africa. **Neighbors:** Libya, Algeria on N, Mali, Upper Volta on W, Benin, Nigeria on S, Chad on E. **Topography:** Mostly arid desert and mountains. A narrow savanna in the S and the Niger R. basin in the SW contain most of the population. **Capital:** Niamey. **Cities** (1978 est.): Niamey 130,299, (fluctuates with nomad migration in dry season).

Government: Head of state: Pres. Seyni Kountche; b. 1931; in office: Apr. 15, 1974. **Local divisions:** 7 departments. **Armed forces:** regulars 2,150; para-military 1,800.

Economy: Chief crops: Peanuts, cotton. **Minerals:** Uranium (5th largest reserves in the world). **Per capita arable land:** 7.4 acres. **Meat prod.** (1978): beef: 24,000 metric tons; lamb: 24,000 metric tons. **Electricity prod.** (1977): 70.00 mln. kwh. **Labor force:** 90% agric.

Finance: Currency: CFA franc (Apr. 1981: 262.70 = $1 US). **Gross domestic product** (1978 est.): $1.3 bln. **Per capita income** (1978 est.): $250. **Imports** (1977): $196 mln.; partners (1978): Fr. 41%, U.K. 8%, Jap. 8%, U.S. 7%. **Exports** (1977): $160 mln.; partners (1978): Fr. 75%, Nigeria 11%, W. Ger. 6%. **National budget** (1977): $148.6 million. **International reserves less gold** (Jan. 1981): $124.5 mln. **Gold:** 11,000 oz t. **Consumer prices** (change in 1980): 10.3%.

Transport: Motor vehicles: in use (1976): 9,900 passenger cars, 11,800 comm. vehicles.

Communications: Radios: 145,000 in use (1970). **Telephones in use** (1977): 8,147. **Daily newspaper circ.** (1977): 3,000; 1 per 1,000 pop.

Health: Life expectancy at birth (1975): 39.4 male; 42.5 female. **Births** (per 1,000 pop. 1975): 50.8. **Deaths** (per 1,000 pop. 1975): 23.4. **Natural increase** (1975): 2.7%. **Hospital beds** (per 100,000 pop 1977): 69. **Physicians** (per 100,000 pop. 1977): 2. **Infant mortality** (per 1,000 live births 1978): 162.

Education (1977): **Literacy:** 5%. **Pop. 5-19:** in school: 11%, Teachers per 1,000: 3. **PQLI:** 16.

Niger was part of ancient and medieval African empires. European explorers reached the area in the late 18th century. The French colony of Niger was established 1900-22, after the defeat of Tuareg fighters, who had invaded the area from the N a century before. The country became independent Aug. 3, 1960. The next year it signed a bilateral agreement with France retaining close economic and cultural ties, which have continued. Hamani Diori, Niger's first president, was ousted in a 1974 coup. Drought and famine struck in 1973-74, and again in 1975, and half the country's livestock died.

Nigeria

Federal Republic of Nigeria

People: Population (1980 est.): 77,080,000. **Pop. density:** 216.09 per sq. mi. **Ethnic groups:** Yoruba 18%, Ibo 18%, Hausa-Fulani 32%, 250 others. **Languages:** English (official), Hausa, Yoruba, Ibo, others. **Religions:** Moslems 47% (in N), Christians 34% (in S), others.

Geography: Area: 356,699 sq. mi., more than twice the size of California. **Location:** On the S coast of W. Africa. **Neighbors:** Benin on W, Niger on N, Chad, Cameroon on E. **Topography:** 4 E-W regions divide Nigeria: a coastal mangrove swamp 10-60 mi. wide, a tropical rain forest 50-100 mi. wide, a plateau of savanna and open woodland, and semidesert in the N. **Capital:** Lagos. **Cities:** (1978 est.): Lagos 1,060,848; Ibadan 847,000; Ogbomosho 432,000; Kano 399,000.

Government: Head of state: Pres. Alhaji Shehu Shagari; b.

Apr. 25, 1925; in office: Oct. 1, 1979. **Local divisions:** 19 states, Federal Capital Territory. **Armed forces:** regulars 173,000; reserves 2,000.

Economy: Industries: Food processing, assembly of vehicles and other equipment. **Chief crops:** Cocoa (main export crop), tobacco, palm products, peanuts, cotton, soybeans. **Minerals:** Oil, gas, coal, iron, limestone, columbium, tin. **Crude oil reserves** (1980): 17.4 bln. bbls. **Other resources:** Timber, rubber, hides. **Per capita arable land:** 0.8 acres. **Meat prod.** (1978): beef: 197,000 metric tons; pork: 36,000 metric tons; lamb: 106,000 metric tons. **Fish catch** (1977): 506,000 metric tons. **Electricity prod.** (1978): 3.50 bln. kwh. **Labor force:** 75% agric., 10% ind., commerce and services.

Finance: Currency: Naira (Apr. 1981: .57 = $1 US). **Gross domestic product** (1978): $43 bln. **Per capita income** (1978): $523. **Imports** (1980): $15.79 bln.; partners (1977): UK 22%, W. Ger. 16%, U.S. 11%, Jap. 11%. **Exports** (1980): $26.76 bln.; partners (1977): U.S. 40%, Neth. Ant. 15%, Neth. 11%, UK 8%. **Tourist receipts** (1977): $60 mln. **National budget** (1978): $8.89 bln. revenues; $6.50 bln. expenditures. **International reserves less gold** (Mar. 1981): $9.73 bln. **Gold:** 629,000 oz t. **Consumer prices** (change in 1979): 11.2%.

Transport: Railway traffic (1974): 785 mln. passenger-km; 972 mln. net ton-km. **Motor vehicles:** in use (1973): 150,000 passenger cars, 82,000 comm. vehicles. **Civil aviation:** 852 mln. passenger-km (1977); 6 mln. freight ton-km (1977). **Chief ports:** Port Harcourt, Bonny, Lagos.

Communications: Television sets: 105,000 licensed (1976), 14,000 manuf. (1976). **Radios:** 5.1 mln. licensed (1976), 112,000 manuf. (1976). **Telephones in use** (1978): 128,352. **Daily newspaper circ.** (1976): 527,000.

Health: Life expectancy at birth (1966): 37.2 male; 36.7 female. **Births** (per 1,000 pop. 1975): 50.3. **Deaths** (per 1,000 pop. 1975): 19.7. **Natural increase** (1975): 3.1%. **Hospital beds** (per 100,000 pop. 1977): 80. **Physicians** (per 100,000 pop. 1977): 7.

Education (1977): **Literacy:** 25%. **Pop. 5-19:** in school: 22%, teachers per 1,000: 7. **PQLI:** 28.

Early cultures in Nigeria date back to at least 700 BC. From the 12th to the 14th centuries, more advanced cultures developed in the Yoruba area, at Ife, and in the north, where Moslem influence prevailed.

Portuguese and British slavers appeared from the 15th-16th centuries. Britain seized Lagos, 1861, during an anti-slave trade campaign, and gradually extended control inland until 1900. Nigeria became independent Oct. 1, 1960, and a republic Oct. 1, 1963.

On May 30, 1967, the Eastern Region seceded, proclaiming itself the Republic of Biafra, plunging the country into civil war. Casualties in the war were est. at over 1 million, including many "Biafrans" (mostly Ibos) who died of starvation despite international efforts to provide relief. The secessionists, after steadily losing ground, capitulated Jan. 12, 1970. Within a few years, the Ibos were reintegrated into national life, but mistrust among the regions persists.

Under "indigenization" programs, various industries were to be run by majority Nigerian control by 1979. Oil revenues have made possible a massive economic development program, largely using private enterprise, but agriculture has lagged. Nigeria nationalized British Petroleum's facilities, July, 1979.

Nigeria led in the formation of the Economic Community of West African States, 1975, linking 15 countries.

After 13 years of military rule, the nation experienced a peaceful return to civilian government, Oct., 1979.

Norway

Kingdom of Norway

People: Population (1980 est.): 4,090,000. **Age distrib. (%):** 0–14: 23.5; 15–59: 57.2; 60+: 19.6. **Pop. density:** 32.67 per sq. mi. **Urban** (1977): 44.2%. **Ethnic groups:** Germanic (Nordic, Alpine, Baltic), minority Lapps. **Languages:** Norwegian (official), Lapp. **Religions:** Lutherans 95%.

Geography: Area: 125,181 sq. mi., slightly larger than New Mexico. **Location:** Occupies the W part of Scandinavian peninsula in NW Europe (extends farther north than any European land). **Neighbors:** Sweden, Finland, USSR on E. **Topography:** A highly indented coast is lined with tens of thousands of islands. Mountains and plateaus cover most of the country, which is only

25% forested. **Capital:** Oslo. **Cities** (1978 est.): Oslo 461,437; Bergen 212,308.

Government: Head of state: King Olav V, b. July 2, 1903; in office: Sept. 21, 1957. **Head of government:** Prime Min. Gro Harlem Brundtland, b. Apr. 20, 1939; in office: Feb. 3, 1981. **Local divisions:** Oslo and 19 fylker (counties). **Armed forces:** regulars 39,000; reserves 160,000.

Economy: Industries: Paper, shipbuilding, engineering, metals, chemicals, food processing shipping. **Chief crops:** Grains, potatoes, fruits. **Minerals:** Oil, copper, pyrites, nickel, iron, zinc, lead. **Crude oil reserves** (1980): 5.75 bln. bbls. **Other resources:** Forests. **Per capita arable land:** 0.5 acres. **Meat prod.** (1978): beef: 72,000 metric tons; pork: 80,000 metric tons; lamb: 19,000 metric tons. **Fish catch** (1977): 3.6 mln. metric tons. **Electricity prod.** (1978): 81.11 bln. kwh. **Crude steel prod.** (1979): 891,000 metric tons. **Labor force:** 17% agric.; 24% manuf.

Finance: Currency: Krone (Apr. 1981: 5.55 = $1 US). **Gross domestic product** (1980): $57.32 bln. **Per capita income** (1978): $7,949. **Imports** (1980): $16.96 bln.; partners (1978): Swed. 18%, W. Ger. 14%, UK 12%, U.S. 7%. **Exports** (1980): $18.49 bln.; partners (1978): UK 37%, Swed. 11%, W. Ger. 8%, Den. 6%. **Tourists** (1977): 447,800; receipts: $478 mln. **National budget** (1976): $7.59 bln. revenues; $7.99 bln. expenditures. **International reserves less gold** (Apr. 1981): $5.94 bln. **Gold:** 1.18 mln. oz t. **Consumer prices** (change in 1980): 10.7%.

Transport: Railway traffic (1978): 2.71 bln. passenger-km; 2.06 bln. net ton-km. **Motor vehicles:** in use (1977): 1.11 mln. passenger cars, 161,900 comm. vehicles. **Civil aviation:** 3,792 mln. passenger-km (1978); 145 mln. freight ton-km (1978). **Chief ports:** Bergen, Stavanger, Oslo, Tonsberg.

Communications: Television sets: 1.09 mln. licensed (1976), 108,000 manuf. (1975). **Radios:** 1.29 mln. licensed (1976), 111,000 manuf. (1973). **Telephones in use** (1978): 1,562,500. **Daily newspaper circ.** (1977): 1,740,000; 430 per 1,000 pop.

Health: Life expectancy at birth (1977): 72.12 male; 78.42 female. **Births** (per 1,000 pop. 1980): 12.5. **Deaths** (per 1,000 pop. 1980): 10.0. **Natural increase** (1978): .3%. **Hospital beds** (per 100,000 pop. 1977): 1,481. **Physicians** (per 100,000 pop. 1977): 186. **Infant mortality** (per 1,000 live births 1977): 9.2.

Education (1977): **Literacy:** 99%. **Pop. 5-19:** in school: 69%, teachers per 1,000: 46. **PQLI:** 97.

The first supreme ruler of Norway was Harald the Fairhaired who came to power in 872 AD. Between 800 and 1000, Norway's Vikings raided and occupied widely dispersed parts of Europe.

The country was united with Denmark 1381-1814, and with Sweden, 1814-1905. In 1905, the country became independent with Prince Charles of Denmark as king.

Norway remained neutral during World War I. Germany attacked Norway Apr. 9, 1940, and held it until liberation May 8, 1945. The country abandoned its neutrality after the war, and joined the NATO alliance. Norway, a member of the European Free Trade Assoc., rejected membership in the Common Market in a 1972 referendum.

Abundant hydroelectric resources provided the base for Norway's industrialization, producing one of the highest living standards in the world.

Despite an almost total lack of unemployment and an increasing labor shortage, Norway has refused to admit more than a small number of foreign workers.

Norway's merchant marine is the world's fourth largest.

Norway and the Soviet Union have disputed their territorial waters boundary in the Barents Sea, north of the 2 countries' common border.

Petroleum output from oil and mineral deposits under the continental shelf raised state revenues; new refinery facilities opened in 1979, and new offshore fields were discovered.

In Feb. 1981, Gro Harlem Brundtland became Norway's new Prime Minister, the first woman in the post in the country's history.

Svalbard is a group of mountainous islands in the Arctic O., c. 23,957 sq. mi., pop. varying seasonally from 1,500 to 3,500. The largest, Spitsbergen (formerly called West Spitsbergen), 15,060 sq. mi., seat of governor, is about 370 mi. N of Norway. By a treaty signed in Paris, 1920, major European powers recognized the sovereignty of Norway, which incorporated it in 1925. Both Norway and the USSR mine rich coal deposits. Mt. Newton

(Spitsbergen) is 5,633 ft. tall.

Oman

Sultanate of Oman

People: Population (1980 est.): 890,000. **Pop. density:** 10.85 per sq. mi. **Ethnic groups:** Arab 88%, Baluchi 4%, Persian 3%, Indian 2%, African 2%. **Languages:** Arabic (official), Persian, Urdu, others. **Religions:** Ibadi Moslems 50%, Sunni Moslems 25%, some Hindus.

Geography: Area: 82,000 sq. mi., the size of Kansas. **Location:** On SE coast of Arabian peninsula. **Neighbors:** United Arab Emirates, Saudi Arabia, South Yemen on W. **Topography:** Oman has a narrow coastal plain up to 10 mi. wide, a range of barren mountains reaching 9,900 ft., and a wide, stony, mostly waterless plateau, avg. alt. 1,000 ft. Also the tip of the Ruus-al-Jebal peninsula controls access to the Persian Gulf. **Capital:** Muscat. **Cities** (1975 est.): Matrah 20,000; Muscat 7,000.

Government: Head of state: Sultan Qaboos bin Said; b. Nov. 18, 1942; in office: July 23, 1970. **Local divisions:** 1 province, 9 regions, and districts. **Armed forces:** regulars 19,200; para-military 3,300.

Economy: Chief crops: Dates, fruits vegetables, wheat, frankincense. **Minerals:** Oil. **Crude oil reserves** (1980): 2.40 bln. bbls. **Per capita arable land:** 0.05 acres. **Fish catch** (1977): 198,000 metric tons. **Electricity prod.** (1977): 550.00 mln. kwh. **Labor force:** 83% agric.

Finance: Currency: Rial Omani (Apr. 1981: .35 = $1 US). **Gross domestic product** (1979): $3.39 bln. **Per capita income** (1976): $2,400. **Imports** (1979): $1.25 bln.; partners: UK 21%, UAE 16%, Jap. 16%, W. Ger. 6%. **Exports** (1980): $3.29 bln.; partners: Jap. 57%, U.S. 15%, Nor. 7%, Neth. 6%. **National budget** (1979): $2.00 bln. revenues: $1.88 bln. expenditures. **International reserves less gold** (Jan. 1981): $1.16 bln. **Gold:** 217,000 oz t.

Transport: Chief ports: Matrah, Muscat.

Communications: Telephones in use (1978): 13,068.

Health: Hospital beds (per 100,000 pop. 1977): 173. **Physicians** (per 100,000 pop. 1977): 49.

Education (1977): **Literacy:** 50%. **Pop. 5-19:** in school: 25%, teachers per 1,000: 13. **PQLI:** 33.

A long history of rule by other lands, including Portugal in the 16th century, ended with the ouster of the Persians in 1744. By the early 19th century, Muscat and Oman was one of the most important countries in the region, controlling much of the Persian and Pakistan coasts, and ruling far-away Zanzibar, which was separated in 1861 under British mediation.

British influence was confirmed in a 1951 treaty, and Britain helped supress an uprising by traditionally rebellious interior tribes against control by Muscat in the 1950s. Enclaves on the Pakistan coast were sold to that country in 1958.

On July 23, 1970, Sultan Said bin Taimur was overthrown by his son. The new sultan changed the nation's name to Sultanate of Oman. He launched a domestic development program, and battled leftist rebels in the southern Dhofar area to their defeat, Dec. 1975. Warfare was resumed, 1979.

Oil, discovered in 1964, has been the major source of income for the sultanate.

Economic and military aid accords with the U.S. gave U.S. forces access to air and naval bases around the Indian O., 1980.

Pakistan

Islamic Republic of Pakistan

People: Population (1980 est.): 81,500,000. **Pop. density:** 237.78 per sq. mi. **Urban** (1972): 25.5%. **Ethnic groups:** Punjabi 66%, Sindhi 13%, Pushtun (Iranian) 8.5%, Urdu 7.6%, Baluchi 2.5%, others. **Languages:** Urdu, English are both official. **Religions:** Muslim 97%, Christians 1.4%, Hindus 1.5%.

Geography: Area: 342,750 sq. mi., larger than Texas. **Location:** In W part of South Asia. **Neighbors:** Iran on W, Afghanistan, China on N, India on E. **Topography:** The Indus R. rises in the Hindu Kush and Himalaya mtns. in the N (highest is K2, or Godwin Austen, 28,250 ft., 2d highest in world); then flows over 1,000 mi. through fertile valley and empties into Arabian Sea. Thar Desert, Eastern Plains flank Indus Valley. **Capital:** Islamabad. **Cities** (1972 cen.): Karachi 3,498,634; Lahore 2,165,372; Lyallpur 822,263; Hyderabad 628,310; Rawalpindi 615,392.

Government: Head of state and head of government: Pres. Mohammad Zia ul-Haq; b. 1924; in office: Sept. 16, 1978 (state), July 5, 1977 (govt.). **Local divisions:** Federal capital and 4 provinces with elected legislatures. **Armed forces:** regulars 429,000; reserves 513,000.

Economy: Industries: Textiles, cement, paper, sugar, chemicals, fertilizers, surgical instruments. **Chief crops:** Rice, wheat, cotton, oilseeds, tobacco, sugar. **Minerals:** Sulphur, gypsum, salt, chromite, cement, oil, gas, asbestos, antimony, magnesite, silica. **Crude oil reserves** (1980): 200 mln. bbls. **Other resources:** Wool. **Per capita arable land:** 0.6 acres. **Meat prod.** (1978): beef: 331,000 metric tons; lamb: 239,000 metric tons. **Fish catch** (1977): 248,500 metric tons. **Electricity prod.** (1977): 11.05 bln. kwh. **Labor force:** 60% agric.; 16% ind.

Finance: Currency: Rupee (Apr. 1981: 9.90 = $1 US). **Gross domestic product** (1980): $23.22 bln. **Per capita income** (1980): $280. **Imports** (1980): $5.35 bln.; partners (1978): Jap. 13%, U.S. 11%, UK 9%, W. Ger. 8%. **Exports** (1980): $2.62 bln.; partners (1978): Jap. 9%, Iran 8%, UK 7%, HK 6%. **Tourists** (1977): 220,400; receipts: $61 mln. **National budget** (1978): $2.54 bln. revenues; $3.11 bln. expenditures. **International reserves less gold** (Apr. 1981): $1.08 bln. **Gold:** 1.82 mln. oz t. **Consumer prices** (change in 1980): 11.7%.

Transport: Railway traffic (1978): 13.98 bln. passenger-km; 7.8 bln. net ton-km. **Motor vehicles:** in use (1975): 196,100 passenger cars, 91,700 comm. vehicles. **Civil aviation:** 4,644 mln. passenger-km (1978); 200 mln. freight ton-km (1978). **Chief ports:** Karachi.

Communications: Television sets: 350,000 in use (1976). **Radios:** 1.20 mln. licensed (1976). **Telephones in use** (1975): 240,000. **Daily newspaper circ.** (1976): 965,000.

Health: Life expectancy at birth (1962): 53.72 male; 48.80 female. **Births** (per 1,000 pop. 1968): 36. **Deaths** (per 1,000 pop. 1968): 12. **Natural increase** (1968): 2.4%. **Hospital beds** (per 100,000 pop. 1977): 50. **Physicians** (per 100,000 pop. 1977): 25. **Infant mortality** (per 1,000 live births 1979): 142.

Education (1977): **Literacy:** 23%. **Pop. 5-19:** in school: 27%, teachers per 1,000: 9. **PQLI:** 38.

Present-day Pakistan shares the 5,000-year history of the India-Pakistan sub-continent. At present day Harappa and Mohenjo Daro, the Indus Valley Civilization, with large cities and elaborate irrigation systems, flourished c. 4,000-2,500 BC.

Aryan invaders from the NW conquered the region around 1,500 BC, forging a Hindu civilization that dominated Pakistan as well as India for 2,000 years.

Beginning with the Persians in the 6th century BC, and continuing with Alexander the Great and with the Sassanians, successive nations to the west ruled or influenced Pakistan, eventually separating the area from the Indian cultural sphere.

The first Arab invasion, 712 AD, introduced Islam. Under the Mogul empire (1526-1867), Moslems ruled most of India, yielding to British encroachment and resurgent Hindus.

After World War I the Moslems of British India began agitation for minority rights in elections. Mohammad Ali Jinnah (1876-1948) was the principal architect of Pakistan. A leader of the Moslem League from 1916, he worked for dominion status for India; from 1940 he advocated a separate Moslem state.

When the British withdrew Aug. 14, 1947, the Islamic majority areas of India acquired self-government as Pakistan, with dominion status in the Commonwealth. Pakistan was divided into 2 sections, West Pakistan and East Pakistan. The 2 areas were nearly 1,000 mi. apart on opposite sides of India.

Pakistan became a republic in 1956. Pakistan had a National Assembly (legislature) with equal membership from East and West Pakistan, and 2 Provincial Assemblies. In Oct. 1958, Gen. Mohammad Ayub Khan took power in a coup. He was elected president in 1960, reelected in 1965.

As a member of the Central Treaty Organization, Pakistan had been aligned with the West. Following clashes between India and China in 1962, Pakistan made commercial and aid agreements with Communist China. U.S. aid to both Pakistan and India was suspended during the 1966 war over Kashmir but both economic aid and "nonlethal" military aid were resumed in 1966. The embargo was modified in 1973, lifted in 1975.

Ayub resigned Mar. 25, 1969, after several months of violent rioting and unrest, most of it in East Pakistan, which demanded autonomy. The government was turned over to Gen. Agha Mohammad Yahya Khan and martial law was declared; Yahya assumed the presidency.

The Awami League, which sought regional autonomy for East

Pakistan, won a majority in Dec. 1970 elections to a National Assembly which was to write a new constitution. In March, 1971 Yahya postponed the Assembly. Rioting and strikes broke out in the East.

On Mar. 25, 1971, government troops launched attacks in the East. The Easterners, aided by India, proclaimed the independent nation of Bangladesh. In months of widespread fighting, countless thousands were killed. Some 10 million Easterners fled into India.

Full scale war between India and Pakistan had spread to both the East and West fronts by December 3. Pakistan troops in the East surrendered Dec. 16; Pakistan agreed to a cease-fire in the West Dec. 17. On July 3, 1972, Pakistan and India signed a pact agreeing to withdraw troops from their borders and seek peaceful solutions to all problems.

In Aug. 1973 India agreed to release 93,000 Pakistani prisoners held since 1971. The return was completed in April, 1974. Pakistan agreed to repatriate 200,000 Bengali nationals stranded in Pakistan, and agreed to accept some Biharis (non Bengalis) unwanted in Bangladesh. India and Pakistan agreed in 1976 to resume full diplomatic relations.

Zulfikar Ali Bhutto, leader of the Pakistan People's party, which had won the most West Pakistan votes in the Dec. 1970 elections, became president Dec. 20. In 1972 he announced new land reforms and said the government would control management of major industries.

A new constitution adopted Apr. 10, 1973, made Pakistan a federal Islamic republic. Bhutto became prime minister Aug. 14.

Bhutto was overthrown in a military coup July, 1977. Some 300 people had been killed in protests over alleged rigging of parliamentary elections earlier in the year. Convicted of complicity in a 1974 political murder, Bhutto was executed Apr.4, 1979. The new military rulers made concessions to Moslem conservatives.

Relations with the U.S. were strained, 1979, when the U.S. embassy in Islamabad was stormed and burned and 2 Americans were killed, Nov. 21st, along with attacks on other U.S. installations. But by Apr. 1981, the U.S., pressured by the Soviet threat in Afghanistan, agreed to a five-year economic and military aid program with Pakistan.

Panama

Republic of Panama

People: Population (1980 est.): 1,940,000. **Age distrib.** (%): 0–14: 43.4; 15–59: 51.0; 60+: 5.7. **Pop. density:** 66.20 per sq. mi. **Urban** (1978): 56.6%. **Ethnic groups:** Mestizo 70%, West Indian 14%, Caucasian 10%, Indian 6%. **Languages:** Spanish (official), English. **Religions:** Roman Catholics 93%, Protestants 6%.

Geography: Area: 29,306 sq. mi., slightly larger than West Virginia. **Location:** In Central America. **Neighbors:** Costa Rica on W., Colombia on E. **Topography:** 2 mountain ranges run the length of the isthmus. Tropical rain forests cover the Caribbean coast and eastern Panama. **Capital:** Panama. **Cities** (1978 est.): Panama 439,310; San Miguelito 146,310, Colon 85,600.

Government: Head of state and head of government: Pres. Aristides Royo; b. Aug. 14, 1940; in office: Oct. 11, 1978. **Local divisions:** 9 provinces, 1 territory. **Armed forces:** paramilitary 11,000.

Economy: Industries: Oil refining, shipping, international banking. **Chief crops:** Bananas, pineapples, cocoa, coconuts, sugar. **Minerals:** Cement, clay, salt, copper. **Other resources:** Forests (mahogany), shrimp. **Per capita arable land:** 0.6 acres. **Meat prod.** (1978): beef: 52,000 metric tons; pork: 6,000 metric tons. **Fish catch** (1977): 228,000 metric tons. **Electricity prod.** (1978): 1.26 bln. kwh. **Labor force:** 40% agric., 33% ind. and commerce.

Finance: Currency: Balboa (Apr. 1981: 1.00 = $1 US). **Gross domestic product** (1979): $2.84 bln. **Per capita income** (1979): $1,116. **Imports** (1979): $1.19 bln.; partners (1977): U.S. 31%, Ecuador 15%, Venez. 8%, Saudi Ar. 7%. **Exports** (1980): $337 mln.; partners (1977): U.S. 45%, Canal Zone 10%, W. Ger. 8%, Neth. 5%. **Tourists** (1977): 361,900; receipts: $145 mln. **National budget** (1980): $695 mln. revenues; $818 mln. expenditures. **International reserves less gold** (Mar. 1981): $80.4 mln. **Consumer prices** (change in 1980): 13.8%.

Transport: Motor vehicles: in use (1975): 66,200 passenger cars, 19,600 comm. vehicles. **Chief ports:** Balboa, Cristobal,

Puerto Armuelles.

Communications: Television sets: 186,000 in use (1976). **Radios:** 270,000 in use (1976). **Telephones in use** (1978): 156,668. **Daily newspaper circ.** (1976): 136,000; 79 per 1,000 pop.

Health: Life expectancy at birth (1970): 64.26 male; 67.50 female. **Births** (per 1,000 pop. 1980): 26.8. **Deaths** (per 1,000 pop. 1975): 6.9. **Natural increase** (1975): 2.8%. **Hospital beds** (per 100,000 pop. 1977): 386. **Physicians** (per 100,000 pop. 1977): 78. **Infant mortality** (per 1,000 live births 1979): 29.

Education (1977): **Literacy:** 82%. **Pop. 5-19:** in school: 68%, teachers per 1,000: 24. **PQLI:** 81.

The coast of Panama was sighted by Rodrigo de Bastidas, sailing with Columbus for Spain in 1501, and was visited by Columbus in 1502. Vasco Nunez de Balboa crossed the isthmus and "discovered" the Pacific O. Sept. 13, 1513. Spanish colonies were ravaged by Francis Drake, 1572-95, and Henry Morgan, 1660-71. Morgan destroyed the old city of Panama which had been founded in 1519. Freed from Spain, Panama joined Colombia in 1821.

Panama declared its independence from Colombia Nov. 3, 1903, with U.S. recognition. U.S. naval forces deterred action by Colombia. On Nov. 18, 1903, Panama granted use, occupation and control of the Canal Zone to the U.S. by treaty, ratified Feb. 26, 1904. *(See also Panama Canal.)*

Rioting began Jan. 9, 1964, in a dispute over the flying of the U.S. and Panamanian flags and terms of the 1903 treaty. At least 21 Panamanians and 3 U.S. soldiers died in the rioting.

In 1967 new treaties were proposed, but Panama rejected them in 1970. In Feb. 1974 the U.S. and Panama agreed to negotiate a new treaty which would give the U.S. the right to operate and protect the canal for a certain period, with Panama sharing in the revenues, and would also set a date for final transfer of jurisdiction to Panama. Opposition by U.S. senators stalled the talks.

The U.S. and Panama initialed two treaties in 1977 that would provide for a gradual takeover by Panama of the canal, and withdrawal of U.S. troops, to be completed by 1999. U.S. payments would be substantially increased in the interim. The permanent neutrality of the canal would also be guaranteed. The treaties were ratified by the U.S. Senate in 1978.

After ruling single-handedly for a decade, Gen. Omar Torrijos Herrera abruptly handed over the government to former Education Minister Aristides Royo, Oct. 1978.

Due to easy Panama ship regulations and strictures in the U.S., merchant tonnage registered in Panama since World War II ranks high in size. Similarly easy financial regulations have made Panama a center for international banking.

Inflation, unemployment, and uncertainty over the canal have recently marred a record of economic growth and social improvement from 1950 to 1973.

Japan and Panama agreed, Mar. 1980, on a feasibility study for a second Panama Canal, large enough to accomodate fully-loaded 300,000-ton tankers.

Papua New Guinea

People: Population (1980 est.): 3,080,000. **Age distrib.** (%): 0–14: 43.8; 15–59: 50.3; 60+: 11.4. **Pop. density:** 17.28 per sq. mi. **Urban** (1976): 12.9%. **Ethnic groups:** Papuans (in S and interior), Melanesian (N,E), pygmies, minorities of Chinese, Australians, Polynesians. **Languages:** Melanesian Pidgin, Police Motu, English, 750 local languages. **Religions:** Protestants 33%, Roman Catholic 18%, local religions.

Geography: Area: 178,260 sq. mi., slightly larger than California. **Location:** Occupies eastern half of island of New Guinea. **Neighbors:** Indonesia (West Irian) on W, Australia on S. **Topography:** Thickly forested mtns. cover much of the center of the country, with lowlands along the coasts. Included are some of the nearby islands of Bismarck and Solomon groups, including Admiralty Is., New Ireland, New Britain, and Bougainville. **Capital:** Port Moresby. **Cities** (1976 cen.): Port Moresby (met.) 113,449.

Government: Head of state: Queen Elizabeth II, represented by Gov. Gen. Tore Lokoloko, b. Sept. 21, 1930; in office: Mar. 1, 1977. **Head of government:** Prime Min. Julius Chan; b. Aug. 29, 1939; in office: Mar. 13, 1980. **Local divisions:** National capital and 19 provinces with elected legislatures. **Armed forces:** regulars 3,500.

Economy: Chief crops: Coffee, coconuts, cocoa. **Minerals:**

Gold, copper, silver, gas. **Per capita arable land:** 0.01 acres. **Meat prod.** (1978): pork: 22,000 metric tons. **Fish catch** (1977): 39,900 metric tons. **Electricity prod.** (1977): 1.12 bln. kwh. **Labor force:** 53% agric., 17% ind. and commerce, 10% services.

Finance: Currency: Kina (Apr. 1981: .67 = $1 US). **Gross domestic product** (1979): $2.27 bln. **Per capita income** (1978): $480. **Imports** (1979): $939 mln.; partners (1977): Austral. 43%, Jap. 17%, Sing. 10%. **Exports** (1980): $1.07 bln.; partners (1977): Jap. 25%, W. Ger. 19%, Austral. 12%, U.S. 10%. **National budget** (1978): $366.6 mln. **International reserves less gold** (Mar. 1981): $350.08 mln. **Gold:** 62,000 oz t. **Consumer prices** (change in 1980): 12.0%.

Transport: Motor vehicles: in use (1976): 17,700 passenger cars, 19,200 comm. vehicles. **Chief ports:** Port Moresby, Lae.

Communications: Telephones in use (1978): 37,848. **Daily newspaper circ.** (1977) 25,000: 9 per 1,000 pop.

Health: Life expectancy at birth (1975): 47.5 male; 47.0 female. **Births** (per 1,000 pop. 1975): 42.0. **Deaths** (per 1,000 pop. 1975): 17.5. **Natural increase** (1975): 2.5%. **Hospital beds** (per 100,000 pop. 1977): 469. **Physicians** (per 100,000 pop. 1977): 7.

Education (1977): **Literacy:** 32%. **Pop. 5-19:** in school: 28%, teachers per 1,000: 10. **PQLI:** 43.

Human remains have been found in the interior of New Guinea dating back at least 10,000 years and possibly much earlier. Successive waves of peoples probably entered the country from Asia through Indonesia. Europeans visited in the 15th century, but land claims did not begin until the 19th century, when the Dutch took control of the western half of the island.

The southern half of eastern New Guinea was first claimed by Britain in 1884, and transferred to Australia in 1905. The northern half was claimed by Germany in 1884, but captured in World War I by Australia, which was granted a League of Nations mandate and then a UN trusteeship over the area. The 2 territories were administered jointly after 1949, given self-government Dec. 1, 1973, and became independent Sept. 16, 1975. Australia promised $1 billion in aid for the 5 years starting 1976-77, and pledged assistance in defense and foreign affairs.

The indigenous population consists of a huge number of tribes, many living in almost complete isolation with mutually unintelligible languages.

A secession movement in copper-rich Bougainville led to violence in 1973 and 1976. Indonesian border incursions were reported in 1978.

A series of strikes besieged the country, 1979. Tribal warfare in the western highlands took an est. 400 lives; a state of emergency was proclaimed.

Paraguay

Republic of Paraguay

People: Population (1979 est.): 3,117,000. **Age distrib. (%):** 0-14: 45.1; 15-59: 49.7; 60+: 5.2. **Pop. density:** 18.4 per sq. mi. **Urban** (1975): 39.6%. **Ethnic groups:** Mestizos 95%, small Caucasian, Indian, Negro minorities. **Languages:** Spanish, 75%, Guarani. **Religions:** Roman Catholics 95%, Mennonites.

Geography: Area: 157,047 sq. mi., the size of California. **Location:** One of the 2 landlocked countries of S. America. **Neighbors:** Bolivia on N, Argentina on S, Brazil on E. **Topography:** Paraguay R. bisects the country. To E are fertile plains, wooded slopes, grasslands. To W is the Chaco plain, with marshes and scrub trees. Extreme W is arid. **Capital:** Asunción. **Cities** (1978 est.): Asunción 434,928, Encarnación.

Government: Head of state: Pres. Alfredo Stroessner; b. Nov. 3, 1912; in office: Aug. 15, 1954. **Local divisions:** 16 departments. **Armed forces:** regulars 15,500; para-military 4,000.

Economy: Industries: Food processing, wood products. **Chief crops:** Corn, wheat, cotton, beans, peanuts, tobacco, citrus fruits, yerba mate. **Minerals:** Iron, manganese, limestone. **Other resources:** Forests. **Per capita arable land:** 0.8 acres. **Meat prod.** (1978): beef: 134,000 metric tons; pork: 61,000 metric tons. **Electricity prod.** (1977): 626.00 mln. kwh. **Labor force:** 49% agric., 28% ind. and commerce, 19% service.

Finance: Currency: Guarani (Apr. 1981 126.00 = $1 US). **Gross domestic product** (1979): $3.42 bln. **Per capita income** (1979 est.): $1,038. **Imports** (1980): $615 mln.; partners (1978): Braz. 20%, Arg. 15%, Algeria 11%, UK 10%. **Exports** (1980): $310 mln.; partners (1978): W. Ger. 15%, Jap. 13%, Neth. 10%, Arg. 9%. **Tourist receipts** (1977): $35 mln. **National budget** (1978): $321 mln. revenues; $301 mln. expenditures. **International reserves less gold** (Apr. 1981): $801.5 mln. **Gold:** 35,000 oz t. **Consumer prices** (change in 1980): 22.3%.

Transport: Railway traffic (1977): 23 mln. passenger-km; 17 mln. net ton-km. **Motor vehicles:** in use (1971): 16,000 passenger cars, 14,000 comm. vehicles. **Chief ports:** Asuncion.

Communications: Television sets: 55,000 in use (1976). **Radios:** 180,000 in use (1976). **Telephones in use** (1977): 41,644. **Daily newspaper circ.** (1976): 106,000; 39 per 100,000 pop.

Health: Life expectancy at birth (1975): 60.3 male; 63.6 female. **Births** (per 1,000 pop. 1975): 39.8. **Deaths** (per 1,000 pop. 1975): 8.9. **Natural increase** (1975): 3.1%. **Hospital beds** (per 100,000 pop. 1977): 135. **Physicians** (per 100,000 pop. 1977): 77. **Infant mortality** (per 1,000 live births 1979): 84.2.

Education (1977): **Literacy:** 82%. **Pop. 5-19:** in school: 52%, teachers per 1,000: 24. **PQLI:** 75.

The Guarani Indians were settled farmers speaking a common language before the arrival of Europeans.

Visited by Sebastian Cabot in 1527 and settled as a Spanish possession in 1535, Paraguay gained its independence from Spain in 1811. It lost much of its territory to Brazil, Uruguay, and Argentina in the War of the Triple Alliance, 1865-1870. Large areas were won from Bolivia in the Chaco War, 1932-35.

Gen. Alfredo Stroessner has ruled since 1954. Suppression of the opposition and decimation of small Indian groups has been charged by international rights groups.

The first stages of a large hydroelectric project were completed in 1968-70. In 1973 Brazil and Paraguay agreed to build a 10-million kilowatt hydroelectric plant, largest in the world, at Itaipu of the Parana R. Income from the project fueled an economic boom in 1977-78. Other major hydroelectric power generator projects are in beginning stages.

Peru

Republic of Peru

People: Population (1980 est.): 17,780,000. **Age distrib. (%):** 0-14: 44.2; 15-59: 50.6; 60+: 5.2. **Pop. density:** 35.83 per sq. mi. **Urban** (1975): 62.5%. **Ethnic groups:** Indians 45%, Mestizos 37%, Caucasians 15%, blacks, Asians. **Languages:** Spanish, Quechua both official, Aymara; 30% speak no Spanish. **Religions:** Roman Catholics over 90%.

Geography: Area: 496,222 sq. mi., five-sixths the size of Alaska. **Location:** On the Pacific coast of S. America. **Neighbors:** Ecuador, Colombia on N, Brazil, Bolivia on E, Chile on S. **Topography:** An arid coastal strip, 10 to 100 mi. wide, supports much of the population thanks to widespread irrigation. The Andes cover 27% of land area. The uplands are well-watered, as are the eastern slopes reaching the Amazon basin, which covers half the country with its forests and jungles. **Capital:** Lima. **Cities** (1972 cen.): Lima 2,833,609; Arequipa 302,316.

Government: Head of state: Pres. Fernando Belaunde Terry; b. Oct. 7, 1912; in office: July 28, 1980. **Head of government:** Prime Min. Manuel Ulloa; in office: July 28, 1980. **Local divisions:** 23 departments, 1 province. **Armed forces:** regulars 92,000; para-military 25,000.

Economy: Industries: Fish meal, steel. **Chief crops:** Cotton, sugar, coffee, rice, potatoes, beans, corn, barley, tobacco. **Minerals:** Copper, lead, molybdenum, silver, zinc, iron, oil. **Crude oil reserves** (1980): 655 mln. bbls. **Other resources:** Wool, sardines. **Per capita arable land:** 0.5 acres. **Meat prod.** (1978): beef: 82,000 metric tons; pork: 70,000 metric tons; lamb: 33,000 metric tons. **Fish catch** (1977): 2.5 mln. metric tons. **Electricity prod.** (1977): 8.56 bln. kwh. **Crude steel prod.** (1979): 436,000 metric tons. **Labor force:** 43% agric.; 21% ind. and mining; 36% gov.

Finance: Currency: Sol (Apr. 1981: 404.86 = $1 US). **Gross domestic product** (1979): $13.59 bln. **Per capita income** (1979): $655. **Imports** (1979): $2.15 bln.; partners (1977): U.S. 29%, Ecu. 10%, Venez. 9%, W. Ger. 7%. **Exports** (1979): $3.59 bln.; partners (1977): U.S. 30%, Jap. 12%, It. 5%. **Tourists** (1977): 264,000; receipts (1977): $113 mln. **National budget** (1978): $1.69 bln. revenues; $2.22 bln. expenditures. **International reserves less gold** (Nov. 1980): $1.92 bln. **Gold:** 2.15 mln. oz t. **Consumer prices** (change in 1980): 59.2%.

Transport: Railway traffic (1976): 528 mln. passenger-km; (1977) 612 mln. net ton-km. **Motor vehicles:** in use (1977):

300,400 passenger cars, 166,200 comm. vehicles; assembled (1975): 21,200 passenger cars; 12,900 comm. vehicles. **Chief ports:** Callao, Chimbate, Mollendo.

Communications: Television sets: 600,000 in use (1976), 100,000 manuf. (1975). **Radios:** 2.07 mln. in use (1976). **Telephones in use** (1978): 402,459. **Daily newspaper circ.** (1977): 828,000; 51 per 1,000 pop.

Health: Life expectancy at birth (1965): 52.59 male; 55.48 female. **Births** (per 1,000 pop. 1975): 41.0. **Deaths** (per 1,000 pop. 1975): 13.6. **Natural increase** (1975): 2.7%. **Hospital beds** (per 100,000 pop. 1977): 184. **Physicians** (per 100,000 pop. 1977): 64. **Infant mortality** (per 1,000 live births 1979): 80.

Education (1977): **Literacy:** 72%. **Pop. 5-19:** in school: 62%, teachers per 1,000: 17. **PQLI:** 65.

The powerful Inca empire had its seat at Cuzco in the Andes covering most of Peru, Bolivia, and Ecuador, as well as parts of Colombia, Chile, and Argentina. Building on the achievements of 800 years of Andean civilization, the Incas had a high level of skill in architecture, engineering, textiles, and social organization.

A civil war had weakened the empire when Francisco Pizarro, Spanish conquistador, began raiding Peru for its wealth, 1532. In 1533 he had the seized ruling Inca, Atahualpa, fill a room with gold as a ransom, then executed him and enslaved the natives.

Lima was the seat of Spanish viceroys until the Argentine liberator, Jose de San Martin, captured it in 1821; Spain was defeated by Simon Bolivar and Antonio J. de Sucre; recognized Peruvian independence, 1824. Chile defeated Peru and Bolivia, 1879-84, and took Tarapaca, Tacna, and Arica; returned Tacna, 1929.

On Oct. 3, 1968, a military coup ousted Pres. Fernando Belaunde Terry. In 1968-74, the military government put through sweeping agrarian changes, and nationalized oil, mining, fishmeal, and banking industries.

Food shortages, escalating foreign debt, and strikes led to another coup, Aug. 29, 1976, and to a slowdown of socialist programs. Labor protests culminated in a general strike in July, 1977. Moderate leftists led in free 1978 voting for a constituent assembly.

After 12 years of military rule, Peru returned to democratic leadership under former Pres. Fernando Belaunde Terry, July 1980. The new government planned to encourage the return of private enterprise to stimulate the inflation-ridden economy.

Peru is normally the world's top fishing nation; it takes about a sixth of total world tonnage, mostly anchovies from the plankton-rich waters of the coastal Peru current. The industry was crippled, 1972, by a disappearance of anchovies from off-shore waters. The government nationalized the industry, 1973. A shift in the ocean currents, 1974, brought at least some of the anchovies back.

Fighting again erupted, Jan. 28, 1981, in the ongoing border dispute between Peru and Ecuador; it was reported that both sides had suffered heavy casualties.

Philippines

Republic of the Philippines

People: Population (1980 est.): 48,400,000. **Age distrib.** (%): 0-14: 42.9; 15-59: 52.5; 60+: 4.6. **Pop. density:** 417.85 per sq. mi. **Urban** (1970): 31.8%. **Ethnic groups:** Malays the large majority, Chinese, Americans, Spanish are minorities. **Languages:** Filipino (based on Tagalog), Spanish, English all official; 90 others spoken. **Religions:** Roman Catholics 85%, Moslems 5%, Philippine Independents 4%, Protestants 3%.

Geography: Area: 115,831 sq. mi., slightly larger than Nevada. **Location:** An archipelago off the SE coast of Asia. **Neighbors:** Nearest are Malaysia, Indonesia on S, Taiwan on N. **Topography:** The country consists of some 7,100 islands stretching 1,100 mi. N-S. About 95% of area and population are on 11 largest islands, which are mountainous, except for the heavily indented coastlines and for the central plain on Luzon. **Capital:** Quezon City (Manila is de facto capital). **Cities** (1978 est.): Manila 1,438,252; Quezon City 994,679; Davao 515,520.

Government: Head of state: Pres. Ferdinand E. Marcos; b. Sept. 11, 1917; in office: Dec. 30, 1965 (pres.), Jan. 17, 1973 (premier). **Head of govt:** Prime Min. Cesar Virta; in office: Apr. 8, 1981. **Local divisions:** 12 regions, 72 provinces, 60 chartered cities. **Armed forces:** regulars 103,000; reserves 124,000.

Economy: Industries: Food processing, clothing, drugs, paper, appliances. **Chief crops:** Hemp, copra, sugar, rice, corn,

pineapple, tobacco. **Minerals:** Chromium, cobalt, copper, gold, nickel, silver, gypsum, sulphur, mercury, phosphates, zinc, iron, coal, manganese. **Crude oil reserves** (1980): 25 mln. bbls. **Other resources:** Forests (42% of area). **Per capita arable land:** 0.3 acres. **Meat prod.** (1978): beef: 142,000 metric tons; pork: 387,000 metric tons; lamb: 6,000 metric tons. **Fish catch** (1977): 1.5 mln. metric tons. **Electricity prod.** (1977): 15.80 bln. kwh. **Crude steel prod.** (1979): 397,000 metric tons. **Labor force:** 57% agric.

Finance: Currency: Peso (Apr. 1981: 7.82 = $1 US). **Gross domestic product** (1980): $35.7 bln. **Per capita income** (1978): $457. **Imports** (1980): $8.15 bln.; partners (1978): Jap. 27%, U.S. 21%, Saudi Ar. 6%. **Exports** (1980): $5.74 bln.; partners (1978): U.S. 33%, Jap. 24%, Neth. 8%. **Tourists** (1977): 730,100; receipts: $311 mln. **National budget** (1980): $4.93 bln. revenues; $5.37 bln. expenditures. **International reserves less gold** (Apr. 1981): $2.53 bln. **Gold:** 1.50 mln. oz t. **Consumer prices** (change in 1980): 17.8%.

Transport: Railway traffic (1978): 621.6 mln. passenger-km; 38.4 mln. net ton-km. **Motor vehicles** in use (1976): 386,200 passenger cars, 281,000 comm. vehicles; assembled (1977): 34,300 passenger cars; 24,400 comm. vehicles. **Civil aviation:** 3,600 mln. passenger-km (1977); 134 mln. freight ton-km (1977). **Chief ports:** Cebu, Manila, Iloilo, Davao.

Communications: Television sets: 800,000 in use (1976), 107,000 manuf. (1976). **Radios:** 1.88 mln. in use (1976), 124,000 manuf. (1976). **Telephones in use** (1978): 567,321. **Daily newspaper circ.** (1976): 919,000.

Health: Life expectancy at birth (1975): 56.9 male; 60.0 female. **Births** (per 1,000 pop. 1975): 41.0. **Deaths** (per 1,000 pop. 1975): 10.3. **Natural increase** (1975): 3.1%. **Hospital beds** (per 100,000 pop. 1977): 146. **Physicians** (per 100,000 pop. 1977): 36. **Infant mortality** (per 1,000 live births 1975): 47.6.

Education (1977): **Literacy:** 85%. **Pop. 5-19:** in school: 55%, teachers per 1,000: 17. **PQLI:** 72.

The Malay peoples of the Philippine islands, whose ancestors probably migrated from Southeast Asia, were mostly hunters, fishers, and unsettled cultivators when first visited by Europeans.

The archipelago was visited by Magellan, 1521. The Spanish founded Manila, 1571. The islands, named for King Philip II of Spain, were ceded by Spain to the U.S. for $20 million, 1898, following the Spanish-American War. U.S. troops suppressed a guerrilla uprising in a brutal 6-year war, 1899-1905.

Japan attacked the Philippines Dec. 8, 1941 (Far Eastern time). Japan conquered the islands in May, 1942. It was ousted by Sept. 1945.

On July 4, 1946, independence was proclaimed in accordance with an act passed by the U.S. Congress in 1934. A republic was established.

A rebellion by Communist-led Huk guerrillas was put down by 1954. But urban and rural political violence periodically reappears.

The Philippines and the U.S. have treaties for U.S. military and naval bases and a 1951 Mutual Defense Treaty. President Ferdinand E. Marcos in 1966 concluded a pact reducing U.S. base leases from 99 to 25 years. Riots by radical youth groups and terrorism by leftist guerrillas and outlaws, increased from 1970. On Sept. 21, 1972, Marcos declared martial law. Ruling by decree, he ordered some land reform and stabilized prices. But opposition was suppressed, and a high population growth rate aggravated poverty and unemployment. Political corruption was believed to be widespread. On Jan. 17, 1973, Marcos proclaimed a new constitution with himself as president. His wife received wide powers in 1978 to supervise planning and development. Diplomatic and trade ties were set with China in 1975 and with the USSR in 1976.

Government troops battled Moslem (Moro) secessionists, 1973-76, in southern Mindanao. Fighting resumed, 1977, after a Libyan-mediated agreement on autonomy was rejected by the region's mainly Christian voters. Casualties have been est. at 50,000, half civilians (10,000 civilians dead). Clashes continued through 1980 when 4 days of arson and bombing caused 19 deaths and 174 injuries.

The archipelago has a coastline of 10,850 mi. Manila Bay, with an area of 770 sq. mi., and a circumference of 120 mi., is the finest harbor in the Far East.

In 1972 and 1974 severe floods destroyed crops in central Luzon. In 1974 the first in a series of flood-control dams, built with U.S. aid, was dedicated. Manufacturing has shown steady gains.

All natural resources of the Philippines belong to the state; their exploitation is limited to citizens of the Philippines or corporations of which 60% of the capital is owned by citizens. In 1946 the right to develop natural resources and to own and operate public utilities until 1974 was extended to U.S. citizens.

Poland
Polish People's Republic

People: Population (1980 est.): 35,580,000. **Age distrib.** (%): 0–14: 23.9; 15–59: 62.7; 60+: 13.5. **Pop. density:** 295.61 per sq. mi. **Urban** (1977): 57.0%. **Ethnic groups:** Polish 98%, Germans, Ukrainians, Byelorussians. **Language:** Polish. **Religions:** Roman Catholics 90%, Protestants 1.5%.

Geography. Area. 120,059 sq. mi. **Location:** On the Baltic Sea in E Central Europe. **Neighbors:** E. Germany on W, Czechoslovakia on S, USSR (Lithuania, Byelorussia, Ukraine) on E. **Topography:** Mostly lowlands forming part of the Northern European Plain. The Carpathian Mts. along the southern border rise to 8,200 ft. **Capital:** Warsaw. **Cities** (1978 est.): Warsaw 1,474,200, Lodz 814,800; Cracow 707,000; Wroclaw 588,700, Poznan 531,600.

Government: Head of state: Pres. Henryk Jablonski; b. Dec. 27, 1909; in office: Mar. 28, 1972. **Head of government:** Premier Wojciech Jaruzelski; in office: Feb. 9, 1981. **Head of Communist Party:** First Sec. Stanislaw Kania; in office: Sept. 6, 1980. **Local divisions:** 49 provinces. **Armed forces:** regulars 317,500; reserves 605,000.

Economy: Industries: Shipbuilding, textiles, chemicals, wood products, metals, autos, aircraft, machinery, cement, aluminum, oil products. **Chief crops:** Grains, potatoes, sugar beets, tobacco, flax. **Minerals:** Coal, copper, silver, zinc, sulphur, salt, cadmium, iron. **Per capita arable land:** 1.0 acres. **Meat prod.** (1979): beef: 730,000 metric tons; pork: 1.84 mln. metric tons; lamb: 18,000 metric tons. **Fish catch** (1977): 665,000 metric tons. **Electricity prod.** (1979): 117.46 bln. kwh. **Crude steel prod.** (1979): 19.2 mln. metric tons. **Labor force:** 28% agric.; 24% manuf.

Finance: Currency: Zloty (Mar. 1980: 33.20 = $1 US). **Net material product** (1978): $57.3 bln. **Per capita income** (1976 est.): $2,500. **Imports** (1979): $17.49 bln.; partners (1979): USSR 31%, E. Ger. 8% W. Ger. 7% Czech. 6%. **Exports** (1979): $16.23 bln.; partners (1979): USSR 35%, E. Ger. 7%, Czech. 7%, W. Ger. 7%. **Tourists** (1977): 10,544,500; receipts (1976): $157 mln. **Consumer prices** (change in 1978): 68%.

Transport: Railway traffic (1979): 45.47 bln. passenger-km; 135.4 bln. net ton-km. **Motor vehicles:** in use (1977): 1.55 mln. passenger cars, 569,000 comm. vehicles; manuf. (1978): 325,200 passenger cars; 69,600 comm. vehicles. **Civil aviation:** 2,314 mln. passenger-km (1979); 18 mln. freight ton-km (1979). **Chief ports:** Gdansk, Gdynia, Szczecin.

Communications: Television sets: 7.5 mln. licensed (Dec. 1978), 920,000 manuf. (1977). **Radios:** 8.5 mln. licensed (Dec. 1978), 2.29 mln. manuf. (1977). **Telephones in use** (1978): 2,925,450. **Daily newspaper circ.** (1977): 8,331,000; 240 per 1,000 pop.

Health: Life expectancy at birth (1976): 66.92 male; 74.55 female. **Births** (per 1,000 pop. 1980): 19.4. **Deaths** (per 1,000 pop. 1980): 9.7. **Natural increase** (1978): 1.0%. **Hospital beds** (per 100,000 pop. 1977): 767. **Physicians** (per 100,000 pop. 1977): 166. **Infant mortality** (per 1,000 live births 1978): 22.4.

Education (1977): **Literacy:** 98%. **Pop. 5-19:** in school: 54%, teachers per 1,000: 27. **PQLI:** 92.

Slavic tribes in the area were converted to Latin Christianity in the 10th century. Poland was a great power from the 14th to the 7th centuries. In 3 partitions (1772, 1793, 1795) it was apportioned among Prussia, Russia, and Austria. Overrun by the Austro-German armies in World War I, its independence, self-declared on Nov.11, 1918, was recognized by the Treaty of Versailles, June 28, 1919. Large territories to the east were taken in war with Russia, 1921.

Nazi Germany and the USSR invaded Poland Sept. 1-27, 1939, and divided the country. During the war, some 6 million Polish citizens were killed by the Nazis, half of them Jews. With Germany's defeat, a Polish government-in-exile in London was recognized by the U.S., but the USSR pressed the claims of a rival group. The election of 1947 was completely dominated by the Communists.

In compensation for 69,860 sq. mi. ceded to the USSR, 1945,

Poland received approx. 40,000 sq. mi. of German territory E of the Oder-Neisse line comprising Silesia, Pomerania, West Prussia, and part of East Prussia.

In 12 years of rule by Stalinists, large estates were abolished, industries nationalized, schools secularized, and Roman Catholic prelates jailed. Farm production fell off. Harsh working conditions caused a riot in Poznan June 28-29, 1956.

A new Politburo, committed to development of a more independent Polish Communism, was named Oct. 1956, with Wladyslaw Gomulka as first secretary of the Communist Party. Collectivization of farms was ended and many collectives were abolished.

In 1968, Poland joined other Soviet bloc nations in invading Czechoslovakia.

In Dec. 1970 workers in port cities rioted because of price rises and new incentive wage rules. On Dec. 20 Gomulka resigned as party leader; he was succeeded by Edward Gierek; the incentive rules were dropped, price rises were revoked. In June 1971 a new 5-year plan was announced, placing more stress on housing and consumer goods production.

Poland was the first Communist state to get most-favored nation trade terms from the U.S. A 10-year W. Germany cooperation pact was signed in 1974.

A law promulgated Feb. 13, 1953, required government consent to high Roman Catholic church appointments. In 1956 Gomulka agreed to permit religious liberty and religious publications, provided the church kept out of politics. In 1961 religious studies in public schools were halted. Government relations with the Church improved in the 1970s. The number of priests and churches was greater in 1971 than in 1939, and 24 seminaries continued to function. Pope John Paul II, born Karol Wojtyla, was elected the first Polish Pope, Oct. 16, 1978.

After 2 months of labor turmoil had crippled the country, the Polish government, Aug. 30, 1980, met the demands of striking workers at the Lenin Shipyard, Gdansk. Among the 21 concessions granted were the right to form independent trade unions and the right to strike — unprecedented political developments in the Soviet bloc. Labor and political unrest continued, however. On several occasions in the Spring of 1981, with Russian troops poised on the Polish border, a Soviet invasion seemed imminent but never materialized.

Portugal
Republic of Portugal

People: Population (1980 est.): 9,930,000. **Age distrib.** (%): 0–14: 27.9; 15–59: 57.9; 60+: 14.3. **Pop. density:** 280.98 per sq. mi. **Ethnic groups:** Homogeneous, with small African minority. **Languages:** Portuguese. **Religions:** Roman Catholics 98%.

Geography: Area: 35,340 sq. mi., slightly smaller than Indiana. **Location:** At SW extreme of Europe. **Neighbors:** Spain on N, E. **Topography:** Portugal N of Tajus R, which bisects the country NE-SW, is mountainous, cool and rainy. To the S there are drier, rolling plains, and a warm climate. **Capital:** Lisbon. **Cities** (1978 est.): Lisbon 829,900; Porto 335,700.

Government: Head of state: Pres. Antonio dos Santos Ramalho Eanes; b. Jan. 25, 1935; in office: July 14, 1976. **Head of government:** Prime Min. Francisco de Sa Carneiro, b. Nov. 14, 1932; in office: Jan. 3, 1980. **Local divisions:** 18 provinces, 2 autonomous districts. **Armed forces:** regulars 60,500; paramilitary 31,850.

Economy: Industries: Textiles, pottery, shipbuilding, oil products, paper, glassware, tourism. **Chief crops:** Grains, corn, rice, grapes, olives, fruits. **Minerals:** Tungsten, uranium, coal, copper, tin, kaolin, gold, iron, manganese. **Other resources:** Forests (world leader in cork production). **Per capita arable land:** 0.8 acres. **Meat prod.** (1978): beef: 81,000 metric tons; pork: 144,000 metric tons; lamb: 26,000 metric tons. **Fish catch** (1977): 310,300 metric tons. **Electricity prod.** (1979): 13.50 bln. kwh. **Crude steel prod.** (1979): 670,000 metric tons. **Labor force:** 31% agric.; 35% ind. and commerce, 34% services.

Finance: Currency: Escudo (Apr. 1981: 59.21 = $1 US). **Gross domestic product** (1979): $20.1 bln. **Per capita income** (1979): $2,000. **Imports** (1979): $6.53 bln.; partners: W. Ger. 14%, U.S. 12%, UK 10%, Fr. 9%. **Exports** (1979): $3.49 bln.; partners: UK 18%, W. Ger. 13%, Fr. 9%, U.S. 7%. **Tourists** (1977): 1,409,600; receipts: $404 mln. **National budget** (1979): $4.13 bln. expenditures. **International reserves less gold** (Mar. 1981): $569 mln. **Gold:** 22.17 mln. oz t. **Consumer prices** (change in 1980): 16.6%.

Transport: Railway traffic (1978): 5.51 bln. passenger-km; 932.4 mln. net ton-km. **Motor vehicles:** in use (1976): 1.03 mln. passenger cars, 288,000 comm. vehicles; assembled (1978): 20,172 passenger cars; 57,324 comm. vehicles. **Civil aviation:** 3,012 mln. passenger-km (1977); 92 mln. freight ton-km (1977). **Chief ports:** Lisbon, Setubal, Leixoes.

Communications: Television sets: 723,000 licensed (1976), 404,000 manuf. (1977). **Radios:** 1.53 licensed (1976), 717,000 manuf. (1977). **Telephones in use** (1978): 1,174,853. **Daily newspaper circ.** (1977): 527,000; 54 per 1,000 pop.

Health: Life expectancy at birth (1974): 65.29 male; 72.03 female. **Births** (per 1,000 pop. 1978): 17.1. **Deaths** (per 1,000 pop. 1978): 9.8. **Natural increase** (1977): .9%. **Hospital beds** (per 100,000 pop. 1977): 528. **Physicians** (per 100,000 pop. 1977): 142. **Infant mortality** (per 1,000 live births 1980): 39.

Education (1977): **Literacy:** 72%, **Pop. 5-19:** in school: 62%, teachers per 1,000: 30. **PQLI:** 80.

Portugal, an independent state since the 12th century, was a kingdom until a revolution in 1910 drove out King Manoel II and a republic was proclaimed.

From 1932 a strong, repressive government was headed by Premier Antonio de Oliveira Salazar. Illness forced his retirement in Sept. 1968; he was succeeded by Marcello Caetano.

On Apr. 25, 1974, the government was seized by a military junta led by Gen. Antonio de Spinola, who was named president.

The new government reached agreements providing independence for Guinea-Bissau, Mozambique, Cape Verde Islands, Angola, and Sao Tome and Principe. Spinola resigned Sept. 30, 1974, in face of increasing pressure from leftist officers. Despite a 64% victory for democratic parties in April 1975, the Soviet-supported Communist party increased its influence. Banks, insurance companies, and other industries were nationalized. A countercoup in November halted this trend. Free elections under the new constitution were held, 1976, with the Socialist party gaining a parliamentary plurality. After 3 years of turmoil the economy and political life were in disarray, despite aid from the U.S. and West European countries.

Azores Islands, in the Atlantic, 740 mi. W. of Portugal, have an area of 904 sq. mi. and a pop. (1975) of 292,000. A 1951 agreement gave the U.S. rights to use defense facilities in the Azores. The **Madeira Islands,** 360 mi. off the NW coast of Africa, have an area of 307 sq. mi. and a pop. (1976) of 270,000. Both groups were offered partial autonomy in 1976.

Macao, area of 6 sq. mi., is an enclave, a peninsula and 2 small islands, at the mouth of the Canton R. in China. Portugal granted broad autonomy in 1976. Pop. (1979 est.): 282,000.

Qatar

State of Qatar

People: Population (1980 est.): 220,000. **Pop. density:** 55.0 per sq. mi. **Ethnic groups:** Arabs 56%, Iranians 23%, Pakistani 7%, others. **Languages:** Arabic (official), Farsi (Persian), English. **Religions:** Moslems 98%.

Geography: Area: 4,000 sq. mi., smaller than Connecticut. **Location:** Occupies peninsula on W coast of Persian Gulf. **Neighbors:** Saudi Arabia on W, United Arab Emirates on S. **Topography:** Mostly a flat desert, with some limestone ridges, vegetation of any kind is scarce. **Capital:** Doha. **Cities** (1978 est.): Doha 130,000, Umm Said, Ruwais.

Government: Head of state and head of government: Amir Khalifa bin Hamad Al-Thani; b. 1932; in office: Feb. 22, 1972 (amir), 1970 (prime min.) **Armed forces:** regulars 4,700.

Economy: Crude oil reserves (1980): 3.76 bln. bbls. **Per capita arable land:** 0.02 acres. **Electricity prod.** (1977): 900 mln. kwh. **Crude steel prod.** (1979): 396,000 metric tons. **Labor force:** 10% agric., 70% ind., services and commerce.

Finance: Currency: Riyal (Apr. 1981: 3.64 = $1 US). **Gross domestic product** (1979 est.): $4.5 bln. **Per capita income** (1979): $18,000. **Imports** (1979): $1.43 bln.; partners: Jap. 20%, W. Ger. 19%, UK 16%, U.S. 10%. **Exports** (1980): $5.65 bln.; partners (1978): Jap. 22%, Fr. 19%, U.S. 13%, Thai. 9%. **National budget** (1979): $3.2 bln. revenues; $2.19 bln. expenditures. **International reserves less gold** (Sept. 1980): $385.0 mln. **Gold:** 449,000 oz t.

Transport: Chief ports: Doha, Musayid.

Communications: Radios: 40,000 in use (1976). **Telephones in use** (1978): 29,703.

Health: Hospital beds (per 100,000 pop. 1977): 389. **Physi-**

cians (per 100,000 pop. 1977): 105.

Education (1977): **Literacy:** 20%. **Pop. 5-19:** in school: 60%, teachers per 1,000: 48. **PQLI:** 32.

Qatar was under Bahrain's control until the Ottoman Turks took power, 1872 to 1915. In a treaty signed 1916, Qatar gave Great Britain responsibility for its defense and foreign relations. After Britain announced it would remove its military forces from the Persian Gulf area by the end of 1971, Qatar sought a federation with other British protected States in the area; this failed and Qatar declared itself independent, Sept. 1 1971.

Qatar's first ruler under independence, Amir Ahmed bin Ali Al-Thani, was replaced by his cousin, Khalifa bin Hamad Al-Thani, Feb. 22, 1972, in a bloodless coup.

Oil revenues give Qatar a per capita income among the highest in the world, but lack of skilled labor hampers development plans.

Romania

Socialist Republic of Romania

People: Population (1980 est.): 22,270,000. **Age distrib.** (%): 0–14: 25.4; 15–59; 60.5; 60 + : 14.2. **Pop. density:** 242.86 per sq. mi. **Urban** (1977): 47.5%. **Ethnic groups:** Romanians 88.1%, Hungarians 9%, Germans 2%, Serbo-Croats, Ukrainians, Russians, Greeks, Turks, Jews. **Languages:** Romanian, Hungarian, German. **Religions:** Orthodox 80%, Roman Catholics 9%, Calvinists, Jewish, Lutherans.

Geography: Area: 91,699 sq. mi., slightly smaller than Oregon. **Location:** In SE Europe on the Black Sea. **Neighbors:** USSR on E (Moldavia) and N (Ukraine), Hungary, Yugoslavia on W, Bulgaria on S. **Topography:** The Carpathian Mts. encase the north-central Transylvanian plateau. There are wide plains S and E of the mountains, through which flow the lower reaches of the rivers of the Danube system. **Capital:** Bucharest. **Cities** (1978 cen.): Bucharest 1,807,044; Timisoara 268,785, Constanta.

Government: Head of state: Pres. Nicolae Ceausescu; b. Jan. 26, 1918; in office, Dec. 9, 1967. **Head of government:** Prime Min. Ilie Verdet; b. 1925; in office; Mar. 30, 1979. **Head of Communist Party:** Pres. Nicolae Ceausescu; in office: Mar. 23, 1965. **Local divisions:** Bucharest and 39 districts. **Armed forces:** regulars 180,500; reserves 502,000.

Economy: Industries: Steel, metals, machinery, oil products, chemicals, textiles, shoes, tourism. **Chief crops:** Corn, wheat, sugar beets, grapes, fruits. **Minerals:** Oil, gas, coal, salt, bauxite, manganese, lead, zinc, gold, silver. **Other resources:** Timber. **Per capita arable land:** 1.1 acres. **Meat prod.** (1978): beef: 287,000 metric tons; pork: 750,000 metric tons; lamb: 72,000 metric tons. **Fish catch** (1977): 150,700 metric tons. **Electricity prod.** (1978): 64.26 bln. kwh. **Crude steel prod. (1979):** 12.9 mln. metric tons. **Labor force:** 40% agric.; 25% ind. and commerce.

Finance: Currency: Leu (Apr. 1981: 4.47 = $1 US). **Gross domestic product** (1978 est.): $67.5 bln. **Per capita income** (1978): $3,100. **Imports** (1979): $11.79 bln.; partners (1977) USSR 19%, W. Ger. 8% E. Ger. 7%, Czech. 5%. **Exports** (1979): $9.72 bln.; partners (1977): USSR 19%, W. Ger. 7%, E Ger. 7%, Czech. 5%. **Tourists** (1977): 3,684,800; receipts (1976): $112 mln. **National budget** (1979): $76 mln. revenues; $75 mln. expenditures. **International reserves less gold** (Dec. 1980): $323 mln. **Gold:** 3.71 mln. oz t.

Transport: Railway traffic (1977): 23.2 bln. passenger-km 70 bln. net ton-km. **Motor vehicles:** in use (1975): 138,000 passenger cars; (1972): 50,000 comm. vehicles; manuf. (1978 81,360 passenger cars; 50,520 comm. vehicles. **Civil aviation** 1,109 mln. passenger-km (1978); 13 mln. freight ton-km (1978 **Chief ports:** Constanta, Galati, Braila.

Communications: Television sets: 2.96 mln. license (1976), 476,000 manuf. (1977). **Radios:** 3.10 mln. license (1976), 730,000 manuf. (1977). **Telephones in use** (1975 1,196,000. **Daily newspaper circ.** (1977): 3,711,000; 171 p 1,000 pop.

Health: Life expectancy at birth (1974-77): 69.3 male; 71 female. **Births** (per 1,000 pop. 1977): 19.6. **Deaths** (per 1,0 pop. 1977): 9.6. **Natural increase** (1977): 1.0%. **Hospital bec** (per 100,000 pop. 1977): 919. **Physicians** (per 100,000 pc 1977): 135. **Infant mortality** (per 1,000 live births 1979): 31.

Education (1977): **Literacy:** 98%. **Pop. 5-19:** in school: 64 teachers per 1,000: 30. **PQLI:** 91.

Romania's earliest known people merged with invading Prot

Thracians, preceding by centuries the Dacians. The Dacian kingdom was occupied by Rome, 106 AD-271 AD; people and language were Romanized. The principalities of Wallachia and Moldavia, dominated by Turkey, were united in 1859, became Romania in 1861. In 1877 Romania proclaimed independence from Turkey, became an independent state by the Treaty of Berlin, 1878, a kingdom, 1881, under Carol I. In 1886 Romania became a constitutional monarchy with a bicameral legislature.

Romania helped Russia in its war with Turkey, 1877-78. After World War I it acquired Bessarabia, Bukovina, Transylvania, and Banat. In 1940 it ceded Bessarabia and Northern Bukovina to the USSR and part of Southern Dobrudja to Bulgaria.

Marshal Ion Antonescu, leader of a militarist movement, forced Romania to join Germany against the USSR in World War II in 1941. In 1944 Antonescu was overthrown by King Michael with Soviet help and Romania joined the Allies.

With occupation by Soviet troops the Communist-headed National Democratic Front displaced the National Peasant party. A People's Republic was proclaimed, Dec. 30, 1947; Michael was forced to abdicate. Land owners were dispossessed; most banks, factories and transportation units were nationalized.

On Aug. 22, 1965, a new constitution proclaimed Romania a Socialist, rather than a People's Republic. Since 1966, Romania has adopted an independent attitude toward the USSR, witnessed by the visit of U.S. Pres. Nixon in Aug. 1969 and Chinese Communist party chief Hua Guofeng in 1978. Romanian Pres. Nicolae Ceausescu visited the U.S. in 1970 and 1973. The U.S. granted most-favored-nation tariff treatment in 1975, and a 10-year U.S. trade pact was signed in 1976. Since 1959, USSR troops have not been permitted to enter Romania. Romania has maintained friendly relations with China, and has refused to sever diplomatic and trade ties with Israel.

Internal policies remain oppressive. Ethnic Hungarians have protested cultural and job discrimination.

Romania has become industrialized, but lags in consumer goods and in personal freedoms. All industry is state owned, and state farms and cooperatives own over 90% of arable land. Romania is one of the few countries in Europe self-sufficient in oil, though reserves have been depleted.

A major earthquake struck Bucharest in March, 1977, killing over 1,300 people and causing extensive damage to housing and industry.

Rwanda

Republic of Rwanda

People: Population (1980 est.): 5,050,000. **Age distrib. (%):** 0–14: 50.8; 15–59: 46.2; 60+: 3.0. **Pop. density:** 496.61 per sq. mi. **Urban** (1974): 3.5%. **Ethnic groups:** Hutu 89%, Tutsi 10%, Twa (pygmies) 1%. **Languages:** French, Kinyarwandu (both official), Swahili. **Religions:** Roman Catholics 45%, Protestants 9%, Moslems 1%.

Geography: Area: 10,169 sq. mi., the size of Maryland. **Location:** In E central Africa. **Neighbors:** Uganda on N, Zaire on W, Burundi on S, Tanzania on E. **Topography:** Grassy uplands and hills cover most of the country, with a chain of volcanoes in the NW. The source of the Nile R. has been located in the headwaters of the Kagera (Akagera) R., SW of Kigali. **Capital:** Kigali. **Cities** (1977 est.): Kigali 89,950.

Government: Head of state: Pres. Juvenal Habyarimana; b. Mar. 8, 1937; in office: July 5, 1973. **Local divisions:** 10 prefectures. **Armed forces:** regulars 3,750; para-military 1,200.

Economy: Chief crops: Coffee, cotton, tea, pyrethrum, tobacco. **Minerals:** Tin, gold, wolframite. **Per capita arable land:** 0.4 acres. **Electricity prod.** (1977): 149 mln. kwh. **Labor force:** 95% agric.

Finance: Currency: Franc (Apr. 1981: 92.84 = $1 US). **Gross domestic product** (1978): $890 mln. **Per capita income** (1978): $178. **Imports** (1979): $192 mln.; partners (1977): Belg. 21%, Jap. 12%, Kenya 11%, W. Ger. 8%. **Exports** (1980): $72 mln.; partners (1977): Kenya 81%, Belg. 6%. **National budget** (1980): $82.3 mln. revenues; $58.8 mln. expenditures. **International reserves less gold** (Apr. 1981): $169.59 mln. **Gold:** 4,000 oz t. **Consumer prices** (change in 1980): 7.2%.

Transport: Motor vehicles: in use (1975): 6,500 passenger cars, 4,800 comm. vehicles.

Communications: Radios: 70,000 in use (1976), 17,000 manuf. (1976). **Telephones in use** (1978): 4,543. **Daily newspaper circ.** (1977): 200; 0.1 per 1,000 pop.

Health: Life expectancy at birth (1975): 41.8 male; 45.0 female. **Births** (per 1,000 pop. 1970): 51.0. **Deaths** (per 1,000 pop. 1970): 22.0. **Natural increase** (1970): 2.9%. **Hospital beds** (per 100,000 pop. 1977): 154. **Physicians** (per 100,000 pop. 1977): 13. **Infant mortality** (per 1,000 live births 1970): 127.

Education (1977): **Literacy:** 25%. **Pop. 5-19:** in school: 27%, teachers per 1,000: 6. **PQLI:** 32.

For centuries, the Tutsi (an extremely tall people) dominated the Hutus (90% of the population). A civil war broke out in 1959 and Tutsi power was ended. A referendum in 1961 abolished the monarchic system.

Rwanda, which had been part of the Belgian UN trusteeship of Rwanda-Urundi, became independent July 1, 1962. The government was overthrown in a 1973 military coup. Rwanda is one of the most densely populated countries in Africa. All available arable land is being used, and is being subject to erosion. The government has carried out economic and social improvement programs, using foreign aid and volunteer labor on public works projects.

Saint Lucia

People: Population (1979 est.): 121,000. **Age distrib. (%):** 0–20: 49.6; 21–64: 42.7; 65+: 7.7. **Pop. density:** 462.18 per sq. mi. **Ethnic groups:** African or mulatto 97%, white 3%. **Languages:** English (official), French patois. **Religions:** Mainly Roman Catholic.

Geography: Area: 238 sq. mi., about one-fifth the size of Rhode Island. **Location:** In Eastern Caribbean, 2d largest of the Windward Is. **Neighbors:** Martinique to N, St. Vincent to SW. **Topography:** Mountainous, volcanic in origin; Soufriere, a volcanic crater, in the S. Wooded mountains run N-S to Mt. Gimie, 3,145 ft., with streams through fertile valleys. **Capital:** Castries. **City:** Castries (1979 est.): 45,000.

Government: Head of state: Queen Elizabeth II, represented by Gov.-Gen. Boswell Williams; in office: June 19, 1980. **Head of government:** Prime Min. Allan Louisy, b. 1916; in office: July 4, 1979. **Local divisions:** Rural community councils.

Economy: Industries: Agriculture, tourism, construction, manufacturing. **Chief crops:** Bananas, coconuts, cocoa, citrus fruits, spices. **Other resources:** Forests. **Per capita arable land:** 0.1 acres. **Electricity prod.** (1977): 50.00 mln. kwh. **Labor force:** 40% agric.

Finance: Currency: East Caribbean dollar (Mar. 1980: 2.70 = $1 US). **Gross domestic product** (1978): $73.67 mln. **Per capita income** (1978): $698. **Imports** (1979): $72 mln.; partners: UK 25%, U.S. 20%, Trin./Tob. 15%, Can. 12%. **Exports** (1979): $35 mln.; partners: UK 45%, Lee-Wind-Is. 17%, Trin.-/Tob. 12%, Barb. 8%. **Tourists** (1977): 137,100; receipts (1975): $3.9 mln. **National budget** (1977-78 est.): $18.4 mln. revenues; $17.2 mln. expenditures. **Consumer prices** (change in 1978): 11%.

Transport: Motor vehicles: in use (1976): 3,700 passenger cars, 1,800 comm. vehicles. **Chief ports:** Castries, Vieux Fort.

Communications: Television sets: 1,700 in use (1975). **Radios:** 82,000 in use (1976). **Telephones in use** (1978): 7,157. **Daily newspaper circ.** (1976): 4,000; 36 per 1,000 pop.

Health: Life expectancy at birth (1961): 55.13 male; 58.47 female. **Births** (per 1,000 pop. 1975): 35.0. **Deaths** (per 1,000 pop. 1975): 7.3. **Natural increase** (1975): 2.8%. **Pop. per hospital bed** (1975): 202. **Pop. per physician** (1975): 4,231. **Infant mortality** (per 1,000 live births 1975): 36.5.

Education: Pop. 5–19: in school (1975): 34,178. **PQLI:** 63.

St. Lucia was ceded to Britain by France at the Treaty of Paris, 1814. Self government was granted with the West Indies Act, 1967. Independence was attained Feb. 22,.1979.

Primarily an agricultural economy, St. Lucia is undertaking an ambitious development program, including an oil transshipment terminal and free-port zone being built by U.S. oil company Amerada Hess. Aid has come from the Caribbean Community and Venezuela.

Saint Vincent and the Grenadines

People: Population (1980 est.): 120,000. **Pop. density:** 800 per sq. mi. **Ethnic groups:** Mainly of African or mixed origin; also, some Asians, Europeans, and Caribs. **Languages:** English. **Religions:** Methodists, Anglicans, Roman Catholics.

Geography: Area: 150 sq. mi., about twice the size of Washington, D.C. **Location:** In the eastern Caribbean, St. Vincent (133 sq. mi.) and the northern islets of the Grenadines form a part of the Windward chain. **Neighbors:** St. Lucia to N, Barbados to E, Grenada to S. **Topography:** St. Vincent is volcanic, with a ridge of thickly-wooded mountains running its length; Soufriere, rising in the N, erupted in Apr. 1979. **Capital:** Kingstown. **Cities** (1978): Kingstown 25,000.

Government: Head of state: Queen Elizabeth II, represented by Gov.-Gen. Sir Sydney Douglas Gun-Munro; b. Nov. 29, 1916; in office: Jan. 1, 1977. **Head of government:** Robert Milton Cato; b. June 3, 1915; in office: Dec. 11, 1974.

Economy: Industries: Agriculture, tourism. **Chief crops:** Bananas, arrowroot, coconuts. **Per capita arable land:** 0.3 acres. **Electricity prod.** (1977): 20 mln. kwh. **Labor force:** 30% agric.

Finance: Currency: East Caribbean dollar (May 1980: 2.70 = $1 US). **Per capita income** (1979): $250. **Imports** (1979): $36 mln.; partners (1974): UK 30%, Trin./Tob. 15%, Can. 13%, U.S. 9%. **Exports** (1979): $15 mln.; partners (1974): UK 66%, Barb. 15%, Trin./Tob. 9%. **Tourists** (1977): 42,000; receipts (1977): $5.44 mln. **National budget** (1979): $12 mln. revenues; $11.6 mln. expenditures.

Transport: Motor vehicles: in use (1976): 3,500 passenger cars, 800 comm. vehicles. **Chief ports:** Kingstown.

Communications: Telephones in use (1978): 5,302.

Health: Life expectancy at birth (1961): 58.46 male; 59.67 female. **Births** (per 1,000 pop. 1977): 31. **Deaths** (per 1,000 pop. 1973): 10.0. **Natural increase** (1973): 2.2%. **Pop. per hospital bed** (1972): 170. **Infant mortality** (per 1,000 pop. under 1 yr. 1977): 55.

Education (1979): **Literacy:** 95%. **Pop. 5–19:** in school (1975): 26,938; per teacher: 18.5. **PQLI:** 67.

Columbus landed on St. Vincent on Jan. 22, 1498 (St. Vincent's Day). Britain and France both laid claim to the island in the 17th and 18th centuries; the Treaty of Versailles, 1783, finally ceded it to Britain. Associated State status was granted 1969; independence was attained Oct. 27, 1979.

The entire economic life of St. Vincent, dependent upon few crops and tourism, was devastated by the eruption of Mt. Soufriere, Apr. 13, 1979.

In Sept. 1980, St. Vincent was admitted as the 153rd member of the United Nations.

Samoa

People: Population (1980 est.): 160,000. **Age distrib.** (%): 0–14: 50.4; 15–59: 45.4; 60+: 4.3. **Pop. density:** 141.22 per sq. mi. **Urban** (1978): 21.3%. **Ethnic groups:** Samoans (Polynesians) 88%, Euronesians (mixed) 10%, Europeans, other Pacific Islanders. **Languages:** Samoan, English both official. **Religions:** Protestants 75%, Roman Catholics 20%.

Geography: Area: 1,133 sq. mi., the size of Rhode Island. **Location:** In the S. Pacific O. **Neighbors:** Nearest are Fiji on W, Tonga on S. **Topography:** Main islands, Savai'i (660 sq. mi.) and Upolu (430 sq. mi.), both ruggedly mountainous, and small islands Manono and Apolima. **Capital:** Apia. **Cities** (1978 est.): Apia (met.) 32,616.

Government: Head of state: King Malietoa Tanumafili II; b. Jan. 4, 1913; in office: Jan. 1, 1962. **Head of government:** Prime Min. Taisi Tufuga Tupuola Efi; b. Mar. 1, 1938; in office: Mar. 24, 1976. **Local divisions:** 24 districts.

Economy: Chief crops: Cocoa, coconuts, bananas, taro, coffee, bark cloth. **Other resources:** Hardwoods, fish. **Per capita arable land:** 0.9 acres. **Electricity prod.** (1977): 25.00 mln. kwh. **Labor force:** 67% agric.

Finance: Currency: Tala (Jan. 1981: .94 = $1 US). **Gross domestic product** (1976 est.): $50 mln. **Per capita income** (1976): $320. **Imports** (1979): $74 mln.; partners (1977): NZ 29% Austral. 17%, Jap. 15%, U.S. 9%. **Exports** (1979): $18 mln.; partners (1977): NZ 16%, W. Ger. 46%, U.S. 10%, Neth. 10%. **Tourists** (1977): 22,000; receipts (1976): $3 mln. **International reserves less gold** (Mar. 1980): $1.63 mln. **Consumer prices** (change in 1979): 10.8%.

Transport: Motor vehicles: in use (1976): 1,300 passenger cars, 1,900 comm. vehicles. **Chief ports:** Apia, Asau.

Communications: Radios: 50,000 in use (1975). **Telephones in use** (1978): 3,810.

Health: Life expectancy at birth (1966): 60.8 male; 65.2 female. **Births** (per 1,000 pop. 1978): 20.0. **Deaths** (per 1,000 pop. 1978): 2.8. **Natural increase** (1978): 1.7%. **Pop. per hos-**

pital bed (1977): 214. **Pop. per physician** (1977): 2,884. **Infant mortality** (per 1,000 live births 1978): 10.4. **PQLI:** 84.

Western Samoa was a German colony, 1899 to 1914, when New Zealand landed troops and took over. It became a New Zealand mandate under the League of Nations and, in 1945, a New Zealand UN Trusteeship.

An elected local government took office in Oct. 1959 and the country became fully independent Jan. 1, 1962. New Zealand has continued economic aid and educational assistance.

The country's name was changed to Samoa in 1977.

San Marino
Most Serene Republic of San Marino

People: Population (1979 est.): 21,000. **Age distrib.** (%): 0–14: 23.9; 15–59: 61.3; 60+: 14.8. **Pop. density:** 833.33 per sq. mi. **Urban** (1970): 92.4%. **Ethnic groups:** Sanmarinese. **Languages:** Italian. **Religions:** Roman Catholics predominate.

Geography: Area: 24 sq. mi. **Location:** In N central Italy near Adriatic coast. **Neighbors:** Completely surrounded by Italy. **Topography:** The country lies on the slopes of Mt. Titano. **Capital:** San Marino. **City** (1978 est.): San Marino 4,628.

Government: Head of state: Prime Minister Captain Regent: Giordano Bruno Reffi; in office: Oct. 1, 1980. **Local divisions:** 9 sectors. **Armed forces:** 180-man ceremonial army.

Economy: Industries: Postage stamps, tourism, woolen goods, paper, cement, ceramics. **Per capita arable land:** 0.1 acres.

Finance: Currency: Lira. **Tourists** (1977): 2,564,500.

Communications: Television sets: 4,000 licensed (1976). **Radios:** 6,000 licensed (1976). **Telephones in use** (1978): 6,276. **Daily newspaper circ.** (1976): 1,300; 65 per 1,000 pop.

Births (per 1,000 pop. 1977): 14.2. **Deaths** (per 1,000 pop. 1977): 6.9. **Natural increase** (1977): .8%. **Infant mortality** (per 1,000 live births 1977): 24.1.

San Marino claims to be the oldest state in Europe and to have been founded in the 4th century. A communist-led coalition ruled 1947-57; a similar coalition took power in 1978. It has had a treaty of friendship with Italy since 1862.

Sao Tome and Principe
Democratic Republic of Sao Tome and Principe

People: Population (1980 est.): 90,000. **Pop. density:** 241.94 per sq. mi. **Ethnic groups:** Portuguese-African mixture, African minority (Angola, Mozambique immigrants). **Languages:** Portuguese. **Religions:** Christians 80%.

Geography: Area: 372 sq. mi., slightly larger than New York City. **Location:** In the Gulf of Guinea about 125 miles off W Central Africa. **Neighbors:** Gabon, Equatorial Guinea on E. **Topography:** Sao Tome and Principe islands, part of an extinct volcano chain, are both covered by lush forests and croplands. **Capital:** Sao Tome. **Cities** (1976 est.): Sao Tome 20,000.

Government: Head of state and head of government: Pres. Manuel Pinto da Costa, b. 1910; in office: July 12, 1975. **Local divisions:** 2 provinces, 12 counties.

Economy: Chief crops: Coffee, cocoa, coconut products, cinchona. **Per capita arable land:** 0.03 acres. **Electricity prod.** (1977): 8.00 mln. kwh.

Finance: Currency: Dobra (Sept. 1979): 34.70 = $1 US) **Gross domestic product** (1976 est.): $40 mln. **Per capita income** (1976): $270. **Imports** (1979): $22 mln.; partners (1975) Port. 61%, Angola 13%. **Exports** (1979): $27 mln.; partners (1975): Neth. 52%, Port. 33%, W. Ger. 8%.

Transport: Motor vehicles: in use (1973): 1,600 passenger cars, 400 comm. vehicles. **Chief ports:** Sao Tome, Santo Antonio.

Communications: Radios: 20,000 in use (1976).

Health: Births (per 1,000 pop. 1972): 45.0. **Deaths** (per 1,000 pop. 1972): 11.2. **Natural increase** (1972): 3.4%. **Pop. per hospital bed** (1976): 160. **Pop. per physician** (1973): 6,666 **Infant mortality** (per 1,000 live births 1972): 64.3.

The islands were uninhabited when discovered in 1471 by the Portuguese, who brought the first settlers — convicts and exile Jews. Sugar planting was replaced by the slave trade as the chief economic activity until coffee and cocoa were introduced in the 19th century.

Portugal agreed, 1974, to turn the colony over to the Gabon-based Movement for the Liberation of Sao Tome and Principe, which proclaimed as first president its East German-trained leader Manuel Pinto da Costa. Independence came July 12, 1975.

Low cocoa prices, the emigration of most of the 1,000 whites, and the repatriation of Cape Verdean plantation foremen stymied the economy.

Saudi Arabia
Kingdom of Saudi Arabia

People: Population (1979 est.): **9,292,000. Pop. density:** 9.01 per sq. mi. **Ethnic groups:** Arab tribes, immigrants from other Arab and Muslim countries. **Languages:** Arabic. **Religions:** Muslim 00%.

Geography: Area: 873,000 sq. mi., one-fourth the size of the U.S. **Location:** Occupies most of Arabian Peninsula in Middle East. **Neighbors:** Kuwait, Iraq, Jordan on N, Yemen, South Yemen, Oman on S, United Arab Emirates, Qatar on E. **Topography:** The highlands on W, up to 9,000 ft., slope as an arid, barren desert to the Persian Gulf. **Capital:** Riyadh. **Cities** (1974 cen.): Riyadh 666,840; Jidda 561,104; Mecca 366,801.

Government: Head of state and head of government: King Khalid ibn Abdul Aziz Al Saud; b. 1913; in office: Mar. 28, 1975. **Effective head of government:** Dep. Prime Min. Fahd ibn Abdul Aziz Al Saud, b. 1922; in office: Mar. 28, 1975. **Local divisions:** 6 major and 12 minor provinces. **Armed forces:** regulars 44,500; para-military 26,500.

Economy: Industries: Oil products. **Chief crops:** Dates, wheat, barley, fruit. **Minerals:** Oil, gas, gold, silver, iron. **Crude oil reserves** (1980): 163.35 bln. bbls. **Per capita arable land:** 0.3 acres. **Meat prod.** (1978): beef: 12,000 metric tons, lamb: 35,000 metric tons. **Fish catch** (1977): 18,400 metric tons. **Electricity prod.** (1977): 2.50 bln. kwh. **Labor force:** 40% agric.; 11% ind. and commerce; 12% govt.

Finance: Currency: Riyal (Apr. 1981: 3.36 = $1 US). **Gross domestic product** (1980): $116.16 bln. **Per capita income** (1979): $11,500. **Imports** (1980): $33.06 bln.; partners (1979): EEC, Jap. 62%, US 25%, LDCs 12%. **Exports** (1980): $102.47 bln.; partners (1979): EEC 50%, US 16%, Jap., 15%, LDCs 19%. **Tourist receipts** (1977): $823 mln. **International reserves less gold** (Apr. 1981): $27.18 bln. **Gold:** 4.57 mln. oz t. **Consumer prices** (change in 1980): 3.2%.

Transport: Railway traffic (1974): 72 mln. passenger-km; 66 mln. net ton-km. **Motor vehicles:** in use (1974): 59,400 passenger cars, 52,600 comm. vehicles. **Chief ports:** Jidda, Ad-Dammam, Ras Tannurah.

Communications: Television sets: 130,000 in use (1976). **Radios:** 260,000 in use (1976). **Telephones in use** (1978): 185,000. **Daily newspaper circ.** (1976): 143,000.

Health: Life expectancy at birth (1975): 44.2 male; 46.5 female. **Births** (per 1,000 pop. 1975): 49.5. **Deaths** (per 1,000 pop. 1975): 20.2. **Natural increase** (1975): 2.9%. **Hospital beds** (per 100,000 pop. 1977): 155. **Physicians** (per 100,000 pop. 1977): 60.

Education (1977): **Literacy:** 15%. **Pop. 5-19:** in school: 36%, teachers per 1,000: 22. **PQLI:** 29.

Arabia was united for the first time by Mohammed, in the early 7th century. His successors conquered the entire Near East and North Africa, bringing Islam and the Arabic language. But Arabia itself soon returned to its former status as political and cultural backwater.

Nejd, long an independent state and center of the Wahhabi sect, fell under Turkish rule in the 18th century, but in 1913 Ibn Saud, founder of the Saudi dynasty, overthrew the Turks and captured the Turkish province of Hasa; took the Hejaz in 1925 and by 1926, most of Asir. The discovery of oil by an American oil company in the 1930s transformed the new country.

Crown Prince Khalid was proclaimed king on Mar. 25, 1975, after the assassination of King Faisal. There is no constitution and no parliament. The king exercises authority together with a Council of Ministers. The Islamic religious code is the law of the land. Alcohol and public entertainments are restricted, and women have an inferior legal status.

Saudi units fought against Israel in the 1948 and 1973 Arab-Israeli wars. Many billions of dollars of advanced arms have been purchased from Britain, France, and the U.S., including jet fighters and missiles. Beginning with the 1967 Arab-Israeli war,

Saudi Arabia provided large annual financial gifts to Egypt; aid was later extended to Syria, Jordan, and Palestinian guerrilla groups, as well as to other Moslem countries. The country has aided anti-radical forces in Yemen and Oman.

Faisal played a leading role in the 1973-74 Arab oil embargo against the U.S. and other nations in an attempt to force them to adopt an anti-Israel policy. Saudi Arabia joined most other Arab states, 1979, in condemning Egypt's peace treaty with Israel.

Between 1973 and 1976, Saudi Arabia acquired full ownership of Aramco (Arabian American Oil Co.). Saudi Arabia announced, 1979, it will build a $1 billion causeway linking the island state Bahrain to the Arab mainland. A third 5-year $250 billion development plan was approved in 1980.

The Hejaz contains the holy cities of Islam — Medina where the Mosque of the Prophet enshrines the tomb of Mohammed, who died in the city June 7, 632, and Mecca, his birthplace. More than 600,000 Moslems from 60 nations pilgrimage to Mecca annually. The regime faced its first serious opposition when young Moslem fundamentalists seized the Grand Mosque in Mecca, Nov. 20, 1979. (See Index for Chronology.)

Senegal
Republic of Senegal

People: Population (1980 est.): **5,660,000. Age distrib.** (%): 0-14: 44.2; 15-59: 50.5; 60+: 5.3. **Pop. density:** 74.35 per sq. mi. **Urban** (1971): 31.7%. **Ethnic groups:** Wolof 36%, Folani 17.5%, Sere 16.5%, Toucouleur 9%, Diola 9%, Mandigo 6.5%. **Languages:** French (official), tribal languages. **Religions:** Muslims 75%, Christians 5%.

Geography: Area: 76,124 sq. mi., the size of South Dakota. **Location:** At western extreme of Africa. **Neighbors:** Mauritania on N, Mali on E, Guinea, Guinea-Bissau on S, Gambia surrounded on three sides. **Topography:** Low rolling plains cover most of Senegal, rising somewhat in the SE. Swamp and jungles are in SW. **Capital:** Dakar. **Cities** (1976 cen.): Dakar 798,792; Thies 117,333; Kaolack 106,899.

Government: Head of state: Pres. Leopold Senghor; b. Oct. 9, 1906; in office: Sept. 5, 1960. **Head of government:** Prime Min. Abdou Diouf; b. Sept. 7, 1935; in office: Feb. 26, 1970. **Local divisions:** 8 regions. **Armed forces:** regulars 8,350; para-military 1,600.

Economy: Industries: Food-processing, chemicals, cement. **Chief crops:** Peanuts are chief export; millet, corn, rice. **Minerals:** Phosphates. **Per capita arable land:** 1.1 acres. **Meat prod.** (1978): beef: 36,000 metric tons; pork: 7,000 metric tons; lamb: 10,000 metric tons. **Fish catch** (1977): 288,800 metric tons. **Electricity prod.** (1978): 456.00 mln. kwh. **Labor force:** 70% agric.

Finance: Currency: CFA franc (Apr. 1981: 262.70 = $1 US). **Gross domestic product** (1979): $2.40 bln. **Per capita income** (1975): $342. **Imports** (1979): $755 mln.; partners Fr. 45%, Neth. 7%, It. 6%, U.S. 5%. **Exports** (1979): $477 mln.; partners Fr. 49%, UK 10%, It. 6%, Nigeria 5%. **Tourists** (1977): 168,300; receipts $11 mln. **International reserves less gold** (Jan. 1981): $10.5 mln. **Gold:** 29,000 oz t. **Consumer prices** (change in 1980): 8.8%.

Transport: Railway traffic (1976): 180 mln. passenger-km; 164 mln. net ton-km. **Motor vehicles:** in use (1974): 44,800 passenger cars, 25,000 comm. vehicles. **Chief ports:** Dakar, Saint-Louis.

Communications: Television sets: 2,000 in use (1976). **Radios:** 290,000 in use (1976). **Telephones in use** (1978): 42,105. **Daily newspaper circ.** (1976): 25,000; 5 per 1,000 pop.

Health: Life expectancy at birth (1975): 39.4 male; 42.5 female. **Births** (per 1,000 pop. 1975): 47.0. **Deaths** (per 1,000 pop. 1975): 23.1. **Natural increase** (1975): 2.4%. **Hospital beds** (per 100,000 pop. 1977): 111. **Physicians** (per 100,000 pop. 1977): 2. **Infant mortality** (per 1,000 live births 1960-61): 92.9.

Education (1977): **Literacy:** 10%. **Pop. 5-19:** in school: 21%, teachers per 1,000: 4. **PQLI:** 23.

Portuguese settlers arrived in the 15th century, but French control grew from the 17th century. The last independent Moslem state was subdued in 1893. Dakar became the capital of French West Africa.

Independence as part, along with the Sudanese Rep., of the Mali Federation, came June 20, 1960. Senegal withdrew Aug. 20 that year. French political and economic influence is strong.

A long drought brought famine, 1972-73, and again in 1978.
Senegal is recognized as the most democratic of the French-speaking West African nations. Opposition parties were allowed to form in 1976 and 1979, and free elections were held, 1978.

Seychelles

People: Population (1980 est.): 70,000. **Age distrib.** (%): 0–14: 41.5; 15–59; 49.7; 60 + : 8.8. **Pop. density:** 409.36 per sq. mi. **Urban** (1971): 26.1% **Ethnic groups:** Creoles (mixture of Asians, Africans, and French) predominate. **Languages:** English and French (both official), Creole 94%. **Religions:** Roman Catholics 90%, Protestants 8%, Hindus, Moslems.

Geography: Area: 171 sq. mi. **Location:** In the Indian O. 700 miles NE of Madagascar. **Neighbors:** Nearest are Madagascar on SW, Somalia on NW. **Topography:** A group of 86 islands, about half of them composed of coral, the other half granite, the latter predominantly mountainous. **Capital:** Victoria. **Cities** (1980): Port Victoria 23,000.

Government: Head of state: Pres. France Albert Rene, b. Nov. 16, 1935; in office: June 5, 1977.

Economy: Industries: Food processing. **Chief crops:** Coconut products, cinnamon, vanilla, patchouli. **Other resources:** Guano, shark fins, tortoise shells, fish. **Electricity prod.** (1977): 36.00 mln. kwh. **Labor force:** 18.5% agric.; 19.4% mining, construction; 13.5% public admin., soc. serv.; 11.1% restaurants, hotels.

Finance: Currency: Rupee (Jan. 1981: 6.65 = $1 US). **Gross domestic product** (1979 est.): $86 mln. **Per capita income** (1979): $1,030. **Imports** (1979): $89 mln.; partners UK 27%, Kenya 12%, So. Afr. 9%, Jap. 7%. **Exports** (1979): $18 mln.; partners: Pak. 18%. **National Budget** (1977) $17.51 bln. revenues; $20.40 expenditures. **Tourists** (1977): 50,000; receipts: $22 mln. **International reserves less gold** (Apr. 1981): $15.22 mln. **Consumer prices** (change in 1980): 13.5%.

Transport: Motor vehicles: in use (1977): 3,000 passenger cars, 900 comm. vehicles. **Port:** Victoria.

Communications: Radios: 17,000 in use (1976). **Telephones in use** (1978): 4,560. **Daily newspaper circ.** (1977): 4,000; 65 per 1,000 pop.

Health: Life expectancy at birth (1972): 61.9 male; 68.0 female. **Births** (per 1,000 pop. 1977): 25.9. **Deaths** (per 1,000 pop. 1977): 7.7. **Natural increase** (1977): 1.8%. **Pop. per hospital bed** (1975): 200. **Pop. per physician** (1975): 2,857. **Infant mortality** (per 1,000 live births 1977): 43.2. **PQLI:** 72.

The islands were occupied by France in 1768, and seized by Britain in 1794. Ruled as part of Mauritius from 1814, the Seychelles became a separate colony in 1903. The ruling party had opposed independence as impractical, but pressure from the OAU and the UN became irresistible, and independence was declared June 29, 1976. The first president was ousted in a coup a year later by a socialist leader.

A new Constitution announced Mar. 1979, turned the country into a one-party state. The Seychelles, strategically located in the Indian O., have been courted by the Soviet Union.

Sierra Leone
Republic of Sierra Leone

People: Population (1980 est.): 3,470,000. **Age distrib.** (%): 0–14: 40.6; 15–59: 51.5; 60 + : 7.8. **Pop. density:** 124.26 per sq. mi. **Ethnic groups:** Temne 30%, Mende 30%, Creole 2%. **Languages:** English (official), Krio (pidgin), tribal languages. **Religions:** Animist 70%, Muslims 25%, Christians 5%.

Geography: Area: 27,925 sq. mi., slightly smaller than North Carolina. **Location:** On W coast of W. Africa. **Neighbors:** Guinea on N, E, Liberia on S. **Topography:** The heavily-indented, 210-mi. coastline has mangrove swamps. Behind are wooded hills, rising to a plateau and mountains in the E. **Capital:** Freetown. **Cities** (1980 est.): Freetown 500,000; Bo, Kenema, Makeni.

Government: Head of state and head of government: Pres. Siaka P. Stevens; b. Aug. 24, 1905; in office: Apr. 21, 1971 (state), June 14, 1978 (gov't). **Local divisions:** 3 provinces and one region including Freetown. **Armed forces:** regulars 3,000; para-military 800.

Economy: Industries: Wood products. **Chief crops:** Cocoa, coffee, palm kernels, kola nuts, ginger. **Minerals:** Diamonds, iron ore, bauxite. **Per capita arable land:** 3.0 acres. **Fish catch**

(1977): 80,100 metric tons. **Electricity prod.** (1977): 200 mln. kwh. **Labor force:** 75% agric.; 15% industry, serv.

Finance: Currency: Leone (Apr. 1981: 1.14 = $1 US). **Gross domestic product** (1979): $926 mln. **Per capita income** (1977): $199. **Imports** (1979): $316 mln.; partners (1978): EC 35%, UK 25%, Jap., US, China. **Exports** (1980): $190 mln.; partners (1978): US 40%, UK 30%, Neth. 9%, China 7%. **Tourists** (1977): 24,100; receipts: $4 mln. **National budget** (1978): $153 mln. revenues; $170 mln. expenditures. **International reserves less gold** (Apr. 1981): $20.1 mln. **Consumer prices** (change in 1979): 21.2%.

Transport: Motor Vehicles: in use (1976): 18,900 passenger cars, 6,300 comm. vehicles. **Chief ports:** Freetown, Bonthe.

Communications: Television sets: 8,500 in use (1976). **Radios:** 62,000 in use (1975). **Telephones in use** (1977): 15,060. **Daily newspaper circ.** (1970): 45,000; 18 per 1,000 pop.

Health: Life expectancy at birth (1975): 41.8 male; 45.0 female. **Births** (per 1,000 pop. 1975): 45.6. **Deaths** (per 1,000 pop. 1975): 21.1. **Natural increase** (1975): 2.5%. **Hospital beds** (per 100,000 pop. 1977): 99. **Physicians** (per 100,000 pop. 1977): 6.

Education (1977): **Literacy:** 15%. **Pop. 5-19:** in school: 24%, teachers per 1,000: 9. **PQLI:** 31.

Freetown was founded in 1787 by the British government as a haven for freed slaves. Their descendants, known as Creoles, number more than 60,000.

Successive steps toward independence followed the 1951 constitution. Full independence arrived Apr. 27, 1961. Sierra Leone became a republic Apr. 19, 1971. A one-party state approved by referendum 1978, brought political stability, but 1979 was characterized by inflation, corruption, and dependence upon the International Monetary Fund and creditors.

Singapore
Republic of Singapore

People: Population (1980 est.): 2,390,000. **Age distrib.** (%): 0–14: 29.6; 15–59: 63.4; 60 + : 7.0. **Pop. density:** 10,575.22 per sq. mi. **Ethnic groups:** Chinese 74%, Malays 14%, Indians, Pakistanis 8%. **Languages:** Chinese, Malay, Tamil, English all official. **Religions:** Buddhism, Taoism, Islam, Hinduism, Christianity.

Geography: Area: 226 sq. mi., smaller than New York City. **Location:** Off tip of Malayan Peninsula in S.E. Asia. **Neighbors:** Nearest are Malaysia on N, Indonesia on S. **Topography:** Singapore is a flat, formerly swampy island. The nation includes 40 nearby islets. **Capital:** Singapore. **Cities** (1978 est.): Singapore 2,334,400.

Government: Head of state: Pres. Benjamin H. Sheares; b. Aug. 12, 1907; in office: Jan. 2, 1971. **Head of government:** Prime Min. Lee Kuan Yew; b. Sept. 16, 1923; in office: June 5, 1959. **Armed forces:** regulars 36,000; reserves 45,000.

Economy: Industries: Shipbuilding, oil refining, electronics, banking, textiles, food, rubber, lumber processing, tourism. **Per capita arable land:** 0.002 acres. **Meat prod.** (1978): pork: 41,000 metric tons. **Fish catch** (1977): 15,100 metric tons. **Electricity prod.** (1978): 5.89 bln. kwh. **Crude steel prod.** (1979): 297,000 metric tons. **Labor force:** 2% agric.; 27% manuf.

Finance: Currency: Dollar (Apr. 1981: 2.12 = $1 US). **Gross domestic product** (1980): $9.01 bln. **Per capita income** (1975): $2,279. **Imports** (1980): $24.01 bln.; partners (1978). Jap. 19%, Saudi Ar. 13%, Malay. 13%, U.S. 13%. **Exports** (1980): $19.36 bln., partners (1978): U.S. 16%, Malay. 14% Jap. 10%, HK 7%. **Tourists** (1977): 1,506,700; receipts $300 mln. **National budget** (1980): $2.80 bln. revenues; $2.31 bln. expenditures. **International reserves** (Jan. 1981): $6.64 bln. **Consumer prices** (change in 1980): 8.5%.

Transport: Motor vehicles: in use (1977): 142,100 passenger cars, 54,900 comm. vehicles. **Civil aviation:** 9,756 mln passenger-km (1978); 420 mln. freight ton-km (1978).

Communications: Television sets: 294,000 licensed (1976) **Radios:** 356,000 licensed (1976). **Telephones in use** (1978) 455,120. **Daily newspaper circ.** (1977): 497,000; 215 per 1,00 pop.

Health: Life expectancy at birth (1970): 65.1 male; 70.0 fe male. **Births** (per 1,000 pop. (1980): 17.3. **Deaths** (per 1,00 pop. 1980): 5.2. **Natural increase** (1978): 1.2%. **Hospital bed** (per 100,000 pop. 1977): 371. **Physicians** (per 100,000 po 1977): 78. **Infant mortality** (per 1,000 live births 1978): 12.5.

Education (1977): **Literacy:** 76%. **Pop. 5–19:** in school: 59% teachers per 1,000: 21. **PQLI:** 86.

Founded in 1819 by Sir Thomas Stamford Raffles, Singapore was a British colony until 1959 when it became autonomous within the Commonwealth. On Sept. 16, 1963, it joined with Malaya, Sarawak and Sabah to form the Federation of Malaysia.

Tensions between Malayans, dominant in the federation, and ethnic Chinese, dominant in Singapore, led to an agreement under which Singapore became a separate nation, Aug. 9, 1965.

Singapore is the world's 4th largest port. Manufacturing has surpassed shipping, pushing per capita income to second place in Asia, following Japan. Standards in health, education, and housing are high. International banking has grown.

Formerly democratic, the government has suppressed opposition in recent years.

Solomon Islands

People: Population (1979 est.): 222,000. **Age distrib.** (%): 0–14: 48.4; 15–59: 46.5; 60+: 5.1. **Pop. density:** 18.26 per sq. mi. **Urban** (1976): 9.1%. **Ethnic groups:** A variety of Melanesian groups and mixtures, some Polynesians. **Languages:** Pidgin English, Melanesian, and Papuan languages. **Religions:** Anglican, Catholic, Evangelical, traditional religions.

Geography: Area: 11,500 sq. mi., slightly larger than Maryland. **Location:** Melanesian archipelago in the western Pacific O. **Neighbors:** Nearest is Papua New Guinea on W. **Topography:** 10 large volcanic and rugged islands and 4 groups of smaller ones. **Capital:** Honiara. **Cities:** (1976): Honiara 15,000.

Government: Head of state: Queen Elizabeth II, represented by Gov.-Gen. Baddeley Devesi, b. Oct. 16, 1941, in office: July 7, 1978. **Head of government:** Prime Min. Peter Kenilorea; b. May 23, 1943; in office: July 14, 1976. **Local divisions:** 4 districts.

Economy: Industries: Fish canning. **Chief crops:** Coconuts, cocoa, rice, oil palm. **Other resources:** Forests, marine shell. **Per capita arable land:** 0.6 acres. **Fish catch** (1977): 15,800 metric tons. **Electricity prod.** (1977): 18.00 mln. kwh.

Finance: Currency: Dollar (Mar. 1979: .89 = 1 US). **Gross domestic product** (1976): $64.1 mln. **Per capita income** 1976): $300. **Imports** (1979): $57 mln.; partners (1976): Austral. 36%, Sing. 14%, Jap. 12%, UK 10%. **Exports** (1979): $67 mln.; partners (1976): Jap. 34%, U.S. 26%, UK 13%, Neth. 8%. **Consumer prices** (change in 1976): 4.3%.

Communications: Radios: 11,000 in use (1976). **Telephones in use** (1978): 1,984.

Health: Births (per 1,000 pop. 1969): 36.1. **Deaths** (per 1,000 pop. 1969): 13.0. **Natural increase** (1969): 2.3%. **Infant mortality** (per 1,000 live births 1969): 52.4.

The Solomon Islands were sighted in 1568 by an expedition from Peru. Britain established a protectorate in the 1890s over most of the group, inhabited by Melanesians. The islands saw major World War II battles. Self-government came Jan. 2, 1976, and independence was formally attained July 7, 1978.

Somalia
Somali Democratic Republic

People: Population (1980 est.): 3,650,000. **Pop. density:** 14.83 per sq. mi. **Ethnic groups:** Somalis, related tribes 98.8%, Bantus 1.2%, Arabs, Asian, 1.1%. **Languages:** Somali (official), Arabic, Italian, English. **Religions:** Sunni Muslims 99%.

Geography: Area: 246,155 sq. mi., slightly smaller than Texas. **Location:** Occupies the eastern horn of Africa. **Neighbors:** Djibouti, Ethiopia, Kenya on W. **Topography:** The coastline extends for 1,700 mi. Hills cover the N; the center and S are flat. **Capital:** Mogadishu. **Cities** (1978 est.): Mogadishu 230,000.

Government: Head of state: Pres. Mohammed Siad Barre; b. 1919; in office: Oct. 21, 1969. **Local divisions:** 15 regions. **Armed forces:** regulars 46,500; para-military 29,500.

Economy: Chief crops: Incense, sugar, bananas, sorghum, corn, kapok, gum. **Minerals:** Iron, tin, gypsum, sandstone, bauxite, meerschaum, titanium, uranium. **Per capita arable land:** 0.8 acres. **Meat prod.** (1978): beef: 47,000 metric tons; lamb: 65,000 metric tons. **Fish catch** (1977): 32,600 metric tons. **Electricity prod.** (1977): 45.00 mln. kwh. **Labor force:** 60% agric.

Finance: Currency: Shilling (Apr. 1981: 6.30 = $1 US). **Gross domestic product** (1978 est.): $407 mln. **Per capita income** (1976): $105. **Imports** (1979): $287 mln.; partners: It. 29%, UK 10%, India 9%, W. Ger. 5%. **Exports** (1979): $111 mln.; partners: Saudi Ar. 35%, It. 19%, USSR 9%, Jap. 6%. **Tourist receipts** (1977): $4 mln. **International reserves less gold** (Nov. 1980): $32.7 mln. **Gold:** 19,000 oz t. **Consumer prices** (change in 1980): 58.8%.

Transport: Motor vehicles: in use (1972): 8,000 passenger cars, 8,000 comm. vehicles. **Chief ports:** Mogadishu, Berbera.

Communications: Radios: 69,000 in use (1976). **Daily newspaper circ.** (1970): 4,500; 2 per 1,000 pop.

Health: Life expectancy at birth (1975): 39.4 male; 42.6 female. **Births** (per 1,000 pop. 1975): 47.2. **Deaths** (per 1,000 pop. 1975): 21.6. **Natural increase** (1975): 2.6%. **Hospital beds** (per 100,000 pop. 1977): 179. **Physicians** (per 100,000 pop. 1977): 3.

Education (1977): **Literacy:** 5%. **Pop. 5-19:** in school: 19%, teachers per 1,000: 7. **PQLI:** 34.

Arab trading posts developed into sultanates. The Italian Protectorate of Somalia, acquired from 1885 to 1927, extended along the Indian O. from the Gulf of Aden to the Juba R. The UN in 1949 approved eventual creation of Somalia as a sovereign state and in 1950 Italy took over the trusteeship held by Great Britain since World War II.

British Somaliland was formed in the 19th century in the NW. Britain gave it independence June 26, 1960; on July 1 it joined with the former Italian part to create the independent Somali Republic.

On Oct. 21, 1969, a Supreme Revolutionary Council seized power in a bloodless army and police coup, named a Council of Secretaries of State, to aid it, and abolished the Assembly. In May, 1970, several foreign companies were nationalized.

A severe drought in 1975 killed tens of thousands, and spurred efforts to resettle nomads on collective farms. The U.S. charged in 1975 that Soviet naval facilities at Berbera included a missile storage site.

Somalia has laid claim to Ogaden, the huge eastern region of Ethiopia, peopled mostly by Somalis. Ethiopia battled Somali rebels and accused Somalia of sending troops and heavy arms in 1977. Russian forces were expelled in 1977 in retaliation for Soviet support of Ethiopia. Some 11,000 Cuban troops with Soviet arms defeated Somali army troops and ethnic Somali rebels in Ethiopia, 1978. As many as 1.3 mln. refugees entered Somalia. In June 1981, Pres. Barre offered to meet with Ethiopian leader Col. Mengistu Haile Mariam to seek a solution to the Ogaden dispute.

South Africa
Republic of South Africa

People: Population (1980 est.): 29,290,000. **Age distrib.** (%): 0–14: 41.5; 15–59: 54.5; 60+: 3.8. **Pop. density:** 62.08 per sq. mi. **Urban** (1972): 47.9%. **Ethnic groups:** Afrikaner, English, Zulu, Asian, Xhosa. **Religions:** Bantu Christian 14.5%, Dutch Reformed 14.3%, Methodist 10.7%, Anglican 8.8%, Roman Catholic 6.7%, other Christian 18.4%, Moslems, Hindus, and Jews 4%. **Languages:** Afrikaans, English (both official), Zulu, Xhosa, Tswana, N. and S. Sotho.

Geography: Area: 471,819 sq. mi., four-fifths the size of Alaska. **Location:** At the southern extreme of Africa. **Neighbors:** Namibia (SW Africa), Botswana, Zimbabwe on N, Mozambique, Swaziland on E; surrounds Lesotho. **Topography:** The large interior plateau reaches close to the country's 2,700-mi. coastline. There are few major rivers or lakes; rainfall is sparse in W, more plentiful in E. **Capitals:** Cape Town (legislative). Pretoria (administrative), and Bloemfontein (judicial). **Cities** (1979): Durban 851,000; Cape Town 1,108,000; Johannesburg 1,441,000; Pretoria 563,000.

Government: Head of state: Pres. Marais Viljoen, b. Dec. 2, 1915, in office: June 19, 1979. **Head of government:** Prime Min. Pieter Willem Botha; b. Jan. 12, 1916; in office: Sept. 28, 1978. **Local divisions:** 4 provinces. **Armed forces:** regulars 63,250; reserves 135,000.

Economy: Industries: Steel, tires, motors, textiles, plastics. **Chief crops:** Corn, wool, dairy products, grain, tobacco, sugar, fruit, peanuts, grapes. **Minerals:** Largest world production of gold, chromium, antimony, coal, iron, manganese, nickel, phosphates, tin, uranium, gem diamonds, platinum, copper, vanadium. **Other resources:** Wool. **Per capita arable land:** 1.3 acres. **Meat prod.** (1978): beef: 500,000 metric tons; pork: 90,000 metric tons; lamb: 154,000 metric tons. **Fish catch** (1977): 1.0 mln. metric tons. **Electricity prod.** (1978): 84.77 bln.

kwh. **Crude steel prod.** (1979): 8.9 mln. metric tons. **Labor force:** 30% agric.; 18% ind. and commerce; 35% serv.; 8% mining.

Finance: Currency: Rand (Apr. 1981: .82 = $1 US). **Gross domestic product** (1980): $80.21 bln. **Per capita income** (1978): $1,296. **Imports** (1980): $19.25 bln.; partners (1978): W. Ger. 20%, UK 17%, U.S. 16%, Jap. 13%. **Exports** (1980): $25.69 bln.; partners (1978): U.S. 19%, UK 17%, Jap. 10%, W. Ger. 9%. **Tourist receipts** (1977): $321 mln. **National budget** (1980): $16.06 bln. revenues; $17.64 bln. expenditures. **International reserves less gold** (Apr. 1981): $807 mln. **Gold:** 12.28 mln. oz t. **Consumer prices** (change in 1980): 13.7%.

Transport: Railway traffic (1978): 80.96 bln. net ton-km. **Motor vehicles:** in use (1977): 2.16 mln. passenger cars, 821,200 comm. vehicles; assembled (1977): 131,800 passenger cars; 57,900 comm. vehicles. **Civil aviation:** 7,248 mln. passenger-km (1978): 240 mln. freight ton-km (1978). **Chief ports:** Durban, Cape Town, East London, Port Elizabeth.

Communications: Radios: 2.5 mln. in use (1976), 385,000 manuf. (1977). **Telephones in use** (1978): 2,319,558. **Daily newspaper circ.** (1976): 1,728,000; 66 per 1,000 pop.

Health: Life expectancy at birth (1975): 56.6 male; 59.4 female. **Births** (per 1,000 pop. 1975): 37.7. **Deaths** (per 1,000 pop. 1975): 11.5. **Natural increase** (1975): 2.6%. **Hospital beds** (per 100,000 pop. 1977): 614. **Physicians** (per 100,000 pop. 1977): 6. **Infant mortality** (per 1,000 live births 1979): Africans 94, Indians 37, whites 19.

Education (1977): **Literacy:** 50%. **Pop. 5-19:** in school: 61%, teachers per 1,000: 13. **PQLI:** 60.

Bushmen and Hottentots were the original inhabitants. Bantus, including Zulu, Xhosa, Swazi, and Sotho, had occupied the area from Transvaal to south of Transkei before the 17th century.

The Cape of Good Hope area was settled by Dutch, beginning in the 17th century. Britain seized the Cape in 1806. Many Dutch trekked north and founded 2 republics, the Transvaal and the Orange Free State. Diamonds were discovered, 1867, and gold, 1886. The Dutch (Boers) resented encroachments by the British and others; the Anglo-Boer War followed, 1899-1902. Britain won and, effective May 31, 1910, created the Union of South Africa, incorporating the British colonies of the Cape and Natal, the Transvaal and the Orange Free State. After a referendum, the Union became the Republic of South Africa, May 31, 1961, and withdrew from the Commonwealth.

With the election victory of Daniel Malan's National party in 1948, the policy of separate development of the races, or apartheid, already existing unofficially, became official. This called for separate development, separate residential areas, and ultimate political independence for the whites, Bantus, Asians, and Coloreds. In 1959 the government passed acts providing the eventual creation of several Bantu nations or Bantustans on 13% of the country's land area, though most black leaders have opposed the plan.

Under apartheid, blacks are severely restricted to certain occupations, and are paid far lower wages than are whites for similar work. Only whites may vote or run for public office, and militant white opposition has been curbed. There is an advisory Indian Council, partly elected, partly appointed. In 1969, a Colored People's Representative Council was created. Minor liberalization measures were allowed in the 1970s.

At least 600 persons, mostly Bantus, were killed in 1976 riots protesting apartheid. Black protests continued through 1980 partly fueled by rising unemployment.

In 1963, the Transkei, an area in the SE, became the first of these partially self-governing territories or "Homelands." Transkei became independent on Oct. 26, 1976, Bophuthatswana on Dec. 6, 1977, and Venda on Sept. 13, 1979; none received international recognition.

Bophuthatswana: Population (1976 est.): 2,500,000. **Area:** 15,571 sq. mi., 6 discontinuous geographic units. **Capital:** Mmabatho. **Cities:** (1977 est.): Ga-Rankawa, Mabopane (comb. metro area): 153,000. **Head of state:** Pres. Kgosi Lucas Mangope, b. Dec. 27, 1923; in office: Dec. 6, 1977.

Transkei: Population (1979 est.): 2,200,000. **Area:** 15,831 sq. mi., 3 discontinuous geographic units. **Capital:** Umtata (1978 est.): 30,000. **Head of state:** Pres. Kaiser Matanzima; in office: Feb. 20, 1979. **Head of government:** Prime Min. George Matanzima; in office: Feb. 20, 1979.

Venda: Population (1978 est.): 357,000. **Area:** 2,448 sq. mi., 2 discontinuous geographic units. **Capital:** Thohoyandou. **City:** Makearela (1976 est.): 1,972. **Head of state:** Patrick Mphephu; in office: Sept. 13, 1979.

John Vorster, who dominated South African politics as prime minister for 11 years before becoming president in 1979, resigned his post upon accusations of covering up government misappropriations.

Namibia (South-West Africa)

South-West Africa is a sparsely populated land twice the size of California. Made a German protectorate in 1884, it was surrendered to South Africa in 1915 and was administered by that country under a League of Nations mandate. S. Africa refused to accept UN authority under the trusteeship system.

Other African nations charged S. Africa imposed apartheid, built military bases, and exploited S-W Africa. The UN General Assembly, May 1968, created an 11-nation council to take over administration of S-W Africa and lead it to independence. The council charged that S. Africa had blocked its efforts to visit S-W Africa.

In 1968 the UN General Assembly gave the area the name Namibia. In Jan. 1970 the UN Security Council condemned S. Africa for "illegal" control of the area. In an advisory opinion, June 1971, the International Court of Justice declared S. Africa was occupying the area illegally.

In a 1977 referendum, white voters backed a plan for a multiracial interim government to lead to independence. The Marxist South-West Africa People's Organization rejected the plan, and launched a guerrilla war. Both S. Africa and Namibian rebels agreed to a UN plan for independence by the end of 1978. S. Africa rejected the plan, Sept. 20, 1978, and held elections, without UN supervision, for Namibia's constituent assembly, Dec., that were ignored by the major black opposition parties.

The UN peace plan, proposed 1980, called for a cease-fire and a demilitarized zone 31 miles deep on each side of S-W Africa's borders with Angola and Zambia that would be patrolled by UN peacekeeping forces against guerrilla actions. Impartial elections would follow. In 1981, member nations of The Organization of African Unity pressed their demands for settlement of the issue, and criticized the U.S. and other Western nations for their failure to bring pressure on South Africa.

Most of Namibia is a plateau, 3,600 ft. high, with plains in the N, Kalahari Desert to the E, Orange R. on the S, Atlantic O. on the W. Area is 318,261 sq. mi.; pop. (1980 est.) 1 to 1.25 mln.; capital, Windhoek.

Products include cattle, sheep, diamonds, copper, lead, zinc, fish. People include Namas (Hottentots), Ovambos (Bantus), Bushmen, and others.

Walvis Bay, the only deepwater port in the country, was turned over to South African administration in 1922. S. Africa said in 1978 it would discuss sovereignty only after Namibian independence.

Spain
Spanish State

People: Population (1980 est.): 37,430,000. **Age distrib.** (%): 0-14: 27.6; 15-59: 58.0; 60+: 14.4. **Pop. density:** 192.06 per sq. mi. **Ethnic groups:** Spanish (Castilian, Valencian, Andalusian, Asturian) 72.8%, Catalan 16.4%, Galician 8.2%, Basque 2.3%. **Languages:** Spanish (official), Catalan, Galician (Portuguese dialect), Valencian (Spanish dialect), Basque all legally recognized. **Religions:** Roman Catholicism nearly universal.

Geography: Area: 194,883 sq. mi., the size of Colorado and Wyoming combined. **Location:** In SW Europe. **Neighbors:** Portugal on W. France on N. **Topography:** The interior is a high, arid plateau broken by mountain ranges and river valleys. The NW is heavily watered, the south has lowlands and a Mediterranean climate. **Capital:** Madrid. **Cities** (1978 est.): Madrid 3,520,321; Barcelona 1,809,722; Valencia 713,026; Seville 588,784; Zaragoza 547,317; Bilbao 457,655; Malaga 402,978.

Government: Head of state: King Juan Carlos I de Borbon y Borbon, b. Jan. 5, 1938; in office: Nov. 22, 1975. **Head of government:** Prime Min. Leopoldo Calvo Sotelo; in office: Jan. 30, 1981. **Local divisions:** 50 provinces with appointed governors. **Armed forces:** regulars 321,000; reserves 1,085,000.

Economy: Industries: Machinery, textiles, shoes, paper, autos, ships, cement, tourism. **Chief crops:** Grains, olives, grapes, citrus fruits, onions, almonds, esparto, flax, hemp, pulse, tobacco, cotton, rice. **Minerals:** Mercury, potash, uranium, lead, iron, copper, zinc, coal, cobalt, silver, sulphur, phosphates, oil. **Crude oil reserves** (1980): 150 mln. bbls. **Other resources:** Forests (cork). **Per capita arable land:** 1.1 acres. **Meat prod.**

(1978): beef: 445,000 metric tons; pork: 760,000 metric tons; lamb: 153,000 metric tons. **Fish catch** (1977): 1.5 mln. metric tons. **Electricity prod.** (1978): 99.26 bln. kwh. **Crude steel prod.** (1979): 12.3 mln. metric tons. **Labor force:** 19% agric.; 37% ind. and commerce; 41% serv.

Finance: Currency: Peseta (Apr. 1981: 89.26 = $1 US). **Gross domestic product** (1979): $201 bln. **Per capita income** (1979): $5,500. **Imports** (1980): $34.08 bln.; partners (1978): U.S. 13%, W. Ger. 10%, Saudi Ar. 9%, Fr. 9%. **Exports** (1980): $20.83 bln.; partners (1978): Fr. 17%, W. Ger. 11%, U.S. 9%, UK 6%. **Tourists** (1977): 34,266,700; receipts: $4.00 bln. **National budget** (1980): $31.99 bln. revenues; $33.84 bln. expenditures. **International reserves less gold** (Mar. 1981): $10.83 bln. **Gold** (Feb. 1980): 14.61 mln. oz t. **Consumer prices** (change in 1980): 15.5%.

Transport: Railway traffic (1978): 16.76 bln. passenger-km; 9.72 bln. net ton-km. **Motor vehicles:** in use (1977): 5.94 mln. passenger cars, 1.56 mln. comm. vehicles; manuf. (1978): 988,800 passenger cars; 150,000 comm. vehicles. **Civil aviation:** 14,604 mln. passenger-km (1978): 386 mln. freight ton-km (1978). **Chief ports:** Barcelona, Bilbao, Valencia, Cartagena, Gijon.

Communications: Television sets: 6.64 mln. in use (1976), 631,000 manuf. (1976). **Radios:** 9.3 mln. in use (1976), 363,000 manuf. (1976). **Telephones in use** (1978): 9,527,781. **Daily newspaper circ.** (1977): 4,710,000; 128 per 1,000 pop.

Health: Life expectancy at birth (1970): 69.69 male; 74.96 female. **Births** (per 1,000 pop. 1979): 16.1. **Deaths** (per 1,000 pop. 1979): 7.8. **Natural increase** (1977): 1.0%. **Hospital beds** (per 100,000 pop. 1977): 543. **Physicians** (per 100,000 pop. 1977): 176. **Infant mortality** (per 1,000 live births 1977): 15.6.

Education (1977): **Literacy:** 93%. **Pop. 5-19:** in school: 66%, teachers per 1,000: 28. **PQLI:** 93.

Spain was settled by Iberians, Basques, and Celts, partly overrun by Carthaginians, conquered by Rome c.200 BC. The Visigoths, in power by the 5th century AD, adopted Christianity but by 711 AD lost to the Islamic invasion from Africa. Christian reconquest from the N led to a Spanish nationalism. In 1469 the kingdoms of Aragon and Castile were united by the marriage of Ferdinand II and Isabella I, and the last Moorish power was broken by the fall of the kingdom of Granada, 1492. Spain became a bulwark of Roman Catholicism.

Spain obtained a colonial empire with the discovery of America by Columbus, 1492, the conquest of Mexico by Cortes, and Peru by Pizarro. It also controlled the Netherlands and parts of Italy and Germany. Spain lost its American colonies in the early 19th century. It lost Cuba, the Philippines, and Puerto Rico during the Spanish-American War, 1898.

Primo de Rivera became dictator in 1923. King Alfonso XIII revoked the dictatorship, 1930, but was forced to leave the country 1931. A republic was proclaimed which disestablished the church, curtailed its privileges, and secularized education. A conservative reaction occurred 1933 but was followed by a Popular Front (1936-1939) composed of socialists, communists, republicans, and anarchists.

Army officers under Francisco Franco revolted against the government, 1936. In a destructive 3-yr. war, in which one million were said to have died, Franco received massive help and troops from Italy and Germany, while the USSR, France, and Mexico supported the republic. War ended Mar. 28, 1939. Franco was named caudillo, leader of the nation. Spain was neutral in World War II but its relations with fascist countries caused its exclusion from the UN in 1946. It was admitted in 1955.

In July 1969, Franco and the Cortes designated Prince Juan Carlos as the future king and chief of state. After Franco's death, Nov. 20, 1975, Juan Carlos was sworn in as king. He presided over the formal dissolution of the institutions of the Franco regime. In free elections June 1976, moderates and democratic socialists emerged as the largest parties.

In an unsuccessful attempt at a military coup, Feb. 23, 1981, rightist Civil Guards seized the lower house of Parliament and took most of the country's leaders hostage. The plot collapsed the next day when the army remained loyal to King Juan Carlos.

Catalonia and the Basque country were granted autonomy, 1980, following overwhelming approval in home-rule referendums. Basque extremists, however, continued their violent campaign for independence.

Between 1960 and 1975 Spain changed from an agricultural nation to one of the world's important industrial powers.

The **Balearic Islands** in the western Mediterranean, 1,935 sq. mi., are a province of Spain; they include **Majorca** (Mallorca), with the capital, Palma; **Minorca, Cabrera, Ibiza** and **Formentera.** The **Canary Islands,** 2,807 sq. mi., in the Atlantic W of Morocco, form 2 provinces, including the islands of **Tenerife, Palma, Gomera, Hierro, Grand Canary, Fuerteventura,** and **Lanzarote** with Las Palmas and Santa Cruz thriving ports. **Ceuta** and **Melilla,** small enclaves on Morocco's Mediterranean coast, are part of Metropolitan Spain.

Spain has sought the return of Gibraltar, in British hands since 1704. (*See Index.*)

Sri Lanka

Democratic Socialist Republic of Sri Lanka

People: Population (1980 est.): 14,740,000. **Age distrib.** (%): 0–14: 39.0; 15–59: 54.7; 60+: 6.4. **Pop. density:** 581.87 per sq. mi. **Urban** (1971): 22.4%. **Ethnic groups:** Sinhalese 72%, Tamils 20%, Moors 7%. **Languages:** Sinhala (official), Tamil, English. **Religions:** Buddhists 67%, Hindus 18%, Christians 7.7%, Muslims 7.2%.

Geography: Area: 25,332 sq. mi. **Location:** In Indian O. off SE coast of India. **Neighbors:** India on NW. **Topography:** The coastal area and the northern half are flat; the S-central area is hilly and mountainous. **Capital:** Colombo. **Cities** (1979): Colombo 991,000; Jaffna 118,000; Kandy 103,000; Galle 79,000.

Government: Head of state: Pres. Junius Richard Jayewardene; b. Sept. 17, 1906; in office: Feb. 4, 1978. **Head of government:** Ranasinghe Premadasa, b. June 23, 1924, in office: Feb. 6, 1978. **Local divisions:** 22 districts. **Armed forces:** regulars 13,700; reserves 10,700.

Economy: Industries: Plywood, paper, glassware, ceramics, cement, chemicals, textiles. **Chief crops:** Tea, coconuts, rice, cacao, cinnamon, citronella, tobacco. **Minerals:** Graphite, limestone, iron, ilmenite, monazite, zircon, quartz, precious and semiprecious stones. **Other resources:** Forests, rubber. **Per capita arable land:** 0.2 acres. **Meat prod.** (1978): beef: 19,000 metric tons. **Fish catch** (1977): 138,700 metric tons. **Electricity prod.** (1978): 1.38 bln. kwh. **Labor force:** 53.4% agric.; 27% ind. and commerce; 19.4% serv.

Finance: Currency: Rupee (Apr. 1981: 18.35 = $1 US). **Gross domestic product** (1979): $3.35 bln. **Per capita income** (1978): $168. **Imports** (1980): $2.02 bln.; partners: Jap. 11%, Saudi Ar. 10%, UK 10%, India 9%. **Exports** (1980): $1.08 bln.; partners: UK 7%, U.S. 7%, Jap. 6%, Pak. 5%. **Tourists** (1977): 153,700; receipts: $40 mln. **National budget** (1979): $818 mln. revenues; $1.31 bln. expenditures. **International reserves less gold** (Feb. 1981): $219 mln. **Gold:** 63,000 oz t. **Consumer prices** (change in 1980): 26.2%

Transport: Railway traffic (1978): 3.7 bln. passenger-km; 246 mln. net ton-km. **Motor vehicles:** in use (1976): 93,800 passenger cars, 49,200 comm. vehicles. **Civil aviation:** 413 mln. passenger-km (1977); 2.5 mln. freight ton-km (1977). **Chief ports:** Colombo, Trincomalee, Galle.

Communications: Radios: 800,000 in use (1976), 55,000 manuf. (1976). **Telephones in use** (1978): 74,166.

Health: Life expectancy at birth (1967): 64.8 male; 66.9 female. **Births** (per 1,000 pop. 1972): 29.5. **Deaths** (per 1,000 pop. 1972): 7.7. **Natural increase** (1972): 2.2%. **Hospital beds** (per 100,000 pop. 1977): 296. **Physicians** (per 100,000 pop. 1977): 16. **Infant mortality** (per 1,000 live births 1979): 43.

Education (1977): **Literacy:** 81%. **Pop. 5-19:** in school: 47%, teachers per 1,000: 22. **PQLI:** 81.

The island was known to the ancient world as Taprobane (Greek for copper-colored) and later as Serendip (from Arabic). Colonists from northern India subdued the indigenous Veddahs about 543 BC; their descendants, the Buddhist Sinhalese, still form most of the population. Hindu descendants of Tamil immigrants from southern India account for one-fifth of the population; separatism has grown. Parts were occupied by the Portuguese in 1505 and by the Dutch in 1658. The British seized the island in 1796. As Ceylon it became an independent member of the Commonwealth in 1948. On May 22, 1972, Ceylon became the Republic of Sri Lanka.

Prime Min. W. R. D. Bandaranaike was assassinated Sept. 25, 1959. In new elections, the Freedom Party was victorious under Mrs. Sirimavo Bandaranaike, widow of the former prime minister. In Apr., 1962, the government expropriated British and U.S. oil companies. In Mar. 1965 elections, the conservative United National Party won; the new government agreed to pay compensation for the seized oil companies. The U.S., July 1965, resumed economic aid.

After May 1970 elections, Mrs. Bandaranaike became prime minister again. In 1971 the nation suffered economic problems and terrorist activities by ultra-leftists, thousands of whom were executed. Unemployment and food shortages plagued the nation from 1973 to 1976. Massive land reform and nationalization of foreign-owned plantations was undertaken in the mid-1970s. Mrs. Bandaranaike was ousted in 1977 elections by the United Nationals. A presidential form of government was installed in 1978 to restore stability. The economy made significant gains in 1979 due to liberalization of trade and a concentration of major development projects.

Sudan

Democratic Republic of the Sudan

People: Population (1980 est.): 18,690,000. **Pop. density:** 19.32 per sq. mi. **Urban** (1976): 20.4%. **Ethnic groups:** North: Arabs, Nubians; South: Nilotic; Sudanic, Negro tribes. **Languages:** Arabic (official) 51%, 32 other languages. **Religions:** Muslims 70%, traditional 25%, Christians 5%.

Geography: Area: 967,491 sq. mi., the largest country in Africa, over one-fourth the size of the U.S. **Location:** At the E end of Sahara desert zone. **Neighbors:** Egypt on N, Libya, Chad, Central African Republic on W, Zaire, Uganda, Kenya on S, Ethiopia on E. **Topography:** The N consists of the Libyan Desert in the W, and the mountainous Nubia desert in E, with narrow Nile valley between. The center contains large, fertile, rainy areas with fields, pasture, and forest. The S has rich soil, heavy rain. **Capital:** Khartoum. **Cities** (1973 cen.): Khartoum 333,921; Omdurman 299,401; North Khartoum 150,991; Port Sudan 132,631.

Government: Head of state and head of government: Pres., Prime Min. Gaafar Mohammed Nimeiri; b. Jan. 1, 1930; in office: May 25, 1969 (P.M.: Sept. 10, 1977). **Local divisions:** 15 provinces; the southern 3 have a regional government. **Armed forces:** regulars 62,900; para-military 3,500.

Economy: Industries: Textiles, food processing. **Chief crops:** Gum arabic (principal world source), durra (sorghum), cotton (main export), sesame, peanuts, rice, coffee, sugar cane, tobacco, wheat, dates. **Minerals:** Chrome, gold, copper, white mica, vermiculite, asbestos. **Other resources:** Mahogany. **Per capita arable land:** 1.1 acres. **Meat prod.** (1978): beef: 170,000 metric tons; lamb: 123,000 metric tons; **Fish catch** (1977): 24,700 metric tons. **Electricity prod.** (1977): 810 mln. kwh. **Labor force:** 86% agric.; 14% ind., commerce, serv.

Finance: Currency: Pound (Apr. 1981: .50 = $1 US). **Gross domestic product** (1978 est.): $5.6 bln. **Per capita income** (1978 est.): $320. **Imports** (1980): $1.62 bln.; partners (1977): UK 14%, W. Ger. 12%, Jap. 11%, Iraq 10%. **Exports** (1980): $543 mln.; partners (1977): It. 12%, India 9%, China 9%, Jap. 8%. **Tourists** (1977): 36,700; receipts: $11 mln. **National Budget** (1978): $1.13 bln. revenues; $1.48 bln. expenditures. **International reserves less gold** (Mar. 1981): $33.6 mln. **Consumer prices** (change in 1980): 25.4%.

Transport: Railway traffic (1973): 2.3 bln. net ton-km. **Motor vehicles:** in use (1972): 29,200 passenger cars, 21,200 comm. vehicles. **Civil aviation:** 556 mln. passenger-km (1977); 10 mln. freight ton-km (1977). **Chief ports:** Port Sudan.

Communications: Television sets: 100,000 in use (1975). **Radios:** 1.3 mln. licensed (1975). **Telephones in use** (1978): 62,297. **Daily newspaper circ.** (1976): 26,000.

Health: Life expectancy at birth (1975): 43.0 male; 45.0 female. **Births** (per 1,000 pop. 1975): 45.8. **Deaths** (per 1,000 pop. 1975): 20.2 **Natural increase** (1975): 2.6%. **Hospital beds** (per 100,000 pop. 1977): 100. **Physicians** (per 100,000 pop. 1977): 50. **Infant mortality** (per 1,000 live births 1979): 141.

Education (1977): **Literacy:** 20%. **Pop. 5-19:** in school: 26%, teachers per 1,000: 8. **PQLI:** 32.

Northern Sudan, ancient Nubia, was settled by Egyptians in antiquity, and was converted to Coptic Christianity in the 6th century. Arab conquests brought Islam in the 15th century.

In the 1820s Egypt took over the Sudan, defeating the last of earlier empires, including the Fung. In the 1880s a revolution was led by Mohammed Ahmed who called himself the Mahdi (leader of the faithful) and his followers, the dervishes.

In 1898 an Anglo-Egyptian force crushed the Mahdi's successors. In 1951 the Egyptian Parliament abrogated its 1899 and 1936 treaties with Great Britain, and amended its constitution,

Oct. 16, to provide for a separate Sudanese constitution.

Sudan voted for complete independence as a parliamentary government effective Jan. 1, 1956. Gen. Ibrahim Abboud took power 1958, but resigned under pressure, 1964.

In 1969, in a second military coup, a Revolutionary Council took power, but a civilian premier and cabinet were appointed; the government announced it would create a socialist state. The northern 12 provinces are predominantly Arab-Moslem and have been dominant in the central government. The 3 southern provinces are Negro and predominantly pagan. A 1972 peace agreement gave the South regional autonomy.

The government nationalized a number of businesses in May 1970. An attempted communist coup in July 1971 failed, leading to a temporary diplomatic break with the USSR. Soviet arms shipments were announced in 1975, but relations later deteriorated and U.S. ties improved.

Diplomatic relations with the U.S., broken by Sudan during the 1967 Arab-Israeli war, were restored in 1972.

On Mar. 2, 1973, the U.S. ambassador and the charge d'affaires and a Belgian diplomat were slain in Khartoum by 8 Palestinian terrorists. The 8 were freed and turned over to a Palestinian liberation group in Egypt.

Sudan charged Libya with aiding an unsuccessful coup in Sudan in 1976. Sudan has backed the Eritrean separatist movement in neighboring Ethiopia.

Economic problems plagued the nation, 1979, and were aggravated by the influx of an est. 500,000 Ethiopian and Ugandan refugees.

Suriname

People: Population (1979 est.): 404,000. **Pop. density:** 5.85 per sq. mi. **Ethnic groups** Creole 31%, East Indian 37%, Javanese 15.3%, Bush Negro 2.6%, Amerindians, Chinese. **Languages:** Dutch (official), Sranan Tongo (Creole) universal, English, others. **Religions:** Muslims, Hindus, Roman Catholics, Protestants, Jews, Moravians.

Geography: Area: 63,251 sq. mi., slightly larger than Georgia. **Location:** On N shore of S. America. **Neighbors:** Guyana on W, Brazil on S, French Guiana on E. **Topography:** A flat Atlantic coast, where dikes permit agriculture. Inland is a forest belt; to the S, largely unexplored hills cover 75% of the country. **Capital:** Paramaribo. **Cities** (1979): Paramaribo 150,000; Nickerie, Paranam, Moengo.

Government: Head of state: Prime Min. Chin A. Sen; in office: Aug. 14, 1980. **Head of government:** Prime Min. Henck R. Chin A Sen; in office: Mar. 1980. **Local divisions:** 9 districts.

Economy: Industries: Aluminum. **Chief crops:** Rice, sugar, fruits. **Minerals:** Bauxite. **Other resources:** Forests, shrimp. **Per capita arable land:** 0.2 acres. **Electricity prod.** (1977): 1.42 bln. kwh. **Labor force:** 29% agric.; 15% ind. and commerce.

Finance: Currency: Guilder (Apr. 1981: 1.79 = $1 US). **Gross domestic product** (1977): $529 mln. **Per capita income** (1977): $1,240. **Imports** (1979): $411 mln.; partners: U.S. 31%, Neth. 21%, Trin./Tob. 14%, Jap. 7%. **Exports** (1979): $444 mln.; partners: U.S. 40%, Nor. 14%, Neth. 11%, UK 8%. **Tourists** (1975): 54,700; receipts: $10 mln. **National budget** (1976): $160 mln. revenues; $238 mln. expenditures. **International reserves less gold** (Apr. 1981): $227.81 mln. **Gold** 54,000 oz t. **Consumer prices** (change in 1979): 14.9%.

Transport: Motor vehicles: in use (1976): 28,800 passenger cars, 10,200 comm. vehicles. **Chief ports:** Paramaribo, Nieuw Nickerie.

Communications: Television sets: 38,000 in use (1976). **Radios:** 112,000 in use (1976). **Telephones in use** (1978): 20,787. **Daily newspaper circ.** (1977): 33,000; 74 per 1,000 pop.

Health: Life expectancy at birth (1963): 62.5 male; 66.7 female. **Births** (per 1,000 pop. 1966): 36.9. **Deaths** (per 1,000 pop. 1966): 7.2. **Natural increase** (1966): 3.0%. **Pop. per hospital bed** (1975): 184. **Pop. per physician** (1974): 2,030. **Infant mortality** (per 1,000 live births 1966): 30.4. **PQLI:** 83.

The Netherlands acquired Suriname in 1667 from Britain, in exchange for New Netherlands (New York). The 1954 Dutch constitution raised the colony to a level of equality with the Netherlands and the Netherlands Antilles. In the 1970s the Dutch government pressured for Suriname independence, which came Nov. 25, 1975, despite objections from East Indians and some Bush Negroes. Some 40% of the population (mostly East Indians) emigrated to the Netherlands in the months before ind pendence. The Netherlands promised $1.5 billion in aid for the first decade of independence.

A military coup staged by non-commissioned officers, Feb. 1980, installed civilians to its ruling National Military Council.

Swaziland
Kingdom of Swaziland

People: Population (1980 est.): 550,000. **Age distrib.** (%): 0–14: 48.3; 15–59: 47.4; 60+: 4.3. **Pop. density:** 82.03 per sq. mi. **Urban** (1973): 7.9%. **Ethnic groups:** Swazi 90%, Zulu 2.3%, European 2.1%, other African, non-African groups. **Languages:** siSwati, English, (both official). **Religions:** Christians 60%, animist.

Geography: Area: 6,705 sq. mi., slightly smaller than New Jersey. **Location:** In southern Africa, near Indian O. coast. **Neighbors:** South Africa on N, W, S, Mozambique on E. **Topography:** The country descends from W-E in broad belts, becoming more arid in the lowveld region, then rising to a plateau in the E. **Capital:** Mbabane. **Cities** (1980): Mbabane 25,000; Manzini 25,000.

Government: Head of state: King Sobhuza II; b. July 22, 1899; in office: 1921. **Head of government:** Prime Min. Maphevu Dlamini; in office: Mar. 31, 1976. **Local divisions:** 4 districts, 2 municipalities.

Economy: Industries: Wood pulp. **Chief crops:** Corn, cotton, rice, pineapples, sugar, citrus fruits. **Minerals:** Asbestos, iron, coal. **Other resources:** Forests. **Per capita arable land:** 0.7 acres. **Meat prod.** (1978): beef: 15,000 metric tons. **Electricity prod.** (1977): 173.00 mln. kwh. **Labor force:** 60% agric.; 8% ind. and commerce; 9% serv.

Finance: Currency: Lilangeni (Apr. 1981: .82 = $1 US). **Gross domestic product** (1977): $313 mln. **Per capita income** (1977 est.): $530. **Imports** (1979): $355 mln.; partners (1975): So. Afr., UK. **Exports** (1979): $219 mln.; partners (1975): UK, U.S., So. Afr., Jap. **National budget** (1978): $114 mln. revenues; $128 mln. expenditures. **International reserves less gold** (Mar. 1981): $163.46 mln. **Consumer prices** (change in 1980): 17.7%.

Transport: Motor vehicles: in use (1976): 7,900 passenger cars, 7,100 comm. vehicles.

Communications: Radios: 60,000 in use (1976). **Telephones in use** (1978): 9,190. **Daily newspaper circ.** (1976): 5,000; 10 per 1,000 pop.

Health: Life expectancy at birth (1975): 41.8 male; 45 female. **Births** (per 1,000 pop. 1975): 48.3. **Deaths** (per 1,000 pop. 1975): 21.2. **Natural increase** (1975): 2.7%. **Hospital beds** (per 100,000 pop. 1977): 345. **Physicians** (per 100,000 pop. 1977): 11. **Infant mortality rate** (per 1,000 live births 1980): 156.

Education (1977): **Literacy:** 36%. **Pop. 5-19:** in school: 72%, teachers per 1,000: 21. **PQLI:** 43.

The royal house of Swaziland traces back 400 years, and is one of Africa's last ruling dynasties. The Swazis, a Bantu people, were driven to Swaziland from lands to the N by the Zulus in 1820. Their autonomy was later guaranteed by Britain and Transvaal, with Britain assuming control after 1903. Independence came Sept. 6, 1968. In 1973 the king repealed the constitution and assumed full powers.

A new Parliament was opened, 1979. Under the new constitution political parties were forbidden; Parliament's role in government was limited to debate and advice.

Fertile lands and mineral resources have aided development. About 8,000 Swazis hold jobs in South Africa, which has a customs union with Swaziland. The population is homogeneous, except for 6,000 whites who dominate the economy.

Sweden
Kingdom of Sweden

People: Population (1980 est.): 8,310,000. **Age distrib.** (%): 0-14: 20.6; 15-59: 58.2; 60+: 21.2. **Pop. density:** 47.85 per sq. mi. **Urban** (1975): 82.7%. **Ethnic groups:** Swedish 93%, Finnish 3%, Lapps, European immigrants. **Languages:** Swedish, Finnish. **Religions:** Lutherans (official) 95%, other Protestants 5%.

Geography: Area: 173,665 sq. mi., larger than California. **Location:** On Scandinavian Peninsula in N. Europe. **Neighbors:** Norway on W, Denmark on S (across Kattegat), Finland on E. **Topography:** Mountains along NW border cover 25% of Swe-

den, flat or rolling terrain covers the central and southern areas, which includes several large lakes. **Capital:** Stockholm. **Cities** (1978 est.): Stockholm 661,258; Goteborg 442,410; Malmo 240,220.

Government: Head of state: King Carl XVI Gustaf; b. Apr. 30, 1946; in office: Sept. 19, 1973. **Head of government:** Prime Min. Thorbjorn Falldin; b. Apr. 24, 1926; in office: Oct. 11, 1979. **Local divisions:** 24 lan (counties). **Armed forces:** regulars 65,900; reserves 500,000.

Economy: Industries: Steel, machinery, instruments, autos, shipbuilding, shipping, paper. **Chief crops:** Grains, potatoes, sugar beets. **Minerals:** Zinc, iron, lead, copper, gold, silver. **Other resources:** Forests (half the country); yield one fourth exports. **Per capita arable land:** 0.9 acres. **Meat prod.** (1978): beef: 148,000 metric tons; pork: 306,000 metric tons; lamb: 5,000 metric tons. **Fish catch** (1977): 182,100 metric tons. **Electricity prod.** (1978): 90.18 bln. kwh. **Crude steel prod.** (1979): 4.7 mln. metric tons. **Labor force:** 5% agric.; 45% ind. and commerce, 40% serv.

Finance: Currency: Krona (Apr. 1981: 4.76 = $1 US). **Gross domestic product** (1979): $101.49 bln. **Per capita income** (1978): $9,274. **Imports** (1980): $33.44 bln.; partners (1978): W. Ger. 18%, UK 11%, U.S. 7%, Den. 7%. **Exports** (1980): $30.92 bln.; partners (1978): UK 11%, W. Ger. 11%, Nor. 10%, Den. 9%. **National budget** (1979): $39.99 bln. revenues; $44.00 bln. expenditures. **International reserves less gold** (Apr. 1981): $4.09 bln. **Gold:** 6.07 mln. oz t. **Consumer prices** (change in 1980): 13.7%.

Transport: Railway traffic (1978): 5.56 bln. passenger-km; 14.76 bln. net ton-km. **Motor vehicles:** in use (1976): 2.88 mln. passenger cars, 162,400 comm. vehicles; manuf. (1978): 258,000 passenger cars; (1975): 49,200 comm. vehicles. **Civil aviation:** 4,068 mln. passenger-km (1978): 203 mln. freight ton-km (1978). **Chief ports:** Goteborg, Stockholm, Malmo.

Communications: Television sets: 2.98 mln. licensed (1976), 367,000 manuf. (1976). **Radios:** 3.2 mln. licensed (1976), 159,000 manuf. (1976). **Telephones in use** (1978): 5,930,276. **Daily newspaper circ.** (1977): 4,358,000; 528 per 1,000 pop.

Health: Life expectancy at birth (1976): 72.10 male; 77.75 female. **Births** (per 1,000 pop. 1980): 11.7. **Deaths** (per 1,000 pop. 1980): 11.0. **Natural increase** (1978): 0.4%. **Hospital beds** (per 100,000 pop. 1977): 1,496. **Physicians** (per 100,000 pop. 1977): 178. **Infant mortality** (per 1,000 live births (1978): 7.7.

Education (1977): **Literacy:** 99%. **Pop. 5-19:** in school: 72%, teachers per 1,000: 46. **PQLI:** 98.

The Swedes have lived in present-day Sweden for at least 5,000 years, longer than nearly any other European people. Gothic tribes from Sweden played a major role in the disintegration of the Roman Empire. Other Swedes helped create the first Russian state in the 9th century.

The Swedes were Christianized from the 11th century, and a strong centralized monarchy developed. A parliament, the Riksdag, was first called in 1435, the earliest parliament on the European continent, with all classes of society represented.

Swedish independence from rule by Danish kings (dating from 1397) was secured by Gustavus I in a revolt, 1521-23; he built up the government and military and established the Lutheran Church. In the 17th century Sweden was a major European power, gaining most of the Baltic seacoast, but its international position subsequently declined.

The Napoleonic wars, in which Sweden acquired Norway (it became independent 1905), were the last in which Sweden participated. Armed neutrality was maintained in both world wars.

Over 4 decades of Social Democratic rule was ended in 1976 parliamentary elections. Although 90% of the economy is in private hands, the government holds a large interest in water power production and the railroads are operated by a public agency.

Consumer cooperatives are in extensive operation and also are important in agriculture and housing. Per capita GNP, 1977, was among the highest in the world.

The U.S. and Sweden in 1974 ended a 15-month diplomatic "freeze" and exchanged ambassadors.

Swedish voters in a national referendum, Mar. 1980, voted to support limited expansion of nuclear energy.

A labor crisis of strikes locking out more than 800,000 workers, May 1980, brought the country to an industrial standstill and shattered its image of labor tranquillity.

Switzerland

Swiss Confederation

People: Population (1979 est.): 6,343,000. **Age distrib.** (%): 0–14: 21.0; 15–59: 61.1; 60+: 17.9. **Pop. density:** 397.72 per sq. mi. **Urban** (1970): 54.6%. **Ethnic groups:** Defined by mother tongue. **Languages:** German 65%, French 18%, Italian 12%, Romansch 1%. (all official). **Religions:** Roman Catholic 49.4%, Protestant 47.8%, Jewish 0.3%.

Geography: Area: 15,941 sq. mi., as large as Mass., Conn., and R.I., combined. **Location:** In the Alps Mts. in Central Europe. **Neighbors:** France on W., Italy on S, Austria on E, W. Germany on N. **Topography:** The Alps cover 60% of the land area, the Jura, near France, 10%. Running between, from NE to SW, are midlands, 30%. **Capital:** Bern. **Cities** (1978 est.): Zurich 379,600; Basel 185,300; Geneva 150,100; Bern 145,500.

Government: Head of government: Pres. Georges-Andre Chevallaz; b. Feb. 7, 1915; in office: Jan. 1 Dec. 31, 1980. **Local divisions:** 20 full cantons, 6 half cantons. **Armed forces:** regulars 18,500; reserves 621,500.

Economy: Industries: Machinery, machine tools, steel, instruments, watches, textiles, foodstuffs (cheese, chocolate), chemicals, drugs, banking, tourism. **Chief crops:** Grains, potatoes, sugar beets, vegetables, tobacco. **Minerals:** Salt. **Other resources:** Hydro power potential. **Per capita arable land:** 0.1 acres. **Meat prod.** (1978): beef: 150,000 metric tons; pork: 263,000 metric tons. **Electricity prod.** (1978): 42.10 bln. kwh. **Crude steel prod.** (1979): 886,000 metric tons. **Labor force:** 44% ind. and commerce, 8% agric., 52.5% serv.; 4.3% gvt.

Finance: Currency: Franc (Apr. 1981: 2.02 = $1 US). **Gross domestic product** (1979): $97.4 bln. **Per capita income** (1979): $15,455. **Imports** (1980): $36.36 bln.; partners (1978): W. Ger. 29%, Fr. 12%, It. 10%, U.S. 8%. **Exports** (1980): $29.64 bln.; partners (1978): W. Ger. 18%, Fr. 9%, It. 7%, U.S. 7%. **Tourists** (1977): 8,341,400; receipts: $1.94 bln. **National budget** (1979): $8.21 bln. revenues; $9.59 bln. expenditures. **International reserves less gold** (Apr. 1981): $11.20 bln. **Gold:** 83.28 mln. oz t. **Consumer prices** (change in 1980): 4.0%.

Transport: Railway traffic (1978): 9.3 bln. passenger-km; 9.3 bln. net ton-km. **Motor vehicles:** in use (1977): 1.93 mln. passenger cars, 154,000 comm. vehicles. **Civil aviation:** 10,152 mln. passenger-km (1978); 431 mln. freight ton-km (1978).

Communications: Television sets: 1.81 mln. licensed (1976). **Radios:** 2.11 mln. licensed (1976). **Telephones in use** (1978): 4,145,169. **Daily newspaper circ.** (1977): 2,622,000; 414 per 1,000 pop.

Health: Life expectancy at birth (1977): 71.8 male; 76.22 female. **Births** (per 1,000 pop. 1980): 11.9. **Deaths** (per 1,000 pop. 1980): 9.2. **Natural increase** (1978): .2%. **Hospital beds** (per 100,000 pop. 1977): 1,141. **Physicians** (per 100,000 pop. 1977): 201. **Infant mortality** (per 1,000 live births 1977): 9.8.

Education (1977): **Literacy:** 99%. **Pop. 5–19:** in school: 62%; teachers per 1,000: 45. **PQLI:** 96.

Switzerland, the Roman province of Helvetia, is a federation of 23 cantons (20 full cantons and 6 half cantons), 3 of which in 1291 created a defensive league and later were joined by other districts. Voters in the French-speaking part of Canton Bern voted for self-government, 1978; Canton Jura was created Jan. 1, 1979.

In 1648 the Swiss Confederation obtained its independence from the Holy Roman Empire. The cantons were joined under a federal constitution in 1848, with large powers of local control retained by each canton.

Switzerland has maintained an armed neutrality since 1815, and has not been involved in a foreign war since 1515. It is not a member of NATO or the UN. However, the Cabinet took steps, Mar. 28, 1979, to recommend Swiss membership in the UN. Switzerland is a member of several UN agencies and of the European Free Trade Assoc. and has ties with the EC. It is also the seat of many UN and other international agencies.

Switzerland is a leading world banking center; stability of the currency brings funds from many quarters. Some 20% of all workers are foreign residents.

Syria

Syrian Arab Republic

People: Population (1980 est.): 8,980,000. **Age distrib.** (%): 0–14: 48.9; 15–59: 44.9; 60+: 6.2. **Pop. density:** 125.60 per sq. mi. **Urban** (1978): 48.8%. **Ethnic groups:** Arabs, Kurds 6.3%, Armenians 2.8%, Turks, Circassians, Assyrians. **Languages:** Arabic (official), French, Kurdish, Armenian, English. **Religions:** Muslims (Sunni, Alawi, Druze) 88%, Christians 12%.

Geography: Area: 71,498 sq. mi., the size of North Dakota. **Location:** At eastern end of Mediterranean Sea. **Neighbors:** Lebanon, Israel on W, Jordan on S, Iraq on E, Turkey on N. **Topography:** Syria has a short Mediterranean coastline, then stretches E and S with fertile lowlands and plains, alternating with mountains and large desert areas. **Capital:** Damascus. **Cities** (1978 est.): Damascus 1,142,000; Aleppo 878,000; Homs 306,000.

Government: Head of state: Pres. Hafez al-Assad; b. Mar. 1930; in office: Feb. 22, 1971. **Head of government:** Prime Min. Abdul Rauf Qasim; in office: Jan. 16, 1980. **Local divisions:** Damascus and 13 provinces. **Armed forces:** regulars 227,500; reserves 102,500.

Economy: Industries: Oil products, textiles, cement, tobacco, glassware, sugar, brassware. **Chief crops:** Cotton, grain, olives, fruits, vegetables. **Minerals:** Oil, phosphate, gypsum. **Crude oil reserves** (1980): 2.00 bln. bbls. **Other resources:** Wool. **Per capita arable land:** 1.6 acres. **Meat prod.** (1978): beef: 14,000 metric tons; lamb: 60,000 metric tons. **Electricity prod.** (1977): 2.04 bln. kwh. **Labor force:** 51% agric.; 15% manuf.

Finance: Currency: Pound (Apr. 1981: 3.93 = $1 US). **Gross domestic product** (1979): $9.14 bln. **Per capita income** (1975): $702. **Imports** (1979): $3.33 bln.; partners: W. Ger. 11%, Fr. 8%, It. 8%, Iraq 7%. **Exports** (1979): $1.64 bln.; partners: Fr. 10%, W. Ger. 10%, USSR 9%, Neth. 9%. **Tourists** (1977): 681,100; receipts: $110 mln. **International reserves less gold** (Nov. 1980): $408 mln. **Gold** (Dec. 1979): 833,000 oz t. **Consumer prices** (change in 1980): 19.0%.

Transport: Railway traffic (1978): 321.6 mln. passenger-km; 270 mln. net ton-km. **Motor vehicles:** in use (1976): 62,800 passenger cars, 55,900 comm. vehicles. **Chief ports:** Latakia, Tartus.

Communications: Television sets: 230,000 in use (1976), 55,000 manuf. (1977). **Radios:** 1.37 mln. in use (1970). **Telephones in use** (1978): 193,044. **Daily newspaper circ.** (1976): 65,000.

Health: Life expectancy at birth (1970): 54.49 male; 58.73 female. **Births** (per 1,000 pop. 1975): 46.5. **Deaths** (per 1,000 1975): 13.6. **Natural increase** (1975): 3.3%. **Hospital beds** (per 100,000 pop. 1977): 104. **Physicians** (per 100,000 pop. 1977): 39. **Infant mortality** (per 1,000 live births 1976): 15.3.

Education (1977): **Literacy:** 45%. **Pop. 5–19:** in school: 59%, teachers per 1,000: 20. **PQLI:** 57.

Syria contains some of the most ancient remains of civilization. It was the center of the Seleucid empire, but later became absorbed in the Roman and Arab empires. Ottoman rule prevailed for 4 centuries, until the end of World War I.

The state of Syria was formed from former Turkish districts, made a separate entity by the Treaty of Sevres 1920 and divided into the states of Syria and Greater Lebanon. Both were administered under a French League of Nations mandate 1920-1941.

Syria was proclaimed a republic by the occupying French Sept. 16, 1941, and exercised full independence effective Jan. 1, 1944. French troops left in 1946. Syria joined in the Arab invasion of Israel in 1948.

Syria joined with Egypt in Feb. 1958 in the United Arab Republic but seceded Sept. 30, 1961. The Socialist Baath party and military leaders seized power in Mar. 1963. The Baath, a pan-Arab organization, became the only legal party. The government has been dominated by members of the minority Alawite sect, many of whom were assassinated in 1977-78.

In the Arab-Israeli war of June 1967, Israel seized and occupied the Golan Heights area inside Syria, from which Israeli settlements had for years been shelled by Syria.

Syria aided Palestinian guerrillas fighting Jordanian forces in Sept. 1970 and, after a renewal of that fighting in July 1971, broke off relations with Jordan. But by 1975 the 2 countries had entered a military coordination pact.

Syria received large shipments of arms from the USSR in 1972-73 and on Oct. 6, 1973, Syria joined Egypt in an attack on Israel. Arab oil states agreed in 1974 to give Syria $1 billion a year to aid anti-Israel moves. Military supplies used or lost in the 1973 war were replaced by the USSR in 1974 and increased shipments of planes, tanks, and missiles were reported in 1978. U.S. economic aid has been extended. Some 30,000 Syrian troops entered Lebanon in 1976 to mediate in a civil war, and fought Palestinian guerrillas and, later, fought Christian militiamen. Syrian troops again battled Christian forces in Lebanon, Apr. 1981, ending a ceasefire that had been in place.

Tanzania
United Republic of Tanzania

People: Population (1980 est.) 17,400,000. **Pop. density:** 47.96 per sq. mi. **Urban** (1973): 7.3%. **Ethnic groups:** Sukuma 12.6%, Maleonde 4%, 130 other tribes (most Bantu); Europeans, Arabs, Asians. **Languages:** Swahili, English are official. **Religions:** Moslems 30%, Christians 30%, Traditional 40%.

Geography: Area: 362,820 sq. mi., more than twice the size of California. **Location:** On coast of E. Africa. **Neighbors:** Kenya, Uganda on N, Rwanda, Burundi, Zaire on W, Zambia, Malawi, Mozambique on S. **Topography:** Hot, arid central plateau, surrounded by the lake region in the W, temperate highlands in N and S, the coastal plains. Mt. Kilimanjaro, 19,340 ft., is highest in Africa. **Capital:** Dar-es-Salaam. **Cities** (1978 cen.): Dar-es-Salaam 870,020.

Government: Head of state: Pres. Julius Kambarage Nyerere; b. Mar. 1922; in office: Apr. 26, 1964. **Head of government:** Edward M. Sokoine, b. 1938; in office: Feb. 13, 1977. **Local divisions:** 21 regions (4 on Zanzibar), Dar-es-Salaam. **Armed forces:** regulars 51,700; para-military 36,400.

Economy: Industries: Food processing, clothing. **Chief crops:** Sisal, cotton, coffee, tea, tobacco. **Minerals:** Diamonds, gold, salt, tin, mica. **Other resources:** Hides. **Per capita arable land:** 0.6 acres. **Meat prod.** (1978): beef: 131,000 metric tons; lamb: 30,000 metric tons. **Fish catch** (1977): 250,000 metric tons. **Electricity prod.** (1978): 696.00 mln. kwh. **Labor force:** 90% agric.

Finance: Currency: Shilling (Feb. 1981: 8.23 = $1 US). **Gross domestic product** (1979): $4.56 bln. **Per capita income** (1978): $253. **Imports** (1979): $1.10 bln.; partners (1976): UK 12%, Kenya 11%, Iran 9%, W. Ger. 8%. **Exports** (1979): $544 mln.; partners (1976): W. Ger. 14%, UK 13%, U.S. 9%, Sing. 7%. **Tourists** (1977): 93,000; receipts: $9 mln. **National budget** (1979): $828.2 mln. revenues; $1.44 bln. expenditures. **International reserves less gold** (Feb. 1981): $15.4 mln. **Consumer prices** (change in 1980): 30.2%.

Transport: Motor vehicles: in use (1977): 43,600 passenger cars, 46,400 comm. vehicles. **Chief ports:** Dar-es-Salaam, Tanga.

Communications: Radios: 300,000 in use (1976), 177,000 manuf. (1975). **Telephones in use** (1978): 74,264. **Daily newspaper circ.** (1977): 133,000; 8 per 1,000 pop.

Health: Life expectancy at birth (1967): 40 male; 41 female. **Births** (per 1,000 pop. 1967): 47.0. **Deaths** (per 1,000 pop. 1967): 22.0. **Natural increase** (1967): 2.5%. **Hospital beds** (per 100,000 pop. 1977): 206. **Physicians** (per 100,000 pop. 1977): 20. **Infant mortality** (per 1,000 live births 1967): 160-165.

Education (1977): Literacy: 37%. **Pop. 5–19:** in school: 36%, teachers per 1,000: 7. **PQLI:** 50.

The Republic of Tanganyika in E. Africa and the island Republic of Zanzibar, off the coast of Tanganyika, joined into a single nation, the United Republic of Tanzania, Apr. 26, 1964. Zanzibar retains internal self-government. In 1973 Dodoma, in the country's center, was named the future capital.

Tanganyika. Arab colonization and slaving began in the 8th century AD; Portuguese sailors explored the coast by about 1500. Other Europeans followed.

In 1885 Germany established German East Africa of which Tanganyika formed the bulk. It became a League of Nations mandate and, after 1946, a UN trust territory, both under Britain. It became independent Dec. 9, 1961, and a republic within the Commonwealth a year later.

In 1967 the government set on a socialist course; it nationalized all banks and many industries. The government also ordered that Swahili, not English, be used in all official business. Nine million people have been moved into cooperative villages.

Tanzania exchanged invasion attacks with Uganda, 1978-79. Tanzanian forces drove Idi Amin from Uganda, Mar., 1979.

Zanzibar, the Isle of Cloves, lies 23 mi. off the coast of Tanganyika; its area is 640 sq. mi. The island of **Pemba,** 25 mi. to the NE, area 380 sq. mi., is included in the administration. The total population (1978 cen.) is 475,655.

Chief industry is the production of cloves and clove oil of which Zanzibar and Pemba produce the bulk of the world's supply.

Zanzibar was for centuries the center for Arab slave-traders. Portugal ruled for 2 centuries until ousted by Arabs around 1700. Zanzibar became a British Protectorate in 1890; independence came Dec. 10, 1963. Revolutionary forces overthrew the Sultan Jan. 12, 1964. The new government ousted American and British diplomats and newsmen, slaughtered thousands of Arabs, and nationalized farms. Union with Tanganyika followed, 1964. The ruling parties of Tanganyika and Zanzibar were united in 1977, as political tension eased; but a movement for greater autonomy began, 1979.

Thailand
Kingdom of Thailand

People: Population (1979 est.): 46,687,000. **Age distrib.** (%): 0–14: 42.8; 15–59: 52.3; 60+: 4.9. **Pop. density:** 227.26 per sq. mi. **Urban** (1970): 13.2%. **Ethnic groups:** Thais 75%, Chinese 14%, Malays 3%, Khmers, Soais, Karens, Indians. **Languages:** Thai, Chinese. **Religions:** Buddhists 94%, Moslems 4%, Christians 0.6%.

Geography: Area: 198,455 sq. mi., three-fourths the size of Texas. **Location:** On Indochinese and Malayan Peninsulas in S.E. Asia. **Neighbors:** Burma on W, Laos on N, Cambodia on E, Malaysia on S. **Topography:** A plateau dominates the NE third of Thailand, dropping to the fertile alluvial valley of the Chao Phraya R. in the center. Forested mountains are in N, with narrow fertile valleys. The southern peninsula region is covered by rain forests. **Capital:** Bangkok. **Cities** (1977 cen.): Bangkok (met.): 4,178,000; Thonburi 627,989.

Government: Head of state: King Bhumibol Adulyadej; b. Dec. 5, 1927; in office: June 9, 1946. **Head of government:** Prime Min. Prem Tinsulanonda; in office: Mar. 3, 1980. **Local divisions:** 72 provinces. **Armed forces:** regulars 216,000; reserves 500,000.

Economy: Industries: Auto assembly, drugs, textiles, electrical goods. **Chief crops:** Rice (a major export), corn tapioca, jute, sugar, coconuts, tobacco, pepper, peanuts, beans, cotton. **Minerals:** Antimony, tin (5th largest producer), tungsten, iron, manganese, gas. **Crude oil reserves** (1979): 200 bbls. **Other resources:** Forests (teak is exported), rubber. **Per capita arable land:** 0.9 acres. **Meat prod.** (1978): beef: 211,000 metric tons; pork: 152,000 metric tons. **Fish catch** (1977): 2.2 mln. metric tons. **Electricity prod.** (1977): 11.69 bln. kwh. **Crude steel prod.** (1979 est.): 400,000 metric tons. **Labor force:** 76% agric.; 7% manuf.

Finance: Currency: Baht (Apr. 1981: 20.78 = $1 US). **Gross domestic product** (1980): $21.84 bln. **Per capita income** (1978): $444. **Imports** (1978): $9.22 bln.; partners : Jap. 31%, U.S. 14%, Saudi Ar. 6%, W. Ger. 6%. **Exports** (1980): $6.51 bln.; partners : Jap. 20%, Neth. 15%, U.S. 11%, Sing. 8%. **Tourists** (1977): 1,220,700; receipts: $211 mln. **National budget** (1978): $3.20 bln. revenues; $3.85 bln. expenditures. **International reserves less gold** (Apr. 1981): $1.27 bln. **Gold:** 2.49 mln. oz t. **Consumer prices** (change in 1980): 19.7%.

Transport: Railway traffic (1977): 5.63 bln. passenger-km; 2.51 bln. net ton-km. **Motor vehicles:** in use (1975): 266,100 passenger cars, 266,700 comm. vehicles; assembled (1976): 15,000 passenger cars; (1974): 8,600 comm. vehicles. **Civil aviation:** 4,200 mln. passenger-km (1978); 140 mln. freight ton-km (1978). **Chief ports:** Bangkok, Sattahip.

Communication: Television sets: 761,000 in use (1976), 90,000 manuf. (1976). **Radios:** 5.5 mln. in use (1975). **Telephones in use** (1978): 366,862. **Daily newspaper circ.** (1970): 749,000; 21 per 1,000 pop.

Health: Life expectancy at birth (1960): 53.6 male; 58.7 female. **Births** (per 1,000 pop. 1975): 39.6. **Deaths** (per 1,000 pop. 1975): 10.5. **Natural increase** (1975): 2.9%. **Hospital beds** (per 100,000 pop. 1977): 121. **Physicians** (per 100,000 pop. 1977): 12. **Infant mortality** (per 1,000 live births 1976): 25.5.

Education (1977): Literacy: 82%. **Pop. 5-19:** in school: 47%, teachers per 1,000: 16. **PQLI:** 75.

Thais began migrating from southern China in the 11th century. Thailand is the only country in SE Asia never taken over by a European power, thanks to King Mongkut and his son King Chulalongkorn who ruled from 1851 to 1910, modernized the country, and signed trade treaties with both Britain and France.

A bloodless revolution in 1932 limited the monarchy.

Japan occupied the country in 1941. After the war, Thailand followed a pro-West foreign policy. Some 11,000 Thai troops fought in S. Vietnam, but were withdrawn by 1972.

Clashes with Laos and especially with Cambodia have continued to 1980. Tribal and political rebels have conducted guerrilla fighting in the NE and extreme S, 1965-80. Vietnamese infantry were at the Thai-Cambodia border, June 1980.

The military took over the government in a bloody 1976 coup. Kriangsak Chomanan, prime minister since a 1977 military coup, resigned, Feb. 1980, under opposition over soaring inflation, oil price increases, labor unrest and growing crime.

The fertile land yields a rice surplus. Foreign investment has been encouraged.

Togo

Republic of Togo

People: Population (1979 est.): 2,544,000. **Age distrib.** (%): 0-14: 49.8; 15-59: 44.6; 60 + :5.6.**Pop. density:** 93 per sq. mi. **Urban** (1974): 15.2%. **Ethnic groups:** Ewe 20%, Mina 6%, Kabye 14%. **Languages:** French (official), others. **Religions:** Animist 60%, Roman Catholics 18%, Protestants 6.5%, Muslims 9%.

Geography: Area: 21,853 sq. mi., slightly smaller than West Virginia. **Location:** On S coast of W. Africa. **Neighbors:** Ghana on W, Upper Volta on N, Benin on E. **Topography:** A range of hills running SW-NE splits Togo into 2 savanna plains regions. **Capital:** Lomé. **Cities** (1979 est.): Lomé 130,000.

Government: Head of state: Pres. Gnassingbe Eyadema; b. Dec. 26, 1937; in office: Apr. 14, 1967. **Local divisions:** 19 circumscriptions. **Armed forces:** regulars 3,250; para-military 1,400.

Economy: Industries: Textiles, shoes. **Chief crops:** Coffee, cocoa, palm kernels, copra, cotton, kapok, peanuts. **Minerals:** Phosphates. **Per capita arable land:** 2.3 acres. **Electricity prod.** (1978): 67.20 mln. kwh. **Labor force:** 78% agric.; 22% industry.

Finance: Currency: CFA franc (Apr. 1981: 262.70 = $1 US). **Gross domestic product** (1978): $765.5 mln. **Per capita income** (1978): $319. **Imports** (1979): $518 mln.; partners (1977): Fr. 34%, U.K 10%, W. Ger. 9%, U.S. 8%. **Exports** (1979): $219 mln.; partners (1977): Neth. 32%, Fr. 21%, W. Ger. 12%, Pol. 8%. **International reserves less gold** (Jan. 1981): $80.3 mln. **Gold:** 13,000 oz t. **Consumer prices** (change in 1979): 7.5%.

Transport: Railway traffic (1976): 91.2 mln. passenger-km; 37.7 mln. net ton-km. **Motor vehicles:** in use (1974): 13,000 passenger cars, 7,000 comm. vehicles. **Chief ports:** Lome.

Communications: Radios: 52,000 in use (1976). **Telephones in use** (1978): 4,749. **Daily newspaper circ.** (1976): 7,000; 3 per 1,000 pop.

Health: Life expectancy at birth (1961): 31.6 male; 38.5 female. **Births** (per 1,000 pop. 1975): 49.1 **Deaths** (per 1,000 pop. 1975): 21.0. **Natural increase** (1975): 2.8%. **Hospital beds** (per 100,000 pop. 1977): 143. **Physicians** (per 100,000 pop. 1977): 6. **Infant mortality** (per 1,000 live births 1975): 127. **Education** (1977): Literacy: 18%. **Pop. 5-19:** in school: 55%, teachers per 1,000: 10. **PQLI:** 27.

The Ewe arrived in southern Togo several centuries ago. The country later became a major source of slaves. Germany took control from 1884 on. France and Britain administered Togoland as UN trusteeships. The French sector became the republic of Togo Apr. 27, 1960.

The population is divided between Bantus in the S and Hamitic tribes in the N. Togo has actively promoted regional integration, as a means of stimulating the backward economy.

Tonga

Kingdom of Tonga

People: Population (1980 est.): 100,000. **Age distrib.** (%): 0-14: 44.4; 15-59: 50.5; 60 + :5.1. **Pop. density:** 370.37 per sq. mi. **Ethnic groups:** Tongans 98%, other Polynesian, European. **Languages:** Tongan, English. **Religions:** Methodists, Anglicans, Roman Catholics, Seventh Day Adventists, Mormons.

Geography: Area: 270 sq. mi., smaller than New York City. **Location:** In western Pacific O. **Neighbors:** Nearest is Fiji, on W, New Zealand, on S. **Topography:** Tonga comprises 150 volcanic and coral islands, 45 inhabited. **Capital:** Nuku'alofa. **Cities**

(1976 cen.): Nuku'alofa (met.) 18,312.

Government: Head of state: King Taufa'ahau Tupou IV; b. July 4, 1918; in office: Dec. 16, 1965. **Head of government:** Prime Min. Fatafehi Tu'ipelehake; b. Jan. 7, 1922; in office: Dec. 16, 1965. **Local divisions:** 3 island districts.

Economy: Industries: Tourism. **Chief crops:** Coconut products, bananas are exported. **Other resources:** Fish. **Per capita arable land:** 0.4 acres. **Electricity prod.** (1977): 7.00 mln. kwh. **Labor force:** 75% agric.

Finance: Currency: Pa'anga (Sept. 1979: .89 = $1 US). **Gross domestic product** (1976 est.): $40 mln. **Per capita income** (1976): $430. **Imports** (1979): $29 mln.; partners: N Z 37%, Austral. 28%, Jap. 7%, UK 6%. **Exports** (1979): $7 mln.; partners (1978): Neth. 29%, N Z 22%, UK 21%, W. Ger. 11%. **Tourists** (1975): 70,000; receipts: $3 mln. **Consumer prices** (change in 1976): 7.1%.

Transport: Motor vehicles: in use (1974): 1,000 passenger cars, 400 comm. vehicles. **Chief ports:** Nuku'alofa.

Communications: Radios: 15,000 in use (1976). **Telephones in use** (1978): 1,285.

Health: Births (per 1,000 pop. 1976): 13.0. **Deaths** (per 1,000 pop. 1976): 1.9. **Natural increase** (1976): 1.1%. **Pop. per hospital bed** (1976): 300. **Pop. per physician** (1976): 3,000. **Infant mortality** (per 1,000 live births 1976): 20.5.

The islands were first visited by the Dutch in the early 17th century. A series of civil wars ended in 1845 with establishment of the Tupou dynasty. In 1900 Tonga became a British protectorate. On June 4, 1970, Tonga became completely independent and a member of the Commonwealth. Tonga suffered from a severe balance of payments problem, 1979.

Trinidad and Tobago

People: Population (1979 est.): 1,150,000. **Age distrib.** (%): 0-14: 38.0; 15-59: 55.4; 60 + : 6.6. **Pop. density:** 570.71 per sq. mi. **Urban** (1970): 49.4%. **Ethnic groups:** Negroes 43%, East Indians 36%, white 2%, Chinese 1%, mixed 16%. **Languages:** English, Hindi. **Religions:** Roman Catholics 36%, Protestants 30%, Hindus 23%, Muslims 6%.

Geography: Area: 1,980 sq. mi., the size of Delaware. **Location:** Off eastern coast of Venezuela. **Neighbors:** Nearest is Venezuela on SW. **Topography:** Three low mountain ranges cross Trinidad E-W, with a well-watered plain between N and Central Ranges. Parts of E and W coasts are swamps. Tobago, 116 sq. mi., lies 20 mi. NE. **Capital:** Port-of-Spain. **Cities** (1975 est.): Port-of-Spain (met.) 250,000; San Fernando 50,000.

Government: Head of state: Pres. Ellis E. I. Clarke; b. Dec. 28, 1917; in office: July 31, 1976. **Head of government:** Prime Min. Eric E. Williams; b. Sept. 25, 1911; in office: Sept. 24, 1956. **Local divisions:** 8 counties, Ward of Tobago, 3 municipalities.

Economy: Industries: Oil products, rum, cement, tourism. **Chief crops:** Sugar, cocoa, coffee, citrus fruits, bananas. **Minerals:** Asphalt, oil, **Crude oil reserves** (1980): 700 mln. bbls. **Per capita arable land:** 0.1 acres. **Electricity prod.** (1978): 1.62 bln. kwh. **Labor force:** 13% agric., 50% manuf.

Finance: Currency: Dollar (Apr. 1981: 2.40 = $1 US). **Gross domestic product** (1978): $3.93 bln. **Per capita income** (1976): $2,090. **Imports** (1980): $3.16 bln.; partners (1977): Saudi Ar. 22%, U.S. 21%, Indo. 14%, UK 13%. **Exports** (1980): $3.98 bln.; partners (1977): U.S. 69%. **Tourists** (1976): 158,700; receipts: $87 mln. **National budget** (1972): $275.47 mln. revenues; $295.89 mln. expenditures. **International reserves less gold** (Apr. 1981): $2.85 bln. **Gold:** 54,000 oz t. **Consumer prices** (change in 1980): 17.5%.

Transport: Motor vehicles: in use (1977): 117,700 passenger cars, 32,000 comm. vehicles; assembled (1978): 13,752 passenger cars; 2,412 comm. vehicles. **Civil aviation:** 678 mln. passenger-km (1978); 13 mln. freight ton-km (1978). **Chief ports:** Port-of-Spain.

Communications: Television sets: 110,000 in use (1976); 13,000 manuf. (1977). **Radios:** 270,000 licensed (1976), 15,000 manuf. (1977). **Telephones in use** (1978): 74,908. **Daily newspaper circ.** (1976): 144,000.

Health: Life expectancy at birth (1970): 64.08 male; 68.1 female. **Births** (per 1,000 pop. 1978): 25.3. **Deaths** (per 1,000 pop. 1978): 6.6. **Natural increase** (1978): 1.9%. **Hospital beds** (per 100,000 pop. 1977): 445. **Physicians** (per 100,000 pop. 1977): 54. **Infant mortality** (per 1,000 pop. 1978): 28.6.

Education (1977): **Literacy:** 92%. **Pop. 5-19:** in school: 48%; teachers per 1,000: 22. **PQLI:** 87.

Columbus sighted Trinidad in 1498. A British possession since 1802, Trinidad and Tobago won independence Aug. 31, 1962. It became a republic in 1976. The People's National Movement party has held control of the government since 1956.

The nation is one of the most prosperous in the Caribbean, but unemployment usually averages 13%. Oil production has increased with offshore finds. Middle Eastern oil is refined and exported, mostly to the U.S.

Tunisia

Republic of Tunisia

People: Population (1980 est.): 6,360,000. **Age distrib.** (%) 0–14: 43.0 15–59: 50.9, 60+: 5.8. **Pop. density:** 100.35 per sq. mi. **Ethnic groups:** Arabs, small Berber minority; Europeans 1%. **Languages:** Arabic, French. **Religions:** Islam nearly universal.

Geography: Area: 63,378 sq. mi., slightly larger than Florida. **Location:** On N coast of Africa. **Neighbors:** Algeria on W, Libya on E. **Topography:** The N is wooded and fertile. The central coastal plains are given to grazing and orchards. The S is arid, approaching Sahara Desert. **Capital:** Tunis. **Cities** (1977): Tunis 1,000,000, Sousse, Sfax, Bizerte.

Government: Head of state: Pres. Habib Bourguiba; b. Aug. 3, 1903; in office: July 25, 1957. **Head of government:** Prime Min. Mohamed Mzali; b. Dec. 23, 1925; in office: Apr. 23, 1980. **Local divisions:** 13 governorates. **Armed forces:** regulars 22,300; para-military 2,500.

Economy: Industries: Food processing, textiles, clothing, leather, oil products, construction materials, tourism. **Chief crops:** Grains, dates, olives, citrus fruits, figs, vegetables, grapes. **Minerals:** Phosphates, iron, oil, lead, zinc. **Crude oil reserves** (1980): 2.25 bln. bbls. **Per capita arable land:** 1.3 acres. **Meat prod.** (1978): beef: 35,000 metric tons; lamb: 43,000 metric tons. **Fish catch** (1977): 38,400 metric tons. **Electricity prod.** (1978): 1.79 bln. kwh. **Crude steel prod.** (1979 est.): 150,000 metric tons. **Labor force:** 45% agric.; 19% industry; 10% serv.

Finance: Currency: Dinar (Apr. 1981: 4.91 = $1 US). **Gross domestic product** (1978): $5.89 bln. **Per capita income** (1978) $934. **Imports** (1980): $3.54 bln.; partners (1978): Fr. 34%, W. Ger. 12%, It. 10%. **Exports** (1980): $2.20 bln.; partners (1978): It. 16%, Fr. 16%, W. Ger. 16%, Gr. 9%. **Tourists** (1977): 1,016,000; receipts: $323 mln. **National budget** (1978): $1.92 bln. revenues; $2.08 bln. expenditures. **International reserves less gold** (Apr. 1981): $520.2 mln. **Gold:** 187,000 oz t. **Consumer prices** (change in 1980): 10.0%.

Transport: Railway traffic (1978): 705.6 mln. passenger-km; 1.37 bln. net ton-km. **Motor vehicles:** in use (1975): 102,600 passenger cars, 67,000 comm. vehicles; assembled (1978): 2,124 passenger cars; 4,848 comm. vehicles. **Civil aviation:** 1,182 mln. passenger-km (1978); 11 min. freight ton-km (1978). **Chief ports:** Tunis, Sfax, Bizerte.

Communications: Television sets: 208,000 in use (1976), 53,000 manuf. (1977). **Radios:** 810,000 in use (1976), 71,000 manuf. (1977). **Telephones in use** (1978): 144,116. **Daily newspaper circ.** (1976): 232,000.

Health: Life expectancy at birth (1975): 54.0 male; 56.0 female. **Births** (per 1,000 pop. 1978): 34.1. **Deaths** (per 1,000 pop. 1975): 12.5. **Natural increase** (1975): 2.4%. **Hospital beds** (per 100,000 pop. 1977): 229. **Physicians** (per 100,000 pop. 1977): 4. **Infant mortality** (per 1,000 pop. under 1 yr. 1975): 125.

Education (1977): **Literacy:** 40%. **Pop. 5-19:** in school: 50%, teachers per 1,000: 16. **PQLI:** 49.

Site of ancient Carthage, and a former Barbary state under the suzerainty of Turkey, Tunisia became a protectorate of France under a treaty signed May 12, 1881. The nation became independent Mar. 20, 1956, and ended the monarchy the following year. Habib Bourguiba has headed the country since independence.

Although Tunisia is a member of the Arab League, Bourguiba in the 1960s urged negotiations to end Arab-Israeli disputes and was denounced by other members. In 1966 he broke relations with Egypt but resumed them after the 1967 Arab-Israeli war. He again urged negotiations with Israel in June 1973.

Dozens were killed in rioting and labor violence in 1978, protesting wage curbs.

Tunisia survived a Libyan-engineered raid against the southern mining center of Gafsa, Jan. 1980. A liberal-minded government undertook steps to ease the blocked political situation.

Turkey

Republic of Turkey

People: Population (1980 est.): 45,360,000. **Age distrib.** (%): 0–14: 40.0; 15–59: 52.6; 60+: 7.2. **Pop. density:** 150.50 per sq. mi. **Urban** (1977): 44.6%. **Ethnic groups:** Turks 90%, Kurds 7%, Arabs 1.2%, Circassians, Greeks, Armenians, Georgians, Jews. **Languages:** Turkish, Kurdish, Arabic. **Religions:** Muslims 98%, Christians, Jews.

Geography: Area: 301,380 sq. mi., twice the size of California. **Location:** Occupies Asia Minor, between Mediterranean and Black Seas. **Neighbors:** Bulgaria, Greece on W, USSR (Georgia, Armenia) on N, Iran on E, Iraq, Syria on S. **Topography:** Central Turkey has wide plateaus, with hot, dry summers and cold winters. High mountains ring the interior on all but W, with more than 20 peaks over 10,000 ft. Rolling plains are in W; mild, fertile coastal plains are in S, W. **Capital:** Ankara. **Cities** (1979 est.): Istanbul 3,900,000; Ankara 2,600,000; Izmir 1,700,000; Adana 1,000,000.

Government: Head of state: Acting Pres. Ihsan Sabri Caglayangil; b. 1908; in office: Apr. 7, 1980. **Head of government:** Prime Min. Bulent Ulusu; in office: Sept. 20, 1980. **Local divisions:** 67 provinces, with appointed governors. **Armed forces:** regulars 566,000; reserves 425,000.

Economy: Industries: Silk, textiles, steel, shoes, furniture, cement, paper, glassware, appliances. **Chief crops:** Tobacco (6th largest producer), cereals, cotton, olives, figs, nuts, sugar, opium gums. **Minerals:** Antimony, chromium, mercury, borate, copper, molybdenum, magnesite, asbestos. **Crude oil reserves** (1980): 125 mln. bbls. **Other resources:** Wool, silk, forests. **Per capita arable land:** 1.4 acres. **Meat prod.** (1978): beef: 240,000 metric tons; lamb: 384,000 metric tons. **Fish catch** (1977): 155,300 metric tons. **Electricity prod.** (1978): 21.60 bln. kwh. **Crude steel prod.** (1979): 2.4 mln. metric tons. **Labor force:** 55.8% agric.; 17.2% ind. and commerce; 17% serv.; 10% govt.

Finance: Currency: Lira (Apr. 1981: 99.18 = $1 US). **Gross domestic product** (1980): $50.63 bln. **Per capita income** (1978 est.): $1,140 **Imports** (1979): $5.07 bln.; partners (1978): W. Ger. 16%, Fr. 8%, It. 6%, U.S. 6%. **Exports** (1979): $2.44 bln.; partners (1978): W. Ger. 22%, It. 8%, U.S. 7%, Fr. 6%. **Tourists** (1977): 1,661,400; receipts: $205 mln. **National budget** (1978): $3.83 bln. revenues; $4.31 bln. expenditures. **International reserves less gold** (Jan. 1981): $1.31 bln. **Gold:** 3.77 mln. oz t. **Consumer prices** (change in 1980): 110.2%.

Transport: Railway traffic (1978): 5.6 bln. passenger-km; 5.7 bln. net ton-km. **Motor vehicles:** in use (1976): 471,500 passenger cars, 230,800 comm. vehicles; assembled (1978): 54,120 passenger cars; 35,784 comm. vehicles. **Civil aviation:** 2,220 mln. passenger-km (1977); 19 mln. freight ton-km (1977). **Chief ports:** Istanbul, Izmir, Mersin, Samsun.

Communications: Television sets: 1.7 mln. in use (1976), 684,000 manuf. (1977). **Radios:** 4.2 mln. licensed (1976), 324,000 manuf. (1977). **Telephones in use** (1978): 1,378,620.

Health: Life expectancy at birth (1966): 53.7 male; 53.7 female. **Births** (per 1,000 pop. 1967): 39.6. **Deaths** (per 1,000 pop. 1967): 14.6. **Natural increase** (1967): 2.5%. **Hospital beds** (per 100,000 pop.1977): 195. **Physicians** (per 100,000 pop. 1977): 56. **Infant mortality** (per 1,000 pop. under 1 yr. 1967): 153.

Education (1977): **Literacy:** 60%. **Pop. 5-19:** in school: 49%, teachers per 1,000: 15. **PQLI:** 60.

Ancient inhabitants of Turkey were among the worlds first agriculturalists. Such civilizations as the Hittite, Phrygian, and Lydian flourished in Asiatic Turkey (Asia Minor), as did much of Greek civilization. After the fall of Rome in the 5th century, Constantinople was the capital of the Byzantine Empire for 1,000 years. It fell in 1453 to Ottoman Turks, who ruled a vast empire for over 400 years.

Just before World War I, Turkey, or the Ottoman Empire, ruled what is now Syria, Lebanon, Iraq, Jordan, Israel, Arabia, Yemen, and islands in the Aegean Sea.

Turkey joined Germany and Austria in World War I and its defeat resulted in loss of much territory and fall of the sultanate. A republic was declared Oct. 29, 1923. The Caliphate (spiritual leadership of Islam) was renounced 1924. Martial law, imposed in 1971, was ended in 1973 and political life is active and free.

Long embroiled with Greece over Cyprus, off Turkey's south coast, Turkey invaded the island July 20, 1974, after Greek officers seized the Cypriot government as a step toward unification with Greece. Turkey sought a new government for Cyprus, with Greek Cypriot and Turkish Cypriot zones. In reaction to Turkey's moves, the U.S. Congress cut off military aid in 1975. Turkey, in turn, suspended the use of most U.S. bases. A new base accord was tentatively reached in March, 1976 and aid was restored in 1978. Turkey and the USSR signed a nonaggression pact in 1978.

In June, 1971, Turkey agreed to stop all opium poppy production, in return for $37.5 million in economic aid from the U.S. In 1974 it announced it would resume opium production, with U.S. and U.N. controls, for medical use only.

Religious and ethnic tensions and active left and right extremists have caused endemic violence. Martial law was in effect from 1979, in approx. one-third of the nation's provinces. In Jan. 1981, the military rulers ousted high-level civilian officials.

Tuvalu

People: Population (1979 est.): 7,400. **Pop. density:** 700 per sq. mi. **Ethnic group:** Polynesian. **Languages:** Tuvaluan, English. **Religions:** mainly Protestant.

Geography: Area: 10 sq. mi., less than one-half the size of Manhattan. **Location:** 9 islands forming a NW-SE chain 360 mi. long in the SW Pacific O. **Neighbors:** Nearest are Samoa on SE, Fiji on S. **Topography:** The islands are all low-lying atolls, nowhere rising more than 15 ft. above sea level, composed of coral reefs. **Capital:** Funafuti (pop. 1979): 2,200.

Government: Head of state: Queen Elizabeth II, represented by Gov.-Gen. Fiatau Penitala Teo, b. July 23, 1911; in office: Oct. 1, 1978. **Head of government:** Prime Min. Toarlipi Lauti, b. Nov. 20, 1928; in office: Sept. 9, 1977. **Local divisions:** 8 island councils on the permanently inhabited islands.

Economy: Industries: Copra. **Chief crops:** Coconuts. **Labor force:** Approx. 1,500 Tuvaluans work overseas in the Gilberts' phosphate industry, or as overseas seamen.

Finance: Currency: Australian dollar. **Imports** (1979): $1.83 mln. **Exports** (1979): $276,047; partners: UK.

Transport: Chief port: Funafuti.

Health: (including former Gilbert Is.) **Life expectancy at birth** (1962): 56.9 male; 59.0 female. **Births** (per 1,000 pop. 1971): 22.3. **Deaths** (per 1,000 pop. 1971): 6.5. **Natural increase** (1971): 1.6%. **Infant mortality** (per 1,000 pop. under 1 yr. 1971): 48.9.

Education: Pop. 5–19: in school (1976): 1,794.

The Ellice Islands separated from the British Gilbert and Ellice Islands colony, 1975, and became independent Tuvalu Oct. 1, 1978. Under a Treaty of Friendship, pending ratification by the U.S. Senate, the U.S. relinquishes its claims to Funafuti, Nukufetau, Nukulailai (Nukulaelae), and Nurakita (Niulakita).

The only cash crop, copra, was devastated by hurricane damage, 1972. Britain is committed to providing extensive economic aid. Australian funding has provided for a marine training school and a deep-sea wharf.

Uganda

Republic of Uganda

People: Population (1979 est.): 13,225,000. **Age distrib.** (%): 0–14: 46.1; 15–59: 47.9; 60+: 5.8. **Pop. density:** 140.23 per sq. mi. **Urban** (1972): 7.1%. **Ethnic groups:** Bantu, Nilotic, Nilo-Hamitic, Sudanic tribes. **Languages:** English (official), Swahili (national), Luganda, others. **Religions:** Christians 50%, Moslems 6%, others.

Geography: Area: 91,134 sq. mi., slightly smaller than Oregon. **Location:** In E. Central Africa. **Neighbors:** Sudan on N, Zaire on W, Rwanda, Tanzania on S, Kenya on E. **Topography:** Most of Uganda is a high plateau 3,000-6,000 ft. high, with high Ruwenzori range in W (Mt. Margherita 16,750 ft.), volcanoes in SW, NE is arid, W and SW rainy. Lakes Victoria, Edward, Albert form much of borders. **Capital:** Kampala. **Cities** (1969 cen.): Kampala (met.) 330,700.

Government: Head of state: Pres. Milton Obote; assumed full control Sept. 17, 1980; elections held Dec. 1980. **Head of government:** Chmn. military commission Paulo Muwenga; in office: May 12, 1980. **Local divisions:** 10 provinces. **Armed forces:** regulars 21,000 (pre-invasion).

Economy: Chief Crops: Coffee (68% of 1973 earnings), cot-

ton, tea, corn, peanuts, sisal, oil seeds, tobacco, sugar. **Minerals:** Copper, tin. **Per capita arable land:** 0.7 acres. **Meat prod.** (1978): beef: 72,000 metric tons; lamb: 13,000 metric tons. **Fish catch** (1977): 178,600 metric tons. **Electricity prod.** (1978): 720.00 mln. kwh. **Labor force:** 90% agric.

Finance: Currency: Shilling (Jan. 1981: 7.72 = $1 US). **Gross domestic product** (1978): $8.36 bln. **Per capita income** (1978): $240. **Imports** (1978): $255 mln.; partners: Kenya 57%, UK 9%, W. Ger. 9%, It. 6%. **Exports** (1979): $426 mln.; partners: U.S. 38%, UK 17%, Neth. 6%, Fr. 5%. **Tourists** (1974): 10,300; receipts (1977): $1 mln. **National budget** (1972): $214.45 mln. revenues; $341.69 mln. expenditures. **International reserves less gold** (Apr. 1981): $45.3 mln. **Consumer prices** (change in 1978): 36.5%.

Transport: Motor vehicles: in use (1974): 27,000 passenger cars, 8,900 comm. vehicles.

Communications: Television sets: 71,000 in use (1976). **Radios:** 250,000 in use (1976). **Telephones** in use (1978): 48,884. **Daily newspaper circ.** (1976): 35,000; 3 per 1,000 pop.

Health: Life expectancy at birth (1975): 48.3 male; 51.7 female. **Births** (per 1,000 pop. 1975): 44.9. **Deaths** (per 1,000 pop. 1975): 16.0. **Natural increase** (1975): 2.9%. **Hospital beds** (per 100,000 pop. 1977): 157. **Physicians** (per 100,000 pop. 1977): 20. **Infant mortality** (per 1,000 live births 1975): 160.

Education (1977): **Literacy:** 25%. **Pop. 5-19:** in school: 27%, teachers per 1,000: 8. **PQLI:** 42.

Britain obtained a protectorate over Uganda in 1894. The country became independent Oct. 9, 1962, and a republic within the Commonwealth a year later. In 1967, the traditional kingdoms, including the powerful Buganda state, were abolished and the central government strengthened.

Gen. Idi Amin seized power from Prime Min. Milton Obote in 1971. As many as 300,000 of his opponents were reported killed in subsequent years. Amin was named president for life in 1976.

In 1972 Amin expelled nearly all of Uganda's 45,000 Asians. In 1973 the U.S., Canada, and Norway ended economic aid programs; the U.S. withdrew all diplomatic personnel.

A June 1977 Commonwealth conference condemned the Amin government for its "disregard for the sanctity of human life."

Amid worsening economic and domestic crises, Uganda's troops exchanged invasion attacks with long-standing foe Tanzania, 1978 to 1979. Tanzanian forces, coupled with Ugandan exiles and rebels, ended the dictatorial rule of Amin, Apr. 11, 1979. Two coups followed the provisional government of Yusufu Lule.

The U.S. reopened its embassy, reinstated economic aid, and ended its trade embargo in 1979.

Four governments have been in power since Amin fled. The present one is led by Milton Obote who took office in Dec. 1980. But the country remains in utter economic and social chaos, and signs of repression, reminiscent of the Amin regime, have begun to reappear.

Union of Soviet Socialist Republics

People: Population (1980 est.): 266,670,000. **Age distrib.** (%): 0–19: 36.7; 20-59: 50.5; 60+: 12.7. **Pop. density:** 30.83 per sq. mi. **Urban** (1979): 62%. **Ethnic groups:** Russians 53%, Ukrainians 17%, Uzbeks 4%, Byelorussians 4%, 150 others. **Languages:** Slavic (Russian, Ukrainian, Byelorussian, Polish), Altaic (Turkish, etc.), other Indo-European, Uralian, Caucasian. **Religions:** Russian Orthodox 18%, Moslems 9%, other Orthodox, Protestants, Jews, Buddhists.

Geography: Area: 8,649,490 sq. mi., the largest country in the world, nearly 2½ times the size of the U.S. **Location:** Stretches from E. Europe across N Asia to the Pacific O. **Neighbors:** Finland, Poland, Czechoslovakia, Hungary, Romania on W, Turkey, Iran, Afghanistan, China, Mongolia, N. Korea on S. **Topography:** Covering one-sixth of the earth's land area, the USSR contains every type of climate except the distinctly tropical, and has a varied topography.

The European portion is a low plain, grassy in S, wooded in N with Ural Mtns. on the E. Caucasus Mts. on the S. Urals stretch N-S for 2,500 mi. The Asiatic portion is also a vast plain, with mountains on the S and in the E; tundra covers extreme N, with forest belt below; plains, marshes are in W, desert in SW. **Capital:** Moscow. **Cities** (1979 cen.): Moscow 7,831,000; Leningrad 4,073,000; Kiev 2,144,000; Tashkent 1,779,000; Kharkov 1,444,000; Gorky 1,344,000; Novosibirsk 1,312,000; Minsk

1,262,000; Kuibyshev 1,216,000; Sverdlovsk 1,211,000; Dnepropetrovsk 1,066,000; Tbilisi 1,066,000; Odessa 1,046,000; Chelyabinsk 1,031,000; Baku 1,022,000; Donetsk 1,021,000; Yerevan 1,019,000; Omsk, 1,014,000.

Government: Head of state: Pres. Leonid I. Brezhnev; b. Dec. 19, 1906; in office: June 16, 1977. **Head of government:** Premier Nikolai A. Tikhonov; b. May 1, 1905; in office: Oct. 23, 1980. **Head of Communist Party:** Gen. Sec. Leonid Brezhnev; in office: Oct. 14, 1964. **Local divisions:** 15 union republics, within which are 20 autonomous republics, 6 krays (territories), 120 oblasts (regions), 8 autonomous oblasts, 10 national areas. **Armed forces:** regulars 3,658,000; reserves 5,000,000; paramilitary 460,000.

Economy: Industries: Steel, machinery, machine tools, vehicles, chemicals, cement, textiles, appliances, paper. **Chief crops:** Grain, cotton, sugar beets, potatoes, vegetables, sunflowers. **Minerals:** Iron (41% of world reserves), manganese (88%), mercury, potash, antimony, bauxite, cobalt, chromium, copper, coal (58%), gold, lead, molybdenum, nickel, phosphates (30%), silver, tin, tungsten, zinc, oil (59%), potassium salts (54%). **Crude oil reserves** (1980): 67.00 bln. bbls. **Other resources:** Forests (25% of world reserves). **Per capita arable land:** 2.1 acres. **Meat prod.** (1978): beef: 7.1 mln. metric tons; pork: 5.1 mln. metric tons; lamb: 885,000 metric tons. **Fish catch** (1977): 9.4 mln. metric tons. **Electricity prod.** (1979): 1,239 bln. kwh. **Crude steel prod.** (1979): 149.0 mln. metric tons. **Labor force:** 23% agric.; 38% manuf. & constr.

Finance: Currency: Ruble (Sept. 22, 1981: .64 = $1 US). **Net material product** (1978): $278.9 bln. **Per capita income** (1976): $2,600. **Imports** (1980): $59.19 bln.; partners (1980): E. Ger. 10%, Pol. 10%, Czech. 8%, Bulg. 8%. **Exports** (1980): $66.29 bln.; partners (1980): E. Ger. 10%, Pol. 9%, Bulg. 8%, Czech. 8%. **National budget** (1980 est): $388.75 bln. revenues; $388.28 bln. expenditures. **Tourists** (1977): 4,399,800. **Consumer prices** (change in 1979): 0.7%.

Transport: Railway traffic (1978): 332.4 bln. passenger-km; 3,426 bln. net ton-km. **Motor vehicles:** in use (1977): 6.64 mln. passenger cars, 6.33 mln. comm. vehicles; manuf. (1977): 1.28 mln. passenger cars; 781,200 comm. vehicles. **Civil aviation** (international only): 8.4 bln. passenger-km (1978); 270 mln. freight ton-km (1978). **Chief ports:** Leningrad, Odessa, Murmansk, Kaliningrad, Archangelsk, Riga, Vladivostock.

Communications: Television sets: 60 mln. in use (Dec. 1979), 7.07 mln. manuf. (1977). **Radios:** 122.5 mln. in use (1975), 8.65 mln. manuf. (1977). **Telephones in use** (1978): 19.6 mln. **Daily newspaper circ.** (1977): 102,462,000; 396 per 1,000 pop.

Health: Life expectancy at birth (1972): 64 male; 74 female. **Births** (per 1,000 pop. 1977): 18.1. **Deaths** (per 1,000 pop. 1976): 9.6. **Natural increase** (1976): .9%. **Hospital beds** (per 100,000 pop. 1977): 1,213. **Physicians** (per 100,000 pop. 1977): 346. **Infant mortality** (per 1,000 live births 1974): 27.7.

Education (1977): Literacy: 99%. **Pop. 5-19:** in school: 58%, teachers per 1,000: 37. **PQLI:** 92.

The USSR is nominally a federation consisting of 15 union republics, the largest being the Russian Soviet Federated Socialist Republic. Important positions in the republics are filled by centrally chosen appointees, often ethnic Russians.

Beginning in 1939 the USSR by means of military action and negotiation overran contiguous territory and independent republics, including all or part of Lithuania, Latvia, Estonia, Poland, Czechoslovakia, Romania, Germany, Tannu Tuva, and Japan. The union republics are:

Republic	Area sq. mi.	Pop. (cen. 1979)
Russian SFSR	6,593,391	137,552,000
Ukrainian SSR	232,046	49,757,000
Uzbek SSR	158,069	15,391,000
Kazakh SSR	1,064,092	14,685,000
Byelorussian SSR	80,154	9,559,000
Azerbaijan SSR.	33,436	6,028,000
Georgian SSR	26,911	5,016,000
Moldavian SSR	13,012	3,948,000
Tadzhik SSR	54,019	3,801,000
Kirghiz SSR	76,642	3,529,000
Lithuanian SSR	26,173	3,399,000
Armenian SSR	11,306	3,031,000
Turkmen SSR.	188,417	2,759,000
Latvian SSR.	24,695	2,521,000
Estonian SSR	17,413	1,466,000

The **Russian Soviet Federated Socialist Republic** contains over 50% of the population of the USSR and includes 76% of its territory. It extends from the old Estonian, Latvian, and Finnish borders and the Byelorussian and Ukrainian lines on the W, to the shores of the Pacific, and from the Arctic on the N to the Black and Caspian seas and the borders of Kazakh SSR, Mongolia, and Manchuria on the S. Siberia encompasses a large part of the RSFSR area. Capital: Moscow.

Parts of eastern and western Siberia have been transformed by steel mills, huge dams, oil and gas industries, electric railroads, and highways.

The **Ukraine**, the most densely populated of the republics, borders on the Black Sea, with Poland, Czechoslovakia, Hungary, and Romania on the W and SW. Capital: Kiev.

The Ukraine contains the arable black soil belt, the chief wheat-producing section of the Soviet Union. Sugar beets, potatoes, and livestock are important.

The Donets Basin has large deposits of coal, iron and other metals. There are chemical and machine industries and salt mines.

Byelorussia (White Russia). Capital: Minsk. Chief industries include machinery, tools, appliances, tractors, clocks, cameras, steel, cement, textiles, paper, leather, glass. Main crops are grain, flax, potatoes, sugar beets.

Azerbaijan boasts near Baku, the capital, important oil fields. Its natural wealth includes deposits of iron ore, cobalt, etc. A high-yield winter wheat is grown, as are fruits. It produces iron, steel, cement, fertilizers, synthetic rubber, electrical and chemical equipment. It borders on Iran and Turkey.

Georgia, in the western part of Transcaucasia, contains the largest manganese mines in the world. There are rich timber resources and coal mines. Basic industries are food, textiles, iron, steel. Grain, tea, tobacco, fruits, grapes are grown. Capital: Tbilisi (Tiflis). Despite massive party and government purges since 1972, illegal private enterprise and Georgian nationalist feelings persist; attempts to repress them have led to violence.

Armenia is mountainous, sub-tropical, extensively irrigated. Copper, zinc, aluminum, molybdenum, and marble are mined. Instrument making is important. Capital: Erevan.

Uzbekistan, most important economically of the Central Asia republics, produces 67% of USSR cotton, 50% of rice, 33% of silk, 34% of astrakhan, 85% of hemp. Industries include iron, steel, cars, tractors, TV and radio sets, textiles, food. Mineral wealth includes coal, sulphur, copper, and oil. Capital: Tashkent.

Turkmenistan in Central Asia, produces cotton, maize, carpets, chemicals. Minerals: oil, coal, sulphur, barite, lime, salt, gypsum. The Kara Kum desert occupies 80% of the area. Capital: Ashkhabad.

Tadzhikistan borders on China and Afghanistan. Over half the population are Tadzhiks, mostly Moslems, speaking an Iranian dialect. Chief occupations are farming and cattle breeding. Cotton, grain, rice, and a variety of fruits are grown. Heavy industry, based on rich mineral deposits, coal and hydroelectric power, has replaced handicrafts. Capital: Dushanbe.

Kazakhstan extends from the lower reaches of the Volga in Europe to the Altai Mtns. on the Chinese border. It has vast deposits of coal, oil, iron, tin, copper, lead, zinc, etc. Fish for its canning industry are caught in Lake Balkhash and the Caspian and Aral seas. The capital is Alma-Ata. About 50% of the population is Russian or Ukrainian, working in the virgin-grain lands opened up after 1954, and in the growing industries.

Kirghizia is the eastern part of Soviet Central Asia, on the frontier of Xinjiang, China. The people breed cattle and horses and grow tobacco, cotton, rice, sugar beets. Industries include machine and instrument making, chemicals. Capital: Frunze.

Moldavia, in the SW part of the USSR, is a fertile black earth plain bordering Romania and includes Bessarabia. It is an agricultural region that grows grains, fruits, vegetables, and tobacco. Textiles, wine, food and electrical equipment industries have been developed. Capital: Kishinev. The region was taken from Romania in 1940; the people speak Romanian.

Lithuania, on the Baltic, produces cattle, hogs, electric motors, and appliances. The capital is Vilnius (Vilna). **Latvia** on the Baltic and the Gulf of Riga, has timber and peat resources est. at 3 bln. tons. In addition to agricultural products it produces rubber goods, dyes, fertilizers, glassware, telephone apparatus, TV and radio sets, railroad cars. Capital: Riga.

Estonia, also on the Baltic, has textiles, shipbuilding, timber, roadmaking and mining equipment industries and a shale oil refining industry. Capital: Tallinn. The 3 Baltic states were provinces of imperial Russia before World War I, were independent nations between World Wars I and II, but were conquered by Russia in 1940. The U.S. has never formally recognized the takeover.

Economy. Almost all legal economic enterprises are state-owned. There were 29,600 collective farms in 1976, along with 18,064 larger state farms. A huge illegal black market plays an important role in distribution; illegal private production and service firms are periodically exposed.

The USSR is incalculably rich in natural resources; distant Siberian reserves are being exploited with Japanese assistance. Its heavy industry is 2d only to the U.S. It leads the world in oil and steel production. Consumer industries have lagged comparatively. Agricultural output has expanded, but in poor crop years the USSR has been forced to make huge grain purchases from the West. Shortages and rationing of basic food products periodically occur.

Exports include petroleum and its products, iron and steel, rolled non-ferrous metals, industrial plant equipment, arms, lumber, cotton, asbestos, gold, manganese, and others. 55% of its trade is with Communist nations, 33% with the West, which supplies advanced technology. The USSR had a $4 billion trade deficit with the West in 1976, financed by gold sales, long-term loans, and a trade surplus with East Europe and underdeveloped countries. Debt to the West reached $14.4 billion by 1977.

Industrial growth in 1979 dropped, due to short falls in oil, coal, and steel industries, as well as the worst grain harvest since 1975.

History. Slavic tribes began migrating into Russia from the W in the 5th century AD. The first Russian state, founded by Scandinavian chieftains, was established in the 9th century, centering in Novgorod and Kiev.

In the 13th century the Mongols overran the country. It recovered under the grand dukes and princes of Muscovy, or Moscow, and by 1480 freed itself from the Mongols. Ivan the Terrible was the first to be formally proclaimed Tsar (1547). Peter the Great (1682-1725), extended the domain and in 1721, founded the Russian Empire.

Western ideas and the beginnings of modernization spread through the huge Russian empire in the 19th and early 20th centuries. But political evolution failed to keep pace.

Military reverses in the 1905 war with Japan and in World War I led to the breakdown of the Tsarist regime. The 1917 Revolution began in March with a series of sporadic strikes for higher wages by factory workers. A provisional democratic government under Prince Georgi Lvov was established but was quickly followed in May by the second provisional government, led by Alexander Kerensky. The Kerensky government and the freely-elected Constituent Assembly were overthrown in a Communist coup led by Vladimir Ilyich Lenin Nov. 7.

Lenin's death Jan. 21, 1924, resulted in an internal power struggle from which Joseph Stalin eventually emerged the absolute ruler of Russia. Stalin secured his position at first by exiling opponents, but from the 1930s to 1953, he resorted to a series of "purge" trials, mass executions, and mass exiles to work camps. These measures resulted in millions of deaths, according to most estimates.

Germany and the USSR signed a non-aggression pact Aug. 1939; Nazi forces launched a massive invasion of the Soviet Union, June 1941. Notable heroic episode was the "900 days" siege of Leningrad, lasting to Jan. 1944, and causing 1,000,000 deaths; the city was never taken. Russian winter counterthrusts, 1941 to '42 and 1942 to '43, stopped the German advance. Turning point was the failure of German troops to take and hold Stalingrad, Sept. 1942 to Feb. 1943. With British and U.S. Lend-Lease aid and sustaining great casualties, the Russians drove the Axis from eastern Europe and the Balkans in the next 2 years.

After Stalin died, Mar. 5, 1953, Nikita Khrushchev was elected first secretary of the Central Committee. In 1956 he condemned Stalin. "De-Stalinization" of the country on all levels was effected after Stalin's body was removed from the Lenin-Stalin tomb in Moscow.

Under Khrushchev the open antagonism of Poles and Hungarians toward domination by Moscow was brutally suppressed in 1956. He advocated peaceful co-existence with the capitalist countries, but continued arming the USSR with nuclear weapons. He aided the Cuban revolution under Fidel Castro but withdrew Soviet missiles from Cuba during confrontation by U.S. Pres. Kennedy, Sept.-Oct. 1962.

The USSR, the U.S., and Great Britain initialed a joint treaty July 25, 1963, banning above-ground nuclear tests.

Khrushchev was suddenly deposed, Oct. 1964, and replaced as party first secretary by Leonid I. Brezhnev, and as premier by Aleksei N. Kosygin.

In 1968, the U.S. and USSR joined 59 other nations in signing a treaty to bar spread of nuclear weapons.

In Aug. 1968 Russian, Polish, East German, Hungarian, and Bulgarian military forces invaded Czechoslovakia to put a curb on liberalization policies of the Czech government. The USSR declared it had a duty to intervene in nations where socialism was "imperiled" according to the "Brezhnev Doctrine."

The USSR in 1971 continued heavy arms shipments to Egypt. In July 1972 Egypt ordered most of the 20,000 Soviet military personnel in that country to leave. When Egypt and Syria attacked Israel in Oct. 1973, the USSR launched huge arms airlifts to the 2 Arab nations. In 1974, the Soviet replenished the arms used or lost by the Syrians in the 1973 war, and continued some shipments to Egypt.

Massive Soviet military aid to North Vietnam in the late 1960s and early 1970s helped assure Communist victories throughout Indo-China. Soviet arms aid and advisers were sent to several African countries in the 1970s, including Algeria, Angola, Somalia, and Ethiopia.

In 1972, the U.S. and USSR reached temporary agreements to freeze intercontinental missiles at their current levels, to limit defensive missiles to 200 each and to cooperate on health, environment, space, trade, and science. The U.S. and USSR, June 18, 1979, signed a strategic arms treaty limiting both nations to the same maximum number of long-range bombers and missiles.

Meanwhile, under Brezhnev, dissident intellectuals were repressed and purge-type trials resumed.

On Aug. 1, 1975, 35 countries of Europe and North America signed a European security pact tacitly approving current boundaries and urging freer movement of people and ideas. Most members of Russian groups set up to monitor the pact were jailed in a 1978 crackdown.

A limitation on grain sales, imposed by Pres. Carter, Jan. 4, 1980, in response to the Soviet invasion of Afghanistan, was lifted, Apr. 24, 1981, by the Reagan administration.

More than 130,000 Jews and over 40,000 ethnic Germans were allowed to emigrate from the USSR in the 1970s, following pressure from the West. Many leading figures in the arts also left the country.

Government. The Communist Party leadership dominates all areas of national life. A Politburo of 14 full members and 8 candidate members makes all major political, economic, and foreign policy decisions. Party membership in 1978 was reported to be over 16,000,000.

United Arab Emirates

People: Population (1979 est.): 900,000. **Pop. density:** 28.13 per sq. mi. **Ethnic groups:** Arabs 72%, Iranians, Pakistanis and Indians 26%. **Languages:** Arabic (official), Persian, English, Hindi, Urdu. **Religions:** Moslems 96.7%, Christians 1.3%.

Geography: Area: 32,000 sq. mi., the size of Maine. **Location:** On the S shore of the Persian Gulf. **Neighbors:** Qatar on N, Saudi Ar. on W, S, Oman on E. **Topography:** A barren, flat coastal plain gives way to uninhabited sand dunes on the S. Hajar Mtns. are on E. **Capital:** Abu Dhabi. **Cities** (1979 est.): Dubai; Abu Dhabi 300,000; Dubai, Sharjah.

Government: Head of state: Pres. Zayed bin Sultan Al Nahyan, b. 1923; in office: Dec. 2, 1971. **Head of government:** Prime Min. Rashid bin Saeed Al Maktoum; in office: June 25, 1979. **Local divisions:** 7 autonomous emirates: Abu Dhabi, Ajman, Dubai, Fujaira, Ras al-Khaimah, Sharjah, Umm al-Qaiwain. **Armed forces:** regulars 25,150.

Economy: Chief crops: Vegetables, dates, limes. **Minerals:** Oil. **Crude oil reserves** (1980): 29.4 bln. bbls. **Per capita arable land:** 0.02 acres. **Fish catch** (1977): 64,400 metric tons. **Electricity prod.** (1977): 700.00 mln. kwh. **Labor force:** 5% agric.;85% ind. and commerce; 5% serv.; 5% gvt.

Finance: Currency: Dirham (Apr. 1981: 3.67 = $1 US). **Gross domestic product** (1979) $9.43 bln. **Per capita income** (1979 est.) $16,000. **Imports** (1980): $16 bln.; partners (1977): Jap. 19%, U.K. 18%, U.S. 11%, W. Ger. 9%. **Exports** (1980): $20.69 bln.; partners (1977): Jap. 26%, U.S. 16%, Fr. 12%, Neth. 7%. **International reserves less gold** (Apr. 1981): $2.35 bln. **Gold:** 617,000 oz t.

Transport: Chief ports: Dubai, Abu Dhabi.

Communications: Radios: 55,000 in use (1975). **Telephones in use** (1978): 96,847. **Daily newspaper circ.,** (1977): 2,000, 8 per 1,000 pop.

Health: Hospital beds (per 100,000 pop. 1977): 228. **Physicians** (per 100,000 pop. 1977): 130.

Education (1977): **Literacy:** 21%. **Pop. 5-19:** in school: 35%, teachers per 1,000: 24. **PQLI:** 35.

The 7 "Trucial Sheikdoms" gave Britain control of defense and foreign relations in the 19th century. They merged to become an independent state Dec. 2, 1971.

The Abu Dhabi Petroleum Co. was fully nationalized in 1975. Oil revenues have given the UAE one of the highest per capita GNPs in the world. International banking has grown in recent years.

United Kingdom of Great Britain and Northern Ireland

People: Population (1979 est.): 55,901,000. **Age distrib.** (%): 0–4: 22.9; 15–59: 57.4; 60+: 19.7. **Pop. density:** 592.48 per sq. mi. **Urban** (1973): Eng. & Wales: 77.7%, N. Ire.: 54.7%, Scot. (1974): 70.0%. **Ethnic groups:** English 81.5%, Scottish 9.6%, Irish 2.4, Welsh 1.9%, Ulster 1.8%; West Indian, Indian, Pakistani over 2%; others. **Languages:** English nearly universal, Welsh spoken in western Wales; Gaelic. **Religions:** Church of England 55%, Roman Catholics 10%, Presbyterians 3%, Methodists 1%, Jews 1%, other Protestants, Hindus, Muslims.

Geography: Area: 94,214 sq. mi., slightly smaller than Oregon. **Location:** Off the NW coast of Europe, across English Channel, Strait of Dover, and North Sea. **Neighbors:** Ireland to W, France to SE. **Topography:** England is mostly rolling land, rising to Uplands of southern Scotland; Lowlands are in center of Scotland, granite Highlands are in N. Coast is heavily indented, especially on W. British Isles have milder climate than N Europe, due to the Gulf Stream, and ample rainfall. Severn, 220 mi., and Thames, 215 mi., are longest rivers. **Capital:** London. **Cities** (1978 est.): London 7,028,200; Birmingham 1,058,800; Glasgow 832,097; Leeds 744,500; Sheffield 588,000; Liverpool 539,700; Manchester 490,000; Edinburgh 463,923; Bradford 458,900; Bristol 416,300; Belfast 357,600.

Government: Head of state: Queen Elizabeth II; b. Apr. 21, 1926; in office: Feb. 6, 1952. **Head of government:** Prime Min. Margaret Thatcher; b. Oct. 13, 1925; in office: May 4, 1979. **Local divisions:** England and Wales: 47 non-metro counties, 6 metro counties, Greater London; Scotland: 9 regions, 3 island areas; N. Ireland: 26 districts. **Armed forces:** regulars 322,891; reserves 257,640.

Economy: Industries: Steel, metals, vehicles, shipbuilding, shipping, banking, insurance, appliances, textiles, chemicals, electronics, aircraft, machinery, scientific instruments, distilling. **Chief crops:** Grains, sugar beets, fruits, vegetables. **Minerals:** Coal, tin, oil, gas, limestone, iron, salt, clay, chalk, gypsum, lead, silica. **Crude oil reserves** (1980): 15.4 bln. bbls. **Per capita arable land:** 0.3 acres. **Meat prod.** (1978): beef: 970,000 metric tons; pork: 800,000 metric tons; lamb: 235,000 metric tons. **Fish catch** (1977): 1 mln. metric tons. **Electricity prod.** (1978): 287.74 bln. kwh. **Crude steel prod.** (1979): 21.6 mln. metric tons. **Labor force:** 1.6% agric.; 55.2% ind. and commerce; 28.5% serv.; 70% govt.

Finance: Currency: Pound (Apr. 1981: .47 = $1 US). **Gross domestic product** (1979): $405.09 bln. **Per capita income** (1978): $4,955. **Imports** (1980): $119.91 bln.; partners (1979): W. Ger. 12%, U.S. 10%, Fr. 8%, Neth. 7%. **Exports** (1980): $115.18 bln.; partners (1979): U.S. 9%, W. Ger. 10%, Fr. 7%, Neth. 7%. **Tourists** (1977): 11,490,000; receipts $3.81 bln. **National budget** (1979): $134.63 bln. revenues; $149.28 bln. expenditures. **International reserves less gold** (Apr. 1981): $20.27 bln. **Gold:** 18.84 mln. oz t. **Consumer prices** (change in 1980): 18.0%.

Transport: Railway traffic (1978): 30.7 bln. passenger-km; 19.98 bln. net ton-km. **Motor vehicles:** in use (1979): 14.92 mln. passenger cars, 1.82 mln. comm. vehicles; manuf. (1978): 1.22 mln. passenger cars; 384,000 comm. vehicles. **Civil aviation:** 47,004 mln. passenger-km (1979): 1,247 mln. freight ton-km (1979). **Chief ports:** London, Liverpool, Glasgow, Southampton, Cardiff, Belfast.

Communications: Television sets: 18.27 mln. licensed (Dec. 1979), 2.18 mln. manuf. (1977). **Radios:** 40.0 mln. licensed (Dec. 1977), 891,000 manuf. (1977). **Telephones in use** (1978): 23,182,239. **Daily newspaper circ.** (1977): 22,900,000; 410 per

1,000 pop.

Health: Life expectancy at birth: (1970): 67.8 male; 73.8 female. **Births:** (per 1,000 pop. 1980): 13.5. **Deaths:** (per 1,000 pop. 1980): 12.0. **Natural increase:** (1977): .01%. **Hospital beds** (per 100,000 pop. 1977): 894. **Physicians** (per 100,000 pop. 1977): 153. **Infant mortality:** (per 1,000 live births 1977): 14.0.

Education (1977): **Literacy:** 99%. **Pop. 5-19:** in school: 83%, teachers per 1,000: 45. **PQLI:** 94.

The United Kingdom of Great Britain and Northern Ireland comprises England, Wales, Scotland, and Northern Ireland.

Queen and Royal Family. The ruling sovereign is Elizabeth II of the House of Windsor, born Apr. 21, 1926, elder daughter of King George VI. She succeeded to the throne Feb. 6, 1952, and was crowned June 2, 1953. She was married Nov. 20, 1947, to Lt. Philip Mountbatten, born June 10, 1921, former Prince of Greece. He was created Duke of Edinburgh, Earl of Merioneth, and Baron Greenwich, and given the style H.R.H., Nov. 19, 1947; he was given the title Prince of the United Kingdom and Northern Ireland Feb. 22, 1957. Prince Charles Philip Arthur George, born Nov. 14, 1948, is the Prince of Wales and heir apparent.

Parliament is the legislative governing body for the United Kingdom, with certain powers over dependent units. It consists of 2 houses: The **House of Lords** includes 763 hereditary and 314 life peers and peeresses, certain judges, 2 archbishops and 24 bishops of the Church of England. Total membership is over 1,000. The **House of Commons** has 635 members, who are elected by direct ballot and divided as follows: England 516; Wales 36; Scotland 71; Northern Ireland 12.

Resources and Industries. Great Britain's major occupations are manufacturing and trade. Metals and metal-using industries contribute more than 50% of the exports. Of about 60 million acres of land in England, Wales and Scotland, 46 million are farmed, of which 17 million are arable, the rest pastures.

Large oil and gas fields have been found in the North Sea. Commercial oil production began in 1975; self-sufficiency is expected by the early 1980s with projected output of 2 million barrels a day. There are large deposits of coal; 1977-78 output was 119 million tons.

The railroads, nationalized since 1948, have been reduced in total length, with a basic network, Dec. 1978, of 11,123 mi. The merchant marine totaled 49,700,000 gross registered tons in July 1978, comprising nearly 7.5% of active world shipping.

The world's first power station using atomic energy to create electricity for civilian use began operation Oct. 17, 1956, at Calder Hall in Cumbria.

Britain imports all of its cotton, rubber, sulphur, 80% of its wool, half of its food and iron ore, also certain amounts of paper, tobacco, chemicals. Manufactured goods made from these basic materials have been exported since the industrial age began. Main exports are machinery, chemicals, woolen and synthetic textiles, clothing, autos and trucks, iron and steel, locomotives, ships, jet aircraft, farm machinery, drugs, radio, TV, radar and navigation equipment, scientific instruments, arms, whisky.

Religion and Education. The Church of England is Protestant Episcopal. The queen is its temporal head, with rights of appointments to archbishoprics, bishoprics, and other offices. There are 2 provinces, Canterbury and York, each headed by an archbishop. About 48% of the population is baptized into the Church, less than 10% is confirmed. Most famous church is Westminster Abbey (1050-1760), site of coronations, tombs of Elizabeth I, Mary of Scots, kings, poets, and of the Unknown Warrior.

Other major religious affiliations represented in the UK: Roman Catholics, Methodists, Jews, Baptists, United Reformed Church (Congregational and Presbyterian), Calvinistic Methodist (Presbyterian) Church of Wales, Unitarians, Society of Friends, Mormons, Church of Christ Scientist, The Presbyterian Church in Ireland, The Church of Scotland (Presbyterian), Hindus, Moslems.

Education is free and compulsory from 5 to 16. The most celebrated British universities are Oxford and Cambridge, each dating to the 13th century. There are 40 other universities.

History. Britain was part of the continent of Europe until about 6,000 BC, but migration of peoples across the English Channel continued long afterward. Celts arrived 2,500 to 3,000 years ago. Their language survives in Welsh, Cornish, and Gaelic enclaves.

England was added to the Roman Empire in 43 AD. After the withdrawal of Roman legions in 410, waves of Jutes, Angles, and Saxons arrived from German lands. They contended with Danish raiders for control from the 8th through 11th centuries.

The last successful invasion was by French-speaking Normans in 1066, who united the country with their dominions in France.

Opposition by nobles to royal authority forced King John to sign the Magna Carta in 1215, a guarantee of rights and the rule of law. In the ensuing decades, the foundations of the parliamentary system were laid.

English dynastic claims to large parts of France led to the Hundred Years War, 1338-1453, and the defeat of England. A long civil war, the War of the Roses, lasted 1455-85, and ended with the establishment of the powerful Tudor monarchy. A distinct English civilization flourished. The economy prospered over long periods of domestic peace unmatched in continental Europe. Religious independence was secured when the Church of England was separated from the authority of the Pope in 1534.

Under Queen Elizabeth I, Britain became a major naval power, leading to the founding of colonies in the new world and the expansion of trade with Europe and the Orient. Scotland was united with England when James VI of Scotland was crowned James I of England in 1603.

A struggle between Parliament and the Stuart kings led to a bloody civil war, 1642-49, and the establishment of a republic under the Puritan Oliver Cromwell. The monarchy was restored in 1660, but the "Glorious Revolution" of 1688 confirmed the sovereignty of Parliament: a Bill of Rights was granted 1689.

In the 18th century, parliamentary rule was strengthened. Technological and entrepreneurial innovations led to the Industrial Revolution. The 13 North American colonies were lost, but replaced by growing empires in Canada and India. Britain's role in the defeat of Napoleon, 1815, strengthened its position as the leading world power.

The extension of the franchise in 1832 and 1867, the formation of trade unions, and the development of universal public education were among the drastic social changes which accompanied the spread of industrialization and urbanization in the 19th century. Large parts of Africa and Asia were added to the empire during the reign of Queen Victoria, 1837-1901.

Though victorious in World War I, Britain suffered huge casualties and economic dislocation. Ireland became independent in 1921, and independence movements became active in India and other colonies.

The country suffered major bombing damage in World War II, but held out against Germany singlehandedly for a year after the fall of France in 1940.

Industrial growth continued in the postwar period, but Britain lost its leadership position to other powers. Labor governments passed socialist programs nationalizing some basic industries and expanding social security. Nearly all of the empire was given independence. Britain joined the NATO alliance and, in 1973, the European Communities (Common Market).

Wales

The Principality of Wales in western Britain has an area of 8,016 sq. mi. and a population (est. 1977) of 2,768,200. Cardiff is the capital, pop. (1977 est.) 278,900.

England and Wales are administered as a unit. Less than 20% of the population of Wales speak both English and Welsh; about 32,000 speak Welsh solely. Welsh nationalism is advocated by a segment. A 1979 referendum rejected, 4-1, the creation of an elected Welsh Assembly.

Early Anglo-Saxon invaders drove Celtic peoples into the mountains of Wales, terming them Waelise (Welsh, or foreign). There they developed a distinct nationality. Members of the ruling house of Gwynedd in the 13th century fought England but were crushed, 1283. Edward of Caernarvon, son of Edward I of England, was created Prince of Wales, 1301.

Scotland

Scotland, a kingdom now united with England and Wales in Great Britain, occupies the northern 37% of the main British island, and the Hebrides, Orkney, Shetland and smaller islands. Length, 275 mi., breadth approx. 150 mi., area, 30,405 sq. mi., population (est. 1977) 5,195,600.

The Lowlands, a belt of land approximately 60 mi. wide from the Firth of Clyde to the Firth of Forth, divide the farming region of the Southern Uplands from the granite Highlands of the North, contain 75% of the population and most of the industry. The Highlands, famous for hunting and fishing, have been opened to industry by many hydroelectric power stations.

Edinburgh, pop. (1978 est.) 463,929, is the capital. Glasgow,

pop. (1978 est.) 832,097, is Britain's greatest industrial center. It is a shipbuilding complex on the Clyde and an ocean port. Aberdeen, pop. (1978 est.) 208,340, NE of Edinburgh, is a major port, center of granite industry, fish processing, and North Sea oil exploitation. Dundee, pop. (1978 est.) 192,765, NE of Edinburgh, is an industrial and fish processing center. About 90,000 persons speak Gaelic as well as English.

History. Scotland was called Caledonia by the Romans who battled early Pict and Celtic tribes and occupied southern areas from the 1st to the 4th centuries. Missionaries from Britain introduced Christianity in the 4th century; St. Columba, an Irish monk, converted most of Scotland in the 6th century.

The Kingdom of Scotland was founded in 1018. William Wallace and Robert Bruce both defeated English armies 1297 and 1314, respectively.

In 1603 James VI of Scotland, son of Mary, Queen of Scots, succeeded to the throne of England as James I, and effected the Union of the Crowns. In 1707 Scotland received representation in the British Parliament, resulting from the union of former separate Parliaments. Its executive in the British cabinet is the Secretary of State for Scotland. The growing Scottish National Party urges independence. A 1979 referendum on the creation of an elected Scotland Assembly was defeated.

There are 8 universities. Memorials of Robert Burns, Sir Walter Scott, John Knox, Mary, Queen of Scots draw many tourists, as do the beauties of the Trossachs, Loch Katrine, Loch Lomond and abbey ruins.

Industries. Engineering products are the most important industry, with growing emphasis on office machinery, autos, electronics and other consumer goods. Oil has been discovered offshore in the North Sea, stimulating on-shore support industries.

Scotland produces fine woolens, worsteds, tweeds, silks, fine linens and jute. It is known for its special breeds of cattle and sheep. Fisheries have large hauls of herring, cod, whiting. Whisky is the biggest export.

The Hebrides are a group of c. 500 islands, 100 inhabited, off the W coast. The Inner Hebrides include **Skye, Mull,** and **Iona,** the last famous for the arrival of St. Columba, 563 AD. The Outer Hebrides include **Lewis** and **Harris.** Industries include sheep raising and weaving. The **Orkney Islands,** c. 90, are to the NE. The capital is Kirkwall, on Pomona Is. Fish curing, sheep raising and weaving are occupations. NE of the Orkneys are the 200 **Shetland Islands,** 24 inhabited, home of Shetland pony. The Orkneys and Shetlands have become centers for the North Sea oil industry.

Northern Ireland

Six of the 9 counties of Ulster, the NE corner of Ireland, constitute Northern Ireland, with the parliamentary boroughs of Belfast and Londonderry. Area 5,463 sq. mi., 1978 est. pop. 1,540,000, capital and chief industrial center, Belfast, (1978 est.) 357,600.

Industries. Shipbuilding, including large tankers, has long been an important industry, centered in Belfast, the largest port. Linen manufacture is also important, along with apparel, rope, and twine. Growing diversification has added engineering products, synthetic fibers, and electronics. They are large numbers of cattle, hogs, and sheep, potatoes, poultry, and dairy foods are also produced.

Government. An act of the British Parliament, 1920, divided Northern from Southern Ireland, each with a parliament and government. When Ireland became a dominion, 1921, and later a republic, Northern Ireland chose to remain a part of the United Kingdom. It elects 12 members to the British House of Commons.

During 1968-69, large demonstrations were conducted by Roman Catholics who charged they were discriminated against in voting rights, housing, and employment. The Catholics, a minority comprising about a third of the population, demanded abolition of property qualifications for voting in local elections. Violence and terrorism intensified, involving branches of the Irish Republican Army (outlawed in the Irish Republic), Protestant groups, police, and up to 15,000 British troops.

A succession of Northern Ireland prime ministers pressed reform programs but failed to satisfy extremists on both sides. Over 2,000 were killed in over 10 years of bombings and shootings through Mar. 1980, some in England itself. Britain suspended the Northern Ireland parliament Mar. 30, 1972, and imposed direct British rule. A coalition government was formed in 1973 when moderates won election to a new one-house Assembly. But a Protestant general strike overthrew the government in

1974. Direct rule continued in 1978, after the failure of a constitutional convention to achieve a settlement.

The turmoil and agony of Northern Ireland was dramatized in 1981 by the deaths of imprisoned Irish nationalist hunger strikers in Maze Prison near Belfast. On May 5, Robert Sands, elected a Member of Parliament, April 10, died on his 66th day without food. As of July 13, five other inmates had starved themselves to death in an attempt to achieve status as political prisoners, but the British government refused to yield to their demands.

Education and Religion. Northern Ireland is 2/3 Protestant, 1/3 Roman Catholic. Education is compulsory through age 15. There are 2 universities and 24 technical colleges.

Channel Islands

The Channel Islands, area 75 sq. mi., cen. pop 1977 131,027 off the NW coast of France, the only parts of the one-time Dukedom of Normandy belonging to England, are **Jersey, Guernsey** and the dependencies of Guernsey — **Alderney, Brechou, Great Sark, Little Sark, Herm, Jethou and Lihou.** Jersey and Guernsey have separate legal existences and lieutenant governors named by the Crown. The islands were the only British soil occupied by German troops in World War II.

Isle of Man

The Isle of Man, area 227 sq. mi., 1979 est. pop. 64,000, is in the Irish Sea, 20 mi. from Scotland, 30 mi. from Cumberland. It is rich in lead and iron. The island has its own laws and a lieutenant governor appointed by the Crown. The Tynwald (legislature) consists of the Legislative Council, partly elected, and House of Keys, elected. Capital: Douglas. Farming, tourism, fishing (kippers, scallops) are chief occupations. Man is famous for the Manx tailless cat.

Gibraltar

Gibraltar, a dependency on the southern coast of Spain, guards the entrance to the Mediterranean. The Rock has been in British possession since 1704. The Rock is 2.75 mi long, 3/4 of a mi. wide and 1,396 ft. in height; a narrow isthmus connects it with the mainland. Est. pop. 1979, 29,000.

In 1966 Spain called on Britain to give "substantial sovereignty" of Gibraltar to Spain and imposed a partial blockade. In 1967, residents voted 12,138 for remaining under Britain, 44 for returning to Spain. A new constitution, May 30, 1969, gave an elected House of Assembly more control in domestic affairs. A UN General Assembly resolution requested Britain to end Gibraltar's colonial status by Oct. 1, 1969. No settlement has been reached.

British West Indies

Swinging in a vast arc from the coast of Venezuela NE, then N and NW toward Puerto Rico are the Windward and Leeward Islands, forming a coral and volcanic barrier sheltering the Caribbean from the open Atlantic. Many of the islands are self-governing British possessions. Universal suffrage was instituted 1951-54; ministerial systems were set up 1956-1960.

Moving northward from the southern end of the arc lie the former British **Windward Islands. St. Vincent and the Grenadines** gained full independence from UK in 1979; **St. Lucia** became independent earlier that year; and **Dominica** gained independence in 1978 *(See Index).*

Further north, in the **Leeward Islands,** are **Montserrat** (1977 pop. 12,160, area 32 sq. mi., capital Plymouth), **Antigua** (1979 pop. 74,000, area 171 sq. mi., capital St. John's), and **St. Kitts (St. Christopher)-Nevis-Anguilla,** 3 islands (1979 pop. 57,000, area 136 sq. mi., capital Basseterre on St. Kitts). Nearby are the small **British Virgin Islands.**

Britain granted self-government to 5 of these islands (exception, Montserrat) and island groups in 1967-1969; each became an Associated State, with Britain controlling foreign affairs and defense.

Anguilla declared its independence from St. Kitts June 16, 1967. A 1976 constitution provides for an autonomous elected government. Area 35 sq. mi., pop. 6,500.

The three **Cayman Islands,** a dependency, lie S of Cuba, NW of Jamaica. Pop. is 16,000 (1979), most of it on Grand Cayman. It is a free port; in the 1970s Grand Cayman became a tax-free refuge for foreign funds and branches of many Western banks were opened there. Total area 93 sq. mi., capital Georgetown.

The **Turks and Caicos Islands,** at the SE end of the Bahama chain, are a separate possession. There are about 30 islands, only 6 inhabited, 1979 pop. est. 7,000, area 166 sq. mi., capital Grand Turk. Salt, crayfish and conch shells are the main exports.

Bermuda

Bermuda is a British dependency governed by a royal governor and an Assembly, dating from 1620, the oldest legislative body among British dependencies. Capital is Hamilton.

It is a group of 360 small islands of coral formation, 20 inhabited, comprising 21 sq. mi. in the western Atlantic, 580 mi. E of North Carolina. Pop., 1980 cen., was 54,893 (about 61% of African descent). Density is high.

The police commissioner was shot to death in 1972. Gov. Richard Sharples and an aide were slain by gunmen in 1973. Racial hostility increased with the 1977 execution of two blacks convicted of the killings.

The U.S. has air and naval bases under long-term lease, and a NASA tracking station

Bermuda boasts many resort hotels, serving over 500,000 visitors a year. The government raises most revenue from import duties. Exports: lilies, drugs, cosmetics.

Belize

Belize (formerly called British Honduras) is in Central America facing the Caribbean to the E, with Mexico on the N and Guatemala on the W. Pop. (1980 cen.) 144,657, area 8,866 sq. mi., capital Belmopan.

Internal self-government was granted by Britain in 1964.

The area has long been claimed by Guatemala, but also was promised independence by Britain. In Apr. 1968, a mediator proposed that British Honduras be made independent but have close association with Guatemala. The proposal was rejected by Belize. Britain moved several hundred troops to Belize in 1977 to counter Guatemalan "bellicosity."

Main export is sugar, along with citrus fruits, mahogany and other hardwoods, chicle, seafood.

South Atlantic

Falkland Islands and Dependencies, a British dependency, lies 300 mi. E of the Strait of Magellan at the southern end of South America.

The Falklands or Islas Malvinas include about 200 islands, area 4,700 sq. mi., pop. (1977 est.) 2,000. Sheep-grazing is the main industry; wool is the principal export. There are indications of large oil and gas deposits. The islands are also claimed by Argentina though 97% of inhabitants are of British origin. **South Georgia,** area 1,450 sq. mi., and the uninhabited **South Sandwich Is.** are dependencies of the Falklands.

British Antarctic Territory, south of 60° S lat., was made a separate colony in 1962 and comprises mainly the **South Shetland Islands,** the **South Orkneys** and **Graham's Land.** A chain of meteorological stations is maintained.

St. Helena, an island 1,200 mi. off the W coast of Africa and 1,800 E of South America, has 47 sq. mi. and est. pop., 1979 of 6,000. Flax, lace and rope making are the chief industries. After Napoleon Bonaparte was defeated at Waterloo the Allies exiled him to St. Helena, where he lived from Oct. 16, 1815, to his death, May 5, 1821. Capital is Jamestown.

Tristan da Cunha is the principal of a group of islands of volcanic origin, total area 40 sq. mi., half way between the Cape of Good Hope and South America. A volcanic peak 6,760 ft. high erupted in 1961. The 262 inhabitants were removed to England, but most returned in 1963. The islands are dependencies of St. Helena.

Ascension is an island of volcanic origin, 34 sq. mi. in area, 700 mi. NW of St. Helena, through which it is administered. It is a communications relay center for Britain, and has a U.S. satellite tracking center. Est. pop., 1976, was 1,179, half of them communications workers. The island is noted for sea turtles.

Asia and Indian Ocean

Brunei was between 1888 and 1971 a protected sultanate. It is on the N side of the Island of Borneo, between the Malaysian states of Sarawak and Sabah. Its area is 2,226 sq. mi., the size of Delaware, with population (1979 est.) 213,000, two-thirds Malay and indigenous races, one-third Chinese descent.

A 1959 constitution was amended, 1965, to provide for general elections to the Legislative Council. There is a sultan and a British high commissioner. A 1971 agreement gave Brunei full self-government, with Britain responsible for foreign affairs. Independence was set for 1983.

Brunei's rich Seria oilfield provides tax revenues well in excess of expenditures. Rubber is also exported.

Hong Kong is a Crown Colony at the mouth of the Canton R. in China, 90 mi. S of Canton. Its nucleus is Hong Kong Is., 35½ sq. mi., acquired from China 1841, on which is located Victoria, the capital. Opposite is Kowloon Peninsula, 3 sq. mi. and Stonecutters is., ¼ sq. mi., added, 1860. An additional 355 sq. mi. known as the New Territories, a mainland area and islands, were leased from China, 1898, for 99 years. Total area of the colony is 398 sq. mi., with a population, 1979 est., of 4,900,000 including fewer than 20,000 British. From 1949 to 1962 Hong Kong absorbed more than a million refugees from the mainland. The flow of refugees continued into the 1970s.

Hong Kong harbor was long an important British naval station and one of the world's great trans-shipment ports. Britain announced in 1975 a reduction of its garrison to 6,400 men.

Principal industries are textiles and apparel (39% of exports); also tourism, shipbuilding, iron and steel, fishing, cement, and small manufactures. Total exports exceeded $11 billion in 1978.

Spinning mills, among the best in the world, and low wages compete with textiles elsewhere and have resulted in the protective measures in some countries. Hong Kong also has a booming electronics industry.

British Indian Ocean Territory was formed Nov. 1965, embracing islands formerly dependencies of Mauritius or Seychelles: the Chagos Archipelago (including Diego Garcia), Aldabra, Farquhar and Des Roches. The latter 3 were transferred to Seychelles, which became independent in 1976. Area 22 sq mi.; pop. 1977 est. 2,000. In 1973 the U. S. Navy established a communications station on Diego Garcia and in 1975 began constructing a naval base.

Pacific Ocean

Pitcairn Island is in the Pacific, halfway between South America and Australia. The island was discovered in 1767 by Carteret but was not inhabited until 23 years later when the mutineers of the Bounty landed there. The area is 18 sq. mi. and pop. 1978, was 68. It is a British colony and is administered by a British Representative in New Zealand and a local Council. The uninhabited islands of **Henderson, Ducie** and **Oeno** are in the Pitcairn group.

The **Gilbert Islands** became independent in 1979 (*see Index for Kiribati*).

Tuvalu, formerly called the Ellice Islands, became independent in 1978 (*see Index*).

United States of America

People: Population (1980 cen.): 226,504,825. **Age distrib.**(%): 0–14: 23.9; 15–59: 61.0; 60+: 15.2. **Pop. density:** 62.43 per sq. mi. **Urban** (1970): 73.5%. **Cities** (1975 est.): New York 7,481,613; Chicago 3,099,391; Los Angeles 2,727,399; Philadelphia 1,815,808; Houston 1,397,562; Detroit 1,335,085.

Armed forces: regulars 2,022,000; reserves 797,000.

Economy: Minerals: Coal, copper, lead, molybdenum, phosphates, uranium, bauxite, gold, iron, mercury, nickel, potash, silver, tungsten, zinc. **Crude oil reserves** (1980): 26.50 bln. bbls. **Per capita arable land:** 2.1 acres. **Meat prod.** (1978): beef: 11.33 mln. metric tons; pork: 6.13 mln. metric tons; lamb: 155,000 metric tons. **Fish catch** (1977): 3.1 mln. metric tons. **Electricity prod.** (1978): 2,211 bln. kwh. **Crude steel prod.** (1979): 123.3 mln. metric tons.

Finance: Gross domestic product (1980): $2,576.6 bln. **Per capita income** (1978): $8,612. **Imports** (1980): $252.99 bln.; partners (1978): Can. 19%, Jap. 14%, W. Ger. 6%. **Exports** (1980): $220.71 bln.; partners (1978): Can. 20%, Jap. 9%, W. Ger. 5%, UK 5%. **Tourists** (1977): 18,609,800; receipts $6.16 bln. **National budget** (1980): $533.04 bln. revenues; $600.86 bln. expenditures and lending. **International reserves less gold** (Apr. 1981): $18.54 bln. **Gold:** 264.2 mln. oz t. **Consumer prices** (change in 1980): 13.5%.

Transport: Railway traffic (1978): 16.5 bln. passenger-km; 1,252.8 bln. net ton-km. **Motor vehicles:** in use (1976): 109.0 mln. passenger cars, 26.15 mln. comm. vehicles; manuf. (1978): 9.17 mln. passenger cars; 3.71 mln. comm. vehicles. **Civil aviation:** 359,628 mln. passenger-km (1978); 10,080 mln. freight ton-km (1978).

Communications: Television sets: 121.1 mln. in use (1975), 7.86 mln. manuf. (1977). **Radios:** 402 mln. in use (1975), 12.49 mln. manuf. (1977). **Telephones in use** (1978): 162,076,000. **Daily newspaper circ.** (1977): 62,159,000; 287 per 1,000 pop.

Health: Life expectancy at birth (1975): 68.7 male; 76.5 female. **Births** (per 1,000 pop. 1980): 16.2. **Deaths** (per 1,000 pop. 1980): 8.9. **Natural increase** (1977): .7%. **Hospital beds** (per 100,000 pop. 1977): 630. **Physicians** (per 100,000 pop. 1977): 176. **Infant mortality** (per 1,000 live births 1977): 14.0. **Education** (1977): **Literacy:** 99%. **Pop. 5-19:** in school: 85%,

teachers per 1,000: 43. **PQLI:** 95.

Upper Volta

Republic of Upper Volta

People: Population (1980 est.): 6,910,000. **Pop. density:** 65.27 per sq. mi. **Ethnic groups:** Voltaic groups (Mossi, Bobo), Mande. **Languages:** French (official), More, Sudanic tribal languages. **Religions:** Moslems 20%, Roman Catholics 5%, others.

Geography: Area: 105,869 sq. mi., the size of Colorado. **Location:** In W. Africa, S of the Sahara. **Neighbors:** Mali on NW, Niger on NE, Benin, Togo, Ghana, Ivory Coast on S. **Topography:** Landlocked Upper Volta is in the savannah region of W. Africa. The N is arid, hot, and thinly populated. **Capital:** Ouagadougou. **Cities** (1978): Ouagadougou 200,000; Bobo-Dioulasso 150,000; Koudougou 60,000.

Government: Head of state: Pres. Aboubacar Sangoule Lamizana; b. 1916; in office: Jan. 3, 1966. **Head of government:** Prime Min. Joseph Conombo; in office: July 16, 1978. **Local divisions:** 10 departments. **Armed forces:** regulars 4,070; para-military 1,850.

Economy: Chief crops: Cotton, rice, peanuts, karite, grain, corn. **Minerals:** Manganese, gold, diamonds. **Per capita arable land:** 2.1 acres. **Meat prod.** (1978): beef: 22,000 metric tons; lamb: 12,000 metric tons. **Electricity prod.** (1977): 70.00 mln. kwh. **Labor force:** 95% agric.; 5% industry, serv., commerce.

Finance: Currency: CFA franc (Apr. 1981: 262.70 = $1 US). **Gross domestic product** (1976 est.): $500 mln. **Per capita income** (1976): $75. **Imports** (1979): $300 mln.; partners (1977): Fr. 45%, Ivory Coast 13%, U.S. 9%, W. Ger. 6%. **Exports** (1979): $76 mln.; partners (1977): Ivory Coast 32%, Den. 22%, Neth. 11%, Fr. 7%. **Tourists** (1977): 23,000; receipts (1975): $2 mln. **International reserves less gold** (Jan. 1981): $65.8 mln. **Gold:** 11,000 oz t. **Consumer prices** (change in 1980): 12.2%.

Transport: Motor vehicles: in use (1975): 9,500 passenger cars, 10,100 comm. vehicles.

Communications: Television sets: 6,000 in use (1975). **Radios:** 105,000 in use (1976). **Telephones in use** (1978): 3,564. **Daily newspaper circ.** (1976): 1,500; 0.2 per 1,000 pop.

Health: Life expectancy at birth (1961): 32.1 male; 31.1 female. **Births** (per 1,000 pop. 1975): 47.9. **Deaths** (per 1,000 pop. 1975): 23.2. **Natural increase** (1975): 2.5%. **Hospital beds** (per 100,000 pop. 1977): 57. **Physicians** (per 100,000 pop. 1977): 3. **Infant mortality** (per 1,000 live births 1975): 182. **Education** (1977): **Literacy:** 7%. **Pop. 5-19:** in school: 7%, teachers per 1,000: 2. **PQLI:** 17.

The Mossi tribe entered the area in the 11th to 13th centuries. Their kingdoms ruled until defeated by the Mali and Songhai empires.

French control came by 1896, but Upper Volta was not finally established as a separate territory until 1947. Full independence came Aug. 5, 1960, and a pro-French government was elected. A 1966 coup established the current regime. Free multi-party presidential and parliamentary elections were held in 1978.

Several hundred thousand farm workers migrate each year to Ivory Coast and Ghana. A long drought brought famine in 1973-74; renewed drought occurred in 1977-78.

Uruguay

Oriental Republic of Uruguay

People: Population (1979 est.): 2,910,000. **Age distrib.** (%): 0–14: 27.0; 15–59: 58.7; 60+: 14.3. **Pop. density:** 41.72 per sq. mi. **Urban** (1975): 83.0%. **Ethnic groups:** Caucasians (Iberians, Italians) 85-90%, mestizos 5-10%, mulatto and Negro 3-5%. **Languages:** Spanish. **Religions:** Roman Catholics 66%, Jews 2%, Protestants 2%, other 30%.

Geography: Area: 68,548 sq. mi., the size of Washington State. **Location:** In southern S. America, on the Atlantic O. **Neighbors:** Argentina on W, Brazil on N. **Topography:** Uruguay is composed of rolling, grassy plains and hills, well-watered by rivers flowing W to Uruguay R. **Capital:** Montevideo. **Cities** (1979 est.): Montevideo 1,500,000.

Government: Head of state: Pres. Aparicio Mendez Manfredini; b. Aug. 24, 1904; in office: Sept. 1, 1976. **Local divisions:** 19 departments. **Armed forces:** regulars 27,500; para-military 2,200.

Economy: Industries: Meat-packing, metals, textiles, wine, cement, oil products. **Chief crops:** Corn, wheat, citrus fruits, rice, oats, linseed. **Per capita arable land:** 1.6 acres. **Meat prod.** (1978): beef: 354,000 metric tons; pork: 16,000 metric tons; lamb: 35,000 metric tons. **Fish catch** (1977): 48,400 metric tons. **Electricity prod.** (1977): 3.04 bln. kwh. **Crude steel prod.** (1979): 14,000 metric tons. **Labor force** 8% agric.; 34% ind. and commerce; 10% serv.; 25% gvt.

Finance: Currency: New Peso (Mar. 1981: 10.44 = $1 US). **Gross domestic product** (1980): $9.86 bln. **Per capita income** (1978): $1,710. **Imports** (1977): $164 bln.; partners (1977): Braz. 13%, Arg. 12%, U.S. 10%, Iraq 9%. **Exports** (1980): $1.06 bln.; partners (1977): Braz. 19%, U.S. 17%, W. Ger. 12%, Neth. 7%. **Tourists** (1976): 491,700; receipts (1977): $180 mln. **National budget** (1979): $1.30 bln. revenues; $1.24 bln. expenditures. **International reserves less gold** (Feb. 1981): $501 mln. **Gold:** 3.95 mln. oz t. **Consumer prices** (change in 1980): 63.5%.

Transport: Railway traffic (1977): 389 mln. passenger-km; 307 mln. net ton-km. **Motor vehicles:** in use (1976): 127,100 passenger cars, 104,200 comm. vehicles. **Civil aviation:** 74 mln. passenger-km (1977); 288,000 freight ton-km (1977). **Chief ports:** Montevideo.

Communications: Television sets: 355,000 in use (1976). **Radios:** 1.6 mln. in use (1976). **Telephones in use** (1978): 268,026.

Health: Life expectancy at birth (1964): 65.51 male; 71.56 female. **Births** (per 1,000 pop. 1976): 20.9. **Deaths** (per 1,000 pop. 1976): 10.2. **Natural increase** (1976): 1.1%. **Hospital beds** (per 100,000 pop. 1977): 418. **Physicians:** (per 100,000 pop. 1977): 139. **Infant mortality** (per 1,000 live births 1976): 45.9.

Education (1977): **Literacy:** 94%. **Pop. 5-19:** in school: 60%; teachers per 1,000: 34. **PQLI:** 87.

Spanish settlers did not begin replacing the indigenous Charrua Indians until 1624. Portuguese from Brazil arrived later, but Uruguay was attached to the Spanish Viceroyalty of Rio de la Plata in the 18th century. Rebels fought against Spain beginning in 1810. An independent republic was declared Aug. 25, 1825.

Liberal governments adopted socialist measures as far back as 1911. More than a third of the workers are employed by the state, which owns the power, telephone, railroad, cement, oil-refining and other industries. Social welfare programs are among the most advanced in the world.

Uruguay's standard of living was one of the highest in South America, and political and labor conditions among the freest. Economic stagnation, inflation, plus floods, drought in 1967 and a general strike in 1968 brought attempts by the government to strengthen the economy through a series of devaluations of the peso and wage and price controls. But inflation continued. The cost of living rose 1,200% between 1968 and 1976.

Tupamaros, leftist guerrillas drawn from the upper classes, increased terrorist actions in 1970; a U.S. police adviser was slain in Aug. In 1971 the guerrillas kidnaped and, after 8 months, freed the British ambassador. Violence continued and in Feb. 1973 Pres. Juan Maria Bordaberry agreed to military control of his administration. In June he abolished Congress and set up a Council of State in its place. By 1974 the military had apparently defeated the Tupamaros, using severe repressive measures. The economic decline continued. Bordaberry was removed by the military in a 1976 coup. Elections were promised for 1981.

Vanuatu

Republic of Vanuatu

People: Population (Jan. 1979): 112,600. **Population density:** 19.58 per sq. mi. **Ethnic groups:** Melanesian, European, Polynesian, Micronesian. **Languages:** Bislama (national), French and English both official. **Religions:** Presbyterian, Anglican, Roman Catholicism, animism.

Geography: Area: 5,750 sq. mi. **Location:** SW Pacific, 1,200 mi NE of Brisbane, Australia. **Topography:** dense forest with narrow coastal strips of cultivated land. **Capital:** Vila. **Cities:** Santo, Farari, Lenakel.

Government: Head of state: Pres. Ati George Sokomanu; in office: July 30, 1980. **Head of gov't:** Prime Min. Father Walter Lini; in office: July 30, 1980.

Economy: Industries: Fish-freezing, meat canneries, tourism. **Chief crops:** Copra, cocoa, coffee. **Minerals:** Manganese. **Other resources:** Forests, cattle.

Finance: Currency: Australian dollar and Vanuatu franc (Sept. 22, 1979: VFr 64 = $1 US). **Imports** (1979): $40 mln.; partners (1977): Aus. 30%, Fr. 25%, Japan 8%. **Exports** (1979): $50 mln.; partners (1977): Fr. 43%, U.S. 28%, Japan 15%.

Education: Education not compulsory, but 85-90% of children of primary school age—approximately 22,500 pupils in 1977—attend primary schools.

The Anglo-French condominium of the New Hebrides, administered jointly by France and Great Britain since 1906, became the independent Republic of Vanuatu on July 30, 1980.

Vatican

State of Vatican City

People: Population (1979 est.): 1,000. **Ethnic groups:** Italians, Swiss. **Languages:** Italian, Latin. **Religion:** Roman Catholicism.

Geography: Area: 108.7 acres. **Location:** In Rome, Italy. **Neighbors:** Completely surrounded by Italy. **Currency:** Lira.

The popes for many centuries, with brief interruptions, held temporal sovereignty over mid-Italy (the so-called Papal States), comprising an area of some 16,000 sq. mi., with a population in the 19th century of more than 3 million. This territory was incorporated in the new Kingdom of Italy, the sovereignty of the pope being confined to the palaces of the Vatican and the Lateran in Rome and the villa of Castel Gandolfo, by an Italian law, May 13, 1871. This law also guaranteed to the pope and his successors a yearly indemnity of over $620,000. The allowance, however, remained unclaimed.

A Treaty of Conciliation, a concordat and a financial convention were signed Feb. 11, 1929, by Cardinal Gasparri and Premier Mussolini. The documents established the independent state of Vatican City, and gave the Catholic religion special status in Italy. The treaty (Lateran Agreement) was made part of the Constitution of Italy (Article 7) in 1947. Italy and the Vatican reached preliminary agreement in 1976 on revisions of the concordat, that would eliminate Roman Catholicism as the state religion and end required religious education in Italian schools.

Vatican City includes St. Peter's, the Vatican Palace and Museum covering over 13 acres, the Vatican gardens, and neighboring buildings between Viale Vaticano and the Church. Thirteen buildings in Rome, outside the boundaries, enjoy extraterritorial rights; these buildings house congregations or officers necessary for the administration of the Holy See.

The legal system is based on the code of canon law, the apostolic constitutions and the laws especially promulgated for the Vatican City by the pope. The Secretariat of State represents the Holy See in its diplomatic relations. By the Treaty of Conciliation the pope is pledged to a perpetual neutrality unless his mediation is specifically requested. This, however, does not prevent the defense of the Church whenever it is persecuted. A total of 84 nations maintain diplomatic representatives in Vatican City. The U.S. does not have an official ambassador.

The present sovereign of the State of Vatican City is the Supreme Pontiff John Paul II, Karol Wojtyla, born in Wadowice, Poland, May 18, 1920, elected Oct. 16, 1978 (the first non-Italian to be elected pope in 456 years), in succession to John Paul I, Albino Luciani, who died Sept. 28, 1978, after serving as pope only 34 days.

Venezuela

Republic of Venezuela

People: Population (1979 est.): 14,529,000. **Age distrib.** (%): 0–14: 42.8; 15–59: 52.4; 60+: 4.8. **Pop. density:** 37.26 per sq. mi. **Urban** (1977): 75.1%. **Ethnic groups:** Mestizo 70%, white (Spanish, Portuguese, Italian) 20%, Negro 8%, Indian 2%. **Languages:** Spanish (official), Indian languages 2%. **Religions:** Roman Catholics 96%, Protestants 2%.

Geography: Area: 352,143 sq. mi., more than twice the size of California. **Location:** On the Caribbean coast of S. America. **Neighbors:** Colombia on W, Brazil on S, Guyana on E. **Topography:** Flat coastal plain and Orinoco Delta are bordered by Andes Mtns. and hills. Plains, called llanos, extend between mountains and Orinoco. Guyana Highlands and plains are S of Orinoco, which stretches 1,700 mi. and drains 80% of Venezuela. **Capital:** Caracas. **Cities** (1978): Caracas 2,800,000; Maracaibo 845,000; Barquisimeto 459,000; Valencia 471,000. **Government: Head of state:** Pres. Luis Herrera Campins; b. May 4, 1925; in office: Mar. 12, 1979. **Local divisions:** 20 states, 2 federal territories, federal district. **Armed forces:** regulars 41,500; para-military 10,000.

    Economy: Industries: Steel, oil products, textiles, containers, tobacco, paper, tires, shoes. **Chief crops:** Coffee, cocoa, fruits, sugar. **Minerals:** Oil (5th largest producer), iron (extensive reserves and production), gold, copper, salt, coal, nickel, manganese, asbestos, diamonds, mica. **Crude oil reserves** (1980): 17.87 bln. bbls. **Per capita arable land:** 0.9 acres. **Meat prod.** (1978): beef: 282,000 metric tons; pork: 91,000 metric tons; lamb: 10,000 metric tons. **Fish catch** (1977): 152,200 metric tons. **Electricity prod.** (1977): 23.05 bln. kwh. **Crude steel prod.** (1979): 1.5 mln. metric tons. **Labor force:** 20% agric.; 20% ind. and commerce; 54% petroleum, mining.

    Finance: Currency: Bolivar (Apr. 1981: 4.29 = $1 US). **Gross domestic product** (1979): $48.97 bln. **Per capita income** (1978):. $2,772. **Imports** (1980): $11.39 bln.; partners (1977): U.S. 39%, W. Ger. 12%, Jap. 11%, It. 6%. **Exports** (1980): $18.77 bln.; partners (1977): U.S. 36%, Neth. Ant. 18%, Can. 12%. **Tourists** (1977): 652,400; receipts: $261 mln. **National budget** (1979): $11.65 bln. revenues; $10.73 bln. expenditures. **International reserves less gold** (Apr. 1981): $8.48 bln. **Gold:** 11.46 mln. oz t. **Consumer prices** (change in 1980): 21.6%.

    Transport: Railway traffic (1971): 42 mln. passenger-km; 15 mln. net ton-km. **Motor vehicles:** in use (1975): 955,200 passenger cars, 369,400 comm. vehicles; assembled (1976): 97,000 passenger cars; 66,000 comm. vehicles. **Civil aviation:** 3,012 mln. passenger-km (1977); 118 mln. freight ton-km (1977). **Chief ports:** Maracaibo, La Guaira, Puerto Cabello.

    Communications: Television sets: 1.43 mln. in use (1976), 86,000 manuf. (1972). **Radios:** 5.03 mln. in use (1976), 74,000 manuf. (1972). **Telephones in use** (1978): 847,318. **Daily newspaper circ.** (1977): 2,263,000; 178 per 1,000 pop.

    Health: Life expectancy at birth (1961): 66.41 male; 66.41 female. **Births** (per 1,000 pop. 1975): 36.2. **Deaths** (per 1,000 pop. 1975): 7.1. **Natural increase** (1975): 2.9%. **Hospital beds** (per 100,000 pop. 1977): 292. **Physicians** (per 100,000 pop. 1977): 107. **Infant mortality** (per 1,000 live births 1977): 40.4.

    Education (1977): **Literacy:** 82%. **Pop. 5-19:** in school: 58%, teachers per 1,000: 19. **PQLI:** 79.

    Columbus first set foot on the South American continent on the peninsula of Paria, Aug. 1498. Alonso de Ojeda, 1499, found Lake Maracaibo, called the land Venezuela, or Little Venice, because natives had houses on stilts. Venezuela was under Spanish domination until 1821. The republic was formed after secession from the Colombian Federation in 1830.

    Military strongmen ruled Venezuela for most of the 20th century. They promoted the oil industry; some social reforms were implemented. Since 1959, the country has enjoyed progressive, democratically-elected governments.

    Venezuela helped found the Organization of Petroleum Exporting States (OPEC). The government, Jan. 1, 1976, nationalized the oil industry with compensation. Development has begun of the Orinoco tar belt, believed to contain the world's largest oil reserves. Oil production rose 11% in 1979, as a result of the decline in Iranian oil exports.

    Construction is booming, including a new $3.8 billion city, Ciudad Guyana, 300 mi. SE of Caracas. Oil profits help finance the extensive industrial development. Government efforts at income redistribution were thwarted by inflation in 1974-5, but public works and welfare programs in slum areas have improved.

    Foreign investment is being encouraged.

Vietnam

Socialist Republic of Vietnam

People: Population (1980 est.): 52,300,000. **Pop. density:** 413.65 per sq. mi. **Ethnic groups:** Vietnamese 85–90%, Chinese 2%, remainder Muong, Thai, Meo, Khmer, Man, Cham. **Languages:** Vietnamese (official), French, Chinese, English, Khmer. **Religions:** Buddhists, Confucians, and Taoists most numerous, Roman Catholics, animists, Muslims, Protestants.

    Geography: Area: 126,436 sq. mi., the size of New Mexico. **Location:** On the E coast of the Indochinese Peninsula in SE Asia. **Neighbors:** China on N, Laos, Cambodia on W. **Topography:** Vietnam is long and narrow, with a 1,400-mi. coast. About 24% of country is readily arable, including the densely settled Red R. valley in the N, narrow coastal plains in center, and the wide, often marshy Mekong R. Delta in the S. The rest consists of semi-arid plateaus and barren mountains, with some stretches of tropical rain forest. **Capital:** Hanoi. **Cities** (1976 cen.): Ho Chi Minh City 1,845,000; Haiphong 1,515,000; Hanoi 597,000; Da Nang, Hue, Nha Trang, Vinh.

    Government: Head of state: Acting Pres. Nguyen Hau Tho; in office: Mar. 30, 1980. **Head of government:** Prime Min. Pham Van Dong; b. 1906; in office: Sept. 20, 1955. **Head of Communist Party:** First Sec. Le Duan; b. 1907; in office: Sept. 10, 1960. **Local divisions:** 36 provinces. **Armed forces:** regulars 1,023,000; para-military 1,570,000.

    Economy: Industries: Food processing, textiles, machine building, mining, cement, chemical fertilizers, glass, tires. **Chief crops:** Rice, rubber, fruits and vegetables, corn, manioc, sugarcane, fish. **Minerals:** Phosphates, coal, iron, manganese, bauxite, apatite, chromate. **Other resources:** Forests. **Per capita arable land:** 0.2 acres. **Meat prod.** (1978): beef: 93,000 metric tons; pork: 457,000 metric tons. **Fish catch** (1977): 1 mln. metric tons. **Electricity prod.** (1975): 1.32 bln. kwh. **Labor force:** 70% agric.; 8% ind. and commerce.

    Finance: Currency: Dong (Sept. 1979: 2.18 = $1 US). **Gross domestic product** (1978): $7.6 mln. **Per capita income** (1978): $150. **Imports** (1978 est.): $1.5 bln.; partners: USSR 30%, Jap. 16%, Fr. 7%, It. 5%. **Exports** (1978 est.): $416 mln.; partners: USSR 54%, Jap. 11%.

    Transport: Railway traffic (1973): 170 mln. passenger-km; 1.00 mln. net ton-km. **Motor vehicles:** in use (S. Vietnam only) (1974): 70,000 passenger cars, 100,000 comm. vehicles. **Chief ports:** Ho Chi Minh City, Haiphong, Da Nang, Cam Ranh.

    Communications: Radios: 2.6 in use (1974), 87,000 manuf. (South only) (1973). **Daily newspaper circ.** (1977): 250,000; 5 per 1,000 pop.

    Health: Life expectancy at birth (1975): 43.2 male; 46.0 female. **Births** (per 1,000 pop. 1975): 41.0. **Deaths** (per 1,000 pop. 1975): 19.8. **Natural increase** (1975): 2.12%. **Hospital beds** (per 100,000 pop. 1977): 343. **Physicians** (per 100,000 pop. 1977): 18.

    Education (1977): **Literacy:** 75%. **Pop. 5-19:** in school: 62%, teachers per 1,000: 24. **PQLI:** 59.

    Vietnam's recorded history began in Tonkin before the Christian era. Settled by Viets from central China, Vietnam was held by China, 111 BC-939 AD, and was a vassal state during subsequent periods. Vietnam defeated the armies of Kublai Khan, 1288. Conquest by France began in 1858 and ended in 1884 with the protectorates of Tonkin and Annam in the N. and the colony of Cochin-China in the S.

    In 1940 Vietnam was occupied by Japan; nationalist aims gathered force. A number of groups formed the Vietminh (Independence) League, headed by Ho Chi Minh, communist guerrilla leader. In Aug. 1945 the Vietminh forced out Bao Dai, former emperor of Annam, head of a Japan-sponsored regime. France, seeking to reestablish colonial control, battled communist and nationalist forces, 1946-1954, and was finally defeated at Dienbienphu, May 8, 1954. Meanwhile, on July 1, 1949, Bao Dai had formed a State of Vietnam, with himself as chief of state, with French approval. Communist China backed Ho Chi Minh.

    A cease-fire accord signed in Geneva July 21, 1954, divided Vietnam along the Ben Hai R. It provided for a buffer zone, withdrawal of French troops from the North and elections to determine the country's future. Under the agreement the communists gained control of territory north of the 17th parallel, 22 provinces with area of 62,000 sq. mi. and 13 million pop., with its capital at Hanoi and Ho Chi Minh as president. South Vietnam came to comprise the 39 southern provinces with approx. area of 65,000 sq. mi. and pop. of 12 million. Some 900,000 North Vietnamese fled to South Vietnam. Neither South Vietnam nor the U.S. signed the agreement.

    On Oct. 26, 1955, Ngo Dinh Diem, premier of the interim government of South Vietnam, proclaimed the Republic of Vietnam and became its first president.

    The Democratic Republic of Vietnam, established in the North, adopted a constitution Dec. 31, 1959, based on communist principles and calling for reunification of all Vietnam. Pres. Ho Chi Minh, re-elected July 15, 1960, by unanimous vote of the National Assembly, had held office since 1945. He died Sept. 3, 1969.

North Vietnam sought to take over South Vietnam beginning in 1954. Fighting persisted from 1956, with the communist Vietcong, aided by North Vietnam, pressing war in the South and South Vietnam receiving U.S. aid. Northern aid to Vietcong guerrillas was intensified in 1959, and large-scale troop infiltration began in 1964, with Russian and Chinese arms assistance. Large Northern forces were stationed in border areas of Laos and Cambodia.

A serious political conflict arose in the South in 1963 when Buddhists denounced authoritarianism and brutality. This paved the way for a military coup Nov. 1-2, 1963, which overthrew Diem. Several military coups followed. In elections Sept. 3, 1967, Chief of State Nguyen Van Thieu was chosen president.

In 1964, the U.S. began air strikes against North Vietnam. Beginning in 1965, the raids were stepped up and U.S. troops became combatants. U.S. troop strength in Vietnam, which reached a high of 543,400 in Apr. 1969, was ordered reduced by U.S. President Nixon in a series of withdrawals, beginning in June 1969. U.S. bombings were resumed in 1972-73.

A ceasefire agreement was signed in Paris Jan. 27, 1973 (EST), by the U.S., North and South Vietnam, and the Vietcong. It was never implemented. U.S. aid was curbed in 1974 by the U.S. Congress. Heavy fighting continued for two years throughout Indochina.

Massive numbers of North Vietnamese troops, aided by tanks, launched attacks against remaining government outposts in the Central Highlands in the first months of 1975. Government retreats turned into a rout, and the Saigon regime surrendered April 30. Conquest of the country was effectively completed within days.

A Provisional Revolutionary Government assumed control, aided by officials and technicians from Hanoi, and first steps were taken to transform society along communist lines. All businesses and farms were to be collectivized by 1979.

The U.S. accepted over 165,000 Vietnamese fleeing the new regime, while scores of thousands more sought refuge in other countries.

The war's toll included — Combat deaths: U.S. 46,079; South Vietnam over 200,000; other allied forces 5,225. Civilian casualties were over a million. Displaced war refugees in South Vietnam totaled over 6.5 million.

After the fighting ended, 8 Northern divisions remained stationed in the South, while Southern forces of over 900,000 were demobilized, adding to severe economic problems. Over 1 million urban residents and 260,000 Montagnards were resettled in the countryside by 1978, the first of 10 million scheduled for forced resettlement. An unknown number were sent to long-term re-education camps, including thousands of adherents of the Hoa Hao sect. A 1977 crop failure caused food shortages; the south remained more prosperous than the north.

The first National Assembly of both parts of the country met June 24, 1976. The country was officially reunited July 2, 1976. The Northern capital, flag, anthem, emblem, and currency were applied to the new state. Nearly all major government posts went to officials of the former Northern government, and thousands of Northern officials were sent south.

Heavy fighting with Cambodia took place, 1977-80, amid mutual charges of aggression and atrocities against civilians. Increasing numbers of Vietnamese civilians, ethnic Chinese, escaped the country, via the sea, or the overland route across Cambodia.

Relations with China soured as 140,000 ethnic Chinese left Vietnam charging discrimination; China cut off economic aid. Reacting to Vietnam's invasion of Cambodia, China attacked 4 Vietnamese border provinces, Feb., 1979, instigating heavy fighting.

Yemen

Yemen Arab Republic

People: Population (1980 est.): **5,930,000. Pop. density:** 78.76 per sq. mi. **Ethnic groups:** Arabs, some Negroids. **Languages:** Arabic. **Religions:** Sunni Moslems 50%, Shiite Moslems 50%.

Geography: Area: 75,290 sq. mi., slightly smaller than South

Dakota. **Location:** On the southern Red Sea coast of the Arabian Peninsula. **Neighbors:** Saudi Arabia on NE, South Yemen on S. **Topography:** A sandy coastal strip leads to well-watered fertile mountains in interior. **Capital:** Sanaa. **Cities** (1979): Sanaa 250,000; Taiz, Hodeida.

Government: Head of state: Pres. Ali Abdullah Saleh, b. 1942; in office: July 17, 1978. **Head of government:** Prime Min. Abdul Aziz Abdul-Ghani; in office: Jan. 16, 1975. **Local divisions:** 11 governorates. **Armed forces:** regulars 36,600; paramilitary 20,000.

Economy: Industries: Textiles, cement. **Chief crops:** Wheat, sorghum, qat, fruits, coffee, cotton. **Minerals:** Salt. **Crude oil reserves** (1978): 370 mln. bbls. **Per capita arable land:** 0.7 acres. **Meat prod.** (1978): beef: 14,000 metric tons; lamb: 50,000 metric tons. **Fish catch** (1977): 17,500 metric tons. **Electricity prod.** (1977): 65.00 mln. kwh. **Labor force:** 55% agric.; 4% ind. and commerce; 16% serv.

Finance: Currency: Rial (Apr. 1981: 4.56 = $1 US). **Gross domestic product** (1977-78): $2.7 bln. **Per capita income** (1977-78): $475. **Imports** (1979): $1.49 bln.; partners (1976): Saudi Ar. 12%, Jap. 10%, India 7%, Austral. 7%. **Exports** (1979): $14 mln.; partners (1976): China 33%, S. Yemen 25%, It. 19%, Saudi Ar. 15%. **International reserves less gold** (Mar. 1981): $1.05 bln. **Gold:** 7,000 oz t. **Consumer prices** (change in 1977): 24.8%.

Transport: Chief ports: Al-Hudaydah, Al-Mukha.

Communications: Radios: 90,000 in use (1976). **Daily newspaper circ.** (1970): 56,000; 10 per 1,000 pop.

Health: Life expectancy at birth (1975): 37.3 male; 38.7 female. **Births** (per 1,000 pop. 1975): 48.7. **Deaths** (per 1,000 pop. 1975): 26.3. **Natural increase** (1975): 2.2%. **Hospital beds** (per 100,000 pop. 1977): 58. **Physicians** (per 100,000 pop. 1977): 8.

Education (1977): **Literacy:** 12%. **Pop. 5-19:** in school: 15%, teachers per 1,000: 4. **PQLI:** 27.

Yemen's territory once was part of the ancient kindgom of Sheba, or Saba, a prosperous link in trade between Africa and India. A Biblical reference speaks of its gold, spices and precious stones as gifts borne by the Queen of Sheba to King Solomon.

Yemen became independent in 1918, after years of Ottoman Turkish rule, but remained politically and economically backward. Imam Ahmed ruled 1948-1962. The king was reported assassinated Sept. 26, 1962, and a revolutionary group headed by Brig. Gen. Abdullah al-Salal declared the country to be the Yemen Arab Republic.

The Imam Ahmed's heir, the Imam Mohamad al-Badr, fled to the mountains where tribesmen joined royalist forces; internal warfare between them and the republican forces continued. Egypt sent 70,000 troops to aid the republicans; Saudi Arabia supported the royalists with military aid. About 150,000 people were killed in the fighting.

After its defeat in the June 1967 Arab-Israeli war, Egypt announced it would withdraw its troops from Yemen; the last of them left Nov. 29, 1967; Saudi Arabia said it would stop aiding the royalists.

This was accompanied by a bloodless coup Nov. 5, 1967. Fighting continued between the republican and royalist forces. Saudi Arabia announced in Feb. 1968 it was renewing its aid to the royalists.

In April 1970 hostilities ended with an agreement between Yemen and Saudi Arabia and appointment of several royalists to the Yemen government.

There were border skirmishes with forces of the People's Democratic Republic of Yemen in 1972-73. The U.S. and Yemen in 1972 resumed diplomatic relations, broken by Yemen after the 1967 Arab-Israeli war.

On June 13, 1974, an Army group, led by Col. Ibrahim al-Hamidi, seized the government. Hamidi pursued close Saudi and U.S. ties; he was killed in 1977 by unknown assassins. His successor was murdered, reportedly by pro-South Yemen forces or by the S. Yemen government.

The People's Democratic Republic of Yemen went to war with Yemen on Feb. 24, 1979. Swift Arab mediation led to a ceasefire and a mutual withdrawal of forces, Mar. 19th. An Arab League-sponsored agreement between North and South Yemen on unification of the 2 countries was signed Mar. 29th.

There are periodic droughts. Per capita GNP is among the lowest in the world. A prolonged drought has forced imports of food. The remittances from 400,000 Yemenis living in Arab oil countries provide most of foreign earnings.

South Yemen

People's Democratic Republic of Yemen

People: Population (1979 est.): 1,863,000. **Age distrib. (%):** 0–14: 49.4; 15–59: 45.5; 60+: 5.5. **Pop. density:** 16.67 per sq. mi. **Urban** (1973): 33.3%. **Ethnic groups:** Arabs, 75%, Indians 11%, Somalis 8%, others. **Languages:** Arabic. **Religions:** Muslims (Sunni) 91%, Christians 4%, Hindus 3.5%.

Geography: Area: 111,000 sq. mi., the size of Nevada. **Location:** On the southern coast of the Arabian Peninsula. **Neighbors:** Yemen on W, Saudi Arabia on N, Oman on E. **Topography:** The entire country is very hot and very dry. A sandy coast rises to mountains which give way to desert sands. **Capital:** Aden. **Cities** (1978 est.): Aden 271,590.

Government: Head of state: Pres. Ali Nasir Muhammad al-Hasani; in office: Apr. 21, 1980. **Head of Communist Party:** Sec. Gen. Ali Nasir Muhammad Al-Hasani; in office: April 21, 1980. **Local divisions:** 6 governorates. **Armed forces:** regulars 20,800; para-military 15,000.

Economy: Industries: Transshipment. **Chief crops:** Cotton (main export), grains. **Per capita arable land:** 0.3 acres. **Meat prod.** (1978) lamb: 11,000 metric tons. **Fish catch** (1977): 161,700 metric tons. **Electricity prod.** (1977) 180.00 mln. kwh. **Labor force:** 43.8% agric.; 28% ind. and commerce; 28% serv.

Finance: Currency: Dinar (Apr. 1981: .35 = $1 US). **Gross domestic product** (1977 est.): $550 mln. **Per capita income** (1977): $310. **Imports** (1979) $480 mln.; partners (1976): Kuw. 17%, Jap. 13%, Qatar 9%, UK 7%. **Exports** (1979): $250 mln.; partners (1976): Can. 75%, Jap. 7%. **Tourists** (1976): 18,000; receipts (1974): $4 mln. **National budget** (1977): $101 mln. revenues; $137 mln. expenditures. **International reserves less gold** (Mar. 1981): $249.28 mln. **Gold:** 42,000 oz t. **Consumer prices** (change in 1978): 7.1%.

Transport: Motor vehicles: in use (1976): 11,900 passenger cars, 10,500 comm. vehicles. **Chief ports:** Aden.

Communications: Television sets: 32,000 in use (1976). **Radios:** 100,000 in use (1976). **Daily newspaper circ.** (1976): 4,000; 12 per 1,000 pop.

Health: Life expectancy at birth (1975): 40.6 male; 42.4 female. **Births** (per 1,000 pop. 1975): 48.2 **Deaths** (per 1,000 pop. 1975): 23.1. **Natural increase** (1975): 2.5%. **Hospital beds** (per 100,000 pop. 1977): 154. **Physicians** (per 100,000 pop. 1977): 11. **Infant mortality rate** (per 1,000 live births in 1980): 114.

Education (1977): **Literacy:** 20%. **Pop. 5-19:** in school: 41%, teachers per 1,000: 16. **PQLI:** 32.

Aden, mentioned in the Bible, has been a port for trade in incense, spice and silk between the East and West for 2,000 years. British rule began in 1839. Aden provided Britain with a controlling position at the southern entrance to the Red Sea.

A war for independence began in 1963. The National Liberation Front (NLF) and the Egypt-supported Front for the Liberation of Occupied South Yemen, waged a guerrilla war against the British and local dynastic rulers. The 2 groups vied with each other for control. The NLF won out. Independence came Nov. 30, 1967. In 1969, the left wing of the NLF seized power and inaugurated a thorough nationalization of the economy and regimentation of daily life.

The new government broke off relations with the U.S. and nationalized some foreign firms. Aid has been furnished by the USSR and China, with the USSR supplying most military aid.

In 1972-73 there were border skirmishes with forces of the Yemen Arab Republic. South Yemen aided leftist guerrillas in neighboring Oman. Relations with Saudi Arabia later improved. S. Yemen troops fought in Ethiopia against Eritrean rebels in 1978; 500 Cuban troops and some Soviet facilities were reported in Yemen.

Pres. Salem Robaye Ali, who had tried to improve relations with Yemen, Saudi Arabia, Oman, and the U.S., was executed after a bloody coup June 1978. The new ruling faction was accused by N. Yemen of the murder of N. Yemen's president 2 days earlier. N. Yemen, Egypt, and Saudi Arabia froze ties with S. Yemen in July.

The People's Democratic Republic of Yemen went to war with Yemen on Feb. 24, 1979. Swift Arab mediation led to a cease-fire and a mutual withdrawal of forces, Mar. 19th. An Arab League-sponsored agreement between North and South Yemen on unification of the 2 countries was signed Mar. 29th.

The Port of Aden is the country's most valuable resource, but

with the closing of the Suez Canal after the Arab-Israeli War in June 1967, the port lost much of its business. The canal was reopened in 1975.

Socotra, the largest island in the Arabian Sea, Kamaran, an island in the Red Sea near the coast of North Yemen, and Perim, an island in the strait between the Gulf of Aden and the Red Sea, are controlled by South Yemen.

Yugoslavia

Socialist Federal Republic of Yugoslavia

People: Population (1980 est.): 22,340,000. **Age distrib. (%):** 0–14: 25.6; 15-59: 61.6; 60+: 12.7. **Pop. density:** 226.19 per sq. mi. **Urban** (1971): 38.6%. **Ethnic groups:** Serbs 40%, Croats 22%, Slovenes 8%, Macedonians 6%, Bosnian Moslems 6%, Albanians 2%, Montenegrin Serbs 2%, Hungarians 2%, Turks 1%. **Languages:** Serbo-Croatian, Macedonian, Slovene (all official), Albanian, Hungarian. **Religions:** Orthodox 50%, Roman Catholics 30%, Moslems 10%, Protestants 1%.

Geography: Area: 98,766 sq. mi., the size of Wyoming. **Location:** On the Adriatic coast of the Balkan Peninsula in SE Europe. **Neighbors:** Italy on W, Austria, Hungary on N, Romania, Bulgaria on E, Greece, Albania on S. **Topography:** The Dinaric Alps run parallel to the Adriatic coast, which is lined by offshore islands. Plains stretch across N and E river basins. S and NW are mountainous. **Capital:** Belgrade. **Cities** (1980 est.): Belgrade 1,300,000; Zagreb 700,000; Skopje 440,000; Sarajevo 400,000; Ljubljana 300,000.

Government: Head of state: Pres. Sergej Kraigher; in office: May 15, 1981. **Head of government:** Prime Min. Veselin Djuranovic; b. May 17, 1925; in office: Feb. 4, 1977; **Head of Communist Party:** H. E. Cvijetin Mijatovic; in office: May 15, 1980. **Local divisions:** 6 republics: Serbia, Croatia, Slovenia, Bosnia-Herzegovina, Macedonia, Montenegro; 2 autonomous provinces: Vojvodina, Kosovo. **Armed forces:** regulars 259,000; reserves, para-military 500,000.

Economy: Industries: Steel, chemicals, wood products, cement, textiles, tourism. **Chief crops:** Corn, grains, tobacco, sugar beets. **Minerals:** Antimony, bauxite, lead, mercury, coal, iron, copper, chrome, manganese, zinc, salt. **Crude oil reserves** (1980): 275 mln. bbls. **Per capita arable land:** 0.8 acres. **Meat prod.** (1978): beef: 340,000 metric tons; pork: 656,000 metric tons; lamb: 61,000 metric tons. **Fish catch:** (1977): 60,900 metric tons. **Electricity prod.** (1978): 51.35 bln. kwh. **Crude steel prod.** (1979): 3.5 mln. metric tons. **Labor force:** 48% agric.; 52% ind. and commerce. manuf.

Finance: Currency: Dinar (Apr. 1981: 32.92 = $1 US). **Gross domestic product** (1979 est.): $69 bln. **Per capita income:** $3,109. **Imports** (1980): $15.08 bln.; partners (1978): W. Ger. 18%, USSR 14%, It. 8%, U.S. 6%. **Exports** (1980): $9.10 bln.; partners (1978): USSR 25%, It. 9%, W. Ger. 8%, U.S. 7%. **Tourists** (1977): 5,625,100; receipts: $841 mln. **National budget** (1977): $9.45 bln. revenues; $10.11 bln. expenditures. **International reserves less gold** (Apr. 1981): $1.25 bln. **Gold:** 1.86 mln. oz t. **Consumer prices** change in 1980): 29.9%.

Transport: Railway traffic (1978): 10.4 bln. passenger-km; 23.38 bln. net ton-km. **Motor vehicles:** in use (1977): 1.92 mln. passenger cars, 199,200 comm. vehicles; manuf. (1978): 193,200 passenger cars; 62,400 comm. vehicles. **Civil aviation:** 2,724 mln. passenger-km (1978); 29 mln. freight ton-km (1978). **Chief ports:** Rijeka, Split, Dubrovnik.

Communications: Television sets: 3.5 mln. licensed (1976), 427,000 manuf. (1977). **Radios:** 4.5 mln. licensed (1976), 187,000 manuf. (1977). **Telephones in use** (1978): 1,555,663. **Daily newspaper circ.** (1977): 2,085,000; 96 per 1,000 pop.

Health: Life expectancy at birth (1972): 65.42 male; 70.22 female. **Births** (per 1,000 pop. 1980): 17.0. **Deaths** (per 1,000 pop. 1980): 9.0. **Natural increase** (1978): .9%. **Hospital beds** (per 100,000 pop. 1977): 603. **Physicians** (per 100,000 pop. 1977): 131. **Infant mortality** (per 1,000 live births 1977): 33.6

Education (1977): **Literacy:** 85%. **Pop. 5–19:** in school: 60%, teachers per 1,000: 26. **PQLI:** 84.

Serbia, which had since 1389 been a vassal principality of Turkey, was established as an independent kingdom by the Treaty of Berlin, 1878. Montenegro, independent since 1389, also obtained international recognition in 1878. After the Balkan wars Serbia's boundaries were enlarged by the annexation of Old Serbia and Macedonia, 1913.

When the Austro-Hungarian empire collapsed after World War I, the Kingdom of the Serbs, Croats, and Slovenes was formed from the former provinces of Croatia, Dalmatia, Bosnia, Herzegovina, Slovenia, Voyvodina and the independent state of Montenegro. The name was later changed to Yugoslavia.

Nazi Germany invaded in 1941. Many Yugoslav partisan troops continued to operate. Among these were the Chetniks led by Draja Mikhailovich, who fought other partisans led by Josip Broz, known as Marshal Tito. Tito, backed by the USSR and Britain from 1943, was in control by the time the Germans had been driven from Yugoslavia in 1945. Mikhailovich was executed July 17, 1946, by the Tito regime.

A constituent assembly proclaimed Yugoslavia a republic Nov. 29, 1945. It became a federated republic Jan. 31, 1946, and Marshal Tito, a communist, became head of the government.

The Stalin policy of dictating to all communist nations was rejected by Tito. He accepted economic aid and military equipment from the U.S. and received aid in foreign trade also from France and Great Britain. Tito also supported the liberal government of Czechoslovakia in 1968 before the Russian invasion, but he paid a friendship visit to Moscow in 1972.

A separatist movement among Croatians, 2d to the Serbs in numbers, brought arrests and a change of leaders in the Croatian Republic in Jan. 1972. Violence by extreme Croatian nationalists and fears of Soviet political intervention have led to restrictions on political and intellectual dissent, which had previously been freer than in other East European countries. Serbians, Montenegrins, and Macedonians use Cyrillic, Croatians and Slovenians use Latin letters. Croatia and Slovenia have been the most prosperous republics.

Most industry is socialized and private enterprise is restricted to small-scale production. Since 1952 workers are guaranteed a basic wage and a share in cooperative profits. Management of industrial enterprises is handled by workers' councils. Farmland is 85% privately owned but farms are restricted to 25 acres.

Beginning in 1965, reforms designed to decentralize the administration of economic development and to force industries to produce more efficiently in competition with foreign producers were introduced.

Yugoslavia has developed considerable trade with Western Europe as well as with Eastern Europe. Money earned by Yugoslavs working temporarily in Western Europe helps pay for imports. Unemployment and inflation became serious in 1975. The U.S. agreed in 1977 to expand arms sales.

Pres. Tito died May 4, 1980; with his death, the post as head of the Collective Presidency and also that as head of the League of Communists became a rotating system of succession among the members representing each republic and autonomous province.

Zaire

Republic of Zaire

People: Population (1979 est.): 28,090,000. **Pop. density:** 30.66 per sq. mi. **Urban** (1977): 30.3%. **Ethnic groups:** Mostly Bantus: Luba 18%, Mongo 17%, Kongo 12%, Ruanda 10%, others. **Languages:** French (official), others. **Religions:** Roman Catholics, Protestants, syncretic sects 60%, Moslems 1%, others.

Geography: Area: 905,063 sq. mi., one-fourth the size of the U.S. **Location:** In central Africa. **Neighbors:** Congo on W, Central African Republic, Sudan on N, Uganda, Rwanda, Burundi, Tanzania on E, Zambia, Angola on S. **Topography:** Zaire includes the bulk of the Zaire (Congo) R. Basin. The vast central region is a low-lying plateau covered by rain forest. Mountainous terraces in the W, savannas in the S and SE, grasslands toward the N, and the high Ruwenzori Mtns. on the E surround the central region. A short strip of territory borders the Atlantic O. The Zaire R. is 2,718 mi. long. **Capital:** Kinshasa. **Cities** (1978 est.): Kinshasa 2,008,352; Kananga 601,239; Luluabourg 506,033.

Government: Head of state: Pres. Mobutu Sese Seko; b. Oct. 14, 1930; in office: Nov. 25, 1965. **Head of government:** Nguzu Karl-i-Bond; in office: Aug. 27, 1980. **Local divisions:** 8 regions, capital district. **Armed forces:** regulars 20,500; paramilitary 35,000.

Economy: Chief crops: Coffee, cotton, rice, sugar cane, bananas, plantains, coconuts, manioc, mangoes, tea, cacao, palm oil. **Minerals:** Cobalt (two-thirds of world output), copper, cadmium, gold, silver, tin, germanium, zinc, iron, tungsten, manganese, uranium, radium. **Crude oil reserves** (1980): 135 mln. bbls. **Other resources:** Forests, rubber, ivory. **Per capita arable land:** 0.5 acres. **Meat prod.** (1978): beef: 22,000 metric tons; pork: 29,000 metric tons; lamb: 9,000 metric tons. **Fish catch** (1977): 107,000 metric tons. **Electricity prod.** (1977): 4.10 bln. kwh. **Labor force:** 78% agric.

Finance: Currency: Zaire (Mar. 1981: 3.11 = $1 US). **Gross domestic product** (1979): $6.16 bln. **Per capita income** (1975): $127. **Imports** (1980): $835 mln.; partners (1977): Belg. 20%, U.S. 12%, W. Ger. 11%, Fr. 9%. **Exports** (1980): $1.63 bln.; partners (1977): Belg. 22%, UK 19%, It. 11%, Gr. 9%. **Tourists** (1977): 24,500; receipts (1976): $11 mln. **National budget** (1978): $886 mln. revenues; $1.8 bln. expenditures. **International reserves less gold** (Apr. 1981): $99.10 mln. **Gold:** 319,000 oz t. **Consumer prices** (change in 1980): 36.8%.

Transport: Railway traffic (1976): 467 mln. passenger-km; 2.20 bln. net ton-km. **Motor vehicles:** in use (1974): 84,800 passenger cars, 76,400 comm. vehicles; assembled (1975): 2.11 mln. comm. vehicles. **Civil aviation:** 662 mln. passenger-km (1977); 41 mln. freight ton-km (1977). **Chief ports:** Matadi, Boma.

Communications: Television sets: 7,000 in use (1976). **Radios:** 2.45 mln. in use (1974). **Telephones in use** (1977): 48,000. **Daily newspaper circ.** (1976): 45,000; 9 per 1,000 pop.

Health: Life expectancy at birth (1975): 41.9 male; 45.1 female. **Births** (per 1,000 pop. 1975): 46.8. **Deaths** (per 1,000 pop. 1975): 20.7. **Natural increase** (1975): 2.6%. **Hospital beds** (per 100,000 pop. 1977): 291. **Physicians** (per 100,000 pop. 1977): 2. **Infant mortality** (per 1,000 live births 1975): 104.

Education (1977): Literacy: 30%. **Pop. 5-19:** in school: 45%, teachers per 1,000: 11. **PQLI:** 32.

The earliest inhabitants of Zaire may have been the pygmies, followed by Bantus from the E and Nilotic tribes from the N. The large Bantu Bakongo kingdom ruled much of Zaire and Angola when Portuguese explorers visited in the 15th century.

Leopold II, king of the Belgians, formed an international group to exploit the Congo in 1876. In 1877 Henry M. Stanley explored the Congo and in 1878 the king's group sent him back to organize the region and win over the native chiefs. The Conference of Berlin, 1884-85, organized the Congo Free State with Leopold as king and chief owner. Exploitation of native laborers on the rubber plantations caused international criticism and led to granting of a colonial charter, 1908.

Belgian and Congolese leaders agreed Jan. 27, 1960, that the Congo would become independent June 30. In the first general elections, May 31, the National Congolese movement of Patrice Lumumba won 35 of 137 seats in the National Assembly. He was appointed premier June 21, and formed a coalition cabinet.

Widespread violence caused Europeans and others to flee. Katanga, rich in minerals, seceded from the republic July 11, but ended the secession in 1963. The UN Security Council Aug. 9, 1960, called on Belgium to withdraw its troops and sent a UN contingent. President Kasavubu removed Lumumba as premier. Lumumba fought for control backed by Ghana, Guinea and India; he was murdered in 1961.

The last UN troops left the Congo June 30, 1964, and Moise Tshombe became president.

On Sept. 7, 1964, leftist rebels set up a "People's Republic" in Stanleyville. Tshombe hired foreign mercenaries and sought to rebuild the Congolese Army. In Nov. and Dec. 1964 rebels slew scores of white hostages and thousands of Congolese; Belgian paratroops, dropped from U.S. transport planes, rescued hundreds. By July 1965 the rebels had lost their effectiveness.

In 1965 Gen. Joseph D. Mobutu was named president. He later changed his name to Mobutu Sese Seko. On July 1 he renamed Leopoldville, Kinshasa; Stanleyville, Kisangani; and Elisabethville, Lubumbashi.

The country changed its name to Republic of Zaire on Oct. 27, 1971; in 1972 Zairians with Christian names were ordered to change them to African names.

In 1969-74, political stability under Mobutu was reflected in improved economic conditions. In 1974 most foreign-owned businesses were ordered sold to Zaire citizens, but in 1977 the government asked the original owners to return. A fall in copper prices in 1975 brought a surge in foreign debt and economic difficulties, causing political unrest, which continued through 1980.

In 1977, a force of Zairians, apparently trained by Cubans, invaded Shaba province (Katanga) from Angola. Zaire repelled the attack, with the aid of Egyptian pilots and 1,500 Moroccan troops flown in by France. The U.S. sent "nonlethal" supplies.

But many Belgian and other European mining experts failed to return after a second unsuccessful invasion from Angola in May 1978, suppressed by French, Belgian, and Moroccan troops.

prices hurt the economy in the late 1970s, but was partly offset by increased Western aid.

Drought in 1979 caused further shortage of food supplies; the economy further deteriorated.

Zambia

Republic of Zambia

People: Population (1979 est.): 5,649,000. **Age distrib.** (%): 0–14: 46.5; 15–59: 49.3; 60+: 4.1. **Pop. density:** 18.82 per sq. mi. **Urban** (1978): 39.3%. **Ethnic groups:** Africans 99%, mostly Bantu tribes, Europeans and Asians 1%. **Languages:** English (official), 70 local languages and dialects. **Religions:** Christians 15%, animists.

Geography: Area: 290,724 sq. mi., larger than Texas. **Location:** In southern central Africa. **Neighbors:** Zaire on N, Tanzania, Malawi, Mozambique on E, Zimbabwe, Namibia on S, Angola on W. **Topography:** Zambia is mostly high plateau country covered with thick forests, and drained by several important rivers, including the Zambezi. **Capital:** Lusaka. **Cities** (1978 est.): Lusaka 559,000; Kitwe 310,000; Ndola 291,000.

Government: Head of state: Pres. Kenneth David Kaunda; b. Apr. 28, 1924; in office: Oct. 24, 1964. **Head of government:** Prime Min. Daniel Lisulo; in office: June 16, 1978. **Local divisions:** 9 provinces. **Armed forces:** regulars 14,300; paramilitary 1,200.

Economy: Chief crops: Corn, tobacco, peanuts, cotton, sugar. **Minerals:** Cobalt, copper, zinc, gold, lead, vanadium, manganese, coal. **Other resources:** Rubber, ivory. **Per capita arable land:** 2.3 acres. **Meat prod.** (1978): beef: 28,000 metric tons; pork: 11,000 metric tons. **Fish catch** (1977): 53,700 metric tons. **Electricity prod.** (1978): 7.88 bln. kwh. **Labor force:** 57% agric.; 43% ind. and commerce.

Finance: Currency: Kwacha (Jan. 1981: .82 = $1 US). **Gross domestic product** (1979): $3.24 bln. **Per capita income** (1978): $414. **Imports** (1979): $904 mln.; partners (1977): UK 23%, Saudi Ar. 12%, W. Ger. 12%, U.S. 11%. **Exports** (1979): $1.41 bln.; partners (1977): Jap. 17%, UK 16%, W. Ger. 14%, It. 10%. **Tourists** (1976): 56,200; receipts (1977): $12 mln. **National budget** (1979): $753 mln. revenues; $973 mln. expenditures. **International reserves less gold** (Mar. 1981): $49.7 mln. **Gold:** 217,000 oz t. **Consumer prices** (change in 1980): 11.4%.

Transport: Motor vehicles: in use (1976): 93,500 passenger cars, 78,400 comm. vehicles. **Civil aviation:** 499 mln. pasenger-km (1977); 33 mln. freight ton-km (1977).

Communications: Television sets: 25,000 in use (1976). **Radios:** 110,000 in use (1976), 28,000 manuf. (1977). **Telephones in use** (1978): 54,475. **Daily newspaper circ.** (1976): 101,000; 20 per 1,000 pop.

Health: Life expectancy at birth (1975): 44.3 male; 47.5 female. **Births** (per 1,000 pop. 1975): 49.6. **Deaths** (per 1,000 pop. 1975): 19.1. **Natural increase** (1975): 3.1%. **Hospital beds** (per 100,000 pop. 1977): 366. **Physicians** (per 100,000 pop. 1977): 5. **Infant mortality** (per 1,000 live births 1978): 160.

Education (1977): Literacy: 49%. **Pop. 5-19:** in school: 52%, teachers per 1,000: 12. **PQLI:** 41.

As Northern Rhodesia, the country was under the administration of the South Africa Company, 1889 until 1924, when the office of governor was established, and, subsequently, a legislature. The country became an independent republic within the Commonwealth Oct. 24, 1964.

After the white government of Rhodesia declared its independence from Britain Nov. 11, 1965, relations between Zambia and Rhodesia became strained and use of their jointly owned railroad was disputed.

Britain gave Zambia an extra $12 million aid in 1966 after imposing an oil embargo on Rhodesia, and Zambia set up a temporary airlift to carry copper out from its mines and gasoline in. In Aug. 1968 a 1,058-mi. pipeline was completed, bringing oil from Tanzania. In 1973 a truck road to carry copper to Tanzania's port of Dar es Salaam was completed with U.S. aid. A railroad, built with Chinese aid across Tanzania, reached the Zambian border in 1974.

As part of a program of government participation in major industries, a government corporation in 1970 took over 51% of the ownership of 2 foreign-owned copper mining companies, paying with bonds. Privately-held land and other enterprises were nationalized in 1975, as were all newspapers. Decline in copper

Zimbabwe

People: Population (1980 est.): 7,360,000. **Age distrib.** (%): 0–14: 49.2; 15–59: 47.8; 60+: 3.0. **Pop. density:** 48.96 per sq. mi. **Urban** (1978): 19.6%. **Ethnic groups:** Shona 77%, Ndebele 19%, white 3%, Coloreds and Asians. **Languages:** English (official), Shona, Ndebele. **Religions:** Christians and part Christians 75%, Moslems.

Geography: Area: 150,333 sq. mi., nearly as large as California. **Location:** In southern Africa. **Neighbors:** Zambia on N, Botswana on W, S. Africa on S, Mozambique on E. **Topography:** Rhodesia is high plateau country, rising to mountains on eastern border, sloping down on the other borders. **Capital:** Salisbury. **Cities** (1979 est.): Salisbury (met.) 650,000; Bulawayo (met.) 358,000.

Government: Head of state: Pres. Cannan Banana, b. Mar. 5, 1936; in office: Apr. 18, 1980. **Head of government:** Prime Min. Robert G. Mugabe; b. Apr. 14, 1928; in office: Apr. 18, 1980. **Local divisions:** 7 provinces. **Armed forces:** regulars 21,500; para-military 52,500.

Economy: Industries: Clothing, chemicals, light industries. **Chief crops:** Tobacco, sugar, cotton, corn, tea. **Minerals:** Chromium, gold, nickel, asbestos, copper, iron, coal. **Per capita arable land:** 0.9 acres. **Meat prod.** (1978): beef: 150,000 metric tons; pork: 11,000 metric tons; lamb: 10,000 metric tons. **Electricity prod.** (1978): 4.51 bln. kwh. **Crude steel prod.** (1979): 740,000 metric tons. **Labor force:** 35% agric.; 30% ind. and commerce; 20% serv.; 15% gvt.

Finance: Currency: Dollar (1976: 1 = $1.54 US). **Gross domestic product** (1979 est.): $3.4 bln. **Per capita income** (1979 est.): White $8,000, African $240-$500. **Imports** (1979): $937 mln.; partners (1965): US 30%, So. Afr. 23%, U.S. 7%, Jap. 6%. **Exports** (1979): $1.15 bln.; partners (1965): Zamb. 25%, UK 22%, So. Afr. 10%, W. Ger. 9%. **Consumer prices** (change in 1977): 11.9%.

Transport: Railway traffic (1978): 4.87 bln. net ton-km. **Motor vehicles:** in use (1974): 180,000 passenger cars, 70,000 comm. vehicles.

Communications: Television sets: 72,000 in use (1976). **Radios:** 255,000 in use (1976). **Telephones in use** (1978): 196,750. **Daily newspaper circ.** (1976): 78,000; 12 per 1,000 pop.

Health: Life expectancy at birth (1975): 49.8 male; 53.3 female. **Births** (per 1,000 pop. 1975): 47.5. **Deaths** (per 1,000 pop. 1975): 14.9. **Natural increase** (1975): 3.3%. **Hospital beds** (per 100,000 pop. 1977): 258. **Physicians** (per 100,000 pop. 1977): 9. **Infant mortality** (per 1,000 live births 1975): 122.

Education (1977): **Literacy:** 30%. **Pop. 5-19:** in school: 39%, teachers per 1,000: 11. **PQLI:** 46.

Britain took over the area as Southern Rhodesia in 1923 from the British South Africa Co. (which, under Cecil Rhodes, had conquered the area by 1897) and granted internal self-government. Under a 1961 constitution, voting was restricted to maintain whites in power. On Nov. 11, 1965, Prime Min. Ian D. Smith announced his country's unilateral declaration of independence. Britain termed the act illegal, and demanded Rhodesia broaden voting rights to provide for eventual rule by the majority Africans.

Urged by Britain, the UN imposed sanctions, including embargoes on oil shipments to Rhodesia. Some oil and gasoline reached Rhodesia, however, from South Africa and Mozambique, before the latter became independent in 1975. In May 1968, the UN Security Council ordered a trade embargo.

A new constitution came into effect, Mar. 2, 1970, providing for a republic with a president and prime minister. The election law effectively prevented full black representation through income tax requirements.

A proposed British-Rhodesian settlement was dropped in May 1972 when a British commission reported most Rhodesian blacks opposed it. Intermittent negotiations between the government and various black nationalist groups failed to prevent increasing skirmishes. By mid-1978, over 6,000 soldiers and civilians had been killed. Rhodesian troops battled guerrillas within Mozambique and Zambia. An "internal settlement" signed Mar.

1978 in which Smith and 3 popular black leaders share control until transfer of power to the black majority was rejected by guerrilla leaders.

In the country's first universal-franchise election, Apr. 21, 1979, Bishop Abel Muzorewa's United African National Council gained a bare majority control of the black-dominated parliament. Britain's Thatcher government, 1979, began efforts to nor-

malize its relationship with Zimbabwe. A British cease-fire was accepted by all parties, Dec. 5th; elections were held in 1980. Independence was finally achieved Apr. 18, 1980. Factional fighting broke out, Feb. 1981, but was quelled quickly, easing fears of a civil war.

Zimbabwe was admitted as the 154th member of the United Nations, Sept. 20, 1980.

United Nations

The 36th regular session of the United Nations General Assembly was scheduled to open in September, 1981. *See Chronology for developments at UN sessions during 1981.*

UN headquarters are in New York, N.Y., between First Ave. and Roosevelt Drive and E. 42d St. and E. 48th St. The General Assembly Bldg., Secretariat, Conference and Library bldgs. are interconnected. A new UN office building-hotel was opened in New York in 1976.

A European office at Geneva includes Secretariat and agency staff members. Other offices of UN bodies and related organizations are scattered throughout the world.

The UN has a post office originating its own stamps. *See Index for Postal Information.*

Proposals to establish an organization of nations for maintenance of world peace led to the United Nations Conference on International Organization at San Francisco, Apr. 25-June 26, 1945, where the charter of the United Nations was drawn up. It was signed June 26 by 50 nations, and by Poland, one of the original 51, on Oct. 15, 1945. The charter came into effect Oct. 24, 1945, upon ratification by the permanent members of the Security Council and a majority of other signatories.

Roster of the United Nations
(As of July 1981)

The 154 members of the United Nations, with the years in which they became members.

Member	Year	Member	Year	Member	Year	Member	Year
Afghanistan	1946	Dominican Rep.	1945	Lesotho	1966	Sao Tome e Principe	1975
Albania	1955	Ecuador	1945	Liberia	1945	Saudi Arabia	1945
Algeria	1962	Egypt[2]	1945	Libya	1955	Senegal	1960
Angola	1976	El Salvador	1945	Luxembourg	1945	Seychelles	1976
Argentina	1945	Equatorial Guinea	1968	Madagascar (Malagasy)	1960	Sierra Leone	1961
Australia	1945	Ethiopia	1945	Malawi	1964	Singapore[1]	1965
Austria	1955	Fiji	1970	Malaysia[1]	1957	Solomon Islands	1978
Bahamas	1973	Finland	1955	Maldives	1965	Somalia	1960
Bahrain	1971	France	1945	Mali	1960	South Africa[5]	1945
Bangladesh	1974	Gabon	1960	Malta	1964	Spain	1955
Barbados	1966	Gambia	1965	Mauritania	1961	Sri Lanka	1955
Belgium	1945	Germany, East	1973	Mauritius	1968	Sudan	1956
Benin	1960	Germany, West	1973	Mexico	1945	Suriname	1975
Bhutan	1971	Ghana	1957	Mongolia	1961	Swaziland	1968
Bolivia	1945	Greece	1945	Morocco	1956	Sweden	1946
Botswana	1966	Grenada	1974	Mozambique	1975	Syria[2]	1945
Brazil	1945	Guatemala	1945	Nepal	1955	Tanzania[3]	1961
Bulgaria	1955	Guinea	1958	Netherlands	1945	Thailand	1946
Burma	1948	Guinea-Bissau	1974	New Zealand	1945	Togo	1960
Burundi	1962	Guyana	1966	Nicaragua	1945	Trinidad & Tobago	1962
Byelorussia	1945	Haiti	1945	Niger	1960	Tunisia	1956
Cambodia (Kampuchea)	1955	Honduras	1945	Nigeria	1960	Turkey	1945
Cameroon	1960	Hungary	1955	Norway	1945	Uganda	1962
Canada	1945	Iceland	1946	Oman	1971	Ukraine	1945
Cape Verde	1975	India	1945	Pakistan	1947	USSR	1945
Central Afr. Rep.	1960	Indonesia[6]	1950	Panama	1945	United Arab Emirates	1971
Chad	1960	Iran	1945	Papua New Guinea	1975	United Kingdom	1945
Chile	1945	Iraq	1945	Paraguay	1945	United States	1945
China[4]	1945	Ireland	1955	Peru	1945	Upper Volta	1960
Colombia	1945	Israel	1949	Philippines	1945	Uruguay	1945
Comoros	1975	Italy	1955	Poland	1945	Venezuela	1945
Congo	1960	Ivory Coast	1960	Portugal	1955	Vietnam	1977
Costa Rica	1945	Jamaica	1962	Qatar	1971	Yemen	1947
Cuba	1945	Japan	1956	Romania	1955	Yemen, South	1967
Cyprus	1960	Jordan	1955	Rwanda	1962	Yugoslavia	1945
Czechoslovakia	1945	Kenya	1963	Saint Lucia	1979	Zaire	1960
Denmark	1945	Kuwait	1963	Saint Vincent and the		Zambia	1964
Djibouti	1977	Laos	1955	Grenadines	1980	Zimbabwe	1980
Dominica	1978	Lebanon	1945	Samoa (Western)	1976		

(1) Malaya joined the UN in 1957. In 1963, its name was changed to Malaysia following the accession of Singapore, Sabah, and Sarawak. Singapore became an independent UN member in 1965. (2) Egypt and Syria were original members of the UN. In 1958, the United Arab Republic was established by a union of Egypt and Syria and continued as a single member of the UN. In 1961, Syria resumed its separate membership. (3) Tanganyika was a member of the United Nations from 1961 and Zanzibar was a member from 1963. Following the ratification in 1964 of Articles of Union between Tanganyika and Zanzibar, the United Republic of Tanganyika and Zanzibar continued as a single member of the United Nations, later changing its name to United Republic of Tanzania. (4) The General Assembly voted in 1971 to expel the Chinese government on Taiwan and admit the Peking government in its place. (5) The General Assembly rejected the credentials of the South African delegates in 1974, and suspended the country from the Assembly. (6) Indonesia withdrew from the UN in 1965 and rejoined in 1966.

Organization

The text of the UN Charter, and further information, may be obtained from the Office of Public Information, United Nations, N.Y.

General Assembly. The General Assembly is composed of representatives of all the member nations. Each nation is

entitled to one vote.

The General Assembly meets in regular annual sessions

and in special session when necessary. Special sessions are convoked by the Secretary General at the request of the Security Council or of a majority of the members of the UN.

On important questions a two-thirds majority of members present and voting is required; on other questions a simple majority is sufficient.

The General Assembly must approve the budget and apportion expenses among members. A member in arrears will have no vote if the amount of arrears equals or exceeds the amount of the contributions due for the preceeding two full years.

Security Council. The Security Council consists of 15 members, 5 with permanent seats. The remaining 10 are elected for 2-year terms by the General Assembly; they are not eligible for immediate reelection.

Permanent members of the Council: China, France, USSR, United Kingdom, United States.

Non-permanent members are Ireland, Japan, Panama, Spain and Uganda (until Dec. 31, 1982); East Germany, Mexico, Niger, Philippines, and Tunisia (until Dec. 31, 1981).

The Security Council has the primary responsiblity within the UN for maintaining international peace and security. The Council may investigate any dispute that threatens international peace and security.

Any member of the UN at UN headquarters may participate in its discussions and a nation not a member of UN may appear if it is a party to a dispute.

Decisions on procedural questions are made by an affirmative vote of 9 members. On all other matters the affirmative vote of 9 members must include the concurring votes of all permanent members; it is this clause which gives rise to the so-called "veto." A party to a dispute must refrain from voting.

The Security Council directs the various truce supervisory forces deployed in the Middle East, India-Pakistan, and Cyprus.

Economic and Social Council. The Economic and Social Council consists of 54 members elected by the General Assembly for 3-year terms of office. The council is responsible under the General Assembly for carrying out the functions of the United Nations with regard to international economic, social, cultural, educational, health and related matters. The council meets usually twice a year.

Trusteeship Council. The administration of trust territories is under UN supervision. The only remaining trust territory is the Pacific Islands, administered by the U.S.

Secretariat. The Secretary General is the chief administrative officer of the UN. He may bring to the attention of the Security Council any matter that threatens international peace. He reports to the General Assembly.

Kurt Waldheim (Austria), secretary general, was reelected to a 2d 5-year term beginning Jan. 1, 1977.

The 1980-81 program budget was $1.25 billion, exclusive of trust funds, special contributions, and expenses for the Specialized or the Related Organizations.

The US contributes 25% of the regular budget, the Soviet Union 11.33%, Japan 8.66%, W. Germany 7.74%, and France, China, and Britain about 5% each.

International Court of Justice. The International Court of Justice is the principal judicial organ of the United Nations. All members are *ipso facto* parties to the statute of the Court, as are three nonmembers — Liechtenstein, San Marino, and Switzerland. Other states may become parties to the Court's statute.

The jurisdiction of the Court comprises cases which the parties submit to it and matters especially provided for in the charter or in treaties. The Court gives advisory opinions and renders judgments. Its decisions are only binding between the parties concerned and in respect to a particular dispute. If any party to a case fails to heed a judgment, the other party may have recourse to the Security Council.

The 15 judges are elected for 9-year terms by the General Assembly and the Security Council. Retiring judges are eligible for re-election. The Court remains permanently in session, except during vacations. All questions are decided by majority. The Court sits in The Hague, Netherlands.

Judges: 9-year term in office ending 1988: Robert Ago, Italy. Richard Baxter, U.S. Abdullah Ali, Egypt. Platon D. Morozov, USSR. Jose Sette Camara, Brazil. **9-year term in office ending 1985:** Taslim Olawala Elias, Nigeria, Hermann Mosier, W. Germany. Shigeru Oda, Japan. Salah El Dine Tarazi, Syria. Manfred Lachs, Poland. **9-year term in office ending 1982:** Isaac Forster, Senegal. Andre Gros, France. Jose Maria Ruda, Argentina. Nagendra Singh, India. Sir Humphrey Waldock, Britain.

The president until 1982 is Sir Humphrey Waldock, the vice president is Nagendra Singh.

Specialized and Related Agencies

These agencies are autonomous, with their own memberships and organs which have a functional relationship or working agreements with the UN. (Headquarters, number of member nations.)

International Labor Org. (ILO) aims to promote social justice, employment, and sound industrial relations; improve labor conditions and living standards. (Geneva, 145)

Food & Agriculture Org. (FAO) aims to increase production from farms, forests, and fisheries; improve distribution, marketing, and nutrition; better conditions for rural people. (Rome, 147)

United Nations Educational, Scientific, & Cultural Org. (UNESCO) aims to promote collaboration among nations in the fields of education, science, and culture and communication. (Paris, 155; one associate)

World Health Org. (WHO) aims to aid the attainment of the highest possible level of health. (Geneva, 157)

International Monetary Fund (IMF) aims to promote international monetary co-operation and currency stabilization. (Washington, D.C., 141)

International Civil Aviation Org. (ICAO) promotes international civil aviation standards and regulations. (Montreal, 148)

Universal Postal Union (UPU) aims to perfect postal services and promote international collaboration. (Berne, 162)

International Telecommunication Union (ITU) sets up international regulations of radio, telegraph, telephone and space radio-communications. Allocates radio frequencies. (Geneva, 155)

World Meteorological Org. (WMO) aims to co-ordinate and improve world meteorological work, and promotes operational hydrology. (Geneva, 154)

Intergovernmental Maritime Consultative Org. (IMCO) aims to promote co-operation on technical matters affecting international shipping. (London, 121)

World Intellectual Property Organization (WIPO) seeks to protect, through international cooperation, literary, industrial, scientific, and artistic works, i.e. "intellectual property." (Geneva, 116)

International Atomic Energy Agency (IAEA) aims to promote the safe, peaceful uses of atomic energy. (Vienna, 110)

General Agreement on Tariffs and Trade (GATT) is the only treaty setting rules for world trade. Provides a forum for settling trade disputes and negotiating trade liberalization. (Geneva, 86; 1 provisional, 30 de facto)

International Bank for Reconstruction and Development (World Bank) provides loans and technical assistance for economic development projects in developing member countries; encourages cofinancing for projects from other public and private sources, both bilateral and multilateral (Washington, D.C., 134). **International Development Association (IDA),** an affiliate of the Bank, provides funds for development projects on concessionary terms to the poorer developing member countries. (Washington, D.C., 121)

International Finance Corporation (IFC) promotes the growth of the private sector in developing member countries; encourages the development of local capital markets; stimulates the international flow of private capital. (Washington, D.C., 119)

Ambassadors and Envoys

As of May 1981.

The address of foreign embassies to the United States is Washington, D.C. The address of U.S. embassies abroad is simply the appropriate foreign capital. The following countries are not listed due to suspension of diplomatic relations with the U.S.: Albania[1], Angola[2], Cambodia[3], Republic of China (Taiwan)[4], Cuba[5], Iran[6], Iraq,[7], Vietnam[3], South Yemen[3].

Countries	Envoys from United States	Envoys to United States
Afghanistan	*Vacant*	Salem M. Spartak, Chargé
Algeria	*Vacant*	Redha Malek, Amb.
Argentina	Harry W. Shlaudeman, Amb.	Jorge A. Aja Espil, Amb.
Australia	*Vacant*	Nicholas F. Parkinson, Amb.
Austria	*Vacant*	Karl Herbert Schober, Amb.
Bahamas	*Vacant*	Reginald L. Wood, Amb.
Bahrain	Peter A. Sutherland, Amb.	Abdulaziz Abdulrahman Buali, Amb.
Bangladesh	Jane A. Coon, Amb.[9]	Tabarak Husain, Amb.
Barbados	*Vacant*	Charles A. J. Skeete, Amb.
Belgium	Charles H. Price, Amb.[9]	J. Raoul Schoumaker, Amb.
Benin	*Vacant*	Thomas S. Boya, Amb.
Bolivia	*Vacant*	*Vacant*
Botswana	Horace G. Dawson Jr., Amb.	Moteane J. Melamu, Amb.
Brazil	Robert Marion Sayre, Amb.	Antonio F.A. da Silveira, Amb.
Bulgaria	Jack Richard Perry, Amb.	Stoyan I. Zhulev, Amb.
Burma	Patricia M. Byrne, Amb.	U Kyaw Khaing, Amb.
Burundi	Frances D. Cook, Amb.	Simon Sabimbona, Amb.
Cameroon	Joann Thompson, Chargé	Benoit Bindzi, Amb.
Canada	*Vacant*	Peter M. Towe, Amb.
Cape Verde	Peter Jon de Vos, Amb.	Jose Luis Fernandes Lopes, Chargé
Centr. African Rep.	Arthur H. Woodruff, Amb.	Jacques Topand Makombo, Amb.
Chad[10]	Donald R. Norland, Amb.	Mahamat Ali Adoum, Chargé
Chile	George W. Landau, Amb.	Jose Miguel Barros, Amb.
China, People's Rep.	*Vacant*	Chai Zemin, Amb.
Colombia	Thomas D. Boyatt, Amb.	Jorge Mario Eastman, Amb.
Comoros	Fernando E. Rondon, Amb.	Henri Jux Ratsimbazafy, Chargé
Congo	William L. Swing, Amb.	Nicolas Mondjo, Amb.
Costa Rica	Francis J. McNeil, Amb.	Jose Rafael Echeverria, Amb.
Cyprus	Galen L. Stone, Amb.	Andrew J. Jacovides, Amb.
Czechoslovakia	*Vacant*	Jaromir Johanes, Amb.
Denmark	*Vacant*	Otto R. Borch, Amb.
Djibouti	Jerrold M. North, Amb.	Salah Hadji Farah, Amb.
Dominica	*Vacant*	Charles Skete, Amb.
Dominican Republic	Robert L. Yost, Amb.	Rafael Molina Morillo
Ecuador	Raymond E. González, Amb.	Ricardo Crespo-Zaldumbide, Amb.
Egypt	Alfred L. Atherton Jr., Amb.	Ashraf A. Ghorbal, Amb.
El Salvador	Dean R. Hinton, Amb.	Roberto Jimenez Ortiz, Chargé
Equatorial Guinea	Joann Thompson, Chargé	Don Carmelo Nvono-Nca M. Oluy, Amb.
Estonia[8]		Ernst Jaakson, Consul General
Ethiopia	*Vacant*	Tesfaye Demeke, Chargé
Fiji	William Bodde Jr., Amb.	Filipe N. Bole, Amb.
Finland	James E. Goodby, Amb.	Jaakko Iloniemi, Amb.
France	Arthur A. Hartman, Amb.	Francois de Laboulaye, Amb.
Gabon	Arthur T. Tienken, Amb.	Aboubakar Bokoko, Amb.
Gambia, The.	Larry G. Piper, Amb.	Ousman A. Sallah, Amb.
Germany, East.	Herbert S. Okun, Amb.	Horst Grunert, Amb.
Germany, West	Arthur F. Burns, Amb.	Peter Hermes, Amb.
Ghana	Thomas W.M. Smith, Amb.	Joseph K. Baffour-Senkyire, Amb.
Greece	Robert J. McCloskey, Amb.	John A. Tzounis, Amb.
Grenada	*Vacant*	Bernard K. Radix, Amb.
Guatemala	*Vacant*	Felipe D. Monterroso, Amb.
Guinea	Allen C. Davis, Amb.	Mamady Lamine Conde, Amb.
Guinea-Bissau	Peter Jon de Vos, Amb.	*Vacant*
Guyana	George B. Roberts Jr., Amb.	Laurence E. Mann, Amb.
Haiti	*Vacant*	Josette Philippeaux, Chargé
Honduras	Jack R. Binns, Amb.	Federico A. Poujol, Amb.
Hungary	Harry E. Bergold Jr., Amb.	Ferenc Esztergalyos, Amb.
Iceland	Richard A. Ericson Jr., Amb.	Hans G. Andersen, Amb.
India	*Vacant*	K. R. Narayanan, Amb.
Indonesia	Edward E. Masters, Amb.	D. Ashari, Amb.
Ireland	William V. Shannon, Amb.	Sean Donlon, Amb.
Israel	Samuel W. Lewis, Amb.	Ephraim Evron, Amb.
Italy	Maxwell M. Raab, Amb.[9]	Paolo Pansa Cedronio, Amb.
Ivory Coast	Nancy V. Rawls, Amb.	Timothee N'Guetta Ahoua, Amb.
Jamaica	Loren E. Lawrence, Amb.	Keith Johnson, Amb.
Japan	Michael J. Mansfield, Amb.	Yoshio Okawara, Amb.
Jordan	*Vacant*	Al-Sharif Fawaz Sharaf, Amb.
Kenya	William C. Harrop, Amb.	John P. Mbogua, Amb.
Kiribati	William Bodde Jr., Min.	*Vacant*
Korea, South	William H. Gleysteen Jr., Amb.	Yong Shik Kim, Amb.
Kuwait	Francois M. Dickman, Amb.	Shaikh S. N. Al-Sabah, Amb.
Laos	*Vacant*	Khamtan Ratanavong, Chargé
Latvia[8]		Anatol Dinbergs, Chargé
Lebanon	John G. Dean, Amb.	Khalil Itani, Amb.
Lesotho	John R. Clingerman, Amb.	'M'alineo N. Tau, Amb.
Liberia	William Swing, Amb.[9]	Joseph Saye Guannu, Amb.
Libya[11]	*Vacant*	*Vacant*.
Lithuania[8]		Stasys A. Backis, Chargé
Luxembourg	James G. Lowenstein, Amb.	Adrien Meisch, Amb.
Madagascar	Fernando E. Rondon, Amb.	Henri Jux Ratsimbazafy, Chargé

Countries	Envoys from United States	Envoys to United States
Malawi	John A. Burroughs Jr., Amb.	Nelson T. Mizere, Amb.
Malaysia	Barbara M. Watson, Amb.	Zain Azraai, Amb.
Maldives	Donald R. Toussaint, Amb.	*Vacant*
Mali	*Vacant*	Maki K. A. Tall, Amb.
Malta	*Vacant*	Emanuel C. Farrugia, Chargé
Mauritania	*Vacant*	Abdellah Ould Daddah, Amb.
Mauritius	Robert C. Gordon, Amb.	Chitmansing Jesseramsing, Chargé
Mexico	John A. Gavin, Amb.	Hugo B. Margain, Amb.
Morocco	*Vacant*	Ali Bengelloun, Amb.
Mozambique	*Vacant*	*Vacant*
Nauru	Philip H. Alston Jr., Amb.	T.W. Star, Amb.
Nepal	Phillip R. Trimble, Amb.	Bhekh B. Thapa, Chargé
Netherlands	Geri M. Joseph, Amb.	Jan Hendrik Lubbers, Amb.
New Zealand	*Vacant*	Thomas Francis Gill, Chargé
Nicaragua	Lawrence A. Pezzullo, Amb.	Arturo J. Cruz, Amb.
Niger	James K. Bishop, Amb.	Andre Wright, Amb.
Nigeria	Stephen Low, Amb.	Olujimi Jolaoso, Amb.
Norway	*Vacant*	Knut Hedemann, Amb.
Oman	John Countryman, Amb.[9]	Sadek J. Sulaiman, Amb.
Pakistan	Arthur W. Hummel Jr., Amb.	Najmuddin A. Shaikh, Amb.
Panama	Ambler H. Moss Jr., Amb.	Juan Jose Amado, Amb.
Papua New Guinea	Harvey J. Feldman, Amb.	Kubulan Los, Amb.
Paraguay	Lyle F. Lane, Amb.	Mario Lopez Escobar, Amb.
Peru	Edwin G. Corr, Amb.	Fernando Schwalb, Amb.
Philippines	Richard W. Murphy, Amb.	Eduardo Z. Romualdez, Amb.
Poland	Francis J. Meehan, Amb.	Romuald Spasowski, Amb.
Portugal	Richard J. Bloomfield, Amb.	Pedro R. de Menezes, Chargé
Qatar	Charles E. Marthinsen, Amb.	Abdelkader B. Al-Ameri, Amb.
Romania	O. Rudolph Aggrey, Amb.	Nicolae Ionescu, Amb.
Rwanda	Harry R. Melone	Bonaventure Ubalijoro, Amb.
St. Lucia	*Vacant*	Barry B.L. Auguste
Samoa	Anne C. Martindell, Amb.	Charles Skete, Amb.
Sao Tome and Principe	Arthur T. Tienken, Amb.	*Vacant*
Saudi Arabia	*Vacant*	Faisal Alhegelan, Amb.
Senegal	Charles W. Bray, Amb.[9]	Andre Coulbary, Amb.
Seychelles	William C. Harrop, Amb.	*Vacant*
Sierra Leone	Theresa Ann Healy, Amb.	Ahmed A. Seray-Wurie, Chargé
Singapore	Harry E. T. Thayer, Amb.	Punch Coomaraswamy, Amb.
Solomon Islands	Harvey J. Feldman, Amb.	Francis Bugotu, Amb.
Somalia	Donald K. Petterson, Amb.	Mohamud Haji Nur, Amb.
South Africa	William B. Edmondson, Amb.	Donald B. Sole, Amb.
Spain	Terence A. Todman, Amb.	José Llado, Amb.
Sri Lanka	Donald R. Toussaint, Amb.	W.S. Karunaratne, Amb.
Sudan	C. William Kontos, Amb.	Omer Salih Eissa, Amb.
Suriname	John J. Crowley Jr., Amb.	Henricus A. F. Heidweiller, Amb.
Swaziland	Richard C. Matheron, Amb.	Norman M. Vilakati, Chargé
Sweden	*Vacant*	Wilhelm Wachtmeister, Amb.
Switzerland	Richard D. Vine, Amb.	Anton Hegner, Amb.
Syria	Talcott W. Seelye, Amb.	Abdul Hassib Istwani, Chargé
Tanzania	*Vacant*	Paul Bomani, Amb.
Thailand	Morton I. Abramowitz, Amb.	Prok Amaranand, Amb.
Togo	Marilyn P. Johnson, Amb.	Yao Grunitzky, Amb.
Tonga	William Bodde Jr., Amb.	'Inoke F. Faletau, Amb.
Trinidad and Tobago	Irving G. Cheslaw, Amb.	Victor C. McIntyre, Amb.
Tunisia	Stephen W. Bosworth, Amb.	Ali Hedda, Amb.
Turkey	James W. Spain, Amb.	Sukru Elekdag, Amb.
Tuvalu	William Bodde Jr., Amb.	Ionatana Ionatana, Amb.
Uganda	Gordon R. Beyer, Amb.	Aloysius R. Kabiritsi, Chargé
USSR	Jack F. Matlock, Chargé	Anatoliy F. Dobrynin, Amb.
United Arab Emirates	William D. Wolle, Amb.	Saeed Al-Shamsi, Chargé
United Kingdom	John J. Louis Jr., Amb.	Nicholas Henderson, Amb.
Upper Volta	*Vacant*	Telesphore Yaguibou, Amb.
Uruguay	*Vacant*	Jorge Pacheco Areco, Amb.
Venezuela	William H. Luers, Amb.	Marcial Perez-Chiriboga, Amb.
Yemen Arab Rep.	George M. Lane, Amb.	Yahya M. Al-Mutawakel, Amb.
Yugoslavia	*Vacant*	Budimir Loncar, Amb.
Zaire	Robert B. Oakley	Kasongo Mutuale, Amb.
Zambia	Frank G. Wisner II, Amb.	Putteho M. Ngonda, Amb.
Zimbabwe	Robert V. Keeley, Amb.	Elleck K. Mashingaidze, Amb.

Ambassadors at Large: Vernon Walters, Daniel J. Terra.

Special Missions Headed by Ambassadors

U.S. Mission to North Atlantic Treaty Organization, Brussels—W. Tapley Bennett Jr.
U.S. Mission to the European Communities, Brussels—Thomas O. Enders
U.S. Mission to the International Atomic Energy Agency, Vienna—Vacant
U.S. Mission to the United Nations, New York—Jeane J. Kirkpatrick
U.S. Mission to the European Office of the UN, Geneva—Gerald B. Helman
U.S. Mission to the Organization for Economic Cooperation and Development, Paris—Abraham Katz[9]
U.S. Mission to the Organization of American States, Washington—William Middendorf
United Nations Educational, Scientific, and Cultural Organization, Paris—*Vacant*
Council of the International Civic Aviation Organization, Montreal—John E. Downs

(1) Relations severed in 1939. (2) Post temporarily closed in 1975. (3) U.S. embassy closed in 1975. (4) U.S. severed relations in 1978. (5) Relations severed in 1961; limited ties restored in 1977. (6) U.S. severed relations on Apr. 7, 1980. (7) Relations severed in 1967, limited staff returned in 1972; Belgium protects U.S. interests. (8) U.S. does not officially recognize 1940 annexation by USSR. (9) Nominated. (10) All embassy working activities were suspended and all American personnel were withdrawn, Mar. 24, 1980. (11) All embassy working activities were suspended and all American personnel were withdrawn, May 2, 1980. U.S. closed the Libyan mission in Wash., DC, May 6, 1981.

Major International Organizations

Association of Southeast Asian Nations (ASEAN), was formed in 1967 to promote political and economic cooperation among the non-communist states of the region. Members are Indonesia, Malaysia, Philippines, Singapore, Thailand. Annual ministerial meetings set policy; a central Secretariat in Jakarta and 11 permanent committees work in trade, transportation, communications, agriculture, science, finance, and culture.

The Commonwealth, originally called the British Commonwealth of Nations, is an association of nations and dependencies loosely joined by a common interest based on having been parts of the old British Empire. The British monarch is the symbolic head of the Commonwealth.

There are 44 self-governing independent nations in the Commonwealth, plus various colonies and protectorates. As of June 1981, the members were the United Kingdom of Great Britain and Northern Ireland and 14 other nations recognizing the British monarch, represented by a governor-general, as their head of state: Australia, Bahamas, Barbados, Canada, Fiji, Grenada, Jamaica, Mauritius, New Zealand, Papua New Guinea, St. Lucia, St. Vincent and the Grenadines, Solomon Islands, and Tuvalu (a special member); and 28 countries with their own heads of state: Bangladesh, Botswana, Cyprus, Dominica, The Gambia, Ghana, Guyana, India, Kenya, Kiribati, Lesotho, Malawi, Malaysia, Malta, Nauru (a special member), Nigeria, Samoa, Seychelles, Sierra Leone, Singapore, Sri Lanka, Swaziland, Tanzania, Tonga, Trinidad and Tobago, Uganda, Zambia, Zimbabwe and Vanuatu. In addition various Caribbean dependencies take part in certain Commonwealth activities.

The Commonwealth facilitates consultation among member states through meetings of prime ministers and finance ministers, and through a permanent Secretariat. Members consult on economic, scientific, educational, financial, legal, and military matters, and try to coordinate policies.

European Communities (EC) is the collective designation of three organizations with common membership: the European Economic Community (Common Market), the European Coal and Steel Community, and the European Atomic Energy Community. The 10 full members are: Belgium, Denmark, France, West Germany, Greece, Ireland, Italy, Luxembourg, Netherlands, United Kingdom. Portugal and Spain applied in 1977 for membership. Another 61 nations in Africa, the Caribbean, and the Pacific are affiliated under the Lomé Convention.

A merger of the 3 communities executives went into effect July 1, 1967, though the component organizations date back to 1951 and 1958. A Council of Ministers, a Commission, a European Parliament, and a Court of Justice comprise the permanent structure. The communities aim to integrate their economies, coordinate social developments, and ultimately, bring about political union of the democratic states of Europe.

European Free Trade Association (EFTA), consisting of Austria, Iceland, Norway, Portugal, Sweden, Switzerland and associated member Finland, was created Jan. 4, 1960, to gradually reduce customs duties and quantitative restrictions between members on industrial products. By Dec. 31, 1966, all tariffs and quotas had been eliminated. The United Kingdom and Denmark withdrew to become members of EC Jan. 1, 1973 at which time EFTA members entered into free trade agreements with the EC. All industrial customs barriers between the two blocs were removed July 1, 1976.

League of Arab States (The Arab League) was created Mar. 22, 1945, by Egypt, Iraq, Jordan, Lebanon, Saudi Arabia, Syria, and Yemen. Joining later were Algeria, Bahrain, Djibouti, Kuwait, Libya, Mauritania, Morocco, Oman, Qatar, Somalia, Sudan, Tunisia, United Arab Emirates and South Yemen. The Palestine Liberation Org. has been admitted as a full member. The League fosters cultural, economic, and communication ties and mediates disputes among the Arab states; it represents Arab states in certain international negotiations, and coordinates a military, economic, and diplomatic offensive against Israel. As a result of Egypt signing a peace treaty with Israel, the League, Mar. 1979, suspended Egypt's membership and transferred the League's headquarters from Cairo to Tunis.

North Atlantic Treaty Org. (NATO) was created by treaty (signed Apr. 4, 1949; in effect Aug. 24, 1949) among Belgium, Canada, Denmark, France, Iceland, Italy, Luxembourg, the Netherlands, Norway, Portugal, the United Kingdom, and the U.S. Greece, Turkey, and West Germany have joined since. The members agreed to settle disputes by peaceful means; to develop their individual and collective capacity to resist armed attack; to regard an attack on one as an attack on all, and to take necessary action to repel an attack under Article 51 of the United Nations Charter.

The NATO structure consists of a Council and a Military Committee of 3 commands (Allied Command Europe, Allied Command Atlantic, Allied Command Channel) and the Canada-U.S. Regional Planning Group.

Following announcement in 1966 of nearly total French withdrawal from the military affairs of NATO, organization hq. moved, 1967, from Paris to Brussels. In August, 1974, Greece announced a total withdrawal of armed forces from NATO, in response to Turkish intervention in Cyprus. Nevertheless, Greece has continued to participate in NATO military planning activities.

Organization of African Unity (OAU), formed May 25, 1963, by 30 African countries (50 by 1980) to coordinate cultural, political, scientific and economic policies; to end colonialism in Africa; and to promote a common defense of members' independence. It holds annual conferences of heads of state, has a council of foreign ministers meeting at least twice a year, a secretary-general and a mediation-arbitration commission. Hq. is in Addis Ababa, Ethiopia.

Organization of American States (OAS) was formed in Bogota, Colombia, in 1948. Hq. is in Washington, D.C. It has a Permanent Council, Inter-American Economic and Social Council, and Inter-American Council for Education, Science and Culture, a Juridical Committee and a Commission on Human Rights. The Permanent Council can call meetings of foreign ministers to deal with urgent security matters. A General Assembly meets annually. A secretary general and assistant are elected for 5-year terms. There are 28 members, each with one vote in the various organizations: Argentina, Barbados, Bolivia, Brazil, Chile, Colombia, Costa Rica, Cuba, Dominica, Dominican Republic, Ecuador, El Salvador, Grenada, Guatemala, Haiti, Honduras, Jamaica, Mexico, Nicaragua, Panama, Paraguay, Peru, St. Lucia, Suriname, Trinidad & Tobago, U.S., Uruguay, Venezuela. In 1962, the OAS excluded Cuba from OAS activities but not from membership.

Organization for Economic Cooperation and Development (OECD) was established Sept. 30, 1961 to promote economic and social welfare in member countries, and to stimulate and harmonize efforts on behalf of developing nations. Nearly all the industrialized "free market" countries belong, with Yugoslavia as an associate member. OECD collects and disseminates economic and environmental information. Members in 1981 were: Australia, Austria, Belgium, Canada, Denmark, Finland, France, West Germany, Greece, Iceland, Ireland, Italy, Japan, Luxembourg, Netherlands, New Zealand, Norway, Portugal, Spain, Sweden, Switzerland, Turkey, United Kingdom, United States. Hq. is in Paris.

Organization of Petroleum Exporting Countries (OPEC) was created Nov. 14, 1960 at Venezuelan initiative. The group has been successful in determining world oil prices, and in advancing members' interests in trade and development dealings with industrialized oil-consuming nations. Members in 1981 were Algeria, Ecuador, Gabon, Indonesia, Iran, Iraq, Kuwait, Libya, Nigeria, Qatar, Saudi Arabia, United Arab Emirates, Venezuela.

Warsaw Treaty Organization (Warsaw Pact) was created May 14, 1955, as a mutual defense alliance by Albania, Bulgaria, Czechoslovakia, East Germany, Hungary, Poland, Romania, and the USSR. Hq. is in Moscow. It provides for a unified military command; if one member is attacked, the others will aid it with all necessary steps including armed force; joint maneuvers are held; there is a Political Consultative Committee and a Committee of Defense Ministers. Albania was barred from meetings in 1962, withdrew in 1968.

U.S. Aid to Foreign Nations

Source: Bureau of Economic Analysis, U.S. Commerce Department

Figures are for calendar year 1980, and are in millions of dollars. (*Less than $500,000.) Data shown by country exclude the military supplies and services furnished under the Foreign Assistance Act and direct Defense Department appropriations. Data shown include credits which have been extended to private entities in the country specified.

Grants are largely outright gifts for which no payment is expected or which at most involve an obligation on the part of the receiver to extend aid to the U.S. or other countries to achieve a common objective.   Net grants and credits take into account all known returns to the U.S. government, including reverse grants, returns of grants, and payments of principal. A minus sign (—) indicates that the total of these returns to the U.S. is greater than the total of grants or credits.

Other assistance represents the transfer of U.S. farm products in exchange for foreign currencies, less the government's disbursements of the currencies as grants, credits, or for purchases.

Amounts do not include investments in international financial institutions in 1980 as follows: Asian Development Bank, $53 million; Inter-American Development Bank, $233 million; International Development Assn., $476 million; International Bank for Reconstruction and Development, $16 million; International Finance Corp., $22 million.

	Total	Net grants	Net credits	Net other		Total	Net grants	Net credits	Net other
TOTAL	10,015	5,431	4,656	-72	Cape Verde	6	6	—	—
					Cen. African Rep.	2	2	—	—
Military grants	1,533	1,533	—	—	Chad	6	6	—	—
Other grants, credits, ass't.	8,482	3,298	4,656	-72	Congo	2	1	1	—
Western Europe	394	44	351	(*)	Djibouti	3	3	—	—
Austria	14	—	14	—	Ethiopia	20	22	-1	(*)
Belgium-Luxembourg	52	—	52	—	Gabon	-4	1	-5	—
Denmark	15	—	15	—	Gambia	4	4	—	—
Finland	9	—	9	(*)	Ghana	16	13	2	1
France	-31	—	-31	—	Guinea	7	6	3	-1
Germany, West	-14	—	-14	—	Guinea-Bissau	2	2	—	—
Iceland	5	—	5	(*)	Ivory Coast	27	2	26	(*)
Ireland	(*)	—	(*)	—	Kenya	50	20	30	—
Italy	184	6	179	—	Lesotho	20	20	—	—
Netherlands	-27	—	-27	—	Liberia	30	25	5	—
Norway	-52	—	-52	—	Malawi	4	3	1	—
Portugal	-99	26	-125	(*)	Mali	25	23	1	—
Spain	159	12	147	(*)	Mauritania	17	17	—	—
Sweden	5	—	5	—	Mauritius	4	1	3	—
Switzerland	-9	—	-9	—	Morocco	39	21	20	-2
United Kingdom	178	—	178	—	Mozambique	17	7	10	—
Yugoslavia	22	—	22	(*)	Niger	10	10	(*)	—
Atomic EC	-5	—	-5	—	Nigeria	-3	(*)	-3	—
Other & unspecified	-12	(*)	-12	—	Rwanda	7	7	(*)	(*)
Eastern Europe	-285	—	-267	-18	Senegal	37	32	5	(*)
Hungary	-4	—	-4	—	Sierra Leone	9	7	2	—
Poland	-243	—	-225	-18	Somalia	67	50	17	(*)
Romania	-23	—	-23	—	Sudan	73	40	34	(*)
Soviet Union	-14	—	-14	—	Swaziland	11	7	4	—
Near East & South Asia	4,582	1,516	3,110	-44	Tanzania	30	23	7	—
Afghanistan	4	2	2	—	Togo	6	7	(*)	—
Bangladesh	174	110	64	—	Tunisia	50	8	48	-6
Cyprus	17	21	-4	—	Uganda	14	14	(*)	—
Egypt	1,466	185	1,317	-36	Upper Volta	30	30	—	—
Greece	-52	—	-52	(*)	Zaire	144	11	133	1
India	164	164	-2	2	Zambia	42	11	31	—
Israel	1,849	678	1,172	(*)	Zimbabwe	26	26	—	—
Jordan	160	27	133	(*)	Other & unspecified	64	62	2	—
Lebanon	18	(*)	14	(*)	**Western Hemisphere**	677	302	376	-1
Nepal	16	19	(*)	-3	Argentina	-30	(*)	-30	—
Oman	13	—	13	—	Bahamas	-2	—	-2	—
Pakistan	65	32	38	-5	Barbados	1	(*)	1	—
Saudi Arabia	4	—	4	—	Bermuda	-1	—	-1	—
Sri Lanka (Ceylon)	55	13	42	(*)	Bolivia	29	33	-3	(*)
Syria	22	9	15	-2	Brazil	-28	3	-31	(*)
Turkey	525	169	356	(*)	Canada	95	—	95	—
Yemen (Sana)	16	15	(*)	—	Cayman Islands	-1	—	-1	—
Other & unspecified	67	68	-1	—	Chile	-68	10	-77	-2
East Asia & Pacific	830	262	568	-1	Colombia	6	8	-2	(*)
China-Taiwan	388	(*)	388	—	Costa Rica	3	3	1	—
Fiji	2	2	—	—	Dominican Republic	30	9	21	—
Hong Kong	10	(*)	10	—	Ecuador	16	5	11	—
Indonesia	137	38	103	-3	El Salvador	49	30	18	—
Japan	-49	—	-49	(*)	Guatemala	15	10	5	—
Kampuchea	40	40	—	—	Guyana	3	2	1	—
Korea (So.)	101	2	97	2	Haiti	36	27	8	—
Malaysia	-10	1	-11	—	Honduras	20	10	10	—
New Zealand	-4	—	-4	—	Jamaica	12	5	7	—
Philippines	32	37	-4	(*)	Mexico	180	12	168	—
Singapore	25	—	25	—	Nicaragua	78	6	73	—
Thailand	31	15	15	—	Panama	4	7	-3	—
Trust Terr. Pacific	107	107	—	—	Paraguay	-1	3	-4	—
Other & unspecified	19	19	(*)	(*)	Peru	-2	26	-28	—
Africa	1,095	589	514	-8	St. Vincent	1	—	1	—
Algeria	125	—	125	—	Suriname	-1	—	-1	—
Angola	8	8	(*)	—	Trinidad-Tobago	89	—	89	—
Benin	2	2	1	—	Uruguay	-3	(*)	-3	—
Botswana	16	16	—	—	Venezuela	18	(*)	18	—
Burundi	5	5	—	(*)	Other & unspecified	128	93	36	—
Cameroon	25	10	15	—	**Intl. orgs. & unspecified**	1,180	1,185	-4	—

Military Expenditures and Social Conditions

Source: World Military and Social Expenditures 1980 by Ruth Leger Sivard; copyright © 1980 by World Priorities Inc., Box 1003, Leesburg, VA 22075.

1977

Country	Military public expenditures per capita		Military public expenditures per soldier[1]		Economic-social standing[2]
	Rank	U.S. $	Rank	U.S. $	Avg. Rank[3]
Afghanistan	116	4	134	527	133
Albania	47	55	102	2,915	55
Algeria	63	28	69	5,962	75
Angola	—	—	—	—	112
Argentina	52	46	44	9,254	33
Australia	20	184	10	36,914	11
Austria	39	73	32	14,892	11
Bahrain	29	112	29	18,000	38
Bangladesh	132	1	123	1,606	133
Barbados	116	4	126	1,000	36
Belgium	14	255	16	29,128	17
Benin	124	3	84	4,500	119
Bolivia	82	12	106	2,652	78
Botswana	—	—	—	—	86
Brazil	76	16	64	6,752	54
Bulgaria	42	68	89	4,020	26
Burma	111	5	131	900	115
Burundi	124	3	119	1,857	129
Cambodia	—	—	—	—	116
Cameroon	106	6	49	8,333	104
Canada	22	167	6	48,513	7
Central African Rep.	116	4	45	9,000	127
Chad	106	6	81	4,800	137
Chile	53	45	72	5,577	47
China	71	22	73	5,570	82
China, Taiwan	33	90	97	3,270	62
Colombia	103	7	103	2,877	69
Congo	67	25	78	5,143	90
Costa Rica	92	9	95	3,600	50
Cuba	53	45	112	2,275	42
Cyprus	58	41	108	2,500	51
Czechoslovakia	25	126	41	10,470	20
Denmark	17	207	14	30,086	4
Dominican Rep.	80	14	90	4,000	67
Ecuador	66	26	51	8,042	63
Egypt	28	119	33	13,409	85
El Salvador	85	11	59	7,143	79
Equatorial Guinea	71	22	126	1,000	105
Ethiopia	111	5	121	1,824	140
Fiji	103	7	90	4,000	48
Finland	32	92	40	10,950	9
France	11	281	15	29,705	10
Gabon	61	29	29	18,000	57
Gambia	—	—	—	—	121
East Germany	19	190	26	20,248	14
West Germany	10	282	11	35,417	6
Ghana	57	42	110	2,333	95
Greece	23	164	52	7,615	32
Guatemala	85	11	80	4,857	77
Guinea	116	4	96	3,500	125
Guyana	88	10	90	4,000	60
Haiti	127	2	119	1,857	117
Honduras	92	9	111	2,288	88
Hungary	40	69	58	7,165	29
Iceland	—	—	—	—	8
India	111	5	105	2,739	114
Indonesia	96	8	82	4,753	107
Iran	15	222	23	22,965	64
Iraq	24	138	46	8,862	66
Ireland	50	52	39	11,400	21
Israel	2	1,045	22	23,031	22
Italy	34	88	31	15,109	24
Ivory Coast	96	8	36	12,000	97
Jamaica	85	11	68	6,000	46
Japan	44	60	18	28,824	11
Jordan	40	69	101	2,985	81
Kenya	88	10	28	18,500	100
No. Korea	45	59	115	2,080	82
So. Korea	49	53	98	3,175	69
Kuwait	6	659	7	74,700	23
Laos	92	9	133	612	132
Lebanon	67	25	63	8,900	53
Lesotho	—	—	—	—	99
Liberia	116	4	124	1,400	102
Libya	27	125	37	11,724	33
Luxembourg	35	81	17	29,000	18
Madagascar	111	5	67	4,000	101
Malawi	124	3	53	7,500	128
Malaysia	51	49	42	9,953	58
Mali	116	4	65	6,500	138
Malta	75	21	60	7,000	33
Mauritania	60	30	67	6,143	125
Mauritius	132	1	126	1,000	58
Mexico	92	9	71	5,615	60
Mongolia	38	78	90	4,000	52
Morocco	59	38	47	8,600	98
Mozambique	111	5	107	2,579	130
Nepal	132	1	132	750	136
Netherlands	13	273	13	34,346	15
New Zealand	37	79	27	18,923	18
Nicaragua	71	22	54	7,429	68
Niger	127	2	90	4,000	135
Nigeria	63	28	48	8,502	103
Norway	12	276	19	28,615	3
Oman	4	844	5	52,846	74
Pakistan	82	12	113	2,152	119
Panama	96	8	118	1,875	42
Papua New Guinea	96	8	55	7,333	91
Paraguay	88	10	122	1,706	71
Peru	70	23	76	5,386	65
Philippines	82	12	74	5,556	92
Poland	30	108	35	12,202	27
Portugal	45	59	43	9,729	42
Qatar	1	1,257	4	60,000	30
Romania	53	45	75	5,400	31
Rwanda	116	4	88	4,250	124
Saudi Arabia	3	939	1	115,436	66
Senegal	96	8	55	7,333	118
Sierra Leone	127	2	100	3,000	122
Singapore	21	179	38	11,472	37
Somalia	88	10	126	1,000	131
South Africa	36	80	8	38,891	72
Spain	48	54	66	6,359	28
Sri Lanka	127	2	116	2,000	84
Sudan	80	14	85	4,385	109
Swaziland	127	2	126	1,000	87
Sweden	9	325	9	38,826	1
Switzerland	18	206	3	68,421	2
Syria	25	126	86	4,347	80
Tanzania	96	8	60	7,000	108
Thailand	79	15	99	3,133	89
Togo	103	7	77	5,333	110
Trinidad & Tobago	106	6	60	7,000	42
Tunisia	65	27	57	7,273	76
Turkey	43	63	70	5,807	73
Uganda	96	8	83	4,619	110
USSR	8	348	20	24,490	24
United Arab Emirates	5	822	21	24,346	49
UK	16	213	12	35,074	16
U.S.	7	465	7	48,337	5
Upper Volta	116	4	104	2,750	139
Uruguay	71	22	109	2,370	38
Venezuela	56	43	34	13,386	40
Vietnam	76	16	125	1,301	93
Yemen	76	16	116	2,000	123
So. Yemen	67	25	114	2,095	106
Yugoslavia	31	96	50	8,065	40
Zaire	106	6	79	5,000	112
Zambia	106	6	24	21,429	95
Zimbabwe	84	29	25	20,300	93

(1) "Soldier" represents all members of the armed forces. (2) Represents average ranks for Gross National Product per capita, education (encompassing public expenditures per capita, school-age population per teacher, percent school-age population in school, percent women in total university enrollment, literacy rate), and health (encompassing public expenditures per capita, population per physician, population per hospital bed, infant mortality rate, life expectancy). (3) Rank shows the standing of the country among those in the table. The rank order is repeated if more than one country has the same figure.

Population of World's Largest Urban Areas

The ranking below represents one attempt at comparing the world's largest urban areas, taking into account, where necessary and within the limits of available data, urban development extending outward from the principal city named in the table.

City proper is a large locality with legally fixed boundaries and an administratively recognized urban status which is usually characterized by some form of local government. Urban agglomeration has been defined as comprising the city proper and also the suburban fringe or thickly settled territory living outside of, but adjacent to, the city boundaries. U-Urban agglomeration; C-City proper.

New York, N.Y. (est. 1977)	U 16,962,000
Mexico City, Mexico (est. 1978)	U 13,993,866
Tokyo, Japan (est. 1977)	U 11,695,150
Los Angeles-Long Beach, Cal. (est. 1977)	U 10,605,000
Shanghai, China (est. 1978)	U 10,000,000
Buenos Aires, Argentina (est. 1978)	U 9,749,000
Paris, France (census, 1975)	U 8,547,625
Peking, China (est. 1978)	U 8,000,000
Moscow, USSR (est. 1978)	U 7,909,000
Chicago, Ill. (est. 1977)	U 7,662,000
Sao Paulo, Brazil (est. 1975)	C 7,198,608
Calcutta, India (census, 1971)	U 7,031,382
Tianjin, China (est. 1978)	C 7,000,000
London, England (est. 1977)	U 6,970,100
Seoul, S. Korea (census, 1975)	C 6,879,464
Chongqing, China (est. 1977)	C 6,000,000
Bombay, India (census, 1971)	C 5,970,575
Philadelphia, Pa. (est. 1977)	U 5,627,000
Cairo, Egypt (census, 1976)	C 5,084,463
Canton, China (est. 1977)	C 5,000,000
Rio de Janeiro, Brazil (est. 1975)	C 4,857,716
San Francisco-Oakland, Cal. (est. 1977)	U 4,693,000
Detroit, Mich. (est. 1977)	U 4,620,000
Hong Kong (est. 1978)	C 4,610,000
Jakarta, Indonesia (census, 1971)	U 4,576,009
Manila, Philippines (est. 1975)	U 4,500,000
Teheran, Iran (census, 1966)	C 4,496,159
Leningrad, USSR (est. 1978)	U 4,480,000
Shenyang, China (est. 1977)	C 4,400,000
Luta, China (est. 1977)	C 4,200,000
Bangkok, Thailand (est. 1975)	C 4,178,000
Boston, Mass. (est. 1977)	U 3,898,000
Istanbul, Turkey (est. 1975)	U 3,864,493
Santiago, Chile (est. 1978)	U 3,691,548
Delhi-New Delhi, India (census, 1971)	U 3,647,023
Madrid, Spain (est. 1974)	C 3,520,320
Wuhan, China (est. 1977)	C 3,500,000
Karachi, Pakistan (census, 1972)	C 3,498,634
Lima, Peru (census, 1972)	U 3,302,523
Madras, India (census, 1971)	C 3,169,930
Berlin, E. and W. (both est. 1977)	C 3,038,224
Washington, D.C.-Md.-Va. (est. 1977)	U 3,033,000
Sydney, Australia (census, 1976)	U 3,021,982
Nanking, China (est. 1977)	C 3,000,000
Rome, Italy (est. 1977)	C 2,897,505
Cleveland, Oh. (est. 1977)	U 2,874,000
Bogota, Colombia (census, 1973)	C 2,855,065
Toronto, Ontario, Canada (census, 1976)	U 2,803,101
Montreal, Quebec, Canada (census, 1976)	U 2,802,485
Osaka, Japan (est. 1977)	C 2,723,752
Houston, Tex. (est. 1977)	U 2,708,000
Yokohama, Japan (est. 1977)	C 2,694,569
Manchester, England (est. 1977)	U 2,674,800
Dallas-Ft. Worth, Tex. (est. 1977)	U 2,673,000
Melbourne, Australia (census, 1976)	U 2,604,035
Caracas, Venezuela (est. 1976)	U 2,576,000
Ankara, Turkey (est. 1975)	U 2,572,562
Pusan, S. Korea (census, 1975)	C 2,450,125
St. Louis, Mo. (est. 1977)	U 2,380,000
Guadalajara, Mexico (est. 1976)	U 2,343,034
Singapore (est. 1978)	U 2,334,400
Alexandria, Egypt (census, 1976)	C 2,318,655

U.S. Passport, Visa, and Health Requirements

Source: Passport Services, U.S. State Department and U.S. Public Health Service

Passports are issued by the United States Department of State to citizens and nationals of the United States for the purpose of documenting them for foreign travel and identifying them as Americans.

How to Obtain a Passport

An applicant for a passport who has never been previously issued a passport in his own name, must execute an application in person before (1) a passport agent; (2) a clerk of any federal court or state court of record or a judge or clerk of any probate court, accepting applications; (3) a postal employee designated by the postmaster at a Post Office which has been selected to accept passport applications; or (4) a diplomatic or consular officer of the U.S. abroad. Effective Jan. 1981, it is no longer possible to include family members of any age in a U.S. passport. All persons are required to obtain individual passports in their own name.

A passport previously issued to the applicant, or one in which he was included, will be accepted as proof of citizenship in lieu of the following documents. A person born in the United States shall present his birth certificate. To be acceptable, the certificate must show the given name and surname, the date and place of birth and that the birth record was filed shortly after birth. A delayed birth certificate (a record filed more than one year after the date of birth) is acceptable provided that it shows that the report of birth was supported by acceptable secondary evidence of birth.

If no primary evidence is not obtainable, a notice from the registrar shall be submitted stating that no birth record exists. The notice shall be accompanied by the best obtainable secondary evidence such as a baptismal certificate, a certificate of circumcision, or a hospital birth record.

A person in the U.S. who has been issued a passport in his own name within the last eight years may obtain a new passport by filling out, signing and mailing a passport by mail application together with his previous passport, two identical signed photographs and the established fee to the nearest Passport Agency or to the Passport Services in Wash., D.C. If; however, an applicant is applying for a passport for the first time, or his prior passport was issued before his 18th birthday, he must execute a passport application in person.

A naturalized citizen should present his naturalization certificate. A person born abroad claiming citizenship through either a native-born or naturalized citizen must submit a certificate of citizenship issued by the Immigration and Naturalization Service; or a Consular Report of Birth or Certification of Birth issued by the Dept. of State. If one of the above documents has not been obtained, he must submit evidence of citizenship of the parent(s) through whom citizenship is claimed and evidence which would establish the parent/child relationship. Additionally, if through birth to American parent(s), parents' marriage certificate plus an affidavit from parent(s) showing periods and places of residence or physical presence in the U.S. and abroad, specifying periods spent abroad in the employment of the U.S. government, including the armed forces, or with certain international organizations; if through naturalization of parents, evidence of admission to the U.S. for permanent residence.

Under certain conditions, married women must present evidence of marriage. Special laws govern women married prior to Mar. 3, 1931 and should be investigated.

Aliens — An alien leaving the U.S. must request passport facilities from his home government. He must have a permit from his local Collector of Internal Revenue, and if he wishes to return he should request a re-entry permit from the Immigration and Naturalization Service if it is required.

Contract Employees — Persons traveling because of a contract with the Government must submit with their applications letters from their employer stating position, destination and purpose of travel, armed forces contract number, and expiration date of contract when pertinent.

Photographs and Fees

Photographs — Identical photographs, sufficiently recent (normally taken within the past six months) to be a good likeness, both signed by the applicant, must accompany the passport application. An individual photograph of the passport bearer is required at all times.

Fees — The passport fee is $10. A fee of $5 shall be charged for execution of the application. No execution fee is payable where a passport is applied for by mail. All applicants must pay the passport fee and, where applicable, the execution fee unless specifically exempted by law.

The loss or theft of a valid passport is a serious matter and should be reported in writing immediately to the Passport Services, Dept. of State, Wash., D.C. 20524, or to the nearest passport agency, or to the nearest consular office of the U.S. when abroad.

Foreign Regulations

A visa, usually rubber stamped in a passport by a representative of the country to be visited, certifies that the bearer of the passport is permitted to enter that country for a certain purpose and length of time. Visa information can be obtained by writing directly to foreign consular officials.

Health Information

Smallpox — Some countries require an International Certificate of Vaccination against smallpox. Vaccination is not required for direct travel from the U.S. to most other countries.

Yellow Fever — A few African countries require vaccination of all travelers. A number of countries require vaccination if travelers arrive from infected or endemic areas. Vaccination is recommended for travel to infected areas and for travel outside the urban areas of countries in the endemic zones.

Cholera — A few countries require vaccination if travelers arrive from infected areas. Mozambique and Niger require vaccination of all travelers.

Plague — Vaccination is not indicated for most travelers to countries reporting cases of plague, particularly if their travel is limited to urban areas with modern hotels.

Malaria — There is a risk in the Caribbean, Central and South America, Africa, the Middle and Far East, and the Indian subcontinent. Travelers are strongly advised to seek information from their health department or private physician.

Return to the United States — No vaccinations are required to return to the United States from any country.

Vaccination Information — Yellow fever vaccine must be obtained at an officially designated Center, and the Certificate, valid for 10 years, must be stamped by the Center, The location of Centers is available from local health departments. Other vaccinations may be obtained from licensed physicians.

Travelers are advised to contact their local health department, physician, or agency that advises international travelers 2 weeks prior to departure to obtain the most current information.

Passports Issued and Renewed

Source: Bureau of Consular Affairs, U.S. State Department

Passports are actual count; other data based on sample.

Item	1960	1970[5]	1975	1976	1977	1978	1979	1980
New and renewed passports...	853,087	2,219,159	2,334,359	2,816,683	3,107,122	3,234,471	3,169,999	3,020,468
Object of Travel[1]								
Government	115,910	146,169	131,739	134,883	153,992	142,901	146,879	135,868
Nongovernment	737,177	2,072,990	2,123,960	2,529,290	2,388,540	2,641,690	2,404,090	2,331,630
Personal reasons[2]	321,590	1,791,330	376,400	602,980	1,005,630	1,567,880	1,540,690	1,246,130
Pleasure[3]	350,897	216,700	1,315,600	1,511,060	1,102,250	821,070	552,580	829,680
Business[4]	24,540	39,940	273,110	272,600	190,890	163,770	202,450	161,520
Education	31,240	20,230	132,490	125,590	78,550	75,440	92,980	79,550
Religion	6,780	3,350	22,450	13,690	9,160	11,090	13,590	10,970
Health	1,460	640	1,510	1,500	1,090	980	610	990
Other	670	800	2,400	1,870	970	1,460	1,190	2,790
Not stated	NA	NA	78,660	152,510	564,590	449,880	619,030	552,970
First area designation:								
Africa	8,440	18,790	32,930	35,390	33,980	24,020	22,430	28,538
Australia and Oceania	35,220	51,210	96,300	106,540	108,280	95,670	107,180	126,420
Europe	669,662	1,910,169	1,611,410	1,990,993	2,291,942	2,535,381	2,392,029	2,192,858
Far East	55,960	116,730	154,660	180,090	187,130	170,010	187,820	198,868
North, Central, and South America	58,935	72,410	317,980	347,020	316,590	263,240	317,610	333,220
Middle-East	24,670	48,890	121,010	156,530	169,060	145,870	142,830	140,010
World Tour	200	960	60	120	140	280	100	570
Sex of passport recipients:								
Male	419,615	1,123,620	1,128,050	1,353,610	1,496,250	1,555,200	1,543,490	1,497,200
Female	433,472	1,095,539	1,206,309	1,463,073	1,610,872	1,679,271	1,626,509	1,523,268
Citizenship of passport recipients:								
Native	710,172	2,072,560	2,039,690	2,458,050	2,853,290	2,916,840	2,799,810	2,797,780
Naturalized	142,915	146,599	294,669	358,633	253,832	317,631	370,189	222,688

(1) Data not entirely comparable because of changes in classifications in 1961. (2) Includes "Personal business," "Join husband." "Accompany husband," "Business and pleasure," "Visit family." (3) Includes "Sightsee," "Vacation," "Visit," and "Tourist." (4) Includes applications formerly listed under "Employment" and "Commercial business." (5) Legislation effective Aug. 26, 1968 eliminated passport renewals.

Customs Exemptions and Advice to Travelers

United States residents returning after a stay abroad of at least 48 hours are, generally speaking, granted customs exemptions of $300 each. The duty-free articles must accompany the traveler at the time of his return, must be for his personal or household use, must have been acquired as an incident of his trip, and must be properly declared to Customs. Not more than one liter of alcoholic beverages may be included in the $300 exemption.

If a U.S. resident arrives directly or indirectly from American Samoa, Guam, or the Virgin Islands of the United States, his purchase may be valued up to $600 fair retail value, but not more than $300 of the exemption may be applied to the value of articles acquired elsewhere than in such insular possessions, and 4 liters of alcoholic beverages may be included in his exemption, but not more than 1 liter of such beverages may have been acquired elsewhere than in the designated islands.

In either case, the exemption for alcoholic beverages is accorded only when the returning resident has attained 21 years of age at the time of his arrival. One hundred cigars and 200 cigarettes may be included (except Cuban products) in either exemption. Cuban cigars may be included if obtained in Cuba and all articles acquired there do not exceed $100 in retail value.

The $300 or $600 exemption may be granted only if the exemption, or any part of it, has not been used within the preceding 30-day period and your stay abroad was for at least 48 hours. The 48-hour absence requirement does not apply if you return from Mexico or the Virgin Islands of the United States.

Bona fide gifts costing no more than $25 fair retail value or $40 from American Samoa, Guam, or Virgin Islands, may be mailed to friends at home duty-free; addressee cannot receive in a single day gifts exceeding the $25 limit.

U.S. Immigration Law
Source: Immigration and Naturalization Service, U.S. Justice Department

The Immigration and Nationality Act as amended by the Act of October 3, 1965, and the Immigration and Nationality Amendments of 1976 (P.L. 94-571) "marked the final end of an immigration quota system based on nationality." The latter amendments eliminated inequities in the existing law regarding the admission of immigrants from countries in the Western Hemisphere. The seven-category preference system, the 20,000 per-country limit, and the provisions for adjustment of status, all of which were in effect for Eastern Hemisphere countries, were extended to the Western Hemisphere.

The Immigration and Nationality Act, as amended, provides for the numerical limitation of most immigration. Not subject to any numerical limitations are immigrants classified as immediate relatives who are spouses or children of U.S. citizens, or parents of citizens who are 21 years of age or older; returning residents; certain former U.S. citizens; ministers of religion; and certain long-term U.S. government employees.

Numerical Limitation of Immigrants
Immigration to the U.S. is numerically limited to 270,000 per year. Within this quota there is an annual limitation of 20,000 for each country. The colonies and dependencies of foreign states are limited to 600 per year, chargeable to the country limitation of the mother country.

Visa Categories
Applicants for immigration are classified as either preference or nonpreference. The preference visa categories are based on certain relationships to persons in the U.S., i.e., unmarried sons and daughters over 21 of U.S. citizens, spouses and unmarried sons and daughters of resident aliens, married sons and daughters of U.S. citizens, brothers and sisters of U.S. citizens 21 or over (first, 2d, 4th, and 5th preference, respectively); members of the professions or persons of exceptional ability in the sciences and arts whose services are sought by U.S. employers (3d preference); and

skilled and unskilled workers in short supply (6th preference); refugees (7th preference). Spouses and children of preference applicants are entitled to the same preference if accompanying or following to join such persons.

Except for refugee status, preference status is based upon approved petitions, filed with the Immigration and Naturalization Service, by the appropriate relative or employer (or in the 3d preference by the alien himself).

Other immigrants not within one of the above-mentioned preference groups may qualify as nonpreference applicants and receive only those visa numbers not needed by preference applicants.

Labor Certification
The Act of October 3, 1965, established new controls to protect the American labor market from an influx of skilled and unskilled foreign labor. Prior to the issuance of a visa, the would-be 3d, 6th, and nonpreference immigrant must obtain the Secretary of Labor's certification, establishing that there are not sufficient workers in the U.S. at the alien's destination who are able, willing, and qualified to perform the job; and that the employment of the alien will not adversely affect the wages and working conditions of workers in the U.S. similarly employed; or that there is satisfactory evidence that the provisions of that section do not apply to the alien's case.

Extension of Adjustment of Status
The Act of October 3, 1965, excluded Western Hemisphere natives from adjusting their status to permanent residence under Section 245 of the Immigration and Nationality Act which allows a nonimmigrant alien to adjust to permanent resident without leaving the U.S. to secure a visa. The 1976 Amendments restored the adjustment of status provision to Western Hemisphere natives, and declared ineligible for adjustment of status aliens who are not defined as immediate relatives and who accept unauthorized employment prior to filing their adjustment application.

Immigrants Admitted from All Countries
Fiscal Year Ends June 30 through 1976, Sept. 30 thereafter

Year	Number	Year	Number	Year	Number	Year	Number
1820	8,385	1881-1890 . . .	5,246,613	1951-1960 . . .	2,515,479	1976	398,613
1821-1830 . . .	143,439	1891-1900 . . .	3,687,564	1961-1970 . . .	3,321,777	1976 July-Sept.	103,676
1831-1840 . . .	599,125	1901-1910 . . .	8,795,386	1971	370,478	1977	462,315
1841-1850 . . .	1,713,251	1911-1920 . . .	5,735,811	1972	384,685	1978	601,442
1851-1860 . . .	2,598,214	1921-1930 . . .	4,107,209	1973	400,063	1979	460,348
1861-1870 . . .	2,314,824	1931-1940 . . .	528,431	1974	394,861	1820-1979 . . .	49,125,413
1871-1880 . . .	2,812,191	1941-1950 . . .	1,035,039	1975	386,194		

Naturalization: How to Become an American Citizen
Source: The Federal Statutes

A person who desires to be naturalized as a citizen of the United States may obtain the necessary application form as well as detailed information from the nearest office of the Immigration and Naturalization Service or from the clerk of a court handling naturalization cases.

An applicant must be at least 18 years old. He must have been a lawful resident of the United States continuously for 5 years. For husbands and wives of U.S. citizens the period is 3 years in most instances. Special provisions apply to certain veterans of the Armed Forces.

An applicant must have been physically present in this country for at least half of the required 5 years' residence.

Every applicant for naturalization must:

(1) demonstrate an understanding of the English language, including an ability to read, write, and speak words in ordinary usage in the English language (persons physically unable to do so, and persons who, on the date of their examinations, are over 50 years of age and have been lawful permanent residents of the United States for 20 years or more are exempt).

(2) have been a person of good moral character, attached to the principles of the Constitution, and well disposed to the good order and happiness of the United States for five years just before filing the petition or for whatever other period of residence is required in his case and continue to be such a person until admitted to citizenship; and

(3) demonstrate a knowledge and understanding of the fundamentals of the history, and the principles and form of government, of the U.S.

The petitioner also is obliged to have two credible citizen witnesses. These witnesses must have personal knowledge of the applicant.

When the applicant files his petition he pays the court clerk $25. At the preliminary hearing he may be represented by a lawyer or social service agency. There is a 30-day wait. If action is favorable, there is a final hearing before a judge, who administers the following oath of allegiance:

I hereby declare, on oath, that I absolutely and entirely renounce and abjure all allegiance and fidelity to any foreign prince, potentate, state or sovereignty, to whom or which I have heretofore been a subject or citizen; that I will support and defend the Constitution and laws of the United States of America against all enemies, foreign and domestic; that I will bear true faith and allegiance to the same; that I will bear arms on behalf of the United States when required by the law; that I will perform noncombatant service in the armed forces of the United States when required by the law; that I will perform work of national importance under civilian direction when required by the law; and that I take this obligation freely without any mental reservation or purpose of evasion; so help me God.

Sources: Population: Bureau of the Census (April, 1981 summary, including armed forces personnel in each state but excluding such personnel stationed overseas); area: Geography Division, Bureau of the Census; Value added by manufacture: Bureau of the Census; lumber production: Commerce Department; mineral production: Bureau of Mines; commercial fish-landings: Marine Fisheries Service; per capita income: Bureau of Economic Analysis, Commerce Department; forested land: Department of Agriculture, Forest Service; unemployment: Bureau of Labor Statistics; energy production: Energy Department; education: Education Department; construction valuation: Dodge Construction Potentials, McGraw-Hill Information Systems Company.

Alabama

Heart of Dixie, Cotton State

People. Population (1980): 3,890,061; **rank:** 21. **Pop. density:** 76.7 per sq. mi. **Urban** (1970): 58.4%. **Racial distrib.** (1980): 73.7% White; 26.3% Black; Hispanic 33,100. **Major ethnic groups:** German, English, Italian, Polish. **Net migration** (1970-79): +75,000.

Geography. Total area: 51,609 sq. mi.; **rank:** 29. **Land area:** 50,708 sq. mi. **Acres forested land:** 21,361,100. **Location:** in the east south central U.S., extending N-S from Tenn. to the Gulf of Mexico; east of the Mississippi River. **Climate:** long, hot summers; mild winters; generally abundant rainfall. **Topography:** coastal plains inc. Prairie Black Belt give way to hills, broken terrain; highest elevation, 2,407 ft. **Capital:** Montgomery.

Economy. Principal industries: pulp and paper, apparel, textiles, primary metals, lumber and wood, food processing, fabricated metals, automotive tires. **Principal manufactured goods:** cast iron and plastic pipe, ships, paper products, chemicals, steel, mobile homes, fabrics, poultry processing. **Value added by manufacture** (1978): $9.7 bln. **Agriculture: Chief crops:** soybeans, cotton, peanuts, corn, hay, wheat, pecans, peaches, potatoes, tomatoes. **Livestock:** 1.92 mln. cattle; 800,000 hogs/pigs; 20.7 mln. poultry. **Timber/lumber** (1979): pine, hardwoods; 1.56 bln. bd. ft. **Minerals** (1979): natural gas, bituminous coal, crude petroleum, accounting for 80% of the $1.9 bln. total mineral value for raw materials. Also, cement and stone. **Commercial fishing** (1980): $51 mln. **Chief ports:** Mobile. **Value of construction** (1980): $1.9 bln. **Employment distribution:** 26.7% manuf.; 20% trade; 15% serv. **Per capita income** (1980): $7,484. **Unemployment** (1980): 8.8%. **Tourism** (1979): tourists spent $2.2 bln.

Finance. No. banks (1979): 317; **No. savings and loan assns.** (1978): 61.

Federal government. No. federal civilian employees (Mar. 1980): 56,107. **Avg. salary:** $19,858. **Notable federal facilities:** George C. Marshall NASA Space Center, Huntsville; Maxwell AFB, Montgomery; Ft. Rucker, Ozark; Ft. McClellan, Anniston; Natl. Fertilizer Development Center, Muscle Shoals.

Energy. Electricity production (1980, mwh, by source): Hydroelectric: 9.38 mln. Mineral: 45.4 mln. Nuclear: 23.5 mln.

Education. No. schools: 1,582 elem. and second.; 58 higher ed. **Avg. salary, public school teachers** (1980): $13,312.

State data. Motto: We dare defend our rights. **Flower:** Camellia. **Bird:** Yellowhammer. **Tree:** Southern pine. **Song:** Alabama. **Entered union** Dec. 14, 1819; rank, 22d. **State fair** at: Birmingham; early Oct.

History. First Europeans were Spanish explorers in the early 1500s. The French made the first permanent settlement, on Mobile Bay, 1701-02; later, English settled in the northern areas. France ceded the entire region to England at the end of the French and Indian War, 1763, but Spanish Florida claimed the Mobile Bay area until U. S. troops took it, 1813. Gen. Andrew Jackson broke the power of the Creek Indians, 1814, and they were removed to Oklahoma. The Confederate States were organized Feb. 4, 1861, at Montgomery, the first capital.

Tourist attractions. Jefferson Davis' "first White House" of the Confederacy; Ivy Green, Helen Keller's birthplace at Tuscumbia; statue of Vulcan near Birmingham; George Washington Carver Museum at Tuskegee Institute; Alabama Space and Rocket Center at Huntsville. At Russell Cave National Monument, near Bridgeport, may be seen a detailed record of occupancy by humans from about 10,000 BC to 1650 AD.

Famous Alabamians include Hank Aaron, Tallulah Bankhead, Hugo L. Black, George Washington Carver, Nat King Cole, William C. Handy, Helen Keller, Harper Lee, Joe Louis, John Hunt Morgan, Jesse Owens, Booker T. Washington, Hank Williams.

Chamber of Commerce: 468 S. Perry St., P.O. Box 76, Montgomery, AL 36101.

Alaska

No official nickname

People. Population (1980): 308,455; **rank:** 50. **Pop. density:** 0.54 per sq. mi. **Urban** (1970): 48.4%. **Major ethnic groups:** Anglo-Saxons, Alaska natives (Eskimos, Aleuts and Indians). **Net migration** (1970-79): +47,000.

Geography. Total area: 589,757 sq. mi.; **rank:** 1. **Land area:** 569,600 sq. mi. **Acres forested land:** 119,114,900. **Location:** NW corner of North America, bordered on east by Canada. **Climate:** SE, SW, and central regions, moist and mild; far north extremely dry. Extended summer days, winter nights, throughout. **Topography:** includes Pacific and Arctic mountain systems, central plateau, and Arctic slope. Mt. McKinley, 20,320 ft., is the highest point in North America. **Capital:** Juneau.

Economy. Principal industries: oil, gas. **Principal manufactured goods:** fish products, lumber and pulp, furs. **Value added by manufacture** (1978): $546.8 mln. **Agriculture: Chief crops:** barley, hay, silage, potatoes, lettuce, milk, eggs. **Livestock:** 8,300 cattle; 800 hogs/-pigs; 6,500 sheep; 28,000 poultry. **Timber/lumber:** spruce, yellow cedar, hemlock. **Minerals** (1979): crude petroleum, natural gas, sand and gravel. Total mineral production valued at $5.7 bln. **Commercial fishing** (1979): $597 mln. **Chief ports:** Skagway, Juneau, Sitka, Valdez, Wrangell. **International airports at:** Anchorage, Fairbanks, Juneau. **Value of construction** (1980): $643 mln. **Employment distribution:** 27.9% gvt.; 16.1% serv. 9% transp. **Per capita income** (1980): $12,406. **Unemployment** (1980): 9.6%. **Tourism** (1979): out-of-state visitors spent $650 mln.

Finance. No. banks (1979): 12; **No. savings and loan assns.:** (1978): 4.

Federal government. No. federal civilian employees (Mar. 1980): 13,660. **Avg. salary:** $22,443.

Energy. Electricity production (1980, mwh, by source): Hydroelectric: 538,951 Mineral: 2.6 mln.; Nuclear: —.

Education. No. schools: 420 elem. and second.; 16 higher ed. **Avg. salary, public school teachers** (1980): $26,173.

State data. Motto: North to the future. **Flower:** Forget-me-not. **Bird:** Willow ptarmigan. **Tree:** Sitka spruce. **Song:** Alaska's Flag. **Entered union:** Jan. 3, 1959; rank, 49th. **State fair at:** Palmer; late Aug.—early Sept.

History. Vitus Bering, a Danish explorer working for Russia, was the first European to land in Alaska, 1741. Alexander Baranov, first governor of Russian America, set up headquarters at Archangel, near present Sitka, in 1799. Secretary of State William H. Seward in 1867 bought Alaska from Russia for $7.2 million, a bargain some called "Seward's Folly." In 1896 gold was discovered and the famed Gold Rush was on.

Tourist attractions: Glacier Bay National Monument, Mt. McKinley National Park, one of North America's great wildlife sanctuaries, Pribilof Islands fur seal rookeries, restored St. Michael's Russian Orthodox Cathedral, Sitka.

Famous Alaskans include Carl Eielson, Ernest Gruening, Joe Juneau, Sydney Laurence, James Wickersham.

Chamber of Commerce: 200 N. Franklin St., Juneau, AK 99801.

1854. Long Apache wars did not end until 1886, with Geronimo's surrender.

Tourist attractions. The Grand Canyon of the Colorado, an immense, vari-colored fissure 217 mi. long, 4 to 13 mi. wide at the brim, 4,000 to 5,500 ft. deep; the Painted Desert, extending for 30 mi. along U.S. 66; the Petrified Forest; Canyon Diablo, 225 ft. deep and 500 ft. wide; Meteor Crater, 4,150 ft. across, 570 ft. deep, made by a prehistoric meteor. Also, London Bridge at Lake Havasu City.

Famous Arizonans include Cochise, Geronimo, Barry Goldwater, Zane Grey, George W. P. Hunt, Helen Jacobs, Percival Lowell, William H. Pickering, Morris Udall, Stewart Udall, Frank Lloyd Wright.

Chamber of Commerce: 2701 E. Camelback Rd. Phoenix, AZ 85016.

Arizona

Grand Canyon State

People. Population (1980): 2,717,866; **rank:** 29. **Pop. density:** 23.9 per sq. mi. **Urban** (1970): 79.6%. **Racial distrib. (1980):** 82.4% White; 2.7% Black; 14.8% Other (includes American Indians); Hispanic 440,915. **Major ethnic groups:** Mexican, German, English, Italian. **Net migration** (1970-79): +464,000.

Geography. Total area: 113,909 sq. mi.; **rank:** 6. **Land area:** 113,417 sq. mi. **Acres forested land:** 18,493,900. **Location:** in the southwestern U.S. **Climate:** clear and dry in the southern regions and northern plateau; high central areas have heavy winter snows. **Topography:** Colorado plateau in the N, containing the Grand Canyon; Mexican Highlands running diagonally NW to SE; Sonoran Desert in the SW. **Capital:** Phoenix.

Economy: Principal industries: manufacturing, tourism, mining, agriculture. **Principal manufactured goods:** electronics, printing and publishing, foods, primary and fabricated metals, aircraft and missiles, apparel. **Value added by manufacture** (1978): $3.9 bln. **Agriculture: Chief crops:** cotton, sorghum, barley, corn, wheat, sugar beets, citrus fruits. **Livestock:** 1.14 mln. cattle; 99,000 hogs/pigs; 490,000 sheep; 565,000 poultry. **Timber/lumber** (1978): pine, fir, spruce; 383 mln. bd. ft. **Minerals** (1979): copper (prod. valued at $1.9 bln. 75% of total mineral production), gold, silver, molybdenum, sand and gravel, lime. **International airports at:** Phoenix, Tucson, Yuma. **Value of construction** (1980): $3.1 bln. **Employment distribution** (1979): 24.1% trade, 20.3% gvt., 19.5% serv., 14.7% manuf. **Per capita income** (1980): $8,649. **Unemployment** (1980): 6.7% **Tourism** (1980): tourists spent $4.0 bln.

Finance. No. banks: (1979): 27; **No. savings and loan assns.** (1978): 16.

Federal government: No. federal civilian employees (Mar. 1979): 31,608. **Avg. salary:** $18,118. **Notable federal facilities:** Williams, Luke, Davis-Monthan AF bases; Ft. Huachuca Army Base; Yuma Proving Grounds.

Energy. Electricity production (1980, mwh, by source): Hydroelectric: 9.8 mln.; Mineral: 27.0 mln.; Nuclear: —.

Education. No. schools: 1,053 elem. and second.; 23 higher ed. **Avg. salary, public school teachers** (1980): $15,835.

State data. Motto: Ditat Deus (God enriches). **Flower:** Blossom of the Seguaro cactus. **Bird:** Cactus wren. **Tree:** Paloverde. **Song:** Arizona. **Entered union** Feb. 14, 1912; rank, 48th. **State fair** at: Phoenix; late Oct.–early Nov.

History. Marcos de Niza, a Franciscan, and Estevan, a black slave, explored the area, 1539. Eusebio Francisco Kino, Jesuit missionary, taught Indians Christianity and farming, 1690-1711, left a chain of missions. Spain ceded Arizona to Mexico, 1821. The U. S. took over at the end of the Mexican War, 1848. The area below the Gila River was obtained from Mexico in the Gadsden Purchase,

Arkansas

Land of Opportunity

People. Population (1980): 2,285,513; **rank:** 33. **Pop. density:** 43.9 per sq. mi. **Urban** (1970): 50%. **Racial distrib.** (1980): 66.1% White; 16.3% Black; Hispanic 17,873. **Major ethnic groups:** German, English, Italian, Polish. **Net migration** (1970-80): +136,000.

Geography. Total area: 53,104 sq. mi.; **rank:** 27. **Land area:** 51,945 sq. mi. **Acres forested land:** 18,281,500. **Location:** in the west south-central U.S. **Climate:** long, hot summers, mild winters; generally abundant rainfall. **Topography:** eastern delta and prairie, southern lowland forests, and the northwestern highlands, which include the Ozark Plateaus. **Capital:** Little Rock.

Economy. Principal industries: manufacturing, agriculture, tourism. **Principal manufactured goods:** poultry products, forestry products, aluminum, electric motors, transformers, garments, shoes, bricks, fertilizer, petroleum products. **Value added by manufacture** (1978): $5.5 bln. **Agriculture:** Chief crops: soybeans, rice, cotton, hay, wheat, sorghum, tomatoes, strawberries. **Livestock:** 2 mln. cattle; 400,000 hogs/pigs; 4,900 sheep; 40.3 mln. poultry. **Timber/lumber** (1979): oak, hickory, gum, cypress, pine; 75 mln. bd. ft. **Minerals** (1979): bauxite, bromine, and vanadium prod. 1st in U.S. Also natural gas, crude petroleum. Total mineral production valued at $667.9 mln. **Commercial fishing** (1980): $5.2 mln. **Chief ports:** Little Rock, Pine Bluff, Osceola, Helena, Fort Smith, Van Buren, Camden. **Value of construction** (1980): $1.25 bln. **Employment distribution:** 26.5% manuf.; 19.8% trade; 13.5% serv.; 8.9% agric. **Per capita income** (1980): $7,180. **Unemployment** (1980): 7.6% **Tourism** (1977): out-of-state visitors spent $1.1 bln.

Finance. No. banks (1979): 261; **No. savings and loan assns.** (1978): 75.

Federal government. No. federal civilian employees (Mar. 1980): 15,407. **Avg. salary:** $17,878. **Notable federal facilities:** Nat'l. Center for Toxicological Research, Jefferson; Pine Bluff Arsenal.

Energy. Electricity production (1980, mwh, by source): Hydroelectric: 1.7 mln.; Mineral: 10.1 mln.; Nuclear: 7.8 mln.

Education. No. schools: 1,286 elem. and second.; 34 higher ed. **Avg. salary, public school teachers** (1980): $12,419.

State data. Motto: Regnat Populus (The people rule). **Flower:** Apple Blossom. **Bird:** Mockingbird. **Tree:** Pine. **Song:** Arkansas. **Entered union:** June 15, 1836; rank, 25th. **State fair at:** Little Rock; late Sept.- early Oct.

History. First European explorers were de Soto, 1541, Jolliet, 1673; La Salle, 1682. First settlement was by the French under Henri de Tonty, 1686, at Arkansas Post. In 1762 the area was ceded by France to Spain, then back again in 1800, and was part of the Louisiana Purchase by the U.S. in 1803. Arkansas seceded from the Union in 1861, only after the Civil War began, and more than 10,000 Arkansans fought on the Union side.

Tourist attractions. Hot Springs National Park, water ranging from 95° to 147°F; Blanchard Caverns, near Mountain View, are among the nation's largest; Crater of Diamonds, near Murfreesboro, only U.S. diamond mine.

Famous Arkansans include Hattie Caraway, "Dizzy" Dean, Orval Faubus, James W. Fulbright, Douglas MacArthur, John L. McClellan, James S. McDonnel, Winthrop Rockefeller, Edward Durell Stone, Archibald Yell.

Chamber of Commerce: 911 Wallace Bldg., Little Rock, AR 72201.

California
Golden State

People. Population (1980): 23,668,562; **rank:** 1. **Pop. density:** 151.3 per sq. mi. **Urban** (1970): 90.9%. **Racial distrib.** (1980): 76.1% White; 7.6% Black; 16.1% Other (includes American Indians, Asian Americans, and Pacific Islanders); Hispanic 4,543,770. **Major ethnic groups:** English, German, Italian, Russian. **Net migration** (1970-80): +1,462,000.

Geography. Total area 158,693 sq. mi.; **rank:** 3. **Land area:** 156,361 sq. mi. **Acres forested land:** 40,152,100. **Location:** on western coast of the U.S. **Climate:** moderate temperatures and rainfall along the coast; extremes in the interior. **Topography:** long mountainous coastline; central valley; Sierra Nevada on the east; desert basins of the southern interior; rugged mountains of the north. **Capital:** Sacramento.

Economy. Principal industries: agriculture, aerospace, manufacturing, construction, recreation. **Principal manufactured goods:** foods, primary and fabricated metals, machinery, electric and electronic equipment, chemicals and allied products. **Value added by manufacture** (1978): $62.5 bln. **Agriculture:** Chief crops: cotton, grapes, dairy products, lettuce, eggs, tomatoes, nursery products, nuts, apricots, avocados, citrus fruits, barley, rice, olives. **Livestock** (1980): 4.6 mln. cattle; 180,000 hogs/pigs; 1 mln. sheep; 83.1 mln. poultry. **Timber/lumber** (1979): fir, pine, redwood, oak; 3.9 bln. bd. ft. **Minerals** (1977): crude petroleum, natural gas, and natural gas liquids 69% of total value mineral production, $4.1 bln. **Commercial fishing** (1979): $227.5 mln. **Chief ports:** Long Beach, San Diego, Oakland, San Francisco, Sacramento, Stockton. **International airports at:** Los Angeles, San Francisco. **Value of construction** (1980): $17.6 bln. **Employment distribution** (1980): 23.0% trade; 20.0% serv.; 17.9% gvt. **Per capita income** (1980): $10,856. **Unemployment** (1980): 6.8% **Tourism** (1976): out-of-state visitors spent $12.4 bln.

Finance. Notable industries: banking, insurance, real estate, investment. **No. banks** (1979): 257; **No. savings and loan assns.** (1978): 170.

Federal government. No. federal civilian employees (Mar. 1980): 265,057. **Avg. salary:** $19,206. **Notable federal facilities:** Vandenberg, Beale, Travis, McClellan AF bases, San Francisco Mint.

Energy. Electricity production (1980, mwh, by source): Hydroelectric: 40.7 mln.; Mineral: 89.5 mln.; Nuclear: 4.9 mln.

Education. No. schools: 9,023 elem. and second.; 262 higher ed. **Avg. salary, public school teachers** (1980): $19,450.

State Data. Motto: Eureka (I have found it). **Flower:** Golden poppy. **Bird:** California valley quail. **Tree:** California redwood. **Song:** I Love You, California. **Entered Union** Sept. 9, 1850; **rank,** 31st. **State fair** at: Sacramento; late Aug.—early Sept.

History. First European explorers were Cabrillo, 1542, and Drake, 1579. First settlement was the Spanish Alta California mission at San Diego, 1769, first in a string founded by Franciscan Father Junipero Serra. U. S. traders and settlers arrived in the 19th century and staged the abortive Bear Flag Revolt, 1846; the Mexican War began later in 1846 and U.S. forces occupied California; Mexico ceded the province to the U.S., 1848, the same year the Gold Rush began.

Tourist attractions. Scenic regions are Yosemite Valley; Lassen and Sequoia-Kings Canyon national parks; Lake Tahoe; the Mojave and Colorado deserts; San Francisco Bay; and Monterey Peninsula. Oldest living things on earth are believed to be a stand of Bristlecone pines in the Inyo National Forest, est. to be 4,600 years old. The world's tallest tree, the Howard Libbey redwood, 362 ft. with a girth of 44 ft., stands on Redwood Creek, Humboldt County.

Also, Palomar Observatory; Disneyland; J. Paul Getty Museum, Malibu; Tournament of Roses and Rose Bowl.

Famous Californians include Luther Burbank, John C. Fremont, Bret Harte, Wm. R. Hearst, Jack London, Aimee Semple McPherson, John Muir, William Saroyan, Junipero Serra, Leland Stanford, John Steinbeck, Earl Warren.

Chamber of Commerce: 455 Capitol Mall, Sacramento, CA 95814.

Colorado
Centennial State

People. Population (1980): 2,888,834; **rank:** 28. **Pop. density:** 27.8 per sq. mi. **Urban** (1970): 78.5%. **Racial distrib.** (1980): 88.9% White; 3.5% Black; Hispanic 339,300. **Major ethnic groups:** German, Russian, English, Italian. **Net migration** (1970-80): +668,811.

Geography. Total area: 104,247 sq. mi.; **rank:** 8. **Land area:** 103,766 sq. mi. **Acres forested land:** 22,271,000. **Location:** in west central U.S. **Climate:** low relative humidity, abundant sunshine, wide daily, seasonal temperatures ranges; alpine conditions in the high mountains. **Topography:** eastern dry high plains; hilly to mountainous central plateau; western Rocky Mountains of high ranges alternating with broad valleys and deep, narrow canyons. **Capital:** Denver.

Economy. Principal industries: manufacturing, government, mining, tourism, agriculture, aerospace, electronics equipment. **Principal manufactured goods:** computer equipment, instruments, foods, machinery, aerospace products, rubber, steel. **Value added by manufacture** (1979): $6.14 bln. **Agriculture:** Chief crops: corn, wheat, hay, sugar beets, barley, potatoes, apples, peaches, pears, soy beans. **Livestock** (1979): 3.1 mln. cattle; 330,000 hogs/pigs; 795,000 sheep; 6,450,000 poultry. **Timber/lumber** (1979): oak, ponderosa pine, Douglas fir; 330.8 mln. bd. ft. **Minerals** (1980): molybdenum, uranium, coal, natural gas, petroleum. Total mineral production valued at $2.3 bln. **International airports at:** Denver. **Value of construction** (1980): $2.7 bln. **Employment distribution** (1979): 21.2% trade; 17.1% serv.; 16.7% gvt.; 12.8% manuf. **Per capita income** (1980): $9,964. **Unemployment** (1980): 5.6% **Tourism** (1979): out-of-state visitors spent $890 mln.

Finance. No. banks (1979): 410; **No. savings and loan assns.** (1978): 48.

Federal government. No. federal civilian employees (Mar. 1980): 42,304. **Avg. salary:** $19,769. **Notable federal facilities:** U.S. Air Force Academy; U.S. Mint; Ft. Carson, Lowry AFB; Solar Energy Research Institute; U.S. Rail Transport. Test Center; N. Amer. Aerospace Defense Command.

Energy. Electricity production (1980, mwh, by source): Hydroelectric: 1.7 mln.; Mineral: 21.2 mln.; Nuclear: 666,719.

Education. No. schools: 1,435 elem. and second.; 41 higher ed. **Avg. salary, public school teachers** (1979): $16,205.

State data. Motto: Nil Sine Numine (Nothing without Providence). **Flower:** Rocky Mountain columbine. **Bird:** Lark bunting. **Tree:** Colorado blue spruce. **Song:** Where the Columbines Grow. **Entered union** Aug. 1, 1876; **rank** 38th. **State fair** at: Pueblo; last week in Aug.

History. Early civilization centered around Mesa Verde 2,000 years ago. The U.S. acquired eastern Colorado in the Louisiana Purchase, 1803; Lt. Zebulon M. Pike explored the area, 1806, discovering the peak that bears his name. After the Mexican War, 1846-48, U.S. immigrants settled in the east, former Mexicans in the south.

Tourist attractions. Rocky Mountain National Park; Garden of the Gods; Great Sand Dunes and Dinosaur national monuments; Pikes Peak and Mt. Evans highways; Mesa Verde National Park (pre-historic cliff dwellings); 35 major ski areas. The Grand Mesa tableland comprises Grand Mesa Forest, 659,584 acres, with 200 lakes stocked with trout.

Famous Coloradans include Frederick Bonfils, William N. Byers, M. Scott Carpenter, Jack Dempsey, Douglas Fairbanks, Lowell Thomas, Byron R. White, Paul Whiteman.

Tourist information: Dept. of Local Affairs, 1313 Sherman St., Denver, CO 80203.

Connecticut

Constitution State, Nutmeg State

People. Population (1980): 3,107,576; **rank:** 25. **Pop. density:** 639.1 per sq. mi. **Urban** (1970): 77.4%. **Racial distrib.** (1980): 90.0% White; 6.9% Black; Hispanic 124,499. **Major ethnic groups:** Italian, Polish, English, Irish. **Net migration** (1970-79): −37,000.

Geography. Total area: 5,009 sq. mi.; **rank:** 48. **Land area:** 4,862 sq. mi. **Acres forested land:** 1,860,800. **Location:** New England state in the northeastern corner of the U.S. **Climate:** moderate; winters avg. slightly below freezing, warm, humid summers. **Topography:** western upland, the Berkshires, in the NW, highest elevations; narrow central lowland N-S; hilly eastern upland drained by rivers. **Capital:** Hartford.

Economy. Principal industries: manufacturing, retail trade, government, services. **Principal manufactured goods:** aircraft engines and parts, submarines, copper wire and tubing, silverware, helicopters, bearings, cutlery, machine tools. **Value added by manufacture** (1978): $12.2 bln. **Agriculture: Chief crops:** tobacco, hay, apples, potatoes, nursery stock. **Livestock:** 104,000 cattle; 11,000 hogs/pigs; 5,400 sheep; 5.9 mln. poultry. **Timber/lumber** (1977): oak, birch, beech, maple; 43 mln. bd. ft. **Minerals** (1980): stone, sand and gravel. Total mineral production valued at $62.8 mln. **Commercial fishing** (1979): $6.9 mln. **Chief ports:** New Haven, Bridgeport, New London. **International airports at:** Windsor Locks. **Value of construction** (1980): $1.4 bln. **Employment distribution:** 31% manuf.; 19% serv. **Per capita income** (1980): $11,445. **Unemployment** (1980): 5.8% **Tourism** (1976): out-of-state visitors spent $1 bln.

Finance. Notable industries: insurance, finance, banking. **No. banks** (1979): 65; **No. savings and loan assns.** (1978): 38.

Federal Government. No. federal civilian employees (Mar. 1980): 17,157. **Avg. salary:** $19,124. **Notable federal facilities:** U.S. Coast Guard Academy; U.S. Navy Submarine Base.

Energy Electricity production (1980, mwh, by source): Hydroelectric: 249,819; Mineral: 12.6 mln.; Nuclear: 11.8 mln.

Education. No. schools: 1,408 elem. and second.; 47 higher ed. **Avg. salary, public school teachers** (1979): $16,475.

State data. Motto: Qui Transtulit Sustinet (He who transplanted still sustains). **Flower:** Mountain laurel. **Bird:** American robin. **Tree:** White oak. **Song:** Yankee Doodle Dandy. **Fifth** of the 13 original states to ratify the Constitution, Jan. 9, 1788.

History. Adriaen Block, Dutch explorer, was the first European visitor, 1614. By 1634, settlers from Plymouth Bay started colonies along the Connecticut River and in 1637 defeated the Pequot Indians. In the Revolution, Connecticut men fought in most major campaigns and turned back British raids on Danbury and other towns, while Connecticut privateers captured British merchant ships.

Tourist attractions. Winchester Gun Museum, Yale University's Art Gallery, Peabody Museum, all in New Haven; Mystic Seaport, Mystic, a recreated 19th century seaport village; P.T. Barnum Museum, Bridgeport.

Famous "Nutmeggers" include Ethan Allen, Phineas T. Barnum, Samuel Colt, Jonathan Edwards, Nathan Hale, Katharine Hepburn, Isaac Hull, J. Pierpont Morgan, Israel Putnam, Harriet Beecher Stowe, Mark Twain, Noah Webster, Eli Whitney.

Chamber of Commerce: Suite 1202, 60 Washington St., Hartford, CT 06106.

Delaware

First State, Diamond State

People. Population (1980): 595,225; **rank:** 47. **Pop. density:** 300.3 per sq. mi. **Urban** (1970): 72.2%. **Racial distrib.** (1980): 82.0% White; 16.1% Black; Hispanic 9,671. **Major ethnic groups:** Italian, English, Polish, German. **Net migration** (1970-80): +7,470.

Geography. Total area: 2,057 sq. mi.; **rank:** 49. **Land area:** 1,982 sq. mi. **Acres forested land:** 391,800. **Location:** occupies the Delmarva Peninsula on the Atlantic coastal plain. **Climate:** moderate. **Topography:** Piedmont plateau to the N, sloping to a near sea-level plain. **Capital:** Dover.

Economy. Principal industries: chemistry, agriculture, poultry, shellfish, tourism, auto assembly, food processing, transportation equipment. **Principal manufactured goods:** nylon, apparel, luggage, foods, cash registers, autos, processed meats and vegetables, railroad and aircraft equipment. **Value added by manufacture** (1978): $2.01 bln. **Agriculture: Chief crops:** soybeans, corn, potatoes, mushrooms, greenhouse and dairy products, grain, hay. **Livestock:** 31,000 cattle; 50,000 hogs/pigs; 1,700 sheep; 850,000 poultry. **Timber/Lumber:** 408 mln. bd. ft. **Minerals** (1978): Sand and gravel. Total mineral production valued at $2.2 mln. **Commercial fishing** (1979): $638,000. **Chief ports:** Wilmington. **International airports at:** Philadelphia/Wilmington. **Value of construction** (1980): $324 mln. **Employment distribution:** 70.7% serv.; 27.6% manuf. **Per capita income** (1980): $10,195. **Unemployment** (1980): 7.7%. **Tourism** (1977): out-of-state visitors spent $313 mln.

Finance. No. banks (1979): 20; **No. savings and loan assns.** (1978): 18.

Federal government. No. federal civilian employees (Mar. 1980): 4,292. **Avg. salary:** $18,661. **Notable federal facilities:** Dover Air Force Base, Federal Wildlife Refuge, Bombay Hook.

Energy. Electricity production (1980, mwh, by source): Hydroelectric: —; Mineral: 6.6 mln.; Nuclear: —.

Education. No. schools: 254 elem. and second.; 10 higher ed. **Avg. salary, public school teachers** (1980): $16,148.

State data. Motto: Liberty and independence. **Flower:** Peach blossom. **Bird:** Blue hen chicken. **Tree:** American holly. **Song:** Our Delaware. **First** of original 13 states to ratify the Constitution, Dec. 7, 1787. **State fair at:** Harrington; end of July.

History. The Dutch first settled in Delaware near present Lewes, 1631, but were wiped out by Indians. Swedes settled at present Wilmington, 1638; Dutch settled anew, 1651, near New Castle and seized the Swedish settlement, 1655, only to lose all Delaware and New Netherland to the British, 1664.

Tourist attractions. Ft. Christina Monument, the site of founding of New Sweden; John Dickinson "Penman of the Revolution" home, Dover; Henry Francis du Pont Winterthur Museum; Hagley Museum, Wilmington; Old Swedes (Trinity Parish) Church, erected 1698, is the oldest Protestant church in the U.S. still in use.

Famous Delawareans include Thomas F. Bayard, Henry Seidel Canby, E. I. du Pont, John P. Marquand, Howard Pyle, Caesar Rodney.

Chamber of Commerce: 1102 West St., Wilmington, DE 19081.

Florida

Sunshine State

People. Population (1980): 9,739,992; **rank:** 7. **Pop. density:** 180.0 per sq. mi. **Urban** (1970): 80.5%. **Racial distrib.** (1980): 83.9% White; 13.7% Black; Hispanic 857,898. **Major ethnic groups:** German, English, Italian, Russian. **Net migration** (1970-79): +2,948,574.

Geography. Total area: 58,560 sq. mi.; **rank:** 22. **Land area:** 54,090 sq. mi. **Acres forested land:** 17,039,700. **Location:** peninsula jutting southward 500 mi. bet. the Atlantic and the Gulf of Mexico. **Climate:** subtropical N of Bradenton-Lake Okeechobee-Vero Beach line; tropical S of line. **Topography:** land is flat or rolling; highest point is 345 ft. in the NW. **Capital:** Tallahassee.

Economy. Principal industries: services, trade, gvt., agriculture, tourism, manufacturing, aerospace, food processing, chemical, finance, insurance, real estate, construction. **Principal manufactured goods:** metal products, paper, electronics equip., transp. equipment. **Value added by manufacture** (1980): $11.2 bln. **Agriculture. Chief crops:** citrus fruits, vegetables, sugarcane, avocados, watermelons, peanuts, cotton, tobacco, strawberries, peaches. **Livestock** (1981): 2.8 mln. cattle; 370,000 hogs/pigs; 4,500 sheep; 12 mln. poultry. **Timber/lumber** (1980): pine, oak, cypress, palm; 468 mln. bd. ft. **Minerals** (1979): petroleum, stone, phosphate rock. Total mineral production valued at $1.9 bln. **Commercial fishing** (1980): $116.5 mln. **Chief ports:** Tampa, Jacksonville, Miami, Pensacola. **International airports at:** Miami, Tampa, Jacksonville, Orlando, Ft. Lauderdale, W. Palm Beach. **Value of construction** (1980): $12.9 bln. **Per capita income** (1980): $8,987. **Unemployment** (1980): 6.0% **Tourism** (1980): out-of-state visitors spent $16 bln.

Finance. No. banks (1979): 585; **No. savings and loan assns.** (1978): 122.

Federal government. No. federal civilian employees (Mar. 1980): 71,920. **Avg. salary:** $19,219. **Notable federal facilities:** John F. Kennedy Space Center, Cape Canaveral; Eglin Air Force Base.

Energy. Electricity production (1980, mwh, by source): Hydroelectric: 214,621; Mineral: 78.9 mln.; Nuclear: 16.7 mln.

Education. No. schools: 2,695 elem. and second.; 77 higher ed. **Avg. salary, public school teachers** (1980): $14,149.

State data. Motto: In God we trust. **Flower:** Orange blossom. **Bird:** Mockingbird. **Tree:** Sabal palmetto palm. **Song:** Swanee River. **Entered union** Mar. 3, 1845; rank, 27th. **State fair** at: Tampa; Feb.

History. First European to see Florida was Ponce de Leon, 1513. France established a colony, Fort Caroline, on the St. Johns River, 1564; Spain settled St. Augustine, 1565, and Spanish troops massacred most of the French. Britain's Francis Drake burned St. Augustine, 1586. Britain held the area briefly, 1763-83, returning it to Spain. After Andrew Jackson led a U.S. invasion, 1818, Spain ceded Florida to the U.S., 1819. The Seminole War, 1835-42, resulted in removal of most Indians to Oklahoma. Florida seceded from the Union, 1861, was readmitted, 1868.

Tourist attractions. Miami, with the nation's greatest concentration of luxury hotels at Miami Beach; St. Augustine, oldest city in U.S.; Walt Disney World, an entertainment and vacation development near Orlando, Kennedy Space Center, Cape Canaveral.

Everglades National Park, 3d largest of U.S. national parks, preserves the beauty of the vast Everglades swamp. Castillo de San Marcos, St. Augustine, is a national monument. Also, the Ringling Museum of Art, and the Ringling Museum of the Circus, both in Sarasota.

Famous Floridians include Henry M. Flagler, James Weldon Johnson, MacKinlay Kantor, Henry B. Plant, Marjorie Kinnan Rawlings, Joseph W. Stilwell, Charles P. Summerall.

Chamber of Commerce: P.O. Box 5497, Tallahassee, FL 32301.

Georgia

Empire State of the South, Peach State

People. Population (1980): 5,464,265; **rank:** 13. **Pop. density:** 94.0 per sq. mi. **Urban** (1970): 60.3%. **Racial distrib.** (1980): 72.2% White; 26.8% Black; Hispanic 61,261. **Major ethnic groups:** German, English, Russian, Italian. **Net migration** (1970-79): +128,000.

Geography. Total area: 58,876 sq. mi.; **rank:** 21. **Land area:** 58,073 sq. mi. **Acres forested land:** 25,256,100. **Location:** South Atlantic state. **Climate:** maritime tropical air masses dominate in summer; continental polar air masses in winter; east central area drier. **Topography:** most southurly of the Blue Ridge Mtns. cover NE and N central; central Piedmont extends to the fall line of rivers; coastal plain levels to the coast flatlands. **Capital:** Atlanta.

Economy. Principal industries: manufacturing, forestry, agriculture, chemicals. **Principal manufactured goods:** textiles, transportation equipment, foods, clothing, paper and wood products, chemical products, cigarettes. **Value added by manufacture** (1978): $13.9 bln. **Agriculture: Chief crops:** cotton, peanuts, tobacco, pecans, peaches, rye, corn, soybeans. **Livestock** (1978): 1.85 mln. cattle; 1.59 mln. hogs/pigs; 3,200 sheep; 38.6 mln. poultry. **Timber/lumber** (1978): pine, hardwood; 1.3 bln. bd. ft. **Minerals** (1978): clay, crushed stone, and cement accounted for 91% of the total mineral production (valued at $577 mln.). **Commercial fishing** (1979): $27.7 mln. **Chief ports:** Savannah, Brunswick. **International airports at:** Atlanta. **Value of construction** (1980): $3.8 bln. 3.8 bln. Employment distribution: 25.2% manuf.; 22% trade; 14.2% serv. **Per capita income** (1980): $8,000. **Unemployment** (1980): 6.4% **Tourism** (1979): tourists spent $2.2 bln.

Finance. No. banks (1979): 439; **No. savings and loan assns.** (1978): 96.

Federal government. No. federal civilian employees (Mar. 1980): 70,724. **Avg. salary:** $18,966. **Notable federal facilities:** Robins AFB; Fts. Benning, Gordon, McPherson; Nat'l. Law Enforcement Training Ctr., Glynco.

Energy. Electricity production (1980, mwh, by source): Hydroelectric: 4.3 mln.; Mineral: 50.5 mln.; Nuclear: 8.4 mln.

Education. No. schools: 2,057 elem. and second.; 82 higher ed. **Avg. salary, public school teachers** (1980): $14,027.

State data. Motto: Wisdom, justice and moderation. **Flower:** Cherokee rose. **Bird:** Brown thrasher. **Tree:** Live oak. **Song:** Georgia On My Mind. **Fourth** of the 13 original states to ratify the Constitution, Jan. 2, 1788.

History. Gen. James Oglethorpe established the first settlements, 1733, for poor and religiously-persecuted Englishmen. Oglethorpe defeated a Spanish army from Florida at Bloody Marsh, 1742. In the Revolution, Georgians seized the Savannah armory, 1775, and sent the munitions to the Continental Army; they fought seesaw campaigns with Cornwallis' British troops, twice liberating Augusta and forcing final evacuation by the British from Savannah, 1782.

Tourist attractions. The Little White House in Warm Springs where Pres. Franklin D. Roosevelt died Apr. 12, 1945, 2,500-acre Callaway Gardens; Jekyll Island State Park, the restored 1850s farming community of Westville; Dahlonega, site of America's first gold rush; Stone Mountain, and Six Flags Over Georgia.

Okefenokee in the SE is one of the largest swamps in the U.S., a wetland wilderness and peat bog covering 660 sq. mi. A large part of it is a National Wildlife Refuge, a home for wild birds, alligators, bear, deer.

Famous Georgians include James Bowie, Erskine Caldwell, Lucius D. Clay, Ty Cobb, John C. Fremont, Joel Chandler Harris, Martin Luther King Jr., Sidney Lanier, Margaret Mitchell, Joseph Wheeler.

Chamber of Commerce: 1200 Commerce Bldg., Atlanta, GA 30303.

Hawaii

Aloha State

People. Population (1980): 965,000; **rank:** 40. **Pop. density:** 150.1 per sq. mi. **Urban** (1970): 83.1%. **Racial distrib.** (1980): 33.0% White; 1.7% Black; 65.1% Other (includes Asian Americans and Pacific Islanders); Hispanic 71,479. **Major ethnic groups:** Caucasian, part-Hawaiian, Japanese, Filipino, Chinese. **Net migration.** (1970-79): +36,200.

Geography. Total area: 6,450 sq. mi.; **rank:** 47. **Land area:** 6,425 sq. mi. **Acres forested land:** 1,986,000. **Location:** Hawaiian Islands lie in the North Pacific, 2,397 mi. SW from San Francisco. **Climate:** temperate, mountain regions cooler; Mt. Waialeale, on Kauai, wettest spot in the U.S. annual rainfall 486.1 in. **Topography:** islands are tops of a chain of submerged volcanic mountains; active volcanoes: Mauna Loa, Kilauea. **Capital:** Honolulu.

Economy. Principal industries: tourism, government, sugar refining, agriculture, aquaculture, fishing, motion pictures, manufacturing. **Principal manufactured goods:** sugar, canned pineapple, clothing, foods. **Value added by manufacture** (1978): $598.2 mln. **Agriculture: Chief crops:** sugar, pineapples, macadamia nuts, fruits, coffee, vegetables and melons. **Livestock:** 213,000 cattle; 53,000 hogs/pigs; 1.3 mln. poultry. **Minerals** (1979): Portland cement, stone. Total mineral production valued at $55 mln. **Commercial fishing** (1980): $12 mln. **Chief ports:** Honolulu, Port Allen, Kahului, Hilo. **International airports at:** Honolulu. **Value of construction** (1980): $1.1 bln. **Employment distribution:** 66.7% among gvt., construct., trade; 23.9% serv. **Per capita income** (1980): $9,787. **Unemployment** (1980): 5.0%. **Tourism** (1979): visitors spent $3.9 bln.

Finance. No. banks (1979): 12; **No. savings and loan assns.** (1978): 7.

Federal government. No. federal civilian employees (Mar. 1980): 23,401. **Avg. salary:** $20,527. **Notable federal facilities:** Pearl Harbor Naval Shipyard; Hickam AFB; Schofield Barracks.

Energy. Electricity production (1980, mwh, by source): Hydroelectric: 19,756; Mineral: 6.48 mln.; Nuclear: —.

Education. No. schools: 322 elem. and second.; 12 higher ed. **Avg. salary, public school teachers** (1980): $18,339.

State data. Motto: The life of the land is perpetuated in righteousness. **Flower:** Hibiscus. **Bird:** Hawaiian goose. **Tree:** Candlenut. **Song:** Hawaii Ponoi. **Entered union** Aug. 21, 1959; rank, 50th. **State fair** at: Honolulu; late May through mid-June.

History. Polynesians from islands 2,000 mi. to the south settled the Hawaiian Islands, probably about 700 A.D. First European visitor was British Capt. James Cook, 1778. Missionaries arrived, 1820, taught religion, reading and writing. King Kamehameha III and his chiefs created the first Constitution and a Legislature which set up a public school system. Sugar production began in 1835, it became the dominant industry. In 1893, Queen Liliuokalani was deposed, followed, 1894, by a republic headed by Sanford B. Dole. Annexation by the U.S. came in 1898.

Tourist attractions. Natl. Memorial Cemetery of the Pacific, USS Arizona Memorial, Pearl Harbor; Hawaii Volcanoes, Haleakala National Parks, Kilauea; Polynesian Cultural Center, Diamond Head, Waikiki Beach, Oahu.

Famous Islanders include John A. Burns, Father Joseph Damien, Sanford Dole, Hiram L. Fong, Daniel K. Inouye, Duke Kahanamoku, Queen Liliuokalani, Queen Kaahumanu, Bernice Pauahi Bishop, Bette Midler.

Chamber of Commerce: Dillingham Bldg., 735 Bishop St., Honolulu, HI 96813.

Idaho

Gem State

People. Population (1980): 943,935; **rank:** 41. **Pop.**

density: 11.4 per sq. mi. **Urban** (1970): 54.1%. **Racial distrib.** (1980): 95.5% White; 0.3% Black; Hispanic 36,615. **Major ethnic groups:** English, German, Swedish, Norwegian. **Net migration** (1970-80): +129,027.

Geography. Total area: 83,557 sq. mi.; **rank:** 13. **Land area:** 82,677 sq. mi. **Acres forested land:** 21,726,600. **Location:** Pacific Northwest-Mountain state bordering on British Columbia. **Climate:** tempered by Pacific westerly winds; drier, colder, continental clime in SE; altitude an important factor. **Topography:** Snake R. plains in the S; central region of mountains, canyons, gorges (Hells Canyon, 7,000 ft., deepest in N.A.); subalpine northern region. **Capital:** Boise.

Economy. Principal industries: agriculture, manufacturing, tourism, lumber, mining, electronics. **Principal manufactured goods:** processed foods, lumber and wood products, chemical products, primary metals, fabricated metal products, machinery. **Value added by manufacture** (1980): $1.8 bln. **Agriculture: Chief crops:** potatoes, peas, sugar beets, alfalfa seed, wheat, hops, barley, plums and prunes, mint, onions, corn, cherries, apples, trout. **Livestock:** 1.86 mln. cattle; 110,000 hogs/pigs; 468,000 sheep; 1.023 mln. poultry. **Timber/lumber** (1978): yellow, white pine; Douglas fir; white spruce; 2.0 bln. bd. ft. **Minerals** (1979): silver, phosphate rock, lead, zinc, sand and gravel. Total mineral production valued at $415 mln. **Commercial fishing** (1979): $35,000. **Chief ports:** Lewiston. **International airports at:** Boise. **Value of construction** (1980) $649 mln. **Employment distribution:** 20.1% trade; 8.7% agric.; 15% serv.; 13.5% manuf. **Per capita income** (1980): $8,126. **Unemployment** (1980): 7.9% **Tourism** (1976): out-of-state visitors spent $540 mln.

Finance. No. banks (1979): 27; **No. savings and loan assns.** (1978): 12.

Federal government. No. federal civilian employees (Mar. 1980): 8,059. **Avg. salary:** $19,433. **Notable federal facilities:** Ida. Nat'l. Engineering Lab, Idaho Falls; Nat'l. Reactor Testing Sta., Upper Snake River Plains.

Energy. Electricity production (1980, mwh, by source): Hydroelectric: 9.5 mln.; Mineral: 4,234; Nuclear —.

Education: No. schools: 596 elem. and second.; 9 higher ed. **Avg. salary, public school teachers** (1980): $13,615.

State data. Motto: Esto Perpetua (It is perpetual). **Flower:** Syringa. **Bird:** Mountain bluebird. **Tree:** White pine. **Song:** Here We Have Idaho. **Entered union** July 3, 1890; rank, 43d. **State fair** at: Boise and Blackfoot; late Aug.—early Sept.

History. Exploration of the Idaho area began with Lewis and Clark, 1805-06. Next came fur traders, setting up posts, 1809-34, and missionaries, establishing missions, 1830s-1850s. Mormons made their first permanent settlement at Franklin, 1860. Idaho's Gold Rush began that same year, and brought thousands of permanent settlers. Strangest of the Indian Wars was the 1,300-mi. trek in 1877 of Chief Joseph and the Nez Perce tribe, pursued by troops that caught them a few miles short of the Canadian border. In 1890, Idaho adopted a progressive Constitution and became a state.

Tourist attractions. Hells Canyon, deepest gorge in N.A.; Craters of the Moon; Sun Valley, year-round resort in the Sawtooth Mtns.; Crystal Falls Cave; Shoshone Falls; Lava Hot Springs; Lake Pend Oreille; Lake Coeur d'Alene.

Famous Idahoans include William E. Borah, Fred T. Dubois, Chief Joseph, Sacagawea.

Chamber of Commerce: P.O. Box 389, Boise, ID 83701.

Illinois

The Inland Empire

People. Population (1980): 11,418,461; **rank:** 5. **Pop. density:** 204.8 per sq. mi. **Urban** (1970): 83%. **Racial distrib.** (1980): 80.7% White; 14.6% Black; Hispanic

635,525. **Major ethnic groups:** German, Polish, Italian, English, Russian. **Net migration** (1970-79): −542,000.

Geography. Total area: 56,400 sq. mi.; **rank:** 24. **Land area:** 55,748 sq. mi. **Acres forested land:** 3,810,400. **Location:** east-north central state; western, southern, and eastern boundaries formed by Mississippi, Ohio, and Wabash Rivers, respectively. **Climate:** temperate; typically cold, snowy winters, hot summers. **Topography:** prairie and fertile plains throughout; open hills in the southern region. **Capital:** Springfield.

Economy. Principal industries: manufacturing, wholesale and retail trade, agriculture, services. **Principal manufactured goods:** machinery, electric and electronic equipment, foods, primary and fabricated metals, chemical products, printing and publishing. **Value added by manufacture** (1978): $44.8 bln. **Agriculture: Chief crops:** corn, soybeans, wheat, oats, hay. **Livestock** (1979): 2.85 mln. cattle; 6.55 mln. hogs/pigs; 167,000 sheep; 17.6 mln. poultry. **Timber/lumber** (1978): cottonwood, gum, walnut; 221 mln. bd. ft. **Minerals** (1977): mineral fuels (coal, natural gas, petroleum) accounted for 75% of the total $1.7 bln. mineral production. Also stone, sand and gravel, cement. **Commercial fishing** (1979): $1.0 mln. **Chief ports:** Chicago. **International airports at:** Chicago. **Value of construction** (1980): $5.3 bln. **Employment distribution:** 24% manuf.; 17% serv.; 2% agric. **Per capita income** (1980): $10,658. **Unemployment** (1980) 8.3%. **Tourism** (1975): out-of-state visitors spent $3.7 bln.

Finance. Notable industries: insurance, real estate. **No. banks** (1979): 1,288; **No. savings and loan assns.** (1978): 387.

Federal government. No. federal civilian employees (Mar. 1980): 89,287. **Avg. salary:** $18,999. **Notable federal facilities:** Fermi Nat'l. Accelerator Lab; Argonne Nat'l. Lab; Ft. Sheridan; Rock Island; Great Lakes, Rantoul, Scott Field.

Energy. Electricity production (1980, mwh, by source): Hydroelectric: 121,476; Mineral: 75.5 mln.; Nuclear: 27.7 mln.

Education. No. schools: 5,592 elem. and second.; 154 higher ed. **Avg. salary, public school teachers** (1980): $17,781.

State data. Motto: State sovereignty—national union. **Flower:** Native violet. **Bird:** Cardinal. **Tree:** White oak. **Song:** Illinois. **Entered union** Dec. 3, 1818; **rank,** 21st. **State fair** at: Springfield; mid-Aug.

History: Fur traders were the first Europeans in Illinois, followed shortly, 1673, by Jolliet and Marquette, and, 1680, La Salle, who built a fort near present Peoria. First settlements were French, at Fort St. Louis on the Illinois River, 1692, and Kaskaskia, 1700. France ceded the area to Britain, 1763; Amer. Gen. George Rogers Clark, 1778, took Kaskaskia from the British without a shot. Defeat of Indian tribes in Black Hawk War, 1832, and railroads in 1850s, inspired immigration.

Tourist attractions: Lincoln shrines at Springfield, New Salem, Sangamon; Cahokia Mounds, E. St. Louis; Starved Rock State Park; Crab Orchard Wildlife Refuge; Mormon settlement at Nauvoo; Fts. Kaskaskia, Chartres, Massac (parks).

Famous Illinoisans include Jane Addams, William Jennings Bryan, Stephen A. Douglas, James T. Farrell, Ernest Hemingway, Edgar Lee Masters, Carl Sandburg, Adlai Stevenson, Frank Lloyd Wright.

Chamber of Commerce: 20 N. Wacker Dr., Chicago, IL 60606.

Indiana

Hoosier State

People. Population (1980): 5,490,179; **rank:** 12. **Pop. density:** 152.0 per sq. mi. **Urban** (1970): 64.9%. **Racial distrib.** (1980): 91.1% White; 7.5% Black; Hispanic 87,020. **Major ethnic groups:** German, Polish, English, Mexican. **Net migration** (1970-79): −150,000.

Geography. Total area: 36,291 sq. mi.; **rank:** 38. **Land area:** 36,097 sq. mi. **Acres forested land:** 3,942,900. **Location:** east north-central state; Lake Michigan on northern border. **Climate:** 4 distinct seasons with a temperate climate. **Topography:** hilly southern region; fertile rolling plains of central region; flat, heavily glaciated north; dunes along Lake Michigan shore. **Capital:** Indianapolis.

Economy. Principal industries: manufacturing, wholesale and retail trade, agriculture, government, services. **Principal manufactured goods:** primary and fabricated metals, transportation equipment, electrical and electronic equipment, non-electrical machinery, chemical products, foods. **Value added by manufacture** (1978): 25.6 bln. **Agriculture: Chief crops:** corn, wheat, soybeans, hay. **Livestock** (1980): 1.85 mln. cattle; 4.9 mln. hogs/pigs; 165,000 sheep; 20.5 mln. poultry. **Timber/lumber** (1977): oak, tulip, beech, sycamore; 166 mln. bd. ft. **Minerals** (1979): mineral fuels, esp. coal; sand, gravel, stone; total $829.0 mln. mineral production. **Commercial fishing** (1979): $66,000. **Chief ports:** Lake Michigan facility, east of Gary, Southwind Maritime Centre at Mt. Vernon. **International airports at:** Indianapolis. **Value of construction** (1980): $2.7 bln. **Employment distribution** (1980): 30.8% manuf.; 22.4% trade; 15.8% serv. **Per capita income** (1980): $8,978. **Unemployment** (1980). 9.6%. **Tourism** (1978): tourists spent $1.9 bln.

Finance. No. banks (1979): 406; **No. savings and loan assns.** (1978): 166.

Federal government. No. federal civilian employees (Mar. 1980): 33,734 **Avg. salary:** $18,692. **Notable federal facilities:** Naval Avionics Ctr.; Ft. Benjamin Harrison; Grissom AFB; Navy Weapons Support Ctr., Crane.

Energy. Electricity production (1980 mwh, by source): Hydroelectric: 474,392 Mineral: 70.1 mln.; Nuclear: —.

Education. No. schools: 2,540 elem. and second.; 66 higher ed. **Avg. salary, public school teachers** (1980): $15,078.

State data. Motto: Crossroads of America. **Flower:** Peony. **Bird:** Cardinal. **Tree:** Tulip poplar. **Song:** On the Banks of the Wabash, Far Away. **Entered union** Dec. 11, 1816; rank, 19th. **State fair** at: Indianapolis; mid-Aug.

History: Pre-historic Indian Mound Builders of 1,000 years ago were the earliest known inhabitants. A French trading post was built, 1731-32, at Vincennes and La Salle visited the present South Bend area, 1679 and 1681. France ceded the area to Britain, 1763. During the Revolution, American Gen. George Rogers Clark captured Vincennes, 1778, and defeated British forces 1779; at war's end Britain ceded the area to the U.S. Miami Indians defeated U.S. troops twice, 1790, but were beaten, 1794, at Fallen Timbers by Gen. Anthony Wayne. At Tippecanoe, 1811, Gen. William H. Harrison defeated Tecumseh's Indian confederation.

Tourist attractions. Lincoln, George Rogers Clark memorials; Wyandotte Cave; Vincennes, Tippecanoe sites; Indiana Dunes; Hoosier Nat'l. Forest; Benjamin Harrison Home.

Famous "Hoosiers" include Ambrose Burnside, Hoagy Carmichael, Eugene V. Debs, Theodore Dreiser, Paul Dresser, Cole Porter, Gene Stratton Porter, Ernie Pyle, James Whitcomb Riley, Booth Tarkington, Lew Wallace, Wendell L. Willkie, Wilbur Wright.

Chamber of Commerce: Board of Trade Building, Indianapolis, IN 46204.

Iowa

Hawkeye State

People. Population (1980): 2,913,387 **rank:** 27. **Pop. density:** 52.0 per sq. mi. **Urban** (1970): 57.2%. **Racial distrib.** (1980): 97.4% White; 1.4% Black; Hispanic 15,852. **Major ethnic groups:** German, Scandinavian, English, Dutch. **Net migration** (1970-80): −60,491.

Geography. Total area: 56,290 sq. mi.; **rank:** 25. **Land area:** 55,941 sq. mi. **Acres forested land:** 1,561,300. **Location:** Midwest state bordered by Mississippi R. on the E and Missouri R. on the W. **Climate:** humid, continental.

Topography: Watershed from NW to SE; soil especially rich and land level in the N central counties. **Capital:** Des Moines.

Economy. Principal industries: manufacturing, agriculture. **Principal manufactured goods:** tires, farm machinery, electronic products, appliances, office furniture, chemicals, fertilizers, auto accessories. **Value added by manufacture** (1978): $9.8 bln. **Agriculture: Chief crops:** silage and grain corn, soybeans, oats, hay. **Livestock** (1979): 2.9 mln. cattle; 21.8 mln. hogs/pigs; 222,000 sheep; 7.7 mln. poultry. **Timber/lumber:** red cedar. **Minerals** (1980): cement, stone, and sand and gravel accounted for 93% of the total $248 mln. production. **Commercial fishing** (1980): $1.1 mln. **Value of construction** (1980): 1.6 bln. **Employment distribution:** 22.2% trade; 19.3% manuf.; 16.5% serv.; 16.4% gvt. **Per capita income** (1980): $9,178. **Unemployment** (1980): 5.7%. **Tourism** (1978): tourists spent $1.27 bln.

Finance. No. banks (1979): 657; **No. savings and loan assns.** (1978): 78.

Federal government. No. federal civilian employees (Mar. 1980): 14,283. **Avg. salary:** $18,668.

Energy. Electricity production (1980, mwh, by source): Hydroelectric: 944,849; Mineral: 18.2 mln.; Nuclear: 2.5 mln.

Education. No. schools: 2,153 elem. and second.; 62 higher ed. **Avg. salary, public school teachers** (1980): $15,340.

State data. Motto: Our liberties we prize and our rights we will maintain. **Flower:** Wild rose. **Bird:** Eastern goldfinch. **Tree:** Oak. **Song:** The Song of Iowa. **Entered union** Dec. 28, 1846; rank, 29th. **State fair** at: Des Moines; mid-to-late Aug.

History. A thousand years ago several groups of prehistoric Indian Mound Builders dwelt on Iowa's fertile plains. Marquette and Jolliet gave France its claim to the area, 1673. It became U.S. territory through the 1803 Louisiana Purchase. Indian tribes were moved into the area from states further east, but by mid-19th century were forced to move on to Kansas. Before and during the Civil War, Iowans strongly supported Abraham Lincoln and became traditional Republicans.

Tourist attractions. Herbert Hoover birthplace and library, West Branch; Effigy Mounds Nat'l. Monument, Marquette, a pre-historic Indian burial site; Davenport Municipal Art Gallery's collection of Grant Wood's paintings and memorabilia.

Famous Iowans include James A. Van Allen, Marquis Childs, Buffalo Bill Cody, Susan Glaspell, James Norman Hall, Harry Hansen, Billy Sunday, Carl Van Vechten, Henry Wallace, Meredith Willson, Grant Wood.

Tourist information: Travel Development Council, 250 Jewett Bldg., Des Moines, IA 50319.

Kansas
Sunflower State

People. Population (1980): 2,363,208; **rank:** 32. **Pop. density:** 28.8 per sq. mi. **Urban** (1970): 66.1%. **Racial distrib.** (1980): 91.7% White; 5.3% Black; Hispanic 63,333. **Major ethnic groups:** German, Russian, English, Mexican. **Net migration** (1970-79): −4,000.

Geography. Total area: 82,264 sq. mi.; **rank:** 14. **Land area:** 81,787 sq. mi. **Acres forested land:** 1,344,400. **Location:** West North Central state, with Missouri R. on E. **Climate:** temperate but continental, with great extremes bet. summer and winter. **Topography:** hilly Osage Plains in the E; central region level prairie and hills; high plains in the W. **Capital:** Topeka.

Economy. Principal industries: agriculture, machinery, mining, aerospace. **Principal manufactured goods:** processed foods, aircraft, petroleum products, farm machinery. **Value added by manufacture** (1978): $6.1 bln. **Agriculture: Chief crops:** wheat, sorghum, corn, hay. **Livestock:** 6.4 mln. cattle; 1.9 mln. hogs/pigs; 200,000 sheep; 2.14 mln. poultry. **Timber/lumber:** oak, walnut. **Minerals** (1980): petroleum, natural gas liquids, cement,

salt, stone, sand and gravel. Total mineral production $3.5 bln. **Commercial fishing** (1980): $9 mln. **Chief ports:** Kansas City. **International airports at:** Wichita. **Value of construction** (1980): $1.87 bln. **Employment distribution** (1980): 18.6% trade; 15.6% manuf.; 15.5% gvt.; 14.1% serv. **Per capita income** (1980): $9,958. **Unemployment** (1980): 4.4% **Tourism** (1978): out-of-state visitors spent $1.1 bln.

Finance. No. banks (1979): 617; **No. savings and loan assns.** (1978): 83

Federal government. No. federal civilian employees (Mar. 1980): 19,260. **Avg. salary:** $18,608. **Notable federal facilities:** McConnell AFB; Fts. Riley, Leavenworth.

Energy. Electricity production (1980, mwh, by source): Hydroelectric: 8,304; Mineral: 25.1 mln.; Nuclear: —.

Education. No. schools: 1,801 elem. and second.; 52 higher ed. **Avg. salary, public school teachers** (1980): $13,690.

State data. Motto: Ad Astra per Aspera (To the stars through difficulties). **Flower:** Native sunflower. **Bird:** Western meadowlark. **Tree:** Cottonwood. **Song:** Home on the Range. **Entered union** Jan. 29, 1861; rank, 34th. **State fair** at: Hutchinson; 2d week of Sept.

History. Coronado marched through the Kansas area, 1541; French explorers came next. The U.S. took over in the Louisiana Purchase, 1803. In the pre-war North-South struggle over slavery, so much violence swept the area it was called Bleeding Kansas. Railroad construction after the war made Abilene and Dodge City terminals of large cattle drives from Texas.

Tourist attractions. Eisenhower Center and "Place of Meditation," Abilene; Agricultural Hall of Fame and National Ctr., Bonner Springs, displays farm equipment; Dodge City; Ft. Scott.

Famous Kansans include Thomas Hart Benton, John Brown, Walter P. Chrysler, Amelia Earhart, Cyrus Holliday, Gen. Hugh Johnson, Walter Johnson, Alf Landon, Brock Pemberton, Robert Stroud.

Chamber of Commerce: 500 First National Tower, One Townsite Plaza, Topeka, KS 66603.

Kentucky
Bluegrass State

People. Population (1980): 3,661,433 **rank:** 23. **Pop. density:** 92.3 per sq. mi. **Urban** (1970): 52.3%. **Racial Distrib.** (1980): 92.3% White; 7.1% Black; Hispanic (1970): 11,112. **Major ethnic groups:** German, English, Italian, Irish. **Net migration** (1970-79): +91,000.

Geography. Total area: 40,395 sq. mi.; **rank:** 37. **Land area:** 39,650 sq. mi. **Acres forested land:** 12,160,800. **Location:** east south central state, bordered on N by Illinois, Indiana, Ohio; on E by West Virginia and Virginia; in S by Tennessee; on W by Missouri. **Climate:** moderate, with plentiful rainfall. **Topography:** mountainous in E; rounded hills of the Knobs in the N; Bluegrass, heart of state; wooded rocky hillsides of the Pennyroyal; Western Coal Field; the fertile Purchase the SW. **Capital:** Frankfort.

Economy. Principal industries: manufacturing, coal mining, construction, agriculture. **Principal manufactured goods:** whiskey, textiles, cigarettes, steel products, trucks. **Value added by manufacture** (1978): $10.8 bln. **Agriculture: Chief crops:** tobacco, soybeans, corn, wheat, hay, fruit. **Livestock:** 2.7 mln. cattle; 1.3 mln. hogs/pigs; 21,000 sheep; 3.5 mln. chickens. **Timber/lumber** (1977): hardwoods, pines; 412 mln. bd. ft. **Minerals** (1979): fossil fuels accounted for 98% of the total $4 bln. mineral production. **Commercial fishing** (1978): $923,000. **Chief ports:** Paducah, Louisville, Covington, Owensboro, Ashland. **International airports at:** Covington. **Value of construction** (1980): $2.19 bln. **Employment distribution:** manuf. 23.9%; trade 21.5%; gvt. 18.5%; serv. 16.4%. **Per capita income** (1980): $7,718. **Unemployment** (1980): 8.1% **Tourism** (1978): tourists spent $1.2 bln.

Finance. No. banks (1979): 343; **No. savings and**

loan assns. (1978): 105.

Federal government. No. federal civilian employees (Mar. 1980): 30,688. **Avg. salary:** $17,514. **Notable federal facilities:** U.S. Gold Bullion Depository; Ft. Knox; Addiction Research Center and Federal Correction Institution, Lexington.

Energy. Electricity production (1980, mwh, by source): Hydroelectric: 2.9 mln.; Mineral: 54.1 mln.; Nuclear: —.

Education. No. schools: 1,677 elem. and second.; 42 higher ed. **Avg. salary, public school teachers** (1980): $14,480.

State data. Motto: United we stand, divided we fall. **Flower:** Goldenrod. **Bird:** Cardinal. **Tree:** Kentucky coffee tree. **Song:** My Old Kentucky Home. **Entered union** June 1, 1792; rank, 15th. **State fair** at: Louisville.

History. Kentucky was the first area west of the Alleghenies settled by American pioneers; first permanent settlement, Harrodsburg, 1774. Daniel Boone blazed the Wilderness Trail through the Cumberland Gap and founded Boonesboro, 1775. Indian attacks, spurred by the British, were unceasing until, during the Revolution, Gen. George Rogers Clark captured British forts in Indiana and Illinois, 1778. In 1792, after Virginia dropped its claims to the region, Kentucky became the 15th state.

Tourist attractions. Kentucky Derby and accompanying festivities, Louisville; Land Between the Lakes Nat'l. Recreation Area encompassing Kentucky Lake and Lake Barkley; Mammoth Cave with 150 mi. of passageways, 200-ft. high rooms, blind fish, and Echo River, 360 ft. below ground; Old Ft. Harrod State Park; Lincoln birthplace, Hodgenville; My Old Kentucky Home, Bardstown.

Famous Kentuckians include Alben Barkley, Daniel Boone, Louis D. Brandeis, Kit Carson, Henry Clay, Jefferson Davis, John Fox Jr., Thomas Hunt Morgan, Elizabeth Madox Roberts, Robert Penn Warren.

Chamber of Commerce: Versailles Rd., P.O. Box 817, Frankfort, KY 40601.

Louisiana

Pelican State

People. Population (1980): 4,203,972; **rank:** 18. **Pop. density:** 93.5 per sq. mi. **Urban** (1970): 66.1%. **Racial distrib.** (1980): 69.2% White; 29.4% Black; Hispanic 99,105. **Major ethnic groups:** Italian, German, English, French. **Net migration** (1970-79): +34,000.

Geography. Total area: 48,523 sq. mi.; **rank:** 31. **Land area:** 44,930 sq. mi. **Acres forested land:** 14,558,100. **Location:** south central Gulf Coast state. **Climate:** subtropical, affected by continental weather patterns. **Topography:** lowlands of marshes and Mississippi R. flood plain; Red R. Valley lowlands; upland hills in the Florida Parishes; average elevation, 100 ft. **Capital:** Baton Rouge.

Economy. Principal industries: wholesale and retail trade, government, manufacturing, construction, transportation, mining. **Principal manufactured goods:** chemical products, foods, transportation equipment, electronic equipment, apparel, petroleum products. **Value added by manufacture** (1978): $10.8 bln. **Agriculture: Chief crops:** soybean, sugarcane, rice, corn, cotton, sweet potatoes, melons, pecans. **Livestock:** 1.3 mln. cattle; 150,000 hogs/pigs; 13,000 sheep; 3.5 mln. poultry. **Timber/lumber** (1978): pines, hardwoods, oak; 2.2 bln. bd. ft. **Minerals** (1978): mineral fuels (natural gas, liquified petroleum gases, crude petroleum, natural gasoline and cycle products), sulfur, lime, salt, sand and gravel. Total mineral production valued at $12 bln. **Commercial fishing** (1979): $198.5 mln. **Chief ports:** New Orleans, Baton Rouge, Lake Charles, S. Louisiana Port Commission at La Place. **International airports at:** New Orleans. **Value of construction** (1980): $3.27 bln. **Employment distribution:** 24.1% trade; 18.2% gvt.; 16.8% serv.; 14.6% manuf.; 8.4% constr. **Per capita income** (1980): $8,282. **Unemployment** (1980): 6.7% **Tourism** (1980): out-of-state visitors spent $2.15 bln.

Finance. Notable industries: finance, insurance, real estate. **No. banks** (1979): 262; **No. savings and loan assn.** (1978): 122.

Federal government. No. federal civilian employees (Mar. 1980): 27,471. **Avg. salary:** $17,974. **Notable federal facilities:** Barksdale, England, Ft. Polk military bases; Strategic Petroleum Reserve, New Orleans; Michoud Assembly Plant, New Orleans; U.S. Public Service Hospital, Carville.

Energy. Electricity production (1980, mwh, by source): Hydroelectric: —; Mineral: 45.7 mln.; Nuclear: —.

Education. No. schools: 1,878 elem. and second.; 32 higher ed. **Avg. salary, public school teachers** (1980): $13,770.

State data. Motto: Union, justice and confidence. **Flower:** Magnolia. **Bird:** Eastern brown pelican. **Tree:** Cypress. **Song:** Give Me Louisiana. **Entered union** Apr. 30, 1812; rank, 18th. **State fair** at: Shreveport; Oct.

History. The area was first visited, 1530, by Cabeza de Vaca and Panfilo de Narvaez. The region was claimed for France by LaSalle, 1682. First permanent settlement was by French at Fort St. Jean Baptiste (now Natchitoches), 1717. France ceded the region to Spain, 1762, took it back, 1800, and sold it to the U.S., 1803, in the Louisiana Purchase. During the Revolution, Spanish Louisiana aided the Americans. Admitted to statehood, 1812, Louisiana was the scene of the Battle of New Orleans, 1815.

Louisiana Creoles are descendants of early French and/or Spanish settlers. About 4,000 Acadians, French settlers in Nova Scotia, Canada, were forcibly transported by the British to Louisiana in 1755 (an event commemorated in Longfellow's *Evangeline*) and settled near Bayou Teche; their descendants became known as Cajuns. Another group, the Islenos, were descendants of Canary Islanders brought to Louisiana by a Spanish governor in 1770. Traces of Spanish and French survive in local dialects.

Tourist attractions. Mardi Gras, French Quarter, Superdome, Dixieland jazz, all New Orleans; Battle of New Orleans site; Longfellow-Evangeline Memorial Park.

Famous Louisianians include Louis Armstrong, Pierre Beauregard, Judah P. Benjamin, Braxton Bragg, Grace King, Huey Long, Leonidas K. Polk, Henry Miller Shreve, Edward D. White Jr.

Chamber of Commerce: P.O. Box 3988, Baton Rouge, LA 70821.

Maine

Pine Tree State

People. Population (1980): 1,124,660; **rank:** 38. **Pop. density:** 36.3 per sq. mi. **Urban** (1970): 50.8%. **Racial distrib.** (1980): 98.3% White; 0.3% Black; Hispanic 5,005. **Major ethnic groups:** English, Irish, Italian, German. **Net migration** (1970-80): +74,000.

Geography. Total area: 33,215 sq. mi.; **rank:** 39. **Land area:** 30,920 sq. mi. **Acres forested land:** 17,718,300. **Location:** New England state at northeastern tip of U.S. **Climate:** Southern interior and coastal, influenced by air masses from the S and W; northern clime harsher, avg. +100 in. snow in winter. **Topography:** Appalachian Mtns. extend through state; western borders have rugged terrain; long sand beaches on southern coast; northern coast mainly rocky promontories, peninsulas, fjords. **Capital:** Augusta.

Economy. Principal industries: manufacturing, services, trade, government, agriculture, fisheries, forestry. **Principal manufactured goods:** paper and wood products, textiles, leather, processed foods. **Value added by manufacture** (1978): $2.6 bln. **Agriculture: Chief crops:** potatoes ($93.8 mln.), apples, blueberries, sweet corn, peas, beans. **Livestock:** 133,401 cattle; 9,326 hogs/pigs; 11,008 sheep; 9.2 mln. poultry. **Timber/lumber** (1979): pine, spruce, fir; 409 mln. bd. ft. **Minerals** (1980): sand and gravel, cement, zinc, stone, copper. Total mineral production valued at $49.7 mln. **Commercial fishing** (1980): $92.7 mln. **Chief ports:** Searsport, Portland. **International airports at:** Portland, Bangor. **Value of con-**

struction (1980): $537 mln. **Employment distribution** (1979): 23.6% manuf.; 18.4% trade; 19.9% gvt.; 17.8% serv. **Per capita income** (1980): $7,052. **Unemployment** (1980): 7.7% **Tourism** (1979): out-of-state visitors spent $478.6 mln.

Finance. No. banks (1979): 41; **No. savings and loan assns.** (1978): 21.

Federal government. No. federal civilian employees (Mar. 1980): 7,241. **Avg. salary:** $18,188. **Notable federal facilities:** Kittery Naval Shipyard; Brunswick Naval Air Station; Loring Air Force Base.

Energy. Electricity production (1980, mwh, by source): Hydroelectric: 1.4 mln.; Mineral: 2.01 mln.; Nuclear: 4.4 mln.

Education. No. schools: 847 elem. and second.; 27 higher ed. **Avg. salary, public school teachers** (1980): $12,450.

State data. Motto: Dirigo (I direct) **Flower:** White pine cone and tassel. **Bird:** Chickadee. **Tree:** Eastern white pine. **Song:** State of Maine Song. **Entered union** Mar. 15, 1820; rank, 23d.

History. Maine's rocky coast was explored by the Cabots, 1498-99. French settlers arrived, 1604, at the St. Croix River; English, 1607, on the Kennebec. In 1691, Maine was made part of Massachusetts. In the Revolution, a Maine regiment fought at Bunker Hill; a British fleet destroyed Falmouth (now Portland), 1775, but the British ship Margaretta was captured near Machiasport. In 1820, Maine broke off from Massachusetts, became a separate state.

Tourist attractions. Acadia Nat'l. Park, Bar Harbor, on Mt. Desert Is.; Bath Iron Works and Marine Museum; Boothbay (Harbor) Railway Museum; Sugarloaf/USA Ski Area; Ogunquit, Portland, York.

Famous "Down Easters" include James G. Blaine, Cyrus H.K. Curtis, Hannibal Hamlin, Longfellow, Sir Hiram and Hudson Maxim, Edna St. Vincent Millay, Kate Douglas Wiggin, Ben Ames Williams.

Chamber of Commerce: 477 Congress St., Portland, ME 04111.

eral facilities: U.S. Naval Academy, Annapolis; Natl. Agric. Research Cen.; Ft. George C. Meade, Aberdeen Proving Ground.

Energy. Electricity production (1980, mwh, by source): Hydroelectric: 1.26 mln.; Mineral: 19.0 mln.; Nuclear: 10.9 mln.

Education. No. schools: 1,681 elem. and second.; 54 higher ed. **Avg. salary, public school teachers** (1980): $17,589.

State data. Motto. Fatti Maschii, Parole Femine (Manly deeds, womanly words). **Flower:** Black-eyed susan. **Bird:** Baltimore oriole. **Tree:** White oak. **Song:** Maryland, My Maryland. **Seventh** of the original 13 states to ratify Constitution, Apr. 28, 1788. **State fair** at: Timonium; end-Aug. to Sept. 7.

History. Capt. John Smith first explored Maryland, 1608. William Claiborne set up a trading post on Kent Is. in Chesapeake Bay, 1631. Britain granted land to Cecilius Calvert, Lord Baltimore, 1632; his brother led 200 settlers to St. Marys River, 1634. The bravery of Maryland troops in the Revolution, as at the Battle of Long Island, won the state its nickname, The Old Line State. In the War of 1812, when a British fleet tried to take Fort McHenry, Marylander Francis Scott Key, 1814, wrote The Star-Spangled Banner.

Tourist Attractions. Racing events include the Preakness, at Pimlico track, Baltimore; the International at Laurel Race Course; the John B. Campbell Handicap at Bowie. Also Annapolis yacht races; Ocean City summer resort; restored Ft. McHenry, Baltimore, near which Francis Scott Key wrote The Star-Spangled Banner; Antietam Battlefield, 1862, near Hagerstown; South Mountain Battlefield, 1862; Edgar Allan Poe house, Baltimore; The State House, Annapolis, 1772, the oldest still in use in the U.S.

Famous Marylanders include Benjamin Banneker, Francis Scott Key, H.L. Mencken, William Pinkney, Upton Sinclair, Roger B. Taney, Charles Willson Peale.

Chamber of Commerce: 60 West St., Annapolis, MD 21401.

Maryland
Old Line State, Free State

People. Population (1980): 4,216,446; rank: 17. **Pop. density:** 426.2 per sq. mi. **Urban** (1970): 76.6%. **Racial distrib.** (1980): 74.9% White; 22.7% Black; Hispanic 64,740. **Major ethnic groups:** German, Italian, Russian, English, Polish. **Net migration** (1970-80): +48,000.

Geography. Total area: 10,577 sq. mi.; rank: 42. **Land area:** 9,891 sq. mi. **Acres forested land:** 2,653,200. **Location:** Middle Atlantic state stretching from the Ocean to the Allegheny Mtns. **Climate:** continental in the west; humid subtropical in the east. **Topography:** Eastern Shore of coastal plain and Maryland Main of coastal plain, piedmont plateau, and the Blue Ridge, separated by the Chesapeake Bay. **Capital:** Annapolis.

Economy. Principal industries: food, manufacturing, tourism. **Principal manufactured goods:** food and kindred products, primary metals, electric and electronic equipment. **Value added by manufacture** (1978): $7.7 bln. **Agriculture:** Chief crops: tobacco, corn, soybeans. **Livestock:** 380,000 cattle; 235,000 hogs/pigs; 18,000 sheep; 1.87 mln. poultry. **Timber/lumber** (1978): hardwoods; 213.1 mln. bd. ft. **Minerals** (1978): coal, stone, sand and gravel. Total value of mineral production; $217 mln. **Commercial fishing** (1979): $35 mln. **Chief ports:** Baltimore. **International airports at:** Baltimore. **Value of construction** (1980): 3.0 bln. **Employment distribution:** 24% government; 23.8% wholesale and retail trade; 19.9% services and mining. **Per capita income** (1980): $10,322. **Unemployment** (1980): 6.4%. **Tourism** (1980): tourists spent $13 bln.

Finance. No. banks (1979): 102; **No. savings and loan assns.** (1978): 206.

Federal government. No. federal civilian employees (Mar. 1980): 118,271. **Avg. salary:** $21,183. **Notable fed-**

Massachusetts
Bay State, Old Colony

People. Population (1980): 5,737,037; rank: 11. **Pop. density:** 733.0 per sq. mi. **Urban** (1970): 84.6%. **Racial distrib.** (1980): 93.4% White; 3.8% Black; Hispanic 141,043. **Major ethnic groups:** Canadian, Italian, Irish, English, Polish. **Net migration** (1970-79): −145,225.

Geography. Total area: 8,257 sq. mi.; rank: 45. **Land area:** 7,826 sq. mi. **Acres forested land:** 2,952,300. **Location:** New England state along Atlantic seaboard. **Climate:** temperate, with colder and drier clime in western region. **Topography:** jagged indented coast from Rhode Island around Cape Cod; flat land yields to stony upland pastures near central region and gentle hilly country in west; except in west, land is rocky, sandy, and not fertile. **Capital:** Boston.

Economy. Principal industries: manufacturing, services, trade, finance-insurance-real estate. **Principal manufactured goods** (1980): electronics, machinery, instruments, fabricated metals, printing and publishing. **Value added by manufacture** (1978): $18.6 bln. **Agriculture:** Chief crops: nursery, greenhouse products, cranberries, fruits, tobacco, corn, potatoes. **Livestock** (1979): 90,159 cattle; 41,466 hogs/pigs; 13,594 sheep; 22,397 horses, ponies; 1.9 mln. poultry. **Timber/lumber** (1980): white pine, oak, other hard woods; 240 mln. bd. ft. **Minerals** (1979): sand and gravel, stone. Total value of mineral production $92.5 mln. **Commercial fishing** (1979): $175.5 mln. **Chief ports:** Boston, Fall River, Salem, New Bedford-Fairhaven. **International airport at:** Boston. **Value of construction** (1980): $2.7 bln. **Employment distribution** (1980): 29.0% manuf.; 28.8% serv.; 26.7% trade. **Per capita income** (1980): $9,992. **Unemployment** (1980): 5.6%. **Tourism** (1976): out-of-state visitors spent $2.6 bln.

Finance. No. banks (1979): 149; **No. savings and loan assns.** (1978): 165.

Federal government. No. federal civilian employees (Mar. 1980): 50,580. **Avg. salary:** $18,967. **Notable federal facilities:** Ft. Devens; U.S. Custom House, Boston; Q.M. Laboratory, Natick.

Energy. Electricity production (1980, mwh, by source): Hydroelectric: 95,506; Mineral: 31.5 mln.; Nuclear: 3.2 mln.

Education. No. schools: 2,838 elem. and second.; 119 higher ed. **Avg. salary, public school teachers** (1980): $17,000.

State data. Motto: Ense Petit Placidam Sub Libertate Quietem (By the sword we seek peace, but peace only under liberty). **Flower:** Mayflower. **Bird:** Chickadee. **Tree:** American elm. **Song:** All Hail to Massachusetts. **Sixth** of the original 13 states to ratify Constitution, Feb. 6, 1788.

History. The Pilgrims, seeking religious freedom, made their first settlement at Plymouth, 1620; the following year they gave thanks for their survival with the first Thanksgiving Day. Indian opposition reached a high point in King Philip's War, 1675-76, won by the colonists. Demonstrations against British restrictions set off the "Boston Massacre," 1770, and Boston "tea party," 1773. First bloodshed of the Revolution was at Lexington, 1775.

Tourist attractions. Cape Cod with Provincetown artists' colony; Berkshire Music Festival, Tanglewood; Boston "Pops" concerts; Museum of Fine Arts, Arnold Arboretum, both Boston; Jacob's Pillow Dance Festival, West Becket; historical Shaker Village, Old Sturbridge, Lexington, Concord, Salem, Plymouth Rock.

Famous "Bay Staters" include Samuel Adams, Louisa May Alcott, Horatio Alger, Clara Barton, Emily Dickinson, Emerson, Hancock, Hawthorne, Oliver W. Holmes, Winslow Homer, Elias Howe, Samuel F.B. Morse, Poe, Revere, Sargent, Thoreau, Whistler, Whittier.

Chamber of Commerce: None.

loan assns. (1978): 65.

Federal government. No. federal civilian employees (Mar. 1980): 46,194. **Avg. salary:** $18,912. **Notable federal facilities:** Isle Royal, Sleeping Bear Dunes national parks.

Energy. Electricity production (1980, mwh, by source): Hydroelectric: 1.0 mln; Mineral: 57.8 mln.; Nuclear: 15.8 mln.

Education. No. schools: 4,785 elem. and second.; 96 higher ed. **Avg. salary, public school teachers** (1980): $19,456.

State data. Motto: Si Quaeris Peninsulam Amoenam Circumspice (If you seek a pleasant peninsula, look about you). **Flower:** Apple blossom. **Bird:** Robin. **Tree:** White pine. **Song:** Michigan, My Michigan. **Entered union** Jan. 26, 1837; rank, 26th. **State fair** at: Detroit, Aug.–early Sept; Upper Peninsula (Escanaba) Aug. 18–23, 1981.

History. French fur traders and missionaries visited the region, 1616, set up a mission at Sault Ste. Marie, 1641, and a settlement there, 1668. The whole region went to Britain, 1763. During the Revolution, the British led attacks from the area on American settlements to the south until Anthony Wayne defeated their Indian allies at Fallen Timbers, Ohio, 1794. The British returned, 1812, seized Ft. Mackinac and Detroit. Oliver H. Perry's Lake Erie victory and William H. Harrison's troops, who carried the war to the Thames River in Canada, 1813, freed Michigan once more.

Tourist attractions. Henry Ford Museum, Greenfield Village, reconstruction of a typical 19th cent. American village, both in Dearborn; Michigan Space Ctr., Jackson; Tahquamenon (Hiawatha) Falls; DeZwaan windmill and Tulip Festival, Holland; "Soo Locks," St. Marys Falls Ship Canal, Sault Ste. Marie.

Famous Michiganders include George Custer, Paul de Kruif, Thomas Dewey, Edna Ferber, Henry Ford, Edgar Guest, Betty Hutton, Robert Ingersoll, Will Kellogg, Danny Thomas, Stewart Edward White.

Chamber of Commerce: 501 S. Capitol Ave., Suite 500, Lansing, MI 48933.

Michigan

Great Lake State, Wolverine State

People. Population (1980): 9,258,344; **rank:** 8. **Pop. density:** 162.9 per sq. mi. **Urban** (1970): 73.8%. **Racial distrib.** (1980): 84.9% White; 12.9% Black; Hispanic 162,388. **Major ethnic groups:** Polish, German, English, Italian. **Net migration** (1970-79): −300,000.

Geography. Total area: 58,216 sq. mi.; **rank:** 23. **Land area:** 56,817 sq. mi. **Acres forested land:** 19,270,400. **Location:** east north central state bordering on 4 of the 5 Great Lakes, divided into an Upper and Lower Peninsula by the Straits of Mackinac, which link lakes Michigan and Huron. **Climate:** well-defined seasons tempered by the Great Lakes. **Topography:** low rolling hills give way to northern tableland of hilly belts in Lower Peninsula; Upper Peninsula is level in the east, with swampy areas; western region is higher and more rugged. **Capital:** Lansing.

Economy. Principal industries: manufacturing, mining, agriculture, food processing, tourism, fishing. **Principal manufactured goods:** automobiles, machine tools, chemicals, foods, primary metals and metal products, plastics. **Value added by manufacture** (1978): $41.8 bln. **Agriculture: Chief crops:** corn, winter wheat, soybeans, dry beans, oats, hay, sugar beets, honey, asparagus, sweet corn, apples, cherries, grapes, peaches, blueberries, flowers. **Livestock:** 1.31 mln. cattle; 960,000 hogs/pigs; 132,000 sheep; 8 mln. poultry. **Timber/lumber** (1977): hickory, ash, oak, hemlock; 350 mln. bd. ft. **Minerals** (1979): crude petroleum, iron ore, cement, natural gas, stone, sand and gravel. Total mineral production valued at $2.33 bln. **Commercial fishing** (1979): $3.6 mln. **Chief ports:** Detroit, Muskegon, Sault Ste. Marie. **International airports at:** Detroit. **Value of construction** (1980): $4.13 bln. **Employment distribution:** 32% manuf.; 17% serv.; **Per capita income** (1980): $9,847. **Unemployment** (1980): 12.6% **Tourism** (1976): out-of-state visitors spent $3.8 bln.

Finance. No. banks (1979): 372; **No. savings and**

Minnesota

North Star State, Gopher State

People. Population (1980): 4,077,148; **rank:** 20. **Pop. density:** 51.4 per sq. mi. **Urban** (1970): 66.4%. **Racial distrib.** (1980): 96.5% White; 1.3% Black; Hispanic 32,124. **Major ethnic groups:** German, Swedish, Norwegian. **Net migration** (1970-79): +16,000.

Geography. Total area: 84,068 sq. mi.; **rank:** 12. **Land area:** 79,289 sq. mi. **Acres forested land:** 16,709,200. **Location:** north central state bounded on the E by Wisconsin and Lake Superior, on the N by Canada, on the W by the Dakotas, and on the S by Iowa. **Climate:** northern part of state lies in the moist Great Lakes storm belt; the western border lies at the edge of the semi-arid Great Plains. **Topography:** central hill and lake region covering approx. half the state; to the NE, rocky ridges and deep lakes; to the NW, flat plain; to the S, rolling plains and deep river valleys. **Capital:** St. Paul.

Economy. Principal industries: agri business, forest products, mining, manufacturing, tourism. **Principal manufactured goods:** food processing, non-electrical machinery, chemicals, paper, electric and electronic equipment, printing and publishing, instruments, fabricated metal products. **Value added by manufacture** (1978): $10.9 bln. **Agriculture: Chief crops:** corn, soybeans, wheat, sugar beets, sunflowers, barley. **Livestock** (1981): 3.8 mln. cattle; 5.1 mln. hogs/pigs; 295,000 sheep; 38.5 mln. poultry. **Timber/lumber:** needle-leaves and hardwoods. **Minerals** (1980): iron ore (95% of the total $1.74 bln. of mineral production), sand and gravel, stone. **Commercial fishing** (1980): $22.1 mln. **Chief ports:** Duluth, St. Paul, Minneapolis. **International airports at:** Minneapolis-St. Paul. **Value of construction** (1980): $2.7 bln. **Employment distribution** (1980): 22.7% trade; 22.5% manuf.; 19.6% serv.; 17.8% gvt **Per capita in-**

come (1980): $9,519. Unemployment (1980): 5.7%. Tourism (1976): out-of-state visitors spent $900 mln.

Finance. No. banks (1979): 762; No. savings and loan assns. (1978): 62.

Federal government. No. federal civilian employees (Mar. 1980): 23,789. Avg. salary: $19,197.

Energy. Electricity production (1980, mwh, by source): Hydroelectric: 641,617; Mineral: 20.8 mln.; Nuclear: 10.0 mln.

Education. No. schools: 2,173 elem. and second.; 65 higher ed. Avg. salary, public school teachers (1980): $16,750.

State data. Motto: L'Etoile du Nord (The star of the north). Flower: Pink and white lady's-slipper. Bird: Common loon. Tree: Red pine. Song: Hail! Minnesota. Entered union May 11, 1858; rank, 32d. State fair at: Saint Paul; end-Aug. to early Sept.

History. Fur traders and missionaries from French Canada opened the region in the 17th century. Britain took the area east of the Mississippi, 1763. The U.S. took over that portion after the Revolution and in 1803 bought the western area as part of the Louisiana Purchase. The U.S. built present Ft. Snelling, 1820, bought lands from the Indians, 1837. Sioux Indians staged a bloody uprising, 1862, and were driven from the state.

Tourist attractions. Minnehaha Falls, Minneapolis, inspiration for Longfellow's *Hiawatha*; Voyageurs Nat'l. Park, a water wilderness along the Canadian border; Mayo Clinic, Rochester; St. Paul Winter Carnival; the "land of 10,000 lakes" actually has 12,034 lakes over 10 acres in size; many water and winter sports and activities throughout the state.

Famous Minnesotans include F. Scott Fitzgerald, Cass Gilbert, Hubert Humphrey, Sinclair Lewis, Paul Manship, E. G. Marshall, William and Charles Mayo, Walter F. Mondale, Harold Stassen, Thorstein Veblen.

Chamber of Commerce: 200 Hanover Bldg., 480 Cedar St., St. Paul, MN 55101.

Mississippi

Magnolia State

People. Population (1980): 2,520,638; rank: 31. Pop. density: 53.2 per sq. mi. Urban (1970): 44.5%. Racial distrib. (1975): 63.6% White; 35.9% Black; Hispanic (1970): 8,182. Major ethnic groups: German, Italian, English. Net migration (1970-79): +7,000.

Geography. Total area: 47,716 sq. mi.; rank: 32. Land area: 47,296 sq. mi. Acres forested land: 16,715,600. Location: south central state bordered on the W by the Mississippi R. and on the S by the Gulf of Mexico. Climate: semi-tropical, with abundant rainfall, long growing season, and extreme temperatures unusual. Topography: low, fertile delta bet. the Yazoo and Mississippi rivers; loess bluffs stretching around delta border; sandy Gulf coastal terraces followed by piney woods and prairie; rugged, high sandy hills in extreme NE followed by black prairie belt. Pontotoc Ridge, and flatwoods into the north central highlands. Capital: Jackson.

Economy. Principal industries: manufacturing, food processing, seafood, government, wholesale and retail trade, agriculture. Principal manufactured goods: apparel, transportation equipment, lumber and wood products, foods, electrical machinery and equipment. Value added by manufacture (1978): $5.9 bln. Agriculture: Chief crops: soybeans, cotton, rice. 60 Livestock: 1.81 mln. cattle; 440,000 hogs/pigs; 5,400 sheep; 11.5 mln. poultry. Timber/lumber (1978): pine, oak, hardwoods; 1.3 bln. bd. ft. Minerals (1977): crude petroleum and natural gas (85% of total $499 mln. value of mineral production), sand and gravel. Commercial fishing (1979): $33.3 mln. Chief ports: Pascagoula, Vicksburg, Gulfport, Natchez. Value of construction (1980): $1.54 bln. Employment distribution: 28.3% manuf.; 22.8% gvt.; 19.4% trade; 14.2% serv. Per capita income (1980): $6,508. Unemployment (1980): 7.5% Tourism (1976): out-of-state visitors spent $850.5 mln.

Finance. No. banks (1979): 183; No. savings and loan assns. (1978): 60.

Federal government. No. federal civilian employees (Mar. 1980): 24,001. Avg. salary: $18,536. Notable federal facilities: Columbus, Kessler AF bases; Meridian Naval Air Station, NASA/NOAA International Earth Sciences Center.

Energy. Electricity production (1980, mwh, by source): Hydroelectric: —; Mineral 18.4 mln.; Nuclear: —.

Education. No. schools: 1,234 elem. and second.; 46 higher ed. Avg. salary, public school teachers (1980): $11,900.

State data. Motto: Virtute et Armis (By valor and arms). Flower: Magnolia. Bird: Mockingbird. Tree: Magnolia. Song: Go, Mississippi! Entered union Dec. 10, 1817; rank, 20th. State fair at: Jackson; Fall.

History. De Soto explored the area, 1540, discovered the Mississippi River, 1541. La Salle traced the river from Illinois to its mouth and claimed the entire valley for France, 1682. First settlement was the French Ft. Maurepas, near Ocean Springs, 1699. The area was ceded to Britain, 1763; American settlers followed. During the Revolution, Spain seized part of the area and refused to leave even after the U.S. acquired title at the end of the Revolution, finally moving out, 1798. Mississippi seceded 1861. Union forces captured Corinth and Vicksburg and destroyed Jackson and much of Meridian.

Tourist attractions. Vicksburg National Military Park and Cemetery, other Civil War sites; Natchez Trace; Indian mounds; estate pilgrimage at Natchez; Mardi Gras and blessing of the shrimp fleet, Aug., both in Biloxi.

Famous Mississippians include Dana Andrews, William Faulkner, Lucius O.C. Lamar, Elvis Presley, Leontyne Price, Hiram Revels, Eudora Welty.

Chamber of Commerce: P.O. Box 1849, Jackson, MS 39205.

Missouri

Show Me State

People. Population (1980): 4,346,267; rank: 16. Pop. density: 62.9 per sq. mi. Urban (1970): 70.1%. Racial distrib. (1980): 88.3% White; 10.4% Black; Hispanic 51,667. Major ethnic groups: German, Italian, English, Russian. Net migration (1970-79): —16,000.

Geography. Total area: 69,686 sq. mi.; rank: 19. Land area: 68,995 sq. mi. Acres forested land: 12,876,000. Location: West North central state near the geographic center of the conterminous U.S.; bordered on the E by the Mississippi R., on the NW by the Missouri R. Climate: continental, susceptible to cold Canadian air, moist, warm Gulf air, and drier SW air. Topography: Rolling hills, open, fertile plains, and well-watered prairie N of the Missouri R.; south of the river land is rough and hilly with deep, narrow valleys; alluvial plain in the SE; low elevation in the west. Capital: Jefferson City.

Economy. Principal industries: agriculture, manufacturing, aerospace, tourism. Principal manufactured goods: transportation equipment, food and related products, electrical and electronic equipment, chemicals. Value added by manufacture (1978): $15.0 bln. Agriculture: Chief crops: soybeans, corn, wheat, cotton. Livestock: 5.4 mln. cattle; 4.6 mln. hogs/pigs; 123,000 sheep; 7.7 mln. poultry. Timber/lumber: oak, hickory. Minerals (1980): lead, fire clay, zinc, barite, lime cement. Total value of mineral production $1.2 bln. Commercial fishing (1979) $203,000. Chief ports: St. Louis, Kansas City. International airports at: St. Louis, Kansas City. Value of construction (1980): $2.58 bln. Employment distribution: 24% trade; 23% manuf.; 19% serv.; 17% gvt.; 7% transp. Per capita income (1980): $8,846. Unemployment (1980): 7.0%. Tourism (1977): out-of-state visitors spent $2.7 bln.

Finance. Notable industries: banking. No. banks (1979): 727; No. savings and loan assns. (1978): 114.

Federal government. No. federal civilian employees (Mar. 1980): 58,268. Avg. salary: $18,609. Notable fed

eral facilities: Federal Reserve banks, St. Louis, Kansas City; Ft. Leonard Wood, Rolla.

Energy. Electricity production (1980 mwh, by source): Hydroelectric: 558,034; Mineral: 48.3 mln.; Nuclear: —.

Education. No. schools: 2,763 elem. and second.; 84 higher ed. **Avg. salary, public school teachers** (1980): $13,847.

State data. Motto: Salus Populi Suprema Lex Esto (The welfare of the people shall be the supreme law). **Flower:** Hawthorn. **Bird:** Bluebird. **Tree:** Dogwood. **Song:** Missouri Waltz. **Entered union** Aug. 10, 1821; rank, 24th. **State fair** at: Sedalia; 3d week in Aug.

History. DeSoto visited the area, 1541. French hunters and lead miners made the first settlement, c. 1735, at Ste. Genevieve. The U.S. acquired Missouri as part of the Louisiana Purchase, 1803. The fur trade and the Santa Fe Trail provided prosperity; St. Louis became the "jump-off" point for pioneers on their way West. Pro- and anti-slavery forces battled each other there during the Civil War.

Tourist attractions. Mark Twain State Park, Florida; Tom Sawyer and Huckleberry Finn statues, Hannibal; Jesse James birthplace, Excelsior Springs; Pony Express Museum, St. Joseph. The Harry S. Truman Library, near Independence, contains presidential papers and memorabilia. Mr. Truman is buried in the library courtyard.

Famous Missourians include Zoe Akins, Thomas Hart Benton, Omar Bradley, George Washington Carver, Thomas Dooley, T. S. Eliot, Bernarr Macfadden, J. C. Penney; John J. Pershing, Joseph Pulitzer, Sara Teasdale, Mark Twain.

Chamber of Commerce: 400 E. High St., P.O. Box 149, Jefferson City, MO 65101.

Montana

Treasure State

People. Population (1980): 786,690; **rank:** 44. **Pop. density:** 5.4 per sq. mi. **Urban** (1970): 53.4%. **Racial distrib.** (1980): 94.0% White; 0.2% Black; 5.6% Other (includes American Indians); Hispanic 9,974. **Major ethnic groups:** German, Norwegian, Russian, English. **Net migration** (1970-79): +38,000.

Geography. Total area: 147,138 sq. mi.; **rank:** 4. **Land area:** 145,587 sq. mi. **Acres forested land:** 22,559,300. **Location:** Mountain state bounded on the E by the Dakotas, on the S by Wyoming, on the S/SW by Idaho, and on the N by Canada. **Climate:** colder, continental climate with low humidity. **Topography:** Rocky Mtns. in western third of the state; eastern two-thirds gently rolling northern Great Plains. **Capital:** Helena.

Economy. Principal industries: agriculture, mining, manufacturing, tourism. **Principal manufactured goods:** petroleum products, primary metals and minerals, lumber and wood products, farm machinery, processed foods. **Value added by manufacture** (1978): $850 mln. **Agriculture: Chief crops:** wheat, cattle, barley, sheep, sugar beets, hay, flax, oats. **Livestock:** 2.67 mln. cattle; 250,000 hogs/pigs; 595,000 sheep; 965,000 poultry. **Timber/lumber** (1977): Douglas fir, pines, larch; 1.3 bln. bd. ft. **Minerals** (1978): mineral fuels (71% of the total $719 mln. mineral production), copper, silver. **International airports at:** Great Falls. **Value of construction** (1980): $398 mln. **Employment distribution:** 20.5% trade; 20.1% gvt.; 15.9% serv.; 8.9% agric; 6.7% manuf. **Per capita income** (1980): $8,445. **Unemployment** (1980): 6.0%. **Tourism** (1979): out-of-state visitors spent $421.8 mln.

Finance. No. banks (1979): 165; **No. savings and loan assns.** (1978): 15.

Federal government. No. federal civilian employees (Mar. 1980): 9,327. **Avg. salary:** $19,435. **Notable federal facilities:** Malmstrom AFB; Ft. Peck, Hungry Horse, Libby, Yellowtail dams.

Energy. Electricity production (1980, mwh, by source): Hydroelectric: 9.9 mln; Mineral: 5.5 mln.; Nuclear: —.

Education. No. schools: 876 elem. and second.; 13 higher ed. **Avg. salary, public school teachers** (1980): $14,540.

State data. Motto: Oro y Plata (Gold and silver). **Flower:** Bitterroot. **Bird:** Western meadowlark. **Tree:** Ponderosa pine. **Song:** Montana. **Entered union** Nov. 8, 1889; rank, 41st. **State fair** at: Great Falls; end July to early Aug.

History. French explorers visited the region, 1742. The U.S. acquired the area partly through the Louisiana Purchase, 1803, and partly through the explorations of Lewis and Clark, 1805-06. Fur traders and missionaries established posts in the early 19th century. Indian uprisings reached their peak with the Battle of the Little Big Horn, 1876. The coming of the Northern Pacific Railway, 1883, brought population growth.

Tourist attractions. Glacier National Park, on the Continental Divide, is a scenic and recreational wonderland, with 60 glaciers, 200 lakes, and many trout streams.

Also, Museum of the Plains Indian, Blackfeet Reservation near Browning; Custer Battlefield National Cemetery; Flathead Lake, in the NW, Lewis and Clark Cavern, Morrison Cave State Park, near Whitehall.

There are 7 Indian reservations, covering over 5 million acres; tribes are Blackfeet, Crow, Confederated Salish & Kootenai, Assiniboine, Gros Ventre, Sioux, Northern Cheyenne, Chippewa, Cree. Population of the reservations is approximately 25,500.

Famous Montanans include Gary Cooper, Marcus Daly, Chet Huntley, Will James, Myrna Loy, Mike Mansfield, Jeannette Rankin, Charles M. Russell, Brent Musberger.

Chamber of Commerce: 110 Neil Ave., P.O. Box 1730, Helena, MT 59601.

Nebraska

Cornhusker State

People. Population (1980): 1,570,006; **rank:** 35. **Pop. density:** 20.5 per sq. mi. **Urban** (1970): 61.5%. **Racial distrib.** (1980): 94.9% White; 3.1% Black; Hispanic 28,020. **Major ethnic groups:** German, Czechoslovakian, Swedish, Russian. **Net migration** (1970-80): —12,600.

Geography. Total area: 77,227 sq. mi.; **rank:** 15. **Land area:** 76,483 sq. mi. **Acres forested land:** 1,029,100. **Location:** West North Central state with the Missouri R. for a N/NE border. **Climate:** continental semi-arid. **Topography:** till plains of the central lowland in the eastern third rising to the Great Plains and hill country of the north central and NW. **Capital:** Lincoln.

Economy. Principal industries: agriculture, food processing, manufacturing. **Principal manufactured goods:** foods, machinery, electric and electronic equipment, chemicals, primary and fabricated metal products. **Value added by manufacture** (1978): $3.2 bln. **Agriculture: Chief crops:** corn, wheat, sorghum, hay, oats, beans, sugar beets, popcorn, potatoes, soybeans. **Livestock:** 6.95 mln. cattle; 3.9 mln. hogs/pigs; 250,000 sheep; 4.2 mln. poultry. **Minerals** (1980): cement, sand and gravel, natural gas liquids, petroleum. Total mineral production valued at $271.8 mln. **Commercial fishing** (1979): $25,000. **Chief ports:** Omaha, Sioux City, Brownsville, Blair, Plattsmouth, Nebraska City. **Value of construction** (1980): $838 mln. **Employment distribution:** 22.1% trade; 17.6% gvt.; 15.8% serv.; 12.9% manuf. **Per capita income** (1980): $8,914. **Unemployment** (1980): 4.0%. **Tourism** (1980): out-of-state visitors spent over $800 mln.

Finance. No. banks (1979): 461; **No. savings and loan assns.** (1978): 44.

Federal government. No. federal civilian employees (Mar. 1980): 12,502. **Avg. salary:** $19,096. **Notable federal facilities:** Strategic Air Command Base, Omaha.

Energy. Electricity production (1980, mwh, by source): Hydroelectric: 1.3 mln.; Mineral: 9.2 mln.; Nuclear: 5.7 mln.

Education. No. schools: 1,993 elem. and second.; 31 higher ed. **Avg. salary, public school teachers** (1980):

$13,519.

State data. Motto: Equality before the law. **Flower:** Goldenrod. **Bird:** Western meadowlark. **Tree:** Cottonwood. **Song:** Beautiful Nebraska. **Entered union** Mar. 1, 1867; rank, 37th. **State fair** at Lincoln; Sept. 3-12.

History. Spanish and French explorers and fur traders visited the area prior to the Louisiana Purchase, 1803. Lewis and Clark passed through, 1804-06. First permanent settlement was Bellevue, near Omaha, 1823. Many Civil War veterans settled under free land terms of the 1862 Homestead Act; struggles followed between homesteaders and ranchers.

Tourist attractions. Boys Town, founded by Fr. Flanagan, west of Omaha, is a self-contained community of under-privileged and homeless boys. Arbor Lodge State Park, Nebraska City, is a memorial to J. Sterling Morton, founder of Arbor Day. Buffalo Bill Ranch State Historical Park, North Platte, contains Cody's home and memorabilia of his Wild West Show.

Also, Pioneer Village, Minden; Oregon Trail, landmarks, Scotts Bluff National Mountain and Chimney Rock Historic Site.

Famous Nebraskans include Fred Astaire, Charles W. and William Jennings Bryan, Willa Cather, Michael and Edward A. Cudahy, Loren Eiseley, Rev. Edward J. Flanagan, Henry Fonda, Rollin Kirby, Harold Lloyd, Malcolm X, Roscoe Pound.

Chamber of Commerce: 1008 Terminal Bldg., Lincoln, NE 68508.

Nevada

Sagebrush State, Battle Born State

People. Population (1980): 799,184; **rank:** 43. **Pop. density:** 7.2 per sq. mi. **Urban** (1970): 80.9%. **Racial distrib.** (1980): 87.5% White; 6.3% Black; Hispanic 53,786. **Major ethnic groups:** Italian, German, English, Mexican. **Net migration** (1970-80): +310,000.

Geography. Total area: 110,540 sq. mi.; **rank:** 7. **Land area:** 109,889 sq. mi. **Acres forested land:** 7,683,300. **Location:** Mountain state bordered on N by Oregon and Idaho, on E by Utah and Arizona, on SE by Arizona, and on SW/W by California. **Climate:** semi-arid. **Topography:** rugged N-S mountain ranges; southern area is within the Mojave Desert; lowest elevation, Colorado R. Canyon, 470 ft. **Capital:** Carson City.

Economy. Principal industries: tourism, mining, manufacturing, lumber, government, agriculture, warehousing, trucking. **Principal manufactured goods:** gaming devices, electronics, chemicals, forest products, stone-clay-glass products. **Value added by manufacture** (1978): $660.1 mln. **Agriculture: Chief crops:** alfalfa, barley, wheat, oats, cotton. **Livestock:** 570,000 cattle; 8,000 hogs/pigs; 133,000 sheep; 14,000 poultry. **Timber/lumber** (1977): pine, fir, spruce; 19 mln. bd. ft. **Minerals** (1979): gold (3d largest in U.S. with 26% of total output), copper, sand and gravel. Total mineral production valued at $251.2 mln. **International airports** at Las Vegas, Reno. **Value of construction** (1980): $1.1 bln. **Employment distribution:** 42% serv.; 20% trade; 14% gvt. **Per capita income** (1980): $10,458. **Unemployment** (1980): 6.2% **Tourism** (1976): out-of-state visitors spent $1.3 bln.

Finance. No. banks (1979): 9; **No. savings and loan assns.** (1978): 7.

Federal government. No. federal civilian employees (Mar. 1980): 8,640. **Avg. salary:** $19,183. **Notable federal facilities:** Nevada Test Site.

Energy. Electricity production (1980, mwh, by source): Hydroelectric: 2.3 mln.; Mineral: 11.7 mln. Nuclear: —.

Education. No. schools: 287 elem. and second.; 6 higher ed. **Avg. salary, public school teachers** (1980): $16,191.

State data. Motto: All for our country. **Flower:** Sagebrush. **Bird:** Mountain bluebird. **Tree:** Single-leaf pinon. **Song:** Home Means Nevada. **Entered union** Oct. 31, 1864; rank, 36th. **State fair** at Reno; early Sept.

History. Nevada was first explored by Spaniards in 1776. Hudson's Bay Co. trappers explored the north and central region, 1825; trader Jedediah Smith crossed the state, 1826 and 1827. The area was acquired by the U.S., in 1848, at the end of the Mexican War. First settlement, Mormon Station, now Genoa, was est. 1849. In the early 20th century, Nevada adopted progressive measures such as the initiative, referendum, recall, and woman suffrage.

Tourist attractions. Legalized gambling provided the impetus for the development of resort areas Lake Tahoe, Reno, and Las Vegas. Ghost towns, rodeos, trout fishing, water sports and hunting important.

Notable are Helldorado Week in May, Las Vegas; Basque Festival, Elko; Reno Rodeo, 4th of July; Valley of Fire State Park, Overton; Death Valley, on the California border; Lehman Caves National Monument.

Famous Nevadans include Walter Van Tilburg Clark, Sarah Winnemucca Hopkins, John William MacKay, Pat McCarran, William Morris Stewart.

Chamber of Commerce: P.O. Box 3499, Reno, NV 89505.

New Hampshire

Granite State

People. Population (1980): 920,610; **rank:** 42. **Pop. density:** 101.9 per sq. mi. **Urban** (1970): 56.4%. **Racial distrib.** (1980): 98.8% White; 0.4% Black; Hispanic 5,587. **Major ethnic groups:** English, Irish, French, Polish, Italian, German. **Net migration** (1970-79): +101,000.

Geography. Total area: 9,304 sq. mi.; **rank:** 44. **Land area:** 9,027 sq. mi. **Acres forested land:** 5,013,500. **Location:** New England state bounded on S by Massachusetts, on W by Vermont, on N/NW by Canada, on E by Maine and the Atlantic O. **Climate:** highly varied, due to its nearness to high mountains and ocean. **Topography:** low, rolling coast followed by countless hills and mountains rising out of a central plateau. **Capital:** Concord.

Economy. Principal industries: manufacturing, communications, trade, agriculture, mining. **Principal manufactured goods:** leather products, wood and paper products, electrical equipment, machinery, minerals, fabricated metal products. **Value added by manufacture** (1978): $2.7 bln. **Agriculture: Chief crops:** vegetables, dairy products, greenhouse products, hay, apples. **Livestock:** 70,000 cattle; 9,900 hogs/pigs; 8,500 sheep; 950,000 poultry. **Timber/lumber** (1978): white pine, hemlock, oak, birch; 240 mln. bd. ft. **Minerals** (1979): sand and gravel. Total mineral production valued at $23.2 mln. **Commercial fishing** (1980): $9.25 mln. **Chief ports:** Portsmouth. **Value of construction** (1980): $469 mln. **Employment distribution:** 30% manuf.; 31% trade; 7% serv. **Per capita income** (1980): $8,980. **Unemployment** (1980): 4.7%. **Tourism** (1976): out-of-state visitors spent $690.6 mln.

Finance. Notable industries: insurance, banking. **No. banks** (1979): 79; **No. savings and loan assns.** (1978): 17.

Federal government. No. federal civilian employees (Mar. 1980): 13,491. **Avg. salary:** $18,634. **Notable federal facilities:** Pease Air Base, Newington.

Energy. Electricity production (1980, mwh, by source): Hydroelectric: 871,658; Mineral: 5.1 mln.; Nuclear: —.

Education. No. schools: 561 elem. and second.; 24 higher ed. **Avg. salary, public school teachers** (1980): $13,342.

State data. Motto: Live free or die. **Flower:** Purple lilac. **Bird:** Purple finch. **Tree:** White birch. **Song:** Old New Hampshire. **Ninth** of the original 13 states to ratify the Constitution, June 21, 1788.

History. First explorers to visit the New Hampshire area were England's Martin Pring, 1603, and Champlain, 1605. First settlement was Little Harbor, near Rye, 1623 Indian raids were halted, 1759, by Robert Rogers' Rang ers. Before the Revolution, New Hampshire men seized a British fort at Portsmouth, 1774, and drove the royal governor out, 1775. Three regiments served in the Continental Army and scores of privateers raided British shipping.

Tourist attractions. Mt. Washington, highest peak in Northeast, hub of network of trails; Lake Winnipesaukee; White Mt. Natl. Forest; Crawford, Franconia, Pinkham notches in White Mt. region—Franconia famous for the Old Man of the Mountain, described by Hawthorne as the Great Stone Face; the Flume, a spectacular gorge; the aerial tramway on Cannon Mt; the MacDowell Colony, Peterborough, summer haven for writers, composers, artists.

Famous New Hampshirites include Salmon P. Chase, Ralph Adams Cram, Mary Baker Eddy, Daniel Chester French, Robert Frost, Horace Greeley, Sarah Buell Hale, Augustus Saint-Gaudens, Daniel Webster.

Chamber of Commerce: 57 Market St., Manchester, NH 03101.

New Jersey
Garden State

People. Population (1980): 7,364,158; **rank:** 9. **Pop. density:** 979.1 per sq. mi. **Urban** (1970): 88.9%. **Racial distrib.** (1980): 83.2% White; 12.5% Black; Hispanic 491,867. **Major ethnic groups:** Italian, German, Polish. **Net migration** (1970-79): −129,000.

Geography. Total area: 7,836 sq. mi.; **rank:** 46. **Land area:** 7,521 sq. mi. **Acres forested land:** 1,928,400. **Location:** Middle Atlantic state bounded by the N and E by New York and the Atlantic O., on the S and W by Delaware and Pennsylvania. **Climate:** moderate, with marked difference bet. NW and SE extremities. **Topography:** Appalachian Valley in the NW also has highest elevation, High Pt., 1,801 ft.; Appalachian Highlands, flat-topped NE-SW mountain ranges; Piedmont Plateau, low plains broken by high ridges (Palisades) rising 400-500 ft.; Coastal Plain, covering three-fifths of state in SE, gradually rises from sea level to gentle slopes. **Capital:** Trenton.

Economy. Principal industries: manufacturing, trade, services. **Principal manufactured goods:** chemicals, food, petroleum and coal, transportation equipment. **Value added by manufacture** (1978): $40.5 bln. **Agriculture:** Chief crops: tomatoes, blueberries, cranberries, corn, peaches, grains, hay. **Livestock:** 114,000 cattle; 75,000 hogs/pigs; 8,300 sheep; 2.12 mln. poultry. **Timber/lumber** (1977): pine, white cedar, oak, elm; 22.9 mln. bd. ft. **Minerals** (1978): sand and gravel, stone, zinc. Total value of mineral production, $118 mln. **Commercial fishing** (1979): $53.0 mln. **Chief ports:** Newark, Elizabeth, Hoboken, Ameri-Port (Delaware R.). **International airports at:** Newark. **Value of construction** (1980): $3.6 bln. **Employment distribution** (1980): 25.7% manuf.; 2.3% trade; 19.7% serv.; 17.5% gvt. **Per capita income** (1980): $10,755. **Unemployment** (1980): 7.2%. **Tourism** (1978): tourists spent $4.0 bln.

Finance. Notable industries: banking, insurance. **No. banks** (1979): 176; **No. savings and loan assns.** (1978): 17.

Federal government. No. federal civilian employees (Mar. 1980): 61,758. **Avg. salary:** $19,519. **Notable federal facilities:** McGuire AFB Fort Dix; Fort Monmouth; Picatinny Arsenal; Lakewood Naval Air Station, Lakehurst Naval Air Engineering Center.

Energy. Electricity production (1979, mwh, by source): Hydroelectric: —; Mineral: 22.0 mln.; Nuclear: 7.6 mln.

Education. No. schools: 3,164 elem. and second.; 63 higher ed. **Avg. salary, public school teachers** (1980): 17,075.

State Data. Motto: Liberty and prosperity. **Flower:** purple violet. **Bird:** Eastern goldfinch. **Tree:** Red oak. **Third** of the original 13 states to ratify the Constitution, Dec. 18, 1787. **State fair** at: Hamilton Twp., Mercer Co.; 3d week of Sept.

History. The Lenni Lenape (Delaware) Indians had mostly peaceful relations with European colonists who ar-

rived after the explorers Verrazano, 1524, and Hudson, 1609. The Dutch were first; when the British took New Netherland, 1664, the area between the Delaware and Hudson Rivers was given to Lord John Berkeley and Sir George Carteret. New Jersey was the scene of nearly 100 battles, large and small, during the Revolution, including Trenton, 1776, Princeton, 1777, Monmouth, 1778.

Tourist attractions. Grover Cleveland birthplace, Caldwell; Walt Whitman Poetry Center, Camden; Edison Lab National Monument, West Orange; numerous Revolutionary historic sites; Great Adventure amusement park; 127 miles of Atlantic Ocean beaches; Miss America Pageant, Atlantic City; legalized casino gambling, inaugurated 1978, in Atlantic City.

Famous New Jerseyites include Aaron Burr, James Fenimore Cooper, Stephen Crane, Thomas Edison, Alexander Hamilton, Joyce Kilmer, Gen. George McClellan, Thomas Paine, Molly Pitcher, Paul Robeson, Walt Whitman, Alexander Woolcott.

Chamber of Commerce: 5 Commerce St., Newark, NJ 07102.

New Mexico
Land of Enchantment

People. Population (1980): 1,299,968; **rank:** 37. **Pop. density:** 10.7 per sq. mi. **Urban** (1970): 69.8%. **Racial distrib.** (1980): 75.1% White; 1.8% Black; 15.3% Other (includes American Indians); Hispanic 476,089. **Major ethnic groups:** Mexican, German, English. **Net migration** (1970-80): +165,000.

Geography. Total area: 121,666 sq. mi.; **rank:** 5. **Land area:** 121,412 sq. mi. **Acres forested land:** 18,059,800. **Location:** southwestern state bounded by Colorado on the N, Oklahoma, Texas, and Mexico on the E and S, and Arizona on the W. **Climate:** dry, with temperatures rising or falling 5°F with every 1,000 ft. elevation. **Topography:** eastern third, Great Plains; central third Rocky Mtns. (85% of the state is over 4,000 ft. elevation); western third high plateau. **Capital:** Santa Fe.

Economy. Principal industries: extractive industries, tourism, agriculture. **Principal manufactured goods:** foods, electrical machinery, apparel, lumber, printing, transportation equipment. **Value added by manufacture** (1978): $794.9 mln. **Agriculture:** Chief crops: wheat, hay, sorghum, grain, onions, cotton, corn. **Livestock:** 1.72 mln. cattle; 72,000 hogs/pigs; 578,000 sheep; 1.21 mln. poultry. **Timber/lumber** (1978): Ponderosa pine, Douglas fir; 199 mln. bd. ft. **Minerals** (1978): perlite, potassium salts, uranium each ranked first in U.S. production. Also copper, molybdenum, natural gas, natural gas liquids, pumice, crude petroleum. Total value of mineral production, $3.4 bln. **International airports at:** Albuquerque. **Value of construction** (1980): $1.05 bln. **Employment distribution:** 23.0% serv.; 18.0% agric.; 10% manuf.; 8.9% gvt. **Per capita income** (1980): $7,956. **Unemployment** (1980): 7.4%. **Tourism** (1980): out-of-state visitors spent $987 mln.

Finance. No. banks (1979): 87; **No. savings and loan assns.** (1978): 34.

Federal government. No. federal civilian employees (Mar. 1980): 24,501. **Avg. salary:** $18,574. **Notable federal facilities:** Kirtland, Cannon, Hollomon AF bases; Los Alamos Scientific Laboratory; White Sands Missile Range.

Energy. Electricity production (1980, mwh, by source): Hydroelectric: 94,098; Mineral: 24.5 mln.; Nuclear: —.

Education. No. schools: 694 elem. and second.; 19 higher ed. **Avg. salary, public school teachers** (1980): $14,674.

State data. Motto: Crescit Eundo (It grows as it goes). **Flower:** Yucca. **Bird:** Roadrunner. **Tree:** Piñon. **Song:** O, Fair New Mexico, Asi Es Nuevo Mexico. **Entered union** Jan. 6, 1912; rank, 47th. **State fair** at: Albuquerque; mid-Sept.

History. Franciscan Marcos de Niza and a black slave Estevan explored the area, 1539, seeking gold. First settlements were at San Juan Pueblo, 1598, and Santa Fe, 1610. Settlers alternately traded and fought with the Apaches, Comanches, and Navajos. Trade on the Santa Fe Trail to Missouri started 1821. The Mexican War was declared May, 1846, Gen. Stephen Kearny took Santa Fe, August. In the 1870s, cattlemen staged the famed Lincoln County War in which Billy (the Kid) Bonney played a leading role. Pancho Villa raided Columbus, 1916.

Tourist Attractions. Carlsbad Caverns, a national park, has caverns on 3 levels and the largest natural cave "room" in the world, 1,500 by 300 ft., 300 ft. high; White Sands Natl. Monument, the largest gypsum deposit in the world.

Pueblo ruin from 100 AD, Chaco Canyon; Acoma, the "sky city," built atop a 357-ft. mesa; 19 Pueblo, 4 Navajo, and 2 Apache reservations. Also, ghost towns, dude ranches, skiing, hunting, and fishing.

Famous New Mexicans include Billy (the Kid) Bonney, Kit Carson, Peter Hurd, Archbishop Jean Baptiste Lamy, Bill Mauldin, Georgia O'Keeffe, Kim Stanley, Lew Wallace.

Tourist information: New Mexico Travel Division, Bataan Bldg., Sante Fe, N.M. 87503 (800-545-2040).

New York
Empire State

People. Population (1980): 17,557,288; **rank:** 2. **Pop. density:** 367.0 per sq. mi. **Urban** (1970): 88.9%. **Racial distrib.** (1980): 79.5% White; 13.68% Black; Hispanic (1980): 1,659,245. **Major ethnic groups:** Italian, Russian, Polish, German. **Net migration** (1970-80): −1,431,132.

Geography. Total area: 49,576 sq. mi.; **rank:** 30. **Land area:** 47,831 sq. mi. **Acres forested land:** 17,218,400. **Location:** Middle Atlantic state, bordered by the New England states, Atlantic Ocean, New Jersey and Pennsylvania, Lakes Ontario and Erie, and Canada. **Climate:** variable; the SE region moderated by the ocean. **Topography:** highest and most rugged mountains in the NE Adirondack upland; St. Lawrence-Champlain lowlands extend from Lake Ontario NE along the Canadian border; Hudson-Mohawk lowland follows the flows of the rivers N and W, 10-30 mi. wide; Atlantic coastal plain in the SE; Appalachian Highlands, covering half the state westward from the Hudson Valley, include the Catskill Mtns., Finger Lakes; plateau of Erie-Ontario lowlands. **Capital:** Albany.

Economy. Principal industries: manufacturing, finance, communications, tourism, transportation. **Principal manufactured goods:** books and periodicals, clothing and apparel, pharmaceuticals, machinery, instruments, toys and sporting goods, electronic equipment, automotive and aircraft components. **Value added by manufacture** (1978): $48.3 bln. **Agriculture:** Chief crops: potatoes, apples, corn, grapes, onions, hay. **Products:** milk, eggs, maple syrup, nursery products, poultry, wines. **Livestock:** 1.71 mln. cattle; 140,000 hogs/pigs; 65,000 sheep; 13.4 mln. poultry. **Timber/lumber** (1979): saw log production; 596 mln. bd. ft. **Minerals** (1978): natural gas, sand and gravel, stone, peat, clay. First in emery, ilmenite production. Total value mineral production, $438 mln. **Commercial fishing** (1979): $39.0 mln. **Chief ports:** New York, Buffalo, Albany. **International airports at:** New York, Buffalo, Syracuse, Niagara Falls, Ogdensburg, Sullivan County. **Value of construction** (1980): $5.9 bln. **Employment distribution:** 1.3% agric.; 24% manuf.; 29% serv.; 20% trade. **Per capita income** (1980): $10,143. **Unemployment** (1980): 7.6%. **Tourism** (1979): tourists spent $7 bln.

Finance. Notable industries: banking, trade, security and commodity brokerage and exchange, insurance, real estate. **No. banks** (1979): 302; **No. savings and loan assns.** (1978): 127.

Federal government. No. federal civilian employees (Mar. 1980): 139,111. **Avg. salary:** $18,542. **Notable federal facilities:** West Point Military Academy; Merchant Marine Academy; Ft. Drum; Griffiss, Plattsburgh AF bases; Watervliet Arsenal.

Energy. Electricity production (1980, mwh, by source): Hydroelectric: 26.2 mln.; Mineral: 63.0 mln.; Nu-

clear: 19.2 mln.

Education: No. schools: 6,025 elem. and second.; 286 higher ed. **Avg. salary, public school teachers** (1980): $19,800.

State data. Motto: Excelsior (Ever upward). **Flower:** Rose. **Bird:** Bluebird. **Tree:** Sugar maple. **Eleventh** of the original 13 states to ratify the Constitution, July 26, 1788. **State fair** at: Syracuse, end-Aug. to early Sept.

History. In 1609 Henry Hudson discovered the river that bears his name and Champlain explored the lake, far upstate, which was named for him. Dutch built posts near Albany 1614 and 1624; in 1626 they settled Manhattan. A British fleet seized New Netherland, 1664. Ninety-two of the 300 or more engagements of the Revolution were fought in New York, including the Battle of Bemis Heights-Saratoga, a turning point of the war.

Tourist attractions. New York City; Adirondack and Catskill mtns.; Finger Lakes, Great Lakes; Thousand Islands; Niagara Falls; Saratoga Springs racing and spas; Philipsburg Manor, Sunnyside, the restored home of Washington Irving, The Dutch Church of Sleepy Hollow, all in North Tarrytown; Corning Glass Center and Steuben factory, Corning; Fenimore House, National Baseball Hall of Fame and Museum, both in Cooperstown; Ft. Ticonderoga overlooking lakes George and Champlain.

The Franklin D. Roosevelt National Historic Site, Hyde Park, includes the graves of Pres. and Mrs. Roosevelt, the family home since 1867, the Roosevelt Library. Sagamore Hill, Oyster Bay, the Theodore Roosevelt estate, includes his home.

Famous New Yorkers include Peter Cooper, George Eastman, Julia Ward Howe, Charles Evans Hughes, Henry and William James, Herman Melville, Alfred E. Smith, Elizabeth Cady Stanton, Walt Whitman.

Chamber of Commerce: 150 State St., Albany, NY 12207.

North Carolina
Tar Heel State, Old North State

People. Population (1980): 5,874,429; **rank:** 10. **Pop. density:** 120.3 per sq. mi. **Urban** (1970): 45%. **Racial distrib.** (1980): 75.8% White; 22.4% Black; Hispanic (1980): 56,607. **Major ethnic groups:** German, English. **Net migration** (1970-80): +393,369.

Geography. Total area: 52,586 sq. mi.; **rank:** 28. **Land area:** 48,798 sq. mi. **Acres forested land:** 20,043,300. **Location:** South Atlantic state bounded by Virginia, South Carolina, Georgia, Tennessee, and the Atlantic O. **Climate:** sub-tropical in SE, medium-continental in mountain region; tempered by the Gulf Stream and the mountains in W. **Topography:** coastal plain and tidewater, two-fifths of state, extending to the fall line of the rivers; piedmont plateau, another two-fifths, 200 mi. wide of gentle to rugged hills; southern Appalachian Mtns. contains the Blue Ridge and Great Smoky mtns. **Capital:** Raleigh.

Economy. Principal industries: manufacturing, agriculture, tobacco, tourism. **Principal manufactured goods:** textiles, tobacco products, electrical/electronic equip., chemicals, furniture, food products, non-electrical machinery. **Value added by manufacture** (1978): $20.6 bln. **Agriculture:** Chief crops: tobacco, soybeans, corn, peanuts, small sweet potatoes, grains, vegetables, fruits. **Livestock:** 1.08 mln. cattle; 2.6 mln. hogs/pigs; 8,000 sheep; 20.8 mln. poultry. **Timber/lumber** (1979): yellow pine, oak, hickory, poplar, maple. 1.5 bln. bd. ft. **Minerals** (1980): stone, feldspar, lithium minerals, sand and gravel, scrap mica. Total mineral production valued at $361 mln. **Commercial fishing** (1980): $68.8 mln. **Chief ports:** Morehead City, Wilmington. **Value of construction** (1980): $3.47 bln. **Employment distribution:** 34.5% manuf.; 19.8% trade; 17.2% gvt.; 14.3% serv. **Per capita income** (1980): $7,852. **Unemployment** (1980): 6.6%. **Tourism** (1976): out-of-state visitors spent $2.2 bln.

Finance. No. banks (1979): 83; **No. savings and loan assns.** (1978): 197.

Federal government. No. federal civilian employees (Mar. 1980): 35,299. **Avg. salary:** $18,175. **Notable federal facilities:** Ft. Bragg; Camp LeJeune Marine Base; U.S. EPA Research and Development Labs, Cherry Point Marine Corps Air Station.

Energy. Electricity production (1980, mwh, by source): Hydroelectric: 5.4 mln.; Mineral: 60.8 mln.; Nuclear: 5.7 mln.

Education. No. schools: 2,274 elem. and second.; 126 higher ed. **Avg. salary, public school teachers** (1980): $14,066

State data. Motto: Esse Quam Videri (To be rather than to seem). **Flower:** Dogwood. **Bird:** Cardinal. **Tree:** Pine. **Song:** The Old North State. **Twelfth** of the original 13 states to ratify the Constitution, Nov. 21, 1789. **State fair** at: Raleigh; mid-Oct.

History. The first English colony in America was the first of 2 established by Sir Walter Raleigh on Roanoke Is., 1585 and 1587. The first group returned to England; the second, the "Lost Colony," disappeared without trace. Permanent settlers came from Virginia, c. 1660. Roused by British repressions, the colonists drove out the royal governor, 1775; the province's congress was the first to vote for independence; ten regiments were furnished to the Continental Army. Cornwallis' forces were defeated at Kings Mountain, 1780, and forced out after Guilford Courthouse, 1781.

Tourist attractions. Cape Hatteras and Cape Lookout national seashores; Great Smoky Mtns. (half in Tennessee); Guilford Courthouse and Moore's Creek parks, Revolutionary battle sites; Bennett Place, NW of Durham, where Gen. Joseph Johnston surrendered the last Confederate army to Gen. Wm. Sherman; Ft. Raleigh, Roanoke Is., where Virginia Dare, first child of English parents in the New World, was born Aug. 18, 1587; Wright Brothers National Memorial, Kitty Hawk.

Famous North Carolinians include Richard J. Gatling, Billy Graham, Wm. Rufus King, Dolley Madison, Edward R. Murrow, Enos Slaughter, Moses Waddel.

Tourist information: Division of Travel & Tourism Development, P.O. Box 25249, Raleigh, NC 27611.

assns. (1978): 12.

Federal government. No. federal civilian employees (Mar. 1980): 6,471. **Avg. salary:** $18,348. **Notable federal facilities:** Strategic Air Command bases at Minot, Grand Forks; Northern Prairie Wildlife Research Center; Garrison Dam; Theodore Roosevelt Natl. Park; Grand Forks Energy Research Center; Ft. Union Natl. Historic Site.

Energy. Electricity production (1980, mwh, by source): Hydroelectric: 2.5 mln.; Mineral: 13.3 mln.; Nuclear: —.

Education. No. schools: 831 elem. and second.; 16 higher ed. **Avg. salary, public school teachers** (1980): $13,263.

State data. Motto: Liberty and union, now and forever, one and inseparable. **Flower:** Wild prairie rose. **Bird:** Western Meadowlark. **Tree:** American elm. **Song:** North Dakota Hymn. **Entered union** Nov. 2, 1889; rank, 39th. **State fair** at: Minot; 3d week in July.

History. Pierre La Verendrye was the first French fur trader in the area, 1738, followed later by the English. The U.S. acquired half the territory in the Louisiana Purchase, 1803. Lewis and Clark built Ft. Mandan, spent the winter of 1804-05 there. In 1818, American ownership of the other half was confirmed by agreement with Britain. First permanent settlement was at Pembina, 1812. Missouri River steamboats reached the area, 1832; the first railroad, 1873, bringing many homesteaders. The state was first to hold a presidential primary, 1912.

Tourist attractions. International Peace Garden, a 2,200-acre tract extending across the border into Manitoba, commemorates the friendly relations between the U.S. and Canada; 65,000-acre Theodore Roosevelt National Memorial Park, Badlands, contains the president's Elkhorn Ranch; Ft. Abraham Lincoln State Park and Museum, S of Mandan.

Famous North Dakotans include Maxwell Anderson, Angie Dickinson, John Bernard Flannagan; Louis L'Amour, Peggy Lee, Eric Sevareid, Vilhjalmur Stefansson, Lawrence Welk.

Chamber of Commerce: P.O. Box 2467, Fargo, ND 58102.

North Dakota

Sioux State, Flickertail State

People. Population (1980): 652,695; **rank:** 46. **Pop. density:** 9.4 per sq. mi. **Urban** (1970): 44.3%. **Racial distrib.** (1980): 95.8% White; 0.39% Black; Hispanic (1980): 3,903. **Major ethnic groups** Norwegian, Russian, German. **Net migration** (1970-80): —17,000.

Geography. Total area: 70,665 sq. mi.; **rank:** 17. **Land area:** 69,273 sq. mi. **Acres forested land:** 421,800. **Location:** West North Central state, situated exactly in the middle of North America, bounded on the N by Canada, on the E by Minnesota, on the S by South Dakota, on the W by Montana. **Climate:** continental, with a wide range of temperature and moderate rainfall. **Topography:** Central Lowland in the E comprises the flat Red River Valley and the Rolling Drift Prairie; Missouri Plateau of the Great Plains on the W. **Capital:** Bismarck.

Economy. Principal industries: agriculture, manufacturing. **Principal manufactured goods:** farm equipment, processed foods. **Value added by manufacture** (1978): $485 mln. **Agriculture: Chief crops:** spring wheat, durum, barley, rye, flaxseed, oats, potatoes, soybeans, sugarbeets, sunflowers, hay. **Livestock:** 2 mln. cattle; 370,000 hogs/pigs; 236,000 sheep; 1.5 mln. poultry. **Minerals** (1980): petroleum (70% of the total $935.8 mln. output value), natural gas, natural gas liquids, lignite, salt, lime. **Commercial fishing** (1979): $101,000. **International airports at:** Fargo, Grand Forks, Bismarck, Minot. **Value of construction** (1980): $442 mln. **Employment distribution:** 16.8% agric.; 15.6% serv.; 4.9% manuf. **Per capita income** (1980): $8,556. **Unemployment** (1980): 4.9% **Tourism** (1979): out-of-state visitors spent $196 mln.

Finance No. banks (1979): 175; **No. savings and loan**

Ohio

Buckeye State

People. Population (1980): 10,797,419; **rank:** 6. **Pop. density:** 263.5 per sq. mi. **Urban** (1970): 75.3%. **Racial distrib.** (1980): 88.8% White; 9.9% Black; Hispanic (1980): 119,880. **Major ethnic groups:** German, Italian, Polish, English. **Net migration** (1970-79): —624,000.

Geography. Total area: 41,222 sq. mi.; **rank:** 35. **Land area:** 40,975 sq. mi. **Acres forested land:** 6,146,600. **Location:** East North Central state bounded on the N by Michigan and Lake Erie; on the E and S by Pennsylvania, West Virginia; and Kentucky; on the W by Indiana. **Climate:** temperate but variable; weather subject to much precipitation. **Topography:** generally rolling plain; Allegheny plateau in E; Lake [Erie] plains extend southward; central plains in the W. **Capital:** Columbus.

Economy. Principal industries: manufacturing, tourism, government, trade. **Principal manufactured goods:** transportation equipment, machinery, primary and fabricated metal products. **Value added by manufacture** (1978): $47.6 bln. **Agriculture: Chief crops:** corn, hay, winter wheat, oats, soybeans. **Livestock** (1980): 1.83 mln. cattle; 2.2 mln. hogs/pigs; 320,000 sheep; 12.7 mln. poultry. **Timber/lumber** (1978): oak, ash, maple, walnut, beech; 444 mln. bd. ft. **Minerals** (1979): mineral fuels (82% of the total $1.76 bln. value of mineral production), clays, sand and gravel, stone, gypsum. **Commercial fishing** (1979): $2.2 mln. **Chief ports:** Cleveland, Toledo, Cincinnati, Ashtabula. **International airports at:** Cleveland, Columbus, Dayton. **Value of construction** (1980): $5.1 bln. **Employment distribution:** 27.2% manuf.; 20.8% trade; 17.8% serv.; 14.8% gvt. **Per capita income** (1980): $9,398. **Unemployment** (1980): 8.4%. **Tourism**

(1977): out-of-state visitors spent $3 bln.

Finance. Notable industries: banking, insurance. **No. banks** (1979): 408; **No. savings and loan assns.** (1978): 400.

Federal government. No. federal civilian employees (Mar. 1980): 79,614. **Avg. salary:** $19,921. **Notable federal facilities:** Wright Patterson, Rickenbacker AF bases; Defense Construction Supply Center; Lewis Research Ctr.; Portsmouth Gaseous Diffusion Plant; Mound Laboratory.

Energy. Electricity production (1980, mwh, by source): Hydroelectric: 6,032; Mineral: 119.9 mln.; Nuclear: 2.1 mln.

Education. No. schools: 4,943 elem. and second.; 133 higher ed. **Avg. salary, public school teachers** (1980): $15,187.

State data. Motto: With God, all things are possible **Flower:** Scarlet carnation. **Bird:** Cardinal. **Tree:** Buckeye. **Song:** Beautiful Ohio. **Entered union** Mar. 1, 1803; rank, 17th. **State fair** at: Columbus; mid-Aug.

History. LaSalle visited the Ohio area, 1669. American fur-traders arrived, beginning 1685; the French and Indians sought to drive them out. During the Revolution, Virginians defeated the Indians, 1774, but hostilities were renewed, 1777. The region became U.S. territory after the Revolution. First organized settlement was at Marietta, 1788. Indian warfare ended with Anthony Wayne's victory at Fallen Timbers, 1794. In the War of 1812, Oliver H. Perry's victory on Lake Erie and William H. Harrison's invasion of Canada, 1813, ended British incursions.

Tourist attractions. Memorial City Group National Monuments, a group of 24 prehistoric Indian burial mounds; Neil Armstrong Air and Space Museum, Wapakoneta; Air Force Museum, Dayton; Pro Football Hall of Fame, Canton; birthplaces, homes, and memorials to Ohio's 6 U.S. presidents: Wm. Henry Harrison, U.S. Grant, Garfield, Hayes, McKinley, Harding.

Famous Ohioans include Sherwood Anderson, Neil Armstrong, George Bellows, Ambrose Bierce, Paul Laurence Dunbar, Thomas Edison, John Glenn, Bob Hope, Eddie Rickenbacker, John D. Rockefeller Sr. and Jr., Gen. Wm. Sherman, Orville Wright.

Chamber of Commerce: 17 S. High St., 8th Fl., Columbus, OH 43215.

Chief ports: Catoosa, Muskogee. **International airports at:** Oklahoma City, Tulsa. **Value of construction** (1980): $2.3 bln. **Employment distribution** (1980): 21.3% trade; 17.8% gvt.; 15.8% serv.; 15.1% manuf. **Per capita income** (1980): $9,081. **Unemployment** (1980): 4.8% **Tourism** (1979): tourists spent $1.8 bln.

Finance. No. banks (1979): 496; **No. savings and loan assns.** (1978): 59.

Federal government. No. federal civilian employees (Mar. 1980): 41,630. **Avg. salary:** $18,427. **Notable federal facilities:** Federal Aviation Agency and Tinker AFB, both Oklahoma City; Ft. Sill, Lawton; Altus AFB, Altus; Vance AFB, Enid.

Energy. Electricity production (1980, mwh, by source): Hydroelectric: 1.3 mln.; Mineral: 43.3 mln.; Nuclear: —

Education. No. schools: 1,929 elem. and second.; 43 higher ed. **Avg. salary, public school teachers** (1980): $13,210.

State data. Motto: Labor Omnia Vincit (Labor conquers all things). **Flower:** Mistletoe. **Bird:** Scissortailed flycatcher. **Tree:** Redbud. **Song:** Oklahoma! **Entered union** Nov. 16, 1907; rank, 46th. **State fair** at: Oklahoma City; last week of Sept.

History. Part of the Louisiana Purchase, 1803, Oklahoma was known as Indian Territory (but was not given territorial government) after it became the home of the "Five Civilized Tribes"—Cherokee, Choctaw, Chickasaw, Creek, and Seminole—1828-1846. The land was also used by Comanche, Osage, and other Plains Indians. As white settlers pressed west, land was opened for homesteading by runs and lottery, the first run taking place Apr. 22, 1889. The most famous run was to the Cherokee Outlet, 1893.

Tourist attraction. Will Rogers Memorial, Claremore, contains his collections of saddles, ropes, trophies; his tomb is there. Also, National Cowboy Hall of Fame, Oklahoma City; restored Ft. Gibson Stockade, near Muskogee, the Army's largest outpost in Indian lands; Indian powwows; rodeos; fishing; hunting; Ouachita National Forest.

Famous Oklahomans include Carl Albert, Woody Guthrie, Gen. Patrick J. Hurley, Karl Jansky, Mickey Mantle, Wiley Post, Oral Roberts, Will Rogers, Maria Tallchief, Jim Thorpe.

Chamber of Commerce: 4020 N. Lincoln Blvd., Oklahoma City, OK 73105.

Oklahoma

Sooner State

People. Population (1980): 3,025,266; **rank:** 26. **Pop. density:** 43.9 per sq. mi. **Urban** (1970): 68%. **Racial distrib.** (1980): 85.8% White; 6.76% Black; 5.6% Amer. Ind. **Major ethnic groups:** German, English, Mexican. **Net migration** (1970-80): +294,000.

Geography. Total area: 69,919 sq. mi.; **rank:** 18. **Land area:** 68,782 sq. mi. **Acres forested land:** 8,513,300. **Location:** West South Central state bounded on the N by Colorado and Kansas; on the E by Missouri and Arkansas; on the S and W by Texas and New Mexico. **Climate:** temperate; southern humid belt merging with colder northern continental; humid eastern and dry western zones. **Topography:** high plains predominate the W, hills and small mountains in the E; the east central region is dominated by the Arkansas R. Basin, and the Red R. Plains, in the S. **Capital:** Oklahoma City.

Economy. Principal industries: mineral and energy exploration and production, manufacturing, agriculture. **Principal manufactured goods:** oil field machinery and equipment, non-electrical machinery, food and kindred products, fabricated metal products. **Value added by manufacture** (1978): $5.2 bln. **Agriculture: Chief crops:** wheat, cotton lint, sorghum grain, peanuts, hay, soybeans, cotton seed, barley, oats, pecans. **Livestock:** 5.5 mln. cattle; 370,000 hogs/pigs; 93,000 sheep; 4.96 mln. poultry. **Timber/lumber** (1979): pine, oaks, hickory; 288 mln. bd. ft. **Minerals** (1979): mineral fuels (95% of the total $4 bln. mineral production); gypsum, sand and gravel, stone, feldspar, pumice. **Commercial fishing** (1979): $2.8 mln.

Oregon

Beaver State

People. Population (1980): 2,632,663; **rank:** 30. **Pop. density:** 27.3 per sq. mi. **Urban** (1970): 67.1%. **Racial distrib.** (1980): 94.5% White; 1.4% Black; Hispanic (1980): 65,883. **Major ethnic groups:** German, Scandinavian, English, Russian. **Net migration** (1970-80): +541,130.

Geography. Total area: 96,981 sq. mi.; **rank:** 10. **Land area:** 96,184 sq. mi. **Acres forested land:** 29,810,000. **Location:** Pacific state, bounded on N by Washington; on E by Idaho; on S by Nevada and California; on W by the Pacific. **Climate:** coastal mild and humid climate; continental dryness and extreme temperatures in the interior. **Topography:** Coast Range of rugged mountains; fertile Willamette R. Valley to E and S; Cascade Mtn. Range of volcanic peaks E of the valley; plateau E of Cascades, remaining two-thirds of state. **Capital:** Salem.

Economy. Principal industries: manufacturing, forestry, food processing, agriculture, tourism. **Principal manufactured goods:** lumber, foods, instruments, machinery, fabricated metals, transportation equipment, primary metals. **Value added by manufacture** (1978): $7.1 bln. **Agriculture: Chief crops:** wheat, potatoes, winter pears, filberts, plums, prunes, peppermint oil, blackberries, boysenberries. **Livestock:** 1.75 mln. cattle; 130,000 hogs/pigs; 520,000 sheep; 7.22 mln. poultry. **Timber/lumber** (1978): Douglas fir, hemlock, ponderosa pine; 7.5 bln. bd. ft. **Minerals** (1979): nickel, crushed stone, sand

and gravel, cement, clays, diatomite, lime, pumice, talc. Total mineral production valued at $150 mln. **Commercial fishing** (1979): $66 mln. **Chief ports:** Portland, Astoria, Newport, Coos Bay. **International Airports at:** Portland. **Value of construction** (1980): $1.88 bln. **Employment distribution:** 23.6% trade; 20.9% manuf.; 18.4% govt.; 16.9% serv. **Per capita income** (1980): $9,400. **Unemployment** (1980): 8.2%. **Tourism** (1980): out-of-state visitors spent $1.14 bln.

Finance. No. banks (1979): 80; **No. savings and loan assns.** (1978): 28.

Federal government. No. federal civilian employees (Mar. 1980): 22,396. **Avg. salary:** $19,518. **Notable federal facilities:** Bonneville Power Administration.

Energy. Electricity production (1980, mwh, by source): Hydroelectric: 30.1 mln.; Mineral: 810,222; Nuclear: 5.3 mln.

Education. No. schools: 1,421 elem. and second.; 43 higher ed. **Avg. salary, public school teachers** (1980): $16,015.

State data. Motto: The union. **Flower:** Oregon grape. **Bird:** Western meadowlark. **Tree:** Douglas fir. **Song:** Oregon, My Oregon. **Entered union** Feb. 14, 1859; rank, 33d. **State fair** at: Salem; end-Aug. to early Sept.

History. American Capt. Robert Gray discovered and sailed into the Columbia River, 1792; Lewis and Clark, traveling overland, wintered at its mouth 1805-06; fur traders followed. Settlers arrived in the Willamette Valley, 1834. In 1843 the first large wave of settlers arrived via the Oregon Trail. Early in the 20th century, the "Oregon System," reforms which included the initiative, referendum, recall, direct primary, and woman suffrage, was adopted.

Tourist attractions. Crater Lake National Park, deepest lake in the U.S. (1,932 ft.) in a former volcano, 6 mi. in diameter; Oregon Dunes National Recreation Area; Ft. Clatsop National Memorial includes a replica of the fort in which Lewis and Clark spent the winter of 1805-06. Oregon Caves National Monument contains stone waterfalls. Also skiing, annual Pendleton Round-Up.

Famous Oregonians include Ernest Bloch, Childe Hassam, Ernest Haycox, Chief Joseph, Edwin Markham, Dr. John McLoughlin, Joaquin Miller, Linus Pauling, John Reed, William Simon U'Ren.

Chamber of Commerce: 220 Cottage St., N.E., Salem, OR 97301.

Pennsylvania

Keystone State

People. Population (1980): 11,866,728; **rank:** 4. **Pop. density:** 263.9 per sq. mi. **Urban** (1970): 71.5%. **Racial distrib.** (1980): 89.7% White; 8.8% Black; Hispanic 1980): 154,004. **Major ethnic groups:** Italian, Polish, German, English. **Net migration** (1970-79): −478,000.

Geography. Total area: 45,333 sq. mi.; **rank:** 33. **Land area:** 44,966 sq. mi. **Acres forested land:** 16,825,900. **Location:** Middle Atlantic state, bordered on the E by the Delaware R., on the S by the Mason-Dixon Line; on the W by West Virginia and Ohio; on the N/NE by Lake Erie and New York. **Climate:** continental with wide fluctuations in seasonal temperatures. **Topography:** Allegheny Mtns. run SW to NE, with Piedmont and Coast Plain in the SE triangle; Allegheny Front a diagonal spine across the state's center; N and W rugged plateau falls to Lake Erie lowland. **Capital:** Harrisburg.

Economy. Principal industries: steel, travel, health, apparel, machinery, food & agriculture. **Principal manufactured goods:** primary metals, foods, fabricated metal products, non-electrical machinery, electrical machinery. **Value added by manufacture** (1979): $40.5 bln. **Agriculture: Chief crops:** corn, hay, mushrooms, apples, potatoes, winter wheat, oats, vegetables, tobacco, grapes. **Livestock:** 1.9 mln. cattle; 870,000 hogs/pigs; 85,000 sheep; 20.9 mln. poultry. **Timber/lumber** (1978): pine, spruce, oak, maple; 558 mln. bd. ft. **Minerals** (1978): bituminous coal, anthracite, sand & gravel, limestone. **Com-**

mercial fishing (1979): $251,000. **Chief ports:** Philadelphia, Pittsburgh, Erie. **International airports at:** Philadelphia, Pittsburgh, Erie, Harrisburg. **Value of construction** (1980): $5.1 bln. **Employment distribution:** 27.9% manuf.; 20.8% trades; 20.4% serv.; 15.3% gvt. **Per capita income** (1980): $9,294. **Unemployment** (1980): 7.8%. **Tourism** (1980): out-of-state visitors spent $6.4 bln.

Finance. No. banks (1979): 378; **No. savings and loan assns.** (1978): 400.

Federal government. No. federal civilian employees (Mar. 1980): 114,544. **Avg. salary.** $18,295. **Notable federal facilities:** Army War College, Carlisle; Ships Control Ctr., Mechanicsburg; New Cumberland Army Depot; Philadelphia Navy Yard, Philadelphia.

Energy. Electricity production (1980, mwh, by source): Hydroelectric: 733,573; Mineral: 109.6 mln. Nuclear: 12.0 mln.

Education. No. schools: 5,451 elem. and second.; 178 higher ed. **Avg. salary, public school teachers** (1980): $16,700.

State data. Motto: Virtue, liberty and independence. **Flower:** Mountain laurel. **Bird:** Ruffed grouse. **Tree:** Hemlock. **Second** of the original 13 states to ratify the Constitution, Dec. 12, 1787. **State fair** at: Harrisburg; 2d week in Jan.

History. First settlers were Swedish, 1643, on Tinicum Is. In 1655 the Dutch seized the settlement but lost it to the British, 1664. The region was given by Charles II to William Penn, 1681, Philadelphia (brotherly love) was the capital of the colonies during most of the Revolution, and of the U.S., 1790-1800. Philadelphia was taken by the British, 1777; Washington's troops encamped at Valley Forge in the bitter winter of 1777-78. The Declaration of Independence, 1776, and the Constitution, 1787, were signed in Philadelphia.

Tourist attractions. Independence Hall, Liberty Bell, Carpenters Hall, all in Philadelphia; Valley Forge; Gettysburg battlefield; Amish festivals, Lancaster Cty., Hershey Chocolate World; Pocono Mtns.; Delaware Water Gap; Longwood Gardens, near Kennett Square; Pine Creek Gorge; hunting, fishing, winter sports.

Famous Pennsylvanians include Marian Anderson, Maxwell Anderson, Andrew Carnegie; Stephen Foster, Benjamin Franklin, George C. Marshall, Andrew W. Mellon, Robert E. Peary, Mary Roberts Rinehart, Betsy Ross.

Chamber of Commerce: 222 N. 3d St., Harrisburg, PA 17101.

Rhode Island

Little Rhody, Ocean State

People. Population (1980): 947,154; **rank:** 39. **Pop. density:** 902.9 per sq. mi. **Urban** (1970): 87.1% **Racial distrib.** (1980): 94.6% White; 2.9% Black; Hispanic (1980): 19,707. **Major ethnic groups:** Italian, English, Irish. **Net migration** (1970-79): −27,000.

Geography. Total area: 1,214 sq. mi.; **rank:** 50. **Land area:** 1,049 sq. mi. **Acres forested land:** 404,200. **Location:** New England state. **Climate:** invigorating and changeable. **Topography:** eastern lowlands of Narragansett Basin; western uplands of flat and rolling hills. **Capital:** Providence.

Economy. Principal industries: manufacturing, services. **Principal manufactured goods:** costume jewelry, machinery, textiles, electronics, silverware. **Value added by manufacture** (1978): $2.9 bln. **Agriculture: Chief crops:** potatoes, apples, corn. **Livestock:** 10,000 cattle; 8,700 hogs/pigs; 2,100 sheep; 260,000 poultry. **Timber/lumber:** oak, chestnut. **Minerals** (1980): gem stones, sand and gravel, stone. Total value mineral production, $7.5 mln. **Commercial fishing** (1979): $36.0 mln. **Chief ports:** Providence, Newport, Tiverton. **Value of construction** (1980): $331 mln. **Employment distribution** (1980): 32.1% manuf.; 20.8% serv.; 20.4% trade. **Per capita income** (1980): $9,250. **Unemployment** (1980): 7.2%. **Tourism** (1980): out-of-state visitors spent $375 mln.

Finance. Notable industries: banking, insurance. **No. banks** (1979): 17; **No. savings and loan assns.** (1978): 6.

Federal government. No. federal civilian employees (Mar. 1980): 8,084. **Avg. salary:** $19,183. **Notable federal facilities:** Naval War College.

Energy. Electricity production (1980, mwh, by source): Hydroelectric: 1,265; Mineral: 962,339; Nuclear: —.

Education. No. schools: 431 elem. and second.; 13 higher ed. **Avg. salary, public school teachers** (1980): $17,929.

State data. Motto: Hope. **Flower:** Violet. **Bird:** Rhode Island red. **Tree:** Red maple. **Song:** Rhode Island. **Thirteenth** of original 13 states to ratify the Constitution, May 29, 1790. **State fair** at: E. Greenwich; mid-Aug.

History. Rhode Island is distinguished for its battle for freedom of conscience and action, begun by Roger Williams, founder of Providence, who was exiled from Massachusetts Bay Colony in 1636, and Anne Hutchinson, exiled in 1638. Rhode Island gave protection to Quakers in 1657 and to Jews from Holland in 1658.

The colonists broke the power of the Narragansett Indians in the Great Swamp Fight, 1675, the decisive battle in King Philip's War. British trade restrictions angered the colonists and they burned the British revenue cutter Gaspee, 1772. The colony declared its independence May 4, 1776. Gen. John Sullivan and Lafayette won a partial victory, 1778, but failed to oust the British.

Tourist attractions. Newport mansions; summer resorts and water sports; Touro Synagogue, Newport, 1763; first Baptist church in America, Providence, 1638; Gilbert Stuart birthplace, Saunderstown; Narragansett Indian Fall Festival.

Famous Rhode Islanders include Ambrose Burnside, George M. Cohan, Nelson Eddy, Jabez Gorham, Nathanael Greene, Christopher and Oliver La Farge, Matthew C. and Oliver Perry, Gilbert Stuart.

Chamber of Commerce: 206 Smith St., Providence, RI 02908.

out-of-state visitors spent $2.2 bln.

Finance. No. banks (1979): 85; **No. savings and loan assns.** (1978): 74.

Federal government: No. federal civilian employees (Mar. 1980): 28,196. **Avg. Salary:** $18,051. **Notable federal facilities:** Polaris Submarine Base; Barnwell Nuclear Power Plant; Ft. Jackson.

Energy. Electricity production (1980, mwh, by source): Hydroelectric: 2.9 mln.; Mineral: 21.4 mln.; Nuclear: 17.4 mln.

Education. No. schools: 1,329 elem. and second.; 61 higher ed. **Avg. salary, public school teachers** (1980): $12,947.

State data. Motto: Dum Spiro Spero (While I breathe, I hope). **Flower:** Carolina jessamine. **Bird:** Carolina wren. **Tree:** Palmetto. **Song:** Carolina. **Eighth** of the original 13 states to ratify the Constitution, May 23, 1788. **State fair** at: Columbia; Oct. 16-25.

History. The first English colonists settled, 1670, on the Ashley River, moved to the site of Charleston, 1680. The colonists seized the government, 1775, and the royal governor fled. The British took Charleston, 1780, but were defeated at Kings Mountain that year, and at Cowpens and Eutaw Springs, 1781. In the 1830s, South Carolinians, angered by federal protective tariffs, adopted the Nullification Doctrine, holding a state can void an act of Congress. The state was the first to secede and, in 1861, Confederate troops fired on and forced the surrender of U. S. troops at Ft. Sumter, in Charleston Harbor, launching the Civil War.

Tourist attractions. Restored historic Charleston harbor area and Charleston gardens: Middleton Place, Magnolia, Cypress; other gardens at Brookgreen, Edisto, Glencairn; state parks; coastal islands; shore resorts such as Myrtle Beach; fishing and quail hunting; Ft. Sumter National Monument, in Charleston Harbor; Charleston Museum, est. 1773, is the oldest museum in the U.S..

Famous South Carolinians include James F. Byrnes John C. Calhoun, DuBose Heyward, James Longstreet Francis Marion, Charles Pinckney, John Rutledge Thomas Sumter.

Chamber of Commerce: 1002 Calhoun St., Columbia SC 29201.

South Carolina
Palmetto State

People. Population (1980): 3,119,208; **rank:** 24. **Pop. density:** 103.1 per sq. mi. **Urban** (1970): 47.6%. **Racial distrib.** (1980): 68.8% White; 30.4% Black; Hispanic (1980): 33,414. **Major ethnic groups:** German, English. **Net migration** (1970-80): +270,350.

Geography. Total area: 31,055 sq. mi.; **rank:** 40. **Land area:** 30,225 sq. mi. **Acres forested land:** 12,249,400. **Location:** south Atlantic coast state, bordering North Carolina on the N; Georgia on the SW and W; the Atlantic O. on the E, SE and S. **Climate:** humid sub-tropical. **Topography:** Blue Ridge province in NW has highest peaks; piedmont lies between the mountains and the fall line; coastal plain covers two-thirds of the state. **Capital:** Columbia.

Economy: Principal industries: tourism, textiles, apparel, chemical, agriculture, manufacturing. **Principal manufactured goods:** textiles, chemicals and allied products, non-electrical machinery, apparel and related products. **Value added by manufacture** (1978): $9.4 bln. **Agriculture. Chief crops:** tobacco, soybeans, corn, cotton, peaches, hay, vegetables. **Livestock** (1978): 960,000 cattle; 525,000 hogs/pigs; 1,300 sheep; 8.05 mln. poultry. **Timber/lumber** (1979): pine, oak; 1.2 bln. bd. ft. **Minerals** (1980): cement, stone, limestone, granite, sand and gravel, clays; vermiculite, kaolin, both 2d in U.S. production. Total mineral production valued at $210 mln. **Commercial fishing** (1980): $21.0 mln. **Chief ports:** Charleston, Georgetown. **International airports at:** Charleston, Greenville-Spartanburg. **Value of construction** (1980): $2.5 bln. **Employment distribution** (1980): 33% manuf.; 20% gvt.; 13.3% serv. **Per capita income** (1980): $7,519. **Unemployment** (1980): 6.9%. **Tourism** (1979):

South Dakota
Coyote State, Sunshine State

People. Population (1980): 690,178; **rank:** 45. **Pop density:** 9.0 per sq. mi. **Urban** (1970): 44.6%. **Racial distrib.** (1980): 92.6% White; 0.31% Black; 7.1% Other (includes American Indians); Hispanic (1980): 4,028. **Major ethnic groups:** German, Norwegian, Russian. **Net migration** (1970-80): −26,974.

Geography. Total area: 77,047 sq. mi.; **rank:** 16. **Land area:** 75,955 sq. mi. **Acres forested land:** 1,702,000. **Location:** West North Central state bounded on the N by North Dakota; on the E by Minnesota and Iowa; on the S by Nebraska; on the W by Wyoming and Montana. **Climate:** characterized by extremes of temperature, persistent winds, low precipitation and humidity. **Topography:** Prairie Plains in the E; rolling hills of the Great Plains in the W; the Black Hills, rising 3,500 ft. in the SW corner. **Capital:** Pierre.

Economy: Principal industries: mining, manufacturing, agriculture. **Principal manufactured goods:** processed meats, electrical appliances, occupational health and safety products, computer sub-assemblies. **Value added by manufacture** (1978): $726.1 mln. **Agriculture. Chief crops:** rye, flaxseed, oats, durum, wheat, honey, alfalfa, sunflower seeds. **Livestock** (1980): 4.19 mln. cattle; 1.4 mln. hogs/pigs; 810,000 sheep; 3.32 mln. poultry. **Timber/lumber** (1979): ponderosa pine; 190 mln. bd. ft. **Minerals** (1980 est.): gold (1st in U.S.), crude oil, stone, sand and gravel. Total value mineral production, $238.3 mln. **Commercial fishing** (1979): $309,000. **Value of construction** (1980): $421 mln. **Employment distribution** 15.6% serv.; 13.1% agric.; 8.2% manuf. **Per capita**

come (1980): $7,452. Unemployment (1980): 4.7%. Tourism (1979): out-of-state visitors spent $415 mln.

Finance. No. banks (1979): 155; No. savings and loan assns. (1978): 18.

Federal government. No. federal civilian employees (Mar. 1980): 8,037. Avg. salary: $17,927. Notable federal facilities: Bureau of Indian Affairs.

Energy. Electricity production (1980, mwh, by source): Hydroelectric: 5.7 mln.; Mineral: 2.8 mln.; Nuclear: —.

Education: No. schools: 869 elem. and second.; 18 higher ed. Avg. salary, public school teachers (1980): $12,350.

State data. Motto: Under God, the people rule. Flower: Pasque flower. Bird: Ringnecked pheasant. Tree: Black Hills spruce. Song: Hail, South Dakota. Entered union Nov. 2, 1889; rank, 40th. State fair at: Huron; late Aug.-early Sept.

History. La Verendrye explored the region, 1742-43. Lewis and Clark passed through the area, 1804 and 1806. First American settlement was at Sioux Falls, 1859. Gold was discovered, 1874, on the Sioux Reservation; miners rushed in. The U.S. first tried to stop them, then relaxed its opposition. Custer's defeat by the Sioux followed; the Sioux relinquished the land, 1877 and the "great Dakota Boom" began. A new Indian uprising came in 1890, climaxed by the massacre of Indian families at Wounded Knee.

Tourist attractions. Needles Highway through the Black Hills; Badlands National Monument "moonscape"; Custer State Park's bison and burro herds; Ft. Sisson, a restored army frontier post of 1864; the "Great Lakes of South Dakota," reservoirs created behind Oahe, Big Bend, Ft. Randall, and Gavins Point dams on the Missouri R.

Mount Rushmore, in the Black Hills, has an altitude of 6,200 ft. Sculptured on its granite face are the heads of Washington, Jefferson, Lincoln, and Theodore Roosevelt. These busts by Gutzon Borglum are proportionate to men 465 ft. tall. Rushmore is visited by about 2 million persons annually.

Famous South Dakotans include Crazy Horse, Alvin H. Hansen, Dr. Ernest O. Lawrence, Sacagawea, Sitting Bull.

Chamber of Commerce: P.O. Box 190, Pierre, SD 57501.

Tennessee

Volunteer State

People. Population (1980): 3,835,078; rank: 22. Pop. density: 92.7 per sq. mi. Urban (1970): 58.7%. Racial distrib. (1980): 83.5% White; 15.8% Black; Hispanic (1980): 34,081. Major ethnic groups: German, English, Italian. Net migration (1970-79): +202,500.

Geography. Total area: 42,244 sq. mi.; rank: 34. Land area: 41,328 sq. mi. Acres forested land: 13,160,500. Location: East South Central state bounded on the N by Kentucky and Virginia; on the E by North Carolina; on the S by Georgia, Alabama, and Mississippi; on the W by Arkansas and Missouri. Climate: humid continental to the N; humid sub-tropical to the S. Topography: rugged country in the E; the Great Smoky Mtns. of the Unakas; low ridges of the Appalachian Valley; the flat Cumberland Plateau; slightly rolling terrain and knobs of the Interior Low Plateau, the largest region; Eastern Gulf Coastal Plain to the W, is laced with meandering streams; Mississippi Alluvial Plain, a narrow strip of swamp and flood plain in the extreme W. Capital: Nashville.

Economy. Principal industries: manufacturing, agriculture, tourism, publishing, music. Principal manufactured goods: primary and fabricated metals, foods, electrical and electronic machinery, transportation equipment, apparel. Value added by manufacture (1978): $14.0 bln. Agriculture: Chief crops: soybeans, tobacco, cotton, corn, nursery stock, hay. Livestock: 2.3 mln. cattle; 1.4 mln. hogs/pigs; 12,000 sheep; 5.4 mln. poultry. Timber/-

lumber (1979): red oak, white oak, yellow poplar, hickory; 684 mln. bd. ft. Minerals (1978): bituminous coal, stone, zinc, ball clay, cement. Total value mineral production, $347.5 mln. Commercial fishing (1978): $2.4 mln. Chief ports: Memphis, Nashville, Chattanooga. International airports at: Memphis, Nashville, Chattanooga. Value of construction (1980): $2.76 bln. Employment distribution: 28.4% manuf.; 20.8% trade; 16.9% govt.; 15.4% serv. Per capita income (1980): $7,786. Unemployment (1980): 7.2%. Tourism (1978): out-of-state visitors spent $1.3 mln.

Finance. Notable industries: insurance. No. banks (1979): 352; No. savings and loan assns. (1978): 97.

Federal government. No. federal civilian employees (Mar. 1980): 66,172. Avg. salary: $19,184. Notable federal facilities: Tennessee Valley Authority; Oak Ridge Nat'l. Laboratories.

Energy. Electricity production (1980, mwh, by source): Hydroelectric: 8.7 mln.; Mineral: 50.9 mln.; Nuclear: 518,840.

Education. No. schools: 1,856 elem. and second.; 76 higher ed. Avg. salary, public school teachers (1980): $13,158.

State data. Motto: Agriculture and commerce. Flower: Iris. Bird: Mockingbird. Tree: Tulip poplar. Song: The Tennessee Waltz. Entered union June 1, 1796; rank, 16th. State fair at: Nashville; 3d week of Sept.

History. Spanish explorers first visited the area, 1541. English traders crossed the Great Smokies from the east while France's Marquette and Jolliet sailed down the Mississippi on the west, 1673. First permanent settlement was by Virginians on the Watauga River, 1769. During the Revolution, the colonists helped win the Battle of Kings Mountain, N.C., 1780, and joined other eastern campaigns. The state seceded from the Union 1861, and saw many engagements of the Civil War, but 30,000 soldiers fought for the Union.

Tourist attractions. Natural wonders include Reelfoot Lake, the reservoir basin of the Mississippi R. formed by the 1811 earthquake; Lookout Mountain, Chattanooga; Fall Creek Falls, 256 ft. high; Great Smoky Mountains National Park.

Also, the Hermitage, 13 mi. E of Nashville, home of Andrew Jackson; the homes of presidents Polk and Andrew Johnson; the Parthenon, Nashville, a replica of the Parthenon of Athens; the Grand Old Opry, Nashville.

Famous Tennesseans include Davy Crockett,. David Farragut, William C. Handy, Sam Houston, Cordell Hull, Grace Moore, Dinah Shore, Alvin York.

Tourist Information: Tourist Development Office, 601 Broadway, Nashville, TN 37202.

Texas

Lone Star State

People. Population (1980): 14,228,383; rank: 3. Pop. density: 54.2 per sq. mi. Urban (1970): 79.7%. Racial distrib. (1980): 78.6% White; 12.0% Black; Hispanic (1980): 2,985,643. Major ethnic groups: Mexican, German. Net migration (1970-79): +1,045,000.

Geography. Total area: 267,338 sq. mi.; rank: 2. Land area: 262,134 sq. mi. Acres forested land: 23,279,300. Location: Southwestern state, bounded on the SE by the Gulf of Mexico; on the SW by Mexico, separated by the Rio Grande; surrounding states are Louisiana, Arkansas, Oklahoma, New Mexico. Climate: extremely varied; driest region is the Trans-Pecos; wettest is the NE. Topography: Gulf Coast Plain in the S and SE; North Central Plains slope upward with some hills; the Great Plains extend over the Panhandle, are broken by low mountains; the Trans-Pecos is the southern extension of the Rockies. Capital: Austin.

Economy. Principal industries: petroleum, manufacturing, construction. Principal manufactured goods: machinery, transportation equipment, foods, refined petroleum, apparel. Value added by manufacture (1978): $36.4 bln. Agriculture: Chief crops: cotton, grain sorghum, grains, vegetables, citrus and other fruits, pecans, peanuts. **Livestock:** 13.9 mln. cattle; 800,000 hogs/pigs; 2.25 mln. sheep; 16.8 mln. poultry. **Timber/lumber** (1978): pine, cypress; 950 mln. bd. ft. **Minerals** (1978): petroleum, natural gas, natural gas liquids, cement, sulfur, stone, sand and gravel, lime, salt; total $19.9 bln. **Commercial fishing** (1979): $160 mln. **Chief ports:** Houston, Galveston, Brownsville, Beaumont, Port Arthur, Corpus Christi. **Major International airports at:** Houston, Dallas/Ft. Worth, San Antonio. **Value of construction** (1980): $13.6 bln. **Employment distribution:** 18% manuf.; 17% serv.; 6% transp. **Per capita income** (1980): $9,513. **Unemployment** (1980): 5.3%. **Tourism** (1979): out-of-state visitors spent $4.8 bln.

Finance. No. banks (1979): 1,427; **No. savings and loan assns.** (1978): 320.

Federal government. No. federal civilian employees (Mar. 1980): 134,437. **Avg. salary:** $18,438. **Notable federal facilities:** Fort Hood (Killeen).

Energy. Electricity production (1980, mwh, by source): Hydroelectric: 979,125; Mineral: 149.0 mln.; Nuclear: —.

Education. No. schools: 5,953 elem. and second.; 147 higher ed. **Avg. salary, public school teachers** (1980): $14,157.

State data. Motto: Friendship. **Flower:** Bluebonnet. **Bird:** Mockingbird. **Tree:** Pecan. **Song:** Texas, Our Texas. **Entered union** Dec. 29, 1845; rank, 28th. **State fair** at: Dallas; mid-Oct.

History. Pineda sailed along the Texas coast, 1519; Cabeza de Vaca and Coronado visited the interior, 1541. Spaniards made the first settlement at Ysleta, near El Paso, 1682. Americans moved into the land early in the 19th century. Mexico, of which Texas was a part, won independence from Spain, 1821; Santa Anna became dictator, 1835. Texans rebelled; Santa Anna wiped out defenders of the Alamo, 1836. Sam Houston's Texans defeated Santa Anna at San Jacinto and independence was proclaimed the same year. In 1845, Texas was admitted to the Union.

Tourist attractions. Padre Island National Seashore; Big Bend, Guadalupe Mtns. national parks; The Alamo; Ft. Davis; Six Flags Amusement Park. Named for Pres. Lyndon B. Johnson are a state park, a natl. historic site marking his birthplace, boyhood home, and ranch, all near Johnson City, and a library in Austin.

Famous Texans include Stephen Austin, James Bowie, Carol Burnett, J. Frank Dobie, Sam Houston, Howard Hughes, Mary Martin, Chester Nimitz, Katharine Ann Porter, Sam Rayburn.

Chamber of Commerce: 1004 International Life Bldg., Austin, TX 78701.

(1978 est.): $2.3 bln. **Agriculture: Chief crops:** wheat, hay, apples, peaches, barley, alfalfa seed. **Livestock:** 819,000 cattle; 49,000 hogs/pigs; 627,000 sheep; 5.36 mln. poultry. **Timber/lumber:** aspen, spruce, pine. **Minerals** (1980): crude oil, copper, coal, uranium, gold, natural gas, vanadium, silver, zinc, lead, iron ore, lime, salt. Total value of mineral production valued at $2.0 bln. **International airports at:** Salt Lake City. **Value of construction** (1980): $1.1 bln. **Employment distribution:** 23.6% trade; 22.5% govt., 17.6% serv.; 15.8% manuf. **Per capita income** (1980): $7,485. **Unemployment** (1980): 6.2%. **Tourism** (1978): out-of-state visitors spent $220 mln.

Finance. No. banks (1979): 76; **No. savings and loan assns.** (1978): 16.

Federal government. No. federal civilian employees (Mar. 1980): 33,676. **Avg. salary:** $17,987. **Notable federal facilities:** Hill AFB; Tooele Army Depot, IRS Western Service Center.

Energy. Electricity production (1980, mwh, by source): Hydroelectric: 821,467; Mineral: 11.2 mln.; Nuclear: —.

Education. No. schools: 574 elem. and second.; 14 higher ed. **Avg. salary, public school teachers** (1980): $14,965.

State data. Motto: Industry. **Flower:** Sego lily. **Bird:** Seagull. **Tree:** Blue spruce. **Song:** Utah, We Love Thee. **Entered union** Jan. 4, 1896; rank, 45th. **State fair** at: Salt Lake City; Sept.

History. Spanish Franciscans visited the area, 1776, the first white men to do so. American fur traders followed. Permanent settlement began with the arrival of the Mormons, 1847. They made the arid land bloom and created a prosperous economy, organized the State of Deseret, 1849, and asked admission to the Union. This was not achieved until 1896, after a long period of controversy over the Mormon Church's doctrine of polygamy, which it discontinued in 1890.

Tourist attractions. Temple Square, Mormon Church hdqtrs., Salt Lake City; Great Salt Lake; fishing streams; lakes and reservoirs, numerous winter sports; campgrounds. Natural wonders may be seen at Zion, Canyonlands, Bryce Canyon, Arches, and Capitol Reef national parks; Dinosaur, Rainbow Bridge, Timpanogas Cave, and Natural Bridges national monuments. Also Lake Powell and Flaming Gorge Dam.

Famous Utahans include Maude Adams, Ezra Taft Benson, John Moses Browning, Philo Farnsworth, Osmond Family, Ivy Baker Priest, George Romney, Brigham Young, Loretta Young.

Tourist information: Division of Travel Development, Council Hall, Salt Lake City, UT 84114.

Utah

Beehive State

People. Population (1980): 1,461,037; **rank:** 36. **Pop. density:** 17.7 per sq. mi. **Urban** (1970): 80.4%. **Racial distrib.** (1980): 95% White; —% Black; Hispanic (1980): 60,302. **Major ethnic groups:** English, German, Danish. **Net migration** (1970-80): +149,000.

Geography. Total area: 84,916 sq. mi.; **rank:** 11. **Land area:** 82,096 sq. mi. **Acres forested land:** 15,557,400. **Location:** Middle Rocky Mountain state; its southeastern corner touches Colorado, New Mexico, and Arizona, and is the only spot in the U.S. where 4 states join. **Climate:** arid; yet the SW has a semitropical climate. **Topography:** high Colorado plateau is cut by brilliantly-colored canyons of the SE; broad, flat, desert-like Great Basin of the W; the Great Salt Lake and Bonneville Salt Flats to the NW; Middle Rockies in the NE run E-W; valleys and plateaus of the Wasatch Front. **Capital:** Salt Lake City.

Economy. Principal industries: mining, manufacturing, tourism, trade, services, transportation. **Principal manufactured goods:** guided missiles and parts, electronic components, food products, primary metals, electrical and transportation equipment. **Value added by manufacture**

Vermont

Green Mountain State

People. Population (1980): 511,456; **rank:** 48. **Pop. density:** 55.1 per sq. mi. **Urban** (1970): 32.2%. **Racial distrib.** (1980): 99.0% White; 0.22% Black; Hispanic (1980): 3,304. **Major ethnic groups:** English, Italian, German. **Net migration** (1970-80): +66,724.

Geography. Total area: 9,609 sq. mi.; **rank:** 43. **Land area:** 9,267 sq. mi. **Acres forested land:** 4,511,700. **Location:** northern New England state. **Climate:** temperate, with considerable temperature extremes; heavy snowfall in mountains. **Topography:** Green Mtns. N-S backbone 20-36 mi. wide; avg. altitude 1,000 ft. **Capital:** Montpelier.

Economy. Principal industries: manufacturing, tourism, agriculture, mining, government. **Principal manufactured goods:** machine tools, furniture, scales, books, computer components, skis, fishing rods. **Value added by manufacture** (1978): $1.38 bln. **Agriculture: Chief crops:** apples, maple syrup, hay; also, dairy products. **Livestock:** 320,000 cattle; 6,300 hogs/pigs; 8,000 sheep; 570,000 poultry. **Timber/lumber:** pine, spruce, fir, hemlock. **Minerals** (1979): stone; asbestos (2d in U.S.); talc (1st in U.S.); sand and gravel; gemstones; dimension granite, marble, and slate (2d in U.S.). Total value mineral production, $49.5 mln. **International airports at:** Burlington. **Value of construction** (1980): $251 mln. **Employment distribution:** 22% manuf.; 19% serv.; 14% retail trade. **Per capita income** (1980): $7,839. **Unemployment** (1980): 6.4% **Tourism** (1980): out-of-state visitors spent $450 mln.

Finance. No. banks (1979): 30; **No. savings and loan assns.** (1978): 7.

Federal government. No. federal civilian employees (Mar. 1980): 3,297. **Avg. salary:** $18,716.

Energy. Electricity production (1980, mwh, by source): Hydroelectric: 743,308; Mineral: 48,853; Nuclear: 2.9 mln

Education. No. schools: 443 elem. und second.; 21 higher ed. **Avg. salary, public school teachers** (1980): $12,750.

State data. Motto: Freedom and unity. **Flower:** Red clover. **Bird:** Hermit thrush. **Tree:** Sugar maple. **Song:** Hail, Vermont. **Entered union** Mar. 4, 1791; rank, 14th. **State fair** at: Rutland; early Sept.

History. Champlain explored the lake that bears his name, 1609. First American settlement was Ft. Dummer, 1724, near Brattleboro. Ethan Allen and the Green Mountain Boys captured Ft. Ticonderoga, 1775; John Stark defeated part of Burgoyne's forces near Bennington, 1777. In the War of 1812, Thomas MacDonough defeated a British fleet on Champlain off Plattsburgh, 1814.

Tourist attractions. Year-round outdoor sports, esp. hiking, camping and skiing; there are over 56 ski areas in the state. Popular are the Shelburne Museum; Rock of Ages Tourist Center, Graniteville; Vermont Marble Exhibit, Proctor; Bennington Battleground; Pres. Coolidge homestead, Plymouth; Maple Grove Maple Museum, St. Johnsbury.

Famous Vermonters include Ethan Allen, Adm. George Dewey, John Dewey, Stephen A. Douglas, Dorothy Canfield Fisher, James Fisk.

Chamber of Commerce: P.O. Box 37, Montpelier, VT 05602.

Finance. No. banks (1979): 234; **No. savings and loan assns.** (1978): 85.

Federal government. No. federal civilian employees (Mar. 1980): 133,432. **Avg. salary:** $20,486. **Notable federal facilities:** Pentagon; Naval Sta., Norfolk; Naval Air Sta., Norfolk, Virginia Beach; Naval Shipyard, Portsmouth; Marine Corps Base, Quantico; Langley AFB; NASA at Langley.

Energy. Electricity production (1980, mwh, by source): Hydroelectric: 864,476; Mineral: 21.9 mln.; Nuclear: 11.4 mln.

Education. No. schools: 2,031 elem. and second.; 72 higher ed. **Avg. salary, public school teachers** (1980): $14,025.

State data. Motto: Sic Semper Tyrannis (Thus always to tyrants). **Flower:** Dogwood. **Bird:** Cardinal. **Tree:** Dogwood. **Song:** Carry Me Back to Old Virginia. **Tenth of the** original 13 states to ratify the Constitution, June 26, 1788. **State fair** at: Richmond; late Sept.-early Oct.

History. English settlers founded Jamestown, 1607. Virginians took over much of the government from royal Gov. Dunmore in 1775, forcing him to flee. Virginians under George Rogers Clark freed the Ohio-Indiana-Illinois area of British forces. Benedict Arnold burned Richmond and Petersburg for the British, 1781. That same year, Britain's Cornwallis was trapped at Yorktown and surrendered.

Tourist attractions. Colonial Williamsburg; Busch Gardens; Wolf Trap Farm, near Falls Church; Arlington National Cemetery; Mt. Vernon, home of George Washington; Jamestown Festival Park; Yorktown; Jefferson's Monticello, Charlottesville; Robert E. Lee's birthplace, Stratford Hall, and grave, at Lexington; Appomattox; Shenandoah National Park; Blue Ridge Parkway; Virginia Beach.

Famous Virginians include Richard E. Byrd, James B. Cabell, Patrick Henry, Joseph E. Johnston, Robert E. Lee, Meriwether Lewis and William Clark, John Marshall, Edgar Allan Poe, Walter Reed, Booker T. Washington.

Chamber of Commerce: 611 E. Franklin St., Richmond, VA 23219.

Virginia

Old Dominion

People. Population (1980): 5,346,279; **rank:** 14. **Pop. density:** 134.3 per sq. mi. **Urban** (1970): 63.1%. **Racial distrib.** (1980): 79.1% White; 18.9% Black; Hispanic (1980): 79,873. **Major ethnic groups:** English, German, Italian. **Net migration** (1970-80): +348,200.

Geography. Total area: 40,817 sq. mi.; **rank:** 36. **Land area:** 39,780 sq. mi. **Acres forested land:** 16,417,400. **Location:** South Atlantic state bounded by the Atlantic O. on the E and surrounded by North Carolina, Tennessee, Kentucky, West Virginia, and Maryland. **Climate:** mild and equable. **Topography:** mountain and valley region in the W, including the Blue Ridge Mtns.; rolling piedmont plateau; tidewater, or coastal plain, including the eastern shore. **Capital:** Richmond.

Economy. Principal industries: government, manufacturing, agriculture, tourism, trade. **Principal manufactured goods:** textiles, food processing, apparel, transportation equipment, chemicals. **Value added by manufacture** (1978): $11.9 bln. **Agriculture: Chief crops:** tobacco, hay, corn, peanuts. **Livestock:** 1.62 mln. cattle; 670,000 hogs/pigs; 172,000 sheep; 104 mln. poultry. **Timber/lumber** (1977): pine and hardwoods; 957 mln. bd. ft. **Minerals** (1977): bituminous coal, stone, cement, lime, sand and gravel, zinc. Total value mineral production, $1.3 bln. **Commercial fishing** (1979): $84.6 mln. **Chief ports:** Hampton Roads, Chesapeake Bay. **International airports at:** Norfolk, Dulles, Richmond, Newport News. **Value of construction** (1980): $3.49 bln. **Employment distribution:** 20% manuf.; 21% trade; 18% serv.; 7% gvt. **Per capita income** (1980): $9,435. **Unemployment** (1980): 5.1% **Tourism** (1978): out-of-state visitors spent $2.4 bln.

Washington

Evergreen State

People. Population (1980): 4,130,163; **rank:** 19. **Pop. density:** 62.0 per sq. mi. **Urban** (1970): 72.6%. **Racial distrib.** (1980): 91.4% White; 2.5% Black; Hispanic (1980): 119,986. **Major ethnic groups:** German, English, Norwegian. **Net migration** (1970-79): +296,000.

Geography. Total area: 68,192 sq. mi.; **rank:** 20. **Land area:** 66,570 sq. mi. **Acres forested land:** 23,181,000. **Location:** northwestern coastal state bordered by Canada on the N; Idaho on the E; Oregon on the S; and the Pacific O. on the W. **Climate:** mild, dominated by the Pacific O. and protected by the Rockies. **Topography:** Olympic Mtns. on NW peninsula; open land along coast to Columbia R.; flat terrain of Puget Sound Lowland; Cascade Mtns. region's high peaks to the E; Columbia Basin in central portion; highlands to the NE; mountains to the SE. **Capital:** Olympia.

Economy. Principal industries: transp. equip., lumber and wood products, agriculture, food products. **Principal manufactured goods:** aircraft, lumber and plywood, aluminum, paper, preserved fruits and vegetables, nonelectrical machinery. **Value added by manufacture** (1978): $10.4 bln. **Agriculture: Chief crops:** Wheat, apples, hay, potatoes, barley, hops, pears. **Livestock** (1981): 1.45 mln. cattle; 100,000 hogs/pigs; 80,000 sheep; 6,598 mln. poultry. **Timber/lumber** (1979): Douglas fir, hemlock, cedar, pine; 7.0 bln. bd. ft. **Minerals** (1977): cement, coal, sand and gravel, stone. Total value mineral production, $216 mln. **Commercial fishing** (1979): $97 mln. **Chief ports:** Seattle, Tacoma, Vancouver, Kelso-Longview. **International airports at:** Seattle/Tacoma, Spokane, Yakima, Pasco. **Value of construction** (1980): $4.78 bln. **Employment distribution:** 21.1% trade; 19.3% govt.;

17.1% serv.; **16.4%** manuf. **Per capita income** (1980): $10,363. **Unemployment** (1980): 7.5%. **Tourism** (1978): out-of-state visitors spent $1.9 bln.

Finance. No. banks (1979): 110; **No. savings and loan assns.** (1978): 50.

Federal government. No. federal civilian employees (Mar. 1980): 54,089. **Avg. salary:** $19,807. **Notable federal facilities:** Bonneville Power Admin.; Ft. Lewis; McChord AFB; Hanford Nuclear Reservation; Bremerton Naval Shipyards.

Energy. Electricity production (1980, mwh, by source): Hydroelectric: 82.9 mln.; Mineral: 7.3 mln.; Nuclear: 2.0 mln.

Education. No. schools: 1,933 elem. and second.; 49 higher ed. **Avg. salary, public school teachers** (1980): $18,815.

State data. Motto. Alki (By and by). **Flower:** Western rhododendron. **Bird:** Willow goldfinch. **Tree:** Western hemlock. **Song:** Washington, My Home. **Entered union** Nov. 11, 1889; rank, 42d.

History. Spain's Bruno Hezeta sailed the coast, 1775. American Capt. Robert Gray sailed up the Columbia River, 1792. Canadian fur traders set up Spokane House, 1810; Americans under John Jacob Astor established a post at Fort Okanogan, 1811. Missionary Marcus Whitman settled near Walla Walla, 1836. Final agreement on the border of Washington and Canada was made with Britain, 1846, and gold was discovered in the state's northeast, 1855, bringing new settlers.

Tourist attractions. Mt. Rainier, Olympic, North Cascades national parks; Pacific beaches; outdoor year-round sports; rodeos; Indian reservations.

Famous Washingtonians include Chester Carlson, Bing Crosby, Mary McCarthy, Marcus Whitman, Minoru Yamasaki.

Chamber of Commerce: P.O. Box 658, Olympia, WA 98507.

West Virginia

Mountain State

People. Population (1980): 1,949,644 **rank:** 34. **Pop. density:** 80.9 per sq. mi. **Urban** (1970): 39%. **Racial distrib.** (1980): 96.1% White; 3.3% Black; Hispanic (1980): 12,707. **Major ethnic groups:** Italian, English, German. **Net migration** (1970-79): +28,000.

Geography. Total area: 24,181 sq. mi.; **rank:** 41. **Land area:** 24,070 sq. mi. **Acres forested land:** 11,668,600. **Location:** South Atlantic state bounded on the N by Ohio, Pennsylvania, Maryland; on the S and W by Virginia, Kentucky, Ohio; on the E by Maryland and Virginia. **Climate:** humid continental climate except for marine modification in the lower panhandle. **Topography:** rugged, ranging from hilly to mountainous; Allegheny Plateau in the W, covers two-thirds of the state; mountains here are the highest in the state, over 4,000 ft. **Capital:** Charleston.

Economy. Principal industries: mining, mineral and chemical production, agriculture. **Principal manufactured goods:** synthetic fibers, plastics. **Value added by manufacture** (1978): $4.4 bln. **Agriculture:** Chief crops: apples, peaches, dairy, tobacco, corn. **Chief products:** dairy products. **Livestock:** 570,000 cattle; 62,000 hogs/pigs; 108,000 sheep; 3.1 mln. poultry. **Timber/lumber:** oak, yellow poplar, hickory, walnut, cherry. **Minerals** (1977): bituminous coal, natural gas, crude petroleum, clay, cement, lime, salt. Total value mineral production $3.7 billion. **Commercial fishing** (1980): $21,000. **Chief port:** Huntington. **Value of construction** (1980): $835 mln. **Per capita income** (1980): $7,831. **Unemployment** (1980): 9.4%. **Tourism** (1976): out-of-state visitors spent $771 mln.

Finance. No. banks (1979): 235; **No. savings and loan assns.** (1978): 35.

Federal government. No. federal civilian employees (Mar. 1980): 13,416. **Avg. salary:** $18,230. **Notable federal facilities:** National Radio Astronomy Observatory, Green Bank.

Energy. Electricity production (1980, mwh, by source): Hydroelectric: 423,784; Mineral: 70.3 mln.; Nuclear: —.

Education. No. schools: 1,317 elem. and second.; 28 higher ed. **Avg. salary, public school teachers** (1980): $13,000.

State Data. Motto: Montani Semper Liberi (Mountaineers are always free) **Flower:** Big rhododendron. **Bird:** Cardinal. **Tree:** Sugar maple. **Songs:** The West Virginia Hills; This Is My West Virginia; West Virginia, My Home, Sweet Home. **Entered union** June 20, 1863; rank, 35th. **State fair** at: Lewisburg; 3d week in Aug.

History. Early explorers included George Washington, 1753, and Daniel Boone. The area became part of Virginia and often objected to rule by the eastern part of the state. When Virginia seceded, 1861, the Wheeling Conventions repudiated the act and created a new state, Kanawha, subsequently changed to West Virginia. It was admitted to the Union as such, 1863.

Tourist attractions. Harpers Ferry National Historic Park has been restored to its condition in 1859, when John Brown seized the U.S. Armory. Still standing is the fire-engine house in which Brown and a score of followers were besieged and captured by a force of U.S. Marines under Col. Robert E. Lee.

Also Science and Cultural Center, Charleston; White Sulphur and Berkeley Springs mineral water resorts; state parks and forests; trout fishing; turkey, deer, and bear hunting.

Famous West Virginians include Newton D. Baker, Pearl Buck, John W. Davis, Thomas "Stonewall" Jackson, Dwight Whitney Morrow, Michael Owens.

Chamber of Commerce: P.O. Box 2789, Charleston, WV 25330.

Wisconsin

Badger State

People. Population (1980): 4,705,335; **rank:** 15. **Pop. density:** 86.3 per sq. mi. **Urban** (1970): 65.9%. **Racial distrib.** (1980): 94.4% White; 3.8% Black; Hispanic (1980): 62,981. **Major ethnic groups:** German, Norwegian, Italian. **Net migration** (1970-80): +9,000.

Geography. Total area: 56,154 sq. mi.; **rank:** 26. **Land area:** 54,464 sq. mi. **Acres forested land:** 14,907,700. **Location:** North central state, bounded on the N by Lake Superior and Upper Michigan; on the E by Lake Michigan; on the S by Illinois; on the W by the St. Croix and Mississippi rivers. **Climate:** long, cold winters and short, warm summers tempered by the Great Lakes. **Topography:** narrow Lake Superior Lowland plain met by Northern Highland which slopes gently to the sandy crescent Central Plain; Western Upland in the SW; 3 broad parallel limestone ridges running N-S are separated by wide and shallow lowlands in the SE. **Capital:** Madison.

Economy. Principal industries: manufacturing, trade, services, government, transportation, communications, agriculture, tourism. **Principal manufactured goods:** machinery, foods, fabricated metals, transportation equipment, paper and wood products. **Value added by manufacture** (1978): $18.8 bln. **Agriculture:** Chief crops: corn, beans, beets, peas, hay, oats, cabbage, cranberries. **Chief products:** milk, cheese. **Livestock:** 4.3 mln. cattle, 1.8 mln. milk cows; 1.83 mln. hogs/pigs; 113,000 sheep; 11 mln. poultry. **Timber/lumber:** maple, birch, oak, evergreens. **Minerals** (1980): sand and gravel and crushed stone, dimension stone, taconite, lime. Total value mineral production $142.5 mln. **Commercial fishing** (1980): $3.5 mln. **Chief ports:** Superior, Milwaukee, Green Bay, La Crosse, Kenosha. **International airports** at: Milwaukee. **Value of construction** (1980): $2.27 bln. **Employment distribution** (1980): 28.8% manuf.; 22.6% trade; 18.8% serv.; 16.5% gvt. **Per capita income** (1980): $9,254. **Unemployment** (1980): 7.0% **Tourism** (1979): out-of-state visitors spent $2.4 bln.

Finance. Notable industries: insurance. **No. banks** (1979): 636; **No. savings and loan assns.** (1978): 117.

Federal government. No. federal civilian employees (Mar. 1980): 21,484. **Avg. salary:** $18,490. **Notable federal facilities:** Ft. McCoy.

Energy. Electricity production (1980, mwh, by source): Hydroelectric: 1.8 mln.; Mineral: 26.0 mln.; Nuclear: 9.9 mln.;

Education. No. schools: 3,096 elem and second.; 62 higher ed. **Avg. salary, public school teachers** (1980): $18,180.

State data. Motto: Forward. **Flower:** Wood violet. **Bird:** Robin. **Tree:** Sugar maple. **Song:** On, Wisconsin! **Entered union** May 29, 1848; rank, 30th. **State fair at:** West Allis; mid-Aug.

History. Jean Nicolet was the first European to see the Wisconsin area, arriving in Green Bay, 1634; French missionaries and fur traders followed. The British took over, 1763. The U.S. won the land after the Revolution but the British were not ousted until after the War of 1812. Lead miners came next, then farmers. Railroads were started in 1851, serving growing wheat harvests and iron mines.

Tourist attractions. Old Wade House and Carriage Museum, Greenbush; Villa Louis, Prairie du Chien; Circus World Museum, Baraboo; Wisconsin Dells; Door County peninsula; Chequamegon and Nicolet national forests; Lake Winnebago; numerous lakes for water sports, ice boating and fishing; skiing and hunting.

Famous Wisconsinites include Edna Ferber, King Camp Gillette, Harry Houdini, Robert LaFollette, Alfred Lunt, Joseph R. McCarthy, Spencer Tracy, Thorstein Veblen, Orson Welles, Thornton Wilder, Frank Lloyd Wright.

Tourist information: Wisconsin Assn. of Manufacturers and Commerce, 111 E. Wisconsin Ave., Milwaukee, WI 53202.

$17,537.

State data. Motto: Equal Rights. **Flower:** Indian paintbrush. **Bird:** Meadowlark. **Tree:** Cottonwood. **Song:** Wyoming. **Entered union** July 10, 1890; rank, 44th. **State fair at:** Douglas; end of Aug.

History. Francés Francois and Louis Verendrye were the first Europeans, 1743. John Colter, American, was first to traverse Yellowstone Park, 1807-08. Trappers and fur traders followed in the 1820s. Forts Laramie and Bridger became important stops on the pioneer trail to the West Coast. Indian wars followed massacres of army detachments in 1854 and 1866. Population grew after the Union Pacific crossed the state, 1869. Women won the vote, for the first time in the U.S., from the Territorial Legislature, 1869.

Tourist attractions. Yellowstone National Park, 3,472 sq. mi. in the NW corner of Wyoming and the adjoining edges of Montana and Idaho, the oldest U.S. national park, est. 1872, has some 10,000 geysers, hot springs, mud volcanoes, fossil forests, a volcanic glass (obsidian) mountain, the 1,000-ft.-deep canyon and 308-ft.-high waterfall of the Yellowstone River, and a wide variety of animals living free in their natural habitat.

Also, Grand Teton National Park, with mountains 13,000 ft. high; National Elk Refuge, covering 25,000 acres; Devils Tower, a cluster of rock columns 865 ft. high; Fort Laramie and surrounding areas of pioneer trails; Buffalo Bill Museum, Cody; Cheyenne Frontier Days Celebration, last full week in July, the state's largest rodeo, and world's largest purse.

Famous Wyomingites include James Bridger, Buffalo Bill Cody, Nellie Tayloe Ross.

Tourist information: Travel Commission, Etchepare Circle, Cheyenne, WY 82002.

Wyoming

Equality State

People. Population (1980) 470,816; **rank:** 49. **Pop. density:** 4.8 per sq. mi. **Urban** (1970): 60.5%. **Racial distrib.** (1980): 95.0% White; 0.71% Black; Hispanic (1980): 24,499. **Major ethnic groups:** German, English, Russian. **Net migration** (1970-79): +77,000.

Geography. Total area: 97,914 sq. mi.; **rank:** 9. **Land area:** 97,203 sq. mi. **Acres forested land:** 10,028,300. **Location:** Mountain state lying in the high western plateaus of the Great Plains. **Climate:** semi-desert conditions throughout; true desert in the Big Horn and Great Divide basins. **Topography:** the eastern Great Plains rise to the foothills of the Rocky Mtns.; the Continental Divide crossed the state from the NW to the SE. **Capital:** Cheyenne.

Economy. Principal industries: mining, agriculture, forestry, tourism. **Principal manufactured goods:** refined petroleum products, foods, wood products, stone, clay and glass products. **Value added by manufacture** (1981): $425.6 mln. **Agriculture: Chief crops:** wheat, barley, oats, sugar beets, hay. **Livestock:** 1.34 mln. cattle; 32,000 hogs/pigs; 1.05 mln. sheep; 70,000 poultry. **Timber/lumber** (1979): aspen, yellow pine; 200 mln. bd. ft. **Minerals** (1978): petroleum, sodium carbonate, coal, uranium, natural gas; total $2.6 bln. value of mineral production. **International airports at:** Casper. **Value of construction** (1980): $649 mln. **Employment distribution:** 16% trade; 14% serv.; 12% mining. **Per capita income** (1980): $10,692. **Unemployment** (1980): 3.9%. **Tourism** (1979): out-of-state visitors spent $531 mln.

Finance. No. banks (1979): 94; **No. savings and loan assns.** (1978): 12.

Federal government. No. federal civilian employees (Mar. 1980): 5,406. **Avg. salary:** $18,751. **Notable federal facilities:** Warren AFB; Laramie Energy Research Ctr.

Energy. Electricity production (1980, mwh, by source): Hydroelectric: 1.1 mln., Mineral: 21.2 mln.; Nuclear: —.

Education. No. schools: 411 elem. and second.; 8 higher ed. **Avg. salary, public school teachers** (1980):

District of Columbia

Area: 67 sq. mi. **Population:** (1979): 648,000. **Motto:** Justitia omnibus, Justice for all. **Flower:** American beauty rose. **Tree:** Scarlet oak. **Bird:** Wood thrush. The city of Washington is coextensive with the District of Columbia.

The District of Columbia is the seat of the federal government of the United States. It lies on the west central edge of Maryland on the Potomac River, opposite Virginia. Its area was originally 100 sq. mi. taken from the sovereignty of Maryland and Virginia. Virginia's portion south of the Potomac was given back to that state in 1846.

The 23d Amendment, ratified in 1961, granted residents the right to vote for president and vice president for the first time and gave them 3 members in the Electoral College. The first such votes were cast in Nov. 1964.

Congress, which has legislative authority over the District under the Constitution, established in 1878 a government of 3 commissioners appointed by the president. The Reorganization Plan of 1967 substituted a single commissioner (also called mayor), assistant, and 9-member City Council. Funds were still appropriated by Congress; residents had no vote in local government, except to elect school board members.

In Sept. 1970, Congress approved legislation giving the District one delegate to the House of Representatives. The delegate could vote in committee but not on the House floor. The first was elected 1971.

In May 1974 voters approved a charter giving them the right to elect their own mayor and a 13-member city council; the first took office Jan. 2, 1975. The district won the right to levy its own taxes but Congress retained power to veto council actions, and approve the city's annual budget.

Proposals for a "federal town" for the deliberations of the Continental Congress were made in 1783, 4 years before the adoption of the Constitution that gave the Confederation a national government. Rivalry between northern and southern delegates over the site appeared in the First Congress, 1789. John Adams, presiding officer of the Senate, cast the deciding vote of that body for Germantown, Pa. In 1790 Congress compromised by making Philadelphia the temporary capital for 10 years. The Virginia members of the House wanted a capital on the eastern bank of the Potomac; they were defeated by the Northerners, while the Southerners defeated the Northern attempt to have the nation assume the war debts of the 13 original states, the Assumption Bill fathered by Alexander Hamilton. Hamilton and Jefferson arranged a compromise: the Virginia men voted for the Assumption Bill, and the Northerners conceded the capital to the Potomac. President Washington chose the site in Oct. 1790 and persuaded landowners to sell their holdings to the government at £25, then about $66, an acre. The capital was named Washington.

Washington appointed Pierre Charles L'Enfant, a French engineer who had come over with Lafayette, to plan the capital on an area not over 10 mi. square. The L'Enfant plan, for streets 100 to 110 feet wide and one avenue 400 feet wide and a mile long, seemed grandiose and foolhardy. But Washington endorsed it. When L'Enfant ordered a wealthy landowner to remove his new manor house because it obstructed a vista, and demolished it when the owner refused, Washington stepped in and dismissed the architect. The official map and design of the city was completed by Benjamin Banneker, a distinguished black architect and astronomer, and Andrew Ellicott.

On Sept. 18, 1793, Pres. Washington laid the cornerstone of the north wing of the Capitol. On June 3, 1800, Pres. John Adams moved to Washington and on June 10, Philadelphia ceased to be the temporary capital. The City of Washington was incorporated in 1802; the District of Columbia was created as a municipal corporation in 1871, embracing Washington, Georgetown, and Washington County.

Outlying U.S. Areas

Commonwealth of Puerto Rico

(Estado Libre Asociado de Puerto Rico)

People. Population (1980): 3,187,566. **Pop. density:** 928 per sq. mi. **Urban** (1975): 61.8%. **Racial distribution:** 99% Hispanic. **Net migration** (1979): +6,078.

Geography. Total area: 3,435 sq. mi. **Land area:** 3,421 sq. mi. **Location:** island lying between the Atlantic to the N and the Caribbean to the S; it is easternmost of the West Indies group called the Greater Antilles, of which Cuba, Hispaniola, and Jamaica are the larger units. **Climate:** mild, with a mean temperature of 76°. **Topography:** mountainous throughout three-fourths of its rectangular area, surrounded by a broken coastal plain; highest peak is Cerro de Punta, 4,389 ft. **Capital:** San Juan.

Economy. Principal industries: manufacturing. **Principal manufactured goods:** apparel; petrochemicals; pharmaceuticals; scientific instruments; medical supplies; food products. **Value added by manufacture:** $4.83 bln. **Agriculture: Chief crops:** sugar; plantains; coffee; bananas; yams; taniers; pineapples; pidgeon peas; peppers; tomatoes; pumpkins; coriander; lettuce; tobacco. **Livestock** (1980): 478,989 cattle; 219,611 pigs; 7.4 mln. poultry. **Minerals** (1979): cement, crushed stone, sand and gravel, lime. Total value mineral production, $142 mln. **Commercial fishing:** $7.3 mln. **Chief ports/river shipping:** San Juan, Ponce, Mayaguez, Guayanillá, Yabucoa, Aguirre. **International airports at:** San Juan; Aguadilla. **Value of construction** (1980): $1.3 bln. **Employment distribution:** 24% gvt.; 19% manuf.; 18% trade; 18% serv. **Per capita income** (1980): $3,299. **Unemployment** (1980): 17.0%. **Tourism** (1980): No. out-of-area visitors: 1.67 mln.; $615.4 mln. spent.

Finance. Notable industries: life insurance, mortgage banks, credit unions, retirement fund systems. **Financial institutions** (1979): No. banks: 20; No. savings and loan assns. (1978): 12; Other: 4 retirement fund systems; over 100 credit unions.

Federal government. No. federal civilian employees (Mar. 1977): 8,558. **Federal payroll** (1977): $117.5 mln. **Notable federal facilities:** U.S. Naval Station at Roose-

velt Roads; U.S. Army Salinas Training Area and Ft. Allen; Sabana SECA Communications Center (U.S. Navy).

Energy. Production (1979): Hydroelectric: 11,443 Kwh.

Education. No. schools: 1,841 elem. and second.; 34 higher ed. **Avg. salary, public school teachers** (1978): $8,100.

Misc. Data. Motto. Joannes Est Nomen Ejus (John is his name). **Flower:** Maga. **Bird:** Reinita. **Tree:** Ceiba. **Song:** La Borinquena.

History: Puerto Rico (or Borinquen, after the original Arawak Indian name Boriquen), was discovered by Columbus, Nov. 19, 1493. Ponce de Leon conquered it for Spain, 1509, and established the first settlement at Caparra, across the bay from San Juan.

Sugar cane was introduced, 1515, and slaves were imported 3 years later. Gold mining petered out, 1570. Spaniards fought off a series of British and Dutch attacks; slavery was abolished, 1873. The U.S. took the island during the Spanish-American War, 1898, without any major battle.

General tourist attractions: Ponce Museum of Art; forts El Morro and San Cristobal; Old Walled City of San Juan; Arecibo Observatory; Cordillera Central and state parks; El Yunque Rain Forest; San Juan Cathedral; Porta Coeli Chapel and Museum of Religious Art, San German; Condado Convention Center; Casa Blanca, Ponce de Leon family home, Puerto Rican Family Museum of 16th and 17 centuries and now Fine Arts Centers.

Cultural facilities, festivals, etc.: Festival Casals classical music concerts, mid-June; Puerto Rico Symphony Orchestra at Music Conservatory; Botanical Garden and Museum of Anthropology, Art, and History at the University of Puerto Rico; Institute of Puerto Rican Culture, at the Dominican Convent.

The Commonwealth of Puerto Rico is a self-governing part of the U.S. with a primary Hispanic culture. Puerto Ricans are U.S. citizens and about 1.5 million now live in the continental U.S., although since 1974, a reverse migration flow has resulted in net immigration to the island.

The current commonwealth political status of Puerto Rico gives the island's citizens virtually the same control over their internal affairs as the fifty states of the U.S. However, they do not vote in national elections, although they do vote in national primary elections.

Puerto Rico is represented in Congress solely by a resident commissioner who has a voice but no vote, except in committees.

No federal income tax is collected from residents on income earned from local sources in Puerto Rico.

Puerto Rico's famous "Operation Bootstrap" begun in the late 1940s succeeded in changing the island from "The Poorhouse of the Caribbean" to an area with the highest per capita income in Latin America. This pioneering program encouraged manufacturing and the development of the tourist trade by selective tax exemption, low-interest loans, and other incentives. Despite the marked success of Puerto Rico's development efforts over an extended period of time, per capita income in Puerto Rico is low in comparison to that of the U.S. In calendar year 1980, net transfer payments from the U.S. government to individuals and governments in Puerto Rico totalled $3.277 bln., or 29% of the Gross Domestic Product of $11,105 bln.

Famous Puerto Ricans include: Pablo Casals, Orlando Cepeda, Roberto Clemente, Jose Feliciano, Luis A. Ferre, Jose Ferrer, Dona Felisa Rincon de Gautier, Luis Munoz Marin, Rita Moreno, Adm. Horacio Rivero.

Chamber of Commerce: 100 Tetuan P.O.B. S3789, San Juan, PR 00904.

Guam

Pearl of the Pacific

People. Population (1980): 106,000. **Pop. density:** 521.5 per sq. mi. **Urban** (1970): 25.5%. Native Guamanians, ethnically called chamorros, are basically of Indonesian stock, with a mixture of Spanish and Filipino. In addition to the offical language, they speak the native Chamorro.

Geography. Total area: 212 sq. mi. land, 30 mi. long and 4 to 8.5 mi. wide. **Location:** largest and southernmost of the Mariana Islands in the West Pacific, 3,000 mi. W of Hawaii. **Climate:** tropical, with temperatures from 70° to 90°F; avg. annual rainfall, about 70 in. **Topography:** coralline limestone plateau in the N; southern chain of low volcanic mountains sloping gently to the W, more steeply to coastal cliffs on the E; general elevation, 500 ft.; highest pt., Mt. Lamlam, 1,334 ft. **Capital:** Agana.

Economy. Principal industries: contruction, manufacturing, tourism, petroleum refining, watch assembly, banking. **Principal manufactured goods:** textiles, foods, petroleum products. **Value added by manufacture:** $187.5 million/yr. **Agriculture: Chief crops:** cabbages, eggplants, cucumber, taro, bananas, coconuts, watermelon, yams, avocados, papayas, maize, sweet potatoes, sugar cane. **Livestock:** 1,493 cattle; 10,637 hogs/pigs; 147,875 poultry. **Commercial fishing:** $187,000. **Chief ports:** Apra Harbor. **International airports at:** Tamuning. **Value of construction** (1978): $111.2 mln. **Employment distribution:** 45% gvt.; 13% construct.; 3% manufacturing; 12% services; 18% trade. **Per capita income** (1974): $3,333. **Unemployment** (1978): 26% **Tourism** (1978): No. out-of-area visitors: 232,000.

Finance. Notable industries: insurance, real estate, finance. **No. banks:** 16; **No. savings and loan assns.:** 2.

Federal government. No. federal employees (1976): 6,014. **Notable federal facilities:** Andersen AFB; other naval and air bases, including a nuclear submarine installation and a large ship-repair yard.

Education. No. public schools: 27 elementary; 9 secondary; 1 higher education. **Avg. salary, public school teachers** (1979): $12,684.

Misc. Data. Flower: Puti Tai Nobio (Bougainvillea). **Bird:** Toto (Fruit dove). **Tree:** Ifit (Intsiabijuga). **Song:** Stand Ye Guamanians.

History. Magellan arrived in the Marianas Mar. 6, 1521, and called them the Ladrones (thieves). They were colonized in 1668 by Spanish missionaries who renamed them the Mariana Islands in honor of Maria Anna, queen of Spain. When Spain ceded Guam to the U.S., it sold the other Marianas to Germany. Japan obtained a League of Nations mandate over the German islands in 1919; in Dec. 1941 it seized Guam; the island was retaken by the U.S. in July 1944.

Guam is under the jurisdiction of the Interior Department. It is administered under the Organic Act of 1950, which provides for a governor and a 21-member unicameral legislature, elected biennially by the residents who are American citizens but do not vote for president.

Beginning in Nov., 1970, Guamanians elected their own governor, previously appointed by the U.S. president. He took office in Jan. 1971. In 1972 a U.S. law gave Guam one delegate to the U.S. House of Representatives; the delegate may vote in committee but not on the House floor.

General tourist attractions. annual mid-Aug. Merizo Water Festival; Tarzan Falls; beaches; water sports, duty-free port shopping.

Virgin Islands

St. John, St. Croix, St. Thomas

People. Population (1980): 95,000. **Pop. density:** 757.6 per sq. mi. **Urban** (1970): 25%. **Racial distribution:** 15% White; 85% Black. **Major ethnic groups:** West Indian, Chachas. **Net migration** (1977): +9,000.

Geography. Total area: 133 sq. mi.; **Land area:** 132 sq. mi. **Location:** 3 larger and 50 smaller islands and cays in the S and W of the V.I. group (British V.I. colony to the N and E) which is situated 70 mi. E of Puerto Rico, located W of the Anegada Passage, a major channel connecting the Atlantic O. and the Caribbean Sea. **Climate:** subtropical; the sun tempered by gentle trade winds; hu-

midity is low; average temperature, 78° F. **Topography:** St. Thomas is mainly a ridge of hills running E and W, and has little tillable land; St. Croix rises abruptly in the N but slopes to the S to flatlands and lagoons; St. John has steep, lofty hills and valleys with little level tillable land. **Capital:** Charlotte Amalie, St. Thomas.

Economy. Principal industries: tourism, rum, petroleum refining, bauxite processing, watch assembly, textiles. **Principal manufactured goods:** rum, textiles, pharmaceuticals, perfumes. **Gross Domestic Product** (1977): $500 million. **Agriculture: Chief crops:** truck garden produce. **Minerals:** sand, gravel. **Chief ports:** Cruz Bay, St. John; Frederiksted and Christiansted, St. Croix; Charlotte Amalie, St. Thomas. **International airports on:** St. Thomas, St. Croix. **Value of construction** (1976): $42,300,000. **Per capita income** (1977): $5,000. **Unemployment** (1977): 7.9%. **Tourism** (1977): No. out-of-area visitors: 1,119,726; $152.2 million spent. **No. banks** (1979): 6.

Education: No. public schools: 33 elem. and second.; 1 higher education. **Avg. salary, public school teachers** (1980): $13,575.

Misc. data. Flower: Yellow elder or yellow cedar. **Bird:** Yellow breast. **Song:** Virgin Islands March.

History. The islands were discovered by Columbus in 1493, who named them for the virgins of St. Ursula, the sailor's patron saint. Spanish forces, 1555, defeated the Caribes and claimed the territory; by 1596 the native population was annihilated. First permanent settlement in the U.S. territory, 1672, by the Danes; U.S. purchased the islands, 1917, for defense purposes.

The inhabitants have been citizens of the U.S. since 1927. Legislation originates in a unicameral house of 15 senators, elected for 2 years. The governor, formerly appointed by the U.S. president, was popularly elected for the first time in Nov. 1970. In 1972 a U.S. law gave the Virgin Islands one delegate to the U.S. House of Representatives; the delegate may vote in committee but not in the House.

General tourist attractions. Megen Bay, St. Thomas; duty-free shopping; Virgin Islands National Park, 14,488 acres on St. John of lush growth, beaches, Indian relics, and evidence of colonial Danes.

Chamber of Commerce: for St. Thomas and St. John: P.O. Box 324, St. Thomas, VI 00801; for St. Croix: 17 Church St., Christiansted, St. Croix, VI 00820.

American Samoa

Capital: Fagatogo, Island of Tutuila. **Area:** 76 sq. mi. **Population:** (1978 est.) 31,171. **Motto:** Samoa Muamua le Atua (In Samoa, God Is First). **Song:** Amerika Samoa. **Flower:** Paogo (Ula-fala). **Plant:** Ava.

Blessed with spectacular scenery and delightful South Seas climate, American Samoa is the most southerly of all lands under U. S. ownership. It is an unincorporated territory consisting of 6 small islands of the Samoan group: **Tutuila, Aunu'u, Manu'a Group (Ta'u, Olosega and Ofu),** and **Rose.** Also administered as part of American Samoa is **Swain's Island,** 210 mi. to the NW, acquired by the U.S. in 1925. The islands are 2,600 mi. SW of Honolulu.

American Samoa became U. S. territory by a treaty with the United Kingdom and Germany in 1899. The islands were ceded by local chiefs in 1900 and 1904.

Samoa (Western), comprising the larger islands of the Samoan group, was a New Zealand mandate and UN Trusteeship until it became an independent nation Jan. 1, 1962 *(see Index.)*

Tutuila and Annu'u have an area of 52 sq. mi. Ta'u has an area of 17 sq. mi., and the islets of Ofu and Olosega, 5 sq. mi. with a population of a few thousand. Swain's Island has nearly 2 sq. mi. and a population of about 100.

About 70% of the land is bush. Chief products and exports are fish products, copra, and handicrafts. Taro, bread-fruit, yams, coconuts, pineapples, oranges, and bananas are also produced.

Formerly under jurisdiction of the Navy, since July 1, 1951, it has been under the Interior Dept. On Jan. 3, 1978, the first popularly elected Samoan governor and lieutenant governor were inaugurated. Previously, the governor was appointed by the Secretary of the Interior. American Samoa has a bicameral legislature and an elected delegate to appear before U.S. agencies in Washington. In 1980 the Territory will elect a non-voting delegate to Congress.

The American Samoans are of Polynesian origin. They are nationals of the U.S.; there are more than 15,000 in Hawaii and 90,000 on the U.S. west coast.

Minor Caribbean Islands

Quita Sueño Bank, Roncador and Serrana, lie in the Caribbean between Nicaragua and Jamaica. They are uninhabited. They were to be turned over to Colombia under a 1972 agreement, but this still awaits U.S. Senate action.

Navassa lies between Jamaica and Haiti, covers about 2 sq. mi., is reserved by the U.S. for a lighthouse and is uninhabited.

Wake, Midway, Other Islands

Wake Island, and its sister islands, **Wilkes** and **Peale,** lie in the Pacific Ocean on the direct route from Hawaii to Hong Kong, about 2,000 mi. W of Hawaii and 1,290 mi. E of Guam. The group is 4.5 mi. long, 1.5 mi. wide, and totals less than 3 sq. mi.

The U.S. flag was hoisted over Wake Island, July 4, 1898, formal possession taken Jan. 17, 1899; Wake has been administered by the U.S. Air Force since 1972. Population (1980) was 300.

The **Midway Islands,** acquired in 1867, consist of 2, **Sand** and **Eastern,** in the North Pacific 1,150 mi. NW of Hawaii, with area of about 2 sq. mi., administered by the Navy Dept. Population (1975 est.) was 2,256.

Johnston Atoll, SW of Hawaii, area 1 sq. mi., pop. 300 (1978), is under Air Force control, and **Kingman Reef,** S of Hawaii, is under Navy control.

Howland, Jarvis, and **Baker Islands** south of the Hawaiian group, uninhabited since World War II, are under the Interior Dept.

Palmyra is an atoll SW of Hawaii, 4 sq. mi. Privately owned, it is under the Interior Dept.

Islands Under Trusteeship

The U. S Trust Territory of the Pacific Islands, also called Micronesia, includes 3 major archipelagoes: the **Caroline Islands, Marshall Islands,** and **Mariana Islands** (except **Guam:** see above). There are 2,141 islands, 98 of them inhabited. Total land area is 687 sq. mi., but the islands are scattered over 3 million sq. mi. in the western Pacific N of the equator and E of the Philippines. Population (1978 est.): 136,810.

The Marianas

In process of becoming a U.S. commonwealth were the Northern Mariana Islands, which since 1947 have been part of the Trust Territory of the Pacific Islands, assigned to U.S. administration by the United Nations. The Northern Marianas comprise all the Marianas except Guam, stretching N-S in a 500-mi. arc of tropical islands east of the Philippines and southeast of Japan.

Residents of the islands on June 17, 1975, voted 78% in favor of becoming a commonwealth of the U.S. rather than continuing with the Carolines and Marshalls in the U.S.-UN Trusteeship. On Mar. 24, 1976, U.S. Pres. Ford signed a congressionally-approved commonwealth covenant giving the Marianas control of domestic affairs and giving the U.S. control of foreign relations and defense, and the right to maintain military bases on the islands. The full force of commonwealth status will come into effect at the termination of the trusteeship.

Pres. Carter, on Oct. 24, 1977, approved the Constitution of the Northern Mariana Islands with the effective date of Jan. 9, 1978. In December 1977, the voters of the Northern Marianas elected a governor, lieutenant governor, and members of a bicameral legislature for the new government.

Ferdinand Magellan was the first European to visit the Marianas, 1521. Spain, Germany, and Japan held the islands in turn until World War II when the U.S. seized them in bitter battles on 2 of the main islands, Saipan and Tinian.

Population in 1980 was estimated at 16,600, mostly on Saipan. English is the official language, Roman Catholicism the major religion. The people are descendants of the early Chamorros, Spanish, Japanese, Filipinos, and Mexicans. Land area is 181.9 sq. mi.

Tourism is an important industry; visitors are mostly from Japan. Crops include coconuts, breadfruit, melons and tomatoes.

The Carolines and Marshalls

In 1885, many of the Carolines, Marshalls, and Marianas were claimed by Germany. Others, held by Spain, were sold to Germany at the time of the Spanish-American War, 1898. After the outbreak of World War I, Japan took over the 3 archipelagoes; following that war, League of Nations mandates over them were awarded to Japan.

After World War II, the United Nations assigned them, 1947, as a Trust Territory to be administered by the U.S. They were placed, 1951, under administration of the U.S. Interior Dept.

There is a high commissioner, appointed by the U.S. president. Saipan is the headquarters of the administration. The Congress of Micronesia, an elected legislature with limited powers, held its first meeting, 1965.

In 1969, a commission of the Congress of Micronesia recommended that Micronesia be given internal self-government in free association with the U.S.

A U.S. offer of commonwealth status was rejected by Micronesian leaders in 1970.

The U.S. and three Trust Territory negotiating commissions representing, respectively, the Marshall Islands, Palau, and the Federated States of Micronesia, comprised of Truk, Yap, Ponape and Kosrae, are negotiating a free association arrangement: the three Micronesian areas would enjoy full self-government; the U.S. would retain responsibility for defense. An agreement, initiated in late-1980, is currently under review by the Reagan Administration.

Among the noted islands are the former Japanese strongholds of **Palau, Peleliu, Truk,** and **Yap** in the Carolines; **Bikini** and **Eniwetok,** where U.S. nuclear tests were staged, and **Kwajalein,** another World War II battle scene, all in the Marshalls.

Many of the islands are volcanic with luxuriant vegetation; others are of coral formation. Only a few are self-sustaining. Principal exports are copra, trochus shells, fish products, handicrafts, and vegetables.

Disputed Pacific Islands

In the central Pacific, S and SW of Hawaii lie 25 islands that were claimed by the U.S.; 18 of them were also claimed by the United Kingdom and 7 by New Zealand. **Kiribati** achieved its independence from the U.K. in July, 1979; the U.S. signed a treaty with the Cook Is. on June 11, 1980 and with New Zealand for Tokelau on Dec. 2, 1980, relinquishing claims to the disputed islands. The treaties are pending U.S. Senate ratification.

The **Tuvalu (Ellice) Islands,** including Funafuti, Nukufetau, Nukulailai, and Nurakita, became independent of the UK, Oct. 1, 1978; treaty relinquishing U.S. claim still pending U.S. Senate ratification (*See Index*).

The **Cook Islands,** including Danger, Manahiki, Rakahanga, and Penrhyn (Tongareva), are self-governing in free association with New Zealand. **Tokelau** is a New Zealand territory.

NORTH AMERICAN CITIES

Their History, Business and Industry, Educational Facilities, Cultural Advantages, Tourist Attractions and Transportation

Akron, Ohio

The World Almanac is sponsored in the Akron area by the Akron Beacon Journal, 44 E. Exchange Street, Akron, OH 44328; (216) 375-8111; a Knight-Ridder newspaper; founded 1839; circulation 163,000 daily, 221,000 Sunday; Paul Poorman editor and vice president.

Population: 237,177 (city), 660,233 (SMSA); 5th in state; total employed (Apr., 1981) 277,100; average household effective buying income $21,190.

Area: 56 sq. mi. (city), 413 sq. mi. (metro) on Ohio Canal, 30 mi. south of Lake Erie; founded 1825; Summit County seat.

Industry: home plants of Firestone, Goodyear, Goodrich, General and Goodyear Aerospace employ 24,822, use 40% of entire world rubber supply; other products mfd. in area include auto bodies, salt, clay, matches, rubber toys, road building equipment, missile components.

Transportation: Akron-Canton Airport served by 2 major carriers; Akron Muni Airport; Conrail covers 9 former private rail and trunk lines; birthplace of trucking industry, served by 79 motor common carriers; metro transit system; Greyhound and Continental Trailways; 2 taxicab firms; city bisected east-west and north-south by interstate highway systems.

Communications: 5 TV, one cablevision, and 5 radio stations; 2 public broadcast TV outlets.

New construction: $105.4 million in private investments in 1980 including Goodyear, General Tire, B.F. Goodrich, PPG Industries, Polysar, I.T.T., Continental Baking, and others.

Federal facilities: downtown federal office bldg.; Army Reserve Center; Navy-Marine Reserve Center.

Medical facilities: 7 major hospitals including specialized children's treatment center; State of Ohio Fallsview Psychiatric Hospital; Northeast Ohio Univ. College of Medicine.

Education: Univ. of Akron and School of Law; Kent State Univ.; Firestone Conservatory of Music.

Sports: NBA Cleveland Cavaliers play in nearby Richfield Township Coliseum; Firestone Country Club, home of the World Series of Golf; 35,000-seat Akron Rubber Bowl; Derby Downs, home of the All-American Soap Box Derby; home of the annual PBA $100,000 Firestone Tournament of Champions.

Cultural attractions: E. J. Thomas Performing Arts Center; Blossom Music Center, summer home of the Cleveland Orchestra; Stan Hywet mansion; Akron Art Institute; Akron Symphony Orchestra, Akron Civic Theater.

Other attractions: Akron Zoological Park; John Brown Home; Simon Perkins Mansion; Railway Museum.

Accommodations: nearly 2,900 quality hotel and motel rooms in the metro area.

Further information: Akron Regional Development Board, or Akron Convention and Visitors Bureau, both 1 Cascade Plaza, Akron, OH 44308.

Albuquerque, New Mexico

The World Almanac is sponsored in the Albuquerque area by The Albuquerque Tribune, 717 Silver Avenue S.W., Albuquerque, NM 87102; phone (505) 842-2371; founded June 22, 1922 by Carl Magee; a Scripps-Howard Newspaper since Sept. 24, 1923; circulation 45,000; editor William Tanner; sponsors Tribune Annual Spelling Bee.

Population: 331,767 (city), 419,700 (county), 448,798 (SMSA); first in state; total employed 190,900 (1980).

Area: 87.1 sq. mi. on Rio Grande and interstates 40, 25, and U.S. 66; Bernalillo County seat.

Industry: electronics with Signetics, Sperry Flight Systems, GTE-Lenkurt, Gulton, Sparton, Sandia Laboratories, General Electric, Digital Equipment Corp., Pertec, Honeywell, Intel; medical with Ethicon; clothing with Levi Strauss, Pioneer Wear.

Commerce: retail sales $2.3 billion; per capita income $8,760; financial resources $2.2 billion in 12 banks, $1.3 billion in 6 savings and loan assns.

Transportation: Santa Fe Railway, Amtrak; Continental Trailways and Greyhound bus lines; Albuquerque Int'l Airport, hub for 10 airlines, average 693 air movements daily.

Communications: 5 TV, 21 radio stations, 3 TV cable systems.

New construction: value of building permits $241 million in 1980, down from $304 million in 1979.

Medical facilities: 9 major hospitals.

Cultural facilities: symphony orchestra, light opera, 55 art galleries, 5 museums, 8 library branches, 16 legitimate theaters.

Educational facilities: Univ. of New Mexico, Univ. of Albuquerque, Technical-Vocational Institute; 107 public schools.

Recreational facilities: Sandia Peak ski area with longest tramway in North America; Rio Grande Zoo, Cibola National Forest, 12 golf courses, 31 swimming pools, 115 free city tennis courts, 102 private courts, 165 city parks.

Convention facilities: downtown convention center with underground parking facility and 300-room hotel; 90 motels and hotels.

Sports: Dukes baseball, Univ. of New Mexico athletic activities.

History: founded Feb. 7, 1706; named for Duke of Albuquerque, viceroy of New Spain.

Further information: Chamber of Commerce, 401 2d NW, Albuquerque, NM 87102.

Allentown, Pennsylvania

The World Almanac is sponsored in the Allentown-Bethlehem-Easton area by Call-Chronicle Newspapers, 101 North 6th Street, Allentown, PA 18105; phone (215) 820-6500; Call founded 1883, daily circulation The Morning Call 118,616, Weekender 117,938, Sunday 153,221; Sunday 157,000; publisher Bernard C. Stinner, president Roy Follett, exec. editor Lawrence J. Hyams; sponsors newspaper-in-the-classroom, newsprint recycling, college finance seminars, forum 1040, youth run.

Population: Allentown 103,758, Bethlehem 70,419, SMSA 637,109, 3d in state; total employed 275,200.

Area: 1,490 sq. mi. (metro) in eastern Pa. at Lehigh and Delaware rivers; Lehigh County seat.

Industry: Bethlehem Steel Corp., 2d largest in U.S.; home offices for Mack Truck Inc., Air Products & Chemicals, Martin Guitar, Rodale Press, New Jersey Zinc Co., Allen Products (ALPO); area leads in textile production; transistor developed in Western Electric here. Other industries include Kraft Foods, F.&M. Schaefer Brewing Co., American Can Co. (Dixie), Durkee Foods.

Commerce: 3d largest Pa. market; metro retail sales over $2.7 billion; average family buying power $23,200.

Transportation: 3 major rail lines, 5 bus lines; 9 federal and state highways intersect area; jet airport serves some 600,000 passengers annually on 5 airlines.

Communications: 4 TV and 12 radio stations.

Medical facilities: 6 major hospitals.

Cultural facilities: Allentown Art Museum (including Kress Renaissance and Baroque collection), Bethlehem Bach Choir, Allentown Symphony, 7 theater groups (plus 2 summer and several college theater groups); Allentown Band is oldest continuing concert band in U.S.; 10 colleges including Lehigh Univ., Muhlenberg, Cedar Crest, and Lafayette.

Other attractions: center of "Pennsylvania Dutch" area, covered bridges; 1,400-acre park system; 1,170-acre game preserve, pre-Cambrian mountain range, access to Appalachian Trail, many historic houses, Allentown Fair, Kutztown Folk Festival, Liberty Bell Shrine, Bavarian Festival at

Barnesville. Drum Corps Int'l Eastern Championship; new Hilton Hotel.

Sports: fishing, game hunting, auto racing at Pocono Raceway, Lehigh Valley Jets basketball, Olympic bicycle velodrome at Trexlertown, Pennsylvania Stoners soccer.

History: settled in 1600s by Germans seeking religious freedom; Allentown founded 1762; hiding place for Liberty Bell during Revolutionary War; GAR founded Flag Day here 1906; one of 5 First Defender Companies in Civil War.

Further information: Chambers of Commerce in Allentown: 462 Walnut Street, 18105; Bethlehem: 11 W. Market Street, 18018; Easton: 157 S. 4th Street, 18042.

Amarillo, Texas

The World Almanac is sponsored in the Amarillo area by the Amarillo Globe-News, 900 S. Harrison, Amarillo, TX 79166; phone (806) 376-4488; a division of the Southwestern Newspapers Corp., and publisher of Daily News, Globe-Times and Sunday News-Globe; James L. Whyte, vice president and general manager; Jerry Huff, executive editor.

Population: 149,230 city, 173,550 SMSA; total employed 87,000; 3.7% unemployed.

Area: 82 sq. mi. in central panhandle of Texas at junction of Interstate 40 and 27 in Potter and Randall counties; Potter County seat.

Industry: 3-state hub of $10.4 billion agribusiness market including wheat, beef, and produce, value $2.9 billion; ASARCO, Inc. copper refinery, Santa Fe Rail welding plant; Bell Helicopter, Levi Strauss, Iowa Beef Processors, Amarillo Gear, oil and gas, coal burning electricity plant, and Owens-Corning Fiberglas plant.

Commerce: wholesale-retail center for 5-state area; retail sales $1.023 billion; bank resources $1.58 billion, 6 savings and loan assns.

Transportation: served by 6 airlines; 2 railroads, 4 bus lines, 20 truck lines; 2 interstate, 4 federal, and one state highway intersect Amarillo.

Communications: 4 TV, 12 radio stations.

Medical facilities: 9 hospitals including VA facilities in

metro area; mental health centers, speech and hearing center; cancer center (Texas Tech Univ. Medical School branch.

Culture, recreation: Amarillo Symphony, fine arts complex, civic center complex and convention center, 2 dinner theaters, Amarillo Theatre Center (55th year of operation), Alibates National Monument, Lake Meredith, Wonderland Amusement Park and Storyland Zoo, Palo Duro Canyon State Park, Cal Farley's Boys Ranch, summer musical drama "Texas"; regional history museum, Discovery Center Planetarium, 46 parks, central library and 3 branches, 2 colleges, state vocational-technical school, National Helium Monument.

Sports: drag racing, stock car racing, college and high school football, basketball, baseball, wrestling, tennis, and track; Gold Sox baseball; rodeo, motorcycle racing.

History: settled 1887 as railroad crew camp, incorporated 1892; named for yellow lake clay.

Further information: Amarillo Chamber of Commerce, 1000 S. Polk, Amarillo, TX 79101.

Anchorage, Alaska

The World Almanac is sponsored in the Anchorage area by The Anchorage Times, 820 W. 4th Avenue, Anchorage, AK 99501, or P.O. Box 40, Anchorage, AK 99510; phone (907) 279-5622; founded 1915; circulation 48,000(E), 58,000(S); editor-publisher Robert B. Atwood; sponsors Alaska State Spelling Bee, Kodak Photo Contest.

Population: city, borough unified in 1975; total population of new municipality is 173,992.

Area: 927 sq. mi. (census district), at head of Cook Inlet on south central coast.

Industry and commerce: business center for most of Alaska; aviation, oil companies, railroading, shipping, wholesaling, retailing, and national defense activities are largest elements in area's economy.

Transportation: Anchorage International Airport is major refueling stop on transpolar flights; thousands of small planes make city one of country's busiest air traffic centers with 5 airports and 25% of world's seaplanes in area; headquarters of Alaska Railroad; $12 million port.

Communications: 4 TV and 11 radio stations; 2 daily newspapers.

Medical facilities: 4 hospitals.

Federal facilities: Elmendorf AFB, Ft. Richardson.

Cultural facilities: annual Festival of Music; 4 theater groups; fine arts museum; community concert organization, opera company, civic symphony.

Educational facilities: 57 elementary and secondary schools enroll 37,000; Univ. of Alaska, Alaska Pacific Univ.

Recreation: 2 major alpine ski areas; cross-country skiing and bicycling; annual Fur Rendezvous with dogsled races; Iditarod dogsled race to Nome; Chugach National Forest.

Convention facilities: 7 major hotels and motels offer more than 2,800 rooms.

History: founded 1915 as headquarters for Alaska Railroad; twice winner of All America city award, for coping with rapid growth, and for swift recovery from catastrophic 1964 earthquake.

Further information: Chamber of Commerce, 415 F Street; or Convention and Visitors Bureau, 201 E 3d Avenue, both Anchorage, AK 99501.

Atlanta, Georgia

The World Almanac is sponsored in the Atlanta area by The Atlanta Journal and Constitution, 72 Marietta Street, Atlanta, GA 30303; phone (404) 526-5151; circulation, The Atlanta Constitution (morn.) 215,130, The Atlanta Journal (eve.) 204,424, combined daily 419,554, Saturday WEEKEND 437,393, Sunday Journal and Constitution 495,624; member Million Market Newspapers, Inc.; sponsor: The Peachtree Road Race, The Journal-Constitution Tennis Open, The Atlanta Journal 500.

Population: 425,022 (city), 2,010,368 (SMSA), first in state; total employed 931,000 (metro, 1980).

Area: 136 sq. mi. in north central Georgia, on Piedmont plateau of Blue Ridge foothills, 1,050 ft above sea level; 4,326 sq. mi. in 15-county metro area; state capital and Fulton

County seat.

Industry: 431 of Fortune 500 firms operate in Atlanta; Ford, 2 GM assembly plants, Lockheed-Ga. Co.; home base for Coca-Cola, Fuqua, Ind., Delta Air Lines, Equifax, Scripto, Genuine Parts, Simmons Co., Gold Kist, Oxford Ind., Rollins, Inc., Georgia Pacific Corp., National Service Industries, Royal Crown Companies, Life of Georgia.

Commerce: financial, retail, wholesale center of Southeast; massive Merchandise Mart has 2d largest wholesale showroom in U.S. under one roof; 6th Federal Reserve District hdqtrs.; 74 banks, over 385 branches with resources of $9.1 billion (15-county metro); 20 savings and loan associations with 180 branches in metro area with deposits of $5 billion (1980).

Transportation: founded as railroad center; now served by 7 lines of 2 systems; Greyhound and Trailways bus terminal used by 3 companies with 205 buses in and out daily; 15 domestic and international passenger airlines, 4 commuter carriers, 12 freight only carriers; more than 1,800 scheduled flights daily; nonstop passenger service to 156 cities from Hartsfield International Airport, direct flights to 7 international cities including Brussels, London, Amsterdam, Frankfurt, Mexico City, and the Caribbean; 2d busiest airport in world, 40 million passengers (1980) and No. one commuting point in nation's domestic air route pattern. Metropolitan Atlanta Rapid Transit Authority at $2.1 billion, most massive publicly financed project in Southeast since TVA; under construction is 52.9 mi. rapid rail, 8 mi. of rapid busways coordinated with street bus operations; Southeastern hub of 41,000 mi. interstate system with 6 legs of 3 interstate hwys. intersecting 100-acre downtown interchange; 63 mi. hwy. encircles city.

Communications: 8 TV stations, 39 radio stations, 8 cable TV companies; Protestant Radio and TV Center; largest Bell System toll-free dialing area; one of nation's 5 TV and radio network control centers; 10 daily newspapers.

New construction: $2.1 billion MARTA rapid transit system, $100 million Georgia Pacific office bldg., $37.7 million Georgia Power office bldg., $100 million Southern Bell office bldg, total value city building permits (1980) $470 million.

Medical facilities: 56 hospitals with over 12,000 beds (metro), VA hospital; national Center for Disease Control of U.S. Pub. Health Dept., National Cancer Center at Emory Univ. Med. School.

Federal facilities: 34,200 federal, non-military employees (1980); Ft. McPherson, hdqtrs. U.S. Army Forces Command; Ft. Gillem; Dobbins AFB; NAS Atlanta.

Cultural facilities: Memorial Arts Center with museum, symphony orchestra, ballet, School of Art; Civic Center with auditorium-theater-exhibition hall; Callanwolde, multiuse arts center; 29 degree-granting colleges including Ga. Tech, Ga. State Univ., Emory Univ.

Sports: NBA Hawks; NFL Falcons; NL Braves; World Championship Tennis, college football's Peach Bowl, PGA Atlanta Classic, the Atlanta Journal-Constitution Peachtree Road Race, The Atlanta Journal-Constitution Open International Tennis Championships, The Atlanta Journal 500; road, sports car racing, motocross.

Convention facilities: 927,000 convention delegates in 1980; Ga. World Congress Center has largest single display room in U.S. equal to 8 football fields; simultaneous translation facilities; 29,400 hotel/motel rooms, most downtown or near.

History: named 1845; chartered 1847; burned by Union Gen. Sherman 1864.

Further information: Chamber of Commerce, 1300 N. Omni International, Atlanta, GA 30302.

Augusta, Georgia

The World Almanac is sponsored in the Augusta area by the Chronicle-Herald, 725 Broad Street, Augusta, GA 30903; phone (404) 724-0851; Chronicle established in 1785, circulation 56,806, Herald 18,773, Sunday, 82,196; William S. Morris III publisher, E.B. Skinner general manager, David L. Playford managing editor, Herald; W.H. Eanes managing editor, Chronicle.

Population: 47,532 (city), 320,574 (SMSA).

Area: 1,695 sq. mi. (metro: Richmond, Columbia counties, Ga.; Aiken County, S.C.) straddling Savannah River; Augusta County seat.

Industry: diversified; Continental forest industries Du Pont, Procter & Gamble, Lily-Tulip, Olin, Dymo, Monsanto, Columbia Nitrogen, A.E.C., TRW Corp., Owens-Corning, Kendall, Textron, Kimberly-Clark, Hall Printing, G.D. Searle.

Commerce: wholesale, retail center of 17 counties in 2 states; 1980 taxable sales $1.6 billion; per capita income $5,781, household buying income $19,174; 7 banks, 5 savings-loan assns.; distribution center.

Transportation: 5 railroads, 26 truck lines, 2 airlines at modern airport and in-city field for executive planes; Interstate 20, other federal highways.

Communications: 3 TV and 13 radio stations.

Medical facilities: 9 major hospitals, including Eisenhower Memorial at Ft. Gordon, Medical College of Georgia.

Federal facilities: Ft. Gordon and Savannah River (AEC) Plant.

Cultural facilities: Augusta College, Medical College of Ga., Paine College, Univ. of S.C. at Aiken; museum, art gallery, arts council with 25 affiliates; Augusta Symphony, Augusta Opera Assn., Augusta Ballet Co.

Recreational facilities: hunting, fishing, boating, camping; 7 golf courses; home of Masters Golf Tournament.

Convention facilities: 14,570 sq. ft. exhibition hall, 23,000 sq. ft. arena.

History founded as fort 1717; named for wife of Prince of Wales 1735; capital of Georgia 1778.

Further information: Chamber of Commerce of Greater Augusta, 600 Broad Street Plaza, Augusta, GA 30902.

Bakersfield, California

The World Almanac is sponsored in the Bakersfield and Kern County area by The Bakersfield Californian (mornings and Sunday), 1707 Eye Street, Bakersfield, CA 93302; phone (805) 395-7500; founded 1866 as Havilah Courier, christened The Bakersfield Californian 1897; circulation: 75,000 daily, 85,000 Sunday; president Berenice Fritts Koerber, publisher Donald H. Fritts, executive director Alfred T. Fritts, chief executive officer J.K. Stanners, managing editor Owen Kearns Jr.

Population: 105,611 city, 227,806 metro, 412,474 Kern County.

Area: approximately 8,060 square miles in Kern County of which Bakersfield is county seat; in California's San Joaquin Valley.

Industry: oil, gas, agriculture, military; oil valuation $976 million; total agriculture production $799.4 million; Edwards AFB and China Lake Naval Test Station in eastern Kern County.

Commerce: retail sales in Kern $1.5 billion; total bank deposits $1.640 billion.

Transportation: 2 railroads, 3 airlines, 2 bus lines, Interstate

5, Highway 99.

Communications: 3 TV and 12 radio stations; CATV from Los Angeles.

Cultural facilities: symphony orchestra, Cunningham Art Gallery; 4-year state college, city college; community theater.

History: Kern County organized April 2, 1866, from portions of Los Angeles and Tulare counties; discovery of gold on Kern River in 1851 brought influx of settlers; oil discovered in 1865, with major boom in 1909; gold mining town of Havilah first county seat, moved to Bakersfield in 1875.

Baltimore, Maryland

The World Almanac is sponsored in the Baltimore area by The Baltimore Sun, 501 N. Calvert Street, Baltimore, MD 21202; phone (301) 332-6000; founded in 1837; publishes The Sun, The Evening Sun and The Sunday Sun; daily circulation 348,459, Sunday 375,644; president Donald H. Patterson Sr., publisher John R. Murphy, managing editor The Sun Paul A. Banker, managing editor The Evening Sun John M. Lemmon; The Sun has 8 foreign bureaus in addition to its Washington Bureau, and a West Coast correspondent; news & feature stories from all 3 papers are syndicated nationally by The Field News Service.

Population: 786,755 (city), 2,166,308 (SMSA); first in state; 9th in U.S.; 983,033 metro employed.

Area: 91 sq. mi. (city), 2,225 sq. mi. (metro) in central Maryland on Patapsco R., a tributary of Chesapeake Bay.

Industry: highly diversified; most important: steel production, electronic equipment, food processing, transportation equipment, chemical products.

Commerce: $16.7 billion effective buying income in city and 5 surrounding counties; average household EBI $21,796, retail sales over $9.2 billion in 1980; area supports 14 regional shopping malls, over 250 shopping centers, 9 department stores.

Transportation: newly renovated Baltimore-Washington International Airport 9 mi. from downtown; passenger terminal can handle 11 million passengers a year; Harbor Tunnel, Francis Scott Key Bridge carry traffic across harbor; Amtrak; state authorized buses; subway system under construction; major interstate highways allow overnight trucking service to 67 million people; Chessie & Conrail systems.

Port facilities: nation's 3d largest port; furthest inland port on Atlantic Coast; responsible for 170,000 jobs and $4 billion in annual economic impact on state; World Trade Center focal point of port commerce; leading cargoes: ores, coal, petroleum products, grains.

New construction: Central business district rebuilt in last 20 years featuring Charles Center, Hopkins Plaza, Inner Harbor; Inner Harbor area includes: Hyatt Regency Hotel, National Aquarium, Harborplace (2 pavilions of shops and eateries), Mt. Royal District; Md. Concert Center, renovation of Lyric Theatre, Md. Institute College of Art; major shopping malls in Annapolis, Hunt Valley, White Marsh; Coldspring, 375 acre city neighborhood.

Convention facilities: $50-million Inner Harbor Baltimore Convention Center with 115,000 sq. ft. unobstructed exhibition space, 41,000 sq. ft. of meeting space divisible into 26 rooms; Civic Center: 35 meeting rooms, 111,000 sq. ft. exhibit space; both are within walking distance to downtown hotels, approx. 2,100 rooms.

Cultural facilities: Baltimore Symphony Orchestra, Baltimore Ballet Co., Baltimore Opera Co., Baltimore Museum of Art, Walters Art Gallery, Md. Science Center, Morris Mechanic Theatre (pre-Broadway and touring shows), Center Stage (repertory co.), Arena Players, Merriweather Post Pavilion, Md. Historical Society.

Educational facilities: 42 metro colleges & universities including Johns Hopkins Univ. and School of Medicine; Univ. of Md. Professional Schools, Towson State Univ., Morgan State Univ., Peabody Conservatory of Music, U.S. Naval Academy, Goucher College.

Sports & Recreation: Orioles (baseball), Colts (NFL football), Blast (indoor soccer); horse racing at Timonium, Bowie, Laurel, Pimlico (home of Preakness); steeplechase racing features Md. Hunt Cup; Chesapeake Bay offers fishing, boating, yachting, waterfowl hunting; ocean and ski resorts within 3-hour drive.

Communications: 3 daily newspapers (morning, 2 evening), 2 Sunday; 5 TV stations (4 commercial, 1 PBS) plus several cable TV companies operating in the metro area; 33 radio stations.

Other attractions: City Fair, Timonium State Fair in Sept.; Preakness Festival Week in May; ethnic, craft, music festivals through summer; Ft. McHenry Historic Shrine where Francis Scott Key wrote "Star Spangled Banner;" Constellation, first ship in U.S. Navy; Baltimore and Ohio Transportation Museum; Edgar Allen Poe home and grave; Babe Ruth house; Washington Monument, first architectual monument in U.S. to George Washington, in Mt. Vernon Square; Baltimore Streetcar Museum; Cloisters Children's Museum; 142-acre zoo in Druid Hill Park; Little Italy; restored early 19th century rowhouses in Fells Point, Bolton Hill, Seton Hill, Otterbein, Barre Circle; Top of the World observation center; Shot Tower; Lacrosse Hall of Fame; St. Elizabeth Seton's House; Pride of Baltimore clipper ship; Lexington Market; state capital of Annapolis, with nation's highest concentration of 18th century buildings still in use; old mill town of Ellicott City.

History: founded in 1729 by members of the Calvert family, the Lords of Baltimore; one of the 13 original colonies; nation's first railroad (Baltimore & Ohio) built to counter competition from new Erie Canal. Baltimore "firsts" include: first umbrella in U.S.; first investment banking house in U.S.; first commercial ice cream factory; first dental college in the world; first trolleycar & longest service line; Notre Dame, first Catholic women's college; first typesetting machine (Mergenthaler); first telegraph line (Morse) set up from Baltimore to Washington; first Ouija board invented.

Further information: Baltimore Economic Development Corp., 22 Light Street; Baltimore Promotion Council, 1102 St. Paul Street both 21202; Baltimore Convention Bureau, 1 West Pratt Street, Convention Plaza, 21201.

Baton Rouge, Louisiana

The World Almanac is sponsored in the Baton Rouge area by the Morning Advocate and State-Times, 525 Lafayette Street, Baton Rouge, LA 70802 (mailing address: P.O. Box 588, Baton Rouge, LA 70821) phone (504) 383-1111; founded 1842; combined daily circulation 115,968, Sunday 118,573; president Charles P. Manship Jr., publisher Douglas L. Manship, vice president of news and production Richard Palmer, vice president of business and advertising Charles Garvey, executive editor all newspapers Jim Hughes, managing editors: Jack Clark (Morning Advocate), Don Buchanan (State-Times), Art Adams (Sunday Advocate).

Population: 219,486 (city), 495,888 (SMSA); total 1980 SMSA employment 212,000.

Area: 66.3 sq. mi. (city), 472.1 sq. mi (parish), on east bank of Mississippi River, 80 mi. northeast of New Orleans; state capital and East Baton Rouge Parish seat.

Industry: northern anchor of 100-mile long petrochemical complex along the Mississippi River.

Commerce: marketing center for major trade area of over 600,000; bank resources $3.78 billion; 7 banks, 8 savings and loan associations.

Transportation: major transfer point on southern federal interstate system; one airport with 5 airlines; 2 bus lines; 4 railroad trunk lines; Port of Baton Rouge is 4th largest in U.S. with over 79 million tons in 1980.

Communications: 5 TV and 13 radio stations; 2 daily newspapers, 2 weeklies.

Cultural facilities: 6 museums, 4 theaters, symphony, planetarium, observatory, 15 art galleries; "Riverside Centroplex" civic center.

Educational facilities: Louisiana State Univ., founded 1860, center of 8-campus system; Southern Univ., largest Negro land-grant educational institution in the world, founded 1880, center of 3-college system.

Sports: home of LSU Tigers and Southern Jaguars home stadium; football, baseball, basketball, track.

Other attractions: state capitol building, city-parish zoo and arboretum; 113 public parks; major recreational rivers and lakes.

History: called "le Baton Rouge" (French for "red stick") by members of Iberville's exploratory expedition (St. Patrick's Day, 1699) because of presence of a red pole marking boundary between hunting grounds of Houmas and

Bayougoula Indians; first white settlement circa 1719; scene of Revolutionary War battle (1779), 1810 revolt which culminated with the region passing from Spanish and into American hands, and a Civil War battle (1862). Parish is also the location of Port Hudson, scene of the longest continuous siege (48 days) during the Civil War; incorporated 1817; state capital 1849-1862, 1882-present; government structure is a city-parish combination with a mayor-president and city-parish council.

Further information: Chamber of Commerce, P.O. Box 1868, Baton Rouge, LA 70821; Louisiana Tourist Commission, P.O. Box 44291, Capitol Station, Baton Rouge, LA 70804; Baton Rouge Area Convention and Visitors Bureau, P.O. Box 3202, Baton Rouge, LA 70821.

Billings, Montana

The World Almanac is sponsored in the Billings area by the Billings Gazette, 401 N. Broadway, Billings, MT 59101; phone (406) 657-1200; founded 1885; member of Lee Enterprises, Inc. since 1960; circulation daily 60,535, Sunday 62,622; publisher George D. Remington, editor Richard J. Wesnick.

Population: 66,798 (city) 108,035 (county), first in state; total employed 55,600, 4.5% unemployment.
Area: south central Montana on Yellowstone River, 125 mi. from Yellowstone Park; Yellowstone County seat.
Industry: 3 oil refineries, beet sugar refinery, 2 packing plants, 3d largest livestock auction yards in U.S., center for northern Great Plains coal industry; headquarters for oil, minerals and gas companies and related services; district headquarters Burlington Northern Railroad.
Commerce: wholesale-retail center for eastern Montana, northern Wyoming; retail sales (1980) $665 million; 9 banks, 2 savings and loan assns., average spendable family income $16,181.
Transportation: 4 airlines, one railroad, 2 bus lines, 98 motor carriers, interstates 90 and 94; Metro city bus transit.
Communications: 2 TV and 9 radio stations; one weekly, one daily newspaper.
New Construction: total permits, commercial/church/school $5.1 million; residential $9.1 million.

Medical facilities: 2 hospitals, 478 beds, 108 dentists, 200 doctors, 5 nursing homes, Northern Rockies Regional Cancer Treatment Center, Regional Mental Health Center.
Cultural facilities: 10 art galleries, symphony orchestra, 2 western museums, studio theater, theater of performing arts, liberal arts college, private (church related) college, 90 churches, vo-tech program, sheltered workshop, 37 public schools, 10 parochial schools, Center for Handicapped Children, Migrant Children's Program.
Other attractions: big game hunting, fishing, boating, skiing within one hour's drive; snowmobiling, bicycling, saddle clubs; auto & motorcylce clubs, 23 city parks; 2,800 hotel/-motel rooms, Metra civic center for sports and concerts; 5 golf courses.
History: founded 1882 with arrival of Northern Pacific Railroad; named after Frederic Billings, then NP president; now largest city in 500-mile radius.
Further information: Tourist Information Bureau, Billings Chamber of Commerce, P.O. Box 2519, Billings, MT 59103.

Binghamton, New York

The World Almanac is sponsored in the Binghamton area by The Evening Press and The Sun-Bulletin, Vestal Parkway East, Binghamton, NY 13902; phone (607) 798-1234; circulation: evening 66,993, Sunday 82,692, morning 27,735, Saturday morning and holidays 72,701; president and publisher Fred G. Eaton, executive editor William F. Mungo Jr., Evening Press managing editor Michael G. Doll, Sun-Bulletin managing editor Soren W. Nielsen.

Population: 55,860 (city), 301,274 (metro area), 8th among state metro areas; total employed 134,000.
Area: 10.98 sq. mi. at junction of Chenango and Susquehanna rivers; 715 sq. mi. in county; Broome County seat.
Industry: IBM, computers; Singer Co., transportation equipment products and simulators; Endicott Johnson Corp., shoes; General Electric, aircraft electronic equipment; Savin, copiers; Universal Instruments, production assembly equipment; Frito Lay, snack foods; Crowley Food, dairy food processing; Amphenol Cadre, electronic equipment; Chenango Industries, electronic assembly; Vail Ballou Press and Grosset & Dunlap, printing and publication.
Commerce: national headquarters of Security Mutual Life Insurance Co. and Columbian Mutual Life Insurance Co.; 12 banks.
Transportation: 7 airlines, major being USAir, out of Broome County Airport; intersection Interstates 81 & 88 and Route 17; Conrail and Delaware & Hudson freight rail carriers; Greyhound, Short Line, Trailways, Chenango Valley bus lines.

Communications: 4 TV stations, 4 AM, 3 FM radio stations.
Medical facilities: 4 major hospitals.
Cultural facilities: Roberson Center for the Arts and Sciences, Binghamton Museum of Fine Arts, Kopernik Observatory; Tri-Cities Opera, Binghamton Symphony & Choral Society, BC Pops; SUNY-Binghamton—Cider Mill Playhouse, Harpur Jazz & Wind Ensemble, Univ. Orchestra & Chorus, Univ. Art Gallery; Broome Community College.
Other attractions: Veterans Memorial Arena, Oakdale Mall, municipal parks zoo, 2 major state parks on outskirts of city; 3 county parks.
Sports: Binghamton Whalers American Hockey League team; BC Open golf tournament; Pro Bowlers Assn. eastern champion invitational.
History: settled 1800; became rail center by 1848, with roads replacing old Chenango Canal that fed Erie Canal; named for Philadelphia patriot and multi-millionaire William Bingham.
Further information: Broome County Convention and Visitors Bureau, 84 Court Street, Binghamton, NY 13902.

Birmingham, Alabama

The World Almanac is sponsored in the Birmingham area by The Birmingham Post-Herald, 2200 Fourth Avenue N., Birmingham, AL 35202; phone (205) 325-2222; Post founded 1921 by Scripps-Howard Newspapers; Herald founded 1887; circulation, 75,630; editor Angus McEachran, vice president W. H. Metz, managing editor David Brown; major public service projects include Goodfellow Christmas Fund.

Population: 284,413 (city), 834,067 (SMSA); employment 360,660 (metro, 1979).
Area: 89 sq. mi. in north central Alabama; state's largest city; Jefferson County seat.
Industry: heavy manufacturing in metals; U.S. Steel is area's largest employer; U.S. Pipe and Foundry and American Cast Iron Pipe Co. are in top 10 employers; South Central Bell's 5-state headquarters located in city.

Commerce: wholesale-retail center for Alabama; retail sales (1979) $5.4 billion; 14 banks (county), 6 bank holding companies, 7 savings and loan assns.
Transportation: 5 major rail freight lines, Amtrak; Greyhound and Continental Trailways bus lines; Eastern, American, Delta, United, Republic and USAir air lines with modern airport terminal; 75 truck line terminals; 3 interstate highways, I-59 complete, I-65 and I-20 under construction.

Communications: 2 daily newspapers, 3 commercial TV stations, 16 commercial radio stations, one PBS TV and one PBS radio outlet.

Medical facilities: Univ. of Alabama in Birmingham Medical Center covers 60 sq. blocks; heart surgery team brings patients from all over the world; VA hospital, in same complex, is the base of organ transplant program; Baptist Medical Centers have 2 major hospitals; 13 other hospitals.

Cultural facilities: symphony orchestra; Oscar Wells Museum of Art; Civic Opera; 4 resident civic theaters; 2 resident ballet companies.

Education: Samford Univ., Birmingham-Southern, Miles, and Daniel Payne colleges; Jefferson State and Lawson State junior colleges.

Convention facilities: civic center with exhibition hall, theater, music hall, and coliseum; several convention hotels and motels in civic center area.

Sports: nicknamed "Football Capital of the South" for

Univ. of Alabama and Auburn Univ. games played at municipal stadium, Legion Field.

Other attractions: world's 2d largest cast iron statue, Vulcan, mythical god of the forge, overlooks Birmingham from Red Mountain as a symbol of the steel industry; Arlington Shrine, antebellum home that housed federal troops during Civil War; Botanical Gardens complex with Japanese Garden; Jimmie Morgan Zoo; extensive city park system.

History: chartered 1871; soon became known as the "Magic City" because of its rapid growth brought on by the presence of the 3 ingredients in steelmaking — coal, iron ore, and lime; mining died out in recent years and most iron ore is now imported by ship and barge to Birmingport on Warrior River from South America; coal mining, in decline since the 1940s, is on the upswing.

Further information: Chamber of Commerce, 2027 First Avenue N., Birmingham, AL 35202.

Bismarck, North Dakota

The World Almanac is sponsored in western North Dakota by the Bismarck Tribune, 707 Front Avenue, Bismarck, ND 58501; phone (701) 223-2500; founded 1873 as weekly, became daily 1881; circ. 29,750; publisher A.G. Sorlie, editor Charles W. Walk, general manager Sanders Hook, advertising manager James H. Hewitson; major awards include Pulitzer Prize Gold Medal, 1937.

Population: 44,485, 3d in state; total employed 24,010.

Area: 18.5 sq. mi on Missouri River; state capital and Burleigh County seat.

Industry: agriculture, printing, trucking, farm machinery, state government, electric power, manufacturing, concrete products, railroad, insurance, livestock sales rings, lignite coal.

Commerce: retail trade area radius 100 miles, serving 150,000 people; retail sales (1979) $300 million; bank deposits (1980) $751 million; 6 banks, 5 building and loan assns.

Transportation: 2 rail lines; airport, hub for 5 airlines; 6 truck lines, 4 bus lines, U.S. Highways 18 and 83, I-94.

Communications: one daily newspaper; 3 AM, 3 FM radio stations, 3 TV stations.

New construction: 1980 building permits $36 million.

Medical facilities: 2 hospitals, 453 bed capacity, served by 120 MDs.

Federal facilities: federal buildings house 20 offices; 14th Radar Bomb Scoring Detachment.

Cultural facilities: Bismarck Junior College, Mary College; 72,000-volume public library, state library, Elan Gallery, Heritage Center.

Recreation: 30 parks with over 1,450 acres, indoor artificial ice arena, 3 golf courses, 5 swimming pools, playgrounds, tennis courts, YMCA, duck and game hunting, fishing, nearby Fort Lincoln State Park.

Convention facilities: 8,000 seat Civic Center; 1,480 rooms in 18 motels, 5 banquet and meeting facilities for groups 200-1,200.

Other attractions: Dakota Zoo, Garrison Dam, United Tribes of North Dakota Educational Technical Center, state capitol.

History: founded 1872 as Edwinton, a rail town; name changed to Bismarck in 1873 to encourage German investment capital.

Further information: Chamber of Commerce, 412 Sixth Street, Bismarck, ND 58501.

Bloomington, Illinois

The World Almanac is sponsored in Bloomington-Normal and central Illinois by The Daily Pantagraph, 301 W. Washington Street, Bloomington, IL 61701; phone (309) 829-9411; founded 1837 by Jesse W. Fell; circulation 52,788; president Davis U. Merwin; publisher Peter E. Thieriot; editor Harold Liston; general manager William Diesel; managing editor Gene F. Smedley.

Population: 87,500 Bloomington-Normal, 119,149 (McLean County); mid-way between Chicago and St. Louis in central Illinois.

Industry: over 50 industries in county, among major insurance cities in U.S., home offices of State Farm, Country Companies, Union Auto; uniform diversity of nonagricultural employment in all major work force areas; leads nation in corn and soybean production with 1,789 farms in county.

Commerce: 1979 metro retail sales $553 million; per household income $23,572; per household retail sales, $10,546.

Transportation: B-N Airport, 4 bus lines, 6 federal and state highways, 4 railroads, Amtrak, 35 interstate and 23 intrastate motor carriers; Britt Airways.

Communications: 6 radio stations.

Medical facilities: 3 hospitals; Watson-Gailey Foundation Eye Bank.

Cultural facilities: Illinois Wesleyan Univ. in Bloomington; Illinois State Univ. in Normal; 81 churches; home of American Passion Play; B-N Symphony, community players, amateur musical.

History: incorporated 1850; site of A. Lincoln's "Lost Speech" and David Davis mansion; state historical shrine; city's Stevenson family has produced 3 generations of leadership; vice president Adlai E.; governor, presidential candidate and UN Ambassador, Adlai E. II; and former U.S. Senator Adlai E. III.

Further information: Association of Commerce and Industry of McLean County, 210 S. East Street, Bloomington, IL 61701.

Boise, Idaho

The World Almanac is sponsored in the Boise area by the Idaho Statesman, 1200 N. Curtis Road, Boise, ID 83704; phone (208) 377-6200; founded 1864 as Tri-Weekly; daily circulation 56,920, Sunday 70,288; publisher Gary F. Sherlock, managing editor Rod Sandeed; a Gannett newspaper.

Population: 154,735 (city division, 1980), 173,036 (metro area), first in state; total employed 84,500 (metro).

Area: 1,054 sq. mi. on Boise River at foot of Salmon River Mountains; state capital and Ada County seat.

Industry: mobile home and recreational trailer production;

Hewlett-Packard; world headquarters Boise Cascade Corp., Morrison-Knudsen Co., and Albertson Food Stores.

Commerce: wholesale and retail center for southwest Idaho; retail sales $2.5 billion (1980); bank resources $707 million in 6 banks with 27 branches; 4 savings and loan associations, and 7 insurance company offices.

Transportation: 3 major airlines, 2 feeder airlines, one rail freight line, 4 bus lines, 17 common carrier truck lines; Amtrak.

Communications: 4 TV and 9 radio stations.

Medical facilities: 3 major hospital complexes including a Veteran's Administration facility.

Cultural facilities: Boise Philharmonic Orchestra, art gallery, state museum, Boise Little Theatre, public library, Boise State Univ.

Other attractions: 33 parks, Southwestern Idaho Fairgrounds, 2 major recreational lakes, scenic mountain areas; Bogus Basin ski resort offers one of the world's longest illuminated ski runs.

History: founded 1863; named derived from "les bois" (the trees), a description for area used by French fur trappers in 1811.

Further information: Boise Chamber of Commerce, P. O. Box 2368, or Department of Commerce and Development, Idaho Statehouse, both Boise, ID 83701.

Boston, Massachusetts

The World Almanac is sponsored in the Boston area by the Boston Herald American, 300 Harrison Avenue, Boston, MA 02106; phone (617) 426-3000. The Herald American was established June 19, 1972; daily circulation 209,126, Sunday 246,298; publisher James T. Dorris, general manager Dennis Mulligan, editor Donald Forst.

Population: 562,994 (city), 2,759,800 (SMSA).

Area: 46 sq. mi. on Massachusetts Bay; state capital and Suffolk County seat.

Commerce: northeast center for finance and insurance; home office for 50 insurance companies; banking center for New England with total commercial banking deposits of $16.422 billion (1978); accounts for 35% of the nation's mutual fund holdings; retail center for northern New England; major electronics industry and publishing center.

Transportation: terminating point for 2 railroads, Amtrak and Boston & Maine; MBTA (Massachusetts Bay Transportation Authority) provides surface and subway transportation for metropolitan Boston; Massachusetts Port Authority (operates Logan International Airport and the Port of Boston (shipping); 5 interstate highways.

Communications: 21 newspapers (3 daily, 19 weekly), 8 TV and 31 radio stations.

New construction: Copley Place, Lafayette Place, Waterfront Hotel and building rehabilitation, Quincy Market (incl. Faneuil Hall restoration), and the Ritz Carlton hotel-/condominium complex.

Medical facilities: health care is Boston's largest industry in terms of dollars invested; major institutions: Mass. General, Children's, and New England medical centers; Boston City, Beth Israel, Deaconess hospitals; Harvard, Boston Univ., and Tufts medical schools; Lahey Clinic.

Federal facilities: 50 federal agencies employ 45,700 (military facilities not included).

Cultural facilities: Boston Public Library, the Boston Athenaeum, Boston Symphony Orchestra; Boston Pops; Boston Opera Co.; Boston Ballet; Museum of Fine Arts; Museum of

Science/Hayden Planetarium; New England Aquarium; Museum of Transportation; Children's Museum.

Educational facilities: 16 degree-granting institutions in the city and 47 in the metro area, including Harvard, Boston College, Boston Univ., Tufts, M.I.T., Brandeis, Univ. of Mass., Suffolk, Emmanuel, Simmons, and Wentworth Inst.

Recreation: 2,327 acres of city recreation area, includes historic Boston Common and Public Garden; Metropolitan District Commission provides extensive facilities, including beaches and harbor islands.

Convention facilities: 49 hotels equipped to handle conventions; exhibition halls include Commonwealth Pier Exhibition Hall with 168,000 sq. ft. and John B. Hynes Veterans Auditorium in Prudential Center with 154,000 sq. ft. and auditorium seating 5,800.

Sports: professional teams include Red Sox (baseball), the NBA champion Celtics (basketball), New England Patriots (football), Bruins (hockey).

Other attractions: Quincy Market (a reconstruction of the historic Boston marketplace), Faneuil Hall, the "Freedom Trail", a 1½ mile walk through historic Boston; Beacon Hill and Back Bay historical districts; U.S.S. Constitution - "Old Ironsides" - the oldest commissioned ship in the U.S. Navy.

Nicknames: The Hub (of the Universe), Bean Town.

History: capital city of commonwealth, founded 1630; from 1770, Boston was scene of many events leading to American Revolution, including Boston Tea Party on Dec. 16, 1773; incorporated Feb. 23, 1822.

Further information: Boston Chamber of Commerce, 125 High Street, Boston, MA 02110.

Bridgeport, Connecticut

The World Almanac is sponsored in the Bridgeport area by The Bridgeport Post (eve.), The Telegram (morn.), and The Sunday Post; published by The Post Publishing Co., 410 State Street, Bridgeport, CT 06602; phone (203) 333-0161; circulation Post 73,572, Telegram 17,518, Sunday Post 92,306; John E. Pfriem president and general manager, Leonard E. Gilbert managing editor.

Population: 142,546, largest in state; planning region 300,897; 9-town district labor force 551,305.

Area: 17.5 sq. mi. on north shore of Long Island Sound at mouth of the Pequonnock R.; Fairfield County Seat.

Industry: "Industrial Capital of Connecticut;" products include machine tools, ammunition, wiring devices, brass goods, valves, electrical apparatus and appliances; nearby are Sikorsky Aircraft and Avco Lycoming; corporate headquarters: Warnaco, General Electric in Fairfield; Raybestos-Manhattan, and American Chain & Cable in Trumbull.

Commerce: retail sales $2 billion (1980); downtown renewal includes 64-store enclosed shopping complex with Gimbels and Sears stores, 2,000-car parking garage, U.S. Courthouse, 100-unit apartment building for senior citizens and handicapped; $50 million development in planning stage, will include 300-room hotel, executive conference center, cultural and media center.

Transportation: railroad station served by Amtrak, adjacent to multi-transportation center and 500-car parking garage;

city served by Conn. Turnpike (Interstate 95); historic U.S. 1 (Boston Post Road); municipal Sikorsky Memorial Airport; Conrail; 2 national bus lines; summer ferry to Port Jefferson, N.Y.

Medical facilities: 3 general hospitals, state mental health center; municipal convalescent hospital; major Easter Seal rehabilitation center.

Cultural facilities: Univ. of Bridgeport, Fairfield Univ., Sacred Heart Univ., Housatonic Comm. College; Museum of Art, Science, Industry; P. T. Barnum museum; symphony orchestra; city-supported downtown cabaret theater; American Shakespeare theater in adjoining town of Stratford.

Recreational facilities: "The Park City" has 1,200 acres of parks, including Seaside with 2-mile shoreline; zoo; municipal indoor ice-skating rink, 9,000-capacity Jai Alai fronton, summertime community-wide Barnum Festival.

Further information: Bridgeport Area Chamber of Commerce, 180 Fairfield Avenue, Bridgeport, CT 06604.

Buffalo, New York

The World Almanac is sponsored in the Buffalo area by The Buffalo Evening News, One News Plaza, P.O. Box 100, Buffalo, NY 14240; phone (716) 849-4444; circulation 270,000, Sunday 185,000; Warren E. Buffett chairman; Henry Z. Urban publisher and president; Stanford Lipsey vice chairman; Murray B. Light editor and vice president; Richard K. Feather vice president.

Population: 357,870 (city), 1,241,434 (SMSA), 3d in state; hub of broad 8 county area with population of 1,714,400.
Area: 49.6 sq. mi. city, 1,567 sq. mi. metro, at western end of N.Y. State on Lake Erie, Niagara River, and U.S.-Can. boundary; Erie County seat; metro area includes Niagara Falls, Lockport, Tonawanda, N. Tonawanda, Lackawanna.
Industry: 1,063 manufacturing establishments, headquarters for Rich Products, Buffalo Forge, Trico Products, Fisher-Price Toys; large plants for Republic Steel, Bethlehem Steel, Chevrolet, Ford, Westinghouse, Union Carbide.
Commerce: wholesale and financial center for western N.Y.; retail sales $5.5 billion (metro); average income per household after taxes (metro) $15,947; distribution center for northeastern U.S. and Canada; $6.5 billion in trade between U.S. and Canada handled each year; 13 commercial banks, 8 savings banks, 4 savings and loans.
Transportation: Greater Buffalo Int. Airport served by 6 airlines with over 3 million passengers, 160,000 flights (1980); 6 major railroads, 22 freight terminals; about 350 motor carriers; highway system includes New York State Thruway and Kensington Expressway. Direct highway and rail service to all parts of Canada; direct water service to entire Great Lakes-St. Lawrence Seaways system, overseas, and Atlantic seaboard.
Communications: 2 major Buffalo newspapers, 3 additional dailies and one Sunday in surrounding cities; 5 TV, 20 AM and FM radio stations; 4 cable systems.
Cultural facilities: Buffalo Philharmonic in Kleinhans Music Hall; Albright-Knox Art Gallery; Studio Arena theater; Shea's Theater; Museum of Science; Historical Museum; Zoological Gardens (23 acres); Shaw Festival at Niagara-on-the-Lake, Ontario; performing arts center (Artpark) in Lewiston.
Educational facilities: State Univ. at Buffalo (largest unit of state univ.); Niagara Univ., Canisius College; 5 other colleges; several 2-year institutions.
Convention facilities: Memorial Auditorium seats up to 17,000, new Buffalo convention center seats up to 20,000; Niagara Falls Convention Center seats up to 12,000; additional facilities available at several hotels and motels.
Sports: Bills football (NFL), Sabres hockey (NHL), Rich Stadium; Bison baseball. Stallions Soccer [MISL].
Recreation: abundant facilities for all year around sports and activities; near both U.S. and Canada vacationlands.
Other attractions: Niagara Falls and river areas from Buffalo to Lake Ontario; Robert Moses and Adam Beck hydro stations; St. Lawrence Seaway, Welland Canal locks, aquarium (Niagara Falls), Our Lady of Victory Basilica (Lackawanna); Old Fort Niagara; Letchworth and Allegany parks; Darien Lake Fun Country; Naval Park; Buffalo Raceway.
Further information: Chamber of Commerce, 107 Delaware, Buffalo, NY 14202.

Calgary, Alberta, Canada

The World Almanac is sponsored in Calgary and southern Alberta by the Calgary Sun, 830 - 10th Avenue S.W., Calgary, Alberta, T2R 0B1; phone (1-403) 263-7730; known as the Calgary Albertan for 78 years up to Aug. 1, 1980; daily circulation 60,000, Sunday circulation 64,000; publisher Hartley Steward, managing editor Les Pyette, general manager Paul Whitlock.

Population: 560,618.
Area: 235 sq. mi.; elevation 3,440 feet in the foothills of the Rockies, 150 miles north of the Alberta-Montana border.
Industry: 526 oil and gas companies, 519 service and supply companies, 358 energy industry consultant firms, 400 data processing firms, and over 1,000 industrial plants in city; meatpacking, transportation, and fertilizer industries also play a prominent part; manufacturing payroll (1979) $442 million; trading area population over one million; more industrial info. available from Bruce McDonald, director, Business Development, P.O. Box 2100, Calgary, Alberta.
Commerce: retail sales (1979) $3.25 billion; gross income of market area (1979) $7.71 billion; per capita spending in market area (1979) $3,200; no sales or gasoline tax.
Transportation: 2 railways; Greyhound Canadian headquarters; International Airport served by 9 airlines.
Communications: 3 TV stations, 2 cable companies; 5 FM, 5 AM radio stations; 2 daily and 4 weekly newspapers.
Medical facilities: 7 major hospitals, 5 auxiliary hospitals, and one tuberculosis center.
New construction: $1.5 billion in construction in 1980 as oil and gas boom continues.
Cultural facilities: 2,700 seat auditorium; Glenbow Museum; QR Arts Centre; Centennial Planterium; symphony orchestra; performing arts center under construction; live theater groups; ballet troupe; opera company, synchronized swimming group.
Education: 254 schools from elementary through senior high school; Univ. of Calgary, Alberta Vocational Centre, Mount Royal College, Southern Alberta Institute of Technology.
Recreation: One hour drive to 4 major ski resorts in Rocky Mountains; 22 ice arenas, 223 athletic parks, 2 ski areas within city, 14 golf courses.
Sports: Calgary Flames (NHL); Calgary Stampede in July attracts one million people over 10 days; Stampeders, Canadian Football League; Calgary Canucks, Alberta Junior Hockey League; Calgary Wranglers, Western Hockey League; Calgary Expos, baseball; Calgary Outlaws, semi-pro soccer.
Other attractions: Heritage Park reconstructs pioneer life on a lake; Calgary Zoo; Dinosaur Park with life-size models; Calgary Tower; more than 1,500 restaurants.
History: began as R.C.M.P. outpost in 1875; railroad arrived in 1883 as population reached 1,800; discovery of oil during 1914 in Turner Valley started Calgary on road to become Canada's oil capital.
Further information: Chamber of Commerce, 517 Centre Street; Calgary Tourist and Convention Association 1300 - 6th Avenue S.W., Calgary, Alberta.

Charleston, West Virginia

The World Almanac is sponsored in the Charleston area by The Charleston Gazette, 1001 Virginia Street, East, Charleston, WV 25330; phone (304) 348-5140; circulation (morn.) 55,518. (Sun.) 105,942; founded 1873 as the Kanawha Chronicle, became The Charleston Gazette 1898; W. E. Chilton III publisher; Don Marsh editor.

Population: 63,968 (city), 231,414 (county), most populous city, county in state; county labor force, 125,900.
Area: 29.3 sq. mi. at meeting place of the Kanawha and Elk rivers; state capital. Kanawha County seat.
Industry: manufacturing including chemicals and fabricated metals; coal, glass, petroleum products, alloys.
Commerce: wholesale, retail center for West Virginia, So. Ohio, E. Kentucky; county retail sales, $1.2 billion; average family income $19,993.
Transportation: 2 rail freight lines, Amtrak, bus lines, state's busiest airport; barge lines, 3 interstate highways.
Communications: 4 TV and 10 radio stations.

Medical facilities: 6 hospitals, 2 of them major complexes.
Cultural facilities: modern civic center and auditorium, Sunrise Cultural and Art Center, symphony orchestra, Community Music Assn., Light Opera Guild, Kanawha Players, State Museum, Univ. of Charleston, W. Va. Univ.
Other attractions: Coonskin Park, Kanawha State Forest, 6

golf courses, public tennis, International League baseball.
History: first settlement, Fort Lee, 1788; Virginia Assembly established Charles Town 1794; named Charleston 1818.
Further information: Charleston Regional Chamber of Commerce and Development, 818 Virginia Street, East, Charleston, WV 25301.

Charlotte, North Carolina

The World Almanac is sponsored in the Charlotte area by The Charlotte Observer, 600 S. Tryon Street, Charlotte, NC 28233; phone (704) 379-6300; founded 1886 as Charlotte Chronicle; changed to Charlotte Daily Observer, March 1892; sold to Knight Newspapers Inc. 1955; circulation 171,769 daily, 238,470 Sunday; president and publisher Rolfe Neill; editor Rich Oppel.

Population: 314,447 (city), 404,270 (Mecklenburg County), 1.3 million (12-county metro area); labor force 341,400.
Area: 123.4 sq. mi. in Piedmont section of N.C., a plateau extending from the Appalachians to the Coastal Plains.
Industry: over 670 manufacturing companies, industrial chemicals, textiles, food products, machinery, printing and publishing.
Commerce: major trucking center, photographic and data processing center, 1,400 wholesale firms with $11.1 billion sales; retail sales $4.8 billion (Mecklenburg County); average household income $21,571; 15 banks, 11 mortgage banks, 6 building and loan associations.
Transportation: 120 trucking firms; 2 major railway lines; 4 bus lines; 5 airlines with 192 air movements per day.
Communications: 5 TV and 14 radio stations.
Medical facilities: an outstanding center in Southeast, 7 hospitals including 3 large general.
Cultural facilities: Opera Assn.; Charlotte Symphony Orchestra; Oratorio Society; Mint Museum (art); Nature Museum; Spirit Square (facility for all art activities under one

roof); over 400 churches; Discovery Place (museum).
Education: Univ. of N.C. Charlotte; Davidson College; Johnson C. Smith Univ.; Queens College; Central Piedmont Community College; Kings College; Hamilton College.
Convention facilities: Charlotte Coliseum-Auditorium, Civic Center, Trade Mart, Merchandise Mart.
Sports: Charlotte Motor Speedway (NASCAR) with World 600 and National 500 races; Charlotte Observer Marathon; Carolina Lightnin' (pro soccer); Charlotte Orioles (pro baseball).
Other attractions: 2 major recreational lakes; Carowinds (family theme park); climate — four distinct seasons, avg. daily max. temp. 71.2, yearly avg. temp. 60.5; Festival in the Park; Southern Living Show.
History: incorporated 1768, named for Queen Charlotte of England; played major role in American Revolution; was gold mining capital of country before 1849; U.S. Mint built in 1836 to serve gold mining industry.
Further information: Chamber of Commerce, P.O. Box 32785, Charlotte, NC 28232; phone (704) 377-6911.

Chattanooga, Tennessee

The World Almanac is sponsored in the Chattanooga area by the Chattanooga News-Free Press, 400 E. 11th Street, Chattanooga, TN 37401; phone (615) 756-6900; circulation 67,000 daily, 130,000 Sunday; publisher Roy McDonald, president Frank McDonald, senior vice president Everett Allen, vice president and editor Lee Anderson, secretary J. W. Hoback, treasurer Clifford Welch.

Population: 169,565 (city), 420,873 (SMSA); 4th in state; 174,100 employed in labor force.
Area: 2,109.8 sq. mi. metropolitan shopping area at juncture of Tennessee River and north Georgia boundary line; Hamilton County seat.
Industry: about 600 manufacturers employ 57,300, producing more than 1,500 classified products including principal products of textile, fabricated metals, chemicals, primary metals, food products, machinery, apparel, paper products, and leather goods; receipts added by manufacture approximately $1 billion.
Commerce: wholesale and retail center; wholesale sales over $800 million; bank assets $1.2 billion; 9 banks, 2 mortgage banks, 4 savings and loan assns., 3 major life insurance companies.
Transportation: 2 major freight lines, 2 bus lines, 13 federal and state highways; modern municipal airport.
New construction: multi-million-dollar TVA office complex and related downtown redevelopment; arena at Univ. of Tenn. at Chattanooga.

Communications: one cable TV, 5 TV, 20 radio stations; 2 newspapers.
Medical facilities: speech and hearing rehabilitation center; children and adults rehabilitation and education center; Willie D. Miller Eye Center; 11 major hospital complexes including psychiatric facility.
Cultural facilities: Univ. of Tenn. at Chattanooga; 3 liberal arts colleges; state tech community college; state vocational-tech school; symphony orchestra; opera assn., civic chorus, community concert assn., Boys Choir, conservatory of music, Little Theatre, programs and performances at the Tivoli Theater, Memorial Auditorium and Miller Park.
Other attractions: multi-million dollar vacation complex; Chattanooga Choo-Choo, in one of the world's largest restaurants, in restored railroad terminal; recreational lakes, mountains, and museums.
History: explored by DeSoto 1540, settled 1828 at Ross's Landing, incorporated 1839.
Further information: Chattanooga Convention and Visitors Bureau, Civic Forum, Chattanooga, TN.

Chicago, Illinois

The World Almanac is sponsored in the Chicago area by the Chicago Tribune, 435 N. Michigan Avenue, Chicago, IL 60611; phone (312) 222-3232; founded 1847; circulation daily 790,475, Sunday 1,150,540; publisher Stanton R. Cook, editor James D. Squires; major awards include 9 Pulitzer prizes won by staff members.

Population: 3,005,072 (city), 2d largest city in nation; 5,253,190 (Cook County); 7,057,853 (SMSA); 3,710,000 in resident labor force; 4 million suburban residents; est. 19% of U.S. population dwells within a 300 mile radius.
Area: 228.124 sq. mi. (city); 4,657 sq. mi. (metro area).
Industry: metro area is a leader in production of steel, metal products, sausages, cookies, candy, metal furniture, mattresses, envelopes, boxes, inorganic chemicals, soap, paint, gaskets, cans, saws, screws, bolts, barrels, machine tools, blowers, switchgear, radios, TV's, communications equipment,

railroad equipment, and surgical appliances; Chicago (SCA) produces a gross metro product of $112.1 billion, 4.4% of GNP.
Commerce: 14,547 manufacturers in Chicago with sales over $94 billion; 47,197 retailers in metro area with sales over $33.6 billion in 1980; 13,467 wholesalers in metro area with sales over $72.8 billion (1977); 59,206 service establishments in the area do an $8.6 billion business (1977); median household income $22,597; Midwest Stock Exchange markets stocks and bonds; 7th Federal Reserve District Bank;

world's leading grain futures market; Chicago Board of Trade; Mercantile Exchange.

Transportation: 3 major airports with 28 commercial airlines handle over 43.6 million passengers, 724,155 aircraft a year; O'Hare is one of the world's busiest and largest airports handling 851,474 tons of freight and mail; 391,676 trucks registered in the metro area; 51 million tons of manufactured goods shipped out yearly; Chicago trucks service more than 54,000 communities; over 12 major highways, expressways, tollways; 3d largest interstate highway system in nation. Railways ship 512 million tons; 90,000 freight cars per week, 25,000 passengers handled daily through Amtrak headquarters; ships carry 1,099,574 tons of cargo in and out of metro area.

New construction: $213 million in industrial construction on 119 projects in 1980; $1 billion in residential construction activity; $1.7 billion in commercial construction on 818 projects; site of the tallest buildings in the U.S. - John Hancock, the Standard Oil, and Sears Tower buildings.

Convention facilities: 1,115 conventions, 171 trade shows, 16,040 corporate meetings, 2.6 million total attendance;

$993 million income generated.

Educational facilities: 95 institutions of higher learning, including Univ. of Chicago, Illinois Institute of Technology, Loyola Univ., Univ. of Illinois - Circle Campus.

Recreation: 131 forest preserves, 79 city parks, 147 golf courses, 15 athletic parks and race tracks; 35 museums, zoos, and permanent exhibitions; 73 swimming pools; athletic clubs, tennis courts.

Cultural facilities: Art Institute, Museum of Contemporary Art, Museum of Science and Industry; Shedd Aquarium is largest in the world; Adler Planetarium; Lincoln Park and Brookfield zoos; Academy of Science and Historical Society museums.

Sports: NFL Bears, AL White Sox, NL Cubs, NHL Black Hawks, NBA Bulls, NASL Sting.

History: Indians named the area Checagou after area's strong-smelling wild onions; incorporated 1837 with population of 4,170.

Further information: Visitors Bureau and Information Center, Association of Commerce and Industry, 130 S. Michigan Avenue, Chicago, IL 60603.

Cincinnati, Ohio

The World Almanac is sponsored in the Cincinnati area by The Cincinnati Post, a Scripps-Howard Newspaper, 800 Broadway, Cincinnati, OH 45202; phone (513) 352-2000; founded in 1881 by Alfred and Walter Wellman; evening circulation 147,018; editor William R. Burleigh, business manager John L. Feldmann.

Population: 385,457 (city), 1,392,394 (SMSA), 2d in state.

Area: 2,154 sq. mi. (metro) in SW Ohio, SE Ind., and 3 N. central counties in Ky.; Hamilton County seat.

Industry: home of Procter & Gamble, Federated, Kroger, Kenner, Armco Steel, U.S. Shoe, Western Southern, Union Central & Ohio National Life Insurance, Baldwin Piano and Organ, Cincinnati Milacron, Dubois Chemical, Senco Products, Stearns & Foster, Totes, Gibson Cards, GM, Ford, and GE plants; production of jet engines, playing cards, chemicals, cosmetics, machine tools, belts, clothing; printing and publishing.

Communications: 6 TV stations; subscription and cable TV available in some areas; 12 AM, 25 FM radio stations; 28 weekly, 2 daily newspapers.

New construction: Good Samaritan Hospital, 19-story, 507-bed tower is scheduled for completion in 1986; Hyatt Regency is scheduled to break ground for a 500-room downtown hotel; Jewish hospital renovation and addition of 300 beds; Netherland Hilton plans a $25 million renovation; Ford plans to start developing 'a small city' in Clermont county; Public Library addition; expansion of elevated walkways.

Medical facilities: 30 hospitals with 9,652 beds; 192 physicians per 100,000 population; Children's Hospital Medical Center; UC Medical Center where Sabin oral polio vaccine was discovered; Shriners Burn Institute and VA Hospital.

Cultural facilities: Art Museum, Historical Society, Symphony Orchestra, Krohn Conservatory, Lloyd Library, May Festival, Taft Museum, Cincinnati Opera, Arts Consortium, Cincinnati Ballet, Museum of Natural History, Contemporary Arts Center, Playhouse in the Park, UC Observatory, and Northern Kentucky Arts Council.

Educational facilities: Cincinnati, Xavier, Northern Kentucky univs.; Cincinnati Bible, Mount St. Joseph, Edgecliff, Hebrew Union, St. Gregory, Thomas More colleges; 8 technical and 2-year colleges; 47 vocational schools.

Convention facilities: numerous hotels, motels, and restaurants; Convention and Exposition Center; Music Hall; Cincinnati Gardens; Emery and Taft auditoriums; Riverfront Stadium and Riverfront Coliseum.

Sports: Reds NL baseball, Bengals NFL football, Suds softball, River Downs and Latonia race tracks; College Football Hall of Fame.

Other attractions: Cincinnati Zoo, Fountain Square Plaza, Americana and Kings Island amusement parks, Delta Queen and New Mississippi Queen excursion boats.

Further information: Chamber of Commerce, 120 West 5th Street, Cincinnati, OH 45202; phone (513) 579-3100.

Cleveland, Ohio

The World Almanac is sponsored in the Cleveland area by The Cleveland Press, 901 Lakeside Avenue, Cleveland, OH 44114; (216) 623-1111; founded 1878 by E.W. Scripps; sold to Joseph E. Cole Oct. 31, 1980; circulation 302,410; Joseph E. Cole, publisher; Herbert Kamm, editor; Gerald H. Gordon, general manager; Dan Sabol, managing editor; major awards include Pulitzer Prize, Lasker Award, Penney-Missouri Award.

Population: 573,822 (city), 1,895,997 (SMSA), first in state; total employed 905,000 (non-agricultural).

Area: 1,519 sq. mi., SMSA 4 county area; along southern shore of Lake Erie, east and west of Cuyahoga River; Cuyahoga County seat.

Industry: city has been described as "an industrial powerhouse," bills itself "The Best Location in the Nation"; within 600 miles are 12 of the top 20 U.S. markets, 55% of U.S. population, 54% of U.S. households, 56% of U.S. effective buying income, 65% of U.S. manufacturing shipments, 64% of U.S. manufacturing plants, 74% of top 1,000 U.S. industrial corporate headquarters; no single industry dominates economy—metal and steel products are mainstays; manufacturing complex occupied essentially with machinery and tools, fabricated metal products, primary metals, automotive products. Important industries include manufacturing of electric motors, products of petroleum, rubber, plastic, stone clay and glass, chemicals, paints, wearing apparel, measuring instruments, electronic components; food products is $15 billion a year business. Retail sales are more than

$8.5 billion; median income of families is $21,374.

Transportation: Hopkins Airport with more than 6 million passengers each year; Burke Lakefront Airport, 5 minutes from public square and capable of handling intermediate jets; Port of Cleveland visited by more than 23 overseas steamship lines and Great Lakes fleet; largest city on Lake Erie and 3d largest on Great Lakes; Cleveland is only U.S. city with airport-to-downtown rail service; ride takes 20 minutes and costs about $11 less than a cab ride; Amtrak train service.

Communications: Cleveland Press, evening daily, plus Sunday; Plain Dealer, morning daily plus Sunday; numerous foreign language newspapers; 6 TV stations; 16 AM and 20 FM radio stations.

New construction: $50 million Medical Mutual Bldg., $60 million office complex, $26 million State of Ohio Bldg., $60 million National City complex, Medical Mutual Bldg., Superior Square, Statler Hotel conversion to Statler Office Tower.

Cultural facilities: Cleveland Orchestra; Play House, na-

tion's oldest and largest resident professional theater; Museum of Art; Karamu House for interracial arts; Western Reserve Historical Society; Health Museum; Natural Science Museum; Cultural Gardens; zoo; Blossom Music Center; Garden Center; Sea World; aquarium.
Educational facilities: Case Western Reserve Univ., Cuyahoga Community College, John Carroll Univ., Notre Dame, Ursuline, and Dyke colleges; Cleveland State Univ.
Sports: NFL Browns, American League Indians, NBA Cavaliers; golfing, horse and car racing, boating, polo, and hunter trials.
Other attractions: downtown Convention Center is largest city-owned convention facility in U.S., public library is 5th in size of book collection in U.S.; Public Square, hub of city, marked by 52-story Terminal Tower. "The Forest City" is encircled by "Emerald Necklace," 18,500 acres of metropoli-

tan parks; Cleveland Clinic, known for medical research, attracts patients throughout the world; University Hospitals of Cleveland has largest research and care center for cystic fibrosis in country; center of a regional renal transplant program; Metropolitan General Hospital is noted for its neurological and burn clinic; many nationality restaurants, due to large ethnic population (close to 6,000 immigrants each year).

History: settlement established in summer, 1796 by Gen. Moses Cleaveland, was capital of the Western Reserve, became a city in 1836.

Further information: Greater Cleveland Growth Assn., 690 Union Commerce Building, Cleveland, OH 44115; Convention Visitor's Bureau of Greater Cleveland, 1301 E. 6th Street, Cleveland, OH 44114; phone (216) 621-4110.

Columbia, South Carolina

The World Almanac is sponsored in the Columbia area by Columbia Newspapers, Inc., P.O. Box 1333, Columbia, SC 29202; phone (803) 771-6161; circulation, The State (am) 104,921; The Columbia Record (pm) 32,998; The State (Sun.) 124,055 (ABC 3/31/80); Ben R. Morris, publisher and president; R. Sidney Crim, general manager; James W. Holton Jr., assistant general manager and advertising director; William E. Rone, editorial page editor, The State; H. Harrison Jenkins, editorial page editor, The Columbia Record; Thomas N. McLean, executive editor, The State and The Columbia Record.

Population: 99,296 (1980 census), city corporate limits; 2-county metro area (Richland and Lexington) 408,176.
Area: 1,465 sq. mi. (metro area); center of South Carolina near confluence of Broad and Saluda rivers (at Columbia).
Government: state capital with about 100 state agencies, 19 federal agencies; government employees total more than 33,000; Fort Jackson military post numbers over 20,000 personnel.
Industry: more than 50 national firms such as General Electric, Allied Chemical, Continental Can, Burlington, Litton, Bendix, M. Lowenstein, Rockwell Int., Square D, Westinghouse, Colite Ind., Nassau Recycle, Michelin, Mepco Electra, Canron Ltd.; fibers, heavy equipment, electronics, textiles, fertilizer, cement products, and tires. Columbia (SMSA) industrial wages for fiscal 1979 exceeded $314 million; total industrial capital invested exceeded $876 million in fiscal 1979.
Commerce: retail sales (metro, 1979) over $1.48 billion; total effective buying income was $2.55 billion, while the average effective buying income per household was $21,600; 11 commercial (main) banking institutions.
Transportation: Metropolitan Airport with 2 airlines and freight service; 3 rail freight lines, Amtrak; 46 major freight companies; 3 interstate, 6 federal, and 6 state highways.

Communications: 4 TV and 12 radio stations.
Medical facilities: 6 general hospitals, including modern Richland Memorial; William S. Hall Psychiatric Institute; 2 state mental hospitals.
Cultural facilities: Town Theatre, the oldest continuous community theater in nation; 3 other theaters; Museum of Art and Sciences; Gibbes Planetarium; Township Auditorium, home of Artist Series; Dreher Auditorium with Philharmonic Orchestra, City Ballet, Lyric Theatre and Choral Society; Fraser Hall.
Recreation facilities: 13 golf courses; city park system; 2 municipal pools; wide range of hunting activities; Riverbanks Zoological Park, part of 135-acre complex; Lake Murray, water sports.
Sports: Williams-Brice Stadium, home of Univ. of South Carolina Fighting Gamecock football team; Carolina Coliseum for basketball, conventions.
Educational facilities: 31,000-student Univ. of South Carolina; 4 private colleges; Technical Education Center; Lutheran Seminary.
History: established 1786 as state capital; burned in 1865 by Union General Sherman.
Further information: Chamber of Commerce, 1308 Laurel Street, Columbia, SC 29202.

Columbus, Georgia — Phenix City, Alabama

The World Almanac is sponsored in the Columbus, Ga. - Phenix City, Ala., area by the Columbus Enquirer and the Columbus Ledger, 17 W. 12th Street, Columbus, GA 31994; phone (404) 324-5526; combined daily circulation 65,494, Sunday 70,841; Enquirer founded 1828, awarded Pulitzer Prize 1926; Ledger founded 1886, awarded Pulitzer Prize 1955. Published by the R. W. Page Corporation; Glenn Vaughn, president and publisher; Bill Brown, vice-president and executive editor; Rick Kaspar, vice-president and general manager. Owned by Knight-Ridder Newspapers, Inc.

Population: 170,108 (Columbus); 27,012 (Phenix City); 237,901 (metro); 98,600 employed (metro).
Area: 1,100 sq. miles (metro: Muscogee and Chattahoochee counties, Ga.; Russell County, Ala.) straddling the Chattahoochee River.
Industry: major textile production center: Fieldcrest Mills, Inc., Bibb Company, Swift Textiles, Westpoint Pepperell, Columbus Mills; Lummus Industries, Columbus Foundries, Interstate Brands, Union Carbide, TRW, Inc.; Internat'l. hqs. Tom's Foods, Ltd. and Burnham Van Service; lumber products, beverages, concrete, bakery goods, and paper.
Commerce: center of west Georgia—east Alabama finance, agriculture, textiles, hydroelectric power; metro retail sales $914.1 million; avg. household buying income $18,335; 9 banks, 6 savings and loan associations.
Federal facilities: Ft. Benning, world's largest infantry school, $388.9 million annual disbursements.
Transportation: 2 rail, 2 bus lines; Delta, Eastern, Southern airlines; 33 truck lines; Chattahoochee R. is navigable.

Communications: 3 TV and 10 radio stations.
New construction: 180-room Hilton Hotel; Ft. Benning expansion; 417-bed hospital to replace Medical Center; North By-pass; expansions for Swift Textiles, Southeast Canners, SCM Corp.; Pratt-Whitney aircraft plant.
Medical facilities: 5 hospitals.
Cultural facilities: Museum of Arts and Sciences, Springer Theater (state theater of Georgia). Three Arts Theater, Bradley Memorial Library; Columbus College, Chattahoochee Valley Community College.
Sports: Astros, Southern baseball league.
History: Columbus founded 1828; gained early prominence as shipping center for cotton, fish; birthplace of Coca-Cola formula. Phenix City founded 1883, growing from a Creek Indian trading post.
Further information: Columbus Chamber of Commerce, P.O. Box 1200, Columbus, GA 31902, or Phenix City-Russell County Chamber of Commerce, P.O. Box 1326, Phenix City, AL 36867.

Columbus, Ohio

The World Almanac is sponsored in the Columbus area by the Columbus Citizen-Journal, 34 S. Third Street, Columbus, OH 43216; phone (614) 461-5000; Citizen founded 1899, Journal 1811; circ. 114,266 a.m. daily except Sun.; owned by E. W. Scripps Co.; editor Richard R. Campbell, business manager Gregory A. Dembski, managing editor Seymour Raiz.

Population: 564,871 (city), 1,088,973 (SMSA); 2d in state; total employed in SMSA 532,580.

Area: 183.1 sq. mi. city, 552 sq. mi. county, in central Ohio at the confluence of Olentangy and Scioto Rivers; state capital and Franklin County seat.

Industry: highly diversified; 1,015 manufacturers in county (1981) including General Motors, Rockwell International, Western Electric, Bordon, R. G. Barry; planes, missiles, refrigerators, mining machinery, telephones, auto parts; home office of Battelle Memorial Institute with world-wide research laboratories.

Commerce: wholesale, retail center for central, southern Ohio, parts of W. Va., Ky. Retail sales, $4.7 billion; financial assets of 9 banks, 19 savings and loan assns. $40.7 billion; 51 insurance co. home offices, assets $6.2 billion; per capita income (county) $8,532.

Transportation: 155 truck lines, 4 intercity bus lines, 3 railroads, 12 airlines using Port Columbus International with 125 air movements daily; OSU's Don Scott Field capable of handling intermediate jets; 22 major highways.

Communications: 5 TV stations, 19 radio stations and 4 cable TV companies incl. QUBE, the first 2-way system; 2 daily, 19 weekly, 6 monthly newspapers.

Medical facilities: 12 hospitals, medical centers; Children's Hospital leads nation in children admitted; Ohio State Univ. College of Medicine.

Cultural facilities: Ohio Theatre, symphony orchestra, Cultural Arts Center, Bicentennial Park; art museums, Colum-

bus Museum of Art and Sculpture Garden; Players Theatre, 3 professional and 11 community theaters, 4 ballet cos.; public library, 22 branches; Center for Science and Industry, Ohio Historical Center, 19th century village; Columbus Zoo, home of first gorilla born in captivity.

Other attractions: Ohio Expositions Center with its coliseum and Ohio State Fair; German Village, Victorian Village, Ohio Center for conventions; Lynn Street Mall, Park of Roses, world's largest; Ohio Railway Museum, 252 parks, boating, floating amphitheater.

Educational facilities: Ohio State, Capital Univ. and Theo. Sem., Franklin Univ., Ohio Dominican College, Columbus College of Art & Design, Columbus Technical Inst., Ohio Inst. of Technology, Otterbein College.

New construction: Capitol South redevelopment; Port Columbus expansion and renovation; Vantage Industrial Park; 2 Nationwide Plaza; Chemlawn Headquarters; Busch Corp. Center; Galbreath office bldg.

Federal facilities: Defense Construction Supply Center; Confederate cemetery, federal office bldg., Ft. Hayes.

Sports: Ohio Stadium and Franklin County Stadium; Clippers (baseball), Pacesetters (women's football), Beulah Park (thoroughbreds), Scioto Downs (harness); Muirfield Memorial golf tournament; NHRA Spring Nationals.

History: founded 1812 as state capital, named for Christopher Columbus.

Further information: Chamber of Commerce, P. O. Box 1527, Columbus, OH 43216.

Corpus Christi, Texas

The World Almanac is sponsored in the Corpus Christi area by The Caller and The Times, P.O. Box 9136, Corpus Christi, TX 78408; Caller (a.m.) founded 1883; Times (p.m.) founded 1911; merged 1929; Caller circulation 63,311, Times 24,403, Sunday 90,603; publisher Edward H. Harte; general manager James W. Hopson; executive editor Robert E. Rhodes; Caller managing editor John R. Thomas; Times managing editor Bill Duncan.

Population: 231,999; labor force 118,700.

Area: 328 sq. mi. (226 water), 210 miles SW of Houston on Corpus Christi Bay; Nueces County seat.

Industry: oil refineries; offshore oil rig fabrication; chemical, petrochemical, synthetics, aluminum, and zinc plants.

Commerce: Port of Corpus Christi handled 53.5 million tons in 1980; economic hub of south Texas; farming, ranching, oil and gas production, commercial fishing, tourist trade; 14 banks have deposits in excess of $1.3 billion.

Transportation: 6 airlines, 2 bus lines, 3 railroads but no rail passenger service.

Communications: 2 daily newspapers, 6 TV stations (one public service, one Spanish), 15 radio stations.

New construction: permits issued for $187 million in 1980.

Medical facilities: 10 hospitals, including a children's center, with more than 1,400 beds.

Federal facilities: Corpus Christi Naval Air Station is headquarters for Naval Air Training Command; Corpus Christi

Army Depot is army's only complete helicopter overhaul plant; combined payroll more than $109 million.

Cultural facilities: Corpus Christi Museum, Art Museum of South Texas, Japanese Art Museum; symphony, little theater, Del Mar College, Corpus Christi State Univ., Corpus Christi Bayfront Plaza Auditorium and Convention Center.

Recreation: public beaches and fishing piers on the Bay and along Gulf of Mexico on Mustang Island and in 88-mile-long Padre Island National Seashore; surf and charter boat fishing; sailing, city marina with launching ramps; large tennis center, 3 private tennis clubs, 6 golf courses.

History: Spanish explorer Alonzo de Pineda discovered Corpus Christi Bay in 1519; Blas Maria de la Garza Falcon established San Petronilla Ranch on Petronilla Creek about 1765; city grew from a frontier trading post est. in 1839; city incorporated Feb. 16, 1852.

Further information: Corpus Christi Chamber of Commerce, P.O. Box 640, Corpus Christi, TX 78403.

Dallas, Texas

The World Almanac is sponsored in Dallas by The Dallas Morning News, Communications Center, Dallas, TX 75265; phone (214) 745-8222; published by the oldest business in Texas, the News was founded in 1842 by Samuel Bangs; circulation, 345,676 Sunday, 278,746 daily; publisher Joe M. Dealey, president James M. Moroney Jr., vice president, executive editor Burl Osborne. Winner of numerous national awards including Freedoms Foundation, National Headliner and Business in the Arts. Sponsors Teen-age Citizenship Tribute, Fly-the-Flag program, Spelling Bee, Science Fair, Sports Show, Involved Citizen Award, etc.

Population: 904,078 (city), (7th in nation); 1,556,549 (county), Dallas-Fort Worth SMSA 2,964,342; total employed 1.5 million with 4.1% unemployment.

Area: 900 sq. mi. astride Trinity River in north Texas about 75 miles south of Oklahoma border; elevation from 450 to 750 feet; Dallas County seat.

Industry: banking and insurance capital of the Southwest, Dallas ranks 3d among U.S. cities in the number of million-dollar-net-worth companies with 1,119 such firms; 1,925

manufacturing plants shipped $16.2 billion worth of goods during 1979—principally oil field machinery, electronics, food, apparel, soaps and detergents.

Commerce: a $5.5 billion wholesale market; Dallas ranks 15.7 nationally in giftware, home furnishing and floor covering wholesaling, 2d in apparel and toys. Metro retail sales totaled $15.7 billion in 1980, while estimated buying income reached $28.4 billion and bank deposits $25 billion.

Transportation: Dallas-Fort Worth and Love Field airports.

In 1980 DF/W was 4th in the world in air carrier operations with 463,447 and 11 million passengers enplaned; Love Field's air carrier operations totaled 90,818 and 1.7 million passengers enplaned. City is served by 12 major and 6 commuter air lines, 8 railroads, 2 trans-continental bus lines, 45 motor freight lines, 4 taxi companies with 1,000 cabs. Dallas Transit System serves 118,000 people daily on 105 lines, 568 route miles.

Communications: 2 metropolitan daily newspapers, numerous suburban dailies, 4 commercial VHF TV stations, public television, 2 UHF stations, 16 AM and 21 FM radio stations, 2 city magazines.

New construction: $2.28 billion in building permits in 1980; projects include $60 million Galleria shopping mall, $47 million Olympia-York downtown office bldg., $35 million Mobil Oil Research and Development Lab.

Medical facilities: 42 hospitals with 9,100 beds, 403 bassinets. Baylor University Medical Center consistently ranks in the top 10 among the country's "super hospitals."

Cultural facilities: symphony orchestra, civic opera, summer musicals, civic ballet, Sunday concert series — among others — offer varied programs; drama at Dallas Theater Center, Theater Three, National Children's Theater, Repertory Theater, and 4 dinner theaters; 7 museums; SMU's Owens Fine Arts Center with a collection of paintings and sculpture; numerous art galleries.

Education: 150,448 students attend 33 colleges and universities within 33 miles of Dallas; Southern Methodist Univ., the Univ. of Texas at Dallas, Univ. of Dallas, North Texas State, Univ. of Texas at Arlington, Baylor Univ. College of Dentistry, Southwestern Medical School; the Dallas Community College system with over 40,000 students on 7 campuses.

Convention facilities: 3 major convention centers, including expanded Dallas Convention Center with more combined meeting-exhibit space (611,000 sq. ft.) than any other in U.S.; 24,923 air-conditioned hotel rooms. Dallas always among nation's top 3 convention cities. In 1980, 1.69 million people attended 1,587 conventions.

Sports: professional sports include football, baseball, basketball, tennis, golf, hockey, soccer, and rodeo. Cotton Bowl is site of annual New Year's Day football game.

Other attractions: Six Flags Over Texas, Dallas Zoo, Reunion Arena, International Wildlife Park; Fair Park is home of State Fair of Texas 16 days each October; museums of fine arts, health and science, natural history; Hall of State; Garden Center and Music Hall; excellent lakes, golf courses, parks, luxury hotels, and restaurants.

History: first settler was Tennessee frontiersman John Neely Bryan who established a trading post and plotted the townsite in 1844; incorporated 1856; named for Vice-President George Mifflin Dallas. Since 1931, the city has had council-manager form of government. Spectacular population growth began after World War II, when aircraft manufacturing augmented an economy that had been built first on cotton, then on oil, banking, and insurance; diversified economic expansion fed the growth into the 1980s.

Further information: Dallas Chamber of Commerce, Fidelity Union Tower, Dallas, TX 75201.

Dayton, Ohio

The World Almanac is sponsored in the Dayton area by The Journal Herald, 37 S. Ludlow Street, Dayton, OH 45402; phone (513) 225-2421; founded as Dayton Repertory; circulation 101,629; executive editor Arnold Rosenfeld, managing editor William Worth, editorial page editor William Wild, "Day" section editor Mickey Davis.

Population: 203,588 (city), 826,891 (SMSA), 4th in state; total employed 357,500.

Area: 48.71 sq. mi. at junction of Mad, Miami, and Stillwater rivers; Montgomery County seat.

Industry: NCR Corp., General Motors Corp. (Delco Moraine, Delco Products, Delco Air, Inland Mfg. new small diesel truck plant); world headquarters for Frigidaire Co., Standard Register, Monarch Marking Systems, Mead Corp., Duriron Co., Inc., Montsanto Research Corp., Ohio Bell, Dayton Newspapers, Inc. (publishers of The Journal Herald and the Dayton Daily News), Dayton Power and Light; more than 800 other manufacturing facilities.

Commerce: retail sales $3.3 billion; average effective buying household income $22,115.

Transportation: 2 airports, 6 airlines, 2 trunk rail systems, 4 bus lines, county wide Dayton Regional Transit Auth.

Communications: 5 TV, 8 radio stations.

Medical facilities: 12 hospitals, including Wright Patterson AFB Hosp. and a VA facility.

Federal facilities: Wright Patterson AFB, HQ. for Air Force Logistics Command and Aeronautical Systems Div.; Defense Electronics Supply Center, federal bldg., VA center.

Convention facilities: modern downtown convention and exhibition center.

New construction: downtown Arcade, Gem City Savings Assoc. headquarters, Amphitheater (part of the Miami River Corridor Project), Emery Air Freight (Dayton Municipal Airport), Courthouse Plaza (includes dept. store, bank bldg., utilities bldg., Mead Tower world headquarters, and 2 restaurants), General Motors small diesel truck plant, Wright State Business School, and expansion of Sinclair Community College.

Educational facilities: Univ. of Dayton (law school), Wright State Univ. (med. school and new business school); Sinclair, Miami Jacobs jr. colleges; United Theological Seminary, Central State Univ., Wilberforce Univ., Wittenberg Univ.; Cederville, Wilmington, and Antioch colleges.

Cultural facilities: Dayton Art Inst., Philharmonic Orch., opera, ballet, contemporary dance co.; 4 amateur theatrical groups, 2 professional cos.; Diehl band shell, River Corridor Amphitheater, Deeds Carillon, dinner theater.

Sports: Amateur Trapshoot national headquarters, college sports, Bogie Busters Pro/Am golf tourn. for Muscular Sclerosis; Dayton Hydroglobe, 5 amateur soccer teams.

Other attractions: Air Force Museum, Carillon Park, Aviation Hall of Fame, Dayton Air Fair, Old Courthouse Museum, A World A'Fair, Dayton River Corridor Festival, Paul Lawrence Dunbar Home, Wright Bros. Memorial, Oregon Historic District, Cox Arboretum, Aullwood Audubon Center and Farm, Wegerzyn Center.

History: "Birthplace of Aviation."

Further information: Dayton Area Chamber of Commerce, Suite 1980, Winters Bank Tower, 40 North Main Street, Dayton, OH 45423.

Denver, Colorado

The World Almanac is sponsored in the Denver area by the Rocky Mountain News, 400 W. Colfax Avenue, Denver, CO 80204; phone (303) 892-5000; founded 1859 by William N. Byers; circulation daily 288,410, Sunday 306,627; editor Ralph Looney, business manager William W. Fletcher; sponsors Colorado-Wyoming Spelling Bee, Golden Wedding Party, Huck Finn Day, and Showagon.

Population: 491,396 (city), 1,615,442 (SMSA), first in state; total employed 839,700.

Area: 116.4 sq. mi. on S. Platte River at edge of Great Plains near Rocky Mountains; state capital and Denver County seat.

Industry: Mountain Bell, employing 13,700; Adolph Coors Cos., 5th largest U.S. brewer of beer, also glass and metal containers and ceramic parts; Storage Technology Corp., manufacturer of memory parts; Martin Marietta Corp., aerospace research and production; Gates Rubber Co., maker of v-belts and hose; Samsonite Corp., world's largest maker of luggage.

Commerce: largest distribution center in the region embracing one-third of U.S. geographical area; bank deposits $7 billion; 94 banks, 16 savings and loan assns., and 45 insurance co. home offices.

Transportation: 6 major rail freight lines, Amtrak; Continental and Greyhound bus lines; 3 interstate highways intersect city; Stapleton International Airport has 1,000 daily flights, hub for 8 major airlines, home of Frontier Airlines and United Airlines Flight Training Center.

Medical facilities: largest medical center between Kansas City and San Francisco; 17 regional comprehensive cancer centers; Univ. of Colorado Medical Center, National Jewish Hospital, Children's Asthma Research Institute and Hospital (CARIH); 22 major hospitals.

Communications: 8 TV and 35 radio stations.

Federal facilities: largest complex of federal offices outside Washington, D.C., with 40,000 federal employees; site of Department of Energy's Rocky Flats plant, U.S. Mint, Lowry AFB, Air Force Accounting and Finance Center, Fitzsimons Army Medical Center, Army's Rocky Mountain Arsenal.

Cultural facilities: symphony orchestra, 3 non-professional orchestras, 3 choral groups, Denver Art Museum, 15 theater cos.; 3-sq. block convention complex; 12,000-seat Red Rocks outdoor theater; Performing Arts Center.

Educational facilities: Univ. of Colorado; Univ. of Denver; Colorado School of Mines; Colorado Women's, Metropolitan State, Loretto Heights and Regis colleges; Univ. of Colorado School of Medicine, Iliff School of Theology.

Recreational facilities: 150 parks, 8,030 acres of mountain parks, 44 golf courses in metro area; City Park Zoo, 2 amusement parks, many ski areas.

Sports: pro teams include NFL Broncos; Bears, American Association baseball; NBA Nuggets; NHL Rockies.

Other attractions: Museum of Natural History, Gates Planetarium, Botanic Gardens, State Historical Museum.

History: founded 1858 with discovery of gold; fast became supply center for mountain mining camps; named for territorial governor.

Further information: Denver Chamber of Commerce, 1301 Welton Street; Hospitality Center, 225 W. Colfax Avenue, both Denver, CO 80204.

Des Moines, Iowa

The World Almanac is sponsored in Iowa by the Des Moines Register and Tribune, 715 Locust Street, Des Moines, IA 50304; phone (515) 284-8000; founded 1849; circulation evening Tribune 82,035, morning Register 219,582, Sunday Register 405,101; board chairman and publisher David Kruidenier; president and editor Michael Gartner; executive vice president Gary Gerlach; executive editor James Gannon; major awards include 12 Pulitzer prizes.

Population: 191,003 (city), 337,814 (SMSA).

Area: 66 sq. mi., at juncture of Raccoon and Des Moines rivers, south central Iowa. State capital and Polk County seat.

Industry: considered to be 2d largest insurance center in U.S. (56 home companies) and 2d largest tire center with Firestone, Armstrong plants; publishing center — Meredith Co., Better Homes and Gardens, Wallace-Homestead, others; farm implements — North American headquarters of Massey Ferguson, John Deere; lawn and garden equipment, sporting goods, food products, cosmetics, dental equipment, automotive accessories, concrete forms, nozzles, tools; 700 wholesale and jobbing firms; Standard Oil credit card center, bulk mail center.

Commerce: retail sales in metro area $1.917 billion (1980); per capita income $8,930 (1980); average household income, $23,637.

Transportation: enlarged in-city airport, 6 major airlines; 4 bus lines, 3 railroads, 69 truck lines; interstate highways 80 and 35.

New construction: downtown shops, offices; Carrier Insurance bldg., downtown high rise retirement residence; Wall Street Journal printing plant.

Communications: 13 radio, 4 TV stations, cablevision.

Medical facilities: 9 hospitals with 2,700 beds.

Cultural facilities: art center, Center of Science and Industry, community playhouse, drama workshop, Drake Univ., symphony orchestra, Grand View Junior, Area Community, and 2 bible colleges; Univ. of Osteopathic Medicine and Health Sciences, Civic Center Theater, Botanical Center.

Recreation: 1,400 acres of parks, 9 public golf courses, 10 public pools, tennis, YWCA, YMCA; 5,000-acre reservoir.

Other attractions: AAA baseball, Drake Relays, Missouri Valley and Big Eight (Iowa State U.) conferences; 15,000-seat auditorium; boys and girls state basketball tournaments, State Fair, Living History Farms, Children's Zoo, 36-story Ruan Center, tallest in Iowa, Terrace Hill (Governor's Mansion), state capitol and state historical bldg.

History: founded 1843 as a fort to protect rights of Indians; incorporated 1853, became Iowa capital 1857.

Further information: Chamber of Commerce, 8th and High Streets, Des Moines, IA 50309.

Detroit, Michigan

The World Almanac is sponsored in the Detroit area by The Detroit News, 615 Lafayette, Detroit, MI 48231; phone (313) 222-2095; founded 1873 by James E.Scripps; circulation daily 629,553, Sun. 822,875; published by Evening News Assn.: president Peter B. Clark, sr. v.p. Richard Spitzley; Detroit News: president Robert C. Nelson, v.p. and gen. mgr. Gene R. Arehart, v.p. and editor William E. Giles; major awards won include Pulitzer Prize, Nat'l Headliners; over 35 community projects include Science Fair, Bicycle Marathon, Golden Gloves.

Population: 1,203,339 (city) first in state, 6th in U.S.; 4,344,139 (SMSA).

Area: 139.6 sq. mi. on the Detroit River, a Great Lakes connecting link and the world's busiest inland waterway; Wayne County seat.

Industry: "The Motor City"; area plants produce 25% of the nation's cars and trucks, employing more than 195,100. Nonautomotive manufacturing and nonmanufacturing firms employ more than 1.2 million; other products are machine tools, iron products, metal stampings, hardware, industrial chemicals, drugs, paint, wire products.

Commerce: metro median income per household $19,710 (1978); area retail sales $18.8 billion (1979).

Transportation: served by 10 railroads, over 220 intercity truck lines, 19 airlines, and 25 steamship lines serving more than 40 countries.

Communications: 8 TV and 50 radio stations.

New construction: 2.4 acre, Phase II of Renaissance Center, $65 million twin office towers; 3.4 acre, $48 million West Clinical Service Bldg. of Henry Ford Hospital; 3.7 acre, $53 million New Center office-retail bldg.; 21 acre, $42 million Wayne County Jail.

Cultural facilities: symphony orchestra, International Institute, Meadow Brook music and drama programs, Institute of Arts, concert band, and the annual Freedom Festival, celebrating Canada's Dominion Day, July 1, and U.S. Independence Day, July 4.

Educational facilities: 13 colleges and universities in metro area including Wayne State Univ., Univ. of Detroit, and branches of the Univ. of Michigan and Michigan State.

Convention facilities: Cobo Hall and Convention Arena with 500,000 sq. ft. of exhibit space; Joe Louis Arena with 33,000 sq. ft. of exhibition space; more than 23,000 rooms in 350 hotels and motels in greater Detroit (Wayne, Oakland, Macomb counties).

Sports: Tigers baseball (American League), Express (NASL), NFL Lions, NHL Red Wings, NBA Pistons; 6 winter skiing areas within short driving distance.

Other attractions: Chrysler, Ford, American Motors, and General Motors auto plants; Henry Ford Museum and Greenfield Village, Cranbrook Institute (science museum and arts), Belle Isle (1,000 acre park), zoo, public library, historical museum, and Fort Wayne Military Museum.

History: founded 1701 by the Frenchman Cadillac as a strategic frontier fort and trading post, ceded to the British in 1763 and turned over to the U.S. in 1796 as a village of 2,500; reoccupied by the British for a year in the War of 1812. Completion of the Erie Canal in 1825 opened a cheap water transport route from New York to the Northwest and made Detroit an important commercial center. R. E. Olds built Detroit's first auto factory in 1899; and Henry Ford, who handbuilt his first car in 1896, formed his first company in 1899, and the present Ford Motor Co. in 1903. The area's industries made it the "Arsenal of Democracy" in World War II.

Further information: Greater Detroit Chamber of Commerce, 150 Michigan Avenue; and Detroit Public Information Dept., City-County Bldg., both Detroit, MI 48226; and Detroit Convention Bureau, 100 Renaissance Center, Detroit, MI 48243.

Dubuque, Iowa

The World Almanac is sponsored in the Dubuque area by the Dubuque Telegraph-Herald (Mon.-Fri. evenings; Sunday Mornings), 8th and Bluff Streets, P.O. Box 688, Dubuque, IA 52001; phone (319) 588-5611; founded 1836; circulation 39,073 daily, 41,938 Sunday; publisher Norman R. McMullin, executive editor Stephen M. Kent, advertising director Dan Grady.

Population: 62,321 city, 93,637 SMSA.

Area: 23.7 sq. mi. in Dubuque County on the Mississippi River on the eastern boundry of the state; Dubuque County seat; 183 miles west of Chicago; 310 miles north of St. Louis

Commerce: retail sales $423 million (1980), median household income $22,217 (1980).

Medical facilities: 3 hospitals with 697 beds; Iowa's 2d largest medical clinic.

Industry: agriculture, meat processing, industrial tractor manufacturing, millwork, oil handling equipment, pumps, plumbing goods, furniture, paper containers, snow removal equipment, metal tanks and fittings, sheet metal goods; iron, copper, brass, and aluminum castings; medical laboratory equipment, insulation board, chemicals, insecticides, chemical fertilizer, textbook publishing.

Transportation: Illinois Central Gulf, Milwaukee Road, Burlington Northern railroads, Amtrak; 16 motor truck cos., 3 interstate bus lines, intracity bus lines; barge transportation; airport 6.5 miles south of city by Ozark, Mississippi Valley and Mid-Continent airlines, 2 charter services; 5 air freight cos.; city is served by U.S. highways 20, 52, 61, 151, and state highway 3.

Communications: One television station, CATV; 2 AM, 3 FM radio stations; daily, weekly labor, and weekly Catholic newspapers.

Federal facilities: U.S. Post Office and court house; Corps of Engineers Lock and Dam; U.S. Coast Guard.

Cultural facilities: 8 art galleries, symphony orchestra, community theater groups, Carnegie-Stout Public Library.

Education: 13 public elementary schools; 2 public junior high schools; 2 public high schools; 10 parochial elementary schools, one parochial high school; Univ. of Dubuque; Clarke, Loras colleges; vocational-technical school; nurses training school.

Recreation: 24 parks, YM-YWCA, 6 golf courses in county; 3 public swimming pools, 2 nature preserves, ski area; boating, fishing, water skiing, cross country skiing, downhill skiing, ice skating, racquetball.

Convention facilities: Five Flags Civic Center; 17 hotels and motels, 71 restaurants, 22 fast food services; 14 night clubs.

Sports: Blues, Merchants, and Pilots semi-pro baseball; Fighting Saints hockey; city league softball, basketball, volleyball, horseshoes.

Other attractions: 4th Street cable railway, Shot Tower; riverboat museum; Farmers' Market held every Saturday May-October in streets, area wide market selling homegrown and homemade products; Pickett's Brewery, only one in Iowa; architecture from 1870-1910 period; Trappist Monastery 12 miles SW of city.

History: founded by Julien Dubuque who mined lead in the area in 1785; area has been under 5 different flags throughout its history; local government organized in 1837, city charter adopted 1841, council-manager-ward form of government adopted 1980; keystone of the tri-state area of Ia., Ill., and Wis.

Further information: Dubuque Area Chamber of Commerce, 880 Locust Street, Dubuque, IA 52001; phone (319) 583-8246; or Dubuque Information and Referral Service, 1358 Central Avenue, Dubuque, IA 52001, phone (319) 557-8800.

Edmonton, Alberta, Canada

The World Almanac is sponsored in central and northern Alberta by the Edmonton Journal, 10006 - 101 Street, P.O. Box 2421, Edmonton, Alberta, T5J 2S6; phone (403) 425-9120; founded November 11, 1903. A division of Southam Press Limited; circulation 190,000; publisher J. Patrick O'Callaghan; editor Stephen Hume; assistant editor William Thorsell; sponsor Learn to ski, swim, canoe, pan gold, play golf, tennis, racquetball, and Shape Up Fitness programs; Literary Awards, Newspaper in Education.

Population: 534,000 city (1981 est.), 730,325 metro (1981 est.); capital of Alberta, largest Alberta city, 5th in Canada; total metro employed 385,000 (1980 est.).

Area: 263 sq. mi. on North Saskatchewan River.

Industry: 2d largest refining center in Canada, 7000 producing wells; petrochemical facilities include plastics, fertilizers, man made fibers, steel tube mills, 2d largest meat processing center in Canada; serves 2 major oil sands plants to north; prosperous mixed farming area.

Commerce: major supply center for Northwest Territories, Yukon, northeastern B.C., and Canadian Arctic; origin and terminus of 5 oil and natural gas pipelines east and west; retail sales (metro, 1980) $6.3 billion; mfg. shipments (metro, 1980) $4.9 billion; trading area population 1.2 million.

Transportation: crossroads of Yellowhead, Alaska, and Mackenzie highways; Canadian National, Canadian Pacific, Northern Alberta, Great Slave, and Alberta Resources railroads; 4 airports, 8 airlines, 304,349 itinerant movements in 1980; Light Rapid Transit System.

Communications: 13 radio stations including one French station; 4 TV stations including one French station, 2 cable TV networks.

New construction: over $1.7 billion in building permits issued in metro area in 1980.

Medical facilities: 5 general and 5 auxiliary hospitals, 2 rehabilitation centers, 10 nursing homes.

Cultural facilities: Edmonton Symphony Orchestra, Edmonton Art Gallery, Centennial Library, Provincial Museum and Archives, Univ. of Alberta (Canada's 3d largest), Northern Alberta Institute of Technology (Canada's largest technical college), Grant McEwan Community College, Alberta and Edmonton ballet companies. Canada's most active professional theater, housed in the Citadel Theatre complex; Theatre Three, Northern Light professional theaters; Stage West dinner theater; Edmonton Opera, Northern Alberta Jubilee Auditorium, Queen Elizabeth Planetarium, Muttart Conservatory.

Other attractions: Klondike Days, annual celebration of the 1898 Yukon gold rush is held in mid-July; August Heritage Festival; Valley Zoo, Fort Edmonton, Capital City Recreation Park, Hawrelak Park; Alberta Wildlife Park, Polar Park, Elk Island National Park and many lakes nearby.

Sports: CFL Eskimos, NHL Oilers, NASL Drillers, PCL Trappers; 18,000 seat Coliseum, 54,000 seat sport complex and $8.5 million aquatic center built for the 1978 Common-

wealth Games; Kinsmen Field House indoor track seats 4,000; city will host the 1983 World Student Games.
History: Fort Edmonton built in 1795, named after town now a borough of London, England; oil discovered at Leduc

(20 miles south) in 1947 rocketed the city into prominence as one of the world's leading petrochemical centers.
Further information: Chamber of Commerce, 600 Sun Life Place, 10123 - 99 Street, Edmonton, Alta.

El Paso, Texas

The World Almanac is sponsored in the El Paso area by the El Paso Herald-Post, 401 Mills Avenue, El Paso, TX 79999; phone (915) 546-6100; Herald founded 1881, Post 1922, merged (under Scripps-Howard) 1931; circulation 33,346; Harry Moskos editor, Ron Royhab managing editor.

Population: 479,448 (El Paso), with twin city Juarez, Mex., 600,000.
Area: 239 sq. mi. on the western tip of Texas where Rio Grande cuts boundaries of Texas, New Mexico, and Mexico at foot of the Rockies (including Franklin Mtns.); El Paso County seat.
Industry: manufacturing payroll $335.2 million (1980), employment 35,600; clothing largest employer with Billy the Kid, Sun Apparel, Farah, Blue Bell; Juarez-El Paso border in-bond industries at 96 and 36,000 employed including electronic and others such as RCA, GTE Sylvania, Allen Bradley; home of El Paso Natural Gas, ASARCO Inc., Tony Lama Boots, Phelps Dodge, Standard and Texaco refineries, Old El Paso (pet foods), and Ashley's of Texas canned Mexican foods; nut processing, cattle, pecans, cotton and other agriculture.
Commerce: wholesale-retail center for west Texas, New Mexico, northern Mexico; retail sales (1980) $1.7 billion, 22 banks, 6 savings and loans; exports (1980) $1.7 billion, imports $1.4 billion.
Transportation: 5 major rail lines, 8 bus lines, 5 major highways; gateway to Mexico, busiest crossing point in the U.S. with more than 77 million crossings a year; International Airport with 7 airlines with 234,036 flights including military, 955,159 passengers, 14,656 tons of freight (1980).
Communications: 6 TV and 23 radio stations.
New construction: 1980 building permits totaled $257.3 million.

Medical facilities: 16 hospitals with 2,429 beds; area cancer treatment center; Univ. of Texas System School of Nursing, Texas Tech Univ. School of Medicine.
Federal facilities: Ft. Bliss (U.S. Army Air Defense center, Allied Students Missile Center, Sgts. Major Academy), William Beaumont Army Medical Center and McGregor Range, Holloman AFB in New Mexico.
Cultural facilities: Univ. of Texas at El Paso, El Paso Community College, El Paso Symphony, Museum of Art with Kress Collection, Ballet El Paso, opera companies, theater groups, Chamizal National Memorial Theatre, and McKelligon Canyon Pavilion; civic-convention center, public libraries.
Other attractions: annual Sun Carnival and Sun Bowl football game; Terry Bradshaw Cancer Treatment Center Tournament, Tigua Indian community arts and crafts center, missions that pre-date those of the Californias; Old Mesilla Art Colony; horse racing in nearby New Mexico, horse and dog racing in Juarez; ProNaf museum and restaurants in Juarez; zoo, Museum of History, Wilderness Park Museum, Fort Bliss Replica Museum, Hueco Tanks State Park; Guadalupe Mountains and Big Bend national parks within 300 miles; skiing in Ruidoso, N.M. and Carlsbad Caverns within 200 miles; exotic Juarez, Mexico and Pancho Villa country.
Further information: Convention and Visitors Bureau, 5 Civic Center Plaza, El Paso, TX 79901.

Erie, Pennsylvania

The World Almanac is sponsored in the Erie area by The Erie Daily Times, 205 W. 12th Street, Erie, PA 16501; phone (814) 456-8531; founded in 1888; circulation 74,000 daily, 92,000 Sunday; Edward M. Mead, Michael Mead, co-publishers; executive editor Joseph Meagher, managing editor Len Kholos.

Population: 119,123 (city), 279,780 (county), 3d in state; total employed 51,500 (city), 113,300 (county).
Area: 19.53 sq. mi. at tip of northwestern Pa.; Erie County seat.
Commerce: county produces $269 million in exports, highest per capita in Pennsylvania; Erie's retail sales total more than $855 million; tourism—5 miles of beaches, fishing, boating; winter sports with 6 county parks and Presque Isle State Park offering camping, hiking trails, tennis courts, picnic areas, and ball fields; seaport—60 or more oceangoing vessels each year, the only U.S. port of call for the Canadian passenger schooner Challenge; over 506 industrial plants produce machinery and parts, iron and steel forgings, hardware, meters, plastics, paper (Hammermill), furniture, toys; General Electric produces Amtrak passenger trains.
Special awards: (1981) Chamber of Commerce received the Governor's Export Award in the service category, and The American Sterilizer Co. for the industrial sector.
New construction: John E. Lampe marina, public facility which will provide 250 boat stalls, launching ramps, and include a 30 acre park; Erie Insurance Exchange expansion.

Transportation: 5 railroads, Boston-Chicago Amtrak line; airport; 35 trucking companies, 4 bus lines.
Cultural facilities: Penn State Univ. extension; Gannon, Mercyhurst, and Villa Maria colleges; Philharmonic Society, Council of the Arts; theater groups; Erie County Field House for plays, entertainment, and sports; work begun on $8 million Erie Civic Center.
Convention facilities: Erie Hilton, 2 Holiday Inns, 90 other hotels and motels with over 3,200 rooms.
Medical facilities: Hamot Medical Center, Saint Vincent Health Center, VA hospital, Medi-Center, Millcreek Community Hospital, Erie County Geriatric Center, Corry Memorial Hospital, Shriners' Hospital for Crippled Children, Union City Memorial Hospital, Doctors' Osteopathic Hospital, Fairview Medical Center.
History: named after Eriez Indians; site of building of ship Niagara with which Oliver Hazard Perry defeated British in 1813 in Lake Erie battle.
Further information: Chamber of Commerce, 1006 State, Erie, PA 16501.

Evansville, Indiana

The World Almanac is sponsored in southwestern Indiana, western Kentucky, and southeastern Illinois by the Evansville Press, P.O. Box 454, Evansville, IN 47703; phone (812) 464-7600; founded July 2, 1906, by E.W. Scripps and J.C. Harper; circulation 45,600; editor William W. Sorrels, managing editor Tom Tuley.

Population: 130,496 (city), 307,103 (SMSA); 4th in state.
Area: 47 sq. mi. at bend of Ohio River in southwest corner of state; Vanderburgh County seat.
Industry: Whirlpool Corp. plants (refrigeration and air conditioning); Mead Johnson & Co. (pharmaceutical division of Bristol-Myers Co.); Alcoa Warrick Operations (aluminum)

just east of city; 283 manufacturing firms.
Commerce: retail sales $766.5 million (1980); effective buying income per household $15,641 (1980); home offices of CrediThrift of America, Inc.; 4 banks, 6 savings and loan.
Transportation: world headquarters of Atlas Van Lines; 4 railroads, 5 commercial barge lines, 4 interstate bus lines;

Allegheny, Delta, Eastern air lines.

Communications: 2 daily newspapers; 4 TV and 6 radio stations.

New construction: more than $3 billion in commercial and industrial expansion underway including downtown Riverview Commerce Centre bank, hotel and Coal Exchange office building; 120-store Eastland Mall.

Medical facilities: 4 general and mental hospitals; branch of Indiana University Medical School.

Cultural facilities: Philharmonic Orchestra, Museum of Arts and Science, Mesker Zoo, Univ. of Evansville, Indiana State Univ., Evansville; national headquarters of Phi Mu Alpha music fraternity; Abraham Lincoln boyhood home nearby.

Other attractions: new 150-passenger "Spirit of Evansville" riverboat.

Sports: Evansville Triplets baseball of American Assn. (AAA), farm team of Detroit Tigers.

Further information: Chamber of Commerce, Southern Securities Building, Evansville, IN 47708.

Fort Wayne, Indiana

The World Almanac is sponsored in the Fort Wayne area by the Journal-Gazette, 600 W. Main Street, Fort Wayne, IN 46802; phone (219) 461-8333; established June 14, 1899 by consolidation of The Journal and The Daily Gazette; circulation daily 60,471, Sundays 105,346; president-publisher Richard G. Inskeep; secretary-treasurer Naomi Erb; editor Larry W. Allen.

Population: 172,196 (city), 380,439 (SMSA); total employed 173,000 (metro).

Area: 51.96 sq. mi. at confluence of St. Joseph, St. Mary's, and Maumee rivers in NE Ind.; Allen County seat. Allen County is largest of Indiana's 92 counties (671 sq. mi.), and has greatest number of farms in state, 1,858.

Industry: General Electric and International Harvester largest employers; Magnavox, Essex International, and Central Soya home offices; several firms manufacture about 85% of world's diamond wire dies.

Commerce: wholesale and retail center for northeastern Indiana, southeastern Michigan, northwestern Ohio; retail sales (metro) over $1.597 billion; bank deposits $2.189 billion; 5 banks, 4 savings-and-loan assns.; E. B. I. per household (metro) $22,669; 6 life insurance companies, including Lincoln National Life, based here.

Transportation: 2 major rail freight lines, Amtrak; 56 motor freight lines including home-based North American Van, Elway Express, Scott, and Transport Motor; I-69 connects city with Indianapolis and Indiana Toll Road; U.S. 30 dual lane to Chicago; municipal airport; hq. for 122d Tactical Fighter Wing, Indiana Air National Guard; United, Delta, Air Wisconsin airlines.

Communications: 10 radio, 4 TV stations.

Medical facilities: 4 hospitals including VA.

Cultural facilities: Philharmonic Orchestra; Fine Arts and Performing Arts complex; 9 universities and colleges; 3 museums; Foellinger outdoor theater.

Sports: Komet hockey team (IHL) plays at Allen Co. War Memorial Coliseum; annual Mad Anthony celebrities golf.

Other attractions: replica of 3d Fort Wayne (1815); children's zoo, 88 parks and playgrounds, 19 golf courses, 37 shopping centers.

History: first white settlement in Indiana (circa 1692).

Further information: Chamber of Commerce, 826 Ewing Street, Ft. Wayne, IN 46802.

Fort Worth, Texas

Population: city 385,141 (5th in state), county 860,880, Ft. Worth/Dallas SMSA 2,964,342; 441,422 total employed with 4.5% unemployment.

Area: 861 sq. mi. on the Trinity River in north central Texas, about 50 miles from Oklahoma border; Tarrant County seat.

Commerce: diversified manufacturing, including aerospace, plants, food and beverage, mobile homes, autos, medical industries; 1,651 manufacturers; agribusiness related industry and services produces over $22.5 million in agriculture products a year.

Transportation: Dallas-Fort Worth regional airport 24 minutes driving time from downtown; 4th in the world (1980) in air carrier operations with 463,447; 21.9 passengers; 9 major railroads, Amtrak; 41 motor carriers; city-owned local bus service, 2 transcontinental, 2 intrastate bus lines.

Communications: one daily newspaper; 26 area radio stations, 8 area TV stations; weekly and monthly publications, including Fort Worth Magazine.

Medical facilities: 33 hospitals with 4,700 beds; 2 children's hospitals with 200 beds, 4 government hospitals.

Federal facilities: 14 federal agencies; Carswell AFB.

Cultural facilities: Casa Manana, America's first permanent musical arena theater; community theater; symphony, opera, ballet; Texas Boys Choir and Texas Girls Choir; Van Cliburn Piano Competition; Kimbell Art Museum, Amon Carter Museum of Western Art, Fort Worth Museum of Science & History, Fort Worth Art Center.

Education: 8 colleges and universities with more than 53,000 students; 27 other colleges and campuses within 50-mile radius with over 97,000 students; Texas Christian Univ., Univ. of Texas at Arlington; Texas Wesleyan College; Texas College of Osteopathic Medicine; 3 campuses of Tarrant County Junior College; Southwestern Baptist Theological Seminary.

Recreation: Forest Park, Heritage Park, Fort Worth Zoological Park, Trinity Park, Botanic Gardens, Japanese Garden, Water Garden Park, several other parks; 9 municipal golf courses.

Convention facilities: Tarrant County Convention Center; Will Rogers Memorial Center; 145 conventions (1980); 63 hotels and motels with 6,000 rooms.

Sports attractions: Dallas Cowboys football, Texas Rangers baseball, Fort Worth Texans hockey; Colonial National Golf Tournament; TCU football.

Other attractions: Six Flags Over Texas, Fat Stock Show and Rodeo, Miss Texas Pageant, Log Cabin Village, North Fort Worth western historical area; Cowtown Rodeo weekly; Pate Museum of Transportation.

History: Founded 1849 as a frontier Army post on the Chisholm Trail; later became major railroad.

Further information: Chamber of Commerce, 700 Throckmorton, Fort Worth, TX 76102.

Fresno, California

The World Almanac is sponsored in the Fresno area by The Fresno Bee, 1626 E Street, Fresno, CA 93786; phone (209) 441-6111; founded 1922; circulation daily 134,777 Sunday 152,993; president C. K. McClatchy, editor C. K. McClatchy, executive editor Frank McCulloch, managing editor George Gruner.

Population: 218,202 (city), 515,013 (county); total employed 266,800.

Area: one of largest counties in the state, 3,819,456 acres; located in geographical center of the state; Fresno County seat.

Agriculture: leading county in U.S. in farm production, number of farms, and annual value of agriculture production; state's leading county in total value and production of plums, grapes, cantaloupes, barley, turkeys, peaches, boysenberries, figs, nectarines, cotton, alfalfa seed.

Industry: 600 diversified manufacturing establishments; food processing is major industry; 2d in importance is production of beverages, primarily wine, brandy, and spirits; metro retail sales over $2.3 billion.

Transportation: daily service by 9 airlines; Amtrak; freeways connect to all major metropolitan areas in California; served by 23 common truck carriers, one interstate bus line, and 2 mainline railroads with freight handling facilities; U.S. port of entry.

Communications: one public and 6 commercial TV stations, 5 cable TV services, 18 commercial radio stations, and 2 public radio stations.

Medical facilities: 6 general hospitals including a VA installation; a surgical center and a medical school under construction.

Cultural facilities: community philharmonic, opera, ballet and theater; Fresno Art Center, Meux Home Museum, Discovery Center, Kearney Museum, downtown malls with one of the best outdoor art displays in the West.

Recreation: Western Hockey League team, California Baseball League team; golf, tennis, swimming; Yosemite, Sequoia, and Kings Canyon national parks with groves of giant Sequoia trees plus facilities for boating, sailing, hunting,

fishing, skiing, hiking, pack trips and camping.

Other attractions: Duncan Water Gardens, Underground Gardens; Roeding Park with city zoo and children's Storyland; nationally famous rodeo, county fair.

Convention facilities: Convention Center Theatre seats 2,361; Exhibit Hall facilities can accommodate up to 3,500 with banquet capacity of 2,400; 11 meeting rooms, the largest of which will accommodate up to 390, exhibit space of 59,000 sq. ft; Selland Arena has capacity of 7,500, parking for 900 cars; 5,000 hotel and motel rooms.

History: area explored by the Spaniards in the early 1800s and visited by fur trappers before 1840; settlement began when gold miners came in the 1850s; county created Apr. 19, 1856, from parts of Mariposa, Merced, and Tulare counties.

Further information: Fresno City & County Chamber of Commerce, P.O. Box 1469, Fresno, CA 93721.

Greenville, South Carolina

The World Almanac is sponsored in the Greenville County area by The Greenville News and Greenville Piedmont (daily a.m. and p.m. and combined weekend editions), P.O. Box 1688, 305 S. Main Street, Greenville, SC 29602; phone (803) 298-4100; circulation 107,936 daily, 106,017 Sunday (Mar. 1979); chairman of the board and publisher J. Kelly Sisk, president and co-publisher Rhea T. Eskew, executive editor John S. Pittman.

Population: 58,242 city, 287,913 county, 562,934 SMSA; 264,100 SMSA labor force, 6.1% SMSA unemployment.

Area: 789 sq. mi. in county; Greenville is county seat; in South Carolina's Piedmont area; county includes 7 incorporated areas.

Industry: textiles, apparel, tires, fiber production, chemicals, machinery, electronics, food.

Commerce: 1979 retail sales in SMSA $2.39 billion; 1979 bank debits in SMSA $23.8 billion; 1980 per capita income est. $7,344 county.

Transportation: 2 airports (one general aviation), 2 airlines, 2 bus lines, 3 railroads; Interstate 85, US highways 25, 29, 123, 276.

Communications: 5 TV, 15 radio stations, 2 cable TV services; 2 daily, 3 weekly newspapers.

New construction: $1.02 billion industrial development and expansion from 1960 to May 1981, creating more than 33,000 jobs in the county; $30 million downtown hotel-convention center to be completed in 1982; $30 million

Greenville Hospital System expansion; $50 million Daniel International Corp. engineering bldg.

Cultural facilities: Greenville County Museum of Art, Greenville Little Theatre, Warehouse Theatre, Bob Jones Univ. Classic Players, Furman Univ. Guild, Greenville Symphony Orchestra, Bob Jones Univ. Art Museum; 2 four-year univs., two-year college, technical college; more than 400 churches representing 26 faiths.

Medical facilities: 9 hospitals in Greenville Hospital System, St. Francis Community Hospital, Shriners Hospital for Crippled Children.

Sports: Furman Univ. in Southern Conference, nearby Clemson Univ. in Atlantic Coast Conference; 3 stock car tracks in county; boating in upstate lakes.

History: county created by General Assembly 1786, city named Pleasantburg in 1797, Greenville in 1831.

Further information: Greater Greenville Chamber of Commerce, 24 Cleveland Street, P.O. Box 10048, Greenville, SC 29603; (803) 242-1050.

Halifax, Nova Scotia, Canada

The World Almanac is sponsored in Nova Scotia by The Chronicle-Herald and The Mail-Star, 1650 Argyle Street, Halifax, Nova Scotia; phone (902) 426-2811; circulation Chronicle (morning) 72,227, Mail-Star (aft.) 55,959; publisher Graham W. Dennis, president Fred G. Mounce, general manager Frank Huelin, managing editor Ken Foran, treasurer W.D. Coleman.

Population: 280,000, labor force 125,000.

Area: 24.19 sq. mi. on the southeast coast of the province; capital city.

Industry: leading industrial area in Atlantic provinces; establishments include oil refineries, electronic equipment manufacturers, ship yards, metal works, breweries, and fish processing; 3d largest and one of Canada's most diversified scientific research centers.

Commerce: financial center of region, regional head offices of all major banks; retail sales over $970 million, average family income $26,800 (1979); all 3 levels of government constitute employment for 20,583.

Transportation: 2 major passenger-freight lines; 8 container lines call at easternmost commercial port on mainland North America; container port with 3 sea-shore cranes handled 233,000 20-foot equivalent containers with tonnage of 2.1 million (1979); about 533,000 tons break bulk cargo and 14.4 million tons bulk cargo; international airport handled

1.35 million passengers (1979).

Communications: 5 radio, 2 TV stations; 2 daily and one weekly newspapers.

New construction: building permits issued for over $500 million worth of construction for last 3 years.

Education: 12 universities, colleges, tech-voc schools, 9 research institutes; 48 common and 4 private schools.

Medical facilities: 9 hospitals (3 teaching).

Cultural facilities: Atlantic Symphony Orchestra, Rebecca Cohn Auditorium, Pro Life Theater, 6 museums, bus and water tours; over 80 restaurants, 30 cafes.

Parks: 3 major parks (403 acres).

Sports: Halifax Voyageurs of the AHL.

History: founded in 1749 by the English; meeting place of first legislative assembly in Canada (1758).

Further information: Halifax Visitors and Convention Bureau, Suite 508, Market Mall, Scotia Square, Halifax, Nova Scotia B3J 3A5; phone (902) 426-8736.

Hamilton, Ontario, Canada

The World Almanac is sponsored in Hamilton and the Niagara Peninsula by The Spectator (a division of Southam Inc.) 44 Frid Street, Hamilton, Ontario L8N 3G3; phone (416) 526-3333; founded in 1846; circulation 148,401; publisher John D. Muir; general manager Thomas J. McCarthy; executive editor John Doherty; managing editor Alex Beer.

Population: 306,640 (city), 410,045 (Hamilton-Wentworth region.

Area: 54.4 sq. mi. (city), 426 sq. mi. (region) at west end of Lake Ontario.

Industry: 64.4 per cent of Canada's steel is produced at the Steel Company of Canada Ltd., Dominion Foundries and Steel Ltd., and Slater Steel Ltd.; 757 plants in the metro area manufacturing iron and steel products, electrical appliances, agricultural equipment, tires, wire, food products, heavy machinery, chemicals, and textiles.

Commerce: retail sales (1979) $1.712 billion or 2.27 per cent of Canadian total sales; average weekly wage $331.81; disposable income per capita $8,364.

Transportation: Hamilton Street Railway, Canadian National and Canadian Pacific railways as well as Toronto, Hamilton, and Buffalo line; western terminals for GO transit (provincial rapid transit system); provincial highways to Toronto, Windsor, and Buffalo pass through region; city airport 9 miles south at Mount Hope.

Communications: TV station, community programming cable station, 4 radio stations.

New construction: $40 million office bldg., $450 million Dofasco Hot Strip Rolling Mill, $365 million Steel Co. of Canada expansion.

Medical facilities: 5 major hospitals including medical center at McMaster Univ., Hamilton Psychiatric Hospital, St. Peter's Center for chronically ill and geriatric patients.

Educational facilities: McMaster Univ., Mohawk College of Applied Arts and Technology.

Cultural facilities: Hamilton Place theater-auditorium; art gallery; Hamilton Philharmonic Orchestra; Hamilton Players' Guild; Theatre Aquarius; Multicultural Center; public library.

Convention facilities: convention center with 13 meeting rooms, banquet hall seating 1,500, exhibition hall seating 2,500, topped by a 14-story office tower.

Other attractions: Dundurn Castle, restored prime minister's residence circa 1850; Whitehearn, restored Victorian home; Canadian Football Hall of Fame; Royal Botanical Gardens, one of the largest park systems per capita in Canada; Hess Village boutiques and restaurants in old restored homes; hiking on Bruce Trail, winding through region along Niagara Escarpment; $60 million shopping mall.

Sports: Hamilton Tiger-Cats football, 2 municipal golf courses, Royal Hamilton Yacht Club.

History: explorer Sieur de la Salle discovered Hamilton area in 1669; city takes name from George Hamilton, who laid out streets on part of the farm he bought in 1813.

Further information: Chamber of Commerce, 100 King Street W., Suite 830, Hamilton, Ont. L8P 1A2

Hartford, Connecticut

The World Almanac is sponsored in the Hartford metro area by The Hartford Courant (mornings and Sunday), 285 Broad Street, Hartford, CT 06115; phone (203) 241-6200; founded 1764; circulation: 213,101 daily, 287,961 Sunday; publisher and chief executive officer Keith L. McGlade, vice president and treasurer Richard H. King, vice president and director of operations Milton J. Merz Jr., editor and vice president Mark Murphy.

Population: 136,392 city, 726,036 SMSA, 807,766 Hartford County.

Area: approx. 1,524 sq. mi. in metro area.

Industry: insurance, government, defense.

Commerce: retail sales in metro area $4.3 billion; total bank deposits $9.404 billion.

Transportation: 2 railroads, 24 airlines, 8 bus lines; interstate highways I91 (north and south), I84 (east and west) cross in city.

Communications: 3 TV, 20 radio stations; cable TV.

Cultural facilities: Hartford Symphony, Connecticut Opera, Wadsworth Atheneum, Hartford Stage Company, Hartford Ballet, Mark Twain House, Children's Museum.

Educational facilities: Trinity College, Univ. of Hartford, Univ. of Conn. Law School, School of Social Work, and Hartford Branch; Greater Hartford and Manchester community colleges.

Sports: NHL Whalers play in Hartford Civic Center.

History: founded 1636 by Thomas Hooker and group of settlers from Newtown (Cambridge), Mass., became Connecticut's capitol city 1665.

Further information: Chamber of Commerce, 250 Constitution Plaza, Hartford, CT 06103.

Honolulu, Hawaii

The World Almanac is sponsored in Hawaii by The Honolulu Advertiser, P.O. Box 3110, Honolulu, HI 96802; phone (808) 537-2977; founded July 2, 1856, as Pacific Commercial Advertiser by Henry M. Whitney; circulation 83,721 mornings, 201,301 Sunday; president and publisher Thurston Twigg-Smith, editor-in-chief George Chaplin, executive editor Buck Buchwach, managing editor Mike Middlesworth; awards from American Political Science Assn., American Assn. for the Advancement of Science, others.

Population: 762,874; 80% of state population; total employed 298,300.

Area: 595 sq. mi., encompassing Oahu Island; state capital.

Commerce: major destination for U.S., Japanese tourists; persons staying a night or more 3.9 million in 1980, up from 1.8 million a decade earlier; average daily visitor census 96,497 in 1980, up from 36,943 a decade earlier; tourist spending $3 billion in 1980, up from $595 million in 1970; visitor dollars top military spending, $1.3 billion in 1980; sugarcane and pineapple major agriculture export crops; retail sales (statewide) $6.1 billion; total personal income $9.3 billion; per capita personal income $9,787; Pacific basin business and financial center.

Transportation: dependent on ships, planes for most goods; passengers arrive mostly by air; 26 airlines serve airport, 9 domestic carriers, 15 foreign, 2 inter-island.

Communications: 6 TV, 21 radio stations; 3 major daily newspapers.

Medical facilities: 21 civilian acute care hospitals, one military acute care hospital (Tripler Army Medical Center), 7 specialty long-term hospitals; Univ. of Hawaii School of Medicine.

Federal facilities: 7 major military bases, including Pearl Harbor Naval Base.

Cultural facilities: statewide public school system, 230 schools with 164,781 students in 1980; 132 private schools with 37,634 students in 1980; 9-campus Univ. of Hawaii; main campus at Manoa in Honolulu; university stresses oceanography, tropical environment problems and resources, tsunami research, volcanology, inter-race relations; East-West Center, Inc., at Manoa is public education corp. funded by federal government, attracts international students and researchers; Bernice Pauahi Bishop Museum is center for studies of Pacific cultures, houses artifacts, maintains floating square-rigger Falls of Clyde; Polynesian Cultural Center showcases native dances, music, arts; Honolulu Academy of Arts, Iolani Palace.

Recreation: surfing, swimming, sailing, fishing, football, basketball, baseball.

Other attractions: Waikiki Beach, extinct volcano Diamond Head, Arizona Memorial, balmy weather, tradewinds, multi-racial population, cultural diversity, Polynesian heritage.

History: Honolulu ("sheltered bay" in Hawaiian) was a small village when first westerners called aboard 2 British ships in 1786, 8 years after Capt. James Cook became first known European to discover Hawaiian Islands.

Further information: Hawaii Visitors Bureau, 2270 Kalakaua Avenue, Honolulu, HI 96815.

Houston, Texas

The World Almanac is sponsored in the Southwest by The Houston Post, 4747 Southwest Freeway, Houston, TX 77001; phone (713) 621-8000; founded in 1836; circulation daily 347,921, Saturday 366,168, Sunday 419,308; Oveta Culp Hobby, chairman of the board and editor; William P. Hobby, president; awards include Pulitzer Prize, Grand Prix, Editor & Publisher; community events sponsored: Educational Services, Science Engineering Fair, Scholastic Art Awards, Scholastic Writing Awards, travel shows, Houston Post Family Night at the Shrine Circus, the Rodeo, the Ice Capades, the Harlem Globetrotters, the Avon Championship Tennis Circuit, and the Southern Living Cooking Show.

Population: (city) 1,594,086, 5th in nation; 2,891,146 (SMSA); total employed (SMSA) 1.4 million; total wages and salaries (SMSA) $29 billion.
Area: 556 sq. mi. (city) on upper center Gulf Coast prairies, 49 ft. above sea level; Harris County seat; connected to Gulf of Mexico by 50-mile inland waterway, the Ship Channel.
Industry: nation's leading manufacturer in petrochemicals, 5th in machinery manufacturing and first in chemicals and allied products; supplies nation with over 50% petrochemicals, 80% synthetic rubber; produces $74.3 million in agriculture, $16.4 million in soybeans; over 500 firms in underwater, offshore, and oceanographic markets; world's petroleum refining capital.
Commerce: Houston-Galveston SCSA leads South and Southwest in retail sales volume; average spendable family income $25,265; 233 metro banks with resources of $34 billion and deposits of $27 billion; 53 foreign banks.
Transportation: Port of Houston (nation's 3d in tonnage) connects with 250 world ports by over 200 steamship lines, hosts 5,476 ships yearly; 25 major airlines, 2 airports; 5 major rail systems; 50 common-carrier truck lines; 210-mile freeway system; 1,016-mile bus transit system.
Communications: 2 daily newspapers; 29 radio stations; 5 commercial, one educational TV station.
New construction: non-residential contracts awarded $2.4 billion, residential units completed value $2 billion (1980).
Medical facilities: Texas Medical Center includes 26 major institutions on 225 acres; Harris County has 59 hospitals (including VA) with 16,401 beds, 30 ambulances, 3 emergency Life Flight helicopters.
Federal facilities: Lyndon B. Johnson Space Center, $202 million manned-spacecraft center, Ellington AFB.
Cultural facilities: $3 million Alley Theatre and Miller Outdoor Theatre; Houston Symphony Orchestra, Houston Grand Opera, Houston Ballet Foundation perform in $7.5 million Jones Hall for Performing Arts; 30 major art galleries including Museum of Fine Arts (permanent collection valued at $14 million) and Contemporary Art Museum; Houston Public Library, 26 branches; 4 bookmobiles; Harris County Public Library, 17 branches, 2 bookmobiles.

Education: 29 major universities including Rice, Univ. of Houston, Texas Southern; 7 major medical schools including Baylor College of Medicine and Univ. of Texas Health Science Center (8 branches); Houston Independent School District, 7th largest in nation; total enrollment 194,043; 22 school districts in Harris County, total enrollment 483,109; private and parochial school enrollment 30,000.
Recreational facilities: 272 parks, 5 municipal golf courses, 42 municipal swimming pools, 3 tennis centers with 54 courts and 82 neighborhood courts; Astroworld 65-acre amusement park; botanical garden arboretum, Hermann Park and Zoo; 55 community centers, 70 county parks, 70 miles of Gulf beaches in one hour's drive.
Convention facilities: 683 major conventions held in Houston in 1980 with 711,944 delegates attending; hotels and motels have 23,000 rooms; the Astrodome can seat 60,000 for conventions; Astrohall has 550,000 sq. ft.; downtown locations include Albert Thomas Convention Center, 300,000 sq. ft.; Sam Houston Coliseum, 50,000 sq. ft.; Music Hall seats 3,036; Exposition Hall, 83,000 sq. ft. exhibit area.
Sports: Astros baseball, Oilers football, Rockets basketball; sports events centers are Astrodome and Summit.
Climate: temperature moderated by winds from Gulf of Mexico, abundant rainfall; average daily temp. 69.8, total precip. 38.99 inches (1980).
Scientific facilities: one of the top 10 science centers in the nation; over 80 research firms maintain facilities for study in petroleum, chemicals, medicine, earth sciences, aerospace, oceanography.
History: founded 1836 by J.K. and A.C. Allen, city eventually encompassed Old Harrisburg which was an 1826 townsite laid out by John Harris; named for Gen. Sam Houston, commander of the Texas Army, which won independence from Mexico for the Republic of Texas Apr. 21, 1836. Houston was first president of the Republic, later governor of the state of Texas; both Houston and Harrisburg were for brief periods capitals of the republic.
Further information: Houston Convention and Visitor Council, 1522 Main Street; Houston Chamber of Commerce, 1100 Milam, both Houston, TX 77002.

Huntington, West Virginia

The World Almanac is sponsored in the Huntington-Ashland-Ironton area by The Herald-Dispatch (morn.), Huntington Publishing Company, 946 Fifth Avenue, Huntington, WV 25701; member of the Gannett Group; circulation 48,538 Sunday 50,483; publisher and president Harold E. Burdick, controller Ed Burns, executive editor C. Donald Hatfield.

Population: 63,684 (city), 376,100 (5-county metro area); largest city in the state.
Area: 15.86 sq. mi., on Ohio River near where West Virginia, Ohio, and Kentucky meet; Cabell County seat.
Industry: center for coal transport and for hand-crafted glass; leading industries are Ashland Oil, Armco Steel Co., Huntington Alloys, Inc., div. of International Nickel Co.
Commerce: largest port for inland vessels in U.S. handles nearly 20 million tons of materials per year, moved by 7 freight companies; 1978 total retail sales in metro area, $939.9 million.
Transportation: Tri-State Airport, with the longest runway in the state, is served by 2 airlines and 2 commuter airlines; Amtrak; 18 truck lines; urban bus transport system; 2 inter-

state bus lines.
Communications: 4 TV and 14 radio stations.
Cultural facilities: Marshall Univ.; Ashland Community College (Univ. of Kentucky); Huntington Galleries of Art.
Medical facilities: 6 general hospitals with 1,800 total beds; 3 specialty hospitals including a VA hospital.
New construction: $32 million renewal program includes downtown pedestrian shopping plaza, civic center and new city-county library; $18 million Henderson Center sports complex for Marshall Univ. and $125 million enclosed shopping mall; riverfront marina and parkland development being planned.
Further information: Chamber of Commerce, 522 Ninth Street, Huntington, WV 25701.

Indianapolis, Indiana

The World Almanac is sponsored in the Indianapolis area by The Indianapolis Star, The Indianapolis News, 307 N. Pennsylvania Street, Indianapolis, IN 46204; phone (317) 633-1240. News founded 1869, Star 1903; circulation daily Star, 220,292, daily News, 140,576, Sunday Star, 363,201; publisher Eugene S. Pulliam; president William A. Dyer Jr; Star editor John H. Lyst; News editor Dr. Harvey C. Jacobs; Pulitzer prizes-

News, Star; Nat'l. Headliners first prize-Star.

Population: 700,807 (city), 1,161,539 (SMSA); total employed 561,300.
Area: 379.4 sq. mi.; geographic center of state; state capital and Marion County seat.
Industry: over 1,520 diversified manufacturers including plane and auto engines and parts, electronics, pharmaceuticals, machinery; 1980 manufacturing payroll over $2.3 billion.
Commerce: commercial center for Indiana; retail sales $5.8 billion; per capita personal income $9,100; 6 banks with resources over $7.3 billion; home offices of over 60 insurance companies.
Transportation; 11 airlines; Indianapolis International Airport, 5 rail freight lines; Amtrak; 3 interstate bus lines; 65 truck lines; 7 interstate freeway routes.
Communications: 6 TV stations and 18 radio stations.
New construction: projects totalling over $370 million under construction in 1981.
Medical facilities: 17 hospitals, over 6,800 beds.
Federal facilities: Fort Harrison incl. Army Finance and Accounting Center, U.S.A. Admin. Center.
Cultural facilities: Museum of Art and Oldfields Museum of Decorative Arts; Indiana State Museum; Indianapolis Zoo; Children's Museum; Conner Prairie Pioneer Settlement and

Museum of Indiana Heritage; Clowes Hall, home of symphony orch.; Civic Theatre, oldest amateur theatrical group; repertory theater; Starlight Musicals.
Education facilities: Butler Univ., Indiana Central Univ., Marian College, Christian Theological and St. Mauer's seminaries, Purdue-Indiana Univ. at Indianapolis, Indiana Univ. medical center, nation's largest.
Recreation facilities: 13,000 park acres, 16 municipal swimming pools, 12 public golf courses; 18,000-seat domed sports arena, Indianapolis Sports Center.
Convention facilities: Indiana Convention-Exposition Center, Indiana State Fairgrounds.
Sports: home of the Pacers NBA; minor league baseball, soccer, hockey.
Other attractions: Indianapolis 500, Hoosier 100; annual National Drag Racing championships; U.S. open Clay Court championships.
History: important before Civil War, with nation's first union railway station (1853); home of James Whitcomb Riley, Booth Tarkington, and President Benjamin Harrison.
Additional information: Indianapolis Chamber of Commerce, 320 N. Meridian Street, Indianapolis, IN 46204; phone (317) 267-2900.

Jacksonville, Florida

The World Almanac is sponsored in the Jacksonville area by The Florida Times-Union and the Jacksonville Journal, One Riverside Avenue, Jacksonville, FL 32202; phone (904) 359-4111; circulation, Times-Union 152,976, Journal 47,401, combined Saturday 174,107, combined Sunday 197,940; publisher J.J. Daniel, president John A. Tucker; Journal won Pulitzer prize for photography in 1967.

Population: 540,898 (1980); total employment 225,700 (1981).
Area: 827 sq. mi., includes nearly all of Duval Co. in northeast Florida; under one consolidated government.
Industry: diversified economy; banking and insurance center.
Commerce: emphasis on finance distribution; home or regional headquarters for 24 insurance companies; 1980 retail sales $2.6 billion; effective buying income per household $19,458.
Transportation: 3 major railroads and Amtrak; over 40 truck lines; 8 airlines averaging 110 air movements daily; 2 interstate bus lines; the South Atlantic's major domestic distribution center located at Jacksonville Port, handled 15 million tons in 1979.
Communications: 6 TV stations, 2 cable TV systems, and 26 radio stations.
New construction: $422.5 million in building permits issued in 1980.
Medical facilities: 13 general hospitals and one naval hospital with total of 3,300 beds.
Federal facilities: 3 naval stations including the 2d largest

naval complex on East Coast add $556 million yearly to the economy.
Cultural facilities: Cummer Art Gallery, Jacksonville Art Museum, Museum of Arts and Sciences, Brest Planetarium, Marine Science Center, Jacksonville Symphony, Opera Repertory, Ballet Guild, 6 community theaters.
Education: Univ. of North Florida, Jacksonville Univ., Edward Waters, Florida Junior, and Jones colleges.
Sports: Gator Bowl; $400,000 Tournament Players Championships golf tournament; Jacksonville Univ. basketball and baseball; Murjani tennis tournament; pro football, soccer, and baseball.
Other attractions: civic auditorium, coliseum, Jacksonville Zoo, Fort Caroline, Kingsley Plantation; 8 miles of public beaches.
History: founded in 1822 by Isaiah Hart; named for Andrew Jackson; fire in 1901 destroyed 2,368 buildings, left 10,000 homeless; city and county governments merged in 1968 after referendum.
Further information: Chamber of Commerce, 3 Independent Drive, P.O. Drawer 329, Jacksonville, FL 32201; phone (904) 353-0300.

Kalamazoo, Michigan

The World Almanac is sponsored in the Kalamazoo area by The Kalamazoo Gazette, 401 S. Burdick, Kalamazoo, MI 49007; phone (616) 345-3511; founded 1833; circulation daily 61,155, Sunday 68,558; owned and operated by Booth Newspapers, Inc.; president Werner Veit, editor Daniel M. Ryan, manager Ralph H. Bastien Jr.

Population: 79,722 (city), 212,378 (county); total employed (Kalamazoo-Portage SMSA) 134,000.
Area: located equidistant to two of the largest metro areas in nation — Chicago and Detroit, 140 miles away; Kalamazoo County seat.
Industry: paper-making is the traditional industry with 5 large plants; Checker Motors Corp. manufactures cars; Fisher Body Division body stamping plant; Upjohn Co., pharmaceuticals.
Commerce: shopping center for large part of southwestern Michigan; in 1959, city became first in country to close downtown streets and create a pedestrian mall, now known as "Mall City;" 3 banks with combined assets in 1980 of $1 billion, 2 savings and loan assns. with assets over $600 million.

Communications: daily newspaper, one TV, 9 radio stations.
Transportation: 2 railroads provide freight service, Amtrak passenger service; 34 general carriers provide trucking services; airport with freight and passenger service; 3 bus lines.
Cultural facilities: 5 auditoriums offering music and theatrical performances; 5 live arts theaters, art center, symphony orchestra, Kalamazoo Civic Players.
Educational facilities: 3 colleges and one university.
Other attractions: Kalamazoo Nature Center, 83 lakes (county), National Junior Tennis Championships, 2 major hospitals, Kalamazoo Hilton Convention Center, IHL Kalamazoo Wings (hockey).
Further information: Kalamazoo County Chamber of Commerce, 500 W. Crosstown, Kalamazoo, MI 49008, phone (616) 381-4000.

Kansas City, Missouri

Population: 448,159 (city), 1,322,156 (SMSA); total employed 651,100 (SMSA).
Area: 3,341 sq. mi., SMSA, at confluence of Missouri and Kansas rivers in Jackson, Clay, and Platte counties.
Industry: recognized as the world's food capital; sales from farming and agriculture totaled $7.5 billion in 1979; top employers: U.S. government, General Motors, TWA, Bendix, Western Electric, Ford; city is a leading hard wheat center, stocker and feeder market, and is among the top 5 cities in flour production and grain elevator capacity.
Commerce: total retail sales (1980) over $6 billion; bank deposits (1980) $6.84 billion; the center of a 7-county metro area: Jackson, Clay, Platte, Cass, and Ray counties in Missouri; Johnson and Wyandotte counties in Kansas.
Transportation: 12 airlines with 434 scheduled arrivals and departures daily at Kansas City International Airport; 191 truck lines and several barge companies; city is one of the nation's major rail centers.
Communications: 6 TV stations, 14 AM, 19 FM radio stations, 7 daily newspapers in area.
New construction: Crown Center business and apartment complex covers 25 square blocks; $40 million, 750 room Hyatt Regency Hotel; $25 million Bannister Mall Shopping Center.
Cultural facilities: Starlight Theater, nation's 2d largest outdoor theater; William Rockhill Nelson Gallery of Art, among the 10 top American museums with one of the largest Oriental collections outside China; Performing Arts Foundation formed in 1965 to present festival events; Univ. of Missouri at Kansas City; Rockhurst College; Kansas City Art Institute; Univ. of Kansas Medical Center. Within commuting distance are Univ. of Kansas, Park College, William Jewell College, Truman Library in Independence. Linda Hall Library of Science and Technology is one of the largest privately endowed technical reference libraries in the nation.
Recreational facilities: more than 100 parks cover 5,345 acres, including Swope Park, 2d largest in nation, with zoo.
Sports: The American Royal Livestock and Horse Show each fall attracts entries from throughout the country; home of the NFL Chiefs, American League Royals, NBA Kings.
History: Kansas City's beginnings can be traced to a French trading post established in 1821 by Francois Chouteau. It became an important trade and transportation center as the overland routes of the Oregon and Santa Fe trails spread westward. As agricultural production boomed, it became an important market and distribution center for crops from throughout the middle west.

Further information: Chamber of Commerce of Greater Kansas City, 920 Main, Kansas City, MO 64105.

Kitchener-Waterloo, Ontario, Canada

The World Almanac is sponsored in the Kitchener-Waterloo area by the Kitchener-Waterloo Record, 225 Fairway Road S., Kitchener, Ont. N2G 4E5; phone (519) 894-2231; founded 1878; circulation 72,235; president and general manager Paul J. Motz, vice-president and publisher K. A. Baird

Population: 138,271 (Kitchener), 54,157 (Waterloo), 306,775 (Waterloo region); total employed 167,000.
Area: 51.74 sq. mi. (Kitchener) and 25.47 sq. mi. (Waterloo), 65 miles west of Toronto.
Industry: highly diversified industry (500 companies), rubber, plastics, electronics, metal fabrication, brewing, distilling, meat packing, footwear, furniture, food processing, automotive components; Budd Canada Inc., largest autoframe manufacturer in Canada; Arrow Shirt Co., largest shirt making facility under one roof in Canada. Annual gross product exceeds $2.27 billion.
Agricultural: hog and dairy area; Waterloo region's 1,588 farms (247,000 acres) accounted for $120 million production in 1978.
Commerce: wholesale and retail center for area; metro retail sales (1979) $1.27 billion; 10 banks, 63 branches; 15 trust companies, 25 branches; 41 life insurance offices, 29 other insurance offices; Waterloo, "The Hartford of Canada," head office for 6 insurance companies.
Transportation: 2 major rail lines, 34 truck lines, on Ontario's key highway 401; Waterloo-Wellington Airport; 45 mi. from Toronto International.
Communications: one TV and 4 radio stations; one daily, one weekly newspaper.
Medical facilities: 2 major hospitals.
Cultural facilities: symphony orchestra, Kitchener-Waterloo Art Gallery, Doon Pioneer Village; Centre in the Square, 28 mi. from Stratford, home of the Shakespearian Festival.
Educational facilities: Univ. of Waterloo, Wilfrid Laurier Univ., Conestoga College.
Other attractions: nationally-known farmers market; Canada's largest annual Oktoberfest celebration; Woodside, national historic park, boyhood home of W. L. Mackenzie King, Canadian prime minister 21 years.
History: founded 1807 by Pennsylvania German settlers; retains strong Germanic flavor.
Further information: Kitchener Chamber of Commerce, 67 King East; Waterloo Chamber of Commerce, 5 Bridgeport Road W.

Knoxville, Tennessee

The World Almanac is sponsored by The Knoxville News-Sentinel, 204 W. Church Avenue, Knoxville, TN 37901; Sentinel founded in 1886, News in 1921 by Scripps-Howard Newspapers; Sentinel purchased by Scripps-Howard in 1926 and combined with News; circulation 100,626 daily, 158,654 Sunday; president and business manager Roger A. Daley, editor Ralph L. Millett Jr., managing editor Harold E. Harlow.

Population: 183,139 (city), 319,298 (county), 476,517 (metro area), 3d in state; 213,300 total employed in metro area.
Area: 77.6 sq. mi. (city), 528 sq. mi. (county), located almost exact center of that portion of U.S. lying east of the Mississippi River and south of the Great Lakes; Knox County seat.
Industry: major manufacturing industries are chemicals and primary metals; nearly 300 plants representing 51 diversified major industries (coal and zinc mining, marble quarrying, meat packing, electronics, steel fabrication, industrial controls eqpt., furniture, auto safety eqpt., refuse eqpt., apparel), with Aluminum Co. of America, Union Carbide Corp. Nuclear Div. at Oak Ridge; headquarters for Magnovox Consumer Electronics Corp., Matsushita (Panasonic), London Fog, Levi Strauss, Allied Chemicals, Robertshaw-Fulton Controls, Rohm & Haas.
Commerce: wholesale and retail trade center of a multicounty area in east Tennessee, Virginia, Kentucky, and North Carolina; county retail sales (1980) $1.9 billion.
Transportation: 5 airlines, 2 commuter airlines. 2 interstate bus lines, 44 motor freight carriers; L & N and Southern railroads; interstate highways I-40 and I-75 intersect in heart of city, I-640 bypass under construction; Tennessee River barges.
New construction: downtown renewal continues, $172 million expended since 1972; $225 million in Interstate improvements underway; Art and Architecture bldg. nearing completion; $24 million sewer plant; Neyland Stadium (football) enclosed north end to complete bowl and increase seating to 92,000; 1982 World's Fair site preparation ($25 million); London Fog plant ($24 million), Panasonic plant underway.
Cultural facilities: Univ. of Tennessee, Knoxville College, Knoxville Symphony Orchestra, Knoxville Civic Opera, 13 museums, art gallery, auditorium-coliseum; city-county library (616,753 volumes), Zoological Park, University community theater, Clarence Brown Theater, choral society, opera workshop, Lamar House-Bijou Theater.

Sports: Univ. of Tennessee (all major collegiate sports), Knoxville College; Knoxville pro baseball; Golden Gloves boxing arena; Ivy Glenn, training base for professional boxer John Tate.

Other attractions: 1982 World's Fair on theme "Energy Turns The World," May 1-Oct 31; Great Smoky Mountains National Park, 39 miles from Knoxville, offers year-round scenic beauty, skiing in season; within 30 miles of Knoxville, with 9 million visitations annually; 8 TVA lakes, 3,673 miles of shoreline providing fishing, boating, swimming; Oak Ridge, known for its nuclear developments, 22 miles from Knoxville; American Museum of Atomic Energy and Oak Ridge National Lab; Dogwood Arts Festival held each April.

Further Information: Greater Knoxville Chamber of Commerce, P.O. Box 2229, or Knoxvisit, P.O. Box 15012, both Knoxville, TN 37901.

Las Vegas, Nevada

The World Almanac is sponsored in the Las Vegas area by the Las Vegas Review-Journal, P.O. Box 70, 1111 W. Bonanza, Las Vegas, NV 00126; phone (702) 383-0211; founded as a weekly in 1909; purchased 1956 by Donald W. Reynolds, present publisher; member Donrey Media Group; circulation 80,079 weekdays, 97,967 Sundays; general manager William Wright.

Population: 164,674 (city), 462,218 (SMSA), 461,816 (county), first in state; labor force 208,000, total employment 193,200 (county, '80 annual avg.).

Area: 55 sq. mi. (city), 275 sq. mi. (metro), near center of broad desert valley in southern Nevada; 290 mi. NE of Los Angeles, 283 mi. NW of Phoenix, one of 8 joined cities and unincorporated towns (metro); Clark County seat.

Industry: 24 hr. tourism, manufacturing (stone, clay, glass, food, chemicals), warehousing, mining; county employment: manuf. 6,900; mining 500; construction 13,800; transportation/utilities 13,100; wholesale/retail trade 45,300; finance/insurance/real estate 10,200; services 45,300 hotel/-gaming/recreation 70,500; government (excluding military) 34,500.

Commerce: total taxable sales $3.3 billion (county, 1980); average spendable family income $23,480; 6 commercial banks, $3.2 billion total deposits; 7 savings & loans with $1.9 billion savings deposits.

Transportation: McCarran Int'l Airport with 10.5 million passengers in 1980; 15 major carriers, 5 commuter lines, 17 air freight carriers; Union Pacific RR; Amtrak; 15 truck lines; 6 major van lines; 4 bus lines; U.S. highways 93 & 95, Interstate 15.

Communications: 5 TV stations (4 commercial, one PBS); 14 AM, 4 FM radio stations, one PBS; 3 daily newspapers.

Medical facilities: 8 hospitals, 1,679 beds; 20 convalescent and rest homes; 56 clinics.

Federal facilities: Nellis AFB, largest tactical fighter training base in world with 7.5 million acres combined air and ground area, home of Thunderbirds USAF Air Demonstration Squadron; 8,347 military, 1,014 civilian employees, $181 million payroll; Water & Power Resources Service, agency for Dept. of Interior, responsible for water in 17 western states.

Education: 76 elementary, 18 jr. high, 14 high schools, 2 spec. ed., one vo-tech, 32 private and church affiliated schools; one community college; Univ. of Nevada (UNLV).

Cultural facilities: Clark Co. Dist. Library; James R. Dickinson (Univ.) Library with Nevada gaming collections. Las Vegas Art League and Museum; Reed Whipple Cultural Arts Center; Judy Bayley Theatre; Artemus W. Ham Concert Hall; Las Vegas Civic Symphony; Nevada Dance Theatre; City Museum of Archeology; Southern Nevada Museum and Cultural Center; Rainbow Co. Children's Theatre.

Recreation: Lake Mead, Lake Mojave, Hoover Dam, Tule Springs, Valley of Fire, Red Rock Canyon area, Toiyabe National Forest (Mt. Charleston), Rogers Springs, Desert Nat'l Wildlife Range, Colorado River, skiing, boating, fishing, swimming, hiking, camping.

Sports: amateur and professional competition in tennis, golf, auto racing, bowling, basketball, boccie ball, boxing; UNLV sports competitions; Mint 400 Off Road race, Sahara Invitational golf tournament, Alan King tennis classic, WCT Challenge Cup, Pizza Hut basketball invitational, racquet ball.

History: first recorded group to enter the Las Vegas Valley was Antonio Armijo's party in early 1839. Las Vegas, Spanish for "The Meadows," first settled by Europeans in June 1855 by a 30-man Mormon group under William Bringhurst; city of Las Vegas founded May 15, 1905, as a result of public land auction by the railroad.

Further information: Las Vegas Chamber of Commerce, 2301 E. Sahara Avenue, Las Vegas, NV 89104, phone (702) 457-4664; Las Vegas Convention/Visitors Authority, 711 E. Desert Inn Road, Las Vegas, NV 89109, phone (702) 733-2323.

Lethbridge, Alberta, Canada

The World Almanac is sponsored in the Lethbridge area by The Lethbridge Herald, 504 7th Street S., Lethbridge, Alberta; phone (403) 328-4411; founded as a daily in 1907; circulation weekdays 28,712, Saturdays 30,727; publisher Don Doram, managing editor Klaus Pohle.

Population: 54,624.

Area: 25 sq. mi.; located on Oldman River, 60 miles north of Montana border, 130 miles south of Calgary.

Industry: based on agriculture; 3 federally-inspected packing plants slaughtered 30% of the cattle slaughtered in Alberta in 1980; more than one million acres of irrigated farms produce sugar beets, market and processing vegetables, grains; much larger dryland area growing grains and rapeseed; vast ranching and cattle-feeding operations; brewery, distillery, flour mill, food processing plants, oilseed processing plants; foundry, recreation vehicle, mobile home, truck body, boat and farm machinery manufacturing.

Commerce: 1980 retail sales $410 million, 16% more than 1979; 7 banks, 6 trust companies, 3 credit unions, 11 finance companies; 5 major shopping malls; distributing center for area of 155,000 people.

Transportation: CP Rail, 2 bus lines, depots for 50 trucking firms, regional airline to major Alberta cities.

Communications: one newspaper; 2 TV, 3 radio stations.

New construction: building permits totalled $88.3 million in 1980, compared with $59.6 million in 1979; relocation of CP railyards from downtown will free 135 acres for redevelopment in the 1980s.

Medical facilities: 2 general hospitals (plans for new 330-bed hospital), one long-term care hospital, 3 nursing homes, 4 senior citizens retirement lodges.

Education and culture: Lethbridge Agriculture Centre is Canada's 2d largest; Univ. of Lethbridge, Lethbridge Comm. College; Alexander Galt Museum, Nikka Yuko Centennial Japanese Garden, Fort Whoop-Up, replica of historic fort; Lethbridge Symphony Orchestra and Chorus, Bowman Arts Centre, Yates Memorial Centre.

Other attractions: 4 large parks, 5 artificial ice arenas, 3 golf courses, 3 indoor and 2 outdoor swim pools, Sportsplex (arena), exhibition grounds, Sick's Brewery Gardens.

Sports: Lethbridge Dodgers, farm team of L.A. Dodgers; Broncos, Western Canada Jr. Hockey League; Dusters, Continental Basketball League.

History: early coal-mining town; Coalbanks, renamed Lethbridge Oct. 16, 1885, after coal co. official; a whiskey-trader's depot, Fort Whoop-Up was booming 5 mi. south-

west of Lethbridge in 1860s; first settlers came 15 years later, many from the U.S., others from Europe.
Further information: Lethbridge Chamber of Commerce,

309 Canada Trust Building, 304 7th Street S., Lethbridge, Alta. T1J 2G3; Travel and Convention Association of Southern Alberta, 2805 Scenic Drive, Lethbridge, Alta.

Lexington, Kentucky

The World Almanac is sponsored in central and eastern Kentucky by the Lexington Herald-Leader Co., publishers of the Lexington Leader (afternoon daily, circulation 33,963), the Lexington Herald (morning daily, circulation 70,151), and the Sunday Herald-Leader (circulation 111,188), all Knight-Ridder newspapers; publisher and chairman Creed Black, president and general manager Ray Frazier, vice-president and Herald editor John Carroll, vice-president and Leader editor Steve Wilson, vice-president of marketing Lewis Owens, vice-president of production Phil Eaton.

Population: 204,165, 316,098 SMSA.
Area: 283 sq. mi.; 2d largest city in Kentucky, located in central Kentucky, 80 miles east of Louisville, 84 miles south of Cincinnati; Fayette County seat.
Industry: shipping and wholesale center for central and eastern Kentucky; livestock and general farming area; horse breeding and sales; loose leaf tobacco production and market.
Commerce: (1979) retail sales urban-county $1.1 billion, SMSA 1.4 billion; effective buying income per household $22,000; 8 commercial banks with $1.2 billion in deposits; 4 savings and loan assns. with assets of $248 million; 9 mortgage companies.
Transportation: Chesapeake and Ohio, Southern, Louisville and Nashville railroads; 30 motor freight companies; Frontier, Delta, Piedmont, USAir, Air Kentucky airlines; LexTran city bus service.
Communications: newspapers: Lexington Herald (morn.), Lexington Leader (eve.), Sunday Herald-Leader; 3 commercial TV stations, one state educational TV network; CATV; 4 AM, 3 FM radio stations.
New construction: (1980) 5,150 building permits totalling $177 million.
Medical facilities: 4 general hospitals (incl. Univ. of Kentucky Medical Center), 1,505 beds; 5 specialized hospitals with 1,714 beds; 950 physicians, 2,146 registered nurses; 607 LPN's, 222 dentists, 16 optometrists, 250 pharmacists.
Cultural facilities: Lexington Council of the Arts; Lexington

Philharmonic Orchestra; Kentucky Guild of Artists and Craftsmen; Lexington Ballet Co.; Studio Players; Univ. of Kentucky School of Fine Arts; Lexington Opera House; Ashland, home of Henry Clay; Blue Grass Trust for Historic Preservation.
Religion. 197 churches and synagogues representing 34 denominations.
Education: 34 elementary schools; 10 junior, 5 senior high schools; 6 parochial schools; Univ. of Kentucky; Transylvania Univ.; Lexington Theological Seminary; Lexington Baptist College; Lexington Technical Institute, Episcopal Theological Seminary; 9 business and secretarial schools.
Sports and Recreation: Keeneland (thoroughbred racing), The Red Mile (harness racing), Kentucky Horse Park; Univ. of Kentucky basketball and football; 65 neighborhood playgrounds and community parks, 22 motion picture theaters, 8 private country clubs, 4 public golf courses.
Convention facilities: Lexington Convention Center including 23,000-seat Rupp Arena; 32 hotels and motels with 4,500 rooms.
History: incorporated as a township in May of 1781; a leading manufacturing center of the early West for hemp goods, nails, and gunpowder; early site of cotton and furniture factories, breweries and distilleries; known as "Athens of the West" due to Transylvania Univ., first institution of higher learning west of the Allegheny Mountains.
Further information: Greater Lexington Chamber of Commerce, 421 North Broadway, Lexington, KY 40508.

Little Rock, Arkansas

The World Almanac is sponsored in the Little Rock area by the Arkansas Gazette, 112 West Third Street, Little Rock, AR 72203; phone (501) 371-3700; founded 1819 at Arkansas Post, A.T., by Wm. E. Woodruff, moved to Little Rock 1821; circulation 128,740 daily, 154,875 Sunday; Hugh B. Patterson Jr., publisher and president; Carrick H. Patterson, executive editor; J. O. Powell, editorial director; Robert R. Douglas, managing editor; J. R. Williamson, senior vice president; John T. Meriwether, vice president and general manager.

Population: 158,461 (city), 393,781 (SMSA); 182,000 employed (metro, June 1980).
Area: 51 sq. mi. (city), 781.0 sq. mi. (county); state capital and Pulaski County seat.
Industry: (metro) 350 manufacturing plants, employing 30,000 persons, including Allis-Chalmers, Armstrong Rubber Co., Timex, Remington Arms, Jacuzzi Bros., Teletype, Westinghouse, CPC, International, and General Electric.
Commerce: retail sales (est. 1979) $2.1 billion; bank resources (Jan. 1979) $2 billion; 11 banks, 6 building & loan associations, 4 old line insurance companies.
Transportation: 2 railroads, 6 federally certified airlines, 3 interstate bus lines, one inter-city line, 33 truck lines, 12 common carrier barge lines.
Communications: 3 commercial TV, one ETV, 14 radio stations; 2 daily, one weekly newspaper.
Medical facilities: 10 hospitals including UA Medical Sciences campus, 2 VA hospitals, and Ark. State Hospital for Nervous Diseases.
Federal facilities: Little Rock AFB, Tactical Airlift Wing;

Camp Joseph T. Robinson, Arkansas National Guard headquarters and training center; U.S. National Guard Bureau's Non-Commissioned Officers Institute.
Education: Univ. of Arkansas at Little Rock with Schools of Law, Medicine, Nursing, and Pharmacy; UA Graduate Institute of Technology; Philander Smith, Shorter and Arkansas Baptist colleges; 112 public schools; 27 private and special schools.
Cultural facilities: Arkansas Symphony, Arkansas Arts Center, 3 major public libraries, convention center-auditorium-hotel; Arkansas Repertory Theatre; Arkansas Territorial Restoration and Museum of Science & Natural History.
History: French explorer Bernard de la Harpe noted "le petit roche" on his map of the Arkansas River Valley in 1722.
Further information: Greater Little Rock Chamber of Commerce, One Spring Building; Arkansas Parks & Tourist Dept., State Capitol; both Little Rock, AR 72201.

Los Angeles, California

The World Almanac is sponsored in Los Angeles by the Los Angeles Herald Examiner, 1111 S. Broadway, Los Angeles, CA 90015, phone (213) 744-8000; Los Angeles Examiner founded 1903 by Wm. R Hearst, merged Los Angeles Herald Express 1962; circulation 285,099 daily, 303,724 Sunday; Francis L. Dale publisher, James G. Bellows editor, Theodore P. Grassl general manager, David W. Feldman director of sales.

Population: 2,966,763 (city), 7,477,657 (county), 5-county urban area 11 million; first in state, 2d urban area in U.S.; total civilians employed 3.3 million (county, 1979); labor force 3.5 million (county, 1979).

Area: 463.7 sq. mi. on Pacific, 418 mi. south of San Francisco, 145 mi. north of Mexico; Los Angeles County seat; one of 81 cities in county.

Industry: leading aerospace industry with 7 of the top 10 defense contractors in the nation located in the area; center of entertainment industry with more than 600 firms in movie and television entertainment work. Women's clothing, sportswear, electronics, rubber tires, printing, furniture, paper, autos, auto parts, chemicals, manufacturing. Work force (county, 1979): agriculture, forestry, and fishing 21,029; mining 12,037, construction 120,947, transport and utilities 193,007, trade 815,914 (266,176 wholesale, 549,738 retail); finance, insurance, and real estate 226,897, services 782,481, government 386,826, manufacturing 926,791; 2d largest county in mfg. activity, $52.3 million in total shipments. Among top 20 counties in U.S. in agricultural production; farm income $219.3 million (county '79); livestock (dairy, eggs, meat) production $59.6 million; sea fish harvested 490.4 million pounds (county '77).

Commerce: total taxable retail sales $41.7 billion (county '79), $15 billion (city '79); median family income $20,046; personal income $66.6 billion (county '78); 81 banks, 1,131 branches, savings and loans with 746 branches; bank deposits $35.5 billion (June '78); S&L savings $35.8 billion (Mar. '81).

Transportation: Santa Fe, Union Pacific, Southern Pacific railroads; Amtrak; Continental, Greyhound bus lines; Southern California Rapid Transit District serving 2,280 mi. with 3,050 buses plus other local and intercity bus lines; Airport Transit Bus and Gray Line tours; 5.3 million vehicles (county, Dec. '80), one of largest concentrations in nation — 4.0 million autos, 743,629 trucks, 192,902 motorcycles, 345,584 trailers; 156.6 mi. freeway (city) 491.2 (county); airlines (50 commuter, 5 cargo) serving Los Angeles International airport, 523,961 takeoffs and landings, 33.4 million passengers, 881,890 tons cargo ('80); 9 other airports; more than 46 miles of commercial waterfront in Los Angeles-Long Beach Harbor, with value of $26 billion in 1980. 8,600 ships, 90 million tons cargo.

Communications: 19 TV stations (10 UHF, 9 VHF), 71 radio stations, 65 commercial; more than 90 newspapers in English and foreign languages, 14 publishing daily (county).

New construction: residential building permits 27,883 units: single family 8,121; multiple 19,762 (county, '80).

Medical facilities: 822 hospitals and clinics with 80,252 beds, including 180 general care hospitals, 39,154 beds, 22 psychiatric, 2,076 beds, 409 nursing homes, 38,665 beds (county, Mar. '78).

Educational facilities: 1,156 elementary, 190 jr. high, 153 sr. high, 77 continuation, 66 adult, approx. 800 private all levels (county '80); 61 libraries (city) plus 91 others in the county; UCLA, Univ. Southern Cal., California Institute of Technology; Loyola, Marymount, Pepperdine universities; Claremont, Woodbury, Occidental, Whittier, Mt. St. Mary colleges; 21 community colleges; campuses of California State University-Los Angeles, Long Beach, Northridge, Dominguez Hills.

Cultural facilities: 1,838 churches, Huntington Art Gallery and Library, Hollywood Bowl, Greek Theater, Music Center, Mark Taper Forum, Ahmanson Theater, Huntington Hartford Theater, Griffith Park Planetarium, Mt. Wilson and Mt. Palomar observatories; Los Angeles Museum, County Art Museum, UCLA Botanical Gardens, La Brea Tar Pits and natural history museum, Southwest Museum.

Recreational facilities: more than 300 city parks and recreation centers, plus 122 county parks; 14 public golf courses, 15 /public beaches within 35 miles of city center; ocean, mountains, desert, lakes, forests; Disneyland, Marineland, Knott's Berry Farm, Lion County Safari, Universal Movie Studio tour.

Convention facilities: approx. 20,000 hotel rooms (city), 50,000 (county); large convention center.

Sports: collegiate sports including Rose Bowl; pro teams in baseball (Dodgers), basketball (Lakers), hockey (Kings), soccer (Aztecs).

History: discovered 1542 by Portuguese navigator Juan Rodriguez Cabrillo; Mission San Gabriel founded Sept., 1771; city formally founded Sept. 4, 1781 by Spanish colonial governor as El Pueblo de Nuestra Senora la Reina de los Angeles de Porciuncula; inc. April 4, 1850.

Further information: Chamber of Commerce, P.O. Box 3696, Terminal Annex, Los Angeles, CA 90051.

Louisville, Kentucky

The World Almanac is sponsored in Kentucky and southern Indiana by The Courier-Journal and The Louisville Times, 525 West Broadway, Louisville, KY 40202; phone (502) 582-4011; Courier-Journal founded 1868, Times 1884; Courier circulation 186,348, Times 149,423, Sunday 327,565; chairman of the board Barry Bingham Sr., editor and publisher Barry Bingham Jr.; major awards include 8 Pulitzer prizes.

Population: 298,451 (city), 901,970 (SMSA); first in state; total employed 403,500 (SMSA).

Area: 65.2 sq. mi. (city), 1,392 sq. mi. (metro); on southern bank of Ohio River.

Industry and Commerce: 14th in total industrial shipments; famous for baseball bats, cigarettes, railroad repair shops, electrical appliances, farm machinery, motor vehicles, plumbing fixtures, and whiskey; 1,011 manufacturing firms in area; estimated retail sales (Jefferson County, 1980) $3.698 billion.

Transportation: 6 trunk-line railroads, one terminal railroad, 100 inter-city truck lines; 5 barge lines; 2 bus lines; 8 airlines, and 2 municipal airports.

Communications: 20 radio and 4 TV stations, 2 educational.

Medical facilities: 21 hospitals, 6,000 total beds.

Cultural facilities: Louisville Orchestra, Kentucky Opera Association, Art Center Association, J.B. Speed Art Museum; 20 private art galleries, Macauley Theatre, Actors Theatre, The Children's Theatre, Louisville Civic Ballet, Louisville-Jefferson County Youth Orchestra, The Louisville Free Public Library (20 branches); 700 churches, 40 denominations.

Education: 10 colleges and universities, 3 business colleges and technical schools in area.

New construction: First phase of 1.75 million sq. ft. downtown Galleria; $26 million Performing Arts Complex in downtown area to be completed in 1983.

Recreation: 158 public parks, covering more than 7,000 acres.

Convention facilities: Kentucky Fair & Exposition Center, largest ground-level exhibit hall and auditorium complex in North America with 650,000 sq. ft., 20,000-plus seating, parking for 27,000 cars; 100,000 sq. ft. Commonwealth Convention Center in downtown Louisville; Louisville Gardens, downtown, handles up to 7,000.

Sports: Kentucky Derby, held annually at Churchill Downs since 1875; Louisville Downs harness racing.

Other: Belle of Louisville excursion steamboat; Churchill Downs Museum; Louisville Zoo, American Printing House for the Blind; Kentucky Railway Museum; Museum of History and Science; Cave Hill Cemetery.

History: founded by explorer George Rogers Clark in 1778; named after King Louis XVI of France.

Further information: Louisville Area Chamber of Commerce, 300 West Liberty, Louisville, KY 40202.

Lubbock, Texas

The World Almanac is sponsored in the Lubbock area by the Lubbock Avalanche-Journal, 8th Street and Avenue J, Lubbock, TX 79408; phone (806) 762-8844; founded 1900 as Leader, became Avalanche 1908, daily 1921; Plains Journal weekly founded 1923, consolidated 1926; circulation (morn.) 55,997, (eve.) 14,602, (Sat.) 65,951, (Sun.) 78,613; member Southwestern Newspaper Corp.; general manager Robert Norris, editor

Jay Harris.

Population: 173,979 (city), 211,861 (SMSA); 100,210 total employed.

Area: 82.2 sq. mi.; center of South Plains territory of northwest Texas; Lubbock County seat.

Industry: vegetable oils, cotton seed flour, grain sorghum, livestock, petroleum, sand and gravel; 250 manufacturing companies.

Commerce: wholesale and retail center for west Texas and eastern New Mexico; retail sales $2.306 billion; bank resources $1.203 billion; 9 banks.

Transportation: 13 motor freight carriers; 2 major railroads, bus line; Lubbock International Airport, with 6 major airlines averaging 80 flights per day; 6 major federal and state highways.

Communications: 4 TV and 16 radio stations.

Medical facilities: 8 hospitals, Lubbock State School for Mentally Retarded; Texas Tech Medical School.

Federal facilities: Reese AFB, federal building, Federal Aviation Admin., and National Weather Service, U.S. Customs port of entry.

Cultural facilities: symphony orchestra, Theatre Centre; Museum of Texas Tech Univ., Moody Planetarium; Ranching Heritage Center (authentic ranch houses dating to 1835), Lubbock Christian College; Texas Tech Univ., Lubbock Cultural Affairs Council, Lubbock Garden & Arts Center.

Recreational facilities: 55 city parks, 3,000 acres, Mackenzie State Park, state's largest, with Prairie Dog Town; Buffalo Lakes, Canyon Lakes-Parks; 3,200-seat Municipal Auditorium, 10,000-seat Municipal Coliseum, annual Panhandle South Plains Fair; Lubbock Memorial Civic Center, modern convention facility with 200,000 sq. ft. including 44,000 sq. ft. exhibit hall with banquet facilities for 1,400, auditorium seating 1,400.

Sports: Texas Tech, and Lubbock Christian college sports; Tech Jones Stadium, indoor rodeos.

Further information: Chamber of Commerce, P.O. Box 561, Lubbock, TX 79408.

Lynchburg, Virginia

The World Almanac is sponsored in the Lynchburg area by The News and the Daily Advance, PO Box 131, Lynchburg, VA 24505; phone (804) 237-2941; published by Carter Glass & Sons, Publishers, Inc.

Population: 66,743 (city).

Area: 50 sq. mi.

Commerce: retail sales $379 million (1980).

Industry: Babcock & Wilcox, nuclear energy; General Electric, communications systems; Lynchburg Foundry, metal castings; C.B. Fleet, pharmaceuticals; Craddock-Terry, shoes; Meredith Burda, rotogravure printing; Simplimatic Engineering; Limitorque Corp., machinery manufacturer.

Transportation: 20 trucking firms; airport served by Piedmont and Air Virginia airlines; Southern, N&W, and C&O railroads and Amtrak; metropolitan bus fleet.

Communications: WSET television; cablevision; 11 radio stations; The News (morning) and The Daily Advance (afternoon) newspapers.

New construction: $61.1 million in 1980.

Medical facilities: Virginia Baptist Hospital with 313 beds and Lynchburg General Hospital with 270 beds and a 110-bed extended care facility; cooperative agreement between the hospitals prevents duplication of services.

Cultural facilities: Fine Arts Center which offers drama, music, and visual arts year round; Point of Honor Museum, Old Courthouse, Dabney Scott House, Adams House, Miller-Claytor House, Anne Spencer House, Monument Terrace, all historic landmarks; 94 churches representing some 30 faiths; Thomas Road Baptist Church (18,000 members), one of the largest churches in the nation.

Education: 2 high schools, 3 junior high schools, 14 elementary schools with an 18/1 pupil-teacher ratio; Lynchburg, Randolph-Macon Woman's, and Liberty Baptist 4-year colleges.

Recreation: 9 parks covering 343 acres, Blackwater Creek Natural Area (288 acres), 12 horseshoe pits, 2 public swimming pools, 35 tennis courts; city stadium with baseball seating capacity of 4,216 and football capacity of 14,200; 7 playlots; public library with 100,000 items; 18 play areas, 6 senior citizen centers.

Sports: Lynchburg Mets baseball; interscholastic and intercollegiate sports including football, baseball, basketball, swimming, tennis, wrestling, and track; Lynchburg 10-miler for amateur runners is an annual event attracting over 4,000 runners from all over the country.

History: began as a tobacco trading center in the early 1800s; named after John Lynch.

Macon, Georgia

The World Almanac is sponsored in the Macon area by the Macon Telegraph & News, 120 Broadway, Macon, GA 31213; phone (912) 744-4200; acquired by Knight-Ridder Newspapers, Inc., 1969; circulation Telegraph (morn.) 51,781 News (eve.) 19,282, Saturday 66,569, Sunday 85,859. Publisher Bert Struby, general manager Edmund E. Olson, executive editor Billy Watson, News editor Ed Corson.

Population: 116,860 city, 254,623 metro, 4th in state; metro civilian labor force 98,150.

Area: 52 sq. mi., 6 miles northwest of geographical center of Georgia; Bibb County seat.

Industry: Bibb Co., textile industry leader and largest industrial employer, headquartered in area; other textile-related are YKK Zipper Co. of Japan and Texprint; Armstrong Cork Co. acoustical tile plant is one of area's largest; Georgia Kraft container board manufacturer; Brown & Williamson Tobacco Corp.; Keebler Co. cracker manufacturing plant; Georgia Steel Inc., fabricated plate work and structural steel; Inland Container, corrugated shipping containers; Levi Strauss, clothing manufacturer. Kaolin deposits are mined in area; Government Employees Insurance Co. regional office; Boeing, Inc. cargo handling system.

Transportation: Central of Georgia, Southern, Georgia, and Seaboard railroads; 28 motor freight carriers; Intercity Bus Lines; Trailways, Greyhound bus lines; Delta and Atlantic Southeastern airlines.

Medical facilities: Bibb County has 5 hospitals located in Macon with 1,088 beds; the Macon-Bibb County Public Health Department serves Bibb, Jones, and Twiggs counties.

Federal facilities: Robins AFB including Warner Robins Air Logistics Center, 16 miles from Macon, is Georgia's largest employer.

Educational facilities: Wesleyan College, nation's oldest college for women; Mercer Univ. with law school; Macon Junior College.

Other attractions: Ocmulgee National Monument is largest archeological development east of the Mississippi disclosing 6 different Indian group occupancies and restored Indian mounds and lodges; $4.5 million coliseum seats 10,000.

History: Fort Hawkins established in 1806; chartered in 1823, named for Nathaniel Macon of North Carolina.

Further information: Macon Chamber of Commerce, 305 Coliseum Drive, Macon, GA 31201; phone (912) 746-7601.

Madison, Wisconsin

The World Almanac is sponsored in Madison by Madison Newspapers, Inc., publisher of The Capital Times and the Wisconsin State Journal, 1901 Fish Hatchery Road, Madison, WI 53713; phone (608) 252-6100; circulation, Wisconsin State Journal (morn.) 76,479, The Capital Times (eve.) 33,938, combined daily 110,417, Sunday Wisconsin State Journal 127,377.

Population: 170,616 (city), 323,109 (SMSA), 2d in state; metro work force 176,000.

Area: 52 sq. mi. (city), 1,194 sq. mi. (metro/county) in south central Wisconsin; state capital and Dane County seat.

Commerce: home office of 29 insurance firms, 375 industrial firms, 28 banks, 10 savings and loans; 25 major shopping areas; 1980 retail sales $1.5 billion; average effective buying income $22,500; city has AAA financial rating.

Transportation: Dane County Regional Airport serving 700,000 passengers and 5 million lbs. of freight; 3 airlines, 3 railroads, 2 interstate highways (I-90, I-94); 4 bus lines, 30 common carriers, city owned bus system.

Communications: 3 commercial and one public TV stations, commercial (one AM and 3 FM) radio stations; 2 daily and 17 weekly newspapers (metro/county).

Medical facilities: 9 hospitals (5 general, 4 specialized) including Univ. of Wis. and VA; 20 major clinics, approx. 1,200 physicians.

Federal facilities: Forest Products Laboratory, National Fish and Wildlife Laboratory.

Cultural facilities: Dane County Coliseum, Madison Civic Center, 2 art centers, 2 museums, dinner playhouse, 11 drama groups, ballet company, symphony and 7 other music organizations; approx. 330 churches representing 45 denominations.

Education: Univ. of Wisconsin; Edgewood, Madison Business, Madison Area Technical colleges; 35 elementary, 10 middle, 4 high schools, 14 parochial, one vocational-technical; 7 city and 32 university libraries.

Recreation: 5 lakes with total of 18,000 acres of water surface, approx. 4,700 acres of parks; Vilas Zoo, Univ. of Wis. Arboretum, 9 golf courses.

Convention facilities: Dane County Coliseum, 5 major convention size hotels, 55 supper clubs; Greater Madison Convention and Visitor's Bureau (425 W. Washington, Madison, WI 53703).

Sports: Univ. of Wisconsin in Big Ten, football, basketball, hockey and other major sports.

Other attractions: weekly Farmer's Market (May-Oct.), World Dairy Exposition headquarters, annual Winter Spirit Festival, numerous political organizations; All-American city.

Further information: Greater Madison Chamber of Commerce, 625 W. Washington Avenue, Madison, WI 53701; phone (608) 256-8348.

Memphis, Tennessee

The World Almanac is sponsored in the Memphis area by The Memphis Press-Scimitar, 495 Union Avenue, Memphis, TN 38101; phone (901) 529-2500; Scimitar founded 1880 by G.P.M. Turner; Press 1906 by Scripps-McRae League, predecessor of Scripps-Howard Newspapers; circulation 100,119; editor Milton R. Britten, managing editor Van Pritchartt Jr.

Population: 646,356 (city), 909,767 (SMSA); first in state; 389,100 employed.

Area: 290 sq. mi. on east bank of the Mississippi River; Shelby County seat.

Industry: extensive cotton marketing-warehousing and processing of cotton seed into vegetable oil products; headquarters of Holiday Inns Inc., Federal Express Co. (air freight), and Conwood Corp. (tobacco and food products); other large industries include Schering-Plough (drugs), International Harvester (cotton pickers, hay balers), and Firestone (tires).

Commerce: wholesale-retail center for large parts of Tennessee, Arkansas, and Mississippi; retail sales (1980) $3.6 billion; bank deposits $2.7 billion; 9 banks, 5 savings-loan assns.; per capita personal income $7,556.

Transportation: 15 airlines, 42 air freight companies, 5.2 million air passengers (1980); 6 trunk line railroads, 97 motor freight lines, 6 barge lines.

Communications: 5 TV and 24 radio stations, 2 daily newspapers.

Medical facilities: 18 hospitals housing 7,104 beds, 13 full-time clinics, 1,784 doctors, 504 dentists, 13 long-term care facilities housing 3,113 beds.

Federal facilities: Naval Air Station, Naval Air Technical Training Center, Defense Depot Memphis, and Air Force's 164th Air Transport Group.

Cultural facilities: Memphis Symphony Orchestra, opera theater, Theatre Memphis, Brooks Art Gallery, Chucalissa Indian Village & Museum, Memphis Museum; annual performances of Metropolitan Opera.

Educational facilities: Memphis State Univ., Southwestern, LeMoyne-Owen, Christian Brothers colleges; U-T Center for Health Sciences, Shelby State Comm. College, State Technical Institute, Southern College of Optometry, Memphis Academy of Arts, Mid-South Bible College; 160 public elementary-secondary schools, 100 private schools, 22 public library branches offer 1.5 million volumes.

Recreational facilities: Meeman-Shelby Forest state park, 190 other parks, 21 golf courses, 16 public swimming pools, 13 country clubs.

Convention facilities: Cook Convention Center, 1.3 million sq. ft, seating 17,000; 49 hotels & motels with 9,331 total rooms.

Sports: Liberty Bowl, home of Memphis State Univ. football, site of Liberty Bowl game; Mid-South Coliseum, home of MSU basketball team; Memphis Chicks, Southern League baseball; Danny Thomas Memphis Classic golf tournament; Memphis Americans, professional indoor soccer team; U. S. National Indoor Tennis Championships.

Other attractions: Cotton Carnival each May; Mid-South Fair each Sept., Libertyland theme park, Beale St., home of the blues where composer W. C. Handy lived; Mid-America Mall; Graceland, home and burial site of Elvis Presley.

History: DeSoto, exploring Mississippi River, stopped here in 1541; Ft. Adams est. in 1797; Memphis inc. in 1826; yellow fever in 1878 nearly depopulated city, but its population grew back to 64,589 in 1890.

Further information: Memphis Area Chamber of Commerce, 555 Beale Street, Memphis, TN 38103.

Mexico City (Ciudad de Mexico), Mexico

Population: 15,000,000 (1980 est. metro. area).

Area: about 53 sq. mi. within the 573 sq. mi. Federal District (Distrito Federal; population, 1979 est. 9.2 million); in central Mexico at an altitude of 7,349 ft.

Industry and commerce: capital of Mexico; the political and economic hub of the nation; manufactures include steel, automobiles, appliances, textiles, rubber goods, furniture, and electrical equipment; marketing center of Mexico.

Transportation: center of modern highway and rail system; 25-mi. subway system is being extended and will eventually extend 40 to 50 miles; served by most international air lines, Mexico City is 4 hrs. by jet from New York and 3 hrs. from Los Angeles.

Communications: major media center for Mexico and parts of Latin America; major film center.

Cultural facilities: cultural capital of Latin America: Palace of Fine Arts and Ballet Folklorico; National Palace (Diego Rivera murals); National University with over 90,000 students; National Museum of Anthropology; Polyforum Cultural Siqueiros, containing world's largest mural; 4 symphony orchestras; city itself is an architectural exhibit of Aztec ruins, baroque cathedrals, and ultra-modern buildings.

Other attractions: Xochimilco with the "floating gardens" and gondolas; Chapultepec Castle, palace of the French-

supported Emperor and Empress of Mexico, Maximilian and Carlota; 22-ton Aztec Calendar Stone; 2 volcanoes, Popocatepetl (17,887 ft.) and Iztaccihuatl (17,343 ft.); sports centers.
History: traditionally founded 1321 by Aztecs, city was called Tenochtitlan; captured by Spanish under Cortez in

1519 and again in 1521; occupied by the U.S. in 1847 and by the French from 1863 to 1867.
Further information: Mexican National Tourist Council, Mariano Escobedo 726, Mexico, D.F., or 405 Park Avenue, NY 10022; or 9701 Wilshire Boulevard, Beverly Hills, CA 90212.

Miami, Florida

The World Almanac is sponsored in the Miami area by The Miami Herald, 1 Herald Plaza, Miami, FL 33101; phone (305) 350-2111; founded Dec. 1, 1910, by Frank B. Shutts; circulation (1981) 444,860 daily, 545,898 Sunday; chairman James L. Knight, executive editor John McMullan, editor Jim Hampton, managing editor Heath Meriweather; newspaper or staff writers have won or shared in 6 Pulitzer prizes, and numerous other honors.

Population: 346,931 (city), 1,573,817 (SMSA); first in state; total employed in metro area, 621,100 (1980 average).
Area: 53.8 sq. mi. land and water, on Biscayne Bay at mouth of Miami River in southeast Florida; largest of 28 municipalities in Dade County; Dade County seat.
Industry: 5,000 light manufacturing plants; tourism and aviation are mainstays of economy; 779 hotels and motels with 60,069 rooms handle 15 million visitors a year; aviation hub with Eastern (largest industrial employer) headquarter base; winter agriculture center.
Commerce: center of Latin American finance and commerce with more than 100 banks, 16 savings and loan associations, 14 foreign banks, and 15 Edge Act banks; largest concentration of international banks outside New York; annual retail sales total nearly $5 billion; Port of Miami is the largest cruise center in world with 24 liners and 1.7 million passengers (1980); 2 duty-free trade zones, with one million sq. ft. of space.
Transportation: Miami International, served by 109 air carriers, handled more than 22 million travelers in 1980; Seaboard Coast Line, Amtrak, and all-freight Fla. East Coast Railroads operate in Miami, as do Greyhound and Trailways buses; 65 truck lines.
Communications: 6 commercial and 5 educational or closed-circuit TV stations; 31 radio stations.
New construction: $6.8 billion investment in structures incl. $1.2 billion People Mover; downtown Knight Convention Center, The World Trade Center, hotels, office towers, condominiums, restaurants, and stores.
Medical facilities: 41 hospitals, 11,894 beds; 5,362 beds at 39 nursing homes in metro area; 2,975 members of Dade County Medical Association; VA hospital, Jackson Memorial Hospital one of area's leading research facilities.
Federal facilities: Homestead AFB south of Miami with some 8,000 Air Force, Army, and Navy personnel; Federal Aviation Administration; Coast Guard bases; 2 federal hospitals; oceanographic center; 13,700 U.S. employees.
Cultural facilities: Philharmonic, Opera Guild, and other musical groups perform regularly; 18 auditoriums, resident

and touring theatrical productions, 6 major art museums; 29 public libraries; 12 playhouses and 60 night clubs and theater restaurants, some in major hotels; New World Contemporary Festival of the Arts scheduled for June, 1982, headed by Rudolph Bing, sponsored by Greater Miami Opera Assn.
Educational facilities: 6 colleges and universities, plus 3 campuses of Miami-Dade Community College; Univ. of Miami is largest independent institution of higher learning in southeast; Florida International Univ.; public school system has 229,858 students and is the 5th largest in nation.
Recreational facilities: 14 miles of public beach on ocean and bay; 365 parks and playgrounds, 11 stadiums and grandstands, 45 golf courses, 57 marinas with 37,000 boats registered; 105 movie houses, 100 miles of bikeways, 28 bowling alleys.
Convention facilities: Miami Beach convention hall can handle largest conventions; 300 conventions brought more than 86,000 delegates to Miami in 1979; 570 conventions brought 290,000 delegates to Miami Beach in same year.
Sports: pro football Miami Dolphins and Univ. of Miami play in Orange Bowl, which seats 75,000; stadium also hosts Orange Bowl game, Orange Blossom Classic; Miami Stadium is spring home of Baltimore Orioles; parimutuel wagering at 5 horse and greyhound tracks, jai-alai frontons.
Other attractions: balmy subtropical climate with mean annual temperature of 75.3 degrees; 600 Protestant churches; 53 Catholic churches, 55 synagogues; city is bilingual with over 500,000 Latin American residents; one of nation's largest Jewish communities; marine stadium features powerboat and regatta racing; Everglades National Park, 40 miles south of Miami, is virgin wilderness.
History: America's newest big city, Miami had only 3 houses in 1895 in a community called Fort Dallas. Julia Tuttle persuaded Henry Flagler to extend his railroad south from West Palm Beach to stimulate Miami development; city was incorporated in 1896, when railroad arrived.
Further information: Metro-Dade Department of Tourism, 234 West Flagler Street, Miami, FL 33130.

Milwaukee, Wisconsin

The World Almanac is sponsored in the Milwaukee area by The Milwaukee Journal, 333 W. State Street, P.O. Box 661, Milwaukee, WI 53201; phone (414) 224-2000; founded 1882 by Lucius W. Nieman; circulation 332,932 daily, 515,108 Sunday; chairman of the board Donald B. Abert; publisher Warren J. Heyse; president of The Journal Co. Thomas J. McCollow; editor Richard H. Leonard; major awards include 2 Pulitzer prizes to the newspaper and 3 to staff members.

Population: 636,212 (city), 1,392,872 (SMSA); city 18th and metro area 27th in U.S.; total employment 680,800 (metro area).
Area: 95.8 sq. mi. on shore of Lake Michigan, Milwaukee County seat.
Industry: county 10th in U.S. in volume of industrial production, $9 billion (1978); 30% of workers employed in manufacturing; largest U.S. producer of diesel and gasoline engines, outboard motors, motorcycles, tractors, padlocks, beer; 4th largest U.S. automaking center; major producer of electrical equipment, mining, and construction machinery (SMSA); graphic arts and food processing are largest nondurable goods employers; location for 12 "Fortune 500" industries.
Commerce: wholesale and retail trade center for Wisconsin, upper Michigan; total retail sales $6.2 billion (SMSA); wholesale trade $10.4 billion (SMSA). Average household

effective buying income $22,693 (SMSA); metro area is home to 97 banks and 49 savings and loan associations.
Transportation: 7 major rail lines; Amtrak; 9 airlines provide direct service to East and West coasts, South, Southeast, Southwest, and Florida for over 2.9 million passengers annually using Gen. Mitchell Field which has international air arrivals facility; 19 U.S. and foreign-flag ship lines use Milwaukee's St. Lawrence Seaway port which handles more than 2 million tons annually including 1.8 million tons overseas cargo; Port of Milwaukee gateway for 350 cities in 31 states and overseas ports except the Far East. Milwaukee SMSA exports more than $2 billion worth of goods annually; 4 inter-city bus lines, 70 motor freight carriers; I-94, I-43, 5 federal and 14 state highways intersect Milwaukee.
Communications: morning, evening, and Sunday metropolitan newspapers; 5 commercial, 2 educational TV stations; 5 cable TV services, 2 pay TV companies; 29 AM and FM ra-

dio stations.
Medical facilities: 25 major hospitals and medical centers, including 600 bed VA hospital.
Cultural facilities: Milwaukee Symphony, Repertory Theater, opera and operetta companies; Mid-America Ballet; Milwaukee Art Center, Milwaukee museum, 4th largest in U.S.; Univ. of Wisconsin-Milwaukee, Marquette Univ., Medical College of Wisconsin, 8 other colleges and vocational schools; 3-theater Performing Arts Center; complete convention, exhibition arena-auditorium complex; Mitchell Park Conservatory, Milwaukee County Stadium, and Milwaukee County Zoo are parts of 13,000 acre Milwaukee County

park system.
Sports: Brewers (American League), Bucks (NBA); Admirals (Intl. Hockey League); Marquette Univ., Univ. Wisconsin-Milwaukee; Green Bay Packers (NFL) play 3 home games at Milwaukee County Stadium.
History: founded by Solomon Juneau (1818), one of many French trappers in area in early 1800s; incorporated as town 1837, as city 1846, 2 years prior to Wisconsin statehood.
Further information: Metropolitan Milwaukee Association of Commerce, 756 N. Milwaukee Street, Milwaukee, WI 53202.

Minneapolis, Minnesota

Population: 370,951 (city), 2,109,207 (SMSA); first in state, 35th in nation; total employed (city, 1980) 192,217.
Area: 59 sq. mi. (city), 4,000 sq. mi. (10-county metro area) around St. Anthony Falls near junction of Minnesota and Mississippi rivers; Hennepin County seat.
Industry: diverse; major electronics-computer manufacturing center including Honeywell, Control Data, Medtronics; headquarters for nation's 4 largest grain millers, including General Mills, Pillsbury, and International Multifoods.
Commerce: $21,600 median household income; $5.8 billion total retail sales metro area (1980); 24 commercial banks, 6 savings and loan assns.; headquarters for Ninth Federal Reserve District; world trade center, 12th among U.S. metro areas in exports; Mpls. Grain Exchange.
Transportation: 5 trunk railroads; 150 trucking firms; 5 major barge lines headquartered in city; Mpls.-St. Paul International Airport, averaging 600 flights daily.
Communications: 4 commercial, 2 educational TV stations; 39 radio stations.
Medical facilities: 21 hospitals, including a leading heart hospital at Univ. of Minn.

Federal facilities: Farm Credit Administration regional office; FBI regional office; EPA district office, area headquarters HUD.
Cultural facilities: Minnesota Orchestra, 7 art galleries-museums, Tyrone Guthrie Theatre, Walker Art Center, Univ. of Minnesota, Orchestra Hall, Inst. of Arts, Children's Theater.
Sports: Minnesota Twins (American League), Minnesota Vikings (NFL), Minnesota North Stars (NHL), Minnesota Kicks (NASL).
Other attractions: 153 parks, 22 lakes; 57-story IDS Tower; Minnehaha Falls; Mpls. Aquatennial celebration in July; average yearly snowfall, 41 inches.
History: first visited in 1680s by Fr. Louis Hennepin who discovered and named St. Anthony Falls on the Mississippi River; French fur traders used the area in 18th century; inc. 1871. Falls became power source for lumber and milling operations in 19th century.
Further information: Greater Minneapolis Chamber of Commerce Information, 15 S. 5th Street, Minneapolis, MN 55402.

Mobile, Alabama

The World Almanac is sponsored in the Mobile area by The Mobile Press Register, 304 Government Street, Mobile, AL 36630; phone (205) 433-1551; circulation, Register (morn.) 51,050, Press (eve.) 51,296, Sunday, 96,769; Register founded 1813, Press 1928. William J. Hearin publisher and president, Fallon Trotter executive editor, John Fay associate executive editor.

Population: 200,452 (city), 439,941 (SMSA); (metro) 2d city in state; total employed (metro) 161,900.
Area: 142 sq. mi. at head of Mobile Bay; Mobile County seat.
Industry: $300 million-plus Alabama State Docks and the growing oil and natural gas fields in Mobile County have attracted varied industry to city; Mobile fields produced 2.8 million barrels of oil, 3.8 million barrels of condensate and millions of cubic feet of natural gas in 1979; other industry includes paper, timber, chemicals, alumina, paints, aircraft engines, shipbuilding, and metals.
Commerce: wholesale-retail center for large portion of southwest Alabama and southeast Mississippi; county retail sales more than $1.4 billion (1980).
Transportation: served by 4 railroads; one of the great river systems; 3 major airlines, 55 truck lines, and 135 shipping

lines.
Communications: 2 TV, 15 radio stations; cable TV.
Medical facilities: Univ. of South Alabama Medical Center, Cancer Research Center, and 6 modern hospitals.
Cultural facilities: Municipal Auditorium-Theater complex seats 16,000; art gallery, museum, amateur theater, public library and branches; Univ. of South Alabama, Spring Hill and Mobile colleges, and Bishop State Junior College.
Military facilities: Coast Guard base and Coast Guard aviation training center.
Annual attractions: Azalea Trail Run, America's Junior Miss, Senior Bowl football game, and Mardi Gras.
History: founded in 1702 by Jean Baptiste Le Moyne; 6 flags have flown over city since then.
Further information: Chamber of Commerce, P.O. Box 2187, Mobile, AL 36652.

Montgomery, Alabama

The World Almanac is sponsored in the Montgomery area by the Advertiser-Journal, 200 Washington Street, Montgomery, AL 36102; phone (205) 262-1611; Advertiser founded 1828, Journal 1881; circulation Advertiser (morn) 47,823, Journal (eve) 25,013, combined Sunday 75,446; publisher Jim Martin.

Population: 178,157 (city), 273,154 (SMSA).
Area: 128.98 sq. mi. (city), 442 sq. mi. (county); state capital; Montgomery County seat.
Industry: machinery manufacture, glass products, textiles, refrigeration equipment, furniture, food products, paper, and fertilizers; industrial park in East Montgomery.
Commerce: wholesale retail center for 13 counties in central Alabama; SMSA retail sales $1.057 billion; average spendable income $17,066, per capita income $5,651; 7 banks, 5 savings and loan assns.; state docks, 37 trucking lines, 6 insurance co. home offices.
Transportation: 5 major railroads, 3 airlines, 2 national bus

lines, one city bus line; interstates 65 and 85 intersect in the city; Alabama River navigable to the Gulf of Mexico.
Communications: 2 daily, 2 weekly newspapers; 4 TV, 14 radio stations; cable TV.
Medical facilities: 5 general hospitals, VA hospital, Air Force hospital, area mental health hospital, private hospital.
Federal facilities: Maxwell AFB, houses the Air Univ., Gunter Air Force station.
Cultural facilities: Art Guild, Civic Ballet, Little Theatre, Community Concert Series, Museum of Fine Arts, Tumbling Waters Flag Museum; 14 theaters, 19 recreational fa-

cilities, city zoo; 5 major colleges and universities; civic center.

Sports: Blue Gray Football Classic; Southeastern Championship Rodeo; George Lindsay Celebrity Golf Tournament, American Express Tennis Tournament, Blue Gray Tennis Tournament, Alabama River Run, Alabama River Raft Race.

Other attractions: river boat makes regularly scheduled excursions of the Alabama River; State Capitol housed Confederate offices; White House of Confederacy, home of Jefferson Davis; Hank Williams grave site, Dexter Avenue Baptist Church; Fort Tolouse, antebellum town with many colonial mansions and churches.

History: inc. 1819; site of inauguration of Jefferson Davis as president of the Confederate States of America, Feb. 18, 1861.

Further information: Chamber of Commerce, P.O. Box 79, Montgomery, AL 36101.

Montreal, Quebec, Canada

The World Almanac is sponsored in Montreal area by The Gazette, a Southam newspaper, 250 St. Antoine Street, Montreal H2Y 3R7, Quebec, Canada; phone (514) 282-2222; founded 1778 by Fleury Mesplet; circulation 210,000 daily; publisher Robert McConnell, editor Mark Harrison, managing editor Mel Morris, editorial page editor Joan Fraser; sponsors Christmas fund; 16 National Newspaper awards in last 7 years.

Population: 1,214,300 (city), 2,761,000 (metro); after Paris, the 2d largest French-speaking city in the world, 67% French origin, 12% Anglo-Saxon, 21% other origins; Canada's largest urban center.

Area: 68 sq. mi. on an island of 190 sq. mi. in the St. Lawrence River where the Ottawa and Richelieu rivers flow into it at the head of the St. Lawrence Seaway; metro area extends over 1,000 sq. mi.; the 769 ft. Mount Royal dominates the Island which averages 100 ft. above sea level.

Industry: Canada's industrial hub ($7 billion, value of shipments of goods of own manufacturer).

Commerce: total effective buying income $15 billion, headquarters of many of Canada's largest financial institutions, home of the Montreal and Canadian stock exchanges; about 75% of countries have consulates or representatives in Montreal.

Transportation: St. Lawrence Seaway, Port of Montreal; 14 miles long, 42 miles of harbor with 140 berths; Mirabel jetport with multi-million electric train link to downtown planned for 1980's; existing Metro has been expanded to 46 miles; world headquarters of Air Canada, International Civil Aviation Organization, and International Air Transport Association serving 3 major airports; headquarters of Canadian National and Canadian Pacific railways.

Communications: 4 TV stations, 21 radio stations, 4 daily newspapers; headquarters for Bell Canada, CN-CP Telecommunications.

Educational facilities: Concordia University, McGill University, Universite de Montreal, Universite de Quebec.

Cultural facilities: Place des Arts with 3,000 seat hall and 2 theaters, attracting the finest forms of artistic, cultural, and musical entertainment; the Montreal Museum of Fine Arts, the Musee de l'Art Contemporain; some of the world's most beautiful churches, including the Mary Queen of The World Basilica, a half-size replica of St. Peter's in Rome.

Sports: Olympic complex including a 56,000 permanent seat stadium, home of the National Baseball League Expos, the Canadian Football League Alouettes, and the National Soccer Assn. Manic; 7,200 seat Velodrome, 2 50-meter pools, 25-meter diving pool, and a scuba diving pool — 15-meter depth; the Montreal Forum, home of the NHL Canadiens.

Recreational facilities: within an hour of the Laurentien and Eastern townships skiing, hunting, and fishing resort areas; over 5,000 restaurants of all lands; over 100 cinemas, 19 museums, 13 city libraries, the Montreal Botanical Gardens, St. Helen's Island Park, Dow Planetarium, Montreal Municipal Golf Course.

Convention facilities: over 15,000 hotel and motel rooms; full facilities for conventions; new Montreal Convention Centre scheduled for completion in 1982.

Medical facilities: over 80 hospitals with 26,000 beds, including the renowned Montreal Neurological Institute, and the Montreal Children's Hospital.

History: Montreal was first visited by Jacques Cartier in 1535; founded under the name of Ville Marie in 1642; Old Montreal, some 1,000 acres in all, is the largest such restoration in North America and retains the general atmosphere of the 18th century.

Further information: Convention and Visitor's Bureau of Greater Montreal, 1270 Sherbrooke Street W., H3G 1H7; The Montreal Tourist Bureau, 85 Notre Dame Street East, Montreal, Quebec.

Nashville, Tennessee

The World Almanac is sponsored in Nashville by The Tennessean, 1100 Broadway, Nashville, TN 37202; phone (615) 255-1221; founded as The Tennessean in 1907 but incorporated publications date to 1812; circulation daily 134,700, Sunday 236,400; president Amon Carter Evans, publisher John Seigenthaler; 3 Pulitzer prizes, 8 Headliner awards, 3 Sigma Delta Chi awards.

Population: 455,651 in unified metro government, 2d in state.

Area: 533 sq. mi., straddling Cumberland River, in north central part of state; Davidson County seat.

Industry: music (over 50% of U.S. singles are recorded in 40 studio complexes); clothing, headquarters of Genesco, world's largest and most diversified clothing and footwear manufacturer; insurance, 2 of largest U.S. companies located here; world's largest glass plant; chemicals, printing (especially religious materials), aerostructures, tires, air conditioning, heating equipment.

Commerce: retail center for middle Tennessee, south Kentucky; retail sales over $2 billion; bank resources over $4 billion in 8 banks, 109 branches.

Transportation: 9 U.S. highways and 6 branches of the interstate system radiate from Nashville; 10 commercial airlines with over 200 daily flights; 2 railroads, Amtrak; bus service, 73 motor freight lines.

Communications: 5 TV stations (one public), and 22 AM and FM radio stations.

Medical facilities: 18 hospitals, 2 medical schools, VA hospital, speech-hearing center.

Cultural: symphony orchestra; replica of Parthenon with art gallery; public and state libraries; botanic garden and fine arts center, 3 community theaters.

Educational facilities: 17 colleges and universities; 137 public schools, 39 private schools.

Convention facilities: 10,000-seat auditorium; Opryland convention center.

Other attractions: Grand Ole Opry, Opryland U.S.A. (theme park featuring music); Country Music Hall of Fame; Hermitage (home of Andrew Jackson); Belle Meade antebellum mansion.

Recreation facilities: water sports, outdoor activity on Old Hickory and Percy Priest lakes.

History: settled in 1780 as a fort in then western North Carolina; incorporated, 1784, with first written charter west of Alleghenies.

Further information: Chamber of Commerce, 161 4th Avenue N., Nashville, TN 37219.

New Haven, Connecticut

The World Almanac is sponsored in the greater New Haven area by the New Haven Register (founded 1812) and the New Haven Journal-Courier (founded 1755); circulation Register (eve.) 96,526, Sunday 140,372, Journal-Courier (morn.) 37,837; chairman of the board, publisher and editor-in-chief Lionel S. Jackson; president and assistant publisher Lionel S. Jackson Jr.; vp and general manager Brian Thayer; editor (Journal-Courier) Don W. Sharpe; executive editor (Register) Bruce Reynolds.

Population: 126,109 (city), 416,053 (SMSA), 3d in state.

Area: 21.1 sq. mi. southern coast of Conn. on north shore of Long Island Sound; New Haven County seat.

Industry: 1,000 firms in immediate area; principal products are guns, hardware, rubber goods, paper products, machinery, and tools.

Commerce: wholesale-retail center for southern Conn., total retail sales (1979) $2.9 billion; serves 850,000 people within a radius of 25 miles; busy harbor, particularly oil tankers.

Transportation: Conrail, Amtrak Cosmopolitan turbotrain; 25 major truck lines; 14 federal and state highways; Tweed-New Haven Airport served by 3 commuter airlines, limo service to New York and Hartford airports; bus line.

Communications: VHF, 2 UHF TV stations, and 6 radio stations.

Medical facilities: Yale Medical Center, Yale-New Haven Hospital; Hospital of St. Raphael.

Cultural facilities: Yale Univ. Library with over 6 million books, one of the world's largest collections; Yale's Peabody Museum of Natural History, art gallery, and Beinecke Rare Book Library; The Yale Center for British Art, New Haven Colony Historical Society, cultural center, 3 legitimate theaters; New Haven Symphony, Woolsey Hall.

Educational facilities: Yale Univ. and graduate schools; Albertus Magnus, Southern Conn. State, South Central Community, Quinnipiac, Greater New Haven State Technical colleges; Univ. of New Haven.

Recreational facilities: Yale Bowl, Payne-Whitney Gym, Ingalls Rink, The Coliseum; 15 parks including Frederick Brewster's estate, West and East Rock scenic drives, West Rock Nature Center; 7 golf courses, 6 skating rinks.

Convention facilities: coliseum-convention center with 19-story hotel nearby.

Sports: AHL Nighthawks (hockey), West Haven A's (baseball).

History: founded 1638 by Puritans; named after Newhaven in England; incorporated 1638, became a part of Conn. 1662; first mayor was Roger Sherman, signer of Declaration of Independence.

Further information: Greater New Haven Chamber of Commerce, 195 Church Street, New Haven, CT. 06506.

New Orleans, Louisiana

The World Almanac is sponsored in New Orleans by The Times-Picayune-The States-Item, 3800 Howard Avenue, New Orleans, LA 70140; phone (504) 586-3560; founded 1837; editor Charles A. Ferguson; sponsors the Crescent City Classic, Doll and Toy Fund.

Population: 557,482 (city), 1,183,606 (SMSA); first in state; total employed, 480,200 (metro area as of May 1979).

Area: 363.5 sq. mi. of which 199.4 are land.

Industry: Port of New Orleans, 2d largest in nation; volume of business for 1979-80 was record $12.5 billion; tourist business is 2d largest, with $1.3 billion spent in metro area in 1980.

Commerce: trade center for lower Mississippi Valley; metro area bank deposits $5.69 billion as of Dec. 1980; metro savings and loan assets of $4.14 billion as of Mar. 1981; average household income 1980, $23,144; retail sales $4.97 billion in 1980.

Transportation: rail hub with direct lines north, east, and west; Amtrak passenger service to Chicago, Los Angeles; Southern railway to New York; New Orleans International Airport serves airlines, Lakefront Airport commercial aviation; cruise ships to Mexico and Caribbean.

New construction: $145 million, 48-story, 1,200 room Orleans Sheraton Hotel; $100 million, 56-story Place St. Charles Office bldg.; $88 million, 750,000 sq. ft. New Orleans exhibition hall; $66 million, 14-story Hotel Inter Continental New Orleans.

Communications: 4 commercial TV stations and educational channel; 20 radio stations.

Medical facilities: major medical center with 2 schools of medicine; one dental school; Charity Hospital 2d largest in nation; Ochsner Medical Institutions.

Federal facilities: hdqtrs. 5th U. S. Circuit Court of Appeals and 8th Naval District; regional office U. S. Census Bureau, field office U. S. Dept. Agriculture Marketing Service.

Recreation: City Park, 1500 acres with golf, tennis, boating; Audubon Park, 250 acres with golf, tennis, and zoo; Pontchartrain Beach Amusement Park, large lakeside amusement center.

Convention facilities: 22,000 rooms in major hotels; 160,000 sq. ft. exhibition space in Superdome, 134,000 sq. ft. in Rivergate, and 32,500 sq. ft. Municipal Auditorium.

Cultural facilities: Theater for the Performing Arts seats 2,317 for operas, concerts; Municipal Auditorium seats up to 8,000 for special events; museums include New Orleans Museum of Art, Louisiana State Museum, Historic New Orleans Collection, and many small galleries.

Educational facilities: Tulane Univ., Univ. of New Orleans, Loyola Univ., Dillard, Southern Univ. in New Orleans, Xavier, St. Mary's Dominican.

Other attractions: Louisiana Superdome seats 75,000; French Quarter is historic tourist attraction.

Sports: Saints (NFL); Sugar Bowl game on New Year's day.

History: named after the Duke of Orleans, founded in swamp within crescent of the Mississippi River 100 miles from Gulf of Mexico by Jean Baptiste Le Moyne, Sieur de Bienville, in 1718; became capital of Louisiana Territory in 1722, when Adrien de Pauger laid out what is now the French Quarter; became part of U.S. with Louisiana Purchase in 1803.

Further information: Chamber of Commerce of New Orleans Area, 301 Camp Street; Greater New Orleans Tourist and Convention Commission, 334 Royal Street, both New Orleans, LA 70130.

New York City, New York

The World Almanac is sponsored in the greater New York City metropolitan area by the New York Daily News, 220 E. 42d Street, New York, NY 10017, phone (212) 949-1234. New York News Inc. founded June 26, 1919 by Joseph Medill Patterson; circulation daily 1,491,556; Sunday 1,995,702; president and publisher Robert M. Hunt; editor and executive vice president Michael J. O'Neill; executive vice president Henry K. Wurzer; managing editor William L. Umstead; associate editor John J. Smee. Pulitzer Prizes for editorial writing, news photography, cartoon, international and local investigative reporting; sponsors Golden Gloves, National Spelling Bee championship for New York City, and other major school athletic, cultural, and educational events as community service programs.

Population: 7,071,030 (city), 10,543,442 (consolidated area, N.Y. City, Westchester, Nassau, Suffolk counties); first in state and nation; total employed 3,298,400 (1980); per capita personal income $7,496.
Area: 300 sq. mi. at mouth of Hudson River; embraces 5 boroughs — Manhattan, Bronx, Brooklyn, Queens, and Staten Island.
Industry: nation's leader in manufacturing and service industries; produces 10.8% of America's apparel, 7.4% of printing and publishing; 11,321 manufacturing establishments (1980).
Commerce: nation's richest port, handling annual 50 million long tons of maritime cargo; Wall Street, world's largest financial center, with New York and American stock exchanges; wholesale-retail center for New York, New Jersey and southwestern Connecticut; retail sales $24.5 billion (1980); 202 commercial banks, deposits $153.4 billion; 82 savings banks, resources $44.2 billion (1980); World Trade Center, twin 110-story towers.
Transportation: Kennedy International Airport with over 13 million overseas air travelers, handled 760,036 tons of import-export air tonnage (1980); served by 76 scheduled air carriers; LaGuardia Airport served by more than 34 scheduled airlines; 4 heliports. Conrail, Amtrak railroads; 2 major rail terminals, Penn and Grand Central stations; 64 interstate bus lines; subway network covers every borough except Staten Island; ferry and the 4,260-ft. Verrazano-Narrows Bridge (world's longest suspension span) link Staten Island to Manhattan and Brooklyn; 18 bridges connect Manhattan with other boroughs, George Washington Bridge over the Hudson River to New Jersey; 4 tunnels under the Hudson and East rivers.
Communications: 15 TV stations (6 commercial, 2 educational, one municipal, 2 Spanish, 4 CATV); 39 AM and FM radio stations; WPIX-TV and WPIX-FM are broadcast affiliates of The News.
Medical facilities: over 100 hospitals, 5 major medical research centers specialize in cancer, heart diseases, sickle cell anemia, and other research; Sloan-Kettering Institute for Cancer Research; 4 VA hospitals.
Federal facilities: Fort Wadsworth, Staten Island; Governors Island, many federal agencies represented in buildings at Federal Plaza and 90 Church St.
Educational facilities: 29 universities and colleges including medical colleges, law schools, colleges of pharmacy, colleges of dentistry, institutes of art and architecture; 1,000 schools in the public school system; 879 private schools; public libraries total 201.
Cultural facilities: Lincoln Center for the Performing Arts (Philharmonic, Ballet Company, Metropolitan Opera, and other theatrical arts), Carnegie Hall, Brooklyn Academy of Music. Broadway and Off-Broadway alliance for varied theatrical productions; outdoor Delacorte Theatre in Central Park; 65 museums including American Museum of Natural History, Metropolitan Museum of Art, Museum of the Performing Arts, Museum of Modern Art, Whitney Museum, and South Street Seaport Museum.
Other attractions: United Nations; botanic gardens in the Bronx and Brooklyn; Central Park and Prospect Park; Bronx Zoo and 4 other zoos; Hayden Planetarium; The Cloisters; N.Y. Aquarium in Coney Island; 13 municipal golf courses, 535 tennis courts, 37 outdoor 9 indoor swimming pools.
Sports: NBA Knicks, Nets; NHL Rangers and Stanley Cup Champion Islanders; NL Mets and NFL Jets play in Shea Stadium; AL Yankees play in Yankee Stadium; NFL Giants and NASL Cosmos play in Giants Stadium in nearby E. Rutherford, N.J.; Madison Square Garden hosts sports, concerts, ice shows, other events. Thoroughbred racing at Belmont and Aqueduct; harness racing at Roosevelt, Yonkers, and the Meadowlands; area has off-track betting.
History: discovered by Giovanni da Verrazano in 1524; in 1626 Peter Minuit bought the island from the Manhattan Indians for about $24 in goods and trinkets; settlement named New Amsterdam. In 1664, British troops occupied city without resistance and named it New York in honor of the Duke of York, brother of the King. On Jan. 1, 1898, Manhattan and large areas to the NE, E, and S were consolidated into one city of New York.
Further information: Convention and Visitors Bureau, 2 Columbus Circle, New York, NY.

Newport News, Hampton, Williamsburg, Virginia

The World Almanac is sponsored in the Virginia Peninsula area by the Daily Press, Inc., publishers of the Daily Press (mornings and Sunday) and The Times-Herald (evenings except Sunday), 7505 Warwick Boulevard, Newport News, VA 23607; phone (804) 244-8421; The Daily Press, Inc., also operates an AM and FM radio station, WGH, broadcasting popular and classical music.

Population: 363,817 (SMSA).
Area: Newport News, Hampton, and Williamsburg are the key cities in the Newport News—Hampton SMSA that borders Hampton Roads, one of the great waterways of the world, connecting the James River to Chesapeake Bay, and ultimately, to the Atlantic Ocean.
Industry: economic base of the area is the shipbuilding industry; Newport News Shipbuilding is a major contractor to the U.S. Navy and to private-sector shipowners and operators, and is reputed to be the largest shipyard in the world; it employs more than 25,000 production workers at its facility along the James River. Hampton Roads area is the most important coal port in the world; it gathers coal from the Appalachian Mountains and redistributes it by ship to ports around the world; the rising demand for solid hydrocarbons has vastly accelerated movement through the port in the past 2 years; area also is a major source of seafood, particularly crabs and oysters that are plentiful in Chesapeake Bay and its tributary rivers.
Commerce: manufacturing shipments in 1980 exceeded $2.6 billion; in addition to shipbuilding, the principal industries are meat-packing, oil refining, and a complex of technical industries associated with NASA space activities; personal income in 1980 in excess of $3.4 billion, or $8,711 per capita; retail sales (excluding autos, gasoline, and liquor) in excess of $1.4 billion.
Federal facilities: located in the area are the Tactical Command of the U.S. Air Force, Naval Supply and Weapons stations, the Army's training and transportation commands and the training center of the U.S. Coast Guard; NASA's Langley Research Center has maintains an installation on the Peninsula.
Other attractions: based on Colonial Williamsburg, and with the additional attractions of Jamestown, Yorktown, and Busch Gardens, a theme park utilizing the concept of "The Old Country", tourism is a major industry; one million tourists visited Colonial Williamsburg in 1980.
History: Peninsula selected by the first colonists as evidenced by the Jamestown settlement; site of the first capital of Colonial Virginia and the intellectual center of the American Revolution; during the World Wars, area was a major staging area for troops moving overseas and for fleets using Hampton Roads as a base of operations.

Oakland, California

Population: 339,288 (city), employed in Oakland, 180,597.
Area: 53.4 sq. mi.; Alameda County seat.
Industry: food processing, fabricated metal products, transportation equipment, chemicals and paint; Port of Oakland is 2d in containerized cargo; home base for Kaiser Industries.
Commerce: 9,290 retail and wholesale outlets (1980) with taxable sales of $1.8 billion; median income for family, $11,997 per annum.
Transportation: western terminus for Southern Pacific, Santa Fe, and Western Pacific railroads; International Airport is major airfreight terminal and center for supplemental air carriers; headquarters for Bay Area Rapid Transit, underground, underwater 75-mile subway connecting 15 commu-

nities.
Medical facilities: 9 hospitals include Children's Hospital Medical Center, Kaiser Foundation, and the Veterans Administration.
New construction: Pacific Telephone Bldg., Wells Fargo Bldg., Clorox Bldg.; 16 square block city center project, and major downtown garage under construction.
Cultural facilities: museum, half garden, half gallery design, has divisions of natural science, history, and art; symphony, Chinese Community Cultural Center.
Educational facilities: Univ. of California at Berkeley, Mills College, College of Holy Names, Cal. State, Hayward; Chabot, California College of Arts and Crafts, Peralta Community College.

Recreational facilities: 26,000 acre regional park system serving the East Bay; zoo in 100-acre Knowland State Park has large collection of gibbons and aerial tram; Lake Merritt Park includes botanical garden, wildfowl refuge, natural science center, and Children's Fairyland.
Sports: Raiders (football), Athletics (baseball), Golden State Warriors (basketball).
Other attractions: Oakland Coliseum, over 50,000 capacity, for theatrical entertainment, exhibits, conventions, and circus; Jack London Square.
History: area explored in 1772, settled in 1850; incorporated as town in 1852, as city in 1854.
Further information: Chamber of Commerce, 1320 Webster Street, Oakland, CA 94612.

Oklahoma City, Oklahoma

The World Almanac is sponsored in the Oklahoma City area by The Daily Oklahoman and Oklahoma City Times, 500 N. Broadway, Oklahoma City, OK 73125; phone (405) 232-3311; morning Oklahoman founded 1894; evening Times in 1888; Oklahoma Publishing Co., acquired Oklahoman 1903, Times 1916; circulation Oklahoman 181,599, Times 84,457, Saturday Oklahoman & Times 219,608, Sunday Oklahoman 290,256; editor and publisher Edward L. Gaylord, managing editor Jim Standard.

Population: (1980) 403,213 (city) 829,584 (SMSA); largest in state, 3.2% unemployed 1979.
Area: 650 sq. mi. (city), 700 sq. mi. (county), 3,491 sq. mi. (metro area); located in state's center on Canadian River in Oklahoma, Cleveland, Canadian, McClain, and Pottawatomie counties; elev. 1,276 feet; state capital and Oklahoma County seat.
Industry: state's industry, finance, government, energy and agribusiness hub; Oklahoma City Air Logistics Center at Tinker AFB employs 16,000 civilians, 5,000 military; General Motors assembly plant employs 5,700, Western Electric employs 5,500; national headquarters for Kerr-McGee, Hertz, Wilson Foods, Inc., Federal Aviation Agency, T.G. & Y. Stores, Lee Way Motor Freight, Macklanburg-Duncan, Scrivner, Inc., C. R. Anthony, Cain's Coffee Co., Dolese Bros., Globe Life and Accident Insurance, Star Manufacturing Co., Oklahoma Publishing Co., Sirloin Stockade, Braums Ice Cream, L. S. B. Industries, CMI Corp., and Fleming Foods; home of the Interstate Oil Compact Commission.
Commerce: regional, national and international marketing center; average household income $17,868, effective buying income $6.3 billion (metro), consumer retail sales $3.7 billion (metro); banking with $6.9 billion resources, savings and loans with $1.6 billion in assets.
Transportation: interstate highways 35, 40, 44, and 240; federal highways U. S. 62, 66, 77, 81, 270, and 277; extensive expressway development program underway; 5 major bus lines; the Santa Fe, Frisco, and Katy railroads provide rail freight service; 41 truck lines; 9 major airlines service Will Rogers World Airport, plus 3 commuter lines; 160 scheduled flights per day.
Communications: 3 metro daily newspapers, 8 weekly newspapers; 24 radio, 7 TV stations, one education TV channel, 3 subscription TV channels, cable TV.
New construction: building permits $537 million (metro); $360 million in new construction has been completed in the Central Business District Project 1-A, most of which is linked by an all-weather pedestrian system, the Metro Concourse; first units of downtown luxury townhouses and apartments have begun with $300 million in construction projected for the next 5 years.
Medical facilities: Oklahoma Health Center, incl. Univ. of Oklahoma medical schools, VA and 3 other hospitals; Okla-

homa Medical Research Foundation and Dean McGee Eye Institute; 18 hospitals, 9 community health clinics, regional ambulance service.
Cultural facilities: National Cowboy Hall of Fame and Western Heritage Center; Oklahoma Art Center; Artsannex; Artsplace II, Oklahoma Museum of Art, Omniplex, Kirkpatrick Planetarium, Oklahoma Symphony Orchestra, Ballet Oklahoma, Oklahoma Heritage Center, National Softball Hall of Fame, Oklahoma Historical Society, 45th Infantry Division Museum, Firefighters Museum, Field Trial Hall of Fame, Lyric Theater, Oklahoma Theater Center, Oklahoma County libraries with 11 branches and 5 bookmobiles.
Education: 18 institutions of higher education in or near city; Univ. of Oklahoma Health Sciences Center, Oklahoma City Univ., Oklahoma Christian College, Oklahoma State Univ. Tech. Inst., South Oklahoma City Junior College, Midwest Christian College (city); Oscar Rose Junior College, Central State Univ., Univ. of Oklahoma, Bethany Nazarene College, Hillsdale Free Baptist College, St. Gregory's College, Oklahoma Baptist Univ. (metro); 7 vo-tech schools, 138 elementary, 63 secondary schools, 13 private schools.
Recreation: Hefner, Overholser, Stanley Draper, and Hiwassee lakes (city); Lake Thunderbird and Little River State Park (metro); 132 municipal parks, 11 gymnasiums, 24 recreation centers, Oklahoma City Zoo, Martin Park Nature Center, 28 golf courses, 84 public tennis courts, 60 public playgrounds, 12 municipal ball diamonds.
Convention facilities: Myriad Convention Center seats 26,700 in arena plus exhibition halls; Civic Center Music Hall 3,200; State Fairgrounds Arena 16,500; 84 hotels and motels with 8,750 rooms.
Sports: Univ. of Oklahoma in Big 8 Conference; 89ers baseball, Stars hockey.
Annual events: National Finals Rodeo, 7 major horse shows, Miss Rodeo America Pageant, Festival of the Arts, State Fair of Oklahoma, Heritage Hills and Mesta Park home tours, Oklahoma City Powwow, National Academy of Western Art Exhibition and Western Heritage Awards, Junior Livestock Show and Exposition.
History: settled by land run April 22, 1889; became state capital in 1910.
Further information: Oklahoma City Chamber of Commerce, One Santa Fe Plaza, Oklahoma City, OK 73102.

Omaha, Nebraska

Population: (1980) 311,681 city, 566,140 SMSA; first in state; 266,000 civilian labor force.
Area: eastern Nebraska, 92 sq. mi. of rolling hills on west bank of Missouri River; Douglas County seat.
Industry: $3.7 billion annual shipments; Western Electric, 600 others employ 36,000; food processing center; 4th largest livestock market in salable receipts.
Commerce: major trade center, $2.4 billion retail sales; 3,000 retail, 1,200 wholesale firms; $22,297 income per household; 42 banks, $2.5 billion deposits; 12 savings and loans, $3.4 billion assets; 4th largest insurance center in U.S., 44 princi-

pal admin. offices; hqs Union Pacific, InterNorth, Northwestern Bell, ConAgra, Valmont, Peter Kiewit Sons, Hinky Dinky, Brandeis, Richman Gordman, Mutual of Omaha.
Transportation: 9 major airlines; 4th largest rail center, served by 8 major railroads, transcontinental Amtrak; 94 truck lines, Interstate highways 80 and 29, 2 intercity bus, 3 barge lines; 3.3 million tons carried on Missouri River annually; port of entry, foreign trade zone.
Communications: 6 TV channels, 17 radio stations, cable TV.
New construction: 2 15-story office towers, parking garage,

18-story Northwestern Bell headquarters, Kiewit Conference Center, Central Park Mall.
Medical facilities: 14 hospitals, 4,400 acute care beds; 2 medical schools (Nebraska U., Creighton U.), one dental, 7 nursing schools, Eppley Institute for Cancer Research.
Federal facilities: Strategic Air Command's global headquarters, Army Corps of Engineers, Federal Reserve branch.
Cultural facilities: Orpheum performing arts center, symphony orchestra, opera, ballet, 17 theater groups, 15 museums, Joslyn Art Museum's $30 million collection.
Educational facilities: 3 universities, 6 colleges educate 32,000 students; 30 adult education schools.
Recreation: 6,000 acres of public parks include 140 tennis courts, 30 pools, 17 golf courses, 3 marinas, ice rinks.
Sports: Omaha Royals baseball, Ak-Sar-Ben horse racing, NCAA College World Series.
Other attractions: 1,300-acre Fontenelle Forest, Doorly Zoo, Boys Town, President Ford birthsite, Gen. Dodge House; Western Heritage and Aerospace museums; downtown's Old Market; unique 60,000-member Ak-Sar-Ben civic org., Schramm Aquarium. Ranked 10th among 50 largest U.S. cities in quality of life.
History: Lewis and Clark, 1804; Mormon settlement, 1846; capitol of Nebraska territory 1855-67.
Further information: Greater Omaha Chamber of Commerce, 1620 Dodge Street, Omaha, NE 68102.

Orange County, California

The World Almanac is sponsored in Orange County by The Register, 625 N. Grand Avenue, Santa Ana, CA 92711; phone (714) 835-1234; circulation combined daily morning and evening 238,757, Sunday 272,369; founded 1905, purchased in 1935 by R.C. Hoiles, founder of Freedom Newspapers Inc., a 30-daily newspaper group; R.D. Threshie Jr. publisher; H. Christian Anderson general manager; Jim Dean editor; Larry Burkhart director of marketing.

Population: 1,931,570, 2d most populous county in the state, compares with 212,364 in 1950, 2.5 million projected for 1990; county encompasses 26 cities.
Area: 511,040 acres in S. California from Pacific Ocean inland 25 miles to Cleveland National Forest; 42-mile coastline stretches from Long Beach past Huntington Beach surfing, Newport Beach yacht harbor, Laguna Beach art colony, Dana Point small-craft harbor, to San Clemente and Camp Pendleton.
Commerce and Industry: median income (1980) $25,900 (The Register's Consumer Attitude Survey); total personal income $19.4 billion (1979 est.); taxable retail sales (1980) $12.6 billion; automotive purchases led the retail sales category with $2.6 billion in taxable sales in 1980; general merchandise was 2d with $1.36 billion in sales, followed by eating and drinking places with $1.1 billion. The unemployment rate average about 4.2 percent during 1980; among the major employers in Orange County are Rockwell International, Hughes Aircraft, Alpha Beta Co., Beckman Instruments, and Disneyland.
New construction: 14,000 permits were issued for single and multiple family construction during 1980; the median price of a single family home was $136,000 (1980); vacancy factor was 3.4 percent during the year.
Transportation: 8 major freeways, including main Los Angeles-San Diego artery; transit district with countywide routes including freeway commuter buses and Dial-A-Ride in some areas; John Wayne Airport, nation's 2d busiest airport with 613,226 tower operations in 1980.
Communications: local UHF-TV station, 7 VHF-TV stations regionally, over 40 radio stations.
Federal facilities: Marine Corps Air Station at El Toro, Los Alamitos Naval Air Station, Seal Beach Naval Weapons Station, Santa Ana Marine Corps Lighter-Than-Air Station (now used for helicopters, once for dirigibles), federal building in Santa Ana, General Services Administration building, national archives center in Laguna Niguel, Cleveland National Forest, Marine Corps Camp Pendleton in nearby San Diego County.
Medical facilities: Univ. of Cal. medical school at Irvine, 65 hospitals and convalescent hospitals.
Recreation: 781 acres of beaches, more than 13,000 acres for regional parks, 141 scenic sea cliffs, 3 yacht basins, 3 fishing lakes, wilderness campgrounds, 35 golf courses, 21-mile equestrian and bicycle trail along Santa Ana River.
Other attractions: Disneyland, Knott's Berry Farm amusement park, Lion Country Safari, Movieland Wax Museum, Los Alamitos Racetrack; motorcycle park, auto raceway, mid-summer Laguna Beach Art Festival-Pageant of Masters, Santa Ana Zoo, air and car museums, Anaheim Stadium.
Convention facilities: Anaheim Convention Center, Disneyland Convention Center, hotels in Anaheim, Buena Park, Costa Mesa, Irvine, Newport Beach, Santa Ana.
Sports: (AL) Cal. Angels, (NASL) Cal. Surf, (NFL) L.A. Rams; interscholastic sports.
Cultural-Educational facilities: 2 major public universities, one private liberal arts college, 7 community colleges, multiple trade and special interest schools, 507 public K-12 schools; 237 private and church K-12 schools; city and county libraries, symphony orchestra society; 2 master chorales, 6 ballet companies, 32 community theater groups, repertory theater, 4 art museums.
History: first Spanish expedition 1769 by Capt. Gaspar de Portola, who recorded first reported earthquake in the state; county formed March 11, 1889 from Los Angeles County; Glenn Martin tested his first plane near Santa Ana; Madame Modjeska resided in local forest hideaway; Toastmasters International founded in Santa Ana 1924; Howard Hughes set world's speed record in Santa Ana in 1935 with 351 mph airplane flight. Swallows traditionally return each year to Mission San Juan Capistrano on March 19.
Further information: Anaheim Visitor and Convention Center Bureau, 800 W. Katella Avenue, Anaheim, CA, Orange County Chamber of Commerce, One City Boulevard W., Orange, CA.

Orlando, Florida

The World Almanac is sponsored in the Orlando area by the Sentinel Star, 633 N. Orange Avenue, Orlando, FL 32802; phone (305) 420-5000; Sentinel and Evening Star founded as dailies in 1913; merged in 1931; acquired by Tribune Company of Chicago in 1965; combined to create "all day" newspaper in 1973; circulation (ABC Newspaper Publisher's Statement 6 months ending March 31, 1981) 207,621 weekdays, 198,889 Saturday, 248,282 Sunday; president and chief executive officer Harold R. Lifvendahl, editor Stephen R. Vaughn.

Population: 128,394 (city), 694,645 (SMSA); 4th fastest-growing city over 500,000 population; metro employed 302,672 (1981), average unemployment rate 5.9% (1980).
Area: 44 sq. mi. (city); 2,822 sq. mi. (metro); elevation 20 ft. to 190 ft.; only major inland Florida city; Orange County seat.
Commerce: regional transportation, communications, distribution, retail, financial, education, and agriculture center for central Florida; Orlando Foreign Trade Zone; 1980 metro retail sales $3.5 billion; retail sales per household rank 15th among cities over 500,000 population; insurance center with 9 regional offices and 3 national home offices; regional offices for Southern Bell and United Telephone; 24 banks with 112 offices and $2.5 billion in 1980 deposits; 18 savings and loan associations with 74 offices and $1.9 billion in 1980 deposits.
Industry: over 800 manufacturers with 35,000 employees; emerging electronics center (Martin Marietta, Western Elec-

tric, Stromberg-Carlson, Westinghouse, NCR, Qwip, Piezo, General Electric, Burroughs); citrus-processing and packing; food processing; packaging; marine and boat manufacturing. **Agriculture:** center for vegetables, foliage plants, and citrus products shipped nationwide; over one third of Florida's citrus groves located in surrounding east central Florida region.

Tourism: number one tourist destination in the world; Walt Disney World with annual attendance of 14 million; Sea World with annual attendance of 3 million; Six Flag's Stars Hall of Fame; Mystery Fun House; Wet 'n Wild; Wings and Wheels Museum; Church Street Station; Lake Buena Vista; Cypress Gardens; Kennedy Space Center; Ringling Brothers and Barnum & Bailey Circus World; Daytona Beach.

Conventions: major national convention city; over 2000 conventions in 1980 drawing 430,000 delegates; convention expenditures over $90 million; 32,000 first class hotel and motel rooms; Orange County Civic Center with 325,000 sq. ft. of exhibit space scheduled to open in 1982.

Transportation: Orlando International Airport handled 6.5 million passengers in 1980, major U.S. hub airport, new $300 million terminal, 14 commercial airlines; 3 full service general aviation airports; Seaboard Coastline Railroad, Amtrak; Greyhound and Trailways bus lines; 33 common carrier truck lines; 8 freight forwarding companies; Port Canaveral, Jacksonville, Tampa nearest sea ports; I-4 and Florida Turnpike provide access to I-75 and I-95.

Communications: 5 television stations (3 network, 1 independent, 1 public); 24 radio stations (13 AM, 11 FM); 6 cablevision systems with 90,000 subscribers.

New construction: over $3.7 billion in major commercial projects scheduled during next 3 to 5 years including: Walt Disney World's EPCOT $800 million, Western Electric $500 million, Plaza International $300 million, Reedy Creek Resort $180 million, Little England $140 million, Universal Studios $100 million, Central Florida Research Park $100 million, Florida Mall $75 million; 1980 metro residential building permits 13,606.

Education: Univ. of Central Florida, Valencia Community College, Seminole Community College, Rollins College.

Federal facilities: Orlando Naval Training Center supporting 29 commands and activities including Naval Nuclear Power School, military personnel 12,500, civilian personnel 3,000; total local federal disbursements $370 million.

Medical facilities: over 4,000 beds in 17 metro hospitals including Orlando Regional Medical Center and Florida Hospital.

Cultural facilities: Florida Symphony Orchestra, Loch Haven Art Center, John Young Science Center, Orange County Historical Museum, Central Florida Civic Theater, Central Florida Zoological Park, Orlando Public Library System, Morse Gallery of Art.

Sports: Tangerine Bowl football game in 50,000 seat stadium; Minnesota Twins spring training site; Univ. of Central Florida Knights (football, basketball, soccer); Rollins College Tarheels (basketball, soccer); Bay Hill Classic, Walt Disney World National Team Championship, Florida Lady Citrus golf tournaments; Golden South Classic AAU track and field meet; Silver Spurs Rodeo (semi-annual); Ben White Raceway; Sanford-Orlando Kennel Club; Orlando-Seminole Jai-Alai Fronton; Daytona International Speedway.

History: area first settled in 1830's; Orange County established 1845; Orlando incorporated 1875; named for Col. Orlando J. Rees killed in Seminole Indians War.

Additional information: Orlando Area Chamber of Commerce, P.O. Box 1234, Orlando, FL 32802.

Ottawa, Ontario, Canada

Population: 301,567 (city), 738,600 (1979 metro region estimate, including greater Ottawa 556,900 and Hull, Que. 181,700); Canada's 8th largest city, linked with neighboring city of Hull by 5 bridges; labor force (Ottawa-Hull region) 358,000.

Area: 42.5 sq. mi. (city), 1,100 sq. mi. (region) on Ontario-Quebec border at the Chaudiere Falls on the Ottawa River; national capital.

National Capital Region: Ottawa and Hull, occupying 1,800 sq. mi. of eastern Ontario and western Quebec, form the National Capital Region of Canada, administered by the National Capital Commission (NCC), created by Parliament in 1959, which deals directly with 2 provincial governments, 2 regional governments, and 57 municipal jurisdictions.

Industry: major employer (69,446) is the federal government; tourism provides 13,000 jobs; Bell Canada largest private employer.

Commerce: 1980 retail sales $2.8 billion; 1980 per capita disposable income $9,735; 3d largest convention site in Canada with capacity for 5,000; 5,800 hotel-motel rooms in region; exhibit space 60,000 sq. ft. in 3 major hotels, 120,000 sq. ft. in the Civic Centre and 75,700 sq. ft. in the Nepean Sportsplex.

Transportation: Ottawa International Airport, 15 minutes from downtown, ranks as the nation's 9th busiest, more than 100 scheduled flights daily by 6 airlines; surface transportation provided by VIA rail and intercity bus service.

Communications: 2 daily (one in French), 4 weekly newspapers; 6 TV and 14 radio stations.

Education facilities: Carleton Univ., the bi-lingual Univ. of Ottawa, and Algonquin Community College.

Medical facilities: 11 hospitals, many include a public psychiatric unit; bed capacity over 4,000.

Cultural facilities: $45 million National Arts Centre with 2,300-seat opera house-concert hall, and an 800-seat theater; Ottawa Little Theatre.

National museums: National Gallery of Canada, Museum of Man, Museum of Natural Sciences, Museum of Science and Technology, Canadian War Museum, National Aeronautical Collection.

Sports: Ottawa Rough Riders, CFL; Ottawa 67's hockey.

Other attractions: gothic-style Parliament buildings, housing Canada's House of Commons and Senate; during the summer, Changing the Guard ceremony 2 militia regiments; Peace Tower, memorial to Canada's war dead; Central Canada Exhibition; Ottawa's oldest building, the Bytown Museum; Royal Mint; Rideau Canal provides boating facilities in summer, the longest skating rink in the world; 5 miles of the Rideau Canal from downtown Ladies' to Carleton Univ.; the Experimental Farm, 1,200 working acres in the heart of Ottawa; Winter Fair; 80 camping and trailer parks, 7 regional beaches; mountain lake recreation facilities; Gatineau Park (88,218 acres).

History: founded 1827 as Bytown, inc. as Ottawa 1855; named after Outaouac (or Outaouais Indian tribe); chosen as Canada's capital in 1857 by Queen Victoria.

Further information: Canada's Capital Visitors Bureau, 7th Floor, 222 Queen Street, Ottawa, Ont. K1P 5V9.

Pensacola, Florida

The World Almanac is sponsored in the Pensacola area by the Pensacola News-Journal, One News Journal Plaza, Pensacola FL 32501; phone (904) 433-0041; predecessor The Floridian founded in 1821, first daily News 1899, Journal 1898, merged 1924; combined circulation daily 71,550, Sunday 71,699; member Gannett Group; publisher Clifford W. Barnhart, editor J. Earle Bowden.

Population: 57,619 (city), 233,794 (county), 289,782 (metro area).

Area: southern end of 759 sq. mi. Escambia County at westernmost edge of Florida panhandle.

Industry: Monsanto Corp., St. Regis Pulp & Paper Co., Vanity Fair, American Cyanamid, Armstrong Cork, Westinghouse, Air Products, Reichhold Chemicals.

Labor force: civilian 112,400, military 13,000.

Commerce: retail sales $1.2 billion; average family income $12,958; effective buying income over $1.4 billion.

Transportation: 3 airlines, 2 railroads, 2 bus lines, 16 truck lines, intercoastal waterway, interstate 10, 3 U.S. highways.

Communications: 4 TV, 14 radio stations.

New construction: Monsanto expansion, Ellyson Field industrial park development, downtown mall, St. Regis Paper

Co. expansion, port expansion.

Medical facilities: Baptist Hospital, University Hospital, West Florida Hospital, U.S. Naval Hospital, Sacred Heart Hospital.

Federal facilities: Naval Air Station, Corry Field, Saufley Field, Whiting Field, carrier USS Lexington.

Cultural facilities: public library, Historical Museum, T.T. Wentworth Museum, Hispanic Museum, Transportation Museum, Museum of Naval Aviation, Saenger Theater, Art Association, Arts Council, Inc., Oratorio Society.

Educational facilities: Univ. of West Florida, Pensacola Junior College.

Recreation facilities: Pensacola Beach, 6 golf courses.

Sports: Pensacola Open, American Amateur Golf Classic, Virginia Slims tennis, International Bill Fishing Tournament, intercollegiate sports; pari-mutual greyhound racing; American Amateur Tennis Classic, Fiesta Road Run, Sertoma Run, Palafox Place Run.

Events: Fiesta of Five Flags, Mardi Gras, Seafood Festival, Great Gulfcoast Art Festival, July 4th celebration.

Further information: Pensacola Area Chamber of Commerce, 117 West Garden Street, Pensacola, FL 32593; phone (904) 438-4081; Pensacola-Escambia Development Comm., 803 N. Palafox, Pensacola, FL 32501; phone (904) 433-3065.

Philadelphia, Pennsylvania

The World Almanac is sponsored in the Philadelphia area by The Philadelphia Inquirer, 400 N. Broad Street, Philadelphia, PA 19101; phone (215) 854-2000; est. 1829, lineage traced to Pennsylvania Packet, founded 1771; circulation 428,862 daily, 851,376 Sunday; Pulitzer prizes 1975, 1976, 1977, 1978, 1979, 1980; published by Philadelphia Newspapers, Inc.; president Sam S. McKeel; executive editor Eugene L. Roberts Jr.; editor Edwin Guthman; managing editor Gene Foreman; sponsors Delaware Valley Science Fair, Book & Author Luncheons, Old Newsboys' Day, Phila. Distance Run, Head of the Schuylkill Regatta. PNI also publishes the Philadelphia Daily News, afternoon tabloid, at same address; founded 1925; circulation 232,190; editor F. Gilman Spencer; executive editor Zachary Stalberg; managing editor Tom Livingston; sponsors Dragnet rewards program, high school all-star football game, Broad St. Run.

Population: 1,688,210 (city), 4,700,996 (SMSA), 5.9 million (14-co. RTA); 6.8 million (20-co. ADI); employment 2.0 million (metro).

Area: 130 sq. mi. (city), 3,553 sq. mi. (metro); located in southeastern Pa. on Delaware and Schuylkill rivers; 90 mi. from N.Y.C., 136 mi. from Wash., D.C., 60 mi. from Atlantic City; Phila. is county seat (city and co. coextensive).

Industry: over 90% of all U.S. basic industries represented; major center for textiles and apparel, food processing, petroleum (largest oil refining region on East Coast), printing and publishing, instruments, chemicals and pharmaceuticals, finance and insurance; companies headquartered in metro area include Sun Co., IU International, Campbell Soup, Scott Paper, Rohm & Haas, Crown Cork & Seal, Pennwalt, Certain-teed, SmithKline, Thiokol, Penn Mutual Life, INA, ARA Services, Alco Standard, Arco Chemical.

Commerce: 58 comm. banks (metro), $21.5 billion deposits; 7 mutual savings banks, $11.4 billion; retail sales (metro) $18.6 billion; average household income (metro) $24,738.

Transportation: biggest freshwater port in world (50 mi. waterfront); certified foreign trade zone; 2d in intl. cargo among N. Atlantic U.S. ports (67.6 million tons in 1980); 2 modern marine terminals for containerized cargo; rail service by Conrail, Chessie System, and Amtrak; over 250 truck lines; vast highway network, 6 bridges in metro area between Pa. and N.J.; Phila. Intl. Airport handled 9.6 million passengers in 1980 and 117,340 tons of freight through Cargo City facility; area transit (SEPTA) conveyed 267.1 million passengers on subway, el, rail commuter, bus, and streetcar lines in 1980.

Communications: 4 daily newspapers: Inquirer, Bulletin, Daily News, Journal; 24 AM, 29 FM; 6 comm. TV stations, one subscription station; cable TV.

New construction: $308 million center-city RR commuter tunnel (largest public bldg. project in Phila. history); $200 million Gallery II project on Market St. East (125-store mall, 33-story office bldg., and dept. store); $125 million One Logan Sq. complex (incl. 375-room, world-class Four Seasons Hotel); 450-room Hershey Phila. Hotel; 312-room Hotel Rittenhouse; Intl. Airport high-speed line.

Medical facilities: 124 hospitals (metro); 6 medical schools, 2 dental schools, 2 pharmacy schools.

Federal facilities: Phila. Naval Base; Defense Industrial Supply Ctr.; Defense Personnel Support Ctr.; U.S. Navy Aviation Supply Office Compound; Veterans Adm. Ctr.; Internal Revenue Serv. Ctr.; U.S. Mint; Ft. Dix and McGuire AFB (metro).

Cultural facilities: Phila. Orchestra; Pa. Ballet; Opera Co. of Phila.; Acad. of Music; Philadelphia Museum of Art; Franklin Inst.; Pa. Acad. of the Fine Arts; Rodin Museum; University Museum; Acad. of Natural Sciences; Barnes Fdtn.; Mann Music Center; Robin Hood Dell East; theaters: Walnut St. (oldest in U.S.); Shubert, and Forrest; community and summer theaters.

Educational facilities: 54 colleges and universities within 25 mi. of City Hall; University City Science Center (16-acre research complex).

Convention facilities: Civic Center with 383,000 sq. ft. of air-cond. exhibit space; 13,000-seat Convention Hall; over 500 motels/hotels (metro) with 20,000 first-class rooms.

Recreational facilities: over 8,600 acres of parks inc. 4,516-acre Fairmount Park (largest city park in U.S.); hundreds of playgrounds, swimming pools, golf courses, tennis courts, ice-skating rinks; close to seashore, mountains.

Sports: NL Phillies, NFL Eagles and Army-Navy football game (Veterans Stadium); MISL Fever, NBA 76ers and NHL Flyers (Spectrum); Penn Relays (Franklin Field); sculling races (Schuylkill R.); area horse racing (Keystone, Liberty Bell, Brandywine, Delaware Park, Atlantic City); Greater Philadelphia Independence Marathon.

Other attractions: Independence Hall and Liberty Bell (in most historic sq. mi. in U.S.); old city district and Benjamin Franklin Parkway centers of interest; many historic bldgs. preserved, restored or reconstructed; Penn's Landing waterfront dev.; Afro-American Museum; City Hall; Elfreth's Alley; Franklin Court; Society Hill; Fairmount Park mansions; zoo (America's first); Mummers Parade (Jan. 1); Freedom Festival (climaxed by July 4th celebration); Super Sunday festival (Oct.); nearby attractions incl. Valley Forge, Longwood Gardens, Great Adventure, Atlantic City casinos.

1982 Tricentennial—Century IV, year-long celebration of 300th anniversary of the founding of Philadelphia. Hundreds of events and programs throughout year.

History: Wm. Penn founded his "Greene Countrie Towne" as Quaker colony in 1682; gave it Greek name that means "City of Brotherly Love"; national capital 1790-1800; historical shrines incl. Independence Hall, Liberty Bell, Carpenters' Hall, Franklin's grave, Betsy Ross House, Gloria Dei Church, Christ Church, USS Olympia, Fort Mifflin.

Further information: Victor Kendrick, Office of City Representative, 1660 Municipal Services Bldg., Phila., PA 19107, phone (215) 686-3655; Phila. Tourist Bureau, 1525 J.F. Kennedy Boulevard, Phila., PA 19102; phone (215) 864-1976.

Phoenix, Arizona

The World Almanac is sponsored in the Phoenix area by The Phoenix Gazette, 120 East Van Buren Street, Phoenix, AZ 85004; phone (602) 271-8000; founded Oct. 28, 1880, as Arizona Gazette by Charles H. McNeil; circulation 106,220; publisher emeritus Mason Walsh, publisher Darrow Tully, managing editor Alan D. Moyer; sponsors Christmas Fund Drive, Music Memory Programs, Family Symphony Concerts, Phoenix Giants' bat boy contest, tennis clinic, cactus show, and other events.

Population: 764,911 (city), 1,511,552 (SMSA); capital and largest city in state; total employed 644,800.
Area: 325 sq. mi. (city), 9,226 sq. mi. (metro), in south central Arizona.
Industry: electronic equipment manufacturers, Honeywell and Motorola each employ more than 8,000; Arizona divisions of The Garrett Corp., and Sperry Flight Systems each employ more than 5,000; other major employers are Goodyear Aerospace, General Electric, Western Electric Cable, Reynolds Metals, Marathon Steel, Arizona Public Service, Salt River Project, Mountain Bell, Courier Terminal Systems, Spring City Knitting Co., Siemens Corp., Amerco, General Semi-conductor Industries, United Metro, International Metal Products, Greyhound, American Express, and Phoenix Newspapers.
Commerce: wholesale-retail center for state; retail sales (1980) $7.3 billion; effective household buying income $20,947; bank and S&L assets $20.1 billion; 19 banks with 394 area offices, 7 S&Ls with 137 offices in metro area.
Transportation: transportation center of the Southwest; Sky Harbor International Airport served by 14 airlines, 6.6 million passengers (1980); 3 railroads; 2 transcontinental bus lines; 10 transcontinental truck lines; 25 heavy equipment haulers; 34 interstate and 39 intrastate truck lines.
Communications: 8 TV and 35 radio stations.
New construction: (1980) 22,434 new residential building permits; total value of building permits, $1.5 billion.

Medical facilities: Barrow Neurological Institute; 28 general care hospitals, Veterans' Hospital; other special services.
Cultural facilities: art museum, public library, symphony orchestra, Indian museums, zoo, botanical gardens, community and professional theaters; Civic Plaza convention center; Gammage Auditorium.
Federal facilities: Luke AFB, Williams AFB.
Educational facilities: Arizona State Univ., American Graduate School of International Management; 4 community colleges; Maricopa Technical College (vocational); 67 public and parochial high schools.
Sports: 70 golf courses and $300,000 Phoenix Open; inland surfing beach; ice skating rinks; amusement park; pro basketball, baseball teams; auto, greyhound, and horse racing; annual Fiesta Bowl football game.
Other attractions: Frank Lloyd Wright's Taliesin West; Paolo Soleri's Arcosanti; Dons' Club guided tours of Arizona; full calendar of events including state and county fairs and rodeos, horse shows, regattas, polo tournaments.
History: founded 1870, on site of ancient Indian settlement; the Hohokam tribe, which flourished ca. 500-1200 A.D., developed an intricate system of irrigation canals which form the base of the canal system in use today.
Further information: Phoenix and Valley of the Sun Convention and Visitors Bureau, 2701 E. Camelback Road, Phoenix, AZ 85016; or Phoenix Metropolitan Chamber of Commerce, 34 W. Monroe, Suite 900, Phoenix, AZ 85003

Pittsburgh, Pennsylvania

The World Almanac is sponsored in the Pittsburgh area by The Pittsburgh Press, 34 Boulevard of the Allies, Pittsburgh, PA 15230; phone (412) 263-1100; founded June 23, 1884, as Evening Penny Press by Thomas J. Keenan; circulation 250,000 daily, 650,000 Sunday; editor John Troan, business manager William A. Holcombe, executive editor Leo Koeberlein, managing editor Ralph Brem; sponsors Press Old Newsboys Fund for Children's Hospital which raised $2.2 million in 1980.

Population: 423,938 (city), 2,244,620 (4-county metro area), 2d in state and 31st in nation; metro area labor force of 1,035,800 (Apr. 1981), unemployment was 6% (Apr. 1981).
Area: 55.5 sq. mi at juncture of Allegheny and Monongahela rivers which form Ohio River; Allegheny County seat; altitude, 702 feet.
Industry: one-fifth of nation's steelmaking capacity concentrated in metro area; western Pennsylvania mines produce 40 million tons of bituminous coal annually; 6,000 different products made in area; home of world's first full-scale nuclear power plant; world's largest manufacturers of aluminum, steel rolls, rolling mill machinery, air brakes, plate and window glass, and safety equipment; 3d largest headquarters city in nation.
Commerce: retail sales (Allegheny County, 1980) $5.8 billion; exports abroad of products manufactured here totaled $400 in 1979; average household effective buying income (Allegheny County) $20,000.
Transportation: 11 scheduled airlines handled 11.5 million passengers on 292,465 flights at International Airport (1980); 7 railroads; Continental Trailways and Greyhound bus lines; over 400 common carriers; Port Authority Transit vehicles carried 107.5 million passengers (1980) over 176 routes, 5 trolley lines; 9 major highways serve the city; a 4.5 mile busway opened in 1977, and another 6.8 mile busway and $480 million 10.5 mile light rail trolley system, incl. a downtown subway, are under construction.
Communications: 2 daily newspapers; 6 TV (including country's first educational station) and 25 radio stations.
New construction: through Renaissance II, the city will increase its office space by more than 25% and spend approximately $4.5 billion in construction and development during the next 5 years; $32 million convention center opened in 1981; headquarters for PPG Industries and Dravo Corp. in addition to Riverfront Center and Oxford Center are under construction; Greater Pittsburgh International Airport planning expansion. Station Square, Allegheny River Edge Park,

and Grant Street East expansion underway.
Medical facilities: 21 hospitals include Univ. of Pittsburgh Health and Medical complex where Dr. Jonas Salk developed polio vaccine; VA installation.
Federal facilities: Federal Building contains scores of U.S. government offices (information center: 412/644-3456); Army base at Oakdale; Air Force base.
Cultural facilities: Heinz Hall is home of the opera co., ballet, civic light opera, youth symphony and symphony orchestra; 4 community theaters, one legitimate theater; Frick Art Museum; Carnegie Museum and Art Gallery, home of the Pittsburgh International series, a biennial one-man art show offering a $55,000 prize; American Wind Symphony.
Educational facilities: Univ. of Pittsburgh, Duquesne Univ., Point Park, Chatham, Carlow, Robert Morris, and La Roche colleges; Carnegie-Mellon Univ., Community College of Allegheny Co.; 18 Carnegie public libraries, 3 bookmobiles, community libraries.
Sports: Pirates baseball, Steelers football; NHL Penquins.
Other attractions: Highland Park Zoo, children's zoo, Twilight Zoo, aquarium, aviary, Buhl Planetarium, Allegheny Observatory, Phipps Conservatory, Fort Pitt Museum; 2 amusement parks; 2 operating passenger inclines; folk festival; Three Rivers Arts Festival every June; harness racing; river cruises; Civic Arena; Three Rivers Stadium.
History: first hunters and trappers came through in 1714; city dates from Nov. 25, 1758, when English forces under Brig. Gen. John Forbes occupied the ruins of Fort Duquesne, which French soldiers had burned and abandoned, and built a new and bigger fortress called Fort Pitt. When incorporated in 1816, it already had a reputation as a "Smoky City" from factories and coal-burning homes. Massive "Renaissance Plan" has cleared the skies and rebuilt the heart of the city during the past 30 years.
Further information: Chamber of Commerce, 411 Seventh Avenue, Pittsburgh, PA 15219; Convention and Visitors Bureau, 200 Roosevelt Boulevard, Pittsburgh, PA 15222.

Portland, Maine

The World Almanac is sponsored in the Portland area by the Maine Sunday Telegram, 390 Congress, Portland, ME 04104; phone (207) 775-5811; published by Guy Gannett Publishing Co., founded 1921; circulation 120,017; publisher Jean Gannett Hawley, editor John K. Murphy; also publishes morning Press Herald, circulation 57,611 and Evening Express, 30,595.

Population: 61,572 (city), 183,457 (SMSA) (metro area), first in state; total employed 29,800.

Area: 21.6 sq. mi.; peninsula on Casco Bay; Cumberland County seat.

Industry: One of the Atlantic Coast's busiest oil shipping centers, east terminus Montreal pipeline; fishing fleet base, seafood shipping center; landbased products: printed materials, metal, processed food, electronic parts, paper.

Commerce: tourist center, regional retail-wholesale hub, large shopping complex, 1,485 retail, 350 wholesale, 600 service enterprises; retail sales (1980) $448.2 million.

Transportation: municipal jetport, Delta, Bar Harbor airlines; 3 rail freight lines, integrated bus system, Greyhound, Michaud Trailways bus terminals, 35 truck lines; Maine Turnpike, interstate 95 and 295 highways connect to all New England; deep water anchorage, auto ferries year round to Yarmouth, Nova Scotia.

Communications: 3 TV, 5 AM, 6 FM stations.

New construction: 2 office bldgs., art museum, housing for elderly, fish processing complex, parking garage; export-import pier, condominiums.

Medical facilities: medical center, 2 hospitals.

Cultural facilities: symphony orch., Kotzschmar organ, one of world's largest; public, historical libraries; Victorian, art museums; Henry Longfellow home (1785); branch Univ. of Maine, Westbrook College, art, vocational, and business schools; Portland Headlight, oldest lighthouse in country.

Recreation: 18-hole municipal golf course, 9 others in area; scenic cruises; swimming, tennis, fishing within easy travel; scenic parks.

Conventional facilities: civic center, 3 large assembly halls, meeting rooms in modern hotels and motels.

Sports: Maine Mariners hockey (AHL).

Further information: Tourist Bureau, 142 Free Street, Portland, ME.

Portland, Oregon

The World Almanac is sponsored in the Portland area by The Oregon Journal, 1320 SW Broadway, Portland, OR 97201; phone (503) 221-8275; founded Mar. 11, 1902; circulation 105,246; editor Donald J. Sterling Jr., managing editor Peter Thompson.

Population: 366,383 (city), 1,236,294 (SMSA), first in state; total employed, 587,300.

Area: 80 sq. mi., at junction of Columbia and Willamette rivers; Multnomah County seat.

Industry: electrical and electronic industries along with lumber and wood products, food, and paper; ranks first in manufacture of logging, lumbering equipment; home of Louisiana-Pacific (forest products), Tektronix (oscilloscopes), Omark (saw cutting chain), Hyster (lifts, hoists, lumber handling), White Stag, Pendleton, Jantzen (clothing).

Commerce: wholesale-retail center for large part of Oregon, SW Washington; retail sales metro area (1979), $5.46 billion; 18 banks, 9 savings and loan associations.

Transportation: 3 major rail freight lines, Amtrak; Greyhound, Trailways buses; 10th largest freshwater port in U.S., with 27-mile frontage, 29 marine berths; 12 million tons of cargo pass over docks annually; more than 1,400 ships visit annually; hub for 11 airlines, flights to all parts of world; air freight service by Flying Tigers and Federal Express.

Communications: 5 TV and 29 radio stations.

Medical facilities: 17 major hospitals, Univ. of Oregon

Health Sciences Center, VA hospital.

Cultural facilities: art museum, Oregon Symphony Orchestra, Opera Assn., Oregon Historical Society, Portland State Univ., Univ. of Portland, and Lewis & Clark, Reed, Warner Pacific, Judson Baptist, and Concordia colleges.

Other attractions: annual Rose Festival, Rose Show; park system includes Washington Park, Hoyt Arboretum International Rose Test Garden, Amer. Rhododendron Soc. Test Garden, Washington Park Zoo, Oregon Museum of Science and Industry, Forestry Center; Forest Park is largest forest area in a U.S. city's limits. Analysis of 243 population centers in mid-1970s named Portland as "America's Most Liveable City", based on "economic, political, environmental, health and education, and social components."

Sports: Trail Blazers of the NBA play at the Memorial Coliseum; Timbers (soccer) and Beavers (baseball) play at Civic Stadium.

History: chartered 1851 with population of 821; named after Portland, Me., rather than Boston, Mass., on flip of coin by 2 early citizens.

Further information: Chamber of Commerce, 824 SW 5th, Portland, OR 97204.

Providence, Rhode Island

The World Almanac is sponsored in the Providence area by The Providence Journal-Bulletin, 75 Fountain Street, Providence, RI 02902; phone (401) 277-7000; Journal founded 1829, Bulletin 1863, Sunday Journal 1883; circulation, Journal (morn.) 78,634, Bulletin (eve.) 139,687, Sunday Journal 230,800; chairman & chief executive officer John C. A. Watkins, publisher & president Michael P. Metcalf, senior v.p.-operations & admin. Charles P. O'Donnell, v.p. and exec. editor Charles McC Hauser.

Population: 156,804 (city), 917,962 (SMSA); total employed 109,978.

Area: 18.91 sq. mi., at the head of Narragansett Bay in Providence County; state capital.

Industry: jewelry, silverware, plated ware, costume jewelry are largest industries; Textron is based in Providence, 984 manufacturing companies in the city.

Commerce: wholesale-retail center for entire state; retail sales $2.8 billion (metro); median household effective buying income $17,970 (metro); home of Narragansett Capital, largest small business investment company in nation; 2 savings and loan assns., 2 mutual savings banks, one cooperative bank, 6 commercial banks.

Transportation: Amtrak, passenger service between Boston, Providence, New York, and Washington; 3 bus lines; 45 locally-based common carriers and contract truckers; 11 major highways link Providence to every corner of R.I.; 5 major airlines out of T. F. Green Airport in Warwick (15 min. away); port is 3d largest in New England with 25 wharves and docks, 10.5 miles of commercial waterfront on the bay.

Communications: 3 TV and 8 radio stations.

Medical facilities: 7 hospitals; one VA hospital.

Cultural facilities: Trinity Square Repertory Co., R. I. Philharmonic, R. I. School of Design Museum; R. I. Historical Society.

Education: Brown Univ., founded 1764, is 7th oldest college in nation; 7-year M.D. program inaugurated 1973; Providence and R. I. colleges, and R. I. School of Design.

Recreation: one of America's most attractive recreational areas centers around Providence; 69 salt water beaches, 23 fresh water beaches, 50 golf and country clubs, 5 ski areas, 29 yacht clubs, 28 parks, all within 45 minutes of city.

Convention facilities: R.I. Civic Center (seats 12,000).

Sports: America's Cup races since 1930; Newport-Bermuda race starts at Newport every other year.

Other attractions: largest collection of original early American homes of any city; located along Benefit St., they have been preserved by the Providence Preservation Society.

History: founded 1636 by Roger Williams; incorporated 1832; official state name is "Rhode Island and Providence Plantations."

Further information: Chamber of Commerce, 10 Dorrance Street, Providence, RI 02903.

Quebec City, Quebec, Canada

Population: 186,088 (city), 480,500 (metro); oldest city in Canada (1608) and the capital of the province of Quebec.
Area: 30 sq. mi.; natural citadel on north shore of St. Lawrence River at confluence with St. Charles River; 400 miles from Gulf of St. Lawrence; 167 miles east of Montreal; older part is built on a cliff 360 ft. above the St. Lawrence.
Industry: some 300 industrial firms, ranging from primary industry products to a variety of consumer products, employ over 16,000 people; food and beverage, leather footwear and leather products, textiles, apparel, wood products, pulp and paper, printing and publishing, iron and steel products, nonferrous metal and chemical products.
Commerce: total effective buying income $3 billion; Quebec harbor, one of the busiest seaports of Canada, accommodates the largest ocean-going vessels with year-round facilities, an important container terminal; Provincial Government, with more than 15,000 employees. is the largest single employer and consumer in the city.
Transportation: Canadian Pacific and Canadian National railroads; Air Canada, Quebecair, Nordair; bus center.
Communications: 3 TV stations (2 French, one English); 6 radio stations (French), 2 newspapers (French).

Medical facilities: 5 large general hospitals.
Cultural facilities: historic character, cultural appeal and natural beauty make tourism important area of economic activity; annual "Carnaval" in Feb. is internationally known; annual summer festival (July) changes the city into an open theater for numerous artistic events; Expo-Quebec, an annual provincial exhibition (industrial, commercial, and agricultural), draws over 500,000 people a year.
Educational facilities: Laval University, the first in North America; Quebec University; 3 colleges.
Sports: home of NHL Nordiques.
Other attractions: only walled city in North America with fortifications standing today as they were 125 years ago; the Citadel, built from 1823-1832, contains within its walls 25 buildings, including the summer residence of Governor-General of Canada, Parliament buildings (1886), Quebec Museum, Battlefield Park, Ursulines Museum, Seminary (1663), Talon cellars, Notre Dame des Victoires Church, and Tresor Street.
History: founded 1608 by French explorer Samuel de Champlain; cradle of French civilization in America; once the key to the interior of the North American continent.

Raleigh, North Carolina

The World Almanac is sponsored in eastern North Carolina by The News and Observer and The Raleigh Times, 215 S. McDowell Street, Raleigh, NC 27602; phone (919) 829-4500; circulation N&O (morn.) 129,062, Times (eve.) 33,647, N&O Sunday 167,296; publisher Frank Daniels Jr., editorial director Claude Sitton, editor Times A.C. Snow, managing editor N&O Bob Brooks, Times Mike Yopp.

Population: 149,771 (city), 300,833 (county), 525,059 (SMSA area of Wake, Orange, and Durham counties; 3d in state; 154,980 employed (Wake County), 272,700 (metro).
Area: 55 sq. mi. in the geographical center of the state where Piedmont joins coastal plains; alt. 363 ft., temperate climate; state capital and Wake County seat.
Commerce: retail center of eastern N.C.; 1980 retail sales $1.656 billion (city), $2.202 billion (Wake County), $3.225 billion (metro); 16 banks, and 6 savings and loans; average annual income per household $18,745.
Education: 9 colleges; North Carolina State Univ. (Raleigh), Univ. of North Carolina (Chapel Hill), and Duke Univ. (Durham) form Research Triangle; Triangle Park employs 18,000 in all areas of research including toxicological, pharmaceutical, development of telecommunications, fiber, environmental, engineering, and humanities research; metro area has more Ph.Ds per capita than anywhere in the world.
Transportation: 2 rail and 6 bus lines, Amtrak; 275 motor freight companies; airport has 9 airlines carrying 886,848 passengers per year; one interstate, 4 U.S. and 2 state highways into city; city mass transit bus system.
Communications: 4 TV and 15 radio stations; 2 daily newspapers and 10 weeklies.

New construction: $166 million (1980).
Medical facilities: 6 hospitals (1,894 beds); major state mental hospital; 516 Wake County doctors, 173 dentists.
Convention facilities: 33 motels, 3,783 rooms; Civic Center seats 10,000; Dorton Arena, 8,110; Memorial Auditorium, 2,289; Reynolds Coliseum, 12,700; Jane S. McKimmon Center, 3,000.
Cultural facilities: 3 museums, state fairgrounds, state symphony, community college and professional theater groups.
Recreation: 5,200-acre Umstead State Park, Lake Wheeler with 650 acres of water and 60 acres of land; Carter Stadium (45,600 seats); 13 year-round recreation areas or city parks; 600 restaurants.
Sports: ACC football and basketball; pro golf and tennis; annual track and field meets; annual horse shows; 2 major dog shows; annual speedboat regatta; college sports.
History: city of Raleigh was established in 1792 in honor of Sir Walter Raleigh; Andrew Johnson birthplace; Oakwood Historic District preserves large Victorian neighborhoods.
Further information: Raleigh Chamber of Commerce, 411 S. Salisbury Street, Raleigh, NC 27602; phone (919) 833-3005.

Regina, Saskatchewan, Canada

The World Almanac is sponsored in southern Saskatchewan by The Leader-Post, 1964 Park Street, Regina, Sask., S4P 3GA, phone (306) 565-8211; founded 1883 by Nicholas Flood Davin; circulation 69,078; president Michael Sifton, Toronto; executive vice-president Max Macdonald; editor W. Ivor Williams; associate editor C.E.W. Bell; managing editor J.M.F. Swan; business manager William Duffus; advertising manager George Crawford; MacLaren Trophy for editorial page reproduction excellence.

Population: 159,100, first in province; labor force, 79,200.
Area: 37.5 sq. mi., 100 miles north of Canada-U.S. border; provincial capital.
Industry: over 293 manufacturing industries; gross production value (1979) $560 million, 34% of Saskatchewan total.
Commerce: service center for oil, potash; grain production area; retail sales (1980) $831.3 million, 24.3% of province.
Transportation: 2 rail lines, 4 airlines, 3 bus lines, and 125 trucking companies; main Trans-Canada highway bisects; city-run transit system.
Communications: 3 TV, 7 radio stations, cable television.
Medical facilities: 4 major hospitals, 1,485 beds.
Cultural facilities: Saskatchewan Centre of Arts, multipurpose theater-convention center with: Jubilee theater (seats 450) stage, ballroom, reception hall and dining room; Centennial theater (seats 2,029); Hanbidge Hall convention area, 12,200 square feet, 9 meeting rooms, seats 1,600; Regina Symphony; Globe Repertory; Museum Natural History; Norman Mackenzie Art Gallery; RCMP Museum.
Educational facilities: Regina University; 14 collegiates; 97 elementary, 7 specialized schools; Wascana Institute of Applied Arts and Sciences.
Recreation facilities: Saskatchewan Roughriders (Canadian pro football); 154 parks and playgrounds; 8 golf courses; 6 swimming pools; 9 indoor ice rinks.
Other attractions: Wascana Centre, 2,300-acre development, with man-made lake, public buildings, parks, recreation in heart of city; home of Canadian Western Agribition, Canada's major international livestock show.
History: founded 1882, and since that time headquarters for RCMP training depot.
Further information: Regina Chamber of Commerce, 2145 Albert Street, Regina, Sask.

Reno, Nevada

The World Almanac is sponsored in the northern Nevada area by the Nevada State Journal and Reno Evening Gazette, 401 West Second Street, P.O. Box 280, Reno, NV 89520; phone (702) 786-8989; Journal founded 1870, Gazette founded 1876; combined daily circulation 56,538, Sunday 50,624; publisher Robert B. Whittington.

Population: 100,756 (city), 193,623 (county), including Sparks, 2d largest in the state; 1980 labor force 109,300.

Area: 36.8 sq. mi. (including Stead annexation) in northwestern part of the state at the eastern foot of the Sierra Nevadas; Washoe County seat.

Industry: gross gaming revenue for county $455.3 million (1980), netted state taxes of $35.8 million; warehousing continued to grow because of Nevada's liberal free port law with est. 25 million sq. ft. in the county; marriages (35,232) outnumbered divorces (4,023).

Commerce: taxable sales in SMSA (Washoe County) for 1980, $1.7 billion; assessed valuation (city) $1.5 billion, EBI per household $24,657; bank resources $3.6 billion.

Transportation: 17 motor freight lines, 3 freight railroads, Amtrak, 3 commercial bus lines, 12 airlines; airport handled (1980) 2.3 million passengers; U.S. 395 and Interstate 80.

Communications: 3 TV, 12 radio stations, 2 CATV, one satellite TV.

New construction: 127 commercial, 426 residential units totaling $92.1 million assessed valuation (1980).

Medical facilities: 3 hospitals, including VA.

Educational facilities: Univ. of Nevada, Reno, Truckee Meadow Comm. College; public schools with 31,110 students, private/parochial schools with 1,365 students.

Cultural facilities: 1,428 seat Pioneer Theater Auditorium, Atmospherium Planetarium, 8,000 seat Centennial Coliseum, and 350,000 volume library; national air races; Reno Rodeo ($188,400 purse); Nevada Historical Society, Nevada Opera Guild, Reno Philharmonic Orchestra; Sierra Nevada Museum of Art, Sierra Arts Foundation, Reno Little Theatre.

Recreation: 24-hour gambling; world's largest gambling casino; 21 ski resorts within a 1½ hour drive; Lake Tahoe and Pyramid Lake offering fishing, boating, swimming, sunbathing, medium game-hunting, camping; historic Virginia City mining town and tourist attraction within 1/2 hour drive.

Sports: Reno Padres minor league baseball.

History: established 1868 with public auction of land by Central Pacific Railroad Co., known prior as Lake's Crossing; named after Civil War hero General Jesse L. Reno.

Further information: Chamber of Commerce, P.O. Box 3499, Reno, NV 89505; Marketing Department, Reno Newspapers, Inc. P.O. Box 280, Reno, NV 89520.

Richmond, Virginia

The World Almanac is sponsored in the Richmond area by the Richmond Times-Dispatch and News Leader, 333 E. Grace Street, Richmond, VA 23219; phone (804) 649-6000; Times-Dispatch founded 1850 by James A Cowardin, circulation 136,385 daily, 222,273 Sunday; News Leader founded 1896 by Joseph Bryan, circulation 114,412; chairman D. Tennant Bryan; publisher J. Stewart Bryan III; president Alan S. Donnahoe; executive editor John E. Leard; Times-Dispatch managing editor Alf Goodykoontz; News Leader managing editor J.A. Finch.

Population: 219,214 (city), 591,719 (metro area), total employed (non-agricultural) 313,676.

Area: 62.5 sq. mi. (city), located at fall line of James River, 90 miles from Atlantic Ocean; independent city.

Industry: tobacco, with 12,600 workers, and chemicals, with 7,700 are leaders in employment; Philip Morris cigarette plant is world's largest and most modern; printing, publishing, manufacture of paper and allied products, and food.

Commerce: wholesale-retail center for central Virginia; retail sales $2.52 billion in 1979, per capita income $9,741, median effective buying income $19,447, total income (SMSA) $6 billion.

Transportation: 4 major railroads, 5 intercity bus lines, 4 commercial air lines, 3 commuter air lines, 69 motor truck lines; 3 interstate, 6 U.S., and 9 state highways; deepwater terminal accessible to ocean-going ships.

Communications: 4 TV, 26 radio stations; 2 cable TV stations.

Medical facilities: Medical College of Virginia known worldwide for heart and kidney transplants, medical research; 21 other hospitals, including McGuire VA Hospital.

Federal facilities: Defense General Supply Center, Fifth Federal Reserve Bank, U. S. Fourth Circuit Court, Ft. Lee (Quartermaster Corps).

Cultural facilities: Va. Museum and Theater with professional artists make city a center for dramatic, other performing arts; other drama groups; symphony orchestra.

Educational facilities: Virginia Commonwealth Univ. has state's largest enrollment; Univ. of Richmond, Virginia Union Univ., Union Theological Seminary (Presbyterian), Randolph-Macon College.

Recreational facilities: coliseum for athletic, entertainment events; city-owned Mosque auditorium, Parker Field, City Stadium, numerous parks.

Convention facilities: large downtown hotels near Mosque and Coliseum.

Sports: Braves (IL baseball), Rifles (Eastern Hockey League); national ranked track and tennis events.

Other attractions: St. John's Church, scene of Patrick Henry's "Liberty or Death" speech; Virginia Capitol, designed by Thomas Jefferson; White House of the Confederacy; Civil War battlefields.

History: exploration here in 1607 by Capt. John Smith, first settlement 1609, incorporated as town 1742, made Va. capital 1779, Confederate Capital 1861-65; burned 1781 by Benedict Arnold, and 1865 when cotton, tobacco stockpiles fire set by fleeing Confederates spread to city; damaged by floods 1771, 1969, 1972.

Further information: Chamber of Commerce, 201 E. Franklin Street, Richmond, VA 23219.

Roanoke, Virginia

The World Almanac is sponsored in the Roanoke area by the Roanoke Times & World-News, 201-203 Campbell Avenue, Roanoke, VA 24010; phone (703) 981-3000; Times founded 1886, World-News founded 1889; Barton W. Morris Jr., president and publisher; circulation combined daily 118,276, Sunday 120,413.

Population: 100,427 (city), 223,578 (SMSA); labor force 112,910.

Area: 43.25 sq. mi.; SMSA includes Roanoke City, Salem City; Roanoke, Craig, Botetourt counties; located at southern extremity of Shenandoah Valley midway between Maryland and Tennessee.

Industry: 19% of work force in manufacturing; leading firms are General Electric, Eaton Corp., ITT, Singer, Burlington Industries, Mohawk Rubber, Ingersoll Rand.

Commerce: headquarters Shenandoah Life Ins. Co., Estate Life Ins. Co., Appalachian Power Co., Advance Stores, Mick or Mack Groceries; Regional Allstate Ins. Co. offices; Kroger (central warehouse); retail sales metro area (1980) $1.088 billion; average household effective buying income $20,250 (metro area); retail center for 20 counties and parts of W. Va. and N.C.

Transportation: Norfolk & Western Railway Co. headquarters; 2 airlines; Trailways and Greyhound buses; Amtrak north-south Washington, D.C.-West Va.; 30 interstate trucking firms with terminals; highways interstate 81, spur 581, US 11, 460, 220, 221, Blue Ridge Parkway.

Communications: 3 TV and 13 radio stations.

Medical facilities: 4 general, 4 specialty hospitals, VA facility; state hospital.

Cultural facilities: 2 civic centers with auditorium, coliseums and exhibit halls; symphony orchestra, art center, theaters; Roanoke, Hollins, Virginia Western Community, National Business colleges; Va. Polytechnic Inst. and State Univ.; concert and lecture series.

Other attractions: Mill Mt. Park rising 1,000 ft. in center of

city; children's zoo; Transportation and Historical Museum, Smith Mt., Fairy Stone and Claytor Lakes state parks; Natural Bridge, Dixie Caverns, Peaks of Otter.

Sports: baseball; school sports, winter skiing nearby; public recreation and parks programs.

History: formerly named Big Lick, Roanoke, an Indian word for shell money, became a city in 1884 with the linking of the Shenandoah Valley Railroad with Norfolk and Western Railroad.

Further information: Roanoke Valley Chamber of Commerce, 14 West Kirk Avenue, P.O. Box 20, Roanoke, VA 24001.

Rochester, New York

The World Almanac is sponsored in the Rochester area by Gannett Rochester Newspapers, 55 Exchange Street, Rochester, NY 14614; phone (716) 232-7100, circulation Democrat and Chronicle (morn.) 128,539, Times-Union (eve.) 116,144, Democrat and Chronicle (Sunday) 233,343; publisher George Dastyck, executive editor Robert Giles, director of advertising Peter Stegner. Times-Union reporters awarded a 1972 Pulitzer prize; Gannett News Service awarded 1980 Pulitzer prize.

Population: 241,741 (city), 970,313 (SMSA).

Area: 675 sq. mi. (Monroe County) straddling Genesee River on Lake Ontario, 2,966 sq. mi. (metro); Monroe County seat.

Industry: world leader in production of photographic, optical, and scientific instruments with Eastman Kodak (55,800 employees), Xerox (14,000), and Bausch & Lomb (5,000), all founded in Rochester; other fields include machinery, food products, apparel, printing and publishing.

Commerce: retail sales (1980) $4.5 billion; 20 commercial and savings banks; 1980 average household effective buying income $25,553 (metro area).

Transportation: Monroe County Airport with 8 major airlines and several freight companies; rail freight service by 4 lines, Amtrak; Greyhound, Trailways, Bluebird bus lines; Rochester Transit Service; port of Rochester; over 75 motor freight firms.

Communications: 5 TV and 23 radio stations.

New construction: Eastman Kodak, 2 manufacturing plants; Strong Museum.

Medical facilities: one of the nation's most advanced health care centers; 8 general hospitals including Strong Memorial.

Cultural facilities: Eastman Theater, part of Univ. of Rochester's Eastman School of Music, and home of the Philharmonic Orchestra; Memorial Art Gallery; Museum and Science Center, including Strasenburgh Planetarium; George Eastman House of Photography; 3 theater companies.

Educational facilities: 8 private and 2 public 4-year colleges; 3 community colleges.

Recreational facilities: Finger Lakes area with 13 parks, summer and winter sports, golf, tennis, bowling; 16-park Monroe County System including Seneca Park Zoo, Highland Park, Lilac Festival.

Convention facilities: 2d largest used site in NY; War Memorial 7,500 cap., Dome Arena 5,000 cap.; 4,600 hotel & motel rooms.

Sports: International League Red Wings, Baltimore Orioles farm team; AHL Amerks, NASL Lancers; Continental Basketball Assn. Zeniths, American Pro Softball League Express; thoroughbred racing and Finger Lake race track (Canandaigua).

Further information: Chamber of Commerce, 55 St. Paul Street, 14604; Convention and Publicity Bureau, 100 Exchange Street, 14614.

Rockford, Illinois

The World Almanac is sponsored in the Rockford area by the Rockford Newspapers, Inc., 99 E. State Street, Rockford, IL 61105; phone (815) 987-1200; publisher of the Rockford Register Star (daily 80,000) and Sunday Register Star, (85,000); publisher Gary L. Watson; member of the Gannett Group.

Population: 139,712 (city), 250,884 (county), 135,810 work force (county).

Area: 38.104 sq. mi. (city) on Rock River in extreme north central Illinois; Winnebago County seat; 519 sq. mi. (county).

Industry: more than 700 manufacturing establishments; products include machine tools (Sundstrand, Ingersoll Milling Machine, Barber-Colman, Greenlee Bros.), screws and bolts (Rockford Products, Elco, Camcar, National Lock), pharmaceuticals (Warner-Lambert, American Chicle), and paints (Valspar); Chrysler Corp. assembly plant is in nearby Belvidere.

Commerce: retail "magnet" for northern Ill. and southern Wis.; 28 shopping centers including Mall at CherryVale (108 stores); retail sales (1980) $930.5 million (city); 16 commercial banks, resources (1980) $1.096 billion; 5 savings and loan assns., resources (1980) $670.4 million.

Transportation: Amtrak Chicago connection; 4 rail freight lines, 3 bus lines, 43 truck lines; TWA and Ozark Air Lines with Chicago connection; U.S. 51 and 20, interstate 90, Ill. 70, 2 and 173.

Communications: 4 TV, 6 radio stations, one cable TV; 4 weekly newspapers, one daily newspaper.

Medical facilities: 3 hospitals, 2 public supported extended

care facilities.

Cultural facilities: symphony orchestra, concert band, civic theater, 3 choral organizations, 6 legitimate theaters.

Education: 68 public schools (K-12), 27 parochial and private schools (K-12); Rockford College, Rock Valley College (2 years, liberal arts), UI-Rockford School of Medicine, Rockford Business College (2 years).

Recreation: 23 forest preserves, over 100 parks totaling 3,000 acres; one state park, 4 public golf courses, 4 country club courses, 61 public tennis courts, 7 private tennis courts, 2 indoor tennis facilities, 2 private platform tennis facilities, 3 public swimming pools, 7 private swim clubs, 76 baseball diamonds; Riverview Ice House; 2 roller skating rinks.

Agriculture: 192,000 acres tilled farmland (est. value $390 million); 2,400 persons on 775 commercial farms.

Other attractions: Children's Farm, Time Museum, Tinker Swiss Cottage, Rockford Museum, John Erlander Home, Burpee Natural History Museum, Burpee Art Museum, Rockford Council for the Arts and Sciences.

History: founded in 1834 by Germanicus Kent and Thatcher Blake beside fording place across Rock River; incorporated in 1852.

Further information: Rockford Area Chamber of Commerce: 815 E. State Street, Rockford, IL 61101.

Sacramento, California

The World Almanac is sponsored in the Sacramento area by The Sacramento Bee, 21st & Q, Sacramento, CA 95816; phone (916) 446-9211; founded 1857; circulation daily 214,021, Sunday 238,854; president C. K. McClatchy, editor C. K. McClatchy, executive editor Frank McCulloch, managing editor Mike Kidder.

Population: 275,741 (city), 783,381 (county), 1,010,989 (SMSA); total employed 441,200 (SMSA).

Area: 94 sq. mi. (city), 997 sq. mi. (county), 85 mi. northeast of San Francisco in Sacramento Valley, at junction of Sacramento and American rivers; state capital and Sacramento County seat.

Industry: 475 manufacturing plants including Campbell Soup, Procter & Gamble, Cal. Almond Growers Exchange, Del Monte, Teichert Construction, Aerojet-General, Hewlett-Packard, Computer Sciences Corp., and Cal. Farm Bureau Federation.

Commerce: wholesale-retail center for Sacramento Valley; total retail sales $4.9 billion in 1980.

Transportation: 3 county operated airports, including metropolitan airport, plus numerous private airports; $55 million Port of Sacramento gives access to Pacific; 2 mainline transcontinental rail carriers; junction 4 major highways.

Communications: 6 TV and 23 radio stations.

New construction: restoration of Old Sacramento as state and federal historical project, regional sewage treatment plant, Hewlett-Packard factory, General Electric Medical Systems Div., McDonell Douglas Security Park, Signetics Corp., Second Foundation.

Medical facilities: 10 major hospitals, Univ. of California Medical School in nearby Davis.

Federal facilities: 2 large air force bases, army depot, many regional federal offices.

Cultural facilities: Sacramento Community Center complex; symphony orchestra, ballet co., 10 live theaters (including the Music Circus, an in-the-round summer stock theater), the Crocker Art Gallery, and many art shows.

Education: California State Univ.-Sacramento, McGeorge College of Law, Lincoln Univ. Law School, the nearby Univ. of California-Davis, and 3 community colleges.

Recreation: zoo, 95 public parks, 74 playgrounds, 8 public and 4 private golf courses, fishing, hunting, boating, camping, hiking, and skiing in nearby high Sierras; Golden Bear harness racing, American River Parkway bicycle trail, nearby Lake Tahoe.

Other attractions: Sutter's fort, State Capitol, Governor's Mansion, Old Sacramento historical area, Railway Museum; annual events: Camellia Festival, Dixieland Jazz Festival, Golden West track & field meet, Pig Bowl.

History: first permanent settlement founded by John Augustus Sutter Sr. in 1839; James Marshall discovered gold at Sutter's Mill in 1848, 35 mi. northeast, gateway to the Mother Lode Country; Pony Express and Central Pacific Railroad were part of early history.

Further information: Sacramento Metropolitan Chamber of Commerce, 917 7th Street, P.O. Box 1017; phone (916) 443-3771; or Sacramento Area Commerce & Trade Organization, 917 7th Street, P.O. Box 1132, phone (916) 444-2144; both Sacramento, CA 95805.

St. Louis, Missouri

The World Almanac is sponsored in the St. Louis area by the St. Louis Post-Dispatch, 900 N. Tucker Boulevard, St. Louis, MO 63101; phone (314) 622-7000; founded Dec. 12, 1878 by Joseph Pulitzer; circulation 244,599 Mondays through Fridays; 436,298 Sundays (average for 6 months ending March 31, 1981); editor and publisher Joseph Pulitzer Jr., associate editor Michael E. Pulitzer, managing editor David Lipman, contributing editor Evarts A. Graham Jr., vice president and general manager of newspaper operations Glenn Christopher; major awards include 5 Pulitzer prizes to the newspaper and 11 to staff members.

Population: 453,085 (city), 974,815 (county), 2,344,912 (SMSA), 12th in nation in payroll employment (983,700, first quarter, 1981).

Area: 4,935 sq. mi. (metro) just south of confluence of Missouri and Mississippi rivers.

Industry: 2d to Detroit in auto and truck assembly with Ford, GM, and Chrysler plants; headquarters of McDonnell Douglas, aerospace manufacturer; Interco, largest shoe company in U.S.; Anheuser-Busch, world's largest brewer; Monsanto, General Dynamics, Ralston-Purina, Pet, Inc., Chromalloy American, Consolidated Aluminum, Emerson Electric, Brown Group; 3,215 manufacturing concerns employ 234,000 (first quarter of 1981); ranks 10th in nation in number of "Fortune 500" company headquarters.

Commerce: $8.2 billion retail sales (1980 metro); $19,997 median family income; more than 220 banking institutions, total deposits $6.5 billion (Apr., 1981).

Transportation: 11 major airlines with 8.2 million passenger movements (1980); 2d largest rail center in U.S.; 17 trunk line railroads; largest inland port in U.S. handled 22.5 millions tons of cargo in 1978; 9 major highways, 14 motor-bus lines, 350 motor freight lines, 14 barge lines.

Communications: 6 TV and 35 radio stations.

New construction: industrial and commercial contracts totaled $636.2 million, and residential $339.4 million (1980); Lambert International Airport expansion; $40 million computer center for McDonnell-Douglas; $50 million IBM office project.

Medical facilities: 65 hospitals (metro) with 14,651 beds; Washington Univ. and St. Louis Univ. medical schools and affiliated hospitals provide treatment in many areas.

Federal facilities: Military Personnel Records Center, Defense Mapping Agency Aerospace Center, Army Troop Support and Aviation Material Readiness Command, Army Aviation Research & Development Command, Army Logistics Management Systems Agency, Postal Service Data Processing Center, Scott AFB.

Cultural facilities: Art Museum; Museum of Science and Natural History; restored historic homes; symphony orchestra; Loretto-Hilton Repertory Theatre; St. Louis Opera Theater (3-week summer season), American Theater; 4 dinner theaters; Laumeier Sculpture Garden; Municipal Theatre (Muny Opera) offers Broadway shows in big outdoor theater in Forest Park.

Educational facilities: 4 major universities: Washington, St. Louis, Univ. of Missouri at St. Louis, and Southern Illinois Univ. at Edwardsville; 26 colleges and seminaries with over 200 other private schools.

Convention facilities: 16,000 hotel rooms; 90,000 sq. ft. exhibit space in Kiel Auditorium; 240,000 sq. ft. exhibit space in Cervantes Convention Center.

Sports: Busch Stadium home of the Cardinal baseball and football teams; St. Louis Blues (NHL); horse racing at Fairmont Park; St. Louis Steamers, indoor soccer; St. Louis Streak, women's pro basketball.

Recreational facilities: Jefferson National Expansion Memorial with 630-foot Gateway Arch on riverfront; 1,326-acre Forest Park with 3 golf courses, ball fields, floral displays, zoo, McDonnell Planetarium, Steinberg skating rink and Jefferson Memorial displaying Lindbergh trophies; National Museum of Transport; Six Flags, St. Louis; Grant's Farm with President Grant's cabin and animal displays; Missouri Botanical Garden with floral displays, Japanese garden and advanced research display greenhouse, the Climatron; excursion boats, show boat, minesweeper, Army Corps of Engineers museum on riverfront; Dental Health Theater with world's largest model teeth; Maryland Plaza/Central West End, a collection of art galleries, shops, night spots and entertainment; Westport Plaza; the Magic House, a 15-room mansion with scientific "magic" for children.

Other attractions: climate has 4 distinct seasons: spring and autumn warm, winters mild, summers hot with 90-degree temperatures; average temperature 55.9 degrees; average precipitation 35.9 inches; downtown area contains significant architecture including Eads Bridge, Old Post Office, Union Station, Old Courthouse, Old Cathedral, Spanish International Pavilion which now contains a hotel tower; Louis Sullivan's Wainwright Building refurbished as a state office building; and restoration of Laclede's Landing area on riverfront north of Gateway Arch.

History: named for French King Louis IX by fur trapper Pierre Laclede whose trading post became major fur market and gateway to the West; starting point of Lewis and Clark expedition and other explorations.

Further information: Convention and Visitors Bureau, 500 N. Broadway, or Regional Commerce and Growth Assn., 10 S. Broadway, both St. Louis, Mo.

St. Paul, Minnesota

The World Almanac is sponsored in the St. Paul area by the St. Paul Dispatch and Pioneer Press, 55 E. 4th Street, St. Paul, MN 55101; phone (612) 222-5011; founded 1849 as Minnesota Pioneer by James Goodhue; circulation, Pioneer Press (morn M-F) 109,122; Dispatch (eve M-F) 116,552; Pioneer Press/Dispatch (morn Sat.) 183,651; Sunday Pioneer Press, 252,554; Bernard H. Ridder Jr., chairman, Knight-Ridder Newspapers, Inc.; publisher Thomas L. Carlin, executive editor John R. Finnegan, editor William G. Sumner. First newspaper published in Minnesota.

Population: 270,230 (city); 2,109,207 (SMSA) 2d in state; total employed (city, 1980) 141,182.
Area: 55 sq. mi. in eastern Minnesota on banks of Mississippi River close to Minnesota and Wisconsin vacationlands; state capital and Ramsey County seat.
Industry: West Publishing, world's largest law book publisher; international center for electronics and computer technology; Union Stockyards is largest livestock center in nation. Headquarters 3M Co., Am. Hoist & Derrick Co., Burlington Northern RR, Univac, Brown & Bigelow, Whirlpool, Economics Laboratory, Hoerner-Waldorf Corp., St. Paul Companies (insurance).
Commerce: retail sales (1980) $3.4 billion; median household income, $21,800; 25 banks and 6 savings and loan associations.
Transportation: 5 major and 2 regional rail lines, Amtrak; 21 intercity truck firms, 37 terminals; 3 interstate bus lines; 730-mile public transit system; metropolitan airport, hub of 8 commercial airlines, headquarters for Northwest and Republic airlines, averages 600 air movements per day; Downtown Airport; 60 firms operate barges on Mississippi River using a 9-foot channel downtown.
Communications: 4 commercial and 2 educational TV stations; 29 radio stations.
Medical facilities: 12 private hospitals; a 611 bed community hospital and research center: St. Paul-Ramsey Hospital.
Federal facilities: Ft. Snelling; area headquarters for HEW;

district headquarters for IRS, FCC, Immigration and Naturalization Service; U.S. District Court.
Cultural facilities: St. Paul Chamber Orchestra, St. Paul City Ballet, Science Museum of Minn. & Omnitheater. Univ. of Minnesota Institute of Agriculture, Hamline Univ., St. Thomas, St. Catherine, Bethel, Concordia, and Macalester colleges, and William Mitchell College of Law; city school system with 80 public schools and 61 private schools.
Recreational facilities: more than 900 lakes in metro area, 438 tennis courts, 148 swimming beaches, 513 parks, 50 golf courses, 27 ski centers; 52 neighborhood recreation centers, 35 miles of parkways, 100 miles of hiking and biking trails.
Convention facilities: Civic Center with 101,000 sq. ft. exhibit space, seating for 35,000 in 4 main buildings, 15 meeting halls; 50 hotels and motels.
Other attractions: Winter Carnival in Jan., Minnesota State Fair, Como Park Zoo and Conservatory; onyx statue of Indian God of Peace in City Hall, Minnesota Historical Society Museums, Arts & Science Center, Fort Snelling State Park, Minn. Zoological Garden nearby.
History: once called "Pig's Eye" for first settler, Pierre "Pig's Eye" Parrant; changed to St. Paul when Father Lucien Galtier built St. Paul's Chapel 1841; became town 1847, city 1854.
Further information: St. Paul Area Chamber of Commerce, 701 North Central Tower, 445 Minnesota Street, St. Paul, MN 55101.

St. Petersburg, Florida

The World Almanac is sponsored in Florida's Suncoast Area by The St. Petersburg Times and Evening Independent, 490 1st Avenue S., St. Petersburg, FL 33701; phone (813) 893-8111; Times founded 1884, Independent 1906; circulation Times (morn.) 222,336, Independent (evening) 42,346, Sunday Times 277,857; Eugene C. Patterson, editor of The Times and president of The Times Publishing Co.; Robert Stiff, editor, The Independent; John B. Lake, executive vice president and publisher, The Times Publishing Co.

Population: 236,893 (city), 728,409 (Pinellas County), 1,550,035 (SMSA); Pinellas County (Mar. 1981) employment 244,100, unemployment 5.8%.
Industry and Commerce: 3.2 million tourists visited county in 1980; industries include General Electric, Honeywell, Sperry, Eckerd Drugs, Jim Walter Research, All-State Insurance regional office, GTE, Paradyne Corp., ECI, Aircraft Porous Media, VRN, Silor Optical; ABA Industries, county (1980) retail sales $3.5 billion.
Transportation: U.S. 19, 41, and 98 link city to rest of gulf coast Florida; interstates 175, 75, and 4 link St. Petersburg with Tampa, Orlando, and east coast; Tampa International Airport 25 miles from downtown; other airports are St. Petersburg-Clearwater International and Albert Whitted; Amtrak, Seaboard Coast Line railroads; Greyhound and Trailways bus lines.
Communications: 6 TV, 46 radio stations.
Convention and Tourist facilities: over 75,000 units house 160,000 visitors; Bayfront Center seats 8,250 in arena, 2,250 in auditorium; Pinellas restaurants can serve 116,500 people at one time; Disney World 2 hours away.

Medical facilities: 13 major hospitals; Bay Pines veterans complex adding 1,150 new beds; All Children's Hospital.
Cultural facilities: Museum of Fine Arts, Gulf Coast Symphony, Historical Museum, community theaters, Eckerd College Free Institutions Forums; varied musical, theatrical, and dance events at Bayfront Center complex.
Educational facilities: Univ. of South Florida's downtown Bayboro Campus, Stetson College of Law, Eckerd College, St. Petersburg Junior College.
Recreational facilities: 76 parks on 1,800 acres, many with recreational buildings, pools, tennis courts, boat ramps, and picnic areas; municipal and private marinas; deep sea fishing, golf courses, baseball fields.
Sports: St. Louis Cardinals and New York Mets spring training site; greyhound racing, baseball, jai alai, horse racing, NFL football, basketball, pro tennis, boat racing, NASL soccer; LPGA-PGA team golf, LPGA S&H Green Stamps golf classic.
Additional information: St. Petersburg Chamber of Commerce, 225 4th Street S., St. Petersburg, FL 33701.

Salem, Oregon

The World Almanac is sponsored in the Salem area by the Statesman Journal Newspapers, 280 Church Street NE, P.O. Box 13009, Salem, OR 97309; phone (503) 399-6611; publisher of the morning Statesman-Journal; daily circulation 65,297, Sunday 62,161; John H. McMillan, publisher.

Population: 89,233 (city), 249,655 (SMSA).
Area: 32 sq. mi. on the Willamette River in the center of the bountiful Willamette Valley 50 miles south of Portland; 61 miles from Pacific Ocean; state capital, Marion County seat.
Industry: government (over 14,500 state employees), agricul-

ture (over 100 crops), food processing — 2d in nation for fruit, berries, and vegetables; over 15 canneries produced over 10 million cases of canned goods and 260 million pounds of frozen foods; lumber and lumber products; manufacturing (batteries, radios, metal products, feeds, paints, textiles, food processing cans); pulp and paper mill.

Commerce: retail sales (1979) $967 million; med. household income (1979) $15,908; 7 commercial banks, 6 savings & loan associations.

Transportation: 2 rail freight lines, Amtrak; Greyhound, Trailways bus lines, 11 truck lines, Air Oregon.

Communications: one public TV, 6 radio stations, one daily newspaper, one farm weekly newspaper.

Medical facilities: hospital with 2 units, General and Memorial.

Cultural facilities: symphony orchestra, art association, little theater, Bush House museum, Deepwood, Mission Mill museum, Northwest History collection, Willamette Univ., Civic Center.

Education: metro area includes 108 public schools — 89 ele-

mentary, 12 junior highs, 20 high schools, and 15 parochial schools; State Schools for the Blind and Deaf, Chemeketa Community College, Willamette Univ., Western Baptist Bible College, and Oregon College of Education.

Recreation: back-packing, fishing, golf, snow and water skiing, camping, 44 parks in 5 mile radius; hunting for deer, elk, and fowl; Bush Pasture Park; within one hour drive Mt. Hood, Detroit Lake, Oregon Coast, Mt. Jefferson, 9 golf courses in 15 mile radius; 70 tennis courts in area.

Sports: Salem Senators baseball, Northwest League.

History: founded in 1842 by Methodist missionary, Jason Lee.

Further information: Chamber of Commerce, P.O. Box 231, Salem, OR 97308.

Salt Lake City, Utah

The World Almanac is sponsored in the Salt Lake City area by the Salt Lake Tribune, 143 S. Main Street, Salt Lake City, UT 84111; phone (801) 237-2045; founded Apr. 15, 1871; circulation 114,629 daily, 189,311 Sunday; publisher John W. Gallivan; editor Will Fehr; 1957 Pulitzer Prize; civic projects, statewide civic beautification awards; Sub for Santa program; Community Christmas Tree Plantings; Spring Garden Festival; Ski Race; No Champs Tennis and Golf tournaments, Newspaper in Education; Old Fashioned 4th of July.

Population: 163,033 (city), 619,066 (county), 935,280 (SMSA); first in state; 79% of state pop. lives in Wasatch Front Counties of Salt Lake, Davis, Utah, and Weber; state capital and Salt Lake County seat.

Area: nestled in a vast valley (elev. 4,327 ft.) surrounded by Wasatch and Oquirrh mountains.

Industry: labor-force (metro area, 1980 est.) 282,242; average unemployment rate 4.9%; effective buying income $3.9 billion (county, 1979); per family income (county, 1979) $19,194; total construction value (county, 1980) $344.9 million; major employers are Hill AFB (30 miles north), Univ. of Utah, Brigham Young Univ., Granite School District, Kennecott Copper Corp., local defense industries; county has over 900 manufacturing plants; metro area major center for electronics, apparel manufacturing, mining, smelting, refining, distribution, warehousing center of Mountain West; area becoming center for energy resources development operations.

Transportation: 16 air lines, customs office, free-trade zone, International Airport; 22 freight carriers maintain terminals in city; geographic center of 11 western states; hub of central transcontinental highway system; 3 railroads, all major western truck, bus lines.

Communications: 2 daily newspapers, 4 commercial TV stations, 3 cable TV, 2 public TV, Home Box Office TV; 18 radio stations.

New construction: Sheraton Hotel, $62 million; $28 million,

480-room Marriott Hotel; $16.5 million expansion of Salt Palace convention, exhibit center; two 23-story residential condominiums, state office bldg.; 13-story bank bldg.

Medical facilities: 10 hospitals, including Univ. of Utah Medical Center, major research in transplant surgery.

Educational facilities: Univ. of Utah; Westminster, Utah Technical, and LDS Business colleges.

Cultural facilities: Utah Symphony Orchestra, Mormon Tabernacle Choir, Ballet West, Utah Opera Co., Ririe-Woodbury Co., Repertory Dance Theatre, 2 cultural arts halls.

Other attractions: Temple Square, home of 4 million-member Church of Jesus Christ of Latter-Day Saints (Mormons); Salt Palace Civic Auditorium; 700 acres in 22 parks, 25 playgrounds, 10 golf courses, 100 tennis courts; near Great Salt Lake (7 times more salty than ocean); Hogle Zoological Gardens, Kennecott Copper's Bingham mine; 4 well-defined seasons, mean annual temperature 51.0 degrees F.

Sports: 9 major ski resorts; Golden Eagles (Central Hockey League), Salt Lake Gulls baseball; Bonneville Salt Flats, Univ. of Utah in major NCAA sports; Utah Jazz (NBA).

History: founded July 24, 1847 by Brigham Young and contingent of pioneers.

Further information: Chamber of Commerce, 19 E. 2d So.; Utah Travel Council, Council Hall; Salt Lake Valley Visitors and Convention Bureau, West Temple at First South, all Salt Lake City, UT.

San Antonio, Texas

The World Almanac is sponsored in the San Antonio area by the S. A. Express (morning) and S. A. News (evening), P.O. Box 2171, San Antonio, TX 78297; phone (512) 225-7411; circulation daily, Express 81,112, News 73,954, Sunday Express-News 186,815; chairman K. Rupert Murdoch, publisher and editor Charles O. Kilpatrick; Express-News Corp. is a division of News America, Inc.

Population: 785,410 city, 988,800 county, total employed 387,300.

Area: 1,247 sq. mi. (Bexar County); 2 1/2 hours from Gulf Coast and Mexican border.

Industry: 5 military bases include Kelly AFB, largest employer; fast-growing medical industry; diverse manufacturing, tourism, construction, trade, and service industries.

Commerce: center for 100 mile radius retail trade area, livestock production; retail sales (1980) $14.4 billion.

Federal facilities: Kelly AFB, hq. AF Air Security Service; Randolph AFB, hq. Air Training Command & AF Personnel Center; Brooks AFB, hq. AF Aerospace Medical Division; Lackland AFB with Wilford Hall USAF Medical Center; Fort Sam Houston, hq. 5th Army, & Army Health Services Command, Brooke Army Medical Center.

Medical facilities: Univ. of Texas Medical, Dental, Nursing schools; Audie Murphy VA Hospital; Southwest Research Institute; Southwest Foundation of Res. and Educ.

Transportation: International Airport, Stinson air field, 14 major airlines; 3 rail freight, Amtrak; 6 bus lines; 44 common-carrier truck lines; 576 miles of freeway and state high-

ways.

Educational facilities: Univ. of Texas at San Antonio; Trinity, St. Mary's, and Our Lady of the Lake universities; Incarnate Word College; 2 jr. colleges, San Antonio, St. Philip's; permanent extension of National Univ. of Mexico.

Convention facilities: Convention Center with large arena, theater, exhibit, meeting space.

Cultural facilities: symphony orchestra; Institute of Texan Cultures, Mexican Cultural Institute, Witte Museum, McNay Art Institute, San Antonio Museum of Art.

Sports: Spurs (NBA), Dodgers minor league baseball, Charros minor league football; livestock show and rodeo, Texas Open PGA Tournament, Avon Ladies Tennis Tournament.

Other attractions: historic Alamo, old Spanish missions of San Jose, Concepcion, Capistrano, Espada; Hemis Fair Plaza with 750-foot observation tower-restaurant; downtown River Walk; zoo; Fiesta San Antonio, Folklife Festival.

Further information: Greater San Antonio Chamber of Commerce, 602 E. Commerce, P. O. Box 1628, San Antonio, TX 78296.

San Bernardino, California

The World Almanac is sponsored in the San Bernardino area by the Sun, 399 North D Street, San Bernardino, CA 92401; phone (714) 889-9666; Sun founded 1894; daily circulation 79,982, Sunday 87,187; member Gannett chain; publisher William Honeysett, advertising director William Ridenour, editor Wayne C. Sargent.

Population: 118,057 (city), 1,557,080 (2-county metro area).

Area: 47.22 sq. mi. at base of Cajon Pass, 58 miles east of Los Angeles; San Bernardino County seat.

Industry: business and industrial firms include Celotex-Marley, Scott Paper (foam div.), Captive Plastics, Culligan, Edginton Oil, Hanford Foundry, Knudsen Dairy, Mode O'-Day, Pepsi Cola and Seven-Up bottling plants, Santa Fe Railway, TRW Systems, and Terry Industries.

Commerce: trading center for 20,189 sq. mi. San Bernardino county, largest in the nation; retail sales (1979) $938 million; 7 banks, 22 branches; 12 savings and loan assns.; 2 major shopping center complexes, each parking over 5,000 cars.

Transportation: Santa Fe, Southern Pacific, and Union Pacific rail lines, Amtrak; Greyhound and Continental bus lines; major interstate highways leading from Mexico to Canada and West to East Coast; municipal airport and nearby Ontario International Airport.

Communications: 15 radio and one VHF educational TV station; access to 5 Los Angeles channels.

Medical facilities: 3 major hospitals with 995 beds; major research and training center for heart surgery and hip and knee replacement surgery.

Federal facilities: Norton Air Force Base.

Cultural facilities: symphony orchestra, Civic Light Opera, nearby Redlands Bowl (summer concerts); National Orange Show with orange festival every spring; Convention Center-Exhibit Hall complex.

Educational facilities: California State College, junior college, 3 major universities nearby.

New construction: 6 redevelopment project areas with commercial and industrial development sites.

Sports: Little League Western Regional Headquarters.

History: founded 1852 by Mormons who purchased land from Spanish grant holders.

Further information: Chamber of Commerce, 546 West 6th Street, San Bernardino, CA 92401.

San Diego, California

The World Almanac is sponsored in San Diego by The San Diego Union and The Tribune (Copley Newspapers), P.O. Box 191, San Diego, CA 92112; phone (714) 299-3131; Union founded 1868 (pioneer daily of Southwest); circulation, Union (morn.) 207,171, Tribune (eve.) 127,271, Sunday Union 329,820; publisher Helen K. Copley, general manager Al De Bakcsy, Union editor Gerald L. Warren, Tribune editor Neil Morgan.

Population: 876,504 (city), 1,859,623 (SMSA); total civilian employment 696,800.

Area: (county) 4,255 sq. mi.; 70 mi. Pacific Coast, San Clemente to Mexican border.

Industry: tourism, manufacturing, military and agriculture; manufactured products earn $5.9 billion a year; non-military payroll $6.9 billion, military $1 billion; tourist spending over $1 billion; corporations with bases or divisions include Bendix, Burroughs, Control Data, Cubic, General Dynamics, Gulf, Honeywell, International Harvester's Solar division, NCR Corp., Pacific Southwest Airlines, Rohr, Sea World, Teledyne Ryan, TraveLodge, Wickes, Van Camp sea food, Foodmaker (Jack-in-the-Box); aerospace, rapid transit design and manufacture, oceanography, nuclear energy, medicine important; also shipbuilding, tuna fishing, clothing, ocean shipping; among top 20 counties in farm products (avocados, cut flowers, eggs); Marine Corps Recruit Depot, Naval Training Center, North Island and Miramar Naval Air Stations, Naval Electronics Lab and Undersea Center, Marine Corps base at Camp Pendleton.

Transportation: freeway system is state's 2d largest; Amtrak, 11 airlines, bus lines; primary airport Lindbergh Field.

Communications: some 30 TV and radio stations.

Medical facilities: Salk Institute for Biological Studies, Scripps Clinic & Research Foundation; Naval Hospital; many hospitals.

Education and Cultural facilities: San Diego State Univ., U.S. International Univ., Univ. of San Diego, Univ. of California, San Diego (3 colleges and Scripps Institution of Oceanography), Point Loma College; symphony; Old Globe Theatre (functioning reproduction of Shakespeare's Globe Theatre); opera; ballet; Fine Arts and Timken galleries; La Jolla Museum of Contemporary Art.

Other attractions: world famous zoo and wild animal park; Balboa Park, central 1,400 acres containing museums, zoo, Fleet Space Theatre (computerized planetarium), many other attractions; Mission Bay Park includes Sea World; "Old San Diego" state historical park; "Star of India" ship-museum; visits to neighboring Mexico (Tijuana); 70 miles of beaches.

Sports: NFL Chargers; NL Padres; NBA Clippers; NASL Sockers; Holiday Bowl; Andy Williams Open golf tournament; racing at Del Mar, Caliente (Mexico).

Other attractions: climate sunny; summer and winter resort; average temp. 68° in summer, 57° in winter, rainfall mainly December to March; famous "place names" include La Jolla (part of city of San Diego); 70 golf courses including Torrey Pines; large convention facilities; off-shore "whale watching."

History: area discovered 1542 by Cabrillo, founded in 1769 by Father Junipero Serra.

Further information: San Diego Chamber of Commerce, 110 West "C", Suite 1600, San Diego, CA 92101.

San Francisco, California

The World Almanac is sponsored in the San Francisco-Oakland area by The San Francisco Examiner, P.O. Box 3100, Rincon Annex, San Francisco, CA 94119; phone (415) 777-2424; founded June 12, 1865; circulation daily Examiner, 157,206; Sunday Examiner & Chronicle, 633,710; president R. A. Hearst, general manager Jim Sevrens; major awards: Pulitzer Prize, Freedoms Foundation, California Newspaper Publisher's Assn.; Examiner sponsors Golden Gloves, Bay to Breakers Race, Opera in the Park, Senior Citizens Christmas Camp.

Population: 678,974, 3,226,867 (SMSA); total employed 530,100 (city).

Area: 44.6 sq. mi. on the northern tip of a peninsula; San Francisco County seat.

Industry: food products, printing, publishing, fabricated metal products; west's financial capital and administrative center for many of the nation's leading corporations; West Coast operations' headquarters for a majority of the federal agencies; finance, insurance, and real estate; a major port of the Pacific Coast.

Commerce: wholesale-retail employment 107,500; services 144,200; manufacturing 50,100; total wholesale and retail outlets 26,399, taxable sales $4.9 billion; 40 banks with 157 branches; 25 savings and loans with 39 branches; total deposits in banks $24 billion.

Transportation: 37 major airlines serve the Bay Area; International Airport processed 22.2 million passengers, 318,670 metric tons of freight (1980); Municipal Railway (intra-city);

AC-Transit and Bay Area Rapid Transit System (BART) to East Bay cities; Greyhound bus and Southern Pacific Railroad to Peninsula areas; Golden Gate Bridge District bus and ferry service to Marin County; Port of San Francisco services available: LASH, BULK, general cargo, containerization and barge service.

Communications: 2 major newspapers; 118 others serving the Bay Area; 45 radio stations, 7 TV channels received directly, one cable TV system.

Medical facilities: 24 general hospitals with over 7,406 beds, 5 specialty hospitals with over 1,935 beds; 3,033 physicians/surgeons and 772 dentists; Univ. of Cal. Medical Center, with 42 buildings, is a general teaching and research institute and is the largest kidney transplant center in the world.

Cultural facilities: San Francisco Opera, Spring Opera, Western Opera Theater, symphony, ballet, Civic Light Opera, American Conservatory Theater, Japanese Cultural Center, Chinese Cultural Center, International Film Festival; 3 museums, 29 libraries, 540 churches, and 136 theaters.

Educational facilities: 97 public elementary schools; 17 junior high, 11 high schools, and 965 special schools with a combined enrollment of 32,466; Univ. of California, San Francisco; California State Univ., Univ. of San Francisco,

and City College of San Francisco.

New construction: Louise M. Davies Symphony Hall, $28 million home of S.F. Symphony, with 3,000 seating capacity; George R. Moscone Convention Center, 650,000 sq. ft. bldg. on 11 acres.

Recreational facilities: 120 parks and many miniparks, 78 playgrounds, 6 golf courses, numerous tennis courts, 10 swimming pools, 5½ miles of ocean beach, one lake, one fishing pier, Marina small craft harbor and 3 yacht clubs.

Convention facilities: 102 hotels and motels with over 20,000 rooms.

Sports: Candlestick Park, home of the NL Giants and NFL 49ers; pro teams in all major sports.

Other attractions: zoo and 1,013-acre Golden Gate Park containing the California Academy of Sciences, De Young Museum, Japanese Tea Garden, and Arboretum; cable cars, Fisherman's Wharf, Chinatown, the Ferry Building.

History: San Francisco Bay discovered 1769 by Sgt. Jose Ortega; pueblo of Yerba Buena est. 1834, renamed San Francisco on January 3, 1847; inc. April 15, 1850.

Further information: Chamber of Commerce, 465 California Street, San Francisco, CA 94104; San Francisco Convention and Visitors Bureau, 1390 Market Street, San Francisco, CA 94102.

San Jose, California

The World Almanac is sponsored in the San Jose area by The Mercury and News, 750 Ridder Park Drive, San Jose, CA 95190; phone (408) 289-5000; Mercury founded June 20, 1851, News July 23, 1883; combined daily circulation 223,386, Sunday Mercury News 270,063; president and publisher P. Anthony Ridder, editor Robert Ingle.

Population: 636,550 (city), 1,295,071 (metro area coextensive with Santa Clara County); total employed 722,800 (metro, Apr. '81).

Area: broad alluvial 832,256-acre valley at south end of San Francisco Bay; Santa Clara County seat.

Industry: largest county in northern Cal. for manufacturing employment and total wages; called "Silicon Valley" due to high technology semiconductor and other electronics firms; IBM, Hewlett-Packard, Varian Assocs., Intel Corp., National Semiconductor, Memorex, Amdahl, Lockheed Missiles & Space; diversity shown by Ford Motor Co., Spectra Physics, FMC Corp., Syntex; county a major producer of cut flowers; over 50 wineries, many distributing world wide.

Commerce: leading retail trade center of northern Cal., $6.2 billion in 1980; 140 shopping centers; 2d nationally in median household income among U.S. metro areas; 85% earn $10,000 plus annually, 76% earn $15,000 plus, 50% earn $25,000 plus (metro).

Transportation: Municipal Airport served by 8 major airlines, 4 commuter carriers; highway system interconnected with inter-state in north-south, east-west directions; Southern Pacific and Western Pacific railroads; county transit buses link to Bay Area Rapid Transit.

Education: San Jose State, Santa Clara, and Stanford universities, plus several community colleges; 47% of adult population is college educated (metro).

Cultural facilities: 100 year old Symphony, Civic Light Opera; Actors Repertory, Dance and Children's Musical theaters; 2,700 seat Center for Performing Arts; Flint Center; San Jose Historical Museum; Rosicrucian Egyptian Museum, Planetarium, Art Gallery; De Saisset Gallery and Museum; Montalvo Center for the Arts; Triton Museum of Art; New Almaden Mercury Mining Museum.

Sports: Earthquakes (soccer), Missions (minor league baseball); 8 reservoirs with boat ramps, 2 with camping; outlet to S. F. Bay for ocean sports; Amer. and Nat. league football and baseball franchises.

Other attractions: Japanese Tea Gardens; Lick Observatory; Winchester Mystery House; Marriott's Great America.

History: founded 1777, first civil settlement in Cal.; county is one of original 27 in state; first public school in state, San Jose Granary, 1795; first state capitol, Dec. 15, 1849.

Further information: Chamber of Commerce Metro-San Jose, One Paseo de San Antonio, San Jose, CA 95113; phone (408) 998-7000.

San Juan, Puerto Rico

The World Almanac is sponsored in Puerto Rico by the San Juan Star, GPO Box 4187, San Juan, PR 00936; phone (809) 782-4200; founded Nov. 2, 1959; circulation 45,000 daily; 50,000 Sunday; president and general manager John A. Zerbe Jr.; vice president and editor Andrew T. Viglucci; major awards include 1961 Pulitzer Prize for editorial writing; APME citations 1960, 1965; staff awards include 1970 IAPA Mergenthaler Award, 1972 Overseas Press Club Award; National Spelling Bee 1975 champion.

Population: 535,000 (city), 1,200,000 (metro area), first in commonwealth.

Area: 47 sq. mi. in Caribbean, capital city.

Industry: seat of Puerto Rico's tourism industry with 19 luxury hotels and several dozen high rise condominiums. City is also the commercial and shipping hub of the island and is a major stop for cruise ships plying the Caribbean. Major industries are electronics, pharmaceuticals, and computers and computer components. Petrochemical industry represents $1.5 billion in investments. Center of island's rum industry with the Bacardi distillery on San Juan Bay, the largest in the world. More than 75 per cent of all rum sold in U.S. is Puerto Rican rum.

Transportation: San Juan International Airport handles more than 500,000 passengers monthly with 4 major U.S. airlines and 10 foreign lines; Isla Grande Airport handles

small aircraft traffic.

Education: seat of the Rio Piedras campus of the Univ. of Puerto Rico, the public university system, InterAmerican Univ., College of the Sacred Heart, UPR Medical Sciences campus and UPR Law School, World Univ., and several junior and regional colleges.

Federal facilities: Ft. Buchanan army base with 9-hole golf course on grounds; Roosevelt Roads Naval Station.

Cultural facilities and events: The Casals Festival, guided for 18 years by the late Maestro Casals, is an annual June event bringing together some of the world's finest musicians; annual San Juan Carnival, last week in June; the Puerto Rico Institute of Culture is housed in a restored Dominican convent; El Morro, the Spanish-built fortress that guards the entrance to San Juan Harbor; numerous art museums i

Old San Juan; the Puerto Rico Symphony Orchestra in concerts spread over the year; the capitol building and governor's mansion; Palace of Fine Arts.

Convention facilities: Condado Convention Center seats 5,000 for meetings, 3,000 for meals.

New construction: Old City restoration program, Ponce Art Museum.

Sports: Hiram Bithorn Stadium, baseball, track, and outdoor events; Roberto Clemente Coliseum, basketball, box-

ing, and indoor events; soccer, cockfighting arenas (legal).

History: discovered by Columbus on his 2d voyage to the New World in 1493, colonized by Juan Ponce de Leon, Puerto Rico's first Spanish governor; since 1952 a commonwealth freely associated with the United States. Free market with U.S. and same currency, common citizenship.

Further information: Chamber of Commerce, 100 Tetuan Street, Old San Juan; Dept. of Tourism, Banco de Ponce Bldg., Hato Rey, PR.

Santa Ana, California
See Orange County, California

Saskatoon, Saskatchewan, Canada

The World Almanac is sponsored in central and northern Saskatchewan by the Saskatoon Star-Phoenix, 204 Fifth Avenue North, Saskatoon, Sask. S7K 2P1; phone (306) 652-9200; Daily Star and Phoenix founded in 1906 and 1902 respectively, merged in 1928 into the Star-Phoenix; circulation 55,000; publisher, Michael C. Sifton; executive vice-president, James K. Struthers.

Population: 150,000, 2d in province; per capita income $9,920.

Area: 45.38 sq. mi. on the South Saskatchewan River in the central part of the province.

Industry: retail, wholesale, service distribution hub for primary trading area of 250,000 and secondary trading area of 510,000; center of the province's $2 billion mining industry, primarily potash (1980 sales $986 million), oil ($880 million), uranium ($224 million); other major industries include agriculture, meat packing, construction, light manufacturing, and high technology electronics including fibre optics.

Commerce: 1980 retail sales totalled $775.5 million or $5,201 per capita (36% above the national average); unemployment rate in 1980 varied from 3.6% to 5.3%; job opportunities continue to grow at a rate of 3.5% to 4% per year.

Transportation: 4 scheduled airlines, 2 railways, 3 bus lines, several air charter services and numerous freight carriers; airport is the fastest growing in Canada and has international status with flights to the U.S.; Yellowhead highway is easiest access through Rockies from prairies to Pacific.

Communications: one daily newspaper, 2 local TV stations, cable TV with community channel and 4 U.S. stations; 8 radio stations, one farm weekly, one community weekly.

Medical facilities: 3 major hospitals with 1,231 beds; essential health care costs are covered by a government-run medicare program; University Hospital is a teaching hospital.

Educational facilities: Univ. of Saskatchewan, famed for agriculture, space, physics, medicine, veterinary colleges; Kelsey Institute of Applied Arts & Sciences, School for the Deaf, School for Retarded Children, French School.

Cultural facilities: Centennial Auditorium, multi-purpose theater (2,000 seats), convention center (1,800 seats); Western Development Museum houses North America's largest display of antique cars, farm implements, and 1910 Pioneer Village; Mendel Art Gallery; John Diefenbaker Centre, Saskatoon Symphony Orchestra; 4 theater cos.

Recreation: 2,494 acres of parkland, wild animal farm, 5 golf courses, 5 swimming pools, 5 indoor ice rinks, man-made ski mountain, skeet range; variety of resort areas are within easy driving distance.

History: founded 1882 as a Temperance colony, incorporated 1906; named after famous Saskatoon berry found on banks of river; close to battle sites of the Riel rebellion of 1885.

Further information: Board of Trade, Bessborough Hotel, Saskatoon, Sask. S7K 3G8

Savannah, Georgia

The World Almanac is sponsored in the Savannah area by the Savannah News-Press, 111 West Bay Street, Savannah GA 31402; phone (912) 236-9511; publisher of the Savannah Morning News and Evening Press; combined circulation 77,030 daily, 72,961 Sunday; Donald E. Harwood, general manager; Wallace M. Davis Jr., executive editor; Gene Stewart, advertising director.

Population: 141,634 (city), 225,581 (SMSA); SMSA civilian labor force 88,239.

Area: 57 sq. mi. on Savannah River, 18 mi. from Atlantic Ocean; Chatham County seat.

Industry: world's largest pulp-to-paper container plant owned by Union Camp Corp.; Savannah Sugar Refining Corp., nation's 3d largest seller; jet aircraft manufacturer (Gulf Stream American Aviation Corp.); tea packaging (Tetley); fertilizer materials, ship repair, titanium dioxide production (American Cyanamid).

Commerce: hub of "Coastal Empire" economic center of Ga. and 3 S. Carolina counties; the Southeast's leading foreign trade port between Baltimore and New Orleans; served by 97 steamship lines, 36 deep water terminals; retail sales (1980) $1.3 billion; 7 commercial banks, 42 branches; 4 savings and loan assns, 11 branches.

Transportation: 4 rail freight lines, Seaboard Coastline, Southern, Central of Georgia, and Savannah-Atlanta; Amtrak; Greyhound and Trailways bus lines, 74 truck lines; Delta, Eastern, Air Florida Airlines; intercoastal waterway.

Communications: Savannah News-Press, Inc. (daily and Sunday), 3 weekly papers; 4 TV and 14 radio stations.

New construction: Ga. Port Authority's port expansion; Mulberry Inn, Days Inn, Oglethorpe Mall expansion.

Medical facilities: 4 hospitals, Medical Arts Center.

Federal facilities: U. S. Customs House, Ft. Stewart/Hunter assigned the 24th Infantry Division, 19,367 troops, 280,000 acres, 35 mi. so. of city.

Cultural facilities: Savannah Art Assn., Savannah Symphony, Ballet Guild, Little Theatre, Telfair Academy of Arts

and Sciences, Kennedy Fine Arts Center, SSC; Fine Arts Bldg., ASC; Maritime Museum, Fort Pulaski National Monument and Military Museum, Civic Center.

Education: Armstrong State and Savannah State colleges, units of the Univ. System of Georgia; Savannah College of Art & Design; 60 public, 3 vocational-tech, 18 parochial, 10 private, 3 business schools; Skidaway Inst. of Oceanography and Aquarium.

Recreation: 17 theaters; 7 golf courses, 33 public tennis courts; 71 squares, parks, and playgrounds; 3 sports fields; 2 recreation centers; 2 stadiums; 4 fishing piers, 12 boat ramps.

Convention facilities: 8,000 seat auditorium at Civic Center.

Sports: Braves Southern League baseball; Savannah Speedway; SSC Tigers, ASC Pirates.

Annual events: St. Patrick's Day Parade, Oktober Festival, Blessing of the Fleet, Night in Olde Savannah, Arts Festival, Farmer's Market, Christmas Parade, Garden Club Show.

Other attractions: Savannah Science, Ships of the Sea, and Antique Car museums; Fort Jackson, Fort Pulaski, Fort Screven and Tybee Museum, Fort McAllister; downtown historic section; river cruises.

History: mother city of Ga.; Gen. James Oglethorpe and 120 followers settled last of 13 original colonies here; site of Revolutionary War battle, end of Gen. Sherman's Civil War "March to the Sea"; much of the old city is a national historic landmark, largest in the country.

Further information: Savannah Area Chamber of Commerce, Savannah Visitors Center, 301 W. Broad Street, Savannah, GA 31402; phone (912) 233-3069.

Seattle, Washington

The World Almanac is sponsored in the Seattle area by The Seattle Times, Fairview Avenue N. & John Street, P.O. Box 70, Seattle, WA 98111; phone (206) 464-2111; founded 1896 by Alden J. Blethen; circulation 261,432 daily, 344,724 Sunday; publisher John A. Blethen; president W.J. Pennington; senior vice president and general manager Harold G. Fuhrman.

Population: 493,846 (city), 1,600,944 (SMSA); first in state; total employed (metro) 799,100.

Area: 91.6 sq. mi. between Puget Sound and Lake Washington; King County seat.

Industry: headquarters for Boeing, 79,800 employees, world's largest manufacturer of commercial jet aircraft; Port of Seattle has $1 billion current value of properties and facilities including Seattle-Tacoma airport; nation's 4th largest containerized-shipping seaport; area has 42,360 employer units; major industries are transportation products, retail trade, insurance, banking, shipbuilding, wood products, and food products.

Commerce: business center for western Wash. and Alaska; major import-export center for Far East; total retail sales (1980) $8.67 billion; per capita income (1980) $9,300; 41 commercial and savings banks with 310 branches.

Transportation: 3 transcontinental railroads, Amtrak; International Airport served by 19 scheduled airlines, 9 commuter airlines, handled 9.2 million passengers (1980); ferries serve Puget Sound, Canada, and Alaska.

Communications: 5 daily newspapers in metro area; 7 TV, 23 AM and 19 FM stations.

New construction: $537.8 million (city).

Medical facilities: 26 hospitals, including Univ. of Wash. Health Sciences Center, Northwest Kidney Center, and Fred Hutchinson Cancer Research Center.

Educational facilities: Four 4-year colleges: Univ. of Wash., Seattle Univ., Cornish Institute, and Seattle Pacific Univ.; 7 community colleges.

Federal facilities: 13th Naval Dist. Hdqts.; Pacific Marine center, National Oceanic & Atmospheric Admin.; 13th Coast Guard Dist. Hdqts.; many regional offices, 37-story federal office bldg.

Cultural facilities: symphony orchestra, opera association, art museum and 10 other museums, 92 art galleries, 6 professional theater companies.

Recreation: major boating center; salmon and trout fishing; several nearby ski areas; Mt. Rainier, North Cascades, and Olympic National parks within 2-hour drive.

Sports: Breakers (Western Hockey League); Kingdome, concrete-dome stadium, home of NFL Seahawks, AL Mariners, NBA SuperSonics and NASL Sounders.

Other attractions: Seattle Center, site of 1962 world's fair, has 14,000-seat coliseum, 3,100-seat opera house, playhouse, arena, Space Needle, and Pacific Science Center; Seattle Aquarium, Woodland Park Zoo.

History: settled 1851, named for an Indian chief who befriended the settlers; virtually destroyed by fire in 1889, quickly rebuilt; Alaska Gold Rush of 1897 spurred growth and propelled Seattle toward its status as the Northwest's principal city.

Further information: Chamber of Commerce, 215 Columbia Street, Seattle, WA 98104, or Convention and Visitors Bureau, 1815 7th Avenue, 98101.

Sioux Falls, South Dakota

The World Almanac is sponsored in the Sioux Falls area by the Argus Leader, 200 S. Minnesota Avenue, Sioux Falls, SD 57102; phone (605) 331-2200, a Gannett newspaper; founded in 1881; circulation 44,652 daily (A.M.), 55,154 Sunday; publisher and president Larry Fuller.

Population: 81,182 (city), 109,432 (metro); largest in state.

Area: 36 sq. mi. in southeastern South Dakota, located at junction of interstates 29 and 90; Minnehaha County seat.

Industry and Commerce: Sioux Falls stockyards are 3d largest in the U.S.; John Morrell & Co. is the largest employer with 3,200 employees; there are 7 commercial banks, 5 savings and loan assns.; wholesale and retail center for South Dakota, parts of Minnesota and Iowa; yearly retail sales over $6.69 million.

Transportation: served by 5 major highways, 4 bus lines, and 3 rail lines; Joe Foss Field with modern terminal is within 2 miles of business district and has 3 major airlines.

Communication: daily and weekly newspaper, 3 TV and 12 radio stations; state headquarters for Northwestern Bell Telephone Co.

Medical facilities: 4 hospitals with over 1,040 beds, including the Royal C. Johnson Memorial Hospital for war veterans and Crippled Children's Hospital and School.

Federal facilities: Earth Resources Observation Systems Data Center of the U.S. Dept. of Interior.

Cultural and Educational facilities: public library, convention center, Civic Fine Arts Assn., Sioux Falls Symphony, Community Playhouse, Augustana College, Sioux Falls College, North American Baptist Seminary, the SD School for the Deaf, vocational school, 2 business schools, 2 nurses training schools, 28 public and 9 parochial schools; 96 churches.

Recreation: 52 parks, 4 swimming pools, 3 municipal golf courses, Great Plains Zoo, 10,000-seat Arena, 4,000-seat Coliseum, Packer Stadium.

Further information: Chamber of Commerce, 127 E. 10th Street, Sioux Falls, SD 57101.

Spokane, Washington

The World Almanac is sponsored in the Spokane area by the Spokane Daily Chronicle, P.O. Box 2168 Spokane, WA 99210; phone (509) 455-7121; founded 1881; circulation 59,026 daily; published by Cowles Pub. Co., William H. Cowles, 3rd, president; John E. Smithmeyer, general manager; Gordon Coe, managing editor.

Population: 171,300 (city), 341,835 (county); 2d in state; total employed 134,900.

Area: 52.12 sq. mi. centrally located in eastern Washington, 18 miles from the Idaho border; Spokane County seat.

Industry: heavily based on service industries and wholesale and retail trade with 462 manufacturing establishments; 2,544 retail, 717 wholesale, and 2,563 establishments dealing with services; annual payrolls in Spokane County $1.583 billion; effective buying income (1980) for Spokane County $2.8 billion; Kaiser Aluminum and Chemical Corp. has 2 plants, a reduction plant and a rolling mill; area industries include forest products, silver, lead, zinc, and other mining; agriculture, poultry, dairy and meat products, flour and cereals, livestock, processed foods; commercial truck trailer bodies, electrical fixtures, electronic keyboard manufacturing, and plastic products.

Commerce: retail, transportation, and medical center of a 80,000 sq. mi. inland market in eastern Washington, northern Idaho, and western Montana, known as the Inland Empire with a population of more than 1.4 million; retail sales in the Inland Empire $5.9 billion, metro area $1.5 billion; commercial banks, 3 mutual savings banks, and 6 savings and loan assns.

Transportation: 2 transcontinental railroads, Amtrak; International Airport served by 4 major airlines and 2 commuter airlines; 25 motor freight lines.

Communications: 2 daily newspapers; 3 commercial, or public, one cable TV; 11 AM, 10 FM radio stations.

Convention facilities: Riverpark Center, legacy of Expo '7 2,700 seat opera house and 40,000 sq. ft. convention cente Spokane Coliseum capacity 8,000 with 45,000 sq. ft. exhib space; hotels and motels have 3,000 guest rooms.

Medical facilities: 6 major hospitals, 7 specialized hospitals, and Fairchild AFB hospital.
Education facilities: one college, 2 universities, and 2 community colleges.
Federal facilities: Fairchild AFB, federal office bldg.
Cultural facilities: symphony orchestra, opera house, 2 museums, civic theater, arboretum, zoo, northwest Indian center; community concerts, music and allied arts festival.
Recreation: 76 lakes within a 50 mile radius of the city; 12 indoor and 7 outdoor theaters; 11 city swimming pools, 55 public tennis courts, 12 golf courses, 94 public parks, 12 national parks and 15 national forests within a day's drive; 2 snow ski resorts within 1½ hours drive; power and sail boating, hunting, and fishing.
Sports: Spokane Indians, farm club for Seattle Mariners;

35,000 seat Albi football stadium; Playfair horse race track; 8,000 seat Spokane Coliseum for basketball, hockey, and boxing; Spokane Flyers hockey.
Other attractions: city-center Riverfront Park, site of Expo '74 World's Fair, includes IMAX theater, ice rink, children's zoo, gondola ride over river falls, antique carousel, train ride, outdoor amphitheaters, popcorn wagons, and restaurant; average annual rainfall 17.19 inches.
History: Lewis and Clark expedition of 1804-06 through area; first permanent settlers in 1871 attracted to river and falls where they built a house and a sawmill; 2 sq. mi. city of 1,000 people inc. 1881 as Spokane Falls; after Washington gained statehood in 1889, city name changed to Spokane.
Further information: Spokane Area Chamber of Commerce, P.O. Box 2147, Spokane, WA 99210.

Springfield, Illinois

The World Almanac is sponsored in the Springfield area by the State Journal-Register (morn. and eve.), oldest newspaper in Illinois, 313 S. Sixth Street, P.O. Box 219, Springfield, IL 62705; phone (217) 788-8600; circulation 72,878 (Sunday); John P. Clarke publisher, Edward H. Armstrong editor, Patrick Coburn managing editor.

Population: 99,637 (city), 186,104 (SMSA), 4th in state; total employed (annual average) 87,033.
Area: 46.86 sq. mi. on Sangamon River in center of state; state capital and Sangamon County seat.
Commerce: state and federal offices; 11 banks, 8 savings and loan assns., 10 insurance co. home offices; 154 national, regional, and state assns.; 29 civic clubs, 74 social service organizations, 41 women's organizations; annual retail sales $780 million.
Transportation: 5 railroads, 69 truck carriers, one airport; nearby barge facilities.
Communications: 2 TV, 8 radio stations.
Medical facilities: 3 hospitals with 1,629 beds; 358 doctors, 97 dentists, 19 chiropractors; 36 clinics, 29 licensed nursing homes, the Springfield Regional Trauma Center.
Cultural facilities: municipal band, opera, symphony, chorus; Theatre Guild, state museum, Lincoln historical sites, New Salem State Park, Old State Capitol; art associations, summer theater, Springfield Ballet Co., Illinois Coun-

try Opry; Clayville renovated stagecoach stop, arts and crafts festivals, Oliver Parks Telephone Museum, Lincoln Library, Lincoln Memorial Garden, Nelson Recreation Center, Henson Robinson Children's Zoo, Sangamon State Univ. Auditorium, Prairie Capital Convention Center.
Education: Sangamon State Univ., Lincoln Land Community College, Springfield College in Ill., Southern Illinois Univ. School of Medicine, Capital Area Vocational School.
Recreation: 40 parks; swimming, boating, water skiing on Lake Springfield; 4 public golf courses, tennis courts; 2,410 acres in parks.
Special events: Illinois State Fair, Old Capitol Art Fair, International Carillon Festival, Midwest Charity Horse Show, LPGA Rail Golf Classic, Springfield Redbirds baseball; Ethnic Festival, Autumnfest, Photo Fair, Old Capitol Sound and Light Show. Lincolnfest, NCAA Division II Soccer Tournament.
Further information: Greater Springfield Chamber of Commerce, 3 Old State Capitol Plaza, Springfield, IL.

Springfield, Massachusetts

The World Almanac is sponsored in the Springfield area by The Morning Union, the evening Daily News and The Sunday Republican, 1860 Main Street, Springfield, MA 01101, phone (413) 788-1000; Union founded 1864, Daily News 1880, Republican 1824; circulation, Union 72,495, Daily News 75,619, Republican 142,937; publisher David Starr, Union-Republican editor Arnold S. Friedman, Daily News editor Richard C. Garvey.

Population: 152,319 (city), 530,373 (SMSA); 2d in state, 76,081 employed in city.
Area: 33.1 sq. mi. in SW part of state; I-91 and I-90 cross near city; Hampden County seat.
Industry: 231 manufacturing plants produce boxes, children's games, wallets, handguns, plastics, envelopes, hair shampoo, chemicals, paper; among major employers: Monsanto, Milton Bradley, Smith & Wesson, Breck.
Commerce: metro retail sales $1.88 billion; avg. household pendable income $14,703; Mass. Mutual Life Ins. Co. is one of the largest in U.S.; Baystate West, a combined high-rise shopping mall, office-hotel complex.
Transportation: Amtrak, 2 rail lines, 5 bus lines; Bradley International Airport (Hartford-Springfield) 18 miles south; major truck depot.
Communications: 3 TV, 9 radio stations.
Medical facilities: 6 major hospital complexes.
Educational facilities: 21 accredited colleges and universities include Amherst, American International, Hampshire,

Mount Holyoke, Univ. of Massachusetts, Our Lady of the Elms, Smith, Springfield, Western New England (and Law School), Williams, Westfield State, North Adams State, Holyoke and Greenfield community colleges, Springfield Technical Community College.
Cultural facilities: State West Theater, Civic Center and Symphony Hall, quadrangle complex; 2 museums of art, library, natural history museum including planetarium; 145 churches and 7 synagogues; 155 parks; Eastern States Exposition, Tanglewood Music Festival.
Sports: Indians (AHL) hockey; Holyoke Millers baseball; Basketball Hall of Fame; Tip-Off Tourney opens college basketball season in U.S.
History: founded 1636 by William Pynchon; first U.S. musket developed at city's armory (now a U.S. landmark) 1795; Springfield rifle developed in 1903 and produced here (as was the Garand M-1 rifle.)
Further information: Chamber of Commerce, 1500 Main Street, Springfield, MA 01103.

Stockton, California

The World Almanac is sponsored in the San Joaquin County area by the Stockton Record (eves. and Saturday and Sunday mornings), 530 E. Market Street, Stockton, CA 95202; phone (209) 943-6397; founded in 1895; circulation 57,140 daily, 56,342 Sunday; president and publisher Robert P. Uecker, executive editor Philip Bookman, managing editor James S. Hushaw.

Population: 149,779 city, 185,039 metropolitan area, 347,342 county; total county employment 141,000 to 159,000 in 1980.
Area: 1,440 sq. mi. county, 35.13 sq. mi. city; located 80 mi.

east of San Francisco; San Joaquin County seat.
Industry: agriculture, $760 million countywide in 1980; food processing, light manufacturing, Port of Stockton, Sharpe Army Depot, Rough and Ready Island Naval Station.

Commerce: $938 million taxable retail sales city, $1.8 billion county wide in 1980.
New construction: $122 million (city) in 1980
Medical facilities: San Joaquin General Hospital, Dameron, St. Joseph's, Oak Park Community, Stockton State (for mental and physically disabled).
Cultural facilities: 110 churches, Univ. of the Pacific (private), Delta College (2-year public), Humphreys College (private); Pioneer Museum and Haggin Galleries, city/county library, Stockton Civic Theater, Stockton Symphony, ballet troupe, 3 dinner theaters, Stockton Civic Auditorium.
Recreation: city-operated programs include softball leagues, soccer, 3 public golf courses, several private clubs offering golf, tennis, swimming, racquetball, boating facilities; access

to 1,000 miles of San Joaquin-Sacramento River Delta waterways.
Convention facilities: Stockton Civic Auditorium, Hilton Hotel, Holiday Inn
History: founded 1844 by Capt. Charles M. Weber and inc. 1850; San Joaquin County established 1850; city was major transshipment point between San Francisco and the Central Sierra mines during Gold Rush era; most early commerce and industry centered around servicing mining activities; city later became the hub of a thriving agricultural community in the northern San Joaquin Valley and Delta areas.
Further information: Greater Stockton Chamber of Commerce, 1105 N. El Dorado Street, Stockton, CA 95202; phone (209) 466-7066.

Syracuse, New York

The World Almanac is sponsored in the Syracuse area by the Herald-Journal, Clinton Square, P.O. Box 4915, Syracuse, NY, 13221; phone (315) 470-0011; founded Jan. 15, 1877, by Arthur Jenkins; circulation 112,194 daily, 232,703 Sunday Herald-American Post Standard; president Stephen Rogers, editor and publisher Stephen A. Rogers, editor William D. Cotter; sponsors Christmas toy fund.

Population: 170,105 (city), 642,547 (SMSA), (metro), 6th in state; 280,100 employed.
Area: 25.82 sq. mi. near center of state; interstate routes 90 and 81 intersect at Syracuse.
Industry: some 500 manufacturing plants produce electrical and non-electrical machinery, primary metals, food, transportation equipment, chemicals, pharmaceuticals, paper, candles, china; Schlitz brewery, world's largest ever built at one time, located in suburban Lysander, sold to Anheuser-Busch in 1980; major Miller brewery north of city; major employers: General Electric, Carrier Corp., Crucible Steel, Crouse-Hinds, Allied Chemical.
Commerce: retail sales (1981 est.) $2.7 billion; average household spendable income (1981 est.) $22,500.
Transportation: 2 rail freight lines, Amtrak; 3 bus lines, 164

truck lines; 8 airlines.
Communications: 4 TV, 16 radio stations.
Medical facilities: 4 major hospital complexes.
Cultural facilities: Syracuse Univ., State Univ. College of Environmental Science and Forestry, and Le Moyne, Maria Regina, and Onondaga Community colleges; Everson Museum of Art; symphony; $22 million county center.
Sports: Syracuse Univ. football at new 52,000-seat Carrier dome; Chiefs (baseball).
History: first explored 1615 by French; salt deposits led to area development, known as "Salt City;" "crossroads" since Indian days; became city 1847.
Further information: Chamber of Commerce, One MONY Plaza, Syracuse, NY 13202.

Tallahassee, Florida

The World Almanac is sponsored in the north Florida-south Georgia Panhandle area by The Tallahassee Democrat, 227 N. Magnolia Drive, Tallahassee, FL 32302; phone (904) 599-2100; founded 1905; circulation 50,805 (morn), 59,299 Sunday; member Knight-Ridder Newspapers, Inc., W. H. Harwell Jr., president and publisher; Walker Lundy, vice president and executive editor; J. Carrol Dadisman, vice president and general manager.

Population: 81,548 (city) 157,076 (SMSA); total employment 73,500.
Area: 26.14 sq. mi. between Gulf of Mexico and Georgia line; state capital and Leon County seat.
Commerce: 50% of economic base is state and local government; small manufacturers 3.6%; agriculture only 1.1% of economic base; retail-wholesale center serving 17 county area; 3 shopping malls and 22 shopping centers; retail sales (1979) $635 million; effective buying income per household $21,017; 13 commercial banks (resources, $543 million) and 5 savings & loan (resources 3.5 billion).
Transportation: 3 major airlines, 4 commuter flight services, one railroad, 10 motor carriers.
Communications: 13 radio, 2 local TV stations, one local educational TV station.
Educational facilities: Florida State Univ., Florida A & M Univ., Tallahassee Community College, Lively Area Vocational Tech School.
Convention facilities: Tallahassee-Leon County Civic Center, a 300,000 sq. ft. complex opened in 1981 includes a 40,000 sq. ft. exhibition hall, 13,500 seat arena with removable basketball court, 7 meeting rooms (12,000 sq. ft.), full

kitchen facilities to serve 3,000 per meal.
Medical facilities: Tallahassee Memorial Regional Medical Center, Capital Medical Center, Sunland Center (HRS), Ambulatory Centre of Tallahassee.
Recreational facilities: 6 recreation centers, 11 playgrounds, 75 ball fields, 30 tennis courts; salt water fishing in Gulf of Mexico; bass fishing in Lake Jackson; deer, dove, quail, duck, geese hunting; 4 golf courses, PGA Tallahassee Open Invitational.
Other attractions: college athletic events at Florida State Univ. and Florida A & M; symphony, ballet, repertory theater, opera, touring plays, and art exhibits; 1845 historic capital and 22-story capitol tower; Apalachicola National Forest; Junior Museum; Wakulla Springs, Maclay Gardens State Park, LeMoyne Art Gallery, Natural Bridge State Historic Memorial, Florida State Univ. "Flying High" Circus.
History: est. as state capital 1823; Tallahassee means "old town" or "deserted fields" in Creek; area prospered with large plantations and antebellum mansions, many still standing.
Further information: Chamber of Commerce, P.O. Box 1639, Tallahassee, FL 32302; phone (904) 224-8116.

Tampa, Florida

The World Almanac is sponsored in the Tampa Bay area by The Tampa Tribune and The Tampa Times, 202 S. Parker Street, Tampa, FL 33606; phone (813) 272-7711; Times founded in 1893, Tribune 1894; combined circulation 215,840; D.T. Bryan, chairman of the board; A.S. Donnahoe, president; R.F. Pittman Jr., publisher; J.F. Urbanski, vice president/general manager; J. Clendinen, chairman of editorial board; P. Hogan, Tribune managing editor; B. Witwer, Times managing editor.

Population: 271,523 (city), 1,550,035 (SMSA); total employed in county 297,908 (civilian, non-agricultural).
Area: 84.45 sq. mi. (city) 1,062.0 sq. mi. (county) on Gulf of Mexico, halfway between the northern edge and southern tip

of Florida; Hillsborough County seat.
Industry: Port of Tampa is the closest U.S. deepwater port to the Panama Canal and among the largest in the nation; total tonnage for 1980 reached 51.1 million; principal expo

cargo is phosphate; Bone Valley Formation, 30% of world's phosphate production; cigar manufacturing (Cuesta-Rey, Fuenta Arturo, Hav-A-Tampa, Standard); strong shrimp industry, Singleton; beer breweries (Anheuser-Busch and Joseph Schlitz); Florida Steel Corp.; other industries include Jim Walter Corp., General Telephone, Florida Mining & Materials, and Lykes Bros.

Commerce: (1980) county retail sales $3.3 billion; 28 banks with total deposits (1980) of $2.6 billion; 11 savings and loans (1980) $1.3 billion.

Transportation: 5 bus lines, Greyhound, Trailways; 2 railroads, Seaboard Coast Line, Amtrak; 46 trucking lines; junction of I-75 and I-4; Tampa International Airport, 7.7 million passengers in 1980, 16 major airlines and direct flights to Europe; Port of Tampa, 140 steamship lines.

Convention facilities: Curtis Hixon Hall, 7,100 capacity main hall plus 10 other rooms; Tampa hotels and motels have over 10,000 guest rooms and over 125 meeting/banquet rooms with seating from 25 to 1,000.

New construction: Tampa City Center, Westbank, Metropolitan Tower, TECO, Paragon Plaza Phase I, Paragon Plaza Phase II, Saturn Condominium Project, Seddon Island Development, Landmark Hotel, Tampa International Airport expansions, harbor dredging, Busch Gardens expansion, Austin Center, Hyde Park - AMLEA Project, Kings Point Development, One Laurel Place Condominium,

Monte Carlo Condominium, Atrium Condominium, extension of Crosstown Expressway.

Medical facilities: 6 major hospitals.

Federal facilities: MacDill AFB, Federal Bldg.

Cultural facilities: Florida Gulf Coast Symphony, The Tampa Museum, Tampa Theatre, Tampa Ballet Co.; $2.4 million library; Hillsborough County Museum of Science & Industry, community theater, Gasparilla Art Fair.

Education: Univ. of S. Fla., Univ. of Tampa, Florida College, and Hillsborough Comm. College.

Other attractions: Busch Gardens (#2 attraction in attendance in Fla.), Lowry Park Zoo, Ybor City (Latin Quarter); 62 parks, 31 recreation areas, annual Gasparilla Pirate Invasion; site for Florida State Fair.

Sports: NFL Tampa Bay Buccaneers with 71,500 seat stadium (home of Superbowl in 1984), NASL (Soccer) Tampa Bay Rowdies, Tampa Tarpons (farm team for Cincinnati Reds); Cincinnati Reds spring training site; greyhound racing, jai-alai.

History: Fort Brooke est. 1824 on site of present Tampa; inc. 1885.

Further information: Greater Tampa Chamber of Commerce, 801 E. Kennedy Boulevard, Tampa, FL 33602; phone (813) 228-7777.

Toledo, Ohio

The World Almanac is sponsored in the Toledo area by The Blade, 541 Superior Street, Toledo, OH 43660; phone (419) 245-6000; founded 1835; circulation 167,028 daily, 211,721 Sunday; publishers Paul Block Jr. and William Block; associate publisher John D. Willey; editor Bernard Judy; executive editor Robert Hartley; executive news editor Joseph O'Conor; managing editor William Rosenberg.

Population: 354,635 (city), 791,137 (SMSA); total employed 329,300.

Area: 85.3 sq. mi. at juncture of Maumee River and Lake Erie in northwestern Ohio; Lucas County seat.

Industry: glass, headquarters for Owens-Illinois, Owens Corning & Libbey-Owens-Ford; automotive parts, largest producer in nation, home of American Motors Jeep, Toledo Scale, and Schindler Haughton Elevator; largest petroleum refining center between Chicago and the East Coast.

Commerce: Port of Toledo is one of the prime bulk shipping ports on the Great Lakes, handling vast quantities of grain, coal, iron ore, and petroleum products; ranks 3d on Great Lakes and 25th in U.S.; total retail sales $3.37 billion; spendable income per household $23,593.

Transportation: 7 railroads, 6 major airlines, 120 motor freight lines, 2 interstate bus lines; 13 major highways converge here, permitting the rapid flow of goods to almost 60% of the nation's consumers.

New construction: $94 million Owens-Illinois world head-

quarters, $10 million Toledo Trust Co. office bldg.

Communications: 4 TV, 13 radio stations and one cablevision company.

Medical facilities: 10 major hospital complexes, including the Medical College of Ohio Hospital.

Cultural facilities: Museum of Art with largest display of antique glass in the world; Peristyle used for the performing arts; symphony, opera company.

Education: Univ. of Toledo and its Community and Technical College; Michael J. Owens Technical College; Bowling Green State Univ.; Monroe Community College.

Other attractions: Municipal Zoo among top 10 in the nation; modern 2,500 seat Masonic Auditorium, Great Hall.

Sports: Mud Hens, farm club of the Minnesota Twins, at the Lucas County Recreation Center.

History: founded in 1837; took its name from sister city, Toledo, Spain.

Further information: Convention and Vistors Bureau, 218 Huron, Toledo, OH 43604.

Toronto, Ontario, Canada

The World Almanac is sponsored in the metropolitan Toronto area by The Toronto Star, One Yonge Street, Toronto, Ontario, M5E 1E6; phone (416) 367-2000; established 1892, Joseph E. Atkinson, publisher, 1899-1948; circulation daily 481,855, Saturday 800,162, Sunday 390,782; chairman and publisher Beland H. Honderich; president Martin Goodman; editor-in-chief Denis Harvey. Canada's largest newspaper in circulation, display and classified advertising lineage; winner of 45 national newspaper awards and sponsor of the Santa Claus Fund and Fresh Air Fund.

Population: 595,000 (city), 2,914,000 (metro); largest city in Canada, 9th in North America; labor force 1.6 million.

Area: 241 sq. mi. on northwest shore of Lake Ontario; provincial capital.

Industry: Canada's leading commercial and industrial center; 6,000 manufacturing establishments; value of factory shipments (1979) $23.7 billion; principal industries: slaughtering and meat packing, clothing, printing and publishing, machinery, electrical goods, furniture, food products, rubber goods, sheet metal products.

Commerce: retail sales (1980) $10.8 billion; headquarters for Eaton's and Simpson's, Canada's largest department stores; head offices of 25 trust companies and 22 federally chartered banks; including 19 foreign bank subsidiaries Toronto Stock Exchange, 3d in North America, traded shares worth $29 billion in 1980; per capita disposable income $9,688.

Transportation: Transit Commission carries 366 million pas-

sengers annually on 754 miles of routes including 34 miles of subway; 2.5 million tons of cargo carried by 32 lines unloaded (1980) at this major Great Lakes port; 40 airlines handle 13.7 million passengers annually at International Airport.

Communications: 7 TV stations including educational and French-language channels; 10 AM and 8 FM radio stations; 3 daily newspapers, 42 foreign language newspapers.

New construction: value of building permits (1980) $1.2 billion; $50-million expansion-renovation of Royal Ontario Museum (reopens July 1982); $64-million convention center will seat 10,000; $80-million downtown housing-commercial development includes 2,700-seat concert hall scheduled to open fall 1982.

Medical facilities: 40 active-treatment hospitals including renowned Hospital for Sick Children; special treatment centers: Clark Institute for Psychiatry, Addiction Research

Centre, Ontario Crippled Children's Centre, Ontario Centre for the Deaf

Cultural facilities: 65 alternate and cabaret theater groups, including Canada's largest children's theater; National Ballet of Canada and Canadian Opera Company perform in 3,200-seat O'Keefe Centre; symphony orchestra and Mendelssohn Choir at Massey Hall; touring shows at Royal Alexandra Theatre; 82 public libraries, Henry Moore collection of sculptures and drawings in Art Gallery of Ontario.

Education: York and Toronto Univs.; Ryerson Polytechnical Institute, 4 colleges of applied arts and technology, 2 teachers' colleges, Royal Conservatory of Music, Ontario College of Art, Osgoode Hall Law School.

Recreation: Canadian National Exhibition, world's biggest annual fair; Ontario Place, 100 acres of offshore islands with restaurants, marina, and 1,000-seat Cinesphere for film showings; Toronto Islands have 3 yacht clubs, 560 acres of beaches and picnic grounds; Harborfront, 86-acre sports, arts, and entertainment park.

Convention facilities: Canada's top convention center;

292,285 visitors attended 692 conventions in 1980 and spent $111 million; total rooms 19,000.

Sports: 10 public golf courses; thoroughbred and harness racing; NHL Maple Leafs play in 16,435-seat Gardens; Blue Jays AL baseball, Argonauts CFL football, and Blizzard NASL soccer play in 54,000-seat Exhibition Stadium.

Other attractions: Ontario Science Centre, designed for participation and involvement; Black Creek Pioneer Village, living displays of Upper Canada; McMichael collection of paintings by Canada's famed Group of Seven; Metro Zoo has 500 species roaming 5 continental areas covering 700 acres; Canada's Wonderland, 400-acre theme park opened in 1981; CN Tower, world's tallest free-standing structure; Eaton Centre downtown galleria contains 300 shops.

History: town of York founded 1793 on site of French fort as capital of British Colony of Upper Canada; incorporated as city 1834 and named Toronto from Indian word for meeting place.

Further information: Convention and Tourist Bureau, Toronto Eaton Centre, Toronto, Ontario M5B 2H1.

Tucson, Arizona

The World Almanac is sponsored in the Tucson area by The Arizona Daily Star, 4850 S. Park Avenue, PO Box 26807, Tucson, AZ 85726; phone (602) 294-4433; founded 1877 as a weekly; Michael E. Pulitzer, editor and publisher; William J. Woestendiek, executive editor; Frank E. Johnson, managing editor; Stephen E. Auslander, editorial page editor; Frank Delehanty, business manager; Sandra K. Hall, director, special services; Star sponsors Sportsmen's Fund for less-chance youngsters.

Population: 330,537 (city), 531,263 (county); 192,575 employed in county out of total civilian labor force of 204,350.

Area: Sonoran Desert of southern Arizona, elev. 2,500 ft.; Santa Catalina Mts. immediately N and E reach 9,000 ft.; Pima County seat; 60 miles from Mexico.

Industry: Hughes Aircraft, IBM, Gates Learjet, Davis Monthan AFB, aircraft reclamation plants handling surplus craft from DM AFB; electronics, light manufacturing, tourism; center of the "copper circle"—Anaconda, Duval, American Smelting and Refining, Kennecott, Magma, Pima, and other mining operations.

Transportation: International Airport served by most major airlines, with Cochise Airlines within Arizona, and AeroMexico to and from Mexico; 3 smaller airports; 2 national, one local bus line; Southern Pacific Railroad; trucks.

Communications: 2 newspapers; 5 TV and 18 radio stations.

Medical facilities: 9 hospitals including Arizona Health Sciences Center which has teaching hospital.

Climate: dry, mild; freezing temperatures are rare in winter; summer brings some rain and temperature of 100 deg. F.

Culture: Univ. of Arizona, Pima Community College; Tucson Museum of Art, Tucson Symphony, Arizona Theater Co., Tucson Metropolitan Ballet; many musical, drama, and dance groups, dinner theater; Ariz. Opera Co., Southern Ar-

izona Light Opera Company, Tucson Boys Chorus; Los Changuitos Feos mariachi group provide local flavor, plus many ethnic groups.

Convention facilities: convention center accommodates 10,000 theater-style in arena, sit-down functions 5,000, meeting-rooms 1,000 theater-style, music hall 2,300; contiguous exhibit space 64,000 sq. ft. adjacent to hotel.

Sports: Toros, Pacific Coast League farm team of Houston Astros; Cleveland Indians spring training site; Tucson Open golf tournament; various pro tennis tournaments; UA is a member of PAC 10 athletic conference.

Other attractions: Kitt Peak National Observatory is 60 miles from Tucson; UA Flandrau Planetarium, many other astronomical observatories; nationally famous rodeo in Feb.; Arizona-Sonora Desert Museum; Old Tucson; Tucson Festival in Apr., Saguaro National Monument; Nogales, 60 miles away, is nearest major border city in Mexico.

History: Presidio of Tucson est. 1775; Mission San Xavier del Bac founded nearby by Rev. Eusebio Francisco Kino SJ, who first visited area in 1692.

Further information: Tucson Metrop. Chamber of Commerce, PO Box 991, Tucson, AZ 85702; Tucson Convention and Visitors Bureau, 120 W. Broadway, PO Box 27210, Tucson, AZ 85726.

Tulsa, Oklahoma

The World Almanac is sponsored in the Tulsa area by The Tulsa Tribune, 318 S. Main, Tulsa, OK 74102; phone (918) 582-1101; founded 1904 as The Tulsa Democrat (renamed the Tulsa Tribune in 1920); circulation 78,470; editor Jenkin Lloyd Jones; managing editor Gordon Fallis; executive editor Jenkin Lloyd Jones Jr.

Population: 360,919 (city), 678,627 (SMSA); 310,400 employed.

Area: 185,405 sq. mi. on Arkansas River at 96th meridian in Tulsa, Osage, and Rogers counties.

Industry: (1980) manufacturing, which includes aerospace, metal fabrication, and oil, provides jobs for 20% of the SMSA work force; 62,500 mfg. employees, including 41,900 production workers, total payroll $1.21 billion; of these totals 44,531 worked in the city earning $863 million; retail employees 16% SMSA workers, and the service industry employs 19%; top employers are American Airlines, Cities Service, McDonnell Douglas, Rockwell International, Combustion Engineering.

Commerce: retail sales (1980) $2.3 billion; 27 banks, 5 savings and loans; per capita income $10,322.

Transportation: (1980) Tulsa Port of Catoosa, nation's most inland port, head of Arkansas Verdigris navigation channel, barge tonnage 1.9 million tons; 4 rail freight lines, 2 regional bus lines, 2 national bus lines, 30 truck lines, 10 airlines with 2,097,796 passenger movements.

Communications: 2 daily newspapers, 5 TV, 14 radio sta-

tions.

New construction: (1980) building permits valued at $444 million.

Medical facilities: 5 hospitals, Osteopathic College, Univ. of Oklahoma medical school branch.

Federal facilities: District Corps of Engineers, hq Southwestern Power Administration.

Cultural facilities: Univ. of Tulsa, Oral Roberts Univ. Tulsa Junior College; Philharmonic, opera, civic ballet, 4 art museums including Philbrook Art Center, Thomas Gilcrease Institute of American History and Art, Rebecca and Gershon Fenster Gallery of Jewish Art, the Alexandre Hogue Gallery; American Theater Co.

Convention facilities: 436 conventions in 1980 with 201,899 attending.

Sports: Tulsa Roughnecks pro soccer; Tulsa Ice Oilers pro hockey in Central Hockey League; Tulsa Twisters team rodeo; Tulsa Drillers, farm team for Texas Rangers; intercollegiate athletics; 4 public and 7 country club golf courses.

Further information: Metropolitan Tulsa Chamber of Commerce, 616 S. Boston Avenue, Tulsa, OK 74119.

Vancouver, British Columbia, Canada

The World Almanac is sponsored in the Vancouver area by The Vancouver Sun, 2250 Granville Street, Vancouver, B.C., V6H 3G2; phone (604) 732-2111; founded 1886; circulation 246,216; publisher Clark Davey, director of marketing Michael J.B. Alexandor; sponsors world's largest free Salmon Derby, Sun Family Pops Concerts, Sun Tournament of Soccer Champions, and many other community services.

Population: 410,188 (city), 1,805,242 (metro area); first in province, 3d in Canada.

Area: 44 sq. mi. on the Pacific coast at the mouth of the north arm of the Fraser River; scenic beauty of the city accented by the towering, snowcapped Coast Mountains to the north and rich agricultural land to the east and south.

Industry: 98 miles of waterfront, stretching up Burrard Inlet, the largest cargo port on the Pacific and Canada's 2d busiest, with 49.2 million tons handled in 1980; major cargos: grain, lumber, coal, mineral ore, chemicals, and manufactured goods; tourism a major industry with an estimated 11.5 million visitors bringing in $900 million in 1980.

Commerce: retail sales $5.4 billion in 1980; value of shares traded on the Vancouver exchange $4.4 billion in 1980.

Transportation: western terminus of Canada's 2 national railways, Canadian National Railway and Canadian Pacific; headquarters of provincially operated British Columbia Railway, which is linked to the U.S. by Amtrak along the Burlington Northern Railway right-of-way; 3 major long-distance bus carriers, Provincial Stage Lines, Trailways, and Greyhound; International Airport served by 8 major airlines handled more than 7.2 million passengers in 1980.

Communications: 12 AM, 7 FM radio stations; 4 local TV stations; also U.S. network TV outlets.

Medical facilities: General and St. Paul's are largest hospitals; also Shaughnessy in Vancouver, Royal Columbian in New Westminster, Burnaby General, Lion's Gate in North Vancouver, and Riverview Psychiatric Hospital.

Cultural facilities: symphony orchestra, opera assn., several professional theater groups, Centennial and Maritime Museums and Art Gallery; Queen Elizabeth Theatre and The Orpheum are the major art facilities.

Other attractions: Pacific National Exhibition, Gastown, Chinatown, the H.R. MacMillan Planetarium, Bloedel Conservatory, Granville Island Public Market, aquarium; 1,000-acre Stanley Park, zoo, Capilano Suspension Bridge, Van-Dusen Botanical Garden, Park & Tilford Garden, Lynn Canyon Ecology Centre, Heritage Village; 18 golf courses, Grouse Mountain, Cypress Bowl, and Mount Seymour ski areas; Univ. of British Columbia, Simon Fraser Univ.; 18 beaches, fresh and salt water fishing.

Sports: B.C. Lions (CFL football); Canucks (NHL hockey); Whitecaps (NASL soccer); Vancouver Canadians (PCL baseball); Exhibition Park racetrack (thoroughbreds); Cloverdale Raceway (harness racing), and several amateur teams and sports activities.

History: discovered by Spaniards, first mapped 1791; taken possession by Capt. George Vancouver for British 1792; Hudson's Bay Co. post established early 1800s; city incorporated 1886.

Further information: Chamber of Commerce, 1177 West Hastings, Vancouver, B.C.

Washington, District of Columbia

The World Almanac is sponsored in the Washington, D.C. area by The Journal Newspapers, 475 School Street SW; phone (703) 750-2000; the group includes The Montgomery Journal, The Prince George's Journal, The Fairfax Journal, The Arlington Journal, and The Alexandria Journal, which have been published daily since Sept. 14, 1981; John Greenwald, editorial director.

Population: 637,651 (city), 3,045,399 (SMSA including D.C. and parts of Md. and Va.).

Area: 67 sq. mi. (city), 2,812 (metro) at head of tidewater of Potomac R., 30 miles from Chesapeake Bay, 130 miles from Atlantic Ocean, 240 miles from NYC.

Industry: U. S. Capital, federal government employs 361,500 civilian (April, 1981) and 57,764 military personnel (Sept., 1980) total employment 1,633,000 (1980); government related activity, law, journalism, professional and trade assns., unions, lobbying groups, and scientists provide another large portion of employment base; tourism a major industry.

Commerce: metro area per capita income, $11,313 (1979); area retail sales $15.5 billion (1980).

Transportation: circumferential highway; 101-mile rapid rail transit system: 40 miles and 44 stations now open; long distance rail and bus service; National, Dulles, and Baltimore-Washington International airports.

Communications: several national magazines; news bureaus of major newspapers, wire services, and TV networks; 21 FM, 23 AM radio stations; 7 TV stations; 1 daily metropolitan newspaper, over 40 weekly newspapers.

Educational facilities: American, Catholic, District of Columbia, Georgetown, George Washington, and Howard universities, and Gallaudet College; nearby Univ. of Maryland and George Mason Univ.

Medical facilities: major medical research center; National Institutes of Health, Walter Reed Hospital, Bethesda Naval Medical Center; about 40 general and 3 teaching hospitals.

Cultural facilities: Kennedy Center with 4 performance halls and Wolf Trap Farm Park in nearby Vienna, Va., present major concerts, ballet, opera; Arena Stage, Ford's Theatre, National Theater, many community theater groups; Smithsonian Institution; Corcoran Gallery of Art, Library of Congress; D.C. Public Library with 24 branches.

Sports: pro sports include football (Redskins), basketball (Bullets), hockey (Capitals), soccer (Diplomats).

History: named for George Washington and Christopher Columbus; Georgetown in the District of Columbia first settled 1665, then annexed by the city when D.C. created as seat of federal government by Act of Congress 1790.

Further information: Convention and Visitors Association, 1575 I Street, NW, Suite 250, Washington, DC 20005.

West Palm Beach, Florida

The World Almanac is sponsored in Palm Beach County by Palm Beach Newspapers, Inc., 2751 South Dixie Highway, West Palm Beach, FL 33405; phone (305) 833-7411; publisher of The Post and The Evening Times; combined daily circulation 124,770; Sunday, The Post 148,072.

Population: 62,530 (city), 570,300 (metro); total labor force 245,229.

Area: 43.5 sq. mi. (city), 2,023 sq. mi. (metro), in southeast top of Fla.'s "Gold Coast."

Industry: Pratt & Whitney Aircraft, IBM, U.S. Sugar Corp., Atlantic Sugar Assn., Gulf & Western Food Products Co., American Foods Inc., Duda & Sons Corp, Assoc. farms, Rinker Materials Corp., Solitron Devices Inc., NCI Inc., Palm Beach Newspapers Inc., Perry Oceanographics Inc., Rel Reeves Inc., Southern Bell, Florida Power & Light, tourism.

Commerce: 52 general service banks, 16 savings and loans,

total assets $6.45 billion (1980); retail sales $3.60 billion (1980), per capita EBI $8,936 (1980).

Transportation: Palm Beach Intl. Airport; 2 rail freight lines, Amtrak; Greyhound, Trailways bus lines; Palm Beach County Transportation Authority (bus); Sunshine Lines 15 truck lines; Port of Palm Beach for freight shipping.

Communications: 3 TV, 14 radio stations, cable TV; 3 daily newspapers, one winter-season daily, 6 weeklies, society journal magazine, 7 special publications.

Medical facilities: 13 hospitals, 2,264 beds.

Cultural facilities: Society of Four Arts, Henry Morrison

Flagler Museum, Norton Gallery & School of Art, Morikami Museum and Park; 4 community, 2 legitimate, 3 college theaters; West Palm Beach Auditorium, Lion Country Safari.
Education: Florida Atlantic Univ. (Jr. & Sr.), Palm Beach Jr. College, North & South Tech. Ed. centers, Palm Beach Atlantic College.
Sports: West Palm Beach Expos minor league baseball; Atlanta Braves spring training site; greyhound racing, jai-alai fronton, Gold Coast Barracudas semi-pro football, 91 golf

courses, 2 polo fields, county fairgrounds, auto race track; tennis, water sports, and hunting.
History: founded late 1800's by workers and business people associated with the construction of the Royal Poinciana Hotel in Palm Beach by Henry Morrison Flagler who set aside 48 homesites on the shore of Lake Worth; inc. 1894.
Further information: Area Planning Board of Palm Beach County, 2300 Palm Beach Lakes Boulevard, West Palm Beach, FL 33407; Chamber of Commerce, 501 N. Flagler Drive, West Palm Beach, FL 33401.

Wichita, Kansas

The World Almanac is sponsored in the Wichita area by the Wichita Eagle and Beacon Publishing Co., Inc., 825 East Douglas, Wichita, KS 67202; phone (316) 268-6000; founded 1872 as weeklies, became dailies 1884, consolidated 1961; combined to form single morning publication (Wichita Eagle-Beacon) Oct. 1, 1980; circulation 125,656 daily, 177,043 Sunday; Norman Christiansen, president and publisher; Peter Ridder, general manager; Davis Merritt Jr., executive editor; Joe Harper, managing editor.

Population: 1980 census (city) 279,272, first in state; (SMSA) 410,121; employment (1981 first quarter average) 215,900.
Area: (city) 105.25 sq. mi. at juncture of Arkansas and Little Arkansas rivers; Sedgwick County seat.
Industry: 60% of free world general aviation aircraft is manufactured in Wichita; aircraft employment in area: Beech 7,200, Boeing 16,000, Cessna 12,000, Gates Learjet 3,000; other fields: meat processing, flour milling, grain storage, petroleum refining, natural gas, chemicals; largest non-aero manufacturer employer, Coleman Co.
Commerce: wholesale-retail center for large part of Kansas and northern Oklahoma; metro (SMSA) retail sales (1980) $2.4 billion; bank resources $2.3 billion.
Transportation: 4 major rail freight lines, Continental Trailways bus line, 72 truck lines, 9 major highways; Jabara Airport, Mid-Continent Airport, 8 airlines, 62 flights daily, averages 600 air movements per day; National Flying Farmers headquarters.
Communications: 4 TV, 7 AM and 6 FM radio stations; cable TV.
Medical facilities: world's largest speech and hearing rehabilitation center (Institute of Logopedics); 6 hospital complexes including VA installation; 588 doctors.
Federal facilities: McConnell AFB, VA regional office.
Educational facilities: Wichita State Univ., Univ. of Kansas School of Medicine-Wichita, Friends Univ., Kansas Newman College; 91 elementary, 17 jr. high, 13 high schools; 18

special, 17 vocational schools.
Convention facilities: facilities include Kansas Coliseum, 189,000 sq. ft., seating capacity 12,200; Century II Civic Center, 100,000 sq. ft., seating capacity 10,000.
Cultural facilities: Wichita Symphony Orchestra; Omnisphere (planetarium), Wichita Art Museum, Wichita Art Assn. and Childrens Theater, Wichita Music Theater, Crown Uptown Dinner Theater, Marple Theater, Ulrich Museum of Art, American Theatre League, Metropolitan Ballet Co., Mid-America Dance Co., Repertory Arts Assn., Wichita Choral Society, community theater, city library, mid-America All Indian Center; 436 churches.
Other Attractions: Sedgwick County Zoo, FantaSea water amusement park, Joyland Amusement Park, Cow Town (restoration of 1872 Wichita), historical museum; 69 city parks (over 2,808 acres), 2 county parks, recreation lakes, Lake Afton Observatory; National Junior Livestock Show, Wichita River Festival, Wichita Jazz Festival.
Sports: Wichita Aeros, Texas Rangers farm team; Wichita Wind (CHL), Edmonton Oiler farm team; Wichita Wings (MISL); National Baseball Congress (semi-pro); 11 golf courses, 5 tennis clubs, auto racing, polo, raquetball, track and field.
History: founded 1870, became railhead (shipping point) for cattle herds driven up Chisholm Trail; named after Wichita Indians.
Further information: Chamber of Commerce, 350 West Douglas, Wichita, KS 67202.

Wilmington, Delaware

The World Almanac is sponsored in Delaware by The News-Journal Company, Wilmington, DE 19899; phone (302) 573-2000; publisher of The Morning News, Evening Journal (combined circulation 131,347), The News Journal (Saturdays, circulation 116,703) and the Sunday News Journal (circulation 109,631), member Gannett Group; president and publisher, John J. Curley; executive editor, Sidney H. Hurlburt; editor of the editorial page, J. Donald Brandt.

Population: 70,366 (Wilmington), 523,386 (SMSA); Wilmington is largest city in state.
Area: 15.1 sq. mi. at the confluence of the Brandywine, Christina, and Delaware rivers.
Industry: one of the largest chemical and petrochemical centers in the U.S.; autos, utilities, steel; about 400 manufacturing firms; many insurance firms and holding companies.
Commerce: port is major auto importing center; retail sales (SMSA 1980) $2.3 billion, est. 1980 income in SMSA $4.1 billion; state has 12 state-chartered commercial banks, 19 state-chartered savings and loans, 5 national banks, 2 mutual savings banks, 2 federally chartered savings and loans.
Transportation: 2 major railway lines, 3 bus lines, 35 motor freight carriers, airport.
Communications: one public TV station, 6 radio stations.
Medical facilities: Wilmington Medical Center (4 divisions); 2 private hospitals, Alfred I. duPont Institute for children with orthopedic handicaps.
Federal facilities: Dover AFB (Dover).
Cultural attractions: Grand Opera House, Winterthur Museum, Hagley Museum, Old Brandywine Village, Fort Christina Park; Wilmington Symphony Orchestra, Wilmington Opera Society, Wilmington Drama League, Museum of

Natural History; Fort Delaware; Wilmington Institute Free Library.
Education: Univ. of Delaware (Newark); Delaware State College (Dover); Delaware Technical and Community College, Brandywine Junior College, Delaware Law School (Wilmington).
Sports: horse racing at Delaware Park, Brandywine Raceway, Dover Downs, Harrington Raceway (Harrington); auto racing at Dover Downs; Univ. of Delaware football.
Other attractions: Rehoboth Beach; Longwood Gardens and Brandywine River Museum (both in nearby PA); Delaware Art Museum (Wilmington); historic old New Castle; old Dover; Ashland Nature Center; several state parks and recreational areas.
Convention facilities: Wilmington has 2 major hotels.
History: founded as Fort Christina in 1638; named for Queen of Sweden; name changed to Willington in 1731 and then to Wilmington in 1739 in honor of the Earl of Wilmington; it is the first city in the first state of the union.
Further information: Delaware State Chamber of Commerce, 1102 West Street, Wilmington, DE 19801; The News-Journal Co., Promotion/Public Service Dept., Wilmington, DE 19899.

Windsor, Ontario, Canada

The World Almanac is sponsored in Windsor and a large part of southwestern Ontario including Essex, Kent, and Lambton counties by The Windsor Star (ave. circ. 91,000), 167 Ferry Street, Windsor, Ontario, N9A 4M5, a division of Southam Inc.; published daily since 1890 (present name since 1957); publisher Gordon Bullock, general manager A.H. Fast, editor G.C. Morgan.

Population: 198,844 (city), 249,500 (metro), 318,319 (county of Essex); total employed 108,000 (metro).

Area: 46.24 sq. mi. (city), 316.93 sq. mi. (metro), 718.97 sq. mi. (Essex County); one mile across Detroit River from Detroit, Mich.; largest Canadian city on U.S.-Canadian border.

Industry: (1980) investment into manufacturing sector was in excess of $950 million; over 840 manufacturers produced a diversity of products valued at $4.8 billion; Ford Motor Co. is building new Essex engine plant to produce V-6 engines and new aluminum casting plant. General Motors expanding its Windsor transmission plant; companies such as Kelsey Hayes, Gulf & Western, National Auto Rad, and Champion Spark Plug make the most of their location adjacent to Detroit to serve automotive markets in the U.S. and Canada; city is the home of Canadian Club and a major food and beverage processing center; area processing companies include Green Giant, Chun-King, Dainty Rice, Windsor Packers, H.J. Heinz, and Holiday Juice; city is the machine tool center of Canada with 15% of Canada's tool and die makers; the chemical industry produces a wide range of paints and lacquers, metal working compounds, pharmaceuticals, and vitamin preparations.

Commerce: retail sales (metro) $844 million; average weekly earnings $317.79; 5th largest manufacturing center in Canada; 10 banks, 82 branches; 15 trust cos.; 26 finance cos.; 34 credit unions.

Transportation: 6 major railways; 2 major airlines (Nordair, Air Canada); linked to Detroit by vehicular tunnel, rail tunnel, and suspension bridge; western terminus highway 401; over 50 major freight carriers; deep water port; bonded warehouse facilities; municipal bus line, 4 intercity bus lines.

Communications: daily newspaper; 6 radio stations; one TV outlet; access to Detroit's 50 radio and 6 TV outlets; monthly magazine.

New construction: (city) 311 dwelling units; (metro) 490 dwelling units; (Essex County) 728 dwelling units (1980); Windsor's riverfront is Canada's show window to the Midwest U.S. Over $40 million worth of construction now under

way and at least $80 million worth planned to start within the next year; City Centre project will include a 320-room luxury hotel, office tower, apartment tower, retail space, cinema complex, and parking structure; city has invested close to a million dollars in an Ouellette Ave. sidewalk widening and beautification program.

Medical facilities: 4 major hospitals; regional children's center; handicapped children's rehabilitation center.

Educational facilities. Univ. of Windsor, St. Clair College of Applied Arts & Technology.

Cultural facilities: Cleary Auditorium & Convention Centre; Art Gallery of Windsor, Windsor Symphony Orchestra; Multicultural Council of Windsor; Univ. of Windsor Players; Windsor Light Opera Assn.; Windsor Public Library; Essex Hall Theatre; Ontario Film Theatre.

Other attractions: Hiram Walker Historical Museum, Fort Malden Historic Park & Museum; Jackson Park Sunken Gardens; Dieppe Gardens; Coventry Gardens and Peace Fountain, Fox Creek Conservation Area, Heritage Village, Windsor Raceway, Bob-Lo Island Amusement Park, Great Lakes resort area, Ojibway Park, Point Pelee Provincial Park; site of International Freedom Festival and Multicultural Carousel of Nations Festival.

Sports: Spitfire hockey; Windsor Minor Lacrosse Assn., Windsor Yacht Club, several marinas; 7 public golf courses, 2 public curling rinks, 96 parks and playgrounds.

History: originally established by Ottawa and Huron indians, first permanent white settlement around 1750; site of War of 1812; in 1836, citizens chose the name Windsor; became a city with a population of 11,000 in 1892; located at the crossroads of the most highly industrialized areas in Canada and the U.S., it is now the home of not only its original French and British settlers but of people representing every part of the world.

Further information: Chamber of Commerce, 500 Riverside Drive West, Tourist Information, 80 Chatham Street East, Windsor Essex County Development Commission, Place Goyeau, all Windsor, Ontario.

Winnipeg, Manitoba, Canada

The World Almanac is sponsored in the Winnipeg area by the Winnipeg Free Press, 300 Carlton Street, Winnipeg, Man., Canada; phone (204) 943-9331; founded 1872; daily circulation 146,300; publisher Don Nicol, editor John Dafoe, managing editor Murray Burt; the newspaper and its staff have received numerous journalism awards.

Population: 556,372.

Area: 235 sq. mi. surrounding the junction of Red and Assiniboine rivers, near center of North America; capital of the province of Manitoba.

Industry: manufacturing and agriculture are the largest source of jobs; 1,025 establishments, 53,000 employees; value of factory shipments $2.35 billion.

Commerce: retail sales over $1.9 billion in 1979; Winnipeg Commodity Exchange only gold futures market in Canada; headquarters Canada Grains Council, Canadian Grain Commission, Canadian Wheat Board.

Transportation: International Airport served by 10 airlines; 2 national railways; Via-Rail passenger service; one rail line to U.S.; 5 national and regional bus lines; major trucking hub.

Communications: 10 TV channels, 4 stations; 11 radio stations.

New construction: valued at $734.3 million in 1979.

Medical facilities: one of Canada's largest medical teaching centers; research in immunology, transplant-tissue rejection, cancer, blood diseases, respiratory diseases, endocrinology, neo-natal, pre-natal medicine; of Manitoba's 85 active treatment hospitals, 13 are in Winnipeg, including 2 major teaching centers plus Univ. of Manitoba Rh Inst.; 300-plus bed Seven Oaks Hospital opened in 1980.

Federal facilities: passport office, Canada mint.

Cultural facilities: art gallery, Royal Winnipeg Ballet, contemporary dancers, Winnipeg Symphony Orchestra, Manitoba Chamber Orchestra, Manitoba Opera Assn., Manitoba Theatre Center, Cercle Moliere, Museum of Man and Nature, summer Rainbow Stage, Manitoba theater workshop, over 12 amateur theater groups.

Educational facilities: Univ. of Manitoba with 4 affiliated colleges; Univ. of Winnipeg, Red River Community College.

Sports: Blue Bombers (Canadian Football League), Winnipeg Jets (National Hockey League), Assiniboia Downs.

Convention facilities: downtown Winnipeg Convention Center handles up to 5,000 delegates.

Other attractions: major zoo in Assiniboine Park; Red River exhibition, multi-cultural Folklorama festival each summer; folk festival in Birds Hill park; French Canadian winter carnival in St. Boniface; planetarium.

History: first colony, Lord Selkirk Settlers, 1812; inc. Nov. 8, 1873; in 1972, amalgamation of city government replaced 7 cities, 4 urban municipalities, one town and a metropolitan government.

Additional information: Chamber of Commerce, 700-177 Lombard Avenue, Tourist Information, 101 Legislative Building, and Tourist and Convention Association of Manitoba, 226-375 York Avenue.

Winston-Salem, North Carolina

The World Almanac is sponsored in the Piedmont Triad area by the Winston-Salem Journal and The Sentinel, 418-420 N. Marshall Street, Winston-Salem, NC 27102; phone (919) 727-7211; Sentinel founded 1856, Journal 1897; brought under same ownership in 1926; now an affiliate of Media General Inc.; general manager Thomas E. Waldrop, publisher Joe Doster.

Population: 131,885 (city), 243,683 (county); work force in county 159,000.

Area: 61.34 sq. mi. (city), 419 sq. mi. (county), in north central N.C.; Forsyth County seat.

Industry: R. J. Reynolds Industries with diversified interests in tobacco, food, shipping, oil, and packaging; Western Electric Co., Westinghouse, Jos. Schlitz brewery, Hanes Corp., Hanes Dye and Finishing Co., Brenner Industries, Wachovia Corp., and Bahnson Co.

Commerce: total retail sales county (1979) $1.8 billion, part of the Piedmont Triad which with Greensboro and High Point comprise a rapidly growing part of the Piedmont part of N.C.

Transportation: headquarters for Piedmont Airlines at Smith Reynolds Airport; city also served by 4 airlines at Greensboro-High Point-Winston-Salem regional airport; 2 bus lines; 54 carriers of various types.

Communications: 4 TV, 10 radio stations; cable TV.

New construction: 16-story Reynolds Plaza due for completion in 1981-82.

Medical facilities: Bowman Gray School of Medicine of Wake Forest Univ.; Baptist, Forsyth Memorial, and Medical

Park hospitals; other treatment centers.

Cultural facilities: one of the nation's first arts councils formed in 1949; now building Winston Square, cultural center downtown; N.C. School of the Arts, Wake Forest Univ., Salem College, Winston-Salem State Univ.; Old Salem, restoration of town between 1766 and 1830.

Recreation: more than 50 public parks, 10 community centers, 10 public pools; boating and fishing at Winston and Salem lakes; 17 golf courses including Tanglewood.

Convention facilities: Winston-Salem Hyatt hotel complex sits across street from Benton Convention Center; hotels and motels offer more than 2,400 rooms in area.

Sports: Red Sox, farm club of Boston Red Sox; stock car racing; Wake Forest football at Groves stadium; Winston-Salem State football at Bowman Gray Stadium; Atlantic Coast Conference baseball at Memorial Coliseum.

History: Salem founded 1766 by the Moravian Church; Winston founded in 1849 as industrial city; cities merged in 1913.

Further information: Chamber of Commerce, P.O. Box 1408, Winston-Salem, NC 27102.

Yakima, Washington

The World Almanac is sponsored in the Yakima SMSA by the Yakima Herald-Republic (published daily and Sunday), 114 North Fourth Street, Yakima, WA 98909; phone (509) 248-1251; founded 1903 as the Yakima Republic, given present name in 1970; circulation (May, 1980) daily 41,289, Sunday 43,001; publisher James E. Barnhill. The Yakima Herald-Republic is a division of Harte-Hanks Communications, Inc.

Population: 49,825 city, 172,508 SMSA.

Area: 11.78 sq. mi. in south central Washington, 142 miles southeast of Seattle, 146 miles south of Canadian border; altitude 1,052 ft., Yakima County seat.

Industry: food processing, agriculture, timber; first in the nation in production of apples, hops, mint; first in number of fruit trees.

Commerce: (1980) retail sales $719.3 million (SMSA); E.B.I. per household (1980) $18,615; postal receipts (1980) $4 million.

Transportation: Republic Airlines and Cascade Airways; Burlington Northern, Union Pacific railroads, Amtrak; Greyhound; interstate 82, highways 12 and 97.

Communications: daily, weekly newspapers; 4 TV, 10 radio stations.

New construction: 843 building permits totalling over $34 million issued in 1979.

Medical facilities: 3 hospitals with 460 beds, 150 physicians, 11 osteopaths, 64 dentists, 13 optometrists; cardiac surgery at St. Elizabeth's Hospital.

Federal facilities: U.S. Army Firing Center, 409 permanent personnel, trains active and reserve units on 263,131 acres; U.S. Army, Marine, and Navy reserve facilities; U.S. Postal

Service regional center.

Cultural facilities: Yakima Valley Museum, Yakima Valley Regional Library, Allied Arts Council, Yakima Symphony, Little Theater, Capitol Theater; over 95 churches.

Education: Yakima Valley College, J. M. Perry Institute, Yakima Business College; City College; 7 public school districts in and around city, 7 parochial schools, St. Elizabeth Health Sciences Library.

Sports and Recreation: 12 theaters, 5 drive-ins; historic trolleys; hunting and fishing; skiing in Cascade Mountains 45 minutes from city; 4 golf courses, 30 tennis courts, 9 swimming pools, 31 parks; auto racing, horse racing; youth baseball, softball; Central Washington State Fair, Washington State Open Horse Show.

Convention facilities: Yakima Convention Center, over 1,400 motel units.

History: founded Jan. 27, 1886 as North Yakima on route of Northern Pacific Railroad.

Further information: Greater Yakima Chamber of Commerce, P.O. Box 1490, or Yakima V&C Bureau, 10 North 8th Street, both Yakima, WA 98907.

Youngstown, Ohio

The World Almanac is sponsored in the Youngstown area by The Vindicator, Vindicator Square, Youngstown, OH 44501; phone (216) 747-1471; founded 1863 by J. H. Odell; Wm. F. Maag began daily Sept. 25, 1889; daily circulation 100,324, Sunday 156,657; president, publisher, general manager William J. Brown; advertising manager William Mittler; managing editor Ann N. Przelomski.

Population: 115,436 (city), 529,887 (SMSA).

Area: 35 sq. mi. in northeastern Ohio at juncture of Ohio Turnpike, I-80, and Ohio Rt. 11; Mahoning County seat.

Industry: no longer a strong iron and steel center, still some production with Jones & Laughlin Steel Corp., Republic Steel; local steel supplied to big nearby plants of General Motors Packard Electric Div. in Warren and GMAD plant in Lordstown, where Chevrolet vans and other GM models are assembled; GF Business Equipment sells office furnishings world wide; Commercial Shearing does world-wide tunnel frame and hydraulics business; other fabricators use local steel, rubber.

Commerce: wholesale-retail center for large area of northeast Ohio, western Pennsylvania; retail sales of metro area (est.) over $2.1 billion; value added by manufacturing $2.6 billion; average spendable family income $20,006.

Transportation: truck transport center with 113 motor freight terminals; rail lines; airport served by United Airlines, Dade Air Charter, Allegheny Commuter; headquarters for Beckett Aviation, largest fleet of executive aircraft in U.S.

Communications: 4 TV stations, all major networks and PBS; 9 radio stations.

Medical facilities: Northeastern Ohio Univ. College of Medicine, 6 large hospitals in area.

Federal facilities: U.S. Air Force Reserve base flying transports at airport; regional post office; army and navy reserve centers.

Cultural facilities: symphony orchestra with downtown bldg.; ballet guild, Youngstown Playhouse in own modern bldg., Butler Institute of American Art.

Educational facilities: Youngstown State Univ. with graduate program; Penn-Ohio Junior College; Youngstown Col-

lege of Business and Professional Drafting; 55 public and parochial schools; branches of Kent State Univ. in nearby Warren, Salem, and East Liverpool.

Recreational facilities: 10 parks, 44 playgrounds, golf course, 6 swimming pools; Mill Creek Park with 2,383 acres; 4 large reservoirs in area for recreation, many golf courses.

Further information: Youngstown Area Chamber of Commerce, 200 Wick Bldg., Youngstown, OH 44503.

Washington, Capital of the U.S.

The Capitol

The United States Capitol has presented an entirely new east central front since 1961. That portion was extended 32 ft. 6 in. and reproduced in Georgia marble. The extension added 100 rooms and cost $11.4 million. The original wall of Virginia sandstone became an inner wall.

Dr. William Thornton, an amateur architect, submitted a plan for the Capitol in the spring of 1793 that won him $500 and a city lot. The design consisted of a center section topped with a low dome; on either side were wings to accomodate the House and Senate that measured about 126 ft. by 120 ft. George Washington laid the cornerstone Sept. 18, 1793; in Nov. 1800 Congress met in that north or Senate wing. Also housed in that small wing were the Supreme Court, other local courts, and the Library of Congress.

The south, or House wing, was completed in 1807 under the direction of Benjamin H. Latrobe. At the time the Capitol was burned by the British in 1814 the Capitol consisted of these 2 wings joined by a wooden walkway. The interiors were gutted by the fire and nearly 5 years were needed to rebuild the Capitol. It was occupied again in 1819; the central portion with its low copper-covered wooden dome was completed in 1829 by the 3d architect of the Capitol, Charles Bulfinch.

The present Senate and House wings and the iron dome were designed and constructed by Thomas U. Walter, the 4th architect of the Capitol, between 1851-1863. The House moved into its chamber Dec. 16, 1857 and the Senate Jan. 4, 1859. These moves enabled the Supreme Court to occupy the Old Senate Chamber from 1860-1935 when it moved into its own building. The Old Hall of the House became Statuary Hall. Those original chambers have been restored and are open to the public.

The present cast iron dome at its greatest exterior measures 135 ft. 5 in., and it is topped by the bronze Statue of Freedom that stands 19½ ft. and weighs 14,985 pounds. On its base are the words "E Pluribus Unum (Out of Many One). The sculptor was Thomas Crawford and the cost, including casting, $23,796. The Rotunda, covered by the huge dome, measures 96 ft. in diameter. Looking upward 180 ft. into the "eye" of the dome one sees the huge fresco, "Apotheosis of Washington," by Constantino Brumidi. Encircling the rotunda 58 ft. up is a frescoed frieze depicting scenes from the landing of Columbus in 1492 to Kitty Hawk in 1903. It measures 300 ft.

Prayer Room

A nondenominational room where members of Congress may pray and meditate is located off the rotunda. Dominating the room is a stained glass window of George Washington kneeling in prayer at Valley Forge. The prayer room is not open to the public.

National Statuary Hall

Statuary Hall was created in 1864 and occupies the former Old Hall of the House. States were invited to contribute not more than 2 statues of distinguished deceased persons to the collection. Statues now number 93 and it has become necessary to display them throughout the Capitol.

Office Buildings for Members

Members of Congress meet constituents and transact other business in 5 office buildings on Capitol Hill, 2 for the Senate and 3 for the House. The original Senate building, the Richard Brevard Russell Office Building, was completed in 1909, enlarged in 1933; the second Senate building, the Everett McKinley Dirksen Office Building, was constructed in 1958. A subway connects both with the Capitol.

The original House building (1908) was named for former Speaker Joseph G. Cannon (R. Ill.), the second (1933) for former Speaker Nicholas Longworth (R. Oh.), and the third (1964) for former Speaker Sam Rayburn (D. Tex.). The Rayburn Building has underground transportation to the Capitol.

Also on Capitol Hill is the bell tower and statue memorial to

Sen. Robert A. Taft of Ohio (1889-1953). It was erected by popular subscription and dedicated Apr. 14, 1959, by President Eisenhower.

Hours for Visiting

The Capitol is normally open from 9 a.m. to 4:30 p.m. daily, closed Christmas, New Year's Day, and Thanksgiving Day. Should either the House or the Senate remain in session beyond closing time, the wing of the Capitol in use stays open until the session closes.

Tours through the Capitol, including the House and Senate Galleries, are conducted from 9 a.m. to 4 p.m. without charge. It is not necessary to take a tour to see the Capitol. Visitors desiring to hear debate in either chamber for a longer period than the tour allows must obtain a visitor's card from their Senator or Representative.

The White House

The White House, the president's residence, stands on 18 acres on the south side of Pennsylvania Avenue, between the Treasury and the Executive Office Building. The main building 168 by 85-1/2 ft., has 6 floors, with the East Terrace, 135 by 35 ft., leading to the East Wing, a 3-story building, 139 by 82 ft., used for offices and as an entrance for tours. The West Terrace, 174 by 35 ft., contains offices and press facilities, and leads to the West Wing, 3 stories high, 148 by 98 ft., erected in 1902 and enlarged several times since.

The White House was designed by James Hoban, an Irish-born architect, in a competition that paid $500. The main facade resembles the Duke of Leinster's house in Dublin. President Washington chose the site, which was included on the plan of the Federal City prepared by the French engineer, Major Pierre L'Enfant. The cornerstone was laid Oct. 13, 1792. President Washington never lived in the house. President John Adams entered in Nov. 1800, and Mrs. Adams hung her washing in the uncompleted East Room.

The walls are of sandstone, quarried at Aquia Creek, Va. The exterior walls were painted during the course of construction, causing the building to be termed the "White House." For many years, however, it was generally referred to as the "President's House" or the "President's Palace." Thomas Jefferson developed the east and west terraces, which housed one-story offices, woodsheds, and a wine cellar. On Aug. 24, 1814, during Madison's administration, the house was burned by the British. James Hoban rebuilt it by Oct. 1817, for President Monroe to move in.

The south portico was added in 1824 and the north portico in 1829. In 1948 President Truman had a second-floor balcony built into the south portico. In 1948 he had Congress authorize complete rebuilding because the White House was unsafe. During its reconstruction he lived in Blair House, 1651 Pennsylvania Ave. Reconstruction cost $5,761,000. The interior was completely removed, new underpinning 24 ft. deep was placed under the outside walls and a steel frame was built to support the interior.

Visiting Hours

The White House is open from 10 a.m. to 12 noon, Tuesday through Friday, except on Thanksgiving, Christmas, and New Year. Also Saturdays, 10 a.m. to 2 p.m. Jun. 1 through Labor Day, and 10 a.m. to noon Labor Day through May 31. Only the public rooms on the ground floor and state floor may be visited.

President's Guest House

Blair House, the President's Guest House, fronts on Pennsylvania Ave., northwest of the White House grounds. It is supervised by the Dept. of State and is the official residence of heads of state who visit Washington. Built 1824, it was the home of Francis Preston Blair (1791-1876), political leader and Lincoln advisor. President Truman lived there 1948-1952 during rebuilding of the White House, and 2 Puerto Rican fanatics tried to shoot their way in Nov. 1, 1950, killing one guard and wounding 2 others. Restoration and refurnishing began in 1963 and the house was reopened Jan. 14, 1964.

Other Centers of Interest
Arlington National Cemetery

Arlington National Cemetery, on the former Custis estate in Virginia, is the site of the **Tomb of the Unknown Soldier** and the final resting place of John Fitzgerald Kennedy, president of the United States, who was buried there Nov. 25, 1963. A torch burns day and night over his grave. The remains of his brother Sen. Robert F. Kennedy (N.Y.) were interred on June 8, 1968, in an area adjacent. Many other famous Americans are also buried at Arlington, as well as American soldiers from every major war.

Arlington National Cemetery, administered by the Department of the Army, was established June 15, 1864, on land originally the estate of George Washington Parke Custis. The land was part of the District of Columbia from 1791 until 1847, when Arlington County was returned to Virginia.

The Unknown Soldier of World War I was entombed on the east front of the Arlington Memorial Amphitheater Nov. 11, 1921. The tomb is inscribed: *Here rests in honored glory an American soldier known but to God.* The body had been chosen at Chalons-sur-Marne from unidentified dead in Europe. On Memorial Day, May 30, 1958, 2 unidentified servicemen, one of whom died in World War II and one in the Korean War, were placed in crypts beside the first.

As of May 1, 1981, a total of 181,209 interments had been made in Arlington National Cemetery. Among the unknown dead are 2,111 who died on the battlefields of Virginia in the Civil War and 167 who lost their lives when the battleship Maine was blown up in Havana Harbor Feb. 15, 1898. The total of unknown dead interred in Arlington National Cemetery is 4,724. In April, 1980 a columbarium for cremated remains was opened.

Arlington House, The Robert E. Lee Memorial

On a hilltop above the cemetery, stands Arlington House, the Robert E. Lee Memorial, which from 1955 to 1972 was officially called the Custis-Lee Mansion. The house has a portico 60 ft. wide, with 8 Doric columns, and faces the Potomac. With its 2 wings the house extends 140 ft. It was built by George Washington Parke Custis, grandson of Martha Washington and father of Mary Ann Randolph Custis, who married Lee in this house in 1831. Here Lee wrote his resignation from the U.S. Army, Apr. 20, 1861. The house became a military headquarters and was confiscated by the government. The U.S. Supreme Court restored it to the legal heir, George Washington Custis Lee, grandson of the builder, who sold the entire estate (including the mansion) to the Government in 1883 for $150,000. The mansion and grounds are administered by the National Park Service of the Dept. of the Interior.

U.S. Marine Corps War Memorial

North of the National Cemetery, approximately 350 yards, stands the bronze statue of the raising of the United States flag on Iwo Jima, executed by Felix de Weldon from the photograph by Joe Rosenthal, and presented to the nation by members and friends of the U.S. Marine Corps, at a cost of $850,000. It was dedicated Nov. 10, 1954, and is under the administration of the Dept. of the Interior, National Park Service.

Folger Shakespeare Library

The **Folger Shakespeare Library** on Capitol Hill, Washington, D. C., is a research institution devoted to the advancement of learning in the background of Anglo-American civilization in the 16th and 17th centuries and in most aspects of the continental Renaissance. It has the largest collection of Shakespeareana in the world with 79 copies of the First Folio. Its collection of English books printed before 1640 is the largest in the Western Hemisphere. It also has extensive source materials for the history of theater and drama from the Middle Ages to the end of the 19th century, both English and American. The library owns approximately 250,000 books and manuscripts, about half of them rare. It is also the home of a professional acting company and chamber music ensemble.

The library was founded and endowed by Henry Clay Folger, a former president of the Standard Oil Co. of New York, and his wife, Emily Jordan Folger. He left its administration to the trustees of his alma mater, Amherst College. The exhibition gallery and replica Elizabethan Theatre are open free 10 a.m. to 4 p.m. daily; closed federal holidays and on Sundays after Labor Day to April 15.

Library of Congress

Established by and for Congress in 1800, the Library of Congress has extended its services over the years to other Government agencies and other libraries, to scholars, and to the general public,

and it now serves as the national library. Three buildings, the Thomas Jefferson Bldg. (1897), John Adams Bldg. (1939) and James Madison Bldg. (1980), cover 64.6 acres of floor space. The library also occupies 2 other buildings in the metropolitan area.

Dr. Daniel J. Boorstin became the 12th Librarian of Congress Nov. 12, 1975. Today the library's collections contain more than 74 million items, including more than 18 million volumes and pamphlets.

In addition to providing a variety of reference and bibliographic services to other government agencies, the Library of Congress serves as a cataloging and bibliographic center for libraries throughout the country. Its cataloging data is available on printed cards (a service offered since 1901), on magnetic tapes for libraries using computers, and in book catalogs. A program called Cataloging in Publication makes cataloging information available in books themselves so that they can be processed and put into circulation almost immediately after their delivery to libraries.

The library's exhibit halls are open to the public. Guided tours are given every hour from 9 a.m. through 4 p.m. Monday through Friday. Arrangements for groups should be made in advance with the Tour Coordinator.

Thomas Jefferson Memorial

The **Thomas Jefferson Memorial** stands on the south shore of the Tidal Basin in West Potomac park. It is a circular stone structure, with Vermont marble on the exterior and Georgia white marble inside and combines architectural elements of the dome of the Pantheon in Rome and the rotunda designed by Jefferson for the University of Virginia. The central circular chamber, 86¼ ft. in diameter, is dominated by a 19-ft. tall full-length figure of Thomas Jefferson by the American sculptor Rudulph Evans. The architects were John Russell Pope and his associates Otto R. Eggers and Daniel P. Higgins. The Memorial was dedicated by President F. D. Roosevelt Apr. 13, 1943, the 200th anniversary of Jefferson's birth.

On the pediment over the portico is a sculptured group by Adolph A. Weinman showing Jefferson standing before the committee appointed by the Continental Congress to draft the Declaration of Independence. On the interior walls are four panels with inscriptions from Jefferson's writings. On the frieze of the main entablature are Jefferson's lines: "I have sworn upon the altar of God eternal hostility against every form of tyranny over the mind of man."

The memorial is open daily from 8 a.m. to midnight, except Christmas Day. An elevator and curb ramps for the handicapped are in service.

John F. Kennedy Center

John F. Kennedy Center for the Performing Arts, designated by Congress as the National Cultural Center and the official memorial in Washington to President Kennedy, opened September 8, 1971. The white marble building, designed by Edward Durell Stone, houses a 2,300-seat Opera House, a 2,750-seat Concert Hall, the 1,150-seat Eisenhower Theater, the 513-seat Terrace Theater, the 224-seat American Film Institute Theater, a 100-seat laboratory theater, and 3 restaurants. All facilities are in full operation throughout the year. Tours are available daily, free of charge, between 10:00 a.m. and 1:15 p.m.

Lincoln Memorial

The **Lincoln Memorial** in West Potomac Park, on the axis of the Capitol and the Washington Monument, consists of a large marble hall enclosing a heroic statue of Abraham Lincoln in meditation sitting on a large armchair. It was dedicated on Memorial Day, May 30, 1922. The Memorial was designed by Henry Bacon. The statue was made by Daniel Chester French. Murals and ornamentation on the bronze ceiling beams are by Jules Guerin.

The memorial, built on bedrock, is of white Colorado-Yule marble. There are 2 Doric columns at the entrance and 36 others in the colonnade. The frieze above the 36 columns bears the names of the 36 states existing at the time of Lincoln's death. On the attic parapet are recorded names of the 48 states existing in 1922.

Inside are 3 memorials to Lincoln. The seated figure of Lincoln is 19 ft. from head to foot and the classic armchair is 12½ ft. tall. Over the back of the chair a flag is draped in marble. The statue was fashioned out of 28 blocks of Georgia white marble. On the north wall is inscribed the Second Inaugural Address. On the south wall is the Gettysburg Address.

The memorial is open daily from 8 a.m. to midnight, except Christmas Day. A new elevator for the handicapped is in service.

Mount Vernon

Mount Vernon on the south bank of the Potomac, 16 miles below Washington, D. C., is part of a large tract of land in northern

Virginia which was originally included in a royal grant made to Lord Culpepper, who in 1674 granted 5,000 acres to Nicholas Spencer and John Washington. The division between Spencer and Washington put John Washington's son Lawrence in possession of the Washington half in 1690. Later it became the property of Lawrence Washington's son Augustine, the father of George Washington.

The present house is an enlargement of one apparently built on the site of an earlier one by Augustine Washington, who lived there 1735-1738. His son Lawrence came there in 1743, when he renamed the plantation Mount Vernon in honor of Admiral Vernon under whom he had served in the West Indies. Lawrence Washington died in 1752 and was succeeded as proprietor of Mount Vernon by his half-brother, George Washington.

Washington brought his wife, Martha Dandridge Custis, to Mount Vernon in 1759, having previously enlarged the house from 1-1/2 to 2-1/2 stories. Just before the Revolution he planned additions, and when he was called away to war his kinsman Lund Washington supervised the work, which was completed after Washington returned in 1783. During the Revolution Washington visited Mount Vernon only twice, on the way to and from Yorktown in 1781. In 1789 he left to become president and lived in New York and Philadelphia, with brief visits to the plantation. He came back in 1797 and died in Mount Vernon Dec. 14, 1799. He was buried in the old family vault. He had made plans for a new burial vault and this was built in 1831. Both his remains and those of Martha, who died in 1802, were transferred there.

Mount Vernon was left to Washington's nephew, U.S. Supreme Court Justice Bushrod Washington, and by him to his nephew, John Augustine Washington, whose son, John A. Washington Jr., was the last private owner. In 1853 Miss Ann Pamela Cunningham of South Carolina organized the Mount Vernon Ladies' Assn., which bought the mansion and 200 acres, since extended to just under 500 acres. The Association reassembled original Washington furniture and repaired the buildings. It restored the kitchen garden, flower garden, and experimental botanical garden, reconstructed the greenhouse, and built a museum. Several trees planted by Washington still exist, and the boxwood dates from 1798. The Association preserves house and tomb with the visitor's fee.

National Arboretum

The National Arboretum, one of Washington's great showplaces, occupies 444 acres in the northeastern section of the city. Collections of azaleas, magnolias, hollies, cherries, crabapples, conifers, and ferns and wildflowers are prime attractions. The National Herb Garden and National Bonsai Collection are special attractions in the nation's only federally-supported gardens.

The Arboretum is open every day of the year except Christmas. The visiting hours are 8 a.m. to 5 p.m. Monday through Friday and 10 a.m. to 5 p.m. on Saturday and Sunday.

National Archives

The Declaration of Independence, the Constitution of the United States, and the Bill of Rights are on permanent display in the National Archives Exhibition Hall. They are sealed in glass-and-bronze cases.

The National Archives holds the permanently valuable federal records of the United States government, 1774 to the present. As a research institution, it is designed to preserve these records and make them available to scholars, students, writers, and the general public.

The National Archives and Records Service is a part of the General Services Administration. Through the Office of Presidential Libraries it administers the Herbert Hoover Library at West Branch, Iowa, the Franklin D. Roosevelt Library at Hyde Park, N.Y., the Harry S. Truman Library at Independence, Mo., the Dwight D. Eisenhower Library at Abilene, Kan., the John Fitzgerald Kennedy Library at Boston, Mass., the Lyndon Baines Johnson Library at Austin, Tex., and the Gerald Ford Library to be built in Ann Arbor, Mich., and museum to stand in Grand Rapids. For research information, call 202-523-3218; for visitor information, 202-523-3000.

National Gallery of Art

The National Gallery of Art, situated in an area bounded by Constitution Avenue and the Mall, between Third and Seventh Streets, was established by Joint Resolution of Congress Mar. 24, 1937, and opened Mar. 17, 1941. Although technically a bureau of the Smithsonian Institution, the gallery is an autonomous organization governed by its own board of trustees. The chairman of the board is the chief justice of the United States. Other members are the secretaries of state and of the treasury, the secretary of the

Smithsonian Institution, and 5 distinguished private citizens.

The collections comprise gifts of over 300 donors (none of the works were acquired with Government funds) and cover the American and various European schools of art from the 13th century to the present.

The building was erected with funds given by Andrew W. Mellon, who also gave his collection of 126 paintings and 26 pieces of sculpture, which included such masterpieces as Raphael's Alba Madonna, the Niccolini-Cowper Madonna, and St. George and the Dragon, van Eyck's Annunciation, Botticelli's Adoration of the Magi, and 9 Rembrandts.

The gallery's Education Department gives daily talks on the gallery's collection. The Extension Service lends films and slide programs to schools, colleges, and civic groups in more than 4,000 communities in the United States and Canada. Nearly all of the gallery's services are available to the public free of charge.

The National Gallery is in the process of moving into its new East Building, which adjoins the original West Building.

Open daily except Christmas and New Year's, from 10 a.m. to 5 p.m. Monday through Saturday and noon to 9 p.m. Sunday. During the summer open Monday through Saturday 10 a.m. to 9 p.m., noon to 9 p.m. on Sunday.

The Pentagon

The Pentagon, headquarters of the Department of Defense, is the world's largest office building, with 3 times the floor space of the Empire State Building in New York. Situated in Arlington, Va., it houses more than 23,000 employees in offices that occupy 3,707,745 square feet.

The Pentagon was completed Jan. 15, 1943, at a cost of about $83 million. It covers 34 acres, is 5 stories high and consists of 5 rings of buildings connected by 10 corridors, with a 5-acre pentagonal court in the center. Each of the outermost sides of the building is 921 ft. long and the perimeter is 7/8's of a mile. Total length of the corridors is 17½ miles.

Tours are available Monday through Friday (excluding federal holidays), and start every 30 minutes at the Concourse. The first tour begins at 9 a.m. and the last at 3:30 p.m. Walk-ins are welcome. During the summer tourist season, tours are conducted every 15 minutes. For goups of 15 or more, reservations are required. Call 202-695-1776 for information.

Smithsonian Institution

The Smithsonian Institution is one of the world's great historical, scientific, educational, and cultural establishments. It comprises numerous facilities, mostly in the metropolitan Wash., D.C., area. It was founded by an Act of Congress in 1846, pursuant to a bequest of James Smithson, a British scholar-scientist, to the United States to found at Washington "an establishment for the increase and diffusion of knowledge among men." The Smithsonian, ever since its founding, has been a center for basic scientific research; it engages in programs of education and it is also the largest museum-gallery complex in the world. More than 24 million persons visit its halls annually.

Among the Smithsonian's components are the Anacostia Neighborhood Museum, Arts and Industries Building, Freer Gallery of Art, Hirshhorn Museum and Sculpture Garden, Natl. Museum of American History, Natl. Museum of Natural History, Natl. Museum of Man, Natl. Air and Space Museum, Natl. Museum of American Art, Museum of African Art, Natl. Portrait Gallery, Natl. Zoological Park, Smithsonian Associates, Smithsonian Institution Traveling Exhibition Service.

Washington Monument

The Washington Monument is a tapering shaft or obelisk of white marble, 555 ft., 5-1/8 inches in height and 55 ft., 1-1/2 inches square at base. Eight small windows, 2 on each side, are located at the 500-ft. level, where Washington points of interest are indicated.

The capstone weighs 3,300 lbs. and was placed Dec. 6, 1884. The monument was dedicated Feb. 21, 1885, and opened Oct. 9, 1888. It weighs 81,120 tons. It is dressed with white Maryland marble in 2-ft. courses. The first 150 ft. are backed by rubble masonry. From that point to 452 ft. Maine granite was used as backing, and above 452 ft. marble was used. The face of the monument is primarily marble from Maryland. Set into the interior wall are 190 memorial stones from states, foreign countries, and organizations. An iron stairway has 50 landings and 898 steps. A modern elevator takes sightseers to the 500-ft. level in one minute, compared with 12 "precarious minutes" in 1888.

The Monument is open 7 days a week, 9 a.m. to 5 p.m. Extended summer hours are 8 a.m. to 12 midnight. It is closed Christmas Day.

Cherry Blossom Time

Cherry blossom time in Washington is looked upon as the opening of spring. The famous cherry trees encircle the Tidal Basin in West Potomac Park and for 2 miles line the roadside in East Potomac Park. A gift by the Mayor of Tokyo to the city of Washington, the original 3,000 trees were propagated from the trees on the Arawaka River in a suburb of Tokyo. The first trees were planted by Mrs. William Howard Taft, wife of the president, and by Viscountess Chinda, wife of the Japanese Ambassador, Mar. 27, 1912. The trees are usually in full blossom the first week in April.

Notable Tall Buildings in North American Cities

Height from sidewalk to roof, including penthouse and tower if enclosed as integral part of structure; actual number of stories beginning at street level. Asterisks (*) denote buildings still under construction Jan. 1982.

City	Hgt. ft.	Stories
Akron, Oh.		
First National Tower Bldg.	330	28
Akron Center.	321	24
Albany, N.Y.		
Office Tower, So. Mall	589	44
State Office Building	388	34
Agency (4 bldgs.), So. Mall.	310	23
Atlanta, Ga.		
Peachtree Center Plaza Hotel	723	71
Georgia Pacific Tower, 123 Peachtree	697	51
Southern Bell Telephone, 675 W. Peachtree	677	47
First National Bank, 2 Peachtree	556	44
Equitable Building, 100 Peachtree	453	34
101 Marietta Tower, 101 Marietta St.	446	36
Peachtree Summit No. 1	406	31
North Avenue Tower, 310 North Ave.	403	26
Tower Place, 3361 Piedmont Road	401	29
National Bank of Georgia	390	32
Richard B. Russell, Federal Bldg.	383	26
Atlanta Hilton Hotel	383	32
Peachtree Center Harris Bldg.	382	31
Southern Bell Telephone	380	. . .
Trust Company Bank	377	28
Coastal States Insurance	377	27
Peachtree Center Cain Building	376	30
Peachtree Center Building	374	31
Life of Georgia Tower	371	29
Georgia Power Tower, 333 Piedmont	349	24
Peachtree Center South	332	27
Gas Light Tower, 235 Peachtree	331	27
Hyatt Regency Hotel, 265 Peachtree	330	23
100 Colony Square, 1175 Peachtree	328	25
Georgia Power Building	318	22
Colony Square Hotel, 180 14th St.	310	28
Austin, Tex.		
Austin National Bank	328	26
American Bank	313	21
State Capitol	309	. . .
Univ. of Texas Admin. Bldg.	307	29
J. Frank Dobie Univ. Center	299	29
Baltimore, Md.		
U.S. Fidelity & Guaranty Co.	529	40
Maryland National Bank Bldg.	509	34
World Trade Center Bldg.	405	32
Saint-Paul Apartments Bldg.	385	37
Arlington Federal Savings and Loan Assn. Bldg.	370	28
Blaustein Building	370	30
Charles Plaza Apts. So.	350	31
Charles Center South.	330	26
Tower Bldg.	330	16
Baltimore Arts Tower	319	15
First National Bank of Maryland	315	22
Lord Baltimore Hotel	315	24
Mercantile-Safe Deposit and Trust Co.	315	21
Charles Plaza Apts. No.	315	28
Baltimore Hilton Hotel.	302	29
One Charles Center Bldg.	301	24
Baltimore Gas and Electric Co. Bldg.	300	22
Chesapeake & Potomac Telephone Co.	300	16
Baton Rouge, La.		
State Capitol	460	34
American Bank Bldg.	310	25
Hilton Hotel.	290	28
Birmingham, Ala.		
First Natl. Southern Natural Bldg.	390	30
South Central Bell Hdqts. Bldg.	390	30
City Federal Bldg.	325	27
Cabana Motel	287	21

City	Hgt. ft.	Stories
Boston, Mass.		
John Hancock Tower	790	60
Prudential Tower	750	52
Federal Reserve Bldg.	604	32
Boston Co. Bldg., Court St.	601	41
First National Bank of Boston	591	37
Shawmut Bank Bldg.	520	38
Sixty State St.	509	38
Employers Commercial Employees Bldg.	507	40
New England Merch. Bank Bldg.	500	40
U.S. Custom House.	496	32
John Hancock Bldg.	495	26
State St. Bank Bldg.	477	34
One Hundred Summer St.	450	33
McCormack Bldg.	401	22
Keystone Custodian Funds.	400	32
Saltonstall Office Bldg.	396	22
Harbor Towers (2 bldgs.)	396	40
John F. Kennedy Bldg.	387	24
Longfellow Towers (2 bldgs.)	380	38
Federal Bldg. & Post Office	345	22
Suffolk County Courthouse.	330	19
Jamaicaway Towers	320	30
Sheraton-Boston Hotel	310	29
Buffalo, N.Y.		
Marine Midland Center	529	40
City Hall	378	32
Rand Bldg., not incl. 40-ft. beacon	351	29
Main Place Tower	350	26
One M&T Plaza	317	21
Liberty Bank	305	23
Calgary, Alta.		
Calgary Tower	626	. . .
Scotia Centre	504	38
*Nova Bldg., 801 7th Ave. SW.	500	37
Two Bow Valley Square	468	39
Fifth & Fifth Bldg.	460	35
Oxford Square North	463	34
Shell Tower	460	34
Oxford Square South	449	33
*Four Bow Valley Square	441	37
Esso Plaza (twin towers)	435	34
Family Life Bldg.	410	33
*Pan Canadian Bldg., 150 9th Ave. SW.	410	28
Norcen Tower	408	33
Sun Oil Bldg.	397	34
Western Centre	385	40
Three Bow Valley Square	382	33
Mobil Tower	369	29
*Sun Life Bldg. (twin towers)	374	28
A.G.T. Tower, 411 1st St. SE.	366	28
One Palliser Square.	350	28
Mount Royal House	330	34
Standard Life Bldg.	327	25
Place Concorde (twin towers)	321	36
Bow Valley Inn.	320	25
Charlotte, N.C.		
NCNB Plaza, 101 S. Tryon	503	40
First Union Plaza	433	32
Wachovia Center, 400 S. Tryon	420	32
Southern National Center, 200 S. College	300	32
City National Center, 200 S. Tryon	299	18
Chicago, Ill.		
Sears Tower (world's tallest).	1,454	110
Standard Oil (Indiana).	1,136	80
John Hancock Center.	1,127	100
Water Tower Place (a)	859	74
First Natl. Bank	850	60
IBM Bldg.	695	52
Daley Center.	662	31
Lake Point Tower	645	70
Board of Trade, incl. 81 ft. statue	605	44
Prudential Bldg., 130 E. Randolph.	601	41
Antenna tower, 311 ft., makes total.	912	. . .

City	Hgt. ft.	Stories	City	Hgt. ft.	Stories
1000 Lake Shore Plaza Apts.	590	55	Plaza of the Americas.	332	25
Marina City Apts., 2 buildings	588	61	Park Central No. 3.	327	20
Mid Continental Plaza.	580	50	Adolphus Tower.	327	27
Pittsfield, 55 E. Washington St.	557	38	Bell Telephone Bldg.	326	23
Kemper Insurance Bldg.	555	45	**Dayton, Oh.**		
Newberry Plaza, State & Oak	553	56	Winters Bank Bldg.	404	30
Harbor Point	550	54	Mead Tower, 10 W. 2d St.	365	28
LaSalle Natl. Bank, 135 S. LaSalle St.	535	44	Centre City Office Bldg.	297	21
One LaSalle Street	530	49	Hulman Bldg.	295	23
111 E. Chestnut St.	529	56	Grant-Deneau Bldg.	290	22
River Plaza, Rush & Hubbard	524	56	**Denver, Col.**		
Pure Oil, 35 E. Wacker Drive.	523	40	Argo Tower.	600	42
United Ins. Bldg., 1 E. Wacker Dr.	522	41	Anaconda Tower.	580	40
Lincoln Tower, 75 E. Wacker Dr.	519	42	One Denver Place.	467	35
Carbide & Carbon, 230 N. Mich.	503	37	Amoco Bldg., 17th Ave. & Broadway	450	36
Walton Colonnade.	500	44	Brooks Towers, 1020 15th St.	420	42
LaSalle-Wacker, 221 N. LaSalle St.	491	41	First of Denver Plaza	415	32
Amer. Nat'l Bank, 33 N. LaSalle St.	479	40	Energy Center 1.	404	29
Bankers, 105 W. Adams St.	476	41	Colorado Nat'l. Bank, 17th & Curtis	389	26
Brunswick Bldg.	475	37	First National Bank	385	28
Continental Companies.	475	45	Security Life Bldg.	384	33
American Furniture Mart	474	24	Energy Plaza, 1125 17th St.	370	28
Sheraton Hotel, 505 N. Mich. Ave.	471	42	Lincoln Center.	366	30
Playboy Bldg., 919 N. Mich. Ave.	468	37	Denver Natl. Bank Plaza	363	29
188 Randolph Tower	465	45	Western Fed. Savings.	357	27
Tribune Tower, 435 N. Mich. Ave.	462	36	Colorado State Bank	352	26
Chicago Marriott, Mich. & Ohio Sts.	460	45	Executive Tower.	350	30
(a) World's tallest reinforced concrete bldg.			Larimer Place	335	32
Cincinnati, Oh.			410 Building	335	24
Carew Tower	568	49	Mountain Bell, 17th & Curtis	330	21
Central Trust Tower	504	33	D&F Tower.	330	20
Netherland Hilton	372	31	Great West Plaza (twin towers)	325	29
Dubois Tower, 5th & Walnut	420	32	Prudential Tower Plaza	322	25
Central Trust Center	355	27	Barclay Towers	314	30
First Natl. Bank Center	351	26	**Des Moines, Ia.**		
Stouffer's North Tower	350	33	Ruan Center	457	36
Kroger Bldg.	320	25	Financial Center, 7th & Walnut.	345	25
Federated Bldg.	317	21	Equitable Bldg.	318	19
Cleveland, Oh.			**Detroit, Mich.**		
Terminal Tower	708	52	Detroit Plaza Hotel	720	71
Erieview Plaza Tower	529	40	City Natl. Bank Bldg., 637 Griswold	557	47
Justice Center, 1250 Ontario.	420	26	*15000 Town Center Dr.	554	40
Federal Bldg.	419	32	Guardian, 500 Griswold.	485	40
Cleveland Trust Tower No. 1.	383	29	Renaissance Center (4 bldgs.)	479	39
Ohio-Bell Telephone	365	22	Book Tower, 1227 Wash. Blvd.	472	35
Cleveland State Univ. Towers	319	21	13000 Town Center Dr.	443	32
Central Natl. Bank Bldg.	305	23	Cadillac Tower, 51 Cadillac Sq.	437	40
Diamond Shamrock Bldg.	300	23	David Stott, 1150 Griswold	436	38
CEI Bldg.	300	22	Mich. Cons. Gas Co. Bldg.	430	32
Columbus, Oh.			Fisher, W. Grand Blvd. & 2d St.	420	28
State Office Tower, 30 E. Broad.	624	42	J. L. Hudson Bldg.	397	28
LeVeque-Lincoln Tower, 50 W. Broad.	555	47	McNamara Federal Office Bldg.	393	27
OneNationwide Plaza	485	40	Detroit Bank & Trust Bldg., 6438 Woodward	374	27
Borden Bldg., 180 E. Broad	438	34	American Center	374	27
Franklin Cty. Municipal Courts Bldg.	357	19	Top of Troy Bldg.	374	27
Columbus Center, 100 E. Broad.	357	20	Detroit Bank & Trust Bldg., 211 W. Fort.	370	28
Ohio Bell Bldg., 150 E. Gay St.	346	26	Edison Plaza.	365	25
88 E. Broad St.	324	20	Woodward Tower	358	34
BancOhio Plaza, 155 E. Broad.	317	25	Buhl, 535 Griswold	350	26
Dallas, Tex.			Ford Bldg.	346	25
First International Bldg.	710	56	Michigan Bell Telephone	340	19
*Arco Bldg., 1601 Bryan St.	660	49	1st Federal Savings & Loan	338	23
Placid Oil, 1600 Pacific Ave.	645	50	Pontchartrain Motor Hotel	336	23
First National Bank	625	52	Commonwealth Bldg.	325	25
Republic Bank Tower	598	50	1300 Lafayette East.	325	30
*First City Center, 1700 Pacific Ave.	595	49	**Edmonton, Alta.**		
Olympia York, 1999 Bryan St.	562	37	AGT Tower, 10020-100 St.	441	34
Reunion Tower.	560	50	CN Tower, 1004-104 Ave.	365	26
Southland Life Tower	550	42	Toronto Dominion Tower	325	27
Diamond Shamrock, 717 N. Harwood St.	550	34	Oxford Tower	325	29
2001 Bryan St.	512	40	Sun Life Bldg.	320	25
Republic Bank Bldg., not incl. 150-ft. ornamental tower	452	36	Edmonton House	315	34
One Main Place	445	34	**Fort Wayne, Ind.**		
LTV Tower	434	31	One Summit Square, 911 S. Calhoun.	442	27
Mercantile Natl. Bank Bldg., not incl. 115-ft. weather beacon	430	31	Ft. Wayne Natl. Bank	339	26
			Lincoln Natl. Bank	312	23
Mobil Bldg.	430	31	**Fort Worth, Tex.**		
Fidelity Union Tower	400	33	Ft. Worth Natl. Bank.	454	37
One Dallas Centre	386	30	Continental Natl. Bank Bldg.	380	30
Southwestern Bell Toll Bldg.	372	22	First National Bank, 500 W. 7th	300	21
Court House & Fedl. Office Bldg.	362	16	One Tandy Center	300	20
Mercantile Dallas Bldg.	360	22	Two Tandy Center.	300	20
Sheraton Hotel.	352	38	**Hamilton, Ont.**		
Hyatt Regency, 303 Reunion Blvd.	343	30	Century Twenty One	418	43
Elm Place, 1005-09 Elm St.	341	22	Stelco Tower.	339	25
Main Tower.	336	26			

City	Hgt. ft.	Stories	City	Hgt. ft.	Stories
The Olympia	321	33	**Hull, Ont.**		
Harrisburg, Pa.			Les Terrasses De La Chaudiere	383	30
State Office Tower #2	334	21	Place Du Portage, Phase 1	333	24
City Towers	291	25	Place Du Portage, Phase 2	281	20
Hartford, Conn.			**Indianapolis, Ind.**		
Travelers Ins. Co. Bldg.	527	34	American United Life Ins. Co.	533	37
Hartford Plaza	420	22	Indiana Natl. Bank Tower	504	37
Hartford Natl. Bank & Trust	360	26	City-County Bldg.	377	26
*One Commercial Plaza	349	27	Merchants Plaza/Hyatt Regency Hotel . .	328	26
One Financial Plaza, 755 Main.	335	26	Indiana Bell Telephone	320	20
One Corporate Center	305	23	Blue Cross-Blue Shield Bldg.	302	18
Honolulu, Ha.			Riley Towers (2 bldgs.)	294	30
Ala Moana Hotel.	390	38	**Jacksonville, Fla.**		
Pacific Trade Center	360	30	Independent Life & Accident Ins. Co. . .	535	37
*Ana Nanala Apt.	350	41	Gulf Life Ins. Co. Bldg.	432	28
*Honolulu Tower.	350	40	Prudential Ins. Co. of America	295	22
*Lakeside Development	350	40	Blue Cross-Blue Shield	287	20
*Tapa Tower.	350	40	**Jersey City, N.J.**		
Discovery Bay	350	42	Medical Center (5 bldgs.; 332 ft., 294 ft., 274 ft., (2) 273 ft.)		
Hyatt Regency Waikiki	350	39	**Kansas City, Mo.**		
Hemmeter Center	350	39	Kansas City Power and Light Bldg. . . .	476	32
Mehelani Waikiki Lodge.	350	43	City Hall	443	29
Regency Tower, 2525 Date St.	350	42	Federal Office Bldg.	413	35
Regency Tower #2.	350	43	Commerce Tower	402	32
Yacht Harbor Towers	350	40	Southwest Bell Telephone Bldg.	394	27
Canterbury Place	350	40	Pershing Road Associates	352	28
Iolani Towers.	350	38	A. T. & T. Long Line Bldg.	331	20
Diamond Head Tower.	350	38	Bryant Bldg.	319	26
Ala Wai Sunset	350	44	Federal Reserve Bldg.	311	21
Century Center	350	41	City Center Square, 1100 Main	302	30
Pacific Beach Hotel	350	43	Holiday Inn	300	28
Waikiki Ala Wai Waterfront	350	43	**Las Vegas, Nev.**		
Waikiki Lodge II	350	43	Las Vegas Hilton	375	30
Chateau Waikiki	349	39	MGM Grand	362	26
Rainbow Plaza	348	37	Landmark Hotel	356	31
Waikiki Beach Tower	347	39	Sundance Hotel	322	33
2121 Ala Wai Blvd.	347	41	Sahara Hotel	294	24
Royal Kuhio	346	39	**Little Rock, Ark.**		
Century Square	344	36	First National Bank	454	33
Waipuna	343	38	Worthen Bank & Trust	375	28
Ioloni Court Tower.	341	40	Union National Bank.	331	24
Waikiki Banyon.	341	36	Tower Bldg.	300	18
Waikiki Sunset Makai	341	37	**Los Angeles, Cal.**		
*Hale Kaheka	337	38	United Cal. Bank.	858	62
The Villa on Eaton Square	335	37	Security Pacific Natl. Bank	738	55
Houston, Tex.			*Crocker Center, 313 S. Grand	718	55
Texas Commerce Tower	1,002	75	Atlantic Richfield Plaza (2 bldgs.)	699	52
*Allied Bank Plaza, 1000 Louisiana . . .	970	71	"J" Square, 444 S. Flower	625	49
First International Plaza.	748	55	Crocker-Citizen Plaza.	620	42
*Three Houston Center, 1301 McKinney .	725	52	Century Plaza Towers (2 bldgs.).	571	44
One Shell Plaza			Union Bank Square	516	41
(not incl. 285 ft. TV tower)	714	50	City Hall	454	28
Capital Natl. Bank Plaza	685	50	Equitable Life Bldg.	454	34
One Houston Center	678	47	Occidental Life Bldg.	452	32
First City Tower	664	49	Mutual Benefit Life Ins. Bldg.	435	31
1100 Milam Bldg.	651	47	Broadway Plaza	414	33
Exxon Bldg.	606	44	1900 Ave. of Stars	398	27
Two Houston Center	570	40	1 Wilshire Bldg.	395	28
Dresser Tower.	550	40	*The Evian, 10490 Wilshire Blvd.	390	31
Pennzoil, 700 Milam (2 bldgs.)	523	36	Bonaventure Hotel, 404 S. Figueroa . . .	367	34
Two Allen Center	521	36	Cal. Fed. Savings & Loan Bldg.	363	24
Entex Bldg.	518	35	Century City Office Bldg.	363	24
Tenneco Bldg.	502	33	Bunker Hill Towers	349	32
Conoco Tower	465	32	International Industries Plaza.	347	24
One Allen Center	452	34	City Natl. Bank Bldg.	344	24
Summit Tower West	441	31	Wilshire West Plaza	327	24
Coastal Tower	441	31	**Louisville, Ky.**		
*Four Leafs Towers (2 bldgs.)	400	40	First Natl. Bank	512	40
Gulf Bldg.	428	37	Citizen's Plaza	420	30
First City Natl. Bank.	410	32	Galt House	325	25
Houston Lighting & Power	410	27	Louisville Trust Bldg.	312	24
Neils Esperson Bldg.	409	31	**Memphis, Tenn.**		
Hyatt Regency Houston	401	34	100 N. Main Bldg.	430	37
Houston Natural Gas Bldg.	386	28	Commerce Square	396	31
*Amoco Center, 501 Westlake Blvd. . . .	382	28	Sterick Bldg.	365	31
Bank of the Southwest	369	24	Clark, 5100 Poplar	365	32
Sheraton-Lincoln Hotel	352	28	First Natl. Bank Bldg.	332	28
Two Shell Plaza	341	26	Hyatt Regency	329	28
American General Life	337	25	Lowenstein's Towers	296	25
Transco.	333	25	Lincoln American Life Tower	290	22
Four Seasons Hotel, 1300 Lamar	330	29	**Miami, Fla.**		
Allied Chemical Bldg.	328	25	One Biscayne Corp.	456	40
609 Fannin Bldg.	325	22	First Federal Savings & Loan	375	32
Holiday Inn	325	30	Dade County Court House	357	27
Post Oak Central 2	321	24	New World Center.	340	30
Three Post Oak Central	321	24			
Capital Natl. Bank	320	21			

City	Hgt. ft.	Stories	City	Hgt. ft.	Stories
Plaza Venetia	332	33	Woolworth, 233 Broadway	792	60
Flagler Center Bldg.	318	25	1 Penn Plaza	764	57
Omni International Hotel	296	29	Exxon, 1251 Ave. of Americas	750	54
Milwaukee, Wis.			1 Liberty Plaza	743	50
First Wis. Center & Office Tower	625	42	Citibank	741	57
City Hall	350	9	One Astor Plaza	730	54
Wisconsin Telephone Co.	313	19	Union Carbide Bldg., 270 Park Ave.	707	52
Marine Plaza Bldg.	288	22	General Motors Bldg.	705	50
Allen-Bradley Co.	280	17	Metropolitan Life, 1 Madison Ave.	700	50
Minneapolis, Minn.			500 5th Ave.	697	60
			9 W. 57th St.	688	50
IDS Center	775	57	Chem. Bank, N.Y. Trust Bldg.	687	50
Pillsbury Bldg., 200 S. 6th St.	529	40	55 Water St.	687	53
Foshay Tower, not including 163-ft.			Chanin, Lexington Ave. & 42d St.	680	56
antenna tower.	447	32	Gulf & Western Bldg.	679	44
Hennepin County Government Center	403	24	Marine Midland Bldg., 140 Bway.	677	52
First Natl. Bank Bldg.	366	28	McGraw Hill, 1221 Ave. of Am.	674	51
Municipal Building	355	14	Lincoln, 60 E. 52d Street	673	53
North Western Bell Telephone	350	26	1633 Broadway	670	48
100 Washington Square	340	22	*725 5th Ave.	664	56
Cedar-Riverside	337	39	American Brands, 245 Park Ave.	648	47
Dain Tower	311	26	*A. T. & T. Tower, 570 Madison Ave.	648	37
Montreal, Que.			General Electric, 570 Lexington	640	50
			Irving Trust, 1 Wall St.	640	50
Place Victoria	624	47	345 Park Ave.	634	44
Place Ville Marie	616	42	Grace Plaza, 1114 Ave. of Am.	630	50
Canadian Imperial Bank			1 New York Plaza	630	50
of Commerce	604	43	Home Insurance Co. Bldg.	630	44
Le Complexe Desjardins			N.Y. Telephone, 1095 Ave. of Am.	630	40
La Tour du Sud	498	40	888 7th Ave.	628	42
La Tour du L'Est.	428	32	1 Hammarskjold Plaza	628	50
La Tour du Nord	355	27	Waldorf-Astoria, 301 Park Ave.	625	47
La Tour Laurier	425	36	Burlington House, 1345 Ave. of Am.	625	50
C.I.L. House	429	32	Olympic Tower, 645 5th Ave.	620	51
Chateau Champlain Hotel	420	38	10 E. 40th St.	620	48
Port Royal Apts.	400	33	*101 Park Ave.	618	50
Royal Bank Tower.	397	22	New York Life, 51 Madison Ave.	615	40
Sun Life Bldg.	390	26	Penney Bldg., 1301 Ave. of Am.	609	46
Banque Canadienne National	390	32	*IBM, 590 Madison Ave.	603	41
Place du Canada	372	33	560 Lexington Ave.	600	46
Hydro Quebec	360	27	Celanese Bldg., 1211 Ave. of Am.	592	45
Alexis Nihon Plaza.	331	33	U.S. Court House, 505 Pearl St.	590	37
Bell Telephone.	324	22	Federal Bldg., Foley Square	587	41
Le Cartier Apts.	320	32	Time & Life, 1271 Ave. of Am.	587	47
Nashville, Tenn.			Cooper Bregstein Bldg., 1250 Bway.	580	40
Natl. Life & Acc. Ins. Co.	452	31	1185 Ave. of Americas	580	42
Nashville Life & Casualty Tower	409	30	Municipal, Park Row & Centre St.	580	34
James K. Polk State Office Bldg.	383	32	1 Madison Square Plaza	576	42
First American Natl. Bank	354	28	Westvaco Bldg. 299 Park Ave.	574	42
Hyatt Regency.	300	28	Socony Mobil Bldg., East 42d St.	572	45
Third Natl. Bank Bldg.	292	20	Sperry Rand Bldg., 1290 Ave. of Am.	570	43
Andrew Jackson State Office Bldg.	286	17	600 3d Ave.	570	42
Newark, N.J.			Helmsley Bldg., 230 Park Ave.	565	35
National Newark & Essex Bank	465	36	1 Bankers Trust Plaza	565	40
Raymond-Commerce	448	36	Palace Hotel, Madison & 51st St.	563	51
Park Plaza Bldg.	400	26	30 Broad St.	562	48
Prudential Corporate Bldg.	369	27	Sherry-Netherland, 5th Ave. & 59th St.	560	40
Prudential Ins. Co., 753 Broad St.	360	26	Continental Can, 633 3d Ave.	557	39
Western Electric Bldg.	359	31	Sperry & Hutchinson, 330 Madison	555	39
Gateway 1	359	31	Galleria, 117 E. 57th St.	552	57
American Insurance Company	326	21	Interchem Bldg., 1133 Ave. of Am.	552	45
Raymond Plaza West	310	26	*151 E. 44th St.	550	42
Prudential Ins. Co., 213 Washington St.	300	15	N.Y. Telephone, 323 Bway.	550	45
New Orleans, La.			919 3d Ave.	550	47
			Burroughs Bldg., 605 3d Ave.	550	44
One Shell Square	697	51	Bankers Trust, 33 E. 48 St.	547	41
Plaza Tower	531	45	Transportation Bldg., 225 Bway.	546	45
Marriott Hotel	450	42	Equitable, 120 Broadway	545	42
Canal Place One	439	32	1 Brooklyn Bridge Plaza	540	42
Bank of New Orleans	438	31	Equitable Life, 1285 Ave. of Am.	540	42
Int'l. Trade Mart Bldg.	407	33	Ritz Tower, Park Ave. & 57th St.	540	41
225 Baronne St.	362	28	Bankers Trust, 6 Wall St.	540	39
Hyatt-Regency Hotel, Poydras Plaza	360	25	1166 Ave. of Americas	540	44
Hibernia Bank Bldg.	355	23	1700 Broadway	533	41
1250 Poydras Plaza.	341	24	Downtown Athletic Club, 19 West St.	530	45
New Orleans Hilton, Intl. River Center	340	29	Nelson Towers, 7th Ave. & 34th St.	525	45
American Bank Bldg.	330	23	767 3d Ave.	525	39
Pan American Life Bldg.	323	27	Hotel Pierre, 5th Ave. & 61st St.	525	44
New York, N.Y.			House of Seagram, 375 Park Ave.	525	38
World Trade Center (2 towers)	1,350	110	*7 World Trade Center	525	40
Empire State, 34th St. & 5th Ave.	1,250	102	Random House, 825 3d Ave.	522	40
TV tower, 222 ft., makes total	1,472		3 Park Ave.	522	42
Chrysler, Lexington Ave. & 43d St.	1,046	77	North American Plywood, 800 3d Ave.	520	41
American International Bldg., 70 Pine St.	950	67	Du Mont Bldg., 515 Madison Ave.	520	42
40 Wall Tower	927	71	26 Broadway	520	31
Citicorp Center.	914	46	Newsweek Bldg., 444 Madison Ave.	518	43
RCA Bldg., Rockefeller Center	850	70	Sterling Drug Bldg., 90 Park Ave.	515	41
1 Chase Manhattan Plaza	813	60	First National City Bank.	515	41
Pan Am Bldg., 200 Park Ave.	808	59	Bank of New York, 48 Wall St.	513	32

City	Hgt. ft.	Stories
Navarre, 512 7th Ave.	513	43
Williamsburg Savings Bank, Bklyn.	512	42
ITT—American, 437 Madison Ave.	512	40
International, Rockefeller Center	512	41
1407 Broadway Realty Corp.	512	44
United Nations, 405 E. 42 St.	505	39
Park Vendome Tower.	505	48
2 New York Plaza.	504	40
22 E. 40th St.	503	43
60 Broad St.	503	39
Sheraton Centre.	501	51
World Apparel Center, 1411 Bway.	501	42
Oakland, Cal.		
Ordway Bldg., 2150 Valdez St.	404	28
Kaiser Bldg.	390	28
Clorox Bldg.	330	24
City Hall	319	15
Tribune Tower	305	21
United Cal. Bank Bldg.	297	18
Blue Cross Bldg.	296	21
Oklahoma City, Okla.		
Liberty Tower	500	36
First National Bank	493	33
City National Bank Tower.	440	32
Two Galleria Tower	425	32
Kerr-McGee Center	393	30
Mid America Plaza	362	19
Fidelity Plaza.	310	15
Southwestern Bell Telephone	303	15
Omaha, Neb.		
Woodmen Tower	469	30
Northwestern Bell Telephone Hdqrs.	334	16
Masonic Manor	320	22
First Natl. Bank	295	22
Ottawa, Ont.		
Place de Ville, Tower C.	368	29
R.H. Coats Bldg.	326	27
Place Bell Canada.	318	26
DBS Tower.	308	26
Holiday Inn	308	28
Parliament Bldgs., Peace Tower.	303	. . .
Skyline Hotel.	286	25
L'Esplanade Laurier (2 towers)	285	22
Philadelphia, Pa.		
City Hall Tower, incl. 37-ft.		
statue of Wm. Penn.	548	7
1818 Market St.	500	40
Fidelity Mutual Life Ins. Bldg.	490	38
Phila. Saving Fund Society	490	39
Central Penn Natl. Bank	490	36
Centre Square.	490	40
Industrial Valley Bank Bldg.	482	32
Philadelphia National Bank	475	25
2000 Market St. Bldg.	435	29
Atlantic Richfield Tower, Centre Square	412	33
Fidelity Bank Bldg.	410	30
Two Girard Plaza	404	30
Lewis Tower, 15th & Locust	397	33
Fifteen Hundred Locust	390	44
Philadelphia Electric Co.	384	27
INA Annex, 1600 Arch St.	383	27
Academy House, 1420 Locust St.	377	37
Penn Mutual Life.	375	20
The Drake, 15th & Spruce	375	33
Medical Tower, 255 So. 17th.	364	33
State Bldg., 1400 Spring Garden	351	18
United Engineers, 17th & Ludlow	344	20
Packard, 15th & Chestnut	340	25
Inquirer Building	340	18
Dorchester	339	32
Transportation Centre.	336	18
Franklin-Plaza Hotel.	333	30
Land Title, Broad & Chestnut	331	22
Suburban Station Bldg.	330	21
Phoenix, Ariz.		
Valley National Bank	483	40
Arizona Bank Downtown	407	31
First National Bank	372	27
United Bank Plaza, 3334 N. Central.	356	27
First Federal Savings Bldg.	341	26
Regency Apts.	297	21
Pittsburgh, Pa.		
U.S. Steel Bldg.	841	64
*Dravo Tower	725	54
*PPG Tower	623	40
*One Oxford Centre	615	46

City	Hgt. ft.	Stories
Gulf, 7th Ave. and Grant St.	582	44
University of Pittsburgh	535	42
Mellon Bank Bldg.	520	41
1 Oliver Plaza	511	39
Grant, Grant St. at 3rd Ave.	485	40
Koppers, 7th Ave. and Grant	475	34
Equibank Bldg.	445	34
Pittsburgh National Bldg.	424	30
Alcoa Bldg., 425 Sixth Ave.	410	30
*Liberty Tower.	358	29
Westinghouse Bldg.	355	23
Oliver, 535 Smithfield St.	347	25
Gateway Bldg. No. 3	344	24
Centre City Tower.	341	26
Federal Bldg., 1000 Liberty Ave.	340	23
Bell Telephone, 416 7th Ave.	339	21
Hilton Hotel.	333	22
Frick, 437 Grant St.	330	20
Portland, Ore.		
First Natl. Bank of Oregon	538	41
Georgia Pacific Bldg.	367	27
Providence, R.I.		
Industrial National Bank.	420	26
Rhode Island Hospital Trust Tower	410	30
40 Westminster Bldg.	301	24
Richmond, Va.		
Federal Reserve Bank	393	21
First & Merchants Natl. Bank.	313	26
City Hall	310	18
One James River Plaza.	302	21
Rochester, N.Y.		
Xerox Tower.	443	30
Lincoln First Tower	390	26
Eastman Kodak Bldg.	360	19
First Federal Bank Plaza	305	22
St. Louis, Mo.		
Gateway Arch	630	. . .
Mercantile Trust Bldg.	550	37
1st National Bank/IBM	515	35
Laclede Gas. Bldg., 8th & Olive	400	30
S.W. Bell Telephone Bldg.	398	31
Civil Courts.	387	13
Queeny Tower.	321	24
Counsil House Plaza	320	30
Park Plaza Hotel.	310	30
Pierre Laclede Tower.	309	24
Stauffer's Riverfront Inn, 3rd St.	301	22
St. Paul, Minn.		
First Natl. Bank Bldg., incl.		
100-ft. sign.	517	32
Osborn Bldg.	368	20
Kellogg Square Apts.	366	32
Northwestern Bell Telephone Bldg.	340	15
American National Bank Bldg.	335	25
North Central Tower	328	27
Minn. Mutual Life Center	315	21
St. Paul Cathedral.	307	. . .
Conwed Tower	305	25
Salt Lake City, Ut.		
L.D.S. Church Office Bldg.	420	30
Beneficial Life Tower	351	27
City & County Bldg.	290	. . .
State Capitol	285	. . .
Univ. Club Bldg.	277	24
Commercial Security Bank Towers	275	20
San Antonio, Tex.		
Tower of the Americas	622	. . .
Tower Life	404	30
Nix Professional Bldg.	375	23
Natl. Bank of Commerce	310	24
First Natl. Bank Tower	302	20
Frost Bank Tower	300	21
Alamo National Bldg.	288	23
Milam Bldg.	280	20
San Diego, Cal.		
California First Bank.	388	27
Wickes Bldg.	340	25
Financial Square.	339	24
Central Federal	320	22
Union Bank	320	22
Little America Westgate Hotel	303	19
San Diego Gas & Electric Bldg.	293	21
San Francisco, Cal.		
Transamerica Pyramid	853	48
Bank of America.	778	52

City	Hgt. ft.	Stories	City	Hgt. ft.	Stories
Embarcadero Center, No. 4	570	45	Royal Trust Tower (TD Centre)	600	46
Security Pacific Bank	569	45	Royal Bank Plaza—South Tower	589	41
One Market Plaza, Spear St.	565	43	Manulife Centre	545	53
Wells Fargo Bldg.	561	43	*Confederation Square	540	43
Standard Oil, 575 Market St.	551	39	Two Bloor West	486	34
Shaklee Bldg., 444 Market	537	38	*Exchange Tower	480	36
Aetna Life	529	38	Commerce Court North	476	34
First & Market Bldg.	529	38	Simpson Tower	473	33
Metropolitan Life	524	38	Sun Life Centre	470	35
Hilton Hotel	493	46	Cadillac-Fairview Bldg., 10 Queen St.	465	36
Pacific Gas & Electric	492	34	Palace Pier (2 bldgs.)	452	46
Union Bank	487	37	Continental Bank Bldg.	450	35
Pacific Insurance	476	34	Sheraton Centre	443	43
Bechtel Bldg., Fremont St.	475	33	Hudson's Bay Centre	442	35
333 Market Bldg.	474	33	Leaside Towers (2 bldgs.)	423	44
Hartford Bldg.	465	33	Commercial Union Tower (TD Centre)	420	32
Mutual Benefit Life	438	32	Maple Leaf Mills Tower	419	30
Russ Bldg.	435	31	Plaza 2 Hotel	415	41
Pacific Telephone Bldg.	435	26	Royal York Hotel	399	27
Embarcadero Center, No. 3	412	31	390 Bay St.	394	31
Levi Strauss	412	31	Royal Bank Plaza—North Tower	387	26
Cal. State Automobile Assn.	399	29	Eaton Tower	385	29
Alcoa Bldg.	398	27	*Maclean-Hunter Bldg.	380	30
St. Francis Hotel	395	32	Harborside Apts.	380	39
Shell Bldg.	386	29	Harbour Castle Hilton, East	374	35
595 Market Bldg.	379	30	*Sun Life Bldg.	370	28
Del Monte	378	28	Travellers Tower	369	27
Great Western Savings	359	26	York Centre	360	27
Union Square Hyatt House Hotel	355	35	3 Massey Square	354	38
Equitable Life Bldg.	355	25	Harbour Castle Hilton, West	353	35
Fox Plaza	354	29	Mowat Block	349	24
International Bldg.	350	22	Toronto Professional Tower	346	26
450 Sutter Street	343	26	L'Apartel at Harbour Square	344	36
Cathedral Apts.	340	21	Sutton Place Hotel	340	32
Royal Towers	330	24	Richmond-Adelaide Centre	340	26
Fairmont Hotel	330	29	50 Cordova Ave.	340	36
Seattle, Wash.			Provincial Court Bldg.	340	5
Seattle-1st Natl. Bank Bldg.	609	50	**Tulsa, Okla.**		
Space Needle	605		Bank of Oklahoma Tower	667	52
Seafirst 5th Ave. Plaza	543	42	1st National Tower	516	41
Bank of Cal., 900 4th Ave.	536	42	4th Natl. Bank of Tulsa	412	33
Rainer Bank Tower, 4th & Univ.	514	42	320 South Boston Bldg.	400	24
Smith Tower	500	42	Cities Service Bldg.	388	28
Federal Office Bldg.	487	37	Univ. Club Tower	377	32
Pacific Northwest Bell	466	33	Philtower	343	24
One Union Square	456	38	**Vancouver, B.C.**		
1111 3d Ave. Bldg.	454	35	Harbour Centre (incl. 100 ft. pylon)	581	32
Washington Plaza	397	40	Royal Bank Tower	468	37
Financial Center	389	30	Scotiabank Tower	451	36
Fourth & Blanchard Bldg.	360	24	Canada Trust Tower, 1055 Melville	450	35
Park Hilton Hotel	352	33	T-D Bank Tower	410	31
Safeco Plaza	325	22	200 Granville Square	403	30
Norton Bldg.	310	21	Bentall III, 595 Burrand	399	31
Springfield, Mass.			Sheraton-Landmark Hotel	394	41
Valley Bank Tower	370	29	Hyatt Regency Vancouver	357	36
Chestnut Towers	290	34	Hotel Vancouver	352	22
Syracuse, N.Y.			Oceanic Plaza	342	26
State Tower	315	22	Board of Trade Tower	342	26
Tampa, Fla.			MacMillan-Bloedel Bldg.	340	28
Tampa City Center	537	39	Guinness Tower	328	23
First Financial Tower	458	36	Marine Bldg.	321	21
Exchange Natl. Bldg.	280	22	Pacific Centre III, 607 Granville	315	24
Toledo, Oh.			Four Seasons Hotel	311	30
Owens-Illinois Corp. Headquarters	411	32	Martello Tower	300	31
Owens-Corning Fiberglas Tower	400	30	**Wilmington, Del.**		
Ohio Citizens Bank Bldg.	368	27	Hercules Tower	287	23
*City-County State Office Bldg.	300	22	American Life Ins. Co. Bldg.	282	21
Toledo Trust Bldg.	288	21	**Winnipeg, Man.**		
Toronto, Ont.			Richardson Bldg., 375 Main	406	32
CN Tower, World's tallest			Commodity Exchange Tower	393	32
self-supporting structure	1,821		55 Nassau St.	356	38
First Canadian Place	952	72	North Star Inn	272	30
Commerce Court West	784	57	**Winston-Salem, N.C.**		
Toronto-Dominion Tower (TD Centre)	758	56	Wachovia Bldg.	410	30
			Reynolds Bldg.	315	21

Tall Buildings in Other Cities

Figures denote number of stories. Height in feet is in parentheses.

Cape Canaveral, Fla., Vehicle Assembly Bldg., 40 (552); Allentown, Pa., Power & Light Bldg., 23 (320); Amarillo, Tex., American Natl. Bank, 33 (374); Bethlehem, Pa., Martin Tower, 21 (332); Charleston, W. Va., Kanawha Valley Bldg., 20 (384); Cuyahoga Falls, Oh., Cathedral Tower Restaurant, 60 (554); Frankfort, Ky., Capital Plaza Office Tower, 28 (338); Galveston, Tex., American National Ins., 20 (358); Greenville, S.C., Daniel Bldg., 22 (305); Halifax, N.S., Fenwick Towers, 31 (300); Knoxville, Tenn., United American Bank, 30 (400); Lansing, Mich., Michigan Natl. Tower, 25 (300, not including antenna tower); Lexington, Ky., Kinkaid Tower, 22 (333); Lincoln, Neb., State Capitol (432); Mobile, Ala., First Natl. Bank, 33 (420); New Haven, Conn., Knights of Columbus Hqs. (319); Niagara Falls, Ont., Skylon, (520) So. Bend Ind., American National Bank Bldg., 25 (312); Tacoma, Wash., Washington Plaza, 23 (290); Tallahassee, Fla., State Capitol Tower, 22 (345).

HISTORY

Memorable Dates in U.S. History

1492
Christopher Columbus and crew sighted land **Oct. 12** in the present-day Bahamas.

1497
John Cabot explored northeast coast to Delaware.

1513
Juan Ponce de Leon explored Florida coast.

1524
Giovanni da Verrazano led French expedition along coast from Carolina north to Nova Scotia; entered New York harbor.

1539
Hernando de Soto landed in Florida **May 28**; crossed Mississippi River, **1541.**

1540
Francisco Vazquez de Coronado explored Southwest north of Rio Grande. Hernando de Alarcon reached Colorado River, Don Garcia Lopez de Cardenas reached Grand Canyon. Others explored California coast.

1565
St. Augustine, Fla. founded by Pedro Menendez. Razed by Francis Drake **1586.**

1579
Francis Drake claimed California for Britain. Metal plate, found **1936,** thought to be left by Drake, termed probable hoax **1979.**

1607
Capt. John Smith and 105 cavaliers in 3 ships landed on Virginia coast, started first permanent English settlement in New World at **Jamestown, May 13.**

1609
Henry Hudson, English explorer of Northwest Passage, employed by Dutch, sailed into New York harbor in **Sept.,** and up Hudson to Albany. The same year, **Samuel de Champlain** explored Lake Champlain just to the north.
Spaniards settled **Santa Fe., N.M.**

1619
House of Burgesses, first representative assembly in New World, elected **July 30** at Jamestown, Va.
First Negro laborers — indentured servants — in English N. American colonies, landed by Dutch at Jamestown in **Aug.** Chattel slavery legally recognized, **1650.**

1620
Plymouth Pilgrims, Puritan separatists from Church of England, some living in Holland, left Plymouth, England **Sept. 15** on Mayflower. Original destination Virginia, they reached Cape Cod **Nov. 19,** explored coast; 103 passengers landed **Dec. 21** (Dec. 11 Old Style) at Plymouth. Mayflower Compact was agreement to form a government and abide by its laws. Half of colony died during harsh winter.

1624
Dutch left 8 men from ship New Netherland on **Manhattan Island** in **May.** Rest sailed to Albany.

1626
Peter Minuit bought Manhattan for Dutch from Man-a-hat-a Indians **May 6** for trinkets valued at $24.

1634
Maryland founded as Catholic colony with religious tolerance.

1636
Harvard College founded **Oct. 28,** now oldest in U.S., Grammar school, compulsory education established at Boston.
Roger Williams founded Providence, R.I., **June,** as a democratically ruled colony with separation of church and state. Charter was granted, **1644.**

1654
First Jews arrived in New Amsterdam.

1660
British Parliament passed **Navigation Act,** regulating colonial commerce to suit English needs.

1664
Three hundred **British troops Sept. 8** seized New Netherland from Dutch, who yield peacefully. Charles II granted province of New Netherland and city of New Amsterdam to brother, Duke of York; both renamed New York. The Dutch recaptured the colony **Aug. 9, 1673,** but ceded it to Britain **Nov. 10, 1674.**

1676
Nathaniel Bacon led planters against autocratic British Gov. Berkeley, burned Jamestown, Va. Bacon died, 23 followers executed.
Bloody **Indian war** in New England ended **Aug. 12.** King Philip, Wampanoag chief, and many Narragansett Indians killed.

1682
Robert Cavelier, Sieur de La Salle, claimed lower Mississippi River country for France, called it Louisiana **Apr. 9.** Had French outposts built in Illinois and Texas, **1684.** Killed during mutiny **Mar. 19, 1687.**

1683
William Penn signed treaty with Delaware Indians and made payment for Pennsylvania lands.

1692
Witchcraft delusion at Salem (now Danvers) Mass. inspired by preaching; 19 persons executed.

1696
Capt. William Kidd, American hired by British to fight pirates and take booty, becomes pirate. Arrested and sent to England, where he was hanged **1701.**

1699
French settlements made in Mississippi, Louisiana.

1704
Indians attacked Deerfield, Mass. **Feb. 28-29,** killed 40, carried off 100.
Boston News Letter, first regular newspaper, started by John Campbell, postmaster. (*Publick Occurences* was suppressed after one issue **1690.**)

1709
British-Colonial troops captured French fort, Port Royal, Nova Scotia, in **Queen Anne's War 1701-13.** France yielded Nova Scotia by treaty **1713.**

1712
Slaves revolted in New York **Apr. 6.** Six committed suicide, 21 were executed. Second rising, **1741;** 13 slaves hanged, 13 burned, 71 deported.

1716
First theater in colonies opened in Williamsburg, Va.

1728
Pennsylvania Gazette founded by Samuel Keimer in Philadelphia. Benjamin Franklin bought interest **1729.**

1732
Benjamin Franklin published first *Poor Richard's Almanac;* published annually to 1757.

1735
Freedom of the press recognized in New York by acquittal of John Peter Zenger, editor of *Weekly Journal,* on charge of libeling British Gov. Cosby by criticizing his conduct in office.

1740-41
Capt. Vitus Bering, Dane employed by Russians, reached Alaska.

1744
King George's War pitted British and colonials vs. French. Colonials captured Louisburg, Cape Breton Is. **June 17, 1745.** Returned to France **1748** by Treaty of Aix-la-Chapelle.

1752
Benjamin Franklin, flying kite in thunderstorm, proved

lightning is electricity **June 15;** invented lightning rod.
1754
French and Indian War (in Europe called 7 Years War, started 1756) began when French occupied Ft. Duquesne (Pittsburgh). British moved Acadian French from Nova Scotia to Louisiana **Oct. 1755.** British captured Quebec **Sept. 18, 1759** in battles in which French Gen. Montcalm and British Gen. Wolfe were killed. Peace signed **Feb. 10 1763.** French lost Canada and American Midwest. British tightened colonial administration in North America.
1764
Sugar Act placed duties on lumber, foodstuffs, molasses and rum in colonies.
1765
Stamp Act required revenue stamps to help defray cost of royal troops. Nine colonies, led by New York and Massachusetts at Stamp Act Congress in New York **Oct. 7-25, 1765,** adopted Declaration of Rights opposing taxation without representation in Parliament and trial without jury by admiralty courts. Stamp Act repealed **Mar. 17, 1766.**
1767
Townshend Acts levied taxes on glass, painter's lead, paper, and tea. In 1770 all duties except on tea were repealed.
1770
British troops fired **Mar. 5** into Boston mob, killed 5 including **Crispus Attucks,** a Negro, reportedly leader of group; later called **Boston Massacre.**
1773
East India Co. tea ships turned back at Boston, New York, Philadelphia in **May.** Cargo ship burned at Annapolis **Oct. 14,** cargo thrown overboard at **Boston Tea Party Dec. 16.**
1774
"Intolerable Acts" of Parliament curtailed Massachusetts self-rule; barred use of Boston harbor till tea was paid for.
First Continental Congress held in Philadelphia **Sept. 5-Oct. 26;** protested British measures, called for civil disobedience.
Rhode Island abolished slavery.
1775
Patrick Henry addressed Virginia convention, **Mar. 23** said "Give me liberty or give me death."
Paul Revere and William Dawes on night of **Apr. 18** rode to alert patriots that British were on way to Concord to destroy arms. At Lexington, Mass. **Apr. 19** Minutemen lost 8 killed. On return from Concord British took 273 casualties.
Col. Ethan Allen (joined by Col. Benedict Arnold) captured Ft. **Ticonderoga, N.Y. May 10;** also Crown Point. Colonials headed for **Bunker Hill,** fortified Breed's Hill, Charlestown, Mass., repulsed British under Gen. William Howe twice before retreating **June 17;** British casualties 1,000; called Battle of Bunker Hill. Continental Congress **June 15** named **George Washington** commander-in-chief.
1776
France and Spain each agreed **May 2** to provide one million livres in arms to Americans.
In Continental Congress **June 7,** Richard Henry Lee (Va.) moved "that these united colonies are and of right ought to be free and independent states." Resolution adopted July 2. **Declaration of Independence** approved **July 4.**
Col. Moultrie's batteries at **Charleston, S.C.** repulsed British sea attack **June 28.**
Washington, with 10,000 men, lost **Battle of Long Island Aug. 27,** evacuated New York.
Nathan Hale executed as spy by British **Sept. 22.**
Brig. Gen. Arnold's **Lake Champlain** fleet was defeated at Valcour **Oct. 11,** but British returned to Canada. Howe failed to destroy Washington's army at **White Plains Oct. 28.** Hessians captured Ft. Washington, Manhattan, and 3,000 men **Nov. 16;** Ft. Lee, N.J. **Nov. 18.**
Washington in Pennsylvania, recrossed **Delaware River Dec. 25-26,** defeated 1,400 Hessians at Trenton, N.J. **Dec. 26.**
1777
Washington defeated Lord Cornwallis at **Princeton Jan.**

3. Continental Congress adopted Stars and Stripes. *See Flag article.*
Maj. Gen. John Burgoyne with 8,000 from Canada captured Ft. **Ticonderoga July 6.** Americans beat back Burgoyne at Bemis Heights **Oct. 7** and cut off British escape route. Burgoyne surrendered 5,000 men at **Saratoga N.Y. Oct. 17.**
Marquis de Lafayette, aged 20, made major general.
Articles of Confederation and Perpetual Union adopted by Continental Congress **Nov. 15**
France recognized independence of 13 colonies **Dec. 17.**
1778
France signed treaty of aid with U.S. **Feb. 6.** Sent fleet; British evacuated Philadelphia in consequence **June 18.**
1779
John Paul Jones on the *Bonhomme Richard* defeated *Serapis* in British North Sea waters **Sept. 23.**
1780
Charleston, S.C. fell to the British **May 12,** but a British force was defeated near **Kings Mountain, N.C. Oct. 7** by militiamen.
Benedict Arnold found to be a traitor **Sept. 23.** Arnold escaped, made brigadier general in British army.
1781
Bank of North America incorporated in Philadelphia **May 26.**
Cornwallis, harrassed by U.S. troops, retired to **Yorktown, Va.** Adm. De Grasse landed 3,000 French and stopped British fleet in Hampton Roads. Washington and Rochambeau joined forces, arrived near Williamsburg **Sept. 26.** When siege of Cornwallis began **Oct. 6,** British had 6,000, Americans 8,846, French 7,800. **Cornwallis surrendered Oct. 19.**
1782
New British cabinet agreed **in March** to recognize U.S. independence. Preliminary agreement signed in Paris **Nov. 30.**
1783
Massachusetts Supreme Court **outlawed slavery** in that state, noting the words in the state Bill of Rights "all men are born free and equal."
Britain, U.S. signed **peace treaty Sept. 3** (Congress ratified it **Jan. 14, 1784).**
Washington ordered army disbanded Nov. 3, bade farewell to his officers at Fraunces Tavern, N.Y. City **Dec. 4.**
Noah Webster published *American Spelling Book,* great bestseller.
1784
First successful daily newspaper, **Pennsylvania Packet & General Advertiser,** published **Sept. 21.**
1786
Delegates from 5 states at **Annapolis, Md. Sept. 11-14** asked Congress to call convention in Philadelphia to write practical constitution for the 13 states.
1787
Shays's Rebellion, of debt-ridden farmers in Massachusetts, failed **Jan. 25.**
Northwest Ordinance adopted **July 13** by Continental Congress. Determined government of Northwest Territory north of Ohio River, west of New York; 60,000 inhabitants could get statehood. Guaranteed freedom of religion, support for schools, no slavery.
Constitutional convention opened at Philadelphia **May 25** with George Washington presiding. Constitution adopted by delegates **Sept. 17;** ratification by 9th state, New Hampshire, **June 21, 1788,** meant adoption; declared in effect **Mar. 4, 1789.**
1789
George Washington chosen president by all electors voting (73 eligible, 69 voting, 4 absent); John Adams, vice president, 34 votes. **Feb. 4.** First Congress met at Federal Hall, N.Y. City; regular sessions began **Apr. 6.** Washington inaugurated there **Apr. 30.** Supreme Court created by Federal Judiciary Act **Sept. 24.**
1790
Congress met in Philadelphia **Dec. 6,** new temporary Cap-

ital.

1791

Bill of Rights went into effect **Dec. 15.**

1792

Gen. **"Mad" Anthony Wayne** made commander in Ohio-Indiana area, trained "American Legion"; established string of forts. Routed Indians at Fallen Timbers on Maumee River **Aug. 20, 1794**, checked British at Fort Miami, Ohio.

1793

Eli Whitney invented **cotton gin**, reviving southern slavery.

1794

Whiskey Rebellion, west Pennsylvania farmers protesting liquor tax of **1791**, was suppressed by 15,000 militiamen **Sept. 1794**. Alexander Hamilton used incident to establish authority of the new federal government in enforcing its laws.

1795

U.S. bought peace from **Algiers and Tunis** by paying $800,000, supplying a frigate and annual tribute of $25,000 **Nov. 28.**

Gen. **Wayne** signed peace with Indians at Fort Greenville.

Univ. of North Carolina became first operating state university.

1796

Washington's Farewell Address as president delivered **Sept. 19.** Gave strong warnings against permanent alliances with foreign powers, big public debt, large military establishment and devices of "small, artful, enterprising minority" to control or change government.

1797

U.S. **frigate United States** launched at Philadelphia **July 10;** Constellation at Baltimore **Sept. 7;** Constitution (Old Ironsides) at Boston **Sept. 20.**

1798

War with France threatened over French raids on U.S. shipping and rejection of U.S. diplomats. Congress voided all treaties with France, ordered Navy to capture French armed ships. Navy (45 ships) and 365 privateers captured 84 French ships. USS Constellation took French warship Insurgente **1799**. Napoleon stopped French raids after becoming First Consul.

1801

Tripoli declared war June 10 against U.S., which refused added tribute to commerce-raiding Arab corsairs. Land and naval campaigns forced Tripoli to conclude **peace June 4, 1805.**

1803

Supreme Court, in **Marbury v. Madison** case, for the first time overturned a U.S. law **Feb. 24.**

Napoleon, who had recovered Louisiana from Spain by secret treaty, sold all of **Louisiana**, stretching to Canadian border, to U.S., for $11,250,000 in bonds, plus $3,750,000 indemnities to American citizens with claims against France. U.S. took title **Dec. 20.** Purchases doubled U.S. area.

1804

Lewis and Clark expedition ordered by Pres. Jefferson to explore what is now northwest U.S. Started from St. Louis **May 14;** ended **Sept. 23, 1806.** Sacajawea, an Indian woman, served as guide.

Vice Pres. **Aaron Burr**, after long political rivalry, **shot Alexander Hamilton** in a duel **July 11** in Weehawken, N.J.; Hamilton died the next day.

1807

Robert Fulton made first practical steamboat trip; left N.Y. City **Aug. 17**, reached Albany, 150 mi., in 32 hrs.

1808

Slave importation outlawed. Some 250,000 slaves were illegally imported 1808-1860.

1811

William Henry Harrison, governor of Indiana, defeated Indians under the Prophet, in battle of Tippecanoe **Nov. 7.**

Cumberland Road begun at Cumberland, Md.; became important route to West.

1812

War of 1812 had 3 main causes: Britain seized U.S. ships trading with France; Britain seized 4,000 naturalized U.S. sailors by **1810**; Britain armed Indians who raided western border. U.S. stopped trade with Europe **1807** and **1809**. Trade with Britain only was stopped, **1810.**

Unaware that Britain had raised the blockade 2 days before, **Congress declared war June 18** by a small majority. The West favored war, New England opposed it. The British were handicapped by war with France.

U.S. naval victories in 1812 included: USS Essex captured Alert **Aug. 13;** USS Constitution destroyed Guerriere **Aug. 19;** USS Wasp took Frolic **Oct. 18;** USS United States defeated Macedonian off Azores **Oct. 25;** Constitution beat Java **Dec. 29.** British captured Detroit **Aug. 16.**

1813

Commodore **Oliver H. Perry** defeated British fleet at Battle of Lake Erie, **Sept. 10.** U.S. victory at Battle of the Thames, Ont., **Oct. 5**, broke Indian allies of Britain, and made Detroit frontier safe for U.S. But Americans failed in Canadian invasion attempts. York (Toronto) and Buffalo were burned.

1814

British landed in Maryland in August, defeated U.S. force **Aug. 24, burned Capitol** and White House. Maryland militia stopped British advance **Sept. 12.** Bombardment of Ft. McHenry, Baltimore, for 25 hours, **Sept. 13-14,** by British fleet failed; Francis Scott Key wrote words to **Star Spangled Banner.**

U.S. won naval Battle of **Lake Champlain Sept. 11.** Peace treaty signed at Ghent **Dec. 24.**

1815

Some 5,300 British, unaware of peace treaty, attacked U.S. entrenchments near **New Orleans, Jan. 1.** British had over 2,000 casualties, Americans lost 71.

U.S. flotilla finally ended piracy by **Algiers, Tunis, Tripoli** by **Aug. 6.**

1816

Second Bank of the U.S. chartered.

1817

Rush-Bagot treaty signed **Apr. 28-29;** limited U.S., British armaments on the Great Lakes.

1819

Spain cedes **Florida** to U.S. **Feb. 22.**

American steamship Savannah made first part steam-powered, part sail-powered crossing of Atlantic, Savannah, Ga. to Liverpool, Eng., 29 days.

1820

Henry Clay's **Missouri Compromise** bill passed by Congress **May 3.** Slavery was allowed in Missouri, but not elsewhere west of the Mississippi River north of 36° 30' latitude (the southern line of Missouri). Repealed **1854.**

1821

Emma Willard founded Troy Female Seminary, first U.S. women's college.

1823

Monroe Doctrine enunciated **Dec. 2,** opposing European intervention in the Americas.

1824

Pawtucket, R.I. weavers strike in first such action by women.

1825

Erie Canal opened; first boat left Buffalo **Oct. 26,** reached N.Y. City **Nov. 4.** Canal cost $7 million but cut travel time one-third, shipping costs nine-tenths; opened Great Lakes area, made N.Y. City chief Atlantic port.

John Stevens, of Hoboken, N.J., built and operated first experimental steam **locomotive** in U.S.

1828

South Carolina **Dec. 19** declared the right of state **nullification of federal laws**, opposing the "Tariff of Abominations."

Noah Webster published his *American Dictionary of the English Language.*

Baltimore & Ohio first U.S. passenger railroad, was begun **July 4.**

1830
Mormon church organized by Joseph Smith in Fayette, N.Y. **Apr. 6.**

1831
Nat Turner, Negro slave in Virginia, led local slave rebellion, killed 57 whites in **Aug.** Army called in, Turner captured, tried, and hanged.

1832
Black Hawk War (Ill.-Wis.) **Apr.-Sept.** pushed Sauk and Fox Indians west across Mississippi.

South Carolina convention passed **Ordinance of Nullification** in Nov. against permanent tariff, threatening to withdraw from the Union. Congress **Feb. 1833** passed a compromise tariff act, whereupon South Carolina repealed its act.

1833
Oberlin College, first in U.S. to adopt coeducation; refused to bar students on account of race, **1835.**

1835
Texas proclaimed right to secede from Mexico; Sam Houston put in command of Texas army, **Nov. 2-4.**

Gold discovered on **Cherokee land** in Georgia. Indians forced to cede lands **Dec. 20** and to cross Mississippi.

1836
Texans besieged in Alamo in San Antonio by Mexicans under Santa Anna **Feb. 23-Mar. 6;** entire garrison killed. Texas independence declared, **Mar. 2.** At San Jacinto **Apr. 21** Sam Houston and Texans defeated Mexicans.

Marcus Whitman, H.H. Spaulding and wives reached Fort Walla Walla on Columbia River, Oregon. **First white women to cross plains.**

Seminole Indians in Florida under Osceola began attacks **Nov. 1,** protesting forced removal. The unpopular 8-year war ended **Aug. 14, 1842;** Indians were sent to Oklahoma. War cost the U.S. 1,500 soldiers.

1841
First emigrant **wagon train for California,** 47 persons, left Independence, Mo. **May 1,** reached Cal. **Nov. 4.**

Brook Farm commune set up by New England transcendentalist intellectuals. Lasts to **1846.**

1842
Webster-Ashburton Treaty signed **Aug. 9,** fixing the U.S.-Canada border in Maine and Minnesota.

First use of **anesthetic** (sulphuric ether gas).

Settlement of Oregon begins via **Oregon Trail.**

1844
First message over first **telegraph line** sent **May 24** by inventor Samuel F.B. Morse from Washington to Baltimore: "What hath God wrought!"

1845
Texas Congress **voted for annexation** to U.S. **July 4.** U.S. Congress admits Texas to Union **Dec. 29.**

1846
Mexican War. Pres. James K. Polk ordered Gen. Zachary Taylor to seize disputed Texan land settled by Mexicans. After border clash, U.S. declared war **May 13;** Mexico **May 23.** Northern Whigs opposed war, southerners backed it.

Bear flag of Republic of California raised by American settlers at Sonoma **June 14.**

About 12,000 U.S. troops took Vera Cruz **Mar. 27, 1847,** Mexico City **Sept. 14, 1947.** By **treaty, Feb. 1848,** Mexico ceded claims to Texas, California, Arizona, New Mexico, Nevada, Utah, part of Colorado. U.S. assumed $3 million American claims and paid Mexico $15 million.

Treaty with Great Britain **June 15** set **boundary in Oregon** territory at 49th parallel (extension of existing line). Expansionists had used slogan "54° 40′ or fight."

Mormons, after violent clashes with settlers over polygamy, left Nauvoo, Ill. for West under Brigham Young, settled **July 1847** at Salt Lake City, Utah.

Elias Howe invented **sewing machine.**

1847
First **adhesive U.S. postage stamps** on sale **July 1;** Benjamin Franklin 5¢, Washington 10¢.

Ralph Waldo Emerson published first book of poems; Henry Wadsworth Longfellow published *Evangeline.*

1848
Gold discovered Jan. 24 in California; 80,000 prospectors emigrate in **1849.**

Lucretia Mott and Elizabeth Cady Stanton lead **Seneca Falls, N.Y. Women's Rights Convention July 19-20.**

1850
Sen. Henry Clay's **Compromise of 1850** admitted California as 31st state **Sept. 9,** slavery forbidden; made Utah and New Mexico territories without decision on slavery; made Fugitive Slave Law more harsh; ended District of Columbia slave trade.

1851
Herman Melville's *Moby Dick,* Nathaniel Hawthorne's *House of the Seven Gables* published.

1852
Uncle Tom's Cabin, by Harriet Beecher Stowe, published.

1853
Commodore Matthew C. Perry, U.S.N., received by Lord of Toda, Japan **July 14;** negotiated treaty to open Japan to U.S. ships.

1854
Republican party formed at Ripon, Wis. **Feb. 28.** Opposed Kansas-Nebraska Act (became law **May 30**) which left issue of slavery to vote of settlers.

Henry David Thoreau published *Walden.*

1855
Walt Whitman published *Leaves of Grass.*

First railroad train crossed Mississippi on the river's first bridge, Rock Island, Ill.-Davenport, Ia. **Apr. 21.**

1856
Republican party's first nominee for president, **John C. Fremont,** defeated. Abraham Lincoln made 50 speeches for him.

Lawrence, Kan. sacked **May 21** by slavery party; abolitionist John Brown led anti-slavery men against Missourians at **Osawatomie, Kan. Aug. 30**

1857
Dred Scott decision by U.S. Supreme Court **Mar. 6** held, 6-3, that a Negro slave did not become free when taken into a free state, Congress could not bar slavery from a territory, and Negroes could not be citizens.

1858
First **Atlantic cable** completed by Cyrus W. Field **Aug. 5;** cable failed **Sept. 1.**

Lincoln-Douglas debates in Illinois **Aug. 21-Oct. 15.**

1859
First commercially productive **oil well,** drilled near Titusville, Pa., by Edwin L. Drake **Aug. 27.**

Abolitionist **John Brown** with 21 men seized U.S. Armory at **Harpers Ferry** (then Va.) **Oct. 16.** U.S. Marines captured raiders, killing several. Brown was hanged for treason by Virginia **Dec. 2.**

1860
New England shoe-workers, 20,000, strike, win higher wages.

Abraham Lincoln, Republican, elected president in **4-way** race.

First **Pony Express** between Sacramento, Cal. and St. Joseph, Mo. started **Apr. 3;** service ended **Oct. 24, 1861** when first transcontinental telegraph line was completed.

1861
Seven southern states set up **Confederate States of America Feb. 8,** with Jefferson Davis as president. Confederates fired on **Ft. Sumter** in Charleston, S.C. **Apr. 12,** captured it **Apr. 14.**

President Lincoln called for 75,000 volunteers **Apr. 15.** By **May,** 11 states had seceded. Lincoln blockaded southern ports **Apr. 19,** cutting off vital exports, aid.

Confederates repelled Union forces at first **Battle of Bull Run July 21.**

First **transcontinental telegraph** was put in operation.

1862
Homestead Act was approved **May 20;** it granted free

family farms to settlers.

Land Grant Act approved **July 7,** providing for public land sale to benefit agricultural education; eventually led to establishment of state university systems.

Union forces were victorious in western campaigns, took **New Orleans.** Battles in East were inconclusive.

1863

Lincoln issued **Emancipation Proclamation Jan. 1,** freeing "all slaves in areas still in rebellion."

The entire **Mississippi River** was in Union hands by July 4. Union forces won a major victory at **Gettysburg, Pa. July 1-July 4.** Lincoln read his **Gettysburg Address Nov. 19.**

Draft riots in N.Y. City killed about 1,000, including Negroes who were hung by mobs **July 13-16.** Rioters protested provision allowing money payment in place of service. Such payments were ended 1864.

1864

Gen. Sherman marched through Georgia, taking Atlanta **Sept. 1,** Savannah **Dec. 22.**

Sand Creek massacre of Cheyenne and Arapaho Indians **Nov. 29** in a raid by 900 cavalrymen who killed 150-500 men, women, and children; 9 soldiers died. The tribes were awaiting surrender terms when attacked.

1865

Robert E. Lee surrendered 27,800 Confederate troops to Grant at Appomattox Court House, Va. **Apr. 9.** J.E. Johnston surrendered 31,200 to Sherman at Durham Station, N.C. **Apr. 18.** Last rebel troops surrendered **May 26.**

President **Lincoln was shot Apr. 14** by John Wilkes Booth in Ford's Theater, Washington; died the following morning. Booth was reported dead **Apr. 26.** Four co-conspirators were hung **July 7.**

Thirteenth Amendment, abolishing slavery, took effect **Dec. 18.**

1866

First post of the **Grand Army of the Republic** formed **Apr. 6;** was a major national political force for years. Last encampment, **Aug. 31, 1949,** attended by 6 of the 16 surviving veterans.

Ku Klux Klan formed secretly in South to terrorize Negros who voted. Disbanded **1869-71.** A second Klan was organized **1915.**

Congress took control of southern Reconstruction, backed freedmen's rights.

1867

Alaska sold to U.S. by Russia for $7.2 million **Mar. 30** through efforts of Sec. of State William H. Seward.

Horatio Alger published first book, *Ragged Dick.*

The **Grange** was organized **Dec 4,** to protect farmer interests.

1868

The World Almanac, a publication of the *New York World,* appeared for the first time.

Pres. **Andrew Johnson** tried to remove Edwin M. Stanton, secretary of war; was impeached by House **Feb. 24** for violation of Tenure of Office Act; acquitted by Senate **March-May.** Stanton resigned.

1869

Financial **"Black Friday"** in New York **Sept. 24;** caused by attempt to "corner" gold.

Transcontinental railroad completed; golden spike driven at Promontory, Utah **May 10** marking the junction of Central Pacific and Union Pacific.

Knights of Labor formed in Philadelphia. By **1886,** it had 700,000 members nationally.

Woman suffrage law passed in Territory of Wyoming **Dec. 10.**

1871

Great fire destroyed Chicago Oct. 8-11; loss est. at $196 million.

1872

Amnesty Act restored civil rights to citizens of the South **May 22** except for 500 Confederate leaders.

Congress founded first national park — **Yellowstone** in Wyoming.

1873

First U.S. **postal card** issued **May 1.**

Banks failed, panic began in **Sept.** Depression lasted 5 years.

"Boss" William Tweed of N.Y. City convicted of stealing public funds. He died in jail in **1878.**

Bellevue Hospital in N.Y. City started the first **school of nursing.**

1875

Congress passed **Civil Rights Act Mar. 1** giving equal rights to Negroes in public accommodations and jury duty. Act invalidated in **1883** by Supreme Court.

First **Kentucky Derby** held **May 17** at Churchill Downs, Louisville, Ky.

1876

Samuel J. Tilden, Democrat, received majority of popular votes for president over **Rutherford B. Hayes,** Republican, but 22 electoral votes were in dispute; issue left to Congress. Hayes given presidency in **Feb., 1877** after Republicans agree to end Reconstruction of South.

Col. **George A. Custer** and 264 soldiers of the 7th Cavalry killed **June 25** in "last stand," Battle of the Little Big Horn, Mont., in Sioux Indian War.

Mark Twain published *Tom Sawyer.*

1877

Molly Maguires, Irish terrorist society in Scranton, Pa. mining areas, broken up by hanging of 11 leaders for murders of mine officials and police.

Pres. Hayes sent troops in violent national **railroad strike.**

1878

First commercial **telephone** exchange opened, New Haven, Conn. **Jan. 28.**

1879

F.W. Woolworth opened his first five-and-ten store in Utica, N.Y. **Feb. 22.**

Henry George published *Progress & Poverty,* advocating single tax on land.

1881

Pres. **James A. Garfield shot** in Washington, D.C. **July 2;** died **Sept. 19.**

Booker T. Washington founded Tuskegee Institute for Negroes.

Helen Hunt Jackson published *A Century of Dishonor* about mistreatment of Indians.

1883

Pendleton Act, passed **Jan. 16,** reformed federal civil service.

Brooklyn Bridge opened **May 24.**

1886

Haymarket riot and bombing, evening of **May 4,** followed bitter labor battles for 8-hour day in Chicago; 7 police and 4 workers died, 66 wounded. Eight anarchists found guilty. Gov. John P. Altgeld denounced trial as unfair.

Geronimo, Apache Indian, finally surrendered **Sept. 4.**

American Federation of Labor (AFL) formed **Dec. 8** by 25 craft unions.

1888

Great blizzard in eastern U.S. **Mar. 11-14;** 400 deaths.

1889

Johnstown, Pa. flood May 31; 2,200 lives lost.

1890

First execution by **electrocution:** William Kemmler **Aug. 6** at Auburn Prison, Auburn, N.Y., for murder.

Battle of Wounded Knee, S.D. Dec. 29, the last major conflict between Indians and U.S. troops. About 200 Indian men, women, and children, and 29 soldiers were killed.

Castle Garden closed as N.Y. immigration depot; **Ellis Island** opened **Dec. 31,** closed **1954.**

Sherman Antitrust Act begins federal effort to curb monopolies.

Jacob Riis published *How the Other Half Lives,* about city slums.

1892

Homestead, Pa., strike at Carnegie steel mills; 7 guards and 11 strikers and spectators shot to death **July 6;** setback for unions.

1893

Financial panic began, led to 4-year depression.

1894

Thomas A. **Edison's kinetoscope** (motion pictures) (invented **1887**) given first public showing **Apr. 14** in N.Y. City.

Jacob S. Coxey led 500 unemployed from the Midwest into Washington, D.C. **Apr. 29.** Coxey was arrested for trespassing on Capitol grounds.

1896

William Jennings Bryan delivered "Cross of Gold" speech at Democratic National Convention in Chicago **July 8.**

Supreme Court, in **Plessy v. Ferguson,** approved racial segregation under the "separate but equal" doctrine.

1898

U.S. **battleship Maine** blown up **Feb. 15** at Havana, 260 killed.

U.S. **blockaded Cuba Apr. 22** in aid of independence forces. Spain declared **war Apr. 24.** U.S. destroyed Spanish fleet in Philippines **May 1,** took Guam **June 20.**

Puerto Rico taken by U.S. **July 25-Aug. 12.** Spain agreed **Dec. 10** to cede Philippines, Puerto Rico, and Guam, and approved independence for Cuba.

U.S. annexed independent republic of **Hawaii.**

1899

Filipino insurgents, unable to get recognition of independence from U.S., started guerrilla war **Feb. 4.** Crushed with capture **May 23, 1901** of leader, Emilio Aguinaldo.

U.S. declared **Open Door Policy** to make China an open international market and to preserve its integrity as a nation.

John Dewey published *School and Society,* backing progressive education.

1900

Carry Nation, Kansas anti-saloon agitator, began raiding with hatchet.

U.S. helped suppress **"Boxers"** in Peking.

1901

Pres. William **McKinley was shot Sept. 6** by an anarchist, Leon Czolgosz; died **Sept. 14.**

1903

Treaty between U.S. and Colombia to have U.S. dig **Panama Canal** signed **Jan. 22,** rejected by Colombia. Panama declared independence with U.S. support **Nov. 3;** recognized by Pres. Theodore Roosevelt **Nov. 6.** U.S., Panama signed canal treaty **Nov. 18.**

Wisconsin set first **direct primary** voting system **May 23.**

First **automobile trip** across U.S. from San Francisco to New York **May 23-Aug. 1.**

First successful flight in heavier-than-air mechanically propelled airplane by **Orville Wright Dec. 17** near Kitty Hawk, N.C., 120 ft. in 12 seconds. Fourth flight same day by **Wilbur Wright,** 852 ft. in 59 seconds. Improved plane patented **May 22, 1906.**

Jack London published *Call of the Wild.*

Great Train Robbery, pioneering film, produced.

1904

Ida Tarbell published muckraking *History of Standard Oil.*

1905

First **Rotary Club** of local businessmen founded in Chicago.

1906

San Francisco earthquake and fire **Apr. 18-19** left 452 dead, $350 million damages.

Pure Food and Drug Act and Meat Inspection Act both passed **June 30.**

1907

Financial panic and depression started **Mar. 13.**

First round-world cruise of U.S. **"Great White Fleet";** 16 battleships, 12,000 men.

1909

Adm. Robert E. Peary reached **North Pole Apr. 6** on 6th attempt, accompanied by Matthew Henson, a black, and 4 Eskimos.

National Conference on the Negro convened **May 30,** leading to founding of the National Association for the Advancement of Colored People.

1910

Boy Scouts of America founded **Feb. 8.**

1911

Supreme Court dissolved **Standard Oil Co.**

First **transcontinental airplane flight** (with numerous stops) by C.P. Rodgers, New York to Pasadena, **Sept. 17-Nov. 5;** time in air 82 hrs., 4 min.

1912

U.S. sent marines **Aug. 14** to **Nicaragua,** which was in default of loans to U.S. and Europe.

1913

N.Y. Armory Show introduced modern art to U.S. public **Feb. 17.**

U.S. **blockaded Mexico** in support of revolutionaries.

Charles Beard published his *Economic Interpretation of the Constitution.*

Federal Reserve System was authorized **Dec. 23,** in a major reform of U.S. banking and finance.

1914

Ford Motor Co. raised basic wage rates from $2.40 for 9-hr. day to $5 for 8-hr. day **Jan. 5.**

When U.S. sailors were arrested at Tampico **Apr. 9,** Atlantic fleet was sent to **Veracruz,** occupied city.

Pres. Wilson proclaimed **U.S. neutrality** in the European war **Aug. 4.**

The **Clayton Antitrust Act** was passed **Oct. 15,** strengthening federal anti-monopoly powers.

1915

First **telephone talk,** New York to San Francisco, **Jan. 25** by Alexander Graham Bell and Thomas A. Watson.

British ship **Lusitania** sunk **May 7** by German submarine; 128 American passengers lost (Germany had warned passengers in advance). As a result of U.S. campaign, Germany issued apology and promise of payments **Oct. 5.** Pres. Wilson asked for a military fund increase **Dec. 7.**

U.S. troops landed in **Haiti July 28.** Haiti became a virtual U.S. protectorate under **Sept. 16** treaty.

1916

Gen. John J. **Pershing entered Mexico** to pursue Francisco (Pancho) Villa, who had raided U.S. border areas. Forces withdrawn **Feb. 5, 1917.**

Rural Credits Act passed **July 17,** followed by Warehouse Act. **Aug. 11;** both provided financial aid to farmers.

Bomb exploded during **San Francisco** Preparedness Day parade **July 22,** killed 10. Thomas J. Mooney, labor organizer, and Warren K. Billings, shoe worker, were convicted; both pardoned in **1939.**

U.S. bought **Virgin Islands** from Denmark **Aug. 4.**

U.S. established military government in the **Dominican Republic Nov. 29.**

Trade and loans to **European Allies** soared during the year.

John Dewey published *Democracy in Education.*

Carl Sandburg published *Chicago Poems.*

1917

Germany, suffering from British blockade, declared almost unrestricted **submarine warfare Jan. 31.** U.S. cut diplomatic ties with Germany **Feb. 3,** and formally declared war **Apr. 6.**

Conscription law was passed **May 18.** First U.S. troops arrived in Europe **June 26.**

The **18th (Prohibition)** Amendment to the Constitution was submitted to the states by Congress **Dec. 18.** On **Jan. 16, 1919,** the 36th state (Nebraska) ratified it. Franklin D. Roosevelt, as 1932 presidential candidate, endorsed repeal; 21st Amendment repealed 18th; ratification completed **Dec. 5, 1933.**

1918

Over one million **American troops** were in Europe by July. War ended **Nov. 11.**

Influenza epidemic killed an estimated 20 million worldwide, 548,000 in U.S.

1919

First **transatlantic flight**, by U.S. Navy seaplane, left Rockaway, N.Y. **May 8,** stopped at Newfoundland, Azores, Lisbon **May 27.**

Boston police strike Sept. 9; National Guard breaks strike.

Sherwood Anderson published *Winesburg, Ohio.*

About 250 **alien radicals** were deported **Dec. 22.**

1920

In national **Red Scare**, some 2,700 Communists, anarchists, and other radicals were arrested **Jan.-May.**

Senate refused **Mar. 19** to ratify the **League of Nations** Covenant.

Nicola Sacco, 29, shoe factory employee and radical agitator, and **Bartolomeo Vanzetti**, 32, fish peddler and anarchist, accused of killing 2 men in Mass. payroll holdup **Apr. 15.** Found guilty **1921.** A 6-year worldwide campaign for release on grounds of want of conclusive evidence and prejudice failed. Both were executed **Aug. 23, 1927.** Vindicated July 19, 1977 by proclamation of Mass. Gov. Dukakis.

First regular licensed **radio broadcasting** begun **Aug. 20.**

Wall St., N.Y. City, bomb explosion killed 30, injured 100, did $2 million damage **Sept. 16.**

Sinclair Lewis' *Main Street,* F. Scott Fitzgerald's *This side of Paradise* published.

1921

Congress sharply curbed **immigration,** set national quota system **May 19.**

Joint Congressional resolution declaring **peace with Germany, Austria, and Hungary** signed **July 2** by Pres. Harding; treaties were signed in **Aug.**

Limitation of Armaments Conference met in Washington **Nov. 12 to Feb. 6, 1922.** Major powers agreed to curtail naval construction, outlaw poison gas, restrict submarine attack on merchantmen, respect integrity of China. Ratified **Aug. 5, 1925.**

Ku Klux Klan began revival with violence against blacks in North, South, and Midwest.

1922

Violence during **coal-mine strike** at Herrin, Ill., **June 22-23** cost 36 lives, 21 of them non-union miners.

Reader's Digest founded.

1923

First **sound-on-film** motion picture, "Phonofilm" was shown by Lee de Forest at Rivoli Theater, N.Y. City, beginning in **April.**

1924

Law approved by Congress **June 15** making all **Indians** citizens.

Nellie Tayloe Ross elected governor of Wyoming **Nov. 9** after death of her husband **Oct. 2;** installed **Jan. 5, 1925,** first woman governor. **Miriam (Ma) Ferguson** was elected governor of Texas **Nov. 9;** installed **Jan. 20, 1925.**

George Gershwin wrote *Rhapsody in Blue.*

1925

John T. Scopes found guilty of having taught evolution in Dayton, Tenn. high school, fined $100 and costs **July 24.**

1926

Dr. Robert H. Goddard demonstrated practicality of **rockets Mar. 16** at Auburn, Mass. with first liquid fuel rocket; rocket traveled 184 ft. in 2.5 secs.

Air Commerce Act passed, providing federal aid for airlines and airports.

1927

About 1,000 **marines landed in China Mar. 5** to protect property in civil war. U.S. and British consulates looted by nationalists **Mar. 24.**

Capt. **Charles A. Lindbergh** left Roosevelt Field, N.Y. **May 20** alone in plane Spirit of St. Louis on first New York-Paris nonstop flight. Reached Le Bourget airfield **May 21,** 3,610 miles in 33 ½ hours.

The Jazz Singer, with **Al Jolson,** demonstrated part-talking pictures in N.Y. City **Oct. 6.**

Show Boat opened in New York **Dec. 27.**

O. E. Rolvaag published *Giants in the Earth.*

1929

"St. Valentine's Day massacre" in Chicago **Feb. 14;** gangsters killed 7 rivals.

Farm price stability aided by **Agricultural Marketing Act,** passed **June 15.**

Albert B. Fall, former sec. of the interior, was convicted of accepting a bribe of $100,000 in the leasing of the Elk Hills (Teapot Dome) naval oil reserve; sentenced **Nov. 1** to $100,000 fine and year in prison.

Stock Market crash Oct. 29 marked end of postwar prosperity as stock prices plummeted. Stock losses for 1929-31 estimated at $50 billion; worst American depression began.

Thomas Wolfe published *Look Homeward, Angel.* William Faulkner published *The Sound and the Fury.*

1930

London **Naval Reduction Treaty** signed by U.S., Britain, Italy, France, and Japan **Apr. 22;** in effect **Jan. 1, 1931;** expired **Dec. 31, 1936.**

Hawley-Smoot Tariff signed; rate hikes slash world trade.

1931

Empire State Building opened in N.Y. City **May 1.**

Pearl Buck published *The Good Earth.*

1932

Reconstruction Finance Corp. established **Jan. 22** to stimulate banking and business. Unemployment stood at 12 million.

Charles Lindbergh Jr. kidnaped Mar. 1, found dead **May 12.**

Bonus March on Washington **May 29** by World War I veterans demanding Congress pay their bonus in full. Army, under Gen. Douglas MacArthur, disbanded the marchers on Pres. Hoover's orders.

1933

All banks in the U.S. were ordered closed by Pres. Roosevelt **Mar. 6.**

In the "100 days" special session, **Mar. 9—June 16,** Congress passed **New Deal** social and economic measures.

Gold standard dropped by U.S.; announced by Pres. Roosevelt **Apr. 19,** ratified by Congress **June 5.**

Prohibition ended in the U.S. as 36th state ratified 21st Amendment **Dec. 5.**

U.S. foreswore armed intervention in **Western Hemisphere** nations **Dec. 26.**

1934

U.S. troops pull out of **Haiti Aug. 6.**

1935

Comedian **Will Rogers** and aviator Wiley Post **killed Aug. 15** in Alaska plane crash.

Social Security Act passed by Congress **Aug. 14.**

Huey Long, Senator from Louisiana and national political leader, was **assassinated Sept. 8.**

Porgy and Bess, George Gershwin opera on American Negro theme, opened **Oct. 10** in N.Y. City.

Committee for Industrial Organization (CIO) formed to expand industrial unionism **Nov. 9.**

1936

Boulder Dam completed.

Margaret Mitchell published *Gone With the Wind.*

1937

Amelia Earhart Putnam, aviator, and co-pilot Fred Noonan lost **July 2** near Howland Is. in the Pacific.

Pres. Roosevelt asked for 6 additional Supreme Court justices; "packing" plan defeated.

Auto, steel labor unions won first big contracts.

1938

Naval Expansion Act passed **May 17.**

National minimum wage enacted **June 28.**

Orson Welles radio dramatization of *War of the Worlds* caused nationwide scare **Oct. 30.**

1939
Pres. Roosevelt asked **defense budget hike Jan. 5, 12.**

N.Y. **World's Fair** opened **Apr. 30,** closed **Oct. 31;** reopened **May 11, 1940,** and finally closed **Oct. 21.**

Einstein alerts FDR to **A-bomb** opportunity in **Aug. 2** letter.

U.S. declares its neutrality in European war **Sept. 5.**

Roosevelt proclaimed a limited **national emergency Sept. 8,** an unlimited emergency **May 27, 1941.** Both ended by Pres. Truman **Apr. 28, 1952.**

John Steinbeck published *Grapes of Wrath.*

1940
U.S. authorized sale of **surplus war material** to Britain **June 3;** announced transfer of 50 overaged destroyers **Sept. 3.**

First **peacetime draft** approved **Sept. 14.**

Richard Wright published *Native Son.*

1941
The **Four Freedoms** termed essential by Pres. Roosevelt in speech to Congress **Jan. 6;** freedom of speech and religion, freedom from want and fear.

Lend-Lease Act signed **Mar. 11,** providing $7 billion in military credits for Britain. Lend-Lease for USSR approved in **Nov.**

U.S. occupied **Iceland July 7.**

The **Atlantic Charter,** 8-point declaration of principles, issued by Roosevelt and Winston Churchill **Aug. 14.**

Japan attacked **Pearl Harbor,** Hawaii, 7:55 a.m. **Dec. 7,** 19 ships sunk or damaged, 2,300 dead. U.S. declared war on Japan **Dec. 8,** on Germany and Italy **Dec. 11** after those countries declared war.

1942
Federal government forcibly moved 110,000 **Japanese-Americans** (including 75,000 U.S. citizens) from West Coast to detention camps. Exclusion lasted 3 years.

Battle of **Midway June 3-6** was Japan's first major defeat.

Marines landed on **Guadalcanal Aug. 7;** last Japanese not expelled until **Feb. 9, 1943.**

U.S., Britain invaded North Africa **Nov. 8.**

First **nuclear chain reaction** (fission of uranium isotope U-235) produced at Univ. of Chicago, under physicists Arthur Compton, Enrico Fermi, others **Dec. 2.**

1943
All war contractors barred from **racial discrimination May 27.**

Pres. Roosevelt signed **June 10** the pay-as-you-go income tax bill. Starting **July 1** wage and salary earners were subject to a **paycheck withholding** tax.

Race riot in Detroit June 21; 34 dead, 700 injured. Riot in Harlem section of N.Y. City; 6 killed.

U.S. troops invaded **Italy Sept. 9.**

Marines advanced in **Gilbert Is. in Nov.**

1944
U.S., Allied forces invaded Europe at **Normandy June 6.**

G.I. Bill of Rights signed **June 22,** providing veterans benefits.

U.S. forces landed on **Leyte,** Philippines **Oct. 20.**

1945
Yalta Conference met in the Crimea, USSR, **Feb. 3-11.** Roosevelt, Churchill, and Stalin agreed Russia would enter war against Japan.

Marines landed on **Iwo Jima Feb. 19;** U.S. forces invaded **Okinawa Apr. 1.**

Pres. Roosevelt, 63, died of cerebral hemorrhage in Warm Springs, Ga. **Apr. 12.**

Germany surrendered May 7.

First **atomic bomb,** produced at Los Alamos, N.M., exploded at Alamogordo, N.M. **July 16.** Bomb dropped on **Hiroshima Aug. 6,** on **Nagasaki Aug. 9.** Japan surrendered **Aug. 15.**

U.S. forces entered **Korea** south of 38th parallel to displace Japanese **Sept. 8.**

Gen. Douglas MacArthur took over supervision of Japan **Sept. 9.**

1946
Strike by 400,000 **mine workers** began **Apr. 1;** other industries followed.

Philippines given independence by U.S. **July 4.**

1947
Truman Doctrine: Pres. Truman asked Congress to aid Greece and Turkey to combat Communist terrorism **Mar. 12.** Approved **May 15.**

United Nations Security Council voted unanimously **Apr. 2** to place under **U.S. trusteeship** the Pacific islands formerly mandated to Japan.

Jackie Robinson on Brooklyn Dodgers **Apr. 11,** the first black to play in major league baseball.

Taft-Hartley Labor Act curbing strikes was vetoed by Truman **June 20;** Congress overrode the veto.

Proposals later known as the **Marshall Plan,** under which the U.S. would extend aid to European countries, were made by Sec. of State George C. Marshall **June 5.** Congress authorized some $12 billion in next 4 years.

1948
USSR began a land **blockade of Berlin's** Allied sectors **Apr. 1.** This blockade and Western counter-blockade were lifted **Sept. 30, 1949,** after British and U.S. planes had lifted 2,343,315 tons of food and coal into the city.

Organization of American States founded **Apr. 30.**

Alger Hiss, former State Dept. official, indicted **Dec. 15** for perjury, after denying he had passed secret documents to Whittaker Chambers for transmission to a communist spy ring. His second trial ended in conviction **Jan. 21, 1950,** and a sentence of 5 years in prison.

Kinsey Report on Sexuality in the Human Male published.

1949
U.S. troops withdrawn from **Korea June 29.**

North Atlantic Treaty Organization **(NATO)** established **Aug. 24** by U.S., Canada, and 10 West European nations, agreeing that "an armed attack against one or more of them in Europe and North America shall be considered an attack against all."

Mrs. I. Toguri D'Aquino **(Tokyo Rose** of Japanese wartime broadcasts) was sentenced **Oct. 7** to 10 years in prison for treason. Paroled **1956,** pardoned **1977.**

Eleven leaders of **U.S. Communist party** convicted **Oct. 14,** after 9-month trial in N.Y. City, of advocating violent overthrow of U.S. government. Ten defendants sentenced to 5 years in prison each and the 11th, to 3 years. Supreme Court upheld the convictions **June 4, 1951.**

1950
U.S. **Jan 14** recalled all consular officials from **China** after the latter seized the American consulate general in Peking.

Masked bandits robbed **Brink's Inc.,** Boston express office, **Jan. 17** of $2.8 million, of which $1.2 million was in cash. Case solved **1956,** 8 sentenced to life.

Pres. Truman authorized production of **H-bomb Jan. 31.**

United Nations asked for troops to restore Korea peace **June 25.**

Truman ordered Air Force and Navy to Korea **June 27** after North Korea invaded South. Truman approved ground forces, air strikes against North **June 30.**

U.S. sent 35 military advisers to South Vietnam **June 27,** and agreed to provide military and economic aid to anti-Communist government.

Army seized all railroads Aug. 27 on Truman's order to prevent a general strike; roads returned to owners in **1952.**

U.S. **forces landed** at Inchon **Sept. 15;** UN force took Pyongyang **Oct. 20,** reached China border **Nov. 20,** China sent troops across border **Nov. 26.**

Two members of a **Puerto Rican nationalist** movement tried to kill Pres. Truman **Nov. 1.** (see Assassinations)

U.S. **Dec. 8** banned shipments to **Communist China** and to Asiatic ports trading with it.

1951

Sen. **Estes Kefauver** led Senate investigation into organized crime. Preliminary report **Feb. 28** said gambling take was over $20 billion a year.

Julius Rosenberg, his wife, Ethel, and Morton Sobell, all U.S. citizens, were found guilty **Mar. 29** of conspiracy to commit wartime espionage. Rosenbergs sentenced to death, Sobell to 30 years. Rosenbergs **executed June 19, 1953.** Sobell released **Jan. 14, 1969.**

Gen. **Douglas MacArthur** was removed from his Korea command **Apr. 11** for making unauthorized policy statements.

Korea cease-fire talks began in July; lasted 2 years. **Fighting ended July 27, 1953.**

Tariff concessions by the U.S. to the Soviet Union, Communist China, and all communist-dominated lands were suspended **Aug. 1.**

The U.S., **Australia,** and **New Zealand** signed a mutual security pact **Sept. 1.**

Transcontinental television inaugurated **Sept. 4** with Pres. Truman's address at the Japanese Peace Treaty Conference in San Francisco.

Japanese Peace Treaty signed in San Francisco **Sept. 8** by U.S., Japan, and 47 other nations.

J.D. Salinger published *Catcher in the Rye.*

1952

U.S. **seizure of nation's steel mills** was ordered by Pres. Truman **Apr. 8** to avert a strike. Ruled illegal by Supreme Court **June 2.**

Peace contract between West Germany, U.S., Great Britain, and France was signed **May 26.**

The last racial and ethnic barriers to naturalization were removed, **June 26-27,** with the passage of the **Immigration and Naturalization Act of 1952.**

First **hydrogen device** explosion **Nov. 1** at Eniwetok Atoll in Pacific.

1953

Pres. Eisenhower announced **May 8** that U.S. had given France $60 million for **Indochina War.** More aid was announced in **Sept.** In **1954** it was reported that three fourths of the war's costs were met by U.S.

1954

Nautilus, first atomic-powered submarine, was launched at Groton, Conn. **Jan. 21.**

Five members of Congress were wounded in the House **Mar. 1** by 4 **Puerto Rican independence supporters** who fired at random from a spectators' gallery.

Sen. **Joseph McCarthy** led televised hearings **Apr. 22-June 17** into alleged Communist influence in the Army.

Racial segregation in public schools was unanimously ruled unconstitutional by the Supreme Court **May 17,** as a violation of the 14th Amendment clause guaranteeing equal protection of the laws.

Southeast Asia Treaty Organization **(SEATO)** formed by collective defense pact signed in Manila **Sept. 8** by the U.S., Britain, France, Australia, New Zealand, Philippines, Pakistan, and Thailand.

Condemnation of Sen. **Joseph R. McCarthy** (R., Wis.) voted by Senate, 67-22 **Dec. 2** for contempt of a Senate elections subcommittee, for abuse of its members, and for insults to the Senate during his Army investigation hearings.

1955

U.S. agreed **Feb. 12** to help train **South Vietnamese** army. Supreme Court ordered **"all deliberate speed"** in integration of public schools **May 31.**

A **summit meeting** of leaders of U.S., Britain, France, and USSR took place **July 18-23** in Geneva, Switzerland.

Rosa Parks refused **Dec. 1** to give her seat to a white man on a bus in Montgomery, Ala. Bus segregation ordinance

declared unconstitutional by a federal court following boycott and NAACP protest.

Merger of America's 2 largest labor organizations was effected **Dec. 5** under the name American Federation of Labor and Congress of Industrial Organizations. The merged **AFL-CIO** had a membership estimated at 15 million.

1956

Massive resistance to Supreme Court desegregation rulings was called for **Mar. 12** by 101 Southern congressmen.

Federal-Aid **Highway Act** signed **June 29,** inaugurating interstate highway system.

First transatlantic **telephone cable** went into operation **Sept. 25.**

1957

Congress approved first **civil rights bill** for Negroes since Reconstruction **Apr. 29,** to protect voting rights.

National Guardsmen, called out by Arkansas Gov. Orval Faubus **Sept. 4,** barred 9 Negro students from entering previously all-white Central High School in **Little Rock.** Faubus complied **Sept. 21** with a federal court order to remove the National Guardsmen. The Negroes entered school **Sept. 23** but were ordered to withdraw by local authorities because of fear of mob violence. Pres. Eisenhower sent federal troops **Sept. 24** to enforce the court's order.

Jack Kerouac published *On the Road,* beatnik journal.

1958

First U.S. earth satellite to go into orbit, **Explorer I,** launched by Army **Jan. 31** at Cape Canaveral, Fla.; discovered Van Allen radiation belt.

Five thousand U.S. Marines sent to **Lebanon** to protect elected government from threatened overthrow **July-Oct.**

First domestic **jet airline** passenger service in U.S. opened by National Airlines **Dec. 10** between New York and Miami.

1959

Alaska admitted as 49th state **Jan. 3; Hawaii** admitted **Aug. 21.**

St. Lawrence Seaway opened **Apr. 25.**

The **George Washington,** first U.S. ballistic-missile submarine, launched at Groton, Conn. **June 9.**

N.S. **Savannah,** world's first atomic-powered merchant ship, launched **July 21** at Camden, N.J.

Soviet Premier **Khrushchev** paid unprecedented visit to U.S. **Sept. 15-27,** made transcontinental tour.

1960

A wave of **sit-ins** began **Feb. 1** when 4 Negro college students in Greensboro, N.C. refused to move from a Woolworth lunch counter when they were denied service. By **Sept. 1961** more than 70,000 students, whites and blacks, had participated in sit-ins.

U.S. launched first **weather satellite,** Tiros I, **Apr. 1.**

Congress approved a strong **voting rights act Apr. 21.**

A **U-2 reconnaisance plane** of the U.S. was shot down in the Soviet Union **May 1.** The incident led to cancellation of an imminent Paris summit conference.

Mobs attacked U.S. embassy in **Panama Sept. 17** in dispute over flying of U.S. and Panamanian flags.

U.S. announced **Dec. 15** it backed rightist group in **Laos,** which took power the next day.

1961

The U.S. severed diplomatic and consular relations with **Cuba Jan. 3,** after disputes over nationalizations of U.S. firms, U.S. military presence at Guantanamo base, etc.

Invasion of Cuba's **"Bay of Pigs" Apr. 17** by Cuban exiles trained, armed, and directed by the U.S., attempting to overthrow the regime of Premier Fidel Castro, was repulsed.

Commander Alan B. Shepard Jr. was rocketed from Cape Canaveral, Fla., 116.5 mi. above the earth in a Mercury capsule **May 5** in the first U.S. manned sub-orbital space flight.

1962

Lt. Col. John H. Glenn Jr. became the first American in orbit **Feb. 20** when he circled the earth 3 times in the Mercury capsule **Friendship 7.**

Pres. Kennedy said **Feb. 14** U.S. military advisers in Vietnam would fire if fired upon.

Supreme Court **Mar. 26** backed **one-man one-vote** apportionment of seats in state legislatures.

First U.S. **communications satellite** launched in **July.**

James Meredith became first black student at Univ. of Mississippi **Oct. 1** after 3,000 troops put down riots.

A Soviet **offensive missile buildup in Cuba** was revealed **Oct. 22** by Pres. Kennedy, who ordered a naval and air quarantine on shipment of offensive military equipment to the island. Kennedy and Soviet Premier Khrushchev reached agreement **Oct. 28** on a formula to end the crisis. Kennedy announced **Nov. 2** that Soviet missile bases in Cuba were being dismantled.

Rachel Carson's *Silent Spring* launched environmentalist movement.

1963

Supreme Court ruled **Mar. 18** that all **criminal defendants** must have counsel and that illegally acquired evidence was not admissible in state as well as federal courts.

Supreme Court ruled, 8-1, **June 17** that laws requiring **recitation of the Lord's Prayer** or Bible verses in public schools were unconstitutional.

A limited **nuclear test-ban treaty** was agreed upon **July 25** by the U.S., Soviet Union and Britain, barring all nuclear tests except underground.

Washington demonstration by 200,000 persons **Aug. 28** in support of **Negro demands** for equal rights. Highlight was speech in which Dr. Martin Luther King said: "I have a dream that this nation will rise up and live out the true meaning of its creed, 'We hold these truths to be self-evident: that all men are created equal.' "

South Vietnam Pres. **Ngo Dinh Diem assassinated Nov. 2;** U.S. had earlier withdrawn support.

Pres. John F. Kennedy was shot and fatally wounded by an assassin **Nov. 22** as he rode in a motorcade through downtown Dallas, Tex. Vice Pres. Lyndon B. Johnson was inaugurated president shortly after in Dallas. Lee Harvey Oswald was arrested and charged with the murder. Oswald was shot and fatally wounded **Nov. 24** by Jack Ruby, 52, a Dallas nightclub owner, who was convicted of murder **Mar. 14, 1964** and sentenced to death. Ruby died of natural causes **Jan. 3, 1967** while awaiting retrial.

U.S. troops in **Vietnam** totalled over 15,000 by year-end; aid to South Vietnam was over $500 million in **1963.**

1964

Panama suspended relations with U.S. **Jan. 9** after riots. U.S. offered **Dec. 18** to negotiate a new canal treaty.

Supreme Court ordered **Feb. 17** that **congressional districts** have equal populations.

U.S. reported **May 27** it was sending military planes to **Laos.**

Omnibus **civil rights bill** passed **June 29** banning discrimination in voting, jobs, public accommodations, etc.

Three **civil rights workers** were reported missing in Mississippi **June 22;** found buried **Aug. 4.** Twenty-one white men were arrested. On **Oct. 20, 1967,** an all-white federal jury convicted 7 of conspiracy in the slayings.

U.S. Congress **Aug. 7** passed **Tonkin Resolution,** authorizing presidential action in Vietnam, after North Vietnam boats reportedly attacked 2 U.S. destroyers **Aug. 2.**

Congress approved War on Poverty bill **Aug. 11.**

The **Warren Commission** released **Sept. 27** a report concluding that Lee Harvey Oswald was solely responsible for the Kennedy assassination.

1965

Pres. Johnson in **Feb.** ordered continuous **bombing of** North Vietnam below 20th parallel.

Some 14,000 U.S. troops sent to **Dominican Republic** during civil war **Apr. 28.** All troops withdrawn by following year.

New **Voting Rights Act** signed **Aug. 6.**

Los Angeles riot by blacks living in **Watts** area resulted in death of 35 persons and property damage est. at $200 million **Aug. 11-16.**

Water Quality Act passed **Sept. 21** to meet pollution, shortage problems.

National origins quota system of **immigration** abolished **Oct. 3.**

Massive **electric power failure** blacked out most of northeastern U.S, parts of 2 Canadian provinces the night of **Nov. 9-10.**

U.S. forces in **South Vietnam** reached 184,300 by year-end.

1966

U.S. forces began firing into **Cambodia May 1.**

Bombing of Hanoi area of North Vietnam by U.S. planes began **June 29.** By Dec. 31, 385,300 U.S. troops were stationed in South Vietnam, plus 60,000 offshore and 33,000 in Thailand.

Medicare, government program to pay part of the medical expenses of citizens over 65, began **July 1.**

Edward Brooke (R, Mass.) elected **Nov. 8** as first Negro U.S. senator in 85 years.

1967

Black representative **Adam Clayton Powell** (D, N.Y.) was denied **Mar. 1** his seat in Congress because of charges he misused government funds. Reelected in 1968, he was seated, but fined $25,000 and stripped of his 22 years' seniority.

Pres. Johnson and Soviet Premier Aleksei Kosygin met **June 23 and 25** at **Glassboro State College** in N.J.; agreed not to let any crisis push them into war.

Black riots in **Newark, N.J. July 12-17** killed some 26, injured 1,500; over 1,000 arrested. In Detroit, Mich., **July 23-30** at least 40 died; 2,000 injured, and 5,000 left homeless by rioting, looting, burning in city's black ghetto. Quelled by 4,700 federal paratroopers and 8,000 National Guardsmen.

Thurgood Marshall sworn in **Oct. 2** as first black U.S. Supreme Court Justice. Carl B. Stokes (D, Cleveland) and Richard G. Hatcher (D, Gary, Ind.) were elected first black mayors of major U.S. cities **Nov. 7.**

By December 475,000 U.S. troops were in **South Vietnam,** all North Vietnam was subject to bombing. Protests against the war mounted in U.S. during year.

1968

USS Pueblo and 83-man crew seized in Sea of Japan **Jan. 23** by North Koreans; 82 men released **Dec. 22.**

"Tet offensive": Communist troops attacked Saigon, 30 province capitals **Jan. 30,** suffer heavy casualties.

Pres. Johnson curbed bombing of North Vietnam **Mar. 31.** Peace talks began in Paris **May 10.** All bombing of North is halted **Oct. 31.**

Martin Luther King Jr., 39, assassinated Apr. 4 in Memphis, Tenn. James Earl Ray, an escaped convict, pleaded guilty to the slaying, was sentenced to 99 years.

Sen. **Robert F. Kennedy** (D, N.Y.) 42, shot **June 5** in Hotel Ambassador, Los Angeles, after celebrating presidential primary victories. Died **June 6.** Sirhan Bishara Sirhan, Jordanian, convicted of murder.

1969

Expanded four-party **Vietnam peace talks** began **Jan. 18.** U.S. force peaked at 543,400 in April. Withdrawal started **July 8.** Pres. Nixon set Vietnamization policy **Nov. 3.**

A car driven by Sen. **Edward M. Kennedy** (D, Mass.) plunged off a bridge into a tidal pool on Chappaquiddick Is., Martha's Vineyard, Mass. **July 18.** The body of Mary Jo Kopechne, a 28-year-old secretary, was found drowned in the car.

U.S. astronaut **Neil A. Armstrong,** 38, commander of the Apollo 11 mission, became the first man to set foot on the moon July 20. Air Force Col. Edwin E. Aldrin Jr. accompanied Armstrong.

Anti-Vietnam War **demonstrations reached peak** in U.S.; some 250,000 marched in Washington, D.C. **Nov. 15.**

Massacre of hundreds of civilians at **Mylai,** South Vietnam in 1968 incident was reported **Nov. 16.**

1970

United Mine Workers official **Joseph A. Yablonski**, his wife, and their daughter were found shot **Jan. 5** in their Clarksville, Pa. home. UMW chief W. A. (Tony) Boyle was later convicted of the killing.

A federal jury **Feb. 18** found the defendants in the **"Chicago 7"** trial innocent of conspiring to incite riots during the 1968 Democratic National Convention. However, 5 were convicted of crossing state lines with intent to incite riots.

Millions of Americans participated in anti-pollution demonstrations **Apr. 22** to mark the first **Earth Day**.

U.S. and South Vietnamese forces crossed **Cambodian** borders **Apr. 30** to get at enemy bases. Four students were killed **May 4** at Kent St. Univ. in Ohio by National Guardsmen during a protest against the war.

Two **women generals**, the first in U.S. history, were named by Pres. Nixon **May 15.**

A **postal reform** measure was signed **Aug. 12**, creating an independent U.S. Postal Service, thus relinquishing governmental control of the U.S. mails after almost 2 centuries.

1971

Charles Manson, 36, and 3 of his followers were found guilty **Jan. 26** of first-degree murder in the 1969 slaying of actress Sharon Tate and 6 others.

U.S. air and artillery forces aided a 44-day incursion by South Vietnam forces into **Laos** starting **Feb. 8.**

A Constitutional Amendment lowering the **voting age to 18** in all elections was approved in the Senate by a vote of 94-0 **Mar. 10**. The proposed 26th Amendment got House approval by a 400-19 vote **Mar. 23**. Thirty-eighth state ratified **June 30.**

A court-martial jury of 6 officers Mar. 29, after 13 days deliberation, convicted **Lt. William L. Calley Jr.** of premeditated murder of 22 South Vietnamese at Mylai on **Mar. 16, 1968**. He was sentenced to life imprisonment **Mar. 31**. Sentence was reduced to 20 years **Aug. 20.**

Publication of classified **Pentagon papers** on the U.S. involvement in Vietnam was begun **June 13** by the New York Times. In a 6-3 vote, the U.S. Supreme Court **June 30** upheld the right of the Times and the Washington Post to publish the documents under the protection of the First Amendment.

U.S., Japan signed treaty **June 17** for return of **Okinawa I.**, seized during World War II.

Pres. Nixon began a sweeping new economic program **Aug. 15** imposing a 90-day **wage, price, and rent freeze**. He also devalued the dollar by cutting its tie with gold.

More than 1,000 N.Y. State troopers and police stormed the **Attica State Correctional Facility** where 1,200 inmates held 38 guards hostage **Sept. 13**, ending a 4-day rebellion in the maximum-security prison; 9 hostages, 28 convicts killed in the assault.

U.S. bombers struck massively in North Vietnam for 5 days starting **Dec. 26**, in retaliation for alleged violations of agreements reached prior to the 1968 bombing halt. U.S. forces at year-end were down to 140,000.

1972

Pres. Nixon arrived in **Peking Feb. 21** for an 8-day visit to China, which he called a "journey for peace." The unprecedented visit ended with a joint communique pledging that both powers would work for "a normalization of relations."

By a vote of 84 to 8, the Senate approved **Mar. 22** a Constitutional Amendment banning **discrimination against women** because of their sex and sent the measure to the states for ratification.

North Vietnamese forces launched the biggest attacks in 4 years across the demilitarized zone **Mar. 30**. The U.S. responded **Apr. 15** by resumption of bombing of Hanoi and Haiphong after a 4-year lull.

Nixon announced **May 8** the mining of **North Vietnam ports**. Last U.S. combat troops left **Aug. 11.**

Alabama Gov. George C. Wallace, campaigning at a Laurel, Md. shopping center **May 15**, was shot and seriously wounded as he greeted a large crowd. Arthur H. Bremer, 21,

was sentenced Aug. 4 to 63 years for shooting Wallace and 3 bystanders.

In the first visit of a U.S. president to Moscow, Nixon arrived **May 22** for a week of summit talks with Kremlin leaders which culminated in a landmark **strategic arms pact**.

Five men were arrested **June 17** for breaking into the offices of the Democratic National Committee in the **Watergate** office complex in Washington, D.C.

The White House announced **July 8** that the U.S. would sell to the USSR at least $750 million of **American wheat**, corn, and other grains over a period of 3 years. But the USSR bought most of it in 1st year.

Less than 2 weeks after Sen. **Thomas F. Eagleton** received the Democratic vice-presidential nomination, he confirmed **July 25** reports that he had undergone electroshock therapy on 2 occasions years before. He withdrew as the nominee **July 31.**

1973

Five of seven defendants in the **Watergate** break-in trial pleaded guilty **Jan. 11 and 15**, and the other 2 were convicted **Jan. 30.**

All state laws that limited a woman's right to an **abortion** during the first 3 months of pregnancy were overturned **Jan. 22** by the U.S. Supreme Court 7-2.

Four-party **Vietnam peace pacts** were signed in Paris **Jan. 27**, and North Vietnam released some 590 U.S. prisoners by **Apr. 1**. Last U.S. troops left **Mar. 29.**

The **end of the military draft** was announced **Jan. 27** by Defense Sec. Melvin R. Laird.

China and the U.S. agreed **Feb. 22** to set up permanent liaison offices in each other's country.

Some 200-300 members of the militant American Indian Movement **Feb. 27** seized the trading post and church at historic **Wounded Knee** on the Oglala Sioux Reservation in South Dakota.

Top Nixon aides H.R. Haldeman, John D. Ehrlichman, and John W. Dean, and Attorney General Richard Kleindienst **resigned Apr. 30** amid charges of White House efforts to obstruct justice in the Watergate case.

Soviet leader Leonid Brezhnev visited the U.S. **June 16-25**, and signed 9 cooperation agreements with the U.S.

The Senate Armed Services Committee **July 16** began a probe into allegations that the U.S. Air Force had made 3,500 secret **B-52 raids** into **Cambodia** in 1969 and 1970.

John Dean, former Nixon counsel, told Senate hearings **June 25** that Nixon, his staff and campaign aides, and the Justice Department all had conspired to cover up Watergate facts. Nixon refused July 23 to release **tapes** of relevant White House conversations. Some tapes were turned over to the court **Nov. 26.**

The U.S. officially ceased bombing in **Cambodia** at midnight **Aug. 14** in accord with a June Congressional action.

Vice Pres. **Spiro T. Agnew Oct. 10 resigned** and pleaded "nolo contendere" (no contest) to charges of tax evasion on payments made to him by Maryland contractors. Agnew was sentenced to 3 years probation and fined $10,000. Gerald Rudolph Ford **Oct. 12** became first appointed vice president under the 25th Amendment; sworn in **Dec. 6.**

A total ban on **oil exports** to the U.S. was imposed by Arab oil-producing nations **Oct. 19-21** after the outbreak of an Arab-Israeli war. The ban was lifted **Mar. 18, 1974.**

Atty. Gen. Elliot Richardson resigned, and his deputy William D. Ruckelshaus and Watergate Special Prosecutor Archibald Cox were fired by Pres. Nixon **Oct. 20** when Cox threatened to secure a judicial ruling that Nixon was violating a court order to turn tapes over to Watergate case Judge John Sirica.

Leon Jaworski, conservative Texas Democrat, was named **Nov. 1** by the Nixon administration to be special prosecutor to succeed Archibald Cox.

Congress overrode **Nov. 7** Nixon's veto of the **war powers** bill which curbed the president's power to commit armed forces to hostilities abroad without Congressional approval.

1974

Herbert W. Kalmbach, Pres. Nixon's personal lawyer and fundraiser, pleaded guilty **Feb. 25** to promising a contributor an ambassadorship for a $100,000 contribution.

Impeachment hearings were opened **May 9** against Nixon by the House Judiciary Committee.

Ex-Atty. Gen. **Richard G. Kleindienst** pleaded guilty May 16 to a misdemeanor charge that he did not testify accurately and fully before a Congressional committee probing handling of an ITT anti-trust settlement.

John D. Ehrlichman and 3 **White House "plumbers"** were found guilty **July 12** of conspiring to violate the civil rights of Dr. Lewis Fielding, formerly psychiatrist to Pentagon Papers leaker Daniel Ellsberg, by breaking into his Beverly Hills, Cal. office.

The U.S. Supreme Court ruled, 8-0, **July 24** that Nixon had to turn over **64 tapes** of White House conversations sought by Watergate Special Prosecutor Leon Jaworski.

The House Judiciary Committee, in televised hearings **July 24-30,** recommended 3 **articles of impeachment** against Nixon. The first, voted 27-11 **July 27,** charged Nixon with taking part in a criminal conspiracy to obstruct justice in the Watergate cover-up. The second, voted 28-10 **July 29,** charged he "repeatedly" failed to carry out his constitutional oath in a series of alleged abuses of power. The third, voted 27-17 **July 30,** accused him of unconstitutional defiance of committee subpoenas. The House of Representatives voted without debate **Aug. 20,** by 412-3, to accept the committee report, which included the recommended impeachment articles.

Ex-presidential counsel **John W. Dean 3d** was sentenced **Aug. 2** to 1-3 years, on his plea of guilty of conspiring to obstruct justice.

Nixon resigned Aug. 9. His support began eroding **Aug. 5** when he released 3 tapes, admitting he originated plans to have the FBI stop its probe of the Watergate break-in for political as well as national security reasons.

An **unconditional pardon** to ex-Pres. Nixon for all federal crimes that he "committed or may have committed" while president was issued by Pres. Gerald Ford **Sept. 8.**

Charges that the Central Intelligence Agency **(CIA)** abused its powers by massive domestic operations were published **Dec. 21.**

1975

Found guilty of **Watergate** cover-up charges **Jan. 1** were ex-Atty. Gen. John N. Mitchell, ex-presidential advisers H.R. Haldeman and John D. Ehrlichman.

U.S. civilians were evacuated from **Saigon Apr. 29** as communist forces completed takeover of South Vietnam.

U.S. merchant ship **Mayaguez** and crew of 39 seized by Cambodian forces in Gulf of Siam **May 12.** In rescue operation, U.S. Marines attacked Tang Is., planes bombed air base; Cambodia surrendered ship and crew; U.S. losses were 15 killed in battle and 23 dead in a helicopter crash.

Congress voted $405 million for South **Vietnam refugees May 16;** 140,000 were flown to the U.S.

Illegal **CIA operations,** including records on 300,000 persons and groups, infiltration of agents into black, anti-war and political movements, monitoring of overseas phone calls, mail surveillance, and drug-testing, were described by a "blue-ribbon" panel headed by Vice Pres. Rockefeller **June 10.** Information on assassination plots against foreign leaders was ordered withheld by Pres. Ford.

William L. Calley's court-martial conviction for the murder of 22 Vietnamese, overturned in lower courts, was reinstated by the U.S. Court of Appeals in New Orleans **Sept. 10.**

FBI agents captured **Patricia (Patty) Hearst,** kidnaped **Feb. 4, 1974,** in San Francisco **Sept. 18** with others. She was indicted for bank robbery; a San Francisco jury convicted her **Mar. 20, 1976.**

1976

Payments abroad of $22 million in bribes by Lockheed Aircraft Corp. to sell its planes were revealed **Feb. 4** by a Senate subcommittee. Lockheed admitted payments in Japan, Turkey, Italy, and Holland.

A mechanical respirator that had been keeping **Karen Anne Quinlan,** 22, alive for 11 months could be turned off, the New Jersey Supreme Court ruled **Mar. 31;** her parents had asked the ruling so that Karen might die "with grace and dignity." The respirator was disconnected but Karen did not die.

The U.S. celebrated its **Bicentennial July 4,** marking the 200th anniversary of its independence with festivals, parades, and N.Y. City's Operation Sail, a gathering of tall ships from around the world viewed by 6 million persons.

A mystery ailment **"legionnaire's disease"** killed 29 persons who attended an American Legion convention **July 21-24** in Philadelphia. The cause was found to be a bacterium, it was reported **June 18, 1977.**

The **Viking II** lander set down on **Mars' Utopia Plains Sept. 3,** following the successful landing by Viking I **July 20.**

1977

Pres. Jimmy Carter **Jan. 27** pardoned most Vietnam War **draft evaders,** who numbered some 10,000.

A natural **gas shortage** caused by severe winter weather led Congress **Feb. 2** to approve an emergency federal allocation program.

Convicted murderer **Gary Gilmore** was executed by a Utah firing squad **Jan. 17,** in the first exercise of capital punishment anywhere in the U.S. since **1967.** Gilmore had opposed all attempts to delay the execution.

Carter signed an act **Aug. 4** creating a new Cabinet-level **Energy Department.**

Carter announced **Sept. 21** that budget director Bert Lance, a personal friend, had resigned due to pressure over his disputed private financial practices.

1978

Sen. **Hubert H. Humphrey** (D., Minn.), 66, lost a battle with cancer **Jan. 13,** after 32 years of public service, including 4 years as vice-president of the United States.

A crippling 105-day strike by the 160,000-member **United Mineworker's Union** ended **Apr. 4** with final ratification of a new contract; Pres. Carter had invoked the Taft-Hartley Act, **Mar. 6,** to attempt to end the strike, but the miners ignored the order and began going back to work **Mar. 25,** only after a contract agreement was announced.

Pres. Carter's decision, announced **Apr. 7,** to "defer production" of the controversial **neutron bomb,** drew criticism and the resignation from the Army **Apr. 28** of Maj. Gen. John K. Singlaub.

U.S. Senate voted **Apr. 18** to turn over the **Panama Canal** to Panama on Dec. 31, 1999, by a vote of 68-32, ending several months of heated debate; an earlier vote **(Mar. 16)** had given approval to a treaty guaranteeing the area's neutrality after the year 2000.

California voters **June 6** approved (by a 65% majority) the **Proposition 13** initiative to cut property taxes in the state by 57%, thus severely limiting government spending.

The U.S. Supreme Court **June 28** voted 5-4 not to allow a firm quota system in affirmative action plans and ordered that **Alan Bakke** be admitted to a California medical school; Bakke, a white, had contended that he was a victim of "reverse discrimination"; the Court did uphold affirmative action programs that were more "flexible" in nature.

The **House Select Committee on Assassinations** opened hearings **Sept. 6** into assassinations of Pres. Kennedy and Martin Luther King Jr.; the committee recessed **Dec. 30** after concluding conspiracies likely in both cases, but with no further hard evidence for further prosecutions.

Congress passed the Humphrey-Hawkins **"full employment"** Bill **Oct. 15,** which set national goal of reducing unemployment to 4% by 1983, while reducing inflation to 3% in same period; Pres. Carter signed bill, **Oct. 27.**

1979

A major accident occurred, **Mar. 28,** at a nuclear reactor on **Three Mile Island** near Middletown, Pa. Radioactive gases escaped through the plant's venting system and a large hydrogen gas bubble formed in the top of the reactor containment vessel. Although the reactor cooled and the crisis was declared over **Apr. 9,** the clean-up was estimated to take 4 years.

In the worst disaster in U.S. aviation history, an American Airlines **DC-10 jetliner** lost its left engine and crashed shortly after takeoff in Chicago, **May 25,** killing 275 people.

A new **mobile intercontinental missile system,** called MX, was approved, **June 7,** by Pres. Carter. The $30-billion weapons system was designed to counter the ability of the Soviet Union's weapons to eliminate American land-based Minutemen missiles. On **Sept. 7,** Carter approved a "racetrack" scheme of circular roadways for the deployment of the missiles.

Pope John Paul II, Oct. 1-6, visited the U.S. and reaffirmed traditional Roman Catholic teachings.

The federal government announced, **Nov. 1,** a $1.5 billion loan-guarantee plan to aid the nation's 3d largest automaker, **Chrysler Corp.,** which had reported a loss of $460.6 million for the 3d quarter of 1979.

Some 90 people, including 63 Americans, were taken hostage, **Nov. 3,** at the **American embassy in Teheran,** Iran, by militant students who demanded the return of former Shah Mohammad Reza Pahlavi, who was undergoing medical treatment in New York City. Pres. Carter, **Nov. 12,** suspended all Iranian oil imports to the U.S. and, **Nov. 14,** froze all official Iranian assets in American banks. After some of the hostages were released, 50 Americans at the embassy and 3 U.S. diplomats at the Iranian Foreign Ministry remained in captivity.

1980

Citing "an extremely serious threat to peace," Pres. Carter announced, **Jan. 4,** a series of **punitive measures against the USSR,** most notably an embargo on the sale of grain and high technology, in retaliation for the Soviet invasion of Afghanistan.

Eight Americans were killed and 5 wounded, **Apr. 24,** in an ill-fated attempted to **rescue and hostages** held by Iranian **militants** at the U.S. Embassy in Teheran. In the wake of the aborted attempt, Sec. of State Cyrus Vance resigned, **Apr.**

28, and was succeeded by Sen. Edmund Muskie. The incident evidenced U.S. anguish and frustration over the fate of the hostages, and by year's end, 52 Americans remained in captivity.

Pledging that the U.S. would "provide an open heart and open arms," Pres. Carter, **May 5,** offered **a haven to the thousands of refugees** seeking to leave Cuba. In the next 5 months, the "freedom flotilla" carried over 125,000 Cubans to U.S. shores where many Americans feared further strain on their already battered economy and job market.

Wreaking death and general devastation on southwestern Washington and northern Oregon, **Mt. St. Helens erupted, May 18,** in a violent blast estimated to be 500 times as powerful as the Hiroshima atomic bomb. The blast, followed by others on **May 25** and **June 12,** left 25 confirmed dead, at least 40 missing, and economic losses estimated at nearly $3 billion.

In protest of the Soviet Union's invasion of Afghanistan, the **U.S. Olympic Committee** voted, **Apr. 12,** not to attend the Moscow Summer Olympics. The games were held amid a storm of controversy and the most widely observed boycott in the history of the competition, but some 65 nations, led by the U.S., did not participate.

In a sweeping victory, **Nov. 4, Ronald Wilson Reagan** was elected 40th President of the United States, defeating incumbent Jimmy Carter. The stunning GOP victory extended to the U.S. Congress where Republicans gained control of the Senate and wrested 33 House seats from the Democrats.

With 11 children known dead, 4 missing, and no solid leads in any of the cases, frustrated **Atlanta** officials announced, **Nov. 6,** that 5 top homicide detectives were being sent to the city to assist local authorities in their investigation.

Former Beatle **John Lennon** was shot and killed, **Dec. 8,** outside his apartment building on New York City's Upper West Side. Charged in the slaying was Mark David Chapman, a professed Beatle fan and former psychiatric patient.

For events of 1981 and late 1980,
See Chronology

Paleontology: The History of Life

All dates are approximate, and are subject to change based on new fossil finds or new dating techniques; but the sequence of events is generally accepted. Dates are in years before the present.

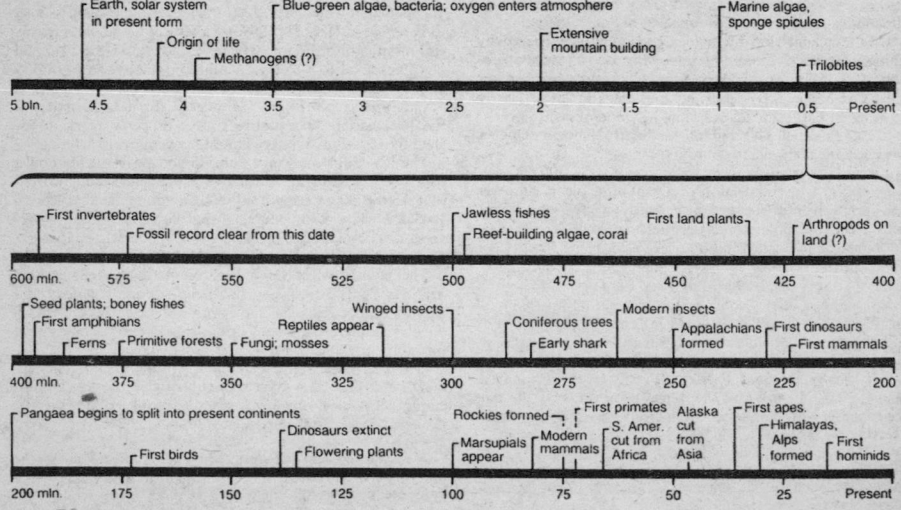

100 Years Ago

With the addition of Italy as the 3d signatory of an 1879 German-Austrian treaty, the Triple Alliance was formed on May 20, 1882. Under the terms of the accord, each party agreed to come to the other's defense should a member be attacked.

The strength of the alliance would be tested repeatedly in the years preceding World War I until, in 1914, Italy would refuse to join her allies against France and, the following year, side with the Entente powers.

British Occupy Cairo

A British naval fleet, under the command of Sir Beauchamp Seymour, bombarded Alexandria, Egypt, on July 11, 1882, in the culmination of a continuing effort to undermine Ahmed Arabi's growing nationalist power base. Soon afterward, British troops landed to protect the Suez Canal from the rebellious Egyptian nationals. On Sept. 13, at the Battle of Tel el-Kebir, Sir Garnet Wolseley defeated the Egyptian nationalists and, two days later, the British occupied Cairo.

United States Enacts Immigration Laws

The year marked a major revision in United States immigration policy. The principle of selection in immigration policy was first introduced with the enactment of a law excluding paupers, convicts, and defectives from entering the U.S. Prior to 1882, immigration into the United States was, essentially, open and unregulated.

Also in 1882, the 1880 Chinese Exclusion Act, barring the entry of Chinese laborers for 10 years, took effect.

Scientific Advances

German bacteriologist Robert Koch succeeded in isolating the tubercle bacillus, thus revolutionizing the treatment of tuberculosis. Koch's findings, along with those of other bacteriologists, would lead to the modern germ theory of disease.

Another German, Fredrich August Johannes Loffler, discovered the bacilli of swine fever, swine erysipelas, and glanders. Austrian physician Josef Breuer documented the effectiveness of hypnosis, a success he would report to his colleague, Sigmund Freud. Together they would write *Studies in Hysteria* (1895).

On Jan. 12, electric power illuminated sections of London for the first time; the following September in New York City, Thomas Edison inaugurated commercial transmission of electricity in the office of financier J.P. Morgan. The year also saw the world's first electric fan, electric flatiron, and electrically-illuminated Christmas tree. And German engineer Gottlieb Daimler invented a gas-powered internal combustion engine. Daimler would install such an engine on a bicycle in 1885, found the Daimler Motor Company in 1890, and develop the Mercedes automobile.

C.S. Parnell Released

Irish political leader C.S. Parnell was released from Kilmainham Prison after he agreed to halt the landowners boycott, stop inciting his compatriots, and cooperate with the Liberal Party. Four days later, Lord Fredrick Cavendish and Thomas Burke were murdered in Dublin's Phoenix Park, but Parnell disavowed responsibility.

Hatfield-McCoy Feud Erupts

The 1882 election-day shooting of Ellison Hatfield ignited what was tantamount to open warfare between the Hatfield and McCoy families of West Virginia and Kentucky. The feud, which traced its roots back to the Civil War, would continue for years until Kentucky authorities finally quelled the situation in 1888. Some of the major events precipitating the bloodbath included the following: William Anderson — "Devil Anse" — Hatfield (brother of Ellison) killed Harmon McCoy during the Civil War; Johnse Hatfield (son of Ellison) attempted to elope with Rosanna McCoy (Randall's daughter), and in retaliation Ellison Hatfield (brother

of "Devil Anse") was shot and killed; three of Randall McCoy sons — captured earlier by an Anse Hatfield posse — were murdered in retaliation for Ellison's murder.

Jesse James Shot

A fugitive since the days of the Civil War, Jesse James was shot and killed on Apr. 3 by fellow gang members Charles and Robert Ford.

James first gained notoriety as a 16-year-old member of the Confederate guerrilla forces with his brilliant marksmanship and daring. He surrendered at the war's end, but was declared an outlaw nevertheless. In 1866, James joined with his brother Frank and organized a band of armed robbers. In the next 16 years, they left a legacy of bold—and often ruthless—crimes in their wake.

By 1882, James, using the alias Thomas Howard, was living quietly in St. Joseph, Mo., when Governor Thomas T. Crittenden offered a $10,000 reward for his capture. Induced by the reward offer, the Fords shot and instantly killed Jesse at his home.

Achievements in the Arts

Edouard Manet's *Bar at the Folies Bergere*, Paul Cezanne's *Self-Portrait*, and John Singer Sargent's *Mr. and Mrs. John W. Field* were among the notable achievements in the visual arts in 1882. In theater, playwright Henrik Ibsen's *Ghosts* premiered at Chicago's Arrone Turner Hall on May 20 and Lillie Langtry—"Jersey Lily"—was introduced to American audiences in the Nov. 6 performance of Tom Taylor's *An Unequal Match*, held in New York's Wallack's Theater. Operatic premieres in 1882 included the Feb. 2 performance of *The Snow Maiden* with music by Nikolai Rimsky-Korsakov, the July 26 performance of Richard Wagner's *Parsifal*, and the Nov. 25 performances (premiered simultaneously in New York and London) of Gilbert and Sullivan's *Iolanthe*.

Peter Ilyich Tchaikovsky's *1812 Overture* was first performed in 1882 as was Bedrich Smetana's *Ma Vlast*, a symphonic cycle that includes *The Moldau*.

Jumbo the Elephant Arrives in America

Jumbo the elephant, the "largest elephant in or out of captivity" according to his new owner P.T. Barnum, made his American debut at New York's Madison Square Garden on Apr. 10. A major attraction at London's Royal Zoological Gardens for 17 years, the animal was sold amid a storm of protests throughout England. Barnum purchased the 6.5 ton elephant (Barnum claimed it weighed 10.5 tons) for $10,000 to perform in the Barnum & Bailey's Circus. In 1885, many mourned Jumbo's death when the animal was killed by a freight train on the Grand Trunk Railway, Ontario.

Notable Quotes of 1882

"I have nothing to declare but my genius," declared Irish essayist Oscar Wilde upon his arrival in New York to begin a year-long lecture tour through North America.

"When a dog bites a man that is not news, but when a man bites a dog that is news," trumpeted John B. Bogart, city editor of the *New York Sun*.

"The public be damned," uttered railroad entrepreneur William H. Vanderbilt in defense of his decision to eliminate the high-speed *Chicago Limited*. "I am working for my stockholders," insisted Vanderbilt. "If the public want(s) the train, why don't they pay for it?"

Births and Deaths

The list of notable persons born in 1882 includes Franklin D. Roosevelt, novelists Virginia Woolf and James Joyce, French painter Georges Braque, Hollywood film producer Samuel Goldwyn, and Russian composer Igor Stravinsky Charles Darwin died in 1882, as did Dante Gabriel Rossetti, English novelist Anthony Trollope, and American authors H.W. Longfellow and Ralph Waldo Emerson.

WORLD HISTORY

by Barry Youngerman

Prehistory: Our Ancestors Take Over

Homo sapiens. The precise origins of *homo sapiens*, the species to which all humans belong, are subject to broad speculation based on a small number of fossils, genetic and anatomical studies, and the geological record. But nearly all scientists agree that we evolved from ape-like primate ancestors in a process that began millions of years ago.

Current theories say the first hominid (human-like primate) was *Ramapithecus*, who emerged 12 million years ago. Its remains have been found in Asia, Europe, and Africa. Further development was apparently limited to Africa, where 2 lines of hominids appeared some 5 or 6 million years ago. One was *Australopithecus*, a tool-maker and social animal, who lived from perhaps 4 to 3 million years ago, and then apparently became extinct.

The 2nd was a human line, *Homo habillus*, a large-brained specimen that walked upright and had a dextrous hand. *Homo habillus* lived in semi-permanent camps and had a food-gathering and sharing economy.

Homo erectus, our nearest ancestor, appeared in Africa perhaps 1.75 million years ago, and began spreading into Asia and Europe soon after. It had a fairly large brain and a skeletal structure similar to ours. *Homo erectus* learned to control fire, and probably had primitive language skills. The final brain development to *Homo sapiens* and then to our sub-species *Homo sapiens sapiens* occurred between 500,000 and 50,000 years ago, over a wide geographic area and in many different steps and recombinations. All humans of all races belong to this sub-species.

The spread of mankind into the remaining habitable continents probably took place during the last ice age up to 100,000 years ago: to the Americas across a land bridge from Asia, and to Australia across the Timor Straits.

Earliest cultures. A variety of cultural modes — in tool-making, diet, shelter, and possibly social arrangements and spiritual expression, arose as early mankind adapted to different geographic and climatic zones.

Three basic tool-making traditions are recognized by archeologists as arising and often coexisting from one million years ago to the near past: the *chopper tradition*, found largely in E. Asia, with crude chopping tools and simple flake tools; the *flake tradition*, found in Africa and W. Europe, with a variety of small cutting and flaking tools, and the *biface tradition*, found in all of Africa, W. and S. Europe, and S. Asia, producing pointed hand axes chipped on both faces. Later biface sites yield more refined axes and a variety of other tools, weapons, and ornaments using bone, antler, and wood as well as stone.

Only sketchy evidence remains for the different stages in man's increasing control over the environment. Traces of 400,000-year-old covered wood shelters have been found at Nice, France. Scraping tools at Neanderthal sites (200,000-30,000 BC in Europe, N. Africa, the Middle East and Central Asia) suggest the treatment of skins for clothing. Sites from all parts of the world show seasonal migration patterns and exploitation of a wide range of plant and animal food sources.

Painting and decoration, for which there is evidence at the Nice site, flourished along with stone and ivory sculpture after 30,000 years ago; 60 caves in France and 30 in Spain show remarkable examples of wall painting. Other examples have been found in Africa. Proto-religious rites are suggested by these works, and by evidence of ritual cannibalism by Peking Man, 500,000 BC, and of ritual burial with medicinal plants and flowers by Neanderthals at Shanidar in Iraq.

The Neolithic Revolution. Sometime after 10,000 BC, among widely separated human communities, a series of dramatic technological and social changes occurred that are summed up as the Neolithic Revolution. The cultivation of previously wild plants encouraged the growth of permanent settlements. Animals were domesticated as a work force and food source. The manufacture of pottery and cloth began. These techniques permitted a huge increase in world population and in human control over the earth.

No region can safely claim priority as the "inventor" of these techniques. Dispersed sites in Cen. and S. America, S.E. Europe, and the Middle East show roughly contemporaneous (10-8,000 BC) evidence of one or another "neolithic" trait. Dates near 6-3,000 BC have been given for E. and S. Asian, W. European, and sub-Saharan African neolithic remains. The variety of crops — field grains, rice, maize, and roots, and the varying mix of other traits suggest that the revolution occurred independently in all these regions.

History Begins: 4000 - 1000 BC

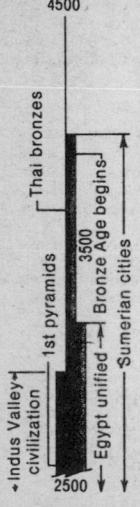

Near Eastern cradle. If history began with writing, the first chapter opened in Mesopotamia, the Tigris-Euphrates river valley. Clay tablets with pictographs were used by the Sumerians to keep records after 4000 BC. A cuneiform (wedge shaped) script evolved by 3000 BC as a full syllabic alphabet. Neighboring peoples adapted the script to their own language.

Sumerian life centered, from 4000 BC, on large cities (Eridu, Ur, Uruk, Nippur, Kish, Lagash) organized around temples and priestly bureaucracies, with the surrounding plains watered by vast irrigation works and worked with traction plows. Sailboats, wheeled vehicles, potters wheels, and kilns were used. Copper was smelted and tempered in Sumeria from c4000 BC and bronze was produced not long after. Ores, as well as precious stones and metals were obtained through long-distance ship and caravan trade. Iron was used from c2000 BC. Improved ironworking, developed partly by the **Hittites**, became widespread by 1200 BC.

Sumerian political primacy passed among cities and their kingly dynasties. Semitic-speaking peoples, with cultures derived from the Sumerian, founded a succession of dynasties that ruled in Mesopotamia and neighboring areas for most of 1800 years; among them the **Akkadians** (first under Sargon c2350 BC), the **Amorites** (whose laws, codified by **Hammurabi**, c1792-1750 BC, have Biblical parallels), and the **Assyrians**, with interludes of rule by the Hittites, Kassites, and Mitanni, all possibly Indo-Europeans. The political and cultural center of gravity shifted northwest with each successive empire.

Mesopotamian learning, maintained by scribes and preserved by successive rulers in vast libraries, was not abstract or theoretical. Algebraic and geometric problems could be solved on a practical basis in construction, commerce, or administration. Systematic lists of astronomical phenomena, plants, animals and stones were kept; medical texts listed ailments and their herbal cures.

The Sumerians worshipped anthropomorphic gods representing natural forces — Anu, god of heaven; Enlil (Ea), god of water. Epic poetry related these and other gods in a hierarchy. Sacrifices were made at **ziggurats** — huge stepped temples. Gods were thought to control all events, which could be foretold using oracular materials. This religious pattern persisted into the first millenium BC.

The Syria-Palestine area, site of some of the earliest urban remains (Jericho, 7000 BC), and of the recently uncovered **Ebla** civilization (fl. 2500 BC), experienced Egyptian cultural and political influence along with Mesopotamian. The **Phoenician** coast was an active commercial center. A phonetic alphabet was invented here before 1600 BC. It became the ancestor of all European, Middle Eastern, Indian, S.E.

Asian, Ethiopian, and Korean alphabets.
Regional commerce and diplomacy were aided by the use of Akkadian as a *lingua franca*, later replaced by Aramaic.

Egypt. Agricultural villages along the Nile were united by 3300 BC into two kingdoms, Upper and Lower Egypt, unified under the Pharaoh Menes c3100 BC; Nubia to the south was added 2600 BC. A national bureaucracy supervised construction of canals and monuments (**pyramids** starting 2700 BC). Brilliant First Dynasty achievements in architecture, sculpture and painting, set the standards and forms for all subsequent Egyptian civilization and are still admired. **Hieroglyphic writing** appeared by 3400 BC, recording a sophisticated literature including romantic and philosophical modes after 2300 BC.
An ordered hierarchy of gods, including totemistic animal elements, was served by a powerful priesthood in Memphis. The pharaoh was identified with the falcon god Horus. Later trends were the belief in an afterlife, and the quasi-monotheistic reforms of **Akhenaton** (c1379-1362 BC).
After a period of conquest by Semitic Hyksos from Asia (c1700-1500 BC), the New Kingdom established an empire in Syria. Egypt became increasingly embroiled in Asiatic wars and diplomacy. Eventually it was conquered by Persia in 525 BC, and it faded away as an independent culture.

India. An urban civilization with a so-far-undeciphered writing system stretched across the Indus Valley and along the Arabian Sea c3000-1500 BC. Major sites are Harappa and **Mohenjo-Daro** in Pakistan, well-planned geometric cities with underground sewers and vast granaries. The entire region (600,000 sq. mi.) may have been ruled as a single state. Bronze was used, and arts and crafts were highly developed. Religious life apparently took the form of fertility cults.
Indus civilization was probably in decline when it was destroyed by **Aryan invaders** from the northwest, speaking an Indo-European language from which all the languages of Pakistan, north India and Bangladesh descend. Led by a warrior aristocracy whose legendary deeds are recorded in the **Rig Veda,** the Aryans spread east and south, bringing their pantheón of sky gods, elaborate priestly (Brahmin) ritual, and the beginnings of the caste system; local customs and beliefs were assimilated by the conquerors.

Europe. On Crete, the bronze-age **Minoan civilization** emerged c2500 BC. A prosperous economy and richly decorative art (e.g. at Knossos palace) was supported by seaborne commerce. Mycenae and other cities in Greece and Asia Minor (e.g. **Troy**) preserved elements of the culture to c1100 BC. Cretan Linear A script, c2000-1700 BC, is undeciphered; Linear B, c1300-1200 BC, records a Greek dialect.
Possible connection between Minoan-Mycenaean monumental stonework, and the great megalithic monuments and tombs of W. Europe, Iberia, and Malta (c4000-1500 BC) is unclear.

China. Proto-Chinese neolithic cultures had long covered northern and southeastern China when the first large political state was organized in the north by the **Shang dynasty** c1500 BC. Shang kings called themselves Sons of Heaven, and presided over a cult of human and animal sacrifice to ancestors and nature gods. The Chou dynasty, starting c1100 BC, expanded the area of the Son of Heaven's dominion, but feudal states exercised most temporal power.
A writing system with 2,000 different characters was already in use under the Shang, with **pictographs** later supplemented by phonetic characters. The system, with modifications, is still in use, despite changes in spoken Chinese.
Technical advances allowed urban specialists to create fine ceramic and jade products, and bronze casting after 1500 BC was the most advanced in the world.
Bronze artifacts have recently been discovered in northern Thailand dating to 3600 BC, hundreds of years before similar Middle Eastern finds.

Americas. Olmecs settled on the Gulf coast of Mexico, 1500 BC, and soon developed the first civilization in the Western Hemisphere. Temple cities and huge stone sculpture date to 1200 BC. A rudimentary calendar and writing system existed. Olmec religion, centering on a jaguar god, and art forms influenced all later Meso-American cultures.
Neolithic ceremonial centers were built on the Peruvian desert coast, c2000 BC.

Classical Era of Old World Civilizations

Greece. After a period of decline during the Dorian Greek invasions (1200-1000 BC), Greece and the Aegean area developed a unique civilization. Drawing upon Mycenaean traditions, Mesopotamian learning (weights and measures, lunisolar calendar, astronomy, musical scales), the Phoenician alphabet (modified for Greek), and Egyptian art, the revived **Greek city-states** saw a rich elaboration of intellectual life. Long-range commerce was aided by metal coinage (introduced by the Lydians in Asia Minor before 700 BC); colonies were founded around the Mediterranean and Black Sea shores (Cumae in Italy 760 BC, Massalia in France c600 BC).
Philosophy, starting with Ionian speculation on the nature of matter and the universe (Thales c634-546), and including mathematical speculation (Pythagoras c580-c500), culminated in Athens in the rationalist idealism of **Plato** (c428-347) and **Socrates** (c470-399); the latter was executed for alleged impiety. Aristotle (384-322) united all fields of study in his system. The arts were highly valued. Architecture culminated in the **Parthenon** in Athens (438, sculpture by Phidias); poetry and drama (Aeschylus 525-456) thrived. Male beauty and strength, a chief artistic theme, were enhanced at the gymnasium and the national games at Olympia.
Ruled by local tyrants or oligarchies, the Greeks were never politically united, but managed to resist inclusion in the Persian Empire (Darius defeated at Marathon 490 BC, Xerxes at Salamis, Plataea 479 BC). Local warfare was common; the **Peloponnesian Wars,** 431-404 BC, ended in Sparta's victory over Athens. Greek political power waned, but classical Greek cultural forms spread thoughout the ancient world from the Atlantic to India.

Hebrews. Nomadic Hebrew tribes entered Canaan before 1200 BC, settling among other Semitic peoples speaking the same language. They brought from the desert a **monotheistic faith** said to have been revealed to Abraham in Canaan c1800 BC and to Moses at Mt. Sinai c1250 BC, after the Hebrews' escape from bondage in Egypt. David (ruled 1000-961 BC) and Solomon (ruled 961-922 BC) united the Hebrews in a kingdom that briefly dominated the area. Phoenicians to the north established colonies

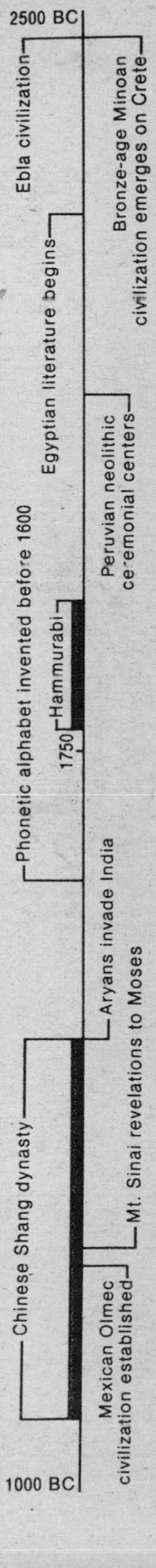
2500 BC
Ebla civilization
Bronze-age Minoan civilization emerges on Crete
Egyptian literature begins
Peruvian neolithic ceremonial centers
Phonetic alphabet invented before 1600
Hammurabi
1750
Aryans invade India
Mt. Sinai revelations to Moses
Chinese Shang dynasty
Mexican Olmec civilization established
1000 BC

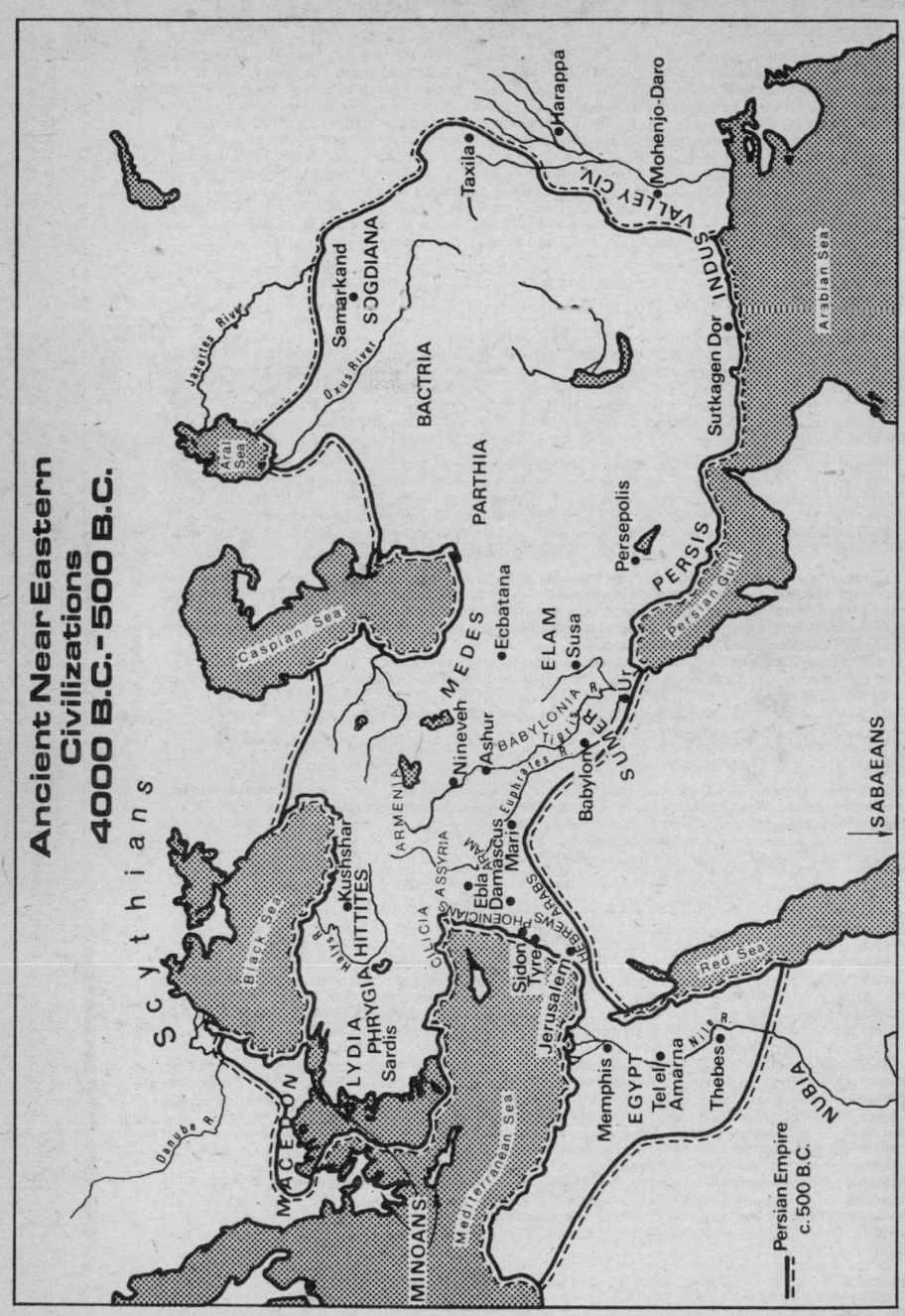

Ancient Near Eastern
Civilizations
4000 B.C.-500 B.C.

Persian Empire
c. 500 B.C.

around the E. and W. Mediterranean (**Carthage** c814 BC) and sailed into the Atlantic.

A temple in Jerusalem became the national religious center, with sacrifices performed by a hereditary priesthood. Polytheistic influences, especially the fertility cult of Baal, were opposed by **prophets** (Elijah, Amos, Isaiah).

Divided into **two kingdoms** after Solomon, the Hebrews were unable to resist the revived Assyrian empire, which conquered Israel, the northern kingdom in 722 BC. Judah, the southern kingdom, was conquered in 586 BC by the Babylonians under Nebuchadnezzar II. But with the fixing of most of the Biblical canon by the mid-fourth century BC, and the emergence of rabbis, arbiters of law and custom, Judaism successfully survived the loss of Hebrew autonomy. A Jewish kingdom was revived under the Hasmoneans (168-42 BC).

China. During the **Eastern Chou** dynasty (770-256 BC), Chinese culture spread east to the sea and south to the Yangtze. Large feudal states on the periphery of the empire contended for pre-eminence, but continued to recognize the Son of Heaven (king), who retained a purely ritual role enriched with courtly music and dance. In the Age of Warring States (403-221 BC), when the first sections of the **Great Wall** were built, the Ch'in state in the West gained supremacy, and finally united all of China.

Iron tools entered China c500 BC, and casting techniques were advanced, aiding agriculture. Peasants owned their land, and owed civil and military service to nobles. Cities grew in number and size, though barter remained the chief trade medium.

Intellectual ferment among noble scribes and officials produced the Classical Age of Chinese literature and philosophy. **Confucius** (551-479 BC) urged a restoration of a supposedly harmonious social order of the past through proper conduct in accordance with one's station and through filial and ceremonial piety. The *Analects*, attributed to him, are revered throughout East Asia. **Mencius** (d. 289 BC) added the view that the Mandate of Heaven can be removed from an unjust dynasty. The Legalists sought to curb the supposed natural wickedness of people through new institutions and harsh laws; they aided the Ch'in rise to power. The Naturalists emphasized the balance of opposites — yin, yang — in the world. **Taoists** sought mystical knowledge through meditation and disengagement.

India. The political and cultural center of India shifted from the Indus to the Ganges River Valley. Buddhism, Jainism, and mystical revisions of orthodox Vedism all developed around 500-300 BC. The *Upanishads*, last part of the *Veda*, urged escape from the illusory physical world. Vedism remained the preserve of the priestly Brahmin caste. In contrast, **Buddhism**, founded by Siddarta Gautama (c563-c483 BC), appealed to merchants in the growing urban centers, and took hold at first (and most lastingly) on the geographic fringes of Indian civilization. The classic Indian epics were composed in this era: The *Ramayana* around 300 BC, the *Mahabharata* over a period starting 400 BC.

Northern India was divided into a large number of monarchies and aristocratic republics, probably derived from tribal groupings, when the Magadha kingdom was formed in Bihar c542 BC. It soon became the dominant power. The **Maurya dynasty**, founded by Chandragupta c321 BC, expanded the kingdom, uniting most of N. India in a centralized bureaucratic empire. The third Mauryan king, **Asoka** (ruled c274-236) conquered most of the subcontinent: he converted to Buddhism, and inscribed its tenets on pillars throughout India. He downplayed the caste system and tried to end expensive sacrificial rites.

Before its final decline in India, Buddhism developed the popular worship of heavenly Bodhisatvas (enlightened beings), and produced a refined architecture (stupa—shrine—at Sanchi 100 AD) and sculpture (Gandhara reliefs 1-400 AD).

Persia. Aryan peoples (Persians, Medes) dominated the area of present Iran by the beginning of the first millenium BC. The prophet **Zoroaster** (born c628 BC) introduced a dualistic religion in which the forces of good (Ahura Mazda, Lord of Wisdom) and evil (Ahiram) battle for dominance; individuals are judged by their actions and earn damnation or salvation. Zoroaster's hymns (*Gathas*) are included in the *Avesta*, the Zoroastrian scriptures. A version of this faith became the established religion of the Persian Empire, and probably influenced later monotheistic religions.

Africa. Nubia, periodically occupied by Egypt since the third millenium, ruled Egypt c750-661, and survived as an independent Egyptianized kingdom (**Kush;** capital Meroe) for 1,000 years.

The Iron Age Nok culture flourished c500 BC-200 AD on the Benue Plateau of **Nigeria.**

Americas. The Chavin culture controlled north Peru from 900-200 BC. Its ceremonial centers, featuring the jaguar god, survived long after. Chavin architecture, ceramics, and textiles influenced other Peruvian cultures.

Mayan civilization began to develop in Central America in the 5th century BC.

Great Empires Unite the Civilized World: 400 BC - 400 AD

Persia and Alexander. Cyrus, ruler of a small kingdom in Persia from 559 BC, united the Persians and Medes within 10 years, conquered Asia Minor and Babylonia in another 10. His son Cambyses and grandson **Darius** (ruled 522-486) added vast lands to the east and north as far as the Indus Valley and Central Asia, as well as Egypt and Thrace. The whole empire was ruled by an international bureaucracy and army, with Persians holding the chief positions. The resources and styles of all the subject civilizations were exploited to create a rich syncretic art.

The Hellenized kingdom of Macedon, which under Phillip II dominated Greece, passed to his son **Alexander** in 336 BC. Within 13 years, Alexander conquered all the Persian dominions. Imbued by his tutor Aristotle with Greek ideals, Alexander encouraged Greek colonization, and Greek-style cities were founded throughout the empire (e.g. Alexandria, Egypt). After his death in 323 BC, wars of succession divided the empire into three parts — Macedon, Egypt (ruled by the **Ptolemies**), and the Seleucid Empire.

In the ensuing 300 years (the **Hellenistic Era**), a cosmopolitan Greek-oriented culture permeated the ancient world from W. Europe to the borders of India, absorbing native elites everywhere.

Hellenistic philosophy stressed the private individual's search for happiness. The Cynics followed Diogenes (c372-287), who stressed satisfaction of animal needs and contempt for social convention. Zeno (c335-c263) and the Stoics exalted reason, identified it with virtue, and counseled an ascetic disregard for misfortune. The Epicureans tried to build lives of moderate pleasure without political or emotional

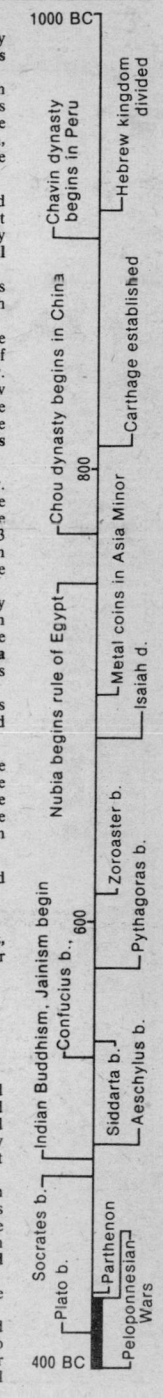

1000 BC

Chavin dynasty begins in Peru

Hebrew kingdom divided

Chou dynasty begins in China

Carthage established

800

Nubia begins rule of Egypt

Metal coins in Asia Minor

Isaiah d.

Zoroaster b.

Pythagoras b.

600

Confucius b.

Indian Buddhism, Jainism begin

Socrates b.

Plato b.

Siddarta b.

Aeschylus b.

Parthenon

Peloponnesian Wars

400 BC

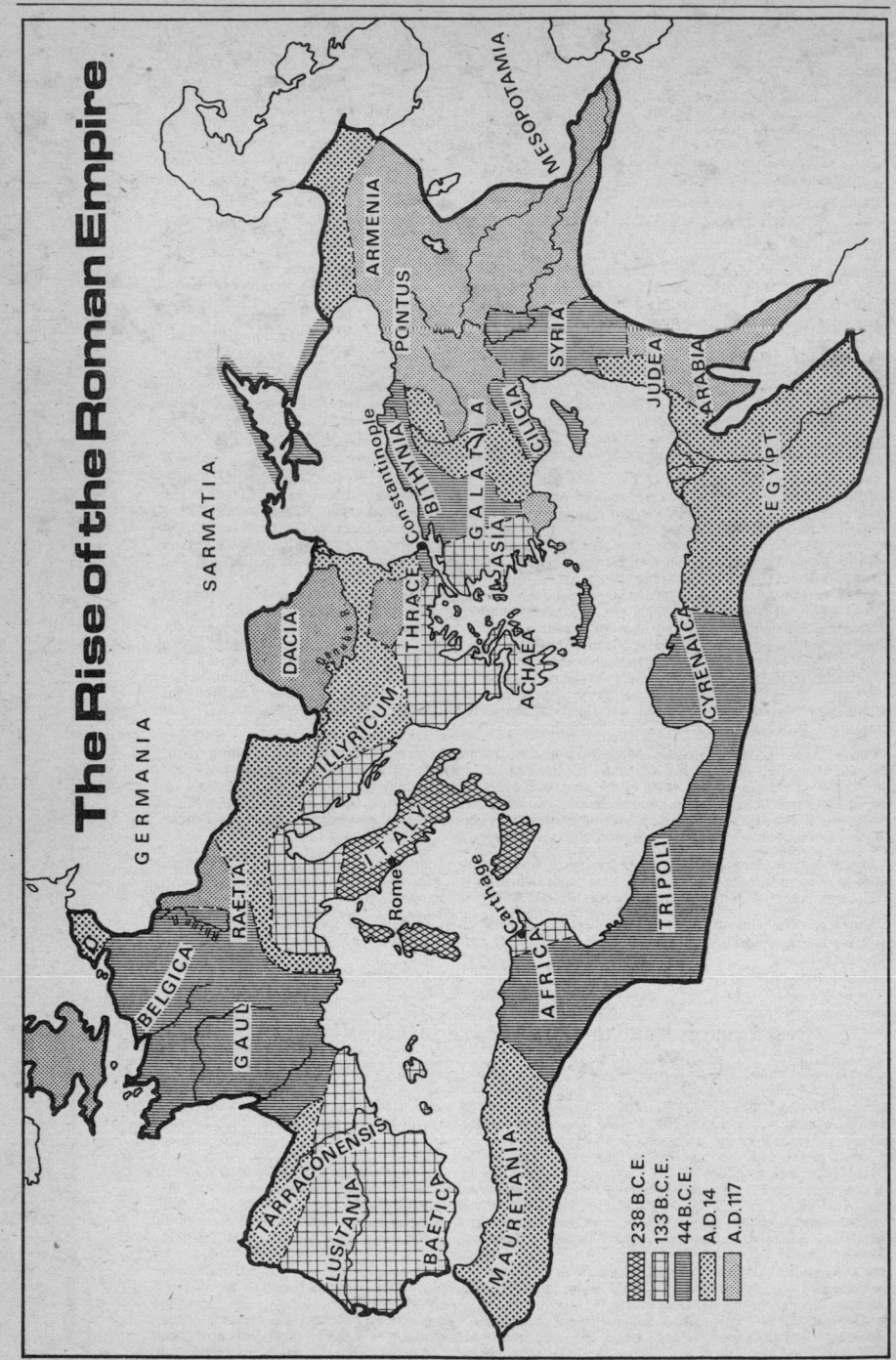

The Rise of the Roman Empire

238 B.C.E.
133 B.C.E.
44 B.C.E.
A.D. 14
A.D. 117

involvement. Hellenistic arts imitated life realistically, especially in sculpture and literature (comedies of Menander, 342-292).

The sciences thrived, especially at Alexandria, where the Ptolemies financed a great library and museum. Fields of study included mathematics (**Euclid's** geometry, c300 BC; Menelaus' non-Euclidean geometry, c100 AD); astronomy (heliocentric theory of Aristarchus, 310-230 BC; Julian calendar 45 BC; Ptolemy's *Almagest,* c150 AD); geography (world map of Eratosthenes, 276-194 BC); hydraulics (**Archimedes,** 287-212 BC); medicine (Galen, 130-200 AD), and chemistry. Inventors refined uses for siphons, valves, gears, springs, screws, levers, cams, and pulleys.

A restored Persian empire under the **Parthians** (N. Iranian tribesmen) controlled the eastern Hellenistic world 250 BC-229 AD. The Parthians and the succeeding Sassanian dynasty (229-651) fought with Rome periodically. The **Sassanians** revived Zoroastrianism as a state religion, and patronized a nationalistic artistic and scholarly renaissance.

Rome. The city of Rome was founded, according to legend, by Romulus in 753 BC. Through military expansion and colonization, and by granting citizenship to conquered tribes, the city annexed all of Italy south of the Po in the 100-year period before 268 BC. The Latin and other Italic tribes were annexed first, followed by the Etruscans (a civilized people north of Rome) and the Greek colonies in the south. With a large standing army and reserve forces of several hundred thousand, Rome was able to defeat Carthage in the 3 **Punic Wars,** 264-241, 218-201, 149-146 (despite the invasion of Italy by Hannibal, 218), thus gaining Sicily and territory in Spain and North Africa.

New provinces were added in the East, as Rome exploited local disputes to conquer Greece and Asia Minor in the 2d century BC, and Egypt in the first (after the defeat and suicide of **Antony and Cleopatra,** 30 BC). All the Mediterranean civilized world up to the disputed Parthian border was now Roman, and remained so for 500 years. Less civilized regions were added to the Empire: Gaul (conquered by Julius Caesar, 56-49 BC), Britain (43 AD) and Dacia NE of the Danube (117 AD).

The original aristocratic republican government, with democratic features added in the fifth and fourth centuries BC, deteriorated under the pressures of empire and class conflict (**Gracchus** brothers, social reformers, murdered 133, 121; slave revolts 135, 73). After a series of civil wars (Marius vs. Sulla 88-82, Caesar vs. Pompey 49-45, triumvirate vs. Caesar's assassins 44-43, Antony vs. Octavian 32-30), the empire came under the rule of a deified monarch (first emperor, **Augustus,** 27 BC-14 AD). Provincials (nearly all granted citizenship by Caracalla, 212 AD) came to dominate the army and civil service. Traditional Roman law, systematized and interpreted by independent jurists, and local self-rule in provincial cities were supplanted by a vast tax-collecting bureaucracy in the 3d and 4th centuries. The legal rights of women, children, and slaves were strengthened.

Roman innovations in **civil engineering** included water mills, windmills, and rotary mills, and the use of cement that hardened under water. Monumental architecture (baths, theaters, apartment houses) relied on the arch and the dome. The network of roads (some still standing) stretched 53,000 miles, passing through mountain tunnels as long as 3.5 miles. Aqueducts brought water to cities, underground sewers removed waste.

Roman art and literature were derivative of Greek models. Innovations were made in sculpture (naturalistic busts and equestrian statues), decorative wall painting (as at Pompeii), satire (Juvenal, 60-127), history (Tacitus 56-120), prose romance (Petronius, d. 66 AD). Violence and torture dominated mass public amusements, which were supported by the state.

India. The **Gupta** monarchs reunited N. India c320 AD. Their peaceful and prosperous reign saw a revival of Hindu religious thought and Brahmin power. The old Vedic traditions were combined with devotion to a plethora of indigenous deities (who were seen as manifestations of Vedic gods). **Caste lines** were reinforced, and Buddhism gradually disappeared. The art (often erotic), architecture, and literature of the period, patronized by the Gupta court, are considered to be among India's finest achievements (Kalidasa, poet and dramatist, fl. c400). Mathematical innovations included the use of zero and decimal numbers. Invasions by White Huns from the NW destroyed the empire c550.

Rich cultures also developed in S. India in this era. Emotional Tamil religious poetry aided the Hindu revival. The Pallava kingdom controlled much of S. India c350-880, and helped spread Indian civilization to S.E. Asia.

China. The Ch'in ruler Shih Huang Ti (ruled 221-210 BC), known as the First Emperor, centralized political authority in China, standardized the written language, laws, weights, measures, and coinage, and conducted a census, but tried to destroy most philosophical texts. The **Han dynasty** (206 BC-220 AD) instituted the Mandarin bureaucracy, which lasted for 2,000 years. Local officials were selected by examination in the Confucian classics and trained at the imperial university and at provincial schools. The invention of **paper** facilitated this bureaucratic system. Agriculture was promoted, but the peasants bore most of the tax burden. Irrigation was improved; water clocks and sundials were used; astronomy and mathematics thrived; landscape painting was perfected.

With the expansion south and west (to nearly the present borders of today's China), trade was opened with India, S.E. Asia, and the Middle East, over sea and caravan routes. Indian missionaries brought Mahayana Buddhism to China by the first century AD, and spawned a variety of sects. Taoism was revived, and merged with popular superstitions. Taoist and Buddhist monasteries and convents multiplied in the turbulent centuries after the collapse of the Han dynasty.

The One God Triumphs: 1-750 AD

Christianity. Religions indigenous to particular Middle Eastern nations became international in the first 3 centuries of the Roman Empire. Roman citizens worshipped **Isis** of Egypt, **Mithras** of Persia, **Demeter** of Greece, and the great mother **Cybele** of Phrygia. Their cults centered on mysteries (secret ceremonies) and the promise of an afterlife, symbolized by the death and rebirth of the god. Judaism, which had begun as the national cult of Judea, also spread by emigration and conversion. It was the only ancient religion west of India to survive.

Christians, who emerged as a distinct sect in the second half of the 1st century AD, revered **Jesus,** a Jewish preacher said to have been killed by the Romans at the request of Jewish authorities in Jerusalem c30 AD. They considered him the Savior (Messiah, or Christ) who rose from the dead and could grant

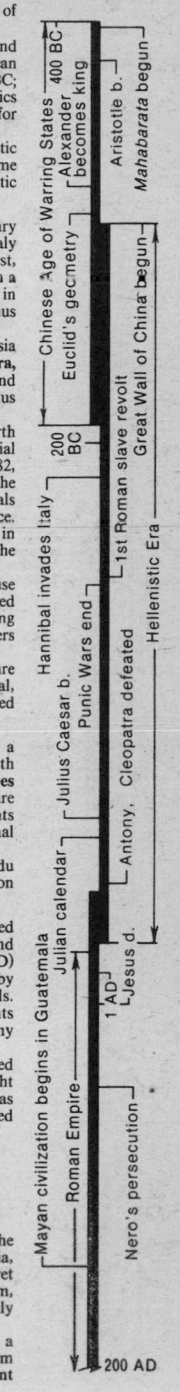

Chinese Age of Warring States

400 BC — Alexander becomes king

Aristotle b.

Mahabharata begun

Euclid's geometry

Great Wall of China begun

200 BC

Hannibal invades Italy

1st Roman slave revolt

Hellenistic Era

Julius Caesar b.

Punic Wars end

Antony, Cleopatra defeated

Mayan civilization begins in Guatemala

Julian calendar

Roman Empire

1 AD — Jesus d.

Nero's persecution

200 AD

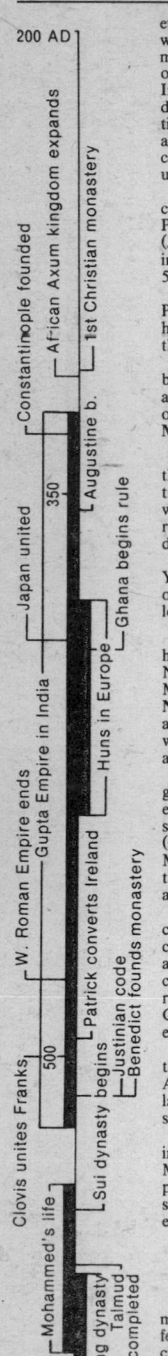

eternal life to the faithful, despite their sinfulness. They believed he was an incarnation of the one god worshipped by the Jews, and that he would return soon to pass final judgment on the world. The missionary activities of such early leaders as **Paul of Tarsus** spread the faith, at first mostly among Jews or among quasi-Jews attracted by the Pauline rejection of such difficult Jewish laws as circumcision. Intermittent persecution, as in Rome under Nero in 64 AD, on grounds of suspected disloyalty, failed to disrupt the Christian communities. Each congregation, generally urban and of plebeian character, was tightly organized under a leader (bishop) elders (presbyters or priests), and assistants (deacons). Stories about Jesus (the Gospels) and the early church (Acts) were written down in the late first and early 2d centuries, and circulated along with letters of Paul. An authoritative canon of these writings was not fixed until the 4th century.

A school for priests was established at Alexandria in the second century. Its teachers (**Origen** c182-251) helped define Christian doctrine and promote the faith in Greek-style philosophical works. Pagan Neoplatonism was given Christian coloration in the works of Church Fathers such as Augustine (354-430). Christian hermits, often drawn from the lower classes, began to associate in monasteries, first in Egypt (St. Pachomius c290-345), then in other eastern lands, then in the West (**St. Benedict's rule,** 529). Popular adoration of saints, especially Mary, mother of Jesus, spread.

Under **Constantine** (ruled 306-337), Christianity became in effect the established religion of the Empire. Pagan temples were expropriated, state funds were used to build huge churches and support the hierarchy, and laws were adjusted in accordance with Christian notions. Pagan worship was banned by the end of the fourth century, and severe restrictions were placed on Judaism.

The newly established church was rocked by doctrinal disputes, often exacerbated by regional rivalries both within and outside the Empire. Chief heresies (as defined by church councils backed by imperial authority) were **Arianism,** which denied the divinity of Jesus; **Donatism,** which rejected the convergence of church and state and denied the validity of sacraments performed by sinful clergy; and the **Monophysite** position denying the dual nature of Christ.

Judaism. First century Judaism embraced several sects, including: the **Sadducees,** mostly drawn from the Temple priesthood, who were culturally Hellenized; the **Pharisees,** who upheld the full range of traditional customs and practices as of equal weight to literal scriptural law, and elaborated synagogue worship; and the **Essenes,** an ascetic, millenarian sect. Messianic fervor led to repeated, unsuccessful rebellions against Rome (66-70, 135). As a result, the Temple was destroyed, and the population decimated.

To avoid the dissolution of the faith, a program of codification of law was begun at the academy of Yavneh. The work continued for some 500 years in Palestine and Babylonia, ending in the final redaction of the **Talmud** (c600), a huge collection of legal and moral debates, rulings, liturgy, Biblical exegesis, and legendary materials.

Islam. The earliest Arab civilization emerged by the end of the 2d millenium BC in the watered highlands of Yemen. Seaborne and caravan trade in frankincense and myrrh connected the area with the Nile and Fertile Crescent. The Minaean, Sabean (Sheba), and Himyarite states successively held sway. By Mohammed's time (7th century AD), the region was a province of Sassanian Persia. In the North, the **Nabataean kingdom** at Petra and the kingdom of Palmyra were first Aramaicized and then Romanized, and finally absorbed like neighboring Judea into the Roman Empire. Nomads shared the central region with a few trading towns and oases. Wars between tribes and raids on settled communities were common, and were celebrated in a poetic tradition that by the 6th century helped establish a classic literary Arabic.

In 611 **Mohammed,** a wealthy 40-year-old Arab of Mecca, had a revelation from Allah, the one true god, calling on him to repudiate pagan idolatry. Drawing on elements of Judaism and Christianity, and eventually incorporating some Arab pagan traditions (such as reverence for the black stone at the kaaba shrine in Mecca), Mohammed's teachings, recorded in the **Koran,** forged a new religion, Islam (submission to Allah). Opposed by the leaders of Mecca, Mohammed made a *hejira* (migration) to Medina to the north in 622, the beginning of the Moslem lunar calendar. He and his followers defeated the Meccans in 624 in the *jihad* (holy war), and by his death (632), nearly all the Arabian peninsula accepted his religious and secular leadership.

Under the first two **caliphs** (successors) Abu Bakr (632-34) and Oman (634-44), Moslem rule was confirmed over Arabia. Raiding parties into Byzantine and Persian border areas developed into campaigns of conquest against the two empires, which had been weakened by wars and by disaffection among subject peoples (including Coptic and Syriac Christians opposed to the Byzantine orthodox church). Syria, Palestine, Egypt, Iraq, and Persia all fell to the inspired Arab armies. The Arabs at first remained a distinct minority, using non-Moslems in the new administrative system, and tolerating Christians, Jews, and Zoroastrians as self-governing "Peoples of the Book," whose taxes supported the empire.

Disputes over the succession, and puritan reaction to the wealth and refinement that empire brought to the ruling strata, led to the growth of schismatic movements. The followers of Mohammed's son-in-law Ali (assassinated 661) and his descendants became the founders of the more mystical Shi'ite sect, still the largest non-orthodox Moslem sect. The Karijites, puritanical, militant, and egalitarian, persist as a minor sect to the present.

Under the **Ummayad** caliphs (661-750), the boundaries of Islam were extended across N. Africa and into Spain. Arab armies in the West were stopped at Tours in 732 by the Frank **Charles Martel.** Asia Minor, the Indus Valley, and Transoxiana were conquered in the East. The vast majority of the subject population gradually converted to Islam, encouraged by tax and career privileges. The Arab language supplanted the local tongues in the central and western areas, but Arab soldiers and rulers in the East eventually became assimilated to the indigenous languages.

New Peoples Enter History: 400-900

Barbarian invasions. Germanic tribes infiltrated S and E from their Baltic homeland during the 1st millenium BC, reaching S. Germany by 100 BC and the Black Sea by 214 AD. Organized into large federated tribes under elected kings, most resisted Roman domination and raided the empire in time of civil war (Goths took Dacia 214, raided Thrace 251-269). German troops and commanders came to dominate the Roman armies by the end of the 4th century. **Huns,** invaders from Asia, entered Europe 372, driving more Germans into the western empire. Emperor Valens allowed Visigoths to cross the Danube 376. Huns under Attila (d. 453) raided Gaul, Italy, Balkans. The western empire, weakened by overtaxation and social stagnation, was overrun in the 5th century. Gaul was effectively lost 406-7, Spain 409, Britain 410, Africa 429-39. Rome itself was sacked 410 by Visigoths under Alaric, 455 by Vandals. The last western emperor, Romulus Augustulus, was deposed 476 by the Germanic chief Odoacer.

Celts. Celtic cultures, which in pre-Roman times covered most of W. Europe, were confined almost entirely to the British Isles after the Germanic invasions. **St. Patrick** completed the conversion of Ireland (c457-92). A strong monastic tradition took hold. Irish monastic missionaries in Scotland, England, and the continent (Columba c521-597; Columban c543-615) helped restore Christianity after the Germanic invasions. The monasteries became renowned centers of classic and Christian learning, and presided over the recording of a Christianized Celtic mythology, elaborated by secular writers and bards. An intricate decorative art style developed, especially in book illumination (Lindisfarne Gospels, c700, Book of Kells, 8th century).

Successor states. The Visigoth kingdom in Spain (from 419) and much of France (to 507) saw a continuation of much Roman administration, language, and law (Breviary of Alaric 506), until its destruction by the Moslems, 711. The Vandal kingdom in Africa, from 429, was conquered by the Byzantines, 533. Italy was ruled in succession by an Ostrogothic kingdom under Byzantine suzerainty 489-554, direct Byzantine government, and the German Lombards (568-774). The latter divided the peninsula with the Byzantines and the papacy under the dynamic reformer Pope Gregory the Great (590-604) and his successors.

King Clovis (ruled 481-511) united the Franks on both sides of the Rhine, and after his conversion to orthodox Christianity, defeated the Arian Burgundians (after 500) and Visigoths (507) with the support of the native clergy and the papacy. Under the **Merovingian** kings a feudal system emerged: power was fragmented among hierarchies of military landowners. Social stratification, which in late Roman times had acquired legal, hereditary sanction, was reinforced. The Carolingians (747-987) expanded the kingdom and restored central power. **Charlemagne** (ruled 768-814) conquered nearly all the Germanic lands, including Lombard Italy, and was crowned Emperor by Pope Leo III in Rome in 800. A centuries-long decline in commerce and the arts was reversed under Charlemagne's patronage. He welcomed Jews to his kingdom, which became a center of Jewish learning (Rashi 1040-1105). He sponsored the "Carolingian Renaissance" of learning under the Anglo-Latin scholar Alcuin (c732-804), who reformed church liturgy.

Byzantine Empire. Under Diocletian (ruled 284-305) the empire had been divided into 2 parts to facilitate administration and defense. Constantine founded **Constantinople,** 330, (at old Byzantium) as a fully Christian city. Commerce and taxation financed a sumptuous, orientalized court, a class of hereditary bureaucratic families, and magnificent urban construction (Hagia Sophia, 532-37). The city's fortifications and naval innovations (Greek fire) repelled assaults by Goths, Huns, Slavs, Bulgars, Avars, Arabs, and Scandinavians. Greek replaced Latin as the official language by c700. Byzantine art, a solemn, sacral, and stylized variation of late classical styles (mosaics at S. Vitale, Ravenna, 526-48) was a starting point for medieval art in E. and W. Europe.

Justinian (ruled 527-65) reconquered parts of Spain, N. Africa, and Italy, codified Roman law (*codex Justinianus*), 529, was medieval Europe's chief legal text), closed the Platonic Academy at Athens and ordered all pagans to convert. Lombards in Italy, Arabs in Africa retook most of his conquests. The Isaurian dynasty from Anatolia (from 717) and the Macedonian dynasty (867-1054) restored military and commercial power. The Iconoclast controversy (726-843) over the permissibility of images, helped alienate the Eastern Church from the papacy.

Arab Empire. Baghdad, founded 762, became the seat of the **Abbasid** Caliphate (founded 750), while Ummayads continued to rule in Spain. A brilliant cosmopolitan civilization emerged, inaugurating an Arab-Moslem golden age. Arab lyric poetry revived; Greek, Syriac, Persian, and Sanskrit books were translated into Arabic, often by Syriac Christians and Jews, whose theology and Talmudic law, respectively, influenced Islam. The arts and music flourished at the court of **Harun al-Rashid** (786-809), celebrated in *The Arabian Nights.* The sciences, medicine, and mathematics were pursued at Baghdad, Cordova, and Cairo (founded 969). Science and Aristotelian philosophy culminated in the systems of Avicenna (980-1037), Averroes (1126-98), and Maimonides (1135-1204), a Jew; all influenced later Christian scholarship and theology. The Islamic ban on images encouraged a sinuous, geometric decorative tradition, applied to architecture and illumination. A gradual loss of Arab control in Persia (from 874) led to the capture of Baghdad by Persians, 945. By the next century, Spain and N. Africa were ruled by Berbers, while Turks prevailed in Asia Minor and the Levant. The loss of political power by the caliphs allowed for the growth of non-orthodox trends, especially the mystical **Sufi** tradition (theologian Ghazali, 1058-1111).

Africa. Immigrants from Saba in S. Arabia helped set up the **Axum** kingdom in Ethiopia in the 2d century (their language, Ge'ez, is preserved by the Ethiopian Church). In the 4th century, when the kingdom became Christianized, it defeated Kushite Meroe and expanded into Yemen. Axum was the center of a vast ivory trade; it controlled the Red Sea coast until c1100. Arab conquest in Egypt cut Axum's political and economic ties with Byzantium.

The Iron Age entered W. Africa by the end of the 1st millenium BC. **Ghana,** the first known sub-Saharan state, ruled in the upper Senegal-Niger region c400-1240, controlling the trade of gold from mines in the S to trans-Sahara caravan routes to the N. The **Bantu** peoples, probably of W. African origin, began to spread E and S perhaps 2000 years ago, displacing the Pygmies and Bushmen of central

Japan. The advanced Neolithic Yayoi period, when irrigation, rice farming, and iron and bronze casting techniques were introduced from China or Korea, persisted to c400 AD. The myriad Japanese states were then united by the **Yamato** clan, under an emperor who acted as the chief priest of the animistic **Shinto** cult. Japanese political and military intervention in Korea by the 6th century quickened a Chinese cultural invasion, bringing Buddhism, the Chinese language (which long remained a literary and governmental medium), Chinese ideographs and Buddhist styles in painting, sculpture, literature, and architecture (7th c. Horyu-ji temple at Nara). The Taika Reforms, 646, tried to centralize Japan according to Chinese bureaucratic and Buddhist philosophical values, but failed to curb traditional Japanese decentralization. A nativist reaction against the Buddhist **Nara period** (710-94) ushered in the

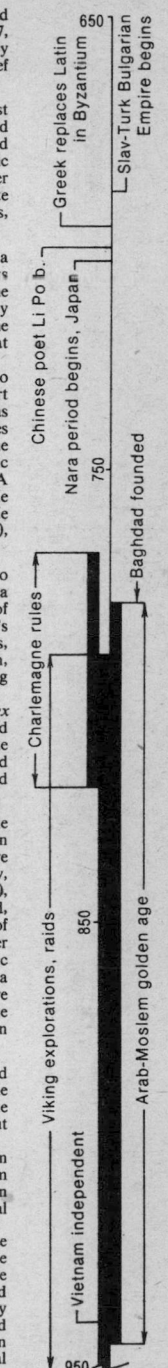

Timeline (650–950):
Greek replaces Latin in Byzantium — Slav-Turk Bulgarian Empire begins — 650
Chinese poet Li Po b. — Nara period begins, Japan — Baghdad founded — 750
Charlemagne rules — Viking explorations, raids — Arab-Moslem golden age — 850
Vietnam independent — 950

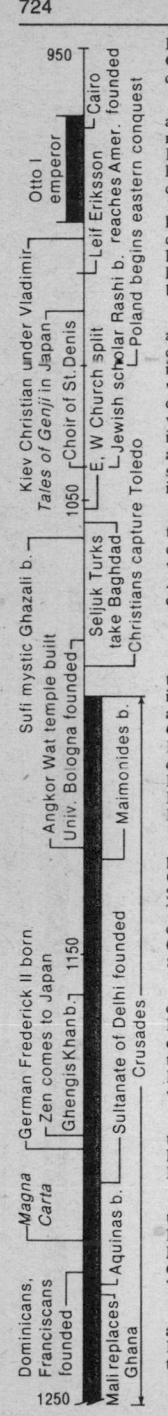

950

1050

1150

1250

Otto I emperor — Cairo
Leif Eriksson
Kiev Christian under Vladimir
Tales of Genji in Japan
Choir of St. Denis
Poland begins eastern conquest
Jewish scholar Rashi b. reaches Amer. founded
E, W Church split
Christians capture Toledo
Sufi mystic Ghazali b.
Angkor Wat temple built
Univ. Bologna founded
Seljuk Turks take Baghdad
Maimonides b.
German Frederick II born
Zen comes to Japan
Ghengis Khan b.
Sultanate of Delhi founded
Crusades
Magna Carta
Aquinas b.
Dominicans, Franciscans founded
Mali replaces Ghana

Heian period (794-1185) centered at the new capital, Kyoto. Japanese elegance and simplicity modified Chinese styles in architecture, scroll painting, and literature; the writing system was also simplified. The courtly novel *Tale of Genji* (1010-20) testifies to the enhanced role of women.

Southeast Asia. The historic peoples of southeast Asia began arriving some 2500 years ago from China and Tibet, displacing scattered aborigines. Their agriculture relied on rice and tubers (yams), which they may have introduced to Africa. Indian cultural influences were strongest; literacy and Hindu and Buddhist ideas followed the southern India-China trade route. From the southern tip of Indochina, the kingdom of **Funan** (1st-7th centuries) traded as far west as Persia. It was absorbed by Chenla, itself conquered by the **Khmer Empire** (600-1300). The Khmers, under Hindu god-kings (Suryavarman II, 1113-c1150), built the monumental Angkor Wat temple center for the royal phallic cult. The **Nam-Viet** kingdom in Annam, dominated by China and Chinese culture for 1,000 years, emerged in the 10th century, growing at the expense of the Khmers, who also lost ground in the NW to the new, highly-organized **Thai** kingdom. On Sumatra, the **Srivijaya** Empire at Palembang controlled vital sea lanes (7th to 10th centuries). A Buddhist dynasty, the Sailendras, ruled central **Java** (8th-9th centuries), building at Borobudur one of the largest stupas in the world.

China. The short-lived Sui dynasty (581-618) ushered in a period of commercial, artistic, and scientific achievement in China, continuing under the **T'ang** dynasty (618-906). Such inventions as the magnetic compass, gunpowder, the abacus, and printing were introduced or perfected. Medical innovations included cataract surgery. The state, from the cosmopolitan capital, Ch'ang-an, supervised foreign trade which exchanged Chinese silks, porcelains, and art works for spices, ivory, etc., over Central Asian caravan routes and sea routes reaching Africa. A golden age of poetry bequeathed tens of thousands of works to later generations (Tu Fu 712-70, Li Po 701-62). Landscape painting flourished. Commercial and industrial expansion continued under the **Northern Sung** dynasty (960-1126), facilitated by paper money and credit notes. But commerce never achieved respectability; government monopolies expropriated successful merchants. The population, long stable at 50 million, doubled in 200 years with the introduction of early-ripening rice and the double harvest. In art, native Chinese styles were revived.

Americas. An Indian empire stretched from the Valley of Mexico to Guatemala, 300-600, centering on the huge city **Teotihuacan** (founded 100 BC). To the S, in Guatemala, a high **Mayan** civilization developed, 150-900, around hundreds of rural ceremonial centers. The Mayans improved on Olmec writing and the calendar, and pursued astronomy and mathematics (using the idea of zero). In S. America, a widespread pre-Inca culture grew from **Tiahuanaco** near Lake Titicaca (Gateway of the Sun, c700).

Christian Europe Regroups and Expands: 900-1300

Scandinavians. Pagan Danish and Norse **(Viking)** adventurers, traders, and pirates raided the coasts of the British Isles (Dublin founded c831), France, and even the Mediterranean for over 200 years beginning in the late 8th century. Inland settlement in the W was limited to Great Britain (King Canute, 994-1035) and Normandy, settled under Rollo, 911, as a fief of France. Other Vikings reached Iceland (874), Greenland (c986), and probably N. America (Leif Eriksson c1000). Norse traders **(Varangians)** developed Russian river commerce from the 8th-11th centuries, and helped set up a state at Kiev in the late 9th century. Conversion to Christianity occurred during the 10th century, reaching Sweden 100 years later. Eleventh century Norman bands conquered S. Italy and Sicily. Duke **William of Normandy** conquered England, 1066, bringing continental feudalism and the French language, essential elements in later English civilization.

East Europe. Slavs inhabited areas of E. Central Europe in prehistoric times, and reached most of their present limits by c850. The first Slavic states were in the Balkans (Slav-Turk **Bulgarian Empire**, 680-1018) and Moravia (628). Missions of St. Cyril (whose Greek-based Cyrillic alphabet is still used by S. and E. Slavs) converted Moravia, 863. The Eastern Slavs, part-civilized under the overlordship of the Turkish-Jewish **Khazar** trading empire (7th-10th centuries), gravitated toward Constantinople by the 9th century. The **Kievan state** adopted Eastern Christianity under Prince Vladimir, 989. King Boleslav I (992-1025) began **Poland's** long history of eastern conquest. The Magyars **(Hungarians)** in Europe since 896, accepted Latin Christianity, 1001.

Germany. The German kingdom that emerged after the breakup of Charlemagne's Empire remained a confederation of largely autonomous states. The Saxon Otto I, king from 936, established the **Holy Roman Empire** of Germany and Italy in alliance with Pope John XII, who crowned him emperor, 962; he defeated the Magyars, 955. Imperial power was greatest under the **Hohenstaufens** (1138-1254), despite the growing opposition of the papacy, which ruled central Italy and the Lombard League cities. Frederick II (1194-1250) improved administration, patronized the arts; after his death German influence was removed from Italy.

Christian Spain. From its northern mountain redoubts, Christian rule slowly migrated south through the 11th century, when Moslem unity collapsed. After the capture of **Toledo** (1085), the kingdoms of Portugal, Castile, and Aragon undertook repeated crusades of reconquest, finally completed in 1492. Elements of Islamic civilization persisted in recaptured areas, influencing all W. Europe.

Crusades. Pope Urban II called, 1095, for a crusade to restore Asia Minor to Byzantium and conquer the Holy Land from the Turks. Some 10 crusades (to 1291) succeeded only in founding 4 temporary Frankish states in the Levant. The 4th crusade sacked Constantinople, 1204. In Rhineland (1096), England (1290), France (1306), Jews were massacred or expelled, and wars were launched against Christian heretics (**Albigensian** crusade in France, 1229). Trade in eastern luxuries expanded, led by the Venetian naval empire.

Economy. The agricultural base of European life benefitted from improvements in **plow design** c1000, and by draining of lowlands and clearing of forests, leading to a rural population increase. Towns grew in N. Italy, Flanders, and N. Germany (Hanseatic League). Improvements in **loom design** permitted factory textile production. **Guilds** dominated urban trades from the 12th century. Banking (centered in Italy, 12th-15th century) facilitated long-distance trade.

The Church. The split between the Eastern and Western churches was formalized in 1054. W. and

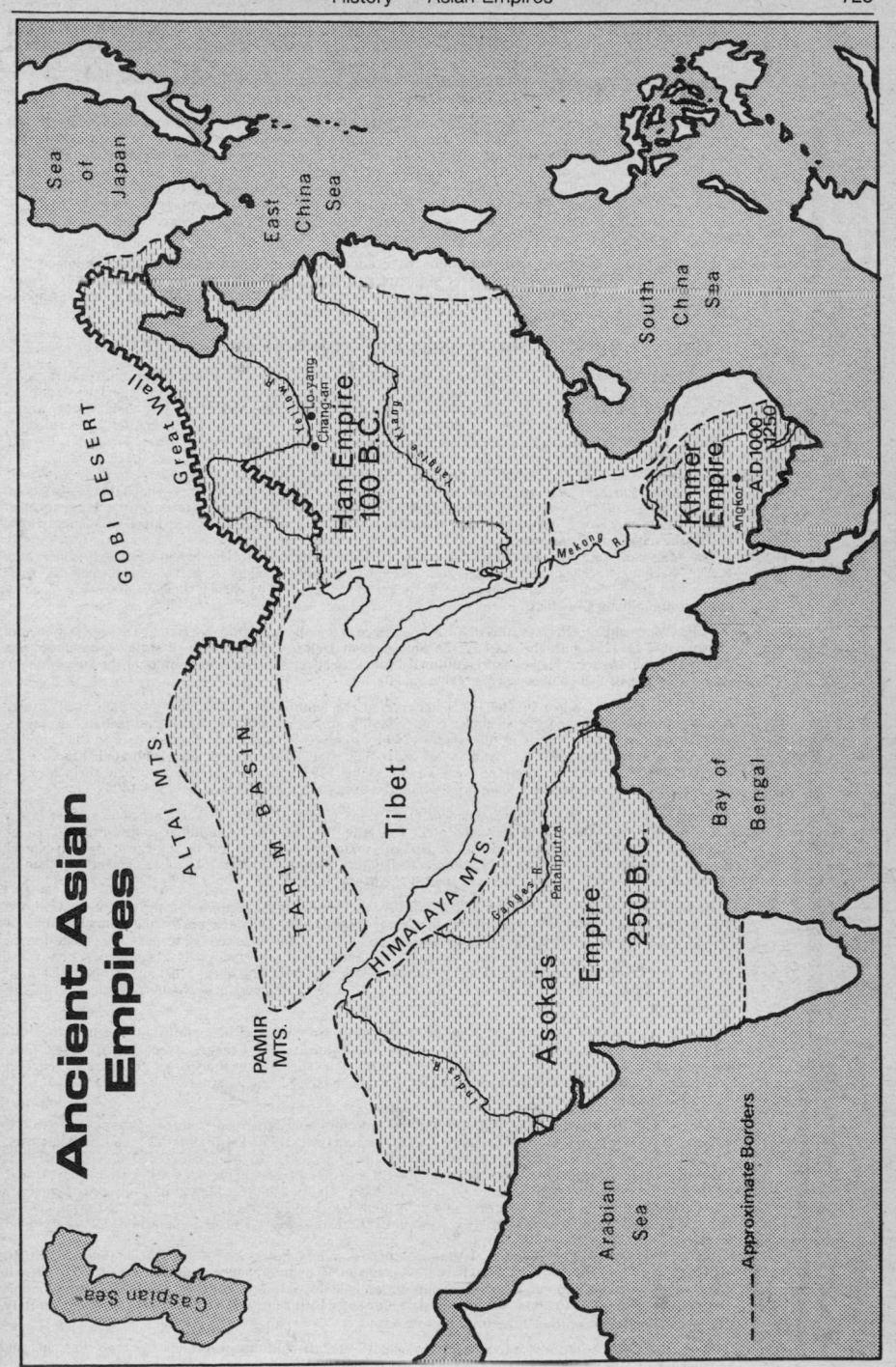

Ancient Asian Empires

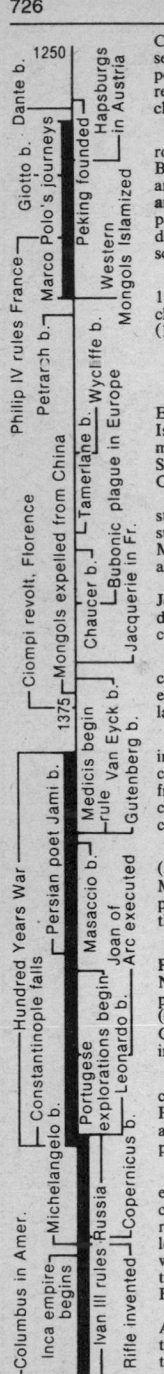

Central Europe was divided into 500 bishoprics under one united hierarchy, but conflicts between secular and church authorities were frequent (German **Investiture Controversy,** 1075-1122). Clerical power was first strengthened through the international monastic reform begun at Cluny, 910. Popular religious enthusiasm often expressed itself in heretical movements (Waldensians from 1173), but was channelled by the **Dominican** (1215) and **Franciscan** (1223) friars into the religious mainstream.

Arts. **Romanesque** architecture (11th-12th centuries) expanded on late Roman models, using the rounded arch and massed stone to support enlarged basilicas. Painting and sculpture followed Byzantine models. The literature of chivalry was exemplified by the epic (Chanson de Roland, c1100) and by courtly love poems of the troubadours of Provence and minnesingers of Germany. **Gothic architecture** emerged in France (choir of St. Denis, c1040) and spread as French cultural influence predominated in Europe. Rib vaulting and pointed arches were used to combine soaring heights with delicacy, and freed walls for display of stained glass. Exteriors were covered with painted relief sculpture and elaborate architectural detail.

Learning. Law, medicine, and philosophy were advanced at independent **universities** (Bologna, late 11th century), originally corporations of students and masters. Twelfth century translations of Greek classics, especially Aristotle, encouraged an analytic approach. Scholastic philosophy, from Anselm (1033-1109) to Aquinas (1225-74) attempted to reconcile reason and revelation.

Apogee of Central Asian Power; Islam Grows: 1250-1500

Turks. Turkic peoples, of Central Asian ancestry, were a military threat to the Byzantine and Persian Empires from the 6th century. After several waves of invasions, during which most of the Turks adopted Islam, the **Seljuk Turks** took Baghdad, 1055. They ruled Persia, Iraq, and, after 1071, Asia Minor, where massive numbers of Turks settled. The empire was divided in the 12th century into smaller states ruled by Seljuks, Kurds (**Saladin** c1137-93), and Mamelukes (a military caste of former Turk, Kurd, and Circassian slaves), which governed Egypt and the Middle East until the Ottoman era (c1290-1922).

Osman I (ruled c1290-1326) and succeeding sultans united Anatolian Turkish warriors in a militaristic state that waged holy war against Byzantium and Balkan Christians. Most of the Balkans had been subdued, and Anatolia united, when **Constantinople fell,** 1453. By the mid-16th century, Hungary, the Middle East, and North Africa had been conquered. The Turkish advance was stopped at Vienna, 1529, and at the naval battle of Lepanto, 1571, by Spain, Venice, and the papacy.

The Ottoman state was governed in accordance with orthodox Moslem law. Greek, Armenian, and Jewish communities were segregated, and ruled by religious leaders responsible for taxation; they dominated trade. State offices and most army ranks were filled by slaves through a system of child conscription among Christians.

India. Mahmud of Ghazni (971-1030) led repeated Turkish raids into N. India. Turkish power was consolidated in 1206 with the start of the **Sultanate at Delhi.** Centralization of state power under the early Delhi sultans went far beyond traditional Indian practice. Moslem rule of most of the subcontinent lasted until the British conquest some 600 years later.

Mongols. Genghis Khan (c1162-1227) first united the feuding Mongol tribes, and built their armies into an effective offensive force around a core of highly mobile cavalry. He and his immediate successors created the largest land empire in history; by 1279 it stretched from the east coast of Asia to the Danube, from the Siberian steppes to the Arabian Sea. East-West trade and contacts were facilitated (Marco Polo c1254-1324). The western Mongols were Islamized by 1295; successor states soon lost their Mongol character by assimilation. They were briefly reunited under the Turk Tamerlane (1336-1405).

Kublai Khan ruled China from his new capital Peking (founded 1264). Naval campaigns against Japan (1274, 1281) and Java (1293) were defeated, the latter by the Hindu-Buddhist maritime kingdom of Majapahit. The **Yuan** dynasty made use of Mongols and other foreigners (including Europeans) in official posts, and tolerated the return of Nestorian Christianity (suppressed 841-45) and the spread of Islam in the South and West. A native reaction expelled the Mongols, 1367-68.

Russia. The Kievan state in Russia, weakened by the decline of Byzantium and the rise of the Catholic Polish-Lithuanian state, was overrun by the Mongols, 1238-40. Only the northern trading republic of Novgorod remained independent. The grand dukes of Moscow emerged as leaders of a coalition of princes that eventually defeated the Mongols, by 1481. With the fall of Constantinople, the **Tsars** (Caesars) at Moscow (from Ivan III, ruled 1462-1505) set up an independent Russian Orthodox Church. Commerce failed to revive. The isolated Russian state remained agrarian, with the peasant class falling into serfdom.

Persia. A revival of Persian literature, using the Arab alphabet and literary forms, began in the 10th century (epic of Firdausi, 935-1020). An art revival, influenced by Chinese styles, began in the 12th. Persian cultural and political forms, and often the Persian language, were used for centuries by Turkish and Mongol elites from the Balkans to India. Persian mystics from Rumi (1207-73) to Jami (1414-92) promoted **Sufism** in their poetry.

Africa. Two Berber dynasties, imbued with Islamic militance, emerged from the Sahara to carve out empires from the Sahel to central Spain — the **Almoravids,** c1050-1140, and the fanatical **Almohads,** c1125-1269. The Ghanaian empire was replaced in the upper Niger by Mali, c1230-c1340, whose Moslem rulers imported Egyptians to help make **Timbuktu** a center of commerce (in gold, leather, slaves) and learning. The Songhay empire (to 1590) replaced Mali. To the S, forest kingdoms produced refined art works (Ife terra cotta, **Benin** bronzes). Other Moslem states in Nigeria (Hausas) and Chad originated in the 11th century, and continued in some form until the 19th century European conquest. Less developed Bantu kingdoms existed across central Africa.

Some 40 Moslem Arab-Persian trading colonies and city-states were established all along the E. African coast from the 10th century (Kilwa, Mogadishu). The interchange with Bantu peoples produced the **Swahili** language and culture. Gold, palm oil, and slaves were brought from the interior, stimulating the growth of the Monamatapa kingdom of the Zambezi (15th century). The Christian Ethiopian empire (from 13th century) continued the traditions of Axum.

Southeast Asia. Islam was introduced into Malaya and the Indonesian islands by Arab, Persian, and

Indian traders. Coastal Moslem cities and states (starting before 1300), enriched by trade, soon dominated the interior. Chief among these was the **Malacca** state, on the Malay peninsula, c1400-1511.

Arts and Statecraft Thrive in Europe: 1350-1600

Italian Renaissance & humanism. Distinctive Italian achievements in the arts in the late Middle Ages (Dante, 1265-1321, Giotto, 1276-1337) led to the vigorous new styles of the Renaissance (14th-16th centuries). Patronized by the rulers of the quarreling petty states of Italy (Medicis in Florence and the papacy, c1400-1737), the plastic arts perfected realistic techniques, including **perspective** (Masaccio, 1401-28, Leonardo 1452-1519). Classical motifs were used in architecture and increased talent and expense were put into secular buildings. The Florentine dialect was refined as a national literary language (Petrarch, 1304-74). Greek refugees from the E strengthened the respect of humanist scholars for the classic sources (Bruni 1370-1444). Soon an international movement aided by the spread of **printing** (Gutenberg c1400-1468), **humanism** was optimistic about the power of human reason (Erasmus of Rotterdam, 1466-1536, Thomas More's *Utopia*, 1516) and valued individual effort in the arts and in politics (Machiavelli, 1469-1527).

France. The French monarchy, strengthened in its repeated struggles with powerful nobles (Burgundy, Flanders, Aquitaine) by alliances with the growing commercial towns, consolidated bureaucratic control under Philip IV (ruled 1285-1314) and extended French influence into Germany and Italy (popes at Avignon, France, 1309-1417). The **Hundred Years War**, 1338-1453, ended English dynastic claims in France (battles of Crécy, 1346, Poitiers, 1356; Joan of Arc executed, 1431). A French Renaissance, dating from royal invasions of Italy, 1494, 1499, was encouraged at the court of Francis I (ruled 1515-47), who centralized taxation and law. French vernacular literature consciously asserted its independence (La Pleiade, 1549).

England. The evolution of England's unique political institutions began with the Magna Carta, 1215, by which King John guaranteed the privileges of nobles and church against the monarchy and assured jury trial. After the Wars of the Roses (1455-85), the **Tudor dynasty** reasserted royal prerogatives (Henry VIII, ruled 1509-47), but the trend toward independent departments and ministerial government also continued. English trade (wool exports from c1340) was protected by the nation's growing maritime power (**Spanish Armada** destroyed, 1588).

English replaced French and Latin in the late 14th century in law and literature (Chaucer, 1340-1400) and English translation of the Bible began (Wycliffe, 1380s). Elizabeth I (ruled 1558-1603) presided over a confident flowering of poetry (Spenser, 1552-99), drama (**Shakespeare**, 1552-1616), and music.

German Empire. From among a welter of minor feudal states, church lands, and independent cities, the Hapsburgs assembled a far-flung territorial domain, based in Austria from 1276. The family held the title Holy Roman Emperor from 1452 to the Empire's dissolution in 1806, but failed to centralize its domains, leaving Germany disunited for centuries. Resistance to Turkish expansion brought Hungary under Austrian control from the 16th century. The Netherlands, Luxembourg, and Burgundy were added in 1477, curbing French expansion.

The Flemish painting tradition of naturalism, technical proficiency, and bourgeois subject matter began in the 15th century (Jan Van Eyck, 1366-1440), the earliest northern manifestation of the Renaissance. **Durer** (1471-1528) typified the merging of late Gothic and Italian trends in 16th century German art. Imposing civic architecture flourished in the prosperous commercial cities.

Spain. Despite the unification of Castile and Aragon in 1479, the 2 countries retained separate governments, and the nobility, especially in Aragon and Catalonia, retained many privileges. Spanish lands in Italy (Naples, Sicily) and the Netherlands entangled the country in European wars through the mid-17th century, while explorers, traders, and conquerors built up a Spanish empire in the Americas and the Philippines.

From the late 15th century, a **golden age** of literature and art produced works of social satire (plays of Lope de Vega, 1562-1635; Cervantes, 1547-1616), as well as spiritual intensity (El Greco, 1541-1614; Velazquez, 1599-1660).

Black Death. The bubonic plague reached Europe from the E in 1348, killing as much as half the population by 1350. Labor scarcity forced a rise in wages and brought greater freedom to the peasantry, making possible **peasant uprisings** (Jacquerie in France, 1358, Wat Tyler's rebellion in England, 1381). In the *ciompi* revolt, 1378, Florentine wage earners demanded a say in economic and political power.

Explorations. Organized European maritime exploration began, seeking to evade the Venice-Ottoman monopoly of eastern trade and to promote Christianity. Expeditions from Portugal beginning 1418 explored the west coast of Africa, until **Vasco da Gama** rounded the Cape of Good Hope in 1497 and reached India. A Portuguese trading empire was consolidated by the seizure of Goa, 1510, and Malacca, 1551. Japan was reached in 1542. Spanish voyages (**Columbus**, 1492-1504) uncovered a new world, which Spain hastened to subdue. Navigation schools in Spain and Portugal, the development of large sailing ships (carracks), and the invention of the rifle, c1475, aided European penetration.

Mughals and Safavids. East of the Ottoman empire, two Moslem dynasties ruled unchallenged in the 16th and 17th centuries. The Mughal empire in India, founded by Persianized Turkish invaders from the NW under Babur, dates from their 1526 conquest of Delhi. The dynasty ruled most of India for over 200 years, surviving nominally until 1857. **Akbar** (ruled 1556-1605) consolidated administration at his glorious court, where Urdu (Persian-influenced Hindi) developed. Trade relations with Europe increased. Under Shah Jahan (1629-58), a secularized art fusing Hindu and Moslem elements flourished in miniature painting and architecture (**Taj Mahal**). Sikhism, founded c1519, combined elements of both faiths. Suppression of Hindus and Shi'ite Moslems in S India in the late 17th century weakened the empire.

Fanatical devotion to the Shi'ite sect characterized the Safavids of Persia, 1502-1736, and led to hostilities with the Sunni Ottomans for over a century. The prosperity and strength of the empire are evidenced by the mosques at its capital, **Isfahan**. The dynasty enhanced Iranian national consciousness.

China. The Ming emperors, 1368-1644, the last native dynasty in China, wielded unprecedented personal power, while the Confucian bureaucracy began to suffer from inertia. European trade (Portugese

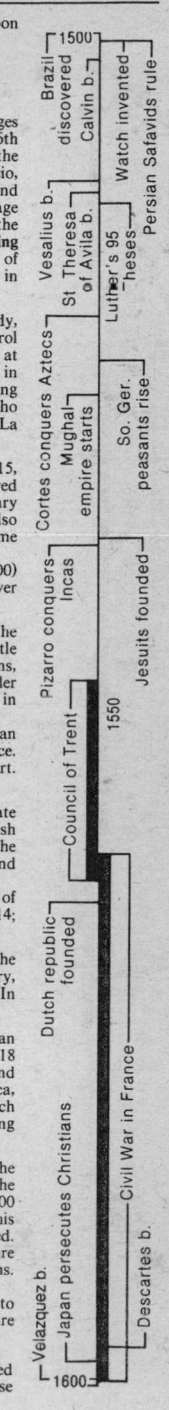

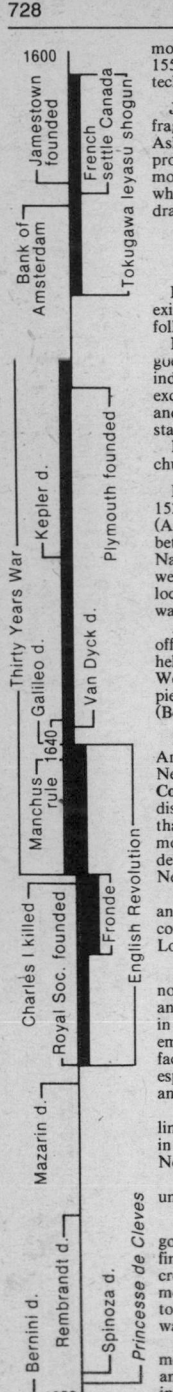

1600

Jamestown founded

French settle Canada

Tokugawa Ieyasu shogun

Bank of Amsterdam

Kepler d.

Plymouth founded

Thirty Years War

Galileo d.

Van Dyck d.

Manchus rule — 1640

English Revolution

Charles I killed

Fronde

Royal Soc. founded

Mazarin d.

Bernini d.

Rembrandt d.

Spinoza d.

Princesse de Cleves

1680

monopoly through **Macao** from 1557) was strictly controlled. Jesuit scholars and scientists (Matteo Ricci 1552-1610) introduced some Western science; their writings familiarized the West with China. Chinese technological inventiveness declined from this era, but the arts thrived, especially painting and ceramics.

Japan. After the decline of the first hereditary shogunate (chief generalship) at **Kamakura** (1185-1333), fragmentation of power accelerated, as did the consequent social mobility. Under Kamakura and the Ashikaga shogunate, 1338-1573, the daimyos (lords) and samurai (warriors) grew more powerful and promoted a martial ideology. Japanese pirates and traders plied the China coast. Popular Buddhist movements included the nationalist Nichiren sect (from c1250) and **Zen** (brought from China, 1191), which stressed meditation and a disciplined esthetic (tea ceremony, landscape gardening, judo, Noh drama).

Reformed Europe Expands Overseas: 1500-1700

Reformation begun. Theological debate and protests against real and perceived clerical corruption existed in the medieval Christian world, expressed by such dissenters as Wycliffe (c1320-84) and his followers, the Lollards, in England, and **Huss** (burned as a heretic, 1415) in Bohemia.

Luther (1483-1546) preached that only faith could lead to salvation, without the mediation of clergy or good works. He attacked the authority of the Pope, rejected priestly celibacy, and recommended individual study of the Bible (which he translated, c1525). His 95 Theses (1517) led to his excommunication (1520). **Calvin** (1509-64) said God's elect were predestined for salvation; good conduct and success were signs of election. Calvin in Geneva and Knox (1505-72) in Scotland erected theocratic states.

Henry VIII asserted English national authority and secular power by breaking away from the Catholic church, 1534. Monastic property was confiscated, and some Protestant doctrines given official sanction.

Religious wars. A century and a half of religious wars began with a South German peasant uprising, 1524, repressed with Luther's support. Radical sects—democratic, pacifist, millennarian—arose (Anabaptists ruled Muenster, 1534-35), and were suppressed violently. Civil war in France from 1562 between **Huguenots** (Protestant nobles and merchants) and Catholics ended with the 1598 Edict of Nantes tolerating Protestants (revoked 1685). Hapsburg attempts to restore Catholicism in Germany were resisted in 25 years of fighting; the 1555 Peace of Augsburg guarantee of religious independence to local princes and cities was confirmed only after the **Thirty Years War**, 1618-48, when much of Germany was devastated by local and foreign armies (Sweden, France).

A Catholic Reformation, or **counter-reformation**, met the Protestant challenge, clearly defining an official theology at the Council of Trent, 1545-63. The **Jesuit** order, founded 1534 by Loyola (1491-1556), helped reconvert large areas of Poland, Hungary, and S. Germany and sent missionaries to the New World, India, and China, while the Inquisition helped suppress heresy in Catholic countries. A revival of piety appeared in the devotional literature (Theresa of Avila, 1515-82) and the grandiose Baroque art (Bernini, 1598-1680) of Roman Catholic countries.

Scientific Revolution. The late nominalist thinkers (Ockham, c1300-49) of Paris and Oxford challenged Aristotelian orthodoxy, allowing for a freer scientific approach. But metaphysical values, such as the Neoplatonic faith in an orderly, mathematical cosmos, still motivated and directed subsequent inquiry. **Copernicus** (1473-1543) promoted the heliocentric theory, which was confirmed when Kepler (1571-1630) discovered the mathematical laws describing the orbits of the planets. The Christian-Aristotelian belief that heavens and earth were fundamentally different collapsed when **Galileo** (1564-1642) discovered moving sunspots, irregular moon topography, and moons around Jupiter. He and **Newton** (1642-1727) developed a mechanics that unified cosmic and earthly phenomena. To meet the needs of the new physics, Newton and Leibnitz (1646-1716) invented calculus, Descartes (1596-1650) invented analytic geometry.

An explosion of observational science included the discovery of blood circulation (Harvey, 1578-1657) and microscopic life (Leeuwenhoek, 1632-1723), and advances in anatomy (Vesalius, 1514-64, dissected corpses) and chemistry (Boyle, 1627-91). Scientific research institutes were founded: Florence, 1657, London (**Royal Society**), 1660, Paris, 1666. Inventions proliferated (Savery's steam engine, 1696).

Arts. Mannerist trends of the high Renaissance (**Michelangelo**, 1475-1564) exploited virtuosity, grace, novelty, and exotic subjects and poses. The notion of artistic genius was promoted, in contrast to the anonymous medieval artisan. Private connoisseurs entered the art market. These trends were elaborated in the 17th century **Baroque** era, on a grander scale. Dynamic movement in painting and sculpture was emphasized by sharp lighting effects, use of rich materials (colored marble, gilt), realistic details. Curved facades, broken lines, rich, deep-cut detail, and ceiling decoration characterized Baroque architecture, especially in Germany. Monarchs, princes, and prelates, usually Catholic, used Baroque art to enhance and embellish their authority, as in royal portraits by Velazquez (1599-1660) and Van Dyck (1599-1641).

National styles emerged. In France, a taste for rectilinear order and serenity (Poussin, 1594-1665), linked to the new rational philosophy, was expressed in classical forms. The influence of **classical values** in French literature (tragedies of Racine, 1639-99) gave rise to the "battle of the Ancients and Moderns." New forms included the essay (Montaigne, 1533-92) and novel (*Princesse de Cleves*, La Fayette, 1678).

Dutch painting of the 17th century was unique in its wide social distribution. The Flemish tradition of undemonstrative realism reached its peak in **Rembrandt** (1606-69) and Vermeer (1632-75).

Economy. European economic expansion was stimulated by the new trade with the East, New World gold and silver, and a doubling of population (50 mln. in 1450, 100 mln. in 1600). New business and financial techniques were developed and refined, such as joint-stock companies, insurance, and letters of credit and exchange. The Bank of Amsterdam, 1609, and the Bank of England, 1694, broke the old monopoly of private banking families. The rise of a business mentality was typified by the spread of clock towers in cities in the 14th century. By the mid-15th century, portable clocks were available; the first watch was invented in 1502.

By 1650, most governments had adopted the **mercantile system**, in which they sought to amass metallic wealth by protecting their merchants' foreign and colonial trade monopolies. The rise in prices and the new coin-based economy undermined the craft guild and feudal manorial systems. Expanding industries, such as clothweaving and mining, benefitted from technical advances. Coal replaced disappearing wood as the chief fuel; it was used to fuel new 16th century blast furnaces making cast iron.

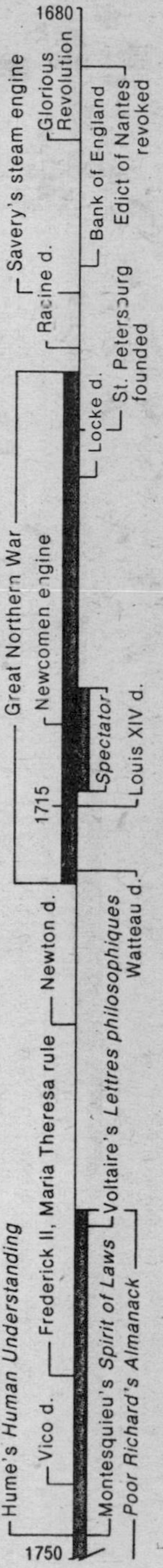
1680
Savery's steam engine
Glorious Revolution
Bank of England
Edict of Nantes revoked
Racine d.
St. Petersburg founded
Locke d.
Great Northern War
Newcomen engine
Spectator
Louis XIV d.
1715
Newton d.
Watteau d.
Voltaire's Lettres philosophiques
Frederick II, Maria Theresa rule
Hume's Human Understanding
Vico d.
Montesquieu's Spirit of Laws
Poor Richard's Almanack
1750

New World. The **Aztecs** united much of the Mesoamerican culture area in a militarist empire by 1519, from their capital, Tenochtitlan (pop. 300,000), which was the center of a cult requiring enormous levels of ritual human sacrifice. Most of the civilized areas of S. America were ruled by the centralized **Inca Empire** (1476-1534), stretching 2,000 miles from Ecuador to N.W. Argentina. Lavish and sophisticated traditions in pottery, weaving, sculpture, and architecture were maintained in both regions.

These empires, beset by revolts, fell in 2 short campaigns to gold-seeking Spanish forces based in the Antilles and Panama. **Cortes** took Mexico, 1519-21; **Pizarro** Peru, 1531-35. From these centers, land and sea expeditions claimed most of N. and S. America for Spain. The Indian high cultures did not survive the impact of Christian missionaries and the new upper class of whites and mestizos. In turn, New World silver, and such Indian products as potatoes, tobacco, corn, peanuts, chocolate, and rubber exercised a major economic influence on Europe. While the Spanish administration intermittently concerned itself with the welfare of Indians, the population remained impoverished at most levels, despite the growth of a distinct South American civilization. European diseases reduced the native population.

Brazil, which the Portuguese discovered in 1500 and settled after 1530, and the Caribbean colonies of several European nations developed a plantation economy where sugar cane, tobacco, cotton, coffee, rice, indigo, and lumber were grown commercially by slaves. From the early 16th to the late 19th centuries, some 10 million Africans were transported to **slavery** in the New World.

Netherlands. The urban, Calvinist northern provinces of the Netherlands rebelled against Hapsburg Spain, 1568, and founded an oligarchic mercantile republic. Their strategic control of the Baltic grain market enabled them to exploit Mediterranean food shortages. Religious refugees — French and Belgian Protestants, Iberian Jews — added to the cosmopolitan commercial talent pool. After Spain absorbed Portugal in 1580, the Dutch seized Portuguese possessions and created a vast, though generally short-lived commercial empire in Brazil, the Antilles, Africa, India, Ceylon, Malacca, Indonesia, and Taiwan, and challenged or supplanted Portuguese traders in China and Japan.

England. Anglicanism became firmly established under Elizabeth I after a brief Catholic interlude under "Bloody Mary," 1553-58. But religious and political conflicts led to a rebellion by Parliament, 1642. Roundheads (Puritans) defeated Cavaliers (Royalists); Charles I was beheaded, 1649. The new **Commonwealth** was ruled as a military dictatorship by Cromwell, who also brutally crushed an Irish rebellion, 1649-51. Conflicts within the Puritan camp (democratic Levelers defeated 1649) aided the Stuart restoration, 1660, but Parliament was permanently strengthened and the peaceful **"Glorious Revolution"**, 1688, advanced political and religious liberties (writings of Locke, 1632-1704). British privateers (Drake, 1540-96) challenged Spanish control of the New World, and penetrated Asian trade routes (Madras taken, 1639). N. American colonies (Jamestown, 1607, Plymouth, 1620) provided an outlet for religious dissenters.

France. Emerging from the religious civil wars in 1628, France regained military and commercial great power status under the ministries of **Richelieu** (1624-42), Mazarin (1643-61), and Colbert (1662-83). Under Louis XIV (ruled 1643-1715) royal absolutism triumphed over nobles and local *parlements* (defeat of Fronde, 1648-53). Permanent colonies were founded in Canada (1608), the Caribbean (1626), and India (1674).

Sweden. Sweden seceded from the Scandinavian Union in 1523. The thinly-populated agrarian state (with copper, iron, and timber exports) was united by the Vasa kings, whose conquests by the mid-17th century made Sweden the dominant Baltic power. The empire collapsed in the Great Northern War (1700-21).

Poland. After the union with Lithuania in 1447, Poland ruled vast territories from the Baltic to the Black Sea, resisting German and Turkish incursions. Catholic nobles failed to gain the loyalty of the Orthodox Christian peasantry in the East; commerce and trades were practiced by German and Jewish immigrants. The bloody 1648-49 cossack uprising began the kingdom's dismemberment.

China. A new dynasty, the **Manchus,** invaded from the NE and seized power in 1644, and expanded Chinese control to its greatest extent in Central and Southeast Asia. Trade and diplomatic contact with Europe grew, carefully controlled by China. New crops (sweet potato, maize, peanut) allowed an economic and population growth (300 million pop. in 1800). Traditional arts and literature were pursued with increased sophistication (*Dream of the Red Chamber,* novel, mid-18th century).

Japan. Tokugawa Ieyasu, shogun from 1603, finally unified and pacified feudal Japan. Hereditary daimyos and samurai monopolized government office and the professions. An urban merchant class grew, literacy spread, and a cultural renaissance occurred (haiku of Basho, 1644-94). Fear of European domination led to persecution of Christian converts from 1597, and stringent isolation from outside contact from 1640.

Philosophy, Industry, and Revolution: 1700-1800

Science and Reason. Faith in human reason and science as the source of truth and a means to improve the physical and social environment, espoused since the Renaissance (Francis Bacon, 1561-1626), was bolstered by scientific discoveries in spite of theological opposition (**Galileo's forced retraction,** 1633). Descartes applied the logical method of mathematics to discover "self-evident" scientific and philosophical truths, while Newton emphasized induction from experimental observation.

The challenge of reason to traditional religious and political values and institutions began with **Spinoza** (1632-77), who interpreted the Bible historically and called for political and intellectual freedom.

French philosophes assumed leadership of the **"Enlightenment"** in the 18th century. Montesquieu (1689-1755) used British history to support his notions of limited government. Voltaire's (1694-1778) diaries and novels of exotic travel illustrated the intellectual trends toward secular ethics and relativism. Rousseau's (1712-1778) radical concepts of the **social contract** and of the inherent goodness of the common man gave impetus to anti-monarchical republicanism. The *Encyclopedia,* 1751-72, edited by Diderot and d'Alembert, designed as a monument to reason, was largely devoted to practical technology.

In England, ideals of political and religious liberty were connected with empiricist philosophy and science in the followers of Locke. But the extreme **empiricism of Hume** (1711-76) and Berkeley

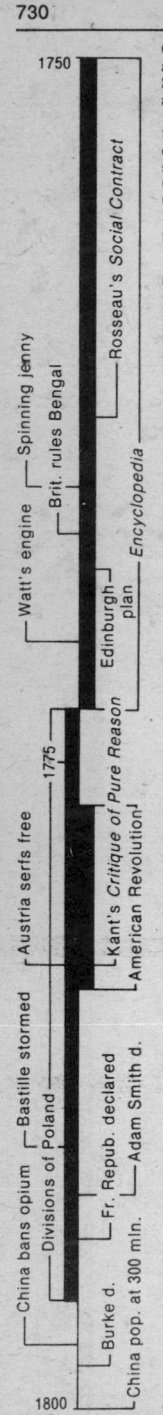

(1685-1753) posed limits to the identification of reason with absolute truth, as did the evolutionary approach to law and politics of Burke (1729-97) and the utilitarianism of Bentham (1748-1832). Adam Smith (1723-90) and other **physiocrats** called for a rationalization of economic activity by removing artificial barriers to a supposedly natural free exchange of goods.

Despite the political disunity and backwardness of most of Germany, German writers participated in the new philosophical trends popularized by Wolff (1679-1754). **Kant's** (1724-1804) **idealism,** unifying an empirical epistemology with *a priori* moral and logical concepts, directed German thought away from skepticism. Italian contributions included work on electricity by Galvani (1737-98) and Volta (1745-1827), the pioneer **historiography of Vico** (1668-1744), and writings on penal reform by Beccaria (1738-94). The American Franklin (1706-90) was celebrated in Europe for his varied achievements.

The growth of the **press** (*Spectator,* 1711-14) and the wide distribution of realistic but sentimental **novels** attested to the increase of a large bourgeois public.

Arts. Rococo art, characterized by extravagant decorative effects, asymmetries copied from organic models, and artificial pastoral subjects, was favored by the continental aristocracy for most of the century (Watteau, 1684-1721), and had musical analogies in the ornamentalized polyphony of late Baroque. The **Neoclassical** art after 1750, associated with the new scientific archeology, was more streamlined, and infused with the supposed moral and geometric rectitude of the Roman Republic (David, 1748-1825). In England, **town planning** on a grand scale began (Edinburgh, 1767).

Industrial Revolution in England. Agricultural improvements, such as the sowing drill (1701) and livestock breeding, were implemented on the large fields provided by enclosure of common lands by private owners. Profits from agriculture and from colonial and foreign trade (1800 volume, £ 54 million) were channelled through hundreds of banks and the **Stock Exchange** (founded 1773) into new industrial processes.

The Newcomen steam pump (1712) aided coal mining. Coal fueled the new efficient steam engines patented by Watt in 1769, and coke-smelting produced cheap, sturdy iron for machinery by the 1730s. The **flying shuttle** (1733) and **spinning jenny** (1764) were used in the large new cotton textile factories, where women and children were much of the work force. Goods were transported cheaply over **canals** (2,000 miles built 1760-1800).

Central and East Europe. The monarchs of the three states that dominated eastern Europe — Austria, Prussia, and Russia — accepted the advice and legitimation of philosophes in creating more modern, centralized institutions in their kingdoms, enlarged by the division of Poland (1772-95).

Under **Frederick II** (ruled 1740-86) Prussia, with its efficient modern army, doubled in size. State monopolies and tariff protection fostered industry, and some legal reforms were introduced. Austria's heterogeneous realms were legally unified under **Maria Theresa** (ruled 1740-80) and **Joseph II** (1780-90). Reforms in education, law, and religion were enacted, and the Austrian serfs were freed (1781). With its defeat in the Seven Years' War in 1763, Austria lost Silesia and ceased its active role in Germany, but was compensated by expansion to the E and S (Hungary, Slavonia, 1699, Galicia, 1772).

Russia, whose borders continued to expand in all directions, adopted some Western bureaucratic and economic policies under **Peter I** (ruled 1682-1725) and **Catherine II** (ruled 1762-96). Trade and cultural contacts with the West multiplied from the new Baltic Sea capital, **St. Petersburg** (founded 1703).

American Revolution. The British colonies in N. America attracted a mass immigration of religious dissenters and poor people throughout the 17th and 18th centuries, coming from all parts of the British Isles, Germany, the Netherlands, and other countries. The population reached 3 million whites and blacks by the 1770s. The small native population was decimated by European diseases and wars with and between the various colonies. British attempts to control colonial trade, and to tax the colonists to pay for the costs of colonial administration and defense clashed with traditions of local self government, and eventually provoked the colonies to rebellion. (*See American Revolution in Index.*)

French Revolution. The growing French middle class lacked political power, and resented aristocratic tax privileges, especially in light of liberal political ideals popularized by the American Revolution. Peasants lacked adequate land and were burdened with feudal obligations to nobles. Wars with Britain drained the treasury, finally forcing the king to call the **Estates-General** in 1789 (first time since 1614), in an atmosphere of food riots (poor crop in 1788).

Aristocratic resistance to absolutism was soon overshadowed by the reformist Third Estate (middle class), which proclaimed itself the **National Constituent Assembly** June 17 and took the "Tennis Court oath" on June 20 to secure a constitution. The storming of the **Bastille** July 14 by Parisian artisans was followed by looting and seizure of aristocratic property throughout France. Assembly reforms included abolition of class and regional privileges, a Declaration of Rights, suffrage by taxpayers (75% of males), and the **Civil Constitution of the Clergy** providing for election and loyalty oaths for priests. A republic was declared Sept. 22, 1792, in spite of royalist pressure from Austria and Prussia, which had declared war in April (joined by Britain the next year). Louis XVI was beheaded Jan. 21, 1793, Queen Marie Antoinette was beheaded Oct. 16, 1793.

Royalist uprisings in La Vendee and the S and military reverses led to a **reign of terror** in which tens of thousands of opponents of the Revolution and criminals were executed. Radical reforms in the **Convention** period (Sept. 1793-Oct. 1795) included the abolition of colonial slavery, economic measures to aid the poor, support of public education, and a short-lived de-Christianization.

Division among radicals (execution of Hebert, March 1794, Danton, April, and Robespierre, July) aided the ascendance of a moderate **Directory,** which consolidated military victories. **Napoleon Bonaparte** (1769-1821), a popular young general, exploited political divisions and participated in a coup Nov. 9, 1799, making himself first consul (dictator).

India. Sikh and Hindu rebels (Rajputs, Marathas) and Afghans destroyed the power of the Mughals during the 18th century. After France's defeat in the Seven Years War, 1763, Britain was the chief European trade power in India. Its control of inland **Bengal and Bihar** was recognized by the Mughal shah in 1765, who granted the **British East India Co.** (under Clive, 1727-74) the right to collect land revenue there. Despite objections from Parliament (1784 India Act) the company's involvement in local wars and politics led to repeated acquisitions of new territory. The company exported Indian textiles, sugar, and indigo.

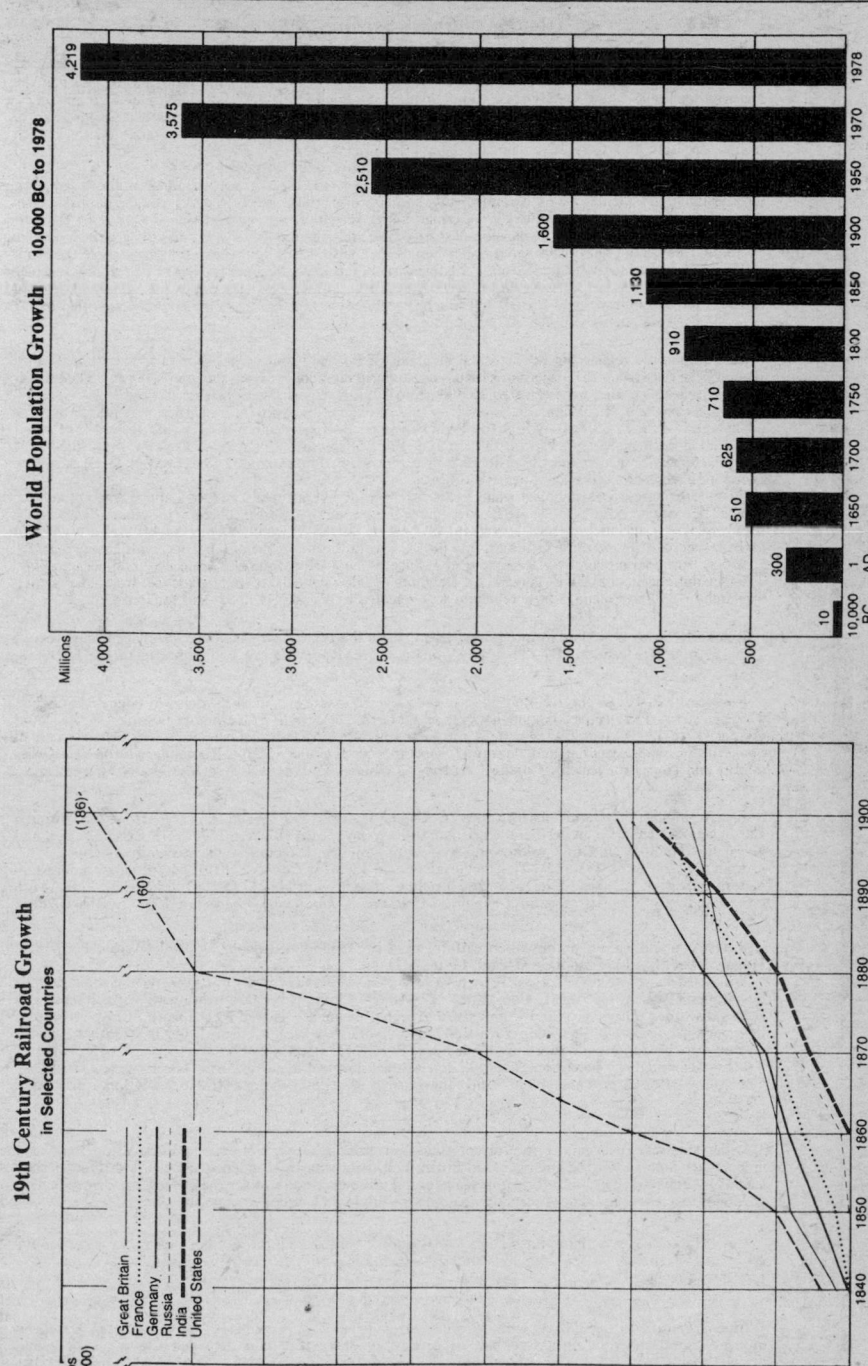

World Population Growth 10,000 BC to 1978

Millions

4,219 — 1978
3,575 — 1970
2,510 — 1950
1,600 — 1900
1,130 — 1850
910 — 1800
710 — 1750
625 — 1700
510 — 1650
300 — 1 AD
10 — 10,000 BC

19th Century Railroad Growth
in Selected Countries

Miles (1,000)

Great Britain ....
France ....
Germany ———
Russia — — —
India ████
United States — — —

(186)
(160)

Change Gathers Steam: 1800-1840

French ideals and empire spread. Inspired by the ideals of the French Revolution, and supported by the expanding French armies, new republican regimes arose near France: the **Batavian** Republic in the Netherlands (1795-1806), the **Helvetic** Republic in Switzerland (1798-1803), the **Cisalpine** Republic in N. Italy (1797-1805), the **Ligurian** Republic in Genoa (1797-1805), and the **Parthenopean** Republic in S. Italy (1799). A Roman Republic existed briefly in 1798 after Pope Pius VI was arrested by French troops. In Italy and Germany, new nationalist sentiments were stimulated both in imitation of and reaction to France (anti-French and anti-Jacobin peasant uprisings in Italy, 1796-9).

From 1804, when Napoleon declared himself emperor, to 1812, a succession of military victories (Austerlitz, 1805, Jena, 1806) extended his control over most of Europe, through puppet states (**Confederation of the Rhine** united W. German states for the first time and **Grand Duchy of Warsaw** revived Polish national hopes), expansion of the empire, and alliances.

Among the lasting reforms initiated under Napoleon's absolutist reign were: establishment of the Bank of France, centralization of tax collection, codification of law along Roman models (*Code Napoleon*), and reform and extension of secondary and university education. In an 1801 concordat, the papacy recognized the effective autonomy of the French Catholic Church. Some 400,000 French soldiers were killed in the Napoleonic Wars, along with 600,000 foreign troops.

Last gasp of old regime. France's coastal blockade of Europe (**Continental System**) failed to neutralize Britain. The disastrous 1812 invasion of Russia exposed Napoleon's overextension. After an 1814 exile at Elba, Napoleon's armies were defeated at Waterloo, 1815, by British and Prussian troops.

At the **Congress of Vienna**, the monarchs and princes of Europe redrew their boundaries, to the advantage of Prussia (in Saxony and the Ruhr), Austria (in Illyria and Venetia), and Russia (in Poland and Finland). British conquest of Dutch and French colonies (S. Africa, Ceylon, Mauritius) was recognized, and France, under the restored Bourbons, retained its expanded 1792 borders. The settlement brought 50 years of international peace to Europe.

But the Congress was unable to check the advance of liberal ideals and of nationalism among the smaller European nations. The 1825 **Decembrist uprising** by liberal officers in Russia was easily suppressed. But an independence movement in **Greece**, stirred by commercial prosperity and a cultural revival, succeeded in expelling Ottoman rule by 1831, with the aid of Britain, France, and Russia.

A constitutional monarchy was secured in France by an **1830 revolution;** Louis Philippe became king. The revolutionary contagion spread to **Belgium,** which gained its independence from the Dutch monarchy, 1830; to **Poland,** whose rebellion was defeated by Russia, 1830-31; and to Germany.

Romanticism. A new style in intellectual and artistic life began to replace Neo-classicism and Rococo after the mid-18th century. By the early 19th, this style, Romanticism, had prevailed in the European world.

Rousseau had begun the reaction against excessive rationalism and skepticism; in education (*Emile,* 1762) he stressed subjective spontaneity over regularized instruction. In Germany, Lessing (1729-81) and Herder (1744-1803) favorably compared the German folk song to classical forms, and began a cult of Shakespeare, whose passion and "natural" wisdom was a model for the Romantic *Sturm und Drang* (storm and stress) movement. **Goethe's** *Sorrows of Young Werther* (1774) set the model for the tragic, passionate genius.

A new interest in **Gothic architecture** in England after 1760 (Walpole, 1717-97) spread through Europe, associated with an aesthetic Christian and mystic revival (Blake, 1757-1827). Celtic, Norse, and German mythology and folk tales were revived or imitated (Macpherson's Ossian translation, 1762, Grimm's *Fairy Tales,* 1812-22). The medieval revival (Scott's *Ivanhoe,* 1819) led to a new interest in history, stressing national differences and organic growth (Carlyle, 1795-1881; Michelet, 1798-1874), corresponding to theories of natural evolution (Lamarck's *Philosophie zoologique,* 1809, Lyell's *Geology,* 1830-33).

Revolution and war fed an obsession with freedom and conflict, expressed by poets (**Byron,** 1788-1824, **Hugo,** 1802-85) and philosophers (**Hegel,** 1770-1831).

Wild gardens replaced the formal French variety, and painters favored rural, stormy, and mountainous landscapes (**Turner,** 1775-1851; **Constable,** 1776-1837). Clothing became freer, with wigs, hoops, and ruffles discarded. Originality and genius were expected in the life as well as the work of inspired artists (Murger's *Scenes from Bohemian Life,* 1847-49). Exotic locales and themes (as in "Gothic" horror stories) were used in art and literature (Delacroix, 1798-1863, **Poe,** 1809-49).

Music exhibited the new dramatic style and a breakdown of classical forms (Beethoven, 1770-1827). The use of folk melodies and modes aided the growth of distinct national traditions (Glinka in Russia, 1804-57).

Latin America. Haiti, under the former slave **Toussaint L'Ouverture,** was the first Latin American independent state, 1800. All the mainland Spanish colonies won their independence 1810-24, under such leaders as **Bolivar** (1783-1830). Brazil became an independent empire under the Portuguese prince regent, 1822. A new class of military officers divided power with large landholders and the church.

United States. Heavy immigration and exploitation of ample natural resources fueled rapid economic growth. The spread of the franchise, public education, and antislavery sentiment were signs of a widespread democratic ethic.

China. Failure to keep pace with Western arms technology exposed China to greater European influence, and hampered efforts to bar imports of opium, which had damaged Chinese society and drained wealth overseas. In the **Opium War,** 1839-42, Britain forced China to expand trade opportunities and to cede Hong Kong.

Timeline (left margin):

1800
- Haiti indep.
- Hugo b.
- Dix b.
- Mill b.
- Lamarck's *Philosophie Zoologique*
- Napoleon emperor
- Congress of Vienna
1815
- Scott's *Ivanhoe*
- Grimm's *Fairy Tales*
- Byron d.
- Brazil indep.
- S. Amer. colonies win indep.
- Decembrist uprising
- Blake d.
- Volta d.
- Beethoven d.
1830
- Greek indep. movement
- Belgian indep.
- 1st Eng. reform bill
- 1st Brit. Factory Act.
- Brit. Emp. slavery banned
- Brook Farm, Mass.
- Opium War
- Telegraph perfected by Morse
1845

Triumph of Progress: 1840-80

Idea of Progress. As a result of the cumulative scientific, economic, and political changes of the preceding eras, the idea took hold among literate people in the West that continuing growth and improvement was the usual state of human and natural life.

Darwin's statement of the **theory of evolution** and survival of the fittest (*Origin of Species*, 1859), defended by intellectuals and scientists against theological objections, was taken as confirmation that progress was the natural direction of life. The controversy helped define popular ideas of the dedicated scientist and ever-expanding human knowledge of and control over the world (Foucault's demonstration of earth's rotation, 1851, Pasteur's germ theory, 1861).

Liberals following Ricardo (1772-1823) in their faith that unrestrained competition would bring continuous economic expansion sought to adjust political life to the new social realities, and believed that unregulated competition of ideas would yield truth (Mill, 1806-73). In England, successive reform bills (1832, 1867, 1884) gave representation to the new industrial towns, and extended the franchise to the middle and lower classes and to Catholics, Dissenters, and Jews. On both sides of the Atlantic, reformists tried to improve conditions for the mentally ill (Dix, 1802-87), women (Anthony, 1820-1906), and prisoners. Slavery was barred in the British Empire, 1833; the United States, 1865; and Brazil, 1888.

Socialist theories based on ideas of human perfectibility or historical progress were widely disseminated. Utopian socialists like Saint-Simon (1760-1825) envisaged an orderly, just society directed by a technocratic elite. A model factory town, New Lanark, Scotland, was set up by utopian Robert Owen (1771-1858), and utopian communal experiments were tried in the U.S. (Brook Farm, Mass., 1841-7). Bakunin's (1814-76) anarchism represented the opposite utopian extreme of total freedom. Marx (1818-83) posited the inevitable triumph of socialism in the industrial countries through a historical process of class conflict.

Spread of industry. The technical processes and managerial innovations of the English industrial revolution spread to Europe (especially Germany) and the U.S., causing an explosion of industrial production, demand for raw materials, and competition for markets. Inventors, both trained and self-educated, provided the means for larger-scale production (Bessemer steel, 1856, sewing machine, 1846). Many inventions were shown at the 1851 London Great Exhibition at the Crystal Palace, whose theme was universal prosperity.

Local specialization and long-distance trade were aided by a revolution in transportation and communication. Railroads were first introduced in the 1820s in England and the U.S. Over 150,000 miles of track had been laid worldwide by 1880, with another 100,000 miles laid in the next decade. Steamships were improved (*Savannah* crossed Atlantic, 1819). The telegraph, perfected by 1844 (Morse), connected the Old and New Worlds by cable in 1866, and quickened the pace of international commerce and politics. The first commercial telephone exchange went into operation in the U.S. in 1878.

The new class of industrial workers, uprooted from their rural homes, lacked job security, and suffered from dangerous overcrowded conditions at work and at home. Many responded by organizing trade unions (legalized in England, 1824; France, 1884). The U.S. Knights of Labor had 700,000 members by 1886. The First International, 1864-76, tried to unite workers internationally around a Marxist program. The quasi-Socialist Paris Commune uprising, 1871, was violently suppressed. Factory Acts to reduce child labor and regulate conditions were passed (1833-50 in England). Social security measures were introduced by the Bismarck regime in Germany, 1883-89.

Revolutions of 1848. Among the causes of the continent-wide revolutions were an international collapse of credit and resulting unemployment, bad harvests in 1845-7, and a cholera epidemic. The new urban proletariat and expanding bourgeoisie demanded a greater political role. Republics were proclaimed in France, Rome, and Venice. Nationalist feelings reached fever pitch in the Hapsburg empire, as Hungary declared independence under Kossuth, a Slav Congress demanded equality, and Piedmont tried to drive Austria from Lombardy. A national liberal assembly at Frankfurt called for German unification.

But riots fueled bourgeois fears of socialism (Marx and Engels' 1848 *Communist Manifesto*) and peasants remained conservative. The old establishment — The Papacy, the Hapsburgs (using Croats and Romanians against Hungary), the Prussian army — was able to rout the revolutionaries by 1849. The French Republic succumbed to a renewed monarchy by 1852 (Emperor Napoleon III).

Great nations unified. Using the "blood and iron" tactics of Bismarck from 1862, Prussia controlled N. Germany by 1867 (war with Denmark, 1864, Austria, 1866). After defeating France in 1870 (loss of Alsace-Lorraine), it won the allegiance of S. German states. A new **German Empire** was proclaimed, 1871. **Italy**, inspired by Mazzini (1805-72) and Garibaldi (1807-82), was unified by the reformed Piedmont kingdom through uprisings, plebiscites, and war.

The U.S., its area expanded after the 1846-47 Mexican War, defeated a secession attempt by slave states, 1861-65. The Canadian provinces were united in an autonomous **Dominion of Canada**, 1867. Control in **India** was removed from the East India Co. and centralized under British administration after the 1857-58 Sepoy rebellion, laying the groundwork for the modern Indian State. Queen Victoria was named Empress of India, 1876.

Europe dominates Asia. The Ottoman Empire began to collapse in the face of Balkan nationalisms and European imperial incursions in N. Africa (Suez Canal, 1869). The Turks had lost control of most of both regions by 1882. Russia completed its expansion south by 1884 (despite the temporary setback of the Crimean War with Turkey, Britain, and France, 1853-56) taking Turkestan, all the Caucasus, and Chinese areas in the East and sponsoring Balkan Slavs against the Turks. A succession of reformist and reactionary regimes presided over a slow modernization (serfs freed, 1861). Persian independence suffered as Russia and British India competed for influence.

China was forced to sign a series of unequal treaties with European powers and Japan. Overpopulation and an inefficient dynasty brought misery and caused rebellions (Taiping, Moslems) leaving tens of millions dead. Japan was forced by the U.S. (Commodore Perry's visits, 1853-54) and Europe to end its isolation. The Meiji restoration, 1868, gave power to a Westernizing oligarchy. Intensified empire-building gave Burma to Britain, 1824-86, and Indo-China to France, 1862-95. Christian missionary activity followed imperial and trade expansion in Asia.

Respectability. The fine arts were expected to reflect and encourage the progress of morals and

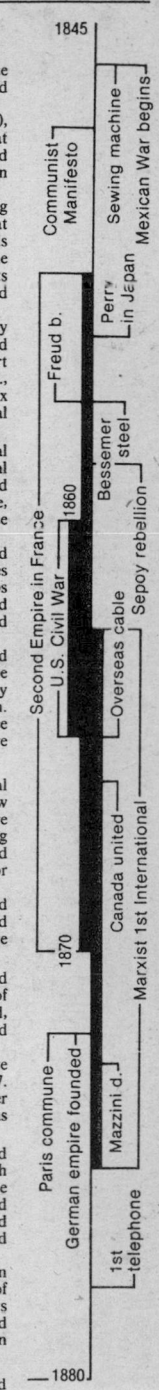

1845

Communist Manifesto

Freud b.

Sewing machine

Perry in Japan   Mexican War begins

Second Empire in France

U.S. Civil War   1860

Bessemer steel

Overseas cable   Sepoy rebellion

Canada united

Marxist 1st International

Paris commune   1870

Mazzini d.

German empire founded

1st telephone

1880

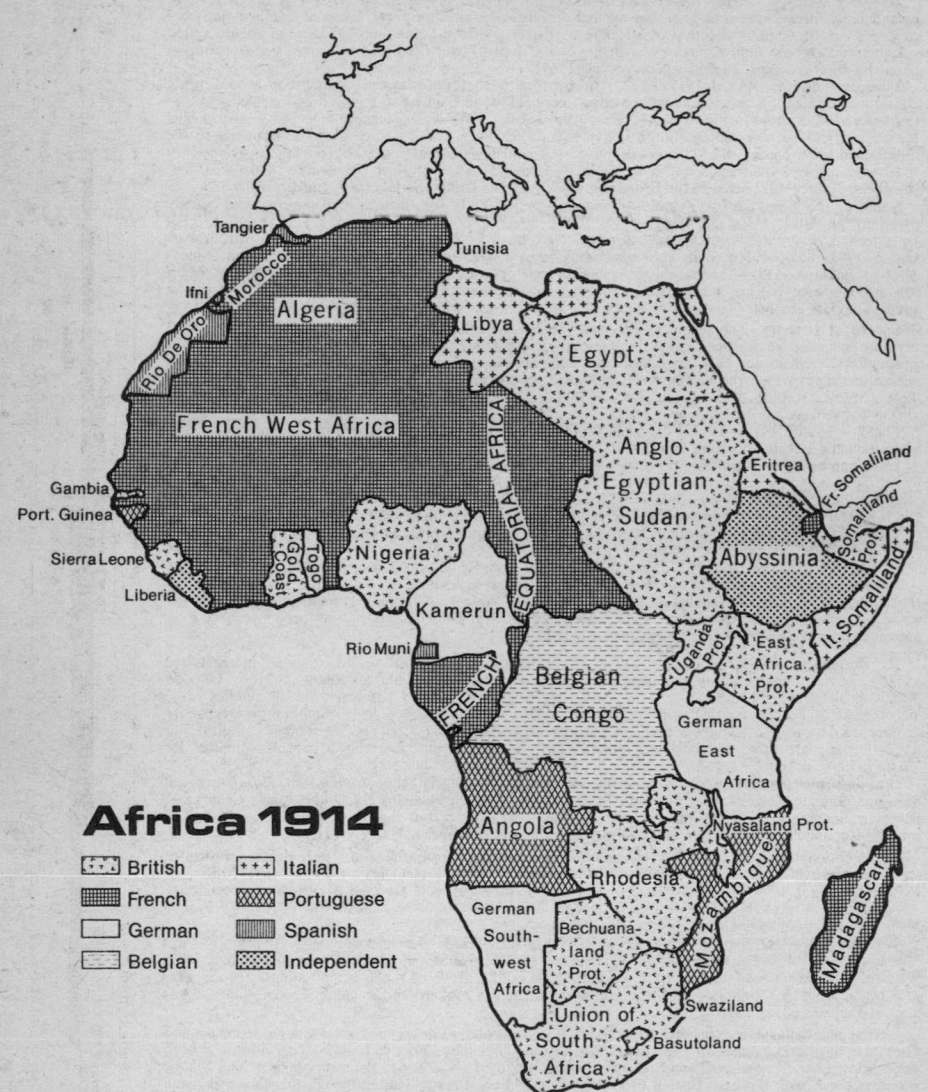

Tangier
Tunisia
Ifni
Rio De Oro
Morocco
Algeria
Libya
Egypt
French West Africa
Anglo Egyptian Sudan
Eritrea
Fr. Somaliland
Gambia
Port. Guinea
Sierra Leone
Liberia
Togo
Gold Coast
Nigeria
EQUATORIAL AFRICA
Abyssinia
Somaliland Prot.
Kamerun
It. Somaliland
Rio Muni
FRENCH
Uganda Prot.
East Africa Prot.
German East Africa
Belgian Congo

Africa 1914

Angola
Nyasaland Prot.
German South-west Africa
Rhodesia
Bechuana-land Prot.
Mozambique
Madagascar
Swaziland
Union of South Africa
Basutoland

	British		Italian
	French		Portuguese
	German		Spanish
	Belgian		Independent

manners among the different classes. "Victorian" prudery, exaggerated delicacy, and familial piety were heralded by **Bowdler's** expurgated edition of Shakespeare (1818). Government-supported mass education inculcated a work ethic as a means to escape poverty (Horatio Alger, 1832-99).

The official **Beaux Arts** school in Paris set an international style of imposing public buildings (Paris Opera, 1861-74, Vienna Opera, 1861-69) and uplifting statues (Bartholdi's *Statue of Liberty*, 1885). Realist painting, influenced by photography (Daguerre, 1837), appealed to a new mass audience with social or historical narrative (Wilkie, 1785-1841, Poynter, 1836-1919) or with serious religious, moral, or social messages (pre-Raphaelites, Millet's Angelus, 1858) often drawn from ordinary life. The **Impressionists** (Pissarro, 1830-1903, Renoir, 1841-1919) rejected the central role of serious subject matter in favor of a colorful and sensual depiction of a moment, but their sunny, placid depictions of bourgeois scenes kept them within the respectable consensus.

Realistic **novelists** presented the full panorama of social classes and personalities, but retained sentimentality and moral judgment (Dickens, 1812-70, Eliot, 1819-80, Tolstoy, 1828-1910, Balzac, 1799-1850).

Veneer of Stability: 1880-1900

Imperialism triumphant. The vast **African** interior, visited by European explorers (Barth, 1821-65, Livingstone, 1813-73) was conquered by the European powers in rapid, competitive thrusts from their coastal bases after 1880, mostly for domestic political and international strategic reasons. W. African Moslem kingdoms (Fulani), Arab slave traders (Zanzibar), and Bantu military confederations (Zulu) were alike subdued. Only Christian Ethiopia (defeat of Italy, 1896) and Liberia resisted successfully. France (W. Africa) and Britain ("Cape to Cairo," Boer War, 1899-1902) were the major beneficiaries. The ideology of "the white man's burden" (Kipling, *Barrack Room Ballads*, 1892) or of a "civilizing mission" (France) justified the conquests.

West European foreign capital investments soared to nearly $40 billion by 1914, but most was in E. Europe (France, Germany) the Americas (Britain) and the white colonies. The foundation of the modern interdependent world economy was laid, with cartels dominating raw material trade.

An industrious world. Industrial and technological proficiency characterized the 2 new great powers — Germany and the U.S. Coal and iron deposits enabled Germany to reach second or third place status in iron, steel, and shipbuilding by the 1900s. German electrical and chemical industries were world leaders. The U.S. post-civil war boom (interrupted by "panics," 1884, 1893, 1896) was shaped by massive immigration from S. and E. Europe from 1880, government subsidy of railroads, and huge private monopolies (Standard Oil, 1870, U.S. Steel, 1901). The **Spanish-American War,** 1898 (Philippine rebellion, 1899-1901) and the Open Door policy in China (1899) made the U.S. a world power.

England led in **urbanization** (72% by 1890), with **London** the world capital of finance, insurance, and shipping. Electric subways (London, 1890), sewer systems (Paris, 1850s), parks, and bargain department stores helped improve living standards for most of the urban population of the industrial world.

Asians assimilate. Asian reaction to European economic, military, and religious incursions took the form of imitation of Western techniques and adoption of Western ideas of progress and freedom. The Chinese "self-strengthening" movement of the 1860s and 70s included rail, port, and arsenal improvements and metal and textile mills. Reformers like **K'ang Yu-wei** (1858-1927) won liberalizing reforms in 1898, right after the European and Japanese "scramble for concessions."

A universal education system in Japan and importation of foreign industrial, scientific, and military experts aided Japan's unprecedented rapid modernization after 1868, under the authoritarian Meiji regime. Japan's victory in the **Sino-Japanese War,** 1894-95, put Formosa and Korea in its power.

In India, the British alliance with the remaining princely states masked reform sentiment among the Westernized urban elite; higher education had been conducted largely in English for 50 years. The **Indian National Congress,** founded in 1885, demanded a larger government role for Indians.

"Fin-de-siecle" sophistication. **Naturalist** writers pushed realism to its extreme limits, adopting a quasi-scientific attitude and writing about formerly taboo subjects like sex, crime, extreme poverty, and corruption (Flaubert, 1821-80, Zola, 1840-1902, Hardy, 1840-1928). Unseen or repressed psychological motivations were explored in the clinical and theoretical works of **Freud** (1856-1939) and in the fiction of Dostoevsky (1821-81), James (1843-1916), Schnitzler (1862-1931) and others.

A contempt for bourgeois life or a desire to shock a complacent audience was shared by the French **symbolist** poets (Verlaine, 1844-96, Rimbaud, 1854-91), neo-pagan English writers (Swinburne, 1837-1909), continental dramatists (Ibsen, 1828-1906) and satirists (Wilde, 1854-1900). **Nietzsche** (1844-1900) was influential in his elitism and pessimism.

Post-impressionist art neglected long-cherished conventions of representation (Cezanne, 1839-1906) and showed a willingness to learn from primitive and non-European art (Gauguin, 1848-1903, Japanese prints).

Racism. Gobineau (1816-82) gave a pseudo-biological foundation to modern racist theories, which spread in the latter 19th century along with **Social Darwinism,** the belief that societies are and should be organized as a struggle for survival of the fittest. The Medieval period was interpreted as an era of natural Germanic rule (Chamberlain, 1855-1927) and notions of superiority were associated with German national aspirations (Treitschke, 1834-96). **Anti-Semitism,** with a new racist rationale, became a significant political force in Germany (Anti-Semitic Petition, 1880), Austria (Lueger, 1844-1910), and France (Dreyfus case, 1894-1906).

Last Respite: 1900-1909

Alliances. While the peace of Europe (and its dependencies) continued to hold (1907 **Hague Conference** extended the rules of war and international arbitration procedures), imperial rivalries, protectionist trade practices (in Germany and France), and the escalating arms race (British *Dreadnought* battleship launched, Germany widens Kiel canal, 1906) exacerbated minor disputes (German-French Moroccan "crises", 1905, 1911).

Security was sought through alliances: **Triple Alliance** (Germany, Austria-Hungary, Italy) renewed

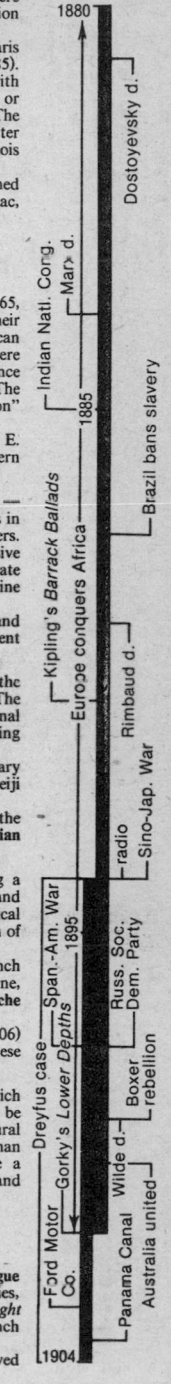

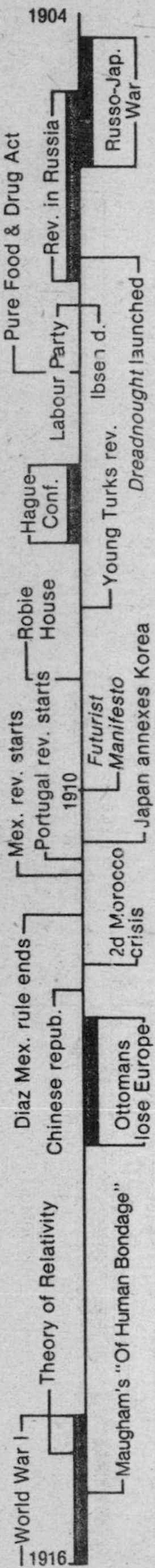
1904
Russo-Jap. War
Rev. in Russia
Pure Food & Drug Act
Labour Party
Ibsen d.
Dreadnought launched
Hague Conf.
Young Turks rev.
Robie House
Futurist Manifesto
Japan annexes Korea
Mex. rev. starts
Portugal rev. starts
1910
2d Morocco crisis
Diaz Mex. rule ends
Chinese repub.
Ottomans lose Europe
Theory of Relativity
Maugham's "Of Human Bondage"
World War I
1916

1902, 1907; Anglo-Japanese Alliance, 1902; Franco-Russian Alliance, 1899; **Entente Cordiale** (Britain, France) 1904; Anglo-Russian Treaty, 1907; German-Ottoman friendship.

Ottomans decline. The inefficient, corrupt Ottoman government was unable to resist further loss of territory. Nearly all European lands were lost in 1912 to Serbia, Greece, Montenegro, and Bulgaria. Italy took Libya and the Dodecanese islands the same year, and Britain took Kuwait, 1899, and the Sinai, 1906. The **Young Turk** revolution in 1908 forced the sultan to restore a constitution, introduced some social reform, industrialization, and secularization.

British Empire. British trade and cultural influence remained dominant in the empire, but constitutional reforms presaged its eventual dissolution: the colonies of **Australia** were united in 1901 under a self-governing commonwealth. **New Zealand** acquired dominion status in 1907. The old Boer republics joined Cape Colony and Natal in the self-governing **Union of South Africa** in 1910.

The 1909 Indian Councils Act enhanced the role of elected province legislatures in **India.** The Moslem League, founded 1906, sought separate communal representation.

East Asia. Japan exploited its growing industrial power to expand its empire. Victory in the 1904-05 war against Russia (naval battle of Tsushima, 1905) assured Japan's domination of **Korea** (annexed 1910) and Manchuria (took Port Arthur 1905).

In China, central authority began to crumble (empress died, 1908). Reforms (Confucian exam system ended 1905, modernization of the army, building of railroads) were inadequate and secret societies of reformers and nationalists, inspired by the Westernized **Sun Yat-sen** (1866-1925) fomented periodic uprisings in the south.

Siam, whose independence had been guaranteed by Britain and France in 1896, was split into spheres of influence by those countries in 1907.

Russia. The population of the Russian Empire approached 150 million in 1900. Reforms in education, law, and local institutions (*zemstvos*), and an industrial boom starting in the 1880s (oil, railroads) created the beginnings of a modern state, despite the autocratic tsarist regime. Liberals (1903 Union of Liberation), Socialists (Social Democrats founded 1898, Bolsheviks split off 1903), and populists (Social Revolutionaries founded 1901) were periodically repressed, and national minorities persecuted (anti-Jewish pogroms, 1903, 1905-6).

An industrial crisis after 1900 and harvest failures aggravated poverty in the urban proletariat, and the 1904-05 defeat by Japan (which checked Russia's Asian expansion) sparked the revolution of 1905-06. A **Duma** (parliament) was created, and an agricultural reform (under Stolypin, prime minister 1906-11) created a large class of landowning peasants (kulaks).

The world shrinks. Developments in transportation and communication and mass population movements helped create an awareness of an interdependent world. Early **automobiles** (Daimler, Benz, 1885) were experimental, or designed as luxuries. Assembly-line mass production (Ford Motor Co., 1903) made the invention practicable, and by 1910 nearly 500,000 motor vehicles were registered in the U.S. alone. **Heavier-than-air flights** began in 1903 in the U.S. (Wright brothers), preceded by glider, balloon, and model plane advances in several countries. Trade was advanced by improvements in **ship design** (gyrocompass, 1907), speed (Lusitania crossed Atlantic in 5 days, 1907), and reach (Panama Canal begun, 1904).

The first transatlantic **radio** telegraphic transmission occurred in 1901, 6 years after Marconi discovered radio. Radio transmission of human speech had been made in 1900. Telegraphic transmission of photos was achieved in 1904, lending immediacy to news reports. **Phonographs,** popularized by Caruso's recordings (starting 1902) made for quick international spread of musical styles (ragtime). **Motion pictures,** perfected in the 1890s (Dickson, Lumiere brothers), became a popular and artistic medium after 1900; newsreels appeared in 1909.

Emigration from crowded European centers soared in the decade: 9 million migrated to the U.S., and millions more went to Siberia, Canada, Argentina, Australia, South Africa, and Algeria. Some 70 million Europeans emigrated in the century before 1914. Several million Chinese, Indians, and Japanese migrated to Southeast Asia, where their urban skills often enabled them to take a predominant economic role.

Social reform. The social and economic problems of the poor were kept in the public eye by realist fiction writers (Dreiser's *Sister Carrie,* 1900; Gorky's *Lower Depths,* 1902; Sinclair's *Jungle,* 1906), journalists (U.S. **muckrakers** — Steffens, Tarbell) and artists (Ashcan school). Frequent labor strikes and occasional assassinations by anarchists or radicals (Austrian Empress, 1898; King Umberto I of Italy, 1900; U.S. Pres. McKinley, 1901; Russian Interior Minister Plehve, 1904; Portugal's King Carlos, 1908) added to social tension and fear of revolution.

But democratic reformism prevailed. In Germany, Bernstein's (1850-1932) **revisionist Marxism,** downgrading revolution, was accepted by the powerful Social Democrats and trade unions. The British Fabian Society (the Webbs, Shaw) and the Labour Party (founded 1906) worked for reforms such as social security and union rights (1906), while women's suffragists grew more militant. U.S. **progressives** fought big business (Pure Food and Drug Act, 1906). In France, the 10-hour work day (1904) and separation of church and state (1905) were reform victories, as was universal suffrage in Austria (1907).

Arts. An unprecedented period of experimentation, centered in France, produced several new **painting** styles: fauvism exploited bold color areas (Matisse, *Woman with Hat,* 1905); expressionism reflected powerful inner emotions (the Brücke group, 1905); cubism combined several views of an object on one flat surface (Picasso's *Demoiselles,* 1906-07); futurism tried to depict speed and motion (Italian Futurist Manifesto, 1910). **Architects** explored new uses of steel structures, with facades either neo-classical (Adler and Sullivan in U.S.); curvilinear Art Nouveau (Gaudi's Casa Mila, 1905-10); or functionally streamlined (Wright's Robie House, 1909).

Music and **Dance** shared the experimental spirit. Ruth St. Denis (1877-1968) and Isadora Duncan (1878-1927) pioneered modern dance, while Diaghilev in Paris revitalized classic ballet from 1909. Composers explored atonal music (Debussy, 1862-1918) and dissonance (Schönberg, 1874-1951), or revolutionized classical forms (Stravinsky, 1882-71), often showing jazz or folk music influences.

War and Revolution: 1910-1919

War threatens. Germany under Wilhelm II sought a political and imperial role consonant with its industrial strength, challenging Britain's world supremacy and threatening France, still resenting the loss of Alsace-Lorraine. Austria wanted to curb an expanded Serbia (after 1912) and the threat it posed to its own Slav lands. Russia feared Austrian and German political and economic aims in the Balkans and Turkey. An accelerated arms race resulted: the German standing army rose to over 2 million men by 1914. Russia and France had over a million each, Austria and the British Empire nearly a million each. Dozens of enormous battleships were built by the powers after 1906.

The **assassination of Austrian Archduke Ferdinand** by a Serbian, June 28, 1914, was the pretext for war. The system of alliances made the conflict Europe-wide; Germany's invasion of Belgium to outflank France forced Britain to enter the war. Patriotic fervor was nearly unanimous among all classes in most countries.

World War I. German forces were stopped in France in one month. The rival armies dug **trench networks**. Artillery and improved machine guns prevented either side from any lasting advance despite repeated assaults (600,000 dead at **Verdun**, Feb.-July 1916). Poison gas, used by Germany in 1915, proved ineffective. Over one million U.S. troops tipped the balance after mid-1917, forcing Germany to sue for peace.

In the East, the Russian armies were thrown back (battle of **Tannenberg**, Aug. 20, 1914) and the war grew unpopular. An allied attempt to relieve Russia through Turkey failed (**Gallipoli** 1916). The new Bolshevik regime signed the capitulatory Brest-Litovsk peace in March, 1918. Italy entered the war on the allied side, Apr. 1915, but was pushed back by Oct. 1917. A renewed offensive with Allied aid in Oct.-Nov. 1918 forced Austria to surrender.

The British Navy successfully blockaded Germany, which responded with submarine U-boat attacks; **unrestricted submarine warfare** against neutrals after Jan. 1917 helped bring the U.S. into the war. Other battlefields included Palestine and Mesopotamia, both of which Britain wrested from the Turks in 1917, and the African and Pacific colonies of Germany, most of which fell to Britain, France, Australia, Japan, and South Africa.

From 1916, the civilian population and economy of both sides were mobilized to an unprecedented degree. Over 10 million soldiers died (May 1917 French mutiny crushed). *For further details, see 1978 and earlier editions of The World Almanac.*

Settlement. At the **Versailles conference** (Jan.-June 1919) and in subsequent negotiations and local wars (Russian-Polish War 1920), the map of Europe was redrawn with a nod to U.S. Pres. Wilson's principle of self-determination. Austria and Hungary were separated and much of their land was given to Yugoslavia (formerly Serbia), Romania, Italy, and the newly independent Poland and Czechoslovakia. Germany lost territory in the West, North, and East, while Finland and the Baltic states were detached from Russia. Turkey lost nearly all its Arab lands to British-sponsored Arab states or to direct French and British rule.

A huge **reparations** burden and partial demilitarization were imposed on Germany. Wilson obtained approval for a League of Nations, but the U.S. Senate refused to allow the U.S. to join.

Russian revolution. Military defeats and high casualties caused a contagious lack of confidence in Tsar Nicholas, who was forced to abdicate, Mar. 1917. A liberal provisional government failed to end the war, and massive desertions, riots, and fighting between factions followed. A moderate socialist government under Kerensky was overthrown in a violent **coup by the Bolsheviks** in Petrograd under Lenin, who disbanded the elected Constituent Assembly, Nov. 1917.

The Bolsheviks brutally suppressed all opposition and ended the war with Germany, Mar. 1918. **Civil war** broke out in the summer between the Red Army, including the Bolsheviks and their supporters, and monarchists, anarchists, nationalities (Ukrainians, Georgians, Poles) and others. Small U.S., British, French and Japanese units also opposed the Bolsheviks, 1918-19 (Japan in Vladivostok to 1922). The civil war, anarchy, and pogroms devastated the country until the 1920 Red Army victory. The wartime total monopoly of political, economic, and police power by the Communist Party leadership was retained.

Other European revolutions. An unpopular monarchy in **Portugal** was overthrown in 1910. The new republic took severe anti-clerical measures, 1911.

After a century of Home Rule agitation, during which **Ireland** was devastated by famine (one million dead, 1846-47) and emigration, republican militants staged an unsuccessful uprising in Dublin, Easter 1916. The execution of the leaders and mass arrests by the British won popular support for the rebels. The Irish Free State, comprising all but the 6 northern counties, achieved dominion status in 1922.

In the aftermath of the world war, radical revolutions were attempted in Germany (**Spartacist** uprising Jan. 1919), **Hungary** (Kun regime 1919), and elsewhere. All were suppressed or failed for lack of support.

Chinese revolution. The Manchu Dynasty was overthrown and a republic proclaimed, Oct. 1911. First president Sun Yat-sen resigned in favor of strongman Yuan Shih-k'ai. Sun organized the parliamentarian **Kuomintang** party.

Students launched protests May 4, 1919 against League of Nations concessions in China to Japan. Nationalist, liberal, and socialist ideas and political groups spread. The **Communist Party** was founded 1921. A communist regime took power in Mongolia with Soviet support in 1921.

India restive. Indian objections to British rule erupted in nationalist riots as well as in the non-violent tactics of Gandhi (1869-1948). Nearly 400 unarmed demonstrators were shot at **Amritsar**, Apr. 1919. Britain approved limited self-rule that year.

Mexican revolution. Under the long Diaz dictatorship (1876-1911) the economy advanced, but Indian and mestizo lands were confiscated, and concessions to foreigners (mostly U.S.) damaged the middle class. A **revolution in 1910** led to civil wars and U.S. intervention (1914, 1916-17). Land reform and a more democratic constitution (1917) were achieved.

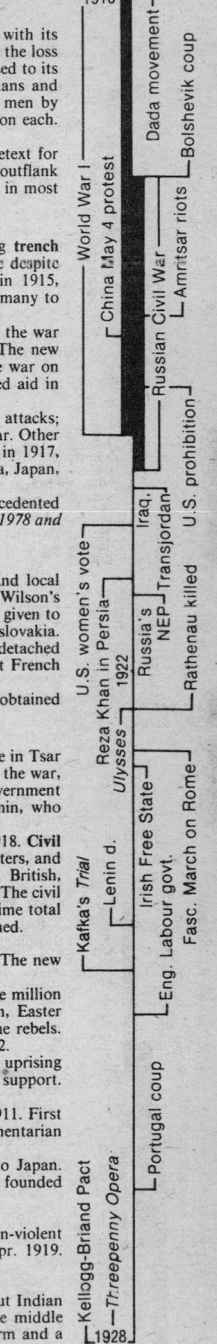

1916 — Dada movement — Bolshevik coup
World War I — China May 4 protest — Russian Civil War — Amritsar riots
U.S. prohibition
Iraq., Transjordan — Rathenau killed
U.S. women's vote — NEP — 1922
Reza Khan in Persia — Russia's
Ulysses
Irish Free State — Fasc. March on Rome
Kafka's Trial — Lenin d.
Eng. Labour govt.
Portugal coup
Kellogg-Briand Pact — Threepenny Opera
1928

The Aftermath of War: 1920-29

U.S. Easy credit, technological ingenuity, and war-related industrial decline in Europe caused a long economic boom, in which ownership of the new products — autos, phones, radios — became democratized. Prosperity, an increase in women workers, women's suffrage (1920) and drastic change in fashion (flappers, mannish bob for women, clean-shaven men), created a wide perception of social change, despite prohibition of alcoholic beverages (1919-33). Union membership and strikes increased. Fear of radicals led to Palmer raids (1919-20) and Sacco/Vanzetti case (1921-27).

Europe sorts itself out. Germany's liberal **Weimar constitution** (1919) could not guarantee a stable government in the face of rightist violence (Rathenau assassinated 1922) and Communist refusal to cooperate with Socialists. Reparations and allied occupation of the Rhineland caused staggering inflation which destroyed middle class savings, but economic expansion resumed after mid-decade, aided by U.S. loans. A sophisticated, innovative culture developed in architecture and design (Bauhaus, 1919-28), film (Lang, *M*, 1931), painting (Grosz), music (Weill, *Threepenny Opera*, 1928), theater (Brecht, *A Man's a Man*, 1926), criticism (Benjamin), philosophy (Jung), and fashion. This culture was considered decadent and socially disruptive by rightists.

England elected its first labor governments (Jan. 1924, June 1929). A 10-day general strike in support of coal miners failed, May 1926. In **Italy**, strikes, political chaos and violence by small Fascist bands culminated in the Oct. 1922 Fascist March on Rome, which established Mussolini's dictatorship. Strikes were outlawed (1926), and Italian influence was pressed in the Balkans (Albania a protectorate 1926). A conservative dictatorship was also established in **Portugal** in a 1926 military coup.

Czechoslovakia, the only stable democracy to emerge from the war in Central or East Europe, faced opposition from Germans (in the Sudetenland), Ruthenians, and some Slovaks. As the industrial heartland of the old Hapsburg empire, it remained fairly prosperous. With French backing, it formed the Little Entente with Yugoslavia (1920) and **Romania** (1921) to block Austrian or Hungarian irredentism. **Hungary** remained dominated by the landholding classes and expansionist feeling. Croats and Slovenes in **Yugoslavia** demanded a federal state until King Alexander proclaimed a dictatorship (1929). Poland faced nationality problems as well (Germans, Ukrainians, Jews); Pilsudski ruled as dictator from 1926. The Baltic states were threatened by traditionally dominant ethnic Germans and by Soviet-supported communists.

An economic collapse and famine in **Russia**, 1921-22, claimed 5 million lives. The New Economic Policy (1921) allowed land ownership by peasants and some private commerce and industry. Stalin was absolute ruler within 4 years of Lenin's 1924 death. He inaugurated a brutal collectivization program 1929-32, and used foreign communist parties for Soviet state advantage.

Internationalism. Revulsion against World War I led to pacifist agitation, the Kellogg-Briand Pact renouncing aggressive war (1928), and **naval disarmament** pacts (Washington, 1922, London, 1930). But the League of Nations was able to arbitrate only minor disputes (Greece-Bulgaria, 1925).

Middle East. Mustafa Kemal (Ataturk) led **Turkish** nationalists in resisting Italian, French, and Greek military advances, 1919-23. The sultanate was abolished 1922, and elaborate reforms passed, including secularization of law and adoption of the Latin alphabet. Ethnic conflict led to persecution of **Armenians** (over 1 million dead in 1915, 1 million expelled), Greeks (forced Greek-Turk population exchange, 1923), and Kurds (1925 uprising).

With evacuation of the Turks from **Arab** lands, the puritanical Wahabi dynasty of eastern Arabia conquered present Saudi Arabia, 1919-25. British, French, and Arab dynastic and nationalist maneuvering resulted in the creation of two more Arab monarchies in 1921: Iraq and Transjordan (both under British control), and two French mandates: Syria and Lebanon. Jewish immigration into British-mandated **Palestine**, inspired by the Zionist movement, was resisted by Arabs, at times violently (1921, 1929 massacres).

Reza Khan ruled **Persia** after his 1921 coup (shah from 1925), centralized control, and created the trappings of a modern state.

China. The Kuomintang under **Chiang Kai-shek** (1887-1975) subdued the warlords by 1928. The Communists were brutally suppressed after their alliance with the Kuomintang was broken in 1927. Relative peace thereafter allowed for industrial and financial improvements, with some Russian, British, and U.S. cooperation.

Arts. Nearly all bounds of subject matter, style, and attitude were broken in the arts of the period. **Abstract** art first took inspiration from natural forms or narrative themes (Kandinsky from 1911), then worked free of any representational aims (Malevich's suprematism, 1915-19, Mondrian's geometric style from 1917). The **Dada** movement from 1916 mocked artistic pretension with absurd collages and constructions (Arp, Tzara, from 1916). Paradox, illusion, and psychological taboos were exploited by **surrealists** by the latter 1920s (Dali, Magritte). Architectural schools celebrated industrial values, whether vigorous abstract constructivism (Tatlin, *Monument to 3rd International*, 1919) or the machined, streamlined **Bauhaus** style, which was extended to many design fields (Helvetica type face).

Prose writers explored revolutionary narrative modes related to dreams (Kafka's *Trial*, 1925), internal monologue (Joyce's *Ulysses*, 1922), and word play (Stein's *Making of Americans*, 1925). Poets and novelists wrote of modern alienation (Eliot's *Waste Land*, 1922) and aimlessness (Lost Generation).

Sciences. Scientific specialization prevailed by the 20th century. Advances in knowledge and technological aptitude increased with the geometric increase in the number of practitioners. Physicists challenged common-sense views of causality, observation, and a mechanistic universe, putting science further beyond popular grasp (Einstein's general theory of relativity, 1915; Bohr's quantum mechanics, 1913; Heisinger's uncertainty principle, 1927).

1928

India salt march
Stock market crash
Smoot-Hawley Tariff

Alfonso leaves Spain

Japan seizes Manchuria

Gandhi's fast

Hitler dictator
International Style

1933

FDR in office

Hitler takes Rhineland
Nuremberg Laws

Long March in China

Fr. Popular Front
Italy takes Ethiopia
Japan invades China
Civil War in Spain

1938

Rise of the Totalitarians: 1930-39

Depression. A worldwide financial panic and economic depression began with the Oct. 1929 U.S. stock market crash and the May 1931 failure of the Austrian Credit-Anstalt. A credit crunch caused international bankruptcies and **unemployment:** 12 million jobless by 1932 in the U.S., 5.6 million in Germany, 2.7 million in England. Governments responded with **tariff restrictions** (Smoot-Hawley Act 1930; Ottawa Imperial Conference, 1932) which dried up world trade. Government public works programs were vitiated by deflationary budget balancing.

Germany. Years of agitation by violent extremists was brought to a head by the Depression. Nazi leader **Hitler** was named chancellor by Pres. Hindenburg Jan. 1933, and given dictatorial power by the Reichstag in Mar. Opposition parties were disbanded, strikes banned, and all aspects of economic, cultural, and religious life brought under central government and Nazi party control and manipulated by sophisticated propaganda. Severe persecution of Jews began (**Nuremberg Laws** Sept. 1935). Many Jews, political opponents and others were sent to concentration camps (Dachau, 1933) where thousands died or were killed. Public works, renewed conscription (1935), arms production, and a 4-year plan (1936) ended unemployment.

Hitler's expansionism started with reincorporation of the Saar (1935), occupation of the **Rhineland** (Mar. 1936), and annexation of Austria (Mar. 1938). At **Munich**, Sept. 1938, an indecisive Britain and France sanctioned German dismemberment of Czechoslovakia.

Russia. Urbanization and education advanced. Rapid industrialization was achieved through successive **5-year-plans** starting 1928, using severe labor discipline and mass forced labor. Industry was financed by a decline in living standards and exploitation of agriculture, which was almost totally collectivized by the early 1930s (*kolkhoz*, collective farm; *sovkhoz*, state farm, often in newly-worked lands). Successive **purges** increased the role of professionals and management at the expense of workers. Millions perished in a series of man-made disasters: elimination of kulaks (peasant land-owners), 1929-34; severe famine, 1932-33; party purges (Great Purge, 1936-38); suppression of nationalities; and poor conditions in labor camps.

Spain. An industrial revolution during World War I created an urban proletariat, which was attracted to socialism and anarchism; Catalan nationalists challenged central authority. The 5 years after King Alfonso left Spain, Apr. 1931, were dominated by tension between intermittent leftist and anti-clerical governments and clericals, monarchists and other rightists. Anarchist and communist rebellions were crushed, but a July, 1936, extreme right rebellion led by Gen. Francisco Franco and aided by Nazi Germany and Fascist Italy succeeded, after a 3-year **civil war** (over 1 million dead in battles and atrocities). The war polarized international public opinion.

Italy. Despite propaganda for the ideal of the Corporate State, few domestic reforms were attempted. An entente with Hungary and Austria, Mar. 1934, a pact with Germany and Japan, Nov. 1937, and intervention by 50-75,000 troops in Spain, 1936-39, sealed Italy's identification with the fascist bloc (anti-Semitic laws after Mar. 1938). Ethiopia was conquered, 1935-37, and **Albania** annexed, Jan. 1939, in conscious imitation of ancient Rome.

East Europe. Repressive regimes fought for power against an active opposition (liberals, socialists, communists, peasants, Nazis). Minority groups and Jews were restricted within national boundaries that did not coincide with ethnic population patterns. In the destruction of **Czechoslovakia, Hungary** occupied southern Slovakia (Mar. 1938) and Ruthenia (Mar. 1939), and a pro-Nazi regime took power in the rest of Slovakia. Other boundary disputes (e.g. Poland-Lithuania, Yugoslavia-Bulgaria, Romania-Hungary) doomed attempts to build joint fronts against Germany or Russia. Economic depression was severe.

East Asia. After a period of liberalism in **Japan,** nativist militarists dominated the government with peasant support. Manchuria was seized, Sept. 1931-Feb. 1932, and a puppet state set up (Manchukuo). Adjacent Jehol (inner Mongolia) was occupied in 1933. China proper was invaded July 1937; large areas were conquered by Oct. 1938.

In **China** Communist forces left Kuomintang-besieged strongholds in the South in a Long March (1934-35) to the North. The Kuomintang-Communist civil war was suspended Jan. 1937 in the face of threatening Japan.

The democracies. The Roosevelt Administration, in office Mar. 1933, embarked on an extensive program of social reform and economic stimulation, including protection for labor unions (heavy industries organized), social security, public works, wages and hours laws, assistance to farmers. Isolationist sentiment (1937 Neutrality Act) prevented U.S. intervention in Europe, but military expenditures were increased in 1939.

French political instability and polarization prevented resolution of economic and international security questions. The **Popular Front** government under Blum (June 1936-Apr. 1938) passed social reforms (40-hour week) and raised arms spending. National coalition governments ruled Britain from Aug. 1931, brought some economic recovery, but failed to define a consistent foreign policy until Chamberlain's government (from May 1937), which practiced deliberate **appeasement** of Germany and Italy.

India. Twenty years of agitation for autonomy and then for independence (Gandhi's **salt march,** 1930) achieved some constitutional reform (extended provincial powers, 1935) despite Moslem-Hindu strife. Social issues assumed prominence with peasant uprisings (1921), strikes (1928), Gandhi's efforts for untouchables (1932 "fast unto death"), and social and agrarian reform by the provinces after 1937.

Arts. The streamlined, geometric design motifs of Art Deco (from 1925) prevailed through the 1930s. Abstract art flourished (Moore sculptures from 1931) alongside a new realism related to social and political concerns (**Socialist Realism** the official Soviet style from 1934; Mexican muralists Rivera, 1886-1957, and Orozco, 1883-1949), which was also expressed in fiction and poetry (Steinbeck's *Grapes of Wrath*, 1939; Sandburg's *The People, Yes*, 1936). Modern architecture (*International Style*, 1932) was unchallenged in its use of man-made materials (concrete, glass), lack of decoration, and monumentality (Rockefeller Center, 1929-40). U.S.-made films captured a world-wide audience with their larger-than-life fantasies (*Gone with the Wind*, 1939).

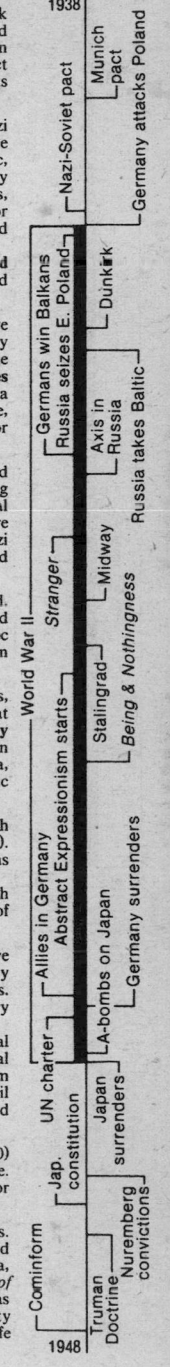

War, Hot and Cold: 1940-49

War in Europe. The Nazi-Soviet non-agression pact (Aug. '39) freed Germany to attack Poland (Sept.). Britain and France, who had guaranteed Polish independence, declared war on Germany. Russia seized East Poland (Sept.), attacked Finland (Nov.) and took the Baltic states (July '40). Mobile German forces staged "blitzkrieg" attacks Apr.-June, '40, conquering neutral Denmark, Norway, and the low countries and defeating France; 350,000 British and French troops were evacuated at **Dunkirk** (May). The Battle of Britain, June-Dec. '40, denied Germany air superiority, German-Italian campaigns won the Balkans by Apr. '41. Three million Axis troops **invaded Russia** June '41, marching through the Ukraine to the Caucasus, and through White Russia and the Baltic republics to Moscow and Leningrad.

Russian winter counterthrusts, '41-'42 and '42-'43 stopped the German advance (Stalingrad Sept. '42-Feb. '43). With British and U.S. Lend-Lease aid and sustaining great casualties, the Russians drove the Axis from all E. Europe and the Balkans in the next 2 years. Invasions of N. Africa (Nov. '42), Italy (Sept. '43), and Normandy (June '44) brought U.S., British, Free French and allied troops to Germany by spring '45. Germany surrendered May 7, 1945.

War in Asia-Pacific. Japan occupied Indochina Sept. '40, dominated Thailand Déc. '41, attacked Hawaii, the Philippines, Hong Kong, Malaya Dec. 7, 1941. Indonesia was attacked Jan. '42, Burma conquered Mar. 42. Battle of **Midway** (June '42) turned back the Japanese advance. "Island-hopping" battles (Guadalcanal Aug. '42-Jan. '43, Leyte Gulf Oct. '44, Iwo Jima Feb. Mar. '45, Okinawa Apr. '45) and massive bombing raids on Japan from June '44 wore out Japanese defenses. Two U.S. atom bombs, dropped Aug. 6 and 9, forced Japan to surrender Aug. 14, 1945. *For further details, see 1978 and earlier editions of The World Almanac.*

Atrocities. The war brought 20th-century cruelty to its peak. Nazi murder camps (Auschwitz) systematically killed 6 million Jews. Gypsies, political opponents, sick and retarded people, and others deemed undesirable were murdered by the Nazis, as were vast numbers of Slavs, especially leaders. German bombs killed 70,000 English civilians. Some 100,000 Chinese civilians were killed by Japanese forces in the capture of Nanking. Severe retaliation by the Soviet army, E. European partisans, Free French and others took a heavy toll. U.S. and British bombing of Germany killed hundreds of thousands, as did U.S. bombing of Japan (80-200,000 at Hiroshima alone). Some 45 million people lost their lives in the war.

Home front. All industries were reoriented to war production and support, and rationing was universal. Science was harnessed for the war effort, yielding such innovations as radar, jet planes, and synthetic materials. Unscathed U.S. industry, partly staffed by women, helped decide the war.

Settlement. The United Nations charter was signed in San Francisco June 26, 1945 by 50 nations. The International Tribunal at Nuremberg convicted 22 German leaders for war crimes Sept. '46, 23 Japanese leaders were convicted Nov. '48. Postwar border changes included large gains in territory for the USSR, losses for Germany, a shift westward in Polish borders, and minor losses for Italy. Communist regimes, supported by Soviet troops, took power in most of E. Europe, including Soviet-occupied Germany (GDR proclaimed Oct. '49). Japan lost all overseas lands.

Recovery. Basic political and social changes were imposed on Japan and W. Germany by the western allies (Japan constitution Nov. '46, W. German basic law May '49). U.S. Marshall Plan aid ($12 billion '47-'51) spurred W. European economic recovery after a period of severe inflation and strikes in Europe and the U.S. The British Labour Party introduced a national health service and nationalized basic industries in 1946.

Cold War. Western fears of further Soviet advances (Cominform formed Oct. '47, Czechoslovakia coup, Feb. '48, Berlin blockade Apr.'48-Sept. '49) led to formation of NATO. Civil War in Greece and Soviet pressure on Turkey led to U.S. aid under the Truman Doctrine (Mar. '47). Other anti-communist security pacts were the Org. of American States (Apr. '48) and Southeast Asia Treaty Org. (Sept. '54). A new wave of Soviet purges and repression intensified in the last years of Stalin's rule, extending to E. Europe (Slansky trial in Czechoslovakia, 1951). Only Yugoslavia resisted Soviet control (expelled by Cominform, June '48; U.S. aid, June '49).

China, Korea. Communist forces emerged from World War II strengthened by the Soviet takeover of industrial Manchuria. In 4 years of fighting, the Kuomintang was driven from the mainland; the People's Republic was proclaimed Oct. 1, 1949. Korea was divided by Russian and U.S. occupation forces. Separate republics were proclaimed in the 2 zones Aug.-Sept. '48.

India. India and Pakistan became independent dominions Aug. 15, 1947. Millions of Hindu and Moslem refugees were created by the partition; riots, 1946-47, took hundreds of thousands of lives; Gandhi himself was assassinated Jan. '48. Burma became completely independent Jan. '48; Ceylon took dominion status in Feb.

Middle East. The UN approved partition of Palestine into Jewish and Arab states. Israel was proclaimed May 14, 1948. Arabs rejected partition, but failed to defeat Israel in war, May '48-July '49. Immigration from Europe and the Middle East swelled Israel's Jewish population. British and French forces left Lebanon and Syria, 1946. Transjordan occupied most of Arab Palestine.

Southeast Asia. Communists and others fought against restoration of French rule in Indochina from 1946; a non-communist government was recognized by France Mar. '49, but fighting continued. Both Indonesia and the Philippines became independent, the former in 1949 after 4 years of war with Netherlands, the latter in 1946. Philippine economic and military ties with the U.S. remained strong; a communist-led peasant rising was checked in '48.

Arts. New York became the center of the world art market; abstract expressionism was the chief mode (Pollock from '43, de Kooning from '47). Literature and philosophy explored existentialism (Camus' *Stranger*, 1942, Sartre's *Being and Nothingness*, 1943). Non-western attempts to revive or create regional styles (Senghor's Negritude, Mishima's novels) only confirmed the emergence of a universal culture. Radio and phonograph records spread American popular music (swing, bebop) around the world.

Timeline (left margin, 1948–1958):

- 1948
- Israel indep.
- Gandhi killed
- Burma independent
- China People's Rep.
- Ger. Dem. Rep.
- Indonesia indep.
- Lonely Crowd
- Indochina War
- Egypt rev.
- Korean War
- H-bomb
- Stalin d.
- McCarthy censured
- Peron ousted
- Bandung conf.
- SEATO founded
- Suez War
- Hungary rev.
- On the Road
- Ghana indep.
- Sputnik
- EEC Treaty
- 1958

The American Decade: 1950-59

Polite decolonization. The peaceful decline of European political and military power in Asia and Africa accelerated in the 1950s. Nearly all of **N. Africa** was freed by 1956, but France fought a bitter war to retain Algeria, with its large European minority, until 1962. **Ghana**, independent 1957, led a parade of new black African nations (over 2 dozen by 1962) which altered the political character of the UN. Ethnic disputes often exploded in the new nations after decolonization (UN troops in Cyprus 1964; **Nigeria** civil war 1967-70). Leaders of the new states, mostly sharing socialist ideologies, tried to create an Afro-Asian bloc (Bandung Conf. 1955), but Western economic influence and U.S. political ties remained strong (Baghdad Pact, 1955).

Trade. World trade volume soared, in an atmosphere of monetary stability assured by international accords (**Bretton Woods** 1944). In Europe, economic integration advanced (**European Economic Community** 1957, European Free Trade Association 1960). Comecon (1949) coordinated the economies of Soviet-bloc countries.

U.S. Economic growth produced an abundance of consumer goods (9.3 million motor vehicles sold, 1955). Suburban housing tracts changed life patterns for middle and working classes (Levittown 1946-51). **Eisenhower's** landside election victories (1952, 1956) reflected consensus politics. Censure of McCarthy (Dec. '54) curbed the political abuse of anti-communism. A system of alliances and military bases bolstered U.S. influence on all continents. Trade and payments surpluses were balanced by overseas investments and foreign aid ($50 billion, 1950-59).

USSR. In the "thaw" after Stalin's death in 1953, relations with the West improved (evacuation of Vienna, Geneva summit conf., both 1955). Repression of scientific and cultural life eased, and many prisoners were freed or rehabilitated culminating in **de-Stalinization** (1956). Khrushchev's leadership aimed at consumer sector growth, but farm production lagged, despite the virgin lands program (from 1954). The 1956 Hungarian revolution, the 1960 U-2 spy plane episode, and other incidents renewed East-West tension and domestic curbs.

East Europe. Resentment of Russian domination and Stalinist repression combined with nationalist, economic and religious factors to produce periodic violence. East Berlin workers rioted in 1953, Polish workers rioted in Poznan, June 1956, and a broad-based revolution broke out in Hungary, Oct. 1956. All were suppressed by Soviet force or threats (at least 7,000 dead in Hungary). But Poland was allowed to restore private ownership of farms, and a degree of personal and economic freedom returned to Hungary. Yugoslavia experimented with worker self-management and a market economy.

Korea. The 1945 division of Korea left industry in the North, which was organized into a militant regime and armed by Russia. The South was politically disunited. Over 60,000 North Korean troops invaded the South June 25, 1950. The U.S., backed by the UN Security Council, sent troops. UN troops reached the Chinese border in Nov. Some 200,000 Chinese troops crossed the Yalu River and drove back UN forces. Cease-fire in July 1951 found the opposing forces near the original 38th parallel border. After 2 years of sporadic fighting, an armistice was signed July 27, 1953. U.S. troops remained in the South, and U.S. economic and military aid continued. The war stimulated rapid economic recovery in Japan. *For details, see 1978 and earlier editions of The World Almanac.*

China. Starting in 1952, industry, agriculture, and social institutions were forcibly collectivized. As many as several million people were executed as Kuomintang supporters or as class and political enemies. The Great Leap Forward, 1958-60, unsuccessfully tried to force the pace of development by substituting labor for investment.

Indochina. Ho's forces, aided by Russia and the new Chinese Communist government, fought French and pro-French Vietnamese forces to a standstill, and captured the strategic Dienbienphu camp in May, 1954. The Geneva Agreements divided Vietnam in half pending elections (never held), and recognized Laos and Cambodia as independent. The U.S. aided the anti-Communist Republic of Vietnam in the South.

Middle East. Arab revolutions placed leftist, militantly nationalist regimes in power in Egypt (1952) and Iraq (1958). But Arab unity attempts failed (United Arab Republic joined Egypt, Syria, Yemen 1958-61). Arab refusal to recognize Israel (Arab League economic blockade began Sept. 1951) led to a permanent state of war, with repeated incidents (Gaza, 1955). Israel occupied Sinai, Britain and France took the Suez Canal, Oct. 1956, but were replaced by the UN Emergency Force. The Mossadegh government in Iran nationalized the British-owned oil industry May 1951, but was overthrown in a U.S.-aided coup Aug. 1953.

Latin America. Dictator Juan Peron, in office 1946, enforced land reform, some nationalization, welfare state measures, and curbs on the Roman Catholic Church, but crushed opposition. A Sept. 1955 coup deposed Peron. The 1952 revolution in Bolivia brought land reform, nationalization of tin mines, and improvement in the status of Indians, who nevertheless remained poor. The Batista regime in Cuba was overthrown, Jan. 1959, by Fidel Castro, who imposed a communist dictatorship, aligned Cuba with Russia, improved education and health care. A U.S.-backed anti-Castro invasion (Bay of Pigs, Apr. 1961) was crushed. Self-government advanced in the British Caribbean.

Technology. Large outlays on research and development in the U.S. and USSR focussed on military applications (H-bomb in U.S. 1952, USSR 1953, Britain 1957, intercontinental missiles late 1950s). Soviet launching of the Sputnik satellite, Oct. 1957, spurred increases in U.S. science education funds (National Defense Education Act).

Literature and letters. Alienation from social and literary conventions reached an extreme in the theater of the absurd (Beckett's *Waiting for Godot* 1952), the "new novel" (Robbe-Grillet's *Voyeur* 1955), and avant-garde film (Antonioni's *L'Avventura* 1960). U.S. Beatniks (Kerouac's *On the Road* 1957) and others rejected the supposed conformism of Americans (Riesman's *Lonely Crowd* 1950).

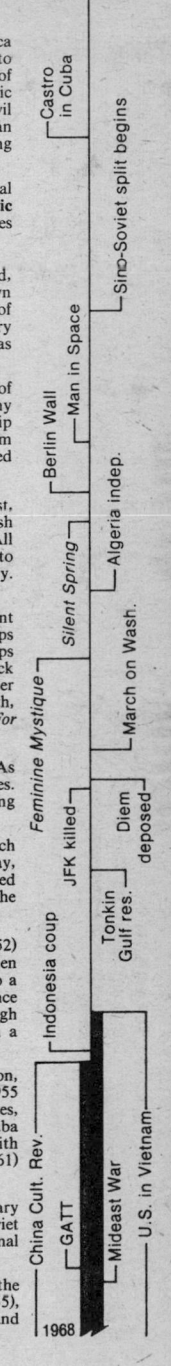

1958

Castro in Cuba

Sino-Soviet split begins

Berlin Wall

Man in Space

Algeria indep.

Silent Spring

March on Wash.

Feminine Mystique

JFK killed

Diem deposed

Indonesia coup

Tonkin Gulf res.

China Cult. Rev.

GATT

Mideast War

U.S. in Vietnam

1968

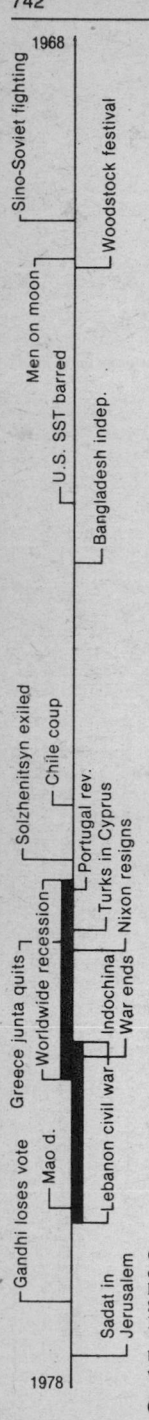

1968

Sino-Soviet fighting

Woodstock festival

Men on moon

U.S. SST barred

Bangladesh indep.

Solzhenitsyn exiled

Chile coup

Portugal rev.

Turks in Cyprus

Nixon resigns

Greece junta quits

Worldwide recession

Indochina War ends

Lebanon civil war

Mao d.

Gandhi loses vote

Sadat in Jerusalem

1978

Rising Expectations: 1960-69

Economic boom. The longest sustained economic boom on record spanned almost the entire decade in the capitalist world; the closely-watched GNP figure doubled in the U.S. 1960-70, fueled by Vietnam War-related budget deficits. The **General Agreement on Tariffs and Trade**, 1967, stimulated West European prosperity, which spread to peripheral areas (Spain, Italy, E. Germany). Japan became a top economic power ($20 billion exports 1970). Foreign investment aided the industrialization of Brazil. Soviet 1965 economic reform attempts (decentralization, material incentives) were limited; but growth continued.

Reform and radicalization. A series of political and social reform movements took root in the U.S., later spreading to other countries with the help of ubiquitous U.S. film and television programs and heavy overseas travel (2.2 million U.S. passports issued 1970). Blacks agitated peaceably and with partial success against segregation and poverty (1963 March on Washington, 1964 **Civil Rights Act**); but some urban ghettos erupted in extensive riots (Watts, 1965; Detroit, 1967; King assassination, Apr. 4, 1968). New concern for the poor (Harrington's *Other America*, 1963) led to Pres. Johnson's **"Great Society"** programs (Medicare, Water Quality Act, Higher Education Act, all 1965). Concern with the environment surged (Carson's *Silent Spring*, 1962). **Feminism** revived as a cultural and political movement (Friedan's *Feminine Mystique*, 1963, National Organization for Women founded 1966) and a movement for homosexual rights emerged (Stonewall riot, in NYC, 1969).

Opposition to U.S. involvement in Vietnam, especially among university students (**Moratorium** protest Nov. '69) turned violent (Weatherman Chicago riots Oct. '69). New Left and Marxist theories became popular, and membership in radical groups swelled (Students for a Democratic Society, Black Panthers). Maoist groups, especially in Europe, called for total transformation of society. In France, students sparked a nationwide strike affecting 10 million workers May-June '68, but an electoral reaction barred revolutionary change.

Arts and styles. The boundary between fine and popular arts were blurred by Pop Art (Warhol) and rock musicals (Hair, 1968). Informality and exaggeration prevailed in fashion (beards, miniskirts). A non-political "counterculture" developed, rejecting traditional bourgeois life goals and personal habits, and use of marijuana and hallucinogens spread (Woodstock festival Aug. '68). Indian influence was felt in music (Beatles), religion (Ram Dass), and fashion.

Science. Achievements in space (men on moon July '69) and electronics (lasers, integrated circuits) encouraged a faith in scientific solutions to problems in agriculture ("green revolution"), medicine (heart transplants 1967) and other areas. The harmful effects of science, it was believed, could be controlled (1963 nuclear weapon test ban treaty, 1968 non-proliferation treaty).

China. Mao's revolutionary militance caused disputes with Russia under "revisionist" Khrushchev, starting 1960. The two powers exchanged fire in 1969 border disputes. China used force to capture areas disputed with India, 1962. The "Great Proletarian Cultural Revolution" tried to impose a utopian egalitarian program in China and spread revolution abroad; political struggle, often violent, convulsed China 1965-68.

Indochina. Communist-led guerrillas aided by N. Vietnam fought from 1960 against the S. Vietnam government of Ngo Dinh Diem (killed 1963). The U.S. military role increased after the 1964 Tonkin Gulf incident. U.S. forces peaked at 543,400, Apr. '69. Massive numbers of N. Viet troops also fought. Laotian and Cambodian neutrality were threatened by communist insurgencies, with N. Vietnamese aid, and U.S. intrigues. *For details, see 1978 and earlier editions of The World Almanac.*

Third World. A bloc of authoritarian leftist regimes among the newly independent nations emerged in political opposition to the U.S.-led Western alliance, and came to dominate the conference of nonaligned nations (Belgrade 1961, Cairo 1964, Lusaka 1970). Soviet political ties and military bases were established in Cuba, Egypt, Algeria, Guinea, and other countries, whose leaders were regarded as revolutionary heros by opposition groups in pro-Western or colonial countries. Some leaders were ousted in coups by pro-Western groups—Zaire's Lumumba (killed 1961), Ghana's Nkrumah (exiled 1966), and Indonesia's Sukarno (effectively ousted 1965 after a Communist coup failed).

Middle East. Arab-Israeli tension erupted into a brief war June 1967. Israel emerged as a major regional power. Military shipments before and after the war brought much of the Arab world into the Soviet political sphere. Most Arab states broke U.S. diplomatic ties, while Communist countries cut their ties to Israel. Intra-Arab disputes continued: Egypt and Saudi Arabia supported rival factions in a bloody Yemen civil war 1962-70; Lebanese troops fought Palestinian commandos in 1969.

East Europe. To stop the large-scale exodus of citizens, E. German authorities built a fortified wall across Berlin Aug. '61. Soviet sway in the Balkans was weakened by Albania's defiance of China (USSR broke ties Dec. '61) and Romania's assertion of industrial and foreign policy autonomy in 1964. Liberalization in Czechoslovakia, spring 1968, was crushed by troops of 5 Warsaw Pact countries. West German treaties with Russia and Poland, 1970, facilitated the transfer of German technology and confirmed post-war boundaries.

Disillusionment: 1970-79

U.S.: Caution and neoconservatism. A relatively sluggish economy, energy and resource shortages (natural gas crunch 1975, gasoline shortage 1979), and environmental problems contributed to a "**limits of growth**" philosophy that affected politics (Cal. Gov. Brown). Suspicion of science and technology killed or delayed major projects (supersonic transport dropped 1971, DNA recombination curbed 1976, Seabrook A-plant protests 1977-78) and was fed by the Three Mile Island nuclear reactor accident in Mar. '79.

Mistrust of big government weakened support for government reform plans among liberals. School busing and racial quotas were opposed (**Bakke decision** June '78); the Equal Rights Amendment for women languished; civil rights for homosexuals were opposed (Dade County referendum June '77).

U.S. defeat in **Indochina** (evacuation Apr. '75), revelations of Central Intelligence Agency misdeeds (Rockefeller Commission report June '75), and the **Watergate** scandals (Nixon quit Aug. '74) reduced faith in U.S. moral and material capacity to influence world affairs. Revelations of Soviet crimes (Solzhenitsyn's *Gulag Archipelago* from 1974) and Russian intervention in Africa aided a revival of anti-Communist sentiment.

Economy sluggish. The 1960s boom faltered in the 1970s; a severe recession in the U.S. and Europe 1974-75 followed a huge oil price hike Dec. '73. Monetary instability (U.S. cut ties to gold Aug. '71), the decline of the dollar, and **protectionist** moves by industrial countries (1977-78) threatened trade. Business investment and spending for research declined. Severe inflation plagued many countries (25% in Britain, 1975; 18% in U.S., 1979).

China picks up pieces. After the 1976 deaths of Mao and Chou, a power struggle for the leadership succession was won by pragmatists. A nationwide purge of orthodox Maoists was carried out, and the. "**Gang of Four**", led by Mao's widow Chiang Ching, was arrested.

The new leaders freed over 100,000 political prisoners, and reduced public adulation of Mao. Political and trade ties were expanded with Japan, Europe, and the U.S. in the late 1970's, as relations worsened with Russia, Cuba, and Vietnam (4-week invasion by China in 1979). Ideological guidelines in industry, science, education, and the armed forces, which the ruling faction said had caused chaos and decline, were reversed (bonuses to workers, Dec. '77; exams for college entrance, Oct. '77). Severe restrictions on cultural expression were eased (Beethoven ban lifted Mar. '77)

Europe. European unity moves (EEC-EFTA trade accord 1972) faltered as economic problems appeared (Britain floated pound 1972; France floated franc 1974). Germany and Switzerland curbed guest workers from S. Europe. Greece and Turkey quarreled over Cyprus (Turks intervened 1974) and Aegean oil rights.

All of non-Communist Europe was under democratic rule after free elections were held in **Spain** June '76, 7 months after the death of Franco. The conservative, colonialist regime in **Portugal** was overthrown Apr. '74. In **Greece**, the 7-year-old military dictatorship yielded power in 1974. Northern Europe, though ruled mostly by Socialists (**Swedish** Socialists unseated 1976, after 44 years in power), turned conservative. The **British** Labour government imposed wage curbs 1975, and suspended nationalization schemes. Terrorism in **Germany** (1972 Munich Olympics killings) led to laws curbing some civil liberties. **French** "new philosophers" rejected leftist ideologies, and the shaky Socialist-Communist coalition lost a 1978 election bid.

Religion back in politics. The improvement in Moslem countries' political fortunes by the 1950s (with the exception of Central Asia under Soviet and Chinese rule), and the growth of Arab oil wealth, was followed by a resurgence of traditional piety. **Libyan** dictator Qaddafi mixed strict Islamic laws with socialism in his militant ideology and called for an eventual Moslem return to Spain and Sicily. The illegal Moslem Brotherhood in **Egypt** was accused of violence, while extreme Moslem groups bombed theaters, 1977, to protest secular values.

In **Turkey**, the National Salvation Party was the first Islamic group to share power (1974) since secularization in the 1920s. Religious authorities, such as Ayatollah Ruholla Khomeini, led the **Iranian** revolution and religiously motivated Moslems took part in the insurrection in Saudi Arabia that briefly seized the Grand Mosque in Mecca in 1979. Moslem puritan opposition to **Pakistan** Pres. Bhutto helped lead to his overthrow July '77. However, Moslem solidarity could not prevent Pakistan's eastern province (**Bangladesh**) from declaring independence, Dec. '71, after a bloody civil war.

Moslem and Hindu resentment against coerced sterilization in **India** helped defeat the Gandhi government, which was replaced Mar. '77 by a coalition including religious Hindu parties and led by devout Hindu Desai. Moslems in the southern **Philippines**, aided by Libya, conducted a long rebellion against central rule from 1973.

Evangelical Protestant groups grew in numbers and prosperity in the U.S. ("**born again**" Pres. Carter elected 1976), and the Catholic charismatic movement obtained respectability. A revival of interest in Orthodox Christianity occurred among **Russian** intellectuals (Solzhenitsyn). The secularist **Israeli** Labor party, after decades of rule, was ousted in 1977 by conservatives led by Begin, an observant Jew; religious militants founded settlements on the disputed West Bank, part of Biblically-promised Israel. U.S. Reform Judaism revived many previously discarded traditional practices.

The Buddhist Soka Gakkai movement launched the Komeito party in Japan, 1964, which became a major opposition party in 1972 and 1976 elections.

Old-fashioned religious wars raged intermittently in **N. Ireland** (Catholic vs. Protestant, 1969-   ) and **Lebanon** (Christian vs. Moslem, 1975-   ), while religious militancy complicated the Israel-Arab dispute (1973 Israel-Arab war. In spite of a **1979 peace treaty between Egypt and Israel** which looked forward to a resolution of the Palestinian issue, increased religious militancy on the West Bank made such a resolution seem unlikely.

Latin America. Repressive conservative regimes strengthened their hold on most of the continent, with the violent coup against the elected Allende government in **Chile**, Sept. '73, the 1976 military coup in **Argentina**, and coups against reformist regimes in **Bolivia**, 1971 and 1979, and **Peru**, 1976. In Central America, increasing liberal and leftist militancy led to the ouster of the Somoza regime of Nicaragua in 1979 and civil conflict in El Salvador.

Indochina. Communist victory in Vietnam, Cambodia, and Laos by May '75 did not bring peace. Attempts at radical social reorganization left over one million dead in Cambodia during 1975-78 and caused hundreds of thousands of ethnic Chinese and others to flee Vietnam ("boat people," 1979). The Vietnamese invasion of Cambodia swelled the refugee population and contributed to widespread starvation in that devastated country.

Russian expansion. Soviet influence, checked in some countries (troops ousted by Egypt 1972) was projected further afield, often with the use of Cuban troops (Angola 1975-   , Ethiopia 1977-   ), and aided by a growing navy, merchant fleet, and international banking ability. Detente with the West — 1972 Berlin pact, 1970 strategic arms pact (**SALT**) — gave way to a more antagonistic relationship in the late 1970s, exacerbated by the Soviet invasion of Afghanistan in 1979.

Africa. The last remaining European colonies were granted independence (**Spanish Sahara** 1976, **Djibouti** 1977) and, after 10 years of civil war and many negotiation sessions, a black government took over Zimbabwe (Rhodesia) in 1979; white domination remained in **S. Africa**. Great power involvement in local wars (Russia in **Angola, Ethiopia**; France in **Chad, Zaire, Mauritania**) and the use of tens of thousands of Cuban troops was denounced by some African leaders as neocolonialism. Ethnic or tribal clashes made Africa the chief world locus of sustained warfare in the late 1970s.

Arts. Traditional modes in painting, architecture, and music, pursued in relative obscurity for much of the 20th century, returned to popular and critical attention in the 1970s. The pictorial emphasis in neorealist and photorealist painting, the return of many architects to detail, decoration, and traditional natural materials, and the concern with ordered structure in musical composition were, ironically, novel experiences for artistic consumers after the exhaustion of experimental possibilities. However, these more conservative styles coexisted with modernist works in an atmosphere of variety and tolerance.

Some Notable Marine Disasters Since 1850
(Figures indicate estimated lives lost)

1854, Mar.—City of Glasgow; British steamer missing in North Atlantic; 480.

1854, Sept. 27—Arctic; U.S. (Collins Line) steamer sunk in collision with French steamer Vesta near Cape Race; 285-351.

1856, Jan. 23—Pacific; U.S. (Collins Line) steamer missing in North Atlantic; 186-286.

1858, Sept. 23—Austria; German steamer destroyed by fire in North Atlantic; 471.

1860, Feb. 19—Hungarian; British steamer wrecked at Cape Sable; 237.

1863, Apr. 27—Anglo-Saxon; British steamer wrecked at Cape Race; 238.

1865, Apr. 27—Sultana; a Mississippi River steamer blew up near Memphis, Tenn; 1,400.

1869, Oct. 27—Stonewall; steamer burned on Mississippi River below Cairo, Ill.; 200.

1870, Jan. 25—City of Boston; British (Inman Line) steamer vanished between New York and Liverpool; 177.

1870, Oct 19—Cambria; British steamer wrecked off northern Ireland; 196.

1872, Nov. 7—Mary Celeste; U.S. half-brig sailed from New York for Genoa; found abandoned in Atlantic 4 weeks later in mystery of sea; crew never heard from; loss of life unknown.

1873, Jan. 22—Northfleet; British steamer foundered off Dungeness, England; 300.

1873, Apr. 1—Atlantic; British (White Star) steamer wrecked off Nova Scotia; 585.

1873, Nov. 23—Ville du Havre; French steamer, sunk after collision with British sailing ship Loch Earn; 226.

1875, May 7—Schiller; German steamer wrecked off Scilly Isles; 312.

1875, Nov. 4—Pacific; U.S. steamer sunk after collision off Cape Flattery; 236.

1878, Sept. 3—Princess Alice; British steamer sank after collision in Thames; 700.

1878, Dec. 18—Byzantin; French steamer sank after Dardanelles collision; 210.

1881, May 24—Victoria; steamer capsized in Thames River, Canada; 200.

1883, Jan. 19—Cimbria; German steamer sunk in collision with British steamer Sultan in North Sea; 389.

1887, Nov. 15—Wah Yeung; British steamer burned at sea; 400.

1890, Feb. 17—Duburg; British steamer wrecked, China Sea; 400.

1890, Sept. 19—Ertogrul; Turkish frigate foundered off Japan; 540.

1891, Mar. 17—Utopia; British steamer sank in collision with British ironclad Anson off Gibraltar; 562.

1895, Jan. 30—Elbe; German steamer sank in collision with British steamer Craithie in North Sea; 332.

1895, Mar. 11—Reina Regenta; Spanish cruiser foundered near Gibraltar; 400.

1898, Feb. 15—Maine; U.S. battleship blown up in Havana Harbor; 266.

1898, July 4—La Bourgogne; French steamer sunk in collision with British sailing ship Cromartyshire off Nova Scotia; 549.

1904, June 15—General Slocum; excursion steamer burned in East River, New York City; 1,030.

1904, June 28—Norge; Danish steamer wrecked on Rockall Island, Scotland; 620.

1906, Aug. 4—Sirio; Italian steamer wrecked off Cape Palos, Spain; 350.

1908, Mar. 23—Matsu Maru; Japanese steamer sank in collision near Hakodate, Japan; 300.

1909, Aug. 1—Waratah; British steamer, Sydney to London, vanished; 300.

1910, Feb. 9—General Chanzy; French steamer wrecked off Minorca, Spain; 200.

1911, Sept. 25—Liberté; French battleship exploded at Toulon; 285.

1912, Apr. 14-15—Titanic; British (White Star) steamer hit iceberg in North Atlantic; 1,503.

1912, Sept. 28—Kichemaru; Japanese steamer sank off Japanese coast; 1,000.

1914, May 29—Empress of Ireland; British (Canadian Pacific) steamer sunk in collision with Norwegian collier in St. Lawrence River; 1,014.

1915, May 7—Lusitania; British (Cunard Line) steamer torpedoed and sunk by German submarine U. 20 off Ireland; 1,198.

1915, July 24—Eastland; excursion steamer capsized in Chicago River; 812.

1916, Feb. 26—Provence; French cruiser sank in Mediterranean; 3,100.

1916, Mar. 3—Principe de Asturias; Spanish steamer wrecked near Santos, Brazil; 558.

1916, Aug. 29—Hsin Yu; Chinese steamer sank off Chinese coast; 1,000.

1917, Dec. 6—Mont Blanc, Imo; French ammunition ship and Belgian steamer collided in Halifax Harbor; 1,600.

1918, Apr. 25—Kiang-Kwan Chinese steamer sank in collision off Hankow; 500.

1918, July 12—Kawachi; Japanese battleship blew up in Tokayama Bay; 500.

1918, Oct. 25—Princess Sophia; Canadian steamer sank off Alaskan coast; 398.

1919, Jan. 17—Chaonia; French steamer lost in Straits of Messina, Italy; 460.

1919, Sept. 9—Valbanera; Spanish steamer lost off Florida coast; 500.

1921, Mar. 18—Hong Kong; steamer wrecked in South China Sea; 1,000.

1922, Aug. 26—Niitaka; Japanese cruiser sank in storm off Kamchatka, USSR; 300.

1927, Oct. 25—Principessa Mafalda; Italian steamer blew up, sank off Porto Seguro, Brazil; 314.

1934, Sept. 8—Morro Castle; U.S. steamer, Havana to New York, burned off Asbury Park, N.J.; 125.

1939, May 23—Squalus; U.S. submarine sank off Portsmouth, N.H.; 26.

1939, June 1—Thetis; British submarine, sank in Liverpool Bay; 99.

1942, Feb. 18—Truxton and Pollux; U.S. destroyer and cargo ship ran aground, sank off Newfoundland; 204.

1942, Oct. 2—Curacao; British cruiser sank after collision with liner Queen Mary; 335.

1947, Jan. 19—Himera; Greek steamer hit a mine off Athens; 392.

1947, Apr. 16—Grandcamp; French freighter exploded in Texas City, Tex., Harbor, starting fires; 510.

1952, Apr. 26—Hobson and Wasp; U.S. destroyer and aircraft carrier collided in Atlantic; 176.

1953, Jan. 31—Princess Victoria; British ferry foundered off northern Irish coast; 134.

1954, Sept. 26—Toya Maru; Japanese ferry sank in Tsugaru Strait, Japan; 1,172.

1956, July 26—Andrea Doria and Stockholm; Italian liner and Swedish liner collided off Nantucket; 51.

1957, July 14—Eshghabad; Soviet ship ran aground in Caspian Sea; 270.

1961, Apr. 8—Dara; British liner burned in Persian Gulf; 212.

1961, July 8—Save; Portuguese ship ran aground off Mozambique; 259.

1963, Apr. 10—Thresher; U.S. Navy atomic submarine sank in North Atlantic; 129.

1964, Feb. 10—Voyager, Melbourne; Australian destroyer sank after collision with Australian aircraft carrier Melbourne off New South Wales; 82.

1968, Jan. 25—Dakar; Israeli submarine vanished in Mediterranean; 69.

1968, Jan. 27—Minerve; French submarine vanished in Mediterranean; 52.

1968, May 21—Scorpion; U.S. nuclear submarine sank in Atlantic near Azores; 99.

1969, June 2—Evans; U.S. destroyer cut in half by Australian carrier Melbourne, S. China Sea; 74.

1970, Mar. 4—Eurydice; French submarine sank in Mediterranean near Toulon; 57.

1970, Dec. 15—Namyong-Ho; South Korean ferry sank in Korea Strait; 308.

1974, May 1— Motor launch capsized off Bangladesh; 250.

1974, Sept. 26— Soviet destroyer burned and sank in Black Sea; est. 200.

1975, Aug. 9— Two Chinese riverboats collided and sank near Canton; c.500.

1976, Oct. 20—George Prince and Frosta; ferryboat and Norwegian tanker collided on Mississippi R. at Luling, La.; 77.

1976, Dec. 25—Patria; Egyptian liner caught fire and sank in the Red Sea; c. 100.

1977, Jan. 11—Grand Zenith; Panamanian-registered tanker sank off Cape Cod, Mass.; 38.

1977, Jan. 17—Spanish freighter collided with launch in Barcelona, Spain harbor; 46.

1979, Jan. 8—Betelgeuse; French oil tanker exploded in Bantry Bay, Ire.; 50.

1979, Aug. 14—23 yachts competing in Fastnet yacht race sunk or abandoned during storm in S. Irish Sea; 18.

1980, Jan. 28—Blackthorn; U.S. Coast Guard vessel sunk in collision with oil tanker in Tampa Bay; 23.

1981, Jan. 27—Tamponas II; Indonesian passenger ship caught fire and sank in Java Sea; 580.

Major Earthquakes

Magnitude of earthquakes (Mag.), distinct from deaths or damage caused, is measured on the Richter scale, on which each higher number represents a tenfold increase in energy measured in ground motion. Adopted in 1935, the scale has been applied in the following table to earthquakes as far back as reliable seismograms are available.

Date	Place	Deaths	Mag.	Date	Place	Deaths	Mag.
526 May 20	Syria, Antioch	250,000	N.A.	1950 Aug. 15	India, Assam	1,530	8.7
856	Greece, Corinth	45,000	"	1953 Mar. 18	NW Turkey	1,200	7.2
1057	China, Chihli	25,000	"	1956 June 10-17	N. Afghanistan	2,000	7.7
1268	Asia Minor, Cilicia	60,000	"	1957 July 2	Northern Iran	2,500	7.4
1290 Sept. 27	China, Chihli	100,000	"	1957 Dec. 13	Western Iran	2,000	7.1
1293 May 20	Japan, Kamakura	30,000	"	1960 Feb. 29	Morocco, Agadir	12,000	5.8
1531 Jan. 26	Portugal, Lisbon	30,000	"	1960 May 21-30	Southern Chile	5,000	8.3
1556 Jan. 24	China, Shaanxi	830,000	"	1962 Sept. 1	Northwestern Iran	12,230	7.1
1667 Nov.	Caucasia, Shemaka	80,000	"	1963 July 26	Yugoslavia, Skopje	1,100	6.0
1693 Jan. 11	Italy, Catania	60,000	"	1964 Mar. 27	Alaska	114	8.5
1730 Dec. 30	Japan, Hokkaido	137,000	"	1966 Aug. 19	Eastern Turkey	2,520	6.0
1737 Oct. 11	India, Calcutta	300,000	"	1968 Aug. 31	Northeastern Iran	12,000	7.4
1755 June 7	Northern Persia	40,000	"	1970 Mar. 28	Western Turkey	1,086	7.4
1755 Nov. 1	Portugal, Lisbon	60,000	8.75*	1970 May 31	Northern Peru	66,794	7.7
1783 Feb. 4	Italy, Calabria	30,000	N.A.	1971 Feb. 9	Cal., San Fernando Valley	65	6.5
1797 Feb. 4	Ecuador, Quito	41,000	N.A.				
1822 Sept. 5	Asia Minor, Aleppo	22,000	N.A.	1972 Apr. 10	Southern Iran	5,057	6.9
1828 Dec. 28	Japan, Echigo	30,000	"	1972 Dec. 23	Nicaragua	5,000	6.2
1868 Aug. 13-15	Peru and Ecuador	40,000	"	1974 Dec. 28	Pakistan (9 towns)	5,200	6.3
1875 May 16	Venezuela, Colombia	16,000	"	1975 Sept. 6	Turkey (Lice, etc.)	2,312	6.8
1896 June 15	Japan, sea wave	27,120	"	1976 Feb. 4	Guatemala	22,778	7.5
1906 Apr. 18-19	Cal., San Francisco	452	8.3	1976 May 6	Northeast Italy	946	6.5
1906 Aug. 16	Chile, Valparaiso	20,000	8.6	1976 June 26	New Guinea, Irian Jaya	443	7.1
1908 Dec. 28	Italy, Messina	83,000	7.5	1976 July 28	China, Tangshan	800,000	8.2
1915 Jan. 13	Italy, Avezzano	29,980	7.5	1976 Aug. 17	Philippines, Mindanao	8,000	7.8
1920 Dec. 16	China, Gansu	100,000	8.6	1976 Nov. 24	Eastern Turkey	4,000	7.9
1923 Sept. 1	Japan, Tokyo	99,330	8.3	1977 Mar. 4	Romania, Bucharest, etc.	1,541	7.5
1927 May 22	China, Nan-Shan	200,000	8.3	1977 Aug. 19	Indonesia	200	8.0
1932 Dec. 26	China, Gansu	70,000	7.6	1977 Nov. 23	Northwestern Argentina	100	8.2
1933 Mar. 2	Japan	2,990	8.9	1978 June 12	Japan, Sendai	21	7.5
1934 Jan. 15	India, Bihar-Nepal	10,700	8.4	1978 Sept. 16	Northeast Iran	25,000	7.7
1935 May 31	India, Quetta	30,000	7.5	1979 Sept. 12	Indonesia	100	8.1
1939 Jan. 24	Chile, Chillan	28,000	8.3	1979 Dec. 12	Colombia, Equador	800	7.9
1939 Dec. 26	Turkey, Erzincan	30,000	7.9	1980 Oct. 10	Northwestern Algeria	4,500	7.5
1946 Dec. 21	Japan, Honshu	2,000	8.4	1980 Nov. 23	Southern Italy	4,800	7.2
1948 June 28	Japan, Fukui	5,131	7.3				
1949 Aug. 5	Ecuador, Pelileo	6,000	6.8				

(*) estimated from earthquake intensity. (N.A.) not available.

Floods, Tidal Waves

Date	Location	Deaths	Date	Location	Deaths
1887	Huang He River, China	900,000	1967 Jan. 18-24	Eastern Brazil	894
1889 May 31	Johnstown, Pa.	2,200	1967 Mar. 19	Rio de Janeiro, Brazil	436
1900 Sept. 8	Galveston, Tex.	5,000	1968 Aug. 7-14	Gujarat State, India	1,000
1903 June 15	Heppner, Ore.	325	1968 Oct. 7	Northeastern India	780
1911	Chang Jiang River, China	100,000	1969 Mar. 17	Mundau Valley, Alagoas, Brazil	218
1913 Mar. 25-27	Ohio, Indiana	732	1969 Aug. 25	Western Virginia	189
1915 Aug. 17	Galveston, Tex.	275	1969 Sept. 15	South Korea	250
1928 Mar. 13	Collapse of St. Francis Dam, Santa Paula, Cal.	450	1969 Oct. 1-8	Tunisia	500
1928 Sept. 13	Lake Okeechobee, Fla.	2,000	1970 May 20	Central Romania	160
1931 Aug.	Huang He River, China	3,700,000	1970 July 22	Himalayas, India	500
1937 Jan. 22	Ohio, Miss. Valleys	250	1971 Feb. 26	Rio de Janeiro, Brazil	130
1939	Northern China	200,000	1972 Feb. 26	Buffalo Creek, W. Va.	118
1947	Honshu Island, Japan	1,900	1972 June 9	Rapid City, S.D.	236
1951 Aug.	Manchuria	1,800	1972 Aug. 7	Luzon Is., Philippines	454
1953 Jan. 31	Western Europe	2,000	1974 Mar. 29	Tubaro, Brazil	1,000
1954 Aug. 17	Farahzad, Iran	2,000	1974 Aug. 12	Monty-Long, Bangladesh	2,500
1955 Oct. 7-12	India, Pakistan	1,700	1975 Jan. 11	Southern Thailand	131
1959 Nov. 1	Western Mexico	2,000	1976 June 5	Teton Dam collapse, Ida.	11
1959 Dec. 2	Frejus, France	412	1976 July 31	Big Thompson Canyon, Col.	130
1960 Oct. 10	Bangladesh	6,000	1976 Nov. 17	East Java, Indonesia	136
1960 Oct. 31	Bangladesh	4,000	1977 July 19-20	Johnstown, Pa.	68
1962 Feb. 17	German North Sea coast	343	1978 June-Sept.	Northern India	1,200
1962 Sept. 27	Barcelona, Spain	445	1979 Jan.-Feb.	Brazil	204
1963 Oct. 9	Dam collapse, Vaiont, Italy	1,800	1979 July	Lomblem Is., Indonesia	539
1966 Nov. 4-6	Florence, Venice, Italy	113	1979 Aug. 11	Morvi, India	5,000-15,000
			1980 Feb. 13-22	So. Cal., Ariz.	26

Some Major Tornadoes Since 1925

Source: National Climatic Center, NOAA, U.S. Commerce Department

Date	Place	Deaths	Date	Place	Deaths
1925 Mar. 18	Mo., Ill. Ind.	689	1927 May 9	Arkansas, Poplar Bluff, Mo.	92
1926 Nov. 25	Belleville to Portland, Ark.	53	1927 Sept. 29	St. Louis, Mo.	72
1927 Apr. 12	Rock Springs, Tex.	74	1929 Apr. 25	SE-Central Ga.	40

Date			Place	Deaths	Date			Place	Deaths
1930	May	6	Hill & Ellis Co., Tex.	41	1957	May	20	Kan., Mo.	48
1932	Mar.	21	Ala. (series of tornadoes)	268	1958	June	4	Northwestern Wisconsin	30
1936	Apr.	5	Tupelo, Miss.	216	1959	Feb.	10	St. Louis, Mo.	21
1936	Apr.	6	Gainesville, Ga.	203	1960	May	5, 6	SE Oklahoma, Arkansas	30
1938	Sept.	29	Charleston, S.C.	32	1965	Apr.	11	Ind., Ill., Oh., Mich., Wis.	271
1942	Mar.	16	Central to NE Miss.	75	1966	Mar.	3	Jackson, Miss.	57
1942	Apr.	27	Rogers & Mayes Co., Okla.	52	1966	Mar.	3	Mississippi, Alabama	61
1944	June	23	Oh., Pa., W. Va., Md.	150	1967	Apr.	21	Illinois	33
1945	Apr.	12	Okla.-Ark.	102	1968	May	15	Arkansas	34
1947	Apr.	9	Tex., Okla. & Kan.	169	1969	Jan.	23	Mississippi	32
1948	Mar.	19	Bunker Hill & Gillespie, Ill.	33	1971	Feb.	21	Mississippi delta	110
1949	Jan.	3	La. & Ark.	58	1973	May	26-7	South, Midwest (series)	47
1952	Mar.	21	Ark., Mo., Tenn. (series)	208	1974	Apr.	3-4	Ala., Ga., Tenn., Ky., Oh.	350
1953	May	11	Waco, Tex.	114	1977	Apr.	1	Southeast Bangladesh	600
1953	June	8	Flint to Lakeport, Mich.	116	1977	Apr.	4	Ala., Miss., Ga.	22
1953	June	9	Worcester and vicinity, Mass.	90	1978	Apr.	16	Orissa, India	500
1953	Dec.	5	Vicksburg, Miss.	38	1979	Apr.	10	Tex., Okla.	60
1955	May	25	Udall, Kan.	80	1980	June	3	Grand Island, Neb. (series)	4

Hurricanes, Typhoons, Blizzards, Other Storms

Names of hurricanes and typhoons in italics—H.—hurricane; T.—typhoon

Date	Location	Deaths	Date	Location	Deaths
1888 Mar. 11-14	Blizzard, Eastern U.S.	400	1965 June 1-2	Windstorm, Bangladesh	30,000
1900 Sept. 8	H., Galveston, Tex.	6,000	1965 Sept. 7-10	H.*Betsy*, Fla., Miss., La.	74
1926 Sept. 16-22	H., Fla., Ala.	372	1965 Dec. 15	Windstorm, Bangladesh	10,000
1926 Oct. 20	H., Cuba	600	1966 June 4-10	H.*Alma*, Honduras, SE U.S.	51
1928 Sept. 12-17	H., W. Indies, Fla.	4,000	1966 Sept. 24-30	H.*Inez*, Carib., Fla., Mex.	293
1930 Sept. 3	H., San Domingo	2,000	1967 July 9	T.*Billie*, Japan	347
1938 Sept. 21	H., New England	600	1967 Sept. 5-23	H.*Beulah*, Carib., Mex., Tex.	54
1942 Oct. 15-16	H., Bengal, India	11,000	1967 Dec. 12-20	Blizzard, Southwest, U.S.	51
1944 Sept. 12-16	H., N.C. to New Eng.	389	1968 Nov. 18-28	T.*Nina*, Philippines	63
1953 Sept. 25-27	T., Vietnam, Japan	1,300	1969 Aug. 17-18	H.*Camille*, Miss., La.	256
1954 Aug. 30	H.*Carol*, Northeast U.S.	68	1970 July 30-		
1954 Oct. 12-13	H.*Hazel*, Eastern, U.S., Haiti	347	Aug. 5	H.*Celia*, Cuba, Fla., Tex.	31
1955 Aug. 12-13	H.*Connie*, Carolinas, Va., Md.	43	1970 Aug. 20-21	H.*Dorothy*, Martinique	42
1955 Aug. 18-19	H.*Diane*, Eastern U.S.	400	1970 Sept. 15	T.*Georgia*, Philippines	300
1955 Sept. 19	H.*Hilda*, Mexico	200	1970 Oct. 14	T.*Sening*, Philippines	583
1955 Sept. 22-28	H.*Janet*, Caribbean	500	1970 Oct. 15	T.*Titang*, Philippines	526
1956 Feb. 1-29	Blizzard, Western Europe	1,000	1970 Nov. 13	Cyclone, Bangladesh	300,000
1957 June 27-30	H.*Audrey*, La., Tex.	430			(est.)
1958 Feb. 15-16	Blizzard, NE U.S.	171	1971 Aug. 1	T.*Rose*, Hong Kong	130
1959 Sept. 17-19	T.*Sarah*, Far East.	2,000	1972 June 19-29	H.*Agnes*, Fla. to N.Y.	118
1959 Sept. 26-27	T.*Vera*, Honshu, Japan.	4,466	1972 Dec. 3	T.*Theresa*, Philippines	169
1960 Sept. 4-12	H.*Donna*, Caribbean, E. U.S.	148	1973 June-Aug.	Monsoon rains in India	1,217
1961 Oct. 31	H.*Hattie*, Br. Honduras	400	1974 June 11	Storm*Dinah*, Luzon Is., Philip.	71
1962 Feb. 17	Flooding, German Coast.	343	1974 July 11	T.*Gilda*, Japan, S. Korea.	108
1962 Sept. 27	Flooding, Barcelona, Spain	445	1974 Sept. 19-20	H.*Fifi*, Honduras	2,000
1963 May 28-29	Windstorm, Bangladesh	22,000	1974 Dec. 25	Cyclone leveled Darwin, Aus.	50
1963 Oct. 4-8	H.*Flora*, Cuba, Haiti	6,000	1975 Sept. 13-27	H.*Eloise*, Caribbean, NE U.S.	71
1964 Oct. 4-7	H.*Hilda*, La., Miss., Ga.	38	1976 May 20	T.*Olga*, floods, Philippines	215
1964 June 30	T.*Winnie*, N. Philippines	107	1977 July 25, 31	T.*Thelma*, T.*Vera*, Taiwan	39
1964 Sept. 5	T.*Ruby*, Hong Kong and China	735	1978 Oct. 27	T.*Rita*, Philippines	c. 400
1964 Sept. 14	Flooding, central S. Korea.	563	1979 Aug. 30-		
1964 Nov. 12	Flooding, S. Vietnam	7,000	Sept. 7	H.*David*, Caribbean, E U.S.	1,100
1965 May 11-12	Windstorm, Bangladesh	17,000	1980 Aug. 4-11	H.*Allen*, Caribbean, Texas.	272

Record Oil Spills

Name, place	Date	Cause	Tons
Ixtoc I oil well, southern Gulf of Mexico	June 3, 1979	Blowout	600,000
Atlantic Empress & Aegean Captain, off Trinidad & Tobago	July 19, 1979	Collision	300,000
Amoco Cadiz, near Portsall, France	March 16, 1978	Grounding	223,000
Torrey Canyon, off Land's End, England	March 18, 1967	Grounding	119,000
Sea Star, Gulf of Oman	Dec. 19, 1972	Collision	115,000
Urquiola, La Coruna, Spain	May 12, 1976	Grounding	100,000
Hawaiian Patriot, northern Pacific	Feb. 25, 1977	Fire.	99,000
Othello, Tralhavet Bay, Sweden	March 20, 1970	Collision	60,000-100,000
Jacob Maersk, Porto do Leixoes, Portugal	Jan. 29, 1975	Grounding	84,000
Wafra, Cape Agulhas, South Africa	Feb. 27, 1971	Grounding	63,000
Epic Colacotroni, Caribbean	May, 1975	Grounding	57,000

Other Notable Oil Spills

Source: Conservation Division, U.S. Geological Survey, U.S. Interior Department

Name, place	Date	Cause	Gallons
World Glory, off South Africa	June 13, 1968	Hull failure	13,524,000
Keo, off Massachusetts	Nov. 5, 1969	Hull failure	8,820,000
Storage tank, Sewaren, N.J.	Nov. 4, 1969	Tank rupture	8,400,000
Ekofisk oil field, North Sea	Apr. 22, 1977	Well blowout	8,200,000
Argo Merchant, Nantucket, Mass.	Dec. 15, 1976	Grounding	7,700,000
Pipeline, West Delta, La.	Oct. 15, 1967	Dragging anchor	6,720,000
Tanker off Japan	Nov. 30, 1971	Ship broke in half	6,258,000

Explosions

Date		Location	Deaths	Date		Location	Deaths
1910	Oct. 1	Los Angeles Times Bldg.,	21	1962	Mar. 3	Gasoline truck, Syria	31
1913	Mar. 7	Dynamite, Baltimore harbor	55	1962	Oct. 3	Telephone Co. office, N. Y. City	23
1915	Sept. 27	Gasoline tank car, Ardmore, Okla.	47	1963	Jan. 2	Packing plant, Terre Haute, Ind.	16
1917	Apr. 10	Munitions plant, Eddystone, Pa.	133	1963	Mar. 9	Dynamite plant, S. Africa	45
1917	Dec. 6	Halifax Harbor, Canada	1,654	1963	Mar. 9	Steel plant, Belecke, W. Germany	19
1918	May 18	Chemical plant, Oakdale, Pa.	193	1963	Aug. 13	Explosives dump, Gauhiti, India	32
1918	July 2	Explosives, Split Rock, N.Y.	50	1963	Oct. 31	State Fair Coliseum, Indianapolis	73
1918	Oct. 4	Shell plant, Morgan Station, N.J.	64	1964	July 23	Bone, Algeria, harbor munitions	100
1919	May 22	Food plant, Cedar Rapids, Ia.	44	1965	Mar. 4	Gas pipeline, Natchitoches, La.	17
1920	Sept. 16	Wall Street, New York, bomb	30	1965	Aug. 9	Missile silo, Searcy, Ark.	53
1924	Jan. 3	Food plant, Pekin, Ill.	42	1965	Oct. 21	Bridge, Tila Bund, Pakistan	80
1928	April 13	Dance hall, West Plains, Mo.	40	1965	Oct. 30	Cartagena, Colombia	48
1937	Mar. 18	New London, Tex., school	294	1965	Nov. 24	Armory, Keokuk, Ia.	20
1940	Sept. 11	Hercules Powder, Kenvil, N.J.	51	1966	Oct. 13	Chemical plant, La Calle, Que.	11
1942	June 5	Ordnance plant, Elwood, Ill.	49	1967	Feb. 17	Chemical plant, Hawthorne, N.J.	11
1944	Apr. 14	Bombay, India, harbor	700	1967	Dec. 25	Apartment bldg., Moscow	20
1944	July 17	Port Chicago, Cal., pier	322	1968	Apr. 6	Sports store, Richmond, Ind.	43
1944	Oct. 21	Liquid gas tank, Cleveland	135	1970	Apr. 8	Subway construction, Osaka, Japan	73
1947	Apr. 16	Texas City, Tex., pier	561	1971	June 24	Tunnel, Sylmar, Cal.	17
1948	July 28	Farben works, Ludwigshafen, Ger.	184	1971	June 28	School, fireworks, Pueblo, Mex.	13
1950	May 19	Munitions barges, S. Amboy, N. J.	30	1971	Oct. 21	Shopping center, Glasgow, Scot.	20
1956	Aug. 7	Dynamite trucks, Cali, Colombia	1,100	1973	Feb. 10	Liquified gas tank, Staten Is., N.Y.	40
1958	Apr. 18	Sunken munitions ship, Okinawa	40	1975	Dec. 27	Chasnala, India, mine	431
1958	May 22	Nike missiles, Leonardo, N.J.	10	1976	Apr. 13	Lapua, Finland, munitions works	45
1959	Apr. 10	World War II bomb, Philippines	38	1977	Nov. 11	Freight train, Iri, S. Korea	57
1959	June 28	Rail tank cars, Meldrin, Ga.	25	1977	Dec. 22	Grain elevator, Westwego, La.	35
1959	Aug. 7	Dynamite truck, Roseburg, Ore.	13	1978	Feb. 24	Derailed tank car, Waverly, Tenn.	12
1959	Nov. 2	Jamuri Bazar, India, explosives	46	1978	July 11	Propylene tank truck, Spanish	
1959	Dec. 13	Dortmund, Ger., 2 apt. bldgs.	26			coastal campsite	150
1960	Mar. 4	Belgian munitions ship, Havana	100	1980	Oct. 23	School, Ortuella, Spain	64
1960	Oct. 25	Gas, Windsor, Ont., store	11	1981	Feb. 13	Sewer system, Louisville, Ky.	0
1962	Jan. 16	Gas pipeline, Alberta, Canada	19				

Fires

Date		Location	Deaths	Date		Location	Deaths
1845	May	Theater, Canton, China	1,670	1961	Jan. 6	Thomas Hotel, San Francisco	20
1871	Oct. 8	Chicago, $196 million loss	250	1961	May 15	Tenement, Hong Kong	25
1871	Oct. 8	Peshtigo, Wis., forest fire	1,182	1961	Dec. 8	Hospital, Hartford, Conn.	16
1876	Dec. 5	Brooklyn (N.Y.), theater	295	1961	Dec. 17	Circus, Niteroi, Brazil.	323
1877	June 20	St. John, N. B., Canada	100	1963	May 4	Theater, Diourbel, Senegal	64
1881	Dec. 8	Ring Theater, Vienna	850	1963	Nov. 18	Surfside Hotel, Atlantic City, N.J.	25
1887	May 25	Opera Comique, Paris	200	1963	Nov. 23	Rest home, Fitchville, Oh.	63
1887	Sept. 4	Exeter, England, theater	200	1963	Dec. 29	Roosevelt Hotel, Jacksonville, Fla.	22
1894	Sept. 1	Hinckley, Minn., forest fire	413	1964	May 8	Apartment building, Manila	30
1897	May 4	Charity bazaar, Paris.	150	1964	Dec. 18	Nursing home, Fountaintown, Ind.	20
1900	June 30	Hoboken, N. J., docks	326	1965	Mar. 1	Apartment, LaSalle, Canada	28
1902	Sept. 20	Church, Birmingham, Ala.	115	1966	Mar. 11	Numata, Japan, 2 ski resorts	31
1903	Dec. 30	Iroquois Theater, Chicago	602	1966	Aug. 13	Melbourne, Australia, hotel	29
1908	Jan. 13	Rhoads Theater, Boyertown, Pa.	170	1966	Sept. 12	Anchorage, Alaska, hotel	14
1908	Mar. 4	School, Collinwood, Oh.	176	1966	Oct. 17	N. Y. City bldg. (firemen)	12
1911	Mar. 25	Triangle factory, N. Y. City	145	1966	Dec. 7	Erzurum, Turkey, barracks	68
1913	Oct. 14	Colliery, Mid Glamorgan, Wales	439	1967	Feb. 7	Restaurant, Montgomery, Ala.	25
1918	Apr. 13	Norman Okla., state hospital	38	1967	May 22	Store, Brussels, Belgium	322
1918	Oct. 12	Cloquet, Minn., forest fire	400	1967	July 16	State prison, Jay, Fla.	37
1919	June 20	Mayaguez Theater, San Juan.	150	1968	Jan. 6	Brooklyn, N. Y., tenement	13
1923	May 17	School, Camden, S. C.	76	1968	Feb. 26	Shrewsbury, England, hospital	22
1924	Dec. 24	School, Hobart, Okla.	35	1968	May 11	Vijayawada, India, wedding hall.	58
1929	May 15	Clinic, Cleveland, Oh.	125	1968	Nov. 18	Glasgow, Scotland, factory	24
1930	Apr. 21	Penitentiary, Columbus, Oh.	320	1969	Jan. 26	Victoria Hotel, Dunnville, Ont.	13
1931	July 24	Pittsburgh, Pa., home for aged	48	1969	Dec. 2	Nursing home, Notre Dame, Can.	54
1938	May 16	Atlanta, Ga., Terminal Hotel.	35	1970	Jan. 9	Nursing home, Marietta, Oh.	27
1940	Apr. 23	Dance hall, Natchez, Miss.	198	1970	Mar. 20	Hotel, Seattle, Wash.	19
1942	Nov. 28	Cocoanut Grove, Boston	491	1970	Nov. 1	Dance hall, Grenoble, France	145
1942		Hostel, St. John's, Newfoundland	100	1970	Nov. 5	Nursing home, Pointe-aux-	
1943	Sept. 7	Gulf Hotel, Houston	55			Trembles, Que.	17
1944	July 6	Ringling Circus, Hartford.	168	1970	Dec. 20	Hotel, Tucson, Arizona.	28
1946	June 5	LaSalle Hotel, Chicago	61	1971	Mar. 6	Psychiatric clinic, Burghoezli,	
1946	Dec. 7	Winecoff Hotel, Atlanta	119			Switzerland	28
1946	Dec. 12	New York, ice plant, tenement	37	1971	Apr. 20	Hotel, Bangkok, Thailand	24
1949	Apr. 5	Hospital, Effingham, Ill.	77	1971	Oct. 19	Nursing home, Honesdale, Pa.	15
1950	Jan. 7	Davenport, Ia., Mercy Hospital	41	1971	Dec. 25	Hotel, Seoul, So. Korea	162
1953	Mar. 29	Largo, Fla., nursing home	35	1972	May 13	Osaka, Japan, nightclub	116
1953	Apr. 16	Chicago, metalworking plant	35	1972	July 5	Sherborne, England, hospital	30
1957	Feb. 17	Home for aged, Warrenton, Mo.	72	1973	Feb. 6	Paris, France, school.	21
1958	Mar. 19	New York City loft building	24	1973	Nov. 6	Fukui, Japan, train	28
1958	Dec. 1	Parochial school, Chicago	95	1973	Nov. 29	Kumamoto, Japan, department	
1958	Dec. 16	Store, Bogota, Colombia	83			store	107
1959	June 23	Resort hotel, Stalheim, Norway	34	1973	Dec. 2	Seoul, Korea, theater	50
1960	Mar. 14	Pusan, Korea, chemical plant	68	1974	Feb. 1	Sao Paulo, Brazil, bank building	189
1960	July 14	Mental hospital, Guatemala City	225	1974	June 30	Port Chester, N. Y., discotheque	24
1960	Nov. 13	Movie theater, Amude, Syria	152				

Date			Location	Deaths	Date			Location	Deaths
1974	Nov.	3	Seoul; So. Korea, hotel discotheque	88	1978	Jan.	28	Kansas City, Coates House Hotel	16
1975	Dec.	12	Mina, Saudi Arabia, tent city	138	1979	Dec.	31	Chapais, Quebec, social club	42
1976	Oct.	24	Bronx, N.Y., social club	25	1980	May	20	Kingston, Jamaica, nursing home	157
1977	Feb.	25	Rossiya Hotel, Moscow	45	1980	Nov.	21	MGM Grand Hotel, Las Vegas	84
1977	May	28	Southgate, Ky., nightclub	164	1980	Dec.	4	Stouffer Inn, Harrison, N.Y.	26
1977	June	9	Abidjan, Ivory Coast nightclub	41	1981	Jan.	9	Keansburg, N.J., boarding home	30
1977	June	26	Columbia, Tenn., jail	42	1981	Feb.	10	Las Vegas Hilton	8
1977	Nov.	14	Manila, PI, hotel	47	1981	Feb.	14	Dublin, Ireland, discotheque	44

Major U.S. Railroad Wrecks

Source: Office of Safety, Federal Railroad Administration

Date			Location	Deaths	Date			Location	Deaths
1876	Dec.	29	Ashtabula, Oh.	92	1923	Sept.	27	Lockett, Wy.	31
1880	Aug.	11	Mays Landing, N. J.	40	1925	June	16	Hackettstown, N. J.	50
1887	Aug.	10	Chatsworth, Ill.	81	1925	Oct.	27	Victoria, Miss.	21
1888	Oct.	10	Mud Run, Pa.	55	1926	Sept.	5	Waco, Col.	30
1896	July	30	Atlantic City, N. J.	60	1928	Aug.	24	I.R.T. subway, Times Sq., N. Y.	18
1903	Dec.	23	Laurel Run, Pa.	53	1938	June	10	Saugus, Mont.	47
1904	Aug.	7	Eden, Col.	96	1939	Aug.	12	Harney, Nev.	24
1904	Sept.	24	New Market Tenn.	56	1940	Aug.	19	Little Falls, N. Y.	31
1906	Mar.	16	Florence, Col.	35	1940	July	31	Cuyahoga Falls, Oh.	43
1906	Oct.	28	Atlantic City, N. J.	40	1943	Aug.	29	Wayland, N. Y.	27
1906	Dec.	30	Washington, D. C.	53	1943	Sept.	6	Frankford Junction, Philadelphia, Pa.	79
1907	Jan.	2	Volland, Kan.	33	1943	Dec.	16	Between Rennert and Buie, N. C.	72
1907	Jan.	19	Fowler, Ind.	29	1944	July	6	High Bluff, Tenn.	35
1907	Feb.	16	New York, N.Y.	22	1944	Aug.	4	Near Stockton, Ga.	47
1907	Feb.	23	Colton, Cal.	26	1944	Sept.	14	Dewey, Ind.	29
1907	July	20	Salem, Mich.	33	1944	Dec.	31	Bagley, Utah	50
1910	Mar.	1	Wellington, Wash.	96	1945	Aug.	9	Michigan, N. D.	34
1910	Mar.	21	Green Mountain, Ia.	55	1946	Apr.	25	Naperville, Ill.	45
1911	Aug.	25	Manchester, N. Y.	29	1947	Feb.	18	Gallitzin, Pa.	24
1912	July	4	East Corning, N. Y.	39	1950	Feb.	17	Rockville Centre, N. Y.	31
1912	July	5	Ligonier, Pa.	23	1950	Sept.	11	Coshocton, Oh.	33
1914	Aug.	5	Tipton Ford, Mo.	43	1950	Nov.	22	Richmond Hill, N. Y.	79
1916	Sept.	15	Lebanon, Mo.	28	1951	Feb.	6	Woodbridge, N. J.	84
1916	Mar.	29	Amherst, Oh.	27	1951	Nov.	12	Wyuta, Wyo.	17
1917	Feb.	27	Mount Union, Pa.	20	1951	Nov.	25	Woodstock, Ala.	17
1917	Sept.	28	Kellyville, Okla.	23	1953	Mar.	27	Conneaut, Oh.	21
1917	Dec.	20	Shepherdsville, Ky.	46	1956	Jan.	22	Los Angeles, Cal.	30
1918	June	22	Ivanhoe, Ind.	68	1956	Feb.	28	Swampscott, Mass.	13
1918	July	9	Nashville, Tenn.	101	1956	Sept.	5	Springer, N. M.	20
1918	Nov.	2	Brooklyn, N. Y., Malbone St. Tunnel	97	1957	June	11	Vroman, Col.	12
1919	Jan.	12	South Byron, N. Y.	22	1958	Sept.	15	Elizabethport, N. J.	48
1919	July	1	Dunkirk, N. Y.	12	1960	Mar.	14	Bakersfield, Cal.	14
1919	Dec.	20	Onawa, Maine	23	1962	July	28	Steelton, Pa.	19
1921	Feb.	27	Porter, Ind.	37	1966	Dec.	28	Everett, Mass.	13
1921	Dec.	5	Woodmont, Pa.	27	1971	June	10	Salem, Ill.	11
1922	Aug.	5	Sulphur Spring, Mo.	34	1972	Oct.	30	Chicago, Ill.	45
1922	Dec.	13	Humble, Tex.	22	1977	Jan.	4	Chicago, Ill., elevated train	11

World's worst train wreck occurred Dec. 12, 1917, Modane, France, passenger train derailed, 543 killed.

Some Notable Aircraft Disasters Since 1937

Date			Aircraft	Site of accident	Deaths
1937	May	6	German zeppelin Hindenburg	Burned at mooring, Lakehurst, N.J.	36
1944	Aug.	23	U.S. Air Force B-24	Hit school, Freckelton, England	76[1]
1945	July	28	U.S. Army B-25	Hit Empire State bldg., N.Y.C.	14[1]
1947	May	30	Eastern Air Lines DC-4	Crashed near Ft. Deposit, Md.	53
1952	Dec.	20	U.S. Air Force C-124	Fell, burned, Moses Lake, Wash.	87
1953	Mar.	3	Canadian Pacific Comet Jet	Karachi, Pakistan	11[2]
1953	June	18	U.S. Air Force C-124	Crashed, burned near Tokyo	129
1955	Nov.	1	United Air Lines DC-6B	Exploded, crashed near Longmont, Col.	44[3]
1956	June	20	Venezuelan Super-Constellation	Crashed in Atlantic off Asbury Park, N.J.	74
1956	June	30	TWA Super-Const., United DC-7	Collided over Grand Canyon, Arizona	128
1960	Dec.	16	United DC-8 jet, TWA Super-Const.	Collided over N.Y. City	134[4]
1962	Mar.	4	Br. Caledonian Airlines DC-7C	Crashed near Douala, Cameroon	111
1962	Mar.	16	Flying Tiger Super-Const.	Vanished in Western Pacific	107
1962	June	3	Air France Boeing 707 jet	Crashed on takeoff from Paris	130
1962	June	22	Air France Boeing 707 jet	Crashed in storm, Guadeloupe, W.I.	113
1963	June	3	Chartered Northw. Airlines DC-7	Crashed in Pacific off British Columbia	101
1963	Nov.	29	Trans-Canada Airlines DC-8F	Crashed after takeoff from Montreal	118
1965	May	20	Pakistani Boeing 720-B	Crashed at Cairo, Egypt, airport	121
1966	Jan.	24	Air India Boeing 707 jetliner	Crashed on Mont Blanc, France-Italy	117
1966	Feb.	4	All-Nippon Boeing 727	Plunged into Tokyo Bay	133
1966	Mar.	5	BOAC Boeing 707 jetliner	Crashed on Mount Fuji, Japan	124
1966	Dec.	24	U.S. military-chartered CL-44	Crashed into village in So. Vietnam	129[1]
1967	Apr.	20	Swiss Britannia turboprop	Crashed at Nicosia, Cyprus	126
1967	July	19	Piedmont Boeing 727, Cessna 310	Collided in air, Hendersonville, N.C.	82
1968	Apr.	20	S. African Airways Boeing 707	Crashed on takeoff, Windhoek, SW Africa	122
1968	May	3	Braniff International Electra	Crashed in storm near Dawson, Tex.	85
1969	Mar.	16	Venezuelan DC-9	Crashed after takeoff from Maracaibo, Venezuela	155[5]
1969	Mar.	20	United Arab Ilyushin-18	Crashed at Aswan airport, Egypt	87
1969	June	4	Mexican Boeing 727	Rammed into mountain near Monterrey, Mexico	79
1969	Dec.	8	Olympia Airways DC-6B	Crashed near Athens in storm	93
1970	Feb.	15	Dominican DC-9	Crashed into sea on takeoff from Santo Domingo	102

Date		Aircraft	Site of accident	Deaths
1970	July 3	British chartered jetliner.	Crashed near Barcelona, Spain.	112
1970	July 5	Air Canada DC-8.	Crashed near Toronto International Airport	108
1970	Aug. 9	Peruvian turbojet.	Crashed after takeoff from Cuzco, Peru	101[1]
1970	Nov. 14	Southern Airways DC-9	Crashed in mountains near Huntington, W. Va. . . .	75[6]
1971	July 30	All-Nippon Boeing 727 and Japanese Air Force F-86	Collided over Morioka, Japan	162[7]
1971	Aug. 11	Soviet Aeroflot Tupolev-104	Crashed at Irkutsk airport, USSR.	97
1971	Sept. 4	Alaska Airlines Boeing 727	Crashed into mountain near Juneau, Alaska	111
1972	Mar. 14	Danish Airliner	Crashed near Dubai, United Arab Emirates	112
1972	Aug. 14	E. German Ilyushin-62	Crashed on take-off East Berlin.	156
1972	Oct. 13	Aeroflot Ilyushin-62	E. German airline crashed near Moscow	176
1972	Dec. 3	Chartered Spanish airliner	Crashed on take-off, Canary Islands	155
1972	Dec. 29	Eastern Airlines Lockheed Tristar . . .	Crashed on approach to Miami Int'l. Airport.	101
1973	Jan. 22	Chartered Boeing 707.	Burst into flames during landing, Kano Airport, Nigeria . . .	176
1973	Apr. 10	British Vanguard turboprop	Crashed during snowstorm at Basel, Switzerland .	104
1973	June 3	Soviet Supersonic TU-144	Exploded in air near Goussainville, France	14[8]
1970	July 11	Brazilian Boeing 707.	Crashed on approach to Orly Airport, Paris	122
1973	July 31	Delta Airlines jetliner.	Crashed, landing in fog at Logan Airport, Boston . .	89
1973	Dec. 23	French Caravelle jet	Crashed in Morocco	106
1974	Jan. 31	Pan American Boeing 707 jet	Crashed in Pago Pago, American Samoa	96
1974	Mar. 3	Turkish DC-10 jet	Crashed at Ermenonville near Paris	346
1974	Apr. 23	Pan American 707 jet	Crashed in Bali, Indonesia	107
1974	Sept. 8	TWA 707 jet	Crashed in Ionian Sea off Greece, after bomb explosion Arab guerrilla group claimed responsibility	80
1974	Dec. 1	TWA-727	Crashed in storm, Upperville, Va.	92
1974	Dec. 4	Dutch-chartered DC-8.	Crashed in storm near Colombo, Sri Lanka	191
1975	Apr. 4	Air Force Galaxy C-58.	Crashed near Saigon, So. Vietnam, after takeoff with load of orphans	172
1975	June 24	Eastern Airlines 727 jet	Crashed in storm, JFK Airport, N.Y. City.	113
1975	Aug. 3	Chartered 707	Hit mountainside, Agadir, Morocco	168
1976	Sept. 10	British Airways Trident, Yugoslav DC-9 .	Collided near Zagreb, Yugoslavia	176
1976	Sept. 19	Turkish 727	Hit mountain, southern Turkey	155
1976	Oct. 6	Cuban DC-8	Crashed near Barbados after bomb explosion	73
1976	Oct. 12	Indian Caravelle jet	Crashed after takeoff, Bombay airport.	95
1976	Oct. 13	Bolivian 707 cargo jet	Crashed in Santa Cruz, Bolivia	100[9]
1976	Dec. 28	Aeroflot TU-104	Crashed at Moscow's Sheremetyevo airport	72
1977	Jan. 13	Aeroflot TU-104	Exploded and crashed at Alma-Ata, Central Asia . .	90
1977	Mar. 27	KLM 747, Pan American 747	Collided on runway, Tenerife, Canary Islands	581
1977	Nov. 19	TAP Boeing 727	Crashed on Madeira	130
1977	Dec. 4	Malaysian Boeing 737.	Hijacked, then exploded in mid-air over Straits of Johore .	100
1977	Dec. 13	U.S. DC-3.	Crashed after takeoff at Evansville, Ind.	29[10]
1978	Jan. 1	Air India 747	Exploded, crashed into sea off Bombay	213
1978	Mar. 16	Bulgarian TU-134	Crashed at Vratsa, Bulgaria	73
1978	Sept. 25	Boeing 727, Cessna 172	Collided in air, San Diego, Cal.	150
1978	Nov. 15	Chartered DC-8	Crashed near Colombo, Sri Lanka	183
1979	May 25	American Airlines DC-10	Crashed after takeoff at O'Hare Intl. Airport, Chicago .	275[11]
1979	Aug. 17	Two Soviet Aeroflot jetliners	Collided over Ukraine	173
1979	Oct. 31	Western Airlines DC-10	Mexico City Airport.	74
1979	Nov. 26	Pakistani Boeing 707	Crashed near Jidda, Saudi Arabia	156
1979	Nov. 28	New Zealand DC-10.	Crashed into mountain in Antarctica	257
1980	Mar. 14	Polish Ilyushin 62	Crashed making emergency landing, Warsaw	87[12]
1980	Aug. 19	Saudi Arabian Tristar	Crashed attempting emergency landing, Riyadh . . .	301

(1) Including those on the ground and in buildings. (2) First fatal crash of commercial jet plane. (3) Caused by bomb planted by John G. Graham in insurance plot to kill his mother, a passenger. (4) Including all 128 aboard the planes and 6 on ground. (5) Killed 84 on plane and 71 on ground. (6) Including 43 Marshall U. football players and coaches. (7) Airliner-fighter crash, pilot of fighter parachuted to safety, was arrested for negligence. (8) First supersonic plane crash killed 6 crewmen and 8 on the ground; there were no passengers. (9) Crew of 3 killed; 97, mostly children, killed on ground. (10) Including U. of Evansville basketball team. (11) Highest death toll in U.S. aviation history. (12) Including 22 members of U.S. boxing team.

Principal U.S. Mine Disasters

Source: Bureau of Mines, U.S. Interior Department

Note: Prior to 1968, only disasters with losses of 50 or more lives are listed; since 1968, all disasters in which 5 or more people were killed are listed. Only fatalities to mining company employees are included. All Bituminous-coal mines unless otherwise noted.

Date	Location	Deaths	Date	Location	Deaths
1855 Mar.	Coalfield, Va.	55	1908 Dec. 29	Switchback, W. Va.	50
1867 Apr. 3	Winterpock, Va.	69	1909 Jan. 12	Switchback, W. Va.	67
1869[1] Sept. 6	Plymouth, Pa.	110	1909 Nov. 13	Cherry, Ill.	259
1883 Feb. 16	Braidwood, Ill.	69	1910 Jan. 31	Primero, Col.	75
1884 Jan. 24	Crested Butte, Col.	59	1910 May 5	Palos, Ala.	90
1884 Mar. 13	Pocahontas, Va.	112	1910 Oct. 8	Starkville, Col.	56
1891 Jan. 27	Mount Pleasant, Pa.	109	1910 Nov. 8	Delagua, Col.	79
1892 Jan. 7	Krebs, Okla.	100	1911 Apr. 7	Throop, Pa.	72
1895 Mar. 20	Red Canyon, Wy.	60	1911 Apr. 8	Littleton, Ala.	128
1896[1] June 28	Pittston, Pa.	58	1911 Dec. 9	Briceville, Tenn.	84
1900 Jan. 1	Scofield, Ut.	200	1912 Mar. 20	McCurtain, Okla.	73
1902 May 19	Coal Creek, Tenn.	184	1912 Mar. 26	Jed, W. Va.	83
1902 July 10	Johnstown, Pa.	112	1913 Apr. 23	Finleyville, Pa.	96
1903 June 30	Hanna, Wy.	169	1913 Oct. 22	Dawson, N.M.	263
1904 Jan. 25	Cheswick, Pa.	179	1914 Apr. 28	Eccles, W. Va.	181
1905 Feb. 20	Virginia City, Ala.	112	1914 Oct. 27	Royalton, Ill.	52
1907 Jan. 29	Stuart W. Va.	84	1915 Mar. 2	Layland, W. Va.	112
1907 Dec. 6	Monongah, W. Va.	361	1917 Apr. 27	Hastings, Col.	121
1907 Dec. 16	Yolande, Ala.	57	1917[2] June 8	Butte, Mon.	163
1907 Dec. 19	Jacobs Creek, Pa.	239	1917 Aug. 4	Clay, Ky.	62
1908 Mar. 28	Hanna, Wy.	59	1919[1] June 5	Wilkes-Barre, Pa.	92
1908 Nov. 28	Marianna, Pa.	154	1922 Nov. 6	Spangler, Pa.	77

Date	Location	Deaths	Date	Location	Deaths
1922 Nov. 22	Dolomite, Ala.	90	1940 Jan. 10	Bartley, W. Va.	91
1923 Feb. 8	Dawson, N.M.	120	1940 Mar. 16	St. Clairsville, Oh.	72
1923 Aug. 14	Kemmerer, Wy.	99	1940 July 15	Portage, Pa.	63
1924 Mar. 8	Castle Gate, Ut.	171	1942 May 12	Osage, W. Va.	56
1924 Apr. 28	Benwood, W. Va.	119	1943 Feb. 27	Washoe, Mon.	74
1925 Feb. 20	Sullivan, Ind.	52	1944 July 5	Belmont, Oh.	66
1925 May 27	Coal Glen, N.C.	53	1947 Mar. 25	Centralia, Ill.	111
1925 Dec. 10	Acmar, Ala.	53	1951 Dec. 21	West Frankfort, Ill.	119
1926 Jan. 13	Wilburton, Okla.	91	1968[3] Mar. 6	Calumet, La.	21
1926[2] Nov. 3	Ishpeming, Mich.	51	1968 Nov. 20	Farmington, W. Va.	78
1927 Apr. 30	Everettville, W. Va.	97	1970 Dec. 30	Hyden, Ky.	38
1928 May 19	Mather, Pa.	195	1972[2] May 2	Kellogg, Ida.	91
1929 Dec. 17	McAlester, Okla.	61	1976 Mar. 9, 11	Oven Fork, Ky.	26
1930 Nov. 5	Millfield, Oh.	79	1977 Mar. 1	Tower City, Pa.	9
1932 Dec. 23	Moweaqua, Ill.	54	1981 Apr. 15	Redstone, Col.	15

(1) Anthracite mine. (2) Metal mine. (3) Nonmetal mine.
World's worst mine disaster killed 1,549 workers in Honkeiko Colliery in Manchuria Apr. 25, 1942.

Historic Assassinations Since 1865

1865—Apr. 14. U. S. Pres. Abraham Lincoln, shot in Washington, D. C.; died Apr. 15.
1881—Mar. 13. Alexander II, of Russia—July 2. U. S. Pres. James A. Garfield, Washington; died Sept. 19.
1900—July 29. Umberto I, king of Italy.
1901—Sept. 6. U. S. Pres. William McKinley in Buffalo, N. Y., died Sept. 14. Leon Czolgosz executed for the crime Oct. 29.
1913—Feb. 23. Mexican Pres. Francisco, I, Madero and Vice Pres. Jose Pino Suarez.—Mar. 18. George, king of Greece.
1914—June 28. Archduke Francis Ferdinand of Austria-Hungary and his wife in Sarajevo, Bosnia (later part of Yugoslavia), by Gavrillo Princip.
1916—Dec. 30. Grigori Rasputin, politically powerful Russian monk.
1918—July 12. Grand Duke Michael of Russia, at Perm.—July 16. Nicholas II, abdicated as czar of Russia; his wife, the Czarina Alexandra, their son, Czarevitch Alexis, and their daughters, Grand Duchesses Olga, Tatiana, Marie, Anastasia, and 4 members of their household were executed by Bolsheviks at Ekaterinburg.
1920—May 20. Mexican Pres. Gen. Venustiano Carranza in Tlaxcalantongo.
1922—Aug. 22. Michael Collins, Irish revolutionary.
1923—July 20. Gen. Francisco "Pancho" Villa, ex-rebel leader, in Parral, Mexico.
1928—July 17. Gen. Alvaro Obregon, president-elect of Mexico, in San Angel, Mexico.
1933—Feb. 15. In Miami, Fla. Joseph Zangara, anarchist, shot at Pres.-elect Franklin D. Roosevelt, but a woman seized his arm, and the bullet fatally wounded Mayor Anton J. Cermak, of Chicago, who died Mar. 6. Zangara was electrocuted on Mar. 20, 1933.
1934—July 25. In Vienna, Austrian Chancellor Engelbert Dollfuss by Nazis.
1935—Sept. 8. U. S. Sen. Huey P. Long, shot in Baton Rouge, La., by Dr. Carl Austin Weiss, who was slain by Long's bodyguards.
1940—Aug. 20. Leon Trotsky (Lev Bronstein), 63, exiled Russian war minister, near Mexico City. Killer identified as Ramon Mercador del Rio, a Spaniard, served 20 years in Mexican prison.
1948—Jan. 30. Mohandas K. Gandhi, 78, shot in New Delhi, India, by Nathuran Vinayak Godse.—Sept. 17. Count Folke Bernadotte, UN mediator for Palestine, ambushed in Jerusalem.
1951—July 20. King Abdullah ibn Hussein of Jordan.
1956—Sept. 21. Pres. Anastasio Somoza of Nicaragua, in Leon; died Sept. 29.
1957—July 26. Pres. Carlos Castillo Armas of Guatemala, in Guatemala City by one of his own guards.
1958—July 14. King Faisal of Iraq; his uncle, Crown Prince Abdul Illah, and July 15, Premier Nuri as-Said, by rebels in Baghdad.
1959—Sept. 25. Prime Minister Solomon Bandaranaike of Ceylon, by Buddhist monk in Colombo.
1961—Jan. 17. Ex-Premier Patrice Lumumba of the Congo, in Katanga Province—May 30. Dominican dictator Rafael Leonidas

Trujillo Molina shot to death by assassins near Ciudad Trujillo.
1963—June 12. Medgar W. Evers, NAACP's Mississippi field secretary, in Jackson, Miss.—Nov. 2. Pres. Ngo Dinh Diem of the Republic of Vietnam and his brother, Ngo Dinh Nhu, in a military coup.—Nov. 22. U. S. Pres. John F. Kennedy fatally shot in Dallas, Tex.; accused Lee Harvey Oswald murdered while awaiting trial.
1965—Jan. 21. Iranian premier Hassan Ali Mansour fatally wounded by assassin in Teheran; 4 executed.—Feb. 21. Malcolm X, black nationalist, fatally shot in N. Y. City; 3 sentenced to life.
1966—Sept. 6. Prime Minister Hendrik F. Verwoerd of South Africa stabbed to death in parliament at Capetown by drifter later ruled insane.
1968—Apr. 4. Rev. Dr. Martin Luther King Jr. fatally shot in Memphis, Tenn.; James Earl Ray sentenced to 99 years.—June 5. Sen. Robert F. Kennedy (D-N. Y.) fatally shot in Los Angeles; Sirhan Sirhan, resident alien, convicted of murder.
1969—July 5. Tom Mboya, Kenya's minister of economic planning and development, in Nairobi.
1971—Nov. 28. Jordan Prime Minister Wasfi Tal, in Cairo, by Palestinian guerrillas.
1973—Mar. 2. U. S. Ambassador Cleo A. Noel Jr., U. S. Charge d'Affaires George C. Moore and Belgian Charge d'Affaires Guy Eid tortured and killed by Palestinian guerrillas in Khartoum, Sudan.
1974—Aug. 15. Mrs. Park Chung Hee, wife of president of So. Korea, hit by bullet meant for her husband.—Aug. 19. U. S. Ambassador to Cyprus, Rodger P. Davies, killed by sniper's bullet in Nicosia.
1975—Feb. 11. Pres. Richard Ratsimandrava, of Madagascar, machine-gunned in Tananarive.—Mar. 25. King Faisal of Saudi Arabia shot by nephew Prince Musad Abdel Aziz, in royal palace, Riyadh.—Aug. 15. Bangladesh Pres. Sheik Mujibur Rahman and wife and son killed in army coup.
1976—Feb. 13. Nigerian head of state, Gen. Murtala Ramat Mohammed, slain by self-styled "young revolutionaries."
1977—Mar. 16. Kamal Jumblat, Lebanese Druse chieftain, was shot and killed on a mountain road near Beirut.—Mar. 18. Congo Pres. Marien Ngouabi shot in Brazzaville.
1978—July 9. Former Iraqi Premier Abdul Razak Al-Naif shot in London.
1979—Feb. 14. U.S. Ambassador Adolph Dubs shot and killed by Afghan Moslem extremists in Kabul.—Mar. 30. British Tory MP Airey Neave killed when bomb in his car exploded. IRA claimed responsibility.—Aug. 27. Lord Mountbatten, WW2 hero, and 2 others were killed when a bomb exploded on his fishing boat off the coast of Co. Sligo, Ire. The IRA claimed responsibility.—Oct. 26. So. Korean President Park Chung Hee and 6 bodyguards fatally shot by Kim Jae Kyu, head of Korean CIA, and 5 aides in Seoul.
1980—Apr. 12. Liberian President William R. Tolbert slain in military coup.—Sept. 17. Former Nicaraguan President Anastasio Somoza Debayle and 2 others shot in Paraguay.

Assassination Attempts

1910—Aug. 6. N. Y. City Mayor William J. Gaynor shot and seriously wounded by discharged city employee.
1912—Oct. 14. Former U. S. President Theodore Roosevelt shot and seriously wounded by demented man in Milwaukee.
1950—Nov. 1. In an attempt to assassinate President Truman, 2 men identified as members of a Puerto Rican nationalist movement—Griselio Torresola and Oscar Collazo—tried to shoot their way into Blair House. Torresola was killed, and a guard, Pvt. Leslie Coffelt was fatally shot. Collazo, wounded, recovered and was tried and convicted Mar. 7. 1951 for the murder of Coffelt. His

death sentence was commuted to life imprisonment by President Truman; sentence commuted by Pres. Carter, Sept. 1979.
1970—Nov. 27. Pope Paul VI unharmed by knife-wielding assailant dressed as priest who attempted to attack him in Manila airport.
1972—May 15. Alabama Gov. George Wallace shot in Laurel, Md. by Arthur Bremer; seriously crippled.
1972—Dec. 7. Mrs. Ferdinand E. Marcos, wife of the Philippine president, was stabbed and seriously injured in Pasay City, Philip-

pines.

1975—Sept. 5. Pres. Gerald R. Ford was unharmed when a Secret Service agent grabbed a pistol aimed at him by Lynette (Squeaky) Fromme, a Charles Manson follower, in Sacramento.

1975—Sept. 22. Pres. Gerald R. Ford escaped unharmed when Sara Jane Moore, a political activist, fired a revolver at him.

1980—Apr. 14. Indian Prime Minister Indira Gandhi was unharmed when a man threw a knife at her in New Delhi.

1981—Jan. 16. Irish political activist Bernadette Devlin McAlis-

key and her husband were shot and seriously wounded by 3 members of a protestant paramilitary group in Co. Tyrone, Ire.

1981—Mar. 30. Pres. Ronald Reagan, Press Secy. James Brady, Secret Service agent Timothy J. McCarthy, and Washington, D.C. policeman Thomas Delahanty were shot and seriously wounded by John W. Hinckley Jr. in Washington, D.C.

1981—May 13. Pope John Paul II and 2 bystanders were shot and wounded by Mehmet Ali Agca, an escaped Turkish murderer, in St. Peter's Square, Rome.

Major Kidnapings

Edward A. Cudahy Jr., 16, in Omaha, Neb., **Dec. 18, 1900.** Returned Dec. 20 after $25,000 paid. Pat Crowe confessed.

Robert Franks, 13, in Chicago, **May 22, 1924**, by 2 youths, Richard Loeb and Nathan Leopold, who killed boy. Demand for $10,000 ignored. Loeb died in prison, Leopold paroled 1958, freed 1963.

Charles A. Lindbergh Jr., 20 mos. old, in Hopewell, N.J., **Mar. 1, 1932;** found dead May 12. Ransom of $50,000 was paid to man identified as Bruno Richard Hauptmann, 35, paroled German convict who entered U.S. illegally. Hauptmann passed ransom bill and $14,000 marked money was found in his garage. He was convicted after spectacular trial at Flemington, and electrocuted in Trenton, N.J., prison, Apr. 3. 1936.

William A. Hamm Jr., 39, in St. Paul, **June 15, 1933.** $100,000 paid. Alvin Karpis given life, paroled in 1969.

Charles F. Urschel, in Oklahoma City, **July 22, 1933.** Released July 31 after $200,000 paid. George (Machine Gun) Kelly and 5 others given life.

George Weyerhaeuser, 9, in Tacoma, Wash., **May 24, 1935.** Returned home June 1 after $200,000 paid. Kidnappers given 20 to 60 years.

Charles Mattson, 10, in Tacoma, Wash., **Dec. 27, 1936.** Found dead Jan. 11, 1937. Kidnaper asked $28,000, failed to contact.

Arthur Fried, in White Plains, N.Y., **Dec. 4, 1937.** Body not found. Two kidnapers executed.

Robert C. Greenlease, 6, son of a Kansas City, Mo. motor car dealer, taken from school **Sept. 28, 1953**, and held for $600,000. Body found Oct. 7, when Mrs. Bonnie Brown Heady and Carl A. Hall were arrested. They pleaded guilty and were executed.

Peter Weinberger, 32 days old, Westbury, N.Y., **July 4, 1956**, for $2,000 ransom, not paid. Child found dead. Angelo John LaMarca, 31, convicted, executed.

Cynthia Ruotolo, 6 wks old, taken from carriage in front of Hamden, Conn. store **Sept. 1, 1956.** Body found in lake.

Lee Crary, 8 in Everett, Wash., **Sept. 22, 1957**, $10,000 ransom, not paid. He escaped after 3 days, led police to George E. Collins, who was convicted.

Eric Peugeot, 4, taken from playground at St. Cloud golf course, Paris, **Apr. 12, 1960.** Released unharmed 3 days later after payment of undisclosed sum. Two sentenced to prison.

Frank Sinatra Jr., 19, from hotel room in Lake Tahoe, Cal., **Dec. 8, 1963.** Released **Dec. 11** after his father paid $240,000 ransom. John W. Irwin, Barry W. Keenan and Joseph C. Amsler sentenced to prison; most of ransom recovered.

Barbara Jane Mackle, 20, abducted **Dec. 17, 1968**, from Atlanta, Ga., motel, was found unharmed 3 days later, buried in a coffin-like wooden box 18 inches underground, after her father had paid $500,000 ransom; Gary Steven Krist sentenced to life, Ruth Eisenmann-Schier to 7 years; most of ransom recovered.

Anne Katherine Jenkins, 22, abducted **May 10, 1969**, from her Baltimore apartment, freed 3 days later after her father paid $10,000 ransom.

Mrs. Roy Fuchs, 35, and 3 children held hostage 2 hours, **May 14, 1969**, in Long Island, N. Y., released after her husband, a bank manager, paid kidnapers $129,000 in bank funds; 4 men arrested, ransom recovered.

C. Burke Elbrick, U.S. ambassador to Brazil, kidnaped by revolutionaries in Rio de Janeiro **Sept. 4, 1969;** released 3 days later after Brazil yielded to kidnaper's demands to publish manifesto and release 15 political prisoners.

Patrick Dolan, 18, found shot to death near Sao Paulo, Brazil, **Nov. 5, 1969**, after he was kidnaped and $12,500 paid.

Sean M. Holly, U.S. diplomat, in Guatemala **Mar. 6, 1970;** freed 2 days later upon release of 3 terrorists from prison.

Lt. Col. Donald J. Crowley, U.S. air attache, in Dominican Republic **Mar. 24, 1970;** released after government allowed 20 prisoners to leave the country.

Count Karl von Spreti, W. German ambassador to Guatemala, **Mar. 31, 1970;** slain after Guatemala refused demands for $700,000 and release of 22 prisoners.

Pedro Eugenio Aramburu, former Argentine president, by terrorists **May 29, 1970;** body found July 17.

Rudy V. Martinez, Guatemalan coffee exporter, by terrorists **Apr. 23, 1970;** released on payment of large ransom.

Ehrenfried von Holleben, W. German ambassador to Brazil, by terrorists **June 11, 1970;** freed after release of 40 prisoners.

Daniel A. Mitrione, U.S. diplomat, **July 31, 1970**, by terrorists in Montevideo, Uruguay; body found Aug. 10 after government rejected demands for release of all political prisoners.

Aloysio Dias Gomide, Brazilian vice consul, in Montevideo, **July 31, 1970;** released Feb. 1, 1971, after wife paid ransom estimated at over $250,000.

James R. Cross, British trade commissioner, **Oct. 5, 1970**, by French Canadian separatists in Quebec; freed Dec. 3 after 3 kidnapers and relatives flown to Cuba by government.

Pierre Laporte, Quebec Labor Minister, by separatists **Oct. 10, 1970;** body found Oct. 18.

Giovanni E. Bucher, Swiss ambassador **Dec. 7, 1970**, by revolutionaries in Rio de Janeiro; freed Jan. 16, 1971, after Brazil released 70 political prisoners.

Geoffrey Jackson, British ambassador, in Montevideo, **Jan. 8, 1971**, by Tupamaro terrorists. Held as ransom for release of imprisoned terrorists, he was released Sept. 9, after the prisoners escaped.

Ephraim Elrom, Israel consul general in Istanbul, **May 17, 1971.** Held as ransom for imprisoned terrorists, he was found dead May 23.

Mrs. Virginia Piper, 49 abducted **July 27, 1972**, from her home in suburban Minneapolis; found unharmed near Duluth 2 days later after her husband paid $1 million ransom to the kidnapers.

Victor E. Samuelson, Exxon executive, **Dec. 6, 1973**, in Campana, Argentina, by Marxist guerrillas, freed Apr. 29, 1974, after payment of record $14.2 million ransom.

J. Paul Getty 3d, 17, grandson of the U.S. oil mogul, released by kidnapers **Dec. 15, 1973**, in southern Italy after family paid $2.8 million ransom.

Patricia (Patty) Hearst, 19, taken from her Berkeley, Cal., apartment **Feb. 4, 1974.** Symbionese Liberation Army demanded her father, Randolph A. Hearst, publisher, give millions to poor. Hearst offered $2 million in food; the Hearst Corp. offered $4 million worth. Kidnapers objected to way food was distributed. Patricia, in message, said she had joined SLA; she was identified by FBI as taking part in a San Francisco bank holdup, **Apr. 15;** she claimed, in message, she had been coerced. Again identified by FBI in a store holdup, **May 16**, she was classified by FBI as "an armed, dangerous fugitive." FBI, **Sept. 18, 1975**, captured Patricia and others in San Francisco; they were indicted on various charges. Patricia for bank robbery. A San Francisco jury convicted her, **Mar. 20, 1976.** She was released from prison under executive clemency, **Feb. 1, 1979.** In 1978, William and Emily Harris were sentenced to 10 years to life for the Hearst kidnaping.

J. Reginald Murphy, 40, an editor of *Atlanta* (Ga.) *Constitution*, kidnaped **Feb. 20, 1974**, freed **Feb. 22** after payment of $700,000 ransom by the newspaper. Police arrested William A. H. Williams, a contractor; most of the money was recovered.

J. Guadalupe Zuno Hernandez, 83, father-in-law of Mexican President Luis Echeverria Alvarez, seized by 4 terrorists **Aug. 28, 1974;** government refused to negotiate; he was released **Sept. 8.**

E. B. Reville, Hepzibah, Ga., banker, and wife Jean, kidnaped **Sept. 30, 1974.** Ransom of $30,000 paid. He was found alive; Mrs. Reville was found dead of carbon monoxide fumes in car trunk Oct. 2.

Jack Teich, Kings Point, N.Y., steel executive, seized **Nov. 12, 1974;** released **Nov. 19** after payment of $750,000.

Samuel Bronfman, 21, heir to Seagram liquor fortune, allegedly abducted **Aug. 9, 1975**, in Purchase, N.Y.; $2.3 million ransom paid by father, Edgar. FBI and N.Y.C. police found Samuel **Aug. 17** in Brooklyn, N.Y., apartment, recovered ransom, and arrested Mel Patrick Lynch, a city fireman, and Dominic Byrne, a limousine operator. Two found not guilty of kidnap, but convicted of extortion after they claimed Sam masterminded ransom plot.

Hanns-Martin Schleyer, a West German industrialist, was kidnaped in Cologne, **Sept. 5, 1977** by armed terrorists. His driver and 3 of his police guards were killed in the terrorist action. Schleyer was found dead, **Oct. 19**, in an abandoned car shortly after 3 jailed terrorist leaders of the Baader-Meinhof gang were found dead in their prison cells near Stuttgart, West Germany.

Aldo Moro, former Italian premier, kidnaped in Rome, **Mar. 16, 1978**, by left-wing terrorists. Five of his bodyguards killed during abduction. Moro's bullet-ridden body was found in a parked car, **May 9**, in Rome. Six members of the Red Brigades arrested, charged, June 5, with complicity in the kidnaping.

ASTRONOMY AND CALENDAR

Edited by Dr. Kenneth L. Franklin, Astronomer
American Museum-Hayden Planetarium

Celestial Events Highlights, 1982

(All times are Greenwich Mean Time)

This year sees 7 eclipses occur, the maximum number. There are 4 of the sun and 3 of the moon. None of the solar eclipses is noteworthy, but the lunar eclipses are each total. They may be seen by anyone anywhere the moon is above the horizon. Although no bright stars are occulted this year, Neptune is covered by the moon a dozen times, and Mercury, Venus, and Mars each have one lunar encounter. Treat notice of these in the tables as an indication that the moon and that particular planet are quite close in the sky. The months of June and July find the moon quite busy, accounting for 3 eclipses and 7 occultations, including one each of the asteroids Vesta (June 12) and Ceres (July 2).

Mars, Jupiter, and Saturn are visible sometime during the night hours until October, when Saturn and Jupiter get lost in the solar glare, and Mars, while visible, just fades into the distance by year's end.

The Perseid meteor shower is served better by the moon this year and is even more worthy of attention than we have noted in the last few years. Although the Eta Aquarids will be hurt by moonlight, these and the better placed Orionids, both suspected of a Halley comet connection, should be watched before comet Halley makes its reappearance in 1985. The satisfying Geminids are free of lunar light this year. Bundle up and watch the fireballs.

January

Mercury may be found low in the western twilight by midmonth. Always difficult to see at best, it will be impossible by the 25th.

Venus is in inferior conjunction this month and is lost to view until February.

Mars is the westernmost planet in the eastern sky at dawn, appearing like a reddish first magnitude star. It is getting brighter all month.

Jupiter is the easternmost planet in the eastern sky at dawn, and the brightest, appearing like a star nearly minus second magnitude. It is getting brighter all month.

Saturn is the middle planet in the eastern sky at dawn, looking like a star of first magnitude, getting brighter all month.

Moon is at perigee, on the 8th, in total eclipse on the 9th, at apogee, the 20th, occults Neptune, the 21st, and eclipses the sun, on the 25th.

Jan. 3—Quadrantid meteor shower fine after midnight.
Jan. 4—Earth at perihelion, 91.4 million miles from the sun.
Jan. 9—Lunar eclipse.
Jan. 16—Mercury, greatest elongation, East 19°.
Jan. 19—Sun enters Capricornus.
Jan. 21—Venus in inferior conjunction.
Jan. 25—Solar eclipse.

February

Mercury begins the month in inferior conjunction, but is increasingly visible in the dawn sky by month's end. At greatest elongation on the 26th, 27° west of the sun, it will be fairly low at sunrise.

Venus becomes increasingly prominent in the dawn sky, attaining greatest brilliancy by the 25th, minus 4.3 magnitude.

Mars approaches Saturn, but backs away in retrograde motion beginning on the 21st.

Jupiter begins its retrograde motion on the 24th.

Saturn begins its retrograde motion on the 1st.

Moon is at perigee, on the 5th, apogee, the 17th, and occults Neptune, the 18th.

Feb. 1—Mercury, inferior conjunction, Saturn stationary, begins retrograde motion.
Feb. 10—Venus stationary, resumes direct motion.
Feb. 12—Mercury stationary, resumes direct motion.
Feb. 16—Sun enters Aquarius.
Feb. 21—Mars stationary, begins retrograde motion.
Feb. 24—Jupiter stationary, begins retrograde motion.

Feb. 25—Venus at greatest brilliancy.
Feb. 26—Mercury at greatest elongation, west 27°.

March

Mercury remains in the morning sky, but increasingly difficult to see.

Venus is most prominent in the morning sky in the east.

Mars continues to brighten, rising before midnight.

Jupiter is getting brighter, keeping ahead of Mars in the visibility race.

Saturn continues to brighten, but is a poor third.

Moon is at perigee, on the 4th, apogee, on the 17th, occults Neptune, the 17th, and at perigee again on the 29th.

Mar. 11—Sun enters Pisces.
Mar. 20—Equinox, Spring begins.
Mar. 31—Mars at opposition.

April

Mercury is in superior conjunction, the 11th, thus invisible all month.

Venus is at greatest elongation, 46° west of the sun on the 1st.

Mars begins to fade from its minus 1.2 magnitude, attained at the first of the month, but is prominent all night long.

Jupiter is at opposition, the 26th, and stays at minus 2 magnitude all month long.

Saturn is at opposition, the 9th, and at its brightest, plus 0.5 magnitude.

Moon is at apogee, and occults Neptune on the 14th, at perigee, the 25th.

Apr. 1—Venus at greatest elongation, 46° west.
Apr. 5—Mars at closest approach to Earth.
Apr. 9—Saturn at opposition.
Apr. 11—Mercury in superior conjunction.
Apr. 15—Pluto at opposition.
Apr. 18—Sun enters Aries.
Apr. 22—Lyrid meteor shower free from moonlight disturbance.
Apr. 26—Jupiter at opposition.

May

Mercury may be seen in the western evening sky by the ninth, when it is 21° east of the sun.

Venus is still prominent in the east before dawn.

Mars resumes its direct motion, on the 21st, a nice evening object.

Jupiter fades, but not noticeably this month.

Saturn fades slowly all month.

Moon is at apogee, and occults Neptune, the 11th, and at perigee, on the 24th.

May 5—Eta Aquarids should be observed despite lunar interference.

May 9—Mercury at greatest elongation, 21° east.

May 13—Sun enters Taurus.

May 21—Mercury stationary, begins retrograde.

May 24—Uranus at opposition.

June

Mercury, in inferior conjunction on the first, may be visible by month's end when it is 22° west of the sun. It is occulted by the moon, the 20th.

Venus remains prominent in the morning sky.

Mars, fading noticeably, draws closer to Saturn all month.

Jupiter resumes its direct motion, the 28th.

Saturn resumes its direct motion, the 19th.

Moon occults Neptune, and is at apogee, on the 7th, occults Mercury, the 20th, eclipses the sun and is at perigee, on the 21st.

June 1—Mercury is in inferior conjunction.

June 13—Mercury stationary, resumes direct motion.

June 17—Neptune at opposition.

June 19—Saturn stationary.

June 20—Sun enters Gemini.

June 21—Solar eclipse; solstice, summer begins.

June 26—Mercury at greatest elongation, 22° west.

June 28—Jupiter stationary.

July

Mercury, visible briefly for the first week, remains invisible for the rest of the month, being in superior conjunction, the 25th.

Venus rapidly approaching the morning horizon, growing more difficult to find.

Mars passes 3° south of Saturn, the 10th, becoming fainter all month.

Jupiter continues to dominate the evening sky, fading almost imperceptibly all month.

Saturn is passed by Mars on the 10th, and is the fainter of the two.

Moon occults Neptune, on the 4th, is at perigee on the 5th, in eclipse on the 6th, occults Venus on the 18th, is a perigee on the 19th, eclipses the sun on the 20th, and occults Neptune on the 31st.

July 4—Earth is a aphelion, 94.6 million miles away.

July 6—Lunar eclipse.

July 20—Solar eclipse; sun enters Cancer.

July 25—Mercury in superior conjunction.

July 29—Delta Aquarid meteor shower distinguished by moonlight.

August

Mercury is visible in the west at dusk by the end of the month.

Venus puts in its last appearance in the morning sky, becoming increasingly difficult to see by month's end.

Mars passes 2° south of Jupiter, on the 10th, appearing as a star of 0.8 magnitude.

Jupiter stays at minus 1.5 magnitude nearly all month, visible in the west in the evening.

Saturn looks like a first magnitude star, west of Jupiter with evening twilight.

Moon is at apogee, on the 1st, perigee, on the 17th, occults Neptune, on the 28th, and at apogee, on the 29th.

Aug. 10—Mars and Jupiter in conjunction; sun enters Leo.

Aug. 11-13—Perseid meteor shower. Watch this one. The moon is in last quarter, rising about midnight, but not bright. There may be fireballs.

September

Mercury is 27° east of the sun on the 6th, but fairly close to the western horizon after sunset, but now is the time to look.

Venus is now virtually invisible, lost in the sun's glare.

Mars holds its brightness to about first magnitude all month, streaking to about 30° east of Jupiter by month's end.

Jupiter remains prominent in the western sky in the evening.

Saturn vanishes by the end of the month.

Moon is at perigee, on the 13th, occults Neptune, on the 24th, and is at apogee, on the 25th.

Sept. 6—Mercury is at greatest elongation, 27° east.

Sept. 16—Sun enters Virgo.

Sept. 19—Mercury stationary, begins retrograde motion.

Sept. 23—Equinox, Autumn begins.

October

Mercury starts the month in inferior conjunction and remains virtually a prisoner of the morning twilight all month.

Venus is completely lost for the month.

Mars continues its eastward march, remaining in the western sky after sunset, looking like a first magnitude star.

Jupiter by month's end dives into the western twilight ending its year-long domination of the night sky.

Saturn, in conjunction on the 18th, is lost all month.

Moon is at perigee, on the 9th, occults Neptune, on the 21st, and is at apogee, on the 23rd.

Oct. 2—Mercury in inferior conjunction.

Oct. 10—Mercury stationary, begins direct motion.

Oct. 17—Mercury at greatest elongation, 18° west.

Oct. 20—Pluto in conjunction.

Oct. 21—Orionid meteor shower may be associated with Halley's comet, which is due to return to the sun Feb. 9, 1986.

There is no moon to interfere with observatories this month.

Oct. 30—Sun enters Libra.

November

Mercury is in superior conjunction, on the 19th, so is lost all month.

Venus is in superior conjunction, on the 4th, and is lost all month.

Mars has won the sole evening planet position, remaining about 3 hours behind the sun.

Jupiter is in conjunction, on the 13th, so is lost to view.

Saturn is increasingly prominent in the morning sky.

Moon is at perigee, on the 4th, occults Neptune, on the 18th, Mars on the 19th, and is at apogee, on the 20th.

Nov. 4—Venus in superior conjunction.

Nov. 13—Jupiter in conjunction.

Nov. 19—Mercury in superior conjunction.

Nov. 22—Sun enters Scorpius.

Nov. 29—Sun enters Ophiuchus.

December

Mercury may be seen by month's end in western sky after sunset.

Venus remains hidden by the sun's glare.

Mars is still in the western sky after sunset.

Jupiter emerges into the morning darkness.

Saturn continues its stately march away from the dawn.

Moon is at perigee, on the 2nd, eclipses the sun, on the 15th, is at apogee, on the 18th, is in eclipse and at perigee, on the 30th.

Dec. 13—Geminid meteor shower, free of moonlight, is worth a ton of hours of observation. Note occasional fire-balls.

Dec. 15—Solar eclipse.

Dec. 16—Sun enters Sagittarius.

Dec. 19—Neptune in conjunction.

Dec. 22—Solstice, winter begins.

Dec. 30—Lunar eclipse; Mercury at greatest elongation, 20° east.

Planets and the Sun

The planets of the solar system, in order of their distance from the sun, are Mercury, Venus, Earth, Mars, Jupiter, Saturn, Uranus, Neptune and Pluto. Both Uranus and Neptune are visible through good field glasses, but Pluto is so distant and so small that only large telescopes or long exposure photographs can make it visible.

Since Mercury and Venus are nearer to the sun than is the earth, their motions about the sun are seen from the earth as wide swings first to one side of the sun and then to the other, although they are both passing continuously around the sun in orbits that are almost circular. When their passage takes them either between the earth and the sun, or beyond the sun as seen from the earth, they are invisible to us. Because of the laws which govern the motions of planets about the sun, both Mercury and Venus require much less time to pass between the earth and the sun than around the far side of the sun, so their periods of visibility and invisibility are unequal.

The planets that lie farther from the sun than does the earth may be seen for longer periods of time and are invisible only when they are so located in our sky that they rise and set about the same time as the sun when, of course, they are overwhelmed by the sun's great brilliance. None of the planets has any light or radiant heat of its own but each shines only by reflecting sunlight from its surface. Mercury and Venus, because they are between the earth and the sun, show phases very much as the moon does. The planets farther from the sun are always seen as full, although Mars does occasionally present a slightly gibbous phase — like the moon when not quite full.

The planets move rapidly among the stars because they are very much nearer to us. The stars are also in motion, some of them at tremendous speeds, but they are so far away that their motion does not change their apparent positions in the heavens sufficiently for anyone to perceive that change in a single lifetime. The very nearest star is about 7,000 times as far away as the most distant planet.

Visible Planets of the Solar System

Mercury, Venus, Mars, Jupiter and Saturn

Mercury

Mercury, nearest planet to the sun, is the second smallest of the nine planets known to be orbiting the sun. Its diameter is 3,100 miles and its mean distance from the sun is 36,000,000 miles.

Mercury moves with great speed in its journey about the sun, averaging about 30 miles a second to complete its circuit in 88 of our days. Mercury rotates upon its axis over a period of nearly 59 days, thus exposing all of its surface periodically to the sun. It is believed that the surface passing before the sun may have a temperature of about 800° F., while the temperature on the side turned temporarily away from the sun does not fall as low as might be expected. This night temperature has been described by Russian astronomers as "room temperature" — possibly about 70°. This would contradict the former belief that Mercury did not possess an atmosphere, for some sort of atmosphere would be needed to retain the fierce solar radiation that strikes Mercury. A shallow but dense layer of carbon dioxide would produce the "greenhouse" effect, in which heat accumulated during exposure to the sun would not completely escape at night. The actual presence of a carbon dioxide atmosphere is in dispute.

This uncertainty about conditions upon Mercury and its motion arise from its shorter angular distance from the sun as seen from the earth, for Mercury is always too much in line with the sun to be observed against a dark sky, but is always seen during either morning or evening twilight.

Mariner 10 made 3 passes by Mercury in 1974 and 1975. A large fraction of the surface was photographed from varying distances, revealing a degree of cratering similar to that of the moon. An atmosphere of hydrogen and helium may be made up of gases of the solar wind temporarily concentrated by the presence of Mercury. The discovery of a weak but permanent magnetic field was a surprise. It has been held that both a fluid core and rapid rotation were necessary for the generation of a planetary magnetic field. Mercury may demonstrate these conditions to be unnecessary, or the field may reveal something about the history of Mercury.

Venus

Venus, slightly smaller than the earth, moves about the sun at a mean distance of 67,000,000 miles in 225 of our days. Its synodical revolution — its return to the same relationship with the earth and the sun, which is a result of the combination of its own motion and that of the earth — is 584 days. Every 19 months, then, Venus will be nearer to the earth than any other planet of the solar system. The planet is covered with a dense, white, cloudy atmosphere that conceals whatever is below it. This same cloud reflects sunlight efficiently so that when Venus is favorably situated, it is the third brightest object in the sky, exceeded only by the sun and the moon.

Spectral analysis of sunlight reflected from Venus' cloud tops has shown features that can best be explained by identifying the material of the clouds as sulphuric acid (oil of vitriol). Infrared spectroscopy from a balloon-borne telescope nearly 20 miles above the earth's surface gave indications of a small amount of water vapor present in the same region of the atmosphere of Venus. In 1956, radio astronomers at the Naval Research Laboratories in Washington, D. C., found a temperature for Venus of about 600° F., in marked contrast to minus 125° F., previously found at the cloud tops. Subsequent radio work confirmed a high temperature and produced evidence for this temperature to be associated with the solid body of Venus. With this peculiarity in mind, space scientists devised experiments for the U.S. space probe Mariner 2 to perform when it flew by in 1962. Mariner 2 confirmed the high temperature and the fact that it pertained to the ground rather than to some special activity of the atmosphere. In addition, Mariner 2 was unable to detect any radiation belts similar to the earth's so-called Van Allen belts. Nor was it able to detect the existence of a magnetic field even as weak as 1/100,000 of that of the earth.

In 1967, a Russian space probe, Venera 4, and the American Mariner 5 arrived at Venus within a few hours of each other. Venera 4 was designed to allow an instrument package to land gently on the planet's surface via parachute. It ceased transmission of information in about 75 minutes when the temperature it read went above 500° F. After considerable controversy, it was agreed that it still had 20 miles to go to reach the surface. The U.S. probe, Mariner 5, went around the dark side of Venus at a distance of about 6,000 miles. Again, it detected no significant magnetic field but its radio signals passed to earth through Venus' atmosphere twice — once on the night side and once on the day side. The results are startling. Venus' atmosphere is nearly all carbon dioxide and must exert a pressure at the planet's surface of up to 100 times the earth's normal sea-level pressure of one atmosphere. Since the earth and Venus are about the same size, and were presumably formed at the same time by the same general process from the same mixture of chemical elements, one is faced with the question: which is the planet with the unusual history — earth or Venus?

Radar astronomers using powerful transmitters as well as sensitive receivers and computers have succeeded in determining the rotation period of Venus. It turns out to be 243 days clockwise — in other words, contrary to the spin of most of the other planets and to its own motion around the sun. If it were exactly 243.16 days, Venus would always present the same face toward the earth at every inferior conjunction. This rate and sense of rotation allows a "day" on Venus of 117.4 earth days. Any part of Venus will receive sunlight on its clouds for over 58 days and will be in darkness for 58 days. Recent radar observations have shown surface features below the clouds. Large craters, continent-sized highlands, and extensive, dry "ocean" basins have been identified.

Mariner 10 passed Venus before traveling on to Mercury in 1974. The carbon dioxide molecule found in such abundance in the atmosphere is rather opaque to certain ultraviolet wavelengths, enabling sensitive television cameras to take pictures of the Venusian cloud cover. Photos radioed to earth show a spiral pattern in the clouds from equator to the poles.

In December, 1978, two U. S. Pioneer probes arrived at Venus. One went into orbit about Venus, the other split into 5 separate probes targeted for widely-spaced entry points to sample different conditions. The instrumentation ensemble was selected on the basis of previous missions that had shown the range of conditions to be studied. The probes confirmed expected high surface temperatures and high winds aloft. Winds of about 200 miles per hour, there, may account for the transfer of heat into the night side in spite of the low rotation speed of the planet. Surface winds were light at the time, however. Atmosphere and cloud chemistries were examined in detail, providing much data for continued analysis. The probes detected 4 layers of clouds and more light on the surface than expected solely from sunlight. This light allowed Russian scientists to obtain at least two photos showing rocks on the surface. Sulphur seems to play a large role in the chemistry of Venus, and reactions involving sulphur may be responsible for the glow. To learn more about the weather and atmospheric circulation on Venus, the orbiter takes daily photos of the daylight side cloud cover. It confirms the cloud pattern and its circulation shown by Mariner 10. The ionosphere shows large variability. The orbiter's radar operates in 2 modes: one, for ground elevation variability, and the second for ground reflectivity in 2 dimensions, thus "imaging" the surface. Radar maps of the entire planet that show the features mentioned above have been produced.

Mars

Mars is the first planet beyond the earth, away from the sun. Mars' diameter is about 4,200 miles, although a determination of the radius and mass of Mars by the space-probe, Mariner 4, which flew by Mars on July 14, 1965 at a distance of less than 6,000 miles, indicated that these dimensions were slightly larger than had been previously estimated. While Mars' orbit is also nearly circular, it is somewhat more eccentric than the orbits of many of the other planets, and Mars is more than 30 million miles farther from the sun in some parts of its year than it is at others. Mars takes 687 of our days to make one circuit of the sun, traveling at about 15 miles a second. Mars rotates upon its axis in almost the same period of time that the earth does — 24 hours and 37 minutes. Mars' mean distance from the sun is 141 million miles, so that the temperature on Mars would be lower than that on the earth even if Mars' atmosphere were about the same as ours. The atmosphere is not, however, for Mariner 4 reported that atmospheric pressure on Mars is between 1% and 2% of the earth's atmospheric pressure. This thin atmosphere appears to be largely carbon dioxide. No evidence of free water was found.

There appears to be no magnetic field about Mars. This would eliminate the previous conception of a dangerous radiation belt around Mars. The same lack of a magnetic field would expose the surface of Mars to an influx of cosmic radiation about 100 times as intense as that on earth.

Deductions from years of telescopic observation indicate that 5/8ths of the surface of Mars is a desert of reddish rock, sand, and soil. The rest of Mars is covered by irregular patches that appear generally green in hues that change through the Martian year. These were formerly held to be some sort of primitive vegetation, but with the findings of Mariner 4 of a complete lack of water and oxygen, such growth does not appear possible. The nature of the green areas is now unknown. They may be regions covered with volcanic salts whose color changes with changing temperatures and atmospheric conditions, or they may be gray, rather than green. When large gray areas are placed beside large red areas, the gray areas will appear green to the eye.

Mars' axis of rotation is inclined from a vertical to the plane of its orbit about the sun by about 25° and therefore Mars has seasons as does the earth, except that the Martian seasons are longer because Mars' year is longer. White caps form about the winter pole of Mars, growing through the winter and shrinking in summer. These polar caps are now believed to be both water ice and carbon dioxide ice. It is the carbon dioxide that is seen to come and go with the seasons. The water ice is apparently in many layers with dust between them, indicating climatic cycles.

The canals of Mars have become more of a mystery than they were before the voyage of Mariner 4. Markings forming a network of fine lines crossing much of the surface of Mars have been seen there by men who have devoted much time to the study of the planet, but no canals have shown clearly enough in previous photographs to be universally accepted. A few of the 21 photographs sent back to earth by Mariner 4 covered areas crossed by canals. The pictures show faint, ill-defined, broad, dark markings, but no positive identification of the nature of the markings.

Mariners 6 & 7 in 1969 sent back many more photographs of higher quality than those of the pioneering Mariner 4. These pictures showed cratering similar to the earlier views, but in addition showed 2 other types of terrain. Some regions seemed featureless for many square miles, but others were chaotic, showing high relief without apparent organization into mountain chains or craters.

Mariner 9, the first artificial body to be placed in an orbit about Mars, has transmitted over 10,000 photographs covering 100% of the planet's surface. Preliminary study of these photos and other data shows that Mars resembles no other planet we know. Using terrestrial terms, however, scientists describe features that seem to be clearly of volcanic origin. One of these features is Nix Olympica, apparently a caldera whose outer slopes are over 300 miles in diameter. Some features may have been produced by cracking (faulting) of the surface and the sliding of one region over or past another. Many craters seem to have been produced by impacting bodies such as may have come from the nearby asteroid belt. Features near the south pole may have been produced by glaciers that are no longer present. Flowing water, nonexistent on Mars at the present time, probably carved canyons, one 10 times longer and 3 times deeper than the Grand Canyon.

Although the Russians landed a probe on the Martian surface, it transmitted for only 20 seconds. In 1976, the U.S. landed 2 Viking spacecraft on the Martian surface. The landers had devices aboard to perform chemical analyses of the soil in search of evidence of life. The results have been inconclusive. The 2 Viking orbiters have returned the best pictures yet of Martian topographic features. Many features can be explained only if Mars once had large quantities of flowing water.

Mars' position in its orbit and its speed around that orbit in relation to the earth's position and speed bring Mars fairly close to the earth on occasions about two years apart and then move Mars and the earth too far apart for accurate observation and photography. Every 15-17 years, the close approaches are especially favorable to close observation.

Mars has 2 satellites, discovered in 1877 by Asaph Hall. The outer satellite, Deimos, revolves around Mars in about 31 hours. The inner satellite, Phobos, whips around Mars in a little more than 7 hours, making 3 trips around the planet each Martian day. Mariner and Viking photos show these bodies to be irregularly shaped and pitted with numerous craters. Phobos also shows a system of linear grooves, each about 1/3-mile across and roughly parallel. Phobos measures about 8 by 12 miles and Deimos about 5 by 7.5 miles in size.

Jupiter

Jupiter is the largest of the planets. Its equatorial diameter is 88,000 miles, 11 times the diameter of the earth. Its polar diameter is about 6,000 miles shorter. This is an equilibrium condition resulting from the liquidity of the planet and its extremely rapid rate of rotation: a Jupiter day is only 10 earth hours long. For a planet this size, this rotational speed is amazing, and it moves a point on Jupiter's equator at a speed of 22,000 miles an hour, as compared with 1,000 miles an hour for a point on the earth's equator. Jupiter is at an average distance of 480 million miles from the sun and takes almost 12 of our years to make one complete circuit of the sun.

The only directly observable chemical constituents of Jupiter's atmosphere are methane (CH_4) and ammonia (NH_3), but it is reasonable to assume the same mixture of elements available to make Jupiter as to make the sun. This would mean a large fraction of hydrogen and helium must be present also, as well as water (H_2O). The temperature at the tops of the clouds may be about minus 260° F. The clouds are probably ammonia ice crystals, becoming ammonia droplets lower down. There may be a space before water ice crystals show up as clouds: in turn, these become water droplets near the bottom of the entire cloud layer. The total atmosphere may be only a few hundred miles in depth, pulled down by the surface gravity (= 2.64 times earth's) to a relatively thin layer. Of course, the gases become denser with depth until they may turn into a slush or a slurry. Perhaps there is no surface — no real interface between the gaseous atmosphere and the body of Jupiter. Pioneers 10 and 11 provided evidence for considering Jupiter to be almost entirely liquid hydrogen. Long before a rocky core about the size of the earth is reached, hydrogen mixed with helium becomes a liquid metal at very high temperature. Jupiter's cloudy atmosphere is a fairly good reflector of sunlight and makes it appear far brighter than any of the stars.

Fourteen of Jupiter's 16 or more satellites have been found through earth-based observations. Four of the moons are large and bright, rivaling our own moon and the planet Mercury in diameter, and may be seen through a field glass. They move rapidly around Jupiter and their change of position from night to night is extremely interesting to watch. The other satellites are much smaller and in all but one instance much farther from Jupiter and cannot be seen except through powerful telescopes. The 4 outermost satellites are revolving around Jupiter clockwise as seen from the north, contrary to the motions of the great majority of the satellites in the solar system and to the direction of revolution of the planets around the sun. The reason for this retrograde motion is not known, but one theory is that Jupiter's tremendous gravitational power may have captured 4 of the minor planets or asteroids that move about the sun between Mars and Jupiter, and that these would necessarily revolve backward. At the great distance of these bodies from Jupiter — some 14 million miles — direct motion would result in decay of the orbits, while retrograde orbits would be stable. Jupiter's mass is more than twice the mass of all the other planets put together, and accounts for Jupiter's tremendous

gravitational field and so, probably, for its numerous satellites and its dense atmosphere.

In December, 1973, Pioneer 10 passed about 80,000 miles from the equator of Jupiter and was whipped into a path taking it out of our solar system in about 50 years. In December, 1974, Pioneer 11 passed within 30,000 miles of Jupiter, moving roughly from south to north, over the poles.

Photographs from both encounters were useful at the time but were far surpassed by those of Voyagers I and II. Thousands of high resolution multi-color pictures show rapid variations of features both large and small. The Great Red Spot exhibits internal counterclockwise rotation. Much turbulence is seen in adjacent material passing north or south of it. The satellites Amalthea, Io, Europa, Ganymede, and Callisto were photographed, some in great detail. Each is individual and unique, with no similarities to other known planets or satellites. Io has active volcanoes that probably have ejected material into a doughnut-shaped ring enveloping its orbit about Jupiter. This is not to be confused with the thin flat disk-like ring closer to Jupiter's surface. Now that such a ring has been seen by the Voyagers, older uncertain observations from Earth can be reinterpreted as early sightings of this structure.

Saturn

Saturn, last of the planets visible to the unaided eye, is almost twice as far from the sun as Jupiter, almost 900 million miles. It is second in size to Jupiter but its mass is much smaller. Saturn's specific gravity is less than that of water. Its diameter is about 71,000 miles at the equator; its rotational speed spins it completely around in a little more than 10 hours, and its atmosphere is much like that of Jupiter, except that its temperature at the top of its cloud layer is at least 100° lower. At about 300° F. below zero, the ammonia would be frozen out of Saturn's clouds. The theoretical construction of Saturn resembles that of Jupiter; it is either all gas, or it has a small dense center surrounded by a layer of liquid and a deep atmosphere.

Until Pioneer 11 passed Saturn in September 1979 only 10 satellites of Saturn were known. Since that time, the situation is quite confused. Added to data interpretations from the fly-by are earth-based observations using new techniques while the rings are edge-on and virtually invisible. It was hoped that the Voyager I fly-by in November 1980 would help sort out the system. It is now believed that Saturn has at least 16 satellites, some sharing orbits. The Saturn satellite system is still confused.

Saturn's ring system begins about 7,000 miles above the visible disk of Saturn, lying above its equator and extending about 35,000 miles into space. The diameter of the ring system, including Saturn itself, is about 170,000 miles; the rings are estimated to be no thicker than 10 miles. In 1973, radar observation showed the ring particles to be large chunks of material averaging a meter on a side.

Voyager I observations showed the rings to be considerably more complex than had been believed, so much so that interpretation will take much time. To the untrained eye, the Voyager photographs could be mistaken for pictures of a colorful phonograph record.

Uranus

Voyager II, after passing Saturn in August 1981, heads for a rendezvous with Uranus in 1986. Uranus, discovered by Sir William Herschel on Mar. 13, 1781, lies at a distance of 1.8 billion miles from the sun, taking 84 years to make its circuit around our star. Uranus has a diameter of about 32,000 miles and spins once in about 15.5 hours. One of the most fascinating features of Uranus is how far it is tipped over. Its north pole lies 98° from being directly up and down to its orbit plane. Thus, its seasons are extreme. If the sun rises at the north pole, it will stay up for 42 years; then it will set and the north pole will be in darkness (and winter) for 42 years.

Uranus has 5 satellites (known to date) whose orbits lie in the plane of the planet's equator. In that plane there are also 9 rings, discovered in 1978. Virtually invisible from Earth, the rings were found by observers watching Uranus pass before a star. As they waited, they saw their photoelectric equipment register a short eclipse of the star, then another, and another. Then the planet occulted the star as expected. After the star came out from behind Uranus, the star winked out several more times. Subsequent observations and analyses indicate 9 narrow, nearly opaque, rings circling Uranus.

The structure of Uranus is subject to some debate. Basically, however, it may have a rocky core surrounded by a thick icy mantle on top of which is a crust of hydrogen and helium that gradually becomes an atmosphere. Perhaps Voyager II will shed some light on this problem.

Neptune

Neptune, currently the most distant planet from the sun (until 1989), lies at an average distance of 2.8 billion miles. Having a diameter of about 31,000 miles and a rotation period of 18.2 hours, it is a virtual twin of Uranus. It is significantly more dense than Uranus, however, and this increases the debate over its internal structure. Neptune circles the sun in 164 years in a nearly circular orbit.

Neptune has 3 satellites, the third being found in 1981. The largest, Triton, is in a retrograde orbit suggesting that it was captured rather than being co-eval with Neptune. Triton is sufficiently large to raise significant tides on Neptune which will one day, say 100 million years from now, cause Triton to come close enough to Neptune for it to be torn apart. It is not known now if Neptune has rings, but it will have when Triton is torn apart. Nereid was found in 1949, and is in a long looping orbit suggesting it, too, was captured. The orbit of the third body is under analysis at this writing.

As with the other giant planets, Neptune is emitting more energy than it receives from the sun. These excesses are thought to be cooling from internal heat sources and from the heat of the formation of the planets.

Little is known of Neptune beyond its distance, but Voyager II, if all continues to operate, will send us pictures and observations in 1989.

Pluto

Although Pluto on the average stays about 5,900 billion miles from the sun, its orbit is so eccentric that it is now approaching its minimum distance of 4.4 billion miles, less than the current distance of Neptune. Thus Pluto, until 1999, is temporarily planet number 8 from the sun. At its mean distance, Pluto takes 247.7 years to circumnavigate the sun. Until recently that was about all that was known of Pluto.

About a century ago, a hypothetical planet was believed to lie beyond Neptune and Uranus. Little more than a guess, a mass of one Earth was assigned to the mysterious body and mathematical searches were begun. Amid some controversy about the validity of the predictive process, Pluto was found nearly where it was predicted to be. It was found by Clyde Tombaugh at the Lowell Observatory in Flagstaff, Ariz., in 1930.

At the U.S. Naval Observatory, also in Flagstaff, on July 2, 1978, James Christy obtained a photograph of Pluto that was distinctly elongated. Repeated observations of this shape and its variation were convincing evidence of the discovery of a satellite of Pluto. Now named Charon, it may be 500 miles across, at a distance of over 10,000 miles, and taking 6.4 days to move around Pluto, the same length of time Pluto takes to rotate once. Gravitational laws allow these interactions to give us the mass of Pluto as 0.0017 of the Earth and a diameter of 1,500 miles. This makes the density about the same as that of water.

It is now clear that Pluto, the body found by Tombaugh, could not have influenced Neptune and Uranus to go astray. Theorists are again at work looking for a new planet X.

Greenwich Sidereal Time for 0ʰ GMT, 1982

(Add 12 hours to obtain Right Ascension of Mean Sun)

Date		h	m	Date		h	m	Date		h	m	Date		h	m
Jan.	1	06	41.3	Apr.	1	12	36.1	July	10	19	10.4	Oct.	8	01	05.2
	11	07	20.7		11	13	15.6		20	19	49.8		18	01	44.6
	21	08	00.1		21	13	55.0		30	20	29.2		28	02	24.1
	31	08	39.6	May	1	14	34.4	Aug.	9	21	08.6	Nov.	7	03	03.5
Feb.	10	09	19.0		11	15	13.8		19	21	48.1		17	03	42.9
	20	09	58.4		21	15	53.2		29	22	27.5		27	04	22.3
Mar.	2	10	37.8		31	16	32.7	Sept.	8	23	06.9	Dec.	7	05	01.8
	12	11	17.3	June	10	17	12.1		18	23	46.4		17	05	41.2
	22	11	57.6		20	17	51.5		28	00	25.8		27	06	20.6
					30	18	31.0								

Astronomical Signs and Symbols

☉	The Sun	⊕	The Earth	♅	Uranus	☐	Quadrature
☾	The Moon	♂	Mars	♆	Neptune	☍	Opposition
☿	Mercury	♃	Jupiter	♇	Pluto	☊	Ascending Node
♀	Venus	♄	Saturn	☌	Conjunction	☋	Descending Node

Two heavenly bodies are in "conjunction" (☌) when they are due north and south of each other, either in Right Ascension (with respect to the north celestial pole) or in Celestial Longitude (with respect to the north ecliptic pole). If the bodies are seen near each other, they will rise and set at nearly the same time. They are in "opposition" (☍) when their Right Ascensions differ by exactly 12 hours, or their Celestial Longitudes differ by 180°. One of the two objects in opposition will rise while the other is setting. "Quadrature" (☐) refers to the arrangement when the coordinates of two bodies differ by exactly 90°. These terms may refer to the relative positions of any two bodies as seen from the earth, but one of the bodies is so frequently the sun that

mention of the sun is omitted; otherwise both bodies are named. The geocentric angular separation between sun and object is termed "elongation." Elongation is limited only for Mercury and Venus; the "greatest elongation" for each of these bodies is noted in the appropriate tables and is approximately the time for longest observation. When a planet is in its "ascending" (☊) or "descending" (☋) node, it is passing northward or southward, respectively, through the plane of the earth's orbit, across the celestial circle called the ecliptic. The term "perihelion" means nearest to the sun, and "aphelion," farthest from the sun. An "occultation" of a planet or star is an eclipse of it by some other body, usually the moon.

Planetary Configurations, 1982

Greenwich Mean Time (0 designates midnight; 12 designates noon)

Mo	D. h. m.			
Jan.	4 11	-		⊕ at perihelion
	8 06	-	☌ * ♄	♄ 5° N of Spica
	9 14	-	☌ ☿ ♀	☿ 5° S
	20	-	☍ ☽ ☉	Lunar eclipse
	15 19	-	☌ ♂ ☽	♂ 3° S
	16 12	-		☿ Gr Elong 19° E
	13	-	☌ ♄ ☽	♄ 3° S
	17 20	-	☌ ♃ ☽	♃ 4° S
	21 10	-	☌ ♀ ☉	Inferior
	25 05	-	☌ ☽ ☉	Eclipse
Feb.	1 04	-	☌ ☿ ☉	Inferior
	12 16	-	☌ ♂ ☽	♂ 2° S
	22	-	☌ ♄ ☽	♄ 3° S
	14 00		☌ ♃ ☽	♃ 4° S
	20 16	-	☌ ♀ ☽	♀ 7° N
	21 15	-	☌ ☿ ☽	☿ 2° N
	25 01	-		♀ Greatest brilliancy
	08	-	☌ * ♄	♄ 5° N of Spica
	26 11	-		☿ Gr elong 27° N
Mar.	11 22	-	☌ ♂ ☽	♂ 2° S
	12 05	-	☌ ♄ ☽	♄ 3° S
	13 17	-	☌ ♃ ☽	♃ 4° S
Mar.	20 22 56			Vernal equinox; Spring begins
	21 14	-	☌ ♀ ☽	♀ 5° N
	24 01	-	☌ ☿ ☽	☿ 2° N
	31 10	-	☍ ♂ ☉	
Apr.	1 18	-		♀ Gr elong 4.6° W
	5 07	-		♂ closest to ⊕
	7 13	-	☌ ♂ ☽	♂ 2° S
	8 10	-	☌ ♄ ☽	♄ 2° S
	9 02	-	☍ ♄ ☉	
	9 21	-	☌ ♃ ☽	♃ 3° S
	11 18	-	☌ ☿ ☉	Superior
	15 21	-	☍ ♇ ☉	
	20 06	-	☌ ♀ ☽	♀ 4° N
	26 00	-	☍ ♃ ☉	
May	4 05	-	☌ ♂ ☽	♂ 3° S
	5 13	-	☌ ♄ ☽	♄ 3° S
	6 21	-	☌ ♃ ☽	♃ 4° S
	9 00	-		☿ Gr elong 21° E
	10 14	-	☌ * ☿	☿ 8° N of Aldebaran
	20 02	-	☌ ♀ ☽	♀ 3° N
	24 03	-	☍ ♂ ☉	
	31 13	-	☌ ♂ ☽	♂ 5° S
June	1 16	-	☌ ♄ ☽	♄ 3° S
	1 20	-	☌ ☿ ☉	Inferior
	2 21	-	☌ ♃ ☽	♃ 4° S
	17 05	-	☍ ♆ ☉	
	18 23	-	☌ ♀ ☽	♀ 2° N
	20 02	-	☌ ☿ ☽	☿ 1°.1 S, occultation
	21 12	-	☌ ☽ ☉	Eclipse
	17 23			Summer solstice; Summer begins
	23 03	-	☌ * ☿	☿ 1°.7 N of Aldebaran
	26 14	-		☿ Gr elong 22° W
	28 12	-	☌ ♂ ☽	♂ 6° S
	21	-	☌ ♄ ☽	♄ 3° S
	30 01	-	☌ ♃ ☽	♃ 4° S
July	4 01	-	☌ * ♀	♀ 4° N of Aldebaran
	13	-		⊕ at aphelion
	6 08	-	☍ ☽ ☉	Eclipse
	10 00	-	☌ ♂ ♄	♂ 3° S
	18 19	-	☌ ♀ ☽	♀ 0°.6 N, occultation
	20 19	-	☌ ☽ ☉	Eclipse
	21 19	-	☌ * ♂	♂ 1°.6 N of Spica
	25 08	-	☌ ☿ ☉	Superior
	26 07	-	☌ ♄ ☽	♄ 3° S
	22	-	☌ ♂ ☽	♂ 6° S
	27 10	-	☌ ♃ ☽	♃ 4° S
Aug.	8 04	-	☌ * ☿	☿ 1°. 0 N of Regulus
	9 16	-	☌ * ♀	♀ 7° S of Pollux
	10 01	-	☌ ♂ ♃	♂ 2° S
	17 14	-	☌ ♀ ☽	♀ 1°.4 S
	20 15	-	☌ ☿ ☽	☿ 5° S
	22 20	-	☌ ♄ ☽	♄ 3° S
	24 01	-	☌ ♃ ☽	♃ 4° S
	15	-	☌ ♂ ☽	♂ 6° S
Sept.	6 04	-		☿ Gr elong 27° E
	7 09	-	☌ * ♀	♀ 0°.7 N of Regulus
	19 10	-	☌ ♄ ☽	♄ 3° S
	20 19	-	☌ ♃ ☽	♃ 4° S
	21 04	-	☌ * ♄	♄ 5° N of Spica
	22 13	-	☌ ♂ ♅	♂ 1°.5 S
	14	-	☌ ♂ ☽	♂ 5° S
	23 08 46			Autumnal equinox; Autumn begins
Oct.	2 05	-	☌ ☿ ☉	Inferior
	3 01	-	☌ * ♂	♂ 3° N of Antares
	15 11	-	☌ ☿ ☽	☿ 4° S
	17 18	-		☿ Gr elong 18° W
	18 15	-	☌ ♃ ☽	♃ 3° S
	18 21	-	☌ ♄ ☉	
	20 14	-	☌ ♇ ☉	
	21 17	-	☌ ♂ ☽	♂ 3° S
	29 04	-	☌ * ☿	☿ 4° N of Spica
Nov.	1 06	-	☌ ☿ ♄	☿ 0°.7 S
	4 02	-	☌ ♀ ☉	Superior
	13 14	-	☌ ♃ ☉	
	19 18	-	☌ ☿ ☉	Superior
	21	-	☌ ♂ ☽	♂ 0°.5 S occultation
	27 11	-	☌ ♅ ☉	
Dec.	11 02	-	☌ ♄ ☽	♄ 3° S
	13 05	-	☌ ♃ ☽	♃ 2° S
	15 09	-	☌ ☽ ☉	Eclipse
	19 00	-	☌ ♆ ☉	
	01	-	☌ ♂ ☽	♂ 1°.6 N
	22 04 39			Winter solstice; Winter begins
	30 12	-	☍ ☽ ☉	Eclipse
	19	-		☿ Gr elong 70° E

Planetary Configurations, 1983

Mo	D. h. m.			
Jan.	2 16	-		⊕ at perihelion
	7 10	-	☌ ☿ ♀	☿ 2° N
	12	-	☌ ♄ ☽	♄ 2° S
	9 22	-	☌ ♃ ☽	♃ 2° S
	15 19	-	☌ ♀ ☽	♀ 1°.8 N
	16 03	-	☌ ☿ ☉	Inferior
	17 04	-	☌ ♂ ☽	♂ 3° N
Feb.	3 21	-	☌ ♄ ☽	♄ 2° S
	6 13	-	☌ ♃ ☽	♃ 1°.5 S
	8 20	-		☿ Gr elong 26° W
	10 15	-	☌ ☿ ☽	☿ 2° N
	15 02	-	☌ ♀ ☽	♀ 4° N
	06	-	☌ * ♂	♂ 5° N of Antares
	17 05	-	☌ * ♃	♃ 5° N of Antares
	17 14	-	☌ ♃ ♅	♃ 0°.8 N
	18 22	-	☌ ♀ ♂	♀ 0°.5 S
Mar.	3 06	-	☌ ♄ ☽	♄ 1°.7 S
	6 03	-	☌ ♃ ☽	♃ 1°.0 S occultation
	16 06	-	☌ ♂ ☽	♂ 5° N
	17 06	-	☌ ♀ ☽	♀ 5° N
	21 04 39			Vernal equinox; Spring begins
	26 11	-	☌ ☿ ☉	Superior
	30 14	-	☌ ♄ ☽	♄ 1°.5 S
Apr.	2 13	-	☌ ♃ ☽	♃ 0°.6 S occultation
	9 12	-	☌ ☿ ♂	☿ 1°.4 N
	14 15	-	☌ ☿ ☽	☿ 6° N
	18 18	-	☍ ♇ ☉	
	21 08	-		☿ Gr elong 70° E
	21 19	-	☍ ♄ ☉	
	26 19	-	☌ ♄ ☽	♄ 1°.6 S
	29 19	-	☌ ♃ ☽	♃ 0°.6 S occultation

Rising and Setting of Planets, 1982

Greenwich Mean Time (0 designates midnight)

1982		20° N. Latitude		30° N. Latitude		40° N. Latitude		50° N. Latitude		60° N. Latitude	
		Rise	Set	Rise	Set	Rise	Set	Rise	Set	Rise	Set
						Venus, 1982						
Jan.	1	7:46	18:56	8:01	18:41	8:19	18:23	8:45	17:57	9:26	17:16
	11	6:53	18:08	7:06	17:55	7:22	17:39	7:44	17:17	8:19	16:42
	21	5:48	17:07	6:00	16:54	6:15	16:40	6:35	16:19	7:08	15:46
	31	4:45	16:04	4:57	15:52	5:12	15:37	5:32	15:17	6:05	14:45
Feb.	10	3:57	15:14	4:09	15:02	4:25	14:46	4:46	14:25	5:20	13:51
	20	3:25	14:41	3:39	14:28	3:55	14:12	4:17	13:49	4:53	13:13
Mar.	2	3:07	14:21	3:20	14:08	3:37	13:51	4:00	13:28	4:37	12:51
	12	2:56	14:11	3:09	13:58	3:26	13:42	3:48	13:19	4:24	12:43
	22	2:50	14:08	3:02	13:56	3:17	13:41	3:38	13:20	4:11	12:47
Apr.	1	2:46	14:10	2:57	13:59	3:10	13:46	3:28	13:28	3:56	13:00
	11	2:43	14:14	2:51	14:06	3:01	13:56	3:15	13:42	3:37	13:20
	21	2:39	14:21	2:45	14:15	2:52	14:00	3:01	13:59	3:15	13:45
May	1	2:36	14:28	2:38	14:26	2:41	14:23	2:45	14:19	2:51	14:13
	11	2:33	14:36	2:32	14:37	2:30	14:38	2:29	14:40	2:26	14:43
	21	2:30	14:45	2:25	14:50	2:19	14:55	2:12	15:03	2:00	15:15
	31	2:28	14:55	2:19	15:03	2:09	15:13	1:56	15:27	1:35	15:48
June	10	2:27	15:06	2:15	15:18	2:01	15:32	1:41	15:52	1:10	16:23
	20	2:29	15:19	2:14	15:34	1:55	15:52	1:30	16:18	0:48	16:59
	30	2:33	15:32	2:15	15:50	1:53	16:12	1:23	16:43	0:31	17:34
July	10	2:40	15:46	2:20	16:06	1:56	16:31	1:21	17:06	0:21	18:06
	20	2:50	16:00	2:30	16:21	2:03	16:47	1:26	17:24	0:20	18:30
	30	3:03	16:13	2:42	16:34	2:16	17:00	1:39	17:37	0:33	18:43
Aug.	9	3:18	16:24	2:58	16:44	2:33	17:09	1:58	17:44	0:58	18:44
	19	3:33	16:32	3:16	16:50	2:54	17:12	2:23	17:43	1:31	18:34
	29	3:49	16:38	3:34	16:53	3:16	17:11	2:51	17:36	2:10	18:17
Sept.	8	4:04	16:41	3:53	16:52	3:39	17:06	3:20	17:25	2:51	17:54
	18	4:18	16:42	4:11	16:49	4:02	16:58	3:50	17:10	3:32	17:29
	28	4:32	16:42	4:29	16:45	4:25	16:49	4:20	16:54	4:12	17:01
Oct.	8	4:45	16:41	4:47	16:40	4:48	16:38	4:50	16:36	4:53	16:33
	18	4:59	16:40	5:05	16:35	5:12	16:28	5:21	16:19	5:35	16:05
	28	5:14	16:41	5:24	16:31	5:35	16:19	5:52	16:03	6:17	15:37
Nov.	7	5:29	16:43	5:43	16:29	6:00	16:12	6:24	15:49	7:01	15:11
	17	5:46	16:48	6:04	16:31	6:25	16:09	6:55	15:39	7:45	14:49
	27	6:04	16:56	6:24	16:36	6:49	16:11	7:45	15:35	8:27	14:33
Dec.	7	6:21	17:08	6:43	16:46	7:11	16:19	7:51	15:39	9:02	14:28
	17	6:38	17:23	7:00	17:00	7:29	16:32	8:10	15:51	9:24	14:36
	27	6:52	17:39	7:14	17:18	7:41	16:50	8:20	16:11	9:30	15:01
						Mars, 1982						
Jan.	1	23:08	11:07	23:08	11:06	23:09	11:06	23:10	11:05	23:11	11:04
	11	22:45	10:40	22:46	10:38	22:48	10:36	22:51	10:33	22:55	10:29
	21	22:20	10:11	22:22	10:08	22:25	10:05	22:29	10:01	22:36	9:54
	31	21:51	9:40	21:54	9:37	21:58	9:33	22:04	9:27	22:12	9:19
Feb.	10	21:19	9:06	21:13	9:13	21:27	8:58	21:33	8:52	21:43	8:42
	20	20:43	8:29	20:36	8:36	20:51	8:21	20:57	8:15	21:07	8:05
Mar.	2	20:01	7:49	19:55	7:55	20:09	7:41	20:15	7:35	20:24	7:26
	12	19:14	7:04	19:09	7:09	19:20	6:57	19:25	6:52	19:33	6:45
	22	18:22	6:15	18:18	6:18	18:26	6:10	18:30	6:07	18:35	6:02
Apr.	1	17:26	5:23	17:25	5:25	17:28	5:21	17:30	5:20	17:32	5:17
	11	16:31	4:31	16:31	4:31	16:31	4:31	16:31	4:31	16:30	4:32
	21	15:38	3:41	15:39	3:39	15:36	3:42	15:35	3:44	15:33	3:46
May	1	14:50	2:54	14:52	2:52	14:47	2:56	14:45	2:58	14:42	3:01
	11	14:07	2:11	14:09	2:09	14:04	2:13	14:03	2:15	14:00	2:18
	21	13:30	1:32	13:31	1:31	13:28	1:33	13:27	1:34	13:26	1:35
	31	12:57	0:56	12:57	0:57	12:57	0:56	12:58	0:55	12:58	0:55
June	10	12:28	0:24	12:26	0:26	12:32	0:21	12:34	0:19	12:37	0:15
	20	12:03	23:54	11:59	23:59	12:09	23:48	12:14	23:44	12:21	23:37
	30	11:41	23:27	11:34	23:34	11:50	23:17	11:58	23:10	12:08	22:59
July	10	11:21	23:01	11:11	23:11	11:34	22:48	11:44	22:38	11:59	22:22
	20	11:03	22:37	10:50	22:50	11:20	22:19	11:33	22:06	11:53	21:46
	30	10:47	22:14	10:31	22:31	11:08	21:53	11:25	21:36	11:50	21:11
Aug.	9	10:32	21:53	10:13	22:13	10:58	21:27	11:18	21:08	11:49	20:37
	19	10:20	21:34	9:57	21:57	10:50	21:03	11:13	20:40	11:50	20:03
	29	10:08	21:16	9:42	21:42	10:43	20:41	11:09	20:14	11:53	19:30
Sep.	8	9:58	20:59	9:28	21:28	10:37	20:20	11:07	19:50	11:58	18:59
	18	9:49	20:45	9:17	21:17	10:32	20:02	11:05	19:28	12:03	18:30
	28	9:41	20:32	9:06	21:06	10:27	19:45	11:04	19:08	12:09	18:03
Oct.	8	9:33	20:20	8:57	20:57	10:23	19:31	11:02	18:51	12:14	17:40
	18	9:27	20:11	8:49	20:49	10:18	19:19	11:00	18:38	12:16	17:22
	28	9:20	20:03	8:42	20:42	10:13	19:10	10:55	18:28	12:14	17:09
Nov.	7	9:14	19:56	8:35	20:35	10:06	19:04	10:49	18:22	12:07	17:03
	17	9:07	19:51	8:29	20:29	9:58	19:00	10:39	18:18	11:55	17:03
	27	8:59	19:46	8:23	20:23	9:48	18:57	10:27	18:18	11:37	17:08
Dec.	7	8:50	19:42	8:16	20:10	9:36	18:57	10:12	18:21	11:14	17:18
	17	8:40	19:38	8:09	20:09	9:22	18:57	9:54	18:25	10:49	17:30
	27	8:29	19:34	8:02	20:02	9:06	18:58	9:34	18:30	10:20	17:43
						Jupiter, 1982						
Jan.	1	1:12	12:36	1:23	12:25	1:36	12:12	1:54	11:54	2:23	11:26
	11	0:39	12:01	0:50	11:50	1:04	11:36	1:22	11:18	1:52	10:48
	21	0:04	11:26	0:16	11:14	0:30	11:00	0:49	10:41	1:20	10:10
	31	23:29	10:49	23:40	10:38	23:55	10:23	0:14	10:04	0:46	9:32
Feb.	10	22:52	10:12	23:04	10:00	23:18	9:46	23:38	9:26	0:10	8:54
	20	22:14	9:34	22:26	9:22	22:40	9:07	23:00	8:47	23:32	8:15
Mar.	2	21:34	8:54	21:46	8:42	22:01	8:28	22:21	8:08	22:52	7:36

		20° N. Latitude		30° N. Latitude		40° N. Latitude		50° N. Latitude		60° N. Latitude	
		Rise	Set	Rise	Set	Rise	Set	Rise	Set	Rise	Set
	12	20:53	8:14	21:05	8:02	21:19	7:48	21:39	7:28	22:10	6:57
	22	20:11	7:32	20:23	7:21	20:37	7:07	20:56	6:47	21:27	6:16
Apr.	1	19:28	6:50	19:39	6:39	19:53	6:25	20:12	6:06	20:42	5:36
	11	18:44	6:07	18:54	5:56	19:08	5:42	19:26	5:24	19:55	4:55
	21	17:59	5:23	18:09	5:13	18:22	5:00	18:40	4:42	19:08	4:14
May	1	17:14	4:39	17:24	4:29	17:36	4:17	17:53	4:00	18:20	3:33
	11	16:29	3:56	16:39	3:46	16:51	3:34	17:07	3:18	17:33	2:52
	21	15:45	3:13	15:54	3:03	16:06	2:52	16:22	2:35	16:40	2:11
	31	15:01	2:30	15:11	2:21	15:22	2:10	15:37	1:54	16:01	1:30
June	10	14:19	1:48	14:28	1:39	14:39	1:28	14:54	1:13	15:18	0:50
	20	13:38	1:08	13:47	0:59	13:58	0:48	14:13	0:33	14:36	0:09
	30	12:58	0:28	13:07	0:19	13:18	0:08	13:33	23:53	13:56	23:30
July	10	12:20	23:49	12:29	23:40	12:40	23:29	12:55	23:14	13:19	22:50
	20	11:42	23:11	11:52	23:02	12:03	22:50	12:19	22:35	12:43	22:11
	30	11:06	22:34	11:16	22:25	11:28	22:13	11:44	21:57	12:09	21:32
Aug.	9	10:31	21:58	10:41	21:48	10:53	21:36	11:10	21:19	11:36	20:53
	19	9:57	21:23	10:08	21:12	10:20	21:00	10:38	20:42	11:05	20:15
	29	9:24	20:48	9:35	20:37	9:48	20:24	10:07	20:06	10:35	19:37
Sept.	8	8:52	20:14	9:03	20:03	9:17	19:49	9:36	19:33	10:06	19:00
	18	8:20	19:40	8:32	19:29	8:47	19:14	9:07	18:54	9:39	18:22
	28	7:49	19:07	8:02	18:55	8:17	18:40	8:38	18:19	9:12	17:45
Oct.	8	7:19	18:35	7:32	18:22	7:48	18:06	8:10	17:44	8:45	17:08
	18	6:49	18:03	7:02	17:49	7:19	17:32	7:42	17:09	8:20	16:32
	28	6:19	17:31	6:33	17:17	6:51	17:00	7:15	16:35	7:54	15:55
Nov.	7	5:49	16:59	6:04	16:44	6:22	16:26	6:48	16:01	7:29	15:19
	17	5:20	16:28	5:35	16:12	5:54	15:53	6:20	15:27	7:04	14:43
	27	4:50	15:56	5:06	15:40	5:26	15:20	5:53	14:53	6:38	14:08
Dec.	7	4:20	15:25	4:37	15:08	4:57	14:48	5:26	14:19	6:13	13:32
	17	3:50	14:53	4:07	14:36	4:28	14:15	4:58	13:46	5:47	12:57
	27	3:20	14:22	3:38	14:04	3:59	13:43	4:30	13:12	5:20	12:22
Saturn, 1982											
Jan.	1	0:09	11:52	0:14	11:47	0:20	11:42	0:28	11:34	0:40	11:21
	11	23:32	11:14	23:37	11:09	23:43	11:02	23:52	10:54	0:05	10:40
	21	22:53	10:36	22:59	10:30	23:05	10:24	23:14	10:15	23:27	10:02
	31	22:14	9:57	22:20	9:51	22:26	9:45	22:35	9:36	22:48	9:23
Feb.	10	21:35	9:17	21:40	9:12	21:46	9:05	21:55	8:57	22:08	8:44
	20	20:54	8:37	20:59	8:32	21:05	8:26	21:14	8:17	21:27	8:04
Mar.	2	20:13	7:56	20:18	7:51	20:24	7:45	20:32	7:37	20:44	7:25
	12	19:31	7:15	19:36	7:10	19:42	7:05	19:49	6:57	20:01	6:45
	22	18:49	6:34	18:53	6:29	18:59	6:24	19:06	6:16	19:18	6:05
Apr.	1	18:06	5:52	18:11	5:48	18:16	5:43	18:23	5:36	18:33	5:25
	11	17:24	5:10	17:28	5:06	17:32	5:01	17:39	4:55	17:49	4:45
	21	16:41	4:28	16:45	4:25	16:49	4:20	16:55	4:14	17:05	4:04
May	1	15:58	3:47	16:02	3:43	16:06	3:39	16:12	3:33	16:21	3:24
	11	15:16	3:05	15:20	3:02	15:24	2:58	15:29	2:52	15:38	2:44
	21	14:35	2:24	14:38	2:21	14:42	2:17	14:47	2:12	14:55	2:04
	31	13:54	1:43	13:57	1:40	14:01	1:36	14:06	1:31	14:13	1:24
June	10	13:13	1:03	13:16	1:00	13:20	0:56	13:25	0:51	13:25	0:51
	20	12:34	0:23	12:37	0:20	12:40	0:17	12:45	0:12	12:53	0:04
	30	11:19	23:19	11:27	23:10	11:19	23:19	11:36	23:01	11:19	23:19
July	10	11:16	23:05	11:20	23:02	11:24	22:58	11:29	22:53	11:37	22:45
	20	10:39	22:27	10:42	22:24	10:46	22:20	10:52	22:14	11:01	22:05
	30	10:02	21:49	10:05	21:46	10:10	21:41	10:16	21:35	10:25	21:26
Aug.	9	9:25	21:12	9:29	21:08	9:34	21:04	9:41	20:57	9:50	20:47
	19	8:50	20:35	8:54	20:31	8:59	20:26	9:06	20:19	9:16	20:08
	29	8:14	19:59	8:19	19:54	8:24	19:49	8:32	19:41	8:43	19:30
Sept.	8	7:39	19:23	7:44	19:18	7:50	19:12	7:58	19:04	8:10	18:51
	18	7:04	18:47	7:10	18:41	7:16	18:35	7:25	18:26	7:38	18:13
	28	6:30	18:11	6:36	18:05	6:42	17:58	6:52	17:49	7:06	17:34
Oct.	8	5:56	17:35	6:02	17:29	6:09	17:22	6:19	17:12	6:34	16:56
	18	5:21	17:00	5:28	16:53	5:36	16:45	5:46	16:35	6:03	16:18
	28	4:47	16:24	4:54	16:17	5:02	16:09	5:14	15:58	5:31	15:40
Nov.	7	4:13	15:49	4:20	15:41	4:29	15:33	4:41	15:21	4:59	15:02
	17	3:38	15:13	3:46	15:05	3:55	14:56	4:08	14:44	4:27	14:24
	27	3:04	14:37	3:12	14:29	3:21	14:20	3:34	14:07	3:55	13:46
Dec.	7	2:29	14:01	2:37	13:53	2:47	13:43	3:01	13:31	3:22	13:08
	17	1:53	13:25	2:02	13:16	2:12	13:06	2:26	12:52	2:48	12:30
	27	1:18	12:48	1:26	12:40	1:37	12:29	1:51	12:15	2:14	11:52

Aurora Borealis and Aurora Australis

The Aurora Borealis, also called the Northern Lights, is a broad display of rather faint light in the northern skies at night. The Aurora Australis, a similar phenomenon, appears at the same time in southern skies. The aurora appears in a wide variety of forms. Sometimes it is seen as a quiet glow, almost foglike in character; sometimes as vertical streamers in which there may be considerable motion; sometimes as a series of luminous expanding arcs. There are many colors, with white, yellow, and red predominating.

The auroras are most vivid and most frequently seen at about 20 degrees from the magnetic poles, along the northern coast of the North American continent and the eastern part of the northern coast of Europe. They have been seen as far south as Key West and as far north as Australia and New Zealand, but rarely.

While the cause of the auroras is not known beyond question, there does seem to be a definite correlation between auroral displays and sun-spot activity. It is thought that atomic particles expelled from the sun by the forces that cause solar flares speed through space at velocities of 400 to 600 miles per second. These particles are entrapped by the earth's magnetic field, forming what are termed the Van Allen belts. The encounter of these clouds of the solar wind with the earth's magnetic field weakens the field so that previously trapped particles are allowed to impact the upper atmosphere. The collisions between solar and terrestrial atoms result in the glow in the upper atmosphere called the aurora. The glow may be vivid where the lines of magnetic force converge near the magnetic poles.

The auroral displays appear at heights ranging from 50 to about 600 miles and have given us a means of estimating the extent of the earth's atmosphere.

The auroras are often accompanied by magnetic storms whose forces, also guided by the lines of force of the earth's magnetic field, disrupt electrical communication.

The Planets and the Solar System

Planet	Mean daily motion "	Orbital velocity miles per sec.	Sidereal revolution days	Synodical revolution days	Dist. from sun in millions of mi. Max.	Min.	Dist. from Earth in millions of mi. Max.	Min.	Light at' perihelion	aphelion
Mercury ..	14732.420	29.75	87.9693	115.9	43.403	28.597	136	50	10.58	4.59
Venus ...	5767.668	21.76	224.7009	583.9	67.726	66.813	161	25	1.94	1.89
Earth....	3548.192	18.51	365.2564	—	94.555	91.445	—	—	1.03	0.97
Mars ...	1886.519	14.99	686.9796	779.9	154.936	128.471	248	35	0.524	0.360
Jupiter ...	298.993	8.12	4332.1248	398.9	507.046	460.595	600	368	0.0408	0.0336
Saturn ...	119.718	5.99	10825.863	378.1	937.541	838.425	1031	745	0.01230	0.00984
Uranus ..	41.978	4.23	30676.15	369.7	1859.748	1699.331	1953	1606	0.00300	0.00250
Neptune ..	21.493	3.38	59911.13	367.5	2821.686	2760.386	2915	2667	0.00114	0.00109
Pluto	14.116	2.95	90824.2	366.7	4551.386	2756.427	4644	2663	0.00114	0.00042

Light at perihelion and aphelion is solar illumination in units of mean illumination at Earth.

Planet	Mean longitude of:* ascending node ° ' "	perihelion ° ' "	Inclination* of orbit to ecliptic ° ' "	Mean distance**	Eccentricity of orbit	Mean longitude at the epoch* ° ' "
Mercury....	48 06 43	77 09 50	7 00 16	0.387100	0.205630	111 13 00
Venus.....	76 30 54	131 33 36	3 23 40	0.723330	0.006788	176 09 15
Earth		102 28 59		0.999990	0.016734	292 45 52
Mars	49 24 47	335 44 38	1 51 00	1.523633	0.093382	260 50 43
Jupiter	100 16 44	14 51 43	1 18 21	5.20488	0.047777	193 46 07
Saturn.....	113 30 22	95 26 20	2 29 10	9.57501	0.053616	183 50 50
Uranus	73 59 49	175 01 05	0 46 20	19.2390	0.050521	233 41 36
Neptune ...	131 31 59	42 16 48	1 46 23	30.1733	0.004505	263 59 39
Pluto	110 02 17	223 14 31	17 08 11	39.9022	0.256387	211 50 01

*Consistent for the standard Epoch: 1981 July 15.0 Ephemeris Time **Astronomical units

Sun and planets	Semi-diameter at unit distance ' "	at mean least dist. "	in miles mean s.d.	Volume ⊕=1.	Mass. ⊕=1.	Density ⊕=1.	Axial rotation d.	h.	m.	s.	Gravity at surface ⊕=1.	Reflecting power Pct.	Probable temperature °F.
Sun......	15 59.62	—	432560	1303730	332830	0.26	24	16	48		27.9	—	+ 10,000
Mercury ...	3.37	5.45	1505	0.054	0.0554	0.98	59				0.37	0.06	+ 620
Venus	8.46	30.50	3762	0.880	0.8150	0.94	244.3 (R)				0.88	0.72	+ 900
Earth.....	—	—	3960	1.000	1.000	1.00	23	56	4		1.00	0.39	+ 72
Moon.....	2.40	16 43.00	1080	0.020	0.0123	0.61	27	7	43	12	0.17	0.07	— 10
Mars	4.68	8.94	2107	0.149	0.1075	0.72	24	37	23		0.38	0.16	— 10
Jupiter	98.37	23.43	44270	1316.	317.84	0.24	9	50	30		2.64	0.70	— 240
Saturn	82.80	9.76	37300	755.	95.147	0.13	10	14			1.15	0.75	— 300
Uranus	32.90	1.80	15200	52.	14.54	0.29	10	49 (R)			1.15	0.90	— 340
Neptune ...	31.10	1.06	15600	57.	17.23	0.30	18	12			1.12	0.82	— 370
Pluto*.....	1.80	0.06	800	0.008	0.0016	0.19	6	9			0.04	0.14	?

*Much of this information is too new to be verified, but observers at the U.S. Naval Observatory have derived values similar to these after having discovered that Pluto has a satellite. It apparently revolves about Pluto in a period equal to Pluto's rotation period. (R) retrograde of Venus and Uranus.

Seven Eclipses in 1982

Greenwich Mean Time

First Eclipse

A total eclipse of the moon, January 9. Generally invisible in North America, seen best in Europe, Africa, and Asia.

Circumstances of the Eclipse

Moon enters penumbra ..	Jan. 9,	17:14.8
Moon enters umbra	9,	18:13.6
Total eclipse begins	9,	19:16.6
Middle of eclipse......	9,	19:55.8
Total eclipse ends	9,	20:35.0
Moon leaves umbra	9,	21:38.1
Moon leaves penumbra ..	9,	22:36.9
Magnitude of eclipse....		1.337

Second Eclipse

A partial eclipse of the sun, January 25, seen throughout Antarctica, except the Palmer Peninsula, and most of New Zealand.

Circumstances of the Eclipse

Eclipse begins	Jan. 25,	02:49.8
Greatest eclipse	25,	04:42.0
Eclipse ends	25,	06:34.3
Magnitude of greatest eclipse		0.566

Third Eclipse

A partial eclipse of the sun, June 21, seen in the South Atlantic Ocean and South Africa.

Circumstances of the Eclipse

Eclipse begins	June 21,	10:27.8
Greatest eclipse	21,	12:03.7

Eclipse ends	21,	13:39.6
Magnitude of greatest eclipse		0.617

Fourth Eclipse

A total eclipse of the moon, July 6, seen in Australia, New Zealand, the Pacific Ocean, most of South America, and most of North America.

Circumstances of the Eclipse

Moon enters penumbra ..	July 6,	4:22.2
Moon enters umbra	6,	5:32.8
Total eclipse begins	6,	6:37.7
Middle of eclipse......	6,	7:30.9
Total eclipse ends	6,	8:24.1
Moon leaves umbra	6,	9:29.0
Moon leaves penumbra ..	6,	10:39.6
Magnitude of eclipse....		1.722

Fifth Eclipse

A partial eclipse of the sun, July 20, visible over the Arctic regions, western Europe, and eastern Siberia.

Circumstances of the Eclipse

Eclipse begins	July 20,	17:18.7
Greatest eclipse	20,	18:43.8
Eclipse ends	20,	20:09.1
Magnitude of greatest eclipse		0.464

Sixth Eclipse

A partial eclipse of the sun, December 15, visible from

western Europe to northern India, including North Africa and the Arabian peninsula.

and eastern Asia.

Circumstances of the Eclipse

Eclipse begins	Dec. 15,	7:21.9
Greatest eclipse	15,	9.31.2
Eclipse ends	15,	11:40.7

Seventh Eclipse

A total eclipse of the moon, December 30, visible from North America, Pacific Ocean, Arctic regions, Australia,

Circumstances of the Eclipse

Moon enters penumbra . .	Dec. 30,	8:51.9
Moon enters umbra	30,	9:50.4
Total eclipse begins	30,	10:58.2
Middle of the eclipse. . . .	30,	11:28.7
Total eclipse ends	30,	11:59.3
Moon leaves umbra	30,	13:07.1
Moon leaves penumbra . .	30,	14:05.5
Magnitude of the eclipse. .		1.188

Star Tables

These tables include stars of visual magnitude 2.5 and brighter. Co-ordinates are for the epoch Jan. 0.432, 1981. Where no parallax figures are given, the trigonometric parallax figure is smaller than the margin for error and the distance given is obtained by indirect methods. Stars of variable magnitude designated by v.

To find the time when the star is on meridian, subtract R.A.M.S. of the sun table on page 757 from the star's right ascension, first adding 24h to the latter, if necessary. Mark this result P.M., if less than 12h; but if greater than 12, subtract 12h and mark the remainder A.M.

Star	Magnitude	Parallax "	Light yrs.	Right ascension h. m.	Declination ° '	Star	Magnitude	Parallax "	Light yrs.	Right ascension h. m.	Declination ° '
α Andromedae (Alpheratz)	2.06	0.02	90	0 07.4	+28 59	β Ursae Majoris (Merak)	2.37	0.04	78	11 00.7	+56 29
β Cassiopeiae	2.26v	0.07	45	0 08.2	+59 03	α Ursae Majoris (Dubhe)	1.81	0.03	105	11 02.6	+61 51
α Phoenicis	2.39	0.04	93	0 25.3	−42 25	β Leonis (Denebola)	2.14	0.08	43	11 48.1	+14 41
α Cassiopeiae (Schedir)	2.22	0.01	150	0 39.4	+56 26	γ Ursae Majoris (Phecda)	2.44	0.02	90	11 52.8	+53 48
β Ceti	2.02	0.06	57	0 42.6	−18 05	α Crucis	1.39		370	12 25.5	−63 00
γ Cassiopeiae	2.13v	0.03	96	0 55.6	+60 37	γ Crucis	1.69		220	12 30.1	−57 00
β Andromedae	2.02	0.04	76	1 08.7	+35 31	γ Centauri	2.17		160	12 40.5	−48 51
α Eridani (Achernar)	0.51	0.02	118	1 37.0	−57 20	β Crucis	1.28v		490	12 46.5	−59 35
γ Andromedae	2.14		260	2 02.7	+42 14	ε Ursae Majoris (Alioth)	1.79v	0.01	68	12 53.2	+56 04
α Arietis	2.00	0.04	76	2 06.1	+23 22	ζ Ursae Majoris (Mizar)	2.26	0.04	88	13 23.2	+55 01
α Ursae Min. (Pole Star)	1.99v		680	2 12.7	+89 11	α Virginis (Spica)	0.91v	0.02	220	13 24.2	−11 04
ο Ceti	2.00v	0.01	103	2 18.4	−3 04	ε Centauri	2.33v		570	13 38.7	−53 22
β Persei (Algol)	2.06v	0.03	105	3 06.9	+40 53	η Ursae Majoris (Alkaid)	1.87		210	13 46.8	+49 24
α Persei	1.80	0.03	570	3 23.0	+49 48	β Centauri	0.63v	0.02	490	14 02.5	−60 17
α Tauri (Aldebaran)	0.86v	0.05	68	4 34.8	+16 28	θ Centauri	2.04	0.06	55	14 05.6	−36 17
β Orionis (Rigel)	0.14v		900	5 13.6	−8 13	α Bootis (Arcturus)	−0.06	0.09	36	14 14.8	+19 17
α Aurigae (Capella)	0.05	0.07	45	5 15.3	+45 59	η Centauri	2.39v		390	14 34.3	−42 04
γ Orionis (Bellatrix)	1.64	0.03	470	5 24.1	+6 20	α Centauri	0.01	0.75	4.3	14 38.3	−60 45
β Tauri (El Nath)	1.65	0.02	300	5 25.1	+28 36	α Lupi	2.32v		430	14 40.7	−47 18
δ Orionis	2.20v		1500	5 31.0	−0 19	ε Bootis	2.37	0.01	103	14 44.2	+27 09
ε Orionis	1.70		1600	5 35.2	−1 13	β Ursae Minoris	2.07	0.03	105	14 50.7	+74 14
ζ Orionis	1.79	0.02	1600	5 39.8	−1 57	α Coronae Borealis	2.23v	0.04	76	15 33.9	+26 47
κ Orionis	2.06	0.01	2100	5 46.9	−9 41	δ Scorpii	2.34		590	15 59.2	−22 34
α Orionis (Betelgeuse)	0.41v		520	5 54.1	+7 24	α Scorpii (Antares)	0.92v	0.02	520	16 28.2	−26 23
β Aurigae	1.86	0.04	88	5 58.1	+44 57	α Trianguli Australis	1.93	0.02	82	16 46.6	−69 00
α Canis Majoris	1.96	0.01	750	6 21.9	−17 57	ε Scorpii	2.28	0.05	66	16 48.9	−34 16
α Carinae (Canopus)	−0.72	0.02	98	6 23.5	−52 41	η Ophiuchi	2.43	0.05	69	17 09.3	−15 42
γ Geminorum	1.93	0.03	105	6 36.6	+16 25	λ Scorpii	1.60v		310	17 32.3	−37 05
α Canis Majoris (Sirius)	−1.47	0.38	8.7	6 44.3	−16 41	α Ophiuchi	2.09	0.06	58	17 34.0	+12 34
ε Canis Majoris	1.48		680	6 57.9	−28 57	θ Scorpii	1.86	0.02	650	17 36.0	−42 59
δ Canis Majoris	1.85		2100	7 07.6	−26 22	κ Scorpii	2.39v		470	17 41.2	−39 01
η Canis Majoris	2.46		2700	7 23.3	−29 16	γ Draconis	2.21	0.02	108	17 56.2	+51 29
α Geminorum (Castor)	1.97	0.07	45	7 33.4	+31 56	ε Sagittarii	1.81	0.02	124	18 22.9	−34 24
α Canis Minoris (Procyon)	0.37	0.29	11.3	7 38.3	+5 16	α Lyrae (Vega)	0.04	0.12	26.5	18 36.3	+38 46
β Geminorum (Pollux)	1.16	0.09	35	7 44.2	+28 04	σ Sagittarii	2.12		300	18 54.1	−26 19
ζ Puppis	2.23		2400	8 02.9	−39 57	α Aquilae (Altair)	0.77	0.20	16.5	19 49.9	+8 49
γ Velorum	1.88		520	8 08.9	−47 17	γ Cygni	2.22		750	20 21.5	+40 12
ε Carinae	1.90		340	8 22.1	−59 27	α Pavonis	1.95		310	20 24.2	−56 48
δ Velorum	1.95	0.04	76	8 44.2	−54 38	α Cygni (Deneb)	1.26		1600	20 40.8	+45 13
λ Velorum	2.24	0.02	750	9 07.3	−43 21	ε Cygni	2.46	0.04	74	20 45.3	+33 54
β Carinae	1.67	0.04	86	9 13.0	−69 38	α Cephei	2.44	0.06	52	21 18.1	+62 30
ι Carinae	2.25		750	9 16.6	−59 12	ε Pegasi	2.38		780	21 43.3	+9 47
κ Velorum	2.49	0.01	470	9 21.5	−54 56	α Gruis	1.76	0.05	64	22 07.0	−47 03
α Hydrae	1.98	0.02	94	9 26.7	−8 35	β Gruis	2.17v		280	22 41.5	−46 59
α Leonis (Regulus)	1.36	0.04	84	10 07.4	+12 04	α Piscis Austrinis (Fomalhaut)	1.15	0.14	22.6	22 56.6	−29 43
γ Leonis	1.99	0.02	90	10 18.9	+19 56	β Pegasi	2.50v	0.02	210	23 02.8	+27 59
						α Pegasi	2.50	0.03	109	23 03.8	+15 06

Astronomical Constants; Speed of Light

The following astronomical constants were adopted in 1968, in accordance with the resolutions and recommendations of the International Astronomical Union (Hamburg 1964): Velocity of light, 299,792.5 kilometers per second, or about 186,282.3976 statute miles per second: solar parallax, 8'.794: constant of nutation, 9'.210; and constant of aberration, 20'.496.

Morning and Evening Stars 1982
Greenwich Mean Time

	Morning	Evening		Morning	Evening
Jan.	Venus (to Jan. 21)	Mercury			Saturn
	Mars	Venus (from Jan. 21)	July	Mercury (to July 25)	Mercury (from July 25)
	Jupiter				Mars
	Saturn			Venus	Jupiter
Feb.	Mercury (from Feb. 1)	Mercury (to Feb. 1)			Saturn
	Venus		Aug.	Venus	Mercury
	Mars				Mars
	Jupiter				Jupiter
	Saturn				Saturn
Mar.	Mercury		Sept.	Venus	Mercury
	Venus				Mars
	Mara				Jupiter
	Jupiter				Saturn
	Saturn		Oct.	Mercury (from Oct. 2)	Mercury (to Oct. 2)
Apr.	Mercury (to Apr. 11)	Mercury (from Apr. 11)		Venus	Mars
	Venus	Mars			Jupiter
	Jupiter (to Apr. 26)	Jupiter (from Apr. 26)		Saturn (from Oct. 18)	Saturn (to Oct. 18)
	Saturn (to Apr. 9)	Saturn (from Apr. 9)	Nov.	Mercury (to Nov. 19)	Mercury (from Nov. 19)
May	Venus	Mercury		Venus (to Nov. 4)	Venus (from Nov. 4)
		Mars		Jupiter (from Nov. 13)	Mars
		Jupiter		Saturn	Jupiter (to Nov. 13)
		Saturn	Dec.	Jupiter	Mercury
June	Mercury (from June 1)	Mercury (to June 1)		Saturn	Venus
	Venus	Mars			Mars
		Jupiter			

Comet Table 1980-1986

Name	Year of first known perihelion	Due to return		Period in years	Peri-helion dist.	Aphe-lion dist.	Inclina-tion to ecliptic degree	Long. of ascend. node degree	From asc. node to perihelion degree
Brooks II	1889	Nov.	1980	6.88	1.84	5.39	6	176	198
Harrington	1953	Nov.	1980	6.80	1.58	5.59	9	119	233
Reinmuth I	1928	Nov.	1980	7.63	2.00	5.75	8	121	9
Encke	1786	Dec.	1980	3.30	0.34	4.02	12	334	186
Tuttle	1790	Jan.	1981	13.77	1.02	10.47	54	270	207
Reinmuth II	1947	Feb.	1981	6.74	1.94	5.20	7	296	45
Borrelly	1905	Feb.	1981	6.76	1.32	5.84	30	75	353
Schwassmann-Wachmann II	1929	Feb.	1981	6.51	2.14	4.83	4	126	357
West-Kohoutek-Ikemara*	1975	Mar.	1981	6.11	1.40	5.29	30	85	358
Neujmin II	1916	May	1981	5.43	1.34	4.84	11	328	194
Finlay	1886	June	1981	6.95	1.10	6.19	4	42	322
Stephan-Oterma	1867	Oct.	1981	38.84	1.60	21.34	18	79	358
Swift-Gehrels	1889	Nov.	1981	9.23	1.35	7.44	9	314	84
Slaughter-Burnham	1958	Nov.	1981	11.62	2.54	7.72	8	346	44
Gehrels II*	1973	Nov.	1981	7.94	2.35	5.61	7	216	183
Kearns-Kwee	1963	Dec.	1981	9.01	2.23	6.43	9	315	131
Oterma	1942	Jan.	1982	7.88	3.39	4.53	4	155	355
Perrine-Mrkos	1896	Apr.	1982	6.72	1.27	5.85	18	240	166
Gale	1927	June	1982	10.99	1.18	8.70	12	67	209
Swift-Tuttle*	1862	Aug.	1982	119.98	0.96	47.69	114	139	153
Gunn	1969	Nov.	1982	6.80	2.45	4.74	10	68	198
Arend	1951	Dec.	1982	7.76	1.82	6.02	22	358	45
Neujmin III	1929	Dec.	1982	10.57	1.98	7.66	4	150	147
Vaisala I	1939	Dec.	1982	11.28	1.87	8.19	12	135	50
Kojima*	1970	Feb.	1983	6.19	1.63	5.11	4	291	178
Pons-Winneke	1819	Mar.	1983	6.34	1.25	5.60	22	93	172
Harrington-Abell	1954	Sept.	1983	7.19	1.77	5.68	17	146	338
Kohoutek	1975	Apr.	1986	5.67	1.56	4.80	5	274	169
Halley	240 B.C.	May	1986	76.1	0.59	35.3	162	58	112

*One appearance only.

Most of the comets in the table will not be seen except by professional astronomers or by well-equipped amateurs. At any given time, these observers may be able to follow about a half dozen comets of which the public is unaware. An easily seen comet is rare, one or two every ten to fifteen years.

Comets are named for their discoverers, up to three independent observers being so honored. If a comet becomes unusual, it may be well-known by these names. Usually, however, a preliminary designation is used: the year followed by a letter of the alphabet assigned in the order of discovery during that year. About two years later after any likely late discoveries, comets are given their permanent designation which states the year of their perihelion passage and a Roman numeral giving the order of passage during that year. Well-known periodic comets receive these designations at each appearance, but the literature and the Comet Table will continue to identify them by their discoverers' names.

Largest Telescopes Are in Northern Hemisphere

Most of the world's major astronomical installations are in the northern hemisphere, while many of astronomy's major problems are found in the southern sky. This imbalance has long been recognized and is being remedied.

In the northern hemisphere the largest reflector is the 236-inch mirror at the Special Astrophysical Observatory in the Caucasus in the Soviet Union. The largest reflectors in the U.S. include 3 in California: at Palomar Mtn., 200 inches; at Lick Observatory, Mt. Hamilton, 120 inches; and at Mt. Wilson Observatory, 100 inches. Also in the U.S. are a 158 inch reflector at Kitt Peak, Arizona, dedicated in June 1973, and a 107-inch telescope at the McDonald Observatory on

Mt. Locke in Texas. A telescope at the Crimean Astrophysical Observatory in the Soviet Union has a 104-inch mirror.

Placed in service in 1975 were three large reflectors for the southern hemisphere. Associated Universities for Research in Astronomy (AURA), the operating organization of Kitt Peak National Observatory, dedicated the 158-inch reflector (twin of the telescope on Kitt Peak) at Cerro Tololo International Observatory, Chile; the European Southern Observatory has a 141-inch reflector at La Silla, Chile; and the Anglo-Australian telescope, 152 inches in diameter, is at Siding Spring Observatory in Australia.

Optical Telescopes

Optical astronomical telescopes are of two kinds, refracting and reflecting. In the first, light passes through a lens which brings the light rays into focus, where the image may be examined after being magnified by a second lens, the eyepiece, or directly photographed.

The reflector consists of a concave parabolic mirror, generally of Pyrex or now of a relatively heat insensitive material, cervit, coated with silver or aluminum, which reflects the light rays back toward the upper end of the telescope, where they are either magnified and observed by the eyepiece or, as in the case of the refractors, photographed. In most reflecting telescopes, the light is reflected again by a secondary mirror and comes to a focus after passing through a hole in the side of the telescope, where the eye-piece or camera is located, or after passing through a hole in the center of the primary mirror.

World's Largest Refractors

Location and diameter in inches

Yerkes Obs., Williams Bay, Wis.	40
Lick Obs., Mt. Hamilton, Cal.	36
Astrophys. Obs., Potsdam, E. Germany	32
Paris Observatory, Meuden, France	32
Allegheny Obs., Pittsburgh, Pa.	30
Univ. of Paris, Nice, France	30
Royal Greenwich Obs., Herstmonceux, England	28
Union Obs., Johannesburg, South Africa	26.5
Universitats-Sternwarte, Vienna, Austria	26.5
University of Virginia	26
Obs., Academy of Sciences, Pulkova, USSR	26
Astronomical Obs., Belgrade, Yugoslavia	26
Leander McCormick Obs., Charlottesville, Va.	26
Obs. Mitaka, Tokyo-to, Japan	26
US Naval Obs., Washington, D.C.	26
Mt. Stromlo Obs., Canberra, Australia	26

World's Largest Reflectors

Special Astrophysical Obs., Zelenchukskaya, USSR	236
Hale Obs., Palomar Mtn., Cal.	200, 100, 60
Mt. Hopkins (SAO), Ariz.	176*, 60

Kitt Peak National Obs., Tucson, Ariz.	158, 84, 60
Cerro Tololo, Chile	158, 60
Siding Spring, Australia	153
La Silla, Chile	141, 60
Lick Obs., Mt. Hamilton, Cal.	120
McDonald Obs., Fort Davis, Tex.	107, 82
Crimean Astrophys. Obs., Nauchny, USSR	104
Byurakan Obs., Armenia S.S.R.	102
Royal Greenwich Obs., Herstmonceux, England	98
Steward Obs., Tucson, Ariz.	90
Mauna Kea Obs., Univ. of Hawaii, Ha.	88, 84
Shemakha Astroph. Obs., Azerbaijan S.S.R.	79
Saint Michel l'Observatoire, (Basses Alpes), Fr.	77
Haute Provence, France	76, 60
Tokyo Obs., Japan	74
Mt. Stromlo, Australia	74
David Dunlap Obs., Ont., Canada	74
Helwan Obs., Helwan, Egypt	74
Astrophys. Obs., Kamogata, Okayama-ken, Japan	74
Sutherland, South Africa	74
Dominion Astrophys. Obs., Victoria, B.C.	73
Perkins Obs., Flagstaff, Ariz.	72
Obs., Padua Univ., Asiago, Italy	72
Agassiz Station Harvard Obs., Cambridge, Mass.	61
National Obs., Bosque Alegre Sta., Argentina	61
U.S. Naval Obs., Flagstaff, Ariz.	61
Catalina Mtn., Ariz.	61
Arizona Univ. Obs., Tucson, Ariz.	60
Boyden Obs., Bloemfontein, South Africa	60
Mt. Haleakala, Ha.	60
Figl Astroph. Obs., Vienna, Austria	60
Mt. Wilson Obs., Pasadena, Cal.	60

*Multiple mirror telescope, equivalent aperture.

Major U.S. Planetariums

Academy Planetarium, U.S. Air Force Academy
Adler Planetarium, Chicago, Ill.
American Museum-Hayden Planetarium, N.Y.C.
Buhl Planetarium, Pittsburgh, Pa.
Charles Hayden Planetarium, Boston, Mass.
Einstein Spacearium, Washington, D.C.
Fels Planetarium, Philadelphia, Pa.
Fernbank Science Center Planetarium, Altanta, Ga.
Griffith Planetarium, Los Angeles, Cal.
La. Arts and Science Planetarium, Baton Rouge, La.
McDonnell Planetarium, St. Louis, Mo.
Morehead Planetarium, Chapel Hill, N.C.
Morrison Planetarium, San Francisco, Cal.
Robert T. Longway Planetarium, Flint, Mich.
Strassenburgh Planetarium, Rochester, N.Y.

The Sun

The sun, the controlling body of our solar system, is a star whose dimensions cause it to be classified among stars as average in size, temperature, and brightness. Its proximity to the earth makes it appear to us as tremendously large and bright. A series of thermo-nuclear reactions involving the atoms of the elements of which it is composed produces the heat and light that make life possible on earth.

The sun has a diameter of 864,000 miles and is distant, on the average, 92,900,000 miles from the earth. It is 1.41 times as dense as water. The light of the sun reaches the earth in 499.012 seconds or slightly more than 8 minutes. The average solar surface temperature has been measured by several indirect methods which agree closely on a value of 6,000° Kelvin or about 10,000° F. The interior temperature of the sun is about 35,000,000 F.°.

When sunlight is analyzed with a spectroscope, it is found to consist of a continuous spectrum composed of all the colors of the rainbow in order, crossed by many dark lines. The "absorption lines" are produced by gaseous materials in the atmosphere of the sun. More than 60 of the natural terrestrial elements have been identified in the sun, all in gaseous form because of the intense heat of the sun.

Spheres and Corona

The radiating surface of the sun is called the **photosphere**, and just above it is the **chromosphere**. The chromosphere is visible to the naked eye only at times of total solar eclipses, appearing then to be a pinkish-violet layer with occasional great prominences projecting above its general level. With proper instruments the chromosphere can be seen or photographed whenever the sun is visible without waiting for a total eclipse. Above the chromosphere is the **corona**, also visible to the naked eye only at times of total eclipse. Instruments also permit the brighter portions of the corona to be studied whenever conditions are favorable. The pearly light of the corona surges millions of miles from the sun. Iron, nickel, and calcium are believed to be principal contributors to the composition of the corona, all in a state of extreme attenuation and high ionization that indicates temperatures on the order of a million degrees Fahrenheit.

Sunspots

There is an intimate connection between sunspots and the corona. At times of low sunspot activity, the fine streamers of the corona will be much longer above the sun's equator than over the polar regions of the sun, while during high sunspot activity, the corona extends fairly evenly outward from all regions of the sun, but to a much greater distance in space. Sunspots are dark, irregularly-shaped regions whose diameters may reach tens of thousands of miles. The average life of a sunspot group is from two to three weeks, but there have been groups that have lasted for more than a year, being carried repeatedly around as the sun rotated upon its

axis. The record for the duration of a sunspot is 18 months. Sunspots reach a low point every 11.3 years, with a peak of activity occurring irregularly between two successive minima.

The sun is 400,000 times as bright as the full moon and gives the earth 6 million times as much light as do all the other stars put together. Actually, most of the stars that can be easily seen on any clear night are brighter than the sun.

The Moon

The moon completes a circuit around the earth in a period whose mean or average duration is 27 days 7 hours 43.2 minutes. This is the moon's sidereal period. Because of the motion of the moon in common with the earth around the sun, the mean duration of the lunar month — the period from one new moon to the next new moon — is 29 days 12 hours 44.05 minutes. This is the moon's synodical period.

The mean distance of the moon from the earth according to the American Ephemeris is 238,857 miles. Because the orbit of the moon about the earth is not circular but elliptical, however, the maximum distance from the earth that the moon may reach is 252,710 miles and the least distance is 221,463 miles. All distances are from the center of one object to the center of the other.

The moon's diameter is 2,160 miles. If we deduct the radius of the moon, 1,080 miles, and the radius of the earth, 3,963 miles, from the minimum distance or perigee, given above, we shall have for the nearest approach of the bodies' surfaces 216,420 miles.

The moon rotates on its axis in a period of time exactly equal to its sidereal revolution about the earth — 27.321666 days. The moon's revolution about the earth is irregular because of its elliptical orbit. The moon's rotation, however, is regular and this, together with the irregular revolution, produces what is called "libration in longitude" which permits us to see first farther around the east side and then farther

around the west side of the moon. The moon's variation north or south of the ecliptic permits us to see farther over first one pole and then the other of the moon and this is "libration in latitude." These two libration effects permit us to see a total of about 60% of the moon's surface over a period of time. The hidden side of the moon was photographed in 1959 by the Soviet space vehicle Lunik III. Since then many excellent pictures of nearly all of the moon's surface have been transmitted to earth by Lunar Orbiters launched by the U.S.

The tides are caused mainly by the moon, because of its proximity to the earth. The ratio of the tide-raising power of the moon to that of the sun is 11 to 5.

Harvest Moon and Hunter's Moon

The Harvest Moon, the full moon nearest the Autumnal Equinox, ushers in a period of several successive days when the moon rises soon after sunset. This phenomenon gives farmers in temperate latitudes extra hours of light in which to harvest their crops before frost and winter come. The 1982 Harvest Moon falls on Oct. 3. Harvest moon in the south temperate latitudes falls on Mar. 9.

The next full moon after Harvest Moon is called the Hunter's Moon, accompanied by a similar phenomenon but less marked; — Nov. 1, northern hemisphere; May 8, southern hemisphere.

Moon's Perigee and Apogee, 1982

	Perigee						Apogee				
Day	Hour GMT	EST	Day	Hour GMT	EST	Day	Hour GMT	EST	Day	Hour GMT	EST
Jan. 8	12	07	July 19	21	16	Jan. 20	12	07	Aug. 1	10	05
Feb. 5	14	09	Aug. 17	02	21*	Feb. 17	08	03	Aug. 29	00	19*
Mar. 4	05	00	Sept. 13	18	13	Mar. 17	05	00	Sept. 25	19	14
Mar. 29	06	01	Oct. 9	01	20*	Apr. 14	00	19*	Oct. 23	15	10
Apr. 25	21	16	Nov. 4	10	05	May 11	15	10	Nov. 20	11	06
May 24	03	22*	Dec. 2	11	06	June 7	23	18	Dec. 18	02	21*
June 21	12	07	Dec. 30	22	17	July 5	01	20*			
*Previous day											

The Zodiac

The sun's apparent yearly path among the stars is known as the **ecliptic**. The zone 16° wide, 8° on each side of the ecliptic, is known as the **zodiac**. Inside of this zone are the apparent paths of the sun, moon, earth, and major planets. Beginning at the point on the ecliptic which marks the position of the sun at the vernal equinox, and thence proceeding eastward, the zodiac is divided into twelve signs of 30° each, as shown herewith.

These signs are named from the twelve constellations of the zodiac with which the signs coincided in the time of the astronomer Hipparchus, about 2,000 years ago. Owing to the precession of the equinoxes, that is to say, to the retrograde motion of the equinoxes along the ecliptic, each sign in the zodiac has, in the course of 2,000 years, moved backward 30° into the constellation west of it; so that the sign Aries is now in the constellation Pisces, and so on. The ver-

nal equinox will move from Pisces into Aquarius about the middle of the 26th century. The signs of the zodiac with their Latin and English names are as follows:

Spring	1.	♈	Aries.	The Ram.
	2.	♉	Taurus.	The Bull.
	3.	♊	Gemini.	The Twins.
Summer	4.	♋	Cancer.	The Crab.
	5.	♌	Leo.	The Lion.
	6.	♍	Virgo.	The Virgin.
Autumn	7.	♎	Libra.	The Balance.
	8.	♏	Scorpio.	The Scorpion.
	9.	♐	Sagittarius.	The Archer.
Winter	10.	♑	Capricorn.	The Goat.
	11.	♒	Aquarius.	The Water Bearer.
	12.	♓	Pisces.	The Fishes.

The Earth: Size, Computation of Time, Seasons

Size and Dimensions

The earth is the fifth largest planet and the third from the sun. Its mass is 6 sextillion, 588 quintillion short tons. Using the parameters of an ellipsoid adopted by the International Astronomical Union in 1964 and recognized by the International Union of Geodesy and Geophysics in 1967, the length of the equator is 24,901.55 miles, the length of a meridian is

24,859.82 miles, the equatorial diameter is 7,926.41 miles, and the area of this reference ellipsoid is approximately 196,938,800 square miles.

The earth is considered a solid, rigid mass with a dense core of magnetic, probably metallic material. The outer part of the core is probably liquid. Around the core is a thick shell or mantle of heavy crystalline rock which in turn is covered by a thin crust forming the solid granite and basalt base of the continents and ocean basins. Over broad areas of the earth's surface the crust has a thin cover of sedimentary rock such as sandstone, shale, and limestone formed by weathering of the earth's surface and deposition of sands, clays, and plant and animal remains.

The temperature in the earth increases about 1°F. with every 100 to 200 feet in depth, in the upper 100 kilometers of the earth, and the temperature near the core is believed to be near the melting point of the core materials under the conditions at that depth. The heat of the earth is believed to be derived from radioactivity in the rocks, pressures developed within the earth, and original heat (if the earth in fact was formed at high temperatures).

Atmosphere of the Earth

The earth's atmosphere is a blanket composed of nitrogen, oxygen, and argon, in amounts of about 78, 21, and 1% by volume. Also present in minute quantities are carbon dioxide, hydrogen, neon, helium, krypton, and xenon.

Water vapor displaces other gases and varies from nearly zero to about 4% by volume. The height of the ozone layer varies from approximately 12 to 21 miles above the earth. Traces exist as low as 6 miles and as high as 35 miles. Traces of methane have been found.

The atmosphere rests on the earth's surface with the weight equivalent to a layer of water 34 ft. deep. For about 300,000 ft. upward the gases remain in the proportions stated. Gravity holds the gases to the earth. The weight of the air compresses it at the bottom, so that the greatest density is at the earth's surface. Pressure, as well as density, decreases as height increases because the weight pressing upon any layer is always less than that pressing upon the layers below.

The temperature of the air drops with increased height until the tropopause is reached. This may vary from 25,000 to 60,000 ft. The atmosphere below the tropopause is the troposphere; the atmosphere for about twenty miles above the tropopause is the stratosphere, where the temperature generally increases with height except at high latitudes in winter. A temperature maximum near the 30-mile level is called the stratopause. Above this boundary is the mesosphere where the temperature decreases with height to a minimum, the mesopause, at a height of 50 miles. Extending above the mesosphere to the outer fringes of the atmosphere is the thermosphere, a region where temperature increases with height to a value measured in thousands of degrees Fahrenheit. The lower portion of this region, extending from 50 to about 400 miles in altitude, is characterized by a high ion density, and is thus called the ionosphere. The outer region is called exosphere; this is the region where gas molecules traveling at high speed may escape into outer space, above 600 miles.

Latitude, Longitude

Position on the globe is measured by means of meridians and parallels. Meridians, which are imaginary lines drawn around the earth through the poles, determine longitude. The meridian running through Greenwich, England, is the prime meridian of longitude, and all others are either east or west. Parallels, which are imaginary circles parallel with the equator, determine latitude. The length of a degree of longitude varies as the cosine of the latitude. At the equator a degree is 69.171 statute miles; this is gradually reduced toward the poles. Value of a longitude degree at the poles is zero.

Latitude is reckoned by the number of degrees north or south of the equator, an imaginary circle on the earth's surface everywhere equidistant between the two poles. According to the IAU Ellipsoid of 1964, the length of a degree of latitude is 68.708 statute miles at the equator and varies slightly north and south because of the oblate form of the globe; at the poles it is 69.403 statute miles.

Computation of Time

The earth rotates on its axis and follows an elliptical orbit around the sun. The rotation makes the sun appear to move across the sky from East to West. It determines day and night and the complete rotation, in relation to the sun, is called the apparent or true solar day. This varies but an average determines the mean solar day of 24 hours.

The mean solar day is in universal use for civil purposes. It may be obtained from apparent solar time by correcting

observations of the sun for the equation of time, but when high precision is required, the mean solar time is calculated from its relation to sidereal time. These relations are extremely complicated, but for most practical uses, they may be considered as follows:

Sidereal time is the measure of time defined by the diurnal motion of the vernal equinox, and is determined from observation of the meridian transits of stars. One complete rotation of the earth relative to the equinox is called the sidereal day. The mean sidereal day is 23 hours, 56 minutes, 4,091 seconds of mean solar time.

The Calendar Year begins at 12 o'clock precisely local clock time, on the night of Dec. 31-Jan. 1. The day and the calendar month also begin at midnight by the clock. The interval required for the earth to make one absolute revolution around the sun is a sidereal year; it consisted of 365 days, 6 hours, 9 minutes, and 9.5 seconds of mean solar time (approximately 24 hours per day) in 1900, and is increasing at the rate of 0.0001-second annually.

The Tropical Year, on which the return of the seasons depends, is the interval between two consecutive returns of the sun to the vernal equinox. The tropical year consists of 365 days, 5 hours, 48 minutes, and 46 seconds in 1900. It is decreasing at the rate of 0.530 seconds per century.

In 1956 the unit of time interval was defined to be identical with the second of Ephemeris Time, 1/31,556,925.9747 of the tropical year for 1900 January 0d 12th hour E.T. A physical definition of the second based on a quantum transition of cesium (atomic second) was adopted in 1964. The atomic second is equal to 9,192,631,770 cycles of the emitted radiation. In 1967 this atomic second was adopted as the unit of time interval for the Intern'l System of Units.

The Zones and Seasons

The five zones of the earth's surface are Torrid, lying between the Tropics of Cancer and Capricorn; North Temperate, between Cancer and the Arctic Circle; South Temperate, between Capricorn and the Antarctic Circle; The Frigid Zones, between the polar Circles and the Poles.

The inclination or tilt of the earth's axis with respect to the sun determines the seasons. These are commonly marked in the North Temperate Zone, where spring begins at the vernal equinox, summer at the summer solstice, autumn at the autumnal equinox and winter at the winter solstice.

In the South Temperate Zone, the seasons are reversed. Spring begins at the autumnal equinox, summer at the winter solstice, etc.

If the earth's axis were perpendicular to the plane of the earth's orbit around the sun there would be no change of seasons. Day and night would be of nearly constant length and there would be equable conditions of temperature. But the axis is tilted 23° 27' away from a perpendicular to the orbit and only in March and September is the axis at right angles to the sun.

The points at which the sun crosses the equator are the equinoxes, when day and night are most nearly equal. The points at which the sun is at a maximum distance from the equator are the solstices. Days and nights are then most unequal.

In June the North Pole is tilted 23° 27' toward the sun and the days in the northern hemisphere are longer than the nights, while the days in the southern hemisphere are shorter than the nights. In December the North Pole is tilted 23° 27' away from the sun and the situation is reversed.

The Seasons in 1982

In 1981 the 4 seasons will begin as follows: add one hour to EST for Atlantic Time; subtract one hour for Central, two hours for Mountain, 3 hours for Pacific, 4 hours for Yukon, 5 hours for Alaska-Hawaii and six hours for Bering Time. Also shown in Greenwich Mean Time.

		Date	GMT	EST
Vernal Equinox	Spring	Mar. 20	22:56	17:56
Summer Solstice	Summer	June 21	17:23	12:23
Autumnal Equinox	Autumn	Sept. 23	08:46	03:46
Winter Solstice	Winter	Dec. 22	04:39	23:39*

*Previous day

Poles of The Earth

The geographic (rotation) poles, or points where the earth's axis of rotation cuts the surface, are not absolutely fixed in the body of the earth. The pole of rotation describes an irregular curve about its mean position.

Two periods have been detected in this motion: (1) an annual period due to seasonal changes in barometric pressure, load of ice and snow on the surface and to other phenomena of seasonal character; (2) a period of about 14 months due to the shape and constitution of the earth.

In addition there are small but as yet unpredictable irregularities. The whole motion is so small that the actual pole at any time remains within a circle of 30 or 40 feet in radius centered at the mean position of the pole.

The pole of rotation for the time being is of course the pole having a latitude of 90° and an indeterminate longitude.

Magnetic Poles

The **north magnetic pole** of the earth is that region where the magnetic force is vertically downward and the **south magnetic pole** that region where the magnetic force is vertically upward. A compass placed at the magnetic poles experiences no directive force.

There are slow changes in the distribution of the earth's magnetic field. These changes were at one time attributed in part to a periodic movement of the magnetic poles around the geographical poles, but later evidence refutes this theory and points, rather, to a slow migration of "disturbance" foci over the earth.

There appear shifts in position of the magnetic poles due to the changes in the earth's magnetic field. The center of the area designated as the north magnetic pole was estimated to be in about latitude 70.5° N and longitude 96° W in 1905; from recent nearby measurements and studies of the secular changes, the position in 1970 is estimated as latitude 76.2° N and longitude 101° W. Improved data rather than actual motion account for at least part of the change.

The position of the south magnetic pole in 1912 was near 71° S and longitude 150° E; the position in 1970 is estimated at latitude 66° S and longitude 139.1° E.

The direction of the horizontal components of the magnetic field at any point is known as magnetic north at that point, and the angle by which it deviates east or west of true north is known as the magnetic declination, or in the mariner's terminology, the **variation of the compass.**

A compass without error points in the direction of magnetic north. (In general this is *not* the direction of the magnetic north pole.) If one follows the direction indicated by the north end of the compass, he will travel along a rather irregular curve which eventually reaches the north magnetic pole (though not usually by a great-circle route). However, the action of the compass should not be thought of as due to any influence of the distant pole, but simply as an indication of the distribution of the earth's magnetism at the place of observation.

Rotation of The Earth

The **speed of** rotation of the earth about its axis has been found to be slightly variable. The variations may be classified as:

(A) **Secular.** Tidal friction acts as a brake on the rotation and causes a slow secular increase in the length of the day, about 1 millisecond per century.

(B) **Irregular.** The speed of rotation may increase for a number of years, about 5 to 10, and then start decreasing. The maximum difference from the mean in the length of the day during a century is about 5 milliseconds. The accumulated difference in time has amounted to approximately 44 seconds since 1900. The cause is probably motion in the interior of the earth.

(C) **Periodic.** Seasonal variations exist with periods of one year and six months. The cumulative effect is such that each year the earth is late about 30 milliseconds near June 1 and is ahead about 30 milliseconds near Oct. 1. The maximum seasonal variation in the length of the day is about 0.5 millisecond. It is believed that the principal cause of the annual variation is the seasonal change in the wind patterns of the Northern and Southern Hemispheres. The semiannual variation is due chiefly to tidal action of the sun, which distorts the shape of the earth slightly.

The secular and irregular variations were discovered by comparing time based on the rotation of the earth with time based on the orbital motion of the moon about the earth and of the planets about the sun. The periodic variation was determined largely with the aid of quartz-crystal clocks. The introduction of the cesium-beam atomic clock in 1955 made it possible to determine in greater detail than before the nature of the irregular and periodic variations.

Astronomical Twilight—Meridian of Greenwich

Date 1982	20° Begin h m	20° End h m	30° Begin h m	30° End h m	40° Begin h m	40° End h m	50° Begin h m	50° End h m	60° Begin h m	60° End h m
Jan. 1	5 16	6 50	5 30	6 35	5 45	6 21	6 00	6 07	6 18	5 49
11	5 19	6 56	5 33	6 43	5 46	6 30	6 00	6 17	6 15	6 01
21	5 21	7 01	5 32	6 51	5 43	6 40	5 55	6 30	6 06	6 18
Feb. 1	5 21	7 07	5 29	6 58	5 38	6 51	5 45	6 44	5 51	6 38
11	5 18	7 11	5 24	7 05	5 29	7 01	5 32	6 59	5 32	7 01
21	5 13	7 15	5 17	7 12	5 17	7 12	5 16	7 14	5 09	7 23
Mar. 1	5 08	7 18	5 08	7 19	5 06	7 21	4 59	7 29	4 44	7 45
11	5 00	7 21	4 58	7 24	4 50	7 32	4 38	7 46	4 12	8 12
21	4 52	7 24	4 45	7 32	4 33	7 44	4 14	8 04	3 37	8 43
Apr. 1	4 42	7 28	4 31	7 39	4 14	7 57	3 47	8 25	2 53	9 21
11	4 32	7 32	4 18	7 47	3 56	8 09	3 20	8 47	2 03	10 10
21	4 23	7 36	4 04	7 54	3 37	8 23	2 52	9 11	0 37	11 47
May 1	4 14	7 41	3 52	8 04	3 19	8 37	2 22	9 39		
11	4 08	7 46	3 41	8 13	3 03	8 53	1 49	10 09		
21	4 02	7 52	3 32	8 22	2 48	9 07	1 13	10 46		
June 1	3 58	7 58	3 26	8 30	2 36	9 20	0 21	11 52		
11	3 56	8 03	3 22	8 36	2 29	9 30				
21	3 57	8 06	3 22	8 40	2 28	9 35				
July 1	3 59	8 07	3 25	8 41	2 30	9 35				
11	4 03	8 06	3 30	8 39	2 40	9 30				
21	4 08	8 03	3 39	8 33	2 52	9 18	1 12	11 23		
Aug. 1	4 15	7 56	3 48	8 23	3 09	9 01	1 49	10 20		
11	4 20	7 50	3 56	8 13	3 22	8 46	2 21	9 46		
21	4 24	7 41	4 05	8 01	3 34	8 27	2 47	9 15		
Sept. 1	4 29	7 31	4 14	7 46	3 51	8 08	3 13	8 43	1 40	10 02
11	4 32	7 20	4 20	7 33	4 02	7 50	3 33	8 16	2 36	9 12
21	4 35	7 11	4 26	7 19	4 14	7 31	3 52	7 52	3 11	8 31
Oct. 1	4 38	7 02	4 33	7 05	4 25	7 13	4 10	7 28	3 41	7 54
11	4 40	6 53	4 40	6 53	4 35	6 58	4 26	7 05	4 07	7 23
21	4 43	6 47	4 45	6 44	4 45	6 43	4 41	6 46	4 32	6 55
Nov. 1	4 46	6 41	4 52	6 34	4 56	6 30	4 58	6 27	4 56	6 27
11	4 50	6 38	4 59	6 28	5 06	6 21	5 13	6 14	5 17	6 08
21	4 55	6 36	5 06	6 25	5 16	6 15	5 26	6 04	5 37	5 52
Dec. 1	5 00	6 37	5 13	6 24	5 25	6 11	5 38	5 58	5 53	5 42
11	5 06	6 40	5 20	6 26	5 34	6 12	5 48	5 57	6 06	5 38
21	5 11	6 45	5 25	6 30	5 39	6 16	5 55	6 00	6 15	5 40
31	5 15	6 50	5 30	6 35	5 44	6 21	6 00	6 06	6 18	5 48

Latitude, Longitude, and Altitude of North American Cities

Source: National Oceanic and Atmospheric Administration, U.S. Commerce Department for geographic positions.
Source for Canadian cities: Geodetic Survey of Canada, Dept. of Energy, Mines, and Resources.
Altitudes U.S. Geological Survey and various sources. *Approx. altitude at downtown business area U.S.; in Canada at city hall except where (a) is at tower of major airport.

City	Lat. N °	'	"	Long. W °	'	"	Alt.* feet
Abilene, Tex.	32	27	05	99	43	51	1710
Akron, Oh.	41	05	00	81	30	44	874
Albany, N.Y.	42	39	01	73	45	01	20
Albuquerque, N.M.	35	05	01	106	39	05	4,945
Allentown, Pa.	40	36	11	75	28	06	255
Alert, N.W.T.	82	29	50	62	21	15	95
Altoona, Pa.	40	30	55	78	24	03	1,180
Amarillo, Tex.	35	12	27	101	50	04	3,685
Anchorage, Alas.	61	10	00	149	59	00	118
Ann Arbor, Mich.	42	16	59	83	44	52	880
Asheville, N.C.	35	35	42	82	33	26	1,985
Ashland, Ky.	38	28	36	82	38	23	536
Atlanta, Ga.	33	45	10	84	23	37	1,050
Atlantic City, N.J.	39	21	32	74	25	53	10
Augusta, Ga.	33	28	20	81	58	00	143
Augusta, Me.	44	18	53	69	46	29	45
Austin, Tex.	30	16	09	97	44	37	505
Bakersfield, Cal.	35	22	31	119	01	18	400
Baltimore, Md.	39	17	26	76	36	45	20
Bangor, Me.	44	48	13	68	46	18	20
Baton Rouge, La.	30	26	58	91	11	00	57
Battle Creek, Mich.	42	18	58	85	10	48	820
Bay City, Mich.	43	36	04	83	53	15	595
Beaumont, Tex.	30	06	20	94	06	09	20
Belleville, Ont.	44	09	42	77	23	11	257
Bellingham, Wash.	48	45	34	122	28	36	60
Berkeley, Cal.	37	52	10	122	16	17	40
Bethlehem, Pa.	40	37	16	75	22	34	235
Billings, Mon.	45	47	00	108	30	04	3,120
Biloxi, Miss.	30	23	48	88	53	00	20
Binghamton, N.Y.	42	06	03	75	54	47	865
Birmingham, Ala.	33	31	01	86	48	36	600
Bismarck, N.D.	46	48	23	100	47	17	1,674
Bloomington, Ill.	40	28	58	88	59	36	800
Boise, Ida.	43	37	07	116	11	58	2,704
Boston, Mass.	42	21	24	71	03	25	21
Bowling Green, Ky.	36	59	41	86	26	33	510
Brandon, Man.	49	51	00	99	57	00	1,265(a)
Brantford, Ont.	43	07	30	80	15	30	705(a)
Brattleboro, Vt.	42	51	06	72	33	48	300
Bridgeport, Conn.	41	10	49	73	11	22	10
Brockton, Mass.	42	05	02	71	01	25	130
Brownsville, Tex.	25	54	07	97	29	58	35
Buffalo, N.Y.	42	52	52	78	52	21	585
Burlington, Ont.	43	19	33	79	47	57	284
Burlington, Vt.	44	28	34	73	12	46	110
Butte, Mon.	46	01	06	112	32	11	5,765
Calgary, Alta.	51	02	46	114	03	24	3,427
Cambridge, Mass.	42	22	01	71	06	22	20
Camden, N.J.	39	56	41	75	07	14	30
Canton, Oh.	40	47	50	81	22	37	1,030
Carson City, Nev.	39	10	00	119	46	00	4,680
Cedar Rapids, Ia.	41	58	01	91	39	53	730
Central Islip, N.Y.	40	47	24	73	12	00	80
Champaign, Ill.	40	07	05	88	14	48	740
Charleston, S.C.	32	46	35	79	55	53	9
Charleston, W.Va.	38	21	01	81	37	52	601
Charlotte, N.C.	35	13	44	80	50	45	720
Charlottetown, P.E.I.	46	14	07	63	07	49	31
Chattanooga, Tenn.	35	02	41	85	18	32	675
Cheyenne, Wy.	41	08	09	104	49	07	6,100
Chicago, Ill.	41	52	28	87	38	22	595
Churchill, Man.	58	45	15	94	10	00	94(a)
Cincinnati, Oh.	39	06	07	84	30	35	550
Cleveland, Oh.	41	29	51	81	41	50	660
Colorado Springs	38	50	07	104	49	16	5,980
Columbia, Mo.	38	57	03	92	19	46	730
Columbia, S.C.	34	00	02	81	02	00	190
Columbus, Ga.	32	28	07	84	59	24	265
Columbus, Oh.	39	57	47	83	00	17	780
Concord, N.H.	43	12	22	71	32	25	290
Corpus Christi, Tex.	27	47	51	97	23	45	35
Dallas, Tex.	32	47	09	96	44	37	435
Dartmouth, N.S.	44	39	50	63	34	08	24
Davenport, Ia.	41	31	19	90	34	33	590
Dawson, Yukon	64	03	30	139	26	00	1,211(a)
Dayton, Oh.	39	45	32	84	11	43	574
Daytona Beach, Fla.	29	12	44	81	01	10	7
Decatur, Ill.	39	50	42	88	56	47	682
Denver, Col.	39	44	58	104	59	22	5,280
Des Moines, Ia.	41	35	14	93	37	00	805
Detroit, Mich.	42	19	48	83	02	57	585
Dodge City, Kan.	37	45	17	100	01	09	2,480
Dubuque, Ia.	42	29	55	90	40	08	620
Duluth, Minn.	46	46	56	92	06	24	610
Durham, N.C.	36	00	00	78	54	45	405

City	Lat. N °	'	"	Long. W °	'	"	Alt.* feet
Eau Claire, Wis.	44	48	31	91	29	49	790
Edmonton, Alta.	53	32	43	113	29	21	2,186
El Paso, Tex.	31	45	36	106	29	11	3,695
Elizabeth, N.J.	40	39	43	74	12	59	21
Enid, Okla.	36	23	40	97	52	35	1,240
Erie, Pa.	42	07	15	80	04	57	685
Eugene, Ore.	44	03	16	123	05	30	422
Eureka, Cal.	40	48	08	124	09	46	45
Evansville, Ind.	37	58	20	87	34	21	385
Fairbanks, Alas.	64	48	00	147	51	00	448
Fall River, Mass.	41	42	06	71	00	10	40
Fargo, N.D.	46	52	30	96	47	18	900
Flagstaff, Ariz.	35	11	36	111	39	06	6,900
Flint, Mich.	43	00	50	83	41	33	750
Ft. Smith, Ark.	35	23	10	94	25	36	440
Fort Wayne, Ind.	41	04	21	85	08	26	790
Fort Worth, Tex.	32	44	55	97	19	44	670
Fredericton, N.B.	45	57	47	66	38	38	29
Fresno, Cal.	36	44	12	119	47	11	285
Gadsden, Ala.	34	00	57	86	00	41	555
Gainesville, Fla.	29	38	56	82	19	19	175
Gallup, N.M.	35	31	30	108	44	30	6,540
Galveston, Tex.	29	18	10	94	47	43	5
Gary, Ind.	41	36	12	87	20	19	590
Grand Junction, Col.	39	04	06	108	33	54	4,590
Grand Rapids, Mich.	42	58	03	85	40	13	610
Great Falls, Mon.	47	29	33	111	18	23	3,340
Green Bay, Wis.	44	30	48	88	00	50	590
Greensboro, N.C.	36	04	17	79	47	25	839
Greenville, S.C.	34	50	50	82	24	01	966
Guelph, Ont.	43	32	35	80	15	54	1,065
Gulfport, Miss.	30	22	04	89	05	36	20
Halifax, N.S.	44	38	54	63	34	30	60
Hamilton, Ont.	43	15	20	79	52	30	329
Hamilton, Oh.	39	23	59	84	33	47	600
Harrisburg, Pa.	40	15	43	76	52	59	365
Hartford, Conn.	41	46	12	72	40	49	40
Helena, Mon.	46	35	33	112	02	24	4,155
Hilo, Hawaii	19	43	30	155	05	24	40
Holyoke, Mass.	42	12	29	72	36	36	115
Honolulu, Ha.	21	18	22	157	51	35	21
Houston, Tex.	29	45	26	95	21	37	40
Hull, Que.	45	25	42	75	42	41	185
Huntington, W.Va.	38	25	12	82	26	33	565
Huntsville, Ala.	34	44	18	86	35	19	640
Indianapolis, Ind.	39	46	07	86	09	46	710
Iowa City, Ia.	41	39	37	91	31	53	685
Jackson, Mich.	42	14	43	84	24	22	940
Jackson, Miss.	32	17	56	90	11	06	298
Jacksonville, Fla.	30	19	44	81	39	42	20
Jersey City, N.J.	40	43	50	74	03	56	20
Johnstown, Pa.	40	19	35	78	55	03	1,185
Joplin, Mo.	37	05	26	90	42	11	990
Juneau, Alas.	58	18	12	134	24	30	50
Kalamazoo, Mich.	42	17	29	85	35	14	755
Kansas City, Kan.	39	07	04	94	38	24	750
Kansas City, Mo.	39	04	56	94	35	20	750
Kenosha, Wis.	42	35	43	87	50	11	610
Key West, Fla.	24	33	30	81	48	12	5
Kingston, Ont.	44	13	53	76	28	48	264
Kitchener, Ont.	43	26	58	80	29	12	1,100
Knoxville, Tenn.	35	57	39	83	55	07	890
Lafayette, Ind.	40	25	11	86	53	39	550
Lancaster, Pa.	40	02	25	76	18	29	355
Lansing, Mich.	42	44	01	84	33	15	830
Laredo, Tex.	27	30	22	99	30	30	440
La Salle, Que.	45	25	45	73	39	30	110
Las Vegas, Nev.	36	10	20	115	08	37	2,030
Laval, Que.	45	33	05	73	44	42	142
Lawrence, Mass.	42	42	16	71	10	08	65
Lethbridge, Alta.	49	41	38	112	49	58	2,985
Lexington, Ky.	38	02	50	84	29	46	955
Lihue, Hawaii	21	58	48	159	22	30	210
Lima, Oh.	40	44	35	84	06	20	865
Lincoln, Neb.	40	48	59	96	42	15	1,150
Little Rock, Ark.	34	44	42	92	16	37	286
London, Ont.	42	59	17	81	14	03	822
Long Beach, Cal.	33	46	14	118	11	18	35
Lorain, Oh.	41	28	05	82	10	49	610
Los Angeles, Cal.	34	03	15	118	14	28	340
Louisville, Ky.	38	14	47	85	45	49	450
Lowell, Mass.	42	38	25	71	19	14	100
Lubbock, Tex.	33	35	05	101	50	33	3,195

City	Lat. N °	'	"	Long. W °	'	"	Alt.* Feet
Macon, Ga.	32	50	12	83	37	36	335
Madison, Wis.	43	04	23	89	22	55	860
Manchester, N.H.	42	59	28	71	27	41	175
Marshall, Tex.	32	33	00	94	23	00	410
Memphis, Tenn.	35	08	46	90	03	13	275
Meriden, Conn.	41	32	06	72	47	30	190
Mexico City, Mexico	19	25	45	99	07	00	7,347
Miami, Fla.	25	46	37	80	11	32	10
Milwaukee, Wis.	43	02	19	87	54	15	635
Minneapolis, Minn.	44	58	57	93	15	43	815
Minot, N.D.	48	14	09	101	17	38	1,550
Mississauga, Ont.	43	33	00	79	35	00	260(a)
Mobile, Ala.	30	41	36	88	02	33	5
Moline, Ill.	41	30	31	90	30	49	585
Moncton, N.B.	46	05	18	64	46	41	38
Montgomery, Ala.	32	22	33	86	18	31	160
Montpelier, Vt.	44	15	30	72	34	41	485
Montreal, Que.	45	30	33	73	33	14	90
Moose Jaw, Sask.	50	23	34	105	32	04	1,784
Muncie, Ind.	40	11	28	85	23	16	950
Nashville, Tenn.	36	09	33	86	46	55	450
Natchez, Miss.	31	33	48	91	23	30	210
Newark, N.J.	40	44	14	74	10	19	55
New Bedford, Mass.	41	38	13	70	55	41	15
New Britain, Conn.	41	40	08	72	46	59	200
New Haven, Conn.	41	18	25	72	55	30	40
New Orleans, La.	29	56	53	90	04	10	5
New York, N.Y.	40	45	06	73	59	39	55
Niagara Falls, N.Y.	43	05	34	79	03	26	570
Niagara Falls, Ont.	43	06	22	79	03	51	590
Nome, Alas.	64	30	00	165	25	00	25
Norfolk, Va.	36	51	10	76	17	21	10
North Bay, Ont.	46	18	35	79	27	45	670
Oakland, Cal.	37	48	03	122	15	54	25
Ogden, Ut.	41	13	31	111	58	21	4,295
Oklahoma City	35	28	26	97	31	04	1,195
Omaha, Neb.	41	15	42	95	56	14	1,040
Orlando, Fla.	28	32	42	81	22	38	70
Oshawa, Ont.	43	53	46	78	51	57	350
Ottawa, Ont.	45	26	24	75	41	42	185
Paducah, Ky.	37	05	13	88	35	56	345
Pasadena, Cal.	34	08	44	118	08	41	830
Paterson, N.J.	40	55	01	74	10	21	100
Pensacola, Fla.	30	24	51	87	12	56	15
Peoria, Ill.	40	41	42	89	35	33	470
Peterborough, Ont.	44	18	32	78	19	13	673
Philadelphia, Pa.	39	56	58	75	09	21	100
Phoenix, Ariz.	33	27	12	112	04	28	1,090
Pierre, S.D.	44	22	18	100	20	54	1,480
Pittsburgh, Pa.	40	26	19	80	00	00	745
Pittsfield, Mass.	42	26	53	73	15	14	1,015
Pocatello, Ida.	42	51	38	112	27	01	4,460
Port Arthur, Tex.	29	52	30	93	56	15	10
Portland, Me.	43	39	33	70	15	19	25
Portland, Ore.	45	31	06	122	40	35	77
Portsmouth, N.H.	43	04	30	70	45	24	20
Portsmouth, Va.	36	50	07	76	18	14	10
Prince Rupert, B.C.	54	19	00	130	19	00	125(a)
Providence, R.I.	41	49	32	71	24	41	80
Provo, Ut.	40	14	06	111	39	24	4,550
Pueblo, Col.	38	16	-17	104	36	33	4,690
Quebec City, Que.	46	48	51	71	12	30	163
Racine, Wis.	42	43	49	87	47	12	630
Rapid City, S.D.	44	04	52	103	13	11	3,230
Raleigh, N.C.	35	46	38	78	38	21	365
Reading, Pa.	40	20	09	75	55	40	265
Regina, Sask.	50	27	02	104	36	30	1,894(a)
Reno, Nev.	39	31	27	119	48	40	4,490
Richmond, Va.	37	32	15	77	26	09	160
Roanoke, Va.	37	16	13	79	56	44	905
Rochester, Minn.	44	01	21	92	28	03	990
Rochester, N.Y.	43	09	41	77	36	21	515
Rockford, Ill.	42	16	07	89	05	48	715
Sacramento, Cal.	38	34	57	121	29	41	30
Saginaw, Mich.	43	25	52	83	56	05	595
St. Catharines, Ont.	43	09	30	79	14	30	362(a)
St. Cloud, Minn.	45	34	00	94	10	24	1,040
Saint John, N.B.	45	16	22	66	03	48	27
St. John's, Nfld.	47	34	00	52	43	30	200(a)
St. Joseph, Mo.	39	45	57	94	51	02	850
St. Louis, Mo.	38	37	45	90	12	22	455
St. Paul, Minn.	44	57	19	93	06	07	780
St. Petersburg, Fla.	27	46	18	82	38	19	20
Salem, Ore.	44	56	24	123	01	59	155

City	Lat. N °	'	"	Long. W °	'	"	Alt.* Feet
Salina, Kan.	38	50	36	97	36	46	1,229
Salt Lake City, Ut.	40	45	23	111	53	26	4,390
San Angelo, Tex.	31	27	39	100	26	03	1,845
San Antonio, Tex.	29	25	37	98	29	06	650
San Bernardino, Cal.	34	06	30	117	17	28	1,080
San Diego, Cal.	32	42	53	117	09	21	20
San Francisco, Cal.	37	46	39	122	24	40	65
San Jose, Cal.	37	20	16	121	53	24	90
San Juan, P.R.	18	27	00	66	04	15	35
Santa Barbara, Cal.	34	25	18	119	41	55	100
Santa Cruz, Cal.	36	58	18	122	01	18	20
Santa Fe, N.M.	35	41	11	105	56	10	6,950
Sarasota, Fla.	27	20	05	82	32	30	20
Saskatoon, Sask.	52	07	49	106	39	35	1,587
Sault Ste. Marie, Ont.	46	30	24	84	20	04	589
Savannah, Ga.	32	04	42	81	05	37	20
Schenectady, N.Y.	42	48	42	73	55	42	245
Scranton, Pa.	41	24	00	76	39	44	725
Seattle, Wash.	47	36	32	122	20	12	10
Sheboygan, Wis.	43	45	03	87	42	52	630
Sherbrooke, Que.	45	24	00	71	53	30	625(a)
Sheridan, Wy.	44	47	55	106	57	10	3,740
Shreveport, La.	32	30	46	93	44	58	204
Sioux City, Ia.	42	29	46	96	24	30	1,110
Sioux Falls, S.D.	43	32	35	96	43	35	1,395
Somerville, Mass.	42	23	15	71	06	07	13
South Bend, Ind.	41	40	33	86	15	01	710
Spartanburg, S.C.	34	57	03	81	56	06	875
Spokane, Wash.	47	39	32	117	25	33	1,890
Springfield, Ill.	39	47	58	89	38	51	610
Springfield, Mass.	42	06	21	72	35	32	85
Springfield, Mo.	37	13	03	93	17	32	1,300
Springfield, Oh.	39	55	38	83	48	29	980
Stamford, Conn.	41	03	09	73	32	24	35
Ctoubonville, Oh.	40	21	42	80	36	53	660
Stockton, Cal.	37	57	30	121	17	10	20
Sudbury, Ont.	46	29	24	80	59	24	917(a)
Superior, Wis.	46	43	14	92	06	07	630
Sydney, N.S.	46	08	30	60	11	00	50
Syracuse, N.Y.	43	03	04	76	09	14	400
Tacoma, Wash.	47	14	59	122	26	15	110
Tallahassee, Fla.	30	26	30	84	16	56	150
Tampa, Fla.	27	56	58	82	27	25	15
Terre Haute, Ind.	39	28	03	87	24	26	496
Texarkana, Tex.	33	25	48	94	02	30	324
Thunder Bay, Ont.	48	22	56	89	14	46	616
Toledo, Oh.	41	39	14	83	32	39	585
Topeka, Kan.	39	03	16	95	40	23	930
Toronto, Ont.	43	39	10	79	23	00	300
Trenton, N.J.	40	13	14	74	46	13	35
Trois-Rivieres, Que.	46	21	00	72	33	00	115(a)
Troy, N.Y.	42	43	45	73	40	58	35
Tucson, Ariz.	32	13	15	110	58	08	2,390
Tulsa, Okla.	36	09	12	95	59	34	804
Urbana, Ill.	40	06	42	88	12	06	
Utica, N.Y.	43	06	12	75	13	33	415
Vancouver, B.C.	49	18	56	123	04	44	141
Victoria, B.C.	48	25	43	123	21	48	57
Waco, Tex.	31	33	12	97	08	00	405
Walla Walla, Wash.	46	04	08	118	20	24	936
Washington, D.C.	38	53	51	77	00	33	25
Waterbury, Conn.	41	33	13	73	02	31	260
Waterloo, Ia.	42	29	40	92	20	20	850
West Palm Beach, Fla.	26	42	36	80	03	07	15
Wheeling, W. Va.	40	04	03	80	43	20	650
Whitehorse, Yukon	60	43	15	135	03	15	2,305(a)
White Plains, N.Y.	41	02	00	73	45	48	220
Wichita, Kan.	37	41	30	97	20	16	1,290
Wichita Falls, Tex.	33	54	34	98	29	28	945
Wilkes-Barre, Pa.	41	14	32	75	53	17	640
Wilmington, Del.	39	44	46	75	32	51	135
Wilmington, N.C.	34	14	14	77	56	58	35
Windsor, Ont.	42	18	56	83	02	10	603
Winnipeg, Man.	49	53	56	97	08	23	762
Winston-Salem, N.C.	36	05	52	80	14	42	860
Worcester, Mass.	42	15	37	71	48	17	475
Yakima, Wash.	46	36	09	120	30	39	1,060
Yellowknife, N.W.T.	62	28	15	114	22	00	674(a)
Yonkers, N.Y.	40	55	55	73	53	54	10
York, Pa.	39	57	35	76	43	36	370
Youngstown, Oh.	41	05	57	80	39	02	840
Yuma, Ariz.	32	42	54	114	37	24	160
Zanesville, Oh.	39	56	18	82	00	30	720

World Cities

City	Lat. N °	'	"	Long. W °	'	"	Alt.* Feet
London, UK (Greenwich)	51	30	00N	0	0	0	245
Paris, France	48	50	14N	2	20	14E	300
Berlin, Germany	52	32	00N	13	25	00E	110
Rome, Italy	41	53	00N	12	30	00E	95
Warsaw, Poland	52	15	00N	21	00	00E	360
Moscow, USSR	55	45	00N	37	42	00E	394
Athens, Greece	37	58	00N	23	44	00E	300
Jerusalem, Israel	31	47	00N	35	13	00E	2,500
Johannesburg, So. Afr.	26	10	00S	28	02	00E	5,740
New Delhi, India	28	38	00N	77	12	00E	770
Peking, China	39	54	00N	116	28	00E	600
Rio de Janeiro, Brazil	22	53	43S	43	13	22W	30
Tokyo, Japan	35	45	00N	139	45	00E	30
Sydney, Australia	33	52	00S	151	12	00E	25

Calendar Adjustment Tables

These tables enable you to determine sun and moon rise and set times at your specific location. To find sunrise and sunset times, use steps A and C only; use all 3 steps for moonrise and moonset times.

A. Find your latitude and longitude or that of a nearby city on pages 768-769. Strike off the figure in the tens column from your latitude, find the remainder at the left of Table A, and mark it. Find the nearest longitude at the left of Table B and mark it. Now, for the day you wish, find the times of the event in the calendar tables in the columns for the latitude to your south and your north. Subtract the southern time from the northern time. Find the nearest tens of minutes to your answer in a column head in Table A. Run down the column to the latitude row you have marked. Add the number you find there (or subtract, if your answer is negative) to the southern time.

B. Find the time of the event for the next day at the southern latitude. Subtract the time for the present day from the time for the next day. In Table B find the column headed by the nearest tens of this answer. Run down the column to the proper longitude row. Add this number to the step A answer.

C. To determine actual clock time, subtract the nearest time zone meridian used in your area from your longitude. (These are: Atlantic, 60°; Eastern, 75°; Central, 90°; Mountain, 105°; Pacific, 120°; Alaska-Hawaii, 150°.) Change this to degrees and decimals of a degree (divide the minutes by

60 and add this decimal to the degrees) and multiply by 4. Write this number on this page for future use and add it (or subtract it, if minus) to the step B answer. If you are on Daylight Time, add one hour.

Example: Find the approximate time of moonrise for Aug. 5, 1982 in Sheboygan, Wis., latitude 43°45', longitude 87°42', or 87.7°. A resident there should mark row 3°40' in Table A and row 90° in Table B.

A. Calendar time for 50° 19:50
   Calendar time for 40° 20:17
   Difference: North minus South −27 min.
   Table A for 3°40' and 30 min. 11
   Thus, subtract 11 min. from 20:17   20.06

B. Calendar time for Aug. 6 20:22
   Calendar time for Aug. 5 19:50
   Difference, Aug. 6-Aug. 5 +32 min.
   Table B for 90 and 32 min. 8 min.
   Add to answer A :08 + 20.06   20:14

C. Sheboygan longitude 87.7
   CST meridian 90.0
   Difference: 2.3' east for earlier than CST 2.3 × 4 = 9.2 minutes to be subtracted: 20.05 (Add 1 hour for daylight time: 21:05 CDT)

Table A: Latitude Adjustment

Lat.	Diff in Min. 10	20	30	40	50	60	70	80	90	100	110	120
0° 20	0	1	1	1	2	2	2	3	3	3	4	4
40	1	1	2	3	3	4	5	5	6	7	7	8
1 00	1	2	3	4	5	6	7	8	9	10	11	12
20	1	3	4	5	7	8	9	11	12	13	15	16
40	2	3	5	7	8	10	12	13	15	17	18	20
2 00	2	4	6	8	10	12	14	16	18	20	22	24
20	2	5	7	9	12	14	16	19	21	23	26	28
40	3	5	8	11	13	16	19	21	24	27	29	32
3 00	3	6	9	12	15	18	21	24	27	30	33	36
20	3	7	10	13	17	20	23	27	30	33	37	40
40	4	7	11	15	18	22	26	29	33	37	40	44
4 00	4	8	12	16	20	24	28	32	36	40	44	48
20	4	9	13	17	22	26	30	35	39	43	48	52
40	5	9	14	19	23	28	33	37	42	47	51	56
5 00	5	10	15	20	25	30	35	40	45	50	55	60
20	5	11	16	21	27	32	37	43	48	53	59	64
40	6	11	17	23	28	34	40	45	51	57	62	68
6 00	6	12	18	24	30	36	42	48	54	60	66	72
20	6	13	19	25	32	38	44	51	57	63	70	76
40	7	13	20	27	33	40	47	53	60	67	73	80
7 00	7	14	21	28	35	42	49	56	63	70	77	84
20	7	15	22	29	37	44	51	59	66	73	81	88
40	8	15	23	31	38	46	54	61	69	77	84	92
8 00	8	16	24	32	40	48	56	64	72	80	88	96
20	8	17	25	33	42	50	58	67	75	83	92	100
40	9	17	26	35	43	52	61	69	78	87	95	104
9 00	9	18	27	36	45	54	63	72	81	90	99	108
20	9	19	28	37	47	56	65	75	84	93	103	112
40	10	19	29	39	48	58	68	77	87	97	106	116

Table B: Longitude Adjustment

Long.	Diff. in Min. 10	20	30	40	50	60	70	80	90	100	110	120
50°	1	3	4	6	7	8	10	11	12	14	15	17
55	2	3	5	6	8	9	11	12	14	15	17	18
60	2	3	5	7	8	10	12	13	15	17	18	20
65	2	4	5	7	9	11	13	14	16	18	20	22
70	2	4	6	8	10	12	14	16	18	19	21	23
75	2	4	6	8	10	12	15	17	19	21	23	25
80	2	4	7	9	11	13	16	18	20	22	24	27
85	2	5	7	9	12	14	16	19	21	24	26	28
90	2	5	8	10	12	15	18	20	22	25	28	30
95	3	5	8	11	13	16	18	21	24	26	29	32
100	3	6	8	11	14	17	19	22	25	28	31	33
105	3	6	9	12	15	18	20	23	26	29	32	35
110	3	6	9	12	15	18	21	24	28	31	34	37
115	3	6	10	13	16	19	22	26	29	32	35	38
120	3	7	10	13	17	20	23	27	30	33	37	40
125	4	7	10	14	17	21	24	28	31	35	38	42
130	4	7	11	14	18	22	25	29	32	36	40	43
135	4	8	11	15	19	22	26	30	34	38	41	45
140	4	8	12	16	19	23	27	31	35	39	43	47
145	4	8	12	16	20	24	28	32	36	40	44	48
150	4	8	12	17	21	25	29	33	38	42	46	50
155	4	9	13	17	22	26	30	34	39	43	47	52
160	4	9	13	18	22	27	31	36	40	44	49	53
165	5	9	14	18	23	28	32	37	41	46	50	55
170	5	9	14	19	24	28	33	38	42	47	52	57

1st Month   January, 1982   31 days

Greenwich Mean Time

NOTE: Light figures indicate Sun. **Dark** figures indicate **Moon.** *Degrees are North Latitude.*

CAUTION: Must be converted to local time. For instruction see page 770.

Day of month / week / year	Sun on meridian / Moon phase	20° Rise Sun/Moon	20° Set Sun/Moon	30° Rise Sun/Moon	30° Set Sun/Moon	40° Rise Sun/Moon	40° Set Sun/Moon	50° Rise Sun/Moon	50° Set Sun/Moon	60° Rise Sun/Moon	60° Set Sun/Moon
	h m s	h m	h m	h m	h m	h m	h m	h m	h m	h m	h m
1 Fr	12 03 18	06 35	17 32	06 56	17 11	07 22	16 45	07 59	16 09	09 02	15 05
1		10 57	22 58	11 05	22 52	11 14	22 46	11 28	22 30	11 45	22 22
2 Sa	12 03 46	06 35	17 33	06 56	17 12	07 22	16 46	07 59	16 10	09 02	15 06
2		11 37	23 53	11 40	23 51	11 44	23 51	11 49	23 49	11 56	23 47
3 Su	12 04 14	06 35	17 34	06 56	17 13	07 22	16 47	07 59	16 11	09 01	15 08
3	04 45 ☽	12 17		12 15		12 14		12 11		12 08	
4 Mo	12 04 41	06 36	17 34	06 56	17 14	07 22	16 48	07 58	16 12	09 00	15 10
4		12 59	00 49	12 52	00 53	12 45	00 58	12 35	01 04	12 24	01 14
5 Tu	12 05 09	06 36	17 35	06 57	17 14	07 22	16 49	07 58	16 13	09 00	15 11
5		13 43	01 48	13 33	01 57	13 20	02 07	13 02	02 22	12 35	02 45
6 We	12 05 35	06 36	17 35	06 57	17 15	07 22	16 50	07 58	16 14	08 59	15 13
6		14 32	02 50	14 17	03 03	13 59	03 19	13 34	03 42	12 54	04 18
7 Th	12 06 02	06 36	17 36	06 57	17 16	07 22	16 51	07 58	16 15	08 58	15 15
7		15 26	03 54	15 08	04 11	14 45	04 33	14 14	05 02	13 21	05 52
8 Fr	12 06 28	06 36	17 36	06 57	17 16	07 22	16 52	07 57	16 16	08 57	15 16
8		16 25	05 00	16 05	05 20	15 39	05 45	15 03	06 20	14 02	07 20
9 Sa	12 06 53	06 37	17 37	06 57	17 17	07 22	16 53	07 56	16 18	08 56	15 18
9	19 53 ○	17 28	06 05	17 07	06 26	16 41	06 52	16 04	07 29	15 00	08 33
10 Su	12 07 18	06 37	17 38	06 57	17 18	07 22	16 54	07 56	16 19	08 55	15 20
10		18 33	07 07	18 13	07 27	17 49	07 52	17 15	08 27	16 17	09 27
11 Mo	12 07 42	06 37	17 38	06 57	17 19	07 22	16 55	07 55	16 20	08 54	15 22
11		19 36	08 03	19 20	08 21	18 59	08 43	18 31	09 13	17 44	10 03
12 Tu	12 08 05	06 38	17 39	06 57	17 20	07 22	16 56	07 55	16 22	08 52	15 24
12		20 37	08 54	20 24	09 08	20 09	09 26	19 48	09 49	19 13	10 24
13 We	12 08 28	06 38	17 40	06 57	17 20	07 21	16 57	07 54	16 24	08 51	15 27
13		21 34	09 39	21 26	09 49	21 16	10 02	21 02	10 18	20 41	10 44
14 Th	12 08 51	06 38	17 40	06 57	17 21	07 21	16 58	07 54	16 25	08 50	15 28
14		22 28	10 21	22 25	10 26	22 20	10 33	22 14	10 43	22 04	10 57
15 Fr	12 09 13	06 38	17 41	06 57	17 22	07 20	16 59	07 53	16 26	08 48	15 31
15		23 20	10 59	23 21	11 00	23 21	11 02	23 23	11 05	23 24	11 08
16 Sa	12 09 34	06 38	17 42	06 56	17 23	07 20	17 00	07 52	16 28	08 46	15 34
16	23 58 ☾		11 35		11 33		11 30		11 26		11 19
17 Su	12 09 54	06 38	17 42	06 56	17 24	07 19	17 01	07 52	16 30	08 45	15 36
17		00 10	12 12	00 15	12 05	00 21	11 57	00 29	11 46	00 42	11 29
18 Mo	12 10 14	06 38	17 43	06 56	17 25	07 19	17 02	07 51	16 31	08 43	15 38
18		01 00	12 48	01 09	12 38	01 20	12 25	01 35	12 08	01 58	11 41
19 Tu	12 10 33	06 38	17 44	06 56	17 26	07 18	17 03	07 50	16 32	08 41	15 40
19		01 50	13 26	02 02	13 12	02 18	12 55	02 39	12 32	03 13	11 55
20 We	12 10 52	06 38	17 44	06 56	17 26	07 18	17 04	07 49	16 34	08 40	15 43
20		02 40	14 07	02 55	13 50	03 15	13 29	03 42	13 00	04 27	12 13
21 Th	12 11 09	06 38	17 45	06 55	17 27	07 18	17 06	07 48	16 36	08 38	15 46
21		03 30	14 50	03 48	14 31	04 11	14 07	04 44	13 33	05 39	12 37
22 Fr	12 11 26	06 38	17 46	06 55	17 28	07 17	17 07	07 47	16 37	08 36	15 48
22		04 21	15 36	04 41	15 16	05 06	14 50	05 42	14 14	06 44	13 11
23 Sa	12 11 43	06 38	17 46	06 55	17 29	07 16	17 08	07 46	16 39	08 34	15 50
23		05 11	16 26	05 32	16 05	05 58	15 39	06 35	15 02	07 40	13 57
24 Su	12 11 58	06 38	17 47	06 54	17 30	07 16	17 10	07 44	16 40	08 32	15 53
24		06 01	17 17	06 21	16 58	06 46	16 33	07 22	15 57	08 24	14 56
25 Mo	12 12 13	06 37	17 48	06 54	17 31	07 15	17 11	07 43	16 42	08 30	15 56
25	04 56 ●	06 48	18 11	07 07	17 53	07 30	17 31	08 03	17 00	08 57	16 07
26 Tu	12 12 27	06 37	17 48	06 54	17 32	07 14	17 12	07 42	16 44	08 28	15 58
26		07 33	19 05	07 49	18 50	08 09	18 32	08 37	18 07	09 21	17 25
27 We	12 12 40	06 37	17 49	06 54	17 33	07 13	17 13	07 41	16 46	08 26	16 00
27		08 16	20 00	08 29	19 49	08 45	19 35	09 06	19 16	09 39	18 46
28 Th	12 12 52	06 36	17 50	06 53	17 34	07 12	17 14	07 40	16 47	08 24	16 03
28		08 58	20 54	09 06	20 47	09 17	20 39	09 31	20 28	09 53	20 10
29 Fr	12 13 03	06 36	17 50	06 52	17 35	07 12	17 15	07 38	16 48	08 21	16 06
29		09 37	21 49	09 42	21 46	09 47	21 44	09 54	21 40	10 05	21 34
30 Sa	12 13 14	06 36	17 51	06 52	17 35	07 11	17 16	07 37	16 50	08 19	16 08
30		10 17	22 44	10 17	22 47	10 17	22 50	10 17	22 54	10 17	23 00
31 Su	12 13 24	06 36	17 52	06 51	17 36	07 10	17 17	07 36	16 52	08 17	16 11
31		10 57	23 41	10 50	23 48	10 47	23 57	10 40		10 28	

2nd Month   February, 1982   28 Days

Greenwich Mean Time

NOTE: Light figures indicate Sun. **Dark** figures indicate **Moon.** *Degrees are North Latitude.*

CAUTION: Must be converted to local time. For instruction see page 770.

Day of month / week / year	Sun on meridian / Moon phase (h m s)	20° Rise Sun/Moon	20° Set Sun/Moon	30° Rise Sun/Moon	30° Set Sun/Moon	40° Rise Sun/Moon	40° Set Sun/Moon	50° Rise Sun/Moon	50° Set Sun/Moon	60° Rise Sun/Moon	60° Set Sun/Moon
1 Mo / 32	12 13 33	06 36	17 52	06 50	17 37	07 09	17 18	07 34	16 54	08 14	16 14
	14 28))	11 40		11 31		11 20		11 05	00 09	10 42	00 27
2 Tu / 33	12 13 41	06 35	17 52	06 50	17 38	07 08	17 20	07 32	16 55	08 12	16 16
		12 25	00 40	12 12	00 51	11 56	01 06	11 33	01 25	10 08	01 57
3 We / 34	12 10 40	06 35	17 53	06 49	17 39	07 07	17 21	07 31	16 57	08 10	16 19
		13 15	01 41	12 58	01 56	12 37	02 16	12 08	02 43	11 21	03 28
4 Th / 35	12 13 54	06 34	17 54	06 48	17 40	07 06	17 22	07 30	16 59	08 08	16 22
		14 10	02 44	13 50	03 02	13 26	03 26	12 51	03 59	11 53	04 36
5 Fr / 36	12 14 00	06 34	17 54	06 48	17 40	07 05	17 24	07 28	17 00	08 05	16 24
		15 09	03 47	14 49	04 08	14 22	04 33	13 45	05 10	12 42	06 13
6 Sa / 37	12 14 05	06 33	17 55	06 47	17 41	07 04	17 25	07 26	17 02	08 02	16 26
		16 12	04 49	15 52	05 09	15 26	05 35	14 50	06 12	13 48	07 15
7 Su / 38	12 14 09	06 33	17 55	06 47	17 42	07 03	17 26	07 25	17 04	08 00	16 29
		17 15	05 47	16 57	06 06	16 35	06 30	16 03	07 03	15 10	7 58
8 Mo / 39	12 14 12	06 33	17 56	06 46	17 43	07 02	17 27	07 23	17 06	07 58	16 32
	07 57 ○	18 17	06 40	18 03	06 56	17 45	07 16	17 20	07 43	16 39	08 27
9 Tu / 40	12 14 14	06 32	17 56	06 46	17 44	07 00	17 28	07 22	17 08	07 55	16 34
		19 17	07 28	19 07	07 40	18 54	07 55	18 36	08 16	18 09	08 47
10 We / 41	12 14 16	06 32	17 57	06 45	17 44	06 59	17 30	07 20	17 09	07 52	16 37
		20 14	08 12	20 08	08 20	20 01	08 30	19 51	08 43	19 36	09 02
11 Th / 42	12 14 16	06 32	17 57	06 44	17 45	06 58	17 31	07 18	17 11	07 50	16 40
		21 08	08 52	21 06	08 58	21 05	09 00	21 03	09 06	20 59	9 15
12 Fr / 43	12 14 16	06 31	17 58	06 43	17 46	06 57	17 32	07 16	17 13	07 47	16 42
		22 00	09 31	22 03	09 30	22 07	09 29	22 12	09 27	22 20	09 25
13 Sa / 44	12 14 16	06 30	17 58	06 42	17 46	06 56	17 33	07 14	17 14	07 44	16 45
		22 51	10 08	22 58	10 03	23 07	09 57	23 20	09 48	23 39	09 36
14 Su / 45	12 14 14	06 30	17 59	06 41	17 47	06 54	17 34	07 13	17 16	07 42	16 48
		23 42	10 45	23 53	10 36		10 25		10 10		9 47
15 Mo / 46	12 14 12	06 29	17 59	06 40	17 48	06 53	17 35	07 11	17 18	07 39	16 50
	20 21 ((		11 23		11 10	00 07	10 55	00 26	10 33	00 56	10 09
16 Tu / 47	12 14 09	06 28	18 00	06 39	17 49	06 52	17 36	07 09	17 20	07 36	16 53
		00 32	12 02	00 55	11 47	01 05	11 27	01 30	11 00	02 11	10 16
17 We / 48	12 14 05	06 28	18 00	06 38	17 50	06 50	17 38	07 08	17 21	07 34	16 56
		01 22	12 45	01 40	12 26	02 02	12 03	02 33	11 31	03 24	10 38
18 Th / 49	12 14 01	06 27	18 01	06 38	17 51	06 49	17 39	07 06	17 23	07 31	16 58
		02 13	13 30	02 33	13 09	02 57	12 44	03 32	12 08	04 32	11 07
19 Fr / 50	12 13 56	06 27	18 01	06 37	17 52	06 48	17 40	07 04	17 25	07 28	17 01
		03 04	14 18	03 24	13 57	03 50	13 31	04 27	12 53	05 32	11 48
20 Sa / 51	12 13 51	06 26	18 02	06 36	17 53	06 47	17 41	07 02	17 26	07 25	17 04
		03 53	15 09	04 14	14 48	04 40	14 22	05 17	13 46	06 21	12 43
21 Su / 52	12 13 44	06 26	18 02	06 35	17 54	06 46	17 42	07 00	17 28	07 22	17 06
		04 42	16 02	05 01	15 43	05 26	15 19	06 00	14 46	06 58	13 50
22 Mo / 53	12 13 37	06 25	18 03	06 34	17 54	06 44	17 44	06 58	17 30	07 20	17 08
		05 28	16 56	05 45	16 40	06 07	16 20	06 36	15 52	07 25	15 06
23 Tu / 54	12 13 30	06 24	18 03	06 33	17 55	06 43	17 45	06 56	17 31	07 17	17 11
	21 13 ●	06 12	17 51	06 26	17 39	06 44	17 24	07 07	17 02	07 45	16 28
24 We / 55	12 13 22	06 24	18 03	06 32	17 56	06 42	17 46	06 54	17 33	07 14	17 14
		06 55	18 47	07 05	18 39	07 17	18 29	07 34	18 15	08 00	17 52
25 Th / 56	12 13 13	06 23	18 03	06 31	17 57	06 40	17 47	06 52	17 34	07 11	17 16
		07 36	19 43	07 42	19 39	07 49	19 34	07 59	19 28	08 13	19 18
26 Fr / 57	12 13 03	06 22	18 04	06 30	17 57	06 38	17 48	06 50	17 36	07 08	17 18
		08 16	20 39	08 18	20 40	08 19	20 41	08 21	20 43	08 25	20 46
27 Sa / 58	12 12 53	06 22	18 04	06 29	17 57	06 37	17 49	06 48	17 38	07 05	17 21
		08 57	21 36	08 54	21 42	08 50	21 49	08 44	21 59	08 36	22 14
28 Su / 59	12 12 43	06 21	18 04	06 28	17 58	06 36	17 47	06 46	17 40	07 02	17 24
		09 39	22 35	09 31	22 45	09 22	22 58	09 09	23 16	08 49	23 44

3rd Month   March, 1982   31 Days

Greenwich Mean Time

NOTE: Light figures indicate Sun. **Dark** figures indicate **Moon.** *Degrees are North Latitude.*

CAUTION: Must be converted to local time. For instruction see page 770.

Day of month / week / year	Sun on meridian **Moon** phase (h m s)	20° Rise Sun/**Moon**	20° Set Sun/**Moon**	30° Rise Sun/**Moon**	30° Set Sun/**Moon**	40° Rise Sun/**Moon**	40° Set Sun/**Moon**	50° Rise Sun/**Moon**	50° Set Sun/**Moon**	60° Rise Sun/**Moon**	60° Set Sun/**Moon**
1 Mo 60	12 12 32	06 20	18 05	06 26	17 50	06 04	17 52	06 44	17 42	07 00	17 26
		10 24	**23 35**	**10 11**	**23 49**	**09 56**		**09 36**		**09 04**	
2 Tu 61	12 12 20 22 15 ☽	06 20	18 06	06 25	17 59	06 32	17 53	06 42	17 43	06 57	17 28
		11 12		**10 55**		**10 36**	**00 08**	**10 08**	**00 33**	**09 24**	**01 14**
3 We 62	12 12 08	06 19	18 06	06 24	18 00	06 31	17 54	06 40	17 45	06 54	17 31
		12 04	**00 36**	**11 45**	**00 54**	**11 21**	**01 17**	**10 48**	**01 49**	**09 52**	**02 42**
4 Th 63	12 11 55	06 18	18 06	06 23	18 01	06 30	17 55	06 38	17 46	06 51	17 34
		13 00	**01 38**	**12 39**	**01 58**	**12 13**	**02 24**	**11 37**	**03 00**	**10 33**	**04 02**
5 Fr 64	12 11 42	06 17	18 06	06 22	18 02	06 28	17 56	06 36	17 48	06 48	17 36
		14 00	**02 39**	**13 39**	**03 00**	**13 13**	**03 26**	**12 36**	**04 03**	**11 31**	**05 08**
6 Sa 65	12 11 29	06 16	18 07	06 21	18 02	06 26	17 57	06 34	17 50	06 45	17 39
		15 01	**03 36**	**14 42**	**03 56**	**14 18**	**04 21**	**13 44**	**04 56**	**12 46**	**05 56**
7 Su 66	12 11 15	06 15	18 07	06 20	18 03	06 25	17 58	06 32	17 51	06 42	17 42
		16 02	**04 30**	**15 46**	**04 48**	**15 26**	**05 09**	**14 58**	**05 39**	**14 11**	**06 28**
8 Mo 67	12 11 00	06 14	18 07	06 19	18 04	06 24	17 59	06 30	17 53	06 39	17 44
		17 02	**05 19**	**16 50**	**05 33**	**16 34**	**05 50**	**16 13**	**06 14**	**15 39**	**06 51**
9 Tu 68	12 10 46 20 45 ◯	06 14	18 08	06 18	18 04	06 22	18 00	06 28	17 54	06 36	17 46
		17 59	**06 04**	**17 52**	**06 14**	**17 42**	**06 26**	**17 28**	**06 42**	**17 07**	**07 08**
10 We 69	12 10 30	06 13	18 08	06 16	18 05	06 20	18 01	06 25	17 56	06 33	17 49
		18 55	**06 46**	**18 51**	**06 51**	**18 47**	**06 58**	**18 42**	**07 07**	**18 33**	**07 20**
11 Th 70	12 10 15	06 12	18 08	06 15	18 06	06 19	18 02	06 23	17 58	06 30	17 51
		19 48	**07 25**	**19 49**	**07 26**	**19 51**	**07 27**	**19 53**	**07 29**	**19 56**	**07 31**
12 Fr 71	12 09 59	06 11	18 08	06 14	18 06	06 17	18 03	06 21	18 00	06 27	17 54
		20 40	**08 02**	**20 46**	**07 59**	**20 53**	**07 55**	**21 02**	**07 50**	**21 16**	**07 42**
13 Sa 72	12 09 43	06 10	18 09	06 12	18 07	06 16	18 04	06 19	18 01	06 24	17 56
		21 32	**08 40**	**21 41**	**08 32**	**21 53**	**08 23**	**22 10**	**08 11**	**22 36**	**07 52**
14 Su 73	12 09 26	06 10	18 10	06 11	18 08	06 14	18 05	06 17	18 02	06 21	17 58
		22 23	**09 18**	**22 36**	**09 07**	**22 53**	**08 53**	**23 16**	**08 34**	**23 53**	**08 04**
15 Mo 74	12 09 10	06 09	18 10	06 10	18 08	06 12	18 06	06 15	18 04	06 18	18 01
		23 14	**09 57**	**23 30**	**09 42**	**23 51**	**09 24**		**08 59**		**08 19**
16 Tu 75	12 08 53	06 08	18 10	06 09	18 09	06 10	18 07	06 13	18 06	06 15	18 04
			10 38		**10 21**		**09 59**	**00 20**	**09 28**	**01 08**	**08 38**
17 We 76	12 08 34 17 15 ☾	06 07	18 10	06 08	18 10	06 09	18 08	06 10	18 08	06 12	18 06
		00 05	**11 22**	**00 24**	**11 03**	**00 48**	**10 58**	**01 21**	**10 03**	**02 19**	**09 04**
18 Th 77	12 08 18	06 06	18 11	06 07	18 10	06 08	18 10	06 08	18 09	06 09	18 08
		00 55	**12 09**	**01 16**	**11 48**	**01 42**	**11 22**	**02 19**	**10 44**	**03 23**	**09 39**
19 Fr 78	12 08 01	06 05	18 11	06 06	18 11	06 06	18 11	06 06	18 11	06 06	18 11
		01 45	**12 58**	**02 06**	**12 38**	**02 33**	**12 11**	**03 10**	**11 34**	**04 16**	**10 28**
20 Sa 79	12 07 43	06 04	18 11	06 05	18 11	06 04	18 12	06 04	18 12	06 03	18 14
		02 34	**13 50**	**02 54**	**13 31**	**03 19**	**13 06**	**03 55**	**12 31**	**04 57**	**11 30**
21 Su 80	12 07 26	06 04	18 12	06 04	18 12	06 02	18 13	06 02	18 14	06 00	18 16
		03 20	**14 44**	**03 39**	**14 27**	**04 02**	**14 05**	**04 34**	**13 34**	**05 28**	**12 42**
22 Mo 81	12 07 08	06 03	18 12	06 02	18 12	06 01	18 14	05 59	18 16	05 57	18 18
		04 05	**15 39**	**04 21**	**15 25**	**04 40**	**15 07**	**05 07**	**14 42**	**05 50**	**14 02**
23 Tu 82	12 06 50	06 02	18 12	06 01	18 13	05 59	18 15	05 57	18 17	05 54	18 21
		04 49	**16 35**	**05 01**	**16 24**	**05 15**	**16 12**	**05 35**	**15 54**	**06 07**	**15 27**
24 We 83	12 06 32	06 01	18 12	06 00	18 14	05 58	18 16	05 55	18 18	05 51	18 24
		05 30	**17 31**	**05 38**	**17 25**	**05 48**	**17 18**	**06 00**	**17 09**	**06 20**	**16 54**
25 Th 84	12 06 14 10 17 ●	06 00	18 13	05 58	18 14	05 56	18 17	05 53	18 20	05 48	18 26
		06 12	**18 28**	**06 15**	**18 27**	**06 19**	**18 26**	**06 24**	**18 25**	**06 32**	**18 22**
26 Fr 85	12 05 56	05 59	18 13	05 57	18 15	05 54	18 18	05 51	18 22	05 45	18 28
		06 53	**19 26**	**06 51**	**19 31**	**06 49**	**19 36**	**06 47**	**19 42**	**06 43**	**19 53**
27 Sa 86	12 05 38	05 58	18 13	05 56	18 15	05 53	18 19	05 49	18 23	05 42	18 31
		07 35	**20 26**	**07 29**	**20 35**	**07 21**	**20 46**	**07 11**	**21 01**	**06 55**	**21 25**
28 Su 87	12 05 19	05 57	18 13	05 55	18 16	05 51	18 20	05 47	18 25	05 39	18 33
		08 20	**21 28**	**08 09**	**21 41**	**07 56**	**21 58**	**07 37**	**22 21**	**07 09**	**22 59**
29 Mo 88	12 05 01	05 56	18 14	05 54	18 16	05 50	18 21	05 44	18 26	05 36	18 36
		09 08	**22 30**	**08 53**	**22 47**	**08 34**	**23 09**	**08 08**	**23 40**	**07 27**	
30 Tu 89	12 04 43	05 56	18 14	05 52	18 17	05 48	18 22	05 42	18 28	05 33	18 38
		10 00	**23 33**	**09 41**	**23 53**	**09 18**		**08 46**		**07 53**	**00 31**
31 We 90	12 04 25	05 55	18 14	05 51	18 18	05 46	18 23	05 40	18 30	05 30	18 40
		10 55		**10 34**		**10 09**	**00 18**	**09 32**	**02 00**	**08 29**	**1 55**

4th Month   April, 1982   30 Days

Greenwich Mean Time

NOTE: Light figures indicate Sun. **Dark** figures indicate **Moon.** *Degrees are North Latitude.*

CAUTION: Must be converted to local time. For instruction see page 770.

Day of month / week / year	Sun on meridian / Moon phase (h m s)	20° Rise Sun/Moon	20° Set Sun/Moon	30° Rise Sun/Moon	30° Set Sun/Moon	40° Rise Sun/Moon	40° Set Sun/Moon	50° Rise Sun/Moon	50° Set Sun/Moon	60° Rise Sun/Moon	60° Set Sun/Moon
1 Th	12 04 07	05 54	18 14	05 50	18 18	05 44	18 22	05 38	18 32	05 27	18 42
91	05 08 ☽	11 54	00 34	11 33	00 55	11 06	01 22	10 28	02 00	09 22	03 06
2 Fr	12 03 49	05 53	18 14	05 48	18 19	05 43	18 24	05 36	18 33	05 24	18 45
92		12 54	01 32	12 34	01 53	12 09	02 19	11 33	02 55	10 32	03 58
3 Sa	12 03 37	05 52	18 15	06 47	10 20	05 42	18 25	05 33	18 35	05 20	18 48
93		13 54	02 26	13 37	02 45	13 15	03 08	12 44	03 40	11 53	04 34
4 Su	12 03 14	05 51	18 15	05 46	18 20	05 40	18 27	05 31	18 36	05 17	18 50
94		14 53	03 16	14 39	03 31	14 22	03 50	13 58	04 16	13 19	04 58
5 Mo	12 02 56	05 50	18 15	05 45	18 21	05 38	18 28	05 29	18 38	05 14	18 52
95		15 50	04 01	15 41	04 12	15 29	04 26	15 12	04 45	14 46	05 05
6 Tu	12 02 39	05 50	18 16	05 44	18 22	05 37	18 29	05 27	18 39	05 11	18 55
96		16 45	04 42	16 40	04 49	16 34	04 58	16 25	05 10	16 11	05 28
7 We	12 02 21	05 49	18 16	05 43	18 22	05 36	18 30	05 25	18 40	05 08	18 58
97		17 39	05 21	17 38	05 24	17 37	05 28	17 36	05 32	17 34	05 39
8 Th	12 02 04	05 48	18 16	05 42	18 23	05 34	18 31	05 23	18 42	05 05	19 00
98	10 18 ◯	18 31	05 59	18 35	05 57	18 39	05 56	18 46	05 53	18 56	05 49
9 Fr	12 01 48	05 47	18 16	05 41	18 23	05 32	18 32	05 21	18 44	05 02	19 02
99		19 22	06 36	19 31	06 30	19 40	06 23	19 54	06 14	20 16	05 59
10 Sa	12 01 31	05 46	18 16	05 40	18 24	05 30	18 33	05 18	18 45	05 00	19 05
100		20 14	07 14	20 26	07 04	20 41	06 52	21 01	06 35	21 35	06 10
11 Su	12 01 15	05 46	18 17	05 38	18 24	05 29	18 34	05 16	18 46	04 57	19 08
101		21 05	07 52	21 21	07 39	21 40	07 22	22 07	06 59	22 52	06 23
12 Mo	12 00 59	05 45	18 17	05 37	18 25	05 27	18 35	05 14	18 48	04 54	19 10
102		21 57	08 33	22 15	08 16	22 38	07 55	23 11	07 27		06 40
13 Tu	12 00 43	05 44	18 17	05 36	18 26	05 26	18 36	05 12	18 50	04 51	19 13
103		22 47	09 16	23 08	08 57	23 34	08 33		07 59	00 06	07 02
14 We	12 00 28	05 44	18 18	05 35	18 26	05 24	18 37	05 10	18 52	04 48	19 15
104		23 38	10 02	23 59	09 41		09 15	00 10	08 37	01 14	07 33
15 Th	12 00 13	05 43	18 18	05 34	18 27	05 22	18 38	05 08	18 53	04 45	19 18
105			10 50		10 28	00 26	10 02	01 04	09 23	02 12	08 16
16 Fr	11 59 58	05 42	18 18	05 33	18 28	05 21	18 39	05 06	18 55	04 42	19 20
106	12 42 ☾	00 26	11 40	00 47	11 20	01 14	10 45	01 52	10 17	02 57	09 12
17 Sa	11 59 44	05 41	18 19	05 32	18 28	05 20	18 40	05 04	18 56	04 39	19 22
107		01 13	12 32	01 33	12 14	01 58	11 50	02 32	11 17	03 31	10 20
18 Su	11 59 30	05 40	18 19	05 30	18 29	05 18	18 41	05 02	18 58	04 36	19 2
108		01 58	13 26	02 16	13 10	02 37	12 50	03 07	12 22	03 55	11 3
19 Mo	11 59 16	05 40	18 20	05 29	18 30	05 17	18 42	05 00	19 00	04 33	19 2
109		02 41	14 20	02 55	14 08	03 12	13 53	03 36	13 32	04 13	12 5
20 Tu	11 59 03	05 39	18 20	05 28	18 30	05 16	18 43	04 58	19 01	04 30	19 3
110		03 23	15 16	03 33	15 03	03 45	14 58	04 02	14 44	04 27	14 2
21 We	11 58 51	05 38	18 20	05 27	18 31	05 14	18 44	04 56	19 02	04 27	19 3
111		04 04	16 12	04 10	16 09	04 16	16 05	04 25	16 00	04 39	15 5
22 Th	11 58 39	05 38	18 20	05 26	18 32	05 13	18 45	04 54	19 04	04 24	19 3
112		04 45	17 10	04 46	17 12	04 47	17 14	04 48	17 17	04 50	17 2
23 Fr	11 58 27	05 37	18 21	05 25	18 32	05 12	18 46	04 52	19 06	04 22	19 3
113	20 29 ●	05 27	18 10	05 23	18 17	05 18	18 26	05 11	18 37	05 01	18 5
24 Sa	11 58 16	05 36	18 21	05 24	18 33	05 10	18 47	04 50	19 07	04 19	19 4
114		06 11	19 13	06 02	19 24	05 51	19 39	05 37	19 59	05 14	20 3
25 Su	11 58 05	05 35	18 21	05 23	18 34	05 08	18 48	04 48	19 08	04 16	19 4
115		06 59	20 17	06 45	20 33	06 29	20 53	06 06	21 21	05 30	22 0
26 Mo	11 57 54	05 34	18 21	05 22	18 34	05 07	18 49	04 46	19 10	04 13	19 4
116		07 51	21 22	07 33	21 42	07 11	22 06	06 41	22 40	05 52	23 4
27 Tu	11 57 44	05 34	18 22	05 21	18 35	05 06	18 50	04 45	19 12	04 10	19 4
117		08 47	22 26	08 27	22 48	08 01	23 14	07 25	23 52	06 24	
28 We	11 57 35	05 33	18 22	05 20	18 35	05 04	18 51	04 43	19 13	04 07	19 4
118		09 46	23 27	09 25	23 49	08 58		08 19		07 12	00 0
29 Th	11 51 26	05 32	18 22	05 19	18 36	05 03	18 52	04 41	19 15	04 04	19 1
119		10 48		10 27		10 01	00 15	09 23	00 53	08 18	01 5
30 Fr	11 57 18	05 32	18 23	05 18	18 36	05 02	18 53	04 39	19 16	04 02	19 5
120	12 07 ☽	11 49	00 24	11 30	00 43	11 07	01 08	10 34	01 42	09 38	02 5

5th Month   May, 1982   31 days

Greenwich Mean Time

NOTE: Light figures indicate Sun. **Dark** figures indicate **Moon**. *Degrees are North Latitude.*

CAUTION: Must be converted to local time. For instruction see page 770.

Day of month / week / year	Sun on meridian / Moon phase (h m s)	20° Rise Sun/Moon	20° Set Sun/Moon	30° Rise Sun/Moon	30° Set Sun/Moon	40° Rise Sun/Moon	40° Set Sun/Moon	50° Rise Sun/Moon	50° Set Sun/Moon	60° Rise Sun/Moon	60° Set Sun/Moon
Sa 121	11 57 10	05 31	18 24	05 18	18 37	05 00	18 54	04 37	19 18	03 59	19 56
		12 48	01 15	12 33	01 31	12 14	01 52	11 48	02 21	11 04	03 07
Su 122	11 57 03	05 30	18 24	05 17	18 38	04 59	18 55	04 35	19 20	03 56	19 59
		13 46	02 01	13 34	02 14	13 21	02 30	13 01	02 51	12 31	03 25
Mo 123	11 56 54	05 30	18 24	05 16	18 38	04 58	18 56	04 34	19 22	03 54	20 02
		14 41	02 43	14 34	02 51	14 25	03 02	14 14	03 17	13 06	03 39
Tu 124	11 56 49	05 29	18 24	05 15	18 39	04 57	18 57	04 32	19 23	03 51	20 04
		15 33	03 22	15 31	03 26	15 28	03 32	15 25	03 39	15 19	03 50
We 125	11 56 44	05 28	18 25	05 14	18 40	04 56	18 58	04 30	19 24	03 48	20 06
		16 25	03 59	16 27	03 59	16 30	03 59	16 34	03 59	16 39	03 59
Th 126	11 56 38	05 28	18 25	05 13	18 40	04 55	18 59	04 29	19 26	03 46	20 09
		17 16	04 35	17 23	04 31	17 31	04 26	17 42	04 19	17 59	04 08
Fr 127	11 56 34	05 28	18 25	05 12	18 41	04 54	19 00	04 27	19 28	03 43	20 12
		18 07	05 12	18 18	05 04	18 31	04 53	18 49	04 40	19 18	04 18
Sa 128	11 56 30	05 27	18 26	05 12	18 42	04 52	19 01	04 26	19 29	03 40	20 14
	00 45 ○	18 58	05 50	19 13	05 38	19 31	05 23	19 56	05 02	20 37	04 30
Su 129	11 56 26	05 26	18 26	05 11	18 42	04 51	19 02	04 24	19 30	03 38	20 16
		19 50	06 30	20 07	06 14	20 29	05 54	21 00	05 28	21 53	04 44
Mo 130	11 56 23	05 26	18 27	05 10	18 43	04 50	19 03	04 22	19 32	03 35	20 19
		20 41	07 12	21 01	06 53	21 26	06 30	22 02	05 58	23 04	05 03
Tu 131	11 56 21	05 26	18 27	05 09	18 44	04 49	19 04	04 20	19 33	03 33	20 22
		21 32	07 56	21 53	07 36	22 20	07 10	22 58	06 33		05 30
We 132	11 56 19	05 25	18 28	05 08	18 44	04 48	19 05	04 19	19 34	03 30	20 24
		22 21	08 44	22 43	08 22	23 10	07 55	23 48	07 16	00 06	06 08
Th 133	11 56 18	05 24	18 28	05 08	18 45	04 47	19 06	04 18	19 36	03 28	20 26
		23 09	09 33	23 29	09 12	23 55	08 45		08 07	00 57	06 59
Fr 134	11 56 17	05 24	18 28	05 07	18 45	04 46	19 07	04 16	19 37	03 26	20 29
		23 54	10 24		10 04		09 39	00 31	09 04	01 34	08 02
Sa 135	11 56 17	05 24	18 28	05 06	18 46	04 45	19 08	04 15	19 38	03 24	20 31
			11 16	00 12	10 59	00 35	10 37	01 07	10 06	02 01	09 15
Su 136	11 56 17	05 24	18 29	05 06	18 46	04 44	19 09	04 14	19 40	03 21	20 34
	05 11 ☾	00 37	12 09	00 52	11 55	01 12	11 38	01 38	11 13	02 21	10 33
Mo 137	11 56 18	05 23	18 30	05 06	18 47	04 43	19 10	04 12	19 42	03 18	20 36
		01 18	13 03	01 30	12 53	01 44	12 40	02 04	12 23	02 35	11 56
Tu 138	11 56 20	05 23	18 30	05 05	18 48	04 42	19 11	04 11	19 43	03 16	20 38
		01 58	13 58	02 06	13 52	02 15	13 45	02 28	13 35	02 47	13 20
We 139	11 56 22	05 23	18 30	05 04	18 48	04 41	19 12	04 10	19 44	03 14	20 40
		02 38	14 54	02 41	14 53	02 45	14 52	02 50	14 50	02 58	14 48
Th 140	11 56 25	05 22	18 31	05 04	18 49	04 40	19 12	04 08	19 46	03 12	20 42
		03 18	15 52	03 16	15 56	03 15	16 01	03 12	16 08	03 08	16 19
Fr 141	11 56 29	05 22	18 32	05 03	18 50	04 40	19 13	04 07	19 47	03 10	20 45
		04 01	16 53	03 54	17 02	03 46	17 13	03 36	17 29	03 20	17 53
Sa 142	11 56 33	05 22	18 32	05 03	18 50	04 39	19 14	04 06	19 48	03 08	20 47
		04 46	17 56	04 35	18 10	04 21	18 28	04 02	18 52	03 33	19 31
Su 143	11 56 37	05 22	18 32	05 02	18 51	04 38	19 15	04 05	19 49	03 06	20 49
	04 40 ●	05 37	19 03	05 21	19 21	05 01	19 43	04 35	20 15	03 52	21 09
Mo 144	11 56 42	05 22	18 32	05 02	18 52	04 38	19 16	04 04	19 50	03 04	20 51
		06 32	20 10	06 13	20 30	05 48	20 57	05 15	21 34	04 19	22 39
Tu 145	11 56 48	05 21	18 33	05 01	18 52	04 38	19 17	04 02	19 52	03 02	20 53
		07 32	21 15	07 10	21 36	06 44	22 04	06 06	22 43	05 00	23 51
We 146	11 56 54	05 21	18 33	05 01	18 53	04 37	19 18	04 01	19 53	03 00	20 55
		08 35	22 15	08 13	22 36	07 46	23 02	07 08	23 38	06 00	
Th 147	11 57 00	05 21	18 34	05 01	18 54	04 36	19 19	04 00	19 54	02 56	20 57
		09 39	23 10	09 19	23 28	08 54	23 51	08 19		07 18	00 41
Fr 148	11 57 07	05 20	18 34	05 00	18 54	04 36	19 20	04 00	19 56	02 56	20 59
		10 41	23 59	10 24		10 03		09 34	00 22	08 45	01 13
Sa 149	11 57 14	05 20	18 34	05 00	18 55	04 35	19 20	03 59	19 57	02 55	21 01
	20 07 ☽	11 40		11 28	00 14	11 12	00 32	10 50	00 56	10 15	01 34
Su 150	11 57 22	05 20	18 35	05 00	18 55	04 34	19 21	03 58	19 58	02 53	21 03
		12 37	00 42	12 23	00 53	12 18	01 06	12 04	01 23	11 42	01 49
Mo 151	11 57 30	05 20	18 35	05 00	18 56	04 34	19 22	03 57	19 59	02 52	21 05
		13 30	01 23	13 26	01 29	13 22	01 36	13 15	01 46	13 06	02 01

6th Month   June, 1982   30 days

Greenwich Mean Time

NOTE: Light figures indicate Sun. **Dark** figures indicate **Moon.** *Degrees are North Latitude.*

CAUTION: Must be converted to local time. For instruction see page 770.

Day of month / week / year	Sun on meridian / Moon phase (h m s)	20° Rise Sun / Moon	20° Set Sun / Moon	30° Rise Sun / Moon	30° Set Sun / Moon	40° Rise Sun / Moon	40° Set Sun / Moon	50° Rise Sun / Moon	50° Set Sun / Moon	60° Rise Sun / Moon	60° Set Sun / Moon
1 Tu 152	11 57 39	05 20	18 36	05 00	18 56	04 34	19 22	03 56	20 00	02 50	21 0
		14 22	02 01	14 23	02 02	14 24	02 04	14 25	02 07	14 27	02 1
2 We 153	11 57 48	05 20	18 36	04 59	18 56	04 33	19 23	03 56	20 01	02 48	21 0
		15 13	02 37	15 10	02 34	15 24	02 31	15 33	02 26	15 46	02 1
3 Th 154	11 57 57	05 20	18 36	04 59	18 57	04 33	19 24	03 55	20 02	02 47	21 1
		16 03	03 13	16 13	03 06	16 24	02 58	16 40	02 46	17 05	02 2
4 Fr 155	11 58 07	05 20	18 36	04 59	18 57	04 32	19 24	03 54	20 03	02 46	21 1
		16 54	03 50	17 07	03 39	17 24	03 26	17 46	03 07	18 23	02 3
5 Sa 156	11 58 17	05 20	18 37	04 58	18 58	04 32	19 25	03 54	20 04	02 44	21 1
		17 45	04 29	18 02	04 14	18 22	03 56	18 51	03 31	19 40	02 5
6 Su 157	11 58 28 / 15 59 ○	05 20	18 38	04 58	18 58	04 31	19 26	03 52	20 04	02 43	21 1
		18 36	05 10	18 56	04 52	19 20	04 30	19 54	03 59	20 53	03
7 Mo 158	11 58 38	05 20	18 38	04 58	18 59	04 31	19 26	03 52	20 05	02 42	21 1
		19 27	05 53	19 48	05 33	20 15	05 08	20 53	04 33	21 59	03
8 Tu 159	11 58 50	05 20	18 38	04 58	19 00	04 31	19 27	03 52	20 06	02 41	21
		20 17	06 40	20 39	06 18	21 06	05 51	21 45	05 13	22 55	04
9 We 160	11 59 01	05 20	18 38	04 58	19 00	04 31	19 28	03 52	20 06	02 40	21
		21 06	07 28	21 27	07 07	21 53	06 39	22 31	06 01	23 37	04
10 Th 161	11 59 12	05 20	18 39	04 58	19 01	04 31	19 28	03 51	20 07	02 39	21
		21 51	08 19	22 11	07 58	22 35	07 32	23 09	06 55		05
11 Fr 162	11 59 24	05 20	18 39	04 58	19 01	04 31	19 29	03 51	20 08	02 38	21
		22 35	09 11	22 52	08 52	23 12	08 29	23 41	07 56	00 07	07
12 Sa 163	11 59 36	05 20	18 39	04 58	19 01	04 31	19 29	03 51	20 09	02 38	21
		23 16	10 03	23 29	09 47	23 46	09 28		09 01	00 28	08
13 Su 164	11 59 49	05 20	18 40	04 58	19 02	04 30	19 30	03 50	20 10	02 37	21
		23 55	10 55		10 44		10 29	00 08	10 09	00 44	09
14 Mo 165	12 00 01 / 18 06 ☾	05 20	18 40	04 58	19 02	04 30	19 30	03 50	20 10	02 36	21
			11 48	00 05	11 41	00 16	11 31	00 32	11 18	00 57	10
15 Tu 166	12 00 14	05 20	18 40	04 58	19 02	04 30	19 30	03 50	20 11	02 36	21
		00 34	12 42	00 39	12 39	00 45	12 35	00 54	12 30	01 07	12
16 We 167	12 00 27	05 20	18 39	04 58	19 02	04 30	19 30	03 50	20 11	02 36	21
		01 12	13 37	01 13	13 39	01 14	13 41	01 15	13 44	01 17	13
17 Th 168	12 00 40	05 20	18 39	04 58	19 03	04 30	19 31	03 50	20 12	02 36	21
		01 52	14 35	01 48	14 41	01 43	14 50	01 37	15 01	01 27	15
18 Fr 169	12 00 53	05 21	18 41	04 59	19 04	04 31	19 32	03 50	20 12	02 35	21
		02 35	15 35	02 26	15 47	02 15	16 01	02 01	16 21	01 39	16
19 Sa 170	12 01 06	05 21	18 41	04 59	19 04	04 31	19 32	03 50	20 12	02 35	21
		03 22	16 40	03 09	16 56	02 52	17 16	02 29	17 44	01 54	18
20 Su 171	12 01 19	05 21	18 41	04 59	19 04	04 31	19 32	03 50	20 12	02 35	21
		04 14	17 46	03 57	18 06	03 35	18 31	03 04	19 06	02 15	20
21 Mo 172	12 01 32 / 11 52 ●	05 22	18 42	05 00	19 04	04 32	19 33	03 51	20 13	02 36	21
		05 12	18 54	04 51	19 15	04 26	19 42	03 50	20 21	02 48	21
22 Tu 173	12 01 45	05 22	18 42	05 00	19 04	04 32	19 33	03 51	20 13	02 36	21
		06 15	19 58	05 53	20 20	05 26	20 47	04 47	21 25	03 38	21
23 We 174	12 01 58	05 22	18 42	05 00	19 04	04 32	19 33	03 51	20 13	02 36	21
		07 20	20 58	06 59	21 18	06 33	21 42	05 56	22 16	04 50	23
24 Th 175	12 02 11	05 22	18 42	05 00	19 04	04 32	19 33	03 51	20 13	02 36	21
		08 26	21 52	08 07	22 08	07 44	22 28	07 12	22 55	06 17	23
25 Fr 176	12 02 24	05 22	18 42	05 00	19 04	04 32	19 33	03 52	20 13	02 37	21
		09 29	22 39	09 14	22 51	08 56	23 06	08 31	23 26	07 50	23
26 Sa 177	12 02 37	05 23	18 43	05 01	19 05	04 33	19 33	03 52	20 13	02 38	21
		10 28	23 22	10 18	23 29	10 06	23 39	09 48	23 51	09 21	
27 Su 178	12 02 50	05 23	18 43	05 01	19 05	04 33	19 33	03 52	20 13	02 38	21
		11 24		11 19		11 12		11 03		10 48	00
28 Mo 179	12 03 02 / 05 52 ☽	05 23	18 43	05 01	19 05	04 34	19 33	03 53	20 13	02 39	21
		12 18	00 01	12 17	00 04	12 16	00 08	12 14	00 13	12 12	00
29 Tu 180	12 03 14	05 24	18 43	05 02	19 05	04 34	19 33	03 54	20 13	02 40	2
		13 09	00 38	13 13	00 37	13 17	00 35	13 23	00 33	13 33	00
30 We 181	12 03 27	05 24	18 43	05 02	19 05	04 34	19 32	03 54	20 13	02 41	0
		14 00	01 14	14 08	01 09	14 18	01 02	14 31	00 53	14 52	00

7th Month   July, 1982   31 Days

Greenwich Mean Time

NOTE: Light figures indicate Sun. **Dark** figures indicate **Moon**. *Degrees are North Latitude.*

CAUTION: Must be converted to local time. For instruction see page 770.

Day of month / week / year	Sun on meridian · Moon phase (h m s)		20° Rise	20° Set	30° Rise	30° Set	40° Rise	40° Set	50° Rise	50° Set	60° Rise	60° Set
1 Th / 182	12 03 38	Sun	05 24	18 43	05 02	19 05	04 35	19 33	03 55	20 13	02 42	21 25
		Moon	14 50	01 51	15 02	01 41	15 17	01 29	15 38	01 13	16 11	00 48
2 Fr / 183	12 03 50	Sun	05 24	18 43	05 02	19 05	04 36	19 33	03 56	20 12	02 43	21 24
		Moon	15 41	02 29	15 57	02 15	16 16	01 59	16 43	01 36	17 28	01 00
3 Sa / 184	12 04 01	Sun	05 24	18 44	05 03	19 05	04 36	19 32	03 56	20 12	02 44	21 24
		Moon	16 32	03 09	16 51	02 52	17 14	02 31	17 47	02 02	18 42	01 15
4 Su / 185	12 04 12	Sun	05 25	18 44	05 04	19 05	04 36	19 32	03 57	20 12	02 45	21 23
		Moon	17 23	03 51	17 44	03 32	18 10	03 08	18 47	02 34	19 51	01 36
5 Mo / 186	12 04 23	Sun	05 25	18 44	05 04	19 05	04 37	19 32	03 57	20 11	02 46	21 22
		Moon	18 14	04 57	18 35	04 16	19 03	03 49	19 42	03 12	20 51	02 06
6 Tu / 187	12 04 33 · 07 32 ○	Sun	05 26	18 44	05 04	19 05	04 37	19 32	03 58	20 11	02 48	21 21
		Moon	19 03	05 25	19 24	05 03	19 51	04 36	20 30	03 57	21 37	02 48
7 We / 188	12 04 43	Sun	05 26	18 44	05 05	19 04	04 38	19 32	03 59	20 10	02 49	21 20
		Moon	19 50	06 15	20 10	05 54	20 35	05 27	21 10	04 49	22 11	03 43
8 Th / 189	12 04 53	Sun	05 26	18 43	05 06	19 04	04 38	19 31	04 00	20 10	02 50	21 18
		Moon	20 34	07 07	20 52	06 47	21 14	06 23	21 44	05 49	22 35	04 49
9 Fr / 190	12 05 02	Sun	05 27	18 43	05 06	19 04	04 39	19 31	04 01	20 09	02 52	21 17
		Moon	21 16	07 59	21 30	07 42	21 48	07 22	22 13	06 53	22 52	06 04
10 Sa / 191	12 05 11	Sun	05 27	18 43	05 06	19 04	04 40	19 30	04 02	20 08	02 54	21 16
		Moon	21 55	08 51	22 06	08 38	22 19	08 22	22 37	07 59	23 06	07 23
11 Su / 192	12 05 19	Sun	05 28	18 43	05 07	19 04	04 40	19 30	04 03	20 08	02 56	21 14
		Moon	22 33	09 43	22 40	09 34	22 48	09 23	22 59	09 08	23 16	08 43
12 Mo / 193	12 05 28	Sun	05 28	18 43	05 08	19 03	04 41	19 30	04 04	20 07	02 57	21 12
		Moon	23 11	10 36	23 13	10 31	23 16	10 25	23 20	10 17	23 26	10 05
13 Tu / 194	12 05 35	Sun	05 28	18 43	05 08	19 03	04 42	19 29	04 05	20 06	02 59	21 11
		Moon	23 49	11 29	23 47	11 29	23 44	11 29	23 41	11 29	23 35	11 29
14 We / 195	12 05 42 · 03 47 ☾	Sun	05 28	18 43			04 43	19 28	04 06	20 05	03 01	21 09
		Moon		12 24		12 29		12 34		12 42	23 46	12 54
15 Th / 196	12 05 49	Sun	05 29	18 42	05 09	19 02	04 44	19 28	04 07	20 04	03 03	21 08
		Moon	00 29	13 21	00 23	13 31	00 14	13 42	00 03	13 59	23 59	14 24
16 Fr / 197	12 05 55	Sun	05 30	18 42	05 10	19 02	04 44	19 27	04 08	20 03	03 05	21 06
		Moon	01 13	14 22	01 01	14 36	00 47	14 53	00 28	15 18		15 57
17 Sa / 198	12 06 01	Sun	05 30	18 42	05 10	19 02	04 45	19 27	04 09	20 02	03 07	21 04
		Moon	02 01	15 25	01 45	15 44	01 25	16 06	00 59	16 38	00 16	17 31
18 Su / 199	12 06 06	Sun	05 30	18 42	05 10	19 02	04 46	19 26	04 10	20 01	03 09	21 02
		Moon	02 54	16 31	02 35	16 52	02 11	17 18	01 37	17 55	00 42	19 00
19 Mo / 200	12 06 11	Sun	05 30	18 42	05 11	19 01	04 46	19 26	04 12	20 00	03 11	21 00
		Moon	03 54	17 37	03 32	17 59	03 05	18 26	02 27	19 05	01 21	20 14
20 Tu / 201	12 06 15 · 18 57 ●	Sun	05 31	18 41	05 11	19 00	04 47	19 25	04 13	19 59	03 13	20 58
		Moon	04 58	18 40	04 36	19 00	04 09	19 26	03 30	20 03	02 22	21 06
21 We / 202	12 06 19	Sun	05 31	18 41	05 12	19 00	04 48	19 24	04 14	19 58	03 15	20 56
		Moon	06 04	19 37	05 44	19 55	05 19	20 17	04 44	20 48	03 43	21 39
22 Th / 203	12 06 22	Sun	05 32	18 41	05 12	19 00	04 49	19 23	04 15	19 57	03 18	20 54
		Moon	07 10	20 29	06 53	20 43	06 32	21 00	06 04	21 24	05 15	22 01
23 Fr / 204	12 06 24	Sun	05 32	18 40	05 13	19 00	04 50	19 22	04 16	19 56	03 20	20 52
		Moon	08 13	21 15	08 00	21 30	07 45	21 36	07 24	21 52	06 51	22 16
24 Sa / 205	12 06 26	Sun	05 32	18 40	05 14	18 59	04 51	19 22	04 18	19 54	03 22	20 50
		Moon	09 12	21 57	09 05	22 02	08 55	22 08	08 43	22 16	08 23	22 28
25 Su / 206	12 06 29	Sun	05 33	18 40	05 14	18 58	04 52	19 21	04 19	19 53	03 24	20 48
		Moon	10 08	22 36	10 06	22 36	10 02	22 37	09 58	22 37	09 51	22 38
26 Mo / 207	12 06 28	Sun	05 33	18 40	05 15	18 58	04 53	19 20	04 20	19 52	03 26	20 46
		Moon	11 02	23 13	11 04	23 09	11 06	23 04	11 10	22 57	11 15	22 47
27 Tu / 208	12 06 28 · 18 22 ☽	Sun	05 34	18 40	05 16	18 57	04 54	19 19	04 22	19 50	03 28	20 44
		Moon	11 54	23 50	12 01	23 42	12 08	23 32	12 19	23 18	12 36	22 57
28 We / 209	12 06 28	Sun	05 34	18 39	05 16	18 56	04 54	19 18	04 23	19 49	03 31	20 41
		Moon	12 45		12 56		13 09		13 27	23 40	13 56	23 08
29 Th / 210	12 06 27	Sun	05 34	18 39	05 17	18 56	04 55	19 17	04 24	19 48	03 33	20 39
		Moon	13 36	00 28	13 51	00 16	14 09	00 01	14 34		15 14	23 22
30 Fr / 211	12 06 25	Sun	05 34	18 38	05 18	18 55	04 56	19 16	04 26	19 47	03 35	20 36
		Moon	14 27	01 07	14 45	00 52	15 07	00 32	15 38	00 05	16 30	23 41
31 Sa / 212	12 06 22	Sun	05 35	18 38	05 18	18 54	04 57	19 15	04 27	19 45	03 38	20 34
		Moon	15 19	01 49	15 39	01 31	16 04	01 07	16 39	00 35	17 42	

8th Month   August, 1982   31 Days

Greenwich Mean Time

NOTE: Light figures indicate Sun. **Dark** figures indicate **Moon.** *Degrees are North Latitude.*

CAUTION: Must be converted to local time. For instruction see page 770.

In each day block the first (light) line gives Sun values; the second (dark) line gives Moon values.

Day of month / week / year	Sun on meridian / Moon phase (h m s)	20° Rise	20° Set	30° Rise	30° Set	40° Rise	40° Set	50° Rise	50° Set	60° Rise	60° Set
1 Su	12 06 19	05 36	18 38	05 18	18 54	04 58	19 14	04 28	19 44	03 40	20 32
213		16 09	02 34	16 31	02 13	16 58	01 47	17 36	01 10	18 45	00 07
2 Mo	12 06 16	05 36	18 37	05 19	18 53	04 59	19 13	04 30	19 42	03 42	20 29
214		16 59	03 21	17 21	02 59	17 48	02 32	18 27	01 53	19 35	00 44
3 Tu	12 06 11	05 36	18 37	05 20	18 52	05 00	19 12	04 32	19 40	03 44	20 26
215		17 47	04 10	18 07	03 49	18 33	03 22	19 10	02 43	20 13	01 35
4 We	12 06 07	05 36	18 36	05 20	18 52	05 01	19 11	04 33	19 38	03 46	20 24
216	22 34 ○	18 32	05 02	18 51	04 42	19 14	04 17	19 46	03 41	20 40	02 39
5 Th	12 06 01	05 37	18 36	05 21	18 51	05 02	19 11	04 34	19 37	03 49	20 22
217		19 15	05 54	19 31	05 37	19 50	05 15	20 17	04 44	21 00	03 52
6 Fr	12 05 55	05 37	18 35	05 22	18 50	05 03	19 09	04 36	19 35	03 51	20 19
218		19 56	06 47	20 08	06 33	20 22	06 15	20 42	05 51	21 14	05 10
7 Sa	12 05 48	05 37	18 34	05 22	18 49	05 04	19 08	04 38	19 33	03 54	20 16
219		20 34	07 40	20 42	07 30	20 52	07 17	21 05	06 59	21 25	06 31
8 Su	12 05 41	05 38	18 34	05 23	18 48	05 04	19 06	04 39	19 32	03 56	20 14
220		21 12	08 32	21 16	08 26	21 20	08 19	21 26	08 09	21 35	07 53
9 Mo	12 05 33	05 38	18 33	05 24	18 47	05 05	19 05	04 40	19 30	03 58	20 11
221		21 50	09 25	21 49	09 24	21 48	09 22	21 46	09 20	21 44	09 16
10 Tu	12 05 25	05 38	18 32	05 24	18 46	05 06	19 04	04 42	19 28	04 01	20 08
222		22 28	10 19	22 23	10 22	22 16	10 26	22 07	10 32	21 54	10 40
11 We	12 05 16	05 38	18 32	05 24	18 46	05 07	19 03	04 43	19 26	04 04	20 05
223		23 10	11 14	23 00	11 22	22 47	11 32	22 31	11 46	22 05	12 07
12 Th	12 05 06	05 38	18 31	05 25	18 44	05 08	19 02	04 44	19 24	04 06	20 02
224	11 08 ☾	23 54	12 12	23 40	12 25	23 22	12 40	22 58	13 02	22 20	13 34
13 Fr	12 04 56	05 39	18 30	05 26	18 43	05 09	19 00	04 46	19 23	04 08	20 00
225			13 13		13 29		13 50	23 32	14 19	22 41	15 07
14 Sa	12 04 46	05 39	18 30	05 26	18 42	05 10	18 59	04 47	19 21	04 11	19 57
226		00 44	14 16	00 26	14 36	00 03	15 00		15 36	23 13	16 37
15 Su	12 04 35	05 40	18 29	05 27	18 41	05 11	18 58	04 48	19 19	04 13	19 55
227		01 39	15 19	01 18	15 41	00 52	16 08	00 16	16 47		17 51
16 Mo	12 04 23	05 40	18 28	05 28	18 40	05 12	18 56	04 50	19 17	04 16	19 52
228		02 39	16 22	02 17	16 44	01 50	17 11	01 11	17 49	00 02	18 55
17 Tu	12 04 11	05 40	18 28	05 28	18 39	05 13	18 54	04 52	19 15	04 18	19 49
229		03 43	17 21	03 22	17 41	02 56	18 05	02 18	18 39	01 12	19 33
18 We	12 03 58	05 41	18 27	05 29	18 39	05 14	18 53	04 53	19 13	04 20	19 47
230		04 49	18 15	04 30	18 31	04 07	18 51	03 35	19 19	02 40	20 00
19 Th	12 03 45	05 41	18 26	05 30	18 38	05 15	18 52	04 54	19 11	04 22	19 44
231	02 45 ●	05 53	19 04	05 39	19 10	05 21	19 30	04 56	19 50	04 15	20 22
20 Fr	12 03 31	05 42	18 26	05 30	18 37	05 16	18 50	04 56	19 09	04 25	19 42
232		06 55	19 48	06 45	19 56	06 33	20 04	06 16	20 16	05 50	20 30
21 Sa	12 03 17	05 42	18 25	05 31	18 35	05 17	18 48	04 58	19 07	04 28	19 39
233		07 54	20 29	07 49	20 32	07 43	20 35	07 34	20 39	07 21	20 44
22 Su	12 03 03	05 42	18 24	05 31	18 34	05 18	18 47	04 59	19 05	04 30	19 37
234		08 50	21 08	08 50	21 06	08 50	21 03	08 50	21 00	08 50	20 55
23 Mo	12 02 48	05 42	18 23	05 32	18 33	05 19	18 46	05 00	19 03	04 32	19 34
235		09 44	21 46	09 49	21 40	09 54	21 32	10 02	21 20	10 14	21 09
24 Tu	12 02 32	05 42	18 22	05 32	18 32	05 20	18 44	05 02	19 01	04 35	19 32
236		10 37	22 52	10 46	22 14	10 57	22 00	11 12	21 42	11 37	21 28
25 We	12 02 16	05 43	18 22	05 32	18 31	05 21	18 43	05 04	18 59	04 38	19 29
237		11 29	23 04	11 42	22 49	11 58	22 31	12 21	22 07	12 57	21 54
26 Th	12 02 00	05 43	18 21	05 33	18 30	05 22	18 41	05 05	18 57	04 40	19 27
238	09 49 ☽	12 21	23 45	12 37	23 27	12 58	23 05	13 27	22 35	14 16	22 28
27 Fr	12 01 43	05 43	18 20	05 34	18 29	05 23	18 40	05 06	18 55	04 42	19 24
239		13 12		13 31		13 56	23 43	14 30	23 08	15 30	23 18
28 Sa	12 01 26	05 44	18 19	05 34	18 28	05 24	18 38	05 08	18 53	04 44	19 22
240		14 03	00 29	14 24	00 09	14 51		15 29	23 48	16 36	
29 Su	12 01 08	05 44	18 18	05 35	18 26	05 24	18 36	05 10	18 51	04 47	19 19
241		14 53	01 15	15 15	00 54	15 43	00 26	16 22		17 32	23 40
30 Mo	12 00 50	05 44	18 17	05 36	18 25	05 25	18 35	05 11	18 49	04 49	19 17
242		15 42	02 04	16 03	01 42	16 30	01 15	17 08	00 36	18 14	
31 Tu	12 00 32	05 44	18 16	05 36	18 24	05 26	18 34	05 12	18 47	04 52	19 14
243		16 28	02 55	16 48	02 34	17 12	02 08	17 46	01 31	18 44	00 42

9th Month   September, 1982   30 Days

Greenwich Mean Time

NOTE: Light figures indicate Sun. **Dark** figures indicate **Moon.** *Degrees are North Latitude.*

CAUTION: Must be converted to local time. For instruction see page 770.

Day of month week year	Sun on meridian / Moon phase	20° Rise	20° Set	30° Rise	30° Set	40° Rise	40° Set	50° Rise	50° Set	60° Rise	60° Set
1 We 244	12 00 13	05 44	18 16	05 37	18 23	05 27	18 32	05 14	18 45	04 54	19 05
		17 12	03 47	17 29	03 29	17 50	03 05	18 10	02 32	10 06	01 06
2 Th 245	11 59 54	05 45	18 15	05 38	18 22	05 28	18 30	05 16	18 43	04 56	19 02
		17 54	04 40	18 07	04 25	18 23	04 06	18 46	03 39	19 22	02 54
3 Fr 246	11 59 35	05 45	18 14	05 38	18 21	05 29	18 29	05 17	18 41	04 59	18 59
	12 28 ○	18 33	05 34	18 43	05 22	18 54	05 08	19 10	04 47	19 34	04 15
4 Sa 247	11 59 15	05 45	18 13	05 38	18 20	05 30	18 28	05 18	18 39	05 01	18 56
		19 12	06 27	19 17	06 20	19 23	06 11	19 31	05 58	19 44	05 38
5 Su 248	11 58 55	05 46	18 12	05 39	18 18	05 31	18 26	05 20	18 36	05 04	18 53
		19 50	07 21	19 50	07 18	19 51	07 14	19 52	07 10	19 53	07 02
6 Mo 249	11 58 35	05 46	18 11	05 40	18 17	05 32	18 24	05 22	18 34	05 06	18 50
		20 29	08 15	20 24	08 17	20 19	08 19	20 13	08 22	20 02	08 27
7 Tu 250	11 58 15	05 46	18 10	05 40	18 16	05 33	18 23	05 23	18 32	05 08	18 47
		21 09	09 10	21 00	09 17	20 49	09 25	20 35	09 36	20 13	09 54
8 We 251	11 57 54	05 46	18 09	05 40	18 15	05 34	18 21	05 24	18 30	05 10	18 44
		21 52	10 07	21 39	10 19	21 23	10 33	21 01	10 52	20 26	11 23
9 Th 252	11 57 34	05 46	18 08	05 41	18 14	05 35	18 20	05 26	18 28	05 12	18 41
		22 40	11 07	22 23	11 22	22 01	11 42	21 32	12 09	20 44	12 54
10 Fr 253	11 57 13	05 46	18 08	05 42	18 12	05 36	18 18	05 28	18 25	05 15	18 38
	17 19 ☾	23 32	12 08	23 12	12 27	22 46	12 51	22 11	13 25	21 11	14 23
11 Sa 254	11 56 52	05 46	18 07	05 42	18 11	05 37	18 16	05 29	18 23	05 17	18 35
			13 10		13 31	23 39	13 58	23 01	14 37	21 52	15 44
12 Su 255	11 56 31	05 46	18 06	05 42	18 10	05 38	18 14	05 30	18 21	05 20	18 32
		00 29	14 11	00 07	14 33		15 01		15 40	22 53	16 50
13 Mo 256	11 56 10	05 46	18 05	05 43	18 08	05 38	18 12	05 32	18 18	05 22	18 28
		01 30	15 10	01 08	15 31	00 41	15 57	00 02	16 33		17 35
14 Tu 257	11 55 49	05 47	18 04	05 44	18 07	05 39	18 11	05 34	18 16	05 24	18 25
		02 33	16 04	02 13	16 22	01 48	16 44	01 13	17 15	00 12	18 05
15 We 258	11 55 28	05 47	18 03	05 44	18 06	05 40	18 09	05 35	18 14	05 27	18 22
		03 36	16 54	03 20	17 08	02 59	17 25	02 31	17 49	01 43	18 26
16 Th 259	11 55 06	05 47	18 02	05 44	18 05	05 41	18 08	05 36	18 12	05 29	18 19
		04 38	17 40	04 26	17 49	04 11	18 01	03 51	18 16	03 17	18 40
17 Fr 260	11 54 45	05 48	18 01	05 45	18 04	05 42	18 06	05 38	18 10	05 32	18 16
	12 09 ●	05 38	18 22	05 31	18 26	05 22	18 32	05 09	18 40	04 50	18 51
18 Sa 261	11 54 24	05 48	18 00	05 46	18 02	05 43	18 04	05 40	18 08	05 34	18 13
		06 35	19 02	06 33	19 02	06 30	19 01	06 26	19 01	06 20	19 01
19 Su 262	11 54 03	05 48	17 59	05 46	18 01	05 44	18 03	05 41	18 06	05 36	18 10
		07 31	19 40	07 33	19 36	07 36	19 30	07 41	19 22	07 48	19 10
20 Mo 263	11 53 41	05 48	17 58	05 47	18 00	05 45	18 01	05 42	18 04	05 38	18 07
		08 25	20 19	08 32	20 10	08 41	19 58	08 53	19 43	09 13	19 20
21 Tu 264	11 53 20	05 48	17 58	05 48	17 58	05 46	18 00	05 44	18 02	05 41	18 04
		09 18	20 58	09 30	20 45	09 44	20 29	10 04	20 06	10 36	19 31
22 We 265	11 52 59	05 49	17 57	05 48	17 57	05 47	17 58	05 45	17 59	05 44	18 01
		10 11	21 39	10 26	21 23	10 46	21 02	11 13	20 33	11 57	19 46
23 Th 266	11 52 48	05 49	17 56	05 49	17 56	05 48	17 57	05 47	17 57	05 46	17 58
		11 04	22 22	11 22	22 03	11 45	21 38	12 18	21 04	13 15	20 06
24 Fr 267	11 52 17	05 49	17 55	05 50	17 55	05 49	17 54	05 48	17 55	05 48	17 55
		11 55	23 08	12 16	22 47	12 42	22 20	13 20	21 42	14 26	20 35
25 Sa 268	11 51 56	05 50	17 54	05 50	17 54	05 50	17 53	05 50	17 52	05 50	17 52
	04 07 ☽	12 46	23 56	13 08	23 34	13 36	23 06	14 15	22 26	15 26	21 15
26 Su 269	11 51 35	05 50	17 53	05 51	17 52	05 51	17 52	05 52	17 50	05 53	17 49
		13 35		13 57		14 25	23 58	15 04	23 19	16 14	22 10
27 Mo 270	11 51 15	05 50	17 52	05 51	17 51	05 52	17 50	05 53	17 48	05 55	17 46
		14 22	00 46	14 43	00 25	15 09		15 45		16 48	23 33
28 Tu 271	11 50 54	05 50	17 51	05 52	17 50	05 53	17 48	05 54	17 46	05 57	17 43
		15 07	01 38	15 25	01 18	15 48	00 53	16 19	00 18	17 12	
29 We 272	11 50 34	05 50	17 50	05 52	17 48	05 54	17 46	05 56	17 44	06 00	17 40
		15 49	02 31	16 04	02 14	16 23	01 52	16 48	01 22	17 29	00 32
30 Th 273	11 50 14	05 51	17 49	05 52	17 47	05 55	17 45	05 58	17 41	06 02	17 37
		16 30	03 24	16 41	03 11	16 54	02 54	17 13	02 31	17 42	01 53

10th Month   October, 1982   31 Days

Greenwich Mean Time

NOTE: Light figures indicate Sun. **Dark** figures indicate **Moon.** *Degrees are North Latitude.*

CAUTION: Must be converted to local time. For instruction see page 770.

Day of month / week / year	Sun on meridian / Moon phase	20° Rise Sun/Moon	20° Set Sun/Moon	30° Rise Sun/Moon	30° Set Sun/Moon	40° Rise Sun/Moon	40° Set Sun/Moon	50° Rise Sun/Moon	50° Set Sun/Moon	60° Rise Sun/Moon	60° Set Sun/Moon
		h m	h m	h m	h m	h m	h m	h m	h m	h m	h m
1 Fr 274	11 49 55	05 51	17 48	05 53	17 46	05 56	17 43	05 59	17 39	06 04	17 34
		17 09	04 17	17 16	04 08	17 24	03 57	17 35	03 41	17 52	03 16
2 Sa 275	11 49 35	05 51	17 47	05 54	17 45	05 57	17 42	06 00	17 37	06 06	17 31
		17 47	05 12	17 50	05 07	17 52	05 01	17 56	04 53	18 01	04 41
3 Su 276	11 49 16 01 08 ○	05 52	17 46	05 54	17 44	05 58	17 40	06 02	17 35	06 09	17 28
		18 26	06 06	18 24	06 07	18 21	06 07	18 17	06 07	18 10	06 07
4 Mo 277	11 48 57	05 52	17 46	05 55	17 42	05 59	17 38	06 04	17 33	06 12	17 25
		19 07	07 02	18 59	07 08	18 51	07 14	18 39	07 22	18 20	07 36
5 Tu 278	11 48 39	05 52	17 45	05 55	17 41	06 00	17 37	06 05	17 31	06 14	17 22
		19 50	08 00	19 38	08 10	19 23	08 23	19 03	08 40	18 32	09 07
6 We 279	11 48 21	05 52	17 44	05 56	17 40	06 01	17 35	06 07	17 29	06 16	17 19
		20 37	09 00	20 20	09 15	20 00	09 33	19 33	09 58	18 48	10 40
7 Th 280	11 48 03	05 52	17 44	05 56	17 38	06 02	17 34	06 08	17 26	06 19	17 16
		21 28	10 02	21 08	10 21	20 44	10 44	20 09	11 16	19 12	12 12
8 Fr 281	11 47 45	05 53	17 43	05 57	17 37	06 03	17 32	06 10	17 24	06 22	17 13
		22 24	11 05	22 02	11 26	21 34	11 52	20 56	12 30	19 48	13 37
9 Sa 282	11 47 29 23 26 ☾	05 53	17 42	05 58	17 36	06 04	17 30	06 12	17 22	06 24	17 10
		23 23	12 06	23 01	12 29	22 33	12 57	21 53	13 27	20 42	14 48
10 Su 283	11 47 12	05 53	17 41	05 58	17 35	06 05	17 28	06 14	17 20	06 26	17 07
			13 05		13 27	23 38	13 54	23 00	14 32	21 55	15 38
11 Mo 284	11 46 56	05 54	17 40	05 59	17 34	06 06	17 27	06 15	17 18	06 28	17 04
		00 25	14 00	00 04	14 19		14 43		15 16	23 22	16 12
12 Tu 285	11 46 41	05 54	17 39	06 00	17 33	06 07	17 26	06 16	17 16	06 31	17 01
		01 27	14 50	01 09	15 05	00 46	15 24	00 15	15 51		16 33
13 We 286	11 46 26	05 54	17 38	06 00	17 32	06 08	17 24	06 18	17 14	06 33	16 58
		02 28	15 35	02 14	15 48	01 56	16 00	01 32	16 19	00 54	16 48
14 Th 287	11 46 11	05 54	17 37	06 01	17 31	06 09	17 22	06 20	17 12	06 36	16 55
		03 27	16 17	03 17	16 24	03 06	16 32	02 50	16 43	02 25	16 59
15 Fr 288	11 45 58	05 54	17 36	06 02	17 30	06 10	17 21	06 21	17 10	06 38	16 53
		04 24	16 57	04 19	16 59	04 14	17 01	04 06	17 04	03 55	17 09
16 Sa 289	11 45 44	05 55	17 36	06 02	17 29	06 11	17 20	06 22	17 08	06 40	16 49
		05 19	17 35	05 19	17 33	05 20	17 29	05 21	17 25	05 22	17 17
17 Su 290	11 45 31 00 04 ●	05 55	17 35	06 03	17 28	06 12	17 18	06 24	17 06	06 43	16 46
		06 13	18 14	06 18	18 06	06 25	17 57	06 34	17 45	06 48	17 26
18 Mo 291	11 45 19	05 56	17 34	06 04	17 27	06 14	17 16	06 26	17 04	06 46	16 43
		07 07	18 53	07 17	18 41	07 29	18 27	07 46	18 07	08 13	17 37
19 Tu 292	11 45 08	05 56	17 34	06 04	17 26	06 15	17 14	06 28	17 02	06 48	16 40
		08 00	19 33	08 14	19 18	08 32	18 58	08 56	18 32	09 36	17 49
20 We 293	11 44 57	05 57	17 33	06 05	17 24	06 15	17 14	06 29	17 00	06 50	16 38
		08 54	20 16	09 11	19 57	09 33	19 34	10 04	19 01	10 56	18 06
21 Th 294	11 44 46	05 57	17 32	06 06	17 23	06 16	17 12	06 31	16 58	06 53	16 35
		09 46	21 01	10 07	20 40	10 32	20 13	11 09	19 36	12 12	18 31
22 Fr 295	11 44 37	05 57	17 32	06 06	17 22	06 17	17 11	06 32	16 56	06 56	16 32
		10 38	21 48	11 00	21 26	11 28	20 58	12 07	20 17	13 18	19 06
23 Sa 296	11 44 28	05 58	17 31	06 07	17 21	06 18	17 10	06 34	16 54	06 58	16 30
		11 28	22 37	11 50	22 15	12 19	21 47	12 59	21 07	14 12	19 55
24 Su 297	11 44 19	05 58	17 30	06 08	17 20	06 20	17 08	06 36	16 52	07 00	16 27
		12 16	23 28	12 37	23 07	13 05	22 41	13 43	22 03	14 51	20 57
25 Mo 298	11 44 12 00 08 ☽	05 58	17 30	06 08	17 19	06 21	17 07	06 37	16 50	07 03	16 24
		13 01		13 21		13 45	23 38	14 20	23 05	15 18	22 09
26 Tu 299	11 44 05	05 58	17 29	06 09	17 18	06 22	17 06	06 39	16 48	07 06	16 21
		13 44	00 20	14 01	00 01	14 21		14 50		15 36	23 27
27 We 300	11 43 58	05 59	17 28	06 10	17 18	06 23	17 04	06 40	16 46	07 08	16 18
		14 24	01 12	14 38	00 57	14 54	00 38	15 16	00 11	15 50	
28 Th 301	11 43 53	06 00	17 28	06 10	17 17	06 24	17 03	06 42	16 45	07 11	16 16
		15 03	02 05	15 12	01 54	15 23	01 40	15 38	01 20	16 01	00 49
29 Fr 302	11 43 48	06 00	17 27	06 11	17 16	06 25	17 02	06 44	16 43	07 14	16 13
		15 42	02 59	15 46	02 52	15 52	02 43	15 59	02 31	16 10	02 13
30 Sa 303	11 43 44	06 00	17 27	06 12	17 15	06 26	17 01	06 46	16 41	07 16	16 11
		16 20	03 53	16 20	03 51	16 20	03 48	16 19	03 44	16 19	03 38
31 Su 304	11 43 41	06 01	17 26	06 12	17 14	06 28	17 00	06 48	16 40	07 19	16 06
		17 00	04 49	16 55	04 52	16 47	04 55	16 40	05 00	16 28	05 00

11th Month   November, 1982   30 Days

Greenwich Mean Time

NOTE: Light figures indicate Sun. **Dark** figures indicate **Moon**. *Degrees are North Latitude.*

CAUTION: Must be converted to local time. For instruction see page 770.

Day of month / week / year	Sun on meridian / Moon phase	Body	20° Rise	20° Set	30° Rise	30° Set	40° Rise	40° Set	50° Rise	50° Set	60° Rise	60° Set
1 Mo / 305	11 43 38 / 12 57 ○	Sun	06 02	17 26	06 13	17 14	06 29	16 58	06 49	16 38	07 22	16 05
		Moon	17 43	05 47	17 33	05 55	17 21	06 04	17 04	06 18	16 38	06 39
2 Tu / 306	11 43 36	Sun	06 02	17 25	06 14	17 13	06 30	16 57	06 51	16 36	07 24	16 02
		Moon	18 29	06 47	18 15	07 00	17 56	07 16	17 32	07 38	16 52	08 14
3 We / 307	11 43 35	Sun	06 02	17 24	06 15	17 12	06 31	16 56	06 52	16 34	07 26	16 00
		Moon	19 20	07 50	19 01	08 08	18 38	08 29	18 06	08 59	17 12	09 50
4 Th / 308	11 43 35	Sun	06 03	17 24	06 16	17 12	06 32	16 55	06 54	16 32	07 29	15 57
		Moon	20 16	08 55	19 54	09 16	19 28	09 42	18 50	10 18	17 44	11 23
5 Fr / 309	11 43 36	Sun	06 04	17 23	06 16	17 11	06 33	16 54	06 56	16 31	07 32	15 54
		Moon	21 16	09 59	20 53	10 21	20 35	10 50	19 44	11 30	18 32	12 42
6 Sa / 310	11 43 37	Sun	06 04	17 23	06 17	17 10	06 34	16 53	06 57	16 29	07 34	15 52
		Moon	22 18	11 00	21 57	11 23	21 29	11 51	-20 50	12 30	19 41	13 41
7 Su / 311	11 43 40	Sun	06 04	17 23	06 18	17 09	06 35	16 52	06 59	16 28	07 36	15 50
		Moon	23 21	11 57	23 02	12 17	22 38	12 43	22 04	13 18	21 06	14 19
8 Mo / 312	11 43 43 / 06 38 ☾	Sun	06 05	17 22	06 19	17 08	06 36	16 50	07 00	16 26	07 39	15 48
		Moon		12 49		13 06	23 48	13 27	23 21	13 56	22 37	14 43
9 Tu / 313	11 43 47	Sun	06 06	17 22	06 20	17 08	06 38	16 49	07 02	16 24	07 42	15 45
		Moon	00 22	13 35	00 07	13 48		14 04		14 25		14 59
10 We / 314	11 43 52	Sun	06 06	17 22	06 21	17 07	06 39	16 48	07 04	16 23	07 44	15 43
		Moon	01 21	14 17	01 10	14 25	00 56	14 36	00 38	14 46	00 08	15 10
11 Th / 315	11 43 58	Sun	06 06	17 22	06 22	17 06	06 40	16 47	07 06	16 22	07 47	15 41
		Moon	02 17	14 57	02 11	15 00	02 04	15 05	01 53	15 10	01 37	15 19
12 Fr / 316	11 44 05	Sun	06 07	17 22	06 22	17 06	06 42	16 46	07 08	16 20	07 50	15 38
		Moon	03 12	15 34	03 11	15 33	03 09	15 32	03 07	15 30	03 04	15 28
13 Sa / 317	11 44 12	Sun	06 08	17 21	06 23	17 05	06 43	16 46	07 09	16 17	07 52	15 36
		Moon	04 06	16 12	04 09	16 06	04 13	15 59	04 19	15 50	04 28	15 36
14 Su / 318	11 44 21	Sun	06 08	17 21	06 24	17 05	06 44	16 45	07 11	16 18	07 55	15 34
		Moon	04 58	16 50	05 07	16 40	05 17	16 27	05 30	16 10	05 52	15 45
15 Mo / 319	11 44 30 / 15 10 ●	Sun	06 08	17 21	06 25	17 04	06 45	16 44	07 12	16 17	07 58	15 32
		Moon	05 51	17 29	06 04	17 15	06 19	16 57	06 41	16 34	07 15	15 56
16 Tu / 320	11 44 40	Sun	06 09	17 20	06 26	17 04	06 46	16 44	07 14	16 16	08 00	15 30
		Moon	06 45	18 10	07 01	17 53	07 21	17 31	07 50	17 00	08 37	16 10
17 We / 321	11 44 51	Sun	06 10	17 20	06 26	17 03	06 47	16 43	07 16	16 14	08 02	15 27
		Moon	07 38	18 54	07 57	18 34	08 22	18 08	08 56	17 32	09 56	16 31
18 Th / 322	11 45 03	Sun	06 10	17 20	06 27	17 03	06 48	16 42	07 17	16 13	08 05	15 25
		Moon	08 30	19 41	08 52	19 19	09 19	18 51	09 58	18 11	11 08	17 01
19 Fr / 323	11 45 15	Sun	06 11	17 20	06 28	17 02	06 49	16 41	07 18	16 12	08 07	15 23
		Moon	09 21	20 30	09 44	20 07	10 12	19 38	10 53	18 58	12 07	17 44
20 Sa / 324	11 45 29	Sun	06 12	17 20	06 29	17 02	06 50	16 40	07 20	16 10	08 10	15 21
		Moon	10 10	21 20	10 32	20 58	11 00	20 31	11 40	19 51	12 52	18 41
21 Su / 325	11 45 43	Sun	06 12	17 19	06 30	17 01	06 52	16 40	07 22	16 09	08 12	15 19
		Moon	10 56	22 11	11 17	21 51	11 43	21 26	12 20	20 51	13 23	19 49
22 Mo / 326	11 45 58	Sun	06 13	17 19	06 31	17 01	06 53	16 39	07 23	16 08	08 14	15 57
		Moon	11 40	23 03	11 58	22 46	12 20	22 25	12 52	21 55	13 44	21 05
23 Tu / 327	11 46 14 / 20 05 ☽	Sun	06 14	17 19	06 32	17 00	06 54	16 38	07 24	16 07	08 16	15 15
		Moon	12 20	23 54	12 35	23 41	12 53	23 25	13 19	23 02	13 59	22 24
24 We / 328	11 46 30	Sun	06 14	17 19	06 32	17 00	06 55	16 38	07 26	16 06	08 19	15 14
		Moon	12 59		13 10		13 23		13 42		14 10	23 46
25 Th / 329	11 46 48	Sun	06 15	17 19	06 33	17 00	06 56	16 37	07 28	16 06	08 22	15 12
		Moon	13 36	00 46	13 43	00 37	13 51	00 26	14 02	00 10	14 19	
26 Fr / 330	11 47 06	Sun	06 15	17 19	06 34	17 00	06 57	16 37	07 29	16 05	08 24	15 10
		Moon	14 14	01 39	14 16	01 34	14 19	01 29	14 22	01 21	14 27	01 09
27 Sa / 331	11 47 25	Sun	06 16	17 19	06 35	17 00	06 58	16 37	07 30	16 04	08 26	15 09
		Moon	14 52	02 23	14 50	02 33	14 46	02 33	14 42	02 34	14 36	02 34
28 Su / 332	11 47 44	Sun	06 16	17 19	06 36	17 00	06 59	16 36	07 32	16 04	08 28	15 08
		Moon	15 33	03 29	15 25	03 34	15 16	03 40	15 04	03 49	14 45	04 03
29 Mo / 333	11 48 04	Sun	06 17	17 19	06 36	17 00	07 00	16 36	07 34	16 03	08 30	15 00
		Moon	16 17	04 28	16 05	04 38	15 49	04 51	15 29	05 08	14 57	05 36
30 Tu / 334	11 48 25	Sun	06 18	17 19	06 37	17 00	07 01	16 36	07 35	16 02	08 32	15 13
		Moon	17 06	05 30	16 49	05 45	16 28	06 04	16 00	06 30	15 13	07 14

12th Month   December, 1982   31 days

Greenwich Mean Time

NOTE: Light figures indicate Sun. **Dark** figures indicate **Moon.** *Degrees are North Latitude.*

CAUTION: Must be converted to local time. For instruction see page 770.

Light figures = Sun, dark figures = Moon (Sun row first, Moon row second for each day).

Day of month / week / year	Sun on meridian / Moon phase (h m s)	20° Rise	20° Set	30° Rise	30° Set	40° Rise	40° Set	50° Rise	50° Set	60° Rise	60° Set
1 We	11 48 47	06 18	17 19	06 38	17 00	07 02	16 36	07 36	16 02	08 34	15 04
335	00 21 ○	18 01	06 36	17 41	06 55	17 29	07 19	17 15	07 53	16 39	08 52
2 Th	11 49 09	06 19	17 20	06 38	17 00	07 03	16 36	07 38	16 01	08 36	15 03
336		19 01	07 42	18 39	08 04	18 11	08 32	17 30	09 11	16 19	10 22
3 Fr	14 49 32	06 20	17 20	06 39	17 00	07 04	16 35	07 39	16 00	08 38	15 01
337		20 05	08 48	19 43	09 10	19 15	09 39	18 34	10 20	17 22	11 33
4 Sa	11 49 56	06 20	17 20	06 40	17 00	07 05	16 35	07 40	16 00	08 40	15 00
338		21 11	09 49	20 50	10 10	20 24	10 37	19 48	11 15	18 44	12 20
5 Su	11 50 20	06 21	17 20	06 41	17 00	07 06	16 35	07 41	16 00	08 42	14 59
339		22 14	10 44	21 58	11 03	21 36	11 26	21 07	11 57	20 17	12 50
6 Mo	15 50 44	06 22	17 20	06 42	17 00	07 07	16 35	07 42	16 00	08 44	14 58
340		23 15	11 34	23 03	11 48	22 47	12 06	22 26	12 30	21 51	13 08
7 Tu	15 51 10	06 22	17 21	06 42	17 00	07 08	16 35	07 44	15 59	08 45	14 57
341	15 33 ☾		12 18		12 28	23 56	12 40	23 43	12 56	23 22	13 21
8 We	11 51 35	06 23	17 21	06 43	17 00	07 09	16 35	07 45	15 59	08 47	14 56
342		00 13	12 58	00 06	13 03		13 09		13 18		13 31
9 Th	11 52 02	06 24	17 21	06 44	17 01	07 10	16 35	07 46	15 59	08 48	14 55
343		01 08	13 36	01 06	13 36	01 02	13 37	00 57	13 38	00 50	13 39
10 Fr	11 52 29	06 24	17 22	06 44	17 00	07 10	16 35	07 47	15 58	08 50	14 54
344		02 02	14 13	02 04	14 09	02 06	14 04	02 09	13 57	02 14	13 46
11 Sa	11 52 56	06 25	17 22	06 45	17 01	07 11	16 35	07 48	15 58	08 52	14 54
345		02 54	14 50	03 01	14 41	03 09	14 31	03 20	14 17	03 37	13 55
12 Su	11 53 23	06 25	17 22	06 46	17 01	07 12	16 35	07 49	15 58	08 53	14 54
346		03 46	15 28	03 57	15 15	04 11	15 00	04 30	14 38	05 00	14 05
13 Mo	11 53 51	06 26	17 22	06 47	17 01	07 13	16 35	07 50	15 58	08 54	14 53
347		04 39	16 08	04 54	15 52	05 12	15 31	05 38	15 03	06 21	14 17
14 Tu	11 54 20	06 26	17 22	06 48	17 02	07 14	16 36	07 51	15 58	08 56	14 53
348		05 31	16 51	05 50	16 31	06 13	16 07	06 45	15 33	07 41	14 35
15 We	11 54 49	06 27	17 23	06 48	17 02	07 14	16 36	07 49	15 58	08 57	14 53
349	09 18 ●	06 24	17 36	06 45	17 14	07 11	16 47	07 49	16 09	08 56	15 01
16 Th	11 55 18	06 28	17 23	06 49	17 02	07 15	16 36	07 52	15 58	08 58	14 53
350		07 15	18 24	07 38	18 01	08 06	17 33	08 47	16 52	10 00	15 38
17 Fr	11 55 47	06 28	17 24	06 50	17 02	07 16	16 36	07 53	15 59	08 59	14 53
351		08 05	19 14	08 28	18 52	08 56	18 24	09 37	17 43	10 50	16 30
18 Sa	11 56 16	06 29	17 24	06 50	17 03	07 16	16 37	07 54	15 59	09 00	14 54
352		08 53	20 05	09 14	19 44	09 41	19 18	10 19	18 41	11 26	17 35
19 Su	11 56 46	06 30	17 25	06 51	17 03	07 17	16 37	07 54	16 00	09 00	14 54
353		09 37	20 56	09 56	20 38	10 20	20 15	10 54	19 43	11 50	18 49
20 Mo	11 57 15	06 30	17 25	06 51	17 04	07 18	16 37	07 55	16 00	09 01	14 54
354		10 18	21 48	10 34	21 33	10 54	21 14	11 22	20 49	12 07	20 06
21 Tu	11 57 45	06 30	17 26	06 52	17 04	07 18	16 38	07 56	16 01	09 02	14 54
355		10 57	22 38	11 09	22 28	11 25	22 14	11 46	21 55	12 19	21 26
22 We	11 58 15	06 31	17 26	06 52	17 05	07 19	16 38	07 56	16 01	09 02	14 55
356		11 34	23 29	11 42	23 23	11 53	23 15	12 07	23 03	12 29	22 49
23 Th	11 58 45	06 32	17 27	06 53	17 06	07 20	16 39	07 57	16 02	09 02	14 56
357	14 17 ☽	12 10		12 14		12 19		12 26		12 37	
24 Fr	11 59 15	06 32	17 27	06 53	17 06	07 20	16 39	07 57	16 02	09 03	14 56
358		12 47	00 21	12 46	00 19	12 46	00 16	12 45	00 13	12 44	00 08
25 Sa	11 59 45	06 32	17 28	06 54	17 06	07 20	16 40	07 57	16 03	09 03	14 57
359		13 25	01 14	13 20	01 17	13 13	01 20	13 05	01 25	12 53	01 32
26 Su	12 00 14	06 33	17 28	06 54	17 07	07 20	16 40	07 58	16 04	09 04	14 58
360		14 06	02 09	13 56	02 17	13 44	02 27	13 27	02 40	13 02	03 00
27 Mo	12 00 44	06 34	17 29	06 55	17 08	07 21	16 41	07 58	16 04	09 04	14 58
361		14 51	03 08	14 36	03 21	14 18	03 37	13 54	03 58	13 15	04 33
28 Tu	12 01 14	06 34	17 29	06 55	17 08	07 21	16 42	07 58	16 05	09 04	14 59
362		15 42	04 11	15 23	04 28	15 00	04 50	14 28	05 20	13 35	06 10
29 We	12 01 43	06 34	17 30	06 55	17 09	07 21	16 43	07 58	16 06	09 04	15 00
363		16 39	05 17	16 18	05 38	15 51	06 04	15 13	06 41	14 06	07 44
30 Th	12 02 12	06 34	17 30	06 56	17 10	07 22	16 44	07 58	16 06	09 04	15 02
364	11 33 ○	17 43	06 25	17 20	06 47	16 51	07 16	16 11	07 56	14 57	09 03
31 Fr	12 02 41	06 35	17 31	06 56	17 10	07 22	16 44	07 59	16 07	09 03	15 03
365		18 50	08 30	18 22	07 52	18 01	08 20	17 22	09 00	16 12	10 1

Julian and Gregorian Calendars; Leap Year

Calendars based on the movements of sun and moon have been used since ancient times, but none has been perfect. The Julian calendar, under which western nations measured time until 1582 A.D., was authorized by Julius Caesar in 46 B.C., the year 709 of Rome. His expert was a Greek, Sosigenes. The Julian calendar, on the assumption that the true year was 365 1/4 days long, gave every fourth year 366 days. The Venerable Bede, an Anglo-Saxon monk, announced in 730 A.D. that the 365 1/4-day Julian year was 11 min., 14 sec. too long, making a cumulative error of about a day every 128 years, but nothing was done about it for over 800 years.

By 1582 the accumulated error was estimated to have amounted to 10 days. In that year Pope Gregory XIII decreed that the day following Oct. 4, 1582, should be called Oct. 15, thus dropping 10 days.

However, with common years 365 days and a 366-day leap year every fourth year, the error in the length of the year would have recurred at the rate of a little more than 3 days every 400 years. So 3 of every 4 centesimal years (ending in 00) were made common years, not leap years. Thus 1600 was a leap year, 1700, 1800 and 1900 were not, but 2000 will be. Leap years are those divisible by 4 except centesimal years, which are common unless divisible by 400.

The Gregorian calendar was adopted at once by France, Italy, Spain, Portugal and Luxembourg. Within 2 years most German Catholic states, Belgium and parts of Switzerland and the Netherlands were brought under the new calendar, and Hungary followed in 1587. The rest of the Netherlands, along with Denmark and the German Protestant states made the change in 1699-1700 (German Protestants retained the old reckoning of Easter until 1776).

The British Government imposed the Gregorian calendar on all its possessions, including the American colonies, in 1752. The British decreed that the day following Sept. 2, 1752, should be called Sept. 14, a loss of 11 days. All dates preceding were marked O.S., for Old Style. In addition New Year's Day was moved to Jan. 1 from Mar. 25. (e.g., under the old reckoning, Mar. 24, 1700 had been followed by Mar. 25, 1701.) George Washington's birth date, which was Feb. 11, 1731, O.S., became Feb. 22, 1732, N.S. In 1753 Sweden too went Gregorian, retaining the old Easter rules until 1844.

In 1793 the French Revolutionary Government adopted a calendar of 12 months of 30 days each with 5 extra days in September of each common year and a 6th extra day every 4th year. Napoleon reinstated the Gregorian calendar in 1806.

The Gregorian system later spread to non-European regions, first in the European colonies, then in the independent countries, replacing traditional calendars at least for official purposes. Japan in 1873, Egypt in 1875, China in 1912 and Turkey in 1917 made the change, usually in conjunction with political upheavals. In China, the republican government began reckoning years from its 1911 founding — e.g., 1948 was designated the year 37. After 1949, the Communists adopted the Common, or Christian Era year count, even for the traditional lunar calendar.

In 1918 the revolutionary government in Russia decreed that the day after Jan. 31, 1918, Old Style, would become Feb. 13, 1918, New Style. Greece followed in 1923. (In Russia the Orthodox Church has retained the Julian calendar, as have various Middle Eastern Christian sects.) For the first time in history, all major cultures have been brought under one calendar.

To change from the Julian to the Gregorian calendar, add 10 days to dates Oct. 5, 1582, through Feb. 28, 1700; after that date add 11 days through Feb. 28, 1800; 12 days through Feb. 28, 1900; and 13 days through Feb. 28, 2100.

Julian Calendar

To find which of the 14 calendars printed on pages 784-785 applies to any year, starting Jan. 1, under the Julian system, find the century for the desired year in the three left-hand columns below; read across. Then find the year in the four top rows; read down. The number in the intersection is the calendar designation for that year.

Year (last two figures of desired year)														
01 02 03 04	05 06 07 08	09 10 11 12	13 14 15 16	17 18 19 20	21 22 23 24	25 26 27 28								
29 30 31 32	33 34 35 36	37 38 39 40	41 42 43 44	45 46 47 48	49 50 51 52	53 54 55 56								
57 58 59 60	61 62 63 64	65 66 67 68	69 70 71 72	73 74 75 76	77 78 79 80	81 82 83 84								
Century	00 85 86 87	88 89 90 91	92 93 94 95	96 97 98 99										

Century			Year columns →																			
0	700	1400	12	7	1	2	10	5	6	7	8	3	4	5 13	2	3	2 11	6 7	1	9	4 5 6 14	2 3 4 12
100	800	1500	11	6	7	1	9	4	5	6	14	2	3	4 12	7	1	2 10	5 6	7	8	3 4 5 13	1 2 3 11
200	900	1600	10	5	6	7	8	3	4	5	13	1	2	3 11	6	7	1 9	4 5	6	14	2 3 4 12	7 1 2 10
300	1000	1700	9	4	5	6	14	2	3	4	12	7	1	2 10	5	6	7 8	3 4	5	13	1 2 3 11	6 7 1 9
400	1100	1800	8	3	4	5	13	1	2	3	11	6	7	1 9	4	5	6 14	2 3	4	12	7 1 2 10	5 6 7 8
500	1200	1900	14	2	3	4	12	7	1	2	10	5	6	7 8	3	4	5 13	1 2	3	11	6 7 1 9	4 5 6 14
600	1300	2000	13	1	2	3	11	6	7	1	9	4	5	6 14	2	3	4 12	7 1	2	10	5 6 7 8	3 4 5 13

Gregorian Calendar

Pick desired year from table below or on page 784 (for years 1800 to 2059). The number shown with each year shows which calendar to use for that year, as shown on pages 784-785 (The Gregorian calendar was inaugurated Oct. 15, 1582. From that date to Dec. 31, 1582, use calendar 6.)

1583-1802

1583 . . 7	1603 . . 4	1623 . . 1	1643 . . 5	1663 . . 2	1683 . . 6	1703 . . 2	1723 . . 6	1743 . . 3	1763 . . 7	1783 . . 4
1584 . . 8	1604 . . 12	1624 . . 9	1644 . . 13	1664 . . 10	1684 . . 14	1704 . . 10	1724 . . 14	1744 . . 11	1764 . . 8	1784 . . 12
1585 . . 3	1605 . . 7	1625 . . 4	1645 . . 1	1665 . . 5	1685 . . 2	1705 . . 5	1725 . . 2	1745 . . 6	1765 . . 3	1785 . . 7
1586 . . 4	1606 . . 1	1626 . . 5	1646 . . 2	1666 . . 6	1686 . . 3	1706 . . 6	1726 . . 3	1746 . . 7	1766 . . 4	1786 . . 1
1587 . . 5	1607 . . 2	1627 . . 6	1647 . . 3	1667 . . 7	1687 . . 4	1707 . . 7	1727 . . 4	1747 . . 1	1767 . . 5	1787 . . 2
1588 . . 13	1608 . . 10	1628 . . 14	1648 . . 11	1668 . . 8	1688 . . 12	1708 . . 8	1728 . . 12	1748 . . 9	1768 . . 13	1788 . . 10
1589 . . 1	1609 . . 5	1629 . . 2	1649 . . 6	1669 . . 3	1689 . . 7	1709 . . 3	1729 . . 7	1749 . . 4	1769 . . 1	1789 . . 5
1590 . . 2	1610 . . 6	1630 . . 3	1650 . . 7	1670 . . 4	1690 . . 1	1710 . . 4	1730 . . 1	1750 . . 5	1770 . . 2	1790 . . 6
1591 . . 3	1611 . . 7	1631 . . 4	1651 . . 1	1671 . . 5	1691 . . 2	1711 . . 5	1731 . . 2	1751 . . 6	1771 . . 3	1791 . . 7
1592 . . 11	1612 . . 8	1632 . . 12	1652 . . 9	1672 . . 13	1692 . . 10	1712 . . 13	1732 . . 10	1752 . . 14	1772 . . 11	1792 . . 8
1593 . . 6	1613 . . 3	1633 . . 7	1653 . . 4	1673 . . 1	1693 . . 5	1713 . . 1	1733 . . 5	1753 . . 2	1773 . . 6	1793 . . 3
1594 . . 7	1614 . . 4	1634 . . 1	1654 . . 5	1674 . . 2	1694 . . 6	1714 . . 2	1734 . . 6	1754 . . 3	1774 . . 7	1794 . . 4
1595 . . 1	1615 . . 5	1635 . . 2	1655 . . 6	1675 . . 3	1695 . . 7	1715 . . 3	1735 . . 7	1755 . . 4	1775 . . 1	1795 . . 5
1596 . . 9	1616 . . 13	1636 . . 10	1656 . . 14	1676 . . 11	1696 . . 8	1716 . . 11	1736 . . 8	1756 . . 12	1776 . . 9	1796 . . 13
1597 . . 4	1617 . . 1	1637 . . 5	1657 . . 2	1677 . . 6	1697 . . 3	1717 . . 6	1737 . . 3	1757 . . 7	1777 . . 4	1797 . . 1
1598 . . 5	1618 . . 2	1638 . . 6	1658 . . 3	1678 . . 7	1698 . . 4	1718 . . 7	1738 . . 4	1758 . . 1	1778 . . 5	1798 . . 2
1599 . . 6	1619 . . 3	1639 . . 7	1659 . . 4	1679 . . 1	1699 . . 5	1719 . . 1	1739 . . 5	1759 . . 2	1779 . . 6	1799 . . 3
1600 . . 14	1620 . . 11	1640 . . 8	1660 . . 12	1680 . . 9	1700 . . 6	1720 . . 9	1740 . . 13	1760 . . 10	1780 . . 14	1800 . . 4
1601 . . 2	1621 . . 6	1641 . . 3	1661 . . 7	1681 . . 4	1701 . . 7	1721 . . 4	1741 . . 1	1761 . . 5	1781 . . 2	1801 . . 5
1602 . . 3	1622 . . 7	1642 . . 4	1662 . . 1	1682 . . 5	1702 . . 1	1722 . . 5	1742 . . 2	1762 . . 6	1782 . . 3	1802 . . 6

Perpetual Calendar

The number shown for each year indicates which Gregorian calendar to use. For 1583-1802, or for Julian calendar, see page 783. For years 1803-1820, use numbers for 1983-2000, respectively.

1821...2	1847...6	1873...4	1899...1	1925...5
1822...3	1848...14	1874...5	1900...2	1926...6
1823...4	1849...2	1875...6	1901...3	1927...7
1824...12	1850...3	1876...14	1902...4	1928...8
1825...7	1851...4	1877...2	1903...5	1929...3
1826...1	1852...12	1878...3	1904...13	1930...4
1827...2	1853...7	1879...4	1905...1	1931...5
1828...10	1854...1	1880...12	1906...2	1932...13
1829...5	1855...2	1881...7	1907...3	1933...1
1830...6	1856...10	1882...1	1908...11	1934...2
1831...7	1857...5	1883...2	1909...6	1935...3
1832...8	1858...6	1884...10	1910...7	1936...11
1833...3	1859...7	1885...5	1911...1	1937...6
1834...4	1860...8	1886...6	1912...9	1938...7
1835...5	1861...3	1887...7	1913...4	1939...1
1836...13	1862...4	1888...8	1914...5	1940...9
1837...1	1863...5	1889...3	1915...6	1941...4
1838...2	1864...13	1890...4	1916...14	1942...5
1839...3	1865...1	1891...5	1917...2	1943...6
1840...11	1866...2	1892...13	1918...3	1944...14
1841...6	1867...3	1893...1	1919...4	1945...2
1842...7	1868...11	1894...2	1920...12	1946...3
1843...1	1869...6	1895...3	1921...7	1947...4
1844...9	1870...7	1896...11	1922...1	1948...12
1845...4	1871...1	1897...6	1923...2	1949...7
1846...5	1872...9	1898...7	1924...10	1950...1

1951...2	1977...7	2003...4	2029...4	2055...6
1952...10	1978...1	2004...12	2030...5	2056...14
1953...5	1979...2	2005...7	2031...6	2057...2
1954...6	1980...10	2006...1	2032...14	2058...3
1955...7	1981...5	2007...2	2033...7	2059...4
1956...8	1982...6	2008...10	2034...1	2060...12
1957...3	1983...7	2009...5	2035...2	2061...7
1958...4	1984...8	2010...6	2036...10	2062...1
1959...5	1985...3	2011...7	2037...5	2063...2
1960...13	1986...4	2012...8	2038...6	2064...10
1961...1	1987...5	2013...3	2039...7	2065...5
1962...2	1988...13	2014...4	2040...8	2066...6
1963...3	1989...1	2015...5	2041...3	2067...7
1964...11	1990...2	2016...13	2042...4	2068...8
1965...6	1991...3	2017...1	2043...5	2069...3
1966...7	1992...11	2018...2	2044...13	2070...4
1967...1	1993...6	2019...3	2045...1	2071...5
1968...9	1994...7	2020...11	2046...2	2072...13
1969...4	1995...1	2021...6	2047...3	2073...1
1970...5	1996...9	2022...7	2048...11	2074...2
1971...6	1997...4	2023...1	2049...6	2075...3
1972...14	1998...5	2024...9	2050...7	2076...11
1973...2	1999...6	2025...4	2051...1	2077...6
1974...3	2000...14	2026...5	2052...9	2078...7
1975...4	2001...2	2027...6	2053...4	2079...1
1976...12	2002...3	2028...14	2054...5	2080...9

The remainder of the page consists of fourteen numbered reference calendars (1 through 14), each showing the twelve months (January through December) with day-of-week columns S M T W T F S.

Perpetual Calendar grid (reference numbers and months):

7 / 1983
JANUARY · FEBRUARY · MARCH · APRIL · MAY · JUNE · JULY · AUGUST · SEPTEMBER · OCTOBER · NOVEMBER · DECEMBER

8
JANUARY · FEBRUARY · MARCH · APRIL · MAY · JUNE · JULY · AUGUST · SEPTEMBER · OCTOBER · NOVEMBER · DECEMBER

9
JANUARY · FEBRUARY · MARCH · APRIL · MAY · JUNE · JULY · AUGUST · SEPTEMBER · OCTOBER · NOVEMBER · DECEMBER

10
JANUARY · FEBRUARY · MARCH · APRIL · MAY · JUNE · JULY · AUGUST · SEPTEMBER · OCTOBER · NOVEMBER · DECEMBER

11
JANUARY · FEBRUARY · MARCH · APRIL · MAY · JUNE · JULY · AUGUST · SEPTEMBER · OCTOBER · NOVEMBER · DECEMBER

12
JANUARY · FEBRUARY · MARCH · APRIL · MAY · JUNE · JULY · AUGUST · SEPTEMBER · OCTOBER · NOVEMBER · DECEMBER

13
JANUARY · FEBRUARY · MARCH · APRIL · MAY · JUNE · JULY · AUGUST · SEPTEMBER · OCTOBER · NOVEMBER · DECEMBER

14
JANUARY · FEBRUARY · MARCH · APRIL · MAY · JUNE · JULY · AUGUST · SEPTEMBER · OCTOBER · NOVEMBER · DECEMBER

Each calendar block is headed by the weekday columns S M T W T F S.

The Julian Period

How many days have you lived? To determine this, you must multiply your age by 365, add the number of days since your last birthday until today, and account for all leap years. Chances are your answer would be wrong. Astronomers, however, find it convenient to express dates and long time intervals in days rather than in years, months and days. This is done by placing events within the Julian period.

The Julian period was devised in 1582 by Joseph Scaliger and named after his father Julius (not after the Julian calendar). Scaliger had Julian Day (JD) #1 begin at noon, Jan. 1, 4713 B. C., the most recent time that three major chronological cycles began on the same day — 1) the 28-year solar cycle, after which dates in the Julian calendar (e.g., Feb. 11)

return to the same days of the week (e.g., Monday); 2) the 19-year lunar cycle, after which the phases of the moon return to the same dates of the year; and 3) the 15-year indiction cycle, used in ancient Rome to regulate taxes. It will take 7980 years to complete the period, the product of 28, 19, and 15.

Noon of Dec. 31, 1981, marks the beginning of JD 2,444,970; that many days will have passed since the start of the Julian period. The JD at noon of any date in 1982 may be found by adding to this figure the day of the year for that date, which is given in the left hand column in the chart below. Simple JD conversion tables are used by astronomers.

Days Between Two Dates

Table covers period of two ordinary years. Example—Days between Feb. 10, 1979 and Dec. 15, 1980; subtract 41 from 714; answer is 673 days. For leap year, such as 1980, one day must be added: final answer 674.

Date	Jan.	Feb.	Mar.	April	May	June	July	Aug.	Sept.	Oct.	Nov.	Dec.
1	1	32	60	91	121	152	182	213	244	274	305	335
2	2	33	61	92	122	153	183	214	245	275	306	336
3	3	34	62	93	123	154	184	215	246	276	307	337
4	4	35	63	94	124	155	185	216	247	277	308	338
5	5	36	64	95	125	156	186	217	248	278	309	339
6	6	37	65	96	126	157	187	218	249	279	310	340
7	7	38	66	97	127	158	188	219	250	280	311	341
8	8	39	67	98	128	159	189	220	251	281	312	342
9	9	40	68	99	129	160	190	221	252	282	313	343
10	10	41	69	100	130	161	191	222	253	283	314	344
11	11	42	70	101	131	162	192	223	254	284	315	345
12	12	43	71	102	132	163	193	224	255	285	316	346
13	13	44	72	103	133	164	194	225	256	286	317	347
14	14	45	73	104	134	165	195	226	257	287	318	348
15	15	46	74	105	135	166	196	227	258	288	319	349
16	16	47	75	106	136	167	197	228	259	289	320	350
17	17	48	76	107	137	168	198	229	260	290	321	351
18	18	49	77	108	138	169	199	230	261	291	322	352
19	19	50	78	109	139	170	200	231	262	292	323	353
20	20	51	79	110	140	171	201	232	263	293	324	354
21	21	52	80	111	141	172	202	233	264	294	325	355
22	22	53	81	112	142	173	203	234	265	295	326	356
23	23	54	82	113	143	174	204	235	266	296	327	357
24	24	55	83	114	144	175	205	236	267	297	328	358
25	25	56	84	115	145	176	206	237	268	298	329	359
26	26	57	85	116	146	177	207	238	269	299	330	360
27	27	58	86	117	147	178	208	239	270	300	331	361
28	28	59	87	118	148	179	209	240	271	301	332	362
29	29	—	88	119	149	180	210	241	272	302	333	363
30	30	—	89	120	150	181	211	242	273	303	334	364
31	31	—	90	—	151	—	212	243	—	304	—	365

Date	Jan.	Feb.	Mar.	April	May	June	July	Aug.	Sept.	Oct.	Nov.	Dec.
1	366	397	425	456	486	517	547	578	609	639	670	700
2	367	398	426	457	487	518	548	579	610	640	671	701
3	368	399	427	458	488	519	549	580	611	641	672	702
4	369	400	428	459	489	520	550	581	612	642	673	703
5	370	401	429	460	490	521	551	582	613	643	674	704
6	371	402	430	461	491	522	552	583	614	644	675	705
7	372	403	431	462	492	523	553	584	615	645	676	706
8	373	404	432	463	493	524	554	585	616	646	677	707
9	374	405	433	464	494	525	555	586	617	647	678	708
10	375	406	434	465	495	526	556	587	618	648	679	709
11	376	407	435	466	496	527	557	588	619	649	680	710
12	377	408	436	467	497	528	558	589	620	650	681	711
13	378	409	437	468	498	529	559	590	621	651	682	712
14	379	410	438	469	499	530	560	591	622	652	683	713
15	380	411	439	470	500	531	561	592	623	653	684	714
16	381	412	440	471	501	532	562	593	624	654	685	715
17	382	413	441	472	502	533	563	594	625	655	686	716
18	383	414	442	473	503	534	564	595	626	656	687	717
19	384	415	443	474	504	535	565	596	627	657	688	718
20	385	416	444	475	505	536	566	597	628	658	689	719
21	386	417	445	476	506	537	567	598	629	659	690	720
22	387	418	446	477	507	538	568	599	630	660	691	721
23	388	419	447	478	508	539	569	600	631	661	692	722
24	389	420	448	479	509	540	570	601	632	662	693	723
25	390	421	449	480	510	541	571	602	633	663	694	724
26	391	422	450	481	511	542	572	603	634	664	695	725
27	392	423	451	482	512	543	573	604	635	665	696	726
28	393	424	452	483	513	544	574	605	636	666	697	727
29	394	—	453	484	514	545	575	606	637	667	698	728
30	395	—	454	485	515	546	576	607	638	668	699	729
31	396	—	455	—	516	—	577	608	—	669	—	730

Lunar Calendar, Chinese New Year, Vietnamese Tet

The ancient Chinese lunar calendar is divided into 12 months of either 29 or 30 days (compensating for the fact that the mean duration of the lunar month is 29 days, 12 hours, 44.05 minutes). The calendar is synchronized with the solar year by the addition of extra months at fixed intervals.

The Chinese calendar runs on a sexagenary cycle, i.e., 60 years. The cycles 1876-1935 and 1936-1995, with the years grouped under their twelve animal designations, are printed below. The Year 1982 is found in the eleventh column, under Dog, and is known as a "Year of the Dog." Readers can find the animal name for the year of their birth, marriage, etc., in the same chart. (Note: the first 3-7 weeks of each of the western years belong to the previous Chinese year and animal designation.)

Both the western (Gregorian) and traditional lunar calendars are used publicly in China, and two New Year's celebrations are held. On Taiwan, in overseas Chinese communities, and in Vietnam, the lunar calendar has been used only to set the dates for traditional festivals, with the Gregorian system in general use.

The four-day Chinese New Year, Hsin Nien, and the three-day Vietnamese New Year festival, Tet, begin at the first new moon after the sun enters Aquarius. The day may fall, therefore, between Jan. 21 and Feb. 19 of the Gregorian calendar. Jan. 25, 1982 marks the start of the new Chinese year. The date is fixed according to the date of the new moon in the Far East. Since this is west of the International Date Line the date may be one day later than that of the new moon in the United States.

Rat	Ox	Tiger	Hare (Rabbit)	Dragon	Snake	Horse	Sheep (Goat)	Monkey	Rooster	Dog	Pig
1876	1877	1878	1879	1880	1881	1882	1883	1884	1885	1886	1887
1888	1889	1890	1891	1892	1893	1894	1895	1896	1897	1898	1899
1900	1901	1902	1903	1904	1905	1906	1907	1908	1909	1910	1911
1912	1913	1914	1915	1916	1917	1918	1919	1920	1921	1922	1923
1924	1925	1926	1927	1928	1929	1930	1931	1932	1933	1934	1935
1936	1937	1938	1939	1940	1941	1942	1943	1944	1945	1946	1947
1948	1949	1950	1951	1952	1953	1954	1955	1956	1957	1958	1959
1960	1961	1962	1963	1964	1965	1966	1967	1968	1969	1970	1971
1972	1973	1974	1975	1976	1977	1978	1979	1980	1981	1982	1983
1984	1985	1986	1987	1988	1989	1990	1991	1992	1993	1994	1995

Chronological Eras, 1982

The year 1982 of the Christian Era comprises the latter part of the 206th and the beginning of the 207th year of the independence of the United States of America.

Era	Year	Begins in 1982	Era	Year	Begins in 1982
Byzantine	7491	Sept. 14	Japanese	2642	Jan. 1
Jewish	5743	Sept. 18 (sunset)	Grecian (Seleucidae)	2294	Sept. 14 or Oct. 14
Olympiads (First year of Olympiad 690)	2758	July 2	Diocletian	1699	Sept. 11
			Indian (Saka)	1904	Mar. 22
Roman (Ab Urbe Condita)	2735	Jan. 14	Mohammedan (Hegira)	1403	Oct. 19
Nabonassar (Babylonian)	2731	Apr. 28			

Chronological Cycles, 1982

Dominical Letter	C	Golden Number (Lunar Cycle)	VII	Roman Indiction	5
Epact	25	Solar Cycle	3	Julian Period (year of)	6695

Standard Time Differences — North American Cities

At 12 o'clock noon, Eastern Standard Time, the standard time in N.A. cities is as follows:

City	Time		City	Time		City	Time	
Akron, Oh.	12.00	Noon	Frankfort, Ky.	12.00	Noon	Pierre, S.D.	11.00	A.M.
Albuquerque, N.M.	10.00	A.M.	Galveston, Tex.	11.00	A.M.	Pittsburgh, Pa.	12.00	Noon
Atlanta, Ga.	12.00	Noon	Grand Rapids, Mich.	12.00	Noon	Portland, Me.	12.00	Noon
Austin, Tex.	11.00	A.M.	Halifax, N.S.	1.00	P.M.	Portland, Ore.	9.00	A.M.
Baltimore, Md.	12.00	Noon	Hartford, Conn.	12.00	Noon	Providence, R.I.	12.00	Noon
Birmingham, Ala.	11.00	A.M.	Helena, Mon.	10.00	A.M.	*Regina, Sask.	11.00	A.M.
Bismarck, N.D.	11.00	A.M.	*Honolulu, Ha.	7.00	A.M.	Reno, Nev.	9.00	A.M.
Boise, Ida.	10.00	A.M.	Houston, Tex.	11.00	A.M.	Richmond, Va.	12.00	Noon
Boston, Mass.	12.00	Noon	*Indianapolis, Ind.	12.00	Noon	Rochester, N.Y.	12.00	Noon
Buffalo, N.Y.	12.00	Noon	Jacksonville, Fla.	12.00	Noon	Sacramento, Cal.	9.00	A.M.
Butte, Mon.	10.00	A.M.	Juneau, Alas.	9.00	A.M.	St. John's, Nfld.	1.30	P.M.
Calgary, Alta.	10.00	A.M.	Kansas City, Mo.	11.00	A.M.	St. Louis, Mo.	11.00	A.M.
Charleston, S.C.	12.00	Noon	Knoxville, Tenn.	12.00	Noon	St. Paul, Minn.	11.00	A.M.
Charleston, W.Va.	12.00	Noon	Lexington, Ky.	12.00	Noon	Salt Lake City, Ut.	10.00	A.M.
Charlotte, N.C.	12.00	Noon	Lincoln, Neb.	11.00	A.M.	San Antonio, Tex.	11.00	A.M.
Charlottetown, P.E.I.	1.00	P.M.	Little Rock, Ark.	11.00	A.M.	San Diego, Cal.	9.00	A.M.
Chattanooga, Tenn.	12.00	Noon	Los Angeles, Cal.	9.00	A.M.	San Francisco, Cal.	9.00	A.M.
Cheyenne, Wy.	10.00	A.M.	Louisville, Ky.	12.00	Noon	Santa Fe, N.M.	10.00	A.M.
Chicago, Ill.	11.00	A.M.	*Mexico City	11.00	A.M.	Savannah, Ga.	12.00	Noon
Cleveland, Oh.	12.00	Noon	Memphis, Tenn.	11.00	A.M.	Seattle, Wash.	9.00	A.M.
Colorado Spr., Col.	10.00	A.M.	Miami, Fla.	12.00	Noon	Shreveport, La.	11.00	A.M.
Columbus, Oh.	12.00	Noon	Milwaukee, Wis.	11.00	A.M.	Sioux Falls, S.D.	11.00	A.M.
Dallas, Tex.	11.00	A.M.	Minneapolis, Minn.	11.00	A.M.	Spokane, Wash.	9.00	A.M.
*Dawson, Yuk.	9.00	A.M.	Mobile, Ala.	11.00	A.M.	Tampa, Fla.	12.00	Noon
Dayton, Oh.	12.00	Noon	Montreal, Que.	12.00	Noon	Toledo, Oh.	12.00	Noon
Denver, Col.	10.00	A.M.	Nashville, Tenn.	11.00	A.M.	Topeka, Kan.	11.00	A.M.
Des Moines, Ia.	11.00	A.M.	New Haven, Conn.	12.00	Noon	Toronto, Ont.	12.00	Noon
Detroit, Mich.	12.00	Noon	New Orleans, La.	11.00	A.M.	*Tucson, Ariz.	10.00	A.M.
Duluth, Minn.	11.00	A.M.	New York, N.Y.	12.00	Noon	Tulsa, Okla.	11.00	A.M.
El Paso, Tex.	10.00	A.M.	Nome, Alas.	6.00	A.M.	Vancouver, B.C.	9.00	A.M.
Erie, Pa.	12.00	Noon	Norfolk, Va.	12.00	Noon	Washington, D.C.	12.00	Noon
Evansville, Ind.	11.00	A.M.	Okla. City, Okla.	11.00	A.M.	Wichita, Kan.	11.00	A.M.
Fairbanks, Alas.	7.00	A.M.	Omaha, Neb.	11.00	A.M.	Wilmington, Del.	12.00	Noon
Flint, Mich.	12.00	Noon	Peoria, Ill.	11.00	A.M.	Winnipeg, Man.	11.00	A.M.
*Fort Wayne, Ind.	12.00	Noon	Philadelphia, Pa.	12.00	Noon			
Fort Worth, Tex.	11.00	A.M.	*Phoenix, Ariz.	11.00	A.M.			

*Cities with an asterisk do not observe daylight savings time. During much of the year, it is necessary to add one hour to the cities which do observe daylight savings time to get the proper time relation.

Standard Time Differences—World Cities

The time indicated in the table is fixed by law and is called the legal time, or, more generally, Standard Time. Use of Daylight Saving Time varies widely. *Indicates morning of the following day. At 12.00, Eastern Standard Time, the standard time (in 24-hour time) in foreign cities is as follows:

City	Time	City	Time	City	Time	City	Time
Alexandria	19 00	Copenhagen	18 00	Lima	12 00	Santiago (Chile)	13 00
Amsterdam	18 00	Dacca	23 00	Lisbon	18 00	Seoul	2 00*
Athens	19 00	Delhi	22 30	Liverpool	17 00	Shanghai	1 00*
Auckland	5 00*	Dublin	17 00	London	17 00	Singapore	00 30*
Baghdad	20 00	Gdansk	18 00	Madrid	18 00	Stockholm	18 00
Bangkok	0 00	Geneva	18 00	Manila	1 00*	Sydney (Australia)	3 00*
Belfast	17 00	Havana	12 00	Melbourne	3 00*	Tashkent	23 00
Berlin	18 00	Helsinki	19 00	Montevideo	14 00	Teheran	20 30
Bogota	12 00	Ho Chi Minh City	1 00*	Moscow	20 00	Tel Aviv	19 00
Bombay	22 30	Hong Kong	1 00*	Nagasaki	2 00*	Tokyo	2 00*
Bremen	18 00	Istanbul	19 00	Oslo	18 00	Valparaiso	13 00
Brussels	18 00	Jakarta	0 00	Paris	18 00	Vladivostok	3 00*
Bucharest	19 00	Jerusalem	19 00	Peking	1 00*	Vienna	18 00
Budapest	18 00	Johannesburg	19 00	Prague	18 00	Warsaw	18 00
Buenos Aires	14 00	Karachi	22 00	Rangoon	23 30	Wellington (N.Z.)	5 00*
Calcutta	22 30	Le Havre	18 00	Rio De Janeiro	14 00	Yokohama	2 00*
Cape Town	19 00	Leningrad	20 00	Rome	18 00	Zurich	18 00
Caracas	13 00						

Standard Time, Daylight Saving Time, and Others

Source: Defense Mapping Agency Hydrographic Center; Department of Transportation; National Bureau of Standards; U.S. Naval Observatory

Standard Time

Standard time is reckoned from Greenwich, England, recognized as the Prime Meridian of Longitude. The world is divided into 24 zones, each 15° of arc, or one hour in time apart. The Greenwich meridian (0°) extends through the center of the initial zone, and the zones to the east are numbered from 1 to 12 with the prefix "minus" indicating the number of hours to be subtracted to obtain Greenwich Time.

Westward zones are similarly numbered, but prefixed "plus" showing the number of hours that must be added to get Greenwich Time. While these zones apply generally to sea areas, it should be noted that the Standard Time maintained in many countries does not coincide with zone time. A graphical representation of the zones is shown on the Standard Time Zone Chart of the World published by the Defense Mapping Agency Hydrographic Center, Washington, DC 20390.

The United States and possessions are divided into eight Standard Time zones, as set forth by the Uniform Time Act of 1966, which also provides for the use of Daylight Saving Time therein. Each zone is approximately 15° of longitude in width. All places in each zone use, instead of their own local time, the time counted from the transit of the "mean sun" across the Standard Time meridian which passes near the middle of that zone.

These time zones are designated as Atlantic, Eastern, Central, Mountain, Pacific, Yukon, Alaska-Hawaii, and Bering, and the time in these zones is basically reckoned from the 60th, 75th, 90th, 105th, 120th, 135th, 150th, 165th meridians west of Greenwich. The line wanders to conform to local geographical regions. The time in the various zones is earlier than Greenwich Time by 4, 5, 6, 7, 8, 9, 10, and 11 hours respectively.

24-Hour Time

24-hour time is widely used in scientific work throughout the world. In the United States it is used also in operations of the Armed Forces. In Europe it is used in preference to the 12-hour a.m. and p.m. system. With the 24-hour system the day begins at midnight and hours are numbered 0 through 23.

International Date Line

The Date Line is a zig-zag line that approximately coincides with the 180th meridian, and it is where each calendar day begins. The date must be advanced one day when crossing in a westerly direction and set back one day when crossing in an easterly direction.

The line is deflected between north latitude 48° and 75°, so that all Asia lies to the west of it.

Daylight Saving Time

Daylight Saving Time is achieved by advancing the clock one hour. Under the Uniform Time Act, which became effective in 1967, all states, the District of Columbia, and U.S. possessions were to observe Daylight Saving Time beginning at 2 a.m. on the last Sunday in April and ending at 2 a.m. on the last Sunday in October. Any state could, by law, exempt itself; a 1972 amendment to the act authorized states split by time zones to take that into consideration in exempting themselves. Arizona, Hawaii, Puerto Rico, the Virgin Islands, American Samoa, and part of Indiana are now exempt. Some local zone boundaries in Kansas, Texas, Florida, Michigan, and Alaska have been modified in the last several years by the Dept. of Transportation, which oversees the act. To conserve energy Congress put most of the nation on year-round Daylight Saving Time for two years effective Jan. 6, 1974 through Oct. 26, 1975; but a further bill, signed in October, 1974, restored Standard Time from the last Sunday in that month to the last Sunday in February, 1975. At the end of 1975, Congress failed to renew this temporary legislation and the nation returned to the older end-of April to end-of October DST system.

Legal or Public Holidays, 1982

Technically there are no national holidays in the United States; each state has jurisdiction over its holidays, which are designated by legislative enactment or executive proclamation. In practice, however, most states observe the federal legal public holidays, even though the President and Congress can legally designate holidays only for the District of Columbia and for federal employees.

Federal legal public holidays are: New Year's Day, Washington's Birthday, Memorial Day, Independence Day, Labor Day, Columbus Day, Veterans Day, Thanksgiving, and Christmas.

Chief Legal or Public Holidays

When a holiday falls on a Sunday or a Saturday it is usually observed on the following Monday or preceding Friday. For some holidays, government and business closing practices vary. In most states, the office of the Secretary of State can provide details of holiday closings.

Jan. 1 (Friday) — New Year's Day. All the states.

Feb. 12 (Friday) — Lincoln's Birthday. Alas., Calif., Conn., Fla., Ill., Ind., Ia., Kan., Md., Mo., Mont., N.M., N.Y., Ut., Vt., Wash., W. Va. It is celebrated in Arizona on Feb. 8, in Del. and Ore. on Feb. 1.

Feb. 15 (3d Monday in Feb.) — Washington's Birthday. All the states. In several states the holiday is called Presidents' Day or Washington-Lincoln Day.

Apr. 9 — Good Friday. Observed in all the states. A legal or public holiday in Conn., Del., Fla., Ha., Ind., Ky., La., Md., N.J., and Tenn.

May 31 (last Monday in May) — Memorial Day. All the states except Miss. and S.C.

July 5 (Monday) — Independence Day. All the states.

Sept. 6 (1st Mon. in Sept.) — Labor Day. All the states.

Oct. 11 (2d Mon. in Oct.) — Columbus Day. Ariz., Calif., Conn., D.C., Fla., Ga., Ha., Id., Ill., Ind., Kan., Me., Mass., Minn., Mo., Mont., Nev., N.H., N.J., N.M., N.Y., N.C., Oh., Pa., R.I., S.D., Tenn., Tex., Vt., Va., W. Va., Wis., Wyo., P.R. Observed on Oct. 12 in Md. and Okla.

Nov. 2 (1st Tues. after 1st Mon. in Nov.) — General Election Day. Del., Fla., Ga., Ha., Ill., Ind., La., Md., Mo., Mont., N.H., N.J., N.Y., N.D., Pa., Tenn., Va., Wis., Wyo.

Nov. 11 (Thursday) — Armistice Day (Veterans' Day). All the states.

Nov. 25 (4th Thurs. in Nov.) — Thanksgiving Day. All the states. The day after Thanksgiving is also celebrated as a full or partial holiday in some states.

Dec. 24 (Friday) — Christmas. All the states. The Monday after Christmas is also celebrated as a holiday in some states in 1982.

Other Legal or Public Holidays

Dates are for 1982 observance, when known.

Jan. 10 — Volunteer Fireman Day (2nd Sunday in Jan.). In New Jersey.

Jan. 15 — Martin Luther King's Birthday. Conn., D.C., Fla., Ga., Ill., La., Md., Mass., Mich., N.J., Oh., Pa., S.C. Many schools and black groups in other states also observe the day.

Jan. 18 — Robert E. Lee's Birthday. Ala., Ark., Fla., Ga., La., Miss., N.C., S.C.; Lee-Jackson Day in Va., Confederate Heroes Day in Tex.

Mar. 2 — Texas Independence Day. In that state.

Mar. 3 — Town Meeting Day (1st Tuesday in Mar.) In Vt.

Mar. 25 — Maryland Day. In that state.

Mar. 26 — Prince Jonah Kuhio Kalanianaole Day. In Ha.

Mar. 29 — Seward's Day. In Alas.

Apr. 12 — Anniversary of signing Halifax Resolves. In N.C.

Apr. 19 — Patriot's Day. In Mass., Me.

Apr. 26 — Confederate Memorial Day. In Fla., Ga., Miss.

May 10 — Confederate Memorial Day. In N.C.
May 18 — Primary Election Day. In Pa.

June 3 — Confederate Memorial Day. In La. Jefferson Davis's Birthday in Fla., Ga., celebrated in Miss. on the first Mon. in June (June 7 in 1982).

June 11 — King Kamehameha I Day. In Ha.

June 14 — Flag Day. Observed in all states; a legal holiday in Pa.

June 17 — Bunker Hill Day. In Boston and Suffolk County, Mass.

July 24 — Pioneer Day. In Ut.

Aug. 1 — American Family Day. (2nd Monday in August). In Ariz.

Aug. 9 — Victory Day (2d Monday in August). In Ariz.
Aug. 16 — Bennington Battle Day. In Vt.
Aug. 20 — Admission Day (3d Friday in August). In Ha.
Aug. 27 — Lyndon Johnson's Birthday. In Tex.

Sept. 9 — Admission Day. In Calif.
Sept. 13 — Defenders' Day. In Md.
Sept. 14 — Primary Election Day. In Wis.

Oct. 18 — Alaska Day. In that state.
Oct. 31 — Nevada Day. In that state.

Nov. 1 — All Saints' Day. In La.
Nov. 27 — Day after Thanksgiving. Fla., Me., Minn., Neb., N.H., Wash.

Dec. 27 — Monday after Christmas. Ark., Fla., Ky., Miss., Mo.

Days Usually Observed

American Indian Day (Sept. 24 in 1982). Always fourth Friday in September.

Arbor Day. Tree-planting day. First observed April 10, 1872, in Nebraska. Now observed in every state in the Union except Alaska (often on the last Friday in April). A legal holiday in Utah (always last Friday in April), and in Nebraska (April 22).

Armed Forces Day (May 15 in 1982). Always third Saturday in that month, by presidential proclamation. Replaced Army, Navy, and Air Force Days.

Bill of Rights Day, Dec. 15. By Act of Congress. Bill of Rights took effect Dec. 15, 1791.

Bird Day. Often observed with Arbor Day.

Child Health Day (Oct. 4 in 1982). Always first Monday in October, by presidential proclamation.

Citizenship Day, Sept. 17. President Truman, Feb. 29, 1952, signed bill designating Sept. 17 as annual Citizenship Day. It replaced I Am An American Day, formerly 3rd Sunday in May and Constitution Day, formerly Sept. 17.

Easter Monday (Apr. 12 in 1982). A statutory day in Canada.

Easter Sunday (Apr. 11 in 1982).

Elizabeth Cady Stanton Day, Nov. 12. Birthday of pioneer leader for equal rights for women.

Epiphany (Jan. 6 in 1982). Observed in Puerto Rico.

Father's Day (June 20, in 1982). Always third Sunday in that month.

Flag Day, June 14. By presidential proclamation. It is a legal holiday in Pennsylvania.

Forefathers' Day, Dec. 21. Landing on Plymouth Rock, in 1620. Is celebrated with dinners by New England societies especially "Down East."

Four Chaplains Memorial Day, Feb. 3.

Gen. Douglas MacArthur Day, Jan. 26. A memorial day in Arkansas.

Gen. Pulaski Memorial Day, Oct. 11. Native of Poland and Revolutionary War hero; died (Oct. 11, 1779) from wounds received at the seige of Savannah, Ga. Observed officially in Indiana.

Georgia Day, Feb. 12. Observed in that state. Commemorates landing of first colonists in 1733.

Grandparent's Day (Sept. 12 in 1982). Always first Sunday after Labor Day. Legislated in 1979.

Groundhog Day, Feb. 2. A popular belief is that if the groundhog sees his shadow this day, he returns to his burrow and winter continues 6 weeks longer.

Halloween, Oct. 31. The evening before All Saints or All-Hallows Day. Informally observed in the U.S. with masquerading and pumpkin-decorations. Traditionally an occasion for children to play pranks.

Loyalty Day, May 1. By act of Congress.

Mardi Gras Day (Feb. 23 in 1982). Observed in Louisiana.

May Day. Name popularly given to May 1st. Celebrated as Labor Day in most of the world, and by some groups in the U.S. Observed in many schools as a Spring Festival.

Minnesota Day, May 11. In that state.

Mother's Day (May 9 in 1982). Always second Sunday in that month. First celebrated in Philadelphia in 1908. Mother's Day has become an international holiday.

National Day of Prayer. By presidential proclamation each year on a day other than a Sunday.

National Freedom Day, Feb. 1. To commemorate the signing of the Thirteenth Amendment, abolishing slavery, Feb. 1, 1865. By presidential proclamation.

National Maritime Day, May 22. First proclaimed 1935 in commemoration of the departure of the SS Savannah, from Savannah, Ga., on May 22, 1819, on the first successful transatlantic voyage under steam propulsion. By presidential proclamation.

Oregon's Admission to the Union, Feb. 14. Observed in that state.

Pan American Day, Apr. 14. In 1890 the First International Conference of American States, meeting in Washington, was held on that date. A resolution was adopted which resulted in the creation of the organization known today as the Pan American Union. By presidential proclamation.

Primary Election Day. Observed usually only when presidential or general elections are held.

Reformation Day, Oct. 31. Observed by Protestant groups.

Sadie Hawkins Day (Nov. 13 in 1982). First Saturday after November 11.

St. Patrick's Day, Mar. 17. Observed by Irish Societies, especially with parades.

St. Valentine's Day, Feb. 14. Festival of a martyr beheaded at Rome under Emperor Claudius. Association of this day with lovers has no connection with the saint and probably had its origin in an old belief that on this day birds begin to choose their mates.

Susan B. Anthony Day, Feb. 15. Birthday of a pioneer crusader for equal rights for women.

United Nations Day, Oct. 24. By presidential proclamation, to commemorate founding of United Nations.

Verrazano Day, Apr. 7. Observed by New York State, to commemorate the probable discovery of New York harbor by Giovanni da Verrazano in April, 1524.

Victoria Day (May 18 in 1981). Birthday of Queen Victoria, a statutory day in Canada, celebrated the first Monday before May 25.

Francis Willard Day, Sept. 28. Observed in Minnesota to honor the educator and temperance leader.

Will Rogers Day, Nov. 4. In Oklahoma.

World Poetry Day, Oct. 15.

Wright Brothers Day, Dec. 17. By presidential designation, to commemorate first successful flight by Orville and Wilbur Wright, Dec. 17, 1903.

Other Holidays, Anniversaries, Events — 1982

Jan. 20, 1937	— Franklin D. Roosevelt inaugurated for second term as U.S. President.
Feb. 11 (Thurs.)	— National Inventors' Day.
Feb. 24	— Ash Wednesday.
Mar. 20 (Sat.)	— Spring begins.
Apr. 1 (Thurs.)	— April Fool's Day.
Apr. 3, 1882	— Jesse James dies at age 34 of a gunshot wound by a fellow outlaw.
Apr. 8 (Thurs.)	— Passover begins.
Apr. 9	— Good Friday.
May 8 (Sat.)	— Armed Forces Day.
June 21 (Mon.)	— Summer begins.
June 24 (Thurs.)	— San Juan Day, in Puerto Rico, St. Jean Day in Quebec.
June 26 (Sat.)	— United Nations Charter Day.
July 1 (Thurs.)	— Dominion Day, or Canada Day.
July 14 (Wed.)	— Bastille Day in France.
Aug. 6 (Fri.)	— Hiroshima Day.
Aug. 25 (Wed.)	— Puerto Rico Constitution Day.
Sept. 3, 1957	— At Little Rock, Ark., national guards block black students from entering Central High School.
Sept. 9, 1957	— Civil Rights Act sets up a commission to investigate infringements of voting and other rights.
Sept. 17 (Thurs.)	— Mexican Independence Day.
Sept. 18 (Sat.)	— Rosh Hashanah.
Sept. 23 (Thurs.)	— Autumn begins.
Sept. 27 (Mon.)	— Yom Kippur.
Oct. 21-22, 1967	— Huge march on Washington protesting Vietnam War.
Nov. 5 (Fri.)	— Guy Fawkes Day in Britain.
Nov. 19 (Fri.)	— Discovery of Puerto Rico Day.
Dec. 11 (Sat.)	— Chanukkah.
Dec. 12 (Sun.)	— Fiesta of Our Lady of Gaudalupe in Mexico.
Dec. 21 (Tues.)	— Winter begins.
Dec. 27 (Mon.)	— Boxing Day in the British Commonwealth of Nations.

The Meaning of "One Inch of Rain"

An acre of ground contains 43,560 square feet. Consequently, a rainfall of 1 inch over 1 acre of ground would mean a total of 6,272,640 cubic inches of water. This is equivalent of 3,630 cubic feet.

As a cubic foot of pure water weights about 62.4 pounds, the exact amount varying with the density, it follows that the weight of a uniform coating of 1 inch of rain over 1 acre of surface would be 226,512 pounds, or about 113 short tons. The weight of 1 U.S. gallon of pure water is about 8.345 pounds. Consequently a rainfall of 1 inch over 1 acre of ground would mean 27,143 gallons of water.

Temperature-Humidity (Discomfort) Index

The temperature-humidity index, THI, is a measure of summertime human discomfort resulting from the combined effects of temperature and humidity. (The THI may be calculated by adding wet-bulb and dry-bulb temperatures, multiplying the sum by 0.4 and adding 15.)

The following chart shows the combinations of temperature degrees and humidity percentages which produce discomfort for most persons (the equivalent of a THI value of 75) and those which produce acute discomfort for almost everyone (equivalent to a THI of 80).

Discomfort temp.-humid.	Acute discomfort temp.-humid.	Discomfort temp.-humid.	Acute discomfort temp.-humid.	Discomfort temp.-humid.	Acute discomfort temp.-humid.
75°—100%	81°—100%	82°—49%	88°—54%	90°—14%	96°—20%
76°— 91%	82°— 93%	83°—43%	89°—49%	91°—10%	97°—16%
77°— 82%	83°— 86%	84°—38%	90°—43%	92°— 7%	98°—13%
78°— 75%	84°— 78%	85°—33%	91°—38%	93°— 5%	99°—11%
79°— 68%	85°— 71%	86°—29%	92°—34%	94°— 3%	100°— 8%
80°— 61%	86°— 65%	87°—25%	93°—30%	95°— 1%	101°— 6%
81°— 55%	87°— 59%	88°—20%	94°—26%	96°— 1%	102°— 3%
		89°—17%	95°—23%	97°— 1%	103°— 1%

From 95 degrees up there is discomfort at any humidity. When the temperature is over 102 degrees there is acute discomfort at any humidity.

Tides and Their Causes

Source: National Oceanic and Atmospheric Administration, U.S. Commerce Department

The tides are a natural phenomenon involving the alternating rise and fall in the large fluid bodies of the earth caused by the combined gravitational attraction of the sun and moon. The combination of these two variable force influences produce the complex recurrent cycle of the tides. Tides may occur in both oceans and seas, to a limited extent in large lakes, the atmosphere, and, to a very minute degree, in the earth itself. The period between succeeding tides varies as the result of many factors and force influences.

The tide-generating force represents the difference between (1) the centrifugal force produced by the revolution of the earth around the common center-of-gravity of the earth-moon system and (2) the gravitational attraction of the moon acting upon the earth's overlying waters. Since, on the average, the moon is only 238,857 miles from the earth compared with the sun's much greater distance of 93,000,000 miles, this closer distance outranks the much smaller mass of the moon compared with that of the sun, and the moon's tide-raising force is, accordingly, 2⅓ times that of the sun.

The effect of the tide-generating forces of the moon and sun acting tangentially to the earth's surface (the so-called "tractive force") tends to cause a maximum accumulation of the waters of the oceans at two diametrically opposite positions on the surface of the earth and to withdraw compensating amounts of water from all points 90° removed from the positions of these tidal bulges. As the earth rotates beneath the maxima and minima of these tide-generating forces, a sequence of two high tides, separated by two low tides, ideally is produced each day.

Twice in each lunar month, when the sun, moon, and earth are directly aligned, with the moon between the earth and the sun (at new moon) or on the opposite side of the

earth from the sun (at full moon), the sun and the moon exert their gravitational force in a mutual or additive fashion. Higher high tides and lower low tides are produced. These are called *spring* tides. At two positions 90° in between, the gravitational forces of the moon and sun — imposed at right angles—tend to counteract each other to the greatest extent, and the range between high and low tides is reduced. These are called *neap* tides. This semi-monthly variation between the spring and neap tides is called the *phase inequality*.

The inclination of the moon's orbit to the equator also produces a difference in the height of succeeding high tides and in the extent of depression of succeeding low tides which is known as the *diurnal inequality*. In extreme cases, this phenomenon can result in only one high tide and one low tide each day.

The actual amount of the uplift of the waters in the deep ocean may amount to only one or two feet. However, as this tide approaches shoal waters and its effects are augmented the tidal range may be greatly increased. In Nova Scotia along the narrow channel of the Bay of Fundy, the range of tides or difference between high and low waters, may reach 43 1/2 feet or more (under spring tide conditions) due to resonant amplification.

At New Orleans, the periodic rise and fall of the tide varies with the state of the Mississippi, being about 10 inches at low stage and zero at high. The Canadian Tide Tables for 1972 gave a maximum range of nearly 50 feet at Leaf Basin, Ungava Bay.

In every case, actual high or low tide can vary considerably from the average due to weather conditions such as strong winds, abrupt barometric pressure changes, or prolonged periods of extreme high or low pressure.

The Average Rise and Fall of Tides

Places	Ft.	In.	Places	Ft.	In.	Places	Ft.	In.
Baltimore, Md.	1	1	Mobile, Ala.	1	6	San Diego, Cal.	4	1
Boston, Mass.	9	6	New London, Conn.	2	7	Sandy Hook, N.J.	4	7
Charleston, S.C.	5	2	Newport, R.I.	3	6	San Francisco, Cal.	4	0
Colon, Panama	1	1	New York, N.Y.	4	6	Savannah, Ga.	7	5
Eastport, Me.	18	2	Old Pt. Comfort, Va.	2	6	Seattle, Wash.	7	7
Galveston, Tex.	1	5	Philadelphia, Pa.	5	11	Tampa, Fla.	2	10
Halifax, N.S.	4	5	Portland, Me.	9	0	Vancouver, B.C.	10	6
Key West, Fla.	1	4	St. John's, Nfld.	2	7	Washington, D.C.	2	11

Speed of Winds in the U.S.

Source: National Oceanic and Atmospheric Administration, U.S. Commerce Department
Miles per hour — average through 1980. High through 1980. Wind velocities in true values.

Station	Avg.	High	Station	Avg.	High	Station	Avg.	High
Albuquerque, N.M.	9.0	90	Helena, Mont.	7.9	73	New York, N.Y.(c)	9.4	70
Anchorage, Alas.	6.7	61	Honolulu, Ha.	11.8	67	Omaha, Neb.	10.8	109
Atlanta, Ga.	9.1	70	Jacksonville, Fla.	11.3	84	Pensacola, Fla.	8.4	53
Bismarck, N.D.	10.4	72	Key West, Fla.	11.2	122	Philadelphia, Pa.	9.6	73
Boston, Mass.	12.6	61	Knoxville, Tenn.	7.2	73	Pittsburgh, Pa.	9.3	58
Buffalo, N.Y.	12.3	91	Little Rock, Ark.	8.1	65	Portland, Ore.	7.9	88
Cape Hatteras, N.C.	11.4	(b)110	Louisville, Ky.	8.4	61	Rochester, N.Y.	9.8	73
Chattanooga, Tenn.	6.3	82	Memphis, Tenn.	9.1	46	St. Louis, Mo.	9.5	(b)60
Chicago, Ill.	10.4	60	Miami, Fla.	9.2	(a)74	Salt Lake City, Ut.	8.8	71
Cincinnati, Oh.	7.1	49	Minneapolis, Minn.	10.5	92	San Diego, Cal.	6.7	51
Cleveland, Oh.	10.8	74	Mobile, Ala.	9.1	(b)63	San Francisco, Cal.	10.5	58
Denver, Col.	9.0	56	Montgomery, Ala.	6.7	72	Savannah, Ga.	8.0	66
Detroit, Mich.	10.2	46	Mt. Washington, N.H.	35.0	231	Spokane, Wash.	8.7	59
Fort Smith, Ark.	7.6	58	Nashville, Tenn.	7.9	73	Toledo, Oh.	9.5	72
Galveston, Tex.	11.0	(d)100	New Orleans, La.	8.3	(b)98	Washington, D.C.	9.3	78

(a) Highest velocity ever recorded in Miami area was 132 mph, at former station in Miami Beach in September, 1926. (b) Previous location. (c) Data for Central Park, Battery Place data through 1960, avg. 14.5, high 113. (d) Recorded before anemometer blew away. Estimated high 120.

Men's Names Added to Hurricane List

U.S. government agencies responsible for weather and related communications have used girls' names to identify major tropical storms since 1953. A U.S. proposal that both male and female names be adopted for hurricanes, starting in 1979, was accepted by a committee of the World Meteorological Organization.

Names assigned to Atlantic hurricanes, 1982 — Alberto,

Beryl, Chris, Debby, Ernesto, Florence, Gilbert, Helene, Isaac, Joan, Keith, Leslie, Michael, Nadine, Oscar, Patty, Rafael, Sandy, Tony, Valerie, William.

Names assigned to Eastern Pacific hurricanes, 1982 — Aletta, Bud, Carlotta, Daniel, Emilia, Fabio, Gilma, Hector, Iva, John, Kristy, Lane, Miriam, Norman, Olivia, Paul, Rosa, Sergio, Tara, Vicente, Willa.

National Weather Service Watches and Warnings

Source: National Weather Service, NOAA, U.S. Commerce Department

National Weather Service forecasters issue a Tornado Watch for a specific area where it is reasonably possible that tornadoes may occur during the valid time of the watch. A Watch is to alert people to watch for tornado activity and listen for a Tornado Warning. A Tornado Warning means that a tornado has been sighted or indicated by radar, and that safety precautions should be taken at once. A Hurricane Watch means that an existing hurricane poses a threat to coastal and inland communities in the area specified by the Watch. A Hurricane Warning means hurricane force winds and/or dangerously high water and exceptionally high waves are expected in a specified coastal area within 24 hours.

Tornado—A violent rotating column of air pendant from a thundercloud, usually recognized as a funnel-shaped vortex accompanied by a loud roar. With rotating winds est. up to 300 mph., it is the most destructive storm. Tornado paths have varied in length from a few feet to nearly 300 miles (avg. 5 mi.); diameter from a few feet to over a mile (average 220 yards); average forward speed, 25-40 mph.

Cyclone—An atmospheric circulation of winds rotating counterclockwise in the northern hemisphere and clockwise in the southern hemisphere. Tornadoes, hurricanes, and the lows shown on weather maps are all examples of cyclones having various sizes and intensities. Cyclones are usually accompanied by precipitation or stormy weather.

Hurricane—A severe cyclone originating over tropical ocean waters and having winds 74 miles an hour or higher. (In the western Pacific, such storms are known as typhoons.) The area of strong winds takes the form of a circle or an oval, sometimes as much as 500 miles in diameter. In the lower latitudes hurricanes usually move toward the west or northwest at 10 to 15 mph. When the center approaches 25° to 30° North Latitude, direction of motion often changes to northeast, with increased forward speed.

Blizzard—A severe weather condition characterized by low temperatures and by strong winds bearing a great amount of snow (mostly fine, dry snow picked up from the ground). The National Weather Service specifies, for blizzard, a wind of 35 miles an hour or higher, temperatures 20°F. or lower, and sufficient falling and/or blowing snow to reduce visibility to less than $\frac{1}{4}$ of a mile. For "severe blizzard" wind speeds of 45 mph or more, temperature near or below 10°F., and visibility reduced by snow to near zero.

Monsoon—A name for seasonal winds (derived from Arabic "mausim," a season). It was first applied to the winds over the Arabian Sea, which blow for six months from northeast and six months from southwest, but it has been extended to similar winds in other parts of the world. The monsoons are strongest on the southern and eastern sides of Asia.

Flood—The condition that occurs when water overflows the natural or artificial confines of a stream or other body of water, or accumulates by drainage over low-lying areas.

National Weather Service Marine Warnings and Advisories

Small Craft Advisory: A Small Craft Advisory alerts mariners to sustained (exceeding two hours) weather and/or sea conditions either present or forecast, potentially hazardous to small boats. Hazardous conditions may include winds of 18 to 33 knots and/or dangerous wave or inlet conditions. It is the responsibility of the mariner, based on his experience and size or type of boat, to determine if the conditions are hazardous. When a mariner becomes aware of a Small Craft Advisory, he should immediately obtain the latest marine forecast to determine the reason for the Advisory.

Gale Warning indicates that winds within the range 34 to 47 knots are forecast for the area.

Storm Warning indicates that winds 48 knots and above, no matter how high the speed, are forecast for the area.

However, if the winds are associated with a tropical cyclone (hurricane), the storm warning indicates that winds within the range 48 to 63 knots are forecast.

Hurricane Warning indicates that winds 64 knots and above are forecast for the area.

Primary sources of dissemination are commercial radio, TV, U.S. Coast Guard Radio stations, and NOAA VHF-FM broadcasts. These broadcasts on 162.40 and 162.55 MHz can usually be received 20-40 miles from the transmitting antenna site, depending on terrain and quality of the receiver used. Where transmitting antennas are on high ground, the range is somewhat greater, reaching 60 miles or more.

Wind Chill Table

Source: National Oceanic and Atmospheric Administration, U.S. Commerce Department

Both temperature and wind cause heat loss from body surfaces. A combination of cold and wind makes a body feel colder than the actual temperature. The table shows, for example, that a temperature of 20 degrees Fahrenheit, plus a wind of 20 miles per hour, causes a body heat loss equal to that in minus 10 degrees with no wind. In other words, the wind makes 20 degrees feel like minus 10.

Top line of figures shows actual temperatures in degrees Fahrenheit. Column at left shows wind speeds.

MPH	35	30	25	20	15	10	5	0	−5	−10	−15	−20	−25	−30	−35	−40	−45
5	33	27	21	19	12	7	0	−5	−10	−15	−21	−26	−31	−36	−42	−47	−52
10	22	16	10	3	−3	−9	−15	−22	−27	−34	−40	−46	−52	−58	−64	−71	−77
15	16	9	2	−5	−11	−18	−25	−31	−38	−45	−51	−58	−65	−72	−78	−85	−92
20	12	4	−3	−10	−17	−24	−31	−39	−46	−53	−60	−67	−74	−81	−88	−95	−103
25	8	1	−7	−15	−22	−29	−36	−44	−51	−59	−66	−74	−81	−88	−96	−103	−110
30	6	−2	−10	−18	−25	−33	−41	−49	−56	−64	−71	−79	−86	−93	−101	−109	−116
35	4	−4	−12	−20	−27	−35	−43	−52	−58	−67	−74	−82	−89	−97	−105	−113	−120
40	3	−5	−13	−21	−29	−37	−45	−53	−60	−69	−76	−84	−92	−100	−107	−115	−123
45	2	−6	−14	−22	−30	−38	−46	−54	−62	−70	−78	−85	−93	−102	−109	−117	−125

(Wind speeds greater than 45 mph have little additional chilling effect.)

Explanation of Normal Temperatures

Normal temperatures listed in the tables on pages 793 and 795 are based on records of the National Weather Service for the 30-year period from 1941-1970 inclusive. To obtain the average maximum or minimum temperature for any month, the daily temperatures are added; the total is then divided by the number of days in that month.

The normal maximum temperature for January, for example, is obtained by adding the average maximums for Jan., 1941, Jan., 1942, etc., through Jan., 1970. The total is then divided by 30. The normal minimum temperature is obtained in a similar manner by adding the average minimums for each January in the 30-year period and dividing by 30. The normal temperature for January is one half of the sum for the normal maximum and minimum temperatures for that month. The mean temperature for any one day is one-half the total of the maximum and minimum temperatures for that day.

Monthly Normal Temperature and Precipitation

Source: National Oceanic and Atmospheric Administration, U.S. Commerce Department

These normals are based on records for the 30-year period 1941 to 1970 inclusive. See explanation on page 792. For stations that did not have continuous records from the same instrument site for the entire 30 years, the means have been adjusted to the record at the present site.

Airport station; *city office stations. T, temperature in Fahrenheit; P, precipitation in inches; L, less than .05 inch.

	Jan.		Feb.		Mar.		Apr.		May		June		July		Aug.		Sept.		Oct.		Nov.		Dec.	
Station	T.	P.	T.	P.	T.	P.	T.	P.	T.	P.	T.	P.	T.	P.	T.	P.	T.	P.	T.	P.	T.	P.	T.	P.
Albany, N.Y.	22	2.2	24	2.1	33	2.6	47	2.7	58	3.3	68	3.0	72	3.1	70	2.9	62	3.1	51	2.6	40	2.8	26	2.9
Albuquerque, N.M.	35	0.3	40	0.4	46	0.5	56	0.5	65	0.5	75	0.5	79	1.4	77	1.3	70	0.8	58	0.8	45	0.3	36	0.5
Anchorage, Alas.	12	0.8	18	0.8	24	0.6	35	0.6	46	0.6	55	1.1	58	2.1	56	2.3	48	2.4	35	1.4	21	1.0	13	1.1
Asheville, N.C.	38	3.4	39	3.6	46	4.7	56	3.5	64	3.3	71	4.0	74	4.9	73	4.5	67	3.6	57	3.3	46	2.9	39	3.6
Atlanta, Ga.	42	4.3	45	4.4	51	5.8	61	4.6	69	3.7	76	3.7	78	4.9	78	3.5	72	3.2	62	2.5	51	3.4	44	4.2
Baltimore, Md.	33	2.9	35	2.8	43	3.7	54	3.1	64	3.6	72	3.8	77	4.1	75	4.2	69	3.1	57	2.8	46	3.1	35	3.3
Barrow, Alas.	-15	0.2	-19	0.2	-15	0.2	-1	0.2	19	0.2	33	0.4	39	0.9	38	1.0	30	0.6	15	0.6	-1	0.3	-12	0.2
Birmingham, Ala.	44	4.8	47	5.3	53	6.2	63	4.6	71	3.6	77	4.0	80	5.2	79	4.3	74	3.6	63	2.6	52	3.7	46	5.2
Bismarck, N.D.	8	0.5	14	0.4	25	0.7	43	1.4	54	2.2	64	3.6	71	2.2	69	2.0	58	1.3	47	0.8	29	0.6	16	0.5
Boise, Ida.	29	1.5	36	1.2	41	1.0	49	1.1	57	1.3	65	1.1	75	0.2	72	0.3	63	0.4	52	0.8	40	1.3	32	1.4
Boston, Mass.	29	3.7	30	3.5	38	4.0	49	3.5	59	3.5	68	3.2	73	2.7	71	3.5	65	3.2	55	3.0	45	4.5	33	4.2
Buffalo, N.Y.	24	2.9	24	2.6	32	2.9	45	3.2	55	3.0	66	2.2	70	2.9	68	3.5	62	3.3	52	3.0	40	3.7	28	3.0
Burlington, Vt.	17	1.7	19	1.7	29	1.9	43	2.6	55	3.0	65	3.5	70	3.5	67	3.7	59	3.1	49	2.7	37	2.9	23	2.2
Caribou, Me.	11	2.0	13	2.1	24	2.2	37	2.4	50	3.0	60	3.4	65	4.0	62	3.8	54	3.5	44	3.3	31	3.5	16	2.6
Charleston, S.C.	49	2.9	51	3.3	57	4.8	65	3.0	72	3.8	78	6.3	80	8.2	80	6.4	75	5.2	66	3.1	56	2.1	49	3.1
Chicago, Ill.	24	1.9	27	1.6	37	2.7	50	3.8	60	3.4	71	4.0	75	4.1	74	3.1	66	3.0	55	2.6	40	2.2	29	2.1
Cincinnati, Oh.*	32	3.4	34	3.0	43	4.1	55	3.9	64	4.0	73	3.9	76	4.0	75	3.0	68	2.7	58	2.2	45	3.1	34	2.9
Cleveland, Oh.	27	2.6	28	2.2	36	3.1	48	3.5	58	3.5	68	3.3	71	3.5	70	3.0	64	2.8	54	2.6	42	2.8	30	2.4
Columbus, Oh.	28	2.9	30	2.3	39	3.4	51	3.7	61	4.1	70	4.1	74	4.2	72	2.9	65	2.4	54	1.9	42	2.7	31	2.4
Dallas-Ft. Worth, Tex.	45	1.8	49	2.4	55	2.5	65	4.3	73	4.5	81	3.1	85	1.8	85	2.3	78	3.2	68	2.7	56	2.0	48	1.8
Denver, Col.	30	0.6	33	0.7	37	1.2	48	1.9	57	2.6	66	1.9	73	1.8	72	1.3	63	1.1	52	1.1	39	0.8	33	0.4
Des Moines, Ia.	19	1.1	24	1.1	34	2.3	50	2.9	61	4.2	71	4.9	75	3.3	73	3.3	64	3.1	54	2.1	38	1.4	25	1.1
Detroit, Mich.	26	1.9	27	1.8	35	2.3	48	3.1	58	3.4	69	3.0	73	3.0	72	3.0	65	2.3	54	2.5	41	2.3	30	2.2
Dodge City, Kan.	31	0.5	35	0.6	41	1.1	54	1.7	64	3.1	74	3.3	79	3.1	78	2.6	69	1.7	58	1.7	43	0.6	33	0.5
Duluth, Minn.	9	1.2	12	0.9	24	1.8	39	2.6	49	3.4	59	4.4	66	3.7	64	3.8	54	3.1	45	2.3	28	1.7	14	1.4
Eureka, Cal.*	47	7.4	48	5.2	48	4.8	50	3.0	53	2.1	55	0.7	56	0.1	57	0.3	57	0.7	54	3.2	52	6.8	49	6.0
Fairbanks, Alas.	-12	0.6	-3	0.5	10	0.5	29	0.3	47	0.7	59	1.4	61	1.9	55	2.2	44	1.1	25	0.7	3	0.7	-10	0.7
Fresno, Cal.	45	1.8	50	1.7	54	1.6	60	1.2	67	0.3	74	0.1	81	L	78	L	74	0.1	64	0.4	54	1.2	46	1.7
Galveston, Tex.*	54	3.0	56	2.7	61	2.6	69	2.6	76	3.2	81	4.1	83	4.4	83	4.4	80	5.6	73	2.8	64	3.2	57	3.7
Grand Junction, Col.	27	0.6	34	0.6	41	0.8	52	0.8	62	0.6	71	0.6	79	0.5	75	1.1	67	0.8	55	0.9	40	0.6	30	0.6
Gr. Rapids, Mich.	23	1.9	25	1.5	33	2.5	47	3.4	57	3.2	67	3.4	72	3.1	70	2.5	62	3.3	52	2.6	39	2.8	27	2.2
Hartford, Conn.	25	3.3	27	3.2	36	3.8	48	3.8	58	3.5	68	3.5	73	3.4	70	3.9	63	3.6	53	3.0	41	4.3	28	4.1
Helena, Mon.	18	0.6	25	0.4	31	0.7	43	0.9	52	1.8	59	2.4	68	1.0	66	1.0	56	1.0	45	0.6	32	0.6	23	0.6
Honolulu, Ha.	72	4.4	72	2.5	73	3.2	75	1.4	77	1.0	79	0.3	80	0.6	81	0.8	80	0.7	79	1.5	77	3.0	74	3.7
Houston, Tex.	52	3.6	55	3.5	61	2.7	69	3.5	76	5.1	81	4.5	83	4.1	83	4.4	79	4.7	71	4.1	61	4.0	55	4.0
Huron, S.D.	13	0.4	18	0.8	29	1.1	46	2.0	57	2.8	67	3.8	74	2.2	72	2.0	61	1.8	50	1.5	32	0.7	19	0.5
Indianapolis, Ind.	28	2.9	31	2.4	40	3.8	52	3.9	62	4.1	72	4.2	75	3.7	73	2.8	66	2.9	56	2.5	42	3.1	31	2.7
Jackson, Miss.	47	4.5	50	4.6	56	5.6	66	4.7	73	4.4	79	3.4	82	4.3	81	3.6	76	3.0	66	2.2	55	3.9	49	5.0
Jacksonville, Fla.	55	2.8	56	3.6	61	3.6	68	3.1	74	3.2	79	6.3	81	7.4	81	7.9	78	7.8	71	4.5	61	1.8	55	2.6
Juneau, Alas.	24	3.9	28	3.4	32	3.6	39	3.0	47	3.3	53	2.9	56	4.7	54	5.0	49	6.9	42	7.9	33	5.5	27	4.5
Kansas City, Mo.	27	1.3	32	1.3	41	2.6	54	3.5	64	4.3	73	5.6	78	4.4	77	3.8	68	4.2	58	3.2	42	1.5	31	1.5
Knoxville, Tenn.	41	4.7	43	4.7	50	4.9	60	3.6	68	3.3	76	3.6	78	4.7	77	3.2	72	2.8	61	2.7	49	3.6	42	4.5
Lander, Wyo.	20	0.5	26	0.7	31	1.2	43	2.4	53	2.6	61	1.9	71	0.6	69	0.4	58	1.1	47	1.2	32	0.9	23	0.5
Little Rock, Ark.	40	4.2	43	4.4	50	4.9	62	5.3	70	5.3	78	3.5	81	3.4	81	3.0	73	3.6	62	3.0	50	3.9	42	4.1
Los Angeles, Cal.*	57	3.0	58	2.8	59	2.2	62	1.3	65	0.1	68	L	73	L	74	L	73	0.2	68	0.3	63	2.0	58	2.2
Louisville, Ky.	33	3.5	36	3.5	44	5.1	56	4.1	65	4.2	73	4.1	77	3.8	76	3.0	69	2.9	58	2.4	45	3.3	36	3.3
Marquette, Mich.*	18	1.5	20	1.5	27	1.9	40	2.6	50	2.9	60	3.4	66	3.1	66	3.0	57	3.5	49	2.4	34	3.0	24	2.0
Memphis, Tenn.	41	4.9	44	4.7	51	5.1	63	5.4	71	4.4	79	3.5	82	3.5	80	3.3	74	3.0	63	2.6	51	3.9	43	4.7
Miami, Fla.	67	2.2	68	2.0	71	2.1	75	3.6	78	6.1	81	9.0	82	6.9	83	6.7	82	8.7	78	8.2	72	2.7	68	1.6
Milwaukee, Wis.	19	1.6	23	1.1	31	2.2	45	2.8	54	2.9	65	3.6	70	3.4	69	2.7	61	3.0	51	2.0	37	2.0	24	1.8
Minneapolis, Minn.	12	0.7	17	0.8	28	1.7	45	2.0	57	3.4	67	3.9	72	3.7	70	3.1	60	2.7	50	1.8	32	1.2	19	0.9
Mobile, Ala.	51	4.7	54	4.8	59	7.1	68	5.6	75	4.5	80	6.1	82	8.9	82	6.9	78	6.6	69	2.6	59	3.4	53	5.9
Moline, Ill.	22	1.7	26	1.3	36	2.6	51	3.8	61	3.9	71	4.4	75	4.6	73	3.4	65	3.8	54	2.7	39	1.9	27	1.8
Nashville, Tenn.	38	4.8	41	4.4	49	5.0	60	4.1	69	4.1	77	3.4	80	3.8	79	3.2	72	3.1	61	2.2	48	3.5	40	4.5
Newark, N.J.	31	2.9	33	3.0	41	3.9	52	3.4	62	3.6	71	3.0	76	4.0	75	4.3	68	3.4	58	2.8	46	3.6	35	3.5
New Orleans, La.	53	4.5	56	4.8	61	5.5	69	4.2	75	4.2	80	4.7	82	6.7	82	5.3	78	5.6	70	2.3	60	3.9	55	5.1
New York, N.Y.*	32	2.7	33	2.9	41	3.7	52	3.3	62	3.5	72	3.0	77	3.7	75	4.0	68	3.3	59	2.9	47	3.8	36	3.5
Nome, Alas.	6	0.9	5	0.8	7	0.8	19	0.7	35	0.7	46	1.0	50	2.4	49	3.6	42	2.4	29	1.4	16	1.0	4	0.7
Norfolk, Va.	41	3.4	41	3.3	48	3.4	58	2.7	67	3.3	75	3.6	78	5.7	77	5.9	72	4.2	62	3.1	52	2.9	42	3.1
Okla. City, Okla.	37	1.1	41	1.3	48	2.1	60	3.5	68	5.2	77	4.2	82	2.7	81	2.6	73	3.6	62	2.6	49	1.4	40	1.3
Omaha, Neb.	23	0.8	28	1.0	37	1.6	52	3.0	63	4.1	72	4.9	77	3.7	76	4.0	66	3.3	56	1.9	40	1.1	28	0.8
Parkersburg, W.Va.*	33	3.1	35	2.8	43	3.8	55	3.5	64	3.6	72	4.0	75	4.3	74	3.3	67	2.8	57	2.1	45	2.5	35	2.8
Philadelphia, Pa.	32	2.8	34	2.6	42	3.7	53	3.3	63	3.4	72	3.7	77	4.1	75	4.1	68	3.0	57	2.5	46	3.4	35	3.3
Phoenix, Ariz.	51	0.7	55	0.6	60	0.8	68	0.3	76	0.1	85	0.1	91	0.8	89	1.2	84	0.7	72	0.5	60	0.5	53	0.8
Pittsburgh, Pa.	28	2.8	29	2.4	38	3.6	50	3.4	60	3.6	69	3.5	72	3.8	70	3.2	64	2.5	53	2.5	41	2.5	31	2.5
Portland, Me.	22	3.4	23	3.5	32	3.6	43	3.3	53	3.3	62	3.1	68	2.6	66	2.6	59	3.1	49	3.3	39	4.9	26	4.1
Portland, Ore.	38	5.9	43	4.1	46	3.6	51	2.2	57	2.1	62	1.6	67	0.5	67	0.8	62	1.6	54	3.6	45	5.6	41	6.0
Providence, R.I.	28	3.5	29	3.5	37	4.0	47	3.7	57	3.5	66	2.7	72	2.9	70	3.9	63	3.3	54	3.3	43	4.5	32	4.1
Raleigh, N.C.	41	3.2	42	3.3	49	3.4	60	3.1	67	3.3	74	3.7	78	5.1	77	4.9	71	3.8	60	2.8	50	2.8	41	3.1
Rapid City, S.D.	22	0.5	26	0.6	31	1.0	45	2.1	55	2.8	64	3.7	73	2.1	72	1.5	61	1.2	50	0.9	35	0.5	27	0.4
Reno, Nev.	32	1.2	37	0.9	40	0.7	47	0.5	55	0.7	62	0.4	69	0.3	67	0.2	60	0.2	50	0.4	40	0.7	33	1.1
Richmond, Va.	38	2.9	39	3.0	47	3.4	58	2.8	67	3.4	74	3.5	78	5.6	76	5.1	70	3.6	59	2.9	49	3.2	39	3.2
St. Louis, Mo.	31	1.9	35	2.1	43	3.0	57	3.9	66	3.9	75	4.4	79	3.7	77	2.9	70	2.9	59	2.8	45	2.5	35	2.0
Salt Lake City, Ut.	28	1.3	33	1.2	40	1.6	49	2.1	58	1.5	66	1.3	77	0.7	75	0.9	65	0.7	52	1.2	39	1.3	30	1.4
San Antonio, Tex.	51	1.7	55	2.1	61	1.5	70	2.5	76	3.1	82	2.8	85	1.7	85	2.4	79	3.7	71	2.8	60	1.8	53	1.5
San Diego, Cal.	55	1.9	57	1.5	58	1.6	61	0.8	63	0.2	66	0.1	70	L	71	0.1	70	0.1	66	0.3	61	1.3	57	1.7
San Francisco, Cal.	48	4.4	51	3.0	53	2.5	55	1.6	58	0.4	62	0.1	63	L	63	L	64	0.2	61	1.0	55	2.3	50	4.0
San Juan, P.R.	75	3.7	75	2.5	76	2.0	78	3.4	79	6.5	81	5.6	81	6.4	81	7.0	81	6.1	81	5.6	79	5.5	77	4.7
Sault Ste. Marie, Mich.*	14	1.9	15	1.5	24	1.7	38	2.2	49	3.0	59	3.3	64	2.6	63	3.1	55	3.9	46	2.9	33	3.3	20	2.4
Savannah, Ga.	50	2.9	52	2.9	58	4.4	66	2.9	73	4.2	79	5.9	81	7.9	81	6.5	76	5.6	67	2.8	57	1.9	50	3.3
Seattle, Wash.	38	5.8	42	4.2	44	3.6	49	2.5	55	1.7	60	1.5	65	0.7	64	1.1	60	2.0	52	3.9	45	5.9	41	5.9
Spokane, Wash.	25	2.5	32	1.7	38	1.5	46	1.1	55	1.5	62	1.4	70	0.4	68	0.6	60	0.8	48	1.4	36	2.2	29	2.4
Springfield, Mo.	33	1.7	37	2.2	44	3.0	57	4.3	65	4.9	74	4.7	78	3.6	77	2.9	69	4.1	59	3.4	46	2.3	36	2.5
Syracuse, N.Y.	24	2.7	25	2.8	33	3.0	47	3.1	57	3.0	67	3.1	72	3.1	70	3.5	63	2.7	53	3.1	41	3.3	28	3.1
Tampa, Fla.	60	2.3	62	2.9	66	3.9	72	2.1	77	2.4	81	6.5	82	8.4	82	8.0	81	6.4	75	2.5	67	1.8	62	2.2
Trenton, N.J.*	32	2.8	33	2.7	41	3.8	52	3.2	62	3.4	71	3.2	76	4.7	74	4.2	67	3.2	57	2.5	46	3.3	35	3.3
Washington, D.C.	36	2.6	37	2.5	45	3.3	56	2.9	66	3.7	75	3.5	79	4.1	77	4.7	71	3.1	60	2.7	48	2.9	37	3.0
Wilmington, Del.	32	2.9	34	2.8	42	3.7	52	3.2	62	3.4	71	3.2	76	4.3	74	4.0	68	3.4	57	2.6	46	3.5	35	3.3

Annual Climatological Data

Source: National Oceanic and Atmospheric Administration, U.S. Commerce Department

1979 Station	Elev. ft	Temperature °F Highest	Date	Lowest	Date	Precipitation Total (in.)	Greatest in 24 hrs	Date	Sleet or snow Total (in.)	Greatest in 24 hrs	Date	Fastest Wind MPH	Date	No. of days Clear	Cloudy	Prec. .01 in. or more	Snow, sleet 1 in. or more
Albany, N.Y.	275	95	7/14	-19	2/18	37.14	2.18	7/26	46.0	6.5	1/7-8	44	9/14	68	195	129	13
Albuquerque, N.M.	5311	105	7/14	8	1/30	10.35	0.85	5/20	14.5	3.0	2/16	47	8/19	172	92	59	5
Anchorage, Alas.	114	79	7/3	-16	12/31	21.15	0.96	7/24-25	77.6	13.3	3/17-18	52	2/14	76	231	139	26
Asheville, N.C.	2140	92	8/9	4	1/3	57.44	3.31	11/1-2	23.0	8.6	2/18	37	12/17	103	165	128	6
Atlanta, Ga.	1010	97	8/7	10	1/3	54.71	5.58	4/12-13	4.6	4.2	2/17-18	35	7/18	95	180	115	1
Baltimore, Md.	148	94	8/10	-3	2/10	58.98	4.41	9/5-6	39.2	20.0	2/18-19	44	1/18	104	168	127	7
Barrow, Alas.	31	70	8/24	-42	2/6	3.01	0.30	7/4	15.3	1.1	10/6	37	4/22	71	167	83	2
Birmingham, Ala.	620	99	7/5	12	1/9	69.70	—		T		—					113	0
Bismarck, N.D.	1647	95	7/8	-30	2/11	11.81	0.84	8/20-21	59.0	8.9	2/22	47	5/19	87	174	89	18
Boise, Ida.	2838	102	7/17	-13	1/30	12.07	1.61	8/13	25.2	4.0	11/25-26	40	10/19	112	164	98	8
Boston, Mass.	15	95	6/16	-3	2/11	44.17	2.72	1/20-21	19.7	4.2	1/17	45	1/25	103	163	131	7
Buffalo, N.Y.	705	90	7/20	-18	2/18	43.74	4.94	9/13-14	116.5	20.1	12/30-31	49	12/7	58	227	177	31
Burlington, Vt.	332	93	7/25	-30	2/12	31.56	1.64	9/6-7	62.4	10.4	1/7-8	40	12/15	58	213	154	18
Charleston, S.C.	40	98	8/7	20	2/10	57.98	6.40	9/4-5	1.8	1.7	2/17-18	38	9/4	110	157	117	1
Charleston, W. Va.	1016	91	8/9	1	2/11	48.87	1.97	9/20-21	54.4	7.2	2/18-19	35	1/14	67	204	183	17
Chicago, Ill.	607	92	8/7	-19	1/15	38.04	2.84	8/17-18	56.9	16.5	1/13	58	4/5	70	191	127	15
Cincinnati, Oh.	869	92	8/8	-9	2/5	52.76	4.54	9/13-14	31.9	5.4	1/27-28	35	6/20	83	197	141	11
Cleveland, Oh.	777	91	8/7	-9	2/11	39.84	2.49	5/24-25	38.6	6.9	2/26	40	4/6	59	237	159	11
Columbus, Oh.	812	90	8/7	-7	2/17	49.17	4.86	9/13-14	35.1	6.6	2/12	48	3/13	64	214	146	10
Concord, N.H.	342	94	7/14	-16	2/13	41.27	2.38	5/24-25	55.5	10.6	1/13-14	41	12/8	82	184	135	15
Dallas, Tex.	551	103	6/30	13	1/2	32.42	1.99	5/3	2.5	1.3	1/29	53	1/19	133	142	85	1
Denver, Col.	5283	99	8/6	-11	1/1	20.36	1.68	8/9-10	90.9	14.0	11/19-20	40	12/5	132	130	94	27
Des Moines, Ia.	938	97	8/7	-19	2/9	31.84	2.25	6/27	38.0	7.7	1/12-13	56	8/9	106	163	102	12
Detroit, Mich.	633	92	8/7	-11	1/15	33.04	3.08	7/11	28.4	4.8	1/13-14	56	4/5	80	192	135	11
Dodge City, Kan.	2582	101	7/8	-12	1/14	23.62	2.82	7/22-23	23.8	3.8	1/12-13	55	1/22	150	112	88	9
Duluth, Minn.	1428	88	7/11	-32	1/11	30.92	3.25	5/9-10	66.6	7.7	2/22-23	41	6/3	58	206	147	22
Fairbanks, Alas.	436	82	7/24	-51	2/7	10.33	0.76	7/5-6	42.9	6.2	1/30-31	30	12/4	81	203	119	16
Fresno, Cal.	328	111	8/1	26	12/28	9.95	0.92	1/14-15	T	T	3/13	29	5/5	182	105	52	0
Galveston, Tex.	7	92	8/6	23	1/2	59.35	13.01	7/25-26	0.0	0.0	—	49	1/20	—	—	114	0
Grand Rapids, Mich.	784	90	8/7	-21	1/11	34.62	1.80	12/24-25	71.8	10.9	1/13-14	49	4/5	68	226	141	22
Helena, Mont.	3828	98	8/5	-25	1/30	10.39	1.78	6/18-19	47.9	6.0	4/23	45	4/6	91	167	84	11
Honolulu, Ha.	7	93	10/11	57	1/3	16.93	2.73	2/3-4	0.0	0.0	—	34	12/31	76	99	89	0
Houston, Tex.	96	97	6/30	17	1/2	58.97	7.09	9/19-20	T	T	11/23	37	5/22	115	152	111	0
Huron, S.D.	1281	106	6/14	-25	1/5	15.95	1.51	4/11	42.4	6.3	1/26	42	3/13	102	160	92	16
Indianapolis, Ind.	792	92	8/8	-16	2/5	44.60	4.35	7/12-13	38.7	8.3	2/25-26	42	3/30	86	196	151	10
Jackson, Miss.	291	98	7/5	13	1/9	92.75	8.42	4/11-12	T	T	2/17	40	7/6	129	150	112	0
Jacksonville, Fla.	26	96	7/4	19	1/3	61.78	3.81	9/9-10	0.0	0.0	—	34	8/5	93	149	128	0
Juneau, Alas.	12	80	8/23	-10	2/13	49.29	2.59	11/19-20	101.0	9.4	12/17					195	29
Kansas City, Mo.	973	94	8/7	-12	2/5	31.75	1.79	6/7-8	21.5	5.6	1/12-13	36	10/20	114	151	103	8
Lander, Wyo.	5563	101	8/5	-31	1/31	11.51	1.75	5/1-2	123.5	20.2	4/10-11	61	12/4	112	134	64	24
Little Rock, Ark.	257	98	7/4	10	2/9	64.49	—		11.2		—					103	5
Los Angeles, Cal.	97	103	6/10	34	1/29	13.52	1.70	3/26-27	0.0	0.0	—	45	10/28	143	99	39	0
Louisville, Ky.	477	95	8/8	0	1/15	59.80	5.46	7/25-26	20.4	4.7	2/18	38	2/22	87	186	135	5
Marquette, Mich.	1415	89	7/12	-34	2/17	40.92	—		180.7		—		42	4/6			184	47
Memphis, Tenn.	258	97	7/4	9	2/9	70.89	3.64	4/1-2	10.4	3.3	2/6-7	46	4/11	123	157	119	5
Miami, Fla.	7	94	6/4	40	1/3	60.11	16.21	4/24-25	0.0	0.0	—	37	9/25	72	135	123	0
Milford, Ut.	5028	101	8/4	-24	1/30	7.55	0.77	3/27-28	46.1	5.1	1/5-6	45	5/5	163	105	64	17
Milwaukee, Wis.	672	94	8/7	-16	1/15	30.87	2.03	4/25-26	52.4	12.6	1/12-13	52	12/24	80	184	131	11
Minneapolis, Minn.	834	96	8/6	-28	1/11	31.07	2.29	8/20-21	46.2	5.0	2/20-21	38	4/5	82	183	116	15
Mobile, Ala.	211	97	7/5	18	2/10	79.25	8.55	9/12-13	T	T	1/29	63	9/12	101	157	116	0
Moline, Ill.	582	94	8/7	-27	1/2	34.50	2.49	8/19-20	37.9	15.1	1/12-13	49	4/11	90	164	122	12
Nashville, Tenn.	590	95	8/20	-3	2/10	70.12	6.68	9/13-14	27.5	8.3	2/6-7	32	9/13	100	178	133	7
New Orleans, La	4	97	7/5	23	1/3	60.24	5.25	2/5-6	T	T	1/29	44	7/11	103	163	111	0
New York, N.Y.	132	95	8/10	0	2/18	52.13	3.91	1/20-21	30.2	12.7	2/19	52	9/6	—	—	129	7
Nome, Alas.	13	73	6/4	-31	12/29	22.06	1.05	7/22-23	65.0	8.7	11/14-15	46	1/14	105	202	152	20
Norfolk, Va.	24	98	8/10	14	2/18	64.96	4.36	9/5-6	13.7	6.7	2/18	46	8/8	93	160	111	3
Oklahoma City, Okla.	1285	97	8/10	-3	2/9	41.12	4.76	7/5-6	10.1	6.1	2/6	45	1/23	148	126	86	2
Omaha, Neb.	1309	98	6/14	-17	2/16	28.30	2.57	10/30	32.5	6.1	3/3	37	12/7	119	139	99	12
Philadelphia, Pa.	5	94	7/13	-2	2/11	52.79	2.70	1/20-21	44.7	14.3	2/18-19	50	11/26	87	187	143	10
Phoenix, Ariz.	1110	117	6/26	29	1/30	6.80	1.08	1/16-17	0.0	0.0	—	53	8/11	201	79	36	0
Pittsburgh, Pa.	1137	88	8/8	-12	2/11	40.56	2.09	8/10-11	37.5	6.1	2/18-19	41	4/6	62	209	166	13
Portland, Me.	43	92	5/9	-13	2/18	61.15	3.59	4/27	73.3	27.1	1/17-18	35	4/6	89	186	145	14
Portland, Ore.	21	104	7/16	14	1/1	35.75	1.67	12/1-2	3.0	1.1	2/3	44	4/12	73	220	148	1
Providence, R.I.	51	92	7/13	-7	2/14	58.19	6.71	8/3-4	15.1	4.5	2/7-8	38	12/8	95	175	130	6
Raleigh, N.C.	434	98	8/8	8	2/10	45.37	2.57	9/4-5	17.6	10.4	2/18-19	29	1/21	113	146	107	4
Rapid City, S.D.	3162	103	6/13	-23	1/14	13.99	1.24	7/3-4	19.8	3.6	1/11-12	57	8/30	108	149	91	7
Reno, Nev.	4404	102	7/18	1	1/1	6.03	1.02	12/23-24	14.3	2.6	1/15	49	10/25	139	115	53	6
Richmond, Va.	164	97	8/10	-8	2/10	57.12	3.25	9/21-22	20.2	10.9	2/18-19	43	8/8	102	173	119	4
Rochester, N.Y.	547	95	7/23	-19	2/18	34.90	3.54	9/13-14	117.9	11.3	2/1	60	4/6	55	225	186	33
St. Louis, Mo.	535	98	7/14	-10	2/9	29.48	4.91	4/10-11	25.5	4.7	1/26-27	40	3/14	96	173	119	9
Salt Lake City, Ut.	4221	104	8/4	-8	1/31	8.70	1.08	10/19-20	50.6	7.3	12/21-22	40	2/14	135	160	80	17
San Antonio, Tex.	788	98	10/3	15	1/2	36.64	3.87	6/1	T	T	11/22	48	7/10	99	151	99	0
San Diego, Cal.	13	101	6/4	40	1/29	11.62	2.64	1/30-31	0.0	0.0	—	28	10/29	140	121	46	0
San Francisco, Cal.	8	100	9/12	31	1/29	24.57	2.86	12/23-24	T	T	1/15	35	8/27	153	123	67	0
Sault Ste. Marie, Mich.	721	90	7/12	-35	2/17	43.35	2.69	8/7	138.7	11.5	4/5-6	47	4/6	72	212	170	40
Savannah, Ga.	46	99	7/4	20	1/3	61.92	6.80	9/4-5	T	T	2/18	58	9/4	100	177	127	0
Seattle, Wash.	400	98	7/16	20	1/1	32.26	2.61	12/14-15	2.1	1.2	12/15	38	2/13	63	205	129	1
Sioux City, Ia.	1095	99	6/14	-21	2/1	32.49	4.55	10/29-30	29.8	5.9	3/3-4	54	7/30	106	156	102	11
Spokane, Wash.	2357	102	7/20	-22	1/1	14.35	0.92	10/8-9	44.8	6.1	1/9-10	45	2/6	101	185	104	18
Springfield, Mo.	1268	94	8/8	-17	2/9	48.94	4.01	6/23	25.7	4.4	1/27	45	10/30	123	160	107	10
Syracuse, N.Y.	410	93	7/15	-26	2/18	38.53	2.33	9/6	89.1	9.4	3/11-12	48	4/6	56	222	173	30
Tampa, Fla.	19	94	7/3	28	1/3	66.46	11.84	5/7-8	0.0	0.0	—	39	5/8	104	157	104	0
Trenton, N.J.	56	93	7/13	-1	2/18	53.68	3.16	1/20-21	33.2	8.5	2/18-19	54	9/6	92	190	133	9
Washington, D.C.	10	97	8/10	6	2/18	47.33	3.69	9/5-6	34.9	18.7	2/18-19	49	1/18	88	181	126	5
Williston, N.D.	1899	103	6/13	-30	7/16	11.25	1.17	6/27-28	38.9	7.2	4/12	44	3/12	86	156	74	13
Wilmington, Del.	74	94	8/10	-6	2/18	53.31	2.51	8/2-3	43.6	14.0	2/18-19	35	8/2	87	184	136	11

*To get partly cloudy days deduct the total of clear and cloudy days from 365 (1 yr.). T—trace. (1) Date shown is the starting date of the storm (in some cases it lasted more than one day).

Normal Temperatures, Highs, Lows, Precipitation

Source: National Oceanic and Atmospheric Administration, U.S. Commerce Department

These normals are based on records for the thirty-year period 1941-1970. (See explanation on page 792.) The extreme temperatures (through 1980) are listed for the stations shown and may not agree with the states records shown on page 796.

Airport stations; * designates city office stations. The minus (−) sign indicates temperatures below zero. Fahrenheit thermometer registration.

State	Station	Normal temperature				Extreme temperature		Normal annual precipitation (inches)
		January		July				
		Max.	Min.	Max.	Min.	Highest	Lowest	
Alabama	Mobile	61	41	91	73	104	7	66.98
Alabama	Montgomery	58	37	91	72	105	5	49.86
Alaska	Juneau	29	18	64	48	90	−22	54.67
Arizona	Phoenix	65	38	105	78	118	17	7.05
Arkansas	Little Rock	50	29	93	70	108	−5	48.52
California	Los Angeles*	67	47	83	64	110	28	14.05
California	San Francisco	55	41	71	54	106	20	19.53
Colorado	Denver	44	16	87	59	104	−30	15.51
Connecticut	Hartford	33	16	84	61	102	−26	43.37
Delaware	Wilmington	40	24	86	66	102	−6	40.25
Dist. of Col.	Washington	44	28	88	69	103	1	38.89
Florida	Jacksonville	65	45	90	72	105	12	54.47
Florida	Key West	76	66	89	80	95	46	39.99
Florida	Miami	76	59	89	76	98	31	59.80
Georgia	Atlanta	51	33	87	69	103	−3	48.34
Hawaii	Honolulu	79	65	87	73	93	53	22.90
Idaho	Boise	37	21	91	59	111	−23	11.50
Illinois	Chicago-Midway	32	17	84	65	104	−19	34.44
Indiana	Indianapolis	36	20	85	65	104	−20	38.74
Iowa	Des Moines	28	11	85	65	105	−24	30.85
Iowa	Dubuque	26	9	82	61	99	−28	40.27
Kansas	Wichita	41	21	92	70	113	−12	30.58
Kentucky	Louisville	42	25	87	66	105	−20	43.11
Louisiana	New Orleans	62	44	90	73	100	14	56.77
Maine	Portland	31	12	79	57	103	−39	40.80
Maryland	Baltimore	42	25	87	67	102	−7	40.46
Massachusetts	Boston	36	23	81	65	102	−12	42.52
Michigan	Detroit-City	32	19	83	63	105	−16	30.96
Michigan	Sault Ste. Marie*	22	6	75	53	98	−35	31.70
Minnesota	Minn.-St. Paul	21	3	82	61	104	−34	25.94
Mississippi	Jackson	58	36	93	71	103	6	49.19
Missouri	St. Louis	40	23	88	69	106	−14	35.89
Montana	Helena	28	8	84	52	105	−42	11.38
Nebraska	Omaha	33	12	89	66	114	−22	30.18
Nevada	Winnemucca	41	16	91	51	106	−34	8.47
New Hampshire	Concord	31	10	83	57	102	−37	36.17
New Jersey	Atlantic City	41	24	85	65	106	−11	45.46
New Mexico	Albuquerque	47	24	92	65	105	−17	7.77
New Mexico	Roswell	55	21	95	64	107	−9	10.61
New York	Albany	30	13	84	60	100	−28	33.36
New York	New York-La Guardia	38	26	84	69	107	−2	41.61
No. Carolina	Charlotte	52	32	88	69	104	−3	42.72
No. Carolina	Raleigh	51	30	88	67	105	−1	42.54
No. Dakota	Bismarck	19	−3	84	57	109	−44	16.16
Ohio	Cincinnati-Abbe	40	24	87	66	109	−17	40.03
Ohio	Cleveland	33	20	82	61	103	−19	34.99
Oklahoma	Oklahoma City	48	26	93	70	108	−4	31.37
Oregon	Portland	44	33	79	55	107	−3	37.61
Pennsylvania	Harrisburg	38	23	87	65	107	−8	36.47
Pennsylvania	Philadelphia	40	24	87	67	104	−5	39.93
Rhode Island	Block Island	37	25	76	63	92	−4	40.51
So. Carolina	Charleston	60	37	89	71	103	8	52.12
So. Dakota	Huron	23	2	87	61	112	−39	19.44
So. Dakota	Rapid City	34	10	86	59	110	−27	17.12
Tennessee	Nashville	48	29	90	69	107	−15	46.00
Texas	Amarillo	49	23	91	66	108	−14	20.28
Texas	Galveston*	59	48	87	79	101	8	42.20
Texas	Houston	63	42	94	73	102	17	48.19
Utah	Salt Lake City	37	19	93	61	107	−30	15.17
Vermont	Burlington	26	8	81	59	101	−30	32.54
Virginia	Norfolk	49	32	87	70	103	5	44.68
Washington	Seattle-Tacoma	43	33	75	54	99	0	38.79
Washington	Spokane	31	20	84	55	108	−25	17.42
West Virginia	Parkersburg*	41	24	86	65	106	−27	38.44
Wisconsin	Madison	25	8	81	59	104	−37	30.25
Wisconsin	Milwaukee	27	11	80	59	101	−24	29.07
Wyoming	Cheyenne	38	15	84	55	100	−34	14.65
Puerto Rico	San Juan	82	69	87	75	96	60	59.15

Mean Annual Snowfall (inches) based on record through 1979: Boston, Mass. 43; Sault Ste. Marie, Mich., 112; Albany, N.Y. 65.8; Rochester, N.Y. 89.1; Burlington, Vt., 79.1; Cheyenne, Wyo., 52.6; Juneau, Alas. 106.1.

Wettest Spot: Mount Waialeale, Ha., on the island of Kauai, is the rainiest place in the world, according to the National Geographic Society, with an average annual rainfall of 460 inches.

Highest Temperature: A temperature of 136° F. observed at Azizia, Tripolitania in Northern Africa on Sept. 13, 1922, is generally accepted as the world's highest temperature recorded under standard conditions.

The record high in the United States was 134° in Death Valley, Cal., July 10, 1913.

Lowest Temperature: A record low temperature of −126.9° F. (−88.3° C.) was recorded at the Soviet Antarctic station Vostok on Aug. 24, 1960.

The record low in the United States was −80° at Prospect Creek, Alas., Jan. 23, 1971.

The lowest official temperature on the North American continent was recorded at 81 degrees below zero in February, 1947, at a lonely airport in the Yukon called Snag.

These are the meteorological champions—the official temperature extremes—but there are plenty of other claimants to thermometer fame. However, sun readings are unofficial records, since meteorological data to qualify officially must be taken on instruments in a sheltered and ventilated location.

Record Temperatures by States Through 1980

Source: National Oceanic and Atmospheric Administration, U.S. Commerce Department

State	Lowest °F	Highest	Latest date	Station	Approximate elevation in feet
Alabama	−27		Jan. 30, 1966	New Market	725
		112	Sept. 5, 1925	Centerville	345
Alaska	−79.8		Jan. 23, 1971	Prospect Creek Camp	1,100
		100	June 27, 1915	Fort Yukon	*419
Arizona	−40		Jan. 7, 1971	Hawley Lake	8,180
		127	July 7, 1905	Parker	345
Arkansas	−29		Feb. 13, 1905	Pond	1,250
		120	Aug. 10, 1936	Ozark	396
California	−45		Jan. 20, 1937	Boca	5,532
		134	July 10, 1913	Greenland Ranch	−178
Colorado	−60		Feb. 1, 1951	Taylor Park	9,206
		118	July 11, 1888	Bennett	5,484
Connecticut	−32		Feb. 16, 1943	Falls Village	585
		105	July 22, 1926	Waterbury	409
Delaware	−17		Jan. 17, 1893	Millsboro	20
		110	July 21, 1930	Millsboro	20
Dist. of Col.	−15		Feb. 11, 1899	Washington	112
		106	July 20, 1930	Washington	112
Florida	−2		Feb. 13, 1899	Tallahassee	193
		109	June 29, 1931	Monticello	207
Georgia	−17		Jan. 27, 1940	CCC Camp F-16	1,000
		113	May 27, 1978	Greenville	860
Hawaii	14		Jan. 2, 1961	Haleakala, Maui	9,750
		100	Apr. 27, 1931	Pahala	850
Idaho	−60		Jan. 16, 1943	Island Park Dam	6,285
		118	July 28, 1934	Orofino	1,027
Illinois	−35		Jan. 22, 1930	Mount Carroll	817
		117	July 14, 1954	E. St. Louis	410
Indiana	−35		Feb. 2, 1951	Greensburg	954
		116	July 14, 1936	Collegeville	672
Iowa	−47		Jan. 12, 1912	Washta	1,157
		118	July 20, 1934	Keokuk	614
Kansas	−40		Feb. 13, 1905	Lebanon	1,812
		121	July 24, 1936	Alton (near)	1,651
Kentucky	−34		Jan. 28, 1963	Cynthiana	719
		114	July 28, 1930	Greensburg	581
Louisiana	−16		Feb. 13, 1899	Minden	194
		114	Aug. 10, 1936	Plain Dealing	268
Maine	−48		Jan. 19, 1925	Van Buren	510
		105	July 10, 1911	North Bridgton	450
Maryland	−40		Jan. 13, 1912	Oakland	2,461
		109	July 10, 1936	Cumberland and Frederick	623-325
Massachusetts	−34		Jan. 18, 1957	Birch Hill Dam	840
		107	Aug. 2, 1975	Chester and New Bedford	120-640
Michigan	−51		Feb. 9, 1934	Vanderbilt	785
		112	July 13, 1936	Mio	963
Minnesota	−59		Feb. 16, 1903	Pokegama Dam	1,280
		114	July 6, 1936	Moorhead	904
Mississippi	−19		Jan. 30, 1966	Corinth	420
		115	July 29, 1930	Holly Springs	600
Missouri	−40		Feb. 13, 1905	Warsaw	700
		118	July 14, 1954	Warsaw and Union	687-560
Montana	−70		Jan. 20, 1954	Rogers Pass	5,470
		117	July 5, 1937	Medicine Lake	1,950
Nebraska	−47		Feb. 12, 1899	Camp Clarke	3,700
		118	July 24, 1936	Minden	2,169
Nevada	−50		Jan. 8, 1937	San Jacinto	5,200
		122	June 23, 1954	Overton	1,240
New Hampshire	−47		Jan. 1934	Mt. Washington	6,262
		106	July 4, 1911	Nashua	125
New Jersey	−34		Jan. 5, 1904	River Vale	70
		110	July 10, 1936	Runyon	18
New Mexico	−50		Feb. 1, 1951	Gavilan	7,350
		116	July 14, 1934	Orogrande	4,171
New York	−52		Feb. 9, 1934	Stillwater Reservoir	1,670
		108	July 22, 1926	Troy	35
North Carolina	−29		Jan. 30, 1966	Mt. Mitchell	6,525
		109	Sept. 7, 1954	Weldon	81
North Dakota	−60		Feb. 15, 1936	Parshall	1,929
		121	July 6, 1936	Steele	1,857
Ohio	−39		Feb. 10, 1899	Milligan	800
		113	July 21, 1934	Gallipolis (near)	673
Oklahoma	−27		Jan. 18, 1930	Watts	958
		120	July 26, 1943	Tishmoningo	670
Oregon	−54		Feb. 10, 1933	Seneca	4,700
		119	Aug. 10, 1938	Pendleton	1,074
Pennsylvania	−42		Jan. 5, 1904	Smethport	1,469
		111	July 10, 1936	Phoenixville	100
Rhode Island	−23		Jan. 11, 1942	Kingston	100
		104	Aug. 2, 1975	Providence	51
South Carolina	−20		Jan. 18, 1977	Caesar's Head	3,100
		111	June 28, 1954	Camden	170
South Dakota	−58		Feb. 17, 1936	McIntosh	2,277
		120	July 5, 1936	Gannvalley	1,750

State	Lowest °F	Highest	Latest date	Station	Approximate elevation in feet
Tennessee	−32		Dec. 30, 1917	Mountain City	2,471
		113	Aug. 9, 1930	Perryville	377
Texas	−23		Feb. 8, 1933	Seminole	3,275
		120	Aug. 12, 1936	Seymour.	1,291
Utah.	−50		Jan. 5, 1913	Strawberry Tunnel	7,650
		116	June 28, 1892	Saint George	2,880
Vermont	−50		Dec. 30, 1933	Bloomfield.	915
		105	July 4, 1911	Vernon	310
Virginia	−29		Feb. 10, 1899	Monterey	3,008
		110	July 15, 1954	Balcony Falls	725
Washington	−48		Dec. 30, 1968	Mazama.	2,120
	48		Dec. 30, 1968	Winthrop.	1,755
		118	Aug. 5, 1961	Ice Harbor Dam	475
West Virginia.	−37		Dec. 30, 1917	Lewisburg	2,200
		112	July 10, 1936	Martinsburg	435
Wisconsin	−54		Jan. 24, 1922	Danbury	908
		114	July 13, 1936	Wisconsin Dells.	900
Wyoming	−63		Feb. 9, 1933	Moran.	6,770
		114	July 12, 1900	Basin.	3,500

Canadian Normal Temperatures, Highs, Lows, Precipitation

Source: Atmospheric Environment Service, Environment Canada

These normals are based on varying periods of record over the thirty-year period 1941 to 1970 inclusive. Extreme temperatures are based on varying periods of record for each station through 1980. Airport station; * designates city office stations. The minus (−) sign indicates temperatures below zero. Celsius thermometer registration.

Province	Station	Normal January Max.	Normal January Min.	Normal July Max.	Normal July Min.	Extreme Highest	Extreme Lowest	Precipitation normal annual (millimeters)
Alberta	Calgary	−5	−17	24	10	36	−45	437
Alberta	Edmonton (Industrial Airport)	−10	−19	23	12	34	−48	446
British Columbia	Prince George	−7	−16	22	8	34	−50	621
British Columbia	Victoria	6	2	20	11	35	−16	657
British Columbia	Vancouver.	5	0	22	13	33	−18	1068
Manitoba	Churchill	−24	−31	17	7	33	−45	397
Manitoba	Winnipeg	−13	−23	26	14	41	−45	535
Newfoundland	Gander	−2	−10	22	11	36	−27	1078
Newfoundland	St. John's	−1	−7	20	10	31	−23	1511
New Brunswick	Fredericton	−4	−14	26	13	37	−37	1060
New Brunswick.	Moncton	−3	−13	25	13	37	−32	1099
New Brunswick.	Saint John.	−2	−13	22	11	34	−37	1400
Nova Scotia	Halifax	−2	−10	23	13	34	−26	1396
Nova Scotia	Sydney	−1	−8	23	13	35	−25	1341
Ontario	Ottawa	−6	−16	26	15	38	−36	851
Ontario	Sudbury	−8	−18	25	13	36	−38	835
Ontario	Toronto	−1	−8	27	17	41	−33	790
Ontario	Windsor	−1	−8	28	17	38	−26	836
Prince Edward Island . . .	Charlottetown	−3	−11	23	14	34	−28	1128
Quebec	Montreal	−5	−14	26	16	36	−38	941
Quebec	Quebec City	−7	−16	25	13	36	−36	1089
Quebec	Val-d'Or	−11	−23	23	11	34	−44	902
Saskatchewan	Prince Albert	−15	−27	25	11	38	−50	389
Saskatchewan	Regina	−12	−23	26	12	43	−50	398
Northwest Territories . . .	Alert*	−28	−36	7	1	20	−49	156
Northwest Territories . . .	Yellowknife	−24	−33	21	11	32	−51	250
Yukon Territory	Dawson*	−25	−32	22	9	35	−58	325
Yukon Territory	Whitehorse*	−15	−23	20	8	34	−52	260

Canadian Low and High Temperature Records Through 1980

Source: Atmospheric Environment Service, Environment Canada

Province	Lowest °C	Highest	Latest date	Station	Approximate elevation in meters
Alberta	−61		Jan. 11, 1911	Fort Vermillion	278
		42	July 12, 1886	Medicine Hat.	721
British Columbia	−59		Jan. 31, 1947	Smith River.	673
		44	July 17, 1941	Chinook Cove	404
		44	July 17, 1941	Lillooet	290
		44	July 17, 1941	Lytton.	183
Manitoba	−53		Jan. 9, 1899	Norway House.	219
		44	July 12, 1936	Emerson	241
Newfoundland	−49		Mar. 7, 1968	Twin Falls	457
		42	Aug. 11, 1914	Northwest River.	61
New Brunswick	−47		Feb. 1, 1955	Sisson Dam	278
		39	Aug. 19, 1935	Rexton.	6
Nova Scotia	−41		Jan. 31, 1920	Upper Stewiacke	23
		38	Aug. 19, 1935	Collegeville.	76
Ontario	−58		Jan. 23, 1935	Iroquois Falls.	244
		42	July 13, 1936	Fort Frances.	354
Prince Edward Island . .	−37		Jan. 26, 1884	Kilmahumaig	6
		37	Aug. 19, 1935	Charlottetown	22
Quebec	−54		Feb. 5, 1923	Doucet	376
		40	Aug. 15, 1928	Bark Lake	365
Saskatchewan	−57		Feb. 1, 1893	Prince Albert	436
		45	July 5, 1937	Midale	582
		45	July 5, 1937	Yellow Grass	570
North West Territories .	−57		Dec. 26, 1917	Fort Smith	202
		39	July 18, 1941	Fort Smith	207
Yukon Territory	−63		Feb. 3, 1947	Snag	586
		35	June 18, 1950	Mayo	495

Canadian Normal Temperature and Precipitation

Source: Atmospheric Environment Service, Environment Canada

Normal refers to the mean daily temperature and total monthly precipitation based on varying periods of record over the thirty-year period 1941 to 1970 inclusive. In most cases no adjustment factor was used.

Airport station; *designates city office stations. T, temperature in Celsius; P, precipitation in millimeters.

Station	Jan. T	Jan. P	Feb. T	Feb. P	Mar. T	Mar. P	Apr. T	Apr. P	May T	May P	June T	June P	July T	July P	Aug. T	Aug. P	Sept. T	Sept. P	Oct. T	Oct. P	Nov. T	Nov. P	Dec. T	Dec. P
Calgary, Alta.	−11	17	−7	20	−4	20	3	30	9	50	13	92	17	68	15	56	11	35	6	19	−3	16	−8	15
Charlottetown, P.E.I.	−7	111	−7	95	−3	85	2	82	9	82	14	83	18	73	18	93	14	86	9	97	3	126	−4	116
Churchill, Man.	−28	14	−27	13	−20	18	−11	24	−2	28	6	40	12	49	12	58	6	52	−1	40	−12	40	−22	20
Dawson, Yukon*	−29	19	−23	16	−14	13	−2	9	8	22	14	37	16	53	13	51	6	28	−3	27	−17	25	−25	26
Edmonton, Alta.	−15	25	−11	20	−5	17	4	23	11	37	15	75	18	83	16	72	11	36	5	19	−4	19	−11	21
Fredericton, N.B.	−9	95	−8	93	2	69	4	74	11	81	16	79	19	68	18	88	13	82	8	88	2	109	−6	114
Frobisher Bay, N.W.T.	−26	24	−25	28	−22	21	−14	22	−3	23	4	38	8	53	7	58	2	43	−5	42	−12	37	−20	26
Halifax, N.S.	−6	137	−7	128	−2	104	3	108	9	99	15	79	18	80	18	108	14	95	9	118	4	163	−3	179
Hamilton, Ont.*	−5	66	−4	60	0	66	7	78	13	72	19	71	22	72	21	77	17	71	11	69	5	67	−2	67
Kitchener, Ont.*	−7	61	−6	56	−1	71	7	71	13	83	18	81	21	89	20	79	16	73	10	71	3	78	−4	74
London, Ont.	−6	76	−6	65	−1	72	7	78	12	75	18	81	21	81	20	73	16	79	10	74	3	83	−4	87
Moncton, N.B.	−8	107	−8	100	−3	93	3	84	10	80	15	91	19	80	18	80	14	73	8	91	2	113	−5	109
Montreal, Que.	−10	76	−9	71	−2	71	6	74	13	67	19	83	21	85	20	87	15	80	9	75	2	87	−7	86
Ottawa, Ont.	−11	60	−10	57	−3	61	6	68	12	70	18	73	21	81	19	82	15	79	9	66	1	79	−8	77
Quebec City, Que.	−12	86	−11	77	−4	69	3	75	11	81	16	102	19	108	18	103	13	106	7	82	0	100	−9	101
Regina, Sask.	−17	18	−14	17	−8	18	3	23	11	41	15	83	19	58	18	50	12	36	5	19	−5	18	−13	16
Saint John, N.B.	−7	145	−8	131	−3	105	3	112	9	102	14	95	17	89	16	99	13	103	8	110	3	154	−5	157
St. John's, Nfld.	−4	145	−4	156	−2	133	1	114	6	99	10	89	15	83	15	113	12	112	7	139	4	161	−1	167
Saskatoon, Sask.	−19	18	−15	18	−9	17	3	21	11	34	15	57	19	53	17	45	11	33	5	19	−6	19	−14	18
Sault Ste. Marie, Ont.	−11	81	−11	55	−5	57	3	56	9	85	15	88	18	72	18	67	13	95	8	79	1	106	−6	94
Toronto, Ont.	−4	63	−4	57	1	66	8	67	13	73	19	63	22	81	21	67	17	61	11	62	5	67	−2	64
Vancouver, B.C.	2	147	4	117	6	94	9	61	12	48	15	45	17	30	17	37	14	61	10	122	6	141	4	165
Victoria, B.C.	4	107	6	76	7	49	9	34	12	21	14	21	16	12	16	20	14	33	11	74	7	95	5	115
Whitehorse, Yukon.	−19	19	−13	14	−8	15	0	11	7	14	12	29	14	33	12	36	8	29	1	20	−9	22	−16	20
Windsor, Ont.	−4	55	−3	52	1	66	8	81	14	83	20	84	22	83	21	82	17	61	12	63	4	62	−2	64
Winnipeg, Man.	−18	24	−16	19	−8	26	3	37	11	57	17	80	20	80	19	74	13	53	7	35	−4	27	−14	23
Yellowknife, N.W.T.	−29	14	−26	12	−19	12	−8	10	4	14	12	17	16	33	14	36	7	28	−1	31	−14	24	−24	19

Canadian Annual Climatological Data

Source: Atmospheric Environment Service, Environment Canada

Station (1979)	Elev. meters	Temperature (Celsius) Highest	Date D/Mo.	Lowest	Date D/Mo.	Precipitation Total (mm)	Greatest in 24 hrs.	Date D/Mo.	Snowfall Total (cm)	Greatest in 24 hrs.	Date D/Mo.	Fastest wind Km/h	Date D/Mo.	No. of days Precip., measurable	Snow, sleet
Calgary, Alta.	1084	34.3	21/7	−33.1	15/12	284.6	26.0	20/6	129.9	9.4	14/12	96	sev.	108	106
Charlottetown, P.E.I.	55	29.8	16/6	−23.9	12/2	1513.5	70.0	17/7	194.5	15.0	14/1	83	sev.	180	102
Churchill, Man.	29	33.8	7/7	−45.4	13/2	340.9	20.2	1/8	175.1	17.0	5/3	80	sev.	156	101
Dawson, Yukon	369	29.5	25/7	−55.8	11/2	350.2	23.5	18/7	125.0	12.0	19/3	52	29/11	99	32
Edmonton, Alta.	671	30.5	19/7	−40.1	15/2	429.5	23.9	14/6	119.0	16.8	9/12	106	13/6	126	103
Fredericton, N.B.	20	34.1	16/6	−26.7	17/1	1520.6	58.0	13/8	188.0	16.4	26/2		6/5	176	60
Frobisher, N.W.T.	34	18.0	12/7	−44.7	17/2	636.7	40.4	1/9	290.2	24.9	10/11	130	12/3	170	116
Halifax, N.S.	145	30.4	16/6	−22.4	18/2	1746.4	75.8	5/8	80.8	7.5	18/1	83	sev.	255	85
Hamilton, Ont.	237	31.0	15/7	−25.5	17/2	918.1	38.8	14/9	143.4	29.2	9/4	119	6/4	206	78
Moncton, N.B.	71	30.9	16/6	−25.3	18/2	1583.7	73.6	17/7	238.5	19.4	26/2	82	19/3	190	93
Montreal, Que.	36	32.3	14/7	−28.5	18/2	922.5	81.9	14/9	151.5	32.8	21/1	117	6/10	171	81
Ottawa, Ont.	114	32.8	14/7	−29.3	11/2	1111.3	63.0	14/9	205.7	30.0	21/1	89	16/6	164	96
Quebec, Que.	73	32.0	25/7	−30.1	17/2	1340.9	78.0	16/7	244.0	31.4	26/1	65	sev.	227	93
Regina, Sask.	577	36.2	13/6	−36.6	13/1	286.1	20.6	21/6	134.8	23.2	12/4	126	17/4	216	132
St. John, N.B.	109	30.2	16/6	−23.8	18/2	1974.6	78.0	8/1	176.0	14.8	26/2	93	14/3	193	54
St. John's, Nfld.	140	29.6	4/8	−18.6	21/2	1491.7	47.6	27/12	243.2	35.5	9/1	120	11/12	221	76
Saskatoon, Sask.	501	34.3	19/7	−39.7	15/2	336.5	28.3	21/6	112.7	13.6	13/2	98	1/8	123	69
Sault Ste. Marie, Ont.	192	31.4	4/7	−38.7	17/2	1097.0	59.1	7/8	300.1	27.0	6/4	89	6/4	222	124
Thunder Bay, Ont.	199	33.8	21/7	−39.0	16/1	670.0	34.4	10/5	222.1	18.0	22/3	82	5/9	219	117
Toronto, Ont.	111	30.4	16/6	−24.7	17/2	873.6	41.8	24/1	177.5	27.0	1/12	108	6/4	200	70
Vancouver, B.C.	2	28.7	17/7	−11.2	1/1	986.1	87.5	17/2	52.4	4.0	26/1	85	9/12	175	15
Victoria, B.C.	69	32.1	16/7	−10.8	1/1	780.7	70.2	17/12	16.7	7.3	2/2	59	14/12	160	8
Waterloo/Wellington, Ont.	314	31.1	14/7	−29.2	18/2	928.4	36.2	23/8	124.4	11.9	4/4	83	sev.	176	57
Whitehorse, Yukon	703	27.5	25/8	−45.2	12/2	256.6	17.4	7/7	96.0	8.2	2/3	74	21/11	212	118
Windsor, Ont.	190	33.9	7/8	−21.6	6/1	888.0	61.2	9/7	83.7	8.4	13/1	100	5/4	145	41
Winnipeg, Man.	239	34.0	13/6	−38.8	16/2	471.5	40.8	1/8	127.8	8.8	13/3	93	1/8	140	76
Yellowknife, N.W.T.	205	30.2	1/8	−46.8	13/2	204.9	14.2	20/8	143.3	11.2	28/5	67	sev.	105	85

sev. - several

Speed of Winds in Canada

Source: Atmospheric Environment Service, Environment Canada

Kilometers-per-hour average in most cases is for the period of record 1955 to 1972. High is based on varying periods of record dependent on the origin of the station through 1980.

Station	Avg.	High	Station	Avg.	High	Station	Avg.	High
Calgary, Alta.	21.4	105	London, Ont.	16.4	101	Sault Ste. Marie, Ont.	15.3	89
Charlottetown, P.E.I.	19.3	103	Moncton, N.B.	18.7	100	Thunder Bay, Ont.	14.2	81
Churchill, Man.	25.2	126	Montreal, Que.	15.8	82	Toronto, Ont.	17.2	90
Dawson, Yukon.	6.7	52	Ottawa, Ont.	15.1	87	Vancouver, B.C.	12.1	89
Edmonton, Alta.	14.9	71	Quebec City, Que.	16.7	109	Victoria, B.C.	17.7	109
Fredericton, N.B.	14.2	81	Regina, Sask.	21.5	97	Whitehorse, Yukon.	15.1	81
Frobisher Bay, N.W.T.	16.6	129	Saint John, N.B.	19.0	97	Windsor, Ont.	17.1	92
Halifax, N.S.	18.3	97	Saint John's, Nfld.	24.3	137	Winnipeg, Man.	19.3	90
Hamilton, Ont.	12.8	66	Saskatoon, Sask.	17.9	105	Yellowknife, N.W.T.	16.1	72

ENVIRONMENT

Estimated Total Pollution Control Expenditures

Source: Council on Environmental Quality (billions of 1979 dollars). Does not include research, conservation, and enhancement programs.

Pollutant/source	1979 O&M[1]	1979 Annual Capital costs[2]	1979 Total annual costs[3]	1988 O&M[1]	1988 Annual Capital costs[2]	1988 Total annual costs[3]	Cumulative 1979-88 O&M[1]	Cumulative 1979-88 Capital costs[2]	Cumulative 1979-88 Total costs[3]
Air pollution									
Public	1.7	.4	2.1	2.8	.7	3.5	22.5	5.3	27.8
Private									
Mobile[3]	3.2	4.9	8.1	3.7	11.0	14.7	32.1	83.7	115.8
Industrial	2.5	2.9	5.	3.9	5.1	9.0	32.5	41.5	74.0
Utilities	6.3	3.5	9.8	8.5	6.5	15.0	71.1	50.1	121.2
Subtotal	**13.7**	**11.7**	**25.4**	**18.9**	**23.3**	**42.2**	**158.2**	**180.6**	**338.8**
Water pollution									
Public	3.7	8.2	11.9	5.4	14.2	19.6	45.4	99.7	145.1
Private									
Industrial	4.4	3.2	7.6	6.4	5.1	11.5	52.4	41.1	93.5
Utilities	.4	.5	.9	.4	1.1	1.5	3.6	7.8	11.4
Subtotal	**8.5**	**11.9**	**20.4**	**12.2**	**20.4**	**32.6**	**101.4**	**148.6**	**250.0**
Solid Waste									
Public	1.7	.3	2.0	2.5	.6	3.1	21.8	5.3	27.1
Private	4.5	.7	5.2	7.5	.6	9.1	61.3	12.5	73.8
Subtotal	**6.2**	**1.0**	**7.2**	**10.0**	**2.2**	**12.2**	**83.1**	**17.8**	**100.9**
Toxic Substances[5]	.1	.2	.3	.5	.6	1.1	3.6	4.6	8.2
Drinking Water	.3	.4	.7	.5	.8	1.3	5.3	5.2	10.5
Noise[5]	<.05	.1	.1	.6	1.1	1.6	2.6	4.3	6.9
Pesticides	.1	<.05	.1	.1	<.05	.1	1.6	.1	1.7
Land Reclamation	.4	1.3	1.7	.4	1.4	1.8	4.5	13.5	18.0
Total	**29.3**	**26.6**	**55.9**	**43.2**	**49.7**	**92.9**	**360.3**	**374.7**	**735.0**

(1) Operating and maintenance costs. (2) Interest and depreciation. (3) O&M plus capital costs. (4) Less than 0.05. (5) Incremental and total costs are assumed to be the same. (NA) Not available.

Investment for Pollution Control by U.S. Industries

Source: Bureau of Economic Analysis, U.S. Commerce Department
(billions of dollars)

	1980 Air	1980 Water	1980 Solid waste	1980 Total	1980 Percent of investment[2]	1981[1] Air	1981[1] Water	1981[1] Solid waste	1981[1] Total	1981[1] Percent of investment[2]
All industries[3]	**5.07**	**3.28**	**0.85**	**9.20**	**3.11**	**5.57**	**3.45**	**0.98**	**10.00**	**3.07**
Manufacturing	**2.88**	**2.09**	**.55**	**5.52**	**4.77**	**3.26**	**2.44**	**64**	**6.34**	**4.88**
Durable goods	1.42	.69	.15	2.27	3.85	1.47	.80	.22	2.48	3.73
Primary metals	.67	.26	.04	.98	12.71	.76	.28	.07	1.11	13.54
Blast furnaces, steel works	.41	.19	.01	.61	18.54	.46	19	.02	.66	20.18
Nonferrous metals	.17	.07	.03	.27	8.68	.23	.08	.05	.36	10.03
Fabricated metals	.02	.03	.01	.07	2.36	.03	.05	.01	.08	2.46
Electrical machinery	.07	.06	.02	.16	1.66	.11	.09	.03	.23	1.91
Machinery, except elec.	.07	.07	.01	.15	1.29	.09	.08	.01	.19	1.36
Transportation equipment	.31	.17	.04	.52	2.86	.19	.20	.06	.44	2.29
Motor vehicles	.25	.12	.02	.39	4.30	.13	.13	.03	.30	3.30
Aircraft	.04	04	.02	.10	1.42	.05	.05	.02	.12	1.57
Stone, clay, and glass	.21	.03	.01	.25	6.54	.21	.04	.02	.26	6.67
Other durables	.07	.06	.01	.14	2.75	.09	.06	.02	.17	2.88
Nondurable goods	1.46	1.40	.40	3.25	5.71	1.80	1.64	.43	3.86	6.09
Food including beverage	.08	.18	.02	.27	3.65	.10	.16	.03	.30	3.79
Textiles	.05	.02	A	.07	4.32	.05	.03	A	.08	4.65
Paper	.16	.16	.07	.39	5.73	.18	.17	.08	.43	6.39
Chemicals	.32	.32	.10	.73	5.79	.36	.34	.11	.81	6.18
Petroleum	.83	.69	.19	1.71	8.26	1.06	.91	.18	2.15	8.54
Rubber	.02	.01	.01	.03	1.73	.03	.02	.01	.06	2.61
Other nondurables	.01	.02	.01	.04	.66	.02	.01	.01	.05	.78
Nonmanufacturing	**2.19**	**1.20**	**.30**	**3.69**	**2.05**	**2.31**	**1.01**	**.34**	**3.66**	**1.87**
Mining	.17	.22	.10	.48	3.55	.20	.21	.08	.49	3.09
Transportation	.05	.06	.01	.11	.91	.05	.06	.01	.13	1.01
Railroad	.01	.03	A	.04	.94	.01	.03	A	.05	1.14
Air Transportation	A	A	0	.01	.25	.01	A	A	.01	.24
Other transportation	.03	.03	.01	.07	1.83	.03	.03	.01	.06	1.38
Public utilities	1.86	.88	.15	2.88	8.13	1.92	.69	.20	2.81	7.34
Electric	1.82	.86	.14	2.82	10.03	1.86	.68	.20	2.74	9.06
Gas and other	.04	.02	A	.07	.96	.05	.02	A	.07	.87
Trade and serv.	.09	.04	.04	.17	.20	.11	.03	.04	.19	.22
Communication, commercial, and other	.03	.01	A	.04	.11	.03	.01	.01	.04	.01

(1) Planned. (2) Pollution control as a percent of total plant and equipment investment. (3) Excludes agricultural business; real estate operators; medical, legal, educational, and cultural services; and nonprofit organizations. (4) Includes trade, service, construction, finance, and insurance. (A) Less than $5 million.

Environmental Quality Index

Source: National Wildlife Federation.
Adapted from the Feb.-Mar., 1981 issue of *National Wildlife Magazine*.

In 1969, the National Wildlife Federation began to record an index of environmental quality which measures progress or decline in 7 environmental areas. The index represents the judgment of environmental protection experts and advocates influenced by very high standards of environmental quality.

Wildlife: In 1979, America's wildlife enjoyed its best year in more than a decade. In 1980, unfortunately, the decade's downward trend resumed—due primarily to habitat loss. According to the Environmental Protection Agency, nearly 2 million acres of U.S. habitat will be lost annually between now and the year 2000. The implications for wildlife are staggering: nearly half of the 200,000 square miles of wetlands that once existed in the lower 48 states have now been lost, and gone are 20 million of the 25 million acres of hardwood bottoms along the lower Mississippi River. Against this backdrop the outlook for curing the land and water wildlife needs to survive is further dimmed by the growing resistance to "bureaucratic regulations" and other environmental constraints aimed at slowing the habitat drain. This was manifested in several confrontations over energy and water development plans that would affect wildlife. But one bright spot did stand out in an otherwise dismal picture for 1980. Congress passed, and the president signed, a bill authorizing up to $5 million annually to help states pay for nongame and other wildlife conservation plans.

Minerals: Oil again dominated the minerals scene in 1980, as it has every year since the 1973 Arab embargo. And once again, analysts argued about how much of it the country has left in the ground. The big oil companies continue to claim that substantial reserves still remain to be discovered, while environmentalists warned that we have used a large percentage—some believe as much as 75 percent—of our proved reserves. Environmentalists were also concerned with the government's continuing emphasis on enormously expensive, environmentally disruptive technological breakthroughs such as the synthetic fuels program, particularly at a time when Americans were showing an ever-increasing commitment to conservation. For much of 1980, U.S. oil imports ran 20 percent behind the 1979 level. Overall, the economy's energy efficiency has increased a remarkable 10 percent since 1973. But still, the U.S., representing only 6 percent of the world's population, continued to consume one-third of all oil used in 1980.

Air: Air quality continued to improve in many parts of the country in 1980, with some 2 dozen urban areas showing a 35 percent decline in the number of unhealthy days, but politics made uncertain the prospects for further progress. Throughout the year, federal air-pollution standards drew heavy criticism from industrial representatives, as well as from White House economists. To diffuse mounting pressure to soften their rules, the EPA rolled back some deadlines. The slumping U.S. auto industry received yet another year reprieve on 3 exhaust standards—this despite the results of the EPA's own 7-city study, which found that many recently built cars are creating 3 to 5 times more emissions than they were designed to produce. And in a controversial decision, Ohio's utilities were given more time to burn local supplies of high-sulphur coal without installing costly scrubbers. This decision concerned environmentalists who pointed to evidence that acid rain has increased fiftyfold in the last 25 years over the eastern half of the country.

Water: Since the Clean Water Act was passed 9 years ago, many lakes and rivers in the U.S. have become swimmable and fishable again as sources of direct pollution have been curtailed. But in recent years, a new, equally appalling threat has come to light: the contamination of the nation's ground water supplies. In 1980, a House subcommittee released a list of 2,100 places around the nation where industrial wastes may be contaminating ground water supplies. If this is the case, it would affect at least half the population. According to the EPA, the U.S. is generating nearly 80 billion pounds of hazardous chemical wastes annually, but only 10 percent is being disposed of properly. For this reason, the EPA issued regulations designed to stem the flow of hazardous wastes. The cost of compliance is high, but so is the cost wreacked upon society by uncontrolled dumping. Notes Eckardt C. Beck of the EPA, "Once ground water becomes polluted, it can stay that way for decades."

Forest: A decline in the U.S. construction industry kept the demand for timber low in 1980, but consumption is expected to increase from the 13.3 billion cubic feet used in 1976 to 20.3 billion in 1990 to 28.3 billion in 2030. And while it was not a good year for timber interests, conservationists saw ominous signs in the increasing interest in wood as a fuel source, and in the possible impact that tightening government budgets could have on recreation,

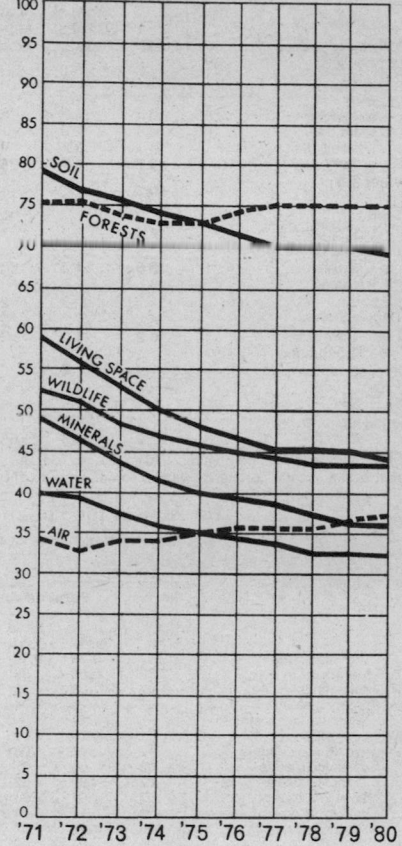

wildlife and watershed protection in public forests. Encouraging was the federal government's proposal to reserve approximately 15.4 million acres of national forests as wilderness, and to provide more incentives to increase production on private lands, thereby lessening the dependence on national forests.

Living Space: U.S. living space declined further in both quality and quantity in 1980. The National Park Service reported that overburdened parks are deteriorating because of overcrowding and pollution, and water projects continued to claim pristine areas. But particularly disturbing was the advent of a grass-roots movement known as the "Sagebrush Rebellion"—an attempt to transfer federal lands to state ownership. Conservationists are concerned that the states would find the cost of properly managing the land too high, and that environmental laws would be circumvented.

Soil: The U.S. is losing valuable farmland at an alarming rate——approximately one million acres per year—to urban sprawl, highways, and other development. It is estimated that in the next 20 years, the nation may pave over another section of agricultural land equal to the size of Indiana. The problem: farmers, who depend on the sale of crops to pay their mortgages, simply cannot compete with the prices developers offer for land. There is still no nationwide policy to protect prime farmlands. And the problem is exacerbated by ongoing land erosion—about 4 billion tons of American soil are lost annually.

U.S. Forest Land by State and Region

Source: Forest Service, U.S. Agriculture Department, 1979.

State or region	Land area (1,000 acres)	Area forested	Percent forested	State or region	Land area (1,000 acres)	Area forested	Percent forested
Connecticut	3,081	1,861	60	Arkansas	33,091	18,282	55
Maine	19,729	17,718	90	Florida	33,994	17,040	50
Massachusetts	5,007	2,952	59	Georgia	36,796	25,256	69
New Hampshire	5,731	5,013	87	Louisiana	28,409	14,558	51
Rhode Island	664	404	61	Mississippi	29,930	16,716	56
Vermont	5,907	4,512	76	North Carolina	30,956	20,043	65
New England	**40,119**	**32,460**	**81**	Oklahoma	43,728	8,513	19
Delaware	1,233	392	32	South Carolina	19,143	12,249	64
Maryland	6,289	2,653	42	Tennessee	26,290	13,161	50
New Jersey	4,775	1,928	40	Texas	167,283	23,279	14
New York	30,357	17,218	57	Virginia	25,286	16,417	65
Pennsylvania	29,592	16,836	50	**South**	**474,906**	**185,514**	**39**
West Virginia	15,334	11,669	76	Alaska	362,485	119,145	33
Mid Atlantic	**87,813**	**50,686**	**58**	California	99,847	40,152	48
Michigan	30,634	19,270	63	Hawaii	4,109	1,986	40
Minnesota	50,382	16,709	33	Oregon	61,356	29,810	49
North Dakota	43,939	422	1	Washington	42,456	23,181	55
South Dakota	48,381	1,702	4	**Pacific Coast**	**570,253**	**214,274**	**38**
Wisconsin	34,616	14,908	43	Arizona	72,580	18,494	25
Lake States	**207,952**	**53,011**	**25**	Colorado	66,283	22,271	34
Illinois	35,442	3,810	11	Idaho	52,676	21,726	41
Indiana	22,951	3,943	17	Montana	92,826	22,559	24
Iowa	35,634	1,561	4	Nevada	70,295	7,683	11
Kansas	52,127	1,344	3	New Mexico	77,669	18,060	23
Kentucky	25,282	12,161	48	Utah	52,505	15,557	30
Missouri	43,868	12,876	29	Wyoming	62,055	10,028	16
Nebraska	48,828	1,029	2	**Rocky Mountain**	**546,959**	**136,378**	**25**
Ohio	26,121	6,147	24				
Central	**241,425**	**42,871**	**18**	**Total U.S.**	**2,169,427**	**'715,194**	**33**
Alabama	32,231	21,361	66				

(1) Of this total, 482,486,000 acres are of commercial quality (137 million acres are government owned); 20,664,000 acres are productive but reserved (land set aside by statute); 4,626,000 acres are deferred for possible reserve status; and 228,782,000 acres are unproductive or awaiting survey.

Major U.S. and Canadian Public Zoological Parks

Source: World Almanac questionnaire, 1981; budget, metro population, and attendance are in millions. (A) designates Park has not provided up-to-date information. (b) includes capital improvements.

Zoo	Budget	Metro pop.	Atten- dance	Acres	Species	Major Attractions
San Diego	$24.0	1.0	3.1	100	824	Loalas, pygmy chimps, Skyfari aerial tramway, parrots, koalas, red pandas.
Bronx (N.Y.C.)	16.0	11.5	2.0	252	600	Wild Asia, children's zoo, Reptile House.
San Diego (Wild Animal Park)	10.0	1.7	1.0	1,800	293	Canine show, bird and elephant show, monorail.
Brookfield (Chicago)	9.0	7.8	1.7	180	503	Porpoise show, predator ecology, baboon island.
National (Wash. D.C.)	8.0	3.0	2.8	167	550	Lion/Tiger complex, Beaver Valley, giant pandas.
Washington Park (Portland)	6.5 ᵇ	1.1	0.7	62	162	Asian elephants, musk oxen, Humboldt penguins.
Calgary	6.4	0.6	0.7	204	320	Exotic vertebrates, prehistoric park.
Milwaukee	6.2	1.5	1.0	185	785	Predator/prey exhibits, barless enclosures.
Toronto (A)	6.2	2.1	1.1	710	407	Canadian Domain ride, exotic plants and birds.
St. Louis	6.0	2.5	2.0	84	630	Big cat country, herpetarium, primate house.
Minnesota	5.9	2.0	1.0	500	250	Sky, whales/sealife, tropics and discovery trails.
Detroit	5.6	4.0	0.9	122	300	Penguinarium, walk-through aviary bldg., great ape house.
Philadelphia	5.5	5.0	1.1	42	525	Reptiles, African plains, hummingbirds.
Los Angeles	3.5	8.0	1.6	113	525	California Condor, Mountain Tapir, Monkey-eating eagle.
Oklahoma City	3.9	0.5	0.6	160	435	African plains, Patagonian cliffs, Galapagos Isl.
Cincinnati	3.3	1.4	1.0	67	556	White tigers, insect world, outdoor gorilla display.
San Antonio	2.8	1.0	0.9	29	711	Whooping cranes, rare antelopes, white rhinoceros, gelada baboons.
Lincoln Park (Chicago)	2.7	7.0	4.0	35	387	Great ape collection, farm in the zoo.
Buffalo	2.5	1.0	0.4	24	251	Rhino yard, tropical gorilla exhibit, children's zoo.
Columbus	2.4	1.0	0.6	92	609	Gorilla and reptile collection, giraffe complex.
San Francisco	2.4	4.0	1.0	125	350	World's largest natural gorilla habitat.
Woodland Park (Seattle)	2.3	1.4	0.9	90	335	Nocturnal house, N. E. swamp and marsh.
Denver	2.2	1.5	1.0	76	324	Bird world, Bighorn and Dall sheep exhibit.
Phoenix	2.0	1.8	0.6	125	266	Arabian oryx herd, children's zoo, Arizona exhibit.
Houston	1.8	2.5	2.0	45	528	Gorilla habitat, tropical bird house, Kipp aquarium.
Cleveland	1.8	2.5	0.5	127	400	Primate and cat bldg., moated bears.
Dallas	1.8	0.9	0.6	50	562	Reptile, hoofed animals exhibit.
Arizona-Sonora Desert Museum (Tucson)	1.8	0.5	0.5	12	236	Earth science center, sunset desert demo.
Baltimore	1.7	1.5	0.4	142	281	Largest black-footed penguin colony in U.S.
Pittsburgh	1.5	1.0	0.6	75	374	Twilight zoo, AquaZoo, Children's zoo train.
Louisville	1.4	0.9	0.4	58	183	Siberian tiger exhibit, polar bear exhibit.
Kansas City	1.3	1.3	0.6	65	150	Great apes, great cats, tropical habitat aviary.

Mammals: Orders and Major Families

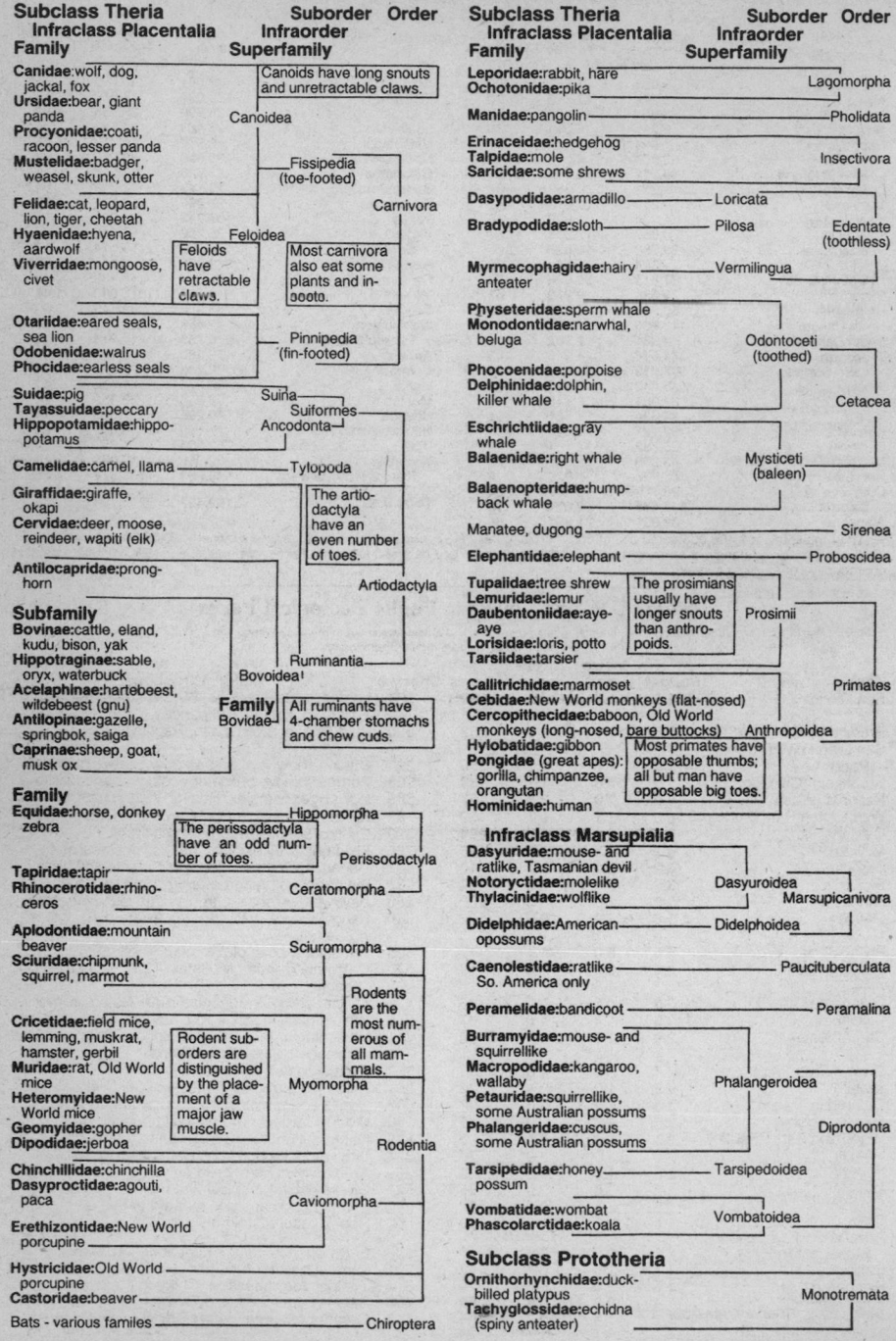

Subclass Theria
Infraclass Placentalia
Family   Suborder   Order
Infraorder
Superfamily

Canidae:wolf, dog, jackal, fox
Ursidae:bear, giant panda
Procyonidae:coati, racoon, lesser panda
Mustelidae:badger, weasel, skunk, otter

Canoids have long snouts and unretractable claws.

Canoidea

Fissipedia (toe-footed)

Carnivora

Felidae:cat, leopard, lion, tiger, cheetah
Hyaenidae:hyena, aardwolf
Viverridae:mongoose, civet

Feloidea

Feloids have retractable claws.

Most carnivora also eat some plants and insects.

Otariidae:eared seals, sea lion
Odobenidae:walrus
Phocidae:earless seals

Pinnipedia (fin-footed)

Suidae:pig
Tayassuidae:peccary
Hippopotamidae:hippopotamus

Suina
Suiformes
Ancodonta

Camelidae:camel, llama — Tylopoda

Giraffidae:giraffe, okapi
Cervidae:deer, moose, reindeer, wapiti (elk)

The artiodactyla have an even number of toes.

Antilocapridae:pronghorn

Artiodactyla

Subfamily
Bovinae:cattle, eland, kudu, bison, yak
Hippotraginae:sable, oryx, waterbuck
Acelaphinae:hartebeest, wildebeest (gnu)
Antilopinae:gazelle, springbok, saiga
Caprinae:sheep, goat, musk ox

Ruminantia
Bovoidea[1]

Family
Bovidae

All ruminants have 4-chamber stomachs and chew cuds.

Family
Equidae:horse, donkey, zebra

Hippomorpha

The perissodactyla have an odd number of toes.

Perissodactyla

Tapiridae:tapir
Rhinocerotidae:rhinoceros

Ceratomorpha

Aplodontidae:mountain beaver
Sciuridae:chipmunk, squirrel, marmot

Sciuromorpha

Rodents are the most numerous of all mammals.

Cricetidae:field mice, lemming, muskrat, hamster, gerbil
Muridae:rat, Old World mice
Heteromyidae: New World mice
Geomyidae:gopher
Dipodidae:jerboa

Rodent suborders are distinguished by the placement of a major jaw muscle.

Myomorpha

Rodentia

Chinchillidae:chinchilla
Dasyproctidae:agouti, paca

Caviomorpha

Erethizontidae: New World porcupine

Hystricidae: Old World porcupine
Castoridae:beaver

Bats - various familes — Chiroptera

Subclass Theria
Infraclass Placentalia
Family   Suborder   Order
Infraorder
Superfamily

Leporidae:rabbit, hare
Ochotonidae:pika

Lagomorpha

Manidae:pangolin — Pholidata

Erinaceidae:hedgehog
Talpidae:mole
Saricidae:some shrews

Insectivora

Dasypodidae:armadillo — Loricata
Bradypodidae:sloth — Pilosa

Edentate (toothless)

Myrmecophagidae:hairy anteater — Vermilingua

Physeteridae:sperm whale
Monodontidae:narwhal, beluga

Odontoceti (toothed)

Phocoenidae:porpoise
Delphinidae:dolphin, killer whale

Cetacea

Eschrichtidae:gray whale
Balaenidae:right whale

Mysticeti (baleen)

Balaenopteridae:humpback whale

Manatee, dugong — Sirenea

Elephantidae:elephant — Proboscidea

Tupaiidae:tree shrew
Lemuridae:lemur
Daubentoniidae:aye-aye
Lorisidae:loris, potto
Tarsiidae:tarsier

The prosimians usually have longer snouts than anthropoids.

Prosimii

Primates

Callitrichidae:marmoset
Cebidae: New World monkeys (flat-nosed)
Cercopithecidae:baboon, Old World monkeys (long-nosed, bare buttocks)
Hylobatidae:gibbon
Pongidae: (great apes): gorilla, chimpanzee, orangutan
Hominidae:human

Most primates have opposable thumbs; all but man have opposable big toes.

Anthropoidea

Infraclass Marsupialia

Dasyuridae:mouse- and ratlike, Tasmanian devil
Notoryctidae:molelike
Thylacinidae:wolflike

Dasyuroidea

Marsupicanivora

Didelphidae: American opossums — Didelphoidea

Caenolestidae:ratlike So. America only — Paucituberculata

Peramelidae:bandicoot — Peramalina

Burramyidae:mouse- and squirrellike
Macropodidae:kangaroo, wallaby
Petauridae:squirrellike, some Australian possums
Phalangeridae:cuscus, some Australian possums

Phalangeroidea

Diprodonta

Tarsipedidae:honey possum — Tarsipedoidea

Vombatidae:wombat
Phascolarctidae:koala

Vombatoidea

Subclass Prototheria

Ornithorhynchidae:duck-billed platypus
Tachyglossidae:echidna (spiny anteater)

Monotremata

Some Endangered Species in North America

Source: U.S. Fish and Wildlife Service, U.S. Interior Department

Common name	Scientific name	Range
Mammals		
Virginia big-eared bat	Plecotus townsendii virginianus	U.S. (Ky., W.V., Va.)
Columbian white-tailed deer	Odocoileus virginianus leucurus	U.S. (Wa., Or.)
San Joaquin kit fox	Vulpes macrotis mutica	U.S. (Cal.)
Salt marsh harvest mouse	Reithrodontomys raviventris	U.S. (Cal.)
Florida panther	Felis concolor coryi	U.S. (Southeast)
Utah prairie dog	Cynomys parvidens	U.S. (Ut.)
Morro Bay kangaroo rat	Dipodomys heermanni	U.S. (Cal.)
Delmarva Peninsula fox squirrel	Sciurus niger cinereus	U.S. (DelMarVa Peninsula to SE Pa.)
West Indian manatee	Trichechus manatus	U.S. (Southeast), Caribbean, So. Amer.
Red wolf	Canis rufus	U.S. (Southeast to Tex.)
Birds		
Masked bobwhite (quail)	Colinus virginianus ridgwayi	U.S. (Ariz.), Mexico
California condor	Gymnogyps californianus	U.S. (Rocky Mtns. east to Carolinas), Canada, Mexico
Whooping crane	Grus americana	U.S., Canada
Eskimo curlew	Numenius borealis	Alaska and N. Canada to Argentina
Bald eagle	Haliaeetus leucocephalus	U.S. (most states), Canada
American peregrine falcon	Falco peregrinus anatum	Canada to Mexico
Arctic peregrine falcon	Falco peregrinus tundrius	Alas. to Greenland, south to Argentina
Aleutian Canada goose	Branta canadensis leucopareia	U.S. (Ark., Cal., Or., Wa.), Japan
Brown pelican	Pelecanus occidentalis	U.S. (Carolinas to Tex., Cal.), West Indies, Central and S. America
Attwater's greater prairie chicken	Tympanuchus cupido attwateri	U.S. (Tex.)
Bachman's warbler (wood)	Vermivora bachmanii	U.S., Cuba
Kirtland's warbler (wood)	Dendroica kirtlandii	U.S., Canada, Bahama Is.
Ivory-billed woodpecker	Campephilus principalis	U.S. (Southcentral and Southeast), Cuba
Reptiles		
American alligator	Alligator mississippiensis	U.S. (Fla.), Mexico, South and Central America, Carribean
American crocodile	Crocodylus acutus	U.S. (Fla.) to So. Amer.
Island night lizard*	Xantusia riversiana	U.S. (Cal.)
Eastern indigo snake*	Drymarchon corais couperi	U.S. (Al., Fl., Ga., Ms., S.C.)

*Threatened rather than endangered

Some Other Endangered Species in the World

Source: U.S. Fish and Wildlife Service, U.S. Interior Department

Common name	Scientific name	Range
Mammals		
Giant sable antelope	Hippotragus niger variani	Angola
African elephant*	Loxodonta africana	Africa
Saudi Arabian gazelle	Gazella dorcas saudiya	Israel, Iraq, Jordan, Saudi Arabia, Syria, Kuwait
Brown hyena	Hyaena brunnea	Southern Africa
Red kangaroo*	Macropus rufs	Australia
Leopard	Panthera pardus	Africa, India, SE Asia
Black howler monkey*	Alouatta pigra	Mexico, Guatamala, Belize
Ocelot	Felis pardalis	C. and S. America
Thin-spined porcupine	Chaetomys subspinosus	Brazil
Tiger	Panthera tigris	Asia
Banded hare wallaby	Lagostrophus fasciatus	Australia
Gray whale	Eschrichtius robustus	N. Pacific Ocean
Wild yak	Bos grunniens mutus	China (Tibet), India
Mountain zebra	Equus zebra zebra	South Africa
Birds		
Indigo macaw	Anodorhynchus leari	Brazil
West African ostrich	Struthio camelus spatzi	Spanish Sahara
Anjouan scops owl	Otus rutilus capnodes	Indian Ocean: Comoro Island
Golden parakeet	Aratinga guarouba	Brazil
Australian parrot	Geopsittacus occidentalis	Australia

*Threatened rather than endangered

Young of Animals Have Special Names

The young of many animals, birds and fish have come to be called by special names. A young eel, for example, is an elver. Many young animals, of course, are often referred to simply as infants, babies, younglets, or younglings.

bunny: rabbit.
calf: cattle, elephant, antelope, rhino, hippo, whale, etc.

cheeper: grouse, partridge, quail.
chick, chicken: fowl.
cockerel: rooster.

codling, sprag: codfish.
colt: horse (male).
cub: lion, bear, shark, fox, etc.

cygnet: swan.
duckling: duck.
eaglet: eagle.
elver: eel.
eyas: hawk, others.
fawn: deer.
filly: horse (female).
fingerling: fish generally.
flapper: wild fowl.
fledgling: birds generally.
foal: horse, zebra, others.
fry: fish generally.

gosling: goose.
heifer: cow.
joey: kangaroo, others.
kid: goat.
kit: fox, beaver, rabbit, cat.
kitten, kitty, catling: cats, other fur-bearers.
lamb, lambkin, cosset, hog: sheep.
leveret: hare.
nestling: birds generally.
owlet: owl.
parr, smolt, grilse: salmon.

piglet, shoat, farrow, suckling: pig.
polliwog, tadpole: frog.
poult: turkey.
pullet: hen.
pup: dog, seal, sea lion, fox.
puss, pussy: cat.
spike, blinker, tinker: mackerel.
squab: pigeon.
squeaker: pigeon, others.
whelp: dog, tiger, beasts of prey.
yearling: cattle, sheep, horse, etc.

Speeds of Animals

Source: Natural History magazine, March 1974.
Copyright © The American Museum of Natural History, 1974.

Animal	Mph	Animal	Mph	Animal	Mph
Cheetah	70	Mongolian wild ass	40	Human	27.89
Pronghorn antelope	61	Greyhound	39.35	Elephant	25
Wildebeest	50	Whippet	35.50	Black mamba snake	20
Lion	50	Rabbit (domestic)	35	Six-lined race runner	18
Thomson's gazelle	50	Mule deer	35	Wild turkey	15
Quarterhorse	47.5	Jackal	35	Squirrel	12
Elk	45	Reindeer	32	Pig (domestic)	11
Cape hunting dog	45	Giraffe	32	Chicken	9
Coyote	43	White-tailed deer	30	Spider (Tegenaria atrica)	1.17
Gray fox	42	Wart hog	30	Giant tortoise	0.17
Hyena	40	Grizzly bear	30	Three-toed sloth	0.15
Zebra	40	Cat (domestic)	30	Garden snail	0.03

Most of these measurements are for maximum speeds over approximate quarter-mile distances. Exceptions are the lion and elephant, whose speeds were clocked in the act of charging; the whippet, which was timed over a 200-yard course; the cheetah over a 100-yard distance; man for a 15-yard segment of a 100-yard run (of 13.6 seconds); and the black mamba, six-lined race runner, spider, giant tortoise, three-toed sloth, and garden snail, which were measured over various small distances.

Gestation, Longevity, and Incubation of Animals

Longevity figures were supplied by Ronald T. Reuther. They refer to animals in captivity; the potential life span of animals is rarely attained in nature. Maximum longevity figures are from the Biology Data Book, 1972. Figures on gestation and incubation are averages based on estimates by leading authorities.

Animal	Gestation (day)	Average longevity (years)	Maximum longevity (yrs., mos.)	Animal	Gestation (day)	Average longevity (years)	Maximum longevity (yrs., mos.)
Ass	365	12	35-10	Leopard	98	12	19-4
Baboon	187	20	35-7	Lion	100	15	25-1
Bear: Black	219	18	36-10	Monkey (rhesus)	164	15	—
Grizzly	225	25	—	Moose	240	12	—
Polar	240	20	34-8	Mouse (meadow)	21	3	—
Beaver	122	5	20-6	Mouse (dom. white)	19	3	3-6
Buffalo (American)	278	15	—	Opossum (American)	14-17	1	—
Bactrian camel	406	12	29-5	Pig (domestic)	112	10	27
Cat (domestic)	63	12	28	Puma	90	12	19
Chimpanzee	231	20	44-6	Rabbit (domestic)	31	5	13
Chipmunk	31	6	8	Rhinoceros (black)	450	15	—
Cow	284	15	30	Rhinoceros (white)	—	20	—
Deer (white-tailed)	201	8	17-6	Sea lion (California)	350	12	28
Dog (domestic)	61	12	20	Sheep (domestic)	154	12	20
Elephant (African)	—	35	60	Squirrel (gray)	44	10	—
Elephant (Asian)	645	40	70	Tiger	105	16	26-3
Elk	250	15	26-6	Wolf (maned)	63	5	—
Fox (red)	52	7	14	Zebra (Grant's)	365	15	—
Giraffe	425	10	33-7				
Goat (domestic)	151	8	18	**Incubation time (days)**			
Gorilla	257	20	39-4	Chicken 21			
Guinea pig	68	4	7-6	Duck. 30			
Hippopotamus	238	25	—	Goose. 30			
Horse	330	20	46	Pigeon. 18			
Kangaroo	42	7	—	Turkey. 26			

A Collection of Animal Collectives

The English language boasts an abundance of names to describe groups of things, particularly pairs or aggregations of animals. Some of these words have fallen into comparative disuse, but many of them are still in service, helping to enrich the vocabularies of those who like their language to be precise, who tire of hearing a group referred to as "a bunch of," or who enjoy the sound of words that aren't over-worked.

band of gorillas
bed of clams, oysters
bevy of quail, swans
brace of ducks
brood of chicks
cast of hawks
cete of badgers
charm of goldfinches
chattering of choughs
cloud of gnats

clowder of cats
clutch of chicks
clutter of cats
colony of ants
congregation of plovers
covey of quail, partridge
cry of hounds
down of hares
drift of swine
drove of cattle, sheep

exaltation of larks
flight of birds
flock of sheep, geese
gaggle of geese
gam of whales
gang of elks
grist of bees
herd of elephants
hive of bees
horde of gnats

husk of hares
kindle or kendle of kittens
knot of toads
leap of leopards
leash of greyhounds, foxes
litter of pigs
mob of kangaroos
murder of crows
muster of peacocks
mute of hounds

nest of vipers	**school** of fish	**sounder** of boars, swine	**troop** of kangaroos,
nest, nide of pheasants	**sedge** or **siege** of cranes	**span** of mules	monkeys
pack of hounds, wolves	**shoal** of fish, pilchards	**spring** of teals	**volery** of birds
pair of horses	**skein** of geese	**swarm** of bees	**watch** of nightingales
pod of whales, seals	**skulk** of foxes	**team** of ducks, horses	**wing** of plovers
pride of lions	**sleuth** of bears	**tribe** or **trip** of goats	**yoke** of oxen

Major Venomous Animals

Snakes

Coral snake - 2 to 4 ft. long, in Americas south of Canada; bite is nearly painless; very slow onset of paralysis, difficulty breathing; mortality high without anti-venin.

Rattlesnake - 2 to 8 ft. long, throughout W. Hemisphere. Rapid onset of symptoms of severe pain, swelling; mortality low, but amputation of affected limb is sometimes necessary; anti-venin. Probably high mortality for Mojave rattler.

Cottonmouth water moccasin - less than 6 ft. long, wetlands of southern U.S. from Virginia to Texas. Rapid onset of symptoms of severe pain, swelling; mortality low, but tissue destruction, caused by the venom's effect on the blood, can be extensive; anti-venin.

Copperhead - less than 4 ft. long, from New England to Texas; pain and swelling; very seldom fatal.

Fer-de-lance - up to 7 ft. long, Martinique only; venom attacks nerves and blood; probably high mortality.

Bushmaster - up to 9 ft. long, jungles of C. and S. America; few bites recorded; probably low mortality.

Yellow-beard - up to 7 ft. long, from tropical Mexico to Brazil; severe tissue damage common; low mortality; anti-venin.

Asian pit vipers - from 2 to 5 ft. long throughout Asia; reactions and mortality vary but most bites cause tissue damage and mortality is generally low.

Sharp-nosed pit viper - up to 5 ft. long, in eastern China and Indo-China; the most toxic of Asian pit vipers; very rapid onset of swelling and tissue damage, internal bleeding; moderate mortality; anti-venin.

Boomslang - under 6 ft. long, in African savannahs; rapid onset of nausea and dizziness, often followed by slight recovery and then sudden death from internal hemorrhaging; bites rare, mortality high; anti-venin.

European vipers - from 1 to 3 ft. long; bleeding and tissue damage; mortality low; anti-venins.

Puff adder - up to 5 ft. long, fat; south of the Sahara and throughout the Middle East; rapid large swelling, great pain, dizziness; moderate mortality often from internal bleeding; anti-venin.

Gaboon viper - over 6 ft. long, fat; 2-inch fangs; south of the Sahara; massive tissue damage, internal bleeding; mortality rate not clear.

Saw-scaled or carpet viper - up to 2 ft. long, in dry areas from India to Africa; severe bleeding, fever; high mortality, venom 3 times more toxic than common cobra's; anti-venin.

Desert horned viper - in dry areas of Africa and western Asia; swelling and tissue damage; low mortality; anti-venin.

Russel's viper or tic-palonga - over 5 ft. long, throughout Asia; internal bleeding; mortality rate not clear; bite reports common; anti-venin.

Black mamba - up to 14 ft. long, fast-moving; S. and C. Africa; rapid onset of dizziness, difficulty breathing, erratic heart-beat; mortality high, nears 100% without anti-venin.

Kraits - in S. Asia; rapid onset of sleepiness; numbness; kraits are among the most lethal snakes in the world with up to 50% mortality even with anti-venin treatment.

Common or Asian cobra - 4 to 8 ft. long, throughout S. Asia; considerable tissue damage, sometimes paralysis; mortality probably not more than 10%; anti-venin.

King cobra - up to 16 ft. long, large hood; throughout S. Asia; rapid swelling, dizziness, loss of consciousness, difficulty breathing, erratic heart-beat; mortality varies sharply with amount of venom involved, most bites involve non-fatal amounts; anti-venin.

Yellow or Cape cobra - 7 ft. long, in southern Africa; most toxic venom of any cobra; rapid onset of swelling, breathing and cardiac difficulties; mortality high without treatment; anti-venin.

Ringhals, or spitting cobra - 5 ft. and 7 ft. long; southern Africa; squirt venom through holes in front of fangs as a defense; venom is severely irritating and can cause blindness.

Australian brown snakes - very slow onset of symptoms of cardiac or respiratory distress; moderate mortality; anti-venin.

Tiger snake - 2 to 6 ft. long, S. Australia; pain, numbness, mental disturbances with rapid onset of paralysis; may be the most deadly of all land snakes though anti-venin is quite effective.

Death adder - less than 3 ft. long, Australia; rapid onset of faintness, cardiac and respiratory distress; at least 50% mortality without anti-venin.

Taipan - up to 11 ft. long, in Australia and New Guinea; rapid paralysis with severe breathing difficulty; mortality nears 100% without anti-venin.

Sea snakes - throughout Pacific and Indian oceans except NE Pacific; almost painless bite, variety of muscle pain, paralysis; mortality rate about 15%, many bites are not envenomed; some anti-venins.

Notes: Not all snake bites by venomous snakes are actually envenomed; for a variety of reasons, the snake may be temporarily lacking in venom or fail to inject it. Any animal bite, however, carries the danger of tetanus and no bite by a venomous snake should go untreated. Anti-venins are not certain cures; they are only an aid in the treatment of bites. Mortality rates above are for envenomed bites; low mortality, up to 5% result in death; moderate, up to 15%; high, over 15%. Even in cases in which the victim recovers fully, prolonged hospitalization and extensive, continuous medical procedures are usually required.

Lizards

Gila monster - up to 30 inches long with heavy body and tail, in high desert in southwest U.S. and N. Mexico; immediate severe pain followed by vomiting, thirst, difficulty swallowing, weakness approaching paralysis; mortality very low with medical treatment, otherwise high; anti-venin.

Mexican beaded lizard - similar to Gila monster, Mexican west-coast; reaction and mortality rate similar to Gila monster; anti-venin.

Insects

Ants, bees, wasps, hornets, etc. All have global distribution. Usual reaction is piercing pain in area of sting. Never directly fatal, except in cases of massive multiple stings. Many people suffer allergic reactions - swelling, rashes, partial paralysis –and a few may die within minutes from severe sensitivity to the venom (anaphylactic shock).

Spiders, scorpions

Black widow - small, round-bodied with hour-glass marking; the widow and its relatives are found around the world in tropical and temperate zones; sharp pain, weakness, clammy skin, muscular rigidity, breathing difficulty and, in small children, convulsions; low mortality.

Brown recluse or fiddleback - small, oblong body; can be found anywhere in U.S. today; slow onset of pain and severe ulceration at place of bite; in severe cases fever, nausea, and stomach cramps; ulceration may last months; very low mortality.

Atrax **spiders** - several varieties, often large, found in Australia; slow onset of breathing and circulation difficulties; low mortality.

Tarantulas - large, hairy spiders found around the world; American tarantulas, and probably all others, are **harmless**, though their bite may cause some pain and swelling.

Scorpions - crab-like body with stinger in tail, various sizes, many varieties throughout tropical and subtropical areas; various symptoms may include severe pain spreading from the wound, numbness, severe emotional agitation, cramps; severe reactions include vomiting, diarrhea, respiratory failure; moderate, perhaps high, mortality, particularly in children; anti-venins.

Sea Life

Sea wasps - jellyfish, with tentacles up to 30 ft. long, in the South Pacific; very rapid onset of circulatory problems; high mortality largely because of the speed of toxic reaction; anti-venin.

Portuguese man-of-war - jellyfish-like, with tentacles up to 70 ft. long, in most warm water areas; immediate severe pain; not fatal, though shock may cause death in a rare case.

Octopi - global distribution, usually in warm waters; all varieties produce venom but only a few can cause death; rapid onset of paralysis with breathing difficulty.

Stingrays - several varieties of differing sizes, found in tropical and temperate seas and some fresh water; severe pain, rapid onset of nausea, vomiting, breathing difficulties; wound area may ulcerate, gangrene may appear; seldom fatal.

Stonefish - brownish fish which lies motionless as a rock on bottom in shallow water; throughout S. Pacific and Indian oceans; extraordinary pain, rapid paralysis; low mortality.

Cone-shells - molluscs in small, beautiful shells in the S. Pacific and Indian oceans; shoot barbs into victims; paralysis; low mortality.

American Kennel Club Registrations

	Rank 1980	1980	Rank 1979	1979		Rank 1980	1980	Rank 1979	1979
Poodles	1	95,250	1	94,950	Gordon Setters	69	1,170	64	1,140
Doberman Pinschers	2	79,908	2	80,363	Rhodesian Ridgebacks	70	1,168	68	1,029
Cocker Spaniels	3	76,113	3	65,685	Soft-Coated Wheaten				
German Shepherd Dogs	4	58,865	4	57,683	Terriers	71	981	7	797
Labrador Retrievers	5	52,398	5	46,077	Bullmastiffs	72	918	70	804
Golden Retrievers	6	44,100	6	38,060	Australian Terriers	73	770	72	784
Beagles	7	35,091	7	35,374	Welsh Terriers	74	748	73	691
Miniature Schnauzers	8	34,962	9	32,666	Bearded Collies	75	653	76	588
Dachshunds	9	33,881	8	32,777	Standard Schnauzers	76	648	74	687
Shetland Sheepdogs	10	28,325	10	25,943	Salukis	77	627	75	619
Yorkshire Terriers	11	24,665	12	22,458	Papillons	78	613	78	576
Lhasa Apsos	12	24,477	11	22,714	Belgian Sheepdogs	79	584	77	584
Collies	13	21,477	13	21,210	Kerry Blue Terriers	80	576	81	499
English Springer					Italian Greyhounds	81	500	80	515
Spaniels	14	21,370	15	20,071	Giant Schnauzers	82	540	82	496
Siberian Huskies	15	20,884	16	19,876	Manchester Terriers	83	492	79	534
Pekingese	16	18,859	17	17,992	Pointers	84	427	85	398
Shih Tzu	17	17,957	20	16,042	Belgian Tervuren	85	422	83	452
Pomeranians	18	17,341	19	16,184	Tibetan Terriers	86	387	86	343
Basset Hounds	19	17,151	23	14,930	Bernese Mountain Dogs	87	380	89	318
Brittany Spaniels	20	17,146	18	17,038	Puli	88	375	87	341
Chihuahuas	21	16,239	21	15,512	Japanese Chin	89	373	84	411
Irish Setters	22	14,938	14	20,912	American Water Span-				
Boxers	23	14,901	24	13,250	iels	90	363	93	282
Chow Chows	24	14,589	26	11,739	Welsh Corgis (Cardigan)	91	361	87	341
Great Danes	25	14,330	22	15,322	Bedlington Terriers	92	336	91	311
Boston Terriers	26	11,636	27	11,125	Black and Tan Coon-				
Old English Sheepdogs	27	10,758	25	12,081	hounds	93	333	92	302
German Shorthaired					Irish Terriers	94	305	90	316
Pointers	28	10,670	28	10,579	Staffordshire Bull Terri-				
Samoyeds	29	8,430	29	8,653	ers	95	260	94	257
Alaskan Malamutes	30	7,642	31	7,377	Briards	96	250	95	246
Maltese	31	7,324	33	6,806	Lakeland Terriers	97	219	99	192
Airedale Terriers	32	6,898	34	6,594	Border Terriers	98	207	104	163
West Highland White					Dandie Dinmont Terriers	99	197	99	192
Terriers	33	6,824	38	6,210	Kuvaszok	99	197	102	180
Bulldogs	34	6,712	35	6,566	Flat-Coated Retrievers	101	194	98	200
Cairn Terriers	35	6,561	37	6,262	Norwich Terriers	102	190	97	205
Scottish Terriers	36	6,334	36	6,343	Skye Terriers	103	171	101	190
Afghan Hounds	37	6,122	32	6,833	Brussels Griffons	104	170	106	156
Keeshonden	38	6,081	39	5,850	French Bulldogs	105	170	106	156
St. Bernards	39	5,908	30	7,444	Scottish Deerhounds	106	155	103	174
Pugs	40	5,731	42	5,497	Welsh Springer Spaniels	107	148	96	224
Dalmatians	41	5,585	41	5,558	Greyhounds	108	137	105	157
Norwegian Elkhounds	42	5,374	40	5,794	Komondorok	109	135	112	102
Weimaraners	43	4,714	43	4,605	Wirehaired Pointing Grif-				
Rottweilers	44	4,701	46	3,286	fons	109	135	108	131
Fox Terriers (Smooth					Irish Water Spaniels	111	114	110	110
and Wire)	45	3,000	44	3,762	Sealyham Terriers	112	108	109	112
Chesapeake Bay Re-					Norfolk Terriers	113	95	111	106
trievers	46	3,828	45	3,460	Clumber Spaniels	114	90	115	76
Bichons Frises	47	2,651	50	2,146	Affenpinschers	115	85	114	87
Silky Terriers	48	2,640	47	2,565	Curly-Coated Retrievers	116	79	120	27
Welsh Corgis (Pem-					English Toy Spaniels	117	76	116	71
broke)	49	2,445	49	2,216	Ibizan Hounds	118	68	112	102
Akitas	50	2,279	51	1,878	Foxhounds (American)	119	51	117	70
Newfoundlands	51	2,147	48	2,345	Belgian Malinois	120	48	118	60
Vizslas	52	1,837	52	1,737	Field Spaniels	121	32	120	27
Miniature Pinschers	53	1,817	54	1,428	Harriers	122	32	122	21
Bloodhounds	54	1,709	53	1,671	Otter Hounds	123	29	119	30
Australian Cattle Dogs	55	1,685	—	—	Sussex Spaniels	124	10	123	14
Schipperkes	56	1,462	56	1,353	Foxhounds (English)	125	0	124	6
Bouviers des Flandres	57	1,389	57	1,345					
English Setters	58	1,370	61	1,263	**Total Registrations:**		**1,011,799**		**965,250**
Basenjis	59	1,348	55	1,393					
Whippets	60	1,323	59	1,296					
Borzois	61	1,309	60	1,283					
Great Pyrenees	62	1,267	57	1,345					
English Cocker Spaniels	63	1,232	63	1,156					
American Staffordshire									
Terriers	64	1,228	66	1,072					
Bull Terriers	65	1,222	67	1,042					
Mastiffs	66	1,198	65	1,097					
Irish Wolfhounds	67	1,192	62	1,189					
German Wirehaired									
Pointers	68	1,171	69	978					

Dogs Registered by Groups	1980	1979
Sporting breeds	253,649	234,250
Hound breeds	107,100	105,050
Working breeds	294,050	287,850
Terrier breeds	73,550	69,300
Toy breeds	114,450	106,300
Non-sporting breeds	169,000	162,500
	1,011,799	965,250

Cat Breeds

There are 27 cat breeds recognized: abyssinian, american shorthair, balinese, birman, bombay, burmese, colorpoint shorthair, egyptian mau, exotic shorthair, havana brown, himalayan, japanese bobtail, korat, leopard cat, lilac foreign shorthair, maine coon cat, manx, ocicat, oriental shorthair, persian, rex, russian blue, scottish fold, siamese, sphynx, turkish angora, wirehair shorthair.

WEIGHTS AND MEASURES

Source: National Bureau of Standards, U.S. Commerce Department

U.S. Moving, Inch by 25.4 mm, to Metric System

On July 2, 1971, following the report of a metric conversion study committee, Commerce Secy. Maurice H. Stans recommended a gradual U.S. changeover during a 10-year period at the end of which the U.S. would be predominantly, but not exclusively, on the metric system. The Metric Conversion Act of 1975, signed Dec. 23, 1975, declared a national policy of coordinating voluntary increasing use of the Metric System and established a U. S. Metric Board to coordinate the change over.

Currently conversion to metric is confined to the following industries: automotive, construction and farm equipment, computer, and bottling. In addition, with encouragement of the U.S. Education Department, our school systems are emphasizing teaching of the metric system.

The International System of Units

Two systems of weights and measures exist side by side in the United States today, with roughly equal but separate legislative sanction: the U.S. Customary System and the International (Metric) System. Throughout U.S. history, the Customary System (inherited from, but now different from, the British Imperial System) has been, as its name implies, customarily used; a plethora of federal and state legislation has given it, through implication, standing as our primary weights and measures system. However, the Metric System (incorporated in the scientists' new SI or Systeme International d'Unites) is the only system that has ever received specific legislative sanction by Congress. The "Law of 1866" reads:

It shall be lawful throughout the United States of America to employ the weights and measures of the metric system; and no contract or dealing, or pleading in any court, shall be deemed invalid or liable to objection because the weights or measures expressed or referred to therein are weights or measures of the metric system.

Over the last 100 years, the Metric System has seen slow, steadily increasing use in the United States and, today, is of importance nearly equal to the Customary System.

On Feb. 10, 1964, the National Bureau of Standards issued the following bulletin:

Henceforth it shall be the policy of the National Bureau of Standards to use the units of the International System (SI), as adopted by the 11th General Conference on Weights and Measures (October 1960), except when the use of these units would obviously impair communication or reduce the usefulness of a report.

What had been the Metric System became the International System (SI), a more complete scientific system.

Seven units have been adopted to serve as the base for the International System as follows: **length**—meter; **mass**—kilogram; **time**—second; **electric current**—ampere; **thermodynamic temperature**—kelvin; **amount of substance**—mole; and **luminous intensity**—candela.

Prefixes

The following prefixes, in combination with the basic unit names, provide the multiples and submultiples in the International System. For example, the unit name "meter," with the prefix "kilo" added, produces "kilometer," meaning "1,000 meters."

Prefix	Symbol	Multiples and submultiples	Equivalent	Prefix	Symbol	Multiples and submultiples	Equivalent
exa	E	10^{18}	quintillionfold	deci	d	10^{1}	tenth part
peta	P	10^{15}	quadrillionfold	centi	c	10^{2}	hundredth part
tera	T	10^{12}	trillionfold	milli	m	10^{3}	thousandth part
giga	G	10^{9}	billionfold	micro	mu	10^{6}	millionth part
mega	M	10^{6}	millionfold	nano	n	10^{9}	billionth part
kilo	k	10^{3}	thousandfold	pico	p	10^{12}	trillionth part
hecto	h	10^{2}	hundredfold	femto	f	10^{15}	quadrillionth part
deka	da	10	tenfold	atto	a	10^{18}	quintillionth part

Tables of Metric Weights and Measures

Linear Measure

10 millimeters (mm)	= 1 centimeter (cm)
10 centimeters	= 1 decimeter (dm) = 100 millimeters
10 decimeters	= 1 meter (m) = 1,000 millimeters
10 meters	= 1 dekameter (dam)
10 dekameters	= 1 hectometer (hm) = 100 meters
10 hectometers	= 1 kilometer (km) = 1,000 meters

Area Measure

100 square millimeters (mm²)	= 1 square centimeter (cm²)
10,000 square centimeters	= 1 square meter (m²) = 1,000,000 square millimeters
100 square meters	= 1 are (a)
100 ares	= 1 hectare (ha) = 10,000 square meters
100 hectares	= 1 square kilometer (km²) = 1,000,000 square meters

Fluid Volume Measure

10 milliliters (mL)	= 1 centiliter (cL)
10 centiliters	= 1 deciliter (dL) = 100 milliliters
10 deciliters	= 1 liter (L) = 1,000 milliliters
10 liters	= 1 dekaliter (daL)
10 dekaliters	= 1 hectoliter (hL) = 100 liters
10 hectoliters	= 1 kiloliter (kL) = 1,000 liters

Cubic Measure

1,000 cubic millimeters (mm³)	= 1 cubic centimeter (cm³)
1,000 cubic centimeters	= 1 cubic decimeter (dm³) = 1,000,000 cubic millimeters
1,000 cubic decimeters	= 1 cubic meter (m³) = 1 stere = 1,000,000 cubic centimeters = 1,000,000,000 cubic millimeters

Weight

10 milligrams (mg)	= 1 centigram (cg)
10 centigrams	= 1 decigram (dg) = 100 milligrams
10 decigrams	= 1 gram (g) = 1,000 milligrams
10 grams	= 1 dekagram (dag)
10 dekagrams	= 1 hectogram (hg) = 100 grams
10 hectograms	= 1 kilogram (kg) = 1,000 grams
1,000 kilograms	= 1 metric ton (t)

Table of U.S. Customary Weights and Measures

Linear Measure

12 inches (in)	= 1 foot (ft)	40 rods	= 1 furlong (fur) = 220 yards = 660 feet
3 feet	= 1 yard (yd)	8 furlongs	= 1 survey mile (mi) = 1,760 yards = 5,280 feet
5 ½ yards	= 1 rod (rd), pole, or perch (16 ½ feet)	3 miles	= 1 league = 5,280 yards = 15,840 feet
		6076.11549 feet	= 1 International Nautical Mile

Liquid Measure

When necessary to distinguish the liquid pint or quart from the dry pint or quart, the word "liquid" or the abbreviation "liq" should be used in combination with the name or abbreviation of the liquid unit.

4 gills	= 1 pint (pt)	= 28.875 cubic inches
2 pints	= 1 quart (qt)	= 57.75 cubic inches
4 quarts	= 1 gallon (gal)	= 231 cubic inches = 8 pints = 32 gills

Area Measure

Squares and cubes of units are sometimes abbreviated by using "superior" figures. For example, ft² means square foot, and ft³ means cubic foot.

144 square inches	= 1 square foot (ft²)	
9 square feet	= 1 square yard (yd²)	= 1,296 square inches
30 ¼ square yards	= 1 square rod (rd²)	= 272 ¼ square feet
160 square rods	= 1 acre	= 4,840 square yards = 43,560 square feet
640 acres	= 1 square mile (mi²)	
1 mile square	= 1 section (of land)	
6 miles square	= 1 township	= 36 sections = 36 square miles

Cubic Measure

1 cubic foot (ft³)	= 1,728 cubic inches (in³)
27 cubic feet	= 1 cubic yard (yd³)

Gunter's or Surveyors' Chain Measure

7.92 inches (in)	= 1 link
100 links	= 1 chain (ch) = 4 rods = 66 feet
80 chains	= 1 survey mile (mi) = 320 rods = 5,280 feet

Troy Weight

24 grains	= 1 pennyweight (dwt)
20 pennyweights	= 1 ounce troy (oz t) = 480 grains
12 ounces troy	= 1 pound troy (lb t) = 240 pennyweights = 5,760 grains

Dry Measure

When necessary to distinguish the dry pint or quart from the liquid pint or quart, the word "dry" should be used in combination with the name or abbreviation of the dry unit.

2 pints (pt)	= 1 quart (qt) = 67.2006 cubic inches
8 quarts	= 1 peck (pk) = 537.605 cubic inches = 16 pints
4 pecks	= 1 bushel (bu) = 2,150.42 cubic inches = 32 quarts

Avoirdupois Weight

When necessary to distinguish the avoirdupois ounce or pound from the troy ounce or pound, the word "avoirdupois" or the abbreviation "avdp" should be used in combination with the name or abbreviation of the avoirdupois unit.

(The "grain" is the same in avoirdupois and troy weight.)

27 ¹¹/₃₂ grains	= 1 dram (dr)
16 drams	= 1 ounce (oz) = 437 ½ grains
16 ounces	= 1 pound (lb) = 256 drams = 7,000 grains
100 pounds	= 1 hundredweight (cwt)*
20 hundredweights	= 1 ton = 2,000 pounds*

In "gross" or "long" measure, the following values are recognized.

112 pounds	= 1 gross or long hundredweight*
20 gross or long hundredweights	= 1 gross or long ton = 2,240 pounds*

*When the terms "hundredweight" and "ton" are used unmodified, they are commonly understood to mean the 100-pound hundredweight and the 2,000-pound ton, respectively; these units may be designated "net" or "short" when necessary to distinguish them from the corresponding units in gross or long measure.

Tables of Equivalents

In this table it is necessary to distinguish between the "international" and the "survey" foot. The international foot, defined in 1959 as exactly equal to 0.3048 meter, is shorter than the old survey foot by approximately 6 parts in 10 million. The survey foot is still used in data expressed in feet in geodetic surveys within the U.S. In this table the survey foot is italicized.

When the name of a unit is enclosed in brackets thus, [1 hand], this indicates (1) that the unit is not in general current use in the United States, or (2) that the unit is believed to be based on "custom and usage" rather than on formal definition.

Equivalents involving decimals are, in most instances, rounded off to the third decimal place except where they are exact, in which cases these exact equivalents are so designated.

Lengths

1 angstrom (A)	0.1 nanometer (exactly) / 0.000 1 micron (exactly) / 0.000 000 1 millimeter (exactly) / 0.000 000 004 inch
1 cable's length	120 fathoms (exactly) / 720 *feet* (exactly) / 219 meters
1 centimeter (cm)	0.3937 inch
1 chain (ch) (Gunter's or surveyors)	66 *feet* (exactly) / 20.1168 meters
1 chain (engineers)	100 feet / 30.48 meters (exactly)
1 decimeter (dm)	3.937 inches
1 degree (geographical)	364,566.929 feet / 69.047 miles (avg.) / 111.123 kilometers (avg.)
-of latitude	68.078 miles at equator / 69.043 miles at poles
-of longitude	69.171 miles
1 dekameter (dam)	32.808 feet
1 fathom	6 *feet* (exactly) / 1.8288 meters (exactly)
1 foot (ft)	0.3048 meters (exactly)
1 furlong (fur)	10 chains (surveyors) (exactly) / 660 *feet* (exactly) / ⅛ survey mile (exactly) / 201.168 meters
[1 hand] (height measure for horses from ground to top of shoulders)	4 inches
1 inch (in)	2.54 centimeters (exactly)
1 kilometer (km)	0.621 mile / 3,281.5 feet
1 league (land)	3 survey miles (exactly) / 4.828 kilometers
1 link (Gunter's or surveyors)	7.92 inches (exactly) / 0.201 meter
1 link engineers	1 foot / 0.305 meter
1 meter (m)	39.37 inches / 1.094 yards
1 micron (u) [the Greek letter mu]	0.001 millimeter (exactly) / 0.000 039 37 inch
1 mil	0.001 inch (exactly) / 0.025 4 millimeter (exactly)
1 mile (mi) (survey or land)	5,280 *feet* (exactly) / 1.609 kilometers
1 international nautical mile (INM)	1.852 kilometers (exactly) / 1.150779 survey miles / 6,076.11549 feet
1 millimeter (mm)	0.039 37 inch
1 nanometer (nm)	0.001 micron (exactly) / 0.000 000 039 37 inch
1 pica (typography)	12 points
1 point (typography)	0.013 837 inch (exactly) / 0.351 millimeter
1 rod (rd), pole, or perch	16 ½ *feet* (exactly) / 5.029 meters
1 yard (yd)	0.9144 meter (exactly)

Areas or Surfaces

1 acre	43,560 square *feet* (exactly) / 4,840 square yards / 0.405 hectare
1 are (a)	119.599 square yards / 0.025 acre

(*continued*)
1 bolt (cloth measure):

length	100 yards (on modern looms)
width	{ 42 inches (usually, for cotton) 60 inches (usually, for wool)
1 hectare (ha) . . . . 2.471 acres
[1 square (building)] . . . . 100 square feet
1 square centimeter (cm²) . . . . 0.155 square inch
1 square decimeter (dm²) . . . . 15.500 square inches
1 square foot (ft²) . . . . 929.030 square centimeters
1 square inch (in²) . . . . 6.4516 square centimeters (exactly)
1 square kilometer (km²)	{ 247.105 acres 0.386 square mile
1 square meter (m²)	{ 1.196 square yards 10.764 square feet
1 square mile (mi²) . . . . 258.999 hectares
1 square millimeter (mm²) . . . . 0.002 square inch
1 square rod (rd²) sq. pole, or sq. perch . . . . 25.293 square meters
1 square yard (yd²) . . . . 0.836 square meter

Capacities or Volumes

1 barrel (bbl) liquid . . . . 31 to 42 gallons°

°There are a variety of "barrels," established by law or usage. For example: federal taxes on fermented liquors are based on a barrel of 31 gallons; many state laws fix the "barrel for liquids" as 31 ½ gallons; one state fixes a 36-gallon barrel for cistern measurement; federal law recognizes a 40-gallon barrel for "proof spirits"; by custom, 42 gallons comprise a barrel of crude oil or petroleum products for statistical purposes, and this equivalent is recognized "for liquids" by 4 states.

1 barrel (bbl), standard, for fruits, vegetables, and other dry commodities except dry cranberries	{ 7,056 cubic inches 105 dry quarts 3.281 bushels, struck measure
1 barrel (bbl), standard, cranberry	{ 5,826 cubic inches 86⁴⁵/₆₄ dry quarts 2.709 bushels, struck measure
1 board foot (lumber measure) . .	a foot-square board 1 inch thick
1 bushel (bu) (U.S.) (struck measure)	{ 2,150.42 cubic inches (exactly) 35.238 liters
[1 bushel, heaped (U.S.)]	{ 2,747.715 cubic inches 1.278 bushels, struck measure°

°Frequently recognized as 1¼ bushels, struck measure.

[1 bushel (bu) (British Imperial) (struck measure)]	{ 1.032 U.S. bushels struck measure 2,219.36 cubic inches
1 cord (cd) firewood . . . . 128 cubic feet (exactly)
1 cubic centimeter (cm³) . . . . 0.061 cubic inch
1 cubic decimeter (dm³) . . . . 61.024 cubic inches
1 cubic inch (in³)	{ 0.554 fluid ounce 4.433 fluid drams 16.387 cubic centimeters
1 cubic foot (ft³)	{ 7.481 gallons 28.317 cubic decimeters
1 cubic meter (m³) . . . . 1.308 cubic yards
1 cubic yard (yd³) . . . . 0.765 cubic meter
1 cup, measuring	{ 8 fluid ounces (exactly) ½ liquid pint (exactly)
[1 dram, fluid (fl dr) (British)]	{ 0.961 U.S. fluid dram 0.217 cubic inch 3.552 milliliters
1 dekaliter (dal)	{ 2.642 gallons 1.135 pecks
1 gallon (gal) (U.S.)	{ 231 cubic inches (exactly) 3.785 liters 0.833 British gallon 128 U.S. fluid ounces (exactly)
[1 gallon (gal) British Imperial] . .	{ 277.42 cubic inches 1.201 U.S. gallons 4.546 liters 160 British fluid ounces (exactly)
1 gill (gi)	{ 7.219 cubic inches 4 fluid ounces (exactly) 0.118 liter
1 hectoliter (hl)	{ 26.418 gallons 2.838 bushels
1 liter (l) (1 cubic decimeter exactly)	{ 1.057 liquid quarts 0.908 dry quart 61.025 cubic inches

1 milliliter (ml) (1 cu cm exactly)	{ 0.271 fluid dram 16.231 minims 0.061 cubic inch
1 ounce, liquid (U.S.)	{ 1.805 cubic inches 29.573 milliliters 1.041 British fluid ounces
[1 ounce, fluid (fl oz) (British)]	{ 0.961 U.S. fluid ounce 1.734 cubic inches 28.412 milliliters
1 peck (pk) . . . . 8.810 liters
1 pint (pt), dry	{ 33.600 cubic inches 0.551 liter
1 pint (pt), liquid	{ 28.875 cubic inches (exactly) 0.473 liter
1 quart (qt) dry (U.S.)	{ 67.201 cubic inches 1.101 liters 0.969 British quart
1 quart (qt) liquid (U.S.) . . .	{ 57.75 cubic in (exactly) 0.946 liter 0.833 British quart
[1 quart (qt) (British)]	{ 69.354 cubic inches 1.032 U.S. dry quarts 1.201 U.S. liquid quarts
tablespoon	{ 3 teaspoons°(exactly) 4 fluid drams ½ fluid ounce (exactly)
1 teaspoon	{ ⅓ tablespoon°(exactly) 1⅓ fluid drams°

°The equivalent "1 teaspoon—1⅓ fluid drams" has been found by the bureau to correspond more closely with the actual capacities of "measuring" and silver teaspoons than the equivalent "1 teaspoon—1 fluid dram" which is given by many dictionaries.

Weights or Masses

1 assay ton°° (AT) . . . . 29.167 grams

°°Used in assaying. The assay ton bears the same relation to the milligram that a ton of 2,000 pounds avoirdupois bears to the ounce troy; hence the weight in milligrams of precious metal obtained from one assay ton of ore gives directly the number of troy ounces to the net ton.

1 bale (cotton measure)	{ 500 pounds in U.S. 750 pounds in Egypt
1 carat (c)	{ 200 milligrams (exactly) 3.086 grains
1 dram avoirdupois (dr avdp) gamma, see microgram	{ 27¹¹/₃₂ (=27.344) grains 1.772 grams
1 grain . . . . 64.799 milligrams
1 gram	{ 15.432 grains 0.035 ounce, avoirdupois
1 hundredweight, gross or long°°° (gross cwt)	{ 112 pounds (exactly) 50.802 kilograms
1 hundredweight, net or short (cwt. or net cwt.)	{ 100 pounds (exactly) 45.359 kilograms
1 kilogram (kg) . . . . 2.205 pounds
1 microgram (µg [The Greek letter mu in combination with the letter g]) . . . . . 0.000001 gram (exactly)
1 milligram (mg) . . . . 0.015 grain
1 ounce, avoirdupois (oz avdp)	{ 437.5 grains (exactly) 0.911 troy ounce 28.350 grams
1 ounce, troy (oz t)	{ 480 grains (exactly) 1.097 avoirdupois ounces 31.103 grams
1 pennyweight (dwt) . . . . 1.555 grams
1 pound, avoirdupois (lb avdp)	{ 7,000 grains (exactly) 1.215 troy pounds 453.592 37 grams (exactly)
1 pound, troy (lb t)	{ 5,760 grains (exactly) 0.823 avoirdupois pound 373.242 grams
1 ton, gross or long°°° (gross ton)	{ 2,240 pounds (exactly) 1.12 net tons (exactly) 1.016 metric tons

°°°The gross or long ton and hundredweight are used commercially in the United States to only a limited extent, usually in restricted industrial fields. These units are the same as British "ton" and "hundredweight."

1 ton, metric (t)	{ 2,204.623 pounds 0.984 gross ton 1.102 net tons
1 ton, net or short (sh ton) . .	{ 2,000 pounds (exactly) 0.893 gross ton 0.907 metric ton

Tables of Interrelation of Units of Measurement

Units of length and area of the international and survey measures are included in the following tables. Units unique to the survey measure are italicized. See pg 808, Tables of Equivalents, 1st para.

1 international foot	= 0.999 998 survey foot (exactly)
1 survey foot	= 1200/3937 meter (exactly)
1 international foot	= 12 × 0.0254 meter (exactly)

Bold face type indicates exact values

Units of Length

Units	Inches	*Links*	Feet	Yards	*Rods*	*Chains*	Miles	cm	Meters
1 inch=	1	0.126 263	0.083 333	0.027 778	0.005 051	0.001 263	0.000 016	**2.54**	**0.025 4**
1 *link* =	**7.92**	1	**0.66**	0.22	0.04	0.01	0.000 125	20.117	0.201 168
1 foot=	**12**	1.515 152	1	0.333 333	0.060 606	0.015 152	0.000 189	**30.48**	**0.304 8**
1 yard=	**36**	4.545 45	**3**	1	0.181 818	0.045 455	0.000 568	**91.44**	**0.914 4**
1 *rod*=	**198**	**25**	**16.5**	**5.5**	1	0.25	0.003 125	502.92	5.029 2
1 *chain*=	**792**	**100**	**66**	**22**	**4**	1	0.012 5	2011.68	20.116 8
1 mile=	**63 360**	**8000**	**5280**	**1760**	**320**	**80**	1	160 934.4	1609.344
1 cm=	0.3937	0.049 710	0.032 808	0.010 936	0.001 988	0.000 497	0.000 006	1	**0.01**
1 meter=	39.37	4.970 960	3.280 840	1.093 613	0.198 838	0.049 710	0.000 621	**100**	1

Units of Area

Units	Sq. inches	*Sq. links*	Sq. feet	Sq. yards	*Sq. rods*	*Sq. chains*
1 sq. inch=	1	.015 942 3	0.006 944	0.000 771 605	0.000 025 5	0.000 001 594
1 sq. *link*=	62.726 4	1	**0.435 6**	0.0484	0.0016	**0.000 1**
1 sq. foot=	**144**	2.295 684	1	0.111 111 1	0.003 673 09	0.000 229 568
1 sq. yard=	**1296**	20.661 16	**9**	1	0.033 057 85	0.002 066 12
1 sq. *rod*=	**39 204**	**625**	272.25	30.25	1	**0.062 5**
1 sq. *chain*=	**627 264**	**10 000**	4 356	484	16	1
1 *acre*=	**6 272 640**	**100 000**	43 560	4 840	160	10
1 sq. mile=	**4 014 489 600**	**64 000 000**	27 878 400	3 097 600	102 400	6400
1 sq. cm=	0.155 000 3	0.002 471 05	0.001 076	0.000 119 599	0.000 003 954	0.000 000 247
1 sq. meter=	1550.003	24.710 44	10.763 91	1.195 990	0.039 536 70	0.002 471 044
1 *hectare*=	15 500 031	247 104	107 639.1	11 959.90	395.367 0	24.710 44

Units	*Acres*	Sq. miles	Sq. cm	Sq. meters	*Hectares*
1 sq. inch=	0.000 000 159 423	0.000 000 000 249 10	6.451 6	0.000 645 16	0.000 000 065
1 sq. *link*=	**0.000 01**	**0.000 000 015 625**	404.685 642 24	0.040 468 56	0.000 004 047
1 sq. foot=	0.000 022 956 84	0.000 000 035 870 06	929.034 1	0.092 903 41	0.000 009 290
1 sq. yard=	0.000 206 611 6	0.000 000 322 830 6	8 361.273 6	**0.836 127 36**	0.000 083 613
1 sq. *rod*=	**0.006 25**	0.000 000 765 625	252 929.5	25.292 95	0.002 529 295
1 *acre*=	**0.1**	**0.001 562 5**	4 046 873	404.687 3	0.040 468 73
1 sq. mile=	**640**	1	25 899 881 103	2 589 988.11	258.998 811 034
1 sq. cm=	0.000 000 024 711	0.000 000 000 038 610	**0.000 1**	**0.000 1**	**0.000 000 01**
1 sq. meter=	0.000 247 104 4	0.000 000 386 102 2	**10 000**	1	**0.0001**
1 *hectare*=	2.471 044	0.003 861 006	**100 000 000**	**10 000**	1

Units of Mass Not Greater than Pounds and Kilograms

Units	Grains	Pennyweights	Avdp drams	Avdp ounces
1 grain=	1	0.041 666 67	0.036 571 43	0.002 285 71
1 pennyweight=	**24**	1	0.877 714 3	0.054 857 14
1 dram avdp=	**27.343 75**	1.139 323	1	**0.062 5**
1 ounce avdp=	**437.5**	18.229 17	**16**	1
1 ounce troy=	**480**	**20**	17.554 29	1.097 143
1 pound troy=	**5760**	**240**	210.651 4	13.165 71
1 pound avdp=	**7000**	291.666 7	**256**	**16**
1 milligram=	0.015 432	0.000 643 015	0.000 564 383	0.000 035 274
1 gram=	15.432 36	0.643 014 9	0.564 383 4	0.035 273 96
1 kilogram=	15 432.36	643.014 9	564.383 4	35.273 96

Units	Troy ounces	Troy pounds	Avdp pounds	Milligrams	Grams	Kilograms
1 grain=	0.002 083 33	0.000 173 611	0.000 142 857	64.798 91	0.064 798 91	0.000 064 799
1 pennyw't.=	**0.05**	0.004 166 667	0.003 428 571	1555.173 84	1.555 173 84	0.001 555 174
1 dram avdp=	0.056 966 15	0.004 747 179	0.003 906 25	1771.845 195	1.771 845 195	0.001 771 845
1 oz avdp=	0.911 458 3	0.075 954 86	**0.062 5**	28 349.523 125	28.349 523 125	0.028 349 52
1 oz troy=	1	0.083 333 333	0.068 571 43	31 103.476 8	31.103 476 8	0.031 103 48
1 lb troy=	**12**	1	0.822 857 1	373 241.721 6	373.241 721 6	0.373 241 722
1 lb avdp=	14.583 33	1.215 278	1	453 592.37	453.592 37	**0.453 592 37**
1 milligram=	0.000 032 151	0.000 002 679	0.000 002 205	1	0.001	0.000 001
1 gram=	0.032 150 75	0.002 679 229	0.002 204 623	**1000**	0.001	**0.000 001**
1 kilogram=	32.150 75	2.679 229	2.204 623	**1 000 000**	**1000**	1

Units of Mass Not Less than Avoirdupois Ounces

Units	Avdp oz	Avdp lb	Short cwt	Short tons	Long tons	Kilograms	Metric tons
1 oz av=	1	0.0625	0.000 625	0.000 031 25	0.000 027 902	0.028 349 523	0.000 028 350
1 lb av=	**16**	1	0.01	0.000 5	0.000 446 429	**0.453 592 37**	0.000 453 592
1 sh cwt=	**1 600**	**100**	1	0.05	0.044 642 86	45.359 237	0.045 359 237
1 sh ton=	**32 000**	**2000**	**20**	1	0.892 857 1	907.184 74	0.907 184 74
1 long ton=	**35 840**	**2240**	**22.4**	**1.12**	1	1016.046 908 8	1.016 046 909
1 kg=	35.273 96	2.204 623	0.022 046 23	0.001 102 311	0.000 984 207	1	**0.001**
1 metric ton=	35 273.96	2 204.623	22.046 23	1.102 311	0.984 206 5	**1000**	1

(continued)

Units of Volume

Units	Cubic inches	Cubic feet	Cubic yards	Cubic cm	Cubic dm	Cubic meters
1 cubic inch =	1	0.000 578 704	0.000 021 433	16.387 064	0.016 387	0.000 016 387
1 cubic foot =	1728	1	0.037 037 04	28 316.846 592	28.316 847	0.028 316 847
1 cubic yard =	46 656	27	1	764 554.857 984	764.554 858	0.764 554 858
1 cubic cm =	0.061 023 74	0.000 035 315	0.000 001 308	1	0.001	0.000 001
1 cubic dm =	61.023 74	0.035 314 67	0.001 307 951	1 000	1	0.001
1 cubic meter =	61 023.74	35.314 67	1.307 951	1 000 000	1000	1

Units of Capacity (Liquid Measure)

Units	Minims	Fluid drams	Fluid ounces	Gills	Liquid pt
1 minim =	1	0.016 666 7	0.002 083 33	0.000 520 833	0.000 130 208
1 fluid dram =	60	1	0.125	0.031 25	0.007 812 5
1 fluid ounce =	480	8	1	0.25	0.062 5
1 gill =	1920	32	4	1	0.25
1 liquid pint =	7680	128	16	4	1
1 liquid quart =	15 360	256	32	8	2
1 gallon =	61 440	1024	128	32	8
1 cubic inch =	265.974	4.432 900	0.554 112 6	0.138 528 1	0.034 632 03
1 cubic foot =	459 603.1	7 660.052	957.506 5	239.376 6	59.844 16
1 milliliter =	16.230 73	0.270 512 18	0.033 814 02	0.008 453 506	.002 113 376
1 liter =	16 230.73	270.512 18	33.814 02	8.453 506	2.113 376

Units	Liquid quarts	Gallons	Cubic inches	Cubic feet	Liters
1 minim =	0.000 065 104 17	0.000 016 276 04	0.003 759 766	0.000 002 175 790	0.000 061 611 52
1 flu. dram =	0.003 906 25	0.000 976 562 5	0.225 585 9	0.000 130 547 4	0.003 696 691
1 fluid oz =	0.031 25	0.007 812 5	1.804 687 5	0.001 044 379	0.029 573 53
1 gill =	0.125	0.031 25	7.218 75	0.004 177 517	0.118 294 118
1 liquid pt =	0.5	0.125	28.875	0.016 710 07	0.473 176 473
1 liquid qt =	1	0.25	57.75	0.033 420 14	0.946 352 946
1 gallon =	4	1	231	0.133 680 6	3.785 411 784
1 cubic in. =	0.017 316 02	0.004 329 004	1	0.000 578 703 7	0.016 387 064
1 cubic foot =	29.922 08	7.480 519	1728	1	28.316 846 592
1 liter =	1.056 688	0.264 172 05	61.023 74	0.035 314 67	1

Units of Capacity (Dry Measure)

Units	Dry pints	Dry quarts	Pecks	Bushels	Cubic in.	Liters
1 dry pint =	1	0.5	0.062 5	0.015 625	33.600 312 5	0.550 610 47
1 dry quart =	2	1	0.125	0.031 25	67.200 625	1.101 220 9
1 peck =	16	8	1	0.25	537.605	8.809 767 5
1 bushel =	64	32	4	1	2150.42	35.239 07
1 cubic inch =	0.029 761 6	0.014 880 8	0.001 860 10	0.000 465 025	1	0.016 387 06
1 liter =	1.816 166	0.908 083	0.113 510 37	0.028 377 59	61.023 74	1

Miscellaneous Measures

Caliber—the diameter of a gun bore. In the U.S., caliber is traditionally expressed in hundredths of inches, eg. .22 or .30. In Britain, caliber is often expressed in thousandths of inches, eg. .270 or .465. Now, it is commonly expressed in millimeters, eg. the 7.62 mm. M14 rifle and the 5.56 mm. M16 rifle. Heavier weapons' caliber has long been expressed in millimeters, eg. the 81 mm. mortar, the 105 mm. howitzer (light), the 155 mm. howitzer (medium or heavy).

Naval guns' caliber refers to the barrel length as a multiple of the bore diameter. A 5-inch, 50-caliber naval gun has a 5-inch bore and a barrel length of 250 inches.

Carat, karat—a measure of the amount of alloy per 24 parts in gold. Thus 24-carat gold is pure; 18-carat gold is one-fourth alloy.

Decibel (db)—a measure of the relative loudness or intensity of sound. A 20-decibel sound is 10 times louder than a 10-decibel sound; 30 decibels is 100 times louder; 40 decibels is 1,000 times louder, etc. One decibel is the smallest difference between sounds detectable by the human ear. A 140-decibel sound is painful.

10 decibels	– a light whisper
20	– quiet conversation
30	– normal conversation
40	– light traffic
50	– typewriter, loud conversation
60	– noisy office
70	– normal traffic, quiet train
80	– rock music, subway
90	– heavy traffic, thunder
100	– jet plane at takeoff

Em—a printer's measure designating the square width of any given type size. Thus, an em of 10-point type is 10 points. An en is half an em.

Gauge—a measure of shotgun bore diameter. Gauge numbers originally referred to the number of lead balls of the gun barrel diameter in a pound. Thus, a 16 gauge shotgun's bore was smaller than a 12-gauge shotgun's. Today, an international agreement assigns millimeter measures to each gauge, eg:

Gauge	Bore diameter in mm.
6	23.34
10	19.67
12	18.52
14	17.60
16	16.81
20	15.90

Horsepower—the energy needed to lift 550 pounds one foot in one second, or to lift 33,000 pounds one foot in one minute. Equivalent to 746 watts or 2,546.0756 btu.

Quire—25 sheets of paper

Ream—500 sheets of paper

Electrical Units

The **watt** is the unit of power (electrical, mechanical, thermal, etc.). Electrical power is given by the product of the voltage and the current.

Energy is sold by the **joule**, but in common practice the billing of electrical energy is expressed in terms of the kilowatt-hour, which is 3,600,000 joules or 3.6 megajoules.

The **horsepower** is a non-metric unit sometimes used in mechanics. It is equal to 746 watts.

The **ohm** is the unit of electrical resistance and represents the physical property of a conductor which offers a resistance to the flow of electricity, permitting just 1 ampere to flow at 1 volt of pressure.

Simple Interest Table

	Time	4%	5%	6%	7%	8%	9%	10%	11%	12%	13%	14%
$1.00	1 month........	$.003	$.004	$.005	$.005	$.006	.008	.008	.009	.010	.011	.012
..	2 months......	.007	.008	.010	.011	.013	.015	.017	.018	.020	.022	.023
..	3.......	.010	.013	.015	.017	.020	.023	.025	.028	.030	.033	.035
..	6.......	.020	.025	.030	.035	.040	.045	.050	.055	.060	.065	.070
..	12.......	.040	.050	.060	.070	.080	.090	.100	.110	.120	.130	.140
$100.00	1 day	.011	.013	.016	.019	.022	.025	.027	.030	.033	.036	.038
..	2 days.....	.022	.027	.032	.038	.044	.049	.055	.060	.066	.071	.077
..	3......	.033	.041	.050	.058	.067	.074	.082	.090	.099	.107	.115
..	4......	.045	.053	.066	.077	.089	.099	.110	.121	.132	.142	.153
..	5......	.056	.069	.082	.097	.111	.123	.137	.151	.164	.178	.192
..	6......	.067	.083	.100	.116	.133	.148	.164	.181	.197	.214	.230
..	1 month	.334	.416	.500	.583	.667	.750	.833	.917	1.000	1.083	1.167
..	2 months ...	.667	.832	1.000	1.166	1.333	1.500	1.667	1.833	2.000	2.167	2.333
..	3........	1.000	1.250	1.500	1.750	2.000	2.250	2.500	2.750	3.000	3.250	3.500
..	6........	2.000	2.500	3.000	3.500	4.000	4.500	5.000	5.500	6.000	6.500	7.000
..	12........	4.000	5.000	6.000	7.000	8.000	9.000	10.000	11.000	12.000	13.000	14.000

Ancient Measures

Biblical
Cubit = 21.8 inches
Omer = 0.45 peck
3.964 liters
Ephah = 10 omers
Shekel = 0.497 ounce
14.1 grams

Greek
Cubit = 18.3 inches
Stadion = 607.2 or 622 feet
Obolos = 715.38 milligrams
Drachma = 4.2923 grams
Mina = 0.9463 pounds
Talent = 60 mina

Roman
Cubit = 17.5 inches
Stadium = 202 yards
As, libra, = 325.971 grams,
pondus .71864 pounds

Weight of Water

1	cubic inch.............	.0360	pound	1	imperial gallon.........	10.0	pounds
12	cubic inches...........	.433	pound	11.2	imperial gallons.........	112.0	pounds
1	cubic foot............	62.4	pounds	224	imperial gallons.........	2240.0	pounds
1	cubic foot............	7.48052	U.S. gal	1	U.S. gallon............	8.33	pounds
1.8	cubic feet............	112.0	pounds	13.45	U.S. gallons...........	112.0	pounds
35.96	cubic feet............	2240.0	pounds	269.0	U.S. gallons...........	2240.0	pounds

Density of Gases and Vapors

Source: National Bureau of Standards (kilograms per cubic meter)

Gas	Wgt.	Gas	Wgt.	Gas	Wgt.
Acetylene...........	1.171	Ethylene...........	1.260	Methyl fluoride........	1.545
Air.............	1.293	Fluorine............	1.696	Mono methylamine	1.38
Ammonia..........	.759	Helium............	.178	Neon............	.900
Argon............	1.784	Hydrogen...........	.090	Nitric oxide..........	1.341
Arsene...........	3.48	Hydrogen bromide.....	3.50	Nitrogen...........	1.250
Butane-iso..........	2.60	Hydrogen chloride......	1.639	Nitrosyl chloride.......	2.99
Butane-n..........	2.519	Hydrogen-iodide.......	5.724	Nitrous oxide.........	1.997
Carbon dioxide.......	1.977	Hydrogen selenide.....	3.66	Oxygen...........	1.429
Carbon monoxide......	1.250	Hydrogen sulfide......	1.539	Phosphine..........	1.48
Carbon oxysulfide.....	2.72	Krypton...........	3.745	Propane...........	2.020
Chlorine..........	3.214	Methane...........	.717	Silicon tetrafluoride.....	4.67
Chlorine monoxide.....	3.89	Methyl chloride.......	2.25	Sulfur dioxide........	2.927
Ethane...........	1.356	Methyl ether.........	2.091	Xenon............	5.897

Temperature Conversion Table

The numbers in **bold face type** refer to the temperature either in degrees Celsius or Fahrenheit which are to be converted. If converting from degrees Fahrenheit to Celsius, the equivalent will be found in the column on the left, while if converting from degrees Celsius to Fahrenheit the answer will be found in the column on the right.

For temperatures not shown. To convert Fahrenheit to Celsius subtract 32 degrees and multiply by 5, divide by 9; to convert Celsius to Fahrenheit, multiply by 9, divide by 5 and add 32 degrees.

Celsius		Fahrenheit	Celsius		Fahrenheit	Celsius		Fahrenheit
− 273.2	− 459.7	....	− 17.8	0	32	35.0	95	203
− 184	− 300	....	− 12.2	10	50	36.7	98	208.4
− 169	− 273	− 459.4	− 6.67	20	68	37.8	100	212
− 157	− 250	− 418	− 1.11	30	86	43	110	230
− 129	− 200	− 328	4.44	40	104	49	120	248
− 101	− 150	− 238	10.0	50	122	54	130	266
− 73.3	− 100	− 148	15.6	60	140	60	140	284
− 45.6	− 50	− 58	21.1	70	158	66	150	302
− 40.0	− 40	− 40	23.9	75	167	93	200	392
− 34.4	− 30	− 22	26.7	80	176	121	250	482
− 28.9	− 20	− 4	29.4	85	185	149	300	572
− 23.3	− 10	14	32.2	90	194			

Water boils at 212° Fahrenheit at sea level. For every 550 feet above sea level, boiling point of water is lower by about 1° Fahrenheit. Methyl alcohol boils at 148° Fahrenheit. Average human oral temperature, 98.6° Fahrenheit. Water freezes at 32° Fahrenheit. Although "Centigrade" is still frequently used, the International Committee on Weights and Measures and the National Bureau of Standards have recommended since 1948 that this scale be called "Celsius."

Breaking the Sound Barrier; Speed of Sound

The prefix Mach is used to describe supersonic speed. It derives from Ernst Mach, a Czech-born German physicist, who contributed to the study of sound. When a plane moves at the speed of sound it is Mach 1. When twice the speed of sound it is Mach 2. When it is near but below the speed of sound its speed can be designated at less than Mach 1, for example, Mach .90. Mach is defined as "in jet propulsion, the ratio of the velocity of a rocket or a jet to the velocity of sound in the medium being considered."

When a plane passes the sound barrier—flying faster than sound travels—listeners in the area hear thunderclaps, but pilots do not hear them.

Sound is produced by vibrations of an object and is transmitted by alternate increase and decrease in pressures that radiate outward through a material media of molecules —somewhat like waves spreading out on a pond after a rock has been tossed into it.

The frequency of sound is determined by the number of times the vibrating waves undulate per second, and is measured in cycles per second. The slower the cycle of waves, the lower the sound. As frequencies increase, the sound is higher.

Sound is audible to human beings only if the frequency falls within a certain range. The human ear is usually not sensitive to frequencies of less than 20 vibrations per second, or more than about 20,000 vibrations per second—although this range varies among individuals. Anything at a pitch higher than the human ear can hear is termed ultrasonic.

Intensity or loudness is the strength of the pressure of these radiating waves, and is measured in decibels. The human ear responds to intensity in a range from zero to 120 decibels. Any sound with pressure over 120 decibels is painful.

The speed of sound is generally placed at 1,088 ft. per second at sea level at 32°F. It varies in other temperatures and in different media. Sound travels faster in water than in air, and even faster in iron and steel. If in air it travels a mile in 5 seconds, it does a mile under water in 1 second, and through iron in ⅓ of a second. It travels through ice cold vapor at approximately 4,708 ft. per sec., ice-cold water, 4,938; granite, 12,960; hardwood, 12,620; brick, 11,960; glass, 16,410 to 19,690; silver, 8,658; gold, 5,717.

Colors of the Spectrum

Color, an electromagnetic wave phenomenon, is a sensation produced through the excitation of the retina of the eye by rays of light. The colors of the spectrum may be produced by viewing a light beam refracted by passage through a prism, which breaks the light into its wave lengths.

Customarily, the primary colors of the spectrum are thought of as those 6 monochromatic colors which occupy relatively large areas of the spectrum: red, orange, yellow, green, blue, and violet. However, Sir Isaac Newton named a 7th, indigo, situated between blue and violet on the spectrum. Aubert estimated (1865) the solar spectrum to contain approximately 1,000 distinguishable hues of which according to Rood (1881) 2 million tints and shades can be distinguished; Luckiesh stated (1915) that 55 distinctly different hues have been seen in a single spectrum.

By many physicists only 3 primary colors are recognized: red, yellow, and blue (Mayer, 1775); red, green, and violet (Thomas Young, 1801); red, green, and blue (Clerk Maxwell, 1860).

The color sensation of black is due to complete lack of stimulation of the retina, that of white to complete stimulation. The infra-red and ultra-violet rays, below the red (long) end of the spectrum and above the violet (short) end respectively, are invisible to the naked eye. Heat is the principal effect of the infra-red rays and chemical action that of the ultra-violet rays.

Common Fractions Reduced to Decimals

8ths	16ths	32ds	64ths		8ths	16ths	32ds	64ths		8ths	16ths	32ds	64ths	
			1	.015625				23	.359375				45	.703125
		1	2	.03125	3	6	12	24	.375			23	46	.71875
			3	.046875				25	.390625				47	.734375
	1	2	4	.0625				13 26	.40625	6	12	24	48	.75
			5	.078125				27	.421875				49	.765625
		3	6	.09375		7	14	28	.4375			25	50	.78125
			7	.109375				29	.453125				51	.796875
1	2	4	8	.125				15 30	.46875			13 26	52	.8125
			9	.140625				31	.484375				53	.828125
		5	10	.15625	4	8	16	32	.5			27	54	.84375
			11	.171875				33	.515625				55	.859375
	3	6	12	.1875				17 34	.53125	7	14	28	56	.875
			13	.203125				35	.546875				57	.890625
		7	14	.21875		9	18	36	.5625			29	58	.90625
			15	.234375				37	.578125				59	.921875
2	4	8	16	.25				19 38	.59375			15 30	60	.9375
			17	.265625				39	.609375				61	.953125
		9	18	.28125	5	10	20	40	.625			31	62	.96875
			19	.296875				41	.640625				63	.984375
	5	10	20	.3125				21 42	.65625	8	16	32	64	1.
			21	.328125				43	.671875					
		11	22	.34375		11	22	44	.6875					

Spirits Measures

Pony	0.5 jigger			For champagne only:	
Shot	0.666 jigger	Quart	32 shots	Rehoboam	3 magnums
	1.0 ounce		1.25 fifth	Methuselah	4 magnums
Jigger	1.5 shot		2 quarts	Salmanazar	6 magnums
	16 shots	Magnum	2.49797 bottles	Balthazar	8 magnums
Pint	0.625 fifth		(wine)	Nebuchadnezzar .	10 magnums
	25.6 shots	For champagne and brandy only:			
	1.6 pints		6.4 pints	Wine bottle (standard):	
Fifth	0.8 quart	Jeroboam	1.6 magnum		0.800633 quart
	0.75706 liter		0.8 gallon	. . . .	0.7576778 liter

Mathematical Formulas

To find the CIRCUMFERENCE of a:

Circle — Multiply the diameter by 3.14159265 (usually 3.1416).

To find the AREA of a:

Circle — Multiply the square of the diameter by .785398 (usually .7854).

Rectangle — Multiply the length of the base by the height.

Sphere (surface) — Multiply the square of the radius by 3.1416 and multiply by 4.

Square — Square the length of one side.

Trapezoid — Add the two parallel sides, multiply by the height and divide by 2.

Triangle — Multiply the base by the height and divide by 2.

To find the VOLUME of a:

Cone — Multiply the square of the radius of the base by 3.1416, multiply by the height, and divide by 3.

Cube — Cube the length of one edge.

Cylinder — Multiply the square of the radius of the base by 3.1416 and multiply by the height.

Pyramid — Multiply the area of the base by the height and divide by 3.

Rectangular Prism — Multiply the length by the width by the height.

Sphere — Multiply the cube of the radius by 3.1416, multiply by 4 and divide by 3.

Playing Cards and Dice Chances

Poker Hands

Hand	Number possible	Odds against
Royal flush	4	649,739 to 1
Other straight flush	36	72,192 to 1
Four of a kind	624	4,164 to 1
Full house	3,744	693 to 1
Flush	5,108	508 to 1
Straight	10,200	254 to 1
Three of a kind	54,912	46 to 1
Two pairs	123,552	20 to 1
One pair	1,098,240	4 to 3 (1.37 to 1)
Nothing	1,302,540	1 to 1
Total	**2,598,960**	

Dice
(Probabilities of consecutive winning plays)

No. consecutive wins	By 7, 11 or point	No. consecutive wins	By 7, 11 or point
1	244 in 495	6	1 in 70
2	6 in 25	7	1 in 141
3	3 in 25	8	1 in 287
4	1 in 17	9	1 in 582
5	1 in 34		

Dice
(probabilities on 2 dice)

Total	Odds against (Single toss)	Total	Odds against (Single toss)
2	35 to 1	8	31 to 5
3	17 to 1	9	8 to 1
4	11 to 1	10	11 to 1
5	8 to 1	11	17 to 1
6	31 to 5	12	35 to 1
7	5 to 1		

Pinochle Auction
(Odds against finding in "widow" of 3 cards)

Open places	Odds against	Open places	Odds against
1	5 to 1	4	3 to 2 for
2	2 to 1	5	2 to 1 for
3	Even		

Bridge
The odds—against suit distribution in a hand of 4-4-3-2 are about 4 to 1, against 5-4-2-2 about 8 to 1, against 6-4-2-1 about 20 to 1, against 7-4-1-1 about 254 to 1, against 8-4-1-0 about 2,211 to 1, and against 13-0-0-0 about 158,753,389,899 to 1.

Measures of Force and Pressure

Dyne = force necessary to accelerate a 1-gram mass 1 centimeter per second per second = 0.000072 poundals

Poundal = force necessary to accelerate a 1-pound mass 1 foot per second per second = 13,825.5 dynes = 0.138255 newtons

Newton = force which, applied for 1 second, will give a velocity of 1 meter per second to a 1-kilogram mass = 100 dynes per square centimeter = 100 microbars = 7.233 poundals

Pascal (pressure) = 1 newton per square meter = 0.020885 pound per square foot

Atmosphere (air pressure at sea level) = 2,116.102 pounds per square foot = 14.6952 pounds per square inch = 1.0332 kilograms per square centimeter = 101,323 newtons per square meter.

Large Numbers

U.S.	Number of zeros	French British, German	U.S.	Number of zeros	French British, German
million	6	million	sextillion	21	1,000 trillion
billion	9	milliard	septillion	24	quadrillion
trillion	12	billion	octillion	27	1,000 quadrillion
quadrillion	15	1,000 billion	nonillion	30	quintillion
quintillion	18	trillion	decillion	33	1,000 quintillion

Roman Numerals

I	–	1	VI	–	6	XI	–	11	L	–	50	CD	–	400	X	–	10,000
II	–	2	VII	–	7	XIX	–	19	LX	–	60	D	–	500	L	–	50,000
III	–	3	VIII	–	8	XX	–	20	XC	–	90	CM	–	900	C	–	100,000
IV	–	4	IX	–	9	XXX	–	30	C	–	100	M	–	1,000	D	–	500,000
V	–	5	X	–	10	XL	–	40	CC	–	200	V	–	5,000	M	–	1,000,000

Chemical Elements, Discoverers, Atomic Weights

Atomic weights, based on the exact number 12 as the assigned atomic mass of the principal isotope of carbon, carbon 12, are provided through the courtesy of the International Union of Pure and Applied Chemistry and Butterworth Scientific Publications.

For the radioactive elements, with the exception of uranium and thorium, the mass number of either the isotope of longest half-life (*) or the better known isotope (**) is given.

Chemical element	Symbol	Atomic number	Atomic weight	Year discov.	Discoverer
Actinium	Ac	89	227*	1899	Debierne
Aluminum	Al	13	26.9815	1825	Oersted
Americium	Am	95	243*	1944	Seaborg, et al.
Antimony	Sb	51	121.76	1450	Valentine
Argon	Ar	18	39.948	1894	Rayleigh, Ramsay
Arsenic	As	33	74.9216	13th c.	Albertus Magnus
Astatine	At	85	210*	1940	Corson, et al.
Barium	Ba	56	137.34	1808	Davy
Berkelium	Bk	97	249**	1949	Thompson, Ghiorso, Seaborg
Beryllium	Be	4	9.0122	1790	Vauquelin
Bismuth	Bi	83	208.980	15th c.	Valentine
Boron	B	5	10.811a	1808	Gay-Lussac, Thenard
Bromine	Br	35	79.904b	1826	Balard
Cadmium	Cd	48	112.40	1817	Stromeyer
Calcium	Ca	20	40.08	1808	Davy
Californium	Cf	98	251**	1950	Thompson, et al.
Carbon	C	6	12.01115a	B.C.	
Cerium	Ce	58	140.12	1803	Klaproth
Cesium	Cs	55	132.905	1860	Bunsen, Kirchhoff
Chlorine	Cl	17	35.453b	1774	Scheele
Chromium	Cr	24	51.996b	1797	Vauquelin
Cobalt	Co	27	58.9332	1735	Brandt
Copper	Cu	29	63.546b	B.C.	
Curium	Cm	96	247*	1944	Seaborg, James, Ghiorso
Dysprosium	Dy	66	162.50	1886	Boisbaudran
Einsteinium	Es	99	254*	1952	Ghiorso, et al.
Erbium	Er	68	167.26	1843	Mosander
Europium	Eu	63	151.96	1901	Demarcay
Fermium	Fm	100	257*	1953	Ghiorso, et al.
Fluorine	F	9	18.9984	1771	Scheele
Francium	Fr	87	223*	1939	Perey
Gadolinium	Gd	64	157.25	1886	Marignac
Gallium	Ga	31	69.72	1875	Boisbaudran
Germanium	Ge	32	72.59	1886	Winkler
Gold	Au	79	196.967	B.C.	
Hafnium	Hf	72	178.49	1923	Coster, Hevesy
Hahnium	Ha	105	262*	1970	Ghiorso, et al.
Helium	He	2	4.0026	1868	Janssen, Lockyer
Holmium	Ho	67	164.930	1878	Soret, Delafontaine
Hydrogen	H	1	1.00797a	1766	Cavendish
Indium	In	49	114.82	1863	Reich, Richter
Iodine	I	53	126.9044	1811	Courtois
Iridium	Ir	77	192.2	1804	Tennant
Iron	Fe	26	55.847b	B.C.	
Krypton	Kr	36	83.80	1898	Ramsay, Travers
Lanthanum	La	57	138.91	1839	Mosander
Lawrencium	Lr	103	256*	1961	Ghiorso, T. Sikkeland, A.E. Larsh, and R.M. Latimer
Lead	Pb	82	207.19	B.C.	
Lithium	Li	3	6.939	1817	Arfvedson
Lutetium	Lu	71	174.97	1907	Welsbach, Urbain
Magnesium	Mg	12	24.312	1829	Bussy
Manganese	Mn	25	54.9380	1774	Gahn
Mendelevium	Md	101	258*	1955	Ghiorso, et al.
Mercury	Hg	80	200.59	B.C.	
Molybdenum	Mo	42	95.94	1782	Hjelm
Neodymium	Nd	60	144.24	1885	Welsbach
Neon	Ne	10	20.183	1898	Ramsay, Travers
Neptunium	Np	93	237*	1940	McMillan, Abelson
Nickel	Ni	28	58.71	1751	Cronstedt
Niobium¹	Nb	41	92.906	1801	Hatchett
Nitrogen	N	7	14.0067	1772	Rutherford
Nobelium	No	102	255*	1958	Ghiorso, et al.
Osmium	Os	76	190.2	1804	Tennant
Oxygen	O	8	15.9994a	1774	Priestley, Scheele
Palladium	Pd	46	106.4	1803	Wollaston
Phosphorus	P	15	30.9738	1669	Brand
Platinum	Pt	78	195.09	1735	Ulloa
Plutonium	Pu	94	242**	1940	Seaborg, et al.
Polonium	Po	84	210**	1898	P. and M. Curie
Potassium	K	19	39.102	1807	Davy
Praseodymium	Pr	59	140.907	1885	Welsbach
Promethium	Pm	61	147**	1945	Glendenin, Marinsky, Coryell
Protactinium	Pa	91	231*	1917	Hahn, Meitner
Radium	Ra	88	226*	1898	P. & M. Curie, Bemont
Radon	Rn	86	222*	1900	Dorn
Rhenium	Re	75	186.2	1925	Noddack, Tacke, Berg
Rhodium	Rh	45	102.905	1803	Wollaston
Rubidium	Rb	37	85.47	1861	Bunsen, Kirchhoff
Ruthenium	Ru	44	101.07	1845	Klaus
Rutherfordium	Rf	104	261*	1969	Ghiorso, et al.

Chemical element	Symbol	Atomic number	Atomic weight	Year discov.	Discoverer
Samarium	Sm	62	150.35	1879	Boisbaudran
Scandium	Sc	21	44.956	1879	Nilson
Selenium	Se	34	78.96	1817	Berzelius
Silicon	Si	14	28.086a	1823	Berzelius
Silver	Ag	47	107.868b	B.C.	
Sodium	Na	11	22.9898	1807	Davy
Strontium	Sr	38	87.62	1790	Crawford
Sulfur	S	16	32.064a	B.C.	
Tantalum	Ta	73	180.948	1802	Ekeberg
Technetium	Tc	43	99**	1937	Perrier and Segre
Tellurium	Te	52	127.60	1782	Von Reichenstein
Terbium	Tb	65	158.924	1843	Mosander
Thallium	Tl	81	204.37	1861	Crookes
Thorium	Th	90	232.038	1828	Berzelius
Thulium	Tm	69	168.934	1879	Cleve
Tin	Sn	50	118.69	B.C.	
Titanium	Ti	22	47.90	1791	Gregor
Tungsten (Wolfram)	W	74	183.85	1783	d'Elhujar
Uranium	U	92	238.03	1789	Klaproth
Vanadium	V	23	50.942	1830	Sefstrom
Xenon	Xe	54	131.30	1898	Ramsay, Travers
Ytterbium	Yb	70	173.04	1878	Marignac
Yttrium	Y	39	88.905	1794	Gadolin
Zinc	Zn	30	65.37	B.C.	
Zirconium	Zr	40	91.22	1789	Klaproth

(1) Formerly Columbium. (a) Atomic weights so designated are known to be variable because of natural variations in isotopic composition. The observed ranges are: hydrogen±0.0001; boron±0.003; carbon±0.005; oxygen±0.0001; silicon±0.001; sulfur±0.003. (b) Atomic weights so designated are believed to have the following experimental uncertainties: chlorine±0.001; chromium±0.001; iron±0.003; bromine±0.001; silver±0.001; copper±0.001.

Inventions and Scientific Discoveries

Invention	Date	Inventor	Nation.
Adding machine	1642	Pascal	French
Adding machine	1885	Burroughs	U.S.
Addressograph	1892	Duncan	U.S.
Aerosol spray	1941	Goodhue	U.S.
Air brake	1868	Westinghouse	U.S.
Air conditioning	1911	Carrier	U.S.
Air pump	1650	Guericke	German
Airplane, automatic pilot	1929	Green	U.S.
Airplane, experimental	1896	Langley	U.S.
Airplane jet engine	1939	Ohain	German
Airplane with motor	1903	Wright bros.	U.S.
Airplane, hydro	1911	Curtiss	U.S.
Airship	1852	Giffard	French
Airship, rigid dirigible	1900	Zeppelin	German
Arc tube	1923	Alexanderson	U.S.
Autogyro	1920	de la Cierva	Spanish
Automobile, differential gear	1885	Benz	German
Automobile, electric	1892	Morrison	U.S.
Automobile, exp'mtl	1875	Marcus	Austrian
Automobile, gasoline	1887	Daimler	German
Automobile, gasoline	1892	Duryea	U.S.
Automobile magneto	1897	Bosch	German
Automobile muffler	...	Maxim, H.P.	U.S.
Automobile self-starter	1911	Kettering	U.S.
Automobile, steam	1889	Roper	U.S.
Babbitt metal	1839	Babbitt	U.S.
Bakelite	1907	Baekeland	Belg., U.S.
Balloon	1783	Montgolfier	French
Barometer	1643	Torricelli	Italian
Bicycle, modern	1884	Starley	English
Bifocal lens	1780	Franklin	U.S.
Block signals, railway	1867	Hall	U.S.
Bomb, depth	1916	Tait	U.S.
Bottle machine	1903	Owens	U.S.
Braille printing	1829	Braille	French
Burner, gas	1855	Bunsen	German
Calculating machine	1823	Babbage	English
Camera—see also Photography			
Camera, Kodak	1888	Eastman, Walker	U.S.
Camera, Polaroid Land	1948	Land	U.S.
Car coupler	1873	Janney	U.S.
Carburetor, gasoline	1876	Daimler	German
Card time recorder	1894	Cooper	U.S.
Carding machine	1797	Whittemore	U.S.
Carpet sweeper	1876	Bissell	U.S.
Cash register	1879	Ritty	U.S.
Cathode ray tube	1878	Crookes	English
Cellophane	1911	Brandenberger	Swiss
Celluloid	1870	Hyatt	U.S.

Invention	Date	Inventor	Nation.
Cement, Portland	1845	Aspdin	English
Chronometer	1735	Harrison	English
Circuit breaker	1925	Hilliard	U.S.
Clock, pendulum	1657	Huygens	Dutch
Coaxial cable system	1929	Affel, Espen-sched	U.S.
Coke oven	1893	Hoffman	Austrian
Compressed air rock drill	1871	Ingersoll	U.S.
Comptometer	1887	Felt	U.S.
Computer, automatic sequence	1939	Aiken et al.	U.S.
Condenser microphone (telephone)	1920	Wente	U.S.
Corn, hybrid	1917	Jones	U.S.
Cotton gin	1793	Whitney	U.S.
Cream separator	1880	DeLaval	Swedish
Cultivator, disc	1878	Mallon	U.S.
Cystoscope	1877	Nitze	German
Dental plate, rubber	1855	Goodyear	U.S.
Diesel engine	1895	Diesel	German
Dynamite	1866	Nobel	Swedish
Dynamo, continuous current	1860	Picinotti	Italian
Dynamo, hydrogen cooled	1915	Schuler	U.S.
Electric battery	1800	Volta	Italian
Electric fan	1882	Wheeler	U.S.
Electrocardiograph	1903	Einthoven	Dutch
Electroencephalograph	1929	Berger	German
Electromagnet	1824	Sturgeon	English
Electron spectrometer	1944	Deutsch, Elliott, Evans	U.S.
Electron tube multigrid	1913	Langmuir	U.S.
Electroplating	1805	Brugnatelli	Italian
Electrostatic generator	1929	Van de Graaff	U.S.
Elevator brake	1852	Otis	U.S.
Elevator, push button	1922	Larson	U.S.
Engine, automobile	1879	Benz	German
Engine, coal-gas 4-cycle	1877	Otto	German
Engine, compression ignition	1883	Daimler	German
Engine, electric ignition	1880	Benz	German
Engine, gas, compound	1926	Eickemeyer	U.S.
Engine, gasoline	1872	Brayton, Geo.	U.S.
Engine, gasoline	1886	Daimler	German
Engine, steam, piston	1705	Newcomen	English
Engine, steam, piston	1769	Watt	Scottish
Engraving, half-tone	1893	Ives	U.S.

Invention	Date	Inventor	Nation.
Filament, tungsten	1915	Langmuir	U.S.
Flanged rail	1831	Stevens	U.S.
Flatiron, electric	1882	Seeley	U.S.
Furnace (for steel)	1861	Siemens	German
Galvanometer	1820	Sweigger	German
Gas discharge tube	1922	Hull	U.S.
Gas lighting	1792	Murdoch	Scottish
Gas mantle	1885	Welsbach	Austrian
Gasoline (lead ethyl)	1922	Midgley	U.S.
Gasoline, cracked	1913	Burton	U.S.
Gasoline, high octane	1930	Ipatieff	Russian
Geiger counter	1913	Geiger	German
Glass, laminated safety	1909	Benedictus	French
Glider	1853	Cayley	English
Gun, breechloader	1811	Thornton	U.S.
Gun, Browning	1918	Browning	U.S.
Gun, magazine	1875	Hotchkiss	U.S.
Gun, silencer	1909	Maxim, H.P.	U.S.
Guncotton	1846	Schoenbein	German
Gyrocompass	1911	Sperry	U.S.
Gyroscope	1852	Foucault	French
Harvester-thresher	1888	Matteson	U.S.
Helicopter	1939	Sikorsky	U.S.
Hydrometer	1768	Baume	French
Ice-making machine	1851	Gorrie	U.S.
Iron lung	1928	Drinker, Shaw	U.S.
Kaleidoscope	1817	Brewster	English
Kinetoscope	1887	Edison	U.S.
Lacquer, nitrocellulose	1921	Flaherty	U.S.
Lamp, arc	1879	Brush	U.S.
Lamp, incandescent	1879	Edison	U.S.
Lamp, incand., frosted	1924	Pipkin	U.S.
Lamp, incand., gas	1916	Langmuir	U.S.
Lamp, Klieg	1911	Kliegl, A.&J.	U.S.
Lamp, mercury vapor	1912	Hewitt	U.S.
Lamp, miner's safety	1816	Davy	English
Lamp, neon	1915	Claude	French
Lathe, turret	1845	Fitch	U.S.
Launderette	1934	Cantrell	U.S.
Lens, achromatic	1758	Dollond	English
Lens, fused bifocal	1908	Borsch	U.S.
Leydenjar (condenser)	1745	von Kleist	German
Lightning rod	1752	Franklin	U.S.
Linoleum	1860	Walton	English
Linotype	1885	Mergenthaler	U.S.
Lock, cylinder	1865	Yale	U.S.
Locomotive, electric	1851	Vail	U.S.
Locomotive, exp'mtl	1801	Trevithick	English
Locomotive, exp'mtl	1812	Fenton et al	English
Locomotive, exp'mtl	1813	Hedley	English
Locomotive, exp'mtl	1814	Stephenson	English
Locomotive practical	1829	Stephenson	English
Locomotive, 1st U.S.	1830	Cooper, P.	U.S.
Loom, power	1785	Cartwright	English
Loudspeaker, dynamic	1924	Rice, Kellogg	U.S.
Machine gun	1861	Gatling	U.S.
Machine gun, improved	1872	Hotchkiss	U.S.
Machine gun (Maxim)	1883	Maxim, H.S.	U.S., Eng.
Magnet, electro	1828	Henry	U.S.
Mantle, gas	1885	Welsbach	Austrian
Mason jar	1858	Mason, J.	U.S.
Match, friction	1827	John Walker	English
Mercerized textiles	1843	Mercer, J.	English
Meter, induction	1888	Shallenberger	U.S.
Metronome	1816	Malzel	Austrian
Micrometer	1636	Gascoigne	English
Microphone	1877	Berliner	U.S.
Microscope, compound	1590	Janssen	Dutch
Microscope, electronic	1931	Knoll, Ruska	German
Microscope, field ion.	1951	Mueller	Germany
Monitor, warship	1861	Ericsson	U.S.
Monotype	1887	Lanston	U.S.
Motor, AC	1892	Tesla	U.S.
Motor, induction	1887	Tesla	U.S.
Motorcycle	1885	Daimler	German
Movie machine	1894	Jenkins	U.S.
Movie, panoramic	1952	Waller	U.S.
Movie, talking	1927	Warner Bros.	U.S.
Mower, lawn	1868	Hilis	U.S.
Mowing machine	1831	Manning	U.S.
Neoprene	1930	Carothers	U.S.
Nylon synthetic	1930	Carothers	U.S.

Invention	Date	Inventor	Nation.
Nylon	1937	Du Pont lab	U.S.
Oil cracking furnace	1891	Gavrilov	Russian
Oil filled power cable	1921	Emanueli	Italian
Oleomargarine	1868	Mege-Mouries	French
Ophthalmoscope	1851	Helmholtz	German
Paper machine	1809	Dickinson	U.S.
Parachute	1785	Blanchard	French
Pen, ballpoint	1888	Loud	U.S.
Pen, fountain	1884	Waterman	U.S.
Pen, steel	1780	Harrison	English
Pendulum	1581	Galileo	Italian
Percussion cap	1814	Shaw	U.S.
Phonograph	1877	Edison	U.S.
Photo, color	1892	Ives	U.S.
Photo film, celluloid	1887	Goodwin	U.S.
Photo film, transparent	1870	Eastman, Goodwin	U.S.
Photoelectric cell	1895	Elster	German
Photographic paper	1898	Baekeland	U.S.
Photography	1835	Talbot	English
Photography	1837	Daguerre	French
Photography	1839	Niepce	French
Photophone	1880	Bell	U.S.
Phototelegraphy	1925	Bell Labs	U.S.
Piano	1709	Cristofori	Italian
Piano, player	1863	Fourneaux	French
Pin, safety	1849	Hunt	U.S.
Pistol (revolver)	1835	Colt	U.S.
Plow, cast iron	1797	Newbold	U.S.
Plow, disc	1896	Hardy	U.S.
Pneumatic hammer	1890	King	U.S.
Powder, smokeless	1863	Schultze	German
Printing press, rotary	1846	Hoe	U.S.
Printing press, web	1865	Bullock	U.S.
Propeller, screw	1804	Stevens	U.S.
Propeller, screw	1837	Ericsson	Swedish
Punch card accounting	1884	Hollerith	U.S.
Radar	1922	Taylor, Young	U.S.
Radio amplifier	1907	De Forest	U.S.
Radio beacon	1928	Donovan	U.S.
Radio crystal oscillator	1918	Nicolson	U.S.
Radio receiver, cascade tuning	1913	Alexanderson	U.S.
Radio receiver, heterodyne	1913	Fessenden	U.S.
Radio transmitter triode modulation	1914	Alexanderson	U.S.
Radio tube-diode	1905	Fleming	English
Radio tube oscillator	1915	De Forest	U.S.
Radio tube triode	1907	De Forest	U.S.
Radio, signals	1895	Marconi	Italian
Radio, magnetic detector	1902	Marconi	Italian
Radio FM 2-path	1929	Armstrong	U.S.
Rayon	1883	Swan	English
Razor, electric	1931	Schick	U.S.
Razor, safety	1895	Gillette	U.S.
Reaper	1834	McCormick	U.S.
Record, cylinder	1887	Bell, Tainter	U.S.
Record, disc	1887	Berliner	U.S.
Record, long playing	1948	Goldmark	U.S.
Record, wax cylinder	1888	Edison	U.S.
Refrigerants, low-boiling fluorine compound	1930	Midgely and co-workers	U.S.
Refrigerator car	1868	David	U.S.
Resin, synthetic	1931	Hill	English
Rifle, repeating	1860	Spencer	U.S.
Rocket engine	1929	Goddard	U.S.
Rubber, vulcanized	1839	Goodyear	U.S.
Saw, band	1808	Newberry	English
Saw, circular	1777	Miller	English
Searchlight, arc	1915	Sperry	U.S.
Sewing machine	1846	Howe	U.S.
Shoe-sewing machine	1860	McKay	U.S.
Shrapnel shell	1784	Shrapnel	English
Shuttle, flying	1733	Kay	English
Sleeping-car	1858	Pullman	U.S.
Slide rule	1620	Oughtred	English
Soap, hardwater	1928	Bertsch	German
Spectroscope	1859	Kirchoff, Bunsen	German
Spectroscope (mass)	1918	Dempster	U.S.
Spinning jenny	1767	Hargreaves	English
Spinning mule	1779	Crompton	English
Steamboat, exp'mtl	1783	Jouffroy	French

Invention	Date	Inventor	Nation.
Steamboat, exp'mtl	1785	Fitch	U.S.
Steamboat, exp'mtl	1787	Rumsey	U.S.
Steamboat, exp'mtl	1788	Miller	Scottish
Steamboat, exp'mtl	1803	Fulton	U.S.
Steamboat, exp'mtl	1804	Stevens	U.S.
Steamboat, practical	1802	Symington	Scottish
Steamboat, practical	1807	Fulton	U.S.
Steam car	1770	Cugnot	French
Steam turbine	1884	Parsons	English
Steel	1856	Bessemer	English
Steel alloy	1891	Harvey	U.S.
Steel alloy, high-speed	1901	Taylor, White	U.S.
Steel, electric	1900	Heroult	French
Steel, manganese	1884	Hadfield	English
Steel, stainless	1916	Brearley	English
Stereoscope	1838	Wheatstone	English
Stethoscope	1819	Laennec	French
Stethoscope, binaural	1840	Cammann	U.S.
Stock ticker	1870	Edison	U.S.
Storage battery, rechargeable	1859	Plante	French
Stove, electric	1896	Hadaway	U.S.
Submarine	1891	Holland	U.S.
Submarine, even keel	1894	Lake	U.S.
Submarine, torpedo	1776	Bushnell	U.S.
Tank, military	1914	Swinton	English
Tape recorder, magnetic	1899	Poulsen	Danish
Telegraph, magnetic	1837	Morse	U.S.
Telegraph, quadruplex	1874	Edison	U.S.
Telegraph, railroad	1887	Woods	U.S.
Telegraph, wireless high frequency	1896	Marconi	Italian
Telephone	1876	Bell	U.S.-Can.
Telephone amplifier	1912	De Forest	U.S.
Telephone, automatic	1891	Stowger	U.S.
Telephone, radio	1902	Poulsen, Fessenden	U.S.
Telephone, radio	1906	De Forest	U.S.
Telephone, radio, l. d	1915	AT&T	U.S.
Telephone, recording	1898	Poulseon	Danish
Telephone, wireless	1899	Collins	U.S.
Telescope	1608	Lippershey	Neth.
Telescope	1609	Galileo	Italian
Telescope, astronomical	1611	Kepler	German
Teletype	1928	Morkrum, Kleinschmidt	U.S.
Television, iconoscope	1923	Zworykin	U.S.
Television, electronic	1927	Farnsworth	U.S.
Television, (mech. scanner)	1926	Baird	Scottish
Thermometer	1593	Galileo	Italian
Thermometer	1710	Reaumur	French
Thermometer, mercury	1714	Fahrenheit	German
Time recorder	1890	Bundy	U.S.
Time, self-regulator	1918	Bryce	U.S.
Tire, double-tube	1845	Thomson	English
Tire, pneumatic	1888	Dunlop	Irish
Toaster, automatic	1918	Strite	U.S.
Tool, pneumatic	1865	Law	English
Torpedo, marine	1804	Fulton	U.S.
Tractor, crawler	1900	Holt	U.S.
Transformer A.C.	1885	Stanley	U.S.
Transistor	1947	Shockley, Brattain, Bardeen	U.S.
Trolley car, electric	1884	Van DePoele,	
	-87	Sprague	U.S.
Tungsten, ductile	1912	Coolidge	U.S.
Turbine, gas	1899	Curtis, C.G.	U.S.
Turbine, hydraulic	1849	Francis	U.S.
Turbine, steam	1896	Curtis, C.G.	U.S.
Type, movable	1450	Gutenberg	German
Typewriter	1868	Soule, Glidden	U.S.
Vacuum cleaner, electric	1907	Spangler	U.S.
Washer, electric	1907	Hurley Co.	U.S.
Welding, atomic hydrogen	1924	Langmuir, Palmer	U.S.
Welding, electric	1877	Thomson	U.S.
Wind tunnel	1923	Munk	U.S.
Wire, barbed	1874	Glidden	U.S.
Wire, barbed	1875	Haisn	U.S.
X-ray tube	1913	Coolidge	U.S.
Zipper	1891	Judson	U.S.

Discoveries and Innovations: Chemistry, Physics, Biology, Medicine

	Date	Discoverer	Nation.
Acetylene gas	1892	Wilson	U.S.
ACTH	1949	Armour & Co.	U.S.
Adrenalin	1901	Takamine	Japanese
Aluminum, electrolytic process	1886	Hall	U.S.
Aluminum, isolated	1825	Oersted	Danish
Analine dye	1856	Perkin	English
Anesthesia, ether	1842	Long	U.S.
Anesthesia, local	1885	Koller	Austrian
Anesthesia, spinal	1898	Bier	German
Anti-rabies	1885	Pasteur	French
Antiseptic surgery	1867	Lister	English
Antitoxin, diphtheria	1891	Von Behring	German
Argyrol	1901	Barnes	U.S.
Arsphenamine	1910	Ehrlich	German
Aspirin	1889	Dresser	German
Atabrine	. . .	Mietzsch, et al.	German
Atomic numbers	1913	Moseley	English
Atomic theory	1803	Dalton	English
Atomic time clock	1947	Libby	U.S.
Atom-smashing theory	1919	Rutherford	English
Aureomycin	1948	Duggar	U.S.
Bacitracin	1945	Johnson, et al.	U.S.
Bacteria (described)	1676	Leeuwenhoek	Dutch
Barbital	1903	Fischer	German
Bleaching powder	1798	Tennant	English
Blood, circulation	1628	Harvey	English
Bordeaux mixture	1885	Millardet	French
Bromine from sea	1924	Edgar Kramer	U.S.
Calcium carbide	1888	Wilson	U.S.
Calculus	1670	Newton	English
Camphor synthetic	1896	Haller	French
Canning (food)	1804	Appert	French
Carbomycin	1952	Tanner	U.S.
Carbon oxides	1925	Fisher	German
Chlorine	1810	Davy	English
Chloroform	1831	Guthrie, S.	U.S.
Chloromycetin	1947	Burkholder	U.S.
Classification of plants and animals	1735	Linnaeus	Swedish
Cocaine	1860	Niermann	German
Combustion explained	1777	Lavoisier	French
Conditioned reflex	1914	Pavlov	Russian
Conteben	1950	Belmisch, Mietzsch, Domagk	German
Cortisone	1936	Kendall	U.S.
Cortisone, synthesis	1946	Sarett	U.S.
Cosmic rays	1910	Gockel	Swiss
Cyanimide	1905	Frank, Caro.	German
Cyclotron	1930	Lawrence	U.S.
DDT	1874	Zeidler	German
(not applied as insecticide until 1939)			
Deuterium	1932	Urey, Brickwedde, Murphy	U.S.
DNA (structure)	1951	Crick	English
		Watson	U.S.
		Wilkins	English
Electric resistance (law)	1827	Ohm	German
Electric waves	1888	Hertz	German
Electrolysis	1852	Faraday	English
Electromagnetism	1819	Oersted	Danish
Electron	1897	Thomson, J.	English
Electron diffraction	1936	Thomson, G.	English
		Davisson	U.S.
Electroshock treatment	1938	Cerletti, Bini	Italian
Erythromycin	1952	McGuire	U.S.
Evolution, natural selection	1858	Darwin	English
Falling bodies, law	1590	Galileo	Italian

	Date	Discoverer	Nation.
Gases, law of combining volumes	1808	Gay-Lussac	French
Geometry, analytic	1619	Descartes	French
Gold (cyanide process for extraction)	1887	MacArthur, Forest	British
Gravitation, law	1687	Newton	English
Holograph	1948	Gabor	British
Human heart transplant	1967	Barnard	S. African
Indigo, synthesis of	1880	Baeyer	German
Induction, electric	1830	Henry	U.S.
Insulin	1922	Banting, Best, Macleod	Canadian
Intelligence testing	1905	Binet, Simon	French
Isinazid	1952	Hoffman-La-Roche	U.S.
		Domagk	German
Isotopes, theory	1912	Soddy	English
Laser (light amplification by stimulated emission of radiation)	1958	Townes, Schawlow	U.S.
Light, velocity	1675	Roemer	Danish
Light, wave theory	1690	Huygens	Dutch
Lithography	1796	Senefelder	Bohemian
Lobotomy	1935	Egas Moniz	Portuguese
LSD-25	1943	Hoffman	Swiss
Mendelian laws	1866	Mendel	Austrian
Mercator projection (map)	1568	Mercator (Kremer)	Flemish
Methanol	1925	Patard	French
Milk condensation	1853	Borden	U.S.
Molecular hypothesis	1811	Avogadro	Italian
Motion, laws of	1687	Newton	English
Neomycin	1949	Waksman, Lechevalier	U.S.
Neutron	1932	Chadwick	English
Nitric acid	1648	Glauber	German
Nitric oxide	1772	Priestley	English
Nitroglycerin	1846	Sobrero	Italian
Oil cracking process	1891	Dewar	U.S.
Oxygen	1774	Priestley	English
Ozone	1840	Schonbein	German
Paper, sulfite process	1867	Tilghman	U.S.
Paper, wood pulp, sulfate process	1884	Dahl	German
Penicillin	1929	Fleming	English
practical use	1941	Florey, Chain	English
Periodic law and table of elements	1869	Mendeleyev	Russian
Planetary motion, laws	1609	Kepler	German
Plutonium fission	1940	Kennedy, Wahl, Seaborg, Segre	U.S.

	Date	Discoverer	Nation.
Polymixin	1947	Ainsworth	English
Positron	1932	Anderson	U.S.
Proton	1919	Rutherford	English
Psychoanalysis	1900	Freud	Austrian
Quantum theory	1900	Planck	German
Quasars	1963	Matthews, Sandage	U.S.
Quinine synthetic	1918	Rabe	German
Radioactivity	1896	Becquerel	French
Radium	1898	Curie, Pierre	French
		Curie, Marie	Pol.-Fr.
Relativity theory	1905	Einstein	German
Reserpine	1949	Jal Vaikl	Indian
Salvarsan (606)	1910	Ehrlich	German
Schick test	1913	Schick	U.S.
Silicon	1823	Berzelius	Swedish
Streptomycin	1945	Waksman	U.S.
Sulfadiazine	1940	Roblin	U.S.
Sulfanilamide	1934	Domagk	German
Sulfanilamide theory	1908	Gelmo	German
Sulfapyridine	1938	Ewins, Phelps	English
Sulfathiazole		Fosbinder, Walter	U.S.
Sulfuric acid	1831	Phillips	English
Sulfuric acid, lead	1746	Roebuck	English
Terramycin	1950	Finlay, et al.	U.S.
Tuberculin	1890	Koch	German
Uranium fission (theory)	1939	Hahn, Meitner, Strassmann	German
		Bohr	Danish
		Fermi	Italian
		Einstein, Pegran, Wheeler	U.S.
Uranium fission, atomic reactor	1942	Fermi, Szilard	U.S.
Vaccine, measles	1954	Enders, Peebles	U.S.
Vaccine, polio	1953	Salk	U.S.
Vaccine, polio, oral	1955	Sabin	U.S.
Vaccine, rabies	1885	Pasteur	French
Vaccine, smallpox	1796	Jenner	English
Vaccine, typhus	1909	Nicolle	French
Van Allen belts, radiation	1958	Van Allen	U.S.
Vitamin A	1913	McCollum, Davis	U.S.
Vitamin B	1916	McCollum	U.S.
Vitamin C	1912	Holst, Froelich	Norwegian
Vitamin D	1922	McCollum	U.S.
Wassermann test	1906	Wassermann	German
Xerography	1938	Carlson	U.S.
X-ray	1895	Roentgen	German

Copyright Law of The United States

Source: Copyright Office, Library of Congress

Original works of authorship in any tangible medium of expression are entitled to protection under the copyright law (Title 17 of the United States Code). The law came into effect on January 1, 1978 (Public Law 94-553, 90 Stat. 2541); it superseded the Copyright Act of 1909, as amended. Before the 1976 Act, there had been only three general revisions of the original copyright law of 1790, namely those of 1831, 1870, and 1909.

Categories of Works

Copyright protection under the new law extends to original works of authorship fixed in any tangible medium of expression, now known or later developed, from which they can be perceived, reproduced, or otherwise communicated, either directly or with the aid of a machine or device. Works of authorship include books, periodicals and other literary works, musical compositions with accompanying lyrics, dramas and dramatico-musical compositions, pantomimes and choreographic works, motion pictures and other audiovisual works, and sound recordings.

The owner of a copyright is given the exclusive right to reproduce the copyrighted work in copies or phonorecords and distribute them to the public by sale, rental, lease, or lending. The owner of a copyright also enjoys the exclusive right to make derivative works based upon the copyrighted work, to perform the work publicly if it be a literary, musical, dramatic, or choreographic work, a pantomime, motion picture, or other audiovisual work, and in the case of literary, musical, dramatic, and choreographic works, pantomimes, and pictorial, graphic, or sculptural works, including the individual images of a motion picture or other audiovisual work, to display the copyrighted work publicly. All of these rights are subject to certain specified exceptions, including the so-called judicial doctrine of "fair use," which is included in the law for the first time.

The act also provides special provisions permitting compulsory licensing for the recording and distribution of phonorecords of nondramatic musical compositions, noncommercial transmissions by public broadcasters of published musical, pictorial, sculptural, and graphic works, performances of copyrighted nondramatic music by means of jukeboxes, and the secondary transmission of copyrighted works on cable television systems.

Single National System

The law establishes a single national system of statutory protection for all copyrightable works fixed in tangible form, whether published or unpublished. Before Jan. 1, 1978 unpublished works were entitled to protection under the common law of the various states while published works came under the Federal statute.

Registration of a claim to copyright in any work, whether published or unpublished, may be made voluntarily at any time during the copyright term by the owner of the copyright or of any exclusive right in the work. Registration is not a condition of copyright protection, but is a prerequisite to an infringement suit. Subject to certain exceptions, the remedies of statutory damages and attorney's fees are not available for those infringements occurring before registration. Even if registration is not made, copies or phonorecords of works published in the U.S. with notice of copyright are required to be deposited for the collections of the Library of Congress. This deposit requirement is not a condition of protection, but does render the copyright owner subject to penalties for failure to deposit after a demand by the Register of Copyrights.

Duration of Copyright

For works created on or after Jan. 1, 1978, copyright subsists from their creation for a term consisting of the life of the author and 50 years after the author's death. For works made for hire, and for anonymous and pseudonymous works (unless the author's identity is revealed in Copyright Office records), the term is 100 years from creation or 75 years from first publication, whichever is shorter.

The law retains for works that were under statutory protection on January 1, 1978, the 28 year term of copyright from first publication (or from registration in some cases), renewable by certain persons for a second term of protection of 47 years. Copyrights in their first 28-year term on Jan. 1, 1978, have to be renewed in order to be protected for the full maximum term of 75 years. Copyrights in their second term on Jan. 1, 1978 were automatically extended to last for a total term of 75 years.

For works that had been created before the law came into effect but had neither been published nor registered for copyright before Jan. 1, 1978, the term of copyright is generally computed in the same way as for new works: the life-plus-50 or 75/100-year terms will apply. However, all works in this category are guaranteed at least 25 years of statutory protection. The law specifies that copyright in a work of this kind will not expire before Dec. 31, 2002, and if the work is published before that date the term is extended by another 25 years, through the end of the year 2027.

Notice of Copyright

Under the 1909 copyright law the copyright notice was the most important requirement for obtaining copyright protection for a published work. For published works, all copies had to bear the prescribed notice from the time of first publication. If a work was published before Jan. 1, 1978 without the required notice, copyright protection was lost permanently and cannot be regained.

The present copyright law requires a notice on copies or phonorecords of sound recordings that are distributed to the public. Errors and omissions, however, do not immediately result in forfeiture of the copyright and can be corrected within prescribed time limits. Innocent infringers misled by an omission or error in the notice generally are shielded from liability.

The notice of copyright required on all visually perceptible copies published in the U.S. or elsewhere under the 1976 Act consists of the symbol © (the letter C in a circle), the word "Copyright," or the abbreviation "Copr.," and the year of first publication, and the name of the owner of copyright in the work. Example: © 1981 JOHN DOE

The notice must be affixed in such manner and location as to give reasonable notice of the claim of copyright.

The notice of copyright prescribed for all published phonorecords of sound recordings consists of the symbol ℗ (the letter P in a circle), the year of first publication of the sound recording, and the name of the owner of copyright in the

sound recording, placed on the surface of the phonorecord, or on the phonorecord label or container in such manner and location as to give reasonable notice of the claim of copyright. Example: ℗ 1981 DOE RECORDS, INC.

Manufacturing Requirements

Under the 1909 Act certain works had to be manufactured in the U.S. to receive copyright protection. The present law does not make manufacture in the U.S. a condition of protection; additionally, it narrows the coverage of the manufacturing provisions, permits the importation of 2,000 copies manufactured abroad instead of the previous limit of 1,500 copies, and equates manufacture in Canada with manufacture in the U.S. Even the narrower requirement is scheduled to terminate on July 1, 1982.

The manufacturing requirements of the law apply as a general rule only to the copies of a work that consists "preponderantly of a nondramatic literary material that is in the English language." They do not extend to dramatic, musical, pictorial, or graphic works; foreign language, bilingual, or multilingual works; public domain material; or works consisting preponderantly of material not subject to the manufacturing provision.

Under the statute, compliance with the manufacturing requirements does not constitute a condition of copyright, but, in cases where the requirements are not satisfied, the rights with respect to reproduction and the distribution of copies are limited as against certain infringers. Even if copies are imported or distributed in violation of the law, there is no effect on the copyright owner's right to make and distribute phonorecords of the work, to make derivative works including dramatizations and motion pictures, and to perform or display the work publicly.

International Protection

The U.S. has copyright relations with more than 70 countries, under which works of American authors are protected in those countries, and the works of their authors are protected in the U.S. The basic feature of this protection is "national treatment," under which the alien author is treated by a country in the same manner that it treats its own authors. Relations exist by virtue of bilateral agreements or through the Buenos Aires Convention or the Universal Copyright Convention. U.S. legislation implementing the latter convention, which became effective Sept. 16, 1955, gives the works of foreign authors the benefit of exemptions from the manufacturing requirements of the U.S. copyright law, provided the works are first published abroad with a copyright notice including the symbol © , the name of the copyright owner and the year date of first publication, and that the work either is by an "author" who is a citizen or subject of a foreign country which belongs to the Convention or is first published in a foreign member country. Conversely, works of U.S. authors are exempt from certain burdensome requirements in particular foreign member countries.

Works published on or after Jan. 1, 1978, are subject to protection under the copyright statute if, on the date of first publication, one or more of the authors is a national or domiciliary of the U.S., or is a national, domiciliary, or sovereign authority of a foreign nation that is a party to a copyright treaty to which the United States is also a party, or is a stateless person, regardless of domicile, or if the work is first published either in the U.S. or in a foreign nation that, on the date of first publication is a party to the Universal Copyright Convention. All unpublished works are protected here regardless of the citizenship or domicile of the author.

A U.S. author may obtain copyright protection in all countries that are members of the Universal Copyright Convention (UCC). In member countries, where no formalities are required, the works of U.S. authors are protected automatically. Member countries whose laws impose formalities protect U.S. works if all published copies bear a convention notice which consists of the symbol ©, together with the name of the copyright owner and the year date of publication. Example: © JOHN DOE 1981.

Further information and application forms may be obtained free of charge by writing to the Copyright Office, The Library of Congress, Washington, D.C. 20559.

Off-Beat News Stories of 1981

If this is Vermont, it must be Tuesday — "I don't want the job," said Mrs. Allard, a grandmother of six, after her first day driving a school bus. She had become confused in the maze of interstate exchanges outside of Boston. Eight hours and 75 miles later, she found herself in Greenfield, Mass., while police in eastern Massachusetts searched frantically for the wayward driver and her charges, Jeff Mason, 10, and Ronald McGaunn, 11. The epic finally ended when the bus ran out of gas, and Mrs. Allard couldn't pay the bill for towing.

"I still don't believe it," a dazed Mrs. Allard moaned. "They thought I was kidnapping the children. For cripe's sake, I have six grandchildren!"

And what about the boys? Were they frightened by the ordeal? "They said they liked this bus driver, because they didn't want to go to school anyway," snapped Mrs. Allard.

Birds, Atlantic City style — The Golden Nugget has donated 6 valuable tropical birds, worth $10,000, to the Philadelphia Zoo, a spokesperson for the Atlantic City-based casino announced recently. Well, actually, the casino is getting rid of the uncooperative tweeters because they refused to chirp and sing, and thus failed to fulfill their obligation to entertain guests. "Visitors frequently found them dozing on their perches in their 3-story cage in the Victorian-style lobby, and they hardly ever sang," noted spokesperson Muriel Harris.

But, despair not. The Golden Nugget has come up with a solution in keeping with Atlantic City tradition. We've hired a special-effects expert from Disneyland," Mrs. Harris said. "He'll create mechanical birds that will walk, warble and chirp to create the proper esthetic setting."

At the bleep, leave your name, number and swearword — Paul White, founder of Curseaholics Anonymous, has announced that his organization will cease operations because he has been getting too many obscene phone calls. White founded the organization when he lost his job as a parking lot attendant after he hurled an object at a woman who had cursed him. Many problems had beset Mr. White in his efforts to help people stop using swearwords, but all were surmountable save the reluctance of the swearing public to take the organization seriously. Of the 2,000 calls received on his special "cursers' hot line," half were from individuals who merely wanted to deliver profane messages.

She only needs experience — Ellen Israel, a New York City-based real estate broker, knew that hard times were upon the auto industry and that the auto makers would be hankering for cash. Armed with this insight, she called Ford's real estate department and subsequently consummated her first transaction — a $40 million sale of the auto maker's 19-story office building on West 57th Street in Manhattan. "I've only been in the business a year, but I knew Ford needed the money," said the 23-year-old broker. Ms. Israel vacationed in Aruba this year.

Lawnmower assault rate up in 1981 — "Guilty," pleaded Frank Karnes, 39, to the charges against him. His offense: shooting his lawnmower, an act that violated statutes prohibiting the use of firearms in populated areas and, consequently, cost Karnes $65. It seems that Karnes opened up on his recalcitrant grass cutter when it refused to start: "I got angry at the mower so I went in the house and got my gun. I went back out and shot five rounds into the mower."

Can't win department — George Smith of Baldwin, L.I., probably would prefer not to hear speeches about equal justice for all under the law. The 61-year-old dealer of "pornographic" magazines was charged with consumer fraud when the Nassau County District Attorney discovered that Mr. Smith's mail offerings, advertised as pornographic "European magazines," were too "tame" to constitute hard-core pornography, and too small (six wallet-size photos for $21.50) to be called magazines. And if Mr. Smith had delivered as promised? "If it had turned out to be hard-core pornography, he would have been in violation of obscenity laws," the D.A. stated. "And as it is, he's in violation of fraud statutes."

Lowell Ferguson update — The third annual "Lowell Ferguson Day," will fall on Saturday, July 31, 1982. Lowell Ferguson, you may recall, is the Western Airlines pilot who inadvertently landed his 727 at the small municipal airport in Buffalo, Wyo., thinking he was touching down at Sheridan, 35 miles away. It marked the first time a jet aircraft of any size had landed in Buffalo.

To mark the occasion, local officials scheduled the first "Lowell Ferguson Day" in 1979, with the planned guest of honor to be none other than Captain Ferguson himself. "I talked to him on the phone and he seemed anxious to come back," explained a Chamber of Commerce official. "Then we got a letter saying he wouldn't come. I guess the airline wanted to forget the whole thing."

Undaunted, Buffalo residents proceeded with plans for the second anniversary celebration last year, complete with prizes. And as an extra precaution, in the event the captain again failed to show, anyone named Lowell Ferguson was eligible for the booty.

Gay mice, deaf pigs — Researchers at the Aegean University in Izmir, Turkey, have discovered that disco music causes homosexuality in mice and deafness in pigs. And the recently released study warns that the findings may have strong implications for humans: "The researchers think that there is a caveat in these studies for human beings as well." No explanation was offered as to how mice were judged resistent to deafness or why pigs kept their sexual identity.

Fun city — Sir Isaac Newton was born there, Oliver Cromwell his first important battle nearby, and, most recently, its locals can boast that Prime Minister Margaret Thatcher is one of their own. But perhaps Grantham's greatest claim to fame lies in its recent recognition as the most boring place in Britain. Grantham won the BBC's Golden Yawn Award, designating it as the town whose inhabitants found living there the most tedious. "The only thing that ever came out of Grantham was the A1 (the main highway linking the town with London)," boasted one local. Another offered, "I suppose it is boring, but there are some places just as boring, I imagine."

We interrupt our regularly scheduled program — "We've taken steps to be sure it never happens again. We are going to cut into the Christian Broadcasting Network 15 minutes early to avoid this in the future," said Orlando Brillante, regional manager of the Florida TV cable system. "It" was a power loss in an antenna that resulted in the transmission of New York's Escapade programming—a blue movie channel —instead of the regularly scheduled Christian Network telecast. As a result, viewers were "treated" to nude women on their screens in place of Oral Roberts' trademark opening song, "Something Good is Going to Happen to You." According to Mr. Brillante, his company, which serves 125,000 customers, received only one complaint about the change in programming.

Oh, by the way, about your stolen car — Orlando, Fla., police found Larry Lorenzen's stolen car only 8 hours after it had been reported missing. Unfortunately, Mr. Lorenzen didn't hear the good news until 14 months later. "They let it sit there in a body shop for over a year without telling me. How can this happen?"

According to police, the problem was the result of a computer mixup, but that explanation didn't assuage the anger of either Lorenzen or Arnie Linneman, the owner of the body shop to which the car was towed and where it accrued $2,300 in storage fees. Meanwhile, the insurance company refused to pay any more than 2 weeks of Linneman's storage fees, claiming that he had failed to file the proper claim forms. "They can claim all they want, but this car isn't leaving until I get a settlement from somebody," Linneman growled.

And although Lorenzen was paid for his loss, he's still mad. "Sure, they really tried to find me. Right in plain view on the floorboard were a whole bunch of business cards with my name and work number printed on them."

Let your fingers do the walking — The angry people at the Elliott-Hamil Funeral Home in Abilene, Tex., will probably ask for a refund on the Yellow Pages advertisement they placed recently. Seems that a mixup — Southwestern Bell calls it a computer error — resulted in the Funeral Home's listing appearing under "Frozen Foods — Wholesale."

SPORTS OF 1981

Olympic Games Records

The modern Olympic Games, first held in Athens, Greece, in 1896, were the result of efforts by Baron Pierre de Coubertin, a French educator, to promote interest in education and culture, also to foster better international understanding through the universal medium of youth's love of athletics.

His source of inspiration for the Olympic Games was the ancient Greek Olympic Games, most notable of the four Panhellenic celebrations. The games were combined patriotic, religious, and athletic festivals held every four years. The first such recorded festival was that held in 776 B.C., the date from which the Greeks began to keep their calendar by "Olympiads," or four-year spans between the games.

The first Olympiad is said to have consisted merely of a 200-yard foot race near the small city of Olympia, but the games gained in scope and became demonstrations of national pride. Only Greek citizens — amateurs — were permitted to participate. Winners received laurel, wild olive, and palm wreaths and were accorded many special privileges. Under the Roman emperors, the games deteriorated into professional carnivals and circuses. Emperor Theodosius banned them in 394 A.D.

Baron de Coubertin enlisted 9 nations to send athletes to the first modern Olympics in 1896; now more than 100 nations compete. Winter Olympic Games were started in 1924.

In 1980, 62 nations, including the United States, Canada, W. Germany, and Japan, refused to participate in the games in protest against the Soviet invasion of Afghanistan.

Sites and Unofficial Winners of Games

1896 Athens (U.S.)	**1920** Antwerp (U.S.)	**1948** London (U.S.)	**1968** Mexico City (U.S.)
1900 Paris (U.S.)	**1924** Paris (U.S.)	**1952** Helsinki (U.S.)	**1972** Munich (USSR)
1904 St. Louis (U.S.)	**1928** Amsterdam (U.S.)	**1956** Melbourne (USSR)	**1976** Montreal (USSR)
1906 Athens (U.S.)*	**1932** Los Angeles (U.S.)	**1960** Rome (USSR)	**1980** Moscow (USSR)
1908 London (U.S.)	**1936** Berlin (Germany)	**1964** Tokyo (U.S.)	**1984** Los Angeles (scheduled)
1912 Stockholm (U.S.)			

*Games not recognized by International Olympic Committee. Games 6 (1916), 12 (1940), and 13 (1944) were not celebrated. East and West Germany began competing separately in 1968.

Olympic Games Champions, 1896—1980

(*Indicates Olympic Records)

Track and Field — Men

60-Meter Run
1900	Alvin Kraenzlein, United States	7s*
1904	Archie Hahn, United States	7s*

100-Meter Run
1896	Thomas Burke, United States	12s
1900	Francis W. Jarvis, United States	10.8s
1904	Archie Hahn, United States	11s
1908	Reginald Walker, South Africa	10.8s
1912	Ralph Craig, United States	10.8s
1920	Charles Paddock, United States	10.8s
1924	Harold Abrahams, Great Britain	10.6s
1928	Percy Williams, Canada	10.8s
1932	Eddie Tolan, United States	10.3s
1936	Jesse Owens, United States	10.3s
1948	Harrison Dillard, United States	10.3s
1952	Lindy Remigino, United States	10.4s
1956	Bobby Morrow, United States	10.5s
1960	Armin Hary, Germany	10.2s
1964	Bob Hayes, United States	10.0s
1968	Jim Hines, United States	9.9s*
1972	Valeri Borzov, USSR	10.14s
1976	Hasely Crawford, Trinidad	10.06s
1980	Allan Wells, Great Britain	10.25s

200-Meter Run
1900	Walter Tewksbury, United States	22.2s
1904	Archie Hahn, United States	21.6s
1908	Robert Kerr, Canada	22.4s
1912	Ralph Craig, United States	21.7s
1920	Allan Woodring, United States	22s
1924	Jackson Scholz, United States	21.6s
1928	Percy Williams, Canada	21.8s
1932	Eddie Tolan, United States	21.2s
1936	Jesse Owens, United States	20.7s
1948	Mel Patton, United States	21.1s
1952	Andrew Stanfield, United States	20.7s
1956	Bobby Morrow, United States	20.6s
1960	Livio Berruti, Italy	20.5s
1964	Henry Carr, United States	20.3s
1968	Tommie Smith, United States	19.8s*
1972	Valeri Borzov, USSR	20.00s
1976	Donald Quarrie, Jamaica	20.23s
1980	Pietro Mennea, Italy	20.19s

400-Meter Run
1896	Thomas Burke, United States	54.2s
1900	Maxey Long, United States	49.4s
1904	Harry Hillman, United States	49.2s
1908	Wyndham Halswelle, Great Britain, walkover	50s
1912	Charles Reidpath, United States	48.2s
1920	Bevil Rudd, South Africa	49.6s
1924	Eric Liddell, Great Britain	47.6s
1928	Ray Barbuti, United States	47.8s
1932	William Carr, United States	46.2s
1936	Archie Williams, United States	46.5s
1948	Arthur Wint, Jamaica, B W I	46.2s
1952	George Rhoden, Jamaica, B W I	45.9s
1956	Charles Jenkins, United States	46.7s
1960	Otis Davis, United States	44.9s
1964	Michael Larrabee, United States	45.1s
1968	Lee Evans, United States	43.8s*
1972	Vincent Matthews, United States	44.66s
1976	Alberto Juantorena, Cuba	44.26s
1980	Viktor Markin, USSR	44.60s

800-Meter Run
1896	Edwin Flack, Great Britain	2m. 11s
1900	Alfred Tysoe, Great Britain	2m. 1.4s
1904	James Lightbody, United States	1m. 56s
1908	Mel Sheppard, United States	1m. 52.8s
1912	James Meredith, United States	1m. 51.9s
1920	Albert Hill, Great Britain	1m. 53.4s
1924	Douglas Lowe, Great Britain	1m. 52.4s
1928	Douglas Lowe, Great Britain	1m. 51.8s
1932	Thomas Hampson, Great Britain	1m. 49.8s
1936	John Woodruff, United States	1m. 52.9s
1948	Mal Whitfield, United States	1m. 49.2s
1952	Mal Whitfield, United States	1m. 49.2s
1956	Thomas Courtney, United States	1m. 47.7s
1960	Peter Snell, New Zealand	1m. 46.3s
1964	Peter Snell, New Zealand	1m. 45.1s
1968	Ralph Doubell, Australia	1m. 44.3s
1972	Dave Wottle, United States	1m. 45.9s
1976	Alberto Juantorena, Cuba	1m. 43.50s*
1980	Steve Ovett, Great Britain	1m. 45.40s

1,500-Meter Run
1896	Edwin Flack, Great Britain	4m. 33.2s
1900	Charles Bennett, Great Britain	4m. 6s

1904	James Lightbody, United States	4m. 5.4s
1908	Mel Sheppard, United States	4m. 3.4s
1912	Arnold Jackson, Great Britain	3m. 56.8s
1920	Albert Hill, Great Britain	4m. 1.8s
1924	Paavo Nurmi, Finland	3m. 53.6s
1928	Harry Larva, Finland	3m. 53.2s
1932	Luigi Beccali, Italy	3m. 51.2s
1936	Jack Lovelock, New Zealand	3m. 47.8s
1948	Henri Eriksson, Sweden	3m. 49.8s
1952	Joseph Barthel, Luxemburg	3m. 45.2s
1956	Ron Delany, Ireland	3m. 41.2s
1960	Herb Elliott, Australia	3m. 35.6s
1964	Peter Snell, New Zealand	3m. 38.1s
1968	Kipchoge Keino, Kenya	3m. 34.9s*
1972	Pekka Vasala, Finland	3m. 36.3s
1976	John Walker, New Zealand	3m. 39.17s
1980	Sebastian Coe, Great Britain	3m. 38.4s

3,000-Meter Steeplechase

1920	Percy Hodge, Great Britain	10m. 0.4s
1924	Willie Ritola, Finland	9m. 33.6s
1928	Toivo Loukola, Finland	9m. 21.8s
1932	Volmari Iso-Hollo, Finland	10m. 33.4s
	(About 3,450 mtrs. extra lap by error)	
1936	Volmari Iso-Hollo, Finland	9m. 3.8s
1948	Thure Sjoestrand, Sweden	9m. 4.6s
1952	Horace Ashenfelter, United States	8m. 45.4s
1956	Chris Brasher, Great Britain	8m. 41.2s
1960	Zdzislaw Krzyszkowiak, Poland	8m. 34.2s
1964	Gaston Roelants, Belgium	8m. 30.8s
1968	Amos Biwott, Kenya	8m. 51s
1972	Kipchoge Keino, Kenya	8m. 23.6s
1976	Anders Garderud, Sweden	8m. 08.2s*
1980	Bronislaw Malinowski, Poland	8m. 09.7s

5,000-Meter Run

1912	Hannes Kolehmainen, Finland	14m. 36.6s
1920	Joseph Guillemot, France	14m. 55.6s
1924	Paavo Nurmi, Finland	14m. 31.2s
1928	Willie Ritola, Finland	14m. 38s
1932	Lauri Lehtinen, Finland	14m. 30s
1936	Gunnar Hockert, Finland	14m. 22.2s
1948	Gaston Reiff, Belgium	14m. 17.6s
1952	Emil Zatopek, Czechoslovakia	14m. 6.6s
1956	Vladimir Kuts, USSR	13m. 39.6s
1960	Murray Halberg, New Zealand	13m. 43.4s
1964	Bob Schul, United States	13m. 48.8s
1968	Mohamed Gammoudi, Tunisia	14m. 05.0s
1972	Lasse Viren, Finland	13m. 26.4s
1976	Lasse Viren, Finland	13m. 24.76s
1980	Miruts Yifter, Ethiopia	13m. 21.0s*

10,000-Meter Run

1912	Hannes Kolehmainen, Finland	31m. 20.8s
1920	Paavo Nurmi, Finland	31m. 45.8s
1924	Willie Ritola, Finland	30m. 23.2s
1928	Paavo Nurmi, Finland	30m. 18.8s
1932	Janusz Kusocinski, Poland	30m. 11.4s
1936	Ilmari Salminen, Finland	30m. 15.4s
1948	Emil Zatopek, Czechoslovakia	29m. 59.6s
1952	Emil Zatopek, Czechoslovakia	29m. 17.0s
1956	Vladimir Kuts, USSR	28m. 45.6s
1960	Pytor Bolotnikov, USSR	28m. 32.2s
1964	Billy Mills, United States	28m. 24.4s
1968	Naftali Temu, Kenya	29m. 27.4s
1972	Lasse Viren, Finland	27m. 38.4s*
1976	Lasse Viren, Finland	27m. 40.38s
1980	Miruts Yifter, Ethiopia	27m. 42.7s

Marathon

1896	Spiridon Loues, Greece	2h. 58m. 50s
1900	Michel Teato, France	2h. 59m. 45s
1904	Thomas Hicks, United States	3h. 28m. 53s
1908	John J. Hayes, United States	2h. 55m. 18.4s
1912	Kenneth McArthur, South Africa	2h. 36m. 54.8s
1920	Hannes Kolehmainen, Finland	2h. 32m. 35.8s
1924	Albin Stenroos, Finland	2h. 41m. 22.6s
1928	A.B. El Ouafi, France	2h. 32m. 57s
1932	Juan Zabala, Argentina	2h. 31m. 36s
1936	Kitei Son, Japan	2h. 29m. 19.2s
1948	Delfo Cabrera, Argentina	2h. 34m. 51.6s
1952	Emil Zatopek, Czechoslovakia	2h. 23m. 03.2s
1956	Alain Mimoun, France	2h. 25m.
1960	Abebe Bikila, Ethiopia	2h. 15m. 16.2s
1964	Abebe Bikila, Ethiopia	2h. 12m. 11.2s
1968	Mamo Wolde, Ethiopia	2h. 20m. 26.4s
1972	Frank Shorter, United States	2h. 12m. 19.8s
1976	Waldemar Cierpinski, E. Germany	2h. 09m. 55s*
1980	Waldemar Cierpinski, E. Germany	2h. 11m. 03s

10,000-Meter Cross-Country

1920	Paavo Nurmi, Finland	27m. 15s*
1924	Paavo Nurmi, Finland	32m. 54.8s

20-Kilometer Walk

1956	Leonid Spirine, USSR	1h. 31m. 27.4s
1960	Vladimir Golubnichy, USSR	1h. 34m. 7.2s
1964	Kenneth Mathews, Great Britain	1h. 29m. 34.0s
1968	Vladimir Golubnichy, USSR	1h. 35m. 58.4s
1972	Peter Frenkel, E. Germany	1h. 26m. 42.4s
1976	Daniel Bautista, Mexico	1h. 24m. 40.6s
1980	Maurizio Damilano, Italy	1h. 23m. 35.5s*

50-Kilometer Walk

1932	Thomas W. Green, Great Britain	4h. 50m. 10s
1936	Harold Whitlock, Great Britain	4h. 30m. 41.4s
1948	John Ljunggren, Sweden	4h. 41m. 52s
1952	Giuseppe Dordoni, Italy	4h. 28m 07.8s
1956	Norman Read, New Zealand	4h. 30m. 42.8s
1960	Donald Thompson, Great Britain	4h. 25m. 30s
1964	Abdon Pamich, Italy	4h. 11m. 11.4s
1968	Christoph Hohne, E. Germany	4h. 20m. 13.6s
1972	Bern Kannenberg, W. Germany	3h. 56m. 11.6s
1980	Hartwig Gauter, E. Germany	3h. 49m. 24.0s*

110-Meter Hurdles

1896	Thomas Curtis, United States	17.6s
1900	Alvin Kraenzlein, United States	15.4s
1904	Frederick Schule, United States	16s
1908	Forrest Smithson, United States	15s
1912	Frederick Kelly, United States	15.1s
1920	Earl Thomson, Canada	14.8s
1924	Daniel Kinsey, United States	15s
1928	Sydney Atkinson, South Africa	14.8s
1932	George Saling, United States	14.6s
1936	Forrest Towns, United States	14.2s
1948	William Porter, United States	13.9s
1952	Harrison Dillard, United States	13.7s
1956	Lee Calhoun, United States	13.5s
1960	Lee Calhoun, United States	13.8s
1964	Hayes Jones, United States	13.6s
1968	Willie Davenport, United States	13.3s
1972	Rod Milburn, United States	13.24s*
1976	Guy Drut, France	13.30s
1980	Thomas Munkelt, E. Germany	13.39s

200-Meter Hurdles

1900	Alvin Kraenzlein, United States	25.4s
1904	Harry Hillman, United States	24.6s*

400-Meter Hurdles

1900	J.W.B. Tewksbury, United States	57.6s
1904	Harry Hillman, United States	53s
1908	Charles Bacon, United States	55s
1920	Frank Loomis, United States	54s
1924	F. Morgan Taylor, United States	52.6s
1928	Lord Burghley, Great Britain	53.4s
1932	Robert Tisdall, Ireland	51.8s
1936	Glenn Hardin, United States	52.4s
1948	Roy Cochran, United States	51.1s
1952	Charles Moore, United States	50.8s
1956	Glenn Davis, United States	50.1s
1960	Glenn Davis, United States	49.3s
1964	Rex Cawley, United States	49.6s
1968	Dave Hemery, Great Britain	48.1s
1972	John Akii-Bua, Uganda	47.82s
1976	Edwin Moses, United States	47.64s*
1980	Volker Beck, E. Germany	48.70s

Standing High Jump

1900	Ray Ewry, United States	5ft. 5 in.
1904	Ray Ewry, United States	4ft. 11 in.
1908	Ray Ewry, United States	5ft. 2 in.
1912	Platt Adams, United States	5ft. 4 1-4 in.*

Running High Jump

1896	Ellery Clark, United States	5ft. 11 1-4 in.
1900	Irving Baxter, United States	6ft. 2 4-5 in.
1904	Samuel Jones, United States	5ft. 11 in.
1908	Harry Porter, United States	6ft. 3 in.
1912	Alma Richards, United States	6ft. 4 in.
1920	Richard Landon, United States	6ft. 4 1-4 in.
1924	Harold Osborn, United States	6ft. 6 in.
1928	Robert W. King, United States	6ft. 4 3-8 in.
1932	Duncan McNaughton, Canada	6ft. 5 5-8 in.
1936	Cornelius Johnson, United States	6ft. 7 15-16 in.
1948	John L. Winter, Australia	6ft. 6 in.
1952	Walter Davis, United States	6ft. 8.32 in.
1956	Charles Dumas, United States	6ft. 11 1-4 in.
1960	Robert Shavlakadze, USSR	7ft. 1 in.

1964	Valery Brumel, USSR.	7ft. 1 3-4 in.
1968	Dick Fosbury, United States	7ft. 4 1-4 in.
1972	Yuri Tarmak, USSR.	7ft. 3 3-4 in.
1976	Jacek Wszola, Poland	7ft. 4 1-2 in.
1980	Gerd Wessig, E. Germany	7ft. 8 3-4 in.*

Standing Broad Jump

1900	Ray Ewry, United States	10ft. 6 2-5 in.
1904	Ray Ewry, United States.	11ft. 4 7-8 in.*
1908	Ray Ewry, United States	10ft. 11 1-4 in.
1912	Constantin Tsicilitras, Greece.	11ft. 3-4 in.

Long Jump

1896	Ellery Clark, United States	20ft. 9 3-4 in.
1900	Alvin Kraenzlein, United States.	23ft. 6 7-8 in.
1904	Myer Prinstein, United States	24ft. 1 in.
1908	Frank Irons, United States	24ft. 6 1-2 in.
1912	Albert Gutterson, United States.	24ft. 11 1-4 in.
1920	William Pettersson, Sweden	23ft. 5 1-2 in.
1924	DeHart Hubbard, United States	24ft. 5 1-8 in.
1928	Edward B. Hamm, United States.	25ft. 4 3-4 in.
1932	Edward Gordon, United States	25ft, 3-4 in.
1000	Jesse Owens, United States	26ft. 5 5-16 in.
1948	William Steele, United States	25ft. 8 in.
1952	Jerome Biffle, United States.	24ft. 10 in.
1956	Gregory Bell, United States.	25ft. 8 1-4 in.
1960	Ralph Boston, United States	26ft. 7 3-4 in.
1964	Lynn Davies, Great Britain	26ft. 5 3-4 in.
1968	Bob Beamon, United States.	29ft. 2 1-2 in.*
1972	Randy Williams, United States	27ft. 1-2 in.
1976	Arnie Robinson, United States	27ft. 4 1-2 in.
1980	Lutz Dombrowski, E. Germany	28ft. 1-4 in.

400-Meter Relay

1912	Great Britain	42.4s
1920	United States	42.2s
1924	United States	41s
1928	United States	41s
1932	United States	40s
1936	United States	39.8s
1948	United States	40.6s
1952	United States	40.1s
1956	United States	39.5s
1960	Germany (U.S. disqualified)	39.5s
1964	United States	39.0s
1968	United States	38.2s
1972	United States	38.19s*
1976	United States	38.33s
1980	USSR.	38.26s

1,600-Meter Relay

1908	United States.	3m. 27.2s
1912	United States.	3m. 16.6s
1920	Great Britain	3m. 22.2s
1924	United States	3m. 16s
1928	United States	3m. 14.2s
1932	United States	3m. 8.2s
1936	Great Britain	3m. 9s
1948	United States	3m. 10.4s
1952	Jamaica, B.W.I.	3m. 03.9s
1956	United States	3m. 04.8s
1960	United States	3m. 02.2s
1964	United States	3m. 00.7s
1968	United States	2m. 56.1s*
1972	Kenya.	2m. 59.8s
1976	United States	2m. 59.52s
1980	USSR.	3m. 01.1s

Pole Vault

1896	William Hoyt, United States.	10ft. 9 3-4 in.
1900	Irving Baxter, United States.	10ft. 9 7-8 in.
1904	Charles Dvorak, United States	11ft. 6 in.
1908	A. C. Gilbert, United States	
	Edward Cook Jr., United States.	12ft. 2 in.
1912	Harry Babcock, United States.	12ft. 11 1-2 in.
1920	Frank Foss, United States.	13ft. 5 in.
1924	Lee Barnes, United States.	12ft. 11 1-2 in.
1928	Sabin W. Carr, United States.	13ft. 9 3-8 in.
1932	William Miller, United States.	14ft. 1 7-8 in.
1936	Earle Meadows, United States	14ft. 3 1-4 in.
1948	Guinn Smith, United States.	14ft. 1 1-4 in.
1952	Robert Richards, United States.	14ft. 11 1-8 in.
1956	Robert Richards, United States.	14ft. 11 1-2 in.
1960	Don Bragg, United States.	15ft. 5 1-8 in.
1964	Fred Hansen, United States	16ft. 8 3-4 in.
1968	Bob Seagren, United States.	17ft. 8 1-2 in.
1972	Wolfgang Nordwig, E. Germany	18ft. 1-2 in.
1976	Tadeusz Slusarski, Poland	18ft. 1-2 in.
1980	Wladyslaw Kozakiewicz, Poland	18ft. 11 1-2 in.*

16-lb. Hammer Throw

1900	John Flanagan, United States	167ft. 4 in.
1904	John Flanagan, United States	168ft. 1 in.
1908	John Flanagan, United States	170ft. 4 1-4 in.
1912	Matt McGrath, United States	179ft. 7 1-8 in.
1920	Pat Ryan, United States	173ft. 5 5-8 in.
1924	Fred Tootell, United States	174ft. 10 1-8 in.
1928	Patrick O'Callaghan, Ireland	168ft. 7 1-2 in.
1932	Patrick O'Callaghan, Ireland.	176ft. 11 1-8 in.
1936	Karl Hein, Germany.	185ft. 4 in.
1948	Imre Nemeth, Hungary	183ft. 11 1-2 in.
1952	Jozsef Csermak, Hungary	197ft. 11 9-16 in.
1956	Harold Connolly, United States.	207ft. 3 1-2 in.
1960	Vasily Rudenkov, USSR.	220ft. 1 5-8 in.
1964	Romuald Klim, USSR.	228ft. 9 1-2 in.
1968	Gyula Zsivotsky, Hungary	240ft. 8 in.
1972	Anatoli Bondarchuk, USSR	248ft. 8 in.
1976	Yuri Syedykh, USSR	254ft. 4 in.
1980	Yuri Syedykh, USSR	268ft. 4 1-2 in.*

Discus Throw

1896	Robert Garrett, United States	95ft. 7 1-2 in.
1900	Rudolf Bauer, Hungary	118ft. 2.9-10 in.
1904	Martin Sheridan, United States.	128ft. 10 1-2 in.
1908	Martin Sheridan, United States	134ft. 2 in.
1912	Armas Taipale, Finland.	148ft. 4 in.
	Both hands—Armas Taipale, Finland. .	271ft. 10 1-4 in.
1920	Elmer Niklander, Finland	146ft. 7 1-4 in.
1924	Clarence Houser, United States	151ft. 5 1-8 in.
1928	Clarence Houser, United States	155ft. 3 in.
1932	John Anderson, United States	162ft. 4 7-8 in.
1936	Ken Carpenter, United States.	165ft. 7 3-8 in.
1948	Adolfo Consolini, Italy	173ft. 2 in.
1952	Sim Iness, United States	180ft. 6.85 in.
1956	Al Oerter, United States	184ft. 10 1-2 in.
1960	Al Oerter, United States	194ft. 2 in.
1964	Al Oerter, United States.	200ft. 1 1-2 in.
1968	Al Oerter, United States	212ft. 6 1-2 in.
1972	Ludvik Danek, Czechoslovakia	211ft. 3 in.
1976	Mac Wilkins, United States	221ft. 5.4 in.*
1980	Viktor Rashchupkin, USSR	218ft. 8 in.

Standing Hop, Step, and Jump

| 1900 | Ray Ewry, United States. . . . . | 34ft. 8 1-2 in.* |
| 1904 | Ray Ewry, United States . . . . | 34ft. 7 1-4 in. |

Triple Jump

1896	James Connolly, United States.	45ft.
1900	Myer Prinstein, United States.	47ft. 4 1-4 in.
1904	Myer Prinstein, United States	47 ft.
1908	Timothy Aheame, Great Britain	48ft. 11 1-4 in.
1912	Gustaf Lindblom, Sweden.	48ft. 5 1-8 in.
1920	Vilho Tuulos, Finland	47ft. 6 7-8 in.
1924	Archie Winter, Australia	50ft. 11 1-4 in.
1928	Mikio Oda, Japan	49ft. 11 in.
1932	Chuhei Nambu, Japan	51ft. 7 in.
1936	Naoto Tajima, Japan	52ft. 5 7-8 in.
1948	Arne Ahman, Sweden.	50ft. 6 1-4 in.
1952	Adhemar de Silva, Brazil	53ft. 2 9-16 in.
1956	Adhemar de Silva, Brazil	53ft. 7 1-2 in.
1960	Jozef Schmidt, Poland	55ft. 1 3-4 in.
1964	Jozef Schmidt, Poland	55ft. 3 1-4 in.
1968	Viktor Saneev, USSR	57ft. 3-4 in.*
1972	Viktor Saneev, USSR	56ft. 11 in.
1976	Viktor Saneev, USSR	56ft. 8 3-4 in.
1980	Jaak Uudmae, USSR	56ft. 11 1-8 in.

16-lb. Shot Put

1896	Robert Garrett, United States	36ft. 9 3-4 in.
1900	Robert Sheldon, United States	46ft. 3 1-8 in.
1904	Ralph Rose, United States	48ft. 7 in.
1908	Ralph Rose, United States	46ft. 7 1-2 in.
1912	Pat McDonald, United States	50ft. 4 in.
	Both hands—Ralph Rose,	
	United States.	90ft. 5 1-2 in.
1920	Ville Porhola, Finland	48ft. 7 1-8 in.
1924	Clarence Houser, United States	49ft. 2 1-2 in.
1928	John Kuck, United States	52ft. 3-4 in.
1932	Leo Sexton, United States	52ft. 6 3-16 in.
1936	Hans Woellke, Germany	53ft. 1 3-4 in.
1948	Wilbur Thompson, United States	56ft. 2 in.
1952	Parry O'Brien, United States	57ft. 1 7-16 in.
1956	Parry O'Brien, United States	60ft. 11 in.
1960	William Nieder, United States	64ft. 6 3-4 in.
1964	Dallas Long, United States	66ft. 8 1-4 in.
1968	Randy Matson, United States	67ft. 4 3-4 in.
1972	Wladyslaw Komar, Poland	69ft. 6 in.
1976	Udo Beyer, E. Germany	69ft. 3-4 in.
1980	Vladimir Kiselyov, USSR.	70ft. 1-2 in.*

Javelin Throw

1908	Erik Lemming, Sweden	178ft. 7 1-2 in.
	Held in middle—Erik Lemming,	
	Sweden	179ft. 10 1-2 in.
1912	Erik Lemming, Sweden	198ft. 11 1-4 in.
	Both hands, Julius Saaristo,	
	Finland	358ft. 11 7-8 in.
1920	Jonni Myrra, Finland	215ft. 9 3-4 in.
1924	Jonni Myrra, Finland	206ft. 6 3-4 in.
1928	Eric Lundquist, Sweden	218ft. 6 1-8 in.
1932	Matti Jarvinen, Finland	238ft. 7 in.
1936	Gerhard Stoeck, Germany	235ft. 8 5-16 in.
1948	Kaj Rautavaara, Finland	228ft. 10 1-2 in.
1952	Cy Young, United States	242ft. 0.79 in.
1956	Egil Danielsen, Norway	281ft. 2 1-4 in.
1960	Viktor Tsibulenko, USSR	277ft. 8 3-8 in.
1964	Pauli Nevala, Finland	271ft. 2 1-2 in.
1968	Janis Lusis, USSR	295ft. 7 1-4 in.
1972	Klaus Wolfermann, W. Germany	296ft. 10 in.
1976	Miklos Nemeth, Hungary	310ft. 4 in.*
1980	Dainis Kula, USSR	299ft. 2 3-8 in.

Decathlon

1912	Hugo Wieslander, Sweden	7,724.49 pts.
1920	Helge Lovland, Norway	6,804.35 pts.
1924	Harold Osborn, United States	7,710.77 pts.
1928	Paavo Yrjola, Finland	8,053.29 pts.
1932	James Bausch, United States	8,462.23 pts.
1936	Glenn Morris, United States	7,900 pts.
1948	Robert Mathias, United States	7,139 pts.
1952	Robert Mathias, United States	7,887 pts.
1956	Milton Campbell, United States	7,937 pts.
1960	Rafer Johnson, United States	8,392 pts.
1964	Willi Holdorf, Germany	7,887 pts.
1968	Bill Toomey, United States	8,193 pts.
1972	Nikola Avilov, USSR	8,454 pts.
1976	Bruce Jenner, United States	8,618 pts.*
1980	Daley Thompson, Great Britain	8,495pts.

Former point systems used prior to 1964.

Track and Field—Women

100-Meter Run

1928	Elizabeth Robinson, United States	12.2s
1932	Stella Walsh, Poland	11.9s
1936	Helen Stephens, United States	11.5s
1948	Francina Blankers-Koen, Netherlands	11.9s
1952	Marjorie Jackson, Australia	11.5s
1956	Betty Cuthbert, Australia	11.5s
1960	Wilma Rudolph, United States	11.0s*
1964	Wyomia Tyus, United States	11.4s
1968	Wyomia Tyus, United States	11.0s*
1972	Renate Stecher, E. Germany	11.07s
1976	Annegret Richter, W. Germany	11.08s*
1980	Ludmila Kondratyeva, USSR	11.6s

200-Meter Run

1948	Francina Blankers-Koen, Netherlands	24.4s
1952	Marjorie Jackson, Australia	23.7s
1956	Betty Cuthbert, Australia	23.4s
1960	Wilma Rudolph, United States	24.0s
1964	Edith McGuire, United States	23.0s
1968	Irena Szewinska, Poland	22.5s
1972	Renate Stecher, E. Germany	22.40s
1976	Barbel Eckert, E. Germany	22.37s
1980	Barbel Wockel, E. Germany	22.03*

400-Meter Run

1964	Betty Cuthbert, Australia	52s
1968	Colette Besson, France	52s
1972	Monika Zehrt, E. Germany	51.08s
1976	Irena Szewinska, Poland	49.29s
1980	Marita Koch, E. Germany	48.88s*

800-Meter Run

1928	Lina Radke, Germany	2m. 16.8s
1960	Ludmila Shevcova, USSR	2m. 4.3s
1964	Ann Packer, Great Britain	2m. 1.1s
1968	Madeline Manning, United States	2m. 0.9s
1972	Hildegard Flack, W. Germany	1m. 58.6s
1976	Tatyana Kazankina, USSR	1m. 54.94
1980	Nadezhda Olizayrenko, USSR	1m. 53.5s*

1,500-Meter Run

1972	Ludmila Bragina, USSR	4m. 01.4s
1976	Tatyana Kazankina, USSR	4m. 05.48s
1980	Tatyana Kazankina, USSR	3m. 56.6s*

400-Meter Relay

1928	Canada	48.4s
1932	United States	47.0s
1936	United States	46.9s
1948	Netherlands	47.5s
1952	United States	45.9s
1956	Australia	44.5s
1960	United States	44.5s
1964	Poland	43.6s
1968	United States	42.8s
1972	West Germany	42.81s
1976	East Germany	42.55s
1980	East Germany	41.60s*

1,600-Meter Relay

1972	East Germany	3m. 23s
1976	East Germany	3m. 19.23s*
1980	USSR	3m. 20.02s

80-Meter Hurdles

1932	Mildred Didrikson, United States	11.7s
1936	Trebisonda Villa, Italy	11.7s
1948	Francina Blankers-Koen, Netherlands	11.2s
1952	Shirley Strickland de la Hunty, Australia	10.9s
1956	Shirley Strickland de la Hunty, Australia	10.7s
1960	Irina Press, USSR	10.8s
1964	Karen Balzer, Germany	10.5s
1968	Maureen Caird, Australia	10.3s*

100-Meter Hurdles

1972	Annelie Ehrhardt, E. Germany	12.59
1976	Johanna Schaller, E. Germany	12.77s
1980	Vera Komisova, USSR	12.56s*

High Jump

1928	Ethel Catherwood, Canada	5ft. 3 in.
1932	Jean Shiley, United States	5ft. 5 1-4 in.
1936	Ibolya Csak, Hungary	5ft. 3 in.
1948	Alice Coachman, United States	5ft. 6 1-8 in.
1952	Esther Brand, South Africa	5ft. 5 3-4 in.
1956	Mildred L. McDaniel, United States	5ft. 9 1-4 in.
1960	Iolanda Balas, Romania	6ft. 3-4 in.
1964	Iolanda Balas, Romania	6ft. 2 3-4 in.
1968	Miloslava Reskova, Czechoslovakia	5ft. 11 3-4 in.
1972	Ulrike Meyfarth, W. Germany	6ft. 3 1-4 in.
1976	Rosemarie Ackermann, E. Germany	6ft. 3 3-4 in.
1980	Sara Simeoni, Italy	6ft. 5 1-2 in.*

Discus Throw

1928	Helena Konopacka, Poland	129ft. 11 7-8 in.
1932	Lillian Copeland, United States	133ft. 2 in.
1936	Gisela Mauermayer, Germany	156ft. 3 3-16 in.
1948	Micheline Ostermeyer, France	137ft. 6 1-2 in.
1952	Nina Romaschkova, USSR	168ft. 8 1-2 in.
1956	Olga Fikotova, Czechoslovakia	176ft. 1 1-2 in.
1960	Nina Ponomareva, USSR	180ft. 8 1-4 in.
1964	Tamara Press, USSR	187ft. 10 1-2 in.
1968	Lia Manoliu, Romania	191ft. 2 1-2 in.
1972	Faina Melnik, USSR	218ft. 7 in.
1976	Evelin Schlaak, E. Germany	226ft. 4 1-2 in.
1980	Evelin Jahl, E. Germany	229ft. 6 1-4 in.*

Javelin Throw

1932	Mildred Didrikson, United States	143ft. 4 in.
1936	Tilly Fleischer, Germany	148ft. 2 3-4 in.
1948	Herma Bauma, Austria	149ft. 6 in.
1952	Dana Zatopkova, Czechoslovakia	165ft. 7 in.
1956	Inessa Janzeme, USSR	176ft. 8 in.
1960	Elvira Ozolina, USSR	183ft. 8 in.
1964	Mihaela Penes, Romania	198ft. 7 1-2 in.
1968	Angela Nemeth, Hungary	198ft. 1-2 in.
1972	Ruth Fuchs, E. Germany	209ft. 7 in.
1976	Ruth Fuchs, E. Germany	216ft. 4 in.
1980	Maria Colon, Cuba	224ft. 5 in.*

Shot Put (8lb., 13oz.)

1948	Micheline Ostermeyer, France	45ft. 1 1-2 in.
1952	Galina Zybina, USSR	50ft. 1 1-2 in.
1956	Tamara Tishkyevich, USSR	54ft. 5 in.
1960	Tamara Press, USSR	56ft. 9 7-8 in.
1964	Tamara Press, USSR	59ft. 6 1-4 in.
1968	Margitta Gummel, E. Germany	64ft. 4 in.
1972	Nadezhda Chizova, USSR	69ft.

| 1976 | Ivanka Christova, Bulgaria. | 69ft. 5 in. |
| 1980 | Ilona Slupianek, E. Germany | 73ft. 6 1-4 in.* |

Long Jump

1948	Olga Gyarmati, Hungary	18ft. 8 1-4 in.
1952	Yvette Williams, New Zealand	20ft. 5 3-4 in.
1956	Elzbieta Krzeskinska, Poland	20ft. 9 3-4 in.
1960	Vyera Krepkina, USSR	20ft. 10 3-4 in.
1964	Mary Rand, Great Britain	22ft. 2 1-4 in.
1968	Viorica Viscopoleanu, Romania	22ft. 4 1-2 in.
1972	Heidemarie Rosendahl, W. Germany	22ft. 3 in.

| 1976 | Angela Voigt, E. Germany | 22ft. 2 1-2 in. |
| 1980 | Tatyana Kolpakova, USSR | 23ft. 2 in.* |

Pentathlon

1964	Irina Press, USSR	5,246 pts.
1968	Ingrid Becker, W. Germany	5,098 pts.
1972	Mary Peters, England	4,801 pts.
1976	Sigrun Siegl, E. Germany	4,745 pts.
1980	Nadyezhda Tkachenko, USSR	5,083pts.*

Former point system, 1964–1968

Swimming—Men

100-Meter Freestyle

1896	Alfred Hajos, Hungary	1:22.2
1904	Zoltan de Halmay, Hungary (100 yards)	1:02.8
1908	Charles Daniels, U.S.	1:05.6
1912	Duke P. Kahanamoku, U.S.	1:03.4
1920	Duke P. Kahanamoku, U.S.	1:01.4
1924	John Weissmuller, U.S.	59.0
1928	John Weissmuller, U.S.	58.6
1932	Yasuji Miyazaki, Japan	58.2
1936	Ferenc Csik, Hungary	57.6
1948	Wally Ris, U.S.	57.3
1952	Clark Scholes, U.S.	57.4
1956	Jon Henricks, Australia	55.4
1960	John Devitt, Australia	55.2
1964	Don Schollander, U.S.	53.4
1968	Mike Wenden, Australia	52.2
1972	Mark Spitz, U.S.	51.22'
1976	Jim Montgomery, U.S.	49.99*
1980	Jorg Woithe, E. Germany	50.40

200-Meter Freestyle

1968	Mike Wenden, Australia	1:55.2
1972	Mark Spitz, U.S.	1:52.78
1976	Bruce Furniss, U.S.	1:50.29
1980	Sergei Kopliakov, USSR	1:49.81*

400-Meter Freestyle

1904	C. M. Daniels, U.S. (440 yards)	6:16.2
1908	Henry Taylor, Great Britain	5:36.8
1912	George Hodgson, Canada	5:24.4
1920	Norman Ross, U.S.	5:26.8
1924	John Weissmuller, U.S.	5:04.2
1928	Albert Zorilla, Argentina	5:01.6
1932	Clarence Crabbe, U.S.	4:48.4
1936	Jack Medica, U.S.	4:44.5
1948	William Smith, U.S.	4:41.0
1952	Jean Boiteux, France	4:30.7
1956	Murray Rose, Australia	4:27.3
1960	Murray Rose, Australia	4:18.3
1964	Don Schollander, U.S.	4:12.2
1968	Mike Burton, U.S.	4:09.0
1972	Brad Cooper, Australia	4:00.27
1976	Brian Goodell, U.S.	3:51.93
1980	Vladimir Salnikov, USSR	3:51.31*

1,500-Meter Freestyle

1908	Henry Taylor, Great Britain	22:48.4
1912	George Hodgson, Canada	22:00.0
1920	Norman Ross, U.S.	22:23.2
1924	Andrew Charlton, Australia	20:06.6
1928	Arne Borg, Sweden	19:51.8
1932	Kusuo Kitamura, Japan	19:12.4
1936	Noboru Terada, Japan	19:13.7
1948	James McLane, U.S.	19:18.5
1952	Ford Konno, U.S.	18:30.0
1956	Murray Rose, Australia	17:58.9
1960	Jon Konrads, Australia	17:19.6
1964	Robert Windle, Australia	17:01.7
1968	Mike Burton, U.S.	16:38.9
1972	Mike Burton, U.S.	15:52.58
1976	Brian Goodell, U.S.	15:02.40
1980	Vladimir Salnikov, USSR	14:58.27*

400-Meter Medley Relay

1960	United States	4:05.4
1964	United States	3:58.4
1968	United States	3:54.9
1972	United States	3:48.16
1976	United States	3:42.22*
1980	Australia	3:45.70

400-Meter Freestyle Relay

1964	United States	3:33.2
1968	United States	3:31.7
1972	United States	3:26.42*

800-Meter Freestyle Relay

1908	Great Britain	10:55.6
1912	Australia	10:11.6
1920	United States	10:04.4
1924	United States	9:53.4
1928	United States	9:36.2
1932	Japan	8:58.4
1936	Japan	8:51.5
1948	United States	8:46.0
1952	United States	8:31.1
1956	Australia	8:23.6
1960	United States	8:10.2
1964	United States	7:52.1
1968	United States	7:52.3
1972	United States	7:35.78
1976	United States	7:23.22*
1980	USSR	7:23.50

100-Meter Backstroke

1904	Walter Brack, Germany (100 yds.)	1:16.8
1908	Arno Bieberstein, Germany	1:24.6
1912	Harry Hebner, U.S.	1:21.2
1920	Warren Kealoha, U.S.	1:15.2
1924	Warren Kealoha, U.S.	1:13.2
1928	George Kojac, U.S.	1:08.2
1932	Masaji Kiyokawa, Japan	1:08.6
1936	Adolph Kiefer, U.S.	1:05.9
1948	Allen Stack, U.S.	1:06.4
1952	Yoshi Oyakawa, U.S.	1:05.4
1956	David Thiele, Australia	1:02.2
1960	David Thiele, Australia	1:01.9
1968	Roland Matthes, E. Germany	58.7
1972	Roland Matthes, E. Germany	56.58
1976	John Naber, U.S.	55.49*
1980	Bengt Baron, Sweden	56.53

200-Meter Backstroke

1964	Jed Graef, U.S.	2:10.3
1968	Roland Matthes, E. Germany	2:09.6
1972	Roland Matthes, E. Germany	2:02.82
1976	John Naber, U.S.	1:59.19*
1980	Sandor Wladar, Hungary	2:01.93

100-Meter Breaststroke

1968	Don McKenzie, U.S.	1:07.7
1972	Nobutaka Taguchi, Japan	1:04.94
1976	John Hencken, U.S.	1:03.11*
1980	Duncan Goodhew, Great Britain	1:03.34

200-Meter Breaststroke

1908	Frederick Holman, Great Britain	3:09.2
1912	Walter Bathe, Germany	3:01.8
1920	Haken Malmroth, Sweden	3:04.4
1924	Robert Skelton, U.S.	2:56.6
1928	Yoshiyuki Tsuruta, Japan	2:48.8
1932	Yoshiyuki Tsuruta, Japan	2:45.4
1936	Tetsuo Hamuro, Japan	2:42.5
1948	Joseph Verdeur, U.S.	2:39.3
1952	John Davies, Australia	2:34.4
1956	Masura Furukawa, Japan	2:34.7
1960	William Mulliken, U.S.	2:37.4
1964	Ian O'Brien, Australia	2:27.8
1968	Felipe Munoz, Mexico	2:28.7
1972	John Hencken, U.S.	2:21.55

| 1976 | David Wilkie, Great Britain | 2:15.11* |
| 1980 | Robertas Zulpa, USSR | 2:15.85 |

100-Meter Butterfly

1968	Doug Russell, U.S.	55.9
1972	Mark Spitz, U.S.	54.27*
1976	Matt Vogel, U.S.	54.35
1980	Par Arvidsson, Sweden	54.92

200-Meter Butterfly

1956	William Yorzyk, U.S.	2:19.3
1960	Michael Troy, U.S.	2:12.8
1964	Kevin J. Berry, Australia	2:06.6
1968	Carl Robie, U.S.	2:08.7
1972	Mark Spitz, U.S.	2:00.70
1976	Mike Bruner, U.S.	1:59.23*
1980	Sergel Fesenko, USSR	1:59.76

200-Meter Individual Medley

| 1968 | Charles Hickcox, U.S. | 2:12.0 |
| 1972 | Gunnar Larsson, Sweden | 2:07.17* |

400-Meter Individual Medley

1964	Dick Roth, U.S.	4:45.4
1968	Charles Hickcox, U.S.	4:48.4
1972	Gunnar Larsson, Sweden	4:31.98
1976	Rod Strachan, U.S.	4:23.68
1980	Aleksandr Sidorenko, USSR	4:22.89*

Springboard Diving — Points

| 1908 | Albert Zurner, Germany | 85.5 |
| 1912 | Paul Guenther, Germany | 79.23 |

1920	Louis Kuehn, U.S.	675.00
1924	Albert White, U.S.	696.40
1928	Pete Desjardins, U.S.	185.04
1932	Michael Galitzen, U.S.	161.38
1936	Richard Degener, U.S.	161.57
1948	Bruce Harlan, U.S.	163.64
1952	David Browning, U.S.	205.29
1956	Robert Clotworthy, U.S.	159.56
1960	Gary Tobian, U.S.	170.00
1964	Kenneth Sitzberger, U.S.	159.90
1968	Bernie Wrightson, U.S.	170.15
1972	Vladimir Vasin, USSR	594.09
1976	Phil Boggs, U.S.	619.52
1980	Aleksandr Portnov, USSR	905.02

Platform Diving — Points

1904	Dr. G.E. Sheldon, U.S.	12.75
1908	Hjalmar Johansson, Sweden	83.75
1912	Erik Adlerz, Sweden	73.94
1920	Clarence Pinkston, U.S.	100.67
1924	Albert White, U.S.	487.30
1928	Pete Desjardins, U.S.	98.74
1932	Harold Smith, U.S.	124.80
1936	Marshall Wayne, U.S.	113.58
1948	Sammy Lee, U.S.	130.05
1952	Sammy Lee, U.S.	156.28
1956	Joaquin Capilla, Mexico	152.44
1960	Robert Webster, U.S.	165.56
1964	Robert Webster, U.S.	148.58
1968	Klaus Dibiasi, Italy	164.18
1972	Klaus Dibiasi, Italy	504.12
1976	Klaus Dibiasi, Italy	600.51
1980	Falk Hoffmann, E. Germany	835.65

Swimming—Women

100-Meter Freestyle

1912	Fanny Durack, Australia	1:22.2
1920	Ethelda Bleibtrey, U.S.	1:13.6
1924	Ethel Lackie, U.S.	1:12.4
1928	Albina Osipowich, U.S.	1:11.0
1932	Helene Madison, U.S.	1:06.8
1936	Hendrika Mastenbroek, Holland	1:05.9
1948	Greta Anderson, Denmark	1:06.3
1952	Katalin Szoke, Hungary	1:06.3
1956	Dawn Fraser, Australia	1:02.0
1960	Dawn Fraser, Australia	1:01.2
1964	Dawn Fraser, Australia	59.5
1968	Jan Henne, U.S.	1:00.0
1972	Sandra Neilson, U.S.	58.59
1976	Kornelia Ender, E. Germany	55.65
1980	Barbara Krause, E. Germany	54.79*

200-Meter Freestyle

1968	Debbie Meyer, U.S.	2:10.5
1972	Shane Gould, Australia	2:03.56
1976	Kornelia Ender, E. Germany	1:59.26
1980	Barbara Krause, E. Germany	1:58.33*

400-Meter Freestyle

1924	Martha Norelius, U.S.	6:02.2
1928	Martha Norelius, U.S.	5:42.8
1932	Helene Madison, U.S.	5:28.5
1936	Hendrika Mastenbroek, Netherlands	5:26.4
1948	Ann Curtis, U.S.	5:17.8
1952	Valerie Gyenge, Hungary	5:12.1
1956	Lorraine Crapp, Australia	4:54.6
1960	Susan Chris von Saltza, U.S.	4:50.6
1964	Virginia Duenkel, U.S.	4:43.3
1968	Debbie Meyer, U.S.	4:31.8
1972	Shane Gould, Australia	4:19.04
1976	Petra Thuemer E. Germany	4:09.89
1980	Ines Diers, E. Germany	4:08.76*

800-Meter Freestyle

1968	Debbie Meyer, U.S.	9:24.0
1972	Keena Rothhammer, U.S.	8:53.68
1976	Petra Thuemer, E. Germany	8:37.14
1980	Michelle Ford, Australia	8:28.90*

100-Meter Backstroke

1924	Sybil Bauer, U.S.	1:23.3
1928	Marie Braun, Netherlands	1:22.0
1932	Eleanor Holm, U.S.	1:19.4
1936	Dina Senff, Netherlands	1:18.9
1948	Karen Harup, Denmark	1:14.4
1952	Joan Harrison, South Africa	1:14.3
1956	Judy Grinham, Great Britain	1:12.9
1960	Lynn Burke, U.S.	1:09.3
1964	Cathy Ferguson, U.S.	1:07.7
1968	Kaye Hall, U.S.	1:06.2
1972	Melissa Belote, U.S.	1:05.78
1976	Ulrike Richter, E. Germany	1:01.83
1980	Rica Reinisch, E. Germany	1:00.86*

200-Meter Backstroke

1968	Pokey Watson, U.S.	2:24.8
1972	Melissa Belote, U.S.	2:19.19
1976	Ulrike Richter, E. Germany	2:13.43
1980	Rica Reinisch, E. Germany	2:11.77*

100-Meter Breaststroke

1968	Djurdjica Bjedov, Yugoslavia	1:15.8
1972	Cathy Carr, U.S.	1:13.58
1976	Hannelore Anke, E. Germany	1:11:16
1980	Ute Geweniger, E. Germany	1:10.22*

200-Meter Breaststroke

1924	Lucy Morton, Great Britain	3:32.2
1928	Hilde Schrader, Germany	3:12.6
1932	Clare Dennis, Australia	3:06.3
1936	Hideko Maehata, Japan	3:03.6
1948	Nelly Van Vliet, Netherlands	2:57.2
1952	Eva Szekely, Hungary	2:51.7
1956	Ursula Happe, Germany	2:53.1
1960	Anita Lonsbrough, Great Britain	2:49.5
1964	Galina Prozumenschikova, USSR	2:46.4
1968	Sharon Wichman, U.S.	2:44.4
1972	Beverly Whitfield, Australia	2:41.71
1976	Marina Koshevaia, USSR	2:33.35
1980	Lina Kachushite, USSR	2:29.54*

200-Meter Individual Medley

| 1968 | Claudia Kolb, U.S. | 2:24.7 |
| 1972 | Shane Gould, Australia | 2:23.07* |

400-Meter Individual Medley

1964	Donna de Varona, U.S.	5:18.7
1968	Claudia Kolb, U.S.	5:08.5
1972	Gail Neall, Australia	5:02.97
1976	Ulrike Tauber, E. Germany	4:42.77
1980	Petra Schneider, E. Germany	4:36.29*

100-Meter Butterfly

1956	Shelley Mann, U.S.	1:11.0
1960	Carolyn Schuler, U.S.	1:09.5
1964	Sharon Stouder, U.S.	1:04.7
1968	Lynn McClements, Australia	1:05.5
1972	Mayumi Aoki, Japan	1:03.34
1976	Kornelia Ender, E. Germany	1:00.13*
1980	Caren Metschuck, E. Germany	1:00.42

200-Meter Butterfly

1968	Ada Kok, Netherlands	2:24.7
1972	Karen Moe, U.S.	2:15.57
1976	Andrea Pollack, E. Germany	2:11.41
1980	Ines Geissler, E. Germany	2:10.44*

400-Meter Medley Relay

1960	United States	4:41.1
1960	United States	4:33.9
1968	United States	4:28.3
1972	United States	4:20.75
1976	East Germany	4:07.95
1980	East Germany	4:06.67*

400-Meter Freestyle Relay

1912	Great Britain	5:52.8
1920	United States	5:11.6
1924	United States	4:58.8
1928	United States	4:47.6
1932	United States	4:38.0
1936	Netherlands	4:36.0
1948	United States	4:29.2
1952	Hungary	4:24.4
1956	Australia	4:17.1
1960	United States	4:08.9
1964	United States	4:03.8
1968	United States	4:02.5

1972	United States	3:55.19
1976	United States	3:44.82
1980	East Germany	3:42.71*

Springboard Diving

		Points
1920	Aileen Riggin, U.S.	539.90
1924	Elizabeth Becker, U.S.	474.50
1928	Helen Meany, U.S.	78.62
1932	Georgia Coleman U.S.	87.52
1936	Marjorie Gestring, U.S.	89.27
1948	Victoria M. Draves, U.S.	108.74
1952	Patricia McCormick, U.S.	147.30
1956	Patricia McCormick, U.S.	142.36
1960	Ingrid Kramer, Germany	155.81
1964	Ingrid Engel-Kramer, Germany	145.00
1968	Sue Gossick, U.S.	150.77
1972	Micki King, U.S.	450.03
1976	Jenni Chandler, U.S.	506.19
1980	Irina Kalinina, USSR	725.91

Platform Diving

		Points
1912	Greta Johansson, Sweden	39.90
1920	Stefani Fryland-Clausen, Denmark	34.60
1924	Caroline Smith, U.S.	166.00
1928	Elizabeth B. Pinkston, U.S.	31.60
1932	Dorothy Poynton, U.S.	40.26
1936	Dorothy Poynton Hill, U.S.	33.93
1948	Victoria M. Draves, U.S.	68.87
1952	Patricia McCormick, U.S.	79.37
1956	Patricia McCormick, U.S.	84.85
1960	Ingrid Kramer, Germany	91.28
1964	Lesley Bush, U.S.	99.80
1968	Milena Duchkova, Czech.	109.59
1972	Ulrika Knape, Sweden	390.00
1976	Elena Vaytsekhouskaya, USSR	406.59
1980	Martina Jaschke, E. Germany	596.25

22d Summer Olympics

Moscow, USSR, July 19-Aug. 3, 1980

Final Medal Standings

(nations in alphabetical order)

	Gold	Silver	Bronze	Total		Gold	Silver	Bronze	Total
Australia	2	2	5	9	Italy	8	3	4	15
Austria	1	3	1	5	Jamaica	0	0	3	3
Belgium	1	0	0	1	Korea, North	0	3	2	5
Brazil	2	0	2	4	Lebanon	0	0	1	1
Britain	5	7	9	21	Mexico	0	1	3	4
Bulgaria	8	16	16	40	Mongolia	0	2	2	4
Cuba	8	7	5	20	Poland	3	14	14	31
Czechoslovakia	2	2	9	13	Romania	6	6	13	25
Denmark	2	1	2	5	Spain	1	3	2	6
Ethiopia	2	0	2	4	Sweden	3	3	6	12
Finland	3	1	4	8	Switzerland	2	0	0	2
France	6	5	3	14	Tanzania	0	2	0	2
Germany, East	47	36	43	126	USSR	80	70	47	197
Greece	1	0	2	3	Uganda	0	1	0	1
Guyana	0	0	1	1	Venezuela	0	1	0	1
Holland	0	1	3	4	Yugoslavia	2	3	4	9
Hungary	7	10	15	32	Zimbabwe	1	0	0	1
India	1	0	0	1	Duplicate medals awarded in some events				
Ireland	0	1	1	2					

Olympic Information

Symbol: Five rings or circles, linked together to represent the sporting friendship of all peoples. The rings also symbolize the 5 continents—Europe, Asia, Africa, Australia, and America. Each ring is a different color—blue, yellow, black, green, and red.

Flag: The symbol of the 5 rings on a plain white background.

Motto: "Citius, Altius, Fortius." Latin meaning "faster, higher, braver," or the modern interpretation "swifter, higher, stronger". The motto was coined by Father Didon, a French educator, in 1895.

Creed: "The most important thing in the Olympic Games is not to win but to take part, just as the most important thing in life is not the triumph but the struggle. The essential thing is not to have conquered but to have fought well."

Oath: An athlete of the host country recites the following at the opening ceremony. "In the name of all competitors I promise that we will take part in these Olympic Games, respecting and abiding by the rules which govern them, in the true spirit of sportsmanship for the glory of sport and the honor of our teams." Both the oath and the creed were composed by Pierre de Coubertin, the founder of the modern Games.

Flame: Symbolizes the continuity between the ancient and modern Games. The modern version of the flame was adopted in 1936. The torch used to kindle the flame is first lit by the sun's rays at Olympia, Greece, and then carried to the site of the Games by relays of runners. Ships and planes are used when necessary.

Winter Olympic Games Champions, 1924-1980

Sites and Unofficial Winners of Games

1924 Chamonix, France (Norway)	**1952** Oslo, Norway (Norway)	**1972** Sapporo, Japan (USSR)
1928 St. Moritz, Switzerland (Norway)	**1956** Cortina d'Ampezzo, Italy (USSR)	**1976** Innsbruck, Austria (USSR)
1932 Lake Placid, N.Y. (U.S.)	**1960** Squaw Valley, Cal. (USSR)	**1980** Lake Placid, N.Y. (E. Germany)
1936 Garmisch-Partenkirchen (Norway)	**1964** Innsbruck, Austria (USSR)	**1984** Sarajevo, Yugoslavia (scheduled)
1948 St. Moritz (Sweden)	**1968** Grenoble, France (Norway)	

Biathlon

10 Kilometers

	Time
1980 Frank Ulrich, E. Germany	0£:10.60

20 Kilometers

	Time
1960 Klas Lestander, Sweden	1:33:21.6
1964 Vladimir Melanin, USSR	1:20:26.8
1968 Magnar Solberg, Norway	1:13:45.9
1972 Magnar Solberg, Norway	1:15:55.50
1976 Nikolai Kruglov, USSR	1:14:12.26
1980 Anatoly Alabyev, USSR	1:08:16.31

40-Kilometer Relay

	Time
1968 USSR, Norway, Sweden	2:13:02
1972 USSR, Finland, E. Germany	1:51:44
1976 USSR, Finland, E. Germany	1:57:55.64
1980 USSR, E. Germany, W. Germany (30 km.)	1:34:03.27

Bobsledding

4-Man Bob

(Driver in parentheses)	Time
1924 Switzerland (Edward Scherrer)	5:45.54
1928 United States (William Fiske) (5-man)	3:20.50
1932 United States (William Fiske)	7:53.68
1936 Switzerland (Pierre Musy)	5:19.85
1948 United States (Edward Rimkus)	5:20.10
1952 Germany (Andreas Ostler)	5:07.84
1956 Switzerland (Frank Kapus)	5:10.44
1964 Canada (Victor Emery)	4:14.46
1968 Italy (Eugenio Monti) (2 races)	2:17.39
1972 Switzerland (Jean Wicki)	4:43.07
1976 E. Germany (Meinhard Nehmer)	3:40.43
1980 E. Germany (Meinhard Nehmer)	3:59.92

2-Man Bob

	Time
1932 United States (Hubert Stevens)	8:14.74
1936 United States (Ivan Brown)	5:29.29
1948 Switzerland (F. Endrich)	5:29.20
1952 Germany (Andreas Ostler)	5:24.54
1956 Italy (Dalla Costa)	5:30.14
1964 Great Britain (Antony Nash)	4:21.90
1968 Italy (Eugenio Monti)	4:41.54
1972 W. Germany (Wolfgang Zimmerer)	4:47.07
1976 E. Germany (Meinhard Nehmer)	3:40.43
1980 Switzerland (Erich Schaerer)	4:09.36

Figure Skating

Men's Singles

1908 Ulrich Sachow, Sweden
1920 Gillis Grafstrom, Sweden
1924 Gillis Grafstrom, Sweden
1928 Gillis Grafstrom, Sweden
1932 Karl Schaefer, Austria
1936 Karl Schaefer, Austria
1948 Richard Button, U.S.
1952 Richard Button, U.S.
1956 Hayes Alan Jenkins, U.S.
1960 David W. Jenkins, U.S.
1964 Manfred Schnelldorfer, Germany
1968 Wolfgang Schwartz, Austria
1972 Ondrej Nepela, Czechoslovakia
1976 John Curry, Great Britain
1980 Robin Cousins, Great Britain

Women's Singles

1908 Madge Syers, Great Britain
1920 Magda Julin-Mauroy, Sweden
1924 Heima von Szabo-Planck, Austria
1928 Sonja Henie, Norway
1932 Sonja Henie, Norway
1936 Sonja Henie, Norway
1948 Barbara Ann Scott, Canada
1952 Jeanette Altwegg, Great Britain
1956 Tenley Albright, U.S.
1960 Carol Heiss, U.S.
1964 Sjoukje Dijkstra, Netherlands

1968 Peggy Fleming, U.S.
1972 Beatrix Schuba, Austria
1976 Dorothy Hamill, U.S.
1980 Anett Poetzsch, E. Germany

Pairs

1908 Anna Hubler & Heinrich Burger, Germany
1920 Ludovika & Walter Jakobsson, Finland
1924 Helene Engelman & Alfred Berger, Austria
1928 Andree Joly & Pierre Brunet, France
1932 Andree Joly & Pierre Brunet, France
1936 Maxie Herber & Ernest Baier, Germany
1948 Micheline Lannoy & Pierre Baugniet, Belgium
1952 Ria and Paul Falk, Germany
1956 Elisabeth Schwarz & Kurt Oppelt, Austria
1960 Barbara Wagner & Robert Paul, Canada
1964 Ludmila Beloussova & Oleg Protopopov, USSR
1968 Ludmila Beloussova & Oleg Protopopov, USSR
1972 Irina Rodnina & Alexei Ulanov, USSR
1976 Irina Rodnina & Aleksandr Zaitzev, USSR
1980 Irina Rodnina & Aleksandr Zaitzev, USSR

Ice Dancing

1976 Ludmila Pakhomova & Aleksandr Gorshkov, USSR
1980 Natalya Linichuk & Gennadi Karponosov, USSR

Alpine Skiing

Men's Downhill

	Time
1948 Henri Oreiller, France	2:55.0
1952 Zeno Colo, Italy	2:30.8
1956 Anton Sailer, Austria	2:52.2
1960 Jean Vuarnet, France	2:06.0
1964 Egon Zimmermann, Austria	2:18.16
1968 Jean Claude Killy, France	1:59.85
1972 Bernhard Russi, Switzerland	1:51.43
1976 Franz Klammer, Austria	1:45.73
1980 Leonhard Stock, Austria	1:45.50

Men's Giant Slalom

	Time
1952 Stein Eriksen, Norway	2:25.0
1956 Anton Sailer, Austria	3:00.1
1960 Roger Staub, Switzerland	1:48.3
1964 Francois Bonlieu, France	1:46.71
1968 Jean Claude Killy, France	3:29.28
1972 Gustavo Thoeni, Italy	3:09.62
1976 Heini Hemmi, Switzerland	3:26.97
1980 Ingemar Stenmark, Sweden	2:40.74

Men's Slalom

	Time
1948 Edi Reinalter, Switzerland	2:10.3
1952 Othmar Schneider, Austria	2:00.0
1956 Anton Sailer, Austria	194.7 pts.
1960 Ernst Hinterseer, Austria	2:08.9
1964 Josef Stiegler, Austria	2:11.13
1968 Jean Claude Killy, France	1:39.73
1972 Francesco Fernandez Ochoa, Spain	1:49.27
1976 Piero Gros, Italy	2:03.29
1980 Ingemar Stenmark, Sweden	1:44.26

Women's Downhill

	Time
1948 Heidi Schlunegger, Switzerland	2:28.3
1952 Trude Jochum-Beiser, Austria	1:47.1
1956 Madeline Berthod, Switzerland	1:40.7
1960 Heidi Biebl, Germany	1:37.6
1964 Christi Haas, Austria	1:55.39
1968 Olga Pall, Austria	1:40.87
1972 Marie Therese Nadig, Switzerland	1:36.68
1976 Rosi Mittermaier, W. Germany	1:46.16
1980 Annemarie Proell Moser, Austria	1:37.52

Women's Giant Slalom

	Time
1952 Andrea Mead Lawrence, U.S.	2:06.8
1956 Ossi Reichert, Germany	1:56.5
1960 Yvonne Ruegg, Switzerland	1:39.9
1964 Marielle Goitschel, France	1:52.24

1968 Nancy Greene, Canada		1:51.97
1972 Marie Therese Nadig, Switzerland		1:29.90
1976 Kathy Kreiner, Canada		1:29.13
1980 Hanni Wenzel, Liechtenstein (2 runs)		2:41.66

Women's Slalom		Time
1948 Gretchen Fraser, U.S.		1:57.2
1952 Andrea Mead Lawrence, U.S.		2:10.6
1956 Renee Colliard, Switzerland		112.3 pts.
1960 Anne Heggtveigt, Canada		1:49.6
1964 Christine Goitschel, France		1:29.86
1968 Marielle Goitschel, France		1:25.86
1972 Barbara Cochran, U.S.		1:31.24
1976 Rosi Mittermaier, W. Germany		1:30.54
1980 Hanni Wenzel, Liechtenstein		1:25.09

Nordic Skiing

Men's Cross-Country Events

15 kilometers (9.3 miles)	Time
1924 Thorleif Haug, Norway	1:14:31
1928 Johan Grottumsbraaten, Norway	1:37:01
1932 Sven Utterstrom, Sweden	1:23:07
1936 Erik-August Larsson, Sweden	1:14:38
1948 Martin Lundstrom, Sweden	1:13:50
1952 Hallgeir Brenden, Norway	1:01:34
1956 Hallgeir Brenden, Norway	49:39.0
1960 Haakon Brusveen, Norway	51:55.0
1964 Eero Maentyranta, Finland	50:54.1
1968 Harald Groenningen, Norway	47:54.2
1972 Sven-Ake Lundback, Sweden	45:28.24
1976 Nikolai Bajukov, USSR	43:58.47
1980 Thomas Wassberg, Sweden	41:57.63
(Note: approx. 18-km. course 1924-1952)	

30 kilometers (18.6 miles)	Time
1956 Veikko Hakulinen, Finland	1:44:06.0
1960 Sixten Jernberg, Sweden	1:51:03.9
1964 Eero Maentyranta, Finland	1:30:50.7
1968 Franco Nones, Italy	1:35:39.2
1972 Vyacheslav Vedenin, USSR	1:36:31.15
1976 Sergei Savaliev, USSR	1:30:29.38
1980 Nikolai Zimyatov, USSR	1:27:02.80

50 kilometers (31 miles)	Time
1924 Thorleif Haug, Norway	3:44:32.0
1928 Per Erik Hedlund, Sweden	4:52:03.0
1932 Veli Saarinen, Finland	4:28:00.0
1936 Elis Viklund, Sweden	3:30:11.0
1948 Nils Karlsson, Sweden	3:47:48.0
1952 Veikko Hakulinen, Finland	3:33:33.0
1956 Sixten Jernberg, Sweden	2:50:27.0
1960 Kalevi Hamalainen, Finland	2:59:06.3
1964 Sixten Jernberg, Sweden	2:43:52.6
1968 Ole Ellefsaeter, Norway	2:28:45.8
1972 Paal Tyldum, Norway	2:43:14.75
1976 Ivar Formo, Norway	2:37:30.05
1980 Nikolai Zimyatov, USSR	2:27:24.60

40-km. Cross-Country Relay	Time
1936 Finland, Norway, Sweden	2:41:33.0
1948 Sweden, Finland, Norway	2:32:08.0
1952 Finland, Norway, Sweden	2:20:16.0
1956 USSR, Finland, Sweden	2:15:30.0
1960 Finland, Norway, USSR	2:18:45.6
1964 Sweden, Finland, USSR	2:18:34.6
1968 Norway, Sweden, Finland	2:08:33.5
1972 USSR, Norway, Switzerland	2:04:47.94
1976 Finland, Norway, USSR	2:07:59.72
1980 USSR, Norway, Finland	1:57:03.46

Combined Cross-Country & Jumping	Points
1924 Thorleif Haug, Norway	453.800
1928 Johan Grottumsbraaten, Norway	427.800
1932 Johan Grottumsbraaten, Norway	446.200
1936 Oddbjorn Hagen, Norway	430.300
1948 Heikki Hasu, Finland	448.800
1952 Simon Slattvik, Norway	451.621
1956 Sverre Stenersen, Norway	455.000
1960 Georg Thoma, Germany	457.952
1964 Tormod Knutsen, Norway	469.280
1968 Franz Keller, W. Germany	449.040
1972 Ulrich Wehling, E. Germany	413.340
1976 Ulrich Wehling, E. Germany	423.390
1980 Ulrich Wehling, E. Germany	432.200

Ski Jumping (90 meters)	Points
1924 Jacob Thams, Norway	227.5
1928 Alfred Andersen, Norway	230.5

1932 Birger Ruud, Norway		228.0
1936 Birger Ruud, Norway		232.0
1948 Petter Hugsted, Norway		228.1
1952 Anders Bergmann, Norway		226.0
1956 Antti Hyvarinen, Finland		227.0
1960 Helmut Recknagel, Germany		227.2
1964 Toralf Engan, Norway		230.7
1968 Vladimir Beloussov, USSR		231.3
1972 Wojiech Fortuna, Poland		219.9
1976 Karl Schnabl, Austria		234.8
1980 Jouko Tormanen, Finland		231.5

Ski Jumping (70 meters)	Points
1964 Veikko Kankkonen, Finland	229.9
1968 Jiri Raska, Czechoslovakia	216.5
1972 Yukio Kasaya, Japan	244.2
1976 Hans Aschenbach, E. Germany	252.0
1980 Anton Innauer, Austria	266.3

Women's Events

5 kilometers (approx. 3.1 miles)	Time
1964 Claudia Boyarskikh, USSR	17:50.5
1968 Toini Gustafsson, Sweden	16:45.2
1972 Galina Koulacova, USSR	17:00.50
1976 Helena Takalo, Finland	15:48.69
1980 Raisa Smetanina, USSR	15:06.92

10 kilometers	Time
1952 Lydia Wideman, Finland	41:40.0
1956 Lyubov Kosyreva, USSR	38:11.0
1960 Maria Gusakova, USSR	39:46.6
1964 Claudia Boyarskikh, USSR	40:24.3
1968 Toini Gustafsson, Sweden	36:46.5
1972 Galina Koulacova, USSR	34:17.82
1976 Raisa Smetanina, USSR	30:13.41
1980 Barbara Petzold, E. Germany	30:31.54

15-km. Cross-Country Relay	Time
1956 Finland, USSR, Sweden	1:09:01.0
1960 Sweden, USSR, Finland	1:04:21.4
1964 USSR, Sweden, Finland	59:20.2
1968 Norway, Sweden, USSR	57:30.0
1972 USSR, Finland, Norway	48:46.1
1976 USSR, Finland, E. Germany (20 km.)	1:07:49.75
1980 E. Germany, USSR, Norway (20 km.)	1:02:11.10

Ice Hockey

1920 Canada, U.S., Czechoslovakia	
1924 Canada, U.S., Great Britain	
1928 Canada, Sweden, Switzerland	
1932 Canada, U.S., Germany	
1936 Great Britain, Canada, U.S.	
1948 Canada, Czechoslovakia, Switzerland	
1952 Canada, U.S., Sweden	
1956 USSR, U.S., Canada	
1960 U.S., Canada, USSR	
1964 USSR, Sweden, Czechoslovakia	
1968 USSR, Czechoslovakia, Canada	
1972 USSR, U.S., Czechoslovakia	
1976 USSR, Czechoslovakia, W. Germany	
1980 U.S., USSR, Sweden	

Luge

Men's Singles	Time
1964 Thomas Keohler, Germany	3:26.77
1968 Manfred Schmid, Austria	2:52.48
1972 Wolfgang Scheidel, E. Germany	3:27.58
1976 Detlef Guenther, E. Germany	3:27.688
1980 Bernhard Glass, E. Germany	2:54.796

Men's Doubles	Time
1964 Austria	1:41.62
1968 E. Germany	1:35.85
1972 Italy, E. Germany (tie)	1:28.35
1976 E. Germany	1:25.604
1980 E. Germany	1:19.331

Women's Singles	Time
1964 Ortun Enderlein, Germany	3:24.67
1968 Erica Lechner, Italy	2:28.66
1972 Anna M. Muller, E. Germany	2:59.18
1976 Margit Schumann, E. Germany	2:50.621
1980 Vera Zozulya, USSR	2:36.537

Speed Skating

Men's Events

500 meters (approx. 547 yds.)	Time
1924 Charles Jewtraw, U.S.	0:44.0
1928 Clas Thunberg, Finland &	
Bernt Evensen, Norway (tie)	0:43.4
1932 John A. Shea, U.S.	0:43.4
1936 Ivar Ballangrud, Norway	0:43.4
1948 Finn Helgesen, Norway	0:43.1
1952 Kenneth Henry, U.S.	0:43.2
1956 Evgeniy Grishin, USSR	0:40.2
1960 Evgeniy Grishin, USSR	0:40.2
1964 Terry McDermott, U.S.	0:40.1
1968 Erhard Keller, W. Germany	0:40.3
1972 Erhard Keller, W. Germany	0:39.44
1976 Evgeny Kulikov, USSR	0:39.17
1980 Eric Heiden, U.S.	0:38.03

1,000 meters	Time
1976 Peter Mueller, U.S.	1:19.32
1980 Eric Heiden, U.S.	1:15.18

1,500 meters	Time
1924 Clas Thunberg, Finland	2:20.8
1928 Clas Thunberg, Finland	2:21.1
1932 John A. Shea, U.S.	2:57.2
1936 Charles Mathiesen, Norway	2:19.2
1948 Sverre Farstad, Norway	2:17.6
1952 Hjalmar Andersen, Norway	2:20.4
1956 Evgenly Grishin, &	
Yuri Mikhailov, both USSR (tie)	2:08.6
1960 Roald Edgar Aas, Norway &	
Evgeniy Grishin, USSR (tie)	2:10.4
1964 Ants Anston, USSR	2:10.3
1968 Cornelis Verkerk, Netherlands	2:03.4
1972 Ard Schenk, Netherlands	2:02.96
1976 Jan Egil Storholt, Norway	1:59.38
1980 Eric Heiden, U.S.	1:55.44

5,000 meters	Time
1924 Clas Thunberg, Finland	8:39.0
1928 Ivar Ballangrud, Norway	8:50.5
1932 Irving Jaffee, U.S.	9:40.8
1936 Ivar Ballangrud, Norway	8:19.6
1948 Reidar Liaklev, Norway	8:29.4
1952 Hjalmar Andersen, Norway	8:10.6
1956 Boris Shilkov, USSR	7:48.7
1960 Viktor Kosichkin, USSR	7:51.3
1964 Knut Johannesen, Norway	7:38.4
1968 F. Anton Maier, Norway	7:22.4

	Time
1972 Ard Schenk, Netherlands	7:23.61
1976 Sten Stensen, Norway	7:24.48
1980 Eric Heiden, U.S.	7:02.29

10,000 meters	Time
1924 Julius Skutnabb, Finland	18:04.8
1928 Event not held, thawing of ice	
1932 Irving Jaffee, U.S.	19:13.6
1936 Ivar Ballangrud, Norway	17:24.3
1948 Ake Seyffarth, Norway	17:26.3
1952 Hjalmar Andersen, Norway	16:45.8
1956 Sigvard Ericsson, Sweden	16:35.9
1960 Knut Johannesen, Norway	15:46.6
1964 Jonny Nilsson, Sweden	15:50.1
1968 Jonny Hooglin, Sweden	15:23.6
1972 Ard Schenk, Netherlands	15:01.3
1976 Piet Kleine, Netherlands	14:50.59
1980 Eric Heiden, U.S.	14:28.13

Women's Events

500 meters	Time
1960 Helga Haase, Germany	0:45.9
1964 Lydia Skoblikova, USSR	0:45.0
1968 Ludmila Titova, USSR	0:46.1
1972 Anne Henning, U.S.	0:43.44
1976 Sheila Young, U.S.	0:42.76
1980 Karin Enke, E. Germany	0:41.78

1,000 meters	Time
1960 Klara Guseva, USSR	1:34.1
1964 Lydia Skoblikova, USSR	1:33.2
1968 Caroline Geijssen, Netherlands	1:32.6
1972 Monika Pflug, W. Germany	1:31.40
1976 Tatiana Averina, USSR	1:28.43
1980 Natalya Petruseva, USSR	1:24.10

1,500 meters	Time
1960 Lydia Skoblikova, USSR	2:52.2
1964 Lydia Skoblikova, USSR	2:22.6
1968 Kaija Mustonen, Finland	2:22.4
1972 Dianne Holum, U.S.	2:20.85
1976 Galina Stepanskaya, USSR	2:16.58
1980 Anne Borckink, Netherlands	2:10.95

3,000 meters	Time
1960 Lydia Skoblikova, USSR	5:14.3
1964 Lydia Skoblikova, USSR	5:14.9
1968 Johanna Schut, Netherlands	4:56.2
1972 Stien Baas-Kaiser, Netherlands	4:52.14
1976 Tatiana Averina, USSR	4:45.19
1980 Bjoerg Eva Jensen, Norway	4:32.13

Winter Olympic Medal Winners in 1980

Lake Placid, N.Y., Feb. 12-24

	Gold	Silver	Bronze	Total		Gold	Silver	Bronze	Total
Austria	3	2	2	7	Italy	0	2	0	2
Bulgaria	0	0	1	1	Japan	0	1	0	1
Canada	0	1	1	2	Liechtenstein	2	2	0	4
Czechoslovakia	0	0	1	1	Netherlands	1	2	1	4
Finland	1	5	3	9	Norway	1	3	6	10
France	0	0	1	1	Sweden	3	0	1	4
Germany, East	9	7	7	23	Switzerland	1	1	3	5
Germany, West	0	2	3	5	USSR	10	6	6	22
Great Britain	1	0	0	1	United States	6	4	2	12
Hungary	0	1	0	1					

Westminster Kennel Club

Year	Best-in-show	Breed	Owner
1969	Ch. Glamoor Good News	Skye terrier	Walter & Mrs. Adele F. Goodman
1970	Ch. Arriba's Prima Donna	Boxer	Dr. & Mrs. P. J. Pagano & Dr. Theodore S. Fickles
1971	Ch. Chinoe's Adamant James	English springer spaniel	Dr. Milton Prickett
1972	Ch. Chinoe's Adamant James	English springer spaniel	Dr. Milton Prickett
1973	Ch. Acadia Command Performance	Poodle	Mrs. Jo Ann Sering & Edward B. Jenner
1974	Ch. Gretchenhof Columbia River	German pointer	Dr. Richard Smith
1975	Ch. Sir Lancelot of Barvan	Old English sheepdog	Mr. & Mrs. Ronald Vanword
1976	Ch. Jo-Ni's Red Baron of Crofton	Lakeland terrier	Virginia Dickson
1977	Ch. Dersade Bobby's Girl	Sealyham terrier	Dorothy Wyrner
1978	Ch. Cede Higgens	Yorkshire terrier	Barbara & Charles Switzer
1979	Ch. Oak Tree's Irishtocrat	Irish water spaniel	Anne E. Snelling
1980	Ch. Sierra Cinnar	Siberian husky	Kathleen Kanzler
1981	Ch. Dhandy Favorite Woodchuck	Pug	Robert Houslohner

World Record Fish Caught by Rod and Reel

Source: International Game Fish Association.
Records confirmed to June, 1981

Saltwater Fish

Species	Weight	Where Caught	Date	Angler
Albacore	88 lbs. 2 oz.	Pt. Mogan, Canary Islands	Nov. 19, 1977	Siegried Dickemann
Amberjack, Greater	149 lbs.	Bermuda	June 21, 1964	Peter Simons
Barracuda, great	83 lbs.	Lagos, Nigeria	Jan. 13, 1952	K.J.W. Hackett
Bass, black sea	8 lbs. 12 oz.	Oregon Inlet, N.C.	Apr. 21, 1979	Joe W. Mizelle Sr.
Bass, giant sea	563 lbs. 8 oz.	Anacaba Island, Cal.	Aug. 20, 1968	James D. McAdam Jr.
Bass, striped	72 lbs.	Cuttyhunk, Mass.	Oct. 10, 1969	Edward J. Kirker
Bluefish	31 lbs. 12 oz.	Hatteras Inlet, N.C.	Jan. 30, 1972	James M. Hussey
Bonefish	19 lbs.	Zululand, S. Africa	May 26, 1962	Brian W. Batchelor
Bonito, Atlantic	16 lbs. 12 oz.	Canary Islands	Dec. 6, 1980	Rolf Fredderies
Bonito, Pacific	23 lbs. 8 oz.	Victoria, Mahe Seychelles	Feb. 19, 1975	Anne Cochain
Cobia	110 lbs. 5 oz.	Mombasa, Kenya	Sept. 8, 1964	Eric Tinworth
Cod	98 lbs. 12 oz.	Isle of Shoals, N.H.	June 8, 1969	Alphonse Bielevich
Conger	39 lbs. 7 oz.	Pornichet-La Baule, France	May 26, 1980	Jean-Claude Guilmineau
Dolphin	87 lbs.	Papagallo Gulf, Costa Rica	Sept. 25, 1976	Manual Salazar
Drum, black	113 lbs. 1 oz.	Lewes, Del.	Sept. 15, 1975	Gerald Townsend
Drum, red	90 lbs.	Rodanthe, N.C.	Nov. 7, 1973	Elvin Hooper
Flounder, summer	22 lbs. 7 oz.	Montauk, N.Y.	Sept. 15, 1975	Charles Nappi
Halibut, Atlantic	234 lbs.	Scrabster, Scotland	Aug. 7, 1979	Colin Booth
Halibut, California	37 lbs. 8 oz.	San Diego, Cal.	July 22, 1979	William E. Williams
Halibut, Pacific	165 lbs. 8 oz.	Sullivan Bay, B.C.	July 17, 1979	Stephanie Pollard
Jack, crevalle	51 lbs.	Lake Worth, Fla.	June 20, 1978	Stephen Schwenk
Jack, horse-eye	22 lbs.	Miami Beach, Fla.	Aug. 26, 1980	Donald Ball
Jewfish	680 lbs.	Fernandina Beach, Fla.	May 20, 1961	Lynn Joyner
Kawakawa	26 lbs.	Merimbula, Australia	Jan. 26, 1980	Wally Elfring
Mackerel, king	90 lbs.	Key West, Fla.	Feb. 16, 1976	Norton Thomton
Marlin, Atlantic blue	1,282 lbs.	St. Thomas, Virgin Islands	Aug. 6, 1977	Larry Martin
Marlin, black	1,560 lbs.	Cabo Blanco, Peru	Aug. 4, 1953	A. C. Glassell Jr.
Marlin, Pacific blue	1,153 lbs.	Guam	Aug. 21, 1969	Greg Perez
Marlin, striped	417 lbs. 8 oz.	Cavalli Islands, New Zealand	Jan. 14, 1977	Phillip Bryers
Marlin, white	181 lbs. 14 oz.	Vitoria, Brazil	Dec. 8, 1979	Evandro Luiz Caser
Permit	51 lbs. 8 oz.	Lake Worth, Fla.	Apr. 28, 1978	William M. Kenney
Pollack	16 lbs. 1 oz.	Plymouth, England	Aug. 13, 1978	Peter J. Peck
Pollock	46 lbs. 7 oz.	Brielle, N.J.	May 26, 1975	John Tomes Holton
Pompano, African	41 lbs. 8 oz.	Ft. Lauderdale, Fla.	Feb. 15, 1979	Wayne Sommers
Roosterfish	114 lbs.	La Paz, Mexico	June 1, 1960	Abe Sackheim
Runner, rainbow	33 lbs. 10 oz.	Clarion Is., Mexico	Mar. 14, 1976	Ralph A. Mikkelsen
Sailfish, Atlantic	128 lbs. 1 oz.	Luanda, Angola	Mar. 27, 1974	Harm Steyn
Sailfish, Pacific	221 lbs.	Santa Cruz Is., Ecuador	Feb. 12, 1947	C. W. Stewart
Seabass, white	83 lbs. 12 oz.	San Felipe, Mexico	Mar. 31, 1953	L.C. Baumgardner
Seatrout, spotted	16 lbs.	Mason's Beach, Va.	May 28, 1977	William Katko
Shark, blue	437 lbs.	Catherine Bay, N.S.W. Australia	Oct. 2, 1976	Peter Hyde
Shark, hammerhead	717 lbs.	Jacksonville Beach, Fla.	July 27, 1980	Richard E. Morse
Shark, man-eater or white	2,664 lbs.	Ceduna, Australia	Apr. 21, 1959	Alfred Dean
Shark, porbeagle	465 lbs.	Cornwall, England	July 23, 1976	Jorge Potier
Shark, shortfin mako	1,080 lbs.	Montauk, N.Y.	Aug. 26, 1979	James Melanson
Shark, thresher	739 lbs.	Tutukaka, New Zealand	Feb. 17, 1975	Brian Galvin
Shark, tiger	1,780 lbs.	Cherry Grove, S.C.	June 14, 1964	Walter Maxwell
Skipjack, black	14 lbs. 8 oz.	Baja, Mexico	May 24, 1977	Lorraine Carlton
Snapper, Cubera	16 lbs. 12 oz.	Miami Beach, Fla.	Feb. 27, 1980	Richard A. Klein
Snook	53 lbs. 10 oz.	Costa Rica	Oct. 18, 1978	Gilbert Ponzi
Spearfish	90 lbs. 13 oz.	Madeira Island, Portugal	June 2, 1980	Joseph Larkin
Swordfish	1,182 lbs.	Iquique, Chile	May 7, 1953	L. Marron
Tanguigue	85 lbs. 6 oz.	Rottnest Is., W. Australia	May 5, 1978	Barry Wrightson
Tarpon	283 lbs.	Lake Maracaibo, Venezuela	Mar. 19, 1956	M. Salazar
Tautog	21 lbs. 6 oz.	Cape May, N.J.	June 12, 1954	R.N. Sheafer
Trevally, lowly	116 lbs.	Pago Pago, Amer. Samoa	Feb. 20, 1978	William G. Foster
Tuna, Atlantic bigeye	375 lbs. 8 oz.	Ocean City, Md.	Aug. 26, 1977	Cecil Browne
Tuna, blackfin	42 lbs.	Bermuda	June 2, 1978	Alan J. Card
Tuna, bluefin	1,496 lbs.	Aulds Cove, Nova Scotia	Oct. 26, 1979	Ken Fraser
Tuna, dog-tooth	194 lbs.	Korea	Sept. 27, 1980	Kim Chul
Tuna, longtail	60 lbs.	Bermagui, N.S.W., Australia	Mar. 17, 1975	N.N. Webster
Tuna, Pacific bigeye	435 lbs.	Cabo Blanco, Peru	Apr. 17, 1957	Dr. Russel Lee
Tuna, skipjack	39 lbs. 15 oz.	Walker Cay, Bahamas	Jan. 21, 1952	F. Drowley
	40 lbs.	Mauritius	Apr. 19, 1971	Joseph Caboche Jr.
Tuna, southern bluefin	256 lbs. 13 oz.	Tasmania, Australia	May 29, 1979	Rodney J. Beard
Tuna, yellowfin	388 lbs. 12 oz.	San Benedicto Island, Mexico	Apr. 1, 1977	Curt Wiesenhutter
Tunny, little	27 lbs.	Key Largo, Fla.	Apr. 20, 1976	William E. Allison
Wahoo	149 lbs.	Cay Cay, Bahamas	June 15, 1962	John Pirovano
Weakfish	17 lbs. 14 oz.	Rye, N.Y.	May 31, 1980	William Herold
Yellowtail, California	71 lbs. 15 oz.	Alijos Rocks, Mexico	June 24, 1979	Michael Carpenter
Yellowtail, southern	111 lbs.	Bay of Islands, New Zealand	June 11, 1961	A.F. Plim

Freshwater Fish

Species	Weight	Where caught	Date	Angler
Bass, largemouth	22 lbs. 4 oz.	Montgomery Lake, Ga.	June 2, 1932	George W. Perry
Bass, peacock	21 lbs.	Orinoco River, Colombia	Feb. 6, 1981	David Orndorf
Bass, redeye	8 lbs. 3 oz.	Flint River, Ga.	Oct. 23, 1977	David A. Hubbard

Species	Weight	Where caught	Date	Angler
Bass, rock	3 lbs.	York River, Ont.	Aug. 1, 1974	Peter Gulgin
Bass, smallmouth	11 lbs. 15 oz.	Dale Hollow Lake, Ky.	July 9, 1955	David L. Hayes
Bass, spotted	8 lbs. 15 oz.	Lewis Smith Lake, Ala.	Mar. 18, 1978	Philip Terry Jr.
Bass, striped	59 lbs. 12 oz.	Colorado River, Ariz.	May 26, 1977	Frank Smith
Bass, white	5 lbs. 9 oz.	Colorado River, Tex.	Mar. 31, 1977	David Cordill
	5 lbs. 6 oz.	Grenada, Miss.	Apr. 21, 1979	William Mulvihill
Bass, whiterock	20 lbs.	Savannah River, Ga.	May 5, 1977	Don Raley
Bass, yellow	2 lbs. 4 oz.	Lake Monroe, Ind.	Mar. 27, 1977	Donald L. Stalker
Bluegill	4 lbs. 12 oz.	Ketona Lake, Ala.	Apr. 9, 1950	T.S. Hudson
Bowfin	21 lbs. 8 oz.	Florence, S.C.	Jan. 29, 1980	Robert Harmon
Buffalo, bigmouth	70 lbs. 5 oz.	Bastrop, La.	Apr. 21, 1980	Delbert Sisk
Buffalo, smallmouth	51 lbs.	Lawrence, Kan.	May 2, 1979	Scott Butler
Bullhead, black	8 lbs.	Lake Waccabuc, N.Y.	Aug. 1, 1951	Kani Evans
Bullhead, brown	5 lbs. 8 oz.	Veal Pond, Ga.	May 22, 1975	Jimmy Andrews
Bullhead, yellow	3 lbs.	Nelson Lake, Wis.	May 8, 1977	Mark Nessman
Burbot	18 lbs. 4 oz.	Pickford, Mich.	Jan. 31, 1980	Thomas Courteman
Carp	55 lbs. 5 oz.	Clearwater Lake, Minn.	July 10, 1952	Frank J. Ledwein
Catfish, blue	97 lbs.	Missouri River, S.D.	Sept. 16, 1959	E.B. Elliott
Catfish, channel	58 lbs.	Santee-Cooper Res., S.C.	July 7, 1964	W.B. Whaley
Catfish, flathead	79 lbs. 8 oz.	White River, Ind.	Aug. 13, 1966	Glenn T. Simpson
Catfish, white	10 lbs. 5 oz.	Raritan River, N.J.	June 23, 1976	Lewis W. Lomerson
Char, Arctic	29 lbs. 11 oz.	Arctic River, N.W.T.	Aug. 21, 1968	Jeanne P. Branson
Crappie, black	6 lbs.	Westwago, La.	Nov. 28, 1969	Lettie T. Robertson
Crappie, white	5 lbs. 3 oz.	Enid Dam, Miss.	July 31, 1957	Fred L. Bright
Dolly Varden	32 lbs.	Lake Pend Oreille, Ida.	Oct. 27, 1949	N.L. Higgins
Drum, freshwater	54 lbs. 8 oz.	Nickajack Lake, Tenn.	Apr. 20, 1972	Benny E. Hull
Gar, alligator	279 lbs.	Rio Grande River, Tex.	Dec. 2, 1951	Bill Valverde
Gar, Florida	4 lbs.	Hillsborough, Fla.	Apr. 13, 1980	Ron Haynes
Gar, longnose	50 lbs. 5 oz.	Trinity River, Tex.	July 30, 1954	Townsend Miller
Gar, shortnose	3 lbs. 5 oz.	Lake Francis Case, S.D.	June 9, 1977	J. Pawlowski
Grayling, Arctic	5 lbs. 15 oz.	Katseyedie River, N.W.T.	Aug. 16, 1967	Jeanne P. Branson
Huchen	70 lbs. 12 oz.	Carinthia, Austria	Jan. 1, 1980	Martin Esterl
Kokanee	6 lbs. 9 oz.	Priest Lake, Ida.	June 9, 1975	Jerry Verge
Muskellunge	69 lbs. 15 oz.	St. Lawrence River, N.Y.	Sept. 22, 1957	Arthur Lawton
Muskellunge, tiger	51 lbs. 3 oz.	Lac Vieux-Desert, Wis., Mich.	July 16, 1919	John Knobla
Perch, white	4 lbs. 12 oz.	Messalonskee Lake, Me.	June 4, 1949	Mrs. Earl Small
Perch, yellow	4 lbs. 3 oz.	Bordentown, N.J.	May, 1865	Dr. C.C. Abbot
Pickerel, chain	9 lbs. 6 oz.	Homerville, Ga.	Feb. 17, 1961	Baxley McQuaig Jr.
Pike, northern	62 lbs. 8 oz.	Rickenbach, Switzerland	June 15, 1979	Jurg Notzli
Redhorse, northern	3 lbs. 11 oz.	Missouri River, S.D.	May 26, 1977	Philip Laumeyer
Redhorse, silver	5 lbs. 14 oz.	Shelbyville, Ind.	Oct. 20, 1980	Ernest Harley Jr.
Salmon, Atlantic	79 lbs. 2 oz.	Tana River, Norway	1928	Henrik Henriksen
Salmon, chinook	93 lbs.	Kelp Bay, Alas.	June 24, 1977	Howard C. Rider
Salmon, chum	27 lbs. 3 oz.	Raymond Cove, Alas.	June 11, 1977	Robert A. Jahnke
Salmon, coho	31 lbs.	Cowichan Bay, B.C.	Oct. 11, 1947	Mrs. Lee Hallberg
Salmon, pink	12 lbs. 8 oz.	Morse, Kenai rivers, Alas.	Aug. 17, 1974	Steven A. Lee
Sauger	8 lbs. 12 oz.	Lake Sakakawea, N.D.	Oct. 6, 1971	Mike Fischer
Shad, American	9 lbs. 4 oz.	Delaware River, Pa.	Apr. 26, 1979	J. Edward Whitman
Splake	16 lbs. 12 oz.	Island Lake, Col.	Sept. 14, 1973	Del Canty
Sturgeon	407 lbs.	Sacramento River, Cal.	May 10, 1979	Raymond Pihenger
Sunfish, green	2 lbs. 2 oz.	Stockton Lake, Mo.	June 18, 1971	Paul M. Dilley
Sunfish, redbreast	1 lb. 8 oz.	Suwannee River, Fla.	Apr. 30, 1977	Tommy D. Cason Jr.
Sunfish, redear	4 lbs. 8 oz.	Chase City, Va.	June 19, 1970	Maurice E. Ball
Trout, brook	14 lbs. 8 oz.	Nipigon River, Ont.	July 1916	Dr. W.J. Cook
Trout, brown	35 lbs. 15 oz.	Nahuel Huapi, Argentina	Dec. 16, 1952	Eugenio Cavaglia
Trout, cutthroat	41 lbs.	Pyramid Lake, Nev.	Dec. 1925	J. Skimmerhorn
Trout, golden	11 lbs.	Cook's Lake, Wyo.	Aug. 5, 1948	Charles S. Reed
Trout, lake	65 lbs.	Great Bear Lake, N.W.T.	Aug. 8, 1970	Larry Daunis
Trout, rainbow	42 lbs. 2 oz.	Bell Island, Alas.	June 22, 1970	David Robert White
Trout, tiger	20 lbs. 13 oz.	Lake Michigan, Wis.	Aug. 12, 1978	Pete Friedland
Walleye	25 lbs.	Old Hickory Lake, Tenn.	Aug. 1, 1960	Mabry Harper
Warmouth	2 lbs. 2 oz.	Douglas Swamp, S.C.	May 19, 1973	Willie Singletary
Whitefish, lake	13 lbs. 1 oz.	Meaford, Ont.	Apr. 28, 1978	Denis Bouchard
Whitefish, mountain	5 lbs.	Athabasca River, Alta.	June 3, 1963	Orville Welch
Whitefish, round	3 lbs. 4 oz.	Leland Harbor, Mich.	Nov. 2, 1977	Vernon Bauer

Canadian Interuniversity Athletic Union Champions

	Basketball	Football	Hockey	Soccer	Swimming, Diving	Volleyball	Wrestling
1967	Windsor	Alberta	Toronto	—	Toronto	British Columbia	—
1968	Waterloo Lutheran	Queen's	Alberta	—	Toronto	Ottawa	—
1969	Windsor	Manitoba	Toronto	—	Toronto	Winnipeg	—
1970	British Columbia	Manitoba	Toronto	—	Toronto	Montreal	Alberta
1971	Acadia	Western Ontario	Toronto	—	Toronto	Winnipeg	Alberta
1972	British Columbia	Alberta	Toronto	Alberta	McGill	Winnipeg	Alberta
1973	St. Mary's	St. Mary's	Toronto	Loyola	Toronto	Winnipeg	O.U.A.A.
1974	Guelph	Western Ontario	Waterloo	British Columbia	Toronto	Winnipeg	O.U.A.A.
1975	Waterloo	Ottawa	Alberta	Victoria	Toronto	Sherbrooke	O.U.A.A.
1976	Manitoba	Western Ontario	Toronto	Concordia	Toronto	British Columbia	O.U.A.A.
1977	Acadia	Western Ontario	Toronto	York	Waterloo	Winnipeg	O.U.A.A.
1978	St. Mary's	Queen's	Alberta	Manitoba	Waterloo	Manitoba	O.U.A.A.
1979	St. Mary's	Acadia	Alberta	Alberta	Waterloo	Saskatchewan	O.U.A.A.
1980	Victoria	Alberta	Alberta	New Brunswick	Toronto	Manitoba	Lakehead
1981	Victoria		Moncton		Toronto	Alberta	Guelph

National Hockey League, 1980-81

Final Standings

Lester Patrick Division

Club	W	L	T	Pts	GF	GA
N.Y. Islanders	48	18	14	110	355	260
Philadelphia	41	24	15	97	313	249
Calgary	39	27	14	92	329	298
N.Y. Rangers	30	36	14	74	312	317
Washington	26	36	18	70	286	317

Charles F. Adams Division

Club	W	L	T	Pts	GF	GA
Buffalo	39	20	21	99	327	250
Boston	37	30	13	87	316	272
Minnesota	35	28	17	87	291	263
Quebec	30	32	18	78	314	318
Toronto	28	37	15	71	322	367

Conn Smythe Division

Club	W	L	T	Pts	GF	GA
St. Louis	45	18	17	107	352	281
Chicago	31	33	16	78	304	315
Vancouver	28	32	20	76	289	301
Edmonton	29	35	16	74	328	327
Colorado	22	45	12	57	258	344
Winnipeg	9	57	14	32	246	400

James Norris Division

Club	W	L	T	Pts	GF	GA
Montreal	45	22	13	103	332	232
Los Angeles	43	24	13	99	337	290
Pittsburgh	30	37	13	73	302	345
Hartford	21	41	18	60	292	372
Detroit	19	43	18	56	252	339

Stanley Cup Playoff Results

N.Y. Islanders defeated Toronto 3 games to 0.
N.Y. Rangers defeated Los Angeles 3 games to 1.
Edmonton defeated Montreal 3 games to 0.
Minnesota defeated Boston 3 games to 0.
Calgary defeated Chicago 3 games to 0.
Buffalo defeated Vancouver 3 games to 0.
St. Louis defeated Pittsburgh 3 games to 2.
Philadelphia defeated Quebec 3 games to 2.

Minnesota defeated Buffalo 4 games to 1.
N.Y. Rangers defeated St. Louis 4 games to 2.
N.Y. Islanders defeated Edmonton 4 games to 2.
Calgary defeated Philadelphia 4 games to 3.
N.Y. Islanders defeated N.Y. Rangers 4 games to 0.
Minnesota defeated Calgary 4 games to 2.
N.Y. Islanders defeated Minnesota 4 games to 1.

Leading Scorers

Player, team	GP	G	A	Pts
Wayne Gretzky, Edmonton	80	55	109	164
Marcel Dionne, Los Angeles	80	58	77	135
Kent Nilsson, Calgary	80	49	82	131
Mike Bossy, N.Y. Islanders	79	68	51	119
Dave Taylor, Los Angeles	72	47	65	112
Peter Stastny, Quebec	77	39	70	109
Charlie Simmer, Los Angeles	65	56	49	105
Mike Rogers, Hartford	80	40	65	105
Bernie Federko, St. Louis	78	31	73	104
Jacques Richard, Quebec	78	52	51	103

Player, team	GP	G	A	Pts
Rick Middleton, Boston	80	44	59	103
Bryan Trottier, N.Y. Islanders	73	31	72	103
Dennis Maruk, Washington	80	50	47	97
Wilf Paiement, Toronto	77	40	57	97
Wayne Babych, St. Louis	78	54	42	96
Darryl Sittler, Toronto	80	43	53	96
Mike Gartner, Washington	80	48	46	94
Bobby Smith, Minnesota	78	29	64	93
Rick Kehoe, Pittsburgh	80	55	33	88
Blake Dunlop, St. Louis	80	20	67	87

Goaltending Leaders

(Best personal goals against average)

Goalie, team	GP	MIN	GA	Avg
Richard Sevigny, Montreal	33	1777	71	2.40
Rick St. Croix, Philadelphia	27	1567	65	2.49

Goalie, team	GP	MIN	GA	Avg
Pete Peeters, Philadelphia	40	2333	115	2.96
Don Edwards, Buffalo	45	2700	133	2.96

(Most wins)

Goalie, team	GP	MIN	W	L	T
Mario Lessard, Los Angeles	64	3746	35	18	11
Mike Liut, St. Louis	61	3570	33	14	13
Tony Esposito, Chicago	66	3935	29	23	14

Goalie, team	GP	MIN	W	L	T
Rogie Vachon, Boston	53	3021	25	19	6
Greg Millen, Pittsburgh	63	3721	25	27	10

Stanley Cup Champions

1928	New York	1939	Boston	1950	Detroit	1961	Chicago
1929	Boston	1940	New York	1951	Toronto	1962	Toronto
1930	Montreal	1941	Boston	1952	Detroit	1963	Toronto
1931	Montreal	1942	Toronto	1953	Montreal	1964	Toronto
1932	Toronto	1943	Detroit	1954	Detroit	1965	Montreal
1933	New York	1944	Montreal	1955	Detroit	1966	Montreal
1934	Chicago	1945	Toronto	1956	Montreal	1967	Toronto
1935	Montreal Maroons	1946	Montreal	1957	Montreal	1968	Montreal
1936	Detroit	1947	Toronto	1958	Montreal	1969	Montreal
1937	Detroit	1948	Toronto	1959	Montreal	1970	Boston
1938	Chicago	1949	Toronto	1960	Montreal	1971	Montreal

1972	Boston
1973	Montreal
1974	Philadelphia
1975	Philadelphia
1976	Montreal
1977	Montreal
1978	Montreal
1979	Montreal
1980	N.Y. Islanders
1981	N.Y. Islanders

Conn Smythe Trophy (MVP in Playoffs)

1965	Jean Beliveau, Montreal	1971	Ken Dryden, Montreal	1977	Guy Lafleur, Montreal
1966	Roger Crozier, Detroit	1972	Bobby Orr, Boston	1978	Larry Robinson, Montreal
1967	Dave Keon, Toronto	1973	Yvan Cournoyer, Montreal	1979	Bob Gainey, Montreal
1968	Glenn Hall, St. Louis	1974	Bernie Parent, Philadelphia	1980	Bryan Trottier, N.Y. Islanders
1969	Serge Savard, Montreal	1975	Bernie Parent, Philadelphia	1981	Butch Goring, N.Y. Islanders
1970	Bobby Orr, Boston	1976	Reg Leach, Philadelphia		

NHL Trophy Winners

	Ross Trophy Leading scorer		Norris Trophy Best defenseman		Calder Trophy Best rookie
1981	Wayne Gretzky, Edmonton	1981	Randy Carlyle, Pittsburgh	1981	Peter Stastny, Quebec
1980	Marcel Dionne, Los Angeles	1980	Larry Robinson, Montreal	1980	Ray Bourque, Boston
1979	Bryan Trottier, N.Y. Islanders	1979	Denis Potvin, N.Y. Islanders	1979	Bob Smith, Minnesota
1978	Guy Lafleur, Montreal	1978	Denis Potvin, N.Y. Islanders	1978	Mike Bossy, N.Y. Islanders
1977	Guy Lafleur, Montreal	1977	Larry Robinson, Montreal	1977	Willi Plett, Atlanta
1976	Guy Lafleur, Montreal	1976	Denis Potvin, N.Y. Islanders	1976	Bryan Trottier N.Y. Islanders
1975	Bobby Orr, Boston	1975	Bobby Orr, Boston	1975	Eric Vail, Atlanta
1974	Phil Esposito, Boston	1974	Bobby Orr, Boston	1974	Denis Potvin, N.Y. Islanders
1973	Phil Esposito, Boston	1973	Bobby Orr, Boston	1973	Steve Vickers, N.Y. Rangers
1972	Phil Esposito, Boston	1972	Bobby Orr, Boston	1972	Ken Dryden, Montreal
1971	Phil Esposito, Boston	1971	Bobby Orr, Boston	1971	Gil Perreault, Buffalo
1970	Bobby Orr, Boston	1970	Bobby Orr, Boston	1970	Tony Esposito, Chicago
1969	Phil Esposito, Boston	1969	Bobby Orr, Boston	1969	Danny Grant, Minnesota
1968	Stan Mikita, Chicago	1968	Bobby Orr, Boston	1968	Derek Sanderson, Boston
1967	Stan Mikita, Chicago	1967	Harry Howell, N.Y. Rangers	1967	Bobby Orr, Boston
1966	Bobby Hull, Chicago	1966	Jacques Laperriere, Montreal	1966	Brit Selby, Toronto
1965	Stan Mikita, Chicago	1965	Pierre Pilote, Chicago	1965	Roger Crozier, Detroit
1964	Stan Mikita, Chicago	1964	Pierre Pilote, Chicago	1964	Jacques Laperriere, Montreal

	Hart Trophy MVP		Vezina Trophy Leading goalie		Lady Byng Trophy Sportsmanship
1981	Wayne Gretzky, Edmonton	1981	Sevigny, Herron, Larocque, Montreal	1981	Rick Kehoe, Pittsburgh
1980	Wayne Gretzky, Edmonton	1980	Edwards, Sauve, Buffalo	1980	Wayne Gretzky, Edmonton
1979	Bryan Trottier, N.Y. Islanders	1979	Dryden, Larocque, Montreal	1979	Bob MacMillan, Atlanta
1978	Guy Lafleur, Montreal	1978	Dryden, Larocque, Montreal	1978	Butch Goring, Los Angeles
1977	Guy Lafleur, Montreal	1977	Dryden, Larocque, Montreal	1977	Marcel Dionne, Los Angeles
1976	Bobby Clarke, Philadelphia	1976	Ken Dryden, Montreal	1976	Jean Ratelle, Boston
1975	Bobby Clarke, Philadelphia	1975	Bernie Parent, Philadelphia	1975	Marcel Dionne, Detroit
1974	Phil Esposito, Boston	1974	Tony Esposito, Chicago	1974	John Bucyk, Boston
1973	Bobby Clarke, Philadelphia		Bernie Parent, Philadelphia	1973	Gilbert Perreault, Buffalo
1972	Bobby Orr, Boston	1973	Ken Dryden, Montreal	1972	Jean Ratelle, N.Y. Rangers
1971	Bobby Orr, Boston	1972	Esposito, Smith, Chicago	1971	John Bucyk, Boston
1970	Bobby Orr, Boston	1971	Giacomin, Villemure,	1970	Phil Goyette, St. Louis
1969	Phil Esposito, Boston		N.Y. Rangers	1969	Alex Devecchio, Detroit
1968	Stan Mikita, Chicago	1970	Tony Esposito, Chicago	1968	Stan Mikita, Chicago
1967	Stan Mikita, Chicago	1969	Hall, Plante, St. Louis	1967	Stan Mikita, Chicago
1966	Bobby Hull, Chicago	1968	Worsley, Vachon, Montreal	1966	Alex Devecchio, Detroit
1965	Bobby Hull, Chicago	1967	Hall, De Jordy, Chicago	1965	Bobby Hull, Chicago
1964	Jean Beliveau, Montreal	1966	Hodge, Worsley, Montreal	1964	Ken Wharram, Chicago
		1965	Sawchuck, Bower, Toronto		
		1964	Charlie Hodge, Montreal		

Frank Selke Trophy (best defensive forward)—1978-81, Bob Gainey, Montreal.

Players in the Hockey Hall of Fame

Exhibition Place, Toronto, Ont.

Abel, Sid	Coulter, Art	Hay, George	Maxwell, Fred	Ruttan, Jack
Adams, Jack	Cowley, Bill	Hern, Riley	McGee, Frank	Sawchuck, Terry
Apps, Syl	Crawford, Rusty	Hextall, Bryan	McGimsie, Billy	Scanlan, Fred
Armstrong, George	Darragh, Jack	Holmes, Hap	McNamara, George	Schmidt, Milt
Bailey, Ace	Davidson, Scotty	Hooper, Tom	Moore, Dickie	Schriner, Sweeney
Bain, Donald	Day, Hap	Horner, Red	Moran, Patrick	Seibert, Earl
Baker, Hobey	Delvecchio, Alex	Horton, Tim	Morenz, Howie	Seibert, Oliver
Barry, Marty	Denneny, Cy	Howe, Gordie	Mosienko, Bill	Shore, Eddie
Bathgate, Andy	Drillon, Gordon	Howe, Syd	Nighbor, Frank	Siebert, Babe
Beliveau, Jean	Drinkwater, Charles	Howell, Harry	Noble, Reginald	Simpson, Joe
Benedict, Benny	Dunderdale, Tommy	Hutton, John	Oliver, Harry	Smith, Alf
Bentley, Doug	Durnan, Bill	Hyland, Harry	Orr, Bobby	Smith, Hooley
Bentley, Max	Dutton, Red	Irvin, James	Patrick, Lester	Smith, Tommy
Blake, Toe	Dye, Babe	Jackson, Busher	Patrick, Lynn	Stanley, Allan
Boon, Dickie	Farrell, Arthur	Johnson, Moose	Phillips, Tom	Stanley, Barney
Bouchard, Butch	Foyston, Frank	Johnson, Ching	Pilote, Pierre	Stewart, Jack
Boucher, Frank	Fredrickson, Frank	Johnson, Tom	Pitre, Pit	Stewart, Nels
Boucher, Buck	Gadsby, Bill	Joliat, Aurel	Plante, Jacques	Stuart, Bruce
Bower, John	Gardiner, Chuck	Keats, Gordon	Pratt, Babe	Stuart, Hod
Bowie, Russell	Gardiner, Herb	Kelly, Red	Primeau, Joe	Taylor, Cyclone
Brimsek, Frank	Gardner, Jimmy	Kennedy, Ted	Pronovost, Marcel	Trihey, Harry
Broadbent, Punch	Geoffrion, Boom Boom	Lach, Elmer	Pulford, Harvey	Thompson, Tiny
Broda, Turk	Gerard, Eddie	Lalonde, Newsy	Quakenbush, Bill	Vezina, Georges
Bucyk, Johnny	Gilmour, Billy	Laviolette, Jack	Rankin, Frank	Walsh, Martin
Burch, Billy	Goodfellow, Ebbie	Lehman, Hugh	Rayner, Chuck	Walker, Jack
Cameron, Harry	Goheen, Moose	LeSueur, Percy	Reardon, Ken	Watson, Harry
Clancy, King	Grant, Mike	Lindsay, Ted	Richard, Henri	Westwick, Harry
Clapper, Dit	Green, Shorty	Lumley, Harry	Richard, Rocket	Weiland, Cooney
Cleghorn, Sprague	Griffis, Silas	Mackay, Duncan	Richardson, George	Whitcroft, Fred
Colville, Neil	Hainsworth, George	Mahovlich, Frank	Roberts, Gordon	Wilson, Phat
Conacher, Charlie	Hall, Glenn	Mantha, Sylvio	Ross, Arthur	Worsley, Gump
Connell, Alex	Hall, Joe	Malone, Joe	Russell, Blair	Worters, Roy
Cook, Bill	Harvey, Doug	Marshall, Jack	Russell, Ernie	

NHL All Star Team, 1981

First team	Position	Second team
Mike Liut, St. Louis	Goalie	Mario Lessard, Los Angeles
Denis Potvin, N.Y. Islanders	Defense	Larry Robinson, Montreal
Randy Carlyle, Pittsburgh	Defense	Ray Bourque, Boston
Wayne Gretzky, Edmonton	Center	Marcel Dionne, Los Angeles
Mike Bossy, N.Y. Islanders	Right Wing	Dave Taylor, Los Angeles
Charlie Simmer, Los Angeles	Left Wing	Bill Barber, Philadelphia

WHA Champions and Trophy Winners

Avco World Trophy Playoff winner		Gordie Howe Trophy MVP		Hunter Trophy Leading scorer	
1973	New England Whalers	1973	Bobby Hull, Winnipeg	1973	Andre Lacroix, Philadelphia
1974	Houston Aeros	1974	Gordie Howe, Houston	1974	Mike Walton, Minnesota
1975	Houston Aeros	1975	Bobby Hull, Winnipeg	1975	Andre Lacroix, San Diego
1976	Winnipeg Jets	1976	Maro Tardif, Quebec	1976	Marc Tardif, Quebec
1977	Quebec Nordiques	1977	Robbie Ftorek, Phoenix	1977	Real Cloutier, Quebec
1978	Winnipeg Jets	1978	Marc Tardif, Quebec	1978	Marc Tardif, Quebec
1979	Winnipeg Jets	1979	Dave Dryden, Edmonton	1979	Real Cloutier, Quebec

NCAA Hockey Champions

1948	Michigan	1957	Colorado College	1966	Michigan State	1975	Michigan Tech
1949	Boston College	1958	Denver	1967	Cornell	1976	Minnesota
1950	Colorado College	1959	North Dakota	1968	Denver	1977	Wisconsin
1951	Michigan	1960	Denver	1969	Denver	1978	Boston Univ.
1952	Michigan	1961	Denver	1970	Cornell	1979	Minnesota
1953	Michigan	1962	Michigan Tech	1971	Boston Univ.	1980	North Dakota
1954	Rensselaer Poly	1963	North Dakota	1972	Boston Univ	1981	Wisconsin
1955	Michigan	1964	Michigan	1973	Wisconsin		
1956	Michigan	1965	Michigan Tech	1974	Minnesota		

Professional Sports Arenas

The seating capacity of sports arenas can vary depending on the event being presented. The figures below are the normal seating capacity for basketball. (*) indicates hockey seating capacity.

Name, location	Capacity	Name, location	Capacity
Allen County War Memorial, Ft. Wayne	*8,022	Mid-South Coliseum, Memphis	11,065
Arizona Veteran's Memorial Coliseum, Phoenix	12,660-*12,474	Milwaukee Arena	10,938-*8,000
Astrohall, Houston	10,000	Mobile Municipal Auditorium	13,100
Baltimore Civic Center	13,043-*10,200	Montreal Forum	*16,074
Boston Garden	15,320-*14,673	Myriad, Oklahoma City	*13,263
Buffalo Memorial Auditorium	17,900-*16,433(a)	Nassau Veterans Memorial Coliseum, Uniondale, N.Y.	*15,105
Capital Centre, Landover, Md.	19,035-*18,130	Norfolk Scope, Va.	10,600-*9,364
Charlotte Coliseum	11,666-*9,575	Northlands Coliseum, Edmonton	*17,046
Checkerdome, St. Louis	20,000-*17,967	Oakland Coliseum Arena	13,237
Chicago Stadium	17,374-*17,100	Olympia Stadium, Detroit	*16,673
Cincinnati Gardens	11,650-*10,606	Omaha Civic Auditorium	9,144
Cobo Hall, Detroit	11,147	The Omni, Atlanta	15,785-*15,191
The Coliseum, Richfield Township, Oh.	19,548	Ottawa Civic Center	*9,355
Convention Center, San Antonio	10,146	Pacific Coliseum, Vancouver, B.C.	*15,613
Cow Palace, San Francisco	14,500-*12,195	Penn Palestra, Philadelphia	9,200
Fairgrounds Coliseum, Indianapolis	9,479	Pittsburgh Civic Arena	*16,033
Freedom Hall, Louisville, Ky.	16,613	Portland Memorial Coliseum	12,666-*10,500
Greensboro Coliseum	15,500-*13,280	Providence Civic Center	11,619-*10,730
Halifax Metro Centre	*9,549	Quebec Coliseum	*15,300
Hampton Roads Coliseum, Va.	10,000-*8,200	Reunion Arena, Dallas	17,761
Hartford Civic Center	*14,510	Richmond Coliseum, Va.	10,700-*8,400
HemisFair Arena, San Antonio	15,693	Riverfront Coliseum, Cincinnati	*15,794
Hersheypark Arena, Pa.	*7,286	St. Paul Civic Center, Minn.	*15,594
International Amphitheatre, Chicago	9,000	Salt Palace, Salt Lake City	12,143-*10,640
Jefferson County Coliseum, Birmingham, Ala.	*16,753	San Diego Sports Arena	13,871-*13,039
Joe Louis Sports Arena, Detroit	*19,275	Seattle Center Coliseum	14,098
Kansas Coliseum, Wichita	*8,906	Silverdome, Pontiac, Mich.	22,366
Kemper Memorial Arena, Kansas City	16,642	Spectrum, Philadelphia	18,276-*17,077
Kiel Auditorium, St. Louis	10,574	Springfield Civic Center, Mass.	*7,455
Kingdome, Seattle	40,192	Stampede Corral, Calgary, Alta	*6,492
Los Angeles Forum	17,505-*16,005	The Summit, Houston	15,676-*15,256
Los Angeles Sports Arena	15,333-*11,325	Tarrant County Convention Center, Ft. Worth	13,500
Louisiana Superdome	47,284	Tingley Coliseum, Albuquerque	*12,000
Madison Square Garden, New York	19,591-*17,500	Uline Arena, Washington, D. C.	11,000
Maple Leaf Gardens, Toronto	17,000-*16,485(a)	Veterans Memorial Audit., Des Moines	15,000
Market Square Arena, Indianapolis	17,032-*15,861	Veterans Memorial Coliseum, New Haven	*8,871
McNichols Sports Arena, Denver	17,251-*16,399	Winnipeg Arena	*15,250
Meadowlands Arena, E. Rutherford, N.J.	20,000-*19,100	Winston-Salem Memorial Coliseum	9,020
Met. Sports Center, Bloomington, Minn.	*15,184	(a) includes standees	

Figure Skating Champions

National Champions | World Champions

Men	Women	Year	Men	Women
Richard Button	Tenley Albright	1952	Richard Button, U.S.	Jacqueline du Bief, France
Hayes Jenkins	Tenley Albright	1953	Hayes Jenkins, U.S.	Tenley Albright, U.S.
Hayes Jenkins	Tenley Albright	1954	Hayes Jenkins, U.S.	Gundi Busch, W. Germany
Hayes Jenkins	Tenley Albright	1955	Hayes Jenkins, U.S.	Tenley Albright, U.S.
Hayes Jenkins	Tenley Albright	1956	Hayes Jenkins, U.S.	Carol Heiss, U.S.
Dave Jenkins	Carol Heiss	1957	Dave Jenkins, U.S.	Carol Heiss, U.S.
Dave Jenkins	Carol Heiss	1958	Dave Jenkins, U.S.	Carol Heiss, U.S.
Dave Jenkins	Carol Heiss	1959	Dave Jenkins, U.S.	Carol Heiss, U.S.
Dave Jenkins	Carol Heiss	1960	Alain Giletti, France	Carol Heiss, U.S.
Bradley Lord	Laurence Owen	1961	none	none
Monty Hoyt	Barbara Roles Pursley	1962	Don Jackson, Canada	Sjoukje Dijkstra, Neth.
Tommy Litz	Lorraine Hanlon	1963	Don McPherson, Canada	Sjoukje Dijkstra, Neth.
Scott Allen	Peggy Fleming	1964	Manfred Schnelldorfer, W. Germany	Sjoukje Dijkstra, Neth.
Gary Visconti	Peggy Fleming	1965	Alain Calmat, France	Petra Burka, Canada
Scott Allen	Peggy Fleming	1966	Emmerich Danzer, Austria	Peggy Fleming, U.S.
Gary Visconti	Peggy Fleming	1967	Emmerich Danzer, Austria	Peggy Fleming, U.S.
Tim Wood	Peggy Fleming	1968	Emmerich Danzer, Austria	Peggy Fleming, U.S.
Tim Wood	Janet Lynn	1969	Tim Wood, U.S.	Gabriele Seyfert, E. Germany
Tim Wood	Janet Lynn	1970	Tim Wood, U.S.	Gabriele Seyfert, E. Germany
John Misha Petkevich	Janet Lynn	1971	Ondrej Nepela, Czech.	Beatrix Schuba, Austria
Ken Shelley	Janet Lynn	1972	Ondrej Nepela, Czech.	Beatrix Schuba, Austria
Gordon McKellen Jr.	Janet Lynn	1973	Ondrej Nepela, Czech.	Karen Magnussen, Canada
Gordon McKellen Jr.	Dorothy Hamill	1974	Jan Hoffmann, E. Germany	Christine Errath, E. Germany
Gordon McKellen Jr.	Dorothy Hamill	1975	Sergei Volkov, USSR	Dianne de Leeuw, Neth.-U.S.
Terry Kubicka	Dorothy Hamill	1976	John Curry, Gt. Britain	Dorothy Hamill, U.S.
Charles Tickner	Linda Fratianne	1977	Vladimir Kovalev, USSR	Linda Fratianne, U.S.
Charles Tickner	Linda Fratianne	1978	Charles Tickner, U.S.	Anett Potzsch, E. Germany
Charles Tickner	Linda Fratianne	1979	Vladimir Kovalev, USSR	Linda Fratianne, U.S.
Charles Tickner	Linda Fratianne	1980	Jan Hoffmann, E. Germany	Anett Potzsch, E. Germany
Scott Hamilton	Elaine Zayak	1981	Scott Hamilton, U.S.	Denise Biellmann, Switzerland

World Pairs and Dancing Champions in 1981

Irina Vorobieva and Igor Lisovsky of the Soviet Union won the 1981 world pairs figure skating championship in Hartford, Conn. Jayne Torvill and Christopher Dean of Great Britain triumphed in ice dancing.

Canadian National Figure Skating Champions

Year	Men	Women	Year	Men	Women
1964	Charles Snelling	Petra Burka	1973	Toller Cranston	Karen Magnussen
1965	Donald Knight	Petra Burka	1974	Toller Cranston	Lynn Nightingale
1966	Donald Knight	Petra Burka	1975	Toller Cranston	Lynn Nightingale
1967	Donald Knight	Valerie Jones	1976	Toller Cranston	Lynn Nightingale
1968	Jay Humphrey	Karen Magnussen	1977	Ron Shaver	Lynn Nightingale
1969	Jay Humphrey	Linda Carbonetto	1978	Brian Pockar	Heather Kemkaran
1970	David McGillivray	Karen Magnussen	1979	Brian Pockar	Janet Morissey
1971	Toller Cranston	Karen Magnussen	1980	Brian Pockar	Heather Kemkaren
1972	Toller Cranston	Karen Magnussen	1981	Brian Orser	Tracey Wainman

Curling Champions

Source: North American Curling News

World Champions

Year	Country, skip	Year	Country, skip	Year	Country, skip
1966	Canada, Ron Northcott	1972	Canada, Crest Melesnuk	1977	Sweden, Ragnar Kamp
1967	Scotland, Chuck Hay	1973	Sweden, Kjell Oscarius	1978	United States, Bob Nichols
1968	Canada, Ron Northcott	1974	United States, Bud Somerville	1979	Norway, Kristian Soerum
1969	Canada, Ron Northcott	1975	Switzerland, Otto Danieli	1980	Canada, Rich Folk
1970	Canada, Don Duguid	1976	United States, Bruce Roberts	1981	Switzerland, Jurg Tanner
1971	Canada, Don Duguid				

U.S. Men's Champions

Year	State, skip	Year	State, skip	Year	State, skip
1966	North Dakota, Joe Zbacnik	1972	North Dakota, Bob LaBonte	1977	Minnesota, Bruce Roberts
1967	Washington, Bruce Roberts	1973	Massachusetts, Barry Blanchard	1978	Wisconsin, Bob Nichols
1968	Wisconsin, Bud Somerville	1974	Wisconsin, Bud Somerville	1979	Minnesota, Scotty Baird
1969	Wisconsin, Bud Somerville	1975	Washington, Ed Risling	1980	Minnesota, Paul Pustover
1970	North Dakota, Art Tallackson	1976	Minnesota, Bruce Roberts	1981	Wisconsin, Somerville-Nichols
1971	North Dakota, Dale Dalziel				

U.S. Ladies Champions

Year	State, skip	Year	State, skip	Year	State, skip
1978	Wisconsin, Sandy Robarge	1980	Washington, Sharon Kozai	1981	Washington, Nancy Langley
1979	Washington, Nancy Langley				

College Basketball

Final Conference Standings, 1980–81

East Coast
Eastern Division

	Conference W	L	All Games W	L
American U.	11	0	24	5
Temple	9	2	19	7
St. Joseph's	9	2	22	7
La Salle	8	3	14	13
Drexel	6	5	14	13
Hofstra	5	6	12	15

Western Division

	W	L	W	L
Lafayette	8	8	15	13
Rider	8	8	14	14
Bucknell	6	10	12	16
Lehigh	6	10	14	12
Delaware	3	13	6	19
W. Chester	2	14	7	20

Big East

	W	L	W	L
Boston College	10	4	21	6
Georgetown	9	5	20	11
Connecticut	8	6	19	8
Villanova	8	6	19	10
St. John's	8	6	17	10
Syracuse	6	8	18	11
Seton Hall	4	10	11	16
Providence	3	11	10	18

ECAC
Northern Division

	W	L	W	L
Northeastern	23	5	—	—
Holy Cross	19	9	—	—
Vermont	16	12	—	—
Maine	14	14	—	—
Boston Univ.	13	14	—	—
Niagara	11	15	—	—
Canisius	11	15	—	—
Colgate	11	18	—	—
New Hampshire	7	19	—	—

Metro Division

	W	L	W	L
Fordham	19	8	—	—
St. Peter's	17	9	—	—
Long Island	18	10	—	—
Siena	17	10	—	—
Wagner	16	11	—	—
Iona	15	14	—	—
Fairleigh Dickinson	13	13	—	—
Fairfield	13	13	—	—
St. Francis (N.Y.)	10	16	—	—
Army	7	19	—	—
Manhattan	6	19	—	—

Southern Division

	W	L	W	L
James Madison	20	8	—	—
Old Dominion	18	9	—	—
St. Francis (Pa.)	17	10	—	—
William & Mary	16	12	—	—
Richmond	15	14	—	—
Towson St.	13	14	—	—
George Mason	10	16	—	—
Navy	9	16	—	—
Robert Morris	9	18	—	—
Baltimore	5	20	—	—
Catholic	4	20	—	—

Eastern Eight

	W	L	W	L
Rhode Island	10	3	21	7
Duquesne	10	3	20	9
West Virginia	9	4	20	8
Pittsburgh	8	5	18	11
Rutgers	7	6	16	14
St. Bonaventure	6	7	14	13
George Washington	4	9	8	19
Massachusetts	0	13	3	24

Ivy League

	W	L	W	L
Penn	13	1	20	6
Princeton	13	1	17	9
Harvard	9	5	16	10
Brown	5	9	9	17
Columbia	5	9	9	17
Cornell	4	10	7	19
Yale	4	10	7	19
Dartmouth	3	11	10	16

Mid-Eastern

	W	L	W	L
N. Carolina A & T	7	3	21	6
Florida A & M	6	4	16	11
Howard	6	4	16	11
Bethune-Cookman	4	6	13	14
S. Carolina St.	4	6	11	15
Delaware St.	3	7	8	18

Mid-American

	W	L	W	L
Toledo	10	6	20	8
Ball St.	10	6	20	9
W. Michigan	10	6	15	12
Bowling Green	10	6	15	12
N. Illinois	10	6	17	12
E. Michigan	8	8	13	14
Miami (Ohio)	6	10	11	15
Ohio Univ.	6	10	7	20
Cent. Michigan	5	11	12	14
Kent St.	5	11	7	19

Ohio Valley

	W	L	W	L
W. Kentucky	12	2	21	6
Murray St.	10	4	17	11
Middle Tenn.	9	5	18	9
Austin Peay	7	7	14	13
E. Kentucky	7	7	10	16
Akron	5	9	8	17
Morehead St.	5	10	11	13
Tennessee Tech.	2	13	6	20

Southland

	W	L	W	L
Lamar	8	2	24	4
Louisiana Tech.	7	3	20	10
Texas-Arlington	7	3	20	7
SW Louisiana	6	4	14	13
Arkansas St.	2	8	12	15
McNeese St.	0	10	11	20

Trans-America

	W	L	W	L
Houston Baptist	9	3	18	10
NE Louisiana	8	4	14	13
Mercer	7	4	17	11
Centenary	7	5	16	12
Samford	5	6	11	17
Ark.-Little Rock	5	6	13	12
NW Louisiana	5	7	11	16
Hardin Simmons	4	8	9	18
Georgia Southern	2	9	5	23

Midwestern City

	W	L	W	L
Xavier, Ohio	8	3	12	13
Loyola, Ill.	7	4	13	15
Oklahoma City	7	4	13	15
Evansville	6	5	19	9
Oral Roberts	6	5	10	16
Detroit	1	5	9	18
Butler	1	10	5	22

Missouri Valley

	W	L	W	L
Wichita St.	12	4	23	6
Tulsa	11	5	21	7
Creighton	11	5	21	8
Bradley	10	6	18	9
Drake	10	6	18	10
W. Texas St.	7	9	16	11
New Mexico St.	7	9	10	17
Indiana St.	4	12	9	18
S. Illinois	0	16	7	20
Illinois St.	0	0	16	11

Big 10

	W	L	W	L
Indiana	14	4	21	9
Iowa	13	5	21	6
Illinois	12	6	20	7
Purdue	10	8	17	10
Minnesota	9	9	17	10
Ohio St.	9	9	14	13
Michigan	8	10	16	11
Michigan St.	7	11	13	14
Wisconsin	5	13	11	15
Northwestern	3	15	9	18

Metro

	W	L	W	L
Louisville	11	1	21	8
Florida St.	7	5	17	11
Cincinnati	6	6	16	13
Virginia Tech	6	6	15	13
Memphis St.	5	7	13	14
Tulane	4	8	12	15
St. Louis	3	9	9	18

Southern

	W	L	W	L
Tenn-Chattanooga	11	5	21	8
Davidson	11	5	13	13
Appalachian St.	11	5	20	9
E. Tennessee St.	9	7	13	14
W. Carolina	9	7	18	10
Furman	8	8	11	16
Marshall	7	8	17	10
VMI	3	13	4	23
Citadel	2	13	9	16

Sun Belt

	W	L	W	L
Va. Commonwealth	9	3	23	4
S. Alabama	9	3	23	5
Ala.-Birmingham	9	3	21	8
S. Florida	7	5	18	10
Jacksonville	4	8	8	19
N.C.-Charlotte	3	9	9	18
Georgia St.	1	11	4	23

ACC

	W	L	W	L
Virginia	13	1	25	3
North Carolina	10	4	25	7
Wake Forest	9	5	22	6
Maryland	8	6	20	9
Clemson	6	8	20	10
Duke	6	8	15	12
N. Carolina St.	4	10	14	13
Georgia Tech	0	14	4	23

Southeastern

	W	L	W	L
Louisiana St.	17	1	28	3
Kentucky	15	3	22	5
Tennessee	12	6	20	7
Alabama	10	8	17	10
Georgia	9	9	18	11
Mississippi	8	10	16	13
Vanderbilt	7	11	15	14
Florida	5	13	12	16
Auburn	4	14	11	16
Mississippi St.	3	15	8	19

Big 8

	W	L	W	L
Missouri	10	4	22	9
Kansas St.	9	5	21	8
Nebraska	9	5	15	12
Kansas	9	5	22	7
Oklahoma St.	8	6	18	9
Colorado	5	9	16	12
Oklahoma	4	10	9	18
Iowa St.	2	12	9	18

Southwest

	W	L	W	L
Arkansas	13	3	22	7
Houston	10	6	21	8
Baylor	10	6	15	12
Texas Tech.	8	8	15	13
Texas A & M	8	8	15	12
Texas	7	9	15	15
Rice	7	9	12	15
TCU	6	10	11	18
So. Methodist	3	13	7	20

Western Athletic

	W	L	W	L
Utah	13	3	24	4
Wyoming	13	3	23	5
Brigham-Young	12	4	22	6
Texas-El Paso	9	7	17	11
San Diego St.	8	8	15	12
Hawaii	7	9	14	13
New Mexico	6	10	11	15
Air Force	3	13	9	18
Colorado St.	1	15	3	24

	Confer-ence W L	All Games W L		Confer-ence W L	All Games W L	Major Independents W L
Pac-10			**West Coast Athletic**			DePaul 27 1
Oregon St.	17 1	26 1	San Francisco	11 3	23 6	Notre Dame 22 5
Arizona St.	16 2	24 3	Pepperdine.	11 3	16 11	So.Mississippi 21 5
UCLA	13 5	20 6	Gonzaga	9 5	19 8	Stetson. 18 8
Southern Cal.	9 9	14 13	Portland	7 7	17 10	Cleveland St. 18 9
Washington.	8 10	14 13	Santa Clara	7 7	14 13	Dayton 17 9
Arizona	8 10	13 14	Loyola	5 9	9 19	Marquette 18 10
Oregon	6 12	13 14	San Diego	3 11	10 16	Pan American 18 10
California	5 13	13 14	St. Mary's	3 11	9 18	Penn St. 17 10
Stanford	5 13	9 18				S. Carolina. 17 10
Washington St.. . . .	3 15	10 17				Nevada-Las Vegas 16 12
						North Texas St. 15 12
PCAA			**Big Sky**			N.Car.-Wilmington. 13 13
Fresno St.	12 2	25 3	Idaho	12 2	25 3	New Orleans. 13 14
San Jose St.	10 4	21 8	Montana	11 3	19 9	East Carolina 12 14
Cal-Irvine	9 5	17 10	Montana St.	11 3	16 11	Valparaiso 12 15
Long Beach St. . . .	9 5	15 13	Idaho St.	6 8	12 14	Campbell. 11 15
Utah St..	5 9	12 16	Nevada-Reno	5 9	11 15	Baptist 10 19
Santa Barbara	5 9	11 16	Weber St.	5 9	8 19	No.Iowa 8 18
Pacific.	4 10	14 13	Boise St.	4 10	7 19	Portland St. 7 21
Fullerton St.	2 12	4 23	N. Arizona	2 12	8 17	Nicholls St.. . . . . 6 22

NCAA Basketball Championships in 1981

East

First round—Brigham Young 60, Princeton 51; James Madison 61, Georgetown 55; Virginia Commonwealth 85, LIU 69; Villanova 90, Houston 72.

Second round—Brigham Young 78, UCLA 55; Notre Dame 54, James Madison 45; Virginia 54, Villanova 50; Tennessee 58, Virginia Commonwealth 56.

Semifinals—Brigham Young 51, Notre Dame 50; Virginia 62, Tennessee 48.

Championship—Virginia 74, Brigham Young 60.

Mideast

First round—Ala. Birmingham 93, W. Kentucky 68; Boston College 93, Ball State 90; Maryland 81, Tenn.-Chattanooga 69; St. Joseph's 59, Creighton 57.

Second round—Ala.-Birmingham 69, Kentucky 62; Boston College 67, Wake Forest 64; Indiana 99, Maryland 64; St. Joseph's 49, DePaul 48.

Semifinals—Indiana 87, Ala.-Birmingham 72; St. Joseph's 42, Boston College 41.

Championship—Indiana 78, St. Joseph's 46.

West

First round—Kansas State 64, San Francisco 60; Northeastern 55, Fresno State 53; Pittsburgh 70, Idaho 69; Wyoming 78, Howard 43.

Second round—Illinois 67, Wyoming 65; Kansas State 50, Oregon State 48; North Carolina 74, Pittsburgh 57; Utah 94, Northeastern 69.

Semifinals—Kansas State 57, Illinois 52; North Carolina 61, Utah 56.

Championship—North Carolina 82, Kansas State 68.

Midwest

First round—Arkansas 73, Mercer 67; Kansas 69, Mississippi 66; Lamar 71, Missouri 67; Wichita State 95, Southern Univ. 70.

Second round—Arkansas 74, Louisville 73; Louisiana State 100, Lamar 78; Kansas 88, Arizona State 71; Wichita State 60, Iowa 56.

Semifinals—Louisiana State 72, Arkansas 56; Wichita State 66, Kansas 65.

Championship—Louisiana State 96, Wichita State 85.

National Semifinals

North Carolina 78, Virginia 65.
Indiana 67, Louisiana State 49.

Championship

Indiana 63, North Carolina 50.

NCAA Division I Champions

Year	Champion	Year	Champion	Year	Champion	Year	Champion
1939	Oregon	1950	CCNY	1961	Cincinnati	1972	UCLA
1940	Indiana	1951	Kentucky	1962	Cincinnati	1973	UCLA
1941	Wisconsin	1952	Kansas	1963	Loyola (Chi.)	1974	No. Carolina State
1942	Stanford	1953	Indiana	1964	UCLA	1975	UCLA
1943	Wyoming	1954	La Salle	1965	UCLA	1976	Indiana
1944	Utah	1955	San Francisco	1966	Texas Western	1977	Marquette
1945	Oklahoma A&M	1956	San Francisco	1967	UCLA	1978	Kentucky
1946	Oklahoma A&M	1957	North Carolina	1968	UCLA	1979	Michigan State
1947	Holy Cross	1958	Kentucky	1969	UCLA	1980	Louisville
1948	Kentucky	1959	California	1970	UCLA	1981	Indiana
1949	Kentucky	1960	Ohio State	1971	UCLA		

National Invitation Tournament Champions

Year	Champion	Year	Champion	Year	Champion	Year	Champion
1938	Temple	1949	San Francisco	1960	Bradley	1971	North Carolina
1939	Long Island Univ.	1950	CCNY	1961	Providence	1972	Maryland
1940	Colorado	1951	Brigham Young	1962	Dayton	1973	Virginia Tech
1941	Long Island Univ.	1952	LaSalle	1963	Providence	1974	Purdue
1942	West Virginia	1953	Seton Hall	1964	Bradley	1975	Princeton
1943	St. John's	1954	Holy Cross	1965	St. John's	1976	Kentucky
1944	St. John's	1955	Duquesne	1966	Brigham Young	1977	St. Bonaventure
1945	De Paul	1956	Louisville	1967	Southern Illinois	1978	Texas
1946	Kentucky	1957	Bradley	1968	Dayton	1979	Indiana
1947	Utah	1958	Xavier (Ohio)	1969	Temple	1980	Virginia
1948	St. Louis	1959	St. John's	1970	Marquette	1981	Tulsa

NCAA Division II Champions

Year	Champion	Year	Champion	Year	Champion	Year	Champion
1966	Kentucky Wesleyan	1970	Philadelphia Textile	1974	Morgan State	1978	Cheyney State
1967	Winston-Salem	1971	Evansville	1975	Old Dominion	1979	North Alabama
1968	Kentucky Wesleyan	1972	Roanoke	1976	Puget Sound	1980	Virginia Union
1969	Kentucky Wesleyan	1973	Kentucky Wesleyan	1977	Tennessee-Chattanooga	1981	Florida Southern

Pro Rodeo Championship Standings in 1980

Event	Winner	Money won	Event	Winner	Money won
All Around	Paul Tierney, Rapid City, S.D.	$105,568	Steer Wrestling	Butch Myers, Welda, Kan.	44,708
Saddle Bronc	Clint Johnson, Spearfish, S.D.	44,711	Team Roping	Tee Woolman, Llano, Tex.	49,983
Bareback	Bruce Ford, Kersey, Col.	69,362	Steer Roping	Guy Allen, Santa Anna, Tex.	20,567
Bull Riding	Don Gay, Mexquite, Tex.	60,639			
Calf Roping	Roy Cooper, Durant, Okla.	77,027			

Pro Rodeo Cowboy All Around Champions

Year	Winner	Money won	Year	Winner	Money won
1963	Dean Oliver, Boise, Ida.	$31,329	1973	Larry Mahan, Dallas, Tex.	$64,447
1964	Dean Oliver, Boise, Ida.	31,150	1974	Tom Ferguson, Miami, Okla.	66,929
1965	Dean Oliver, Boise, Ida.	33,163	1975	Leo Camarillo, Oakdale, Cal.	50,300
1966	Larry Mahan, Brooks, Ore.	40,358		Tom Ferguson, Miami, Okla.	50,300
1967	Larry Mahan, Brooks, Ore.	51,996	1976	Tom Ferguson, Miami, Okla.	87,908
1968	Larry Mahan, Salem, Ore.	49,129	1977	Tom Ferguson, Miami, Okla.	76,730
1969	Larry Mahan, Brooks, Ore.	57,726	1978	Tom Ferguson, Miami, Okla.	103,734
1970	Larry Mahan, Brooks, Ore.	41,493	1979	Tom Ferguson, Miami, Okla.	96,272
1971	Phil Lyne, George West, Tex.	49,245	1980	Paul Tierney, Rapid City, S.D.	105,568
1972	Phil Lyne, George West, Tex.	60,852			

Chess

Chess dates back to antiquity. Its exact origin is unknown. The strongest players of their time, and therefore regarded by later generations as world champions, were Francois Philidor, France; Alexandre Deschappelles, France; Louis de la Bourdonnais, France; Howard Staunton, England; Adolph Anderssen, Germany and Paul Morphy, United States. In 1866 Wilhelm Steinitz of Czechoslovakia defeated Adolph Anderssen and claimed the title of world champion. The official world champions, since the title was first used follow:

1866-1894 Wilhelm Steinitz, Austria		**1937-1946** Dr. Alexander A. Alekhine, USSR		**1961-1963** Mikhail Botvinnik, USSR	
1894-1921 Dr. Emanuel Lasker, Germany				**1963-1969** Tigran Petrosian, USSR	
1921-1927 Jose R. Capablanca, Cuba		**1948-1957** Mikhail Botvinnik, USSR		**1969-1972** Boris Spassky, USSR	
1927-1935 Dr. Alexander A. Alekhine, Russia		**1957-1958** Vassily Smysolv, USSR		**1972-1975** Bobby Fischer, U.S. (a)	
		1958-1959 Mikhail Botvinnik, USSR		**1975** Anatoly Karpov, USSR	
1935-1937 Dr. Max Euwe, Netherlands		**1960-1961** Mikhail Tal, USSR			

(a) Defaulted championship after refusal to accept International Chess Federation rules for a championship match, April 1975.

United States Champions

Unofficial champions		Official champions					
1857-1871 Paul Morphy		**1894** Jackson Showalter		**1948-1951** Herman Steiner		**1972-1973** Robert Byrne	
1871-1876 George Mackenzie		**1894-1895** Albert Hodges		**1951-1954** Larry Evans		**1973-1974** Lubomir Kavalek,	
1876-1880 James Mason		**1895-1897** Jackson Showalter		**1954-1957** Arthur Bisguier		John Grefe	
1880-1889 George Mackenzie		**1897-1909** Harry Pillsbury		**1957-1961** Bobby Fischer		**1974-1977** Walter Browne	
1889-1890 S. Lipschutz		**1909-1936** Frank Marshall		**1961-1962** Larry Evans		**1978-1980** Lubomir Kavalek	
1890 Jackson Showalter		**1936-1944** Samuel Reshevsky		**1962-1968** Bobby Fischer		**1980** (tie) Larry Evans,	
1890-1891 Max Judd		**1944-1946** Arnold Denker		**1968-1969** Larry Evans		Larry Christiansen,	
1891-1892 Jackson Showalter		**1946-1948** Samuel Reshevsky		**1969-1972** Samuel Reshevsky		Walter Browne	
1892-1894 S. Lipschutz							

James E. Sullivan Memorial Trophy Winners

The James E. Sullivan Memorial Trophy, named after the former president of the AAU and inaugurated in 1930, is awarded annually by the AAU to the athlete who "by his or her performance, example and influence as an amateur, has done the most during the year to advance the cause of sportmanship."

Year	Winner	Sport	Year	Winner	Sport	Year	Winner	Sport
1930	Bobby Jones	Golf	1947	John Kelly Jr.	Rowing	1964	Don Schollander	Swimming
1931	Barney Berlinger	Track	1948	Robert Mathias	Track	1965	Bill Bradley	Basketball
1932	Jim Bausch	Track	1949	Dick Button	Skating	1966	Jim Ryun	Track
1933	Glen Cunningham	Track	1950	Fred Wilt	Track	1967	Randy Matson	Track
1934	Bill Bonthron	Track	1951	Rev. Robert Richards	Track	1968	Debbie Meyer	Swimming
1935	Lawson Little	Golf	1952	Horace Ashenfelter	Track	1969	Bill Toomey	Track
1936	Glenn Morris	Track	1953	Dr. Sammy Lee	Diving	1970	John Kinsella	Swimming
1937	Don Budge	Tennis	1954	Mal Whitfield	Track	1971	Mark Spitz	Swimming
1938	Don Lash	Track	1955	Harrison Dillard	Track	1972	Frank Shorter	Track
1939	Joe Burk	Rowing	1956	Patricia McCormick	Diving	1973	Bill Walton	Basketball
1940	Greg Rice	Track	1957	Bobby Joe Morrow	Track	1974	Rick Wohlhuter	Track
1941	Leslie MacMitchell	Track	1958	Glen Davis	Track	1975	Tim Shaw	Swimming
1942	Cornelius Warmerdam	Track	1959	Parry O'Brien	Track	1976	Bruce Jenner	Track
1943	Gilbert Dodds	Track	1960	Rafer Johnson	Track	1977	John Naber	Swimming
1944	Ann Curtis	Swimming	1961	Wilma Rudolph Ward	Track	1978	Tracy Caulkins	Swimming
1945	Doc Blanchard	Football	1962	James Beatty	Track	1979	Kurt Thomas	Gymnastics
1946	Arnold Tucker	Football	1963	John Pennel	Track	1980	Eric Heiden	Speed Skating

Notable Sports Personalities

Henry Aaron, b. 1934: Milwaukee-Atlanta outfielder hit record 755 home runs; led NL 4 times.

Kareem Abdul-Jabbar, b. 1947: Milwaukee, L.A. Lakers center; MVP 6 times; leading scorer twice.

Grover Cleveland Alexander, (1887-1950): pitcher won 374 NL games; pitched 16 shutouts, 1916.

Muhammad Ali, b. 1942; 3-time heavyweight champion.

Mario Andretti, b. 1940; U.S. Auto Club national champ 3 times: won Indy 500, 1969, 1981; Grand Prix champ, 1978.

Eddie Arcaro, b. 1916: jockey rode 4,779 winners including the Kentucky Derby 5 times; the Preakness and Belmont Stakes 6 times each.

Henry Armstrong, b. 1912: boxer held feather-, welter-, light-weight titles simultaneously, 1937-38.

Arthur Ashe, b. 1943: U.S. singles champ, 1968, Wimbledon champ, 1975.

Red Auerbach, b. 1917: coached Boston Celtics to 9 NBA championships.

Ernie Banks, b. 1931: Chicago Cubs slugger hit 512 NL homers; twice MVP.

Roger Bannister, b. 1929: Briton ran first sub 4-minute mile, May 6, 1954.

Rick Barry, b. 1944: NBA scoring leader, 1967; ABA, 1969.

Sammy Baugh, b. 1914: Washington Redskins quarterback held numerous records upon retirement after 16 pro seasons.

Elgin Baylor, b. 1934: L.A. Lakers forward; 1st team all-star 10 times.

Bob Beamon, b. 1946: long jumper won 1968 Olympic gold medal with record 29 ft. 2½ in.

Jean Beliveau, b. 1931: Montreal Canadiens center scored 507 goals; twice MVP.

Johnny Bench, b. 1947: Cincinnati Reds catcher; MVP twice; led league in home runs twice, RBIs 3 times.

Patty Berg, b. 1918: won over 80 golf tournaments: AP Woman Athlete-of-the-Year 3 times.

Yogi Berra, b. 1925: N.Y. Yankees catcher; MVP 3 times; played in 14 World Series.

Raymond Berry, b. 1933: Baltimore Colts receiver caught 631 passes.

George Blanda, b. 1927: quarterback, kicker; 26 years as active player, scoring record 2,002 points.

Bjorn Borg, b. 1956: led Sweden to first Davis Cup, 1975; Wimbledon champion, 5 times.

Julius Boros, b. 1920: won U.S. Open, 1952, 1963; PGA champ, 1968.

Jack Brabham, b. 1926: Grand Prix champ 3 times.

George Brett, b. 1953: Kansas City Royals 3d baseman led AL in batting, 1976, 1980; MVP, 1980.

Lou Brock, b. 1939: St. Louis Cardinals outfielder stole record 118 bases, 1974; record 937 career; led NL 8 times.

Jimmy Brown, b. 1936: Cleveland Browns fullback ran for record 12,312 career yards; MVP 3 times.

Don Budge, b. 1915: won numerous amateur and pro tennis titles, "grand slam," 1938.

Maria Bueno, b. 1939: U.S. singles champ 4 times; Wimbledon champ 3 times.

Mike Burton, b. 1947: swimmer won 1968, 1972 Olympic 1,500 meter freestyle.

Dick Butkus, b. 1942: Chicago Bears linebacker twice chosen best NFL defensive player.

Dick Button, b. 1929: figure skater won 1948, 1952 Olympic gold medals; world titlist, 1948-52.

Walter Camp, (1859-1925): Yale football player, coach, athletic director; established many rules; promoted All-America designations.

Roy Campanella, b. 1921: Brooklyn Dodgers catcher; MVP 3 times.

Earl Campbell, b. 1955: Houston Oilers running back; NFL MVP 1978-1980.

Rod Carew, b. 1945: Minnesota Twins infielder won 7 batting titles; MVP, 1977.

Steve Carlton, b. 1944: NL pitcher won 20 games 5 times, Cy Young award 3 times.

Billy Casper, b. 1931: PGA Player-of-the-Year 3 times; U.S. Open champ twice.

Steve Cauthen, b. 1960: jockey; rode triple crown winner Affirmed, 1978.

Wilt Chamberlain, b. 1936: center scored NBA career record 31,419 points; MVP 4 times.

Jim Clark, (1936-1968): world driving champ twice; won Indy 500, 1965.

Bobby Clarke, b. 1949: Philadelphia Flyers center led team to 2 Stanley Cup championships; MVP 3 times.

Roberto Clemente, (1934-1972): Pittsburgh Pirates outfielder won 4 batting titles; MVP, 1966.

Ty Cobb, (1886-1961): Detroit Tigers outfielder had record .367 lifetime batting average, 4,191 hits, 12 batting titles.

Sebastian Coe, b. 1956: Briton set record in 800 meters, 1,500 meters, and mile, 1979.

Nadia Comaneci, b. 1961: Romanian gymnast won 3 gold medals, achieved 7 perfect scores, 1976 Olympics.

Maureen Connolly, (1934-1969): won tennis "grand slam," 1953; AP Woman-Athlete-of-the-Year 3 times.

Jimmy Connors, b. 1952: U.S. singles champ 3 times.

James J. Corbett, (1866-1933): heavyweight champion, 1892-97; credited with being the first "scientific" boxer.

Margaret Smith Court, b. 1942: Australian won U.S. singles championship 5 times; Wimbledon champ 3 times.

Bob Cousy, b. 1928: Boston Celtics guard led team to 6 NBA championships; MVP, 1957.

Stanley Dancer, b. 1927: harness racing driver drove Hambletonian winner 3 times, Little Brown Jug winner 4 times.

Dizzy Dean, (1911-1974): colorful pitcher for St. Louis Cardinals "Gashouse Gang" in the 30s; MVP, 1934.

Jack Dempsey, b. 1895: heavyweight champion, 1919-26.

Joe DiMaggio, b. 1914: N.Y. Yankees outfielder hit safely in record 56 consecutive games, 1941; MVP 3 times.

Leo Durocher, b. 1906: colorful manager of Dodgers, Giants, and Cubs; won 3 NL pennants.

Gertrude Ederle, b. 1906: first woman to swim English Channel, broke existing men's record, 1926.

Julius Erving, b. 1950: MVP and leading scorer in ABA 3 times; NBA MVP, 1981.

Phil Esposito, b. 1942: scored record 76 goals and 152 points in 1970-71; NHL scoring leader 5 times.

Chris Evert-Lloyd, b. 1954: U.S. singles champ 5 times, Wimbledon champ twice.

Ray Ewry, (1873-1937): track and field star won 8 gold medals, 1900, 1904, and 1908 Olympics.

Juan Fangio, b. 1911: Argentine World Grand Prix champion 5 times.

Bob Feller, b. 1918: Cleveland Indians pitcher won 266 games; pitched 3 no-hitters, 12 one-hitters.

Peggy Fleming, b. 1948: world figure skating champion, 1966-68; gold medalist 1968 Olympics.

Whitey Ford, b. 1928: N.Y. Yankees pitcher won record 10 World Series games.

Dick Fosbury, b. 1947: high jumper won 1968 Olympic gold medal; developed the "Fosbury Flop."

George Foster, b. 1951: Cincinnati Reds outfielder hit 52 home runs, selected MVP, 1977; led NL RBI's, 1976-78.

Jimmy Foxx, (1907-1967): Red Sox, Athletics slugger; MVP 3 times; triple crown, 1933.

A.J. Foyt, b. 1935: won Indy 500 4 times; U.S. Auto Club champ 6 times.

Dawn Fraser, b. 1937: Australian swimmer won Olympics 100-meter freestyle 3 times.

Joe Frazier, b. 1944: heavyweight champion, 1970-73.

Lou Gehrig, (1903-1941): N.Y. Yankees 1st baseman played record 2,130 consecutive games, MVP, 1936.

George Gervin, b. 1952: leading NBA scorer, 1978-80.

Althea Gibson, b. 1927: twice U.S. and Wimbledon singles champ.

Bob Gibson, b. 1935: St. Louis Cardinals pitcher won Cy Young award twice; struck out NL record 3,117 batters.

Frank Gifford, b. 1930: N.Y. Giants back; MVP 1956.

Pancho Gonzalez, b. 1928: World professional tennis champ, 8 years.

Otto Graham, b. 1921: Cleveland Browns quarterback; all-pro 4 times.

Red Grange, b 1903: All-America at Univ. of Illinois; played for Chicago Bears, 1925-35.

Joe Greene, b. 1946: Pittsburgh Steelers lineman; twice NFL outstanding defensive player.

Wayne Gretzky, b. 1961: Edmonton Oilers center led NHL in scoring, 1981; MVP, 1980, 1981.

Lefty Grove, (1900-1975): pitcher won 300 AL games; 20-game winner 8 times.

Walter Hagen, (1892-1969): won PGA championship 5 times. British Open 4 times.

George Halas, b. 1895: founder-coach of Chicago Bears; won 5 NFL championships.

Bill Hartack, b. 1932: jockey rode 5 Kentucky Derby winners.

Doug Harvey, b. 1930: Montreal Canadiens defenseman; Norris Trophy 7 times.

Bill Haughton, b. 1923: harness racing driver won Little Brown Jug 4 times, Hambletonian 4 times.

John Havlicek, b. 1940: Boston Celtics forward scored over 26,000 NBA points.

Eric Heiden, b. 1958: speed skater won 5 1980 Olympic gold medals.

Carol Heiss, b. 1940: world champion figure skater 5 consecutive years, 1956-60; won 1960 Olympic gold medal.

Sonja Henie, (1912-1969): world champion figure skater 1927-36; Olympic gold medalist 1928, 1932, 1936.

Ben Hogan, b. 1912: won 4 U.S. Open championships, 2 PGA, 2 Masters.

Willie Hoppe, (1887-1959): won some 50 world billiard titles.

Larry Holmes, b. 1949: WBC heavyweight champ 1978- .

Rogers Hornsby, (1896-1963): NL 2d baseman batted record .424 in 1924; twice won triple crown; batting leader 6 consecutive years, 1920-25.

Paul Hornung, b. 1935: Green Bay Packers runner-placekicker scored record 176 points, 1960.

Gordie Howe, b. 1928: hockey forward holds NHL career records in goals, assists, and points; NHL MVP 6 times, leading scorer 6 times.

Carl Hubbell, b. 1903: N.Y. Giants pitcher; 20-game winner 5 consecutive years, 1933-37.

Bobby Hull, b. 1939: NHL all-star 10 times, WHA all-star 4 times.

Catfish Hunter, b 1946: pitched perfect game, 1968; 20-game winner 5 times.

Don Hutson, b. 1913: Green Bay Packers receiver caught NFL record 99 touchdown passes.

Reggie Jackson, b. 1946: slugger led AL in home runs 3 times; MVP, 1973; hit 5 World Series home runs, 1977.

Bruce Jenner, b. 1949: decathlon gold medalist, 1976.

Jack Johnson, (1878-1946): heavyweight champion, 1910-15.

Rafer Johnson, b. 1935: decathlon gold medalist, 1960.

Walter Johnson, (1887-1946): Washington Senators pitcher won 414 games.

Bert Jones, b. 1951: Baltimore Colts quarterback; MVP, 1976.

Bobby Jones, (1902-1971): won "grand slam of golf" 1930; U.S. Amateur champ 5 times, U.S. Open champ 4 times.

Deacon Jones, b. 1938: L.A. Rams lineman; twice NFL outstanding defensive player.

Sonny Jurgensen, b. 1934: quarterback named all-pro 5 times; completed record 288 passes, 1967.

Duke Kahanamoku, (1890-1968): swimmer won 1912, 1920 Olympic gold medals in 100-meter freestyle.

Harmon Killebrew, b. 1936: Minnesota Twins slugger led AL in home runs 6 times.

Jean Claude Killy, b. 1943: French skier won 3 1968 Olympic gold medals.

Ralph Kiner, b. 1922: Pittsburgh Pirates slugger led NL in home runs 7 consecutive years, 1946-52.

Billie Jean King, b. 1943: U.S. singles champ 4 times; Wimbledon champ 6 times.

Olga Korbut, b. 1956: Soviet gymnast won 3 1972 Olympic gold medals.

Sandy Koufax, b. 1935: Dodgers pitcher won Cy Young award 3 times; lowest ERA in NL, 1962-66; pitched 4 no-hitters, one a perfect game.

Jack Kramer, b. 1921: twice U.S. singles champ.

Guy Lafleur, b. 1951: Montreal Canadiens forward led NHL in scoring 3 times; MVP, 1977, 1978.

Tom Landry, b. 1924: Dallas Cowboys head coach since 1960.

Rod Laver, b. 1938: Australian won tennis "grand slam," 1962, 1969; Wimbledon champ 4 times.

Sugar Ray Leonard, b. 1956: WBC welterweight champ, 1979-80.

Vince Lombardi, (1913-1970): Green Bay Packers coach led, team to 5 NFL championships and 2 Super Bowl victories.

Johnny Longden, b. 1907: jockey rode 6,032 winners.

Joe Louis, (1914-1981): 1914: heavyweight champion, 1937-49.

Sid Luckman, b. 1916: Chicago Bears quarterback led team to 4 NFL championships, MVP, 1943.

Fred Lynn, b. 1952: Outfielder led AL in batting, 1979; AL MVP, 1975.

Connie Mack, (1862-1956): Philadelphia Athletics manager, 1901-50; won 9 pennants, 5 championships.

Bill Madlock, b. 1951: NL batting leader, 1975 and 1976.

Mickey Mantle, b. 1931: N.Y. Yankees outfielder; triple crown, 1956; 18 World Series home runs.

Alice Marble, b. 1913: U.S. singles champ 4 times.

Rocky Marciano, (1923-1969): heavyweight champion, 1952-56; retired undefeated.

Roger Maris, b. 1934: N.Y. Yankees outfielder hit record 61 home runs, 1961; MVP, 1960 and 1961.

Billy Martin, b. 1928: baseball manager led N.Y. Yankees to World Series title, 1977.

Eddie Mathews, b. 1931: Milwaukee-Atlanta 3d baseman hit 512 career home runs.

Christy Mathewson, (1880-1925): N.Y. Giants pitcher won 373 games.

Bob Mathias, b. 1930: decathlon gold medalist, 1948, 1952.

Willie Mays, b. 1931: N.Y.-S.F. Giants center fielder hit 660 home runs; twice MVP.

Bob McAdoo, b. 1951: leading NBA scorer, 1974-76; MVP, 1975.

John McEnroe, b. 1959: U.S. singles champ, 1978, 1980; Wimbledon champ, 1981.

John McGraw, (1873-1934): N.Y. Giants manager led team to 10 pennants, 3 championships.

Debbie Meyer, b. 1952: swimmer won 200-, 400-, and 800- meter freestyle events, 1968 Olympics.

George Mikan, b. 1924: Minneapolis Lakers center selected in a 1950 AP poll as the greatest basketball player of the first half of the 20th century.

Stan Mikita, b. 1940: Chicago Black Hawks center led NHL in scoring 4 times; MVP twice.

Archie Moore, b. 1913: world light-heavyweight champion, 1952-62.

Howie Morenz, (1902-1937): Montreal Canadiens forward chosen in a 1950 Canadian press poll as the outstanding hockey player of the first half of the 20th century.

Joe Morgan, b. 1943: National League MVP, 1975, 1976.

Thurman Munson, (1947-1979): N.Y. Yankees catcher; MVP, 1976.

Isaac Murphy, (1856-1896): jockey rode 3 Kentucky Derby winners.

Stan Musial, b. 1920: St. Louis Cardinals star won 7 NL batting titles; MVP 3 times; NL record 3,630 hits.

Bronko Nagurski, b. 1908: Chicago Bears fullback and tackle; gained over 4,000 yds. rushing.

Joe Namath, b. 1943: quarterback passed for record 4,007 yds., 1967.

Byron Nelson, b. 1912: won 11 consecutive golf tournaments in 1945, ending the year with record 19 victories; twice Masters and PGA titlist.

Ernie Nevers, (1903-1976): Stanford star selected the best college fullback to play between 1919-1969, in a poll of the Football Writers Assn.; played pro football and baseball.

John Newcombe, b. 1943: Australian twice U.S. singles champ; Wimbledon titlist 3 times.

Jack Nicklaus, b. 1940: PGA Player-of-the-Year, 1967, 1972; leading money winner 7 times.

Chuck Noll, b. 1931: Pittsburgh Steelers coach led team to 4 Super Bowl titles.

Paavo Nurmi, (1897-1973): Finnish distance runner won 6 Olympic gold medals, 1920, 1924, 1928.

Al Oerter, b. 1936: discus thrower won gold medal at 4 consecutive Olympics, 1956-68.

Barney Oldfield, (1878-1946): turn-of-the-century auto racer.

Bobby Orr, b. 1948: Boston Bruins defenseman; Norris Trophy 8 times; led NHL in scoring twice, assists 5 times.

Mel Ott, (1909-1958): N.Y. Giants outfielder hit 511 home runs; led NL 6 times.

Jesse Owens, (1913-1980): track and field star won 4 1936 Olympic gold medals.

Satchel Paige, b. 1906: pitcher starred in Negro leagues, 1924-48; entered major leagues at age 42.

Arnold Palmer, b. 1929: golf's first $1 million winner; won 4 Masters, 2 British Opens.

Jim Palmer, b. 1945: Baltimore Orioles pitcher; Cy Young award 3 times; 20-game winner 7 times.

Dave Parker, b. 1951: Pittsburgh Pirates outfielder led NL in batting, 1977, 1978; MVP, 1978.

Floyd Patterson, b. 1935: twice heavyweight champion.

Walter Payton, 1954: Chicago Bears running back ran for game record 275 yards, 1977; leading NFC rusher, 1976-80.

Pele, b. 1940: Brazilian soccer star scored 1,281 goals during 22-year career.

Bob Pettit, b. 1932: Milwaukee-St. Louis Hawks forward was first NBA player to score 20,000 points; twice NBA scoring leader.

Richard Petty, b. 1937: NASCAR national champ 6 times; 7-times Daytona 500 winner.

Laffit Pincay Jr., b. 1946: leading money-winning jockey, 1970-74, 1979.

Jacques Plante, b. 1929: goalie, 7 Vezina trophies; first goalie to wear a mask in a game.

Gary Player, b. 1935: South African won the Masters, U.S. Open, PGA, and twice the British Open.

Annemarie Proell Moser, b. 1953: Austrian skier won the World Cup championship 5 times; 1980 Olympic gold medalist.

Willis Reed, b. 1942: N.Y. Knicks center; MVP, 1970; playoff MVP, 1970, 1973.

Jim Rice, b. 1953: Boston Red Sox outfielder led AL in home runs, 1977-78; MVP 1978.

Maurice Richard, b. 1921: Montreal Canadiens forward scored 544 regular season goals, 82 playoff goals.

Branch Rickey, (1881-1965): executive instrumental in breaking baseball's color barrier, 1947; initiated farm system, 1919.

Oscar Robertson, b. 1938: guard averaged career 25.7 points per game; record 9,887 career assist; MVP, 1964.

Brooks Robinson, b. 1937: Baltimore Orioles 3d baseman played in 4 World Series; MVP, 1964.

Frank Robinson, b. 1935: slugger MVP in both NL and AL; triple crown winner, 1966; first black manager in majors.

Jackie Robinson, (1919-1972): broke baseball's color barrier with Brooklyn Dodgers, 1947; MVP, 1949.

Larry Robinson, b. 1951: Montreal Canadiens defenseman won Norris trophy, 1977, 1980.

Sugar Ray Robinson, b. 1920: middleweight champion 5 times, welterweight champion.

Knute Rockne, (1883-1931): Notre Dame football coach, 1918-31; revolutionized game by stressing forward pass.

Pete Rose, b. 1942: won 3 NL batting titles; has over 3,300 hits; hit safely in 44 consecutive games, 1978; set record for most NL hits, 1981.

Wilma Rudolph, b. 1940: sprinter won 3 1960 Olympic gold medals.

Bill Russell, b. 1934: Boston Celtics center led team to 11 NBA titles; MVP 5 times; first black coach of major pro sports team.

Babe Ruth, (1895-1948): N.Y. Yankees outfielder hit 60 home runs, 1927; 714 lifetime; led AL 11 times.

Johnny Rutherford, b. 1938: auto racer won Indy 500 3 times.

Nolan Ryan, b. 1947: pitcher struck out record 383 batters, 1973; pitched 4 no-hitters.

Jim Ryun, b. 1947: runner set records for the mile and 1,500 meters, 1967.

Gene Sarazen, b. 1902: won PGA championship 3 times, U.S. Open twice; developer of sand wedge.

Gale Sayers, b. 1943: Chicago Bears back twice led NFC in rushing.

Mike Schmidt, b. 1949: Phillies 3d baseman led NL in home runs, 1974-76, 1980; NL, World Series MVP, 1980.

Tom Seaver, b. 1944: NL pitcher won Cy Young award 3 times.

Willie Shoemaker, b. 1931: jockey rode 3 Kentucky Derby and 5 Belmont Stakes winners; leading career money winner.

Eddie Shore, b. 1902; Boston Bruins defenseman; MVP 4 times, first-team all-star 7 times.

Al Simmons, (1902-1956): AL outfielder had lifetime .334 batting average.

O.J. Simpson, b. 1947: running back rushed for record 2,003 yds., 1973; AFC leading rusher 4 times.

George Sisler, (1893-1973): St. Louis Browns 1st baseman had record 257 hits, 1920; batted .340 lifetime.

Sam Snead, b. 1912: PGA and Masters champ 3 times each.

Peter Snell, b. 1938: New Zealand runner won 800-meter race, 1960, 1964 Olympics.

Warren Spahn, b. 1921: pitcher won 363 NL games; 20-game winner 13 times; Cy Young award, 1957.

Tris Speaker, (1885-1958): AL outfielder batted .344 over 22 seasons; hit record 793 career doubles.

Mark Spitz, b. 1950: swimmer won 7 1972 Olympic gold medals.

Amos Alonzo Stagg, (1862-1965): coached Univ. of Chicago football team for 41 years, including 5 undefeated seasons; introduced huddle, man-in-motion, and end-around play.

Willie Stargell, b. 1941: Pittsburgh Pirate slugger chosen NL, World Series MVP, 1979.

Bart Starr, b. 1934: Green Bay Packers quarterback led team to 5 NFL titles and 2 Super Bowl victories.

Roger Staubach, b. 1942: Dallas Cowboys quarterback; leading NFC passer 5 times.

Casey Stengel, (1890-1975): managed Yankees to 10 pen-

nants, 7 championships, 1949-60.

Jackie Stewart, b. 1939: Scot auto racer retired with record 27 Grand Prix victories.

John L. Sullivan, (1858-1918): last bareknuckle heavyweight champion, 1882-1892.

Fran Tarkenton, b. 1940: quarterback holds career passing records for touchdowns, completions, yardage.

Gustave Thoeni, b. 1951: Italian 4-time world alpine ski champ.

Jim Thorpe, (1888-1953): football All-America, 1911, 1912; won pentathlon and decathlon, 1912 Olympics; played major league baseball for 6 seasons.

Bill Tilden, (1893-1953): U.S. singles champ 7 times; played on 11 Davis Cup teams.

Y.A. Tittle, b. 1926: N.Y. Giants quarterback; MVP, 1961, 1963.

Lee Trevino, b. 1939: won the U.S. and British Open championships twice.

Gene Tunney, (1897-1978): heavyweight champion, 1926-28.

Wyomia Tyus, b. 1945: sprinter won 1964, 1968 Olympic 100-meter dash.

Johnny Unitas, b. 1933: Baltimore Colts quarterback passed for over 40,000 yds.; MVP, 1957, 1967.

Al Unser, b. 1939: Indy 500 winner, 3 times.

Bobby Unser, b. 1934: Indy 500 winner, 1968, twice U.S. Auto Club national champ.

Norm Van Brocklin, b. 1926: quarterback passed for game record 554 yds., 1951; MVP, 1960.

Honus Wagner, (1874-1955): Pittsburgh Pirates shortstop won 8 NL batting titles.

Joe Walcott, b. 1914: heavyweight champion, 1951-52.

Mickey Walker, b. 1901: colorful welter- and middleweight champion of the 20s and 30s.

Bill Walton, b. 1952: led Portland Trail Blazers to NBA championship, 1977; MVP, 1978.

Tom Watson, b. 1949: leading money-winning golfer, 1977-80.

Johnny Weissmuller, b. 1903: swimmer won 52 national championships, 5 Olympic gold medals; set 67 world records.

Jerry West, b. 1938: L.A. Lakers guard had career average 27 points per game; first team all-star 10 times.

Kathy Whitworth, b. 1939: women's golf leading money winner 4 times; first woman to earn over $300,000.

Ted Williams, b. 1918: Boston Red Sox outfielder won 6 batting titles; last major leaguer to hit over .400: .406 in 1941: .344 lifetime batting average.

Helen Wills, b. 1906: winner of 7 U.S., 8 British, 4 French women's singles titles.

John Wooden, b. 1910: coached UCLA basketball team to 10 national championships.

Mickey Wright, b. 1935: won LPGA championship 4 times, Vare Trophy 5 times; twice AP Woman-Athlete-of-the-Year.

Carl Yastrzemski, b. 1939: Boston Red Sox slugger won 3 batting titles, triple crown, 1967.

Cy Young, (1867-1955): pitcher won record 511 major league games.

Babe Didrikson Zaharias, (1914-1956): track star won 2 1932 Olympic gold medals; won numerous golf tournaments.

Emil Zatopek, b. 1922: Czech distance runner won 5,000- and 10,000-meter and marathon, 1952 Olympics.

U.S. National Alpine Championships in 1981

Men's Downhill—Doug Powell, U.S.
Men's Slalom—Steve Mahre, U.S.
Men's Giant Slalom—Phil Mahre, U.S.

Women's Downhill—Holly Flanders, U.S.
Women's Slalom—Christin Cooper, U.S.
Women's Giant Slalom—Tamara McKinney, U.S.

The World Cup Winners

Men		Women		Nation's Cup	
1967	Jean Claude Killy, France	1967	Nancy Greene, Canada	1967	France
1968	Jean Claude Killy, France	1968	Nancy Greene, Canada	1968	France
1969	Karl Schranz, Austria	1969	Gertrud Gabl, Austria	1969	Austria
1970	Karl Schranz, Austria	1970	Michele Jacot, France	1970	France
1971	Gustavo Thoeni, Italy	1971	Annemarie Proell, Austria	1971	France
1972	Gustavo Thoeni, Italy	1972	Annemarie Proell, Austria	1972	France
1973	Gustavo Thoeni, Italy	1973	Annemarie Proell, Austria	1973	Austria
1974	Piero Gros, Italy	1974	Annemarie Proell, Austria	1974	Austria
1975	Gustavo Thoeni, Italy	1975	Annemarie Proell, Austria	1975	Austria
1976	Ingemar Stenmark, Sweden	1976	Rose Mittermaier, W. Germany	1976	Italy
1977	Ingemar Stenmark, Sweden	1977	Lise-Marie Morerod, Austria	1977	Austria
1978	Ingemar Stenmark, Sweden	1978	Hanni Wenzel, Liechtenstein	1978	Austria
1979	Peter Luescher, Switzerland	1979	Annemarie Proell Moser, Austria	1979	Austria
1980	Andreas Wenzel, Liechtenstein	1980	Hanni Wenzel, Liechtenstein	1980	Austria
1981	Phil Mahre, U.S.	1981	Marie-Theres Nadig, Switzerland	1981	Switzerland

Professional Sports Directory

Baseball

Commissioner's Office
75 Rockefeller Plaza
New York, NY 10019

National League

National League Office
1 Rockefeller Plaza
New York, NY 10020

Atlanta Braves
PO Box 4064
Atlanta, GA 30302

Chicago Cubs
Wrigley Field
Chicago, IL 60613

Cincinnati Reds
100 Riverfront Stadium
Cincinnati, OH 45202

Houston Astros
Astrodome
P.O. Box 288
Houston, TX 77001

Los Angeles Dodgers
Dodger Stadium
1000 Elysian Park Ave.
Los Angeles, CA 90012

Montreal Expos
PO Box 500, Station M
Montreal, Que. H1V 3P2

New York Mets
William A. Shea Stadium
Roosevelt Ave. & 126th St.
Flushing, NY 11368

Philadelphia Phillies
PO Box 7575
Philadelphia, PA 19101

Pittsburgh Pirates
600 Stadium Circle
Pittsburgh, PA 15212

St. Louis Cardinals
Busch Memorial Stadium
250 Stadium Plaza
St. Louis, MO 63102

San Diego Padres
PO Box 2000
San Diego, CA 92120

San Francisco Giants
Candlestick Park
San Francisco, CA 94124

American League

American League Office
280 Park Ave.
New York, NY 10017

Baltimore Orioles
Memorial Stadium
Baltimore, MD 21218

Boston Red Sox
24 Yawkey Way
Boston, MA 02215

California Angels
Anaheim Stadium
2000 State College Blvd.
Anaheim, CA 92806

Chicago White Sox
Comiskey Park
Dan Ryan & 35th St.
Chicago, IL 60616

Cleveland Indians
Cleveland Stadium
Cleveland, OH 44114

Detroit Tigers
Tiger Stadium
Detroit, MI 48216

Kansas City Royals
Harry S. Truman Sports Complex
PO Box 1969
Kansas City, MO 64141

Milwaukee Brewers
Milwaukee County Stadium
Milwaukee, WI 53214

Minnesota Twins
Metropolitan Stadium
8001 Cedar Ave.
Bloomington, MN 55420

New York Yankees
Yankee Stadium
Bronx, NY 10451

Oakland A's
Oakland-Alameda County
Coliseum
Oakland, CA 94621

Seattle Mariners
PO Box 4100
Seattle, WA 98104

Texas Rangers
Arlington Stadium
PO Box 1111
Arlington, TX 76010

Toronto Blue Jays
Box 7777
Adelaide St. PO
Toronto, Ont. M5C 2K7

National Basketball Association

League Office
Olympic Tower
645 5th Ave.
New York, NY 10022

Atlanta Hawks
100 Techwood Drive NW
Atlanta, GA 30303

Boston Celtics
Boston Garden
North Station
Boston, MA 02114

Chicago Bulls
333 North Michigan Ave.
Chicago, IL 60601

Cleveland Cavaliers
The Coliseum
2923 Streetsboro Rd.
Richfield, OH 44286

Dallas Mavericks
Reunion Arena
777 Sports St.
Dallas, TX 75247

Denver Nuggets
McNichols Sports Arena
1635 Clay St.
Denver, CO 80204

Detroit Pistons
Pontiac Silverdome
1200 Featherstone
Pontiac, MI 48057

Golden State Warriors
Oakland Coliseum Arena
Oakland, CA 94621

Houston Rockets
The Summit
Houston, TX 77046

Indiana Pacers
Market Square Center
151 N. Delaware
Indianapolis, IN 46204

Kansas City Kings
1800 Genessee
Kansas City, MO 64102

Los Angeles Lakers
The Forum
3900 W. Manchester Blvd.
or PO Box 10
Inglewood, CA 90306

Milwaukee Bucks
901 North 4th St.
Milwaukee, WI 53203

New Jersey Nets
185 E. Union Ave.
E. Rutherford, NJ 07073

New York Knickerbockers
Madison Square Garden Center
4 Pennsylvania Plaza
New York, NY 10001

Philadelphia 76ers
Veterans Stadium
PO Box 25040
Philadelphia, PA 19147

Phoenix Suns
PO Box 1369
Phoenix, AZ 85001

Portland Trail Blazers
Lloyd Bldg.
700 NE Multnomah St.
Portland, OR 97232

San Antonio Spurs
HemisFair Arena
P.O. Box 530
San Antonio, TX 78292

San Diego Clippers
San Diego Sports Arena
3500 Sports Arena Blvd.
San Diego, CA 92110

Seattle SuperSonics
419 Occidental South
Seattle, WA 98104

Utah Jazz
Salt Palace
100 SW Temple
Salt Lake City, UT 84101

Washington Bullets
1 Harry S. Truman Dr.
Landover, MD 20786

National Hockey League

League Headquarters
960 Sun Life Bldg.
Montreal, Quebec H3B 2W2

Boston Bruins
150 Causeway St.
Boston, MA 02114

Buffalo Sabres
Memorial Auditorium
Buffalo, NY 14202

Calgary Flames
P.O. Box 1540
Station M
Calgary, Alta. T2P 3B9

Chicago Black Hawks
1800 W. Madison St.
Chicago, IL 60612

Colorado Rockies
McNichols Sports Arena
Denver, CO 80204

Detroit Red Wings
600 Civic Center Drive
Detroit, MI 48226

Edmonton Oilers
Northlands Coliseum
Edmonton, Alta. T5B 4M9

Hartford Whalers
One Civic Center Plaza
Hartford, CT 06103

Los Angeles Kings
PO Box 10
The Forum
Inglewood, CA 90306

Minnesota North Stars
7901 Cedar Ave. S.
Bloomington, MN 55420

Montreal Canadiens
2313 St. Catherine St., West
Montreal, Quebec H3H 1N2

New York Islanders
Nassau Coliseum
Uniondale, NY 11553

Philadelphia Flyers
The Spectrum
Pattison Place
Philadelphia, PA 19148

Quebec Nordiques
5555 3ieme Ave. Ouest
Charlesbourg, Que. G1H 6R1

Vancouver Canucks
100 North Renfrew St.
Vancouver, B.C. V5K 3N7

St. Louis Blues
5700 Oakland Ave.
St. Louis, MO 63110

Washington Capitals
Capital Centre
Landover, MD 20786

New York Rangers
Madison Square Garden
4 Pennsylvania Plaza
New York, NY 10001

Pittsburgh Penguins
Civic Arena
Pittsburgh, PA 15219

Toronto Maple Leafs
60 Carlton St.
Toronto, Ont. M5B 1L1

Winnipeg Jets
15-1430 Maroons Road
Winnipeg, Man. R3G 0L5

National Football League

League Office
410 Park Avenue
New York, NY 10022

Denver Broncos
5700 Logan St.
Denver, CO 80216

Minnesota Vikings
7110 France Ave. So.
Edina, MN 55435

Pittsburgh Steelers
Three Rivers Stadium
Pittsburgh, PA 15212

Atlanta Falcons
Suwanee Road
Suwanee, GA 30174

Detroit Lions
1200 Featherstone Rd.
Box 4200
Pontiac, MI 48057

New England Patriots
Schaefer Stadium
Foxboro, MA 02035

St. Louis Cardinals
200 Stadium Plaza
St. Louis, MO 63102

Baltimore Colts
P.O. Box 2000
Owings Mills, MD 21117

Green Bay Packers
1265 Lombardi Ave.
Green Bay, WI 54303

New Orleans Saints
1500 Poydras St.
New Orleans, LA 70112

San Diego Chargers
San Diego Stadium
P.O. Box 20666
San Diego, CA 92120

Buffalo Bills
1 Bills Drive
Orchard Park, NY 14127

Houston Oilers
P.O. Box 1516
Houston, TX 77001

New York Giants
Giants Stadium
E. Rutherford, NJ 07073

San Francisco 49ers
711 Nevada St.
Redwood City, CA 94061

Chicago Bears
55 E. Jackson Blvd.
Chicago, IL 60604

Cincinnati Bengals
200 Riverfront Stadium
Cincinnati, OH 45202

Kansas City Chiefs
1 Arrowhead Drive
Kansas City, MO 64129

New York Jets
598 Madison Ave.
New York, NY 10022

Seattle Seahawks
5305 Lake Washington Blvd.
Kirkland, WA 98033

Cleveland Browns
Cleveland Stadium
Cleveland, OH 44114

Los Angeles Rams
2327 W. Lincoln Ave.
Anaheim, CA 92801

Oakland Raiders
7850 Edgewater Drive
Oakland, CA 94621

Tampa Bay Buccaneers
1 Buccaneer Place
Tampa, FL 33607

Dallas Cowboys
6116 North Central Expressway
Dallas, TX 75206

Miami Dolphins
330 Biscayne Blvd.
Miami, FL 33132

Philadelphia Eagles
Veterans Stadium
Philadelphia, PA 19148

Washington Redskins
PO Box 17247
Dulles Intl. Airport
Washington, DC 20041

North American Soccer League

League Office
1133 Ave. of the Americas
Suite 3500
New York, NY 10036

Dallas Tornado
6116 N. Central Expwy.
Dallas, TX 75206

Le Manic de Montreal
1259 Berri St.
Suite 400
Montreal, Que. H2L 4C6

Seattle Sounders
419 Occidental South
Seattle, WA 98104

Edmonton Drillers
Suite 200
10736-107 Ave.
Edmonton, Alta. T5H 0W6

Atlanta Chiefs
PO Box 5015
Atlanta, GA 30302

New York Cosmos
75 Rockefeller Plaza
New York, NY 10019

Tampa Bay Rowdies
1410 N. W. Shore Blvd.
Tampa, FL 33607

Ft. Lauderdale Strikers
1350 North East 56th St.
Ft. Lauderdale, FL 33334

Calgary Boomers
3715 Edmonton Trail NE
Calgary, Alta. T2E 3P3

Portland Timbers
910 Southwest 18th
Portland, OR 97205

Toronto Blizzard
Exhibition Stadium
Toronto, Ont. M6K 3C3

California Surf
PO Box 4
Anaheim, CA 92803

Jacksonville Teamen
1350 North East 56 St.
Ft. Lauderdale, FL 33334

Los Angeles Aztecs
7362 Santa Monica Blvd.
Los Angeles, CA 90046

San Diego Sockers
San Diego Stadium
9449 Friars Road
San Diego, CA 92108

Tulsa Roughnecks
PO Box 35190
Tulsa, OK 75135

Chicago Sting
Suite 1525
333 N. Michigan Ave.
Chicago, IL 60601

Minnesota Kicks
7200 France Ave. So.
Minneapolis, MN 55435

San Jose Earthquakes
800 Charcot Ave.
Suite 100
San Jose, CA 95131

Vancouver Whitecaps
3683 E. Hastings St.
Vancouver, B.C. V5K 2B1

USA Amateur Boxing Federation National Championships

Concord, Cal., May 18-23, 1981

106 lbs.—Jesse Benavides, Corpus Christi, Tex.
112 lbs.—Fred Perkins, U.S. Army.
119 lbs.—Richard Savage, W. Monroe, La.
125 lbs.—Guadalupe Suarez, Corpus Christi, Tex.
132 lbs.—Joe Manley, U.S. Army.
139 lbs.—James Mitchell, U.S. Army.

147 lbs.—Darryl Robinson, Houston, Tex.
156 lbs.—James Rayford, U.S. Navy.
165 lbs.—Michael Grogan, Atlanta, Ga.
178 lbs.—Alex DeLucia, Portland, Ore.
201 lbs.—Mark Mahone, U.S. Navy.
Over 201 lbs.—Tyrone Biggs, Philadelphia, Pa.

National Basketball Association, 1980-81

Final Standings

Eastern Conference

Atlantic Division

Club	W	L	Pct	GB
Boston	62	20	.756	.....
Philadelphia	62	20	.756	.....
New York	50	32	.610	12
Washington	39	43	.476	23
New Jersey	24	58	.293	38

Central Division

Club	W	L	Pct	GB
Milwaukee	60	22	.732	.....
Chicago	45	37	.549	15
Indiana	44	38	.537	16
Atlanta	31	51	.378	29
Cleveland	28	54	.341	32
Detroit	21	61	.256	39

Western Conference

Midwest Division

Club	W	L	Pct	GB
San Antonio	52	30	.634	.....
Houston	40	42	.488	12
Kansas City	40	42	.488	12
Denver	37	45	.451	15
Utah	28	54	.341	24
Dallas	15	67	.183	37

Pacific Division

Club	W	L	Pct	GB
Phoenix	57	25	.695	.....
Los Angeles	54	28	.659	3
Portland	45	37	.549	12
Golden State	39	43	.476	18
San Diego	36	46	.439	21
Seattle	34	48	.415	23

NBA Playoff Results

Philadelphia defeated Indiana 2 games to 0.
Chicago defeated New York 2 games to 0.
Houston defeated Los Angeles 2 games to 1.
Kansas City defeated Portland 2 games to 1.
Boston defeated Chicago 4 games to 0.
Philadelphia defeated Milwaukee 4 games to 3.

Houston defeated San Antonio 4 games to 3.
Kansas City defeated Phoenix 4 games to 3.
Houston defeated Kansas City 4 games to 1.
Boston defeated Philadelphia 4 games to 3.
Boston defeated Houston 4 games to 2.

NBA Champions 1947-1981

Year	Eastern Conference	Western Conference	Winner	Runner-up
1947	Washington	Chicago	Philadelphia	Chicago
1948	Philadelphia	St. Louis	Baltimore	Philadelphia
1949	Washington	Rochester	Minneapolis	Washington
1950	Syracuse	Minneapolis	Minneapolis	Syracuse
1951	Philadelphia	Minneapolis	Rochester	New York
1952	Syracuse	Rochester	Minneapolis	New York
1953	New York	Minneapolis	Minneapolis	New York
1954	New York	Minneapolis	Minneapolis	Syracuse
1955	Syracuse	Ft. Wayne	Syracuse	Ft. Wayne
1956	Philadelphia	Ft. Wayne	Philadelphia	Ft. Wayne
1957	Boston	St. Louis	Boston	St. Louis
1958	Boston	St. Louis	St. Louis	Boston
1959	Boston	St. Louis	Boston	Minneapolis
1960	Boston	St. Louis	Boston	St. Louis
1961	Boston	St. Louis	Boston	St. Louis
1962	Boston	Los Angeles	Boston	Los Angeles
1963	Boston	Los Angeles	Boston	Los Angeles
1964	Boston	San Francisco	Boston	San Francisco
1965	Boston	Los Angeles	Boston	Los Angeles
1966	Philadelphia	Los Angeles	Boston	Los Angeles
1967	Philadelphia	San Francisco	Philadelphia	San Francisco
1968	Philadelphia	St. Louis	Boston	Los Angeles
1969	Baltimore	Los Angeles	Boston	Los Angeles
1970	New York	Atlanta	New York	Los Angeles

Year	Atlantic	Central	Midwest	Pacific	Winner	Runner-up
1971	New York	Baltimore	Milwaukee	Los Angeles	Milwaukee	Baltimore
1972	Boston	Baltimore	Milwaukee	Los Angeles	Los Angeles	New York
1973	Boston	Baltimore	Milwaukee	Los Angeles	New York	Los Angeles
1974	Boston	Capital	Milwaukee	Los Angeles	Boston	Milwaukee
1975	Boston	Washington	Chicago	Golden State	Golden State	Washington
1976	Boston	Cleveland	Milwaukee	Golden State	Boston	Phoenix
1977	Philadelphia	Houston	Denver	Los Angeles	Portland	Philadelphia
1978	Philadelphia	San Antonio	Denver	Portland	Washington	Seattle
1979	Washington	San Antonio	Kansas City	Seattle	Seattle	Washington
1980	Boston	Atlanta	Milwaukee	Los Angeles	Los Angeles	Philadelphia
1981	Boston	Milwaukee	San Antonio	Phoenix	Boston	Houston

NBA All League Team in 1981

First team	Position	Second team
Julius Erving, Philadelphia	Forward	Marquis Johnson, Milwaukee
Larry Bird, Boston	Forward	Adrian Dantley, Utah
Kareem Abdul-Jabbar, Los Angeles	Center	Moses Malone, Houston
Dennis Johnson, Phoenix	Guard	Otis Birdsong, Kansas City
George Gervin, San Antonio	Guard	Nate Archibald, Boston

Final Statistics

Individual Scoring Leaders

(Minimum: 70 games played or 1400 points)

	G	FG	FT	Pts	Avg
Dantley, Utah	80	909	632	2452	30.7
Malone, Houston	80	806	609	2222	27.8
Gervin, San Antonio	82	850	512	2221	27.1
Abdul-Jabbar, Los Angeles	80	836	423	2095	26.2
Thompson, Denver	77	734	489	1967	25.5
Birdsong, Kansas City	71	710	317	1747	24.6
Erving, Philadelphia	82	794	422	2014	24.6
Mitchell, Cleveland	82	853	302	2012	24.5
Free, Golden State	65	516	528	1565	24.1
English, Denver	81	768	390	1929	23.8
Wilkes, Los Angeles	81	786	254	1827	22.6
King, Golden State	81	731	307	1771	21.9
Issel, Denver	80	614	519	1749	21.9
Drew, Atlanta	67	500	454	1454	21.7
Newlin, New Jersey	79	632	414	1688	21.4
Bird, Boston	82	719	283	1741	21.2
Griffith, Utah	81	716	229	1671	20.6
Ma. Johnson, Milwaukee	76	636	269	1541	20.3
Cartwright, New York	82	619	408	1646	20.1
R. Williams, New York	79	616	312	1560	19.7

Field Goal Percentage Leaders

(Minimum: 300 FG made)

	FG	FGA	Pct
Gilmore, Chicago	547	816	.670
Dawkins, Philadelphia	423	697	.607
Maxwell, Boston	441	750	.588
King, Golden State	731	1244	.588
Abdul-Jabbar, Los Angeles	836	1457	.574
Washington, Portland	325	571	.569
Dantley, Utah	909	1627	.559
Cartwright, New York	619	1118	.554
Nater, San Diego	517	935	.553
Ma. Johnson, Milwaukee	636	1153	.552

Free Throw Percentage Leaders

(Minimum: 125 FT made)

	FT	FTA	Pct
Murphy, Houston	206	215	.958
Sobers, Chicago	231	247	.935
Newlin, New Jersey	414	466	.888
Spanarkel, Dallas	375	423	.887
Bridgeman, Milwaukee	213	241	.884
Long, Detroit	160	184	.870
Criss, Atlanta	185	214	.864
Bird, Boston	283	328	.863
McKinney, Denver	162	188	.862
Bates, Portland	170	199	.854

3-Pt. Field Goal Leaders

(Minimum: 25 made)

	FG	FGA	Pct
Taylor, San Diego	44	115	.383
Williams, San Diego	48	141	.340
Hassett, Golden State	53	156	.340
Bratz, Cleveland	57	169	.337
Bibby, San Diego	32	95	.337
Grevey, Washington	45	136	.331

Assists Leaders

(Minimum: 70 games or 400 assists)

	G	No	Avg
Porter, Washington	81	734	9.1
Nixon, Los Angeles	79	696	8.8
Ford, Kansas City	66	580	8.8
Richardson, New York	79	627	7.9
Archibald, Boston	80	618	7.7
Lucas, Golden State	66	464	7.0
Ransey, Portland	80	555	6.9
Cheeks, Philadelphia	81	560	6.9
Davis, Indiana	76	490	6.2
Higgs, Denver	72	408	5.7

Rebound Leaders

(Minimum: 70 games or 800 rebounds)

	G	Off	Def	Tot	Avg
Malone, Houston	80	474	706	1180	14.8
Nater, San Diego	82	295	722	1017	12.4
Smith, Golden State	82	433	561	994	12.1
Bird, Boston	82	191	704	895	10.9
Sikma, Seattle	82	184	668	852	10.4
Carr, Cleveland	81	260	575	835	10.3
Abdul-Jabbar, Los Angeles	80	197	624	821	10.3
Gilmore, Chicago	82	220	608	828	10.1
C. Jones, Philadelphia	81	200	613	813	10.0
Hayes, Washington	81	235	554	789	9.7

Steals Leaders

(Minimum: 70 games or 125 steals)

	G	No	Avg
Johnson, Los Angeles	37	127	3.43
Richardson, New York	79	232	2.94
Buckner, Milwaukee	82	197	2.40
Cheeks, Philadelphia	81	193	2.38
R. Williams, New York	79	185	2.34
Bradley, Indiana	82	186	2.27
Erving, Philadelphia	82	173	2.11
Lee, Detroit	82	166	2.02
Reid, Houston	82	163	1.99
Bird, Boston	82	161	1.96

Blocked Shots Leaders

(Minimum: 70 games or 100 blocked shots)

	G	No	Avg
G. Johnson, San Antonio	82	278	3.39
Rollins, Atlanta	40	117	2.93
Abdul-Jabbar, Los Angeles	80	228	2.85
Parish, Boston	82	214	2.61
Gilmore, Chicago	82	198	2.41
Catchings, Milwaukee	77	184	2.39
Tyler, Detroit	82	180	2.20
Thompson, Portland	79	170	2.15
Poquette, Utah	82	174	2.12
Hayes, Washington	81	171	2.11

1981 NBA Player Draft

The following are the first round picks of the National Basketball Assn.

Dallas—Mark Aquirre, DePaul
Detroit—Isiah Thomas, Indiana
New Jersey—Buck Williams, Maryland
Atlanta—Al Wood, North Carolina
Seattle—Danny Vranes, Utah
Chicago—Orlando Woolridge, Notre Dame
Kansas City—Steve Johnson, Oregon State
San Diego—Tom Chambers, Utah
Dallas—Rolando Blackman, Kansas State
New Jersey—Albert King, Maryland
Washington—Frank Johnson, Wake Forest
Detroit—Kelly Tripucka, Notre Dame

Utah—Dan Schayes, Syracuse
Indiana—Herb Williams, Ohio State
Portland—Jeff Lamp, Virginia
Portland—Darnell Valentine, Kansas
Kansas City—Kevin Loder, Alabama State
New Jersey—Ray Tolbert, Indiana
Los Angeles—Mike McGee, Michigan
Phoenix—Larry Nance, Clemson
Milwaukee—Alton Lister, Arizona State
Philadelphia—Franklin Edwards, Cleveland State
Boston—Charles Bradley, Wyoming

NBA Team Statistics in 1980-81

Offense

Team	Field Goals			Free Throws			Rebounds			Scoring	
	Made	Att	Pct	Made	Att	Pct	Off	Def	Tot	Pts	Avg
Denver	3784	7960	.475	2388	3051	.783	1325	2497	3822	9986	121.8
Milwaukee	3722	7472	.498	1802	2340	.770	1261	2408	3669	9267	113.1
San Antonio	3571	7276	.491	2052	2668	.769	1304	2582	3886	9209	112.3
Philadelphia	3636	7073	.514	1865	2427	.768	1091	2618	3709	9156	111.7
Los Angeles	3780	7382	.512	1540	2113	.729	1165	2491	3656	9117	111.2
Portland	3741	7535	.496	1573	2191	.718	1243	2388	3631	9080	110.7
Phoenix	3587	7326	.490	1810	2430	.745	1234	2490	3724	9019	110.0
Boston	3581	7099	.504	1781	2369	.752	1155	2424	3579	9008	109.9
Golden State	3560	7284	.489	1826	2513	.727	1403	2366	3769	9006	109.8
Chicago	3457	6903	.501	1985	2563	.774	1227	2475	3702	8937	109.0
Houston	3573	7335	.487	1711	2223	.770	1216	2347	3563	8878	108.3
New York	3505	7255	.483	1783	2386	.747	1137	2205	3342	8849	107.9
Indiana	3491	7245	.482	1815	2540	.715	1325	2267	3592	8827	107.6
Kansas City	3572	7151	.500	1576	2206	.714	1037	2450	3487	8769	106.9
New Jersey	3477	7314	.475	1780	2371	.751	1092	2374	3466	8768	106.9
San Diego	3477	7283	.477	1651	2246	.735	1169	2144	3313	8737	106.5
Cleveland	3556	7609	.467	1486	1909	.778	1258	2243	3501	8670	105.7
Washington	3549	7517	.472	1499	2072	.723	1155	2533	3688	8662	105.6
Atlanta	3291	6866	.479	2012	2590	.777	1201	2224	3425	8604	104.9
Seattle	3343	7145	.468	1813	2376	.763	1167	2434	3601	8531	104.0
Dallas	3204	6928	.462	1868	2487	.751	1109	2177	3286	8322	101.5
Utah	3332	6825	.488	1595	2080	.767	962	2325	3287	8301	101.2
Detroit	3236	6986	.463	1689	2330	.725	1201	2111	3312	8174	99.7

Defense

Allowed by	Field Goals			Rebounds			Miscellaneous		Scoring		
	Made	Att	Pct	Off	Def	Tot	Steals	Blk Sh	Pts	Avg	Dif
Philadelphia	3307	7337	.451	1286	2287	3573	818	379	8512	103.8	+7.9
Boston	3372	7296	.462	1192	2174	3366	736	351	8526	104.0	+5.9
Phoenix	3368	7221	.466	1160	2284	3444	912	401	8567	104.5	+5.5
Washington	3518	7491	.470	1204	2638	3842	739	469	8661	105.6	even
Seattle	3453	7421	.465	1247	2357	3604	747	387	8666	105.7	−1.7
Milwaukee	3311	7220	.459	1265	2209	3474	735	400	8680	105.9	+7.2
Detroit	3499	6869	.509	1090	2396	3486	793	585	8692	106.0	−6.3
Indiana	3457	7071	.489	1246	2407	3653	695	439	8712	106.2	+1.4
New York	3555	7092	.501	1147	2457	3604	689	452	8716	106.3	+1.6
Kansas City	3424	7117	.481	1138	2510	3648	717	383	8768	106.9	even
Chicago	3527	7209	.489	1145	2096	3241	784	441	8775	107.0	+2.0
Utah	3430	7018	.489	1154	2440	3594	596	406	8784	107.1	−5.9
Los Angeles	3581	7701	.465	1378	2274	3652	754	357	8802	107.3	+3.9
Houston	3617	7341	.493	1177	2367	3544	689	367	8851	107.9	+0.4
Atlanta	3401	6867	.495	1207	2318	3525	748	555	8858	108.0	−3.1
San Diego	3508	6951	.505	1091	2377	3468	683	392	8867	108.1	−1.6
San Antonio	3581	7582	.472	1214	2177	3391	700	481	8973	109.4	+2.9
Portland	3584	7351	.488	1249	2419	3668	802	422	9007	109.8	+0.9
Dallas	3622	7060	.513	1173	2498	3671	713	480	9011	109.9	−8.4
Cleveland	3608	7174	.503	1158	2499	3657	681	454	9068	110.6	−4.9
Golden State	3631	7204	.504	1137	2210	3347	714	386	9103	111.0	−1.2
New Jersey	3612	7159	.505	1059	2499	3558	815	502	9262	113.0	−6.1
Denver	4059	8017	.506	1320	2680	4000	704	547	10025	122.3	−0.5

NBA Most Valuable Player

1956	Bob Pettit, St. Louis	1969	Wes Unseld, Baltimore
1957	Bob Cousy, Boston	1970	Willis Reed, New York
1958	Bill Russell, Boston	1971	Lew Alcindor, Milwaukee
1959	Bob Pettit, St. Louis	1972	Kareem Abdul-Jabbar (Alcindor), Milwaukee
1960	Wilt Chamberlain, Philadelphia	1973	Dave Cowens, Boston
1961	Bill Russell, Boston	1974	Kareem Abdul-Jabbar, Milwaukee
1962	Bill Russell, Boston	1975	Bob McAdoo, Buffalo
1963	Bill Russell, Boston	1976	Kareem Abdul-Jabbar, Los Angeles
1964	Oscar Robertson, Cincinnati	1977	Kareem Abdul-Jabbar, Los Angeles
1965	Bill Russell, Boston	1978	Bill Walton, Portland
1966	Wilt Chamberlain, Philadelphia	1979	Moses Malone, Houston
1967	Wilt Chamberlain, Philadelphia	1980	Kareem Abdul-Jabbar, Los Angeles
1968	Wilt Chamberlain, Philadelphia	1981	Julius Erving, Philadelphia

NBA Rookie of the Year

1954	Don Meineke, Ft. Wayne	1964	Jerry Lucas, Cincinnati	1973	Bob McAdoo, Buffalo
1955	Ray Felix, Baltimore	1965	Willis Reed, New York	1974	Ernie DiGregorio, Buffalo
1956	Maurice Stokes, Rochester	1966	Rick Barry, San Francisco	1975	Keith Wilkes, Golden State
1957	Tom Heinsohn, Boston	1967	Dave Bing, Detroit	1976	Alvan Adams, Phoenix
1958	Woody Sauldsberry, Philadelphia	1968	Earl Monroe, Baltimore	1977	Adrian Dantley, Buffalo
1959	Elgin Baylor, Minnesota	1969	Wes Unseld, Baltimore	1978	Walter Davis, Phoenix
1960	Wilt Chamberlain, Philadelphia	1970	Lew Alcindor, Milwaukee	1979	Phil Ford, Kansas City
1961	Oscar Robertson, Cincinnati	1971	Dave Cowens, Boston;	1980	Larry Bird, Boston
1962	Walt Bellamy, Chicago		Geoff Petrie, Portland (tie)	1981	Darrell Griffith, Utah
1963	Terry Dischinger, Chicago	1972	Sidney Wicks, Portland		

NBA Scoring Leaders

Year	Scoring champion	Pts	Avg	Year	Scoring champion	Pts	Avg
1947	Joe Fulks, Philadelphia	1,389	23.2	1965	Wilt Chamberlain, San Fran., Phila.	2,534	34.7
1948	Max Zaslofsky, Chicago	1,007	21.0	1966	Wilt Chamberlain, Philadelphia	2,649	33.5
1949	George Mikan, Minneapolis	1,698	28.3	1967	Rick Barry, San Francisco	2,775	35.6
1950	George Mikan, Minneapolis	1,865	27.4	1968	Dave Bing, Detroit	2,142	27.1
1951	George Mikan, Minneapolis	1,932	28.4	1969	Elvin Hayes, San Diego	2,327	28.4
1952	Paul Arizin, Philadelphia	1,674	25.4	1970	Jerry West, Los Angeles	2,309	31.2
1953	Neil Johnston, Philadelphia	1,564	22.3	1971	Lew Alcindor, Milwaukee	2,596	31.7
1954	Neil Johnston, Philadelphia	1,759	24.4	1972	Kareem Abdul-Jabar (Alcindor),		
1955	Neil Johnston, Philadelphia	1,631	22.7		Milwaukee	2,822	34.8
1956	Bob Pettit, St. Louis	1,849	25.7	1973	Nate Archibald, Kansas City-Omaha	2,719	34.0
1957	Paul Arizin, Philadelphia	1,817	25.6	1974	Bob McAdoo, Buffalo	2,261	30.6
1958	George Yardley, Detroit	2,001	27.8	1975	Bob McAdoo, Buffalo	2,831	04.5
1959	Bob Pettit, St. Louis	2,105	29.2	1976	Bob McAdoo, Buffalo	2,427	31.1
1960	Wilt Chamberlain, Philadelphia	2,707	37.9	1977	Pete Maravich, New Orleans	2,273	31.1
1961	Wilt Chamberlain, Philadelphia	3,033	38.4	1978	George Gervin, San Antonio	2,232	27.2
1962	Wilt Chamberlain, Philadelphia	4,029	50.4	1979	George Gervin, San Antonio	2,365	29.6
1963	Wilt Chamberlain, San Francisco	3,586	44.8	1980	George Gervin, San Antonio	2,585	33.1
1964	Wilt Chamberlain, San Francisco	2,948	36.5	1981	Adrian Dantley, Utah	2,452	30.7

NBA All-Defensive Team in 1981

First team	Position	Second team
Bobby Jones, Philadelphia	Forward	Dan Roundfield, Atlanta
Caldwell Jones, Philadelphia	Forward	Kermit Washington, Los Angeles
Kareem Abdul-Jabbar, Los Angeles	Center	George Johnson, San Antonio
Michael Ray Richardson, New York	Guard	Quinn Buckner, Milwaukee
Dennis Johnson, Phoenix	Guard	(tie) Dudley Bradley, Indiana
		Michael Cooper, Los Angeles

Basketball Hall of Fame

Springfield, Mass.

Players

Arizin, Paul
Baylor, Elgin
Beckman, John
Borgmann, Bennie
Brennan, Joseph
Barlow, Thomas
Chamberlain, Wilt
Cooper, Charles
Cousy, Bob
Davies, Bob
DeBernardi, Forrest
Dehnert, Dutch
Endacott, Paul
Foster, Bud
Friedman, Max
Fulks, Joe
Gale, Lauren
Gola, Tom
Gruenig, Ace
Hagan, Cliff
Hanson, Victor
Holman, Nat
Hyatt, Chuck
Johnson, William
Krause, Moose
Kurland, Bob

Lapchick, Joe
Lucas, Jerry
Luisetti, Hank
McCracken, Branch
McCracken, Jack
Macauley, Ed
Mikan, George
Murphy, Stretch
Page, Pat
Pettit, Bob
Phillip, Andy
Pollard, Jim
Robertson, Oscar
Roosma, John S.
Russell, Honey
Russell, Bill
Schayes, Adolph
Schmidt, Ernest
Schommer, John
Sedran, Barney
Sharman, Bill
Steinmetz, Christian
Thompson, Cat
Vandivier, Fuzzy
Wachter, Edward
West, Jerry
Wooden, John

Coaches

Auerbach, Red
Barry, Sam
Blood, Ernest
Cann, Howard
Carlson, Dr. H. C.
Carnevale, Ben
Dean, Everett
Diddle, Edgar
Drake, Bruce
Gill, Slats
Hickey, Edgar
Hobson, Howard
Iba, Hank
Julian, Alvin
Keaney, Frank
Keogan, George
Lambert, Ward
Litwack, Harry
Loeffler, Kenneth
Lonborg, Dutch
McCutchan, Arad
McGuire, Frank
McLendon, John
Meyer, Ray
Meanwell, Dr. W. E.
Newell, Pete
Rupp, Adolph

Sachs, Leonard
Shelton, Everett
Wooden, John

Referees

Enright, James
Hepbron, George
Hoyt, George
Kennedy, Matthew
Nucatola, John
Quigley, Ernest
Shirley, J. Dallas
Tobey, David
Walsh, David

Contributors

Allen, Phog
Bee, Clair
Brown, Walter
Bunn, John
Douglas, Bob
Fisher, Harry
Gottlieb, Edward
Gulick, Dr. L. H.
Harrison, Lester
Hepp, Dr. Ferenc
Hickox, Edward

Hinkle, Tony
Irish, Ned
Jones, R. W.
Kennedy, Walter
Liston, Emil
Mokray, Bill
Morgan, Ralph
Morgenweck, Frank
Naismith, Dr. James
O'Brien, John
Olsen, Harold
Podoloff, Maurice
Porter, H. V.
Reid, William
Ripley, Elmer
St. John, Lynn
Saperstein, Abe
Schabinger, Arthur
Stagg, Amos Alonzo
Taylor, Chuck
Tower, Oswald
Trester, Arthur
Wells, Clifford

Teams

First Team
Original Celtics
Buffalo Germans
Renaissance

American Basketball Association, 1968-1976

Champions

	Regular season		Playoffs	
Year	Eastern division	Western division	Winner	Runner-up
1968	Pittsburgh	New Orleans	Pittsburgh	New Orleans
1969	Indiana	Oakland	Oakland	Indiana
1970	Indiana	Denver	Indiana	Los Angeles
1971	Virginia	Indiana	Utah	Kentucky
1972	Kentucky	Utah	Indiana	New York
1973	Carolina	Utah	Indiana	Kentucky
1974	New York	Utah	New York	Utah
1975	Kentucky	Denver	Kentucky	Indiana
1976		Denver	New York	Denver

Scoring Leaders

Year	Leader	Pts	Avg	Year	Leader	Pts	Avg
1968	Connie Hawkins, Pittsburgh	1,875	26.7	1973	Julius Erving, Virginia	2,268	31.9
1969	Rick Barry, Oakland	1,190	34.0	1974	Julius Erving, New York	2,299	27.3
1970	Spencer Haywood, Denver	2,519	29.9	1975	George McGinnis, Indiana	2,353	29.7
1971	Dan Issel, Kentucky	2,480	29.8	1976	Julius Erving, New York	2,462	29.3
1972	Charlie Scott, Virginia	2,524	34.5				

College Football Stadiums

School	Capacity	School	Capacity
Alabama, Univ. of (Denny Stad.), University, Ala.	59,000	New Mexico, Univ. Stad., Albuquerque	30,646
Arizona State Univ. (Sun Devil), Tempe	70,311	North Carolina St. U. (Carter Stad.), Raleigh	45,600
Arizona, Univ. of (Arizona Stad.), Tucson	57,000	North Carolina, Univ. of (Kenan Stad.)	49,500
Arkansas, Univ. of (Razorback Stad.) Fayetteville	41,500	Northern Illinois Univ. (Huskie Stad.), DeKalb	20,257
Auburn Univ. (Jordan Hare Stad.), Auburn, Ala.	71,863	Northwestern Univ. (Dyche Stad.), Evanston, Ill.	48,500
Baylor Univ. Stad., Waco, Tex.	48,000	Notre Dame Stad., South Bend, Ind.	59,075
Boston Coll. (Alumni Stad.), Boston, Mass.	32,000	Ohio State Univ. (Ohio Stad.), Columbus	83,112
Bowling Green State Univ. (Doyt Perry Field)	23,272	Oklahoma State (Lewis Stad.), Stillwater	50,588
Brigham Young Univ. Stad., Provo, Ut.	30,000	Oklahoma, Univ. of (Owen Field), Norman	71,186
Cal., Univ. of (Memorial Stad.), Berkeley	76,780	Oregon St. Univ. (Parker Stad.), Corvallis	40,593
Cincinnati, Univ. of (Nippert), Oh.	25,270	Oregon, Univ. of (Autzen Stad.), Eugene	42,000
Citadel (Johnson Hagood Stad.), Charleston, S.C.	22,500	Pacific, Univ. of the (Pacific Memorial), Stockton, Cal.	30,000
Clemson Univ. (Memorial Stad.), S.C.	53,306	Penn. State Univ. (Beaver Stad.)	83,017
Colorado St. Univ. (Hughes Stad.), Ft. Collins	30,000	Penn., Univ. of (Franklin Field), Phila.	60,546
Colorado, Univ. of (Folsom Field), Boulder	52,005	Pittsburgh, Univ. of (Pitt. Stad.), Pa.	56,500
Columbia Univ. (Baker Field), N.Y., N.Y.	32,000	Princeton, (Palmer Stad.), Princeton, N.J.	45,725
Cornell (Schoellkopf Crescent), Ithaca, N.Y.	27,000	Purdue, (Ross-Ade Stad.), Lafayette, Ind.	69,250
Dartmouth Coll. (Memorial Field), Hanover, N.H.	20,416	Rice Stad., Houston, Texas	70,000
Delaware, Univ. of (Delaware Stad.), Newark	21,919	Rutgers Stad., New Brunswick, N.J.	23,000
Duke Univ., (Wade Stad.), Durham, N.C.	40,078	So. Carolina, Univ. of (Williams-Brice), Columbia	54,406
E. Carolina Univ. (Ficklen Stad.), Greenville, N.C.	35,000	So. Illinois Univ. (McAndrew Stad.), Carbondale	20,100
Eastern Kentucky (Hanger Field), Richmond	20,000	So. Miss., Univ. of (Roberts Stad.), Hattiesburg	33,000
Florida State, (Campbell Stad.), Tallahassee	51,095	Southwestern La., Univ. of (Cajun Field), Lafayette	24,610
Florida, Univ. of (Florida Field), Gainesville	62,000	Stanford Stad., Stanford, Cal.	84,892
Georgia Tech. (Grant Field), Atlanta	58,121	Syracuse Univ., (Carrier Dome), N.Y.	50,000
Georgia, Univ. of (Sanford Stad.), Athens	59,200	Tenn., Univ. of (Neyland Stad.), Knoxville	90,150
Harvard Stad., Boston, Mass.	37,289	Texas A. & M. Univ. (Kyle Field), College Station	71,600
Hawaii, Univ. of (Aloha Stad.), Honolulu	50,000	Texas Christian Univ. (TCU-Amon Carter Stad.)	46,000
Holy Cross (Fitton Field), Worcester, Mass.	25,000	Texas-El Paso (Sun Bowl)	30,000
Illinois, Univ. of (Memorial Stad.), Urbana	71,229	Texas Tech. Univ. (Jones Stad.), Lubbock	47,000
Indiana St. (Memorial Stad.), Terre Haute	20,500	Texas, Univ. of (Memorial Stad.), Austin	80,000
Indiana Univ. (Memorial Stad.), Bloomington	52,354	Tulsa, Univ. of (Skelly Stad.), Okla.	40,235
Iowa State Stad., Ames	50,000	U.S. Air Force Acad. (Falcon Stad.), Col.	49,668
Iowa, Univ. of (Kinnick Stad.), Iowa City	60,200	U.S. Military Academy (Michie Stad.), West Point, N.Y.	39,480
Kansas State Univ. Stad., Manhattan	42,000	U.S. Naval Academy (Navy-Marine Corps Mem. Stad.)	
Kansas, Univ. of (Memorial Stad.), Lawrence	51,500	Annapolis, Md.	28,000
Kent State Univ. (Dix Stad.), Kent, Oh.	28,883	Utah State Univ. (Romney Stad.), Logan	30,000
Kentucky, Univ. of (Commonwealth), Lexington	58,000	Utah, Univ. of (Robert Rice Stad.), Salt Lake City	30,000
La. State Univ. (Tiger Stad.), Baton Rouge	76,092	Vanderbilt (Dudley Stad.), Nashville	34,694
Louisiana Tech. Univ. (Joe Aillet Stad.), Ruston	22,500	Virginia Tech. (Lane Stad.), Blacksburg	52,500
Maryland, Univ. of (Byrd), College Park	45,000	Virginia, Univ. of (Scott Stad.), Charlottesville	42,000
Memphis State (Liberty Bowl)	50,180	Wake Forest (Groves Stad.), Winston-Salem, N.C.	31,000
Michigan State Univ. (Spartan Stad.), E. Lansing	76,000	Washington State Univ. (Clarence D. Martin)	39,000
Michigan, Univ. of (Mich. Stad.), Ann Arbor	101,701	Washington, Univ. of (Husky Stad.), Seattle	58,946
Minnesota, Univ. of (Memorial Stad.), Minneapolis	56,725	West Texas State Univ. (Kimbrough Stad.), Canyon	30,000
Mississippi St. Univ. (Scott Field)	35,000	West Virginia Univ. (Mountaineer Field)	50,000
Mississippi, Univ. of (Hemingway Stad.)	35,000	Western Mich. Univ. (Waldo Stad.), Kalamazoo	24,500
Missouri, Univ. of (Faurot Field), Columbia	75,000	Wichita State Univ. (Cessna Stad.)	31,500
Nebraska, Univ. of (Memorial Stad.), Lincoln	76,400	Wisconsin, Univ. of (Camp Randall), Madison	77,280
Nevada-Las Vegas, Univ. of (Silver Bowl)	32,000	Wyoming, Univ. of (Memorial), Laramie	33,500
New Mexico State Univ. (Memorial Stad.), Las Cruces	30,000	Yale Bowl, New Haven, Conn.	70,874

Heisman Trophy Winners

Awarded annually to the nation's outstanding college football player.

Year	Winner	Year	Winner	Year	Winner
1935	Jay Berwanger, Chicago, HB	1951	Richard Kazmaier, Princeton, HB	1967	Gary Beban, UCLA, QB
1936	Larry Kelley, Yale, E	1952	Billy Vessels, Oklahoma, HB	1968	O. J. Simpson, USC, RB
1937	Clinton Frank, Yale, QB	1953	John Lattner, Notre Dame, HB	1969	Steve Owens, Oklahoma, RB
1938	David O'Brien, Tex. Christian, QB	1954	Alan Ameche, Wisconsin, FB	1970	Jim Plunkett, Stanford, QB
1939	Nile Kinnick, Iowa, QB	1955	Howard Cassady, Ohio St., HB	1971	Pat Sullivan, Auburn, QB
1940	Tom Harmon, Michigan, HB	1956	Paul Hornung, Notre Dame, QB	1972	Johnny Rodgers, Nebraska, RB-R
1941	Bruce Smith, Minnesota, HB	1957	John Crow, Texas A & M, HB	1973	John Cappelletti, Penn State, RB
1942	Frank Sinkwich, Georgia, HB	1958	Pete Dawkins, Army, HB	1974	Archie Griffin, Ohio State, RB
1943	Angelo Bertelli, Notre Dame, QB	1959	Billy Cannon, La. State, HB	1975	Archie Griffin, Ohio State, RB
1944	Leslie Horvath, Ohio State, QB	1960	Joe Bellino, Navy, HB	1976	Tony Dorsett, Pittsburgh, RB
1945	Felix Blanchard, Army, FB	1961	Ernest Davis, Syracuse, HB	1977	Earl Campbell, Texas, RB
1946	Glenn Davis, Army, HB	1962	Terry Baker, Oregon State, QB	1978	Billy Sims, Oklahoma, RB
1947	John Lujack, Notre Dame, QB	1963	Roger Staubach, Navy, QB	1979	Charles White, USC, RB
1948	Doak Walker, SMU, HB	1964	John Huarte, Notre Dame, QB	1980	George Rogers, So. Carolina, RB
1949	Leon Hart, Notre Dame, E	1965	Mike Garrett, USC, HB		
1950	Vic Janowicz, Ohio State, HB	1966	Steve Spurrier, Florida, QB		

Annual Results of Major Bowl Games

(Note: Dates indicate the year that the game was played.)

Rose Bowl, Pasadena

1902 Michigan 49, Stanford 0
1916 Wash. State 14, Brown 0
1917 Oregon 14, Pennsylvania 0
1918-19 Service teams
1920 Harvard 7, Oregon 6
1921 California 28, Ohio State 0
1922 Wash. & Jeff. 0, California 0
1923 So. California 14, Penn State 3
1924 Navy 14, Washington 14
1925 Notre Dame 27, Stanford 10
1926 Alabama 20, Washington 19
1927 Alabama 7, Stanford 7
1928 Stanford 7, Pittsburgh 6
1929 Georgia Tech 8, California 7
1930 So. California 47, Pittsburgh 14
1931 Alabama 24, Wash. State 0
1932 So. California 21, Tulane 12
1933 So. California 35, Pittsburgh 0
1934 Columbia 7, Stanford 0
1935 Alabama 29, Stanford 13
1936 Stanford 7, So. Methodist 0
1937 Pittsburgh 21, Washington 0
1938 California 13, Alabama 0

1939 So. California 7, Duke 3
1940 So. California 14, Tennessee 0
1941 Stanford 21, Nebraska 13
1942 Oregon St. 20, Duke 16
(at Durham)
1943 Georgia 9, UCLA 0
1944 So. California 29, Washington 0
1945 So. California 25, Tennessee 0
1946 Alabama 34, So. California 14
1947 Illinois 45, UCLA 14
1048 Michigan 49, So. California 0
1949 Northwestern 20, California 14
1950 Ohio State 17, California 14
1951 Michigan 14, California 6
1952 Illinois 40, Stanford 7
1953 So. California 7, Wisconsin 0
1954 Mich. State 28, UCLA 20
1955 Ohio State 20, So. California 7
1956 Mich. State 17, UCLA 14
1957 Iowa 35, Oregon St. 19
1958 Ohio State 10, Oregon 7
1959 Iowa 38, California 12

1960 Washington 44, Wisconsin 8
1961 Washington 17, Minnesota 7
1962 Minnesota 21, UCLA 3
1963 So. California 42, Wisconsin 37
1964 Illinois 17, Washington 7
1965 Michigan 34, Oregon St. 7
1966 UCLA 14, Mich. State 12
1967 Purdue 14, So. California 13
1968 Southern Cal 14, Indiana 3
1969 Ohio State 27, Southern Cal 16
1970 Southern Cal 10, Michigan 3
1971 Stanford 27, Ohio State 17
1972 Stanford 13, Michigan 12
1973 So. California 42, Ohio State 17
1974 Ohio State 42, So. California 21
1975 So California 18, Ohio State 17
1976 UCLA 23, Ohio State 10
1977 So. California 14, Michigan 6
1978 Washington 27, Michigan 20
1979 So. California 17, Michigan 10
1980 So. California 17, Ohio State 16
1981 Michigan 23, Washington 6

Orange Bowl, Miami

1933 Miami (Fla.) 7, Manhattan 0
1934 Duquesne 33, Miami (Fla.) 7
1935 Bucknell 26, Miami (Fla.) 0
1936 Catholic U. 20, Mississippi 19
1937 Duquesne 13, Miss. State 12
1938 Auburn 6, Mich. State 0
1939 Tennessee 17, Oklahoma 0
1940 Georgia Tech 21, Missouri 7
1941 Miss. State 14, Georgetown 7
1942 Georgia 40, TCU 26
1943 Alabama 37, Boston Col. 21
1944 LSU 19, Texas A&M 14
1945 Tulsa 26, Georgia Tech 12
1946 Miami (Fla.) 13, Holy Cross 6
1947 Rice 8, Tennessee 0
1948 Georgia Tech 20, Kansas 14
1949 Texas 41, Georgia 28

1950 Santa Clara 21, Kentucky 13
1951 Clemson 15, Miami (Fla.) 14
1952 Georgia Tech 17, Baylor 14
1953 Alabama 61, Syracuse 6
1954 Oklahoma 7, Maryland 0
1955 Duke 34, Nebraska 7
1956 Oklahoma 20, Maryland 6
1957 Colorado 27, Clemson 21
1958 Oklahoma 48, Duke 21
1959 Oklahoma 21, Syracuse 6
1960 Georgia 14, Missouri 0
1961 Missouri 21, Navy 14
1962 LSU 25, Colorado 7
1963 Alabama 17, Oklahoma 0
1964 Nebraska 13, Auburn 7
1965 Texas 21, Alabama 17

1966 Alabama 39, Nebraska 28
1967 Florida 27, Georgia Tech 12
1968 Oklahoma 26, Tennessee 24
1969 Penn State 15, Kansas 14
1970 Penn State 10, Missouri 3
1971 Nebraska 17, Louisiana St. 12
1972 Nebraska 38, Alabama 6
1973 Nebraska 40, Notre Dame 6
1974 Penn State 16, Louisiana St. 9
1975 Notre Dame 13, Alabama 11
1976 Oklahoma 14, Michigan 6
1977 Ohio State 27, Colorado 10
1978 Arkansas 31, Oklahoma 6
1979 Oklahoma 31, Nebraska 24
1980 Oklahoma 24, Florida St. 7
1981 Oklahoma 18, Florida St. 17

Sugar Bowl, New Orleans

1935 Tulane 20, Temple 14
1936 TCU 3, LSU 2
1937 Santa Clara 21, LSU 14
1938 Santa Clara 6, LSU 0
1939 TCU 15, Carnegie Tech 7
1940 Texas A&M 14, Tulane 13
1941 Boston Col. 19, Tennessee 13
1942 Fordham 2, Missouri 0
1943 Tennessee 14, Tulsa 7
1944 Georgia Tech 20, Tulsa 18
1945 Duke 29, Alabama 26
1946 Oklahoma A&M 33, St. Mary's 13
1947 Georgia 20, No. Carolina 10
1948 Texas 27, Alabama 7
1949 Oklahoma 14, No. Carolina 6
1950 Oklahoma 35, LSU 0

1951 Kentucky 13, Oklahoma 7
1952 Maryland 28, Tennessee 13
1953 Georgia Tech. 24, Mississippi 7
1954 Georgia Tech 42, West Virginia 19
1955 Navy 21, Mississippi 0
1956 Georgia Tech 7, Pittsburgh 0
1957 Baylor 13, Tennessee 7
1958 Mississippi 39, Texas 7
1959 LSU 7, Clemson 0
1960 Mississippi 21, LSU 0
1961 Mississippi 14, Rice 6
1962 Alabama 10, Arkansas 3
1963 Mississippi 17, Arkansas 13
1964 Alabama 12, Mississippi 7
1965 LSU 13, Syracuse 10
1966 Missouri 20, Florida 18

1967 Alabama 34, Nebraska 7
1968 LSU 20, Wyoming 13
1969 Arkansas 16, Georgia 2
1970 Mississippi 27, Arkansas 22
1971 Tennessee 34, Air Force 13
1972 Oklahoma 40, Auburn 22
*1972 (Dec.) Oklahoma 14, Penn State 0
1973 Notre Dame 24, Alabama 23
1974 Nebraska 13, Florida 10
1975 Alabama 13, Penn State 6
1977 (Jan.) Pittsburgh 27, Georgia 3
1978 Alabama 35, Ohio State 6
1979 Alabama 14, Penn State 7
1980 Alabama 24, Arkansas 9
1981 Georgia 17, Notre Dame 10
*Penn St. awarded game by forfeit

Cotton Bowl, Dallas

1937 TCU 16, Marquette 6
1938 Rice 28, Colorado 14
1939 St. Mary's 20, Texas Tech 13
1940 Clemson 6, Boston Col. 3
1941 Texas A&M 13, Fordham 12
1942 Alabama 29, Texas A&M 21
1943 Texas 14, Georgia Tech 7
1944 Randolph Field 7, Texas 7
1945 Oklahoma A&M 34, TCU 0
1946 Texas 40, Missouri 27
1947 Arkansas 0, LSU 0
1948 So. Methodist 13, Penn State 13
1949 So. Methodist 21, Oregon 13
1950 Rice 27, No. Carolina 13
1951 Tennessee 20, Texas 14

1952 Kentucky 20, TCU 7
1953 Texas 16, Tennessee 0
1954 Rice 28, Alabama 6
1955 Georgia Tech 14, Arkansas 6
1956 Mississippi 14, TCU 13
1957 TCU 28, Syracuse 27
1958 Navy 20, Rice 7
1959 TCU 0, Air Force 0
1960 Syracuse 23, Texas 14
1961 Duke 7, Arkansas 6
1962 Texas 12, Mississippi 7
1963 LSU 13, Texas 0
1964 Texas 28, Navy 6
1965 Arkansas 10, Nebraska 7
1966 LSU 14, Arkansas 7

1967 Georgia 24, So. Methodist 9
1968 Texas A&M 20, Alabama 16
1969 Texas 36, Tennessee 13
1970 Texas 21, Notre Dame 17
1971 Notre Dame 24, Texas 11
1972 Penn State 30, Texas 6
1973 Texas 17, Alabama 13
1974 Nebraska 19, Texas 3
1975 Penn State 41, Baylor 20
1976 Arkansas 31, Georgia 10
1977 Houston 30, Maryland 21
1978 Notre Dame 38, Texas 10
1979 Notre Dame 35, Houston 34
1980 Houston 17, Nebraska 14
1981 Alabama 30, Baylor 2

Sun Bowl, El Paso

1936 Hardin Simmons 14, New Mex. St. 14	1950 Texas Western 33, Georgetown 20	1965 Georgia 7, Texas Tech 0
1937 Hardin-Simmons 34, Texas Mines 6	1951 West Texas St. 14, Cincinnati 13	1966 Texas Western 13, TCU 12
1938 West Virginia 7, Texas Tech 6	1952 Texas Tech 25, Col. Pacific 14	1967 Wyoming 28, Florida St. 20
1939 Utah 26, New Mexico 0	1953 Col. Pacific 26, Miss. Southern 7	1968 UTex El Paso 14, Mississippi 7
1940 Catholic U. 0, Arizona St. 0	1954 Texas Western 37, Miss.	1969 Auburn 34, Arizona 10
1941 Western Reserve 26, Arizona St. 13	Southern 14	1969 (Dec.) Nebraska 45, Georgia 6
1942 Tulsa 6, Texas Tech 0	1955 Texas Western 47, Florida St. 20	1970 Georgia Tech. 17, Texas Tech. 9
1943 2d Air Force 13, Hardin-Simmons 7	1956 Wyoming 21, Texas Tech 14	1971 LSU 33, Iowa State 15
1944 Southwestern (Tex.) 7,	1957 Geo. Washington 13, Tex.	1972 North Carolina 32, Texas Tech 28
New Mexico 0	Western 0	1973 Missouri 34, Auburn 17
1945 Southwestern (Tex.) 35, U. of	1958 Louisville 34, Drake 20	1974 Mississippi St. 26, No. Carolina 24
Mex. 0	1959 Wyoming 14, Hardin-Simmons 6	1975 Pittsburgh 33, Kansas 19
1946 New Mexico 34, Denver 24	1960 New Mexico St. 28, No. Texas St. 8	1977 (Jan.) Texas A&M 37, Florida 14
1947 Cincinnati 38, Virginia Tech 6	1961 New Mexico St. 20, Utah State 13	1977 (Dec.) Stanford 24, Louisiana St. 14
1948 Miami (O.) 13, Texas Tech 12	1962 Villanova 17, Wichita 9	1978 Texas 42, Maryland 0
1949 West Virginia 21, Texas Mines 12	1963 West Texas St. 15, Ohio U. 14	1979 Washington 14, Texas 7
	1964 Oregon 21, So. Methodist 14	1980 Nebraska 31, Mississippi St. 17

Gator Bowl, Jacksonville

1946 Wake Forest 26, So. Carolina 14	1958 Tennessee 3, Texas A&M 0	1969 (Dec.) Florida 14, Tenn. 13
1947 Oklahoma 34, N.C. State 13	1959 Mississippi 7, Florida 3	1971 (Jan.) Auburn 35, Mississippi 28
1948 Maryland 20, Georgia 20	1960 Arkansas 14, Georgia Tech 7	1972 Georgia 7, N. Carolina 3
1949 Clemson 24, Missouri 23	1961 Florida 13, Baylor 12	1973 Auburn 24, Colorado 3
1950 Maryland 20, Missouri 7	1962 Penn State 30, Georgia Tech 15	1973 (Dec.) Tex. Tech. 28, Tenn. 19
1951 Wyoming 20, Wash. & Lee 7	1963 Florida 17, Penn State 7	1974 Auburn 27, Texas 3
1952 Miami (Fla.) 14, Clemson 0	1964 No. Carolina 35, Air Force 0	1975 Maryland 13, Florida 0
1953 Florida 14, Tulsa 13	1965 Florida St. 36, Oklahoma 19	1976 Notre Dame 20, Penn State 9
1954 Texas Tech 35, Auburn 13	1966 Georgia Tech 31, Texas Tech 21	1977 Pittsburgh 34, Clemson 3
1955 Auburn 33, Baylor 13	1967 Tennessee 18, Syracuse 12	1978 Clemson 17, Ohio State 15
1956 Vanderbilt 25, Auburn 13	1968 Penn State 17, Florida St. 17	1979 No. Carolina 17, Michigan 15
1957 Georgia Tech 21, Pittsburgh 14	1969 Missouri 35, Alabama 10	1980 Pittsburgh 37, So. Carolina 9

Bluebonnet Bowl, Houston

1959 Clemson 23, TCU 7	1967 Colorado 31, Miami (Fla.) 21	1974 N. Carolina St. 31, Houston 31
1960 Texas 3, Alabama 3	1968 SMU 28, Oklahoma 27	1975 Texas 38, Colorado 21
1961 Kansas 33, Rice 7	1969 Houston 36, Auburn 7	1976 Nebraska 27, Texas Tech 24
1962 Missouri 14, Georgia Tech 10	1970 Oklahoma 24, Alabama 24	1977 USC 47, Texas A&M 28
1963 Baylor 14, LSU 7	1971 Colorado 29, Houston 17	1978 Stanford 25, Georgia 22
1964 Tulsa 14, Mississippi 7	1972 Tennessee 24, Louisiana St. 17	1979 Purdue 27, Tennessee 22
1965 Tennessee 27, Tulsa 6	1973 Houston 47, Tulane 7	1980 No. Carolina 16, Texas 7
1966 Texas 19, Mississippi 0		

Peach Bowl, Atlanta

1968 LSU 31, Florida St. 27	1973 Georgia 17, Maryland 16	1977 N. Carolina St. 24, Iowa St. 14
1969 West Virginia 14, S. Carolina 3	1974 Vanderbilt 6, Texas Tech. 6	1978 Purdue 41, Georgia Tech. 21
1970 Arizona St. 48, N. Carolina 26	1975 W. Virginia 13, No. Carolina St. 10	1979 Baylor 24, Clemson 18
1971 Mississippi 41, Georgia Tech. 18	1976 Kentucky 21, North Carolina 0	1981 (Jan.) Miami 20, Virginia Tech. 10
1972 N. Carolina St. 49, W. Va. 13		

Tangerine Bowl, Orlando

1968 Richmond 49, Ohio 42	1973 Miami, Ohio 16, Florida 7	1977 Florida St. 40, Texas Tech 17
1969 Toledo 56, Davidson 33	1974 Miami, Ohio 21, Georgia 10	1978 N. Carolina St. 30, Pittsburgh 17
1970 Toledo 40, William & Mary 12	1975 Miami, Ohio 20, South Carolina 7	1979 Louisiana St. 34, Wake Forest 10
1971 Toledo 28, Richmond 3	1976 Okla. St. 49, Brigham Young 21	1980 Florida 35, Maryland 20
1972 Tampa 21, Kent State 18		

Liberty Bowl, Memphis

1959 Penn State 7, Alabama 0	1967 N.C. State 14, Georgia 7	1974 Tennessee 7, Maryland 3
1960 Penn State 41, Oregon 12	1968 Mississippi 34, Va. Tech 17	1975 USC 20, Texas A&M 0
1961 Syracuse 15, Miami 14	1969 Colorado 47, Alabama 33	1976 Alabama 36, UCLA 6
1962 Oregon State 6, Villanova 0	1970 Tulane 17, Colorado 3	1977 Nebraska 27, N. Carolina 17
1963 Miss. State 16, N.C. State 12	1971 Tennessee 14, Arkansas 13	1978 Missouri 20, Louisiana St. 15
1964 Utah 32, West Virginia 6	1972 Georgia Tech 31, Iowa State 30	1979 Penn St. 9, Tulane 6
1965 Mississippi 13, Auburn 7	1973 No. Carolina St. 31, Kansas 18	1980 Purdue 28, Missouri 25
1966 Miami (Fla.) 14, Va. Tech 7		

Fiesta Bowl, Phoenix

1971 Arizona St. 45, Flordia St. 38	1975 Arizona St. 17, Nebraska 14	1978 UCLA 10, Arkansas 10
1972 Arizona St. 49, Missouri 35	1976 Oklahoma 41, Wyoming 7	1979 Pittsburgh 16, Arizona 10
1973 Arizona St. 28, Pittsburgh 7	1977 Penn St. 42, Arizona St. 30	1980 Penn St. 31, Ohio St. 19
1974 Okla. St. 16, Brigham Young 6		

Other Bowl Games in 1980

Amos Alonzo Stagg Bowl—Dayton 63, Ithaca (N.Y.) 0.
Zia Bowl—Cal Poly-San Luis Obispo 21, Eastern Illinois 13.
Independence Bowl—Southern Mississippi 16, McNeese State 14.

Garden State Bowl—Houston 35, Navy 0.
Holiday Bowl—Brigham Young 46, Southern Methodist 45.
Camellia Bowl—Boise State 31, Eastern Kentucky 29.
Hall of Fame Bowl—Arkansas 35, Tulane 15.

College Football Teams

Division I Teams

Team	Nickname	Team colors	Conference	Coach	1980 record (W-L-T)
Air Force	Falcons	Blue & silver	Western Athletic	Ken Hatfield	2-10-1
Akron	Zips	Blue & Gold	Ohio Valley	Jim Dennison	3-7-1
Alabama	Crimson Tide	Crimson & white	Southeastern	Paul Bryant	9-2-0
Alcorn State	Braves	Purple & gold	Southwestern	Marino Casem	6-4-0
Appalachian State	Mountaineers	Black & gold	Southern	Mike Working	6-4-1
Arizona	Wildcats	Red & blue	Pacific Ten	Larry Smith	5-6-0
Arizona State	Sun Devils	Maroon & gold	Pacific Ten	Darryl Rogers	7-4-0
Arkansas	Razorbacks	Cardinal & white	Southwest	Lou Holtz	6-5-0
Arkansas State	Indians	Scarlet & black	Southland	Lawrence Lacewell	2-9-0
Army	Cadets	Black, gold, gray	Independent	Ed Cavanaugh	3-7-1
Auburn	Tigers	Orange & blue	Southeastern	Pat Dye	5-6-0
Austin Peay State	Governors	Scarlet & white	Ohio Valley	Emory Hale	7-4-0
Ball State	Cardinals	Cardinal & white	Mid-American	Dwight Wallace	6-5-0
Baylor	Bears	Green & gold	Southwest	Grant Teaff	10-2-0
Bethune-Cookman	Wildcats	Maroon & gold	Mid-Eastern	Bobby Frazier	5-4-1
Boise State	Broncos	Orange & Blue	Big Sky	Jim Criner	10-3-0
Boston College	Eagles	Maroon & gold	Independent	Jack Bicknell	7-4-0
Boston Univ.	Terriers	Scarlet & white	Yankee	Rick Taylor	9-2-0
Bowling Green St.	Falcons	Orange & brown	Mid-American	Denny Stolz	4-7-0
Brigham Young	Cougars	Royal blue & white	Western Athletic	LaVell Edwards	12-1-0
Brown	Bruins, Bears	Brown, cardinal, white	Ivy	John Anderson	6-4-0
Bucknell	Bisons	Orange & blue	Independent	Bob Curtis	6-4-0
California	Golden Bears	Blue & gold	Pacific Ten	Roger Theder	3-8-0
Central Michigan	Chippewas	Maroon & gold	Mid-American	Herb Deromedi	9-2-0
Cincinnati	Bearcats	Red & black	Independent	Mike Gottfried	2-9-0
Citadel	Bulldogs	Blue & white	Southern	Art Baker	7-4-0
Clemson	Tigers	Purple & orange	Atlantic Coast	Danny Ford	6-5-0
Colgate	Red Raiders	Maroon	Independent	Fred Dunlap	5-4-1
Colorado State	Rams	Green & gold	Western Athletic	Sarkis Arslanian	6-4-1
Colorado	Buffaloes	Silver & gold	Big Eight	Chuck Fairbanks	1-10-0
Columbia	Lions	Blue & white	Ivy	Bob Naso	1-9-0
Connecticut	Huskies	Blue & white	Yankee	Walt Nadzak	7-3-0
Cornell	Big Red	Carnelian & white	Ivy	Bob Blackman	5-5-0
Dartmouth	Big Green	Dartmouth green	Ivy	Joe Yukica	4-6-0
Davidson	Wildcats	Red & black	Independent	Ed Farrell	5-5-0
Delaware	Fightin' Blue Hens	Blue & gold	Independent	Harold Raymond	9-2-0
Delaware State	Hornets	Red & blue	Mid-Eastern	Joe Purzycki	2-9-0
Drake	Bulldogs	Blue & white	Missouri Valley	Chuck Shelton	8-3-0
Duke	Blue Devils	Royal blue & white	Atlantic Coast	Red Wilson	2-9-0
East Carolina	Pirates	Purple & gold	Independent	Ed Emory	4-7-0
East Tennessee St.	Buccaneers	Blue & gold	Southern	Jack Carlisle	2-9-0
Eastern Illinois	Panthers	Blue & Gray	Mid-Continent	Darrell Mudra	11-3-0
Eastern Kentucky	Colonels	Maroon & white	Ohio Valley	Roy Kidd	10-3-0
Eastern Michigan	Hurons	Green & white	Mid-American	Mike Stock	1-9-0
Florida	Gators	Orange & blue	Southeastern	Charley Pell	8-4-0
Florida A&M	Rattlers	Orange & green	Mid-Eastern	Rudy Hubbard	5-6-0
Florida State	Seminoles	Garnet & gold	Independent	Bobby Bowden	10-2-0
Fresno State	Bulldogs	Cardinal & blue	Pacific Coast	Jim Sweeney	5-6-0
Fullerton, Cal. State	Titans	Blue, orange, white	Pacific Coast	Gene Murphy	4-7-0
Furman	Paladins	Purple & white	Southern	Dick Sheridan	9-1-1
Georgia	Bulldogs	Red & black	Southeastern	Vince Dooley	12-0-0
Georgia Tech	Yellow Jackets	Old gold & white	Atlantic Coast	Bill Curry	1-9-1
Grambling State	Tigers	Black & gold	Southwestern	Eddie Robinson	10-2-0
Harvard	Crimson	Crimson	Ivy	Joe Restic	7-3-0
Hawaii	Rainbow Warriors	Green & white	Western Athletic	Dick Tomey	8-3-0
Holy Cross	Crusaders	Royal purple	Independent	Rick Carter	3-8-0
Houston	Cougars	Scarlet & white	Southwest	Bill Yeoman	7-5-0
Howard	Bison	Blue & white	Mid-Eastern	Floyd Keith	6-2-2
Idaho	Vandals	Silver & gold	Big Sky	Jerry Davitch	6-5-0
Idaho State	Bengals	Orange & black	Big Sky	Dave Kragthorpe	6-5-0
Illinois	Fighting Illini	Orange & blue	Big Ten	Mike White	3-7-1
Illinois State	Redbirds	Red & white	Missouri Valley	Bob Otolski	4-7-0
Indiana	Fightin' Hoosiers	Cream & crimson	Big Ten	Lee Corso	6-5-0
Indiana State	Sycamores	Blue & white	Missouri Valley	Dennis Raetz	6-5-0
Iowa	Hawkeyes	Old gold & black	Big Ten	Hayden Fry	4-7-0
Iowa State	Cyclones	Cardinal & gold	Big Eight	Donnie Duncan	6-5-0
Jackson State	Tigers	Blue & white	Southwestern	W.C. Gorden	8-3-0
James Madison	Dukes	Purple & gold	Independent	Challace McMillin	4-6-0
Kansas	Jayhawks	Crimson & blue	Big Eight	Don Fambrough	4-5-2
Kansas State	Wildcats	Purple & white	Big Eight	Jim Dickey	3-8-0
Kent State	Golden Flashes	Blue & gold	Mid-American	Ed Chlebek	3-8-0
Kentucky	Wildcats	Blue & white	Southeastern	Fran Curci	3-8-0
Lafayette	Leopards	Maroon & white	Independent	Bill Russo	3-7-0
Lamar	Cardinals	Red & white	Southland	Larry Kennan	3-8-0
Lehigh	Engineers	Brown & white	Independent	John Whitehead	9-1-2
Long Beach, Cal. State	Forty-Niners	Brown & gold	Pacific Coast	Dave Currey	8-3-0
Louisiana State	Fighting Tigers	Purple & gold	Southeastern	Jerry Stovall	7-4-0
Louisiana Tech	Bulldogs	Red & blue	Southland	Billy Brewer	5-6-0
Louisville	Cardinals	Red, black, white	Independent	Bob Weber	5-6-0
Maine	Black Bears	Blue & white	Yankee	Ron Rogerson	4-7-0
Marshall	Thundering Herd	Green & white	Southern	Sonny Randle	2-8-1

Team	Nickname	Team colors	Conference	Coach	1980 record (W-L-T)
Maryland	Terps	Red & white	Atlantic Coast	Jerry Claiborne	8-4-0
Massachusetts	Minutemen	Maroon & white	Yankee	Robert Pickett	7-3-0
McNeese State	Cowboys	Blue & gold	Southland	Ernie Duplechin	10-2-0
Memphis State	Tigers	Blue & gray	Independent	Rex Dockery	2-9-0
Miami (Fla.)	Hurricanes	Orange, green, white	Independent	Howard Schnellenberger	9-3-0
Miami (Ohio)	Redskins	Red & white	Mid-American	Tom Reed	5-6-0
Michigan	Wolverines	Maize & blue	Big Ten	Bo Schembechler	10-2-0
Michigan State	Spartans	Green & white	Big Ten	Frank Waters	3-8-0
Middle Tennessee St.	Blue Raiders	Blue & white	Ohio Valley	Boots Donnelly	2-8-0
Minnesota	Gophers	Maroon & gold	Big Ten	Joe Salem	5-6-0
Mississippi	Rebels	Red & blue	Southeastern	Steve Sloan	3-8-0
Mississippi State	Bulldogs	Maroon & white	Southeastern	Emory Bellard	9-3-0
Miss. Valley State	Delta Devils	Green & white	Southwestern	Archie Cooley	5-5-0
Missouri	Tigers	Old gold & black	Big Eight	Warren Powers	8-4-0
Montana	Grizzlies	Copper, silver, gold	Big Sky	Larry Donovan	3-7-0
Montana State	Bobcats	Blue & gold	Big Sky	Sonny Lubick	4-6-0
Morehead State	Eagles	Blue & gold	Ohio Valley	Steve Loney	4-7-0
Murray State	Racers	Blue & gold	Ohio Valley	Frank Beamer	9-2-0
Navy	Midshipmen	Navy blue & gold	Independent	George Welsh	8-4-0
Nebraska	Cornhuskers	Scarlet & cream	Big Eight	Tom Osborne	10-2-0
Nevada-Las Vegas	Rebels	Scarlet & gray	Independent	Tony Knap	7-4-0
Nevada-Reno	Wolf Pack	Silver & blue	Big Sky	Chris Ault	6-4-1
New Hampshire	Wildcats	Blue & white	Yankee	Bill Bowes	6-4-0
New Mexico	Lobos	Cherry & silver	Western Athletic	Joe Morrison	4-7-0
New Mexico State	Aggies	Crimson & white	Missouri Valley	Gil Krueger	3-7-1
Nicholls St.	Colonels	Red & grey	Independent	William Jackson	2-9-0
North Carolina	Tar Heels	Blue & white	Atlantic Coast	Dick Crum	11-1-0
North Carolina A & T	Aggies	Blue & gold	Mid-Eastern	Jim McKinley	9-3-0
North Carolina State	Wolfpack	Red & white	Atlantic Coast	Monte Kiffin	6-5-0
North Texas State	Mean Green, Eagles	Green & white	Independent	Bob Tyler	6-5-0
Northeast Louisiana	Indians	Maroon & gold	Independent	Pat Collins	7-4-0
Northeastern	Huskies	Red & black	Independent	Pat Pawlak	2-9-0
Northern Arizona	Lumberjacks	Blue & gold	Big Sky	Dwain Painter	5-6-0
Northern Illinois	Huskies	Cardinal & black	Mid-American	Bill Mallory	7-4-0
Northern Iowa	Panthers	Purple & Old Gold	Mid-Continent	Stan Sheriff	7-4-0
Northwestern	Wildcats	Purple & white	Big Ten	Dennis Green	0-11-0
Northwestern State	Demons	Burnt orange, purple, white	Independent	A.L. Williams	8-3-0
Notre Dame	Fighting Irish	Gold & blue	Independent	Gerry Faust	9-2-1
Ohio State	Buckeyes	Scarlet & gray	Big Ten	Earle Bruce	9-3-0
Ohio Univ	Bobcats	Green & white	Mid-American	Brian Burke	6-5-0
Oklahoma	Sooners	Crimson & cream	Big Eight	Barry Switzer	10-2-0
Oklahoma State	Cowboys	Orange & black	Big Eight	Jimmy Johnson	3-7-1
Oregon	Ducks	Green & yellow	Pacific Ten	Rich Brooks	6-3-2
Oregon State	Beavers	Orange & black	Pacific Ten	Joe Avezzano	0-11-0
Pacific	Tigers	Orange & black	Pacific Coast	Bob Toledo	4-8-0
Penn State	Nittany Lions	Blue & white	Independent	Joe Paterno	10-2-0
Pennsylvania	Red & Blue, Quakers	Red & blue	Ivy	Jerry Berndt	1-9-0
Pittsburgh	Panthers	Gold & blue	Independent	Jackie Sherrill	11-1-0
Prairie View A & M	Panthers	Purple & gold	Southwestern	Cornelius Cooper	2-8-0
Princeton	Tigers	Orange & black	Ivy	Frank Navarro	6-4-0
Purdue	Boilermakers	Old gold & black	Big Ten	Jim Young	9-3-0
Rhode Island	Rams	Blue & white	Yankee	Bob Griffin	2-9-0
Rice	Owls	Blue & gray	Southwest	Ray Alborn	5-6-0
Richmond	Spiders	Red & blue	Independent	Dal Shealy	5-6-0
Rutgers	Scarlet Knights	Scarlet	Independent	Frank Burns	7-4-0
San Diego State	Aztecs	Scarlet & black	Western Athletic	Doug Scovil	4-8-0
San Jose State	Spartans	Blue, gold & white	Pacific Coast	Jack Elway	7-4-0
South Carolina	Fighting Gamecocks	Garnet & black	Independent	Jim Carlen	8-4-0
South Carolina State	Bulldogs	Garnet & blue	Mid-Eastern	Bill Davis	10-1-0
Southeastern La.	Lions	Green & gold	Independent	Oscar Lofton	8-2-0
Southern	Jaguars	Blue & gold	Southwestern	Otis Washington	4-6-1
Southern California	Trojans	Cardinal & gold	Pacific Ten	John Robinson	8-2-1
Southern Illinois	Salukis	Maroon & white	Missouri Valley	Rey Dempsey	3-8-0
Southern Methodist	Mustangs	Red & blue	Southwest	Ron Meyer	8-4-0
Southern Mississippi	Golden Eagles	Black & gold	Independent	Bobby Collins	9-3-0
Southwestern La.	Ragin' Cajuns	Vermillion & white	Southland	Sam Robertson	7-4-0
Stanford	Cardinals	Cardinal & white	Pacific Ten	Paul Wiggin	6-5-0
Syracuse	Orangemen	Orange	Independent	Dick MacPherson	5-6-0
Temple	Owls	Cherry & white	Independent	Wayne Hardin	4-7-0
Tennessee	Volunteers	Orange & white	Southeastern	John Majors	5-6-0
Tenn.-Chattanooga	Moccasins	Navy blue & gold	Southern	Bill Oliver	8-3-0
Tennessee State	Tigers	Blue & white	Independent	John A. Merritt	9-1-0
Tennessee Tech	Golden Eagles	Purple & gold	Ohio Valley	Don Wade	4-7-0
Texas	Longhorns	Orange & white	Southwest	Fred Akers	7-5-0
Texas-Arlington	Mavericks	Royal blue & white	Southland	Bud Elliott	3-8-0
Texas-El Paso	Miners	Orange & white	Western Athletic	Bill Michael	1-11-0
Texas A & M	Aggies	Maroon & white	Southwest	Tom Wilson	4-7-0
Texas Christian	Horned Frogs	Purple & white	Southwest	F.A. Dry	1-10-0
Texas Southern	Tigers	Maroon & gray	Southwestern	Joe Redmond	2-9-0
Texas Tech	Red Raiders	Scarlet & black	Southwest	Jerry Moore	5-6-0
Toledo	Rockets	Blue & gold	Mid-American	Chuck Stobart	4-7-0
Tulane	Green Wave	Olive green & sky blue	Independent	Vince Gibson	7-5-0
Tulsa	Golden Hurricane	Blue, red, gold	Missouri Valley	John Cooper	8-3-0
UCLA	Bruins	Navy blue & gold	Pacific Ten	Terry Donahue	9-2-0

Team	Nickname	Team colors	Conference	Coach	1980 record (W-L-T)
Utah State	Aggies	Navy blue & white	Pacific Coast	Bruce Snyder	6-5-0
Utah	Utes	Crimson & white	Western Athletic	Wayne Howard	5-5-1
Vanderbilt	Commodores	Black & gold	Southeastern	George MacIntyre	2-9-0
Virginia	Cavaliers	Orange & blue	Atlantic Coast	Dick Bestwick	4-7-0
VMI	Keydets	Red, white & yellow	Southern	Bob Thalman	3-7-1
Virginia Tech	Gobblers	Orange & maroon	Independent	Bill Dooley	8-4-0
Wake Forest	Demon Deacons	Old gold & black	Atlantic Coast	Al Groh	5-6-0
Washington	Huskies	Purple & gold	Pacific Ten	Don James	9-3-0
Washington State	Cougars	Crimson & gray	Pacific Ten	Jim Walden	4-7-0
Weber State	Wildcats	Purple & white	Big Sky	Mike Price	4-7-0
West Texas State	Buffaloes	Maroon & white	Missouri Valley	Bill Yung	5-6-0
West Virginia	Mountaineers	Old gold & blue	Independent	Don Nehlen	6-6-0
Western Carolina	Catamounts	Purple & white	Southern	Bob Waters	3-7-1
Western Illinois	Leathernecks	Purple & Gold	Mid-Continent	Pete Rodriguez	4-6-0
Western Kentucky	Hilltoppers	Red & white	Ohio Valley	Jimmy Feix	9-1-0
Western Michigan	Broncos	Brown & gold	Mid-American	Elliot Uzelac	7-4-0
Wichita State	Shockers	Gold & black	Missouri Valley	Willie Jeffries	5-5-1
William & Mary	Indians	Green, gold, silver	Independent	Jimmye Laycock	2-9-0
Wisconsin	Badgers	Cardinal & white	Big Ten	Dave McClain	4-7-0
Wyoming	Cowboys	Brown & yellow	Western Athletic	Al Kincaid	6-5-0
Yale	Bulldogs, Elis	Yale blue & white	Ivy	Carmen Cozza	8-2-0
Youngstown St.	Penguins	Scarlet & white	Mid-Continent	Bill Narduzzi	2-8-1

Selected Division 2 and 3 Teams

Team	Nickname	Team colors	Conference	Coach	Record
Alma	Scots	Maroon & cream	Michigan	Phil Brooks	2-6-0
Amherst	Lord Jeffs	Purple & white	Little Three	James Ostendarp	2-6-0
Baldwin-Wallace	Yellow Jackets	Brown & gold	Ohio	Bob Packard	9-1-0
Beloit	Buccaneers	Gold & blue	Midwest	Ed DeGeorge	4-4-1
Bowdoin	Polar Bears	White	CCB	Jim Lentz	5-3-0
Butler	Bulldogs	Blue & white	Heartland	Bill Sylvester	4-6-0
Carleton	Knights	Maize & blue	Midwest	Bob Sullivan	6-3-0
Cheyney State	Wolves	Blue & white	Pennsylvania	Andy Hinson	4-5-1
Chico, Cal. St.	Wildcats	Cardinal & white	Far Western	Dick Trimmer	5-5-0
Coast Guard	Cadets, Bears	Blue & white	Independent	Larry Rutledge	2-8-0
Coe	Kohawks	Crimson & gold	Midwest	Roger Schlegel	5-4-0
Dayton	Flyers	Red & blue	Independent	Mike Kelly	14-0-0
Denison	Big Red	Red & white	Ohio	Keith Piper	4-4-1
Duquesne	Dukes	Red & blue	Independent	Dan McCann	4-5-0
Emory & Henry	Wasps	Blue & gold	Old Dominion	Larry Bales	2-8-0
Evansville	Purple Aces	Purple & white	Heartland	Randy Rodgers	3-8-0
John Carroll	Blue Streaks	Blue & gold	Presidents	Don Stupica	4-5-0
Kalamazoo	Hornets	Orange & black	Michigan	Ed Baker	2-5-0
Kenyon	Lords	Purple & white	Ohio	Tom McHugh	3-6-0
Knox	Siwash	Purple & gold	Midwest	Joe Campanelli	3-6-0
Lawrence	Vikings	Navy & white	Midwest	Ron Roberts	8-1-0
Middlebury	Panthers	Blue & white	Independent	Mickey Heinecken	6-1-1
Millsaps	Majors	Purple & white	Independent	Harper Davis	9-0-0
Morgan State	Bears	Blue & orange	Independent	Tom Morris	4-7-0
Mt. Union	Purple Raiders	Purple & white	Ohio	Ken Wable	5-4-0
Muhlenberg	Mules	Cardinal & gray	Middle Atlantic	Ralph Kirchenheiter	8-1-0
North Dakota State	Bison	Yellow & green	North Central	Don Morton	6-4-0
North Dakota	Sioux	Green & white	North Central	Pat Behms	6-4-0
Northern Michigan	Wildcats	Old gold & green	Mid-Continent	Bill Rademacher	9-1-0
Ohio Northern	Polar Bears	Orange & black	Ohio	A. Wallace Hood	6-2-1
Ohio Wesleyan	Battling Bishops	Red & black	Ohio	Jack Fouts	2-6-1
Olivet	Comets	Red & white	Michigan	Ron Lynch	2-6-0
Puget Sound	Loggers	Green & gold	Independent	Ron Simonson	6-3-0
Ripon	Redmen	Crimson & white	Midwest	Wayne Phillips	5-4-0
Rochester	Yellow Jackets	Yellow & blue	Independent	Pat Stark	3-5-1
St. Cloud State	Huskies	Red & black	Northern	Mike Simpson	6-4-0
St. Lawrence	Saints	Scarlet & brown	ICAC	Andy Talley	5-4-0
St. Norbert	Green Knights	Green & gold	Independent	Larry Van Alstine	3-6-0
St. Olaf	Oles	Black & gold	Minn. IAC	Tom Porter	6-4-0
Santa Clara	Broncos	Cardinal & white	Independent	Pat Malley	8-2-0
Slippery Rock	Rockets, The Rock	Green & white	Pennsylvania	Bob DeSpirito	4-5-0
So. Dakota State	Jackrabbits	Yellow & blue	North Central	John Gregory	3-8-0
South Dakota	Coyotes	Vermilion & white	North Central	Dave Triplett	5-6-0
Southern Oregon	Red Raiders	Red & black	Evergreen	Chuck Mills	2-7-0
Swarthmore	Little Quakers	Garnet	Middle Atlantic	Tom Lapinski	4-5-0
Thiel	Tomcats	Blue & gold	President's Athletic	Wayne Petrarca	4-5-0
Towson State	Tigers	Gold & white	Independent	Phil Albert	5-5-0
Trenton State	Lions	Blue & gold	New Jersey State	Eric Hamilton	8-1-1
Tufts	Jumbos	Blue & brown	Independent	Vic Gatto	6-2-0
Upsala	Vikings	Blue & gray	Middle Atlantic	Pat Briante	3-6-1
Valparaiso	Crusaders	Brown & gold	Heartland	Bill Koch	3-6-1
Wash. & Jeff.	Presidents	Red & black	Presidents Athletic	Pat Mondock	2-7-0
Wash. & Lee	Generals	Royal blue, white	Old Dominion	Gary Fallon	6-4-0
Wayne State	Tartars	Green & gold	Great Lakes	Dave Farris	5-4-0
Wesleyan	Cardinals	Red & black	Little Three	Bill MacDermott	5-3-0
West Chester St.	Golden Rams	Purple & gold	Independent	Otto Kneidinger	5-4-1
Wilkes	Colonels	Navy & gold	Middle Atlantic	Roland Schmidt	3-6-0
Williams	Ephmen	Purple	Little Three	Robert Odell	5-2-1
Wittenberg	Tigers	Red & white	Ohio	Dave Maurer	8-1-0
Wooster	Fighting Scots	Black & gold	Ohio	Tom Hollman	6-2-1

College Football Conference Champions

	Atlantic Coast		Ivy League		Big Eight		Big Ten
1967	Clemson	1967	Yale	1967	Oklahoma	1967	Indiana, Purdue, Minn.
1968	No. Carolina St.	1968	Yale, Harvard	1968	Kansas, Oklahoma	1968	Ohio State
1969	So. Carolina	1969	Princeton, Dartmouth, Yale	1969	Missouri, Nebraska	1969	Michigan, Ohio State
1970	Wake Forest	1970	Dartmouth	1970	Nebraska	1970	Ohio State
1971	North Carolina	1971	Dartmouth, Cornell	1971	Nebraska	1971	Michigan
1972	North Carolina	1972	Dartmouth	1972	Nebraska	1972	Ohio State, Michigan
1973	No. Carolina St.	1973	Dartmouth	1973	Oklahoma	1973	Ohio State, Michigan
1974	Maryland	1974	Yale, Harvard	1974	Oklahoma	1974	Ohio State, Michigan
1975	Maryland	1975	Harvard	1975	Oklahoma, Nebraska	1975	Ohio State
1976	Maryland	1976	Yale, Brown	1976	Oklahoma, Colorado,	1976	Michigan, Ohio State
1977	North Carolina	1977	Yale		Oklahoma State	1977	Michigan, Ohio State
1978	Clemson	1978	Dartmouth	1977	Oklahoma	1978	Michigan St., Michigan
1979	No. Carolina St.	1979	Yale	1978	Nebraska, Oklahoma	1979	Ohio State
1980	North Carolina	1980	Yale	1979	Oklahoma	1980	Michigan
				1980	Oklahoma		

	Mid-America		Missouri Valley		Southeastern		Southwest
1967	Toledo, Ohio Univ.	1967	North Texas	1967	Tennessee	1967	Texas A&M
1968	Ohio Univ.	1968	Memphis State	1968	Georgia	1968	Texas, Arkansas
1969	Toledo	1969	Memphis State	1969	Tennessee	1969	Texas
1970	Toledo	1970	Louisville	1970	Louisiana State	1970	Texas
1971	Toledo	1971	Memphis State	1971	Alabama	1971	Texas
1972	Kent State	1972	Louisville, W. Texas,	1972	Alabama	1972	Texas
1973	Miami		Drake	1973	Alabama	1973	Texas
1974	Miami	1973	No. Texas St., Tulsa	1974	Alabama	1974	Baylor
1975	Miami	1974	Tulsa	1975	Alabama	1975	Texas A&M, Texas,
1976	Ball State	1975	Tulsa	1976	Georgia		Arkansas
1977	Miami	1976	Tulsa, N. Mexico St.	1977	Alabama	1976	Houston
1978	Ball State	1977	W. Texas St.	1978	Alabama	1977	Houston
1979	Central Michigan	1978	N. Mexico St.	1979	Alabama	1978	Houston
1980	Central Michigan	1979	W. Texas St.	1980	Georgia	1979	Houston, Arkansas
		1980	Tulsa, Wichita St.			1980	Baylor

	Pacific Ten		Southern		Western Athletic		Pacific Coast
1967	USC	1967	West Virginia	1967	Wyoming	1969	San Diego State
1968	USC	1967	West Virginia	1968	Wyoming	1970	Long Beach State
1969	USC	1968	Richmond	1969	Arizona State	1972	San Diego State
1970	Stanford	1969	Richmond, Davidson	1970	Arizona State	1973	San Diego State
1971	Stanford	1970	William & Mary	1971	Arizona State	1974	San Diego State
1972	USC	1971	Richmond	1972	Arizona State	1975	San Jose State
1973	USC	1972	East Carolina	1973	Arizona State, Arizona	1976	San Diego State
1974	USC	1973	East Carolina	1974	Brigham Young	1977	Fresno State
1975	UCLA, Cal.	1974	VMI	1975	Arizona State	1978	Utah St., San Jose St.
1976	USC	1975	Richmond	1976	Wyoming, Brigham Young	1979	San Jose St.
1977	Washington	1976	East Carolina	1977	Brigham Young, Arizona St.	1980	Long Beach State
1978	USC	1977	Tenn.-Chattanooga	1978	Brigham Young		
1979	USC	1978	Tenn.-Chattanooga,	1979	Brigham Young		
1980	Washington		Furman	1980	Brigham Young		
		1979	Tenn.-Chattanooga				
		1980	Furman				

National College Football Champions

The NCAA recognizes as unofficial national champion the team selected each year by the AP (poll of writers) and the UPI (poll of coaches). When the polls disagree both teams are listed. The AP poll originated in 1936 and the UPI poll in 1950.

1936	Minnesota	1948	Michigan	1959	Syracuse	1970	Nebraska, Texas
1937	Pittsburgh	1949	Notre Dame	1960	Minnesota	1971	Nebraska,
1938	Texas Christian	1950	Oklahoma	1961	Alabama	1972	Southern Cal.
1939	Texas A&M	1951	Tennessee	1962	Southern Cal.	1973	Notre Dame, Alabama
1940	Minnesota	1952	Michigan State	1963	Texas	1974	Oklahoma, So. Cal.
1941	Minnesota	1953	Maryland	1964	Alabama	1975	Oklahoma
1942	Ohio State	1954	Ohio State, UCLA	1965	Alabama, Mich. State	1976	Pittsburgh
1943	Notre Dame	1955	Oklahoma	1966	Notre Dame	1977	Notre Dame
1944	Army	1956	Oklahoma	1967	Southern Cal.	1978	Alabama, So. Cal.
1945	Army	1957	Auburn, Ohio State	1968	Ohio State	1979	Alabama
1946	Notre Dame	1958	Louisiana State	1969	Texas	1980	Georgia
1947	Notre Dame						

Outland Awards

Honoring the outstanding interior lineman selected by the Football Writers' Association of America.

1946	George Connor, Notre Dame, T	1958	Zeke Smith, Auburn, G	1970	Jim Stillwagon, Ohio State, LB
1947	Joe Steffy, Army, G	1959	Mike McGee, Duke, T	1971	Larry Jacobson, Nebraska, DT
1948	Bill Fischer, Notre Dame, G	1960	Tom Brown, Minnesota, G	1972	Rich Glover, Nebraska, MG
1949	Ed Bagdon, Michigan St., G	1961	Merlin Olsen, Utah State, T	1973	John Hicks, Ohio State, G
1950	Bob Gain, Kentucky, T	1962	Bobby Bell, Minnesota, T	1974	Randy White, Maryland, DE
1951	Jim Weatherall, Oklahoma, T	1963	Scott Appleton, Texas, T	1975	Leroy Selmon, Oklahoma, DT
1952	Dick Modzelewski, Maryland, T	1964	Steve Delong, Tennessee, T	1976	Ross Browner, Notre Dame, DE
1953	J. D. Roberts, Oklahoma, G	1965	Tommy Nobis, Texas, G	1977	Brad Shearer, Texas, DT
1954	Bill Brooks, Arkansas, G	1966	Loyd Phillips, Arkansas, T	1978	Greg Roberts, Oklahoma, G
1955	Calvin Jones, Iowa, G	1967	Ron Yary, Southern Cal, T	1979	Jim Ritcher, No. Carolina St., C
1956	Jim Parker, Ohio State, G	1968	Bill Stanfill, Georgia, T	1980	Mark May, Pittsburgh, OT
1957	Alex Karras, Iowa, T	1969	Mike Reid, Penn State, DT		

All-Time Division 1-A Percentage Leaders

(Classified as Division 1 for last 15 years; including bowl games; ties computed as half won and half lost.)

		Years	Won	Lost	Tied	Pct	Bowl Games W	L	T
1.	Notre Dame	92	616	166	39	.774	7	3	0
2.	Yale	108	709	202	53	.763	0	0	0
3.	Michigan	101	623	207	31	.742	5	7	0
4.	Alabama	86	576	197	41	.733	18	13	3
5.	Texas	88	595	218	29	.724	14	11	2
6.	Princeton	111	637	231	47	.722	0	0	0
7.	Southern Cal	88	535	198	48	.716	19	6	0
8.	Oklahoma	86	547	203	48	.716	15	6	1
9.	Ohio State	91	553	221	48	.702	6	0	0
10.	Harvard	106	638	260	46	.700	1	0	0
11.	Tennessee	84	528	235	45	.681	11	12	0
12.	Penn State	94	558	253	39	.679	11	6	2
13.	Nebraska	91	548	264	39	.667	11	8	0
14.	Miami (O.)	92	479	238	35	.660	5	1	0
15.	Dartmouth	99	528	263	40	.659	0	0	0
16.	Army	91	515	256	48	.658	1	0	0
17.	Louisiana State	87	493	261	41	.646	10	11	1
18.	Minnesota	96	493	270	40	.639	1	2	0
19.	Arizona State	66	355	197	21	.638	6	4	1
20.	Michigan State	84	446	257	39	.627	2	2	0
21.	Pennsylvania	104	616	360	40	.626	0	1	0
22.	Georgia	87	484	288	49	.619	10	9	1
23.	Colorado	91	473	285	31	.619	4	6	0
24.	Stanford	74	415	249	45	.617	7	5	1
25.	Washington	91	449	271	47	.616	4	5	1

Longest Division 1-A Winning Streaks

Wins	Team	Years	Ended by	Score
47	Oklahoma	1953-57	Notre Dame	7-0
39	Washington	1908-14	Oregon State	0-0
37	Yale	1890-93	Princeton	6-0
37	Yale	1887-89	Princeton	10-0
35	Toledo	1969-71	Tampa	21-0
34	Pennsylvania	1894-96	Lafayette	6-4
31	Oklahoma	1948-50	Kentucky	13-7
31	Pittsburgh	1914-18	Cleveland Naval Reserve	10-9
31	Pennsylvania	1896-98	Harvard	10-0
30	Texas	1968-70	Notre Dame	24-11
29	Michigan	1901-03	Minnesota	6-6
28	Alabama	1978-80	Mississippi State	6-3
28	Oklahoma	1973-75	Kansas	23-3
28	Michigan State	1950-53	Purdue	6-0
27	Nebraska	1901-04	Colorado	6-0
26	Cornell	1921-24	Williams	14-7
26	Michigan	1903-05	Chicago	2-0
25	Michigan	1946-49	Army	21-7
25	Army	1944-46	Notre Dame	0-0
25	Southern Cal	1931-33	Oregon State	0-0

U.S. Weightlifting Federation National Championships in 1981

San Francisco, Cal., June 6-7, 1981 (men); Waterloo, Ia., May 23, 1981 (women)
(Note: lifts are in kilograms; one kilogram = 2.2 lbs.)

Senior Men

114 lbs.—Wrenn Norvell, Sayre Park WLC, **157.5 kg.**
123 lbs.—Albert Hood, Los Angeles Naturite, **217.5 kg.**
132 lbs.—Phil Sanderson, York BBC, **240 kg.**
148 lbs.—Cal Schake, Butler WLC, **290 kg.**
165 lbs.—Fred Lowe, York BBC, **315 kg.**
181 lbs.—Val Balison, York BBC, **327.5 kg.**
198 lbs.—Kevin Winter, Sports Palace, **342.5 kg.**
220 lbs.—Ken Clark, Sports Palace, **350 kg.**
242 lbs.—Guy Carlton, York BBC, **360 kg.**
Over 242 lbs.—Jerome Hannan, Colorado Connection, **392.5 kg.**
Team champion—York Barbell Club, York, Pa.

Senior Women

97 lbs.—Joette Weber, Kokomo, Ind., **72.5 kg.**
105.8 lbs.—Quin Burgess, Newnan, Ga., **87.5 kg.**
114 lbs.—Mary Beth Cervenak, Malmstrom AFB, Mont., **115 kg.**
123 lbs.—Lisa Semm, Batavia, Ill., **77.5 kg.**
132 lbs.—Kim Besuden, W. Lafayette, Ind., **102.5 kg.**
148¾ lbs.—Judy Glenney, Farmington, N.M., **172.5 kg.**
165¼ lbs.—Karyn Bastiansen, New York, N.Y., **145 kg.**
181¾ lbs.—Karen Weaver, W. Lafayette, Ind., **85 kg.**
Over 181¾ lbs.—Lorna Griffin, Huntington Beach, Cal., **167.5 kg.**

NCAA Wrestling Champions

Year	Champion	Year	Champion	Year	Champion	Year	Champion	Year	Champion
1961	Oklahoma State	1966	Oklahoma State	1970	Iowa State	1974	Iowa State	1978	Iowa
1962	Oklahoma State	1967	Michigan State	1971	Oklahoma State	1975	Iowa	1979	Iowa
1963	Oklahoma	1968	Oklahoma State	1972	Iowa State	1976	Iowa	1980	Iowa
1964	Oklahoma State	1969	Iowa State	1973	Iowa State	1977	Iowa State	1981	Iowa
1965	Iowa State								

Kentucky Derby

Churchill Downs, Louisville, Ky.; inaugurated 1875; distance 1-1/4 miles; 1-1/2 miles until 1896. 3-year olds.
Times—seconds in fifths.

Year	Winner	Jockey	Trainer	Wt.	Second	Winner's share	Time
1907	Pink Star	A. Minder	W. H. Fizer	117	Zal	$4,850	2:12.3
1908	Stone Street	A. Pickens	J. W. Hall	117	Sir Cleges	4,850	2:15.1
1909	Wintergreen	V. Powers	C. Mack	117	Miami	4,850	2:08.1
1910	Donau	F. Herbert	G. Ham	117	Joe Morris	4,850	2:06.2
1911	Meridian	G. Archibald	A. Ewing	117	Governor Gray	4,850	2:05.
1912	Worth	C. H. Shilling	F. M. Taylor	117	Duval	4,850	2:09.2
1913	Donerail	R. Goose	T. P. Hayes	117	Ten Point	5,475	2:04.4
1914	Old Rosebud	J. McCabe	F. D. Weir	114	Hodge	9,125	2:03.2
1915	Regret*	J. Notter	J. Rowe Sr.	112	Pebbles	11,450	2:05.2
1916	George Smith	J. Loftus	H. Hughes	117	Star Hawk	16,600	2:04.3
1917	Omar Khayyam	C. Borel	C. T. Patterson	117	Ticket	9,750	2:04.
1918	Exterminator	W Knapp	H. McDaniel	114	Escoba	14,700	2:10.4
1919	Sir Barton	J. Loftus	H. G. Bedwell	112	Billy Kelly	20,825	2:09.4
1920	Paul Jones	T. Rice	W. Garth	126	Upset	30,375	2:09.
1921	Behave Yourself	C. Thompson	H. J. Thompson	126	Black Servant	38,450	2:04.1
1922	Morvich	A. Johnson	F. Burlew	126	Bet Mosie	46,775	2:04.3
1923	Zev	E. Sande	D. J. Leary	126	Martingale	53,600	2:05.2
1924	Black Gold	J. D. Mooney	H. Webb	126	Chilhowee	52,775	2:05.1
1925	Flying Ebony	E. Sande	W. B. Duke	126	Captain Hal	52,950	2:07.3
1926	Bubbling Over	A. Johnson	H. J. Thompson	126	Bagenbaggage	50,075	2:03.4
1927	Whiskery	L. McAtee	F. Hopkins	126	Osmand	51,000	2:06.
1928	Reigh Count	C. Lang	B. S. Michell	126	Misstep	55,375	2:10.2
1929	Clyde Van Dusen	L. McAtee	C. Van Dusen	126	Naishapur	53,950	2:10.4
1930	Gallant Fox	E. Sande	J. Fitzsimmons	126	Gallant Knight	50,725	2:07.3
1931	Twenty Grand	C. Kurtsinger	J. Rowe Jr.	126	Sweep All	48,725	2:01.4
1932	Burgoo King	E. James	H. J. Thompson	126	Economic	52,350	2:05.1
1933	Brokers Tip	D. Meade	H. J. Thompson	126	Head Play	48,925	2:06.4
1934	Cavalcade	M. Garner	R. A. Smith	126	Discovery	28,175	2:04.
1935	Omaha	W. Saunders	J. Fitzsimmons	126	Roman Soldier	39,525	2:05.
1936	Bold Venture	I. Hanford	M. Hirsch	126	Brevity	37,725	2:03.3
1937	War Admiral	C. Kurtsinger	G. Conway	126	Pompoon	52,050	2:03.1
1938	Lawrin	E. Arcaro	B. A. Jones	126	Dauber	47,050	2:04.4
1939	Johnstown	J. Stout	J. Fitzsimmons	126	Challedon	46,350	2:03.2
1940	Gallahadion	C. Bierman	R. Waldron	126	Bimelech	60,150	2:05.
1941	Whirlaway	E. Arcaro	B. A. Jones	126	Staretor	61,275	2:01.2
1942	Shut Out	W. D. Wright	J. M. Gaver	126	Alsab	64,225	2:04.2
1943	Count Fleet	J. Longden	G. D. Cameron	126	Blue Swords	60,275	2:04.
1944	Pensive	C. McCreary	B. A. Jones	126	Broadcloth	64,675	2:04.1
1945	Hoop, Jr.	E. Arcaro	I. H. Parke	126	Pot o'Luck	64,850	2:07.
1946	Assault	W. Mehrtens	M. Hirsch	126	Spy Song	96,400	2:06.3
1947	Jet Pilot	E. Guerin	T. Smith	126	Phalanx	92,160	2:06.3
1948	Citation	E. Arcaro	B. A. Jones	126	Coaltown	83,400	2:05.2
1949	Ponder	S. Brooks	B. A. Jones	126	Capot	91,600	2:04.1
1950	Middleground	W. Boland	M. Hirsch	126	Hill Prince	92,650	2:01.3
1951	Count Turf	C. McCreary	S. Rutchick	126	Royal Mustang	98,050	2:02.3
1952	Hill Gail	E. Arcaro	B. A. Jones	126	Sub Fleet	96,300	2:01.3
1953	Dark Star	H. Moreno	E. Hayward	126	Native Dancer	90,050	2:02.
1954	Determine	R. York	W. Molter	126	Hasty Road	102,050	2:03.
1955	Swaps	W. Shoemaker	M. A. Tenney	126	Nashua	108,400	2:01.4
1956	Needles	D. Erb	H. L. Fontaine	126	Fabius	123,450	2:03.2
1957	Iron Liege	W. Hartack	H. A. Jones	126	Gallant Man	107,950	2:02.1
1958	Tim Tam	I. Valenzuela	H. A. Jones	126	Lincoln Road	116,400	2:05.
1959	Tomy Lee	W. Shoemaker	F. Childs	126	Sword Dancer	119,650	2:02.1
1960	Venetian Way	W. Hartack	V. Sovinski	126	Bally Ache	114,850	2:02.2
1961	Carry Back	J. Sellers	J. A. Price	126	Crozier	120,500	2:04.
1962	Decidedly	W. Hartack	H. Luro	126	Roman Line	119,650	2:00.2
1963	Chateaugay	B. Baeza	J. Conway	126	Never Bend	108,900	2:01.4
1964	Northern Dancer	W. Hartack	H. Luro	126	Hill Rise	114,300	2:00.
1965	Lucky Debonair	W. Shoemaker	F. Catrone	126	Dapper Dan	112,000	2:01.1
1966	Kauai King	D. Brumfield	H. Forrest	126	Advocator	120,500	2:02.
1967	Proud Clarion	R. Ussery	L. Gentry	126	Barbs Delight	119,700	2:00.3
1968	Dancer's Image (a)	R. Ussery	H. Forrest	126	Forward Pass	122,600	2:02.1
1969	Majestic Prince	W. Hartack	J. Longden	126	Arts and Letters	113,200	2:01.4
1970	Dust Commander	M. Manganello	D. Combs	126	My Dad George	127,800	2:03.2
1971	Canonero II	G. Avila	J. Arias	126	Jim French	145,500	2:03.1
1972	Riva Ridge	R. Turcotte	L. Laurin	126	No Le Hace	140,300	2:01.4
1973	Secretariat	R. Turcotte	L. Laurin	126	Sham	155,050	1:59.2
1974	Cannonade	A. Cordero	W. C. Stephens	126	Hudson County	274,000	2:04.
1975	Foolish Pleasure	J. Vasquez	L. Jolley	126	Avatar	209,611	2:02.
1976	Bold Forbes	A. Cordero	L. Barrea	126	Honest Pleasure	165,200	2:01.3
1977	Seattle Slew	J. Cruquet	W. H. Turner Jr.	126	Run Dusty Run	214,700	2:02.1
1978	Affirmed	S. Cauthen	L. Barrera	126	Alydar	186,900	2:01.1
1979	Spectacular Bid	R. Franklin	G. Delp	126	General Assembly	228,650	2:02.2
1980	Genuine Risk*	J. Vasquez	L. Jolley	126	Rumbo	250,550	2:02
1981	Pleasant Colony	J. Velasquez	J. Campo	126	Woodchopper	317,200	2:02

(a) Dancer's Image was disqualified from purse money after tests disclosed that he had run with a pain-killing drug, phenylbutazone, in his system. All wagers were paid on Dancer's Image. Forward Pass was awarded first place money.

The Kentucky Derby has been won five times by two jockeys, Eddie Arcaro, 1938, 1941, 1945, 1948 and 1952; and Bill Hartack, 1957, 1960, 1962, 1964 and 1969; and three times by each of three jockeys, Isaac Murphy, 1884, 1890, and 1891; Earle Sande, 1923, 1925 and 1930, and Willie Shoemaker, 1955, 1959, 1965. *Regret and Genuine Risk are the only fillies to win the Derby.

Preakness

Pimlico, Baltimore, Md.; inaugurated 1873; 1 3-16 miles, 3 yr. olds. Time—seconds in fifths.

Year	Winner	Jockey	Trainer	Wt.	Second	Winner's share	Time
1943	Count Fleet	J. Longden	G.D. Cameron	126	Blue Swords	$43,190	1:57.2
1944	Pensive	C. McCreary	B.A. Jones	126	Platter	60,075	1:59.1
1945	Polynesian	W.D. Wright	M. Dixon	126	Hoop Jr.	66,170	1:58.4
1946	Assault	W. Mehrtens	M. Hirsch	126	Lord Boswell	96,620	2:01.2
1947	Faultless	D. Dodson	H.A. Jones	126	On Trust	98,005	1:59
1948	Citation	E. Arcaro	H.A. Jones	126	Vulcan's Forge	91,870	2:02.2
1949	Capot	T. Atkinson	J.M. Gaver	126	Palestinian	79,985	1:56
1950	Hill Prince	E. Arcaro	J.H. Hayes	126	Middleground	56,115	1:59.1
1951	Bold	E. Arcaro	P.M. Burch	126	Counterpoint	83,110	1:56.2
1952	Blue Man	C. McCreary	W.C. Stephens	126	Jampol	86,135	1:57.2
1953	Native Dancer	E. Guerin	W.C. Winfrey	126	Jamie K	66,200	1:57.4
1954	Hasty Road	J. Adams	H. Trotsek	126	Correlation	91,600	1:57.2
1955	Nashua	E. Arcaro	J. Fitzsimmons	126	Saratoga	67,550	1:54.3
1956	Fabius	W. Hartack	H.A. Jones	126	Needles	84,250	1:58.2
1957	Bold Ruler	E. Arcaro	J. Fitzsimmons	126	Iron Liege	65,250	1:56.1
1958	Tim Tam	I. Valenzuela	H.A. Jones	126	Lincoln Road	97,900	1:57.1
1959	Royal Orbit	W. Harmatz	R. Cornell	126	Sword Dancer	136,200	1:57
1960	Bally Ache	R. Ussery	H.J. Pitt	126	Victoria Park	121,000	1:57.3
1961	Carry Back	J. Sellers	J.A. Price	126	Globemaster	126,200	1:57.3
1962	Greek Money	J.L. Rotz	V.W. Raines	126	Ridan	135,800	1:56.1
1963	Candy Spots	W. Shoemaker	M.A. Tenney	126	Chateaugay	127,500	1:56.1
1964	Northern Dancer	W. Hartack	H. Luro	126	The Scoundrel	124,200	1:56.4
1965	Tom Rolfe	R. Turcotte	F.Y. Whiteley Jr.	126	Dapper Dan	128,100	1:56.1
1966	Kauai King	D. Brumfield	H. Forrest	126	Stupendous	129,000	1:55.2
1967	Damascus	W. Shoemaker	F.Y. Whiteley Jr.	126	In Reality	141,500	1:55.1
1968	Forward Pass	I. Valenzuela	H. Forrest	126	Out of the Way	142,700	1:56.4
1969	Majestic Prince	W. Hartack	J. Longden	126	Arts and Letters	129,500	1:55.3
1970	Personality	E. Belmonte	J.W. Jacobs	126	My Dad George	151,300	1:56.1
1971	Canonero II	G. Avila	J. Arias	126	Eastern Fleet	137,400	1:54
1972	Bee Bee Bee	E. Nelson	D.W. Carroll	126	No Le Hace	135,300	1:55.3
1973	Secretariat	R. Turcotte	L. Laurin	126	Sham	129,900	1:54.2
1974	Little Current	M. Rivera	L. Rondinello	126	Neopolitan Way	156,000	1:56.3
1975	Master Derby	D. McHargue	W.E. Adams	126	Foolish Pleasure	158,100	1:56.2
1976	Elocutionist	J. Lively	P.T. Adwell	126	Play The Red	129,700	1:55
1977	Seattle Slew	J. Cruquet	W.H. Turner Jr.	126	Iron Constitution	138,600	1:54.2
1978	Affirmed	S. Cauthen	L. Barrera	126	Alydar	136,200	1:54.2
1979	Spectacular Bid	R. Franklin	G. Delp	126	Golden Act	165,300	1:54.1
1980	Codex	A. Cordero	D.W. Lucas	126	Genuine Risk	180,600	1:54.1
1981	Pleasant Colony	J. Velasquez	J. Campo	126	Bold Ego	270,800	1:54.3

Belmont Stakes

Elmont, N.Y.; inaugurated 1867; 1 1/2 miles, 3 year olds. Time—seconds in fifths.

Year	Winner	Jockey	Trainer	Wt.	Second	Winner's share	Time
1943	Count Fleet	J. Longden	G.D. Cameron	126	Fairy Manhurst	$35,340	2:28.1
1944	Bounding Home	G.L. Smith	M. Brady	126	Pensive	55,000	2:32.1
1945	Pavot	E. Arcaro	O. White	126	Wildlife	52,675	2:30.1
1946	Assault	W. Mehrtens	M. Hirsch	126	Natchez	75,400	2:30.4
1947	Phalanx	R. Donoso	S. Veitch	126	Tide Rips	78,900	2:29.2
1948	Citation	E. Arcaro	H.A. Jones	126	Better Self	77,700	2:28.1
1949	Capot	T. Atkinson	J.M. Gaver	126	Ponder	60,900	2:30.1
1950	Middleground	W. Boland	M. Hirsch	126	Lights Up	61,350	2:28.3
1951	Counterpoint	D. Gorman	S. Veitch	125	Battlefield	82,000	2:29
1952	One Count	E. Arcaro	O. White	126	Blue Man	82,400	2:30.1
1953	Native Dancer	E. Guerin	W.C. Winfrey	126	Jamie K.	82,500	2:28.3
1954	High Gun	E. Guerin	M. Hirsch	126	Fisherman	89,000	2:30.4
1955	Nashua	E. Arcaro	J. Fitzsimmons	126	Blazing Count	83,700	2:29
1956	Needles	D. Erb	H. Fontaine	126	Career Boy	83,600	2:29.4
1957	Gallant Man	W. Shoemaker	J. Nerud	126	Inside Tract	77,300	2:26.3
1958	Cavan	P. Anderson	T.J. Barry	126	Tim Tam	73,440	2:30.1
1959	Sword Dancer	W. Shoemaker	J.E. Burch	126	Bagdad	93,525	2:28.2
1960	Celtic Ash	W. Hartack	T.J. Barry	126	Venetian Way	96,785	2:29.3
1961	Sherluck	B. Baeza	H. Young	126	Globemaster	104,900	2:29.1
1962	Jaipur	W. Shoemaker	W.F. Mulholland	126	Admiral's Voyage	109,550	2:28.4
1963	Chateaugay	B. Baeza	J.P. Conway	126	Candy Spots	101,700	2:30.1
1964	Quadrangle	M. Ycaza	J.E. Burch	126	Roman Brother	110,850	2:28.2
1965	Hail to All	J. Sellers	E. Yowell	126	Tom Rolfe	104,150	2:28.2
1966	Amberoid	W. Boland	L. Laurin	126	Buffle	117,700	2:29.3
1967	Damascus	W. Shoemaker	F.Y. Whiteley Jr.	126	Cool Reception	104,950	2:28.4
1968	Stage Door Johnny	H. Gustines	J.M. Gaver	126	Forward Pass	117,700	2:27.1
1969	Arts and Letters	B. Baeza	J.E. Burch	126	Majestic Prince	104,050	2:28.4
1970	High Echelon	J.L. Rotz	J.W. Jacobs	126	Needles N Pens	115,000	2:34
1971	Pass Catcher	W. Blum	E. Yowell	126	Jim French	97,710	2:30.2
1972	Riva Ridge	R. Turcotte	L. Laurin	126	Ruritania	93,950	2:28
1973	Secretariat	R. Turcotte	L. Laurin	126	Twice A Prince	90,120	2:24
1974	Little Current	M. Rivera	L. Rondinello	126	Jolly Johu	101,970	2:29.1
1975	Avatar	W. Shoemaker	A.T. Doyle	126	Foolish Pleasure	116,160	2:28.1
1976	Bold Forbes	A. Cordero	Laz Barrera	126	McKenzie Bridge	116,850	2:29
1977	Seattle Slew	J. Cruquet	W.H. Turner Jr.	126	Run Dusty Run	109,080	2:29.3
1978	Affirmed	S. Cauthen	Laz Barrera	126	Alydar	110,580	2:26.4
1979	Coastal	R. Hernandez	D.A. Whiteley	126	Golden Act	161,400	2:28.3
1980	Temperence Hill	E. Maple	J. Cantey	126	Genuine Risk	176,220	2:29.4
1981	Summing	G. Martens	Luis Barrera	126	Highland Blade	170,580	2:29

Annual Leading Money-Winning Horses

Year	Horse	Dollars	Year	Horse	Dollars	Year	Horse	Dollars
1944	Pavot	179,040	1957	Round Table	600,383	1970	Personality	444,049
1945	Busher	273,735	1958	Round Table	662,780	1971	Riva Ridge	503,263
1946	Assault	424,195	1959	Sword Dancer	537,004	1972	Droll Roll	471,633
1947	Armed	376,325	1960	Bally Ache	455,045	1973	Secretariat	860,404
1948	Citation	709,470	1961	Carry Back	565,349	1974	Chris Evert	551,063
1949	Ponder	321,825	1962	Never Bend	402,969	1975	Foolish Pleasure	716,278
1950	Noor	346,940	1963	Candy Spots	604,481	1976	Forego	491,701
1951	Counterpoint	250,525	1964	Gun Bow	580,100	1977	Seattle Slew	641,370
1952	Crafty Admiral	277,255	1965	Buckpasser	568,096	1978	Affirmed	901,541
1953	Native Dancer	513,425	1966	Buckpasser	669,078	1979	Spectacular Bid	1,279,334
1954	Determine	328,700	1967	Damascus	817,941	1980	Temperance Hill	1,130,452
1955	Nashua	752,550	1968	Forward Pass	546,674			
1956	Needles	440,850	1969	Arts and Letters	555,604			

Annual Leading Jockey—Money Won

Year	Jockey	Dollars	Year	Jockey	Dollars	Year	Jockey	Dollars
1950	Eddie Arcaro	1,410,160	1961	Willie Shoemaker	2,690,819	1971	Laffit Pincay Jr.	3,784,377
1951	Willie Shoemaker	1,329,890	1962	Willie Shoemaker	2,916,844	1972	Laffit Pincay Jr.	3,225,827
1952	Eddie Arcaro	1,859,591	1963	Willie Shoemaker	2,526,925	1973	Laffit Pincay Jr.	4,093,492
1953	Willie Shoemaker	1,784,187	1964	Willie Shoemaker	2,649,553	1974	Laffit Pincay Jr.	4,251,060
1954	Willie Shoemaker	1,876,760	1965	Braulio Baeza	2,582,702	1975	Braulio Baeza	3,695,198
1955	Eddie Arcaro	1,864,796	1966	Braulio Baeza	2,951,022	1976	Angel Cordero Jr.	4,709,500
1956	Bill Hartack	2,343,955	1967	Braulio Baeza	3,088,888	1977	Steve Cauthen	6,151,750
1957	Bill Hartack	3,060,501	1968	Braulio Baeza	2,835,108	1978	Darrel McHargue	6,029,885
1958	Willie Shoemaker	2,961,693	1969	Jorge Velasquez	2,542,315	1979	Laffit Pincay Jr.	8,193,535
1959	Willie Shoemaker	2,843,133	1970	Laffit Pincay Jr.	2,626,526	1980	Chris McCarron	7,663,300
1960	Willie Shoemaker	2,123,961						

Leading Money-Winning Horses

As of May, 1981

Horse, year foaled	Sts.	1st	2d	3d	Dollars	Horse, year foaled	Sts.	1st	2d	3d	Dollars
Spectacular Bid, 1976	30	26	2	1	2,781,607	Temperance Hill, 1977	22	10	3	1	1,326,322
Affirmed, 1975	29	22	5	1	2,393,818	Secretariat, 1970	21	16	3	1	1,316,808
Kelso, 1957	63	39	12	2	1,977,896	Nashua, 1952	30	22	4	1	1,288,565
Forego, 1970	57	34	9	7	1,938,957	Ancient Title, 1970	57	24	11	9	1,252,791
Round Table, 1954	66	43	8	5	1,749,869	Susan's Girl, 1969	63	29	14	11	1,251,667
Exceller, 1973	33	15	5	6	1,654,002	Carry Back, 1958	61	21	11	11	1,241,165
John Henry, 1975	56	24	12	6	1,619,630	Foolish Pleasure, 1972	26	16	4	3	1,216,705
Dahlia, 1970	48	15	3	7	1,543,139	Seattle Slew, 1974	17	14	2	0	1,208,726
Buckpasser, 1963	31	25	4	1	1,462,014	Damascus, 1964	32	21	7	3	1,176,781
Allez France, 1970	21	13	3	1	1,386,146						

Eclipse Awards in 1980

Sponsored by the Thoroughbred Racing Assn., Daily Racing Form, and the National Turf Writers Assn.

Horse of the Year—Spectacular Bid
Best 2-year-old colt—Lord Avie
Best 2-year-old filly—Heavenly Cause
Best 3-year-old colt—Temperence Hill
Best 3-year-old filly—Genuine Risk
Best colt, horse, or gelding (4-year-olds & up)—Spectacular Bid
Best filly or mare (4-year-olds & up)—Glorious Song
Best male turf horse—John Henry

Best turf filly or mare—Just A Game 2d
Best sprinter—Plugged Nickle
Best steeplechase horse—Zaccio
Best trainer—Bud Delp
Best jockey—Chris McCarron
Best apprentice jockey—Frank Lovato Jr.
Best owner—Mr. & Mrs. Bertram Firestone
Best breeder—Mrs. Henry D. Paxson

U.S. Thoroughbred Records

Furlongs	Horse, age, weight	Track, state	Date	Time
5	Zip Pocket, 3, 122	Turf Paradise, Ariz.	Apr. 22, 1967	0:55.2
5½	Zip Pocket, 3, 129	Turf Paradise, Ariz.	Nov. 19, 1967	1:01.2
6 (¾ mile)	Grey Papa, 6, 116	Longacres, Wash.	Sept. 4, 1972	1:07.1
6½	Best Hitter, 4, 114	Longacres, Wash.	Aug. 24, 1973	1:13.4
7	Triple Bend, 4, 123	Hollywood, Cal.	May 6, 1972	1:19.4
8 (1 mile)	Dr. Fager, 4, 134	Arlington, Ill.	Aug. 24, 1968	1:32.1
8½	Swaps, 4, 130	Hollywood, Cal.	June 23, 1956	1:39
9	Secretariat, 3, 124	Belmont, N.Y.	Sept. 15, 1973	1:45.2
9½	Riva Ridge, 4, 127	Aqueduct, N.Y.	July 4, 1973	1:52.2
10	Spectacular Bid, 4, 126	Santa Anita, Cal.	Feb. 3, 1980	1:57.4
10½	Tempted, 4, 128	Aqueduct, N.Y.	Oct. 12, 1959	2:09
11	Man o' War, 3, 126	Belmont, N.Y.	June 12, 1920	2:14.1
12 (1½ miles)	Secretariat, 3, 126	Belmont, N.Y.	June 9, 1973	2:24
13	Swaps, 4, 130	Hollywood, Cal.	July 25, 1956	2:38.1
14	Noor, 5, 117	Santa Anita, Cal.	Mar. 4, 1950	2:52.4
16 (2 miles)	Kelso, 7, 124	Aqueduct, N.Y.	Oct. 31, 1964	3:19.1

Triple Crown Turf Winners, Jockeys, and Trainers

(Kentucky Derby, Preakness, and Belmont Stakes)

Year	Horse	Jockey	Trainer	Year	Horse	Jockey	Trainer
1919	Sir Barton	J. Loftus	H. G. Bedwell	1946	Assault	Mehrtens	M. Hirsch
1930	Gallant Fox	E. Sande	J. Fitzsimmons	1948	Citation	E. Arcaro	H.A. Jones
1935	Omaha	W. Sanders	J. Fitzsimmons	1973	Secretariat	R. Turcotte	L. Laurin
1937	War Admiral	C. Kurtsinger	G. Conway	1977	Seattle Slew	J. Cruguet	W.H. Turner Jr.
1941	Whirlaway	E. Arcaro	B.A. Jones	1978	Affirmed	S. Cauthen	L.S. Barrera
1943	Count Fleet	J. Longden	G.D. Cameron				

Estimated Earnings of Athletes

The actual amount of money paid by a club to an athlete is known only to the club, the athlete, his agent, and the IRS. The following salary and earnings figures have been taken from published sources, reliable, but not official. The figures do not include outside income, such as fees for personal appearances and commercial endorsements. The earnings of boxers are difficult to determine. As much as 1/3 of their earnings may go to their managers. They also have large training expenses. Larry Holmes and Sugar Ray Leonard can earn as much as $4 million for a single fight.

Athlete	Dollars	Athlete	Dollars
Dave Winfield, baseball	1,500,000	Reggie Jackson, baseball	580,000
Fred Lynn, baseball	1,200,000	Mike Schmidt, baseball	560,000
Eddie Murray, baseball	1,000,000	Cale Yarborough, auto racing (1980)	537,357
Nolan Ryan, baseball	1,000,000	Larry Hisle, baseball	530,000
Phil Niekro, baseball (mostly deferred payments)	1,000,000	Bert Blyleven, baseball	500,000
Moses Malone, basketball	1,000,000	Gorman Thomas, baseball	500,000
George Brett, baseball	1,000,000	Ed Farmer, baseball	495,000
Kareem Abdul-Jabbar, basketball	1,000,000	Sparky Lyle, baseball	480,000
Otis Birdsong, basketball	900,000	Oscar Gamble, baseball	475,000
Dave Parker, baseball	900,000	John McEnroe, tennis (as of 7/10/81)	474,600
Rod Carew, baseball	900,000	Tommy John, baseball	470,000
Andre Dawson, baseball	800,000	Robin Yount, baseball	470,000
James Edwards, basketball	800,000	Bob Lanier, basketball	450,000
Scott Wedman, basketball	800,000	Rich Gossage, baseball	450,000
Darrell Porter, baseball	800,000	Rick Cerone, baseball	440,000
Ron Leflore, baseball	800,000	Joe Rudi, baseball	440,000
Don Sutton, baseball	775,000	Dave Goltz, baseball	425,000
Chris McCarron, horse racing (1980)	766,330	Johnny Bench, baseball	420,000
Gus Williams, basketball	750,000	Martina Navratilova, tennis (as of 7/10/81)	404,281
Steve Carlton, baseball	750,000	Rennie Stennett, baseball	400,000
Pete Rose, baseball	745,000	Archie Manning, football	379,000
David Thompson, basketball	650,000-750,000	Bobby Allison, auto racing (as of 7/10/81)	363,670
Rick Burleson, baseball	700,000	Dan Pastorini, football	358,000
Claudell Washington, baseball	700,000	Gil Perreault, hockey	350,000
Bruce Sutter, baseball	700,000	Tom Watson, golf (as of 7/3/81)	338,842
Jim Rice, baseball	700,000	Ray Floyd, golf (as of 7/3/81)	327,754
Vida Blue, baseball	700,000	Chris Evert-Lloyd, tennis (as of 7/10/81)	303,555
George Foster, baseball	700,000	Mario Andretti, auto racing (as of 7/10/81)	301,479
Julius Erving, basketball	500,000-700,000	Tony Esposito, hockey	300,000
Ted Simmons, baseball	665,000	Giorgio Chinaglia, soccer	283,000
Larry Bird, basketball	650,000	Bert Jones, football	275,000
Walter Payton, football	600,000	Brad Park, hockey	265,000
Steve Kemp, baseball	600,000	Franz Beckenbauer, soccer	250,000
Roy Smalley, baseball	600,000	Steve Bartkowski, football	230,000
Keith Hernandez, baseball	600,000	Jack Ham, football	230,000
Craig Swan, baseball	600,000	Lee Roy Selmon, football	218,000
Marcel Dionne, hockey	600,000	Wayne Gretzky, hockey	150,000
Magic Johnson, basketball	600,000	Earl Anthony, bowling (as of 7/10/81)	126,305
Dale Earnhardt, auto racing (1980)	588,925	Nancy Lopez-Melton, golf (as of 6/12/81)	102,474
Carlton Fisk, baseball	580,000		

Intercollegiate Rowing Association Championship

Lake Onondaga, Syracuse, N.Y. (3 miles)

Year	Winner	Time	Year	Winner	Time	Year	Winner	Time
1960	California	15:57.0	1968	Penn (a)	6:15.6	1975	Wisconsin (a)	6:08.2
1961	California	16:49.2	1969	Penn (a)	6:30.4	1976	California (a)	6:31.0
1962	Cornell	17:02.9	1970	Washington (a)	6:39.3	1977	Cornell (a)	6:32.4
1963	Cornell	17:24.0	1971	Cornell (a)	6:06.0	1978	Syracuse (a)	6:39.5
1964	California (a)	6:31.1	1972	Penn (a)	6:22.6	1979	Brown (a)	6:26.4
1965	Navy	16:51.3	1973	Wisconsin (a)	6:21.0	1980	Navy (a)	6:46.0
1966	Wisconsin	16:03.4	1974	Wisconsin (a)	6:33.0	1981	Cornell (a)	5:57.3
1967	Penn	16:15.9						

(a) race at 2,000 meters

Tour de France in 1981

Bernard Hinault of France won the Tour de France, the world's most prestigious bicycle endurance race, for the 3d time in 4 years on July 19, 1981. The race covered 2,436 miles from Frankfurt, Germany to Paris. Lucien Van Impe of Belgium finished second.

Boxing Champions by Classes

As of Aug., 1981 the only universally accepted title holder was in the middleweight division. The following are the recognized champions of the World Boxing Association and the World Boxing Council.

	WBA	WBC
Heavyweight	Mike Weaver, Los Angeles, Cal.	Larry Holmes, Easton, Pa.
Light Heavyweight	Michael Spinks, St. Louis, Mo.	Matthew Saad Muhammad, Philadelphia, Pa.
Middleweight	Marvin Hagler, Brockton, Mass.	Marvin Hagler, Brockton, Mass.
Jr. Middleweight	Alub Kalule, Denmark	Maurice Hope, England
Welterweight	Thomas Hearns, Detroit, Mich.	Sugar Ray Leonard, Palmer Park, Md.
Jr. Welterweight	Aaron Pryor, Cincinnati, Oh.	Saoul Mamby, New York, N.Y.
Lightweight	Sean O'Grady, Oklahoma City, Okla.	Alexis Arguello, Coral Gables, Fla.
Jr. Lightweight	Sammy Serrano, Puerto Rico	Cornelius Boza-Edwards, England
Featherweight	Eusebio Pedroza, Panama	Salvadore Sanchez, Mexico
Jr. Featherweight	Sergio Palma, Argentina	Wilfredo Gomez, Puerto Rico
Bantamweight	Jeff Chandler, Philadelphia, Pa.	Lupe Pintor, Mexico
Flyweight	Luis Ibarra, Panama	Shoji Oguma, Japan

Ring Champions by Years

*Abandoned title

Heavyweights

1882-1892	John L. Sullivan (a)	1925-1926	Paul Berlenbach
1892-1897	James J. Corbett (b)	1926-1927	Jack Delaney*
1897-1899	Robert Fitzsimmons	1927-1929	Tommy Loughran*
1899-1905	James J. Jeffries (c)	1930-1934	Maxey Rosenbloom
1905-1906	Marvin Hart	1934-1935	Bob Olin
1906-1908	Tommy Burns	1935-1939	John Henry Lewis*
1908-1915	Jack Johnson	1939	Melio Bettina*
1915-1919	Jess Willard	1939-1941	Billy Conn*
1919-1926	Jack Dempsey	1941	Anton Christoforidis (won NBA title)
1926-1928	Gene Tunney*	1941-1948	Gus Lesnevich, Freddie Mills
1928-1930	vacant	1948-1950	Freddie Mills
1930-1932	Max Schmeling	1950-1952	Joey Maxim
1932-1933	Jack Sharkey	1952-1960	Archie Moore
1933-1934	Primo Carnera	1961-1962	vacant
1934-1935	Max Baer	1962-1963	Harold Johnson
1935-1937	James J. Braddock	1963-1965	Willie Pastrano
1937-1949	Joe Louis*	1965-1966	Jose Torres
1949-1951	Ezzard Charles	1966-1968	Dick Tiger
1951-1952	Joe Walcott	1968-1974	Bob Foster*, John Conteh (WBA)
1952-1956	Rocky Marciano*	1975-1977	John Conteh (WBC), Miguel Cuello (WBC),
1956-1959	Floyd Patterson		Victor Galindez (WBA)
1959-1960	Ingemar Johansson	1978	Mike Rossman (WBA), Mate Parlov (WBC),
1960-1962	Floyd Patterson		Marvin Johnson (WBC)
1962-1964	Sonny Liston	1979	Victor Galindez (WBA), Matthew Saad Mu-
1964-1967	Cassius Clay* (Muhammad Ali) (d)		hammad (WBC)
1970-1973	Joe Frazier	1980	Eddie Mustava Muhammad (WBA)
1973-1974	George Foreman	1981	Michael Spinks (WBA)
1974-1978	Muhammad Ali		
1978-1979	Leon Spinks (e), Muhammad Ali*		**Middleweights**
1978	Ken Norton (WBC), Larry Holmes (WBC)		
1979	John Tate (WBA)	1884-1891	Jack "Nonpareil" Dempsey
1980	Mike Weaver (WBA)	1891-1897	Bob Fitzsimmons*
		1897-1907	Tommy Ryan*

(a) London Prize Ring (bare knuckle champion).
(b) First Marquis of Queensberry champion.
(c) Jeffries abandoned the title (1905) and designated Marvin Hart and Jack Root as logical contenders and agreed to referee a fight between them, the winner to be declared champion. Hart defeated Root in 12 rounds (1905) and in turn was defeated by Tommy Burns (1906) who immediately laid claim to the title. Jack Johnson defeated Burns (1908) and was recognized as champion. He clinched the title by defeating Jeffries in an attempted comeback (1910).
(d) Title declared vacant by the World Boxing Assn. and other groups in 1967 after Clay's refusal to fulfill his military obligation. Joe Frazier was recognized as champion by New York, 5 other states, Mexico, and So. America. Jimmy Ellis was declared champion by the World Boxing Assn. Frazier KOd Ellis, Feb. 16, 1970.
(e) After Spinks defeated Ali, the WBC recognized Ken Norton as champion. Norton subsequently lost his title to Larry Holmes.

		1907-1908	Stanley Ketchel, Billy Papke
		1908-1910	Stanley Ketchel
		1911-1913	vacant
		1913	Frank Klaus, George Chip
		1914-1917	Al McCoy
		1917-1920	Mike O'Dowd
		1920-1923	Johnny Wilson
		1923-1926	Harry Greb
		1926-1931	Tiger Flowers, Mickey Walker
		1931-1932	Gorilla Jones (NBA)
		1932-1937	Marcel Thil
		1938	Al Hostak (NBA), Solly Krieger (NBA)
		1939-1940	Al Hostak (NBA)
		1941-1947	Tony Zale
		1947-1948	Rocky Graziano
		1948	Tony Zale, Marcel Cerdan
		1949-1951	Jake LaMotta

Light Heavyweights

1903	Jack Root, George Gardner	1951	Ray Robinson, Randy Turpin,
1903-1905	Bob Fitzsimmons		Ray Robinson*
1905-1912	Philadelphia Jack O'Brien*	1953-1955	Carl (Bobo) Olson
1912-1916	Jack Dillon	1955-1957	Ray Robinson
1916-1920	Battling Levinsky	1957	Gene Fullmer, Ray Robinson, Carmen
1920-1922	George Carpentier		Basilio
1922-1923	Battling Siki	1958	Ray Robinson
1923-1925	Mike McTigue	1959	Gene Fullmer (NBA); Ray Robinson (N.Y.)
		1960	Gene Fullmer (NBA); Paul Pender (New
			York and Mass.)
		1961	Gene Fullmer (NBA); Terry Downes
			(New York, Mass., Europe)

1962	Gene Fullmer, Dick Tiger (NBA), Paul Pender (New York and Mass.)*
1963	Dick Tiger (universal).
1963-1965	Joey Giardello
1965-1966	Dick Tiger
1966-1967	Emile Griffith
1967	Nino Benvenuti
1967-1968	Emile Griffith
1968-1970	Nino Benvenuti
1970-1977	Carlos Monzon*
1977-1978	Rodrigo Valdez
1978-1979	Hugo Corro
1979-1980	Vito Antuofermo
1980	Alan Minter, Marvin Hagler

Welterweights

1892-1894	Mysterious Billy Smith
1894-1896	Tommy Ryan
1896	Kid McCoy*
1900	Rube Ferns, Matty Matthews
1901	Rube Ferns
1901-1904	Joe Walcott
1904-1906	Dixie Kid, Joe Walcott, Honey Mellody
1907-1911	Mike Sullivan
1911-1915	vacant
1915-1919	Ted Lewis
1919-1922	Jack Britton
1922-1926	Mickey Walker
1926	Pete Latzo
1927-1929	Joe Dundee
1929	Jackie Fields
1930	Jack Thompson, Tommy Freeman
1931	Freeman, Thompson, Lou Brouillard
1932	Jackie Fields
1933	Young Corbett, Jimmy McLarnin
1934	Barney Ross, Jimmy McLarnin
1935-1938	Barney Ross
1938-1940	Henry Armstrong
1940-1941	Fritzie Zivic
1941-1946	Fred Cochrane
1946-1946	Marty Servo*; Ray Robinson (a)
1946-1950	Ray Robinson*
1951	Johnny Bratton (NBA)
1951-1954	Kid Gavilan
1954-1955	Johnny Saxton
1955	Tony De Marco, Carmen Basilio
1956	Carmen Basilio, Johnny Saxton, Carmen Basilio
1957	Carmen Basilio*
1958-1960	Virgil Akins, Don Jordan
1960	Benny Paret
1961	Emile Griffith, Benny Paret
1962	Emile Griffith
1963	Luis Rodriguez, Emilo Griffith
1964-1966	Emile Griffith*
1966-1969	Curtis Cokes
1969-1970	Jose Napoles, Billy Backus
1971-1975	Jose Napoles
1975-1976	John Stracey (WBC), Angel Espada (WBA)
1976-1979	Carlos Palomino (WBC), Jose Cuevas (WBA)
1979	Wilfredo Benitez (WBC), Sugar Ray Leonard (WBC)
1980	Roberto Duran (WBC), Thomas Hearns (WBA), Sugar Ray Leonard (WBC)

(a) Robinson gained the title by defeating Tommy Bell in an elimination agreed to by the NY Commission and the NBA. Both claimed Robinson waived his title when he won the middleweight crown from LaMotta in 1951, Gavilan defeated Bratton in an elimination to find a successor.

Lightweights

1896-1899	Kid Lavigne
1899-1902	Frank Erne
1902-1908	Joe Gans
1908-1910	Battling Nelson
1910-1912	Ad Wolgast
1912-1914	Willie Ritchie
1914-1917	Freddie Welsh
1917-1925	Benny Leonard*
1925	Jimmy Goodrich, Rocky Kansas
1926-1930	Sammy Mandell
1930	Al Singer, Tony Canzoneri
1930-1933	Tony Canzoneri
1933-1935	Barney Ross*
1935-1936	Tony Canzoneri
1936-1938	Lou Ambers
1938	Henry Armstrong
1939	Lou Ambers
1940	Lew Jenkins
1941-1943	Sammy Angott
1944	S. Angott (NBA), J. Zurita (NBA)
1945-1951	Ike Williams (NBA: later universal)
1951-1952	James Carter
1952	Lauro Salas, James Carter
1953-1954	James Carter
1954	Paddy De Marco; James Carter
1955	James Carter; Bud Smith
1956	Bud Smith, Joe Brown
1956-1962	Joe Brown
1962-1965	Carlos Ortiz
1965	Ismael Laguna
1965-1968	Carlos Ortiz
1968-1969	Teo Cruz
1969-1970	Mando Ramos
1970	Ismael Laguna, Ken Buchanan (WBA)
1971	Mando Ramos (WBC), Pedro Carrasco (WBC)
1972-1979	Roberto Duran* (WBA)
1972	Pedro Carrasco (WBC), Mando Ramos (WBC), Chango Carmona (WBC), Rodolfo Gonzalez (WBC)
1974-1976	Guts Ishimatsu (WBC)
1976-1977	Esteban De Jesus (WBC)
1979	Jim Watt (WBC), Ernesto Espana (WBA)
1980	Hilmer Kenty (WBA)
1981	Alexis Arguello (WBC); Sean O'Grady (WBA)

Featherweights

1892-1900	George Dixon (disputed)
1900-1901	Terry McGovern, Young Corbett*
1901-1912	Abe Attell
1912-1923	Johnny Kilbane
1923	Eugene Criqui, Johnny Dundee
1923-1925	Johnny Dundee*
1925-1927	Kid Kaplan*
1927-1928	Benny Bass, Tony Canzoneri
1928-1929	Andre Routis
1929-1932	Battling Battalino*
1932-1934	Tommy Paul (NBA)
1933-1936	Freddie Miller
1936-1937	Petey Sarron
1937-1938	Henry Armstrong*
1938-1940	Joey Archibald (b)
1942-1948	Willie Pep
1948-1949	Sandy Saddler
1949-1950	Willie Pep
1950-1957	Sandy Saddler*
1957-1959	Hogan (Kid) Bassey
1959-1963	Davey Moore
1963-1964	Sugar Ramos
1964-1967	Vicente Saldivar*
1968-1971	Paul Rojas (WBA), Sho Saijo (WBA)
1971	Antonio Gomez (WBA), Kuniaki Shibada (WBC)
1972	Ernesto Marcel* (WBA), Clemente Sanchez* (WBC), Jose Legra (WBC)
1973	Eder Jofre (WBC)
1974	Ruben Olivares (WBA), Alexis Arguello (WBA), Bobby Chacon (WBC)
1975	Ruben Olivares (WBC), David Kotey (WBC)
1976	Danny Lopez (WBC)
1977	Rafael Ortega (WBA)
1978	Cecilio Lastra (WBA), Eusebio Pedrosa (WBA)
1980	Salvador Sanchez (WBC)

(b) After Petey Scalzo knocked out Archibald (Dec. 5, 1938) in an overweight match and was refused a title bout, the NBA named Scalzo champion. The NBA title succession was: Petey Scalzo, 1938-1941; Richard Lemos, 1941; Jackie Wilson, 1941-1943; Jackie Callura, 1943; Phil Terranova, 1943-1944; Sal Bartolo, 1944-1946.

History of Heavyweight Championship Bouts

*Title Changed Hands

1889—July 8—John L. Sullivan def. Jake Kilrain, 75, Richburg, Miss. Last championship bare knuckles bout.

*1892—Sept. 7—James J. Corbett def. John L. Sullivan, 21, New Orleans. Big gloves used for first time.

1894—Jan. 25—James J. Corbett KOd Charley Mitchell, 3, Jacksonville, Fla.
*1897—Bob Fitzsimmons def. James J. Corbett, 14, Carson City, Nev.
*1899—June 9—James J. Jeffries def. Bob Fitzsimmons, 11, Coney Island, N.Y.
1899—Nov. 3—James J. Jeffries def. Tom Sharkey, 25, Coney Island, N.Y.
1900—May 11—James J. Jeffries KOd James J. Corbett, 23, Coney Island, N.Y.
1901—Nov. 15—James J. Jeffries KOd Gus Ruhlin, 5, San Francisco.
1902—July 25—James J. Jeffries KOd Bob Fitzsimmons, 8, San Francisco.
1903—Aug. 14—James J. Jeffries KOd James J. Corbett, 10, San Francisco.
1904—Aug. 26—James J. Jeffries KOd Jack Monroe, 2, San Francisco.
*1905—James J. Jeffries retired, July 3—Marvin Hart KOd Jack Root, 12, Reno. Jeffries refereed and presented the title to the victor. Jack O'Brien also claimed the title.
*1906—Feb. 23—Tommy Burns def. Marvin Hart, 20, Los Angeles.
1906—Nov. 28—Philadelphia Jack O'Brien and Tommy Burns, 20, draw, Los Angeles.
1907—May 8—Tommy Burns def. Jack O'Brien, 20, Los Angeles.
1907—July 4—Tommy Burns KOd Bill Squires, 1, Colma, Cal.
1907—Dec. 2—Tommy Burns KOd Gunner Moir, 10, London.
1908—Feb. 10—Tommy Burns KOd Jack Palmer, 4, London.
1908—March 17—Tommy Burns KOd Jem Roche, 1, Dublin.
1908—April 18—Tommy Burns KOd Jewey Smith, 5, Paris.
1908—June 13—Tommy Burns KOd Bill Squires, 8, Paris.
1908—Aug. 24—Tommy Burns KOd Bill Squires, 13, Sydney, New South Wales.
1908—Sept. 2—Tommy Burns KOd Bill Lang, 2, Melbourne, Australia.
*1908—Dec. 26—Jack Johnson KOd Tommy Burns, 14, Sydney, Australia. Police halted contest.
1909—May 19—Jack Johnson and Jack O'Brien, 6, draw, Philadelphia.
1909—June 30—Jack Johnson and Tony Ross, 6, draw, Pittsburgh.
1909—Sept. 9—Jack Johnson and Al Kaufman, 10, draw, San Francisco.
1909—Oct. 16—Jack Johnson KOd Stanley Ketchel, 12, Colma, Cal.
1910—July 4—Jack Johnson KOd Jim Jeffries, 15, Reno, Nev. Jeffries came back from retirement.
1912—July 4—Jack Johnson def. Jim Flynn, 9, Las Vegas, N.M. Contest stopped by police.
1913—Nov. 28—Jack Johnson KOd Andre Spaul, 2, Paris.
1913—Dec. 9—Jack Johnson and Jim Johnson, 10, draw, Paris. Bout called a draw when Jack Johnson declared he had broken his arm.
1914—June 27—Jack Johnson def. Frank Moran, 20, Paris.
*1915—April 5—Jess Willard KOd Jack Johnson, 26, Havana, Cuba.
1916—March 25—Jess Willard and Frank Moran, 10, draw, New York.
*1919—July 4—Jack Dempsey KOd Jess Willard, Toledo, Oh. Willard failed to answer bell for 4th round.
1920—Sept. 6—Jack Dempsey KOd Billy Miske, 3, Benton Harbor, Mich.
1920—Dec. 14—Jack Dempsey KOd Bill Brennan, 12, New York.
1921—July 2—Jack Dempsey KOd George Carpentier, 4, Boyle's Thirty Acres, Jersey City, N.J. Carpentier had held the so-called white heavyweight title since July 16, 1914, in a series established in 1913, after Jack Johnson's exile in Europe late in 1912.
1923—July 4—Jack Dempsey def. Tom Gibbons, 15, Shelby, Mont.
1923—Sept. 14—Jack Dempsey KOd Luis Firpo, 2, New York.
*1926—Sept. 23—Gene Tunney def. Jack Dempsey, 10, Philadelphia.
1927—Sept. 22—Gene Tunney def. Jack Dempsey, 10, Chicago.
1928—July 26—Gene Tunney KOd Tom Heeney, 11, New York; soon afterward he announced his retirement.
*1930—June 12—Max Schmeling def. Jack Sharkey, 4, New York. Sharkey fouled Schmeling in a bout which was generally considered to have resulted in the election of a successor to Gene Tunney, New York.
1931—July 3—Max Schmeling KOd Young Stribling, 15, Cleveland.
*1932—June 21—Jack Sharkey def. Max Schmeling, 15, New York.

*1933—June 29—Primo Carnera KOd Jack Sharkey, 6, New York.
1933—Oct. 22—Primo Carnera def. Paulino Uzcudun, 15, Rome.
1934—March 1—Primo Carnera def. Tommy Loughran, 15, Miami.
*1934—June 14—Max Baer KOd Primo Carnera, 11, New York.
*1935—June 13—James J. Braddock def. Max Baer, 15, New York.
*1937—June 22—Joe Louis KOd James J. Braddock, 8, Chicago.
1937—Aug. 30—Joe Louis def. Tommy Farr, 15, New York.
1938—Feb. 23—Joe Louis KOd Nathan Mann, 3, New York.
1938—April 1—Joe Louis KOd Harry Thomas, 5, New York.
1938—June 22—Joe Louis KOd Max Schmeling, 1, New York.
1939—Jan. 25—Joe Louis KOd John H. Lewis, 1, New York.
1939—April 17—Joe Louis KOd Jack Roper, 1, Los Angeles.
1939—June 28—Joe Louis KOd Tony Galento, 4, New York.
1939—Sept. 20—Joe Louis KOd Bob Pastor, 11, Detroit.
1940—February 9—Joe Louis def. Arturo Godoy, 15, New York.
1940—March 29—Joe Louis KOd Johnny Paycheck, 2, New York.
1940—June 20—Joe Louis KOd Arturo Godoy, 8, New York.
1940—Dec. 16—Joe Louis KOd Al McCoy, 6, Boston.
1941—Jan. 31—Joe Louis KOd Red Burman, 5, New York.
1941—Feb. 17—Joe Louis KOd Gus Dorzaio, 2, Philadelphia.
1941—March 21—Joe Louis KOd Abe Simon, 13, Detroit.
1941—April 8—Joe Louis KOd Tony Musto, 9, St. Louis.
1941—May 23—Joe Louis def. Buddy Baer, 7, Washington, D.C., on a disqualification.
1941—June 18—Joe Louis KOd Billy Conn, 13, New York.
1941—Sept. 29—Joe Louis KOd Lou Nova, 6, New York.
1942—Jan. 9—Joe Louis KOd Buddy Baer, 1, New York.
1942—March 27—Joe Louis KOd Abe Simon, 6, New York.
1946—June 19—Joe Louis KOd Billy Conn, 8, New York.
1946—Sept. 18—Joe Louis KOd Tami Mauriello, 1, New York.
1947—Dec. 5—Joe Louis def. Joe Walcott, 15, New York.
1948—June 25—Joe Louis KOd Joe Walcott, 11, New York.
*1949—June 22—Following Joe Louis' retirement Ezzard Charles def. Joe Walcott, 15, Chicago, NBA recognition only.
1949—Aug. 10—Ezzard Charles KOd Gus Lesnevich, 7, New York.
1949—Oct. 14—Ezzard Charles KOd Pat Valentino, 8, San Francisco; clinched American title.
1950—Aug. 15—Ezzard Charles KOd Freddy Beshore, 14, Buffalo.
1950—Sept. 27—Ezzard Charles def. Joe Louis in latter's attempted comeback, 15, New York; universal recognition.
1950—Dec. 5—Ezzard Charles KOd Nick Barone, 11, Cincinnati.
1951—Jan. 12—Ezzard Charles KOd Lee Oma, 10, New York.
1951—March 7—Ezzard Charles def. Joe Walcott, 15, Detroit.
1951—May 30—Ezzard Charles def. Joey Maxim, light heavyweight champion, 15, Chicago.
*1951—July 18—Joe Walcott KOd Ezzard Charles, 7, Pittsburgh.
1952—June 5—Joe Walcott def. Ezzard Charles, 15, Philadelphia.
*1952—Sept. 23—Rocky Marciano KOd Joe Walcott, 13, Philadelphia.
1953—May 15—Rocky Marciano KOd Joe Walcott, 1, Chicago.
1953—Sept. 24—Rocky Marciano KOd Roland LaStarza, 11, New York.
1954—June 17—Rocky Marciano def. Ezzard Charles, 15, New York.
1954—Sept. 17—Rocky Marciano KOd Ezzard Charles, 8, New York.
1955—May 16—Rocky Marciano KOd Don Cockell, 9, San Francisco.
1955—Sept. 21—Rocky Marciano KOd Archie Moore, 9, New York. Marciano retired undefeated, Apr. 27, 1956.
*1956—Nov. 30—Floyd Patterson KOd Archie Moore, 5, Chicago.
1957—July 29—Floyd Patterson KOd Hurricane Jackson, 10, New York.
1957—Aug. 22—Floyd Patterson KOd Pete Rademacher, 6, Seattle.
1958—Aug. 18—Floyd Patterson KOd Roy Harris, 12, Los Angeles.
1959—May 1—Floyd Patterson KOd Brian London, 11, Indianapolis.
*1959—June 26—Ingemar Johansson KOd Floyd Patterson, 3, New York.

*1960—June 20—Floyd Patterson KOd Ingemar Johansson, 5, New York. First heavyweight in boxing history to regain title.
1961—Mar. 13—Floyd Patterson KOd Ingemar Johansson, 6, Miami Beach.
1961—Dec. 4—Floyd Patterson KOd Tom McNeeley, 4, Toronto.
*1962—Sept. 25—Sonny Liston KOd Floyd Patterson, 1, Chicago.
1963—July 22—Sonny Liston KOd Floyd Patterson, 1, Las Vegas.
*1964—Feb. 25—Cassius Clay KOd Sonny Liston, 7, Miami Beach.
1965—May 25—Cassius Clay KOd Sonny Liston, 1, Lewiston, Maine.
1965—Nov. 11—Cassius Clay KOd Floyd Patterson, 12, Las Vegas.
1966—Mar. 29—Cassius Clay def. George Chuvalo, 15, Toronto.
1966—May 21—Cassius Clay KOd Henry Cooper, 6, London.
1966—Aug. 6—Cassius Clay KOd Brian London, 3, London.
1966—Sept. 10—Cassius Clay KOd Karl Mildenberger, 12, Frankfurt, Germany.
1966—Nov. 14—Cassius Clay KOd Cleveland Williams, 3, Houston.
1967—Feb. 6—Cassius Clay def. Ernie Terrell, 15, Houston.
1967—Mar. 22—Cassius Clay KOd Zora Folley, 7, New York.
Clay was stripped of his title by the WBA and others for refusing military service.
*1970—Feb. 16—Joe Frazier KOd Jimmy Ellis, 5, New York.
1970—Nov. 18—Joe Frazier KOd Bob Foster, 2, Detroit.
1971—Mar. 8—Joe Frazier def. Cassius Clay (Muhammad Ali), 15, New York.
1972—Jan. 15—Joe Frazier KOd Terry Daniels, 4, New Orleans.
1972—May 25—Joe Frazier KOd Ron Stander, 5, Omaha.
*1973—Jan. 22—George Foreman KOd Joe Frazier, 2, Kingston, Jamaica.
1973—Sept. 1—George Foreman KOd Joe Roman, 1, Tokyo.
1974—Mar. 3—George Foreman KOd Ken Norton, 2, Caracas.
*1974—Oct. 30—Muhammad Ali KOd George Foreman, 8, Zaire.
1975—Mar. 24—Muhammad Ali KOd Chuck Wepner, 15, Cleveland.
1975—May 16—Muhammad Ali KOd Ron Lyle, 11, Las Vegas.
1975—June 30—Muhammad Ali def. Joe Bugner, 15, Malaysia.
1975—Oct. 1—Muhammad Ali KOd Joe Frazier, 14, Manila.
1976—Feb. 20—Muhammad Ali KOd Jean-Pierre Coopman, 5, San Juan.
1976—Apr. 30—Muhammad Ali def. Jimmy Young, 15, Landover, Md.
1976—May 25—Muhammad Ali KOd Richard Dunn, 5, Munich.
1976—Sept. 28—Muhammad Ali def. Ken Norton, 15, New York.
1977—May 16—Muhammad Ali def. Alfredo Evangelista, 15, Landover, Md.
1977—Sept. 29—Muhammad Ali def. Earnie Shavers, 15, New York.
*1978—Feb. 15—Leon Spinks def. Muhammad Ali, 15, Las Vegas.
*1978—Sept. 15—Muhammad Ali def. Leon Spinks, 15, New Orleans. Ali retired in 1979.

(Bouts when title changed hands only)

*1978—June 9—(WBC) Larry Holmes def. Ken Norton, 15, Las Vegas.
*1980—Mar. 31—(WBA) Mike Weaver KOd John Tate, 15, Knoxville.

Sports on Television

Source: Sports 1980, A.C. Nielsen Co.

	Household rating %	% Viewing audience			
		Men	Women	Teens	Children
Football					
NFL Superbowl	44.4	50	32	9	9
ABC-NFL (Monday evening)	20.2	59	28	7	6
CBS-NFL	15.7	56	28	9	7
NBC-NFL	15.2	56	27	8	9
College bowl games	17.1	52	32	8	8
College All-Star games	12.0	54	28	8	10
NCAA regular season	11.8	56	26	8	10
Baseball					
World Series	32.6	50	38	6	6
All-Star game	26.8	49	32	12	7
Regular season	8.0	52	32	8	8
Horse racing					
Average all	8.6	43	44	7	6
Basketball					
NBA average	6.0	53	28	11	8
NCAA average	7.6	56	28	8	8
Bowling					
Pro tour	8.5	43	43	6	8
Auto racing	6.0	49	35	8	8
Golf					
Tournaments	4.3	52	37	5	6
Tennis					
Wimbledon	6.6	51	35	7	7
Tournament average	4.8	47	41	7	5
Multi-sports series					
ABC Wide World of Sports	10.8	45	36	9	10
CBS Sports Spectacular	5.9	46	35	8	11
Sportsworld	5.5	48	33	8	11

American Power Boat Assn. Gold Cup Champions

Year	Boat	Driver	Year	Boat	Driver
1970	Miss Budweiser	Dean Chenoweth	1976	Miss U.S.	Tom D'Eath
1971	Miss Madison	Jim McCormick	1977	Atlas Van Lines	Bill Muncey
1972	Atlas Van Lines	Bill Muncey	1978	Atlas Van Lines	Bill Muncey
1973	Miss Budweiser	Dean Chenoweth	1979	Atlas Van Lines	Bill Muncey
1974	Pay'N Pak	George Henley	1980	Miss Budweiser	Dean Chenoweth
1975	Pay 'N Pak	George Henley	1981	Miss Budweiser	Dean Chenoweth

American Bowling Congress Championships in 1981

78th Tournament, Memphis, Tenn.

Regular Division

Individual

1. Rob Vital, Lancaster, Pa. 247, 268, 265 — 780.
2. Frank Huspen, Chicago, Ill. 269, 269, 236 — 774.
3. Ron Guelden, Shreveport, La. 223, 267, 280 — 770.

Runners-up — Bill Lillard, Houston, Tex., 749; Mike Russell, Westminster, Cal. 748; Bob Chamberlain, Detroit, Mich., 736; Jim Lindquist, Minneapolis, Minn., 731; Rod Toft, St. Paul, Minn., 730; Ted Hannahs, Cambridge, Oh., 727; Jim Kontos, Munster, Ind., 726.

All Events

1. Rod Toft, St. Paul, Minn. 650, 727, 730 — 2,107.
2. Jim Kontos, Munster, Ind. 658, 713, 726 — 2,097.
3. Bill Lillard, Houston, Tex. 645, 691, 749 — 2,085.

Runners-up — John Eiss, Bloomington, Minn., 2,074; Paul Aarestad, Minneapolis, Minn., 2,072; Len Cianciolo, Detroit, Mich., 2,069; Rich Wonders, Racine, Wis., 2,063; Ted Hannahs, Cambridge, Oh., 2,055; Mike Steinback, Chicago, Ill. 2,033; Bill Netzhammer, Ames, Ia., 2,030.

Doubles

1. (Tie) Jim Kontos, Munster, Ind. 233, 244, 236 — 713 & Al Bruder, Chicago, Ill. 178, 225, 246 — 649; Bob Blaney, Cambridge, Oh. 237, 214, 224 — 675 & Ted Hannahs, Cambridge, Oh. 221, 243, 223 — 687; aggregate — 1,362.

Team

1. Strachota's Milshore Bowl, Milwaukee, Wis. — Glenn Mueller 190, 200, 222 — 612; Don Gazzana 205, 206, 215 — 626; Jim Hanke 217, 228, 223 — 668; Ross Rittberg 235, 246, 205 — 686; Gary Odekirk 202, 209, 185 — 596; aggregate — 3,188.

2. Western Bowl, Indianapolis, Ind. — Steve Robbins 216, 200, 214 — 630; Ken Mitchell 147, 213, 255 — 615; Larry McGinty 151, 192, 234 — 577; Scott Maker 288, 170, 207 — 665; Steve Waggoner 243, 246, 210 — 699; aggregate — 3,186.

Booster Division

Team

1. Robey Tire, Ann Arbor, Mich. — Arvil Patton 179, 127, 201 — 507; Gary Colby 215, 173, 178 — 566; William Stander 202, 169, 216 — 587; Harold Stander 198, 235, 189 — 622; James Colby 192, 187, 172 — 551; aggregate — 2,833.

2. The Agony of Defeat, Flagstaff, Ariz. — Bob Lawrence 148, 231, 182 — 561; Elmer Samuelson 221, 213, 159 — 593; Gerry Soo Hoo 192, 175, 161 — 528; Dan Blailock 179, 147, 232 — 558; James Shallman 211, 190, 170 — 571; aggregate — 2,811.

Other Bowling Championships in 1981

U.S. Open — Men — Houston, Tex., Feb. 1-7; Marshall Holman, Medford, Ore., average 220, prize $21,000. Women — Rockford, Ill., Apr. 27 — May 2; Donna Adamek, Duarte, Cal.; average 205, prize $10,000.

National Intercollegiate Championships — Men — Memphis, Tenn., May 16; doubles — Tim Lundberg, Kansas State and Randy Homer, Southwest (Mo.) Baptist College; Singles — Bud Loveall, West Texas State; all events — Bob Worrall, Northern Arizona. Women — Baltimore, Md., May 6; doubles — Michele Citro, Penn State and Carol Palangio, Robert Morris (Pa.); singles, Linda Pinter, Michigan State; all events — Michele Citro, Penn State.

National Collegiate Team Championship — St. Louis, Mo., May 7-9; men — Arizona State; women — Arizona State.

Masters Bowling Tournament Champions

Year	Winner	Runner-up	W-L	Avg
1971	Jim Godman Lorain, Oh.	Don Johnson, Detroit	9-1	229
1972	Bill Beach, Sharon, Pa.	Jim Godman, Lorain, Oh.	8-1	220
1973	Dave Soutar, Gilroy, Cal.	Dick Ritger, Hartford, Wis.	7-0	218
1974	Paul Colwell, Tucson	Steve Neff, Sarasota, Fla.	7-0	234
1975	Ed Ressler Jr., Allentown, Pa.	Sam Flanagan, Parkersburg, W. Va.	9-1	213
1976	Nelson Burton Jr., St. Louis	Steve Carson, Oklahoma City	7-0	220
1977	Earl Anthony, Tacoma, Wash.	Jim Godman, Lorain, Oh.	7-0	218
1978	Frank Ellenburg, Mesa, Ariz.	Earl Anthony, Tacoma, Wash.	8-1	200
1979	Doug Myers, El Toro, Cal.	Bill Spigner, Hamden, Conn.	7-1	202
1980	Neil Burton, St. Louis, Mo.	Mark Roth, North Arlington, N.J.	7-1	206
1981	Randy Lightfoot, St. Charles, Mo.	Skip Tucker, Merritt Island, Fla.	7-1	218

All-Time Records for League and Tournament Play

Type of record	Holder of record	Year	Score	Competition
High team total	Budweiser Beer, St. Louis	1958	3,858	League
High team game	C. T. Maintenance, Berea, Oh.	1981	1,353	League
High doubles total	Nelson Burton Jr., Billy Walden, St. Louis	1970	1,614	Tournament
High doubles game	Jesse Foley and Wendell Cromer, Shreveport, La.	1976	598*	League
High individual total	Albert Brandt, Lockport, N.Y.	1939	886	League
High all events score	Denny Campbell, Chicago	1976	2,314	Tournament

* In 4-person league.

Record Averages for Consecutive Tournaments

No. in row	Holder of record	Span	Games	Average
Two	Jim Godman, Lorain, Oh.	1974-75	18	228.78
Three	Jim Godman, Lorain, Oh.	1974-76	27	223.96
Four	Jim Godman, Lorain, Oh.	1974-77	36	219.44
Five	Jim Godman, Lorain, Oh.	1973-77	45	216.33
Ten	Bob Strampe, Detroit	1961-70	111	211.10

Official Records of Annual ABC Tournaments

Type of record	Holder of record	Year	Score
High team total	Ace Mitchell Shur-Hooks, Akron	1966	3,357
High team game	Falstaff Beer, San Antonio	1958	1,226
High doubles score	John Klares-Steve Nagy, Cleveland	1952	1,453
High doubles game	Tommy Hudson, Akron, Ohio-Les Zikes, Chicago	1976	558
High singles total	Mickey Higham, Kansas City, Mo.	1977	801
High all events score	Jim Godman, Lorain, Oh.	1974	2,184
High team all events	Cook County Tobacco, Chicago, Ill.	1981	9,695
High life-time pin total	Bill Doehrman, Ft. Wayne	1908-1981	109,398

Bowlers with 6 or More Sanctioned 300 Games

Elvin Mesger, Sullivan, Mo.	27	George Pappas, Charlotte, N.C.	10	Bob Ramirez, Los Angeles	7
George Billick, Old Forge, Pa.	17	Boss Bosco, Akron	9	Don McCune, Munster, Ind.	7
Dick Weber, St. Louis	17	Mickey Higham, Kansas City, Mo.	9	Don Glover, Rosenberg, Tex.	7
Don Johnson, Las Vegas	16	Al Savas, Milwaukee	9	Mark Sutter, St. Louis	7
Dave Soutar, Gilroy, Cal.	16	Lou Foxie, Paterson, N.J.	9	Salvatore Bivona, Paterson, N.J.	6
Ron Graham, Louisville	15	Jerry Woji, Stockton, Cal.	9	Lou Campi, Dumont, N.J.	6
Al Faragalli, Wayne, N.J.	14	Tom Hennessey, St. Louis	9	Ed Davis, Milford, N.J.	6
Don Carter, Miami, Fla.	13	Russell Field, San Jose, Cal.	9	*Bill Flynn, Cleveland	6
John Wilcox Jr., Shavertown, Pa.	13	Roger Fink, Lodi, Cal.	9	Sam Garofalo, St. Louis	6
Ray Bluth, St. Louis	12	Howard Holmes, Los Angeles	8	Joe Joseph, Lansing, Mich.	6
Walter Ward, Cleveland	12	Dennis Wright, Milwaukee	8	Pete Kozloski, Plains, Pa.	6
Casey Jones, Plymouth, Wis.	12	Ray Eklund, Milwaukee	8	Vince Lucci, Trenton, N.J.	6
Dennis Soper, Tustin, Cal.	12	Walter King, Detroit	8	Steve Nagy, Cleveland	6
Dave Williams, Sebastopol, Cal.	12	Junie McMahon, Lodi, N.J.	8	Frank Pollak, Pittsburgh	0
Keith Orton, Brigham City, Ut	12	Bud Hom, Los Angeles	8	Robert Pinkalla, Milwaukee	6
David Forcier, Providence R.I.	12	Jim Godman, Lorain, Oh.	8	Harold Schaeffer, St. Louis	6
*Hank Marino, Milwaukee	11	Don Dubro, St. Louis	8	Harry Smith, Rochester, N.Y.	6
Frank Clause, Old Forge, Pa.	11	Joe Donato, Schenectady, N.Y.	7	Bob Strampe, Detroit	6
Ed Lubanski, Detroit	11	Eddie Botten, Union City, N.J.	7	Jerry Tharp, St. Louis	6
Pat Patterson, St. Louis	11	Dick Hoover, Akron	7	George Tomek, Plymouth, Pa.	6
Norm Meyers, St. Louis, Mo.	11	Ken McKenzie, Dallas	7	Stephen Tomek, Plymouth, Pa.	6
Jim Ewald, Louisville, Ky.	11	Ray Schanen, Milwaukee	7	William Capleton, Prospect Park, N.J.	6
Mike Durbin, Lorain, Oh.	10	Wayne Pinkalla, Milwaukee	7		

*Bowled two 300 games in official 3-game series.

Women's International Bowling Congress Champions

Individual	All events	Year	2-woman teams	5-woman teams
Barbara Leicht, Albany, N.Y. 689	Virginia Norton, South Gate, Cal. . . . 1,821	1975	Jennette James, Oyster Bay, Dawn Raddatz, Northport, N.Y. 1,234	Atlanta Bowling Center (Ga.) Buffalo, N.Y. 2,836
Beverly Shonk, Canton, Oh. 686	Betty Morris, Stockton, Cal. 1,866	1976	Georgene Cordes-Shirley Sjostrom, Bloomington, Minn.; Eloise Vacco-Debbie Rainone, Cleveland Hts., Oh. (tie). . . 1,232	PWBA 1, Oklahoma City, Okla. 2,839
Akiko Yamaga, Tokyo, Japan. . . . 714	Akiko Yamaga, Tokyo, Japan 1,895	1977	Ozella Houston-Dorothy Jackson, Detroit, Mich. 1,234	Allgauer's Restaurant Chicago, Ill. 2,818
Mae Bolt, Berwyn, Ill. 709	Annese Kelly, New York, N.Y. . . . 1,896	1978	Barbara Shelton-Annese Kelly, New York, N.Y. 1,211	Cook County Vending, Chicago, Ill. 2,956
Betty Morris, Stockton, Cal. 699	Betty Morris, Stockton, Cal. 1,945	1979	Mary Ann Deptula-Geri Beattie, Warren, Dearborn Hts., Mich. . 1,314	Alpine Lanes, Euless, Tex. 3,096
Betty Morris, Stockton, Cal. . . . 674	Cheryl Robinson, Van Nuys, Cal. 1,848	1980	Carol Lee-Dawn Raddatz, Hempstead, E. Northport, N.Y. 1,247	All Japan, Tokyo, Japan 3,014
Virginia Norton, So. Gate, Cal. . . . 672	Virginia Norton, So. Gate, Cal. 1,905	1981	Nikki Gianulias-Donna Adamek, Vallejo, Duarte, Cal. 1,305	Earl Anthony's Dublin Bowl, Dublin Oh. 2,963

Sanctioned 300 Games During 1980-81 Season

Pat Adams, Felton, Cal.; Nancy Anderson, San Luis Obispo, Cal.; Debbie Benach, Canton, Oh.; Debbie Bennett, Akron, Oh.; Judith Boenisch, Tucson, Ariz.; Susan Brehm, Amelia, Oh.; Pam Buckner, Reno, Nev.; Sharon Caldwell, Tampa, Fla.; Linda Chiaradio, Westerly, R.I.; Jane Cloud, North Highlands, Cal.; Janet Colner, Downey, Cal.; Doris Covington, Conroe, Tex.; JoAnne Crawford, Granville, N.Y.; Mary Cummings, Vestal, N.Y.; Rita Dalton, San Antonio, Tex.; Connie deJong, Boulder Creek, Cal.; Judi Donaldson, Phoenix, Ariz.; Jacqueline Esquivel, Romeoville, Ill.; Judy Farley, Princeton, Ill.; Betty Ganter, Wilmington, Del.; Mary Gardner, San Carlos, Cal. (2); Toni Gillard, Beverly, Oh.; Cara Gorman, San Jose, Cal.; Peg Gorman, San Jose, Cal.; Judy Gossett, Redwood City, Cal.; Nancy Grove, North Huntingdon, Pa.; Sharon Harnstrom, Bellflower, Cal.; Connie Heard, Houston, Tex.; Sandra Hearne, San Francisco, Cal.; Regi Hills, St. Peters, Mo.; Jackie Hopkins, Marion, Ind.; Virginia Johnson, Broken Arrow, Okla.; Nancy Joyce, New Hartford, N.Y.; Annese Kelly, New York, N.Y.; Linda Kelly, Union, Oh.; Pamela Kiesel, Throop, Pa.; Olga Krubsack, Nekoosa, Wis.; Susan Kvasnicka, Berwyn, Ill.; Lois Lebkuecher, East Meadow, N.Y.; Marcia Leininger, LaCrosse, Wis.; Lil Lookingbill, Champaign, Ill.; Kelli Luster, Canyon Country, Cal.; Jeanne Maiden, Willowick, Oh. (2); Cindy Martens, Altamont, Ill.; Cindy Mason, Sunnyvale, Cal.; BettyJo McDermott, Creston, Oh.; Reita McDonough, Tyler, Tex.; Martha McGowan, San Diego, Cal.; MaryLou McKay, Tarentum, Pa.; Mary McLaughlin, Pittsburgh, Pa.; Mary Michel, Van Nuys, Cal.; Dana Miller, Albuquerque, N.M.; Karla Myers, Moline, Ill.; Jenny Olson, Arvada, Col.; Betty Remmick, Lakewood, Col.; Sue Reynolds, Akron, Oh.; Joyce Richardson, Widefield, Col.; Beverly Rios, San Diego, Cal.; Lou Rolfingsmeyer, St. Louis, Mo.; Shirley Schinke, Jamestown, N.D.; Patricia Schubert, Jefferson, Oh.; Mary Sharp, Akron, Oh.; Karen Shonkwiler, Mansfield, Oh.; Donna Sipniewski, Dayton, Oh.; Shirley Spalding, Albuquerque, N.M.; Susan Stiriz, Hialeah, Fla.; Linda Syvertsen, St. Louis, Mo.; Janice Thompson, LaCrosse, Wis.; Carolyn Trump, Akron, Oh.; Mari Kae Weed, Juneau, Alas.; Donna Zuniga, Tulsa, Okla.

Most Sanctioned 300 Games

Betty Morris, Stockton, Cal.	5	Pat Adams, Felton, Cal.	3	Cindy Mason, Sunnyvale, Cal.	3
Jeanne Maiden, Willowick, Oh.	4	Debbie Bennett, Akron, Oh.	3	Carolyn Trump, Akron, Oh.	3
Beverly Ortner, Tucson, Ariz.	4	Sylvia Wene Martin, Philadelphia, Pa.	3		

PBA Winter Tour, 1981

Date	Event	Winner	Winner's share
Jan. 10	Miller High Life Classic, Anaheim, Cal.	Steve Martin	$21,000
Jan. 17	Showboat Invitational, Las Vegas, Nev.	Mark Roth	21,000
Jan. 24	Alameda Open, Alameda, Cal.	Bob Handley	12,000
Jan. 31	Quaker State Open, Grand Prairie, Tex.	Marshall Holman	20,000
Feb. 7	BPAA U.S. Open, Houston, Tex.	Marshall Holman	21,000
Feb. 14	Rolaids Open, St. Louis, Mo.	Earl Anthony	16,000
Feb. 21	AMF MagicScore Open, Peoria, Ill.	Earl Anthony	20,000
Feb. 28	Cleveland Open, No. Olmsted, Oh.	Mal Acosta	13,000
Mar. 7	PBA National Championship, Toledo, Oh.	Earl Anthony	21,000
Mar. 14	Miller High Life Open, Milwaukee, Wis.	Mike Durbin	21,000
Mar. 21	King Louie Open, Overland Park, Kan.	Marshall Holman	13,000
Mar. 28	True Value Open, Miami, Fla.	Bo Bowden	21,000
Apr. 4	Fair Lanes Open, Baltimore, Md.	Wayne Webb	13,000
Apr. 11	Long Island Open, Garden City, N.Y.	Earl Anthony	13,000
Apr. 18	Greater Hartford Open, Hartford, Conn.	Wayne Webb	12,000
Apr. 25	Firestone Tournament of Champions, Akron, Oh.	Steve Cook	30,000

Leading Averages in 1980

(400 or more games in PBA tournaments)

Pos.	Name, City	Tournaments	Games	Pinfall	Average
1.	Earl Anthony, Dublin, Cal.	18	656	143,359	218.535
2.	Mark Roth, Little Silver, N.J.	28	898	194,801	216.928
3.	Tom Baker, Buffalo, N.Y.	26	876	187,497	214.038
4.	Joe Berardi, Pearl River, N.Y.	20	665	142,011	213.550
5.	Nelson Burton Jr., St. Louis, Mo.	23	709	151,368	213.495
6.	Mike Aulby, Indianapolis, Ind.	34	1,031	219,115	212.527
7.	Jay Robinson, Van Nuys, Cal.	27	765	162,523	212.448
8.	Gary Dickinson, Ft. Worth, Tex.	17	504	106,998	212.298
9.	John Petraglia, Staten Island, N.Y.	21	591	125,466	212.294
10.	Wayne Webb, Rehoboth, Mass.	32	1,055	223,458	211.809
11.	George Pappas, Charlotte, N.C.	30	966	204,434	211.629
12.	Mal Acosta, Fremont, Cal.	26	744	157,435	211.606
13.	Tommy Hudson, Akron, Oh.	27	766	162,077	211.589
14.	Dennis Lane, Kingsport, Tenn.	27	774	163,744	211.556
15.	Dave Frame, Baldwin Park, Cal.	27	740	156,532	211.530

Firestone Tournament of Champions

This is professional bowling's richest tournament and has been held each year since its inception in 1965, in Akron, Oh., the home of the Professional Bowlers Association. First prize is $30,000.

Year	Winner	Year	Winner	Year	Winner	Year	Winner
1965	Billy Hardwick	1970	Don Johnson	1974	Earl Anthony	1978	Earl Anthony
1966	Wayne Zahn	1971	Johnny Petraglia	1975	Dave Davis	1979	George Pappas
1967	Jim Stefanich	1972	Mike Durbin	1976	Marshall Holman	1980	Wayne Webb
1968	Dave Davis	1973	Jim Godman	1977	Mike Berlin	1981	Steve Cook
1969	Jim Godman						

Leading PBA Averages by Year

Year	Bowler	Tournaments	Average	Year	Bowler	Tournaments	Average
1962	Don Carter, St. Louis, Mo.	25	212.844	1972	Don Johnson, Akron, Oh.	30	215.290
1963	Billy Hardwick, Louisville, Ky.	26	210.346	1973	Earl Anthony, Tacoma, Wash.	29	215.799
1964	Ray Bluth, St. Louis, Mo.	27	210.512	1974	Earl Anthony, Tacoma, Wash.	28	219.394
1965	Dick Weber, St. Louis, Mo.	19	211.895	1975	Earl Anthony, Tacoma, Wash.	30	219.060
1966	Wayne Zahn, Atlanta, Ga.	27	208.663	1976	Mark Roth, New York, N.Y.	28	215.970
1967	Wayne Zahn, Atlanta, Ga.	29	212.342	1977	Mark Roth, New York, N.Y.	28	218.174
1968	Jim Stefanich, Joliet, Ill.	33	211.895	1978	Mark Roth, North Arlington, N.J.	25	219.834
1969	Bill Hardwick, Louisville, Ky.	33	212.957	1979	Mark Roth, North Arlington, N.J.	26	221.662
1970	Nelson Burton Jr., St. Louis, Mo.	32	214.908	1980	Earl Anthony, Dublin, Cal.	18	218.535
1971	Don Johnson, Akron, Oh.	31	213.977				

PBA Leading Money Winners

Total winnings are from PBA, ABC Masters, and BPAA All-Star tournaments only, and do not include numerous other tournaments or earnings from special television shows and matches.

Year	Bowler	Dollars	Year	Bowler	Dollars	Year	Bowler	Dollars
1960	Don Carter	22,525	1967	Dave Davis	54,165	1974	Earl Anthony	99,585
1961	Dick Weber	26,280	1968	Jim Stefanich	67,377	1975	Earl Anthony	107,585
1962	Don Carter	49,972	1969	Billy Hardwick	64,160	1976	Earl Anthony	110,833
1963	Dick Weber	46,333	1970	Mike McGrath	52,049	1977	Mark Roth	105,583
1964	Bob Strampe	33,592	1971	Johnny Petraglia	85,065	1978	Mark Roth	134,500
1965	Dick Weber	47,674	1972	Don Johnson	56,648	1979	Mark Roth	124,517
1966	Wayne Zahn	54,720	1973	Don McCune	69,000	1980	Wayne Webb	116,700

World Track and Field Records

As of Sept. 1, 1981

*Indicates pending record; a number of new records await confirmation. The International Amateur Atheletic Federation, the world body of track and field, recognizes only records in metric distances except for the mile.

Men's Records

Running

Event	Record	Holder	Country	Date	Where made
100 meters	9.95 s.	Jim Hines	U.S.	Oct. 14, 1968	Mexico City
200 meters	19.72 s.	Pietro Mennea	Italy	Sept. 12, 1979	Mexico City
400 meters	43.86 s.	Lee Evans	U.S.	Oct. 18, 1968	Mexico City
800 meters	*1 m., 41.72 s.	Sebastian Coe	Gr. Britain	June, 1981	Florence, Italy
1,000 meters	*2 m., 12.18 s.	Sebastian Coe	Gr. Britain	July, 1981	Oslo
1,500 meters	3 m., 31.36 s.	Steve Ovett	Gr. Britain	Aug. 27, 1980	Koblenz, W. Germany
1 mile	*3m., 47.33 s.	Sebastian Coe	Gr. Britain	Aug. 28, 1981	Brussels
2,000 meters	4 m., 51.4 s.	John Walker	New Zealand	June 30, 1976	Oslo
3,000 meters	7 m., 32.1 s.	Henry Rono	Kenya	June 27, 1978	Oslo
5,000 meters	13 m., 08.4 s.	Henry Rono	Kenya	Apr. 8, 1978	Berkeley, Cal.
10,000 meters	27 m., 22.47 s.	Henry Rono	Kenya	June 11, 1978	Vienna
20,000 meters	57 m., 24.2 s.	Jos Hermens	Netherlands	May 1, 1976	Netherlands
25,000 meters	1 hr., 14 m., 12 s.	Bill Rodgers	U.S.	Feb. 21, 1979	Saratoga, Cal.
30,000 meters	1 hr., 31 m., 30.4 s.	Jim Adler	Gr. Britain	Sept. 5, 1970	London
3,000 meter stpl	8 m., 05.4 s.	Henry Rono	Kenya	May 13, 1978	Seattle

Hurdles

110 meters	*12.93 s.	Renaldo Nehemiah	U.S.	Aug. 19, 1981	Zurich
400 meters	47.13 s.	Edwin Moses	U.S.	July 3, 1980	Milan, Italy

Relay Races

400 mtrs.	38.03 s.	National team (Collins, Riddick, Wiley, Williams)	U.S.	Sept. 3, 1977	Dusseldorf
800 mtrs. (4×200)	1 m., 20.3 s.	USC	U.S.	May 27, 1978	Tempe, Ariz.
1,600 mtrs. (4×400)	2 m., 56.1 s.	National team (Matthews, Freeman, James, Evans)	U.S.	Oct. 20, 1968	Mexico City
3,200 mtrs. (4×800)	7 m., 08.1 s.	National team	USSR	Aug. 12, 1978	USSR

Field Events

Event	Record	Holder	Country	Date	Where made
High jump	7 ft., 8¾ in.	Gerd Wessig	E. Germany	Aug. 1, 1980	Moscow
Long jump	29 ft., 2½ in.	Bob Beamon	U.S.	Oct. 18, 1968	Mexico City
Triple jump	58 ft., 8¼ in.	Joao de Oliveira	Brazil	Oct. 15, 1975	Mexico City
Pole vault	*19 ft., ¾ in.	Vladimir Polyakov	USSR	June, 1981	Tbilisi, USSR
16 lb. shot put.	72 ft., 8 in.	Udo Beyer	E. Germany	July 6, 1978	Sweden
Discus throw	233 ft., 5 in.	Wolfgang Schmidt	E. Germany	Aug. 9, 1978	E. Berlin
Javelin throw	311 ft., 4 in.	Ferenc Paragi	Hungary	Apr. 23, 1980	Tata, Hungary
16 lb. hammer throw	268 ft., 4 in.	Yuri Sedykh	USSR	July 31, 1980	Moscow
Decathlon	8,649 pts.	Guido Kratschmer	W. Germany	June 13-14, 1980	W. Germany

Walking

2 hours	17 mi., 881 yds.	Jose Marin	Spain	Apr. 8, 1979	Barcelona
30,000 mtrs.	2 h., 8 min.	Jose Marin	Spain	Apr. 8, 1979	Barcelona
50,000 mtrs.	3 hr., 41 m., 39 s.	Raul Gonzales	Mexico	May 25, 1978	Norway

Women's Records

Running

100 meters	10.88 s.	Marlies Gohr	E. Germany	July 1, 1977	Dresden
200 meters	21.71 s.	Marita Koch	E. Germany	June 10, 1979	E. Berlin
400 meters	48.60 s.	Marita Koch	E. Germany	Aug. 4, 1979	Turin, Italy
800 meters	1 m., 53.42 s.	Nadezhda Olizarenko	USSR	July 27, 1980	Moscow
1,500 meters	3 m., 52.47 s.	Tatyana Kazankina	USSR	Aug. 13, 1980	Zurich
1 mile	4 m., 21.68 s.	Mary Decker	U.S.	Jan. 26, 1980	Auckland, N.Z.
3,000 meters	8 m., 27.12 s.	Ludmila Bragina	USSR	Aug. 7, 976	College Park, Md.

Hurdles

110 meters	12.36 s.	Grazyna Rabsztyn	Poland	June 13, 1980	Warsaw
400 meters	54.28 s.	Karin Rossley	E. Germany	May 17, 1980	E. Germany

Relay Races

400 mtrs. (4×100)	41.60 s.	National team	E. Germany	Aug. 1, 1980	Moscow
800 mtrs. (4×200)	1 m., 28.15 s.	National team	E. Germany	Aug. 9, 1980	E. Germany
1,600 mtrs. (4×400)	3 m., 19.23 s.	National team	E. Germany	July 31, 1976	Montreal
3,200 mtrs. (4×800)	7 m., 52.35 s.	National team	USSR	Aug. 16, 1976	USSR

Field Events

Event	Record	Holder	Country	Date	Where made
High jump	6 ft., 7 in.	Sara Simeoni	Italy	Aug. 31, 1978	Prague
Shot put	73 ft., 8 in.	Ilona Slupianek	E. Germany	May 11, 1980	Potsdam
Long jump	23 ft., 3¼ in.	Vilma Bardauskiene	USSR	Aug. 29, 1978	Prague
Discus throw	235 ft., 7 in.	Maria Vergova	Bulgaria	July 13, 1980	Sofia
Javelin	*235 ft., 10 in.	Antoaneta Todorova	Bulgaria	Aug. 15, 1981	Yugoslavia
Pentathlon	5,083 pts.	Nadyezhda Tkachenko	USSR	July 24, 1980	Moscow

U.S. Track and Field Indoor Records

As of Aug., 1981

*Indicates pending record; a number of new records await confirmation. The International Amateur Federation, the world body of track and field, does not recognize world indoor records.

Men's Records

Running

Event	Record	Holder	Date	Where made
50 meters	5.72	Ray James	Feb. 10, 1980	Syracuse, N.Y.
60 yards	*6.04	Stanley Floyd	Jan., 1981	. . .
60 meters	6.38	Houston McTear	Jan. 5, 1980	Long Beach, Cal.
100 yards	9.54	Harvey Glance	Feb. 16, 1980	Houston
300 yards	*29.26	Terron Wright	Feb., 1981	Bloomington, Ind.
300 meters	34.25	Vince Jones	Mar. 3, 1979	Normal, Ill.
500 yards	54.4	Lee Evans	Jan. 8, 30, 1971	Idaho and Maryland
500 motors	1:02	Stan Vinson	Feb. 11, 1978	Louisville
600 yards	1:07.6	Marty McGrady	Feb. 27, 1970	New York City
600 meters	1:18.3	Mark Winzenried	Feb. 2, 1972	Louisville
800 meters	1:47.4	Ted Nelson	Apr. 7, 1965	Berlin
1,000 yards	*2:04.9	Don Paige	Feb., 1981	New York City
1,000 meters	2:20.3	Don Paige	Jan. 20, 1979	New York City
1,500 meters	3:38.3	Steve Scott	Feb. 16, 1979	San Diego
One mile	3:53	Steve Scott	Feb. 15, 1980	Los Angeles
2,000 meters	*4:58.6	Steve Scott	Feb., 1981	Louisville
3,000 meters	7:45.2	Steve Scott	Jan. 5, 1980	Long Beach, Cal.
2 miles	8:20.4	Steve Prefontaine	Feb. 17, 1974	San Diego
3 miles	13:06.7	Bruce Bickford	Feb. 29, 1980	New York City
5,000 meters	13:41	Glenn Howard	Feb. 8, 1975	Louisville
50-yd. hurdles	*5.98	Renaldo Nehemiah	Feb., 1981	Toronto
60-m. hurdles	7.62	Renaldo Nehemiah	Feb. 11, 1979	Montreal

Field Events

Event	Record	Holder	Date	Where made
High jump	*7 ft. 7 3/4 in.	Jeff Woodard	Feb., 1981	New York City
Pole vault	18 ft. 5 1/2 in.	Dan Ripley	Mar. 3, 1979	Ft. Worth
Long jump	*27 ft. 10 1/4 in.	Carl Lewis	Feb., 1981	Ft. Worth
Triple jump	56 ft.	Ron Livers	Feb. 2, 1980	Albuquerque
Shot put	72 ft. 2 3/4 in.	George Woods	Feb. 8, 1974	Inglewood, Cal.

Women's Records

Running

Event	Record	Holder	Date	Where made
50 yards	*5.83	Evelyn Ashford	Feb., 1981	Toronto
50 meters	6.26	Evelyn Ashford	Feb. 23, 1980	Daly City, Cal.
60 yards	*6.65	Evelyn Ashford	Jan., 1981	Albuquerque
60 meters	7.04	Evelyn Ashford	Jan. 5, 1980	Long Beach, Cal.
220 yards	*23.27	Chandra Cheeseborough	Feb., 1981	New York City
300 yards	34.07	Rosalyn Bryant	Feb. 2, 1980	Lincoln, Neb.
300 meters	38.56	Wanda Hooker	Mar. 8, 1980	Columbia, Mo.
400 meters	53.31	Gwen Gardner	Feb. 8, 1980	New York City
440 yards	53.92	Rosalyn Bryant	Feb. 29, 1980	New York City
500 yards	1:03.3	Rosalyn Bryant	Feb. 18, 1977	San Diego
500 meters	1:11.7	Delisa Watson	Feb. 9, 1980	Louisville
600 yards	1:19.3	Robin Campbell	Feb. 15, 1974	Toronto
600 meters	1:28.8	Christine Mullen	Mar. 8, 1980	Columbia, Mo.
800 meters	1:58.9	Mary Decker	Feb. 22, 1980	San Diego
880 yards	1:58.9	Mary Decker	Feb. 22, 1980	San Diego
1,000 yards	2:23.8	Mary Decker	Feb. 3, 1978	Inglewood, Cal.
1,000 meters	2:40.2	Francie Larrieu	Jan. 18, 1975	Los Angeles
1,500 meters	4:00.8	Mary Decker	Feb. 8, 1980	New York City
One mile	4:28.5	Francie Larrieu	Mar. 3, 1975	Richmond, Va.
3,000 meters	8:57.6	Jan Merrill	Mar. 5, 1978	Montreal
2 miles	*9:38.1	Francie Larrieu	Feb., 1981	New York City
50-yd. hurdles	6.37	Deby La Plante	Feb. 10, 1978	Toronto
50-m. hurdles	6.95	Candy Young	Feb. 3, 1979	Edmonton
60-yd. hurdles	7.47	Stephanie Hightower	Feb. 8, 1980	New York City
60-m hurdles	8.17	Stephanie Hightower (3 times)	Feb., Mar., 1980	. . .

Field Events

Event	Record	Holder	Date	Where made
High Jump	*6 ft. 4 3/4 in.	Joni Huntley	Feb., 1981	New York City
Shot put	61 ft. 2 1/4 in.	Maren Seidler	Jan. 20, 1978	W. Germany
Long jump	21 ft. 4 3/4 in.	Martha Watson	Mar. 16, 1973	Richmond, Va.
		Martha Watson	Jan. 16, 1976	Los Angeles
		Kathy McMillan	Feb. 19, 1976	Greensboro, N.C.

Evolution of the World Record for the One-Mile Run

The table below shows how the world record for the one-mile has been lowered in the past 117 years.

Year	Individual, country	Time	Year	Individual, country	Time
1864	Charles Lawes, Britain	4:56	1942	Arne Andersson, Sweden	4:06.2
1865	Richard Webster, Britain	4:36.5	1942	Gunder Haegg, Sweden	4:04.6
1868	William Chinnery, Britain	4:29	1943	Arne Andersson, Sweden	4:02.6
1868	W. C. Gibbs, Britain	4:28.8	1944	Arne Andersson, Sweden	4:01.6
1874	Walter Slade, Britain	4:26	1945	Gunder Haegg, Sweden	4:01.4
1875	Walter Slade, Britain	4:24.5	1954	Roger Bannister, Britain	3:59.4
1880	Walter George, Britain	4:23.2	1954	John Landy, Australia	3:58
1882	Walter George, Britain	4:21.4	1957	Derek Ibbotson, Britain	3:57.2
1882	Walter George, Britain	4:19.4	1958	Herb Elliott, Australia	3:54.5
1884	Walter George, Britain	4:18.4	1962	Peter Snell, New Zealand	0:54.4
1894	Fred Bacon, Scotland	4:18.2	1964	Peter Snell, New Zealand	3:54.1
1895	Fred Bacon, Scotland	4:17	1965	Michel Jazy, France	3:53.6
1895	Thomas Connett, U.S.	4:15.6	1966	Jim Ryun, U.S.	3:51.3
1911	John Paul Jones, U.S.	4:15.4	1967	Jim Ryun, U.S.	3:51.1
1913	John Paul Jones, U.S.	4:14.6	1975	Filbert Bayi, Tanzania	3:51
1915	Norman Taber, U.S.	4:12.6	1975	John Walker, New Zealand	3:49.4
1923	Paavo Nurmi, Finland	4:10.4	1979	Sebastian Coe, Britain	3:49
1931	Jules Ladoumegue, France	4:09.2	1980	Steve Ovett, Britain	3:48.8
1933	Jack Lovelock, New Zealand	4:07.6	1981	Sebastian Coe, Britain	3:48.53
1934	Glenn Cunningham, U.S.	4:06.8	1981	Steve Ovett, Britain	3:48.40
1937	Sydney Wooderson, Britain	4:06.4	1981	Sebastian Coe, Britain	3:47.33
1942	Gunder Haegg, Sweden	4:06.2			

Track and Field Events in 1981

74th Annual Millrose Games

New York, N.Y., Feb. 6, 1981

Men

60 Yds.—Stanley Floyd, Houston, Tex. **Time—0:06.15.**
60-Yd. High Hurdles—Renaldo Nehemiah, Athletic Attic. **Time—0:06.98.**
400 Meters—Bert Cameron, Univ. of Texas-El Paso. **Time—0:47.68.**
500 Yds.—Ed Yearwood, Long Island Alliance. **Time—0:55.5.**
600 Yds.—Anthony Tufariello, Villanova. **Time—1:09.07.**
800 Meters—Peter Lamashon, Univ. of Texas-El Paso. **Time—1:50.02.**
1,000 Yds.—Don Paige, Athletic Attic. **Time—2:04.09.**
One Mile—Eamonn Coughlan, Ireland. **Time—3:53.**
5,000 Meters—Suleiman Nyambui, Univ. of Texas-El Paso. **Time—13:20.3.**

One-Mile Walk—Evan Fox, New York AC. **Time—6:13.05.**
Pole Vault—Brad Pursley, Abilene Christian. **17 ft. 9 in.**
High Jump—Jeff Woodard, Philadelphia Pioneer. **7 ft. 6 in.**

Women

60 Yds.—Chandra Cheeseborough, Tenn. State. **Time—0:06.06.**
60-Yd. Hurdles—Benita Fitzgerald, Univ. of Tenn. **Time—0:07.80.**
400 Meters—June Griffith, Adelphi. **Time—0:53.08.**
800 Meters—Robin Campbell, Stanford TC. **Time—2:07.03.**
1,500 Meters—Maggie Keyes, Cal. Poly State. **Time—4:14.09.**
High Jump—Joni Huntley, Pacific Coast Club. **6 ft. 4¾ in.**

TAC/USA Indoor Championships

New York, N.Y., Feb. 27, 1981

Men

60 Yds.—Stanley Floyd, unattached. **Time—0:06.15.**
60-Yd. Hurdles—Alejandro Casanas, Cuba. **Time—0:07.14.**
440 Yds.—Ed Yearwood, Long Island Alliance TC. **Time—0:48.12.**
600 Yds.—Mike Solomon, Philadelphia Pioneer Club. **Time—1:10.31.**
1,000 Yds.—Bill Martin, Athletics West. **Time—2:08.37.**
One Mile—Steve Scott, Sub-4 TC. **Time—3:57.3.**
3 Miles—Eamonn Coghlan, New York AC. **Time—12:54.80.**
High Jump—Jeff Woodard, unattached. **7 ft. 7¾ in.**
Pole Vault—Thierry Vigneron, France. **18 ft. 4½ in.**
Long Jump—Larry Myricks, Athletic Attic. **26 ft. 8¼ in.**
Triple Jump—Mike Marlow, Stars & Stripes TC. **54 ft. 6½ in.**
Shot Put—Brian Oldfield, Univ. of Chicago TC. **69 ft. 4 in.**
35 Lb. Weight Throw—Ed Kania, Pacific Coast Club. **73 ft. 4 in.**

Team champion—Philadelphia Pioneer Club.

Women

60 Yds.—Evelyn Ashford, unattached. **Time—0:06.63.**
60-Yd. Hurdles—Benita Fitzgerald, Tennessee. **Time—0:07.72.**
220 Yds.—Chandra Cheeseborough, Tenn. State. **Time—0:23.27.**
440 Yds.—Diane Dixon, Atoms TC. **Time—0:55.38.**
880 Yds.—Delisa Walton, Tennessee. **Time—2:05.1.**
One Mile—Jan Merrill, Age Group AA. **Time—4:34.03.**
2 Miles—Francie Larrieu, Pacific Coast Club. **Time—9:38.1.**
High Jump—Joni Huntley, Pacific Coast Club. **6 ft. 1¼ in.**
Long Jump—Ana Alexander, Cuba. **20 ft. 9¾ in.**
Shot Put—Marita Walton, Maryland. **52 ft. 11 in.**
Team champion—Tenn. State.

Toronto Star — Maple Leaf Indoor Games

Toronto, Ont., Feb. 13, 1981

Men

50 Yds.—Carl Lewis, Houston Tex. **Time—0:05.31.**
50-Yd. Hurdles—Ronaldo Nehemiah, D.C. International. **Time—0:05.98.**
600 Meters—Mark Enyeart, Pacific Coast Club. **Time—1:18.57.**
1,000 Meters—Mike Boit, Kenya. **Time—2:22.59.**
One Mile—Eamonn Coghlan, Ireland. **Time—3:55.63.**
5,000 Meters—Suleiman Nyambui, Tanzania. **Time—13:44.08.**

Pole Vault—Brad Bursley, Abilene Christian Univ. **17 ft. 6 in.**

Women

50 Yds.—Evelyn Ashford, Los Angeles, Calif. **Time—0:05.83.**
50-Yd. Hurdles—Benita Fitzgerald, Univ. of Tenn. **Time—0:06.72.**
600 Meters—Lorna Forde, New York Atoms. **Time—1:30.63.**
1,500 Meters—Jan Merrill, New London A.C. **Time—4:17.62.**

USA/Mobil Outdoor Track & Field Championships

Sacramento, Cal., June 19-21, 1981

Men

100 Meters—Carl Lewis, Santa Monica TC. **Time—0:10.13.**
200 Meters—Jeff Phillips, Philadelphia Pioneer Club. **Time—0:20.36.**
400 Meters—Cliff Wiley, DC International. **Time—0:44.70.**
800 Meters—James Robinson, Inner City AC. **Time—1:45.53.**
1,500 Meters—Sydney Maree, Athletic Attic. **Time—3:35.02.**
3,000-Meter Steeplechase—Henry Marsh, Athletics West. **Time—8:30.7.**
5,000 Meters—Matt Centrowitz, New York AC. **Time—13:28.86.**
10,000 Meters—Alberto Salazar, Athletics West. **Time—28:39.33.**
110-Meter Hurdles—Greg Foster, Shaklee TC. **Time—0:13.39.**
400-Meter Hurdles—Edwin Moses, unattached. **Time—0:47.59.**
5,000-Meter Walk—Ray Sharp, Athletic Attic. **Time—20:47.52.**
High Jump—Tyke Peacock, Modesto JC. **7 ft. 4½ in.**
Pole Vault—Billy Olsen, Pacific Coast Club. **18 ft. 2½ in.**
Long Jump—Carl Lewis, Santa Monica TC. **28 ft. 3½ in.**
Triple Jump—Willie Banks, Athletics West. **57 ft. 7½ in.**
Shot Put—Dave Laut, Athletics West. **70 ft. 10½ in.**
Discus—Ben Plucknett, Southern Cal Striders. **226 ft. 5 in.**
Hammer Throw—Richard Olsen, New York AC. **235 ft. 10 in.**

Javelin—Bruce Kennedy, Pacific Coast Club. **276 ft. 8 in.**

Women

100 Meters—Evelyn Ashford, Medalist TC. **Time—0:11.07.**
200 Meters—Evelyn Ashford. **Time—0:22.30.**
400 Meters—Denean Howard, Shaklee TC. **Time—0:51.79.**
800 Meters—Madeline Manning, Oral Roberts TC. **Time—1:58.50.**
1,500 Meters—Jan Merrill, Age Group AA. **Time—4:14.62.**
3,000 Meters—Brenda Webb, Athletics West. **Time—9:04.54.**
10,000 Meters—Joan Benoit, Athletics West. **Time—33:37.5.**
100-Meter Hurdles—Stephanie Hightower, Los Angeles Naturite TC. **Time—0:13.09.**
400-Meter Hurdles—Sandy Myers, Los Angeles Naturite TC. **Time—0:56.43.**
5,000-Meter Walk—Susan Liers-Westerfield, Island TC. **Time—24:26.7.**
High Jump—Pam Spencer, Los Angeles Naturite TC. **6 ft. 4¾ in.**
Long Jump—Jodi Anderson, Los Angeles Naturite TC. **22 ft. ¼ in.**
Shot Put—Denise Wood, Knoxville TC. **55 ft. 5¾ in.**
Discus—Leslie Deniz, Sun Devil Sports. **182 ft. 9 in.**
Javelin—Karin Smith, Medalist TC. **208 ft. 2 in.**

Lacrosse Champions in 1981

NCAA Division I Championship

At Princeton, N.J., May 30—North Carolina 14, Johns Hopkins 13.

Semi-finals

Johns Hopkins 10, Virginia 6; North Carolina 17, Navy 8.

Quarter Finals

Johns Hopkins 19, Maryland 14; Virginia 16, Massachusetts 12; North Carolina 13, Syracuse 6; Navy 16, Army 10.

NCAA Division II Championship

At Garden City, N.Y., May 17—Adelphi 17, Loyola (Md.) 14.

NCAA Division III Championship

At Geneva, N.Y., May 24—Hobart 10, Cortland (N.Y.) 8.

All-Star College Game

At Syracuse, N.Y., June 13—North 20, South 18.

U.S. Club Lacrosse Association Championship

At Garden City, N.Y., June 14—Long Island L.C. 21, Mt. Washington (Md.) 12.

Junior College Lacrosse Championship

At Catonsville, Md., June 10—SUNY-Farmingdale 18, Nassau (N.Y.) C.C. 8.

Coach of the Year

Division I—Willie Scroggs, North Carolina.
Division II—Jay Connor, Loyola (Md.)
Division III—Dave Urick, Hobart.

USILA Division I All America Team

Attack: Jeff Cook (Johns Hopkins), Syd Abernethy (Navy), Mike Burnett (North Carolina).
Midfield: Brendan Schneck (Johns Hopkins), Peter Schmitz (Massachusetts), Tom Donahue (Syracuse), Doug Hall (North Carolina).
Defense: Bob Henry (Army), Mike McLaughlin (Navy), Jeff McKee (Syracuse).
Goalie: Tom Sears (North Carolina).
  Note: 4 midfielders selected for the 3 midfield positions.

Second Team

Attack: Peter Worstell (Maryland), Jim Weller (Massachusetts), Lee Vosburgh (Massachusetts).
Midfield: John Fay (New Hampshire), Norm Engelke (Cornell), Steve Kraus (Virginia), Peter Voelkel (North Carolina).
Defense Lance Schneck (Johns Hopkins), Mike Sotir (Virginia), Gary Burns (North Carolina).
Goalie: Ron Aviles (N.C. State).
  Note: 4 midfielders selected for the 3 midfield positions.

Association for Intercollegiate Athletics for Women

Division I Championship—University Park, Pa. May 16—Maryland 5, Ursinus 4.
Division II Championship—Delaware 8, Lehigh 4.
Division III Championship—Trenton 7, Franklin & Marshall 6.

AIAW Division I All-Championship Team

Candy Finn (Penn State), Sandy Lanahan (Maryland), Francesca DenHartog (Harvard), Traci Davis (Ursinus), Debbie Tweed (Ursinus), Jackie Williams (Maryland), Laura LeMire (Maryland), Lauries Holmes (Ursinus), Gina Buggy (Ursinus), Chris Sailer (Harvard), Tracy Andrews (Rhode Island), Lori Moxley (Maryland), Cara Eisenberg (James Madison), Judy Strong (Massachusetts), Sue Darwin (Ursinus), Mindy Jacobs (Temple).

U.S. Squash Racquets Association Amateur Champions

1961	Henri R. Salaun	1967	Samuel P. Howe 3d	1972	Victor Niederhoffer	1977	Thomas E. Page
1962	Samuel P. Howe 3d	1968	Colin Adair	1973	Victor Niederhoffer	1978	Michael Desaulniers
1963	Benjamin H. Heckscher	1969	Anil Nayar	1974	Victor Niederhoffer	1979	Mario Sanchez
1964	Ralph E. Howe	1970	Anil Nayar	1975	Victor Niederhoffer	1980	Michael Desaulniers
1965	Stephen T. Vehslage	1971	Colin Adair	1976	Peter Briggs	1981	Mark Alger
1966	Victor Niederhoffer						

National Football League

Final 1980 Standings

National Conference

Eastern Division

Club	W	L	T	Pct	PF	PA
Philadelphia	12	4	0	.750	384	222
Dallas	12	4	0	.750	454	311
Washington	6	10	0	.375	251	293
St. Louis	5	11	0	.313	299	350
N.Y. Giants	4	12	0	.250	249	427

Central Division

Club	W	L	T	Pct	PF	PA
Minnesota	9	7	0	.563	317	308
Detroit	9	7	0	.503	334	272
Chicago	7	9	0	.438	304	264
Green Bay	5	10	1	.344	231	371
Tampa Bay	5	10	1	.344	271	341

Western Division

Club	W	L	T	Pct	PF	PA
Atlanta	12	4	0	.750	405	272
Los Angeles	11	5	0	.688	424	289
San Francisco	6	10	0	.375	320	415
New Orleans	1	15	0	.063	289	487

American Conference

Eastern Division

Club	W	L	T	Pct	PF	PA
Buffalo	11	5	0	.688	320	260
New England	10	6	0	.625	441	325
Miami	8	8	0	.500	266	305
Baltimore	7	9	0	.438	355	387
N.Y. Jets	4	12	0	.250	302	395

Central Division

Club	W	L	T	Pct	PF	PA
Cleveland	11	5	0	.688	357	310
Houston	11	5	0	.688	295	251
Pittsburgh	9	7	0	.563	352	313
Cincinnati	6	10	0	.375	244	312

Western Division

Club	W	L	T	Pct	PF	PA
San Diego	11	5	0	.688	418	327
Oakland	11	5	0	.688	364	306
Denver	8	8	0	.500	310	323
Kansas City	8	8	0	.500	319	336
Seattle	4	12	0	.250	291	408

NFC playoffs—Dallas 34, Los Angeles 13; Dallas 30, Atlanta 27; Philadelphia 31, Minnesota 16; Philadelphia 20, Dallas 7.
AFC playoffs—Oakland 27, Houston 7; Oakland 14, Cleveland 12; San Diego 20, Buffalo 14; Oakland 34, San Diego 27.
Championship game—Oakland 27, Philadelphia 10.

Oakland Defeats Philadelphia in Super Bowl

The Oakland Raiders won their second Super Bowl championship by defeating the Philadelphia Eagles 27-10 on Jan. 25, 1981 at the Superdome in New Orleans. Jim Plunkett of the Raiders was chosen the game's most valuable player.

Score by Periods

Oakland	14	0	10	3—27
Philadelphia	0	3	0	7—10

Scoring

Oakland—Branch 2 yd. pass from Plunkett (Bahr kick).
Oakland—King 80 yd. pass from Plunkett (Bahr kick).
Philadelphia—Franklin 30 yd. field goal.
Oakland—Branch 29 yd. pass from Plunkett (Bahr kick).
Oakland—Bahr 46 yd. field goal.
Philadelphia—Krepfle 8 yd. pass from Jaworski (Franklin kick).
Oakland—Bahr 35 yd. field goal.

Individual Statistics

Rushing—Oakland, van Eeghen 19-80, King 6-18, Jensen 3-12, Plunkett 3-9, Whittington 3-minus 2. Philadelphia, Montgomery 16-44, Harris 7-14, Giammona 1-7, Harrington 1-4, Jaworski 1-0.
Passing—Oakland, Plunkett 13-21-0-261. Philadelphia, Jaworski 18-38-3-291.
Receiving—Oakland, Branch 5-67, Chandler 4-77, King 2-93, Chester 2-24, Philadelphia, Montgomery 6-91, Carmichael 5-83, Smith 2-59, Krepfle 2-16, Spagnola 1-22, Parker 1-19, Harris 1-1.
Interceptions—Oakland, Martin 3-44.
Kickoff returns—Oakland, Matthews 2-29, Moody 1-19. Philadelphia, Campfield 5-87.

Team Statistics

	Oakland	Philadelphia
First downs	17	19
Rushes-yards	34-117	26-69
Passing yards	260	291
Return yards	45	20
Passes	13-21-0	18-38-3
Punts	3-42	3-37
Fumbles-lost	0-0	1-1
Penalties-yards	5-37	6-57
Field goals	2-3	1-2
Time of possession	29:49	30:11

Super Bowl

Year	Winner	Loser	Site
1967	Green Bay Packers, 35	Kansas City Chiefs, 10	Los Angeles Coliseum
1968	Green Bay Packers, 33	Oakland Raiders, 14	Orange Bowl, Miami
1969	New York Jets, 16	Baltimore Colts, 7	Orange Bowl, Miami
1970	Kansas City Chiefs, 23	Minnesota Vikings, 7	Tulane Stadium, New Orleans
1971	Baltimore Colts, 16	Dallas Cowboys, 13	Orange Bowl, Miami
1972	Dallas Cowboys, 24	Miami Dolphins, 3	Tulane Stadium, New Orleans
1973	Miami Dolphins, 14	Washington Redskins, 7	Los Angeles Coliseum
1974	Miami Dolphins, 24	Minnesota Vikings, 7	Rice Stadium, Houston
1975	Pittsburgh Steelers, 16	Minnesota Vikings, 6	Tulane Stadium, New Orleans
1976	Pittsburgh Steelers, 21	Dallas Cowboys, 17	Orange Bowl, Miami
1977	Oakland Raiders, 32	Minnesota Vikings, 14	Rose Bowl, Pasadena
1978	Dallas Cowboys, 27	Denver Broncos, 10	Superdome, New Orleans
1979	Pittsburgh Steelers, 35	Dallas Cowboys, 31	Orange Bowl, Miami
1980	Pittsburgh Steelers, 31	Los Angeles Rams, 19	Rose Bowl, Pasadena
1981	Oakland Raiders, 27	Philadelphia Eagles, 10	Superdome, New Orleans

George Halas Trophy Winners

The Halas Trophy, named after football coach George Halas, is awarded annually to the outstanding defensive player in football in a poll conducted by Murray Olderman of Newspaper Enterprise Assn.

1966	Larry Wilson, St. Louis	1971	Carl Eller, Minnesota	1976	Jerry Sherk, Cleveland
1967	Deacon Jones, Los Angeles	1972	Joe Greene, Pittsburgh	1977	Harvey Martin, Dallas
1968	Deacon Jones, Los Angeles	1973	Alan Page, Minnesota	1978	Randy Gradishar, Denver
1969	Dick Butkus, Chicago	1974	Joe Greene, Pittsburgh	1979	Lee Roy Selmon, Tampa Bay
1970	Dick Butkus, Chicago	1975	Curley Culp, Houston	1980	Lester Hayes, Oakland

National Football League Champions

	East	West	
Year	Winner (W.L.T.)	Winner (W.L.T.)	Playoff
1933	New York Giants (11-3-0)	Chicago Bears (10-2-1)	Chicago Bears 23, New York 21
1934	New York Giants (8-5-0)	Chicago Bears (13-0-0)	New York 30, Chicago Bears 13
1935	New York Giants (9-3-0)	Detroit Lions (7-3-2)	Detroit 26, New York 7
1936	Boston Redskins (7-5-0)	Green Bay Packers (10-1-1)	Green Bay 21, Boston 6
1937	Washington Redskins (8-3-0)	Chicago Bears (9-1-1)	Washington 28, Chicago Bears 21
1938	New York Giants (8-2-1)	Green Bay Packers (8-3-0)	New York 23, Green Bay 17
1939	New York Giants (9-1-1)	Green Bay Packers (9-2-0)	Green Bay 27, New York 0
1940	Washington Redskins (9-2-0)	Chicago Bears (8-3-0)	Chicago Bears 73, Washington 0
1941	New York Giants (8-3-0)	Chicago Bears (10-1-1)(a)	Chicago Bears 37, New York 9
1942	Wash. Redskins (10-1-1)	Chicago Bears (11-0-0)	Washington 14, Chicago Bears 6
1943	Wash. Redskins (6-3-1)(a)	Chicago Bears (8-1-1)	Chicago Bears, 41, Washington 21
1944	New York Giants (8-1-1)	Green Bay Packers (8-2-0)	Green Bay 14, New York 7
1945	Wash. Redskins (8-2-0)	Cleveland Rams (9-1-0)	Cleveland 15, Washington 14
1946	New York Giants (7-3-1)	Chicago Bears (8-2-1)	Chicago Bears 24, New York 14
1947	Philadelphia Eagles (8-4-0)(a)	Chicago Cardinals (9-3-0)	Chicago Cardinals 28, Philadelphia 21
1948	Philadelphia Eagles (9-2-1)	Chicago Cardinals (11-1-0)	Philadelphia 7, Chicago Cardinals 0
1949	Philadelphia Eagles (11-1-0)	Los Angeles Rams (8-2-2)	Philadelphia 14, Los Angeles 0
1950	Cleveland Browns (10-2-0)(a)	Los Angeles Rams (9-3-0)(a)	Cleveland 30, Los Angeles 28
1951	Cleveland Browns (11-1-0)	Los Angeles Rams (8-4-0)	Los Angeles 24, Cleveland 17
1952	Cleveland Browns (8-4-0)	Detroit Lions (9-3-0)(a)	Detroit 17, Cleveland 7
1953	Cleveland Browns (11-1-0)	Detroit Lions (10-2-0)	Detroit 17, Cleveland 16
1954	Cleveland Browns (9-3-0)	Detroit Lions (9-2-1)	Cleveland 56, Detroit 10
1955	Cleveland Browns (9-2-1)	Los Angeles Rams (8-3-1)	Cleveland 38, Los Angeles 14
1956	New York Giants (8-3-1)	Chicago Bears (9-2-1)	New York 47, Chicago Bears 7
1957	Cleveland Browns (9-2-1)	Detroit Lions (8-4-0)(a)	Detroit 59, Cleveland 14
1958	New York Giants (9-3-0)(a)	Baltimore Colts (9-3-0)	Baltimore 23, New York 17(b)
1959	New York Giants (10-2-0)	Baltimore Colts (9-3-0)	Baltimore 31, New York 16
1960	Philadelphia Eagles (10-2-0)	Green Bay Packers (8-4-0)	Philadelphia 17, Green Bay 13
1961	New York Giants (10-3-1)	Green Bay Packers (11-3-0)	Green Bay 37, New York 0
1962	New York Giants (12-2-0)	Green Bay Packers (13-1-0)	Green Bay 16, New York 7
1963	New York Giants (11-3-0)	Chicago Bears (11-1-2)	Chicago 14, New York 10
1964	Cleveland Browns (10-3-1)	Baltimore Colts (12-2-0)	Cleveland 27, Baltimore 0
1965	Cleveland Browns (11-3-0)	Green Bay Packers (10-3-1)(a)	Green Bay 23, Cleveland 12
1966	Dallas Cowboys (10-3-1)	Green Bay Packers (12-2-0)	Green Bay 34, Dallas 27

(a) Won divisional playoff. (b) Won at 8:15 sudden death overtime period.

Year	Conference	Division	Winner (W-L-T)	Playoff
1967	East	Century	Cleveland (9-5-0)	Dallas 52, Cleveland 14
		Capitol	Dallas (9-5-0)	
	West	Central	Green Bay (9-4-1)	Green Bay 28, Los Angeles 7
		Coastal	Los Angeles (11-1-2)(a)	Green Bay 21, Dallas 17
1968	East	Century	Cleveland (10-4-0)	Cleveland 31, Dallas 20
		Capitol	Dallas (12-2-0)	
	West	Central	Minnesota (8-6-0)	Baltimore 24, Minnesota 14
		Coastal	Baltimore (13-1-0)	Baltimore 34, Cleveland 0
1969	East	Century	Cleveland (10-3-1)	Cleveland 38, Dallas 14
		Capitol	Dallas (11-2-1)	
	West	Central	Minnesota (12-2-0)	Minnesota 23, Los Angeles 20
		Coastal	Los Angeles (11-3-0)	Minnesota 27, Cleveland 7
1970	American	Eastern	Baltimore (11-2-1)	Baltimore 17, Cincinnati 0
		Central	Cincinnati (8-6-0)	Oakland 21, Miami 14
		Western	Oakland (8-4-2)	Baltimore 27, Oakland 17
	National	Eastern	Dallas (10-4-0)	Dallas 5, Detroit 0
		Central	Minnesota (12-2-0)	San Francisco 17, Minnesota 14
		Western	San Francisco (10-3-1)	Dallas 17, San Francisco 10
1971	American	Eastern	Miami (10-3-1)	Miami 27, Kansas City 24
		Central	Cleveland (9-5-0)	Baltimore 20, Cleveland 3
		Western	Kansas City (10-3-1)	Miami 21, Baltimore 0
	National	Eastern	Dallas (11-3-0)	Dallas 20, Minnesota 12
		Central	Minnesota (11-3-0)	San Francisco 24, Washington 20
		Western	San Francisco (9-5-0)	Dallas 14, San Francisco 3
1972	American	Eastern	Miami (14-0-0)	Miami 20, Cleveland 14
		Central	Pittsburgh (11-3-0)	Pittsburgh 13, Oakland 7
		Western	Oakland (10-3-1)	Miami 21, Pittsburgh 17
	National	Eastern	Washington (11-3-0)	Washington 16, Green Bay 3
		Central	Green Bay (10-4-0)	Dallas 30, San Francisco 28
		Western	San Francisco (8-5-1)	Washington 26, Dallas 3
1973	American	Eastern	Miami (12-2-0)	Miami 34, Cincinnati 16
		Central	Cincinnati (10-4-0)	Oakland 33, Pittsburgh 14
		Western	Oakland (9-4-1)	Miami 27, Oakland 10
	National	Eastern	Dallas (10-4-0)	Dallas 27, Los Angeles 16
		Central	Minnesota (12-2-0)	Minnesota 27, Washington 20
		Western	Los Angeles (12-2-0)	Minnesota 27, Dallas 10
1974	American	Eastern	Miami (11-3-0)	Oakland 28, Miami 26
		Central	Pittsburgh (10-3-1)	Pittsburgh 32, Buffalo 14
		Western	Oakland (12-2-0)	Pittsburgh 24, Oakland 13
	National	Eastern	St. Louis (10-4-0)	Minnesota 30, St. Louis 14
		Central	Minnesota (10-4-0)	Los Angeles 19, Washington 10
		Western	Los Angeles (10-4-0)	Minnesota 14, Los Angeles 10
1975	American	Eastern	Baltimore (10-4-0)	Pittsburgh 28, Baltimore 10
		Central	Pittsburgh (12-2-0)	Oakland 31, Cincinnati 28
		Western	Oakland (11-3-0)	Pittsburgh 16, Oakland 10
	National	Eastern	St. Louis (11-3-0)	Dallas 17, Minnesota 14

(continued)

(continued)

Year	Conference	Division	Winner (W-L-T)	Playoff
		Central	Minnesota (12-2-0)	Los Angeles 35, St. Louis 23
		Western	Los Angeles (12-2-0)	Dallas 37, Los Angeles 7
1976	American	Eastern	Baltimore (11-3-0)	Pittsburgh 40, Baltimore 14
		Central	Pittsburgh (10-4-0)	Oakland 24, New England 21
		Western	Oakland (13-1-0)	Oakland 24, Pittsburgh 12
	National	Eastern	Dallas (11-3-0)	Minnesota 35, Washington 20
		Central	Minnesota (11-2-1)	Los Angeles 14, Dallas 12
		Western	Los Angeles (10-3-1)	Minnesota 24, Los Angeles 13
1977	American	Eastern	Baltimore (10-4-0)	Oakland 37, Baltimore 31
		Central	Pittsburgh (9-5-0)	Denver 34, Pittsburgh 21
		Western	Denver (12-2-0)	Dallas 37, Chicago 7
	National	Eastern	Dallas (12-2-0)	Minnesota 14, Los Angeles 7
		Central	Minnesota (9-5-0)	Denver 20, Oakland 17
		Western	Los Angeles (10-4-0)	Dallas 23, Minnesota 6
1978	American	Eastern	New England (11-5-0)	Pittsburgh 33, Denver 10
		Central	Pittsburgh (14-2-0)	Houston 31, New England 14
		Western	Denver (10-6-0)	Pittsburgh 34, Houston 5
	National	Eastern	Dallas (12-4-0)	Dallas 27, Atlanta 20
		Central	Minnesota (8-7-1)	Los Angeles 34, Minnesota 10
		Western	Los Angeles (12-4-0)	Dallas 28, Los Angeles 0
1979	American	Eastern	Miami (10-6-0)	Houston 17, San Diego 14
		Central	Pittsburgh (12-4-0)	Pittsburgh 34, Miami 14
		Western	San Diego (12-4-0)	Pittsburgh 27, Houston 13
	National	Eastern	Dallas (11-5-0)	Tampa Bay 24, Philadelphia 17
		Central	Tampa Bay (10-6-0)	Los Angeles 21, Dallas 19
		Western	Los Angeles (9-7-0)	Los Angeles 9, Tampa Bay 0
1980	American	Eastern	Buffalo (11-5-0)	San Diego 20, Buffalo 14
		Central	Cleveland (11-5-0)	Oakland 14, Cleveland 12
		Western	San Diego (11-5-0)	Oakland 34, San Diego 27
	National	Eastern	Philadelphia (12-4-0)	Philadelphia 31, Minnesota 16
		Central	Minnesota (9-7-0)	Dallas 30, Atlanta 27
		Western	Atlanta (12-4-0)	Philadelphia 20, Dallas 7

1980 NFL Individual Leaders

National Football Conference

Passing[1]

	Att	Comp	Pct Comp	Yards	Avg Gain	TD	Pct TD	Int	Rating Points
Jaworski, Philadelphia	451	257	57.0	3529	7.82	27	6.0	12	90.9
Ferragamo, Los Angeles	404	240	59.4	3199	7.92	30	7.4	19	89.7
Bartkowski, Atlanta	463	257	55.5	3544	7.65	31	6.7	16	88.0
Montana, San Francisco	273	176	64.5	1795	6.58	15	5.5	9	87.8
Danielson, Detroit	417	244	58.5	3223	7.73	13	3.1	11	82.6
Manning, New Orleans	509	309	60.7	3716	7.30	23	4.5	20	81.8
White, Dallas	436	260	59.6	3287	7.54	28	6.4	25	80.8
Theismann, Washington	454	262	57.7	2962	6.52	17	3.7	16	75.1
Kramer, Minnesota	522	299	57.3	3582	6.86	19	3.6	23	72.1
Dickey, Green Bay	478	278	58.2	3529	7.38	15	3.1	25	70.0
Williams, Tampa Bay	521	254	48.8	3396	6.52	20	3.8	16	69.7
Hart, St. Louis	425	228	53.6	2946	6.93	16	3.8	20	68.7
DeBerg, San Francisco	321	186	57.9	1998	6.22	12	3.7	17	66.5
Evans, Chicago	278	148	53.2	2039	7.33	11	4.0	16	66.1
Simms, N.Y. Giants	402	193	48.0	2321	5.77	15	3.7	19	58.9

Rushing

	Att	Yds	Avg	TD
Payton, Chicago	317	1460	4.6	6
Anderson, St. Louis	301	1352	4.5	9
Andrews, Atlanta	265	1308	4.9	4
Sims, Detroit	313	1303	4.2	13
Dorsett, Dallas	278	1185	4.3	11
Cain, Atlanta	235	914	3.9	8
Brown, Minnesota	219	912	4.2	8
Ivery, Green Bay	202	831	4.1	3
Bryant, Los Angeles	183	807	4.4	3
Montgomery, Philadelphia	193	778	4.0	8

Punt Returns

	No	Yds	Avg	TD
Johnson, Atlanta	23	281	12.2	0
Solomon, San Francisco	27	298	11.0	2
Green, St. Louis	16	168	10.5	1
Jones, Dallas	54	548	10.1	0
Nelms, Washington	48	487	10.1	0
Smith, Atlanta	27	262	9.7	0
Williams, Detroit	27	259	9.6	0
Bell, St. Louis	21	195	9.3	0
Sciarra, Philadelphia	36	330	9.2	0
Henry, Philadelphia	26	222	8.5	0

Receiving

	No	Yds	Avg	TD
Cooper, San Francisco	83	567	6.8	4
Clark, San Francisco	82	991	12.1	8
Lofton, Green Bay	71	1226	17.3	4
Rashad, Minnesota	69	1095	15.9	5
Tilley, St. Louis	68	966	14.2	6
Chandler, New Orleans	65	975	15.0	6
Young, Minnesota	64	499	7.8	2
Brown, Minnesota	62	623	10.0	2
Hill, Dallas	60	1055	17.6	8
Monk, Washington	58	797	13.7	3

Kickoff Returns

	No	Yds	Avg	TD
Mauti, New Orleans	31	798	25.7	0
Williams, Chicago	27	666	24.7	1
Owens, San Francisco	31	726	23.4	1
Green, St. Louis	32	745	23.3	0
Rogers, New Orleans	41	930	22.7	0
Jones, Dallas	32	720	22.5	0
Payton, Minnesota	53	1184	22.3	0
Davis, Tampa Bay	44	951	21.6	0
Kane, Detroit	23	495	21.5	0
Suhey, Chicago	19	406	21.4	0

Interceptions

	No	Yds	TD
Cromwell, Los Angeles	8	140	1
Richardson, Atlanta	7	139	0
Parrish, Washington	7	13	0
Lavender, Washington	6	96	1
Wilson, Philadelphia	6	79	0
Murphy, Washington	6	58	0
Allen, Detroit	6	38	0
Turner, Minnesota	6	22	0
Hunter, Detroit	6	20	0
Perry, Los Angeles	5	115	1

Scoring-Kicking

	XP-XPA	FG-FGA	Pts
Murray, Detroit	35-36	27-42	116
Mazzetti, Atlanta	46-49	19-27	103
Corral, Los Angeles	51-52	16-30	99
Franklin, Philadelphia	48-48	16-31	96
Septien, Dallas	59-60	11-17	92
Danmeier, Minnesota	33-38	16-26	81
Moseley, Washington	27-30	18-33	81
Yepremian, Tampa Bay	31-32	16-23	79
Wersching, San Francisco	33-39	15-19	78
Danelo, N.Y. Giants	27-28	16-24	75

Punting

	No	Yds	Avg
Jennings, New York Giants	94	4211	44.8
Blanchard, Tampa Bay	88	3722	42.3
Skladany, Detroit	72	3036	42.2
Swider, St. Louis	99	4111	41.5
Miller, San Francisco	77	3152	40.9
White, Dallas	71	2903	40.9
Parsons, Chicago	79	3207	40.6
Corral, Los Angeles	76	3002	39.5
Erxleben, New Orleans	89	3499	39.3
Runager, Philadelphia	75	2947	39.3

Scoring-Touchdowns

	TD	Rush	Pass	Other	Pts
Sims, Detroit	16	13	3	0	96
Dorsett, Dallas	11	11	0	0	66
Brown, Minnesota	10	8	2	0	60
Gray, N.Y. Giants	10	0	10	0	60
Montgomery, Philadelphia	10	8	2	0	60
Solomon, San Francisco	10	0	8	2	60
Anderson, St. Louis	9	9	0	0	54
Cain, Atlanta	9	8	1	0	54
Carmichael, Philadelphia	9	0	9	0	54
Cooper, San Francisco	9	5	4	0	54

American Conference

Passing[1]

	Att	Comp	Pct Comp	Yards	Avg Gain	TD	Pct TD	Int	Rating Points
Sipe, Cleveland	554	337	60.8	4132	7.46	30	5.4	14	91.4
Fouts, San Diego	589	348	59.1	4715	8.01	30	5.1	24	84.6
Morton, Denver	301	183	60.8	2150	7.14	12	4.0	13	77.9
Fuller, Kansas City	320	193	60.3	2250	7.03	10	3.1	12	76.1
Jones, Baltimore	446	248	55.6	3134	7.03	23	5.2	21	75.5
Bradshaw, Pittsburgh	424	218	51.4	3339	7.88	24	5.7	22	75.1
Ferguson, Buffalo	439	251	57.2	2805	6.39	20	4.6	18	74.6
Grogan, New England	306	175	57.2	2475	8.09	18	5.9	22	73.1
Plunkett, Oakland	320	165	51.6	2299	7.18	18	5.6	16	72.8
Zorn, Seattle	488	276	56.6	3346	6.86	17	3.5	20	72.4
Stabler, Houston	457	293	64.1	3202	7.01	13	2.8	28	68.6
Anderson, Cincinnati	275	166	60.4	1778	6.47	6	2.2	13	67.1
Woodley, Miami	327	176	53.8	1850	5.66	14	4.3	17	63.2
Todd, N.Y. Jets	479	264	55.1	3329	6.95	17	3.5	30	62.4
Thompson, Cincinnati	234	115	49.1	1324	5.66	11	4.7	12	61.0

(1) At least 192 passes needed to qualify. Leader based on percentage of completions, touchdown passes, interceptions, and average yards.

Rushing

	Att	Yds	Avg	TD
Campbell, Houston	373	1934	5.2	13
Cribbs, Buffalo	306	1185	3.9	11
Pruitt M., Cleveland	249	1034	4.2	6
van Eeghen, Oakland	222	838	3.8	5
Muncie, N.O.-S.D.	175	827	4.7	6
Ferguson, New England	211	818	3.9	2
Dickey, Baltimore	176	800	4.5	11
Harris, Pittsburgh	208	789	3.8	4
Calhoun, New England	200	787	3.9	9
King, Oakland	172	761	4.4	4

Interceptions

	No	Yds	TD
Hayes, Oakland	13	273	1
Barbaro, Kansas City	10	163	0
Schroy, N.Y. Jets	8	91	1
Shell, Pittsburgh	7	135	0
Freeman, Buffalo	7	107	1
Tatum, Houston	7	100	0
Breeden, Cincinnati	7	91	0
Harris, Kansas City	7	54	0
Small, Miami	7	46	0
Ray, N.Y. Jets	6	132	1

Receiving

	No	Yds	Avg	TD
Winslow, San Diego	89	1290	14.5	9
Jefferson, San Diego	82	1340	16.3	13
Joiner, San Diego	71	1132	15.9	4
Largent, Seattle	66	1064	16.1	6
Pruitt M., Cleveland	63	471	7.5	0
McCullum, Seattle	62	874	14.1	6
Carr, Baltimore	61	924	15.1	5
Barber, Houston	59	712	12.1	5
Butler, Buffalo	57	832	14.6	6
Nathan, Miami	57	588	10.3	5

Scoring-Touchdowns

	TD	Rush	Pass	Other	Pts
Campbell, Houston	13	13	0	0	78
Dickey, Baltimore	13	11	2	0	78
Jefferson, San Diego	13	0	13	0	78
Cribbs, Buffalo	12	11	1	0	72
Chandler, Oakland	10	0	10	0	60
Calhoun, New England	9	9	0	0	54
Smith, Pittsburgh	9	0	9	0	54
Winslow, San Diego	9	0	9	0	54
Francis, New England	8	0	8	0	48
Branch, Oakland	7	0	7	0	42

Punting

	No	Yds	Avg
Prestridge, Denver	70	3075	43.9
Guy, Oakland	71	3099	43.6
Roberts, Miami	77	3279	42.6
Ramsey, N.Y. Jets	73	3096	42.4
Weaver, Seattle	67	2798	41.8

	No	Yds	Avg
McInally, Cincinnati	83	3390	40.8
Colquitt, Pittsburgh	61	2483	40.7
Parsley, Houston	67	2727	40.7
Grupp, Kansas City	84	3317	39.5
Partridge, San Diego	60	2347	39.1

Punt Returns

	No	Yds	Avg	TD
Smith, Kansas City	40	581	14.5	2
James, New England	33	331	10.0	1
Bell, Pittsburgh	34	339	10.0	0
Fuller, San Diego	30	298	9.9	0
Upchurch, Denver	37	353	9.5	0
Matthews, Oakland	48	421	8.8	0
Harper, N.Y. Jets	28	242	8.6	0
Lewis, Seattle	41	349	8.5	1
Haynes, New England	17	140	8.2	0
Roaches, Houston	47	384	8.2	0

Scoring-Kicking

	XP-XPA	FG-FGA	Pts
Smith, New England	51-51	26-34	129
Benirschke, San Diego	46-48	24-36	118
Steinfort, Denver	32-33	26-34	110
Bahr, Oakland	41-44	19-37	98
Lowery, Kansas City	37-37	20-26	97
Bahr, Pittsburgh	39-42	19-28	96
Herrera, Seattle	33-33	20-31	93
Cockroft, Cleveland	39-44	16-26	87
Fritsch, Houston	26-27	19-24	83
Mike-Mayer, Baltimore	43-46	12-23	79

Kickoff Returns

	No	Yds	Avg	TD
Ivory, New England	36	992	27.6	1
Lewis, Seattle	25	585	23.4	0
Brunson, Denver	40	923	23.1	0
Wright, Cleveland	25	576	23.0	0
Carson, Kansas City	40	917	22.9	0

	No	Yds	Avg	TD
Glasgow, Baltimore	33	743	22.5	0
Pollard, Pittsburgh	22	494	22.5	0
Bessillieu, Miami	40	890	22.3	0
Harper, N.Y. Jets	49	1070	21.8	0
Hall, Cleveland	32	691	21.6	0

NEA All-NFL Team in 1980

Chosen by team captains, team representatives, and coaches of the 28 NFL teams in a poll conducted by Newspaper Enterprise Assn.

First team	Offense	Second team
James Lofton, Green Bay	Wide receiver	Harold Carmichael, Philadelphia
John Jefferson, San Diego	Wide receiver	Stanley Morgan, New England
Kellen Winslow, San Diego	Tight end	Ozzie Newsome, Cleveland
Mike Kenn, Atlanta	Tackle	Leon Gray, Houston
Dan Dierdorf, St. Louis	Tackle	Marvin Powell, New York Jets
John Hannah, New England	Guard	Doug Wilkerson, San Diego
Herbert Scott, Dallas	Guard	David Scott, Atlanta
Mike Webster, Pittsburgh	Center	Rich Saul, Los Angeles
Brian Sipe, Cleveland	Quarterback	Steve Bartkowski, Atlanta
Walter Payton, Chicago	Running back	Ottis Anderson, St. Louis
Earl Campbell, Houston	Running back	Billy Sims, Detroit
Ed Murray, Detroit	Placekicker	Fred Steinfort, Denver

First team	Defense	Second team
Art Still, Kansas City	End	Jack Youngblood, Los Angeles
Lee Roy Selmon, Tampa Bay	End	Dave Hampton, Chicago
Randy White, Dallas	Tackle	Fred Smerlas, Buffalo
Gary Johnson, San Diego	Tackle	Charles Johnson, Philadelphia
Jack Lambert, Pittsburgh	Middle linebacker	Randy Gradishar, Denver
Ted Hendricks, Oakland	Linebacker	Jack Ham, Pittsburgh
Robert Brazile, Houston	Linebacker	Matt Blair, Minnesota
Lester Hayes, Oakland	Corner back	Mike Haynes, New England
Lemar Parrish, Washington	Corner back	Pat Thomas, Los Angeles
Donnie Shell, Pittsburgh	Safety	Randy Logan, Philadelphia
Nolan Cromwell, Los Angeles	Safety	Gary Barbaro, Kansas City
Dave Jennings, New York Giants	Punter	Ray Guy, Oakland

Pro Football Hall of Fame

Canton, Ohio

Herb Adderley	Art Donovan	Clarke Hinkle	George McAfee	Andy Robustelli
Lance Alworth	Paddy Driscoll	Elroy Hirsch	Hugh McElhenny	Art Rooney
Morris (Red) Badgro	Bill Dudley	Cal Hubbard	John (Blood) McNally	Gale Sayers
Cliff Battles	Turk Edwards	Lamar Hunt	Mike Michalske	Joe Schmidt
Sammy Baugh	Weeb Ewbank	Don Hutson	Wayne Millner	Bart Starr
Chuck Bednarik	Tom Fears	Deacon Jones	Ron Mix	Ernie Stautner
Bert Bell	Ray Flaherty	Walt Kiesling	Lenny Moore	Ken Strong
Raymond Berry	Len Ford	Frank (Bruiser) Kinard	Marion Motley	Joe Stydahar
Charles Bidwell	Dr. Daniel Fortmann	Curly Lambeau	Bronko Nagurski	Jim Taylor
George Blanda	Bill George	Dick (Night Train) Lane	Greasy Neale	Jim Thorpe
Jim Brown	Frank Gifford	Yale Lary	Ernie Nevers	Y. A. Tittle
Paul Brown	Otto Graham	Dante Lavelli	Ray Nitschke	George Trafton
Roosevelt Brown	Red Grange	Bobby Layne	Leo Nomellini	Charlie Trippi
Dick Butkus	Forrest Gregg	Tuffy Leemans	Jim Otto	Emlen Tunnell
Tony Canadeo	Lou Groza	Bob Lilly	Steve Owen	Clyde (Bulldog) Turner
Joe Carr	Joe Guyon	Vince Lombardi	Clarence (Ace) Parker	Norm Van Brocklin
Guy Chamberlin	George Halas	Sid Luckman	Jim Parker	Steve Van Buren
Jack Christiansen	Ed Healey	Link Lyman	Joe Perry	Johnny Unitas
Dutch Clark	Mel Hein	Tim Mara	Pete Pihos	Bob Waterfield
George Connor	Pete Henry	Gino Marchetti	Hugh (Shorty) Ray	Bill Willis
Jim Conzelman	Arnold Herber	George Marshall	Dan Reeves	Larry Wilson
Willie Davis	Bill Hewitt	Ollie Matson	Jim Ringo	Alex Wojciechowicz

National Football Conference Leaders

(National Football League prior to 1970)

Passing / Pass-Receiving

Player, team	Atts	Com	YG	TD	Year	Player, team	Ct	YG	TD
Bart Starr, Green Bay	272	163	2,144	4	1964	Johnny Morris, Chicago	93	1,200	10
Rudy Bukich, Chicago	312	176	2,641	20	1965	Dave Parks, San Francisco	80	1,344	12
Bart Starr, Green Bay	251	156	2,257	3	1966	Charlie Taylor, Washington	72	1,119	12
Sonny Jurgensen, Washington	508	288	3,747	16	1967	Charlie Taylor, Washington	70	990	9
Earl Morrall, Baltimore	317	182	2,909	17	1968	Clifton McNeil, San Francisco	71	944	7
Sonny Jurgensen, Washington	422	274	3,102	15	1969	Dan Abramowicz, New Orleans	73	1,015	7
John Brodie, San Francisco	378	223	2,941	24	1970	Dick Gordon, Chicago	71	1,026	13
Roger Staubach, Dallas	211	126	1,882	15	1971	Bob Tucker, Giants	59	791	4
Norm Snead, N.Y. Giants	325	196	2,307	17	1972	Harold Jackson, Philadelphia	62	1,048	4
Roger Staubach, Dallas	286	179	2,428	23	1973	Harold Carmichael, Philadelphia	67	1,116	9
Sonny Jurgensen, Washington	167	107	1,185	11	1974	Charles Young, Philadelphia	63	696	3
Fran Tarkenton, Minnesota	425	273	2,294	25	1975	Chuck Foreman, Minnesota	73	691	9
James Harris, Los Angeles	158	91	1,460	8	1976	Drew Pearson, Dallas	58	806	6
Roger Staubach, Dallas	361	210	2,620	18	1977	Ahmad Rashad, Minnesota	51	681	2
Roger Staubach, Dallas	413	231	3,190	25	1978	Rickey Young, Minnesota	88	704	5
Roger Staubach, Dallas	461	267	3,586	27	1979	Ahmad Rashad, Minnesota	80	1,156	9
Ron Jaworski, Philadelphia	451	257	3,529	27	1980	Earl Cooper, San Francisco	83	567	4

Scoring / Rushing

Player, team	TD	PAT	FG	Pts	Year	Player, team	Yds	Atts	TD
Lenny Moore, Baltimore	20	0	0	120	1964	Jimmy Brown, Cleveland	1,446	280	7
Gale Sayers, Chicago	22	0	0	132	1965	Jimmy Brown, Cleveland	1,544	289	17
Bruce Gossett, Los Angeles	0	29	28	113	1966	Gale Sayers, Chicago	1,231	229	8
Jim Bakken, St. Louis	0	36	27	117	1967	Leroy Kelly, Cleveland	1,205	235	11
Leroy Kelly, Cleveland	20	0	0	120	1968	Leroy Kelly, Cleveland	1,239	248	16
Fred Cox, Minnesota	0	43	26	121	1969	Gayle Sayers, Chicago	1,032	236	8
Fred Cox, Minnesota	0	35	30	125	1970	Larry Brown, Washington	1,125	237	5
Curt Knight, Washington	0	27	29	114	1971	John Brockington, Green Bay	1,105	216	4
Chester Marcol, Green Bay	0	29	33	128	1972	Larry Brown, Washington	1,216	285	8
David Ray, Los Angeles	0	40	30	130	1973	John Brockington, Green Bay	1,144	265	3
Chester Marcol, Green Bay	0	19	25	94	1974	Larry McCutcheon, Los Angeles	1,109	236	3
Chuck Foreman, Minnesota	22	0	0	132	1975	Jim Otis, St. Louis	1,076	269	5
Mark Moseley, Washington	0	31	22	97	1976	Walter Payton, Chicago	1,390	311	13
Walter Payton, Chicago	16	0	0	96	1977	Walter Payton, Chicago	1,852	339	14
Frank Corrall, Los Angeles	0	31	29	118	1978	Walter Payton, Chicago	1,395	333	11
Mark Moseley, Washington	0	39	25	114	1979	Walter Payton, Chicago	1,610	369	14
Ed Murray, Detroit	0	35	27	116	1980	Walter Payton, Chicago	1,460	317	6

American Football Conference Leaders

(American Football League prior to 1970)

Passing / Pass-Receiving

Player, team	Atts	Com	YG	TD	Year	Player, team	Ct	YG	TD
Len Dawson, Kansas City	354	199	2,879	18	1964	Charlie Hennigan, Houston	101	1,561	8
Jack Hadl, San Diego	348	174	2,798	21	1965	Lionel Taylor, Denver	85	1,131	6
Len Dawson, Kansas City	284	159	2,527	10	1966	Lance Alworth, San Diego	73	1,383	13
Daryle Lamonica, Oakland	425	220	3,228	20	1967	George Sauer, N.Y. Jets	75	1,189	6
Len Dawson, Kansas City	224	131	2,109	9	1968	Lance Alworth, San Diego	68	1,312	10
Greg Cook, Cincinnati	197	106	1,845	11	1969	Lance Alworth, San Diego	64	1,003	4
Daryle Lamonica, Oakland	356	179	2,516	22	1970	Marlin Briscoe, Buffalo	57	1,036	8
Bob Griese, Miami	263	145	2,089	19	1971	Fred Biletnikoff, Oakland	61	929	9
Earl Morrall, Miami	150	83	1,360	11	1972	Fred Biletnikoff, Oakland	58	802	7
Ken Stabler, Oakland	260	163	1,997	14	1973	Fred Willis, Houston	57	371	1
Ken Anderson, Cincinnati	328	213	2,667	18	1974	Lydell Mitchell, Baltimore	72	544	2
Ken Anderson, Cincinnati	377	228	3,169	21	1975	Reggie Rucker, Cleveland	60	770	3
						Lydell Mitchell, Baltimore	60	554	4
Ken Stabler, Oakland	291	194	2,737	27	1976	MacArthur Lane, Kansas City	66	686	1
Bob Griese, Miami	307	180	2,252	22	1977	Lydell Mitchell, Baltimore	71	620	4
Terry Bradshaw, Pittsburgh	368	207	2,915	28	1978	Steve Largent, Seattle	71	1,168	8
Dan Fouts, San Diego	530	332	4,082	24	1979	Joe Washington, Baltimore	82	750	3
Brian Sipe, Cleveland	554	337	4,132	30	1980	Kellen Winslow, San Diego	89	1,290	9

Scoring / Rushing

Player, team	TD	PAT	FG	Pts	Year	Player, team	Yds	Atts	TD
Gino Cappelletti, Boston	7	36	25	155	1964	Cookie Gilchrist, Buffalo	981	230	6
Gino Cappelletti, Boston	9	27	17	132	1965	Paul Lowe, San Diego	1,121	222	7
Gino Cappelletti, Boston	6	35	16	119	1966	Jim Nance, Boston	1,458	299	11
George Blanda, Oakland	0	56	20	116	1967	Jim Nance, Boston	1,216	269	7
Jim Turner, N.Y. Jets	0	43	34	145	1968	Paul Robinson, Cincinnati	1,023	238	8
Jim Turner, N.Y. Jets	0	33	32	129	1969	Dick Post, San Diego	873	182	6
Jan Stenerud, Kansas City	0	26	30	116	1970	Floyd Little, Denver	901	209	3
Garo Yepremian, Miami	0	33	28	117	1971	Floyd Little, Denver	1,133	284	6
Bobby Howfield, N.Y. Jets	0	40	27	121	1972	O.J. Simpson, Buffalo	1,251	292	6
Roy Gerela, Pittsburgh	0	36	29	123	1973	O.J. Simpson, Buffalo	2,003	332	12
Roy Gerela, Pittsburgh	0	33	20	93	1974	Otis Armstrong, Denver	1,407	263	9
O.J. Simpson, Buffalo	23	0	0	138	1975	O.J. Simpson, Buffalo	1,817	329	16
Toni Linhart, Baltimore	0	49	20	109	1976	O.J. Simpson, Buffalo	1,503	290	8
Errol Mann, Oakland	0	39	20	99	1977	Mark van Eeghen, Oakland	1,273	324	7
Pat Leahy, N.Y. Jets	0	41	22	107	1978	Earl Campbell, Houston	1,450	302	13
John Smith, New England	0	46	23	115	1979	Earl Campbell, Houston	1,697	368	19
John Smith, New England	0	51	26	129	1980	Earl Campbell, Houston	1,934	373	13

1981 NFL Player Draft

The following are the first round picks of the National Football League

Team	Player	Pos.	College	Team	Player	Pos.	College
1—New Orleans	George Rogers	RB	South Carolina	16—Detroit	Mark Nichols	WR	San Jose St.
2—N.Y. Giants	Lawrence Taylor	LB	North Carolina	17—Pittsburgh	Keith Gary	DE	Oklahoma
3—N.Y. Jets	Freeman McNeil	RB	UCLA	18—Baltimore	Donnell Thomp-		
4—Seattle	Kenny Easley	DB	UCLA		son	DT	North Carolina
5—St. Louis	E.J. Junior	LB	Alabama	19—New England	Brian Holloway	OT	Stanford
6—Green Bay	Rich Campbell	QB	California	20—Washington	Mark May	OT	Pittsburgh
7—Tampa Bay	Hugh Green	LB	Pittsburgh	21—Oakland	Ted Watts	DB	Texas Tech
8—San Francisco	Ronnie Lott	DB	USC	22—Cleveland	Hanford Dixon	DB	So. Mississippi
9—Los Angeles	Mel Owens	LB	Michigan	23—Oakland	Curt Marsh	OT	Washington
10—Cincinnati	David Verser	WR	Kansas	24—San Diego	James Brooks	RB	Auburn
11—Chicago	Keith Van Horne	OT	USC	25—Atlanta	Bobby Butler	DB	Florida St
12—Baltimore	Randy McMillan	RB	Pittsburgh	26—Dallas	Howard Richards	OT	Missouri
13—Miami	David Overstreet	RB	Oklahoma	27—Philadelphia	Leonard Mitchell	DE	Houston
14—Kansas City	Willie Scott	TE	USC	28—Buffalo	Booker Moore	RB	Penn State
15—Denver	Dennis Smith	DB	USC				

Jim Thorpe Trophy Winners

The winner of the Jim Thorpe Trophy, named after the athletic great, is picked by Murray Olderman of Newspaper Enterprise Assn. in a poll of players from the 28 NFL teams. It goes to the most valuable NFL player and is the oldest and highest professional football award.

Year	Player, team	Year	Player, team
1955	Harlon Hill, Chicago Bears	1968	Earl Morrall, Baltimore Colts
1956	Frank Gifford, N.Y. Giants	1969	Roman Gabriel, Los Angeles Rams
1957	John Unitas, Baltimore Colts	1970	John Brodie, San Francisco 49ers
1958	Jim Brown, Cleveland Browns	1971	Bob Griese, Miami Dolphins
1959	Charley Conerly, N.Y. Giants	1972	Larry Brown, Washington Redskins
1960	Norm Van Brocklin, Philadelphia Eagles	1973	O.J. Simpson, Buffalo Bills
1961	Y.A. Tittle, N.Y. Giants	1974	Ken Stabler, Oakland Raiders
1962	Jim Taylor, Green Bay Packers	1975	Fran Tarkenton, Minnesota Vikings
1963	(tie) Jim Brown, Cleveland Browns,	1976	Bert Jones, Baltimore Colts
	and Y.A. Tittle, N.Y. Giants	1977	Walter Payton, Chicago Bears
1964	Lenny Moore, Baltimore Colts	1978	Earl Campbell, Houston Oilers
1965	Jim Brown, Cleveland Browns	1979	Earl Campbell, Houston Oilers
1966	Bart Starr, Green Bay Packers	1980	Earl Campbell, Houston Oilers
1967	John Unitas, Baltimore Colts		

Bert Bell Memorial Trophy Winners

The Bert Bell Memorial Trophy, named after the former NFL commissioner, is awarded annually to the outstanding rookies in a poll conducted by Murray Olderman of Newspaper Enterprise Assn.

1964	Charlie Taylor, Washington, WR	1973	AFC: Boobie Clark, Cincinnati, RB
1965	Gale Sayers, Chicago, RB		NFC: Chuck Foreman, Minnesota, RB
1966	Tommy Nobis, Atlanta, LB	1974	Don Woods, San Diego, RB
1967	Mel Farr, Detroit, RB	1975	AFC: Robert Brazile, Houston, LB
1968	Earl McCullouch, Detroit, WR		NFC: Steve Bartkowski, Atlanta, QB
1969	Calvin Hill, Dallas, RB	1976	AFC: Mike Haynes, New England, CB
1970	Raymond Chester, Oakland, TE		NFC: Sammy White, Minnesota, WR
1971	AFC: Jim Plunkett, New England, QB	1977	Tony Dorsett, Dallas, RB
	NFC: John Brockington, Green Bay, RB	1978	Earl Campbell, Houston, RB
1972	AFC: Franco Harris, Pittsburgh, RB	1979	Ottis Anderson, St. Louis, RB
	NFC: Willie Buchanon, Green Bay, DB	1980	Billy Sims, Detroit, RB

Football Stadiums

See index for major league baseball seating capacity, and college stadiums.

Name, location	Capacity	Name, location	Capacity
Anaheim Stadium, Anaheim, Cal.	69,000	Los Angeles Memorial Coliseum	93,761
Arrowhead Stadium, Kansas City, Mo.	78,198	Louisiana Superdome, New Orleans	71,330
Atlanta-Fulton County Stadium	60,756	Metropolitan Stadium, Bloomington, Minn.	48,446
Astrodome, Houston, Tex.	50,000	Mile High Stadium, Denver, Col.	75,103
Baltimore Memorial Stadium	60,763	Milwaukee County Stadium	55,958
Buffalo War Memorial Stadium	46,206	Mississippi Memorial Stadium, Jackson	61,000
Busch Memorial Stadium, St. Louis	51,392	Oakland-Alameda County Coliseum	54,615
Candlestick Park, San Francisco, Cal.	61,115	Orange Bowl, Miami, Fla.	75,289
Cleveland Municipal Stadium	80,385	Pontiac Silverdome, Mich.	80,638
Columbus (Ga.) Memorial Stadium	35,000	Rich Stadium, Buffalo, N.Y.	80,020
Cotton Bowl, Dallas, Tex.	72,000	Riverfront Stadium, Cincinnati, Oh.	59,754
Franklin Field, Philadelphia, Pa.	60,546	Rose Bowl, Pasadena, Cal.	106,721
Gator Bowl, Jacksonville, Fla.	70,000	Rubber Bowl, Akron, Oh.	35,007
Giants Stadium, E. Rutherford, N.J.	76,500	San Diego Stadium	52,596
John F. Kennedy Stadium, Philadelphia, Pa.	105,000	Schaefer Stadium, Foxboro, Mass.	61,279
Robert F. Kennedy Memorial Stadium, Wash., D.C.	55,031	Shea Stadium, New York, N.Y.	60,000
Kezar Stadium, San Francisco, Cal.	59,636	Soldier Field, Chicago, Ill.	57,959
Kingdome, Seattle, Wash.	64,752	Sugar Bowl, New Orleans, La.	80,982
Ladd Memorial Stadium, Mobile, Ala.	40,605	Tampa Stadium, Tampa, Fla.	72,126
Lambeau Field, Green Bay, Wis.	56,267	Texas Stadium, Dallas, Tex.	65,101
Legion Field, Birmingham, Ala.	72,000	Three Rivers Stadium, Pittsburgh, Pa.	50,350
Liberty Bowl, Memphis, Tenn.	50,180	Veterans Stadium, Philadelphia, Pa.	71,464

All-Time Pro Football Records

NFL, AFL, and All-American Football Conference
(as of Sept. 5, 1981)

Leading Lifetime Rushers

Player	League	Yrs	Att	Yards	Avg	Player	League	Yrs	Att	Yards	Avg
Jim Brown	NFL	9	2,359	12,312	5.2	Lydell Mitchell	NFL	9	1,675	6,534	3.9
O.J. Simpson	AFL-NFL	11	2,404	11,236	4.7	Lawrence McCutcheon	NFL	9	1,487	6,440	4.3
Joe Perry	AAFC-NFL	16	1,929	9,723	5.0	Floyd Little	AFL-NFL	9	1,641	6,323	3.8
Franco Harris	NFL	9	2,220	9,352	4.2	Don Perkins	NFL	8	1,500	6,217	4.1
Jim Taylor	NFL	10	1,941	8,597	4.4	Ken Willard	NFL	10	1,622	6,105	3.8
Walter Payton	NFL	6	1,865	8,386	4.5	Calvin Hill	NFL	11	1,448	6,060	4.2
Larry Csonka	AFL-NFL	11	1,891	8,081	4.3	Chuck Foreman	NFL	8	1,556	5,950	3.8
Leroy Kelly	NFL	10	1,727	7,274	4.2	Larry Brown	NFL	8	1,530	5,875	3.8
John Riggins	NFL	9	1,666	6,822	4.1	Steve Van Buren	NFL	8	1,320	5,860	4.3
John Henry Johnson	NFL-AFL	13	1,571	6,803	4.3	Bill Brown	NFL	14	1,649	5,838	3.4

Most Yards Gained, Season — 2,003, O.J. Simpson, Buffalo Bills, 1973.
Most Yards Gained, Game — 275, Walter Payton, Chicago Bears vs. Minnesota Vikings, Nov. 20, 1977.
Most Games, 100 Yards or more, Season — 11, O.J. Simpson, Buffalo Bills, 1973; Earl Campbell, Houston Oilers, 1979.
Most Games, 100 Yards or more, Career — 58, Jim Brown, Cleveland Browns, 1957-1965.
Most Games, 200 Yards or more, Career — 6, O.J. Simpson, Buffalo Bills, 1969-1977; San Francisco 49ers, 1978.
Most Touchdowns Rushing, Career — 106, Jim Brown, Cleveland Browns, 1957-1965.
Most Touchdowns Rushing, Season — 19, Jim Taylor, Green Bay Packers, 1962; Earl Campbell, Houston Oilers, 1979.
Most Touchdowns Rushing, Game — 6, Ernie Nevers, Chicago Cardinals vs. Chicago Bears, Nov. 8, 1929.
Most Rushing Attempts, Season — 373, Earl Campbell, Houston Oilers, 1980.
Most Rushing Attempts, Game — 41, Franco Harris, Pittsburgh vs. Cincinnati, Oct. 17, 1976.
Longest run from Scrimmage — 97 yds., Andy Uram, Green Bay vs. Chicago Cardinals, Oct. 8, 1939; Bob Gage, Pittsburgh vs. Chicago Bears, Dec. 4, 1949. (Both scored touchdown).

Leading Lifetime Passers
(Minimum 1,500 attempts)

Player	League	Yrs	Att	Comp	Yds	Pts*	Player	League	Yrs	Att	Comp	Yds	Pts*
Otto Graham	AAFC-NFL	10	2,626	1,464	23,584	86.8	Frank Ryan	NFL	13	2,133	1,090	16,042	77.7
Roger Staubach	NFL	11	2,958	1,685	22,700	83.5	Bob Griese	AFL-NFL	14	3,429	1,926	25,092	77.3
Sonny Jurgensen	NFL	18	4,262	2,433	32,224	82.8	Brian Sipe	NFL	7	2,191	1,239	15,207	76.9
Len Dawson	NFL-AFL	19	3,741	2,136	28,711	82.6	Dan Fouts	NFL	8	2,594	1,489	19,454	75.5
Fran Tarkenton	NFL	18	6,467	3,686	47,003	80.5	Norm Van Brocklin	NFL	12	2,895	1,553	23,611	75.3
Bart Starr	NFL	16	3,149	1,808	24,718	80.3	Sid Luckman	NFL	12	1,744	904	14,686	75.0
Bert Jones	NFL	8	2,038	1,138	14,569	79.2	Don Meredith	NFL	9	2,308	1,170	17,199	74.7
Ken Stabler	AFL-NFL	11	2,938	1,779	22,280	78.2	Roman Gabriel	NFL	15	4,495	2,365	29,429	74.5
Johnny Unitas	NFL	18	5,186	2,830	40,239	78.2	Y.A. Tittle	AAFC-NFL	17	4,395	2,427	33,070	74.4
Ken Anderson	NFL	10	3,060	1,736	21,808	78.0	Earl Morrall	NFL	21	2,689	1,379	20,809	74.2

*Rating points based on performances in the following categories: Percentage of completions, percentage of touchdown passes, percentage of interceptions, and average gain per pass attempt.

Most Yards Gained, Season — 4,715, Dan Fouts, San Diego Chargers, 1980.
Most Yards Gained, Game — 554, Norm Van Brocklin, Los Angeles Rams vs. New York Yankees, Sept. 18, 1951 (27 completions in 41 attempts).
Most Touchdowns Passing, Career — 342, Fran Tarkenton, Minnesota Vikings, 1961-65; N.Y. Giants, 1967-71; Minnesota Vikings, 1972-78.
Most Touchdown Passing, Season — 36, George Blanda, Houston Oilers, 1961 and Y.A. Tittle, N.Y. Giants, 1963.
Most Touchdown Passing, Game — 7, Sid Luckman, Chicago Bears vs. New York Giants, Nov. 14, 1943; Adrian Burk, Philadelphia Eagles vs. Washington Redskins, Oct. 17, 1954; George Blanda, Houston Oilers vs. New York Titans, Nov. 19, 1961; Y.A. Tittle, New York Giants vs. Washington Redskins, Oct. 28, 1962; Joe Kapp, Minnesota Vikings vs. Baltimore Colts, Sept. 28, 1969.
Most Passing Attempts, Season — 589, Dan Fouts, San Diego Chargers, 1980.
Most Passing Attempts, Game — 68, George Blanda, Houston Oilers vs. Buffalo Bills, Nov. 1, 1964 (37 completions).
Most Passes Completed, Season — 348, Dan Fouts, San Diego Chargers, 1980.
Most Passes Completed, Game — 42, Richard Todd, N.Y. Jets vs. San Francisco 49ers, Sept. 21, 1980.
Most Consecutive Passes Completed — 17, Bert Jones, Baltimore Colts vs. N.Y. Jets, Dec. 15, 1974.

Leading Lifetime Receivers

Player	League	Yrs	No	Yds	Avg	Player	League	Yrs	No	Yds	Avg
Charley Taylor	NFL	13	649	9,110	14.0	Jackie Smith	NFL	16	488	7,991	16.4
Don Maynard	AFL-NFL	15	633	11,834	18.7	Art Powell	AFL-NFL	10	479	8,046	16.8
Ray Berry	NFL	13	631	9,275	14.7	Boyd Dowler	NFL	12	474	7,270	15.4
Fred Biletnikoff	AFL-NFL	14	589	8,974	15.2	Harold Carmichael	NFL	9	455	6,895	15.2
Lionel Taylor	AFL	10	567	7,195	12.7	Pete Retzlaff	NFL	11	452	7,412	16.4
Lance Alworth	AFL-NFL	11	542	10,266	18.9	Roy Jefferson	NFL	12	451	7,539	16.7
Harold Jackson	NFL	13	532	9,577	18.0	Carroll Dale	NFL	14	438	8,271	18.9
Bobby Mitchell	NFL	11	521	7,954	15.3	Haven Moses	AFL-NFL	13	433	7,845	18.1
Billy Howton	NFL	12	503	8,459	16.8	Paul Warfield	NFL	13	427	8,565	20.1
Tommy McDonald	NFL	12	495	8,410	17.0	Mike Ditka	NFL	12	427	5,812	13.6
Don Hutson	NFL	11	488	7,991	16.4						

Most Yards Gained, Season — 1,746, Charley Hennigan, Houston Oilers, 1961.
Most Yards Gained, Game — 303, Jim Benton, Cleveland Rams vs. Detroit Lions, Nov. 22, 1945 (10 receptions).
Most Pass Receptions, Season — 101, Charley Hennigan, Houston Oilers, 1964.
Most Pass Receptions, Game — 18, Tom Fears, Los Angeles Rams vs. Green Bay Packers, Dec. 3, 1950 (189 yards).
Most Consecutive Games, Pass Receptions — 127, Harold Carmichael, Philadelphia Eagles, 1972-1980.
Most Touchdown Passes, Career — 99, Don Hutson, Green Bay Packers, 1935-1945.
Most Touchdown Passes, Season — 17, Don Hutson, Green Bay Packers, 1942; Elroy Hirsch, Los Angeles Rams, 1951; Bill Groman, Houston Oilers, 1961.
Most Touchdown Passes, Game — 5, Bob Shaw, Chicago Cardinals vs. Baltimore Colts, Oct. 2, 1950.
Most Consecutive Games, Touchdown Passes — 11, Elroy Hirsch, Los Angeles Rams, 1950-1951; Buddy Dial, Pittsburgh Steelers, 1959-1960.

Leading Lifetime Scorers

Player	League	Yrs	TD	PAT	FG	Total	Player	League	Yrs	TD	PAT	FG	Total
George Blanda	NFL-AFL	26	9	943	335	2,002	Lou Michaels	NFL	13	1	386	187	955*
Lou Groza	AAFC-NFL	21	1	810	264	1,608	*Includes safety.						
Jim Turner	AFL-NFL	16	1	521	304	1,439	Roy Gerela	AFL-NFL	11	0	351	184	903
Jim Bakken	NFL	17	0	534	282	1,380	Bobby Walston	NFL	12	46	365	80	881
Fred Cox	NFL	15	0	519	282	1,365	Pete Gogolak	AFL-NFL	10	0	344	173	863
Jan Stenerud	AFL-NFL	14	0	397	282	1,243	Errol Mann	NFL	11	0	315	177	846
Gino Cappelletti	AFL	11	42	350	176	1,130	Don Hutson	NFL	11	105	172	7	823
Don Cockroft	NFL	13	0	432	216	1,080	Mark Moseley	NFL	10	0	262	170	772
Garo Yepremian	AFL-NFL	13	0	438	208	1,062	Paul Hornung	NFL	9	62	190	66	760
Bruce Gossett	NFL	11	0	374	219	1,031	Jim Brown	NFL	9	126	0	0	756
Sam Baker	NFL	15	2	428	179	977							

Most Points, Season — 176, Paul Hornung, Green Bay Packers, 1960 (15 TD's, 41 PAT's, 15 FG's).
Most Points, Game — 40, Ernie Nevers, Chicago Cardinals vs. Chicago Bears, Nov. 28, 1929 (6 TD's, 4 PAT's).
Most Touchdowns, Season — 23, O.J. Simpson, Buffalo Bills, 1975 (16 rushing, 9 pass receptions).
Most Touchdowns, Game — 6, Ernie Nevers, Chicago Cardinals vs. Chicago Bears, Nov. 28, 1929 (6 rushing); Dub Jones, Cleveland Browns vs. Chicago Bears, Nov. 25, 1951 (4 rushing, 2 pass receptions); Gale Sayers, Chicago Bears vs. San Francisco 49ers, Dec. 12, 1965 (4 rushing, 1 pass reception, 1 punt return).
Most Points After Touchdown, Season — 64, George Blanda, Houston Oilers, 1961 (65 attempts).
Most Consecutive Points After Touchdown — 234, Tommy Davis, San Francisco 49ers, 1959-1965.
Most Field Goals, Game — 7, Jim Bakken, St. Louis Cardinals vs. Pittsburgh Steelers, Sept. 24, 1967.
Most Field Goals, Season — 34, Jim Turner, New York Jets, 1968 and 1969.
Most Field Goals Attempted, Season — 49, Bruce Gossett, Los Angeles Rams, 1966; Curt Knight, Washington Redskins, 1971.
Most Field Goals Attempted, Game — 9, Jim Bakken, St. Louis Cardinals vs. Pittsburgh Steelers, Sept. 24, 1967 (7 successful).
Most Consecutive Field Goals — 20, Garo Yepremian, Miami Dolphins, 1978, New Orleans Saints, 1979.
Most Consecutive Games, Field Goal — 31, Fred Cox, Minnesota Vikings, 1968-1970.
Longest Field Goal — 63 yds., Tom Dempsey, New Orleans Saints vs. Detroit Lions, Nov. 8, 1970.
Highest Field Goal Completion Percentage, Season (14 attempts) — 88.46, Lou Groza, Cleveland Browns, 1953 (23 FG's in 26 attempts).

Pass Interceptions

Most Passes Had Intercepted, Game — 8, Jim Hardy, Chicago Cardinals vs. Philadelphia Eagles, Sept. 24, 1950 (39 attempts).
Most Passes Had Intercepted, Season — 42, George Blanda, Houston Oilers, 1962 (418 attempts).
Most Passes Had Intercepted, Career — 277, George Blanda, Chicago Bears, 1949-1958; Houston Oilers, 1960-1966; Oakland Raiders, 1967-1975 (4,000 attempts).
Most Consecutive Passes Attempted Without Interception — 294, Bart Starr, Green Bay Packers, 1964-1965.
Most Interceptions By, Season — 14, Dick Lane, Los Angeles Rams, 1952.
Most Interceptions By, Career — 81, Paul Krause, Washington Redskins, 1964-67; Minnesota Vikings, 1968-79.
Most Consecutive Games, Passes Intercepted By — 8, Tom Morrow, Oakland Raiders, 1962 (4), 1963 (4).
Most Touchdowns Scored via Pass Interceptions, Lifetime — 9, Ken Houston, Houston Oilers, 1967 (2); 1968 (2); 1969; 71 (4).

Punting

Highest Punting Average, Career (300 punts) — 45.10, Sam Baugh, Washington Redskins, 1937-1952 (338 punts).
Highest Punting Average, Season (20 punts) — 51.3, Sam Baugh, Washington Redskins, 1940 (35 punts).
Longest Punt — 98 yds., Steve O'Neal, New York Jets vs. Denver Broncos, Sept. 21, 1969.

Kickoff Returns

Most Yardage Returning Kickoffs, Career — 6,922, Ron Smith, Chicago Bears, 1965; Atlanta Falcons, 1966-67; Los Angeles Rams, 1968-69; Chicago Bears, 1970-72; San Diego Chargers, 1973; Oakland Raiders, 1974.
Most Yardage Returning Kickoffs, Season — 1,317, Bobby Jancik, Houston Oilers, 1963.
Most Yardage Returning Kickoffs, Game — 294, Wally Triplett, Detroit Lions vs. Los Angeles Rams, Oct. 29, 1950 (4 returns).
Most Touchdowns Scored via Kickoff Returns, Career — 6, Ollie Matson, Chicago Cardinals, 1952 (2), 1954, 1956, 1958 (2); Gale Sayers, Chicago Bears, 1965, 1966 (2), 1967 (3); Travis Williams, Green Bay Packers, 1967 (4), 1969; Los Angeles Rams, 1971.
Most Touchdowns Scored via Kickoff Returns, Season — 4, Travis Williams, Green Bay Packers, 1967; Cecil Turner, Chicago Bears, 1970.
Most Touchdowns Scored via Kickoff Returns, Game — 2, Tim Brown, Philadelphia Eagles vs. Dallas Cowboys, Nov. 6, 1966; Travis Williams, Green Bay Packers vs. Cleveland Browns, Nov. 12, 1967.
Most Kickoff Returns, Career — 275, Ron Smith, Chicago Bears, 1965; Atlanta Falcons, 1966-67; Los Angeles Rams, 1968-69; Chicago Bears, 1970-72; San Diego Chargers, 1973; Oakland Raiders, 1974.
Most Kickoff Returns, Season — 55, Bruce Harper, New York Jets, 1978, 1979; David Turner, Cincinnati Bengals, 1979.
Longest Kickoff Return — 106 yds., Al Carmichael, Green Bay Packers vs. Chicago Bears, October 7, 1956; Noland Smith, Kansas City vs. Denver, Dec. 17, 1967; Roy Green, St. Louis Cardinals vs. Dallas Cowboys, Oct. 21, 1979 (all scored TD).

Punt Returns

Most Yardage Returning Punts, Career — 2,651, Rick Upchurch, Denver Broncos, 1975-1980.
Most Yardage Returning Punts, Season — 655, Neal Colzie, Oakland Raiders, 1975.
Most Yardage Returning Punts, Game — 205, George Atkinson, Oakland Raiders vs. Buffalo Bills, Sept. 15, 1968.
Most Touchdowns Scored via Punt Returns, Career — 8, Jack Christiansen, Detroit Lions, 1951 (4), 1952 (2), 1954, 1956.
Most Punt Returns, Career — 258, Emlen Tunnell, New York Giants, 1948-1958; Green Bay Packers, 1959-1961.
Most Punt Returns, Season — 70, Danny Reece, Tampa Bay Buccaneers, 1979.
Longest Punt Return — 98 yards, Gil LeFebvre, Cincinnati Reds vs. Brooklyn Dodgers, Dec. 3, 1933; Charles West, Minnesota Vikings vs. Washington Redskins, Nov. 3, 1968; Dennis Morgan, Dallas Cowboys vs. St. Louis Cardinals, Oct. 13, 1974 (all scored TD).

Miscellaneous Records

Most Fumbles, Season — 17, Dan Pastorini, Houston Oilers, 1973.
Most Fumbles, Game — 7, Len Dawson, Kansas City Chiefs vs. San Diego Chargers, Nov. 15, 1964.
Longest Winning Streak (regular season) — 17 games, Chicago Bears, 1933-1934.
Longest Undefeated Streak (includes tie games) — 29 games, Cleveland Browns, 1047 1040 (won 27, tied 2).
Most Seasons, Active Player — 26, George Blanda, Chicago Bears, 1949-1958; Houston Oilers, 1960-1966 and Oakland, 67-75.

American Football League

Year	Eastern Division	Western Division	Playoff
1960	Houston Oilers (10-4-0)	L. A. Chargers (10-4-0)	Houston 24, Los Angeles 16
1961	Houston Oilers (10-3-1)	San Diego Chargers (12-2-0)	Houston 10, San Diego 3
1962	Houston Oilers (11-3-0)	Dallas Texans (11-3-0)	Dallas 20, Houston 17(b)
1963	Boston Patriots (8-6-1)(a)	San Diego Chargers (11-3-0)	San Diego 51, Boston 10
1964	Buffalo Bills (12-2-0)	San Diego Chargers (8-5-1)	Buffalo 20, San Diego 7
1965	Buffalo Bills (10-3-1)	San Diego Chargers (9-2-3)	Buffalo 23, San Diego 0
1966	Buffalo Bills (9-4-1)	Kansas City Chiefs (11-2-1)	Kansas City 31, Buffalo 7
1967	Houston Oilers (9-4-1)	Oakland Raiders (13-1-0)	Oakland 40, Houston 7
1968	New York Jets (11-3-0)	Oakland Raiders (12-2-0)(a)	New York 27, Oakland 23
1969	New York Jets (10-4-0)	Oakland Raiders (12-1-1)	Kansas City 17, Oakland 7(c)

(a) won divisional playoff (b) won at 2:45 of second overtime. (c) Kansas City defeated Jets to make playoffs.

Canadian Football League

Final 1980 Standings

Eastern Conference

	W	L	T	PF	PA	Pts
Hamilton Tiger–Cats	8	7	1	332	377	17
Montreal Alouettes	8	8	0	356	375	16
Ottawa Rough Riders	7	9	0	353	393	14
Toronto Argonauts	6	10	0	334	358	12

Western Conference

	W	L	T	PF	PA	Pts
Edmonton Eskimos	13	3	0	505	281	26
Winnipeg Blue Bombers	10	6	0	394	387	20
Calgary Stampeders	9	7	0	407	355	18
B.C. Lions	8	7	1	381	351	17
Saskatchewan Roughriders	2	14	0	284	469	4

East semifinal—Montreal 25, Ottawa 21.
West semifinal—Winnipeg 32, Calgary 14.
East final—Hamilton 24, Montreal 13.

West final—Edmonton 34, Winnipeg 24.
Championship (Grey Cup)—Edmonton 48, Hamilton 10.

Canadian Football League (Grey Cup)

Winners of Eastern and Western divisions meet in championship game for Grey Cup (donated by Governor-General Earl Grey in 1909). Canadian football features 3 downs, 110-yard field, and each team can have 12 players on field at one time.

1949	Montreal Alouettes 28, Calgary Stampeders 15	1965	Hamilton Tiger-Cats 22, Winnipeg Blue Bombers 16
1950	Toronto Argonauts 13, Winnipeg Blue Bombers 0	1966	Saskatchewan Roughriders 29, Ottawa Rough Riders 14
1951	Ottawa Rough Riders 21, Saskatchewan Roughriders 14	1967	Hamilton Tiger-Cats 24, Saskatchewan Roughriders 1
1952	Toronto Argonauts 21, Edmonton Eskimos 11	1968	Ottawa Rough Riders 24, Calgary Stampeders 21
1953	Hamilton Tiger-Cats 12, Winnipeg Blue Bombers 6	1969	Ottawa Rough Riders 29, Saskatchewan Roughriders 11
1954	Edmonton Eskimos 26, Montreal Alouettes 25	1970	Montreal Alouettes 23, Calgary Stampeders 10
1955	Edmonton Eskimos 34, Montreal Alouettes 19	1971	Calgary Stampeders 14, Toronto Argonauts 11
1956	Edmonton Eskimos 50, Montreal Alouettes 27	1972	Hamilton Tiger-Cats 13, Saskatchewan Roughriders 10
1957	Hamilton Tiger-Cats 32, Winnipeg Blue Bombers 7	1973	Ottawa Rough Riders 22, Edmonton Eskimos 18
1958	Winnipeg Blue Bombers 35, Hamilton Tiger-Cats 28	1974	Montreal Alouettes 20, Edmonton Eskimos 7
1959	Winnipeg Blue Bombers 21, Hamilton Tiger-Cats 7	1975	Edmonton Eskimos 9, Montreal Alouettes 8
1960	Ottawa Rough Riders 16, Edmonton Eskimos 6	1976	Ottawa Rough Riders 23, Saskatchewan Roughriders 20
1961	Winnipeg Blue Bombers 21, Hamilton Tiger-Cats 14	1977	Montreal Alouettes 41, Edmonton Eskimos 6
1962	Winnipeg Blue Bombers 28, Hamilton Tiger-Cats 27	1978	Edmonton Eskimos 20, Montreal Alouettes 13
1963	Hamilton Tiger-Cats 21, British Columbia Lions 10	1979	Edmonton Eskimos 17, Montreal Alouettes 9
1964	British Columbia Lions 34, Hamilton Tiger-Cats 24	1980	Edmonton Eskimos 48, Hamilton Tiger-Cats 10

Table Tennis in 1980-81

U.S. National Table Tennis Closed

Las Vegas, Nev., Dec. 11-14, 1980

Men's Singles — Dan Seemiller, Pittsburgh, Pa.
Women's singles — Heja Lee, Las Vegas, Nev.
Mixed Doubles — Rick Seemiller & Cheryl Dadian, Pittsburgh Pa., & Milwaukee, Wis.

Women's Doubles — Heja Lee & Angie Sistrunk, Las Vegas, Nev. & San Diego, Cal.
Men's Doubles — Dan & Rick Seemiller, Pittsburgh, Pa.

36th World Table Tennis Championships

Novi Sad, Yugoslavia, Apr. 14-26, 1981

Men's Singles — Guo Yuehua, China.
Women's Singles — Tong Ling, China.
Mixed Doubles — Xie Saike & Huang Junqun, China.
Women's Doubles — Cao Yanhua & Zhang Deying, China.

Men's Doubles — Cai Zhenhua & Li Zhenshi, China.
Men's team (Swaythling Cup) — China.
Women's team (Corbillon Cup) — China.

U.S. National Table Tennis Open

Princeton, N.J., June 17-21, 1981

Men's Singles — Xie Saike, China.
Women's Singles — Tong Ling, China.
Mixed Doubles — Cai Zhenhua & Zhang Deying, China.
Women's Doubles — An Hae Sook & Hwang Nam Sook, South Korea.

Men's Doubles — Kim Wan & Yoo Si Hung, South Korea.
Men's team — China.
Women's team — China.

Golf Records

United States Open

Year	Winner	Year	Winner	Year	Winner	Year	Winner
1899	Willie Smith	1920	Edward Ray	1940	Lawson Little	1963	Julius Boros
1900	Harry Vardon	1921	Jim Barnes	1941	Craig Wood	1964	Ken Venturi
1901	Willie Anderson	1922	Gene Sarazen	1942-45	(Not played)	1965	Gary Player
1902	L. Auchterlonie	1923	Bobby Jones*	1946	Lloyd Mangrum	1966	Billy Casper
1903	Willie Anderson	1924	Cyril Walker	1947	L. Worsham	1967	Jack Nicklaus
1904	Willie Anderson	1925	Willie MacFarlane	1948	Ben Hogan	1968	Lee Trevino
1905	Willie Anderson	1926	Bobby Jones*	1949	Cary Middlecoff	1969	Orville Moody
1906	Alex Smith	1927	Tommy Armour	1950	Ben Hogan	1970	Tony Jacklin
1907	Alex Ross	1928	John Farrell	1951	Ben Hogan	1971	Lee Trevino
1908	Fred McLeod	1929	Bobby Jones*	1952	Julius Boros	1972	Jack Nicklaus
1909	George Sargent	1930	Bobby Jones*	1953	Ben Hogan	1973	Johnny Miller
1910	Alex Smith	1931	Wm. Burke	1954	Ed Furgol	1974	Hale Irwin
1911	John McDermott	1932	Gene Sarazen	1955	Jack Fleck	1975	Lou Graham
1912	John McDermott	1933	John Goodman*	1956	Cary Middlecoff	1976	Jerry Pate
1913	Francis Ouimet*	1934	Olin Dutra	1957	Dick Mayer	1977	Hubert Green
1914	Walter Hagen	1935	Sam Parks Jr.	1958	Tommy Bolt	1978	Andy North
1915	Jerome Travers*	1936	Tony Manero	1959	Billy Casper	1979	Hale Irwin
1916	Chick Evans*	1937	Ralph Guldahl	1960	Arnold Palmer	1980	Jack Nicklaus
1917-18	(Not played)	1938	Ralph Guldahl	1961	Gene Littler	1981	David Graham
1919	Walter Hagen	1939	Byron Nelson	1962	Jack Nicklaus		

*Amateur

U.S. Women's Open Golf Champions

Year	Winner	Year	Winner	Year	Winner	Year	Winner
1948	"Babe" Zaharias	1957	Betsy Rawls	1966	Sandra Spuzich	1974	Sandra Haynie
1949	Louise Suggs	1958	Mickey Wright	1967	Catherine Lacoste*	1975	Sandra Palmer
1950	"Babe" Zaharias	1959	Mickey Wright	1968	Susie Maxwell Berning	1976	JoAnne Carner
1951	Betsy Rawls	1960	Betsy Rawls	1969	Donna Caponi	1977	Hollis Stacy
1952	Louise Suggs	1961	Mickey Wright	1970	Donna Caponi	1978	Hollis Stacy
1953	Betsy Rawls	1962	Marie Lindstrom	1971	JoAnne Carner	1979	Jerilyn Britz
1954	"Babe" Zaharias	1963	Mary Mills	1972	Susie Maxwell Berning	1980	Amy Alcott
1955	Fay Crocker	1964	Mickey Wright	1973	Susie Maxwell Berning	1981	Pat Bradley
1956	Mrs. K. Cornelius	1965	Carol Mann				

*Amateur

Masters Golf Tournament Champions

Year	Winner	Year	Winner	Year	Winner	Year	Winner
1934	Horton Smith	1948	Claude Harmon	1960	Arnold Palmer	1971	Charles Coody
1935	Gene Sarazen	1949	Sam Snead	1961	Gary Player	1972	Jack Nicklaus
1936	Horton Smith	1950	Jimmy Demaret	1962	Arnold Palmer	1973	Tommy Aaron
1937	Byron Nelson	1951	Ben Hogan	1963	Jack Nicklaus	1974	Gary Player
1938	Henry Picard	1952	Sam Snead	1964	Arnold Palmer	1975	Jack Nicklaus
1939	Ralph Guldahl	1953	Ben Hogan	1965	Jack Nicklaus	1976	Ray Floyd
1940	Jimmy Demaret	1954	Sam Snead	1966	Jack Nicklaus	1977	Tom Watson
1941	Craig Wood	1955	Cary Middlecoff	1967	Gay Brewer Jr.	1978	Gary Player
1942	Byron Nelson	1956	Jack Burke	1968	Bob Goalby	1979	Fuzzy Zoeller
1943-1945	(Not played)	1957	Doug Ford	1969	George Archer	1980	Severiano Ballesteros
1946	Herman Keiser	1958	Arnold Palmer	1970	Billy Casper	1981	Tom Watson
1947	Jimmy Demaret	1959	Art Wall Jr.				

Professional Golfer's Association Championships

Year	Winner	Year	Winner	Year	Winner	Year	Winner
1920	Jock Hutchison	1936	Denny Shute	1952	James Turnesa	1967	Don January
1921	Walter Hagen	1937	Denny Shute	1953	Walter Burkemo	1968	Julius Boros
1922	Gene Sarazen	1938	Paul Runyan	1954	Melvin Harbert	1969	Ray Floyd
1923	Gene Sarazen	1939	Henry Picard	1955	Doug Ford	1970	Dave Stockton
1924	Walter Hagen	1940	Byron Nelson	1956	Jack Burke	1971	Jack Nicklaus
1925	Walter Hagen	1941	Victor Ghezzi	1957	Lionel Hebert	1972	Gary Player
1926	Walter Hagen	1942	Sam Snead	1958	Dow Finsterwald	1973	Jack Nicklaus
1927	Walter Hagen	1944	Bob Hamilton	1959	Bob Rosburg	1974	Lee Trevino
1928	Leo Diegel	1945	Byron Nelson	1960	Jay Hebert	1975	Jack Nicklaus
1929	Leo Diegel	1946	Ben Hogan	1961	Jerry Barber	1976	Dave Stockton
1930	Tommy Armour	1947	Jim Ferrier	1962	Gary Player	1977	Lanny Wadkins
1931	Tom Creavy	1948	Ben Hogan	1963	Jack Nicklaus	1978	John Mahaffey
1932	Olin Dutra	1949	Sam Snead	1964	Bob Nichols	1979	David Graham
1933	Gene Sarazen	1950	Chandler Harper	1965	Dave Marr	1980	Jack Nicklaus
1934	Paul Runyan	1951	Sam Snead	1966	Al Geiberger	1981	Larry Nelson
1935	Johnny Revolta						

Canadian Open Golf Champions

Year	Winner	Year	Winner	Year	Winner	Year	Winner
1946	George Fazio	1955	Arnold Palmer	1964	Kel Nagle	1973	Tom Weiskopf
1947	Bobby Locke	1956	Doug Sanders	1965	Gene Littler	1974	Bobby Nichols
1948	C.W. Congdon	1957	George Bayer	1966	Don Massengale	1975	Tom Weiskopf
1949	E.J. Harrison	1958	Wes Ellis Jr.	1967	Billy Casper	1976	Jerry Pate
1950	Jim Ferrier	1959	Doug Ford	1968	Bob Charles	1977	Lee Trevino
1951	Jim Ferrier	1960	Art Wall, Jr.	1969	Tommy Aaron	1978	Bruce Lietzke
1952	John Palmer	1961	Jacky Cupit	1970	Kermit Zarley	1979	Lee Trevino
1953	Dave Douglas	1962	Ted Kroll	1971	Lee Trevino	1980	Bob Gilder
1954	Pat Fletcher	1963	Doug Ford	1972	Gay Brewer	1981	Peter Oosterhuis

Professional Golf Tournaments in 1981

Date	Event	Winner	Score	Prize
Jan. 11	Tucson Open	Johnny Miller	265	$54,000
Jan. 25	Phoenix Open	David Graham	268	54,000
Feb. 2	Bing Crosby National Pro-Am, Pebble Beach, Cal.	John Cook	*209	40,000
Feb. 8	San Diego Open	Bruce Lietzke	*278	45,000
Feb. 15	Hawaiian Open, Honolulu	Hale Irwin	265	58,500
Feb. 22	Glenn Campbell-Los Angeles Open	Johnny Miller	270	54,000
Mar. 1	Bay Hill Classic, Orlando, Fla.	Andy Bean	266	54,000
Mar. 8	American Motors Inverrary Classic, Lauderhill, Fla.	Tom Kite	274	54,000
Mar. 15	Doral Open, Miami, Fla.	Ray Floyd	273	45,000
Mar. 23	Tournament Players Championship, Ponte Vedra Beach, Fla.	Ray Floyd	285	72,000
Mar. 29	Heritage Classic, Hilton Head, S.C.	Bill Rogers	278	54,000
Apr. 5	Greater Greensboro Open, N.C.	Larry Nelson	*281	54,000
Apr. 12	Masters Tournament, Augusta, Ga.	Tom Watson	208	60,000
Apr. 19	Tournament of Champions, Carlsbad, Cal.	Lee Trevino	273	54,000
Apr. 26	New Orleans Open	Tom Watson	270	63,000
May 4	Houston Open	Ron Streck	198	47,250
May 10	Byron Nelson Classic, Dallas, Tex.	Bruce Lietzke	*281	54,000
May 17	Colonial National Tournament, Ft. Worth, Tex.	Fuzzy Zoeller	274	54,000
May 23	Memorial Tournament, Dublin, Oh.	Keith Fergus	284	63,000
May 31	Kemper Open, Bethesda, Md.	Craig Stadler	270	72,000
June 7	Atlanta Classic	Tom Watson	277	54,000
June 14	Westchester Classic, Harrison, N.Y.	Ray Floyd	275	72,000
June 21	U.S. Open, Ardmore, Pa.	David Graham	273	55,000
June 28	Danny Thomas-Memphis Classic	Jerry Pate	274	54,000
July 5	Western Open, Oak Brook, Ill.	Ed Fiori	277	54,000
July 12	Greater Milwaukee Open	Jay Haas	274	45,000
July 19	Quad Cities Open, Coal Valley, Ill.	Dave Barr	*270	36,000
July 26	Anheuser-Busch Classic, Williamsburg, Va.	John Mahaffey	276	54,000
Aug. 2	Canadian Open, Oakville, Ont.	Peter Oosterhuis	280	76,500
Aug. 9	PGA Championship, Duluth, Ga.	Larry Nelson	273	80,000
Aug. 16	Greater Hartford Open	Hubie Green	264	54,000
Aug. 23	Buick Open, Grand Blanc, Mich.	Hale Irwin	*277	63,000
Aug. 30	World Series of Golf, Akron, Oh.	Bill Rogers	275	100,000
Sept. 6	B.C. Open, Endicott, N.Y.	Jay Haas	270	45,000
Sept. 13	Pleasant Valley Classic, Sutton, Mass.	Jack Renner	273	54,000

Women

Date	Event	Winner	Score	Prize
Feb. 1	Deer Creek Championship, Deerfield, Fla.	Sandra Palmer	284	$15,000
Feb. 8	Elizabeth Arden Champsionship, N. Miami Beach, Fla.	Sally Little	*283	18,750
Feb. 22	Bent Tree Classic, Sarasota, Fla.	Amy Alcott	276	22,500
Mar. 8	Arizona Copper Tournament, Tucson, Ariz.	Nancy Lopez-Melton	278	18,750
Mar. 15	Sun City Classic, Sun City, Ariz.	Patty Hayes	277	15,000
Mar. 22	Desert Inn Pro-Am, Las Vegas, Nev.	Donna Caponi	286	30,000
Mar. 29	Women's Kemper Open, Costa Mesa, Cal.	Pat Bradley	284	26,250
Apr. 5	Colgate-Dinah Shore, Rancho Mirage, Cal.	Nancy Lopez-Melton	277	37,500
Apr. 12	American Defender Open, Raleigh, N.C.	Donna Caponi	208	18,750
Apr. 19	Lady Citrus, Orlando, Fla.	Beth Daniel	*209	15,000
Apr. 26	Birmingham Classic, Birmingham, Ala.	Beth Solomon	*206	15,000
May 3	Women's International, Hilton Head, S.C.	Sally Little	*287	18,750
May 10	Lady Michelob, Roswell, Ga.	Amy Alcott	209	18,750
May 17	Coca-Cola Classic, Paramus, N.J.	Kathy Whitworth	*211	18,750
May 24	Corning Classic, Corning, N.Y.	Kathy Hite	282	18,750
May 31	Golden Lights Classic, Greenwich, Conn.	Cathy Reynolds	285	18,750
June 7	McDonald's Open, Malvern, Pa.	Sandra Post	282	22,500
June 14	LPGA Championship, Kings Island, Oh.	Donna Caponi	280	22,500
June 21	Lady Keystone Open, Hershey, Pa.	JoAnne Carner	203	18,750
July 5	Peter Jackson Classic, Dorion, Que.	Jan Stephenson	278	30,000
July 12	Mayflower Classic, Indianapolis, Ind.	Debbie Austin	279	22,500
July 19	WUI Classic, Jericho, N.Y.	Donna Caponi	282	18,750
July 26	U.S. Women's Open, La Grange, Ill.	Pat Bradley	279	22,000
Aug. 9	West Virginia Classic, Wheeling, W. Va.	Hollis Stacey	*212	18,750
Aug. 16	Mary Kay Classic, Dallas, Tex.	Jan Stephenson	198	23,250
Aug. 23	World Championship of Women's Golf, Shaker Heights, Oh.	Beth Daniel	284	50,000
Aug. 30	Columbia Savings Classic, Denver, Col.	JoAnne Carner	278	22,500
Sept. 13	United Virginia Bank Classic, Suffolk, Va.	Jan Stephenson	205	18,750

*Won playoff.

British Open Golf Champions

Year	Winner	Year	Winner	Year	Winner	Year	Winner
1914	Harry Vardon	1933	Denny Shute	1953	Ben Hogan	1968	Gary Player
1915-19	(Not played)	1934	Henry Cotton	1954	Peter Thomson	1969	Tony Jacklin
1920	George Duncan	1935	Alf Perry	1955	Peter Thomson	1970	Jack Nicklaus
1921	Jock Hutchison	1936	Alf Padgham	1956	Peter Thomson	1971	Lee Trevino
1922	Walter Hagen	1937	T.H. Cotton	1957	Bobby Locke	1972	Lee Trevino
1923	Arthur Havers	1938	R.A. Whitcombe	1958	Peter Thomson	1973	Tom Weiskopf
1924	Walter Hagen	1939	Richard Burton	1959	Gary Player	1974	Gary Player
1925	Jim Barnes	1940-45	(Not played)	1960	Ken Nagle	1975	Tom Watson
1926	Bobby Jones	1946	Sam Snead	1961	Arnold Palmer	1976	Johnny Miller
1927	Bobby Jones	1947	Fred Daly	1962	Arnold Palmer	1977	Tom Watson
1928	Walter Hagen	1948	Henry Cotton	1963	Bob Charles	1978	Jack Nicklaus
1929	Walter Hagen	1949	Bobby Locke	1964	Tony Lema	1979	Severiano
1930	Bobby Jones	1950	Bobby Locke	1965	Peter Thomson		Ballesteros
1931	Tommy Armour	1951	Max Faulkner	1966	Jack Nicklaus	1980	Tom Watson
1932	Gene Sarazen	1952	Bobby Locke	1967	Roberto de Vicenzo	1981	Bill Rogers

U.S. Amateur

Year	Winner	Year	Winner	Year	Winner	Year	Winner
1914	Francis Ouimet	1931	Francis Ouimet	1950	Sam Urzetta	1966	Gary Cowan
1915	Robert Gardner	1932	Ross Somerville	1951	Billy Maxwell	1967	Bob Dickson
1916	Chick Evans Jr.	1933	George Dunlap Jr.	1952	Jack Westland	1968	Bruce Fleisher
1917-18	(not played)	1934	Lawson Little	1953	Gene Littler	1969	Steve Melnyk
1919	Davidson Herron	1935	Lawson Little	1954	Arnold Palmer	1970	Lanny Wadkins
1920	Chick Evans Jr.	1936	John Fischer	1955	Harvie Ward	1971	Gary Cowan
1921	Jesse Guilford	1937	John Goodman	1956	Harvie Ward	1972	Vinnie Giles
1922	Jess Sweetser	1938	Willie Turnesa	1957	Hillman Robbins	1973	Craig Stadler
1923	Max Marston	1939	Bud Ward	1958	Charles Coe	1974	Jerry Pate
1924	Bobby Jones	1940	Dick Chapman	1959	Jack Nicklaus	1975	Fred Ridley
1925	Bobby Jones	1941	Bud Ward	1960	Deane Beman	1976	Bill Sander
1926	George Von Elm	1942-45	(not played)	1961	Jack Nicklaus	1977	John Fought
1927	Bobby Jones	1946	Ted Bishop	1962	Labron Harris Jr.	1978	John Cook
1928	Bobby Jones	1947	Skee Riegel	1963	Deane Beman	1979	Mark O'Meara
1929	Harrison Johnston	1948	Willie Turnesa	1964	Bill Campbell	1980	Hal Sutton
1930	Bobby Jones	1949	Charles Coe	1965	Robert Murphy Jr.	1981	Nathaniel Crosby

Women's U.S. Amateur

Year	Winner	Year	Winner	Year	Winner	Year	Winner
1914	Mrs. H. A. Jackson	1931	Helen Hicks	1950	Beverly Hanson	1966	JoAnne Carner
1915	Mrs. C. H. Vanderbeck	1932	Virginia Van Wie	1951	Dorothy Kirby	1967	Lou Dill
1916	Alexa Stirling	1933	Virginia Van Wie	1952	Jackie Pung	1968	JoAnn Carner
1917-18	(not played)	1934	Virginia Van Wie	1953	Mary Faulk	1969	Catherine Lacoste
1919	Alexa Stirling	1935	Glenna C. Vare	1954	Barbara Romack	1970	Martha Wilkinson
1920	Alexa Stirling	1936	Pamela Barton	1955	Pat Lesser	1971	Laura Baugh
1921	Marion Hollins	1937	Mrs. J. A. Page	1956	Marlene Stewart	1972	Mary Budke
1922	Glenna Collett	1938	Patty Berg	1957	JoAnne Gunderson	1973	Carol Semple
1923	Edith Cummings	1939	Betty Jameson	1958	Anne Quast	1974	Cynthia Hill
1924	Mrs. D.C. Hurd	1940	Betty Jameson	1959	Barbara McIntire	1975	Beth Daniel
1925	Glenna Collett	1941	Mrs. Frank New	1960	JoAnne Gunderson	1976	Donna Horton
1926	Mrs. G. Stetson	1942-45	(not played)	1961	Anne Q. Decker	1977	Beth Daniel
1927	Mrs. M. Horn	1946	"Babe" Zaharias	1962	JoAnne Gunderson	1978	Cathy Sherk
1928	Glenna Collett	1947	Louise Suggs	1963	Anne Q. Welts	1979	Carolyn Hill
1929	Glenna Collett	1948	Grace Lenczyk	1964	Barbara McIntire	1980	Juli Inkster
1930	Glenna Collett	1949	Dorothy Porter	1965	Jean Ashley	1981	Juli Inkster

PGA Hall of Fame

Established in 1940 to honor those who have made outstanding contributions to the game by their lifetime playing ability.

Anderson, Willie	Dudley, Edward	Hutchison Sr., Jock	Runyan, Paul
Armour, Tommy	Dutra, Olin	Jones, Bob	Sarazen, Gene
Barnes, Jim	Evans, Chick	Little, W. Lawson	Shute, Denny
Berg, Patty	Farrell, Johnny	Mangrum, Lloyd	Smith, Alex
Boros, Julius	Ford, Doug	McDermott, John	Smith, Horton
Brady, Mike	Ghezzi, Vic	McLeod, Fred	Smith, MacDonald
Burke, Billy	Guldahl, Ralph	Middlecoff, Cary	Snead, Sam
Burke Jr., Jack	Hagen, Walter	Nelson, Byron	Travers, Jerry
Cooper, Harry	Harbert, M. R. (Chick)	Ouimet, Francis	Travis, Walter
Cruickshank, Bobby	Harper, Chandler	Palmer, Arnold	de Vicenzo, Roberto
Demaret, Jimmy	Harrison, E. J.	Picard, Henry	Wood, Craig
Diegel, Leo	Hogan, Ben	Revolta, Johnny	Zaharias, Mildred (Babe)

PGA Leading Money Winners

Year	Player	Dollars	Year	Player	Dollars	Year	Player	Dollars
1945	Byron Nelson	52,511	1957	Dick Mayer	65,835	1969	Frank Beard	175,223
1946	Ben Hogan	42,556	1958	Arnold Palmer	42,407	1970	Lee Trevino	157,037
1947	Jimmy Demaret	27,936	1959	Art Wall Jr.	53,167	1971	Jack Nicklaus	244,490
1948	Ben Hogan	36,812	1960	Arnold Palmer	75,262	1972	Jack Nicklaus	320,542
1949	Sam Snead	31,593	1961	Gary Player	64,540	1973	Jack Nicklaus	308,362
1950	Sam Snead	35,758	1962	Arnold Palmer	81,448	1974	Johnny Miller	353,201
1951	Lloyd Mangrum	26,088	1963	Arnold Palmer	128,230	1975	Jack Nicklaus	323,149
1952	Julius Boros	37,032	1964	Jack Nicklaus	113,284	1976	Jack Nicklaus	266,438
1953	Lew Worsham	34,002	1965	Jack Nicklaus	140,752	1977	Tom Watson	310,653
1954	Bob Toski	65,819	1966	Billy Casper	121,944	1978	Tom Watson	362,429
1955	Julius Boros	65,121	1967	Jack Nicklaus	188,988	1979	Tom Watson	462,636
1956	Ted Kroll	72,835	1968	Billy Casper	205,168	1980	Tom Watson	530,808

LPGA Leading Money Winners

Year	Winner	Dollars	Year	Winner	Dollars	Year	Winner	Dollars
1954	Patty Berg	16,011	1963	Mickey Wright	31,269	1972	Kathy Whitworth	65,063
1955	Patty Berg	16,492	1964	Mickey Wright	29,800	1973	Kathy Whitworth	82,854
1956	Marlene Hagge	20,235	1965	Kathy Whitworth	28,658	1974	JoAnne Carner	87,094
1957	Patty Berg	16,272	1966	Kathy Whitworth	33,517	1975	Sandra Palmer	94,805
1958	Beverly Hanson	12,629	1967	Kathy Whitworth	32,937	1976	Judy Rankin	150,734
1959	Betsy Rawls	26,774	1968	Kathy Whitworth	48,379	1977	Judy Rankin	122,890
1960	Louise Suggs	16,892	1969	Carol Mann	49,152	1978	Nancy Lopez	189,813
1961	Mickey Wright	22,236	1970	Kathy Whitworth	30,235	1979	Nancy Lopez	215,987
1962	Mickey Wright	21,641	1971	Kathy Whitworth	41,101	1980	Beth Daniel	231,000

Ryder Cup Matches

United States vs. Great Britain — Professional (biennial)
Series standing — United States 20, Great Britain 3, 1 tie

Series record		**Series record**	
1955	United States 8; Great Britain 4	1969	United States 16; Great Britain 16
1957	Great Britain 7; United States 4	1971	United States 18½; Great Britain 13½
1959	United States 8½; Great Britain 3½	1973	Great Britain 13; United States 10
1961	United States 14½; Great Britain 9½	1975	United States 21; Great Britain 11
1963	United States 23; Great Britain 9	1977	United States 12½; Great Britain 7½
1965	United States 19½; Great Britain 12½	1979	United States 17; Great Britain-Ireland 11
1967	United States 23½; Great Britain 8½	1981	United States 18½; Great Britain-Ireland 9½

International Walker Cup Golf Match

United States vs. Great Britain — Men's Amateur (biennial)
Series standing — United States, 25, Great Britain 2, 1 tie

Series record		**Series record**	
1955	United States 10; Great Britain 2	1969	United States 10; Great Britain 8
1957	United States 10; Great Britain 2	1971	Great Britain 13; United States 11
1959	United States 9; Great Britain 3	1973	United States 14; Great Britain 10
1961	United States 11; Great Britain 1	1975	United States 15½; Great Britain 8½
1963	United States 9; Great Britain 3	1977	United States 16; Great Britain 8
1965	United States 11; Great Britain 11	1979	United States 15½; Great Britain-Ireland 8½
1967	United States 13; Great Britain 7	1981	United States 15; Great Britain-Ireland 9

International Curtis Cup Golf Match

United States vs. Great Britain (plus Ireland) — Women's Amateur (biennial)
Series standing — United States 17, Great Britain 2, 2 ties

Series record		**Series record**	
1954	United States 6; Great Britain 3	1968	United States 10½; Great Britain 7½
1957	Great Britain 5; United States 4	1970	United States 11½; Great Britain 6½
1959	Great Britain 4½; United States 4½	1972	United States 10; Great Britain 8
1960	United States 6½; Great Britain 2½	1974	United States 13; Great Britain 5
1962	United States 8; Great Britain 1	1976	United States 11½; Great Britain 6½
1964	United States 10½; Great Britain 7½	1978	United States 12; Great Britain 6
1966	United States 13; Great Britain 5	1980	United States 13; Great Britain 5

Contract Bridge Championships for North America in 1980-81

Source: American Contract Bridge League, Memphis, Tenn.

Fall Championships

Lancaster, Pa., Nov. 14 - 23, 1980

Open Teams (Board-A-Match) Reisinger Trophy — Malcolm Brachman, Bobby Goldman, Dallas, Tex.; Paul Soloway, Seattle, Wash.; Eddie Kantar, Los Angeles, Cal.; Michael Lawrence, Berkeley, Cal.; Ron Andersen, New York, N.Y.

North American Swiss Teams — (tie) — Judy Rich, Philip M. Cowan, New York, N.Y.; Rich DeMartino, Riverside, Conn., Steve Becker, Cos Cob, Conn.; Dale Beers, Cromwell, Conn., William Epperson, Ridgefield, N.J., Dave Furman, Lansdowne, Pa., Dave Treitel, Stamford, Conn.

Blue Ribbon Pairs — Allan Stauber, Poughkeepsie, N.Y., and Warren Rosner, Nanuet, N.Y.

Life Master Men's Pairs — Jan and Craig Janitschke, Denver, Col.

Life Master Women's Pairs — Claire Tornay, New York, N.Y., and Kathie Cappelletti, Alexandria, Va.

Mixed Pairs — Jeff and Patty Meckstroth, Reynoldsburg, Oh.

Rookie Pairs — Sunny Ngan and Peter Ngan, Willowdale, Ont.

Most master points in tournament — Jeff Meckstroth.

Spring Championships

Detroit, Mich., Mar., 1981

Vanderbilt Trophy Open Teams — B. J. Becker, Ron Rubin, Edgar Kaplan, Michael Becker, all New York, N.Y., and Norman Kay, Narberth, Pa.

Men's Board-A-Match Teams — Joseph Silver, Montreal Ont., Neil Chambers, Vancouver, B.C., Allan Stauber, Poughkeepsie, N.Y., and Marty Bergen, White Plains, N.Y.

Women's Knock-Out Teams — Jo Morse, Silver Spring, Md., Evelyn Levitt, Wilmington, Del., Helen Utegaard, Carmichael, Cal., Pat Lapides, San Diego, Cal., Sandi Leavitt, Lincolnwood, Ill., and June Deutsch, Chicago, Ill.

Open Pairs — Dan Gertsman, Buffalo, N.Y., and Marc Nathan, Miami, Fla.

Men's Pairs — Allan Stauber, Poughkeepsie, N.Y., and Warren Rosner, Nanuet, N.Y.

Women's Pairs — Emma Jean Hawes, Ft. Worth, Tex. and Dorothy Truscott, New York, N.Y.

Grand National Pairs — Robert and Helen Blakey, Columbia, Md.

Most master points for tournament — Allan Stauber.

Summer Championships

Boston, Mass., July, 1981

Spingold Master Teams — Ralph Katz, Steubenville, Oh., Allan Stauber, Poughkeepsie, N.Y., Warren Rosner, Nanuet, N.Y., John Sutherlin, San Francisco, Cal., Ron Gerard, White Plains, N.Y., and Larry Cohen, Mt. Vernon, N.Y.

Grand National Teams — Eddie Wold, Ira Chorush, Houston, Tex., Dr. George Rosenkranz, Mexico City, Mex., Mike Passell, Dallas, Tex., James Jacoby, Richardson, Tex.

Master Mixed Teams — Ralph Katz, Steubenville, Oh., Esta Van Zandt, Houston, Tex., Doug and Sandra Fraser, Mount Royal, Que., Paul Lewis, Las Vegas, Nev., and Linda Peterson, San Bruno, Cal.

Life Master Pairs — Steve Weinstein and Fred Stewart, Accord, N.Y.

Most master points for tournament — Ralph Katz.

Tennis

USTA National Champions

Men's Singles

Year	Champion	Final opponent	Year	Champion	Final opponent
1920	Bill Tilden	William Johnston	1951	Frank Sedgman	E. Victor Seixas Jr.
1921	Bill Tilden	Wallace Johnston	1952	Frank Sedgman	Gardnar Mulloy
1922	Bill Tilden	William Johnston	1953	Tony Trabert	E. Victor Seixas Jr.
1923	Bill Tilden	William Johnston	1954	E. Victor Seixas Jr.	Rex Hartwig
1924	Bill Tilden	William Johnston	1955	Tony Trabert	Ken Rosewall
1925	Bill Tilden	William Johnston	1956	Ken Rosewall	Lewis Hoad
1926	Rene Lacoste	Jean Borotra	1957	Malcolm Anderson	Ashley Cooper
1927	Rene Lacoste	Bill Tilden	1958	Ashley Cooper	Malcolm Anderson
1928	Henri Cochet	Francis Hunter	1959	Neale A. Fraser	Alejandro Olmedo
1929	Bill Tilden	Francis Hunter	1960	Neale A. Fraser	Rod Laver
1930	John Doeg	Francis Shields	1961	Roy Emerson	Rod Laver
1931	H. Ellsworth Vines	George Lott	1962	Rod Laver	Roy Emerson
1932	H. Ellsworth Vines	Henri Cochet	1963	Rafael Osuna	F. A. Froehling 3d
1933	Fred Perry	John Crawford	1964	Roy Emerson	Fred Stolle
1934	Fred Perry	Wilmer Allison	1965	Manuel Santana	Cliff Drysdale
1935	Wilmer Allison	Sidney Wood	1966	Fred Stolle	John Newcombe
1936	Fred Perry	Don Budge	1967	John Newcombe	Clark Graebner
1937	Don Budge	Baron G. von Cramm	1968	Arthur Ashe	Tom Okker
1938	Don Budge	C. Gene Mako	1969	Rod Laver	Tony Roche
1939	Robert Riggs	S. Welby Van Horn	1970	Ken Rosewall	Tony Roche
1940	Don McNeill	Robert Riggs	1971	Stan Smith	Jan Kodes
1941	Robert Riggs	F. L. Kovacs	1972	Ilie Nastase	Arthur Ashe
1942	F. R. Schroeder Jr.	Frank Parker	1973	John Newcombe	Jan Kodes
1943	Joseph Hunt	Jack Kramer	1974	Jimmy Connors	Ken Rosewall
1944	Frank Parker	William Talbert	1975	Manuel Orantes	Jimmy Connors
1945	Frank Parker	William Talbert	1976	Jimmy Connors	Bjorn Borg
1946	Jack Kramer	Thomas Brown Jr.	1977	Guillermo Vilas	Jimmy Connors
1947	Jack Kramer	Frank Parker	1978	Jimmy Connors	Bjorn Borg
1948	Pancho Gonzales	Eric Sturgess	1979	John McEnroe	Vitas Gerulaitis
1949	Pancho Gonzales	F. R. Schroeder Jr.	1980	John McEnroe	Bjorn Borg
1950	Arthur Larsen	Herbert Flam	1981	John McEnroe	Bjorn Borg

Women's Singles

Year	Champion	Final opponent	Year	Champion	Final opponent
1936	Alice Marble	Helen Jacobs	1959	Maria Bueno	Christine Truman
1937	Anita Lizana	Pauline Betz	1960	Darlene Hard	Maria Bueno
1938	Alice Marble	Louise Brough	1961	Darlene Hard	Ann Haydon
1939	Alice Marble	Louise Brough	1962	Margaret Smith	Darlene Hard
1940	Alice Marble	Margaret Osborne	1963	Maria Bueno	Margaret Smith
1941	Sarah Palfrey Cooke	Pauline Betz	1964	Maria Bueno	Carole Graebner
1942	Pauline Betz	Jadwiga Jedrzejowska	1965	Margaret Smith	Billie Jean Moffitt
1943	Pauline Betz	Nancye Wynne	1966	Maria Bueno	Nancy Richey
1944	Pauline Betz	Helen Jacobs	1967	Billie Jean King	Ann Haydon Jones
1945	Sarah P. Cooke	Helen Jacobs	1968	Virginia Wade	Billie Jean King
1946	Pauline Betz	Doris Hart	1969	Margaret Court	Nancy Richey
1947	Louise Brough	Margaret Osborne	1970	Margaret Court	Rosemary Casals
1948	Margaret Osborne duPont	Louise Brough	1971	Billie Jean King	Rosemary Casals
1949	Margaret Osborne duPont	Doris Hart	1972	Billie Jean King	Kerry Melville
1950	Margaret Osborne duPont	Doris Hart	1973	Margaret Court	Evonne Goolagong
1951	Maureen Connolly	Shirley Fry	1974	Billie Jean King	Evonne Goolagong
1952	Maureen Connolly	Doris Hart	1975	Chris Evert	Evonne Goolagong
1953	Maureen Connolly	Doris Hart	1976	Chris Evert	Evonne Goolagong
1954	Doris Hart	Louise Brough	1977	Chris Evert	Wendy Turnbull
1955	Doris Hart	Patricia Ward	1978	Chris Evert	Pam Shriver
1956	Shirley Fry	Althea Gibson	1979	Tracy Austin	Chris Evert Lloyd
1957	Althea Gibson	Louise Brough	1980	Chris Evert Lloyd	Hana Mandlikova
1958	Althea Gibson	Darlene Hard	1981	Tracy Austin	Martina Navratilova

Mixed Doubles

Year	Champions	Year	Champions
1950	Mrs. M. O. duPont—Kenneth MacGregor	1966	Donna Floyd Fales—Owen Davidson
1951	Doris Hart—Frank Sedgman	1967	Billie Jean King—Owen Davidson
1952	Doris Hart—Frank Sedgman	1968	Mary Ann Eisel—Peter Curtis
1953	Doris Hart—E. Victor Seixas Jr.	1969	Margaret S. Court—Marty Riessen
1954	Doris Hart—E. Victor Seixas Jr.	1970	Margaret S. Court—Marty Riessen
1955	Doris Hart—E. Victor Seixas Jr.	1971	Billie Jean King—Owen Davidson
1956	Mrs. M. O. duPont—Ken Rosewall	1972	Margaret S. Court—Marty Riessen
1957	Althea Gibson—Kurt Nielsen	1973	Billie Jean King—Owen Davidson
1958	Mrs. M. O. duPont—Neale Fraser	1974	Pam Teeguarden—Geoff Masters
1959	Mrs. M. O. duPont—Neale Fraser	1975	Rosemary Casals—Dick Stockton
1960	Mrs. M. O. duPont—Neale Fraser	1976	Billie Jean King—Phil Dent
1961	Margaret Smith—Robert Mark	1977	Betty Stove—Frew McMillan
1962	Margaret Smith—Fred Stolle	1978	Betty Stove—Frew McMillan
1963	Margaret Smith—Kenneth Fletcher	1979	Greer Stevens—Bob Hewitt
1964	Margaret Smith—John Newcombe	1980	Wendy Turnbull—Marty Riessen
1965	Margaret Smith—Fred Stolle	1981	Anne Smith—Kevin Curren

Men's Doubles

Year	Champions	Year	Champions
1925	R. Norris Williams—Vincent Richards	1954	E. Victor Seixas Jr.—Tony Trabert
1926	R. Norris Williams—Vincent Richards	1955	Kosei Kamo—Atsushi Miyagi
1927	Bill Tilden—Francis Hunter	1956	Lewis Hoad—Ken Rosewall
1928	George Lott—John Hennessey	1957	Ashley Cooper—Neale Fraser
1929	George Lott—John Doeg	1958	Hamilton Richardson—Alejandro Olmedo
1930	George Lott—John Doeg	1959	Neale A. Fraser—Roy Emerson
1931	Wilmer Allison—John Van Ryn	1960	Neale A. Fraser—Roy Emerson
1932	H. Ellsworth Vines—Keith Gledhill	1961	Dennis Ralston—Chuck McKinley
1933	George Lott—Lester Stoefen	1962	Rafael Osuna—Antonio Palafox
1934	George Lott—Lester Stoefen	1963	Dennis Ralston—Chuck McKinley
1935	Wilmer Allison—John Van Ryn	1964	Dennis Ralston—Chuck McKinley
1936	Don Budge—C. Gene Mako	1965	Roy Emerson—Fred Stolle
1937	Baron G. von Cramm—Henner Henkel	1966	Roy Emerson—Fred Stolle
1938	Don Budge—C. Gene Mako	1967	John Newcombe—Tony Roche
1939	Adrian Quist—John Bromwich	1968	Robert Lutz—Stan Smith
1940	Jack Kramer—Frederick Schroeder Jr.	1969	Fred Stolle—Ken Rosewall
1941	Jack Kramer—Frederick Schroeder Jr.	1970	Pierre Barthes—Nicki Pilic
1942	Gardnar Mulloy—William Talbert	1971	John Newcombe—Roger Taylor
1943	Jack Kramer—Frank Parker	1972	Cliff Drysdale—Roger Taylor
1944	Don McNeill—Robert Falkenburg	1973	John Newcombe—Owen Davidson
1945	Gardnar Mulloy—William Talbert	1974	Bob Lutz—Stan Smith
1946	Gardnar Mulloy—William Talbert	1975	Jimmy Connors—Ilie Nastase
1947	Jack Kramer—Frederick Schroeder Jr.	1976	Marty Riessen—Tom Okker
1948	Gardnar Mulloy—William Talbert	1977	Bob Hewitt—Frew McMillan
1949	John Bromwich—William Sidwell	1978	Stan Smith—Bob Lutz
1950	John Bromwich—Frank Sedgman	1979	John McEnroe—Peter Fleming
1951	Frank Sedgman—Kenneth McGregor	1980	Bob Lutz—Stan Smith
1952	Mervyn Rose—E. Victor Seixas Jr.	1981	John McEnroe—Peter Fleming
1953	Rex Hartwig—Mervyn Rose		

Women's Doubles

Year	Champions	Year	Champions
1938	Alice Marble—Mrs. Sarah P. Fabyan	1960	Darlene Hard—Maria Bueno
1939	Alice Marble—Mrs. Sarah P. Fabyan	1961	Darlene Hard—Lesley Turner
1940	Alice Marble—Mrs. Sarah P. Fabyan	1962	Maria Bueno—Darlene Hard
1941	Mrs. S. P. Cooke—Margaret Osborne	1963	Margaret Smith—Robyn Ebbern
1942	A. Louise Brough—Margaret Osborne	1964	Billie Jean Moffitt—Karen Susman
1943	A. Louise Brough—Margaret Osborne	1965	Carole C. Graebner—Nancy Richey
1944	A. Louise Brough—Margaret Osborne	1966	Maria Bueno—Nancy Richey
1945	A. Louise Brough—Margaret Osborne	1967	Rosemary Casals—Billie Jean King
1946	A. Louise Brough—Margaret Osborne	1968	Maria Bueno—Margaret S. Court
1947	A. Louise Brough—Margaret Osborne	1969	Francoise Durr—Darlene Hard
1948	A. Louise Brough—Mrs. M. O. du Pont	1970	M. S. Court—Judy Tegart Dalton
1949	A. Louise Brough—Mrs. M. O. du Pont	1971	Rosemary Casals—Judy Togart Dalton
1950	A. Louise Brough—Mrs. M. O. du Pont	1972	Francoise Durr—Betty Stove
1951	Doris Hart—Shirley Fry	1973	Margaret S. Court—Virginia Wade
1952	Doris Hart—Shirley Fry	1974	Billie Jean King—Rosemary Casals
1953	Doris Hart—Shirley Fry	1975	Margaret Court—Virginia Wade
1954	Doris Hart—Shirley Fry	1976	Linky Boshoff—Ilana Kloss
1955	A. Louise Brough—Mrs. M. O. du Pont	1977	Betty Stove—Martina Navratilova
1956	A. Louise Brough—Mrs. M. O. du Pont	1978	Martina Navratilova—Billie Jean King
1957	A. Louise Brough—Mrs. M. O. du Pont	1979	Betty Stove—Wendy Turnbull
1958	Darlene Hard—Jeanne Arth	1980	Billie Jean King—Martina Navratilova
1959	Darlene Hard—Jeanne Arth	1981	Anne Smith—Kathy Jordan

NCAA Tennis Champions

Year	Singles	College	Doubles	College
1969	Joaquin Loyo Mayo	USC	Joaquin Loyo Mayo—Marcelo Lara	USC
1970	Jeff Borowiak	UCLA	Pat Cramer—Luis Garcia	Miami (Fla.)
1971	Jimmy Connors	UCLA	Jeff Borowiak—Haroon Rahim	UCLA
1972	Dick Stockton	Trinity (Tex.)	Sandy Mayer—Roscoe Tanner	Stanford
1973	Sandy Mayer	Stanford	Sandy Mayer—Jim Delaney	Stanford
1974	John Whitlinger	Stanford	John Whitlinger—Jim Delaney	Stanford
1975	Billy Martin	UCLA	Butch Walts—Bruce Manson	USC
1976	Bill Scanlon	Trinity	Peter Fleming—Ferdi Taygan	UCLA
1977	Matt Mitchell	Stanford	Bruce Manson—Chris Lewis	USC
1978	John McEnroe	Stanford	Bruce Nichols—John Austin	UCLA
1979	Kevin Curren	Texas	Erick Iskersky—Ben McKown	Trinity
1980	Robert Van't Hof	USC	Mel Purcell—Rodney Harman	Tennessee
1981	Tim Mayotte	Stanford	Carl Richter—David Pate	Texas Christian

Clay Court Champions

Year	Champion	Year	Champion	Year	Champion	Year	Champion
1958	Bernard Bartzen	1964	Dennis Ralston	1970	Cliff Richey	1976	Jimmy Connors
1959	Bernard Bartzen	1965	Dennis Ralston	1971	Zeljko Franulovic	1977	Manuel Orantes
1960	Barry MacKay	1966	Cliff Richey	1972	Bob Hewitt	1978	Jimmy Connors
1961	Bernard Bartzen	1967	Arthur Ashe	1973	Manuel Orantes	1979	Jimmy Connors
1962	Chuck McKinley	1968	Clark Graebner	1974	Jimmy Connors	1980	Jose-Luis Clerc
1963	Chuck McKinley	1969	Zeljko Franulovic	1975	Manuel Orantes	1981	Jose-Luis Clerc

British Champions, Wimbledon

Inaugurated 1877

Men's Singles

Year	Champion	Final opponent	Year	Champion	Final opponent
1933	Jack Crawford	Ellsworth Vines	1960	Neale Fraser	Rod Laver
1934	Fred Perry	Jack Crawford	1961	Rod Laver	Chuck McKinley
1935	Fred Perry	Gottfried von Cramm	1962	Rod Laver	Martin Mulligan
1936	Fred Perry	Gottfried von Cramm	1963	Chuck McKinley	Fred Stolle
1937	Donald Budge	Gottfried von Cramm	1964	Roy Emerson	Fred Stolle
1938	Donald Budge	Wilfred Austin	1965	Roy Emerson	Fred Stolle
1939	Bobby Riggs	Elwood Cooke	1966	Manuel Santana	Dennis Ralston
1940-45	not held		1967	John Newcombe	Wilhelm Bungert
1946	Yvon Petra	Geoff E. Brown	1968	Rod Laver	Tony Roche
1947	Jack Kramer	Tom P. Brown	1969	Rod Laver	John Newcombe
1948	Bob Falkenburg	John Bromwich	1970	John Newcombe	Ken Rosewall
1949	Ted Schroeder	Jaroslav Drobny	1971	John Newcombe	Stan Smith
1950	Budge Patty	Fred Sedgman	1972	Stan Smith	Ilie Nastase
1951	Dick Savitt	Ken McGregor	1973	Jan Kodes	Alex Metreveli
1952	Frank Sedgman	Jaroslav Drobny	1974	Jimmy Connors	Ken Rosewall
1953	Vic Seixas	Kurt Nielsen	1975	Arthur Ashe	Jimmy Connors
1954	Jaroslav Drobny	Ken Rosewall	1976	Bjorn Borg	Ilie Nastase
1955	Tony Trabert	Kurt Nielsen	1977	Bjorn Borg	Jimmy Connors
1956	Lew Hoad	Ken Rosewall	1978	Bjorn Borg	Jimmy Connors
1957	Lew Hoad	Ashley Cooper	1979	Bjorn Borg	Roscoe Tanner
1958	Ashley Cooper	Neale Fraser	1980	Bjorn Borg	John McEnroe
1959	Alex Olmedo	Rod Laver	1981	John McEnroe	Bjorn Borg

Women's Singles

Year	Champion	Year	Champion	Year	Champion	Year	Champion
1946	Pauline Betz	1955	Louise Brough	1964	Maria Bueno	1973	Billie Jean King
1947	Margaret Osborne	1956	Shirley Fry	1965	Margaret Smith	1974	Chris Evert
1948	Louise Brough	1957	Althea Gibson	1966	Billie Jean King	1975	Billie Jean King
1949	Louise Brough	1958	Althea Gibson	1967	Billie Jean King	1976	Chris Evert
1950	Louise Brough	1959	Maria Bueno	1968	Billie Jean King	1977	Virginia Wade
1951	Doris Hart	1960	Maria Bueno	1969	Ann Haydon-Jones	1978	Martina Navratilova
1952	Maureen Connolly	1961	Angela Mortimer	1970	Margaret Court	1979	Martina Navratilova
1953	Maureen Connolly	1962	Karen Hantze-Susman	1971	Evonne Goolagong	1980	Evonne Goolagong
1954	Maureen Connolly	1963	Margaret Smith	1972	Billie Jean King	1981	Chris Evert Lloyd

French Open Champions   Australian Open

Men	Women	Year	Men	Women
Roy Emerson	Françoise Durr	1967	Roy Emerson	Nancy Richey
Ken Rosewall	Nancy Richey	1968	Bill Bowrey	Billie Jean King
Rod Laver	Margaret Smith Court	1969	Rod Laver	Margaret Smith Court
Jan Kodes	Margaret Smith Court	1970	Arthur Ashe	Margaret Smith Court
Jan Kodes	Evonne Goolagong	1971	Ken Rosewall	Margaret Smith Court
Andres Gimeno	Billie Jean King	1972	Ken Rosewall	Virginia Wade
Ilie Nastase	Margaret Court	1973	John Newcombe	Margaret Court
Bjorn Borg	Chris Evert	1974	Jimmy Connors	Evonne Goolagong
Bjorn Borg	Chris Evert	1975	John Newcombe	Evonne Goolagong
Adriano Panatta	Sue Barker	1976	Mark Edmondson	Evonne Goolagong
Guillermo Vilas	Mima Jausovec	1977	Roscoe Tanner	Kerry Reid
Bjorn Borg	Virginia Ruzici	1978	Vitas Gerulaitis	Evonne Goolagong
Bjorn Borg	Chris Evert Lloyd	1979	Guillermo Vilas	Chris O'Neill
Bjorn Borg	Chris Evert Lloyd	1980	Guillermo Vilas	Barbara Jordan
Bjorn Borg	Hana Mandlikova	1981	Brian Teacher	Kim Warwick

WCT World Series of Tennis in 1981

Dates	Event, city	Singles winner	Doubles winners
Jan. 19-25	The Copa Monterrey, Monterrey, Mexico	Johan Kriek	Kevin Curran-Steve Denton
Jan. 26-Feb. 1	U.S. Pro Indoor Championships, Philadelphia, Pa.	Roscoe Tanner	Marty Riessen-Sherwood Stewart
Feb. 2-8	United Virginia Bank Tennis Classic, Richmond, Va.	Yannick Noah	Tim Gullikson-Bernard Mitton
Mar. 9-15	WCT Belgian Indoor Championships Challenge Du Parc, Brussels, Belgium	Jimmy Connors	Sandy Mayer-Frew McMillan
Mar. 16-22	ABN Wereldtennis Toernoor 1981, Rotterdam, Netherlands	Jimmy Connors	Fritz Buehning-Ferdi Taygan
Mar. 23-29	The Cuore Tennis Cup, Milan, Italy	John McEnroe	Brian Gottfried-Raul Ramirez
Mar. 30-Apr. 5	The Trevira Cup 1981, Frankfurt, Germany	John McEnroe	Brian Teacher-Butch Walts
Apr. 6-12	The River Oaks/Houston National Bank Tournament, Houston, Tex.	Guillermo Vilas	Mark Edmondson-Sherwood Stewart

WCT Finals

Dallas, Tex., Apr. 27-May 3, 1981

Quarterfinals
John McEnroe def. Sandy Mayer 7-5, 6-4, 6-3.
Brian Gottfried def. Sammy Giammalva 7-5, 6-3, 6-1.
Johan Kriek def. Wojtek Fibak 7-5, 3-6, 6-1, 6-4.
Roscoe Tanner def. Vijay Amritraj 6-2, 1-6, 2-6, 7-6 (8-6), 6-4.

Semifinals
McEnroe def. Gottfried 6-3, 6-4, 6-1.
Kriek def. Tanner 7-6 (7-2), 6-3, 4-6, 0-6, 6-4.
Final
McEnroe def. Kriek 6-1, 6-2, 6-4.

Tournament of Champions

Forest Hills, N.Y., May 2-10, 1981

Quarterfinals	Semifinals
Kirmayr def. Taroczy 4-6, 7-6(15-13), 7-6(7-3).	Kirmayr def. Fibak 6-2, 6-4.
Fibak def. Teltscher 2-6, 6-3, 6-3.	Dibbs def. Pecci 7-6(7-4), 6-3.
Pecci def. Purcell 6-2, 6-2.	**Final**
Dibbs def. Clerc 7-5, 6-4.	Dibbs def. Kirmayr 6-3, 6-2.

Davis Cup Challenge Round

Year	Result	Year	Result	Year	Result
1900	United States 5, British Isles 0	1928	France 4, United States 1	1957	Australia 3, United States 2
1901	(not played)	1929	France 3, United States 2	1958	United States 3, Australia 2
1902	United States 3, British Isles 2	1930	France 4, United States 1	1959	Australia 3, United States 2
1903	British Isles 4, United States 1	1931	France 3, Great Britain 2	1960	Australia 4, Italy 1
1904	British Isles 5, Belgium 0	1932	France 3, United States 2	1961	Australia 5, Italy 0
1905	British Isles 5, United States 0	1933	Great Britain 3, France 2	1962	Australia 5, Mexico 0
1906	British Isles 5, United States 0	1934	Great Britain 4, United States 1	1963	United States 3, Australia 2
1907	Australia 3, British Isles 2	1935	Great Britain 5, United States 0	1964	Australia 3, United States 2
1908	Australasia 3, United States 2	1936	Great Britain 3, Australia 2	1965	Australia 4, Spain 1
1909	Australasia 5, United States 0	1937	United States 4, Great Britain 1	1966	Australia 4, India 1
1910	(not played)	1938	United States 3, Australia 2	1967	Australia 4, Spain 1
1911	Australasia 5, United States 0	1939	Australia 3, United States 2	1968	United States 4, Australia 1
1912	British Isles 3, Australasia 2	1940-45	(not played)	1969	United States 5, Romania 0
1913	United States 3, British Isles 2	1946	United States 5, Australia 0	1970	United States 5, W. Germany 0
1914	Australasia 3, United States 2	1947	United States 4, Australia 1	1971	United States 3, Romania 2
1915-18	(not played)	1948	United States 5, Australia 0	1972	United States 3, Romania 2
1919	Australasia 4, British Isles 1	1949	United States 4, Australia 1	1973	Australia 5, United States 0
1920	United States 5, Australasia 0	1950	Australia 4, United States 1	1974	South Africa (default by India)
1921	United States 5, Japan 0	1951	Australia 3, United States 2	1975	Sweden 3, Czech. 2
1922	United States 4, Australasia 1	1952	Australia 4, United States 1	1976	Italy 4, Chile 1
1923	United States 4, Australasia 1	1953	Australia 3, United States 2	1977	Australia 3, Italy 1
1924	United States 5, Australasia 0	1954	United States 3, Australia 2	1978	United States 4, Great Britain 1
1925	United States 5, France 0	1955	Australia 5, United States 0	1979	United States 5, Italy 0
1926	United States 4, France 1	1956	Australia 5, United States 0	1980	Czechoslovakia 4, Italy 1
1927	France 3, United States 2				

Water Ski Champions in 1981

Source: American Water Ski Assn.

39th Annual National Water Ski Championships

Du Quoin, Ill., Aug. 19-23, 1981

Men's Open Overall—Carl Roberge, Orlando, Fla., 3,370 points.
Men's Open Slalom—Bob LaPoint, Castro Valley, Cal., 57 buoys.
Men's Open Tricks—Cory Pickos, Eagle Lake, Fla., 8,660 points.
Men's Open Jumping—Sammy Duvall, Greenville, S. C., 182 feet.
Women's Open Overall—Cyndi Benzel, Newberry Springs, Cal., 3,435 points.
Women's Open Slalom—Cindy Todd, Pierson, Fla., 58¼ buoys.
Women's Open Tricks—Barbara Cleveland, Hawthorne, Fla., 5,050 points.
Women's Open Jumping—Linda Giddens, Eastman, Ga., 128 feet.
Senior Men's Overall—Dr. J. D. Morgan, Lake Wales, Fla., 2,917 points.
Senior Men's Slalom—Ken White, Bynum, Tex., 51½ buoys.

Senior Men's Tricks—Greg Wilson, St. Marys, Oh., 4,840 points.
Senior Men's Jumping—Dr. J. D. Morgan, 127 feet.
Senior Women's Overall—Thelma Salmas, Lantana, Fla., 2,466 points.
Senior Women's Slalom—Thelma Salmas, 40 buoys.
Senior Women's Tricks—Scarlett Dwyer, Calistoga, Cal., 2,330 points.
Senior Women's Jumping—Thelma Salmas, 97 feet.
Boys' Overall—Chris Swann, Winter Park, Fla., 2,535 points.
Boys' Slalom—Chris Swann, 49½ buoys.
Boys' Tricks—Tory Baggiano, Montgomery Ala., 5,880 points.
Boys' Jumping—Danny Zeisler, Sandy Hook, Conn., 125 feet.
Girls' Overall—Jennifer Leachman, Parkersburg, Oh., 2,874 points.
Girls' Slalom—Jennifer Leachman, 55½ buoys.
Girls' Tricks—Sally Monnier, 5,330 points.
Girls' Jumping—Jennifer Leachman, 109 feet.

23d Annual Masters Tournament

Callaway Gardens, Ga., July 11-12, 1981

Men's Overall—Mike Hazelwood, London, England, 2,737 points.
Men's Slalom—Carl Roberge, Orlando, Fla., 55½ buoys.
Men's Tricks—Cory Pickos, Eagle Lake, Fla., 8,940 points.
Men's Jumping—Mike Hazelwood, 184 feet.
Women's Overall—Judy McClintock, Streetsville, Ont., Can-

ada, 2,804 points.
Women's Slalom—Cindy Todd, Pierson, Fla., 55 buoys.
Women's Tricks—Ana Maria Carrasco, Caracas, Venezuela, 6,610 points.
Women's Jumping—Linda Giddens, Eastman, Ga., 130 feet.

17th World Water Ski Championships

Chertsey, Surrey, England, Sept. 1-6, 1981

Men's Overall—Sammy Duvall, U.S., 2,717.65 points.
Men's Slalom—Andy Mapple, Great Britain, 66.75 buoys (2 rounds).
Men's Tricks—Cory Pickos, U.S., 17,260 points (2 rounds).
Men's Jumping—Mike Hazelwood, Great Britain, 115.70 meters (2 rounds).
Women's Overall—Karin Roberge, U.S., 2,794.31 points.

Women's Slalom—Cindy Todd, U.S., 57.75 buoys (2 rounds).
Women's Tricks—Ana Maria Carrasco, Venezuela, 12,750 points (2 rounds).
Women's Jumping—Deena Brush, U.S., 77.60 meters (2 rounds).
Team results—U.S., 8,519.86 points; Australia, 7,777.03 points; Great Britain, 7,665.97 points.

Trotting and Pacing Records

Source: Martin J. Evans, U.S. Trotting Assn.; records to Aug. 15, 1981

Trotting Records

Asterisk (*) denotes record was made against the clock. Times—seconds in fifths.

One mile records (mile track)

All-age — *1:54.4 — Nevele Pride, Indianapolis, Ind., Aug. 31, 1969; Lindy's Crown, DuQuoin, Ill., Aug. 30, 1980.
Two-year-old — 1:57 — Brisco Hanover, Du Quoin, Ill., Sept. 2, 1977.
Three-year-old — 1:55 — Speedy Somolli and Florida Pro, Du Quoin, Ill., Sept. 2, 1978.

(Half-mile track)

All-age — 1:56.4 — Nevele Pride, Saratoga Springs, N.Y., Sept. 6, 1969.
Two-year-old — 2:00.1 — Ayres, Delaware, Oh., 1963.
Three-year-old — 1:58.3 — Songcan, Delaware, Oh., 1972.

(Five Eighth-mile track)

All-Age — 1:57.1 — Lindy's Crown, Wilmington, Del., July 27, 1980.
Two-year-old — 2:00.1 — Smokin Yankee, Laurel, Md., Sept. 10, 1980.
Three-year-old — 1:58 — Keystone Sister, Meadow Lands, Pa., Aug. 14, 1981.

Pacing Records

One mile records (mile track)

All-age — *1:49.1 — Niatross, Lexington, Ky., Oct. 1, 1980.
Two-year-old — 1:54 — French Chef, Indianapolis, Ind., Aug. 22, 1980.
Three-year-old — *1:49.1 — Niatross, Lexington, Ky., Oct. 1, 1980.

(Half-mile track)

All age — 1:54.4 — Niatross, Delaware, Oh., Sept. 18, 1980.
Two-year-old — 1:57.2 — Slapstick, Louisville, Ky., Sept. 6, 1980.
Three-year-old — 1:54.4 — Niatross, Delaware, Oh., Sept. 18, 1980.

(Five Eighth-mile track)

All-age — 1:53.2 — Storm Damage, Washington, Pa., Aug. 6, 1980.
Two-year-old — 1:56.1 — French Chef, Columbus, Oh., Sept. 6, 1980.
Three-year-old — 1:53.2 — Storm Damage, Washington, Pa., Aug. 6, 1980.

The Hambletonian (3-year-old trotters)

Year	Winner	Driver	Purse	Year	Winner	Driver	Purse
1947	Hoot Mon	S.F. Palin	$46,267	1965	Egyptian Candor	Del Cameron	$122,245
1948	Demon Hanover	Harrison Hoyt	59,941	1966	Kerry Way	Frank Ervin	122,540
1949	Miss Tilly	Fred Egan	69,791	1967	Speedy Streak	Del Cameron	122,650
1950	Lusty Song	Del Miller	75,209	1968	Nevele Pride	Stanley Dancer	116,190
1951	Mainliner	Guy Crippen	95,263	1969	Lindy's Pride	Howard Beissinger	124,910
1952	Sharp Note	Bion Shively	87,637	1970	Timothy T.	John Simpson Sr.	143,630
1953	Helicopter	Harry Harvey	117,118	1971	Speedy Crown	Howard Beissinger	128,770
1954	Newport Dream	Del Cameron	106,830	1972	Super Bowl	Stanley Dancer	119,090
1955	Scott Frost	Joe O'Brien	86,863	1973	Flirth	Ralph Baldwin	144,710
1956	The Intruder	Ned Bower	98,591	1974	Christopher T	Bill Haughton	160,150
1957	Hickory Smoke	John Simpson Sr.	111,126	1975	Bonefish	Stanley Dancer	232,192
1958	Emily's Pride	Flave Nipe	106,719	1976	Steve Lobell	Bill Haughton	263,524
1959	Diller Hanover	Frank Ervin	125,284	1977	Green Speed	Bill Haughton	284,131
1960	Blaze Hanover	Joe O'Brien	144,590	1978	Speedy Somolli	Howard Beissinger	241,280
1961	Harlan Dean	James Arthur	131,573	1979	Legend Hanover	George Sholty	300,000
1962	A.C. Os Viking	Sanders Russell	116,312	1980	Burgomeister	Bill Haughton	293,570
1963	Speedy Scot	Ralph Baldwin	115,549	1981	Shiaway St. Pat	Ray Remmen	838,000
1964	Ayres	John Simpson Sr.	115,281				

Annual Leading Money-Winning Horses

Trotters

Year	Horse	Dollars	Year	Horse	Dollars	Year	Horse	Dollars
1954	Katie Key	84,867	1963	Speedy Scot	144,403	1972	Super Bowl	437,108
1955	Scott Frost	186,101	1964	Speedy Scot	235,710	1973	Spartan Hanover	262,023
1956	Scott Frost	85,851	1965	Dartmouth	252,348	1974	Delmonica Hanover	252,165
1957	Hoot Song	114,877	1966	Noble Victory	210,696	1975	Savoir	351,385
1958	Emily's Pride	118,830	1967	Carlisle	231,243	1976	Steve Lobell	338,770
1959	Diller Hanover	149,897	1968	Nevele Pride	427,440	1977	Green Speed	584,405
1960	Su Mac Lad	159,662	1969	Lindy's Pride	323,997	1978	Speedy Somolli	362,404
1961	Su Mac Lad	245,750	1970	Fresh Yankee	359,002	1979	Chiola Hanover	553,058
1962	Duke Rodney	206,113	1971	Fresh Yankee	293,960	1980	Classical Way	350,410

Pacers

Year	Horse	Dollars	Year	Horse	Dollars	Year	Horse	Dollars
1954	Red Sails	66,615	1963	Overtrick	208,833	1972	Albatross	459,921
1955	Adios Harry	98,900	1964	Race Time	199,292	1973	Sir Dalrae	307,354
1956	Adios Harry	129,912	1965	Bret Hanover	341,784	1974	Armbro Omaha	345,146
1957	Torpid	113,982	1966	Bret Hanover	407,534	1975	Silk Stockings	336,312
1958	Belle Action	167,887	1967	Romulus Hanover	277,636	1976	Keystone Ore	539,762
1959	Bye Bye Byrd	199,933	1968	Rum Customer	355,618	1977	Governor Skipper	522,148
1960	Bye Bye Byrd	187,612	1969	Overcall	373,150	1978	Abercrombie	703,260
1961	Adios Butler	180,250	1970	Most Happy Fella	387,239	1979	Hot Hitter	826,542
1962	Henry T. Adios	220,302	1971	Albatross	558,009	1980	Niatross	1,414,313

Leading Money-Winning Horses

(As of Aug. 15, 1981)

Trotters				Pacers			
Bellino II	$1,960,945	Fresh Yankee	$1,294,252	Niatross	$2,019,213	Rum Customer	$1,001,548
Ideal Du Gazeau	1,744,357	Hadol du Vivier	1,263,121	Rambling Willie	1,926,602	Cardigan Bay	1,000,837
Un De Mai	1,660,627	Keystone Pioneer	1,071,927	Albatross	1,201,470	Abercrombie	984,391
Eleazar	1,465,454	Roquepine	956,161	Land Grant	1,092,560	Hot Hitter	963,574
Savoir	1,365,145	Green Speed	953,013	Governor Skipper	1,039,756	McKinzie Almahurst	936,130

Harness Horse of the Year

(Chosen by the U.S. Trotting Assn. and the U.S. Harness Writers Assn.)

1948	Rodney	1956	Scott Frost	1964	Bret Hanover	1972	Albatross
1949	Good Time	1957	Torpid	1965	Bret Hanover	1973	Sir Dalrae
1950	Proximity	1958	Emily's Pride	1966	Bret Hanover	1974	Delmonica Hanover
1951	Pronto Don	1959	Bye Bye Byrd	1967	Nevele Pride	1975	Savior
1952	Good Time	1960	Adios Butler	1968	Nevele Pride	1976	Keystone Ore
1953	Hi Lo's Forbes	1961	Adios Butler	1969	Nevele Pride	1977	Green Speed
1954	Stenographer	1962	Su Mac Lad	1970	Fresh Yankee	1978	Abercrombie
1955	Scott Frost	1963	Speedy Scot	1971	Albatross	1979	Niatross
						1980	Niatross

Leading Drivers

Races Won

Year	Driver		Year	Driver		Year	Driver		Year	Driver	
1958	Bill Haughton	176	1964	Bob Farrington	312	1970	Herve Filion	486	1976	Herve Filion	445
1959	William Gilmour	165	1965	Bob Farrington	310	1971	Herve Filion	543	1977	Herve Filion	441
1960	Del Insko	156	1966	Bob Farrington	283	1972	Herve Filion	605	1978	Herve Filion	423
1961	Bob Farrington	201	1967	Bob Farrington	277	1973	Herve Filion	445	1979	Ron Waples	443
1962	Bob Farrington	203	1968	Herve Filion	407	1974	Herve Filion	637	1980	Herve Filion	474
1963	Donald Busse	201	1969	Herve Filion	394	1975	Daryl Buse	360			

Money Won

Year	Driver	Dollars	Year	Driver	Dollars	Year	Driver	Dollars
1957	Bill Haughton	586,950	1965	Bill Haughton	889,943	1973	Herve Filion	2,233,302
1958	Bill Haughton	816,659	1966	Stanley Dancer	1,218,403	1974	Herve Filion	3,474,315
1959	Bill Haughton	711,435	1967	Bill Haughton	1,305,773	1975	Carmine Abbatiello	2,275,093
1960	Del Miller	567,282	1968	Bill Haughton	1,654,172	1976	Herve Filion	2,241,045
1961	Stanley Dancer	674,723	1969	Del Insko	1,635,463	1977	Herve Filion	2,551,058
1962	Stanley Dancer	760,343	1970	Herve Filion	1,647,837	1978	Carmine Abbatiello	3,344,457
1963	Bill Haughton	790,086	1971	Herve Filion	1,915,945	1979	John Campbell	3,308,984
1964	Stanley Dancer	1,051,538	1972	Herve Filion	2,473,265	1980	John Campbell	3,732,306

Little Brown Jug (3-year-old pacers)

Delaware, Oh.

Year	Winner	Driver	Purse	Year	Winner	Driver	Purse
1957	Torpid	John Simpson Sr.	$73,528	1969	Laverne Hanover	Billy Haughton	$109,731
1958	Shadow Wave	Joe O'Brien	65,252	1970	Most Happy Fella	Stanley Dancer	100,110
1959	Adios Butler	Clint Hodgins	76,582	1971	Nansemond	Herve Filion	102,944
1960	Bullet Hanover	John Simpson Sr.	66,510	1972	Strike Out	Keith Waples	104,916
1961	Henry T. Adios	Stanley Dancer	70,069	1973	Melvin's Woe	Joe O'Brien	120,000
1962	Lehigh Hanover	Stanley Dancer	75,038	1974	Armbro Omaha	Billy Haughton	132,630
1963	Overtrick	John Patterson Sr.	68,294	1975	Seatrain	Ben Webster	147,813
1964	Vicar Hanover	Billy Haughton	66,590	1976	Keystone Ore	Stanley Dancer	153,799
1965	Bret Hanover	Frank Ervin	71,447	1977	Gov. Skipper	John Chapman	150,000
1966	Romeo Hanover	George Sholty	74,616	1978	Happy Escort	Bill Popfinger	186,760
1967	Best of All	James Hackett	84,778	1979	Hot Hitter	Herve Filion	226,455
1968	Rum Customer	Billy Haughton	104,226	1980	Niatross	Clint Galbraith	207,000
				1981	Fan Hanover(A)	Glen Garnsey	243,779

(A) First filly to win the Little Brown Jug.

AAU Wrestling Champions in 1981

Freestyle

105.5 lbs.—Bill Rosado, Sunkist Kids.
114.5 lbs.—Joe Gonzales, Sunkist Kids.
125.5 lbs.—John Azevedo, Sunkist Kids.
136.5 lbs.—Lee Roy Smith, Cowboy Wrestling Club.
149.5 lbs.—Andrew Rein, Wisconsin Wrestling Club.
163 lbs.—David Schultz, Oklahoma Underdogs.
180.5 lbs.—Dan Zilverberg, Sunkist Kids.
198 lbs.—Eric Wais, Oklahoma Underdogs.
220 lbs.—Greg Gibson, U.S. Marines.
Heavyweight—Jimmy Jackson, Sunkist Kids.
Outstanding wrestler—David Schultz.
Team—Sunkist Kids.

Greco-Roman

105.5 lbs.—T. J. Jones, U.S. Navy.
114.5 lbs.—Wilfredo Leivia, U.S. Marine Corps.
125.5 lbs.—Dan Mello, U.S. Marine Corps.
136.5 lbs.—Abdurrahim Kuzu, Nebraska Olympic Club.
149.5 lbs.—Doug Yeats, Canada.
163 lbs.—David Schultz, Oklahoma Underdogs.
180.5 lbs.—Dan Chandler, Twin City WC.
198 lbs.—Mike Houck, Minnesota WC.
220 lbs.—Jeff Blatnick, Adirondack 3-Style WC.
Heavyweight—Ron Carlisle, U.S. Marine Corps.
Outstanding wrestler—Jeff Blatnick.
Team—U.S. Marine Corps.

Rifle and Pistol Individual Championships in 1981

Source: National Rifle Assn.

National Outdoor Rifle and Pistol Championships

Pistol — SFC Joseph J. Pascarella, 2651-134X.
Civilian Pistol — Donald L. Hamilton, 2630-114X.
Regular Service — MSG Bonnie Harmon, 2645-148X.
Police Pistol — John L. Farley, 2609-100X.
Woman Pistol — SP5 Ruby E. Fox, 2572-79X.
Senior Pistol — Robert V. Coghe, 2563-72X.
Collegiate Pistol — Bernt L. Oydna, 2535-76X.
Junior Pistol — Kenneth O. Swanson, 2526-58X.
Smallbore Rifle Prone — Mary E. Stidworthy, 6391-530X.
Civilian Smallbore Rifle Prone — David Ross, 3d, 6388-495X.
Woman Smallbore Rifle Prone — Mary E. Stidworthy, 6391-530X.
Senior Smallbore Rifle Prone — Richard F. Hanson, 6375-483X.
Collegiate Smallbore Rifle Prone — Mary E. Stidworthy, 6391-530X.
Smallbore Rifle Position — Lones W. Wigger Jr., 2086.
Civilian Smallbore Rifle Position — David B. Lyman, 2050.
Woman Smallbore Rifle Position — Gloria K. Parmentier, 2056.
Senior Smallbore Rifle Position — Donald W. Burtis, 1855.
Collegiate Smallbore Rifle Position — Danny K. Wigger, 1987.
High Power Rifle — David I. Boyd, 2d, 2369-087X
High Power Civilian — Carl R. Bernosky, 2368-106X.
High Power Service — David I. Boyd, 2d, 2369-087X.
High Power Woman — Noma J. McCullough, 2339-083X.
High Power Junior — Mark R. Liebetrau, 2355-080X.
High Power Senior — Creighton Audette, 2327-061X.
High Power Collegiate — Dan Sutton, 2325-074X.

U. S. NRA International Shooting Championships

English Match — Lones W. Wigger Jr., 1779.
Smallbore Three Position — Lones W. Wigger Jr., 3472.
Air Rifle — John A. Rost, 1737.
Ladies Air Rifle — Karen E. Monez, 1162.
Woman Standard Rifle Prone — Marsha A. Beasley, 1759.
Woman Standard Rifle Three Position — Wanda R. Jewell, 1721.
Free Pistol — Darius Young, 1673.
Air Pistol — Donald C. Nyord, 1732.
Woman Air Pistol — Sallie L. Carroll, 1112.
Center Fire Pistol — Darius Young, 1773.
Rapid Fire Pistol — Allyn W. Johnson, 1765.
Standard Pistol — Darius Young, 1736.
Woman Smallbore Pistol — Sallie L. Carrol, 1716.

National Indoor Rifle and Pistol Championships

Conventional Rifle — Lones W. Wigger Jr., 800.
International Rifle — Lones W. Wigger Jr., 1182.
NRA 3-Position Rifle — Lones W. Wigger Jr., 1175.
Woman Conventional Rifle — Karen E. Monez, 798.
Woman NRA 3-Position Rifle — Karen E. Monez, 1167.
Woman International Rifle — Karen E. Monez, 1163.
Conventional Pistol — Guigno D. Carapellotti, 884.
Woman Conventional Pistol — SP5 Ruby E. Fox, 855.
International Free Pistol — Steve F. Reiter, 562.
International Standard Pistol — Donald L. Hamilton, 580.
Woman International Free Pistol — Patricia A. Graham, 527.
Woman International Standard Pistol — Elinor A. Collins, 534.
Air Rifle — Lones W. Wigger Jr., 584.
Woman Air Rifle — Barbara S. Mann, 576.
Air Pistol — Toivo Koehler, 574.
Woman Air Pistol — Jeanne E. David, 529.

National Skeet Shoot Championships in 1981

High Overall - 550 targets

Champion — Louis Hulgan, McCalla, Ala., 548.
Women — Stanka Petrovich, Roselle, N.J., 542.
Industry — John Hancock, Stone Mountain, Ga., 544.
Veteran — Frank Laudano, Port Arthur, Tex., 519.
Sub-senior — T. J. Maddox, Macon, Ga., 542.
Senior — Carl Sorensen, Racine, Wis., 537.
Junior — J. C. Martin, Laredo, Tex., 541.
Collegiate — Jeff Sizemore, Corpus Christie, Tex., 543.

.410 Bore - 100 targets

Champion — Wayne Mayes, Cleveland, Tenn., 100.
Women — Conni Place, Bloomfield Hills, Mich., 97.
Industry — John Hancock, Stone Mountain, Ga., 98.
Veteran — Tom Sanfilipo, Fairfield, Cal., 92.
Sub-senior — Boyd Wickman, Des Moines, Ia., 98.
Senior — Howard Posson, Arcadia, Cal., 97.
Junior — Earl Mitchell, Austin, Tex., 97.
Collegiate — Jeff Sizemore, Corpus Christie, Tex., 99.

28 Gauge - 100 targets

Champion — Dave Starrett, New Boston, Oh., 100.
Women — Ila Hill, Birmingham, Mich., 100.
Industry — Ken Sedlecky, Plano, Tex., 99.
Veteran — Barbee Ponder Jr., Amite, La., 96.
Sub-senior — Ila Hill, 100.
Senior — Jim Leer, San Antonio, Tex., 99.
Junior — Tal Sprinkles, Roundrock, Tex., 100.
Collegiate — Todd Bender, San Antonio, Tex., 100.

20 Gauge - 100 targets

Champion — Chip Youngblood, Fort Lauderdale, Fla., 100.
Women — Stanka Petrovich, Roselle, N.J., 100.
Industry — Asa Oliver, Plano, Tex., 100.
Veteran — Don Tyler, Fort Walton Beach, Fla., 97.
Sub-senior — Jesse Briley, Houston, Tex., 100.
Senior — Carl Sorensen, Racine, Wis., 99.
Junior — Bobby Wrenn, Punta Gorda, Fla., 99.
Collegiate — Stanka Petrovich, Roselle, N.J., 100.

12 Gauge - 250 targets

Champion — John Shima, San Antonio, Tex., 250.
Women — Stanka Petrovich, Roselle, N.J., 247.
Industry — Ken Sedlecky, Plano, Tex., 249.
Veteran — Frank Laudano, Port Arthur, Tex., 244.
Sub-senior — T. J. Maddox, Macon, Ga., 250.
Senior — Carl Sorensen, Racine, Wis., 250.
Junior — Tal Sprinkles, Roundrock, Tex., 250.
Collegiate — Jeff Sizemore, Corpus Christie, Tex., 250.

12 Champion of Champions - 100 targets

Champion — John Shima, San Antonio, Tex., 100.
Women — Conni Place, Bloomfield Hills, Mich., 99.
Veteran — Barbee Ponder, Amite, La., 99.
Sub-senior — Boyd Wickman, Des Moines, Ia., 100.
Senior — Clarence Johnson, Louisville, Ky., 99.
Junior — Randy Borth, Wentzville, Mo., 96.
Collegiate — Preston Douglass, San Antonio, Tex., 99.

All-American Derby in 1981

Higheasterjet won the $1 million All-American Derby on Aug. 30, 1981 at Ruidoso Downs, N.M. The 3-year-old, owned by G.D. Highsmith of LaGrange, Tex., became the first quarter horse to reach $1 million in career earnings. He ran the 440 yards in 21.93 seconds.

U.S. Outdoor Diving Championships in 1981

Greg Louganis won the men's one-meter and 3-meter diving titles at the U.S. outdoor championships in Mission Viejo, Cal. Bruce Kimball won the 10-meter title.

The women's titles were won by Kelly McCormick (one-meter), Megan Neyer (3-meter), and Debbie Rush (10-meter).

World Swimming Records

As of Sept., 1981

Effective June 1, 1969, FINA recognizes only records made over a 50-meter course.

Men's Records

Freestyle

Distance	Time	Holder	Country	Where made	Date
100 Meters	0:49.36	Rowdy Gaines	U.S.	Austin, Tex.	Apr., 1981
200 Meters	1:49.16	Rowdy Gaines	U.S.	Austin, Tex.	Apr. 11, 1980
400 Meters	3:50.49	Peter Szmidt	Canada	Ontario, Canada	July, 1980
800 Meters	7:56.43	Vladimir Salnikov	USSR	Minsk	Mar. 23, 1979
1,500 Meters	14:58.27	Vladimir Salnikov	USSR	Moscow	July, 1980

Breaststroke

100 Meters	1:02.86	Gerald Moerken	W. Germany	Jonkoping, Sweden	Aug. 17, 1977
200 Meters	2:15.11	David Wilkie	Gt. Britain	Montreal	July 24, 1976

Butterfly

100 Meters	0:53.81	William Paulus	U.S.	Austin, Tex.	Apr., 1981
200 Meters	1:58.01	Craig Beardsley	U.S.	Kiev, USSR	Aug., 1981

Backstroke

100 Meters	0:55.49	John Naber	U.S.	Montreal	July 19, 1976
200 Meters	1:59.19	John Naber	U.S.	Montreal	July 24, 1976

Individual Medley

200 Meters	2:02.78	Alex Baumann	Canada	Heidelberg, W. Germany	July, 1981
400 Meters	4:20.05	Jesse Vassallo	U.S., Puerto Rico	W. Berlin	Aug. 22, 1978

Freestyle Relays

400 M. (4×100)	3:19.74	Babashoff, Gaines, McCagg, Montgomery	U.S.	W. Berlin	Aug. 22, 1978
800 M. (4×200)	7:20.83	Forrester, Furniss, Gaines, Hackett	U.S.	W. Berlin	Aug. 24, 1978

Medley Relays

400 M. (4×100)	3:42.22	Hencken, Naber, Montgomery, Vogel	U.S.	Montreal	July 22, 1976

Women's Records

Freestyle

100 Meters	0:54.79	Barbara Krause	E. Germany	Moscow	July, 1980
200 Meters	1:58.43	Cynthia Woodhead	U.S.	San Juan, P.R.	Aug., 1979
400 Meters	4:06.28	Tracey Wickham	Australia	W. Berlin	Aug. 24, 1978
800 Meters	8:18.77	Cynthia Woodhead	U.S.	Paris	Feb. 8, 1980
1,500 Meters	16:04.49	Kim Linehan	U.S.	Ft. Lauderdale, Fla.	Aug. 19, 1979

Breaststroke

100 Meters	1:08.60	Ute Geweniger	E. Germany	Yugoslavia	Sept., 1981
200 Meters	2:27.32	Tracy Caulkins	U.S.	Paris	Feb. 7, 1981

Butterfly

100 Meters	0:57.93	Mary T. Meagher	U.S.	Brown Deer, Wis.	Aug. 16, 1981
200 Meters	2:05.96	Mary T. Meagher	U.S.	Brown Deer, Wis.	Aug. 13, 1981

Backstroke

100 Meters	1:00.86	Rica Reinisch	E. Germany	Moscow	July, 1980
200 Meters	2:11.77	Rica Reinisch	E. Germany	Moscow	July, 1980

Individual Medley

200 Meters	2:11.73	Ute Geweniger	E. Germany	E. Berlin	July 5, 1981
400 Meters	4:36.29	Petra Schneider	E. Germany	Moscow	July, 1980

Freestyle Relays

400 M. (4×100)	3:42.71	National Team	E. Germany	Moscow	July, 1980

Medley Relays

400 M. (4×100)	4:06.67	National Team	E. Germany	Moscow	July, 1980

U.S. Outdoor Swimming Championships in 1981

Brown Deer, Wis., Aug. 13-16, 1981

Men

50-Meter Freestyle—Robin Leamy, Western Samoa. Time—0:22.54.
100-Meter Freestyle—Chris Cavanaugh, Saratoga, Cal. Time—0:50.71.
200-Meter Freestyle—Dave Larson, Gainesville, Fla. Time—1:50.86.
400-Meter Freestyle—Jeff Float. Time—3:54.99.
800-Meter Freestyle—Doug Towne, Tucson, Ariz. Time—8:05.07.
1,500-Meter Freestyle—Max Metzker, Australia. Time—15:23.86.
100-Meter Breaststroke—Nick Nevid, Elm Grove, Wis. Time—1:03.80.
200-Meter Breaststroke—Nick Nevid, Elm Grove, Wis. Time—2:19.27.
100-Meter Backstroke—Rich Carey, Mt. Kisco, N.Y. Time—0:56.58.
200-Meter Backstroke—Jesse Vassallo, Mission Viejo, Cal. Time—2:01.50.
100-Meter Butterfly—Matt Gribble, Miami, Fla. Time—0:54.15.
200-Meter Butterfly—Craig Beardsley, Harrington Park, N.J. Time—1:59.01.
200-Meter Individual Medley—Bill Barrett, Mission Viejo, Cal. Time—2:03.26.
400-Meter Individual Medley—Jesse Vassallo, Mission Viejo, Cal. Time—4:20.33.
800-Meter Freestyle Relay—Florida Aquatic Time—7:30.23.

Women

100-Meter Freestyle—Jill Sterkel, Hacienda Hts., Cal. Time—0:56.25.
200-Meter Freestyle—Marybeth Linzmeier, Mission Viejo, Cal. Time—2:00.05.
400-Meter Freestyle—Tiffany Cohen, Mission Viejo, Cal. Time—4:09.88.
800-Meter Freestyle—Marybeth Linzmeier. Time—8:27.80.
1,500 Meter Freestyle—Marybeth Linzmeier, Time—16:16.86.
100-Meter Breaststroke—Tracy Caukins, Nashville, Tenn. Time—1:10.77.
200-Meter Breaststroke—Tracy Caukins. Time—2:32.48.
100-Meter Backstroke—Theresa Andrews, Annapolis, Md. Time—1:03.04.
200-Meter Backstroke—Libby Kinkead, West Chester, Pa. Time—2:15.13.
100-Meter Butterfly—Mary T. Meagher, Louisville, Ky. Time—0:57.93.
200-Meter Butterfly—Mary T. Meagher. Time—2:05.96.
200-Meter Individual Medley—Tracy Caukins. Time—2:14.18.
400-Meter Individual Medley—Tracy Caukins. Time—4:43.66.
800-Meter Freestyle Relay—Mission Viejo. Time—8:07.44.

3d National Sports Festival

Syracuse, N.Y., July, 1981

Boxing

106 lbs.—Jesse Benevides, North Carolina.
112 lbs.—Fred Perkins, Ft. Bragg, N.C.
119 lbs.—Richard Savage, West Monroe, La.
125 lbs.—Ben Marquez, Denver, Col.
132 lbs.—Vincent Pazienza, Cranston, R.I.
139 lbs.—Vincent Webb, University City, Mo.
147 lbs.—Mark Breland, New York, N.Y.
156 lbs.—Alfred Mayes, St. Louis, Mo.
165 lbs.—Randy Smith, Chicago, Ill.
178 lbs.—Johnny Williams, Chicago, Ill.
Heavyweight—Mark Mahone, Norfolk, Va.
172 lbs.—Breet Barron, San Francisco, Cal.
189 lbs.—Hector Estevez, Miami, Fla.
209 lbs.—Miguel Tudela, Alhambra, Cal.
Over 209 lbs.—Brad Moss, Gilroy, Cal.
Open Division—Dewey Mitchell, Seven Springs, Fla.

Women

134 lbs.—Robin Chapman, Cranford, N.J.
158 lbs.—Corinne Shigemoto, Santa Clara, Cal.

Canoe-Kayak

500-Meter Kayak—David Halpren, Seattle, Wash.
500-Meter Canoe—Bret Young, Hastings, N.Y.
500-Meters Pairs—Rod and Rusty McLain, Gloversville, N.Y.
500-Meters Kayak Pairs—Gus Peterson, Agoura, Cal. and Terry Kent, Rochester, N.Y.
1,000-Meters Kayak—David Halpren.
1,000-Meters Canoe—Rod McLain.
1,000-Meters Kayak Pairs—Terry Kent and Gus Peterson.
1,000-Meters Canoe Pairs—Tom Smith, New York, N.Y. and Bret Young.

Women

500-Meter Kayak—Linda Dragan, Washington, D.C.
500-Meter Kayak Pairs—Carol Toeppner, Costa Mesa, Cal. and Shelis Canover, Hadley, Mass.

Cycling—Men

100-Kilometer—John Beckman, Beaverton, Ore.
64.8-Kilometer Criterium—Len Nitz, New York, N.Y.

Women

50-Kilometer—Connie Carpenter, Madison, Wis.
28.8-Kilometer Criterium—Jacque Bradley, Ames, Ia.

Diving—Men

100-Meters—Greg Louganis, Mission Viejo, Cal.
300-Meters—Dave Burgering, Mission Viejo, Cal.

Women

100-Meters—Chris Seufert, Ann Arbor, Mich.
300-Meters—Chris Seufert.

Judo—Men

132 lbs.—Doug Tono, Chicago, Ill.
156 lbs.—Mike Swain, Bridgewater, N.J.
143 lbs.—Craig Agena, Aurora, Col.

Figure Skating

Ice Dancing—Elisa Spitz, Short Hills, N.Y. and Scott Gregory, Wilmington, Del.
Pairs—Kitty and Peter Carruthers, Burlington, Mass.
Men's Singles—Scott Hamilton, Denver, Col.
Women's Singles—Rosalynn Summers, Edmonds, Wash.

Roller Skating—Men

Artistic Figures—Tony St. Jacques, Virginia Beach, Va.
Artistic Singles—Tim McGuire, Flint, Mich.
500 Meters—Donnie Van Patter, Little Rock, Ark.
1,000 Meters—Ray Sharp, N. Little Rock, Ark.
1,500 Meters—Ray Sharp.
3,000 Meters—Tom Peterson, Tacoma, Wash.

Women

Artistic Figures—Anna Conklin, Bakersfield, Cal.
Artistic Singles—Tina Kneisley, Brighton, Minn.
1,000 Meters—Beverly Calhoun, Hampton, Va.
1,500 Meters—Mary Hohl Barriere, Cincinnati, Oh.
3,000 Meters—Mary Hohl Barriere.
Free Dance—Charles Kirchner, Riverside, N.J. and Linda Todd, Cherry Hill, N.J.
Mixed Pairs—Paul Price, Howell, Mich. and Tina Kneisley.

Rowing

Single Sculls (Men)—John Biglow, Bellevue, Wash.
Single Sculls (Women)—Cathleen Thaxton, San Diego, Cal.

Shooting—Men

Air Rifle—John Rost, Cincinnati, Oh.
English Match—Kurt Fitz-Randolph, Palm Bay, Fla.
Free Pistol—Eric Buljung, Ft. Benning, Ga.
International Trap—Dayne Johnson, Ft. Worth, Tex.
International Skeet—Sai Chiang, San Francisco, Cal.
Free Rifle—Philip Whitworth, Fairmont, W. Va.
Rapid Fire Pistol—Rojelio Cirredondo, Columbus, Ga.

Air Pistol—Eric Buljung.

Women

Small Bore—Ruby Fox, Parker, Ariz.
Air Rifle—Ethel Ann Alves, New Castle, Del.
Standard Rifle—Pat Spurgin, Fairmont, W. Va.

Speed Skating—Men

500 Meters—Steve Merrifield, Canoga Park, Cal.
1,500 Meters—Steve Merrifield.
1,000 Meters—Steve Merrifield.

Women

500 Meters—Gloria Bogacki, E. Park Ridge, Ill.
1,000 Meters—Gloria Bogacki.
1,500 Meters—Gloria Bogacki.

Swimming—Men

100-Meter Freestyle—Robin Leamy, Palos Verdes, Cal.
200-Meter Freestyle—Mike Heath, Dallas, Tex.
400-Meter Freestyle—Doug Towne, Tucson, Ariz.
1,600-Meter Freestyle—Paul Budd, Memphis, Tenn.
100-Meter Butterfly—Dave Cowell, Belpre, Ore.
200-Meter Butterfly—John Denny, Ft. Wayne, Ind.
100-Meter Backstroke—Rick Carey, Mt. Kisco, N.Y.
200-Meter Backstroke—Rick Carey.
100-Meter Breaststroke—Bill Barrett, Alpharetta, Ga.
200-Meter Breaststroke—John Moffet, Balboa, Cal.
200-Meter Individual Medley—Bill Barrett.

Women

100-Meter Freestyle—Susie Thayer, Barstow, Fla.
200-Meter Freestyle—Mary Wayte, Mercer Island, Wash.
400-Meter Freestyle—Sabrina Sagehorn, Martinez, Cal.
800-Meter Freestyle—Susan Andra, Wichita, Kan.
100-Meter Backstroke—Theresa Andrews, Annapolis, Md.
200-Meter Backstroke—Mary Wayte.
100-Meter Breaststroke—Terri Baxter, Palo Alto, Cal.
200-Meter Breaststroke—Polly Winde, Elliot City, Pa.
100-Meter Butterfly—Melanie Buddmeyer, Pittsburgh, Pa.
200-Meter Butterfly—Sara Linke, Walnut Creek, Cal.
200-Meter Individual Medley—Patty Gavin, Ardmore, Pa.
400-Meter Individual Medley—Patty Gavin.

Synchronized Swimming

Solo—Tracie Ruiz, Bothell, Wash.
Duet—Candy Costie and Tracie Ruiz, Bothell, Mich.
Figure—Tracie Ruiz.

Fencing

Foil—Helk Hamberzumian, San Francisco, Cal.
Foil (Women)—Ilona Maskal, Rutherford, N.J.
Epee—Bob Nieman, San Antonio, Tex.
Sabre—Peter Westbrook, New York, N.Y.

Tennis

Singles (Men)—Gus Anderson, Salinas, Cal.
Singles (Women)—Robin White, San Jose, Cal.
Doubles (Women)—Julie Grummell, Longview, Wash. and Robin White.
Doubles (Men)—Randy Vigmostad, Greenlawn, N.Y. and Fred Perrin, Southampton, N.Y.
Mixed Doubles—Andy Winterbauer, Mercer Island, Wash. and Julie Grummell.

Track and Field—Men

100 Meters—James Sanford, Los Angeles, Cal.
200 Meters—Dwayne Evans, Tempe, Ariz.
400 Meters—Tony Darden, Reno, Nev.
800 Meters—James Robinson, Berkeley, Cal.
1,500 Meters—Tom Byers, Eugene, Ore.
3,000 Meter Steeplechase—Henry Marsh, Eugene, Ore.
5,000 Meters—Craig Virgin, Lebanon, Ill.
10,000 Meters—Grey Meyer, Holliston, Mass.
20-Kilometer Walk—Todd Scully, Blacksburg, Va.
50-Kilometer Walk—Vince O'Sullivan, New York, N.Y.
High Jump—Greg Seay, Oklahoma City, Okla.
Pole Vault—Dave Volz, Bloomington, Ind.
Long Jump—Larry Myricks, Clinton, Miss.
Triple Jump—David McFadgen, Petersburg, Va.

110 Meter High Hurdles—Renaldo Nehemiah, Scotch Plains, N.J.
400 Meter High Hurdles—Andre Phillips, Los Angeles, Cal.
Shot Put—Brian Oldfield, Los Angeles, Cal.
Discus—John Powell, Los Angeles, Cal.
Hammer Throw—Dave McKenzie, Sacramento, Cal.
Javelin—Bob Roggy, Eugene, Ore.
Decathlon—Brian Mondschein, Huntington Beach, Cal.
Marathon—Gary Tuttle, Ventura, Cal.

Women

100 Meters—Evelyn Ashford, Los Angeles, Cal.
200 Meters—Florence Griffith, Los Angeles, Cal.
400 Meters—Denean Howard, Granada Hills, Cal.
800 Meters—Madeline Manning-Mimms, Clarksville, Tenn.
1,500 Meters—Cincy Bremser, Madison, Wis.
3,000 Meters—Kim Gallagher, Upper Darby, Pa.
Marathon—Laura Dewald, Arlington, Va.
100-Meter Hurdles—Stephanie Hightower, Columbus, Oh.
400-Meter Hurdles—Edna Brown, Philadelphia, Pa.
High Jump—Pam Spencer, Northridge, Cal.
Long Jump—Kathy McMillan-Ray, Clarkesville, Tenn.
Shot Put—Denise Wood, Montclair, N.J.
Discus—Denise Wood.
Javelin—Patty Kearney, Eugene, Ore.
Heptathlon—Cindy Gariner, Lebanon, Ore.

Weightlifting

114 lbs.—Richard Stoner, Butler, Pa.
123 lbs.—Brian Miyamoto, Hawaii.
132 lbs.—Joe Widdel, Waterloo, Ia.
148 lbs.—Don Abrahamson, Winter Park, Fla.
165 lbs.—Mark Levell, Chicago, Ill.
181 lbs.—Curt White, Charles, Ill.
198 lbs.—Kevin Winter, San Jose, Cal.
220 lbs.—Ken Clark, Pacifica, Cal.
242 lbs.—Guy Carlton, Colorado Springs, Col.
Over 242 lbs.—Mario Martinez, Salinas, Cal.

Wrestling—Greco-Roman

106 lbs.—Jeff Clark, Voorheesville, N.Y.
115 lbs.—Gil Sanchez, Cheyenne, Wyo.
123 lbs.—Kevin Allen, Clarendon, Vt.
132 lbs.—John Placek, Schenectady, N.Y.
143 lbs.—William Taylor, Portland, Ore.
154 lbs.—John Cardi, Ballston Spa, N.Y.
165 lbs.—Jacob Sabo, Granville, N.Y.
178 lbs.—Ab Brown, Casper, Wyo.
192 lbs.—Scott Sabo, Granville, N.Y.
Unlimited lbs.—Gary Albright, Billings, Mont.

Wrestling—Freestyle

106 lbs.—Joe Gallardo, Corona, Cal.
115 lbs.—Matt Campbell, Havre, Mont.
123 lbs.—James Jordan, St. Paris, Oh.
132 lbs.—Marc Sprague, Portland, Ore.
143 lbs.—Scott Duncan, Marian, Oh.
154 lbs.—John DeHart, Chesterton, Ind.
165 lbs.—Howard Lawson, Piacentia, Cal.
178 lbs.—Paul Diekel, Whitehall, N.J.
192 lbs.—Todd Wychoff, New London, Oh.
Unlimited lbs.—Dave Koplovitz, Schenectady, N.Y.

Other Winners

Archery—Men: Darrell Pace, Cincinnati, Oh.; Women: Ruth Rowe, Gaithersburg, Md.
Baseball—East.
Basketball—Men: West; Women: South.
Equestrian—Dressage: Lendon Gray, Dixmont, Ma.; Jumping—Katherine Giffort, Elnora, N.Y.
Gymnastics, All-Around—Men: Brian Meeker; Women: Beth Pope.
Hockey—Great Lakes.
Modern Pentathlon—Brian Davies, San Antonio, Tex.
Soccer—East.
Softball—Men: Peterbilt Western; Women: Sun City Saints.
Volleyball—Men: East; Women: West.
Water Polo—East.
Yachting—East.

Little League World Series in 1981

Taiwan won the 1981 Little League World Series by defeating Tampa (Fla.) 4-2 at Williamsport, Pa. The victory was Taiwan's 5th consecutive championship and their 10th world title in the past 13 years.

Members of National Baseball Hall of Fame and Museum

The shrine of organized baseball, dedicated June 12, 1939, is located in Cooperstown, N. Y.

Alexander, Grover Cleveland	Connolly, Thomas H.	Grove, Lefty	Lindstrom, Fred	Ruffing, Red
Anson, Cap	Connor, Roger	Hafey, Chick	Lloyd, Pop	Rusie, Amos
Averill, Earl	Coveleski, Stan	Haines, Jesee	Lopez, Al	Ruth, Babe
Appling, Luke	Crawford, Sam	Hamilton, Bill	Lyons, Ted	Schalk, Ray
Baker, Home Run	Cronin, Joe	Harridge, Will	Mack, Connie	Sewell, Joe
Bancroft, Dave	Cummings, Candy	Harris, Bucky	MacPhail, Larry	Simmons, Al
Banks, Ernie	Cuyler, Kiki	Hartnett, Gabby	Mantle, Mickey	Sisler, George
Barrow, Edward G.	Dean, Dizzy	Heilmann, Harry	Manush, Henry	Snider, Duke
Beckley, Jake	Delahanty, Ed	Herman, Billy	Maranville, Rabbit	Spahn, Warren
Bell, Cool Papa	Dickey, Bill	Hooper, Harry	Marquard, Rube	Spalding, Albert
Bender, Chief	DiHigo, Martin	Hornsby, Rogers	Mathews, Eddie	Speaker, Tris,
Berra, Yogi	DiMaggio, Joe	Hoyt, Waite	Mathewson, Christy	Stengel, Casey
Bottomley, Jim	Duffy, Hugh	Hubbard, Cal	Mays, Willie	Terry, Bill
Boudreau, Lou	Evans, Billy	Hubbell, Carl	McCarthy, Joe	Thompson, Sam
Bresnahan, Roger	Evers, John	Huggins, Miller	McCarthy, Thomas	Tinker, Joe
Brouthers, Dan	Ewing, Buck	Irvin, Monte	McGinnity, Joe	Traynor, Pie
Brown (Three Finger), Mordecai	Faber, Urban	Jennings, Hugh	McGraw, John	Vance, Dazzy
Bulkeley, Morgan C.	Feller, Bob	Johnson, Byron	McKechnie, Bill	Waddell, Rube
Burkett, Jesse C.	Flick, Elmer H.	Johnson, William (Rudy)	Medwick, Joe	Wagner, Honus
Campanella, Roy	Ford, Whitey	Johnson, Walter	Mize, Johnny	Wallace, Roderick
Carey, Max	Foster, Andrew	Joss, Addie	Musial, Stan	Walsh, Ed.
Cartwright, Alexander	Foxx, Jimmy	Kaline, Al	Nichols, Kid	Waner, Lloyd
Chadwick, Henry	Frick, Ford	Keefe, Timothy	O'Rourke, James	Waner, Paul
Chance, Frank	Frisch, Frank	Keeler, William	Ott, Mel	Ward, John
Charleston, Oscar	Galvin, Pud	Kelley, Joe	Paige, Satchel	Weiss, George
Chesbro, John	Gehrig, Lou	Kelly, George	Pennock, Herb	Welch, Mickey
Clarke, Fred	Gehringer, Charles	Kelly, King	Plank, Ed	Wheat, Zach
Clarkson, John	Gibson, Bob	Kiner, Ralph	Radbourne, Charlie	Williams, Ted
Clemente, Roberto	Gibson, Josh	Klein, Chuck	Rice, Sam	Wilson, Hack
Cobb, Ty	Giles, Warren	Klem, Bill	Rickey, Branch	Wright, George
Cochrane, Mickey	Gomez, Lefty	Koufax, Sandy	Rixey, Eppa	Wright, Harry
Collins, Eddie	Goslin, Goose	Lajoie, Napoleon	Roberts, Robin	Wynn, Early
Collins, James	Greenberg, Hank	Landis, Kenesaw M.	Robinson, Jackie	Yawkey, Tom
Combs, Earle	Griffith, Clark	Lemon, Bob	Robinson, Wilbert	Young, Cy
Comiskey, Charles A.	Grimes, Burleigh	Leonard, Buck	Roush, Edd	Youngs, Ross
Conlan, Jocko				

All-Star Baseball Games, 1933-1981

Year	Winner	Score	Location	Year	Winner	Score	Location
1933	American	4-2	Chicago	1959	American	5-3	Los Angeles
1934	American	9-7	New York	1960	National	5-3	Kansas City
1935	American	4-1	Cleveland	1960	National	6-0	New York
1936	National	4-3	Boston	1961	National (3)	5-4	San Francisco
1937	American	8-3	Washington	1961	Called-Rain	1-1	Boston
1938	National	4-1	Cincinnati	1962	National (3)	3-1	Washington
1939	American	3-1	New York	1962	American	9-4	Chicago
1940	National	4-0	St. Louis	1963	National	5-3	Cleveland
1941	American	7-5	Detroit	1964	National	7-4	New York
1942	American	3-1	New York	1965	National	6-5	Minnesota
1943*	American	5-3	Philadelphia	1966	National (3)	2-1	St. Louis
1944*	National	7-1	Pittsburgh	1967	National (4)	2-1	Anaheim
1945	(not played)			1968*	National	1-0	Houston
1946	American	12-0	Boston	1969	National	9-3	Washington
1947	American	2-1	Chicago	1970*	National (2)	5-4	Cincinnati
1948	American	5-2	St. Louis	1971*	American	6-4	Detroit
1949	American	11-7	New York	1972*	National	4-3	Atlanta
1950	National (1)	4-3	Chicago	1973*	National	7-1	Kansas City
1951	National	8-3	Detroit	1974*	National	7-2	Pittsburgh
1952	National	3-2	Philadelphia	1975*	National	6-3	Milwaukee
1953	National	5-1	Cincinnati	1976*	National	7-1	Philadelphia
1954	American	11-9	Cleveland	1977*	National	7-5	New York
1955	National (2)	6-5	Milwaukee	1978*	National	7-3	San Diego
1956	National	7-3	Washington	1979*	National	7-6	Seattle
1957	American	6-5	St. Louis	1980*	National	4-2	Los Angeles
1958	American	4-3	Baltimore	1981*	National	5-4	Cleveland
1959	National	5-4	Pittsburgh				

(1) 14 innings, (2) 12 innings, (3) 10 innings, (4) 15 innings *Night game.

Major League Perfect Games Since 1900

Year	Player	Clubs	Score	Year	Player	Clubs	Score
1904	Cy Young	Boston vs. Phil. (AL)	3-0	1964	Jim Bunning	Phil. vs. N.Y. Mets (NL)	6-0
1908	Addie Joss	Cleveland vs. Chicago (AL)	1-0	1965	Sandy Koufax	Los Angeles vs. Chic. (NL)	1-0
1917	Ernie Shore (a)	Boston vs. Wash. (AL)	4-0	1968	Jim Hunter	Oakland vs. Minn. (AL)	4-0
1922	Charles Robertson	Chicago vs. Detroit (AL)	2-0	1981	Len Barker	Cleveland vs. Toronto (AL)	3-0
1956	Don Larson (b)	N.Y. Yankees vs. Brooklyn	2-0				

(a) Babe Ruth, the starting pitcher, was ejected from the game after walking the first batter. Shore replaced him and the base-runner was out stealing. Shore retired the next 26 batters. (b) World Series.

Major League Pennant Winners, 1901–1981

National League					American League				
Year	Winner	Won	Lost	Pct	Manager	Year	Winner	Won	Lost	Pct	Manager
---	---	---	---	---	---	---	---	---	---	---	---
1901	Pittsburgh	90	49	.647	Clarke	1901	Chicago	83	53	.610	Griffith
1902	Pittsburgh	103	36	.741	Clarke	1902	Philadelphia	83	53	.610	Mack
1903	Pittsburgh	91	49	.650	Clarke	1903	Boston	91	47	.659	Collins
1904	New York	106	47	.693	McGraw	1904	Boston	95	59	.617	Collins
1905	New York	105	48	.686	McGraw	1905	Philadelphia	92	56	.622	Mack
1906	Chicago	116	36	.763	Chance	1906	Chicago	93	58	.616	Jones
1907	Chicago	107	45	.704	Chance	1907	Detroit	92	58	.613	Jennings
1908	Chicago	99	55	.643	Chance	1908	Detroit	90	63	.588	Jennings
1909	Pittsburgh	110	42	.724	Clarke	1909	Detroit	98	54	.645	Jennings
1910	Chicago	104	50	.675	Chance	1910	Philadelphia	102	48	.680	Mack
1911	New York	99	54	.647	McGraw	1911	Philadelphia	101	50	.669	Mack
1912	New York	103	48	.682	McGraw	1912	Boston	105	47	.691	Stahl
1913	New York	101	51	.664	McGraw	1913	Philadelphia	96	57	.627	Mack
1914	Boston	94	59	.614	Stallings	1914	Philadelphia	99	53	.651	Mack
1915	Philadelphia	90	62	.592	Moran	1915	Boston	101	50	.669	Carrigan
1916	Brooklyn	94	60	.610	Robinson	1916	Boston	91	63	.591	Carrigan
1917	New York	98	56	.636	McGraw	1917	Chicago	100	54	.649	Rowland
1918	Chicago	84	45	.651	Mitchell	1918	Boston	75	51	.595	Barrow
1919	Cincinnati	96	44	.686	Moran	1919	Chicago	88	52	.629	Gleason
1920	Brooklyn	93	60	.604	Robinson	1920	Cleveland	98	56	.636	Speaker
1921	New York	94	56	.614	McGraw	1921	New York	98	55	.641	Huggins
1922	New York	93	61	.604	McGraw	1922	New York	94	60	.610	Huggins
1923	New York	95	58	.621	McGraw	1923	New York	98	54	.645	Huggins
1924	New York	93	60	.608	McGraw	1924	Washington	92	62	.597	Harris
1925	Pittsburgh	95	58	.621	McKechnie	1925	Washington	96	55	.636	Harris
1926	St. Louis	89	65	.578	Hornsby	1926	New York	91	63	.591	Huggins
1927	Pittsburgh	94	60	.610	Bush	1927	New York	110	44	.714	Huggins
1928	St. Louis	95	59	.617	McKechnie	1928	New York	101	53	.656	Huggins
1929	Chicago	98	54	.645	McCarthy	1929	Philadelphia	104	46	.693	Mack
1930	St. Louis	92	62	.597	Street	1930	Philadelphia	102	52	.622	Mack
1931	St. Louis	101	53	.656	Street	1931	Philadelphia	107	45	.704	Mack
1932	Chicago	90	64	.584	Grimm	1932	New York	107	47	.695	McCarthy
1933	New York	91	61	.599	Terry	1933	Washington	99	53	.651	Cronin
1934	St. Louis	95	58	.621	Frisch	1934	Detroit	101	53	.656	Cochrane
1935	Chicago	100	54	.649	Grimm	1935	Detroit	93	58	.616	Cochrane
1936	New York	91	62	.597	Terry	1936	New York	102	51	.667	McCarthy
1937	New York	95	57	.625	Terry	1937	New York	102	52	.662	McCarthy
1938	Chicago	89	63	.586	Hartnett	1938	New York	99	53	.651	McCarthy
1939	Cincinnati	97	57	.630	McKechnie	1939	New York	106	45	.702	McCarthy
1940	Cincinnati	100	53	.654	McKechnie	1940	Detroit	90	64	.584	Baker
1941	Brooklyn	100	54	.649	Durocher	1941	New York	101	53	.656	McCarthy
1942	St. Louis	106	48	.688	Southworth	1942	New York	103	51	.669	McCarthy
1943	St. Louis	105	49	.682	Southworth	1943	New York	98	56	.636	McCarthy
1944	St. Louis	105	49	.682	Southworth	1944	St. Louis	89	65	.578	Sewell
1945	Chicago	98	56	.636	Grimm	1945	Detroit	88	65	.575	O'Neill
1946	St. Louis	98	58	.628	Dyer	1946	Boston	104	50	.675	Cronin
1947	Brooklyn	94	60	.610	Shotton	1947	New York	97	57	.630	Harris
1948	Boston	91	62	.595	Southworth	1948	Cleveland	97	58	.626	Boudreau
1949	Brooklyn	97	57	.630	Shotton	1949	New York	97	57	.630	Stengel
1950	Philadelphia	91	63	.591	Sawyer	1950	New York	98	56	.636	Stengel
1951	New York	98	59	.624	Durocher	1951	New York	98	56	.636	Stengel
1952	Brooklyn	96	57	.627	Dressen	1952	New York	95	59	.617	Stengel
1953	Brooklyn	105	49	.682	Dressen	1953	New York	99	52	.656	Stengel
1954	New York	97	57	.630	Durocher	1954	Cleveland	111	43	.721	Lopez
1955	Brooklyn	98	55	.641	Alston	1955	New York	96	58	.623	Stengel
1956	Brooklyn	93	61	.604	Alston	1956	New York	97	57	.630	Stengel
1957	Milwaukee	95	59	.617	Haney	1957	New York	98	56	.636	Stengel
1958	Milwaukee	92	62	.597	Haney	1958	New York	92	62	.597	Stengel
1959	Los Angeles	88	68	.564	Alston	1959	Chicago	94	60	.610	Lopez
1960	Pittsburgh	95	59	.617	Murtaugh	1960	New York	97	57	.630	Stengel
1961	Cincinnati	93	61	.604	Hutchinson	1961	New York	109	53	.673	Houk
1962	San Francisco	103	62	.624	Dark	1962	New York	96	66	.593	Houk
1963	Los Angeles	99	63	.611	Alston	1963	New York	104	57	.646	Houk
1964	St. Louis	93	69	.574	Keane	1964	New York	99	63	.611	Berra
1965	Los Angeles	97	65	.599	Alston	1965	Minnesota	102	60	.630	Mele
1966	Los Angeles	95	67	.586	Alston	1966	Baltimore	97	63	.606	Bauer
1967	St. Louis	101	60	.627	Schoendienst	1967	Boston	92	70	.568	Williams
1968	St. Louis	97	65	.599	Schoendienst	1968	Detroit	103	59	.636	Smith

National League

	East					West					Playoff
Year	Winner	W	L	Pct	Manager	Winner	W	L	Pct	Manager	winner
1969	N.Y. Mets	100	62	.617	Hodges	Atlanta	93	69	.574	Harris	New York
1970	Pittsburgh	89	73	.549	Murtaugh	Cincinnati	102	60	.630	Anderson	Cincinnati
1971	Pittsburgh	97	65	.599	Murtaugh	San Francisco	90	72	.556	Fox	Pittsburgh
1972	Pittsburgh	96	59	.619	Virdon	Cincinnati	95	59	.617	Anderson	Cincinnati
1973	N.Y. Mets	82	79	.509	Berra	Cincinnati	99	63	.611	Anderson	New York
1974	Pittsburgh	88	82	.543	Murtaugh	Los Angeles	102	60	.630	Alston	Los Angeles
1975	Pittsburgh	92	69	.571	Murtaugh	Cincinnati	108	54	.667	Anderson	Cincinnati
1976	Philadelphia	101	61	.623	Ozark	Cincinnati	102	60	.630	Anderson	Cincinnati
1977	Philadelphia	100	61	.621	Ozark	Los Angeles	98	64	.605	Lasorda	Los Angeles

Year	Winner	East W	L	Pct	Manager	West Winner	W	L	Pct	Manager	Playoff winner
1978	Philadelphia .	90	72	.556	Ozark	Los Angeles . . .	95	67	.586	Lasorda	Los Angeles
1979	Pittsburgh. . .	98	64	.605	Tanner	Cincinnati.	90	71	.559	McNamara	Pittsburgh
1980	Philadelphia .	91	71	.562	Green	Houston	93	70	.571	Virdon	Philadelphia
1981(a)	Philadelphia .	34	21	.618	Green	Los Angeles . . .	36	21	.632	Lasorda	(c)
1981(b)	Montreal . . .	30	23	.566	Williams, Fanning	Houston	33	20	.623	Virdon	Los Angeles

American League

Year	Winner	East W	L	Pct	Manager	West Winner	W	L	Pct	Manager	Playoff winner
1969	Baltimore . . .	109	53	.673	Weaver	Minnesota	97	65	.599	Martin	Baltimore
1970	Baltimore . . .	108	54	.667	Weaver	Minnesota	98	64	.605	Rigney	Baltimore
1971	Baltimore . . .	101	57	.639	Weaver	Oakland	101	60	.627	Williams	Baltimore
1972	Detroit	86	70	.551	Martin	Oakland	93	62	.600	Williams	Oakland
1973	Baltimore . . .	97	65	.599	Weaver	Oakland	94	68	.580	Williams	Oakland
1974	Baltimore . . .	91	71	.562	Weaver	Oakland	90	72	.556	Dark	Oakland
1975	Boston	95	65	.594	Johnson	Oakland	98	64	.605	Dark	Boston
1976	New York . . .	97	62	.610	Martin	Kansas City . . .	90	72	.556	Herzog	New York
1977	New York . . .	100	62	.617	Martin	Kansas City . . .	102	60	.630	Herzog	New York
1978	New York . . .	100	63	.613	Martin, Lemon	Kansas City . . .	92	70	.568	Herzog	New York
1979	Baltimore . . .	102	57	.642	Weaver	California	88	74	.543	Fregosi	Baltimore
1980	New York . . .	103	59	.636	Howser	Kansas City . . .	97	65	.599	Frey	New York
1981(a)	New York . . .	34	22	.607	Michael	Oakland	37	23	.617	Martin	(d)
1981(b)	Milwaukee . . .	31	22	.585	Rodgers	Kansas City . . .	30	23	.566	Frey, Howser	New York

(a) First half; (b) Second half; (c) Montreal and Los Angeles won the divisional playoffs; (d) New York and Oakland won the divisional playoffs.

Baseball Stadiums

National League

Team		Home run distances (ft.) LF	Center	RF	Seating capacity
Atlanta Braves.	Atlanta-Fulton County Stadium . . .	330	402	330	52,194
Chicago Cubs	Wrigley Field. . . .	355	400	353	37,741
Cincinnati Reds	Riverfront Stadium	330	404	330	52,392
Houston Astros	Astrodome	340	406	340	45,000
Los Angeles Dodgers	Dodger Stadium	330	395	330	56,000
Montreal Expos	Olympic Stadium	325	404	325	59,984
New York Mets	Shea Stadium	338	410	338	55,300
Philadelphia Phillies	Veterans Stadium	330	408	330	65,454
Pittsburgh Pirates	Three Rivers Stadium	335	400	335	54,499
St. Louis Cardinals	Busch Memorial Stadium. . . .	330	414	330	50,222
San Diego Padres	San Diego Stadium	330	420	330	51,362
San Francisco Giants	Candlestick Park	335	410	335	58,000

American League

Team		LF	Center	RF	Seating capacity
Baltimore Orioles	Memorial Stadium. . . .	309	405	309	52,862
Boston Red Sox	Fenway Park	315	390	302	33,536
California Angels	Anaheim Stadium	333	404	333	67,335
Chicago White Sox	Comiskey Park	352	445	352	44,492
Cleveland Indians	Cleveland Stadium	320	400	320	76,685
Detroit Tigers	Tiger Stadium	340	440	325	52,687
Kansas City Royals	Royals Stadium	330	410	330	40,628
Milwaukee Brewers	Milwaukee County Stadium	320	402	315	53,192
Minnesota Twins	Metropolitan Stadium	343	402	330	45,919
New York Yankees	Yankee Stadium	312	417	310	57,545
Oakland A's	Oakland-Alameda County Coliseum . . .	330	400	330	50,255
Seattle Mariners	Kingdome	316	410	316	59,438
Texas Rangers	Arlington Stadium	330	400	330	41,284
Toronto Blue Jays	Exhibition Stadium	330	400	330	43,737

Cy Young Award Winners

Year	Player, club	Year	Player, club	Year	Player, club
1956	Don Newcombe, Dodgers	1969	(NL) Tom Seaver, Mets	1975	(NL) Tom Seaver, Mets
1957	Warren Spahn, Braves		(AL) (tie) Dennis McLain, Tigers		(AL) Jim Palmer, Orioles
1958	Bob Turley, Yankees		Mike Cuellar, Orioles	1976	(NL) Randy Jones, Padres
1959	Early Wynn, White Sox	1970	(NL) Bob Gibson, Cardinals		(AL) Jim Palmer, Orioles
1960	Vernon Law, Pirates		(AL) Jim Perry, Twins	1977	(NL) Steve Carlton, Phillies
1961	Whitey Ford, Yankees	1971	(NL) Ferguson Jenkins, Cubs		(AL) Sparky Lyle, Yankees
1962	Don Drysdale, Dodgers		(AL) Vida Blue, A's	1978	(NL) Gaylord Perry, Padres
1963	Sandy Koufax, Dodgers	1972	(NL) Steve Carlton, Phillies		(AL) Ron Guidry, Yankees
1964	Dean Chance, Angels		(AL) Gaylord Perry, Indians	1979	(NL) Bruce Sutter, Cubs
1965	Sandy Koufax, Dodgers	1973	(NL) Tom Seaver, Mets		(AL) Mike Flanagan, Orioles
1966	Sandy Koufax, Dodgers		(AL) Jim Palmer, Orioles	1980	(NL) Steve Carlton, Phillies
1967	(NL) Mike McCormick, Giants	1974	(NL) Mike Marshall, Dodgers		(AL) Steve Stone, Orioles
	(AL) Jim Lonborg, Red Sox		(AL) Jim (Catfish) Hunter, A's		
1968	(NL) Bob Gibson, Cardinals				
	(AL) Dennis McLain, Tigers				

Home Run Leaders

National League		American League	
Year	**HR**	**Year**	**HR**
1921 George Kelly, New York	23	1921 Babe Ruth, New York	59
1922 Rogers Hornsby, St. Louis	42	1922 Ken Williams, St. Louis	39
1923 Cy Williams, Philadelphia	41	1923 Babe Ruth, New York	41
1924 Jacques Fournier, Brooklyn	27	1924 Babe Ruth, New York	46
1925 Rogers Hornsby, St. Louis	39	1925 Bob Meusel, New York	33
1926 Hack Wilson, Chicago	21	1926 Babe Ruth, New York	47
1927 Hack Wilson, Chicago; Cy Williams, Philadelphia	30	1927 Babe Ruth, New York	60
1928 Hack Wilson, Chicago; Jim Bottomley, St. Louis	31	1928 Babe Ruth, New York	54
1929 Charles Klein, Philadelphia	43	1929 Babe Ruth, New York	46
1930 Hack Wilson, Chicago	56	1930 Babe Ruth, New York	49
1931 Charles Klein, Philadelphia	31	1931 Babe Ruth, Lou Gehrig, New York	46
1932 Charles Klein, Philadelphia, Mel Ott, New York	38	1932 Jimmy Foxx, Philadelphia	58
1933 Charles Klein, Philadelphia	28	1933 Jimmy Foxx, Philadelphia	48
1934 Collins, St. Louis; Mel Ott, New York	35	1934 Lou Gehrig, New York	49
1935 Walter Berger, Boston	34	1935 Jimmy Foxx, Philadelphia, Hank Greenberg, Detroit	36
1936 Mel Ott, New York	33	1936 Lou Gehrig, New York	49
1937 Mel Ott, New York, Joe Medwick, St. Louis	31	1937 Joe DiMaggio, New York	46
1938 Mel Ott, New York	36	1938 Hank Greenberg, Detroit	58
1939 John Mize, St. Louis	28	1939 Jimmy Foxx, Boston	35
1940 John Mize, St. Louis	43	1940 Hank Greenberg, Detroit	41
1941 Dolph Camilli, Brooklyn	34	1941 Ted Williams, Boston	37
1942 Mel Ott, New York	30	1942 Ted Williams, Boston	36
1943 Bill Nicholson, Chicago	29	1943 Rudy York, Detroit	34
1944 Bill Nicholson, Chicago	33	1944 Nick Etten, New York	22
1945 Tommy Holmes, Boston	28	1945 Vern Stephens, St. Louis	24
1946 Ralph Kiner, Pittsburgh	23	1946 Hank Greenberg, Detroit	44
1947 Ralph Kiner, Pittsburgh; John Mize, New York	51	1947 Ted Williams, Boston	32
1948 Ralph Kiner, Pittsburgh; John Mize, New York	40	1948 Joe DiMaggio, New York	39
1949 Ralph Kiner, Pittsburgh	54	1949 Ted Williams, Boston	43
1950 Ralph Kiner, Pittsburgh	47	1950 Al Rosen, Cleveland	37
1951 Ralph Kiner, Pittsburgh	42	1951 Gus Zernial, Chicago-Philadelphia	33
1952 Ralph Kiner, Pittsburgh; Hank Sauer, Chicago	37	1952 Larry Doby, Cleveland	32
1953 Ed Mathews, Milwaukee	47	1953 Al Rosen, Cleveland	43
1954 Ted Kluszewski, Cincinnati	49	1954 Larry Doby, Cleveland	32
1955 Willie Mays, New York	51	1955 Mickey Mantle, New York	37
1956 Duke Snider, Brooklyn	43	1956 Mickey Mantle, New York	52
1957 Hank Aaron, Milwaukee	44	1957 Roy Sievers, Washington	42
1958 Ernie Banks, Chicago	47	1958 Mickey Mantle, New York	42
1959 Ed Mathews, Milwaukee	46	1959 Rocky Colavito, Cleveland, Harmon Killebrew, Washington	42
1960 Ernie Banks, Chicago	41	1960 Mickey Mantle, New York	40
1961 Orlando Cepeda, San Francisco	46	1961 Roger Maris, New York	61
1962 Willie Mays, San Francisco	49	1962 Harmon Killebrew, Minnesota	48
1963 Hank Aaron, Milwaukee, Willie McCovey, San Francisco	44	1963 Harmon Killebrew, Minnesota	45
1964 Willie Mays, San Francisco	47	1964 Harmon Killebrew, Minnesota	49
1965 Willie Mays, San Francisco	52	1965 Tony Conigliaro, Boston	32
1966 Hank Aaron, Atlanta	44	1966 Frank Robinson, Baltimore	49
1967 Hank Aaron, Atlanta	39	1967 Carl Yastrzemski, Boston, Harmon Killebrew, Minn.	44
1968 Willie McCovey, San Francisco	36	1968 Frank Howard, Washington	44
1969 Willie McCovey, San Francisco	45	1969 Harmon Killebrew, Minnesota	49
1970 Johnny Bench, Cincinnati	45	1970 Frank Howard, Washington	44
1971 Willie Stargell, Pittsburgh	48	1971 Bill Melton, Chicago	33
1972 Johnny Bench, Cincinnati	40	1972 Dick Allen, Chicago	37
1973 Willie Stargell, Pittsburgh	44	1973 Reggie Jackson, Oakland	32
1974 Mike Schmidt, Philadelphia	36	1974 Dick Allen, Chicago	32
1975 Mike Schmidt, Philadelphia	38	1975 George Scott, Milwaukee; Reggie Jackson, Oakland	36
1976 Mike Schmidt, Philadelphia	38	1976 Graig Nettles, New York	32
1977 George Foster, Cincinnati	52	1977 Jim Rice, Boston	39
1978 George Foster, Cincinnati	40	1978 Jim Rice, Boston	46
1979 Dave Kingman, Chicago	48	1979 Gorman Thomas, Milwaukee	45
1980 Mike Schmidt, Philadelphia	48	1980 Reggie Jackson, New York; Ben Oglivie, Milwaukee	41
1981 Mike Schmidt, Philadelphia	31	1981 Bobby Grich, California; Tony Armas, Oakland; Dwight Evans, Boston; Eddie Murray, Baltimore	22

All-time Major League Record (154-game Season)—60—Babe Ruth, New York Yankees (A), 1927. **(162-game Season)—61**—Roger Maris, New York Yankees, 1961. Prior to the 1931 season a batted ball that bounced into the stands was a home run (now a ground-rule double). None of Babe Ruth's record 60 homers bounced into the stands.

Runs Batted In Leaders

National League		American League	
Year	**RBI**	**Year**	**RBI**
1946 Enos Slaughter, St. Louis	130	1946 Hank Greenberg, Detroit	127
1947 John Mize, New York	138	1947 Ted Williams, Boston	114
1948 Stan Musial, St. Louis	131	1948 Joe DiMaggio, New York	155
1949 Ralph Kiner, Pittsburgh	127	1949 Ted Williams, Vern Stephens, Boston	159
1950 Del Ennis, Philadelphia	126	1950 Walt Dropo, Vern Stephens, Boston	144
1951 Monte Irvin, New York	121	1951 Gus Zernial, Chicago-Philadelphia	129
1952 Hank Sauer, Chicago	121	1952 Al Rosen, Cleveland	105
1953 Roy Campanella, Brooklyn	142	1953 Al Rosen, Cleveland	145
1954 Ted Kluszewski, Cincinnati	141	1954 Larry Doby, Cleveland	126
1955 Duke Snider, Brooklyn	136	1955 Ray Boone, Detroit, Jack Jensen, Boston	116
1956 Stan Musial, St. Louis	109	1956 Mickey Mantle, New York	130
1957 Hank Aaron, Milwaukee	132	1957 Roy Sievers, Washington	114
1958 Ernie Banks, Chicago	129	1958 Jack Jensen, Boston	122
1959 Ernie Banks, Chicago	143	1959 Jack Jensen, Boston	112
1960 Hank Aaron, Milwaukee	126	1960 Roger Maris, New York	112

Year		RBI	Year		RBI
1961	Orlando Cepeda, San Francisco	142	1961	Roger Maris, New York	142
1962	Tommy Davis, Los Angeles	153	1962	Harmon Killebrew, Minnesota	126
1963	Hank Aaron, Milwaukee	130	1963	Dick Stuart, Boston	118
1964	Ken Boyer, St. Louis	119	1964	Brooks Robinson, Baltimore	118
1965	Deron Johnson, Cincinnati	130	1965	Rocky Colavito, Cleveland	108
1966	Hank Aaron, Atlanta	127	1966	Frank Robinson, Baltimore	122
1967	Orlando Cepeda, St. Louis	111	1967	Carl Yastrzemski, Boston	121
1968	Willie McCovey, San Francisco	105	1968	Ken Harrelson, Boston	109
1969	Willie McCovey, San Francisco	126	1969	Harmon Killebrew, Minnesota	140
1970	Johnny Bench, Cincinnati	148	1970	Frank Howard, Washington	126
1971	Joe Torre, St. Louis	137	1971	Harmon Killebrew, Minnesota	119
1972	Johnny Bench, Cincinnati	125	1972	Dick Allen, Chicago	113
1973	Willie Stargell, Pittsburgh	119	1973	Reggie Jackson, Oakland	117
1974	Johnny Bench, Cincinnati	129	1974	Jeff Burroughs, Texas	118
1975	Greg Luzinski, Philadelphia	120	1975	George Scott, Milwaukee	109
1976	George Foster, Cincinnati	121	1976	Lee May, Baltimore	109
1977	George Foster, Cincinnati	149	1977	Larry Hisle, Minnesota	119
1978	George Foster, Cincinnati	120	1978	Jim Rice, Boston	139
1979	Dave Winfield, San Diego	118	1979	Don Baylor, California	139
1980	Mike Schmidt, Philadelphia	121	1980	Cecil Cooper, Milwaukee	122
1981	Mike Schmidt, Philadelphia	91	1981	Eddie Murray, Baltimore	78

Batting Champions

National League

Year	Player	Club	Pct.
1919	Edd Roush	Cincinnati	.321
1920	Rogers Hornsby	St. Louis	.370
1921	Rogers Hornsby	St. Louis	.397
1922	Rogers Hornsby	St. Louis	.401
1923	Rogers Hornsby	St. Louis	.384
1924	Rogers Hornsby	St. Louis	.424
1925	Rogers Hornsby	St. Louis	.403
1926	Eugene Hargrave	Cincinnati	.353
1927	Paul Waner	Pittsburgh	.380
1928	Rogers Hornsby	Boston	.387
1929	Lefty O'Doul	Philadelphia	.398
1930	Bill Terry	New York	.401
1931	Chick Hafey	St. Louis	.349
1932	Lefty O'Doul	Brooklyn	.368
1933	Charles Klein	Philadelphia	.368
1934	Paul Waner	Pittsburgh	.362
1935	Arky Vaughan	Pittsburgh	.385
1936	Paul Waner	Pittsburgh	.373
1937	Joe Medwick	St. Louis	.374
1938	Ernie Lombardi	Cincinnati	.342
1939	John Mize	St. Louis	.349
1940	Debs Garms	Pittsburgh	.355
1941	Pete Reiser	Brooklyn	.343
1942	Ernie Lombardi	Boston	.330
1943	Stan Musial	St. Louis	.357
1944	Dixie Walker	Brooklyn	.357
1945	Phil Cavarretta	Chicago	.355
1946	Stan Musial	St. Louis	.365
1947	Harry Walker	Philadelphia	.363
1948	Stan Musial	St. Louis	.376
1949	Jackie Robinson	Brooklyn	.342
1950	Stan Musial	St. Louis	.346
1951	Stan Musial	St. Louis	.355
1952	Stan Musial	St. Louis	.336
1953	Carl Furillo	Brooklyn	.344
1954	Willie Mays	New York	.345
1955	Richie Ashburn	Philadelphia	.338
1956	Hank Aaron	Milwaukee	.328
1957	Stan Musial	St. Louis	.351
1958	Richie Ashburn	Philadelphia	.350
1959	Hank Aaron	Milwaukee	.355
1960	Dick Groat	Pittsburgh	.325
1961	Roberto Clemente	Pittsburgh	.351
1962	Tommy Davis	Los Angeles	.346
1963	Tommy Davis	Los Angeles	.326
1964	Roberto Clemente	Pittsburgh	.339
1965	Roberto Clemente	Pittsburgh	.329
1966	Matty Alou	Pittsburgh	.342
1967	Roberto Clemente	Pittsburgh	.357
1968	Pete Rose	Cincinnati	.335
1969	Pete Rose	Cincinnati	.348
1970	Rico Carty	Atlanta	.366
1971	Joe Torre	St. Louis	.363
1972	Billy Williams	Chicago	.333
1973	Pete Rose	Cincinnati	.338
1974	Ralph Garr	Atlanta	.353
1975	Bill Madlock	Chicago	.354
1976	Bill Madlock	Chicago	.339
1977	Dave Parker	Pittsburgh	.338
1978	Dave Parker	Pittsburgh	.334
1979	Keith Hernandez	St. Louis	.344
1980	Bill Buckner	Chicago	.324
1981	Bill Madlock	Pittsburgh	.341

American League

Year	Player	Club	Pct.
1919	Ty Cobb	Detroit	.384
1920	George Sisler	St. Louis	.407
1921	Harry Heilmann	Detroit	.394
1922	George Sisler	St. Louis	.420
1923	Harry Heilmann	Detroit	.403
1924	Babe Ruth	New York	.378
1925	Harry Heilmann	Detroit	.393
1926	Henry Manush	Detroit	.378
1927	Harry Heilmann	Detroit	.398
1928	Goose Goslin	Washington	.379
1929	Lew Fonseca	Cleveland	.369
1930	Al Simmons	Philadelphia	.381
1931	Al Simmons	Philadelphia	.390
1932	Dale Alexander	Detroit-Boston	.367
1933	Jimmy Foxx	Philadelphia	.356
1934	Lou Gehrig	New York	.363
1935	Buddy Myer	Washington	.349
1936	Luke Appling	Chicago	.388
1937	Charlie Gehringer	Detroit	.371
1938	Jimmy Foxx	Boston	.349
1939	Joe DiMaggio	New York	.381
1940	Joe DiMaggio	New York	.352
1941	Ted Williams	Boston	.406
1942	Ted Williams	Boston	.356
1943	Luke Appling	Chicago	.328
1944	Lou Boudreau	Cleveland	.327
1945	George Stirnweiss	New York	.309
1946	Mickey Vernon	Washington	.353
1947	Ted Williams	Boston	.343
1948	Ted Williams	Boston	.369
1949	George Kell	Detroit	.343
1950	Billy Goodman	Boston	.354
1951	Ferris Fain	Philadelphia	.344
1952	Ferris Fain	Philadelphia	.327
1953	Mickey Vernon	Washington	.337
1954	Roberto Avila	Cleveland	.341
1955	Al Kaline	Detroit	.340
1956	Mickey Mantle	New York	.353
1957	Ted Williams	Boston	.388
1958	Ted Williams	Boston	.328
1959	Harvey Kuenn	Detroit	.353
1960	Pete Runnels	Boston	.320
1961	Norm Cash	Detroit	.361
1962	Pete Runnels	Boston	.326
1963	Carl Yastrzemski	Boston	.321
1964	Tony Oliva	Minnesota	.323
1965	Tony Oliva	Minnesota	.321
1966	Frank Robinson	Baltimore	.316
1967	Carl Yastrzemski	Boston	.326
1968	Carl Yastrzemski	Boston	.301
1969	Rod Carew	Minnesota	.332
1970	Alex Johnson	California	.328
1971	Tony Oliva	Minnesota	.337
1972	Rod Carew	Minnesota	.318
1973	Rod Carew	Minnesota	.350
1974	Rod Carew	Minnesota	.364
1975	Rod Carew	Minnesota	.359
1976	George Brett	Kansas City	.333
1977	Rod Carew	Minnesota	.388
1978	Rod Carew	Minnesota	.333
1979	Fred Lynn	Boston	.333
1980	George Brett	Kansas City	.390
1981	Carney Lansford	Boston	.336

National League Records in 1981

First-half standings

Eastern Division

Club	W	L	Pct.	GB
Philadelphia	34	21	.618	...
St. Louis	30	20	.600	1½
Montreal	30	25	.545	4
Pittsburgh	25	23	.521	5½
New York	17	34	.333	15
Chicago	15	37	.288	17½

Western Division

Club	W	L	Pct.	GB
Los Angeles	36	21	.632	...
Cincinnati	35	21	.625	½
Houston	28	29	.491	8
Atlanta	25	29	.463	9½
San Francisco	27	32	.458	10
San Diego	23	33	.411	12½

Second-half standings

Eastern Division

Club	W	L	Pct	GB
Montreal	30	20	.600	...
St. Louis	29	23	.558	½
Philadelphia	25	27	.481	4½
New York	24	28	.462	5½
Chicago	23	28	.451	6
Pittsburgh	21	33	.389	9½

Western Division

Club	W	L	Pct	GB
Houston	33	20	.623	...
Cincinnati	31	21	.590	1½
San Francisco	29	23	.588	3½
Los Angeles	27	26	.509	6
Atlanta	25	27	.481	7½
San Diego	18	36	.333	15½

National League Playoffs

Divisional

Houston 3, Los Angeles 1.
Houston 1, Los Angeles 0.
Los Angeles 6, Houston 1.
Los Angeles 2, Houston 1.

Los Angeles 4, Houston 0.
Montreal 3, Philadelphia 1.
Montreal 3, Philadelphia 1.
Philadelphia 6, Montreal 2.

Philadelphia 6, Montreal 5.
Montreal 3, Philadelphia 0.
League
Los Angeles 5, Montreal 1.

Montreal 3, Los Angeles 0.
Montreal 4, Los Angeles 1.
Los Angeles 7, Montreal 1.
Los Angeles 2, Montreal 1.

Club Batting

Club	Pct.	AB	R	H	HR	SB
Philadelphia	.273	3665	491	1002	69	103
Cincinnati	.267	3637	464	972	64	58
St. Louis	.265	3537	464	936	50	88
Los Angeles	.262	3751	450	984	82	73
Pittsburgh	.257	3576	407	920	55	122
Houston	.257	3693	394	948	45	81
San Diego	.256	3757	382	963	32	83
San Francisco	.250	3766	427	941	63	89
New York	.248	3493	348	868	57	103
Montreal	.246	3591	443	883	81	138
Atlanta	.243	3642	395	886	64	98
Chicago	.236	3546	370	838	57	72

Club Pitching

Club	ERA	CG	IP	H	R	BB	SO
Houston	2.66	23	990	842	331	300	610
Los Angeles	3.01	26	997	904	356	302	603
San Francisco	3.28	8	1009	970	414	393	561
Montreal	3.30	20	975	902	394	268	520
Atlanta	3.45	11	968	936	416	330	471
New York	3.55	7	926	906	432	336	490
Pittsburgh	3.56	11	942	953	425	346	492
St. Louis	3.63	11	943	902	417	290	388
San Diego	3.72	9	1002	1013	455	414	492
Cincinnati	3.73	25	966	863	440	393	593
Chicago	4.01	6	957	983	483	388	532
Philadelphia	4.05	19	960	967	472	347	580

Individual Batting (at least 70 at-bats); Individual Pitching (at least 35 innings)

*Rookie; †Bats or pitches lefthanded; ‡Switch hitter

Atlanta Braves

Batting	Pct.	G	AB	R	H	HR	RBI	SB
Washington†	.291	85	320	37	93	5	37	12
Horner	.277	79	300	42	83	15	42	2
Chambliss†	.272	107	404	44	110	8	51	4
*Linares	.265	78	253	27	67	5	25	8
Benedict	.264	90	295	26	78	5	35	1
*Harper	.260	40	73	9	19	2	8	5
Asselstine†	.256	56	86	8	22	2	10	1
Butler†	.254	40	126	17	32	0	4	9
Murphy	.247	104	369	43	91	13	50	14
Hubbard	.235	99	361	39	85	6	33	4
Miller†	.231	50	134	29	31	0	7	23
Ramirez	.218	95	307	30	67	2	20	7
Royster	.204	64	93	13	19	0	9	7
Pocoroba‡	.180	57	122	4	22	0	8	0

Pitching	W	L	ERA	G	IP	H	BB	SO
Camp	9	3	1.78	48	76	68	12	47
Garber	4	6	2.59	35	59	49	20	34
*Mahler	8	6	2.81	34	112	109	43	54
McWilliams†	2	1	3.08	6	38	31	8	23
Niekro	7	7	3.11	22	139	120	56	62
Montefusco	2	3	3.51	26	77	75	27	34
Perry	8	9	3.93	23	151	182	24	60
Boggs	3	13	4.09	25	143	140	54	81
Walk	1	4	4.60	12	43	41	23	16
Hanna	2	1	6.43	20	35	45	23	22

Chicago Cubs

Batting	Pct.	G	AB	R	H	HR	RBI	SB
Buckner†	.311	106	421	45	131	10	75	5
Henderson	.293	82	287	32	84	5	35	5
Durham†	.290	87	328	42	95	10	35	25
Morales	.286	84	245	27	70	1	25	1
*Waller	.268	30	71	10	19	3	13	2
*Davis	.256	56	180	14	46	4	21	0
Blackwell‡	.234	58	158	21	37	1	11	2
Cruz	.229	53	109	15	25	7	15	2
Dillard	.218	53	119	18	26	2	11	0
Reitz	.215	82	260	10	56	2	28	0
Bonds	.215	45	163	26	35	6	19	5
DeJesus	.194	106	403	49	78	0	13	21
Strain	.189	25	74	7	14	0	1	0
*Tabler	.188	35	101	11	19	1	5	0
Tyson‡	.185	50	92	6	17	2	8	1
Thompson†	.165	57	115	8	19	0	8	2

Pitching	W	L	ERA	G	IP	H	BB	SO
Eastwick	0	1	2.30	30	43	43	15	24
Capilla†	1	0	3.18	42	51	52	34	28
Reuschel	4	7	3.45	13	86	87	23	53
*Smith	3	6	3.49	40	67	57	31	50
Bird	4	5	3.60	12	75	72	16	34
*Martz	5	7	3.67	33	108	103	49	32
Krukow	9	9	3.69	25	144	146	55	101
Griffin	2	5	4.50	16	52	64	9	20
McGlothen	1	4	4.75	20	55	71	28	26
Tidrow	3	10	5.04	51	75	73	30	39
Kravec†	1	6	5.08	24	78	80	39	50
Caudill	1	5	5.83	30	71	87	31	45

Cincinnati Reds

Batting	Pct.	G	AB	R	H	HR	RBI	SB
Griffey†	.311	101	396	65	123	2	34	12
Nolan†	.309	81	236	25	73	1	26	1
Bench	.309	52	178	14	55	8	25	0
Concepcion	.306	106	421	57	129	5	67	4
Foster	.295	108	414	64	122	22	90	4
Collins‡	.272	95	360	63	98	3	23	26
Oester‡	.271	105	354	45	96	5	42	2
Knight	.259	106	386	43	100	6	34	2
Driessen‡	.236	82	233	35	55	7	33	2
O'Berry‡	.180	55	111	6	20	1	5	0
Landestoy‡	.153	47	85	8	13	0	5	5

Pitching	W	L	ERA	G	IP	H	BB	SO
Price†	6	1	2.50	41	54	42	10	41
Seavor	14	2	2.55	23	166	120	66	87
Soto	12	9	3.29	25	175	142	61	151
Hume	9	4	3.44	51	68	63	31	27
*Berenyi	9	6	3.50	21	126	97	77	106
Pastore	4	9	4.02	22	132	125	35	81
Moskau	2	1	4.91	27	55	54	32	32
LaCoss	4	7	6.12	20	78	102	30	22

Houston Astros

Batting	Pct.	G	AB	R	H	HR	RBI	SB
Howe	.296	103	361	43	107	3	36	1
*Pittman	.281	52	135	11	38	0	7	4
Thon	.274	49	95	13	26	0	3	6
Garcia	.272	48	136	9	37	0	15	2
Cedeno	.271	82	306	42	83	5	34	12
Ashby‡	.271	83	255	20	69	4	33	0
Cruz†	.267	107	409	53	109	13	55	5
Scott‡	.264	100	401	49	106	4	39	18
Reynolds†	.260	87	323	43	84	4	31	3
Puhl†	.251	96	350	43	88	3	28	22
Heep†	.250	33	96	6	24	0	11	0
Garner	.248	87	294	35	73	1	26	10
Pujols	.239	40	117	5	28	1	14	1
Walling†	.234	65	158	23	37	5	23	2
Woods	.209	54	110	10	23	0	12	2

Pitching	W	L	ERA	G	IP	H	BB	SO
Ryan	11	5	1.69	21	149	99	68	140
Sambito†	5	5	1.83	49	64	43	22	41
Knepper†	9	5	2.18	22	157	128	38	75
Sutton	11	9	2.60	23	159	132	29	104
D. Smith	5	3	2.76	42	75	54	23	52
Niekro	9	9	2.82	24	166	150	47	77
Ruhle	4	6	2.91	20	102	97	20	39
LaCorte	4	2	3.64	37	42	41	21	40

Los Angeles Dodgers

Batting	Pct.	G	AB	R	H	HR	RBI	SB
Baker	.320	103	400	48	128	9	49	10
Monday†	.315	66	130	24	41	11	25	1
Guerrero	.300	98	347	46	104	12	48	5
Cey	.288	85	312	42	90	13	50	0
Garvey	.283	110	431	63	122	10	64	3
*Sax	.277	31	119	15	33	2	9	5
Scioscia†	.276	93	290	27	80	2	29	0
Landreaux†	.251	99	390	48	98	7	41	18
Thomas‡	.248	80	218	25	54	4	24	7
Russell	.233	82	262	20	61	0	22	2
Yeager	.209	42	86	5	18	3	7	0
Lopes	.206	58	214	35	44	5	17	20
Johnstone†	.205	61	83	8	17	3	6	0

Pitching	W	L	ERA	G	IP	H	BB	SO
Hooton	11	6	2.28	23	142	124	33	74
Reuss†	10	4	2.29	22	153	138	27	51
*Valenzuela†	13	7	2.48	25	192	140	61	180
Howe†	5	3	2.50	41	54	51	18	32
*Stewart	4	3	2.51	32	43	40	14	29
Welch	9	5	3.45	23	141	141	41	88
Sutcliffe	2	2	4.02	14	47	41	20	16
Goltz	2	7	4.09	26	77	83	25	48
Castillo	2	4	5.29	34	51	50	24	35

Montreal Expos

Batting	Pct.	G	AB	R	H	HR	RBI	SB
Cromartie†	.304	99	358	41	109	6	42	2
*Raines‡	.304	88	313	61	95	5	37	71
Dawson	.302	103	394	71	119	24	64	26
*Francona†	.274	34	95	10	26	1	8	1

Batting	Pct.	G	AB	R	H	HR	RBI	SB
Carter	.251	100	374	48	94	16	68	1
Parrish	.244	97	349	42	85	8	44	0
Milner†	.237	65	135	12	32	5	18	0
*Wallach	.236	71	212	19	50	4	13	0
Speier	.225	96	307	33	69	2	25	1
White‡	.218	59	119	11	26	3	11	5
Phillips†	.214	48	84	6	18	0	4	1
Scott‡	.205	95	336	43	69	0	26	30

Pitching	W	L	ERA	G	IP	H	BB	SO
Fryman†	5	3	1.88	35	43	38	14	25
Reardon	3	0	2.19	43	70	48	21	49
Gullickson	7	9	2.81	22	157	142	34	115
Lee†	5	6	2.93	31	89	90	14	34
Sanderson	9	7	1.98	22	137	122	31	77
Burris	9	7	3.04	22	136	117	41	52
Rogers	12	8	3.41	22	161	149	41	87
Sosa	1	2	3.69	32	-39	46	8	18
Jackson†	2	2	3.77	45	43	44	19	21
Lea	5	4	4.64	16	64	63	26	31
Bahnsen	2	1	4.96	25	49	45	24	28

New York Mets

Batting	Pct.	G	AB	R	H	HR	RBI	SB
Youngblood	.350	43	143	16	50	4	25	2
Staub†	.317	70	161	9	51	5	21	1
*Brooks	.307	98	358	34	110	4	38	9
Bailor	.284	51	81	11	23	0	8	2
*Wilson†	.271	92	328	49	89	3	14	24
Stearns	.271	80	273	25	74	1	.24	12
Trevino	.262	56	149	17	39	0	10	3
Taveras	.230	84	283	30	65	0	11	16
Mazzilli‡	.228	95	324	36	74	6	34	17
Flynn	.222	105	325	24	72	1	20	1
Kingman	.221	100	353	40	78	22	59	6
Cubbage†	.213	67	80	9	17	1	4	0
Valentine	.208	70	245	23	51	8	36	0
Jorgensen†	.205	86	122	8	25	3	15	4

Pitching	W	L	ERA	G	IP	H	BB	SO
Falcone†	5	3	2.56	35	95	84	36	56
*Leach	1	1	2.57	21	35	26	12	16
*Lynch	4	5	2.93	17	80	79	21	57
Allen	7	6	2.96	43	67	64	26	50
Miller	1	0	3.32	23	38	49	15	22
*Searage†	1	0	3.65	26	37	34	17	16
Scott	5	10	3.90	23	136	130	34	54
Zachry	7	14	4.14	24	139	151	56	76
*Harris	3	5	4.43	16	69	65	28	54
Jones†	1	8	4.88	13	59	65	38	14

Philadelphia Phillies

Batting	Pct.	G	AB	R	H	HR	RBI	SB
D. Davis	.333	45	96	12	32	2	19	1
Rose‡	.325	107	431	73	140	0	33	4
Smith	.324	62	176	40	57	2	11	21
Schmidt	.316	102	354	78	112	31	91	12
Matthews	.301	101	359	62	108	9	67	15
Trillo	.287	94	349	37	100	6	36	10
Bowa‡	.283	103	360	34	102	0	31	16
McBride†	.271	58	221	26	60	2	21	5
Maddox	.263	94	323	37	85	5	40	9
Moreland	.255	61	196	16	50	6	37	1
Gross†	.225	83	102	14	23	0	7	2
*Aguayo	.214	45	84	11	18	1	7	1
Boone	.211	76	227	19	48	4	24	2

Pitching	W	L	ERA	G	IP	H	BB	SO
Carlton†	13	4	2.42	24	190	152	62	179
McGraw†	2	4	2.66	34	44	35	14	26
R. Reed	5	3	3.10	39	61	54	17	40
*Bystrom	4	3	3.33	9	54	55	16	24
Christenson	4	7	3.53	20	107	108	30	70
Proly	2	1	3.86	35	63	66	19	19
Noles	2	4	4.19	13	58	57	23	34
Lyle†	9	6	4.44	48	75	85	33	29
Ruthven	12	7	5.14	23	147	162	54	80
Espinosa	3	5	6.08	14	74	98	24	22
*M. Davis†	1	4	7.74	9	43	49	24	29

Pittsburgh Pirates

Batting	Pct.	G	AB	R	H	HR	RBI	SB
Madlock	.341	82	279	35	95	6	45	18
*Pena	.300	66	210	16	63	2	17	1
Easler†	.286	95	339	43	97	7	42	'4
Moreno†	.276	103	434	62	120	1	35	39

Batting	Pct.	G	AB.	R	H	HR	RBI	SB
Lacy	.268	78	213	31	57	2	10	24
Parker†	.258	67	240	29	62	9	48	6
Foli	.247	86	316	32	78	0	20	7
*Ray†	.245	31	102	10	25	0	6	0
Thompson†	.242	86	223	36	54	15	42	0
Berra	.241	81	232	21	56	2	27	11
Nicosia	.231	54	169	21	39	2	18	3
B. Robinson	.216	39	88	8	19	2	8	1
Montanez†	.210	55*	100	8	21	1	6	0

Pitching	W	L	ERA	G	IP	H	BB	SO
Bibby	6	3	2.49	14	94	79	26	48
Tekulve	5	5	2.49	45	65	61	17	34
Solomon	8	6	3.12	22	127	133	27	38
Scurry†	4	5	3.77	27	74	74	40	65
Rhoden	9	4	3.90	21	136	147	53	76
Tiant	2	5	3.95	9	57	54	19	32
*Perez	2	7	3.98	17	86	92	34	46
Homo	1	3	4.50	33	42	47	18	23
D. Robinson	0	3	5.92	16	38	47	23	17

St. Louis Cardinals

Batting	Pct.	G	AB	R	H	HR	RBI	SB
Iorg†	.327	75	217	23	71	2	39	2
Hernandez†	.306	103	376	65	115	8	48	12
Oberkfell†	.293	102	376	43	110	2	45	4
Templeton‡	.288	80	333	47	96	1	33	8
Hendrick	.284	101	394	67	112	18	61	4
Herr‡	.268	103	411	50	110	0	46	23
Lezcano	.266	72	214	26	57	5	28	0
*Landrum	.261	81	119	13	31	0	10	4
Ramsey‡	.258	47	124	19	32	0	9	4
Tenace	.233	58	129	26	30	5	22	0
Porter†	.224	61	174	22	39	6	31	1

Pitching	W	L	ERA	G	IP	H	BB	SO
*Rincon	3	1	1.75	5	36	27	5	13
Sutter	3	5	2.63	48	82	64	24	57
Forsch	10	5	3.19	20	124	106	29	41
Sorensen	7	7	3.28	23	140	149	26	52
Kaat†	6	6	3.40	41	53	60	17	8
*Martin†	8	5	3.41	17	103	85	26	36
Martinez	2	5	3.99	18	97	95	39	34
Shirley†	6	4	4.10	28	79	78	34	36
Andujar	8	4	4.10	20	79	85	23	37
Littell	1	3	4.39	28	41	36	31	22
Sykes†	2	0	4.62	22	37	37	18	14
Bair	4	2	5.07	35	55	55	19	30
Otten	1	0	5.25	24	36	44	20	20

Individual Batting

Leaders 270 or more at bats

Player, club	Pct.	AB	R	H	HR	RBI	SB
Madlock, Pittsburgh	.341	279	35	95	6	45	18
Rose, Philadelphia‡	.325	431	73	140	0	33	4
Baker, Los Angeles	.320	400	48	128	9	49	10
Schmidt, Philadelphia	.316	354	78	112	31	91	12
Buckner, Chicago†	.311	421	45	131	10	75	5
Griffey, Cincinnati†	.311	396	65	123	2	34	12
May, San Francisco†	.310	316	20	98	2	33	1
*Brooks, New York	.307	358	34	110	4	38	9

San Diego Padres

Batting	Pct.	G	AB	R	H	HR	RBI	SB
Evans	.323	54	93	11	30	0	7	2
Salazar	.303	109	400	37	121	3	38	11
Kennedy†	.301	101	382	32	115	2	41	0
*Bonilla	.290	99	369	30	107	1	25	4
Richards†	.288	104	393	47	113	3	42	20
Perkins†	.280	92	254	27	71	2	40	0
Lefebvre†	.256	86	246	31	63	8	31	6
Jones†	.249	105	397	53	99	4	39	7
Smith†	.222	110	450	53	100	0	21	22
Edwards	.214	58	112	13	24	2	13	3
*Bass†	.210	69	176	13	37	4	20	0

Pitching	W	L	ERA	G	IP	H	BB	SO
Lucas†	7	7	2.00	57	90	78	36	53
Urrea	2	2	2.39	38	49	43	28	19
*Boone†	1	0	2.86	37	63	63	21	43
Eichelberger	8	8	3.51	25	141	136	74	81
Littlefield	2	3	3.66	42	64	53	28	21
Wise	4	8	3.77	18	98	116	19	27
*Welsh†	6	7	3.77	22	124	122	41	51
Mura	5	14	4.27	23	139	156	50	70
Curtis†	2	6	5.10	28	67	70	30	31
*Lollar†	2	8	6.08	24	77	87	51	38

San Francisco Giants

Batting	Pct.	G	AB	R	H	HR	RBI	SB
May†	.310	97	316	20	98	2	33	1
Leonard	.290	44	145	21	42	4	29	5
Herndon	.288	96	364	48	105	5	41	15
Clark	.268	99	385	60	103	17	53	1
Evans†	.258	102	357	51	92	12	48	2
Cabell	.255	96	396	41	101	2	36	6
LeMaster	.253	104	324	27	82	0	28	3
Bergman†	.252	69	151	17	38	4	14	2
Martin	.241	72	241	23	58	4	25	6
Morgan†	.240	90	308	47	74	8	31	14
Stennett	.230	38	87	8	20	1	7	2
North†	.221	46	131	22	29	1	12	26

Pitching	W	L	ERA	G	IP	H	BB	SO
Holland†	7	5	2.41	47	101	87	44	78
Blue†	8	6	2.45	18	125	97	54	63
*Breining	5	2	2.54	45	78	66	38	37
Minton	4	5	2.89	55	84	84	36	29
Alexander	11	7	2.90	24	152	156	44	77
Griffin	8	8	3.77	22	129	121	57	83
Lavelle†	2	6	3.82	34	66	58	23	45
Whitson	6	9	4.02	22	123	130	47	65
Ripley	2	4	4.05	19	91	103	27	47

Individual Pitching

Leaders—110 or more innings

Pitcher, club	W	L	ERA	G	IP	H	BB	SO
Ryan, Houston	11	5	1.69	21	149	99	68	140
Knepper, Houston†	9	5	2.18	22	157	128	38	75
Hooton, Los Angeles	11	6	2.28	23	142	124	33	74
Reuss, Los Angeles†	10	4	2.29	22	153	138	27	51
Carlton, Philadelphia†	13	4	2.42	24	190	152	62	179
Blue, San Francisco†	8	6	2.45	18	125	97	54	63
*Valenzuela, L.A.†	13	7	2.48	25	192	140	61	180
Seaver, Cincinnati	14	2	2.55	23	166	120	66	87

Leading Pitchers, Earned-Run Average

National League					American League				
Year	Player, club	G	IP	ERA	Year	Player, club	G	IP	ERA
1966	Sandy Koufax, Los Angeles	41	323	1.73	1966	Gary Peters, Chicago	29	204	2.03
1967	Phil Niekro, Atlanta	46	207	1.87	1967	Joe Horlen, Chicago	35	258	2.06
1968	Bob Gibson, St. Louis	34	305	1.12	1968	Luis Tiant, Cleveland	34	258	1.60
1969	Juan Marichal, San Francisco	37	300	2.10	1969	Dick Bosman, Washington	31	193	2.19
1970	Tom Seaver, New York	37	291	2.81	1970	Diego Segui, Oakland	47	162	2.56
1971	Tom Seaver, New York	*36	286	1.76	1971	Vida Blue, Oakland	39	312	1.82
1972	Steve Carlton, Philadelphia	41	346	1.98	1972	Luis Tiant, Boston	43	179	1.91
1973	Tom Seaver, New York	36	290	2.07	1973	Jim Palmer, Baltimore	38	296	2.40
1974	Buzz Capra, Atlanta	39	217	2.28	1974	Catfish Hunter, Oakland	41	318	2.49
1975	Randy Jones, San Diego	37	285	2.24	1975	Jim Palmer, Baltimore	39	323	2.09
1976	John Denny, St. Louis	30	207	2.52	1976	Mark Fidrych, Detroit	31	250	2.34
1977	John Candelaria, Pittsburgh	33	231	2.34	1977	Frank Tanana, California	31	241	2.54
1978	Craig Swan, New York	29	207	2.43	1978	Ron Guidry, New York	35	274	1.74
1979	J. R. Richard, Houston	38	292	2.71	1979	Ron Guidry, New York	33	236	2.78
1980	Don Sutton, Los Angeles	32	212	2.21	1980	Rudy May, New York	41	175	2.47
1981	Nolan Ryan, Houston	21	149	1.69	1981	Steve McCatty, Oakland	22	186	2.32

ERA is computed by multiplying earned runs allowed by 9, then dividing by innings pitched.

Most Valuable Player

Baseball Writers' Association

National League

Year	Player, team	Year	Player, team	Year	Player, team
1931	Frank Frisch, St. Louis	1948	Stan Musial, St. Louis	1965	Willie Mays, San Francisco
1932	Charles Klein, Philadelpha	1949	Jackie Robinson, Brooklyn	1966	Roberto Clemente, Pittsburgh
1933	Carl Hubbell, New York	1950	Jim Konstanty, Philadelphia	1967	Orlando Cepeda, St. Louis
1934	Dizzy Dean, St. Louis	1951	Roy Campanella, Brooklyn	1968	Bob Gibson, St. Louis
1935	Gabby Hartnett, Chicago	1952	Hank Sauer, Chicago	1969	Willie McCovey, San Francisco
1936	Carl Hubbell, New York	1953	Roy Campanella, Brooklyn	1970	Johnny Bench, Cincinnati
1937	Joe Medwick, St. Louis	1954	Willie Mays, New York	1971	Joe Torre, St. Louis
1938	Ernie Lombardi, Cincinnati	1955	Roy Campanella, Brooklyn	1972	Johnny Bench, Cincinnati
1939	Bucky Walters, Cincinnati	1956	Don Newcombe, Brooklyn	1973	Pete Rose, Cincinnati
1940	Frank McCormick, Cincinnati	1957	Henry Aaron, Milwaukee	1974	Steve Garvey, Los Angeles
1941	Dolph Camilli, Brooklyn	1958	Ernie Banks, Chicago	1975	Joe Morgan, Cincinnati
1942	Mort Cooper, St. Louis	1959	Ernie Banks, Chicago	1976	Joe Morgan, Cincinnati
1943	Stan Musial, St. Louis	1960	Dick Groat, Pittsburgh	1977	George Foster, Cincinnati
1944	Martin Marion, St. Louis	1961	Frank Robinson, Cincinnati	1978	Dave Parker, Pittsburgh
1945	Phil Cavarretta, Chicago	1962	Maury Wills, Los Angeles	1979	(tie) Willie Stargell, Pittsburgh
1946	Stan Musial, St. Louis	1963	Sandy Koufax, Los Angeles		Keith Hernandez, St. Louis
1947	Bob Elliott, Boston	1964	Ken Boyer, St. Louis	1980	Mike Schmidt, Philadelphia

American League

Year	Player, team	Year	Player, team	Year	Player, team
1931	Lefty Grove, Philadelphia	1948	Lou Boudreau, Cleveland	1965	Zoilo Versalles, Minnesota
1932	Jimmy Foxx, Philadelphia	1949	Ted Williams, Boston	1966	Frank Robinson, Baltimore
1933	Jimmy Foxx, Philadelphia	1950	Phil Rizzuto, New York	1967	Carl Yastrzemski, Boston
1934	Mickey Cochrane, Detroit	1951	Yogi Berra, New York	1968	Denny McLain, Detroit
1935	Henry Greenberg, Detroit	1952	Bobby Shantz, Philadelphia	1969	Harmon Killebrew, Minnesota
1936	Lou Gehrig, New York	1953	Al Rosen, Cleveland	1970	John (Boog) Powell, Baltimore
1937	Charley Gehringer, Detroit	1954	Yogi Berra, New York	1971	Vida Blue, Oakland
1938	Jimmy Foxx, Boston	1955	Yogi Berra, New York	1972	Dick Allen, Chicago
1939	Joe DiMaggio, New York	1956	Mickey Mantle, New York	1973	Reggie Jackson, Oakland
1940	Hank Greenberg, Detroit	1957	Mickey Mantle, New York	1974	Jeff Burroughs, Texas
1941	Joe DiMaggio, New York	1958	Jackie Jensen, Boston	1975	Fred Lynn, Boston
1942	Joe Gordon, New York	1959	Nellie Fox, Chicago	1976	Thurman Munson, New York
1943	Spurgeon Chandler, New York	1960	Roger Maris, New York	1977	Rod Carew, Minnesota
1944	Hal Newhouser, Detroit	1961	Roger Maris, New York	1978	Jim Rice, Boston
1945	Hal Newhouser, Detroit	1962	Mickey Mantle, New York	1979	Don Baylor, California
1946	Ted Williams, Boston	1963	Elston Howard, New York	1980	George Brett, Kansas City
1947	Joe DiMaggio, New York	1964	Brooks Robinson, Baltimore		

Rookie of the Year
Baseball Writers' Association

1947—Combined selection—Jackie Robinson, Brooklyn, 1b
1948—Combined selection—Alvin Dark, Boston, N.L. ss

National League

Year	Player, team	Year	Player, team	Year	Player, team
1949	Don Newcombe, Brooklyn, p	1960	Frank Howard, Los Angeles, of	1971	Earl Williams, Atlanta, c
1950	Sam Jethroe, Boston, of	1961	Billy Williams, Chicago, of	1972	Jon Matlack, New York, p
1951	Willie Mays, New York, of	1962	Ken Hubbs, Chicago, 2b	1973	Gary Matthews, S.F., of
1952	Joe Black, Brooklyn, p	1963	Pete Rose, Cincinnati, 2b	1974	Bake McBride, St. Louis, of
1953	Jim Gilliam, Brooklyn, 2b	1964	Richie Allen, Philadelphia, 3b	1975	John Montefusco, S.F., p
1954	Wally Moon, St. Louis, of	1965	Jim Lefebvre, Los Angeles, 2b	1976	(tie) Butch Metzger, San Diego, p
1955	Bill Virdon, St. Louis, of	1966	Tommy Helms, Cincinnati, 2b		Pat Zachry, Cincinnati, p
1956	Frank Robinson, Cincinnati, of	1967	Tom Seaver, New York, p	1977	Andre Dawson, Montreal, of
1957	Jack Sanford, Philadelphia, p	1968	Johnny Bench, Cincinnati c	1978	Bob Horner, Atlanta, 3b
1958	Orlando Cepeda, S.F., 1b	1969	Ted Sizemore, Los Angeles, 2b	1979	Rick Sutcliffe, Los Angeles, p
1959	Willie McCovey, S.F., 1b	1970	Carl Morton, Montreal, p	1980	Steve Howe, Los Angeles, p

American League

Year	Player, team	Year	Player, team	Year	Player, team
1949	Roy Sievers, St. Louis, of	1960	Ron Hansen, Baltimore, ss	1971	Chris Chambliss, Cleveland, 1b
1950	Walt Dropo, Boston, 1b	1961	Don Schwall, Boston, p	1972	Carlton Fisk, Boston, c
1951	Gil McDougald, New York, 3b	1962	Tom Tresh, New York, if-of	1973	Al Bumbry, Baltimore, of
1952	Harry Byrd, Philadelphia, p	1963	Gary Peters, Chicago, p	1974	Mike Hargrove, Texas, 1b
1953	Harvey Kuenn, Detroit, ss	1964	Tony Oliva, Minnesota, of	1975	Fred Lynn, Boston, of
1954	Bob Grim, New York, p	1965	Curt Blefary, Baltimore, of	1976	Mark Fidrych, Detroit, p
1955	Herb Score, Cleveland, p	1966	Tommie Agee, Chicago, of	1977	Eddie Murray, Baltimore, dh
1956	Luis Aparicio, Chicago, ss	1967	Rod Carew, Minnesota, 2b	1978	Lou Whitaker, Detroit, 2b
1957	Tony Kubek, New York, if-of	1968	Stan Bahnsen, New York, p	1979	(tie) John Castino, Minnesota, 3b
1958	Albie Pearson, Washington, of	1969	Lou Piniella, Kansas City, of		Alfredo Griffin, Toronto, ss
1959	Bob Allison, Washington, of	1970	Thurman Munson, New York, c	1980	Joe Charboneau, Cleveland, of

College World Series in 1981

Arizona State Univ. won the 1981 College World Series by defeating Oklahoma State Univ. 7-4 in the final game at Omaha, Neb. It was the Sun Devils' 5th College World Series title.

American League Records in 1981
First-half standings

Eastern Division					Western Division				
Club	W	L	Pct.	GB	Club	W	L	Pct.	GB
New York	34	22	.607	...	Oakland	37	23	.617	...
Baltimore	31	23	.574	2	Texas	33	22	.600	1½
Milwaukee	31	25	.554	3	Chicago	31	22	.585	2½
Detroit	31	26	.544	3½	California	31	29	.517	6
Boston	30	26	.536	4	Kansas City	20	30	.400	12
Cleveland	26	24	.520	5	Seattle	21	36	.368	14½
Toronto	16	42	.276	19	Minnesota	17	39	.304	18

American League Records in 1981
Second-half standings

Eastern Division					Western Division				
Club	W	L	Pct.	GB	Club	W	L	Pct.	GB
Milwaukee	31	22	.585	...	Kansas City	30	23	.566	...
Boston	29	23	.558	1½	Oakland	27	22	.551	1
Detroit	29	23	.558	1½	Texas	24	26	.480	4½
Baltimore	28	23	.549	2	Minnesota	24	29	.453	6
Cleveland	26	27	.491	5	Seattle	23	29	.442	6½
New York	25	26	.490	5	Chicago	23	30	.434	7
Toronto	21	27	.438	7½	California	20	30	.400	8½

American League Playoffs

Divisional			League
Oakland 4, Kansas City 0.	New York 5, Milwaukee 3.	Milwaukee 2, New York 1.	New York 3, Oakland 1.
Oakland 2, Kansas City 1.	New York 3, Milwaukee 0.	New York 7, Milwaukee 3.	New York 13, Oakland 3.
Oakland 4, Kansas City 1.	Milwaukee 5, New York 3.		New York 4, Oakland 0.

Club Batting

Club	Pct	AB	R	H	HR	SB
Boston	.275	3820	519	1052	90	32
Chicago	.272	3615	476	982	76	86
Texas	.270	3581	452	968	49	46
Kansas City	.267	3560	397	952	61	100
Cleveland	.263	3507	431	922	39	119
Milwaukee	.257	3743	493	961	96	39
Detroit	.256	3600	427	922	65	61
California	.256	3688	476	944	97	44
New York	.252	3529	421	889	100	46
Seattle	.251	3780	426	950	89	100
Baltimore	.251	3516	429	883	88	41
Oakland	.247	3677	458	910	104	98
Minnesota	.240	3676	378	884	47	34
Toronto	.226	3521	329	797	61	66

Club Pitching

Club	ERA	CG	IP	H	R	BB	SO
New York	2.90	16	948	827	343	287	603
Oakland	3.30	60	993	883	403	370	505
Texas	3.40	23	940	851	389	322	488
Chicago	3.47	20	941	891	423	336	529
Detroit	3.53	33	969	840	404	373	476
Kansas City	3.55	24	922	909	405	273	404
Baltimore	3.70	25	940	923	437	347	489
California	3.71	27	971	958	453	323	426
Boston	3.81	19	987	983	481	354	536
Toronto	3.82	20	953	908	466	377	451
Cleveland	3.88	33	931	989	442	311	569
Milwaukee	3.91	11	986	994	459	352	448
Minnesota	3.98	13	980	1021	486	376	500
Seattle	4.23	10	997	1039	521	360	478

Individual Batting (at least 70 at-bats; Individual Pitching (at least 35 innings)
*Rookie; †Bats or pitches lefthanded ‡Switch hitter

Baltimore Orioles

Batting	Pct	G	AB	R	H	HR	RBI	SB
Murray‡	.294	99	378	57	111	22	78	2
Ayala	.279	44	86	12	24	3	13	0
Singleton‡	.278	103	363	48	101	13	49	0
Bumbry†	.273	101	392	61	107	1	27	22
Roenicke	.269	85	219	31	59	3	20	1
Dauer	.263	96	369	41	97	4	38	0
DeCinces	.263	100	346	49	91	13	55	0
Lowenstein†	.249	83	189	19	47	6	20	7
Crowley†	.246	68	134	12	33	4	25	0
Morales	.244	38	86	6	21	2	14	0
Sakata	.227	61	150	19	34	5	15	4
Dwyer†	.224	68	134	16	30	3	10	0
Dempsey	.215	92	251	24	54	6	15	0
Graham†	.176	55	142	7	25	2	11	0
Belanger	.165	64	139	9	23	1	10	2

Pitching	W	L	ERA	G	IP	H	BB	SO
Stewart	4	8	2.33	29	112	89	57	57
T. Martinez†	3	3	2.90	37	59	48	32	50
McGregor†	13	5	3.26	24	160	167	40	82
D. Martinez	14	5	3.32	25	179	173	62	88
Palmer	7	8	3.76	22	127	117	46	35
Stoddard	4	2	3.89	31	37	38	18	32
Flanagan†	9	6	4.19	20	116	108	37	72
Stone	4	7	4.57	15	63	63	27	30
Ford	1	2	6.53	15	40	61	10	12

Boston Red Sox

Batting	Pct	G	Ab	R	H	HR	RBI	SB
Lansford	.336	102	399	61	134	4	52	15
Remy†	.307	88	359	55	110	0	31	9
Evans	.296	108	412	84	122	22	71	3
Miller†	.291	97	316	38	92	2	33	3
*Gedman†	.288	62	205	22	59	5	26	0
Stapleton	.285	93	355	45	101	10	42	0
Rice	.284	108	451	51	128	17	62	2
Perez	.252	84	306	35	77	9	39	0
Yastrzemski†	.246	91	338	36	83	7	53	0
Hoffman	.231	78	242	28	56	1	20	0
Allenson	.223	47	139	23	31	5	25	0
Rudi	.180	49	122	14	22	6	24	0

Pitching	W	L	ERA	G	IP	H	BB	SO
Rainey	0	1	2.70	11	40	39	13	20
Burgmeier†	4	5	2.85	32	60	61	17	35
*Ojeda†	6	2	3.14	10	66	50	25	28
Campbell	1	1	3.19	30	48	45	20	37
Torrez	10	3	3.69	22	127	130	51	54
Stanley	10	8	3.82	35	99	110	38	28
Tanana†	4	10	4.02	24	141	142	43	78
Clear	8	3	4.09	34	77	69	51	82
Eckersley	9	8	4.27	23	154	160	35	79
Tudor†	4	3	4.56	18	79	74	28	44
*Crawford	0	5	4.97	14	58	69	18	29

California Angels

Batting	Pct	G	AB	R	H	HR	RBI	SB
Carew†	.305	93	364	57	111	2	21	16
Grich	.304	100	352	56	107	22	61	2
Burleson	.293	109	430	53	126	5	33	4
Ford	.277	97	375	53	104	15	48	2
Campaneris	.256	55	82	11	21	1	10	5
Clark	.250	34	88	12	22	4	19	0
Downing	.249	93	317	47	79	9	41	1
*Harris†	.247	36	77	5	19	3	9	0
Baylor	.239	103	377	52	90	17	66	3
Hobson	.235	85	268	27	63	4	36	1
Lynn†	.219	76	256	28	56	5	31	1
Ott†	.217	75	258	20	56	2	22	2
Harlow†	.207	45	82	13	17	0	4	1
Beniquez	.181	58	166	18	30	3	13	2

Pitching	W	L	ERA	G	IP	H	BB	SO
Aase	4	4	2.35	39	65	56	24	38
Forsch	11	7	2.94	20	153	143	27	55
Hassler†	4	3	3.20	42	76	72	33	44
*Witt	8	9	3.28	22	129	123	47	75
Renko	8	4	3.44	22	102	93	42	50
Kison	1	1	3.48	11	44	40	14	19
Jefferson	2	4	3.62	26	77	80	24	27
Zahn†	10	11	4.42	25	161	181	43	52
Frost	1	8	5.55	21	47	44	19	16

Detroit Tigers

Batting	Pct	G	AB	R	H	HR	RBI	SB
Gibson	.328	83	290	41	95	9	40	17
Kemp†	.277	105	372	52	103	9	49	9
Jackson	.270	85	270	29	73	5	40	6
Whitaker†	.263	109	335	48	88	5	36	5
Cowens	.261	85	253	27	66	1	18	3
Jones	.259	71	174	19	45	2	19	1
Trammell	.258	105	392	52	101	2	31	10
Peters‡	.256	63	207	26	53	0	15	1
Summers†	.255	64	165	16	42	3	21	1
Parrish	.244	96	348	39	85	10	46	2
Brookens	.243	71	239	19	58	4	25	5
Hebner†	.226	78	226	19	51	5	28	1
Kelleher	.221	61	77	10	17	0	6	0
Wockenfuss	.215	70	172	20	37	9	25	0
Papi	.204	40	93	8	19	3	12	1
*Leach†	.193	54	83	9	16	1	11	0

Pitching	W	L	ERA	G	IP	H	BB	SO
Saucier†	4	2	1.65	38	49	26	21	23
Tobik	2	2	2.70	27	60	47	33	32
Petry	10	9	3.00	23	141	115	57	79
Wilcox	12	9	3.04	24	166	152	52	79
Morris	14	7	3.05	25	198	153	78	97
Lopez	5	3	3.62	29	82	70	31	53
Rozema	5	5	3.63	28	104	99	25	46
Schatzeder†	6	8	6.08	17	71	74	29	20
*Bailey†	1	4	7.30	9	37	45	13	17

Chicago White Sox

Batting	Pct	G	AB	R	H	HR	RBI	SB
Nordhagen	.308	65	208	19	64	6	33	0
Lemon	.302	94	328	50	99	9	50	5
Almon	.301	103	349	46	105	4	41	16
Baines†	.286	82	280	42	80	10	41	6
Bernazard‡	.276	106	384	53	106	6	34	4
Johnson	.276	41	134	10	37	1	15	0
Luzinski	.265	104	378	55	100	21	62	0
Squires†	.265	92	294	35	78	0	25	7
Fisk	.263	96	338	44	89	7	46	3
LeFlore	.246	82	337	46	83	0	24	36
Morrison	.234	90	290	27	68	10	34	3
Pryor	.224	47	76	4	17	0	6	0

Pitching	W	L	ERA	G	IP	H	BB	SO
Lamp	7	6	2.41	27	127	103	43	71
Burns††	10	6	2.64	24	157	139	49	108
Trout†	8	7	3.46	20	125	122	38	54
Hoyt	9	3	3.56	43	91	80	28	60
*Hickey†	0	2	3.68	41	44	38	18	17
Dotson	9	8	3.77	24	141	145	49	73
Barrios	1	3	4.00	8	36	45	14	12
Koosman†	4	13	4.02	27	121	125	41	76
Baumgarten†	5	9	4.06	19	102	101	40	52
Farmer	3	3	4.58	42	53	53	34	42

Kansas City Royals

Batting	Pct	G	AB	R	H	HR	RBI	SB
Hurdle†	.329	28	76	12	25	4	15	0
G. Brett†	.314	89	347	42	109	6	43	14
Wilson†	.303	102	439	54	133	1	32	34
McRae	.272	101	389	38	106	7	36	3
Otis	.269	99	372	49	100	9	57	16
Aikens†	.266	101	349	45	93	17	53	0
Wathan	.252	89	301	24	76	1	19	11
White	.250	94	364	35	91	9	38	4
Quirk†	.250	46	100	8	25	0	10	0
Geronimo†	.246	59	118	14	29	2	13	6
*Motley	.232	42	125	15	29	2	8	1
Washington‡	.227	98	339	40	77	2	29	10

Pitching	W	L	ERA	G	IP	H	BB	SO
Quisenberry	1	4	1.74	40	62	59	15	20
Gura†	11	8	2.72	23	172	139	35	61
Martin	4	5	2.76	29	62	55	29	25
Leonard	13	11	2.99	26	202	202	41	107
*Jones†	3	3	3.20	12	76	74	28	29
Wright	2	3	3.46	17	52	57	21	27
Splittorff†	5	5	4.36	21	99	111	23	48
*Hammaker†	1	3	5.31	10	39	44	12	11
Gale	6	6	5.38	19	102	107	38	47

Cleveland Indians

Batting	Pct	G	AB	R	H	HR	RBI	SB
Hargrove†	.317	94	322	43	102	2	49	5
Diaz	.313	63	182	25	57	7	38	2
Harrah	.291	103	361	64	105	5	44	12
Dilone‡	.290	72	269	33	78	0	19	29
Orta†	.272	88	338	50	92	5	34	4
Bannister	.263	68	232	36	61	1	17	16
Kuiper†	.257	72	206	15	53	0	14	1
*Hayes†	.257	43	109	21	28	1	17	8
Manning†	.244	103	360	47	88	4	33	25
Veryzer	.244	75	221	13	54	0	14	1
Thornton	.239	69	226	22	54	6	30	3
Rosello	.238	43	84	11	20	1	7	0
Hassey†	.232	61	190	8	44	1	25	0
Kelly†	.213	48	75	8	16	1	16	2
Charboneau	.210	48	138	14	29	4	18	1

Pitching	W	L	ERA	G	IP	H	BB	SO
Blyleven	11	7	2.89	20	159	145	40	107
Denny	10	6	3.14	19	146	139	64	94
Spillner	4	4	3.15	32	97	86	39	59
*Brennan	2	2	3.19	7	48	49	14	15
Barker	8	7	3.92	22	154	150	46	127
Monge†	3	5	4.34	31	58	58	21	41
Stanton	3	3	4.40	24	43	43	18	34
Waits†	8	10	4.93	22	126	173	44	51
Garland	3	7	5.79	12	56	89	14	15

Milwaukee Brewers

Batting	Pct	G	AB	R	H	HR	RBI	SB
Cooper†	.320	106	416	70	133	12	60	5
Moore	.301	48	156	16	47	1	9	1
Brouhard	.274	60	186	19	51	2	20	1
Yount	.273	96	377	50	103	10	49	4
Gantner†	.267	107	352	35	94	2	33	3
Molitor	.267	64	251	45	67	2	19	10
Thomas	.259	103	363	54	94	21	65	4
Oglivie†	.243	107	400	53	97	14	72	2
Howell†	.238	76	244	37	58	6	33	0
Hisle	.230	27	87	11	20	4	11	0
Bosley†	.229	42	105	11	24	0	3	2
Simmons‡	.216	100	380	45	82	14	61	0
Money	.216	60	185	17	40	2	14	0
Romero	.198	44	91	6	18	1	10	0

Pitching	W	L	ERA	G	IP	H	BB	SO
Fingers	6	3	1.04	47	78	55	13	61
Easterly†	3	3	3.19	44	62	46	34	31
Vuckovich	14	4	3.54	24	150	137	57	84
Caldwell†	11	9	3.94	24	144	151	38	41
Augustine†	2	4	4.28	27	61	75	18	26
Lerch†	7	9	4.30	23	111	134	43	53
Slaton	5	7	4.38	24	117	120	50	47
Haas	11	7	4.47	24	137	146	40	64
Cleveland	2	3	5.12	35	65	57	30	18
*Keeton	1	0	5.14	17	35	47	11	9

Minnesota Twins

Batting	Pct	G	AB	R	H	HR	RBI	SB
Castino	.268	101	381	41	102	6	36	4
*Ward	.264	85	295	42	78	3	29	5
Smalley‡	.263	56	167	24	44	7	22	0
*Engle	.258	82	248	29	64	5	32	0
Hatcher	.255	99	377	36	96	3	37	3
Wynegar‡	.247	47	150	11	37	0	10	0
Wilfong†	.246	93	305	32	75	3	19	2
Butera	.240	62	167	13	40	0	18	0
Powell†	.239	80	264	30	63	2	25	7
Mackanin	.231	77	225	21	52	4	18	1
*Washington	.226	28	84	8	19	0	5	4
Goodwin†	.225	59	151	18	34	2	17	3
Adams†	.209	72	220	13	46	2	24	0
Sofield†	.176	41	102	9	18	0	5	3

Pitching	W	L	ERA	G	IP	H	BB	SO
Corbett	2	6	2.56	54	88	80	34	60
*Havens†	3	6	3.58	14	78	76	24	43
Erickson	3	8	3.86	14	91	93	31	44
Arroyo	7	10	3.94	23	128	144	34	39
Verhoeven	0	0	3.98	25	52	57	14	16
Redfern	9	8	4.06	24	142	140	52	77
Williams	6	10	4.08	23	150	160	52	76
*Cooper	1	5	4.27	27	59	61	32	33
*O'Connor†	3	2	5.91	28	35	46	30	16

New York Yankees

Batting	Pct	G	AB	R	H	HR	RBI	SB
Milbourne‡	.313	61	163	24	51	1	12	2
Mumphrey‡	.307	80	319	44	98	6	32	13
Winfield	.294	105	388	52	14	13	68	11
Piniella	.277	60	159	16	44	5	18	0
Murcer†	.265	50	117	14	31	6	24	0
Nettles†	.244	103	349	46	85	15	46	0
Cerone	.244	71	234	23	57	2	21	0
Dent	.238	73	227	20	54	7	27	0
Gamble†	.238	80	189	24	45	10	27	0
Jackson†	.237	94	334	33	79	15	54	0
Revering†	.233	76	206	20	48	4	17	0
Randolph	.232	93	357	59	83	2	24	14
Watson	.212	59	156	15	33	6	12	0
Foote	.208	40	125	12	26	6	10	0

Pitching	W	L	ERA	G	IP	H	BB	SO
Gossage	3	2	0.77	32	47	22	14	48
*Righetti†	2	2	2.06	15	105	75	38	89
LaRoche†	4	1	2.49	26	47	38	16	24
John†	9	8	2.64	20	140	135	39	50
Reuschel	4	4	2.66	12	71	75	10	22
Davis	4	5	2.71	43	73	47	25	83
Bird	5	1	2.72	17	53	58	16	28
Guidry†	11	5	2.76	23	127	100	26	104
May†	6	11	4.14	27	148	137	41	79
*Nelson	3	1	4.85	8	39	40	23	16

Oakland A's

Batting	Pct	G	AB	R	H	HR	RBI	SB
Henderson	.319	108	423	89	135	6	35	56
*Drumright†	.291	31	86	8	25	0	11	0
Picciolo	.268	82	179	23	48	4	13	0
McKay‡	.263	79	224	25	59	4	21	4
Armas	.264	109	440	51	115	22	76	5
Johnson	.260	84	273	40	71	17	59	5
*Babitt	.256	54	156	10	40	0	14	5
Murphy†	.251	107	390	58	98	15	60	10
Heath	.236	84	301	26	71	8	30	3
Newman	.231	68	216	17	50	3	15	0
Gross†	.206	82	243	29	50	10	31	2
Stanley	.193	66	145	15	28	0	7	2
Spencer†	.188	79	234	20	44	4	13	1
Page†	.141	34	92	9	13	4	13	2

Pitching	W	L	ERA	G	IP	H	BB	SO
McCatty	14	7	2.32	22	186	140	61	91
Langford	12	10	3.00	24	195	190	58	84
Owchinko†	4	3	3.23	29	39	34	19	26
Jones	4	1	3.39	33	61	51	40	43
Keough	10	6	3.41	19	140	125	45	60
Underwood†	4	6	3.64	25	84	69	38	75
Norris	12	9	3.75	23	173	145	63	78
Kingman	3	6	3.96	18	100	112	32	52

Seattle Mariners

Batting	Pct	G	AB	R	H	HR	RBI	SB
Paciorek	.326	104	405	50	132	14	66	13
Zisk	.311	94	357	42	111	16	43	0
Meyer†	.262	83	252	26	66	3	22	4
Bochte†	.260	99	335	39	87	6	30	1
Cruz‡	.256	94	352	57	90	2	24	43
*Serna	.255	30	94	11	24	4	9	2
Burroughs	.254	89	319	32	81	10	41	0
Bulling	.247	62	154	15	38	2	15	0
Gray	.245	69	208	27	51	13	31	2
Randle‡	.231	82	273	22	63	4	25	11
Simpson†	.222	91	288	32	64	2	30	12
Narron†	.222	76	203	13	45	3	17	0
Anderson	.204	70	162	12	33	2	19	3
*Henderson	.167	59	126	17	21	6	13	2
Auerbach	.155	38	84	12	13	1	6	1
*Edler	.141	29	78	7	11	0	5	3

Pitching	W	L	ERA	G	IP	H	BB	SO
*Stoddard	2	1	2.57	5	35	35	9	22
Andersen	3	3	2.65	41	68	57	18	40
Beattie	3	2	2.96	13	67	59	18	36
Allard	3	2	3.75	7	48	48	8	20
Abbott	4	4	3.95	22	130	127	28	35
Rawley†	4	6	3.97	46	68	64	38	35
*Clark†	2	5	4.35	29	93	92	55	52
Bannister†	9	9	4.46	21	121	128	39	85
Clay	2	7	4.63	22	101	116	42	32
*Gleaton†	4	7	4.76	20	85	88	38	31
Parrott	3	6	5.08	24	85	102	28	43
Drago	4	6	5.50	39	54	71	15	27

Texas Rangers

Batting	Pct	G	AB	R	H	HR	RBI	SB
Stein	.330	53	115	21	38	2	22	1
Oliver†	.309	102	421	53	130	4	55	3
Bell	.294	97	360	44	106	10	64	3
Rivers‡	.286	99	399	62	114	3	26	9
Sample	.283	66	230	36	65	3	25	4
Roberts	.279	72	233	26	65	4	31	3
Sundberg	.277	102	339	42	94	3	28	2
Putnam†	.266	95	297	33	79	8	35	4
Wagner	.259	50	85	15	22	1	14	1
Wills‡	.251	102	410	51	103	2	41	12
Mendoza	.231	88	229	18	53	0	22	2
Grubb†	.231	67	199	26	46	3	26	0

Pitching	W	L	ERA	G	IP	H	BB	SO
Comer	8	2	2.57	36	77	70	31	22
Hough	4	1	2.96	21	82	61	31	69
Medich	10	6	3.08	20	143	136	33	65
Honeycutt††	11	6	3.30	20	128	120	17	40
Darwin	9	9	3.64	22	146	115	57	98
Matlack†	4	7	4.15	17	104	101	41	43
Jenkins	5	8	4.50	19	106	122	40	63

Toronto Blue Jays

Batting	Pct	G	AB	R	H	HR	RBI	SB
Garcia	.252	64	250	24	63	1	13	13
Mayberry†	.248	94	290	34	72	17	43	1
Woods†	.247	85	288	20	71	1	21	3
Iorg	.242	70	215	17	52	0	10	2
Whitt†	.236	74	195	16	46	1	16	5
Moseby†	.233	100	378	36	88	9	43	11
*Bell	.233	60	163	19	38	5	12	3
*Barfield	.232	25	95	7	22	2	9	4
Martinez	.227	45	128	13	29	4	21	1
Bonnell	.220	66	227	21	50	4	28	4
Velez	.213	80	240	32	51	11	28	0
Griffin†	.209	101	388	30	81	0	21	8
Macha	.200	37	85	4	17	0	6	1
Ainge	.187	86	246	20	46	0	14	8
Upshaw†	.171	61	111	15	19	4	10	2

Pitching	W	L	ERA	G	IP	H	BB	SO
Jackson	1	2	2.61	39	62	65	25	27
McLaughlin	1	5	2.85	40	60	55	21	38
Stieb	11	10	3.18	25	184	148	61	89
Garvin†	1	2	3.40	35	53	46	23	25
Leal	7	13	3.67	29	130	127	44	71
Bomback	5	5	3.90	20	90	84	35	33
Todd	2	7	3.95	21	98	94	31	41
Clancy	6	12	4.90	22	125	126	64	56
Berenguer	2	13	5.24	20	91	84	51	49
Willis†	0	4	5.91	20	35	43	20	16

Individual Batting

Leaders—270 or more at bats

Player, club	Pct	AB	R	H	HR	RBI	SB
Lansford, Boston	.336	399	61	134	4	52	15
Gibson, Detroit†	.328	290	41	95	9	40	17
Paciorek, Seattle . . .	.326	405	50	132	14	66	13
Cooper, Milwaukee† . .	.320	416	70	133	12	60	5
Henderson, Oakland . .	.319	423	89	135	6	35	56
Hargrove, Cleveland† . .	.317	322	43	102	2	49	5
G. Brett, Kansas City† . .	.314	347	42	109	6	43	14
Zisk, Seattle	.311	357	42	111	16	43	0

Individual Pitching

Leaders—110 or more innings

Pitcher, club	W	L	ERA	G	IP	H	BB	SO
McCatty, Oakland	14	7	2.32	22	186	140	61	91
Stewart, Baltimore. . . .	4	8	2.33	29	112	89	57	57
Lamp, Chicago	7	6	2.41	27	127	103	43	71
John, New York†	9	8	2.64	20	140	135	39	50
Burns, Chicago†	10	6	2.64	24	157	139	49	108
Gura, Kansas City† . . .	11	8	2.72	23	172	139	35	61
Guidry, New York†	11	5	2.76	23	127	101	26	104
Blyleven, Cleveland . . .	11	7	2.89	20	159	145	40	107

Major League Leaders in 1981

National League

Home Runs
Schmidt, Philadelphia, 31; Dawson, Montreal, 24; Kingman, New York, 22; Foster, Cincinnati, 22; Hendrick, St Louis, 18

RBIs
Schmidt, Philadelphia, 91; Foster, Cincinnati, 90; Buckner, Chicago, 75; Carter, Montreal, 68; Matthews, Philadelphia, 67; Concepcion, Cincinnati, 67.

Stolen Bases
Raines, Montreal, 71; Moreno, Pittsburgh, 39; R. Scott, Montreal, 30; Dawson, Montreal, 26; Collins, Cincinnati, 26; North, San Francisco, 26.

Runs
Schmidt, Philadelphia, 78; Rose, Philadelphia, 73; Dawson, Montreal, 71; Hernandez, St. Louis, 67; Henderick, St. Louis, 67.

Hits
Rose, Philadelphia, 140; Buckner, Chicago, 131; Concepcion, Cincinnati, 129; Baker, Los Angeles, 128; Griffey, Cincinnati, 123.

Doubles
Buckner, Chicago, 35; Jones, San Diego, 34; Concepcion, Cincinnati, 28; Hernandez, St. Louis, 27; Chambliss, Atlanta, 25.

Triples
Reynolds, Houston, 12; Richards, San Diego, 12; Herr, St. Louis, 9; Wilson, New York, 9; Moreno, Pittsburgh, 8; Templeton, St. Louis, 8; Herndon, San Francisco, 8.

Pitching (9 Decisions)
Seaver, Cincinnati, 14-2, .875, 2.54; Carlton, Philadelphia, 13-4, .765, 2.42; Camp, Atlanta, 9-3, .750, 1.78; Reuss, Los Angeles, 10-4, .714, 2.30; Rhoden, Pittsburgh, 9-4, .692, 3.89; Hume, Cincinnati, 9-4, .692, 3.46; Ryan, Houston, 11-5, .688, 1.69; Forsch, St. Louis, 10-5, .667, 3.18.

Strikeouts
Valenzuela, Los Angeles, 180; Carlton, Philadelphia, 179; Soto, Cincinnati, 151; Ryan, Houston, 140; Gullickson, Montreal, 114.

American League

Home Runs
Murray, Baltimore, 22; Evans, Boston, 22; Gldh, California, 22; Armas, Oakland, 22; Thomas, Milwaukee, 21; Luzinski, Chicago, 21.

RBIs
Murray, Baltimore, 78; Armas, Oakland, 76; Oglivie, Milwaukee, 72; Evans, Boston, 71; Winfield, New York, 68.

Stolen Bases
R. Henderson, Oakland, 56; J. Cruz, Seattle, 43; LeFlore, Chicago, 36; Wilson, Kansas City, 34; Dilone, Cleveland, 30.

Runs
R.Henderson, Oakland, 89; Evans, Boston, 84; C. Cooper, Milwaukee, 70; Harrah, Cleveland, 64; Rivers, Texas, 62.

Hits
R. Henderson, Oakland, 135; Lansford, Boston, 134; C. Cooper, Milwaukee, 133; Wilson, Kansas City, 133; Paciorek, Seattle, 132.

Doubles
C. Cooper, Milwaukee, 34; Oliver, Texas, 29; Paciorek, Seattle, 28; G. Brett, Kansas City, 27; Dauer, Baltimore, 26.

Triples
Castino, Minnesota, 9; Baines, Chicago, 7; G. Brett, Kansas City, 7; Wilson, Kansas City, 7; R. Henderson, Oakland, 7.

Pitching (9 Decisions)
Corner, Texas, 8-2, .800, 2.53; Vuckovich, Milwaukee, 14-4, .778, 3.55; Torrez, Boston, 10-3, .769, 3.69; Hoyt, Chicago, 9-3, .750, 3.77; D. Martinez, Baltimore, 14-5, .737, 3.32; Clear, Boston, 8-3, .727, 4.11; McGregor, Baltimore, 13-5, .722, 3.26; Guidry, New York, 11-5, .688, 2.91.

Strikeouts
Barker, Cleveland, 127; Burns, Chicago, 108; Blyleven, Cleveland, 107; Leonard, Kansas City, 105; Guidry, New York, 104.

Triple Crown Winners

Players leading league in batting, runs batted in, and homers in a single season

Year	Player, team	Year	Player, team
1909	Ty Cobb, Detroit Tigers	1937	Joe Medwick, St. Louis Cardinals
1922	Rogers Hornsby, St. Louis Cardinals	1942	Ted Williams, Boston Red Sox
1925	Rogers Hornsby, St. Louis Cardinals	1947	Ted Williams, Boston Red Sox
1933	Jimmy Foxx, Philadelphia Athletics	1956	Mickey Mantle, New York Yankees
1933	Chuck Klein, Philadelphia Phillies	1966	Frank Robinson, Baltimore Orioles
1934	Lou Gehrig, New York Yankees	1967	Carl Yastrzemski, Boston Red Sox

Major League Attendance in 1981

National League

Club	1981 1st Half Average Attendance	2nd Half Average Attendance	1980 Average Attendance
Atlanta	14,771	6,206	13,616
Chicago	9,862	10,792	15,879
Cincinnati	22,402	20,451	29,966
Houston	27,277	25,342	29,208
Los Angeles	46,238	39,527	40,115
Montreal	26,014	33,007	29,442
New York	13,979	14,685	15,685
Philadelphia	32,669	28,032	33,996
Pittsburgh	12,951	9,937	22,253
St. Louis	18,638	19,657	17,314
San Diego	14,337	5,602	14,793
San Francisco	14,094	10,633	14,053
Totals	21,015	19,034	22,837

American League

Club	1981 1st Half Average Attendance	2nd Half Average Attendance	1980 Average Attendance
Baltimore.	22,708	16,729	22,468
Boston	19,394	21,250	24,761
California.	28,795	23,396	28,362
Chicago	25,336	14,721	16,005
Cleveland	21,283	7,353	14,359
Detroit	17,673	24,630	23,491
Kansas City	27,850	26,565	28,256
Milwaukee	19,254	17,174	24,122
Minnesota	7,053	8,819	10,537
New York	32,287	32,043	33,258
Oakland	27,279	22,452	11,230
Seattle.	13,394	8,446	10,453
Texas.	17,908	13,228	15,561
Toronto.	14,717	14,273	18,671
Totals	20,865	17,751	20,269

First Game

Los Angeles	ab	r	h	bi	New York	ab	r	h	bi
Lopes 2b . . .	3	1	0	0	Randolph 2b . .	3	0	0	0
Russell ss . . .	3	0	0	0	Mumphrey cf . .	3	2	2	0
Johnstone ph . .	1	0	1	1	Winfield lf . . .	3	0	0	1
Stewart p. . .	0	0	0	0	Piniella rf . . .	4	1	2	1
Baker lf . . .	2	0	1	0	Watson 1b . . .	3	1	2	3
Garvey 1b . . .	4	0	1	0	Nettles 3b . . .	3	0	0	0
Cey 3b . . .	4	0	1	0	Cerone c . . .	3	0	0	0
Guerrero cf. . .	3	0	0	0	Milbourne ss . .	4	1	0	0
Monday rf . . .	4	0	0	0	Guidry p	2	0	0	0
Yeager c . . .	3	1	1	1	Davis p	0	0	0	0
Landreaux ph . .	1	0	0	0	Gossage p . . .	0	0	0	0
Reuss p . . .	1	0	0	0					
Castillo p . . .	0	0	0	0					
Goltz p . . .	0	0	0	0					
Sax ph . . .	1	0	0	0					
Niedenfuer p . .	0	0	0	0					
Thomas ss . .	0	1	0	0					
Totals	30	3	5	3	Totals	28	5	6	5

```
Los Angeles . . . . . . 0  0  0  0  1  0  0  2  0—3
New York . . . . . . . . 3  0  1  0  0  0  0  x—5
```

DP - Los Angeles 1. LOB - Los Angeles 5, New York 6. 2B - Piniella. HR - Watson (1), Yeager (1). SB - Mumphrey, Piniella. S - Guidry. SF - Baker.

	ip	h	r	er	bb	so
Los Angeles						
Reuss L,0-1 . . .	2 ⅔	5	4	4	0	2
Castillo	1	0	1	1	5	0
Goltz	⅓	0	0	0	0	0
Niedenfuer	3	1	0	0	0	0
Stewart	1	0	0	0	1	0
New York						
Guidry W, 1-0	7	4	1	1	2	6
Davis	0	0	2	2	2	0
Gossage S, 1	2	1	0	0	0	2

PB - Cerone. T - 2:32. A - 56,470.

How runs were scored—Three in Yankees first: Mumphrey singled. Piniella doubled. Watson hit a home run scoring Mumphrey and Piniella.

One in Yankees fourth: Mumphrey singled and stole second. Piniella singled scoring Mumphrey.

One in Yankees fifth: four Yankee batters walked forcing in a run.

One in Dodgers fifth: Yeager hit a home run.

Two in Dodgers eighth: Thomas and Lopes walked. Johnstone singled scoring Thomas. Baker hit a sacrifice fly scoring Lopes.

Second Game

Los Angeles	ab	r	h	bi	New York	ab	r	h	bi
Lopes 2b . . .	3	0	0	0	Mumphrey cf	2	0	0	0
Monday ph . .	1	0	0	0	Milbourne . .	4	0	1	1
Howe p . . .	0	0	0	0	Winfield lf . .	4	0	0	0
Stewart p . .	0	0	0	0	Gamble rf . .	2	0	0	0
Russell ss . .	4	0	1	0	Piniella ph . .	1	0	1	0
Baker lf . . .	4	0	0	0	Brown rf . . .	0	1	0	0
Garvey 1b . .	3	0	2	0	Nettles 3b . .	4	1	2	0
Cey 3b . . .	4	0	0	0	Watson 1b . .	4	0	2	1
Guerrero cf . .	4	0	0	0	Cerone c . . .	2	0	0	0
Landreaux cf	3	0	0	0	Randolph 2b . .	2	1	0	1
Yeager c . .	2	0	0	0	John p . . .	1	0	0	0
Johnstone ph	1	0	0	0	Murcer ph . .	0	0	0	0
Scioscia c . .	0	0	0	0	Gossage p . .	1	0	0	0
Hooton p . .	2	0	0	0					
Forster p. . .	0	0	0	0					
Smith ph . .	1	0	1	0					
Sax 2b . . .	0	0	0	0					
Totals . . .	34	0	4	0	Totals . . .	27	3	6	3

```
Los Angeles . . . . . 0  0  0   0  0  0   0  0  0—0
New York . . . . . . . 0  0  0   1  0  0   2  x—3
```

E - Milbourne, Lopes Stewart. DP - Los Angeles 1. LOB - Los Angeles 6, New York 9. 2B - Milbourne. S - John, Murcer. SF - Randolph.

	ip	h	r	er	bb	so
Los Angeles						
Hooton L,0-1	6	3	1	0	4	1
Forster	1	0	0	0	1	1
Howe	⅓	2	2	2	0	0
Stewart	⅔	1	0	0	1	1
New York						
John W,1-0	7	3	0	0	3	4
Gossage S,2	2	1	0	0	1	3

T - 2:29. A - 56,505.

Third Game

New York	ab	r	h	bi	Los Angeles	ab	r	h	bi
Randolph 2b . .	2	0	0	0	Lopes 2b	4	1	2	0
Mumphrey cf . .	5	0	0	0	Russell ss . . .	5	1	2	0
Winfield lf . . .	3	0	0	0	Baker lf . . .	4	0	0	0
Piniella rf . . .	5	1	1	0	Garvey 1b . . .	4	1	2	0
Watson 1b . . .	4	1	2	2	Cey 3b . . .	2	2	3	3
Cerone c . . .	4	2	2	1	Guerrero cf . .	3	0	1	1
Rodriguez 3b . .	4	0	2	0	Monday rf . . .	2	0	1	0
Milbourne ss . .	2	0	2	1	Thomas rf . . .	1	0	0	0
Righetti p . . .	1	0	0	0	Yeager c . . .	1	0	0	0
Frazier p	1	0	0	0	Scioscia c . . .	3	0	1	0
May p . . .	0	0	0	0	Valenzuela p . .	3	0	0	0
Murcer ph . . .	1	0	0	0					
Davis p	0	0	0	0					
Totals	32	4	9	3	Totals	32	5	11	4

```
New York . . . . . . . . 0  2  2   0  0  0   0  0  0—4
Los Angeles . . . . . 3  0  0   0  2  0   0  0  x—5
```

E—Lopes. DP—Yankees 2, Los Angeles 3. LOB—Yankees 9, Los Angeles 9. 2B—Lopes, Cerone, Watson, Guerrero. HRs—Cey (1), Watson (2), Cerone (1). S—Righetti, Lopes.

	ip	h	r	er	bb	so
Los Angeles						
Valenzuela W, 1-0 . .	9	9	4	4	7	6
New York						
Righetti	2	5	3	3	2	1
Frazier L, 0-1 . . .	2	3	2	2	1	1
May	3	2	0	0	0	2
Davis	1	1	0	0	1	0

HBP—by Righetti (Guerrero). T—3:04. A—56,236.

How runs were scored—Three in Dodgers first: Lopes doubled. Russell singled. Cey hit a home run scoring Lopes and Russell.

Two in Yankees second: Watson hit a home run. Cerone doubled. Milbourne singled scoring Cerone.

Two in Yankees third: Piniella singled. Cerone hit a home run scoring Piniella.

Two in Dodgers fifth: Garvey singled. Cey walked. Guerrero doubled scoring Garvey. Cey scored as Scioscia hit into a double play.

Fourth Game

New York	ab	r	h	bi	Los Angeles	ab	r	h	bi
Randolph 2b . .	5	3	2	1	Lopes 2b	5	2	2	2
Milbourne ss . .	4	1	1	1	Russell ss . . .	5	0	1	1
Winfield lf . . .	4	0	0	0	Garvey 1b . . .	5	1	3	0
Jackson rf . . .	3	2	3	1	Cey 3b . . .	5	0	2	2
Gamble lf . . .	4	1	2	1	Baker lf . . .	5	1	1	0
Brown cf . . .	0	0	0	0	Monday rf . . .	3	1	1	0
Piniella lf . . .	1	0	0	0	Thomas cf . . .	1	0	0	0
Watson 1b . . .	3	0	1	2	Guerrero rf . . .	3	0	2	0
Cerone c . . .	5	0	2	1	Scioscia c . . .	1	1	0	0
Robertson pr . .	0	0	0	0	Yeager c . . .	0	0	0	1
Rodriguez 3b . .	4	0	2	0	Welch p . . .	0	0	0	0
Foote ph . . .	1	0	0	0	Goltz p . . .	0	0	0	0
Reuschel p . . .	2	0	0	0	Landreaux ph . .	1	1	1	0
May p . . .	1	0	0	0	Forster p . . .	0	0	0	0
Davis p	0	0	0	0	Smith ph . . .	1	0	0	0
Frazier . . .	1	0	0	0	Niedenfuer p . .	0	0	0	0
John p . . .	0	0	0	0	Johnstone ph . .	1	1	1	2
Murcer ph . . .	1	0	0	0	Howe p . . .	0	0	0	0
Totals	39	7	13	7	Totals	36	8	14	8

```
New York . . . . . . . 2  1  1   0  0  2   0  1  0—7
Los Angeles . . . . . 0  0  2   0  1  3   2  0  x—8
```

E—Russell, Jackson, Howe. LOB—Yankees 12, Los Angeles 10. 2B—Milbourne, Landreaux, Garvey, Monday. 3B—Randolph. HR—Randolph (1), Johnstone (1), Jackson (1). SB—Winfield, Lopes 2. S—Milbourne, Scioscia, Howe. SF—Watson, Yeager.

	ip	h	r	er	bb	so
New York						
Reuschel	3	6	2	2	1	2
May	1⅓	2	1	1	0	1
Davis	1	2	3	2	1	0
Frazier L, 1-1 . . .	⅔	2	2	2	1	0
John	2	2	0	0	0	2

How runs were scored—One in Yankees fifth: Randolph reached first on an error and was sacrificed to second. Milbourne doubled scoring Randolph.

How runs were scored—One in Yankees fifth: Randolph reached first on an error and was sacrificed to second. Milbourne doubled scoring Randolph.

Two in Yankees eighth: Piniella and Nettles singled. Brown ran for Piniella. Watson singled scoring Brown. Randolph hit a sacrifice fly scoring Nettles.

Los Angeles	ip	h	r	er	bb	so
Welch	0	3	2	2	1	0
Goltz	3	4	2	2	1	2
Forster	1	1	0	0	2	0
Niedenfuer	2	2	0	0	1	0
Howe W, 1-0	3	3	1	1	0	1

T—3:32. A—56,242.

How runs were scored—Two in Yankees first: Randolph tripled. Milbourne doubled scoring Randolph. Winfield walked. Jackson singled. Watson hit a sacrifice fly scoring Milbourne.
One in Yankees second: Randolph hit a home run.
One in Yankees third: Jackson singled. Watson walked. Cerone singled scoring Jackson.
Two in Dodgers third: Landreaux doubled. Lopes singled scoring Landreaux. Garvey singled. Cey grounded out scoring Lopes.
One in Dodgers fifth: Garvey doubled. Cey singled scoring Garvey.
Two in Yankees sixth: Randolph reached first on an error. Jackson walked. Gamble singled scoring Randolph. Watson singled scoring Jackson.
Three in Dodgers sixth: Scioscia walked. Johnstone hit a home run scoring Scioscia. Lopes reached second on an error. Russell singled scoring Lopes.
Two in Dodgers seventh: Baker singled. Monday doubled. Guerrero walked. Yeager hit a sacrifice fly scoring Baker. Lopes singled scoring Monday.
One in Yankees eighth: Jackson hit a home run.

Fifth Game

New York	ab	r	h	bi	Los Angeles	ab	r	h	bi
Randolph 2b	3	0	0	0	Lopes 2b	3	0	0	0
Milbourne ss	4	0	1	0	Russell ss	4	0	0	0
Winfield cf	4	0	1	0	Garvey 1b	4	0	1	0
Jackson rf	4	1	1	0	Cey 3b	2	0	0	0
Gossage p	0	0	0	0	Landreaux cf	0	0	0	0
Watson 1b	3	0	0	0	Baker lf	4	0	0	0
Piniella lf	4	0	2	1	Guerrero rf	3	1	1	1
Brown pr	0	0	0	0	Yeager c	3	1	2	1
Cerone c	4	0	0	0	Thomas cf	3	0	0	0
Rodriguez 3b	3	0	0	0	Reuss p	2	0	0	0
Guidry p	3	0	0	0					
Mumphrey cf	0	0	0	0					
Totals	32	1	5	1	Totals	28	2	4	2

New York . . . . . 0 1 0 0 0 0 0 0—1
Los Angeles . . . . 0 0 0 0 0 0 2 0 x—2

E—Lopes 3. DP—Los Angeles 6. LOB—New York 7, Los Angeles 6. 2B—Jackson, Yeager. HRs—Guerrero (1), Yeager (2). SB—Lopes, Landreaux.

New York	ip	h	r	er	bb	so
Guidry L, 1-1	7	4	2	2	2	9
Gossage	1	0	0	0	1	0
Los Angeles						
Reuss W, 1-1	9	5	1	1	3	6

HBP—by Gossage (Cey). T—2:19. A—56,115.

How runs were scored—One in Yankees second: Jackson doubled. Piniella singled scoring Jackson.
Two in Dodgers seventh: Guerrero hit a home run. Yeager hit a home run.

Sixth Game

Los Angeles	ab	r	h	bi	New York	ab	r	h	bi
Lopes 2b	4	2	1	1	Randolph 2b	3	1	2	1
Russell ss	4	1	2	0	Mumphrey cf	5	0	1	0
Garvey 1b	4	1	1	0	Winfield lf	4	0	0	0
Cey 3b	3	1	2	1	Jackson rf	5	0	0	0
Thomas 3b	2	0	0	1	Watson 1b	5	0	0	0
Baker lf	5	2	2	0	Nettles 2b	3	0	2	0
Guerrero cf	5	1	3	5	Rodriguez 3b	1	1	1	0
Monday rf	3	0	1	0	Cerone c	3	0	0	0
Yeager c	5	0	1	1	Milbourne ss	2	0	0	0
Hooton p	2	1	0	0	John p	1	0	0	0
Landreaux cf	1	0	0	0	Murcer ph	1	0	0	0
Howe p	2	0	0	0	Frazier p	0	0	0	0
					Davis p	0	0	0	0
					Reuschel p	0	0	0	0
					Gamble ph	1	0	0	0
					Piniella ph	1	0	1	1
					May p	0	0	0	0
					Brown ph	1	0	0	0
					Laroche p	0	0	0	0
Totals	40	9	13	9	Totals	35	2	7	2

Los Angeles . . . 0 0 0 1 3 4 0 1 0—9
New York . . . . . 0 0 1 0 0 1 0 0 0—2

E—Milbourne, Nettles, Lopes. LOB—Los Angeles 10, New York 10. 2B—Nettles, Randolph, Guerrero. 3B—Guerrero. HRs—Randolph (1), Guerrero (1). SB—Randolph, Lopes, Russell. S—Russell.

Los Angeles	ip	h	r	er	bb	so
Hooton W, 1-1	5⅓	5	2	2	5	2
Howe S	3⅔	2	0	0	1	3
New York						
John	4	6	1	1	0	2
Frazier L, 0-3	1	4	3	3	0	1
Davis	⅓	1	3	2	2	1
Reuschel	⅔	1	1	0	2	0
May	2	1	1	1	1	2
Laroche	1	0	0	0	0	2

How runs were scored—One in Yankees third: Randolph hit a home run.
One in Dodgers fourth: Baker and Monday singled. Yeager singled scoring Baker.
Three in Dodgers fifth: Lopes singled and was sacrificed to second. Cey singled scoring Lopes. Baker singled. Guerrero tripled scoring Cey and Baker.
Four in Dodgers sixth: Hooton and Lopes walked. Russell singled scoring Hooton. Garvey walked. Thomas grounded out scoring Lopes. Guerrero doubled scoring Russell and Garvey.
One in Yankee sixth: Nettles singled. Rodriguez ran for Nettles. Cerone and Milbourne walked. Piniella singled scoring Rodriguez.
One in Dodgers eighth: Guerrero hit a home run.

World Series Results, 1903-1981

1903 Boston AL 5, Pittsburgh NL 3
1904 No series
1905 New York NL 4, Philadelphia AL 1
1906 Chicago AL 4, Chicago NL 2
1907 Chicago NL 4, Detroit AL 0, 1 tie
1908 Chicago NL 4, Detroit AL 1
1909 Pittsburgh NL 4, Detroit AL 3
1910 Philadelphia AL 4, Chicago NL 1
1911 Philadelphia AL 4, New York NL 2
1912 Boston AL 4, New York NL 3, 1 tie
1913 Philadelphia AL 4, New York NL 1
1914 Boston NL 4, Philadelphia AL 0
1915 Boston AL 4, Philadelphia NL 1
1916 Boston AL 4, Brooklyn NL 1
1917 Chicago AL 4, New York NL 2
1918 Boston AL 4, Chicago NL 2
1919 Cincinnati NL 5, Chicago AL 3
1920 Cleveland AL 5, Brooklyn NL 2
1921 New York NL 5, New York AL 3
1922 New York NL 4, New York AL 0, 1 tie
1923 New York AL 4, New York NL 2
1924 Washington AL 4, New York NL 3
1925 Pittsburgh NL 4, Washington AL 3
1926 St. Louis NL 4, New York AL 3
1927 New York AL 4, Pittsburgh NL 0
1928 New York AL 4, St. Louis NL 0

1929 Philadelphia AL 4, Chicago NL 1
1930 Philadelphia AL 4, St. Louis NL 2
1931 St. Louis NL 4, Philadelphia AL 3
1932 New York AL 4, Chicago NL 0
1933 New York NL 4, Washington AL 1
1934 St. Louis NL 4, Detroit AL 3
1935 Detroit AL 4, Chicago NL 2
1936 New York AL 4, New York NL 2
1937 New York AL 4, New York NL 1
1938 New York AL 4, Chicago NL 0
1939 New York AL 4, Cincinnati NL 0
1940 Cincinnati NL 4, Detroit AL 3
1941 New York AL 4, Brooklyn NL 1
1942 St. Louis NL 4, New York AL 1
1943 New York AL 4, St. Louis NL 1
1944 St. Louis NL 4, St. Louis AL 2
1945 Detroit AL 4, Chicago NL 3
1946 St. Louis NL 4, Boston AL 3
1947 New York AL 4, Brooklyn NL 3
1948 Cleveland AL 4, Boston NL 2
1949 New York AL 4, Brooklyn NL 1
1950 New York AL 4, Philadelphia NL 0
1951 New York AL 4, New York NL 2
1952 New York AL 4, Brooklyn NL 3
1953 New York AL 4, Brooklyn NL 2
1954 New York NL 4, Cleveland AL 0

1955 Brooklyn NL 4, New York AL 3
1956 New York AL 4, Brooklyn NL 3
1957 Milwaukee NL 4, New York AL 3
1958 New York AL 4, Milwaukee NL 3
1959 Los Angeles NL 4, Chicago AL 2
1960 Pittsburgh NL 4, New York AL 3
1961 New York AL 4, Cincinnati NL 1
1962 New York AL 4, San Francisco NL 3
1963 Los Angeles NL 4, New York AL 0
1964 St. Louis NL 4, New York AL 3
1965 Los Angeles NL 4, Minnesota AL 3
1966 Baltimore AL 4, Los Angeles NL 0
1967 St. Louis NL 4, Boston AL 3
1968 Detroit AL 4, St. Louis NL 3
1969 New York NL 4, Baltimore AL 1
1970 Baltimore AL 4, Cincinnati NL 1
1971 Pittsburgh NL 4, Baltimore AL 3
1972 Oakland AL 4, Cincinnati NL 3
1973 Oakland AL 4, New York NL 3
1974 Oakland AL 4, Los Angeles NL 1
1975 Cincinnati NL 4, Boston AL 3
1976 Cincinnati NL 4, New York AL 0
1977 New York AL 4, Los Angeles NL 2
1978 New York AL 4, Los Angeles NL 2
1979 Pittsburgh NL 4, Baltimore AL 3
1980 Philadelphia NL 4, Kansas City AL 2
1981 Los Angeles NL 4, New York AL 2

Baseball Strikes Out

Major league baseball players picked up their bats and gloves and exchanged base lines for picket lines on June 12, 1981. It was the second time that the big leaguers had gone on strike. In 1972, 86 games were cancelled during a dispute between the players and owners over pensions. This time the players walked out over the issue of free-agent compensation.

The owners were dissatisfied with the system that awarded them an amateur draft choice as compensation for losing a player who had opted for free agency and signed with another team. A player is eligible to become a free agent after 6 major league seasons. They insisted that the signing team should compensate the player's old team with a player, or players already playing in the major leagues. The Major League Baseball Association, the players' union, rejected this idea, contending that a team would be less likely to sign a free agent if it had to give up major league players in return.

During the strike, the players' union presented a united front behind their executive director, Marvin Miller. The owners were less united, with some publicly expressing dissatisfaction with Ray Grebey, the head of the owners' bargaining unit. The negotiations were highlighted by the tireless efforts of the federal mediator, Kenneth Moffett, and the intervention of Labor Secretary Raymond J. Donovan. The strike was settled on July 31. It had lasted 49 days and was the longest in the history of professional sports. In total, 712 games were cancelled, or about 34% of the 1981 season.

The strike had a far-reaching economic impact. In major league cities, hotels that housed visiting teams, mass transit that carried fans to and from the games, and stadium employees and concessionaires were hurt by the walkout. Television stations that broadcast baseball games had to scramble to replace the games with movies or syndicated programs. Some stations chose to show minor league games to fill their needs and those of their baseball-starved fans.

The 650 major league players, whose average salary is $173,000 per year, lost an estimated $28 million in salaries during the walkout. The owners, who had armed themselves with a $50 million strike insurance policy from Lloyd's of London and a $15 million strike fund, lost about $116 million.

The final settlement called for a complicated "player pool" concept in which free agents would be divided into three basic groups. Ranking free agents will be those players who are in the top 30% statistically over a 2-year period. Type A players will be those in the top 20%, and Type B players will be those in the next 10%. Another provision of the settlement was service credit for the players during the strike, a key point with the union since service time affects pensions, free agency, and salary arbitration.

The walkout also necessitated major league baseball's first split season. The divisional leaders at the time of the walkout were declared the winners of the "first half" of the season. They would meet the winners of the "second half" of the season in special divisional playoffs.

The fans showed little sympathy for either side. They saw the strike as a dispute between rich players and rich owners, and were angered that they were being denied their favorite summer recreation. They showed their displeasure during the "second season"; attendance was down alarmingly in many cities. The players and owners can only hope that this trend doesn't continue in 1982.

Major League Franchise Shifts and Additions

1953—Boston Braves (N. L.) became Milwaukee Braves. Home attendance, last season in Boston (1952), 281,278; first season in Milwaukee (1953), 1,826,397.

1954—St. Louis Browns (A. L.) became Baltimore Orioles. Home attendance, last season in St. Louis (1953), 297,238; first season in Baltimore (1954), 1,060,910.

1955—Philadelphia Athletics (A. L.) became Kansas City Athletics. Home attendance, last season in Phila. (1954), 627,100; first season in K.C. (1955), 1,393,054.

1958—New York Giants (N. L.) became San Francisco Giants. Home attendance, last season in New York (1957), 653,923; first season in San Francisco (1958), 1,272,625.

1958—Brooklyn Dodgers (N. L.) became Los Angeles Dodgers. Home attendance, last season in Brooklyn (1957), 1,028,258; first season in Los Angeles (1958), 1,845,556.

1961—Washington Senators (A. L.) became Minnesota Twins. Home attendance, last season in Washington (1960), 743,404; first season in Minneapolis-St. Paul (1961), 1,256,722.

1961—Los Angeles Angels (later renamed the California Angels) enfranchised by the American League.

1961—Washington Senators enfranchised by the American League (a new team, replacing the former Washington club, whose franchise was moved to Minneapolis-St. Paul).

1962—Houston Colt .45's (later renamed the Houston Astros) enfranchised by the National League.

1962—New York Mets enfranchised by the National League.

1966—Milwaukee Braves (N. L.) became Atlanta Braves. Home attendance, last season in Milwaukee (1965), 555,584; first season in Atlanta (1966), 1,539,801.

1968—Kansas City Athletics (A. L.) became Oakland Athletics. Home attendance, last season in Kansas City (1967), 652,246; first season in Oakland (1968), 838,501.

1969—Two major leagues each added two teams for totals of 12 and split into two divisions. American League additions: Kansas City Royals and Seattle Pilots; National League additions: Montreal Expos and San Diego Padres.

1970—Seattle franchise shifted to Milwaukee. Club was renamed Milwaukee Brewers.

1971—Washington franchise to Dallas-Fort Worth, with field at Arlington, Tex.

1977—Toronto and Seattle enfranchised by the American League.

All-Time Home Run Leaders

Player	HR	Player	HR	Player	HR	Player	HR
Hank Aaron	755	Billy Williams	426	Tony Perez	357	Graig Nettles	295
Babe Ruth	714	Carl Yastrzemski	426	Dick Allen	351	Dave Kingman	292
Willie Mays	660	Reggie Jackson	425	Lee May	351	Jim Wynn	291
Frank Robinson	586	Duke Snider	407	Ron Santo	342	Robert Johnson	288
Harmon Killebrew	573	Al Kaline	399	John (Boog) Powell	339	Hank Sauer	288
Mickey Mantle	536	Frank Howard	382	Joe Adcock	336	Del Ennis	288
Jimmy Foxx	534	Orlando Cepeda	379	Bobby Bonds	332	Frank Thomas	286
Ted Williams	521	Norm Cash	377	Hank Greenberg	331	Rusty Staub	284
Willie McCovey	521	Rocky Colavito	374	Willie Horton	325	Ken Boyer	282
Ed Mathews	512	Gil Hodges	370	Roy Sievers	318	Ted Kluszewski	279
Ernie Banks	512	Ralph Kiner	369	Mike Schmidt	314	Rudy York	277
Mel Ott	511	Johnny Bench	364	Al Simmons	307	Roger Maris	275
Lou Gehrig	493	Joe DiMaggio	361	Rogers Hornsby	302	George Scott	271
Stan Musial	475	John Mize	359	Chuck Klein	300	Brooks Robinson	268
Willie Stargell	472	Yogi Berra	358	Reggie Smith	296	Vic Wertz	266

Most Home Runs in One Season

Homers	Player, team	Year	Homers	Player, team	Year
61	Roger Maris, New York (AL)	1961	51	Ralph Kiner, Pittsburgh (NL)	1947
60	Babe Ruth, New York (AL)	1927	51	John Mize, New York (NL)	1947
59	Babe Ruth, New York (AL)	1921	51	Willie Mays, New York (NL)	1955
58	Jimmy Foxx, Philadelphia (AL)	1932	50	Jimmy Foxx, Boston (AL)	1938
58	Hank Greenberg, Detroit (AL)	1938	49	Babe Ruth, New York (AL)	1930
56	Hack Wilson, Chicago (NL)	1930	49	Lou Gehrig, New York (AL)	1934
54	Babe Ruth, New York (AL)	1920	49	Lou Gehrig, New York (AL)	1936
54	Babe Ruth, New York (AL)	1928	49	Ted Kluszewski, Cincinnati (NL)	1954
54	Ralph Kiner, Pittsburgh (NL)	1949	49	Willie Mays, San Francisco (NL)	1962
54	Mickey Mantle, New York (AL)	1961	49	Harmon Killebrew, Minnesota (AL)	1964
52	Mickey Mantle, New York (AL)	1956	49	Frank Robinson, Baltimore (AL)	1966
52	Willie Mays, San Francisco (NL)	1965	49	Harmon Killebrew, Minnesota (AL)	1969
52	George Foster, Cincinnati (NL)	1977			

Ten Most Dramatic Sports Events, Nov. 1980—Oct. 1981

Selected by The World Almanac sports staff

—The WBC champion Sugar Ray Leonard knocking out the WBA champion Thomas Hearns in the 14th round to become the undisputed world welterweight champion. Hearns was ahead in the judges' scoring at the time of the knockout.

—Len Barker of the Cleveland Indians pitching a perfect game against the Toronto Blue Jays. It was the 9th major league perfect game since 1900, and the first since 1968.

—John McEnroe defeating Bjorn Borg to win the Wimbledon singles title. Borg had won the title for 5 consecutive years.

—Nolan Ryan of the Houston Astros becoming the first major leaguer to pitch 5 no-hit games. He pitched his 5th no-hitter against the Los Angeles Dodgers.

—Jim Plunkett leading the Oakland Raiders to their 2d Super Bowl championship. He threw 3 touchdown passes and was chosen the game's most valuable player.

—Phil Mahre becoming the first American skier to win a World Cup title. He finished the season with 266 points, compared with 260 points for his chief rival, Ingemar Stenmark of Sweden.

—No. 1 ranked USC defeating No. 2 ranked Oklahoma 28-24, on a touchdown pass from John Mazur to Fred Cornwell with 2 seconds remaining in the game.

—Sebastian Coe and Steve Ovett of Great Britain breaking the world record for the mile 3 times within 2 weeks. Coe's time of 3 minutes, 47.33 seconds finally established the new standard.

—Richard Petty winning the Daytona 500 auto race for the 7th time. He averaged 169.651 mph during the race.

—The Boston Celtics defeating the Philadelphia 76ers in the semifinals to become the 4th team in NBA history to win a playoff series after trailing, 3 games to one. The Celtics went on to win their 14th NBA title.

Softball Tournament Champions in 1981

Source: Amateur Softball Assn.

Men

Super Division — Howard's Western-Steer, Denver, Col.
Major Slow Pitch — Elite Coating, Gordon, Ga.
Major Ind. Slow Pitch — Raffield's Fisheries, Port St. Joe, Fla.
"A" Slow Pitch — Ray Sears, Gambrills, Md
"A" Ind. Slow Pitch — Central Telephone, Hickory, N.C.
Church — First Methodist, Lewisville, Tex.
16-Inch — Budweiser, Harvey, Ill.

Women

Ind. Slow Pitch — Provident Vets, Chattanooga, Tenn.
Major Slow Pitch — Turnboys, Tifton, Ga.
Major Fast Pitch — Orlando Rebels, Orlando, Fla.
"A" Fast Pitch — Montclair 81s, Montclair, N.J.
"A" Slow Pitch — Orlando Stars, Orlando, Fla.
Church — South Main Baptist, Houston, Tex.

Polo Records

U.S. Open

1972	Milwaukee 9, Tulsa 5
1973	Oak Brook 9, Willow Bend 4.
1974	Milwaukee 7, Houston 6.
1975	Milwaukee 14, Tulsa-Dallas 6.
1976	Willow Bend 10, Tulsa 5.
1977	Retama 11, Wilson Ranch 7.
1978	Abercrombie & Kent 7, Tulsa 6.
1979	Retama 6, Huisache 5.
1980	Southern Hills 9, Willow Bend 6.

Silver Cup

1971	Green Hill Farm 8, Milwaukee 6.
1972	Red Doors Farm 10, Sun Ranch 6.
1973	Houston 6, Willow Bend 4.

1974	Houston 7, Willow Bend 6.
1975	Lone Oak-Bunntyco 8, Tulsa 5.
1976	Wilson Ranch 10, Tulsa 8.
1977	Boca Raton 6, Houston 5.
1978	Wilson Ranch 7, Ft. Lauderdale 6.
1979	Retama 7, Willow Bend 6.
1980	Retama 9, Houston 8.

Other tournaments in 1981

Delegate's Cup—Steppenwolf, 8, The Annex 6.
America Cup—Boca Raton 7, Tulsa 6.
North American Cup—Southern Hills 11, Maui 10.
Gold Cup—Boca Raton 12, Rolex A&K 11.
National Copper Cup—Old Pueblo 9, Pima County 3.

Marathons in 1981

Boston Marathon

Toshihiko Seko of Japan covered the traditional distance of 26 miles 385 yards in 2 hours 9 minutes 26 seconds to win the 85th annual Boston Marathon. Craig Virgin of Lebanon, Ill. finished second, and Bill Rodgers, who has won the event 4 times, finished third. Allison Roe of New Zealand was the women's champion, finishing 191st among the 6,400 starters.

New York Marathon

Alberto Salazar of Eugene, Ore. covered the 26 mile-385-yard course in a world record 2 hours 8 minutes 13 seconds to win the New York Marathon for the second consecutive year. Jukka Toivola of Finland finished second. Allison Roe of New Zealand lowered the women's world record for the distance to 2 hours 25 minutes 28 seconds.

North American Soccer League in 1981

Final Standings

Eastern Division

	W	L	GF	GA	Bonus points	Total points
New York	23	9	80	49	64	200
Montreal	15	17	63	57	55	141
Washington	15	17	59	58	51	135
Toronto	7	25	39	82	37	77

Northwest Division

	W	L	GF	GA	Bonus points	Total points
Vancouver	21	11	74	43	62	186
Calgary	17	15	59	54	51	151
Portland	17	15	52	49	45	141
Seattle	15	17	60	62	51	137
Edmonton	12	20	60	79	51	123

Southern Division

	W	L	GF	GA	Bonus points	Total points
Atlanta	17	15	62	60	53	151
Ft. Lauderdale	18	14	54	46	44	144
Jacksonville	18	14	51	46	41	141
Tampa Bay	15	17	63	64	53	139

Central Division

	W	L	GF	GA	Bonus points	Total points
Chicago	23	9	84	50	63	195
Minnesota	19	13	63	57	55	163
Tulsa	17	15	60	49	54	154
Dallas	5	27	27	71	26	54

Western Division

	W	L	GF	GA	Bonus points	Total points
San Diego	21	11	68	49	55	173
Los Angeles	19	13	53	55	48	160
California	11	21	60	77	51	117
San Jose	11	21	44	78	42	108

Total points: Win - 6 points, Loss - 0 points. Bonus points: one point is awarded for each goal scored up to a maximum of 3 per team per game. No bonus points are given for goals scored in overtime or the Shootout.

NASL Playoffs

Quarter finals

Tampa Bay 4, Vancouver 1.
Tampa Bay 1, Vancouver 0.
Ft. Lauderdale 3, Calgary 1.
Ft. Lauderdale 2, Calgary 0.
Minnesota 3, Tulsa 1.
Minnesota 1, Tulsa 0.
Chicago 3, Seattle 2.
Seattle 3, Chicago 0.
Chicago 3, Seattle 2.

Montreal 5, Los Angeles 3.
Los Angeles 3, Montreal 2.
Montreal 2, Los Angeles 1.
Portland 2, San Diego 1.
San Diego 5, Portland 1.
San Diego 2, Portland 0.
Jacksonville 2, Atlanta 1.
Jacksonville 2, Atlanta 1.

Semi-finals

New York 6, Tampa Bay 3.

Tampa Bay 3, New York 2.
New York 2, Tampa Bay 0.
Ft. Lauderdale 3, Minnesota 1.
Ft. Lauderdale 3, Minnesota 0.
Montreal 3, Chicago 2.
Chicago 4, Montreal 2.
Chicago 4, Montreal 2.
Jacksonville 2, San Diego 1.
San Diego 2, Jacksonville 1.
San Diego 3, Jacksonville 1.

Finals

New York 4, Ft. Lauderdale 3.
New York 4, Ft. Lauderdale 1.
San Diego 2, Chicago 1.
Chicago 4, San Diego 1.
Chicago 1, San Diego 0.

Soccer Bowl

Chicago 1, New York 0.

NASL Champions

Year	Champion
1967	Oakland Clippers (NPSL)
1967	Los Angeles Wolves (USA)
1968	Atlanta Chiefs
1969	Kansas City Spurs
1970	Rochester Lancers
1971	Dallas Tornado
1972	New York Cosmos
1973	Philadelphia Atoms
1974	Los Angeles Aztecs
1975	Tampa Bay Rowdies
1976	Toronto Metros
1977	New York Cosmos
1978	New York Cosmos
1979	Vancouver Whitecaps
1980	New York Cosmos
1981	Chicago Sting

Leading Scorers

Player, team	Goals	Assists	Points
Giorgio Chinaglia, New York	29	16	74
Karl-Heinz Granitza, Chicago	19	17	55
Mike Stojanovic, San Diego	23	6	52
Brian Kidd, Atlanta	22	8	52
Franz Gerber, Calgary	20	10	50
Teofilo Cubillas, Ft. Lauderdale	17	10	44
Arno Steffenhagen, Chicago	17	10	44
Gordon Hill, Montreal	16	12	44
Edi Kirschner, Edmonton	17	9	43
Duncan McKenzie, Tulsa	14	15	43

Leading Goalkeepers

Player, team	*Minutes	Goals against	Average
Arnie Mausser, Jacksonville	2,906	39	1.21
Jan van Beveren, Ft. Lauderdale	3,002	43	1.29
Barry Siddall, Vancouver	2,217	33	1.30
Zeljko Bilecki, Tulsa	2,631	39	1.33
Volkmar Gross, San Diego	2,971	45	1.36
Hubert Birkenmeier, New York	2,874	45	1.41
Keith MacRae, Portland	1,714	29	1.52
Jim Brown, Washington	2,872	49	1.54
Bob Rigby, Montreal	2,980	52	1.57
Jack Brand, Seattle	2,024	36	1.60

*At least 1,440 minutes needed to qualify

NASL Leading Scorers

Year	Player, team	G	A	Pts	Year	Player, team	G	A	Pts
1967	Yanko Daucik, Toronto	20	8	48	1977	Steven David, Los Angeles	26	6	58
1968	John Kowalik, Chicago	30	9	69	1978	Giorgio Chinaglia, New York	34	11	79
1969	Kaizer Motaung, Atlanta	16	4	36	1979	Oscar Fabbiani, Tampa Bay	25	8	58
1970	Kirk Apostolidis, Dallas	16	3	35	1980	Giorgio Chinaglia, New York	32	13	77
	Carlos Metidieri, Rochester	14	7	35	1981	Giorgio Chinaglia, New York	29	16	74
1971	Carlos Metidieri, Rochester	19	8	46	1974	Paul Child, San Jose	15	6	36
1972	Randy Horton, New York	9	4	22	1975	Steven David, Miami	23	6	52
1973	Kyle Rote, Jr., Dallas	10	10	30	1976	Giorgio Chinaglia, New York	19	11	49

NASL Leading Goalkeepers

Year	Player, team	GP	G	Avg	Year	Player, team	Minutes	G	Avg
1967	Mirko Stojanovic, Oakland	29	29	1.00	1974	Barry Watling, Seattle	1,800	16	0.80
1968	Ataulfo Sanchez, San Diego	22	19	0.93	1975	Shep Messing, Boston	1,639	17	0.93
1969	Manfred Kammerer, Atlanta	14	15	1.07	1976	Tony Chursky, Seattle	1,981	20	0.91
1970	Lincoln Phillips, Washington	22	21	0.95	1977	Ken Cooper, Dallas	2,100	21	0.90
			Minutes		1978	Phil Parkes, Vancouver	2,650	28	0.95
1971	Mirko Stojanovic, Dallas	1,359	11	0.79	1979	Phil Parkes, Vancouver	2,705	29	0.96
1972	Ken Cooper, Dallas	1,260	12	0.86	1980	Jack Brand, Seattle	2,975	30	0.91
1973	Bob Rigby, Philadelphia	1,157	8	0.62	1981	Arnie Mausser, Jacksonville	2,906	39	1.21

NASL All-Star Team in 1981

First team	Position	Second team
Jan van Beveron, Ft. Lauderdale	Goalkeeper	Hubert Birkenmeier, New York
Frantz Mathieu, Chicago	Defender	Barry Wallace, Tulsa
Wim Rijsbergen, New York	Defender	Kevin Bond, Seattle
Peter Nogly, Edmonton	Defender	Mihalj Keri, Los Angeles
John Gorman, Tampa Bay	Defender	Pierce O'Leary, Vancouver
Teofilo Cubillas, Ft. Lauderdale	Midfielder	Alan Hudson, Seattle
Vladislav Bogicevic, New York	Midfielder	George Best, San Jose
Arno Steffenhagen, Chicago	Midfielder	Peter Lorimer, Vancouver
Giorgio Chinaglia, New York	Forward	Karl-Heinz Granitza, Chicago
Brian Kidd, Atlanta	Forward	Robert Cabanas, New York
Gordon Hill, Montreal	Forward	Franz Gerber, Calgary

The World Cup

The World Cup, emblematic of International soccer supremacy, was won by Argentina on June 25, 1978, with a 3-1 overtime victory over the Netherlands. By winning the championship, Argentina became the fifth host country to emerge as champion since the competition began in 1930. Winners and sites of previous World Cup play follow:

Year	Winner	Site	Year	Winner	Site
1930	Uruguay	Uruguay	1962	Brazil	Chile
1934	Italy	Italy	1966	England	England
1938	Italy	France	1970	Brazil	Mexico City
1950	Uruguay	Brazil	1974	W. Germany	W. Germany
1954	W. Germany	Switzerland	1978	Argentina	Argentina
1958	Brazil	Sweden			

The America's Cup

Competition for the America's Cup grew out of the first contest to establish a world yachting championship, one of the carnival features of the London Exposition of 1851. The race, open to all classes of yachts from all over the world, covered a 60-mile course around the Isle of Wight; the prize was a cup worth about $500, donated by the Royal Yacht Squadron of England, known as the "America's Cup" because it was first won by the United States yacht America. Successive efforts of British and Australian yachtsmen have failed to win the famous trophy, which remains in the United States.

On Sept. 25, 1980, the yacht Freedom defeated the Australian challenger, Australia, for the 4th time in 5 races to keep the symbol of world sailing supremacy in the United States. Freedom was skippered by Dennis Connor of San Diego, Cal.

Winners of the America's Cup

1851	America	1920	Resolute defeated Shamrock IV, England, (3-2)
1870	Magic defeated Cambria, England, (1-0)	1930	Enterprise defeated Shamrock V, England, (4-0)
1871	Columbia (first three races) and Sappho (last two races) defeated Livonia, England, (4-1)	1934	Rainbow defeated Endeavour, England, (4-2)
1876	Madeline defeated Countess of Dufferin, Canada, (2-0)	1937	Ranger defeated Endeavour II, England, (4-0)
1881	Mischief defeated Atalanta, Canada, (2-0)	1958	Columbia defeated Sceptre, England, (4-0)
1885	Puritan defeated Genesta, England, (2-0)	1962	Weatherly defeated Gretel, Australia, (4-1)
1886	Mayflower defeated Galatea, England, (2-0)	1964	Constellation defeated Sovereign, England, (4-0)
1887	Volunteer defeated Thistle, Scotland, (2-0)	1967	Intrepid defeated Dame Pattie, Australia, (4-0)
1893	Vigilant defeated Valkyrie II, England, (3-0)	1970	Intrepid defeated Gretel II, Australia, (4-1)
1895	Defender defeated Valkyrie III, England, (3-0)	1974	Courageous defeated Southern Cross, Australia, (4-0)
1899	Columbia defeated Shamrock, England, (3-0)	1977	Courageous defeated Australia, Australia, (4-0)
1901	Columbia defeated Shamrock II, England, (3-0)	1980	Freedom defeated Australia, Australia, (4-1)
1903	Reliance defeated Shamrock III, England, (3-0)		

Grand Prix Standings in 1981

Driver, Country, Points
Nelson Piquet, Brazil, 50.
Carlos Reutemann, Argentina 49.
Alan Jones, Australia, 46.
Jacques Laffite, France, 44.
Alain Prost, France, 43.
John Watson, Ireland, 27.
Gilles Villeneuve, Canada, 25.

Driver, Country, Points
Elio DeAngelis, Italy, 14.
Hector Rebaque, Mexico, 11.
Rene Arnoux, France, 11.
Eddie Cheever, U.S., 10.
Ricardo Patrese, Italy, 10.
Didier Pironi, France 9.
Nigel Mansell, England, 8.

Driver Country, Points
Bruno Giacornelli, Italy, 7.
Mark Surer, Switzerland, 4.
Mario Andretti, U.S., 3.
Andrea DeCesarls, Italy, 1.
Slim Borgudd, Sweden, 1.
Eliseo Salazar, Chile 1.
Patrick Tambay, France, 1.

Auto Racing

Indianapolis 500 Winners

Year	Winner	Chassis	Engine	MPH	Purse	Runner up
1948	Mauri Rose	Deidt	Offenhauser	119.814	$171,075	Bill Holland
1949	Bill Holland	Deidt	Offenhauser	121.327	179,050	Johnnie Parsons
1950	Johnnie Parsons	Kurtis Kraft	Offenhauser	124.002(a)	201,135	Bill Holland
1951	Lee Wallard	Kurtis Kraft	Offenhauser	126.244	207,650	Mike Nazaruk
1952	Troy Ruttman	Kuzma	Offenhauser	128.922	230,100	Jim Rathmann
1953	Bill Vukovich	Kurtis Kraft 500A	Offenhauser	128.740	246,300	Art Cross
1954	Bill Vukovich	Kurtis Kraft 500A	Offenhauser	130.840	269,375	Jim Bryan
1955	Bob Sweikert	Kurtis Kraft 500C	Offenhauser	128.209	270,400	Tony Bettenhausen
1956	Pat Flaherty	Watson	Offenhauser	128.490	282,052	Sam Hanks
1957	Sam Hanks	Epperly	Offenhauser	135.601	300,252	Jim Rathmann
1958	Jimmy Bryan	Epperly	Offenhauser	133.791	305,217	George Amick
1959	Rodger Ward	Watson	Offenhauser	135.857	338,100	Jim Rathmann
1960	Jim Rathmann	Watson	Offenhauser	138.767	369,150	Rodger Ward
1961	A.J. Foyt	Watson	Offenhauser	139.130	400,000	Eddie Sachs
1962	Rodger Ward	Watson	Offenhauser	140.293	426,152	Len Sutton
1963	Parnelli Jones	Watson	Offenhauser	143.137	494,031	Jim Clark
1964	A.J. Foyt	Watson	Offenhauser	147.350	506,625	Rodger Ward
1965	Jim Clark	Lotus	Ford	151.388	628,399	Parnelli Jones
1966	Graham Hill	Lola	Ford	144.317	691,809	Jim Clark
1967	A.J. Foyt	Coyote	Ford	151.207	737,109	Al Unser
1968	Bobby Unser	Eagle	Offenhauser	152.882	809,627	Dan Gurney
1969	Mario Andretti	Hawk	Ford	156.867	805,127	Dan Gurney
1970	Al Unser	P.J. Colt	Ford	155.749	1,000,002	Mark Donohue
1971	Al Unser	P.J. Colt	Ford	157.735	1,001,604	Peter Revson
1972	Mark Donohue	McLaren	Offenhauser	163.465	1,011,846	Al Unser
1973	Gordon Johncock	Eagle	Offenhauser	159.014(b)	1,011,846	Billy Vukovich
1974	Johnny Rutherford	McLaren	Offenhauser	158.589	1,015,686	Bobby Unser
1975	Bobby Unser	Eagle	Offenhauser	149.213(c)	1,101,322	Johnny Rutherford
1976	Johnny Rutherford	McLaren	Offenhauser	148.725(d)	1,037,775	A.J. Foyt
1977	A.J. Foyt	Coyote	Ford	161.331	1,116,807	Tom Sneva
1978	Al Unser	Lola	Cosworth	161.363	1,145,225	Tom Sneva
1979	Rick Mears	Penske	Cosworth	158.899	1,271,954	A.J. Foyt
1980	Johnny Rutherford	Chaparral	Cosworth	142.862	1,502,425	Tom Sneva
1981	Bobby Unser	Penske	Cosworth	139.085	1,609,375	Mario Andretti

(a) 345 miles. (b) 332.5 miles. (c) 435 miles. (d) 255 miles. Race record—163.465 MPH, Mark Donohue, 1972.

1981 Indianapolis 500 Final Standings

1—Bobby Unser, Albuquerque, N.M., Penske-Cosworth.
2—Mario Andretti, Nazareth, Pa., Wildcat-Cosworth.
3—Vern Schuppan, Australia, McLaren-Cosworth.
4—Kevin Cogan, Redondo Beach, Cal., Phoenix-Cosworth.
5—Geoff Brabham, San Clemente, Cal., Penske-Cosworth.
6—Sheldon Kinser, Bloomington, Ind., Longhorn-Cosworth.
7—Tony Bettenhausen, Indianapolis, Ind., McLaren-Cosworth.
8—Steve Krisiloff, Dana Point, Cal., Penske-Cosworth.
9—Gordon Johncock, Phoenix, Ariz., Wildcat-Cosworth.
10—Dennis Firestone, Gardenia, Cal., Wildcat-Cosworth.

Notable One-Mile Speed Records

Date	Driver	Car	MPH	Date	Driver	Car	MPH
1/26/06	Marriott	Stanley (Steam)	127.659	2/22/33	Campbell	Napier-Campbell	272.109
3/16/10	Oldfield	Benz	131.724	9/ 3/35	Campbell	Bluebird Special	301.13
4/23/11	Burman	Benz	141.732	11/19/37	Eyston	Thunderbolt 1	311.42
2/12/19	DePalma	Packard	149.875	9/16/38	Eyston	Thunderbolt 1	357.5
4/27/20	Milton	Dusenberg	155.046	8/23/39	Cobb	Railton	368.9
4/28/26	Parry-Thomas	Thomas Spl.	170.624	9/16/47	Cobb	Railton-Mobil	394.2
3/29/27	Seagrave	Sunbeam	203.790	8/ 5/63	Breedlove	Spirit of America	407.45
4/22/28	Keech	White Triplex	207.552	10/27/64	Arfons	Green Monster	536.71
3/11/29	Seagrave	Irving-Napier	231.446	11/15/65	Breedlove	Spirit of America	600.601
2/ 5/31	Campbell	Napier-Campbell	246.086	10/23/70	Gabelich	Blue Flame	622.407
2/24/32	Campbell	Napier-Campbell	253.96	10/9/79	Barrett	Budweiser Rocket	638.637*

*not recognized as official by sanctioning bodies.

World Grand Prix Champions

Year	Driver	Year	Driver	Year	Driver
1950	Nino Farina, Italy	1961	Phil Hill, United States	1971	Jackie Stewart, Scotland
1951	Juan Fangio, Argentina	1962	Graham Hill, England	1972	Emerson Fittipaldi, Brazil
1952	Alberto Ascari, Italy	1963	Jim Clark, Scotland	1973	Jackie Stewart, Scotland
1953	Alberto Ascari, Italy	1964	John Surtees, England	1974	Emerson Fittipaldi, Brazil
1954	Juan Fangio, Argentina	1965	Jim Clark, Scotland	1975	Nicki Lauda, Austria
1955	Juan Fangio, Argentina	1966	Jack Brabham, Australia	1976	James Hunt, England
1956	Juan Fangio, Argentina	1967	Denis Hulme, New Zealand	1977	Nikki Lauda, Austria
1957	Juan Fangio, Argentina	1968	Graham Hill, England	1978	Mario Andretti, U.S.
1958	Mike Hawthorne, England	1969	Jackie Stewart, Scotland	1979	Jody Scheckter, So. Africa
1959	Jack Brabham, Australia	1970	Jochen Rindt, Austria	1980	Alan Jones, Australia
1960	Jack Brabham, Australia				

Grand Prix for Formula 1 Cars in 1981

Grand Prix	Winner, car	Grand Prix	Winner, car
Argentine	Nelson Piquet, Brabham	German	Nelson Piquet, Brabham
Austrian	Jacques Laffite, Ligier	Italian	Alain Prost, Renault
Belgian	Carlos Reutemann, Williams	Las Vegas	Alan Jones, Williams
British	John Watson, McLaren	Monaco	Gilles Villeneuve, Ferrari
Brazilian	Carlos Reutemann, Williams	San Marino	Nelson Piquet, Brabham
Canadian	Jacques Laffite, Ligier	South African	Carlos Reutemann, Williams
Dutch	Alain Prost, Renault	Spanish	Gilles Villeneuve, Ferrari
French	Alain Prost, Renault		

United States Auto Club National Champions

Year	Driver	Year	Driver	Year	Driver	Year	Driver
1956	Jimmy Bryan	1962	Rodger Ward	1968	Bobby Unser	1974	Bobby Unser
1957	Jimmy Bryan	1963	A. J. Foyt	1969	Mario Andretti	1975	A. J. Foyt
1958	Tony Bettenhausen	1964	A. J. Foyt	1970	Al Unser	1976	Gordon Johncock
1959	Rodger Ward	1965	Mario Andretti	1971	Joe Leonard	1977	Tom Sneva
1960	A. J. Foyt	1966	Mario Andretti	1972	Joe Leonard	1978	Tom Sneva
1961	A. J. Foyt	1967	A. J. Foyt	1973	Roger McCluskey	1979	A. J. Foyt
						1980	Johnny Rutherford

NASCAR Racing in 1981

Winston Cup Grand National Races

Date	Race, site	Winner	Car	Winnings
Jan. 11	Winston Western 500, Riverside, Cal.	Bobby Allison	Chevrolet	$24,600
Feb. 15	Daytona 500, Daytona Beach, Fla.	Richard Petty	Buick	90,575
Feb. 22	Richmond 400, Richmond, Va.	Darrell Waltrip	Buick	18,800
Mar. 1	Carolina 500, Rockingham, N.C.	Darrell Waltrip	Buick	21,655
Mar. 15	Coca-Cola 500, Atlanta, Ga.	Cale Yarborough	Buick	28,950
Mar. 29	Valleydale 500, Bristol, Tenn.	Darrell Waltrip	Buick	22,450
Apr. 5	Northwestern Bank 400, No. Wilkesboro, N.C.	Richard Petty	Buick	18,850
Apr. 12	CRC Chemicals Rebel 500, Darlington, S.C.	Darrell Waltrip	Buick	23,225
Apr. 26	Virginia 500, Martinsville, Va.	Morgan Shepherd	Pontiac	24,525
May 3	Winston 500, Talladega, Ala.	Bobby Allison	Buick	41,500
May 9	Melting Tool 420, Nashville, Tenn.	Benny Parsons	Ford	15,950
May 24	World 600, Charlotte, N.C.	Bobby Allison	Buick	60,200
June 7	Budweiser Nascar 400, College Station, Tex.	Benny Parsons	Ford	22,750
June 14	Warner W. Hodgdon 400, Riverside, Cal.	Darrell Waltrip	Buick	23,650
June 21	Gabriel 400, Brooklyn, Mich.	Bobby Allison	Buick	24,075
July 11	Busch Nashville 420, Nashville, Tenn.	Darrell Waltrip	Buick	15,700
July 26	Mountain Dew 500, Pocono, Pa.	Darrell Waltrip	Buick	23,640
Aug. 2	Talladega 500, Talladega, Ala.	Ron Bouchard	Buick	38,905
Aug. 16	Champion Spark Plug 400, Brooklyn, Mich.	Richard Petty	Buick	23,750
Aug. 22	Busch 500, Bristol, Tenn.	Darrell Waltrip	Buick	18,800
Sept. 7	Southern 500, Darlington, S.C.	Neil Bonnett	Ford	33,375
Sept. 13	Wrangler Sanforest 400, Richmond, Va.	Benny Parsons	Ford	18,525
Sept. 20	CRC Chemicals 500, Dover, Del.	Neil Bonnett	Ford	19,000

Daytona 500 Winners

Year	Driver, car	Avg. MPH	Year	Driver, car	Avg. MPH
1962	Fireball Roberts, Pontiac	152.529	1972	A. J. Foyt, Mercury	161.550
1963	Tiny Lund, Ford	151.566	1973	Richard Petty, Dodge	157.205
1964	Richard Petty, Plymouth	154.334	1974	Richard Petty, Dodge (c)	140.894
1965	Fred Lorenzen, Ford (a)	141.539	1975	Benny Parsons, Chevrolet	153.649
1966	Richard Petty, Plymouth (b)	160.627	1976	David Pearson, Mercury	152.181
1967	Mario Andretti, Ford	146.926	1977	Cale Yarborough, Chevrolet	153.218
1968	Cale Yarborough, Mercury	143.251	1978	Bobby Allison, Ford	159.730
1969	Lee Roy Yarborough, Ford	160.875	1979	Richard Petty, Oldsmobile	143.977
1970	Pete Hamilton, Plymouth	149.601	1980	Buddy Baker, Oldsmobile	177.602
1971	Richard Petty, Plymouth	144.456	1981	Richard Petty, Buick	169.651

(a) 322.5 miles because of rain. (b) 495 miles because of rain. (c) 450 miles.

Leading Daytona 500 Finishers in 1981

Driver, car	Laps	Winnings	Driver, car	Laps	Winnings
Richard Petty, Buick	200	$90,575	Bill Elliott, Ford	199	$30,615
Bobby Allison, Pontiac	200	84,050	Jody Ridley, Ford	198	29,665
Ricky Rudd, Oldsmobile	200	53,115	Cale Yarborough, Oldsmobile	197	20,325
Buddy Baker, Oldsmobile	200	35,740	Joe Millikan, Buick	197	21,500
Dale Earnhardt, Pontiac	200	37,365	Johnny Rutherford, Pontiac	195	17,285

Grand National Champions (NASCAR)

Year	Driver	Year	Driver	Year	Driver	Year	Driver
1953	Herb Thomas	1960	Rex White	1967	Richard Petty	1974	Richard Petty
1954	Lee Petty	1961	Ned Jarrett	1968	David Pearson	1975	Richard Petty
1955	Tim Flock	1962	Joe Weatherly	1969	David Pearson	1976	Cale Yarborough
1956	Buck Baker	1963	Joe Weatherly	1970	Bobby Isaac	1977	Cale Yarborough
1957	Buck Baker	1964	Richard Petty	1971	Richard Petty	1978	Cale Yarborough
1958	Lee Petty	1965	Ned Jarrett	1972	Richard Petty	1979	Richard Petty
1959	Lee Petty	1966	David Pearson	1973	Benny Parson	1980	Dale Earnhardt

CHRONOLOGY OF THE YEAR'S EVENTS

Reported Month by Month in 3 Categories: National, International, and General — Nov. 1, 1980, to Nov. 1, 1981

NOVEMBER

National

Report Accuses Civiletti and Jimmy and Billy Carter — A Justice Department report, released on Nov. 1 by the special Senate subcommittee investigating the president's brother, Billy Carter, and his relationship with Libya, claimed that Pres. Jimmy Carter had not cooperated fully with the investigation. The report also accused Attorney General Benjamin R. Civiletti of dissembling and Billy Carter of lying under oath. The White House issued a denial.

Reagan Beats Carter In Landslide — Ronald Reagan, the Republican candidate for president, became the first politician to unseat an incumbent president since 1932, winning a majority of the vote in 43 states on Nov. 4. Also going down to defeat were such congressional powers as Senators Birch Bayh (D, Ind.), George McGovern (D, S.D.), Jacob Javits (L, N.Y.), and Congressman John Brademas (D, Ind.), the majority whip. Reagan's victory was so overwhelming that President Carter began his concession speech at 9:50 P.M. EST, before the polls had closed in several of the western states.

F.B.I. Officials Found Guilty — Two former officials of the Federal Bureau of Investigation were found guilty, Nov. 6, of conspiring to violate the constitutional rights of U.S. citizens. W. Mark Felt and Edward S. Miller were convicted of authorizing agents to break into homes secretly and without search warrants while hunting for bomb suspects in the years 1972 and 1973. Five homes in New York and New Jersey, belonging to relatives and acquaintances of members of the Weather Underground, a militant antiwar organization, had been entered illegally. On Dec. 15, the two men were sentenced to pay a fine. Felt's fine was $5,000 and Miller's $3,500.

Reagan Starts White House Transition — Ronald Reagan announced, Nov. 6, that William J. Casey, the former head of the Security and Exchange Commission, would serve as chairman of his Transition Executive Committee, and Edwin Meese as its director. He also vowed to move as swiftly as possible to carry out his economic program, calling for tax cuts, a federal hiring freeze, and reduction in government spending. Reagan indicated that he would not interfere with the lame duck government's activities in such matters as freeing the hostages in Iran or communicating with the Soviets. The president-elect announced, Nov. 12, that he planned to cut the 1981 budget by $13 billion, and that Caspar Weinberger, his top budget advisor, was working on a plan for a $40-billion cut. On Nov. 17, Reagan made his first trip to Washington since his election, visiting with the Republican and Democratic leaderships, cultural and religious leaders, President Carter, and Mayor Marion Barry of Washington, D.C.

Price And Incomes Rise — The Labor Department announced, Nov. 7 that producer prices rose by 0.8% in October. This was equal to a 10.6% compounded annual rate, and followed a September decline of 0.2%. The unemployment rate for October was slightly up—7.6% versus 7.5% in September. It was also predicted that food prices would continue to rise. Sugar, for example, rose 20% in October. According to a Commerce Department report issued on Nov. 8, total personal income for the April-June quarter rose an average of 1.1% from the previous quarter of January-March. However, inflation rose 2.6%, more than outpacing the rise in wages.

More Public Lands In Alaska — On Nov. 12, the House approved and sent to the White House a Senate measure that would make more than 104 million acres of land in Alaska into national parks, wildlife refuges, and national conservation areas. The acreage, which is scattered throughout the state, includes more land than there is in the state of California. As a part of the bill, the William O. Douglas Arctic Wildlife Range on Alaska's North Slope was designated as wilderness in which no development would be permitted. This area is the breeding ground of the last large caribou herds.

Carter Plans For the Future — At a Nov. 12 press conference, President Carter outlined his plans for the future. After the inauguration of Ronald Reagan, he said, he would return to Plains, Ga., to write his memoirs and "live the life of a former president." He intended also "to become a very good fly fisherman," and not to overburden Reagan with advice on how to be president. Carter also denied having any ambition to run for public office again.

Klansmen Freed — Six present or former members of the Ku Klux Klan and American Nazi Party were acquitted, Nov. 17, on 5 counts of first-degree murder and one count of felonious rioting. A jury in Greensboro, N.C. deliberated for 7 days before arriving at their verdict. The charges stemmed from the slaying of 5 members of the Communist Workers Party at their anti-clan rally in the fall of 1979. It was alleged that the defendants had armed themselves and had driven into the crowd at the rally while firing their guns. In Washington, the Justice Department was studying the verdict to investigate the possibility of bringing criminal civil rights charges against the Klansmen.

Havana Airlift Begins — A planeload of 120 Cuban refugees arrived in Miami, Nov. 19. They were among a group of 600 Cubans stranded at the Port of Mariel by Fidel Castro in September when the Cuban leader had ordered a halt to the boatlift that had brought more than 125,000 Cubans to the United States. The refugees were immediately taken to a race track for immigration processing.

Mortgage Rate Rises — The government announced, Nov. 25, that a surge in mortgage rates had pushed consumer prices up 1% in October, and that those prices were at a point 12.6% higher than that of Oct. 1979. In terms of take-home pay, the average worker was able to buy 6% fewer goods than had been possible a year earlier. Housing costs had risen 0.7% in September, but jumped to 1.3% in October. This jump was attributed to a 3.1% rise in October in home financing, taxes, and insurance charges. House prices, themselves, rose 1.5% in that month. Elsewhere, price increases for the month went up as follows: food, 0.8%; gasoline, 0.3%; apparel and upkeep, 0.5%; transportation, 0.8%; and medical care, 0.8%.

Cabinet Selections Hit Snag — William E. Simon, the investment banker and former secretary of the treasury under Pres. Gerald R. Ford, announced, Nov. 28, that he did not want to be considered for a cabinet post in the new administration, citing a reluctance to return to Washington. He had been President-elect Reagan's first choice for the treasury job. At the same time, George P. Shultz, a vice president of a construction company and a former secretary of both the treasury and labor Departments under Pres. Richard M. Nixon, and a leading candidate for secretary of state, sent a message that he did not want to join the Reagan administration.

International

Labor Crisis In Poland — On Nov. 1, the Polish independent trade union organization, Solidarity, led by Lech Walesa, threatened a series of strikes if the Polish Supreme Court did not reverse a lower court ruling ordering the insertion of a clause asserting the supreme role of the Communist Party in dealing with labor in the solidarity charter. Prime Minister Jozef Pinkowski promised a court ruling in 10 days, and Solidarity was given permission to publish its own weekly newspaper and was granted access to state-owned television. The planned strike would begin on Nov. 10 in Warsaw and Gdansk, move to Szczecin and Cracow on Nov. 12, and two days after that to Katowice and other cities. Its purpose would be to dramatize the loyalty of Poland's 13 million workers to Solidarity. On Nov. 7, some workers jumped the gun, as hospital workers struck in Gdansk, Katowice, Warsaw, Stolp, and other cities, and postal workers walked off the job in Gdansk, Poznan, and elsewhere. The Polish Supreme Court, **Nov. 10**, decided to reverse the ruling, saying the lower court had overstepped its authority. The strikes were called off, but Polish Pres. Henryk Jablonski warned that food rationing might be the result of the victory, since laborers had won $3.3 billion in raises, adding to the $20 billion in foreign debts owed by the country. U.S. Secretary of State Edmund Muskie, **Nov. 13**, appealed to President Carter to increase the amount of grain that could be sold on credit to Poland in 1980-81. The increase was to be from $670 million to $900 million. Meanwhile, despite the strike call-off, wildcat strikes had been breaking out all over the country, creating a feeling that Solidarity was not completely able to control the labor force. On **Nov. 15**, Walesa pleaded for calm and reason. Workers in the region where Czestochowa is located demanded the resignation of the provisional governor, Miroslaw Wierzbicki, who sent his resignation to Warsaw, **Nov. 17**. By **Nov. 22**, at least 18 first secretaries in Poland's 49 provinces had been purged and more moderate leaders had replaced them. On **Nov. 24**, Polish railway workers staged a 2-hour strike for wage increases, and the following day miners struck for 2 hours and Solidarity again threatened a general strike. On **Nov. 28**, after long discussions between the government and Solidarity, it was announced that the threatened general strike would be postponed until after a series of talks concerning union demands. These talks were scheduled to begin early in December.

West Germany Cuts Back On Arms Outlay — West Germany announced, **Nov. 1**, that it would not raise its military expenditures as it had promised the North Atlantic Treaty Organization that it would. West Germany has Western Europe's strongest army, and had pledged to raise its expeditures by 3% beyond the projected national inflation rate every year until 1986. This was said to be the only way that NATO could keep up with the military expansion of the Soviet Union.

Farm Confiscation In Zimbabwe — Prime Minister Robert Mugabe of Zimbabwe announced, **Nov. 2**, that his government might have to seize white-owned farms in his country without paying compensation to the owners. Pointing out that there were many blacks who were homeless as a result of the 7-year guerrilla war that had brought him to power, he added that the government did not have the money to resettle them. He also accused Britain of reneging on its promises to send money to help the Zimbabwe government buy land for this resettlement.

Death Sentence Upheld — A South Korean military appeals court, **Nov. 3**, confirmed the death sentence of Kim Dae Jung, who had been convicted of plotting to overthrow the government by instigating student demonstrations. It was alleged that Kim was the leader of Hanmintong, an organization that supports North Korea. He had run for president of South Korea in 1971. On **Nov. 12**, the government of President Chun Doo Hwan announced a political purge that banned more than 800 people from running for public office until June, 1988. Kim's name was high on the list.

Hostage Negotiations Snarled — Iran announced new conditions for the release of the 52 American hostages, and on **Nov. 4** urged the United States to reply through the mass media to their offer. The four main Iranian demands were promises by the U.S. not to interfere in Iranian affairs, to unfreeze Iranian assets in the U.S., to drop financial claims made against Iran, and to move to return the wealth of the late Shah Mohammed Riza Pahlevi. The State Department noted that Iran's conditions required careful analysis and study and that therefore an answer would take time. There was also a question that the United States might not have the legal power to conform to the last two demands. Algeria was selected as the intermediary between the United States and Iran on this matter, and, **Nov. 12**, that country delivered to Iran a secret response from the United States. On **Nov. 20**, State Department confirmed that the U.S. had accepted the 4 conditions in principle, but the United States was still waiting for a formal Iranian request for further clarification of several details. On **Nov. 27**, the Islamic radicals who were keeping the hostages prisoner said that they had handed the Americans over to the government of Iran.

Iran-Iraq War Continues — Iran and Iraq announced, **Nov. 8**, that their armies had clashed in several cities in the Iranian province of Khuzistan, and Iran announced that it had repelled an Iraqi advance outside Abadan. Iraq claimed that 30 Iranian troops had been killed and 2 tanks destroyed at Abadan and 2 gunboats had been sunk in the Shatt-al-Arab waterway. Iran claimed that it had halted the flow of Iraqi oil through the Persian Gulf by destroying Iraq's major oil-export platforms. On **Nov. 9**, President Saddam Hussein of Iraq declared that his country was engaged in a holy war to defend the ideals of the Prophet Mohammed and announced that the prices of gasoline and kerosene would be raised 300% and the distribution of both sugar and electricity would be curtailed. Also on **Nov. 9**, Iran announced a tripling of gasoline prices and restrictions on sugar and electricity. The Iraqi attacks on Abadan were stepped up on **Nov. 12**, and, on **Nov. 16**, the Iraqis claimed to have killed more than 500 Iranian troops in a battle for the town of Susangird in southwest Iran. Kuwait accused Iran of a rocket attack on an area of the country bordering Iraq, and Saudi Arabia offered to go to Kuwait's aid in case of danger.

Earthquakes Hit Southern Italy: Close to 3,000 Killed

A series of earthquakes, centered in Southern Italy, rumbled through the area near Naples, **Nov. 23 and 24**, killing, according to initial reports, at least 350 people and injuring hundreds. Reports of damage came from 29 cities and towns where buildings of up to 5 stories had been reduced to rubble. The epicenter of the quake was at Eboli, 30 miles southeast of Naples.

The main shock was felt at 7:34 P.M. on **Nov. 23**, and was followed by 7 other quakes during the next 6 hours. In Balvano, a Roman Catholic Church caved in during evening services, killing nearly 100 people. In Potenza, 90 miles east of Naples, almost all of the 50,000 residents fled to the hills.

Rescue teams were hampered by road and rail damage and many electricity lines were down. Fires broke out in many towns because stoves had been left on when people left their homes. The quakes, measuring 6.8 on the Richter Scale, were more severe than the 1976 earthquakes in northeastern Italy.

By **Nov. 25**, the death toll had risen to more than 1,000. Casualty figures were still not available from some of the mountain villages. Also on that day, the estimate of the number of quakes involved had risen from 7 to 32. The rescue operations had been joined by thousands of soldiers, firemen, carabinieri, forest guards, local policemen, and Red Cross volunteers. Army trucks delivered tents and campers; helicopters brought plasma and medical supplies; field hospitals were set up.

Meanwhile, in the mountains where most of the destroyed villages and towns were located, temperatures fell below freezing. Pope John Paul II visited 3 towns in the quake area to offer his support and prayers. Aftershocks were still being felt, and the observatory at Messina in Siciliy reported that more than 100 tremors had occurred.

By **Nov. 27**, the slowness and inefficiency of the rescue operations had been so greatly criticized that Interior Minister Virginio Rognoni offered to resign from the cabinet. The resignation was rejected by Prime Minister Arnaldo Forlani, who feared that it would bring down the entire government.

Torrential rains began falling in the quake area, causing landslides that blocked the newly-opened rescue roads. Estimated death tolls ranged from the government's 1,900 to an army estimate of 10,000 in the Province of Avellino alone.

On **Nov. 28**, the Italian Communist Party called for the ouster of Christian Democrats from the government because of the poor handling of rescue operations, which were still being hampered by snow, rain, and high winds. By this time, the number of known dead had reached 2,904 and the number of homeless, in one estimate, was 300,000. One hundred thirty-three towns had been listed as seriously damaged or almost destroyed.

The search for survivors was abandoned on **Nov. 30**, and the work of the rescue teams was directed toward providing vaccination, water, food, clothing and temporary shelter for the survivors. On **Dec. 16**, the official death toll was set at 2,916 people.

Iran, **Nov. 22,** denied the accusation. The battle for Susangird was still being waged on **Nov. 17,** with both sides claiming heavy casualties, and, on **Nov. 22,** Iran accused Iraq of attacking civilians in the town of Gilan with surface-to-surface missiles.

Human Rights Conference Begins — The Madrid Conference to review compliance with the Helsinki accords on European security and human rights, opened, **Nov. 11,** amidst fears that the United States and its allies would have a confrontation with the Soviet Union and some eastern European countries in setting up an agenda. The Soviets had lobbied to limit the time given over to a discussion of such matters as the Soviet invasion of Afghanistan and alleged human rights violations in eastern Europe. On **Nov. 13,** Griffin B. Bell, the head of the U.S. delegation, criticized the Soviets for their Afghanistan intervention and curtailment of human rights. Support for this criticism came from West Germany, Britain, Norway, Switzerland, Sweden, and Luxemburg. Bell also accused the Soviet Union of jamming radio broadcasts, preventing Jewish emigration from the Soviet Union, and the imprisonment of Soviet dissidents. Willy Brandt of West Germany urged the conference to put aside differences and carry détente into the 1980's. On **Nov. 17,** Max M. Kampelman, co-chairman of the U.S. delegation, warned that the Atlantic alliance would not concede military superiority to the Soviets, but that the United States was still willing to negotiate arms control agreements with the Soviet Union.

Guinea-Bissau Government Falls — The government of Pres. Luis de Almedia Cabral of Guinea-Bissau was toppled **Nov. 14,** by nationalist military officers, and 2 members of the government were killed in the coup. The new leaders of the West African country accused the former regime of executing more than 500 political prisoners in 6 years.

Pope Visits West Germany — Pope John Paul II began a 5-day visit to West Germany on **Nov. 15,** and, in Mainz, called upon Roman Catholics to widen their contacts with other Christian churches. He was the first Pope to visit the country in 198 years. On **Nov. 16** and **17,** the Pope conferred with Protestant and Jewish leaders. Although there had been demonstrations in Fulda against the Church's stand on abortion, on the last day of his trip, **Nov. 19,** the Pope celebrated a mass for youth in Munich. At the mass, members of the Federation of German Catholic Youths criticized his stand on priestly celibacy and the participation of women in church services.

Trial In Peking — China, **Nov. 15,** outlined its charges against Mao Zedong's widow, Jiang Qing, and nine other radicals by accusing them of persecuting to death more than 34,000 people during the Cultural Revolution of the 1960's. Jiang was also accused of ordering 40 people dressed as Red Guards to burglarize the houses of 5 famous writers to find material that incriminated her, and then of burning the material. The trial had been postponed for more than a month because Jiang and Zhang Chunqiao, another member of the so-called "Gang of Four," had refused to confess their crimes of arbitrary arrests, imprisonment, and physical abuse. On **Nov. 18,** Zhang and two others, Yao Wenyuan and Wang Hongwen, were accused of plotting an armed rebellion in Shanghai in 1976. The trial began, **Nov. 20,** with the reading of the indictment, which also contained an accusation that they had attempted to kill Mao. On **Nov. 23,** Wu Faxian, a former deputy chief of staff of the armed forces, testified that he had damaged China's Air Force by giving Lin Liguo, a leader of the plot to assasinate Mao, the command of the air force. On **Nov. 24,** Wang and Yao confessed that they had tried to persuade Mao not to name Deng Xiaoping as senior Deputy Prime Minister in 1974, and, on **Nov. 25,** three more of the group testified that they had participated in the plot to kill Mao. Zhang, however, refused to confess, **Nov. 27,** and Jiang denied that she had been in on the plot.

Begin Holds On — By the narrow margin of 3 votes, Prime Minister Begin of Israel won a vote of confidence, **Nov. 19.** Public opinion polls had shown the Labor Party to be leading his coalition, the Likud, because of rapidly rising inflation and a decline in real wages. Two of Begin's former cabinet ministers, Moshe Dayan, a former Foreign Minister, and Ezer Weizman, a former defense minister joined the opposition in the vote. As a result of that vote, Weizman was

ousted from Begin's Herut Party, thus leaving the government without a majority in the Knesset.

Upper Volta's President Ousted — Another African nation lost its president when Sangoule Lamizana, president of Upper Volta, was overthrown, **Nov. 25,** by a group called the Military Committee of Recovery for National Progress, led by Col. Saye Zerbo. Zerbo said that the coup had been necessary because of the political and economic situation of the country, and guaranteed all individual and group freedoms except that of political activity.

Percy Goes to Moscow — Senator Charles H. Percy (R—Ill.), who was expected to be named chairman of the Senate Foreign Relations Committee, met with Soviet Foreign Minister Andrei A. Gromyko in Moscow, **Nov. 28.** He reported that he had told Gromyko that the unratified arms agreement between the United States and the Soviet Union was "dead as a doornail." However, he suggested that a new start be made on the arms accord. In a visit with Leonid I. Brezhnev, he warned the Soviet leader that the use of troops in Poland would be a grave error. On **Nov. 30,** Edwin Meese 3rd, a senior advisor to President-elect Reagan, stated that Washington and Moscow would begin talks on a new arms limitation treaty within a few weeks after Reagan's inauguration on Jan. 20.

General

New Uses For Radar And Sonar — Two United States Navy scientists, Herbert M. Uberall and Guillermo C. Gaunaurd, announced, **Nov. 2,** a new technique for using radar or sonar to identify a distant object. It provides a mathematical way to learn about the shape and composition of an object by reflected, radio, sound, or other types of waves. In its military use, the technique can tell the difference between an enemy soldier and a decoy. In nonmilitary applications, it might be used to tell whether an underground pool contains oil or water, or whether a mass in the brain was fluid or tumor.

News From Saturn — Voyager 1 was approaching Saturn and sending back pictures to be interpreted. On **Nov. 7,** Bradford A. Smith, the leader of the project's photo interpretation team, announced that photographs had identified 95 separate rings surrounding the planet, as compared to the old number of 3, which are the only ones that can be distinuished from earth by small telescopes. The rings were thought to be composed of small icy objects. On **Nov. 8,** a 15th moon of Saturn was discovered and the count of rings was raised to more than 100. By **Nov. 9,** Voyager 1 was within 2.5 million miles of Saturn and gathering speed. New photographs showed contrasting bands of pale yellow, golden brown, and reddish brown running parallel to the planet's equator, as well as jet streams in its hydrogen-helium atmosphere. On **Nov. 11,** the spacecraft crossed the orbit of Saturn's outermost moon and was in the region of the planet's magnetic field. By **Nov. 12,** it was within 77,000 miles of the planet and photos suggested that the number of rings around the planet may run from 500 to 1,000, and that the inner satellites of Saturn are icy gray and white, many of them having craters similar to our own moon.

Disasters — A methane gas explosion occured, **Nov. 7,** in a coal mine near Madison, W. Va., killing 5 miners ... Brush fires that began on **Nov. 16** swept across some 30,000 acres in southern California, forcing thousands to flee and destroying nearly 100 homes. By **Nov. 25,** there were nine major fires burning in five counties involving some 45,000 acres, and, by **Nov. 27,** 70,000 acres were ablaze, 422 homes had been destroyed, and four people were dead. ... A Korean Airlines 747 flying from Los Angeles to Korea crashed in flames at the Seoul airport, **Nov. 19,** killing 8 of the 226 people aboard ... A fire in the MGM Grand Hotel in Las Vegas on **Nov. 21** killed 84 people and injured more than 500 ... Two passenger trains and the uncoupled cars of a freight train were involved in a crash near Lamezia Terme, Italy, **Nov. 21,** that killed 28 passengers.

DECEMBER

National

Prices and Interest Rates Up; Jobless Rate Down — The Commerce Department reported, **Dec. 1,** that the Economic Index went up .9% in October and that this was the smallest gain in 4 months. Building permits for housing, industrial investment, and growth of the money supply after allowance for inflation were down, while liquid assets and prices of certain raw materials were up. But, on **Dec. 4,** the Federal Reserve Board increased from 12% to 13% the basic interest rate that it charges for loans to financial institutions, which caused the nation's larger banks to raise their prime lending rate from 18½% to 19%. By **Dec. 19,** these rates had risen to 21½%. The Labor Department announced, **Dec. 5,** that the unemployment rate had fallen from 7.6% to 7.5% during the month of November, indicating a small economic recovery, but the Bureau of Labor Statistics announced, **Dec. 23,** that consumer prices had risen 1% during that same month. According to the Labor Department, during November it took $25.62 to buy goods and services that could have been purchased for $10 in 1967.

Republican Transition Continues — The Republican senators elected Howard H. Baker Jr. (R. Tenn.) as their majority leader, **Dec. 2.** Baker, who ran unopposed, replaced Sen. Robert C. Byrd (D. W.Va.). President-elect Ronald Reagan announced his first 8 cabinet-level appointments on **Dec. 11,** and the nominees were presented at a joint news conference which was not attended by Reagan. Those selections were: Secretary of the Treasury—Donald T. Regan, chairman of Merrill Lynch & Co.; Secretary of Defense— Caspar W. Weinberger, general counsel and vice president of the Bechtel Power Corp.; Attorney General—William French Smith, senior partner of the law firm Gibson, Dunn & Crutcher and Reagan's personal attorney; Secretary of Commerce—Malcolm Baldrige, chairman of Scoville Inc.; Secretary of Health and Human Services—Sen. Richard S. Schweiker (R. Penn.); Secretary of Transportation—Andrew L. Lewis Jr., a Pennsylvania businessman; Director of the Office of Management and Budget—Rep. David A. Stockman (R. Mich.); and Director of Central Intelligence—William J. Casey, counsel to the law firm Rogers and Wells. Reagan, **Dec. 16,** added 2 more nominees for his cabinet; Secretary of State—Alexander M. Haig Jr., a retired army general and president of the United Technologies Corp.; and Secretary of Labor—Raymond J. Donovan, vice president of the Schiavone Construction Co. Five more nominees were announced by Reagan on **Dec. 22.** They were: Secretary of the Interior—James G. Watt, a lawyer; Secretary of Agriculture—John R. Block, the Illinois Director of Agriculture; Secretary of Housing and Urban Development—Samuel R. Pierce Jr., a lawyer; Secretary of Energy—James B. Edwards, former governor of South Carolina; and U.S. Representative to the United Nations—Jeane J. Kirkpatrick, a professor of government.

House Accepts Waste Cleanup Bill — The House of Representatives, **Dec. 3,** approved a Senate-passed bill to create a $1.6 billion fund that would enable the government to deal with dangerous toxic waste dumps and chemical spills. No provision was made, however, to deal with oil spills or to provide compensation for damage to health or property for the victims of hazardous wastes. The House also passed a bill that set a timetable for developing permanent underground storage places for highly radioactive nuclear waste.

Dohrn Turns Herself In — Bernardine Dohrn, the alleged leader of the radical group Weather Underground, surrendered to Chicago authorities on **Dec. 3,** after 10 years in hiding. She had been arrested in 1970 and indicted for her part in the Weather Underground's violent "Days of Rage" antiwar demonstrations in Chicago in 1969. Dohrn then was freed on bail and did not appear in court after the indictment. At the re-opening of her case, Dohrn pleaded not guilty to the charges of mob action, flight to avoid persecution, and assaulting two policemen. She was released on bail. At her trial on **Jan. 13,** Dohrn was fined $1,500 and placed on 3 years' probation.

Abscam Trials Continue — Reps. Frank Thompson Jr. (D. N.J.) and John M. Murphy (D. N.Y.) were found guilty, **Dec. 3,** of charges stemming from the government's Abscam investigation into political corruption. Thompson was found guilty of bribery and conspiracy and Murphy of conspiracy, conflict of interest, and receiving an unlawful gratuity. Both men had been bribed by undercover agents posing as Arab sheiks and their agents; the taking of the bribes had been secretly videotaped by the FBI.

Percy Talks Stir Controversy — It was disclosed on **Dec.**

5 that messages from the U.S. ambassador to the Soviet Union, Thomas J. Watson Jr., to the State Department indicated that Sen. Charles H. Percy (R. Ill.) had told Soviet leaders that he favored a Palestine state with Yasir Arafat as its leader. Arafat is the head of the Palestine Liberation Organization (PLO). Since Percy was to become the chairman of the Senate Foreign Relations Committee, this announcement stirred anger in the State Department, the Pentagon, and the Reagan transition team. On **Dec. 9,** Sen. Bob Packwood (R. Ore.) criticized Percy in a speech on the Senate floor for his proposal, indicating that "... it's the way to war." And on **Dec. 13,** the FBI began an investigation of what was called an unauthorized disclosure of the cablegrams from Ambassador Watson to the State Department.

Chrysler Still in Economic Trouble — The Chrysler Corp. told the government, **Dec. 8,** that it needed $350 million in additional federal loan guarantees if it were to keep producing vehicles. This was to be in addition to the $800 million previously guaranteed. Treasury Secretary G. William Miller suggested that the company should also try to raise its own additional capital funds. It was proposed that Chrysler could do this by joining forces with another company or by selling a fractional interest in their firm. On **Dec. 12,** Chrysler reacted by asking for freezes on employee wages and supplier parts in order to save $1.5 billion and thus persuade the government to guarantee the loans. Chrysler predicted, **Dec. 17,** that they would lose more than $200 million in the final quarter of the year, thus bringing its 1980 deficit up to $1.7 billion. The prediction prompted Chrysler to increase its requests for federal loan guarantees to $400 million.

Mexico Terminates Fishing Treaties — In a notice announced on **Dec. 28** and delivered to the State Department on **Dec. 29,** the Government of Mexico announced its plans to cancel 2 fishing treaties between itself and the United States. The first was a 1976 agreement that gave the U.S. a quota for snapper and grouper caught in Mexican Gulf and Pacific waters, which would be terminated in one year. The second was a 1977 treaty that permitted Mexico a squid allocation off the eastern seaboard of the U.S., which would be cancelled within 6 months of the delivery of the notice. This notice was seen as a blow to efforts to produce a treaty between the 2 countries on the more important tuna fishing industry. Mexico and the U.S. had been engaged in a "tuna war" since a July embargo on tuna imports from Mexico was imposed by the U.S.

New Governor for Connecticut — William A. O'Neill, the lieutenant governor of Connecticut, was sworn in as governor, **Dec. 31,** following the resignation of Ella T. Grasso. Gov. Grasso was the first woman elected chief executive of a state without having a politician-husband as her predecessor. Grasso decided to resign after it was discovered that she had cancer of the liver, a condition that is usually incurable, and she no longer felt able to endure the rigors of being governor.

International

Elections — Several national elections around the world brought some surprises in December. In a plebiscite in Uruguay, **Dec. 1,** the voters defeated a proposed constitution that would have given the military the power to run the country. This vote against military rule came in the first public elections that had been permitted in 7 years ... In Taiwan the ruling party, the Kuomintang, won the parliamentary elections, **Dec. 7** ... On **Dec. 8,** Gen. António Ramalho Eanes, the president of Portugal, was re-elected, amidst political turmoil following the death of one of the chief vote-getters of his opponent's party, Prime Minister Francisco Sá Carneiro, in a plane crash on **Dec. 4** . . . Milton Obote, the candidate of the Uganda People's Party, was elected president of that country on **Dec. 11** . . . On **Dec. 17,** Forbes Burnham was re-elected president of Guyana, but his opponents charged election fraud.

Peking Trial Continues — Jiang Tengjiao, a former air force commander, confessed, **Dec. 1,** that he had plotted to murder Mao Zedong. Jiang was on trial with 4 other military leaders before one of the Chinese government's 2 special tribunals. The other tribunal was trying the Gang of Four and Mao's political secretary, Chen Boda. On **Dec. 4,** one of the Gang of Four, Mao's widow Jiang Qing, reversed her previous plea of complete innocence and confessed in court that she had personally directed a special group that had persecuted China's former head of state, Liu Shaoqi, and his wife. The prosecution, **Dec. 6**, accused her of ordering the death by torture of 2 teachers in 1967 while trying to force them to give evidence that Liu's wife was an American spy. Jiang was expelled from the courtroom, **Dec. 12**, after she repeatedly yelled at a witness who was testifying against her and, on the next day, the prosecution rested its case against all the defendants except Jiang. She was charged with contempt of court, **Dec. 23**, after she shouted at a panel of judges and prosecutors, calling them "fascists" and Chinese Nationalist agents. She reiterated her plea of innocence on **Dec. 24**, claiming that she had committed the alleged persecutions of Communist Party officials during the Cultural Revolution on the orders of her husband. She then dared the court to sentence her to death in a public execution. The chief prosecutor demanded that she be sentenced to death, and, on **Dec. 29**, she was hauled from the courtroom shouting, "I am prepared to die." This concluded testimony and arguments in the trial; the defendants were not expected to appear in court again until the verdicts and sentences were handed down.

Polish Turmoil Escalates — Stanislaw Kania, the Polish Communist leader, announced **Dec. 1**, that the Soviet Union had granted some $1.3 billion to assist Poland in dealing with its economic crisis, and he accused the new independent trade union, Solidarity, of being in league with anticommunist factions outside the country. That same day, the Soviet army closed to western observers a strip along the East German-Polish border, giving rise to talk of Polish preparations to cope with the Polish labor crisis. On **Dec. 2**, the Polish Communist party dismissed 4 members of the Politburo, consolidating Kania's power, and the White House warned that intervention in Poland by any outside power would affect Soviet-American relations. The Communist Party's Central Committee, **Dec. 4**, asked for an end to the unrest, pleading for the Poles themselves to stay calm and stay on their jobs, and some communist leaders said that if the problem were not handled properly, they would have the right and duty to ask for Soviet military aid as a last resort. The leaders of the Soviet Union and its Eastern European allies held a surprise meeting, **Dec. 5**, in Moscow to discuss the Polish problem, and, alarmed by this Warsaw Pact meeting, Solidarity assured the nation that no further strikes were being planned. In Washington, the Carter administration announced, **Dec. 8**, that military reservists had been called up in the Soviet Union, East Germany, and Czechoslovakia, increasing speculation on the possibility of intervention in Poland on the ploy of military maneuvers. Then, on **Dec. 9**, leaders of a Polish farmers' organization, Rural Solidarity, called for a national meeting to plan a method to force the authorities to recognize the group of some 500,000 members as an independent union. More than 1,000 farmers gathered in Warsaw on **Dec. 14**, but no strike vote was passed. However, some farmers threatened to take their products off the market if they were not recognized as a union. On **Dec. 18**, it was announced that Poland had begun its first meat rationing since World War II, and that the rationing would last until the end of the year. Each person would be limited to 1.1 pounds of prime meat, 1.8 pounds of smoked meat, and 3.3 pounds of lower quality meat until the first of 1981.

Tension Rises Between Jordan and Syria: Lebanon Involved — King Hussein of Jordan, **Dec. 1**, announced that he had asked the U.S. and other western countries to speed their deliveries of arms to his country, warning that 30,000 Syrian troops had been massing near the Jordan border. He himself had deployed 24,000 Jordanian soldiers on his side of the border. The following day, Syria presented a list of demands to Jordan, among them the demand that Hussein pledge to recognize the PLO as the sole representative of the Palestine people. It was also reported that Syria had begun removing some of its troops from the border, allegedly on the advice of the Soviet Union. On **Dec. 3**, Jordan rejected Syria's demands. King Khalid of Saudi Arabia, **Dec. 5**, invited Hussein and President Hafez al-Assad of Syria to Riyadh to talk over their differences, but, on **Dec. 7**, this plan seemed to have failed as reports stated there were 50,000 Syrian soldiers as well as 30,000 Jordanian troops on the border. A Jordanian announcement, **Dec. 10**, told of 36

American made tanks being turned over to them by Iraq as a gesture of thanks for Jordan's help to Iraq in its war with Iran. The tanks had been captured from the Iranian armed forces. That same day, some Syrian troops were being pulled back from the border and Jordan indicated that it would also remove some of its soldiers. On **Dec. 13**, Syrian jets attacked training camps for the Moslem Brotherhood in Jordan, and, on **Dec. 21**, Syrian troops battled with Christian militia forces in Zahle, Lebanon. The Syrians' demand that Lebanese gunmen responsible for killing 5 Syrian soldiers be turned over to them had been ignored. By **Dec. 22**, 10 people had been killed and 21 wounded. A cease-fire was declared on **Dec. 26**.

Terrorist Violence Mounts in El Salvador — Following the killings of 4 U.S. women in El Salvador, the U.S. government, **Dec. 5**, suspended $25 million in new military and economic aid to that nation pending the report of a fact-finding mission led by William D. Rogers, the former assistant secretary of state for inter-American affairs. The bodies of the 4 women, 3 Roman Catholic nuns and a lay worker were found, **Dec. 4**, in a crude grave 25 miles southeast of the capital city, San Salvador. Extreme rightist groups were blamed for the murders, which came in the wake of the **Nov. 27** slayings of 6 prominent leftist leaders, members of the Democratic Revolutionary Front. The responsibility for these deaths had been claimed by a right-wing paramilitary group, the Maximiliano Hernandez Martinez Brigade. As the fact-finding mission arrived in El Salvador, **Dec. 6**, 2 of the 5 members of the nation's ruling junta threatened to resign unless the army purged rightist terrorists from its ranks. On **Dec. 7**, Col. Adolfo Arnoldo Majano, the most liberal of the junta members, was ousted; he had openly feuded with the other members of the junta. The state department, **Dec. 12**, announced that, as a result of the report of the special mission, the U.S. would resume aid only when the military-civilian government was reorganized. On **Dec. 13**, Jose Napoleon Duarte was named the first civilian president of El Salvador in 49 years and the leader of a 4-member junta. He vowed that people responsible for the violence would be dismissed from the government and arrested. The State Department announced on **Dec. 17** that El Salvador would receive $20 million in economic aid, but no money for military aid, and the following day, the Inter-American Development Bank approved $45.4 million in loans for peasant cooperatives to try to combat rural guerilla violence. But, on **Dec. 26**, Fermán Cienfuegos, a top guerrilla commander, predicted that the leftists would mount an offensive against the new government before the inauguration of Ronald Reagan. He also predicted that a real war could break out if Venezuela, Colombia, Guatemala, or Honduras came to Duarte's aid. The next day the leftist guerrillas mounted their offensive against government troops in the north and heavy fighting was under way. Estimates of the guerrilla strength ranged from 2,500 to 10,000 trained troops. On **Dec. 28**, the army commander reported that he had the situation in hand.

Iran-Iraq War Continues — The Iranian government announced, **Dec. 5**, that Iraqi bombers had destroyed a main oil pipeline and that they had retaliated by bombing the Iraqi oil terminal of Fao. On **Dec. 6**, the Iraqis reported that Iranian warplanes had bombed several targets in the Kurdish section of northern Iraq and that the Iraqis had destroyed 4 Iranian planes. Despite the claims, there seemed to be no major changes in positions along the 300-mile front. Iranian jet fighters continued to bomb the oil terminal at Fao and Iraqi planes concentrated on the oil refining city of Avadan on **Dec. 7**, and, on **Dec. 11**, the Iraqis were again predicting that the war would go on a long time. Despite a cease-fire appeal from OPEC, fighting broke out on **Dec. 15** in Iran's highlands and the province of Khuzistan and reports listed the dead as 96 Iranians and 122 Iraqis. By **Dec. 19**, Iraq had halted all pumping from its northern oil fields, and on **Dec. 22**, Iraq claimed to have captured $\frac{1}{3}$ of the oil-producing province of Khuzistan. On **Dec. 26** the Iraqis announced that they had invaded Iran's northwestern province of Kurdistan, which extended the front to the full length of the border.

Brezhnev Visits India — Leonid I. Brezhnev, the president of the Soviet Union, arrived on a state visit to India on **Dec. 8**, and was greeted by Prime Minister Indira Gandhi, her cabinet, and many diplomats. There were anti-Soviet demonstrations in New Delhi and maximum security was placed around the Soviet leader to protect him from the demonstrators who were protesting the Soviet activities in Afghanistan. On **Dec. 13** it was announced that Brezhnev had offered India large-scale aid, including help in mining coal, exploring for oil, refining oil, and building power plants. India was to collaborate with the Soviets in manufacturing transport aircraft.

Tension in Northern Ireland Prisons — Prime Minister Margaret Thatcher of Britain and Prime Minister Charles Haughey of Ireland met, **Dec. 8,** to discuss a hunger strike in 2 Northern Ireland prisons. Seven male prisoners opposing British rule in Northern Ireland had been on a hunger strike for 7 weeks, and for 3 weeks a similar strike had been carried on by 3 women at another prison. Another 6 prisoners at the men's prison had threatened to begin their own fast if they were not granted special political status instead of being treated as common criminals. On **Dec. 18,** the first 7 called off their hunger strike as 2 of them were nearing death by starvation, even though the British government had refused to yield to their demands.

Yugoslavs Offer Broad Arms Proposal in Madrid — The Yugoslav delegation to the 35-nation European security conference in Madrid proposed a disarmament plan, **Dec. 12,** that covered both nuclear and conventional weapons. Because of deteriorating East-West relations, they suggested that a multi-national disarmament conference be held. On **Dec. 19,** the first phase of the conference ended with a warning from the U.S. to the Soviets that an invasion of Poland was not acceptable. Plans were made to reconvene on **Jan. 7,** and it was noted by the delegates that there was a unity of purpose to the first session, at least among the NATO countries, and that the Soviets had been isolated even among neutral and non-aligned countries, especially on the issues of Afghanistan and human rights.

Oil Prices Rise Again — At the OPEC meeting in Denpasar, Indonesia, Saudi Arabia raised its crude oil prices by $2 per barrel, **Dec. 16,** bringing the Saudi's price to the $32 per barrel already charged by the other OPEC nations. Then the oil ministers from the 13 OPEC countries agreed to permit the price to rise as high as $40 per barrel, allowing many members of the group to raise their prices as much as $4 per barrel. It was calculated that this might raise the price of home heating oil in the U.S. 7 cents a gallon. On **Dec. 29,** Libya and Indonesia announced price increases of $3 to $4 per barrel. It was believed widely that Algeria would not only raise its price to $41 per barrel, but would also maintain its surcharge of $3 per barrel, making the total price $44 per barrel. Nigeria raised its price by $3, to $40 per barrel.

Soviet Embassy Attacked — Afghans living in Iran stormed the Soviet Embassy in Teheran, **Dec. 27,** protesting the Soviet intervention in Afghanistan. They broke into the compound, burned a Soviet flag, and then were dispersed by Iranian police. On **Dec. 28,** the Soviet Union delivered a formal protest to Iran asking for the government of that country to make repairs and to beef up security around the embassy, but did not note in the message that the rioters were Afghans.

General

Death Rate Increasing for Youths — It was announced, **Dec. 5,** by the Surgeon General of the U.S., Dr. Julius B. Richmond, that while the overall death rate for all Americans had dropped by 20% from 1960–1978, it had grown by 11% for young people 15 to 24 years old. In the single year of 1977–78, the rate had jumped by 3%. Blamed were deaths from automobile accidents and murders stemming from drug and alcohol abuse and emotional problems. In addition to these statistics, infant mortality had dropped by 47% to 13 deaths per 1,000 live births; motor vehicle deaths were up, and deaths from heart disease were down by 20%.

John Lennon Assassinated — On **Dec. 8,** John Lennon, the singer, composer, and ex-Beatle, was shot down by a former mental patient, Mark David Chapman, outside Lennon's apartment house in New York City. The singer was shot in the back twice after getting out of a taxi, and never regained consciousness. Lennon, 40 years old, who was widely thought to be the most intellectual and outspoken of the singing group, was in the company of his wife, Yoko

Ono, when the killer struck. She was unhurt. The following Sunday, **Dec. 14,** commemorative vigils were held around the world.

Surrogate Mother's Baby Delivered — The second instance of a woman becoming a surrogate mother by delivering a baby belonging to another woman was reported in Knoxville, Tenn., on **Dec. 10.** The surrogate mother had been impregnated by artificial insemination with the sperm of her sister's husband.

Cosmonauts Return Home — Three Russian cosmonauts returned to earth, **Dec. 10,** after a 13-day flight that included repairing and testing the orbiting Soviet space station Salyut 6. This was the 6th manned space flight by the Soviets in 1980 and the first using 3 men since 1971. The cosmonauts had been launched on Nov. 27 and linked up with the space station the next day. They did repairs and maintenance on the station's temperature control, telemetry, and refueling systems. Salyut 6 had been in space for more than 3 years and had been visited by 13 crews, including 7 with astronauts from other countries.

Leonardo Notebook Worth $5 Million — A record was set by Armand Hammer, the industrialist and art collector, on **Dec. 12,** when he bought the Leonardo da Vinci notebook "Of the Nature, Weight, and Movement of Water" for $5,126,000. This was the highest price ever paid at an auction for a manuscript, eclipsing the sale of a Gutenberg Bible in New York in 1978 for $2 million. The 36-page notebook, also known as the Codex of Leicester, was sold in London, and Hammer planned to exhibit it around the world, beginning with a show in London's Royal Academy.

Ancient Fleet Found — In a report from Tokyo, **Dec. 13,** it was claimed that Japanese divers had found the wreckage of Kublai Khan's invasion fleet. The fleet had been driven from Japan's shores and sunk more than 700 years ago by a violent storm. More than 70 wooden hulls had been found submerged in mud to a depth of 6 feet in waters over 80 feet deep in an inlet off the coast of Nagasaki. Also found were a Mongol sword, stone implements used for pounding rice cakes, and a bronze statute of Buddha.

Art Works Stolen in Argentina — The discovery of the theft of more than $25 million worth of paintings and other works was announced, **Dec. 27,** by the National Museum of Fine Arts in Buenos Aires. Among the works were 3 oil paintings by Pierre Auguste Renoir, a watercolor by Paul Cézanne, a pencil drawing by Henri Matisse, and a charcoal pastel by Edgar Degas. Police guessed that the robbery occurred before dawn on Christmas Day and the thieves had entered through holes in the roof made by construction workers who were remodeling the second floor galleries.

Man-Made Heart Keeps Calf Alive — A **Dec. 28** announcement issued by a group of researchers at the University of Utah reported that they had kept a calf alive for 32 weeks with a man-made heart and requested permission to implant a similar device in a human being. A university panel was set up to review the possibility of the human implant. The artificial heart, it was thought, could be used to keep a heart patient alive long enough for surgeons to locate another human heart to be used in a transplant operation. The heart received approval from the University of Utah's College of Medicine, **Jan. 27.**

Disasters — A flash fire at the Stouffer's Inn near White Plains, N.Y. on **Dec. 4,** killed 26 people, most of them corporate executives trapped in meeting rooms . . . Ten people were killed, 8 of them UN employees, when their light plane crashed in Tanzania, **Dec. 5** . . . On **Dec. 19,** 2 earthquakes in Iran killed 26 people and damaged Shiite Moslem shrines in Qum . . . A Colombian jetliner crashed in a desert north of Bogota, **Dec. 21,** and all 68 people on board were killed. The cause was reported to be an explosion in a rear bathroom; an anonymous phone call shortly after the crash informed the airline that a bomb had been placed on board . . . Floods in the Pacific Northwest, it was reported on **Dec. 27,** had washed away more than a dozen homes in Washington and killed 2 people in Oregon.

JANUARY

National

Prices and Employment Up; Index and Productivity Down — Citing an increase in loan demand by business, banks across the country announced, **Jan. 3,** that they would cut their prime rate from 21½% to 20½%. On **Jan. 9**, the Labor Dept. reported that producer prices had risen in Dec. by .6 of 1%, meaning that 1980 finished 11.7% higher than the year before. At the same time, food prices declined slightly. It was also announced that the unemployment rate for December was 7.4% of the nation's work force, little changed from November's 7.5%. The Labor Department's Bureau of Labor Statistics pointed out that the employment situation had not recovered from the sharp slump in the beginning of the year of 1980, having been on a plateau since the month of May. On **Jan. 23**, the Bureau of Labor Statistics released a report on the Consumer Price Index, which had climbed 1.1% in the month of December, making a total rise for the year 1980 of 12.4%, the second consecutive year of double-digit inflation. Not since World War I had there been two such consecutive years. On the other hand, the Commerce Department announced on **Jan. 30** that the economic index which forecasts future economic trends, dropped by .8 of 1% during December, indicating an economic slowdown.

Second Draft Registration Held — On **Jan. 5**, the 2d round of draft registration was conducted. About 1.9 million men born in 1962 were to register with the Selective Service System. In the previous registration period, which covered those men born in 1960 and 1961, some 95% of the eligible did register, and Bernard D. Rostker, the director of the SSS, predicted a higher percentage this time.

Transition Continues — President-elect Ronald Reagan met with Pres. José López Portillo of Mexico on **Jan. 5** to discuss the establishment of a personal relationship to ease tensions and renew the friendship between the two countries. Meeting on the Bridge of Friendship between El Paso, Tex., and Ciudad Juarez, Mex., they clasped arms and left for a 70 minute meeting in the Juarez Museum of Art and History. Details of the meeting were withheld, but it was predicted that the two would meet again between May and July. On **Jan. 7**, Reagan completed his cabinet selections by naming T.H. Bell, the commissioner of higher education in Utah, as secretary of education. The president-elect also announced that he would retain Mike Mansfield, the former Senate majority leader, as the U.S. ambassador to Japan. Pres. Jimmy Carter gave his final State of the Union Message to Congress, **Jan. 16**, warning that the U.S. faces serious problems, such as unemployment, inflation, and a tight world oil market. He also deplored the Soviet threat to the integrity of Poland and defended his SALT treaty with Russia.

Planes Destroyed in Puerto Rico — Nine military jet fighters were destroyed and 2 damaged at the Muñiz Air National Guard Base near San Juan, P.R., **Jan. 12**. A Puerto Rican terrorist group, the Macheteros, claimed the responsibility for setting the time bombs that did the damage. The group, which favors independence for Puerto Rico, announced that it had also ambushed a Navy bus on **Dec. 3, 1979**, killing 3 sailors and wounding 10. The attack on the planes was the most severe ever made against a military installation in Puerto Rico. No one was injured, but the total damage was estimated at $45 million.

Exile Troubles Continue — The FBI announced, **Jan. 16**, that it had arrested 7 anti-Castro Cuban exiles in the Florida Keys, seizing an arsenal of weapons intended for use in an invasion of Cuba. The arms included pipe bombs, hand grenades, semiautomatic rifles, pistols, ammunition, and smokeless powder. The men were accused of conspiracy and violation of a Federal firearms law. On **Jan. 30**, the Immigration and Naturalization Service moved to expel 3,900

Hostages Return to the U.S.: A National Celebration

A terrible chapter in American history came to a close, **Jan. 20**, when the 52 Americans who had been held hostage in Iran for 444 days were flown to freedom. The release was precipitated by an agreement, **Jan. 19**, between the U.S. and Iran, in which the U.S. agreed to return to Iran $8 billion in Iranian assets which the U.S. had frozen following the November 1979 seizure of the hostages and the U.S. embassy in Teheran.

The release of hostages was postponed one day, until just minutes after the inauguration of Ronald Reagan as U.S. president, when a last-minute dispute arose over an appendix to the agreement. Iran had objected that the accord would force Iran to drop any claims on the U.S. beyond the money that the U.S. would transfer into escrow accounts.

In the first stage of their flight to freedom, the 52 Americans were escorted out of Iran by Algerian diplomats aboard an Algerian airliner. Following a refueling stop in Athens, the former hostages were flown to Algiers where they were transferred to the custody of Deputy Secretary of State Warren M. Christopher. The freed Americans then boarded 2 U.S. Air Force planes for the flight to Wiesbaden, West Germany, for debriefing, testing, and rehabilitation in preparation for their return to the U.S. Former Pres. Jimmy Carter, **Jan. 21**, flew to Wiesbaden to welcome the Americans and reported that they had been subjected to acts of barbarism, including beatings, months in solitary confinement, the constant fear of death, and physical and mental mistreatment.

The tortuous path of negotiations leading to the release had begun many months before. In November, Iran announced new conditions for the release of the 52 hostages, and, on **Nov. 4**, urged the U.S. to reply to their offer through the mass media. The 4 main Iranian demands called for U.S. promises not to interfere in Iranian affairs, to unfreeze Iranian assets in the U.S., to drop financial claims against Iran, and to move to return the wealth of the late Shah Mohammed Riza Pahlevi. The State Department responded that Iran's conditions required careful analysis and study and that the U.S. would, therefore, need time to respond. The U.S. also questioned whether it had the legal power to conform to the last two demands.

Algeria was selected as the intermediary between the U.S. and Iran on this matter, and, **Nov. 12**, delivered to Iran a secret response from the U.S. The State Department confirmed, **Nov. 20**, that the U.S. had accepted the 4 conditions in principle, but that the U.S. was still waiting for a formal request from Iran for further clarification of several details. On **Nov. 27**, the Islamic radicals who were holding the hostages prisoner said that they had handed the Americans over to the Iranian government.

The month of December began with high hopes that the hostages would be freed soon. Hojatolislam Hashemi Rafsanjani, speaker of the Iranian Parliament, said, **Dec. 8**, that the dispute over the embassy hostages was much closer to being solved. By **Dec. 13**, Ahmad Azizi, the director of American hostage affairs in the Iranian prime minister's office, said that the U.S. response to the latest 4 Iranian demands made in November had been basically positive, and, **Dec. 14**, he indicated that quick U.S. action on the demands might free the hostages by Christmas.

But on **Dec. 19**, Iran told the U.S. that it must deposit in Algeria the billions of dollars worth of Iranian assets frozen in the U.S. and offer assurance that the U.S. would help in the returning of the wealth of the late Shah. The U.S. argued that although Iran contended that it was owed more than $30 billion, only about $8 billion had been frozen by the U.S. government, and that the U.S. had no control over, or even knowledge of, the extent of the Shah's American wealth. As this time, John H. Trattner, a State Department spokesman, indicated that the hostages would probably not be home by Christmas.

Prime Minister Mohammed Ali Rajai announced, **Dec. 20**, that the main stumbling block in the negotiations was the return of the Shah's wealth. It was proposed that since there was no accurate figure on the amount of the Shah's property, the U.S. should deposit between $5 billion and $10 billion in Algeria and, as the U.S. would find the Shah's property, Iran could draw from the fund an equivalent amount of the value of the property. This amount would then be replenished by the U.S. If no assets were found in the U.S., Iran would be able to take possession of the whole fund. State Department officials had characterized this as a simple ransom and weighed the possibility of halting the exchange discussions until after Ronald Reagan's inauguration.

Rafsanjani, **Dec. 22**, threatened that the hostages would be put on trial as spies if the U.S. did not agree to deposit $24 billion in Algeria to cover the guarantees for both the

Haitians who had entered the US since **Oct. 11, 1980.** The Haitians were expected to appeal the decision on the basis that they were seeking asylum from the Duvalier regime in their native country.

Reagan Inaugurated — Ronald Wilson Reagan became the 40th President of the United States on **Jan. 20.** In his inaugural address, he promised an era of national renewal. He also issued orders for a hiring freeze. The oath of office was administered at 11:57 A.M. in the first inaugural ceremony ever held on the western front of the United States Capitol Building. Reagan, at the age of 69, was the oldest man ever to be sworn in as president, and, in June, would become the oldest man to serve in the office.

Another Victim Found in Atlanta — The body of a 15-year-old boy, Terry Pue, was found strangled on **Jan. 23.** He was thought to be connected with a reign of terror that had existed in Atlanta for the previous 18 months. At least 16 children, ranging from 7 to 15 years old, had disappeared; 13 had been found dead. Terry Pue was the 14th.

Another Abscam Conviction — On **Jan. 26,** former Rep. Richard Kelly (R. Fla.) was found guilty of bribery, conspiracy, and interstate travel in aid of a racketeering enterprise. He was the 6th member or former member of Congress to be convicted in the Abscam trials. Videotapes had shown Kelly taking $25,000 in cash and putting it in his pocket after promising to help 2 Arab sheiks immigrate to the U.S. Sentencing was scheduled for **Feb. 23.**

Supreme Court Permits Trial Television — The U.S. Supreme Court **Jan. 26** unanimously ruled that the various states were free to permit the televising of criminal trials. The justices felt that television does not violate a defendant's right to a fair trial, even when the suspect objects to the cameras. The ruling still left open the right of appeal on the grounds that the trial was unfair or the jurors were prejudiced by a particular type of news coverage. At the time of the decision, 27 states had permitted some form of televised court proceedings, 21 of them in criminal trials, but 10 of the 21 required the consent of the defendant.

Reagan Abolishes Oil Price Controls — President Reagan, **Jan. 28,** abolished the remaining price and allocation controls on domestic oil and gasoline production and distribution. It was predicted that retail gasoline prices would rise by 3 to 5 cents per gallon, and possibly by 12 cents per gallon by the end of the summer and that heating oil prices would climb even higher. The administration pointed out that only 15% of the crude oil processed by U.S. refineries had remained subject to price controls.

President Holds First Press Conference — Ronald Reagan held his first press conference as president in Washington, **Jan. 29.** In it, he ordered a 60-day freeze on pending government regulations. He also announced the elimination of the Council on Wage and Price Stability, the federal agency that had monitored national wage and price increases for 6 years. Reagan warned that his proposed budget cuts, scheduled to be announced by mid-February, would be bigger than anyone has ever attempted. He also repeated his support for a 30% cut in personal tax rates, and the elimination of the Departments of Energy and Education.

International

Hua Ousted — The absence of Hua Guofeng, the Chinese Communist Party Chairman, from a New Year's reception **Jan. 1,** stirred rumors that he had been forced to resign from his post. Because the reception, given by the Central Committee, was unusual in that such affairs are usually sponsored by the government, it was believed that the celebration

Shah's wealth and the frozen Iranian assets.

On **Dec. 24,** President-elect Reagan called the Iranians "nothing better than criminals and kidnappers" and President Carter ruled out the possibility of paying ransom for the release of the hostages. The U.S. asked Algeria to send its team of intermediaries to Washington to discuss the form that the U.S. response to the demands should take.

On Christmas Day, Msgr. Annibale Bugnini, the Papal Nuncio in Iran, and other clergymen held services for the hostages and distributed gifts to them. Although the Iranian press agency claimed that he had met with all the hostages, Msgr. Bugnini said that he had seen only 20 to 30 of them. In a television film transmitted by satellite from Iran, 26 hostages were seen celebrating Christmas with the clergymen. On **Dec. 26,** the Algerian ambassador to Iran announced that he had visited all 52 hostages over Christmas night and that they appeared to be well. Iranian authorities released more films of the hostages, bringing to 43 the number that had been seen on American television.

Iran offered a new plan, **Dec. 27,** calling for the U.S. to turn over to Iran about $9 billion in frozen assets and for Iran to hold the hostages until the rest of the claims were arbitrated, a period of perhaps a year or more. The State Department issued no comment on the new Iranian proposal, but, on **Dec. 28,** President-elect Ronald Reagan called the plan a "ransom" sought by "barbarians" and said it should not be accepted. Also on **Dec. 28,** the U.S. revealed the formal proposals it had been making to the Iranian government. These included the return of $6 billion in frozen assets, the freezing of the Shah's property in the U.S., and an attempt to seek dismissal of court claims once an international commission was set up to deal with private U.S. claims. All of these proposals were contingent on the release of all the hostages at one time.

The U.S. put forth another proposal, **Dec. 30,** setting a deadline for resolving the hostage matter if it were to be done during the Carter administration. The plan provided for the transfer of $5 billion to $6 billion to an Algerian account at the same time the hostages were delivered to Algeria. At the end of the month, the major stumbling block seemed to hinge on negotiations over who would make the first move.

On **Jan. 3,** the Algerian diplomatic intermediaries met with Iranian officials to discuss the U.S. proposal for freeing the hostages, but there was no indication of what the Iranian response was. Then, on **Jan. 9,** Iran raised more questions about the U.S. proposal, about the amount of Iran's frozen assets that it would recover. The U.S., **Jan. 10,** promised Iran $5.5 billion that would be paid on the day that the hostages were freed, and that Iran would probably recover more than 70% of its frozen assets within a few days of the hostages' release.

Azizi announced **Jan. 11,** that his government had accepted the Algerian suggestion that instead of paying $24 billion into Algerian banks, the U.S. would merely guarantee its payment. Two bills were introduced in the Iranian Parliament, one authorizing arbitration of disputes involving Iran's assets and the other nationalizing the wealth of the Shah, but **Jan. 13,** the day when they were to be approved by the Council of Guardians, a group that must approve all legislation passed by the Parliament, the Council could not summon a quorum. The bills were finally passed on **Jan. 14.**

Behzad Nabavi, the Iranian Minister of State for Executive Affairs, announced, **Jan. 15,** that the frozen assets must be deposited in Algerian banks by **Jan. 16,** but U.S. officials said that this was not possible. Nabavi **Jan. 16.** backed off from his statement, saying no obstacle remained in the way of an agreement. On **Jan. 16,** President Carter ordered an exchange transaction of more than $900 million worth of gold with Britain so that the U.S. would have a sufficient supply of the gold in the Bank of England for transfer to Iran. Twelve large American banks agreed, **Jan. 17,** to drop lawsuits seeking repayment of loans owed to them by Iran if Iran agreed to repay a portion of the debt and to settle the rest later.

The U.S., **Jan. 19,** agreed to unfreeze Iran's assets and release its deposits in U.S. banks, and Iran agreed to repay almost all its U.S. bank loans.

In preparation for the big reunion, relatives of the hostages flew to Washington **Jan. 24,** and on **Jan. 25,** the hostages set foot on American soil after their Air Force VC-137 named Freedom One landed at Stewart International Airport, 17 miles from the U.S. Military Academy at West Point, N.Y.

They were joined by their families and taken by bus to the Hotel Thayer on the academy grounds where they were to stay until **Jan. 27.** Along the way they were cheered by some 20,000 people. On **Jan. 27,** they were flown to Washington where President Reagan greeted them on the South Lawn of the White House.

was held purposely without Hua as a signal to the Chinese people that he had been ousted. It was reported, **Jan. 3**, that Deng Xiaoping, deputy chairman of the Communist Party, had taken over Hua's job as head of the Communist Party's Military Commission.

Fighting and Violence Intensifies in El Salvador — A spokesperson of the Unified Revolutionary Directorate in El Salvador predicted, **Jan. 2**, that leftist insurgents would soon open a military offensive to overthrow the government. Claiming a trained guerrilla force of some 5,000 soldiers armed with automatic rifles, mortars, and grenade launchers, Fermán Cienfuegos, a member of the 5-man military command, warned of the coming battle. In violence from the other end of the political spectrum, two Americans were murdered **Jan. 3** by right-wing assassins. Michael P. Hammer and Mark David Pearlman, both working in El Salvador's land redistribution program, were shot in a hotel coffee shop. Meanwhile, heavy fighting broke out between the military and leftists on the mountain slopes on the north west edge of the capital, San Salvador. By **Jan. 5** the military claimed to have killed 27 leftist guerrillas. It was announced, **Jan. 6**, by the U.S. embassy in El Salvador that John J. Sullivan, an American journalist, was missing and was presumed to be the victim of political violence. Leftist guerrillas attacked San Salvador **Jan. 10**, setting off more than 20 explosions in 14 different locations in the city during the 4-hour raid. The civilian-military junta that controls the government imposed a nationwide curfew on **Jan. 11** in the light of leftists' claims that they had begun a "final offensive." Pres. José Napoleón Duarte announced that government troops were in control of the situation, although 300 people had died in the last 24 hours. By **Jan. 13**, more than 500 had been killed, and the guerrillas were attacking several other Salvadorean cities. President Carter authorized the emergency delivery of $5 million in combat equipment, **Jan. 16**, to aid the government of El Salvador in putting down the revolution. The decision was prompted by indications that the guerrillas had been receiving weapons from leftists in other countries. By **Jan. 22** the guerrilla offensive seemed to have stalled as the government troops retook several towns that had been occupied by the leftist forces.

Mideast War Steps Up — Iranian Pres. Abolhassan Bani-Sadr announced, **Jan. 5**, that the Iranian army had mounted a counteroffensive against Iraq. It was claimed that 200 Iraqis had been killed and 500 captured near Ahwaz, and 100 others had been killed in the Gilan region of Iran. These statements, however, were dismissed by U.S. military analysts, and by Iraqi officials who denied **Jan. 8** that there had been any counteroffensive. Bani-Sadr pledged, **Jan. 9**, that Iran would fight on. However, on **Jan. 10**, Iraq said that it had won a 5-day battle for a city in the oil-rich province of Khuzistan, destroying the major portion of an Iranian armored division. By **Jan. 13** the fighting seemed to be diminishing as the Iraqis dug in along the border. On **Jan. 15**, Ayatollah Ruhollah Khomeini called upon the Iranian people to stop criticizing Bani-Sadr for his conduct of the war, and Iran accused the Soviet Union of sending military advisors and arms to Iraq. The Iraqis announced, **Jan. 25**, that they had captured 2 strategic mountain passes in Iran's Kurdistan Province.

Resurgence of Polish Labor Unrest — After a 5-week lull, Polish workers were again agitating for their rights. Workers and farmers in the southeast part of the country staged a 1-hour strike, **Jan. 6**, in protest of governmental harassment, and **Jan. 7**, delegates of the independent trade union, Solidarity, proclaimed a 5-day work week, with Saturdays off and no increase in work loads, no cuts in salaries, and no curtailment of other days off. Mieczyslaw Jagielski, the first deputy prime minister, suggested an alternate plan of just 2 Saturdays off per month or that work loads be increased to compensate for the 5-day week. The Soviet Press Agency, Tass, warned, **Jan. 9**, that a nationwide walkout in Poland would increase the damage to the country's economy. This was the first warning that the Russians had issued since the wave of Polish strikes began during the previous summer. Most of the workers in Poland's heavy industries took Saturday, **Jan. 10**, off. Solidarity estimated that 80% of the factories were shut down that day. Stanislaw Kania, Poland's Communist Party leader, warned farmers, **Jan. 11**, not to try to organize an independent labor union modeled after Solidarity, and on **Jan. 12**, for the first time,

the authorities used force to quell a demonstration by union members. The town hall of Nowy Sacz had been occupied for 3 days by the demonstrators, and policemen with shields were sent into the building to remove the union members peacefully. Marshal Viktor G. Kulikov, the Soviet Commander of the Warsaw Pact arrived, **Jan. 13**, in Warsaw for a meeting with Kania, and this visit was seen as a warning to the Polish unions. However, a 2-hour warning strike was held in Rzeszow, **Jan. 14**, and farmers occupied a meeting hall in that city in support of the farmers' union. A 4-hour strike of Warsaw bus and streetcar workers was held **Jan. 16**, and, on **Jan. 20**, Solidarity called for negotiations with the government over the 5-day work week. Ten cities in Poland were the victims of work stoppages **Jan. 22** when hundreds of thousands of union members walked off the job for up to 4 hours in protest of the government's stand on the 5-day week and the fact that 26 Soviet army divisions were poised on the Polish border. On **Jan. 24**, a Saturday, millions of workers obeyed Solidarity's call to take the day off. By **Jan. 28**, wildcat strikes were being staged all over the country. The government and Solidarity announced, **Jan. 31**, that they had reached an agreement. The government would make 3 out of every 4 Saturdays non-working days, turn over a weekly hour-long television program to the union leadership, and hold talks with the farmers' union.

More Oil Price Rises — Kuwait announced, **Jan. 10**, that it had raised the price of its crude oil by $4 a barrel. This increase, raising the price to $35.50 per barrel, was made retroactive to **Jan. 1**. The United Arab Emirates, the U.S.'s 10th largest supplier, raised its price to $35.56 per barrel, compared to Saudi Arabia's $32 per barrel, the lowest price of the OPEC nations.

Insurrection in Nigeria — At least 1,000 people were killed in 2 weeks as Islamic cult members attacked local authorities in Nigeria with daggers, swords, bows and arrows, it was announced **Jan. 9**. Nigerian officials stated that the revolt was backed by Libya. The government claimed to have killed nearly all of the riotous cult members, followers of Alhaji Mohammadu Marwa, a renegade religious leader.

Bernadette Devlin Shot — Bernadette Devlin McAliskey, the former member of Parliament from Northern Ireland, was shot and seriously wounded, **Jan. 16**. The opponent of what she termed "the British occupation of Northern Ireland" was attacked by armed men who burst into her home 30 miles west of Belfast. Her husband, Michael, was also seriously wounded in the attack, which police said was the work of a Protestant paramilitary group. On **Jan. 21**, terrorists shot and killed Protestant leader Sir Norman Strong and his son in Belfast. Responsibility for the murders was claimed by guerrillas of the Irish Republican Army, who stated that the killings were in reprisal for attacks on nationalist people. Police felt the people alluded to were Bernadette and Michael McAliskey.

Philippine Martial Law Lifted — President Ferdinand E. Marcos of the Philippines ended the state of martial law in his country, **Jan. 17**. He had ruled for 8 years and 4 months under martial law. Marcos apparently canceled martial law in hopes of making relations with the U.S. more friendly, and also in honor of the coming visit of Pope John Paul II. Marcos also freed 341 prisoners and transferred his own legislative powers to the Philippine National Assembly.

Islamic Leaders Meet — Leaders of 37 Moslem nations and the Palestine Liberation Organization convened, **Jan. 25-30**, in Taif, Saudi Arabia. Missing was the 5-member Iranian delegation, which had been instructed by Ayatollah Ruhollah Khomeini to boycott the meeting because President Saddam Hussein of Iraq would be present. Libya also boycotted the meeting in protest of the basing of U.S. surveillance planes in Saudi Arabia, and Afghanistan was barred from the conference because its government was attempting to suppress Moslem rebels. Egypt was also banned from the meeting because of its peace treaty with Israel. In an opening speech read by Crown Prince Fahd, King Khalid of Saudi Arabia urged the group to work to drive Israel out of the Arab territories it has occupied since 1967 and to secure the rights of the Palestinians. UN Secretary General Kurt Waldheim urged, **Jan. 26**, that the delegates help the United Nations mediate the Iraqi-Iranian war. The delegates approved a resolution, **Jan. 27**, that called for immediate withdrawal of Soviet troops from Afghanistan. President Elias Sarkis of Lebanon protested, on **Jan. 28**, that Palestinian military activity in the southern part of his country was in violation of a commitment made to him by the guerrilla movement. He asserted that the Palestinians were using Lebanese bases to attack Israel, which drew Israeli reprisals against Lebanon.

Mao's Widow Sentenced — Jiang Qing, the widow of Mao Zedong, was sentenced to death, **Jan. 25,** for counterrevolutionary crimes during the Cultural Revolution of 1966-76. However, the sentence was suspended for 2 years during which she would be "helped to reform through labor." If she reforms, the court can commute the sentence to life imprisonment. The sentences for the other 3 members of the Gang of Four were also announced. Zhang Chunqiao, the former mayor of Shanghai, received the same sentence as Jiang. Yao Wenyuan, the former head of China's mass communication organizations, was sentenced to 20 years. Wang Hongwen, the former deputy party chairman, was sentenced to life imprisonment. Other defendants received prison sentences of from 16 to 18 years, but since most of them were jailed in 1971, it was ruled that they had already served more than half of their sentences.

South Korea Ends Martial Law — Pres. Chun Doo Hwan of South Korea lifted martial law in his country, **Jan. 24.** This ended 456 days of total or partial military authority, dating back to the assassination of President Park Chung Hee. However, the midnight-to-4 a.m. curfew that had existed since 1945 remained in effect. This ending of martial law was one of a series of actions made by Chun before his visit to Washington to meet President Reagan in February. He also commuted the death sentence of opposition politician Kim Dae Jung to life imprisonment.

General

Mammals Cloned for the First Time — Scientists in Switzerland reported, **Jan. 6,** that they had achieved the first cloning of a mammal, having produced 3 mice. Cloning is the taking of a cell nucleus from a plant or an animal and activating it so that it becomes a complete organism identical to the plant or animal that furnished the original nucleus. The nuclei used in this research came from embryonic mice cell nuclei which were then placed in fertilized eggs from another mouse. The original nuclear material from those eggs was then extracted, leaving only the inserted nucleus. After culturing the eggs for 4 days, they were placed in the wombs of other mice, which then gave birth to the offspring.

Flu Sweeps the Country — Outbreaks of influenza were found all across the country and several areas reported full scale epidemics, the National Center for Disease Control announced **Jan. 8.** Deaths from pneumonia and influenza in 121 cities had exceeded what is called the "epidemic threshold" in the previous 3 weeks. These cities included 26% of the total population of the U.S. Normally 3.5% of the deaths in those cities would have been caused by pneumonia or influenza, but the rate had climbed to 5%, and hospital admissions were up nearly 60%. It seemed that the disease most often contracted was influenza virus A/Bangkok/79, a descendent of the A/Hong Kong virus that caused a national epidemic in the winter of 1968-69.

Grumman Admits Responsibility — The Grumman Corporation, **Jan. 24,** notified officials in 27 cities that it had found a flaw in its Flxible buses that might cause the driver to lose control of the bus. Grumman officials said that the buses should be inspected, and taken out of service if necessary. Grumman promised to repair the defect—a piece that secured the bus's A-frame to the front assembly. New York City's entire fleet of these buses had been taken out of service. Some of the other cities that had purchased a total of 2,600 Flxibles were Hartford, Los Angeles, Chicago, Atlanta, Dallas, Honolulu, and Santa Monica.

Japanese Banks Forgive Chrysler — A large portion of the claims against the Chrysler Corporation were written off, **Jan. 24,** by 7 major Japanese commercial banks. Chrysler had requested an 85% writeoff on the $156 million that it had borrowed from the banks, as a condition laid down by the U.S. Federal Loan Guarantee Board when it approved Chrysler's application for extra loan guarantees totaling $400 million. The Japanese banks felt that they had no alternative, since the auto maker had to be rescued financially.

Endangered Species List De-emphasized — It was learned, **Jan. 30,** that the Interior Department's Office of Endangered Species had been instructed to de-emphasize its efforts to place on its endangered species list animals and plants that are faced with extinction. Instead, it was to concentrate on the "recovery" of species already on the list. It was to reduce by half the number of species to be examined for listing as endangered and spend more time planning to take such steps as moving an affected animal or plant to a less dangerous area.

Disasters — A river boat carrying relatives of Brazilian workers hit a sandbar and sank, **Jan. 8,** in a tributary of the Amazon River; the death toll was at least 230, 50 of them children ... Twenty-four people were killed and 6 were missing in a fire in a Keansburg, N.J. rest home, **Jan. 9** ... An Indonesian passenger ship caught fire in a storm and sank in the Java Sea, **Jan. 27,** killing 87, and little hope was held out for the rescue of the 287 people listed as missing.

FEBRUARY

National

Bilingual Plan Revoked — Secretary of Education T. H. Bell barred proposed regulations that would have required public schools to teach foreign-speaking students in their native languages, **Feb. 2.** The plans would have forced school districts with more than 25 foreign-speaking students to provide instruction in both the foreign language and in English. Bell estimated that the costs of these programs over the next 5 years would have been about $1 billion, and that there were about 3.5 million children in the U. S. who spoke little or no English, 70% of them Hispanic Americans.

Reagan Cuts Synthetic Fuel Projects — It was announced by the Office of Management and Budget, **Feb. 4,** that Pres. Ronald Reagan intended to eliminate 5 large synthetic fuel development projects and slash federal support to the Synthetic Fuels Corporation by about one-third, or $5.3 billion. Thus, the corporation would have to put up 40%, rather than 25%, of the cost of plants to be built to develop these fuels. The total package would represent a federal saving of some $9.1 billion.

Fuel Prices Rise — Three major gasoline and heating oil suppliers, Exxon, Texaco, and Shell, announced new price increases, **Feb. 4.** The increase averaged 9 cents a gallon on heating oil, and it was predicted that prices could reach $1.40 per gallon by the end of the heating season from about 94 cents the previous November. Gasoline prices had risen about 16 cents per gallon since the first of the year, and the prediction was that they might rise to $1.60 per gallon. The Labor Department, **Feb. 13,** blamed these higher fuel costs for the rise of .9% in producer prices in January. In addition, the figures released did not include the effects of President Reagan's **Jan. 28** decontrol of domestic oil. The price index was up 8.9% from a year earlier. The Labor Department also announced that the unemployment rate for the month of January remained steady at about 7.4%.

Senate Votes to Raise Debt Ceiling — On **Feb. 6,** the Senate voted to increase the federal debt limit by $50 billion to $985 billion. Predictions were that the amount voted would not last the fiscal year which ends Sept. 30.

Three Convicted in Miami — Three young black men were declared guilty of murder in the beating deaths of three whites during the Liberty City section of Miami riots of **May, 1980.** They had been charged with three counts of 1st degree murder, but were convicted, **Feb. 6,** on lesser charges. Samuel Lightsey was convicted of 2d degree murder, and Lawrence and Leonard Capers of 3d degree murder. A 4th youth, Patrick Moore, was acquitted. The 3 victims had been dragged from their car and beaten to death after their automobile was stopped by a crowd in Liberty City.

Atlanta Tragedy Continues — Atlanta police began searching, **Feb. 8,** for another young black child, Patrick Baltazar, who had been missing since **Feb. 6.** He was the 18th missing child in the Atlanta area; 15 of the other 17 had been found dead. All of them were between the ages of 7 and 15. On **Feb. 9,** Lee Gooch, a 15-year-old, missing since January, was found alive in Florida, but, **Feb. 13,** 2 more children were found dead, one of them Patrick Baltazar. Although a police team was doggedly sifting evidence, hoping to find a key to the murders, citizens were beginning to complain, accusing the police of not acting fast enough.

of not being experienced enough, and of not utilizing civilian help in a positive way.

As the remains of 2 more youngsters were found on **Feb. 14,** the scope of the investigation was changed with the formation of 35-member investigating team. The presence of identical fibers on 5 of the bodies pointed to the possibility that at least 5 of the children had been killed by the same person. On **Feb. 15,** the skeleton of an 11-year-old boy, Jeffrey Mathis, was identified, raising the total number of victims to 17, with 1 child still missing. Two more sets of remains were found on **Feb. 20.** On **Feb. 21,** Vice Pres. George Bush announced the establishment of a task force to coordinate federal efforts to aid the city's investigation. The Departments of Justice, Education, and Health and Human Services would provide technical aid for the investigation, psychiatric help for the victims' families, and other services.

New Plan to Combat Violent Crime — The Justice Department announced **Feb. 10** that it was developing a package of proposals to increase the federal government's ability to fight violent crime and that the White House was studying a proposal to create a Presidential commission on victims of crime. The Justice Department was studying 5 measures, including making murder for hire a federal offence and allowing judges to consider the safety of a community when setting bail. The other measures called for Congress to establish a victim compensation fund so that victims or their survivors could get up to $50,000 for loss of earnings, for federal law to provide new protections for crime victims and witnesses, and also for federal law to provide an increased or mandatory sentence for crimes involving the use of a weapon or unusual violence.

Heroin Trade Rises — The Federal Drug Enforcement Administration announced, **Feb. 15,** that, despite the hundreds of millions of dollars spent per year in the battle against heroin, only 2% to 5% of the illegal drug traffic was being kept from distribution channels. The prime reason cited was that nothing could be done to curb production of narcotics in Iran, Afghanistan, and parts of Pakistan. In addition, 4 other problems were mentioned: restricted budgets for fighting the traffic, coupled with the inflation of heroin prices have left enforcement officials without funds for undercover investigators to buy drugs; the Carter Administration, according to the officials, was uncommitted to fighting drugs; a lack of long-term planning in the campaign against drug distribution; the ease with which drug dealers obtain release on bail after their arrests.

U.S. Auto Industry Has Worst Year — In an attempt to curb lagging sales, General Motors and Ford announced, **Feb. 17,** that they would institute the largest rebate plans in their history. GM's rebates were to run from $500 to $700 and Ford was to rebate 10% on its middle and large size cars. In so doing they joined the other members of the Big Four, Chrysler and American Motors, in offering these incentives. Chrysler had been offering 7% and American 10%. But when Chrysler reported a loss of $1.71 billion for 1980, **Feb. 27,** the largest loss in American corporate history, it indicated that these plans had not been successful. All of the Big Three, GM, Ford, and Chrysler, had lost money during 1980, adding up to the worst year in U.S. automobile history, totaling an estimated loss of $4.06 billion. Even General Motors, which sold 45.9% of all cars bought in the U.S., had its first full-year loss since 1921.

Drug Use Leveling Off — According to the results of a survey of high school seniors released on **Feb. 18,** the use of illicit drugs by young people in the U.S. ceased to rise in 1980. This was the 1st year since the survey began in 1975 that the upward climb had leveled off, and the number of students admitting to the use of marijuana had actually declined. The leader of the study for the National Institute of Drug Abuse, Dr. Lloyd Johnston, predicted that the rise in drug use among teenagers seemed to be at an end. A similar trend had been reported by the military.

Tax Reduction Proposed — President Reagan urged Congress, **Feb. 18,** to cut the size of the budget. He proposed a $695.5 billion budget for fiscal year 1982 with a $45 billion deficit. The cuts he recommended, which would total $41.4 billion, would affect 83 major programs plus an annual tax cut for individuals of about 10% over the next three years. Only the military budget was to be increased, by $7.2 billion. Hardest hit by the budget cuts would be the arts, transit, the poor, and synthetic fuels. On **Feb. 26,** after he was informed that his advisors had underestimated the growth in federal spending for fiscal year 1982, Reagan ordered further cuts in the budget of from $3 billion to $6 billion. Then, on **Feb. 27,** it was announced that he had decided on an additional budget cut of from $10 billion to $13 billion to achieve his goal of reducing the growth of federal spending and offset the budgetary miscalculation on spending in the next fiscal year.

Agreement Reached on Three Mile Island Case — The owners and builders of the Three Mile Island (Pa.) nuclear reactor settled the claims of thousands of people, **Feb. 21.** These claimants all lived within a 25-mile radius of the plant, and the settlement totaled $25 million. Most of the money would be paid for business losses incurred during the evacuation of the area some 2 years before. It was still possible, however, that other claimants would file suit, individuals for personal injury, and local governments for the added costs of police and other services, for example.

Consumer Price Increases Slow — The Labor Department reported **Feb. 25** that consumer prices rose by 0.7 of 1% in January. Although this represented the 1st time since **Aug. 1980** that the annual increase for the previous year was lower than 10% (it was 9.1%), it was noted that the report had been made too early to register the increase in gasoline and heating oil prices.

International

Aid to El Salvador Rebels Linked to USSR — *The New York Times* reported, **Feb. 6,** that captured rebel documents indicated that the Soviet Union and Cuba had agreed in 1980 to deliver tons of weapons to Marxist guerrillas in El Salvador. According to the *Times,* these weapons were to come from stockpiles of U.S. arms that had been seized in Vietnam and Ethiopia. It had been previously noted that many of the arms captured from the guerrillas had been U.S.-made rifles, mortars, and machine guns. On **Feb. 11,** in response to a U.S. charge that Nicaragua was permitting Cuba to use its territory for shipment of arms to El Salvador, the Nicaraguan Sandinist government urged the Salvadoran rebels to seek a political settlement with the Duarte government in El Salvador. The U.S. charge against Nicaragua had resulted in the cutting off of economic aid to that government. On **Feb. 14** Vladilen M. Vasev, minister counselor of the Soviet Embassy in Washington, denied that the Soviets had supplied arms to the leftists. He did, however, admit that the Soviets had been sending arms to Cuba and Ethiopia without restrictions. The Salvadoran Marxist-led Democratic Revolutionary Front received more pressure from its allies, **Feb. 15,** to negotiate with the ruling junta. Because of the U.S. charge of Soviet intervention, Social Democratic parties in Latin America and Europe, as well as the governments of Nicaragua, Mexico, Panama, and Ecuador had urged this negotiation. Congressional leaders backed a plan for more aid to the Duarte government, **Feb. 17.** The State Department, **Feb. 19,** provided the embassies of friendly governments in Washington with a memorandum stating that the Salvadoran insurgency was a textbook case of indirect armed aggression by the Soviets. The leftist leaders in El Salvador declared that the U.S. had sent 100 military advisors to help the junta in the war. The U.S., however, admitted only to 18. An assessment by the Pentagon, announced **Feb. 20,** said that the army of the Salvadoran government was so ill-prepared to fight that it had no hope of defeating the leftists. Because of that, Secretary of State Alexander M. Haig, Jr. stated that it was even more important to cut off the flow of arms from Cuba and the Soviet Union. On **Feb. 21,** leaders of the guerrillas said that they were short of arms, but that they were trying to re-equip themselves by buying on the black market. They refused to admit that some of their arms had come from Communist countries. West German spokesmen said, **Feb. 22,** that there was a possibility that they might become involved in an attempt to bring the warring factions in El Salvador together for negotiations in Bonn. The State Department declared, **Feb. 23,** that the campaign against Soviet-bloc arms shipments had resulted in a slowing down of the flow of weapons. On **Feb. 24** President Reagan reiterated his support for the junta, although he had no intention of involving the U.S. in the fighting.

New Polish Government Eases Labor Strife — In a move seen as an attempt to increase the military's influence in the face of continued labor unrest, Polish Prime Minister Jozef Pinkowski was replaced, **Feb. 9,** by the Minister of Defense, Gen. Wojciech Jaruzelski. The government and leaders of Solidarity, the independent labor union, had announced, **Feb. 2,** that they had made some progress in ending wildcat strikes in southern Poland. However, talks between the government and wildcat strike leaders had broken down in the province of Bielsko-Biala, **Feb. 4,** and Lech Walesa, the leader of Solidarity, had warned that the Polish workers would stage sit-ins if any force were used on the workers of Bielsko-Biala. The government had yielded, **Feb. 6,** accepting the resignations of the provincial governor and 3 deputies, ending the strike. Gen. Jaruzelski appealed, **Feb. 12,** for 3 months without strikes to let his government have time to deal with the economic crisis. Walesa responded that he agreed in principal with the moratorium, but needed to talk with government representatives before making a final decision. On **Feb. 14,** Walesa met with Deputy Premier Mieczyslaw Rakowski, and indicated that he had approved a 90-day period without strikes. On **Feb. 18,** the government negotiated an end to a 26-day student sit-in at the University of Lodz, granting them the right to have a student union that would not be controlled by the communist party. However, on **Feb. 26,** only one week after the strike respite had gone into effect, 450 students occupied the rector's offices at a teachers college in Olsztyn, protesting inadequate accommodations.

Peru and Ecuador Clash — Foreign ministers of the Organization of American States met in an emergency meeting, **Feb. 2,** to consider the border conflict between Peru and Ecuador. Both countries had called a cease-fire in the Amazon jungle region on the border because of appeals from the U.S., Pope John Paul II, and other Latin American countries. Ecuador asked the OAS to condemn Peru for aggression, and Peru asked for a committee to be sent to investigate an invasion of a border that had been set by a treaty of 1942. Both sides had claimed heavy losses to the other side, but Ecuador claimed that only 2 of its soldiers were killed, and Peru admitted to the loss of 1 man.

Iran-Iraq War Continues — On **Feb. 2,** Iran estimated that its army had killed more than 200 in major counterattacks against Iraqi troops and Kurdish insurgents in Kurdistan Province and Azerbaijan in the last 2 days. On the other side, Iraq claimed that 166 enemy soldiers had been killed and 2 helicopters and a Phantom jet had been shot down. On **Feb. 3,** it was reported that Saudi Arabia and other Persian Gulf countries had been cooperating in the shipment of arms, including tanks, to Iraq in its war against Iran. The prospects for peace were bolstered by a report from a conference of foreign ministers of nonaligned countries in New Delhi, India on **Feb. 9.** Agha Shahi, the Foreign Minister of Pakistan, said that he had received a favorable reaction from Iran to a proposal for a visit to both warring countries by the leaders of 8 Islamic nations and organizations. After a visit by President Saddam Hussein of Iraq to the battlefront in the hills of Ilam, in Iran, **Feb. 10,** Iraqi forces began a local offensive against the Iranians. The Iraqis reported that 163 Iranians were killed, and another report numbered the Iraqi dead at 45. President Abolhassan Bani-Sadr of Iran discussed the principles with former Prime Minister Olof Palme of Sweden, a United Nations envoy, on which agreement could be reached to end the war **Feb. 19.** There was some hope that Iran and Iraq would agree to allow 70 foreign vessels to leave the disputed Shatt al Arab waterway, where they had been trapped since September of 1980. But the Iranians seemed united in backing the refusal to enter peace talks before the Iraqis withdrew from Iran. On **Feb. 28,** the high-level Islamic peace mission arrived in Teheran to attempt to end the war. The group included the Presidents of Bangladesh, Gambia, Guinea, and Pakistan, as well as high-ranking officials of Malaysia, Senegal, Turkey, and the Palestine Liberation Organization. The mission was scheduled to have talks with Bani-Sadr and Ayatollah Ruhollah Khomeini.

Iran Releases Jailed American — Iranian authorities met, **Feb. 4,** with Swiss diplomats to discuss the fate of an American woman who had been held for 9 months in Teheran. The woman was Cynthia B. Dwyer, a freelance journalist from Buffalo, N.Y., who was arrested on **May 5, 1980** and accused of spying for the CIA. Dwyer had gone to Iran in April of 1980 in the hope of writing articles about the situation there. Dwyer was one of 3 Americans still being held in Iran. The others were Mohi Sobhani and Zia Nassri. Sobhani was released **Feb. 4.** On **Feb. 11,** Dwyer was on her way home.

Guerrillas Feuding in Zimbabwe — Prime Minister Robert Mugabe of Zimbabwe vowed, **Feb. 11,** to take harsh action against warring black guerrilla troops. Nineteen people had been killed in ambushes over a period of 4 days. On **Feb. 12,** it was reported that the government had used helicopter gunships and mortars against the insurgents on the outskirts of Bulawayo, and Mugabe threatened to use air force fighter planes against them. More than 100 lives had been lost. The guerrillas had been divided into two factions—those loyal to Mugabe and those loyal to Joshua Nkomo, the Minister of Internal Affairs until he was demoted by Mugabe. By **Feb. 13,** more than 300 people were dead and the Nkomo guerrillas had been crushed.

Lucas Accused in Guatemala — The bullet-riddled bodies of 14 young people, all showing signs of torture, were found east of Guatemala City, **Feb. 15.** Heavy gunfire also erupted in front of the headquarters of the liberal Christian Democratic Party, leaving 1 dead and 3 wounded. On **Feb. 17** Amnesty International accused Guatemalan Pres. Romeo Lucas Garcia of directly supervising an intelligence agency that carried out political assassinations. They estimated that since he took office in June 1978, 5,000 people had been seized without warrant and killed by security forces and that 615 others who had been seized were still missing.

Pope John Paul Travels Again — Pope John Paul II began a trip to the Far East on **Feb. 16** with a mass in a Karachi, Pakistan stadium. Twenty minutes before he reached the stadium, a grenade exploded near a reviewing stand, killing the man, allegedly a Pakistanian Moslem, carrying it and wounding 3 others. The Pope arrived in Manila, on **Feb. 17,** and was greeted at the airport by church leaders and Pres. Ferdinand E. Marcos and his wife. The next day, the Pope delivered a speech on human rights as Marcos sat beside him. In the speech, the Pope praised the lifting of martial law in the Philippines. On **Feb. 18,** still in Manila, the Pope celebrated the beatification of 16 martyrs killed in Japan in the 1630's for their faith, and spoke to the people of one of the slums of Manila. The next day, he was welcomed to Cebu in the Philippines. In 2 separate speeches he restated his views in favor of priestly celibacy and his opposition to abortion. On **Feb. 23,** the Pope made a brief stop in Guam, and then traveled on to Japan, where he visited Emperor Hirohito in Tokyo, **Feb. 24.** On **Feb. 25,** John Paul became the first world leader to visit the atom-bombed cities of Nagasaki and Hiroshima in Japan. While in Nagasaki he asked that Vatican aides examine the possibilities of resuming pastoral work in China and of opening diplomatic relations with Peking.

Coup in Spain Attempted — A group of Civil Guards seized the lower house of the Spanish Parliament, **Feb. 23,** and took most of the county's leaders as hostages. Several of the guardsmen fired long bursts from automatic weapons as they marched into the Congress of Deputies and ordered the legislators to lie on the floor. None of the 347 members and a few senators who were present were reported hurt. Simultaneously, army troops with tanks briefly took over the state-run television station outside Madrid and the head of the military region in the Valencia area proclaimed a state of emergency. By **Feb. 24,** other military units had joined with the Valencia contingent and the Madrid Civil Guard. However, 18 hours after it had begun, the uprising collapsed. Much of the credit for the collapse was given to King Juan Carlos who appeared on television after the station was liberated by loyal troops, denouncing the seizure and pledging his faith in democracy. The Civil Guard released the legislators and then were imprisoned. Their leaders surrendered. The general in Valencia was relieved of his post, as was the army's deputy chief of staff. On **Feb. 27,** more than 1 million people marched through the center of Madrid in support of King Juan Carlos and in condemnation of the attempted takeover. By **March 8,** 80 of the 150 Civil Guards who stormed the parliament had been released from prison.

Mrs. Thatcher Visits U.S. — Prime Minister Margaret Thatcher of Great Britain visited President Reagan in the White House, **Feb. 26.** The leader of Britain's austerity program said that both she and Reagan were determined "to sweep away the restrictions that hold back enterprise." On

Feb. 27, she declared that the free world was counting on Reagan's administration to restore faith in the U.S. dollar and cautioned the president not to be too quick to accept a Soviet proposal for a meeting between himself and the Soviet leader, Leonid I. Brezhnev. On **Feb. 28,** Thatcher promised Britain's support for Reagan's blocking of Soviet encroachment in El Salvador, Africa, and the Persian Gulf.

General

Life Expectancy Lowered in Poor Nations — In a **Feb. 8** report from the Overseas Development Council it was announced that the death rates in developing countries had been increasing. These death rates had been dropping for the last few years and there was hope that they would eventually reach the point where the population of the developing countries would live to be 60 to 65 years old, on average, just as is the case in the industrialized nations. The chief factors cited were a slowdown in economic development and the advances in controlling infectious diseases, which meant that the people were being attacked by diarrheal diseases, respiratory infections, and malnutrition, which are more difficult to control.

Wastes to Be Used to Make Gasohol — United Bio-Fuel Industries announced, **Feb. 15,** that they would build a $60 million plant in Petersburg, Va., to make ethanol from municipal garbage and from agricultural, industrial, and forest wastes. Ethanol, or grain alcohol, can be used to make gasohol, which is usually 1 part alcohol to 9 parts gasoline. It was expected that the plant could produce ethanol at a cost of from 70 cents to $1.15 per gallon.

Fungus Linked to Marijuana — Researchers at the Medical College of Wisconsin in Milwaukee announced, **Feb. 18,** that marijuana contains a common household fungus that could lead to allergic reactions or lung damage when smoked. It also could cause life-threatening infections. The fungus belongs to the aspegillus family and its spores are not damaged by burning.

X-Rays Linked to Heart Diseases — Dr. Genevieve M. Matanoski of the Johns Hopkins University School of Hygiene and Public Health suggested, **Feb. 20,** a possible connection between chronic exposure to X-rays and an increased risk of fatal heart disease. In her study she found that the death rate from heart disease was 29% higher in radiologists than in eye doctors.

Mrs. Harris Found Guilty — Jean S. Harris was convicted in White Plains, N.Y., **Feb. 24,** of murder in the 2d degree. The former headmistress had been accused of the multiple shooting on **Mar. 10, 1980** of her companion and lover for 14 years, Dr. Herman Tarnower, the famed Scarsdale Diet Doctor. In addition, she was convicted on 2 counts of criminal possession of a weapon. Her defense had been that the doctor had died in a struggle over the gun that she had intended for her own suicide. On **March 20,** she was sentenced to a minimum of 15 years to life in prison.

Endangered Species Debated — An international meeting of conservationists and animal traders began on **Feb. 25** in New Delhi, India to discuss restrictions on the international traffic in endangered animals and plants. The discussion centered on revision of the lists of those species whose trade is totally banned and those species whose exports are controlled. The real discussion centered on parrots and whales. Naturalists favored putting all parrots on one list or the other, rather than just a few species. They also wanted to end all commercial whaling.

Disasters — A fire in a circus tent in Bangalore, India killed 66 and injured some 500 people, **Feb. 8** . . . In a stampede after a soccer match in Athens, **Feb. 8,** at least 24 fans were crushed to death . . . Seventy Soviet military officers, including up to 24 admirals and generals, died in a plane crash on the outskirts of Leningrad, **Feb. 13** . . . At least 17 people were killed and 30 injured, **Feb. 14,** in a fire that swept through a 23-story office building in Sao Paulo, Brazil . . . An early morning fire engulfed a Dublin discotheque, **Feb. 14,** killing 44 and injuring 129, many of them teenagers . . . On **Feb. 15,** it was announced that 2 months of heavy rain had flooded nearly 400,000 acres in the vicinity of Butuan, the Philippines, killing 220 and causing sickness in more than 14,000 people . . . The drought and heat waves of 1980 killed more than 1,300 people, it was announced on **Feb. 19** . . . On **Feb. 25** a series of earthquakes hit Athens and the surrounding area, killing 15 and wounding 53.

MARCH

National

Reagan Cuts Budget — In a speech to a conference of the National League of Cities, President Reagan, **Mar. 2,** defended his budget-cutting program and asked that the mayors in the U.S. help him push it through. On **Mar. 10,** he delivered his budget for fiscal 1982 to Congress. It called for a total of $695 billion, with a deficit of $45 billion, and for a reduction in spending of $13.8 billion in addition to the $34.8-billion announced in February for a total of $48.6 billion. Additional budget cuts were to be made in the programs of the Dept. of Agriculture for food and nutrition, the Dept. of Education, the National Oceanic and Atmospheric Administration, the National Science Foundation, NASA, and REA. On **Mar. 18,** the Senate Budget Committee recommended more than $35 billion in cuts, and **Mar. 19,** it unanimously adopted a package of budget cuts totaling $36.4 billion—more than had been recommended by the president.

U.S. to Aid Atlanta Investigations — Pres. Reagan announced, **Mar. 5,** that the federal government would give nearly $1 million in grants to finance mental health and social programs relating to the case of the missing and murdered children in Atlanta. At that time, 19 out of 21 missing black children had been found dead. Also on **Mar. 5,** 2 missing children were found alive and safe. But a 20th body, that of 13-year-old Curtis Walker, was found the next day in the South River, south of Atlanta. By **Mar. 14,** law enforcement officials had reached the conclusion that fewer than half of the dead children had been killed by the same person. On **Mar. 18,** however, activists, saying that the murders were racially motivated, promised to begin armed patrols, despite the warnings of Mayor Maynard Jackson of Atlanta. On **Mar. 31,** the body of 13-year-old Timothy Lyndale Hill was found in the Chattachoochee River.

Prices Up, Unemployment Slightly Down — Producer prices rose 0.8% in February, the Labor Dept. reported on **Mar. 6.** The rise was probably caused by the price increases announced by the OPEC nations in December and January. At the same time, employment in the U.S. rose a bit, with the unemployment rate declining to 7.3% compared to 7.4% during the previous 2 months, according to the Bureau of Labor Statistics. The Consumer Price Index rose 1% during February, it was announced on **Mar. 24,** probably because of the Reagan Administration's decontrol of oil prices.

Three Mile Island Cleanup Continues — Government specialists said, **Mar. 9,** that there was hope that the cleanup of the disabled nuclear reactor at Three Mile Island could be made with very little risk to workers. The job, however, would probably take at least until 1988. A total of $37 million had been budgeted for the job, and the idea of sealing up and abandoning the plant had been rejected, on the grounds that that would make the area a permanent waste disposal site.

Reagan Visits Canada — Demonstrators gathered outside the Canadian Parliament, **Mar. 10,** to protest the U.S. intervention in El Salvador as Pres. Ronald Reagan arrived in Ottawa on his first foreign visit as a president. Meeting with Prime Minister Pierre Elliott Trudeau, Reagan talked about the importance of curbing inflation, aid to El Salvador, and the problem of acid rain. On **Mar. 11,** he addressed Parliament, deploring the Russian invasion of Afghanistan and pledging continuing friendship with Canada. Trudeau, **Mar. 12,** asked that the U.S. administration act to save fish stocks in the Atlantic, since Reagan had scrapped the Canadian treaty which had encompassed a plan to manage and share the fish stocks on the Georges Bank.

Coal Strike Looms — Last minute efforts to avoid a strike of coal miners failed, **Mar. 17,** and a strike was threatened to begin on **Mar. 27.** It would affect 160,000 miners in the coal fields of Appalachia and the Midwest. By **Mar. 19,** 12,000 miners had gone out in wildcat strikes, protesting the industry's plan to run mining shifts on Sundays and claiming that the mine owners wanted them to work 56-hour weeks. The miners also requested changes in the pension plan. On **Mar. 27,** the members of the United Mine Workers rejected a tentative agreement from the Bituminous Coal Operators Association and went on strike. Scattered nonunion mines were shut down as well. The coal companies had offered a pay increase of 36% over 3 years, but eliminated the royalties that they would pay to the union when they bought nonunion coal.

International

U.S. Sends More Advisers to El Salvador — As the political situation in El Salvador remained unstable, the U.S. State Department announced, **Mar. 2**, that it would expand its military assistance to that country by sending 20 additional military advisers and $25 million in military equipment to the Duarte government. The decision evoked immediate protests from Congressional Democrats, chiefly centered on fear that such an action would endanger the prospects for a peaceful solution to El Salvador's internal woes. President Reagan asserted, however, on **Mar. 3**, that there was no likelihood that U.S. armed forces would be sent to the tiny Central American country. On **Mar. 11**, U.S. officials stated that it appeared that leftist guerrillas might be running low on weapons. This decrease was attributed to a decision by Nicaragua and Cuba to reduce their aid to the rebels. An additional 12 U.S. military advisers, all members of the Army's Special Forces, or Green Berets, arrived in El Salvador, **Mar. 22**. This brought the total of advisers to 54, 15 of whom were Green Berets. It was also announced that the Reagan administration would ask for another $60 million in assistance for El Salvador. The Defense Department had announced, **Mar. 20**, that 18 of the 54 military advisers sent to El Salvador would return to the U.S. by July, following the completion of their assignments.

New Party Formed in Britain — Twelve members of Parliament resigned from the Labor Party, **Mar. 2**, and said they would form a new political party—the Social Democrats. The new party immediately became the third-ranking party in the Commons, edging in front of the 11-member Liberal Party contingent. The reason given for the formation of the new party was that the Labor Party was gradually becoming too left-wing. In another political move, Bernadette Devlin McAliskey, the civil rights leader who was recovering from gunshot wounds, announced, **Mar. 21**, that she would run for Parliament.

Pakistani Airliner Hijacked — Three political dissidents hijacked a Pakistani jetliner, **Mar. 2**. Carrying what appeared to be hand grenades, they forced the plane to fly, with 117 people aboard, to Kabul, Afghanistan. The hijackers were demanding the release of 90 Pakistanis that were being held in Karachi as political prisoners. On **Mar. 6**, they killed one of the hostages, a Pakistani diplomat, and set a deadline for the next day to release the prisoners in Pakistan. Two American women and 2 Pakistani men were freed by the hijackers **Mar. 7**, and Pakistan agreed to free 5 of the political prisoners. On **Mar. 9**, the plane was flown to Damascus, Syria, with 116 passengers and 7 crew members still aboard, and one more hostage was released. The hijackers continued their threats to blow up the plane, but on **Mar. 12**, Pakistan agreed to free 55 of the political prisoners. The next day, Libya agreed to take in these prisoners and the hijackers agreed to free their hostages when the prisoners were safe. The hijackers surrendered **Mar. 14**, after 13 days, when the prisoners landed in Aleppo, Syria, instead of Libya. The Syrian government announced, **Mar. 19**, that the hijackers would be allowed to stay in that country until another country agreed to take them in. But Pakistan asked that they be extradited home.

Iran-Iraq War Continues — The Islamic Commission, trying to end the war between Iran and Iraq, decided, **Mar. 3**, that it would carry specific cease-fire proposals to Teheran and Baghdad the following day. They presented their proposals to Ayatollah Ruhollah Khomeini and Pres. Saddam Hussein and then returned to Jidda, Saudi Arabia, to await their replies. On **Mar. 15**, President Hussein of Iraq offered to arm dissident Iranian rebels, indicating that the cease-fire proposals had been rejected. Heavy fighting then

Reagan Wounded in Assassination Attempt

Pres. Ronald Reagan was shot in the chest by a would-be assassin **Mar. 30**, in Washington, D.C., as he walked to his limousine following an address to a labor meeting at the Washington Hilton. The alleged assailant, John W. Hinckley, Jr., rapidly fired several shots before he was overpowered by police officers and secret service men. Also wounded by the burst of gunfire were Presidential Press Secretary James S. Brady, who was critically injured, secret service agent Timothy J. McCarthy, and police officer Thomas K. Delahanty.

Surgeons removed a .22-caliber bullet from the president's left lung and began treating him for lung collapse. Brady had been struck above the left eye, Delahanty in the neck, and McCarthy in the liver.

Vice President George Bush immediately cut short a trip to Texas to return to Washington, D.C., to carry out the necessary presidential duties. In Washington, Secretary of State Alexander M. Haig immediately rushed to the White House Situation Room and asserted over nationwide television that he was in charge of the administration's crisis management plan. The statement caused controversy inasmuch as Bush arrived in Washington within hours of the shooting and was able to take charge of the crisis. Also Haig, in reporting on the president's condition, mistated the presidential order of succession, declaring that the secretary of state rather than the speaker of the House followed the vice-president.

By **March 31**, the doctors admitted that the president, who was making tremendous progress, had been in danger of losing his life immediately after the shooting. He had been having breathing problems, was having chest pains, was spitting up blood, and his blood pressure was low and falling. Nevertheless, he had managed to joke with his wife, Nancy, and the surgeons and nurses. That same day Reagan was able to meet with senior aides and sign a bill eliminating an increase in dairy price supports.

Meanwhile, Brady showed miraculous improvement in his condition. He was conscious and could move his right arm and leg, despite extensive damage to his brain tissue.

On **Apr. 1**, Reagan was moved from the intensive care unit of the hospital to a private room, began to eat solid food, and was in what was termed "good" condition. Brady was able to speak and breathe without the aid of a respirator. McCarthy was listed as "good" and Delahanty was in "serious but stable" condition.

The FBI revealed, **Apr. 2**, that the bullets fired on **Mar. 30** were of an explosive type, and the surgeons who operated on the president had not known that they could have detonated at any time.

On **Apr. 2**, it was admitted that Reagan had lost more blood than had been previously disclosed—about 3.7 quarts, or more than half the amount found in a normal adult body. On that same day, Hinckley was found fit to stand trial after a psychiatric examination.

James S. Brady was able to tell his physician, **Apr. 3**, that he felt fine. It was also announced that he could move the right side of his body almost normally, and some response in the left side had been detected.

By **Apr. 4**, Reagan was able to talk with aids at considerable length, although he was put on antibiotics to improve his breathing and hold down his fever. He was able to leave his bed on **Apr. 7**, and his temperature was described as "near normal." Timothy J. McCarthy was released from the hospital that day, and Brady was able to drink by himself and eat some solid food.

By **Apr. 8**, the president was able to work for some 2 hours a day. The next day his antibiotic dosage was cut. On **Apr. 11**, Reagan was released from the hospital—12 days after he was shot—and returned to the White House. He refused to leave the hospital in a wheelchair, electing to walk out from the lobby to his limousine.

The president's work load was up to 4 or 5 hours per day on **Apr. 18**. Brady underwent another operation on **Apr. 23** to close holes that had allowed air to seep into his brain. Air continued into James Brady's skull, however, and he was confined to a reclining position. On **May 5**, he was operated on again to remove blood clots.

Reagan made his first public appearance since the shooting on **Apr. 28**, speaking to a joint session of Congress to ask approval of his plans for cutting the budget. The speech was interrupted by thunderous applause many times.

broke out **Mar. 19,** and 124 Iranians and 17 Iraqis were killed in the Gilan area of western Kermanshah Province. On **Mar. 21,** the Iraqis launched missile attacks at 2 locations in the oil-rich Iranian province of Khuzistan.

Soviets in Orbit — Tass, the Soviet press agency, announced **Mar. 12,** that the Soviet Union had launched a manned space capsule, the Soyuz T-4. The two astronauts aboard were to effect a linkup with the orbiting Salyut 6 space station.

Great Train Robber Held, Released — Ronald Biggs, who escaped from a British jail in 1970 after being sentenced for taking part in a major train robbery, was reported missing from his Brazilian home, **Mar. 18.** The robbery had involved the theft of $7 million dollars worth of British currency from a London-Glasgow train in 1963. He had been carried out of a Rio De Janeiro restaurant on **Mar. 16** and had not been seen since. On **Mar. 23,** Biggs turned up as a prisoner in Barbados, having been kidnaped by agents of a London-based security company. The Barbadian police freed the 5 kidnapers **March 25,** but held Biggs in jail pending an extradition attempt. Biggs himself was released, **Apr. 23,** and permitted to return to his home in Brazil after a court in Barbados refused his extradition to England.

Two More Hijackings — A Honduran airliner was hijacked by 4 men, **Mar. 27,** and forced to fly from Nicaragua to Panama City. The hijackers demanded that Honduras free 16 jailed Salvadoran leftists. Honduras refused to cooperate, and the hijackers surrendered to Panamanian officials, requesting asylum in Cuba. On **Mar. 29,** hijackers holding an Indonesian jet at the Bangkok airport in Thailand shot and wounded an American hostage when he tried to escape. Fifty-five passengers and crew members remained on the plane. The hijackers were demanding that Indonesia release 20 political prisoners, then raised the number to 80, then 84. On **Mar. 31,** Indonesian commandos rushed the airliner, killed 4 of the 5 hijackers, and freed the hostages. The gun battle lasted but 3 minutes.

Polish Situation Remains Tense — A month of continuing tension and strife, both among workers and farmers, eased slightly, **Mar. 30,** when a last-minute agreement between Solidarity, the Polish workers' union, and the government averted an indefinite general strike scheduled for Mar. 31. On **Mar. 27,** some 13 million Polish workers had gone on a 4-hour warning strike. The day before, Warsaw Pact military maneuvers in and around Poland, which had begun **Mar. 18,** had been extended indefinitely. The White House had expressed concern that the Polish government might crack down on Solidarity or that the Soviet Union might undertake "repressive action" in Poland. The month had started on a low note with reports that Poland was having trouble feeding its citizens. The government cut sugar rations by half, **Mar. 1,** and announced that it would institute meat rationing on April 1. A temporary rationing of butter was also under consideration. Agriculture Minister Jerzy Wojtecki cited as the reason for the rationing the fact that 1980 had been the worst year in the previous 20 for agricultural production, accompanied by a serious decline in the number of livestock. Political tension increased when Polish and Soviet officials met, **Mar. 4,** in Moscow and agreed that the defense of communism in any country was not only a matter for that country, but also for the entire socialist community. This was viewed by many as a resurgence of the Brezhnev Doctrine which holds that communist countries have the right to intervene by force to safeguard communism in Eastern Europe. Signs that the Warsaw Pact would shortly begin military maneuvers in and around Poland heightened concern that armed intervention in Poland was a possibility. Sporadic labor unrest and demonstrations peppered the nation. On **Mar. 9,** 450 farmers met in Poznan in the first national congress of their still unrecognized union. A demonstration by farmers in Bydgoszcz, **Mar. 19,** was broken up by riot police. Many of the farmers, who were seeking to form a union, were hospitalized. The following day, at least 4 2-hour strikes were held in northern cities to protest the harassment. The leaders of Solidarity broke off all talks with Polish authorities and told union members to prepare to go on strike.

General

New Galaxies Reported — Astronomers at the Lick Observatory in California, **Mar. 3,** reported that they had discovered a galaxy estimated to be 10 billion light years away. The farthest galaxy discovered previously was 8 billion light years away. This new galaxy had been observed for a total of 40 hours over a period of 3 years. Over the same time, 3 other galaxies were observed that were almost as distant from the earth. A distance of 10 billion light years means that the light from that source has taken 10 billion years to get to earth.

Whale Trade Curtailed — Delegates from 37 countries attending the Convention on International Trade in Endangered Species of Wild Fauna and Flora in New Delhi, India, voted, **Mar. 6,** to outlaw trade in the products of 3 species of whale. Japan voted against the measure, and the U.S., the USSR, and several other countries abstained. The international trade affected by the ban was the oil, meat, and bones of the sperm, the sei, and the fin whales, which are virtually the only species of whales now hunted commercially. Under the provisions of the treaty, customs officials will now confiscate any products made from the protected wildlife.

Teenage Drinking on Increase — One-third of the nation's high school students are problem drinkers, according to a report released **Mar. 19.** The Research Triangle Institute had conducted a study for the National Institute on Alcohol Use and the National Institute on Drug Abuse and found that 13% more girls than boys were moderate drinkers and 14% more boys than girls were heavy drinkers. The problem drinker was defined as someone who is drunk at least 6 times a year or experiences alcohol-related problems with friends, family, school, the police, or while driving.

Space Shuttle Accident — A countdown rehearsal in Florida for the space shuttle Columbia was delayed because of the death of one technician and injuries to two others **Mar. 19.** The death was caused by a lack of oxygen when the 3 men were exposed to a pure nitrogen atmosphere in an enclosed area around the engines inside the shuttle.

Postal Rates Up — First class postage was increased from 15 cents to 18 cents on **Mar. 22.** The United States Postal Service also said that it would petition the Postal Rate Commission to get a further raise to 20 cents. Postal card rates went from 10 cents to 12 cents, and parcel post rates increased by 13%. The reason given for the rise was that the Postal Service had a current deficit of $306 million, and it needed $3.75 billion more than its current rates brought in just to break even.

Burnett Awarded $1.6 Million — In a libel suit against the *National Enquirer,* actress Carol Burnett was awarded a $1.6 million settlement **Mar. 26.** It was found that the newspaper had lied in 1976, saying that Burnett had been intoxicated at an encounter with then Secretary of State Henry Kissinger at a Washington restaurant. Several other personalities, including Johnny Carson, have suits pending against the tabloid. The Enquirer's lawyers indicated that they would appeal the decision.

The award was cut in half, **May 13,** by Judge Peter Smith of Los Angeles Superior Court. Burnett indicated that she was satisfied with the $800,000 figure and on **June 4** announced that she would give $100,000 each to the University of Hawaii and the University of California at Berkeley for their journalism programs.

Disasters — A train carrying tourists home from an Argentine beach collided, **Mar. 8,** with 2 derailed freight cars, killing 45 and injuring 120 . . . Nineteen people died in a fire in a residential Chicago, Ill., hotel, **Mar. 14** . . . A condominium under construction in Cocoa Beach, Fla. collapsed **Mar. 28,** killing 11 construction workers and injuring 22.

APRIL

National

No End to Coal Strike — The chief negotiator for the Bituminous Coal Operators Association, B. R. Brown, announced, **Apr. 1,** that there were no plans to resume talks with the United Mine Workers who were on strike. And several coal mine owners predicted that it could be weeks before bargaining would begin again. But on **Apr. 10,** Brown agreed to open the talks again. On **Apr. 16,** violence broke out in the West Virginia coal fields when 2 mine union officials were fired upon by 2 coal mine guards. In Kentucky, mine workers on a picket line threw rocks at a coal truck. On **Apr. 24,** snipers attacked a convoy of coal trucks in

Kentucky. And, as there was still no progress toward settlement of the strike, the Federal Department of Energy reported that the 160,000 member walkout had cut the country's coal production by half.

Trouble Increases in Atlanta — Two more bodies were found in the Chattahoochee River near Atlanta, Ga., bringing the total number of black youths reported missing to 24, and the number of bodies found to 22, it was announced **Apr. 2.** The special task force was still hard at work, charting, measuring, and tracing patterns of information. More than 35 investigators were assigned to the cases, and it was said that they believed that one person was responsible for all the crimes. The count rose to 25 on **Apr. 6** when a retarded man missing since **Mar. 30** was added to the list. His body was found in an abandoned apartment building on **Apr. 9.** The body of a 15-year-old boy was found **Apr. 19,** raising the total of known dead to 24, and the body of a 23-year-old man, found **Apr. 21,** increased the tally to 25. On **Apr. 17,** the body of a 21-year-old man was found in the river and the count rose to 26 dead.

Unemployment Steady, Prices and GNP Up — The Labor Department's Bureau of Labor Statistics announced, **Apr. 3,** that the March unemployment rate was at the same level as that of February—7.3%. The total number of unemployed people was 7,764,000. This was taken as a sign that the U.S. economy had remained reasonably strong. Also on **Apr. 3,** the Bureau reported that the Producer Price Index rose by 1.3% in March, making the total year's increase 16.8%. The reason given for the rise was the increase in prices for oil products. The Consumer Price Index was up 0.6% in March, the Labor Department announced **Apr. 23.** This was an important figure as it is the one government statisticians use to calculate the future increase for the year and the resultant cost of living increase for social security recipients. The Commerce Department announced, **Apr. 20,** that the Gross National Product of the U.S. grew by 6.5% during the previous year. The first quarter of 1981 had shown the biggest gain in the GNP since the second quarter of 1978.

Eased Car Standards Proposed — The Reagan Administration suggested, **Apr. 6,** easing or eliminating 35 air quality and safety regulations on automobiles. The proposal was designed to help the domestic auto industry fight Japanese imports. It was calculated that this measure would save U.S. car manufacturers more than $9 billion during the next 5 years. The main things to be eliminated were the most stringent emissions standards, bumper crash-worthiness standards, and the equipping of larger automobiles with air bags.

Crime Increases — The Justice Department's Bureau of Justice Statistics reported, **Apr. 7,** that 30% of the nation's 80.6 million households were victimized by one or more crimes in 1980. Many of these homes experienced crimes every year, but most of these crimes were nonviolent. Higher income homes were more likely to be victimized, and urban and suburban homes were more often burglarized than rural homes. Violent crimes were experienced in 6% of all homes, and these crimes included rape, robbery, and assault. Members of 14% of the households experienced personal larceny away from home, such as purse snatching, pocket picking, and theft. Black and white households were victimized to an almost equal extent.

Space Shuttle Columbia Takes Off — Despite the deaths of two technicians as a result of an accident at the launch pad in March, the Space Shuttle Columbia was sent into orbit **Apr. 12.** The two astronauts aboard, civilian John W. Young and Navy Capt. Robert L. Crippen, soon discovered that some 17 heat-shielding tiles had ripped off the structure, probably during the launch. Fortunately, they were in a non-critical area. Meanwhile, the Columbia's 2 solid propellant booster rockets were retrieved from their ocean landing point by 2 specially built ships. A Soviet trawler that appeared to be attempting to pick up the rockets was warned away by a Coast Guard helicopter. As the astronauts were putting the spacecraft through tests on **April 13,** they received a congratulatory radio call from Vice President George Bush. On **Apr. 14,** the Columbia returned, speeding out of orbit and gliding to a safe, unassisted landing on the desert near Edwards Air Force Base, Calif. On **Apr. 15,** space agency officials reported that the spaceship was in excellent condition, and should be able to make as many as 100 trips into orbit in the future.

Reagan Ends Curb — The 15-month-old curb on exporting grain to the Soviet Union was lifted by President Reagan, **Apr. 24.** Repeating his opposition to the Soviet invasion of Afghanistan, Reagan said that he recognized the curb as being ineffective and harmful to U.S. farmers.

Agnew Ruled to Be Bribe Taker — Former Vice President Spiro T. Agnew, **Apr. 27,** was ordered to repay the state of Maryland a total of $248,735. Maryland Judge Bruce C. Williams ruled that Agnew had taken thousands of dollars in bribe money from contractors while he was governor of that state. He then ordered that $147,500 worth of kickbacks and $101,235 in interest be returned, mentioning that the money really belonged to the people of Maryland. Agnew's lawyers indicated that they would appeal.

Abscam Investigations Wind Down — Rep. Raymond F. Lederer (D., Pa.), in the face of expulsion from Congress, resigned his seat in the House of Representatives, **Apr. 29.** He had been convicted, **Jan. 9,** of accepting a $50,000 bribe in the Abscam operation. On **Apr. 30,** Sen. Harrison A. Williams Jr. (D., N. J.) was convicted of bribery and conspiracy charges connected to the same operation. Williams, the 7th member of Congress to be convicted on Abscam charges, vowed that he would not resign from the Senate. However, he faced up to 15 years in prison, as well as possible expulsion from that body.

International

Iran-Iraq War Continues — The 2d attempt by Islamic leaders to end the Iran-Iraq war was termed a failure, **Apr. 1.** Although the 9-man mission, headed by Pres. Ahmed Sékou Touré of Guinea, met with Iranian leaders in Teheran, **Mar. 30,** and with Iraqi leaders in Baghdad, **Mar. 31,** the talks were fruitless. Iraq insisted that Iran recognize Iraqi sovereignty over the Shatt al Arab waterway, and Iran refused to talk of peace while Iraqi forces were in Iran. But the peace mission announced, **Apr. 2,** that they would send 2 members back for more discussion. On **Apr. 4,** the Islamic Republic Party of Iran demanded the overthrow of Iraq's president, Saddam Hussein, despite the desire of Pres. Abolhassan Bani-Sadr of Iran to take a more moderate path toward ending the war. That day Iranian jet fighters struck 4 air bases inside Iraqi territory, destroying a number of Soviet-built TU-22 long-range bombers, according to Iran's defense minister, Javad Fakuri. On **Apr. 6,** Bani-Sadr called the Islamic peace mission's proposal for a cease-fire vague. Fighting intensified on **Apr. 15** in the southern oil-producing province of Khuzistan.

Thai Generals Stage Abortive Coup — Thai army generals overthrew the one-year-old government of Gen. Prem Tinsulanonda on **Apr. 1,** and established a revolutionary committee under the direction of Gen. Sant Chitpatima. The Thai constitution was abolished and the cabinet and parliament were dissolved. Gen. Prem. was allowed to remain as the commander of the army. On **Apr. 2,** Prem declared that he was still prime minister and that he had the support of King Phumiphol Aduldet. The rebellion ended **Apr. 3,** as thousands of troops loyal to Prem moved into Bangkok. Sant escaped by helicopter, and Prem promised leniency for the rebels. On **Apr. 5,** 100 rebel officers were put under temporary detention pending trial by a military court.

Clashes in Lebanon; Israel Intervenes — Clashes between Syrian troops and Christian militiamen near Zahle, Lebanon, beginning **Apr. 1,** signaled an end to the ceasefire that had been in place. The fighting was the most violent since the 1976 civil war. A group of Roman Catholic clergymen had asked for the removal and replacement of Syrian troops from Lebanon with UN troops. By **Apr. 5,** 136 people had been killed and 500 wounded in Zahle and Beirut. Secretary of State Haig condemned the Syrians, **Apr. 6,** accusing them of brutality. On **Apr. 8,** Pres. Elias Sarkis of Lebanon declared a cease-fire, and the Red Cross sent ambulances to Zahle to evacuate about 20 people who had been wounded there. Israel admitted, **Apr. 14,** that it was giving aid to the Lebanese Christians, and, **Apr. 15,** shelling erupted in Beirut. The southern Lebanese port city of Sidon was attacked by Christian militia forces, **Apr. 19,** and at least 16 people were killed and 60 wounded. On **Apr. 20,** the Beirut airport was shelled by Christian forces and Israeli jet pilots reported accurate hits on guerrilla positions in southern Lebanon. Fighting between Israeli-backed Christian forces and Palestinian guerrillas intensified **Apr. 21,** and at least 11 people were killed and 40 wounded. At the same time, shells and rockets struck many of the sections of Beirut as Syrian forces exchanged fire with Christians. By **Apr. 22,** fighting had broken out not only between Syrians and Christians, but also between two Moslem factions—the Shiites and the Baathists. By **Apr. 25,** the total death toll in Lebanon had risen to 400, and Israeli jets were still bombing southern Lebanese targets. On **Apr. 28,** Israeli jets shot down 2 Syrian helicopters in central Lebanon, and Syria moved antiaircraft missles into the Bekaa Valley in eastern Lebanon to counter the Israeli attacks. This was the first time Israel had intervened in fighting between Syria and Lebanese Christian forces in that area. The intervention raised serious international concern that the Lebanese clashes might escalate to wider fighting.

Soviet Threat to Poland Eases — As the West carefully watched Warsaw Pact military maneuvers in and around Poland during the first week in April, speculation that the Soviet Union might invade Poland to stem internal disquiet grew. On **Apr. 3,** the U.S. State Department issued a warning that any unjustified military action against Poland would not be tolerated. However, on **Apr. 7,** at the 16th Congress of the Czechoslovak Communist Party in Prague, Soviet leader Leonid Brezhnev stated that Poland would be able to solve its own problems. An announcement that Soviet troops would return to their bases followed Brezhnev's speech. But defense ministers of the NATO countries warned the USSR, **Apr. 8,** that military intervention in Poland would harm East-West relations, indicating that they did not believe that the Soviet army manuevers were really over. On **Apr. 25,** U.S. Sec. of State Alexander M. Haig Jr. said that if the Soviets were to invade Poland, the administration would impose a ban on all U.S. trade with the Soviet Union and would reinstate the grain embargo.

US Sub Sinks Japanese Ship — A Japanese freighter and an U.S. nuclear-powered submarine collided in the East China Sea, **Apr. 9,** and the cargo ship sank. Thirteen of the crew of the freighter, the *Nissho Maru*, were rescued by Japanese destroyers from rafts, but the captain and first officer were not recovered. On **Apr. 10,** the U.S. Navy issued a statement of regret, but the Japanese expressed anger that the navy had waited 36 hours before telling the Japanese government of the incident, and that the men on the submarine, the *George Washington*, had made no effort to rescue the survivors. On **Apr. 11,** the navy claimed that the submarine had surfaced, but could not find any survivors nor any sign of the freighter, which had gone down quickly. Some of the survivors, however, claimed that they had seen the sub close by and had waved their hands at an American aircraft circling above them. The U.S. ambassador to Japan, Mike Mansfield, made a formal apology to the Japanese foreign minister, Masayoshi Ito. By **Apr. 20,** the U.S. Navy had accepted liability for the sinking and Japanese lawyers had indicated that a claim of some $4.2 million would be presented.

Riots Break Out in London — Hundreds of youths, most of them black, rioted in the Brixton section of London on the nights of **Apr. 11 and 12.** Stones, bottles, and firebombs were thrown at police, stores were set afire, and many automobiles were overturned and torched. More than 1,000 policemen were sent into the district, and more than 30 of them were sent to the hospital. Two dozen buildings were destroyed, 20 civilians injured, and 200 arrested. The government set up a judicial inquiry, **Apr. 13,** to investigate the causes of the riots. Then, on **Apr. 20,** black youths threw rocks at police during a fair in a north London suburb and another fair in Western London. The police arrested 40 of the rioters. Meanwhile, in 5 coastal cities, youth gangs battled each other and the police. The police reported 153 arrests. The following day a mob of black youths rampaged through East London, breaking windows, overturning cars, and threatening policemen. Eight were taken into custody.

Lévesque Is Winner — Premier René Lévesque and his separatist Parti Québécois were elected to a new term, **Apr. 13.** in the Quebec election. After the election, the party controlled 80 of the 122 seats in the National Assembly against only 42 for the Liberal Party.

Polish Rural Solidarity Formalized — The Polish parliament, **Apr. 16,** recommended the legalization of Rural Solidarity, an independent union of the nation's 3.5 million private farmers. The government acceded, **Apr. 17,** and signed an official agreement with union representatives to grant the union official recognition by May 10.

General

Artificial Skin Developed — Doctors at the Massachusetts General Hospital in Boston reported, **Apr. 23,** that artificial skin had been successfully used to replace skin destroyed by burns. The artificial skin is made of cowhide, shark cartilage, and plastic, and can perform many of the functions of real skin. The use of the artificial skin avoids the need for drugs that suppress the body's immune reactions, and, therefore, does not increase the victim's chances of getting a fatal infection. Ten burn patients had been successfully treated with the new skin, of which 3, it was judged, would surely have died without the treatment.

Laetrile Condemned — It was announced, **Apr. 30,** that a government-sponsored study of the use of the drug, laetrile, by 163 patients with advanced cancer had found that the drug was not effective. Most of these patients had cancer of the colon, lung, or breast, and 104 of them had died since July. The report also mentioned that some 70,000 Americans had tried the drug, which is made from apricot pits, and 22 states have legalized its use. Advocates of the use of laetrile said that these test results proved nothing, charging that the drug used in the study was not pure laetrile.

Artificial Bone Developed — A team of researchers at Harvard University reported, **Apr. 30,** that they had developed a new demineralized bone powder. The substance had been used as implants in patients with birth defects to form bones where none had existed, and to help mend the bones of patients whose fractured bones had failed to heal. Fifty-five implants in 44 patients had been performed in 2½ years, many of them to repair cleft palates and missing or deformed parts of the jaw and face.

Disasters — A tornado hit West Bend, Wis. **Apr. 4,** killing 6, injuring 100, and causing $15 million in damages . . . A British freighter sank in the Pacific about 300 miles off Costa Rica, **Apr. 8,** and 17 were listed as missing . . . A blast in a Carbondale, Col. coal mine, **Apr. 15,** trapped 15 miners, all of whom died . . . Fifteen persons were killed in a midair collision between a commuter airliner and a private plane over northern Colorado, **Apr. 17** . . . Filipino terrorists killed 11 and wounded 155 in a grenade attack on a Roman Catholic cathedral in Davao, **Apr. 19** . . . A Nile tourist boat ran aground and sank **Apr. 22,** killing 6, and injuring 12 . . . Rains, floods, and mudslides in Venezuela, **Apr. 25 and 26,** killed 20 and left 4,000 homeless.

MAY

National

Tragedies in Atlanta Escalate — As little progress was being made in tracking the killer or killers of more than 20 black children in Atlanta, Ga., Atlanta police announced, **May 1,** that they were adopting a new policy in hope of avoiding delays in locating missing persons. The missing persons unit was placed under the command of the task force investigating the murders of the young blacks killed there since July 1979. On **May 7,** a missing 14-year-old boy was found alive, although it had been feared that he had been one of the victims. Muhammad Ali, the former heavyweight boxing champion, announced, **May 9,** that he would donate $400,000 to the reward fund for information leading to the arrest of the killer. The 27th victim was found east of the city, **May 12.** He was a 17-year-old whose body was found only hours after he had been reported missing. On **May 13,** the total rose to 28 when the body of another 17-year-old boy was discovered. The number of volunteers searching for bodies increased to 75, **May 23,** up from 40 the week before, and a new victim, a black man in his late 20s, was found on **May 24.** The number of missing and murdered young blacks rose to 30 on **May 25.** On **May 26,** Lee Patrick Brown, Atlanta's Commissioner of Public Safety, indicated that it was believed that the victims were being selectively chosen, rather than attacked at random.

Extradition Request Signed in Buffalo Killings — The Governor of Georgia, George Busbee, signed an extradition request from the State of New York, **May 2,** for a suspect in the 1980 Buffalo, N.Y. slayings. A 25-year-old white army private, Joseph G. Christopher, a prisoner at Ft. Benning Ga., had been linked with the killings of several black men in Buffalo, N. Y. the previous September. Two nurses from Ft. Benning had testified that Christopher had boasted that he had done the killings. Law enforcement officials said that he had also bragged about killing black men in New York City in December 1980.

Reagan Budget Has Ups and Downs — The House of Representatives adopted a budget, **May 7**, that would curtail federal spending, thereby endorsing Pres. Reagan's plan for a $689 billion budget and projected deficit for the fiscal year 1982. The administration announced, **May 12**, the details for a reduction in Social Security benefits that would sharply reduce the pensions of workers who retire before the age of 65. The payments would be somewhat reduced to those who retire at 65 or older, and the limits on income for the elderly that tended to reduce their pensions would be eliminated. On **May 20**, in the first Congressional rebuff to the new president, the U.S. Senate rejected 2 elements of the program—the cut in payments to early retirees and the reduction in benefits that exceed those necessary to achieve a financially sound system. On **May 21**, the president suggested that Congressional leaders of both parties meet with administration leaders to prepare a bipartisan effort to save Social Security. He stated that he had 3 goals: to preserve the integrity of the Social Security Trust Fund and the system's basic benefit structure; to hold down taxes that support the system; and to eliminate all abuses "that can rob the elderly of their rightful legacy."

Prices Up; Unemployment Steady — The Bureau of Labor Statistics reported, **May 8**, that producer prices had increased only 0.8% in April because there had been smaller rises in the cost of food, gasoline, and heating oil. The Bureau also stated that the U.S. unemployment rate stayed at 7.3% for the third consecutive month, since the economy had created about a half million additional jobs and the number of unemployed people declined slightly. It was announced by the Commerce Dept., **May 19**, that the gross national product had grown at an 8.4% annual rate in the first quarter of 1981. This was the strongest quarterly growth since the spring of 1978, and was a revision of the estimate of 6.5% made in April. Consumer prices in April had risen a mere 0.4%, it was reported by the Labor Dept. **May 22**. This was the lowest monthly increase since Oct. 1977.

Soviet Jetliner Detained — Federal law-enforcement agents stopped a Soviet airplane at Dulles International Airport near Washington, D.C., **May 13**. Several pieces of cargo were seized and examined in a search for evidence of a violation of export law controls. Some radio navigation equipment was confiscated, but it was later learned that the equipment had been properly licensed for export. The USSR promptly protested, saying that the search of the plane was a criminal, barbarous act, a bandit operation, and an insolent provocation. The U.S. State Dept. denied that they had directed the search, but maintained that no violations of diplomatic immunity had occurred, since searches were not made of diplomatic baggage or mail pouches. On the next day, William T. Archey, Acting Commissioner of Customs, admitted to 2 technical violations. On **May 15**, Soviet authorities in Moscow claimed that customs agents had caused nearly $200,000 in damages to the airliner, and they were reserving the right to demand compensation. The State Dept. in Washington said that they had no intention of apologizing to the Soviet Union.

Prison Riots Flare Up — Inmates of the Southern Michigan Prison in Jackson rioted on the morning of **May 22** in protest over an alleged unauthorized lockup prior to a search for hidden weapons. Twenty-four prisoners were injured, most of them by smoke inhalation from fires set by other inmates and one guard was injured by a glass jar that had been thrown at him. One small domitory building was destroyed by fire and several other buildings were damaged. Order was partially restored, but hundreds of prisoners refused to return to their cells and remained in 2 of the prison's courtyards. All but 150 returned to their cells after dark, when they had presented a list of grievances to the warden. By the next day, all the inmates were back in their cells.

In another prison incident also on **May 22**, fights involving some 450 prisoners broke out in the Michigan Reforma-

tory in Ionia. Four guards were reported injured, as were 42 prisoners. Guards and state troopers fired tear gas and herded the inmates back into their cells. The warden said that the inmates would be responsible for cleaning up the mess caused by their 8-hour riot. Three guards were taken hostage, **May 23**, at the Maximum Security Prison near Carson City, Nev. but were later released unharmed. The uprising ended when guards, shooting automatic weapons in the air, herded the prisoners back into their cells. Then, on **May 26**, another riot erupted at Jackson. Some 1,000 inmates, many of them armed with clubs, took over a cell block and set fire to domitories. This riot lasted for 9 1/2 hours, and it took 165 state troopers and 200 prison guards to stop it. Wearing gas masks and armed with rifles, they pushed the rioting inmates back into the cell blocks. At least 21 people were injured. Six guards at the prison walked off the job, **May 28**. Also on May 26, 150 to 200 prisoners started a disturbance at Marquette State Prison in Michigan. They set 3 fires and refused to return to their cells. All of them were later confined to their cells. In yet another flare-up, after 2 days of fighting, 40 inmates were transferred from Sumter Correctional Institution, in Bushnell, Fla., to tougher facilities, **May 26**. Eight inmates and 2 guards had been injured when a group of black prisoners attacked another group of black prisoners, and then a group of black inmates turned on a group of whites.

Butz Pleads Guilty — Former Agriculture Secretary Earl L. Butz pleaded guilty, **May 22**, to a charge of filing a false income tax return in 1978. He admitted, in Federal District Court in Ft. Wayne, Ind., that he had avoided paying taxes on more than half his income of $148,000, chiefly from speaking fees for lectures that he had given that year. Judge Jesse E. Eschbach said that he would need time to study an investigative report before he passed sentence. Butz, who was Secretary of Agriculture in the Nixon and Ford Administrations from 1972 to 1976, could receive up to 5 years in prison and be fined $10,000.

Teamster Boss Indicted — Roy L. Williams, the interim president of the International Brotherhood of Teamsters, along with 4 other men, was indicted, **May 22**, for conspiracy to bribe a senator, Howard W. Cannon (D, Nev.). Williams denied the charges. The accusation was that the conspiracy took place between late 1978 and July, 1979. The accused men were also indicted for wire fraud and traveling interstate to further the plan of bribery. The men allegedly offered Cannon the right to purchase a 5.8-acre plot of land in Las Vegas from the pension fund of the Teamsters Union.

Elderly Population Rises — The Census Bureau reported, **May 23**, that there were 25.5 million people over 65 years of age in the U.S. and that that represented an increase of 28% over the 1970 figure. According to the report, from 1970-1980, the median age in the nation rose from 28 to 30 years of age, partly because the number of elderly people increased and partly because the number of children under 15 dropped from 58 million to 51 million. The change in the distribution of age, it was predicted, would affect the government's allocation of such funds as programs for the elderly and programs for younger people—schools and day-care centers, for example. The figures also showed that there were 6 million more women than men in the U.S.

Highway Deaths Increase — Small automobiles and speeding on the highways were given as the main reasons for the recent increase in highway deaths in a National Highway Traffic Safety Commission report released **May 23**. The commission announced that the number of Americans dying in automobile accidents was again increasing after the sharp decline caused by the imposition of the 55-miles-per-hour speed limit. In 1979, the last year for which statistics were available, small cars were involved in 55% of all fatal crashes, although they represented only 38% of the number of cars on the road. The commission also predicted that auto deaths would increase by 30% by 1990. This would represent a rise from 27,000 to 35,000 per year.

Aircraft Crashes on Carrier Deck — A Marine electronic combat aircraft crashed on the deck of the U.S. Navy aircraft carrier *Nimitz,* **May 26**. It burst into flames, causing a fire that killed 14 men, destroyed 3 fighter planes, and damaged 16 other aircraft. In addition, 48 sailors were injured. The crash occurred during a night training operation. On **May 28**, the *Nimitz* steamed into Norfolk (Va.) Harbor, and despite the memory of the crash, returned to sea, **May 30**, to resume night landing exercises.

Coal Strike Ends — United Mine Workers leaders, **May 29,** approved a new agreement that would give miners a 38% increase in wages and benefits, and, **June 6,** the miners themselves approved the new contract. The agreement ended the 72-day-old strike that had cost the miners more than $50 million a week in wages. Earlier in the month, as the strike had gone into its 7th week, striking coal miners in eastern Ohio had, **May 7,** vandalized nonunion coal trucks at a loading dock along the Ohio River and power had been knocked out at a nonunion mine in eastern Kentucky.

International

Spanish Troubles Mount — Sporadic terrorist activity continued to plague Spain as a 62-year-old Spanish general, Andrés Gonzáles de Suso, was killed by gunmen, **May 4,** in Madrid. A policeman and 2 terrorists were also killed in the incident. One terrorist was captured and identified as a member of the First of October Antifascist Resistance Organization. The group also claimed responsibility for the death of 2 Civil Guards in Barcelona that day. On **May 7,** Basque terrorists bombed the car of Lieut. Gen. Joaquin Valenzuela, a senior military aide to King Juan Carlos, wounding him and killing a colonel and 2 other soldiers in Madrid. Two young men belonging to E.T.A., the Basque separatist organization, had pulled up beside the general's staff car at a red light and put a satchel containing a bomb on the roof. Several weeks later, on **May 23,** 25 heavily armed men seized the Barcelona headquarters of a bank, took 200 people hostage, and demanded the release of 4 officers from prison. The 4 officers had been involved in the attempted governmental takeover in February. The next day, police commandos raided the bank, killed one terrorist, captured the rest, and freed the hostages. The police alleged that at least 2 of the captured men had affiliations with the National Labor Confederation, the main anarchist group in Spain.

Mideast Clash Escalates — U.S. officials expressed concern, **May 4,** that Israel and Syria were moving toward a new confrontation over Lebanon. The U.S. had been unable to persuade Syria to withdraw antiaircraft missiles from Lebanon. When Israel made the same demands, the Syrians rejected them, **May 5,** as "ridiculous." On **May 6,** First Deputy Foreign Minister Georgi M. Korniyenko of the USSR arrived in Syria to discuss the cessation of hostilities. Meanwhile, Kuwait assured Syria of its support against Israel, and Israeli jets were sighted over Lebanon for the first time since Syria had brought in its missiles. And, although urging caution, Korniyenko pledged fresh Soviet military supplies for Syria, **May 8.** On **May 11,** Prime Minister Menachem Begin of Israel announced that Syria had increased the number of antiaircraft batteries in Lebanon and added that the Israeli air force might have no choice but to retaliate. According to the Israeli military command, some missiles were fired at Israeli planes on **May 12,** but no damage was done and the planes returned to base. But Syria announced that one of the planes had indeed been shot down.

On **May 14,** a Syrian missile shot down an Israeli drone—an unmanned photographic reconnaissance craft. Begin increased his demands, **May 21,** calling on Syria to remove its missiles not only from Lebanon, but also from Syrian territory along the Lebanese border. Another Israeli drone was downed **May 22,** and yet another on **May 25.** On **May 27,** Pres. Reagan recalled his special envoy to the Middle East, Philip C. Habib, to consult on what the U.S. should do to try to avert an Israeli-Syrian clash. Habib had been conferring with mideast officials since **May 7,** traveling among Israel, Syria, Lebanon, and Saudi Arabia. The next day Israeli jets destroyed a complex of Libyan antiaircraft missile batteries south of Beirut, and the Lebanese said that the jets had also struck at Palestinian guerrilla encampments in southeastern Lebanon. Lebanese Christian militiamen exchanged heavy rocket and artillery fire with Syrian forces in Zahle, **May 30.**

Bobby Sands Dies — Robert Sands, the imprisoned Irish Republican Army leader and member of Parliament, died, **May 5,** in Maze Prison near Belfast, Northern Ireland, after a 66-day hunger strike. Sands, who was serving a 14-year prison sentence for a firearms violation, was elected to Parliament from Northern Ireland on **Apr. 9,** although he was already in the 6th week of his hunger strike. The purpose of the hunger strike was to force the British government to grant political prisoner status to Irish Nationalist inmates, rather than treating them as common criminals. The weakening Sands had been given the last rites of the Roman Catholic Church on **Apr. 17,** and, on **Apr. 20,** Roman Catholic youths in Londonderry had battled soldiers and police with stones and bottles to show support for the dying man. Five cars were hijacked and a bus was set on fire. The British, however, felt that concessions to Sands would lend political legitimacy to the IRA in their fight to reunite Northern Ireland with Ireland, and Prime Minister Margaret Thatcher had refused, **Apr. 21,** to meet with 3 members of the Irish Parliament who had hoped to discuss Sands' case with her. That day, youths in Londonderry attacked British security forces for the 7th straight day. Sands had refused to see 2 envoys of the European Human Rights Commission, **April 24,** because they wanted to urge him to end his fast. On **Apr. 28,** Pope John Paul II had sent his private secretary, the Rev. John Magee, to meet with Sands. On **May 5,** the day of Sands' death, Thatcher served notice in the British House of Commons that British policy would not be changed concerning Northern Ireland, and that political status would not be granted to convicted criminals. The IRA staged a military funeral for Sands, **May 7,** in Belfast. Several thousand people marched, and thousands more lined the streets along the route of the funeral procession. As violence flared in Londonderry, **May 9,** more than 300 homemade gasoline bombs and bottles filled with sulphuric acid were thrown at police. Twenty-one people were arrested. On **May 12,** Francis Hughes, another IRA hunger striker, died in the Maze prison, and more clashes were reported in Londonderry. The third Irish hunger striker, Raymond

---

Pope John Paul II Shot in St. Peter's Square; Escaped Murderer Seized

Pope John Paul II was shot and seriously wounded, **May 13,** as he was being driven through St. Peter's Square at the Vatican. Standing in the slowly-moving car, surrounded a crowd of some 10,000, the Pope was suddenly struck by 2 pistol bullets and wounded in the abdomen, right arm, and left hand. A militant Turkish terrorist, Mehmet Ali Agca, a convicted murderer, was accused of the crime and taken into custody. In addition to the Pope, two women were also hit by the gunfire.

The Pontiff underwent 5 hours and 25 minutes of surgery, during which parts of his intestine were removed. The 2 women were also treated. Ann Odre, of Buffalo, N.Y., underwent surgery for the removal of a bullet in her chest, and Rose Hill, of Jamaica, underwent treatment for a slight bullet wound in her arm.

The Pope remained on the critical list, **May 14,** and the prognosis was guarded because of the risk of infection. The next day it was reported that the Pope was still in pain, but was regaining strength, although suffering from a slight fever. By **May 16,** although the fever remained, John Paul II had regained some of his normal intestinal activity.

On **May 17,** the Pope left his bed for the first time and was able to record a message that was broadcast to pilgrims and tourists in St. Peter's Square. He forgave his assailant and said that he regarded his own sufferings as an offering to the church and the world. The following day he was moved from the intensive care unit of the hospital to a 4-room private suite.

It was reported by Italian police sources, **May 19,** that Agca had admitted that he had considered killing Queen Elizabeth II of Britain, the Secretary General of the UN, and the President of the European Parliament. That same day, the Pope's temperature dropped to normal and he had his first nourishment by mouth, and, the next day, he had his first walk and first semisolid food.

By **May 23,** the Pontiff was declared out of danger. On **June 3,** exactly 3 weeks after he had been shot, John Paul II walked unaided from the hospital, blessed the crowd that had formed, and was driven home to his apartment in the Vatican. In 20 minutes after his return, he appeared in his white vestments in the window of his apartment overlooking St. Peter's Square and waved to the crowd.

McCreesh, died in Maze Prison, **May 21,** and more violence broke out in Belfast. The following day, Patrick O'Hara became the fourth hunger striker to die at the prison, and U.S. Sen. Edward M. Kennedy (D, Mass.) wrote Prime Minister Thatcher asking that she institute prison reform that would end the hunger strikes. Thatcher paid a 9-hour visit to Northern Ireland, **May 28,** meeting with the commanding officers of the police and the army, but repeated her stand on the granting of political status to those convicted of a crime. On **May 29,** 4 IRA hunger strikers and 5 other prisoners in Maze Prison declared that they would run for seats in the Irish Parliament.

U.S. Expels Libyans — Libya was ordered, **May 6,** to close its diplomatic mission in Washington, D.C., and to remove the mission staff from the country. The Reagan administration had compiled a list of complaints, including alleged efforts by Libyans to kill opponents of the regime of Col. Muammar el-Qaddafi, the Libyan leader, and Libyan incursions in Chad, the Sudan, and Egypt. It was pointed out that this action did not constitute the breaking off of diplomatic relations, but did reduce U.S. and Libyan relations to the lowest level at which diplomatic relations can be maintained.

Suzuki Visits Reagan — Japan's Prime Minister, Zenko Suzuki, began 2 days of talks with Pres. Ronald Reagan, **May 7.** Reagan admitted making a slip on the grain embargo ruling, indicating that Japan should have been consulted before the measure was enacted, and vowed that the U.S. would closely consult with Japan on matters of interest to that country. When Reagan had abruptly rescinded the embargo on grain to the USSR, Japanese businessmen had felt that they had sacrificed in imposing restraints on some exports to the Soviet, and resented the U.S. reversal of policy. Suzuki vowed, **May 8,** even greater efforts to improve Japan's defense capabilities, especially for the patrolling of sea lanes in the western Pacific, providing naval protection for a perimeter of several hundred miles around Japan. The U.S. had feared that these sea lanes were undefended.

Salvadoran Troubles Continue — Six members of El Salvador's armed forces were arrested as suspects in the killing of 3 American nuns and a lay worker in Dec., 1980, it was announced **May 9.** Salvadoran Defense Minister José Guillermo García refused to say which branch of the service they belonged to, but it was reported that they were members of the National Guard. On **May 11,** the Senate Foreign Relations Committee voted to impose restrictions on U.S. military aid to El Salvador unless Pres. Reagan were to certify that the Salvadoran government was making significant progress in improving human rights and making economic and political changes.

Swedish Government Resigns — The coalition government of Swedish Prime Minister Thorbjorn Falldin collapsed, **May 8,** after a dispute over how and when to begin lowering the country's high income tax rates. The coalition had had but a one-vote majority in Parliament. The withdrawal from the coalition of members of the conservative Moderate Party, **May 4,** had paved the way for a vote of no confidence for Falldin. Rather than face this vote, which would require a new election, both Falldin, leader of the Center Party, and Foreign Minister Ola Ullsten, head of the Liberal Party, resigned.

France Elects New President — In an upset victory, Francois Mitterrand, the Socialist Party leader, defeated the incumbent president of France, Valéry Giscard d'Estaing, **May 10.** For the first time since 1958, France had elected a president from the left and the center-left. The following day, as turmoil hit the French financial markets, prices tumbled, the value of the franc dropped, and the price of gold rose. The Finance Ministry sent extra customs officers to airports and border crossings to prevent the smuggling of money and other valuables outside the country. Mitterrand, **May 23,** set June 14 and 21 as dates for elections to the new National Assembly.

Italian Government Resigns Amidst Scandal — Following the disclosure that many prominent Italian public figures, possibly including several cabinet members, belonged to a secret Masonic lodge, the government of Arnaldo Forlani resigned, **May 26.** Justice Minister Adolfo Sarti had resigned, **May 23,** following reports linking him to the lodge. Calling itself Propaganda Due, the Masonic lodge had been linked to currency law violations, fake kidnapings, espio-

nage, and the murder of a journalist. The list of 953 members, released by the government Apr. 21, included the names of cabinet ministers, members of Parliament, judges, and army and police generals.

President of Ecuador Dies — Jaime Roldós Aguilera, the president of Ecuador, was killed in an airplane crash near the Peruvian border, **May 24.** In addition to the president, his wife, Marta, his defense minister, Maj. Gen. Marco Subía Martínez, and 2 military aides were also killed. At age 40, he was the youngest president in the Western Hemisphere, and had been elected in 1979 by the largest margin in Ecuadorean history after 9 years of civilian and military dictatorships.

Turkish Jet Hijacked — A Turkish airliner was hijacked by 4 leftist extremists at the Ankara airport in Turkey, **May 24.** The hijackers forced the plane, carrying 91 passengers and crew members, to fly to Bulgaria. The hijackers threatened to kill 5 U.S. bankers aboard unless they were paid $100,000 and 47 prisoners in Turkish jails were released. When the plane landed at Burgas, Bulgaria, 17 passengers, all of them Turkish citizens, were released and 2 others escaped. On **May 25,** some of the terrorists were overcome by passengers and crew members and the rest were captured by Bulgarian security forces on the ground, after being lured off the plane by promises of holding a news conference. Turkey asked for the extradition of the 4, **May 26.**

Bangladesh Leader Killed — President Ziaur Rahman of Bangladesh was shot and killed, **May 30,** in the city of Chittagong. It was thought that a little-known opposition group, Biplabi Parishad, was responsible for the act, and this group claimed to have taken control of the government of the Chittagong area. The Bangladesh government announced, **June 1,** that it had regained control of Chittagong and that the revolution had been crushed, and rebel troops had fled the city.

General

Billie Jean King Confesses — Billie Jean King, the tennis champion, admitted, **May 1,** that she had had a lesbian relationship with her former secretary, Marilyn Barnett. Her statement came 2 days after Barnett had filed a lawsuit asserting that she was entitled to a portion of King's property. The tennis star also indicated that the relationship had been over for some years, and that she had never promised Barnett financial support or a share in her California home.

The Sinking in Florida — A sinkhole that appeared suddenly in Winter Park, Fla., consumed a frame cottage, 6 imported cars in a car lot, and a camping vehicle, **May 9.** It was reported that the hole was 2 city blocks wide, and still growing. By 5:30 p.m. it was 1,000 feet wide, 170 feet deep, had cut water and power lines, and was growing a rate of a few inches per hour. The cause was an apparent lowering of the underground water table, which caused the soil to dry out and shrink. By evening the house had disappeared, and the dirt had been eaten away around a swimming pool and the backs of adjoining business establishments.

Disasters — A military jet exploded over a western Maryland farm, **May 6,** killing all 27 crew members . . . An Argentine jetliner crashed into the Río de la Plata near the Buenos Aires Metropolitan Airport, **May 7,** during a thunderstorm, killing 30 . . . A collision between a bus and a train in central Java, **May 7,** killed 31 and injured 20 . . . When an electrical spark flew into a pocket of methane in a coal mine near Redstone, Col., an explosion resulted that killed 15 on **May 8** . . . Wind-whipped fire in Mandalay, Burma, **May 10,** destroyed more than 6,000 buildings and left 35,000 homeless. The death count reached 5 . . . Floods swept Austin, Tex., **May 25,** killing 10, with 8 others listed as missing.

JUNE

National

Reagan Budget Maneuvering Continues — Pres. Ronald Reagan promised, **June 1,** to make no compromise in his tax-cutting plan, except for changes in its size and starting date. Reagan said he would delay the starting date from Jan. 1 to Oct. 12, 1981, and would settle for a 5% instead of a 10% cut, in the first year, but would insist on a 10% cut in each of the next 2 years. But, **June 4,** he acceded to some of the demands of Congressional leaders and scaled back his original proposal for tax breaks for businesses by some 30%. He also endorsed, for the first time, tax breaks for individuals such as easing the higher tax rate for married couples and the lowering of gift and estate taxes. A coalition of Republicans and conservative Democrats in the House voted, **June 25,** to allow the president's package to be voted on as one entity, rather than splitting it into 6 separate votes. On **June 26,** the House gave Reagan his second successive victory by adopting his $38.2 billion in budget cuts. The bill then went to a Senate-House conference.

James Earl Ray Stabbed — James Earl Ray, the convicted slayer of the Rev. Martin Luther King Jr., was stabbed 22 times, **June 4** in the Brushy Mountain State Penitentiary in Tennessee. After an hour of surgery involving 77 stitches, Ray was pronounced in good condition. On **June 5,** it was announced that 4 members of a Black Muslim group were suspected of being the attackers.

Lefever Rebuffed — The Senate Foreign Relations Committee, **June 5,** voted that the Senate reject the nomination of Ernest W. Lefever as assistant secretary of state for human rights. Five hours later, Lefever withdrew from consideration for the post. His withdrawal was the first defeat on a Reagan nomination. In a last-ditch effort to show support for his nominee, Reagan, **June 2,** had said that he would not retreat one inch from his endorsement. A tough confirmation fight over the nomination of Lefever had been expected because of his human rights position.

Prices and Unemployment Up — Labor Department officials announced, **June 5,** that unemployment in May had risen from 7.3% to 7.6%—the first significant increase in a year. It was also noted that there was a particularly high number of layoffs in auto manufacturing because of a decrease in car sales. The Labor Department also announced that prices of finished goods rose in May only 0.4 of 1%, an indication, it was said, that inflation was slowing down.

Haitian Deportations Begin — Justice Department officials, **June 5,** directed the Miami authorities to hold deportation hearings of newly arrived Haitians in open court, one case at a time. Miami immigration authorities had been conducting mass deportation proceedings for a week against newly arrived Haitians. These had been held in locked courtrooms with private lawyers barred. Thirty-five cases a day had been processed; 140 Haitians had been through the proceedings, and 25 who said that they were not afraid to return to their homeland had been deported. On **June 6,** it was announced that there was a backlog of 6,000 cases of Haitians facing hearings. The Immigration and Naturalization Service revealed, **June 9,** that 76 other hearings from the previous week had been reviewed and all 76 were to be deported, since their rights had not been violated. But, on **June 10,** the 76, who were scheduled for deportation by charter flight, were granted a reprieve when a Federal District Judge granted a stay until a hearing could be held on a motion to stop the deportations. The motion was filed by the Haitian Refugee Center, Inc. and the American Civil Liberties Union.

Blanton Convicted — Former Tennessee Gov. Ray Blanton and 2 aides were convicted in Federal District Court in Nashville, **June 9,** of extortion, conspiracy and mail fraud. The crimes were committed in 1976 during the Blanton administration and concerned the sale of liquor store licenses. Blanton faced a maximum of 70 years in prison and a $29,000 fine. On **June 10,** Blanton ordered his attorney to file an appeal.

Suspect in Atlanta Slayings Arrested — Atlanta, Ga., police, **June 21,** arrested Wayne B. Williams, a 23-year-old black man, and charged him with the murder of Nathaniel Cater, aged 27, whose body had been found in the Chattahoochee River in May. District Attorney Lewis Slaton guessed that as many as 13 of the other deaths being investigated were similar in nature to the slaying of Cater. Williams' murder case was forwarded to a grand jury, **June 23,** and the district attorney said that he would seek an indictment within 30 days. Earlier in the month, on **June 3,** Atlanta police had taken Williams into custody to be questioned about the killings of 28 young blacks in and near that city. Williams was held through the night, but released the next day without charges being brought against him. On **June 7,** it was indicated that analyses of carpet samples,

sweepings, pieces of clothing, and animal hairs taken from Williams' home showed matchups with fibers found on 9 of the bodies in the case, but, on **June 8,** District Attorney Slaton said that police still lacked sufficient evidence to arrest Williams. Although under constant police surveillance, Williams briefly eluded police, **June 10,** escaping from his home by hiding on the floor of his father's car. He was later found, but not until he had been charged with 5 traffic violations during his disappearance. Williams, **June 12,** filed suit against several newspapers, TV stations, and networks, the mayor, the public safety commissioner of Atlanta, and the heads of law enforcement agencies. He charged that his rights had been violated and his reputation damaged by the publicity he had been given, and asked that the news releases linking him to the killings be stopped. A federal judge ruled, **June 15,** that attorneys for Williams could argue privately for an order barring such publicity.

Supreme Court Rules on Draft — The U.S. Supreme Court ruled, **June 25,** that the Constitution permits Congress to limit draft registration to men. It was also assumed, in the decision, that the Constitution permits such a limitation in the draft itself. The ruling allowed Congress and the administration to revive the draft without including women. The decision outraged feminists, civil libertarians, and opponents of the administration's military position. Previously, a special 3-judge Federal District Court had ruled, July 18, 1980, that male—only registration discriminated between the sexes and was, consequently, in violation of the Fifth Amendment.

International

Crisis in Bangladesh — An army rebellion against the government of Bangladesh collapsed **June 1,** just 2 days after Pres. Ziaur Rahman had been assassinated. The leader of the uprising, Maj. Gen. Manzur Ahmed, was arrested and government troops took control of the southeastern port city of Chittagong, which was the only city to have fallen into the rebels' hands. On **June 2,** the government announced that it had also arrested 20 army officers who had been involved in the plot, and that 3 of them had been killed after being taken into custody. One of them was Gen. Manzur. Abdus Sattar, a 75-year-old jurist, was appointed acting president, and, on **June 4,** promised to hold a presidential election within 180 days.

Aid Pledged to Anti-Libya African Nations — The Reagan Administration announced, **June 2,** that the U.S. would support all African nations that would resist intervention from Libya, citing the presence of Libyan troops in Chad. Libya had intervened in the Chad civil war between followers of Pres. Goukouni Oueddei and those on the side of a former defense minister. The Administration had asked Congress for increases in military aid to neighboring countries of Libya, such as Tunisia, The Sudan, and Egypt.

Mitterrand Takes Charge — President François Mitterrand's new Socialist government raised France's minimum wage by 10%, **June 3,** increased social security benefits, and raised taxes on banks, oil companies, and the rich. On **June 14,** the socialists won by a landslide in the first round of elections for the National Assembly, and, in the final vote **June 20,** scored a sweeping victory, assuring Mitterrand full government power. His first task was to select a cabinet, and on **June 23,** he announced the appointment of 4 members of the Communist Party to the 44-member body.

Fighting Continues in El Salvador — Government troops fought their way up Chichontepec volcano in a battle against 500 leftist guerrillas, **June 5.** The next day it was announced that at least 100 were killed in the fighting. On **June 6,** Argentina agreed to send $15 million in economic aid credits and technical assistance to the Salvadoran government, but they pointed out that none of the aid would be of a military nature. By **June 11,** at least 225 guerrillas and 14 army soldiers had been killed at Chichontepec volcano. And on **June 13,** the guerrillas claimed that they had overrun the northern town of Arcatao and killed 140 government soldiers. This was denied by the army. At least another 10 people were killed in a battle in the port city of La Unión, it was announced **June 28.**

López Portillo Visits Reagan — President José López Portillo of Mexico arrived in Washington, D.C., **June 7,** and after a night's rest, met with Pres. Reagan at the White House. On **June 8,** he agreed in principle to participate with the U.S. in a plan to strengthen the economic and political freedom of the countries in the Caribbean region. On **June 9,** it was announced that progress has been made on a "guest worker" plan to permit 50,000 Mexicans to work in the U.S. Also discussed was a proposal to grant amnesty to 2.7 million Mexicans thought to be living in the U.S. illegally. After a meeting with Sen. Edward M. Kennedy (D., Mass.), López Portillo returned to Mexico City.

Israel Destroys Iraqi Nuclear Plant — Israeli warplanes, **June 7,** bombed and destroyed an Iraqi atomic reactor near Baghdad, killing one French technician. The Israeli government claimed that the reactor would have enabled the Iraqis to manufacture nuclear weapons which could have been used against Israel. Israeli Prime Minister Menachem Begin claimed that the $275-million facility was near completion and if the raid had been postponed for a few months, the bombing would have blanketed Baghdad with radiation. The U.S. immediately condemned the raid, **June 8,** as did the Arab governments. U.S. President Reagan announced, **June 9,** that Congress would be notified that Israel may have violated its arms agreements with the U.S. by using American-made planes in the attack. That same day, the USSR charged that the U.S. was an accomplice in the raid, because the U.S. had armed the Israelis. On **June 10,** the U.S. suspended the shipment of 4 F-16 fighter bombers to Israel because of the possible violation of the arms agreement. Iraq vowed to push their nuclear plans despite the Israel threat, but continued to deny Israeli charges that it had been building nuclear weapons. Arab foreign ministers, as well as officials of the Arab League, **June 11,** called upon the UN to impose binding sanctions on Israel and to condemn the raid on the nuclear reactor center. France and Great Britain joined the Arabs and other Third World countries, **June 15,** in censuring Israel. France demanded that Israel pay reparations to Iraq, and Britain agreed. However, both countries refused to support an arms embargo against the Israelis. President Reagan, **June 16,** said that, in fact, it seemed the Israelis had violated their arms agreement with the U.S., but stated that he was confident that they might have sincerely believed that their action was defensive. The French government, **June 17,** maintained that since French scientists had been working on the French-built Iraqi reactor, the Iraqis could not have built an atomic bomb without detection. U.S. efforts to reach a compromise with Iraq on UN action succeeded when, on **June 19,** the UN Security Council strongly condemned the attack, urged Israel to open its nuclear plants to international inspection, but did not ask for an arms embargo. On **June 21,** Israel rejected the UN Security Council's condemnation. On **June 24,** former Israeli Defense and Foreign Minister Moise Dayan stated that his country had the capacity of producing nuclear weapons and, if the Arabs decided to manufacture them, Israel could do the same in a short time.

Polish Power Struggle — The Polish Communist Party Central Committee, in an emergency session **June 10-11,** retained Stanislaw Kania as their party leader, in a move that was seen as a rebuff of the Soviet Union. The meeting had been triggered by a **June 5** letter from the Soviet Communist Party asserting that the Polish Politburo was not acting strongly enough to stem the tide of counterrevolution and warning that the USSR would not leave Poland alone in the crisis. In the apparent attempt, through the letter, to force reorganization of the Polish leadership, the USSR had criticized Kania by name, as well as Prime Minister Wojciech Jaruzelski. On **June 12,** Jaruzelski dismissed 5 cabinet ministers and merged several other ministries. Jaruzelski also promised to punish those persons who distribute provocative leaflets, use printing presses to publish illegal material, and attached or abused the police.

Marcos Wins — Pres. Ferdinand E. Marcos of the Philippines was reelected, **June 16,** by an overwhelming majority. This was the first voting for president since 1969. Marcos received 86% of the total vote. The other 14% was divided among 12 other candidates, in an election in which 80 to 90% of the electorate voted.

U.S. to Sell Arms to China — Sec. of State Alexander M. Haig Jr. announced, **June 16,** at the end of a 3-day visit to Peking that the U.S. had decided in principle to sell arms to China. Stressing that the 2 countries were friends, but not allies, Haig said that the details of the sale would be worked out when a Chinese military delegation would visit Wash-

ington, D.C., in August. It was expected that antitank weapons and antiaircraft missiles, as well as other defensive weapons, would be the first to be sold.

Bani-Sadr Ousted as Iranian President — The Ayatollah Ruhollah Khomeini, **June 22,** formally removed Abolhassan Bani-Sadr as president of Iran, leaving the clergy in control of the government. The removal was the culmination an intensive month-long attack on Bani-Sadr's power. Bani-Sadr was in hiding and rumored to be attempting to flee to the West. On **June 1,** a special commission established by the Ayatollah had warned Bani-Sadr that he had not only violated the constitution but also the orders of the Ayatollah by refusing to sign bills passed by the parliament. The commission, however, did not recommend legal action against Bani-Sadr. On **June 5,** despite the conviction of his associates that his ouster was near at hand, Bani-Sadr vowed to stay on as president no matter what might occur. Khomeini verbally attacked the president, **June 8,** stating that he would remove any politician who continue to challenge Islamic authorities. The Ayatollah, **June 10,** dismissed Bani-Sadr as chief of Iran's armed forces, and, on the following day, demonstrators roamed through the streets of Teheran, calling for the president's resignation, trial, and execution. The marchers were mobilized by the Party of God, an extremist group. By **June 13,** Bani-Sadr had fled into hiding. However, on **June 14,** Khomeini asserted that the president was still able to carry out his duties, but in an apparent reversal, **June 15,** set a condition that Bani-Sadr could remain in office only if he were to broadcast an apology to the people of Iran for calling on them to resist the clergy-dominated government. By **June 18,** it was suspected that Bani-Sadr had fled Iran. The Iranian parliament, after a 4-day delay, began formal impeachment proceedings against the president. Nineteen people were killed, 200 injured, and 30 arrested in street clashes between rival political factions. On **June 19,** parliament found him unfit for office, and the Iranian prosecutor general ordered him arrested on sight. Following the formal dismissal, the hunt for the former president was stepped up, **June 23,** by arresting and questioning some of his closest friends and aides. It was announced, **June 24,** that a presidential election would be held on **July 24.** By this time, 23 supporters of Bani-Sadr had been executed by firing squads, in addition to 7 members of the Bahai sect that were charged with spying and collecting funds for Israel. On **June 27,** a bomb, hidden in a tape recorder, exploded in the Abouzar Mosque in Teheran, wounding Hojatolislam Ali Khameini, an aide to Ayatollah Khomeini. The following night, Ayatollah Mohammed Beheshti, Iran's chief justice and 73 others were killed by a bomb explosion. The blast occurred while Beheshti was addressing a meeting of the ruling Islamic Republican Party. Senior Islamic clergymen blamed both the U.S. and leftist groups supporting Bani-Sadr for the bombings.

New Government Formed In Italy — Giovanni Spadolini, the head of the small Republican party, **June 28,** was sworn in as the head of a 5-part coalition government in Italy. The government was the first to be led by a premier not to belong to the Christian Democratic party since World War II. The Christian Democrats, however, did hold 15 of the 27 ministerial posts in the new government. The previous government, led by Arnaldo Forlani had resigned over a scandal involving the Propaganda 2, or P2, Masonic lodge. In the ongoing investigation of the scandal, the police had, **June 9,** confiscated the membership lists of more than 500 Masonic lodges belonging to the Grand Orient of Italy, the principal Masonic organization in the country, believed to have more than 15,000 members.

Hau Goufeng Ousted — The handpicked successor of Mao Zedong was replaced, **June 29,** as head of the Chinese Communist Party by Hu Yaobang, a favorite of the senior deputy chairman Deng Xiaoping. Hau, who had come to power 5 years previously, was denounced as being no longer fit because he had made leftist errors and had created a personality cult for himself. The replacement had been expected since Hau volunteered to resign in November 1980. The following day, the Party announced that Mao, who had been its leader for 27 years until his death, had been a brilliant commander, but had made mistakes as the leader of the country, such as emphasizing class struggle and quick results instead of slow modernization and party building.

General

Acupuncture Has New Use — After an 18-month $170,000 federally-financed study at the Haight-Ashbury Free Medical Clinic in San Francisco, it was announced, **June 13**, that acupuncture could be used to treat drug abuse. Acupuncture treatments were given to 460 heroin addicts for 30 minutes per day for up to 21 days. Six months after the end of the treatments, 5% of the addicts were reported to be completely free from heroin use, and 86% had reduced their use of the drug. The acupuncture was used on 2 main points of the ear—one called the "lung" point and the other called "God's Door," which was said to reduce anxiety levels. Dr. Gregory L. Johnson said that the acupuncture treatment worked faster, in those cases where it was effective, then the usual methadone treatment, and cost a third to one-half as much.

Chapman Pleads Guilty — Mark David Chapman pleaded guilty, **June 22**, to killing John Lennon, the former Beatle, in New York City in December 1980. In a closed courtroom proceeding, Chapman, against his lawyers' advice, made his plea when he was promised that his sentence would not exceed 20 years to life imprisonment. Chapman was scheduled to be sentenced on Aug. 24.

Disasters — One dozen tornadoes hit the Denver, Col., area, **June 3**, injuring 46 and destroying 50 homes . . . A 9-car train carrying 500 people fell off a bridge during a storm in the Indian state of Bihar, **June 6**, and, by **June 12**, when rescue operations ceased, 248 bodies had been found and 340 people were still missing . . . An earthquake hit a large part of the southeastern Iranian province of Kerman, **June 11**, leaving a death toll estimated at more than 3,000 . . . On the weekend of **June 13**, at least 20 people were killed in torrential rains coupled with tornadoes in the central and eastern parts of the U.S. stretching from Texas to Maryland . . . Eleven mountain climbers were believed dead after being swept off the face of Mount Ranier in Washington, **June 21**, and buried under up to 70 feet of boulder-sized chunks of ice.

JULY

National

Labor Unions Reunite — The United Automobile Workers labor union rejoined the AFL-CIO, **July 1**, ending a separation that had lasted 13 years. The 1.2 million auto workers thus became the second largest member group of the AFL-CIO, which totals 15 million members. The 1968 rift that occurred was caused by differences of opinion between the then heads of the 2 organizations—Walter Reuther of the UAW and George Meany of the AFL-CIO. Reuther, as a leader of mostly unskilled workers, was a believer in political activism by labor. Meany, as a leader of basically craft unions, had tended to stick to bread-and-butter issues. He also distrusted international labor organizations, which Reuther favored.

White House Protesters Arrested — A total of 80 demonstrators were arrested at the White House, **July 3**, for staging a sitdown protest against the Reagan Administration's budget cuts and involvement with El Salvador. Of that number, 31 were arrested for refusing to leave the White House grounds and the rest were charged with obstructing traffic on Pennsylvania Avenue. Among those arrested was Philip Berrigan, a former Roman Catholic priest and leader of the protests against the Vietnam War ten years before. As of **July 3**, 195 people had been arrested in the series of protests at the White House.

Haitian Refugee Problem Continues — The Justice Dept. announced, **July 6**, that it was willing to hold new hearings for 85 Haitians who had previously been ordered deported. It had been alleged that the 85 had been deprived of their rights when the deportation order was issued. Concern was also expressed by an attorney representing the Haitians for the 1,150 other Haitians being held in the Krome Avenue Detention Camp outside Miami, Fla. Over the **July 18-19** weekend, federal officials began moving several hundred Haitians from the Miami camp to detention centers around the country in an attempt to ease crowding at Krome Avenue. But a spokesman for the Justice Department said that this would not solve the problem, since between 1,000 and

1,500 Haitians arrive in the U.S. by boat each month.

Reagan Nominates Woman for Supreme Court Justice — Pres. Ronald Reagan announced, **July 7**, that he would nominate Sandra Day O'Connor for a seat on the U.S. Supreme Court. O'Connor, a 51-year-old judge on the Arizona Court of Appeals, would, if confirmed, be the first woman to serve on the Supreme Court.

Reagan Backs Loans to 4 Latin American Countries — The Reagan Administration announced, **July 8**, that it favored making loans to Chile, Argentina, Paraguay, and Uruguay. This reversed the Carter Administration's policy of denying loans to these countries because of their positions on human rights. A State Department spokesman declared that there had been significant improvements in the human rights situation in those countries.

Missing Persons Reports Fall in Atlanta — It was announced, **July 8**, that there had been no related killings in Atlanta, Ga., since the arrest of Wayne B. Williams, and the number of missing black youths reported to police had fallen off. But it was pointed out that the cause of the decreased number of reports might have been due to the belief of parents that the 2-year string of slayings was over, and, consequently, they were not so apt to report to the police when a child merely did not return home on time. Williams requested, **July 14**, that he be released on bail, but the motion was denied on **July 15**. On **July 16**, Judge Sam Phillips McKenzie also rejected Williams' requests to appear before the Fulton County Grand Jury and to poll the grand jury to find if any of the members were prejudiced because of news accounts. On **July 17**, Williams was indicted on charges of murdering 2 of the 28 young black people killed in the last 2 years in the Atlanta area. He was charged with murdering Nathaniel Cater, 27, by strangling and asphyxiating him, and with murdering Jimmy Ray Payne, 21, by asphyxiating him with objects and by means which are to the grand jury unknown. The bodies of these two men were found less than a mile apart.

California Fights the Fruit Fly — California agricultural experts confessed an error, **July 9**, when they admitted that they had released hundreds of thousands of Mediterranean fruit flies in the state during the month of June. These flies were thought to be sterile and were released in an attempt to control the medflies biologically. But, according to the experts, they apparently turned out to be fertile and the result was an increase in the reproductive rate among the insects that threatened the state's $1-billion produce crop. Federal officials were considering a quarantine of the entire state. Gov. Edmund G. Brown Jr. ordered extensive aerial spraying with the pesticide malathion, **July 10**, after federal officials had ordered the fumigation of all produce leaving the state. Meanwhile, tens of thousands of people in the infested areas near San Francisco were stripping their gardens of produce and attorneys for several cities were fighting the spraying order. Also, in the face of the commencement of spraying, which was to begin **July 14**, many residents of the Santa Clara Valley were preparing to leave their homes. On **July 12**, it was announced that new infestation of the medfly had been found, and the spraying area had been increased from 97 to 117 square miles. The helicopters that were to be used were being kept at a secret location for fear of sabotage by the anti-spraying forces. The California Supreme Court refused, **July 13**, to bar the pesticide spraying, which was scheduled to begin at 2 a.m. the next day, and, on **July 15**, Gov. Brown asked that California be declared a major disaster area, and that the government give financial aid in the spraying. Meanwhile, more larvae were found outside the target area. On **July 17**, Texas, Alabama, Florida, Mississippi, and South Carolina declared that they would reject California fruits and vegetables that had not been fumigated against the medfly. By **July 18**, the infected area had increased to 150 square miles, and the spraying was almost over. On **July 19**, Secretary of Agriculture John R. Block announced that the federal government would pay half the cost of the spraying. The following day, the first phase of the spraying was completed, and Louisiana, Arkansas, and North Carolina joined in the fruit embargo. But, on **July 23**, a federal court judge ordered Florida to lift its quarantine and 4 other states said they would not enforce theirs. On that day, the second round of spraying began.

CIA Aide Resigns — Max C. Hugel, chief of clandestine operations at the Central Intelligence Agency, resigned, **July**

14, in the face of accusations that he had participated in fraudulent securities transactions in the 1970s. At that time he was the manager of an electronics business, the Brother International Corporation. John H. Stein, a career CIA employee, was appointed to succeed Hugel as deputy director of operations.

Slower Inflation Predicted — The Reagan Administration predicted, **July 15,** that interest rates would decline during the next few months. It was also predicted that an upturn in the economy might not occur until 1982, and that unemployment might be higher by autumn.

Tax Cut Approved — The House of Representatives approved the administration's tax cut bill, **July 29.** The measure provided for 3 years of reductions totalling 25% in individual tax rates and other reductions in business taxes and oil production taxes. This was considered to be a decisive victory for the president over the House Democratic majority, whereas the outcome in the Senate, where the Republicans hold the majority, was never in doubt.

International

Iran Crisis Continues — Fifty Iranian leftist guerrillas were arrested on Teheran, it was announced **July 1,** for plotting to destroy the Parliament building. They were members of the Marxist opposition group called Mujahedeen-i-Khalq, which had been denounced by Ayatollah Ruhollah Khomeini as being responsible for the **June 28** bomb attack which had killed some 70 members of the Islamic Republican Party. It was also announced that some 80 executions had been carried out in the previous 2 weeks against supporters of the self-exiled former president, Abolhassan Bani-Sadr. A story published in a London magazine quoted Bani-Sadr, **July 4,** as saying that Kurdish tribesmen in northwestern Iran had helped shelter him, but it was not known exactly where he was hiding. On the night of **July 5,** 27 more supporters of left-wing groups were executed in Iran, and on **July 7,** 9 more were executed and the British news agency Reuters was ordered to close its bureau in Teheran. A tape recording of a speech by Bani-Sadr urging the people of his country to support him in his opposition to the government was reported, **July 12,** as being circulated in northwest Iran. On **July 13,** 22 persons were put to death on charges of anti-state activities, and 6 others were executed as drug or sex offenders. By **July 15,** the execution toll reached more than 200 and members of Bani-Sadr's disbanded guard corps were ordered to turn in their weapons. The next day, another 200 leftists were arrested in raids in various parts of the country and 4 were put to death. Bani-Sadr arrived in France, **July 29,** and was granted political asylum as long as he refrained from political activity. He had flown there from Teheran the night before in a hijacked Iranian plane, and it was thought that his escape had been arranged by the Mujahedeen group.

Begin Finally Wins — By **July 1,** it appeared that the party of Prime Minister Menachem Begin would gain a slim majority in the Israeli Parliament and he would be able to retain his post and form a coalition government. Israel's religious parties had indicated that they would rather form a coalition with Begin's Likud bloc than with Shimon Peres' Labor Party. On **July 5,** the Likud bloc had taken a 1 seat margin over the Labor Party, and the next day Begin and former foreign minister Moshe Dayan met to talk about the possibility of bringing Dayan's Telem Party into the coalition. Begin announced, **July 8,** that the coalition had been formed and he would begin to form a cabinet.

Hostage Crisis Solution Held Legal — The U.S. Supreme Court ruled, **July 2,** that Presidents Jimmy Carter and Reagan had the legal authority to carry out the arrangements with Iran that led to the freeing of the hostages. That meant that more than $2 billion in Iranian assets could be legally transferred out of the U.S. as planned in the agreement.

Ulster Violence Continues — On **July 2,** the British government proposed the setting up of an advisory council on Northern Ireland that would have representatives of both the Protestant and the Roman Catholic groups as members. Leaders of both groups rejected the idea. The next day, the Rev. Ian Paisley, the Protestant leader, escaped a shooting attempt for which the Irish National Liberation Army claimed credit. He was uninjured. On **July 8,** Joseph McDonnell, a member of the Irish Republican Army, became the fifth hunger striker to die in Maze Prison in Belfast. This death set off new violence in the streets, in which 2 teenagers were killed by British police. On **July 11,** a group of Roman Catholics ended a week-long mediation effort after being rebuffed by both Protestants and Roman Catholics. They had been trying to negotiate with Britain to do something about the 8 remaining hunger strikers in Maze Prison. The rioting resumed, **July 12,** when rioters began showering British troops with acid and gasoline bombs. The next day, after the death of the 6th hunger striker, Martin Hurson, street battles flared again in Northern Ireland. Five policemen were wounded as they were attacked by a group of 30 young men hurling gasoline bombs and rocks. More than 100 milk bottle firebombs were thrown at police in a suburb of Belfast and more than 200 firebombs as well as homemade grenades were thrown in Londonderry. On **July 15** Britain accepted an offer of a fact-finding mission from the International Committee of the Red Cross. The team would try to end the hunger strikes, and would investigate conditions in the Maze Prison, but the hunger strikers insisted in their demands to deal directly with the British government, rather than with the Red Cross. On **July 18,** some 15,000 IRA sympathizers attacked 1,000 policemen who were guarding the British Embassy in Dublin. At least 70 people were injured. By **July 23,** after being rebuffed by the hunger strikers, Red Cross members of the negotiating team dropped their efforts.

Polish Cabinet Reorganized; Landmark Congress Held — In an effort to help his government cope with the country's economic crisis, and just before the arrival of Soviet Foreign Minister Andrei A. Gromyko, Polish Prime Minister Wojciech Jaruzelski, **July 3,** reorganized his cabinet. Eight cabinet ministers were ousted, 5 new ones appointed, and 4 were reassigned. Following his talks with Jaruzelski and the Polish Communist Party leader Stanislaw Kania, Gromyko seemed to lean toward advising the Soviet Union not to interfere with the internal affairs of Poland. On **July 17,** the Polish congress, in a landmark meeting voting for the first time by secret ballot, elected a new central committee, dominated by Kania's centrist bloc. The following day, Kania was re-elected as the party leader. In the 6-day congress, the defeat of party bureaucrats and replacement with little known grass-roots members marked the voting for the committee membership. Prime Minister Jaruzelski, **July 19,** announced that the price of food, coal, natural gas, and housing would have to be increased 110% and wage increases would have to stop. The monthly meat ration was cut 20% by the government, **July 24.**

Riots Erupt in Britain — About 200 white youths rampaged through a west London district, **July 3,** throwing gasoline bombs at policemen and harrassing Asian residents. The disturbance, in which store windows were broken, a garage set on fire, and 64 people hurt, lasted 3 hours. The next day, local officials said that they were sure that the rioters were members of the National Front, a neo-Nazi group. More than 100 policemen were injured, **July 5,** in Liverpool, when they were bombarded with stones and gasoline bombs. On **July 6,** the British government promised new measures to protect the police, and, on **July 8,** Prime Minister Margaret Thatcher pleaded with the British people to halt the epidemic of violence. The following day, the House of Commons erupted in a storm of recrimination, and Thatcher was forced to shout to make herself heard. By **July 11,** violence had erupted in a dozen cities across England. In London alone, 250 arrests were made and 40 people were injured. Firemen were fighting 6 fires in separate sections of the city. The government, **July 12,** announced a package of measures to punish rioters, involving the creation of special courts with increased powers, making parents financially responsible for their children's acts, and setting up a youth employment program. On **July 13,** Thatcher visited Liverpool in an attempt to urge the people there to unite with the police to end urban violence. As she left the town hall, tomatoes and rolls of toilet tissue were thrown at her. That same day, the trouble spread to Scotland, where firebombs were thrown in Dundee. The government announced new measures, **July 14,** permitting police to carry guns loaded with plastic bullets, use armored vehicles, and fire water cannons. Thatcher announced, **July 27,** a package of youth unemployment measures that was expected to cost approximately $1 billion.

Mideast War Continues; Truce Negotiated — The special Arab League peacemaking committee dealing with the continued fighting in Lebanon adjourned, July 5, with a brief statement expressing relief at the easing of tension in Beirut and Zahle. However, on July 8, a joint patrol of Israelis and Lebanese rightists clashed with an Irish battalion of the UN peacekeeping force. On July 10, Israeli jets bombed Palestinian targets in southern Lebanon and 3 people were killed and more than 15 wounded. Another strike occurred on July 12, killing or wounding 25 people. On July 14, Israeli jets shot down a Syrian MIG fighter over southern Lebanon as the Israelis were carrying on another air strike. The next day, in retaliation for the raids, Palestinian guerrillas fired rockets at northern Israeli towns, killing 3 and wounding 25. On July 16, Israeli jets destroyed 5 bridges in Lebanon, closing down several guerrilla supply lines. Israeli jets bombed a densely populated section of Beirut, July 17, and knocked out 3 more bridges in southern Lebanon. The raids left at least 300 dead and more than 800 wounded. That day, Israeli Prime Minister Menachem Begin warned the guerrillas that they could no longer hide amid the civilian populations in Lebanon. On July 20, President Reagan suspended the delivery of 2 shipments of American jet fighter-bombers to Israel because of the escalating level of violence in the Middle East. The shipments were to have included 6 F-16 planes. On July 22, Israeli jets made 4 raids on 2 temporary bridges that had been built to replace the previously destroyed spans. The death toll was estimated at 50 people. In addition, the planes set fire to the oil pipeline delivering crude oil from Saudi Arabia. On July 24, Israeli and Palestinian forces agreed to a cease-fire, negotiated through the efforts of U.S. envoy Philip C. Habib. Israel agreed to halt attacks on Palestinian positions in Lebanon and Palestinians agreed to stop military buildups in southern Lebanon. But, on July 25, radicals in the PLO refused to honor the cease-fire, and fired rockets at the towns of Qlaia and Merj 'Uyon, where the troops of the Israeli-backed militia were headquartered. However, PLO leaders denounced the radicals and, by July 29, it was reported that the radical faction had agreed to observe the truce.

Isabel Perón Freed — After 5 years of house arrest, former Argentine President Isabel Martinez de Perón was freed on parole by a federal court, July 6. The widow of Juan Perón had been overthrown by a military coup in 1976. More than 1,000 of her supporters greeted her as she came out of the courthouse, but they were restrained by some 100 policemen. On July 9, Mrs. Perón left for Spain where she hoped to live.

Vatican in Debt — The Vatican announced, July 15, that its 1981 debt would reach $26 million. This was the first public disclosure of its kind. The statement included an appeal to wealthier Catholic dioceses around the world to increase their contributions to the Curia, which is the government of the Roman Catholic Church. These dioceses were mainly ones in the U.S. and West Germany. Vatican sources also felt that the curtailment of public appearances by Pope John Paul II following his assassination attempt might further hurt church contributions, which had been increased while he was traveling around the world.

Assassin Convicted — The trial of Mehmet Ali Agca, the Turkish citizen who was accused of trying to assassinate Pope John Paul II, opened in Rome on July 20. Agca admitted that he had tried to kill the Pope, but said that Italy had no right to try him, since the crime had been committed on Vatican soil. He also refused to answer questions in court. On July 22, Agca was found guilty of the attempted assassination and was sentenced to life in prison, the first year of which was to be spent in solitary confinement.

Prince Charles Weds Lady Diana — Before 2,500 guests in St. Paul's Cathedral in London, the Prince of Wales married Lady Diana Spencer, July 29. An estimated 700 million people also watched the ceremony on world-wide television. For one of the guests, the occasion was not a happy one. It was announced, July 30, that President Dawda Kairaba Jawara of Gambia was overthrown in a leftist coup while he was in England for the royal wedding.

General

Solar Powered Plane Crosses Channel — After several unsuccessful attempts, a solar-powered airplane crossed the English Channel, July 7. The 210 pound *Solar Challenger* flew from Cormeilles-en-Vexin, France to the Manston Royal Air Force Base in England in 5½ hours, powered by 16,000 photovoltaic cells on its wings, converting the energy of the sun to electricity, which drove the motor. The plane, with a wingspan of 47 feet, made the 165-mile journey at an average speed of about 30 miles per hour at an altitude of 11,000 feet.

New Drug May Control Herpes — It was announced, July 8, that a drug had been developed that may prevent outbreaks of cold sores and genital herpes. These are infections that are nuisances to healthy people but may be fatal to newborn babies or the very ill. Doctors at Johns Hopkins Medical School used the drug, acyclovir, on infections in transplant patients who were chosen because their natural immunity had been suppressed in order to prevent the rejection of the transplanted organs. Ten people who were about to receive bone marrow transplants were given the drug, and ten others were given inactive substitutes. The drug was administered for 18 days. After 84 days, none of those who had been given the drug developed sores, while 7 of the other 10 got herpes infections.

Disasters — Tropical storm Kelly hit the Central Philippines July 1, killing at least 120 in flash floods and mudslides. . . . The death toll in a poisoned liquor epidemic in India rose to 219 on July 8. . . . Walkways in the form of concrete bridges in the Hyatt Regency Hotel in Kansas City, Missouri, collapsed July 17, killing 43 and injuring 150 people. . . . The New China News Agency announced July 25 that 753 people had died, 558 were missing, 28,140 were injured, and 1.5 million were homeless as the result of flooding in Sichuan Province. . . . An Aeroméxico DC-9 bound for Tijuana crashed at the Chihuahua airport, July 28, while trying to land, killing 32 people. . . . An earthquake in southeastern Iran, July 29, killed at least 8,000 people. . . . On July 31, 6 coaches of a passenger train derailed in Pakistan, killing 43 and injuring at least 50 people.

AUGUST

National

Fruit Fly Saga Continues — By Aug. 3, more than $4 million in claims had been filed against the state of California by people who cited damage from the pesticide spraying that the state had conducted against the Mediterranean fruit fly invasion. Most of the claims were for damage to trees and shrubs, although some cited allergic reactions. On Aug. 5, 3 dead medflies were found in East Tampa, Fla., inciting state and federal officials to fear for that state's $2 billion citrus crop. Officials reasoned that if the flies had come from California it indicated that that state's quarantine measures had broken down. Florida began ground-spraying near Tampa, Aug. 7, but a judge refused to allow Florida to reimpose a quarantine on California produce. On Aug. 9, 2 more fertile medflies were found in Florida, and one was found in Livermore, Cal., near the fertile San Joaquin Valley, thus posing a threat to that state's $14 billion fruit and vegetable industry. Aerial spraying of pesticide began on an area around Boulder Creek, Cal., where one fruit fly had been found, on Aug. 13. Then, on Aug. 14, it was found that the medflies were beginning to infest the San Joaquin Valley. Only 3 had been found near Patterson, but experts estimated that for each fly found in an insect trap, at least 500 others were present in the area. Spraying in that area began Aug. 15, and 78 square miles were fumigated. By Aug. 16, 56 flies had been found in the area. By Aug. 25, 5 were found in Los Angeles County, and, on Aug. 26, Japan began requiring fumigation of all food products from California.

Air Traffic Controllers Go Out on Strike — Federal air traffic controllers, Aug. 3, began an illegal nationwide strike, after their union had rejected the government's final offer for a new contract. However, 50 to 60 percent of the 14,200 scheduled daily airline flights were able to operate under supervisors and non-strikers. Pres. Reagan warned the strikers that if they did not return to work by 11 a.m. Aug. 5, they would be fired. Most of the 13,000 striking controllers were determined to defy the back-to-work order, and, on Aug. 5 the Federal Aviation Administration sent out the first dismissal notices, and the president of the Norfolk, Va. unit of the union was ordered to spend 60 days in jail by an Alexandria, Va., judge. Four others were jailed in Kansas City,

Kan. On **Aug. 6,** the International Federation of Air Traffic Controllers Associations asked its 60 member groups to deny clearance to aircraft flying to the U.S. By **Aug. 7,** 521 military air traffic controllers had been assigned to civilian airports and 17 control towers at smaller airports had been closed. Also, Canadian controllers were causing slowdowns in handling aircraft to show their support of the American strikers. By **Aug. 9,** controllers in other countries, including France and New Zealand, were beginning to refuse to clear aircraft for flights to the U.S., and the Canadian controllers had refused to guide American flights over the Western Atlantic. Canadian Transport Minister Jean-Luc Pepin threatened the controllers with dismissal, heavy fines, and jail terms. This broke the boycott in Canada. On **Aug. 14,** the controller's union claimed that there had been 64 instances of near-misses in the sky over Washington, D.C., since the beginning of the strike. Portuguese controllers began a 2-day boycott of flights to and from the U.S., **Aug. 16.** They had been handling 20 percent of the trans-Atlantic travel, but alternate routes were soon set up to avoid the boycott. On **Aug. 17,** the government began officially accepting applications for air traffic controller jobs.

Reagan Endorses Neutron Bomb — Pres. Ronald Reagan decided, **Aug. 6,** to go forward with the full production of neutron weapons. He ordered that the Lance missile and 8-inch artillery shells be furnished with the nuclear material tritium to make complete enhanced-radiation weapons. These weapons produce more radiation and less blast and heat than other nuclear weapons, and are thus able to kill people without damaging their surroundings. Reagan ordered the weapons to be stockpiled only in the U.S., and that, if some were to be sent to Europe, this would be done only after consultation with the countries involved. On **Aug. 10,** Defense Secretary Caspar W. Weinberger said the weapons were already in production, and the U.S. would soon be capable of deploying them overseas within a few hours.

Prices Up, Unemployment, Economic Index Down — The Labor Department reported, **Aug. 7,** that the unemployment rate in the U.S. fell to 7 percent in July. This was the lowest point since April 1980. Producers' prices rose 4 percent in July, the Labor Department announced **Aug. 14.** This was not as much as had been predicted, but, on **Aug. 8,** the Labor Department said that consumer prices had risen 1.2 percent in July. This was the fastest pace for inflation in 16 months. The Commerce Department announced, **Aug. 28,** that the nation's economic index fell by 0.1 of one percent in July. The slightness of the decline was considered encouraging.

Deportation Problems Escalate — Judge Alcee Hastings, **Aug. 10,** rejected an effort to block U.S. immigration officials from holding deportation hearings for Haitian refugees scheduled to be sent to a camp in Puerto Rico. On **Aug. 12,** 125 of the Haitians were transported to a former U.S. Navy base at Juana Diaz, P.R. Pres. Reagan and Gov. Carlos Romero Barceló of P.R. had agreed that they would be detained for no more than one year. Meanwhile Florida sued the government to relieve the congestion at the Miami detention center, which was built to house 815, and at times had held 1,500. On **Aug. 17,** a series of hearings began in Atlanta to consider the cases of about 1,800 Cuban refugees who had entered the U.S. in the 1980 "freedom flotillas." These were the refugees that the Immigration and Naturalization Service had ruled not admissible to this country because of their criminal records. On **Aug. 19,** Federal District Judge Marvin H. Shoob temporarily barred the government from deporting any of the refugees. He also directed that 365 of the refugees were free to leave their detention facility as soon as they could be united with American sponsors. The judge pointed out that the only crime these 365 had committed was entering the U.S. without proper entry papers.

Williams Pleads Not Guilty — Wayne B. Williams entered a plea of not guilty, **Aug. 17,** to charges in the deaths of 2 of the 28 young blacks in Atlanta. Judge Clarence Cooper set a tentative trial date of **Oct. 5,** and Dist. Atty. Lewis Slaton said he would not seek the death penalty.

Reagan Seeks More Budget Cuts — Pres. Reagan conducted a 3-hour review of proposals aimed at achieving at least $75 billion in budget cuts, **Aug. 18.** Others at the meeting were David A. Stockman, director of the Office of Management and Budget, and Treasury Secretary Donald T. Re-

gan. Reagan's advisors had recommended that he cut military spending by from $10 billion to $20 billion per year. Military spending authorizations were scheduled to rise to $226 billion in the next fiscal year, and to $373 billion in the year after that.

Hinckley Indicted — John W. Hinckley Jr. was indicted, **Aug. 24,** by a federal grand jury on charges of attempting to kill President Reagan, **March 30.** He was also indicted for assault with intent to kill James S. Brady, the White House press secretary. The indictment listed 11 other counts, including wounding Secret Service Agent Timothy J. McCarthy and Police Officer Thomas K. Delahanty. A conviction on the attempt to kill the president carries a maximum penalty of life imprisonment.

International

Torrijos Killed — Brig. Gen. Omar Torrijos Herrera, the Commander in Chief of the National Guard of Panama and that country's former president, was killed, **Aug. 1,** in the crash of a Panamanian Air Force plane. He had been the architect of the Panama Canal treaties with the U.S., as well as the man who gave asylum to the deposed Shah of Iran. He was also the person who was most responsible, with help from the Vatican, for convincing the government of Argentina that they should permit Isabel Martínez de Perón to leave for exile in Spain after 5 years of Argentine house arrest.

Hunger Strikes in Ulster Continue — Kevin Lynch, a prisoner at Maze Prison in Belfast, **Aug. 1,** became the 7th hunger striker to die. Meanwhile, the family of another hunger striker, Patrick Quinn, decided that he was not capable of making rational decisions, and had him given nourishment and medical attention. On **Aug. 2,** Kieran Doherty became the 8th prisoner to starve himself to death. Doherty had been elected to the Irish Parliament in June. Gangs of youths in Belfast threw gasoline bombs and stones at soldiers and policemen and two policemen were killed west of Belfast in an Irish Republican Army ambush. Five other men in the prison continued their fast. On the day of Doherty's funeral, **Aug. 4,** rioters in Roman Catholic neighborhoods in Belfast threw bricks, bottles, and gasoline bombs at soldiers and policemen. The security forces then fired plastic bullets to disperse the crowds. The next day, Irish guerrillas set off bombs in 6 cities in Northern Ireland. Car bombs were set off in Belfast, Londonderry, Lisburn, and Armagh, injuring 7 people. The guerrillas issued a statement, **Aug. 7,** calling for reforms in Maze Prison. On **Aug. 8,** Thomas G. McElwee became the 9th hunger striker to die, and more firebombs and stones were thrown. The next day, 2 civilians were killed in a Belfast riot. Patrick Quinn gave up his hunger strike, **Aug. 15,** because of his family's request. The 10th death was that of Michael Devine, on **Aug. 20,** and on **Aug. 22,** 48 were injured in bombings and rioting in Ulster.

Pope Recovers — Physicians announced, **Aug. 1,** that Pope John Paul II had fully recovered from the viral infection he had had since June, and that he was about to undergo a second and final operation on his intestine. On **Aug. 5,** the 45-minute operation was performed, and it was termed a complete success in that his intestine was able to perform normally. The Pope walked out of the hospital, completely recovered, **Aug. 14,** and resumed his duties at the Vatican.

Polish Unrest Continues — The Polish Communist Party's ruling Politburo, **Aug. 1,** warned the Solidarity trade union that further unrest might lead to nationwide conflict. The Prime Minister Wojciech Jaruzelski, **Aug. 2,** held talks with the Military Council to discuss internal defense and security in the face of proposed protests by Solidarity. On **Aug. 3,** Solidarity organized a demonstration protesting food shortages in Poland and the police refused to let the parade pass in front of the headquarters of the Communist Party Central Committee. The resulting blockade was not broken up until **Aug. 5,** but the end of the protest was peaceful. The Polish Government again criticized Solidarity, **Aug. 7,** for its aggressive behavior. On **Aug. 9,** 5,000 Poles marched through the town of Krosno to protest the food shortages, despite Solidarity's urging them not to do so. Stanislaw Kania, the Polish Communist Party leader, said, **Aug. 11,** that further demonstrations could lead to a national tragedy, because they were leading to anarchy. Solidarity called a printers' strike, **Aug. 18,** closing or disrupting most newspapers in Poland. The strike lasted for two days.

More Killings in El Salvador — Eight government soldiers were killed, **Aug. 3,** in El Salvador during fighting with guerrilla forces on the Guazapa volcano, 19 miles north of San Salvador. Also that day the bodies of 7 victims of political violence were found in the San Salvador area. Hector Metón, an official with the office of the UN High Commissioner for Refugees in San Juan, Costa Rica announced, **Aug. 7,** that 305,000 people had fled from El Salvador in the preceding year. Because of the violence and hunger in the country, these Salvadorans had escaped to the U.S., Mexico, Guatemala, Honduras, Nicaragua, Costa Rica, Belize, and Panama. The Commission for Human Rights in Central America reported, **Aug. 12,** that the Salvadoran army had killed 96 unarmed civilians, including 46 children, the previous week. The report also said that the army was using toxic gases, white phosphorous, and bacteriological weapons that had caused the deaths of thousands of children and elderly people. On **Aug. 13,** the guerrilla forces announced that they had overrun a National Guard garrison in the town of Perquín. On **Aug. 25,** leftists attacked a bus with dynamite near San Vicente, killing 5 and wounding 14. The bus had been carrying farm workers and members of a rightist paramilitary group. In addition, 45 more bodies were found along highways that day. At least 26 more bodies were found on Salvadoran highways **Aug. 26,** raising the total to more than 26,000 since October 1979. On **Aug. 28,** Mexico and France recognized the guerrilla forces as a representative political force. The U.S. still supported the ruling junta.

Revolt in Bolivia — Gen. Luis García Meza resigned, **Aug. 4,** as president of Bolivia. Bowing to the demands of rebels in the army, he turned the running of the government over to a military junta, consisting of the commanders of the army, navy, and air force. The rebels had siezed Santa Cruz, Bolivia's second largest city, on **Aug. 3.** On **Aug. 6,** they indicated that they would not obey the orders of the junta to surrender and return to their barracks. The 2 sides reached a compromise, **Aug. 8.** The junta was to remain in power, but officers who had been exiled in the previous year would be permitted to return to Bolivia. On **Aug. 14,** it was announced that Bolivia was on the verge of bankruptcy.

Canadian Postal Strike Ends — Alan Gold, a federal mediator, announced in Ottawa, **Aug. 6,** that an agreement had been reached in the 38-day-old Canadian postal strike. The settlement covered salaries, maternity leaves, paid holidays, and health and safety provisions. After the agreement was approved by the union, the strike officially ended **Aug. 11.**

Portuguese Prime Minister Resigns — Portugal's cabinet announced, **Aug. 10,** that Prime Minister Francisco Pinto Balsemao had resigned. The 3 parties in his political coalition pledged to remain in control of the country. Balsemao cited rifts in his coalition that made it impossible to govern as the cause of his decision. His resignation was formally accepted by President António Ramalho Eanes, **Aug. 11.** On **Aug. 25,** Eanes reappointed Balsemao as Prime Minister, who agreed to form a new cabinet.

Reagan, Sadat Meet — A two-day meeting between Pres. Ronald Reagan and Pres. Anwar el-Sadat of Egypt ended, **Aug. 6,** with Reagan promising Sadat that the U.S. would take an active role in Middle East diplomacy. Stating that he was anxious for the Camp David negotiations to continue between Egypt and Israel, Reagan did not explain further, having decided to wait until after his meetings with Prime Minister Menachem Begin of Israel in September. Sadat indicated that he was pleased with the conference and stated that he was impressed by the U.S.'s ability to secure a ceasefire from the Palestine Liberation Organization.

Reagan Ends Jet Ban — Pres. Ronald Reagan lifted a 10-week-old suspension in the shipment of F-15 and F-16 jet fighters to Israel, **Aug. 17.** This was done despite the fact that the U.S. had not reached a decision on whether Israel had violated its agreement with the U.S. by using its F-16s to bomb the Iraqi nuclear plant in June. Sixteen of the planes were released and it was announced that they would be sent to Israel within a few days.

Navy Planes Down Libyan Jets — The U.S. announced, **Aug. 19,** that 2 Navy F-14 jets had shot down 2 Soviet-built Libyan SU-22's about 60 miles from the coast of Libya after the Libyans had fired upon the U.S. planes. The battle happened during a 2-day U.S. Navy exercise in the Southern Mediterranean. Libya claimed that the battle occurred over its territorial waters, but the U.S. stated that it regarded the area as international waters. Pres. Ronald Reagan, **Aug. 20,** defended the action and called it a case of prompt retaliation that would make American power impressive to the enemies of freedom. On **Aug. 24,** Vice Adm. William H. Rowden, the commander of the Sixth Fleet, announced that American fighters had intercepted Libyan aircraft on 45 occasions during the recent manuevers, but had not fired upon them until provoked by being fired on first.

South Africa Invades Angola — Angolan government officals, **Aug. 24,** annnounced that 2 South African armored columns had crosssed into southern Angola from South-West Africa and were as much as 60 miles into the country. The Angolan government mobilized its troops after the South Africans had attacked guerrilla bases of the SWAPO. Two columns with 32 tanks and 82 other vehicles had crosssed the border. One column occupied the town of Catequero and the other fought in Xangongo. Both had the support of Southern African jets. Twenty-nine insurgents and 4 South Africans had been killed. Prime Minister P. W. Botha of South Africa admitted, **Aug. 26,** that the 2 columns had entered Angola, but denied that it was a full-scale invasion. Officials described it as a "limited" operation, aimed at Angola-based guerrillas fighting for Namibian independence. Angola claimed South Africa was, in fact, trying to establish a "no-man's" land along the Angolan-Namibian border. Angola called for a UN Security Council meeting, **Aug. 27,** to demand the withdrawal of the South African troops, and the Organization of African Unity demanded the expulsion of South Africa from the UN. Meanwhile, fierce fighting was reported in Angola as South African planes bombed N'Giva and Angolan forces engaged one of the South African columns. It was also reported that the South Africans had totally destroyed the town of Xangongo. By **Aug. 29,** the South Africans claimed to have killed 240 Angolans and destroyed radar and antiaircraft installations.

Begin, Sadat Agree to Re-open Talks on West Bank — President Anwar el-Sadat of Egypt and Prime Minister Menachem Begin of Israel, **Aug. 26,** agreed to renew their talks concerning self-rule for the Palestinian Arabs of the West Bank of the Jordan and the Gaza Strip. The announcement was made after a 2-day meeting between the 2 men in Alexandria, the talks were to begin on **Sept. 23.** Earlier in the month, Egypt and Israel, **Aug. 3,** had signed an agreement that would establish a 2,500 member international peace-keeping force in the Sinai. Almost half of the force would consist of U.S. combat troops and civilian observers.

Iranian President, Premier Killed — Iran's newly elected president, Mohammed Ali Rajai, and Prime Minister Mohammed Javad Bahonar were killed, **Aug. 30,** when a bomb exploded in the prime minister's office. Five others were killed and 15 wounded in the attack, which was laid to opposition groups to the Islamic Republican movement. Speaker of the Parliament Hojatolislam Hasheimi Rafsanjani and Chief Justice Ayatollah Moussavi Ardebeli were appointed to presidential committee, **Aug. 31,** to run the country until a special election could be held. In other developments earlier in the month, Abolhassan Bani-Sadr, the deposed president, who was in self-exile in France, announced, **Aug. 3,** that he was considering moving to Australia or Sweden, since the French had threatened him with expulsion if he made any political statements. Because of growing anti-French feelings in Iran, 110 French citizens in that country decided to return home. But, on **Aug. 6,** the first contingent of 62 people was refused permission to leave and the Air France plane that had come for them was not allowed to land. On **Aug. 7,** supporters of Bani-Sadr seized the Iranian Interest Section's building in Washington, D. C. The takeover lasted for an hour and one demonstrator was shot by someone in the building. Police arrested 24 demonstrators. On **Aug. 10,** 57 of the French citizens arrived in Paris from Teheran, and, on **Aug. 12,** 50 more made the same journey. The Iranian state radio reported **Aug. 17** that 23 more leftists had been executed by firing squads, bringing the total to about 500 since the removal of Bani-Sadr. On **Aug. 26,** 26 more were executed.

General

Oldest Sacred Ark Found — American archeologists announced, **Aug. 2,** that they had found a sacred ark in Israel that was older than any yet found. It appeared to have the same functions as arks used in modern synagogues, and was reported to date back to the 3rd century, A.D. The ark was discovered in a ruined synagogue at the site of Nabratein in Upper Galilee, a mile north of the city of Safad. Dr. Eric Meyers of Duke University said that the base stone from the ark was 4.6 ft. long and weighed half a ton.

Gypsy Moth Damage Report — Gypsy Moth caterpillars ate the leaves off trees covering at least 9 million acres in 1981, it was announced **Aug. 8.** The area of devastation reached from Maine to Maryland and was twice the area defoliated in 1980. In New York State alone, 2.4 million acres of trees were damaged.

Saturn Photographed — Voyager 2, the unmanned spacecraft, began sending photographs of Saturn back to Earth, **Aug. 21.** At that time it was 2.8 million miles from Saturn. The photographs indicated that that planet had a jet stream with 1,000 mph winds, bluish storm clouds, and a cloud system that curled into a figure 6.

Disasters — A Taiwanese jetliner exploded and crashed near Sanyi, Taiwan **Aug. 22,** killing 110.

SEPTEMBER

National

Fruit Fly Fight Continues — A new area of California was added to the Mediterranean fruit fly fight, **Sept. 3,** when medflies were found in a 16-square mile section of Pleasenton, about 35 miles southeast of San Francisco. This area was added to the schedule for aerial pesticide spraying. On **Sept. 4,** a new discovery of medflies in Stanislaus County in the San Joaquin Valley, forced an extension of the quarantine. However, good news came from the San Jose area, where a full 6-week life cycle had passed without the discovery of new fruit flies in the area. No fertile medflies were found over the Labor Day weekend and, on **Sept. 8,** the Dept. of Agriculture said that aerial spraying of malathion over 1,200 miles of farmland was showing results, and predicted that the medflies would be eradicated. On **Sept. 9,** it was announced that no fertile flies had been found in the state of California since **Sept. 3,** but officials would not know until late spring 1982 whether or not the fly had been eradicated, since the flies could survive in the larval stage and re-emerge at that time.

Producers' Prices Up, Consumer Prices Up — The Department of Labor announced, **Sept. 4,** that the government's Producer Price Index for finished goods rose only 0.3 of one percent in August. This was attributed to a slight decline in meat and energy prices. Over all, food prices were up only 0.2 of one percent after a 1.5 percent rise in July. On **Sept. 24,** the Labor Department announced that the Consumer Price Index, the most widely followed measure of inflation, rose 0.8 of one percent in August, down from 1.2 percent in July.

Reagan Criticized for Strike Stand — Lane Kirkland, president of the AFL-CIO, asserted, **Sept. 6,** that Pres. Ronald Reagan's tough tactics in handling the air traffic controllers' strike had shown that Reagan was insensitive to the needs of labor. Secretary of Labor Raymond J. Donovan restated the administration's stand on the matter, saying that no amnesty would be granted to the controllers who had been fired for walking off their jobs. The administration had fired the controllers on the grounds that they had violated a no-strike clause in their union contract.

Reagan Cuts Budget Again — Pres. Reagan called for $10 billion to $15 billion more in budget cuts for the next fiscal year, **Sept. 8.** Officials stated that he was making an effort to preserve his goal of a deficit that did not go over $42.5 billion, and that $3 billion of the additional cuts would come from military spending. On **Sept. 12,** the president announced that he would cut his projections for military spending by $20 billion to $21 billion over the next 3 years. It was hoped that this would help to balance the budget by 1984. Reagan, in a television speech to the nation, **Sept. 24,** proposed $13 billion in additional spending cuts and $3 billion in increased taxes for the fiscal year 1982. He also raised his deficit target to $43.1 billion.

Crime Rate Up — The FBI index of reported serious crimes rose by 9 percent in 1980 over the previous year, it

was announced **Sept. 10.** Violent crimes of murder, forcible rape, robbery, and aggravated assault increased 11 percent. All kinds of crime in the bureau's index had increased—murder by 7 percent, forcible rape by 8 percent, robbery by 18 percent, aggravated assault by 7 percent, burglary by 14 per cent, larceny-theft by 8 percent, and motor vehicle theft by 2 percent. There had been 23,044 murders in 1980, and men of ages 20-29 constituted the largest group of murder victims. Of the murders, 45 percent resulted from quarrels and 18 percent occurred as the result of felony activities. On the same day the report was issued, the House Judiciary Committee approved legislation authorizing a $170 million program of federal assistance to local law-enforcement efforts.

Refugees Still a Problem — On **Sept. 10,** 8 more Cuban refugees were released from the federal penitentiary in Atlanta. They left for Michigan and New York, where they had sponsors. This brought the number of released detainees up to 75 during the previous 3 weeks. Pres. Reagan issued an executive order, **Sept. 29,** authorizing the Coast Guard to intercept and turn around ships on the high seas that were suspected of carrying illegal immigrants. Previously the Coast Guard could intercept these vessels only after they had entered U.S. territorial waters.

AWACS Sale in Trouble — Opponents of Pres. Reagan's plans to sell $8.5 billion worth of air warfare equipment to Saudi Arabia said, **Sept. 17,** that a majority of the Senate was against the sale. Included in the list of equipment were 5 Airborne Warning and Control System planes. According to the statement, 51 of the 100 Senators were against the sale, 19 of them Republicans. Secretary of State Alexander M. Haig Jr. said, **Sept. 20,** that at least a dozen of those senators were willing to reconsider their position on the sale. In Jerusalem, Prime Minister Menachem Begin denied a link between the AWACS sale and his agreement with the administration for strategic cooperation, even though some experts felt that it threatened the security of Israel.

Williams Loses Plea — Wayne B. Williams was denied a motion, **Sept. 21,** to have separate trials in the deaths of 2 young black men in Atlanta. This ruling by Judge Clarence Cooper would permit Dist. Att. Lewis Slaton to use evidence in one of the murders to support evidence in the other.

First Woman Joins High Court — The Senate, **Sept. 21,** confirmed the appointment of Sandra Day O'Connor as an associate justice of the U.S. Supreme Court. She was the first woman to be appointed to that body. The vote in the Senate was 99-0, Sen. Max Baucus (D., Mont.) being absent. Justice O'Connor took her seat, **Sept. 25,** after a brief ceremony in the courtroom in which Chief Justice Warren E. Burger administered the oath of office.

Hostages to Be Paid — A presidential commission recommended, **Sept. 21,** that the government pay each of the Americans held hostage in Iran $12.50 per day for their time in captivity, the money to be tax-exempt. Medical and health benefits in an unlimited amount were also recommended for those who were suffering captivity-related disabilities. The total amount to be paid to each person who was held for the full 444 days would be $5,550. Attorney Bryce Clagett said that the amount was not enough and he expected some of the hostages to file suit in the Federal Court of Appeals to claim just compensation. The basis of the suit would be that the hostages were denied the right to sue the country of Iran by an agreement between the U.S. and that country.

International

Disagreement Over El Salvador — Argentine diplomats announced, **Sept. 1,** that their nation would join Colombia and Venezuela in declaring their support for the junta government in El Salvador. It was their hope that this statement would offset the impact of the Mexican-French Aug. 28 declaration of support for the leftist guerrillas. Argentina also expected that other nations would join in the letter of support for the junta.

Angola-South Africa Conflict Continues — According to South African officials on **Sept. 1,** some Soviet army officers had been killed and a Russian sergeant captured in Angola in the war against nationalist guerrillas. The Soviets had been sending development and aid experts to Angola since

1976, but had denied sending any military personnel. The South Africans issued another communique **Sept. 5,** stating that 4 Russians had been killed—2 Soviet lieutenant colonels and 2 women, one of them the wife of the captured sergeant. It was stated that the sergeant and a number of other Russians tried to escape from the Angolan town of N'Giva while it was being attacked by South African troops. Elisio de Figueiredo, the Angolan chief delegate to the UN, stated, **Sept. 9,** that there were 15,000 South African troops in Angola, despite an earlier statement from South Africa that the soldiers were being withdrawn. By that time, more than 700 people had been killed in the fighting. The UN General Assembly, **Sept. 14,** voted 117-0, with 12 abstentions, to isolate South Africa and arm the guerrillas fighting to make South West Africa the independent nation of Namibia. The resolution, however, had no binding force, but it did call on all nations to stop all trade with South Africa. The Soviet Union, **Sept. 19,** finally admitted that South African forces had killed 2 Soviet military specialists and captured a 3rd.

Iran in Political Turmoil — Slain Iranian Prime Minister Mohammed Javad Bahonar was replaced, **Sept. 1,** by Ayatollah Mohammed Riza Mahdavi-Kani, the former Minister of the Interior. In addition, the leader of Friday prayers in Teheran, Hojatolislam Ali Khamenei, was appointed leader of the ruling party. It was also announced that the election of a new president would be held within 50 days. Two gun battles between Iranian revolutionary guards and guerrillas were fought in Teheran, **Sept. 3,** killing 10 guerrillas and one guard. The Iranian Prosecutor General was killed by a' bomb, **Sept. 5.** The prosecutor, Hojatolislam Ali Qoddousi, died 5½ hours after the explosion, and Iran's police chief, Col. Houshang Dastgerdi, died as a result of a previous bomb blast. Then, on **Sept. 11,** Ayatollah Ruhollah Khomeini's personal representative in the province of East Azerbaijan, Ayatollah Assadollah Madani, was killed by a grenade during an outdoor prayer service. Six others were also killed, including the assailant. The latest killings brought the deaths due to explosions since June to more than 200 politicans, clergymen, and fundamentalist supporters of the Khomeini regime and included the president, prime minister, prosecutor general, and chief justice. The leftist People's Mujahdeen was accused by Iranian leaders of being responsible and the Mujahdeen movement responded by issuing a statement saying that the struggle against Ayatollah Khomeini's rule had entered a new phase. On **Sept. 17,** the Iranian state radio announced that 19 more opponents of the government had been executed, and, on **Sept. 20,** 149 more faced firing squads. The next day the count had climbed by 45 more. Fierce fighting broke out, **Sept. 27,** between Mujahdeen guerrillas and revolutionary guards in the streets of Teheran. Teheran radio reported that several persons were killed—policemen, revolutionary guards, and others—and 40 were injured. On **Sept. 29,** Hojatolislam Abdulkarim Hashemi Nejad, a member of Parliament, was killed by a grenade, and 43 more guerrillas were put to death. Iran announced, **Sept. 29,** that its Defense Minister, its Acting Chief of Staff, and 2 other top military leaders were killed in an air crash near Teheran. Sabotage was not suspected.

Letup in Northern Ireland — Matthew Devlin, a hunger striker in Maze Prison in Belfast, **Sept. 4,** ended his fast and accepted food. The solidarity of the Northern Ireland hunger strike was further weakened, **Sept. 6,** when another prisoner was taken off the fast by his mother. John Pickering, another prisoner, joined the hunger strikers, **Sept. 7,** and 2 policemen were killed by an IRA land mine. Bernárd Fox ended his hunger strike, **Sept. 24.**

Sadat Cracks Down on Religious Groups — Pres. Anwar el-Sadat of Egypt, fearing the rise of religious factionalism, deposed the nation's Coptic Pope, **Sept. 5.** Pope Shenuda III was the head of Egypt's 6 million members of the Coptic Orthodox Christian Church. Sadat also criticized certain Islamic organizations, saying that they were trying to increase religious tension in the country. On **Sept. 7,** the Egyptian government announced that it would gradually take over the supervision of 40,000 mosques. Only those religious leaders approved by the government would be allowed to conduct services, and their sermons were not to contain any political statements. As of then, 1,536 people had been arrested as being dissidents—Moslem clerics, Coptic Christian priests, journalists, politicians, lawyers, and professors. On **Sept. 11,**

Egyptian riot police broke up 2 Moslem fundamentalist demonstrations against Sadat's policies concerning mixing politics with religion.

Solidarity Flexes Its Muscles — The independent Polish labor union, Solidarity, announced, **Sept. 6,** that it was planning to expand its role and develop a program to overcome Poland's economic crisis. The group acknowledged that this action might be considered as going beyond the functions of trade unionism. At their convention, the members also asked, **Sept. 10,** that there be free elections, both for parliament and for local legislative bodies, and called for permission to send representatives to polling places. The Polish Politburo, **Sept. 16,** accused the union of pushing Poland toward a national tragedy, and claimed that Solidarity had violated the agreements of August and September 1980 under which it had been formed. On **Sept. 18,** the Polish government warned the union that they were espousing anti-Sovietism, and that the U.S.S.R. might retaliate by reducing its exports of oil, cotton, and natural gas to Poland if Solidarity did not come into line. The Polish Parliament, **Sept. 25,** passed laws that gave workers more influence in the running of factories and other enterprises. Solidarity began the second phase in its national convention in Gdansk, **Sept. 26.** The union had invited 3 representatives of the American AFL-CIO, but these men were not granted visas by the Polish government. The next day a rift appeared in the leadership of the union when some of the rank and file members accused the leadership of compromising with the government over the workers' demand to participate in the running of the factories.

Bomb kills 23 in Lebanon — A bomb exploded, **Sept. 17,** in the southern port city of Sidon, Lebanon, destroying a guerrilla command center of the Palestinian-Lebanese leftist alliance. More than 20 people, most of them civilian passersby, were killed. A Lebanese right-wing underground organization, The Front for Liberation of Lebanon from Aliens, claimed responsibility for the act. In addition to the deaths in the blast at Sidon, 90 more people were wounded. The Liberation Front also claimed responsibility for another bomb blast that day in the northern Lebanese town of Chekka. This exploded outside a cement factory that was run by people with pro-Palestinian and pro-Syrian views.

Belize Becomes Independent — Britain's last colony on the American mainland, Belize, became independent at midnight, **Sept. 20,** amid fireworks, champagne, and reggae music. The country, formerly British Honduras, would still have a contingent of British troops on hand to protect it against possible attack from neighboring Guatemala. Guatemala had refused to recognize Belize's independence, claiming that it was rightfully a part of Guatemala itself.

Iran-Iraq Fighting Flares Again — The Iranian government announced, **Sept. 27,** that its forces had broken the Iraqi siege of Abadan, the oil refinery city in the midst of the war zone between Iraq and Iran. The city had been under almost daily bombardment for almost a year. In a surprise attack by the Iranian troops, more than 600 Iraqis were killed or wounded and 1,500 were captured. Iraq denied the statement, saying that the Iranians had been driven back with heavy losses.

General

Drug May Unclog Arteries After Heart Attacks — Researchers announced, **Sept. 30,** that they had developed a clot-dissolving drug that might protect people from the damage that usually follows heart attacks. The treatment, called intracoronary thrombolysis, consisted of inserting a tube into the heart attack victim's leg, threading it through an artery to the heart, and then releasing the medicine streptokinase, which dissolves the clots that so often block the coronary arteries and starve heart muscles after heart attacks.

Disasters — A pit explosion caused the deaths of 65 Czech coal miners at Zalusi, **Sept. 4**...At least 160 pilot whales beached themselves and died in Tasmania, **Sept. 9**...An Amazon river boat sank in the northern jungle port of Obidos, Brazil, **Sept. 19,** drowning 300...A Turkish Air Force jet fighter crashed near a bivouac area prepared for a NATO exercise near Babaeski, **Sept. 22,** killing the pilot and 25 others on the ground.

OCTOBER

National

House, Senate Committee Reject AWACS Sale — The House of Representatives, **Oct. 14,** by a vote of 301-111, disapproved Reagan's proposed sale of AWACS to Saudi Arabia. Citing a 1974 amendment to the Arms Export Control Act that provides that the two houses of Congress must pass a joint resolution in order to block the sale, the administration continued to urge support on Capitol Hill. On **Oct. 15,** the Senate Foreign Relations Committee voted 9-8 in disapproving the AWACS sale. The vote on the proposal by the full Senate was then postponed until later in the month. This was interpreted as a sign that the administration was unsure that they could avoid a defeat on the issue. Pres. Reagan, at a news conference **Oct. 17,** stated that the U.S. would lose all credibility in the Middle East if it did not go through with the Saudi sale.

U.S. Takes New Stand on Grain Sale to Soviets — After 2 days of talks with Soviet leaders in Moscow, U.S. officials announced, **Oct. 1,** that the U.S. would nearly triple the amount of American wheat and corn that the USSR would be allowed to purchase during the next 12 months. The total amount permissible would be 23 million metric tons, or about 25 million tons. The price for the purchase was estimated to be about $3 billion.

Prices, Unemployment Up — The Bureau of Labor Statistics reported, **Oct. 2,** that the unemployment rate in the U.S. rose to 7.5% in September, due chiefly to an extensive loss of jobs among adults, including an unprecedented layoff of construction workers and school teachers. The September rate was 0.3 of one percent higher than that of the previous month. The Bureau announced, **Oct. 9,** that the government's Consumer Price Index rose by 0.2 of one percent during September, the smallest rise in more than 3 years. The small rise was attributed to both lower prices on some foods and the price-cutting by the automobile manufacturers on their late-1981 models.

Reagan Announces Nuclear Plans — Pres. Ronald Reagan rejected, **Oct. 2,** the plan for shuttling MX missiles among shelters in the western deserts of the U.S. Rather than play a guessing game with a possible enemy as to which silos the missiles were in, Reagan said he favored reinforcing existing silos. He also revived plans to build the B-1 long range bomber, a program that had been canceled by former Pres. Jimmy Carter. It was announced that more powerful and accurate nuclear missiles would be built for Trident submarines.

More Budget Cutting — The administration announced, **Oct. 10,** that by deferring some federal spending, about $1 billion would be saved through Nov. 20. The plan called for reducing the spending level in the period from Oct. 1 to Nov. 20 by 12 percent from the level then operative under a continuing resolution that went into effect when Congress failed to pass major appropriations bills by the start of the fiscal year on Oct. 1. Then, on **Oct. 18,** the administration agreed to trim the $13 billion package of new budget cuts by more than half. Administration and Congressional negotiators agreed to seek $7 billion to $8 billion in new revenues instead of the $3 billion that the White House had suggested. The new plan included seeking $5 billion to $6 billion in new budget cuts from discretionary appropriations, and a trimming in military spending of about $3 billion, rather than the $2 billion that had been planned.

International

Beirut Bomb Kills 83 — An explosion outside the offices of the Palestine Liberation Organization, **Oct. 1,** killed 83 people. A car packed with more than 100 pounds of explosives blew up, tore the facades from 5 buildings and injured more than 250 people, in addition to those who were killed. The Front for the Liberation of Lebanon from Foreigners claimed credit for the bombing and warned that the attacks would go on until no foreigners were left in Lebanon. A spokesman for the P.L.O., Mahmoud Labady, said that the blast signaled a new kind of war with Israel, although the Israelis denied having a hand in the attack.

New Government in Iran, More Executions — Iranians, **Oct. 2,** elected their 2d president in 3 months, Hojatolislam

Ali Khamenei of the Islamic Republican Party. The new president announced that he would retain Ayatollah Mohammed Riza Mahdavi-Kani as prime minister. Khamenei replaced Ali Rajai, who was killed by a bomb explosion on **Aug. 30.** On **Oct. 1,** Ayatollah Ruhollah Kohmeini had appointed Ali Zahirnejad as military commander of Iran to replace Maj. Gen. Valiollah Falahi, who had been killed in a plane crash on **Sept. 29.** On the same day, Abdolhassan Bani-Sadr, the former Iranian president, had announced that he had formed what he called a transitional Iranian government in Paris, hoping that it would soon replace the Islamic fundamentalist goverment in Teheran. He appointed himself provisional president. Reports, **Oct. 3,** said that 30 more opponents of the Khomeini government had been executed, all of them Mujahedeen guerrillas, and, on **Oct. 4,** that 66 more leftist guerrillas had been executed, bringing the total number of executions to about 1,500 since Bani-Sadr had been deposed. On **Oct. 7,** former Prime Minister Mehdi Bazargan astonished the Iranian parliament by condemning the execution of Moslem leftists. On **Oct. 8,** it was reported that the parliament was preparing a bill to expel Bazargan for his criticism, and 26 more were executed in Isfahan, in the central part of Iran. Teheran Radio announced, **Oct. 11,** that 82 leftists had been executed the night before. Khamenei was sworn in as president **Oct. 13,** and vowed to stamp out deviation, liberalism, and American-influenced leftists. The government also announced that 22 more leftists had been executed. Amnesty International's London office reported that by their calculations, 1,800 had been executed since Bani-Sadr was ousted. Leaders of the Bahai Faith in the U.S. accused Iran, **Oct. 17,** of persecuting members of their religious group because of their historical friendship with those of the Jewish faith. Bahais, it was alleged, were losing pensions, jobs, places in the army, and employment in state-owned industry. Bahai places of worship had also been destroyed. On **Oct. 19,** Ali Akbar Vellayti was chosen to replace Ayatollah Mohammed Riza Mahdavi-Kani as Prime Minister of Iran. And 25 more Iranians had been executed.

Ulster Attitude Changes — The Irish hunger strikes in Maze Prison in Belfast, Northern Ireland, were called off, **Oct. 3.** The prisoners announced that they felt that after 10 men had died, the families of the remaining strikers were no longer willing to let others die, and, therefore, the hunger strike would no longer be an effective protest weapon. The next day, the IRA vowed to continue its struggle against the British despite the ending of the prison fasts. The British government, **Oct. 6,** granted the prisoners the right to wear their own clothes at all times, promised to consider reduction in sentences for good behavior, and increased the number of prisoners with whom an inmate could associate in off hours from 25 to 50. The next day the prisoners critcized the new rules, demanding that all the prison time spent in protest be counted toward their sentences, rather than half of the time being applied toward release. The IRA was blamed for 3 bomb explosions in Northern Ireland, **Oct. 9,** in which no one was hurt, and for a bomb that exploded in London **Oct. 10,** killing one and injuring at least 50. Lieut. Gen. Sir Steuart Pringle, the commandant of the Royal Marines, was wounded, **Oct. 17,** when a bomb went off in his car as he drove through London. The IRA claimed responsibility.

Kania Replaced in Poland — Polish Communist party leader Stanislaw Kania was dismissed, **Oct. 18,** and replaced by Prime Minister Wojciech Jaruzelski, a general. Along with the dismissal came a party demand for stronger action to deal with Poland's economic crisis and the "antisocialists" in Solidarity, the Polish labor union. However, in that Jaruzelski was regarded as a moderate, the move was not seen as a signal that the dialogue with Solidarity would be abandoned totally. Earlier in the month, on **Oct. 2,** Lech Walesa had been re-elected chairman of Solidarity. Though he won with only a 55 percent majority, the vote was viewed as support for his moderate policies. The election itself had marked the first time that an institution not sponsored by the Communist party had organized its own national elections anywhere in the Soviet bloc nations. In his victory speech, **Oct. 3,** Walesa said that the union faced a very hard period and warned governmental authorities not to try to exploit Solidarity. On **Oct. 3,** the Polish government announced that the prices of tobacco products and certain foodstuffs would be increased sharply, and Solidarity, **Oct.**

Sadat Assassinated; Egyptian President Mourned by World Leaders

Pres. Anwar el-Sadat of Egypt was shot and killed, **Oct. 6,** by a group of men in uniform during a military parade in Nasser City, near Cairo. As jet fighters flew overhead, 4 men leaped out of a truck towing an artillery piece and walked toward the reviewing stand. Suddenly a grenade exploded and rifles were fired toward the stand. Initially, it was estimated that 10 other persons were killed in the reviewing stand and 38 wounded.

Sadat was rushed to Maadi Military Hospital by helicopter and it was announced several hours later that he had died. Later reports stated that he may have been hit by as many as 5 bullets and shrapnel fragments, and that he had been dead when he arrived at the hospital. It was generally assumed that Vice President Hosni Mubarak would take over the reigns of government, although Mubarak announced that Speaker of Parliament Sufi Abu Taleb would serve as acting president. Mubarak took over the direction of the armed forces.

Security forces immediately began patrolling the streets of Cairo and guarding government buildings. In the U.S., Secretary of State Alexander M. Haig Jr. blamed Islamic fundamentalists for the assassination and said that 6 uniformed men had taken part: a major, an lieutenant, and 4 enlisted men. He also announced that the major and 2 of the enlisted men had been killed by Sadat's guards and the others had been captured.

On **Oct. 7,** the Egyptian parliament named Mubarak as the man to seek the presidency in a soon to be held single-candidate election. Taleb, the acting president, appointed Mubarak prime minister for the interim. The next day, Pres. Ronald Reagan officially invited Mubarak to visit the U.S. in 1982, and former Presidents Richard M. Nixon, Gerald R. Ford, and Jimmy Carter left for Egypt to attend the funeral.

On **Oct. 8,** Egyptian officials announced that apparently only 4 men had been active in the assassination, but it was still not clear how they had been able to get into the parade, leap from the truck at the right moment, and shoot Sadat with almost no opposition from the security guards. A series of photographs showed 3 of the men firing automatic weapons at the reviewing stand and there was no evidence of anyone firing back. It was thought that the guards had been distracted by the jets roaring overhead. It was also announced that the attackers had used submachine guns.

Oct. 9 saw the beginning of 24 hours of clashes between policemen and Moslem fundamentalists in Asyut, Egypt. At least 20 people—14 policemen and 6 fundamentalists—were killed in the fighting in protest of Sadat's and Mubarak's pro-Western policies.

Also on **Oct. 9,** the Egyptian government released preliminary findings concerning the assasination. It was claimed that an army lieutenant, Khaled Ahmed Shawki al-Istanbuli, had organized the plot. Istanbuli's brother, a Moslem extremist, had been arrested in a crackdown on religious extremists on **Sept. 5,** and it was inferred that Istanbuli wanted revenge.

In a ceremony attended by leaders from 80 countries, Sadat was buried, **Oct. 10,** near the reviewing stand where he had been assassinated. His grave was at the Tomb of the Egyptian Unknown Soldier.

On **Oct. 1,** Secretary of State Haig announced that the U.S. was ready to speed up the delivery of arms to Egypt and would take part with Egypt in a joint army exercise. Haig's remarks were prompted by reports of continuing violence in Egypt and were meant to be a pledge to help secure the country for Mubarak. This statement led to the accusation by the USSR, **Oct. 12,** that the U.S. was applying unlawful pressures on the Egyptian government.

The Egyptian government announced, **Oct. 12,** that it had dismissed 18 army officers that were believed to be Moslem religious fanatics. That day, 3 American security experts announced, in Washington, D.C. that they believed that there had been a breakdown of security at the parade grounds when Sadat was murdered. By studying photographs, they concluded that Egyptian security forces appeared confused, outgunned, poorly stationed, and slow to respond.

On **Oct. 13,** one week after the assassination, Egyptians elected Vice President Hosni Mubarak as president. Three days later, Murbarak ordered a nationwide crackdown on Moslem fundamentalists. It was reported that security forces had swept through towns across the country and that thousands of Moslem militants had been arrested.

On **Oct. 18,** the government announced the arrest of 230 members of the Takfir Wahigra, the group of Moslem fundamentalists that was thought to have planned Sadat's assassination. By that time, experts estimated that some 1,500 fundamentalists had been taken into custody.

Pres. Mubarak said, **Oct. 19,** that he believed that a limited network of fanatic plotters was involved in the assassination of Sadat, and that they would be rooted out by wholesale arrests. It was also announced that 134 Egyptian soldiers—30 officers and 104 enlisted men, had been dismissed from the army and transferred to civilian job because of suspected extremist religious leanings. They were, however, not under suspicion as being plotters in Sadat's death. Although Egyptian officials stuck to their story that only 4 men had been involved in the plot, Lieut. Gen. Abdel Halim Abu Ghazala, the Defense Minister, hinted that several others might have been involved.

4, protested the moves because it had not been consulted. Finance Minister Marian Krzak was sent to the union's convention in Gdansk. When he appeared before the convention, Walesa warned him that the union would not be controlled by the government if it insisted on the price increases. The government then announced that liquor prices would be doubled, and that the cost of heating and electrical power would rise the next week. On **Oct. 5,** the government put the price rises into effect on tobacco. That set the price of a pack of cigarettes at about $2, meaning that the average Polish worker would have to work an extra hour just to pay the increase on that pack. This was regarded as a slap in the face to Solidarity, since Walesa had told the government to maintain the previous price levels. On **Oct. 7,** at the Solidarity convention in Gdansk, the union approved a 2-year national program to try to solve the country's economic problems. A suggestion was made that a new retail price system be gradually introduced in order to stabilize the economy. The union also called for a cut in military spending, and threatened a nationwide strike within 2 weeks over the government's consumer price policy. The union's program also demanded a national tribunal to punish members of the previous Communist regime, which was named as the cause of the economic problems of the country. On **Oct. 14,** nearly 12,000 women occupied the textile mills west of Warsaw where they worked to protest food shortages. Also, employees of 17 chemical plants all over the country held a 2-hour warning strike demanding more holidays and benefits. The Polish government and Solidarity agreed **Oct. 15** on a temporary freeze on price increases. This would last until a plan for more compensation of the lowest-paid workers could be worked out.

Socialists Win in Greece — The Greek Socialist Party won a major victory, **Oct. 18,** when their candidate, Andreas Papandreou, was elected president, and they gained a strong majority in the parliament. This ended 35 years of pro-Western conservative rule, and it was thought that there would be a radical change in the foreign policy of the country, given the Socialists' generally negative stance toward membership in NATO and EEC, and resentment of the presence of American military bases in their country.

General

Disasters — Tropical Storm Lydia swept into the northern Pacific coast of Mexico, **Oct. 9,** killing at least 65. . .A 77-foot log protruding from a truck pierced the windshield and door of a school bus in Waynesboro, Miss., **Oct. 12,** killing 3 students and wounding 25. . .Methane gas seeped into a coal mine near Sapporo, Japan, **Oct. 16,** killing 61.

Major Actions During the 97th Congress, 1981

The 97th Congress convened, Jan. 5, 1981. Bills passed and signed, and other major actions during the session, included the following:

Debt Limit Raised. The House, Feb. 5, and Senate, Feb. 6, voted to increase the ceiling on the national debt to $985 billion from the previous limit of $935.1 billion.

Pay Raises Nixed. A 16.8% pay increase for members of Congress, the judiciary, the cabinet and 37,000 high-level government employees, was voted down by the House and Senate, Mar. 12, The proposed pay raise, recommended by Pres. Jimmy Carter, would have died automatically on Mar. 16.

Dairy-Price Support. The Senate passed, Mar. 25, and the president signed, Mar. 31, legislation that canceled a proposed 7 percent increase in dairy-price supports, scheduled to go into effect April 1.

Abscam Scandal Postscripts

Hinson Resigns. Rep. Jon Hinson (R., Miss.) resigned from Congress, Apr. 16, in the wake of his arrest on a morals charge in Washington, DC. U.S. Captiol police arrested, Feb. 4, Hinson and a Library of Congress clerk in a Longworth public restroom and charged them with sodomy.

Lederer Resigns. Rep. Raymond F. Lederer (D., Pa.) resigned, Apr. 29, from the House of Representatives following his conviction in the Abscam scandal on felony bribe-taking charges.

Nerve Gas Amendment. The Senate passed, May 21, a House-approved amendment appropriating $20 million for the production of binary nerve gas weapons. The fiercely contested measure passed 50 to 48.

Abortion Aid Restricted. An amendment further restricting the federal funding of abortions was passed, May 21, in a 52-43 vote. The new restrictions, passed as a rider on a supplemental appropriations bill, eliminated provisions for the federal funding of abortions in cases of rape and incest.

Environmental, Housing Issues

Sewage Cost-Sharing Repealed. A bill that would allow industries to constititutional, sewage treatment facilities without contributing to the cost of building those facilities was passed unanimously, May 28. The measure repealed a provision of the 1980 Clean Water Act.

Clean Air Postponed. In a move designed to aid the ailing U.S. steel industry, the House voted, May 28, to postpone required compliance with clean air laws for prejudices to 3 years. By defering the purchase of expensive anti-pollution equipment, steel companies, it was hoped, could invest in the modernization of aging plants.

Housing. Legislation curtailing federal housing aid to cities that controlled the rents of new housing units — or of old units as they became occupied by new tenants — was passed by the Senate, June 4. In addition, the bill required tenants in subsidized housing to pay up to 30%, versus the current 25%, of their income for rent.

Infant Formula Marketing

Infant Formula Resolutions. The House, June 16, and Senate, June 18, passed separate resolutions that supported the aims of the World Health Organization and, in effect, criticized the Reagan Administration's stand on the marketing of infant formula throughout the world. The United States had cast the only dissenting vote, May 21, when a WHO code, intended to limit aggressive modes of marketing the formula, was passed.

Saccharin Sales Extended. The Senate voted, June 26, to extend until 1983 legislation that prohibited the Food and Drug Administration from removing the artificial sweetener saccharin from the market.

Economic Recovery Program

Tax-cut Legislation Passed. Both houses of Congress passed, July 29, President Reagan's tax-cut legislation. The bill, the largest tax cut in the nation's history, cleared, Aug. 4, and was sent to the White House for the president's signature. It was expected that in fiscal year 1982 the measure would reduce taxes by $37.6 billion, and would save taxpayers $750 billion over the next 5 years.

Reagan Budget Cuts. Following an intensive lobbying effort by the Reagan Administration, the House and Senate gave final approval, July 31, to the President's package of budget cuts, reducing federal spending to $695 billion from the previously planned $730 billion level. Over 200 domestic social programs were affected in the sweeping, highly controversial legislation.

Poland Intervention Resolution. The House passed, July 30, a resolution cautioning against interference and the use of force in resolving Poland's democratization process. Passed by a vote of 410 to 1, the resolution stated that the U.S. would respond to acts of "internal repression or external agression" against the Polish people.

Williams Expulsion Recommended

Abscam. The Senate Select Committee on Ethics recommended unanimously, Aug. 24, the expulsion of Senator Harrison A. Williams from the Senate for his involvement in the Abscam scandal. In recommending expulsion, the committee cited the New Jersey Democrat's "ethically repugnant" conduct in the affair. The committee also recommended that full Senate consideration of the matter be delayed until the Senator's appeal was heard in New Jersey federal court.

O'Connor Nomination Confirmed

Senate Confirms O'Connor Nomination. The Senate, Sept. 21, confirmed the appointment of Sandra Day O'Connor as an associate justice of the U.S. Supreme Court. She was the first woman to be appointed to that body. The vote in the Senate was 99-0, with Senator Max Baucus (D., Mont.) absent.

$1.08 Trillion Debt Limit. The Senate voted, Sept. 29, to raise the federal debt limt to $1.08 trillion. It was the first time the debt limit had been raised over the $1 trillion mark.

AWACS

House Blocks AWACS. By a vote of 301 to 111, the House voted, Oct. 14, to disapprove the proposed sale of Airborne Warning and Control System radar surveillance planes and other air-combat equipment to Saudi Arabia. While both houses of Congress were required to veto the arms deal within 30 days of its formal submission, Oct. 1, to Congress, the Reagan Administration's proposal suffered another setback on Oct. 16, when the Senate Foreign Relations Committee voted 9 to 8 to recommend disapproval of the sale.

Social Security

Social Security Solvency. In a 95 to 0 vote, the Senate approved, Oct. 15, legislation designed to preserve the solvency of the Social Security System. The measure also restored the minimum benefit for current recipients, reversing action taken in August. House approval of the bill was expected within a matter of weeks.

Tobacco Support Preserved. The House voted, Oct. 21, to preserve the tobacco price support program. In a vote of 231 to 184, the House defeated a proposal that would end the 48-year-old program that sets price supports and allocates acreage among growers.

Major Decisions of the U.S. Supreme Court, 1980-81

Among the notable actions in 1980-81, the Supreme Court:

Refused to review, and thus let stand, the decision by an Illinois court that a divorced mother had to relinquish custody of her three children because she was living with a man who was not the children's natural father (Oct. 20, 1980).

Ruled unanimously that the immunity from civil suits accorded to judges could not be extended to private citizens in cases in which a judge and private citizens were accused of conspiring together to violate someone's constitutional rights (Nov. 17, 1980).

Ruled, 5-4, that a Kentucky law requiring public schools to post a copy of the Ten Commandments in every classroom was in violation of the First Amendment (Nov. 17, 1980).

Overturned an earlier decision by the U.S. 2d Circuit Court of Appeals and held, 5-4, that the Organized Crime Control Act of 1970 gave the federal government the right to appeal a criminal sentence it believed to be too lenient (Dec. 9, 1980).

Teen-Age Abortions

Ruled, 6-3, that a state could make it a criminal offense for a physician to perform an abortion on a teen-age girl without first notifying her parents. The majority opinion, however, suggested that such notice was not required if the girl in question was mature and independent (March 23, 1981).

Struck down unanimously a Louisiana law that gave a husband the right to unilaterally dispose of property that he jointly owned with his wife (March 23, 1981).

Statutory Rape

Ruled, 5-4, that statutory rape laws that applied only to males were constitutional, affirming an earlier ruling by the California Supreme Court (March 23, 1981).

Ruled, 6-3, that a defendant who was a member of a racial or ethnic minority did not have the automatic right to have the trial judge question prospective jurors about their possible prejudices (April 21, 1981).

Ruled, 7-2, that law enforcement officials, armed only with an arrest warrant, had no legal right to enter the home of someone other than the person they sought to arrest (April 21, 1981).

Ruled, 7-2, that workers who joined a wildcat strike could not be sued for damages by their employer. The court had ruled in 1962 that a union, but not its individual members, could be sued for breaking no-strike agreements, but had not ruled on whether individual employees could be sued for joining a strike not authorized by the union (May 4, 1981).

Double Jeopardy

Ruled, 5-4, that the constitutional protection against double jeopardy could not be extended to death penalty hearings. Specifically, convicted murderers, sentenced to life imprisonment, could not, in a subsequent retrial, be sentenced to death (May 4, 1981).

"Miranda Rights" Broadened

In what was seen as a broadening of "Miranda rights," ruled unanimously that a defendant suspected of a capital crime could refuse to submit to a psychiatric examination if the testimony of the examining psychiatrist could be used against him in sentencing (May 18, 1981).

Ruled, 8-0, that private pension plans could reduce the benefits of a retired worker by an amount equal to any compensation award received for a job-related disability (May 18, 1981).

Ruled unanimously that a Connecticut prison inmate had been deprived of due process because the state had refused to pay for a blood test with which he might have defended himself in a paternity suit. State law required paternity case defendants to pay for their own blood tests, regardless of their ability to meet the cost (June 1, 1981).

Iranian Assets Transfer

Upheld, unanimously, the authority of Presidents Reagan and Carter to suspend court-approved monetary claims against Iran as a condition of the agreement that freed the U.S. hostages held by the Iranian government. The action cleared the way for the transfer of $2.3 billion in Iranian assets out of the U.S. (June 2, 1981).

Ruled, 5-4, that women who are paid less than men are entitled to sue their employer, even if the jobs performed by the two sexes are not identical (June 8, 1981).

Upheld unanimously a federal law giving the government broad powers to curb the abuses associated with strip mining. The court held that coal mining, in any form, is an interstate activity, and that the Constitution permits Congress to pass legislation to regulate "activities causing air or water pollution or other environmental hazards that may have effects in more than one state" (June 15, 1981).

Ruled, 8-1, that prison authorities could place more than one inmate in cells designed to house one person without violating the constitutional rights on the inmates, if the overall conditions at the prison were adequate (June 15, 1981).

Ruled unanimously that states could restrict the rights of religious groups to sell merchandise and solicit funds in public places (June 22, 1981).

Nixon Wiretapping

Divided, 4-4, and thus technically affirmed a lower court ruling that former President Richard M. Nixon and his top aides — former Attorney General John Mitchell, former White House Chief of Staff H.R. Haldeman and former national security advisor Henry A. Kissinger — had to stand trial in a civil suit over the warrantless wiretapping of ex-national security official Morton Halperin (June 22, 1981).

Ruled, 7-2, that an employer was not obligated to bargain with unions over a decision to shut down part of a company's operation (June 22, 1981).

Upheld, 7-2, a New York law that gave the State Liquor Authority the power to ban topless entertainment in bars that serve alcoholic beverages (June 22, 1981).

Women Excluded from Draft

Ruled 6-3, that the Constitution permitted the exclusion of women from military draft registration and, by extension, from the draft itself. The ruling thus reversed the decision of a three-judge panel that in 1980 had found male-only draft registration unconstitutional. The court's decision was based on deference to Congress' authority over national defense issues. In his dissent, Justice Thurgood Marshall noted that it was "demonstrably false" that "every draftee must be available for assignment to combat." Likewise, Justice Byron R. White saw "no adequate justification" for sex discrimination in the claim that draftees were needed for combat (June 25, 1981).

Ruled, 6-3, that military pension benefits may not become part of a property settlement in a divorce. Since in the case of military families the service member's pension is often the largest economic asset, the ruling placed a significant limit on the financial rights of divorced spouses of military personnel (June 26, 1981).

Ruled, 6-3, that television stations were required to sell "reasonable" amounts of air time to federal office candidates requesting time during political campaigns (July 1, 1981).

Deaths, Nov. 1, 1980—Oct. 31, 1981

A

Addonizio, Hugh, 67; former mayor of Newark, N.J.; 6-term U.S. representative; Red Bank, N.J., Feb. 2.

Agar, Herbert, 83; writer and editor who won the 1933 Pulitzer Prize for history; Sussex, England, Nov. 24.

Algren, Nelson, 72; novelist and short-story writer, *The Man with the Golden Arm;* Sag Harbor, N.Y., May 9.

Allen, Robert S., 80; political columnist, co-founded the "Washington Merry-Go-Round" column; Washington, D.C., Feb. 23.

Amalrik, Andrei, 42; Soviet human rights activist and political exile; nr. Guadalajara, Spain, Nov. 11.

Anderson, Jack Z., 76; U.S. representative from California, 1939-53; Hollister, Cal., Feb. 9.

Aronson, Boris, 81; stage designer who won 6 Tony awards; Nyack, N.Y., Nov. 16.

Astaire, Adele, 83; dancer who starred in Broadway musicals in the 1920s with her brother, Fred Astaire; Phoenix, Jan. 25.

Asther, Nils, 84; Hollywood leading man in the 1920s and 1930s; Stockholm, Oct. 13.

B

Bagnold, Enid, 91; British playwright and novelist, *National Velvet;* London, Mar. 31.

Baldwin, Roger, 97; a founder of the American Civil Liberties Union; Ridgewood, N.J., Aug. 26.

Ball, Edward, 93; businessman who headed the billion-dollar Alfred du Pont Trust; New Orleans, June 24.

Barber, Samuel, 70; composer who won Pulitzer prizes in 1958 and 1963; best known for the opera *Vanessa;* New York, Jan. 23.

Barr Jr., Alfred Hamilton, 79; art scholar who helped develop the Museum of Modern Art in New York City; Salisbury, Conn., Aug. 15.

Battles, Cliff, 70; football hall of fame halfback-quarterback who played in the NFL in the 1930s; Seminole, Fla., Apr. 28.

Beard, Matthew, 56; actor who played Stymie in the "Our Gang" film series, known on TV as "The Little Rascals"; Los Angeles, Jan. 8.

Becker, Frank J., 82; U.S. representative from New York, 1953-65; Lynbrook, N.Y., Sept. 4.

Bennett, Robert Russell, 87; orchestrator of some 300 Broadway musicals; New York, Aug. 18.

Berman, Emile Zola, 78; trial lawyer whose clients included Sirhan Sirhan; New York, July 3.

Betancourt, Romulo, 73; Venezuelan political leader who was twice that country's president; New York, Sept. 28.

Bliss, Ray C., 73; Ohio political leader who helped rebuild the GOP in the mid-1960s; Akron, Aug. 6.

Boehm, Karl, 87; Austrian conductor noted for Mozart, Wagner interpretations; Salzburg, Aug. 14.

Bondi, Beulah, 92; character actress whose career spanned 50 years; Hollywood, Cal., Jan. 12.

Boone, Richard, 63; actor best known for the TV series, "Have Gun, Will Travel"; St. Augustine, Fla., Jan. 11.

Bowling, Alice, 54; singer who appeared for 6 years as the original "Champagne Lady" on the Lawrence Welk TV show;

Dallas, Apr. 25.

Brasselle, Keefe, 58; film actor and TV producer; Downey, Cal., July 7.

Bradley, Gen. Omar, 88; World War II hero and the last U.S. 5-star general; New York, Apr. 8.

Brown, Roy, 56; singer who influenced many leading rock and soul vocalists; Los Angeles, May 25.

Breuer, Marcel, 79; architect and designer who played a major role in shaping 20th century architecture; New York, July 1.

C

Cabot, John Moors, 79; U.S. ambassador to 5 nations between 1954 and 1965; Washington, D.C., Feb. 24.

Carroll, Joe, 65; jazz vocalist who helped popularize "be-bop" singing style; New York, Feb. 1.

Celler, Emanuel, 92; U.S. representative from New York City, 1923-73; New York, Jan. 15.

Chapin, Harry, 38; folk-rock composer and singer; Jericho, N.Y., July 16.

Chayefsky, Paddy, 58; playwright and screenwriter, *Marty, Network;* New York, Aug. 1.

Clair, Rene, 82; French film director; Neuilly, France, Mar. 15.

Clements, Stanley, 55; actor who played a tough street kid in films in the 1940s and 1950s; Los Angeles, Oct. 16.

Cole, Cozy, 71; jazz drummer; Columbus, Oh., Jan. 29.

Connelly, Marc, 90; playwright won 1930 Pulitzer Prize for *The Green Pastures;* New York, Dec. 21.

Cotter, William R., 55; U.S. representative from Connecticut since 1971; East Lyme, Conn., Sept. 8.

Cramer, Polly, 77; writer of "Polly's Pointers" syndicated newspaper column for 20 years; Palm Springs, Cal., May 13.

Cronin, A.J., 84; Scottish physician and author, *The Citadel, The Keys of the Kingdom;* Switzerland, Jan. 6.

Crowther, Bosley, 75; film critic for *The New York Times,* 1940-67; Mt. Kisco, N.Y., Mar. 7.

Curran, Joseph, 75; founder of the National Maritime Union; Boca Raton, Fla., Aug. 14.

D

(Chief) Dan George, 82; American-Indian actor, *Little Big Man;* Vancouver, B.C., Sept. 23.

Daniel, Dan, 91; baseball writer for New York City newspapers for 50 years; Pompano Beach, Fla., July 2.

Darden Jr., Colgate W., 84; Virginia political leader and educator; Norfolk, June 9.

Davis, Jim, 65; actor best known as Jock Ewing in the "Dallas" TV series; Northridge, Cal., Apr. 26.

Day, Dorothy, 83; social activist who founded the Catholic Worker Movement; New York, Nov. 29.

Dayan, Moshe, 66; Israeli soldier and statesman who directed Israel's campaigns in the 1967 and 1973 wars, as well as the Camp David accords; Tel Aviv, Oct. 16.

Dean, Paul "Daffy," 67; major league pitcher in the 1930s; brother of Dizzy Dean; Springdale, Ark., Mar. 17.

Delbruck, Dr. Max, 74; pioneer in modern molecular genetics; Pasadena, Cal., Mar. 9.

Dinkeloo, John G., 63; architect who helped build Dulles International Airport; Fredericksburg, Va., June 15.

DiSalle, Michael V., 73; governor of Ohio, 1959-63; Italy, Sept. 15.

Dixon, Jean, 85; actress who appeared in comedy roles in numerous Broadway plays; New York, Feb. 12.

Doenitz, Adm. Karl, 89; commander of German U-boat campaign during World War II; presided over Germany's surrender; Hamburg, Dec. 24.

Dominick, Peter H., 65; U.S. senator from Colorado, 1963-75; Hobe Sound, Fla., Mar. 18.

Douglas, Donald W., 88; airplane designer whose DC-3 opened the era of mass airline travel; Palm Springs, Cal., Feb. 1.

Douglas, Melvyn, 80; actor who was a popular film leading man in the 1930s; later became a supporting actor winning 2 Oscars; New York, Aug. 4.

Drew, Richard, 81; chemical engineer who invented Scotch tape; Santa Barbara, Cal., Dec. 7.

E

Edwards, Joan, 61; popular singer in the 1940s on "Your Hit Parade" radio show; New York, Aug. 27.

Edwards, Sherman, 61; composer and lyricist for the musical, *1776;* New York, Mar. 30.

Elson, Bob, 76; broadcaster for the White Sox and Cub baseball teams for some 40 years; Chicago, Mar. 10.

Elliot, "Jumbo" Jim, 66; track and field coach at Villanova Univ. since 1935; Juno Beach, Fla., Mar. 22.

Erwin, George "Pee Wee", 68; trumpet and clarinet player with the Miller, Goodman, and Dorsey orchestras; Teaneck, N.J., June 20.

Ethridge, Mark F., 84; journalist who helped build *The Louisville Courier-Journal* and *The Louisville Times* into nationally known newspapers; Moncure, N.C., Apr. 5.

Evans, Madge, 71; actress who starred in films and the theater in the 1930s; Oakland, N.J., Apr. 26.

F

Farrand, Clair L., 85; inventor of the cone radio loudspeaker and holder of some 250 patents; Palm Springs, Cal., Jan. 7.

Fields, Shep, 70; leader of the band known for its "rippling rhythm" sound in the 1930s; Los Angeles, Feb. 23.

Fischetti, John, 64; editorial cartoonist who won the 1969 Pulitzer Prize; Chicago, Nov. 18.

Fisk, James B., physicist who headed a group that pioneered the development of radar during World War II; Elizabethtown, N.J., Aug. 10.

Fitzsimmons, Frank, 73; president of the International Brotherhood of Teamsters; La Jolla, Cal., May 6.

Fletcher, Harvey, 96; physicist whose work resulted in the development of stereophonic sound; Provo, Ut., July 23.

Fox, Carol, 55; co-founder and general manager of the Lyric Opera of Chicago; Chicago, July 21.

Fox, Terry, 22; Canadian marathon runner who competed on an artificial limb after losing his leg to cancer; Vancouver, B.C., June 28.

Fredericka, 63; queen of Greece, 1947-64; later queen mother; Madrid, Feb. 6.

Friedhofer, Hugo, 83; film orchestrator and composer who won 1947 Oscar for *The Best Years of Our Lives;* Hollywood, Cal., May 17.

Frings, Ketti, 61; playwright who won 1958 Pulitzer Prize for dramatization of Thomas Wolfe's *Look Homeward, Angel;* Los Angeles, Feb. 11.

G

Garcia, Sara, 85; Mexican stage and screen actress; Mexico City, Nov. 21.

Gary, Romain, 66; French novelist and diplomat; Paris, Dec. 2.

Gnagy, Jon, 74; artist whose TV program in the 1940s and 1950s taught millions how to draw; Palm Springs, Cal., Mar. 7.

Golden, Harry, 79; newspaper publisher and author, *Only in America;* Charlotte, N.C., Oct. 2.

Grahame, Gloria, 55; actress who appeared in supporting roles in 1940s and 1950s films; New York, Oct. 5.

Grasso, Ella, 61; governor of Connecticut, 1975-80; first woman elected governor in her own right; Hartford, Conn., Feb. 5.

Green, Paul, 87; playwright who won 1927 Pulitzer Prize for *In Abraham's Bosom;* Chapel Hill, N.C., May 4.

Guion, David, 88; composer, "Home on the Range"; Dallas, Oct. 17.

Guyer, Tennyson, 67; U.S. representative from Ohio since 1973; Alexandria, Va., Apr. 12.

H

Haden, Sara, 82; character actress who appeared in some 70 films; Woodland Hills, Cal., Sept. 15.

Hagerty, James C., 71; White House press secretary during the Eisenhower administration; Bronxville, N.Y., Apr. 11.

Haley, Bill, 55; rock-and-roll singer and band leader, "Rock Around the Clock"; Harlingen, Tex., Feb. 9.

Haley, James A., 82; U.S. representative from Florida, 1953-77; Sarasota, Fla., Aug. 6.

Hansford, Pamela, 69; British novelist and playwright; London, June 18.

Hanson, Howard, 84; conductor and composer who won the 1944 Pulitzer Prize for music; Rochester, N.Y., Feb. 26.

Harburg, E.Y., 84; lyricist, *Over the Rainbow, April in Paris;* Los Angeles, Mar. 5.

Hardin, Tim, 39; singer-songwriter popular in the 1960s; Los Angeles, Dec. 29.

Harding, Ann, 79; stage and screen actress popular in the 1930s; Sherman Oaks, Cal., Sept. 1.

Hayden, Russell "Lucky", 68; actor who starred in western films in the 1930s and 1940s; Palm Springs, Cal., June 9.

Hays, Brooks, 83; U.S. representative from Arkansas, 1943-58; Bethesda, Md., Oct. 11.

Hays, Lee, 67; singer and songwriter who co-founded the "Weavers" folk-singing quartet; Tarrytown, N.Y., Aug. 26.

Hendrix, Wanda, 52; actress who starred in films in the 1940s and early 1950s; Burbank, Cal., Feb. 1.

Herridge, Robert, 67; television writer and producer who won 3 Emmys; Woodstock, N.Y., Aug. 14.

Hirshhorn, Joseph, 82; financier and art patron; Washington, D.C., Aug. 31.

Horan, James, 67; novelist and historian of the Old West; New York, Oct. 13.

Howard, Elston, 51; catcher-outfielder for the N.Y. Yankees; American League MVP in 1963; New York, Dec. 14.

Hulme, Kathryn, 81; author of the 1956 best seller *The Nun's Story;* Lihue, Ha., Aug. 27.

Humes, Helen, 68; blues and ballad singer; Santa Monica, Cal., Sept. 13.

I

Ilg, Frances L., 78; pediatrician and author of child behavior books; Manitowish Waters, Wis., July 26.

J

Jaffee, Irving, 74; speed skater who won 2 gold medals at the 1932 Olympics; San Diego, Mar. 20.

Jenkins, Ray H., 83; special counsel during the Army-McCarthy hearings in the 1950s; Knoxville, Tenn., Dec. 26.

Jennings, Williams, 60; sports executive in hockey and golf; Byram, Conn., Aug. 17.

Jensen, Alfred Julio, 77; Guatemalan-born abstract painter; Glen Ridge, N.J., Apr. 4.

Jessel, George, 83; show business personality whose career spanned 7 decades; Los Angeles, May 24.

Johnson, J.C., 84; jazz and pop composer, "The Joint is Jumpin' "; New York, Feb. 27.

Jones, Paul C., 79; U.S. representative from Missouri, 1948-69; Kennett, Mo., Feb. 10.

Joslyn Allyn, 79; character actor in numerous films and some 3,500 radio shows; Woodland Hills, Cal., Jan. 21.

K

Kanner, Dr. Leo, 86; child psychologist and author; Sykesville, Md., Apr. 3.

Kelly, Patsy, 71; actress who appeared in comedy roles in films and the theater; Woodland Hills, Cal., Sept. 24.

Kemper, James, 94; founder of insurance and financial empire; Chicago, Sept. 18.

Kintner, Robert E., 71; media executive who headed both NBC and ABC; Washington, D.C., Dec. 20.

Kipnis, Claude, 42; French-born mime who toured the U.S. with his own company; New York, Feb. 8.

Knight, John S., 87; founder of the Knight newspaper publishing empire; Akron, June 16.

Kondrashin, Kiril, 67; Soviet symphony conductor who defected to the West in 1978; Amsterdam, Mar. 7.

Kosygin, Alexei, 76; Soviet premier, 1964-80; Moscow, Dec. 18.

Kuharich, Joe, 63; football coach of the Philadelphia Eagles in the 1960s; Philadelphia, Jan. 25.

L

Lane, Frank, 85; baseball executive who was general manager for 4 major league teams; Richardson, Tex., Mar. 19.

Lane, Lola, 75; one of the Lane sisters who were Hollywood leading ladies during the 1930s; Santa Barbara, Cal., June 22.

Lape, Esther, 100; social scientist who lead an unsuccessful battle in the 1920s and 1930s for U.S. participation in the World Court; New York, May 17.

Lasker, Edward, 95; chess master who won U.S. Open championship 5 times; New York, Mar. 23.

Lennon, John, 40; singer and composer who is best known as a member of the "Beatles"; New York, Dec. 8.

Leontovich, Mikhail, 78; Soviet nuclear phsyicist; Moscow, Apr. 1.

Lesage, Jean, 68; premier of Quebec, 1960-66; Quebec, Dec. 11.

Levene, Sam, 75; actor who created

legendary stage and screen comedy roles during a 50-year career; New York, Dec. 28.

Levin, Meyer, 75; novelist, *Compulsion;* Israel, July 9.

Lewis, David, 72; Canadian political leader helped found the New Democratic Party; Ottawa, May 24.

Liebman, Max, 78; producer of the popular 1950s TV program "Your Show of Shows"; New York, July 21.

Lilienthal, David E., 81; first chairman of the Atomic Energy Commission; headed the TVA; New York, Jan. 15.

Lindsay, Margaret, 70; actress who appeared in 88 films during her 30-year career; Hollywood, Cal., May 8.

Lindstrom, Fred, 75; baseball hall of famer who played mostly with the N.Y. Giants; Chicago, Oct. 4.

Link, Edwin, 77; inventor of the Link flight simulator used in training over 2 million airmen; Binghamton, N.Y., Sept. 7.

Loeb, William, 75; controversial New Hampshire newspaper publisher; Burlington, Mass., Sept. 13.

Loos, Anita, 88; screenwriter, playwright, and novelist, *Gentlemen Prefer Blondes;* New York, Aug. 18.

Lopokova, Lydia, 88; Russian-born ballerina; widow of John Maynard Keynes; England, June 8.

Louis, Joe, 66; world heavyweight boxing champion, 1937-49; Las Vegas, Apr. 12.

Ludden, Allen, 63; TV game-show host, "G.E. College Bowl," "Password"; Los Angeles, June 9.

M

Marley, Bob, 36; singer who helped popularize reggae music; Miami, May 11.

Marshall, Laurence, 91; founder and president for 38 years of Raytheon Company; Cambridge, Mass., Nov. 5.

Martin, Ross, 61; character actor best known for his role in "The Wild, Wild West" TV series; Ramona, Cal., July 3.

Matthews, Jessie, 74; British musical-comedy singer and dancer; London, Aug. 20.

McCormick, John, 88; U.S. representative from Massachusetts for 42 years; Speaker of the House, 1962-70; Dedham, Mass., Nov. 22.

McEwen, John, 80; Australian political leader; Melbourne, Nov. 20.

McHugh, Frank, 83; supporting actor in numerous films in the 1930s and 1940s; Greenwich, Conn., Sept. 11.

McLuhan, Marshall, 69; Canadian communications theorist and author, *The Medium is the Message;* Toronto, Dec. 31.

McNamara, Margaret, 65; founder of the "Reading is Fundamental" program; wife of Robert S. McNamara; Washington, D.C., Feb. 10.

McQueen, Steve, 50; actor who was one of the most celebrated and highly paid film stars of the 1960s and early 1970s; Juarez, Mexico, Nov. 7.

Meiklejohn, William, 78; Hollywood talent agent credited with discovering Mickey Rooney, Judy Garland, Ronald Reagan; Burbank, Cal., Apr. 26.

Montale, Eugenio, 84; Italian poet who won the 1975 Nobel Prize for literature; Milan, Sept. 12.

Montgomery, Robert, 77; actor starred in films in the 1930s and 1940s; New York, Sept. 27.

Morrison, Paul, 74; set designer for more than 60 Broadway productions; New York, Dec. 29.

Moses, Robert, 92; urban planner known as New York's master builder; Lincoln Center, Shea Stadium, New York

Coliseum; W. Islip, N.Y., July 29.

Mosley, Sir Oswald, 84; British fascist leader in the 1930s; Paris, Dec. 2.

Mueller, Merrill, 64; print and broadcast journalist for some 40 years; Santa Monica, Cal., Dec. 1.

Myers, Carmel, 80; silent screen leading lady; Los Angeles, Nov. 9.

N

Northrop, John Knudsen, 85; aviation design pioneer who founded aeronautical company; Glendale, Cal., Feb. 18.

Noyes, David M., 83; presidential assistant and biographer of President Truman, *Mr. Citizen;* Los Angeles, Aug. 7.

O

O'Connell, Arthur, 73; character actor of the stage and screen; Hollywood, Cal., May 19.

Osborne, John, 74; columnist for *The New Republic* magazine, Washington, D.C., May 2.

P

Patten, Lewis B., 66; author of more than 100 western novels; Denver, May 25.

Peabody, Mary Parkman, 89; civil rights and antiwar activist in the 1960s; Cambridge, Mass., Feb. 6.

Perry, Eleanor, 66; screenwriter whose credits include *David and Lisa* and *Diary of a Mad Housewife;* New York, Mar. 14.

Person, Bernard, 86; journalist who helped found *Facts on File* news digest; Albuquerque, N.M., Mar. 9.

Powell, Wesley, 65; governor of New Hampshire, 1958-62; Hampton Falls, N.H., Jan. 6.

Ponselle, Rosa, 84; dramatic soprano starred at the Metropolitan Opera for 19 years; Stevenson, Md., May 25.

Popov, Dusko, 69; double agent for Great Britain during World War II; model for the fictional spy, James Bond; Opio, France, Aug. 21.

Procope, Russell, 72; clarinetist with the Duke Ellington band for 3 decades; New York, Jan. 21.

R

Raft, George, 85; actor who appeared in over 100 films, usually in tough-guy roles; Hollywood, Cal., Nov. 24.

Rahman, Ziaur, 45; president of Bangladesh; Chittagong, Bangladesh, May 30.

Richter, Karl, 54; German conductor who was famed for his Bach interpretations; Munich, Feb. 16.

Roberts, Rachel, 53; Welsh-born stage and screen actress; Los Angeles, Nov. 26.

Rocha, Glauber, 42; Brazilian film director; Rio de Janeiro, Aug. 22.

Roldos Aguilera, Jaime, 40; president of Ecuador since 1979; nr. Guachanama, Ecuador, May 24.

Roosevelt, John A., 65; youngest son of FDR; New York, Apr. 27.

S

el-Sadat, Anwar, 62; president of Egypt; shared 1978 Nobel Peace Prize; Cairo, Oct. 6.

Sanders, Col. Harland, 90; founder of the Kentucky Fried Chicken fast food chain; Shelbyville, Ky., Dec. 16.

Saroyan, William, 72; novelist and playwright, *The Time of Your Life;* Fresno, Cal., May 18.

Sauter, Eddie, 66; jazz composer, arranger, and orchestra leader; Nyack, N.Y., Apr. 21.

Scott, Hazel, 61; jazz pianist and singer; once married to Adam Clayton Powell Jr.; New York, Oct. 2.

Sharp, Zerna, 91; creator of the "Dick and Jane" reading primers used in U.S. classrooms for 4 decades; Frankfort, Ind., June 17.

Shawkey, Bob, 90; pitcher won 198 major league games mostly for the N.Y. Yankees; Syracuse, N.Y., Dec. 31.

Smith, Joe, 97; partner in the Smith and Dale vaudeville comedy team for 73 years; Englewood, N.J., Feb. 22.

Smythe, Conn, 85; owner of the Toronto Maple Leafs hockey team, 1927-60; Toronto, Nov. 18.

Soong Ching-ling, 90; widow of Sun Yat-sen, the founder of the Chinese Republic; Peking, May 29.

Speer, Albert, 76; Germany's minister of armaments and war production during World War II; London, Sept. 2.

Sutton, Willie "the actor"; bank robber and prison escape artist; Spring Hill, Fla., Nov. 2.

T

Taurog, Norman, 82; Hollywood film director, *Boy's Town;* Rancho Mirage, Cal., Apr. 9.

Teague, Olin, 70; U.S. representative from Texas, 1946-79; Bethesda, Md., Jan. 23.

Thatcher, Torin, 76; actor appeared in the theater and some 70 films; Thousand Oaks, Cal., Mar. 4.

Thomas, Lowell, 89; radio and television broadcaster, author, and world traveler; Pawling, N.Y., Aug. 30.

Thompson, Cecil "Tiny," 77; hockey hall of fame goaltender; Calgary, Feb. 9.

Torrijos Herrera, Gen. Omar, 52; leader of Panama since 1968; Panama, July 31.

Travers, Ben, 94; British author of some 20 plays, 30 films; London, Dec. 18.

Trippe, Juan, 81; international aviation and jet passenger travel pioneer; a founder of Pan Am; New York, Apr. 3.

U

Urey, Harold, 87; scientist whose work led to H-bomb development; won 1934 Nobel Prize in chemistry; La Jolla, Cal., Jan. 5.

V

Vagnozzi, Egidio Cardinal, 74; apostolic delegate to the U.S., 1959-67; Rome, Dec. 26.

Vaughan, Gen. Harry, 87; military aide to President Truman; Ft. Belvoir, Va., May 20.

Vera-Ellen (Rohe), 55; dancer who starred in film musicals in the 1940s and 1950s; Los Angeles, Aug. 30.

Vinson, Carl, 97; U.S. representative from Georgia who served in the House for a record 50 years; Milledgeville, Ga., June 1.

Voskovec, George, 76; character actor best known for his roles on the New York stage; Pearblossom, Cal., July 1.

W

Waldorf, Lynn "Pappy"; football coach at Northwestern Univ. and Univ. of California; Berkeley, Cal., Aug. 15.

Walker, Mickey, 79; boxer who held the world welterweight and middleweight boxing titles; Freehold, N.J., Apr. 28.

Wallace, DeWitt, 91; founder of the "Reader's Digest" magazine; Mt. Kisco, N.Y., Mar. 30.

Walsh, George, 92; silent screen leading man; Pomona, Cal., June 13.

Walsh Raoul, 93; director of more than 100 Hollywood films; Simi Valley, Cal., Dec. 31.

Walsh, Stella, 69; Polish-born sprinter who won Olympic gold medal in 1932; Cleveland, Dec. 4.

Ward, Barbara, 67; British economist and author; Lodsworth, England, May 31.

Warren, Harry, 87; songwriter, "You'll Never Know," "Lullaby of Broadway"; Los Angeles, Sept. 22.

Watts, Richard, 82; New York film and drama critic for 50 years; New York, Jan. 2.

Waugh, Alec, 83; British author, *Island in the Sun;* Tampa, Fla., Sept. 3.

West, Mae, 87; stage and film star who burlesqued sex; wrote much of her own material; Los Angeles, Nov. 22.

Westheimer, Irvin, 101; founder of the Big Brothers organization; Cincinnati, Dec. 30.

Whitehead, Don, 72; journalist won Pulitzer prizes for international reporting in 1951 and 1953; Knoxville, Tenn., Jan. 12.

Wilder, Alec, 73; songwriter, "I'll Be Around," "While We're Young"; Gainesville, Fla., Dec. 24.

Wilkins, Roy, 80; civil rights leader who headed the NAACP for 22 years; New York, Sept. 8.

Williams, Eric, 69; prime minister of Trinidad and Tobago since 1962; Port of Spain, Mar. 29.

Williams, Mary Lou, 71; jazz pianist, arranger, and composer; Durham, N.C., May 28.

Wilson, Edith, 76; actress, jazz and blues singer; portrayed Aunt Jemima in advertisements for 18 years; Chicago, Mar. 31.

Wyler, William, 79; film director who won 3 Oscars for *Mrs. Miniver, The Best Years of Our Lives,* and *Ben Hur;* Beverly Hills, Cal., July 27.

Wyszynski, Stefan Cardinal, 79; Roman Catholic primate of Poland; Warsaw, May 28.

XYZ

Yost, Charles W., 73; U.S. ambassador to the United Nations, 1967-71; Washington, D.C., May 22.

Yukawa, Hideki, 74; Japanese physicist who won 1949 Nobel Prize in physics; Kyoto, Japan, Sept. 8.

Zuckerman, Yitzhak, 66; leader of the Polish resistance movement during World War II; Tel Aviv, June 17.

VITAL STATISTICS

Source: National Center for Health Statistics, U.S. Department of Health and Human Services

January-April 1981 (Provisional Data)

Births

During the first 4 months of 1981 there were 1,164,000 live births, an increase of 3% over the first 4 months of 1980. The birth rate increased 2% to 15.5, and the fertility rate increased 2% to 66.4.

Marriages

For the first 4 months of 1981 a total of 616,000 marriages was reported, yielding a marriage rate of 8.2 per 1,000 population. The number of marriages and the marriage rate were 3 and 3.6% lower, respectively, than the corresponding figures for the first 4 months of 1980.

Divorces

In the 4 months from January through June, a cumulative total of 391,000 divorces was reported, and the divorce rate for the period was 5.2 per 1,000 population. For the number and rate this was an increase of 2.8% and 2.0%, respectively, over the levels recorded in the first 4 months of 1979.

Deaths

For April 1981 the provisional count of deaths totaled 161,000, amounting to a rate of 8.5 deaths per 1,000 population. This rate was 4% lower than the rate of 8.9% for April 1980. Among the 161,000 deaths for April 1981 were 3,500 deaths at ages under 1 year, yielding an infant mortality rate of 12.4 deaths per 1,000 live births. This rate was 3% lower than the rate of 12.8 for April 1980.

The provisional death rate for the 12 months ending with March 1981, 8.8 deaths per 1,000 population, was 2.0% higher than the rate for the 12 months ending with March 1980, 8.6 deaths per 1,000 population.

Provisional Statistics
12 months ending with April

	Number		Rate*	
	1981	1980	1981	1980
Live births	3,627,000	3,524,000	15.9	15.6
Deaths	2,002,000	1,950,000	8.8	8.6
Natural increase.	1,625,000	1,574,000	7.1	7.0
Marriages	2,392,000	2,389,000	10.5	10.6
Divorces	1,193,000	1,180,000	5.2	5.2
Infant deaths. . .	44,600	45,300	12.3	12.8
Population base (in millions)			228.0	225.5

*Per 1,000 population
Note: Rates for 1980 are based on revised population estimates.

Annual Report for the Year 1980 (Provisional Statistics)

Births

During 1980 an estimated 3,598,000 live births occurred in the United States, 4% more than in 1979. The birth rate was 16.2 live births per 1,000 population and the fertility rate was 69.2 live births per 1,000 women aged 15-44 years. These rates were 3 and 2% higher, respectively, than in 1979.

The increase in the number of births and the birth rate in 1979 and 1980 is a result of the growth in the number of women in the childbearing ages as well as the increase in the rate of childbearing. The number of women in the childbearing ages increased 2% between 1979 and 1980.

As a result of natural increase, the excess of births over deaths, 1,612,000 persons were added to the population during 1980. The rate of natural increase was 7.3 persons per 1,000 population compared with 7.1 for 1979. This increase was due to the increase in the birth rate.

Deaths

The provisional count of deaths in the United States during 1980 totaled 1,986,000, resulting in a rate of 8.9 deaths per 1,000 population. This rate was 2.3% higher than the provisional rate of 8.7 for 1979.

Among these deaths were 45,000 deaths at ages under 1 year yielding an infant mortality rate of 12.5 deaths per 1,000 live births. This rate was 3.8% lower than the provisional infant mortality rate for 1979, 13.0 deaths per 1,000 live births.

Marriages and Divorces

According to provisional reports, there were 2,413,000 marriages in 1980. This represented an increase of 2% over the provisional total for 1979 and the 5th consecutive increase in the annual marriage total. The 1980 provisional marriage total was the largest annual number of marriages ever recorded in the United States, exceeding by about 54,000 the previous peak of 2,359,000 recorded in 1979.

In 1980 the provisional marriage rate was 10.9 per 1,000 population. This rate was 2% higher than the provisional rate for 1979. After a steady decline in the period from 1972 to 1976, the marriage rate has increased each year since 1977.

An estimated 1,182,000 divorces were granted in 1980. This was 12,000 (1%) more than the provisional total for 1979 and almost 3 times more than the final total recorded for 1967.

In 1980 the provisional divorce rate was 5.3 per 1,000 population, the same as 1979. The rate of increase slowed during the second half of the seventies after increasing sharply since 1967.

Births and Deaths in the U.S.

Refers only to events occurring within the U.S., including Alaska and Hawaii beginning in 1960. Excludes fetal deaths. Rates per 1,000 population enumerated as of April 1 for 1960, and 1970; estimated as of July 1 for all other years. (p) provisional. (NA) not available. Beginning 1970 excludes births and deaths occurring to nonresidents of the U.S.

Year	Births				Deaths			
	Males	Females	Total number	Rate	Males	Females	Total number	Rate
1955	2,073,719	1,973,576	4,047,295	24.6	872,638	656,079	1,528,717	9.3
1960	2,179,708	2,078,142	4,257,850	23.7	975,648	736,334	1,711,982	9.5
1965	1,927,054	1,833,304	3,760,358	19.4	1,035,200	792,936	1,828,136	9.4
1970	1,915,378	1,816,008	3,731,386	18.4	1,078,478	842,553	1,921,031	9.5
1975	1,613,135	1,531,063	3,144,198	14.8	1,050,819	842,060	1,892,879	8.9
1978	1,709,394	1,623,885	3,333,279	15.3	1,055,290	872,498	1,927,788	8.8
1979	1,791,267	1,703,131	3,494,398	15.8	1,042,960(p)	863,350(p)	1,906,000(p)	8.7
1980(p)	NA	NA	3,598,000	16.2	NA	NA	1,986,000	8.9

Births and Deaths by States

Source: National Center for Health Statistics, U.S. Department of Health and Human Services

State	Births 1980P	Births 1979	Deaths 1980P	Deaths 1979	State	Births 1980P	Births 1979	Deaths 1980P	Deaths 1979
Alabama	62,814	60,628	35,386	34,304	Nebraska	27,851	26,093	14,681	14,116
Alaska	9,368	8,912	1,692	1,639	Nevada	13,156	11,830	6,408	5,842
Arizona	50,173	45,707	21,609	20,385	New Hampshire	13,648	12,830	7,547	7,287
Arkansas	36,863	35,008	22,565	21,554	New Jersey	91,047	91,896	64,727	64,126
California	401,616	363,463	190,251	169,954	New Mexico	25,661	25,570	9,080	8,596
Colorado	50,279	47,813	19,503	19,057	New York	232,491	231,787	167,769	160,937
Connecticut	34,069	36,959	26,597	26,124	North Carolina	85,123	84,388	49,059	47,168
Delaware	9,544	9,123	5,201	5,048	North Dakota	12,939	12,769	5,850	5,566
Dist. of Col.	17,835	20,334	9,165	9,042	Ohio	169,359	164,111	97,779	93,197
Florida	131,922	130,929	106,816	100,767	Oklahoma	60,601	47,214	28,308	27,204
Georgia	95,980	89,446	43,519	42,646	Oregon	43,998	42,984	21,793	21,071
Hawaii	18,277	17,429	5,190	6,061	Pennsylvania	161,025	157,783	123,400	117,269
Idaho	19,495	19,686	6,431	6,061	Rhode Island	12,512	12,235	9,553	9,295
Illinois	186,578	181,218	100,356	100,218	South Carolina	49,805	49,956	24,337	23,736
Indiana	87,906	87,452	46,721	47,153	South Dakota	13,013	12,623	6,462	6,236
Iowa	48,050	47,083	26,714	26,237	Tennessee	73,500	72,261	43,205	41,264
Kansas	39,330	37,100	21,399	20,552	Texas	268,717	265,066	108,586	107,493
Kentucky	60,778	60,182	33,268	32,552	Utah	43,708	42,304	8,556	8,546
Louisiana	79,202	79,413	35,626	34,918	Vermont	7,640	7,396	4,312	4,364
Maine	16,095	15,755	10,857	10,367	Virginia	75,042	73,812	41,889	40,183
Maryland	52,284	50,043	33,337	32,002	Washington	67,972	55,077	32,495	24,496
Massachusetts	73,355	73,104	54,773	52,624	West Virginia	29,277	30,263	19,120	19,140
Michigan	143,007	142,127	74,002	72,480	Wisconsin	74,470	72,818	40,972	38,873
Minnesota	68,848	64,939	33,495	32,592	Wyoming	9,539	8,946	3,062	2,929
Mississippi	47,538	45,913	22,911	22,720					
Missouri	79,623	78,505	49,881	48,558	Total	3,598,000	3,473,000	1,986,000	1,906,000
Montana	13,928	13,803	6,592	6,407	(p) provisional				

Marriages and Divorces by States

Source: National Center for Health Statistics, U.S. Department of Health and Human Services

1980 provisional figures; divorces include reported annulments.

State	Marriages	Divorces	State	Marriages	Divorces	State	Marriages	Divorces
Alabama	49,006	26,856	Louisiana	41,658	NA	Oklahoma	46,509	24,226
Alaska	5,286	3,435	Maine	14,351	6,239	Oregon	23,115	17,925
Arizona	30,230	19,921	Maryland	45,967	16,293	Pennsylvania	95,394	34,853
Arkansas	25,197	21,778	Massachusetts	49,058	16,487	Rhode Island	7,120	3,583
California	218,385	134,268	Michigan	89,606	40,850	South Carolina	53,923	13,810
Colorado	34,078	18,155	Minnesota	37,825	15,132	South Dakota	8,929	2,823
Connecticut	25,761	11,448	Mississippi	28,043	13,458	Tennessee	58,751	30,100
Delaware	4,423	2,313	Missouri	55,518	27,820	Texas	187,118	97,161
Dist. of Col.	5,182	3,473	Montana	8,367	4,963	Utah	17,074	7,957
Florida	110,575	71,409	Nebraska	14,189	6,481	Vermont	5,187	2,522
Georgia	69,416	33,636	Nevada	115,411	13,659	Virginia	60,193	23,608
Hawaii	11,670	4,386	New Hampshire	9,298	5,222	Washington	46,617	28,424
Idaho	13,084	6,643	New Jersey	54,356	25,843	West Virginia	17,451	9,915
Illinois	110,667	50,465	New Mexico	16,324	10,444	Wisconsin	40,953	17,864
Indiana	57,852	NA	New York	141,299	54,224	Wyoming	6,825	3,970
Iowa	27,527	11,757	North Carolina	46,341	28,161			
Kansas	24,928	13,399	North Dakota	6,139	2,142	Total	2,413,000	1,182,000
Kentucky	34,291	16,988	Ohio	99,522	58,225	(NA) not available.		

Marriages, Divorces, and Rates in the U.S.

Source: National Center for Health Statistics, Public Health Service

Data refer only to events occurring within the United States, including Alaska and Hawaii beginning with 1960. Rates per 1,000 population.

Year	Marriages[1] No.	Marriages[1] Rate	Divorces[2] No.	Divorces[2] Rate	Year	Marriages[1] No.	Marriages[1] Rate	Divorces[2] No.	Divorces[2] Rate
1890	570,000	9.0	33,461	0.5	1940	1,595,879	12.1	264,000	2.0
1895	620,000	8.9	40,387	0.6	1945	1,612,992	12.2	485,000	[3]3.5
1900	709,000	9.3	55,751	0.7	1950	1,667,231	11.1	385,144	2.6
1905	842,000	10.0	67,976	0.8	1955	1,531,000	9.3	377,000	2.3
1910	948,166	10.3	83,045	0.9	1960	1,523,000	8.5	393,000	2.2
1915	1,007,595	10.0	104,298	1.0	1965	1,800,000	9.3	479,000	2.5
1920	1,274,476	12.0	170,505	1.6	1970	2,158,802	10.6	708,000	3.5
1925	1,188,334	10.3	175,449	1.5	1975	2,152,662	10.1	1,036,000	4.9
1930	1,126,856	9.2	195,961	1.6	1979	2,331,337	10.6	1,181,000	5.4
1935	1,327,000	10.4	218,000	1.7	1980(p)	2,413,000	10.9	1,182,000	5.3

(1) Includes estimates and marriage licenses for some states for all years. (2) Includes reported annulments. (3) Divorce rates for 1945 based on population including armed forces overseas. (p) provisional.

Deaths and Death Rates for Selected Causes

Source: National Center for Health Statistics, U.S. Department of Health and Human Services

1979 Cause of death (est.)	Number	Rate[1]	1979 Cause of death (est.)	Number	Rate[1]
All causes	1,906,000	866.2	Acute bronchitis and bronchiolitis	470	0.2
Viral hepatitis	650	0.3	Influenza and pneumonia	44,110	20.0
Tuberculosis, all forms	1,980	0.9	Influenza	590	0.3
Septicemia	8,350	3.8	Pneumonia	43,520	19.8
Syphilis and its sequelae	180	0.1	Chronic obstructive pulmonary diseases	49,980	22.7
All other infective and parasitic diseases	3,320	1.5	Chronic and unqualified bronchitis	3,220	1.5
Malignant neoplasms, including			Emphysema	14,070	6.4
neoplasms of lymphatic and			Asthma	2,540	1.2
hematopoietic tissues	403,780	183.5	Ulcer of stomach and duodenum	5,520	2.5
Diabetes mellitus	33,060	15.0	Hernia and intestinal obstruction	5,010	2.3
Meningitis	1,490	0.7	Cirrhosis of liver	29,860	13.6
Major cardiovascular diseases	953,100	433.0	Cholelithiasis, cholecystitis, and cholangitis	2,840	1.3
Diseases of heart	729,210	331.3	Nephritis, nephrosis and nephrotic syn.	16,080	7.3
Active rheumatic fever and chronic			Infections of kidney	3,070	1.4
rheumatic heart disease	7,470	3.4	Hyperplasia of prostate	580	0.3
Hypertensive heart disease and			Congenital anomalies	13,390	6.1
renal disease	23,670	10.7	Certain causes of mortality in early infancy	22,880	10.4
Ischemic heart disease	549,820	249.8	Symptoms and ill-defined conditions	28,210	12.8
Chronic disease of endocardium and			All other diseases	105,350	47.9
other myocardial insufficiency	6,160	2.8	Accidents	105,420	47.9
All other forms of heart disease	142,090	64.6	Motor vehicle accidents	53,990	24.5
Hypertension	6,910	3.1	Suicide	27,640	12.6
Cerebrovascular diseases	169,350	76.9	Homicide	23,040	10.5
Arteriosclerosis	28,650	13.0	All other external causes	3,880	1.8
Other diseases of arteries,					
arterioles, and capillaries	18,980	8.6			

Due to rounding estimates of death, figures may not add to total. Data based on a 10% sampling of all death certificates for a 12-month (Jan.-Dec.) period. (1) Rates per 100,000 population.

Principal Types of Accidental Deaths

Source: National Center for Health Statistics, U.S. Department of Health and Human Services

Year	All types	Motor vehicle	Falls	Burns	Drowning	Firearms	Machinery	Poison gases	Other poisons
1960	93,806	38,137	19,023	7,645	5,232	2,334	1,951	1,253	1,679
1965	108,004	49,163	19,984	7,347	5,485	2,344	2,054	1,526	2,110
1970	114,638	54,633	16,926	6,718	6,391	2,406	...	1,620	3,679
1975	103,030	45,853	14,896	6,071	6,640	2,380	...	1,577	4,694
1978	105,561	52,411	13,690	6,163	5,784	1,806	...	1,737	3,035
Death rates per 100,000 population									
1960	52.1	21.2	10.6	4.3	2.9	1.3	1.1	0.7	0.9
1965	55.8	25.4	10.3	3.8	2.8	1.2	1.1	0.8	1.1
1970	56.4	26.9	8.3	3.3	3.1	1.2	...	0.8	1.8
1975	48.4	21.5	7.0	2.8	3.1	1.1	...	0.7	2.2
1978	48.4	24.0	6.3	2.8	2.7	0.8	...	0.8	1.4

Deaths in Civil Aviation Accidents

Source: National Safety Council

(includes only U.S. carriers)

Year	Total deaths[1]	Passenger deaths in scheduled flights — Domestic No.	Domestic Rate[2]	International No.	International Rate[2]	General aviation deaths Total	Pleasure flying
1960	1,286	297	0.93	10	0.12	787	NA
1965	1,279	205	0.38	21	0.12	1,029	590
1970	1,454	0	0.00	2	0.01	1,310	726
1975	1,448	113	0.09	0	0.00	1,345	863
1979	1,737	262	0.13	61	0.12	1,382	NA
1980(p)	1,389	11	0.01	0	0.00	1,375	NA

(1) Includes some deaths not shown separately—crew members in scheduled operations and persons not in planes killed in airplane accidents. Excludes deaths in military plane accidents. (2) Rates are the number of deaths per 100,000,000 passenger miles. (p) preliminary. NA—not available.

Transportation Accident Passenger Death Rates, 1980

Source: National Safety Council

Kind of transportation	Passenger miles (billions)	Passenger deaths	Rate per 100,000,000 pass. miles	1978-1980 aver. death rate
Passenger automobiles and taxis[1]	2,200.0	29,050	1.32	1.30
Passenger automobiles on turnpikes	46.1	330	0.72	0.71
Buses	85.8	130	0.15	0.15
Intercity buses[2]	17.3	23	0.13	0.05
Railroad passenger trains	11.0	4	0.04	0.07
Scheduled air transport planes (domestic)	221.2	11	0.01	0.04

(1) Drivers of passenger automobiles are considered passengers. (2) Class 1 only, representing 65 per cent of total intercity bus passenger mileage.

Motor Vehicle Traffic Deaths by State

Source: National Safety Council

Place of accidents	Number 1980	Number 1979	Death rate* 1980	Death rate* 1979	Place of accidents	Number 1980	Number 1979	Death rate* 1980	Death rate* 1979
Total U.S.†	52,600	52,800	3.5	3.5					
Alabama	947	1,020	3.2	3.4	Montana	325	332	4.9	5.0
Alaska	87	90	3.5	3.6	Nebraska	396	330	3.5	2.9
Arizona	947	1,030	4.9	5.3	Nevada	346	365	5.9	6.2
Arkansas	587	548	3.6	3.4	New Hampshire	194	184	3.1	2.9
California	5,489	5,503	3.5	3.4	New Jersey	1,191	1,141	2.4	2.3
Colorado	709	691	3.6	3.5	New Mexico	615	650	5.5	5.7
Connecticut	582	576	3.0	3.0	New York	2,619	2,377	3.4	3.1
Delaware	158	121	3.9	3.0	North Carolina	1,514	1,522	3.6	3.6
Dist. of Col.	46	50	1.4	1.5	North Dakota	181	187	2.9	2.4
Florida	2,879	2,637	3.9	3.5	Ohio	2,033	2,281	2.8	3.1
Georgia	1,503	1,523	3.5	3.5	Oklahoma	972	869	3.7	3.2
Hawaii	185	205	3.9	4.3	Oregon	646	675	3.3	3.5
Idaho	329	333	4.4	4.4	Pennsylvania	2,114	2,204	3.0	3.1
Illinois	1,994	2,048	3.1	3.2	Rhode Island	128	125	2.2	2.1
Indiana	1,177	1,309	3.0	3.3	South Carolina	859	900	3.6	3.7
Iowa	626	654	3.3	3.4	South Dakota	228	211	4.1	3.8
Kansas	595	520	3.5	3.0	Tennessee	1,171	1,236	3.5	3.6
Kentucky	825	905	3.0	3.3	Texas	4,424	4,429	4.1	3.9
Louisiana	1,212	1,187	5.2	5.1	Utah	335	330	3.5	3.4
Maine	260	241	3.7	3.4	Vermont	134	163	3.7	4.4
Maryland	782	700	2.8	25	Virginia	1,045	1,014	2.7	2.6
Massachusetts	881	920	2.5	2.6	Washington	985	1,032	3.4	3.5
Michigan	1,772	1,847	2.8	2.8	West Virginia	539	532	4.7	4.6
Minnesota	863	881	3.1	3.2	Wisconsin	985	997	3.0	3.0
Mississippi	697	716	4.1	4.2	Wyoming	244	244	5.2	5.1
Missouri	1,191	1,162	3.5	3.4					

*The death rate is the number of deaths per 100 million vehicle miles. †Includes both traffic and nontraffic motor-vehicle deaths.

Accidental Injuries by Severity of Injury

Source: National Safety Council

1980 Severity of injury	Total*	Motor vehicle	Work	Home[2]	Public[1]
Deaths*	105,000	52,600	13,000	23,000	21,000
Disabling injuries*	10,000,000	2,000,000	2,200,000	3,400,000	2,600,000
Permanent impairments	360,000	150,000	80,000	90,000	60,000
Temporary total disabilities	9,600,000	1,850,000	2,100,000	3,300,000	2,500,000
Certain Costs of Accidental Injuries, 1980 ($ billions)					
Total*	$83.2	$39.3	$30.2	$8.9	$6.4
Wage loss	22.7	11.9	5.0	3.5	3.6
Medical expense	10.3	3.5	3.1	2.3	1.7
Insurance administration	16.6	10.5	5.9	0.1	0.1

*Duplication between motor vehicle, work, and home are eliminated in the total column. (1) Excludes motor vehicle and work accidents in public places. (2) Excessive heat deaths undoubtedly contributed to the increase in home deaths in 1980.

Home Accident Deaths

Source: National Safety Council

Year	Total home	Falls	Fires, burns[2]	Suffo., ingested object	Suffo., mechanical	Poison (solid, liquid)	Poison by gas	Fire-arms	Other
1950	29,000	14,800	5,000	(1)	1,600	1,300	1,250	950	4,100
1955	28,500	14,100	5,400	(1)	1,250	1,150	900	1,100	4,600
1960	28,000	12,300	6,350	1,850	1,500	1,350	900	1,200	2,550
1965	28,500	11,700	6,100	1,300*	1,200	1,700	1,100	1,300	4,100
1970	27,000	9,700	5,600	1,800	1,100	3,000	1,100	1,400	3,300
1975	25,000	8,000	5,000	1,800	800	3,700	1,000	1,300	3,400
1979	22,000	7,000	4,700	2,100	600	2,300	1,000	1,100	3,100
1980	23,000	6,700	4,400	1,800	600	2,200	900	1,100	5,300 [3]

*Data for this year and subsequent years not comparable with previous years due to classification changes. (1) Included in Other. (2) Includes deaths resulting from conflagration, regardless of nature of injury. (3) Includes 1,000 excessive deaths due to summer heat wave.

Pedalcycle Accidents

Since 1935, the National Safety Council reports the number of pedalcycle motor vehicle deaths has almost tripled to 1,200 in 1980. The number of pedalcycles in use, 100.0 million (including sidewalk pedalcycles), is 29 times the number in 1935; so the death rate in 1980 was one-eleventh the rate in 1935. The proportion of deaths occurring to young adults and adults has steadily increased since 1960. Persons 15 years of age and older accounted for more than three-fifths the deaths in 1980 compared to about one-fifth in 1960.

Average Lifetime in the U.S.

Source: National Center for Health Statistics, U.S. Department of Health and Human Services

1979ᵖ Age interval	Number living[1]	Avg. life expect.[2]	1979ᵖ Age interval	Number living[1]	Avg. life expect.[2]
0-1.	100,000	73.8	40-45.	94,740	36.8
1-5.	98,696	73.8	45-50.	93,414	32.3
5-10	98,451	69.9	50-55.	91,356	28.0
10-15.	98,289	65.0	55-60.	88,087	23.9
15-20.	98,108	60.2	60-65.	83,397	20.1
20-25.	97,610	55.5	65-70.	76,550	16.7
25-30.	96,949	50.8	70-75.	67,879	13.5
30-35.	96,282	46.2	75-80.	56,547	10.6
35-40.	95,606	41.5	80-85.	41,923	8.5
			85 and over	26,925	6.8

(1) Of 100,000 born alive, number living at beginning of age interval. (2) Average number of years of life remaining at beginning of age interval.

Years of Life Expected at Birth

Year	Total pop.	Male	Female	Year	Total pop.	Male	Female
1979ᵖ.	73.8	69.9	77.8	1950	68.2	65.6	71.1
1978	73.3	69.5	77.2	1940	62.9	60.8	65.2
1975	72.5	68.7	76.5	1930	59.7	58.1	61.6
1970	70.8	67.1	74.7	1920[1].	54.1	53.6	54.6
1965	70.2	66.8	73.8	1910[1].	50.0	48.4	51.8
1960	69.7	66.6	73.1	1900[1].	47.3	46.3	48.3

(p) Provisional (1) Based on data for death registration states only.

Ownership of Life Insurance in the U.S. and Assets of U.S. Life Insurance Companies

Source: American Council of Life Insurance

Legal Reserve Life Insurance Companies (millions of dollars)

Year	Purchases of life insurance				Insurance in force					Assets
	Ordinary	Group	Industrial	Total	Ordinary	Group	Industrial	Credit	Total	
1940	7,022	747	3,318	11,087	79,346	14,938	20,866	380	115,530	30,802
1950	18,260	6,237	5,492	29,989	149,116	47,793	33,415	3,844	234,168	64,020
1960	56,183	15,328	6,906	78,417	341,881	175,903	39,563	29,101	586,448	119,576
1965	89,643	52,867*	7,302	149,812*	499,638	308,078	39,818	53,020	900,554	158,884
1970	134,802	65,381*	6,612	206,795*	734,730	551,357	38,644	77,392	1,402,123	207,254
1975	207,052	102,659*	6,741	316,452*	1,083,421	904,695	39,423	112,032	2,139,571	289,304
1977	247,453	115,839	6,504	369,796	1,289,321	1,115,047	39,045	139,402	2,582,815	351,722
1978	283,067	125,129	6,015	414,211	1,425,095	1,243,994	38,080	163,081	2,870,250	389,924
1979	329,571	157,906	5,335	492,812	1,585,878	1,419,418	37,794	179,250	3,222,340	432,282
1980	371,114	170,184	3,275	544,573	1,760,474	1,579,355	35,994	165,215	3,541,038	479,210

*Includes Servicemen's Group Life Insurance $27.4 billion in 1965, $16.8 billion in 1970, and $1.7 billion in 1975.

Accidental Deaths by Month and Type, 1978 and 1980

Source: National Safety Council

Month	1980 totals	1978 details by type								
		All types‡	Motor vehicle	Falls	Drowning†	Fires, burns*	Ingest. of food, object	Firearms	Poison (solid, liquid)	Poison by gas
Total	105,000	105,561	52,411	13,690	7,026	6,163	3,063	1,806	3,035	1,737
January	7,700	7,836	2,952	1,388	190	868	299	154	314	254
February	7,000	6,892	2,767	1,092	166	793	244	128	238	229
March	7,600	7,791	3,617	1,080	320	640	260	143	313	177
April	7,950	8,129	4,057	1,135	460	520	237	127	237	134
May	8,600	9,115	4,622	1,083	930	357	243	107	248	107
June	10,100	9,434	4,813	1,057	1,190	315	265	115	253	60
July	11,600	10,484	5,218	1,160	1,520	319	257	130	234	82
August	10,200	9,827	5,185	1,098	980	287	235	145	234	61
September	8,550	9,110	4,941	1,118	580	298	205	131	220	71
October	8,850	9,070	4,972	1,232	300	397	279	181	235	149
November	8,000	8,633	4,622	1,092	180	530	248	232	239	181
December	8,850	9,240	4,645	1,155	210	839	291	213	270	232
Average	8,750	8,797	4,368	1,141	586	514	255	151	253	145

*Includes deaths resulting from conflagration regardless of nature of injury. †Includes drowning in water transport accidents. Some totals partly estimated. ‡ Includes some deaths not shown separately.

Physical Growth Range for Children from 2 to 18 Years

Source: National Center for Health Statistics, U.S. Department of Health and Human Services

Boys

Age	Height in centimeters			Weight in kilograms		
	Shortest 5%	Median height	Tallest 5%	Lightest 5%	Median weight	Heaviest 5%
2	82.5	86.8	94.4	10.49	12.34	15.50
3	89.0	94.9	102.0	12.05	14.62	17.77
4	95.8	102.9	109.9	13.64	16.69	20.27
5	102.0	109.9	117.0	15.27	18.67	23.09
6	107.7	116.1	123.5	16.93	20.69	26.34
7	113.0	121.7	129.7	18.64	22.85	30.12
8	118.1	127.0	135.7	20.40	25.30	34.51
9	122.9	132.2	141.8	22.25	28.13	39.58
10	127.7	137.5	148.1	24.33	31.44	45.27
11	132.6	143.3	154.9	26.80	35.30	51.47
12	137.6	149.7	162.3	29.85	39.78	58.09
13	142.9	156.5	169.8	33.64	44.95	65.02
14	148.8	163.1	176.7	38.22	50.77	72.13
15	155.2	169.0	181.9	43.11	56.71	79.12
16	161.1	173.5	185.4	47.74	62.10	85.62
17	164.9	176.2	187.3	51.50	66.31	91.31
18	165.7	176.8	187.6	53.97	68.88	95.76

Girls

Age	Shortest 5%	Median height	Tallest 5%	Lightest 5%	Median weight	Heaviest 5%
2	81.6	86.8	93.6	9.95	11.80	14.15
3	88.3	94.1	100.6	11.61	14.10	17.22
4	95.0	101.6	108.3	13.11	15.96	19.91
5	101.1	108.4	115.6	14.55	17.66	22.62
6	106.6	114.6	122.7	16.05	19.52	25.75
7	111.8	120.6	129.5	17.71	21.84	29.68
8	116.9	126.4	136.2	19.62	24.84	34.71
9	122.1	132.2	142.9	21.82	28.46	40.64
10	127.5	138.3	149.5	24.36	32.55	47.17
11	133.5	144.8	156.2	27.24	36.95	54.00
12	139.8	151.5	162.7	30.52	41.53	60.81
13	145.2	157.1	168.1	34.14	46.10	67.30
14	148.7	160.4	171.3	37.76	50.28	73.08
15	150.5	161.8	172.8	40.99	53.68	77.78
16	151.6	162.4	173.3	43.41	55.89	80.99
17	152.7	163.1	173.5	44.74	56.69	82.46
18	153.6	163.7	173.6	45.26	56.62	82.47

This table simply gives a general picture for American children at specific age/dates (not the entire age range). When used as a standard, the individual variation in children's growth should not be overlooked. In most cases the height-weight relationship is probably a more valid index of weight status than a weight-for-age assessment.

Average Weight of Americans by Height and Age

Source: Society of Actuaries; from the *1979 Build and Blood Pressure Study*

The figures represent weights in ordinary indoor clothing and shoes, and heights with shoes.

Height	Men						Height	Women					
	20-24	25-29	30-39	40-49	50-59	60-69		20-24	25-29	30-39	40-49	50-59	60-69
5'2"	130	134	138	140	141	140	4'10"	105	110	113	118	121	123
5'3"	136	140	143	144	145	144	4'11"	110	112	115	121	125	127
5'4"	139	143	147	149	150	149	5'0"	112	114	118	123	127	130
5'5"	143	147	151	154	155	153	5'1"	116	119	121	127	131	133
5'6"	148	152	156	158	159	158	5'2"	120	121	124	129	133	136
5'7"	153	156	160	163	164	163	5'3"	124	125	128	133	137	140
5'8"	157	161	165	167	168	167	5'4"	127	128	131	136	141	143
5'9"	163	166	170	172	173	172	5'5"	130	132	134	139	144	147
5'10"	167	171	174	176	177	176	5'6"	133	134	137	143	147	150
5'11"	171	175	179	181	182	181	5'7"	137	138	141	147	152	155
6'0"	176	181	184	186	187	186	5'8"	141	142	145	150	156	158
6'1"	182	186	190	192	193	191	5'9"	146	148	150	155	159	161
6'2"	187	191	195	197	198	196	5'10"	149	150	153	158	162	163
6'3"	193	197	201	203	204	200	5'11"	155	156	159	162	166	167
6'4"	198	202	206	208	209	207	6'0"	157	159	164	168	171	172

The Nation's Hospitals

Source: American Hospital Association

In 1979, there were 6,988 hospitals in the United States registered by the American Hospital Association. These institutions had about 1.36 million beds and reported admitting some 37.8 million inpatients. About $79.8 billion was spent to provide services for both inpatients and outpatients.

State	Hospitals		Beds		Average daily census		Admissions		Expenses ($1,000)	
	Fed.	Non-fed.	Fed.	Non-fed.	Fed.	Non-fed.	Fed.	Non-fed.	Fed.	Non-fed.
Alabama	8	139	2,555	22,790	2,028	17,135	43,086	727,600	138,682	1,084,346
Alaska	9	17	571	1,120	299	672	16,552	37,824	44,296	105,609
Arizona	16	64	1,844	9,876	1,316	7,203	54,632	339,752	145,235	706,207
Arkansas	4	92	1,866	10,880	1,514	7,468	25,105	416,735	83,978	486,310
California	30	578	9,762	104,592	7,321	72,732	215,098	3,120,977	788,299	8,158,237
Colorado	6	93	1,762	13,264	1,436	8,933	41,878	424,920	160,655	787,725
Connecticut . .	5	61	960	17,484	657	13,971	18,848	440,474	66,271	1,103,503
Delaware . . .	2	13	426	3,794	321	3,220	6,529	78,720	21,500	194,353
Dist. of Columbia	3	14	3,620	4,943	3,451	3,839	42,547	166,800	202,704	502,731
Florida	13	238	3,881	52,615	3,127	38,041	102,040	1,585,207	275,043	2,922,928
Georgia	9	180	2,792	28,290	2,168	20,115	56,291	921,033	218,092	1,388,407
Hawaii	1	26	547	3,341	430	2,574	18,320	98,832	53,155	216,609
Idaho	2	49	182	3,567	111	2,379	4,905	129,480	15,309	174,906
Illinois	10	275	5,824	67,711	4,464	51,745	72,601	1,979,208	302,285	4,546,418
Indiana	4	130	1,973	30,362	1,469	23,897	19,476	890,120	80,615	1,581,048
Iowa	3	138	1,558	19,918	1,104	13,575	19,436	557,362	76,496	875,096
Kansas	7	157	1,906	16,493	1,419	11,682	26,535	425,186	91,387	770,249
Kentucky	5	116	1,834	16,747	1,296	13,002	35,531	632,065	116,354	822,318
Louisiana	8	150	2,498	22,651	1,717	15,875	42,474	749,688	134,343	1,159,669
Maine	1	51	642	6,447	533	4,809	6,938	175,786	26,200	337,325
Maryland	9	75	2,997	22,178	2,302	18,301	48,011	525,081	225,064	1,347,651
Massachusetts	7	179	3,699	40,759	2,970	33,177	31,570	908,516	168,158	2,797,561
Michigan	8	231	2,289	47,966	1,746	37,674	36,618	1,456,308	137,061	3,408,348
Minnesota . . .	5	178	1,683	28,949	1,347	20,924	23,519	686,125	91,287	1,302,251
Mississippi . . .	5	111	1,764	14,719	1,466	10,970	30,935	468,435	99,603	571,342
Missouri	7	157	2,985	31,782	2,181	23,769	50,441	912,737	237,383	1,734,925
Montana	6	61	396	4,926	245	3,167	10,062	130,025	23,930	182,685
Nebraska	5	104	883	11,022	665	7,382	20,178	290,153	52,370	478,018
Nevada	4	21	263	2,989	193	2,025	7,257	112,157	23,623	236,435
New Hampshire	2	31	322	4,358	292	3,175	6,797	130,970	22,523	213,086
New Jersey . . .	4	131	2,591	41,152	2,032	33,955	27,432	1,051,988	127,331	2,239,970
New Mexico . . .	11	43	895	5,209	618	3,703	33,397	164,106	74,978	281,689
New York . . .	16	342	9,762	121,678	8,100	105,316	105,525	2,656,801	498,578	7,755,744
North Carolina .	9	150	2,889	30,485	2,280	23,312	50,809	889,046	151,066	1,384,203
North Dakota . .	5	55	414	5,506	273	3,724	11,918	134,505	23,400	204,347
Ohio.	5	234	4,045	59,530	3,173	46,590	43,045	1,821,880	221,985	3,631,462
Oklahoma . . .	12	130	1,103	16,472	802	11,328	41,971	485,741	89,108	778,354
Oregon	2	83	958	10,670	720	7,464	15,831	367,505	54,570	662,338
Pennsylvania . .	11	303	6,020	80,340	4,879	63,585	46,199	1,956,557	265,592	4,497,442
Rhode Island . .	2	19	399	5,759	307	5,002	10,515	136,452	31,798	370,362
South Carolina .	7	82	1,619	15,258	1,095	11,744	40,351	440,306	108,312	637,550
South Dakota .	10	59	1,146	4,448	837	2,751	20,266	123,541	55,762	156,783
Tennessee . . .	5	162	2,807	28,564	2,254	21,977	39,412	934,382	140,029	1,361,616
Texas	24	544	8,514	71,569	6,965	50,142	178,253	2,341,653	587,166	3,596,652
Utah	2	39	487	4,634	356	3,378	12,791	197,444	35,223	294,568
Vermont	1	18	224	2,717	191	2,010	3,693	75,068	16,511	126,997
Virginia	9	125	3,115	28,744	2,451	22,250	68,688	741,890	234,845	1,351,882
Washington . . .	11	114	2,319	13,640	1,782	9,513	51,495	543,477	151,258	884,587
West Virginia . .	5	73	1,134	12,971	934	9,955	18,967	394,659	65,737	582,082
Wisconsin . . .	3	164	2,090	26,624	1,713	19,395	23,996	759,675	107,301	1,450,782
Wyoming	3	28	533	1,998	443	1,132	6,563	64,487	23,304	83,052
Total U.S. . . .	361	6,627	117,348	1,245,501	91,793	951,657	1,985,597	35,816,529	7,265,755	72,530,632

Selected Statistics on State and County Mental Hospitals

Source: National Institute of Mental Health

Year	Total admitted	Net releases	Deaths in hospital	Residents end of year	Expense per patient[1]
1955	178,033	NA	44,384	558,922	$1,116.59
1960	234,791	NA	49,748	535,540	1,702.41
1970	393,174	394,627	30,804	338,592	5,435.38
1975	376,156	391,345	13,401	193,436	13,634.53
1977	414,703	408,667*	9,716	159,523	NA
1978(p).	406,407	NA	9,080	153,544	NA
1979(p).	406,259	NA	7,830	145,616	NA

*Includes estimates. NA-not available. (p)-provisional data. (1) Per average daily resident patient population.

Patients' Expenditures in Mental Hospitals

Source: National Institute of Mental Health

Based on reports of 298 state and county hospitals on the Jan., 1978, Inventory of Mental Health Facilities.

State	No. patients	Tot. expend. ($000)	State	No. patients	Tot. expend. ($000)	State	No. patients	Tot. expend. ($000)	State	No. patients	Tot. expend. ($000)
U.S...	159,405	3,329,351	Ida. ..	190	5,235	Mo. ..	3,904	77,413	Pa. ..	12,235	291,355
Ala. . .	2,196	37,549	Ill. . .	6,049	174,511	Mon. .	490	13,878	R.I. . .	1,354	23,291
Alas. .	102	6,439	Ind. . .	4,019	67,193	Neb.. .	692	20,912	S.C.. .	3,527	39,022
Ariz. .	642	19,143	Ia. . . .	1,180	24,918	Nev. . .	206	7,431	S.D. . .	625	7,995
Ark. . .	351	13,936	Kan. . .	1,253	28,563	N.H. . .	784	19,689	Tenn. .	3,694	55,465
Cal. . .	8,981	103,900	Ky. . . .	800	20,141	N.J. . . .	6,700	140,620	Tex. . .	5,578	109,910
Col. . .	1,151	36,303	La. . . .	2,099	38,290	N.M. . .	312	9,275	Ut. . . .	337	5,930
Conn. .	2,709	50,218	Me. . . .	663	12,201	N.Y. . .	30,122	692,574	Vt. . . .	356	7,954
Del. . .	688	18,535	Md. . . .	4,012	67,028	N.C. . .	4,062	79,453	Va. . . .	5,793	67,090
D.C.. .	2,344	89,107	Mass.. .	4,270	71,767	N.D. . .	615	9,381	Wash..	1,203	20,658
Fla. . .	6,108	78,611	Mich. . .	4,680	150,047	Oh. . . .	6,868	153,285	W. Va.	2,376	20,788
Ga. . .	5,432	113,505	Minn.. .	2,353	41,102	Okla. . .	2,087	34,078	Wis. . .	747	35,587
Ha. . .	135	6,265	Miss.. .	2,407	20,845	Ore...	1,467	27,205	Wy. . .	276	5,865

Patient Care Episodes in Mental Health Facilities

Source: National Institute of Mental Health

Year	Total all facilities[1]	Inpatient services					Outpatient services		
		State & county mental hospitals	Private mental[2] hospitals	Gen. hosp. psychiatric service (non-VA)	VA psychiatric inpatient services	Federally assisted comm. men. health cen.	Federally assisted comm. men. health cen.	Other
1977	6,392,979	574,226	184,189	571,725	217,507	268,966	1,741,729	2,834,637
1975	6,409,477	598,993	165,327	565,696	214,264	246,891	1,584,968	3,033,308
1969	3,572,822	767,115	123,850	535,493	186,913	65,000	291,148	1,603,303
1965	2,636,525	804,926	125,428	519,328	115,843	—	—	1,071,000
1955	1,675,352	818,832	123,231	265,934	88,355	—	—	379,000

(1) In order to present trends on the same set of facilities over this interval, it has been necessary to exclude from this table the following: private psychiatric office practice; psychiatric service modes of all types in hospitals or outpatient clinics of federal agencies other than the VA (e.g., Public Health Service, Indian Health Service, Department of Defense Bureau of Prisons, etc.); inpatient service modes of multiservice facilities not shown in this table; all partial care episodes, and outpatient episodes of VA hospitals. (2) Includes estimates of episodes of care in residential treatment centers for emotionally disturbed children.

Legal Abortions in the U.S.

Source: Center for Disease Control, U.S. Department of Health and Human Services

Legal abortions, according to selected characteristics of the patient.

	1972	1973	1974	1975	1976	1977	1978
Number	586,760	615,831	763,476	854,853	988,267	1,079,430	1,157,776
Age Characteristic	Percent distribution						
Under 20 years.	32.6	32.7	32.7	33.1	32.1	30.8	30.0
20-24 years.	32.5	32.0	31.8	31.9	33.3	34.5	35.0
25 years and over	34.9	35.3	35.6	35.0	34.6	34.7	34.9
Color							
White	77.0	72.5	69.7	67.8	66.6	66.4	67.0
All other	23.0	27.5	30.3	32.2	33.4	33.6	33.0
Marital status							
Married	29.7	27.4	27.4	26.1	24.6	24.3	26.4
Unmarried	70.3	72.6	72.6	73.9	75.4	75.7	73.6
Number of living children							
0	49.4	48.6	47.8	47.1	47.7	53.4	56.6
1	18.2	18.8	19.6	20.2	20.7	19.1	19.2
2	13.3	14.2	14.8	15.5	15.4	14.4	14.1
3	8.7	8.7	8.7	8.7	8.3	7.0	5.9
4	5.0	4.8	4.5	4.4	4.1	3.3	4.2 *
5 or more	5.4	4.9	4.5	4.2	3.8	2.9	—
Location of abortion facility							
In state of residence	56.2	74.8	86.6	89.2	90.0	90.0	93.8
Out of state of residence	43.8	25.2	13.4	10.8	10.0	10.0	6.2
Period of gestation							
Under 9 weeks	34.0	36.1	42.6	44.6	47.0	51.2	53.2
9-10 weeks	30.7	29.4	28.7	28.4	28.0	27.2	26.9
11-12 weeks	17.5	17.9	15.4	14.9	14.4	13.1	12.3
13-15 weeks	8.4	6.9	5.5	5.0	4.5	3.4	4.0
16-20 weeks	8.2	8.0	6.5	6.1	5.1	4.3	3.7
21 weeks and over.	1.0	1.7	1.2	1.0	0.9	0.9	0.9

*Beginning with 1978, 4 or more.

The Nation's Handicapped

Source: National Center for Health Statistics, U.S. Department of Health and Human Services

Persons with Chronic Activity Limitation, by Selected Conditions, Chronic Activity Limitation Status, Age, and Sex.

1979 Activity limitation sex, and age	Number of persons limited in activity (millions)	Selected chronic condition								
		Arthritis, rheuma-tism	Heart condi-tions	Hyper-tension w/o heart involve-ment	Diabetes	Asthma	Impair-ments of back/ spine	Impair-ments of lower extrem-ity or hip	Visual impair-ments	Hearing impair-ments
All degrees of activity limitation		Percent of persons limited in activity because of specified condition								
Both sexes, all ages.	31.5	17.0	16.4	9.2	5.2	4.4	9.4	7.5	4.5	2.6
Under 45 years	10.3	5.1	4.4	3.0	2.3	8.7	14.1	9.8	3.9	3.2
45-64.	10.5	20.1	20.7	12.1	6.9	3.1	9.7	7.0	3.3	1.7
65 and over	10.7	25.3	23.9	12.2	6.3	1.6	4.6	5.8	6.4	2.9
Male, all ages	15.3	11.7	18.1	7.1	4.5	4.6	8.7	8.4	4.9	2.9
Female, all ages	16.2	22.0	14.9	11.1	5.9	4.2	10.0	6.7	4.2	2.3
Limited but not in major activity										
Both sexes, all ages.	8.0	12.5	9.0	6.6	3.9	6.3	8.6	10.1	5.3	4.7
Under 45 years	4.1	4.2	4.1	2.3	1.9	10.3	10.4	13.1	5.3	4.4
45-64.	2.4	18.7	12.6	11.4	6.4	2.6	9.2	7.3	4.0	3.5
65 and over	1.6	24.5	16.2	10.4	5.4	*1.6	3.3	6.4	7.1	7.1
Limited in amount or kind of major activity										
Both sexes, all ages.	15.6	19.0	15.9	9.9	5.0	4.7	11.3	6.6	3.4	2.0
Under 45 years	5.1	5.8	4.3	3.4	2.2	8.9	17.6	7.4	2.6	2.7
45-64.	5.3	22.4	19.9	12.1	6.9	3.6	10.9	6.6	2.5	1.3
65 and over	5.2	28.8	23.3	14.1	5.7	1.7	5.6	5.9	5.0	2.0
Unable to carry on major activity										
Both sexes, all ages.	7.9	17.4	25.0	10.3	7.0	2.0	6.2	6.6	6.1	1.8
Under 45 years	1.1	5.3	5.9	3.8	4.3	*2.2	11.0	8.7	4.6	*1.5
45-64.	2.8	17.1	29.0	12.7	7.4	2.5	7.7	7.4	4.1	*1.0
65 and over	3.9	21.1	27.7	10.4	7.4	1.6	3.7	5.5	8.0	2.4

Covers civilian, noninstitutionalized population. Based on unpublished data from the National Health Interview Survey, National Center for Health Statistics, U.S. Department of Health and Human Services. (1) Ninth Revision of the International Classification of Diseases used for coding in 1979. *Figure does not meet standards of reliability or precision.

Personal Health Care Costs Per Capita in the U.S.

Source: Public Health Service, U.S. Department of Health and Human Services

Age, fiscal year All ages[1]	Total expenditures	Direct payment	Source of payment			
			Third-party payment			
			Total	Private health insurance	Philanthropy and industry	Govern-ment
			Percent distribution			
1970	$312.00	39.9	60.1	24.0	1.6	34.5
1971	341.00	38.6	61.4	24.1	1.7	35.6
1972	376.00	38.6	61.4	23.8	1.6	36.0
1973	411.00	38.6	61.4	23.8	1.5	36.1
1974	464.00	36.1	63.9	24.2	1.5	38.2
1975	531.00	33.4	66.7	25.8	1.4	39.5
1976[3]	594.00	32.6	67.4	26.9	1.4	39.1
1977[3]	663.00	32.8	67.2	26.9	1.4	38.9
1978[3]	736.00	32.5	67.4	27.0	1.3	39.1
1979[3]	826.00	32.8	67.1	26.5	1.3	39.3
1980[2,3]	941.00	32.4	67.5	26.6	1.3	39.6
Under 65 years						
1970	232.50	43.3	56.7	31.0	1.9	23.9
1971	255.09	41.1	58.9	32.6	1.8	24.5
1972	278.23	38.4	61.6	33.0	1.5	26.8
1973	309.45	38.3	61.7	33.2	1.7	26.8
1974[1]	347.87	39.0	61.0	32.3	1.7	27.0
1975[1]	390.79	36.5	63.5	33.3	1.6	28.6
1976[2,3]	437.83	34.9	65.1	34.5	1.7	29.0
1977[2,3]	514.25	31.9	68.1	36.4	2.6	29.1
65 years and over						
1970	828.31	32.6	67.4	5.5	0.5	61.4
1971	925.98	34.2	65.8	5.4	0.5	60.0
1972	1,033.51	35.5	64.5	5.2	0.4	58.9
1973	1,081.35	33.0	67.0	5.4	0.4	61.1
1974[1]	1,109.54	28.0	72.0	5.7	0.5	65.9
1975[1]	1,335.72	26.3	73.7	5.4	0.4	68.0
1976[2,3]	1,521.36	26.5	73.5	5.4	0.4	67.0
1977[2,3]	1,745.17	26.5	73.5	5.8	0.7	67.0

(1) Revised estimates. (2) Preliminary estimates. (3) Data for fiscal year ending Sept. 30; all other data for fiscal year ending June 30.

Suicide Rates

Source: National Center for Health Statistics, U.S. Department of Health and Human Services

(Rates per 100,000 population) (1978)

Age group	Total	Male	Female	Total	White Male	Female	Total	All other Male	Female
Total.	12.5	19.0	6.3	13.4	20.2	6.9	6.9	11.1	3.1
10-14 years . . .	0.8	1.2	0.4	0.9	1.4	0.4	0.5	0.6	0.5
15-19 years . . .	8.0	12.8	3.1	8.7	13.8	3.4	4.5	7.5	1.6
20-24 years . . .	16.9	27.4	6.4	17.5	28.1	6.7	13.8	23.3	5.0
25-29 years . . .	17.6	27.5	7.9	17.9	27.6	8.3	15.4	26.6	5.8
30-34 years . . .	15.7	23.4	8.3	16.2	23.8	8.7	12.2	20.2	5.5
35-39 years . . .	15.6	22.3	9.3	16.2	22.7	9.8	11.9	19.5	5.7
40-44 years . . .	16.1	21.4	11.0	17.2	22.4	12.2	8.4	14.2	3.7
45-49 years . . .	16.7	22.5	11.1	17.8	23.6	12.2	8.7	14.5	3.7
50-54 years . . .	17.6	24.3	11.3	18.7	25.8	12.1	8.4	11.8	5.6
55-59 years . . .	17.8	25.4	10.8	19.1	27.1	11.6	6.4	9.4	3.8
60-64 years . . .	18.6	30.1	8.4	19.7	32.0	8.8	7.6	11.9	3.9
65-69 years . . .	18.0	30.2	8.3	19.4	32.5	9.0	6.2	10.9	2.5
70-74 years . . .	20.0	37.2	7.4	21.1	39.6	7.8	7.5	13.1	3.0
75-79 years . . .	23.1	45.9	8.4	24.3	48.9	8.7	8.8	14.5	4.3
80-84 years . . .	21.8	50.6	6.0	23.2	54.4	6.3	6.9	13.2	2.9
85+ years . . .	18.6	48.3	5.1	20.0	53.1	5.2	6.3	10.3	4.1

U.S. Fires

Source: National Fire Protection Assn.

Fires attended by the public fire service (1980 estimates)

All Fires by Type of Fire

	No. of fires	Property loss
Fires in structures	1,065,000	$5,454,000,000
Fires outside of structures[1] .	86,500	61,000,000
Fires in vehicles[2].	471,500	685,000,000
Fires in brush, grass, wildland[3]	718,500	*
Fires in rubbish[4]	397,000	*
All other fires.	249,500	54,000,000
Total[6].	**2,988,000**	**$6,254,000,000**

Structure Fires by Property Use

	No. of fires	Property loss
Public assembly	29,000	$326,000,000
Educational.	19,500	101,000,000
Institutional	28,000	25,000,000
Residential	757,500	3,042,000,000
One-/2-family dwellings[5]	590,500	2,447,000,000
Apartments	143,500	401,000,000
Hotels, motels	11,500	154,000,000
Other residential	12,000	40,000,000
Stores and offices	62,000	645,000,000
Industry, utility, defense[6] . .	55,000	672,000,000
Storage in structures[6]. . .	65,500	512,000,000
Special structures	48,500	131,000,000
Total[6].	**1,065,000**	**$5,454,000,000**

*No value involved. (1) Includes outside storage, crops, timber, etc. (2) Includes highway vehicles, trains, boats, ships, aircraft, farm vehicles, and construction vehicles. (3) Excludes crops and timber. (4) Includes dumpsters. (5) Includes mobile homes. (6) Since some fires were not reported to the NFPA, the results presented represent only a portion of the total U.S. fires.

Annual Fire Losses in the U.S.

Source: Insurance Services Office

Year	Loss	Year	Loss	Year	Loss	Year	Loss
1940	$285,878,697	1955.	$885,218,000	1970	$2,264,000,000	1978	4,008,000,000
1945	484,274,000	1960	1,107,824,000	1975	3,560,000,000	1979 1979. . .	4,851,000,000
1950	648,909,000	1965	1,455,631,000	1977	$3,764,000,000	1980 (est.). . .	5,579,000,000

Fire Fighters: Deaths and Injuries

Source: International Association of Fire Fighters
U.S. and Canadian professional fire fighters

Year	In line of duty Deaths	Injuries	Occupational diseases[1] Deaths	Retirement	Year	In line of duty Deaths	Injuries	Occupational diseases[1] Deaths	Retirement
1970	115	38,583	233	465	1976	79	49,819	79	673
1972	100	62,682	133	695	1977	79	55,562	84	828
1973	90	62,619	111	702	1978	74	46,668	61	391
1974	100	56,296	107	604	1979	70	45,070	77	348
1975	108	51,312	88	721					

(1) Includes heart and cardiovascular diseases; lung and respiratory diseases; and other occupational diseases.

Active Federal and Non-Federal Doctors (M.D.s) by State

Source: Division of Health Manpower and Facilities Statistics, U.S. Department of Health and Human Services (1978)

	Total	Non-fed.	Fed.		Total	Non-fed.	Fed.		Total	Non-fed.	Fed.
All areas . . .	401,364	381,122	20,242	Kentucky . . .	4,641	4,455	186	Oklahoma. . .	3,651	3,453	198
United States	396,445	377,492	18,953	Louisiana . . .	5,958	5,675	283	Oregon	4,327	4,192	135
Alabama . . .	4,562	4,363	199	Maine	1,631	1,562	69	Pennsylvania .	21,315	20,831	484
Alaska.	558	445	113	Maryland . . .	11,687	9,851	1,836	Rhode Island .	1,921	1,850	71
Arizona	4,569	4,229	340	Mass.	14,732	14,149	583	South Carolina	3,914	3,640	274
Arkansas . . .	2,548	2,423	125	Michigan. . . .	13,742	13,513	229	South Dakota.	753	677	76
California . . .	50,850	47,891	2,959	Minnesota. . .	7,437	7,212	225	Tennessee . .	6,736	6,498	238
Colorado . . .	5,671	5,248	423	Mississippi . .	2,630	2,436	194	Texas	20,570	19,101	1,469
Connecticut . .	7,403	7,222	181	Missouri	7,679	7,448	231	Utah	2,188	2,107	81
Delaware . . .	951	911	40	Montana. . . .	1,027	965	62	Vermont. . . .	999	970	29
D.C.	3,944	3,322	622	Nebraska . . .	2,277	2,198	79	Virginia	8,965	8,114	851
Florida.	16,224	15,456	768	Nevada	911	860	51	Washington . .	7,020	6,460	560
Georgia. . . .	7,471	6,925	546	N.H.	1,418	1,376	42	West Virginia .	2,533	2,419	114
Hawaii.	1,892	1,670	222	New Jersey. .	13,216	12,870	346	Wisconsin . . .	7,017	6,841	176
Idaho	973	928	45	New Mexico. .	1,855	1,696	159	Wyoming . . .	474	440	34
Illinois	20,327	19,704	623	New York . . .	45,570	44,458	1,112	Puerto Rico . .	3,577	3,424	153
Indiana.	6,659	6,549	110	North Carolina	8,350	7,934	416	Outlying areas	1,342	206	1,136
Iowa	3,524	3,424	100	North Dakota .	835	780	55				
Kansas	3,548	3,385	163	Ohio	16,792	16,366	426				

(1) Excludes 8,858 physicians with addresses unknown.

U.S. Health Expenditures

Source: Health Care Financing Administration, U.S. Department of Health and Human Services

	1950	1960	1965	1970	1975	1977	1979	1980[1]
Total (billions)	**$12.7**	**$26.9**	**$43.0**	**$74.7**	**$131.5**	**$170.0**	**$212.2**	**$244.6**
Type of expenditure								
Health services and supplies	11.7	25.2	39.5	69.4	123.2	161.2	202.3	234.1
Hospital care.	3.9	9.9	13.9	27.8	52.1	67.9	85.3	97.3
Physician services	2.7	5.7	8.5	14.3	24.9	31.2	40.6	45.0
Dentist services	1.0	2.0	2.8	4.8	8.2	11.7	13.6	17.9
Nursing home care	.2	.5	2.1	4.7	9.9	13.4	17.8	21.6
Other professional services	.4	.9	1.0	1.6	2.6	3.7	4.7	5.7
Drugs and drug sundries	1.7	3.7	5.8	8.4	11.8	13.8	17.0	18.1
Eyeglasses and appliances.	.5	.8	1.9	2.1	3.0	3.5	4.4	4.7
Expenses for prepayment and administration	.5	1.1	1.5	2.3	3.7	7.8	7.7	11.6
Gov't public health activities	.4	.4	.8	1.4	3.2	4.3	6.0	7.0
Other health services	.5	1.1	1.3	2.1	3.7	4.0	5.2	5.2
Research and medical facilities construction	1.0	1.7	3.5	5.3	8.3	8.7	9.9	10.5
Research.	.1	.7	1.5	1.9	3.2	3.7	4.6	5.2
Construction	.9	1.0	2.0	3.4	5.1	5.0	5.3	5.3

(1) Projected figures

Accidental Deaths by Age, Sex, and Type, 1978

Source: National Safety Council

	All types	Motor vehicle	Falls	Drown-ing	Fires, burns	Ingest. of food, object	Fire-arms	Poison (solid, liquid)	Poison by gas	% Male all types
All ages	**105,561**	**52,411**	**13,690**	**7,026**	**6,163**	**3,063**	**1,806**	**3,035**	**1,737**	**70**
Under 5	4,766	1,551	192	696	896	463	52	81	51	58
5 to 14	6,118	3,130	124	1,010	586	91	297	37	76	69
15 to 24	26,622	19,164	538	2,180	530	168	581	577	525	78
25 to 34	15,533	9,648	502	1,070	542	183	300	778	287	80
35 to 44	9,491	4,926	551	630	502	257	205	432	205	77
45 to 54	9,174	4,166	835	460	667	292	162	420	171	74
55 to 64	9,600	3,882	1,266	450	733	410	112	305	185	70
65 to 74	9,072	3,217	1,852	300	789	483	68	219	110	62
75 & over	15,185	2,727	7,830	230	918	716	29	186	127	47
Sex										
Male.	73,881	38,139	7,181	5,875	3,786	1,765	1,566	1,800	1,260	
Female	31,680	14,272	6,509	1,151	2,377	1,298	240	1,235	477	
Percent male.	70%	73%	52%	84%	61%	58%	87%	59%	73%	

Canadian Motor Vehicle Traffic Deaths

Source: Statistics Canada

Province	Number 1978	Number 1979	Province	Number 1978	Number 1979
Newfoundland.	74	93	Saskatchewan	296	290
Prince Edward Island.	30	33	Alberta.	503	701
Nova Scotia	228	189	British Columbia.	636	738
New Brunswick	224	260	Yukon	16	14
Quebec	1,766	1,789	Northwest Territories	6	6
Ontario	1,450	1,560	**Total**	**5,426**	**5,856**
Manitoba.	198	183			

Federal Bureau of Investigation

The Federal Bureau of Investigation (FBI) is the investigative arm of the Department of Justice, and is located at 9th Street and Pennsylvania Avenue, Northwest, Washington, D.C. 20535. It investigates all violations of Federal law except those specifically assigned to some other agency by legislative action, such violations including counterfeiting, and internal revenue, postal, and customs violations. It also investigates espionage, sabotage, treason, and other matters affecting internal security, as well as kidnaping, transportation of stolen goods across state lines, and violations of the Federal bank and atomic energy laws.

The FBI's Identification Division houses the largest fingerprint repository in the world, with over 175 million fingerprint cards on file. The file is utilized by law enforcement and other governmental authorities throughout the nation to identify persons having arrest records. The file is also available for humanitarian purposes, such as the identification of persons suffering from amnesia and the victims of major disasters.

The FBI has 59 field divisions in the principal cities of the country. (Consult telephone directories for locations and phone numbers.)

An applicant for the position of Special Agent of the FBI must be a citizen of the U.S., at least 23 and under 35 years old, and a graduate of an accredited law school or of an accredited college or university with a major in accounting. In addition, applicants with a four-year degree from an accredited college or university with a major in other academic areas may qualify with three additional years of full-time work experience. Specialized need areas include languages, science, and financial analysis. Those appointed to the Special Agent position must complete an initial training period of 15 weeks at the FBI Academy, Quantico, Virginia.

William H. Webster, a Federal Appeals Court judge from St. Louis, was sworn in as FBI Director for a ten-year term on February 23, 1978. He replaced Clarence M. Kelley.

U.S. Crime Reports

Source: Federal Bureau of Investigation

Offense	Number 1980 Est.	% Change over[1] 1979	1976
Murder	23,040	+7.4	+22.7
Forcible Rape	82,090	+8.0	+44.7
Robbery	548,810	+17.5	+30.6
Aggravated Assault	654,960	+6.6	+33.4
Burglary	3,759,200	+13.9	+21.7
Larceny-theft	7,112,700	+8.1	+13.4
Motor Vehicle theft	1,114,700	+1.6	+16.4

[1]Percent by which the rate of crime per 100,000 population changed in 1980 as compared with 1979 and 1976.

Reported Crime, 1978-79, by Size of Place

Source: 1979 Uniform Crime Reports, Federal Bureau of Investigation

Population group	Crime Index total	Violent crime	Property crime	Murder and non-negligent man-slaughter	Forcible rape	Robbery	Aggravated assault	Burglary	Larceny-theft
Total all agencies: 12,762 agencies; total population 210,488,000:									
1978	10,755,292	1,036,100	9,739,192	18,980	65,315	410,872	540,933	3,006,131	5,769,898
1979	11,675,935	1,141,121	10,534,814	20,678	73,115	458,741	588,587	3,172,429	6,299,644
Percent change	+8.4	+10.1	+8.2	+8.9	+11.9	+11.7	+8.8	+5.5	+9.2
Total cities: 8,878 cities; total population 144,445,000:									
1978	8,697,123	858,993	7,838,130	14,337	51,022	372,472	421,162	2,311,971	4,715,419
1979	9,439,199	949,740	8,489,459	15,954	57,638	416,165	459,983	2,456,548	5,136,418
Percent change	+8.5	+10.6	+8.3	+11.3	+13.0	+11.7	+9.2	+6.3	+8.9
58 cities, 250,000 and over; population 41,674,000:									
1978	3,280,087	465,289	2,814,798	8,406	26,823	248,940	181,120	921,258	1,496,841
1979	3,523,889	515,833	3,008,056	9,606	29,795	278,298	198,134	973,572	1,595,265
Percent change	+7.4	+10.9	+6.9	+14.3	+11.1	+11.8	+9.4	+5.7	+6.6
109 cities, 100,000 to 249,999; population 15,809,000:									
1978	1,138,038	100,075	1,037,963	1,686	7,023	39,599	51,767	315,109	625,540
1979	1,224,904	110,085	1,114,819	1,831	7,824	44,338	56,092	334,307	677,036
Percent change	+7.6	+10.0	+7.4	+8.6	+11.4	+12.0	+8.4	+6.1	+8.2
284 cities, 50,000 to 99,999; population 19,489,000:									
1978	1,192,697	93,929	1,098,768	1,324	5,920	34,267	52,418	321,070	671,900
1979	1,292,395	101,914	1,190,481	1,375	7,049	37,119	56,371	340,599	734,171
Percent change	+8.4	+8.5	+8.3	+3.9	+19.1	+8.3	+7.5	+6.1	+9.3
625 cities, 25,000 to 49,999; population 21,405,000:									
1978	1,149,329	80,891	1,068,438	1,068	4,820	24,229	50,774	290,799	689,665
1979	1,254,420	88,358	1,166,062	1,225	5,547	27,815	53,771	310,531	758,001
Percent change	+9.1	+9.2	+9.1	+14.7	+15.1	+14.8	+5.9	+6.8	+9.9
1,537 cities, 10,000 to 24,999; population 24,067,000:									
1978	1,074,605	66,198	1,008,407	1,040	3,673	16,356	45,129	259,994	675,070
1979	1,192,482	74,989	1,117,493	1,083	4,201	18,561	51,144	282,989	750,020
Percent change	+11.0	+13.3	+10.8	+4.1	+14.4	+13.5	+13.3	+8.8	+11.1
6,265 cities under 10,000; population 22,002,000:									
1978	862,367	52,611	809,756	813	2,763	9,081	39,954	203,741	556,403
1979	951,109	58,561	892,548	834	3,222	10,034	44,471	214,550	621,925
Percent change	+10.3	+11.3	+10.2	+2.6	+16.6	+10.5	+11.3	+5.3	+11.8
Suburban area 5,365 agencies; population 77,585,000:									
1978	3,371,109	244,841	3,126,268	3,974	16,997	66,435	157,435	938,193	1,927,359
1979	3,665,717	267,500	3,398,217	4,249	19,001	74,622	169,628	987,377	2,120,546
Percent change	+8.7	+9.3	+8.7	+6.9	+11.8	+12.3	+7.7	+5.2	+10.0
Rural area 2,852 agencies; population 30,067,000:									
1978	594,828	51,254	543,574	2,169	4,148	5,973	38,964	221,300	285,386
1979	644,084	54,896	589,188	2,117	4,329	6,340	42,110	227,252	321,115
Percent change	+8.3	7.1	+8.4	−2.4	+4.4	+6.1	+8.1	+2.7	+12.5

Reported Crime in Metropolitan Areas, 1979

Source: Compiled by the World Almanac based on 1979 Uniform Crime Reports, F.B.I.

The 25 Standard Metropolitan Statistical Areas listed below are those which appear most frequently among the top 30 cities in per capita reported crime rate for each of 7 kinds of major crime: the 5 listed below plus aggravated assault and auto theft.

The rates are for reported crimes only; they are not an accurate index of crimes actually committed. In many metropolitan areas an unknown number of crimes go unreported by victims. This is especially true of the crimes of rape, burglary, and larceny. Additionally, figures are often distorted for political reasons.

The number in parentheses following the city name indicates the number of categories (including auto theft and aggravated assault) in which the city appears among the top 30.

The numbers in parentheses following crime rate figures give that city's rank in that category of crime. If no number appears, the city is not among the top 30 in that category. The cities are listed in order of the diversity and violence of criminal activity.

Metropolitan areas	Total[1]	Violent[2]	Property[3]	Rate per 100,000 population Murder[4]	Rape	Robbery	Burglary	Larceny
Las Vegas, Nev. (6)	9,417.4 (1)	1,024.4 (7)	8,958.2 (1)	22.4 (3)	67.6 (14)	530.2	3,368.2 (1)	4,769.8 (14)
Miami, Fla. (6)	9,298.3 (5)	1,372.6 (2)	7,925.8 (8)	21.3 (7)	56.8	545.4	2,636.5 (6)	4,626.4 (22)
Reno, Nev. (5)	9,352.9 (4)	661.3	8,691.5 (3)	12.2	72.5 (5)	369.0	2,764.9 (3)	5,206.1 (5)
Savannah, Ga. (5)	8,409.3 (13)	1,047.4 (6)	7,361.9 (17)	13.6	75.5 (4)	295.5	2,199.4 (28)	4,694.7 (18)
Fresno, Cal. (5)	8,339.4 (16)	845.9 (16)	7,493.5 (15)	16.6 (25)	59.3 (27)	310.3	2,615.1 (7)	4,121.5
Atlanta, Ga. (5)	7,811.4 (24)	878.8 (11)	6,932.7 (27)	20.2 (8)	67.9 (12)	404.9	2,244.2 (22)	4,012.9
Los Angeles-Long Beach, Cal. (5)	7,806.3 (25)	1,205.1 (3)	6,601.2	20.0 (11)	71.3 (9)	529.2	2,387.8 (14)	3,156.7
New York, N.Y. (5)	7,805.3 (26)	1,496.1 (1)	6,308.4	19.8 (12)	44.5	926.7	2,216.9 (26)	3,012.0
Sacramento, Cal. (4)	8,812.1 (7)	724.7	8,087.4 (6)	9.9	54.0	303.4	2,388.7 (13)	4,983.5 (10)
Orlando, Fla. (4)	8,689.5 (9)	908.5 (10)	7,781.0 (11)	9.7	67.8 (13)	213.1	2,537.3 (8)	4,799.3 (12)
Gainesville, Fla. (4)	8,489.1 (10)	792.4 (20)	7,696.7 (13)	8.9	71.6 (8)	152.8	2,195.3 (29)	5,139.1(8)
Bakersfield, Cal. (4)	8,477.8 (11)	776.6 (26)	7,701.3 (12)	15.9 (30)	58.6 (30)	229.9	2,243.7 (23)	4,792.0 (13)
Atlantic City, N.J. (4)	8,436.9 (12)	650.1	7,786.8 (10)	7.9	54.2	307.7	2,270.0 (20)	4,662.6 (19)
Stockton, Cal. (4)	8,382.5 (15)	748.9	7,633.7 (14)	20.1 (10)	56.8	284.9	2,503.9 (9)	4,497.0 (26)
Tallahassee, Fla. (4)	8,004.0 (19)	756.9 (30)	7,247.1 (19)	2.1	81.5 (3)	112.6	2,218.9 (25)	4,729.9 (15)
Dallas-Ft. Worth, Tex. (4)	7,787.7 (28)	693.9	7,093.8 (23)	18.3 (20)	60.2 (26)	262.3	2,245.1 (21)	4,258.4
Daytona Beach, Fla. (3)	9,656.4 (2)	818.2 (18)	8,838.2 (2)	12.4	72.3 (6)	260.5	2,751.0 (4)	5,553.9 (1)
W. Palm Beach-Boca Raton, Fla. (3)	9,467.1 (3)	914.8 (9)	8,552.3 (4)	14.1	38.9	247.9	2,743.6 (5)	5,279.8 (3)
San Francisco-Oakland, Cal. (3)	8,218.0 (17)	826.4 (13)	7,355.6 (18)	11.0	56.0	369.2	2,199.9 (27)	4,424.1
New Orleans, La. (3)	7,966.7 (20)	1,094.7 (4)	6,872.0 (28)	26.6 (2)	57.0	561.1	2,045.0	3,978.3
Albuquerque, N.M. (3)	7,853.3 (23)	764.8 (29)	7,070.6 (25)	15.6	64.2 (17)	214.3	2,140.2	4,435.7 (29)
Phoenix, Ariz. (2)	9,013.4 (6)	673.9	8,339.5 (5)	10.2	53.3	228.2	2,319.8 (16)	5,445.9 (2)
Ft. Lauderdale-Hollywood, Fla. (2)	8,776.5 (8)	732.1	8,044.4 (7)	14.1	49.7	322.1	2,318.7 (17)	5,149.9 (7)
Denver-Boulder, Col. (2)	8,043.5 (18)	609.3	7,434.3 (16)	6.9	61.8 (21)	229.5	2,157.3	4,661.1 (20)
Baton Rouge, La. (2)	7,873.5 (22)	788.2 (21)	7,085.3 (24)	13.5	38.8	150.0	2,169.3	4,455.4 (28)

(1) Other metro areas among the top 30 in total reported crime: Tucson, Ariz. (14); Riverside-San Bernardino-Ontario, Cal. (21); Tampa-St. Petersburg, Fla. (30); Wilmington, N.C. (27); Modesto, Cal. (29).

(2) Violent crime includes murder and non-negligent manslaughter, forcible rape, robbery, and aggravated assault. Other metro areas in the top 30 in violent crime are: Baltimore, Md. (5); Columbia, S.C. (8); Flint, Mich. (12); Newark, N.J. (14); Charleston-No. Charleston, S.C. (15); Pueblo, Col. (17); Jacksonville, Fla. (19); Lakeland-Winter Haven, Fla. (22); Detroit, Mich. (23); Tampa, Fla. (24); Little-Rock-No. Little Rock, Ark. (25); Saginaw, Mich. (27); Ft. Myers-Cape Coral, Fla. (28).

(3) Property crime includes burglary, larceny, and auto theft. Other metro areas in the top 30 are: Tucson, Ariz. (9); Riverside-San Bernardino, Cal. (20); Wilmington, N.C. (21); Modesto, Cal. (22); Des Moines, Ia. (26); Lubbock, Tex. (29); Columbia, Mo. (30).

(4) Of the top 30 cities in murder, all but 4 are in the South (14) or in Texas (8), or in California (4). Houston, Tex. is the no. 1 murder city, with a rate of 30.0.

Crime Rates by State

Source: 1979 Uniform Crime Reports, Federal Bureau of Investigation

(Rates per 100,000 population)

State	Total	Violent	Property	Murder	Rape	Robbery	Assault	Burglary	Larceny	Auto theft
Alabama	4,243.8	413.3	3,830.5	13.2	27.5	109.5	263.1	1,287.3	2,223.2	320.1
Alaska	6,203.7	491.1	5,712.6	13.3	71.9	109.6	296.3	1,383.3	3,713.3	616.0
Arizona	7,857.3	593.0	7,264.4	8.9	45.7	175.7	362.6	1,996.6	4,774.5	493.3
Arkansas	3,620.8	366.2	3,254.5	9.1	27.3	74.6	255.3	984.3	2,076.5	193.8
California	7,468.8	811.1	6,657.7	13.0	53.9	333.8	410.3	2,186.8	3,732.6	738.3
Colorado	7,051.1	522.1	6,529.0	5.8	53.1	157.0	306.1	1,794.4	4,253.2	481.4
Connecticut	5,779.6	414.2	5,365.4	4.2	24.1	193.3	192.6	1,548.3	3,113.9	703.2
Delaware	6,525.8	537.3	5,988.5	5.7	27.8	129.4	374.4	1,527.5	3,965.8	495.2
Florida	7,688.1	833.9	6,854.2	12.2	51.6	249.4	520.6	2,154.4	4,267.5	432.3
Georgia	5,416.9	558.7	4,858.2	17.1	43.3	213.7	284.5	1,594.0	2,847.9	416.3
Hawaii	7,247.5	289.7	6,957.8	7.2	32.3	184.5	65.7	1,807.4	4,435.0	715.4
Idaho	4,240.8	288.7	3,952.0	5.4	20.6	43.3	219.4	1,075.0	2,605.2	271.8
Illinois	5,169.2	481.3	4,687.9	10.7	29.4	198.0	243.2	1,189.0	2,961.7	537.2
Indiana	4,601.4	338.0	4,263.4	8.3	31.1	132.7	165.9	1,169.9	2,660.5	433.0
Iowa	4,301.7	181.2	4,120.6	2.2	11.0	50.2	117.7	922.1	2,928.8	269.7
Kansas	4,895.8	353.6	4,542.2	5.5	26.4	102.3	219.4	1,329.8	2,938.9	273.5
Kentucky	3,183.9	248.0	2,935.9	9.5	20.4	92.1	126.1	909.6	1,770.1	256.2
Louisiana	5,358.7	676.3	4,682.4	16.9	38.6	219.4	401.4	1,396.8	2,877.7	407.9
Maine	4,307.3	202.5	4,104.8	2.8	11.9	31.8	155.9	1,147.9	2,719.1	237.9

State	Total	Violent	Property	Murder	Rape	Robbery	Assault	Burglary	Larceny	Auto theft
Maryland	6,294.7	795.5	5,499.1	9.8	39.4	331.2	415.2	1,509.5	3,502.0	487.6
Massachusetts . . .	5,917.9	531.3	5,386.7	3.7	24.8	203.2	299.6	1,604.6	2,637.1	1,144.9
Michigan	6,147.0	614.2	5,532.8	9.1	44.5	219.6	341.1	1,507.5	3,423.2	602.1
Minnesota.	4,392.8	221.0	4,171.8	2.3	21.5	92.5	104.8	1,112.9	2,729.7	329.2
Mississippi	2,960.6	323.6	2,637.0	12.6	21.7	70.7	218.6	973.7	1,496.5	166.8
Missouri.	4,939.8	527.2	4,412.7	11.2	33.6	210.9	271.4	1,446.7	2,555.4	410.6
Montana	4,460.6	224.2	4,236.4	4.2	20.6	33.1	166.3	803.3	3,121.8	311.3
Nebraska	3,993.1	225.9	3,767.2	4.1	21.5	73.5	126.8	813.5	2,680.7	272.9
Nevada	8,831.6	835.6	7,996.0	17.5	59.5	407.5	351.0	2,820.4	4,471.2	704.4
New Hampshire . .	4,578.8	139.9	4,438.9	2.4	17.1	28.6	91.8	1,199.0	2,915.0	324.9
New Jersey.	5,820.6	501.2	5,319.4	6.6	27.8	250.0	216.8	1,601.5	3,021.7	696.2
New Mexico	5,788.5	586.0	5,202.5	12.4	46.9	121.0	405.6	1,481.5	3,363.8	357.2
New York	6,205.1	917.4	5,287.7	11.9	30.6	529.6	345.3	1,746.9	2,836.4	704.5
North Carolina . . .	4,372.5	446.1	3,926.4	10.7	20.3	77.2	337.9	1,296.6	2,406.4	223.4
North Dakota. . . .	2,755.9	61.3	2,694.5	1.5	8.2	9.9	41.7	461.0	2,071.1	162.4
Ohio	5,129.8	457.5	4,672.3	8.1	31.8	194.8	222.8	1,287.2	2,946.2	438.9
Oklahoma	4,703.0	405.2	4,297.8	9.7	33.0	102.6	260.0	1,474.6	2,396.0	427.2
Oregon	6,373.0	545.4	5,827.6	4.2	44.4	130.6	366.2	1,609.9	3,831.5	386.2
Pennsylvania	3,495.4	333.6	3,161.8	6.2	21.6	152.2	153.6	934.9	1,837.6	389.4
Rhode Island	5,769.5	375.1	5,394.4	3.2	15.2	109.7	247.0	1,550.1	3,051.3	793.0
South Carolina . . .	5,066.2	678.3	4,387.8	12.6	34.3	107.6	523.8	1,506.1	2,585.5	296.2
South Dakota. . . .	2,959.8	159.1	2,800.7	2.0	16.4	20.3	120.3	626.4	2,000.3	174.0
Tennessee	4,013.4	414.0	3,599.3	9.8	34.5	166.1	203.6	1,294.7	1,937.2	367.4
Texas	5,925.3	507.9	5,417.3	16.7	45.1	191.8	254.3	1,791.2	3,081.9	544.2
Utah	5,492.0	304.2	5,187.9	4.8	27.9	77.7	193.8	1,178.9	3,673.4	335.6
Vermont.	5,299.2	184.2	5,115.0	1.4	22.9	28.6	131.2	1,577.9	3,200.0	337.1
Virginia	4,361.3	301.0	4,060.3	8.6	27.1	111.6	153.7	1,082.6	2,730.9	246.8
Washington	6,529.5	434.6	6,094.9	4.8	46.4	120.7	262.8	1,783.6	3,876.8	434.5
West Virginia	2,325.3	168.1	2,157.2	6.8	15.5	43.9	101.8	636.8	1,318.2	202.3
Wisconsin.	4,388.0	166.1	4,221.9	3.4	16.1	60.5	86.1	949.3	3,005.9	266.7
Wyoming	4,824.0	350.9	4,473.1	9.1	27.6	42.2	272.0	863.8	3,246.0	363.3

Total Arrest Trends by Sex, 1979

Source: 1979 Uniform Crime Reports, Federal Bureau of Investigation

	Males				Females			
	Total		Under 18		Total		Under 18	
	1979	Per-cent change 1978-79	1979	Per-cent change 1978-79	1979	Per-cent change 1978-79	1979	Per-cent change 1978-79
Total[1]	7,706,753	+ 1.1	1,642,535	− 1.7	1,437,367	− .7	422,577	− 4.4
Murder and non-negligent manslaughter	14,784	+ 2.6	1,446	+ 3.6	2,373	− 1.9	163	+ 6.5
Forcible rape	27,477	+ 9.0	4,254	+ 9.8	210	− 1.9	55	−28.6
Robbery	116,348	+ 2.2	36,851	− .3	9,321	+ 6.0	2,731	+ 1.6
Aggravated assault.	216,624	+ 5.7	32,493	+ 3.4	30,772	+ 3.1	5,617	+ 4.0
Burglary	421,651	− .4	205,514	− 6.8	28,613	+ 1.8	14,355	− .5
Larceny-theft	739,565	+ 6.3	314,530	+ 1.5	322,425	− 1.2	116,142	− 5.2
Motor vehicle theft	126,261	− 1.2	61,503	− 5.1	12,410	+ 3.3	6,998	− .4
Arson	15,656	+ 6.0	7,865	+ 5.2	1,997	− 1.0	835	+ 6.4
Violent crime[1]	375,233	+ 4.7	75,044	+ 1.9	42,676	+ 3.4	8,566	+ 3.0
Property crime	1,303,133	+ 3.3	589,412	− 2.2	365,445	− .8	138,330	− 4.4
Crime Index total	1,678,366	+ 3.6	664,456	− 1.8	408,121	− .4	146,896	− 4.0
Other assaults	375,353	+ 4.2	64,761	+ 4.2	59,302	+ 3.4	16,545	+ 5.8
Forgery and counterfeiting. . .	47,081	− .6	6,835	+ 2.3	21,175	+ 2.6	2,808	+ 1.5
Fraud.	138,519	+ 2.9	5,933	− 3.1	93,331	+11.0	2,120	+ 7.9
Embezzlement	5,728	+ 6.8	739	+14.9	1,950	+ 6.4	223	+ .9
Stolen property, buying, receiving, possessing	91,502	+ 1.3	31,034	− .9	10,996	− 4.8	3,030	+ 3.5
Vandalism	211,372	+ 9.5	115,415	+ 3.1	19,453	+10.1	9,872	+ 7.5
Weapons, carrying, possessing	135,235	+ 6.6	22,537	+10.0	10,758	+ .9	1,430	+11.0
Prost., commercialized vice . .	25,239	− 2.0	1,121	−15.7	53,919	− 3.7	2,057	− 9.9
Sex offenses (except forcible rape and prostitution)	56,306	+ 1.0	10,240	+ 1.5	4,779	− 3.7	805	−19.7
Drug abuse violations	451,637	− 6.0	92,383	−17.3	67,452	−12.3	18,155	−18.7
Gambling	45,605	− 3.8	1,997	+ 7.2	4,755	+ 5.4	85	−13.3
Offenses against family and children	46,279	− 1.2	1,592	−11.6	5,057	5.5	906	− 8.7
Driving under the influence . .	1,082,191	+ 2.7	25,712	+ 7.8	103,022	+ 5.7	2,770	+ 9.0
Liquor laws	316,558	+11.7	105,685	+12.2	54,743	+11.5	29,248	+11.5
Drunkeness	978,775	− 2.7	38,156	+ 5.4	77,288	− 4.2	6,006	+ 3.1
Disorderly conduct	583,932	+ 6.6	101,022	+ 3.0	106,433	+ .7	20,809	+ 1.6
Vagrancy	26,262	− 6.6	3,842	−23.3	7,410	−40.8	813	−14.7
All other offenses (except traffic)	1,290,898	− 3.6	229,160	5.3	225,201	− 2.1	55,777	− 9.9

(1) Totals will not add due to deletion of several minor arrest categories.

Police Roster

Source: Uniform Crime Reports

Police officers and civilian employees in large cities as of Oct. 31, 1979

City	Officer	Civilian	City	Officer	Civilian	City	Officer	Civilian
Anchorage, Alas. . .	249	74	Jacksonville, Fla. . .	955	634	Portland, Ore. . . .	653	183
Atlanta, Ga.	1,116	331	Kansas City, Mo. . .	1,192	517	Rochester, N.Y. . . .	638	190
Baltimore, Md. . . .	3,171	555	Little Rock, Ark. . . .	272	59	Sacramento, Cal. . .	513	179
Birmingham, Ala. . .	684	185	Los Angeles, Cal. . .	6,699	2,299	St. Louis, Mo.	2,002	595
Boston, Mass.	2,187	277	Louisville, Ky.	672	201	St. Petersburg, Fla. .	401	184
Bridgeport, Conn. . .	387	28	Memphis, Tenn. . . .	1,265	388	San Antonio, Tex. . .	1,138	231
Buffalo, N.Y.	1,107	140	Miami, Fla.	674	219	San Diego, Cal. . . .	1,306	355
Chicago, Ill.	13,293	1,949	Milwaukee, Wis. . . .	2,029	252	San Francisco, Cal. .	1,554	567
Cincinnati, Oh. . . .	945	155	Minneapolis, Minn. .	745	93	San Jose, Cal.	762	248
Cleveland, Oh. . . .	1,864	134	Newark, N.J.	1,198	256	Santa Ana, Cal. . . .	283	134
Columbus, Oh. . . .	914	289	New Orleans, La. . .	1,482	502	Seattle, Wash. . . .	966	334
Dallas, Tex.	2,031	562	New York, N.Y.	23,310	5,211	Stockton, Cal.	236	88
Denver, Col.	1,403	283	Norfolk, Va.	588	133	Tampa, Fla.	582	203
Detroit, Mich.	5,006	607	Oakland, Cal.	621	296	Toledo, Oh.	702	79
Ft. Worth, Tex. . . .	677	260	Oklahoma City, Okl.	707	186	Tucson, Ariz.	546	191
Fresno, Cal.	342	113	Omaha, Neb.	553	155	Washington, D.C. . .	4,034	549
Hartford, Conn. . . .	373	69	Pasadena, Cal. . . .	184	125	Wichita, Kan.	381	143
Honolulu, Ha. . . .	1,475	308	Philadelphia, Pa. . .	7,903	845			
Houston, Tex.	3,012	819	Phoenix, Ariz.	1,597	570			
Indianapolis, Ind. . .	996	334	Pittsburgh, Pa. . . .	1,366	40			

1,143 Law Enforcement Officers Killed 1970-1979

Responding to disturbance calls.	181	Investigating suspicious persons and circumstances	92
Burglaries in progress or pursuing suspect.	73	Ambush	112
Robberies in progress or pursuing suspect.	208	Handling mentally deranged	32
Attempting other arrests	244	Traffic pursuits and stops	144
Civil disorders	5		
Handling, transporting, custody of prisoners	52		

Geographically for the period of 1970-1979 the 1,143 officers who were slain in the line of duty were divided in this fashion: Northeast 161; North Central 245; South 503; and West 197. Another 37 officers were killed in outlying territories.

Canada: Criminal Offenses and Crime Rate

Source: Statistics Canada

	1979 Actual offenses	1979 Rate[2]	1980[1] Actual offenses	1980[1] Rate[2]	Percent change in rate
Total criminal code	1,855,271	7,837.57	2,037,635	8,520.54	+ 8.7
Total homicide	1,385	5.85	1,393	5.82	− 0.5
Murder, 1st degree	234	0.99	225	0.94	− 5.1
Murder, 2nd degree.	353	1.49	268	1.12	− 24.8
Manslaughter	39	0.16	97	0.41	+156.3
Infanticide	5	0.02	3	0.01	+ 50.0
Attempted Murder	754	3.19	790	3.30	+ 3.4
Total sexual offenses	12,333	52.10	12,756	53.34	+ 2.4
Rape	2,291	9.68	2,312	9.67	− 0.1
Indecent assaults on female	6,087	25.71	6,519	27.26	+ 6.0
Indecent assaults on male	1,376	5.81	1,312	5.49	− 5.5
Other sexual offenses	2,579	10.90	2,613	10.93	+ 0.3
Total crimes of violence	147,526	623.23	155,354	649.63	+ 4.2
Assaults (not indecent).	112,911	476.99	116,647	487.77	+ 2.3
Robbery	20,899	88.29	24,567	102.73	+ 16.4
Total property crimes	1,186,697	5,013.19	1,330,300	5,562.76	+ 11.0
Breaking & entering.	296,437	1,252.29	348,283	1,456.37	+ 16.3
Theft, motor vehicle.	91,445	386.31	93,664	391.66	+ 1.4
Theft, over $200.	169,950	717.95	224,019	936.75	+ 30.5
Theft, $200 and under	516,184	2,180.61	537,796	2,248.84	+ 3.1
Having stolen goods	20,997	88.70	24,556	102.68	+ 15.8
Fraud.	91,684	387.32	101,982	426.45	+ 10.1
Total other crimes	521,046	2,201.15	551,981	2,308.15	+ 4.9
Prostitution.	1,283	5.42	1,504	6.29	+ 16.1
Gaming and betting.	3,059	12.92	2,695	11.27	− 12.8
Offensive weapons	15,298	64.63	15,853	66.29	+ 2.6
Other criminal code.	501,406	2,118.18	531,929	2,224.30	+ 5.0
Federal statutes-drugs	64,923	274.27	74,003	309.45	+ 12.8
Federal statutes-other	57,634	243.47	45,475	190.16	− 21.9
Provincial statutes (3)	438,204	851.19	448,470	1,875.31	+ 1.3
Municipal by-laws (3)	69,598	294.02	74,135	310.00	+ 5.4
Total all offenses.	2,485,630	10,500.52	2,605,715	10,896.00	+ 3.8

(1) Preliminary data, subject to revision. (2) Rate per 100,000 population. (3) Excluding traffic offenses.

State and Federal Prison Population; Death Penalty

As of Jan. 1, 1980

Source: Bureau of Justice Statistics, U.S. Justice Department

	Prisoners	Maximum length of sentence		Death penalty		
		More than a year	Year or less (and unsentenced)	Under sentence of death	Executions	Death penalty
Federal institutions . . .	26,233	22,450	3,783	0	0	Yes
State institutions	287,850	279,399	8,451	567	2	...
Male	301,156	289,762	11,394	560	2	...
Female.	12,927	12,087	840	7	0	...
Alabama.	5,343	5,343	0	43	0	Yes
Alaska	760	532	228	0	0	No
Arizona.	3,496	3,496	0	22	0	Yes
Arkansas.	2,937	2,937	0	12	0	Yes
California.	22,628	21,258	1,370	25	0	Yes
Colorado.	2,493	2,483	10	0	0	Yes
Connecticut	4,061	2,139	1,922	0	0	Yes
Delaware	1,427	1,096	331	1	0	Yes
Dist. of Columbia	2,973	2,599	374	0	0	No
Florida	20,133	19,792	341	138	1	Yes
Georgia	12,098	11,658	440	71	0	Yes
Hawaii	891	562	299	0	0	No
Idaho	830	830	0	1	0	Yes
Illinois.	11,211	11,165	46	19	0	Yes
Indiana	5,667	5,270	397	3	0	Yes
Iowa	2,214	2,204	10	0	0	No
Kansas.	2,290	2,290	0	0	0	No
Kentucky.	3,691	3,691	0	3	0	Yes
Louisiana.	7,693	7,693	0	2	0	Yes
Maine.	789	641	148	0	0	No
Maryland.	7,860	7,860	0	1	0	Yes
Massachusetts	2,949	2,920	29	0	0	Yes
Michigan	15,054	15,054	0	0	0	No
Minnesota	2,094	2,094	0	0	0	No
Mississippi	3,458	3,375	83	11	0	Yes
Missouri	5,555	5,555	0	2	0	Yes
Montana	722	718	4	3	0	Yes
Nebraska	1,254	1,156	98	8	0	Yes
Nevada.	1,566	1,566	0	7	1	Yes
New Hampshire.	316	316	0	0	0	Yes
New Jersey	5,875	5,562	313	0	0	No
New Mexico	1,547	1,457	90	0	0	Yes
New York	21,158	21,158	0	0	0	Yes
North Carolina.	14,271	13,602	669	8	0	Yes
North Dakota	220	170	50	0	0	No
Ohio	13,353	13,353	0	0	0	No
Oklahoma	4,081	4,081	0	25	0	Yes
Oregon.	3,218	3,215	3	1	0	Yes
Pennsylvania	7,879	7,792	87	4	0	Yes
Rhode Island	746	565	181	0	0	No
South Carolina	7,643	7,115	528	8	0	Yes
South Dakota	562	539	23	0	0	Yes
Tennessee.	6,626	6,626	0	11	0	Yes
Texas	26,522	26,522	0	117	0	Yes
Utah	960	957	3	7	0	Yes
Vermont	411	286	125	0	0	Yes
Virginia	8,449	8,200	249	8	0	Yes
Washington	4,507	4,507	0	5	0	Yes
West Virginia	1,251	1,251	0	0	0	No
Wisconsin	3,650	3,650	0	0	0	No
Wyoming.	498	498	0	1	0	No

U.S. Crime Rate Up 9% in 1979

An estimated 12,152,730 Crime Index offenses, 9 percent more than during 1978, were reported to law enforcement agencies in 1979. Collectively, violent crimes, which comprised 10 percent of the total Crime Index, were up 11 percent and property crimes rose 9 percent. All offenses increased in volume. Among the violent crimes, murder was up 10 percent; rape, 13 percent; robbery, 12 percent; and aggravated assault, 10 percent. Among property crimes, burglary increased 6 percent, larceny 10 percent, and auto theft 11 percent.

Crime Index Trends by Geographic Region 1979 over 1978

(rates per 100,000 population)

Region	Total	Violent	Property	Murder	Rape	Robbery	Assault	Burglary	Larceny	Auto theft
Total	+8.1	+10.0	+7.9	+7.8	+12.0	+10.9	+9.1	+5.3	+8.9	+9.6
Northeast	+9.7	+11.6	+9.4	+10.1	+12.6	+14.7	+8.1	+6.6	+11.2	+8.8
North Central.	+8.0	+8.2	+8.0	+7.0	+15.7	+4.0	+10.6	+5.5	+8.9	+9.3
South	+8.9	+10.5	+8.7	+9.5	+12.4	+15.3	+7.8	+8.4	+8.1	+14.3
West	+5.2	+8.6	+4.9	+7.4	+7.9	+7.4	+9.7	-.4	+7.5	+6.4

POSTAL INFORMATION

U.S. Postal Service

The Postal Reorganization Act, creating a government-owned postal service under the executive branch and replacing the old Post Office Department, was signed into law by President Nixon on Aug. 12, 1970. The service officially came into being on July 1, 1971.

The new U.S. Postal Service is governed by an 11-man Board of Governors. Nine members are appointed to 9-year terms by the president with Senate approval. These 9, in turn, choose a postmaster general, who is no longer a member of the president's cabinet. The board and the new postmaster general choose the 11th member, who serves as deputy postmaster general. A new Postal Rate Commission of 5 members, appointed by the president, recommends postal rates to the governors for their approval.

The first postmaster general under the new system was Winton M. Blount. He resigned Oct. 29, 1971, and was replaced by his deputy, E. T. Klassen, Dec. 7, 1971. Benjamin F. Bailar succeeded him Feb. 16, 1975, and was succeeded by William F. Bolger on March 15, 1978.

As of Oct. 1, 1980, there was a total of 30,326 post offices throughout the U.S. and possessions.

U.S. Domestic Rates (in effect Nov. 1, 1981)

Domestic includes the U.S., territories and possessions, APO and FPO.

First Class

Letters written, and matter sealed against inspection, 20¢ for 1st oz. or fraction, 17¢ for each additional oz. or fraction.
U.S. Postal cards; single 13¢; double 26¢; private postcards, same.
First class includes written matter, namely letters, postal cards, postcards (private mailing cards) and all other matter wholly or partly in writing, whether sealed or unsealed, except manuscripts for books, periodical articles and music, manuscript copy accompanying proofsheets or corrected proofsheets of the same and the writing authorized by law on matter of other classes. Also matter sealed or closed against inspection, bills and statements of accounts.

Greeting Cards

May be sent first class or single piece third class.

Express Mail

Express Mail Service is available for any mailable article up to 70 pounds, and guarantees delivery between major U.S. cities or your money back.

Articles received by 5 p.m. at a postal facility offering Express Mail will be delivered by 3 p.m. the next day or, if you prefer, your shipment can be picked up as early as 10 a.m. the next business day. Rates include insurance, Shipment Receipt, and Record of Delivery at the destination post office.

Consult Postmaster for other Express Mail Services and rates. (The Postal Service will refund, upon application to originating office, the postage for any Express Mail shipments not meeting the service standard except for those delayed by strike or work stoppage.)

Second Class

Single copy mailings by general public 19¢ for first ounce, 35¢ for over 1 to 2 ozs., 45¢ for over 2 to 3 ozs. and 10¢ for each additional ounce up to 8 ozs. Each additional 2 ozs. over 8 ozs., add 10¢.

Third Class

Third class (limit up to but not including 16 ounces): Mailable matter not in 1st and 2d classes.
Single mailing: Greeting cards (sealed or unsealed), small parcels, printed matter, booklets and catalogs, 20¢ the first ounce, 37¢ for over 1 to 2 ozs., 54¢ for over 2 to 3 ozs., 71¢ for over 3 to 4 ozs., 85¢ for over 4 to 6 ozs., 95¢ for over 6 to 8 ozs., $1.05 for over 8 to 10 ozs., $1.15 for over 10 to 12 ozs., $1.25 for over 12 to 14 ozs., $1.35 for over 14 but less than 16 ozs.

Bulk material: books, catalogs of 24 pages or more, seeds, cuttings, bulbs, roots, scions, and plants. 45¢ per pound, 10.9¢ minimum per piece.

Other matter: newsletters, shopper's guides, advertising circulars, 45¢ per pound, 10.9¢ minimum per piece. Separate rates for some nonprofit organizations. Bulk mailing fee, $40 per calendar year. Apply to postmaster for permit. One-time fee for permit imprint, $40.

Parcel Post—Fourth Class

Fourth class or parcel post (16 ounces and over): merchandise, printed matter, etc., may be sealed, subject to inspection.

On parcels weighing less than 15 lbs. and measuring more than 84 inches, but not more than 100 inches in length and girth combined, the minimum postal charge shall be the zone charge applicable to a 15-pound parcel.

Priority Mail

First class mail of more than 12 ounces can be sent "Priority Mail (Heavy Pieces)" service. The most expeditious handling and transportation available will be used for fastest delivery.

Forwarding Addresses

The mailer, in order to obtain a forwarding address, must endorse the envelope or cover "Address Correction Requested." The destination post office then will determine whether a forwarding address has been left on file and provide it for a fee of 25¢.

Priority Mail

Packages weighing up to 70 pounds and exceeding 100 inches in length and girth combined, including written and other material of the first class, whether sealed or unsealed, fractions of a pound being charged as a full pound, except in the 1 to 5 pound weight category where half-pound weight increments apply.

Rates according to zone apply between the U.S. and Puerto Rico and Virgin Islands.

Parcels weighing less than 15 pounds, measuring over 84 inches but not exceeding 100 inches in length and girth combined are chargeable with a minimum rate equal to that for a 15 pound parcel for the zone to which addressed.

Zones	To 1 lb.	1½	2	2½	3	3½	4	4½	5*
1, 2, 3	$2.24	$2.30	$2.54	$2.78	$3.01	$3.25	$3.49	3.73	$3.97
4	2.24	2.42	2.70	2.98	3.25	3.53	3.81	4.09	4.37
5	2.24	2.56	2.88	3.21	3.53	3.85	4.18	4.50	4.83
6	2.34	2.72	3.09	3.47	3.85	4.22	4.60	4.97	5.35
7	2.45	2.87	3.30	3.73	4.16	4.59	5.02	5.45	5.88
8	2.58	3.07	3.57	4.06	4.56	5.05	5.55	6.05	6.54

*Consult postmaster for parcels over 5 lbs.

Special Handling

Third and fourth class parcels will be handled and delivered as expeditiously as practicable (but not special delivery) upon payment, in addition to the regular postage: up to 10 lbs., 75¢; over 10 lbs., $1.30. Such parcels must be endorsed, Special Handling.

Special Delivery

First class mail up to 2 lbs. $2.10, over 2 lbs. and up to 10 lbs., $2.35; over 10 lbs. $3.00. All other classes up to 2 lbs. $2.35, over 2 and up to 10 lbs., $3.00, over 10 lbs. $3.40.

Bound Printed Matter Rates
(Fourth class single piece zone rate)

Weight lbs.	Local	1&2	3	4	5	6	7	8
1.5	$0.69	$0.92	$0.94	$0.97	$1.02	$1.08	$1.16	$1.19
2	.69	.93	.95	.99	1.06	1.14	1.25	1.28
2.5	.69	.93	.96	1.01	1.10	1.20	1.33	1.38
3	.69	.94	.97	1.03	1.14	1.25	1.41	1.47
3.5	.69	.94	.98	1.05	1.17	1.31	1.50	1.56
4	.69	.95	.99	1.07	1.21	1.37	1.58	1.66
4.5	.69	.95	1.00	1.09	1.25	1.42	1.67	1.75
5	.70	.96	1.02	1.12	1.29	1.48	1.75	1.85
6	.70	.96	1.04	1.16	1.36	1.59	1.92	2.03
7	.70	.97	1.06	1.20	1.44	1.71	2.09	2.22
8	.70	.98	1.08	1.24	1.51	1.82	2.25	2.41
9	.70	.99	1.10	1.28	1.59	1.94	2.42	2.59
10	.70	1.00	1.12	1.32	1.66	2.05	2.59	2.78

Zone Mileage

1 . . Up to 50   3 . . 150-300   5 . . 600-1,000   7 . 1,400-1,800
2 . . . 50-150   4 . 300-600   6 . . 1,000-1,400   8 . . over 1,800

Domestic Mail Special Services

Registry — all mailable matter prepaid with postage at the first-class or airmail rate may be registered. The mailer is required to declare the value of mail presented for registration.

Registered Mail

	Insured	Uninsured
$0.00 to $100.	$3.30	$3.25
$100.01 to $500 . . .	3.60	3.55
$500.01 to $1,000 . .	3.90	3.85
$1,000.01 to $2,000 . .	4.20	4.10
$2,000.01 to $3,000 . .	4.50	4.35
$3,000.01 to $4,000 . .	4.80	4.60
$4,000.01 to $5,000 . .	5.10	4.85
$5,000.01 to $6,000 . .	5.40	5.10
$6,000.01 to $7,000 . .	5.70	5.35
$7,000.01 to $8,000 . .	6.00	5.60
$8,000.01 to $9,000 . .	6.30	5.85
$9,000.01 to $10,000 . .	6.60	6.10

Consult postmaster for registry rates above $10,000.

C.O.D.: Unregistered — is applicable to 3d and 4th class matter and sealed domestic mail of any class bearing postage at the 1st class rate. Such mail must be based on bona fide orders or be in conformity with agreements between senders and addressees. **Registered** — for details consult postmaster.

Insurance — is applicable to 3d and 4th class matter. Matter for sale addressed to prospective purchasers who have not ordered it or authorized its sending will not be insured.

Insured Mail

$0.01 to $20.	$0.45
20.01 to 50	0.85
50.01 to 100.	1.25
100.01 to 150	1.70
150.01 to 200	2.05
200.01 to 300	3.45
300.01 to 400	4.70

Liability for insured mail is limited to $400.

Certified mail — service is available for any matter having no intrinsic value on which 1st class or air mail postage is paid. Receipt is furnished at time of mailing and evidence of delivery obtained. The fee is 75¢ ($1.00 restricted delivery) in addition to postage. Return receipt, restricted delivery, and special delivery are available upon payment of additional fees. No indemnity.

Special Fourth Class Rate
(limit 70 lbs.)

First pound or fraction, 63¢ (46¢ if 500 pieces or more of special rate matter are presorted to 5 digit ZIP code or 58¢ if 500 pieces or more are presorted to Bulk Mail Cntrs.); each additional pound or fraction through 7 pounds, 23¢; each additional pound, 14¢. Only following specific articles: books 24 pages or more, at least 22 of which are printed consisting wholly of reading matter or scholarly bibliography containing no advertisement other than incidental announcements of books; 16 millimeter films in final form (except when mailed to or from commercial theaters); printed music in bound or sheet form; printed objective test materials; sound recordings, playscripts, and manuscripts for books, periodicals, and music; printed educational reference charts; loose-leaf pages and binders therefor consisting of medical information for distribution to doctors, hospitals, medical schools, and medical students. Package must be marked "Special 4th Class Rate" stating item contained.

Library Rate (limit 70 lbs.)

First pound 24¢, each additional pound through 7 pounds, 9¢; each additional pound, 6¢. Books when loaned or exchanged between schools, colleges, public libraries, and certain non-profit organizations; books, printed music, bound academic theses, periodicals, sound recordings, other library materials, museum materials (specimens, collections), scientific or mathematical kits, instruments or other devices; also catalogs, guides or scripts for some of these materials. Must be marked "Library Rate".

Postal Union Mail Special Services

Registration — available to practically all countries. Fee $3.25. The maximum indemnity payable — generally only in case of complete loss (of both contents and wrapper) — is $25.20. To Canada only the fee is $3.55 providing indemnity for loss up to $200.

Parcel Post Rate Schedule

1 lb., not exceeding	Local	1 & 2	Zones 3	4	5	6	7	8
2	1.52	1.55	1.61	1.70	1.83	1.99	2.15	2.48
3	1.58	1.63	1.73	1.86	2.06	2.30	2.55	3.05
4	1.65	1.71	1.84	2.02	2.29	2.61	2.94	3.60
5	1.71	1.79	1.96	2.18	2.52	2.92	3.32	4.07
6	1.78	1.87	2.07	2.33	2.74	3.14	3.64	4.54
7	1.84	1.95	2.18	2.49	2.89	3.38	3.95	5.02
8	1.91	2.03	2.30	2.64	3.06	3.63	4.27	5.55
9	1.97	2.11	2.41	2.75	3.25	3.93	4.63	6.08
10	2.04	2.19	2.52	2.87	3.46	4.22	5.00	6.62
11	2.10	2.28	2.60	3.00	3.68	4.51	5.38	7.15
12	2.17	2.36	2.66	3.10	3.89	4.80	5.75	7.69
13	2.21	2.41	2.72	3.19	4.02	4.96	5.95	7.97
14	2.26	2.46	2.78	3.28	4.13	5.12	6.14	8.24
15	2.31	2.51	2.83	3.36	4.25	5.26	6.32	8.48
16	2.35	2.56	2.89	3.44	4.35	5.40	6.49	8.72
17	2.40	2.59	2.94	3.51	4.45	5.53	6.65	8.94
18	2.44	2.64	2.99	3.59	4.55	5.65	6.80	9.15
19	2.48	2.68	3.04	3.66	4.64	5.77	6.94	9.35
20	2.52	2.72	3.10	3.73	4.73	5.89	7.09	9.55

Consult postmaster for parcels over 20 pounds or measuring more than 84 inches, length and girth.

Return receipt —fee is 60¢.

Special delivery — Available to most countries. Consult post office. Fees: for post cards, letter mail, and airmail "other articles," $2.10 up to 2 pounds; over 2 to 10 pounds, $2.35; over 10 pounds, $3.00. For surface "other articles," $2.35, $3.00, and $3.40, respectively.

Marking — an article intended for special delivery service must have affixed to the cover near the name of the country of destination "EXPRESS" (special delivery) label, obtainable at the post office, or it may be marked on the cover boldly in red "EXPRESS" (special delivery).

Special handling — entitles AO surface packages to priority handling between mailing point and U.S. point of dispatch. Fees: 75¢ for packages to 10 pounds, and $1.30 for packages over 10 pounds.

Airmail — there is daily air service to practically all countries.

Prepayment of replies from other countries — a mailer who wishes to prepay a reply by letter from another country may do so by sending his correspondent one or more international reply coupons, which may be purchased at United States post offices. One coupon should be accepted in any country in exchange for stamps to prepay a surface letter of the first unit of weight to the U.S.

Post Office-Authorized 2-Letter State Abbreviations

The abbreviations below are approved by the U.S. Postal Service for use in addresses only. They do not replace the traditional abbreviations in other contexts. The official list follows, including the District of Columbia, Guam, Puerto Rico, the Canal Zone, and the Virgin Islands (all capital letters are used):

Alabama	AL	Hawaii	HI	Missouri	MO	Puerto Rico	PR
Alaska	AK	Idaho	ID	Montana	MT	Rhode Island	RI
American Samoa	AS	Illinois	IL	Nebraska	NE	South Carolina	SC
Arizona	AZ	Indiana	IN	Nevada	NV	South Dakota	SD
Arkansas	AR	Iowa	IA	New Hampshire	NH	Tennessee	TN
California	CA	Kansas	KS	New Jersey	NJ	Texas	TX
Canal Zone	CZ	Kentucky	KY	New Mexico	NM	Trust Territories	TT
Colorado	CO	Louisiana	LA	New York	NY	Utah	UT
Connecticut	CT	Maine	ME	North Carolina	NC	Vermont	VT
Delaware	DE	Maryland	MD	North Dakota	ND	Virginia	VA
Dist. of Col.	DC	Massachusetts	MA	Northern Mariana Is.	CM	Virgin Islands	VI
Florida	FL	Michigan	MI	Ohio	OH	Washington	WA
Georgia	GA	Minnesota	MN	Oklahoma	OK	West Virginia	WV
Guam	GU	Mississippi	MS	Oregon	OR	Wisconsin	WI
				Pennsylvania	PA	Wyoming	WY

Also approved for use in addressing mail are the following abbreviations:

Alley	Aly	Court	Ct	Grove	Grv	Rural	R
Arcade	Arc	Courts	Cts	Heights	Hts	Square	Sq
Boulevard	Blvd	Crescent	Cres	Highway	Hwy	Street	St
Branch	Br	Drive	Dr	Lane	Ln	Terrace	Ter
Bypass	Byp	Expressway	Expy	Manor	Mnr	Trail	Trl
Causeway	Cswy	Extended	Ext	Place	Pl	Turnpike	Tpke
Center	Ctr	Extension	Ext	Plaza	Plz	Viaduct	Via
Circle	Cir	Freeway	Fwy	Point	Pt	Vista	Vis
		Gardens	Gdns	Road	Rd		

Size Standards for Domestic Mail

Minimum Size

Pieces which do not meet the following requirements are prohibited from the mails:

    a. All pieces must be at least .007 of an inch thick, and

    b. All pieces (except keys and identification devices) which are ¼ inch or less thick must be:

        (1) Rectangular in shape,

        (2) At least 3½ inches high, and

        (3) At least 5 inches long.

Note: Pieces greater than ¼ inch thick can be mailed even if they measure less than 3½ by 5 inches.

Nonstandard Mail

All First-Class Mail weighing one ounce or less and all single-piece rate Third-Class mail weighing one ounce or less is nonstandard (and subject to a 9¢ surcharge in addition to the applicable postage and fees) if:

    1. Any of the following dimensions are exceeded:
        Length—11½ inches,
        Height—6⅛ inches,
        Thickness—¼ inch, or

    2. The piece has a height to length (aspect) ratio which does not fall between 1 to 1.3 and 1 to 2.5 inclusive. (The aspect ratio is found by dividing the length by the height. If the answer is between 1.3 and 2.5 inclusive, the piece has a standard aspect ratio.)

Stamps, Envelopes and Postal Cards

Form	Denomination and prices
Single or sheet	1,2,3,4,5,6,10,11,12,13,14,15,16,17,18,20,25,28,30,45 & 50 cents, $1 and $5.
Book	20 at 20¢ = $4.00
Coil of 100	20 cents. (Dispenser to hold coils of 100 stamps may be purchased for 10¢ additional.)
Coils of 500	1,2,3,5,6,9,10,12,13,15,16, & 20 cents and $1.
Coil of 3,000	1,2,3,5,6,9,10,15,16,20 and 25 cents.

Postal Receipts at Large Cities

Fiscal year	Boston	Chicago	Detroit	L.A.	New York	Phila.	St. Louis	Wash., D.C.
1975	$136,453,079	$365,378,795	$84,338,282	$193,229,077	$453,905,277	$134,571,376	$85,591,774	$115,489,343
1976	151,642,227	384,380,826	95,527,250	203,413,409	484,180,727	147,650,431	96,844,188	125,997,649
1977	173,933,702	424,045,237	102,018,571	232,293,590	528,545,213	168,521,442	107,379,762	138,050,517
1978	185,983,338	451,745,664	112,884,557	251,481,356	559,199,925	180,365,543	115,610,668	156,623,025
1979	211,082,724	506,395,438	120,690,772	273,563,824	627,445,984	211,571,818	126,031,314	175,467,893
1980	224,428,760	528,233,991	119,240,818	271,136,828	666,377,778	221,161,624	127,427,555	187,334,312

Other cities for fiscal year 1980: Atlanta, $201,069,490; Baltimore, $105,347,163; Cincinnati, $82,542,643; Cleveland, $125,545,576; Columbus, $107,896,945; Dallas, $209,604,163; Denver, $106,238,760; Houston, $173,684,326; Indianapolis, $108,289,580; Kansas City, $94,023,231; Minneapolis, $145,444,186; Pittsburgh, $103,579,965; San Francisco, $160,278,304; Seattle, $97,969,564.

Air Mail, Parcel Post International Rates

Aerogrammes — 30¢ each to all countries.
Air mail postcards (single) - 28¢ to all countries except Canada and Mexico (13¢)

Country	Rate group (see below)	Air parcel post rates First 4 oz.	Each add'l. 4 oz. or fraction up to first 5 lbs.	Country	Rate group (see below)	Air parcel post rates First 4 oz.	Each add'l. 4 oz. or fraction up to first 5 lbs.
Afghanistan	D	5.40	1.10	Guyana	B	3.80	.70
Albania	C	4.60	.90	Haiti	A	3.00	.50
Algeria	D	5.40	1.10	Honduras	B	3.80	.70
Andorra	B	3.80	.70	Hong Kong	C	4.60	.90
Angola	E	6.20	1.30	Hungary	C	4.60	.90
Argentina	D	5.40	1.10	Iceland	D	5.40	1.10
Ascension	(4)	—	—	India	D	5.40	1.10
Australia	D	5.40	1.10	Indonesia	E	6.20	1.30
Austria	B	3.80	.70	Iran	D	5.40	1.10
Azores	C	4.60	.90	Iraq	D	5.40	1.10
Bahamas	A	3.00	.50	Ireland (Eire)	C	4.60	.90
Bahrain	D	5.40	1.10	Israel	C	4.60	.90
Bangladesh	E	6.20	1.30	Italy	C	4.60	.90
Barbados	B	3.80	.70	Ivory Coast	D	5.40	1.10
Belgium	E	6.20	1.30	Jamaica	A	3.00	.50
Belize	A	3.00	.50	Japan	E	6.20	1.30
Benin	D	5.40	1.10	Jordan	C	4.60	.90
Bermuda	A	3.00	.50	Kampuchea	(5)	—	—
Bhutan	(5)	—	—	Kenya	D	5.40	1.10
Bolivia	B	3.80	.70	Kiribati	B	3.80	.70
Botswana	E	6.20	1.30	Korea, Democratic People's			
Brazil	E	6.20	1.30	Rep. (North)[1]	(5)	—	—
Brunei	D	5.40	1.10	Korea, Rep. of (South)	D	5.40	1.10
Bulgaria	D	5.40	1.10	Kuwait	C	4.60	.90
Burma	D	5.40	1.10	Lao	E	6.20	1.30
Burundi	E	6.20	1.30	Latvia	E	6.20	1.30
Cameroon	C	4.60	.90	Lebanon	C	4.60	.90
Canada[3,6]	(4)	—	—	Leeward Islands	A	3.00	.50
Cape Verde	D	5.40	1.10	Lesotho	E	6.20	1.30
Cayman Islands	A	3.00	.50	Liberia	B	3.80	.70
Central African Rep.	E	6.20	1.30	Libya	C	4.60	.90
Chad	D	5.40	1.10	Lithuania	E	6.20	1.30
Chile	D	5.40	1.10	Luxembourg	B	3.80	.70
China (People's Republic.	D	5.40	1.10	Macao	C	4.60	.90
of)[7]				Madagascar	C	4.60	.90
Colombia	B	3.80	.70	Madeira Islands	B	3.80	.70
Comoros	E	6.20	1.30	Malawi	D	5.40	1.10
Congo	D	5.40	1.10	Malaysia	D	5.40	1.10
Corsica	E	6.20	1.30	Maldives	D	5.40	1.10
Costa Rica	A	3.00	.50	Mali	C	4.60	.90
Cuba	(5)	—	—	Malta	C	4.60	.90
Cyprus	D	5.40	1.10	Martinique	A	3.00	.50
Czechoslovakia	C	4.60	.90	Mauritania	D	5.40	1.10
Denmark	B	3.80	.70	Mauritius	E	6.20	1.30
Djibouti	E	6.20	1.30	Mexico	A	3.00	.50
Dominica	A	3.00	.50	Mongolia	(5)	—	—
Dominican Republic	A	3.00	.50	Morocco	C	4.60	.90
East Timor	(5)	—	—	Mozambique	E	6.20	1.30
Ecuador	B	3.80	.70	Nauru	C	4.60	.90
Egypt	C	4.60	.90	Nepal	D	5.40	1.10
El Salvador	A	3.00	.50	Netherlands	C	4.60	.90
Equatorial Guinea	D	5.40	1.10	Nertherlands Antilles	A	3.00	.50
Estonia	E	6.20	1.30	New Caledonia	D	5.40	1.10
Ethiopia	D	5.40	1.10	New Zealand	D	5.40	1.10
Faeroe Islands	C	4.60	.90	Nicaragua	B	3.80	.70
Falkland Islands	D	5.40	1.10	Niger	D	5.40	1.10
Fiji	B	3.80	.70	Nigeria	C	4.60	.90
Finland	D	5.40	1.10	Norway	D	5.40	1.10
France				Oman	D	5.40	1.10
(including Monaco)	E	6.20	1.30	Pakistan	D	5.40	1.10
French Guiana	C	4.60	.90	Panama	A	3.00	.50
French Polynesia	D	5.40	1.10	Papua New Guinea	D	5.40	1.10
Gabon	D	5.40	1.10	Paraguay	C	4.60	.90
Gambia	B	3.80	.70	Peru	B	3.80	.70
German Democratic				Philippines	D	5.40	1.10
Republic (East Germany)	C	4.60	.90	Pitcairn Islands	B	3.80	.70
Germany, Federal Rep.				Poland	C	4.60	.90
of (West Germany)	C	4.60	.90	Portugal	B	3.80	.70
Ghana	D	5.40	1.10	Qatar	C	4.60	.90
Gibraltar	D	5.40	1.10	Reunion	E	6.20	1.30
Great Britain	C	4.60	.90	Romania	C	4.60	.90
Greece	C	4.60	.90	Rwanda	D	5.40	1.10
Greenland	D	5.40	1.10	St. Helena	B	3.80	.70
Grenada	B	3.80	.70	St. Lucia	A	3.00	.50
Guadeloupe	A	3.00	.50	St. Pierre & Miquelon	A	3.00	.50
Guatemala	A	3.00	.50	St. Thomas & Principe	D	5.40	1.10
Guinea	B	3.80	.70	St. Vincent & The Grena-	A	3.00	.50
Guinea-Bissau	B	3.80	.70	dines			

Country	Rate group (see below)	First 4 oz.	Each add'l. 4 oz. or fraction up to First 5 lbs.	Country	Rate group (see below)	First 4 oz.	Each add'l. 4 oz. or fraction up to First 5 lbs.
Santa Cruz Islands	B	3.80	.70	Tonga	B	3.80	.70
Saudi Arabia	C	4.60	.90	Trinidad & Tobago	B	3.80	.70
Senegal	D	5.40	1.10	Tristan da Cunha	B	3.80	.70
Seychelles	D	5.40	1.10	Tunisia	C	4.60	.90
Sierra Leone	C	4.60	.90	Turkey	C	4.60	.90
Singapore	D	5.40	1.10	Turks & Caicos Islands	A	3.00	.50
Solomon Islands	C	4.60	.90	Tuvalu (Ellice Islands)	B	3.80	.70
Somalia (Southern Region)	D	5.40	1.10	Uganda	D	5.40	1.10
Somalia (Northern Region)	(4)	—	—	USSR[3]	E	6.20	1.30
South Africa	E	6.20	1.30	United Arab Emirates	D	5.40	1.10
Spain	C	4.60	.90	Upper Volta	C	4.60	.90
Sri Lanka	D	5.40	1.10	Uruguay	B	3.80	.70
Sudan	D	5.40	1.10	Vanuatu	B	3.80	.70
Suriname	B	3.80	.70	Vatican City State	C	4.60	.90
Swaziland	D	5.40	1.10	Venezuela	B	3.80	.70
Sweden	D	5.40	1.10	Vietnam[1]	(5)	—	—
Switzerland	B	3.80	.70	Western Samoa	B	3.80	.70
Syria	C	4.60	.90	Yemen Arab Republic	D	5.40	1.10
Taiwan	C	4.60	.90	Yemen, Peoples Democratic Republic of	D	5.40	1.10
Tanzania	E	6.20	1.30	Yugoslavia	C	4.60	.90
Thailand	D	5.40	1.10	Zaire	D	5.40	1.10
Togo	D	5.40	1.10	Zambia	E	6.20	1.30
				Zimbabwe	E	6.20	1.30

Miscellaneous International Rates

Letters and Letter Pkgs (Surface)

Weight steps

Over Lbs.	Over Ozs.	Through Lbs.	Through Ozs.	Canada	Mexico	All other countries
0	0	0	1	$0.20	$0.20	$0.30
0	1	0	2	.37	.37	.47
0	2	0	3	.54	.57	.64
0	3	0	4	.71	.71	.81
0	4	0	5	.88	.88	.98
0	5	0	6	1.05	1.05	1.15
0	6	0	7	1.22	1.22	1.32
0	7	0	8	1.39	1.39	1.49
0	8	0	9	1.56	1.56	2.76
0	9	0	10	1.73	1.73	2.76
0	10	0	11	1.90	1.90	2.76
0	11	0	12	2.07	2.07	2.76
0	12	1	0	2.58	2.58	2.76
1	0	1	8	3.07	3.07	3.78
1	8	2	0	3.57	3.57	4.80
2	0	2	8	4.06	4.06	5.55
2	8	3	0	4.56	4.56	6.30
3	0	3	8	5.05	5.05	7.05
3	8	4	0	5.55	5.55	7.80
4	0	4	8	6.05	...	...
4	8	5	0	6.54	...	...

Maximum limit: 60 pounds to Canada, 4 pounds to Mexico and all other countries.

Letters and Letter Pkgs (Air)

Canada and Mexico: Refer to rates listed under Letter and Letter Pkgs. (Surface). Mail paid at this rate receives First-Class service in the United States and air service in Canada and Mexico.

Colombia, Venezuela, Central America, the Caribbean Islands, Bahamas, Bermuda, St. Pierre & Miquelon: 35 cents per half ounce up to and including 2 ounces; 30 cents each additional half ounce up to and including 32 ounces; 30 cents per additional ounce over 32 ounces.

All Other Countries: 40 cents per half ounce up to and including 2 ounces; 35 cents each additional half ounce up to and including 32 ounces; 35 cents per additional ounce over 32 ounces.

Parcel Post (Surface)

Canada, Mexico, Central America, The Caribbean Islands, Bahamas, Bermuda, St. Pierre and Miquelon; $3.10 for the first 2 pounds and $1.00 each additional pound or fraction.

All Other Countries: $3.25 for the first 2 pounds and $1.05 for each additional pound or fraction.

For Parcel Post air rates, see tables, pages 973-974.

(1) Restrictions apply; consult post office. (2) To facilitate distribution and delivery, include "Union of Soviet Socialist Republics" or "USSR" as part of the address. (3) Small packets weight limit one pound to Canada. (4) No air parcel post service. (5) No parcel post service. (6) No airmail AO or parcel post to Canada; prepare and prepay all airmail packages as letter mail. (7) The continental China postal authorities will not deliver articles unless addressed to show name of the country as "People's Republic of China"; also, only acceptable spelling of capital is "Beijing."

International Mails

Weight and Dimensional Limits and Surface Rates

For air rates and parcel post see pages 973-974

Letters and letter packages: all written matter or correspondence must be sent as letter mail. Weight limit: 4 lbs. to all countries except Canada, which is 60 lbs. **Surface rates:** Canada and Mexico, 20¢ first ounce; 17¢ each additional oz. or fraction through 12 ozs.; eighth-zone priority rates for heavier weights. Countries other than Canada and Mexico, 1 oz., 30¢; over 1 to 2 ozs., 47¢; over 2 to 3 ozs., 64¢; over 3 to 4 ozs., 81¢; over 4 to 5 ozs., 98¢; over 5 to 6 ozs., $1.15; over 6 to 7 ozs., $1.32; over 7 to 8 ozs., $1.49; over 8 ozs. to 1 pound, $2.76; over 1 lb. to 1 lb., 8 ozs., $3.78; over 1 lb., 8 ozs. to 2 lbs., $4.80; over 2 lbs. to 2 lbs., 8 ozs., $5.55; over 2 lbs., 8 ozs. to 3 lbs., $6.30; over 3 lbs. to 3 lbs., 8 ozs., $7.05; over 3 lbs., 8 ozs. to 4 lbs. $7.80. **Air rates:** Canada and Mexico, 20¢ first ounce; 17¢ each additional ounce or fraction to 1 pound. Central America, Colombia, Venezuela, the Caribbean Islands, Bahamas, Bermuda, and St. Pierre and Miquelon, 35¢ per half ounce up to and including 2 ounces; 30¢ each additional half ounce or fraction. All other countries, 40¢ per half ounce up to and including 2 ounces; 35¢ each additional half ounce or fraction. Aerogrammes, which can be folded into the form of an envelope and sent by air to all countries, are available at post offices for 30¢ each.

Note. Mail to Canada and Mexico bearing postage paid at the surface letter rate will receive first class service in the U.S. and airmail service in Canada and Mexico during the Postal Service First Class Mail Service Improvement Program.

Postcards. Surface rates to Canada and Mexico, 13¢; to all other countries, 19¢. By air, Canada and Mexico, 13¢; to all other countries, 28¢. Maximum size permitted, 6 x 4¼ in.; minimum, 5½ x 3½.

Printed matter. To Canada, Mexico and all other countries: 20¢ (Canada and Mexico) and 23¢ (all other countries) the first ounce, 37¢ for 1 to 2 ozs., 54¢ for 2 to 3 ozs., 71¢ for 3 to 4 ozs., 85¢ for 4 to 6 ozs., 95¢ for 6 to 8 ozs., $1.14 for 8 to 10 ozs., $1.36 for 10 to 12 ozs., $1.58 for 12 to 14 ozs., $1.81 for 14 to 18 ozs., $1.94 for 18 to 20 ozs., $2.07 for 20 to 22 ozs., $2.21 for 22 to 24 ozs., $2.35 for 24 to 26 ozs., $2.49 for 26 to 28 ozs., $2.62 for 28 to 30 ozs., $2.76 for 30 to 32 ozs., $3.31 for 2 lbs. to 3 lbs., $3.86 for 3 lbs. to 4 lbs. and 96¢ for each add'l 1 lb. (Consult post office for rates and conditions applying to certain publications mailed by the publishers or by registered news agents.) Consult post office for book rates.

Exceptional weight limits for printed matter. Printed matter may weigh up to 22 lbs. to Argentina, Bolivia, Brazil, Chile, Colombia, Costa Rica, Cuba, Dominican Republic, Ecuador, El Salvador, Guatemala, Haiti, Honduras, Mexico, Nicaragua, Panama, Paraguay, Peru, Spain (including Balearic Islands, and Canary Islands) Surinam, Uruguay, and Venezuela. For other countries, limit for books is 11 lbs., all other prints, 4 lbs.

Matter for the blind. Surface rate free; air service to Canada for matter prepared as letters/letter packages is at the letter rate. (For all other countries, consult postmaster.) Weight limit 15 lbs.

Small packets. Postage rates for small items of merchandise and samples; consult post office for weight limits and requirements for customs declarations. Rates: Canada, Mexico 20¢, all other countries 23¢ for the first ounce; 37¢ for 1 to 2 ozs.; 54¢ for 2 to 3 ozs.; 71¢ for 3 to 4 ozs.; 85¢ for 4 to 6 ozs.; 95¢ for 6 to 8 ozs.; $1.14 for 8 to 10 ozs.; $1.36 for 10 to 12 ozs.; $1.58 for 12 to 14 ozs.; $1.81 for 14 to 16 ozs. (Consult post office for rates for heavier packets.) For other rates, see schedule "Air Service Other Articles" under heading of International Rates for Air Mail and Surface Parcel Post, pages 973-974.

INTELPOST-A USPS International Service Offering

The U.S. Postal Service, in conjunction with several foreign countries is making available to the public a new service offering called INTELPOST. INTELPOST is an acronym for International Electronic Post.

The INTELPOST system is a very high speed digital facsimile network between the United States and participating countries. INTELPOST utilizes existing international postal acceptance and delivery mechanisms for the acceptance and distribution of the INTELPOST original and facsimile documents. The INTELPOST original document and a transmittal form are scanned by a facsimile reader operated by USPS personnel at the INTELPOST transmitting facility and sent via international satellite communications to its destination.

A black and white image of the original document is printed by a facsimile printer operated by foreign postal personnel and is inserted into an INTELPOST envelope for delivery by participating postal administration personnel according to the service offerings available in the particular country.

The cost of an INTELPOST transmission is $5.00 per page including First Class (normal) delivery in the destinating foreign country. If an optional express type delivery service is available and is selected, the cost of such service will be added to the price of the message. Service is currently available to Canada, the United Kingdom and the Netherlands. Several additional countries are in the process of building INTELPOST Centers.

International Parcel Post

For rates see pages 973-974

General dimensional limits — greatest length, 3½ feet; greatest length and girth combined, 6 feet.

Prohibited articles. Before sending goods abroad the mailer should consult the post office that they will not be confiscated or returned because their importation is prohibited or restricted by the country of address.

Packing. Parcels for transmission overseas should be even more carefully packed than those intended for delivery within the continental U.S. Containers should be used which will be strong enough to protect the contents from the weight of other mail, from pressure and friction, climatic changes, and repeated handlings.

Sealing. Registered or insured parcels must be sealed. To some countries the sealing of ordinary (unregistered and uninsured) parcels is optional, and to others compulsory. Consult post office.

Customs declarations and other forms. At least one customs declaration is required for parcel post packages (surface or air) mailed to another country. In addition, to some countries, a dispatch note is required. The forms may be obtained at post offices.

Canadian Postal Rates

(in effect July 1, 1980)

First class letter mail and postcards. Up to 30 grams 17¢, over 30g and up to 50g 26¢, over 50g and up to 100g 38¢, over 100g and up to 150g 56¢, over 150g and up to 200g 74¢, over 200g and up to 250g 91¢, over 250g and up to 300g $1.09, over 300g and up to 350g $1.27, over 350g and up to 400g $1.44, over 400g and up to 450g $1.62, over 450g and up to 500g $1.80.
Parcels (over 500g). **First class** (maximum 30kg) receive priority air service. **Fourth class** (maximum 16kg) receive surface transmission.

The charges given below are for local (short haul) deliveries. A chart showing the cost for deliveries to all other postal zones may be obtained from your local postmaster.

Over/up to	500g/1kg-	1kg/1.5	1.5/2	2/2.5	2.5/3	3/3.5	3.5/4	4/6	6/8	8/10	10/12	12/14
1st class	$1.85	2.05	2.25	2.45	2.65	2.85	3.05	3.35	3.65	4.25	4.55	4.85
4th class	.85	1.00	1.10	1.25	1.35	1.50	1.60	1.80	2.00	2.20	2.40	2.60

Third class. Standard addressed rates (includes greeting cards). Up to 50g 15¢ plus 8¢ for each additional 50g up to a maximum of 500g.
Premium services. Certified mail (proof of delivery service) 90¢ plus postage. Special delivery first class postage plus $1 per item. Money order fee (maximum $200) - 40¢.

To U.S.A., Territories and Possessions

Airmail letters and postcards, up to and including 30g 17¢, from 30g to 50g 30¢ plus approximately 25¢ for each additional 50g up to 500g. Over 500g up to and including 1kg $3.90 with increases up to $52.69 for 30kg.
Surface parcel post. Up to and including 1kg $1.90 plus 55¢ for each additional 500g up to a maximum of 16kg.

QUICK REFERENCE INDEX

First Class Postal Rates in Brief

U.S. Domestic (in effect Nov. 1, 1981)

Letters—20¢ first ounce, 17¢ each additional ounce.
Postal cards—13¢ each (up to 4½ × 6 in.). Double cards, 26¢. Private cards, 13¢; double 26¢.

U.S. International (in effect Nov. 1, 1981)

Letters—(1) Canada (max. weight 60 lbs.) and Mexico (max. weight 4 lbs.), 20¢ first ounce, 17¢ each addl. ounce to 12 ounces; over 12 ounces to 1 pound, $2.58; over 1 pound to 1½ pounds, $3.07; over 1½ to 2 pounds, $3.57; over 2 to 2½ pounds, $4.06; over 2½ to 3 pounds, $4.56; over 3 to 3½ pounds, $5.05; over 3½ to 4 pounds, $5.55; over 4 to 4½ pounds, $6.05; over 4½ to 5 pounds, $6.54. (2) Countries other than Canada and Mexico, 1 ounce, 30¢; over 1 to 2 ounces, 47¢; over 2 to 3 ounces, 64¢; over 3 to 4 ounces, 81¢; over 4 to 5 ounces, 98¢; over 5 to 6 ounces, $1.15; over 6 to 7 ounces $1.32; and over 7 to 8 ounces, $1.49.
Air mail letters—(1) Canada, and Mexico, same as domestic surface rates. (2) Cen. America, Colombia, Venezuela, the Caribbean Is., Bahamas, Bermuda, and St. Pierre and Miquelon, 35¢ per half ounce through 2 ounces; 30¢ each addl. ½ oz. through 32 ounces. (3) All other countries, 40¢ per half ounce through 2 ounces; 35¢ each addl. ½ oz. through 32 ounces.

Aerogrammes—to all countries, 30¢ each.
Postal cards—to Canada and Mexico 13¢ each. To all other countries, 19¢ each.
Air mail postcards—to Canada and Mexico 13¢ each, to other countries 28¢ each.

Canada (in effect July 1, 1980)

Letter mail and postcards—Up to 30g 17¢, 31-50g 26¢, 51-100g 38¢, 101-150g 56¢, 151-200g 74¢, 201-250g 91¢, 251-300g $1.09, 301-350g $1.27, 351-400g $1.44, 401-450g $1.62, 451-500g $1.80.
To U.S.A. territories and possessions—(1) **Airmail letters and postcards**, up to and including 30g 17¢, 30-50g 30¢ plus approx. 25¢ for each additional 50g up to 500g. Over 500g up to and including 1kg $3.90 with increases up to $52.69 for a maximum of 30kg. (2) **Surface parcel post.** Up to and including 1kg $1.90 plus 55¢ for each additional 500g up to a maximum of 16g.